Reverse
Acronyms, Initialisms &
Abbreviations Dictionary

ISSN 0270-4404

Reverse Acronyms, Initialisms & Abbreviations Dictionary

A Companion Volume to *Acronyms, Initialisms & Abbreviations Dictionary*,
with Terms Arranged Alphabetically by Meaning of Acronym, Initialism, or Abbreviation

Covering: Aerospace, Associations, Banking, Biochemistry, Business, Data Processing,
Domestic and International Affairs, Economics, Education, Electronics, Genetics,
Government, Information Technology, Internet, Investment, Labor, Law, Medicine, Military Affairs,
Pharmacy, Physiology, Politics, Religion, Science, Societies, Sports, Technical
Drawings and Specifications, Telecommunications, Trade, Transportation, and Other Fields

25th Edition

Volume 3

Part 2

G-O

Mary Rose Bonk,
Editor

Pamela Dear,
Associate Editor

GALE

DETROIT · LONDON

Editor:	Mary Rose Bonk
Associate Editor:	Pamela Dear
Contributing Editors:	Mildred Hunt
Data Entry Manager:	Eleanor M. Allison
Data Entry Coordinator:	Kenneth Benson
Production Director:	Mary Beth Trimper
Production Assistant:	Deborah Milliken
Graphic Services Manager:	Barbara J. Yarrow
Macintosh Artist:	Gary Leach
Manager, Technical Support Services:	Theresa A. Rocklin
Programmer:	Charles Beaumont

Library of Congress Catalog Card Number 84-643188
ISBN 0-7876-2455-1 (Volume 1 Complete)
ISBN 0-7876-2456-X (Part 1: A-F only)
ISBN 0-7876-2457-8 (Part 2: G-O only)
ISBN 0-7876-2458-6 (Part 3: P-Z only)
ISSN 0270-4404

Printed in the United States of America

Contents

Volume 1
Part 1 A-F

Volume 1
Part 2 G-O

Volume 1
Part 3 P-Z

Gale's publications in the acronyms and abbreviations field include:

Acronyms, Initialisms & Abbreviations Dictionary series:

Acronyms, Initialisms & Abbreviations Dictionary (Volume 1). A guide to acronyms, initialisms, abbreviations, and similar contractions, arranged alphabetically by abbreviation.

Acronyms, Initialisms & Abbreviations Dictionary Supplement (Volume 2). An interedition supplement in which terms are arranged alphabetically both by abbreviation and by meaning.

Reverse Acronyms, Initialisms & Abbreviations Dictionary (Volume 3). A companion to Volume 1 in which terms are arranged alphabetically by meaning of the acronym, initialism, or abbreviation.

Acronyms, Initialisms & Abbreviations Dictionary Subject Guide series:

Computer & Telecommunications Acronyms (Volume 1). A guide to acronyms, initialisms, abbreviations, and similar contractions used in the field of computers and telecommunications in which terms are arranged alphabetically both by abbreviation and by meaning.

Business Acronyms (Volume 2). A guide to business-oriented acronyms, initialisms, abbreviations, and similar contractions in which terms are arranged alphabetically both by abbreviation and by meaning.

International Acronyms, Initialisms & Abbreviations Dictionary series:

International Acronyms, Initialisms & Abbreviations Dictionary (Volume 1). A guide to foreign and international acronyms, initialisms, abbreviations, and similar contractions, arranged alphabetically by abbreviation.

Reverse International Acronyms, Initialisms & Abbreviations Dictionary (Volume 2). A companion to Volume 1, in which terms are arranged alphabetically by meaning of the acronym, initialism, or abbreviation.

Periodical Title Abbreviations series:

Periodical Title Abbreviations: By Abbreviation (Volume 1). A guide to abbreviations commonly used for periodical titles, arranged alphabetically by abbreviation.

Periodical Title Abbreviations: By Title (Volume 2). A guide to abbreviations commonly used for periodical titles, arranged alphabetically by title.

New Periodical Title Abbreviations (Volume 3). An interedition supplement in which terms are arranged alphabetically both by abbreviation and by title.

User's Guide

The following examples illustrate possible elements of entries in *RAIAD:*

① ② ③ ④

Force Aerienne Tactique [*Tactical Air Force*] [*French*] (NATG) ....FATAC

⑤ ⑥

Multiple-Mirror Telescope [*Mount Hopkins, AZ*] [*Jointly operated by Smithsonian Institution and the University of Arizona*] [*Astronomy*].........................MMT

⑦ ⑧

① Meaning or Phrase

② English Translation

③ Language (for non-English entries)

④ Source code (Allows you to verify entries or find additional information. Decoded in the List of Selected Sources)

⑤ Location or Country of origin (Provides geographic identifiers for airports, colleges and universities, libraries, military bases, political parties, radio and television stations, and others)

⑥ Sponsoring organization

⑦ Subject category (Clarifies entries by providing appropriate context)

⑧ Acronym, Initialism, or Abbreviation

The completeness of a listing is dependent upon both the nature of the term and the amount of information provided by the source. If additional information becomes available during future research, an entry is revised.

Arrangement of Entries

Terms are arranged in alphabetical order, according to the meaning of the acronym, initialism, or abbreviation. If a particular translation has more than one initialism representing it, the various choices are then arranged alphabetically. Thus:

Liquid Nitrogen...LIN
Liquid Nitrogen...LN

Articles, conjunctions, prepositions, etc., generally are not considered in the alphabetizing:

Master Switch...MS
Master *of* Textile Chemistry..MTC
Not Less Than..NLT
Not *in* Line *of* Duty..NLD

List of Selected Sources

Each of the sources included in the following list contributed at least 50 terms. It would be impossible to cite a source for every entry because the majority of terms are sent by outside contributors, are uncovered through independent research by the editorial staff, or surface as miscellaneous broadcast or print media references.

For sources used on an ongoing basis, only the latest edition is listed. For most of the remaining sources, the edition that was used is cited. The editors will provide further information about these sources upon request.

Unless further described in an annotation, the publications listed here contain no additional information about the acronym, initialism, or abbreviation cited.

(AABC)   *Catalog of Abbreviations and Brevity Codes*. Washington, DC: U.S. Department of the Army, 1981. [Use of source began in 1969]

(AAG)   *Aerospace Abbreviations Glossary*. Report Number AG60-0014. Prepared by General Dynamics/Astronautics. San Diego, CA: 1962.

(AAGC)   *Acronyms and Abbreviations in Government Contracting*. 2d ed. By Patricia A. Tobin and Joan Nelson Phillips. Washington, DC: George Washington University, 1997.

(AAMN)   *Abbreviations and Acronyms in Medicine and Nursing*. By Solomon Garb, Eleanor Krakauer, and Carson Justice. New York, NY: Springer Publishing Co., 1976.

(ABBR)   *Abbreviations: The Comprehensive Dictionary of Abbreviations and Letter Symbols*. Vol. 1 C. By Edward Wall. Ann Arbor, MI: The Pierian Press, 1984.

(AC)   *Associations Canada 1995/96*. Edited by Ward McBurney. Toronto, Canada: Canadian Almanac & Directory Publishing Co. Ltd., 1995.

(ACII)   *"Acronym and Initials Index."* 7 February 1996. <http://www.ioi.ie/~readout/cl.html> (7 November 1996).

(AD)   *Abbreviations Dictionary*. 8thed. By Ralph De Sola. Boca Raton, FL: CRC Press, 1992.

(ADA)   *The Australian Dictionary of Acronyms and Abbreviations*. 2nd ed. Compiled by David J. Jones. Leura, NSW, Australia: Second Back Row Press Pty. Ltd., 1981.

(ADDR)   *Army Dictionary and Desk Reference*. By Tim Zurick. Harrisburg, PA: Stackpole Books, 1992.

(AEBS)   *Acronyms in Education and the Behavioral Sciences*. By Toyo S. Kawakami. Chicago, IL: American Library Association, 1971.

(AEE)   *American Educators' Encyclopedia*. By Edward L. Dejnozka and David E. Kapel. Westport, CT: Greenwood Press, 1991.

(AF)   *Reference Aid: Abbreviations in the African Press*. Arlington, VA: Joint Publications Research Service, 1979.

(AFIT)   *Compendium of Authenticated Systems and Logistics.* Washington, DC: Air Force Institute of Technology, 1984.

(AFM)   *Air Force Manual of Abbreviations.* Washington, DC: U.S. Department of the Air Force, 1975. [Use of source began in 1969]

(AIA)   *Aviation Insurance Abbreviations, Organisations and Institutions.* By M.J. Spurway. London, England: Witherby & Co. Ltd., 1983.

(AIE)   *Acronyms and Initialisms in Education.* 6th ed. Compiled by John Hutchins. Norwich, England: Librarians of Institutes and Schools of Education, 1995.

(ANA)   *"Abbreviations" - U.S. Navy Dictionary.* 3rd revision. Washington DC: DCP, 1989.

(APTA)   *Australian Periodical Title Abbreviations.* Compiled by David J. Jones. Leura, NSW, Australia: Second Back Row Press Pty. Ltd., 1985.

(ARC)   *Agricultural Research Centres: A World Directory of Organizations and Programmes.* 2 vols. Edited by Nigel Harvey. Harlow, Essex, England: Longman Group, 1983.
   A world guide to official, educational, industrial, and independent research centers which support research in the fields of agriculture, veterinary medicine, horticulture, aquaculture, food science, forestry, zoology, and botany.

(ARCH)   *Dictionary of Architecture and Construction.* Edited by Cyril M. Harris. New York, NY: McGraw-Hill, Inc., 1975.

(ASF)   *Guide to Names and Acronyms of Organizations, Activities, and Projects.* By Food and Agriculture Organization of the United Nations. Fishery Information, Data, and Statistics Service and U.S. National Oceanic and Atmospheric Administration. Aquatic Sciences and Fisheries Information System Reference Series, Number 10, 1982. n.p.

(BABM)   *Bailliere's Abbreviations in Medicine.* 5th ed. By Edwin B. Steen. London, England: Bailliere Tindall, 1984.

(BARN)   *The Barnhart Abbreviations Dictionary.* Edited by Robert K. Barnhart. New York, NY: John Wiley & Sons, Inc., 1995.

(BI)   *British Initials and Abbreviations.* 3rd ed. By Ian H. Wilkes. London, England: Leonard Hill Books, 1971.

(BIB)   *Bibliotech.* Ottawa, Canada: National Library of Canada, 1988-89.

(BJA)   *Biblical and Judaic Acronyms.* By Lawrence Marwick. New York, NY: Ktav Publishing House, Inc., 1979.

(BRI)   *Book Review Index.* 1997 Cumulation. Edited by Beverly Baer. Detroit, MI: Gale Research, 1998.

(BROA)   *Broadcasting and Cable Yearbook 1997.* 2 vol. New Providence, NJ: R.R. Bowker, 1997.

(BTTJ)   *Breaking Through Technical Jargon: A Dictionary of Computer and Automation Acronyms.* By Mark S. Merkow. New York, NY: Van Nostrand Reinhold, 1990.

(BUR)   *Computer Acronyms and Abbreviations Handbook.* Tokyo, Japan: Burroughs Co. Ltd., 1978.

(BYTE) *Byte: The Small Systems Journal.* Peterborough, NH: McGraw-Hill Information Systems, Inc., 1987-89.

(CAAL) *CAAL COMOPTEVFOR Acronym and Abbreviation List.* Norfolk, VA: (CAAL-U) Operational Test and Evaluation Force, 1981.

(CB) *Centres & Bureaux: A Directory of Concentrations of Effort, Information and Expertise.* Edited by Lindsay Sellar. Beckenham, Kent, England: CBD Research Ltd., 1987.
> A guide to British organizations which include the words "centre" or "bureau" in their names. Entries include name and address; telephone and telex numbers; chief official; and a description of the purposes, activities, and services of the organization.

(CDAI) *Concise Dictionary of Acronyms and Initialisms.* By Stuart W. Miller. New York, NY: Facts on File Publications, 1988.

(CDE) *The Computer Desktop Encyclopedia.* By Alan Freedman. New York, NY: AMACOM, 1996.

(CDI) *The Cancer Dictionary.* By Roberta Altman and Michael Sarg, M.D. New York, NY: Facts on File, 1992.

(CED) *Current European Directories.* 2nd ed. Edited by G.P. Henderson. Beckenham, Kent, England: CBD Research, 1981.

(CET) *Communications-Electronics Terminology.* AFM 11-1. Vol. 3. U.S. Department of the Air Force, 1973.

(CINC) *A CINCPAC Glossary of Commonly Used Abbreviations and Short Titles.* By Ltc. J.R. Johnson. Washington, DC: 1968.

(CMD) *Complete Multilingual Dictionary of Computer Terminology.* Compiled by Georges Nania. Chicago, IL: National Textbook Co., 1984.
> Computer-related terms in Spanish, French, Italian, Portuguese, and English. Indexes in French, Italian, Spanish, and Portuguese are also provided.

(CNC) *American National Standard Codes for the Representation of Names of Countries, Dependencies, and Areas of Special Sovereignty for Information Interchange.* U.S. National Bureau of Standards. Washington, DC: Government Printing Office, 1986. [Use of source began in 1977]
> These standard codes, approved by the International Organization for Standardization and the American National Standards Institute, are used in the international interchange of data in many fields.

(CPH) *The Charles Press Handbook of Current Medical Abbreviations.* 3rd ed. Philadelphia, PA: The Charles Press Publishers, Inc., 1991.

(CRD) *Computer-Readable Databases: A Directory and Data Sourcebook.* 6th ed. Edited by Kathleen Young Marcaccio. Detroit, MI: Gale Research, 1990.
> A guide to online databases, offline files available in various magnetic formats, and CD-ROM files. Entries include producer name, address, telephone number, description of coverage, vendors, and contact person.

(CROSS) *Cross-Border Links: A Directory of Organizations in Canada, Mexico, and the United States.* Edited by Ricardo Hernandez and Edith Sanchez. Albuquerque, NM: Inter-Hemispheric Education Resource Center, 1992.

(CSR)   *Computer Science Resources: A Guide to Professional Literature.* Edited by Darlene Myers. White Plains, NY: Knowledge Industry Publications, Inc., 1981.
        Covers several types of computer-related literature including journals, technical reports, directories, dictionaries, handbooks, and university computer center newsletters. Five appendices cover career and salary trends in the computer industry, user group acronyms, university computer libraries, and trade fairs and shows.

(CTT)   *Corporate TrendTrac.* Edited by A. Dale Timpe. Detroit, MI: Gale Research, 1988-89.
        Covers mergers and acquisitions, stock exchange listings and suspensions, company name changes, bankruptcies, liquidations, and reorganizations.

(DA)   *Dictionary of Aviation.* By R. J. Hall and R. D. Campbell. Chicago, IL: St. James Press, 1991.

(DAS)   *Dictionary of Abbreviations and Symbols.* By Edward Frank Allen. London, England: Cassell and Co. Ltd., 1949.

(DAVI)   *The Davis Book of Medical Abbreviations: A Deciphering Guide.* By Sarah Lu Mitchell-Hatton. Philadelphia, PA: F. A. Davis Co., 1991.

(DBA)   *Directory of British Associations.* Edited by G. P. Henderson and S. P. A. Henderson. Beckenham, Kent, England: CBD Research, Ltd., 1990.

(DBQ)   *A Dictionary of British Qualifications.* London, England: Kogan Page Ltd., 1985.

(DCTA)   *Dictionary of Commercial Terms and Abbreviations.* By Alan E. Branch. London, England: Witherby & Co. Ltd., 1984.

(DD)   *The Financial Post Directory of Directors 1997.* Toronto, Canada: The Financial Post, 1996.

(DEN)   *Dictionary of Electronics and Nucleonics.* By L.E.C. Hughes, R. W. B. Stephens and L. D. Brown. New York, NY: Barnes & Noble, 1969.

(DFIT)   *Dictionary of Finance and Investment Terms.* 4th ed. Edited by John Downes and Jordan Elliot Goodman. Hauppauge, NY: Barron's Educational Series, 1995.

(DGA)   *Dictionary of Graphic Arts Abbreviations.* By L. W. Wallis. Rockport, MA: Rockport Publishers, Inc., 1986.

(DHSM)   *Dictionary of Health Services Management.* 2nd ed. By Thomas C. Timmreck. Owings Mills, MD: Rynd Communications, 1987.

(DI)   *The Dictionary of Initials-What They Mean.* Compiled and edited by Harriette Lewis. Kingswood, Surrey, England: Paper Fronts Elliot Right Way Books, 1983.

(DICI)   *The Dictionary of Initials.* By Betsy M. Parks. Secaucus, NJ: Citadel Press, 1981.

(DIT)   *Dictionary of Informatics Terms in Russian and English.* By G. S. Zhdanov, E. S. Kolobrodov, V. A. Polushkin, and A. I. Cherny. Moscow: Nauka, 1971.

(DLA)   *Bieber's Dictionary of Legal Abbreviations.* 3rd ed. By Mary Miles Prince. Buffalo, NY: William S. Hein & Co., 1988.

(DMA)　　*Dictionary of Military Abbreviations: British, Empire, Commonwealth*. By B. K. C. Scott. Hastings, East Sussex, England: Tamarisk Books, 1982.

(DMAA)　　*Dictionary of Medical Acronyms and Abbreviations*. 3rd ed. Edited by Stanley Jablonski. Philadelphia, PA: Hanley & Belfus, Inc., 1998.

(DMC)　　*Webster's New World Dictionary of Media and Communications*. Revised ed. By Richard Weiner. New York, NY: Macmillan, 1996.

(DNAB)　　*Dictionary of Naval Abbreviations*. 3rd ed. Compiled and edited by Bill Wedertz. Annapolis, MD: Naval Institute Press, 1984.

(DOAD)　　*The Dictionary of Advertising.* Edited by Laurence Urdang. Lincolnwood, IL: NTC Business Books, 1986.

(DOG)　　*A Dictionary of Genetics*. 5th ed. By Robert C. King and William D. Stansfield. New York, NY: Oxford University Press, 1997.

(DOGT)　　*"List of Acronyms."* <http://www.em.doe.gov/rtc1994/loa.html> (5 March 1997).

(DOM)　　*The Dictionary of Multimedia: Terms & Acronyms*. By Brad Hansen. Wilsonvillee, OR: Franklin, Beedle & Associates, 1997.

(DOMA)　　*Dictionary of Military Abbreviations.* By Norman Polmar, Mark Warren, and Eric Wertheim. Annapolis, MD: Naval Institute Press, 1994.

(DS)　　*Dictionary of Shipping International Trade Terms and Abbreviations*. 3rd ed. By Alan E. Branch. London, England: Witherby & Co. Ltd., 1986.

(DSA)　　*Dictionary of Sigla and Abbreviations to and in Law Books before 1607*. By William Hamilton Bryson. Charlottesville, VA: University Press of Virginia, 1975.

(DSUE)　　*A Dictionary of Slang and Unconventional English*. 8th ed. By Eric Partridge. New York, NY: Macmillan Publishing Co., 1984.

(DUND)　　*Directory of United Nations Databases and Information Services*. 4th ed. Compiled by the Advisory Committee for the Coordination of Information Systems. New York, NY: United Nations, 1990.
　　　　　A guide to computerized databases and information systems/services. Entries include sponsoring organization, year established, type, scope, coverage, timespan, and contact information.

(DWSG)　　*Defense Weapon Systems Glossary*. By David Trotz. Piscataway, NJ: Target Marketing, 1992.

(EA)　　*Encyclopedia of Associations*. 29th ed. Vol. 1, National Organizations of the U.S. Edited by Carol A. Schwartz and Rebecca L. Turner. Detroit, MI: Gale Research, 1995 (and supplement 1995) [Use of source began in 1960]
　　　　　A guide to trade, professional, and other nonprofit associations that are national and international in scope and membership and that are headquartered in the United States. Entries include name and address; telephone and telex number; chief official; and a description of the purpose, activities, and structure of the organization.

(EAAP) *Encyclopedia of Associations: Association Periodicals.* 3 vols. Edited by Denise M. Allard and Robert C. Thomas. Detroit, MI: Gale Research, 1987.
> A directory of publications issued by all types of national nonprofit organizations in the United States. Entries include title and organization name, address, telephone number; description of periodical, frequency of publication, and price.

(EAIO) *Encyclopedia of Associations: International Organizations.* 29th ed. Edited by Linda Irvin. Detroit, MI: Gale Research, 1995. [Use of source began in 1985]
> A guide to trade, professional, and other nonprofit associations that are national or international in scope and membership and that are headquartered outside the United States. Entries include name and address; principal foreign language name; telephone and telex number; chief official; and a description of the purpose, activities, and structure of the organization.

(ECED) *The European Communities Encyclopedia and Directory 1992.* London, England: Europa Publications Ltd., 1991; distributed in U.S. by Gale Research, Detroit, MI.
> A comprehensive guide to the European Communities. Entries explain widely-used acronyms and include address, telephone, telex, fax numbers and chief officers for EC-level organizations.

(ECII) *Electronics, Computers and Industrial Instrumentation Abbreviations and Acronyms.* Edited by Sergio Sobredo. Miami, FL: Sergio Sobredo Technical Services, 1986.

(ECON) *The Economist.* London, England: The Economist Newspaper Ltd., 1997. [Use of source began in 1988]

(EDAC) *Dictionary of Educational Acronyms, Abbreviations, and Initialisms.* 2nd ed. Edited by James C. Palmer and Anita Y. Colby. Phoenix, AZ: Oryx Press, 1985.

(EE) *Eastern Europe and the Commonwealth of Independent States 1992.* London, England: Europa Publications Ltd., 1992; distributed in U.S. by Gale Research, Detroit, MI.

(EECA) *Dictionary of Electrical, Electronics, and Computer Abbreviations.* By Phil Brown. London, England: Buttersworth, 1985.

(EG) *Environmental Glossary.* 4th ed. Edited by G. William Frick and Thomas F.P. Sullivan. Rockville, MD: Government Institutes, Inc., 1986.

(EGAO) *Encyclopedia of Governmental Advisory Organizations.* 9th ed. Edited by Donna Batten. Detroit, MI: Gale Research, 1994-95 (and supplement, 1995). [Use of source began in 1975]
> A reference guide to permanent, continuing, and ad hoc U.S. presidential advisory committees, interagency committees, and other government-related boards, panels, task forces, commissions, conferences, and other similar bodies serving in a consultative, coordinating, advisory, research, or investigative capacity. Entries include name and address; telephone number, designated federal employee, history, recommendation and findings of the committee, staff size, publications, and subsidiaries. Also includes indexes to personnel, reports, federal agencies, presidential administration, and an alphabetical and keyword index.

(EMRF) *The St. James Encyclopedia of Mortgage & Real Estate Finance.* By James Newell, Albert Santi, and Chip Mitchell. Chicago, IL: St. James Press, 1991.

(EPA) *Glossary of EPA Acronyms.* Washington, DC: Environmental Protection Agency, 1987.

(ERG)   *Environmental Regulatory Glossary*. 5th ed. Edited by G. William Frick and Thomas F. P. Sullivan. Rockville, MD: Government Institutes, Inc., 1990.

(EY)   *The Europa World Year Book 1992*. London: Europa Publications Ltd., 1992. distributed in U.S. by Gale Research, Detroit, MI.
> An annual survey containing detailed information about the political, economic, statistical, and commercial situation of the regions and countries covered.

(FAAC)   *Contractions Handbook*. Changes. U.S. Department of Transportation. Federal Aviation Administration, 1993. [Use of source began in 1969]

(FAAL)   *Location Identifiers*. U.S. Department of Transportation. Federal Aviation Administration. Air Traffic Service, 1982.

(FEA)   *The Far East and Australasia 1987*. 18th ed. London, England: Europa Publications Ltd., 1986; distributed in U.S. by Gale Research, Detroit, MI.
> An annual survey containing detailed information about the political, economic, statistical, and commercial situation of the regions and countries covered.

(FFDE)   *The Facts on File Dictionary of Environmental Science*. By L. Harold Stevenson and Bruce Wyman. New York, NY: Facts on File, 1991.
> Defines terms from disciplines as diverse as biology, chemistry, geology, physics, engineering, meteorology, social science, medicine, and economics.

(GAAI)   *"Glossary of Abbreviations, Acronyms, and Initialisms."* 17 February 1998.
> <http://www.em.doe.gov/idb97/acropdf.html

(GAVI)   *"Glossary of Aviation Acronyms and Abbreviations."*
> <http://olias.arc.nasa.gov/AFO_Acronyms_.html> (5 March 1997).

(GEA)   *Government Economic Agencies of the World: An International Directory of Governmental Organisations Concerned with Economic Development and Planning*. A Keesing's Reference Publication. Edited by Alan J. Day. Harlow, Essex, England: Longman Group Ltd., 1985.
> Covers over 170 countries and territories. Two introductory sections for each area cover economic data and prevailing economic and political conditions. Individual entries provide title, address, and names of chief officials of each agency. Current activities and financial structure of each agency are also detailed. An index of agency officials is provided.

(GFGA)   *Guide to Federal Government Acronyms*. Edited by William R. Evinger. Phoenix, AZ: The Oryx Press, 1989.

(GNE)   *The Green Encyclopedia.* By Irene Franck and David Brownstone. New York, NY: Prentice Hall General Reference, 1992.

(GPO)   *Style Manual*. Washington, DC: Government Printing Office, 1984.Terms are included in Chapter 24, Foreign Languages.

(GRD)   *Government Research Directory*. 8th ed. Edited by Joseph M. Palmisano. Detroit, MI: Gale Research, 1994. (and supplement, 1994).
> A descriptive guide to U.S. government research and development centers, institutes, laboratories, bureaus, test facilities, experiment stations, data collection and analysis centers, and grants management and research coordinating offices in agriculture, business, education, energy, engineering, environment, the humanities, medicine, military science, and basic applied sciences.

(HCT)	*Health Care Terms.* 2nd ed. By Vergil N. and Debora A. Slee. St. Paul, MN: Tringa Press, 1991.
(HGAA)	*The Handy Guide to Abbreviations and Acronyms for the Automated Office.* By Mark W. Greenia. Seattle, WA: Self-Counsel Press Inc., 1986.
(IAA)	*Index of Acronyms and Abbreviations in Electrical and Electronic Engineering.* Compiled by Buro Scientia. New York, NY: VCH Publishers, 1989.
(IBMDP)	*IBM Data Processing Glossary.* 6th ed. White Plains, NY: IBM Corp., 1977.
(ICAO)	*Aircraft Type Designators.* 13th ed. International Civil Aviation Organization, August, 1981.
(ICDA)	*Designators for Aircraft Operating Agencies, Aeronautical Authorities and Services.* 49th ed. International Civil Aviation Organization, June, 1982. Document also includes telephony designators and postal and telegraphic addresses of government civil aviation authorities.
(ICLI)	*Location Indicators.* 51st ed. International Civil Aviation Organization, February, 1987. Document also contains addresses of flight information centers.
(IDOE)	*The Illustrated Dictionary of Electronics.* 6th ed. By Stan Gibilisco. New York, NY: TAB Books, 1994.
(IEEE)	*IEEE Standard Dictionary of Electrical and Electronics Terms.* Edited by Frank Jay. New York, NY: The Institute of Electrical and Electronics Engineers, Inc., 1977, 1984. Includes definitions for thousands of electrical and electronics terms. Each entry includes a numeric source code.
(IIA)	*Index of Initials and Acronyms.* Compiled by Richard Kleiner. New York, NY: Auerbach Publishers, 1971.
(IID)	*Information Industry Directory.* 15th ed. Edited by Annette Novallo. Detroit, MI: Gale Research, 1995. (and supplement, 1995). An international guide to computer-readable databases, database producers, and publishers, online vendors and time-sharing companies, telecommunications networks, and many other information systems and services. Entries include name and address, telephone number, chief official, and a detailed description of the purpose and function of the system or service.
(ILCA)	*Index to Legal Citations and Abbreviations.* By Donald Raistrick. Abingdon, Oxfordshire, England: Professional Books Ltd., 1981.
(IMH)	*International Marketing Handbook.* 2nd ed. Edited by Frank Bair. Detroit, MI: Gale Research, 1985. An in-depth guide to commercial and trade data on 142 countries of the world. Features include a list of European trade fairs and a report on growth markets in Western Europe.
(INF)	*Infantry.* Fort Benning, GA: U.S. Army Infantry Training School, 1996. [Use of source began in 1983]
(IRC)	*International Research Centers Directory 1992-93.* 6th ed. Edited by Annette Piccirelli. Detroit, MI: Gale Research, 1991. A world guide to government, university, independent, nonprofit, and commercial research and development centers, institutes, laboratories, bureaus, test facilities,

experiment stations, and data collection and analysis centers, as well as foundations, councils, and other organizations which support research.

(IRUK) *Industrial Research in the United Kingdom*. 12th ed. Harlow, Essex, England: Longman Group UK Ltd., 1987.
  A guide to all groups conducting or funding research relevant to British industrial development. Entries include name, address, telephone and telex numbers; chief officials; and scope of activities.

(IT) *Information Today: The Newspaper for Users and Producers of Electronic Information Services*. Medford, NJ: Learned Information Inc., 1988-89.

(ITD) *International Tradeshow Directory*. 5th ed. Frankfurt, Germany: M + A Publishers for Fairs, Exhibitions and Conventions Ltd., 1989.
  A guide to trade fairs and exhibitions throughout the world. Entries include event name, dates, frequency, location, description of purpose, profile of exhibitors and attendees.

(IYR) *The 1989-92 International Yacht Racing Rules*. London, England: International Yacht Racing Union, 1989.

(KSC) *A Selective List of Acronyms and Abbreviations*. Compiled by the Documents Department, Kennedy Space Center Library, 1971, 1973.

(LAIN) *Latest Intelligence: An International Directory of Codes Used by Government, Law Enforcement, Military, and Surveillance Agencies*. By James E. Tunnell. Blue Ridge Summit, PA: TAB BOOKS, 1990.

(LCCP) *MARC Formats for Bibliographic Data*. Appendix II. Washington, DC: Library of Congress, 1982.

(LCLS) *Symbols of American Libraries*. 14th ed. Edited by the Enhanced Cataloging Division. Washington, DC: Library of Congress, 1992. [Use of source began in 1980]

(LWAP) *Legal Words and Phrases: Speed Abbreviations*. By Joel Larus. Boston, MA: Aurico Publishing, 1965.

(MAE) *Medical Abbreviations and Eponyms*. By Sheila B. Sloane. Philadelphia, PA: W.B. Saunders Co., 1985.

(MAH) *Medical Abbreviations Handbook*. 2nd ed. Oradell, NJ: Medical Economics Co., Inc., 1983.

(MCD) *Acronyms, Abbreviations, and Initialisms*. Compiled by Carl Lauer. St. Louis, MO: McDonnell Douglas Corp., 1989. [Use of source began in 1969]

(MDG) *Microcomputer Dictionary and Guide*. By Charles J. Sippl. Champaign, IL: Matrix Publishers, Inc., 1975.
  A listing of definitions for over 5,000 microelectronics terms. Seven appendices.

(MEDA) *Medical Acronyms*. 2nd ed. By Marilyn Fuller Delong. Oradell, NJ: Medical Economic Books, 1989.

(MENA) *The Middle East and North Africa 1987*. 33rd ed. London, England: Europa Publications Ltd., 1986; distributed in U.S. by Gale Research, Detroit, MI.
  An annual survey containing detailed information about the political, economic, statistical, and commercial situation of the regions and countries covered.

(MHDB) *McGraw-Hill Dictionary of Business Acronyms, Initials, and Abbreviations.* By Jerry M. Rosenberg. New York, NY: McGraw-Hill, Inc., 1992.

(MHDI) *McGraw-Hill Dictionary of Information Technology and Computer Acronyms, Initials, and Abbreviations.* By Jerry M. Rosenberg. New York, NY: McGraw-Hill, Inc., 1992.

(MHDW) *McGraw-Hill Dictionary of Wall Street Acronyms, Initials, and Abbreviations.* By Jerry M. Rosenberg. New York, NY: McGraw-Hill, Inc., 1992.

(MSA) *Military Standard Abbreviations for Use on Drawings, and in Specifications, Standards, and Technical Documents.* MIL-STD-12D. U.S. Department of Defense, 1981. [Use of source began in 1975]

(MSC) *Annotated Acronyms and Abbreviations of Marine Science Related Activities.* 3rd ed. Revised by Charlotte M. Ashby and Alan R. Flesh. Washington, DC: U.S. Department of Commerce. National Oceanographic and Atmospheric Administration. Environmental Data Service. National Oceanographic Data Center, 1976, 1981.

(MUGU) *The Mugu Book of Acronyms and Abbreviations.* Missile Range, California: Management Engineering Office, 1963, 1964.

(NADA) *The New American Dictionary of Abbreviations.* By Mary A. De Vries. New York, NY: Signet, 1991.

(NASA) *Space Transportation System and Associated Payloads: Glossary, Acronyms, and Abbreviations.* Washington, DC: U.S. National Aeronautics and Space Administration, 1985.

(NATG) *Glossary of Abbreviations Used in NATO Documents.* AAP 15(B), n.p., 1979. [Use of source began in 1976]

(NCC) *NCC The National Centre for Information Technology. Guide to Computer Aided Engineering, Manufacturing and Construction Software.* Manchester, England: NCC Publications. The National Computing Centre Ltd., 1985.
   Includes software classifications and descriptions, names and addresses of suppliers, processor manufacturers, and operating systems.

(NFD) *The NSFRE Fund-Raising Dictionary.* Edited by Barbara R. Levy. New York, NY: John Wiley & Sons, Inc., 1996.

(NFPA) *Standard for Fire Safety Symbols/NFPA170.* Quincy, MA: National Fire Protection Association, 1994.

(NG) *NAVAIR Glossary of Unclassified Common-Use Abbreviated Titles and Phrases.* NAVAIRNOTE 5216 AIR-6031, n.p., July, 1969.

(NGC) *Catalogue of the National Gallery of Canada.* Compiled by National Gallery of Canada. Ottawa, Canada: National Gallery of Canada, 1998.

(NHD) *The New Hacker's Dictionary.* Edited by Eric Raymond. Cambridge, MA: MIT Press, 1991.

(NITA) *Dictionary of New Information Technology Acronyms.* 2nd ed. By Michael Gordon, Alan Singleton, and Clarence Rickards. London, England: Kogan Page, Ltd., 1986.

(NLC) *Symbols of Canadian Libraries.* 12th ed. National Library of Canada. Minister of Supply and Services Canada, 1987.

(NOAA) *NOAA Directives Manual.* 66-13 Acronyms. 1977.

(NQ) *NASDAQ Company Directory.* New York, NY: National Association of Securities Dealers, Inc., 1990. [Use of source began in 1983]
   Entries include company name, SIC code, contact person's name, title, address, and telephone number.

(NRCH) *A Handbook of Acronyms and Initialisms.* Washington, DC: U.S. Nuclear Regulatory Commission. Division of Technical Information and Document Control, 1985.

(NTCM) *NTC's Mass Media Dictionary.* R. Terry Ellmore. Lincolnwood, IL: National Textbook Co., 1991.

(NUCP) *A Dictionary of Nuclear Power and Waste Management with Abbreviations and Acronyms.* Foo-Sun Lau. Letchworth, England: Research Studies Press, Ltd., 1987.

(NVT) *Naval Terminology.* NWP3. Rev. B. U.S. Department of the Navy. Office of the Chief of Naval Operations, 1980. [Use of source began in 1974]
   Includes a section on definitions of naval terminology.

(OA) *Ocran's Acronyms: A Dictionary of Abbreviations and Acronyms Used in Scientific and Technical Writing.* By Emanuel Benjamin Ocran. London, England: Routledge & Kegan Paul Ltd., 1978.

(OAG) *Official Airline Guide Worldwide Edition.* Oak Brook, IL: Official Airlines Guide, Inc., 1984. [Use of source began in 1975]

(OCD) *Oxford Classical Dictionary.* 2nd ed. Edited by N.G. Hammond and H.H. Scullard. London, England: Oxford University Press, 1970.

(OCLC) *OCLC Participating Institutions Arranged by OCLC Symbol.* Dublin, OH: OCLC, 1981.

(ODBW) *The Oxford Dictionary for the Business World.* New York, NY: Oxford University Press, Inc., 1993.

(OICC) *Abbreviations and Acronyms.* Des Moines, IA: Iowa State Occupational Information Coordinating Committee, 1986.

(OLDSS) *Online Database Search Services Directory.* 2nd ed. Edited by Doris Morris Maxfield. Detroit, MI: Gale Research, 1988.
   Provides detailed descriptions of the online information retrieval services offered by libraries, private information firms, and other organizations in the United States and Canada. Entries include name and address, telephone number, and key contact, as well as online systems accessed, frequently searched databases, and access hardware.

(OPSA) *"Official Postal Service Abbreviations."* <http://www.usps.gov/ncsc/lookups/abbr_suffix.txt> (17 December 1996).

(OSI) *OSI Standards and Acronyms.* 3rd ed. Compiled by Adrian V. Stokes. United Kingdom: Stokes, 1991.

(PAZ) *Parenting A to Z.* By Irene M. Franck and David M. Brownstone. New York, NY: HarperCollins Publishers, Inc., 1996.

(PCM) *PC Magazine.* New York, NY: Ziff-Davis Publishing Co., 1997. [Use of source began in 1987]

(PD)   *Political Dissent: An International Guide to Dissident, Extra-Parliamentary, Guerrilla and Illegal Political Movements*. A Keesing's Reference Publication. Compiled by Henry W. Degenhardt. Edited by Alan J. Day. Harlow, Essex, England: Longman Group, 1983.
        Includes the history and aims of approximately 1,000 organizations, with details of their leaderships.

(PDAA) *Pugh's Dictionary of Acronyms and Abbreviations: Abbreviations in Management, Technology and Information Science*. 5th ed. By Eric Pugh. Chicago, IL: American Library Association, 1987.

(PGP)   *Peterson's Graduate Programs in the Humanities, Arts & Social Sciences*. 31st ed. Princeton, NJ: Peterson's 1997.

(PPE)   *Political Parties of Europe*. 2 vols. Edited by Vincent E. McHale. The Greenwood Historical Encyclopedia of the World's Political Parties. Westport, CT: Greenwood Press, 1983.
        One of a series of reference guides to the world's significant political parties. Each guide provides concise histories of the political parties of a region and attempts to detail the evolution of ideology, changes in organization, membership, leadership, and each party's impact upon society.

(PPW)   *Political Parties of the World*. 2nd ed. A Keesing's Reference Publication. Compiled and edited by Alan J. Day and Henry W. Degenhardt. Harlow, Essex, England: Longman Group, 1980, 1984.
        Covers historical development, structure, leadership, membership, policy, publications, and international affiliations. For each country, an overview of the current political situation and constitutional structure is provided.

(PS)   *Popular Science*. New York, NY: Times-Mirror Magazines, Inc., 1995. [Use of source began in 1992]

(RCD)   *Research Centers Directory*. 19th ed. Edited by Thomas J. Cichonski. Detroit, MI: Gale Research, 1994. [Use of source began in 1986]
        A guide to university-related and other nonprofit research organizations carrying on research in agriculture, astronomy and space sciences, behavioral and social sciences, computers and mathematics, engineering and technology, physical and earth sciences and regional and area studies.

(RDA)   *Army RD and A Magazine*. Alexandria, VA: Development, Engineering, and Acquisition Directorate, Army Materiel Command, 1997. [Use of source began in 1979]

(ROG)   *Dictionary of Abbreviations*. By Walter T. Rogers. London, England: George Allen & Co. Ltd., 1913; reprinted by Gale Research, 1969.

(SAA)   *Space-Age Acronyms, Abbreviations and Designations*. 2nd ed. By Reta C. Moser. New York, NY: IFI/Plenum, 1969.

(SAG)   *Stock Abbreviation Guide*. New York, NY: Associated Press. [Database]

(SDI)   *Report to the Congress on the Strategic Defense Initiative*. U.S. Department of Defense. Strategic Defense Initiative Organization, April, 1987.

(SEIS) *Seismograph Station Codes and Characteristics*. Geological Survey. Circular 791. By Barbara B. Poppe, Debbi A. Naab, and John S. Derr. Washington, DC: U.S. Department of the Interior, 1978.

(SLS)   *World Guide to Scientific Associations and Learned Societies/Internationales Verzeichnis Wissenschaftlicher Verbande und Gesellschaften.* 4th ed. Edited by Barbara Verrel. New York, NY: K.G. Saur, 1984.
> A directory of more than 22,000 societies and associations in all fields of science, culture, and technology. International, national, and regional organizations from 150 countries are also included.

(SPSG)   *Security Owner's Stock Guide.* New York, NY: Standard & Poor's Corp., 1994. [Use of source began in 1988]

(SRA)   *State and Regional Associations of the United States.* 9th ed. Edited by Tracey E. Chirico, Buck J. Downs and John J. Russell. Washington, DC: Columbia Books, Inc., 1997.

(SSD)   *Space Station Directory and Program Guide.* Edited and compiled by Melinda Gipson, Jane Glass, and Mary Linden. Arlington, VA: Pasha Publications Inc., 1988.

(TAG)   *Transportation Acronym Guide 1996.* U.S. Department of Transportation. Washington, DC: Bureau of Transportation Statistics, 1996.

(TDOB)   *The Dictionary of Banking.* By Charles J. Woelfel. Chicago, IL: Probus Publishing Company, 1994.

(TEL)   *Telephony's Dictionary.* 2nd ed. By Graham Langley. Chicago, IL: Telephony Publishing Corp., 1986.
> Includes definitions for U.S. and international telecommunications terms. Ten appendices.

(TNIG)   *Telecommunications, Networking and Internet Glossary.* By George S. Machovec. Chicago, IL: American Library Association, 1993.

(TOCD)   *The Official Catholic Directory 1997.* New Providence, NJ: P.J. Kenedy & Sons, 1997.

(TSPED)   *Trade Shows and Professional Exhibits Directory.* 2nd ed. Edited by Robert J. Elster. Detroit, MI: Gale Research, 1987. [Use of source began in 1986]
> A guide to scheduled events providing commercial display facilities including conferences, conventions, meetings, fairs and festivals, etc. Entries include name of trade show; sponsor name, address, and telephone number; attendance figures; principal exhibits; special features; publications; and date and location of shows.

(TSSD)   *Telecommunications Systems and Services Directory.* 4th ed. (and supplement). Edited by John Krol. Detroit, MI: Gale Research, 1989. [Use of source began in 1985]
> An international descriptive guide to telecommunications organizations, systems, and services. Entries include name and address, telephone number, chief official, and a description of the purposes, technical structure, and background of the service or system.

(USDC)   *"Glossary of Acronyms".* U.S. Department of Commerce.
<http://www.pmel.noaa.gov/pubs/acronym.html> (5 March 1997).

(USGC)   *"U.S. Government Commonly Used Abbreviations and Acronyms."*
<http://www.fed.gov/hptext/infohwy/gov_acro.html> (5 March 1997).

(VNW)   *Words of the Vietnam War.* By Gregory R. Clark. Jefferson, NC: McFarland and Co., Inc., 1990.

(VRA)   *VRA Special Bulletin. No. 2, 1987: Standard Abbreviaitons for Image Descriptions for Use in Fine Arts Visual Resources Collections.* Compiled by Nancy S. Schuller. Austin, TX: Visual Resources Association, 1987.

(WDAA)   *Webster's New World Dictionary of Acronyms and Abbreviations.* By Auriel Douglas and Michael Strumpf. New York, NY: Webster's New World, 1989.

(WDMC)   *Webster's New World Dictionary of Media and Communications.* Revised and updated ed. By Richard Weiner. New York, NY: Webster's New World, 1996.

(WGA)   *Webster's Guide to Abbreviations.* Springfield, MA: Merriam-Webster Inc., 1985.

(WYGK)   *HR Words you Gotta Know!* By William R. Tracey. New York: AMACOM, 1994.

Reverse
Acronyms, Initialisms &
Abbreviations Dictionary

G-O

G
By Meaning

G. Allan Roeher Institute, Downsview, Ontario [*Library symbol National Library of Canada*] (NLC) .... OTNIMR
G and A Factor .... GF
G. & A. N. Scott Ltd., Rochdale, United Kingdom [*Library symbol Library of Congress*] (LCLS) .... UkRoS
G & B Automated Equipment Ltd. [*Toronto Stock Exchange symbol*] .... GB
G & B Aviation Ltd. [*British ICAO designator*] (FAAC) .... TNG
G & K Services CI'A' [*NASDAQ symbol*] (TTSB) .... GKSRA
G & K Services, Inc. [*Associated Press*] (SAG) .... G & K
G & L Realty Corp. [*Associated Press*] (SAG) .... G & L Rty
G & L Realty Corp. [*NYSE symbol*] (SPSG) .... GLR
G. D. Searle & Co., Inc., Skokie, IL [*Library symbol Library of Congress*] (LCLS) .... ISkS
G. D. Searle & Co., Inc., Skokie, IL [*OCLC symbol*] (OCLC) .... JAP
G. D. Searle Co. of Canada Ltd., Oakville, Ontario [*Library symbol National Library of Canada*] (BIB) .... OOAKG
G. G. Drayton Club (EA) .... GGDC
G. J. Orphan & Associates [*Telecommunications service*] (TSSD) .... GJOA
G. K. Chesterton Society (EA) .... GKCS
G. K. Hall Co. [*Publisher*] .... GKH
G. W. Hewlett Senior High School, Hewlett, NY [*Library symbol*] [*Library of Congress*] (LCLS) .... NHewSH
GA Financial [*AMEX symbol*] (TTSB) .... GAF
GA Financial, Inc. [*Associated Press*] (SAG) .... GA Fncl
GA Financial, Inc. [*AMEX symbol*] (SAG) .... GAF
GAB Bancorp [*NASDAQ symbol*] (SAG) .... GABC
Gabbart [*Ship's rigging*] (ROG) .... GT
Gabbett. Abridgment of Statute Law [*1812-18*] [*A publication*] (ILCA) .... Gabb Stat L
Gabbett's Criminal Law [*A publication*] (DLA) .... Gabb Cr Law
Gabbs [*Nevada*] [*Seismograph station code, US Geological Survey Closed*] (SEIS) .... GAB
Gabbs, NV [*Location identifier FAA*] (FAAL) .... GAB
Gabbs Resources Ltd. [*Vancouver Stock Exchange symbol*] .... GAB
Gabelli Conv Securities Fd [*NYSE symbol*] (TTSB) .... GCV
Gabelli Convertible Securities Fund [*Associated Press*] (SAG) .... GabCv
Gabelli Convertible Securities Fund [*NYSE symbol*] (SAG) .... GCV
Gabelli Equity Trust [*Associated Press*] (SAG) .... Gabeli
Gabelli Equity Trust, Inc. [*NYSE symbol*] (SPSG) .... GAB
Gabelli Equity Trust, Inc. [*Associated Press*] (SAG) .... Gabelli
Gabelli Global Multimedia Tr [*NYSE symbol*] (TTSB) .... GGT
Gabelli Global Multimedia Trust, Inc. [*Associated Press*] (SAG) .... GabGloM
Gabelli Global Multimedia Trust, Inc. [*Associated Press*] (SAG) .... GabGM
Gabelli Global Multimedia Trust, Inc. [*NYSE symbol*] (SAG) .... GGT
Gabes [*Tunisia*] [*ICAO location identifier*] (ICLI) .... DTTG
Gabexate Mesilate [*A proteolytic enzyme inhibitor*] .... GM
Gabiro [*Rwanda*] [*ICAO location identifier*] (ICLI) .... HRYO
Gable .... GAB
Gable House Estates Ltd. [*British*] .... GHE
Gable Mountain [*Washington*] [*Seismograph station code, US Geological Survey*] (SEIS) .... GBL
Gables Residential Trust [*Associated Press*] (SAG) .... GablRsd
Gables Residential Trust [*NYSE symbol*] (SPSG) .... GBP
Gabon [*MARC geographic area code Library of Congress*] (LCCP) .... f-go--
Gabon [*ANSI two-letter standard code*] (CNC) .... GA
Gabon [*ANSI three-letter standard code*] (CNC) .... GAB
Gabon [*MARC country of publication code Library of Congress*] (LCCP) .... go
Gabon-Air-Transport [*ICAO designator*] (FAAC) .... GRT
Gaborone [*Botswana*] [*Airport symbol*] (OAG) .... GBE
Gaborone Civil Aviation Headquarters [*Botswana*] [*ICAO location identifier*] (ICLI) .... FBHQ
Gaborone Notwane [*Botswana*] [*ICAO location identifier*] (ICLI) .... FBNW
Gaborone/Sir Seretse Khama [*Botswana*] [*ICAO location identifier*] (ICLI) .... FBSK
Gabriel Dumont Institute, Regina, Saskatchewan [*Library symbol National Library of Canada*] (NLC) .... SRGD
Gabriel Garcia Moreno Memorial Association (EA) .... GGMMA
Gabriel Gonzalez Videla [*Antarctica*] [*Seismograph station code, US Geological Survey Closed*] (SEIS) .... GGV
Gabriel Marcel Society (EA) .... GMS
Gabriel Resources, Inc. [*Vancouver Stock Exchange symbol*] .... GBI
Gabriel Richard Institute (EA) .... GRI
Gabu [*Guinea-Bissau*] [*ICAO location identifier*] (ICLI) .... GGGB
Gabungan SB2 Non-Vakcentral [*Federation of Non-Affiliated Trade Unions*] [*Indonesia*] .... GASERBUN
Gabungan Serikat Buruh Indonesia [*Federation of Indonesian Trade Unions*] .... GSBI

Gabungan Serikat Buruh Islam Indonesia [*Federation of Indonesian Islamic Trade Unions*] .... GASBIINDO
Gach Saran [*Iran*] [*Airport symbol*] (AD) .... GAS
Gachsaran [*Iran*] [*ICAO location identifier*] (ICLI) .... OIAH
Gadabout (DSUE) .... GAD
Gader [*Afghanistan*] [*ICAO location identifier*] (ICLI) .... OAGD
Gadjah Mada University [*Indonesia*] .... GMU
Gadolinium [*Chemical element*] .... Gd
Gadolinium Aluminium Perovskite [*Inorganic chemistry*] .... GAP
Gadolinium, Gallium, Garnet G3
Gadolinium, Gallium, Garnet [*Also, G3*] [*Substrate for magnetic film*] .... GGG
Gadolinium Iron Garnet (IEEE) .... GdIG
Gadolinium Molybdate .... GMO
Gadolinium, Scandium, Gallium, Garnet (MCD) .... GSGG
Gadsden [*Alabama*] [*Airport symbol*] (OAG) .... GAD
Gadsden, AL [*Location identifier FAA*] (FAAL) .... DWY
Gadsden, AL [*AM radio station call letters*] .... WAAX
Gadsden, AL [*AM radio station call letters*] .... WGAD
Gadsden, AL [*AM radio station call letters*] .... WMGJ
Gadsden, AL [*Television station call letters*] .... WNAL
Gadsden, AL [*FM radio station call letters*] .... WQEN
Gadsden, AL [*FM radio station call letters*] .... WSGN
Gadsden, AL [*Television station call letters*] .... WTJP
Gadsden Purchase Refund Group [*Formerly, PRI*] [*Defunct*] (EA) .... GPRG
Gadsden State Junior College, Gadsden, AL [*Library symbol Library of Congress*] (LCLS) .... AGS
Gadzooks, Inc. [*NASDAQ symbol*] (SAG) .... GADZ
Gadzooks, Inc. [*Associated Press*] (SAG) .... Gadzks
Gaede Diffusion Pump .... GDP
Gaelic [*Language, etc.*] .... GAEL
Gaelic Athletic Association .... GAA
Gaelic Athletic Association of Australia .... GAA
Gaelic Football and Hurling Association [*Australia*] .... GFHA
Gaelic (Scots) [*MARC language code Library of Congress*] (LCCP) .... gae
Gaffney, SC [*FM radio station call letters*] .... WAGI
Gaffney, SC [*AM radio station call letters*] .... WEAC
Gaffney, SC [*AM radio station call letters*] .... WFGN
Gaffney, SC [*FM radio station call letters*] .... WYFG
Gaffsail [*Ship's rigging*] (ROG) .... GFSL
Gafsa [*Tunisia*] [*ICAO location identifier*] (ICLI) .... DTTF
Gage (IAA) .... G
Gage .... GA
Gage [*Oklahoma*] [*ICAO location identifier*] (ICLI) .... KGAG
Gage Educational Publishing Ltd., Agincourt, ON, Canada [*Library symbol Library of Congress*] (LCLS) .... CaOAgG
Gage Educational Publishing Ltd., Agincourt, Ontario [*Library symbol National Library of Canada*] (NLC) .... OAGG
Gage, OK [*Location identifier FAA*] (FAAL) .... GAG
Gages Documentation Scheduling Committee .... GADSCO
Gagnef [*Sweden ICAO location identifier*] (ICLI) .... ESVG
Gagnoa [*Ivory Coast*] [*ICAO location identifier*] (ICLI) .... DIGA
Gagnoa [*Ivory Coast*] [*Airport symbol*] (OAG) .... GGN
Gagnoa [*Ivory Coast*] [*Airport symbol*] (AD) .... GGQ
Gagnon [*Canada*] [*Airport symbol*] (OAG) .... YGA
Gagnon [*Quebec*] [*Airport symbol*] (AD) .... YNK
Gagnon, PQ [*ICAO location identifier*] (ICLI) .... CYGA
Gahanna, OH [*FM radio station call letters*] .... WCVO
Gaii Institutionum Commentarii [*Gaius' Institutes*] [*A publication*] (DLA) .... Gaii
Gail Borden Public Library, Elgin, IL [*Library symbol Library of Congress*] (LCLS) .... IElg
Gaillac/Lisle Sur Tarn [*France ICAO location identifier*] (ICLI) .... LFDG
Gaily (ABBR) .... GY
Gain (IDOE) .... A
Gain .... G
Gain (NASA) .... GN
Gain Adjuster Adapter .... GAA
Gain Band Merit .... GBM
Gain Bandwidth (DEN) .... GB
Gain Bandwidth .... GBW
Gain Control .... GC
Gain Control Amplifier .... GCA
Gain Control Driver (CET) .... GCD
Gain Control Pulse (IAA) .... GCP
Gain Control Range .... GCR
Gain Factor [*Computer science*] .... GF
Gain Guided LASER (IAA) .... GGL

Gain of Antenna (IEEE) ... GA
Gain Time Constant (MCD) ... GTC
Gain Time Control ... GTC
Gain-Bandwidth Product ... GBP
Gained by Inventory (DNAB) ... GBI
Gained Output Ratio (IEEE) ... GOR
Gainesville [*Florida*] [*Airport symbol*] ... GNV
Gainesville [*Georgia*] [*Airport symbol*] (AD) ... GVL
Gainesville [*Florida*] [*ICAO location identifier*] (ICLI) ... KGNV
Gainesville, FL [*AM radio station call letters*] ... WAJD
Gainesville, FL [*Television station call letters*] ... WCJB
Gainesville, FL [*AM radio station call letters*] ... WGGG
Gainesville, FL [*FM radio station call letters*] ... WJLF
Gainesville, FL [*AM radio station call letters*] ... WLUS
Gainesville, FL [*AM radio station call letters*] ... WRUF
Gainesville, FL [*FM radio station call letters*] ... WRUF-FM
Gainesville, FL [*FM radio station call letters*] ... WUFT
Gainesville, FL [*Television station call letters*] ... WUFT-TV
Gainesville, FL [*AM radio station call letters*] ... WWLO
Gainesville, FL [*FM radio station call letters*] ... WYFB
Gainesville, FL [*FM radio station call letters*] ... WYGC
Gainesville, FL [*FM radio station call letters*] ... WYKS
Gainesville, GA [*Location identifier FAA*] (FAAL) ... FKV
Gainesville, GA [*Location identifier FAA*] (FAAL) ... GVL
Gainesville, GA [*FM radio station call letters*] ... WBCX
Gainesville, GA [*AM radio station call letters*] ... WDUN
Gainesville, GA [*FM radio station call letters*] ... WFOX
Gainesville, GA [*AM radio station call letters*] ... WGGA
Gainesville, GA [*AM radio station call letters*] ... WLBA
Gainesville, GA [*FM radio station call letters*] ... WYAY
Gainesville Junior College [*Later, Cooke County Junior College*] [*Texas*] ... GJC
Gainesville Junior College, Gainesville, GA [*Library symbol*] [*Library of Congress*] (LCLS) ... GGaC
Gainesville Midland Railroad Co. [*AAR code*] ... GM
Gainesville, MO [*FM radio station call letters*] ... KMAC
Gainesville Public Library, Gainesville, FL [*Library symbol Library of Congress*] (LCLS) ... FG
Gainesville, TX [*Location identifier FAA*] (FAAL) ... GLE
Gainesville, TX [*FM radio station call letters*] ... KDGE
Gainesville, TX [*FM radio station call letters*] (RBYB) ... KECS
Gainesville, TX [*AM radio station call letters*] ... KGAF
Gaining Command Program (MCD) ... GCP
Gaining Inventory Managers (AFM) ... GIM
Gaining Major Command [*Military*] (AFM) ... GMAJCOM
Gaining Motor Air Command (MCD) ... GMAC
Gainsco, Inc. [*Associated Press*] (SAG) ... Gainsco
Gainsco, Inc. [*AMEX symbol*] (SPSG) ... GNA
Gait Training [*Orthopedics*] (DAVI) ... GT
Gaithersburg, MD [*Location identifier FAA*] (FAAL) ... GAI
Gaithersburg, MD [*AM radio station call letters*] ... WMET
Gaius Caligula [*of Suetonius*] [*Classical studies*] (OCD) ... Calig
Gaius Gracchus [*of Plutarch*] [*Classical studies*] (OCD) ... G Gracch
Gaius' Institutes [*A publication*] (DLA) ... Gaius
Gaius' Institutes [*A publication*] (DLA) ... Gaius Inst
Gaius, Institutiones [*Second century AD*] [*Classical studies*] (OCD) ... Gai Inst
Gakona, AK [*Location identifier FAA*] (FAAL) ... GAK
Gal/Guy Fridays [*Classified advertising*] ... G/G/FRIS
Gal Oya [*Ceylon*] [*Airport symbol*] (AD) ... GOY
Gala Law [*Scotland*] [*Seismograph station code, US Geological Survey*] (SEIS) ... EGL
Galactic (KSC) ... GAL
Galactic Center ... GC
Galactic Center Lobe ... GCL
Galactic Center Transient [*Astronomy*] ... GCT
Galactic Cosmic Radiation [*or Ray*] ... GCR
Galactic Cosmic Ray Particle ... GCRP
Galactic Hitchhiker's Guild (EA) ... GHG
Galactic Jupiter Probe [*NASA*] ... GJP
Galactic Latitude [*Astronomy*] (BARN) ... b
Galactic Magnetic Field ... GMF
Galactic Plane [*Astronomy*] ... GP
Galactic Probe ... GP
Galactic Radiation and Background (MCD) ... GRAB
Galactic Radiation Experiment Background Satellite [*Navy transit satellite*] ... GREB
Galactic Radio Wave ... GRW
[*The*] **Galactic Society** (EA) ... TGS
Galacticomm Custom Device Interface [*Galacticomm, Inc.*] [*Telecommunications*] ... GCDI
Galactocerebroside [*Biochemistry*] ... GalC
Galactocerebroside [*Biochemistry*] ... GC
Galactokinase [*Also, GALK*] [*An enzyme*] ... GAK
Galactokinase [*Also, GAK*] [*An enzyme*] ... GALK
Galactorrhea-Amenorrhea Syndrome [*Medicine*] (DMAA) ... GAS
Galactosamine [*Biochemistry*] ... GalN
Galactose [*A sugar*] ... Gal
Galactose Elimination Capacity ... GEC
Galactose Oxidase [*An enzyme*] ... GO
Galactose Phosphate Uridyl Transferase [*An enzyme*] (MAE) ... GPUT
Galactose-1-Phosphate [*Organic chemistry*] (DAVI) ... gal-1-P
Galactose-Binding Protein [*Biochemistry*] ... GBP
Galactosemic Allele [*Genetics*] (DAVI) ... Gt^G
Galactosemic Fibroblasts [*Medicine*] ... GSF
Galactosidase Beta (DMAA) ... GLB
Galactosyl [*Biochemistry*] (DAVI) ... GAL
Galactosylceramidase [*An enzyme*] ... GALC
Galactosyltransferase [*An enzyme*] ... GT
Galactosyltransferase Isoenzyme II [*An enzyme*] (DAVI) ... GT II
Galactotransferase [*Cell strain deficient in galactose-1-phosphate uridyltransferase*] ... GALT
Galadi [*Ethiopia*] [*ICAO location identifier*] (ICLI) ... HAGL
GalaGen, Inc. [*Associated Press*] (SAG) ... GalaGen
GalaGen, Inc. [*NASDAQ symbol*] (SAG) ... GGEN
GalaGen Inc. [*NASDAQ symbol*] (TTSB) ... GGEN
Galahad Public Library, Alberta [*Library symbol National Library of Canada*] (NLC) ... AG
Galapagos (Baltra) [*Ecuador*] [*ICAO location identifier*] (ICLI) ... SEGS
Galapagos Islands [*Ecuador*] [*Seismograph station code, US Geological Survey*] (SEIS) ... GIE
Galapagos Islands [*Ecuador*] [*Airport symbol*] (OAG) ... GPS
Galapagos Islands [*MARC geographic area code Library of Congress*] (LCCP) ... pogg--
Galapagos Rift Zone [*Marine science*] (MSC) ... GRZ
Galapagos Spreading Center [*Oceanography*] ... GSC
Galatians [*New Testament book*] ... GA
Galatians [*New Testament book*] ... Ga
Galatians [*New Testament book*] ... Gal
Galatians [*New Testament book*] (BJA) ... Gl
Galatic Radiation and Background ... GRAB
Galax/Hillsville, VA [*Location identifier FAA*] (FAAL) ... HLX
Galax, VA [*AM radio station call letters*] ... WBOB
Galax, VA [*FM radio station call letters*] ... WBRF
Galaxy ... GALXY
Galaxy Airways Ltd. [*Nigeria*] [*ICAO designator*] (FAAC) ... GXY
Galaxy Books [*Oxford University Press*] ... GB
Galaxy Cablevision Ltd. [*Associated Press*] (SAG) ... GalxCbl
Galaxy Cablevision Ltd. [*AMEX symbol*] (SPSG) ... GTV
Galaxy Cablevision L.P. [*AMEX symbol*] (TTSB) ... GTV
Galaxy Foods [*NASDAQ symbol*] (TTSB) ... GALX
Galaxy Foods Co. [*NASDAQ symbol*] (SAG) ... GALX
Galaxy Foods Co. [*Associated Press*] (SAG) ... GlxyFd
Galaxy Industry Ltd. [*Vancouver Stock Exchange symbol*] ... GXY
Galaxy Minerals, Inc. [*Toronto Stock Exchange symbol*] ... GLY
Galaxy Patrol Fan Club (EA) ... GPFC
Galbanum [*Agum*] [*Pharmacology*] (ROG) ... GALB
Galbraith and Meek's Reports [*9-12 Florida*] [*A publication*] (DLA) ... Galb & M
Galbraith and Meek's Reports [*9-12 Florida*] [*A publication*] (DLA) ... Galb & M (Fla)
Galbraith Lake, AK [*Location identifier FAA*] (FAAL) ... GBH
Galbraith Lake Camp, AK [*Location identifier FAA*] (FAAL) ... LCP
Galbraith's Reports [*9-11 Florida*] [*A publication*] (DLA) ... Galb
Galbraith's Reports [*9-12 Florida*] [*A publication*] (DLA) ... Galbraith
Galcaio [*Somalia*] [*ICAO location identifier*] (ICLI) ... HCMR
Gale [*Meteorology*] ... G
Gale and Davison's English Queen's Bench Reports [*1841-43*] [*A publication*] (DLA) ... G & D
Gale and Davison's English Queen's Bench Reports [*1841-43*] [*A publication*] (DLA) ... Gal & Dav
Gale and Davison's English Queen's Bench Reports [*1841-43*] [*A publication*] (DLA) ... Gale & D
Gale and Davison's English Queen's Bench Reports [*1841-43*] [*A publication*] (DLA) ... Gale & D (Eng)
Gale and Davison's English Queen's Bench Reports [*1841-43*] [*A publication*] (DLA) ... Gale & Dav
Gale and Whatley [*later, Gale*] **on Easements** [*A publication*] (ILCA) ... G & Wh Eas
Gale and Whatley [*later, Gale*] **on Easements** [*A publication*] (ILCA) ... Gale & Wh Eas
Gale and Whatley [*later, Gale*] **on Easements** [*A publication*] (DLA) ... Gale & Whatley Easem
Gale Auto Annual [*A publication*] ... GAA
Gale Book of Averages [*A publication*] ... GBOA
Gale Directory of International Publications [*A publication*] ... GDIP
Gale Directory of Publications [*Later, GDPBM*] [*A publication*] ... GDP
Gale Directory of Publications and Broadcast Media [*Formerly, GDP*] [*A publication*] ... GDPBM
Gale Encyclopedia of Multicultural America [*A publication*] ... GEMA
Gale Environmental Almanac [*A publication*] ... GAE
Gale Environmental Almanac [*A publication*] ... GEA
Gale Environmental Sourcebook [*A publication*] ... GES
Gale Global Access [*Also, GGAEA*] ... GGA
Gale Global Access, Encyclopedia of Associations [*Also, GGA*] ... GGAEA
Gale Information Guide Library [*Publication series*] ... GIGL
Gale International Directory of Publications [*A publication*] ... GIDP
Gale on Easements [*A publication*] (DLA) ... Gale
Gale on Easements [*A publication*] (ILCA) ... Gale Eas
Gale Research Co. [*Later, GRI*] ... GRC
Gale Research Co., Detroit, MI [*Library symbol Library of Congress*] (LCLS) ... MiDG
Gale Research, Inc. ... GRI
Gale Research International Ltd. ... GRIL
Galela [*Indonesia*] [*Airport symbol*] (OAG) ... GLX
Galela/Gamarmalamo [*Indonesia*] [*ICAO location identifier*] (ICLI) ... WAMA
Galen [*Second century AD*] [*Classical studies*] (OCD) ... Gal
Galena [*Alaska*] [*Airport symbol*] (OAG) ... GAL
Galena [*Alaska*] [*ICAO location identifier*] (ICLI) ... PAGA
Galena Air Services, Inc. [*ICAO designator*] (FAAC) ... GAS
Galena, AK [*Location identifier FAA*] (FAAL) ... BZP
Galena, AK [*AM radio station call letters*] ... KIYU
Galena, IL [*FM radio station call letters*] ... WJOD
Galerazamba [*Colombia*] [*Seismograph station code, US Geological Survey*] (SEIS) ... GAL

Galerias de Arte y Salas de Exposiciones [Ministerio de Cultura] [Spain Information service or system] (CRD) .... GALE
Galerie d'Art et Centre Culturel, Universite de Sherbrooke, Quebec [Library symbol National Library of Canada] (NLC) .... QSHERUA
Galeries Lafayette [Department store] [Paris, France] ..... GL
Gales and Seaton's Register of Debates in Congress [1824-37] [A publication] (DLA) .... Reg Deb
Gales and Seaton's Register of Debates in Congress [1824-37] [A publication] (DLA) .... Reg Deb (G & S)
Gale's Business Directory [A publication] .... GBD
Gale's English Exchequer Reports [A publication] (DLA) .... G
Gale's English Exchequer Reports [A publication] (DLA) .... Gale
Gale's Literary Index [CD-ROM] .... GLI
Gale's New Forest Decisions [England] [A publication] (DLA) .... Gale
Gale's Statutes [A publication] (DLA) .... Gale Stat
Gale's Statutes [A publication] (DLA) .... Gale's St
Galesburg [Illinois] [Airport symbol] (OAG) .... GBG
Galesburg, IL [FM radio station call letters] .... WAAG
Galesburg, IL [AM radio station call letters] .... WAIK
Galesburg, IL [FM radio station call letters] .... WGBQ
Galesburg, IL [AM radio station call letters] .... WGIL
Galesburg, IL [FM radio station call letters] .... WVKC
Galesburg Memorial Library, Galesburg, MI [Library symbol Library of Congress] (LCLS) .... MiGal
Galesburg Public Library, Galesburg, IL [Library symbol Library of Congress] (LCLS) .... IG
Galey & Lord, Inc. [Associated Press] (SAG) .... GaleyL
Galey & Lord, Inc. [NYSE symbol] (SAG) .... GNL
Galiceno Horse Breeders Association (EA) .... GHBA
Galien Township Public Library, Galien, MI [Library symbol Library of Congress] (LCLS) .... MiGali
Galilean Baptist Mission (EA) .... GBM
Galilean Resources Corp. [Vancouver Stock Exchange symbol] .... GIN
Galileo [Unit of acceleration] .... gal
Galileo [NASA] .... GLL
Galileo Electro-Optics [NASDAQ symbol] (TTSB) .... GAEO
Galileo Electro-Optics Corp. [NASDAQ symbol] (NQ) .... GAEO
Galileo Electro-Optics Corp. [Associated Press] (SAG) .... Galileo
Galileo Number .... Ga
Galileo Probe Mass Spectrometer .... GPMS
Galinhas [Guinea-Bissau] [ICAO location identifier] (ICLI) .... GGGA
Galinsoga Mosaic Virus [Plant pathology] .... GAMV
Galinsoga Mosaic Virus .... GMV
Galion [Ohio] [Airport symbol] (OAG) .... GQQ
Galion, OH [FM radio station call letters] .... WQLX
Galit Resource Corp. [Vancouver Stock Exchange symbol] .... GIC
Gall Bladder [or a patient with an affliction of this organ] [Medicine] .... GB
Gall Bladder Series [Radiography] .... GBS
Gall Bladder Visualization [Medicine] .... GBviz
Galla [MARC language code Library of Congress] (LCCP) .... gal
Gallae [Nut Galls] [Pharmacology] (ROG) .... GALL
Gallagher [Arthur J.] & Co. [NYSE symbol] (SPSG) .... AJG
Gallagher [Arthur J.] & Co. [Associated Press] (SAG) .... Gallagr
Gallagher & Kennedy, P.A., Phoenix, AZ [Library symbol] [Library of Congress] (LCLS) .... AzPhGK
Gallagher Explorations Ltd. [Vancouver Stock Exchange symbol] .... GGR
Gallahad Petroleum [Vancouver Stock Exchange symbol] .... GPL
Gallant Gold Mines Ltd. [Vancouver Stock Exchange symbol] .... GAG
Gallard-Schlesinger [Chemical manufacturing corporation] .... G-S
Gallatin, MO [FM radio station call letters] .... KGOZ
Gallatin, TN [FM radio station call letters] .... WGFX
Gallatin, TN [AM radio station call letters] .... WHIN
Gallatin, TN [FM radio station call letters] .... WMRO
Gallatin, TN [FM radio station call letters] .... WVCP
Gallatin, TN [AM radio station call letters] (RBYB) .... WYXE
Gallaudet College, Kendall Demonstration School, Washington, DC [Library symbol Library of Congress] (LCLS) .... DGC-K
Gallaudet College, Kendall Demonstration School, Washington, DC [OCLC symbol] (OCLC) .... GQK
Gallaudet College, Model Secondary School for the Deaf, Washington, DC [Library symbol Library of Congress] (LCLS) .... DGC-M
Gallaudet College, Montessori School, Washington, DC [OCLC symbol] (OCLC) .... GQM
Gallaudet College, Washington, DC [Library symbol Library of Congress] (LCLS) .... DGC
Gallaudet College, Washington, DC [OCLC symbol] (OCLC) .... GQG
Gallaudet Encyclopedia of Deaf People and Deafness [A publication] .... GEDPD
Gallaudet Information Retrieval Service .... GIRS
Gallaudet on International Law [A publication] (DLA) .... Gall Int L
Gallaudet Research Institute [Gallaudet College] [Research center] (RCD) .... GRI
Gallaudet University (GAGS) .... Gallaudet U
Gallbladder Disease [Gastroenterology] (DAVI) .... GBD
Gallbladder Patient .... GP
Gallbladder Stone [Medicine] .... GBS
Galleon [Spanish vessel] (DS) .... GI
Gallery .... GAL
Gallery (MSA) .... GALL
Gallery (VRA) .... gall
Gallery (ROG) .... GALLY
Gallery .... GLLRY
Gallery of History [NASDAQ symbol] (TTSB) .... HIST
Gallery of History, Inc. [Associated Press] (SAG) .... GallHist
Gallery of History, Inc. [NASDAQ symbol] (SAG) .... HIST
Gallery of Living Catholic Authors [Defunct] (EA) .... GLCA

Gallery Stratford, Ontario [Library symbol National Library of Canada] (NLC) .... OSTAG
Galley (MSA) .... GALY
Galley .... GY
Galley Proof (ADA) .... GP
Galley-Yarn [Crooked] [Slang British] (DSUE) .... GY
Gallia County District Library, Gallipolis, OH [Library symbol Library of Congress] (LCLS) .... OGalG
Galliano, LA [FM radio station call letters] (RBYB) .... WTIX-FM
Gallic .... GA
Gallic Acid Equivalent [Wine analysis] .... GAE
Gallic Aviation [France ICAO designator] (FAAC) .... GLI
Gallick's Reports (French Criminal Cases) [A publication] (DLA) .... Gall Cr Cas
Galliot [Ship's rigging] (ROG) .... G
Gallipoli Society in the United States of America (EA) .... GSUSA
Gallipolis, OH [Location identifier FAA] (FAAL) .... GAS
Gallipolis, OH [AM radio station call letters] .... WJEH
Gallipolis, OH [AM radio station call letters] .... WMGG
Gallison's United States Circuit Court Reports [A publication] (DLA) .... Gal
Gallison's United States Circuit Court Reports [A publication] (DLA) .... Gall
Gallison's United States Circuit Court Reports [A publication] (DLA) .... Gall CCR
Gallison's United States Circuit Court Reports [A publication] (DLA) .... Gallison
Gallison's United States Circuit Court Reports [A publication] (DLA) .... Gallison's Rep
Gallium [Chemical element] .... Ga
Gallium Aluminum Arsenide (SSD) .... GaAlAs
Gallium Arsenide [Semiconductor] .... GaA
Gallium Arsenide [Semiconductor] (IEEE) .... GaAs
Gallium Arsenide [Phosphide Semiconductor] .... GAASD
Gallium Arsenide [Semiconductor] .... GAS
Gallium Arsenide Diode .... GAD
Gallium Arsenide Field-Effect Transistor [Electronics] (LAIN) .... GaAs FET
Gallium Arsenide Field-Effect Transistor (MCD) .... GAFET
Gallium Arsenide Field-Effect Transistor .... GASFET
Gallium Arsenide Illuminator System .... GAIS
Gallium Arsenide Integrated Circuit [Computer chip] .... GAIC
Gallium Arsenide LASER .... GAL
Gallium Arsenide Microwave Diode .... GAMD
Gallium Arsenide Phosphide [Semiconductor] (IEEE) .... GaAsP
Gallium Arsenide Phosphide Photodiode .... Ga-PD
Gallium Experiment .... GALLEX
Gallium Photo Diode .... GDP
Gallium Substituted Yttrium Iron Garnet .... GAYIG
Gallivare [Sweden ICAO location identifier] (ICLI) .... ESNG
Gallivare [Sweden] [Airport symbol] (OAG) .... GEV
Gallon (AAG) .... GAL
Gallon .... gal
Gallon (ODBW) .... gal
Gallon (ODBW) .... gall
Gallon .... GALL
Gallon (MCD) .... GL
Gallon Capacity (WDAA) .... GAL CAP
Gallons of Fuel ["Energy equivalent" abbreviation - biomass agriculture and conversion] [Fuel chemistry] .... GAL
Gallons per Acre per Day [Irrigation] .... GPAD
Gallons per Capita .... GPC
Gallons per Capita per Day .... GPCD
Gallons per Day .... GPD
Gallons per Flush [Plumbing] .... GPF
Gallons per Foot per Day .... GAL/(FT D)
Gallons per Horsepower-Hour .... GAL/(HP H)
Gallons per Hour (MCD) .... GAL/H
Gallons per Hour .... GPH
Gallons per Mile .... GPM
Gallons Per Mile Ratio [DOE] (TAG) .... GPMR
Gallons per Minute .... G/M
Gallons per Minute .... GAL/MIN
Gallons per Minute (IAA) .... GALLSMIN
Gallons per Minute .... GPM
Gallons per Second .... G/S
Gallons per Second .... GAL/S
Gallons per Second .... GPS
Gallons per Square-Foot per Day .... GAL/(FT^2 D)
Gallons per Square-Foot per Day .... GFD
Gallons per Ton .... GPT
Gallop [Cardiology] (DAVI) .... G
Gallop [Music] (ROG) .... GAL
Galloping Acronyms Save Paper .... GASP
Galloping Gourmet [TV program] .... GG
Galloping Pattern Memory .... GALPAT
Galloway [District in Scotland] (ROG) .... GALL
Galloway Boy's Ranch School, Onamia, MN [Library symbol] [Library of Congress] (LCLS) .... MnOnG
Galloway Cattle Society of America (EA) .... GCSA
Gallup [Diocesan abbreviation] [New Mexico] (TOCD) .... GLP
Gallup [New Mexico] [Airport symbol] (OAG) .... GUP
Gallup, NM [FM radio station call letters] (RBYB) .... KFMQ-FM
Gallup, NM [AM radio station call letters] .... KGAK
Gallup, NM [FM radio station call letters] .... KGLP
Gallup, NM [FM radio station call letters] .... KGLX
Gallup, NM [FM radio station call letters] .... KKJI
Gallup, NM [FM radio station call letters] .... KKOR
Gallup, NM [Television station call letters] .... KOFT
Gallup, NM [FM radio station call letters] .... KXXI
Gallup, NM [AM radio station call letters] .... KYVA

Gallup Poll ... GP
Gallup Public Library, Gallup, NM [*OCLC symbol*] (OCLC) ... GAL
Gallup Public Library, Gallup, NM [*Library symbol Library of Congress*] (LCLS) ... NmG
Gallups Island Radio Association (EA) ... GIRA
Gallus-adeno-like [*Avian virus*] ... GAL
Galois Field [*Mathematics*] (IAA) ... GF
Galoob (Lewis) Toys [*NYSE symbol*] (TTSB) ... GAL
Galoob [*Lewis*] **Toys, Inc.** [*NYSE symbol*] (SPSG) ... GAL
Galoob [*Lewis*] **Toys, Inc.** [*Associated Press*] (SAG) ... Galob
Galoob [*Lewis*] **Toys, Inc.** [*Associated Press*] (SAG) ... Galoob
Galoya/Amparai [*Sri Lanka*] [*ICAO location identifier*] (ICLI) ... VCCG
Galpin Society (EA) ... GS
Galt Collegiate Institute, Cambridge, ON, Canada [*Library symbol Library of Congress*] (LCLS) ... CaOGalC
Galt Collegiate Institute, Cambridge, Ontario [*Library symbol National Library of Canada*] (NLC) ... OGAC
Galtaco, Inc. [*Toronto Stock Exchange symbol*] ... GMI
Galva, IL [*FM radio station call letters*] (RBYB) ... WHHK
Galva Township Library, Galva, IL [*Library symbol Library of Congress*] (LCLS) ... IGal
Galva Township Public Library, Galva, IL [*OCLC symbol*] (OCLC) ... ISK
Galvanic [*or Galvanized*] ... GALV
Galvanic Skin Potential [*Physiology*] ... GSP
Galvanic Skin Resistance [*Physiology*] (DAVI) ... GSR
Galvanic Skin Response [*or Reflex*] [*Physiology*] ... GSR
Galvanic Stimulation Rate [*Physiology*] ... GSR
Galvanised Tank Manufacturers' Association [*British*] (BI) ... GTMA
Galvanized (VRA) ... galv
Galvanized [*Metallurgy*] ... GI
Galvanized [*Technical drawings*] ... GV
Galvanized Aircraft ... GAC
Galvanized and Dipped Metal (IAA) ... GAD
Galvanized Corrugated [*Metal industry*] ... GC
Galvanized Improved Plow [*Steel*] ... GIP
Galvanized Iron (ADA) ... gal
Galvanized Iron ... GALVI
Galvanized Iron ... GI
Galvanized or Tinned [*Freight*] ... GALV TND
Galvanized Pipe [*Technical drawings*] ... GP
Galvanized Plain [*Metal industry*] ... GP
Galvanized Steel ... GALVS
Galvanized Steel [*Telecommunications*] ... GS
Galvanized Steel Fastenings ... GF
Galvanized Steel Sheet [*Technical drawings*] ... GSS
Galvanized Steel Strand [*Telecommunications*] (TEL) ... GSS
Galvanized Steel Wire (IAA) ... GSW
Galvanized Steel Wire Rope ... GSWR
Galvanized Ware Manufacturers Council (EA) ... GWMC
Galvanized Wrought Iron (ADA) ... GWI
Galvanizers Association [*British*] (EAIO) ... GA
Galvanizing ... GLVNZNG
Galvannealed ... GALVND
Galvanocutaneous Reaction ... GCR
Galvanomagnetic Method (IAA) ... GMM
Galvanometer ... GALV
Galvanometer ... GALVNM
Galvanometer [*An instrument for detecting and measuring an electric current*] (WDMC) ... galvo
Galvanometer-Mirror Lightbeam ... GML
Galvasay [*Former USSR Seismograph station code, US Geological Survey Closed*] (SEIS) ... GAY
Galveston [*Texas*] ... GALV
Galveston [*Texas*] [*Airport symbol*] (OAG) ... GLS
Galveston Community College, Galveston, TX [*Library symbol Library of Congress*] (LCLS) ... TxGC
Galveston Cotton Exchange and Board of Trade (EA) ... GCEBT
Galveston, Houston & Henderson Railroad Co. [*AAR code*] ... GHH
Galveston Orientation and Amnesia Test [*Medicine*] (DMAA) ... GOAT
Galveston Resources Ltd. [*Toronto Stock Exchange symbol Vancouver Stock Exchange symbol*] ... GAL
Galveston/Scholes Field [*Texas*] [*ICAO location identifier*] (ICLI) ... KGLS
Galveston, TX [*AM radio station call letters*] ... KGBC
Galveston, TX [*AM radio station call letters*] ... KHCB
Galveston, TX [*Television station call letters*] ... KLTJ
Galveston, TX [*FM radio station call letters*] (RBYB) ... KLTP-FM
Galveston, TX [*FM radio station call letters*] ... KQQK
Galveston, TX [*FM radio station call letters*] ... KRTX
Galveston, TX [*Television station call letters*] ... KTMD
Galveston, TX [*Location identifier FAA*] (FAAL) ... SHS
Galveston Wharves [*AAR code*] ... GWF
Galveston-Houston [*Diocesan abbreviation*] [*Texas*] (TOCD) ... GAL
Galvo-Drive Amplifier ... GDA
Galway [*County in Ireland*] (ROG) ... GAL
Galway [*County in Ireland*] ... GALW
Galway [*County in Ireland*] (ROG) ... GWAY
Galway [*Ireland*] [*Airport symbol*] ... GWY
Gam Financial [*NASDAQ symbol*] (TTSB) ... GFIN
Gama Aviation Ltd. [*British ICAO designator*] (FAAC) ... GMA
Gamair Ltd. [*Gambia*] [*ICAO designator*] (FAAC) ... KBS
Gam-Anon International Service Office (EA) ... GAISO
Gamba [*Gabon*] [*Airport symbol*] (OAG) ... GAX
Gambcrest Enterprises Ltd. [*Gambia*] [*ICAO designator*] (FAAC) ... GEL
Gambela [*Ethiopia*] [*Airport symbol*] (OAG) ... GMB
Gambell [*Alaska*] [*Airport symbol*] (OAG) ... GAM
Gambella [*Ethiopia*] [*ICAO location identifier*] (ICLI) ... HAGM
Gambia [*Aircraft nationality and registration mark*] (FAAC) ... C5
Gambia [*MARC geographic area code Library of Congress*] (LCCP) ... f-gm--
Gambia [*Country in West Africa*] (ROG) ... G
Gambia ... GAM
Gambia [*ANSI two-letter standard code*] (CNC) ... GM
Gambia [*MARC country of publication code Library of Congress*] (LCCP) ... gm
Gambia [*ANSI three-letter standard code*] (CNC) ... GMB
Gambia Air Shuttle [*ICAO designator*] (AD) ... GO
Gambia Air Shuttle Ltd. [*ICAO designator*] (FAAC) ... GSH
Gambia Airways [*ICAO designator*] (FAAC) ... GAW
Gambia Labour Union ... GLU
Gambia News Agency (EY) ... GAMNA
Gambia People's Party [*Political party*] (EY) ... GPP
Gambia Regiment [*British military*] (DMA) ... GR
Gambian Socialist Revolutionary Party [*Political party*] (PD) ... GSRP
Gambier Island [*French Polynesia*] [*Airport symbol*] (OAG) ... GMR
Gambier, OH [*FM radio station call letters*] ... WKCO
Gamble and Barlow's Digest [*Ireland*] [*A publication*] (DLA) ... Gamb & Barl
Gamblers Anonymous (EA) ... GA
Gambling and Betting Addiction ... GABA
Gambling Chip Collectors Association (EA) ... GCCA
Gamboa's Introduction to Philippine Law [*A publication*] (DLA) ... Gamboa
Gamboa's Introduction to Philippine Law [*A publication*] (DLA) ... Gamboa Philippine Law
Gambogia [*Gamboge*] [*Pharmacology*] (ROG) ... GAMBOG
Gamboma [*Congo*] [*ICAO location identifier*] (ICLI) ... FCOG
Gamboma [*Congo*] [*Airport symbol*] (AD) ... GMM
Gambro [*A.B.*], **Inc.** [*NASDAQ symbol*] (NQ) ... GAMB
Gambro [*A. B.*], **Inc.** [*Associated Press*] (SAG) ... Gambro
Game ... G
Game Conservancy [*British*] ... GC
Game Conservation International (EA) ... GAMECOIN
Game Financial Corp. [*Associated Press*] (SAG) ... GameFn
Game Financial Corp. [*NASDAQ symbol*] (SAG) ... GFIN
Game Fishing Association of Australia (EERA) ... GFAA
Game Manufacturers Association (EA) ... GAMA
Game Manufacturers Association (EA) ... GMA
Game Meat Processors of Australia ... GMPA
Game on Urban Transport System [*Kins Developments Ltd.*] [*Software package*] (NCC) ... GUTS
Game Oriented Activities for Learning (AIE) ... GOAL
Game Reserve [*State*] (EERA) ... GR
Game Theory ... GT
Game Winning [*Baseball*] ... GW
Gamekeepers' Association of the United Kingdom (BI) ... GAUK
Gameness (DSUE) ... GAM
Games Abroad [*Baseball*] ... GA
Games Ahead [*Baseball*] ... GA
Games at Home [*Baseball*] ... GAH
Games Behind [*Baseball*] ... GB
Games behind Leader [*Baseball*] ... GBL
Games by Position [*Baseball*] ... G by Pos
Games Finished [*Baseball*] ... GF
Games of the New Emerging Forces [*A counter-attraction to the Olympic Games*] [*Indonesia*] ... GANEFO
Games Played [*Sports statistics*] ... G
Games Played [*Sports statistics*] ... GP
Games [*or Matches*] **Played** [*Sports statistics*] ... P
Games Started [*Baseball*] ... GS
Games Taken Out [*Baseball*] ... TO
Gamete Intrafallopian Transfer [*Fertilization technique*] ... GIFT
Gamete Shedding Substance [*Endocrinology*] ... GSS
Gametek, Inc. [*NASDAQ symbol*] (SAG) ... GAME
Gametek, Inc. [*Associated Press*] (SAG) ... Gametek
Game-Tying Goals [*Hockey*] ... GTG
Gamewardens of Vietnam Association (EA) ... GVA
Game-Winning Goals [*Hockey*] ... GWG
Game-Winning Run Batted In [*Baseball*] ... GW-RBI
Gamin Resources, Inc. [*Vancouver Stock Exchange symbol*] ... GAM
Gaming Corporation of America [*Associated Press*] (SAG) ... Gamng
Gaming Corporation of America [*Associated Press*] (SAG) ... GamngCp
Gaming Corp. of America [*NASDAQ symbol*] (SAG) ... GCAM
Gaming Entertainment Television [*Interactive-gambling TV station*] (ECON) ... GET
Gaming Lottery [*NASDAQ symbol*] (TTSB) ... GLCCF
Gaming Lottery Corp. [*Associated Press*] (SAG) ... GamLott
Gaming Lottery Corp. [*NASDAQ symbol*] (SAG) ... GLCCF
Gaming, Random Interfacing, and Problem Structuring (PDAA) ... GRIPS
Gaming World International, Inc. [*Associated Press*] (SAG) ... GamingW
Gaming World International, Inc. [*Associated Press*] (SAG) ... GamW
Gaming World International, Inc. [*NASDAQ symbol*] (SAG) ... GWLD
Gaming World Intl. [*NASDAQ symbol*] (TTSB) ... GWLD
Gaming World Intl. Wrrt'A' [*NASDAQ symbol*] (TTSB) ... GWLDW
Gamma ... G
Gamma (NASA) ... GAM
Gamma [*Subgroup of IgG*] [*Immunology*] ... Gm
Gamma [*Third letter of the Greek alphabet*] (DAVI) ... GM
Gamma Absorption and Radiation Detection Tracking (IAA) ... GARDTRAK
Gamma Activation Materials Assay System [*Mobile laboratory*] ... GAMAS
Gamma Atomic Radiation Detector ... GARD
Gamma Benzene Hexachloride [*Also, BHC, HCH*] [*Insecticide*] ... GBH
Gamma Biologicals [*AMEX symbol*] (TTSB) ... GBL
Gamma Biologicals, Inc. ... Gam
Gamma Biologicals, Inc. [*Associated Press*] (SAG) ... GamaB
Gamma Biologicals, Inc. [*AMEX symbol*] (SPSG) ... GBL

Gamma Cosmic Ray [*Geophysics*] ... GCR
Gamma Dose Detector System ... GDDS
Gamma Energy Analysis [*Nuclear energy*] (NUCP) ... GEA
Gamma Eta Gamma [*Fraternity*] ... GEG
Gamma European System (IAA) ... GES
Gamma Globulin [*Medicine*] ... GG
Gamma Hydroxy Butyrate [*Steroid*] ... GHB
Gamma Incomplete [*Chemistry*] (IAA) ... GAMIC
Gamma Inspection of Grain Integrity ... GIGI
Gamma Large Array Space Telescope [*A collaboration of physics groups*] ... GLAST
Gamma LINAC Instrumentation ... GLI
Gamma Radiation Source ... GRS
Gamma Radiation Spectrometer ... GRS
Gamma Ray [*or Roentgen*] ... GR
Gamma Ray Ablation Sensing System (SAA) ... GRASS
Gamma Ray Amplification ... GRA
Gamma Ray Amplification by Stimulated Emission of Radiation ... GRASER
Gamma Ray and Neutrino Detector Experiment [*Proposed*] [*University of California, Irvine*] ... GRANDE
Gamma Ray Astronomy Observatory ... GRAO
Gamma Ray Astronomy with Spectroscopy and Positioning ... GRASP
Gamma Ray Astrophysics New Imaging Telescope ... GRANITE
Gamma Ray Attenuation Porosity Evaluator ... GRAPE
Gamma Ray Burst ... GRB
Gamma Ray Burst Detector [*Instrumentation*] ... GBD
Gamma Ray Experiment ... GRE
Gamma Ray Explorer (NASA) ... GRE
Gamma Ray Imaging Telescope System ... GRITS
Gamma Ray Inspection ... GRI
Gamma Ray LASER (NATG) ... GASER
Gamma Ray LASER (MCD) ... GRASER
Gamma Ray Logs (IEEE) ... GAMLOGS
Gamma Ray Observatory [*NASA*] (EGAO) ... GRO
Gamma Ray Projector ... GRP
Gamma Ray Spectrometer ... GRS
Gamma Ray Spectrometric Equipment ... GRSE
Gamma Ray Spectrum ... GRS
Gamma Ray Telescope ... GRT
Gamma Ray Tube ... GRT
Gamma Scintillation System (MSA) ... GSS
Gamma Sigma Sigma (EA) ... GSS
Gamma Technology Research Irradiator (ADA) ... GATRI
Gamma Thermometer Interest Group [*Nuclear energy*] (NRCH) ... GTIG
Gamma Theta Upsilon (EA) ... GTU
Gamma-Activated Factor [*Biochemistry*] ... GAF
Gamma-Activated Site [*Biochemistry*] ... GAS
Gamma-Amino-Beta-Hydroxybutyric Acid (DMAA) ... GABOA
Gamma-Amino-beta-hydroxybutyric Acid [*Pharmacology*] ... GABOB
Gamma-Aminobutyric Acid [*Biochemistry*] ... GABA
Gamma-Aminobutyric Acid Alpha Receptor (DMAA) ... GABRA
Gamma-Aminobutyric Acid Transaminase [*Pharmacology*] (DMAA) ... GABA-T
Gamma-Butyrolactone [*Organic chemistry*] ... GBL
Gamma-Electron-Muon [*Particle detector*] ... GEM
Gamma-Glutamyl Carboxylase (DMAA) ... GGC
Gamma-Glutamyl Transpeptidase [*Also, GGT, GT*] [*An enzyme*] (DAVI) ... GGT
Gamma-Glutamyl Transpeptidase [*Also, GGT, GT*] [*An enzyme*] ... GGTP
Gamma-Glutamyltransferase [*Also, GGTP, GT*] [*An enzyme*] ... GGT
Gamma-Glutamyltransferase [*Also, GGT, GGTP*] [*An enzyme*] ... GT
Gamma-Hydroxy-beta-aminobutyric Acid [*Pharmacology*] ... GOBAB
Gamma-Hydroxybutyric Acid [*Organic chemistry*] ... GHB
Gamma-Linoleic Acid [*Organic chemistry*] ... GLA
Gamma-Linolenic Acid ... GLA
Gamma-Ray Imaging Spectrometer ... GRIS
Gamma-Ray Large Area Space [*Proposed, 1996*] ... GLAST
Gamma-Vinyl-GABA [*Biochemistry*] ... GVG
Gammon Theological Seminary, Atlanta, GA [*Library symbol Library of Congress*] (LCLS) ... GAGTh
Gamow-Teller [*Transition*] [*Nuclear physics*] ... GT
Gampel [*Switzerland ICAO location identifier*] (ICLI) ... LSHG
Gamut [*Music*] (ROG) ... G
Gamut [*Music*] (ROG) ... GAM
Gan [*Maldives*] [*ICAO location identifier*] (ICLI) ... VRGN
Ganado High School Library, Ganado, AZ [*Library symbol Library of Congress*] (LCLS) ... AzGaH
Ganado, TX [*FM radio station call letters*] (RBYB) ... KZAM-FM
Gananoque Public Library, Ontario [*Library symbol National Library of Canada*] (NLC) ... OGAN
Ganatra's Criminal Cases [*India*] [*A publication*] (DLA) ... Ganatra
Ganaveh [*Iran*] [*ICAO location identifier*] (ICLI) ... OIBG
Gandajika [*Zaire*] [*ICAO location identifier*] (ICLI) ... FZWC
Gandalf Data Communications Ltd., Ottawa, ON, Canada [*Library symbol Library of Congress*] (LCLS) ... CaOOGDC
Gandalf Data Ltd., Ottawa, Ontario [*Library symbol National Library of Canada*] (NLC) ... OOGDC
Gandalf Technologies [*NASDAQ symbol*] (TTSB) ... GANDF
Gandalf Technologies, Inc. [*Toronto Stock Exchange symbol*] ... GAN
Gandalf Technologies, Inc. [*NASDAQ symbol*] (NQ) ... GANDF
Gandalf Technologies, Inc. [*Associated Press*] (SAG) ... Gandlf
Gander [*Canada*] [*Airport symbol*] (OAG) ... YQX
Gander Automated Air Traffic System ... GAATS
Gander Automated Message Processing System [*ICAO*] (DA) ... GAMPS
Gander Aviation Ltd. [*Canada ICAO designator*] (FAAC) ... GAN
Gander/International, NF [*ICAO location identifier*] (ICLI) ... CYQX
Gander Mountain [*NASDAQ symbol*] (TTSB) ... GNDR
Gander Mountain, Inc. [*Associated Press*] (SAG) ... Gander
Gander Mountain, Inc. [*NASDAQ symbol*] (NQ) ... GNDR
Gander, NF [*AM radio station call letters*] ... CBG
Gander, NF [*AM radio station call letters*] ... CKGA
Gander, NF [*AM radio station call letters*] ... CKXD
Gander, NF [*ICAO location identifier*] (ICLI) ... CZQX
Gander Public Library, Gander, NF, Canada [*Library symbol Library of Congress*] (LCLS) ... CaNfG
Gander Public Library, Newfoundland [*Library symbol National Library of Canada*] (NLC) ... NFG
Ganderkesee-Atlas Aerodrome [*Germany ICAO location identifier*] (ICLI) ... EDWQ
Gandhi Memorial International Foundation (EA) ... GMIF
Gandhi Peace Center (EA) ... GPC
Gandhi Peace Foundation [*India*] (EAIO) ... GPF
Gandhi Society for Human Rights (EA) ... GSHR
Gandulphus [*Flourished, 1160-85*] [*Authority cited in pre-1607 legal work*] (DSA) ... G
Gandulphus [*Flourished, 1160-85*] [*Authority cited in pre-1607 legal work*] (DSA) ... Ga
Gandulphus [*Flourished, 1160-85*] [*Authority cited in pre-1607 legal work*] (DSA) ... Gan
Gandulphus [*Flourished, 1160-85*] [*Authority cited in pre-1607 legal work*] (DSA) ... Gand
Gane Energy Corp. Ltd. [*Toronto Stock Exchange symbol*] ... GNE
Ganes Creek, AK [*Location identifier FAA*] (FAAL) ... GEK
Ganfield [*England*] ... GANF
Gang Punch [*Computer science*] ... GP
Gangaw [*Myanmar*] [*Airport symbol*] (OAG) ... GAW
Gangaw [*Myanmar*] [*ICAO location identifier*] (ICLI) ... VBGG
Ganglion [*Medicine*] ... G
Ganglion [*Medicine*] ... GANG
Ganglion [*or Ganglionic*] [*Neurology*] (DAVI) ... gangl
Ganglion Cell [*Medicine*] ... GC
Ganglion Cell Layer [*Neuroanatomy*] ... GCL
Ganglion Mother Cell [*Cytology*] ... GMC
Ganglion Nodosum [*Neurology*] ... GN
Ganglionic-Blocking Agent [*Medicine*] ... GBA
Gangshan [*China*] [*ICAO location identifier*] (ICLI) ... RCAY
Gannett Co. [*NYSE symbol*] (TTSB) ... GCI
Gannett Co., Inc. [*Associated Press*] (SAG) ... Gannett
Gannett Co., Inc. [*NYSE symbol*] (SPSG) ... GCI
Gannett News Service ... GNS
Gannett Newspaper Foundation ... GNF
Gannett Satellite Information Network ... GANSAT
Gannon University (GAGS) ... Gannon U
Gannon University, Erie, PA [*Library symbol Library of Congress*] (LCLS) ... PErG
Gannon University, Nash Library, Erie, PA [*OCLC symbol*] (OCLC) ... PGU
Gannosu/Brady [*Japan ICAO location identifier*] (ICLI) ... RJFB
Gantos, Inc. [*Associated Press*] (SAG) ... Gantos
Gantos, Inc. [*NASDAQ symbol*] (SAG) ... GTOS
Gantry Test Rack [*Aerospace*] (AAG) ... GTR
Gantt's Digest of Arkansas Statutes [*A publication*] (DLA) ... Gantt Dig
Gantt's Digest of Arkansas Statutes [*A publication*] (DLA) ... Gantts Dig
Ganz [*White Blot*] [*Rorschach*] [*Psychology*] ... G
Ganzer Bogen [*Full Bow*] [*Music*] ... GB
Ganzfeld [*Whole Field*] [*ESP test*] [*German*] ... GZ
Ganzhou [*China*] [*ICAO location identifier*] (ICLI) ... ZSGZ
Ganzlich [*Complete*] [*German*] (BARN) ... ganz
Gao [*Mali*] [*ICAO location identifier*] (ICLI) ... GAGO
Gao [*Mali*] [*Airport symbol*] (OAG) ... GAQ
GAO [*General Accounting Office*] **Atlanta Regional Office, Atlanta, GA** [*OCLC symbol*] (OCLC) ... GAZ
GAO [*General Accounting Office*] **Boston Regional Office, Boston, MA** [*OCLC symbol*] (OCLC) ... GAF
GAO [*General Accounting Office*] **Denver Regional Office, Denver, CO** [*OCLC symbol*] (OCLC) ... GAE
GAO [*General Accounting Office*] **Norfolk Regional Office, Virginia Beach, VA** [*OCLC symbol*] (OCLC) ... GAN
GAO [*General Accounting Office*] **Philadelphia Regional Office, Philadelphia, PA** [*OCLC symbol*] (OCLC) ... GAG
GAO [*General Accounting Office*] **Review and Approval of Accounting Systems Project** (GFGA) ... GRASP
GAO [*General Accounting Office*] **San Francisco Regional Office, San Francisco, CA** [*OCLC symbol*] (OCLC) ... GAR
GAO [*General Accounting Office*] **Seattle Regional Office, Seattle, WA** [*OCLC symbol*] (OCLC) ... GAX
Gaol Delivery [*Legal*] [*British*] (ROG) ... GD
Gaol Delivery Roll (ROG) ... GDR
Gaon (BJA) ... G
Gaoua [*Burkina Faso*] [*ICAO location identifier*] (ICLI) ... DHOG
Gaoual [*Guinea*] [*ICAO location identifier*] (ICLI) ... GUGL
Gaoxiong [*China*] [*ICAO location identifier*] (ICLI) ... RCKH
Gap Conductance (GAAI) ... GAP CON
Gap Detector ... GD
Gap Filler [*RADAR*] ... GF
Gap Filler/Reporting Post ... GFRP
Gap in Cell Cycle [*Cytology*] ... G
Gap, Inc. [*Formerly, Gap Stores, Inc.*] [*Associated Press*] (SAG) ... Gap
Gap, Inc. [*Formerly, Gap Stores, Inc.*] [*NYSE symbol*] (SPSG) ... GPS
Gap Junction [*Cytology*] ... GJ
Gap Media Project [*An association*] (EA) ... GMP
Gap Separation ... GS
Gap/Tallard [*France ICAO location identifier*] (ICLI) ... LFNA
Gap-Filler Control and Reporting Post [*RADAR*] (IAA) ... GFCRP
Gap-Filler Data [*RADAR*] ... GFD

Gap-Filler Input [*RADAR*] ... GFI
Gap-Filler Output [*RADAR*] ... GFO
Gap-Filler RADAR ... GFR
Gap-Filler/Reporting Post [*RADAR*] ... GF/RP
Gap-Filler Satellite [*RADAR*] (NVT) ... GAPSAT
Gap-Filler Satellite Communication System (MCD) ... GAPSATCOM
GAR Memorial Library, West Newbury, MA [*Library symbol Library of Congress*] (LCLS) ... MWn
Gar Wood Society (EA) ... GWS
Garachine [*Panama*] [*Airport symbol*] (OAG) ... GHE
Garage ... G
Garage ... GAR
Garage [*Classified Advertising*] (ADA) ... GRGE
Garage ... GRGE
Garage Door Council (EA) ... GDC
Garage Door Opener (NG) ... GDO
Garage Equipment Association (EAIO) ... GEA
Garage Forecourts [*Public-performance tariff class*] [*British*] ... GF
Garage Keeper's Legal Liability [*Insurance*] ... GKLL
Garaged [*Automotive advertising*] ... GARGD
Garaina [*Papua New Guinea*] [*Airport symbol*] (OAG) ... GAR
Garamond [*Typography*] (DGA) ... GAR
Garamond [*Typography*] (WDAA) ... GARA
Garan, Inc. [*AMEX symbol*] (SPSG) ... GAN
Garan, Inc. [*Associated Press*] (SAG) ... Garan
Garango [*Burkina Faso*] [*ICAO location identifier*] (ICLI) ... DHEN
Garanti Bankasi [*Guarantee Bank*] [*Turkey*] ... GB
Garantie- und Kreditbank [*Guaranty and Credit Bank*] [*Germany*] (EG) ... Garkreba
Garantie- und Kreditbank [*Guaranty and Credit Bank*] [*Germany*] (EG) ... GKB
Garapan-Saipan, MP [*FM radio station call letters*] ... KPXH
Garapan-Saipan, MP [*FM radio station call letters*] ... KPXP
Garapan-Saipan, MP [*FM radio station call letters*] ... KRSI
Garba Tula [*Kenya*] [*ICAO location identifier*] (ICLI) ... HKGT
Garbage (BARN) ... garb
Garbage (MSA) ... GBG
Garbage Collection [*Slang Computer science*] ... GC
Garbage Disposal Unit (ADA) ... GDU
Garbage In, Garbage Out [*Computer science*] ... GIGO
Garbage In Garbage Out [*Computer science*] (ODBW) ... gigo
Garbage Lighter [*Self-propelled*] [*Navy symbol*] ... YG
Garbage Lighter [*Non-self-propelled*] [*Navy symbol*] ... YGN
Garbage: The Independent Environmental Quarterly [*A publication*] (BRI) ... Garbage
Garbage Truck ... GT
Garbell Holdings Ltd. [*Toronto Stock Exchange symbol*] ... GBH
Garbell Research Foundation (MCD) ... GRF
Garberville, CA [*FM radio station call letters*] (RBYB) ... KHUM
Garberville, CA [*FM radio station call letters*] (RBYB) ... KLVG
Garberville, CA [*FM radio station call letters*] ... KMUD
Garberville, CA [*FM radio station call letters*] ... KWEO
Garble (FAAC) ... GRBL
Garbo Industries [*Vancouver Stock Exchange symbol*] ... GRB
Garboard [*Naval architecture*] ... GARBD
Garchy [*France*] [*Seismograph station code, US Geological Survey*] (SEIS) ... GRC
Gardan [*France ICAO aircraft manufacturer identifier*] (ICAO) ... GY
Garde on Evidence [*1830*] [*A publication*] (DLA) ... Gard Ev
Garden (VRA) ... gard
Garden [*Commonly used*] (OPSA) ... GARDEN
Garden [*Commonly used*] (OPSA) ... GARDN
Garden ... GDN
Garden ... GDN
Garden [*Commonly used*] (OPSA) ... GRDEN
Garden (ADA) ... GRDN
Garden Botanika [*NASDAQ symbol*] (TTSB) ... GBOT
Garden Cat Club (EA) ... GCC
Garden Center of Greater Cleveland, Cleveland, OH [*Library symbol Library of Congress*] (LCLS) ... OCIGC
Garden Centers of America (EA) ... GCA
Garden Centres of Australia ... GCA
Garden City [*Kansas*] [*Airport symbol*] (OAG) ... GCK
Garden City [*New York*] [*Airport symbol*] (OAG) ... JHC
Garden City [*Kansas*] [*ICAO location identifier*] (ICLI) ... KGCK
Garden City, GA [*AM radio station call letters*] ... WNMT
Garden City, ID [*FM radio station call letters*] ... KCIX
Garden City Junior High School, Garden City, NY [*Library symbol*] [*Library of Congress*] (LCLS) ... NGcJ
Garden City, KS [*Location identifier FAA*] (FAAL) ... HMB
Garden City, KS [*FM radio station call letters*] ... KANZ
Garden City, KS [*AM radio station call letters*] ... KIUL
Garden City, KS [*FM radio station call letters*] ... KKJQ
Garden City, KS [*Television station call letters*] ... KSNG
Garden City, KS [*Television station call letters*] ... KUPK-TV
Garden City, NY [*FM radio station call letters*] ... WBAU
Garden City, NY [*FM radio station call letters*] ... WDRE
Garden City, NY [*FM radio station call letters*] ... WHPC
Garden City, NY [*Television station call letters*] ... WLIW
Garden City Park School, New Hyde Park, NY [*Library symbol*] [*Library of Congress*] (LCLS) ... NNhpGE
Garden City Public Library, Garden City, ID [*Library symbol*] [*Library of Congress*] (LCLS) ... IdGc
Garden City Public Library, Garden City, MI [*Library symbol Library of Congress*] (LCLS) ... MiGc
Garden City Public Library, Garden City, NY [*Library symbol Library of Congress*] (LCLS) ... NGc
Garden City Senior High School, Garden City, NY [*Library symbol*] [*Library of Congress*] (LCLS) ... NGcSH
[*The*] **Garden City Western Railway Co.** [*AAR code*] ... GCW
Garden Club of America (EA) ... GCA
Garden Club of Australia ... GCA
Garden Fresh Restaurant [*NASDAQ symbol*] (TTSB) ... LTUS
Garden Fresh Restaurant Corp. [*Associated Press*] (SAG) ... GardnFr
Garden Fresh Restaurant Corp. [*NASDAQ symbol*] (SAG) ... LTUS
Garden Grove, CA [*FM radio station call letters*] ... KIKF
Garden Hill Branch, Northumberland County Public Library, Campbellcroft, Ontario [*Library symbol National Library of Canada*] (BIB) ... OCNGH
Garden History Society [*British*] ... GHS
Garden Industry Manufacturers Association [*British*] (DBA) ... GIMA
Garden Industry of America [*Inactive*] (EA) ... GIA
Garden Lake Resources [*Vancouver Stock Exchange symbol*] ... GAR
Garden Point [*Australia Airport symbol*] (OAG) ... GPN
Garden Ridge [*NASDAQ symbol*] (TTSB) ... GRDG
Garden Ridge Corp. [*Associated Press*] (SAG) ... GardnR
Garden Ridge Corp. [*NASDAQ symbol*] (SAG) ... GRDG
Garden Seed Association ... GSA
Garden State Airlines, Inc. [*ICAO designator*] (FAAC) ... GSA
Garden State Bancshares [*Associated Press*] (SAG) ... GardStat
Garden State Bancshares [*NASDAQ symbol*] (SAG) ... GRDN
Garden Supply Dealers National (EA) ... GSDN
Garden Valley District Library, Garden Valley, ID [*Library symbol*] [*Library of Congress*] (LCLS) ... IdGa
Garden Writers Association of America (EA) ... GWAA
Gardener (ROG) ... GARD
Gardener ... GRDNR
[*The*] **Gardeners' Chronicle** [*A publication*] (ROG) ... G CH
Gardenhire's Reports [*14, 15 Missouri*] [*A publication*] (DLA) ... Gardenhire
Gardenia Society of America (EA) ... GSA
Gardenier's New York Reporter [*A publication*] (DLA) ... Gard NY Rep
Gardenier's New York Reporter [*A publication*] (DLA) ... Gard NY Rept
Gardenier's New York Reporter [*A publication*] (DLA) ... Gard NY Rptr
Gardens (BARN) ... Gard
Gardens [*Commonly used*] (OPSA) ... GARDENS
Gardens ... GDNS
Gardens (MCD) ... GDNS
Gardens (DD) ... Gdns
Gardens [*Commonly used*] (OPSA) ... GRDNS
Gardens Elementary School, Pasadena, TX [*Library symbol*] [*Library of Congress*] (LCLS) ... TxPGE
Gardens for All [*Later, National Association for Gardening*] (EA) ... GA
Garde's First Principles of Pleading [*A publication*] (DLA) ... Gard Pl
Gardez [*Afghanistan*] [*ICAO location identifier*] (ICLI) ... OAGZ
Gardiner, ME ... WABK-FM
Gardiner, ME [*AM radio station call letters*] ... WFAU
Gardiner Public Library, Gardiner, ME [*Library symbol Library of Congress*] (LCLS) ... MeGar
Gardiner Resources [*Vancouver Stock Exchange symbol*] ... GER
Gardiners Avenue Elementary School, Levittown, NY [*Library symbol*] [*Library of Congress*] (LCLS) ... NLevGE
Gardner, Carton, and Douglas, Chicago, IL [*Library symbol Library of Congress*] (LCLS) ... ICGCD
Gardner Denver Machinery [*NASDAQ symbol*] (TTSB) ... GDMI
Gardner Denver Machinery, Inc. [*Associated Press*] (SAG) ... GardDen
Gardner Denver Machinery, Inc. [*NASDAQ symbol*] (SAG) ... GDMI
Gardner, MA [*Location identifier FAA*] (FAAL) ... GDM
Gardner, MA [*AM radio station call letters*] ... WGAW
Gardner Museum, Boston, MA [*Library symbol Library of Congress*] (LCLS) ... MBG
Gardner Syndrome [*Medicine*] ... GS
Gardner-Rasheed Feline Sarcoma Virus ... GR-FeSV
Gardner's Books Ltd. [*British*] ... GB
Gardner's Peerage Case, Reported by Le Marchant [*A publication*] (DLA) ... Gardn PC
Gardnerville-Minden, NV [*FM radio station call letters*] ... KGVM
Gardner-Webb College [*Boiling Springs, NC*] ... GWC
Gardner-Webb College, Boiling Springs, NC [*Library symbol Library of Congress*] (LCLS) ... NcBsG
Gardner-Webb College, Boiling Springs, NC [*OCLC symbol*] (OCLC) ... NGW
Gardner-Webb Junior College [*Later, Gardner-Webb College*] [*North Carolina*] ... GWJC
Gardo [*Somalia*] [*Airport symbol*] (OAG) ... GSR
Gardo [*Somalia*] [*ICAO location identifier*] (ICLI) ... HCMG
Garfield County Library, Jordan, MT [*Library symbol*] [*Library of Congress*] (LCLS) ... MtJG
Garfield County Public Library, New Castle, CO [*Library symbol Library of Congress*] (LCLS) ... CoNc
Garfield County System, New Castle, CO [*OCLC symbol*] (OCLC) ... COG
Garfield Elementary School, Brainerd, MN [*Library symbol*] [*Library of Congress*] (LCLS) ... MnBrGE
Garfield Elementary School, Garfield, MN [*Library symbol*] [*Library of Congress*] (LCLS) ... MnGarE
Garfield Elementary School, Houston, TX [*Library symbol*] [*Library of Congress*] (LCLS) ... TxHGfE
Garfield Elementary School, Willmar, MN [*Library symbol*] [*Library of Congress*] (LCLS) ... MnWilGES
Garfield Guardian, Garfield, NJ [*Library symbol Library of Congress*] (LCLS) ... NjGaG
Garfield Memorial Public Library, Clare, MI [*Library symbol Library of Congress*] (LCLS) ... MiCla
Gargarisma [*Gargle*] [*Pharmacy*] ... GARG
Gargarisma [*Gargle*] [*Pharmacy*] (ROG) ... GARGAR

Gargnas [*Sweden ICAO location identifier*] (ICLI) ..... ESUG
Garin Arava (EA) ..... GA
Garissa [*Kenya*] [*Airport symbol*] (OAG) ..... GAS
Garissa [*Kenya*] [*ICAO location identifier*] (ICLI) ..... HKGA
Garland Chrysanthemum Temperate Virus [*Plant pathology*] ..... GCTEV
Garland, TX [*AM radio station call letters*] ..... KPBC
Garland, TX [*Television station call letters*] ..... KUVN
Garlstedt/Clay Kaserne [*Germany ICAO location identifier*] (ICLI) ..... EDOB
Garm [*Former USSR Seismograph station code, US Geological Survey*] (SEIS) ..... GAR
Garment ..... GMT
Garment ..... GRMT
Garment (VRA) ..... grmt
Garment Dyers Guild of America (EA) ..... GDGA
Garment Graphics [*NASDAQ symbol*] (TTSB) ..... GRMN
Garment Graphics, Inc. [*Associated Press*] (SAG) ..... GarG
Garment Graphics, Inc. [*Associated Press*] (SAG) ..... GarmGph
Garment Graphics, Inc. [*NASDAQ symbol*] (SAG) ..... GRMN
Garment Graphics Wrrt'A' [*NASDAQ symbol*] (TTSB) ..... GRMNW
Garment Graphics Wrrt'B' [*NASDAQ symbol*] (TTSB) ..... GRMNZ
Garment Manufacturers' Association [*Australia*] ..... GMA
Garment Salesmen's Guild of New York [*Later, AG*] (EA) ..... GSG
Garments on Hangers [*Shipping*] ..... GOH
Garmersdorf [*Germany ICAO location identifier*] (ICLI) ..... EDZH
Garmisch-Partenkirchen [*Federal Republic of Germany*] [*Seismograph station code, US Geological Survey*] (SEIS) ..... GAP
Garmsar [*Iran*] [*ICAO location identifier*] (ICLI) ..... OIIR
Garnavillo Historical Society, Garnavillo, IA [*Library symbol Library of Congress*] (LCLS) ..... IaGavoHi
Garnavillo, IA [*FM radio station call letters*] ..... KCTN
Garner Leader and Signal and Herald, Garner, IA [*Library symbol Library of Congress*] (LCLS) ..... IaGarL
Garner, NC [*AM radio station call letters*] ..... WRTG
Garner Public Library, Garner, IA [*Library symbol Library of Congress*] (LCLS) ..... IaGar
Garnes Mountain [*Idaho*] [*Seismograph station code, US Geological Survey*] (SEIS) ..... GMI
Garnet Resources [*NASDAQ symbol*] (TTSB) ..... GARN
Garnet Resources Corp. [*NASDAQ symbol*] (NQ) ..... GARN
Garnet Resources Corp. [*Associated Press*] (SAG) ..... Garnet
Garnish [*Automotive engineering*] ..... GARN
Garnish Molding [*Mechanical engineering*] ..... GMLDG
Garnish Public Library, Garnish, NF, Canada [*Library symbol Library of Congress*] (LCLS) ..... CaNfGa
Garnish Public Library, Newfoundland [*Library symbol National Library of Canada*] (NLC) ..... NFGA
Garnishee [*Legal shorthand*] (LWAP) ..... GARNEE
Garnishee Order (DCTA) ..... GARN
Garnishor [*Legal shorthand*] (LWAP) ..... GARNOR
Garnisonsverwendungsfaehig Feld [*Fit for Garrison Duty in the Field*] [*German military - World War II*] ..... GVF
Garnisonsverwendungsfaehig Heimat [*Fit for Garrison Duty in Zone of Interior*] [*German military - World War II*] ..... GVH
Garoua [*Cameroon*] [*ICAO location identifier*] (ICLI) ..... FKKR
Garoua [*Cameroon*] [*Airport symbol*] (OAG) ..... GOU
GARP Activities Office [*Marine science*] (MSC) ..... GAO
GARP [*Global Atmospheric Research Program*] **Atlantic Tropical Experiment** [*National Oceanic and Atmospheric Administration*] ..... GATE
GARP International Sea Trial [*National Science Foundation*] ..... GIST
GARP Operational Control Center [*Marine science*] (MSC) ..... GOCC
Garretson - Elmendorf - Zinov, Architects and Engineers [*San Francisco, CA*] [*Telecommunications service*] (TSSD) ..... GEZ
Garrett Auxiliary Power Division [*Military contractor*] (RDA) ..... GAPD
Garrett Clipper, Garrett, IN [*Library symbol Library of Congress*] (LCLS) ..... InGarC
Garrett Memorial Library, Moulton, IA [*Library symbol Library of Congress*] (LCLS) ..... IaMou
Garrett Public Library, Garrett, IN [*Library symbol Library of Congress*] (LCLS) ..... InGar
Garrett-Evangelical Theological Seminary, Evanston, IL [*Library symbol Library of Congress*] (LCLS) ..... IEG
Garrison (MUGU) ..... GAR
Garrison Adjutant [*Military British*] ..... GA
Garrison Artillery [*British military*] (DMA) ..... GA
Garrison Aviation Ltd. [*Canada ICAO designator*] (FAAC) ..... AHM
Garrison Co. [*British military*] (DMA) ..... GC
Garrison Elementary School, Rockford, IL [*Library symbol*] [*Library of Congress*] (LCLS) ..... IRoGaE
Garrison Engineer [*British military*] (DMA) ..... GE
Garrison Extracts [*Army*] ..... GE
Garrison Hill [*Washington*] [*Seismograph station code, US Geological Survey*] (SEIS) ..... GHW
Garrison, KY [*FM radio station call letters*] ..... WNUU
Garrison Military Police [*British*] ..... GMP
Garrison Orders [*British military*] (DMA) ..... GO
Garrison Quartermaster-Sergeant [*British military*] (DMA) ..... GQMS
Garrison Sergeant-Major [*British*] ..... GSM
Garson Branch, Nickel Centre Public Library, Ontario [*Library symbol National Library of Canada*] (NLC) ..... OGNC
Garter (MSA) ..... GTR
Garter King of Arms ..... GKA
Garter Stitch [*Knitting*] (ADA) ..... GST
Gartner Group, Inc. [*NASDAQ symbol*] (NQ) ..... GART
Gartner Group, Inc. [*Associated Press*] (SAG) ..... Gartner
Gartner Group'A' [*NASDAQ symbol*] (TTSB) ..... GART
Gartner Lee Associates Ltd., Markham, ON, Canada [*Library symbol*] [*Library of Congress*] (LCLS) ..... CaOMaGL
Gartner Lee Associates Ltd., Markham, Ontario [*Library symbol National Library of Canada*] (NLC) ..... OMGL
Garuahi [*Papua New Guinea*] [*Airport symbol*] (OAG) ..... GRH
Garuda Indonesia [*Airline flight code*] (ODBW) ..... GA
Garuda Indonesia PT [*ICAO designator*] (FAAC) ..... GIA
Garuda Indonesian Airways [*ICAO designator*] (AD) ..... GA
Garuda Indonesian Airways Ltd. ..... GIA
Garvan Institute of Medical Research [*Australia*] ..... GIMR
Garvie's Point Museum, Glen Cove, NY [*Library symbol Library of Congress*] (LCLS) ..... NGlcM
Gary [*Diocesan abbreviation*] [*Indiana*] (TOCD) ..... GRY
Gary Community School Corp., Gary, IN [*OCLC symbol*] (OCLC) ..... IGS
Gary Historical and Cultural Society, Gary, IN [*Library symbol Library of Congress*] (LCLS) ..... InGHi
Gary, IN [*Location identifier FAA*] (FAAL) ..... GYY
Gary, IN [*FM radio station call letters*] ..... WGVE
Gary, IN [*AM radio station call letters*] ..... WLTH
Gary, IN [*Television station call letters*] ..... WPWR
Gary, IN [*AM radio station call letters*] ..... WWCA
Gary, IN [*Television station call letters*] ..... WYIN
Gary Morris Fan Club (EA) ..... GMFC
Gary Post-Tribune, Gary, IN [*Library symbol Library of Congress*] (LCLS) ..... InGPT
Gary Public Library, Gary, IN [*OCLC symbol*] (OCLC) ..... IGP
Gary Public Library, Gary, IN [*Library symbol Library of Congress*] (LCLS) ..... InG
Gary School System, Gary, IN [*Library symbol Library of Congress*] (LCLS) ..... InGS
Garyville, LA [*AM radio station call letters*] ..... WCKW
Garza [*Costa Rica*] [*ICAO location identifier*] (ICLI) ..... MRGA
Gas [*Chemistry*] ..... (g)
Gas Acquisition System ..... GAS
Gas Amplification ..... GA
Gas Analysis (NRCH) ..... GA
Gas Analysis Modeling System [*Department of Energy*] (GFGA) ..... GAMS
Gas and Air [*Medicine*] ..... G and A
Gas and Fuel Corp. [*Victoria, Australia*] [*Commercial firm*] ..... GAFCOR
Gas and Fuel Corp. of Victoria [*Australia*] ..... GFCV
Gas and Oxygen [*Medicine*] ..... G & O
Gas Annulus Sizing Program ..... GASP
Gas Anti-Solvent [*Chemical engineering*] ..... GAS
Gas Appliance Engineers Society [*Later, ASGE*] (EA) ..... GAES
Gas Appliance Improvement Network ..... GAIN
Gas Appliance Manufacturers Association (EA) ..... GAMA
Gas Authority of India Ltd. (ECON) ..... GAIL
Gas Bath Heater [*Classified advertising*] (ADA) ..... GBH
Gas Bearing Part ..... GBP
Gas Bearing System (KSC) ..... GBS
Gas Bioassay System [*NASA*] ..... GBS
Gas Centrifuge Enrichment Plant [*Department of Energy*] ..... GCEP
Gas Chromatograph [*or Chromatography*] ..... GC
Gas Chromatograph Intoximeter [*Measure-of-intoxication test for drunk drivers*] ..... GCI
Gas Chromatograph with Electron Capture Detector [*Chemical analysis*] ..... GC/ECD
Gas Chromatography and Mass Spectroscopy ..... GCMS
Gas Chromatography in Biology and Medicine [*British*] ..... GCBM
Gas Chromatography/Infrared ..... GC/IR
Gas Chromatography - Isotope-Ratio Mass Spectrometry [*Chemistry*] ..... GC-IRMS
Gas Chromatography/Low Resolution Mass Spectrometry ..... GC/LRMS
Gas Chromatography/Mass Spectrometry ..... GC/MS
Gas Chromatography plus Fourier Transform Infrared Spectrometry ..... GC/FTIR
Gas Chromatography - Single Ion Current Monitoring (PDAA) ..... GC-SICM
Gas Chromatography with Electron Capture ..... GC-EC
Gas Chromatography with Flame Ionization Detection ..... GC-FID
Gas Chromatography-Nitrogen Phosphorus Detector ..... GC-NPD
Gas City-Mill Township Public Library, Gas City, IN [*Library symbol Library of Congress*] (LCLS) ..... InGc
Gas Cleaning System [*Combustion technology*] ..... GCS
Gas Collection Header (NRCH) ..... GCH
Gas Component Test Stand (MCD) ..... GCTS
Gas Core Nuclear Rocket ..... GCNR
Gas Council [*British*] ..... GC
Gas Council of New South Wales [*Australia*] ..... GCNSW
Gas Cylinder System ..... GCS
Gas Decay Tank (NRCH) ..... GDT
Gas Density Balance [*Medicine*] (DMAA) ..... GDB
Gas Deployed Skirt (MCD) ..... GDS
Gas Discharge Counter ..... GDC
Gas Discharge Display (IAA) ..... GDD
Gas Discharge Gauge ..... GDG
Gas Discharge Lamp ..... GDL
Gas Discharge Tube ..... GDT
Gas Displacement Chromatography ..... GDC
Gas Dragster [*Class of racing cars*] ..... GD
Gas Drainage ..... GD
Gas Dynamic Facility [*Air Force*] ..... GDF
Gas Dynamic LASER ..... GDL
Gas Dynamic Mixing LASER [*Navy*] ..... GDML
Gas Dynamic System ..... GDS
Gas Dynamics Laboratory ..... GDL
Gas Ejection [*Opening*] [*Technical drawings*] ..... GE
Gas, Electric, Telephones [*of GET, Inc., a consumer group*] ..... GET
Gas, Electricity, Water [*Department of Employment*] [*British*] ..... GEW

Gas Energy Management ..... GEM
Gas Engine Management [*Alternative fuel conversion equipment*] ..... GEM
Gas Equipment Manufacturers' Group (IIA) ..... GEM
Gas Evolution Analysis (DICI) ..... GEA
Gas Examiner [*British*] ..... GE
Gas Exchange ..... GEX
Gas Exchange Module [*Cell culture*] ..... GEM
Gas Explosive Simulation Technique [*Air Force*] ..... GEST
Gas Filled (MSA) ..... GF
Gas Filter Correlation [*NASA*] (KSC) ..... GFC
Gas Filter Correlation Radiometer [*NASA*] ..... GFCR
Gas Fission Products Monitor ..... GFPM
Gas Flow Indicator [*NASA*] ..... GFI
Gas Flow Programmer [*Chromatography*] ..... GFP
Gas Flow Radiation Counter [*Nucleonics*] (IAA) ..... GFRC
Gas Frontal Chromatography ..... GFC
Gas Gathering Data File [*Phillips Petroleum*] ..... GGDF
Gas Generator (AAG) ..... GG
Gas Generator Fueled Ramjet (MCD) ..... GGFRJ
Gas Generator Valve (KSC) ..... GGV
Gas High Pressure ..... GHP
Gas Hot Water Service [*Classified advertising*] (ADA) ..... GHWS
Gas Hour Space Velocity [*Chemical engineering*] ..... GHSV
Gas Identification Officer ..... GIO
Gas in Stomach (MAE) ..... GIS
Gas Industries Network Analyzer (PDAA) ..... GINA
Gas Industry Association of Western Australia ..... GIAWA
Gas Industry Salaried Officers' Federation [*Australia*] ..... GISOF
Gas Injection Molding [*Plastic fabrications*] ..... GIM
Gas LASER ..... GL
Gas LASER Discharge Tube ..... GLDT
Gas LASER Tube ..... GLT
Gas Leak Detector ..... GLD
Gas Liquid Phase Transfer Catalysis [*Physical chemistry*] ..... GL-PTC
Gas [*or Grease*] **Lubricated Bearing** ..... GLB
Gas Measurement System ..... GMS
Gas Metal Arc ..... GMA
Gas Metal Arc Cutting [*Welding*] ..... GMAC
Gas Metal Arc Welding ..... GMAW
Gas Metal Arc Welding - Pulsed Arc ..... GMAW-P
Gas Metal Arc Welding - Short Circuiting Arc ..... GMAW-S
Gas Meter ..... GM
Gas Meter Makers' Association [*A union*] [*British*] ..... GMMA
Gas Missile Tube ..... GMT
Gas, Nonpersistent ..... GNP
Gas Oil ..... G
Gas Oil [*Also, G*] [*Petroleum technology*] ..... GO
Gas/Oil Tax Block Summary Record [*IRS*] ..... G/OTBSR
Gas/Oil Tax Program Summary Record [*IRS*] ..... G/OTPSR
Gas Operated (ADA) ..... GO
Gas or Air [*Transportation*] ..... GA
Gas, Oxygen, Ether [*Anesthesiology*] ..... GOE
Gas Particulate Filter Unit (MCD) ..... GPFU
Gas, Persistent ..... GP
Gas Phase Titration ..... GPT
Gas Plasma Display (HGAA) ..... GASP
Gas Plasma Monitor ..... GPM
Gas Power Exchange ..... GPE
Gas Power Transfer (IEEE) ..... GPT
Gas Power Unit (MUGU) ..... GPU
Gas Pressure (MUGU) ..... GP
Gas Pressure Activator (MCD) ..... GPA
Gas Pressure Bending System ..... GPBS
Gas Processors Association (EA) ..... GPA
Gas Processors Suppliers Association (EA) ..... GPSA
Gas Projectile (MCD) ..... GP
Gas Projectile, Extended Range (MCD) ..... GPER
Gas Proof (AABC) ..... GPF
Gas Properties [*NASA computer program*] ..... GASP
Gas Proportional Scintillation Counters [*Spectroscopy*] ..... GPSC
Gas Pump Unit ..... GPU
Gas Quenching Process ..... GQP
Gas Ratio ..... GR
Gas Recycle Hydrogenation [*Petroleum engineering*] ..... GRH
Gas Release and Swelling Subroutine (PDAA) ..... GRASS
Gas Research Institute (EA) ..... GRI
Gas Research Institute, Chicago, IL [*Library symbol*] [*Library of Congress*] (LCLS) ..... ICGR
Gas Research Institute Digest [*Acronym is used as title of publication*] [*A publication*] ..... GRID
Gas Sampling Valve ..... GSV
Gas Scintillation Proportional Counter [*Instrumentation*] ..... GSPC
Gas Servicer (MCD) ..... GS
Gas Servicer Unit (MCD) ..... GSU
Gas Shutoff [*NFPA pre-fire planning symbol*] (NFPA) ..... G
Gas Source Seismic Section Profiler ..... GASSP
Gas Space Heater ..... GSH
Gas Sulfide [*Process for obtaining heavy water*] ..... GS
Gas Surge Header [*Nuclear energy*] (NRCH) ..... GSH
Gas Surge Tank [*Nuclear energy*] (NRCH) ..... GST
Gas Tight ..... GT
Gas Tight High Pressure (IEEE) ..... GTH
Gas to Methanol [*Process developed by ICI*] ..... GTM
Gas Toggle Valve ..... GTV
Gas Toxicity Analysis ..... GTA
Gas Transport LASER ..... GTL
Gas Tube (IAA) ..... GT
Gas Tungsten Arc ..... GTA
Gas Tungsten Arc Cutting [*Welding*] ..... GTAC
Gas Tungsten Arc Weld [*or Welding*] ..... GTAW
Gas Tungsten Arc Welding - Pulsed Arc ..... GTAW-P
Gas Turbine ..... GT
Gas Turbine ..... GTRB
Gas Turbine and Engine Type Designation System ..... GTETDS
Gas Turbine Combined Cycle [*Energy technology*] ..... GTCC
Gas Turbine Compressor ..... GTC
Gas Turbine Compressor and Power Unit (NG) ..... GTCP
Gas Turbine Engine ..... GTE
Gas Turbine Engine-Driven [*Generator*] (RDA) ..... GTED
Gas Turbine Generator ..... GTG
Gas Turbine Generator Set (AABC) ..... GTGS
Gas Turbine High-Temperature Gas-Cooled Reactor [*Nuclear energy*] (NRCH) ..... GT-HTGR
Gas Turbine Laboratory [*MIT*] (MCD) ..... GTL
Gas Turbine Modular Helium Reactor [*Nuclear reactor*] ..... GTMHR
Gas Turbine Power System ..... GTPS
Gas Turbine Power Unit (NG) ..... GTP
Gas Turbine Power Unit (MCD) ..... GTPU
Gas Turbine Ship (IIA) ..... GTS
Gas Turbine Starter (MCD) ..... GTS
Gas Turbine Starting System (NG) ..... GTSS
Gas Turbine Systems Technician, Electrical, Chief [*Navy rating*] (DNAB) ..... GSEC
Gas Turbine Systems Technician, Electrical, Fireman [*Navy rating*] (DNAB) ..... GSEFN
Gas Turbine Systems Technician, Electrical, Fireman Apprentice [*Navy rating*] (DNAB) ..... GSEFA
Gas Turbine Systems Technician, Electrical, First Class [*Navy rating*] (DNAB) GSE1
Gas Turbine Systems Technician, Electrical, Second Class [*Navy rating*] (DNAB) GSE2
Gas Turbine Systems Technician, Electrical, Third Class [*Navy rating*] (DNAB) GSE3
Gas Turbine Systems Technician, Master Chief [*Navy rating*] (DNAB) ..... GSCM
Gas Turbine Systems Technician, Mechanical, Chief [*Navy rating*] (DNAB) ..... GSMC
Gas Turbine Systems Technician, Mechanical, Fireman [*Navy rating*] (DNAB) ..... GSMFN
Gas Turbine Systems Technician, Mechanical, Fireman Apprentice [*Navy rating*] (DNAB) ..... GSMFA
Gas Turbine Systems Technician, Mechanical, First Class [*Navy rating*] (DNAB) GSM1
Gas Turbine Systems Technician, Mechanical, Second Class [*Navy rating*] (DNAB) GSM2
Gas Turbine Systems Technician, Mechanical, Third Class [*Navy rating*] (DNAB) GSM3
Gas Turbine Systems Technician, Senior Chief [*Navy rating*] (DNAB) ..... GSCS
Gas Turbine Test Facility ..... GTTF
Gas Under Pressure ..... GUP
Gas, Undercarriage, Mixture, and Prop [*Checkout procedure*] ..... GUMP
Gas Vent Institute [*Defunct*] (EA) ..... GVI
Gas Ventilation [*Medicine*] (DMAA) ..... GV
Gas Volume [*in Gas Phase*] (DAVI) V
Gas Volume per Unit Time [*Medicine*] (DAVI) V
Gas Wall Oven and Hot Plate [*Classified advertising*] (ADA) ..... GWO & HP
Gas Weld ..... GAS/W
Gas-Analysis Laboratory [*NASA*] ..... GAL
Gas-Analysis Sample Container [*Apollo*] [*NASA*] ..... GASC
Gasar [*Afghanistan*] [*ICAO location identifier*] (ICLI) ..... OAGS
Gas-Assisted Thermal-Enhanced Oil Recovery ..... GATEOR
Gas-Cooled Breeder Reactor [*Nuclear energy*] (NRCH) ..... GBR
Gas-Cooled Breeder Reactor [*Nuclear energy*] ..... GCBR
Gas-Cooled Fast Breeder Reactor ..... GCFBR
Gas-Cooled Fast Reactor ..... GCFR
Gas-Cooled Fast Reactor Experiment (IEEE) ..... GCFRE
Gas-Cooled, Heavy-Water-Moderated Reactor [*Nuclear energy*] (NRCH) ..... GCHWR
Gas-Cooled Loop [*Nuclear energy*] (NRCH) ..... GCL
Gas-Cooled Reactor ..... GCR
Gas-Cooled Reactor Associates (NRCH) ..... GCRA
Gas-Cooled Reactor Experiment (NRCH) ..... GCRE
Gas-Cooled Unit ..... GCU
Gascoyne Junction [*Australia Airport symbol Obsolete*] (OAG) ..... GSC
Gas-Driven Gyro Inertial Platform [*Aerospace*] (AAG) ..... GDGIP
Gas-Driven Intensifier Pump (MCD) ..... GDI
Gaseous and Liquid Effluent [*Nuclear energy*] (NRCH) ..... GALE
Gaseous Axisymmetric Jet ..... GAJ
Gaseous Diffusion Plant [*Nuclear energy*] (NUCP) ..... GDP
Gaseous Discharge Principle ..... GDP
Gaseous Ejection (KSC) ..... GEJ
Gaseous Electronics Conference ..... GEC
Gaseous Emissions Data System [*Environmental Protection Agency*] (GFGA) ..... GEDS
Gaseous Flow Measuring System ..... GFMS
Gaseous Flowmeter Calibration Stand ..... GFCS
Gaseous Helium (KSC) ..... GHE
Gaseous Hydrogen (KSC) ..... GH
Gaseous Hydrogen [*NASA*] (KSC) ..... GH_2
Gaseous Ion LASER ..... GIL
Gaseous Mixture (MSA) ..... GM
Gaseous Nitrogen (PDAA) ..... GAN

Gaseous Nitrogen [*NASA*]	GN₂
Gaseous Nitrogen Flow Measuring System	GNFMS
Gaseous Nitrogen Measuring System	GNMS
Gaseous Nuclear Rocket	GNR
Gaseous Oxygen (MCD)	GO2
Gaseous Oxygen	GOX
Gaseous Oxygen Control Valve (NASA)	GCV
Gaseous RADWASTE System [*Nuclear energy*] (NRCH)	GRS
Gaseous Tritium Light [*Device*] [*Nuclear energy*] (NRCH)	GTL
Gaseous Tritium Light Source [*Nuclear energy*] (MCD)	GTLS
Gaseous Waste Disposal [*System*] [*Nuclear energy*] (NRCH)	GWD
Gaseous Waste Management System [*Nuclear energy*] (NRCH)	GWMS
Gaseous Waste Processing System [*Nuclear energy*] (NRCH)	GWPS
Gaseous Waste System [*Nuclear energy*] (NRCH)	GWS
Gases, Fluids, and Propellants [*NASA*] (NASA)	GF & P
Gas-Filled Counter	GFC
Gas-Filled Hydrophobic Region	GFHR
Gas-Filled Rectifier	GFR
Gas-Filled Rectifying Tube	GFRT
Gas-Fired Oven	GFO
Gas-Freeing System	GF
Gas-Gathering Pipeline	GGP
Gas-Guided Aircraft Rocket	GGAR
Gas-Insulated Flow Tube (NRCH)	GIFT
Gas-Insulated Switchgear	GAS
Gasket [*Technical drawings*]	GKT
Gasket (KSC)	GSKT
Gasket Fabricators Association (EA)	GFA
Gasket Material Expert [*Automotive engineering*]	GMX
Gas-Liquid Chromatography [*Analytical chemistry*]	GLC
Gas-Liquid Partition Chromatography	GLPC
Gas-Liquid Radiochromatography [*Analytical chemistry*]	GLRC
Gaslite Petroleum [*Vancouver Stock Exchange symbol*]	GAE
Gasmata [*Papua New Guinea*] [*Airport symbol*] (OAG)	GMI
Gasoffizier [*Gas Officer*] [*German military - World War II*]	GO
Gas-Oil Contact	GOC
Gas-Oil Ratio (IEEE)	GOR
Gas-Oil Separation Plant	GOSP
Gasoline (AFM)	GAS
Gasoline	GAS
Gasoline	GASO
Gasoline and Automotive Service Dealers Association (EA)	GASDA
Gasoline Barge [*Self-propelled*] [*Navy symbol*]	YOG
Gasoline Barge [*Non-self-propelled*] [*Navy symbol*]	YOGN
Gasoline Direct Injection	GDI
Gasoline Engine	GENG
Gasoline Engine, Close-Coupled	GECC
Gasoline Engine Driven	GED
Gasoline/Ethanol [*Automotive fuel*]	GASOHOL
Gasoline Pump Manufacturers Association (EA)	GPMA
Gasoline Range Organic [*Chemistry*]	GRO
Gasoline Stowage and Fuel System Man [*Navy*]	GA
Gasoline Supply	GS
Gasoline Tanker [*Navy symbol*]	AOG
Gasoline Tanker [*Military Sea Transportation Service*] (CINC)	TAOG
Gasoline Vapor Pressure (GNE)	GVP
Gasoline-Engine Heavy-Duty Vehicle	GHDV
Gasoline-Fueled [*Automotive engineering*]	GF
Gasoline-Grade Tertiary-Butyl Alcohol [*Organic chemistry*]	GTBA
Gasoline-Tolerant Methanol Vehicle [*Chrysler Corp.*] [*Automotive engineering*]	GTMV
GaSonics International [*NASDAQ symbol*] (TTSB)	GSNX
Gasonics International Corp. [*Associated Press*] (SAG)	Gasonics
Gasonics International Corp. [*NASDAQ symbol*] (SAG)	GSNX
Gas-Operated Core	GOC
Gaspar de Calderinis [*Deceased, 1390*] [*Authority cited in pre-1607 legal work*] (DSA)	G de Cal
Gaspar de Calderinis [*Deceased, 1390*] [*Authority cited in pre-1607 legal work*] (DSA)	Gas de Cal
Gaspar de Calderinis [*Deceased, 1390*] [*Authority cited in pre-1607 legal work*] (DSA)	Gas de Cald
Gaspar de Calderinis [*Deceased, 1390*] [*Authority cited in pre-1607 legal work*] (DSA)	Gasp de Cald
Gaspar's Small Cause Court Reports [*Bengal*] [*A publication*] (DLA)	Gaspar
Gaspe [*Canada*] [*Airport symbol*] (OAG)	YGP
Gaspe, PQ [*FM radio station call letters*]	CJRG
Gaspe, PQ [*ICAO location identifier*] (ICLI)	CYGP
Gaspe-Nord, PQ [*Television station call letters*]	CFER-2
Gas-Permeable Membrane	GPM
Gas-Phase Electron Diffraction [*Physics*]	GED
Gas-Plasma [*Computer display panel*]	GP
Gas-Porous Membrane Electrode [*Electrochemistry*]	GPME
Gasschutzunteroffizier [*Gas Noncommissioned Officer*] [*German military - World War II*]	GU
Gas-Scintillation Imaging Spectrometer	GIS
Gas-Shielded Stud Welding (PDAA)	GSSW
Gassim [*Saudi Arabia*] [*Airport symbol*] (OAG)	ELQ
Gassim [*Saudi Arabia*] [*ICAO location identifier*] (ICLI)	OEGS
Gas-Solid Chromatography	GSC
Gas-Solid-Solid Trickle Flow Reactor [*Chemical engineering*]	GSSTFR
Gas-Source Molecular Beam Epitaxy [*Coating technology*]	GSMBE
Gas-to-Cloth [*Ratio*] (FFDE)	G/C
Gaston College, Dallas, NC [*Library symbol Library of Congress*] (LCLS)	NcDalG
Gaston Memorial Hospital, Inc., Medical Library, Gastonia, NC [*Library symbol Library of Congress*] (LCLS)	NcGaH

Gaston, NC [*FM radio station call letters*]	WLGQ
Gastonia, NC [*Location identifier FAA*] (FAAL)	GHJ
Gastonia, NC [*FM radio station call letters*]	WBAV
Gastonia, NC [*AM radio station call letters*]	WGNC
Gastonia, NC [*AM radio station call letters*]	WLTC
Gaston-Lincoln Regional Library, Gastonia, NC [*Library symbol Library of Congress*] (LCLS)	NcGa
Gaston-Lincoln Regional Library, Gastonia, NC [*Library symbol*] [*Library of Congress*] (LCLS)	NcGaL
Gas-to-Particle Conversion Rate [*Physics*]	GPCR
GasTOPS Ltd., Gloucester, ON, Canada [*Library symbol*] [*Library of Congress*]	CaOGIG
GasTOPS Ltd., Gloucester, Ontario [*Library symbol National Library of Canada*] (NLC)	OGG
Gastralia [*Osteology*]	g
Gastric (WDAA)	GAST
Gastric Acid Secretion [*Medicine*] (DMAA)	GAS
Gastric Alcohol Dehydrogenase [*An enzyme*]	GADH
Gastric Analysis	GA
Gastric and Peptic Ulcer [*A laboratory test kit*] [*Medicine*]	GAP
Gastric Antrum [*Medicine*] (DMAA)	GA
Gastric Bypass [*Surgery*]	GBP
Gastric Cancer Area [*Medicine*] (DMAA)	GCA
Gastric Dilatation Volvulus	GDV
Gastric Electrical Activity [*Medicine*] (DMAA)	GEA
Gastric Emptying Half-Time [*Gastroenterology*] (DAVI)	GET₁/²
Gastric Emptying Time [*Medicine*]	GET
Gastric Fistula [*Gastroenterology*] (DAVI)	GF
Gastric Fluid [*Medicine*] (MAE)	GF
Gastric Ileal Bypass [*Medicine*] (DAVI)	GIB
Gastric Inhibitory Peptide [*Gastroenterology*] (DAVI)	GIP
Gastric [*or Gastrin*] Inhibitory Principle [*or Polypeptide*] [*Medicine*]	GIP
Gastric Juice [*Medicine*] (DMAA)	GJ
Gastric Mucosa [*Medicine*]	GM
Gastric Mucosal Blood Flow [*Medicine*]	GMBF
Gastric Outlet Obstruction [*Gastroenterology*] (DAVI)	GOO
Gastric Parietal Cell [*Cytology*] (AAMN)	GPC
Gastric Pressure [*Physiology*]	GP
Gastric Resection [*Medicine*]	GR
Gastric Reservoir Reduction [*Morbid obesity surgical treatment*]	GRR
Gastric Shield [*Medicine*]	GS
Gastric Stress Bleeding [*Medicine*]	GSB
Gastric Ulcer [*Medicine*]	GU
Gastric Volume [*Medicine*] (DMAA)	GV
Gastric Wrap [*Morbid obesity surgical treatment*]	GW
Gastrin [*Biochemistry*]	G
Gastrin [*Gastroenterology*] (DAVI)	GASTRN
Gastrin [*Biochemistry*]	GT
Gastrin-Releasing Peptide [*Endocrinology*]	GRP
Gastrocnemius [*Muscle*] [*Anatomy*]	GASTROC
Gastrocnemius [*A muscle*]	GC
Gastroduodenal Ulcer [*Medicine*] (DMAA)	GDU
Gastroemotional [*Medicine*] (MAE)	GE
Gastroenterological Society of Australia	GSA
Gastroenterologist	GASTRNTRLGST
Gastroenterology [*Medicine*]	GAS
Gastroenterology	GASTRNTRLY
Gastroenterology (DAVI)	Gastro
Gastroenterology [*Medicine*]	GE
Gastroenterology (DAVI)	GI
Gastroenterology Research Group [*Defunct*] (EA)	GRG
Gastroenteropancreatic System [*Medicine*]	GEP
Gastroenterostomy [*Medicine*]	GE
Gastroesophageal [*Medicine*] (CPH)	GE
Gastroesophageal Junction [*Anatomy*] (DAVI)	GEJ
Gastroesophageal Reflux [*See also GERD*] [*Medicine*]	GER
Gastroesophageal Reflux Disease [*Gastroenterology*] (DAVI)	GERD
Gastroesophageal Reflux Disease [*Gastroenterology*] (DAVI)	GRD
Gastrointestinal [*Gastroenterology*] (DAVI)	Gastro
Gastrointestinal [*Medicine*]	GI
Gastrointestinal Absorption Database [*Environmental Protection Agency Information service or system*] (CRD)	GIABS
Gastrointestinal Anastomosis [*Medicine*] (DAVI)	GIA
Gastrointestinal Bacterial Flora [*Medicine*] (MEDA)	GIBF
Gastrointestinal Bleeding [*Medicine*] (DMAA)	GIB
Gastrointestinal Cancer Antigen [*A tumor marker*] (CDI)	GICA
Gastrointestinal Dialysis [*Medicine*]	GID
Gastrointestinal Hemorrhage [*Medicine*] (DMAA)	GIH
Gastrointestinal Hormone [*Endocrinology*]	GIH
Gastrointestinal Infection [*Medicine*]	GII
Gastrointestinal Pathology Club [*Later, GPS*] (EA)	GPC
Gastrointestinal Pathology Society (EA)	GPS
Gastrointestinal Series [*Radiology*]	GIS
Gastrointestinal System [*Gastroenterology*] (DAVI)	GIS
Gastrointestinal Therapeutic System [*Medicine*]	GITS
Gastrointestinal Tract [*Medicine*]	GIT
Gastrointestinal Tract Bleeding [*Medicine*] (DMAA)	GTB
Gastrointestinal Transcription Unit [*Medicine*]	GITU
Gastrointestinal Tumor Study Group [*Oncology*] (DAVI)	GITSG
Gastrojejunostomy [*Surgery*] (DAVI)	GJ
Gastronomia Espanola [*Ministerio de Cultura*] [*Spain Information service or system*] (CRD)	GAST
Gastroplasty [*Medicine*]	GP
Gastroscopy [*Medicine*] (DMAA)	GCY
Gastrostomy [*Gastroenterology*] (DAVI)	GT

Gastrostomy Tube [*Gastroenterology*] (DAVI) .... GT
Gastrotomy Tube [*Gastroenterology*] (DAVI) .... GT
Gas-Water Module Storage [*Nuclear energy*] (NRCH) .... GWMS
Gatari Hutama Air Services PT [*Indonesia*] [*ICAO designator*] (FAAC) .... GHS
Gate [*Electronics*] .... G
Gate (IDOE) .... g
Gate .... GA
Gate Alarm Indicator [*RADAR*] .... GAI
Gate Array Interface Language (NITA) .... GAIL
Gate Assisted Turnoff Thyristor [*NASA*] (NASA) .... GATT
Gate Breakdown Voltage .... GBDV
Gate Breakdown Voltage .... GBV
Gate City, VA [*AM radio station call letters*] .... WGAT
Gate Craft [*Non-self-propelled*] [*Navy symbol*] .... YNG
Gate Driver .... GD
GATE [*GARP Atlantic Tropical Experiment*] **Equatorial Profiling Experiment**
[*Marine science*] (MSC) .... GEPE
Gate Frequency Position Modulation (IAA) .... GFPM
Gate House (NRCH) .... GH
Gate Leads (IEEE) .... GL
Gate Leakage Current .... GLC
Gate Operating System [*Aviation*] (DA) .... GOS
GATE [*GARP Atlantic Tropical Experiment*] **Operational Control Centre**
[*Marine science*] (MSC) .... GOCC
Gate Pulse Amplifier [*Computer science*] (IAA) ...... GPA
Gate Pulse Generator (IAA) .... GPG
Gate Resistance (IDOE) .... R$_G$
Gate Sensitive Thyristor (IAA) .... GST
Gate Stealer Display (MCD) .... GSD
Gate Tube (IAA) .... GT
Gate Turn Off [*Computer science*] .... GTO
Gate Turn Off Thyristor (NITA) .... GTOT
Gate Turnoff Silicon-Controlled Rectifier [*Electronics*] (IAA) ... GTOSCR
Gate Valve (AAG) .... GTV
Gate Valve (DAC) .... GV
Gate-Assignment and Display System [*United Air Lines, Inc.*] ... GADS
Gate-Associated Transistor (MCD) .... GAT
Gate-Controlled Diode (IAA) .... GCD
Gate-Controlled Switch (IAA) .... GCS
Gated Attenuation [*Computer science*] .... GA
Gated Blood Pool [*Hematology*] (DMAA) .... GBP
Gated Image Intensifier Viewer .... GIIV
Gated Memory (IAA) .... GM
Gated Mode Acquisition [*Telecommunications*] (LAIN) ... GMA
Gated Radionuclide Angiography [*Medicine*] (DMAA) ... GRA
Gated Spin Echo [*Nuclear magnetic resonance*] ...... GASPE
Gated Transport Spectroscopy .... GTS
Gated Video Tracker .... GVT
Gated-Diode Crosspoint [*Electronics*] (PDAA) .... GDX
Gate-Dip Oscillator (IDOE) .... gdo
Gated-Off Controlled Rectifier .... GOCR
Gate-Drain Overlapped Device (MCD) .... GOLD
Gate-Drain Voltage (IDOE) .... V$_{GD}$
Gatelink Transceiver Unit [*Aviation*] .... GTU
Gate-Modulated Bipolar Transistor (MCD) .... GAMBIT
Gates [*Germany ICAO location identifier*] (ICLI) .... EDAO
Gates County Library, Gatesville, NC [*Library symbol Library of Congress*]
(LCLS) .... NcGav
Gates MacGinitie Reading Test [*Educational test*] .. GMRT
Gates Memorial Library, Port Arthur, TX [*Library symbol Library of Congress*] (LCLS) ... TxPo
Gates Rubber Co., Technical Library, Denver, CO [*Library symbol Library of Congress*] (LCLS) ... CoDGR
Gates-Chili Senior High School Library, Rochester, NY [*OCLC symbol*]
(OCLC) .... RWG
Gates-Gaudin-Schumann [*Particle size distribution*] .. GGS
Gate-Source Voltage (IDOE) .... V$_{GS}$
Gatesville Public Library, Gatesville, TX [*Library symbol Library of Congress*] (LCLS) ... TxGat
Gatesville, TX [*FM radio station call letters*] .... KRYL
Gate-Turnoff Controlled Rectifier [*Electronics*] (IAA) ... GTCR
Gateway [*Commonly used*] (OPSA) .... GATEWAY
Gateway [*Commonly used*] (OPSA) .... GATEWY
Gateway [*Commonly used*] (OPSA) .... GATWAY
Gateway [*Commonly used*] (OPSA) .... GTWAY
Gateway .... GTWAY
Gateway (MCD) .... GTWY
Gateway (VRA) .... gtwy
Gateway 2000 [*NASDAQ symbol*] (TTSB) .... GATE
Gateway 2000, Inc. [*NASDAQ symbol*] (SAG) .... GATE
Gateway 2000, Inc. [*Associated Press*] (SAG) Gate2000
Gateway Army Ammunition Plant .... GAAP
Gateway Aviation [*Zambia*] [*FAA designator*] (FAAC) .. GTW
Gateway Bancorp, Inc. (Kentucky) [*Associated Press*] (SAG) ... GtwyKY
Gateway Bancorp, Inc. Kentucky [*NASDAQ symbol*] (SAG) ... GWBC
Gateway Bancorp(Ky) [*NASDAQ symbol*] (TTSB) ..... GWBC
Gateway Data Sciences [*NASDAQ symbol*] (TTSB) ... GDSC
Gateway Data Sciences Corp. [*NASDAQ symbol*] (SAG) ... GDSC
Gateway Data Sciences Corp. [*Associated Press*] (SAG) ... GtewayD
Gateway Exchange [*Telecommunications*] .... GE
Gateway Interface Unit (DGA) .... GIU
Gateway National Recreation Area [*New York*] [*Department of the Interior*] ... GNRA
Gateway School, Gateway, CO [*Library symbol Library of Congress*]
(LCLS) .... CoGwGS

Gateway Technical Institute, Elkhorn Campus, Elkhorn, WI [*Library symbol Library of Congress*] (LCLS) ... WKenG-E
Gateway Technical Institute, Kenosha, WI [*Library symbol Library of Congress*] (LCLS) ... WKenG
Gateway Technical Institute, Racine Campus, Racine, WI [*Library symbol Library of Congress*] (LCLS) ... WKenG-R
Gateway to Care .... GTC
Gateway to Educational Materials .... GEM
Gateway to Educational Materials .... GEM
Gateway-to-Gateway Protocol [*Computer science*] (TNIG) ... GGP
Gatha [*Language, etc.*] (ROG) .... GATH
Gather, Alarm, Report, Display, and Evaluate (IAA) ... GARDE
Gatherer, Stitcher, Side Sewer, and Trimmer [*Publishing*] ... GSST
Gathering .... GTHRNG
Gathering of Nations (EA) .... GN
Gathers Alarms, Reports, Displays, and Evaluates ... GARDAE
Gatineau/Hull [*Canada*] [*Airport symbol*] (OAG) ... YND
Gatineau, PQ [*AM radio station call letters*] .... CJRC
Gatineau, PQ [*FM radio station call letters*] .... CKTF
Gatineau, PQ [*ICAO location identifier*] (ICLI) .... CYND
Gating Half-Cycle [*Computer science*] .... GHC
Gating Waveform .... GWF
Gatlinburg, TN [*FM radio station call letters*] ..... WDLY
Gatling Gun .... GG
Gato, CA [*Location identifier FAA*] (FAAL) .... SAN
Gatwick Handling Ltd. [*British ICAO designator*] (FAAC) ... GHL
GATX Corp. [*Formerly, General American Transportation Corp.*] [*Associated Press*] (SAG) ... GATX
GATX Corp. [*Formerly, General American Transportation Corp.*] [*NYSE symbol*] (SPSG) ... GMT
GATX Corp. $2.50 Cv Pfd [*NYSE symbol*] (TTSB) ... GMTPr
GATX Corp. $3.875 cm Cv Pfd [*NYSE symbol*] (TTSB) ... GMTPrA
Gauche [*Chemical conformation*] .... g
Gauche [*Left*] [*French*] .... G
Gaucher's Disease Registry [*National Gaucher Foundation - NGF*]
[*Superseded by*] (EA) .... GDR
Gaudeamus Foundation [*Netherlands*] (EAIO) ...... GF
Gaudium et Spes [*Pastoral Constitution on the Church in the Modern World*]
[*Vatican II document*] .... GS
Gauge .... G
Gauge (WDMC) .... g
Gauge (AAG) .... GA
Gauge [*of needles*] [*Measurement*] (DAVI) .... ga
Gauge .... GE
Gauge .... GGE
Gauge and Toolmakers Association [*British*] (DS) .. GTMA
Gauge Board .... GABD
Gauge Code Number .... GCN
Gauge Control Analyzer .... GCA
Gauge Factor (MCD) .... GF
Gauge Length .... GL
Gauge Man [*Navy*] .... GA
Gauge Pressure (IAA) .... GP
Gauge Pressure Control .... GPC
Gauge Pressure Switch .... GPS
Gauge Repeatability and Reproducibility [*Materials testing*] ... GR & R
Gauge-Invariant Atomic Orbital [*NASA*] .... GIAO
Gauhati [*India*] [*Airport symbol*] (OAG) .... GAU
Gauhati [*India*] [*ICAO location identifier*] (ICLI) .. VEGT
Gaulish [*Language*] (BARN) .... Gaul
Gaultois Public Library, Newfoundland [*Library symbol National Library of Canada*] (BIB) ... NFGAU
Gauribidanur Array [*India*] [*Seismograph station code, US Geological Survey*] (SEIS) ... GBA
Gauss [*Physics*] (DAVI) .... B
Gauss [*Unit of magnetic flux density*] [*Preferred unit is T, Telsa*] ... G
Gauss [*Later, GTT*] [*Federal Republic of Germany*] [*Geomagnetic observatory code*] ... GAS
Gauss [*Unit of magnetic flux density*] .... Gau
Gauss [*Unit of magnetic flux density*] [*Preferred unit is T, Telsa*] ... GS
Gauss Error Function [*Mathematics*] .... GEF
Gauss Hypergeometric Equation [*Mathematics*] .... GHE
Gauss Hypergeometric Function [*Mathematics*] .... GHF
Gauss Quadrature Rule .... GQR
Gaussian Band Limited Channel (NITA) .... GBLIC
Gaussian Cosine Modulation (PDAA) .... GCM
Gaussian Elimination (IEEE) .... GE
Gaussian Fast Multipole Method [*Physics*] .... GFMM
Gaussian Filtered Minimum Shift Keying (MCD) .... GMSK
Gaussian Image Point [*Optics*] .... GIP
Gaussian Lens Formula [*Optics*] .... GLF
Gaussian Mean Shift Keying .... GMSK
Gaussian Noise (IAA) .... GN
Gaussian Noise Generator [*Electronics*] .... GNG
Gaussian Orbitals [*Atomic physics*] .... GO
Gaussian Random Process [*Mathematics*] .... GRP
Gaussian Wave Group [*Physics*] .... GWG
Gaussian-Type Orbitals [*Atomic physics*] .... GTO
Gauss-Jordan Elimination (IEEE) .... GJE
Gave Delivery .... GD
Gavel Clubs (EA) .... GC
Gavin and Hord's Indiana Statutes [*A publication*] (DLA) ... G & H
Gavin and Hord's Revised Indiana Statutes [*A publication*]
(DLA) .... Gav & H Rev St
Gaviota, CA [*Location identifier FAA*] (FAAL) ..... GVO

Gavle [*Sweden*] [*Airport symbol*] (OAG) .... GVX
Gavle/Avan [*Sweden ICAO location identifier*] (ICLI) .... ESKW
Gavle-Sandviken [*Sweden ICAO location identifier*] (ICLI) .... ESSK
Gavotto [*Gavotte*] [*Music*] (ROG) .... GAVA
Gay AA (EA) .... GAA
Gay Academic Union [*Defunct*] (EA) .... GAU
Gay Activists' Alliance [*Defunct*] .... GAA
Gay American Indians (EA) .... GAI
Gay and Lesbian Advocates and Defenders (EA) .... GLAD
Gay and Lesbian Alliance Against Defamation (EA) .... GLAAD
Gay and Lesbian Association of Choruses (EA) .... GALAC
Gay and Lesbian Association of Choruses (EA) .... GLAC
Gay and Lesbian Atheists [*Defunct*] (EA) .... GALA
Gay and Lesbian Caucus (EA) .... GLC
Gay and Lesbian Counselling Service of New South Wales [*Australia*] .... GLCSNSW
Gay and Lesbian Counselling Service of South Australia .... GLCSSA
Gay and Lesbian Democrats of America [*Defunct*] (EA) .... GLDA
Gay and Lesbian History on Stamps Club (EA) .... GLHSC
Gay and Lesbian Information Bureau (IID) .... GLIB
Gay and Lesbian Literature .... GLL
Gay and Lesbian Media Coalition (EA) .... GLMC
Gay and Lesbian Parents Coalition International (EA) .... GLPCI
Gay and Lesbian Press Association (EA) .... GLPA
Gay Black Female [*Classified advertising*] (CDAI) .... GBF
Gay Black Male [*Classified advertising*] (CDAI) .... GBM
Gay Caucus of Members of the American Psychiatric Association [*Later, AGLP*] (EA) .... GCMAPA
Gay Christian Movement [*British*] .... GCM
Gay Community News Prisoner Project [*An association*] (EA) .... GCNPP
Gay Disaster Disease [*Also called AIDS*] (DAVI) .... GDD
Gay Extremists Fighting Fascistic Entertainment Normalcy [*Focus group of Queer Nation*] .... GEFFEN
Gay Fathers Coalition International [*Later, GLPCI*] (EA) .... GFCI
Gay Legal Advice Project [*British*] (DI) .... GLAP
Gay, Lesbian, or Bisexual Employees [*An association*] .... GLOBE
Gay Liberation Front .... GLF
Gay Male [*Classified advertising*] .... GM
Gay Media Task Force (EA) .... GMTF
Gay Men's Health Crisis (EA) .... GMHC
Gay Men's Press [*GMP is now the name of the company*] .... GMP
Gay Men's VD Clinic (EA) .... GMVDC
Gay News Information and Communication Network [*Information service or system*] (IID) .... GNIC
Gay Nurses' Alliance (EA) .... GNA
Gay Parents Legal and Research Group [*Defunct*] (EA) .... GPLRG
Gay People at Columbia [*Later, CGLA*] (EA) .... GPC
Gay Press Association [*Later, GLPA*] (EA) .... GPA
Gay Public Health Workers Caucus [*Later, LGCPHW*] (EA) .... GPHW
Gay Rights National Lobby (EA) .... GRNL
Gay Theatre Alliance [*Defunct*] (EA) .... GTA
Gay Union International [*Paris, France*] (EAIO) .... GUI
Gay Urban Professional [*Lifestyle classification*] .... Guppie
Gay Veterans Association (EA) .... GVA
Gay White Female [*Classified advertising*] (CDAI) .... GWF
Gay White Male [*Classified advertising*] .... GWM
Gaya [*Niger*] [*ICAO location identifier*] (ICLI) .... DRRG
Gaya [*India*] [*ICAO location identifier*] (ICLI) .... VEGY
Gayarre's Annual Reports [*25-28 Louisiana*] [*A publication*] (DLA) .... Gay (LA)
Gayarre's Annual Reports [*25-28 Louisiana*] [*A publication*] (DLA) .... Gayarre
Gaylactic Network [*An association*] (EA) .... GN
Gaylord [*Diocesan abbreviation*] [*Michigan*] (TOCD) .... GAY
Gaylord Circulation Control System [*Information service or system*] (IID) .... GLS
Gaylord Companies, Inc. [*Associated Press*] (SAG) .... Gaylord
Gaylord Companies, Inc. [*Associated Press*] (SAG) .... Gaylrd
Gaylord Companies, Inc. [*NASDAQ symbol*] (SAG) .... GJCO
Gaylord Container Corp. [*Associated Press*] (SAG) .... GaylC
Gaylord Container Corp. [*Associated Press*] (SAG) .... GaylCn
Gaylord Container Corp. Class A [*AMEX symbol*] (SPSG) .... GCR
Gaylord Container Wrrt [*AMEX symbol*] (TTSB) .... GCRWS
Gaylord Container'A' [*AMEX symbol*] (TTSB) .... GCR
Gaylord Cos. [*NASDAQ symbol*] (TTSB) .... GJCO
Gaylord Cos. Wrrt [*NASDAQ symbol*] (TTSB) .... GJCOW
Gaylord Entertainment [*Associated Press*] (SAG) .... GaylEnt
Gaylord Entertainment [*NYSE symbol*] (SPSG) .... GET
Gaylord Entertainment 'A' [*NYSE symbol*] (TTSB) .... GET
Gaylord, MI [*Location identifier FAA*] (FAAL) .... ALV
Gaylord, MI [*Location identifier FAA*] (FAAL) .... GLR
Gaylord, MI [*FM radio station call letters*] .... WKPK
Gaylord, MI [*FM radio station call letters*] .... WMJZ
Gaylord, MI [*FM radio station call letters*] .... WPHN
Gaylord, MI [*AM radio station call letters*] .... WSNQ
Gaylord-Otsego County Public Library, Gaylord, MI [*Library symbol Library of Congress*] (LCLS) .... MiGay
Gayndah [*Australia Airport symbol*] (OAG) .... GAH
Gay-Related Immunodeficiency [*Also, AID, AIDS*] [*Medicine*] .... GRID
Gays and Lesbians of Zimbabwe [*An association*] .... GALZ
Gays and Lesbians Opposing Violence [*An association*] .... GLOV
Gays for Equality .... GFE
Gaz Metropolitain, Inc. [*Toronto Stock Exchange symbol*] .... GZM
Gaz Metropolitain, Montreal, Quebec [*Library symbol National Library of Canada*] (BIB) .... QMGM
Gaza Strip [*MARC geographic area code Library of Congress*] (LCCP) .... awgz--
Gaza Strip [*MARC country of publication code Library of Congress*] (LCCP) .... gz
Gazelle Resources Ltd. [*Vancouver Stock Exchange symbol*] .... GZL
Gazette [*or Gazetteer*] .... GAZ
Gazette .... GAZ
Gazette and Bankrupt Court Reporter [*New York*] [*A publication*] (DLA) .... Gaz & BC Rep
Gazette for Zanzibar and East Africa [*A publication*] (ILCA) .... Gaz Zan EA
Gazette International Networking Institute (EA) .... GINI
Gazette Law Reports [*New Zealand*] [*A publication*] (DLA) .... Gaz LR
Gazette Law Reports [*New Zealand*] [*A publication*] (DLA) .... GLR
Gazette Law Reports [*New Zealand*] [*A publication*] (DLA) .... GLR (NZ)
Gazette. Law Society of Upper Canada [*A publication*] (DLA) .... Gaz L Soc of Upper Can
Gazette of Bankruptcy [*A publication*] (ROG) .... GAZ B
Gazette of Bankruptcy [*A publication*] (DLA) .... Gaz Bank
Gazette of Bankruptcy [*A publication*] (DLA) .... Gaz Bankr
Gazette Reporter and Minden-Shelby News, Neloa, IA [*Library symbol Library of Congress*] (LCLS) .... IaNeoG
Gaziantep [*Turkey*] [*Airport symbol*] (OAG) .... GZT
Gaziantep [*Turkey ICAO location identifier*] (ICLI) .... LTAJ
Gaz-Physique-Orsay Database [*Universite de Paris-Sud*] [*Information service or system*] .... GAPHYOR
Gazpromavia [*Former USSR*] [*FAA designator*] (FAAC) .... GPZ
Gazzam's Digest of Bankruptcy Decisions [*A publication*] (DLA) .... Gaz Bank Dig
GB Air Academy Ltd. [*British ICAO designator*] (FAAC) .... TUT
GB Airways Ltd. [*British ICAO designator*] (FAAC) .... GBL
GB Foods [*Associated Press*] (SAG) .... GB Fds
GB Foods [*NASDAQ symbol*] (TTSB) .... GBFC
GB Foods Corp. [*NASDAQ symbol*] (SAG) .... GBFC
Gbado [*Zaire*] [*ICAO location identifier*] (ICLI) .... FZFV
Gbadolite [*Zaire*] [*ICAO location identifier*] (ICLI) .... FZFD
Gbangbatok [*Sierra Leone*] [*Airport symbol*] (OAG) .... GBK
Gbangbatok [*Sierra Leone*] [*ICAO location identifier*] (ICLI) .... GFGK
GBC Bancorp [*Associated Press*] (SAG) .... GBC Bc
GBC Bancorp [*NASDAQ symbol*] (NQ) .... GBCB
GBC Technologies, Inc. [*Associated Press*] (SAG) .... GBC Tch
GBC Technologies, Inc. [*NASDAQ symbol*] (SAG) .... GBCT
GBX Resources [*Vancouver Stock Exchange symbol*] .... GBX
GC Companies [*Associated Press*] (SAG) .... GC Cos
GC Companies [*NYSE symbol*] (SAG) .... GCX
GC Optronics, Inc. .... GCO
GCA Surveys [*British ICAO designator*] (FAAC) .... SVY
G-Cat Class Association (EA) .... GCCA
GCN/Microfilm, Boston, MA [*Library symbol Library of Congress*] (LCLS) .... GcNM
GCOS Security Module .... GUSER
GCR Hldgs Ltd [*NASDAQ symbol*] (TTSB) .... GCREF
Gdansk [*Poland*] (BARN) .... Gdk
Gdansk [*Poland*] [*Airport symbol*] (OAG) .... GDN
Gdansk/Rebiechowo [*Poland ICAO location identifier*] (ICLI) .... EPGD
GDP [*Guanosine Diphosphate*] **Dissociation Stimulator** [*Biochemistry*] .... GDS
GDSD [*Ground Data Systems Division*] **Staff Support Room** [*NASA*] (NASA) .... GDSSR
Gduei Noar [*Youth Battalions*] [*Israel*] .... GADNA
GE [*General Electric Co.*] **Information Services** [*Information service or system*] (IID) .... GEIS
GE [*General Electric Co.*] **Robot** .... GERO
GE [*General Electric Co.*] **Stockholders' Alliance Against Nuclear Power/ Nuclear Weapons** (EA) .... GESAANP/NW
Geac Computer Corp. Ltd. [*Toronto Stock Exchange symbol*] .... GAC
Geac Computers International, Markham, Ontario [*Library symbol National Library of Canada*] (NLC) .... OMAG
Gear (AAG) .... G
Gear (MSA) .... GR
Gear Assembly .... GA
Gear Down [*Aviation*] .... GD
Gear Lubricant [*Automotive engineering*] .... GL
Gear on Landlord and Tenant [*A publication*] (DLA) .... Gear Landl & T
Gear Rack .... GRK
Gear Ratio .... GR
Gear Reduction Ratio [*Military*] (CAAL) .... GRR
Gear Test Data .... GTD
Gear Train Analyzer .... GTA
Gear Up [*Aviation*] .... GU
Gearbox .... GRBX
Gearcase (MSA) .... GRC
Geared Radial [*Aircraft engine*] .... GR
Geared Roller Test Machine .... GRTM
Gearing (MSA) .... GRG
Gearshaft (MSA) .... GRSHFT
Geary 18 International Yacht Racing Association (EA) .... G18 IYRA
Geauga County Public Library, Chardon, OH [*OCLC symbol*] (OCLC) .... GEC
Geauga County Public Library, Chardon, OH [*Library symbol Library of Congress*] (LCLS) .... OChaG
Gebbies Pass [*New Zealand*] [*Seismograph station code, US Geological Survey*] (SEIS) .... GPZ
Gebhardt-Heriot Foundation for All Cats (EA) .... GHFC
Geboren [*Born*] [*German*] .... GEB
Gebrueder [*Brothers*] [*German*] .... GEB
Gebunden [*Bound*] [*Publishing*] [*German*] .... GEB
GEC Marconi Avionics Ltd. [*British*] [*FAA designator*] (FAAC) .... FFU
GEC Plessey Telecommunications [*British*] (ECON) .... GPT
GEC [*General Electric Company*] **Rectangular Image Data Processor** (NITA) .... GRID
Gecelinus [*Zenzelinus de Cassanis*] [*Deceased, 1334*] [*Authority cited in pre-1607 legal work*] (DSA) .... Ge
Gecelinus [*Zenzelinus de Cassanis*] [*Deceased, 1334*] [*Authority cited in pre-1607 legal work*] (DSA) .... Gecel

Gecelinus [*Zenzelinus de Cassanis*] [*Deceased, 1334*] [*Authority cited in pre-1607 legal work*] (DSA) .... Gen
Gedaagde [*Defendant*] [*Netherlands*] (ILCA) .... Ged
Gedampft [*Muted*] [*Music*] (AD) .... GED
Gedaref [*Sudan*] [*Airport symbol*] (AD) .... GSU
Gedaref/Azaza [*Sudan*] [*ICAO location identifier*] (ICLI) .... HSGF
Geddes Resources Ltd. [*Toronto Stock Exchange symbol*] .... GDD
Gedeh [*Java*] [*Seismograph station code, US Geological Survey Closed*] (SEIS) .... GED
Geehi [*Australia Seismograph station code, US Geological Survey Closed*] (SEIS) .... GEE
GEEIA [*Ground Electronics Engineering Installation Agency*] **Workload Schedule** (AFM) .... GWS
Geelong Air Travel [*ICAO designator*] (AD) .... FK
Geerlings & Wade [*NASDAQ symbol*] (TTSB) .... GEEB
Geerlings & Wade, Inc. [*NASDAQ symbol*] (SAG) .... GEER
Geerlings & Wade, Inc. [*Associated Press*] (SAG) .... GeerlWd
Geeseair [*Canada ICAO designator*] (FAAC) .... GEE
Geevax Ltd. [*British ICAO designator*] (FAAC) .... GVX
Ge'ez (BJA) .... G
Gegechkori [*Former USSR Seismograph station code, US Geological Survey Closed*] (SEIS) .... GEG
Gehalt [*Contents*] [*German*] (ILCA) .... Geh
Geheime Feldpolizei [*Secret Police*] [*German*] .... GFP
Geheime Staats Polizei [*Secret State Police*] [*Germany*] .... GESTAPO
Geheimrat [*Privy Councillor*] [*German*] (ILCA) .... Geh
Gehl Co. [*NASDAQ symbol*] (NQ) .... GEHL
GEICO Corp. [*NYSE symbol*] (SPSG) .... GEC
GEICO Corp. [*Associated Press*] (SAG) .... GEICO
Geiger-Mueller [*Radiation counter*] .... G-M
Geiger-Mueller Counter [*Nucleonics*] (IAA) .... GC
Geiger-Mueller Tube .... GMT
Geigy Pharmaceuticals, Yonkers, NY [*Library symbol Library of Congress*] (LCLS) .... NYG
Geilenkirchen [*Germany ICAO location identifier*] (ICLI) .... EDNG
Geinsheim Staging Activity .... GSA
Geisinger Medical Center, Medical Library, Danville, PA [*OCLC symbol*] (OCLC) .... GEI
Geist Picture Interest Inventory [*Psychology*] (AEBS) .... GPII
Gel Chromatography .... GC
Gel Destainer [*Analytical chemistry*] .... GD
Gel Diffusion Precipitin [*Biochemistry*] (DAVI) .... GDP
Gel Dryer [*Chromatography*] .... GD
Gel Dryer with Clamps [*Chromatography*] .... GDC
Gel Drying Cart [*Chromatography*] .... GDC
Gel Drying System [*Chromatography*] .... GDS
Gel Electrofocusing [*Analytical chemistry*] .... GEF
Gel Electrophoresis [*Analytical chemistry*] .... GE
Gel Filtration Chromatography .... GFC
Gel Frontal Analysis Chromatography .... GELFAC
Gel Permeation Chromatography .... GPC
Gel Supported Precipitation [*Method*] [*Chemistry*] .... GSP
Gel Tube [*Electrophoresis*] .... GT
Gela [*Italy ICAO location identifier*] (ICLI) LICL
Gelaendegaengig [*Having cross-country mobility*] [*German military - World War II*] .... G
Gelatin .... GEL
Gelatin (VRA) .... gel
Gelatin [*Theatrical lighting*] (WDMC) .... gel
Gelatin Glass Negative (VRA) .... GGNG
Gelatin, Glucose, and Veronal Buffer [*Medicine*] (DMAA) .... GGVB
Gelatin Infusion [*Medium*] [*Biochemistry*] (DAVI) .... GI
Gelatin Infusion Medium [*Medicine*] (BABM) .... GI
Gelatin Manufacturers Institute of America (EA) .... GMI
Gelatin Manufacturers Institute of America (EA) .... GMIA
Gelatin Matrix System .... GMS
Gelatin, Resorcinol, and Formaldehyde .... GRF
Gelatin Rigidized Panel .... GRP
Gelatin Silver Print (VRA) .... SGPT
Gelatina Quavis [*In Any Kind of Jelly*] [*Pharmacy*] (ROG) .... GEL QUAV
Gelatin-Agglutination Test [*Clinical chemistry*] .... GAT
Gelatin-Coated Capsule [*Pharmacy*] .... Gelcap
Gelatine and Glue Research Association [*British*] (BI) .... GGRA
Gelatine Manufacturers of Europe (EAIO) .... GME
Gelatine Veronal Buffer (PDAA) .... GVB
Gelatinous Fiber [*Botany*] .... GF
Gelatin-Tellurite-Taurocholate [*Agar*] [*Medicine*] (MEDA) .... GTT
Gelatin-Tellurite-Taurocholate Agar [*Biochemistry*] (DAVI) .... GTT
Gelbray Association [*Later, GI*] (EA) .... GA
Gelbray International (EA) .... GI
Geldart and Maddock's English Chancery Reports [*6 Maddock's Reports*] [*A publication*] (DLA) .... Geld & M
Geldart and Maddock's English Chancery Reports [*6 Maddock's Reports*] [*A publication*] (DLA) .... Geldart
Geldermann Investment Management [*Finance British*] .... GIM
Geldert and Oxley's Nova Scotia Decisions [*7-9 Nova Scotia Reports*] [*1866-75*] [*Canada*] [*A publication*] (DLA) .... NSD
Geldert and Russell's Nova Scotia Reports [*A publication*] (DLA) .... G & R
Geldert and Russell's Nova Scotia Reports [*A publication*] (DLA) .... Geld & R
Gelding [*Thoroughbred racing*] .... G
Gelled Liquid Propellant .... GLP
Gelling Temperature [*Analytical biochemistry*] .... GT
Gelman Sciences [*AMEX symbol*] (TTSB) .... GSC
Gelman Sciences, Inc. [*Associated Press*] (SAG) .... GelmSci
Gelman Sciences, Inc. [*AMEX symbol*] (SPSG) .... GSC

Gelnhausen [*Germany ICAO location identifier*] (ICLI) .... EDFG
GelTex Pharmaceuticals [*NASDAQ symbol*] (TTSB) .... GELX
GelTex Pharmaceuticals, Inc. [*Associated Press*] (SAG) .... GelTex
GelTex Pharmaceuticals, Inc. [*NASDAQ symbol*] (SAG) .... GELX
Gem and Lapidary Council of New South Wales [*Australia*] .... GLCNSW
Gem Public Library, Alberta [*Library symbol National Library of Canada*] (NLC) .... AGE
Gem State Airlines [*ICAO designator*] (AD) .... GG
Gemara (BJA) .... Gem
Gemeente Archief van Amsterdam, Amsterdam, Netherlands [*Library symbol Library of Congress*] (LCLS) .... NeAA
Gemeinde Berlin (BJA) .... GB
Gemeinschaft der Ikonenfreunde [*Society of Friends of Icons - SFI*] (EAIO) .... GI
Gemeinschaft Unabhangiger Beratender Ingenieurbueros [*Association of German Consulting Engineers*] .... GUBI
Gemeisamer Faktor [*General Factor*] [*Rorschach*] [*Psychology*] .... g
Gemena [*Zaire*] [*ICAO location identifier*] (ICLI) .... FZFK
Gemena [*Zaire*] [*Airport symbol*] (OAG) .... GMA
Gemial [*Slovakia*] [*ICAO designator*] (FAAC) .... GML
Geminatae (BJA) .... Gem
Geminate [*Chemistry*] .... gem
Gemini [*Constellation*] .... Gem
Gemini [*Constellation*] .... Gemi
Gemini Agena [*NASA*] (KSC) .... GA
Gemini Agena Launch Vehicle Working Group [*NASA*] (KSC) .... GALVWG
Gemini Agena Target [*NASA*] .... GAT
Gemini Agena Target Vehicle [*NASA*] .... GATV
Gemini Airline [*British*] .... G
Gemini Airlines Ltd. [*Ghana*] [*ICAO designator*] (FAAC) .... GAL
Gemini Atlas/Agena Target Vehicle [*NASA*] (MCD) .... GAATV
Gemini B .... GB
Gemini B Procedures Simulator (MCD) .... GBPS
Gemini Detailed Maneuver Table (IAA) .... GDMT
Gemini Food Corp. [*Toronto Stock Exchange symbol*] .... GFD
Gemini Fund, Inc. [*NYSE symbol*] (SPSG) .... GMI
Gemini Hatch [*NASA*] .... GH
Gemini II [*NYSE symbol*] (TTSB) .... GMI
Gemini II cm Income Shrs [*NYSE symbol*] (TTSB) .... GMIPr
Gemini II Fund, Inc. [*Associated Press*] (SAG) .... GemII
Gemini Inertial Guidance System [*NASA*] (KSC) .... GIGS
Gemini LASER Experiment [*NASA*] (IAA) .... GLE
Gemini Launch Data System [*NASA*] (MCD) .... GLDS
Gemini Launch Vehicle [*NASA*] .... GLV
Gemini Management Panel [*NASA*] (KSC) .... GMP
Gemini Mission Simulator [*NASA*] .... GMS
Gemini Pad Test [*NASA*] (KSC) .... GPT
Gemini Problem Investigation Status [*NASA*] (IEEE) .... GPIS
Gemini Program [*or Project*] **Office** [*NASA*] (KSC) .... GPO
Gemini Program Planning Board [*NASA*] (KSC) .... GPPB
Gemini Reentry Integration Program [*NASA*] .... GRIP
Gemini Slowscan Television [*NASA*] .... GEST
Gemini Spacecraft Project Office [*NASA*] (MCD) .... GSPO
Gemini Stability Improvement Program [*NASA*] .... GEMSIP
Gemini System Trainer [*NASA*] (IAA) .... GST
Gemini Technology, Inc. [*Toronto Stock Exchange symbol Vancouver Stock Exchange symbol*] .... GMT
Geminiano [*Flourished, 1407-09*] [*Authority cited in pre-1607 legal work*] (DSA) .... Gemi
Gemini-Titan [*NASA*] .... GT
Gemini-Titan-Agena [*NASA*] (KSC) .... GTA
Gemmological Association [*British*] (DBA) .... GA
Gemmological Association of Great Britain (BI) .... GAGB
Gemological Institute of America (EA) .... GIA
Gems & Gemology [*A publication*] (EAAP) .... G & G
Gems, Minerals, and Jewelry Study Unit (EA) .... GMJSU
Gemstar International Group Ltd. [*Associated Press*] (SAG) .... Gemstr
Gemstar International Group Ltd. [*NASDAQ symbol*] (SAG) .... GMSTF
Gemstar Intl. [*NASDAQ symbol*] (TTSB) .... GMSTE
Genaire Ltd., Saint Catharines, ON, Canada [*Library symbol Library of Congress*] (LCLS) .... CaOStCGL
Genaire Ltd., St. Catharines, Ontario [*Library symbol National Library of Canada*] (NLC) .... OSTCGL
Genavco Air Ltd. [*British ICAO designator*] (FAAC) .... GEN
Genavia SRL [*Italy ICAO designator*] (FAAC) .... JVA
Genco Industry, Inc. [*Vancouver Stock Exchange symbol*] .... GNI
Gencor Indus [*AMEX symbol*] (TTSB) .... GX
Gencor Industries [*AMEX symbol*] (SAG) .... GX
Gencor Industries, Inc. [*NASDAQ symbol*] (NQ) .... GCOR
Gencor Industries, Inc. [*Associated Press*] (SAG) .... Gencor
GenCorp [*NYSE symbol*] (TTSB) .... GY
GenCorp, Inc. [*Associated Press*] (SAG) .... GenCrp
GenCorp, Inc. [*NYSE symbol*] (SPSG) .... GY
Gendall Air Ltd. [*Canada ICAO designator*] (FAAC) .... GAB
Gendarmerie Nationale [*France ICAO designator*] (FAAC) .... FGN
Gendarmerie Royale du Canada [*Royal Canadian Mounted Police - RCMP*] .... GRC
Gender .... G
Gender .... GEN
Gender Equality in Mathematics and Science .... GEMS
Gender Equality Indicator [*Australia*] .... GEI
Gender Gap [*Refers to women's tendency to vote for Democratic over Republican candidates, a phenomenon noticed by pollsters beginning with the 1980 election*] .... GG
Gender Identity Disorder [*Medicine*] (DMAA) .... GID
Gendis, Inc. [*Toronto Stock Exchange symbol*] .... GDS

Gene Autry International Fan Club (EA) ... GAIFC
Gene Pitney Fan Club (EA) ... GPFC
Gene Stratton-Porter Memorial, Rome City, IN [*Library symbol Library of Congress*] (LCLS) ... InRomS
Gene Summers International Fan Club (EA) ... GSIFC
Gene Transfer Agent [*Genetics*] ... GTA
Gene Vincent and His Blue Caps International Fan Club (EAIO) ... GVHBCIFC
Genealogical and Heraldic Institute of America (EA) ... GHIA
Genealogical Association of English-Speaking Researchers in Europe (EAIO) ... GAESRE
Genealogical Enterprises, Morrow, GA [*Library symbol Library of Congress*] (LCLS) ... GMorGE
Genealogical Forum of Portland, Portland, OR [*Library symbol Library of Congress*] (LCLS) ... OrPGF
Genealogical [*or Geological*] **Information and Name Tabulating System** [*Computer science*] (IEEE) ... GIANT
Genealogical Institute (EA) ... GI
Genealogical Library, Boise, ID [*Library symbol*] [*Library of Congress*] (LCLS) ... IdBG
Genealogical Society Library, Church of Jesue Christ of Latter-Day Saints, Lethbridge, Alberta [*Library symbol National Library of Canada*] (NLC) ... ALCJC
Genealogical Society Library, Church of Jesus Christ of Latter-Day Saints, Burnaby, British Columbia [*Library symbol National Library of Canada*] (NLC) ... BBCJC
Genealogical Society Library, Church of Jesus Christ of Latter-Day Saints, Calgary, Alberta [*Library symbol National Library of Canada*] (NLC) ... ACCJC
Genealogical Society Library, Church of Jesus Christ of Latter-Day Saints, Cardston, Alberta [*Library symbol National Library of Canada*] (NLC)... ACACJC
Genealogical Society Library, Church of Jesus Christ of Latter-Day Saints, Edmonton, Alberta [*Library symbol National Library of Canada*] (NLC) ... AECJC
Genealogical Society Library, Church of Jesus Christ of Latter-Day Saints, Etobicoke, Ontario [*Library symbol National Library of Canada*] (NLC) ... OTCJC
Genealogical Society of Flemish Americans (EA) ... GSFA
Genealogical Society of Pennsylvania (EA) ... GSP
Genealogical Society of Pennsylvania, Philadelphia, PA [*Library symbol Library of Congress*] (LCLS) ... PPGen
Genealogical Society of Santa Cruz County, Santa Cruz, CA [*Library symbol*] [*Library of Congress*] (LCLS) ... CStcrGS
Genealogical Society of Tasmania [*Australia*] ... GST
Genealogical Society of the Northern Territory [*Australia*] ... GSNT
Genealogical Society of Victoria [*Australia*] ... GSV
Genealogische Recherche mit Magnetband-Speicherung [*Organic chemistry coding system*] ... GREMAS
Genealogy ... GEN
Genealogy ... GENEAL
Genealogy Club of America [*Defunct*] (EA) ... GCA
Geneina [*Sudan*] [*ICAO location identifier*] (ICLI) ... HSGN
Genelabs Technologies [*NASDAQ symbol*] (SPSG) ... GNLB
GeneLabs Technologies, Inc. [*Associated Press*] (SAG) ... GeneLTc
GeneMedicine, Inc. [*Associated Press*] (SAG) ... GeneMed
GeneMedicine, Inc. [*NASDAQ symbol*] (SAG) ... GMED
Genentech, Inc. [*Associated Press*] (SAG) ... Genentc
Genentech, Inc. [*NYSE symbol*] (SPSG) ... GNE
General ... G
General (AABC) ... GEN
General (DMAA) ... gen
General (VRA) ... gen
General ... GEN
General (ODBW) ... Gen
General ... GENL
General (WGA) ... GN
General ... GNL
General (ROG) ... GRAL
General ... GRL
General [*Air Force, Army, Marine Corps*] ... O10
General Abridgment of Cases in Equity [*Equity Cases Abridged*] [*1677-1744*] [*A publication*] (DLA) ... Gen Abr Cas Eq
General Acceptance Corp. (MHDW) ... GAC
General Acceptance Corp. [*NASDAQ symbol*] (SAG) ... GACC
General Acceptance Corp. [*Associated Press*] (SAG) ... GnAcpt
General Acceptance Test Software ... GATS
General Access Copy (MHDI) ... GAC
General Access Transportation Extention [*Telecommunications*] (TSSD) ... GATE
General Accident [*British insurance organization*] ... GA
General Account of Advances ... GAA
General Accounting (AAG) ... GA
General Accounting Instructions ... GAI
General Accounting Material (DNAB) ... GAM
General Accounting Office [*of the US government*] ... GAO
General Accounting Office/Community and Economic Development Division ... GAO/CED
General Accounting Office/Federal Personnel and Compensation Division ... GAO/FPCD
General Accounting Office/Financial and General Management Studies Division ... GAO/FGMSD
General Accounting Office General Government Division ... GAO/GGD
General Accounting Office Human Resources Division ... GAO/HRD
General Accounting Office Letter Report [*A publication*] (DLA) ... GAO Let Rep
General Accounting Office/Logistics and Communications Division ... GAO/LCD
General Accounting Office, Los Angeles Region, Los Angeles, CA [*OCLC symbol*] (OCLC) ... GAM
General Accounting Office Mission Analysis and Systems Acquisition Division ... GAO/MASAD
General Accounting Office National Security and International Affairs Division ... GAO/NSIAD
General Accounting Office, Notice of Execution (DNAB) ... GAO NOTE
General Accounting Office/Procurement and Systems Acquisition Division ... GAO/PSAD
General Accounting Office Program Analysis Division ... GAO/PAD
General Accounting Office Program Evaluation and Methodology Division ... GAO/PEMD
General Accounting Office Review ... GAOR
General Accounting Office, Technical Information Sources and Service, Washington, DC [*OCLC symbol*] (OCLC) ... GAO
General Accounting Office, Washington ... GAOW
General Accounting Package (IAA) ... GAP
General Activities (ADA) ... GA
General Activity, Ascendence-Submission, Masculinity-Femininity, Inferiority Feelings, Nervousness [*Psychology*] (AEBS) ... GAMIN
General Activity Simulation Language [*Computer science*] ... GASL
General Activity Simulation Program [*Programming language*] [*1970*] [*Computer science*] (BUR) ... GASP
General Acts of Arkansas [*A publication*] (DLA) ... Ark Acts
General Adaptation Syndrome [*Medicine*] ... GAS
General Address Reading Devices [*Computer science*] ... GARD
General Adjustment Bureau [*Insurance*] ... GAB
General Administration Letter (OICC) ... GAL
General Administration Section [*of a joint military staff; also the officer in charge of this section*] ... J-5
General Administrative Expense [*A budget appropriation title*] ... GAE
General Administrative Network [*Computer linkup*] [*British*] ... GANNET
General Administrative Order ... GAO
General Adverse Reaction [*Noise*] ... GAR
General Advisory Committee [*to the AEC, later, the Energy Research and Development Administration*] ... GAC
General Aerodynamic Lifting Surface (KSC) ... GALS
General Aeronautical Material ... GAM
General Aerospace, Inc. [*Canada ICAO designator*] (FAAC) ... SWK
General Agency Agreement [*Navy*] (AABC) ... GAA
General Agency Check [*Army*] ... GAC
General Agent [*Insurance*] ... GA
General Agents & Managers Association [*Insurance*] ... GAMA
General Agents and Managers Conference of NALU [*Washington, DC*] (EA) ... GAMC
General Agreement on Privileges and Immunities of the Council of Europe (DLA) ... C of E Agr PI
General Agreement on Tariffs and Trade [*Organization, and the concept it represents, concerned with adjustment of tariffs among 73 member nations*] [*See also AGTDC*] [*Switzerland*] [*Also, an information service or system*] ... GATT
General Agreement on Tariffs and Trade (EERA) ... GATT
General Agreement on Trade in Services ... GATS
General Agricultural Officer [*Ministry of Agriculture, Fisheries, and Food*] [*British*] ... GAO
General Agricultural Workers' Union [*Kenya*] ... GAWU
General Air Cargo [*Venezuela*] [*ICAO designator*] (FAAC) ... GAC
General Air Express ... GAE
General Air Services Ltd. [*Nigeria*] [*ICAO designator*] (FAAC) ... NGS
General Air Staff (NATG) ... GAS
General Air Traffic [*Europe-Asia*] ... GAT
General Air Training ... GAT
General Aircraft Ltd. ... GA
General Alert (NATG) ... GA
General Alert Order (NATG) ... GAO
General Alliance of Operative House Painters [*A union*] [*British*] ... GAOHP
General Allied Oil [*Vancouver Stock Exchange symbol*] ... GAZ
General All-Purpose Simulation Package [*McDonnell Douglas Automation Co.*] (MCD) ... GASP
General Alpha-Numeric Direct Access Library Facility [*Search system*] ... GANDALF
General American [*A type of spoken American English*] (BARN) ... GA
General American English ... GAE
General American Investors Co., Inc. [*Associated Press*] (SAG) ... GAInv
General American Investors Co., Inc. [*NYSE symbol*] (SPSG) ... GAM
General American Life Insurance Co. ... GALIC
General Analine & Film Co., General Research Laboratory, Easton, PA [*Library symbol Library of Congress Obsolete*] (LCLS) ... PEG
General Analysis of System Performance (IAA) ... GASP
General Analysis Technique ... GAT
General Analytical Evaluation ... GAE
General Analytical Methods Information Service [*Laboratory of the Government Chemist*] [*British*] (NITA) ... GAMIS
General Analytical Model for Process Analysis (IEEE) ... GRAMPA
General and Administrative ... G & A
General and Complete Disarmament ... GCD
General and Marine Hospital, Health Sciences Library, Owen Sound, ON, Canada [*Library symbol Library of Congress*] (LCLS) ... CaOOwGM
General and Municipal ... G & M
General and Municipal Workers' Union [*British*] ... GMWU
General and Practical Energy Information Data Base (MCD) ... GAP
General and Special Laws of the State of Texas [*A publication*] (DLA) ... Tex Gen Laws
General Anesthesia [*Medicine*] ... GA
General Antenna Package [*COMSAT*] ... GAP
General Anthropology Division (EA) ... GAD
General Appearance [*On physical examination*] [*Medicine*] (DAVI) ... GA
General Application Plan (AFIT) ... GAP
General Applied Science Laboratory ... GASL

General Appraisers' Decisions [*A publication*] (DLA) .... GA
General Aptitude Series [*Test*] .... GAS
General Aptitude Test [*Psychometrics*] .... GAT
General Aptitude Test Battery (DNAB) .... GAPB
General Aptitude Test Battery .... GATB
General Aptitude Test Battery .... GATBY
General Arab Women Federation (EA) .... GAWF
General Arbitration Council of the Textile and Apparel Industries
   (EA) .... GACTAI
General Arbitration Council of the Textile Industry [*Later, GACTAI*]
   (EA) .... GACTI
General Area Time-Based Train Simulator (PDAA) .... GATTS
General Areas of Competence [*Education*] (AIE) .... GAC
General Arrangement (MCD) .... GA
General Arrangements to Borrow [*United Nations*] (EY) .... GAB
General Assembly .... GA
General Assembly Data .... GAD
General Assembly Library, Wellington, New Zealand, [*Library symbol Library of Congress*] (LCLS) .... NzWGAL
General Assembly of International Sports Federations [*Later, GAISF*]
   (EA) .... GAIF
General Assembly of the Presbyterian Church of England (DAS) .... GAPCE
General Assembly of the United Nations .... GA (UN)
General Assembly Official Record [*United Nations*] [*A publication*] (DLA) .... GAOR
General Assembly Program [*Computer science*] .... GAP
General Assembly to Stop the Powerline (EA) .... GASP
General Assessment Tridimensional Analog Computer (IEEE) .... GATAC
General Assignment (ADA) .... GA
General Assistance [*A form of public charity*] .... GA
General Association of General Baptists (EA) .... GAGB
General Association of International Sports Federations [*Formerly, GAIF*]
   (EA) .... GAISF
General Association of Ladies Hairdressers [*British*] (BI) .... GALH
General Association of Municipal Health and Technical Experts (EA).... GAMHTE
General Association of Regular Baptist Churches (EA) .... GARBC
General Asymptotic Composition Program [*Computer science*] .... GEASCOP
General Atomic Co., San Diego, CA [*Library symbol Library of Congress*]
   (LCLS) .... CSdGA
General Atomic In-Pool Loop (SAA) .... GAIL
General Atomic Material Assay System [*Nuclear energy*] (NRCH) .... GAMAS
General Atomics [*Division of General Dynamics Corp.*] .... GA
General Atomics Corporation .... GA
General Attention [*Medicine*] .... GA
General Audiences [*All ages admitted*] [*Movie rating*] .... G
General Audio and Data Communications Ltd. (NITA) .... GADC
General Audit Manual .... GAM
General Automatic Luminosity and X-Y [*Engine technology*] (PDAA) .... GALAXY
General Automation Automatic Recovery Device (IAA) .... GAARD
General Automation, Inc. [*AMEX symbol*] .... GA
General Automation, Inc. [*Associated Press*] (SAG) .... GnAuto
General Automation Users Group Exchange [*Defunct*] (EA) .... GAUGE
General Automotive Support .... GAS
General Average (WDAA) .... G/AV
General Average [*Insurance*] .... GA
General Average (WDAA) .... GEN AV
General Average Certificate [*Business term*] (DS) .... GAC
General Average Contribution [*Marine insurance*] (DS) .... G/A Con
General Average Deposit [*Marine insurance*] (DS) .... G/A Dep
General Avia SpA [*Italy ICAO aircraft manufacturer identifier*] (ICAO) .... GA
General Aviation (EA) .... GA
General Aviation Activity and Avionics [*FAA*] (TAG) .... GAAA
General Aviation Association Australia .... GAAA
General Aviation Authority [*FAA*] (TAG) .... GAA
General Aviation District Office [*FAA*] .... GADO
General Aviation Facilities Planning Group .... GAFPG
General Aviation Flight Guide [*British*] (AIA) .... GAFG
General Aviation Inspection Aids Summary [*FAA*] .... GAIS
General Aviation Manufacturers' and Traders' Association [*British*]
   (DA) .... GAMTA
General Aviation Manufacturers Association (EA) .... GAMA
General Aviation Pilot Education [*Safety project*] .... GAPE
General Aviation Radio Magnetic Indicator .... GARMI
General Aviation Recovery Device .... GARD
General Aviation Services Ltd. [*British ICAO designator*] (ICDA) .... DG
General Aviation Simulator [*Computer science NASA*] .... GAS
General Aviation Technical Training Conference .... GATTC
General Aviation Terminal, Inc. [*Canada ICAO designator*] (FAAC) .... XGA
General Aviation Trainer .... GAT
General Aviation Transponder .... GAT
General Avionics Testbed [*Military*] .... GATB
General Background .... GB
General Banking Terminal System (MHDW) .... GBTS
General Banner Bearer [*Freemasonry*] (ROG) .... GBB
General Bathymetric Chart of the Oceans [*International Hydrographic Bureau*] .... GEBCO
General Bearing Line [*Navy*] (NVT) .... GBL
General Benchmark Program (MHDB) .... GBMP
General Bending Response Program [*Computer*] [*Navy*] .... GBRP
General Binding Corp. .... GBC
General Binding Corp. [*NASDAQ symbol*] (NQ) .... GBND
General Binding Corp. [*Associated Press*] (SAG) .... GnBnd
General Board [*Military judicial or investigative body*] .... GB
General Board .... GBD
General Board of Christian Social Concerns of the Methodist Church
   (EA) .... GBCSCMC

General Broadcast Signaling Virtual Channel [*Telecommunications*]
   (ACRL) .... GBSVC
General Bronze Corp. (MCD) .... GB
General Business (MHDI) .... GB
General Business System (MHDW) .... GBS
General Cable (IAA) .... GC
General Cable PLC [*NASDAQ symbol*] (SAG) .... GCABY
General Cable PLC [*Associated Press*] (SAG) .... GnCable
General Call Preceding a Message [*Amateur Radio*] (BARN) .... QST
General Capital Increase [*Banking*] .... GCI
General Cargo [*Shipping*] (DS) .... GEN CAR
General Cargo Rates [*Business term*] .... GCR
General Catalog of Variable Stars [*Astronomy*] (OA) .... GCVS
General Ceiling Price Regulation (DLA) .... GCPR
General Certificate of Education [*British*] .... GCE
General Certificate of Secondary Education [*British*] .... GCSE
General Certificate of Secondary Education (BARN) .... GCSE
General Certified End User [*Department of Commerce export license*] .... G-CEU
General Chairman-Member Pickwick Club [*From "The Pickwick Papers" by Charles Dickens*] .... GCMPC
General Chemical Indicators [*Database*] [*Probe Economics, Inc.*] [*Information service or system*] (CRD) .... GENCHEM
General Cigarette Workers' Industrial Union [*British*] .... GCWIU
General Cinema Corp. [*Chestnut Hill, MA*] .... GCC
General Circuit Breaker (MHDI) .... GCB
General Circular .... GC
General Circulation Model [*Meteorology*] [*Computer science*] .... GCM
General Civil Engineering Package (IAA) .... GECEP
General Claim Agent .... GCA
General Classification Test [*Military*] .... GCT
General Classification Test/Arithmetic Test/Electronics Technician Selection Test [*Military*] (DNAB) .... GAE
General Clinical Research Center [*University of Vermont*] [*Research center*]
   (RCD) .... CRC
General Clinical Research Center [*Stanford University*] (RCD) .... GCRC
General Clinical Research Center [*University of Virginia*] (RCD) .... GCRC
General Clinical Research Center [*University of Alabama in Birmingham*]
   (RCD) .... GCRC
General Clinical Research Center [*Scripps Clinic and Research Foundation*] .... GCRC
General Clinical Research Center Program Branch [*National Institutes of Health*] .... GCRCPB
General Clinical Service (MAE) .... GCS
General Code [*A publication*] (DLA) .... GC
General Cognitive Index [*Medicine*] (DMAA) .... GCI
General Combining Ability .... GCA
General Commission on Chaplains and Armed Forces Personnel [*Later, NCMAF*] (EA) .... GCC
General Commission on the Status and Role of Women - United Methodist Church (EA) .... GCSRW - UMC
General Committee of the Comite Europeen des Assurances [*France*]
   (EAIO) .... GCCEA
General Commodity Rate [*Shipping*] (DS) .... GCR
General Communication, Inc. [*Anchorage, AK*] [*Telecommunications*]
   (TSSD) .... GCI
General Communication, Inc. [*NASDAQ symbol*] (NQ) .... GNCM
General Communication Routine (IAA) .... GECOR
General Communication Subsystem [*Computer science*] .... GCS
General Communications, Inc. [*Associated Press*] (SAG) .... GnCom
General Communications System [*Sperry Univac*] (NITA) .... GCS
General Communications Vessel [*Navy ship symbol*] [*World War II*] .... AGC
General Compiler (NITA) .... GECOM
General Component Reference (IEEE) .... GCR
General Comprehensive Operating Supervisor [*Computer science*] .... GCOS
General Comprehensive Operating Supervisor [*Computer science*] .... GECOS
General Comprehensive Operating System (NITA) .... GCOS
General Comprehensive Operating System .... GECOS
General Computer Operational System [*NASA*] .... GCOS
General Computer Systems (NITA) .... GCS
General Computer Systems, Inc. .... GCS
General Condition [*Medicine*] .... GC
General Conditions of Contract .... GCOC
General Conference Committee of the National Poultry Improvement Plan
   [*Department of Agriculture*] (EGAO) .... GCCNPIP
General Conference on Weights and Measures (ACII) .... CGPM
General Conference on Weights and Measures .... GCWM
General Constituency Section for Small or Rural Hospitals (EA) .... SSRH
General Consumers Electronics (NITA) .... GCE
General Continuous Wave (IAA) .... GCW
General Contractor [*Technical drawings*] .... GC
General Control .... GC
General Control Approach .... GCA
General Control Unit (MCD) .... GCU
General Corporation for Light Air Transport & Technical Sevices [*Libya*]
   [*ICAO designator*] (FAAC) .... GLT
General Council (IAA) .... GC
General Council and Register of Consultant Herbalists [*British*] (DBA) .... GCRCH
General Council and Register of Naturopaths [*British*] (DBA) .... GCRN
General Council and Register of Osteopaths Ltd. [*British*] .... GCRO
General Council of British Shipping .... GCBS
General Counsel (AAGC) .... DL
General Counsel .... GC
General Counsel (AAGC) .... Gen Con
General Counsel's Memorandum [*Internal Revenue Service*] .... GCM
General Court-Martial .... GCM

General Court-Martial Authority .... GCMA
General Court-Martial Convening Authority [*DoD*] .... GCMCA
General Court-Martial Jurisdiction .... GCMJ
General Court-Martial Order .... GCMO
General Court-Martial Prisoner .... GCMP
General Cover [*Insurance*] .... GC
General Cueing .... GC
General Cybernetics Corp. [*Vancouver Stock Exchange symbol*] .... GCY
General Data Acquisition Unit (MCD) .... GDAU
General Data Analysis and Simulation (IAA) .... GENDA
General Data Analyzer (IAA) .... GEDAN
General Data Comm (NITA) .... GDC
General Data Stream [*Computer science*] .... GDS
General DataComm Industries, Inc. [*NYSE symbol*] (SPSG) .... GDC
General DataComm Industries, Inc. [*Associated Press*] (SAG) .... GnData
General Declassification Schedule (MCD) .... GDS
General Defense Intelligence Program [*DoD*] .... GDIP
General Defense Intelligence Proposed Program [*DoD*] (MCD) .... GDIPP
General Defense Plan [*Formerly, EDP*] [*NATO*] (NATG) .... GDP
General Delivery .... GD
General Delivery (DD) .... GD
General Delivery .... GEN DEL
General Dental Council [*British*] .... GDC
General Dental Practitioner's Association [*British*] .... GDPA
General Depot [*Military*] .... GENDEP
General Design (AAG) .... GD
General Design Criteria (NRCH) .... GDC
General Design Document [*Computer science*] (MHDI) .... GDD
General Design Memorandum [*US Army Corps of Engineers*] .... GDM
General Destination .... G-Dest
General Detail [*Coast Guard*] .... GENDET
General Development .... GD
General Development Corp. (AAG) .... GDC
General Development Map [*or Model*] .... GDM
General Development Order [*Town and country planning*] [*British*] .... GDO
General Development Plan (MUGU) .... GDP
General Diagram .... GD
General Digest [*A publication*] (DLA) .... Gen Dig
General Digest, New Series [*A publication*] (DLA) .... Gen Dig NS
General [*Purpose*] **Digital Computer** .... GDC
General Discharge .... GD
General Disk Programming System [*Computer science*] (IAA) .... GDPS
General Dispensary [*Military*] .... GD
General Dispensary [*Military*] .... GENDISP
General Disposal Authority .... GDA
General Distribution [*Pentagon security classification code*] .... GENDIS
General Douglas McArthur High School, Levittown, NY [*Library symbol*] [*Library of Congress*] (LCLS) .... NLevMH
General Drafting System [*Applied Research of Cambridge Ltd.*] [*Software package*] (NCC) .... GDS
General Duties [*Ranking title*] [*British Women's Royal Naval Service*] .... G
General Duties (Ground) [*British military*] (DMA) .... GD(G)
General Duties Medical Officer .... GDMO
General Duty .... GD
General Dynamics .... GENDYN
General Dynamics/Astronautics .... GD/A
General Dynamics Astronautics .... GDA
General Dynamics/Convair .... GD/C
General Dynamics, Convair .... GDC
General Dynamics/Convair Aerospace Division, Fort Worth, TX [*Library symbol Library of Congress*] (LCLS) .... TxFG
General Dynamics/Convair Aerospace Division, San Diego, CA [*Library symbol Library of Congress*] (LCLS) .... CSdG
General Dynamics/Convair Division (MCD) .... GD/CV
General Dynamics Corp. [*ICAO aircraft manufacturer identifier*] (ICAO) CV
General Dynamics Corp. [*NYSE symbol*] (SPSG) .... GD
General Dynamics Corp. .... GDC
General Dynamics Corp. [*Associated Press*] (SAG) .... GnDyn
General Dynamics Corp., Pomona Division Library, Pomona, CA [*Library symbol Library of Congress*] (LCLS) .... CPomG
General Dynamics/Daingerfield (SAA) .... GD/D
General Dynamics/Electric Boat Division (KSC) .... GD/EB
General Dynamics/Electronics (SAA) .... GD/E
General Dynamics/Fort Worth (KSC) .... GD/FW
General Dynamics/General Atomic (KSC) .... GD/GA
General Dynamics High-Speed Wind Tunnel .... GDHSWT
General Dynamics [*Corp.*] **Land Systems Division** .... GDLS
General Dynamics Land Systems Inc. [*A publication*] (AAGC) .... GDLS
General Dynamics, Pomona Division .... GD/PD
General Dynamics, Quincy Shipbuilding Division, Quincy, MA [*Library symbol Library of Congress*] (LCLS) .... MQG
General Dynamics/Telecommunications .... GD/T
General Economic Forecasts [*Databank*] (NITA) .... GE economic forecasts
General Edit System [*Computer science*] (IAA) .... GES
General Edit System Programming Language (IAA) .... GESPL
General Education Management System [*Computer science*] (IEEE) .... GEMS
General Education Provisions Act [*1970*] .... GEPA
General Educational Development [*Test*] .... GED
General Educational Development Institute (EA) .... GEDI
General Educational Development Program [*Army*] (AABC) .... GEDP
General Educational Development Test .... GEDT
General Educational Services Corp. .... GES
General Edward Lawrence Logan International Airport [*FAA*] (TAG) .... BOS
General Effectiveness Model (DNAB) .... GEM
General Election .... GE
General Election Expenditure Limit [*Federal Election Commission*] .... GEEL
General Electric (NITA) .... GE
General Electric Airborne Guidance (AAG) .... GEAG
General Electric Aircraft Nuclear Propulsion Department (SAA) .... GE-ANPD
General Electric/Apollo Support Division (KSC) .... GE/ASD
General Electric Atomic Power [*or Products*] .... GEAP
General Electric BWR [*Boiling Water Reactor*] **Thermal Analysis Branch** (NRCH) .... GETAB
General Electric Caliber [*Gatling Gun*] .... GECAL
General Electric Canada, Inc. [*Toronto Stock Exchange symbol*] .... GEZ
General Electric Capital Corp. .... GECC
General Electric Capital Exchange [*AMEX symbol*] (SAG) .... GCG
General Electric Capital Exchange [*Associated Press*] (SAG) .... GEC
General Electric Chemical Engineering Calculation System .... GECECS
General Electric Co. [*NYSE symbol*] (SPSG) .... GE
General Electric Co. .... GEC
General Electric Co. [*Associated Press*] (SAG) .... GenEl
General Electric Co. and Fanuc Automation Corp. .... GEF
General Electric Company Computer Services [*British*] (NITA) .... GECCS
General Electric Co., Electronics Park Library, Syracuse, NY [*OCLC symbol*] (OCLC) .... ZUI
General Electric Co., Information Resources Library, Utica, NY [*OCLC symbol*] (OCLC) .... ZUJ
General Electric Co., Knolls Atomic Laboratory, Technical Library, Schenectady, NY [*Library symbol Library of Congress*] (LCLS) .... NSchGEKA
General Electric Co., Light Research Laboratory, Cleveland, OH [*Library symbol Library of Congress*] (LCLS) .... OCIL
General Electric Co., Main Library, Schenectady, NY [*Library symbol Library of Congress*] (LCLS) .... NSchGEM
General Electric Co., Missile and Space Vehicle Department, Aerosciences Laboratory, Philadelphia, PA [*Library symbol Library of Congress*] (LCLS) .... PPGE-M
General Electric Co., Philadelphia, PA [*Library symbol Library of Congress*] (LCLS) .... PPGE
General Electric Co., Pittsfield, MA [*Library symbol Library of Congress*] (LCLS) .... MPG
General Electric Co., R and D Center, Branch Library, Schenectady, NY [*Library symbol Library of Congress*] (LCLS) .... NSchGERB
General Electric Co., Research Laboratory, Schenectady, NY [*Library symbol Library of Congress*] (LCLS) .... NSchGER
General Electric Co., Santa Barbara, CA [*Library symbol Library of Congress*] (LCLS) .... CStbGE
General Electric Co., Silicone Products Department, Waterford, NY [*Library symbol Library of Congress*] (LCLS) .... NWatfG
General Electric Co., Syracuse, NY [*Library symbol Library of Congress*] (LCLS) .... NSyGE
General Electric Co., Traveling Wave Tube Production Section, Palo Alto, CA [*Library symbol Library of Congress*] (LCLS) .... CPaGE
General Electric Co., Utica, NY [*Library symbol Library of Congress*] (LCLS) .... NUtGE
General Electric Co., WMD Technical Library, Wilmington, NC [*Library symbol Library of Congress*] (LCLS) .... NcWGE
General Electric Comprehensive Operating System [*Computer science*] (NHD) .... GECOS
General Electric Computer Analysis Program .... GELAP
General Electric Credit Auto Lease, Inc. .... GECAL
General Electric Detection and Automatic Correction (NASA) .... GEDAC
General Electric Electronic Processor .... GEEP
General Electric Electronic System Evaluator .... GEESE
General Electric Financial Services [*Australia Commercial firm*] .... GEFS
General Electric Flame Site (MUGU) .... GEFS
General Electric Gas [*Process*] .... GEGAS
General Electric General Purpose .... GEPURS
General Electric Guidance System [*Aerospace*] (AAG) .... GEGS
General Electric Hanford Atomic Products Operation (SAA) .... GE-HAPO
General Electric Heavy Military Electronics (IAA) .... GEHME
General Electric Industrial and Power Systems [*Australia Commercial firm*] .... GEIPS
General Electric Information Services Co. [*General Electric Co.*] [*Software manufacturer*] [*Information service or system Telecommunications*] (IID) .... GEISCO
General Electric Inventory Management System (IAA) .... GEIMS
General Electric Laboratory .... GEL
General Electric Light Military Electronics (IAA) .... GELME
General Electric Lighting [*Australia Commercial firm*] .... GEL
General Electric Macro Assembly Language (NASA) .... GMAL
General Electric Magnetically Anchored Gravity System .... GEMAGS
General Electric Manufacturing Simulator (IEEE) .... GEMS
General Electric Measurement and Control .... GE/MAC
General Electric Medical Systems [*Australia Commercial firm*] .... GEMS
General Electric Missile and Space Vehicle Department [*Military*] (IAA) .... GEMSVD
General Electric Motors [*Australia Commercial firm*] .... GEM
General Electric Network [*Computer science*] .... GEN
General Electric Network for Information Exchange [*General Electric Co.*] [*Online information service*] (IID) .... GEnie
General Electric Nose Cone [*Aerospace*] (AAG) .... GENC
General Electric Parts Explosion System .... GEPEXS
General Electric Plastics [*Australia Commercial firm*] .... GEP
General Electric Process Automation Computer .... GEPAC
General Electric Process Design System .... GEPDS
General Electric Programmable Automatic Comparator [*or Computer*] .... GEPAC
General Electric Radio [*or Range*] **Tracking System** [*Aerospace*] .... GERTS
General Electric Range Safety Instrumentation System [*Aerospace*] .... GERSIS
General Electric Reentry Vehicle [*Aerospace*] (AAG) .... GERV

General Electric Remote Terminal Supervisor .... GERTS
General Electric Remote Terminal Supervisor [*Honeywell*] (NITA) .... GRTS
General Electric Remote Terminal System (IEEE) .... GERTS
General Electric Satellite Orbit Control [*Aerospace*] .... GESOC
General Electric Scientific Color Matching (IAA) .... GESCOM
General Electric Self-Adaptive Control System .... GESAC
General Electric Semiconductor .... GES
General Electric Silicones [*Australia Commercial firm*] .... GES
General Electric Six Hundred Users' Association [*Later, HLSUA*] [*Computer science*] .... GESHUA
General Electric Supply Corp. .... GESCO
General Electric Symbolic Assembly Language (IAA) .... GERSAL
General Electric Symbolic Assembly Language (IAA) .... GESAL
General Electric Technical Services Company .... GETSC
General Electric Technical Services Co. (NRCH) .... GETSCO
General Electric Telemetering and Control (IEEE) .... GE/TAC
General Electric Telemetering and Control .... GETAC
General Electric Test Engineering Language [*Computer science*] (IEEE) .... GETEL
General Electric Test Reactor .... GETR
General Electric Time Sharing System (IAA) .... GETSS
General Electric Training Operational Language (MCD) .... GETOL
General Electric Training Operational Logic [*Computer science*] (IEEE) .... GETOL
General Electric Transportation Systems [*Australia Commercial firm*] .... GETS
General Electric Vallecitos Nuclear Center (DOGT) .... GE
General Electric Vallecitos Nuclear Center [*Vallecitos, CA*] (GAAI) .... GEVNC
General Electric Variable Increment Computer .... GEVIC
General Electrical and Mechanical Systems (IAA) .... GEMS
General Electric-ARSD, Sunnyvale, CA [*OCLC symbol*] (OCLC) .... GEA
General Electricity-Generating Board (OA) .... GEGB
General Electrodynamics Corp. (MCD) .... GEC
General Emergency Operations Plan (CINC) .... GEOP
General Employment Enterprises, Inc. [*Associated Press*] (SAG) .... GnEmp
General Employment Enterprises, Inc. [*AMEX symbol*] (SPSG) .... JOB
General Emulation Language .... GEL
General Energy and Materials Balance System [*Chemical engineering*] [*Computer science*] .... GEMS
General Engine Bulletin .... GEB
General Engine Management System .... GEMS
General Engineering Research .... GER
General Engineering Squadron .... GES
General Engineering System .... GENESYS
General Enrollment Manual .... GEM
General Enrollment Plan [*Insurance*] .... GEP
General Entry Permit .... GEP
General Environmental Statement for Mixed Oxide Fuel .... GESMO
General Epitaxial Monolith (IEEE) .... GEM
General Equipment and Packaging Laboratory [*Army*] .... GEPL
General Equipment Command [*Army*] .... GEC
General Equipment Maintenance System [*Software*] [*Diagonal Data Corp.*] [*Automotive engineering*] .... GEMS
General Equipment Test Activity [*Army*] .... GETA
General Equivalency Diploma [*For nongraduates*] .... GED
General Estimates System [*NHTSA*] (TAG) .... GES
General Estimating Equation [*Mathematics*] .... GEE
General Evaluation Equipment .... GEE
General Examination .... GE
General Expenses .... GE
General Export Services Branch [*Department of Trade*] [*British*] .... GESB
General Extrasensory Perception [*Parapsychology*] .... GESP
General Factor (ADA) .... G
General Failure Criteria .... GFC
General Federation of Labor Unions [*Syria*] .... GFLU
General Federation of Trade Unions [*Various countries*] .... GFTU
General Federation of Trade Unions [*British*] (DBA) .... GFTU
General Federation of Women's Clubs (EA) .... GFWC
General File/Record Control [*Honeywell, Inc.*] .... GEFRC
General File/Record Control [*Honeywell, Inc.*] (IAA) .... GFRC
General Fisheries Council for the Mediterranean [*ICSU*] .... GFCM
General Fitness Assessment .... GFA
General Flight Rules [*CAB*] [*A publication*] (DLA) .... GFR
General Flight Work .... GFW
General Foods Corp. (CDAI) .... GF
General Foods Corp., Hoboken, NJ [*Library symbol Library of Congress*] (LCLS) .... NjHoGF
General Foods, Inc., Management Science Department, Don Mills, ON, Canada [*Library symbol*] [*Library of Congress*] (LCLS) .... CaOTGFM
General Foods Ltd., Cobourg, ON, Canada [*Library symbol Library of Congress*] (LCLS) .... CaOCoGF
General Foods Ltd., Cobourg, Ontario [*Library symbol National Library of Canada*] (NLC) .... OCOGF
General Foods Moisture Vapor Transmission .... GFMVT
General Foods Technical Center Library, Tarrytown, NY [*Library symbol Library of Congress*] (LCLS) .... NTaGF
General Foods Technical Center, White Plains, NY [*OCLC symbol*] (OCLC) .... YGF
General Forecasting Program (BUR) .... GFP
General Foreign Policy [*A publication*] .... GFP
General Forestry Assistance .... GFA
General Format Identifier [*Computer science*] (TNIG) .... GFI
General Freight Agent .... GFA
General Freight Department .... GFD
General Freight Office .... GFO
General Freight Traffic Committee - Eastern Railroads .... GFTC-ER
General Function System Requirement .... GFSR
General Functional Description [*Military*] (AABC) .... GFD
General Functional Requirements .... GFR
General George A. Lincoln [*World War II*] .... GAL
General George C. Marshall [*World War II*] .... GCM
General Gonadotropic Activity [*Endocrinology*] (MAE) .... GGA
General Government Division [*GAO*] (AAGC) .... GGD
General Grand Chapter [*Freemasonry*] .... GGC
General Grand High Priest [*Freemasonry*] .... GGHP
General Grant National Memorial .... GEGR
General Growth Properties [*NYSE symbol*] (SPSG) .... GGP
General Growth Properties [*Associated Press*] (SAG) .... GnGrth
General Headquarters [*Military*] (CDAI) .... GH
General Headquarters [*Military*] .... GHQ
General Headquarters Air Force .... GHQAF
General Headquarters Exercise .... GHQS
General Headquarters File [*Army*] .... GHQF
General Health (DMAA) .... GH
General Health Policy Model .... GHPM
General Health Questionnaire [*Personality development test*] [*Psychology*] .... GHQ
General High Altitude Questionnaire (PDAA) .... GHAQ
General Hospital [*Initialism also refers to a TV program*] .... GH
General Hospital Corp., St. John's, Newfoundland [*Library symbol National Library of Canada*] (NLC) .... NFSGH
General Hospital, Nursing Education, St. John's, NF, Canada [*Library symbol Library of Congress*] (LCLS) .... CaNfSGHN
General Hospital of Port Arthur, Thunder Bay, Ontario [*Library symbol National Library of Canada*] (NLC) .... OTBGH
General Hospital of Saranac Lake, Saranac Lake, NY [*Library symbol Library of Congress*] (LCLS) .... NSIH
General Hospital, St. John's, NF, Canada [*Library symbol Library of Congress*] (LCLS) .... CaNfSGH
General Hospital, Sault Ste. Marie, ON, Canada [*Library symbol*] [*Library of Congress*] (LCLS) .... CaOStMGH
General Hospital, Sault Ste. Marie, Ontario [*Library symbol National Library of Canada*] (NLC) .... OSTMGH
General Host Corp. [*NYSE symbol*] (SPSG) .... GH
General Host Corp. [*Associated Press*] (SAG) .... GnHost
General Hotel, Boarding House, and Apartments [*British*] .... HBA
General Household Survey [*Office of Population Census and Surveys*] [*British*] .... GHS
General Housekeeping Area [*NASA*] (NASA) .... GHA
General Housewares Corp. [*NYSE symbol*] (SPSG) .... GHW
General Housewares Corp. [*Associated Press*] (SAG) .... GnHous
General Image Format [*Marine science*] (OSRA) .... GIF
General Image Format (USDC) .... GIF
General Image Processing System .... GYPSY
General Imaging Generator and Interpreter (IAA) .... GIGI
General Immunocompetence [*Immunology*] (DAVI) .... GIC
General Implementation Plan .... GIP
General Improvement Contractors Association (EA) .... GIC
General Incentive for Research and Development [*Canada*] .... GIRD
General Index .... GI
General Indexing in Reciprocal Lattice Space (KSC) .... GIRLS
General Indulgence (ROG) .... GI
General Industrial Equipment Reserve .... GIER
General Industry Advisory Committee .... GIAC
General Industry Applications (MCD) .... GIA
General Infantry [*Soldier*] [*Army*] (DAVI) .... GI
General Inferencing System .... GENISYS
General Information (IAA) .... GI
General Information and Analysis Tool .... GIANT
General Information Booklet [*Navy*] .... GIB
General Information Environment [*Data Dynamics, Inc.*] [*Portland, OR*] [*Telecommunications service*] (TSSD) .... GENIE
General Information Extractor .... GENIE
General Information File Interrogation (PDAA) .... GIFI
General Information Programme (NITA) .... GIP
General Information Programme [*UNESCO*] [*Acronym is based on foreign phrase*] .... PGI
General Information Retrieval and Application System (PDAA) .... GENIRAS
General Information Retrieval System Simulation .... GIRSS
General Information System for Planning (IAA) .... GISP
General Information Test .... GIT
General Input [*Computer science*] (IAA) .... GI
General Input Channel (NITA) .... GIC
General Input/Output Channel .... GIC
General Insertion Protein [*Genetics*] .... GIP
General Inspection [*Military*] (AABC) .... GI
General Inspection/Procurement Inspection (MCD) .... GI/PI
General Inspectorate Section [*European Theater of Operations*] [*World War II*] .... GI Sec
General Installation Dolly .... GID
General Installation Subcontractor .... GIS
General Instruction Book .... GIB
General Instructions for Routing and Reporting Officers .... GIRO
General Instrument Advanced Nitride Technology (IAA) .... GIANT
General Instrument Corp. [*NYSE symbol*] (SPSG) .... GIC
General Instrument Microelectronics [*British*] (NITA) .... GIM
General Instruments .... GI
General Insurance Fund [*Federal Housing Administration*] .... GIF
General Integrated Analytical Triangulation Program [*National Oceanic and Atmospheric Administration*] .... GIANT
General Intelligence .... G
General Intelligence Unit [*US, London*] .... GIU
General Internal FORTRAN Translator [*Computer science*] (IEEE) .... GIFT
General Internal Logic Test (PDAA) .... GILT

General Internal Process [*Computer science*] (IAA) .... GIP
General International Agreement [*Legal term*] (DLA) .... GIA
General Interpretative System for Matrix Operations [*Data processing system used in engineering*] [*Navy*] [*A union*] .... GISMO
General Iron Fitters Association [*A union*] [*British*] .... GIFA
General Issue .... GI
General Journal [*Accounting*] .... GJ
General Kinetics, Inc. [*Associated Press*] (SAG) .... GenKinet
General Kinetics, Inc. [*AMEX symbol*] (SPSG) .... GKI
General Knowledge Test .... GKT
General Labor and Trades .... GLT
General Laboratory Associates .... GLA
General Labourers' Amalgamated Union [*British*] .... GLAU
General Land Office [*Became part of Bureau of Land Management, 1946*] .... GLO
General Language-Operated Decision Implementation System (PDAA) .... GLODIS
General Laws [*A publication*] (DLA) .... GL
General Laws of Mississippi [*A publication*] (DLA) .... Miss Laws
General Laws of Rhode Island [*A publication*] (DLA) .... RI Gen Laws
General Layout Plan (NATG) .... GLP
General Learning Ability .... GLA
General Learning Corp. [*of Time, Inc.*] .... GLC
General Learning Disability .... GLD
General Leaseholds Ltd. [*Toronto Stock Exchange symbol*] .... GLL
General Ledger .... GENLED
General Ledger (AABC) .... GL
General Ledger Account (AFM) .... GLA
General Ledger Account Code .... GLAC
General Ledger, Accounts Payable, and Accounts Receivable [*Accounting*] .... GLAPPAR
General Ledger / Financial Information and Control System .... GL/FICS
General Ledger Identification Code (AFM) .... GLIC
General Ledger Subsidiary Account (AFM) .... GLSA
General Ledger System [*Accounting*] (IAA) .... GLS
General Letter .... GL
General Letter Package (PDAA) .... GLP
General Lew Wallace Studio, Crawfordsville, IN [*Library symbol Library of Congress*] (LCLS) .... InCLW
General Liability [*Insurance*] .... GL
General Licence [*British*] (ROG) .... GEN L
General Light Inter-Reflection Model (PDAA) .... GLIM
General Lighthouse Authority [*British*] .... GLA
General Lighting Service .... GLS
General Lighting System [*Incadescent lighting*] .... GLS
General Line Rate [*Advertising*] .... GLR
General Line School .... GLS
General Linear [*Group theory, mathematics*] .... GL
General Linear Modeling Program [*Computer science*] .... GLIM
General List [*Navy British*] .... G
General List [*Navy British*] (DMA) .... GL
General Livestock Agent .... GLSA
General Loader [*Honeywell*] (NITA) .... GELOAD
General Logic Unit [*Computer chip*] .... GLU
General Machine Test [*Computer science*] (BUR) .... GMT
General Macroassembly Program [*Honeywell, Inc.*] .... GMAP
General Magic, Inc. [*Associated Press*] (SAG) .... GMagic
General Magic, Inc. [*NASDAQ symbol*] (SAG) .... GMGC
General Magnaplate Corp. [*NASDAQ symbol*] (NQ) .... GMCC
General Magnaplate Corp. [*Associated Press*] (SAG) .... GnMag
General Maintenance [*Army*] .... GM
General Maintenance Aptitude [*Military*] (MCD) .... GMA
General Maintenance Aptitude Area [*Military*] (AFIT) .... GM
General Maintenance System [*Computer science*] (BUR) .... GMS
General Management Certificate .... GenManCert
General Management Directive .... GMD
General Management Plan [*National Park Service*] .... GMP
General Manager (WDAA) .... GEN MGR
General Manager .... GM
General Marine Distress .... GMD
General Maritime Stevedores' Union [*Philippines*] .... GMSU
General Marketing Application .... GMA
General Material and Petroleum Activity [*NCAD*] [*Army*] (MCD) .... GMPA
General Material and Petroleum Management Agency (MCD) .... GMPMA
General Material Services .... GMS
General Mathematical Aptitude Test (BARN) .... GMAT
General Matrix Manipulator (OA) .... GMM
General Matrix Program .... GMP
General Maximum Price Regulation [*World War II*] .... GMPR
General Measurement Loop (MCD) .... GML
General Medical (MAE) .... GM
General Medical Council [*British*] .... GMC
General Medical Intelligence (MCD) .... GMI
General Medical Officer [*Navy*] (DNAB) .... GMO
General Medical Practice (WDAA) .... GMP
General Medical Problem .... GM
General Medical Sciences and Atomic Energy Commission .... GeMSAEC
General Medical Services [*British*] .... GMS
General Medical Services Council [*British*] (BI) .... GMSC
General Medicine .... GM
General Medicine and Surgery .... GM & S
General Meetings [*Quakers*] .... GM
General Mental Ability .... GMA
General Merchandise .... GM
General Merchandise Distributors Council [*Colorado Springs, CO*] (EA) .... GMDC
General Merit [*Military*] .... GM
General Methods of Moments [*Statistics*] .... GMM

General Micro Systems Ltd. (NITA) .... GMS
General Microelectronics .... GME
General Microfilm Co., Cambridge, MA [*Library symbol Library of Congress*] (LCLS) .... GmC
General Microwave Corp. [*AMEX symbol*] (SPSG) .... GMW
General Microwave Corp. [*Associated Press*] (SAG) .... GnMicr
General MIDI [*Musical Instrument Digital Interface*] (CDE) .... GM
General Military Course (AFM) .... GMC
General Military Science .... GMS
General Military Subjects Test .... GMST
General Military Training (AFM) .... GMT
General Military Training Office .... GMTO
General Military Training Review Board (AFM) .... GMTRB
General Milk Sales [*Inactive*] [*An association*] (EA) .... GMS
General Mills, Inc. [*NYSE symbol*] (SPSG) .... GIS
General Mills, Inc. [*Associated Press*] (SAG) .... GnMill
General Mills, Incorporated, Minneapolis, MN [*OCLC symbol*] (OCLC) .... GMI
General Mills, Inc., Minneapolis, MN [*Library symbol Library of Congress*] (LCLS) .... MnMGM
General Mitchell International Airport [*FAA*] (TAG) .... MKE
General Mobile Radio Service [*Telecommunications*] (TSSD) .... GMRS
General Mobilization Material Readiness [*DoD*] .... GMMR
General Mobilization Reserve Acquisition Objective [*DoD*] .... GMRAO
General Mobilization Reserve Materiel Objective [*DoD*] .... GMRMO
General Mobilization Reserve Materiel Requirement [*DoD*] .... GMRMR
General Mobilization Reserve Stock [*DoD*] .... GMRS
General Mobilization Reserve Stockage Objective [*DoD*] .... GMRSO
General Mobilization Reserves [*DoD*] .... GMR
General Model (RDA) .... GENMOD
General Modular Redundancy .... GMR
General Monte Carlo Code [*Computer science*] .... GMC
General Mortgage [*Bond*] (MHDW) .... Gen Mtge
General Mortgage [*Bond*] .... GM
General Mortgage Bond .... GMB
General Motors 7.92% Dep Pfd [*NYSE symbol*] (TTSB) .... GMPrD
General Motors 9.12% Dep Pfd [*NYSE symbol*] (TTSB) .... GMPrG
General Motors 9.125% Dep Pfd [*NYSE symbol*] (TTSB) .... GMPrQ
General Motors Acceptance Corp. .... GMAC
General Motors Air Transport System .... GMATS
General Motors Allison Division .... GMAD
General Motors Assembly Division .... GMAD
General Motors Corp. [*NYSE symbol Toronto Stock Exchange symbol*] (SPSG) .... GM
General Motors Corp. [*ICAO designator*] (FAAC) .... GMC
General Motors Corp. [*NYSE symbol*] (SAG) .... GME
General Motors Corp. [*NYSE symbol*] (SAG) .... GMH
General Motors Corp. [*Associated Press*] (SAG) .... GMot
General Motors Corp. [*Associated Press*] (SAG) .... GnMotr
General Motors Corp. and Fanuc Ltd. [*In company name GMF Robotics Corp.*] .... GMF
General Motors Corp., Detroit Diesel Allison Division, Plant 8 Library, Indianapolis, IN [*Library symbol Library of Congress*] (LCLS) .... InID
General Motors Corp., Engineering Library and Information Services, Warren, MI [*Library symbol*] [*Library of Congress*] (LCLS) .... MiWarGME
General Motors Corp., Engineering Staff Library, Warren, MI [*Library symbol Library of Congress*] (LCLS) .... MiWarGMR-E
General Motors Corp., Inland Manufacturing Division, Engineering Library, Dayton, OH [*Library symbol Library of Congress*] (LCLS) .... ODaGMI
General Motors Corp. Research Laboratories [*Warren, MI*] .... GMRL
General Motors Corp., Research Laboratories Division, Warren, MI [*Library symbol Library of Congress*] (LCLS) .... MiWarGMR
General Motors Corp., Research Laboratory, Warren, MI [*OCLC symbol*] (OCLC) .... EYG
General Motors Defense Research Laboratory (MCD) .... GMDRL
General Motors Distribution Ireland Ltd. [*Dublin, Ireland*] .... GMDIL
General Motors Electric Vehicle [*General Motors Corp*] .... GMEV
General Motors Electronic Data Systems (NITA) .... GM/EDS
General Motors Europe .... GME
General Motors Europe - Passenger Cars [*Switzerland*] .... GME-PC
General Motors Hughes Electronics Corp. .... GMHE
General Motors Improvement Project [*Investigating team sponsored by consumer-advocate Ralph Nader*] .... GMIP
General Motors Information System and Communications Activity (HGAA) .... GMISCA
General Motors Institute .... GMI
General Motors Institute - Engineering and Management Institute [*Flint, MI*] .... GMI-EMI
General Motors Overseas Distribution Corp. .... GMODC
General Motors Proving Grounds [*Automotive engineering*] .... GMPG
General Motors Research .... GMR
General Motors Rotary Engine [*Automotive engineering*] .... GMRE
General Motors South African .... GMSA
General Motors Uniform Test Standards [*Automotive engineering*] .... GMUTS
General Motors World Headquarters, General Motors Law Library, Detroit, MI [*Library symbol Library of Congress*] (LCLS) .... MiDGM-L
General Motors-Holden's Ltd. [*Australia*] (ADA) .... GMH
General Municipal Boilermakers' and Allied Trades Union [*British*] .... GMBATU
General N. B. Baker Library, Sutherland, IA [*Library symbol Library of Congress*] (LCLS) .... IaSu
General NAS [*FAA*] (TAG) .... GNAS
General NAS Maintenance Control Center [*FAA*] (TAG) .... GMCC
General National Vocational Qualification [*British*] (ODBW) .... GNVQ
General Nautical Chart [*Navy*] .... GNC
General Naval Staff [*NATO*] (NATG) .... GNS
General Naval Training [*British military*] (DMA) .... GNT

General Neighborhood Renewal Plan ... GNRP
General Noise and Tonal System (NVT) ... GNATS
General Nonlinear Analysis of Two-Dimensional Structures [Computer program] ... GNATS
General Nonlinear Frame Analysis Program [Structures & Computers Ltd.] [Software package] (NCC) ... GENFAP
General Note (MSA) ... GN
General Notice ... GENOT
General Nuclear Engineering Corp. (MCD) ... GNEC
General Numerical Analysis of Transport [Computer program] ... GNAT
General Nursing Assistance (DMAA) ... GNA
General Nursing Care [Medicine] ... GNC
General Nursing Council ... GNC
General Nursing Council for England and Wales ... GNCEW
General Nutrition Co. [Associated Press] (SAG) ... GenNutr
General Nutrition Co. [NASDAQ symbol] (SAG) ... GNCI
General Obligation [Bond] [Business term] ... GO
General Obligation Bonds [Finance] ... GOB
General Ocean Research [Navy ship symbol] ... GOR
General of the Air Force (WGA) ... Gen AF
General of the Army (AABC) ... GA
General Office [or Officer] [Military] ... GO
General Officer Command [US Army Reserve] (AABC) ... GOCOM
General Officer Commanding [Navy] ... GOC
General Officer Commanding Royal Marines [British] ... GOCRM
General Officer Commanding-in-Chief [British] ... GOC-in-C
General Officer Money Allowance [Military] (AABC) ... GOMA
General Officer Product Improvement Review Board ... GOPIRB
General Officer Review (MCD) ... GOR
General Officer Steering Committee [Military] (MCD) ... GOSC
General Officer Steering Group ... GOSG
General Officers Branch [Air Force] ... GOB
General Officers' Protocol Roster ... GOPR
General Officers Review Group [Air Force] ... GORG
General On-Line Query System (MCD) ... GOQS
General Online Stack System (IAA) ... GOLS
General Operating Agency ... GOA
General Operating Committee ... GOC
General Operating Expenses (MCD) ... GOE
General Operating Language [Computer science] (IEEE) ... GOL
General Operating Room ... GOR
General Operating Specification [Air Materiel Command] (AAG) ... GOS
General Operational Plot ... GOP
General Operational Requirement ... GOR
General Operations and Logistics Simulation [Boeing] ... GOALS
General Operator-Computer Interaction (IEEE) ... GOCI
General Optical Council [British] ... GOC
General Optronics Line of Sight Atmospheric Lightwave Communication System [General Optronics Corp.] [Edison, NJ] [Telecommunications service] (TSSD) ... GOALS
General Order ... GO
General Order of Battle ... GOB
General Order of the Commander-in-Chief [British military] (DMA) ... GOCC
General Orders of the English High Court of Chancery [A publication] (DLA) ... Gen Ord Ch
General Ordination Examination ... GOE
General Organization [Identification card used at Madison Square Garden] ... GO
General Organization Analysis Language (IAA) ... GOAL
General Organizational Environment [Computer science] (BUR) ... GEORGE
General Oriental Investments Ltd. [Vancouver Stock Exchange symbol] ... GOI
General Outpost [Army] (AABC) ... GOP
General Outpost Line [Army] ... GOPL
General Overhaul Specification ... GOS
General Overruling Regulation [Office of Price Stabilization] (DLA) ... GOR
General Pair Decomposition (IAA) ... GPD
General Paralysis [or Paresis] [Medicine] ... GP
General Paralysis of the Insane [Literal translation, but also medical slang for eccentricity] ... GPI
General Parametrics Corp. [Associated Press] (SAG) ... GnPara
General Parametrics Corp. [NASDAQ symbol] (NQ) ... GPAR
General Parcel Service, Inc. [Associated Press] (SAG) ... GnPrcl
General Parcel Service, Inc. [Associated Press] (SAG) ... GPrcl
General Parcel Service, Inc. [NASDAQ symbol] (NQ) ... GPSX
General Parcel Svc Wrrt [NASDAQ symbol] (TTSB) ... GPSXW
General Parent Ring System [Proposed chemical classification] ... GPRS
General Parts Explosion System (IAA) ... GPEXS
General Passenger Agent ... GPA
General Passenger Committee - Eastern Railroads [Defunct] (EA) ... GPC-ERR
General Passenger Department ... GPD
General Patents Index [A publication] ... GPI
General Pause [Music] ... GP
General Pavement Studies [FHWA] (TAG) ... GPS
General Payments System ... GPAY
General People's Congress [or Committee] [Libya] [Political party] (PPW) ... GPC
General People's Congress [Yemen] [Political party] (EY) ... GPC
General Performance Appraisals System ... GPAS
General Performance Number ... GPN
General Periodicals Index [Information Access Co.] [Information service or system] (CRD) ... GPI
General Periodicals Ondisc [Database] ... GPO
General Peripheral Controller ... GPC
General Perturbation Theory [Nuclear science] ... GPT
General Petroleum & Mineral Organization [Saudi Arabia state-owned oil company] ... PETROMIN
General Petroleum Corp., Los Angeles, CA [Library symbol Library of Congress] (LCLS) ... CLGP
General Physical Condition [Medicine] ... GPC
General Physics Corp. [Associated Press] (SAG) ... GnPhys
General Physics Corp. [NYSE symbol] (SPSG) ... GPH
General Physique, Upper Extremity, Lower Extremity, Hearing, Eyesight, Mentality, and Personality [Medicine] (DMAA) ... GULHEMP
General Pico [Argentina] [Airport symbol] (OAG) ... GPO
General Pico [Argentina ICAO location identifier] (ICLI) ... SAZG
General Planning Group ... GPG
General Plant Equipment Requirements ... GPER
General Plant Project ... GPP
General Plant Telephone [Nuclear energy] (NRCH) ... GP
General Plant Telephone [Nuclear energy] (GFGA) ... GPT
General Plumbing & Roofing Services [Commercial firm] [British] ... GPRS
General Police Duties [British military] (DMA) ... GPD
General Political Department [China] [Military] ... GPD
General Political Warfare Department [Military] ... GPWD
General Post Office [British Defunct] ... GPO
General Postal Union [Later, UPU] ... GPU
General Practice (WDAA) ... GEN PRAC
General Practice [Medical specialty] (DAVI) ... GP
General Practice Reform Association [Medicine] (DAVI) ... GPRA
General Practitioner [of medicine] ... GP
General Practitioner Obstetrician ... GPO
General Precision Connector (IAA) ... GPC
General Precision Equipment (IAA) ... GPE
General Precision, Inc. ... GPI
General Precision, Inc., Librascope Division, Glendale, CA [Library symbol Library of Congress] (LCLS) ... CGIL
General Precision Laboratory ... GENPRL
General Precision Laboratory ... GPL
General Preferred Tariff [Canada] ... GP
General Preferred Tariff [Canada] ... GPT
General Preventive Medicine ... GPM
General Price Index (WDAA) ... GPI
General Price Level (ADA) ... GPL
General Price Level Accounting (ADA) ... GPLA
General Price-Level Adjusted [Finance] (PDAA) ... GPLA
General Principles [FBI standardized term] ... GP
General Print and Punch (NITA) ... GPP
General Printing Ink (DGA) ... GPI
General Problem Solver [Computer science] ... GPS
General [or Generic] **Problem Statement Simulator** ... GPSS
General Procedure (BABM) ... GEN PROC
General Procedures ... G
General Process Simulation Studies ... GPSS
General Process Simulator ... GPS
General Processing Subsystem (MCD) ... GPS
General Processor ... GP
General Processor Unit ... GPU
General Product (BUR) ... GP
General Product Acceptance Standard [Automotive engineering] ... GPAS
General Professional Education of the Physician [Panel report] [Association of American Medical Colleges] ... GPEP
General Protection [Computer science] (BYTE) ... GP
General Protection Fault [Computer programming] (BYTE) ... GPF
General Protocol Driver (NITA) ... GPD
General Provision ... GP
General Provisions Policy Statement (MCD) ... GPPS
General Public [Merchandising slang] ... GP
General Public Assistance [A form of public charity] ... GPA
General Public License (NHD) ... GPL
General Public Utilities Corp. [NYSE symbol] (SPSG) ... GPU
General Public Utilities Nuclear Corp. (NRCH) ... GPUN
General Public Virus [Computer science] (NHD) ... GPV
General Public Visiting [Navy] (NVT) ... GENVST
General Publication (KSC) ... GP
General Pulaski Heritage Foundation (EA) ... GPHF
General Purchasing Agency [Allied German Occupation Forces] ... GPA
General Purchasing Board ... GPB
General Purchasing Power [Accounting] ... GPP
General Purpose ... GP
General Purpose Associative Processor (PDAA) ... GPAP
General Purpose Automation Executive [IBM] (NITA) ... GPAX
General Purpose Basic [Programming language] (NITA) ... GPB
General Purpose Expert System Shell [Virginia Polytechnic Institute] [General framework for expert systems] (NITA) ... GUESS
General Purpose Frigate ... FGP
General Purpose Interface Adaptor (NITA) ... GPIA
General Purpose Interface Bus ... GPIB
General Purpose Loader (NITA) ... GPL
General Purpose Processor (MHDI) ... GPP
General Purpose Register (NITA) ... GR
General Purpose System Simulator (NITA) ... GPSS
General Purposes Committee [British] (DCTA) ... GPC
General Quarters [General Alert] [Navy] ... GQ
General Radio ... GR
General Radio Discriminator (IAA) ... GRD
General Radio Frequency Fitting (IAA) ... GRFF
General Radio Frequency Meter (IAA) ... GRFM
General Radio Service [Canada] ... GRS
General Railroad and Airline Stabilization Regulations [A publication] (DLA) ... GRASR
General Railway Classification [British] ... GRC

General Railway Signal Co., Library, Rochester, NY [*OCLC symbol*] (OCLC) .... VQN
General Railway Signal Co., Rochester, NY [*Library symbol Library of Congress*] (LCLS) .... NRGR
General Railway Warrants [*US Military Government, Germany*] .... GRW
General Random Audit Sample Selection Technique [*Military*] (AFIT) .... GRASS
General Range Safety Plan [*NASA*] .... GRSP
General Re Corp. [*Associated Press*] (SAG) .... GenlRe
General Re Corp. [*NYSE symbol*] (SPSG) .... GRN
General Reactor Technology (NRCH) .... GRT
General Reader .... GR
General Receptor for Phosphoinositide [*Biochemistry*] .... GRP
General Reciprocating Engine Bulletin [*A publication*] (DNAB) .... GREB
General Reconnaissance [*Marine Corps*] .... GR
General Reconnaissance School [*British military*] (DMA) .... GRS
General Records Schedules [*Military*] (AABC) .... GRS
General Recurrent Grant .... GRG
General Recursive Algebra and Differentiation (IEEE) .... GRAD
General Reduction and Analysis Support Package [*Military*] (CAAL) .... GRASP
General Register [*Computer science*] .... GR
General Register Office [*British*] .... GRO
General Register Office for Births, Deaths, and Marriages [*A publication*] (DLA) .... GROBDM
General Register Set/Stack [*Computer science*] .... GRS
General Relation Based Information Processing System (IAA) .... GRIPS
General Relativity [*Physics*] .... GR
General Remote Terminal Supervisor .... GRTS
General Remote Terminal System (NITA) .... GERTS
General Reporting System .... GRS
General Reports [*Military*] .... GENREP
General Requests for Ground-Based Electronics Equipment [*NASA*] .... GREE
General Research .... GR
General Research Corp. [*Information service or system*] (IID) .... GRC
General Research Corp., Effects Technology, Inc., Santa Barbara, CA [*Library symbol Library of Congress*] (LCLS) .... CStbGR
General Reserve .... GR
General Reserve Engineer Force [*British military*] (DMA) .... GREF
General Resource Allocation and Selection Program [*NASA*] (KSC) .... GRASP
General Retrieval and Information Processor for Humanities Oriented Studies .... GRIPHOS
General Retrieval Inquiry Negotiation Structure .... GRINS
General Retrieval of Information Program [*Computer science*] .... GRIP
General Retrieval of Information Program [*Hoechst Pharmaceutical Research Laboratories*] [*Personal indexing system*] [*British*] (NITA) .... GRIP
General Revenue Sharing [*Office of Revenue Sharing*] .... GRS
General Robotics and Active Sensory Processing Laboratory [*University of Pennsylvania*] [*Research center*] (RCD) .... GRASP Lab
General Roca [*Argentina*] [*Airport symbol*] (OAG) .... GNR
General Rose Memorial Hospital, Medical Library, Denver, CO [*Library symbol Library of Congress*] (LCLS) .... CoDGRM-M
General Routine Order .... GRO
General Routing Optimization System (IAA) .... GEROS
General Rules and Orders, India [*A publication*] (DLA) .... India Gen R & O
General [*Aviation*] **Safety District Office** .... GSDO
General Safety Inspector [*Aviation*] .... GSI
General Salary Order [*United States*] (DLA) .... GSO
General Salary Stabilization Regulations [*United States*] (DLA) .... GSSR
General Sales Manager .... GSM
General Santos [*Philippines*] [*Airport symbol*] (OAG) .... GES
General Satellite (NASA) .... GSAT
General Scanning, Inc. [*Associated Press*] (SAG) .... GenScan
General Scannning, Inc. [*NASDAQ symbol*] (SAG) .... GSCN
General Schedule [*Federal employee job classification GS-1 to GS-18*] .... GS
General Scholarship Test for High School Seniors [*Education*] (AEBS) .... GST
General School Budget (AIE) .... GSB
General Screening Test .... GST
General Sea Harvest [*Vancouver Stock Exchange symbol*] .... GSP
General Search (IAA) .... GS
General Secretariat .... GS
General Secretary .... GS
General Security of Information Agreement .... GSOIA
General Semantic Problem (AAG) .... GSP
General Semantics .... GS
General Semantics Foundation (EA) .... GSF
General Service [*Military*] (MCD) .... GENSER
General Service [*Military*] .... GENSV
General Service [*Literal translation, but used in sense of "excessively keen," or "overly acute"*] [*Army British*] .... GS
General Service Corps [*Military unit*] [*British*] .... GSC
General Service Infantry [*Army*] .... GSI
General Service Launch [*British military*] (DMA) .... GSL
General Service Manager [*Automotive retailing*] .... GSM
General Service Medal [*British*] .... GSM
General Service Recruit [*Navy*] .... GSR
General Service School [*Army*] .... GSS
General Service Test (NATG) .... GST
General Service Truck [*British*] .... GST
General Service Unit [*Marine Corps*] .... GSU
General Service Volunteer Aid Detachment [*British military*] (DMA) .... GSVAD
General Service Wagon [*British military*] (DMA) .... GSW
General Services Acquisition Regulation .... GSAR
General Services Administration [*Washington, DC*] .... GSA
General Services Administration (AAGC) .... GSA
General Services Administration Acquisition Regulations [*A publication*] (AAGC) .... GSAR
General Services Administration/Automated Data and Telecommunications Services (OICC) .... GSA/ADTS
General Services Administration - Board of Contract Appeals .... GSA-BCA
General Services Administration - Civilian Personnel Office .... GSA-CPO
General Services Administration/Federal Property Resources Services (OICC) .... GSA/FPRS
General Services Administration/Federal Supply Services (OICC) .... GSA/FSS
General Services Administration, National Archives and Record Service, Franklin D. Roosevelt Library, Hyde Park, NY [*Library symbol Library of Congress*] (LCLS) .... NHyF
General Services Administration/National Archives and Records Services [*Franklin D. Roosevelt Library*] [*Hyde Park, NY*] (OICC) .... GSA/NARS
General Services Administration - Office of Preparedness .... GSA-OP
General Services Administration/Office of the Federal Register (OICC) .... GSA/OFR
General Services Administration Property Management Regulation [*A publication*] (AAGC) .... GSPMR
General Services Administration - Public Building Service .... GSA-PBS
General Services Administration, Washington, DC [*OCLC symbol*] (OCLC) .... GSA
General Services Board of Contract Appeals .... GSBCA
General Services Building [*Nuclear energy*] (NRCH) .... GSB
General Services Intelligence [*Military*] (CAAL) .... GENSER
General Services Officer .... GSO
General Session of Peace Roll [*British Legal term*] (ROG) .... GSPR
General Sessions (ADA) .... GENSESS
General Sessions .... GS
General Sewing Data .... GSD
General Shoe Corp. [*Acronym now official name of firm*] .... GENESCO
General Short Arc Geodetic Reduction (PDAA) .... GSAGR
General Signal Corp. [*Associated Press*] (SAG) .... GenSignl
General Signal Corp. [*NYSE symbol*] (SPSG) .... GSX
General Simulation Program [*Programming language*] (IEEE) .... GSP
General Simulation System [*Army*] .... GSS
General Situation [*Military*] (NVT) .... GENSIT
General Situation Map [*Military*] (NATG) .... GSM
General Social Survey [*National Opinion Research Center*] .... GSS
General Society of Colonial Wars (EA) .... GSCW
General Society of Mayflower Descendants (EA) .... GSMD
General Society of Mechanics and Tradesmen (EA) .... GSMT
General Society of Mechanics and Tradesmen, New York, NY [*Library symbol Library of Congress*] (LCLS) .... NNMec
General Society of the War of 1812 (EA) .... GSW 1812
General Society, Sons of the Revolution (EA) .... SR
General Solution (OA) .... GS
General Somatic Afferent [*Nerve*] [*Anatomy*] .... GSA
General Somatic Efferent [*Nerve*] [*Anatomy*] .... GSE
General Soviet [*Later, A Group*] [*Division of National Security Agency*] .... GENS
General Specials .... GS
General Specifications (DNAB) .... GENSPECS
General Specifications for Ships (DNAB) .... GSFS
General Speed [*Military*] .... GS
General Spin Orbitals [*Atomic physics*] .... GSO
General Staff [*Military*] .... GS
General Staff Branch [*Army British*] .... G
General Staff Committees on Army National Guard and Army Reserve Policy (AABC) .... GSCARNGARP
General Staff Corps [*Military*] .... GSC
General Staff Council [*Military*] (AABC) .... GSC
General Staff Identification Badge [*Military decoration*] (GFGA) .... G/SIDBAD
General Staff Identification Badge [*Military decoration*] (AABC) .... GSIdentBad
General Staff Interpreter Officer [*Military British*] .... GSIO
General Staff Officer [*Military*] .... GSO
General Staff Operational Requirements [*Army*] (AABC) .... GSOR
General Staff Requirement [*British*] (RDA) .... GSR
General Staff Support (IAA) .... GSS
General Staff Support Large (IAA) .... GSSL
General Staff Support Medium (IAA) .... GSSM
General Staff Target (NATG) .... GST
General Staff, United States Army .... GSUSA
General Staff with Troops [*Army*] .... GST
General Staff with Troops [*Army*] .... GSWT
General Statistics .... GS
General Status Display System [*Graphics system*] (NITA) .... GSDS
General Statutes of Connecticut [*A publication*] (DLA) .... Conn Gen Stat
General Statutes of North Carolina [*A publication*] (DLA) .... NC Gen Stat
General Steam Navigation Co. [*British*] .... GSNC
General Steam Navigation Co. [*Shipping*] [*British*] .... GSNCO
General Steel Casting Corp. .... GSCC
General Stock Ownership Plan .... GSOP
General Storage (IAA) .... GS
General Storekeeper [*Navy*] .... GSK
General Stores Issue Ship [*Navy symbol*] .... AKI
General Stores Issue Ship [*Navy symbol*] .... AKS
General Stores Material [*Navy*] .... GSM
General Stores Material List .... GSML
General Stores Officer .... GSO
General Stores Supply Office .... GSSO
General Strike .... GS
General Strike for Peace .... GSP
General Strike Plan (NATG) .... GSP
General Stud Book [*Horses*] .... GSB
General Studies Association [*British*] .... GSA
General Studies Teachers' Association of New South Wales [*Australia*] .... GSTANSW

General Subjects (MCD) ... GS
General Submarine Officer (DOMA) ... GSO
General Superintendent ... GS
General Supply Depot ... GSD
General Supply Fund ... GSF
General Supply Office ... GSO
General Supply Schedule ... GSS
General Supply Stock Fund [*Air Force*] (AFM) ... GSSF
General Support [*Army*] ... GENSUP
General Support [*Military*] ... GS
General Support Announcement [*Public television*] ... GSA
General Support/Automatic Test Equipment (MCD) ... GS/ATE
General Support/Automatic Test Support System (MCD) ... GS/ATSS
General Support Company [*Army*] (VNW) ... GSC
General Support/Direct Support ... GS/DS
General Support Division [*Air Force*] ... GSD
General Support Equipment [*Military*] (MUGU) ... GSE
General Support Force [*Air Force*] ... GSF
General Support Group [*Army*] (AABC) ... GSG
General Support Maintenance (MCD) ... GSM
General Support Office ... GSO
General Support Reinforcing [*Army*] (AABC) ... GSR
General Support Rocket System ... GSRS
General Support Service Area (MCD) ... GSSA
General Support Supply Activity (MCD) ... GSSA
General Support System ... GSS
General Support Unit [*Army*] (AABC) ... GSU
General Supported Accommodation Program [*New South Wales, Australia*] ... GSAP
General Surgery (AABC) ... GENSURG
General Surgery ... GS
General Surgical Innovations, Inc. [*Associated Press*] (SAG) ... GenSurg
General Surgical Innovations, Inc. [*NASDAQ symbol*] (SAG) ... GSII
General Surveys and Analysis Branch [*Department of Education*] (GFGA) ... GSAB
General Switched Telephone Nertwork [*Telecommunications*] (OSI) ... GSTN
General Synod Measures (ILCA) ... GSM
General Syntactic Processor ... GSP
General Syntax Analyzer [*Sperry UNIVAC*] ... GSA
General System Description [*Military*] (AABC) ... GSD
General system Design [*Computer science*] ... REP
General System Development [*or Design*] (IAA) ... GSD
General System Mobile [*Telephone*] ... GSM
General System Model [*Computer science*] (EERA) ... GSM
General Systems Division [*IBM Corp.*] ... GSD
General Systems Engineering and Technical Direction ... GSETD
General Systems Research Ltd. [*Vancouver Stock Exchange symbol*] ... GSR
General Systems Theory ... GEST
General Systems Theory ... GST
General Tabulation System ... GTS
General Tariff (ADA) ... GT
General Tariff Bureau Inc. Lansing MI [*STAC*] ... GTB
General Teaching Council [*British*] ... GTC
General Teaching Council for School [*British*] ... GTCS
General Technical Advisory Committee [*for fossil energy*] [*Energy Research and Development Administration*] ... GTAC
General Technical Aptitude Area ... GT
General Technical Data Restricted ... GTDR
General/Technical Score [*Standardized test*] [*Military*] (INF) ... GT
General Technical Services, Inc. (MCD) ... GTS
General Technical Services, Inc. ... GTS
General Telecommunications Organization [*Oman*] [*Telecommunications service*] ... GTO
General Telegraph Exchange (IAA) ... GENTEX
General Telephone & Electronics (NITA) ... GT & E
General Telephone and Electronics [*Information service or system*] (IID) ... GTE
General Telephone and Electronics [*Telecommunications company*] [*Stamford, CT*] (WDMC) ... GTE
General Telephone & Electronics Corp. ... GENTEL
General Telephone & Electronics Corp. ... GT & E
General Telephone & Electronics, GTE Sylvania, Inc., Towanda, PA [*Library symbol Library of Congress*] (LCLS) ... PToG
General Telephone & Electronics Laboratories, Inc., Waltham Research Center Library, Waltham, MA [*Library symbol Library of Congress*] (LCLS) ... MWalG
General Telephone and Electronics Practice [*Telecommunications*] (TEL) ... GTEP
General Telephone Call Processing ... GTCP
General Telephone Co. of Florida [*NYSE symbol*] (SPSG) ... GLF
General Telephone Company of Florida (NITA) ... GT/F
General Telephone Co. of the Northwest ... GTNW
General Telephone Equipment (MCD) ... GTE
General Telephone System (IAA) ... GTS
General Term (DLA) ... Gen T
General Terms Agreement (MCD) ... GTA
General Terms and Conditions ... GT & C
General Test ... GT
General Test Plan (AAG) ... GTP
General Test Support (MCD) ... GTS
General Theological Library, Boston, MA [*Library symbol Library of Congress*] (LCLS) ... MBGT
General Theological Seminary [*New York, NY*] ... GTS
General Theological Seminary of the Protestant Episcopal Church, New York, NY [*Library symbol Library of Congress*] (LCLS) ... NNG
General Theological Seminary, St. Mark's Library, New York, NY [*OCLC symbol*] (OCLC) ... VXM
General Theory of Relativity ... GTR
General Time Sharing System [*Computer science*] ... GTSS
General Tool ... GT
General Tool Contract (MCD) ... GTC
General Tool Experimental (MCD) ... GTX
General Track Simulation [*NASA*] (KSC) ... GETS
General Trade Books [*Publishing*] ... GTB
General Traffic and Transportation Manager ... GT & TM
General Traffic Department ... GTD
General Traffic Manager ... GTM
General Training Assistance (ADA) ... GTA
General Training Program ... GTP
General Training System (MHDB) ... GENTRAS
General Transcription Factor [*Genetics*] ... GTF
General Transistor Corp. (AAG) ... GTC
General Transport [*Military*] ... GT
General Transport Administrative Vehicle ... GTAV
General Transportation Importance ... GTI
General Transpose [*Computer science*] ... GTRP
General Triple-Electron Nuclear Double Resonance [*Spectroscopy*] ... GT-ENDOR
General Troubleshooting ... GTS
General Trustco of Canada [*Toronto Stock Exchange symbol*] ... TTG
General Unary Hypothesis Automation (IEEE) ... GUHA
General Union Democratic Students and Patriotic Afghan (EA) ... GUDSPA
General Union of Associations of Loom Overlookers [*British*] (DCTA) ... GUALO
General Union of Bedding Trade Workers [*British*] ... GUBTW
General Union of Bellhangers and Gas Fitters [*British*] ... GUBGF
General Union of Braziers and Sheet Metal Workers [*British*] ... GUBSMW
General Union of Carpenters and Joiners [*British*] ... GUCJ
General Union of Chamber of Commerce, Industry and Agriculture for Arab Countries [*Lebanon*] (EAIO) ... GUCCIAAC
General University Funds (EERA) ... GUF
General Unwanted Energy Rejection Analysis Program [*Air Force*] ... GUERAP
General Upgrade LAN [*Limited Access Network*] **Program** [*Computer science*] (PCM) ... GULP
General Usage Inventory Director (MCD) ... GUIDE
General Utility Library Program [*Computer science*] ... GULP
General Utility Mechanic ... GUM
General Utility Package (MHDB) ... GPACK
General Vice President (WDAA) ... GVP
General Videotex Corp. ... GVC
General Visceral Afferent [*Neurology*] ... GVA
General Visceral Efferent [*Neurology*] ... GVE
General Visual Slope Indicator [*FAA*] (TAG) ... GVGI
General Wage Increase (MCD) ... GWI
General Wage Stabilization Regulations [*United States*] (DLA) ... GWSR
General War Reserves [*Army*] (AABC) ... GWR
General War Subsystem (MCD) ... GWS
General Warning ... GW
General Warranty Deed [*Real estate*] ... WD
General Watch Officer [*Army*] (AABC) ... GWO
General Water-Quality Engineering [*Survey*] [*Army*] (RDA) ... GWQE
General Well-Being [*Medicine*] (DMAA) ... GWB
General Will [*Collectivist theory of government*] ... GW
General Wiring Cables Group [*British*] (DBA) ... GWCG
General with Parents' Consent [*Motion picture rating*] (BARN) ... GP
General within Families (DICI) ... G/F
General Work Area [*NASA*] (NASA) ... GWA
General Work Force Performance Appraisal System [*Marine science*] (OSRA) ... GWPAS
General Work Force Performance Appraisal System (USDC) ... GWPAS
General Workers Professional Unions [*Bulgaria*] ... GWPU
General X-Ray Diagnosis [*Medicine*] ... GXD
General Yardmaster [*Railroading*] ... GYM
General Yielding Fracture Mechanics (OA) ... GYFM
Generale Occidentale [*Commercial firm*] ... GO
GeneralEndotracheal Anesthesia [*Medicine*] (DAVI) ... GETA
Generalised Linear Interactive Modelling System [*Software*] (EERA) ... GLIM
Generalised System of Preferences (ECON) ... GSP
Generalissimo [*Commander-in-Chief*] [*Spanish*] (ROG) ... GENMO
Generalist [*Ecology*] ... G
Generalist Intelligence Officer ... GIO
Generality and Problem Solving ... GPS
Generalized Academic Simulation Program [*Computer science*] (IEEE) ... GASP
Generalized Access Path Method [*Computer science*] (MHDB) ... GAPM
Generalized Activity Network (IEEE) ... GAN
Generalized Aerospace Program (KSC) ... GASP
Generalized Algebraic Translator [*Computer science*] ... GAT
Generalized Algebraic Translator Extended [*Computer science*] ... GATE
Generalized Antisymmetric Potential ... GASP
Generalized Anxiety Disorder [*Medicine*] (DMAA) ... GAD
Generalized Area of Intersection (OA) ... GAI
Generalized Arteriosclerosis [*Medicine*] ... GAS
Generalized Assembly Language [*Computer science*] (MHDB) ... GAL
Generalized Assembly Line Simulator [*General Motors Corp.*] ... GALS
Generalized Assembly System [*Computer science*] (IEEE) ... GASS
Generalized Atomic Polar Tensor [*Physical chemistry*] ... GAPT
Generalized Audit Software [*Computer science*] ... GAS
Generalized Audit Software Package [*Computer science*] (MHDI) ... GASP
Generalized Automatic Method of Matrix Assembly [*Computer science*] (IAA) ... GAMMA
Generalized Auto-Regressive Conditional Heteroskedacity [*Business term*] (ECON) ... GARCH
Generalized Axially-Symmetrical Potential Theory (PDAA) ... GASPT
Generalized Burst Trapping ... GBT

Generalized Burst Trapping Code (PDAA) .... GBTC
Generalized Circuit Analysis Program (IEEE) .... GCAP
Generalized Communication Interface .... GCI
Generalized Compiler [*Computer science*] .... GECOM
Generalized Computer Program .... GCP
Generalized Constant Elasticity of Substitution (PDAA) .. GCES
Generalized Continuum Hypothesis [*Logic*] .... GCH
Generalized Convulsive Status Epilepticus [*Medicine*] (CPH) .. GCSE
Generalized Data Base Management Systems [*Air Force*] .. GDBMS
Generalized Data Base Processor [*Computer science*] (MHDI) ...... GDP
Generalized Data Entry (ADA) .... GDE
Generalized Data Management System [*Computer science*] (BUR) .. GDMS
Generalized Data Reduction, Manipulation, Evaluation ..... GENDARME
Generalized Data Standardizer [*Bureau of the Census*] (GFGA) .. GENSTAN
Generalized Data Structure Definition Facility [*Computer science*]
   (MHDB) .... GDSDF
Generalized Database Interface [*Computer science*] (MHDB) .... GDI
Generalized Database Planning System .... GPLAN
Generalized Database System (NASA) .... GDBS
Generalized Dictionary/Directory System [*Computer science*] (MHDB) .... GD/DS
Generalized Distributor Program [*Computer science*] ... GDP
Generalized Documentation Processor (NASA) .... GDP
Generalized Drawing Primitive .... GDP
Generalized Edit System Programming Language [*Computer science*]
   (PDAA) .... GESPL
Generalized Electronic Troubleshooting (IAA) .... GETS
Generalized Electronics Maintenance Model .... GEMM
Generalized Engine [*Computer science*] .... GENENG
Generalized Entity-Relationship Model (HGAA) .... GERM
Generalized Environmental Impact Statement .... GEIS
Generalized Equipment Reliability Evaluation Procedure .. GEREP
Generalized Equivalent Cylinder (OA) .... GEC
Generalized Estimating Equation (DMAA) .... GEE
Generalized Euclidian Geometry (OA) .... GEG
Generalized Evaluation Model Simulator [*NASA*] .... GEMS
Generalized Fast Transform (PDAA) .... GFT
Generalized Feedback Shift Register [*Mathematics*] .... GFSR
Generalized Feeder [*Ichthyology*] .... G
Generalized File Maintenance System (ADA) .... GFMS
Generalized File Processor .... GFP
Generalized Fire-Control System Maintenance Trainer [*Spacecraft*]
   [*Navy*] .... GFCSMT
Generalized Glandular Enlargement [*Medicine*] .... GGE
Generalized Gradient Approximation [*Mathematics*] ..... GGA
Generalized Hadamand Matrix .... GH-MATRIX
Generalized Human-Machine Interface (MCD) .... GHMI
Generalized Hyperbolic Class .... GHC
Generalized Hypertrophic Neuropathy .... GHN
Generalized Immittance [*or Impedance*] Converter (IEEE) .. GIC
Generalized Information Management [*Language*] .... GIM
Generalized Information Processing System .... GIPSY
Generalized Information Retrieval and Listing System ..... GIRLS
Generalized Information Retrieval Language [*US Defense Nuclear
   Agency*] .... GIRL
Generalized Information System [*IBM Corp.*] .... GIS
Generalized Information System Virtual Storage (IAA) ... GISVS
Generalized Input/Output Controller [*Computer science*] (IEEE) .... GIOC
Generalized Inquiry System [*Computer science*] .... GIS
Generalized Integrated Square Error [*Aeronautics*] .... GISE
Generalized Internal Reference Method [*Statistical procedure*] .. GIRM
Generalized Interrelated Flow Simulation (IEEE) .... GIFS
Generalized Lagrangian Multiplier [*Military*] (AFIT) .. GLM
Generalized Lambda Family [*Statistics*] .... GLF
Generalized Lattice-Point .... GLP
Generalized Least Squares [*Statistics*] .... GLS
Generalized Linear Model [*Statistics*] .... GLM
Generalized Linear Models [*Computer science*] (EERA) .. GLM
Generalized Lymphadenopathy Syndrome [*Medicine*] (DMAA) .. GLS
Generalized Macroprocessor .... GMAP
Generalized Mainline Framework [*Computer science*] .... GMF
Generalized Management Information System .... GMIS
Generalized Markup Language [*Computer science*] .... GML
Generalized Message Control System (BUR) .... GEMCOS
Generalized Minimum Variance [*Control technology*] .... GMV
Generalized Multitasking .... GMT
Generalized Myotonia [*Medicine*] .... GM
Generalized Officer Assignment On-Line System [*Navy*] (NVT) .. GOALS
Generalized One-Boson Exchange Potential .... GOBEP
Generalized Operations (MCD) .... GO
Generalized Organization of Large Databases (PDAA) .... GOLD
Generalized Organization of Large Databases / Set-Theoretic Approach to
   Relations .... GOLD STAR
Generalized Osteoarthritis [*Medicine*] .... GOA
Generalized Overhauser Orbitals [*Atomic physics*] ..... GOO
Generalized Phrase Structure Grammar [*Artificial intelligence*] .. GPSG
Generalized Post-Processor .... GPP
Generalized Preference Scheme [*Tariff policy*] .... GPS
Generalized Pressure Drop Correlation [*Chemical engineering*] .. GPDC
Generalized Process Control Programming [*Computer science*] (IEEE) .. GPCP
Generalized Processor for Command-Oriented Language (DNAB) .. GEPOL
Generalized Production Function [*Industrial economics*] .. GPF
Generalized Programming [*Computer science*] .... GP
Generalized Programming Extended [*Livermore Atomic Research Computer*]
   [*Sperry UNIVAC*] .... GPX
Generalized Programming Language [*Computer science*] ... GPL

Generalized Queue Entry [*Computer science*] .... GQE
Generalized Radial Basis Function [*Mathematics*] ...... GRBF
Generalized Random Extract Device [*Computer science*] .. GRED
Generalized Reactor Analysis Subsystem .... GRASS
Generalized Read and Simulate Program .... GRASP
Generalized Reduced Gradient .... GRG
Generalized Reed-Muller [*Codes*] (IEEE) .... GRM
Generalized Reentry Application Simulation Program [*NASA*] (KSC) .. GRASP
Generalized Reliability and Maintainability Program [*Military*] .. GRAMP
Generalized Reliability and Maintainability Simulator (MCD) .. GRAMS
Generalized Remote Access Database .... GRAD
Generalized Remote Access Database (IEEE) .... GRADB
Generalized Remote Access Database System (IEEE) ..... GRADS
Generalized Remote Acquisition and Sensor Processing .... GRASP
Generalized Report Module Program [*Computer science*] .. GRM
Generalized Retrieval and Storage Program [*Computer science*] .. GRASP
Generalized Retrieval System [*Computer science*] ...... GRS
Generalized Sanarelli-Shwartzman Reaction [*Medicine*] (MAE) .. GSSR
Generalized Schartzman Reaction [*Medicine*] .... GSR
Generalized Sequential Access Method [*Computer science*] .. GSAM
Generalized Sequential Machine [*Computer science*] .... GSM
Generalized Sequential Probability Ratio Test (PDAA) .. GSPRT
Generalized Simulation Language [*Computer science*] (MDG) .. GSL
Generalized Sinusoidal Quantity .... GSQ
Generalized Sort/Merge [*Computer science*] .... GSM
Generalized Standard Addition Method [*Mathematics*] ... GSAM
Generalized Standard Markup Language [*Also, SGML*] .... GSML
Generalized Supervisor Calls [*Computer science*] (IBMDP) .. GSVC
Generalized Syntax-Directed Translation (PDAA) .... GSDT
Generalized System [*Computer program*] (NITA) .... GENESYS
Generalized System of Tariff Preferences [*US Customs Service*] .. GSP
Generalized System of Tariff Preferences [*US Customs Service*] (MHDW) .. GSTP
Generalized Tethered Object System Simulation (SSD) ... GTOSS
Generalized Top-Down Parsing Language .... GTDPL
Generalized Trace Facility [*Computer science*] (MCD) .. GTF
Generalized Transformation Function .... GTF
Generalized Transition State [*Physical chemistry*] .... GTS
Generalized Unified Ammunition Reporting Data System (MCD) .. GUARDS
Generalized Upper Bounding [*Computer science*] .... GUB
Generalized Valence Bond [*Physics*] .... GVB
Generalized Wegener Granulomatosis [*Medicine*] (DMAA) .. GWG
Generalized Weighted Least Squares Estimates [*Statistics*] .. GLSE
Generally (ROG) .... GENLY
Generally .... GENY
Generally Accepted Accounting Principles [*or Procedures*] .. GAAP
Generally Accepted Auditing Standards .... GAAS
Generally Accepted Government Auditing Standards [*A publication*]
   (AAGC) .... GAGAS
Generally Available Control Technology [*Environmental chemistry*] .. GACT
Generally Labeled [*Radioactive compounds*] .... G
Generally Operational Linear Digit-Controlled Biphase Electrical
   Retardance Gate [*IBM Corp.*] .... GOLDBERG
Generally Recognized [*or Regarded*] as Safe [*FDA term*] .. GRAS
Generally Recognized as Safe Petition [*FDA*] .... GRASP
Generally Regarded [*or Recognized*] as Effective [*Medicine*] .. GRAE
Generaloberst [*Full General*] [*German military - World War II*] .. GO
General-Purpose Airborne Simulator .... GPAS
General-Purpose Amphibian [*Military vehicle*] .... GPA
General-Purpose Amplifier .... GPA
General-Purpose Analog Computer (DEN) .... GPAC
General-Purpose Analysis (IEEE) .... GPA
General-Purpose Armor Machine Gun .... GPAM
General-Purpose Array .... GPA
General-Purpose Automatic Test [*Air Force*] .... GPAT
General-Purpose Automatic Test Equipment [*Army*] (RDA) .. GATE
General-Purpose Automatic Test Equipment [*Army*] (MSA) .. GPATE
General-Purpose Automatic Test Set [*Air Force*] (IAA) .. GPATS
General-Purpose Automatic Test Station .... GPATS
General-Purpose Automatic Test System [*Air Force*] .... GPATS
General-Purpose Barbed Tape Obstacle [*Army*] (RDA) ... GPBTO
General-Purpose Buffer .... GPB
General-Purpose Buffer Interface Module [*Computer science*] (MCD) .. GPBIM
General-Purpose Carrier [*Military*] .... GPC
General-Purpose Central Office Concentrator [*Telecommunications*] .. GPCOC
General-Purpose Closed Loop [*Nuclear energy*] (NRCH) .. GPCL
General-Purpose Communications Adapter .... GPCA
General-Purpose Communications Base (MHDB) .... GPCB
General-Purpose Computer .... GPC
General-Purpose Computing Facility (MHDB) .... GPCF
General-Purpose Contouring Program .... GPCP
General-Purpose Control System (IAA) .... GPCS
General-Purpose Controller Processor (IAA) .... GPCP
General-Purpose Crosslinked Polyethylene [*Insulation*] .. GXL
General-Purpose Data .... GPD
General-Purpose Digital Computer .... GPDC
General-Purpose Discipline [*IBM Corp.*] .... GPD
General-Purpose Discrete Simulator (MHDI) .... GPDS
General-Purpose Display System .... GPDS
General-Purpose Electronic Test Equipment (NVT) .... GPETE
General-Purpose English (ADA) .... GPE
General-Purpose Equipment .... GPE
General-Purpose Evaporator [*Nuclear energy*] (NRCH) .. GPE
General-Purpose Financial Statement (WDAA) .... GPFS
General-Purpose Forces .... GPF
General-Purpose Freight Container (DCTA) .... G

General-Purpose Function Code (NVT) ... GPFC
General-Purpose Graphic Language [*Computer science*] (IEEE) ... GPGL
General-Purpose Heat Source [*Nuclear energy*] ... GPHS
General-Purpose Heavy Machine Gun (MCD) ... GPHMG
General-Purpose Input/Output [*Computer science*] ... GPIO
General-Purpose Input/Output Processor [*Computer science*] ... GIOP
General-Purpose Instrument Bus (IAA) ... GPIB
General-Purpose Intelligent Cable (MHDB) ... GPIC
General-Purpose Interactive Programming Language [*Computer science*] (MHDB) ... GIL
General-Purpose Intercomputer [*Test*] (NVT) ... GPIC
General-Purpose Interface ... GPI
General-Purpose Interface Adapter (IEEE) ... GPIA
General-Purpose Interface Bus [*Computer science*] ... GPIB
General-Purpose Inverter (KSC) ... GPI
General-Purpose Keyboard and Display Control [*Computer science*] (MDG) ... GPKD
General-Purpose Laboratory (KSC) ... GPL
General-Purpose Language [*Computer science*] (CSR) ... GPL
General-Purpose Linear Programming [*Computer science*] (IEEE) ... GPLP
General-Purpose Loop [*Nuclear energy*] (NRCH) ... GPL
General-Purpose Machine Gun [*Military*] ... GPMG
General-Purpose Macrogenerator [*Computer science*] (IEEE) ... GPM
General-Purpose Maneuver ... GPM
General-Purpose Microprogram Simulator [*Computer science*] (IEEE) ... GPMS
General-Purpose Missile ... GPM
General-Purpose Mission Equipment (NASA) ... GPME
General-Purpose Module (MHDB) ... GPM
General-Purpose Multiplex System [*Aviation*] ... GPMS
General-Purpose Operating System ... GPOS
General-Purpose Oscilloscope ... GPO
General-Purpose Outlet (ADA) ... GPO
General-Purpose Output [*Space Flight Operations Facility, NASA*] ... GPO
General-Purpose Packet Satellite Network (MHDI) ... GPSN
General-Purpose Programming [*Computer science*] ... GPP
General-Purpose Psychiatric Questionnaire ... GPPQ
General-Purpose Quarter-Ton Military Utility Vehicle ... JEEP
General-Purpose RADAR (MCD) ... GPR
General-Purpose Radio Receiver ... GPRR
General-Purpose Radio Transmitter ... GPRT
General-Purpose Radiometer ... GPR
General-Purpose Receiver ... GPR
General-Purpose Register [*Computer science*] (MDG) ... GPR
General-Purpose Relay ... GPR
General-Purpose Remote Sensor System (PDAA) ... GPRSS
General-Purpose Representative ... GPR
General-Purpose Rocket Furnace - Gradient ... GPRF-G
General-Purpose Rocket Furnace - Isothermal ... GPRF-I
General-Purpose Satellite Communication System (MCD) ... GPSCS
General-Purpose Scientific Document Image Code [*System*] [*National Institute of Standards and Technology*] ... GPSDIC
General-Purpose Scientific Document Writer [*National Institute of Standards and Technology*] ... GPSDW
General-Purpose Shelter ... GPS
General-Purpose Signal Processor ... GPSP
General-Purpose Simulation [*Formerly, Systems Simulator*] [*IBM Corp.*] [*Computer science*] (IAA) ... GPS
General-Purpose Simulation Environment [*Computer science*] ... GPSE
General-Purpose Simulation Language [*Computer science*] (IAA) ... GPSL
General-Purpose Simulation System [*formerly, Systems Simulator*] [*IBM Corp. 1961*] [*Computer science*] ... GPSS
General-Purpose Software Program [*Computer science*] ... GPSP
General-Purpose String Processor (IAA) ... GPSP
General-Purpose Surface-to-Surface Missile [*Army*] ... GPSSM
General-Purpose Tape Routine [*Computer science*] (PCM) ... GPTR
General-Purpose Terminal (IAA) ... GPT
General-Purpose Terminal Interchanges [*Airline communication system*] [*Raytheon Co.*] ... GPTI
General-Purpose Test Equipment (MCD) ... GPTE
General-Purpose Text Editor [*Computer science*] (MHDB) ... GEDIT
General-Purpose Thermoplastic [*Insulation*] ... GPT
General-Purpose Thermoplastic Elastomer [*Insulation*] ... GTE
General-Purpose Tool ... GPT
General-Purpose Transport [*British military*] (DMA) ... GPT
General-Purpose Vehicle ... GPV
General-Purpose Vehicle ... GPVEH
General-Purpose Vessel ... GPV
General-Purpose Video Buffer ... GPVB
General-Purpose Workstation (SSD) ... GPWS
General-Purpose Yard Simulator (PDAA) ... GPYS
General's Branch, Quarter Master's Branch, and Adjutant's Branch [*Main divisions of Staff Duties*] [*Military British*] ... GQ & A
Generals for Peace and Disarmament [*Ittervoort, Netherlands*] (EAIO) ... GPD
General-Use Consumable List [*Military*] ... GUCL
Generate ... GEN
Generate [*News media*] (WDMC) ... gen
Generate (AABC) ... GENR
Generate Character Text [*Computer science*] (IAA) ... GTXT
Generate Operating System [*Computer program*] ... GENOS
Generate Shell [*Computer science*] (PCM) ... GENSH
Generate Target Position [*Military*] (CAAL) ... GTP
Generated Author Language Teaching System (EDAC) ... GALTS
Generated Data File [*Computer science*] ... GEND
Generated Output ... GO
Generated Real-Time Output Operations on Voltage-Controlled Equipment [*Computer science*] ... GROOVE
Generated Repeatable Exams [*Education*] ... GRE
Generated Symbol [*Computer science*] (NHD) ... GENSYM
Generated Target Tracking ... GTT
Generating ... GNRTNG
Generating and Analyzing Networks [*Computer science*] ... GAN
Generating and Assembly Networks (NITA) ... GAN
Generating Item [*Military*] ... G
Generating Power Unit ... GPU
Generating Significant Dose [*Nuclear energy*] (NRCH) ... GSD
Generating Station Protection System [*Nuclear energy*] (NRCH) ... GSPS
Generating Volt Meter (PDAA) ... GVM
Generation (MSA) ... GEN
Generation (BARN) ... genr
Generation ... GNRTN
[*The*] **Generation After** [*An association*] (EA) ... TGA
Generation Breakdown ... GB
Generation Control Function [*Telecommunications*] (TEL) ... GCF
Generation Data Group [*Computer science*] (BUR) ... GDG
Generation Gather Group [*Computer science*] ... GNG
Generation Management Station ... GMS
Generation of Diversity [*Immunology*] ... GOD
Generation of New Ideas (MHDB) ... GNI
Generation, Reduction, and Training Input System (IEEE) ... GRATIS
Generation Review Committee [*Nuclear Regulatory Commission*] (NRCH) ... GRC
Generation Simulation System [*Power systems*] ... GENESIS
Generation Strategy Language [*Computer science*] (IEEE) ... GSL
Generation Time [*Microbiology*] ... GT
Generation Time [*Laboratory Science*] (DAVI) ... Tc
Generation Time (DAVI) ... Tg
Generations [*A publication*] (BRI) ... Generation
Generations for Peace (EA) ... GFP
Generations United (EA) ... GU
Generation-Skipping Transfer Tax ... GST
Generation-Skipping Transfer Tax ... GSTT
Generative Cell [*Botany*] ... GC
Generative Cell Wall [*Botany*] ... GCW
Generator (IDOE) ... g
Generator (IDOE) ... gen
Generator [*Computer science*] (AAG) ... GEN
Generator (IAA) ... GN
Generator ... GNRTR
Generator (FAAC) ... GNTR
Generator Control Breaker ... GCB
Generator Control Panel (DNAB) ... GCP
Generator Control Relay [*Electronics*] (OA) ... GCR
Generator Control Switch (MCD) ... GCS
Generator Control Unit [*Aviation*] (NASA) ... GCU
Generator/Converter Unit ... GCU
Generator Coordinate Method [*Physics*] ... GCM
Generator Development Tools [*Silicon Design Laboratories*] (NITA) ... GDT
Generator Environmental Tester ... GET
Generator Exhaust Signature Suppression (PDAA) ... GESS
Generator Field ... GF
Generator Field ... GFLD
Generator Field Regulator (IAA) ... GFR
Generator for Optimized Application Language (IAA) ... GOAL
Generator Gas [*System*] [*Nuclear energy*] (NRCH) ... GG
Generator Line Contractor (NASA) ... GLC
Generator Lock (CDE) ... genlock
Generator Lorry [*British*] ... GL
Generator of Excitation [*Medicine*] (DMAA) ... GE
Generator Output Voltage ... GOV
Generator Run (IAA) ... GR
Generator, Starter, Alternator, Regulator, and Rectifier Test Stand (MCD) ... GSARRTS
Generator Starter Drive ... GSD
Generator Step-Up Transformer [*Nuclear energy*] (NRCH) ... GSU
Generator Voltage (IDOE) ... V_g
Generator Voltage (IDOE) ... v_g
Generator-Regulator [*Automotive engineering*] ... G/REG
Generators, Power [*JETDS nomenclature*] [*Military*] (CET) ... G
Generic ... GEN
Generic Airborne RADAR System (DWSG) ... GARS
Generic Array Logic [*Computer science*] ... GAL
Generic Code (AFM) ... GC
Generic Control Language [*Computer science*] (TEL) ... GCL
Generic Electronic Module (SSD) ... GEM
Generic Environmental Impact Statement [*or Study*] [*Nuclear energy*] (NRCH) ... GEIS
Generic Environmental Statement [*Nuclear energy*] (NRCH) ... GES
Generic Experiment Module ... GEM
Generic Expert System Building Tool ... GESBT
Generic Failure ... GF
Generic Flow Control [*Telecommunications*] (ACRL) ... GFC
Generic Identifier [*Telecommunications*] (TEL) ... GI
Generic Integrated Maintenance and Diagnostic System (MCD) ... GIMADS
Generic Intelligent Control System ... GISC
Generic Interactive Neural Network Interpreter ... GINNI
Generic Interface for Operations [*Telecommunications*] (ACRL) ... GIO
Generic Macro Expander [*Telecommunications*] (TEL) ... GME
Generic Maintenance Workstation (SSD) ... GMW
Generic Mapping Tools [*Marine science*] (OSRA) ... GMT
Generic Mapping Tools (USDC) ... GMT

Generic Markup Language (NITA) ... GML
Generic Message Orientation System (SSD) ... GMOS
Generic Missile Model (MCD) ... GEMM
Generic Ordnance Ramjet Engine (MCD) ... GORJE
Generic Pharmaceutical Industry Association (EA) ... GPIA
Generic Processing System [*Computer science*] (TEL) ... GPS
Generic RADAR Analysis and Synthesis Program ... GRASP
Generic Retrieval by Magnetic-Tape Storage [*Computer science*] (PDAA) ... GREMAS
Generic Routing Encapsulation [*Computer science*] ... GRE
Generic Run-Time [*Computer science*] ... GRI
Generic Safety Issue (NRCH) ... GSI
Generic Scan Tool [*Automobile service*] ... GST
Generic Scene Simulation Software (EERA) ... GENESSIS
Generic Security Service Application Program Interface ... GSSAPI
Generic Structure Diagram [*Telecommunications*] (TEL) ... GSD
Generic Structure Language ... GENSAL
Generic Transformed Database ... GTDB
Generic Unit (TEL) ... GU
Generic Update System [*Computer science*] ... GUS
Generic User System [*Computer science*] ... GUS
Generous Tit for Tat [*Game strategy*] ... GTFT
Generous Tit-for-Tat [*Animal behavior*] ... GTFT
GENESCO, Inc. [*NYSE symbol*] (SPSG) ... GCO
Genesco, Inc. [*Associated Press*] (SAG) ... Gensco
Genesee & Western Railroad (IIA) ... G & W
[*The*] **Genesee Brewing Co., Inc.** [*NASDAQ symbol*] (NQ) ... GENB
Genesee Community College, Batavia, NY [*Library symbol Library of Congress*] (LCLS) ... NBatC
Genesee Corp. 'B' [*NASDAQ symbol*] (TTSB) ... GENBB
Genesee County Landmark Society, East Bethany, NY [*Library symbol Library of Congress*] (LCLS) ... NEabG
Genesee Hospital, Stabins Health Science Library, Rochester, NY [*OCLC symbol*] (OCLC) ... VQO
Genesee Memorial Hospital, Batavia, NY [*Library symbol Library of Congress*] (LCLS) ... NBatGH
Geneseo, IL [*AM radio station call letters*] ... WGEN
Geneseo, IL [*FM radio station call letters*] ... WGEN-FM
Geneseo Junior/Senior High School Library, Geneseo, NY [*OCLC symbol*] (OCLC) ... RWH
Geneseo, NY [*Location identifier FAA*] (FAAL) ... GEE
Geneseo, NY [*FM radio station call letters*] ... WGSU
Genesis [*Old Testament book*] ... Gen
Genesis [*Old Testament book*] ... Gn
Genesis ... GNSS
Genesis Airways Ltd. [*British*] [*FAA designator*] (FAAC) ... GSS
[*The*] **Genesis Apocryphon from Qumran. Cave One** (BJA) ... 1QApoc
[*The*] **Genesis Apocryphon from Qumran. Cave One** (BJA) ... 1QGen
[*The*] **Genesis Apocryphon from Qumran. Cave One** (BJA) ... ApocGen
[*The*] **Genesis Apocryphon from Qumran. Cave One** (BJA) ... Apocr
Genesis Energy LP [*NYSE symbol*] (SAG) ... GEL
Genesis Energy LP [*Associated Press*] (SAG) ... GensisE
Genesis Health Ventures [*NYSE symbol*] (SPSG) ... GHV
Genesis Health Ventures, Inc. [*Associated Press*] (SAG) ... Genesis
Genesis Health Ventures, Inc. [*Associated Press*] (SAG) ... GenesisH
Genesis Hlth Ventures [*NYSE symbol*] (TTSB) ... GHV
Genesis Information (EA) ... GI
Genesis Institute [*An association*] (EA) ... GI
Genesis of Atlantic Lows Experiment (USDC) ... GALE
Genesis of Atlantic Tropical Lows Experiment [*National Oceanic and Atmospheric Administration*] ... GALE
Genesis Project (EA) ... GP
Genesis Rabbah (BJA) ... GenR
Genesis Rabbah (BJA) ... GenRabb
Genesis Rabbah (BJA) ... GR
Genesis Resource Corp. [*Vancouver Stock Exchange symbol*] ... GES
Genessee and Wyoming, Inc. [*Associated Press*] (SAG) ... GenWyo
Genessee & Wyoming Railroad Co. [*AAR code*] ... GNWR
Genessee Brewing [*NASDAQ symbol*] (SAG) ... GENB
[*The*] **Genessee Brewing Company, Inc.** [*Associated Press*] (SAG) ... GenesCp
Genesse-Wyoming Board of Cooperative Education Services, Batavia, NY [*Library symbol*] [*Library of Congress*] (LCLS) ... NBatGB
Genetic Algorithm [*Computer science*] ... GA
Genetic Amplification with Transverse Sequencing [*Genetics*] ... GAWTS
Genetic Evaluation and Utilization (PDAA) ... GEU
Genetic Hypertension [*Medicine*] (DMAA) ... GH
Genetic Improvement Programs [*Queensland*] (EERA) ... GIP
Genetic Manipulation Advisory Committee (EERA) ... GMAC
Genetic Manipulation Advisory Group [*British*] ... GMAG
Genetic Prediabetes [*Endocrinology*] ... GP
Genetic Resources Action International [*Spain*] ... GRAIN
Genetic Resources/Communication, Information and Documentation System [*Databank*] (NITA) ... GR/CIDS
Genetic Resources Unit (GNE) ... GRU
Genetic Sequences Databank [*Intelligenetics, Inc.*] [*Information service or system*] (IID) ... GENBANK
Genetic Sex Determination [*Biology*] ... GSD
Genetic Stock Identification [*Pisciculture*] ... GSI
Genetic Systems Corp., Seattle, WA [*Library symbol*] [*Library of Congress*] (LCLS) ... WaSGen
Genetic Therapy ... GT
Genetic Toxicity [*Database*] [*Environmental Protection Agency Information service or system*] (CRD) ... GENETOX
Genetic Toxicology Association (EA) ... GTA
Genetic Variance (DAVI) ... V_G
Genetically Directed Representational Difference Analysis ... GDRDA
Genetically Engineered Microorganism ... GEM
Genetically Engineered Organism ... GEO
Genetically Handicapped Persons Program (MEDA) ... GHPP
Genetically Manipulated Organisms (EERA) ... GMOs
Genetically Significant Concentration [*Mutagenesis*] ... GSC
Genetically Significant Dosage [*X-Ray*] ... GSD
Genetically-Manipulated Organism [*Biochemistry*] ... GMO
Genetically-Related Factor [*Immunology*] ... GRF
Genetics ... GEN
Genetics ... GENET
Genetics and Molecular Biology of Industrial Microorganisms [*Conference*] ... GMBIM
Genetics Institute Dep Shrs [*NASDAQ symbol*] (TTSB) ... GENIZ
Genetics Institute, Inc. [*Associated Press*] (SAG) ... Genetl
Genetics Institute, Inc. [*Associated Press*] (SAG) ... GenetInst
Genetics Institute, Inc. [*NASDAQ symbol*] (NQ) ... GENI
Genetics Institute, Inc. ... GI
Genetics Interest Group [*British*] ... GIG
Genetics Society of America (EA) ... GSA
Genetron Marine, Inc. [*Vancouver Stock Exchange symbol*] ... GNM
Geneva [*City in Switzerland*] ... GEN
Geneva [*Switzerland*] [*Airport symbol*] (OAG) ... GVA
Geneva, AL [*AM radio station call letters*] ... WGEA
Geneva, AL [*FM radio station call letters*] ... WRJM
Geneva College, Beaver Falls, PA [*Library symbol Library of Congress*] (LCLS) ... PBfG
Geneva College, Beaver Falls, PA [*OCLC symbol*] (OCLC) ... PGC
Geneva Consultants Registry [*Alpha Systems Resource*] [*Database*] ... GCR
Geneva Convention for the Amelioration of the Condition of the Wounded and Sick in Armed Forces in the Field, 12 August 1949 [*Army*] (AABC) ... GWS
Geneva Convention for the Amelioration of the Condition of the Wounded and Sick in Armed Forces in the Field, 27 July 1929 [*Army*] ... GWS 1929
Geneva Convention for the Amelioration of the Condition of the Wounded, Sick, and Shipwrecked Members of the Armed Forces at Sea, 12 August 1949 [*Army*] (AABC) ... GWS Sea
Geneva Convention on the Continental Shelf (NOAA) ... GCCS
Geneva Convention Relative to Protection of Civilian Persons in Time of War [*Army*] (AABC) ... GC
Geneva Convention Relative to Treatment of Prisoners of War, 12 August 1949 [*Army*] (AABC) ... GPW
Geneva Convention Relative to Treatment of Prisoners of War, 27 July 1929 [*Army*] ... GPW 1929
Geneva Conventions [*Military*] (NVT) ... GENCONV
Geneva Executives Club (EA) ... GEC
Geneva, IL [*AM radio station call letters*] ... WFXW
Geneva Infant Feeding Association ... GIFA
Geneva Informal Meeting [*of International Non-Governmental Organizations*] [*British*] ... GIM
Geneva N. Gallow Elementary School, Levittown, NY [*Library symbol*] [*Library of Congress*] (LCLS) ... NLevGGE
Geneva, NY [*FM radio station call letters*] ... WEOS
Geneva, NY [*FM radio station call letters*] ... WFLK
Geneva, NY [*AM radio station call letters*] ... WGVA
Geneva, OH [*FM radio station call letters*] ... WKKY
Geneva Public Library, Geneva, IN [*Library symbol Library of Congress*] (LCLS) ... InGe
Geneva Radio Regulations ... GRR
Geneva Steel [*Associated Press*] (SAG) ... GnvStl
Geneva Steel Co. [*NYSE symbol*] (SPSG) ... GNV
Geneva Steel Co.'A' [*NYSE symbol*] (TTSB) ... GNV
Geneve [*Switzerland ICAO location identifier*] (ICLI) ... LSAG
Geneve [*Switzerland ICAO location identifier*] (ICLI) ... LSSS
Geneve/Cointrin [*Switzerland ICAO location identifier*] (ICLI) ... LSGG
Genex Resources [*Vancouver Stock Exchange symbol*] ... GNX
GENICOM Corp. [*NASDAQ symbol*] (NQ) ... GECM
GENICOM Corp. [*Associated Press*] (SAG) ... Genicm
Genie Climatique International (EA) ... GCI
Geniki Laiki Rizospastiki Enosis [*General Union of Populists and Radicals*] [*Greek*] (PPE) ... GLRE
Geniki Synomospondia Ergaton Hellados [*General Confederation of Greek Labor*] ... GSEE
Genini II Fund [*NYSE symbol*] (SAG) ... GMI
Genio Populi Romani [*To the Genius of the Roman People*] [*Latin*] ... GPR
Genital ... GEN
Genital [*Medicine*] (DMAA) ... gen
Genital Neoplasm-Papilloma Syndrome [*Medicine*] (DMAA) ... GENPS
Genital Skin Fibroblast [*Medicine*] (DMAA) ... GSF
Genital Tract Infection [*Medicine*] (CPH) ... GTI
Genital Vein ... GV
Genitalia [*Medicine*] ... GENIT
Genitive [*Case*] [*Grammar*] ... G
Genitive [*Case*] [*Grammar*] ... GEN
Genitive [*Case*] [*Grammar*] ... GENIT
Genito-Genital [*Medicine*] ... GG
Genitourinary [*Medicine*] ... GU
Genitourinary Infection [*Medicine*] (PDAA) ... GUI
Genitourinary System [*Medicine*] ... GUS
Genius Loci [*Genius of the Place*] [*Latin*] (ROG) ... GL
Genius Operator Advertising Data Bank [*Gert Richter*] [*Germany Information service or system*] (CRD) ... GO
Geniuses of Distinction Society [*Later, SGD*] (EA) ... GODS
Genk/Zwartberg [*Belgium ICAO location identifier*] (ICLI) ... EBZW
Genl Acceptance [*NASDAQ symbol*] (TTSB) ... GACC

Genl Amer Investors [*NYSE symbol*] (TTSB) ... GAM
Genl Automation [*NYSE symbol*] (TTSB) ... GA
Genl Binding [*NASDAQ symbol*] (TTSB) ... GBND
Genl Cable plc.ADS [*NASDAQ symbol*] (TTSB) ... GCABY
Genl Chemical Group [*NYSE symbol*] (TTSB) ... GCG
Genl Communication'A' [*NASDAQ symbol*] (TTSB) ... GNCMA
Genl DataComm Ind [*NYSE symbol*] (TTSB) ... GDC
Genl Dynamics [*NYSE symbol*] (TTSB) ... GD
Genl Employ Enterpr [*AMEX symbol*] (TTSB) ... JOB
Genl Growth Properties [*NYSE symbol*] (TTSB) ... GGP
Genl Host [*NYSE symbol*] (TTSB) ... GH
Genl Housewares [*NYSE symbol*] (TTSB) ... GHW
Genl Instrument [*NYSE symbol*] (TTSB) ... GIC
Genl Kinetics [*AMEX symbol*] (TTSB) ... GKI
Genl Magnaplate [*NASDAQ symbol*] (TTSB) ... GMCC
Genl Microwave [*AMEX symbol*] (TTSB) ... GMW
Genl Mills [*NYSE symbol*] (TTSB) ... GIS
Genl Motors [*NYSE symbol*] (TTSB) ... GM
Genl Motors Cl'E' [*NYSE symbol*] (TTSB) ... GME
Genl Nutrition [*NASDAQ symbol*] (TTSB) ... GNCI
Genl Parcel Service [*NASDAQ symbol*] (TTSB) ... GPSX
Genl Physics [*NYSE symbol*] (TTSB) ... GPH
Genl Public Util [*NYSE symbol*] (TTSB) ... GPU
Genl Scanning [*NASDAQ symbol*] (TTSB) ... GSCN
Genl Signal [*NYSE symbol*] (TTSB) ... GSX
Genl Surgical Innovations [*NASDAQ symbol*] (TTSB) ... GSII
Genlyte Group, Inc. [*Associated Press*] (SAG) ... Genlyte
Genlyte Group, Inc. [*NASDAQ symbol*] (NQ) ... GLYT
Genoa [*Italy*] [*Seismograph station code, US Geological Survey Closed*] (SEIS) ... GEN
Genoa [*Italy*] [*Airport symbol*] (OAG) ... GOA
Genoa City Public Library, Genoa City, WI [*Library symbol Library of Congress*] (LCLS) ... WGc
Genoa Elementary School, Houston, TX [*Library symbol*] [*Library of Congress*] (LCLS) ... TxHGE
Genoa Nuclear Generating Station (NRCH) ... GNGS
Genoa, Savona, Spezia, Leghorn, Naples, or Civita Vecchia [*Italian ports*] (DS) ... GSSLNCV
Genoa, Savona, Spezia, or Leghorn [*Italian ports*] (DS) ... GSSL
Genome [*Genetics*] ... g
Genome Data Base [*Genetics*] ... GDB
Genome Therapeutics [*NASDAQ symbol*] (TTSB) ... GENE
Genome Therapeutics Corp [*NASDAQ symbol*] (SAG) ... GENE
Genome Therapeutics Corp. [*Associated Press*] (SAG) ... Genome
Genomic Amplification with Transcript Sequencing [*Genetics*] ... GAWTS
Genomic Mismatch Scanning [*Genetic technique*] ... GMS
Genomic Tested [*Genetics*] ... GT
Genomic Thymus [*Genetics*] ... GTH
Genotypic Relative Risk [*Genetics*] ... GRR
Genotypic Sex Determination [*Embryology*] ... GSD
Genova/Sestri [*Italy ICAO location identifier*] (ICLI) ... LIMJ
Genovese Drug Stores, Inc. [*AMEX symbol*] (SPSG) ... GDX
Genovese Drug Stores, Inc. [*Associated Press*] (SAG) ... GenvDr
Genovese Drug Str'A' [*AMEX symbol*] (TTSB) ... GDXA
Genoveva Resources, Inc. [*Vancouver Stock Exchange symbol*] ... GNV
Genprobe Tech [*Vancouver Stock Exchange symbol*] ... GPO
GenRad, Inc. [*NYSE symbol*] (SPSG) ... GEN
GenRad, Inc. [*Associated Press*] (SAG) ... GnRad
GENSER Integration Information Display (MCD) ... GIID
Gensia Inc. [*NASDAQ symbol*] (TTSB) ... GNSA
Gensia Pharmaceuticals, Inc. [*Associated Press*] (SAG) ... Gensia
Gensia Pharmaceuticals, Inc. [*NASDAQ symbol*] (SAG) ... GNSA
Gensia Pharmaceuticals Wrrt [*NASDAQ symbol*] (TTSB) ... GNSAW
Genstar Financial Corp. [*Toronto Stock Exchange symbol*] ... GFC
Genstar Ltd., Montreal, Quebec [*Library symbol National Library of Canada*] (NLC) ... QMGL
Gensym Corp. [*NASDAQ symbol*] (TTSB) ... GNSM
Gent/St. Denijs Westrem [*Belgium ICAO location identifier*] (ICLI) ... EBGT
Genta, Inc. [*Associated Press*] (SAG) ... Genta
Genta, Inc. [*NASDAQ symbol*] (SPSG) ... GNTA
Gentamicin [*Antibacterial compound*] [*Generic form*] ... GE
Gentamicin [*Antibacterial compound*] ... GENT
Gentamicin [*Antibacterial compound*] ... GM
Gentamicin Peak [*Level*] [*Immunology*] (DAVI) ... GENP
Gentamicin Trough [*Level*] [*Immunology*] (DAVI) ... GENT
Gentex Corp. [*Associated Press*] (SAG) ... Gentex
Gentex Corp. [*NASDAQ symbol*] (NQ) ... GNTX
Gentian Violet [*Also, MRC*] [*A dye*] ... GV
Gentil Membre [*Guest of Club Mediterranee, a vacation cooperative*] ... GM
Gentil Organisateur [*Genial Host*] [*Employee of Club Mediterranee, a vacation cooperative*] ... GO
Gentile Air Force Station [*Ohio*] ... GAFS
Gentisic Acid [*Analgesic drug*] ... GA
Gentleman ... GENT
Gentleman [*or Gentlemen*] (ROG) ... GENTN
Gentleman Cadet [*British*] ... GC
Gentleman Friend ... GF
[*A*] **Gentleman of the University of Cambridge** [*Pseudonym used by Owen Manning*] ... AGOTUOC
Gentleman Rider [*Horsemanship*] ... GR
Gentleman Traveller ... GT
Gentleman Usher of the Black Rod [*British*] (ROG) ... GUBR
Gentleman Usher of the Green Rod [*British*] (ROG) ... GUGR
Gentleman Usher of the Red Rod [*British*] (ROG) ... GURR
Gentleman's Left Handed [*Golf club*] ... GLH
Gentleman's Pocket Knife ... GPK
Gentlemen ... GNTLMN
Gentlemen's Right Handed [*Golf club*] ... GRH
Gentner Communications [*NASDAQ symbol*] (TTSB) ... GTNR
Gentner Communications Corp. [*Associated Press*] (SAG) ... Gentnr
Gentner Communications Corp. [*NASDAQ symbol*] (NQ) ... GTNR
Gentner Communications Wrrt [*NASDAQ symbol*] (TTSB) ... GTNRW
Gentra Inc. [*TS, exchange symbol*] (TTSB) ... GTA
Genuine (ADA) ... GEN
Genuine Occupational Qualification (DI) ... GOQ
Genuine Parts [*NYSE symbol*] (TTSB) ... GPC
Genuine Parts Co. [*Associated Press*] (SAG) ... GenuPrt
Genuine Parts Co. [*NYSE symbol*] (SPSG) ... GPC
Genuine Stress Incontinence [*Urology*] (DAVI) ... GSI
Genus [*Biology*] ... GEN
Genus Equity Corp. [*Toronto Stock Exchange symbol*] ... CSQ
Genus Equity Corp. [*Toronto Stock Exchange symbol*] ... GSQ
Genus et Species Nova [*New Genus and Species*] [*Latin*] (DMAA) ... gen et sp nov
Genus, Inc. [*Associated Press*] (SAG) ... Genus
Genus, Inc. [*NASDAQ symbol*] (CTT) ... GGNS
Genus Novum [*New Genus*] [*Latin*] (DAVI) ... gen nov
Genzyme Corp. [*NASDAQ symbol*] (NQ) ... GENZ
Genzyme Corp. [*Associated Press*] (SAG) ... Genzy
Genzyme Corp. [*Associated Press*] (SAG) ... Genzym
Genzyme Corp. [*Associated Press*] (SAG) ... GenzyT
Genzyme Corp. [*Associated Press*] (SAG) ... GenzyTis
Genzyme Corp.-Genl Div [*NASDAQ symbol*] (TTSB) ... GENZ
Genzyme Corp.-Tissue Repair [*NASDAQ symbol*] (TTSB) ... GENZL
Genzyme Corp. Wrrt [*NASDAQ symbol*] (TTSB) ... GENZZ
Genzyme Transgenics [*NASDAQ symbol*] (TTSB) ... GZTC
Genzyme Transgenics Corp. [*Associated Press*] (SAG) ... GenzyTr
Genzyme Transgenics Corp. [*NASDAQ symbol*] (SAG) ... GZTC
Geo. S. Olive & Co. [*Telecommunications service*] (TSSD) ... GSO
Geoanomaly Interactive Data Analysis System (MCD) ... GIDAS
Geo-Assimilated Positioning System [*Navigation systems*] ... GAPS
Geoballistic Input Unit ... GBIU
Geoballistic Input Unit ... GIU
Geocentric Datum of Australia [*Geographic*] (EERA) ... GGDA
Geocentric Dust Cloud ... GDC
Geocentric Pendulum Control ... GPC
Geocentric Solar Ecliptic [*System*] [*NASA*] ... GSE
Geocentric Solar Magnetospheric [*System*] [*NASA*] ... GSM
Geochemical ... GEOCHEM
Geochemical Ocean Section Study [*Marine science*] (OSRA) ... GOESECS
Geochemical Ocean Section Study [*International Decade of Ocean Exploration*] (USDC) ... GOESECS
Geochemical Ocean Sections Study [*Submarine ocean exploration by US for International Decade of Ocean Exploration*] ... GEOSECS
Geochemical Sections Study (USDC) ... GEOSECS
Geochemical Society (EA) ... GS
Geo-Data International [*Vancouver Stock Exchange symbol*] ... GED
Geode Specialty Growers Association (EA) ... GSGA
Geodesic ... GDSC
Geodesic Isotensoid (IEEE) ... GI
Geodesy [*Science of measuring the earth*] (ROG) ... GEOD
Geodesy, Intelligence, and Mapping Research and Development Agency [*Army*] ... GIMRADA
Geodesy Satellite ... GEOSAT
Geodesy Satellite [*Instrument*] (EERA) ... Geosat
Geodetic ... GEOD
Geodetic Communications and Electronics Squadron [*Air Force*] (AFM) ... GCESq
Geodetic Data Center [*Environmental Science Services Administration*] ... GDC
Geodetic Data Reduction ... GDR
Geodetic Data Site ... GDS
Geodetic Distance Measurement ... GDM
Geodetic Earth-Orbiting Satellite ... GEOS
Geodetic Engineer ... Geod E
Geodetic Estimates from Orbital Perturbation of Satellites (IAA) ... GEOPS
Geodetic Estimates from Orbital Perturbations of Satellites ... GEOPS
Geodetic Inertial Survey and Horizontal Alignment (IEEE) ... GEISHA
Geodetic LASER Survey System ... GLASS
Geodetic Observation Satellite ... GEOS
Geodetic Operations Control Center [*NASA*] ... GOCC
Geodetic Optical System ... GOS
Geodetic Receiver ... GEOCEIVER
Geodetic Research and Development Laboratory [*Rockville, MD*] [*Department of Commerce*] (MSC) ... GRDL
Geodetic Satellite ... Geosat
Geodetic Satellite in Polar Geosynchronous Orbit [*NASA*] (NASA) ... GEOPAUSE
Geodetic Satellite Program ... GSP
Geodetic Spacecraft (AAG) ... GSC
Geodetic Stationary Satellite ... GSS
Geodetic Survey Marks Register [*of Western Australia*] [*State*] (EERA) ... GESMAR
Geodetic Survey Squadron [*Air Force*] (AFM) ... GSSq
Geodome Resources Ltd. [*Toronto Stock Exchange symbol Vancouver Stock Exchange symbol*] ... GOE
Geodynamic Experimental Ocean Satellite ... GEOS
Geodynamic Experimental Ocean Satellite (MCD) ... GEOSAT
Geodynamics Corp. [*NASDAQ symbol*] (NQ) ... GDYN
Geodynamics Corp. [*Associated Press*] (SAG) ... Geodyn
Geodynamics LASER Ranging System [*NASA*] ... GLRS
Geoffrion, Leclerc, Inc. [*Toronto Stock Exchange symbol*] ... GFL
Geognosy [*A knowledge of the structure of the earth*] (ROG) ... GEOGNOS
Geographenkalender (BJA) ... GK

Geographia [of Ptolemy] [Classical studies] (OCD) .... Geog
Geographic .... GEO
Geographic Adjustment by Least Squares (PDAA) .... GALS
Geographic Aerospace Search RADAR .... GASSER
Geographic Air Surveys Ltd. [Canada ICAO designator] (FAAC) .... GSL
Geographic and Alphanumeric Display System (MCD) .... GADS
Geographic Applications Program [United States Geological Survey] (IID) .... GAP
Geographic Area Code Index [Bureau of Census] .... GACI
Geographic Base File [Civil Defense] .... GBF
Geographic Base File/Dual Independent Map Encoding [BTS] (TAG).... GBF/DIME
Geographic Cross-Reference Data [Claritas LP] [Information service or system] (CRD) .... GEOBASE
Geographic Data File [LPC, Inc.] [Information service or system] (IID) .... GDF
Geographic Data Management System [Computer science] .... GDMS
Geographic Data Technology, Inc. [Information service or system] (IID) .... GDT
Geographic Design and Implementation System [Australian Capital Territory] (EERA) .... GEODIS
Geographic Digest [A publication British] .... GD
Geographic Distribution .... GD
Geographic Distribution of Federal Funds Information System [Comptroller General of the United States] .... GDFF
Geographic Districting Information System for Maryland [Maryland State Department of State Planning] [Baltimore] [Information service or system] (IID) .... GeoDIS
Geographic Division [Census] (OICC) .... GEO
Geographic Education National Implementation Project [National Geographic Society] .... GENIP
Geographic Enforcement Initiative [Environmental Protection Agency] (EPA) .... GEI
Geographic File [DoD] .... GEOFILE
Geographic Identification Code Scheme [Bureau of the Census] (GFGA) ..... GICS
Geographic Information Mapping and Management System (EERA) ... GIMMS
Geographic Information Retrieval and Analysis System [Department of the Interior] .... GIRAS
Geographic Information System [Computer science] .... GEOIS
Geographic Information System (EERA) .... GIS
Geographic Information System-Mobile .... SM
Geographic Information Systems [Fish and Wildlife Service] (IID) ... GIS
Geographic Intelligence and Topographic System .... GIANT
Geographic Location (NITA) .... GL
Geographic Names Information System [US Geological Survey] [Information service or system] .... GNIS
Geographic Names Information System .... GNIS
Geographic Navigation [Navy] (CAAL) .... GEONAV
Geographic OPAREA [Operating Area] Coordinates (DNAB) .... GOAC
Geographic Point .... GP
Geographic Position Locator [Navigation] .... GPL
Geographic Practice Cost Index [Medicare] .... GPCI
Geographic Reference File [Bureau of the Census] (GFGA) .... GRF
Geographic Reference System [Civil Defense] .... GEOREF
Geographic Resources Analysis Support System [Army] (RDA) ... GRASS
Geographic Resources Center [University of Missouri - Columbia] [Research center] (RCD) .... GRC
Geographic Sciences Laboratory [Fort Belvoir, VA] [United States Army Engineer Topographic Laboratories] (GRD) .... GSL
Geographic Systems Analysis [Information service or system] (IID) ..... GSA
Geographic Systems, Inc. [Information service or system] (IID) ..... GSI
Geographic Systems Laboratory [US Army Engineer Topographic Laboratories] .... GSL
Geographical [A publication] (BRI) .... Geog
Geographical and Topographical Texts of the Old Testament [A publication] (BJA) .... GTT
[The] Geographical Association [British] .... GA
Geographical Association [British] (DBA) .... GA
Geographical Association of Western Australia .... GAWA
Geographical Association Package Exchange (AIE) .... GAPE
Geographical Data of Sweden [Sweden] (EERA) .... GSD
Geographical Education [A publication] .... Geogr Ed
Geographical Field Group [British] .... GFG
Geographical Information Analysis (EERA) .... GIA
Geographical Information Processing System (EERA) .... GIPS
Geographical Inter-University Resource Management Seminar .... GIRMS
Geographical Journal [A publication] (BRI) .... GJ
Geographical Journal (London) [A publication] .... GJL
Geographical Location [Military] (AABC) .... GEOLOC
Geographical Names Register [New South Wales] [State] (EERA) ..... GNR
Geographical Pole .... GP
Geographical Position .... GP
Geographical Reference Points (GAVI) .... GRP
Geographical Resources Analysis Support System [Software] [Computer science] (EERA) .... GRASS
Geographical Section General Staff [British] .... GSGS
Geographical Situation (MCD) .... GEO/SIT
Geographical Society of New South Wales [Australia] ...... GSNSW
Geographical Society of Philadelphia, Philadelphia, PA [Library symbol Library of Congress Obsolete] (LCLS) .... PPGeo
Geographical Specialist Team [Army] (AABC) .... GST
Geographical Survey Institute (EERA) .... GSI
Geographical Teacher [A publication] (ROG) .... GEOG T
Geographically Impossible (ADA) .... GI
Geographically Referenced Data Storage and Retrieval System [Canada] .... GRDSR
Geographically Separated Units [Military] (AFM) .... GSU
Geographically Undesirable [Slang] .... GU
Geographic-Based Information Management System (PDAA) .... GIMS

Geographici Graeci Minores [A publication] (OCD) .... GGM
Geographics, Inc. [Associated Press] (SAG) .... Geogrph
Geographics, Inc. [NASDAQ symbol] (SAG) .... GGIT
Geographics Inc. [NASDAQ symbol] (TTSB) .... GGIT
Geography [Secondary school course] [British] .... G
Geography [or Geographer] (AFM) .... GEOG
Geography (DD) .... Geog
Geography Department, Carleton University, Ottawa, Ontario [Library symbol Obsolete National Library of Canada] (NLC) ...... OOCCG
Geography Department, University of Victoria, British Columbia [Library symbol National Library of Canada] (NLC) .... BVIVG
Geography Remote Sensing Unit [University of California, Santa Barbara].... GRSU
Geography Teachers' Association of South Australia .... GTASA
Geoid-to-Topography Ratio [Planetary science] .... GTR
Geokinetic Data Acquisition System (PDAA) .... GDAS
Geolocation (DOMA) .... GELOC
Geologic Names Committee [US Geological Survey] .... GNC
Geologic Names of the United States [US Geological Survey] [Information service or system] (IID) .... GEONAMES
Geological .... GEOLGCL
Geological Abstracts .... GA
Geological Applications of Remote Sensing .... GARS
Geological Data Center [University of California, San Diego] (IID) ... GDC
Geological Echo Profiler [Oceanography] (MSC) .... GEP
Geological Engineer (WDAA) .... GE ENG
Geological Engineer .... Ge Engr
Geological Engineer .... Geol E
Geological, Exploration and Development Information System [Australia] .... GEDIS
Geological Information Library of Dallas, Dallas, TX [Library symbol] [Library of Congress] (LCLS) .... TxDaGI
Geological Information Systems [University of Oklahoma] [Information service or system] (IID) .... GIS
Geological Laboratory, Saskatchewan Department of Energy and Mines, Regina, Saskatchewan [Library symbol National Library of Canada] (NLC) .... SRSEMG
Geological Long-Range Inclined ASDIC .... GLORIA
Geological Reference File [American Geological Institute] [Bibliographic database] [Information service or system] (IID) .... GEOREF
Geological (Research) Satellite .... GEOS
Geological Science (DD) .... GeolSci
Geological Society [British] (EAIO) .... GS
Geological Society of America (EA) .... GSA
Geological Society of Australia (EERA) .... GSA
Geological Society of London (BARN) .... GSL
Geological Society of Malaysia (EAIO) .... GSM
Geological Survey [Department of the Interior] .... GS
Geological Survey of Alabama, Tuscaloosa, AL [Library symbol] [Library of Congress] (LCLS) .... ATuGS
Geological Survey of Canada [Marine science] (MSC) .... GSC
Geological Survey of Canada Library [Canada Energy Mines and Resources] [UTLAS symbol] .... EMR
Geological Survey of Canada, Ottawa, ON, Canada [Library symbol Library of Congress] (LCLS) .... CaOOG
Geological Survey of Canada [Commission Geologique du Canada] Ottawa, Ontario [Library symbol National Library of Canada] (NLC) .... OOG
Geological Survey of Canada [Commission Geologique du Canada] Vancouver, British Columbia [Library symbol National Library of Canada] (NLC) .... BVAG
Geological Survey of Great Britain and Museum of Practical Geology (BI) .... GSM
Geological Survey of Queensland [Australia] .... GSQ
Geological Survey, Reston [Virginia] [Seismograph station code, US Geological Survey] (SEIS) .... GSR
Geological Survey - Water Resources Division .... GS-WRD
Geologist .... GEO
Geologist .... GEOL
Geologists' Association [British] .... GA
Geology [or Geologist] (AFM) .... GEOL
Geology (DD) .... Geol
Geology .... GEOLGY
Geology Archive [Database on earth science] [British] (NITA) .... GEOARCHIVE
Geomagnetic Airborne Survey System .... GASS
Geomagnetic Daily Variations .... GDV
Geomagnetic Data Center [National Oceanic and Atmospheric Administration] .... GDC
Geomagnetic Electrokinetograph [Equipment for exploring ocean depths] .... GEEK
Geomagnetic Electrokinetograph [Equipment for exploring ocean depths] ...... GEK
Geomagnetic Electrorinetograph .... GER
Geomagnetic Polarity Timescale .... GPTS
Geomagnetic Reversal Time Scale .... GRTS
Geomagnetic Tail Laboratory (MCD) .... GTL
Geomagnetically Induced Current .... GIC
Geomagnetism .... GEOMAG
Geomaque Explorations [TS, exchange symbol] (TTSB) .... GEO
Geomaque Explorations Ltd. [Toronto Stock Exchange symbol] .... GMQ
Geomarine Technology .... GMT
Geomechanics Abstracts [Rock Mechanics Information Service] [Bibliographic database] [British] .... GMA
Geometric and Positional Tolerance [Drafting symbol] .... GPT
Geometric and Technical Draughting [British Olivetti Ltd.] [Software package] (NCC) .... GTD
Geometric and Technical Language [British Olivetti Ltd.] [Software package] (NCC) .... GTL
Geometric Arithmetic Parallel Processor [Computer science] .... GAPP

Geometric Constraint Network (DMAA) .... GCN
Geometric Data Base (DOMA) .... GBD
Geometric Database (MCD) .... GDB
Geometric Degradation of Position [Aerospace] .... GDOP
Geometric Dilution of Precision .... GDOP
Geometric Dimensioning and Tolerancing .... GD & T
Geometric Efficiency (DMAA) .... G
Geometric Information for Targets (MCD) .... GIFT
Geometric Intelligence .... GI
Geometric Math Model (SSD) .... GMM
Geometric Mean .... GM
Geometric Mean [Psychology] .... MG
Geometric Mean Distance .... GMD
Geometric Mean Radii .... GMR
Geometric Mean Time to Repair [Military] (CAAL) .... GMTTR
Geometric Mean Titer [Analytical chemistry] .... GMT
Geometric Modeller [GE CAE International] [Software package] (NCC) .... GEOMOD
Geometric Modelling Project [Software] [British] (NITA) .... GMP
Geometric Modulation Transfer Function (MCD) .... GMTF
Geometric On-Line Definition [Computer science] (PDAA) .... GOLD
Geometric Phase [Mathematics] .... GP
Geometric Position Error (MCD) .... GPE
Geometric Progression .... GP
Geometric Standard Deviation [Statistics] .... GSD
Geometric Standard Error (PDAA) .... GSE
Geometrical Acoustics .... GA
Geometrical and True Positioning Tolerance .... GTPT
Geometrical Optical Analysis of Lens Systems (PDAA) .... GOALS
Geometrical Theory of Diffraction .... GTD
Geometrodynamics .... GMD
Geometry .... GEO
Geometry [or Geometric] .... GEOM
Geometry (MSA) .... GMTRY
Geometry of the Wake Experiment [Military] (MCD) .... GOWEX
Geometry Technology Module [NASA] .... GTM
Geometry-Optimized [Calculations] .... GO
[The] Geon Co. [Associated Press] (SAG) .... Geon Co
Geon Co. [NYSE symbol] (SPSG) .... GON
Geon Process Butadiene .... GPB
Geonic (BJA) .... G
Geophysical .... GEOPHYS
Geophysical .... GEOPHYS
Geophysical Abstracts [A publication] .... GEAB
Geophysical and Polar Research Center [University of Wisconsin] .... GPRC
Geophysical Associates International .... GAI
Geophysical Automatic Tracker Unit .... GATU
Geophysical Data Center .... GDC
Geophysical Data Record .... GDR
Geophysical Data System (EERA) .... GEODAS
Geophysical Engineer .... Gp E
Geophysical Engineer .... Gp Engr
Geophysical Exploration Manned Mobile Submersible .... GEMMS
Geophysical Fluid Dynamics Laboratory [National Oceanic and Atmospheric Administration] .... GFD
Geophysical Fluid Dynamics Laboratory [Princeton, NJ] [National Oceanic and Atmospheric Administration] .... GFDL
Geophysical Fluid Dynamics Program [National Oceanic and Atmospheric Administration] (GFGA) .... GFDP
Geophysical Fluid Flow Cell [Instrumentation] .... GFFC
Geophysical Institute [University of Alaska, Fairbanks] [Research center] .... GI
Geophysical Institute, University of Alaska [Alaska] [Seismograph station code, US Geological Survey Closed] (SEIS) .... GIA
Geophysical Monitoring for Climate Change (EERA) .... GMCC
Geophysical Monitoring for Climatic Change [National Oceanic and Atmospheric Administration] .... GMCC
Geophysical Monitoring Satellite [DoD, NOAA] .... GMS
Geophysical Range Input Detection System .... GRIDS
Geophysical Report [Oil industry term] (DSUE) .... GEO
Geophysical Research Institute [University of New England, Australia] .... GRI
Geophysical Research Letters [A publication] .... GRL
Geophysical Research Mission [Marine science] (OSRA) .... GRM
Geophysical Sciences Laboratory [New York University] .... GSL
Geophysical Service, Inc. .... GSI
Geophysical Survey System [Naval Oceanographic Office] .... GEOSS
Geophysics (DD) .... Geoph
Geophysics and Space Data Bulletin [A publication Air Force] .... GSDB
Geophysics Collection, Geological Survey of Canada [Collection de la Geophysique, Commission Geologique du Canada], Ottawa, Ontario [Library symbol National Library of Canada] (NLC) .... OOO
Geophysics Corp. of America .... GCA
Geophysics Laboratory, University of Toronto, Ontario [Library symbol National Library of Canada] (NLC) .... OTUGL
Geophysics Research Board .... GRB
Geophysics Research Directorate [US] .... GRD
Geopolitical Code [Military] (AFIT) .... GC
Geopolitics (BARN) .... geopol
Geopotential Decameter [Telecommunications] (TEL) .... GPDM
Geopotential Meter .... GPM
Geopotential Research Explorer Mission (MCD) .... GREM
Geopotential Research Mission [NASA] .... GRM
Geopotential Unit .... GPU
Geopposserde [Defendant] [Netherlands Legal term] (DLA) .... Geopp
Georesources, Inc. [NASDAQ symbol] (NQ) .... GEOI
Georesources Inc. [NASDAQ symbol] (TTSB) .... GEOL
Georesources, Inc. [Associated Press] (SAG) .... Geores

Georganne LaPiere Fan Club (EA) .... GLFC
George [Phonetic alphabet] [Royal Navy World War I Pre-World War II] [World War II] (DSUE) .... G
George [South Africa] [Airport symbol] (OAG) .... GRJ
George A. Zeller Zone Center, Professional Library, Peoria, IL [Library symbol Library of Congress] (LCLS) .... IPZ
George Ade Hazeldon Home, Brook, IN [Library symbol Library of Congress] (LCLS) .... InBroA
George Air Force Base [California] (MCD) .... GAFB
George Bernard Shaw [Irish-born playwright, 1856-1950] .... GBS
George C. Marshall Foundation (EA) .... GCMF
George C. Marshall Research Foundation (EA) .... GCMRF
George C. Marshall Space Flight Center [Also known as MSFC] [NASA] .... GCMSC
George C. Marshall Space Flight Center [Also known as MSFC] [NASA] .... GCMSFC
George C. Wallace Community College, Dothan, AL [Library symbol Library of Congress] (LCLS) .... ADoW
George, CA [FM radio station call letters] .... KATJ
George Cross [British] .... GC
George Eastman House [Rochester, NY] .... GEH
George Eastman House, Rochester, NY [Library symbol Library of Congress] (LCLS) .... NRGE
George Emerson's Old Grandmother Rode a Pig Home Yesterday [Mnemonic guide for spelling "geography"] .... GEOGRAPHY
George Fox College [Oregon] .... GFC
George Fox College, Newberg, OR [Library symbol Library of Congress] (LCLS) .... OrNGF
George H. and Laura E. Brown Library, Washington, NC [Library symbol Library of Congress] (LCLS) .... NcWa
George Hail Free Library, Warren, RI [Library symbol Library of Congress] (LCLS) .... RWa
George Hamilton IV and Friends [Defunct] (EA) .... GHFF
George Henry Lewes [Initials used as pseudonym] .... GHL
George Horne [Refers to old news] [Slang] (DSUE) .... GH
George Jackson Elementary School, Jericho, NY [Library symbol Library of Congress] (LCLS) .... NJerJE
George Jones Country Fan Club (EA) .... GJCFC
George Jones Fan Club (EA) .... GJFC
George Junior Republic, Grove City, PA [OCLC symbol] (OCLC) .... PIB
George Khoury Association of Baseball Leagues (EA) .... GKABL
George (King of England) (DLA) .... G
George M. Low Center for Industrial Innovation [Rensselaer Polytechnic Institute] [Research center] (RCD) CII
George MacDonald Society [Lincoln, England] (EAIO) .... GMS
George Marshall Space Flight Center [Huntsville, AL] (IEEE) .... GMSFC
George Mason Bankshares [Commercial firm Associated Press] (SAG) ..... GMason
George Mason Bankshares [NASDAQ symbol] (SAG) .... GMBS
George Mason College [Later, George Mason University], Fairfax, VA [Library symbol Library of Congress] (LCLS) .... ViFGM
George Mason University (GAGS) .... Geo Mason U
George Mason University [Virginia] .... GMU
George Mason University, Fairfax, VA [OCLC symbol] (OCLC) .... VGM
George McCone Memorial County Library, Circle, MT [Library symbol Library of Congress] (LCLS) .... MtCi
George Medal [British] .... GM
George Mercer, Jr., School of Theology, Garden City, NY [Library symbol Library of Congress] (LCLS) .... NGcG
George Michael International Fan Club (EA) .... GMIFC
George on Libel [1812] [A publication] (DLA) .... Geo Lib
George on Partnership [A publication] (DLA) .... George Partn
George Outram & Co. Ltd., Glasgow, United Kingdom [Library symbol Library of Congress] (LCLS) .... UkGO
George/P. W. Botha [South Africa] [ICAO location identifier] (ICLI) .... FAGG
George Peabody College for Teachers [Later, George Peabody College for Teachers of Vanderbilt University] [Tennessee] .... GPCT
George Peabody College for Teachers of Vanderbilt University (GAGS) .... Geo Peabody C
George Pennal Library, St. Joseph's Health Centre, Toronto, Ontario [Library symbol National Library of Canada] (BIB) .... OTSTJ
George Pepperdine College, Los Angeles, CA [Library symbol Library of Congress] (LCLS) .... CLGPC
GEORGE [General Organizational Environment] Remote Terminal Interrogative Environment [Computer science] (IAA) .... GERTIE
George Resources Co. [Vancouver Stock Exchange symbol] .... GGP
George Rogers Clark National Historical Park .... GERO
George S. Houston Memorial Library, Dothan, AL [Library symbol Library of Congress] (LCLS) .... ADo
George Sand Studies (EA) .... GSS
George Simon Kaufman [American playwright, 1889-1961] .... GSK
George Strait Fan Club (EA) .... GSFC
George Takei's Official Worldwide Fan Club [British] (EAIO) .... GTOWFC
George Town [Bahamas] [Airport symbol] (OAG) .... GGT
George Town, Exuma Island [Bahamas] [ICAO location identifier] (ICLI) ...... MYEG
George Washington [US general and president, 1732-1799] .... GW
George Washington Birthplace National Monument .... GEWA
George Washington Carver National Monument .... GWCA
George Washington Memorial Parkway [National Park Service designation] .... GEWP
George Washington School, West Hempstead, NY [Library symbol] [Library of Congress] (LCLS) .... NWhWE
[The] George Washington University (GAGS) .... George Washington U
George Washington University [Washington, DC] .... GW
George Washington University [Washington, DC] .... GWU

George Washington University, Carnegie Endowment for International Peace Collection, Washington, DC [*Library symbol Library of Congress*] (LCLS) .... DGW-C

George Washington University, Law Library, Washington, DC [*Library symbol Library of Congress*] (LCLS) .... DGW-L

George Washington University, Law Library, Washington, DC [*OCLC symbol*] (OCLC) .... GWL

George Washington University, Medical Center, Population Information Program, Washington, DC [*Library symbol Library of Congress*] (LCLS) .... DGW-PIP

George Washington University, Medical Library, Washington, DC [*Library symbol Library of Congress*] (LCLS) .... DGW-M

George Washington University, Medical Library, Washington, DC [*OCLC symbol*] (OCLC) .... GWM

George Washington University, Washington, DC [*Library symbol Library of Congress OCLC symbol*] (LCLS) .... DGW

George William Russell [*Irish poet, 1867-1935*] [*Pseudonym*] .... AE

George Williams College (GAGS) .... Geo Williams C

George Williams College [*Downer's Grove, IL*] .... GWC

George Williams College, Downers Grove, IL [*OCLC symbol*] (OCLC) .... ICF

George Williams College, Downers Grove, IL [*Library symbol Library of Congress*] (LCLS) .... IDowG

George Williams Hooper Foundation [*Research center*] (RCD) .... GWHF

George's Mississippi Digest [*A publication*] (DLA) .... Geo Dig

George's Reports [*30-39 Mississippi*] [*A publication*] (DLA) .... George

Georgetown [*Delaware*] [*Airport symbol*] (AD) .... GED

Georgetown [*Guyana*] [*Airport symbol*] (OAG) .... GEO

Georgetown [*District of Columbia*] [*Seismograph station code, US Geological Survey*] (SEIS) .... GEO

Georgetown (ROG) .... GEORGETN

Georgetown [*Guyana*] [*Airport symbol*] (AD) .... GRG

Georgetown [*Delaware*] [*Seismograph station code, US Geological Survey*] (SEIS) .... GTD

Georgetown [*Australia Airport symbol*] (OAG) .... GTT

Georgetown [*Guyana*] [*ICAO location identifier*] (ICLI) .... SYGC

Georgetown [*Guyana*] [*ICAO location identifier*] (ICLI) .... SYGT

Georgetown Automatic Translator [*Computer science*] .... GAT

Georgetown Branch, Halton Hills Public Libraries, Ontario [*Library symbol National Library of Canada*] (BIB) .... OGEH

Georgetown Clinical Research Institute [*FAA*] .... GCRI

Georgetown College, Georgetown, KY [*Library symbol Library of Congress*] (LCLS) .... KyGeC

Georgetown College (Kentucky) (GAGS) .... Georgetown C

Georgetown College Observatory (MCD) .... GCO

Georgetown Community Unit School District, Georgetown, IL [*Library symbol*] [*Library of Congress*] (LCLS) .... IGeoSD

Georgetown County Memorial Library, Georgetown SC [*Library symbol Library of Congress*] (LCLS) .... ScGeo

Georgetown, DE [*Location identifier FAA*] (FAAL) .... GED

Georgetown, DE [*AM radio station call letters*] .... WSSR

Georgetown, DE [*FM radio station call letters*] .... WZBH

Georgetown District High School, Georgetown, ON, Canada [*Library symbol Library of Congress*] (LCLS) .... CaOGeG

Georgetown District High School, Ontario [*Library symbol National Library of Canada*] (NLC) .... OGEG

Georgetown, KY [*FM radio station call letters*] .... WRVG

Georgetown, KY [*FM radio station call letters*] .... WTKT

Georgetown, KY [*FM radio station call letters*] (RBYB) .... WXZZ

Georgetown, NY [*Location identifier FAA*] (FAAL) .... GGT

Georgetown, OH [*Location identifier FAA*] (FAAL) .... GEO

Georgetown, OH [*FM radio station call letters*] .... WAXZ

Georgetown/Owen Roberts International [*Cayman Islands*] [*ICAO location identifier*] (ICLI) .... MWCR

Georgetown Public Library, Georgetown, IL [*Library symbol Library of Congress*] (LCLS) .... IGeo

Georgetown Public Library, Georgetown, ON, Canada [*Library symbol Library of Congress*] (LCLS) .... CaOGeo

Georgetown Public Library, Ontario [*Library symbol National Library of Canada*] (NLC) .... OGEO

Georgetown Railroad Co. [*AAR code*] .... GRR

Georgetown, SC [*Location identifier FAA*] (FAAL) .... GGE

Georgetown, SC [*AM radio station call letters*] .... WGTN

Georgetown, SC [*AM radio station call letters*] .... WLMC

Georgetown, SC [*FM radio station call letters*] .... WSCA

Georgetown, SC [*FM radio station call letters*] .... WSYN

Georgetown, SC [*FM radio station call letters*] .... WWXM

Georgetown/Timehri Internacional [*Guyana*] [*ICAO location identifier*] (ICLI) .... SYTM

Georgetown Township Library, Jenison, MI [*Library symbol Library of Congress*] (LCLS) .... MiJen

Georgetown, TX [*Location identifier FAA*] (FAAL) .... GUO

Georgetown, TX [*FM radio station call letters*] .... KHFI

Georgetown, TX [*FM radio station call letters*] .... KNNC

Georgetown, TX [*AM radio station call letters*] .... KWTR

Georgetown University [*Washington, DC*] .... GU

Georgetown University (District of Columbia) (GAGS) ...... Georgetown U

Georgetown University, Kennedy Institute, Center for Bioethics, Washington, DC [*Library symbol Library of Congress*] (LCLS) .... DGU-KIE

Georgetown University, Kennedy Institute, Center for Population Research, Washington, DC [*Library symbol Library of Congress*] (LCLS) .... DGU-Pop

Georgetown University Law Center (AAGC) .... GULC

Georgetown University, Law Library, Washington, DC [*Library symbol Library of Congress*] (LCLS) .... DGU-L

Georgetown University, Law Library, Washington, DC [*OCLC symbol*] (OCLC) .... GUL

Georgetown University, Medical Center Library, Washington, DC [*OCLC symbol*] (OCLC) .... GTU

Georgetown University, Medical, Dental, and Nursing Library, Washington, DC [*Library symbol Library of Congress*] (LCLS) .... DGU-M

Georgetown University, Medical Library Processing Center, Washington, DC [*OCLC symbol*] (OCLC) .... MPG

Georgetown University, Science Library, Washington, DC [*Library symbol Library of Congress*] (LCLS) .... DGU-S

Georgetown University, Washington, DC [*Library symbol Library of Congress OCLC symbol*] (LCLS) .... DGU

Georgetown University, Woodstock Theological Center, Washington, DC [*Library symbol Library of Congress*] (LCLS) .... DGU-W

Georgetown Visitation Preparatory School, Washington, DC [*Library symbol Library of Congress*] (LCLS) .... DGVC

Georgia [*Postal code*] (AFM) .... GA

Georgia (ODBW) .... Ga

Georgia [*MARC country of publication code Library of Congress*] (LCCP) .... gau

Georgia [*Obsolete*] (ROG) .... GEO

Georgia [*MARC geographic area code Library of Congress*] (LCCP) .... n-us-ga

Georgia Agricultural Commodity Commission for Peanuts (SRA) .... GACCP

Georgia Air [*Czechoslovakia*] [*ICAO designator*] (FAAC) .... GEA

Georgia & Florida R. R. .... G & F

Georgia & Florida R. R. [*AAR code*] .... GF

Georgia Apartment Association (SRA) .... GAA

Georgia Appeals Reports [*A publication*] (DLA) .... GA App

Georgia Appeals Reports [*A publication*] (DLA) .... GA App (NS)

Georgia Appeals Reports [*A publication*] (DLA) .... GaA

Georgia, Ashburn, Sylvester & Camilla R. R. [*AAR code*] .... GASC

Georgia Association of Broadcasters (SRA) .... GAB

Georgia Association of Christian Schools (SRA) .... GACS

Georgia Association of Convenience Stores (SRA) .... GACS

Georgia Association of Criminal Defense Lawyers (SRA) .... GACDL

Georgia Association of Educational Leaders (SRA) .... GAEL

Georgia Association of Homes and Services for Children (SRA) ..... GAHSC

Georgia Automated Clearing House Association .... GACHA

Georgia Baptist Hospital, Medical Library, Atlanta, GA [*Library symbol Library of Congress*] (LCLS) .... GABH

Georgia Baptist Hospital, School of Nursing, Atlanta, GA [*Library symbol Library of Congress*] (LCLS) .... GABH-N

Georgia Beer Wholesalers Association (SRA) .... GBWA

Georgia Bonded Fibers [*NASDAQ symbol*] (TTSB) .... BOTX

Georgia Bonded Fibers, Inc. [*NASDAQ symbol*] (SAG) .... BOTX

Georgia Bonded Fibers, Inc. [*Associated Press*] (SAG) .... GaBnd

Georgia Business Lawyer (DLA) .... GA Bus Law

Georgia Code, Annotated [*A publication*] (DLA) .... GA Code Ann

Georgia College, Milledgeville, GA [*OCLC symbol*] (OCLC) .... GGC

Georgia College, Milledgeville, GA [*Library symbol Library of Congress*] (LCLS) .... GMiW

Georgia College of Milledgeville (GAGS) .... Georgia C Milledgeville

Georgia Constitution [*A publication*] (DLA) .... GA Const

Georgia Court of Appeals Reports [*A publication*] (AAGC) .... Ga App

Georgia Decisions [*A publication*] (DLA) .... GA Dec

Georgia Decisions [*A publication*] (DLA) .... Geo Dec

Georgia Department of Education, Atlanta, GA [*OCLC symbol*] (OCLC) .... GSL

Georgia Department of Human Resources, Atlanta, GA [*Library symbol Library of Congress*] (LCLS) .... GAHR

Georgia Division, Lockheed Aircraft Corp. .... GELAC

Georgia Gulf Corp. [*Associated Press*] (SAG) .... GaGulf

Georgia Gulf Corp. [*NYSE symbol*] (SPSG) .... GGC

Georgia Historical Society, Savannah, GA [*Library symbol Library of Congress*] (LCLS) .... GHi

Georgia Hospital Association [*Atlanta*] (TSSD) .... GHA

Georgia Hospital Computer Group .... GHCP

Georgia Institute of Technology (GAGS) .... Georgia Inst Tech

Georgia Institute of Technology [*Atlanta*] .... GIT

Georgia Institute of Technology and Technical Information Science (HGAA) .... GATTIS

Georgia Institute of Technology, Atlanta, GA [*Library symbol Library of Congress OCLC symbol*] (LCLS) .... GAT

Georgia Institute of Technology Research Reactor .... GTRR

Georgia Institute of Technology School of Information Science [*Report series code*] (NITA) .... GITIS

Georgia Institute of Technology Technical Information Service (NITA)..... GATTIS

Georgia Law Journal [*A publication*] (DLA) .... GA LJ

Georgia Law Reporter [*A publication*] (DLA) .... GA L Rep

Georgia Law Reporter [*A publication*] (DLA) .... GA Law Reporter

Georgia Lawyer [*A publication*] (DLA) .... GA L

Georgia Library Information Network [*Library network*] .... GLIN

Georgia Mental Health Institute, Atlanta, GA [*Library symbol Library of Congress*] (LCLS) .... GAGM

Georgia Mental Health Institute, Atlanta, GA [*OCLC symbol*] (OCLC) .... GMH

Georgia Military College [*Milledgeville*] .... GMC

Georgia Military College, Milledgeville, GA [*Library symbol Library of Congress*] (LCLS) .... GMiM

Georgia Milk Producers (SRA) .... GMP

Georgia Mining and Mineral Research Institute [*Georgia Institute of Technology*] [*Research center*] (RCD) .... GMMRI

Georgia Motor Trucking Association [*STAC*] .... GAM

[The] Georgia Northern Railway Co. [*AAR code*] .... GANO

[The] Georgia Northern Railway Co. (IIA) .... GN

Georgia Nuclear Aircraft Laboratory (SAA) .... GNAL

Georgia Nuclear Laboratory [*AEC*] .... GNL

Georgia Nurses Association (SRA) .... GNA

Georgia Oilmen's Association (SRA) .... GOA

Georgia Optometric Association (SRA) .... GOA

Georgia Peanut Commission (EA) .... GPC
Georgia Peanut Producers Association (SRA) .... GPPA
Georgia Pecan Growers Association (SRA) .... GPGA
Georgia Pork Producers Association (SRA) .... GPPA
Georgia Power [Associated Press] (SAG) .... GaP
Georgia Power Capital Ltd. [Associated Press] (SAG) .... GaPC
Georgia Power Capital LP [NYSE symbol] (SAG) .... GPE
Georgia Power Capital Trust I [Associated Press] (SAG) ...... GaPC
Georgia Power Capital Trust I [NYSE symbol] (SAG) .... GPE
Georgia Power Co. [Associated Press] (SAG) .... GaPw
Georgia Power Co. [NYSE symbol] (SPSG) .... GPE
Georgia Power Co., Atlanta, GA [Library symbol Library of Congress]
   (LCLS) .... GAGP
Georgia Propane Gas Association (SRA) .... GPGA
Georgia Psychiatric Physicians Association (SRA) .... GPPA
Georgia Public Service Commission Reports [A publication] (DLA) ... GA PSC
Georgia Pwr $1.90'A'Pfd [NYSE symbol] (TTSB) .... GPEPrP
Georgia Pwr $7.72Pfd [NYSE symbol] (TTSB) .... GPEPr
Georgia Pwr $7.80 Pfd [NYSE symbol] (TTSB) .... GPEPrB
Georgia Pwr $1.925'A'Pfd [NYSE symbol] (TTSB) .... GPEPrS
Georgia Pwr $1.9375'A'Pfd [NYSE symbol] (TTSB) .... GPEPrR
Georgia Pwr $1.9875 'A' Pfd [NYSE symbol] (TTSB) .... GPEPrQ
Georgia Railroad Co. [AAR code] .... GA
Georgia Regional Hospital at Atlanta, Atlanta, GA [Library symbol Library of
   Congress] (LCLS) .... GARH
Georgia Reports [A publication] (DLA) .... GA Rep
Georgia Reports [A publication] (DLA) .... GaR
Georgia Reports [A publication] (DLA) .... Geo
Georgia Reports [A publication] (DLA) .... Geo Rep
Georgia Reports [A publication] (DLA) .... Georgia
Georgia Reports [A publication] (DLA) .... Georgia Rep
Georgia Reports, Annotated [A publication] (DLA) .... GA Rep Ann
Georgia Reports, Annotated [A publication] (DLA) .... Michie's GA Repts Ann
Georgia Reports, Supplement [A publication] (DLA) .... GA Sup
Georgia Reports, Supplement [A publication] (DLA) .... GA Supp
Georgia Retardation Center, Atlanta, GA [Library symbol Library of
   Congress] (LCLS) .... GAGR
Georgia Review [A publication] (BRI) .... Ga R
Georgia Satellites International Fan Club (EA) .... GSIFC
Georgia Sessions Laws [A publication] (DLA) .... GA L
Georgia Society of Professional Engineers (SRA) .... GSPE
Georgia Southern & Florida Railway Co. .... GS & F
Georgia Southern & Florida Railway Co. [AAR code] .... GSF
Georgia Southern College, Statesboro, GA [OCLC symbol] (OCLC) ... GPM
Georgia Southern College, Statesboro, GA [Library symbol Library of
   Congress] (LCLS) .... GStG
Georgia Southern Peanut Warehousemen's Association (SRA) ...... GSPWA
Georgia Southern University (GAGS) .... Georgia So U
Georgia Southwestern College, Americus, GA [Library symbol Library of
   Congress] (LCLS) .... GAmG
Georgia Southwestern College, Americus, GA [OCLC symbol] (OCLC) ..... GHA
Georgia State College for Women [Later, Women's College of Georgia]
   (AEBS) .... GSCW
Georgia State Department of Archives and History, Atlanta, GA [Library
   symbol Library of Congress] (LCLS) .... G-Ar
Georgia State Department of Education, Division of Public Library, Library
   for the Blind and Physically Handicapped, Atlanta, GA [Library symbol
   Library of Congress] (LCLS) .... GAE-BPH
Georgia State Department of Education, Division of Public Library
   Services, Atlanta, GA [Library symbol Library of Congress] (LCLS) ... GAE-P
Georgia State Library, Atlanta, GA [Library symbol Library of Congress]
   (LCLS) .... G
Georgia State University (GAGS) .... Georgia St U
Georgia State University, Atlanta, GA [Library symbol Library of Congress]
   (LCLS) .... GASU
Georgia State University, Atlanta, GA [OCLC symbol] (OCLC) .... GSU
Georgia State University, Documents Library, Atlanta, GA [Library symbol]
   [Library of Congress] (LCLS) .... GASU-D
Georgia State University, Instructional Resource Center, Atlanta, GA
   [Library symbol] [Library of Congress] (LCLS) .... GASU-I
Georgia State University, Law Library, Atlanta, GA [Library symbol Library of
   Congress] (LCLS) .... GASU-L
Georgia Supreme Court Reports [A publication] (DLA) .... GA
Georgia Teachers College [Later, Georgia Southern College] (AEBS) ..... GTC
Georgia Tech Language [Computer science] (CSR) .... GTL
Georgia Tech Research Institute [Georgia Institute of Technology] [Research
   center] (RCD) .... GTRI
Georgia Telecommunications Network [Georgia Hospital Association]
   [Atlanta, GA] [Telecommunications] (TSSD) .... TELNET
Georgia Warm Springs Foundation [Later, RWSF] (EA) .... GWSF
Georgia World Congress Center .... GWCC
Georgian [MARC language code Library of Congress] (LCCP) .... geo
Georgian Association in USA (EA) .... GAUSA
Georgian Bay [ICAO designator] (AD) .... UD
Georgian Bay Airways [Canada ICAO designator] (FAAC) .... GBA
Georgian Bay Regional Library, Barrie, ON, Canada [Library symbol Library
   of Congress] (LCLS) .... CaOBaG
Georgian Bay Regional Library, Barrie, Ontario [Library symbol National
   Library of Canada] (NLC) .... OBAG
Georgian Bay Township Public Library, Mactier, Ontario [Library symbol
   National Library of Canada] (BIB) .... OMGB
Georgian College [EDUCATSS] [UTLAS symbol] .... EUJ
Georgian College of Applied Arts and Technology, Barrie, ON, Canada
   [Library symbol Library of Congress] (LCLS) .... CaOBaGC

Georgian College of Applied Arts and Technology, Barrie, Ontario [Library
   symbol National Library of Canada] (NLC) .... OBAGC
Georgian College of Applied Arts and Technology, Learning Resources
   Centre, Orillia, ON, Canada [Library symbol] [Library of Congress]
   (LCLS) .... CaOOrGC
Georgian College Resource Centre, Owen Sound, ON, Canada [Library
   symbol Library of Congress] (LCLS) .... CaOOwGC
Georgian College Resource Centre, Owen Sound, Ontario [Library symbol
   National Library of Canada] (NLC) .... OOWGC
Georgian Court College [Lakewood, NJ] .... GCC
Georgian Court College, Lakewood, NJ [Library symbol Library of
   Congress] (LCLS) .... NjLakG
Georgian Soviet Socialist Republic [MARC geographic area code Library of
   Congress] (LCCP) .... e-ur-gs
Georgian Soviet Socialist Republic .... GeoSSR
Georgian Soviet Socialist Republic [MARC country of publication code Library
   of Congress] (LCCP) .... gsr
Georgiana, AL [FM radio station call letters] .... WWGA
Georgians for Preservation Action [An association] .... GPA
Georgians Unwilling to Surrender [Organization founded by former governor,
   Lester Maddox] .... GUTS
Georgia-Pacific [NYSE symbol] (TTSB) .... GP
Georgia-Pacific Corp. [Associated Press] (SAG) .... GaPac
Georgia-Pacific Corp. [NYSE symbol] (SPSG) .... GP
Georgia-Tennessee Regional Health Commission, Chattanooga, TN [Library
   symbol Library of Congress] (LCLS) .... TCGT
Georgics [of Vergil] [Classical studies] (OCD) .... G
Georgics [Poetry] (ROG) .... GEORG
Georgina Township Public Library, Keswick, ON, Canada [Library symbol
   Library of Congress] (LCLS) .... CaOKes
Georgina Township Public Library, Keswick, Ontario [Library symbol
   National Library of Canada] (NLC) .... OKES
Georgist Registry [An association] (EA) .... GR
Georgius Natta [Flourished, 1477-95] [Authority cited in pre-1607 legal work]
   (DSA) .... Georg Nat
Georgius Rex [King George] .... GR
Georgius Rex et Imperator [George, King and Emperor] .... GR et I
GEOS [Geodetic Earth-Orbiting Satellite] Data Adjustment Program .... GDAP
GEOSAT [Geodetic Satellite] Follow On [Marine science] (OSRA) ..... GFO
GEOSAT [Geodesy Satellite] Follow-On (USDC) .... GFO
GeoScience Corp. [NASDAQ symbol] (TTSB) .... GSCI
Geoscience Data Index for Alberta [Alberta Research Council] [Information
   service or system] (IID) .... GEODIAL
Geoscience Electronics (MCD) .... GE
Geoscience Electronics (MCD) .... GEO
Geoscience Information Society (EA) .... GIS
Geoscience Research Institute .... GRI
Geosciences Information Center [Federal Institute for Geosciences and
   NaturalResources] [Information service or system] (IID) .... GEOFIZ
Geoscientific Resource Data Base [Queensland] [State] (EERA) ...... GRDB
GEOSECS Operations Group [Marine science] (MSC) .... GOG
Geostar Mining Corp. [Vancouver Stock Exchange symbol] .... GMC
Geostationary Communications Satellite [WARC] .... GCS
Geostationary Earth Orbit .... GEO
Geostationary European Meteorological Satellite .... GEMS
Geostationary Launch Vehicle [Indian Space Research Organization] ...... GSLV
Geostationary Meteorological Satellite [Japan] .... GMS
Geostationary Operational Environmental Satellite [National Oceanic and
   Atmospheric Administration] .... GOES
Geostationary Operational Environmental Satellite [Instrument] (EERA) ..... GOES
Geostationary Operational Environmental Satellite Data Collection
   Platform (MSC) .... GOES/DCP
Geostationary Operational Meteorological Satellite [Marine science]
   (OSRA) .... GOMS
Geostationary Orbit (MCD) .... GSO
Geostationary Orbital Earth Satellite (MCD) .... GOES
Geostationary Satellite (PDAA) .... GSS
Geostationary Satellite Launch Vehicle .... GSLV
Geostationary Technology Satellite .... GTS
Geostationary Transfer Orbit [Space technology] .... GTO
Geostatistical Environmental Assessment Software [US Environmental
   Protection Agency] .... GEO-EAS
Geosynchronous [Satellite orbit] (CDE) .... GEO
Geosynchronous Earth Observation System (IEEE) .... GEOS
Geosynchronous Earth Orbit .... GEO
Geosynchronous Earth Orbit Satellites (ACRL) .... GEOS
Geosynchronous Operational Environmental Satellite [NASA] (NASA) ...... GOES
Geosynchronous Orbit .... GSO
Geosynchronous Orbiting Earth Satellite .... GOES
Geosynchronous Solar Electric Propulsion Stage [NASA] (NASA) .... GEOSEPS
Geosynchronous Synthetic Aperture RADAR (IEEE) .... GEOSAR
Geosynchronous Very-High-Resolution Radiometer .... GVHRR
Geotech Capital [Vancouver Stock Exchange symbol] .... GEO
Geotechnical Fabrics Report [A publication] (EAAP) .... GFR
Geotechnical Research Centre [McGill University] [Canada Research center]
   (RCD) .... GRC
Geotek Communications, Inc. [Associated Press] (SAG) .... GeoTk
Geotek Communications, Inc. [NASDAQ symbol] (NQ) .... GOTK
GeoTel Communications Corp. [NASDAQ symbol] (SAG) .... GEOC
GeoTel Communications Corp. [Associated Press] (SAG) .... GeoTICo
Geothermal Energy .... GTE
Geothermal Energy Update [A publication] .... GEU
Geothermal Loop Experimental Facility [Department of Energy] .... GLEF
Geothermal Resource Interactive Temporal Simulation (PDAA) .... GRITS
Geothermal Resources Council (EA) .... GRC

Geothermal World Info Center [*Later, REIC*] (EA) ... GWIC
GeoWaste, Inc. [*NASDAQ symbol*] (SPSG) ... GEOW
GeoWaste, Inc. [*Associated Press*] (SAG) ... GeoWste
GeoWorks [*Associated Press*] (SAG) ... Geoworks
GeoWorks [*NASDAQ symbol*] (SAG) ... GWRX
Geoworks [*NASDAQ symbol*] (TTSB) ... GWRX
Gepanzerte Pioniermaschine [*Armored Engineer Vehicle*] [*General Electric Co.*] [*German*] (MCD) ... GPM
Geraeteausgabestelle [*Equipment distributing point*] [*German military - World War II*] ... GAST
Geraghty & Miller, Inc. ... G & M
Gerald R. Ford Library ... GRFL
Gerald R. Ford Library, Ann Arbor, MI [*Library symbol*] [*Library of Congress*] (LCLS) ... MiAaF
Gerald Rudolf Ford [*US president, 1913-*] ... GRF
Geraldton [*Australia ICAO location identifier*] (ICLI) ... APGN
Geraldton [*Australia Airport symbol*] (OAG) ... GET
Geraldton [*Canada*] [*Airport symbol*] (OAG) ... YGQ
Geraldton (North), ON [*ICAO location identifier*] (ICLI) ... CYGQ
Geraldton, ON [*Television station call letters*] ... CBLAT
Geraldton Public Library, Ontario [*Library symbol National Library of Canada*] (NLC) ... OGER
Gerard P. Weeg Computing Center [*University of Iowa*] [*Research center*] (RCD) ... WCC
Gerard Parizeau Ltee., Montreal, PQ, Canada [*Library symbol Library of Congress*] (LCLS) ... CaQMGP
Gerard Parizeau Ltee, Montreal, Quebec [*Library symbol National Library of Canada*] (NLC) ... QMGP
Gerard Pucelle [*Deceased, 1184*] [*Authority cited in pre-1607 legal work*] (DSA) ... Ger
Gerard's Titles to Real Estate [*A publication*] (DLA) ... Ger Tit
Gerber Oscillogram Amplitude Translator ... GOAT
Gerber Scientific [*NYSE symbol*] (TTSB) ... GRB
Gerber Scientific, Inc. [*Associated Press*] (SAG) ... GerbSc
Gerber Scientific, Inc. [*NYSE symbol*] (SPSG) ... GRB
Gerecht und Volkommen [*Correct and Complete*] [*German*] ... GUV
Gereformeerd Politiek Verbond [*Reformed Political League*] [*Netherlands Political party*] (PPE) ... GPV
Gerequireerde [*Defendant*] [*Netherlands*] (ILCA) ... Gereq
Geriatric ... GERI
Geriatric & Medical Companies [*NASDAQ symbol*] (NQ) ... GEMC
Geriatric & Medical Companies, Inc. [*Associated Press*] (SAG) ... GeriMed
Geriatric & Medl Cos. [*NASDAQ symbol*] (TTSB) ... GEMC
Geriatric Assessment Team [*Medicine*] (DMAA) ... GAT
Geriatric Assessment Unit [*Australia*] ... GAU
Geriatric Authority (DICI) ... GA
Geriatric Care ... GC
Geriatric Chair (DAVI) ... GC
Geriatric Depression Scale [*Medicine*] (DMAA) ... GDS
Geriatric Education and Training Act [*1985*] ... GREAT
Geriatric Evaluation by Relative Rating Instrument [*Medicine*] (DMAA) ... GERRI
Geriatric Evaluation Unit [*Veterans Administration*] (GFGA) ... GEU
Geriatric Mental State [*Medicine*] (DMAA) ... GMS
Geriatric Nurse Clinician (DMAA) ... GNC
Geriatric Nurse Practitioner (DMAA) ... GNP
Geriatric Order of Old Dolls Who Encourage the Generation Gap Singlemindedly [*Tongue-in-cheek teachers' organization*] ... GOOD EGGS
Geriatric Rehabilitation Team [*Australia*] ... GRT
Geriatric Research, Education, and Clinical Center [*Veterans Administration*] ... GRECC
Geriatric Sentence Completion Form [*Personality development test*] [*Psychology*] ... GSCF
Geriatric-Care Manager ... GCM
Geriatrics ... GER
Geriatrics [*Medicine*] (DAVI) ... geri
Geriatrics ... GERIAT
Gericht [*Court*] [*German*] (ILCA) ... G
Gerim (BJA) ... Ger
Gerin, Inc. [*Toronto Stock Exchange symbol*] ... GEN
Gerkang Oktober [*See also GESTAPU*] [*Plot against the government of Indonesia which began on September 30, 1965 and continued into October*] ... GESTOK
Gerkang, September, Tigapuluh [*See also GESTOK*] [*Plot against the government of Indonesia beginning on September 30, 1965*] ... GESTAPU
Gerle Gold Ltd. [*Vancouver Stock Exchange symbol*] ... GGL
Germ [*or Germination*] (WGA) ... GRM
Germ Ring [*Embryology*] ... GR
Germ Warfare ... GW
German [*or Germanic*] ... G
German [*MARC language code Library of Congress*] (LCCP) ... ger
German [*Language, etc.*] ... GER
German [*Language, etc.*] (ROG) ... GERM
German ... GN
German Aerospace Research Establishment (GAVI) ... DLR
German Air Defense Ground Environment ... GEADGE
German Air Force [*German Luftwaffe*] ... GAF
German Air Force [*ICAO designator*] (FAAC) ... GAF
German Air Force Air Defense School (MCD) ... GAFADS
German Air Force Southern Command (MCD) ... GAFSC
German Air Force Tactical Air Command (MCD) ... GAFTAC
German Amer Bancorp [*NASDAQ symbol*] (TTSB) ... GABC
German American Bancorp [*NASDAQ symbol*] (SAG) ... GABC
German American Bancorp [*Associated Press*] (SAG) ... GerABcp
German American National Political Action Committee (EA) ... GANPAC
German American World Society (EA) ... GAWS
German Antarctic Expedition [*1901-03,1911-12,1938-39*] ... GerAE
German Armed Forces Intelligence Agency (MCD) ... GAFIA
German Army (NATG) ... GA
German Army [*ICAO designator*] (FAAC) ... GAM
German Army ... GAR
German Army Material Office ... GAMO
German Army Office ... GAO
German Association for American Studies (EAIO) ... GAAS
German Association for Applied Mathematics and Mechanics ... GAMM
German Atlantic Line [*Steamship*] (MHDB) ... GAL
German Australian Chamber of Industry and Commerce [*Australia*] ... GACIC
German Australian Society of Australia ... GASA
German Books in Print [*A publication*] ... GBiP
German Cargo Services [*ICAO designator*] (FAAC) ... GEC
German Carpet Research Institute [*See also TFI*] (EAIO) ... GCRI
German Chamber of Industry and Commerce in the United Kingdom (EAIO) ... GCICU
German Colonies Collectors Group (EA) ... GCCG
German Convention Bureau (EA) ... GCB
German Democratic Republic [*ANSI two-letter standard code*] (CNC) ... DD
German Democratic Republic [*East Germany*] ... GDR
German Democratic Republic (WDAA) ... GER DEM REP
German Dermatological Society (EAIO) ... GRS
German East Africa [*Obsolete*] (ROG) ... GEA
German Economic and Monetary Union ... GEMU
German External Property Control Commission [*Minden*] [*Allied German Occupation Forces*] ... GEPC
German Federal Republic [*West Germany*] ... GFR
German Foreign Office [*British World War II*] ... GFO
German Genealogical Society of America (EA) ... GGSA
German Historical Institute (EA) ... GHI
German Information Center [*Information service or system*] (IID) ... GIC
German Information System on Food, Agriculture, and Forestry [*Bonn*] [*Information service or system*] (IID) ... FIS-ELF
German Jewish (BJA) ... GJ
German Language Club (EA) ... GLC
German Liaison Office for the Armament Sector [*Military*] ... GLOAS
German Lutheran Conference of North America (EA) ... GLCNA
German Mass Spectrometer ... GEMS
German, Middle High [*MARC language code Library of Congress*] (LCCP) ... gmh
German Military Documents Section [*of AGO, Army*] [*World War II*] ... GMDS
German Mine Supplies Organization [*Allied German Occupation Forces*] ... GMSO
German Minesweeping Administration [*Allied German Occupation Forces*] ... GMSA
German Minimum Economy [*Allied German Occupation Forces*] ... GME
German Ministry of Defense ... GERMDF
German Naval Forces, North Sea Subarea [*NATO*] (NATG) ... GERNORSEA
German Navy [*ICAO designator*] (FAAC) ... GNY
German, Old High [*MARC language code Library of Congress*] (LCCP) ... goh
German Order of Harugari ... GOH
German Patent (IAA) ... GERPAT
German Patent (IAA) ... GP
German Quarterly [*A publication*] (BRI) ... Ger Q
German Reports (MCD) ... GR
German Research Association (EA) ... GRA
German Research Satellite [*NASA*] ... GRS
German Rhine Coordination Directorate [*Allied German Occupation Forces*] ... GRCD
German Roach [*Immunology*] ... GR
German Sanchez Ruiperez [*Founder and chairman of Anaya, a Spanish publishing enterprise*] ... GSR
German Shepherd Dog (DI) ... GSD
German Shepherd Dog Club of America (EA) ... GSDCA
German Shorthaired Pointer Club of America (EA) ... GSPCA
German Silver ... GS
German Silver ... GSIL
German Society of Pennsylvania (EA) ... GSP
German Society of Pennsylvania, Philadelphia, PA [*Library symbol Library of Congress*] (LCLS) ... PPG
German Society of the City of New York (EA) ... GSCNY
German Student Travel Service ... GSTS
German Studies Library Group (EAIO) ... GSLG
German Tactical Truck (MCD) ... GETT
German Teachers' Association [*British*] ... GTA
German Territorial Forces (MCD) ... GTF
German Territorial Southern Command [*NATO*] (NATG) ... GTSC
German Title (NITA) ... GT
German Touring Car Championship ... GTCC
German Translation (MCD) ... GT
German Wine Society [*Canada*] (EAIO) ... GWS
German Wirehaired Pointer Club of America (EA) ... GWPCA
German Workshop on Artificial Intelligence [*A publication*] ... GWAI
German Yearbook of International Law [*A publication*] (DLA) ... German Yb Int'l L
German Yearbook of International Law [*A publication*] (DLA) ... GYIL
German-American Football Association [*Later, CSL*] ... GAFA
German-American Information and Education Association (EA) ... GIEA
German-American Securities Corp. (BARN) ... GASC
Germania [*of Tacitus*] [*Classical studies*] (OCD) ... Germ
Germania Fluggesellschaft Koln [*Germany ICAO designator*] (FAAC) ... GMI
Germania Judaica [*A publication*] (BJA) ... GermJud
Germania Judaica (BJA) ... GJ
Germanic [*MARC language code Library of Congress*] (LCCP) ... gem
Germanic [*Language, etc.*] ... GMC
Germanicus [*15BC-19AD*] [*Classical studies*] (OCD) ... German
Germanischer Lloyd [*Shipping*] (ROG) ... G

Germanischer Lloyd [*German ship classification society*] (DS) ... GL
German-Israeli Foundation [*US and Israel*] ... GIF
Germanistic Society of America (EA) ... GSA
Germanium [*Chemical element*] ... Ge
Germanium Alloy (IAA) ... GA
Germanium Alloy Diffused (IAA) ... GAD
Germanium Junction Diode (IDOE) ... GJD
Germanium Point-Contact (IDOE) ... gpc
Germanium Rectifier ... GR
Germanium Stack Rectifier ... GSR
Germanium Transistor [*Electronics*] (IAA) ... GET
Germanium-Lithium Argon Scanning System (NRCH) ... GLASS
Germans-from-Russia Heritage Society (EA) ... GFRHS
Germans-from-Russia Heritage Society (EA) ... GRHS
German-Texan Heritage Society (EA) ... GTHS
Germantown Laboratories, Inc., Philadelphia, PA [*Library symbol Library of Congress*] (LCLS) ... PPF-G
Germantown Public Library, Germantown, OH [*Library symbol Library of Congress*] (LCLS) ... OGer
Germantown, TN [*FM radio station call letters*] ... WJOI
Germantown, TN [*AM radio station call letters*] ... WNWZ
Germantown, TN [*FM radio station call letters*] ... WOGY
Germantown, TN [*AM radio station call letters*] ... WPLX
Germany [*MARC geographic area code Library of Congress*] (LCCP) ... e-gx--
Germany (WDAA) ... G
Germany (NATG) ... GE
Germany ... GER
Germany (VRA) ... Ger
Germany ... GY
Germany Air Force Technical Order (MCD) ... GAFTO
Germany, East [*MARC geographic area code Library of Congress*] (LCCP) ... e-ge--
Germany, East [*MARC country of publication code Library of Congress*] (LCCP) ... ge
Germany Fund [*NYSE symbol*] (TTSB) ... GER
Germany Fund, Inc. [*NYSE symbol*] (SPSG) ... GER
Germany Fund, Inc. [*Associated Press*] (SAG) ... GerFd
Germany Fund New [*Associated Press*] (SAG) ... GerNew
Germany Philatelic Society (EA) ... GPS
Germany, West [*MARC geographic area code Library of Congress*] (LCCP) ... e-gw--
Germany, West [*MARC country of publication code Library of Congress*] (LCCP) ... gw
Germ-Cell Alkaline Phosphatase (DMAA) ... GCAP
Germersheim [*Germany ICAO location identifier*] (ICLI) ... EDEZ
Germersheim Army Depot (MCD) ... GAD
Germersheim Reserve Storage Activity (MCD) ... GRSA
Germfree [*Medicine*] ... GF
Germinable Propagule [*Botany*] ... GP
Germinal Center [*Immunochemistry*] ... GC
Germinal Center Hyperplasia [*Medicine*] ... GCH
Germinal Center-Forming Unit (DNAB) ... GCFU
Germinal Matrix Hemorrhage [*Medicine*] (DMAA) ... GMH
Germinal Vesicle (PDAA) ... GV
Germinal Vesicle Breakdown [*Cytology*] ... GVBD
Germinating Ray Acoustics Simulation System (MCD) ... GRASS
Germine Diacetate [*Medicine*] (DMAA) ... GDA
Germplasm Resources Information Network [*Department of Agriculture*] [*Beltsville, MD*] ... GRIN
Geroderma Osteodysplastica Hereditaria [*Medicine*] (DMAA) ... GOH
Geron Corp. [*NASDAQ symbol*] (SAG) ... GERN
Geron Corp. [*Associated Press*] (SAG) ... GeronCp
Gerona [*Spain*] [*Airport symbol*] (OAG) ... GRO
Gerona/Costa Brava [*Spain ICAO location identifier*] (ICLI) ... LEGE
Gerontological Apperception Test [*Medicine*] (DMAA) ... GAT
Gerontological Nurse Practitioner ... GNP
Gerontological Society [*Later, GSA*] (EA) ... GS
Gerontological Society of America (EA) ... GSA
Gerontological Society of America (DAVI) ... GSoA
Gerontology [*American Occupational Therapy Association*] ... G
Gerontology [*American Occupational Therapy Association*] ... GER
Gerontology [*or Gerontologist*] [*Geriatrics*] (DAVI) ... Gerontol
Gerontology Research Center [*Department of Health and Human Services*] [*Research center*] ... GRC
Gerontology Research Center, Baltimore, MD [*OCLC symbol*] (OCLC) ... GRL
Gerontology Special Interest Section [*American Occupational Therapy Association*] ... GSS
Gerrish House Society, Grand Harbour, Grand Manan Island, NB, Canada [*Library symbol Library of Congress*] (LCLS) ... CaNBGG
Gerrish-Higgins School District Public Library, Roscommon, MI [*Library symbol Library of Congress*] (LCLS) ... MiRosc
Gerrity O&G Cv Dep Pfd [*NYSE symbol*] (TTSB) ... GOGPr
Gerrity Oil & Gas [*Associated Press*] (SAG) ... Gerrity
Gerrity Oil & Gas [*NYSE symbol*] (SPSG) ... GOG
Gerson Institute (EA) ... GI
Gerstmann-Staussler Syndrome [*Medicine*] ... GSS
Gerstmann-Straeussler-Scheinker Disease [*Medicine*] (DMAA) ... GSSD
Gerstmann-Straussler-Sheinker [*Disease*] ... GSS
Gerund ... GER
Gesammelte Abhandlungen [*A publication*] (BJA) ... GA
Gesammelte Abhandlungen zur Roemischen Religions- und Stadtgeschichte [*A publication*] (OCD) ... Ges Abh
Gesammelte Schriften [*A publication*] (OCD) ... Ges Schr
Gesammelte Studien [*A publication*] (BJA) ... GesStud
Gesammelte Studien zum Alten Testament [*A publication*] (BJA) ... GSAT
Gesammelte Studien zum Alten Testament [*A publication*] (BJA) ... GST
Gesamtdeutsche Partei [*All-German Party*] [*Political party*] (PPE) ... GDP
Gesamtdeutsche Volkspartei [*All-German People's Party*] [*Germany Political party*] (PPE) ... GVP
Gesamtdeutsches Institut, Bonn, Germany [*Library symbol Library of Congress*] (LCLS) ... GyBoGI
Gesamthochschulbibliothek Duisburg, Duisburg, Germany [*Library symbol Library of Congress*] (LCLS) ... GyDuiH
Gesamtverzeichnis Auslaendischer Zeitschriften [*Cumulative List of Foreign Periodicals*] ... GAZ
Gesamtverzeichnis Auslaendischer Zeitschriften und Serien [*Cumulative List of Foreign Periodicals and Serials*] ... GAZS
Gesamtverzeichnis der Kongressschriften [*Union List of Conference Proceedings*] [*Deutsches Bibliotheksinstitut*] [*Germany*] [*Information service or system*] (CRD) ... GKS
Geschichte [*History*] [*German*] (ILCA) ... G
Geschichte [*of Germanicus*] [*Classical studies*] (OCD) ... Gesch
Geschichte [*History*] [*German*] ... GESCH
Geschichte der Griechischen Religion [*A publication*] (OCD) ... GGR
Geschichte der Perser und Araber zur Zeit der Sasaniden [*A publication*] (BJA) ... GPA
Geschichte des Alten Vorderasien [*A publication*] (BJA) ... GAV
Geschichte des Juedischen Volkes im Zeitalter Jesu Christi [*A publication*] (BJA) ... GJV
Geschichte Vorderasien bis zum Hellenismus [*A publication*] (BJA) ... GVA
Geschichtsbetrachtung und Geschichtliche Ueberlieferung bei den Vorexilischen Propheten [*A publication*] (BJA) ... GB
Geschichtsbetrachtung und Geschichtliche Ueberlieferung bei den Vorexilischen Propheten [*A publication*] (BJA) ... GBU
Gesco Industries, Inc. [*Toronto Stock Exchange symbol*] ... GSD
Gesell Developmental Schedules [*Education*] ... GDS
Gesell School Rediness Test (EDAC) ... GSRT
Gesellschaft [*Company*] [*German*] ... GES
Gesellschaft [*Company*] [*German*] (ODBW) ... Ges
Gesellschaft der Freunde der Ikonenkunst (EAIO) ... EIKON
Gesellschaft fuer Arzneipflanzenforschung [*Society for Medicinal Plant Research*] (EA) ... GA
Gesellschaft fuer Bedrohte Voelker [*Society for Threatened Peoples*] (EAIO) ... GfBV
Gesellschaft fuer Betriebswirtschaftliche Information mbH [*Society for Business Information*] [*Germany Database producer*] ... GBI
Gesellschaft Fuer Biochemie Und Molekularbiologie [*Germany*] ... GBM
Gesellschaft fuer Information und Dokumentation - Informationszentrum fuer Informationswissenschaft und -Praxis [*Information Center for Information Science and Information Work*] [*Society for Information and Documentation*] (IID) ... GID-IZ
Gesellschaft fuer Information und Dokumentation mbH [*Society for Information and Documentation*] [*Information service or system*] (IID) ... GID
Gesellschaft fuer Informationsmarkt-Forschung [*Society for Information-Market Research*] [*Database producer*] (IID) ... GIF
Gesellschaft fuer Internationale Geldgeschichte (EAIO) ... GIG
Gesellschaft fuer Kernforschung mbH, Karlsruhe, Germany [*Library symbol Library of Congress*] (LCLS) ... GyKG
Gesellschaft fuer Mathematik und Datenverarbeitung [*Society for Mathematics and Data Processing*] [*Germany Information service or system*] (IID) ... GMD
Gesellschaft fuer Versuchstierkunde - Society of Labortory Animal Science [*Switzerland*] (EAIO) ... GV-SOLAS
Gesellschaft fuer Weltraumforschung [*Society for Space Research*] [*Germany*] ... GFW
Gesellschaft fuer Wirtschaftspublizistik GmbH [*Society for Public Economics*] [*Germany*] (IID) ... GWP
Gesellschaft fuer Zahlungssysteme [*International banking*] [*Germany*] ... GZS
Gesellschaft fur Flugzieldarstellung GmbH [*Germany ICAO designator*] (FAAC) ... GFD
Gesellschaft mit Beschraenkter Haftung [*Limited Liability Company*] [*German*] ... GmbH
Gesellschaft mit Beschraenkter Haftung und Kommanditgesellschaft [*Combined Limited Partnership and Limited Liability Company*] [*German*] ... GmbH & CoKG
Gesellschaft zur Foerderung der Literatur aus Afrika, Asien, und Lateinamerika (EAIO) ... GFLAAL
Gesetz [*Law*] [*German*] (ILCA) ... G
Gesetz Betreffend der Gesellschaft mit Beschraenkter Haftung [*Law Governing Limited Liability Company*] [*German*] (ILCA) ... GmbHG
Gesetz Gegen den Unlauteren Wettbewerb [*Law Against Unfair Competition*] [*German*] (DLA) ... UWG
Gesetz Gegen Wettbewerbsbeschrankungen [*German Law Against Restraint of Competition*] (DLA) ... GWB
Gesetz u. d. Ausgleichs und Schiedsverfahren Arbeitsstreitigkeiten [*Law on Labor Arbitration*] [*German*] (ILCA) ... Arb Ausgl G
Gesetzblatt [*Gazette*] [*German*] (DLA) ... GBI
Gesetzgebungsstand [*Database*] [*Deutscher Bundestag*] [*German*] [*Information service or system*] (CRD) ... GESTA
Gesetzsammlung [*Collection of Statutes, Gazette*] [*German*] (ILCA) ... GS
Gesneriad Hybridizers Association (EA) ... GHA
Gesneriad Research Foundation (EA) ... GRF
Gesneriad Saintpaulia News [*A publication*] ... GSN
Gesneriad Society International (EA) ... GSI
Gesso (VRA) ... ges
Gestair Executive Jet [*Spain ICAO designator*] (FAAC) ... GES
Gestalt Recognition by Asymptotic Differential Equations ... GRADE
Gestational [*Pediatrics*] ... GEST
Gestational Age [*Medicine*] ... GA
Gestational Day ... GD
Gestational Diabetes Mellitus [*Medicine*] ... GDM

Gestational Trophoblastic Disease [*Medicine*] (MAE) ... GTD
Gestational Trophoblastic Neoplasia [*Medicine*] ... GTN
Gestion et Etude des Informations Spectroscopiques Atmospheriques [*Database*] [*Laboratoire de Meteorologie Dynamique du CNRS*] [*French*] [*Information service or system*] (CRD) ... GEISA
Gestioni e Partecipazioni Industriali [*Industrial Management and Participation*] [*Italian government-sponsored agency to aid ailing companies*] ... GEPI
Gestorben [*Died*] [*German*] ... GEST
Gesture [*Theater*] (WDMC) ... gest
Gesture Comprehension Test [*Occupational therapy*] ... GCT
Get a Life ... GAL
Get Away Special (MCD) ... GAS
Get Fresh Crew [*Rap recording group*] ... GFC
Get Off Your After-End [*Slang Bowdlerized version*] ... GOYA
Get Oil Out (EA) ... GOO
Get Out of My Backyard [*Slang*] ... GOOMBY
Get Out of My Emergency Room [*Used as a noun in reference to an elderly, chronically ill patient*] ... GOMER
Get Out the Vote (GNE) ... GOTV
Get Quick Answer [*Communications*] ... GQA
Get Rid of Junk [*Garage sale sign*] ... GROJ
Get Rid of Waste through Team Harmony ... GROWTH
Get Set Day Care Program [*Later, CDCP*] (EA) ... GSDC
Get the Lead Out [*Of GLO week, sponsored by American Oil Co.*] ... GLO
Get-Away-Special Cannister [*NASA*] ... GAS Can
Getchell Gold Corp. [*Associated Press*] (SAG) ... GetchGld
Getchell Gold Corp. [*AMEX symbol*] (SAG) ... GGO
Getchell Resources, Inc. [*Vancouver Stock Exchange symbol*] ... GHS
Geteilt [*Divided*] [*Music*] ... Get
Gethsemani [*Canada*] [*Airport symbol*] (OAG) ... ZGS
Get-Rid-of-Westmoreland-Now [*Secret society whose members were junior Pentagon officers*] (VNW) ... GROWN
Getting Along [*Psychological testing*] ... GA
Getting the Message [*A reading program*] ... GTM
Getty Communications [*NASDAQ symbol*] (SAG) ... GETTY
Getty Communications [*Associated Press*] (SAG) ... GettyCo
Getty Conservation Institute [*Database producer*] (IID) ... GCI
Getty Oil Co., Exploration and Production Research Library, Houston, TX [*Library symbol Library of Congress*] (LCLS) ... TxHTide(Res)
Getty Oil Co., Houston, TX [*Library symbol Library of Congress*] (LCLS) ... TxHTide
Getty Oil Co., Los Angeles, CA [*Library symbol Library of Congress*] (LCLS) ... CLGO
Getty Petroleum [*NYSE symbol*] (TTSB) ... GTY
Getty Petroleum Corp. [*Associated Press*] (SAG) ... Getty
Getty Petroleum Corp. [*NYSE symbol*] (SPSG) ... GTY
Getty Resources Ltd. [*Toronto Stock Exchange symbol*] ... GEY
Gettysburg Battlefield Preservation Association [*Defunct*] (EA) ... GBPA
Gettysburg College, Gettysburg, PA [*OCLC symbol*] (OCLC) ... GDC
Gettysburg College, Gettysburg, PA [*Library symbol Library of Congress*] (LCLS) ... PGC
Gettysburg National Military Park ... GETT
Gettysburg, PA [*AM radio station call letters*] ... WGET
Gettysburg, PA [*FM radio station call letters*] ... WGTY
Gettysburg, PA [*FM radio station call letters*] ... WZBT
Gettysburg Railroad Co. [*AAR code*] ... GETY
Getuigenis [*Roermond/Maaseik*] (BJA) ... Getuig
Getz's Forms in Conveyancing [*A publication*] (DLA) ... Getz F
Geuserland Airways Ltd. [*New Zealand*] [*ICAO designator*] (FAAC) ... GEY
GeV Electron Microtron [*Atomic accelerator*] [*Proposed*] ... GEM
Gevic Arithmetic Simulation Program ... GASP
Gevic Logic Operation Program ... GLOP
Gewehrgranate [*Rifle Grenade*] [*German military - World War II*] ... GG
Gewerblicher Rechtsschutz und Urheberrecht [*A publication*] (ILCA) ... GRUR
Gewerblicher Rechtsschutz und Urheberrecht, Internationaler Teil [*A publication*] (ILCA) ... GRUR Int
GEWEX [*Global Energy and Water Cycle Experiment*] [*Marine science*] (OSRA) ... GAME
GEWEX [*Global Energy and Water Cycle Experiment*] **Cloud System Study** (EERA) ... GCSS
GEWEX [*Global Energy and Water Cycle Experiment*] **Continental-Scale International Project** [*World Climate Research Program*] [*Geoscience*] ... GCIP
GEWEX [*Global Energy and Water Cycle Experiment*] **Water Vapor Project** [*Marine science*] (OSRA) ... GVaP
GEWEX [*Global Energy and Water Cycle Experiment*] **Water Vapor Project** (USDC) ... GVaP
Gewoya [*Papua New Guinea*] [*Airport symbol*] (OAG) ... GEW
Gey's Balanced Salt Solution [*Medium*] [*Cell culture*] ... GBSS
Geyser (ABBR) ... GYSR
GFS Bancorp [*Associated Press*] (SAG) ... GFS Bcp
GFS Bancorp [*NASDAQ symbol*] (SAG) ... GFSB
GFS Bancorp [*NASDAQ symbol*] (TTSB) ... GUPB
GFSB Bancorp, Inc. [*Associated Press*] (SAG) ... GFSB B
GFSB Bancorp, Inc. [*NASDAQ symbol*] (SAG) ... GUPB
GFW Aviation [*Australia*] [*FAA designator*] (FAAC) ... GFW
GH [*General Hospital*] **Questionnaire Club** [*Defunct*] (EA) ... GHQC
Ghaba Central [*Oman*] [*ICAO location identifier*] (ICLI) ... OOGB
Ghadames [*Libya*] [*ICAO location identifier*] (ICLI) ... HLTD
Ghadames [*Libya*] [*Airport symbol*] (OAG) ... LTD
Ghaem Shahr [*Iran*] [*ICAO location identifier*] (ICLI) ... OINI
Ghaen [*Iran*] [*ICAO location identifier*] (ICLI) ... OIMG
Ghamsar [*Iran*] [*ICAO location identifier*] (ICLI) ... OIFC
Ghana [*Aircraft nationality and registration mark*] (FAAC) ... 9G
Ghana [*MARC geographic area code Library of Congress*] (LCCP) ... f-gh--
Ghana [*ANSI two-letter standard code*] (CNC) ... GH
Ghana [*MARC country of publication code Library of Congress*] (LCCP) ... gh
Ghana [*ANSI three-letter standard code*] (CNC) ... GHA
Ghana Airways [*ICAO designator*] (AD) ... GH
Ghana Airways Corp. [*ICAO designator*] (FAAC) ... GHA
Ghana Battalion [*Military*] ... GHANABATT
Ghana Commercial Bank ... GCB
Ghana Democratic Movement [*Political party*] (EY) ... GDM
Ghana Geographical Association. Bulletin [*A publication*] ... GGAB
Ghana Journal of Sociology [*A publication*] ... GJS
Ghana Movement of Freedom and Justice [*Political party*] ... GMFJ
Ghana Navy ... GHN
Ghana News Agency ... GNA
Ghana Publishing Co. ... GPC
Ghana Trades Union Congress ... GTUC
Ghana Water and Sewerage Corp. ... GWSC
Ghanaian Air Force ... GhAF
Ghanian Cocoa Butter ... GCB
Ghanzhou [*China*] [*Airport symbol*] (OAG) ... KOW
Ghanzi [*Botswana*] [*ICAO location identifier*] (ICLI) ... FBGZ
Ghanzi [*Botswana*] [*Airport symbol*] (AD) ... GNZ
Ghardaia [*Algeria*] [*Airport symbol*] (OAG) ... GHA
Ghardaia/Noumerate [*Algeria*] [*ICAO location identifier*] (ICLI) ... DAUG
Gharo [*Pakistan*] [*ICAO location identifier*] (ICLI) ... OPKF
Ghasre Ghand [*Iran*] [*ICAO location identifier*] (ICLI) ... OIZG
Ghasre-Shirin [*Iran*] [*ICAO location identifier*] (ICLI) ... OICG
Ghat [*Libya*] [*Airport symbol*] (OAG) ... GHT
Ghat [*Libya*] [*ICAO location identifier*] (ICLI) ... HLGT
Ghaziabad [*Afghanistan*] [*ICAO location identifier*] (ICLI) ... OAGA
Ghazni [*Afghanistan*] [*ICAO location identifier*] (ICLI) ... OAGN
Ghazvin [*Iran*] [*ICAO location identifier*] (ICLI) ... OIIK
Ghedi [*Italy ICAO location identifier*] (ICLI) ... LIPL
Ghelmeen [*Afghanistan*] [*ICAO location identifier*] (ICLI) ... OAGM
Gheshm Island [*Iran*] [*ICAO location identifier*] (ICLI) ... OIKQ
Ghetto Arts Program [*Later, Urban Arts Corps*] (EA) ... GAP
Ghetto Job Information [*US Employment Service*] [*Department of Labor*] ... GJI
GHI Mortgage Investors [*Vancouver Stock Exchange symbol*] ... GHI
Ghinnir [*Ethiopia*] [*Airport symbol*] (AD) ... GNN
Ghinnir [*Ethiopia*] [*ICAO location identifier*] (ICLI) ... HAGH
Ghir/Karzin [*Iran*] [*ICAO location identifier*] (ICLI) ... OISQ
Ghisonaccia-Alzitone [*France ICAO location identifier*] (ICLI) ... LFKG
Ghom [*Iran*] [*ICAO location identifier*] (ICLI) ... OIIQ
Ghomsheh [*Iran*] [*ICAO location identifier*] (ICLI) ... OIFR
Ghoochan [*Iran*] [*ICAO location identifier*] (ICLI) ... OIMO
Ghose on Mortgages in India [*A publication*] (DLA) ... Ghose Mort
Ghost ... G
Ghost Canceling Reference [*Television technology*] ... GCR
Ghost in Addition to Crew [*Sailing*] ... GAC
Ghost Research Society (EA) ... GRS
Ghost Story Society [*British*] (DBA) ... GSS
Ghriss [*Algeria*] [*ICAO location identifier*] (ICLI) ... DAOV
GHS, Inc. [*Associated Press*] (SAG) ... GHS Inc
GHS, Inc. [*Formerly, Global Health Systems, Inc.*] [*NASDAQ symbol*] (NQ) ... GHSI
Ghuraf [*South Arabia*] [*Airport symbol*] (AD) ... GFX
GI Civil Liberties Defense Committee ... GICLDC
G-I Manpower Management Information System ... GIMMIS
Giallo/Warehouse 59 E [*Libya*] [*ICAO location identifier*] (ICLI) ... HLGL
Giannetti On-Line Psychosocial History [*Personality development test*] [*Psychology*] ... GOLPH
Giannini Controls Corp. (AAG) ... GCC
Giannini Controls Corp., Duarte, CA [*Library symbol Library of Congress*] (LCLS) ... CDuG
Giant ... GNT
Giant Air Shower ... GAS
Giant Attribute Survey ... GAS
Giant Axon [*Neurology*] ... GA
Giant Axon Neuropathy [*Medicine*] (DMAA) ... GAN
Giant Bay Resources Ltd. [*Toronto Stock Exchange symbol*] ... GBY
Giant Cell Arteritis [*Medicine*] ... GCA
Giant Cell Interstitial Pneumonia [*Medicine*] (MAE) ... GIP
Giant Cell Reparative Granuloma [*Oncology*] ... GCRG
Giant Cell Thyroiditis [*Medicine*] (DMAA) ... GTC
Giant Cell Tumor [*Oncology*] ... GCT
Giant Cell Tumor Cells [*A cell line*] ... GCTC
Giant Cement Holding [*NASDAQ symbol*] (TTSB) ... GCHI
Giant Cement Holding, Inc. [*NASDAQ symbol*] (SAG) ... GCHI
Giant Cement Holding, Inc. [*Associated Press*] (SAG) ... GiantCmt
Giant Cerebral Neuron [*Brain anatomy*] ... GCN
Giant Chinchilla Rabbit Association (EA) ... GCRA
Giant Depolarizing Potential [*Neurophysiology*] ... GDP
Giant Depolarizing Synaptic Potential [*Neurochemistry*] ... GDP
Giant Descending Neuron [*Neurology*] ... GDN
Giant Dipole Resonance ... GDR
Giant Dopamine-Containing Cell [*Medicine*] (DMAA) ... GDC
Giant Earth Mover [*Machine*] ... GEM
Giant Follicular Lymphoma [*Medicine*] (DMAA) ... GFL
Giant Foods [*AMEX symbol*] (SAG) ... GFS
Giant Foods [*Associated Press*] (SAG) ... GiantFd
Giant Gaseous Protoplanet [*Planetary science*] ... GGPP
Giant Gastric Ulcer [*Medicine*] ... GGU
GIANT Group [*NYSE symbol*] (TTSB) ... GPO
Giant Group Ltd. [*Associated Press*] (SAG) ... GIANT
Giant Group Ltd. [*NYSE symbol*] (SPSG) ... GPO
Giant Imperial Quart [*of beer*] ... GIQ
Giant Industries [*NYSE symbol*] (SPSG) ... GI
Giant Industries [*Associated Press*] (SAG) ... GiantIn

Giant Interneurons [*Neurology*] .... GI
Giant Lymph Node Hyperplasia [*Medicine*] (DMAA) .... GLH
Giant Lymph Node Hyperplasia [*Medicine*] (DMAA) .... GLNH
Giant Magnetoresistance [*Materials science*] .... GMR
Giant Magnetoresistive (CDE) .... GMR
Giant Melanoma [*Oncology*] .... GM
Giant Meterwave Radio Telescope [*India*] .... GMRT
Giant Molecular Association [*Galactic science*] .... GMA
Giant Molecular Cloud [*Cosmology*] .... GMC
Giant Motor Synapse [*Anatomy*] .... GMS
Giant North Resources Ltd. [*Vancouver Stock Exchange symbol*] .... GNN
Giant On-Line Instrument for the Acquisition and Total Handling of Data (MCD) .... GOLIATH
Giant Pacific Petroleums, Inc. [*Vancouver Stock Exchange symbol*] .... GPP
Giant Papillary Conjunctivitis [*Ophthalmology*] .... GPC
Giant Pigmented Hairy Nevus (DMAA) .... GPHN
Giant Pigmented Melanosome [*Medicine*] (DMAA) .... GPM
Giant Piston Core [*Geology*] .... GPC
Giant Platelet [*Hematology*] (DAVI) .... PLT-G
Giant Pulse .... GP
Giant Pulse LASER .... GPL
Giant Pulse LASER System .... GPLS
Giant Pulse Ruby LASER (IAA) .... GPRL
Giant Ragweed Test [*Medicine*] (DMAA) .... GRW
Giant Reef Petroleums [*Vancouver Stock Exchange symbol*] .... GRP
Giant Reusable Air Blast Simulator [*Air Force*] .... GRABS
Giant Scale Integration (IAA) .... GSI
Giant Schnauzer Club of America (EA) .... GSCA
Giant Serotonin-Containing [*Neuron*] .... GSC
Giant Serotonin-Containing Neuron (BABM) .... GSCN
Giant Serotonin-Containing Neuron [*Medicine*] (DMAA) .... GSN
Giant Slalom [*In Olympics event, Super-G*] .... G
Giant Slalom .... GS
Giant "Y" Boat [*Navy symbol Obsolete*] .... APY
Giant-to-Giant Interneuron Synaptic Potential [*Neurochemistry*] .... GGSP
Giauque's Election Laws [*A publication*] (DLA) .... Giauq El
Gibault High School, Waterloo, IL [*Library symbol Library of Congress*] (LCLS) .... IWatlGHS
Gibb Family Friendship Club (EA) .... GFFC
Gibb River [*Australia Airport symbol Obsolete*] (OAG) .... GBV
Gibberellic Acid [*Also, GA_3*] [*Plant growth hormone*] .... GA
Gibberellin A_3 [*Also, GA*] [*Plant growth hormone*] .... GA_3
Gibbon Ape Leukemia Virus .... GALV
Gibbon Ape Leukemia Virus (DMAA) .... GLV
Gibbon on Nuisances [*A publication*] (DLA) .... Gibbon
Gibbons and Nathans' Equitable Jurisdiction of County Courts [*A publication*] (DLA) .... Gib & Na Eq Jur
Gibbon's Dilapidations and Nuisances [*2nd ed.*] [*1849*] [*A publication*] (DLA) .... Gib Dil
Gibbon's Dilapidations and Nuisances [*2nd ed.*] [*1849*] [*A publication*] (DLA) .... Gib Nui
Gibbon's History of the Decline and Fall of the Roman Empire [*A publication*] (DLA) .... Gibb Rom Emp
Gibbon's History of the Decline and Fall of the Roman Empire [*A publication*] (DLA) .... Gibbon Rom Emp
Gibbon's Law of Fixtures [*1836*] [*A publication*] (DLA) .... Gib Fix
Gibbons' Lex Temporis, Limitations and Prescription [*A publication*] (DLA) .... Gib Lim
Gibbons on Contracts [*A publication*] (DLA) .... Gib Cont
Gibbons on the Civil Law [*A publication*] (DLA) .... Gib Civ L
Gibbons Public Library, Alberta [*Library symbol National Library of Canada*] (NLC) .... AGI
Gibbons Public Library, Gibbons, AB, Canada [*Library symbol*] [*Library of Congress*] (LCLS) .... CaAGi
Gibbon's Reports, New York Surrogate Court [*A publication*] (DLA) .... Gib
Gibbon's Reports, New York Surrogate Court [*A publication*] (DLA) .... Gibb Sur
Gibbon's Reports, New York Surrogate Court [*A publication*] (DLA) .... Gibb Surr
Gibbon's Reports, New York Surrogate Court [*A publication*] (DLA) .... Gibbons
Gibbon's Reports, New York Surrogate Court [*A publication*] (DLA) .... Gibbons (NY)
Gibbonsville Community Library, Gibbonsville, ID [*Library symbol*] [*Library of Congress*] (LCLS) .... IdGi
Gibbs Adsorption Equation [*Physical chemistry*] .... GAE
Gibbs Adsorption Isotherm [*Physical chemistry*] .... GAI
Gibbs & Hill, Inc. (NRCH) .... G & H
Gibbs & Hill, Inc., Standard Safety Analysis Report [*Nuclear energy*] (NRCH) .... GIBBSSAR
Gibbs Construction [*NASDAQ symbol*] (TTSB) .... GBSE
Gibbs Construction, Inc. [*NASDAQ symbol*] (SAG) .... GBSE
Gibbs Construction, Inc. [*Associated Press*] (SAG) .... GibbsC
Gibbs Construction, Inc. [*Associated Press*] (SAG) .... GibbsCn
Gibbs Construction Wrrt [*NASDAQ symbol*] (TTSB) .... GBSEW
Gibbs Energy [*Symbol*] [*IUPAC*] .... G
Gibbs Free Energy [*Physical chemistry*] .... GFE
Gibbs Function [*Preferred term is Gibbs Energy*] .... G
Gibbs' Judicial Chronicle [*A publication*] (DLA) .... Gibbs' Jud Chr
Gibbs' Practical Forms [*A publication*] (DLA) .... Gibbs F
Gibbs' Reports [*2-4 Michigan*] [*A publication*] (DLA) .... Gibbs
Gibbs-Duhem Equation [*Physical chemistry*] .... GDE
Gibbs-Helmholtz Equation [*Physical chemistry*] .... GHE
Gibbsite [*A mineral*] .... Gb
Gibco/Invenex, Grand Island, NY [*Library symbol Library of Congress*] (LCLS) .... NGiG
Gibilmanna [*Sicily*] [*Seismograph station code, US Geological Survey*] (SEIS) .... GIB
Gibraltar [*MARC geographic area code Library of Congress*] (LCCP) .... e-gi--
Gibraltar .... GBZ
Gibraltar [*ANSI two-letter standard code*] (CNC) .... GI
Gibraltar [*MARC country of publication code Library of Congress*] (LCCP) .... gi
Gibraltar [*Airport symbol*] (OAG) .... GIB
Gibraltar [*ANSI three-letter standard code*] (CNC) .... GIB
Gibraltar (ODBW) .... Gib
Gibraltar .... Gibr
Gibraltar [*International civil aircraft marking*] (ODBW) .... VR-G
Gibraltar Airways Ltd. .... GIBAIR
Gibraltar Airways Ltd. [*British ICAO designator*] (ICDA) .... GT
Gibraltar Defence Force [*British military*] (DMA) .... GDF
Gibraltar Democratic Movement [*Political party*] (PPE) .... GDM
Gibraltar Labour Party - Association for the Advancement of Civil Rights [*Political party*] (PPW) .... GLP-AACR
Gibraltar Mediterranean Command [*NATO*] (NATG) .... GIBMED
Gibraltar Mines Ltd. [*Toronto Stock Exchange symbol Vancouver Stock Exchange symbol*] .... GBM
Gibraltar/North Front [*Gibraltar*] [*ICAO location identifier*] (ICLI) .... LXGB
Gibraltar Packaging Group [*Associated Press*] (SAG) .... GibPack
Gibraltar Packaging Group [*NASDAQ symbol*] (TTSB) .... PACK
Gibraltar Packaging Group, Inc. [*NASDAQ symbol*] (SAG) .... PACK
Gibraltar Socialist Labour Party [*Political party*] (PPW) .... GSLP
Gibraltar Steel [*NASDAQ symbol*] (TTSB) .... ROCK
Gibraltar Steel Corp. [*Associated Press*] (SAG) .... GibrStl
Gibraltar Steel Corp. [*NASDAQ symbol*] (SAG) .... ROCK
Gibson Aviation [*ICAO designator*] (FAAC) .... NTC
Gibson City Community Unit School District, Gibson City, IL [*Library symbol*] [*Library of Congress*] (LCLS) .... IGibSD
Gibson City, IL [*FM radio station call letters*] .... WGCY
Gibson Community Hospital, Gibson City, IL [*Library symbol Library of Congress*] (LCLS) .... IGibH
Gibson, Dunn & Crutcher, Los Angeles, CA [*Library symbol Library of Congress*] (LCLS) .... CLGDC
Gibson General Hospital, Trenton, TN [*Library symbol Library of Congress*] (LCLS) .... TTG
Gibson Greetings [*NASDAQ symbol*] (TTSB) .... GIBG
Gibson Greetings, Inc. [*NASDAQ symbol*] (NQ) .... GIBG
Gibson Greetings, Inc. [*Associated Press*] (SAG) .... GibsnG
Gibson Medical Library, St. Mary's of the Lake Hospital, Kingston, Ontario [*Library symbol National Library of Canada*] (NLC) .... OKSMG
(Gibson of) Durie's Decisions, Scotch Court of Session [*1621-42*] [*A publication*] (DLA) .... Gibson
Gibson Spiral Maze [*Psychology*] .... GSM
Gibsonburg, OH [*FM radio station call letters*] .... WYHK
Gibson's Aids to the Examinations [*A publication*] (DLA) .... Gib Aids
Gibsons, BC [*FM radio station call letters*] .... CISC
Gibson's Codex [*A publication*] (DLA) .... Gibs Code
Gibson's Codex Ecclesiastia [*1715*] [*A publication*] (DLA) .... Cod
Gibson's Codex Ecclesiastia [*1715*] [*A publication*] (DLA) .... Cod Jur
Gibson's Codex Juris Civilis [*A publication*] (DLA) .... Cod
Gibson's Codex Juris Ecclesiastia Anglicani [*A publication*] (DLA) .... Gib Cod
Gibson's Edition of Camden's Britannia [*A publication*] (DLA) .... Gibs Camd
Gibson's Law Notes [*1882-84*] [*A publication*] (DLA) .... Gibs LN
Gibson's Law Notice [*1882-84*] [*A publication*] (DLA) .... Gib LN
Gibson's Memoir of Lord Lyndhurst [*A publication*] (DLA) .... Gib Lynd
Gibsons Public Library, British Columbia [*Library symbol National Library of Canada*] (NLC) .... BGI
Gibson's Scottish Decisions [*A publication*] (DLA) .... Gib Dec
Gichner Mobile Shelters (MCD) .... GMS
Giddens Family Associates (EA) .... GFA
Giddings & Lewis [*NASDAQ symbol*] (TTSB) .... GIDL
Giddings & Lewis, Inc. [*NASDAQ symbol*] (NQ) .... GIDL
Giddings & Lewis, Inc. [*Associated Press*] (SAG) .... GidLew
Giddings, TX [*Location identifier FAA*] (FAAL) .... GYB
Giddings, TX [*FM radio station call letters*] (RBYB) .... KANJ-FM
Giddings, TX [*FM radio station call letters*] .... KOKE
Giddings, TX [*FM radio station call letters*] (RBYB) .... KROX-FM
Gideon Family Association (EA) .... GFA
Gideons International (EA) .... GI
Gidley Research Institute [*Research center*] (RCD) .... GRI
Giebelstadt [*Germany ICAO location identifier*] (ICLI) .... EDEU
Giemsa [*Method*] [*Chromosome stain*] .... G
Gier-Dunkle Integrating Sphere .... GDIS
Giessen [*Germany ICAO location identifier*] (ICLI) .... EDIA
GIF [*Graphics Interchange Format*] [*Computer science*] [*Telecommunications*] .... g
Giffard and Hemming's English Chancery Reports [*A publication*] (DLA) .... Giff & H
Giffard's English Vice-Chancellors' Reports [*65-66 English Reprint*] [*A publication*] (DLA) .... Gif
Giffard's English Vice-Chancellors' Reports [*65-66 English Reprint*] [*A publication*] (DLA) .... Giff
Giffard's English Vice-Chancellors' Reports [*65-66 English Reprint*] [*A publication*] (DLA) .... Giff (Eng)
Gifford, FL [*FM radio station call letters*] .... WKQS
Gifhorn [*Germany ICAO location identifier*] (ICLI) .... EDVX
Gift and Decorative Accessories Association of America [*Later, GAA*] (EA) .... GDAA
Gift Association of America (EA) .... GAA
Gift Coupon Programme [*Later, Co-Action*] [*UNESCO*] .... GCP
Gift Lake School, Alberta [*Library symbol National Library of Canada*] (BIB) .... AGLS
Gift Retailers, Manufacturers, and Reps Association (EA) .... GRMRA
Gift Tax (DLA) .... G
Gift Tax (DLA) .... GT

Gift with Purchase ... GWP
Gift With Purchase [*Retail*] (WDMC) ... g-w-p
Gift Wrappings and Tyings Association [*Defunct*] (EA) ... GWTA
Gifted Advocacy Information Network [*Defunct*] (EA) ... GAIN
Gifted & Learning Disabled ... GT/LD
Gifted and Talented [*Education*] ... GT
Gifted and Talented Screening Form [*Educational test*] ... GTSF
Gifted and Taleted Education Program [*California*] (EDAC) ... GATE
Gifted Child Society (EA) ... GCS
Gifted Children's Information Centre [*British*] (CB) ... GCIC
Gifted Children's Pen Pals International (EA) ... GCPPI
Gifted Resources Education Action Team Project (EDAC) ... GREAT
Gifts In Kind America (NFD) ... GIKA
Giftware Manufacturers' Credit Interchange (EA) ... GMCI
Giftware Manufacturers Credit Interchange (EA) ... GMCT
Giftware Manufacturers' Credit Interchange [*Buffalo, NY*] (EA) ... GWCI
Giftwear ... GFTWR
Gifu [*Japan*] [*Seismograph station code, US Geological Survey*] (SEIS) ... GIF
Gifu [*Japan ICAO location identifier*] (ICLI) ... RJNG
Gig Harbor, WA [*FM radio station call letters*] ... KGHP
Giga [*A prefix meaning multiplied by 10^9*] [*SI symbol*] ... G
Giga Electron Volt ... GeV
Giga Floating Operations per Second [*Computer science*] ... GFLOPS
Giga Information Group, Inc. [*Associated Press*] (SAG) ... GigaInfo
Giga Information Group, Inc. [*NASDAQ symbol*] (SAG) ... GIGX
Giga Operations Per Second (NITA) ... GOPS
Gigabecquerel (NUCP) ... GBq
GigaBIT [*Binary Digit*] [*10^9 BITs*] ... Gb
Gigabit (MHDB) ... GBIT
Gigabit Ethernet Alliance [*Telecommunications*] (ACRL) ... GEA
Gigabit Link Module [*Computer science*] ... GLM
GigaBIT [*Binary Digits*] **per Second** [*Transmission rate*] [*Computer science*] (TSSD) ... GBPS
GigaBIT [*Binary Digit*] **per Second** [*Computer science*] (IAA) ... GBS
GigaBIT [*Binary Digits*] **per Second** [*Transmission rate*] [*Computer science*] ... GPS
Gigabits per Second (EERA) ... Gbps
Gigabyte ... G
Gigabyte [*Computer science*] (EERA) ... Gb
Gigabyte [*10^9 bytes*] ... GB
Gigacharacters ... GCH
Gigacycle [*Measurement*] ... Gc
Gigacycles per Second [*IEEE*] ... Gc/s
Gigacycles per Second [*AIP*] ... Gc/sec
Gigacycles per Second (MUGU) ... GCPS
Gigagram ... Gg
Gigahertz [*1,000 megahertz*] ... GHz
Gigahertz [*1,000 megahertz*] [*Preferred form is GHz*] (MCD) ... GZ
Giga-Instructions per Second [*Computer science*] (NHD) ... GIPS
Gigajoule ... GJ
Gigameter ... gm
Gigapascal [*SI unit of pressure*] ... GPa
Gigascale Integration [*Electronics*] ... GSI
Gigaton ... GT
Gigaton ... GTO
gigatonne [*One billion tonnes*] (EERA) ... Gt
Giga-Tronics, Inc. [*NASDAQ symbol*] (NQ) ... GIGA
Giga-Tronics, Inc. [*Associated Press*] (SAG) ... GigaTr
Gigavolt ... GV
Gigawatt ... GW
Gigawatt Electrical ... GWe
Gigawatt Hour [*DOE*] (TAG) ... GWH
Gigawatt Thermal ... GWt
Gigawatt-days ... GWd
Gigawatt-Electric [*DOE*] (TAG) ... GWE
Gigawatt-Hour ... GWh
Gigayear [*A billion years*] ... GYR
Gigi Resources Ltd. [*Vancouver Stock Exchange symbol*] ... GIG
G-III Apparel Group Ltd. [*NASDAQ symbol*] (NQ) ... GIII
Gila Bend, AZ [*Location identifier FAA*] (FAAL) ... GBN
Gila Cliff Dwellings National Monument ... GICL
Gilat Satellite Networks [*NASDAQ symbol*] (TTSB) ... GILTF
Gilat Satellite Networks Ltd. [*Associated Press*] (SAG) ... GilatSat
Gilat Satellite Networks Ltd. [*NASDAQ symbol*] (SAG) ... GILT
Gilbarco Corp. Library, Greensboro, NC [*Library symbol Library of Congress*] (LCLS) ... NcGGil
Gilbert [*Unit of magnetomotive force*] (DAVI) ... F
Gilbert [*A unit of magnetomotive force*] ... G
Gilbert [*A unit of magnetomotive force*] (CET) ... Gb
Gilbert [*A unit of magnetomotive force*] ... Gi
Gilbert [*A unit of magnetomotive force*] ... Gil
Gilbert and Ellice Islands [*Tuvalu*] [*gb (Gilbert Islands) or tu (Tuvalu) used in records cataloged after October 1978*] [*MARC country of publication code*] [*Library of Congress*] (LCCP) ... gn
Gilbert and Ellice Islands [*Tuvalu*] [*MARC geographic area code Library of Congress*] (LCCP) ... pogn--
Gilbert and Sullivan ... G & S
Gilbert and Sullivan Society [*Australia*] ... G & SS
Gilbert and Sullivan Society (EA) ... GSS
Gilbert Assoc'A' [*NASDAQ symbol*] (TTSB) ... GILBA
Gilbert Associates, Inc. ... GAI
Gilbert Associates, Inc. [*NASDAQ symbol*] (NQ) ... GILB
Gilbert Associates, Inc. [*Associated Press*] (SAG) ... GilbtA
Gilbert Associates, Inc., Reading, PA [*Library symbol Library of Congress*] (LCLS) ... PRG
Gilbert Associates, Incorporated, Standard Safety Analysis Report [*Nuclear energy*] (NRCH) ... GAISSAR
Gilbert Associates [*or General Atomic*] **Standard Safety Analysis Report** [*Nuclear energy*] (NRCH) ... GASSAR
Gilbert Hill [*Idaho*] [*Seismograph station code, US Geological Survey Closed*] (SEIS) ... GHI
Gilbert Islands [*gn (Gilbert and Ellice Islands) used in records cataloged before October 1978*] [*MARC country of publication code Library of Congress*] (LCCP) ... gb
Gilbert Islands [*ANSI two-letter standard code Obsolete*] (CNC) ... GE
Gilbert Islands [*ANSI three-letter standard code Obsolete*] (CNC) ... GEL
Gilbert Keith Chesterton [*British journalist and author*] ... GKC
Gilbert M. Simmons Public Library, Kenosha, WI [*Library symbol Library of Congress*] (LCLS) ... WKen
Gilbert M. Smith Herbarium [*Stanford University*] [*Pacific Grove, CA*] ... GMS
Gilbert on Banking [*A publication*] (DLA) ... Gilb Bank
Gilbert on Distress and Replevin [*A publication*] (DLA) ... Gilb Dis
Gilbert on Ejectments [*A publication*] (DLA) ... Gilb Ej
Gilbert on Replevin [*A publication*] (DLA) ... Gilb Repl
Gilbert on Tenures [*A publication*] (DLA) ... Gilb Ten
Gilbert on the Action of Debt [*A publication*] (DLA) ... Gilb Debt
Gilbert on Uses and Trusts [*A publication*] (DLA) ... Gilb Uses
Gilbert Patterson Memorial Public Library, Maxton, NC [*Library symbol Library of Congress*] (LCLS) ... NcMax
Gilbert Public Library, Gilbert, AZ [*Library symbol Library of Congress*] (LCLS) ... AzGi
Gilbert Public Library, Gilbert, MN [*Library symbol*] [*Library of Congress*] (LCLS) ... MnGi
Gilbert-Eveleth Junior High School, Gilbert, MN [*Library symbol*] [*Library of Congress*] (LCLS) ... MnGiJH
Gilbert-Meulengracht Syndrome [*Medicine*] (DMAA) ... GMS
Gilbert's Cases in Law and Equity [*A publication*] (DLA) ... Cas L & Eq
Gilbert's Cases in Law and Equity [*A publication*] (DLA) ... Gil
Gilbert's Cases in Law and Equity [*A publication*] (DLA) ... Gilb
Gilbert's Cases in Law and Equity [*A publication*] (DLA) ... Gilb Cas
Gilbert's Cases in Law and Equity [*A publication*] (DLA) ... Gilb Cas L & Eq
Gilbert's Cases in Law and Equity [*A publication*] (DLA) ... Gilb KB
Gilbert's Common Pleas [*93 English Reprint*] [*A publication*] (DLA) ... Gilb Cas L & Eq (Eng)
Gilbert's Common Pleas [*93 English Reprint*] [*A publication*] (DLA) ... Gilb Com Pl
Gilbert's Common Pleas [*93 English Reprint*] [*A publication*] (DLA) ... Gilb CP
Gilbert's Common Pleas [*93 English Reprint*] [*A publication*] (DLA) ... Gilb PC
Gilbert's English Chancery Reports [*1705-27*] [*A publication*] (DLA) ... Gil
Gilbert's English Chancery Reports [*1705-27*] [*A publication*] (DLA) ... Gilb
Gilbert's English Chancery Reports [*1705-27*] [*A publication*] (DLA) ... Gilb Ch
Gilbert's English Chancery Reports [*1705-27*] [*A publication*] (DLA) ... Gilb Rep
Gilbert's English Chancery Reports [*1705-27*] [*A publication*] (DLA) ... Rep Cas Eq
Gilbert's English Equity Cases [*A publication*] (DLA) ... Eq Cas
Gilbert's English Equity Reports [*1705-27*] [*A publication*] (DLA) ... Eq R
Gilbert's English Equity Reports [*1705-27*] [*A publication*] (DLA) ... Eq Rep
Gilbert's English Equity Reports [*25 English Reprint*] [*1705-27*] [*A publication*] (DLA) ... Gilb Eq
Gilbert's English Equity Reports [*25 English Reprint*] [*1705-27*] [*A publication*] (DLA) ... Gilb Eq (Eng)
Gilbert's English Equity Reports [*1705-27*] [*A publication*] (DLA) ... Gilb Eq Rep
Gilbert's English Exchequer Reports [*A publication*] (DLA) ... Gilb Exch
Gilbert's Executions [*A publication*] (DLA) ... Gilb Ex
Gilbert's Forum Romanum [*A publication*] (DLA) ... Gilb For Rom
Gilbert's Forum Romanum [*A publication*] (DLA) ... Gilb Forum Rom
Gilbert's History and Practice of the Exchequer [*A publication*] (DLA) ... Gilb Exch Pr
Gilbert's History of Common Pleas [*A publication*] (DLA) ... Gilb Hist CP
Gilbert's Law of Devises [*A publication*] (DLA) ... Gilb Dev
Gilbert's Law of Evidence [*A publication*] (DLA) ... Gilb Ev
Gilbert's Law of Evidence [*A publication*] (DLA) ... Gilbert Ev
Gilbert's Lex Praetoria [*A publication*] (DLA) ... Gilb Lex Pr
Gilbert's Railway Law of Illinois [*A publication*] (DLA) ... Gilb RR
Gilbert's Remainders [*A publication*] (DLA) ... Gilb Rem
Gilbert's Reports in Equity [*England*] [*A publication*] (DLA) ... Rep Eq
Gilbert's Syndrome [*Medicine*] ... GS
Gilbert's Treatise on Rents [*A publication*] (DLA) ... Gilb Rents
Gilbert's Uses and Trusts by Sugden [*A publication*] (DLA) ... Gilbert Uses by Sugd
Gilbertus [*Flourished, 13th century*] [*Authority cited in pre-1607 legal work*] (DSA) ... G
Gilbues [*Brazil*] [*Airport symbol*] (AD) ... GLB
Gilchrist's Local Government Cases [*A publication*] (DLA) ... Gilchr
Gild of Ancient Suppliers of Gas Appliances, Skills, Gins, Accessories, and Substances (EA) ... GASGASGAS
Gildersleeve's Reports [*New Mexico*] [*A publication*] (DLA) ... Gild
Gildersleeve's Reports [*New Mexico*] [*A publication*] (DLA) ... Gildersleeve
Gildersleeve's Reports [*New Mexico*] [*A publication*] (DLA) ... Gildersleeve (N Mex)
Gildersleeve's Reports [*New Mexico*] [*A publication*] (DLA) ... Gildr
Gilding (VRA) ... glt
Gilead Sciences [*NASDAQ symbol*] (TTSB) ... GILD
Gilead Sciences, Inc. [*NASDAQ symbol*] (SPSG) ... GILD
Gilead Sciences, Inc. [*Associated Press*] (SAG) ... Gilead
Gileppe [*Belgium*] [*Seismograph station code, US Geological Survey*] (SEIS) ... GIP
Giles [*Australia Seismograph station code, US Geological Survey*] (SEIS) ... GLS
Giles County Hospital, Pulaski, TN [*Library symbol*] [*Library of Congress*] (LCLS) ... TPuGH
Gilfillan's Edition [*1-20 Minnesota*] [*A publication*] (DLA) ... Gil (Minn)
Gilfillan's Reports [*1-20 Minnesota*] [*A publication*] (DLA) ... Gil
Gilfillan's Reports [*1-20 Minnesota*] [*A publication*] (DLA) ... Gilfillan
Gilford, FL [*FM radio station call letters*] (RBYB) ... WBBE-FM
Gilgames (BJA) ... Gilg

Gilgames and the Land of the Living (BJA) .... GLL
Gilgamesh, Enkidu, and the Netherworld (BJA) .... GEN
[*The*] **Gilgamesh Epic and Old Testament Parallels** [*A publication*] (BJA) .... GE
Gilgit [*Pakistan*] [*Airport symbol*] (AD) .... GIL
Gilgit [*Pakistan*] [*Geomagnetic observatory code*] .... GIT
Gilgit [*Pakistan*] [*ICAO location identifier*] (ICLI) .... OPGT
Gill .... GI
Gill [*Oceanography*] (DAVI) .... gl
Gill [*Unit of weight*] .... GL
Gill and Johnson's Maryland Court of Appeals Reports [*1829-42*] [*A publication*] (DLA) .... G & J
Gill and Johnson's Maryland Reports [*A publication*] (DLA) .... G & J (MD)
Gill and Johnson's Maryland Reports [*A publication*] (DLA) .... G & Jo
Gill and Johnson's Maryland Reports [*A publication*] (DLA) .... G & John
Gill and Johnson's Maryland Reports [*A publication*] (DLA) .... Gill & J
Gill and Johnson's Maryland Reports [*A publication*] (DLA) .... Gill and J (Maryland)
Gill and Johnson's Maryland Reports [*A publication*] (DLA) .... Gill & J (MD)
Gill and Johnson's Maryland Reports [*A publication*] (DLA) .... Gill & Johns
Gill and Johnson's Maryland Reports [*A publication*] (DLA) .... GJ
Gill Aviation Ltd. [*British ICAO designator*] (FAAC) .... GIL
Gill, CO [*Location identifier FAA*] (FAAL) .... GLL
Gill Withdrawal Reflex .... GWR
Gillam [*Canada*] [*Airport symbol*] (OAG) .... YGX
Gillam, MB [*FM radio station call letters*] .... CFIL
Gillam, MB [*ICAO location identifier*] (ICLI) .... CYGX
Gillam Municipal Library, Gillam, MB, Canada [*Library symbol Library of Congress*] (LCLS) .... CaMGi
Gillam Municipal Library, Manitoba [*Library symbol National Library of Canada*] (NLC) .... MGI
Gillam-Grant Community Center Library, Bergen, NY [*Library symbol Library of Congress*] (LCLS) .... NBerG
Gilles de la Tourette Syndrome [*Medicine*] (DMAA) .... GTS
Gillespie Public Library, Gillespie, IL [*Library symbol Library of Congress*] (LCLS) .... IGill
Gillette [*Wyoming*] [*Airport symbol*] (OAG) .... GCC
Gillette Co. [*NYSE symbol*] (SAG) .... G
Gillette Co. [*Associated Press*] (SAG) .... Gillete
Gillette Co., Boston R and D Laboratory, Boston, MA [*Library symbol Library of Congress*] (LCLS) .... MBGi
Gillette Co., Boston R and D Laboratory, Boston, MA [*Library symbol*] [*Library of Congress*] (LCLS) .... MBGil
Gillette Co. Research Institute .... GCRI
Gillette State Hospital for Crippled Children, St. Paul, MN [*Library symbol Library of Congress*] (LCLS) .... MnSG
Gillette, WY [*FM radio station call letters*] .... KAML
Gillette, WY [*FM radio station call letters*] .... KGWY
Gillette, WY [*AM radio station call letters*] .... KIML
Gillett's Treatise on Criminal Law and Procedure in Criminal Cases [*A publication*] (DLA) .... Gillett Cr Law
Gilliam Center, Denver, CO [*Library symbol Library of Congress*] (LCLS) .... CoDGC
Gillies Bay [*Canada*] [*Airport symbol*] (OAG) .... YGB
Gilligan's Island Fan Club (EA) .... GIFC
Gillingham [*Municipal borough in England*] .... GILL
Gill-Morrell [*Valve oscillator*] (DEN) .... GM
Gill-Morrell Oscillator .... GMO
Gill's Maryland Court of Appeals Reports [*1843-51*] [*A publication*] (DLA) .... Gill
Gill's Maryland Reports [*A publication*] (DLA) .... Gill (MD)
Gill's Police Court Reports [*Boston, MA*] [*A publication*] (DLA) .... Gill Pol Rep
Gilman & Ciocia, Inc. [*Associated Press*] (SAG) .... GilmC
Gilman & Ciocia, Inc. [*Associated Press*] (SAG) .... GilmnCio
Gilman & Ciocia, Inc. [*NASDAQ symbol*] (SAG) .... GTAX
Gilman & Ciocia Wrrt [*NASDAQ symbol*] (TTSB) .... GTAXW
Gilman's Illinois and Indiana Digest [*A publication*] (DLA) .... Gilm Dig
Gilman's Reports [*6-10 Illinois*] [*A publication*] (DLA) .... Gil
Gilman's Reports [*6-10 Illinois*] [*A publication*] (DLA) .... Gilm
Gilman's Reports [*6-10 Illinois*] [*A publication*] (DLA) .... Gilm (Ill)
Gilman's Reports [*6-10 Illinois*] [*A publication*] (DLA) .... Gilman
Gilmer, TX [*AM radio station call letters*] (RBYB) .... KBNB-AM
Gilmer, TX [*FM radio station call letters*] .... KFRO
Gilmer, TX [*AM radio station call letters*] .... KHYM
Gilmer's Virginia Reports [*21 Virginia*] [*A publication*] (DLA) .... Gil
Gilmer's Virginia Reports [*21 Virginia*] [*A publication*] (DLA) .... Gilm
Gilmer's Virginia Reports [*21 Virginia*] [*1820-21*] [*A publication*] (DLA) .... Gilmer
Gilmer's Virginia Reports [*21 Virginia*] [*A publication*] (DLA) .... Gilmer (VA)
Gilmer's Virginia Reports [*A publication*] (DLA) .... VA
Gilmer's Virginia Reports [*A publication*] (DLA) .... VA R
Gilmore [*Alaska*] [*Also, GLN*] [*Seismograph station code, US Geological Survey*] (SEIS) .... GLM
Gilmore [*Alaska*] [*Also, GLM*] [*Seismograph station code, US Geological Survey*] (SEIS) .... GLN
Gilmore, AR [*Location identifier FAA*] (FAAL) .... GQE
Gilmore City Public Library, Gilmore City, IA [*Library symbol Library of Congress*] (LCLS) .... IaGc
Gilmore Creek [*Alaska*] [*Seismograph station code, US Geological Survey*] (SEIS) .... GIL
Gilmore Oral Reading Test [*Psychology*] (DAVI) .... GORT
Gilmour and Falconer's Cases, Scotch Court of Session [*A publication*] (DLA) .... Gil & Fal
Gilmour and Falconer's Decisions, Scotch Court of Session [*1961-66*] [*A publication*] (DLA) .... Gilm & F
Gilmour and Falconer's Decisions, Scotch Court of Session [*1961-66*] [*A publication*] (DLA) .... Gilm & Fal
Gilmour and Falconer's Reports, Scotch Court of Session [*A publication*] (DLA) .... Gilm & Falc
Gilmour and Falconer's Reports, Scotch Court of Session [*A publication*] (DLA) .... Pres Fal
Gilmour's Reports, Scotch Court of Session [*A publication*] (DLA) .... Gilm
Gilpin's Opinions of the United States Attorneys-General [*A publication*] (DLA) .... Gilp Opin
Gilpin's United States District Court Reports [*A publication*] (DLA) .... Gilp
Gilroy, CA [*AM radio station call letters*] .... KAZA
Gilroy, CA [*FM radio station call letters*] .... KUFX
Gilroy Free Public Library, Gilroy, CA [*Library symbol Library of Congress*] (LCLS) .... CGi
Gilroy Hot Springs [*California*] [*Seismograph station code, US Geological Survey*] (SEIS) .... GHS
Gilt [*Bookbinding*] .... G
Gilt [*Bookbinding*] (ROG) .... GLT
Gilt (VRA) .... glt
Gilt .... GT
Gilt Beveled Edges [*Bookbinding*] .... GBE
Gilt Deckled Edge [*Bookbinding*] .... GDE
Gilt Edges [*Bookbinding*] .... GE
Gilt Head [*Bookbinding*] (ROG) .... GH
Gilt Leaves [*Bookbinding*] (ROG) .... GL
Gilt Lines [*Bookbinding*] (ROG) .... GL
Gilt Marbled Edges [*Bookbinding*] .... GME
Gilt Market Analysis [*MMS International*] [*Information service or system*] (CRD) .... GMA
Gilt Top [*Bookbinding*] .... GT
Gilt Top [*Bookbinding*] (WDMC) .... gt
Gilt Top Edge [*Bookbinding*] .... GTE
Gilt-Edge (WDMC) .... ge
Gilt-Edged Market Maker [*London Stock Exchange*] [*England*] .... GEMM
Gilt-Edged Market Makers' Association [*London Stock Exchange*] [*England*] .... GEMMA
Gilt-Edged Securities [*Business term*] .... GES
Gilze-Rijen [*Netherlands ICAO location identifier*] (ICLI) .... EHGR
Gimbal (KSC) .... GIMB
Gimbal (AAG) .... GMBL
Gimbal Angle (KSC) .... GA
Gimbal Angle Change .... GAC
Gimbal Angle Controller .... GAC
Gimbal Angle Information Failure .... GAIF
Gimbal Angle Loss .... GAL
Gimbal Angle Matching Monitor .... GAMM
Gimbal Angle Rate .... GAR
Gimbal Angle Readout .... GAR
Gimbal Angle Runaway Detector .... GARD
Gimbal Angle Sequencing Transformation Assembly (KSC) .... GASTA
Gimbal Assembly .... GA
Gimbal Assembly Storage System .... GASS
Gimbal Case (KSC) .... GC
Gimbal Drive Actuator [*or Assembly*] (KSC) .... GDA
Gimbal Electronics .... GE
Gimbal Limit Prearming Inhibiting Signal .... GL
Gimbal Mounted Electronics (KSC) .... GME
Gimbal Package .... GP
Gimbal Pickoff Loop .... GPL
Gimbal Platform (AAG) .... GP
Gimbal Point .... GP
Gimbal Position Display (KSC) .... GPD
Gimbal Position Indicator (KSC) .... GPI
Gimbal Positioning .... GIMP
Gimbal Trim System .... GTS
Gimbaled Electrostatic-Gyro Aircraft Navigation System [*Air Force*] .... GEANS
Gimbaled Integral Nozzle .... GIN
Gimbaled Night and Day Sight .... GNADS
Gimbaled Reaction Wheel Scanner .... GRWS
Gimbaled Telescope Assembly (MCD) .... GTA
Gimballess Analytic Inertial Navigation System .... GAINS
Gimballess Inertial Measuring Unit .... GIMU
Gimballess Inertial Reference System .... GIRS
Gimli, MB [*ICAO location identifier*] (ICLI) .... CYGM
Gimo [*Sweden ICAO location identifier*] (ICLI) .... ESKA
Gin and Tonic .... G & T
Gin Cocktail [*Slang*] .... GC
Gin Rectifiers and Distillers Association [*British*] (DBA) .... GRDA
Ginger Alden "Lady Superstar" Fan Club (EA) .... GALSFC
Ginger Ale .... ga
Ginger Lynn Fan Club [*Defunct*] (EA) .... GLFC
Ginger Rogers: The Star Fan Club (EA) .... GRTSFC
Gingerbread .... GNGRBRD
Gingiva (DMAA) .... G
Gingiva [*Gum*] [*Latin*] .... GING
Gingiva Treatment [*Dentistry*] (MAE) .... GT
Gingival [*Dentistry*] .... G
Gingival Fibromatosis-Progressive Deafness Syndrome [*Medicine*] (DMAA) .... GFD
Gingival Index [*Dentistry*] .... GI
Gingival Margin Trimmer [*Medicine*] (DMAA) .... GMT
Gingival-Periodontal Index [*Dentistry*] .... GPI
Gingivectomy [*Dentistry*] (DAVI) CV
Gingivectomy [*Dentistry*] .... GVTY
Gingivoaxial [*Dentistry*] .... GA
Gingivobuccoaxial [*Dentistry*] .... GBA
Gingivolinguoaxial [*Dentistry*] .... GLA
Gingivoplasty [*Dentistry*] .... GPLY
Ginkgo Biloba Extract [*Biochemistry*] .... GBE

Ginkgo Biloba Extract [*Biochemistry*] .... GBX
Ginn, Herbert E., South Portland ME [*STAC*] .... GHE
Ginn Language Development Program (EDAC) .... GLDP
Ginna Nuclear Power Plant (NRCH) .... GNPP
Ginseng Research Institute (EA) .... GRI
Ginzburg-Landau-Abrikosov-Gorkov [*Superconductivity theory*] .... GLAG
Ginzburg's Bible [*New Massoretico-Critical Text of the Hebrew Bible*] [*A publication*] (BJA) .... GB
Ginze Kedem (BJA) .... GK
Giocossamente [*Humorously*] [*Music*] (ROG) .... GIO
Gioia Del Colle [*Italy ICAO location identifier*] (ICLI) .... LIBV
Giotto Extended Mission [*European Space Agency*] .... GEM
Gippsland Agriculture Centre [*Australia*] .... GAC
Gippsland Fruit Growers' Association [*Australia*] .... GFGA
Gippsland Waters Coalition (EERA) .... GWC
[*The*] **Giraffe Project** [*An association*] (EA) .... TGP
Girard College, Philadelphia, PA [*Library symbol Library of Congress Obsolete*] (LCLS) .... PPGi
Girard, KS [*FM radio station call letters*] .... KSEK
Girard Township Library, Girard, IL [*Library symbol Library of Congress*] (LCLS) .... IGir
Girardot/Santiago Vila [*Colorado ICAO location identifier*] (ICLI) .... SKGI
Girard-Point [*Virus*] .... GP
Girard's Will Case Report [*A publication*] (DLA) .... Gir WC
Girder [*Technical drawings*] .... G
Girder [*Technical drawings*] .... GIR
Girdwood, AK [*Location identifier FAA*] (FAAL) .... AQY
Girl Friend [*Slang*] .... GF
Girl Friends (EA) .... GF
Girl Groups Fan Club (EA) .... GGFC
Girl Guides (BARN) .... GG
Girl Guides Association [*British*] .... GGA
Girl Guides Association of Australia .... GGAA
Girl Scouts of America .... GSA
Girl Scouts of Racine County, Racine, WI [*Library symbol Library of Congress*] (LCLS) .... WRacGS
Girl Scouts of the Philippines .... GSP
Girl Scouts of the USA (EA) .... GS
Girl Scouts of the USA (EA) .... GSUSA
Girl Watchers Society - Ankle and Leg Division .... GWS-A & L
Girls and Mathematics and Science Teaching .... GAMAST
Girls and Physical Activity National Newsletter [*A publication*] .... G & PA
Girls Athletic Association [*Local school affiliates of National Girls Athletic Association*] [*Defunct*] .... GAA
Girls Brigade [*British*] (BI) .... GB
Girls' Brigade Australia .... GBA
Girls Clubs of America [*Later, GI*] (EA) .... GCA
Girls' College (ADA) .... GC
Girls' Education in Mathematics, Science, and Technology (AIE) .... GEMSAT
Girls' Friendly Society of the USA (EA) .... GFS
Girls' Friendly Society of the USA (EA) .... GFSUSA
Girls' Grammar School (ADA) .... GGS
Girls, Inc. (EA) .... GI
Girls into Science and Technology [*British*] (DI) .... GIST
Girls' Life Brigade [*British*] .... GLB
Girls Nation (EA) .... GN
Girls' Naval Training Corps [*British*] .... GNTC
Girls' Prepatory School, Chattanooga, TN [*Library symbol*] [*Library of Congress*] (LCLS) .... TCGP
Girls' PROUT [*Progressive Utilization Theory*] (EA) .... GP
Girl's Public Day School Co. [*British*] (ROG) .... GPDSC
Girls' Public Day School Trust [*British*] .... GPDST
Girls Rodeo Association [*Later, WPRA*] (EA) .... GRA
Girls School [*British*] .... G
Girls' School (ADA) .... GS
Girls' School Company Ltd. [*British*] (BI) .... GSC
[*The*] **Girls' School Year Book** [*A publication*] (ROG) .... GSYB
Girls' Schools Association [*British*] .... GSA
Girls' Schools Lawn Tennis Association [*British*] (BI) .... GSLTA
Girls' Service League [*Later, YCL*] (EA) .... GSL
Girls' Technical School (ADA) .... GTS
Girls Together Outrageously [*or Organically*] [*Rock music group*] .... GTO's
Girls' Training Corps [*British*] (DAS) .... GTC
Girls' Venture Corps [*British*] (BI) .... GVC
Girls' Venture Corps Air Cadets [*British*] (DBA) .... GVCAC
Girls Volunteers [*Australia*] .... GV
Giro [*Money Order*] **Credit Transfer** (DI) .... GCT
Giron [*Cuba ICAO location identifier*] (ICLI) .... MUGN
Girouxville Municipal Library, Girouxville, AB, Canada [*Library symbol*] [*Library of Congress*] (LCLS) .... CaAGvM
Girouxville Public Library, Alberta [*Library symbol National Library of Canada*] (NLC) .... AGVM
Girth and Mirth (EA) .... G & M
Girth Breast Height (WGA) .... GBH
Girton College [*Cambridge University*] (DAS) .... GCC
Gisborne [*New Zealand*] [*Airport symbol*] (OAG) .... GIS
Gisborne [*New Zealand*] [*Seismograph station code, US Geological Survey*] (SEIS) .... GNZ
Gisborne [*New Zealand*] [*ICAO location identifier*] (ICLI) .... NZGS
Gisenyi [*Rwanda*] [*ICAO location identifier*] (ICLI) .... HRYG
Gish Biomedical [*NASDAQ symbol*] (TTSB) .... GISH
Gish Biomedical, Inc. [*NASDAQ symbol*] (NQ) .... GISH
Gish Biomedical, Inc. [*Associated Press*] (SAG) .... GishBi
Gismondine [*A zeolite*] .... GIS
Gissar [*Former USSR Seismograph station code, US Geological Survey Closed*] (SEIS) .... GIS
Gissel Bargaining Order [*Labor relations*] (WYGK) .... GBO
Gissing, Glen L., Evansville WI [*STAC*] .... GGL
Gitanair [*Italy ICAO designator*] (FAAC) .... GTA
Gitega [*Burundi*] [*Airport symbol*] (OAG) .... GID
Gitega [*Burundi*] [*ICAO location identifier*] (ICLI) .... HBBE
Gittin (BJA) .... Git
Giustizia e Liberta [*Italy*] [*Political party*] .... GL
Givat Haviva Educational Foundation (EA) .... GHEF
Give (ABBR) .... GV
Give a Pint, Save a Life Society [*World War II organization which encouraged donating blood*] .... GAPSALS
Give Better Address [*Communications*] .... GBA
Give Better Reference [*Communications*] .... GBR
Give Kids the World (EA) .... GKTW
Give Peace Holiday Project (EA) .... GPHP
Give Quick Answer [*Communications*] .... GQA
Give the Devil His Due [*Slang*] .... GTDHD
Give the Gift of Literacy Foundation [*Duxbury, MA*] .... GTGL
Give Up Smoking [*Health Education Council campaign*] [*British*] .... GUS
Giveaway (ABBR) .... GVAWY
Given .... GIV
Given (DAVI) .... GIVN
Given (ABBR) .... GVN
Given Memorial Library, Pinehurst, NC [*Library symbol Library of Congress*] (LCLS) .... NcP
Givenchy [*Couturier*] .... G
Giving (FAAC) .... GVG
Giving and Learning Our Way [*An association*] .... GLOW
Giyani [*South Africa*] [*ICAO location identifier*] (ICLI) .... FAGI
Gizan [*Saudi Arabia*] [*Airport symbol*] (OAG) .... GIZ
Gizan [*Saudi Arabia*] [*ICAO location identifier*] (ICLI) .... OEGN
Gizo [*Solomon Islands*] [*Seismograph station code, US Geological Survey*] (SEIS) .... GIZ
Gizo [*Solomon Islands*] [*Airport symbol*] (OAG) .... GZO
Gizo/Nusatupe, Gizo Island [*Solomon Islands*] [*ICAO location identifier*] (ICLI) .... AGGN
Gjoa Haven [*Canada*] [*Airport symbol*] (OAG) .... YHK
Gjoa Haven, NT [*ICAO location identifier*] (ICLI) .... CYHK
Gjogur [*Iceland*] [*Airport symbol*] (OAG) .... GJR
GKN Group Services Ltd. [*British ICAO designator*] (ICDA) .... KN
Glabella [*Medicine*] (DMAA) .... G
Glabella [*Anatomy*] (ROG) .... GL
Glabrous [*Botany*] (BARN) .... glab
Glace .... GLC
Glacial [*Chemistry*] (DAVI) .... glac
Glacial .... GLAC
Glacial Acrylic Acid [*Organic chemistry*] .... GAA
Glacial Debris Conjugate Region [*Oceanography*] .... GDCR
Glacial Isostatic Adjustment [*Geophysics*] .... GIA
Glacial Isostatic Adjustment [*Geophysics*] .... GIA
Glacial North Atlantic Intermediate Water .... GNAIW
Glacial Pacific Deep Water .... GPDW
Glacial Till Soil [*Agronomy*] .... GT
Glacier (ROG) .... GL
Glacier Bancorp [*NASDAQ symbol*] (TTSB) .... GBCL
Glacier Bancorp, Inc. [*NASDAQ symbol*] (SPSG) .... GBCI
Glacier Bancorp, Inc. [*Associated Press*] (SAG) .... GlcrBc
Glacier Bay National Monument .... GLBA
Glacier County Library, Cut Bank, MT [*Library symbol Library of Congress*] (LCLS) .... MtCG
Glacier County Library, Cut Bank, MT [*Library symbol*] [*Library of Congress*] (LCLS) .... MtCG
Glacier Creek, AK [*Location identifier FAA*] (FAAL) .... KGZ
Glacier National Park .... GLAC
Glacier Water Services [*AMEX symbol*] (TTSB) .... HOO
Glacier Water Services, Inc. [*Associated Press*] (SAG) .... GlcWatr
Glacier Water Services, Inc. [*AMEX symbol*] (SAG) .... HOO
Glacier-Ocean-Atmosphere [*Global system used for modelling*] .... GOA
Glaciofluvial Soil [*Agronomy*] .... GF
Gladewater, TX [*AM radio station call letters*] .... KEES
Gladewater-Kilgore-Longview [*Texas*] [*Airport symbol*] (AD) .... GGG
Gladiator .... GLDTR
Gladiator Fighter Aircraft [*British*] (DSUE) .... GLAD
Gladiator Resources Ltd. [*Vancouver Stock Exchange symbol*] .... GLR
Gladiolus (DSUE) .... GLAD
Gladman Point, NT [*ICAO location identifier*] (ICLI) .... CYUR
Gladstone [*Australia ICAO location identifier*] (ICLI) .... ABGL
Gladstone [*Australia Airport symbol*] (OAG) .... GLT
Gladstone High School, Gladstone, OR [*Library symbol Library of Congress*] (LCLS) .... OrGlHS
Gladstone, MO [*AM radio station call letters*] .... KGGN
Gladstone Public Library, Gladstone, MI [*Library symbol Library of Congress*] (LCLS) .... MiGl
Gladstone Public Library, Gladstone, OR [*Library symbol Library of Congress*] (LCLS) .... OrGl
Gladstone Resources [*Vancouver Stock Exchange symbol*] .... GAD
Gladstone Stream [*New Zealand*] [*Seismograph station code, US Geological Survey*] (SEIS) .... GSP
Gladstone-Dale Law .... GDL
Gladstonian [*Politics, 1868-1894*] [*British*] (ROG) .... G
Gladstonian Liberal [*British*] (ROG) .... GL
Gladwin County Library, Beaverton Branch Library, Beaverton, MI [*Library symbol Library of Congress*] (LCLS) .... MiGlad-B

Gladwin County Library, Gladwin, MI [*Library symbol Library of Congress*] (LCLS) .... MiGlad
Gladwin, MI [*Location identifier FAA*] (FAAL) .... GDW
Gladwin, MI [*AM radio station call letters*] .... WGDN
Gladwin, MI [*FM radio station call letters*] .... WGDN-FM
Gladys MacArthur Memorial Library, Weidman, MI [*Library symbol Library of Congress*] (LCLS) .... MiWeld
Glamis [*California*] [*Seismograph station code, US Geological Survey*] (SEIS) .... GLA
Glamis Gold Ltd. [*Associated Press*] (SAG) .... Glamis
Glamis Gold Ltd. [*Toronto Stock Exchange symbol NYSE symbol*] .... GLG
Glamorgan Imperial Yeomanry [*British military*] (DMA) .... GIY
Glamorganshire [*County in Wales*] .... GLAM
Glamorganshire [*County in Wales*] .... GLAMS
Glamour Stock [*Investment term*] .... GS
Glamour Stock [*Investment term*] .... GLAD
Glancing Angle Deposition [*Coating technology*] .... GLAD
Gland .... gl
Gland Anlage .... GA
Gland Seal [*System*] [*Nuclear energy*] (NRCH) .... GS
Gland Seal Condenser [*Nuclear energy*] (NRCH) .... GSC
Gland Seal Leak Off [*Nuclear energy*] (NRCH) .... GSLO
Gland Steam Condenser [*Nuclear energy*] (NRCH) .... GSC
Gland Steam Regulator [*Nuclear energy*] (NRCH) .... GSR
Glandless Cottonseed Meal [*Animal feed*] .... GCSM
Glands, Goiter, or Stiffness [*Medicine*] .... GG or S
Glands on Calyx Margin [*Botany*] .... CXGLN
Glandula [*Gland*] [*Endocrinology*] (DAVI) .... gland
Glanville's English Election Cases [*A publication*] (DLA) .... Glan El Cas
Glanville's English Election Cases [*A publication*] (DLA) .... Glanv El Cas
Glanzmann Thrombasthenia [*Medicine*] (DMAA) .... GT
Glare Free Gloss [*Paper*] .... GFG
Glare Shield (MCD) .... GLRSHLD
Glas Owners Club (EA) .... GOC
Glas-Aire Indus Grp Ltd [*NASDAQ symbol*] (TTSB) .... GLAR
Glas-Aire Industries Group Ltd. [*NASDAQ symbol*] (SAG) .... GLAR
Glas-Aire Industries Group Ltd. [*Associated Press*] (SAG) .... GlasAire
Glascock's Reports in All the Courts of Ireland [*A publication*] (DLA) .... Glas
Glascock's Reports in All the Courts of Ireland [*A publication*] (DLA) .... Glasc
Glascock's Reports in All the Courts of Ireland [*A publication*] (DLA) .... Glascock
Glasgal Communications [*NASDAQ symbol*] (TTSB) .... GLAS
Glasgal Communications Unit [*NASDAQ symbol*] (TTSB) .... GLASU
Glasgal Communications Wrrt [*NASDAQ symbol*] (TTSB) .... GLASW
Glasgal Communities [*NASDAQ symbol*] (SAG) .... GLAS
Glasgal Communities [*Associated Press*] (SAG) .... Glasgal
Glasgow [*British ICAO location identifier*] (ICLI) .... EGPF
Glasgow [*British ICAO location identifier*] (ICLI) .... EGRA
Glasgow [*Postcode*] (ODBW) .... G
Glasgow [*Montana*] [*Airport symbol*] (OAG) .... GGW
Glasgow [*Scotland*] [*Airport symbol*] (OAG) .... GLA
Glasgow [*Scotland*] .... GLAS
Glasgow [*Scotland*] (ROG) .... GLASG
Glasgow [*Scotland*] .... GLSGW
Glasgow & South-Western [*Railway*] [*Scotland*] .... G & SW
Glasgow & South-Western [*Railway*] [*Scotland*] (ROG) .... GLAS & SW
Glasgow & South-Western Railway [*Scotland*] .... G & SWR
Glasgow City-County Library, Glasgow, MT [*Library symbol Library of Congress*] (LCLS) .... MtGl
Glasgow College of Technology (AIE) .... GCT
Glasgow Coma Score [*Medicine*] .... GCS
Glasgow International Freight Terminal [*Scotland*] (DS) .... GIFT
Glasgow, KY [*Location identifier FAA*] (FAAL) .... BVQ
Glasgow, KY [*Location identifier FAA*] (FAAL) .... GLW
Glasgow, KY [*AM radio station call letters*] .... WCDS
Glasgow, KY [*AM radio station call letters*] .... WCLU
Glasgow, KY [*FM radio station call letters*] .... WGGC
Glasgow, KY [*FM radio station call letters*] (RBYB) .... WOVO-FM
Glasgow, KY [*FM radio station call letters*] .... WWWQ
Glasgow, MT [*Location identifier FAA*] (FAAL) .... GSG
Glasgow, MT [*FM radio station call letters*] .... KLAN
Glasgow, MT [*AM radio station call letters*] .... KLTZ
Glasgow, MT [*Location identifier FAA*] (FAAL) .... MKR
Glasgow Outcome Score [*Medicine*] (DMAA) .... GOS
Glasgow [*Coma*] Scale [*Neurology*] (DAVI) .... GSC
Glasgow School of Art [*Scotland*] .... GSA
Glasgow University Language Centre [*University of Glasgow*] [*British*] (CB) .... GULC
Glasgow Yeomanry Cavalry [*British military*] (DMA) .... GYC
Glasgow-Prestwick [*Scotland*] [*Airport symbol*] (OAG) .... PIK
Glashow-Iliopoulos-Maiani [*Theory in particle physics*] .... GIM
Glashow-Weinberg-Salam Theories [*Physics*] .... GWS
Glashutten [*Austria*] [*Seismograph station code, US Geological Survey*] (SEIS) .... GHA
Glass (AAG) .... G
Glass .... GL
Glass [*Automotive engineering*] .... GLA
Glass (VRA) .... gls
Glass .... GLS
Glass Accumulation Rate [*Oceanography*] .... GAR
Glass and Allied Traders' Association [*British*] (DBA) .... GATA
Glass & Ceramic Division (ACII) .... G&C
Glass and Ceramics Industry Instrumentation Group (ACII) .... GCIIG
Glass and Fiber Resin .... GFR
Glass and Glazing Federation [*British*] .... GGF
Glass Art Society (EA) .... GAS
Glass Bead Rating (MCD) .... GBR

Glass Bell Jar .... GBJ
Glass Block (DAC) .... GB
Glass Block (AAG) .... GLB
Glass Bottle Blowers Association of the United States and Canada [*Later, GPPAW*] .... GBBA
Glass Bowl .... GB
Glass Capillary .... GC
Glass Cloth Tape .... GCT
Glass Container Industry Research Corp. [*An association*] (EA) .... GCIRC
Glass Container Manufacturers Institute [*Later, GPI*] (EA) .... GCMI
Glass Crafts of America [*Defunct*] (EA) .... GCA
Glass Delay Line .... GDL
Glass Development LASER .... GDL
Glass Door (ADA) .... GD
Glass Fabric Tape .... GFT
Glass Factor [*Tissue culture*] .... GF
Glass Fiber .... GF
Glass Fiber [*Technical drawings*] .... GLF
Glass Fiber Reinforced Concrete .... GFRC
Glass Filament Wound (IAA) .... GFW
Glass Filter Covers .... GFC
Glass Glover [*Commercial firm British*] .... GG
Glass House Crops Research Institute [*Agricultural Research Council*] (PDAA) .... GCRL
Glass in Barrels [*Freight*] .... GLB
Glass Insulation Material .... GIM
Glass LASER Rod .... GLR
Glass Lined Tubing .... GLT
Glass Manufacturers Federation .... GMF
Glass Merchants' Association of Western Australia .... GMAWA
Glass Metal (IAA) .... GM
Glass Microballoon (MCD) .... GMB
Glass Microfilter .... GMF
Glass, Molders, Pottery, Plastics, and Allied Workers International Union (EA) .... GMPPAW
Glass Oceanographic Buoy .... GOB
Glass Packaging Institute (EA) .... GPI
Glass Painters' Trade Union [*British*] .... GPTU
Glass Plasma Display [*Electronics*] (BARN) .... GPD
Glass Plate Negative .... GPN
Glass, Pottery, Plastics, and Allied Workers International Union (EA) .... GPPAW
Glass Precision Tubing .... GPT
Glass Probe Thermistor .... GPT
Glass Reinforced [*Organic chemistry*] .... GLARE
Glass Reinforced Thermoplastic .... GRTP
Glass Technical Institute [*Commercial firm*] (EA) .... GTI
Glass Technology and Fabrication Exhibition (TSPED) .... GLASSEX
Glass Tempering Association (EA) .... GTA
Glass Training Ltd. (AIE) .... GTL
Glass Transition .... Tg
Glass Tube (DEN) .... GT
Glass with Embedded Metal and Sulphide [*In interplanetary dust particles*] .... GEMS
Glass-Bonded Mica .... GBM
Glass-Bonded Zeolite .... GBZ
Glassboro, NJ [*FM radio station call letters*] .... WGLS
Glassboro Public Library, Glassboro, NJ [*Library symbol Library of Congress*] (LCLS) .... NjGb
Glassboro State College (GAGS) .... Glassboro St C
Glassboro State College, Glassboro, NJ [*OCLC symbol*] (OCLC) .... NJG
Glassboro State College, Glassboro, NJ [*Library symbol Library of Congress*] (LCLS) .... NjGbS
Glass-Distilled Water [*Medicine*] (DMAA) .... GDW
Glass-Fiber Filter [*Separation technology*] .... GFF
Glass-Fiber Insulation Tubing .... GFIT
Glass-Fiber Material .... GFM
Glass-Fiber Polyethylene Terephthalate [*Plastics technology*] .... GF-PET
Glass-Fiber Pulling [*Materials processing*] .... GFP
Glass-Fiber Reinforced .... GFR
Glass-Fiber Reinforced Concrete .... GRC
Glass-Fiber Reinforced Gypsum [*Substitute wood*] .... GRG
Glass-Fiber Reinforced Thermoplastics (PDAA) .... GRTP
Glass-Fiber-Reinforced Plastic [*Also, GIFRP*] .... GFRP
Glass-Fiber-Reinforced Plastic [*Also, GFRP*] .... GIFRP
Glass-Fiber-Reinforced Thermoplastic (MCD) .... GFRTP
Glass-Fiber-Reinforced Unsaturated Polyester [*Organic chemistry*] .... GUP
Glassfibre Reinforced Cement Association [*British*] .... GRCA
Glassford on Evidence [*A publication*] (DLA) .... Glassf Ev
Glass-Forming Tendency [*Materials science*] .... GFT
Glassine (VRA) .... glsn
Glassine and Greaseproof Manufacturers Association [*Later, API*] (EA) .... GGMA
Glass-Insulated Wire .... GIW
Glass-Ionomer Cement [*Dental material*] .... GIC
Glassmaster Co. [*Associated Press*] (SAG) .... Glassmst
Glassmaster Co. [*NASDAQ symbol*] (SAG) .... GLMA
Glass-Mat Reinforced Thermoplastic [*Automotive engineering*] .... GMT
Glass-Mat Thermoplastic .... GMT
Glass-Polymer Composite (PDAA) .... GPC
Glass-Reinforced .... GR
Glass-Reinforced Composite .... GRC
Glass-Reinforced Plastic [*or Polyester*] .... GRP
Glass-Reinforced Plastic Joint .... GRPJ
Glass-Reinforced Polypropylene (PDAA) .... GRPP
Glass-Reinforced Structural Plastic .... GRSP
Glass-Silicone-Glass [*Electronics*] (DEN) .... GSG

Glass-Steagal Act [*1933*] ... GSA
Glassware ... GLWR
Glassy Carbon ... GC
Glassy Carbon Electrode ... GCE
Glastonbury Bank & Trust Co. [*NASDAQ symbol*] (SAG) ... GLBT
Glastonbury Bank & Trust Co. [*Associated Press*] (SAG) ... Glstnbry
Glatfelter [*P.H.*] **Co.** [*Associated Press*] (SAG) ... Glatflt
Glatfelter [*P. H.*] **Co.** [*AMEX symbol*] (SPSG) ... GLT
Glaube in der 2. Welt [*Faith in the Second World - FSW*] [*An association Switzerland*] (EAIO) ... G2W
Glauben und Wissen (BJA) ... GW
Glaucolacustrine Soil [*Agronomy*] ... GL
Glaucoma ... GLC
Glaucoma Society of the International Congress of Ophthalmology (EA) ... GSICO
Glaucomatous Optic Nerve Damage [*Medicine*] (DMAA) ... GOND
Glaucous [*Botany*] (BARN) ... glau
Glavnaya Geofizicheskaya Observatory [*Main Geophysical Observatory*] [*Former USSR*] ... GGO
Glavnoe Razvedivatelnoe Upravlenie [*Chief Administration for Intelligence*] [*Division of the General Staff of the Soviet Army*] [*Former USSR*] ... GRU
Glavnoe Upravlenie Ispravitel'no-Trudovykh Lagerei [*Main Administration of Corrective Labor Camps*] [*Former USSR*] ... GULAG
Glavnoe Upravlenie Kontrrazvedkoi [*Chief Administration for Counter-intelligence*] [*of the Ministry of War*] [*Former USSR*] [*World War II*] ... GUKR
Glavnoye Upravleniye Mestami Zaklyucheniya [*Main Administration of Places of Detention*] [*Former USSR*] (LAIN) ... GUMZ
Glavnoye Upravleniye Militsii [*Main Administration of Militia*] [*Former USSR*] (LAIN) ... GUM
Glavny Universalny Magazin [*Department store in USSR*] ... GUM
Glaxo, Inc., Durham, NC [*Library symbol*] [*Library of Congress*] (LCLS) ... NcDurG
Glaxo, Inc., Zebulon, NC [*Library symbol*] [*Library of Congress*] (LCLS) ... NcZG
Glaxo Laboratories Ltd. [*Great Britain*] [*Research code symbol*] ... CG
Glaxo Laboratories Ltd. [*Great Britain*] [*Research code symbol*] ... GR
Glaxo Ltd. ADR [*Formerly, Glaxo Holdilngs Ltd. ADR*] [*NYSE symbol*] (SPSG) ... GLX
Glaxo Wellcome PLC [*Associated Press*] (SAG) ... GlaxcWeL
Glaxo Wellcome plc ADR [*NYSE symbol*] (TTSB) ... GLX
Glaze ... GL
Glaze (MSA) ... GLZ
Glaze (VRA) ... glz
Glaze ... GLZ
Glazed (VRA) ... glz
Glazed ... GLZD
Glazed (DGA) ... GZD
Glazed Cement Manufacturers Association Ltd. [*British*] (BI) ... GCMA
Glazed Ceramic Mosaic (DICI) ... GCM
Glazed Concrete Masonry Units [*Technical drawings*] ... GCMU
Glazed Earthenware ... GEW
Glazed Facing Units [*Technical drawings*] ... GFU
Glazed Imitation Parchment ... GIP
Glazed Interior [*Title*] (DICI) ... GI
Glazed Structural Facing Units [*Technical drawings*] ... GSFU
Glazed Structural Tile [*Technical drawings*] ... GST
Glazed Structural Unit [*Technical drawings*] ... GSU
Glazed Structural Unit Base [*Technical drawings*] ... GSUB
Glazed Vitrified Clay ... GVC
Glazed Wall Tile [*Technical drawings*] ... GWT
Glazed Wall Tile Base [*Technical drawings*] ... GWTB
Glazed Wallboard [*Technical drawings*] ... GLWB
Glazed Weatherproof [*Tile*] (DICI) ... GW
Glazounov Society (EA) ... GS
GLE Resources Ltd. [*Vancouver Stock Exchange symbol*] ... GLE
Gleaner Life Insurance Society [*Adrian, MI*] (EA) ... GLIS
Gleason Corp. [*NYSE symbol*] (SPSG) ... GLE
Gleason Corp. [*Associated Press*] (SAG) ... GleasC
Gleaver's Reports [*Jamaica*] [*A publication*] (ILCA) ... GI
Glebe [*Ecclesiastical*] (ROG) ... GL
Gleb-Goldstein Color Sorting Test [*Psychology*] ... GGCST
Gleichen Municipal Library, Alberta [*Library symbol National Library of Canada*] (NLC) ... AGM
Gleichen Municipal Library, Gleichen, AB, Canada [*Library symbol Library of Congress*] (LCLS) ... CaAGM
Glen [*Commonly used*] (OPSA) ... GLEN
Glen ... GLN
Glen ... GLN
Glen Arbor, MI [*FM radio station call letters*] ... WGFN
Glen Arbor, MI [*FM radio station call letters*] (RBYB) ... WTHM-FM
Glen Auden Resources Ltd. [*Toronto Stock Exchange symbol*] ... GAU
Glen Avon [*California*] [*Seismograph station code, US Geological Survey*] (SEIS) ... GAV
Glen Burnie, MD [*AM radio station call letters*] ... WJRO
Glen Burnie, MD [*FM radio station call letters*] ... WWIN
Glen Campbell Fan Club (EA) ... GCFC
Glen Canyon [*Arizona*] [*Seismograph station code, US Geological Survey*] (SEIS) ... GCA
Glen Canyon Environmental Studies [*Department of the Interior*] ... GCES
Glen Canyon National Recreation Area ... GLCA
Glen Carbon Library, Glen Carbon, IL [*Library symbol Library of Congress*] (LCLS) ... IGlca
Glen County Library, Willows, CA [*Library symbol Library of Congress*] (LCLS) ... CWiWCL
Glen Cove [*New York*] [*Seismograph station code, US Geological Survey*] (SEIS) ... GCY
Glen Cove High School, Glen Cove, NY [*Library symbol*] [*Library of Congress*] (LCLS) ... NGlcHS
Glen Cove Middle School, Glen Cove, NY [*Library symbol Library of Congress*] (LCLS) ... NGlcMS
Glen Cove Public Library, Glen Cove, NY [*Library symbol Library of Congress*] (LCLS) ... NGlc
Glen Ellyn, IL [*FM radio station call letters*] ... WDCB
Glen Ellyn Public Library, Glen Ellyn, IL [*Library symbol Library of Congress*] (LCLS) ... IGle
Glen Head Elementary School, Glen Head, NY [*Library symbol Library of Congress*] (LCLS) ... NGlhES
Glen Innes [*Australia Airport symbol*] (OAG) ... GLI
Glen Lake Community Library, Empire, MI [*Library symbol Library of Congress*] (LCLS) ... MiEm
Glen Lake Community Library, Empire, MI [*Library symbol*] [*Library of Congress*] (LCLS) ... MiEmp
Glen Miller Society (EAIO) ... GMS
Glen Mills, PA [*FM radio station call letters*] ... WZZE
Glen Morris Branch, South Dumfries Township Public Library, Ontario [*Library symbol National Library of Canada*] (BIB) ... OGMSD
Glen Oaks Community College, Centreville, MI [*Library symbol Library of Congress*] (LCLS) ... MiCeG
Glen on Registration of Births and Deaths [*A publication*] (DLA) ... Glen Reg
Glen on the Public Health Laws [*A publication*] (DLA) ... Glen Pub H
Glen Ridge Free Public Library, Glen Ridge, NJ [*Library symbol Library of Congress*] (LCLS) ... NjGlri
Glen Robertson Branch, Stormont, Dundas, and Glengarry County Public Library, Ontario [*Library symbol National Library of Canada*] (BIB) ... ORG
Glen Rose, TX [*FM radio station call letters*] (RBYB) ... KCLE
Glenair [*British*] [*FAA designator*] (FAAC) ... MFM
Glenayre Electronics Ltd. [*Toronto Stock Exchange symbol*] ... GLN
Glenayre Technologies [*NASDAQ symbol*] (TTSB) ... GEMS
Glenayre Techs, Inc. [*NASDAQ symbol*] (SAG) ... GEMS
Glenayre Techs, Inc. [*Associated Press*] (SAG) ... Glenayr
Glenborough Realty Trust [*NYSE symbol*] (TTSB) ... GLB
Glenborough Realty Trust, Inc. [*NYSE symbol*] (SAG) ... GLB
Glenborough Realty Trust, Inc. [*Associated Press*] (SAG) ... GlenRT
Glenbow Alberta Institute, Calgary, AB, Canada [*Library symbol Library of Congress*] (LCLS) ... CaACG
Glenbow-Alberta Institute, Calgary, Alberta [*Library symbol National Library of Canada*] (NLC) ... ACG
Glencair Resources, Inc. [*Toronto Stock Exchange symbol*] ... GCR
Glenco International Corp. [*Vancouver Stock Exchange symbol*] ... GCO
Glencoe, AL [*Department of Commerce*] ... WGMZ
Glencoe Hospital, Glencoe, MN [*Library symbol*] [*Library of Congress*] (LCLS) ... MnGGH
Glencoe Middle School, Glencoe, MN [*Library symbol*] [*Library of Congress*] (LCLS) ... MnGMS
Glencoe, MN [*FM radio station call letters*] ... KARP
Glencoe Public High School, Glencoe, MN [*Library symbol*] [*Library of Congress*] (LCLS) ... MnGHS
Glencoe Public Library, Glencoe, IL [*Library symbol Library of Congress*] (LCLS) ... IGlc
Glencoe Public Library, Glencoe, IL [*OCLC symbol*] (OCLC) ... JAH
Glendale, AZ [*AM radio station call letters*] ... KGME
Glendale, AZ [*FM radio station call letters*] ... KKFR
Glendale, AZ [*FM radio station call letters*] (RBYB) ... KOAZ-FM
Glendale, AZ [*FM radio station call letters*] ... KTWC
Glendale, AZ [*Location identifier FAA*] (FAAL) ... LUF
Glendale, AZ [*Location identifier FAA*] (FAAL) ... VCO
Glendale, CA [*AM radio station call letters*] ... KIEV
Glendale, CA [*FM radio station call letters*] ... KSCA
Glendale College, Glendale, CA [*Library symbol Library of Congress*] (LCLS) ... CGlC
Glendale College Library, Glendale, CA [*OCLC symbol*] (OCLC) ... CGN
Glendale Community College, Glendale, AZ [*Library symbol Library of Congress*] (LCLS) ... AzGC
Glendale Co. Operative Bk [*NASDAQ symbol*] (TTSB) ... GLBK
Glendale Co-Operative Bank [*NASDAQ symbol*] (SAG) ... GLBK
Glendale Co-Operative Bank [*Associated Press*] (SAG) ... GlendCo
Glendale Fed Bk Cv'E'Prd [*NYSE symbol*] (TTSB) ... GLNPrE
Glendale Fed Bk FSB Wrrt [*NASDAQ symbol*] (TTSB) ... GDLEW
Glendale Federal Bank [*NYSE symbol*] (SPSG) ... GLN
Glendale Federal Bank Federal Savings Bank [*Associated Press*] (SAG) ... GlenF
Glendale Federal Bank Federal Savings Bank [*Associated Press*] (SAG) ... GlenFed
Glendale Federal Bank FSB [*NASDAQ symbol*] (SAG) ... GDLB
Glendale Federal Bank FSB [*Associated Press*] (SAG) ... GlenF
Glendale Public Library, Glendale, CA [*Library symbol Library of Congress OCLC symbol*] (LCLS) ... CGl
Glendale Resources, Inc. [*Vancouver Stock Exchange symbol*] ... GDU
Glendale Sanitarium and Hospital, Glendale, CA [*Library symbol Library of Congress*] (LCLS) ... CGlS
Glendale, WV [*Location identifier FAA*] (FAAL) ... GWV
Glendalough [*Valley in Ireland*] (ROG) ... GLENDAL
Glendive [*Montana*] [*Airport symbol*] (OAG) ... GDV
Glendive, MT [*FM radio station call letters*] ... KDZN
Glendive, MT [*AM radio station call letters*] ... KGLE
Glendive, MT [*AM radio station call letters*] ... KXGN
Glendive, MT [*Television station call letters*] ... KXGN-TV
Glendive Public Library, Glendive, MT [*Library symbol Library of Congress*] (LCLS) ... MtG
Glendora Public Library, Glendora, CA [*Library symbol Library of Congress*] (LCLS) ... CGle
Gleneden Beach, OR [*FM radio station call letters*] ... KSHL

Glenex Industries, Inc. [*Vancouver Stock Exchange symbol*] ... GXI
Glengyle [*Australia Airport symbol*] (OAG) ... GLG
[*The*] **Glenmary Home Missioners** (TOCD) ... Glmy
Glenmary Research Center (EA) ... GRC
Glenmuick [*New Zealand*] [*Seismograph station code, US Geological Survey Closed*] (SEIS) ... GLE
Glenn A. Jones, MD, Memorial Library, Johnstown, CO [*Library symbol Library of Congress*] (LCLS) ... CoJo
Glenn Miller Birthplace Society (EA) ... GMBS
Glenn Mills School, Glenn Mills, PA [*OCLC symbol*] (OCLC) ... PIG
Glenn R. Frye Memorial Hospital, Hickory, NC [*Library symbol*] [*Library of Congress*] (LCLS) ... NcHyFH
Glennallen, AK [*AM radio station call letters*] ... KCAM
Glennallen, AK [*FM radio station call letters*] (RBYB) ... KXGA
Glenn's Annual Reports [*16-18 Louisiana*] [*A publication*] (DLA) ... Glenn
Glenns Ferry Public Library, Glenns Ferry, ID [*Library symbol*] [*Library of Congress*] (LCLS) ... IdGf
Glennville, GA [*AM radio station call letters*] ... WKIG
Glennville, GA [*FM radio station call letters*] ... WKIG-FM
Glenohumeral [*Joint*] [*Anatomy*] (DAVI) ... GH
Glenohumeral Joint [*Anatomy*] (DAVI) ... GH
Glenrose Provincial General Hospital, Staff Library, Edmonton, AB, Canada [*Library symbol*] [*Library of Congress*] (LCLS) ... CaAEG
Glens [*Commonly used*] (OPSA) ... GLENS
Glens [*Postal Service standard*] (OPSA) ... GLNS
Glens ... GLNS
Glens Falls [*New York*] [*Airport symbol*] (AD) ... GFL
Glens Falls, NY [*Location identifier FAA*] (FAAL) ... GFL
Glens Falls, NY [*AM radio station call letters*] ... WBZA
Glens Falls, NY [*FM radio station call letters*] ... WGFR
Glens Falls, NY [*AM radio station call letters*] ... WWSC
Glens Falls, NY [*FM radio station call letters*] ... WYLR
Glen's Highway Laws [*A publication*] (DLA) ... Glen High
Glenside Free Library, Glenside, PA [*Library symbol Library of Congress*] (LCLS) ... PGl
Glenside Free Library, Glenside, PA [*Library symbol*] [*Library of Congress*] (LCLS) ... PGIL
Glentech International Ltd. [*British*] ... GTI
Glenvet Resources Ltd. [*Vancouver Stock Exchange symbol*] ... GVT
Glenview, IL [*Location identifier FAA*] (FAAL) ... NBU
Glenview, IL [*Location identifier FAA*] (FAAL) ... NZE
Glenview, IL [*FM radio station call letters*] ... WMWA
Glenville State College [*West Virginia*] ... GSC
Glenville State College, Glenville, WV [*Library symbol Library of Congress*] (LCLS) ... WvGlS
Glenway Financial Corp. [*NASDAQ symbol*] (SAG) ... GFCO
Glenway Financial Corp. [*Associated Press*] (SAG) ... Glenway
Glenway Fin'l [*NASDAQ symbol*] (TTSB) ... GFCO
Glenwood and Souris Regional Library, Souris, Manitoba [*Library symbol National Library of Canada*] (NLC) ... MSOG
Glenwood and Souris Regional Library, Souris, MB, Canada [*Library symbol Library of Congress*] (LCLS) ... CaMSoG
Glenwood, AR [*FM radio station call letters*] ... KWXE
Glenwood, AR [*AM radio station call letters*] ... KWXI
Glenwood, AR [*AM radio station call letters*] (RBYB) ... KWXI-AM
Glenwood Landing Elementary School, Glen Head, NY [*Library symbol*] [*Library of Congress*] (LCLS) ... NGlhGE
Glenwood Landing Elementary School, Glenwood Landing, NY [*Library symbol Library of Congress*] (LCLS) ... NGlwES
Glenwood, MN [*FM radio station call letters*] ... KMGK
Glenwood Public Library, Alberta [*Library symbol National Library of Canada*] (NLC) ... AGL
Glenwood Public Library District, Glenwood, IL [*Library symbol Library of Congress*] (LCLS) ... IGlw
Glenwood Public Library, Glenwood, IA [*Library symbol*] [*Library of Congress*] (LCLS) ... IaGle
Glenwood Public Library, Glenwood, MN [*Library symbol*] [*Library of Congress*] (LCLS) ... MnGle
Glenwood Public Library, Glenwood, NF, Canada [*Library symbol Library of Congress*] (LCLS) ... CaNfGl
Glenwood Public Library, Newfoundland [*Library symbol National Library of Canada*] (NLC) ... NFGL
Glenwood Senior High School, Glenwood, MN [*Library symbol*] [*Library of Congress*] (LCLS) ... MnGleSH
Glenwood Springs, CO [*Location identifier FAA*] (FAAL) ... GWS
Glenwood Springs, CO [*FM radio station call letters*] ... KDRH
Glenwood Springs, CO [*AM radio station call letters*] ... KGLN
Glenwood Springs, CO [*FM radio station call letters*] ... KMTS
Glenwood Springs, CO [*Television station call letters*] ... KREG
Glenwood Springs, CO [*FM radio station call letters*] (RBYB) ... KZGO
Glenwood Springs Public Library, Glenwood Springs, CO [*Library symbol Library of Congress*] (LCLS) ... CoGs
Glenwood Springs Public Library, Glenwood Springs, CO [*Library symbol*] [*Library of Congress*] (LCLS) ... CoGsP
Glia Precursor [*Biochemistry*] ... GP
Glial Bundle [*Medicine*] (DMAA) ... GB
Glial Fibrillary Acidic Protein [*Also, GFAP*] [*Biochemistry*] ... GFA
Glial Fibrillary Acidic Protein [*Also, GFA*] [*Biochemistry*] ... GFAP
Glial Growth Factor [*Biochemistry*] ... GGF
Glial Growth Promoting Factor [*Neurology*] ... GGPF
Glial Maturation Factor [*Biochemistry*] ... GMF
Glial-Derived Growth Factor [*Biochemistry*] ... GDNF
Glia-Neuron Cell Adhesion Molecule [*Cytology*] ... GNCAM
Gliatech, Inc. [*NASDAQ symbol*] (SAG) ... GLIA
Gliatech, Inc. [*Associated Press*] (SAG) ... Gliatech
Glicentin [*Biochemistry*] ... GLI
Glidden Co. Research Library, Cleveland, OH [*Library symbol Library of Congress*] (LCLS) ... OClG
Glidden Graphic, Glidden, IA [*Library symbol Library of Congress*] (LCLS) ... IaGliG
Glide and Skip [*Bombing mission*] ... GLIP
Glide Angle [*Aviation*] ... GA
Glide Angle Indicator Light [*Aviation*] (DNAB) ... GAIL
Glide Bomb [*Air Force*] ... GB
Glide Bomb [*Air Force*] ... GLOMB
Glide Bomb Unit [*Air Force*] (MCD) ... GBU
Glide Path [*Aviation*] ... GP
Glide Path Indicator [*Aviation*] (NATG) ... GPI
Glide Path Intercept Point [*Aviation*] ... GPIP
Glide Path Landing System [*Aviation*] (IAA) ... GPLS
Glide Return to Landing Site (NASA) ... GRTLS
Glide Return to Launch Site (MCD) ... GRTLS
Glide Slope [*Aviation*] (NASA) ... GLD
Glide Slope [*Aviation*] (MSA) ... GLS
Glide Slope [*Aviation*] ... GS
Glide Slope Antenna [*Aviation*] ... GSA
Glide Slope Indicator [*Aviation*] ... GSI
Glide Slope Receiver [*Aviation*] ... GSR
Glide Slope Reference Bar [*Aviation*] ... GSRB
Glide Speed Indicator ... GSI
Glidepath [*Slope*] **Station** [*ITU designation*] (CET) ... RLG
Glider ... G
Glider ... GLD
Glider (FAAC) ... GLDR
Glider ... GLI
Glider [*Special*] [*Navy symbol*] ... VLB
Glider Aircraft [*When first letter in Navy aircraft designation*] ... L
Glider Badge [*Military decoration*] ... GliBad
Glider Developments, Inc. [*Vancouver Stock Exchange symbol*] ... GRI
Glider Flight Control Electronics Subsystem ... GFCES
Glider Operational Training Unit [*British military*] (DMA) ... GOTU
Glider Pilot Regiment [*Military unit*] [*British*] ... GPR
Glider Training School [*British military*] (DMA) ... GTS
Gliding Club [*British*] (ADA) ... GC
Gliding Deceleration Technology System ... GDTS
Gliding Horse and Pony Registry (EA) ... GHPR
Gliding School [*British military*] (DMA) ... GS
Glimcher Realty Trust [*Associated Press*] (SAG) ... GlimchRt
Glimcher Realty Trust [*NYSE symbol*] (SPSG) ... GRT
Glimmer Resources, Inc. [*Vancouver Stock Exchange symbol*] ... GME
Glimpse [*Optics*] ... G
Glioma [*Neurology*] (DAVI) ... glio
Gliomatosis Peritonei [*Oncology*] ... GP
Glissando [*Gliding*] [*Music*] (ROG) ... GLIS
Glissando [*Gliding*] [*Music*] ... Gliss
Glitter (VRA) ... glit
Glitter Gold Mines [*Vancouver Stock Exchange symbol*] ... GGM
Gloag and Henderson's Introduction to the Law of Scotland [*7th ed.*] [*1968*] [*A publication*] (DLA) ... Gloag & Henderson
Global ... GLBL
Global ... Glo
Global Address ... GA
Global Address Space (MHDI) ... GAS
Global Air [*Bulgaria*] [*ICAO designator*] (FAAC) ... GLB
Global Air Link [*Nigeria*] [*ICAO designator*] (FAAC) ... GNB
Global Airborne Integrated Navigation System [*Military*] (IAA) ... GAINS
Global Alert System [*Vancouver Stock Exchange symbol*] ... GBA
Global Analyses, Interpretation, and Modeling [*Task Force*] [*Marine science*] (OSRA) ... GAIM
Global Analysis, Interpretation and Modelling [*Climate*] (EERA) ... GAIM
Global Analysis Systems [*Information service or system*] (IID) ... GAS
Global Anxiety Score [*Medicine*] (DMAA) ... GAS
Global Area Coverage [*Meteorology*] ... GAC
Global Area Network (IAA) ... GAN
Global Assessment [*Psychiatric evaluation test*] ... GA
Global Assessment on Soil Degradation (EERA) ... GLASOD
Global Assessment Scale [*Psychiatric evaluation test*] ... GAS
Global Asset Management [*Commercial firm British*] (ECON) ... GAM
Global Assimilation and Prognosis System (EERA) ... GASP
Global Atmosphere Gases Experiment (EERA) ... GAGE
Global Atmosphere Watch [*Marine science*] (OSRA) ... GAW
Global Atmospheric and Aerosol Radiation Study ... GAARS
Global Atmospheric Gases Experiment [*Environmental science*] ... GAGE
Global Atmospheric Measurements Experiment on Tropospheric Aerosols and Gases [*National Science Foundation*] ... GAMETAG
Global Atmospheric Measurements Program [*National Science Foundation*] ... GAMP
Global Atmospheric Research (NOAA) ... GAR
Global Atmospheric Research Program [*Terminated National Science Foundation*] ... GARP
Global Atmospheric Sampling Laboratory (EERA) ... GASLAB
Global Atmospheric Sampling Program [*NASA*] ... GASP
Global Atmospheric Watch (EERA) ... GAW
Global Atmospheric Watch (USDC) ... GAW
Global Auto [*Computer science*] ... GA
Global Automation Information Network [*An association*] ... GAIN
Global Backscatter Experiment [*Marine science*] (OSRA) ... GLOBE
Global Backscatter Experiment [*NASA/MSFC*] ... GLOBE
Global Backscatter Experiment (USDC) ... GLOBE
Global Ballistic Missile Defense ... GBMD
Global Ballistic Transport [*Military*] ... GBT

Global Biodiversity Assessment [Book] (EERA) .... GBA
Global Brain Ischemia .... GBI
Global Burden of Disease .... GBD
Global Casinos [NASDAQ symbol] (SAG) .... GBCS
Global Casinos [Associated Press] (SAG) .... GlbCasn
Global Cerebral Metabolic Rate for Glucose [Brain research] .... GCMRGlc
Global Change and Terrestrial Ecosystems [Marine science] (OSRA) .... GCTE
Global Change and Terrestrial Ecosystems (USDC) .... GCTE
Global Change and the Antarctica (EERA) .... GLOCHANT
Global Change Data and Information System [Marine science] (OSRA) ...... GCDIS
Global Change Data and Information System (USDC) .... GCDIS
Global Change Database Project (EERA) .... GCDP
Global Change Master Director (EERA) .... GCMD
Global Change Research Plan [Program] [Marine science] (OSRA) .... GCRP
Global Change Research Plan/Program (USDC) .... GCRP
Global Change Research Program (EERA) .... GCRP
Global Chart of the World [Air Force] .... GCW
Global Chemical Transport Model [Marine science] (OSRA) .... GCTM
Global Circulation Model [National Center for Atmospheric Research] .... GCM
Global Circulation Models [Climate] (EERA) .... GCM
Global Citizens Association [Quebec, PQ] (EAIO) .... GCA
Global Climate Coalition [A US lobby group] .... GCC
Global Climate Model .... GCM
Global Climate Observing System [Marine science] (OSRA) .... GCOS
Global Climate Observing System (USDC) .... GCOS
Global Climate Perspectives System (USDC) .... GCPS
Global Climate Perspectives System [Marine science] (OSRA) .... GCPS
Global Climatic Change [Marine science] (OSRA) .... GCC
Global Climatic Change (USDC) .... GCC
Global Command and Control System .... GCCS
Global Committee of Parliamentarians on Population and Development
   (EA) .... GCPPD
Global Communications Satellite System .... GCSS
Global Communications System [Air Force] .... GLOBECOM
Global Communications System [Air Force] .... GLOCOM
Global Community Health .... GCH
Global Competitiveness Council [Defunct] (EA) .... GCC
Global Congress of the World's Religions (EA) .... GCWR
Global Control (IAA) .... GC
Global Cooperation for a Better World [Australia] .... GCBW
Global Coral Reef Alliance (EA) .... GCRA
Global Data Administrator (MHDI) .... GDA
Global Data Area .... GDA
Global Data Link .... GDL
Global Data Management System .... GDMS
Global Data Manager .... GDM
Global Data Processing System [World Meteorological Organization] .... GDPS
Global Data Systems [Vancouver Stock Exchange symbol] .... GD
Global Database .... GDB
Global Decision Support System (MCD) .... GDSS
Global Descriptor Table [Computer science] .... GDT
Global Descriptor Table Register [Computer science] (PCM) .... GDTR
Global Deterioration Scale [Medicine] .... GDS
Global Developmental Delay .... GDD
Global Digital Sea Ice Data Bank (USDC) .... GDSIB
Global Digital Sea Ice Data Bank [Marine science] (OSRA) .... GDSIDB
Global Digital Seismic Network .... GDSN
Global Digital Seismograph Network [Earthquake study] .... GDSN
Global DirectMail [NYSE symbol] (TTSB) .... GML
Global Directmail Corp. [Associated Press] (SAG) .... GlbDir
Global Directmail Corp. [NYSE symbol] (SAG) .... GM
Global Directory Agent .... GDA
Global Directory Service .... GDS
Global Distribution Systems .... GDS
Global Education Associates (EA) .... GEA
Global Electronic Mail Service [Electronic Mail Corp. of America] [Old
   Greenwich, CT] [Telecommunications] (TSSD) .... GEMSERVICE
Global Electronic Markets Co. [Joint venture of Citicorp and McGraw-Hill, In c.
   to provide computerized buying, selling, shipping, and insuring services for
   commodities traders] .... GEMCO
Global Energy and Water Cycle Experiment [World Climate Research
   Program] [Geo science] .... GEWEX
Global Energy and Water Cycle Experiment [Marine science] (OSRA) .... GEWEX
Global Energy Balance Archive .... GEBA
Global Energy Balance Archive [A publication] .... GEBA
Global Energy Ltd. [Vancouver Stock Exchange symbol] .... GYC
Global Energy Network International .... GENI
Global Energy Operations & Management Co. .... GEOMAN
Global Engineering Documents [Santa Ana, CA] [Information service or
   system] .... GED
Global Environment Change Report (EERA) .... GECR
Global Environment Facility [Implemented jointly by the World Bank, the
   United Nations Environment Program, and the United Nations Development
   Program] .... GEF
Global Environment Fund [of the World Bank] (EERA) .... GEF
Global Environment Monitoring System [UNEP] [Database producer]
   (IID) .... GEMS
Global Environmental Change [Marine science] (OSRA) ...... GEC
Global Environmental Management Initiative [Environmental science] ...... GEMI
Global Environmental Research Organization .... GERO
Global Environmental Trust Fund [GEF-Core Fund] (EERA) .... GETF
Global Exchange, Inc. .... GXI
Global Family of Operational [Plan] Assessment Report (DOMA) .... GFOAR
Global Finance Information [Information service or system] (IID) ...... GFI
Global Financial Studies .... GFS

Global Focal Sclerosis [Medicine] (DMAA) .... GFS
Global Forcing Contribution [Environmental science] .... GFC
Global Futures Network [India] [India] (EAIO) .... GFN
Global Geospace Science .... GGS
Global Geospace Study [Proposed] [United States, Japan, and Europe] ...... GGS
Global Getra Ltd. [Bulgaria] [ICAO designator] (FAAC) ...... GLJ
Global Government Plus Fund, Inc. [Associated Press] (SAG) ...... GlbGvt
Global Government Plus Fund, Inc. [NYSE symbol] (SPSG) ..... GOV
Global Government Plus Fund Ltd. [Toronto Stock Exchange symbol] .... GGF
Global Health Sciences Fd [NYSE symbol] (TTSB) .... GHS
Global Health Sciences Fund [NYSE symbol] (SPSG) .... GHS
Global Health Sciences Fund [Associated Press] (SAG) ...... GlbHlt
Global High Income Dollar Fund [NYSE symbol] (SPSG) ..... GHI
Global High Income Dollar Fund [Associated Press] (SAG) ...... GlobHi
Global High Inc. Dollar Fd [NYSE symbol] (TTSB) .... GHI
Global High-Visibility Mast .... GHVM
Global Historical Climate Network [Marine science] (OSRA) .... GHCN
Global Historical Climate Network (USDC) .... GHCN
Global Horizontal Sounding Technique [Meteorology] .... GHOST
Global Imaging Networks (DGA) .... GIN
Global Impacts of Applied Microbiology [International conferences] ...... GIAM
Global Improvement Rating (DMAA) .... GIR
Global Indexing System (GNE) .... GIS
Global Industrial and Social Progress Research Institute .... GISPRI
Global Industrial Tech [NYSE symbol] (TTSB) .... GIX
Global Industrial Technologies [NYSE symbol] (SAG) .... GIX
Global Industrial Technologies [Associated Press] (SAG) ...... GlobIndl
Global Industries [NASDAQ symbol] (TTSB) .... GLBL
Global Industries Ltd. [NASDAQ symbol] (SAG) .... GLBL
Global Industries Ltd. [Associated Press] (SAG) .... GlobIInd
Global Infectious Disease and Epidemiology Network .... GIDEON
Global Information and Early Warning System [FAO] [United Nations]
   (DUND) .... GIEWS
Global Information and Telecommunications Industries ..... GITI
Global Information Exchange System (DOMA) .... GLOBIXS
Global Information Network (EA) .... GIN
Global Information Services, Inc. [Flushing, NY] [Telecommunications]
   (TSSD) .... GIS
Global Information System Technology, Inc. (PCM) .... GIST
Global Instrumentation Control System (IAA) .... GICS
Global Integrated Monitoring System (EERA) .... GIMS
Global Integration and Synthesis [Climate change] (EERA) ..... GIAS
Global Intellicom [NASDAQ symbol] (TTSB) .... GBIT
Global Intellicom, Inc. [NASDAQ symbol] (SAG) .... GBIT
Global Intellicom, Inc. [Associated Press] (SAG) .... GlobIInt
Global Intelligence (IEEE) .... GLINT
Global Interdependence Center (EA) .... GIC
Global International Ltd. [Bulgaria] [ICAO designator] (FAAC) ...... GLS
Global Interrogation Recording and Location System (MCD) ...... GIRLS
Global Inventory Modeling and Monitoring Study (EERA) .... GIMMS
Global Investigation of Pollution in the Marine Environment [National
   Science Foundation] .... GIPME
Global Ionospheric Studies .... GIS
Global Issues [Program] [Department of State] .... GIS
Global Jewish Database [Bar-Ilan University] [Information service or system]
   (CRD) .... GJD
Global Land Cover Test Sites [Remote sensing] (EERA) ..... GLCTS
Global Land Information System (EERA) .... GLIS
Global Land Use [NASA] .... GLU
Global Learning (EA) .... GL
Global Learning and Observations to Benefit the Environment [NASA] .... GLOBE
Global Legislators Organization for a Balanced Environment [International
   coalition] .... GLOBE
Global Lending and Overseas Banking Evaluator [Chase Econometrics]
   [Database] .... GLOBE
Global Lightweight Airborne Navigation Computer Equipment .... GLANCE
Global Limb Photometric Scanning Experiment (MCD) ...... GLIMPSE
Global LORAN Navigation Chart [Air Force] .... GLC
Global Low-Orbiting Message Relay [Satellite] .... GLOMR
Global Management Bureau .... GMB
Global Manned Space Flight Network (SAA) .... GMSFN
Global Marine [NYSE symbol] (TTSB) .... GLM
Global Marine, Inc. [NYSE symbol] (SPSG) .... GLM
Global Marine, Inc. [Associated Press] (SAG) .... GlobM
Global Marine, Inc. (NOAA) .... GMI
Global Maritime Distress and Safety System (DA) .... GMDSS
Global Market Information, Inc. [Associated Press] (SAG) ...... GlbMktI
Global Market Information, Inc. [Associated Press] (SAG) ...... GIMkt
Global Market Information, Inc. [NASDAQ symbol] (SAG) ..... GMKT
Global Marketplace .... GM
Global Matching Figures Test [Education] (EDAC) .... GMF
Global Mobile Personal Communications System [International
   Telecommunications Union] [Geneva, Switzerland] (ECON) .... GMPCS
Global Names Information System [Computer science] .... GNIS
Global Natural Res [NYSE symbol] (TTSB) .... GNR
Global Natural Resources, Inc. [Associated Press] (SAG) ...... GlobNR
Global Natural Resources, Inc. [NYSE symbol] (SPSG) ...... GNR
Global Navigation and Planning Chart [Military] .... GNPC
Global Navigation Chart [Military] .... GNC
Global Navigation Satellite System [Military] .... GLONASS
Global Navigation Satellite System .... GNSS
Global Navigation Satellite System .... GNSS
Global Navigation Satellite System .... GNSS
Global Negotiations .... GN's
Global Network Academy [On-line education] [Information retrieval] ...... GNA

Global Network for Environmental Monitoring [*Defunct*] (EA) .... GNEM
Global Network for Monitoring the Biosphere [*Marine science*] (MSC) .... MABNET
Global Network Navigator [*An on-line publication and Internet reference guide*] (ECON) .... GNN
Global Network of Astronomical Telescopes [*Proposed network*] .... GNAT
Global Observations to Benefit the Environment (EERA) .... GLOBE
Global Observing System (EERA) .... GOS
Global Observing Systems [*Weather*] .... GOS
Global Ocean Carriers [*AMEX symbol*] (TTSB) .... GLO
Global Ocean Carriers Ltd. [*Associated Press*] (SAG) .... GlblOcn
Global Ocean Carriers Ltd. [*AMEX symbol*] (CTT) .... GLO
Global Ocean Ecosystem Dynamics or Global Ocean-Ecosystem Coupling (USDC) .... Globec
Global Ocean Euphotic Zone Study [*Marine science*] (OSRA) .... GOEZS
Global Ocean Floor Analysis and Research [*Navy*] .... GOFAR
Global Ocean Flux Study [*Federal government*] .... GOFS
Global Ocean Observation System (ECON) .... GOOS
Global Ocean Surveillance System (IEEE) .... GLOSS
Global Ocean-Atmosphere-Land System [*Program*] [*Marine science*] (OSRA) .... GOALS
Global OCean-Atmosphere-Land System [*Program*] (USDC) .... GOALS
Global Ocean-Atmosphere-Land-Surface Interactions (EERA) .... GOALS
Global Oceanographic and Meteorological Experiment [*Marine science*] (MSC) .... GLOMEX
Global Omnibus Environmental Survey (EERA) .... GOES
Global One Distribution & Merchandising, Inc. [*Associated Press*] (SAG) .... GlblOne
Global One Distribution & Merchandising, Inc. [*NASDAQ symbol*] (SAG).... GOGO
Global Operating System (IAA) .... GOS
Global Options (EA) .... GO
Global Orbiting Navigational Satellite System [*FAA*] (TAG) .... GLONASS
Global Oscillations at Low Frequency [*Aerospace*] .... GOLF
Global Oscillations Network Group [*National Science Foundation*] .... GONG
Global Outdoors, Inc. [*Associated Press*] (SAG) .... GlobOut
Global Outdoors, Inc. [*NASDAQ symbol*] (SAG) .... GLRS
Global Outreach [*An association*] (EA) .... GO
Global Ozone Monitoring by Occultation of Stars [*Marine science*] (OSRA) .... GOMOS
Global Ozone Monitoring Experiment [*Marine science*] (OSRA) .... GOME
Global Ozone Monitoring Radiometer .... GOMR
Global Ozone Observing System (USDC) GO3OS
Global Ozone Observing System [*Marine science*] (OSRA) .... GOOS
Global Partners Income Fd [*NYSE symbol*] (TTSB) .... GDF
Global Partners Income Fund [*NYSE symbol*] (SPSG) .... GDF
Global Partners Income Fund [*Associated Press*] (SAG) .... GlobPart
Global Perspective Country Outlooks [*Global Perspective, Inc.*] [*Information service or system*] (CRD) .... GPCO
Global Perspectives in Education (EA) .... GPE
Global Pharmaceutical Corp. [*Associated Press*] (SAG) .... GlobalPh
Global Pharmaceutical Corp. [*NASDAQ symbol*] (SAG) .... GLPC
Global Plotting Chart [*Air Force*] .... GPC
Global Point Warning [*Military*] .... GPW
Global Position System [*Instrument*] (EERA) .... GPS
Global Position System Consortium (EERA) .... GPSCO
Global Position System Integrity Monitoring [*System*] (EERA) .... GPSIM
Global Positioning Satellite .... GPS
Global Positioning Satellite System .... GPSS
Global Positioning System [*Formerly, NAVSTAR*] [*Air Force*] .... GPS
Global Positioning System/Inertial Navigation System [*Air Force*] .... GPS/INS
Global Positioning System Network Control Center [*Air Force*] (MCD) .... GPS NCC
Global Positioning System Program Contractor [*Air Force*] (MCD) .... GPS PC
Global Positioning System-Active .... GPSA
Global Positioning System-Passive .... GPSP
Global Precipitation Chemistry Project [*Study of rain properties*] .... GPCP
Global Precipitation Climatology Center [*Marine science*] (OSRA) .... GPCC
Global Precipitation Climatology Centre (EERA) .... GPCC
Global Precipitation Climatology Project [*Marine science*] (OSRA) .... GPCP
Global Precision System .... GPS
Global Processing Center (EERA) .... GPC
Global Program Line Editor [*Beagle Bros.*] .... GPLE
Global Program on AIDS [*Acquired Immune Deficiency Syndrome*] [*WHO*] .... GPA
Global Protection against Limited Strike [*Military*] .... GPALS
Global RADAR for Ocean Waves .... GLOW
Global Radio Navigation System [*Aviation*] (DA) .... GRANAS
Global Range Ballistic Missile [*Air Force*] .... GRBM
Global Range Missile [*Air Force*] .... GRM
Global Reach Internet Connection [*Computer science*] .... GRIC
Global Readiness Index .... GRI
Global Reference Atmosphere Model (SSD) .... GRAM
Global Reference Code [*Developed by Smithsonian Institution*] .... GRC
Global Regular Expression and Print [*Computer science*] (CDE) .... grep
Global Regular-Expression Purser [*Computer science*] .... GREP
Global Renewable Energy Services [*Swinden, England*] [*Commercial firm*] .... GRES
Global Res [*NASDAQ symbol*] (TTSB) .... GLRS
Global Rescue Alarm Network [*Program*] [*Navy*] .... GRAN
Global Resource Information Data Base [*UNEP*] [*Nairobi, Kenya*] [*Information service or system*] (IID) .... GRID
Global Resource Information Database [*NASA*] .... GRID
Global Resources, Inc. [*Associated Press*] (SAG) .... GlbRsc
Global Resources, Inc. [*NASDAQ symbol*] (SAG) .... GLRS
Global Resources Information System .... GRIS
Global Roaming Internet Connection [*Computer science*] .... GRIC
Global Satellite Data Acquisition Team [*Marine science*] (OSRA) .... GSAT

Global Satellite Data Acquisition Team (USDC) .... GSAT
Global Schoolhouse [*Computer science Telecommunications*] .... GSH
Global Sea Level Observing System .... GLOSS
Global Sea Level Observing System [*Marine science*] (OSRA) .... GLOSS
Global Sea Surface Temperature Computation .... GOSSTCOMP
Global Severity Index [*Medicine*] (DMAA) .... GSI
Global Shared Resources [*Computer science*] (IBMDP) .... GSR
Global Simulation Control Center .... GSCC
Global Small Cap Fund [*AMEX symbol*] (TTSB) .... GSG
Global Small Cap Fund, Inc. [*Associated Press*] (SAG) .... GlobSml
Global Small Capital Fund [*AMEX symbol*] (SPSG) .... GSG
Global Solar Radiation Index (PDAA) .... GSRI
Global Space Station [*Proposed by NASA and ESA*] .... GSS
Global Space Transport (IAA) .... GST
Global Space-Based Positioning and Navigation System .... GSBPS
Global Spectral Ocean Wave Model .... GSOWM
Global Spill Management [*Associated Press*] (SAG) .... GlbSpill
Global Spill Management, Inc. [*NASDAQ symbol*] (SAG) .... GSMI
Global Spill Mgmt [*NASDAQ symbol*] (TTSB) .... GEGID
Global Strategy Corp. [*Vancouver Stock Exchange symbol*] .... GSY
Global Strategy Fund [*British*] .... GSF
Global Stratotype Section and Point [*Paleontology*] .... GSSP
Global Subsurface System (DWSG) .... GSS
Global Surveillance Station (IAA) .... GSS
Global Surveillance System [*Air Force*] .... GSS
Global System for Mobile Communication [*Computer science*] .... GSM
Global System for Mobiles [*European mobile-phone network*] (ECON) .... GSM
Global System of Trade Preferences [*United Nations Conference on Trade and Development*] [*Proposed*] .... GSTP
Global Systems, Inc. [*ICAO designator*] (FAAC) .... XGS
Global Tape Recording Exchange (EA) .... GTRE
Global Technology Watch [*Information service or system*] (IID) .... GTW
Global Tele Solutions Wrrt [*NASDAQ symbol*] (TTSB) .... GTSTW
Global Telecomm Solutions [*NASDAQ symbol*] (TTSB) .... GTST
Global Telecommunication System [*World Meteorological Organization*] (IID) .... GTS
Global Telecommunications Solutions, Inc. [*Associated Press*] (SAG) .... GlbTel
Global Telecommunications Solutions, Inc. [*Associated Press*] (SAG) .... GlobTele
Global Telecommunications Solutions, Inc. [*NASDAQ symbol*] (SAG) .... GTST
Global Telemedia Intl [*NASDAQ symbol*] (TTSB) .... GTMIE
Global Temperature and Salinity Pilot Project (EERA) .... GTSPP
Global Terrestrial Observing System [*Marine science*] (OSRA) .... GTOS
Global Terrestrial Observing System (USDC) .... GTOS
Global Time and Position [*Navigation systems*] .... GTP
Global Title Translation .... GTL
Global Tomorrow Coalition (GNE) .... GTC
Global Tomorrow Coalition (EA) .... GTC
Global Total Return Fund [*Associated Press*] (SAG) .... GlobTR
Global Tracking [*RADAR*] .... GLOTRAC
Global Tracking Systems .... GTS
Global Transportation Network (DOMA) .... GTN
Global Treasury Services [*Barclays Bank*] [*British*] .... GTS
Global Trend Network (GNE) .... GTN
Global Trends Network [*USA*] (EERA) .... GTN
Global Tropospheric Chemistry Program [*Federal government*] .... GTCP
Global Tropospheric Experiment [*National Oceanic and Atmospheric Administration*] .... GTE
Global University Funding .... GUF
Global Utilization of Streptokinase and Tissue Plasminogen Activator for Occluded Coronary Arteries [*Cardiology study*] .... GUSTO
Global Utilization of Streptokinase and TPA [*Tissue Plasminogen Activator*]for Occluded Arteries [*Comparative study*] .... GUSTO
Global Vegetation Index (MCD) .... GVI
Global Videophone Standard [*Telecommunications*] (CDE) .... GVS
Global Village Commun [*NASDAQ symbol*] (TTSB) .... GVIL
Global Village Communications, Inc. [*NASDAQ symbol*] (SAG) .... GVIL
Global Village Communictions, Inc. [*Associated Press*] (SAG) .... GlbVilag
Global Virtual Private Network [*Computer science*] (CDE) .... GVPN
Global War Avoidance Telecommunications System (MCD) .... GLOWATS
Global Warming International Center [*An association*] (EA) .... GWIC
Global Water (EA) .... GW
Global Weather Central .... GWC
Global Weather Dynamics, Inc. [*ICAO designator*] (FAAC) .... XGW
Global Weather Experiment [*Marine science*] (MSC) .... GWE
Global Weather Facsimile Network (MCD) .... GWFN
Global Women of African Heritage (EA) .... GWAH
Global Yield Fund, Inc. [*NYSE symbol*] (SPSG) .... PGY
Globalink, Inc. [*Associated Press*] (SAG) .... Globlink
Globalink, Inc. [*AMEX symbol*] (SAG) .... GNK
Globally Averaged Surface Temperature (EERA) .... GAST
Globally Unique Identifier (PCM) .... GUID
Globally Unique Identifiers [*Microsoft Corp.*] [*Computer science*] (PCM) .... GUID
Globalstar Telecommunications Ltd. [*Associated Press*] (SAG) .... Globalstr
Globalstar Telecommunications Ltd. [*NASDAQ symbol*] (SAG) .... GSTRF
Globalstar Telecommunictions Ltd. [*Associated Press*] (SAG) .... Globlstr
Global-Warming Factor [*Meteorology*] .... GWF
Global-Warming Index [*Meteorology*] .... GWI
Global-Warming Potential [*Meteorology*] .... GWP
Global-Wide Help and Information Systems [*On-line help system for Mosaic developers*] .... GWHIS
Globe Air Cargo [*Antigua and Barbuda*] [*ICAO designator*] (FAAC) .... GBC
Globe and Mail [*Newspaper databank*] [*Canada*] (NITA) .... GAM
Globe and Mail Data Base [*Info Globe*] [*Information service or system*] (CRD) .... GAM

Globe and Mail, Toronto, ON, Canada [*Library symbol Library of Congress*] (LCLS) ... CaOTGM
Globe and Mail, Toronto, Ontario [*Library symbol National Library of Canada*] (NLC) ... OTGM
Globe, AZ [*Location identifier FAA*] (FAAL) ... GAZ
Globe, AZ [*FM radio station call letters*] (RBYB) ... KHOT
Globe, AZ [*AM radio station call letters*] ... KJAA
Globe, AZ [*FM radio station call letters*] ... KRXS
Globe Ball Valve ... GBV
Globe Business Resources [*NASDAQ symbol*] (TTSB) ... GLBE
Globe Business Resources, Inc. [*NASDAQ symbol*] (SAG) ... GLBE
Globe Business Resources, Inc. [*Associated Press*] (SAG) ... GlbeBus
Globe Encyclopaedia [*A publication*] (ROG) ... Gl Ency
Globe Free Press, Grand Junction, IA [*Library symbol Library of Congress*] (LCLS) ... IaGjG
Globe Mackay Cable and Radio Corp. [*Philippines*] [*Telecommunications*] ... GMCR
Globe Microphone Evaluation ... GME
Globe Stop Valve ... GSV
Globe Thermometer ... GT
Globe Valve (AAG) ... GLV
Globes [*Freight*] ... GLBS
Globetrotters' Club (EAIO) ... GT's
Globe-Union, Inc., Milwaukee, WI [*Library symbol Library of Congress*] (LCLS) ... WMG
Globigerina [*Quality of the bottom*] [*Nautical charts*] ... GI
Globin Insulin ... GI
Globoid Cell Leukodystrophy [*Medicine*] (DMAA) ... GCL
Globular [*Referring to proteins*] [*Biochemistry*] (DAVI) ... G
Globular ... GLOB
Globular Cluster [*Astrophysics*] ... GC
Globular-Fibrous [*Biochemistry*] ... GF
Globulin ... G
Globulin ... GLOB
Globulin/Albumin [*Ratio*] [*Medicine*] (DMAA) ... G/A
Globulin-Albumin [*Biochemistry*] (DAVI) ... G-ALB
Globulin-Binding Insulin [*Medicine*] (DMAA) ... GBI
Globus (BJA) ... GI
Globus Pallidus [*Brain anatomy*] ... GP
Glockenspiel [*Music*] ... GLOCK
Glomerular Basal Lamina [*Medicine*] (DAVI) ... GBL
Glomerular Basement Membrane [*Medicine*] ... GBM
Glomerular Basement Membrane-Reactive Antibodies [*Immunology*] ... GBM-rAb
Glomerular Capillary Wall [*Anatomy*] ... GCW
Glomerular Complement Receptor [*Immunology*] ... GCR
Glomerular Epithelial Cell [*Medicine Medicine*] (DMAA) ... GEC
Glomerular Filtrate [*Medicine*] ... GF
Glomerular Filtration Rate [*Nephrology*] ... GFR
Glomerular Index [*Medicine*] (AAMN) ... GI
Glomerular Nephritis [*Medicine*] ... GN
Glomerular Plasma Flow [*Medicine*] (DMAA) ... GPF
Glomerular Sclerosis [*Medicine*] ... GS
Glomerular-Stimulating Hormone [*Endocrinology*] (MAE) ... GSH
Glomerulocystic Kidney [*Nephrology*] ... GCK
Glomerulo-Tubulo-Nephritis [*Medicine*] ... GITN
Glomerulo-Tubulo-Nephritis [*Medicine*] ... GTN
Glomus intraradices [*A fungus*] ... GI
Glon Kristy Resources [*Vancouver Stock Exchange symbol*] ... GKI
Glons [*Belgium ICAO location identifier*] (ICLI) ... EBGL
Gloom ... G
Gloria [*Glory*] [*Latin*] ... GL
Gloria [*Kyrgyzstan*] [*FAA designator*] (FAAC) ... GLO
Gloria Chandler Recordings [*Record label*] ... Chan
Gloria Loring Fan Club [*Defunct*] (EA) ... GLFC
Gloria Patri [*Glory to the Father*] [*Latin*] ... GP
Glory Explorations [*Vancouver Stock Exchange symbol*] ... GYE
Glosa Education Organisation (EAIO) ... GEO
Glosa International Language Network (EAIO) ... GILN
Gloss (DSA) ... Gl
Gloss (WDMC) ... gl
Gloss (VRA) ... glo
Gloss Low Emission [*Ink*] (DGA) ... GLE
Gloss Low Tack [*Ink*] (DGA) ... GLT
Glossa Ordinaria [*A publication*] (DSA) ... Gl Ord
Glossaria Latina [*A publication*] (OCD) ... Gloss Lat
Glossary (ROG) ... GL
Glossary ... GLOS
Glossary ... GLOSS
Glossary Function List ... GFL
Glossary of EPA [*Environmental Protection Agency*] **Acronyms** [*A publication*] (EPA) ... GEA
Glossary of Merchant Ship Types (MCD) ... GMST
Glossary of Naval Ship Types (MCD) ... GNST
[*A*] **Glossary of the Aramaic Inscriptions** [*A publication*] (BJA) ... GAI
Glossopharyngeal Breathing ... GPB
Glossy (WDMC) ... gl
GLOTRAC [*Global Tracking*] **Adjustment** ... GLAD
Gloucester [*Massachusetts*] [*Seismograph station code, US Geological Survey*] (SEIS) ... GLO
Gloucester [*British depot code*] ... GLO
Gloucester [*City in England*] (ROG) ... GLOSTER
Gloucester [*City in England*] (ROG) ... GLOUC
Gloucester and Bristol [*Diocese*] (ROG) ... G & B
Gloucester and Cheltenham/Staverton [*British ICAO location identifier*] (ICLI) ... EGBJ
Gloucester City Library, Gloucester City, NJ [*Library symbol Library of Congress*] (LCLS) ... NjGl
Gloucester City News, Gloucester City, NJ [*Library symbol Library of Congress*] (LCLS) ... NjGlN
Gloucester County College, Sewell, NJ [*Library symbol Library of Congress*] (LCLS) ... NjSewG
Gloucester County College, Voorhees, NJ [*OCLC symbol*] (OCLC) ... NGC
Gloucester County Historical Society, Woodbury, NJ [*Library symbol Library of Congress*] (LCLS) ... NjWdHi
Gloucester Fisheries Association (EA) ... GFA
Gloucester High School, Ontario [*Library symbol National Library of Canada*] (BIB) ... OGHS
Gloucester Lyceum and Sawyer Free Public Library, Gloucester, MA [*Library symbol Library of Congress*] (LCLS) ... MGl
Gloucester, MA [*FM radio station call letters*] ... WBOQ
Gloucester Master Mariners Association (EA) ... GMMA
Gloucester Public Library, Beriault Branch, Beriault, ON, Canada [*Library symbol*] [*Library of Congress*] (LCLS) ... CaOGB
Gloucester Public Library, E.D. Jones Branch, Gloucester, ON, Canada [*Library symbol*] [*Library of Congress*] (LCLS) ... CaOGEDJ
Gloucester Township [*Blackwood*] **Library, Blackwood, NJ** [*Library symbol Library of Congress*] (LCLS) ... NjBla
Gloucester, VA [*AM radio station call letters*] ... WXGM
Gloucester, VA [*FM radio station call letters*] ... WXGM-FM
Gloucestershire [*County in England*] ... GLOS
Gloucestershire [*County in England*] (ODBW) ... Glos
Gloucestershire [*County in England*] (ROG) ... GLOUC
Gloucestershire [*County in England*] (BARN) ... Gloucester
Gloucestershire [*County in England*] ... GLOUCS
Gloucestershire Regiment [*Military British*] (ROG) ... GLOUC R
Gloucestershire Regiment [*Military unit*] [*British*] ... GR
Gloucestershire Technical Information Service (NITA) ... GTIS
Glove ... GLV
Glove Collector Club (EA) ... GCC
Glover's Municipal Corporations [*A publication*] (DLA) ... Glov Mun Cor
Glovers' Mutual Aid Society [*A union*] [*British*] ... GMAS
Gloversville Free Library, Gloversville, NY [*Library symbol*] [*Library of Congress*] (LCLS) ... NGlo
Gloversville, NY [*AM radio station call letters*] ... WENT
Glovertown Public Library, Glovertown, NF, Canada [*Library symbol Library of Congress*] (LCLS) ... CaNfGlo
Glovertown Public Library, Newfoundland [*Library symbol National Library of Canada*] (NLC) ... NFGLO
Glow Discharge [*Photovoltaic energy systems*] ... GD
Glow Plug ... GLPG
Glow Tube (IAA) ... GT
Glow-Discharge Lamp [*Spectrometry*] ... GDL
Glow-Discharge Lamp Source [*Spectrometry*] ... GDLS
Glow-Discharge Mass Spectroscopy [*or Spectrometry*] ... GDMS
Glow-Discharge Optical Emission Spectroscopy ... GDOES
Glow-Discharge Spectrometry ... GDS
Glowna Komisja Badania Zbrodni Hitlerowskich [*A publication*] (BJA) ... GKBZH
Glowna Zydowska Organizacja Bojowa [*A publication*] (BJA) ... GZOB
Glucagon (DMAA) ... GCG
Glucagon [*Endocrinology*] ... Gg
Glucagon [*Medicine*] (DMAA) ... Gln
Glucagon Receptor (DMAA) ... GCGR
Glucagon-Free Insulin [*Medicine*] (DMAA) ... GFI
Glucagon-Like Immunoreactivity [*or Immunoreactant*] [*Endocrinology*] ... GLI
Glucagon-Like Peptide [*Biochemistry*] ... GLP
Glucinium [*Also, Gl*] [*Old name for chemical element beryllium*] ... G
Glucinium [*Also, G*] [*Old name for chemical element beryllium*] ... Gl
Gluckstadt, MS [*FM radio station call letters*] ... WLIN
Gluckstadt, MS [*FM radio station call letters*] (RBYB) ... WYOY-FM
Glucoamylase [*An enzyme*] ... GA
Glucoamylase Unit [*Of hydrolytic enzyme activity*] ... GAU
Glucocorticoid [*Endocrinology*] ... GC
Glucocorticoid Hormone [*Endocrinology*] ... GCH
Glucocorticoid Receptor (DMAA) ... GCGR
Glucocorticoid Receptor (DMAA) ... GCR
Glucocorticoid Receptor [*Endocrinology*] ... GR
Glucocorticoid Receptor Protein [*Biochemistry*] ... GRP
Glucocorticoid Responsive Element [*Endocrinology*] ... GRE
Glucocorticoid-Remediable Aldosteronism [*Medicine*] ... GRA
Glucoheptanoic Acid [*Biochemistry*] (DAVI) ... GHA
Glucoheptonate [*USAN*] [*Organic chemistry*] ... GLUCEPTATE
Gluconic Acid [*Biochemistry*] ... GlcA
Glucono-delta-Lactone [*Organic chemistry*] ... GDL
Glucophosphate Isomerase [*An enzyme*] ... GPI
(Glucopyranosyl)fluorothymine [*Biochemistry*] ... GFT
Glucosamine [*Biochemistry*] ... GlcN
Glucose [*Also, Glc, GLUC*] [*A sugar*] ... G
Glucose [*Also, G, GLUC*] [*A sugar*] ... Glc
Glucose [*Organic chemistry*] (DAVI) ... GLU
Glucose [*Also, G, Glc*] [*A sugar*] ... GLUC
Glucose/Acetone [*Biochemistry*] (DAVI) ... GA
Glucose and Saline [*Medicine*] ... GS
Glucose Consumption Rate ... GCR
Glucose Controlled Insulin Infusion System [*Medicine*] (DMAA) ... GCIIS
Glucose Electrolyte Solution [*Medicine*] ... GES
Glucose/Galactose Malabsorption [*Medicine*] ... GGM
Glucose in Normal Saline [*Medicine*] ... G/NS
Glucose in Water [*Medicine*] ... G/W
Glucose Infusion Rate [*Physiology*] ... GIR
Glucose Infusion Test [*Diabetes detection*] (CPH) ... GIT

Glucose, Insulin, and Potassium [*Solution*] [*Medicine*] .... GIK
Glucose Insulin Tolerance Test [*Medicine*] .... GITT
Glucose:Nitrogen [*Ratio*] .... G:N
Glucose Oxidase [*Also, GO, GOD*] [*An enzyme*] (AAMN) .... glu ox
Glucose Oxidase [*Also, glu ox, GOD*] [*An enzyme*] .... GO
Glucose Oxidase [*Also, glu ox, GO*] [*An enzyme*] .... GOD
Glucose Oxidase Test [*Organic chemistry*] (DAVI) .... GOT
Glucose Oxidase-Peroxidase [*Also, PGO*] [*Enzyme mixture*] .... GOD-POD
Glucose Phosphate [*Biochemistry*] .... GP
Glucose Phosphorylase B [*An enzyme*] .... GPB
Glucose, Post Prandial [*Clinical chemistry*] .... GLPP
Glucose Regulated Protein [*Biochemistry*] .... GRP
Glucose Therapy [*Medicine*] (DMAA) .... GT
Glucose to Nitrogen Ratio [*Medicine*] (AAMN) .... G/N R
Glucose Tolerance [*Medicine*] .... GT
Glucose Tolerance Factor [*Medicine*] .... GTF
Glucose Tolerance Factor [*Medicine*] (DMAA) .... GTF
Glucose Tolerance Test [*Medicine*] .... GTT
Glucose Transporter [*Biochemistry*] .... GLUT
Glucose Transporter [*Biochemistry*] .... GT
Glucose Turnover [*Physiology*] .... GT
Glucose-1-phosphate [*Biochemistry*] G1P
Glucose-6-Phosphatase [*Organic chemistry*] (DAVI) G-6-Pase
Glucose-6-phosphate Dehydrogenase [*Also, GPD, G6PDH*] [*An enzyme*] G6PD
Glucose-6-phosphate Dehydrogenase [*Also, GPD, G6PD*] [*An enzyme*] G6PDH
Glucose-6-phosphate Dehydrogenase [*Also, G6PD, G6PDH*] [*An enzyme*] .... GPD
Glucose-6-Phosphate Dehydrogenase Enzyme Variant A [*Organic chemistry*] (DAVI) G-6-PDHA
Glucose-Free Dialysate [*Nephrology*] .... GFD
Glucose-Free Hanks [*Solution*] [*Cell incubation medium*] .... GFH
Glucose-L-Phosphate (DMAA) .... GLP
Glucose-Ringer-Phosphate Solution .... GRPS
Glucosidase (DMAA) .... GLUC
Glucosyltransferase (DMAA) .... GTF
Glucuronic Acid [*Also, GlcUA*] [*Biochemistry*] .... GA
Glucuronic Acid [*Also, GA*] [*Biochemistry*] .... GlcUA
Glucuronidase [*An enzyme*] .... GCR
Glucuronidase [*An enzyme*] .... GUS
Glucuronide [*Biochemistry*] (AAMN) .... Glucur
Glucuronosyltransferase [*An enzyme*] .... GT
Glue Line Heating .... GLH
Glue Weld Joint .... GWJ
Gluecksburg [*Germany ICAO location identifier*] (ICLI) .... EDCA
Glued Laminated Wood (PDAA) .... GLULAM
Glumitocin [*Endocrinology*] .... GT
Glutagen Sensitive Enteropathy [*Medicine*] .... GSE
Glutamate [*An amino acid*] (DOG) .... glu
Glutamate Acid Decarboxylase [*An enzyme*] .... GAD
[*The*] **Glutamate Association - United States** (EA) .... TGA
Glutamate Decarboxylase [*An enzyme*] .... GAD
Glutamate Dehydrogenase [*An enzyme*] .... GD
Glutamate Dehydrogenase [*An enzyme*] .... GDH
Glutamate Dehydrogenase (DMAA) .... GLD
Glutamate Dehydrogenase [*Organic chemistry*] .... GLDH
Glutamate Manufacturers Technical Committee (EA) .... GMTC
Glutamate Receptor [*Biochemistry*] .... GluR
Glutamate Receptor Interacting Protein [*Neurochemistry*] .... GRIP
Glutamate Semialdehyde Aminotransferase [*An enzyme*] .... GSA-AT
Glutamate Synthase (BARN) .... GOGAT
Glutamate-Binding Protein [*Biochemistry*] .... GBP
Glutamatesemialdehyde [*Organic chemistry*] .... GSA
Glutamic Acid [*One-letter symbol; see Glu*] [*An amino acid*] .... E
Glutamic Acid [*See also Glu*] [*An amino acid*] .... GA
Glutamic Acid [*Also, E, GA*] [*An amino acid*] .... Glu
Glutamic Acid [*An amino acid*] (DOG) .... glu
Glutamic Acid [*or Glutamine*] [*Also, Z An amino acid*] .... Glx
Glutamic Acid [*or Glutamine*] [*Also, Glx Symbol An amino acid*] .... Z
Glutamic Acid-Alanine-Tyrosine [*Biopolymer*] .... GAT$_{10}$
Glutamic-Oxaloacetic Transaminase [*Also, AAT, ASAT, AST*] [*An enzyme*] .... GOT
Glutamic-Pyruvic Transaminase [*Also, AAT, ALAT, ALT*] [*An enzyme*] .... GPT
Glutamic-Pyruvic Transaminase-C [*An enzyme*] (OA) .... GPT-C
Glutamine [*Also, Q*] [*An amino acid*] (DOG) .... gin
Glutamine [*or Glu(NH$_2$)*] [*Also, Q An amino acid*] .... Gln
Glutamine [*An amino acid*] (DAVI) .... Glu
Glutamine [*An amino acid*] (BARN) .... GluN
Glutamine [*or Gln*] [*Also, Q An amino acid*] .... Glu(NH$_2$)
Glutamine [*An amino acid*] (DAVI) .... GLUTAM
Glutamine [*One-letter symbol; see Gln*] .... Q
Glutamine Synthetase [*Also, GS*] [*An enzyme*] .... GNS
Glutamine Synthetase [*Also, GNS*] [*An enzyme*] .... GS
Glutamine-Transfer Ribonucleic Acid Synthetase .... GlnRS
Glutaminyl-RNA Synthetase [*An enzyme*] .... GlmRS
Glutamyl Transferase [*Liver-function test*] (CPH) .... GT
Glutamyl Transpeptidase [*An enzyme*] .... GT
Glutamyl Transpeptidase [*An enzyme*] .... GTP
Glutamylaminomethylsulfonic Acid [*Biochemistry*] .... GAMSA
Glutamyl(methoxy)naphthylamide [*Biochemistry*] .... GMNA
Glutaraldehyde [*Biochemistry*] .... GA
Glutaraldehyde-Dichromate [*Fixative*] .... GD
Glutathione [*Biochemistry*] .... GSH
Glutathione [*Oxidized*] [*Biochemistry*] .... GSSG
Glutathione Bicarbonate Ringer [*Solution mixture*] .... GBR
Glutathione Peroxidase [*An enzyme*] (MAE) .... GP
Glutathione Peroxidase [*An enzyme*] .... GPx
Glutathione Reductase [*An enzyme*] .... GR
Glutathione Reductase [*An enzyme*] (DAVI) .... GSSG-R
Glutathione S-Transferase [*An enzyme*] .... GST
Glutathione-Insulin Transhydrogenase [*An enzyme*] (MAE) .... GIT
Glutathione-SH [*Reduced glutathione*] [*Biochemistry*] .... GSH
Gluten Intolerance Group [*Later, GIGNA*] (EA) .... GIG
Gluten Intolerance Group of North America (EA) .... GIGNA
Gluten-Free [*Diet*] .... GF
Gluten-Free Diet .... GFD
Gluten-Sensitive Enteropathy [*Medicine*] .... GSE
Gluteus Medius [*Anatomy*] .... GM
Glyceraldehyde [*Biochemistry*] .... Gra
Glyceraldehyde Phosphate [*Biochemistry*] .... GAP
Glyceraldehyde Phosphate Dehydrogenase [*Organic chemistry*] (MAH) .... GAPD
Glyceraldehyde-3-Phosphate [*Biochemistry*] (DAVI) G-3-P
Glyceraldehydephosphate Dehydrogenase [*Also, GPDH*] [*An enzyme*] .... GAPDH
Glycerate-3-Phosphate [*Biochemistry*] (DAVI) .... PG
Glyceric Acid [*Biochemistry*] .... Gri
Glycerin .... GLYC
Glycerin and Water Enema [*Medicine*] .... GWE
Glycerin in Water [*Medicine*] (DHSM) .... Glyc in W
Glycerine .... GLYCN
Glycerine and Oleochemicals Association (EA) .... G & OA
Glycerine Ball Memory .... GBM
Glycerine in Water [*Medicine*] .... GW
Glycerine Producers Association (EA) .... GPA
Glycerinisopropylidene Ether [*Organic chemistry*] .... GIE
Glyceritum [*Glycerite*] (MAE) .... glyc
Glycerol [*Organic chemistry*] (DAVI) .... Gly
Glycerol [*Biochemistry*] .... Gro
Glycerol Dichlorohydrin [*Organic chemistry*] .... GDCH
Glycerol Kinase [*An enzyme*] (MAE) .... GK
Glycerol Kinase Deficiency [*Medicine*] .... GKD
Glycerol Monolaurate [*Food-grade lipid*] [*Pharmacology*] .... GML
Glycerol Triacetate [*Known as Triacetin*] [*Organic chemistry*] .... GTA
Glycerolphosphate Dehydrogenase [*An enzyme*] .... GPDH
Glycerone [*Biochemistry*] .... Grn
Glycerophophas [*Pharmacy*] (ROG) .... GLYCEROPH
Glycerophosphate [*Biochemistry*] .... GP
Glycerophosphate Dehydrogenase (MAE) .... GDH
Glycerophosphate Dehydrogenase .... GPD
Glyceryl Distearate [*Organic chemistry*] .... GD
Glyceryl Guaiacolate [*Expectorant*] (AAMN) .... GG
Glyceryl Methacrylate [*Organic chemistry*] (DAVI) .... GMA
Glyceryl Monooleate [*Organic chemistry*] .... GMO
Glyceryl Monostearate [*Organic chemistry*] .... GMS
Glyceryl Trinitrate [*Also, NG, NTG*] [*Explosive, vasodilator*] .... GTN
Glyceryl Triricinoleate [*Organic chemistry*] .... GTRO
Glycerylphosphorylcholine [*Biochemistry*] .... GPC
Glycerylphosphorylethanolamine [*Biochemistry*] (MAE) .... GPE
Glycidoxycoumarin [*Biochemistry*] .... GOC
Glycidydiisopropylidenexylitol [*Organic chemistry*] .... GDX
Glycidyl Azide Polymer [*Chemistry*] .... GAP
Glycidyl Methacrylate [*Organic chemistry*] .... GMA
Glycidyldiisopropylidenearabitol [*Organic chemistry*] .... GDA
Glycidylisopropylideneglycerol [*Organic chemistry*] .... GIG
Glycinate [*Organic chemistry*] .... gly
Glycine [*One-letter symbol; see Gly*] [*An amino acid*] .... G
Glycine [*Also, G*] [*An amino acid*] .... Gly
Glycine [*An amino acid*] (DOG) .... gly
Glycine Amide Phosphoribosyl Synthetase (DMAA) .... GARS
Glycine Ethyl Ester (MAE) .... GEE
Glycine, Glycine Phenylalanine, Leucine [*A synthetic peptide*] .... GGPL
Glycine Mosaic Virus [*Plant pathology*] .... GMV
Glycine Mottle Virus [*Plant pathology*] .... GMOV
Glycine Receptor [*Organic chemistry*] .... GlyR
Glycine-Buffered Saline [*Microbiology*] .... GBS
Glycinecresol Red [*An indicator*] [*Chemistry*] .... GCR
Glycinenaphthol Violet [*An indicator*] [*Chemistry*] .... GNV
Glycinergic Interplexiform Cell [*Physiology*] .... Gly-IPC
Glycine-Rich Beta-Globulin [*Immunology*] .... GBG
Glycine-Rich Gamma-Glycoprotein [*Immunology*] .... GGG
Glycine-Rich Glycoprotein (DMAA) .... GRG
Glycinethymol Blue [*An indicator*] [*Chemistry*] .... GTB
Glycinxylidide [*Biochemistry*] .... GX
Glycogen [*Biochemistry*] .... G
Glycogen and Fat-Free Solid (DMAA) .... GFFS
Glycogen Phosphorylase [*An enzyme*] .... GP
Glycogen Storage Disease [*Medicine*] .... GSD
Glycogen Synthase Kinase [*An enzyme*] .... GSK
Glycogenic Unit [*Medicine*] .... GU
Glycogenosis Type 1 [*Medicine*] GT1
Glycohemoglobin [*Biochemistry, medicine*] .... GHb
Glycol (KSC) .... GLY
Glycol Dimethacrylate (MCD) .... GDMA
Glycol Dimethyl Ether [*Organic chemistry*] .... GDME
Glycol Dinitrate [*Organic chemistry*] .... GDN
Glycol Methacrylate [*Organic chemistry*] .... GMA
Glycol Trim Console (MCD) .... GTC
Glycol Trim Unit (MCD) .... GTU
Glycolic Acid Oxidase [*An enzyme*] .... GAO
Glycolic Aldehyde Dinitrophenylhydrazone [*Organic chemistry*] .... GADNPH
Glycolipoprotein (DMAA) .... GLP
Glycolyl Phthalate [*Organic chemistry*] .... GP
Glycolytic Substrate .... GS
Glycomacropeptide [*Biochemistry*] .... GMP

Glycophorin A [*Biochemistry*] .... GPA
Glycophorin Binding Protein [*Biochemistry*] .... GBP
Glycoprotein .... GP
Glycoprotein B [*Biochemistry*] .... GPB
Glycoprotein I (DMAA) .... GPI
Glycosaminoglycan [*Biochemistry*] .... GAG
Glycosaminoglycans, Glycoproteins, and Glycolipids Group [*Informal name for organization that later became Society for Complex Carbohydrates*] ...... 4G's
Glycosphingolipid [*Biochemistry*] .... GL
Glycosphingolipid [*Biochemistry*] .... GSL
Glycosylated Hemoglobin [*Clinical chemistry*] .... GHB
Glycosylated Plasma Protein [*Clinical chemistry*] .... GPP
Glycosylated Serum Protein .... GSP
Glycosylated Whole Blood [*Clinical chemistry*] .... GWB
Glycosylation Site Binding Protein [*Biochemistry*] .... GSBP
Glycosyl-Phosphatidylinositol [*Biochemistry*] .... GPI
Glycotyrosine [*Biochemistry*] .... GT
Glycylglycine [*Organic chemistry*] .... GG
Glycyrrhiza [*Licorice*] [*Pharmacology*] (ROG) .... GLYCYRRH
Glyn and Jameson's English Bankruptcy Reports [*1821-28*] [*A publication*] (DLA) .... G & J
Glyn and Jameson's English Bankruptcy Reports [*1821-28*] [*A publication*] (DLA) .... Gl & J
Glyn and Jameson's English Bankruptcy Reports [*1821-28*] [*A publication*] (DLA) .... Glyn & J
Glyn and Jameson's English Bankruptcy Reports [*1821-28*] [*A publication*] (DLA) .... Glyn & J (Eng)
Glyn and Jameson's English Bankruptcy Reports [*1821-28*] [*A publication*] (DLA) .... Glyn & Jam
Glyn Valley Railway [*Formerly, E & GVR*] [*Wales*] .... GVR
Glyndon Elementary School, Glyndon, MN [*Library symbol*] [*Library of Congress*] (LCLS) .... MnGlyE
Glyndon-Felton High School, Glyndon, MN [*Library symbol*] [*Library of Congress*] (LCLS) .... MnGlyHS
Glynn on Water Powers [*A publication*] (DLA) .... Glynn Wat Pow
Glyoxal Bis(guanylhydrazone) [*Organic chemistry*] .... GAG
Glyoxal Bis(o-hydroxyanil) [*An indicator*] [*Chemistry*] .... GBHA
Glyoxalase [*An enzyme*] .... GLO
Glyoxylic Acid [*Biochemistry*] (OA) .... GA
Glyph (VRA) .... gly
Glypototheca (VRA) .... glypto
GMD-Informationszentrum fuer Informationswissenschaft und -Praxis [*GMD Information Center for Information Science and Information Work*] [*Information service or system*] (IID) .... GMD-IZ
Gmelin Formula Index [*Gmelin-Institut fuer Anorganische Chemie und Grenzgebiete*] [*Germany Information service or system*] (CRD) .... GFI
Gmelinite [*A zeolite*] .... GME
GMI Engineering and Management Institute, Flint, MI [*Library symbol Library of Congress*] (LCLS) .... MiFliG
GMIS, Inc. [*NASDAQ symbol*] (SPSG) .... GMIS
GMT [*Greenwich Mean Time*] of Orbital Midnight .... TOM
G-Myeloma Protein [*Biochemistry*] (MAH) .... G-MP
G-Myeloma Proteins [*Biochemistry*] (DAVI) .... G-MP
GN & C [*Guidance, Navigation, and Control*] Flight Test Station (MCD) ..... GNCFTS
GN & C [*Guidance, Navigation, and Control*] Test Station (MCD) .... GNCTS
GN & C [*Guidance, Navigation and Control*] Test Station [*NASA*] (NASA) .... GTS
Gnangara [*Australia Geomagnetic observatory code*] .... GNA
GNC [*Guidance and Navigation Computer*] Dynamic Simulator [*NASA*] (NASA) .... GDS
[*The*] GNI Group, Inc. [*Associated Press*] (SAG) .... GNI
[*The*] GNI Group, Inc. [*NASDAQ symbol*] (NQ) .... GNUC
Gnome Club (EA) .... GC
Gnome Engine [*Hovercraft*] .... GE
Gnome-Rhone [*Aircraft engine*] .... G-R
Gnomes Anonymous [*New Malden, Surrey, England*] (EA) ...... GA
Gnomon [*Munich*] [*A publication*] (BJA) .... Gnom
Gnomonic Tracking Chart [*Air Force*] .... GT
Gnostic Concepts, Inc. [*San Mateo, CA*] [*Database producer*] [*Information service or system*] [*Telecommunications*] (TSSD) .... GCI
Gnotobiote [*Medicine*] (DMAA) .... GN
GnRH [*Gonadotropin Releasing Hormone*] Associated Peptide [*Endocrinology*] .... GAP
Go [*to*] [*Computer science*] [*Telecommunications*] .... g
Go Ahead [*or resume sending*] [*Communications*] .... GA
Go Around (MCD) .... GA
Go for Broke [*Slang*] .... GFB
Go Go's Fan Club [*Defunct*] (EA) .... GGFC
Go Like Hell [*In model name Omni GLH, proposed for Dodge car designed by Carroll Shelby*] .... GLH
Go Long [*Investment term*] .... GL
Go to Heaven [*Name of missionary, "Professor Gotoh," for Worldwide Church of God*] .... GOTOH
Goa [*Panjim*] [*India*] [*Seismograph station code, US Geological Survey*] (SEIS) .... GOA
Goa [*India*] [*Airport symbol*] (OAG) .... GOI
Goa [*India*] [*ICAO location identifier*] (ICLI) .... VAGO
Goal [*A position in lacrosse, soccer, hockey, etc.*] .... G
Goal Attack [*Netball*] .... GA
Goal Attainment Follow-Up Guide (DMAA) .... GAFG
Goal Attainment Scale .... GAS
GOAL [*Ground Operations Aerospace Language*] Automatic Procedure [*NASA*] (NASA) .... GAP
Goal Defence [*Netball*] .... GD
Goal Gradient [*Psychology*] .... GG
Goal Keeper [*Netball*] .... GK

GOAL [*Ground Operations Aerospace Language*] Language Processor (MCD) .... GLP
Goal Post .... GP
GOAL [*Ground Operations Aerospace Language*] Processing Language (MCD) .... GPL
GOAL [*Ground Operations Aerospace Language*] Program Control Block (MCD) .... GPCB
Goal Programming .... GP
Goal Programming Problem .... GPP
Goal Shooter [*Netball*] .... GS
GOAL [*Ground Operations Aerospace Language*] Test Procedure Release Notice [*NASA*] (NASA) .... GPRN
GOAL [*Ground Operations Aerospace Language*] Test Procedure Update Request (MCD) .... GPUR
Goal-Based Evaluation .... GBE
Goal-Directed Programming .... GDP
Goal-Directed Serial Alternation .... GDSA
Goal-Free Evaluation [*Education*] (AEE) .... GFE
Goalkeeper [*Sports*] (BARN) .... G
Goalkeeper (WGA) .... GK
Goal-Oriented Approach to Life Cycle Software .... GOALS
Goal-Oriented Language .... GOL
Goals Against [*Hockey*] .... A
Goals Against [*Hockey*] .... GA
Goals and Timetables (AAGC) .... G&T
Goals For [*Hockey*] .... F
Goals For [*Hockey*] .... GF
Goals-Against Average [*Hockey*] .... AVG
Go-Around (GAVI) .... GAR
Goat [*Veterinary medicine*] .... G
Goat Anti-Mouse Immunoglobulin [*Immunology*] .... GAMIg
Goat Anti-Rabbit [*Also, GARb*] [*Immunology*] .... GAR
Goat Anti-Rabbit [*Also, GAR*] [*Immunology*] .... GARb
Goat Anti-Rabbit Immunoglobulin [*Immunochemistry*] ...... GARI
Goat Antiserum to Rabbit Gamma-Globulin [*Immunology*] .... GARGG
Goat Dairymen's Association [*Australia*] .... GDA
Goat Gamma-Globulin [*Immunology*] .... GGG
Goat Industry Council of Australia .... GICA
Goat Producers Association [*British*] (DBA) .... GPA
Goba [*Ehtiopia*] [*Airport symbol*] (AD) .... GOB
Goba [*Ethiopia*] [*ICAO location identifier*] (ICLI) .... HAGB
Gobabis [*Namibia*] [*ICAO location identifier*] (ICLI) .... FAGB
Gobble (DSUE) .... GOB
Gobel O'Malley Co. [*Entertainer George Gobel's firm; O'Malley is business ma nager*] .... GOMALCO
Gobernador Gordillo [*Argentina ICAO location identifier*] (ICLI) .... SACT
Gobernador Gregores [*Argentina*] [*Airport symbol*] (OAG) ..... GGS
Gobernador Gregores [*Argentina ICAO location identifier*] (ICLI) .... SAWR
Goblin Loose in the Computer Hut [*Computer science*] .... GLITCH
Goch [*Germany ICAO location identifier*] (ICLI) .... EDCC
Goch [*Germany ICAO location identifier*] (ICLI) .... EDNX
Gochnour Idiom Screening Test .... GIST
God Be with You (ROG) .... GOOD-B'YE
God Bless You .... G-B-Y
God Damn .... GD
God Damned Independent [*College slang for student not affiliated with a fraternity or sorority*] .... GDI
God Knows What .... GKW
God Only Knows [*Facetious diagnosis for a puzzling medical case*] .... GOK
God Only Really Knows [*Facetious diagnosis for a puzzling medical case*] .... GORK
Godbolt's English King's Bench Reports [*78 English Reprint*] [*A publication*] (DLA) .... Godb (Eng)
Goddard College (GAGS) .... Goddard C
Goddard College, Plainfield, VT [*Library symbol Library of Congress*] (LCLS) .... VtPlaG
Goddard Communications Center [*NASA*] .... GCC
Goddard Computing Center [*NASA*] .... GCC
Goddard Earth Model [*NASA*] .... GEM
Goddard Experiment Support System [*NASA*] (MCD) .... GES
Goddard Experimental Package [*NASA*] .... GEP
Goddard Flight Space Center [*NASA*] (AAGC) .... GFSC
Goddard High-Resolution Spectrograph .... GHRS
Goddard Institute for Space Studies [*NASA*] .... GI for SS
Goddard Institute for Space Studies [*NASA*] .... GISS
Goddard Kay Rogers Ltd. [*British*] .... GKR
Goddard Laboratory for Atmospheric Sciences (MCD) ...... GLAS
Goddard Laboratory of Atmospheric Sciences [*Marine science*] [*Army*] (OSRA) .... GLAS
Goddard Launch Operations [*NASA*] .... GLO
Goddard Management Instruction [*NASA*] .... GMI
Goddard Mission Control Facility [*NASA*] (KSC) .... GMCF
Goddard Network Control [*NASA*] (MCD) .... GNC
Goddard Network Operations Support [*NASA*] (KSC) .... GNOS
Goddard Network Support Operations [*King's College*] [*Wilkes-Barre, PA*] [*NASA*] (KSC) .... GNSO
Goddard on Easements [*A publication*] (DLA) .... Godd Ease
Goddard on Easements [*A publication*] (DLA) .... Godd Easem
Goddard on Easements [*A publication*] (DLA) .... Goddard
Goddard Optical Research Facility [*Goddard Space Flight Center*] [*NASA*] .... GORF
Goddard Range and Range Data [*NASA*] (KSC) .... GRARD
Goddard Range and Range Rate [*Tracking system*] [*NASA*] ..... GRARR
Goddard Range and Range Rate System [*NASA*] (IAA) .... GRRRS
Goddard Range [*and Range Rate*] Instrumentation Tracking System [*NASA*] (AAG) .... GRITS

Goddard Real Time System [*NASA*] (IAA) .... GRTS
Goddard Research and Engineering Management Exercise [*NASA*] ...... GREMEX
Goddard Satellite Tracking [*NASA*] (MCD) .... GOST
Goddard Space Flight Center [*Greenbelt, MD*] [*NASA*] .... GSFC
Goddard Space Flight Center, Greenbelt, MD [*OCLC symbol*] (OCLC) .... NAG
Goddard Trajectory Determination System [*NASA*] .... GTDS
Gode [*Ethiopia*] [*Airport symbol*] (OAG) .... GDE
Gode [*Ethiopia*] [*ICAO location identifier*] (ICLI) .... HAGO
Godecke AG [*Germany*] [*Research code symbol*] .... Go
Godefroi and Shortt on Railway Companies [*A publication*]
    (DLA) .... Godef & Sh RC
Godefroi and Shortt's Law of Railway Companies [*A publication*]
    (DLA) .... G & Sh RR
Godefroi's Law of Trusts and Trustees [*A publication*] (DLA) .... Godef Trust
Godefroi's Law of Trusts and Trustees [*A publication*] (DLA) .... Godefroi
Godell Memorial Library, Warren, MN [*Library symbol*] [*Library of Congress*]
    (LCLS) .... MnWar
[*The*] Godfather Part III [*Motion picture*] G3
Godfrey, IL [*FM radio station call letters*] .... WLCA
Godfrey Memorial Library, Middletown, CT [*Library symbol Library of Congress*] (LCLS) .... CtMG
Godfrey-Nash [*Forerunner of British HRG and Frazer-Nash automobiles*] .... GN
Godhavn [*Greenland*] [*ICAO location identifier*] (ICLI) .... BGGN
Godhavn [*Greenland*] [*Seismograph station code, US Geological Survey*] (SEIS) .... GDH
Godolphin on Admiralty Jurisdiction [*A publication*] (DLA) .... Godo
Godolphin on Admiralty Jurisdiction [*2nd ed.*] [*1685*] [*A publication*]
    (DLA) .... Godolph Adm Jur
Godolphin's Abridgment of Ecclesiastical Law [*A publication*] (DLA) .... Godo
Godolphin's Ecclesiastical Law [*A publication*] (DLA) .... Godolph Ecc Law
Godolphin's Orphan's Legacy [*A publication*] (DLA) .... Godo
Godolphin's Orphan's Legacy [*A publication*] (DLA) .... Godol
Godolphin's Orphan's Legacy [*A publication*] (DLA) .... Godolph Leg
Godolphin's Orphan's Legacy [*A publication*] (DLA) .... Godolph Orph Leg
Godolphin's Repertorium Canonicum [*A publication*] (DLA) .... Godo
Godolphin's Repertorium Canonicum [*A publication*] (DLA) .... Godolph Rep Can
GODORT [*Government Documents Round Table*] Education Task
    Force .... GODORT ETF
GODORT [*Government Documents Round Table*] Federal Documents Task
    Force .... GODORT FDTF
GODORT [*Government Documents Round Table*] International Documents
    Task Force .... GODORT IDTF
GODORT [*Government Documents Round Table*] Machine-Readable
    Government Information Task Force .... GODORT MRGITF
GODORT [*Government Documents Round Table*] State and Local Documents
    Task Force .... GODORT SLDTF
Gods Narrows [*Canada*] [*Airport symbol*] (OAG) .... YGO
God's Own Medicine [*Also, God's Medicine*] [*Morphine*] [*Slang*] .... GOM
Gods River [*Canada*] [*Airport symbol*] (OAG) .... ZGI
Godson on Patents [*2nd ed.*] [*1840*] [*A publication*] (DLA) .... Gods Pat
Godson's Mining Commissioner's Cases [*Ontario*] [*A publication*]
    (DLA) .... Godson
Godthaab [*Denmark*] [*Airport symbol*] .... GOH
Godthab [*Greenland*] [*ICAO location identifier*] (ICLI) .... BGGH
Goebel Collectors' Club [*Later, MIHC*] (EA) .... GCC
Goebel's Probate Court Cases [*Ohio*] [*A publication*] (DLA) .... Go
Goebel's Probate Court Cases [*Ohio*] [*A publication*] (DLA) .... Goeb
Goebel's Probate Court Cases [*Ohio*] [*A publication*] (DLA) .... Goebel (Ohio)
Goebel's Probate Reports [*Ohio*] [*A publication*] (DLA) .... Goebel
Goebel's Probate Reports [*Ohio*] [*A publication*] (DLA) .... Goebel's Rep
Goebel's Probate Reports [*Ohio*] [*A publication*] (DLA) .... Ohio Prob Ct
Goeppingen [*Germany ICAO location identifier*] (ICLI) .... EDIB
Goerz-Visier [*Bomb sight manufactured by Goerz Co.*] [*German military - World War II*] .... GV
Goes Like Hell - Some More [*In model "GLH-S," Dodge car designed by Carroll Shelby*] [*Facetious translation: "Goes Like Hell - Squared"*] .... GLH-S
Goes Over All Terrain [*Vehicle*] .... GOAT
GOES [*Geostationary Operational Environmental Satellite*] Precipitation Index [*Marine science*] (OSRA) .... GPI
Goetek Communications [*NASDAQ symbol*] (TTSB) .... GOTK
Goethe House, German Cultural Institute, New York, NY [*Library symbol Library of Congress*] (LCLS) .... NNGoe
Goethe Institute (EA) .... GI
Goethe Institute, German Culture Institute, Atlanta, GA [*Library symbol Library of Congress*] (LCLS) .... GAGI
Goethe Society of North America (EA) .... GSNA
Goethite [*A mineral*] .... GO
Goetsenhove [*Belgium ICAO location identifier*] (ICLI) .... EBTN
Goettingen [*Federal Republic of Germany*] [*Geomagnetic observatory code*] ..... GTT
Goettinger Predigt-Meditationen [*A publication*] (BJA) .... GPM
Goettingischer Gelehrte Anzeigen [*A publication*] (OCD) .... Gott Anz
Goffered Edges [*Bookbinding*] (DGA) .... GOF E
Goffs, CA [*Location identifier FAA*] (FAAL) .... GFS
Gofredus de Trano [*Deceased, 1245*] [*Authority cited in pre-1607 legal work*] (DSA) .... G
Gofredus de Trano [*Deceased, 1245*] [*Authority cited in pre-1607 legal work*] (DSA) .... Go
Gofredus de Trano [*Deceased, 1245*] [*Authority cited in pre-1607 legal work*] (DSA) .... God
Gofredus de Trano [*Deceased, 1245*] [*Authority cited in pre-1607 legal work*] (DSA) .... Gof
Gogama Community Library, Ontario [*Library symbol National Library of Canada*] (NLC) .... OGOG
Gogebic Community College [*Ironwood, MI*] .... GCC
Gogerial [*Sudan*] [*ICAO location identifier*] (ICLI) .... HSGO

Goguet's Origin of Laws [*A publication*] (DLA) .... Gog Or
Goiania [*Brazil*] [*Airport symbol*] (OAG) .... GYN
Goiania/Santa Genoveva [*Brazil ICAO location identifier*] (ICLI) .... SBGO
Goilala Air Services [*Australia*] .... GAS
Going Public [*Investment term*] .... GP
Going-Home Money .... GHM
Goings On About Town [*The New Yorker magazine*] (WDMC) .... GOAT
Goirand's French Code of Commerce [*A publication*] (DLA) .... Goir Fr Co
Gokango [*Congo*] [*ICAO location identifier*] (ICLI) .... FCMG
Gokwe [*Zimbabwe*] [*ICAO location identifier*] (ICLI) .... FVGO
Golabi-Rosen Syndrome [*Medicine*] (DMAA) .... GRS
Golay Logic Operating Language .... GLOL
Golay Pneumatic Cell .... GPC
Golay Transform Processor (IAA) .... GTP
Golbalstar Telecommunications [*NASDAQ symbol*] (TTSB) .... GSTRF
Golbandi [*Iran*] [*ICAO location identifier*] (ICLI) .... OIBI
Golconda, IL [*FM radio station call letters*] .... WDXR
Gold [*Chemical Element*] (DOG) .... Au
Gold .... G
Gold (MSA) .... GLD
Gold (VRA) .... go
Gold Banc Corp., Inc. [*NASDAQ symbol*] (SAG) .... GLDB
Gold Banc Corp., Inc. [*Associated Press*] (SAG) .... GoldBnc
Gold Beach, OR [*Location identifier FAA*] (FAAL) .... GOL
Gold Beach, OR [*FM radio station call letters*] .... KGBR
Gold Beaters' Trade Society [*A union*] [*British*] .... GBTS
Gold Belt Air Transport, Inc. [*Canada ICAO designator*] (FAAC) .... GBT
Gold Bevelled Deckle Edges [*Printing*] (DGA) .... GOLD BDE
Gold Bevelled Edges [*Printing*] (DGA) .... GOLD BE
Gold Black [*Ultrafine gold metal particles*] .... GB
Gold Bond [*Bond payable in gold coin*] .... GB
Gold Bondholders Protective Council (EA) .... GBPC
Gold Bridge Development [*Vancouver Stock Exchange symbol*] .... GGD
Gold Canyon Mines, Inc. [*Vancouver Stock Exchange symbol*] .... GCN
Gold Canyon Resources [*Vancouver Stock Exchange symbol*] .... GCU
Gold Clause Agreement [*Shipping*] (DS) .... GCA
Gold Coast [*Later, Ghana*] (ROG) .... GC
Gold Coast [*Australia Airport symbol*] (OAG) .... OOL
Gold Coast Divisional Court Reports [*A publication*] (DLA) .... GCDC
Gold Coast Environment Centre (EERA) .... GCEC
Gold Coast Full Court Selected Judgments [*A publication*] (DLA) .... GC Full Ct
Gold Coast Full Court Selected Judgments [*A publication*] (DLA) .... GCFC
Gold Coast Judgments and the Masai Cases, by King-Farlow [*1915-17*] [*Ghana*] [*A publication*] (DLA) .... KF
Gold Coast Judgments and the Masai Cases, by King-Farlow [*1915-17*] [*Ghana*] [*A publication*] (DLA) .... King-Farlow
Gold Coast Judgments, by Earnshaw [*1909-10*] [*Ghana*] [*A publication*] (DLA) .... Earnshaw
Gold Coast Native Institutions [*A publication*] (DLA) .... Hayford
Gold Coast Regiment [*British military*] (DMA) .... GCR
Gold Coast Selected Judgments of the Divisional Courts [*A publication*] (DLA) .... GC Div Ct
Gold Coast Territorial Force [*British military*] (DMA) .... GCTF
Gold Corp. [*Western Australia*] [*Commercial firm*] .... GC
Gold Coupling Dendrite .... GCD
Gold Cup Resources [*Vancouver Stock Exchange symbol*] .... GSL
Gold Edges [*Printing*] (DGA) .... GOLD E
Gold Exchange Standard .... GES
Gold Field .... GF
Gold Fields of South Africa Ltd. [*NASDAQ symbol*] (NQ) .... GLDF
Gold Fields of South Africa Ltd. [*Associated Press*] (SAG) .... GoldFd
Gold Fields S. Africa ADR [*NASDAQ symbol*] (TTSB) .... GLDFY
Gold Filled Association [*Defunct*] (EA) .... GFA
Gold Film Mercury Detector [*Spectrometry*] .... GFMD
Gold Hill [*California*] [*Seismograph station code, US Geological Survey*] (SEIS) .... GHC
Gold Hill, OR [*FM radio station call letters*] .... KRWQ
Gold Inlay [*Dentistry*] .... G
Gold Institute [*Also known as L'Institut de l'Or*] (EA) .... GI
Gold King Construction [*Vancouver Stock Exchange symbol*] .... GKC
Gold King River [*Alaska*] [*Seismograph station code, US Geological Survey*] (SEIS) .... GKC
Gold Leaf (VRA) .... go lf
Gold Lease (ADA) .... GL
Gold Life Saving Medal [*Military decoration*] .... GLSM
Gold Life-Saving Medal [*Military decoration*] (GFGA) .... GLM
Gold Maple Leaf [*Canadian coin*] .... GML
Gold Mark Minerals [*Vancouver Stock Exchange symbol*] .... GMK
Gold Medal .... GM
Gold Medallist (DAS) .... GM
Gold Mining Association of America .... GMAA
Gold Mountain [*Washington*] [*Seismograph station code, US Geological Survey*] (SEIS) .... GMW
Gold Plated [*Freight*] .... GLD PLTD
Gold Point Resources [*Vancouver Stock Exchange symbol*] .... GOP
Gold Points [*Investment term*] .... GP
Gold Power Resources Corp. [*Vancouver Stock Exchange symbol*] .... GPW
Gold Producers' Association [*Australia*] .... GPA
Gold Prospectors Association of America (EA) .... GPAA
Gold Reserve [*NASDAQ symbol*] (TTSB) .... GLDR
Gold Reserve .... GR
Gold Reserve Corp. [*NASDAQ symbol*] (NQ) .... GLDR
Gold Reserve Corp. [*Associated Press*] (SAG) .... GoldRs
Gold Ridge Resources [*Vancouver Stock Exchange symbol*] .... GRU
Gold Salt Therapy [*Medicine*] (DMAA) .... GST

Gold Seeker Resources Ltd. [*Vancouver Stock Exchange symbol*] .... GSK
Gold Smoke [*Dispersion of ultrafine metal particles*] .... GS
Gold Sodium Thiomalate [*Organic chemistry*] (DAVI) .... GST
Gold Sodium Thiomalate [*Organic chemistry*] (DAVI) .... GSTM
Gold Spring Resources [*Vancouver Stock Exchange symbol*] .... GSJ
Gold Standard [*NASDAQ symbol*] (TTSB) .... GSTD
Gold Standard, Inc. [*Associated Press*] (SAG) .... GldStd
Gold Standard, Inc. [*NASDAQ symbol*] (NQ) .... GSTD
Gold Standards .... GS
Gold Star Lapel Button [*Military decoration*] (AABC) .... GSLB
Gold Star Mothers .... GSM
Gold Star Owners Club (EA) .... GSOC
Gold Star Parents for Amnesty [*Defunct*] (EA) .... GSPA
Gold Star Resources, Inc. [*Vancouver Stock Exchange symbol*] .... GLA
Gold Star Wives of America (EA) .... GSW
Gold Star Wives of America [*Later, GSW*] (EA) .... GSWA
Gold Surface Barrier .... GSB
Gold Texas Resources Ltd. [*Vancouver Stock Exchange symbol*] .... GTX
Gold Thioglucose .... GTG
Gold Torch Resources [*Vancouver Stock Exchange symbol*] .... GTJ
Gold Vapor LASER [*Physics*] .... GVL
Gold Ventures Ltd. [*Vancouver Stock Exchange symbol*] .... GVL
Gold Wing Road Riders Association (EA) .... GWRRA
Golda Meir Memorial Association (EA) .... GMMA
Goldbarg-Rutenberg [*Enzyme unit*] .... G-R
Goldbelt Mines [*Vancouver Stock Exchange symbol*] .... GOT
Goldberg Anorectic Attitude Scale [*Medicine*] (DMAA) .... GAAS
Goldbrae Development Ltd. [*Vancouver Stock Exchange symbol*] .... GOB
Gold-Braid Chaser [*Refers to a woman who dates only officers*] [*Slang
    British*] (DSUE) .... GBC
Goldcorp [*NYSE symbol*] (SAG) .... GG
Goldcorp [*Associated Press*] (SAG) .... GoldcpA
Goldcorp [*Associated Press*] (SAG) .... GoldcpB
Goldcorp, Inc. [*Associated Press*] (SAG) .... Goldcp
Goldcorp Investments Ltd. [*Toronto Stock Exchange symbol*] .... G
Golden [*Colorado School of Mines*] [*Colorado*] [*Seismograph station code, US
    Geological Survey*] (SEIS) .... GLD
Golden [*Philately*] .... gldn
Golden .... GLDN
Golden [*New Mexico*] [*Seismograph station code, US Geological Survey*]
    (SEIS) .... GNM
Golden [*Bergen Park*] [*Colorado*] [*Seismograph station code, US Geological
    Survey*] (SEIS) .... GOL
Golden Acres Elementary School, Pasadena, TX [*Library symbol*] [*Library of
    Congress*] (LCLS) .... TxPGaE
Golden Adit Resources [*Vancouver Stock Exchange symbol*] .... GLQ
Golden Age Records [*Record label*] .... GAR
Golden Air Commuter AB [*Sweden ICAO designator*] (FAAC) .... GAO
Golden American Saddlebred Horse Association (EA) .... GASHA
Golden and District Museum, Golden, British Columbia [*Library symbol
    National Library of Canada*] (NLC) .... BGD
Golden Band Resources [*Vancouver Stock Exchange symbol*] .... GBN
Golden, BC [*AM radio station call letters*] .... CKGR
Golden Bear Golf, Inc. [*Associated Press*] (SAG) .... GldBear
Golden Bear Golf, Inc. [*NASDAQ symbol*] (SAG) .... JACK
Golden Bear Resources Ltd. [*Vancouver Stock Exchange symbol*] .... GBR
Golden Books Family Ent [*NASDAQ symbol*] (TTSB) .... GBFE
Golden Books Family Entertainment, Inc. [*NASDAQ symbol*] (SAG) .... GBFE
Golden Books Family Entertainment, Inc. [*Associated Press*] (SAG) .... GoldBks
[The] Golden Bough [*A publication*] (OCD) .... GB
Golden Cadillac Resources Ltd. [*Vancouver Stock Exchange symbol*] ...... GCD
Golden Chance Resources, Inc. [*Vancouver Stock Exchange symbol*] .... GCH
Golden Circle Ltd. [*Australia Commercial firm*] .... GCL
Golden Common LISP [*List Processor*] [*Artificial intelligence language*] ..... GC LISP
Golden CommPass [*Front-end computer processor*] (PCM) .... GCP
Golden Companions [*An association*] (EA) .... GC
Golden Concord Mining [*Vancouver Stock Exchange symbol*] .... GCC
Golden Crown Resources Ltd. [*Vancouver Stock Exchange symbol*] .... GCS
Golden Dawn [*In occult society name, Hermetic Order of the Golden Dawn*] ...... GD
Golden Dawn Explorations Ltd. [*Vancouver Stock Exchange symbol*] .... GDE
Golden Diamond Travel and Tourism Agency [*Saudi Arabia*] .... GDT
Golden Dividend Resources [*Vancouver Stock Exchange symbol*] .... GOV
Golden Dragon Resources [*Vancouver Stock Exchange symbol*] .... GDQ
Golden Eagle Air Services Ltd. [*Canada ICAO designator*] (FAAC) .... SAJ
Golden Eagle Group [*NASDAQ symbol*] (TTSB) .... GEGP
Golden Eagle Group, Inc. [*NASDAQ symbol*] (SAG) .... GEGP
Golden Eagle Group, Inc. [*Associated Press*] (SAG) .... GldEagl
Golden Eagle Group, Inc. [*Associated Press*] (SAG) .... GldEg
Golden Eagle Group Wrrt [*NASDAQ symbol*] (TTSB) .... GEGPW
Golden Enterprises [*NASDAQ symbol*] (TTSB) .... GLDC
Golden Enterprises, Inc. [*NASDAQ symbol*] (NQ) .... GLDC
Golden Enterprises, Inc. [*Associated Press*] (SAG) .... GoldEn
Golden Exodus [*Vancouver Stock Exchange symbol*] .... GXV
Golden Eye Minerals [*Vancouver Stock Exchange symbol*] .... GOM
Golden Gate Baptist Theological Seminary, Mill Valley, CA [*Library symbol
    Library of Congress*] (LCLS) .... CMIG
Golden Gate College [*California*] .... GGC
Golden Gate College, San Francisco, CA [*Library symbol Library of
    Congress*] (LCLS) .... CSfGG
Golden Gate Explorations [*Vancouver Stock Exchange symbol*] .... GGX
Golden Gate National Recreation Area Advisory Commission [*National Park
    Service*] [*San Francisco, CA*] (EGAO) .... GGNRA
Golden Gate National Recreation Area Advisory Commission [*National Park
    Service*] [*San Francisco, CA*] (EGAO) .... GGNRACAC

Golden Gate Productions [*San Francisco, CA*] [*Telecommunications*]
    (TSSD) .... GGP
Golden Gate University (GAGS) .... Golden Gate U
Golden Gate University Advanced Legal Education Program (DLA) .... GGUALE
Golden Gate University, School of Law, San Francisco, CA [*Library symbol
    Library of Congress*] (LCLS) .... CSfGG-L
Golden Gate Youth Camp, Residents' Library, Golden, CO [*Library symbol
    Library of Congress*] (LCLS) .... CoGG
Golden Glacier [*Vancouver Stock Exchange symbol*] .... GGA
Golden Glory [*Vancouver Stock Exchange symbol*] .... GDG
Golden Gloves Association of America [*Later, GGA of A*] .... GG
Golden Gloves Association of America (EA) .... GGA of A
Golden Gloves Association of America [*Later, GGA of A*] (EA) .... GGAA
Golden Group Explorations, Inc. [*Vancouver Stock Exchange symbol*] ..... GGE
Golden Hat Resources [*Vancouver Stock Exchange symbol*] .... GHA
Golden Hemlock [*Vancouver Stock Exchange symbol*] .... GHE
Golden Hind Ventures Ltd. [*Vancouver Stock Exchange symbol*] .... GHV
Golden Hope Resources, Inc. [*Vancouver Stock Exchange symbol*] .... GHR
Golden Horizon [*Vancouver Stock Exchange symbol*] .... GHZ
Golden Hour Tango .... GHT
Golden Iskut Resources [*Vancouver Stock Exchange symbol*] .... GIS
Golden Isles Financial Holdings, Inc. [*NASDAQ symbol*] (SAG) .... GIFH
Golden Isles Financial Holdings, Inc. [*Associated Press*] (SAG) .... GoldIsl
Golden Isles Finl Hldg [*NASDAQ symbol*] (TTSB) .... GIFH
Golden Isles Finl Hldg Unit [*NASDAQ symbol*] (TTSB) .... GIFHU
Golden Key National Honor Society (EA) .... GKNHS
Golden Key Resources Ltd. [*Vancouver Stock Exchange symbol*] .... GKY
Golden Knight Res [*NASDAQ symbol*] (TTSB) .... GKRVE
Golden Knight Resources, Inc. [*Toronto Stock Exchange symbol Vancouver
    Stock Exchange symbol*] .... GKR
Golden Knight Resources, Inc. [*NASDAQ symbol*] (NQ) .... GKRV
Golden Knight Resources, Inc. [*Associated Press*] (SAG) .... GldKngt
Golden Lake Resources Ltd. [*Vancouver Stock Exchange symbol*] .... GLK
Golden Lion Resources Ltd. [*Vancouver Stock Exchange symbol*] .... GIR
Golden Lion Tamarin [*South American monkey*] .... GLT
Golden Lion Tamarin Management Committee (EA) .... GLTMC
Golden Meadow, LA [*AM radio station call letters*] .... KLEB
Golden Memories of Elvis Fan Club (EA) .... GMEFC
Golden Myra Resources, Inc. [*Toronto Stock Exchange symbol*] .... MRA
Golden Nematode [*A worm*] .... GN
Golden Nevada [*Vancouver Stock Exchange symbol*] .... GVA
Golden Nevada Resources, Inc. [*Toronto Stock Exchange symbol*] .... GVA
Golden News Resources Corp. [*Vancouver Stock Exchange symbol*] .... GDN
Golden North Resource Corp. [*Toronto Stock Exchange symbol Vancouver
    Stock Exchange symbol*] .... GNO
Golden Number [*Number used to fix the date of Easter*] .... GN
Golden Oil Co. [*NASDAQ symbol*] (NQ) .... GOCO
Golden Oil Co. [*Associated Press*] (SAG) .... GoldnOil
Golden Pheasant [*Vancouver Stock Exchange symbol*] .... GPE
Golden Pond Resources [*Vancouver Stock Exchange symbol*] .... GDP
Golden Poultry Co. [*NASDAQ symbol*] (TTSB) .... CHIK
Golden Poultry Co., Inc. [*NASDAQ symbol*] (NQ) .... CHIK
Golden Poultry Co., Inc. [*Associated Press*] (SAG) .... GldPoul
Golden Prairie, SK [*Television station call letters*] CKMC-1
Golden Princess [*Vancouver Stock Exchange symbol*] .... GLP
Golden Pyramid Resources, Inc. [*Vancouver Stock Exchange symbol*] ..... GPR
Golden Quail Res Ltd [*NASDAQ symbol*] (TTSB) .... GQRVF
Golden Quail Resources Ltd. [*Associated Press*] (SAG) .... GldQual
Golden Quail Resources Ltd. [*Vancouver Stock Exchange symbol*] .... GQR
Golden Quail Resources Ltd. [*NASDAQ symbol*] (NQ) .... GQRV
Golden Queen Mining [*Vancouver Stock Exchange symbol*] .... GQM
Golden Range Resources, Inc. [*Toronto Stock Exchange symbol*] .... GOR
Golden Regional Library (J. Lester Trezise Regional Library), Golden, CO
    [*Library symbol Library of Congress*] (LCLS) .... CoGJ-G
Golden Retriever Club of America (EA) .... GRCA
Golden Rim Resources, Inc. [*Vancouver Stock Exchange symbol*] .... GRR
Golden Ring Council of Senior Citizens Clubs [*Defunct*] (EA) .... GRCSCC
Golden Rock Resources Ltd. [*Vancouver Stock Exchange symbol*] .... GRK
Golden Rule [*Freemasonry*] (ROG) .... GR
Golden Rule Foundation (EA) .... GRF
Golden Rule Resources Ltd. [*Toronto Stock Exchange symbol*] .... GNU
Golden Rule Society (EA) .... GRS
Golden Sceptre Resources [*Toronto Stock Exchange symbol Vancouver Stock
    Exchange symbol*] .... GOD
Golden Seal Resources Ltd. [*Vancouver Stock Exchange symbol*] .... GOA
Golden Seven Industry [*Vancouver Stock Exchange symbol*] .... GSU
Golden Seville Resources Ltd. [*Vancouver Stock Exchange symbol*] .... GSV
Golden Shamrock Resources Corp. [*Vancouver Stock Exchange symbol*] .... GS
Golden Shield Resources Ltd. [*Toronto Stock Exchange symbol Vancouver
    Stock Exchange symbol*] .... GLS
Golden Sitka Resources [*Vancouver Stock Exchange symbol*] .... GSZ
Golden Spike National Historic Site .... GOSP
Golden Star Air Cargo Co. Ltd. [*Sudan*] [*ICAO designator*] (FAAC) .... GLD
Golden Star Resources [*AMEX symbol*] (TTSB) .... GSR
Golden Star Resources Ltd. [*Associated Press*] (SAG) .... GldStarR
Golden Star Resources Ltd. [*Toronto Stock Exchange symbol*] .... GSC
Golden Star Resources Ltd. [*AMEX symbol*] (SPSG) .... GSR
Golden State Mutual Life Insurance Co., Los Angeles, CA [*Library symbol
    Library of Congress*] (LCLS) .... CLGS
Golden State Resources [*Vancouver Stock Exchange symbol*] .... GOS
Golden Systems, Inc. [*NASDAQ symbol*] (SAG) .... GLDN
Golden Systems, Inc. [*Associated Press*] (SAG) .... GldnSyst
Golden Tag Resources [*Vancouver Stock Exchange symbol*] .... GOG
Golden Tech Resources Ltd. [*Vancouver Stock Exchange symbol*] .... GTS
Golden Terrace Resource Corp. [*Toronto Stock Exchange symbol*] .... GTR

Golden Titan Resources [*Vancouver Stock Exchange symbol*] .... GN
Golden Treasury Series [*A publication*] .... GTS
Golden Trend Energy [*Vancouver Stock Exchange symbol*] .... GTG
Golden Triangle Ind [*NASDAQ symbol*] (TTSB) .... GTII
Golden Triangle Industries, Inc. [*Associated Press*] (SAG) .... GoldTri
Golden Triangle Industries, Inc. [*NASDAQ symbol*] (SAG) .... GTII
Golden Triangle Royalty & Oil, Inc. [*Associated Press*] (SAG) .... GoldTri
Golden Triangle Royalty & Oil, Inc. [*NASDAQ symbol*] (NQ) .... GTRO
Golden Trio Minerals [*Vancouver Stock Exchange symbol*] .... GIO
Golden Vale Explorations Corp. [*Vancouver Stock Exchange symbol*] .... GLV
Golden Valley Health Center, Golden Valley, MN [*Library symbol Library of
    Congress*] (LCLS) .... MnGvH
Golden Valley Lutheran College, Minneapolis, MN [*Library symbol Library of
    Congress*] (LCLS) .... MnMG
Golden Valley, MN [*AM radio station call letters*] (RBYB) .... KDIZ-AM
Golden Valley, MN [*AM radio station call letters*] .... KQRS
Golden Valley, MN [*FM radio station call letters*] .... KQRS-FM
Golden Valley, MN [*AM radio station call letters*] .... KYCR
Golden West [*ICAO designator*] (AD) .... VF
Golden West Airlines (MHDW) .... GQ
Golden West Airlines [*ICAO designator*] (AD) .... GW
Golden West College, Huntington Beach, CA [*Library symbol Library of
    Congress*] (LCLS) .... CHuG
Golden West College Library, Huntington Beach, CA [*OCLC symbol*]
    (OCLC) .... CGW
Golden West Financial Corp. [*NYSE symbol*] (SPSG) .... GDW
Golden West Financial Corp. [*Associated Press*] (SAG) .... GldWF
Golden West Finl [*NYSE symbol*] (TTSB) .... GDW
Golden West Network [*Australia*] .... GWN
Golden West Subscription Television [*Cable TV programming service*] ..... GWSTV
Golden Zone Resources [*Vancouver Stock Exchange symbol*] .... GZR
Goldenbell Resources, Inc. [*Toronto Stock Exchange symbol Vancouver Stock
    Exchange symbol*] .... GBL
Goldendale, WA [*AM radio station call letters*] .... KLCK
Goldendale, WA [*FM radio station call letters*] .... KYYT
Goldenhar Syndrome [*Medicine*] (DMAA) .... GS
Goldenlode Resources Ltd. [*Vancouver Stock Exchange symbol*] .... GEL
Goldenrod Resources & Technology, Inc. [*Vancouver Stock Exchange
    symbol*] .... GRL
Golder Associates, Mississauga, ON, Canada [*Library symbol*] [*Library of
    Congress*] (LCLS) .... CaOMGA
Golder Associates, Mississauga, Ontario [*Library symbol National Library of
    Canada*] (NLC) .... OMGA
Golder, Brawner & Associates Ltd., Vancouver, BC, Canada [*Library symbol
    Library of Congress*] (LCLS) .... CaBVaGB
Golder Brawner & Associates Ltd., Vancouver, British Columbia [*Library
    symbol National Library of Canada*] (NLC) .... BVAGB
Golder, Thoma & Cressey [*Chicago, IL*] [*Telecommunications service*]
    (TSSD) .... GTC
Goldera Resources, Inc. [*Vancouver Stock Exchange symbol*] .... GDA
Goldesborough's [*or Gouldsborough's*] **English King's Bench Reports**
    [*A publication*] (DLA) .... Gold
Goldesborough's [*or Gouldsborough's*] **English King's Bench Reports**
    [*A publication*] (DLA) .... Goldes
Goldex Mines Ltd. [*Toronto Stock Exchange symbol*] .... GLX
Goldex Resources [*Vancouver Stock Exchange symbol*] .... GXS
Goldfarb Corp. [*Toronto Stock Exchange symbol*] .... GDF
Goldfever Resources Ltd. [*Vancouver Stock Exchange symbol*] .... GFV
Goldfield Corp. [*Associated Press*] (SAG) .... GldFld
Goldfield Corp. [*AMEX symbol*] (SPSG) .... GV
Goldfields Against Serious Pollution [*Australia*] .... GASP
Goldfields Air Navigation [*Australia*] .... GAN
Goldfields Air Services [*Australia ICAO designator*] (FAAC) .... GOS
Goldfields Esperance Development Authority [*Australia*] .... GEDA
Gold-Filled Manufacturers Association [*Later, GFA*] (EA) .... GFMA
Goldfinch [*Ornithology*] .... GF
Goldfinch Mineral Ltd. [*Vancouver Stock Exchange symbol*] .... GFM
Goldfish Society of America (EA) .... GFSA
Goldfish Society of America (EA) .... GSA
Goldflow (AFM) .... GF
Goldhaven Resources Ltd. [*Vancouver Stock Exchange symbol*] .... GHN
Goldhurst Resources [*Vancouver Stock Exchange symbol*] .... GHT
Gold-labelled Antigen Detection [*Medicine*] (DMAA) .... GLAD
Goldlund Mines Ltd. [*Toronto Stock Exchange symbol*] .... GOL
Goldman-Fristoe Test of Articulation [*Education*] .... GFTA
Goldman-Fristoe-Woodcock Test of Auditory Discrimination
    [*Education*] .... G-F-W
Gold-Medal Resources Ltd. [*Vancouver Stock Exchange symbol*] .... GML
Goldneck Summer Squash .... GN
Goldome FSB, Bufflo, NY [*Library symbol*] [*Library of Congress*] (LCLS) ..... NBuGD
Goldpac Investments Ltd. [*Vancouver Stock Exchange symbol*] .... GPK
Gold-Pan Resources, Inc. [*Vancouver Stock Exchange symbol*] .... GPN
Gold-Plating Bath Analyzer and Controller (PDAA) .... GOBAC
Goldpost Resources, Inc. [*Toronto Stock Exchange symbol*] .... GPT
Goldquest Exploration, Inc. [*Toronto Stock Exchange symbol*] .... GQX
Goldreich-Julian [*PULSAR theory*] .... GJ
Goldrich Resources, Inc. [*Vancouver Stock Exchange symbol*] .... GRD
Goldrite Mining [*Vancouver Stock Exchange symbol*] .... GRQ
Goldsboro, NC [*Location identifier FAA*] (FAAL) .... DDX
Goldsboro, NC [*Location identifier FAA*] (FAAL) .... GSB
Goldsboro, NC [*Location identifier FAA*] (FAAL) .... GWW
Goldsboro, NC [*FM radio station call letters*] .... WEQR
Goldsboro, NC [*AM radio station call letters*] .... WFMC
Goldsboro, NC [*AM radio station call letters*] .... WGBR
Goldsboro, NC [*FM radio station call letters*] .... WKTC

Goldsboro, NC [*Television station call letters*] .... WNCN
Goldsboro, NC [*AM radio station call letters*] .... WSSG
Goldsboro/Seymour-Johnson Air Force Base [*North Carolina*] [*ICAO location
    identifier*] (ICLI) .... KGSB
Goldsearch, Inc. [*Vancouver Stock Exchange symbol*] .... GDH
Goldsil Resources Ltd. [*Toronto Stock Exchange symbol Vancouver Stock
    Exchange symbol*] .... GOO
Goldsmith and Guthrie's Appeals Reports [*Missouri*] [*A publication*]
    (DLA) .... G & G
Goldsmith and Guthrie's Appeals Reports [*Missouri*] [*A publication*]
    (DLA) .... G & G (MO)
Goldsmith and Guthrie's Appeals Reports [*Missouri*] [*A publication*]
    (DLA) .... Gold & G
Goldsmith Civic Garden Center, Memphis, TN [*Library symbol Library of
    Congress*] (LCLS) .... TMGG
Goldsmith Minerals [*Vancouver Stock Exchange symbol*] .... GMM
Goldsmiths' and Jewellers' Trade Association [*A union*] [*British*] .... GJTA
Goldsmith's College [*London, England*] .... GC
Goldsmith's Doctrine and Practice of Equity [*6th ed.*] [*1871*] [*A publication*]
    (DLA) .... Golds Eq
Goldsmiths', Silversmiths', and Jewellers' Benevolent Society [*British*] .... GSJBS
Goldstack Resources [*Vancouver Stock Exchange symbol*] .... GOR
Goldstein Golub Kessler [*Commercial firm*] .... GGK
Goldstein-Scheerer Cube Test [*Psychology*] .... GSCT
Goldstein-Scheerer Object Sorting Test [*Psychology*] .... GSOST
Goldstein-Scheerer Stick Test [*Psychology*] .... GSST
Goldstone [*California*] [*Seismograph station code, US Geological Survey*]
    (SEIS) .... GSC
Goldstone, CA [*Spaceflight tracking and data network*] [*NASA*] (NASA) ..... GDS
Goldstone, California [*Spaceflight Tracking and Data Network*] [*NASA*] .... GDX
Goldstone Deep Space Communications Complex [*NASA*] .... GDSCC
Goldstone Duplicate Standard [*Deep Space Instrumentation Facility*]
    [*NASA*] .... GSDS
Goldstone Predict [*Orbit identification*] [*NASA*] .... GLPR
Goldstone Tracking Station [*NASA*] .... GTS
Goldstone-SFOF [*Space Flight Operations Facility*] **Microwave Assembly**
    [*NASA*] .... GSMA
Goldstream Resources Ltd. [*Vancouver Stock Exchange symbol*] .... GSM
Goldteck Mines Ltd. [*Toronto Stock Exchange symbol*] .... GKT
Goldvein, VA [*Television station call letters*] .... WNVT
Goldwater, Barry [*Chemical symbols for gold and water; used to refer to the
    1964 Republican presidential candidate*] .... AuH_2O
Goldways Resources [*Vancouver Stock Exchange symbol*] .... GWY
Goldwest Resources Ltd. [*Vancouver Stock Exchange symbol*] .... GDW
Goldwing Flyers Club (EA) .... GFC
Goldwinn Resources Ltd. [*Vancouver Stock Exchange symbol*] .... GWN
Goldwyn [*Samuel*] **Co.** [*Associated Press*] (SAG) .... GldwSam
Goldwyn [*Samuel*] **Co.** [*AMEX symbol*] (SPSG) .... SG
Goleta, CA [*FM radio station call letters*] .... KMGQ
Goleta National Bank [*NASDAQ symbol*] (SAG) .... GLTB
Goleta National Bank [*Associated Press*] (SAG) .... GoletaN
Golf [*Phonetic alphabet*] [*International*] (DSUE) .... G
Golf Association of Michigan (SRA) .... GAM
Golf Ball Manufacturers Association (EA) .... GBMA
Golf Ball Manufacturers' Conference [*British*] (BI) .... GBMC
Golf Club .... GC
Golf Coaches Association of America (EA) .... GCAA
Golf Collectors' Society (EA) .... GCS
Golf Course Association (EA) .... GCA
Golf Course Builders of America (EA) .... GCBA
Golf Course Operations and Management Programs [*Association of
    Independent Colleges and Schools specialization code*] .... GM
Golf Course Superintendents Association of America (EA) .... GCSAA
Golf Course Superintendents Association of New Jersey (SRA) .... GCSA/NJ
Golf Enterprises [*NASDAQ symbol*] (TTSB) .... GLFE
Golf Enterprises, Inc. [*NASDAQ symbol*] (SAG) .... GLFE
Golf Enterprises, Inc. [*Associated Press*] (SAG) .... Golf Ent
Golf Head Optical Speed Trap [*Golf self-improvement program*] .... GHOST
Golf Manufacturers and Distributors Association (EA) .... GMDA
Golf Products and Components Association [*Defunct*] (EA) .... GPCA
Golf Society [*British*] (DBA) .... GSGB
Golf Technology Holding, Inc. [*Associated Press*] (SAG) .... GolfTech
Golf Technology Holding, Inc. [*NASDAQ symbol*] (SAG) .... SNKE
Golf Training Sys Wrrt [*NASDAQ symbol*] (TTSB) .... GTSXW
Golf Training Systems [*NASDAQ symbol*] (TTSB) .... GTSX
Golf Training Systems, Inc. [*Associated Press*] (SAG) .... GolfTS
Golf Training Systems, Inc. [*Associated Press*] (SAG) .... GolfTSy
Golf Training Systems, Inc. [*NASDAQ symbol*] (SAG) .... GTSX
Golf Training Systems Unit [*NASDAQ symbol*] (TTSB) .... GTSXU
Golf Writers Association of America (EA) .... GWAA
Golfe Air Quebec Ltd. [*Canada ICAO designator*] (FAAC) .... GAQ
Golfing Union of Ireland (EAIO) .... GUI
Golfito [*Costa Rica*] [*Airport symbol*] (OAG) .... GLF
Golfito [*Costa Rica*] [*ICAO location identifier*] (ICLI) .... MRGF
Golgi Apparatus [*Medicine*] (DMAA) .... GA
Golgi Tendon Organ [*Anatomy*] .... GTO
Golgi-Associated Endoplasmic Reticulum Lysosomes .... GERL
Goliad, TX [*FM radio station call letters*] .... KHMC
Goliath Edison Screw .... GES
Goliath Gold Mines Ltd. [*Toronto Stock Exchange symbol Vancouver Stock
    Exchange symbol*] .... GOH
Golmud [*China*] [*Airport symbol*] (OAG) .... GOQ
Golombok Rust Inventory of Sexual Satisfaction [*Test*] [*Psychology*] .... GRISS
Golovin [*Alaska*] [*Airport symbol*] (OAG) .... GLV
Golpaygan [*Iran*] [*ICAO location identifier*] (ICLI) .... OIFG

Golpazari [*Turkey*] [*Also, GPA*] [*Seismograph station code, US Geological Survey*] (SEIS) .... GLP
Golpazari [*Turkey*] [*Also, GLP*] [*Seismograph station code, US Geological Survey*] (SEIS) .... GPA
Goma [*Zaire*] [*ICAO location identifier*] (ICLI) .... FZNA
Goma [*Zaire*] [*Airport symbol*] (OAG) .... GOM
Gomare [*Botswana*] [*ICAO location identifier*] (ICLI) .... FBGM
Gombarts Reducing Agent [*Medicine*] (AAMN) .... GRA
Gombarts Reducing Agent - Negative [*Medicine*] (AAMN) .... GRAN
Gomori Methenamine Silver Stain [*Medicine*] (DMAA) .... GMS
Gomori's Methenamine Silver [*A biological stain*] .... GMS
Gomphrena Virus [*Plant pathology*] .... GV
Gonadal Dysgenesis [*Endocrinology*] .... GD
Gonadal Steroid-Binding Globulin [*Medicine*] (DMAA) .... GBG
Gonadal Steroid-Binding Globulin [*Medicine*] .... GSBG
Gonadotropic Hormone [*Endocrinology*] .... GDH
Gonadotropic Hormone [*Endocrinology*] .... GTH
Gonadotropin [*Endocrinology*] .... Gn
Gonadotropin Enhancing Factor [*Endocrinology*] .... GEF
Gonadotropin-Inhibitory Material [*Endocrinology*] (MAE) .... GIM
Gonadotropin-Releasing Agent [*Endocrinology*] .... GRA
Gonadotropin-Releasing Factor [*Also, GnRH, LH-RF, LH-RH, LH-RH/FSH-RH, LRF, LRH*] [*Endocrinology*] .... GnRF
Gonadotropin-Releasing Factor [*Also, GnRF, GnRH, LH-RF, LH-RH/FSH-RH, LRF, LRH*] [*Endocrinology*] .... GRF
Gonadotropin-Releasing Hormone [*Also, GnRF, LH-RF, LH-RH, LH-RH/FSH-RH, LRF, LRH*] [*Endocrinology*] .... GnRH
Gonadotropin-Releasing Hormone Agonist [*Endocrinology*] .... GnRHA
Gonad-Stimulating Substance [*Endocrinology*] .... GSS
Gonalia [*Papua New Guinea*] [*Airport symbol*] (OAG) .... GOE
Gonbad Ghabous [*Iran*] [*ICAO location identifier*] (ICLI) .... OINK
Gondar [*Ethiopia*] [*Airport symbol*] (OAG) .... GDQ
Gondar [*Ethiopia*] [*ICAO location identifier*] (ICLI) .... HAGN
Gondi [*MARC language code Library of Congress*] (LCCP) .... gon
Gondola .... GOND
Gone for the Day .... GFD
Gone on Arrival [*Police terminology*] (IIA) .... GOA
Gone to Texas [*Sign on doors of New Englanders who had gone West, nineteenth century*] .... GTT
Gone with the Wind [*A novel by Margaret Mitchell; also, a motion picture*] .... GWTW
Gongwer's State Reports [*Ohio*] [*A publication*] (DLA) .... GSR
Gonidial [*With reference to colonies of bacteria*] .... G
Gonif's Molly [*Thief's Girl*] [*Yiddish*] .... GUN MOLL
Goniodysgenesis-Mental Retardation-Short Stature Syndrome [*Medicine*] (DMAA) .... GMS
Goniometer [*JETDS nomenclature*] [*Military*] (CET) .... GO
Goniometer [*RADAR instrument*] (DSUE) .... GONIO
Gonion (DMAA) .... Go
Gonni Air Services Ltd. [*Suriname*] [*ICAO designator*] (FAAC) .... GON
Gonococcal [*Clinical chemistry*] .... GC
Gonococcal Arthritis/Dermatitis Syndrome [*Medicine*] .... GADS
Gonococcal Base [*Broth*] [*Growth medium*] .... GCB
Gonococcal Ophthalmia Neonatorum [*Medicine*] .... GON
Gonococcal Urethritis [*Medicine*] (DMAA) .... GCU
Gonococcal Urethritis [*Medicine*] .... GU
Gonococcus [*Medicine*] (MEDA) .... GN
Gonococcus Filus [*A microorganism*] .... GF
Gonorrhea Case [*Medical slang*] .... GC
Gonorrhea Complement Fixation Test [*Medicine*] .... GCFT
Gonorrheal Invasive Peritonitis [*Medicine*] (DMAA) .... GIP
Gonosomatic Indices .... GSI
Gonvick-Trail Community School, Gonvick, MN [*Library symbol*] [*Library of Congress*] (LCLS) .... MnGonS
Gonville and Caius College [*Cambridge University*] (ROG) .... G & C
Gonville and Caius College [*Cambridge University*] (ROG) .... GCC
Gonzaga Special Report. Public Sector Labor Law [*A publication*] (DLA) .... Gonz Pub Lab L Rep
Gonzaga University (GAGS) .... Gonzaga U
Gonzaga University, Law Library, Spokane, WA [*Library symbol Library of Congress*] (LCLS) .... WaSpG-L
Gonzaga University, Spokane, WA [*Library symbol Library of Congress*] (LCLS) .... WaSpG
Gonzales, CA [*AM radio station call letters*] .... KKMC
Gonzales, CA [*FM radio station call letters*] (RBYB) .... KMBY-FM
Gonzales Gold Mines Ltd. [*Vancouver Stock Exchange symbol*] .... GZG
Gonzales, TX [*AM radio station call letters*] .... KCTI
Gonzales, TX [*FM radio station call letters*] (RBYB) .... KCTI-FM
Good (DAVI) .... G
Good [*Condition*] [*Antiquarian book trade, numismatics, etc.*] .... G
Good (WDMC) .... g
Good .... GD
Good [*Track condition*] [*Thoroughbred racing*] .... GD
Good Agricultural Practice [*Toxicology*] .... GAP
Good American Helping Hands (EA) .... GAHH
Good Automated Laboratory Practice [*Environmental Protection Agency*] .... GALP
Good Average Quality (ADA) .... GAQ
Good Bears of the World (EA) .... GBW
Good Clinical Practice [*Medicine*] .... GCP
Good Company Man [*Theater term*] (DSUE) .... GCM
Good Condition [*Doll collecting*] .... gc
Good Conduct [*Military decoration*] .... GC
Good Conduct Badge [*British*] .... GCB
Good Conduct Discharge .... GCD
Good Conduct Medal [*Military decoration*] .... GCM
Good Conduct Medal [*Military decoration*] (AABC) .... GCMDL

Good Conduct Medal Clasp .... GCMC
Good Counsel College [*New York*] .... GCC
Good Day Sunshine Beatles Fan Club (EA) .... GDSBFC
Good Delivery [*Business term*] .... GD
Good Emergency Mother Substitute [*Pediatrics*] (DAVI) .... GEMS
Good Engineering Practice (EG) .... GEP
Good Evening [*Amateur radio*] .... GE
Good Fair Average [*Insurance*] .... GFA
Good Faith [*Legal shorthand*] (LWAP) .... GF
Good Faith Charitable Organization (EA) .... GFCO
[*The*] Good Food Guide [*A publication British*] .... GFG
Good Gardeners' Association [*British*] .... GGA
Good Gay Poets (EA) .... GGP
Good Government [*A publication*] .... Good Govt
[*The*] Good Guys, Inc. [*NASDAQ symbol*] (NQ) .... GGUY
[*The*] Good Guys, Inc. [*Associated Press*] (SAG) .... GoodGy
Good Hope [*Guyana*] [*ICAO location identifier*] (ICLI) .... SYGH
[*The*] Good Hotel Guide [*A publication British*] .... GHG
Good Housekeeping Check Sheet (AAG) .... GHCS
Good in Bed (DSUE) .... GIB
Good Industrial Large-Scale Practice .... GILSP
Good Industrial Relations Directors [*Meetings sponsored by Master Printers of America*] .... GIRD
Good Intent Society of Galvanizers and Enamellers [*A union*] [*British*] .... GISGE
Good Laboratory Practice [*FDA*] .... GLP
Good Large Scale Practice .... GLSP
Good Luck (MHDB) .... GL
Good Luck and Smooth Sailing [*Slang Military*] (DNAB) .... GLASS
Good Management Practice .... GMP
Good Manufacturing Practice .... GMP
Good Marketable Quality [*Business term*] .... GMQ
Good Mason [*Freemasonry*] (ROG) .... GM
Good Merchantable Brand [*Business term*] .... GMB
Good Morning [*Amateur radio*] .... GM
Good Morning America [*Television program*] .... GMA
Good Morning Britain [*Early morning television program*] [*ITV*] [*British*] .... GMB
Good Neighbour Council of South Australia .... GNCSA
Good Neighbour Council of Tasmania [*Australia*] .... GNCT
Good Neighbour Program [*Australia*] .... GNP
Good News Bible [*Today's English Version*] [*A publication*] (BJA) .... GNB
Good News Mission (EA) .... GNM
Good Night [*Amateur radio*] .... GN
Good Old Friday [*Slang*] .... GOF
Good Ordinary Brand [*Business term*] .... GOB
Good Ordinary Brand [*Business term*] (ODBW) .... gob
Good Outdoor Manners Association (EA) .... GOMA
Good Practice .... GP
Good Practices in Mental Health (PDAA) .... GPMH
Good Sam Recreational Vehicle Club (EA) .... GSRVC
Good Samaritan Auxiliary Hospital, Edmonton, AB, Canada [*Library symbol*] [*Library of Congress*] (LCLS) .... CaAEGSA
Good Samaritan Auxiliary Hospital, Edmonton, Alberta [*Library symbol National Library of Canada*] (NLC) .... AEGSA
Good Samaritan Coalition [*Defunct*] (EA) .... GSC
Good Samaritan Hospital and Medical Center, Portland, OR [*Library symbol Library of Congress*] (LCLS) .... OrPGH
Good Samaritan Hospital, Corvallis, OR [*Library symbol Library of Congress*] (LCLS) .... OrCGSH
Good Samaritan Hospital, Dayton, OH [*Library symbol Library of Congress*] (LCLS) .... ODaGS
Good Samaritan Hospital, Medical Library, Cincinnati, OH [*Library symbol Library of Congress*] (LCLS) .... OCGSH
Good Samaritan Hospital, Medical Library, West Palm Beach, FL [*Library symbol Library of Congress*] (LCLS) .... FWpbG
Good Samaritan Hospital, Seattle, WA [*Library symbol Library of Congress*] (LCLS) .... WaSGS
Good Samaritan Hospital, Seattle, WA [*Library symbol*] [*Library of Congress*] (LCLS) .... WaSGSH
Good Samaritan Hospital, West Islip, NY [*Library symbol Library of Congress*] (LCLS) .... NWiH
Good Shepherd Hospital, Hermiston, OR [*Library symbol Library of Congress*] (LCLS) .... OrHeGS
Good Shepherd Sisters [*Australia*] .... GSS
Good Skiing Conditions .... G
Good Sound Merchantable .... GSM
Good Stuff to Know .... GSTK
Good Templar .... GT
Good This Month [*Business term*] .... GTM
Good This Week [*Business term*] .... GTW
Good Tidings (EA) .... GT
Good Till Canceled [*as in a brokerage order*] .... GTC
Good Times Restaurants [*NASDAQ symbol*] (TTSB) .... GTIM
Good Times Restaurants, Inc. [*Associated Press*] (SAG) .... GoodT
Good Times Restaurants, Inc. [*Associated Press*] (SAG) .... GoodTm
Good Times Restaurants, Inc. [*NASDAQ symbol*] (SAG) .... GTIM
Good Times Restaurants Wrrt [*NASDAQ symbol*] (TTSB) .... GTIMW
Good Times Restaurants Wrrt'B' [*NASDAQ symbol*] (TTSB) .... GTIMZ
Good Visual Field [*Ophthalmology*] (DAVI) .... GVF
Good Will In, Good Will Out [*Computer science*] .... GWIGWO
Good Words [*A publication*] (ROG) .... GW
Goodall City Library, Ogallala, NE [*Library symbol Library of Congress*] (LCLS) .... NbOg
Good-By [*Amateur radio*] .... GB
Goodenough Figure Drawing [*Psychology*] (DAVI) .... GFD
Goodenough-Harris Drawing Test [*Education*] .... G-H

Goodenough-Harris Drawing Test [*Psychology*] (DAVI) .... GHDT
Goodenow Family Association (EA) .... GFA
Goodeve on Railway Companies and Passengers [*A publication*] (DLA) .... Good Ry C
Goodeve on Real Property [*1883-1906*] [*A publication*] (DLA) .... Goodeve
Goodeve's Abstract of Patent Cases [*1785-1883*] [*England*] [*A publication*] (DLA) .... Good Pat
Goodeve's Law of Evidence [*India*] [*A publication*] (DLA) .... Good Ev
Goodfellow Air Force Base [*Texas*] .... GAFB
Goodfellow Technical Training Center [*Military*] .... GTTC
Gooding, ID [*Location identifier FAA*] (FAAL) .... GNG
Gooding, ID [*FM radio station call letters*] (RBYB) .... KAKO
Gooding, ID [*FM radio station call letters*] (RBYB) .... KMXM-FM
Gooding, ID [*AM radio station call letters*] .... KRXR
Gooding Public Library, Gooding, ID [*Library symbol*] [*Library of Congress*] (LCLS) .... IdGo
Gooding Public School District, Gooding, ID [*Library symbol*] [*Library of Congress*] (LCLS) .... IdGoPS
Goodland [*Kansas*] [*Airport symbol*] (OAG) .... GLD
Goodland, KS [*Television station call letters*] .... KBSL
Goodland, KS [*FM radio station call letters*] .... KGCR
Goodland, KS [*FM radio station call letters*] .... KKCI
Goodland, KS [*AM radio station call letters*] .... KLOE
Goodland Public Library (Mitten Memorial Library), Goodland, IN [*Library symbol Library of Congress*] (LCLS) .... InGoo
Goodman & Goodman, Toronto, Ontario [*Library symbol National Library of Canada*] (BIB) .... OTGG
Goodman, WI [*FM radio station call letters*] .... WGAZ
GoodMark Foods [*NASDAQ symbol*] (TTSB) .... GDMK
GoodMark Foods, Inc. [*NASDAQ symbol*] (NQ) .... GDMK
Goodmark Foods, Inc. [*Associated Press*] (SAG) .... Goodmrk
Goodness of Fit (MCD) .... GOF
Goodnews Bay [*Alaska*] [*Airport symbol*] (OAG) .... GNU
Goodnow Library, Sudbury, MA [*Library symbol Library of Congress*] (LCLS) .... MSu
Goodnow Library, Sudbury, MA [*Library symbol*] [*Library of Congress*] (LCLS) .... MSuL
Goodpasture [*Syndrome*] [*Medicine*] (DAVI) .... GP
Goodpasture's Syndrome [*Medicine*] (DAVI) .... GPS
Goodrich and Clincher (ROG) .... G & C
Goodrich, BF Capital [*Associated Press*] (SAG) .... GdrcCa
Goodrich, BF, Co. [*Associated Press*] (SAG) .... Goodrch
[*The*] **Goodrich** [*B.F.*] **Co.** [*Associated Press*] (SAG) .... Gdrich
[*The*] **Goodrich** [*B. F.*] **Co.** [*NYSE symbol*] (SPSG) .... GR
Goodrich Petrol 8% Cv'A'Pfd [*NASDAQ symbol*] (TTSB) .... GDPAP
Goodrich Petroleum [*NYSE symbol*] (SAG) .... GDP
Goodrich Petroleum [*NASDAQ symbol*] (SAG) .... GDPAP
Goodrich Petroleum [*Associated Press*] (SAG) .... GoodrP
Goodrich Petroleum [*Associated Press*] (SAG) .... GoodrPet
Goodrich-Amram Procedural Rules Service [*A publication*] (DLA) .... Goodrich-Amram
Goodridge Public School, Goodridge, MN [*Library symbol*] [*Library of Congress*] (LCLS) .... MnGoos
Goods .... GDS
Goods and Services Tax [*Canadian*] (ODBW) .... GST
Goods and Services Tax [*Canada*] .... GST
Goods in Bad Order .... GBO
Goods in Custody (ADA) .... GIC
Goods on Hand (DS) .... GDH
Goods on Hand (DS) .... GOH
Good-Service Pension [*Navy British*] .... GSP
Good-until-Canceled Order [*Business term*] .... GUC
Goodwell, OK [*FM radio station call letters*] .... KPSU
Goodwill Industries of America (EA) .... GIA
Goodwill Industries Volunteer Services (EA) .... GIVS
Goodwin Institute for Cancer Research [*Nova University*] [*Research center*] (RCD) .... GICR
Goodwin Railroad, Inc. [*AAR code*] .... GWIN
Goodwin's Probate Practice [*A publication*] (DLA) .... Good Pr
Goodwood Data Systems Ltd., Carleton Place, ON, Canada [*Library symbol Library of Congress*] (LCLS) .... CaOCpG
Goodwood Data Systems Ltd., Carleton Place, Ontario [*Library symbol National Library of Canada*] (NLC) .... OCPG
Goodwyn Institute, Memphis, TN [*Library symbol Library of Congress*] (LCLS) .... TMG
Goodyear Aerospace Corp. .... GAC
Goodyear Aircraft and Engineering Corp. .... GAEC
Goodyear Associative Processor [*Computer science*] .... GAP
Goodyear Atomic Corp. (KSC) .... GAT
Goodyear Atomic Corp., Portsmouth, OH [*Library symbol Library of Congress*] (LCLS) .... OPosmG
Goodyear, AZ [*Location identifier FAA*] (FAAL) .... GYR
Goodyear Canada, Inc. [*Toronto Stock Exchange symbol*] .... GT
Goodyear Electronic Differential Analyzer (IAA) .... GEDA
Goodyear Engineering Report (MCD) .... GER
Goodyear Tire & Rub [*NYSE symbol*] (TTSB) .... GT
[*The*] **Goodyear Tire & Rubber Co.** [*Associated Press*] (SAG) .... Goodyear
[*The*] **Goodyear Tire & Rubber Co.** [*NYSE symbol*] (SPSG) .... GT
[*The*] **Goodyear Tire & Rubber Co.** .... GTR
Goodyear Tire & Rubber Co., Akron, OH [*Library symbol Library of Congress*] (LCLS) .... OAkGy
Goodyear Video Network [*Training and motivational program*] .... GVN
Goodyear-Reston-Winthrop [*Publishing group*] .... GRW
Goody's Family Clothing [*Associated Press*] (SAG) .... GdyFam
Goody's Family Clothing [*NASDAQ symbol*] (SPSG) .... GDYS
Goofball [*Barbiturate pill*] .... GB
Goonabad [*Iran*] [*ICAO location identifier*] (ICLI) .... OIMD
Goondiwindi [*Australia Airport symbol*] (OAG) .... GOO
Goose Air Defense Sector .... GADS
Goose and Gander, Society for the Preservation of First Wives and First Husbands (EA) .... GGSPFWFH
Goose Bay [*Canada*] [*Airport symbol*] (OAG) .... YYR
Goose Bay, NF [*AM radio station call letters*] .... CFLN
Goose Bay, NF [*ICAO location identifier*] (ICLI) .... CYYR
Goose Creek, SC [*FM radio station call letters*] .... WSSP
Goose Creek Township Carnegie Library, De Land, IL [*Library symbol Library of Congress*] (LCLS) .... IDelan
Goose Hepatitis Virus [*Medicine*] (DMAA) .... GHV
Goose Management Unit .... GMU
Goose NORAD [*North American Air Defense*] **Sector** (IAA) .... GNS
Goose Red Blood Cell .... GRBC
Goosecreekite [*A zeolite*] .... GOO
GOP Action Committee .... GOPAC
GOP [*Grand Old Party*] **Women's Political Action League** (EA) .... GOPAL
Gopher Tape Armor [*Telecommunications*] (TEL) .... GT
Gora [*Papua New Guinea*] [*Airport symbol*] (OAG) .... GOC
Gorakhpur [*India*] [*Airport symbol*] (OAG) .... GOP
Gorakhpur [*India*] [*ICAO location identifier*] (ICLI) .... VEGK
Goran Capital [*NASDAQ symbol*] (TTSB) .... GNCNF
Goran Capital, Inc. [*NASDAQ symbol*] (SAG) .... GNCN
Goran Capital, Inc. [*Associated Press*] (SAG) .... GoranC
Gorda Cay, Abaco Island [*Bahamas*] [*ICAO location identifier*] (ICLI) .... MYAG
Gorda Ridge Eruption Assessment Team [*Marine science*] (OSRA) .... GREAT
Gordetsky [*G.R.*] **Telecommunications and General Management Consulting** [*San Diego, CA*] [*Telecommunications*] (TSSD) .... GRG
Gordex Minerals Ltd. [*Toronto Stock Exchange symbol*] .... GXM
Gordo Public Library, Gordo, AL [*Library symbol Library of Congress*] (LCLS) .... AGor
Gordon & Breach [*Publisher*] [*British*] .... G & B
Gordon College, Wenham, MA [*Library symbol Library of Congress*] (LCLS) .... MWenhG
Gordon College, Wenham, MA [*Inactive*] [*OCLC symbol*] (OCLC) .... MWN
Gordon Cooper Library, Carbondale, CO [*Library symbol Library of Congress*] (LCLS) .... CoCa
Gordon Diagnostic System (EDAC) .... GDS
Gordon Diagnostic System [*Attention deficit disorder test*] .... GSI
Gordon, E. S., Joplin MO [*STAC*] .... GES
Gordon Environmental Studies Laboratory [*University of Montana*] [*Research center*] (RCD) .... GEVST
Gordon Fraser [*Publisher*] [*British*] .... GF
Gordon, GA [*FM radio station call letters*] .... WALJ
Gordon, GA [*AM radio station call letters*] .... WBNM
Gordon Highlanders [*Military British*] (ROG) .... GORD HIGHRS
Gordon Junior College, Barnesville, GA [*Library symbol*] [*Library of Congress*] (LCLS) .... GBG
Gordon Military College [*Georgia*] .... GMC
Gordon, NE [*Location identifier FAA*] (FAAL) .... GRN
Gordon, NE [*FM radio station call letters*] .... KSDZ
Gordon on the Law of Decedents in Pennsylvania [*A publication*] (DLA) .... Gord Dec
Gordon Personal Inventory [*Psychology*] .... GPI
Gordon Personal Profile [*Psychology*] .... GPP
Gordon Personal Profile and Inventory [*Personality development test*] [*Psychology*] .... GPP-I
Gordon Setter Club of America (EA) .... GSCA
Gordon-Conwell Theological Seminary Library, South Hamilton, MA [*Library symbol Library of Congress*] (LCLS) .... MSohG
Gordon-Conwell Theological Seminary, South Hamilton, MA [*OCLC symbol*] (OCLC) .... BCT
Gordon's Digest of United States Laws [*A publication*] (DLA) .... Gord Dig
Gordon's Reports [*24-26 Colorado and 10-13 Colorado Appeals*] [*A publication*] (DLA) .... Gordon
Gordon's Treason Trials [*A publication*] (DLA) .... Gord Tr
Gordonsville, VA [*Location identifier FAA*] (FAAL) .... GVE
Gordonville, MO [*FM radio station call letters*] .... KCGQ-FM
Gore [*New Zealand*] [*Airport symbol*] (AD) .... GOE
Gore [*Ethiopia*] [*Airport symbol*] (OAG) .... GOR
Gore [*Ethiopia*] [*ICAO location identifier*] (ICLI) .... HAGR
Gore & Storrie Ltd., Toronto, Ontario [*Library symbol National Library of Canada*] (NLC) .... OTGS
Gore Bay, ON [*ICAO location identifier*] (ICLI) .... CYZE
Gore Bay Union Public Library, Ontario [*Library symbol National Library of Canada*] (NLC) .... OGBU
Gore-Brown on Companies [*43rd ed.*] [*1977*] [*A publication*] (DLA).... Gore-B Comp
Gorgan [*Iran*] [*ICAO location identifier*] (ICLI) .... OING
Gorgas Memorial Laboratory [*Panama*] [*Research center*] (RCD) .... GML
Gorge [*Board on Geographic Names*] .... GRGE
Gorgias [*483-376BC*] [*Classical studies*] (OCD) .... Gorg
Gorgias [*of Plato*] [*Classical studies*] (OCD) .... Grg
Gorham Collectors' Guild [*Defunct*] (EA) .... GCG
Gorham, ME [*AM radio station call letters*] .... WLAM
Gorham, ME [*FM radio station call letters*] .... WMPG
Gorham, NH [*FM radio station call letters*] .... WXLQ
Gorham State Teachers College [*Merged with University of Maine*] .... GSTC
Gori [*Former USSR Seismograph station code, US Geological Survey*] (SEIS) .... GOR
Gorilla Foundation (EA) .... GF
Gorilla Sign Language (BYTE) .... GSL
Goris [*Former USSR Seismograph station code, US Geological Survey*] (SEIS) .... GRS

Gorizia [*Italy ICAO location identifier*] (ICLI) .... LIPG
Gorje [*Yugoslavia*] [*Seismograph station code, US Geological Survey Closed*]
(SEIS) .... GRJ
Gorkha [*Nepal*] [*ICAO location identifier*] (ICLI) .... VNGK
Gorman [*TACAN station*] (MCD) .... GMN
Gorman, CA [*Location identifier FAA*] (FAAL) .... GMN
Gorman-Rupp [*AMEX symbol*] (TTSB) .... GRC
Gorman-Rupp Co. [*Associated Press*] (SAG) .... GormRup
Gorman-Rupp Co. [*AMEX symbol*] (SPSG) .... GRC
Gormanston County Meath [*Ireland*] [*ICAO location identifier*] (ICLI) .... EIGM
Gormfelt [*Denmark ICAO location identifier*] (ICLI) .... EKGF
Gorna Orechovitsa [*Bulgaria*] [*ICAO location identifier*] (ICLI) .... LBGO
Gorna Orjachovica [*Bulgaria*] [*Airport symbol*] (OAG) .... GOZ
Gorny [*Former USSR Seismograph station code, US Geological Survey Closed*] (SEIS) .... GOY
Goroka [*Papua New Guinea*] [*ICAO location identifier*] (ICLI) .... AYGA
Goroka [*Papua New Guinea*] [*Airport symbol*] (OAG) .... GKA
Goroka [*Papua New Guinea*] [*Seismograph station code, US Geological Survey Closed*] (SEIS) .... GKA
Goroka [*Papua New Guinea*] [*Seismograph station code, US Geological Survey Closed*] (SEIS) .... GRK
Gorom-Gorom [*Burkina Faso*] [*ICAO location identifier*] (ICLI) .... DHEG
Gorom-Gorom [*Burkina Faso*] [*Airport symbol*] (OAG) .... XGG
Gorontalo [*Indonesia*] [*Airport symbol*] (OAG) .... GTO
Gorontalo/Jalaluddin [*Indonesia*] [*ICAO location identifier*] (ICLI) .... WAMG
Gorron [*France*] [*Seismograph station code, US Geological Survey*] (SEIS) .... GRR
Gosford [*Australia Airport symbol Obsolete*] (OAG) .... GOS
Gosford's Manuscript Reports, Scotch Court of Session [*A publication*] (DLA) .... Gosf
Goshen College, Goshen, IN [*OCLC symbol*] (OCLC) .... IGC
Goshen College, Goshen, IN [*Library symbol Library of Congress*] (LCLS) .... InGo
Goshen, IN [*Location identifier FAA*] (FAAL) .... GSH
Goshen, IN [*FM radio station call letters*] .... WGCS
Goshen, IN [*AM radio station call letters*] .... WKAM
Goshen, IN [*FM radio station call letters*] .... WZOW
Goshen Library and Historical Society, Goshen, NY [*Library symbol Library of Congress*] (LCLS) .... NGos
Goshen News, Goshen, IN [*Library symbol Library of Congress*] (LCLS) .... InGoN
Goshen Public Library, Goshen, IN [*Library symbol Library of Congress*] (LCLS) .... InGoP
Gosling Library, St. John's, Newfoundland [*Library symbol National Library of Canada*] (NLC) .... NFSGO
Gosling Library, St. John's, NF, Canada [*Library symbol Library of Congress*] (LCLS) .... CaNfSGo
Gosnell, AR [*FM radio station call letters*] (RBYB) .... KAMJ
Gospel (ROG) .... GOSP
Gospel .... GSPL
Gospel and the Age Series [*A publication*] .... GAA
Gospel Association for the Blind (EA) .... GAB
Gospel Light Publications [*British*] .... GLP
Gospel Literature International (EA) .... GLINT
Gospel literature Outreach [*Australia*] .... GLO
Gospel Missionary Union (EA) .... GMU
Gospel Music Association (EA) .... GMA
Gospel Music Workshop of America (EA) .... GMWA
Gospel of Peter [*Apocryphal work*] .... G Pet
Gospel of the Hebrews [*Apocryphal work*] .... G Heb
Gospel of Thomas [*Apocryphal work*] .... G Thom
Gospel Recordings (EA) .... GR
Gospel Recordings, Inc. .... GRI
Gospel Truth Association (EA) .... GTA
Gospel-in-Film Service [*Australia*] .... GIFS
Gospelrama Gospel Expo [*An association*] (EA) .... GGE
GOSS [*Integrated Global Ocean Station System*] **Sea Level Project in the Pacific** (USDC) .... ISLP-Pac
Gossamer Hat [*Tall hat*] (ROG) .... GOSS
Gossan Resources [*Vancouver Stock Exchange symbol*] .... GSS
Gossau SG [*Switzerland ICAO location identifier*] (ICLI) .... LSXO
Gossip (DSUE) .... GOS
Gossudarstvenny Obstschessojusny Standart [*All-Union State Standard*] [*Former USSR*] .... GOST
Gossypol Acetic Acid (DMAA) .... GAA
Gosudarstvennaia Biblioteka SSSR Imeni V. I. Lenina [*Lenin State Library of the USSR*], Moscow, Soviet Union [*Library symbol Library of Congress*] (LCLS) .... Ru
Gosudarstvennaia Publichnaia Biblioteka Imeni Saltykova-Shchedrina [*State Saltikov-Shchedrin Public Library*], Leningrad, Soviet Union [*Library symbol Library of Congress*] (LCLS) .... RuL
Gosudarstvennaia Publichnaia Nauchno-Tekhnicheskaia Biblioteka SSSR [*State Public Scientific and Technical Library*], Moscow, Soviet Union [*Library symbol Library of Congress*] (LCLS) .... RuMG
Gosudarstvennaja Planovaja Komissija [*Central Planning Commission*] [*Former USSR*] .... GOSPLAN
Gosudarstvennoe Knigoizdatelstvo [*State Publishing House*] [*Former USSR*] .... GEZ
Gosudarstvennoe Politicheskoe Upravlenie [*Government Political Administration*] [*Soviet secret service organization, also known as OGPU Later, KGB*] .... GPU
Gosudarstvennoe Strakhovanie [*State insurance*] [*Former USSR*] .... GOSSTRAKH
Gosudarstvennyi Institut Zhurnalistiki .... GIZH
Gosudarstvennyi Komitet Oborony [*State Defense Committee*] [*Former USSR World War II*] .... GKO
Gosudarstvennyi Universal'nyi Magazin [*Government Department Store*] [*Moscow*] .... GUM

Gosudarstvennyy Komitet po Nauki i Teknologii [*State Committee for Science and Technology*] [*Former USSR*] (LAIN) .... GKNT
Gosudartsvennaia Publichnaia Biblioteka Ukrainskoi SSR [*State Public Library of the Ukrainian SSR*], Kiev, Soviet Union [*Library symbol Library of Congress*] (LCLS) .... RuUk
Got Ya Again [*Initialism used as name of second successful phony event staged by Washington, DC, law enforcement agents posing as fences*] [*See PFF Inc*] .... GYA
Gotaas-Larsen Shipping Corp. (MHDW) .... GOTLF
Goteborg [*Sweden*] [*Seismograph station code, US Geological Survey Closed*] (SEIS) .... GOT
Goteborg/Eastern Hospital [*Sweden ICAO location identifier*] (ICLI) .... ESHB
Goteborg/Landvetter [*Sweden ICAO location identifier*] (ICLI) .... ESGG
Goteborg/Save [*Sweden ICAO location identifier*] (ICLI) .... ESGP
Goteborgs Hogskolas Arsskrift [*Gothenburg*] [*A publication*] (BJA) .... GotHA
Goteborgs Universititsbibliotek, Goteborg, Sweden [*Library symbol Library of Congress*] (LCLS) .... SwGU
Gotenba [*Japan*] [*Seismograph station code, US Geological Survey Closed*] (SEIS) .... GTN
Gotham Avenue Elementary School, Elmont, NY [*Library symbol*] [*Library of Congress*] (LCLS) .... NEImoGE
Gothenburg [*Sweden*] [*Airport symbol*] (OAG) .... GOT
Gothenburg, NE [*Location identifier FAA*] (FAAL) .... GTE
Gothenburg University Terminal System [*IBM Corp.*] (EECA) .... GUTS
Gothic [*Language, etc.*] (ROG) .... GO
Gothic [*MARC language code Library of Congress*] (LCCP) .... got
Gothic [*Language, etc.*] .... GOTH
Gothic (VRA) .... Goth
Gothic Energy [*NASDAQ symbol*] (TTSB) .... GOTH
Gothic Energy Corp. [*NASDAQ symbol*] (SAG) .... GOTH
Gothic Energy Corp. [*Associated Press*] (SAG) .... GothE
Gothic Energy Corp. [*Associated Press*] (SAG) .... Gothic
Gothic Energy Corp. [*Associated Press*] (SAG) .... GothicEn
Gothic Energy Wrrt [*NASDAQ symbol*] (TTSB) .... GOTHW
Gothic Energy Wrrt [*NASDAQ symbol*] (TTSB) .... GOTHZ
Gothic Letter .... GL
Gott Hilf Mir Elenden [*God Help Miserable Me*] [*Motto of Eleonore, Electress of Brandenburg (1583-1607)*] [*German*] .... GHME
Gott Ist Mein Teil [*God Is My Portion*] [*Motto of Friedrich IV, Duke of Liegnitz (1552-96)*] [*German*] .... GIMT
Gott Ist Mein Trost [*God Is My Comfort*] [*Motto for a number of 16th and 17th century German and Bavarian rulers*] [*German*] .... GIMT
Gott Mein Gut [*God Is My Good*] [*Motto of Karl, Margrave of Baden-Durlach (1529-77); Ernst Friedrich, (1560-1604)*] [*German*] .... GMG
Gott Verlaeszt die Seinen Nicht [*God Forsakes Not His Own*] [*Motto of Dorothee, Duchess of Braunschweig-Wolfenbuttel (1607-34)*] [*German*] .... GVDSN
Gott Wende Alles zum Besten [*May God Turn Everything to the Best*] [*Motto of Amoene Amalie, Princess of Anhalt (d. 1626)*] [*German*] .... GWAZB
Gott Wirds Wohl Schaffen [*God Will Arrange*] [*Motto of Dorothee Auguste, Duchess of Braunschweig (1577-1625)*] [*German*] .... GWWS
Gottes Wille Geschehe [*God's Will Be Done*] [*Motto of Juliane Ursula, Margravine of Baden (d. 1614)*] [*German*] .... GWG
Gottingen [*Federal Republic of Germany*] [*Seismograph station code, US Geological Survey*] (SEIS) .... GTT
Gottlieb Kaylor & Stocks, Ottawa, Ontario [*Library symbol National Library of Canada*] (BIB) .... OOGKS
Gottlieb Textiles .... GOTTEX
Gottschalks, Inc. [*NYSE symbol*] (SPSG) .... GOT
Gottschalks, Inc. [*Associated Press*] (SAG) .... Gotchk
Gottschall's Dayton Superior Court Reports [*Ohio*] [*A publication*] (DLA) .... Gottschall
Gottwaldov [*Former Czechoslovakia*] [*Airport symbol*] (OAG) .... GTW
Gouache (VRA) .... gou
Goucher College (GAGS) .... Goucher C
Goucher College Babylonian Collection (BJA) .... GCBC
Goucher College, Baltimore, MD [*Library symbol Library of Congress*] (LCLS) .... MdBG
Goudsmit's Pandects [*Roman law*] [*A publication*] (DLA) .... Goud Pand
Goudy Society (EA) .... GS
Gough Island [*South Africa*] [*ICAO location identifier*] (ICLI) .... FAGE
Goulais River Community Library, Ontario [*Library symbol National Library of Canada*] (NLC) .... OGOR
Goulburn Island [*Australia Airport symbol Obsolete*] (OAG) .... GBL
Goulburn Valley Airlines [*Australia*] .... GVA
Goulburn Valley Viticultural Association [*Australia*] .... GVVA
Gould and Tucker's Notes on Revised Statutes of United States [*A publication*] (DLA) .... G & T
Gould and Tucker's Notes on Revised Statutes of United States [*A publication*] (DLA) .... Gould & T
Gould Belt [*Galactic science*] .... GB
Gould, Incorporated, Gould Information Center, Cleveland, OH [*Library symbol Library of Congress*] (LCLS) .... OCIGI
Gould, Inc., Ocean Systems Information Center, Cleveland, OH [*OCLC symbol*] (OCLC) .... OGO
Gould Information Center, Cleveland, OH [*OCLC symbol*] (OCLC) .... OGI
Gould Laboratory Materials Research, Cleveland, OH [*OCLC symbol*] (OCLC) .... CIE
Gould League of New South Wales [*Australia*] .... GLNSW
Gould League of Victoria [*Australia*] .... GLV
Gould on the Principles of Pleading in Civil Actions [*A publication*] (DLA) .... Gould Pl
Gould on Waters [*A publication*] (DLA) .... Gould Wat
Gould's Arkansas Digest of Laws [*A publication*] (DLA) .... Gould's Dig
Goulds, FL [*FM radio station call letters*] .... WRTO

Goulds Public Library, Newfoundland [*Library symbol National Library of Canada*] (BIB) .... NFGO
Goulds Pumps [*NASDAQ symbol*] (TTSB) .... GULD
Goulds Pumps, Inc. [*Associated Press*] (SAG) .... GouldP
Goulds Pumps, Inc. [*NASDAQ symbol*] (NQ) .... GULD
Gould's Stenographic Reporter [*Monographic Series*] [*Albany, NY*] [*A publication*] (DLA) .... Gould Sten Rep
Gouldsborough's English King's Bench Reports [*A publication*] (DLA) .... Gould
Gouldsborough's English King's Bench Reports [*A publication*] (DLA) .... Gouldsb
Gouldsborough's English King's Bench Reports [*A publication*] (DLA) .... Gouldsb (Eng)
Goundam [*Mali*] [*ICAO location identifier*] (ICLI) .... GAGM
Goundam [*Mali*] [*Airport symbol*] (OAG) .... GUD
Gourcy [*Burkina Faso*] [*ICAO location identifier*] (ICLI) .... DHCU
Gourd Society of America [*Superseded by AGS*] (EA) .... GSA
Gourde [*Monetary unit*] [*Haiti*] .... G
Gourde [*Monetary unit*] [*Haiti*] .... GDE
Goure [*Niger*] [*ICAO location identifier*] (ICLI) .... DRZG
Gourick's Patent Digest [*1889-91*] [*A publication*] (DLA) .... Gour
Gourlie on General Average [*A publication*] (DLA) .... Gourl Gen Av
Goutte [*Drop*] [*Pharmacy*] .... gutt
Gouvernement de la Republique de l'Angola en Exile [*Government of the Republic of Angola in Exile*] .... GRAE
Gouvernement du Quebec, Ministere de l'Education, Service General des Moyens d'Enseignement, Montreal, PQ, Canada [*Library symbol Library of Congress*] (LCLS) .... CaQMSGME
Gouvernement du Quebec, Service Aerien Gouvernemental [*Canada*] [*FAA designator*] (FAAC) .... QUE
Gouvernement Militaire de la Zone Francaise d'Occupation [*Military Government of the French Zone of Occupation*] [*of Germany*] .... GMZFO
Gouvernement Provisoire de la Republique Algerienne [*Provisional Government of the Algerian Republic*] .... GPRA
Gouverneur, NY [*FM radio station call letters*] .... WGIX
Gouverneur, NY [*AM radio station call letters*] .... WIGS
Govalkot [*India*] [*Seismograph station code, US Geological Survey Closed*] (SEIS) .... GOV
Gove [*Australia ICAO location identifier*] (ICLI) .... ADGV
Gove [*Australia Airport symbol*] (OAG) .... GOV
Govenment Performance and Results Act [*1993*] .... GPRA
Govern (ROG) .... GOV
Govern (ROG) .... GOVN
Governador Valadares [*Brazil*] [*Airport symbol*] (OAG) .... GVR
Governed (ROG) .... GOVD
Governesses Benevolent Institute [*British*] (AIE) .... GBI
Governing (MSA) .... GOVG
Governing Bodies Association [*Organization of school officials*] [*British*] .... GBA
Governing Bodies Association of Public Schools [*British*] .... GBAPS
Governing Body .... GB
Governing Body of Girls' Schools Association [*British*] .... GBGSA
Governing Body of the Church in Wales (DAS) .... GBCW
Governing Council (EERA) .... GC
Governing Council for Environmental Programs [*United Nations*] .... GCEP
Governing Council of the Cat Fancy [*British*] (BI) .... GCCF
Governing International Fisheries Agreements .... GIFA
Governing International Fishing Agreement (MSC) .... GIFA
Government .... G
Government .... GOV
Government (VRA) .... gov
Government (DD) .... govt
Government (AFM) .... GOVT
Government .... GOVT
Government (WDAA) .... GVT
Government Acceptance Test (MCD) .... GAT
Government Accountability Project (EA) .... GAP
Government Accountability Property System (MCD) .... GAPS
Government Accounting Office (MCD) .... GAO
Government Accounting Service [*British*] .... GAS
Government Accumulation Yard .... GAY
Government Acquisition Quality Assurance (MCD) .... GAQA
Government Actuary [*Australia*] .... GA
Government Actuary's Department .... GAD
Government Administrators Association (SRA) .... GAA
Government Advertising Agency [*New South Wales, Australia*] .... GAA
Government Advisory Committee on International Book and Library Programs [*Terminated, 1977*] (EGAO) .... GAC
Government Aerospace Systems Division [*Harris Corp.*] .... GASD
Government Affairs Branch [*European Theater of Operations*] [*World War II*] .... GAB
Government Affairs Foundation [*Defunct*] (EA) .... GAF
Government Agency (AAG) .... GA
Government Agency Arbitrage and Swap System (MHDW) .... GAASS
Government Agricultural Policy and Services for Farmers [*British*] .... GAPSF
Government Aircraft (DNAB) .... GOVAIR
Government Aircraft Facilities .... GAF
Government Aircraft Plant .... GAP
Government and Aeronautical Products Division [*Honeywell, Inc.*] .... GAPD
Government and Industrial (IEEE) .... GI
Government and Industry Team .... GAIT
Government and Legal Affairs Division [*American Occupational Therapy Association*] .... GLAD
Government and Relief in Occupied Areas [*Post-World War II*] .... GARIOA
Government Architect (ADA) .... GA
Government Archives Division [*National Archives of Canada*] [*Information service or system*] (IID) .... GAD
Government Astronomy Administration Round Table .... GAART

Government Authorized Representative .... GAR
Government Bill of Lading .... GBL
Government Bill of Lading .... GBLADING
Government Bill of Lading Office Code (AFIT) .... GBLOC
Government Bill of Lading System .... GOBILS
Government Boat .... G/B
Government Bunkers .... GB
Government Bureau of Standards .... GBS
Government Capital Expenditure [*Economics*] G2
Government Capital Expenditure [*Finance*] .... GCE
Government Civil Aviation Authority [*ICAO designator*] (ICDA) .... YA
Government Clerical Services' Union [*Ceylon*] .... GCSU
Government Code and Cypher School [*Later, GCHQ*] [*Sometimes facetiously translated as Golf, Chess, and Cheese Society*] [*British*] .... GCCS
Government Code Headquarters [*Formerly, GCCS*] [*British*] (INF) .... GCHQ
Government Communications (TEL) .... GC
Government Communications Headquarters [*British*] .... GCHQ
Government Competitive Testing .... GCT
Government Computer Expo (HGAA) .... GCE
Government Computer News .... GCN
Government Concept of Operations (RDA) .... GCO
Government Contract Advisor [*CD-ROM*] [*Published by Clark Boardman*] (AAGC) .... GCA
Government Contract Committee [*Later, OFCCP*] [*Department of Labor*] .... GCC
Government Contract Costs, Pricing and Accounting Report [*A publication*] (AAGC) .... CP&AR
Government Contract Management Association (AAGC) .... GCMA
Government Contract Management Association of America (EA) .... GCMA
Government Contractor .... GC
Government Contractors Subcontractors .... GCS
Government Contracts Program [*George Washington University Law Center*] (DLA) .... GCP
Government Contracts Reporter [*A publication*] (AAGC) .... GCR
Government Contracts Reporter [*Commerce Clearing House*] [*A publication*] (DLA) .... Gov't Cont Rep
Government Contribution .... GC
Government Current Expenditure [*Economics*] G1
Government Data Network [*Telecommunications*] (OSI) .... GDN
Government Data Publications [*Information service or system*] (IID) .... GDP
Government Development Bank of Puerto Rico .... GDB
Government Development Platform [*Marine science*] (OSRA) .... GDP
Government Development Platform (USDC) .... GDP
Government Disclosure Service [*A publication*] (AAGC) .... GDS
Government Document Application Profile [*Telecommunications*] (OSI) .... GDAP
Government Document Publishing Service .... GDPS
Government Documents Catalog Service [*Information service or system*] (IID) .... GDCS
Government Documents Round Table [*American Library Association*] .... GODORT
Government Economic Service [*British*] .... GES
Government EDP [*Electronic Data Processing*] Standards Committee [*Canada*] .... GESC
Government Electronics Division .... GED
Government Electronics Market (IAA) .... GEM
Government Employees Clinic Center [*British*] .... GECC
Government Employees' Compensation Act [*1908*] .... GECA
Government Employees Council [*Later, PED*] (EA) .... GEC
Government Employees Exchange .... GEX
Government Employees Insurance Co. .... GEICO
Government Employees Training Act [*1966*] .... GETA
Government Employees United Against Discrimination [*An association*] .... GUARD
Government Energy Management Program [*Australia*] .... GEMP
Government Evacuation Scheme [*British World War II*] .... GES
Government Excess Baggage Authorization .... GEBA
Government Expenditure [*Economics*] .... G
Government Expenditure [*Economics*] .... Gd
Government Expenditure Management System [*Australia*] .... GEMS
Government Facilities Brochure .... GFB
Government Facilities Request (AAG) .... GFR
Government Final Inspection .... GFI
Government Finance Officers Association of United States and Canada (EA) .... GFOA
Government Finance Statistics (NITA) .... GFS
Government Finance Statistics [*International Monetary Fund*] [*Information service or system*] (CRD) .... GFSY
Government Fiscal Year (MCD) .... GFY
Government Flight Representative .... GFR
Government Fluidic Coordinating Group .... GFCG
Government Form .... GF
Government Free Issue (AABC) .... GFI
Government Funded (BABM) .... GF
Government Furnished Repair Parts .... GFRP
Government Geoscience Database Policy Advisory Committee [*Commonwealth*] (EERA) .... GGDPAC
Government Girl .... GG
Government Gold Mining Areas .... GGMA
Government Grade [*Followed by a number, 1-18; National Security Agency Employee Grade*] .... GG
Government House [*Canada*] .... GH
Government House [*Canada*] (DNAB) .... GOVTHO
Government House, Reference Library, Ottawa, ON, Canada [*Library symbol Library of Congress*] (LCLS) .... CaOOGH
Government Idle Industrial Reserve (AAG) .... GIIR
Government Imprinted Penalty Stationery Society (EA) .... GIPS
Government in the Sunshine Act [*1976*] .... GISA

Government/Industry Technical Liaison Committee [*Australia*] ... GITL
Government Information and Advertising [*New South Wales, Australia*] ... GIA
Government Information Exchange [*Internet*] (AAGC) ... GIX
Government Information Locator Service [*Internet*] (AAGC) ... GILS
Government Information Organization [*Later, NAGC*] ... GIO
Government Information Service (WDAA) ... GIS
Government Information Services [*Republic of Ireland*] ... GIS
Government Information Services Committee [*Special Libraries Association*] ... GISC
Government Information Subcommittee [*American Library Association*] ... GIS
Government Initiated (IEEE) ... GI
Government In-Service Library, Yellowknife, NT, Canada [*Library symbol Library of Congress*] (LCLS) ... CaNWYGI
Government Interface Control Working Group [*Military*] ... GICWG
Government Issue [*Army*] ... GI
Government Issue Technical Inspection (INF) ... GITI
Government Laboratory (BARN) ... GL
Government Land Register [*of Western Australia*] [*State*] (EERA) ... GLR
Government Large Structures Assembly (SSD) ... GLSA
Government Launch Service (SSD) ... GLS
Government Launch Service (Cryogenic) (SSD) ... GLS(C)
Government Libraries Information Network in New South Wales [*Australia*] ... GLINN
Government Library, Government of the Northwest Territories, Yellow knife, Northwest Territories [*Library symbol National Library of Canada*] (NLC) ... NWYGI
Government Logistics Evaluation and Testing (MCD) ... GLET
Government Losses in Shipment Act [*1937*] ... GLISA
Government Lot Acceptance Test [*Military*] (CAAL) ... GLAT
Government Maintenance Depot (MCD) ... GMD
Government Management Information Sciences (EA) ... GMIS
Government Maturity Test (MCD) ... GMT
Government Microcircuit Applications Conference ... GOMAC
Government Minimum Essential Requirements Document ... GMERD
Government Modification Authorization (AAG) ... GMA
Government Motor Vehicle (DNAB) ... GMV
Government National Mortgage Administration (AAGC) ... GNMA
Government National Mortgage Association [*See also GNMA*] ... GINNIE MAE
Government National Mortgage Association [*Nickname: Ginnie Mae*] ... GNMA
Government National Railway Association [*Proposed*] [*Nickname: Ginnie Rae*] ... GNRA
Government Network Management Profile [*National Institute of Standards and Technology*] ... GNMP
Government Nomenclature Equipment (DNAB) ... GNE
Government Obligation [*Economics*] ... GO
Government of Alberta Publications [*Alberta Public Affairs Bureau*] [*Canada Information service or system*] (CRD) ... GAP
Government of American Samoa (MUGU) ... GAS
Government of Bangladesh ... GOB
Government Of Bangladesh ... GOB
Government of Burma (CINC) ... GOB
Government of Ghana ... GOG
Government of Honduras ... GOH
Government of India ... GI
Government of Indonesia ... GOI
Government of Iran ... GOI
Government of Israel (MCD) ... GOI
Government of Israel Furnished Equipment (MCD) ... GOIFE
Government of Israel Trade Center (EA) ... GITC
Government of Italy ... GOI
Government of Japan (CINC) ... GOJ
Government of Korea ... GOK
Government of Malaysia (CINC) ... GOM
Government of New Brunswick, Translation Bureau, Fredericton, NB, Canada [*Library symbol*] [*Library of Congress*] (LCLS) ... CaNBFT
Government of New Zealand ... GNZ
Government of North Vietnam ... GNVN
Government of Pakistan (ECON) ... GOP
Government of Singapore (CINC) ... GOS
Government of Spain ... GOS
Government of Sweden (MCD) ... GOS
Government of the Gambia ... GOTG
Government of the Khmer Republic [*Anticommunist government of Cambodia during the early seventies*] (VNW) ... GKR
Government of the Philippines (CINC) ... GOP
Government of the Republic of China ... GRC
Government of the Ryukyu Islands ... GRI
Government of the Yukon, Department of Economic Development: Mines and Small Business, Whitehorse, YT, Canada [*Library symbol*] [*Library of Congress*] (LCLS) ... CaYWED
Government of the Yukon, Department of Health and Human Resources, Whitehorse, YT, Canada [*Library symbol*] [*Library of Congress*] (LCLS) ... CaYWHHR
Government of the Yukon, Department of Renewable Resources, Whitehorse, YT, Canada [*Library symbol*] [*Library of Congress*] (LCLS) ... CaYWRR
Government of the Yukon, Department of Territorial Affairs, Whitehorse, YT, Canada [*Library symbol Library of Congress*] (LCLS) ... CaYWTA
Government of the Yukon, Library Services Branch, Whitehorse, YT, Canada [*Library symbol Library of Congress*] (LCLS) ... CaYWLS
Government of Tunisia ... GOT
Government of Uganda (ECON) ... GOU
Government of Vietnam ... GVN
Government Off- The Shelf (DOMA) ... GOTS
Government Officials Responsible for Standardization Policies [*Economic Commission for Europe*] [*United Nations*] (PDAA) ... GORSP
Government on Taiwan ... GONT
Government Open Systems Implementation Protocol [*Telecommunications*] ... GOSIP
Government Open Systems Interconnection Profile [*National Institute of Standards and Technology*] (GFGA) ... GOSIP
Government Open Systems Interconnection Profiles Computer science (EERA) ... GOSIP
Government Operations Committee [*US Senate*] ... GO
Government Operations Committee ... GOC
Government Operations Committee [*House and Senate*] (AAGC) ... Gov Ops
Government or Commercial Aircraft (DNAB) ... GOVMERAIR
Government Owned ... GO
Government Packet Network [*Canada*] ... GPN
Government Paper Specification Standards ... GPS
Government Patent Policy Act [*1981*] ... GPPA
Government Patents Board [*Functions transferred to Secretary of Commerce, 1961*] ... GPB
Government Performance and Results Act [*1993*] (RDA) ... GPRA
Government Plant Representative ... GPR
Government Preliminary Evaluation (MCD) ... GPE
Government Preliminary Inspection (MCD) ... GPI
Government Printer [*Queensland, Australia*] ... GOPRINT
Government Printing Office ... GPO
Government Printing Office Bookstore (OICC) ... GPOB
Government Procurement Practices Board [*Proposed*] ... GPPB
Government Procurement Service ... GPS
Government Production and Research Property (SSD) ... GPRP
Government Property ... GP
Government Property Administration (MCD) ... GPA
Government Property Lost or Damaged [*or Destroyed*] ... GPLD
Government Property Register [*of New South Wales*] [*State*] (EERA) ... GPR
Government Property Yard ... GPY
Government Public Relations Association [*Defunct*] ... GPRA
Government Publications [*Northern Territory, Australia*] ... GP
Government Publications Center (SAA) ... GPC
Government Publications, University of Saskatchewan, Saskatoon, Saskatchewan [*Library symbol National Library of Canada*] (NLC) ... SSUGP
Government Purchases ... G
Government Purchases of Goods and Services [*BTS*] (TAG) ... GPGS
Government Purpose Classification ... GPC
Government Purpose Rights (AAGC) ... GPR
Government Quality Assurance (NATG) ... GQA
Government Rate Tender ... GRT
Government Reform and Oversight Committee [*House of Representatives*] (AAGC) ... GRO
Government Regulation (AAG) ... GR
Government Relations Office, Spar Aerospace Ltd., Ottawa, Ontario [*Library symbol National Library of Canada*] (BIB) ... OOSAR
Government Report (AAG) ... GR
Government Report Authorization and Record (AAG) ... GRAR
Government Reports and Topical Announcements [*Later, WGA*] [*National Technical Information Service*] ... GRTA
Government Reports Announcements [*Department of Commerce*] [*Database producer*] ... GRA
Government Reports Announcements and Index [*Department of Commerce A publication*] ... GRAI
Government Reports Index [*Formerly, USGRDR-I*] [*Department of Commerce*] ... GRI
Government Research and Development Reports ... GRR
Government Research Centers Directory [*Later, GRD*] [*A publication*] ... GRC
Government Research Corp. [*Information service or system*] (IID) ... GRC
Government Research Directory [*A publication*] ... GRD
Government Research Index (MCD) ... GRI
Government Research Institute of Formosa ... GRIF
Government Reservation Bureau ... GRB
Government Reserve [*British*] (ADA) ... GR
Government Responsibility (MCD) ... GR
Government Responsibility Action ... GRA
Government Responsibility Authorized (MCD) ... GRA
Government Revenue (MENA) ... gr
Government Rubber [*Synthetic rubber*] (IIA) ... GR
Government Rubber-Acrylonitrile [*Synthetic rubber*] ... GR-A
Government Rubber-Isobutylene [*Synthetic rubber*] ... GR-I
Government Rubber-Styrene [*Also, SBR*] [*Synthetic rubber*] ... GR-S
Government Satellite Services Facility (SSD) ... GSSF
Government Savings Bank [*Australia*] ... GSB
Government Securities Management System [*The Bond Buyer, Inc.*] [*Information service or system*] (IID) ... GSMS
Government Securities Trading [*Computer*] ... GST
Government Security [*Business term*] ... GS
Government Selected Price ... GSP
Government Service ... GS
Government Service Insurance System Employees' Association [*Philippines*] ... GSISEA
Government Services Library, Charlottetown, Prince Edward Island [*Library symbol National Library of Canada*] (NLC) ... PCPL
Government Services Organization (DOMA) ... GSO
Government Solicitor's Office [*Australian Capital Territory*] ... GSO
Government Source Inspection ... GSI
Government Spares Release (MCD) ... GSR
Government Specified Equipment List [*Military*] (CAAL) ... GSEL
Government Sponsored Enterprise [*FNMA*] (EMRF) ... GSE
Government Sponsored Promotion (ADA) ... GSP

Government Staffs [*British*] .... GS
Government Standard Parts .... GSP
Government Standards .... GOV STD
Government Statistical Service [*British*] .... GSS
Government Statistician's Office [*Queensland, Australia*] .... GSO
Government Steam Train [*British*] .... GST
Government Superannuation Office [*Queensland, Australia*] .... GSO
Government Support Date (MCD) .... GSD
Government Technical Report .... GTR
Government Technical Representative .... GTR
Government Technology Productivity .... GTP
Government Technology Services [*NASDAQ symbol*] (SPSG) .... GTSI
Government Technology Services [*Associated Press*] (SAG) .... GvtTch
Government Technology Svcs [*NASDAQ symbol*] (TTSB) .... GTSI
Government Telecommunications Agency [*Canada*] .... GTA
Government Telecommunications Network [*British*] (EECA) .... GTN
Government Telegram (IAA) .... GOVTEL
Government Telegraph Code [*British World War II*] .... GTC
Government Test Facility .... GTF
Government Test Laboratory (MSA) .... GTL
Government Training Centre [*British*] .... GTC
Government Transportation [*or Travel*] **Request** .... GTR
Government Travel Request (MCD) .... GTR
Government Undertaking for Finding Another Way [*Parliamentary slang*] [*British*] (DI) .... GUFFAW
Government Union of Burma .... GUB
Government, University, Industry, Laboratory Development [*Microelectronics*] .... GUILD
Government Use Only (WDAA) .... GUO
Government Vehicle (FAAC) .... GVH
Government Vehicle Pool [*Victoria, Australia*] .... GVP
Government Vehicle Service [*Postal Service*] .... GVS
Government White Paper .... GWP
Government Workers' Trade Union Federation [*Ceylon*] .... GWTUF
Government Workforce Management Unit [*Victoria, Australia*] .... GWMU
Governmental .... GOVTL
Governmental .... GVRNMTL
Governmental Accounting Standards Board [*Stamford, CT*] (EA) .... GASB
Governmental Affairs (DLA) .... GA
Governmental Affairs Institute [*Later, VPS*] (EA) .... GAI
Governmental Defence Council [*British*] .... GDC
Governmental Refuse Collection and Disposal Association (EA) .... GRCDA
Governmental Research Association (EA) .... GRA
Government-Assisted Students .... GAS
Government-Education-Medical .... GEM
Government-Funded Procurement .... GFP
Government-Funded Program .... GFP
Government-Furnished Accessory Equipment .... GFAE
Government-Furnished Aeronautical Equipment (AFM) .... GFAE
Government-Furnished Aeronautical Equipment List (MCD) .... GFAEL
Government-Furnished Aerospace Equipment .... GFAE
Government-Furnished Aircraft Equipment .... GFAE
Government-Furnished Ammunition (MCD) .... GFA
Government-Furnished Articles (KSC) .... GFA
Government-Furnished Baseline .... GFB
Government-Furnished Capital Equipment (MCD) .... GFCE
Government-Furnished Data (NASA) .... GFD
Government-Furnished Documentation (KSC) .... GFD
Government-Furnished Equipment .... GFE
Government-Furnished Equipment and Data .... GFE & D
Government-Furnished Equipment and Material (NRCH) .... GFE & M
Government-Furnished Equipment and Material (IAA) .... GFEAM
Government-Furnished Equipment / Government-Furnished Aircraft Equipment (SAA) .... GFE/GFAE
Government-Furnished Equipment/Information (AAGC) .... GFE/I
Government-Furnished Equipment List (MCD) .... GFEL
Government-Furnished Equipment Records .... GFER
Government-Furnished Equipment Requirements Request .... GFERR
Government-Furnished Facilities (MCD) .... GFF
Government-Furnished Information .... GFI
Government-Furnished Items [*DoD*] .... GFI
Government-Furnished List .... GFL
Government-Furnished Material .... GFM
Government-Furnished Missile .... GFM
Government-Furnished Missile Equipment (AAG) .... GFME
Government-Furnished Parts (AFM) .... GFP
Government-Furnished Property .... GFP
Government-Furnished Property and Material .... GFP/M
Government-Furnished Property and Services (MSA) .... GFP & S
Government-Furnished Property List (MCD) .... GFPL
Government-Furnished Services (KSC) .... GFS
Government-Furnished Software (NASA) .... GFS
Government-Furnished Support Equipment (MCD) .... GFSE
Government-Furnished Support Property (KSC) .... GFSP
Government-Furnished Surplus Material (MCD) .... GFSM
Government-Industry Conference against Chemical Weapons (EERA) .... GICCW
Government-Industry Cooperative Oyster Research Program .... GICORP
Government-Industry Coordinating Committee .... GICC
Government-Industry Data Exchange Program [*Formerly, IDEP*] [*Navy Information service or system*] .... GIDEP
Government-Lent Property (NG) .... GLP
Government-Loaned Equipment (MSA) .... GLE
Government-Loaned Material .... GLM
Government-Operated Civil Engineering Supply Store .... GOCESS
Government-Operated Parts Store .... GOPARS
Government-Owned Aircraft .... GOA
Government-Owned and Maintained [*Telecommunications*] (TEL) .... GOAM
Government-Owned/Commercial-Operated [*Facility*] (AFIT) .... GOCO
Government-Owned/Contractor-Operated [*Facility*] (NG) .... GO/CO
Government-Owned Depot .... GOD
Government-Owned Equipment (MCD) .... GOE
Government-Owned Facility .... GOF
Government-Owned Financial Institution (ADA) .... GFI
Government-Owned/Government-Operated [*Facility*] .... GO/GO
Government-Owned Industrial Equipment (SAA) .... GOIE
Government-Owned Installation .... GOI
Government-Owned Material .... GOM
Government-Owned Material Repair and Reimbursement (MCD) .... GOMR & R
Government-Owned Plant Equipment .... GOPE
Government-Owned/Privately-Operated (GFGA) .... GOPO
Government-Owned Property .... GOP
Government-Owned Terminal .... GOT
Government-Owned Vehicle [*GSA*] (TAG) .... GOV
Government-Purpose License Rights (AAGC) .... GPLR
Governments Division [*Census*] (OICC) .... GOVS
Government's Involvement in Volunteer Efforts Programs .... GIVE
Governments Statute of Local Governments [*A publication*] (DLA) .... Stat Local
Government's Total Contract Cost (AAGC) .... GTCC
Government-Specified Equipment [*Military*] (DNAB) .... GSE
Government-Sponsored Enterprises [*Federal National Mortgage Association, Student Loan Marketing Association, etc.*] .... GSES
Government-University-Industry Research Roundtable [*Academy of Sciences*] .... GUIRR
Government-Wide Index [*Later, USGRDR*] .... GWI
Government-Wide Index to Research and Development .... GWIRD
Government-Wide Quality Assurance Program .... GWQAP
Governo Revolucionario de Angola no Exilio [*Revolutionary Angolan Government-in-Exile*] [*Portuguese*] (PD) .... GRAE
Governor (AFM) .... GOV
Governor (DD) .... gov
Governor .... GOV
Governor .... Govr
Governor (DSUE) .... GV
Governor & Co. of the Bank of Ireland [*Associated Press*] (SAG) .... BkIreInd
Governor & Co. of the Bank of Ireland [*NYSE symbol*] (SAG) .... IRE
Governor General .... GG
Governor Macquarie Tower [*Sydney, New South Wales, Australia*] .... GMT
Governor, Marshall Islands .... GOVMAR
Governor of New South Wales [*Australia*] .... GNSW
Governor of Queensland [*Australia*] .... GQ
Governor of South Australia .... GSA
Governor of Tasmania [*Australia*] .... GT
Governor of Victoria [*Australia*] .... GV
Governor of Western Australia .... GWA
Governor Phillip Tower [*Sydney, New South Wales, Australia*] .... GPT
Governor Steam Valve (IEEE) .... GSV
Governor William Bradford Compact [*An association*] (EA) .... GWBC
Governor-General of Northern Ireland (DAS) .... GGNI
Governor-General's Bodyguard [*British military*] (DMA) .... GGBG
Governor-General's Order [*British military*] (DMA) .... GGO
Governor's Bodyguard [*British military*] (DMA) .... GBG
Governor's Commissioned Officer [*British military*] (DMA) .... GCO
Governors' Conference .... GC
Governor's Foot Guard .... GFG
Governor's Harbour [*Bahamas*] [*Airport symbol*] (OAG) .... GHB
Governor's Harbour, Eleuthera Island [*Bahamas*] [*ICAO location identifier*] (ICLI) .... MYEM
Governor's Horse Guard .... GHG
Governor's Island [*Massachusetts*] (WDAA) .... GOV IS
Governors State University (GAGS) .... Gov St U
Governors State University [*Illinois*] .... GSU
Governors State University Energy Group (EA) .... GSUEG
Governors State University, Park Forest South, IL [*OCLC symbol*] (OCLC) .... IAF
Governors State University, Park Forest South, IL [*Library symbol Library of Congress*] (LCLS) .... IPfsG
Govett & Co. Ltd. [*Associated Press*] (SAG) .... Govett
Govett & Co. Ltd. [*NASDAQ symbol*] (SAG) .... GOVT
Go-Video [*AMEX symbol*] (TTSB) .... VCR
Go-Video, Inc. [*Associated Press*] (SAG) .... GoVd
Go-Video, Inc. [*Associated Press*] (SAG) .... GoVideo
Go-Video, Inc. [*AMEX symbol*] (SPSG) .... VCR
Go-Video Wrrts [*AMEX symbol*] (TTSB) .... VCR.WS
Govone [*Italy ICAO location identifier*] (ICLI) .... LIMQ
Gow on Partnerships [*A publication*] (DLA) .... Gow Part
Gower Federal Service [*Rocky Mountain Mineral Law Foundation*] [*Information service or system*] (CRD) .... GFS
Gowganda Resources, Inc. [*Toronto Stock Exchange symbol Vancouver Stock Exchange symbol*] .... GOW
Gowling & Henderson, Ottawa, Ontario [*Library symbol National Library of Canada*] (NLC) .... OOGOH
Gowling & Henderson, Toronto, ON, Canada [*Library symbol*] [*Library of Congress*] (LCLS) .... CaOTGOH
Gowling & Henderson, Toronto, Ontario [*Library symbol National Library of Canada*] (NLC) .... OTGOH
Gowned (ABBR) .... GWND
Gowns and Towels [*Medicine*] (DMAA) .... G & T
Gowrie News, Gowrie, IA [*Library symbol Library of Congress*] (LCLS) .... IaGow
Gow's English Nisi Prius Cases [*171 English Reprint*] [*A publication*] (DLA) .... Gow

Gow's English Nisi Prius Cases [*171 English Reprint*] [*A publication*] (DLA) ... Gow NP
Gow's English Nisi Prius Cases [*171 English Reprint*] [*A publication*] (DLA) ... Gow NP (Eng)
GOX [*Gaseous Oxygen*] **Vent Arm** (NASA) ... GVA
Goya [*Argentina*] [*Airport symbol*] (OAG) ... OYA
Goya [*Argentina ICAO location identifier*] (ICLI) ... SATG
Goyer Organization of Ideas Test (EDAC) ... GOIT
Goyongo [*Zaire*] [*ICAO location identifier*] (ICLI) ... FZFJ
Gozaisho [*Japan*] [*Seismograph station code, US Geological Survey Closed*] (SEIS) ... GZS
Goz-Beida [*Chad*] [*ICAO location identifier*] (ICLI) ... FTTG
Gozo Party [*Malta*] [*Political party*] (PPE) ... GP
GP Express Airlines, Inc. [*ICAO designator*] (FAAC) ... GPE
GP Financial Corp. [*NASDAQ symbol*] (SAG) ... GNPT
GPC [*General Purpose Computer*] **Interface Adapter** (NASA) ... GIA
GPC [*General Purpose Computer*] **Memory** (NASA) ... GMEM
GPC [*General Purpose Computer*] **Memory** ... G-MEM
GPETE End Item Replacement (NVT) ... GEIR
GPETE Initial Outfitting Requirement [*Military*] (CAAL) ... GIOR
G-Protein-Coupled Receptor [*Biochemistry*] ... GPCR
GPS [*Global Positioning System*] **Aided Targeting System** [*Army*] (DOMA) ... GATS
GPS [*Global Positioning System*] **Guidance Package** ... GGP
GPS [*Global Positioning System*] **Integrity Broadcast** [*Navigation systems*] ... GIB
GPS [*Global Positioning Systems*] **Integrity Channel** [*Navigation systems*] ... GIC
GPz Owners of America [*Defunct*] (EA) ... GPZOA
Graaff Reinet [*South Africa*] [*ICAO location identifier*] (ICLI) ... FAGR
Grab Bar [*Technical drawings*] ... GB
Grab Rod (AAG) ... GR
Grab Sample [*Analytical technique*] ... GS
Grace ... GRC
Grace A. Dow Memorial [*Public*] **Library, Midland, MI** [*Library symbol Library of Congress*] (LCLS) ... MiMid
Grace [*W. R.*] **& Co.** [*NYSE symbol*] (SPSG) ... GRA
Grace [*W.R.*] **& Co.** [*Associated Press*] (SAG) ... Grace
Grace Balloch Memorial Library, Spearfish, SD [*Library symbol Library of Congress*] (LCLS) ... SdSpe
Grace Bible Institute [*Nebraska*] ... GBI
Grace Cancer Drug Center [*Roswell Park Memorial Institute*] [*Research center*] (RCD) ... GCDC
Grace College, Winona Lake, IN [*OCLC symbol*] (OCLC) ... IGR
Grace College, Winona Lake, IN [*Library symbol Library of Congress*] (LCLS) ... InWinG
Grace Contrino Abrams Peace Education Foundation (EA) ... GCAPEF
Grace Dart Hospital Center, Montreal, PQ, Canada [*Library symbol*] [*Library of Congress*] (LCLS) ... CaQMGDH
Grace Dart Hospital Center, Montreal, Quebec [*Library symbol National Library of Canada*] (NLC) ... QMGDH
Grace District Library, Grace, ID [*Library symbol*] [*Library of Congress*] (LCLS) ... IdGr
Grace General Hospital, C. A. Pippy, Jr. Medical Library, St. John's, NF, Canada [*Library symbol Library of Congress*] (LCLS) ... CaNfSGGH
Grace General Hospital, Ottawa, ON, Canada [*Library symbol Library of Congress*] (LCLS) ... CaOOGGH
Grace General Hospital, Ottawa, Ontario [*Library symbol National Library of Canada*] (NLC) ... OOGGH
Grace General Hospital, School of Nursing, St. John's, NF, Canada [*Library symbol Library of Congress*] (LCLS) ... CaNfSGGHN
Grace Hospital, Detroit, MI [*Library symbol Library of Congress*] (LCLS) ... MiDGrH
Grace Hospital, Medical Library, Morganton, NC [*Library symbol*] [*Library of Congress*] (LCLS) ... NcMoGH
Grace Hospital, Winnipeg, Manitoba [*Library symbol National Library of Canada*] (NLC) ... MWGH
Grace Hospital, Winnipeg, MB, Canada [*Library symbol Library of Congress*] (LCLS) ... CaMWGH
Grace of God Movement for the Women of America [*Later, GGMWW*] (EA) ... GGMWA
Grace of God Movement for the Women of the World (EA) ... GGMWW
Grace Period [*Business term*] ... GP
Grace Shepherd School, Hines Creek, Alberta [*Library symbol National Library of Canada*] (BIB) ... AHCGS
Grace (W.R.) [*NYSE symbol*] (TTSB) ... GRA
Graceland College, Lamoni, IA [*Library symbol Library of Congress*] (LCLS) ... IaLG
Graceland College, Lamoni, IA [*OCLC symbol*] (OCLC) ... IOF
Graceland News Fan Club [*Defunct*] (EA) ... GNFC
Grace's Insect [*Growth*] **Medium** [*Microbiology*] ... GIM
Graceville, FL [*FM radio station call letters*] (RBYB) ... WYDA-FM
Graceville Public Library, Graceville, MN [*Library symbol*] [*Library of Congress*] (LCLS) ... MnGra
Gracewood State School and Hospital, Gracewood, GA [*Library symbol Library of Congress*] (LCLS) ... GGraG
Graciosa Bay/Luova, Santa Cruz Islands [*Solomon Islands*] [*ICAO location identifier*] (ICLI) ... AGGL
Graciosa, Graciosa Island [*Portugal ICAO location identifier*] (ICLI) ... LPGR
Graciosa Island [*Azores*] [*Airport symbol*] (OAG) ... GRW
Graco, Inc. [*NYSE symbol*] (SPSG) ... GGG
Graco, Inc. [*Associated Press*] (SAG) ... Graco
Gradatim [*Gradually*] [*Pharmacy*] ... GRAD
Gradational, Calcareous [*Soil*] ... Gc
Gradational, Non-Calcareous [*Soil*] ... Gn
Gradco Systems [*NASDAQ symbol*] (TTSB) ... GRCO
Gradco Systems, Inc. [*Associated Press*] (SAG) ... Gradco
Gradco Systems, Inc. [*NASDAQ symbol*] (NQ) ... GRCO
Grade (ADA) ... G
Grade [*Technical drawings*] ... GD
Grade (KSC) ... GR
Grade (WDMC) ... gr
Grade ... GRDE
Grade Age [*Education*] ... GA
Grade C and Better (DAC) ... C & Btr
Grade Crossing Inventory System [*BTS*] (TAG) ... GCIS
Grade Crossing Protection Device ... GCPD
Grade Level Equivalent [*Educational testing*] ... GLE
Grade Line ... GL
Grade of Service ... GOS
Grade System (AAG) ... GS
Grade Tertiary Butyl Alcohol ... GTBA
Graded [*Medicine*] (DAVI) ... GXD
Graded Assessment in Design and Technology (AIE) ... GADT
Graded Assessment in Science Project (AIE) ... GASP
Graded Base Transistor ... GBT
Graded Exercise (NVT) ... GRADEX
Graded Exercise ... Gx
Graded Exercise Testing ... GXT
Graded Exercixe Electrocardiogram [*Cardiology*] (DAVI) ... GXD EKG
Graded Index [*Optics*] ... GI
Graded Levels of Achievement in Foreign Language Learning (AIE) ... GLAFLL
Graded Program ... GP
Graded Refractive-Index [*Optics*] ... GRIN
Graded Treadmill Exercise Test [*Medicine*] (DMAA) ... GET
Graded-Index Fiber (ACRL) ... GRIN
Gradell Industries, Inc. [*Associated Press*] (SAG) ... Gradell
Gradell Industries, Inc. [*NASDAQ symbol*] (SAG) ... GRDL
Grade-Point Average [*Education*] ... GPA
Gradient (AFM) ... GRAD
Gradient Elution Fractionation ... GEF
Gradient Gel Electrophoresis ... GGE
Gradient Heating Facility ... GHF
Gradient Mixer [*Chromatography*] ... GM
Gradient of Refractive Index [*Optics*] ... GRIN
Gradient Pump Module ... GPM
Gradient Solidification Method [*Optics*] ... GSM
Gradient Wind (NOAA) ... GDWND
Gradient Zone Melting (IAA) ... GZMG
Gradient-Recalled Echo [*Physics*] ... GRE
Grading (WDAA) ... GRAD
Grading ... GRD
Gradual ... GRAD
Gradual ... GRADU
Gradual [*NWS*] (FAAC) ... GRDL
Gradual Dosage Schedule [*Medicine*] (DMAA) ... GDS
Gradual Withdrawal [*Medicine*] (DMAA) ... GW
Gradual-Onset-Rate [*Air Force*] (DOMA) ... GOR
Gradual-Release [*Pharmacy*] ... GR
Graduate ... GR
Graduate (AFM) ... GRAD
Graduate ... GRAD
Graduate Aeronautical Laboratories - California Institute of Technology [*Research center*] (RCD) ... GALCIT
Graduate Aerospace Mechanical Engineering ... GAM
Graduate Aid to Employment (OICC) ... GATE
Graduate and Professional School Financial Aid Service (GAGS) ... GAPSFAS
Graduate Assistant ... GA
Graduate Assistantship Directory [*A publication*] ... GAD
Graduate Business Admission Test ... GBAT
Graduate Center for Materials Research [*University of Missouri - Rolla*] [*Research center*] (RCD) ... MRC
Graduate Certificate ... GradCert
Graduate Certificate in Business [*Australia*] ... GradCertBus
Graduate Certificate in Clinical Instruction [*Australia*] ... GCertClinInstr
Graduate Certificate in Communication [*Australia*] ... GradCertCommunic
Graduate Certificate in Education [*Australia*] ... GCertEd
Graduate Certificate in Educational Studies [*Australia*] ... GCertEdStudies
Graduate Certificate in Finance [*Australia*] ... GradCertFin
Graduate Certificate in Helping Skills [*Australia*] ... GradCertHelpSkills
Graduate Certificate in Human Resource Development [*Australia*] ... GradCertHRD
Graduate Certificate in Industrial Relations [*Australia*] ... GradCertIndRels
Graduate Certificate in Literacy Education [*Australia*] ... GradCertLitEd
Graduate Certificate in Management [*Australia*] ... GradCertMngt
Graduate Certificate in Marketing [*Australia*] ... GradCertMarkt
Graduate Certificate in Mathematics and Mathematics Education [*Australia*] ... GCertMaths & MathEd
Graduate Certificate in Social Administration [*Australia*] ... GCertSocAdmin
Graduate Certificate in Teaching of English to Speakers of Other Languages [*Australia*] ... GradCertTESOL
Graduate Certificate of Museum Management [*Australia*] ... GCertMusMgmt
Graduate Certificate of Scientific and Technical Writing [*Australia*] ... GCertSc & TechWriting
Graduate Certificate of Social Work ... GCSW
Graduate Diploma ... GD
Graduate Diploma (DD) ... GDip
Graduate Diploma for Science Teachers (Geology) ... GradDipGeol
Graduate Diploma in Aboriginal and Islander Education [*Australia*] ... GradDipAbIsEd
Graduate Diploma in Accompaniment [*Australia*] ... GradDipAccom
Graduate Diploma in Accounting [*Australia*] ... GradDipAcc
Graduate Diploma in Accounting ... GradDipAcct
Graduate Diploma in Accounting ... GradDipActng
Graduate Diploma in Administration ... GDA

Graduate Diploma in Administration .... GradDipAdmin
Graduate Diploma in Adult Education and Training [*Australia*] .... GradDipAdultEd & Train
Graduate Diploma in Advanced Accounting .... GradDipAdvAcctg
Graduate Diploma in Alternative Dispute Resolution [*Australia*] .... GradDipAltDispRes
Graduate Diploma in Analytical Chemistry .... GradDipAnalytChem
Graduate Diploma in Antarctic and Southern Ocean Studies [*Australia*] .... GradDipASOS
Graduate Diploma in Applied Communications .... GradDipAppCommunications
Graduate Diploma in Applied Economics [*Australia*] .... GradDipAppEc
Graduate Diploma in Applied History .... GradDipAppHist
Graduate Diploma in Applied Linguistics .... GradDipAppLing
Graduate Diploma in Applied Science [*Australia*] .... GradDipAppSc
Graduate Diploma in Applied Science, General Studies [*Australia*] .... GradDipAppScGenStud
Graduate Diploma in Applied Statistics .... GradDipAppStats
Graduate Diploma in Arts (Children's Literature) [*Australia*] .... GradDipArts(ChLit)
Graduate Diploma in Arts (Counselling) .... GDipA(Couns)
Graduate Diploma in Arts (Welfare Administration) [*Australia*] .... GradDipArts(WelfAdmin)
Graduate Diploma in Asian Law [*Australia*] .... GradDipAsianLaw
Graduate Diploma in Asian Studies .... GradDipAsianStudies
Graduate Diploma in Audiology [*Australia*] .... GradDipAud
Graduate Diploma in Building Project Management .... GradDipBldgProjMgt
Graduate Diploma in Business [*Australia*] .... GradDipBus
Graduate Diploma in Business Administration .... GDBusAd
Graduate Diploma in Business Administration .... GradDipBusAdmin
Graduate Diploma in Business Computing .... GradDipBusComp
Graduate Diploma in Cardio Pulmonary Physiotherapy .... GradDipCPPhty
Graduate Diploma in Child Development .... GDipCD
Graduate Diploma in Children's Literature .... GradDipChildLit
Graduate Diploma in Chiropractic .... GDipCh
Graduate Diploma in Clinical Biochemistry .... GradDipClinBiochem
Graduate Diploma in Clinical Dentistry [*Australia*] .... GradDipClinDent
Graduate Diploma in Clinical Science .... GDipClinSc
Graduate Diploma in Commercial Computing .... GradDipCmlComptg
Graduate Diploma in Commercial Data Processing .... GradDipCommDataProc
Graduate Diploma in Commercial Education [*Australia*] .... GradDipComEd
Graduate Diploma in Communication .... GradDipCommn
Graduate Diploma in Communication Management .... GradDipCommunicationMgt
Graduate Diploma in Community Health .... GDCH
Graduate Diploma in Computer Controlled Systems .... GradDipCompContSys
Graduate Diploma in Computer Studies .... GDipCompSt
Graduate Diploma in Computer Studies .... GradDipCompStud
Graduate Diploma in Computers in Education [*Australia*] .... GradDipCompEd
Graduate Diploma in Computing Science .... GradDipComptgSc
Graduate Diploma in Conflict Resolution [*Australia*] .... GradDipConfRes
Graduate Diploma in Counselling .... GradDipCouns
Graduate Diploma in Curriculum [*Australia*] .... GradDipCurric
Graduate Diploma in Data Analysis .... GradDipDatAnal
Graduate Diploma in Data Processing .... GradDipDP
Graduate Diploma in Demography .... GradDipDemog
Graduate Diploma in Design Studies .... GradDipDesStud
Graduate Diploma in Digital Computer Engineering .... GradDipCompEng
Graduate Diploma in Diplomatic Studies [*Australia*] .... GradDipDiplSt
Graduate Diploma in Drama in Education [*Australia*] .... GradDipDramaEd
Graduate Diploma in Early Childhood Studies [*Australia*] .... GradDipEarlyChildSt
Graduate Diploma in Econometrics .... GradDipEcmetrics
Graduate Diploma in Econometrics [*Australia*] .... GradDipEconom
Graduate Diploma in Economic Development [*Australia*] .... GradDipEconDev
Graduate Diploma in Economic Geology [*Australia*] .... GradDipEconGeol
Graduate Diploma in Economic History .... GradDipEcHist
Graduate Diploma in Economic History [*Australia*] .... GradDipEconHist
Graduate Diploma in Economics .... GDipEc
Graduate Diploma in Economics .... GradDipEc
Graduate Diploma in Economics of Development .... GradDipEcDev
Graduate Diploma in Education .... GradDipEd
Graduate Diploma in Education and Training [*Australia*] .... GradDipEdTrain
Graduate Diploma in Education (Industrial Arts) .... GradDipEd(IndArts)
Graduate Diploma in Education (Technical and Further Education) .... GradDipEd(TAFE)
Graduate Diploma in Educational Administration [*Australia*] .... GradDipEdAdmin
Graduate Diploma in Educational Counseling [*Australia*] .... GradDipEdCouns
Graduate Diploma in Educational Counselling (ADA) .... GradDipEdCouns
Graduate Diploma in Educational Studies .... GDE
Graduate Diploma in Educational Studies .... GradDipEdStudies
Graduate Diploma in Educational Studies Support Teaching [*Australia*] .... GradDipEdStSptTchg
Graduate Diploma in Employment Relations .... GradDipEmpRels
Graduate Diploma in Engineering [*Australia*] .... GradDipE
Graduate Diploma in Engineering [*Australia*] .... GradDipEng
Graduate Diploma in Engineering - Plant Management .... GradDipEng-PlantMgnt
Graduate Diploma in Environmental and Municipal Engineering .... GradDipEnv & MunEng
Graduate Diploma in Environmental Studies [*Australia*] .... GradDipEnvSt
Graduate Diploma in Epidemiology [*Australia*] .... GradDipEpi
Graduate Diploma in Ergonomics .... GDipErg
Graduate Diploma in Exercise and Sport Science .... GDipExerSpSc
Graduate Diploma in Exercise and Sport Sciences .... GradDipExerSportSc
Graduate Diploma in Extension (ADA) .... GDE
Graduate Diploma in Film and Television in Education .... GradDipFilm & Tele in Ed
Graduate Diploma in Finance .... GradDipFin
Graduate Diploma in Fine Art .... GradDipFineArt
Graduate Diploma in Forensic Odontology [*Australia*] .... GradDipForOdont
Graduate Diploma in Gallery Studies [*Australia*] .... GradDipGalSt
Graduate Diploma in Gerontology .... GradDipGeront
Graduate Diploma in Graphic Communication Education [*Australia*] .... GradDipGraphCommEd
Graduate Diploma in Health Administration .... GDipHA
Graduate Diploma in Health Counselling .... GDipHC
Graduate Diploma in Health Information Management .... GradDipHIM
Graduate Diploma in Health Services Management .... GDipHSM
Graduate Diploma in Health Services Management .... GradDipHealthServMgmt
Graduate Diploma in Human Nutrition .... GDipHumNut
Graduate Diploma in Human Physiology and Pharmacology [*Australia*] .... GradDipHumanPhysiol & Pharmacol
Graduate Diploma in Immunology and Microbiology [*Australia*] .... GradDipImmunolMicrobiol
Graduate Diploma in Industrial Design [*Australia*] .... GradDIndDes
Graduate Diploma in Industrial Design .... GradDipIndDes
Graduate Diploma in Industrial Management [*Australia*] .... GDIM
Graduate Diploma in Information Management [*Australia*] .... GradDipInfoMgt
Graduate Diploma in Information Services .... GradDipInfServ
Graduate Diploma in Information Studies .... GradDipInfStudies
Graduate Diploma in Information Technology [*Australia*] .... GradDipInfTech
Graduate Diploma in Intellectual Property Law [*Australia*] .... GradDipIntPropLaw
Graduate Diploma in Internal Auditing .... GradDipAud
Graduate Diploma in International and Commercial Law [*Australia*] .... GradDipIntComLaw
Graduate Diploma in International Law .... GradDipIntLaw
Graduate Diploma in Knowledge Based Systems .... GradDipKnowlBasSys
Graduate Diploma in Labour Relations Law [*Australia*] .... GradDipLabRelLaw
Graduate Diploma in Land Data Management .... GradDipLandDatMan
Graduate Diploma in Land Economy .... GDLE
Graduate Diploma in Landscape Architecture .... GradDipLandArch
Graduate Diploma in Landscape Design .... GradDipLD
Graduate Diploma in Language Teaching [*Australia*] .... GradDipLangTchg
Graduate Diploma in Legal Practice .... GradDipLegalPrac
Graduate Diploma in Legal Studies .... GDipLS
Graduate Diploma in Leisure Studies .... GradDipLeisureStud
Graduate Diploma in Librarianship and Information Studies .... GradDipLibInfStud
Graduate Diploma in Library Science (ADA) .... GDLS
Graduate Diploma in Library Science (ADA) .... GradDipLibSc
Graduate Diploma in Local and Applied History .... GradDipLoc & AppHist
Graduate Diploma in Local Government Engineering .... GradDipLocalGovtEng
Graduate Diploma in Management .... GDipM
Graduate Diploma in Management .... GradDipMgmt
Graduate Diploma in Manipulative Therapy .... GDManTher
Graduate Diploma in Manipulative Therapy .... GradDipManipTh
Graduate Diploma in Marketing .... GradDipMktg
Graduate Diploma in Materials Engineering [*Australia*] .... GradDipMatEng
Graduate Diploma in Mathematical Methods .... GradDipMathMethods
Graduate Diploma in Mathematics Education [*Australia*] .... GradDipMathsEd
Graduate Diploma in Mathematics Science [*Australia*] .... GradDipMathSc
Graduate Diploma in Media Communications and Technology Law [*Australia*] .... GradDipMediaComm & TechLaw
Graduate Diploma in Medical Laboratory Science .... GDipMLS
Graduate Diploma in Mental Health Science [*Australia*] .... GradDipMentHlthSc
Graduate Diploma in Metal Finishing and Surface Protection .... GradDipSurFin
Graduate Diploma in Midwifery [*Australia*] .... GradDipMidwif
Graduate Diploma in Mineral Resources .... GradDipMinRes
Graduate Diploma in Molecular Biology [*Australia*] .... GradDipMolBiol
Graduate Diploma in Movement and Dance [*Australia*] .... GradDipMovement & Dance
Graduate Diploma in Multicultural Studies [*Australia*] .... GradDipMultiStudies
Graduate Diploma in Municipal Engineering [*Australia*] .... GradDipMunEng
Graduate Diploma in Museum Management [*Australia*] .... GradDipMusMgmt
Graduate Diploma in Music [*Australia*] .... GradDipMus
Graduate Diploma in Music (Opera) [*Australia*] .... GradDipMus(Op)
Graduate Diploma in Music (Performance) [*Australia*] .... GradDipMus(Perf)
Graduate Diploma in Music (Repetiteur) [*Australia*] .... GradDipMus(Rep)
Graduate Diploma in Natural Resources Law [*Australia*] .... GradDipNatResourcesLaw
Graduate Diploma in Nursing .... GradDipNurs
Graduate Diploma in Nursing Studies .... GradDipNursStudies
Graduate Diploma in Nutrition and Dietetics .... GradDipNutr & Diet
Graduate Diploma in Occupational Health .... GDOccHlth
Graduate Diploma in Occupational Health and Safety .... GradDipOH & S
Graduate Diploma in Offshore Engineering [*Australia*] .... GradDipOffshEng
Graduate Diploma in Operations Research .... GradDipOR
Graduate Diploma in Organisation Development .... GradDipOrgDev
Graduate Diploma in Paediatric Physiotherapy .... GradDipPaedPhty
Graduate Diploma in Parent Education and Counselling .... GDipPEC
Graduate Diploma in Primary Health .... GDipPHC
Graduate Diploma in Professional Management .... GDipPrfMgt
Graduate Diploma in Project Management [*Australia*] .... GradDipProjMgt
Graduate Diploma in Property .... GradDipProp
Graduate Diploma in Public Accountancy (DD) .... GDPA
Graduate Diploma in Public Accounting (DD) .... GDPA
Graduate Diploma in Public Administration (PGP) .... GDPA
Graduate Diploma in Public Economic Policy .... GradDipPubEcPol
Graduate Diploma in Public Law .... GDipPubL
Graduate Diploma in Public Law .... GradDipPubLaw
Graduate Diploma in Public Policy .... GradDipPubPol
Graduate Diploma in Public Sector Management .... GradDipPSM
Graduate Diploma in Pulp and Paper Technology [*Australia*] .... GradDipPPT
Graduate Diploma in Quality .... GradDipQlty
Graduate Diploma in Quality Technology .... GradDipQualTech
Graduate Diploma in Rehabilitation Counselling .... GradDipRc

Graduate Diploma in Religious Education (PGP) .... GDRE
Graduate Diploma in Safety and Health .... GDSafH
Graduate Diploma in Safety Science .... GDSafS
Graduate Diploma in School Librarianship (ADA) .... GDSL
Graduate Diploma in Science .... GradDipSc
Graduate Diploma in Secretarial Studies .... GradDipSecStud
Graduate Diploma in Social Administration [Australia] .... GradDipSocAdmin
Graduate Diploma in Social Communication (ADA) .... GDSC
Graduate Diploma in Social Ecology [Australia] .... GradDipSocEcol
Graduate Diploma in Southeast Asian Studies .... GradDipSEAsianStud
Graduate Diploma in Special Education [Australia] .... GradDipSpecEd
Graduate Diploma in Sport Science .... GDSSc
Graduate Diploma in Statistics .... GradDipStats
Graduate Diploma in Strategic Studies [Australia] .... GradDipStratSt
Graduate Diploma in Structural Engineering [Australia] .... GradDipStrucEng
Graduate Diploma in Student Welfare [Australia] .... GradDipStudWel
Graduate Diploma in Surveying Practice .... GradDipSurvPrac
Graduate Diploma in Taxation (PGP) .... GDT
Graduate Diploma in Taxation .... GradDipTax
Graduate Diploma in Teacher Librarianship (ADA) .... GDTL
Graduate Diploma in Teacher Librarianship (ADA) .... GradDipTchrLib
Graduate Diploma in Teacher Librarianship (ADA) .... GradDipTeachLib
Graduate Diploma in Teaching (ADA) .... GradDipT
Graduate Diploma in Teaching [Australia] .... GradDipTeach
Graduate Diploma in Technological Entrepreneurship (PGP) .... GDTE
Graduate Diploma in Theology (PGP) .... GDT
Graduate Diploma in Transport and Distribution .... GradDipTrans & Dist
Graduate Diploma in Ultrasonography .... GradDipUltr
Graduate Diploma in Urban and Regional Planning .... GradDipUrb & RegPlan
Graduate Diploma in Urban and Regional Planning .... GradDipURP
Graduate Diploma in Urban Estate Management .... GradDipUEM
Graduate Diploma in Visual Arts .... GradDip(VisArts)
Graduate Diploma in Water Engineering [Australia] .... GradDipWaterEng
Graduate Diploma in Welding Technology .... GradDipWeldTech
Graduate Diploma in Welfare Administration [Australia] .... GradDipWelfAdmin
Graduate Diploma in Women's Health [Australia] .... GradDipWomHlth
Graduate Diploma in Women's Studies [Australia] .... GradDipWomen'sStudies
Graduate Diploma of Arts [Australia] .... GradDipA
Graduate Diploma of Commercial Law [Australia] .... GradDipComLaw
Graduate Diploma of Community Museum Management
  [Australia] .... GradDipComMusMgmt
Graduate Diploma of Community Music [Australia] .... GradDipComMus
Graduate Diploma of Computer Control and Communications
  [Australia] .... GradDipCCC
Graduate Diploma of Computer Science [Australia] .... GradDipCompSc
Graduate Diploma of Family Law [Australia] .... GradDipFamLaw
Graduate Diploma of Fine Arts [Australia] .... GradDipFA
Graduate Diploma of Legal Studies [Australia] .... GradDipLegSt
Graduate Diploma of Material Anthropology [Australia] .... GradDipMatAnth
Graduate Diploma of Melanesian Studies [Australia] .... GradDipMelSt
Graduate Diploma of Museum Curatorship [Australia] .... GradDipMusCur
Graduate Diploma of Psychology [Australia] .... GradDipPsych
Graduate Diploma of Science and Society [Australia] .... GradDipScSoc
Graduate Diploma of the Guildhall School of Music [British] (DBQ) .... GGSM
Graduate Diploma of the London College of Music [British] (DBQ) .... GLCM
Graduate Diploma of Tourism [Australia] .... GradDipTourism
Graduate Division of Applied Mathematics .... GDAM
Graduate Employment and Training [British] .... GET
Graduate Employment and Training Survey (AIE) .... GET
Graduate Engineering Education System .... GENESYS
Graduate Fellowships for Black Americans (EA) .... GFBA
Graduate Grade-Point Average [Higher education] .... GGPA
Graduate in Agriculture .... GA
Graduate in Architecture .... G Arch
Graduate in Arts .... BA
Graduate in Divinity .... GD
Graduate in Law .... GL
Graduate in Letters .... BL
Graduate in Letters .... LB
Graduate in Liberal Arts .... BLA
Graduate in Music of the Royal Northern College of Music [British]
  (DBQ) .... GMusRNCM(Hons)
Graduate in Nursing .... G in N
Graduate in Pharmacy .... G Ph
Graduate in Pharmacy [British] (ROG) .... GP
Graduate in Pharmacy .... Ph G
Graduate in Pharmacy (AAMN) .... Phar G
Graduate in Pharmacy (MEDA) .... Pharm G
Graduate in Pharmacy .... Phm G
Graduate in Science .... B Sc
Graduate in Science .... BS
Graduate Induction Campaign [Australia] .... GIC
Graduate Institute of Technology [University of Arkansas at Little Rock]
  [Research center] (RCD) .... GIT
Graduate Jeweller .... GJ
Graduate Level Specialist Diplomas in Advanced Study in Education,
  College of Preceptors [British] (DBQ) .... DipAse(CofP)
Graduate Library School .... GLS
Graduate Management Admission Council [Los Angeles, CA] (EA) .... GMAC
Graduate Management Admission Test .... GMAT
Graduate Management Association of Australia .... GMAA
Graduate Medical Education [Program] [Army] .... GME
Graduate Medical Education National Advisory Committee [Department of
  Health and Human Services] .... GMENAC
Graduate Member of the Ambulance Service Institute [British] (DBQ) .... GMASI

Graduate Member of the Institute of British Engineers .... Grad Inst BE
Graduate Member of the Institute of Manufacturing [British] (DBQ) .... GradIManf
Graduate Member of the Institute of Mathematics and Its Applications
  [British] (DBQ) .... GradIMA
Graduate Member of the Institute of Physics and the Physical Society
  [British] .... Grad Inst P
Graduate Member of the Institute of Statisticians [British] (DBQ) .... GradIS
Graduate Member of the Institution of Mechanical Engineers
  [British] .... GMI Mech E
Graduate Member of the Non-Destructive Testing Society of Great
  Britain .... Grad MNDTS
Graduate Member of the Royal Institute of Chemistry [British] .... Grad RIC
Graduate Member of the Royal Institute of Chemistry [British] (DBQ) .... GRIC
Graduate Midwife .... Mid G
Graduate Nurse .... GN
Graduate Nurse .... Gr N
Graduate Nurse Transition Program .... GNTP
Graduate of the Birmingham School of Music [British] (DBQ) .... GBSM
Graduate of the British Horological Institute (DBQ) .... GradBHI
Graduate of the British Institute of Non-Destructive Testing
  (DBQ) .... GradInstNDT
Graduate of the Institute of Business and Technical Management [British]
  (DBQ) .... GradInstBTM
Graduate of the Institute of Electrical Engineers [British] (DAS) .... GIEE
Graduate of the Institute of Industrial Security [British] (DBQ) .... GradIISec
Graduate of the Institute of Management Specialists [British] (DBQ) .... GradIMS
Graduate of the Institute of Marketing [British] (DBQ) .... GInstM
Graduate of the Institute of Metal Finishing [British] (DBQ) .... GradIMF
Graduate of the Institute of Metallurgists (BARN) .... Grad IM
Graduate of the Institute of Personnel Management [British] (DBQ) .... GradIPM
Graduate of the Institute of Printing [British] (DBQ) .... GradIOP
Graduate of the Institute of Purchasing and Supply [British] (DBQ) .... GradInstPS
Graduate of the Institute of Supervisory Management [British] (DBQ) .... GradISM
Graduate of the Institute of the Motor Industry [British] (DBQ) .... GIMI
Graduate of the Institution of Automobile Engineers [British] .... GradIAE
Graduate of the Institution of Electrical and Electronics Incorporated
  Engineers [British] (DBQ) .... GradIElecIE
Graduate of the Institution of Electrical and Electronics Incorporated
  Engineers [British] (DBQ) .... Graduate IElecIE
Graduate of the Institution of Electronic and Radio Engineers
  [British] .... Grad IERE
Graduate of the Institution of Mechanical Engineers [British] .... GI Mech E
Graduate of the Institution of Mechanical Engineers [British] .... Grad I Mech E
Graduate of the London School of Tropical Medicine (DAS) .... GLSTM
Graduate of the National Institute of Hardware [British] (DBQ) .... GradNIH
Graduate of the Northern School of Music [Obsolete British] (DBQ) .... GNSM
Graduate of the Plastics and Rubber Institute [British] (DBQ) .... GradPRI
Graduate of the Royal Aeronautical Society [British] .... GR Aero S
Graduate of the Royal Air Force Staff College [British] .... FS
Graduate of the Royal College of Music [British] .... GRCM
Graduate of the Royal Naval Staff College, Greenwich [British] .... NS
Graduate of the Royal Northern College of Music [British] (DBQ) .... GRNCM
Graduate of the Royal Schools of Music [British] .... GRSM
Graduate of the Royal Society of Chemistry [British] (DBQ) .... GRSC
Graduate of the Society of Certified Professionals [British] (DBQ) .... GradSCP
Graduate of the Society of Licensed Aircraft Engineers and Technologists
  [British] (DBQ) .... GradSLAET
Graduate of the Welding Institute [British] (DBQ) .... GradWeldI
Graduate of Trinity College of Music, London .... GTCL
Graduate Opportunities [British] .... GO
Graduate Performance Diploma (PGP) .... GPD
Graduate Practical Nurse .... GPN
Graduate Rabbinical School (BJA) .... GRS
Graduate Record Exam (GAGS) .... GRE
Graduate Record Examination [Higher education] .... GRE
Graduate Record Examinations Board (EA) .... GRE
Graduate Records Examination Board (WDAA) .... GREB
Graduate Reliability Engineering .... GRE
Graduate Research Assistant .... GRA
Graduate Research Center of the Southwest [Later, University of Texas at
  Dallas] .... GRC
Graduate Research Center of the Southwest [Formerly, Southwest Center for
  AdvancedStudies; later, University of Texas at Dallas] .... GRCSW
Graduate Respiratory Therapist .... GRT
Graduate Resume Accumulation and Distribution [Computer science] .... GRAD
Graduate School Foreign Language Test .... GSFLT
Graduate School of Business [University of Chicago] (ECON) .... GSB
Graduate School of Business Administration, Division of Research
  [University of Michigan] [Research center] (RCD) .... DOR
Graduate School of Library Science, McGill University [EDUCATSS]
  [UTLAS symbol] .... EUM
Graduate School of Oceanography [University of Rhode Island] .... GSO
Graduate Science Student Support Postdoctorals Survey [National Science
  Foundation] (GFGA) .... GSSSP
Graduate Search by Computer after Personal Evaluation (AIE) .... GRADSCOPE
Graduate Service Overseas of the National Union of Students [British]
  (AEBS) .... GSO
Graduate Student Loan .... GSL
Graduate Teachers' Association [A union] [British] .... GTA
Graduate Teaching Assistant .... GTA
Graduate Theological Union, Berkeley, CA [Library symbol Library of
  Congress] (LCLS) .... CBGTU
Graduate Theological Union, University of Saskatchewan [UTLAS
  symbol] .... GTU
Graduated Audio Level Adjustment .... GALA

Graduated Combat Capability [*Military*] ..... GCC
Graduated [*or Growing*] **Equity Mortgage** ..... GEM
Graduated Interest Rate [*Finance*] (BARN) ..... GIR
Graduated Length Method [*of learning to ski*] [*Later, Accelerated Length Method*] ..... GLM
Graduated Mobilization Response (DOMA) ..... GMR
Graduated Payment Mortgage [*Sometimes referred to as "Jeep"*] ..... GPM
Graduated Payment Mortgage (DFIT) ..... Jeep
Graduated Pension Scheme [*British*] (BARN) ..... GPS
Graduated Reduction in Tensions [*Cold War term*] ..... GRIT
Graduated-Payment Adjustable Mortgage ..... GPAM
Graduated-Payment Adjustable-Rate Mortgage (WDAA) ..... GPARM
Graduates of Italian Medical Schools (EA) ..... GIMS
Graduation (MSA) ..... GRDTN
Graduation Pledge Alliance [*An association*] (EA) ..... GPA
Graduation Requirement (MCD) ..... GR
Grady on Fixtures [*A publication*] (DLA) ..... Grad Fix
Grady's Hindoo Law of Inheritance [*A publication*] (DLA) ..... Grad Hind Inh
Grady's Indian Codes [*A publication*] (DLA) ..... Grad Ind Co
Grady's Manual of Hindoo Law [*A publication*] (DLA) ..... Grad Hind L
Graeber-Verwaltungsoffizier [*Graves Registration Officer*] [*German military - World War II*] ..... GVO
Graefenberg Array [*Erlangen*] [*Federal Republic of Germany*] [*Seismograph station code, US Geological Survey*] (SEIS) ..... GRF
Graefenberg Spot [*Gynecology*] ..... G (Spot)
Graettinger Public Library, Graettinger, IA [*Library symbol Library of Congress*] (LCLS) ..... IaGra
Graettinger Times, Graettinger, IA [*Library symbol Library of Congress*] (LCLS) ..... IaGraT
Graetz Number [*Physics*] ..... Gz
Graf und Maresch GmbH, Augsburg [*Germany*] [*FAA designator*] (FAAC) ..... DLP
Grafe & Unzer [*Publisher*] [*German*] ..... G & U
Grafenberg Spot [*Medicine*] (DMAA) ..... G
Grafenwoehr [*Germany ICAO location identifier*] (ICLI) ..... EDIC
Graff Electronic Machines Ltd. [*British*] ..... GEM
Graff Pay per View [*NASDAQ symbol*] (SAG) ..... GPPV
Graff Pay per View [*Associated Press*] (SAG) ..... GraffPay
Graffiti [*Slang*] [*British*] ..... GRAF
Graft Coronary Disease [*Cardiology*] (DMAA) ..... GCD
Graft (Polymer) [*Organic chemistry*] ..... g
Graft Versus Host [*Immunology*] ..... GVH
Grafted Rubber Concentrate [*Organic chemistry*] ..... GRC
Grafton [*Australia Airport symbol*] (OAG) ..... GFN
Grafton [*New York*] [*Seismograph station code, US Geological Survey Closed*] (SEIS) ..... GFN
Grafton and Belington Railroad [*Initialism refers to a settlement of Indians who lived near this railroad*] ..... G and B
Grafton & Upton Railroad Co. [*AAR code*] ..... GU
Grafton Group Ltd. [*Toronto Stock Exchange symbol*] ..... GFG
Grafton, ND [*Location identifier FAA*] (FAAL) ..... GAF
Grafton, ND [*AM radio station call letters*] ..... KXPO
Grafton, ND [*FM radio station call letters*] ..... KXPO-FM
Grafton, WV [*AM radio station call letters*] ..... WTBZ
Grafton, WV [*FM radio station call letters*] ..... WTBZ-FM
Graft-Versus Host Disease [*Immunology*] ..... GvHD
Graft-Versus-Host Disease [*Immunology*] ..... GVHD
Graft-Versus-Host Reaction [*Immunology*] ..... GVHR
Graft-Versus-Leukemia [*Medicine*] ..... GvL
Graham and Waterman on New Trials [*A publication*] (DLA) ..... G & W New Tr
Graham and Waterman on New Trials [*A publication*] (DLA) ..... Gra & Wat NT
Graham and Waterman on New Trials [*A publication*] (DLA) ..... Grah & W New Trials
Graham Bond Appreciators Organization [*Defunct*] (EA) ..... GBAO
Graham Brothers Truck and Bus Club (EA) ..... GBTBC
Graham Center [*An association*] (EA) ..... GC
Graham Community Library, Ralston, AB, Canada [*Library symbol*] [*Library of Congress*] (LCLS) ..... CaARGC
Graham Community Library, Ralston, Alberta [*Library symbol National Library of Canada*] (NLC) ..... ARGC
Graham Corp. [*AMEX symbol*] (SPSG) ..... GHM
Graham Corp. [*Associated Press*] (SAG) ..... Graham
Graham County Railroad Co. [*AAR code*] ..... GC
Graham Evangelistic Association, Montreat, NC [*Library symbol Library of Congress*] (LCLS) ..... NcMG
Graham Field Health Products [*NYSE symbol*] (SAG) ..... GFI
Graham, NC [*AM radio station call letters*] ..... WSML
Graham on New Trials [*A publication*] (DLA) ..... Gra N Tr
Graham Owners Club International (EA) ..... GOCI
Graham Public Library, Union Grove, WI [*Library symbol Library of Congress*] (LCLS) ..... WUg
Graham, TX [*Location identifier FAA*] (FAAL) ..... GHX
Graham, TX [*AM radio station call letters*] ..... KSWA
Graham, TX [*FM radio station call letters*] ..... KWKQ
Graham-Field Health [*NYSE symbol*] (TTSB) ..... GFI
Graham-Field Health Products, Inc. [*Associated Press*] (SAG) ..... GrhmFL
Graham-Kendall Memory for Designs Test [*Psychology*] (DAVI) ..... GKMDT
Graham's Practice of the New York Supreme Court [*A publication*] (DLA) ..... Gra Pr
Graham's Reports [*98-107 Georgia*] [*A publication*] (DLA) ..... Gra
Grahamstown [*South Africa*] [*ICAO location identifier*] (ICLI) ..... FAGT
Grahamstown [*South Africa*] [*Airport symbol*] (AD) ..... GHO
Grahamstown [*South Africa*] [*Seismograph station code, US Geological Survey Closed*] (SEIS) ..... GRH
Grahamstown [*South Africa*] [*Seismograph station code, US Geological Survey*] (SEIS) ..... GRM
Graig Cove [*Vanuatu*] [*ICAO location identifier*] (ICLI) ..... NVSF
Grail International Student Center [*Defunct*] (EA) ..... GISC
Grail Movement (EA) ..... GM
Grail Movement of Australia ..... GMA
Grain ..... G
Grain (MCD) ..... GN
Grain (KSC) ..... GR
Grain (WDMC) ..... gr
Grain ..... GRAN
Grain and Feed Dealers National Association [*Later, NGFA*] (EA) ..... GFDNA
Grain and Feed Trade Association of New South Wales [*Australia*] ..... GFTANSW
Grain and Food Trade Association [*British*] ..... GAFTA
Grain Bin Manufacturers Council [*Later, GEMC*] (EA) ..... GBMC
Grain Boundary Dislocation ..... GBD
Grain Boundary Relaxation ..... GBR
Grain Boundary Segregation [*Metallurgy*] ..... GBS
Grain Count [*Measurement of cell labeling*] ..... GC
Grain Cubic (DS) ..... GC
Grain Effect Screenless Halftone [*Printing technique*] ..... GESH
Grain Elevator and Processing Society (EA) ..... GEAPS
Grain Equipment Manufacturers Association (EA) ..... GEMA
Grain Futures Administration [*Superseded by Commodity Exchange Administration, 1936*] ..... GFA
Grain Income Stabilization Plan ..... GISP
Grain Inspection X-Ray Unit (IAA) ..... GIXU
Grain Inventory System [*Department of Agriculture*] (GFGA) ..... GIS
Grain Isolation Liner (MCD) ..... GIL
Grain Legume Advisory Committee [*Australia*] ..... GLAC
Grain Legume Association [*Australia*] ..... GLA
Grain Legume Research Council (EERA) ..... GLRC
Grain Legumes Research Council [*Australia*] ..... GLRC
Grain Marketing Research Laboratory [*Manhattan, KS*] [*Department of Agriculture*] (GRD) ..... GMRL
Grain Neutral Spirits [*Alcohol*] ..... GNS
Grain Pool of Western Australia ..... GPWA
Grain Processing Machinery Manufacturers Association (EA) ..... GPMMA
Grain Products Irradiator [*Nuclear energy*] ..... GPI
Grain Research Committee of Western Australia ..... GRCWA
Grain Research Foundation [*Australia*] ..... GRF
Grain Research Laboratory [*Canadian Grain Commission*] [*Research center*] (RCD) ..... GRL
Grain Services Union ..... GSU
Grain Size Metal (IAA) ..... GS
Grain Sorghum Marketing Board [*New South Wales, Australia*] ..... GSMB
Grain Sorghum Producers Association (EA) ..... GSPA
Grain Transportation Agency [*Winnipeg, MB*] ..... GTA
Grain Valley Associated School District, Grain Valley, MO [*Library symbol*] [*Library of Congress*] (LCLS) ..... MoGvS
Grain-Burning Pattern Regulation (MCD) ..... GBPR
Grain-Burning Pattern Regulation (MCD) ..... GPR
Grain-Consuming Animal Unit [*Agricultural Statistics*] (BARN) ..... GCAU
Grainger [*W.W.*], Inc. [*Associated Press*] (SAG) ..... Graingr
Grainger, [*W. W.*] **Inc.** [*NYSE symbol*] (SPSG) ..... GWW
Grainger (W.W.) [*NYSE symbol*] (TTSB) ..... GWW
Grains (ODBW) ..... gr
Grains Council of Australia (EERA) ..... GCA
Grains Industry Council [*Australia*] ..... GIC
Grains per Anther [*Botany*] ..... G/A
Grains per Foot ..... GPF
Grains per Gallon [*Unit of measure for water hardness*] ..... GPG
Grains Research and Development Corporation [*Commonwealth*] [*State*] (EERA) ..... GRDC
Grajau [*Brazil*] [*Airport symbol*] (AD) ..... GRU
Gral Alvear [*Argentina ICAO location identifier*] (ICLI) ..... SAMA
Gram ..... g
Gram (WDMC) ..... g
Gram (IDOE) ..... gm
Gram ..... GM
Gram (KSC) ..... GR
Gram (ADA) ..... GRM
Gram Atomic Weight (WDAA) ..... G AT WT
Gram Atomic Weight [*Chemistry*] ..... GAW
Gram Calorie ..... GCAL
Gram Calorie (IDOE) ..... gm-cal
Gram Equivalent [*Chemistry*] (IAA) ..... GEQUIV
Gram Equivalent Weight ..... GEW
Gram Force (IAA) ..... GF
Gram Force per Square Centimeter ..... GF/CM^2
Gram Formula Weight [*Chemistry*] ..... GFW
Gram Meter ..... gm-m
Gram Molecular Volume [*Chemistry*] ..... GMV
Gram Molecular Weight [*Chemistry*] ..... GMW
Gram Molecule [*or Molecular*] [*Chemistry*] (IAA) ..... GMOL
Gram Parsons Memorial Foundation (EA) ..... GPMF
Gram per Mile [*Automotive engineering*] ..... g/mi
Gram Percent [*Meaning grams per deciliter*] [*Measurement*] (DAVI) ..... g%
Gram Percent [*Grams per deciliter*] [*Measurement*] (DAVI) ..... Gm%
Grambling, LA [*FM radio station call letters*] ..... KGRM
Grambling State University, Grambling, LA [*Library symbol Library of Congress*] (LCLS) ..... LGra
Grambling State University, Grambling, LA [*OCLC symbol*] (OCLC) ..... LGS
Gram-Calorie (IDOE) ..... g-cal
Gram-Centimeter (AAMN) ..... g-cm
Gram-Centimeter (IDOE) ..... gm-cm
Gram-Force (DMAA) ..... gf
Gramicidin [*Antimicrobial compound*] ..... GRD

Gramicidin A [*Antibiotic*] ... GA
Grammaire du Palmyrenien Epigraphique [*A publication*] (BJA) ... GPE
Grammar ... GR
Grammar [*or Grammatical*] ... GRAM
Grammar [*Copyediting*] (WDMC) ... gram
[*A*] **Grammar of Masoretic Hebrew** [*A publication*] (BJA) ... MH
[*A*] **Grammar of the Hurrian Language** [*A publication*] (BJA) ... GHL
Grammar School [*British*] ... G
Grammar School ... GS
Grammar School for Girls (ADA) ... GSG
Grammaticae Romana Fragmenta [*A publication*] (OCD) ... Gramm Rom Frag
Grammatical Nonalgorithmic Data Description ... GRANADA
Grammatici Latini [*A publication*] (OCD) ... Gramm Lat
Grammatik der Neusyrischen Sprache [*A publication*] (BJA) ... GNsS
Grammatik des Biblische-Aramaeischen [*H. Bauer and P. Leander*] [*A publication*] (BJA) ... BLA
Grammatik des Biblische-Aramaeischen [*H. Bauer and P. Leander*] [*A publication*] (BJA) ... BLe
Grammatik des Biblische-Aramaeischen [*A publication*] (BJA) ... GBA
Grammatik des Christlich-Palaestinischen Aramaeisch [*A publication*] (BJA) ... GCPA
Grammatik des Juedisch-Palaestinischen Aramaeisch [*A publication*] (BJA) ... GJPA
Gramme [*Gram*] [*French*] (ROG) ... GRM
Gram-Meter (MAE) ... g-m
Gram-Molecule (WDAA) ... GM MOL
Gramm-Rudman-Hollings [*Law*] ... GRH
Gramm-Rudman-Hollings Bill [*Proposed deficit-reducing bill, 1985-1986*] ... Grudman
Gramm-Rudman-Hollings Budget Deficit Control Act (AAGC) ... GRH
Gram-Negative [*Also, GRN*] [*Microbiology*] ... GN
Gram-Negative [*Bacteria*] (DAVI) ... gr-
Gram-Negative [*Biochemistry*] (DAVI) ... gram-neg
Gram-Negative [*Also, GN*] [*Microbiology*] ... GRN
Gram-Negative Bacillary Meningitis [*Medicine*] ... GNBM
Gram-Negative Bacillus [*Microbiology*] ... GNB
Gram-Negative Cocci [*Clinical chemistry*] (DAVI) ... G-C
Gram-Negative Diplococci [*Medicine*] (MEDA) ... GND
Gram-Negative Intracellular Diplococci [*Microbiology*] ... GNID
Gram-Negative Rods (DMAA) ... GNR
Gram-Negative Rods [*Biochemistry*] (DAVI) ... G-R
Gram-Negative Sensitivity [*to antibiotics*] ... GNS
Gramola [*Record label*] [*Belgium*] ... Gramo
Gramophone [*Division of Record Corp. of America*] [*Record label*] ... Gram
Gramophone Motor (DEN) ... GM
Gramophone Record Retailers Association [*British*] (BI) ... GRRA
Gramophone Records [*Music or sound effects*] ... GRAMS
Grampian Helicopter Charter Ltd. [*British ICAO designator*] (FAAC) ... GMR
Grampian Region Early Anistreplase Trial [*Cardiology study*] ... GREAT
Gram-Positive [*Also, GRP*] [*Microbiology*] ... GP
Gram-Positive [*Bacteria*] (DAVI) ... gr+
Gram-Positive [*Biochemistry*] (DAVI) ... gram-pos
Gram-Positive [*Also, GP*] [*Microbiology*] ... GRP
Gram-Positive Cocci [*Clinical chemistry*] (DAVI) ... G+C
Gram-Positive Cocci [*Immunology*] (DAVI) ... GPC
Gram-Positive Rods [*Biochemistry*] (DAVI) ... G+R
Grams of Carbon Dioxide Equivalent (EERA) ... gCO2
Grams per Cubic Centimeter ... G/CM^3
Grams per Denier ... GPD
Grams per Gallon (GNE) ... GPG
Grams per Liter ... G/L
Grams per Liter (MAE) ... gm/l
Grams per Mile ... GPM
Grams per Second ... GPS
Grams per Square Centimeter ... G/CM^2
Grams per Square Foot ... G/FT^2
Grams per Square Meter (WDAA) ... GM^2
Grams per Square Meter ... GSM
Grams per Ton ... g/t
Gran Canaria [*Canary Islands*] [*ICAO location identifier*] (ICLI) ... GCLP
Gran Enciclopedia Rialp [*A publication*] ... GER
Gran Premio Romeo [*Alfa Romeo race car*] [*Italian*] ... GPR
Gran Quivira National Monument ... GRQU
Gran Rabinato (BJA) ... GR
Gran Sasso [*Italy ICAO location identifier*] (ICLI) ... LIQI
Gran Sport [*Automobile model designation*] ... GS
Gran Turisimo Americano [*In automobile name Pontiac Firebird GTA*] ... GTA
Gran Turismo [*Grand Touring*] [*Automotive term*] ... GT
Gran Turismo Automatico [*Automobile model designation*] ... GTA
Gran Turismo Berlinetta [*Automobile model designation*] ... GTB
Gran Turismo Cabriolet [*Automobile model designation*] ... GTC
Gran Turismo Europa [*Automobile model designation*] ... GTE
Gran Turismo Experimental [*Grand Touring, Experimental*] [*Automotive term*] ... GTX
Gran Turismo Junior [*Automobile model designation*] ... GTJ
Gran Turismo Omologato [*Grand Touring, Homologated*] [*Automotive engineering*] [*Italian*] ... GTO
Gran Turismo Spider [*Automobile model designation*] ... GTS
Gran Turismo Veloce [*Automobile model designation*] ... GTV
Gran Turismo Zagato [*Automobile model designation*] ... GTZ
Grana Sex Pondere [*Six Grains by Weight*] [*Pharmacy*] (ROG) ... GR VJ POND
Granada [*Spain*] [*Airport symbol*] (OAG) ... GRX
Granada [*Spain ICAO location identifier*] (ICLI) ... LEGR
Granada/Armilla [*Spain ICAO location identifier*] (ICLI) ... LEGA
Granada Aviacion [*Spain ICAO designator*] (FAAC) ... GAV
Granada Exploration Corp. [*Vancouver Stock Exchange symbol*] ... GNA
Granada Public Library, Granada, CO [*Library symbol Library of Congress*] (LCLS) ... CoGra
Granada Public Library, Granada, CO [*Library symbol*] [*Library of Congress*] (LCLS) ... CoGraP
Granatbuechse [*Antitank Grenade Rifle*] [*German*] ... GRB
Granavillo Tribune, Granavillo, IA [*Library symbol Library of Congress*] (LCLS) ... IaGavoT
Granbury, TX [*FM radio station call letters*] (RBYB) ... KMRT-FM
Granbury, TX [*AM radio station call letters*] ... KPAR
Granby, CO [*Location identifier FAA*] (FAAL) ... GNB
Granby, CO [*AM radio station call letters*] ... KRKY
Granby Leader, Granby, PQ, Canada [*Library symbol Library of Congress*] (LCLS) ... CaQGL
Granby Leader Mail Office, Quebec [*Library symbol National Library of Canada*] (NLC) ... QGL
Granby, PQ [*AM radio station call letters*] ... CHEF
Granby Resources Ltd. [*Vancouver Stock Exchange symbol*] ... GNB
Grancamp Resources [*Vancouver Stock Exchange symbol*] ... GCP
GranCare, Inc. [*NYSE symbol*] (SPSG) ... GC
GranCare, Inc. [*Associated Press*] (SAG) ... GranCr
Grand [*Slang term for 1,000 dollars*] ... G
Grand [*Title*] ... GR
Grand ... GRND
Grand ... GRND
Grand Accelerated Space Platform ... GASP
Grand Admiral [*Freemasonry*] (ROG) ... GA
Grand Aerie, Fraternal Order of Eagles (EA) ... FOE
Grand Airways, Inc. [*FAA designator*] (FAAC) ... GND
Grand Airways, Inc. [*ICAO designator*] (FAAC) ... GNV
Grand Aleph Godol (BJA) ... GAG
Grand Alliance for Democracy [*Philippines*] [*Political party*] ... GAD
Grand Almoner [*Freemasonry*] ... GA
Grand American Handicap [*Shooting competition*] ... GAH
Grand Anatolia Project [*Dam system*] [*Turkey*] (ECON) ... GAP
Grand Annual Sojourner [*Freemasonry*] (ROG) ... GAS
Grand Architect [*Freemasonry*] ... GA
Grand Architect of the Universe [*Freemasonry*] (ROG) ... GAOTU
Grand Army of the Republic (GPO) ... GAR
Grand Assistant Conductor [*Freemasonry*] (ROG) ... GAC
Grand Assistant Recording Scribe [*Freemasonry*] (ROG) ... GARS
Grand Avenue Elementary School, Baldwin, NY [*Library symbol*] [*Library of Congress*] (LCLS) ... NBaldGE
Grand Avenue Junior High School, Bellmore, NY [*Library symbol*] [*Library of Congress*] (LCLS) ... NBellmGJ
Grand Award [*Record label*] ... GA
Grand Bahama Auxiliary Air Force Base, Grand Bahama Island [*Bahamas*] [*ICAO location identifier*] (ICLI) ... MYGM
Grand Bahama Island (KSC) ... GBI
Grand Ballon [*France*] [*Seismograph station code, US Geological Survey Closed*] (SEIS) ... GBF
Grand Bank, NF [*Television station call letters*] ... CJOX-1
Grand Bank Public Library, Grand Bank, NF, Canada [*Library symbol Library of Congress*] (LCLS) ... CaNfGB
Grand Bank Public Library, Newfoundland [*Library symbol National Library of Canada*] (NLC) ... NFGB
Grand Banks (FAAC) ... GRBNKS
Grand Bereby/Nero Mer [*Ivory Coast*] [*ICAO location identifier*] (ICLI) ... DIGN
Grand Bounce [*Suspension or dismissal*] [*Slang*] ... GB
Grand Cache, AB [*AM radio station call letters*] ... CKYR-1
Grand Cadence de Tir [*Self-propelled howitzer*] (RDA) ... GCT
Grand Canyon [*Arizona*] ... GC
Grand Canyon [*Arizona*] [*Airport symbol*] (OAG) ... GCN
Grand Canyon [*Arizona*] [*Airport symbol*] (OAG) ... JGC
Grand Canyon Airlines [*ICAO designator*] (AD) ... YE
Grand Canyon Airlines, Inc. [*FAA designator*] (FAAC) ... CVU
Grand Canyon College [*Phoenix, AZ*] ... GCC
Grand Canyon National Park ... GRCA
Grand Captain General [*Freemasonry*] ... GCG
Grand Captain of the Guard [*Freemasonry*] ... GCG
Grand Captain of the Host [*Freemasonry*] ... GCH
Grand Casinos [*NYSE symbol*] (TTSB) ... GND
Grand Casinos, Inc. [*NYSE symbol*] (SAG) ... GND
Grand Casinos, Inc. [*Associated Press*] (SAG) ... GrdCasn
Grand Cayman [*IYRU nationality code*] (IYR) ... CI
Grand Cayman [*West Indies*] [*Airport symbol*] (OAG) ... GCM
Grand Cayman [*Cayman Islands*] [*ICAO location identifier*] (ICLI) ... MWCG
Grand Central [*South Africa*] [*ICAO location identifier*] (ICLI) ... FAGC
Grand Central Rocket Co. (AAG) ... GCR
Grand Central Rocket Co., Redlands, CA [*Library symbol Library of Congress*] (LCLS) ... CRedlG
Grand Centre, AB [*AM radio station call letters*] ... CJCM
Grand Centre Municipal Library, Alberta [*Library symbol National Library of Canada*] (NLC) ... AGCM
Grand Centre Municipal Library, Grand Centre, AB, Canada [*Library symbol Library of Congress*] (LCLS) ... CaAGcM
Grand Cess [*Liberia*] [*Airport symbol*] (OAG) ... GRC
Grand Chancellor ... GC
Grand Chaplain ... GC
Grand Chapter ... GC
Grand Chapter [*Freemasonry*] (ROG) ... GR CHAP
Grand Chapter of Harodim [*Freemasonry*] ... GCH
Grand China Resources Ltd. [*Vancouver Stock Exchange symbol*] ... GCI
Grand Commander ... GC
Grand Commander [*or Commandery*] [*Freemasonry*] ... GCom

Grand Commander of the Knights of Saint Patrick	GCKP
Grand Commander (of the Order) of Spain (ROG)	GCS
Grand Conductor	GC
Grand Coulee [*Washington*] [*Seismograph station code, US Geological Survey Closed*] (SEIS)	GCW
Grand Coulee Public Library, Grand Coulee, WA [*Library symbol Library of Congress*] (LCLS)	WaGc
Grand Coulee, WA [*AM radio station call letters*]	KEYG
Grand Coulee, WA [*FM radio station call letters*]	KEYG-FM
Grand Council [*Freemasonry*] (ROG)	GC
Grand County Public Library, Granby Branch, Granby, CO [*Library symbol Library of Congress*]	CoGranG
Grand County Public Library, Hot Sulphur Springs, CO [*Library symbol Library of Congress*] (LCLS)	CoHsp
Grand Cross	GC
Grand Cross of the French Legion of Honour	GCFLH
Grand Cross (of the Order) of Leopold (ROG)	GCL
Grand Cross, Order of the Niger [*British*]	GCON
Grand Cross, St. Lazarus of Jerusalem (DD)	GCLJ
Grand Deacon [*Freemasonry*]	GD
Grand Deacon of Ceremonies [*Freemasonry*] (ROG)	GDC
Grand Division	GD
Grand Dixence [*Switzerland*] [*Seismograph station code, US Geological Survey*] (SEIS)	DIX
Grand Ducal Highness (ROG)	GDH
Grand Duchess [*or Duke*]	GD
Grand Duchess [*or Duke*] (ROG)	GR D
Grand Duchy	GD
Grand Duke (WGA)	GD
Grand Earl [*Freemasonry*] (ROG)	GE
Grand East [*Freemasonry*] (ROG)	GE
Grand Encampment [*Freemasonry*]	GE
Grand Expert [*Freemasonry*] (ROG)	GE
Grand Ezra [*Freemasonry*] (ROG)	GE
Grand Falls Central Railway Co. Ltd. [*AAR code*]	GFC
Grand Falls Historical Society, Grand Falls, NB, Canada [*Library symbol Library of Congress*] (LCLS)	CaNBGfH
Grand Falls Historical Society, New Brunswick [*Library symbol National Library of Canada*] (NLC)	NBGFH
Grand Falls, NB [*AM radio station call letters*]	CKMV
Grand Falls, NF [*Television station call letters*]	CBNAT
Grand Falls, NF [*Television station call letters*]	CJCN
Grand Falls, NF [*AM radio station call letters*]	CKXG
Grand Falls-Windsor, NF [*AM radio station call letters*]	CBT
Grand Falls-Windsor, NF [*AM radio station call letters*]	CKCM
Grand Financial Scribe [*Freemasonry*] (ROG)	GFS
Grand Fleet [*British military*] (DMA)	GF
Grand Fleet Battle Instructions [*British military*] (DMA)	GFBI
Grand Fleet Battle Orders [*British military*] (DMA)	GFBO
Grand Forks [*North Dakota*] [*Airport symbol*] (OAG)	GFK
Grand Forks [*Canada*] [*Airport symbol Obsolete*] (OAG)	ZGF
Grand Forks Air Defense Sector [*North Dakota*] (SAA)	GFADS
Grand Forks, BC [*AM radio station call letters*]	CKGF
Grand Forks Energy Research Center [*Energy Research and Development Administration*]	GFERC
Grand Forks Energy Technology Center [*Later, University of North Dakota Energy Research Center*] [*Department of Energy*] (GRD)	GFETC
Grand Forks/International [*North Dakota*] [*ICAO location identifier*] (ICLI)	KGFK
Grand Forks Mines [*Vancouver Stock Exchange symbol*]	GFK
Grand Forks, ND [*Location identifier FAA*] (FAAL)	AVA
Grand Forks, ND [*AM radio station call letters*]	KFJM
Grand Forks, ND [*FM radio station call letters*]	KFJM-FM
Grand Forks, ND [*FM radio station call letters*] (RBYB)	KFJY
Grand Forks, ND [*Television station call letters*]	KGFE
Grand Forks, ND [*FM radio station call letters*]	KJKJ
Grand Forks, ND [*AM radio station call letters*]	KKXL
Grand Forks, ND [*FM radio station call letters*]	KKXL-FM
Grand Forks, ND [*AM radio station call letters*]	KNOX
Grand Forks, ND [*FM radio station call letters*]	KNOX-FM
Grand Forks, ND [*Location identifier FAA*] (FAAL)	RDR
Grand Forks Project Office [*Grand Forks, ND*] [*Terminated Department of Energy*] (GRD)	GFPO
Grand Forks Public Library, British Columbia [*Library symbol National Library of Canada*] (NLC)	BGF
Grand Forks Public Library, Grand Forks, ND [*Library symbol Library of Congress*] (LCLS)	NdG
Grand Forks United Hospital, Grand Forks, ND [*Library symbol Library of Congress*] (LCLS)	NdGUH
Grand Format [*Graphic arts*] (DGA)	GF
Grand Gaming Corp. [*NASDAQ symbol*] (SAG)	GGCC
Grand Gaming Corp. [*Associated Press*] (SAG)	Grand
Grand Gaming Corp. [*Associated Press*] (SAG)	GrandG
Grand Gaming Wrrt [*NASDAQ symbol*] (TTSB)	GGCCW
Grand Gorge, NY [*FM radio station call letters*] (RBYB)	WGKR-FM
Grand Guardian [*Freemasonry*]	GG
Grand Gulf Nuclear Station (NRCH)	GGNS
Grand Haven, MI [*AM radio station call letters*]	WGHN
Grand Haven, MI [*FM radio station call letters*]	WGHN-FM
Grand High Priest [*Freemasonry*]	GHP
Grand Inside Sentinel [*Freemasonry*] (ROG)	GIS
Grand Island [*Diocesan abbreviation*] [*Nebraska*] (TOCD)	GI
Grand Island [*Nebraska*] [*Airport symbol*] (OAG)	GRI
Grand Island, NE [*Television station call letters*]	KGIN
Grand Island, NE [*AM radio station call letters*]	KMMJ
Grand Island, NE [*AM radio station call letters*]	KRGI
Grand Island, NE [*FM radio station call letters*]	KRGI-FM
Grand Island, NE [*FM radio station call letters*]	KROA
Grand Island, NE [*FM radio station call letters*]	KSYZ
Grand Island, NE [*Television station call letters*]	KTVG
Grand Island Public Library, Grand Island, NE [*Library symbol Library of Congress*] (LCLS)	NbG
Grand Island Public Library, Grand Island, NE [*Library symbol*] [*Library of Congress*] (LCLS)	NbGi
Grand Isle, LA [*Location identifier FAA*] (FAAL)	GNI
Grand Isle, LA [*Location identifier FAA*] (FAAL)	LEV
Grand Juction Projects Office [*Department of Energy*] [*Grand Juction, CO*] (GAAI)	GJPO
Grand Junction [*Colorado*] [*Airport symbol*] (OAG)	GJT
Grand Junction, CO [*Location identifier FAA*] (FAAL)	FRU
Grand Junction, CO [*FM radio station call letters*]	KBKL
Grand Junction, CO [*AM radio station call letters*] (RBYB)	KBZS-AM
Grand Junction, CO [*FM radio station call letters*]	KCIC
Grand Junction, CO [*AM radio station call letters*]	KEXO
Grand Junction, CO [*TV station call letters*] (RBYB)	KFQX-TV
Grand Junction, CO [*Television station call letters*]	KJCT
Grand Junction, CO [*FM radio station call letters*]	KJOL
Grand Junction, CO [*Television station call letters*]	KJWA
Grand Junction, CO [*Television station call letters*]	KJYE
Grand Junction, CO [*TV station call letters*] (RBYB)	KKCO-TV
Grand Junction, CO [*AM radio station call letters*] (RBYB)	KKGM
Grand Junction, CO [*FM radio station call letters*]	KMKE
Grand Junction, CO [*FM radio station call letters*]	KMSA
Grand Junction, CO [*FM radio station call letters*] (RBYB)	KMXY-FM
Grand Junction, CO [*AM radio station call letters*]	KNZZ
Grand Junction, CO [*AM radio station call letters*]	KPRN
Grand Junction, CO [*AM radio station call letters*]	KQIL
Grand Junction, CO [*AM radio station call letters*]	KQIX
Grand Junction, CO [*Television station call letters*]	KREX
Grand Junction, CO [*FM radio station call letters*] (RBYB)	KRMJ-FM
Grand Junction High School, Grand Junction, CO [*Library symbol Library of Congress*] (LCLS)	CoGjGH
Grand Junction Office [*Grand Junction, CO*] [*Department of Energy*]	GJO
Grand Junction Project Office [*Department of Energy*]	GJPO
Grand Junction Project Office (DOGT)	GJPO
Grand Junction Remedial Action Project [*Department of Energy*] [*Colorado*] (GAAI)	GJRAP
Grand Junior Deacon [*Freemasonry*]	GJD
Grand Junior Warden [*Freemasonry*]	GJW
Grand Jury	GJ
Grand Jury Project (EA)	GJP
Grand Keeper of the Seals [*Freemasonry*]	GKS
Grand King [*Freemasonry*]	GK
Grand Lake Public Library, Grand Lake, CO [*Library symbol Library of Congress*] (LCLS)	CoGl
Grand Larceny	GL
Grand Larousse Encyclopedique [*A publication*]	GLE
Grand Ledge Public Library, Grand Ledge, MI [*Library symbol Library of Congress*] (LCLS)	MiGrl
Grand Ledge Public Library, Grand Ledge, MI [*Library symbol*] [*Library of Congress*] (LCLS)	MiGrlP
Grand Livre du Mois [*Best-selling book of the month*] [*French*]	GLM
Grand Lodge [*Freemasonry*] (ROG)	G LO
Grand Lodge [*Freemasonry*]	GL
Grand Lodge, Ladies Auxiliary, Fraternal Order of Police (EA)	FOP
Grand Lodge of Ancient Free and Accepted Masons of Maryland, Masonic Library, Baltimore, MD [*Library symbol Library of Congress*] (LCLS)	MdBFM
Grand Lodge of Mark Master Masons [*Freemasonry*]	GLMMM
Grand Lodge of New York, F & AM Library and Museum, New York, NY [*Library symbol Library of Congress*] (LCLS)	NNFM
Grand Lodge of Scotland [*Freemasonry*]	GLS
Grand Lodge of the Free and Accepted Masons of the State of Nevada, Reno, NV [*Library symbol Library of Congress*] (LCLS)	NvRFM
Grand Lodge of Vermont, F & AM Library, Burlington, VT [*Library symbol Library of Congress*] (LCLS)	VtBFB
Grand Lodge Order of the Sons of Hermann in Texas [*San Antonio, TX*] (EA)	OSHT
Grand Lot	GL
Grand Mal [*Epilepsy*]	GM
Grand Manan Historical Society, Grand Harbour, Grand Manan Island, New Brunswick [*Library symbol National Library of Canada*] (NLC)	NBGG
Grand Manan Museum, Grand Harbour, Grand Manan Island, New Brunswick, [*Library symbol National Library of Canada*] (NLC)	NBGMM
Grand Manan Museum, Grand Harbour, Grand Manon Island, NB, Canada [*Library symbol*] [*Library of Congress*] (LCLS)	CaNBGMM
Grand Marais, MN [*Location identifier FAA*] (FAAL)	GRM
Grand Marais, MN [*FM radio station call letters*] (RBYB)	KANQ
Grand Marais, MN [*FM radio station call letters*] (RBYB)	WXXZ-FM
Grand Marais Public Library, Grand Marais, MN [*Library symbol*] [*Library of Congress*] (LCLS)	MnGm
Grand Marnier and Amaretto	GRAND AM
Grand Marshal [*Freemasonry*] (ROG)	GM
Grand Master [*Freemasonry*]	GM
Grand Master Key [*Locks*] (ADA)	GMK
Grand Master of the Bath [*British*]	GMB
Grand Master of the Knights of St. Patrick	GMKP
Grand Master of the Order of St. Michael and St. George [*British*]	GMMG
Grand Master of the Order of St. Patrick	GMP
Grand Master of the Order of the British Empire (EY)	GMBE
Grand Master of the Order of the Indian Empire [*British*]	GMIE
Grand Master of the Order of the Star of India [*British*]	GMSI

Grand Master of the Vails [*Freemasonry*] .... GMV
Grand Master's Lodge [*Freemasonry*] (ROG) .... GML
Grand Medal [*Ghana*] .... GM
Grand Met Del L.P. 9.42% Pfd [*NYSE symbol*] (TTSB) .... GRMPrA
Grand Metropolitan ADS [*NYSE symbol*] (SPSG) .... GRM
Grand Metropolitan and Guinness [*Proposed company*] .... GMG
Grand Metropolitan Delaware Ltd. [*Associated Press*] (SAG) .... GrndM
Grand Metropolitan Ltd. [*Associated Press*] (SAG) .... GrndMet
Grand Minister [*Freemasonry*] (ROG) .... GM
Grand Multiparity [*Obstetrics*] .... GM
Grand National [*Automobile racing*] .... GN
Grand National Archery Society [*British*] .... GNAS
Grand National Championship [*Motorcycle racing*] .... GNC
Grand National Curling Club of America .... GNCCA
Grand National Hunt [*British*] .... GNH
Grand National Racing Association (EA) .... GNRA
Grand National Resources, Inc. [*Vancouver Stock Exchange symbol*] .... GAA
Grand National Sportsman [*Car racing division*] .... GNS
Grand Nehemiah [*Freemasonry*] (ROG) .... GN
Grand Offertory Procession in the Sky [*Corporate sobriquet used by novelist William X. Kienzle*] .... GOPITS
Grand Officier de l'Ordre National du Quebec [*Canada*] (DD) .... GOONQ
Grand Old Man [*A venerated man, especially in a specific field*] [*Political slang See also HOM*] .... GOM
Grand Old Party [*The Republican Party*] .... GOP
Grand Old Woman [*England's Queen Victoria*] .... GOW
Grand Ole Opry Fan Club (EA) .... GOOFC
Grand Orator [*Freemasonry*] .... GO
Grand Order of Water Rats [*British*] (BI) .... GOWR
Grand Organist [*Freemasonry*] (ROG) .... GO
Grand Orient [*Freemasonry*] (ROG) .... GO
Grand Outside Sentinel [*Freemasonry*] (ROG) .... GOS
Grand Passion .... GP
Grand Past Master [*Freemasonry*] .... GPM
Grand Past Sojourner [*Freemasonry*] (ROG) .... GPS
Grand Patron [*Freemasonry*] .... GP
Grand Portage Elementary School, Grand Portage, MN [*Library symbol*] [*Library of Congress*] (LCLS) .... MnGpE
Grand Prairie Memorial Library, Grand Prairie, TX [*Library symbol Library of Congress*] (LCLS) .... TxGrp
Grand Prairie, TX [*Location identifier FAA*] (FAAL) .... GPM
Grand Prairie, TX [*AM radio station call letters*] .... KKDA
Grand Prelate [*Freemasonry*] .... GP
Grand Premier Financial, Inc. [*NASDAQ symbol*] (SAG) .... GPFI
Grand Premier Financial, Inc. [*Associated Press*] (SAG) .... GrndPr
Grand Principal Sojourner [*Freemasonry*] .... GPS
Grand Priory of the Knights of the Temple [*Freemasonry*] .... GPKT
Grand Prix .... GP
Grand Prix Association of Long Beach [*NASDAQ symbol*] (SAG) .... GPLB
Grand Prix Association of Long Beach [*Associated Press*] (SAG) .... GrdPrx
Grand Prix Contact Club [*British*] (DBA) .... GPCC
Grand Prix Drivers' Association .... GPDA
Grand Pursuivant [*Freemasonry*] (ROG) .... GP
Grand Quartier-General [*French GHQ*] .... GQG
Grand Rapids [*Minnesota*] [*Airport symbol*] (OAG) .... GPZ
Grand Rapids [*Michigan*] [*Airport symbol*] (OAG) .... GRR
Grand Rapids & Petoskey Railway .... GR & P
Grand Rapids Area Furniture Manufacturers Association (EA) .... GRAFMA
Grand Rapids Area Union List of Serials [*Library network*] .... GRAUL
Grand Rapids Baptist College and Seminary, Grand Rapids, MI [*OCLC symbol*] (OCLC) .... EXB
Grand Rapids Baptist College, Grand Rapids, MI [*Library symbol Library of Congress*] (LCLS) .... MiGrB
Grand Rapids Furniture Market Association [*Inactive*] (EA) .... GRFMA
Grand Rapids Junior College [*Michigan*] .... GRJC
Grand Rapids Junior College, Grand Rapids, MI [*Library symbol Library of Congress*] (LCLS) .... MiGrJC
Grand Rapids/Kent County Cascade [*Michigan*] [*ICAO location identifier*] (ICLI) .... KGRR
Grand Rapids Law Library, Grand Rapids, MI [*Library symbol Library of Congress*] (LCLS) .... MiGrL
Grand Rapids, MI [*Location identifier FAA*] (FAAL) .... CYZ
Grand Rapids, MI [*AM radio station call letters*] .... WBBL
Grand Rapids, MI [*FM radio station call letters*] .... WBCT
Grand Rapids, MI [*FM radio station call letters*] .... WBLU
Grand Rapids, MI [*FM radio station call letters*] .... WBYW
Grand Rapids, MI [*FM radio station call letters*] .... WCSG
Grand Rapids, MI [*AM radio station call letters*] .... WCUZ
Grand Rapids, MI [*FM radio station call letters*] .... WCUZ-FM
Grand Rapids, MI [*FM radio station call letters*] .... WFGR
Grand Rapids, MI [*AM radio station call letters*] .... WFUR
Grand Rapids, MI [*FM radio station call letters*] .... WFUR-FM
Grand Rapids, MI [*AM radio station call letters*] .... WGRD
Grand Rapids, MI [*FM radio station call letters*] .... WGRD-FM
Grand Rapids, MI [*Television station call letters*] .... WGVU
Grand Rapids, MI [*FM radio station call letters*] .... WLAV-FM
Grand Rapids, MI [*FM radio station call letters*] .... WLHT
Grand Rapids, MI [*AM radio station call letters*] .... WOOD
Grand Rapids, MI [*FM radio station call letters*] .... WOOD-FM
Grand Rapids, MI [*Television station call letters*] .... WOOD-TV
Grand Rapids, MI [*AM radio station call letters*] (RBYB) .... WRCV-AM
Grand Rapids, MI [*FM radio station call letters*] .... WVGR
Grand Rapids, MI [*Television station call letters*] .... WXMI
Grand Rapids, MI [*Television station call letters*] .... WZZM
Grand Rapids, Michigan .... GR
Grand Rapids Middle School, Grand Rapids, MN [*Library symbol*] [*Library of Congress*] (LCLS) .... MnGrM
Grand Rapids, MN [*FM radio station call letters*] .... KAXE
Grand Rapids, MN [*FM radio station call letters*] .... KMFY
Grand Rapids, MN [*AM radio station call letters*] .... KOZY
Grand Rapids Public Library [*Michigan*] .... GRPL
Grand Rapids Public Library, Grand Rapids, MI [*OCLC symbol*] (OCLC) .... EXR
Grand Rapids Public Library, Grand Rapids, MI [*Library symbol Library of Congress*] (LCLS) .... MiGr
Grand Rapids Public Library, Grand Rapids, MN [*Library symbol*] [*Library of Congress*] (LCLS) .... MnGr
Grand Rapids Senior HighSchool, Grand Rapids, MN [*Library symbol*] [*Library of Congress*] (LCLS) .... MnGrSH
Grand Recorder [*Freemasonry*] .... GR
Grand Recording Scribe [*Freemasonry*] (ROG) .... GRS
Grand Registrar [*Freemasonry*] (ROG) .... G REG
Grand Registrar [*Freemasonry*] (ROG) .... GR
Grand Ridge Consolidated Community School District 95, Grand Ridge, IL [*Library symbol Library of Congress*] (LCLS) .... IGrSD
[*The*] **Grand River Railway Co.** [*AAR code*] .... GRNR
Grand Royal Arch Captain [*Freemasonry*] .... GRAC
Grand Royal Arch Chapter [*Freemasonry*] (ROG) .... GRAC
Grand Scale Integration (BUR) .... GSI
Grand Scribe [*Freemasonry*] .... GS
Grand Secretary [*Freemasonry*] (ROG) .... G SEC
Grand Secretary [*Freemasonry*] .... GS
Grand Seminaire de Rimouski, Quebec [*Library symbol National Library of Canada*] (NLC) .... QRGS
Grand Seminaire des Saints-Apotres, Sherbrooke, PQ, Canada [*Library symbol Library of Congress*] (LCLS) .... CaQSherG
Grand Seminaire, Montreal, PQ, Canada [*Library symbol Library of Congress*] (LCLS) .... CaQMGS
Grand Seminaire, Montreal, Quebec [*Library symbol National Library of Canada*] (NLC) .... QMGS
Grand Senior Deacon [*Freemasonry*] .... GSD
Grand Senior Warden [*Freemasonry*] (ROG) .... GSW
Grand Sentinel [*Freemasonry*] .... GS
Grand Sentry [*Freemasonry*] .... GS
Grand Slam Home Runs [*Baseball*] .... GSHR
Grand Speed (BARN) .... GS
Grand Standard Bearer [*Freemasonry*] (ROG) .... G ST B
Grand Standard Bearer [*Freemasonry*] .... G STD B
Grand Standard Bearer [*Freemasonry*] (ROG) .... GSB
Grand Steward [*Freemasonry*] .... GS
Grand Superintendent [*Freemasonry*] .... G SUPT
Grand Superintendent of Works [*Freemasonry*] .... GS of W
Grand Sword Bearer [*Freemasonry*] .... G SWD B
Grand Sword-Bearer [*Freemasonry*] .... GSB
Grand Teton Industries, Inc. [*Vancouver Stock Exchange symbol*] .... GTT
Grand Teton National Park .... GRTE
Grand Theft .... GT
Grand Theft Auto (WGA) .... GTA
Grand Tiler [*Freemasonry*] .... GT
Grand Touring [*Automobile model designation*] .... GT
Grand Touring Coupe [*In automobile name Lincoln Mark VII GTC*] .... GTC
Grand Touring Over 3.0 Liters [*Class of racing cars*] .... GTO
Grand Touring Prototype [*Race car designation*] .... GTP
Grand Touring Supreme [*Auto racing*] .... GTS
Grand Touring Under 3.0 Liters [*Class of racing cars*] .... GTU
Grand Toys International [*NASDAQ symbol*] (SAG) .... GRIN
Grand Toys International [*Associated Press*] (SAG) .... GrndToy
Grand Toys International [*Associated Press*] (SAG) .... GrToy
Grand Toys Intl Wrrt [*NASDAQ symbol*] (TTSB) .... GRINW
Grand Traverse Area Sportfishing Association [*Michigan*] .... GTASFA
Grand Traverse Bay, Michigan .... GTB
Grand Traverse Bay Watershed Initiative .... GTBWI
Grand Treasurer [*Freemasonry*] (ROG) .... G TREAS
Grand Treasurer [*Freemasonry*] .... GT
Grand Trunk Pacific Railway .... GTP
Grand Trunk Pacific Railway .... GTPR
Grand Trunk Railroad [*British*] (ROG) .... GTRR
Grand Trunk Railway .... GTR
Grand Trunk Railway .... GTRY
Grand Trunk Western Railroad Co. [*AAR code*] .... GTW
Grand Turk [*British West Indies*] [*Airport symbol*] (OAG) .... GDT
Grand Turk [*British West Indies*] .... GTK
Grand Turk [*Turks and Caicos Islands*] [*ICAO location identifier*] (ICLI) .... MBGT
Grand Turk [*Turks and Caicos Islands*] [*ICAO location identifier*] (ICLI) .... MBJT
Grand Turk Island .... GTI
Grand Ufficiale [*Grand Officer*] (EY) .... GrUff
Grand Un Wrrt Ser 1 [*NASDAQ symbol*] (TTSB) .... GUCOW
Grand Un Wrrt Ser 2 [*NASDAQ symbol*] (TTSB) .... GUCOZ
Grand Unified Force .... GUF
Grand Unified Monopoles [*Cosmology*] .... GUM
Grand Unified Problem Solver .... GUPS
Grand Unified Theory [*Cosmology*] .... GUT
Grand Unified Theory of the Tire .... GUTT
Grand Union [*NASDAQ symbol*] (TTSB) .... GUCO
Grand Union Co. [*Associated Press*] (SAG) .... GrndUn
Grand Union Co. [*NASDAQ symbol*] (SAG) .... GUCO
Grand United Friendly Society [*Australia*] .... GU
Grand United Friendly Society [*Australia*] .... GUFS
Grand United Order of Odd Fellows (EA) .... GUOOF
Grand United Order of Oddfellows [*Australia*] .... GUOO

Grand Valley Public Library, Grand Valley, ON, Canada [*Library symbol*] [*Library of Congress*] (LCLS) ... CaOGRV
Grand Valley Public Library, Ontario [*Library symbol National Library of Canada*] (NLC) ... OGRV
Grand Valley State College, Allendale, MI [*OCLC symbol*] (OCLC) ... EXG
Grand Valley State College, Allendale, MI [*Library symbol Library of Congress*] (LCLS) ... MiAllG
Grand Valley State University [*Michigan*] ... GVSU
Grand View College [*Iowa*] ... GVC
Grand View College, Des Moines, IA [*Library symbol Library of Congress*] (LCLS) ... IaDmG
Grand View College, Des Moines, IA [*OCLC symbol*] (OCLC) ... IWG
Grand Warder [*Freemasonry*] ... GW
Grand Worthy Associate [*Freemasonry*] (ROG) ... GWA
Grand Worthy Chaplain [*Templars*] [*Freemasonry*] (ROG) ... GW CHAP
Grand Worthy Chief [*Templars*] [*Freemasonry*] (ROG) ... GWC
Grand Worthy Chief Templar [*Templars*] [*Freemasonry*] (ROG) ... GWCT
Grand Worthy Deputy Marshal [*Templars*] [*Freemasonry*] (ROG) ... GWDM
Grand Worthy Inside Guard [*Templars*] [*Freemasonry*] (ROG) ... GWIG
Grand Worthy Marshal [*Templars*] [*Freemasonry*] (ROG) ... GWM
Grand Worthy Outside Guard [*Templars*] [*Freemasonry*] (ROG) ... GWOG
Grand Worthy Patriarch [*Freemasonry*] (ROG) ... GWP
Grand Worthy Scribe [*Templars*] [*Freemasonry*] (ROG) ... GWS
Grand Worthy Templar [*Templars*] [*Freemasonry*] (ROG) ... GWT
Grand Worthy Treasurer [*Templars*] [*Freemasonry*] (ROG) ... GW TREAS
Grand Worthy Vice Templar [*Templars*] [*Freemasonry*] (ROG) ... GWVT
Grand-Bourg/Marie-Galante [*French Antilles*] [*ICAO location identifier*] (ICLI) ... TFFM
Grand-Dad's Day Council [*Defunct*] (EA) ... GDC
Granddaughter ... GD
Granddaughter ... Gda
Granddaughter (ROG) ... GRDAU
Granddaughter Of [*Genealogy*] ... GR/D/O
Grande Cache Public Library, Alberta [*Library symbol National Library of Canada*] (NLC) ... AGC
Grande Croix (EY) ... GrCr
Grande Portage [*Vancouver Stock Exchange symbol*] ... GPG
Grande Prairie [*Canada*] [*Airport symbol*] (OAG) ... YQU
Grande Prairie, AB [*Television station call letters*] ... CBXAT
Grande Prairie, AB [*Television station call letters*] ... CBXFT-8
Grande Prairie, AB [*AM radio station call letters*] ... CFGP
Grande Prairie, AB [*Television station call letters*] ... CFRN-1
Grande Prairie, AB [*AM radio station call letters*] ... CJXX
Grande Prairie, AB [*FM radio station call letters*] ... CKUA-4
Grande Prairie, AB [*ICAO location identifier*] (ICLI) ... CYQU
Grande Prairie College, Alberta [*Library symbol National Library of Canada*] (NLC) ... AGPC
Grande Prairie College, Grande Prairie, AB, Canada [*Library symbol Library of Congress*] (LCLS) ... CaAGPC
Grande Prairie Public Library, Alberta [*Library symbol National Library of Canada*] (NLC) ... AGP
Grande Prairie Public Library, Grande Prairie, AB, Canada [*Library symbol*] [*Library of Congress*] (LCLS) ... CaAGP
Grande Prairie Regional College Library [*UTLAS symbol*] ... GPC
Grande Prairie Regional Hospital, Alberta [*Library symbol National Library of Canada*] (NLC) ... AGPH
Grande Prairie Regional Hospital, Grande Prairie, AB, Canada [*Library symbol*] [*Library of Congress*] (LCLS) ... CaAGPH
Grande Puissance Filloux [*World War II*] ... GPF
Grande Ronde Hospital, LaGrande, OR [*Library symbol Library of Congress*] (LCLS) ... OrLgGRH
Grande Tel Technologies [*NASDAQ symbol*] (TTSB) ... GTTIF
Grandes Decisions de la Jurisprudence Administrative [*A publication*] (ILCA) ... GD
GrandeTel Technologies, Inc. [*Associated Press*] (SAG) ... GrandTel
GrandeTel Technologies, Inc. [*NASDAQ symbol*] (SAG) ... GTTIF
Grandex Resources Ltd. [*Vancouver Stock Exchange symbol*] ... GDX
Grandfather ... GF
Grandfather ... GRF
Grandfather-Father-Son [*Computer science*] (PCM) ... GFS
Grandfield, OK [*Location identifier FAA*] (FAAL) ... GFX
Grandioso [*Majestic*] [*Music*] ... GRANDO
Grandma ... GRNDMA
Grandma Lee's, Inc. [*Toronto Stock Exchange symbol*] ... GLI
Grandmet Information Processing [*British*] ... GRIP
Grandmother ... GM
Grandmother (DSUE) ... GRAN
Grandmother ... GRM
Grandmothers for Peace (EA) ... GP
Grandmothers of America in War Service [*World War II*] ... GAWS
Grandnephew (ADA) ... GN
Grandniece (ADA) ... GN
Grand-Orgue [*Great Organ*] [*Music*] ... G
Grand-Orgue [*Great Organ*] [*Music*] ... G Org
Grandpa ... GRNDPA
Grandparents Anonymous (EA) ... GPA
Grandparents Association of America (EA) ... GAA
Grandparents'/Children's Rights (EA) ... GCR
Grandparents Raising Grandchildren (EA) ... GRG
Grandparents Rights Organization (EA) ... GRO
Grands Arrets de la Jurisprudence Civile [*A publication*] (ILCA) ... GA
Grands Ballets Canadiens, Montreal, PQ, Canada [*Library symbol Library of Congress*] (LCLS) ... CaQMGB
Grands Ballets Canadiens, Montreal, Quebec [*Library symbol National Library of Canada*] (NLC) ... QMGB
Grands Toys Intl [*NASDAQ symbol*] (TTSB) ... GRIN
Grandson (ROG) ... GRS
Grandson ... GS
Grandson Of [*Genealogy*] ... GR/S/O
Granduc Mines Ltd. [*Toronto Stock Exchange symbol Vancouver Stock Exchange symbol*] ... GDC
Grandview Colony School, Grande Prairie, Alberta [*Library symbol National Library of Canada*] (BIB) ... AGPGS
Grandview Heights Library, Columbus, OH [*Library symbol Library of Congress*] (LCLS) ... OCoG
Grandview Hospital, Dayton, OH [*Library symbol Library of Congress*] (LCLS) ... ODaGH
Grandview, MO [*Location identifier FAA*] (FAAL) ... GVW
Grandview Personal Care Home, Grandview, MB, Canada [*Library symbol Library of Congress*] (LCLS) ... CaMGPC
Grandview Personal Care Home, Manitoba [*Library symbol National Library of Canada*] (NLC) ... MGPC
Grandview Resources, Inc. [*Toronto Stock Exchange symbol Vancouver Stock Exchange symbol*] ... GND
Grandview/Richards-Gebaur Air Force Base [*Missouri*] [*ICAO location identifier*] (ICLI) ... KGVW
Grandview, WA [*FM radio station call letters*] ... KARY
Grandview, WV [*Television station call letters*] ... WSWP
Grange [*or Manor, a religious residence*] ... GR
Grange Gold Corp. [*Vancouver Stock Exchange symbol*] ... GEG
Granger Resources Corp. [*Vancouver Stock Exchange symbol*] ... GNG
Granger's State Reports [*22-23 Ohio*] [*A publication*] (DLA) ... Granger
Granges Exploration Ltd. [*Toronto Stock Exchange symbol*] ... GEX
Granges, Inc. [*Associated Press*] (SAG) ... Grang
Granges, Inc. [*AMEX symbol Toronto Stock Exchange symbol*] (SPSG) ... GXL
Granges-Gontardes [*France*] [*Seismograph station code, US Geological Survey Closed*] (SEIS) ... GGF
Grangeville, ID [*Location identifier FAA*] (FAAL) ... GVV
Grangeville, ID [*AM radio station call letters*] ... KORT
Grangeville, ID [*FM radio station call letters*] ... KORT-FM
Grangeville Public Library, Grangeville, ID [*Library symbol*] [*Library of Congress*] (LCLS) ... IdGg
Granisle Public Library, British Columbia [*Library symbol National Library of Canada*] (NLC) ... BGR
Granite ... G
Granite (MSA) ... GRAN
Granite (VRA) ... gran
Granite [*Technical drawings*] ... GRN
Granite ... GRNT
Granite Belt Horticultural Research Station [*Australia*] ... GBHRS
Granite Brdcst $1.9375 Cv Pfd [*NASDAQ symbol*] (TTSB) ... GBTVP
Granite Broadcasting [*NASDAQ symbol*] (TTSB) ... GBTVK
Granite Broadcasting Corp. [*NASDAQ symbol*] (SPSG) ... GBTV
Granite Broadcasting Corp. [*Associated Press*] (SAG) ... GranBd
Granite Butte [*Montana*] [*Seismograph station code, US Geological Survey Closed*] (SEIS) ... GBM
Granite City Army Depot (AABC) ... GCAD
Granite City Community Unit 12, Granite City, IL [*Library symbol Library of Congress*] (LCLS) ... IGracCU
Granite City, IL [*AM radio station call letters*] ... WGNU
Granite City, IL [*FM radio station call letters*] ... WKKX
Granite City Public Library, Granite City, IL [*Library symbol Library of Congress*] (LCLS) ... IGrac
Granite Construction [*NASDAQ symbol*] (TTSB) ... GCCO
Granite Construction, Inc. [*NASDAQ symbol*] (SAG) ... GCCO
Granite Construction, Inc. [*Associated Press*] (SAG) ... GrnteC
Granite Creek [*California*] [*Seismograph station code, US Geological Survey*] (SEIS) ... GCC
Granite Cutters' International Association [*Later, Tile, Marble, Terrazzo, Finishers, Shopworkers, and Granite Cutters International Union*] ... GCIA
Granite Cutters' International Association of America (DICI) ... GCIAA
Granite Falls, MN [*FM radio station call letters*] ... KKRC
Granite Falls Municipal Hospital, Granite Falls, MN [*Library symbol*] [*Library of Congress*] (LCLS) ... MnGfH
Granite Falls, NC [*AM radio station call letters*] ... WYCV
Granite Falls Public Library, Granite Falls, MN [*Library symbol*] [*Library of Congress*] (LCLS) ... MnGf
Granite Falls Public Library, Granite Falls, NC [*Library symbol Library of Congress*] (LCLS) ... NcGf
Granite Falls Public School, Granite Falls, MN [*Library symbol*] [*Library of Congress*] (LCLS) ... MnGfPS
Granite Financial, Inc. [*NASDAQ symbol*] (SAG) ... GFNL
Granite Financial, Inc. [*Associated Press*] (SAG) ... GranitFn
Granite Grit Institute of America (EA) ... GGIA
Granite Mountain [*Alaska*] [*Seismograph station code, US Geological Survey*] (SEIS) ... GMA
Granite Mountain [*Utah*] [*Seismograph station code, US Geological Survey*] (SEIS) ... GMU
Granite Point, AK [*Location identifier FAA*] (FAAL) ... GRP
Granite Polishers' and Workers' Union [*British*] ... GPWU
Granite State Bancshares [*NASDAQ symbol*] (TTSB) ... GSBI
Granite State Bankshares, Inc. [*Associated Press*] (SAG) ... GrantSt
Granite State Bankshares, Inc. [*NASDAQ symbol*] (NQ) ... GSBI
Granite Workers' Union [*British*] ... GWU
Graniteville [*South Carolina*] [*Seismograph station code, US Geological Survey Closed*] (SEIS) ... GVS
Granodize ... GRAN
Granolithic ... GRANO
Granolithic Base ... GRB
Granolithic Finish Floor [*Technical drawings*] ... GFF

Granophyric Roof Zone [*Geology*] ... GRZ
Grant ... GR
Grant [*Legal term*] (DLA) ... Gra
Grant [*Legal shorthand*] (LWAP) ... GT
Grant Aid [*Military*] (AFM) ... GA
Grant Aid [*Military*] (AABC) ... GRA
Grant Air Program [*DoD*] (MCD) ... GAP
Grant Application [*Job Training and Partnership Act*] (OICC) ... GA
Grant Application Request (WDAA) ... GAPR
Grant Award [*Job Training and Partnership Act*] (OICC) ... GA
Grant Community Consolidated School District 110, Fairview Heights, IL [*Library symbol Library of Congress*] (LCLS) ... IFhGSD
Grant County Historical Society, Marion, IN [*Library symbol Library of Congress*] (LCLS) ... InMarGHi
Grant, Edge, Robinson, Mead, French, Ackley, Shephard, and Knaggs [*Founders of a town in Michigan's Upper Peninsula that derived its name from the initial letters of their surnames*] ... Germfask
Grant Elementary School, Duluth, MN [*Library symbol*] [*Library of Congress*] (LCLS) ... MnDuGE
Grant Exploration [*Vancouver Stock Exchange symbol*] ... GNT
Grant Geophysical [*NASDAQ symbol*] (TTSB) ... GRNT
Grant Geophysical $2.4375 Cv Pfd [*NASDAQ symbol*] (TTSB) ... GRNTP
Grant Geophysical, Inc. [*NASDAQ symbol*] (SAG) ... GRNP
Grant Geophysical, Inc. [*NASDAQ symbol*] (SPSG) ... GRNT
Grant Geophysical, Inc. [*Associated Press*] (SAG) ... GrntG
Grant Geophysical, Inc. [*Associated Press*] (SAG) ... GrntGeo
Grant Greater Than [*Dialog*] [*Searchable field*] [*Information service or system*] (NITA) ... GG
Grant Information and Control System [*Environmental Protection Agency*] (GFGA) ... GICS
Grant Information System [*Oryx Press*] (IID) ... GIS
Grant Law Library, Davenport, IA [*Library symbol Library of Congress*] (LCLS) ... IaDaGL
Grant Less Than [*Dialog*] [*Searchable fields*] [*Information service or system*] (NITA) ... GL
Grant/Loan Accounting and Management Information System [*Department of Commerce*] (GFGA) ... GLAMIS
Grant MacEwan College, Edmonton, AB, Canada [*Library symbol*] [*Library of Congress*] (LCLS) ... CaAEGMSS
Grant MacEwan Community College, Cromdall Campus Learning Resource Centre, Edmonton, AB,Canada [*Library symbol*] [*Library of Congress*] (LCLS) ... CaAEGMCR
Grant MacEwan Community College, Edmonton, AB, Canada [*Library symbol Library of Congress*] (LCLS) ... CaAEGM
Grant MacEwan Community College, Jasper Place Campus Learning Resource Centre, Edmonton,AB, Canada [*Library symbol*] [*Library of Congress*] (LCLS) ... CaAEGMJP
Grant MacEwan Community College Library Technology Program, Edmonton, AB, Canad a [*OCLC symbol*] (OCLC) ... CGM
Grant MacEwan Community College, Mill Woods Campus Learning Resource Centre, Edmonton, AB, Canada [*Library symbol*] [*Library of Congress*] (LCLS) ... CaAEGMMW
Grant MacEwan Cromdale Campus LRC, Edmonton, Alberta [*Library symbol National Library of Canada*] (NLC) ... AEGMCR
Grant MacEwan Jasper Place Campus LRC, Edmonton, Alberta [*Library symbol National Library of Canada*] (NLC) ... AEGMJP
Grant MacEwan Mill Woods Campus LRC, Edmonton, Alberta [*Library symbol National Library of Canada*] (NLC) ... AEGMMW
Grant MacEwan Seventh Street Plaza Campus, Edmonton, Alberta [*Library symbol National Library of Canada*] (NLC) ... AEGMSS
Grant Maintained School (AIE) ... GMS
Grant, NE [*Location identifier FAA*] (FAAL) ... GGF
Grant Number (NITA) ... GN
Grant of Elchies' Scotch Session Cases [*A publication*] (DLA) ... Grant
Grant of Resident Status ... GORS
Grant on Banking [*A publication*] (DLA) ... Grant Bank
Grant on Corporations [*A publication*] (DLA) ... Grant Corp
Grant Opportunities for Academic Liaison with Industry [*National Science Foundation*] ... GOALI
Grant Parish Library, Colfax, LA [*Library symbol Library of Congress*] (LCLS) ... LColfG
Grant Public Library, Grant, MI [*Library symbol Library of Congress*] (LCLS) ... MiGran
Grant Recipient [*Job Training and Partnership Act*] (OICC) ... GR
Grant Tensor Geophysical Corp. [*Associated Press*] (SAG) ... GrntT
Granted [*Legal term*] (ILCA) ... G
Grantee [*Legal shorthand*] (LWAP) ... GTEE
Grantex Aviation [*British*] [*FAA designator*] (FAAC) ... GTR
Grantham High School, Saint Catharines, ON, Canada [*Library symbol Library of Congress*] (LCLS) ... CaOStCG
Grantham High School, St. Catharines, Ontario [*Library symbol National Library of Canada*] (NLC) ... OSTCG
Grantham, PA [*FM radio station call letters*] ... WVMM
Grant-Illini School 110, Fairview Heights, IL [*Library symbol Library of Congress*] (LCLS) ... IFhGS
Granting ... GRTG
Grant-Maintained Status (ODBW) ... GMS
Grant-Makers for Children and Youth (EA) ... GMCY
Grantmakers for Children, Youth, and Families (NFD) ... GCYF
Grantor [*Legal shorthand*] (LWAP) ... GTOR
Grantor-Retained Income Trust [*Estate planning*] ... GRIT
Grant-Related Expenditure [*British*] ... GRE
Grant-Related Expenditure Assessments [*British*] ... GREA
Grant-Related Poundage [*British*] ... GRP
Grants Administration Division [*Environmental Protection Agency*] ... GAD
Grants Administration Manual [*HEW*] ... GAM
Grant's Cases [*A publication*] (DLA) ... Gr Ca
Grant's Chancery Chamber Reports [*1850-65*] [*Upper Canada*] [*A publication*] (DLA) ... Grant
Grants, Contracts, and General Law Division [*Environmental Protection Agency*] (GFGA) ... GCGLD
Grants Equal to Taxes ... GETT
Grant's Error and Appeal Reports [*A publication*] (DLA) ... E & AUC
Grant's Error and Appeal Reports [*A publication*] (DLA) ... Grant E & A
Grant's Error and Appeal Reports [*A publication*] (DLA) ... Grant Err & App
Grants for Aboriginal Advancement [*Australia*] ... GAA
Grants for Industrial Research and Development (EERA) ... GIRD
Grants/Grants-Milan [*New Mexico*] [*ICAO location identifier*] (ICLI) ... KGNT
Grant's Jamaica Reports [*A publication*] (DLA) ... Gr
Grant's Jamaica Reports [*A publication*] (DLA) ... Grant
Grant's Jamaica Reports [*A publication*] (DLA) ... Grant Jamaica
Grant's Jamaica Reports [*A publication*] (DLA) ... Grant's R
Grants Management Information System [*Department of Health and Human Services*] (GFGA) ... GMIS
Grants, NM [*Location identifier FAA*] (FAAL) ... GNT
Grants, NM [*FM radio station call letters*] ... KAGP
Grants, NM [*AM radio station call letters*] ... KMIN
Grants, NM [*FM radio station call letters*] (RBYB) ... KTHR-FM
Grants, NM [*FM radio station call letters*] ... KZNM
Grants Operations Balance [*Environmental Protection Agency*] (ERG) ... GOB
Grants Pass, OR [*Location identifier FAA*] (FAAL) ... GNA
Grants Pass, OR [*AM radio station call letters*] ... KAGI
Grants Pass, OR [*AM radio station call letters*] ... KAJO
Grants Pass, OR [*FM radio station call letters*] (RBYB) ... KAPK-FM
Grants Pass, OR [*FM radio station call letters*] ... KYJC-FM
Grants Pass, OR [*Location identifier FAA*] (FAAL) ... OOO
Grant's Pennsylvania Cases [*A publication*] (DLA) ... Gr
Grant's Pennsylvania Cases [*A publication*] (DLA) ... Grant
Grant's Pennsylvania Cases [*A publication*] (DLA) ... Grant Cas
Grant's Pennsylvania Cases [*A publication*] (DLA) ... Grant Cas (PA)
Grant's Pennsylvania Cases [*A publication*] (DLA) ... Grant PA
Grant's Pennsylvania Cases [*A publication*] (DLA) ... Grt
Grants to Voluntary Conservation Organisations (EERA) ... GVCO
Grant's Upper Canada Chancery Reports [*A publication*] (DLA) ... Gr
Grant's Upper Canada Chancery Reports [*A publication*] (DLA) ... Grant
Grant's Upper Canada Chancery Reports [*A publication*] (DLA) ... Grant Ch
Grant's Upper Canada Chancery Reports [*A publication*] (DLA) ... Grant Ch (Can)
Grant's Upper Canada Chancery Reports [*A publication*] (DLA) ... Grant UC
Grantsburg, WI [*Location identifier FAA*] (FAAL) ... GTG
Grants-in-Aid ... GIA
Grants-in-Aid of Research ... GIAR
Grantsmanship Center (EA) ... GC
[*The*] **Grantsmanship Center** (EA) ... TGC
Grantsville, MD [*Location identifier FAA*] (FAAL) ... GRV
Grantsville, MD [*FM radio station call letters*] ... WAIJ
Granular ... G
Granular (WDAA) ... GRAN
Granular Activated Carbon ... GAC
Granular Activated Carbon Absorption ... GAC
Granular Boundary Segregation [*Petrology*] ... GBS
Granular Cast [*Medicine*] ... GC
Granular Cyst [*Medicine*] (MAE) ... GC
Granular Diffusion Flame (MCD) ... GDF
Granular Kidney [*Medicine*] (ROG) ... GK
Granular Progenitor Cell [*Medicine*] (DMAA) ... GPC
Granular Quartz Rock (AD) ... quartzite
Granular Snow [*Skiing condition*] ... GR
Granulated (MSA) ... GNLTD
Granulated ... GRANL
Granulation (VRA) ... grnln
Granulation Time ... G/T
Granulation Tissue ... G/T
Granulatus [*Granulated*] [*Pharmacy*] ... GRAN
Granule [*Medicine*] ... GRN
Granule Membrane Protein ... GMP
Granulin (DMAA) ... GRN
Granulocyte [*Hematology*] (DAVI) ... granulo
Granulocyte Activating Mediator [*Immunochemistry*] ... GRAM
Granulocyte Agglutination [*Hematology*] ... GA
Granulocyte Colony-Stimulating Factor Promoter Element (DMAA) ... GPE
Granulocyte Colony-Stimulating Factor Receptor (DMAA) ... GSFR
Granulocyte Cytotoxic [*Hematology*] ... GC
Granulocyte, Erythroid, Macrophage, Megakaryocyte [*Hematology*] ... GEMM
Granulocyte/Macrophage [*Ratio*] [*Hematology*] ... G/M
Granulocyte Turnover Rate [*Hematology*] ... GTR
Granulocyte-Colony Stimulating Factor [*Hematology*] ... G-CSF
Granulocyte-Erythroid (Ratio) [*Hematology*] ... G/E
Granulocyte-Macrophage Colony-Stimulating Activity [*Hematology*] ... GM-CSA
Granulocyte-Macrophage Colony-Stimulating Factor [*Biochemistry*] ... GM-CSF
Granulocytosis-Promoting Factor [*Hematology*] ... GPF
Granuloma Inguinale [*Endocrinology*] (DAVI) ... GI
Granulomatous Angiitis [*Medicine*] ... GA
Granulomatous Angiitis of the Nervous System [*Medicine*] (DMAA) ... GANS
Granulomatous Hypersensitivity [*Medicine*] (DMAA) ... GHR
Granulopoietin [*Hypothetical substance*] [*Hematology*] ... GPO
Granulosa Cells [*Cytology*] ... GC
Granulosis Virus ... GV
Granum [*Grain*] [*Latin*] ... GR
Granum Public Library, Alberta [*Library symbol National Library of Canada*] (NLC) ... AGR

Granville [France] [Airport symbol] (AD) ... GFR
Granville [France ICAO location identifier] (ICLI) ... LFRF
Granville Island Brewing Co. Ltd. [Vancouver Stock Exchange symbol] ... GRV
Granville, OH [FM radio station call letters] ... WDUB
Granville Resources, Inc. [Vancouver Stock Exchange symbol] ... GVR
Grape and Wine Research and Development Corporation (EERA) ... GWRDC
Grape and Wine Research and Development Council [Australia] ... GWRDC
Grape Berry Moth ... GBM
Grape Growers' Association of Western Australia ... GGAWA
Grapefruit Juice [Restaurant slang] ... GJ
Grapel's Sources of the Roman Civil Law [A publication] (DLA) ... Grap Rom Law
Grapel's Translation of the Institutes of Justinian [A publication] (DLA) ... Grap Just
Grapevine Bulgarian Latent Virus [Plant pathology] ... GBLV
Grapevine Chrome Mosaic Virus [Plant pathology] ... GCMV
Grapevine Fan Leaf Virus [Plant pathology] ... GFLV
Grapevine Leafroll-Associated Virus [Plant pathology] ... GLR-AV
Grapevine Virus A [Plant pathology] ... GVA
Grapevine Virus B [Plant pathology] ... GVB
Graph (OA) ... G
Graph Algorithmic Language [Computer science] ... GRAAL
Graph Information Retrieval Language [1970] [Computer science] (CSR) ... GIRL
Graph Isomorphism Tester ... GIT
Graphe de Commande Etape-Transition [State transition command graph] [Computer language] (CDE) ... GRAFCET
Graphed [Quilting] ... G
Graphic ... GRAPH
Graphic (MSA) ... GRPH
Graphic ... GRPHC
Graphic Acids to Packaging Equipment (PDAA) ... GAPE
Graphic Active Device [Computer science] (MHDI) ... GAD
Graphic Adapter Board ... GAB
Graphic Addition to FORTRAN [Computer science] ... GRAF
Graphic Administrative Information System (DNAB) ... GAINS
Graphic Aids for Investigating Networks [NASA] (NASA) ... GAIN
Graphic Ammeter (MSA) ... GA
Graphic Analysis and Correlation Terminal (MCD) ... GACT
Graphic Analysis and Correlation Terminal Fleet Ocean Surveillance Information Facility (DNAB) ... GACTFOSIF
Graphic Analysis of Three-Dimensional Data ... GATD
Graphic Analyzer of Resistance Defects ... GARD
Graphic Animation System for Professionals [Software package] [Paul Mace Software] (PCM) ... GRasp
Graphic Applications Subroutine Package [Computer science] (BUR) ... GASP
Graphic Approach to Numerical Information Processing (IAA) ... GANIP
Graphic Art Club, Toronto [c.1903, SGA from 1912, CSGA from 1923] [Canada] (NGC) ... GAC
Graphic Artists Guild (EA) ... GA
Graphic Artists Guild (EA) ... GAG
Graphic Artists Guild Foundation (EA) ... GAGF
Graphic Arts Advertisers and Exhibitors Council [Defunct] (EA) ... GAAEC
Graphic Arts Advertisers Council [Later, GAAEC] ... GAAC
Graphic Arts Association (SRA) ... GAA
Graphic Arts Association Executives [Defunct] (EA) ... GAAE
Graphic Arts Composing Equipment ... GRACE
Graphic Arts Council of North America (EA) ... GACNA
Graphic Arts Education and Research Foundation (DGA) ... GAERF
Graphic Arts Employers of America (EA) ... GAE
Graphic Arts Equipment and Supply Dealers Association [Defunct] (EA) ... GAESDA
Graphic Arts Guidance Kit ... GAGK
Graphic Arts Industries Association ... GAIA
Graphic Arts International Union [Later, GCIU] ... GAIU
Graphic Arts Literature Abstracts [A publication] ... GALA
Graphic Arts Machinery Association (DGA) ... GAMA
Graphic Arts Manufacturers' Representative Association ... GAMRA
Graphic Arts Marketing Information Service (EA) ... GAMIS
Graphic Arts Merchants' Association of Australia ... GAMAA
Graphic Arts Monthly [A publication] (DGA) ... GAM
Graphic Arts Platemakers Employers' Federation (DGA) ... GAPEA
Graphic Arts Quality (DGA) ... GAQ
Graphic Arts Research Center [Later, T & E Center] [Rochester Institute of Technology] ... GARC
Graphic Arts Research Foundation (EA) ... GARF
Graphic Arts Sales Foundation (EA) ... GASF
Graphic Arts Services Association of New South Wales [Australia] ... GASANSW
Graphic Arts Services Association of Victoria [Australia] ... GASAV
Graphic Arts Show Co., Inc. (DGA) ... GASC
Graphic Arts Spray Manufacturers [Defunct] (EA) ... GASM
Graphic Arts Suppliers Association (EA) ... GASA
Graphic Arts Technical Foundation (EA) ... GATF
Graphic Arts Terminal [Phototypesetting] (NITA) ... GAT
Graphic Arts Trade Association Executives [Later, GAAE] ... GATAE
Graphic Arts Union Employers of America (EA) ... UEA
Graphic Automatic Data Processing System (MCD) ... GADPS
Graphic Codepoint Definition [Telecommunications] ... GCD
Graphic Communications Association (EA) ... GCA
Graphic Communications Computer Association [Printing Industries of America] [Later, GCA] ... GCCA
Graphic Communications, Inc. [Computer science] ... GCI
Graphic Communications International Union (EA) ... GCIU
Graphic Communications Societies Group [British] (NITA) ... GCSG
Graphic Compatibility System [US Military Academy] (NITA) ... GCS
Graphic Compatibility System ... GCS
Graphic Control Center [Touch-activated CRT display] ... GCC
Graphic Controls Corp., Buffalo, NY [Library symbol Library of Congress] (LCLS) ... NBuGC
Graphic Converter Interface [Computer science] (DGA) ... GCI
Graphic Data Entry Unit [Computer science] ... GRAPDEN
Graphic Data Output Area (CMD) ... GDOA
Graphic Data Presentation and Edit (PDAA) ... GADPET
Graphic Data Processing (IAA) ... GRDP
Graphic Data System ... GDS
Graphic Demand Meter ... GD
Graphic Depth Recorder ... GDR
Graphic Design System ... GDS
Graphic Display ... GD
Graphic Display Console (MCD) ... GDC
Graphic Display Interface (MCD) ... GDI
Graphic Display Library ... GDL
Graphic Display Processor ... GDP
Graphic Display Segment ... GDS
Graphic Display Terminal ... GDT
Graphic Display Unit ... GDU
Graphic Drawing Library [Graphic Data Ltd.] [Software package] (NCC) ... GDL
Graphic Engine Monitor (DA) ... GEM
Graphic Environment Operating System [Commodore 64] ... GEOS
Graphic Export Center [Netherlands] ... GEC
Graphic Expression Reading Improvement System ... GERIS
Graphic Finite Element Modeling [Software] [Automotive engineering] ... GRAFEM
Graphic Firing Fan [Weaponry] (INF) ... GFF
Graphic Firing Table [Weaponry] (NATG) ... GFT
Graphic Generator System ... GGS
Graphic Image Pagination System [Penta Systems International] ... GRIPS
Graphic Imaging Specification Language [Printing technology] ... GISL
Graphic Industries [NASDAQ symbol] (TTSB) ... GRPH
Graphic Industries, Inc. [NASDAQ symbol] (NQ) ... GRPH
Graphic Industries, Inc. [Associated Press] (SAG) ... GrphIn
Graphic Information System [Computer databases] ... GIS
Graphic Input Language [Computer science] (PDAA) ... GRAIL
Graphic Input System ... GIS
Graphic Interactive Analytic Network Technique (MCD) ... GIANT
Graphic Interactive Display (IEEE) ... GRID
Graphic Interchange Format [Computer science] ... gif
Graphic Interface for Finite Elements [Graphics data processing] ... GIRAFFE
Graphic Job Processor (MCD) ... GJP
Graphic Kilovolt-Ampere [Meter] (MSA) ... GVA
Graphic Layout and Engineering Aid Method ... GLEAM
Graphic Level Recorder ... GLR
Graphic Library ... GL
Graphic Machine Language ... GML
Graphic Memory Interface Controller [Computer chip] ... GMIC
Graphic Microfilm Corp., Valley Stream, NY [Library symbol Library of Congress] (LCLS) ... GmNY
Graphic Microfilm of New England, Waltham, MA [Library symbol Library of Congress] (LCLS) ... GmNE
Graphic Network Operator Console [Hughes Network Systems, Inc.] ... GNOC
Graphic Numerical Control [Deltacam Systems Ltd.] [Software package] [British] (MCD) ... GNC
Graphic Online Language [Computer science] (IEEE) ... GOLD
Graphic Option Controller (NITA) ... GOC
Graphic Output Circuit Analysis Program ... GOCAP
Graphic Part Programmer (PDAA) ... GPP
Graphic Plan Evaluation Tool (DMAA) ... GPET
Graphic Programming Services [Computer science] (IBMDP) ... GPS
Graphic Read-Only Memory [Computer science] (IAA) ... GROM
Graphic Recording Ammeter (IAA) ... GRA
Graphic Recording Voltmeter (IAA) ... GRV
Graphic Recording Wattmeter (IAA) ... GRW
Graphic Reproduction [A publication] (DGA) ... GR
Graphic Reproduction by Integrated Design ... GRID
Graphic Reproduction Federation (DGA) ... GRF
Graphic Retrieval and Information Display (NASA) ... GRID
Graphic Service Program (IEEE) ... GRASP
Graphic Service Routines [Computer science] (MCD) ... GSR
Graphic Sketch Club, Philadelphia, PA [Library symbol Library of Congress Obsolete] (LCLS) ... PPGraph
Graphic Software Systems Inc. (NITA) ... GSS
Graphic Standards Management Board ... GSMB
Graphic Standards Planning Committee (NITA) ... GSPC
Graphic Stress Telethermometry [Medicine] ... GST
Graphic Structure Input ... GSI
Graphic Subroutine Package [Computer science] ... GSP
Graphic Support Software ... GSS
Graphic Surface Kinetics [Computer program] (KSC) ... GASKET
Graphic Tablet Display [Computer science] (IEEE) ... GTD
Graphic Take-Off Language [Computer science] (PDAA) ... GTOL
Graphic Technician [MARC relator code] [Library of Congress] (LCCP) ... grt
Graphic Text Management System [Computer science] (DGA) ... GTMS
Graphic Training Aid ... GTA
Graphic Training Aids Officer [Army] ... GTAO
Graphic Transform Package (MHDI) ... GTP
Graphic Varmeter ... GRVA
Graphic Video Attributes Controller [Computer chip] ... GVAC
Graphic, Visualization, and Usability Center [Georgia Institute of Technology] ... GVU
Graphic Weather Display System [FAA] (TAG) ... GWDS
Graphical Aid [Computer science] ... GRAID
Graphical Airspace Design Environment [FAA] (TAG) ... GRADE
Graphical Analysis of Program Execution [Computer science] ... GRAPE

Graphical Analysis Procedures for System Simulation (PDAA) .... GAPSS
Graphical Articulted Total Body .... GATB
Graphical Automatic Programming [*Computer science*] .... GAP
Graphical Automatically Programmed Tools [*Computer science*] .... GAPT
Graphical Data Definition Language .... GDDL
Graphical Data Display Manager [*Computer science*] .... GDDM
Graphical Data Entry [*Computer science*] (MUGU) .... GRAPHDEN
Graphical Display and Query Facility [*IBM Corp.*] .... GDQF
Graphical Display System [*Station control and data acquisition*] (IEEE) .... GDS
Graphical Evaluation and Review Technique .... GERT
Graphical Exposure Modeling System [*For estimating pollutants*] .... GEMS
Graphical IBIS [*Issue-Based Information System*] [*Computer science*] (BYTE) .... GIBIS
Graphical Input [*Language*] [*Computer science*] .... GRIN
Graphical Input and Output in FORTRAN [*GST Computer Systems Ltd.*] [*Software package*] [*Computer science*] [*British*] .... GINO-F
Graphical Input of SMILES [*Simplified Molecular Line Editor System*] **Input** .... GRINS
Graphical Input/Output .... GINO
Graphical Interaction [*Language*] [*Computer science*] GRIN-2
Graphical Interactive Network Designer .... GRINDER
Graphical Interactive NMR Analysis [*Computer science*] .... GINA
Graphical Kernel System [*International Standards Organization*] [*Computer science*] .... GKS
Graphical Modeling and Simulation System .... GMSS
Graphical Multi-Meter .... GMM
Graphical Munitions Effects Tables (MCD) .... GMET
Graphical Natural Inference System .... GRANIS
Graphical Operating System Hack [*Computer science*] .... GOSH
Graphical Output Scheme (PDAA) .... GOS
Graphical, Paper and Media Union [*British*] .... GPMU
Graphical PERT [*Program Evaluation and Review Technique*] **Analog** [*Computer science*] (IEEE) .... GPA
Graphical Picture Drawing Language [*Computer science*] (PDAA) .... GPC
Graphical Repair Discard Analysis Procedure Handbook .... GRAPH
Graphical Representation of Language for Temporal Ordering Specification [*Telecommunications*] (OSI) .... GLOTOS
Graphical Rewriting Grammar .... GRG
Graphical User Environment [*Computer science*] .... GUE
Graphical User Interface [*Computer science*] (PCM) .... GUI
Graphical User Interface [*Computer science*] (EERA) .... GUI
Graphical User Interface for Blind People .... GUIB
Graphically Oriented Design and Analysis System [*Computer science*] .... GODAS
Graphically-Aided Mathematical Machine .... GAMMA
Graphic-Oriented Timesharing System [*Computer science*] (IAA) .... GOTS
Graphics (VRA) .... gra
Graphics Access Method (BUR) .... GAM
Graphics Access Method/System Product [*IBM Corp.*] .... GAM/SP
Graphics Action Request (MCD) .... GAR
Graphics Adapter Processor [*Baytec*] .... GAP
Graphics and Administration [*Military*] (GFGA) .... GA
Graphics and/or Media Specialist .... G/MS
Graphics and Sound [*in Apple IIGS*] [*Apple Computer, Inc.*] .... GS
Graphics Application Language (BYTE) .... GAL
Graphics Application Program .... GAP
Graphics Application Program [*Computer science*] (MHDI) .... GAS
Graphics Attachment Support (IAA) .... GAS
Graphics Command Interpreter (IAA) .... GCI
Graphics Communications Terminal .... GCT
Graphics Compatibility Standard [*For image processing*] .... GCS
Graphics Conferencing (MCD) .... GC
Graphics Control Program [*IBM Corp.*] (PCM) .... GCP
Graphics Device Interface .... GDI
Graphics Display List [*Graphic Data Ltd.*] [*Software package*] (NCC) .... GDL
Graphics Display Management System (MCD) .... GDMS
Graphics Engine Interface [*Computer science*] .... GEI
Graphics Engineering and Mapping System [*Navy*] (GFGA) .... GEMS
Graphics Entity and Operation Unification [*Computer science*] .... GEOU
Graphics Environment Manager [*Computer science*] .... GEM
Graphics Finite Element Module [*McDonnell-Douglas Automation Corp.*] .... GFEM
Graphics Flutter Analysis Methods [*Computer science*] .... GFAM
Graphics for the Multipicture System [*Computer graphics*] .... GRAMPS
Graphics Function Monitor [*Tektronix*] (NITA) .... GFM
Graphics Interaction with Proteins [*Computer graphics*] .... GRIP
Graphics Interactive Program (NITA) .... GRIP
Graphics Interactive Programming .... GRIP
Graphics Interactive Programming Language [*McDonnell-Douglas Corp.*] .... GRIP
Graphics Interchange Format [*Computer technology*] .... GIF
Graphics Interface Basic Acceptance Test (MCD) .... GRIBAT
Graphics Language [*Computer science*] (HGAA) .... GICL
Graphics Lathe Module [*McDonnell-Douglas Automation Co.*] .... GLM
[*The*] **Graphics Link Plus** [*Printer software*] [*TerraVision*] (PCM) .... TGL+
Graphics Metafile Resources [*Computer science*] .... GMR
Graphics Mill Module [*McDonnell-Douglas Corp.*] .... GMM
Graphics Mouse Technology (DGA) .... GMT
Graphics Multi-Axis Module [*McDonnell-Douglas Automation Co.*] .... GMAX
Graphics Nesting Processor (MCD) .... GNP
Graphics Nesting Program (MCD) .... GNP
Graphics Network Architecture .... GNA
Graphics Object Content Architecture (CDE) .... GOCA
Graphics Operating System [*Tektronix*] .... GOS
Graphics Package [*Computer science*] (MHDI) .... GP
Graphics Package [*Computer science*] (MHDI) .... GPAC
Graphics Pages per Minute [*Printer technology*] (PCM) .... gppm
Graphics Philately Association (EA) .... GPA
Graphics Postprocessor Module [*McDonnell-Douglas Corp.*] .... GPM
Graphics Preparatory Association (EA) .... GPA
Graphics Processing Unit .... GPU
Graphics Processor .... GP
Graphics Program for Aircraft Design .... GPAD
Graphics Programming Interface [*IBM Corp.*] (PCM) .... GPI
Graphics Schematics Module [*McDonnell-Douglas Corp.*] .... GSM
Graphics Screen Editor (NITA) .... GSE
Graphics Support Processor/Tektronix .... GSPTEK
Graphics System Module .... GSM
Graphics System Processor [*Texas Instruments, Inc.*] [*Computer hardware*] .... GSP
Graphics Terminal .... GT
Graphics Terminal Scheduler (MCD) .... GTS
Graphics Terminal Services .... GTS
Graphics Terminal System .... GTS
Graphics Text Organizer [*Computer science*] .... GTO
Graphics Vendor Control .... GVC
Graphics within Texts (NITA) .... GTX
Graphics-Assisted Management Application [*Computer science*] (BUR) .... GAMA
Graphics-Augmented Structural Post-Processing [*Module*] .... GRASP
Graphics-Oriented Interactive Finite Element Time-Sharing System (PDAA) .... GIFTS
Graphics-Oriented Relational Algebraic Interpreter .... GRAIN
Graphite .... G
Graphite (MSA) .... GPH
Graphite .... Gr
Graphite (VRA) .... grph
Graphite Electrode Contouring Machine (PDAA) .... GEM
Graphite Epoxy (NASA) .... G/E
Graphite Epoxy Motor (MCD) .... GEM
Graphite Fiber Composite .... GFC
Graphite Furnace Atomic Absorption Spectroscopy [*Physics*] .... GFAAS
Graphite Intercalation Compound [*Inorganic chemistry*] .... GIC
Graphite Low-Energy Experimental Pile [*Nuclear reactor*] [*British*] .... GLEEP
Graphite Moderated, Water Cooled (PDAA) .... GMWC
Graphite Oxidation from Reactor Excursion [*Engineering computer code*] .... GORX
Graphite Polyester .... G/P
Graphite Rod Vaporization .... GRV
Graphite-Benzalkonium-Heparin [*Medicine*] (MAE) .... GBH
Graphite-Epoxy Composite Structure (PDAA) .... GECS
Graphite-Fiber Epoxy-Composite .... GFEC
Graphite-Fiber-Reinforced Plastic [*Also, GrFRP*] (NASA) .... GFRP
Graphite-Fiber-Reinforced Plastic [*Also, GFRP*] .... GrFRP
Graphite-Furnace Atomic Absorption [*Spectroscopy*] [*Physics*] .... GFAA
Graphite-Moderated Boiling and Superheating Reactor .... GBSR
Graphite-Reinforced Epoxy .... GRE
Graphitic Oxide .... GO
Graphitized Carbon Black .... GCB
Graphix Zone [*NASDAQ symbol*] (TTSB) .... GZON
Graphix Zone, Inc. [*Associated Press*] (SAG) .... GraphxZn
Graphix Zone, Inc. [*NASDAQ symbol*] (SAG) .... GZON
Graphology (WDAA) .... GRAPH
Grapple Adapter [*Nuclear energy*] (NRCH) .... GA
Grapple Adapter Handling Fixture [*Nuclear energy*] (NRCH) .... GAHF
Grappling and Lock-On Validation .... GALOVAL
Grashof Number [*IUPAC*] .... Gr
Grasonville, MD [*FM radio station call letters*] .... WRNR
Grasp .... Gr
Grasp Objects [*Psychometric test*] .... GO
Grasped Objects Discrimination [*Psychometric test*] .... GOD
Grass [*Botany*] .... G
Grass (ROG) .... GR
Grass [*Maps and charts*] .... GRS
Grass Extract [*Immunology*] .... GR
Grass Mountain [*Washington*] [*Seismograph station code, US Geological Survey*] (SEIS) .... GSM
Grass Pollen [*Immunology*] .... GP
Grass Pollen Count [*Immunology*] .... GPC
Grass Roots [*A publication*] .... Grass R
Grass Roots Art and Community Effort [*Vermont*] .... GRACE
Grass Roots Association (EA) .... GRA
Grass Valley, CA [*FM radio station call letters*] .... KJFA
Grass Valley, CA [*AM radio station call letters*] .... KNCO
Grass Valley, CA [*FM radio station call letters*] .... KNCO-FM
Grass Valley Free Public Library, Grass Valley, CA [*Library symbol Library of Congress*] (LCLS) .... CGr
Grasse River R. R. Corp. [*AAR code*] .... GR
Grassi Block Substitution Test [*Psychology*] .... GBST
Grassland (RDA) .... GRSLND
Grassland Biome [*Ecological biogeographic study*] .... GB
Grassland Heritage Foundation (EA) .... GHF
Grassland Husbandry Adviser [*Ministry of Agriculture, Fisheries, and Food*] [*British*] .... GHA
Grassland Public Library, Alberta [*Library symbol National Library of Canada*] (NLC) .... AGRAS
Grassland Public Library, Grassland, AB, Canada [*Library symbol*] [*Library of Congress*] (LCLS) .... CaAGras
Grassland Research and Serengeti Systems [*Model for simulation*] .... GRASS
Grassland Research Foundation (EA) .... GRF
Grassland Research Institute [*Research center British*] (IRC) .... GRI
Grassland Society of Southern Africa [*See also WVSA*] (EAIO) .... GSSA
Grasslands Ecology Program (EERA) .... GEP

Grasslands National Park, Parks Canada [Parc National Grasslands, Parcs Canada] Val Marie, Saskatchewan [Library symbol National Library of Canada] (NLC) .... SVMPCG
Grass-Model Polygraph .... GMP
Grassroots International (EA) .... GI
Grassroots International (EA) .... GRI
Grater (MSA) .... GRTR
Gratiam Resources [Vancouver Stock Exchange symbol] .... GRS
Gratianus [Flourished, 1151-59] [Authority cited in pre-1607 legal work] (DSA) .... Gra
Gratiarum Actio [of Ausonius] [Classical studies] (OCD) .... Grat Act
Grating (MSA) .... GRTG
Gratio [Tennessee] [Seismograph station code, US Geological Survey] (SEIS) .... GRT
Gratis [Free] [Latin] (ROG) .... GRAT
Gratitude Patient [A nonpaying patient] [Medical slang] .... GP
Grattan's Virginia Reports [A publication] (DLA) .... Grat
Grattan's Virginia Reports [A publication] (DLA) .... Gratt (VA)
Grattan's Virginia Supreme Court Reports [1844-80] [A publication] (DLA) .... Gratt
Gratuity (AABC) .... GRAT
Gratz College, Philadelphia, PA [Library symbol Library of Congress Obsolete] (LCLS) .... PPGratz
Graulhet/Mondragon [France ICAO location identifier] (ICLI) .... LFCQ
Gravatom Projects Ltd. [British] (IRUK) .... GPL
Gravdal [Norway] [Airport symbol] (AD) .... GVD
Grave Record [Genealogy] .... GR
Gravel .... G
Gravel .... GRVL
Gravel .... GRVL
Gravel (KSC) .... GVL
Gravelbourg, SK [AM radio station call letters] CBKF-1
Gravelbourg, SK [Television station call letters] CBKFT-6
Gravelotte [South Africa] [ICAO location identifier] (ICLI) .... FAGV
Gravel-Surface Built-Up Roof [Technical drawings] .... GSBR
Gravenhurst Public Library, Gravenhurst, ON, Canada [Library symbol Library of Congress] (LCLS) .... CaOGra
Gravenhurst Public Library, Ontario [Library symbol National Library of Canada] (NLC) .... OGRA
Grave's Disease [Endocrinology] .... GD
Graves Family Association .... GFA
Graves Public Library, Mendota, IL [Library symbol Library of Congress] (LCLS) .... IMen
Graves Registration [Military] .... GR
Graves Registration [Military] .... GRREG
Graves Registration and Effects Division [Military] .... GRE & E Div
Graves Registration Officer [Military] .... GRO
Graves Registration Service [Military] .... GRS
Gravid [Pregnant] [Medicine] .... GRAV
Gravida [Obstetrics] .... G
Gravida [Obstetrics] (DAVI) .... Gr
Gravida I [Gynecology and obstetrics] (DAVI) .... GI
Gravida Para [Gynecology and obstetrics] (DAVI) .... G/P
Gravida, Para, and Abortus [Gynecology and obstetrics] (DAVI) .... g-p-ab
Gravida, Para, and Abortus [Gynecology and obstetrics] (DAVI) .... GrPAB
Gravida, Para, Multiple Births, Abortions, Live Births [Obstetrics] .... GPMAL
Gravimetric Density .... GD
Gravimetric Volume .... GV
Gravina's De Jure Naturale Gentium, Etc. [A publication] (DLA) .... Grav De Jur Nat Gent
Gravis Computer Peripherals, Inc. [Vancouver Stock Exchange symbol] .... GVP
Gravissimam Educationis [Declaration on Christian Education] [Vatican II document] .... GE
Gravitational .... GRAV
Gravitational Constant [or Newtonian Constant] [Physics] (DAVI) .... G
Gravitational Dipole Moment (PDAA) .... GDM
Gravitational Field Measurements (SAA) .... GFM
Gravitational Mass .... GM
Gravitational Mass Sensor .... GMS
Gravitational Potential Energy [Geophysics] .... GPE
Gravitational Redshift Experiment (SSD) .... GRE
Gravitational Redshift Space Probe [Also, GRAVR] .... GP
Gravitational Redshift Space Probe [Also, GP] .... GRAVR
Gravitational Ulcer [Medicine] .... GU
Gravitationally Stabilized Solar Power System .... GSSPS
Gravito-Inertial Force .... GIF
Gravity [or the force or acceleration produced by it] .... G
Gravity (IDOE) .... g
Gravity .... GR
Gravity (CPH) .... grav
Gravity Association for Universal Scientific Study .... GAUSS
Gravity Cutback (NRCH) .... GCB
Gravity Die-Cast [Automotive engineering] .... GDC
Gravity Eliminated (DAVI) .... G-E
Gravity Gradient (KSC) .... GG
Gravity Gradiometer Mission [NASA] .... GGM
Gravity Independent Photosynthetic Gas Exchanger .... GIPSE
Gravity Measuring System .... GMS
Gravity per Second (KSC) .... G/S
GRAvity PipE no. 4 [Computer science] GRAPE-4
Gravity Probe-B [Experiment to test Einstein's Theory of General Relativity] .... GP-B
Gravity Reference Signal [or System] .... GRS
Gravity Research Foundation (EA) .... GRF
Gravity Sensors System [Navigation] .... GSS
Gravity Settling Culture .... GSC

Gravity Vacuum Tube System [High-speed ground transportation] .... GVT
Gravity-Anchored Space Experiments Satellite (MCD) .... GASES
Gravity-Assisted Space Probe [NASA] .... GASP
Gravity-Controlled Gyro .... GCG
Gravity-Controlled Gyro System .... GCGS
Gravity-Gradient Libration [Damper] .... GGL
Gravity-Gradient Satellite .... GGS
Gravity-Gradient Sensor .... GGS
Gravity-Gradient Stabilization Experiment .... GGSE
Gravity-Gradient Test Satellite [NASA] .... GGTS
Gravity-Gradient Test Satellite .... GIGS
Gravity-Gradient Torque .... GGT
Gravity-Induced Loss of Consciousness [Aviation] .... G-LOC
Gravity-Oriented Test Satellite [NASA] .... GOTS
Gravity-Velocity (MCD) .... G-V
Gravure (VRA) .... grv
Gravure Association of America (EA) .... GAA
Gravure Education Foundation (EA) .... GEF
Gravure Engravers Association (EA) .... GEA
Gravure Engraving Group [British] (DBA) .... GEG
Gravure Research Institute [Later, GAA] (EA) .... GRI
Gravure Technical Association [Later, GAA] (EA) .... GTA
Gray .... GR
Gray [Unit] [Radiation therapy] (DAVI) .... gr
Gray [Thoroughbred racing] .... G
Gray (MSA) .... GRA
Gray (ADA) .... GRY
Gray [Symbol] [SI unit for absorbed dose acceleration] .... Gy
Gray .... GY
Gray and Ductile Iron Founders' Society [Later, Iron Castings Society - ICS] .... GDIFS
Gray Area Systems (MCD) .... GAS
Gray Cast Iron .... GCI
Gray Communications Systems [NYSE symbol] (SAG) .... GCS
Gray Communications Systems [Associated Press] (SAG) .... GrayC
Gray Communications Systems [Associated Press] (SAG) .... GrayCom
Gray Communications Systems [Associated Press] (SAG) .... GryCm
Gray Co., Inc. .... GRACO
Gray Court, SC [FM radio station call letters] .... WSSL
Gray, GA [FM radio station call letters] .... WWIQ
Gray Herbarium [Harvard University] [Cambridge, MA] .... GH
Gray Iron (MSA) .... GI
Gray Iron Founders Society (EA) .... GIFS
Gray, KY [AM radio station call letters] .... WKYZ
Gray Line Sightseeing Association [Commercial firm] (EA) .... GLSA
Gray Oral Reading Tests .... GORT
Gray Oral Reading Tests - Revised [Educational test] .... GORT-R
Gray Panthers (EA) .... GP
Gray Platelet Syndrome [Medicine] (DMAA) .... GPS
Gray-Body Temperature Index [for thermal ecology of lizards] .... GBTI
Gray-Component Replacement [Color reproduction technology] .... GCR
Graydon's Forms of Conveyance [A publication] (DLA) .... Gray Forms
Grayish [Philately] .... grysh
Grayling [Alaska] [Airport symbol] (OAG) .... KGX
Grayling Creek [Montana] [Seismograph station code, US Geological Survey] (SEIS) .... GCR
Grayling, MI [Location identifier FAA] (FAAL) .... GYG
Grayling, MI [AM radio station call letters] .... WGRY
Grayling, MI [FM radio station call letters] (RBYB) .... WGRY-FM
Graymoor Ecumenical Institute (EA) .... GEI
Gray's Country Attorney's Practice [9th ed.] [1869] [A publication] (DLA) .... Gray Att Pr
Grays Harbor College [Washington] .... GHC
Grays Harbor College, Aberdeen, WA [Library symbol Library of Congress] (LCLS) .... WaAG
Gray's Inn [London] [One of the Inns of Court] .... GI
Gray's Massachusetts Reports [A publication] (DLA) .... Gray (Mass)
Gray's Massachusetts Supreme Judicial Court Reports [67-82 Massachusetts] [1854-60] [A publication] (DLA) .... Gray
Gray's Reports [112-22 North Carolina] [A publication] (DLA) .... Gray
Gray's Rule Against Perpetuities [A publication] (DLA) .... Gray Perpetuities
Gray-Saint-Adrien [France ICAO location identifier] (ICLI) .... LFEV
Gray-Scale Sonography [Medicine] .... GSS
Grayson County College, Denison, TX [Library symbol Library of Congress] (LCLS) .... TxDeniG
Grayson Foundation [Later, GJC] (EA) .... GF
Grayson, GA [AM radio station call letters] .... WPLO
Grayson, KY [AM radio station call letters] .... WGOH
Grayson, KY [FM radio station call letters] .... WKCC
Grayson, KY [FM radio station call letters] .... WUGO
Grayson Perceptualization Test [Psychology] .... GPT
Graysonia, Nashville & Ashdown Railroad Co. [AAR code] .... GNA
Grayson-Jockey Club Research Foundation (EA) .... GJC
Graysville, TN [FM radio station call letters] .... WAYB
Gray-Votaw-Rogers [Psychology] (AEBS) .... GVR
Graz [Steiermark] [Austria] [Seismograph station code, US Geological Survey] [Closed] (SEIS) .... GRA
Graz [Austria] [Airport symbol] (OAG) .... GRZ
Graz [Austria ICAO location identifier] (ICLI) .... LOWG
Graz [Austria ICAO location identifier] (ICLI) .... LOXG
Grazhdanskii Vozdushnyi Flot [Civil Air Fleet] [Former USSR] .... GVF
Graziano, R. M., Washington DC [STAC] .... GRM
Graziers' Asociation of South East Queensland [Australia] .... GASEQ
Grazing Capacity [Agriculture] .... GC
Grazing-Incidence Solar Telescope .... GRIST

Grazing-Incidence Spectrometer (PDAA) ... GIS
Grazing-Incidence X-Ray Diffraction ... GIXD
Grazing-Incidence X-Ray Scattering [*Imaging technique*] ... GIXS
Grazioso [*Gracefully*] [*Music*] ... GRAZ
Grazioso [*Gracefully*] [*Music*] ... GRAZO
Grazzanise [*Italy ICAO location identifier*] (ICLI) ... LIRM
GRC International [*Associated Press*] (SAG) ... GRC Int
GRC International [*NYSE symbol*] (SPSG) ... GRH
Grease (MSA) ... GRS
Grease, Artillery/Automotive [*Military*] (INF) ... GAA
Grease Interceptor Trap ... GIT
Grease Monkey Hldg [*NASDAQ symbol*] (TTSB) ... GMHC
Grease Monkey Holding Corp. [*NASDAQ symbol*] (NQ) ... GMHC
Grease Monkey Holding Corp. [*Associated Press*] (SAG) ... GrMonk
Grease Nozzle ... GNOZ
Grease Trap (AAG) ... GT
Great ... G
Great (MCD) ... GR
Great (ROG) ... GRT
Great ... GRT
Great ... GT
Great Amer BackRub [*NASDAQ symbol*] (TTSB) ... RUBB
Great American Airways [*ICAO designator*] (FAAC) ... GRA
Great American Backrub Store, Inc. [*Associated Press*] (SAG) ... GA Back
Great American Backrub Store, Inc. [*NASDAQ symbol*] (SAG) ... RUBB
Great American Bancorp [*NASDAQ symbol*] (TTSB) ... GTPS
Great American Bancorp, Inc. [*Associated Press*] (SAG) ... GA Bcp
Great American Bancorp, Inc. [*NASDAQ symbol*] (SAG) ... GTPS
Great American Dream ... GAD
Great American Management & Investment, Inc. [*NASDAQ symbol*] (NQ) ... GAMI
Great American Management & Investment, Inc. [*Associated Press*] (SAG) ... GtAMg
Great American Shoe Store [*Advertising slogan of Kinney Shoe Corp.*] ... GASS
Great American Station Wagon Owner's Association [*Defunct*] (EA) ... GASWOA
Great American Trials [*A publication*] ... GAT
Great American Truck Racing (EA) ... GATR
Great American Wife and Mother [*Slang*] ... GAWAM
Great Analog Signal Saver ... GASS
Great Annihilator [*Commonwealth - French satellite*] (ECON) ... GRANAT
[*The*] **Great Architect of the Universe** [*Freemasonry*] ... TGAOTU
Great Artesian Basin [*Australia*] ... GAB
Great Artists [*A publication*] ... GA
Great Atl & Pac Tea [*NYSE symbol*] (TTSB) ... GAP
Great Atlantic & Pacific Tea Co., Inc. ... A & P
Great Atlantic & Pacific Tea Co., Inc. [*NYSE symbol*] (SPSG) ... GAP
Great Atlantic & Pacific Tea Co., Inc. [*Associated Press*] (SAG) ... GtAtPc
Great Atlantic Radio Conspiracy (EA) ... GARC
Great Attractor [*Galactic science*] ... GA
Great Australian Bight [*Region*] (EERA) ... GAB
Great Australian Bight Consultative Committee ... GABCC
Great Australian Bight Industry Association (EERA) ... GABIA
Great Australian Bight Trawl Fishery (EERA) ... GAB
Great Barrier [*New Zealand*] [*Seismograph station code, US Geological Survey*] (SEIS) ... GBZ
Great Barrier Airlines [*Airline code*] [*Australia*] ... GB
Great Barrier Island [*Australia Airport symbol*] (OAG) ... GBZ
Great Barrier Island [*New Zealand*] [*Airport symbol*] (AD) ... GTR
Great Barrier Reef (EERA) ... GBR
Great Barrier Reef Consultative Committee [*Australia*] ... GBRCC
Great Barrier Reef Marine Park [*Region*] (EERA) ... GBRMP
Great Barrier Reef Marine Park Authority [*Commonwealth*] (EERA) ... GBRMPA
Great Barrington, MA [*Location identifier FAA*] (FAAL) ... GBR
Great Barrington, MA [*FM radio station call letters*] ... WAMQ
Great Barrington, MA [*AM radio station call letters*] ... WSBS
Great Bay Power [*NASDAQ symbol*] (TTSB) ... GBPW
Great Bay Power Corp. [*NASDAQ symbol*] (SAG) ... GBPW
Great Bay Power Corp. [*Associated Press*] (SAG) ... GrtBay
Great Bay Power Corp. [*Associated Press*] (SAG) ... GrtBayPw
Great Bear Development [*Vancouver Stock Exchange symbol*] ... GBD
Great Bear Foundation (EA) ... GBF
Great Bend [*Kansas*] [*Airport symbol*] (OAG) ... GBD
Great Bend, KS [*Location identifier FAA*] (FAAL) ... HIL
Great Bend, KS [*FM radio station call letters*] ... KHCT
Great Bend, KS [*Television station call letters*] ... KSNC
Great Bend, KS [*AM radio station call letters*] ... KVGB
Great Bend, KS [*FM radio station call letters*] ... KVGB-FM
Great Bend, KS [*FM radio station call letters*] ... KZLS
Great Big Star [*in the movies*] ... GBS
Great Books ... GB
Great Books Foundation (EA) ... GBF
Great Britain [*International automobile identification tag*] ... GB
Great Britain (WGA) ... Gr Br
Great Britain ... Gr Brit
Great Britain (ROG) ... GT BR
Great Britain (WGA) ... Gt Brit
Great Britain and Ireland ... GB & I
Great Britain Collectors Club (EA) ... GBCC
Great Britain Ministry of Aviation ... GBMA
Great Britain Pound [*Banking*] ... GBP
Great British Holiday [*Television movie*] ... GBH
Great British Public ... GBP
Great Bustard Trust [*An association*] (EA) ... GBT
Great Cameron Lake Resources, Inc. [*Vancouver Stock Exchange symbol*] ... GCL
Great Canadian Cider [*Vancouver Stock Exchange symbol*] ... GCE
Great Canadian Oil Sands Ltd. ... GCOS
Great Cardiac Vein [*Medicine*] (DMAA) ... GCV
Great Cardiac Vein Flow [*Medicine*] (DMAA) ... GCVF
Great Central Midland [*or Metropolitan*] **Joint Stock** [*Railroad*] [*British*] (ROG) ... GCMRJS
Great Central Mines [*Vancouver Stock Exchange symbol*] ... GCM
Great Central Mines [*Associated Press*] (SAG) ... GrtCtrl
Great Central Mines [*NASDAQ symbol*] (SAG) ... GTCM
Great Central Mines NL ADS [*NASDAQ symbol*] (TTSB) ... GTCMY
Great Central Railway [*British*] (ROG) ... GC
Great Central Railway [*British*] ... GCR
Great China Airlines [*Taiwan*] [*ICAO designator*] (FAAC) ... GCA
Great Churchmen [*A publication*] ... GC
Great Circle ... GC
Great Circle Distance ... GCD
Great Circle Route (WDAA) ... GCR
Great Circle Track ... GCT
Great Country Bank [*NASDAQ symbol*] (NQ) ... GCBK
Great Country Bank [*Associated Press*] (SAG) ... GCtryB
Great Dane Club of America (EA) ... GDCA
Great Dark Spot [*Image on Neptune*] [*Astronomy*] ... GDS
Great Dark Spot on Neptune [*Astronomy*] ... GDS
Great Dictionary of the Yiddish Language [*Columbia University Department of Linguistics*] [*Information service or system*] (IID) ... GDYL
Great Eastern & Joint Railway [*British*] (ROG) ... GE & JR
Great Eastern Australian Rally [*Cycling*] ... GEAR
Great Eastern Line [*Vancouver Stock Exchange symbol*] ... GTN
Great Eastern Railway [*British*] ... GER
Great Education Reform Act [*1988*] (AIE) ... GERIACT
Great Education Reform Bill [*British*] ... GERBIL
Great Educators [*A publication*] ... GE
Great Exuma [*Bahama Islands*] ... GE
Great Falls [*Montana*] [*Airport symbol*] (OAG) ... GTF
Great Falls [*Montana*] [*ICAO location identifier*] (ICLI) ... KZGT
Great Falls Air Defense Sector [*Montana*] (SAA) ... GLADS
Great Falls/International [*Montana*] [*ICAO location identifier*] (ICLI) ... KGTF
Great Falls/Malmstrom Air Force Base [*Montana*] [*ICAO location identifier*] (ICLI) ... KGFA
Great Falls, MT [*Location identifier FAA*] (FAAL) ... GFA
Great Falls, MT [*FM radio station call letters*] ... KAAK
Great Falls, MT [*FM radio station call letters*] ... KABS
Great Falls, MT [*AM radio station call letters*] ... KEIN
Great Falls, MT [*Television station call letters*] ... KFBB
Great Falls, MT [*FM radio station call letters*] (RBYB) ... KGFC-FM
Great Falls, MT [*FM radio station call letters*] ... KGPR
Great Falls, MT [*FM radio station call letters*] ... KLFM
Great Falls, MT [*AM radio station call letters*] ... KMON
Great Falls, MT [*FM radio station call letters*] ... KMON-FM
Great Falls, MT [*AM radio station call letters*] ... KMSL
Great Falls, MT [*FM radio station call letters*] ... KOOZ
Great Falls, MT [*FM radio station call letters*] ... KQDI-FM
Great Falls, MT [*Television station call letters*] ... KRTV
Great Falls, MT [*Television station call letters*] ... KTGF
Great Falls, MT [*AM radio station call letters*] ... KXGF
Great Falls, MT [*Location identifier FAA*] (FAAL) ... SCL
Great Falls, MT [*Location identifier FAA*] (FAAL) ... SMR
Great Falls Public Library, Great Falls, MT [*Library symbol Library of Congress*] (LCLS) ... MtGr
Great Falls Public Schools, Great Falls, MT [*Library symbol*] [*Library of Congress*] (LCLS) ... MtGrPS
Great Falls-Billings [*Diocesan abbreviation*] [*Montana*] (TOCD) ... GF
Great Financial [*NASDAQ symbol*] (TTSB) ... GTFN
Great Financial Corp. [*Associated Press*] (SAG) ... GrtFncl
Great Financial Corp. [*NASDAQ symbol*] (SAG) ... GTFN
Great Fire [*of London, 1666*] ... GF
Great French Writers [*A publication*] ... GFW
Great Gatsby [*Describes clothing style modeled after the type worn by characters in F. Scott Fitzgerald's novel, "The Great Gatsby"*] ... GG
Great, Grand Master Key [*Locks*] (ADA) ... GGMK
Great Granddaughter ... GGD
Great Grandson ... GGS
Great Gross [*144 dozen*] [*Also, GGR*] ... GG
Great Gross [*144 dozen*] [*Also, GG*] ... GGR
Great Harbour Cay [*Bahamas*] [*Airport symbol*] (OAG) ... GHC
Great Hungarian Plain [*Geology*] ... GHP
[*The*] **Great Ideas Today** [*A publication*] ... GIT
Great Inagua Island [*Bahamas*] [*Airport symbol*] (AD) ... IGA
Great Indian Peninsular R. R. ... GIP
Great Indulgence ... GI
Great Irish Painter [*Reference to Jack B. Yeats, ca. 1905*] ... GIP
Great Jurists of the World, by Sir John MacDonnel and Edward Manson [*1913*] [*A publication*] (DLA) ... GJW
Great Keppel Island [*Australia Airport symbol*] (OAG) ... GKL
Great Lakes [*Vessel load line mark*] ... GL
Great Lakes (MUGU) ... GLAKES
Great Lakes (FAAC) ... GRTLKS
Great Lakes [*MARC geographic area code Library of Congress*] (LCCP) ... nl----
Great Lakes Airlines [*ICAO designator*] (AD) ... GX
Great Lakes and Marine Waters Center [*University of Michigan*] [*Research center*] (RCD) ... GLMWC
Great Lakes Aviation [*NASDAQ symbol*] (TTSB) ... GLUX
Great Lakes Aviation [*ICAO designator*] (AD) ... ZK
Great Lakes Aviation Ltd. [*ICAO designator*] (FAAC) ... GLA
Great Lakes Aviation Ltd. [*NASDAQ symbol*] (SAG) ... GLUX
Great Lakes Aviation Ltd. [*Associated Press*] (SAG) ... GtLkeAv

Great Lakes Basin Commission [*Terminated, 1981*] (EGAO) ... GLBC
Great Lakes Bible College, Lansing, MI [*OCLC symbol*] (OCLC) ... EEG
Great Lakes Bible College, Lansing, MI [*Library symbol Library of Congress*] (LCLS) ... MiLG
Great Lakes Booksellers Association (EA) ... GLBA
Great Lakes Chemical [*NYSE symbol*] (TTSB) ... GLK
Great Lakes Chemical Corp. [*NYSE symbol*] (SPSG) ... GLK
Great Lakes Chemical Corp. [*Associated Press*] (SAG) ... GtLkCh
Great Lakes Club (EA) ... GLC
Great Lakes Coastal Forecasting System [*Marine science*] (OSRA) ... GLCES
Great Lakes Coastal Forecasting System (USDC) ... GLCFS
Great Lakes Colleges Association (EA) ... GLCA
Great Lakes Commission (EA) ... GLC
Great Lakes Ecosystem Restoration and Rehabilitation [*Canada*] (ASF) ... GLERR
Great Lakes Embryo Mortality, Edema, and Deformities Syndrome [*Marine birds*] ... GLEMEDS
Great Lakes Environmental Information Center [*Ann Arbor, MI*] ... GLEDIC
Great Lakes Environmental Information Sharing ... GLEIS
Great Lakes Environmental Research Laboratory [*Ann Arbor, MI*] [*National Oceanic and Atmospheric Administration*] (GRD) ... GLERL
Great Lakes Fish Disease Control Committee [*Canada*] (ASF) ... GLFDCC
Great Lakes Fisheries Laboratory, Ann Arbor, MI [*OCLC symbol*] (OCLC) ... GLF
Great Lakes Fisheries Laboratory, Ann Arbor, MI [*Library symbol Library of Congress*] (LCLS) ... MiAaFL
Great Lakes Fisheries Research Branch [*Canadian Department of Fisheries and Oceans*] [*Research center*] (RCD) ... GLFRB
Great Lakes Fishery Commission [*Canada and United States*] (NOAA) ... GLFC
Great Lakes Fishery Laboratory [*Department of the Interior*] (GRD) ... GLFL
Great Lakes Forecasting System [*Marine science*] (OSRA) ... GLES
Great Lakes Forecasting System (USDC) ... GLFS
Great Lakes Forest Products Ltd. [*Toronto Stock Exchange symbol*] ... GL
Great Lakes Forest Research Centre [*Environment Canada*] [*Research center*] (RCD) ... GLFRC
Great Lakes Forest Research Centre, Canadian Forestry Service [*Centre de Recherches Forestieres des Grands Lacs, Service Canadien des Forets*] **Sault Ste. Marie, Ontario** [*Library symbol National Library of Canada*] (NLC) ... OSTMF
Great Lakes Freight Bureau Inc., Cleveland OH [*STAC*] ... GLB
Great Lakes Group, Inc. [*Toronto Stock Exchange symbol*] ... GLZ
Great Lakes Harbor Association (EA) ... GLHA
Great Lakes Historical Society (EA) ... GLHS
Great Lakes Indian Fish and Wildlife Commission (EA) ... GLIFWC
Great Lakes Information Network ... GLIN
Great Lakes Intercollegiate Athletic Conference ... GLIAC
Great Lakes International Multidisciplinary Program on Crustal Evolution [*Geophysics*] ... GLIMPCE
Great Lakes Laboratory [*State University College at Buffalo*] [*Research center*] (RCD) ... GLL
Great Lakes Licensed Officers' Organization ... GLLO
Great Lakes Lighthouse Keepers Association (EA) ... GLLKA
Great Lakes Maritime Institute (EA) ... GLMI
Great Lakes Megalopolis [*Proposed name for possible "super-city" formed by growth and mergers of other cities*] ... GLM
Great Lakes Mink Association (EA) ... GLMA
Great Lakes National Program Office [*Environmental Protection Agency*] ... GLNPO
Great Lakes Naval Training Center ... GLNTC
Great Lakes Nickel Ltd. [*Toronto Stock Exchange symbol*] ... GTL
Great Lakes Physical Information Analysis Center ... GLPIAC
Great Lakes Pilotage Administration [*Department of Transportation*] ... GLPA
Great Lakes Rules [*Boating*] (DICI) ... GLR
Great Lakes - St. Lawrence Association ... GLASLA
Great Lakes Screw ... GLS
Great Lakes Seaplane Association [*Defunct*] (EA) ... GLSA
Great Lakes Ship Owners Association (EA) ... GLSOA
Great Lakes Sport Fishing Council (EA) ... GLSFC
Great Lakes Sugar Beet Growers (EA) ... GLSBG
Great Lakes United (EA) ... GLU
Great Lakes Water Quality Agreement [*Environmental Protection Agency*] ... GLWQA
Great Lakes Waterways Development Association (EA) ... GLWDA
Great Lakes Wetlands Conservation Action Plan [*Canada*] ... GLWCAP
Great Little Car [*Mazda Motors of America*] ... GLC
Great Little Computer/Small Business System [*Business software*] [*Cumulus Computer Corp.*] (PCM) ... GLC/SBS
Great Masters in Painting and Sculpture [*A publication*] ... GMPS
Great Meteor East [*Nuclear energy*] (NUCP) ... GME
Great Midwestern Conference [*College reports*] ... GMC
Great Minds Think Alike [*Internet language*] (PCM) ... GMTA
Great Musicians [*A publication*] ... GM
Great National Land [*Vancouver Stock Exchange symbol*] ... GNL
Great Neck Library, Great Neck, NY [*Library symbol Library of Congress*] (LCLS) ... NGrn
Great Neck North Middle School, Great Neck, NY [*Library symbol*] [*Library of Congress*] (LCLS) ... NGrnNM
Great Neck South Middle School, Great Neck, NY [*Library symbol Library of Congress*] (LCLS) ... NGrnMS
Great Neck South Senior High School, Great Neck, NY [*Library symbol Library of Congress*] (LCLS) ... NGrnSH
Great New South Wales Bike Ride [*Australia*] ... GNSWBR
Great Nigeria People's Party [*Political party*] (PPW) ... GNPP
Great North of Scotland Railway (ROG) ... GNS
Great North of Scotland Railway ... GNSR
Great Northern Iron Ore Properties [*NYSE symbol*] (SPSG) ... GNI
Great Northern Iron Ore Properties [*Associated Press*] (SAG) ... GNIron
Great Northern of Ireland [*Railway*] (ROG) ... GN of I
Great Northern Petroleums [*Vancouver Stock Exchange symbol*] ... GTP
Great Northern Piccadilly & Brompton Railway [*British*] (ROG) ... GNP & BR
Great Northern Railway (MHDW) ... GN
Great Northern Railway ... GNR
Great Northern Railway ... GNRY
Great Northern Railway Society [*British*] (DBA) ... GNRS
Great Northern Telegraph Co. [*Denmark*] [*Telecommunications*] (TEL) ... GNT
Great Organ [*Music*] ... G ORG
Great Organ [*Music*] ... GO
Great Organ [*Music*] ... Gt
Great Ormond Street Hospital for Children [*British*] (ROG) ... GT ORM H
Great Pacific Industries, Inc. [*Toronto Stock Exchange symbol Vancouver Stock Exchange symbol*] ... GPI
Great Pacific Real Estate Investment Trust, Inc. [*Associated Press*] (SAG) ... GPcRE
Great Pacific Real Estate Investment Trust, Inc. [*AMEX symbol*] (SAG) ... GPR
Great Pacific Resources [*Vancouver Stock Exchange symbol*] ... GEP
Great Peace Journey [*Sweden*] (EAIO) ... GPJ
Great Peace March for Global Nuclear Disarmament [*Defunct*] (EA) ... GPMFGND
Great Peoples [*A publication*] ... GP
Great Pines Water [*NASDAQ symbol*] (TTSB) ... GPWC
Great Pines Water Co. [*NASDAQ symbol*] (SAG) ... GPWC
Great Pines Water Co. [*Associated Press*] (SAG) ... GrtPines
Great Plains [*AAR code*] ... GRIN
Great Plains [*MARC geographic area code Library of Congress*] (LCCP) ... np----
Great Plains Agricultural Council (EA) ... GPAC
Great Plains Coliseum [*Lawton, OK*] ... GPC
Great Plains Conservation Program ... GPCP
Great Plains Development Co. of Canada Ltd., Calgary, AB, Canada [*Library symbol Library of Congress*] (LCLS) ... CaACGP
Great Plains Historical Association [*Later, IGP*] (EA) ... GPHA
Great Plains National Instructional Television Library ... GPNITL
Great Plains Wheat, Inc. (EA) ... GPW
Great Planes Area Vocational Technical School [*Oklahoma*] ... GPAVTS
Great Portland Street [*London*] (DSUE) ... GP
Great Primer ... GP
Great Proletarian Cultural Revolution [*People's Republic of China*] ... GPCR
Great Pyrenees Club of America (EA) ... GPCA
Great Quotations [*A publication*] ... GQ
Great Red Spot [*on planet Jupiter*] ... GRS
Great Renunciation Movement (EA) ... GRM
Great Revolutionary American Standard System [*Book title*] ... GRASS
Great River Library System [*Library network*] ... GRLS
Great River Library System, Quincy, IL [*Library symbol Library of Congress*] (LCLS) ... IQG
Great River Library System, Quincy, IL [*OCLC symbol*] (OCLC) ... ITA
Great River Regional Library, St. Cloud, MN [*Library symbol Library of Congress*] (LCLS) ... MnStclG
Great Roll [*of the Pipe*] [*British*] ... GR
Great Salinity Anomaly [*Marine science*] (OSRA) ... GSA
Great Salt Lake [*Utah*] ... GSL
Great Sand Dunes National Monument ... GRSA
Great Seal [*British*] ... GS
Great Sierra [*ICAO designator*] (AD) ... LT
Great Sitkin [*Alaska*] [*Seismograph station code, US Geological Survey*] (SEIS) ... AD1
Great Smoky Mountains National Park [*Also, GSMNP*] ... GRSM
Great Smoky Mountains National Park [*Also, GRSM*] ... GSMNP
Great Somalia League ... GSL
Great Southern Bancorp [*NASDAQ symbol*] (TTSB) ... GSBC
Great Southern Bancorp, Inc. [*Associated Press*] (SAG) ... GrtSoB
Great Southern Bancorp, Inc. [*Associated Press*] (SAG) ... GrtSoBcp
Great Southern Bancorp, Inc. [*NASDAQ symbol*] (NQ) ... GSBC
Great Southern Development Authority [*Western Australia*] ... GSDA
Great Southwest Corp. ... GSC
Great Southwest Railroad, Inc. [*AAR code*] ... GSW
Great Swamp Research Institute (EA) ... GSRI
Great Thoughts [*A publication*] (ROG) ... GT
Great Toe [*Medicine*] (DMAA) ... GT
Great Train Store [*NASDAQ symbol*] (TTSB) ... GTRN
Great Train Store Wrrt [*NASDAQ symbol*] (TTSB) ... GTRNW
Great Train Stores Co. [*NASDAQ symbol*] (SAG) ... GTRN
Great Train Stores Co. [*Associated Press*] (SAG) ... GtTrain
Great Train Stores Co. [*Associated Press*] (SAG) ... GtTrn
Great Trunk Pacific Railway [*British*] (ROG) ... GTP
Great Universal Stores [*Mail-order firm*] [*British*] ... GUS
Great Universal Stores [*Mail-order firm*] [*British*] ... GUSSIES
Great, Unopposable Commandant of the Realm of Inextinguishable Sagacity [*Rank in Junior Woodchucks organization mentioned in Donald Duck comic by Carl Barks*] ... GUCOTROIS
Great Value [*In automobile name Yugo GV*] ... GV
Great Wall Airlines [*China*] [*ICAO designator*] (FAAC) ... CGW
Great Wall Airlines [*China*] [*ICAO designator*] (FAAC) ... GWA
Great Wall Electr Int. ADS [*NASDAQ symbol*] (TTSB) ... GWALY
Great Wall Electronic International Ltd. [*NASDAQ symbol*] (SAG) ... GWAL
Great Wall Electronic Internationl Ltd. [*Associated Press*] (SAG) ... GrtWall
Great War Prize Cases, by Evans [*England*] [*A publication*] (DLA) ... Pr Ca
Great War Veterans' Association [*Canada*] ... GWVA
Great Warbirds Air Display [*British*] ... GWAD
Great Water Holt (EA) ... GWH
Great West Life Assurance Co., Winnipeg, Manitoba [*Library symbol National Library of Canada*] (NLC) ... MWGW

Great West Life Assurance Co., Winnipeg, MB, Canada [*Library symbol Library of Congress*] (LCLS) ... CaMWGW
Great West Steel Industries Ltd. [*Toronto Stock Exchange symbol Vancouver Stock Exchange symbol*] ... GWS
Great Western & Midland Railway Joint Stock [*British*] (ROG) ... GW & MRJS
Great Western Financial [*Associated Press*] (SAG) ... GtWF
Great Western Financial Corp. [*Associated Press*] (SAG) ... GtWF
Great Western Financial Corp. [*Associated Press*] (SAG) ... GtWFn
Great Western Financial Corp. [*NYSE symbol*] (SPSG) ... GWF
Great Western Petroleum Corp. [*Vancouver Stock Exchange symbol*] ... GWP
[*The*] **Great Western Railway Co.** [*Prior to nationalization*] [*AAR code*] ... GWR
Great Western Society (EA) ... GWS
Great Western Sugar Co., Technical Library, Denver, CO [*Library symbol Library of Congress*] (LCLS) ... CoDGW
Great Westn Fin I 8.25% 'TOPrS' [*NYSE symbol*] (TTSB) ... GWFPrT
Great Westn Finl [*NYSE symbol*] (TTSB) ... GWF
Great Westn Finl 8.30% Dep Pfd [*NYSE symbol*] (TTSB) ... GWFPrA
Great Westn Finl CvDep Pfd [*NYSE symbol*] (TTSB) ... GWFPr
Great Westrn Air, Inc. [*FAA designator*] (FAAC) ... GWA
Great Whale [*Canada*] [*Airport symbol*] (OAG) ... YGW
Great Whale River [*Quebec*] [*Seismograph station code, US Geological Survey Closed*] (SEIS) ... GWC
Great White Spot [*Planetary science*] ... GWS
Great World Resources [*Vancouver Stock Exchange symbol*] ... GWR
Great Writers [*A publication*] ... GW
Great Yarmouth/North Denes [*British ICAO location identifier*] (ICLI) ... EGSD
Great Yarmouth Shipping Co. (MHDW) ... GYSCO
Great-Circle Bearing [*Navigation*] (IAA) ... GCB
Greate Bay Casino [*AMEX symbol*] (SAG) ... GBY
Greate Bay Casino [*Associated Press*] (SAG) ... GrteBayC
Greater ... GRTR
Greater [*Freight*] ... GRTR
Greater (BARN) ... Gtr
Greater Access to Publishing [*British*] ... GAP
Greater [*name of city*] **Alliance to Stop Pollution** ... GASP
Greater Antilles [*MARC geographic area code Library of Congress*] (LCCP) ... nwga--
Greater Blouse and Skirt Contractors Association [*Later, GBSUA*] (EA) ... GBSCA
Greater Blouse, Skirt, and Undergarment Association (EA) ... GBSUA
Greater Britain Movement [*British*] ... GBM
[*The*] **Greater China Fund** [*NYSE symbol*] (SAG) ... GCH
[*The*] **Greater China Fund** [*Associated Press*] (SAG) ... GtChina
Greater Cincinnati Library Consortium [*Library network*] ... GCLC
Greater Cleveland Mathematics Program [*Education*] ... GCMP
Greater Clothing Contractors Association (EA) ... GCCA
Greater Del Valley Svgs [*NASDAQ symbol*] (TTSB) ... GDVS
Greater Delaware Valley Savings Bank [*NASDAQ symbol*] (SAG) ... GDVS
Greater Delaware Valley Savings Bank [*Associated Press*] (SAG) ... GrDelV
Greater East Asia [*Used by Japanese in such terms as War of Greater East Asia and Greater East Asia Co-Prosperity Sphere*] [*World War II*] ... GEA
Greater Ecosystem Alliance (EA) ... GEA
Greater Erie Industrial Development Corp. [*Pennsylvania*] ... GEIDC
Greater Fuel Economy ... GFE
Greater Greensboro [*North Carolina*] **Open** [*Golf tournament*] ... GGO
Greater Hartford [*Connecticut*] **Open** [*Golf tournament*] ... GHO
Greater Hartford Process [*An association*] (EA) ... GHP
Greater Independent Association of National Travel Services (EA) ... GIANTS
Greater Jacksonville [*Florida*] **Open** [*Golf tournament*] ... GJO
Greater Lenora Resources Corp. [*Toronto Stock Exchange symbol Vancouver Stock Exchange symbol*] ... GEN
Greater London [*England*] ... GL
Greater London Council [*Information service or system*] (IID) ... GLC
Greater London Training Board [*British*] (AIE) ... GLTB
Greater Manchester [*County in England*] ... GM
Greater Mekong Sub-Region [*East Asian development zone*] ... GMS
Greater Middle East ... GME
Greater Midwest Regional Medical Library Network [*Illinois, Kentucky, Michigan, Ohio, S. Dakota*] (NITA) ... GMRMLN
Greater New England Society of Inhalation Therapists ... GNESIT
Greater New Orleans Microform Cooperative [*Library network*] ... GNOMAC
Greater New Orleans Microform Cooperative, Tulane University, New Orleans, LA [*Library symbol Library of Congress*] (LCLS) ... LNT-MC
Greater New York Automobile Dealers Association (SRA) ... GNYADA
Greater New York Council for Foreign Students [*Later, English in Action*] ... GNYCFS
[*The*] **Greater New York Savings Bank** [*NASDAQ symbol*] (NQ) ... GRTR
[*The*] **Greater New York Savings Bank** [*Associated Press*] (SAG) ... GtNYSv
Greater North American Aviculturist and Color Bred Judges Association [*Formerly, GNACBJA*] (EA) ... GNAACBJA
Greater North American Color-Bred Judge Association [*Later, GNAACBJA*] (EA) ... GNACBJA
Greater N.Y. Svgs Bk [*NASDAQ symbol*] (TTSB) ... GRTR
Greater Opportunities through Work [*Proposed federal program*] ... GROW
Greater Orlando Area Legal Services [*Florida*] ... GOALS
Greater Pacific Financial Services [*Australia*] ... GPFS
Greater St. Louis Amateur Baseball Hall of Fame (EA) ... GSLABHF
Greater Siamese Cat Club (EA) ... GSCC
Greater Southwest [*Ft. Worth and Dallas, Texas*] [*Airport symbol*] (AD) ... GSW
Greater Super Six Club [*Defunct*] (EA) ... GSSC
Greater Superficial Petrosal Neurectomy [*Neurosurgery*] (DAVI) ... GSPN
Greater Temagami [*Vancouver Stock Exchange symbol*] ... GGT
Greater Than [*FORTRAN*] ... GT
Greater Than Flag (MHDB) ... GTF
Greater than or Equal To [*FORTRAN*] ... GE
Greater Toy Center (EA) ... GTC
Greater Trochanter [*Anatomy*] ... GT
Greater Underwater Propulsive Power [*Type of submarine*] ... GUPPY
Greater Union Organisation [*Australia*] ... GU
Greater Vancouver Library Federation, Burnaby, British Columbia [*Library symbol National Library of Canada*] (NLC) ... BBGVL
Greater Vancouver Regional District, Burnaby, British Columbia [*Library symbol National Library of Canada*] (BIB) ... BBGV
Greater Vancouver Regional District, Planning Development Library, Vancouver, BC, Canada [*Library symbol Library of Congress*] (LCLS) ... CaBVaPD
Greater Victoria Public Library [*UTLAS symbol*] ... GVP
Greater Victoria Public Library, British Columbia [*Library symbol National Library of Canada*] (NLC) ... BVI
Greater Victoria Public Library, Victoria, BC, Canada [*Library symbol Library of Congress*] (LCLS) ... CaBVi
Greater Washington Board of Trade (SRA) ... GWBOT
Greater Washington Society of Association Executives (SRA) ... GWSAE
Greater World Christian Spiritualist Association (EA) ... GWCSA
Greater World Spiritual Centre [*British*] (EAIO) ... GWSC
Greater Yellowstone Coalition (EA) ... GYC
Greater-than-Class-C [*Radioactive waste level definition*] ... GTCC
Greater-than-Lot Quantities ... GLQ
Greatest (ABBR) ... GTST
Greatest Amount of Resources ... GRES
Greatest Axial Linear Dimension ... GALD
Greatest Common Denominator ... GCD
Greatest Common Divisor ... GCD
Greatest Common Factor ... GCF
Greatest Common Measure ... GCM
Greatest Common Multiple (ADA) ... GCM
Greatest Length ... GL
Greatest Overall Coefficient (TEL) ... GOC
Greatest Response Amplitude Probability ... GRAP
Greatest Response Amplitude Probability Data ... GRAPD
Greatest Response Data ... GRD
Greatest Response Probability ... GRP
Greatest Total Resource Demand ... GTRD
Greatest Upper Bound [*Computer science*] ... GUB
Greatly (ABBR) ... GTY
Greatness Is Simplicity [*See also SIG*] ... GIS
Great-West Life Assurance Co. [*Toronto Stock Exchange symbol*] ... GWL
Great-West Lifeco, Inc. [*Toronto Stock Exchange symbol*] ... GWO
Greaves. Criminal Consolidation [*2nd ed.*] [*1862*] [*A publication*] (DLA) ... Greav Cr L
Greaves' Edition of Russell on Crimes [*A publication*] (DLA) ... Greav Russ
Grecian (ROG) ... GR
Greece [*MARC geographic area code Library of Congress*] (LCCP) ... e-gr--
Greece [*ANSI two-letter standard code*] (CNC) ... GR
Greece [*IYRU nationality code*] [*MARC country of publication code Library of Congress*] (LCCP) ... gr
Greece [*ANSI three-letter standard code*] (CNC) ... GRC
Greece (WDAA) ... GRE
Greece (VRA) ... Gre
Greece, NY [*FM radio station call letters*] ... WGMC
Greece-Arcadia Junior/Senior High School Library, Rochester, NY [*OCLC symbol*] (OCLC) ... RWI
Greece-Athena Junior/Senior High School Library, Rochester, NY [*OCLC symbol*] (OCLC) ... RWJ
Greece-Olympia High School Library, Rochester, NY [*OCLC symbol*] (OCLC) ... RWK
Greek ... G
Greek ... GK
Greek ... GR
Greek [*Language, etc.*] ... GRK
Greek American Progressive Association (EA) ... GAPA
Greek, Ancient [*MARC language code Library of Congress*] (LCCP) ... grc
Greek Atomic Energy Commission ... GAEC
Greek Catholic Union of the USA (EA) ... GCUUSA
Greek Church (ROG) ... GC
Greek Cultural and Theatrical Organisation of Australia ... GCTOA
Greek Ex-Servicemen's Association of South Australia ... GESASA
Greek Literary Papyri [*A publication*] (OCD) ... GLP
Greek, Modern [*MARC language code Library of Congress*] (LCCP) ... gre
Greek National Political Society (PPW) ... EPEN
Greek National Tourist Organization (EA) ... GNTO
Greek Odeon [*Record label*] ... GkOd
Greek Organisation of Young Australians ... GOYA
Greek Orthodox Church (BARN) ... GOC
Greek Orthodox Community of Melbourne and Victoria [*Australia*] ... GOCMV
Greek Orthodox Ladies Philoptochos Society (EA) ... GOLPS
Greek Orthodox Theological Review [*A publication*] (BJA) ... GOTR
Greek Orthodox Young Adult League (EA) ... GOYAL
Greek Orthodox Youth of America [*Later, GOYAL*] (EA) ... GOYA
Greek Papyri in the British Museum [*A publication*] (OCD) ... PLondon
Greek Research Reactor ... GRR
Greeley & Hansen, Chicago, IL [*OCLC symbol*] (OCLC) ... IDR
Greeley & Hansen Engineering Library, Chicago, IL [*Library symbol Library of Congress*] (LCLS) ... ICGH
Greeley, CO [*Location identifier FAA*] (FAAL) ... GXY
Greeley, CO [*AM radio station call letters*] ... KFKA
Greeley, CO [*FM radio station call letters*] ... KGLL
Greeley, CO [*AM radio station call letters*] ... KGRE
Greeley, CO [*FM radio station call letters*] ... KUNC
Greeley, CO [*FM radio station call letters*] ... KZDG

Greeley Public Library, Greeley, CO [*Library symbol Library of Congress*] (LCLS) ... CoGr
Greely Public Library, Ontario [*Library symbol National Library of Canada*] (NLC) ... OGRE
Green ... G
Green [*Maps and charts*] ... GN
Green [*Commonly used*] (OPSA) ... GREEN
Green ... GRN
Green (KSC) ... GRN
Green (VRA) ... grn
Green Acres, CA [*FM radio station call letters*] ... KAXL
Green Alliance Senate - New South Wales [*Political party Australia*] ... GA
Green, Amber, Red, Blue [*Priority of the airways*] ... GARB
Green Bag; A Legal Journal [*Boston*] [*A publication*] (DLA) ... Green Bag
Green Bank [*West Virginia*] [*Seismograph station code, US Geological Survey*] (SEIS) ... GBV
Green Bay [*Diocesan abbreviation*] [*Wisconsin*] (TOCD) ... GB
Green Bay [*Wisconsin*] [*Airport symbol*] (OAG) ... GRB
Green Bay & Western Railroad Co. ... GB & W
Green Bay & Western Railroad Co. [*AAR code*] ... GBW
Green Bay Aviation [*ICAO designator*] (AD) ... HE
Green Bay, WI [*Location identifier FAA*] (FAAL) ... SGZ
Green Bay, WI [*Location identifier FAA*] (FAAL) ... TUI
Green Bay, WI [*Television station call letters*] ... WBAY
Green Bay, WI [*AM radio station call letters*] ... WDUZ
Green Bay, WI [*Television station call letters*] ... WFRV
Green Bay, WI [*Television station call letters*] ... WGBA
Green Bay, WI [*FM radio station call letters*] ... WGBW
Green Bay, WI [*AM radio station call letters*] ... WGEE
Green Bay, WI [*FM radio station call letters*] (RBYB) ... WHID
Green Bay, WI [*FM radio station call letters*] ... WIXX
Green Bay, WI [*Television station call letters*] ... WLUK
Green Bay, WI [*AM radio station call letters*] ... WNFL
Green Bay, WI [*FM radio station call letters*] ... WORQ
Green Bay, WI [*FM radio station call letters*] ... WPNE
Green Bay, WI [*Television station call letters*] ... WPNE-TV
Green Bay, WI [*FM radio station call letters*] ... WQLH
Green Belt Act [*Town planning*] [*British*] ... GB
Green Circle Program (EA) ... GCP
Green Coffee Association of New Orleans (EA) ... GCA of NO
Green Coffee Association of New York City (EA) ... GCA
Green [*Daniel*] **Co.** [*NASDAQ symbol*] (NQ) ... DAGR
Green [*Daniel*] **Co.** [*Associated Press*] (SAG) ... GrnDan
Green Cove Springs, FL [*FM radio station call letters*] ... WJBT
Green Currency [*EEC*] ... GC
Green Extension System [*Traffic signal*] (DICI) ... GES
Green Fluorescent Protein [*Biochemistry*] ... GFP
Green Forest Lumber Corp. [*Toronto Stock Exchange symbol*] ... GFT
Green Forest Lumber Ltd. [*Canada ICAO designator*] (FAAC) ... GFL
Green Giant Corp., Le Sueur, MN [*Library symbol Library of Congress*] (LCLS) ... MnLsG
Green Grove Community Library, Nilton Junction, Alberta [*Library symbol National Library of Canada*] (NLC) ... ANJGG
Green Hill School, Staff Library, Chehalis, WA [*Library symbol Library of Congress*] (LCLS) ... WaChehG
Green Hills Aviation [*ICAO designator*] (AD) ... NG
Green Hills Public Library District, Palos Hills, IL [*Library symbol Library of Congress*] (LCLS) ... IPhi
Green Hills Public Library District, Palos Hills, IL [*Library symbol*] [*Library of Congress*] (LCLS) ... IPhiP
Green Indicating Lamp ... GIL
Green [*A. P.*] **Industries, Inc.** [*NASDAQ symbol*] (NQ) ... APGI
Green [*A. P.*] **Industries, Inc.** [*Associated Press*] (SAG) ... GreenAP
Green Island [*Plant pathology*] ... GI
Green Lake Resources Ltd. [*Vancouver Stock Exchange symbol*] ... GLU
Green LASER System ... GLS
Green Leaf Area Index (MCD) ... GLAI
Green Library [*See also BVM*] [*France*] (EAIO) ... GL
Green Light (MSA) ... GL
Green, M. E., Jefferson City MO [*STAC*] ... GME
Green Monkey Kidney Cell ... GMK
Green Mountain Boy [*Pseudonym used by Henry Stevens*] ... GMB
Green Mountain Coffee [*Commercial firm NASDAQ symbol*] (SAG) ... GMCR
Green Mountain Coffee [*Associated Press*] (SAG) ... GrnMtn
Green Mountain College, Poultney, VT [*Library symbol Library of Congress*] (LCLS) ... VtPouG
Green Mountain Junior College [*Vermont*] ... GMJC
Green Mountain Power Corp. [*NYSE symbol*] (SPSG) ... GMP
Green Mountain Power Corp. (NRCH) ... GMPC
Green Mountain Pwr [*NYSE symbol*] (TTSB) ... GMP
Green Mountain Railroad Corp. [*AAR code*] ... GMRC
Green Mountain Textile Overseers Association (EA) ... GMTOA
Green Olive Trade Association (EA) ... GOTA
Green Party of Australia [*Political party*] ... GPA
Green Party of Hungary [*Political party*] (EAIO) ... GPH
[*The*] **Green Party South Australia** [*Political party*] ... GSA
Green Pastures Christian School, St. Cloud, MN [*Library symbol*] [*Library of Congress*] (LCLS) ... MnStclGP
Green Peach Aphid [*Entomology*] ... GPA
Green Phone [*NASA*] (KSC) ... G/P
Green Pulse Width [*Instrumentation*] ... GPW
Green, Red, Orange, White, Blue, Yellow [*Military system of indicating what day of the week food products were made through colored packaging*] ... GROWBY
Green River [*Papua New Guinea*] [*Airport symbol*] (OAG) ... GVI
Green River Community College, Auburn, WA [*Library symbol Library of Congress*] (LCLS) ... WaAuG
Green River Test Complex ... GRTC
Green River, WY [*AM radio station call letters*] ... KUGR
Green Street Financial [*NASDAQ symbol*] (TTSB) ... GSFC
Green Street Financial Corp. [*Associated Press*] (SAG) ... GreenSt
Green Street Financial Corp. [*NASDAQ symbol*] (SAG) ... GSFC
Green Street Joint Venture (EERA) ... GSJV
Green Tea Polyphenol [*Biochemistry*] ... GTP
Green Thumb (EA) ... GT
Green Thumbs [*National Weather Service and Department of Agriculture Extension Service telecommunication system*] ... GT
Green Tobacco Sickness [*Illness resulting from exposure to dissolved nicotine*] ... GTS
Green Tree Financial, Inc. [*NYSE symbol*] (SPSG) ... GNT
Green Tree Finl [*NYSE symbol*] (TTSB) ... GNT
Green Valley [*Plant pathology*] ... GV
Green Valley, AZ [*FM radio station call letters*] (RBYB) ... KFMA-FM
Green Valley, AZ [*FM radio station call letters*] ... KGMS
Green Valley, AZ [*AM radio station call letters*] ... KGVY
Green Valley, AZ [*Television station call letters*] ... KXGR
Green Valley Mine [*Vancouver Stock Exchange symbol*] ... GVY
Green Valley Road [*California*] [*Seismograph station code, US Geological Survey*] (SEIS) ... GVR
Green Valley, WV [*AM radio station call letters*] ... WAMN
Green Weight (WDAA) ... GW
Greenacres, CA [*FM radio station call letters*] ... KRAB
Greenair Hava Tasimaciligi AS [*Turkey*] [*ICAO designator*] (FAAC) ... GRN
Green(A.P.)Indus [*NASDAQ symbol*] (TTSB) ... APGI
Greenbay/Austin Straubel [*Wisconsin*] [*ICAO location identifier*] (ICLI) ... KGRB
Greenberg(William Jr)Desserts [*NASDAQ symbol*] (TTSB) ... BAKE
Greenbriar Corp. [*AMEX symbol*] (TTSB) ... GBR
Greenbriar Corp. [*AMEX symbol*] (SAG) ... GBR
Greenbriar Corp. [*Associated Press*] (SAG) ... Greenbri
Greenbrier [*West Virginia*] [*Airport symbol*] (OAG) ... LWB
Greenbrier College, Lewisburg, WV [*Library symbol Library of Congress*] (LCLS) ... WvLeG
[*The*] **Greenbrier Companies, Inc.** [*NYSE symbol*] (SAG) ... GBX
[*The*] **Greenbrier Companies, Inc.** [*Associated Press*] (SAG) ... Greenbr
Greenbrier Cos. [*NYSE symbol*] (TTSB) ... GBX
Greenbrier County Public Library, Lewisburg, WV [*Library symbol Library of Congress*] (LCLS) ... WvLe
Greenburg, IN [*FM radio station call letters*] ... WRZQ
Greenburg [*William*] **Jr. Desserts & Cafes, Inc.** [*Associated Press*] (SAG) ... WGrnbg
Greenburgh Public Library, Elmsford, NY [*Library symbol Library of Congress*] (LCLS) ... NEI
Greenbush Public Library, Greenbush, MN [*Library symbol*] [*Library of Congress*] (LCLS) ... MnGre
Greenbush Public School, Greenbush, MN [*Library symbol*] [*Library of Congress*] (LCLS) ... MnGreS
Greencastle Banner-Graphic, Greencastle, IN [*Library symbol Library of Congress*] (LCLS) ... InGrBG
Greencastle, IN [*FM radio station call letters*] ... WGRE
Greencastle, IN [*FM radio station call letters*] (RBYB) ... WREB
Greencastle, PA [*FM radio station call letters*] ... WKSL
Greencastle-Putnam County Library, Greencastle, IN [*Library symbol Library of Congress*] (LCLS) ... InGr
Greenclose Aviation Services Ltd. [*British ICAO designator*] (FAAC) ... GCL
Greendale Aviation Co. [*Nigeria*] [*FAA designator*] (FAAC) ... ORE
Greene County Courthouse, Jefferson IA [*Library symbol Library of Congress*] (LCLS) ... IaJGCoC
Greene County District Library, Xenia, OH [*OCLC symbol*] (OCLC) ... GRC
Greene County District Library, Xenia, OH [*Library symbol Library of Congress*] (LCLS) ... OXe
Greene County Historical Society, Inc., Coxsakie, NY [*Library symbol Library of Congress*] (LCLS) ... NCoxHi
Greene County Nuclear Power Plant (NRCH) ... GCNPP
Greene County Public Library, Snow Hill, NC [*Library symbol Library of Congress*] (LCLS) ... NcSn
Greene County Recorder's Office, Bloomfield, IN [*Library symbol Library of Congress*] (LCLS) ... InBlCR
Greene Memorial Hospital, Health Resource Library, Xenia, OH [*Library symbol Library of Congress*] (LCLS) ... OXeGH
Greene Public Library, Greene, IA [*Library symbol Library of Congress*] (LCLS) ... IaGre
Greene Recorder, Greene, IA [*Library symbol Library of Congress*] (LCLS) ... IaGreR
Greenery Rehabilitation Group, Inc. (MHDW) ... GRGI
Greene's Outlines of Roman Law [*A publication*] (DLA) ... Gre Rom Law
Greene's Reports [*7 New York Annotated Cases*] [*A publication*] (DLA) ... Greene
Greeneville, TN [*Location identifier FAA*] (FAAL) ... DYQ
Greeneville, TN [*Location identifier FAA*] (FAAL) ... GCY
Greeneville, TN [*Television station call letters*] ... WEMT
Greeneville, TN [*AM radio station call letters*] ... WGRV
Greeneville, TN [*FM radio station call letters*] ... WIKQ
Greeneville, TN [*AM radio station call letters*] ... WSMG
Greeneville, TX [*Television station call letters*] ... KTAQ
Greenfield [*Massachusetts*] [*Airport symbol*] (AD) ... ORE
Greenfield, CA [*FM radio station call letters*] (RBYB) ... KLOK-FM
Greenfield, CA [*FM radio station call letters*] ... KSEA
Greenfield Community College [*Massachusetts*] ... GCC
Greenfield Community College, Greenfield, MA [*Library symbol Library of Congress*] (LCLS) ... MGrefC

Greenfield Community Unit, District 10, Greenfield, IL [Library symbol Library of Congress] (LCLS) .... IGrefCU
Greenfield Daily Reporter, Greenfield, IN [Library symbol] [Library of Congress] (LCLS) .... InGrefR
Greenfield, IA [Location identifier FAA] (FAAL) .... GFZ
Greenfield, IN [Location identifier FAA] (FAAL) .... GFD
Greenfield, IN [FM radio station call letters] .... WZPL
Greenfield Industries [NASDAQ symbol] (TTSB) .... GEIL
Greenfield Industries, Inc. [NASDAQ symbol] (SAG) .... GFII
Greenfield Industries, Inc. [Associated Press] (SAG) .... Grenfld
Greenfield, MA [AM radio station call letters] .... WGAM
Greenfield, MA [AM radio station call letters] .... WHAI
Greenfield, MA [FM radio station call letters] .... WHAI-FM
Greenfield, MA [FM radio station call letters] .... WRSI
Greenfield, OH [FM radio station call letters] .... WVNU
Greenfield Public Library, Greenfield, IL [Library symbol Library of Congress] (LCLS) .... IGref
Greenfield Public Library, Greenfield, IN [Library symbol Library of Congress] (LCLS) .... InGref
Greenfield, WI [AM radio station call letters] .... WMCS
Greenham Common [British ICAO location identifier] (ICLI) .... EGVI
Greenhood's Doctrine of Public Policy in the Law of Contracts [A publication] (DLA) .... Greenh Pub Pol
Greenhouse .... GRNHS
Greenhouse Action Australia (EERA) .... GAA
Greenhouse Annual [Horticulture] (ROG) .... GA
Greenhouse Biennial [Horticulture] (ROG) .... GB
Greenhouse Coordinating Group [Australia] .... GCG
Greenhouse Corps [Australia] .... GC
Greenhouse Crisis Foundation (EA) .... GCF
Greenhouse Education and Information Program (EERA) .... GEIP
Greenhouse Gas [Climatology] .... GHG
Greenhouse Gas Index .... GGI
Greenhouse Gases (EERA) .... GHG
Greenhouse Information Program Grants Scheme (EERA) .... GIPGS
Greenhouse Perennial [Horticulture] (ROG) .... GP
Greenhouse Plant [Botany] .... G
Greenhouse Shrub [Horticulture] (ROG) .... GS
Greenhouse Suppliers Association (EA) .... GSA
Greenhouse Warming Index [Marine science] (OSRA) .... GWI
Greenhouse Warming Index (USDC) .... GWI
Greenhouse Warming Potential [Environmental chemistry] .... GHWP
Greenhouse Warming Potential (EERA) .... GWP
Greenhow's Law of Shipowners [A publication] (DLA) .... Green Ship
Greenhow's Shipping Law Manual [A publication] (DLA) .... Greenh Sh
Greening Australia (EERA) .... GA
Greening Australia Action .... GAA
Greening Australia Limited (EERA) .... GAL
Greening's Forms of Declarations, Pleadings, Etc. [A publication] (DLA) .... Green Forms
Greenish [Philately] .... grnsh
Greenish Blue .... GB
Greenish Yellow .... GY
Greenland [MARC country of publication code Library of Congress] (LCCP) .... gl
Greenland [ANSI two-letter standard code] (CNC) .... GL
Greenland (BARN) .... Greenl
Greenland [ANSI three-letter standard code] (CNC) .... GRL
Greenland (VRA) .... Grld
Greenland [MARC geographic area code Library of Congress] (LCCP) .... n-gl--
Greenland Base Command .... GBC
Greenland Cruiser .... GC
Greenland Ice Sheet .... GIS
Greenland Ice Sheet Project [National Science Foundation] .... GISP
Greenland Icecore Project [Europe] [Marine science] (OSRA) .... GRIP
Greenland Icesheet Program [Europe] [Marine science] (OSRA) .... GRIP
Greenland Icesheet Program [Europe] (USDC) .... GRIP
Greenland Patrol [Navy] .... GREPAT
Greenlandair Charter AS [Denmark ICAO designator] (FAAC) .... GRC
Greenland-Iceland-Norway [Gap] (DOMA) .... GIN
Greenland-Iceland-United Kingdom [NATO naval defense line] .... GIUK
Greenleaf on Evidence [A publication] (DLA) .... Green Ev
Greenleaf on Evidence [A publication] (DLA) .... Greenl Ev
Greenleaf on Evidence [A publication] (DLA) .... GrEv
Greenleaf on the Testimony of the Evangelists [A publication] (DLA) .... Greenl Test Ev
Greenleaf's Edition of Cruise's Digest of Real Property [A publication] (DLA) .... Green Cruise
Greenleaf's Edition of Cruise's Digest of Real Property [A publication] (DLA) .... Greenl Cr
Greenleaf's Edition of Cruise's Digest of Real Property [A publication] (DLA) .... Greenl Cruise
Greenleaf's Edition of Cruise's Digest of Real Property [A publication] (DLA) .... Greenl Cruise Real Prop
Greenleaf's Over-Ruled Cases [A publication] (DLA) .... Green Ov Cas
Greenleaf's Over-Ruled Cases [A publication] (DLA) .... Greenl Ov Cas
Greenleaf's Reports [1-9 Maine] [A publication] (DLA) .... Gr
Greenleaf's Reports [1-9 Maine] [A publication] (DLA) .... Greenl
Greenlease Kidnapping .... GRENAP
Greenman Brothers, Inc. [AMEX symbol] (SPSG) .... GMN
Greenman Brothers, Inc. [Associated Press] (SAG) .... Grenm
Greenman Technologies [NASDAQ symbol] (TTSB) .... GMTI
Greenman Technologies, Inc. [NASDAQ symbol] (SAG) .... GMTI
Greenman Technologies, Inc. [Associated Press] (SAG) .... Greenman
Greenman Technologies, Inc. [Associated Press] (SAG) .... Grnmn
Greenman Technologies Wrrt [NASDAQ symbol] (TTSB) .... GMTIW

Greenpeace .... GP
Greenpeace Australia .... GPA
Greenpeace International (EA) .... GI
Greenpeace International [Netherlands] (EAIO) .... GPI
Greenpeace USA (EA) .... GPUSA
Greenpoint Financial Corp. [NYSE symbol] (SAG) .... GPT
Greenpoint Financial Corp. [Associated Press] (SAG) .... GrnPtFin
Greenpoint Finl [NYSE symbol] (TTSB) .... GPT
Greenpond [New Jersey] [Seismograph station code, US Geological Survey] (SEIS) .... GPD
[The] Greens [Australia Political party] .... GRE
Greens [Commonly used] (OPSA) .... GREENS
Greens [Political party Australia] .... GRN
Greens [Postal Service standard] (OPSA) .... GRNS
Greens .... GRNS
Green's Bankrupt Law [A publication] (DLA) .... Green BL
Green's Criminal Cases [A publication] (DLA) .... Green Cr Cas
Green's Criminal Cases [A publication] (DLA) .... Green Sc Cr Cas
Green's Criminal Law [England] [A publication] (DLA) .... Green Cr
Green's Criminal Law Reports [A publication] (DLA) .... Green Cr L Rep
Green's Criminal Law Reports [A publication] (DLA) .... Green Cr Law R
Green's Edition of Brice's Ultra Vires [A publication] (DLA) .... Gr Brice
Green's Edition of Brice's Ultra Vires [A publication] (DLA) .... Green Bri
Greens in Lowe [Political party Australia] .... GLO
Greens in Regulation Golf (BARN) .... GIR
Green's New Jersey Law or Equity [A publication] (DLA) .... Green (NJ)
Green's Outlines of Roman Law [A publication] (DLA) .... Green Rom Law
Green's Reports [A publication] (DLA) .... Gr
Green's Reports [A publication] (DLA) .... Green
Green's Reports [Rhode Island] [A publication] (DLA) .... Green (RI)
Green's Scottish Trials for Treason [A publication] (DLA) .... Green Sc Tr
[The] Greens (Western Australia) Inc. .... GWA
Greensboro [Georgia] [Seismograph station code, US Geological Survey] (SEIS) .... GBG
Greensboro Civil Rights Fund [Defunct] (EA) .... GCRF
Greensboro College, Greensboro, NC [Library symbol Library of Congress] (LCLS) .... NcGC
Greensboro, GA [FM radio station call letters] .... WDDK
Greensboro/High Point/West Salem [North Carolina] Reynolds [Airport symbol] (OAG) .... INT
Greensboro/High Point/Winston Salem [North Carolina] [Airport symbol] .... GSO
Greensboro Justice Fund (EA) .... GJF
Greensboro, NC [Location identifier FAA] (FAAL) .... HIH
Greensboro, NC [Location identifier FAA] (FAAL) .... LZY
Greensboro, NC [Location identifier FAA] (FAAL) .... SDJ
Greensboro, NC [Television station call letters] .... WFMY
Greensboro, NC [Television station call letters] .... WGGT
Greensboro, NC [AM radio station call letters] .... WKEW
Greensboro, NC [FM radio station call letters] .... WKSI
Greensboro, NC [Television station call letters] .... WLXI
Greensboro, NC [FM radio station call letters] .... WNAA
Greensboro, NC [AM radio station call letters] .... WPET
Greensboro, NC [FM radio station call letters] .... WQFS
Greensboro, NC [AM radio station call letters] .... WQMG
Greensboro, NC [FM radio station call letters] .... WQMG-FM
Greensboro, NC [AM radio station call letters] (RBYB) .... WTCK-AM
Greensboro, NC [AM radio station call letters] .... WUAG
Greensboro, NC [TV station call letters] (RBYB) .... WUPN-TV
Greensboro, NC [AM radio station call letters] .... WWBG
Greensboro, NC [AM radio station call letters] .... WWWB
Greensboro Public Library, Greensboro, NC [Library symbol Library of Congress] (LCLS) .... NcG
Greensboro Public Library, Greensboro, NC [OCLC symbol] (OCLC) .... NGP
Greensboro Public Schools, Greensboro, NC [Library symbol Library of Congress] (LCLS) .... NcGPS
Greensburg [Diocesan abbreviation] [Pennsylvania] (TOCD) .... GBG
Greensburg, IN [AM radio station call letters] .... WTRE
Greensburg, KY [AM radio station call letters] .... WAKY
Greensburg, KY [FM radio station call letters] .... WGRK
Greensburg, PA [AM radio station call letters] .... WHJB
Greensburg, PA [Television station call letters] .... WPCB
Greensburg, PA [FM radio station call letters] .... WSSZ
Greensburg Public Library, Greensburg, IN [Library symbol Library of Congress] (LCLS) .... InGreb
Greenside Darter [Ichthyology] .... Gd
Greenspond Public Library, Greenspond, NF, Canada [Library symbol Library of Congress] (LCLS) .... CaNfGr
Greenspond Public Library, Newfoundland [Library symbol National Library of Canada] (NLC) .... NFGR
GreenStone Inds Wrrt [NASDAQ symbol] (TTSB) .... STONW
GreenStone Indus [NASDAQ symbol] (TTSB) .... STON
GreenStone Industries, Inc. [Associated Press] (SAG) .... GreenS
GreenStone Industries, Inc. [Associated Press] (SAG) .... GreenStn
GreenStone Industries, Inc. [NASDAQ symbol] (SAG) .... STON
Greenstone Res Ltd [NASDAQ symbol] (TTSB) .... GRERF
Greenstone Resources Ltd. [Toronto Stock Exchange symbol] .... GRE
Greenstone Resources Ltd. [NASDAQ symbol] (NQ) .... GRER
Greenstone Resources Ltd. [Associated Press] (SAG) .... GrnstRs
Greenstone Roberts Adv [NASDAQ symbol] (TTSB) .... GRRI
Greenstone Roberts Advertising, Inc. [Associated Press] (SAG) .... GrnstR
Greenstone Roberts Advertising, Inc. [Associated Press] (SAG) .... GRRI
Greensward Foundation (EA) .... GF
Greentree Energy [Vancouver Stock Exchange symbol] .... GGY
GreenTree Financial Corp. [Associated Press] (SAG) .... GreenTR
Greentree Software [NASDAQ symbol] (TTSB) .... GTSWC

Greentree Software, Inc. [*Associated Press*] (SAG) ... GrntrSft
Greentree Software, Inc. [*NASDAQ symbol*] (NQ) ... GTSW
Greenup, KY [*AM radio station call letters*] ... WLGC
Greenup, KY [*FM radio station call letters*] ... WLGC-FM
Greenup, KY [*FM radio station call letters*] (RBYB) ... WLGC-FM
Greenville [*Mississippi*] [*Airport symbol*] (OAG) ... GLH
Greenville [*Lake Wappapelo*] [*Missouri*] [*Seismograph station code, US Geological Survey*] [*Closed*] (SEIS) ... GRV
Greenville [*North Carolina*] [*Airport symbol*] (OAG) ... PGV
Greenville, AL [*Location identifier FAA*] (FAAL) ... PRN
Greenville, AL [*AM radio station call letters*] ... WGYV
Greenville, AL [*FM radio station call letters*] ... WKXN
Greenville, AL [*FM radio station call letters*] ... WQZX
Greenville & Northern Railway Co. (IIA) ... G & N
Greenville & Northern Railway Co. [*AAR code*] ... GRN
Greenville Area Public Library, Greenville, PA [*Library symbol Library of Congress*] (LCLS) ... PGrev
Greenville College, Greenville, IL [*OCLC symbol*] (OCLC) ... IAG
Greenville College, Greenville, IL [*Library symbol Library of Congress*] (LCLS) ... IGreviC
Greenville County Library, Emporia, VA [*Library symbol Library of Congress*] (LCLS) ... ViEmP
Greenville County Library, Greenville, SC [*Library symbol Library of Congress*] (LCLS) ... ScG
Greenville County Library, Greenville, SC [*OCLC symbol*] (OCLC) ... SGR
Greenville, FL [*Location identifier FAA*] (FAAL) ... GEF
Greenville, GA [*FM radio station call letters*] ... WKZJ
Greenville, IL [*Location identifier FAA*] (FAAL) ... GRE
Greenville, IL [*FM radio station call letters*] ... WGEL
Greenville, IL [*FM radio station call letters*] ... WGRN
Greenville, KY [*Location identifier FAA*] (FAAL) ... GMH
Greenville, KY [*FM radio station call letters*] (RBYB) ... WKYA-FM
Greenville, KY [*FM radio station call letters*] ... WWHK
Greenville/Majors Field [*Texas*] [*ICAO location identifier*] (ICLI) ... KGVT
Greenville, ME [*Location identifier FAA*] (FAAL) ... XQA
Greenville, MI [*FM radio station call letters*] ... WODJ
Greenville, MI [*AM radio station call letters*] ... WPLB
Greenville, MS [*Location identifier FAA*] (FAAL) ... MTQ
Greenville, MS [*FM radio station call letters*] ... WBAQ
Greenville, MS [*AM radio station call letters*] ... WDDT
Greenville, MS [*FM radio station call letters*] ... WDMS
Greenville, MS [*AM radio station call letters*] ... WGVM
Greenville, MS [*AM radio station call letters*] ... WNIX
Greenville, MS [*Television station call letters*] ... WXVT
Greenville, NC [*Location identifier FAA*] (FAAL) ... AQE
Greenville, NC [*AM radio station call letters*] (RBYB) ... WBZQ
Greenville, NC [*AM radio station call letters*] ... WNCT
Greenville, NC [*FM radio station call letters*] ... WNCT-FM
Greenville, NC [*Television station call letters*] ... WNCT-TV
Greenville, NC [*AM radio station call letters*] ... WOOW
Greenville, NC [*Television station call letters*] ... WUNK
Greenville, NC [*Television station call letters*] ... WYDO
Greenville, NC [*FM radio station call letters*] ... WZMB
Greenville, OH [*FM radio station call letters*] ... WDPG
Greenville, OH [*FM radio station call letters*] ... WLSN
Greenville, PA [*FM radio station call letters*] ... WEXC
Greenville, PA [*AM radio station call letters*] ... WGRP
Greenville, PA [*FM radio station call letters*] ... WTGP
Greenville Public Library, Greenville, IL [*Library symbol Library of Congress*] (LCLS) ... IGrevi
Greenville Public Library, Greenville, MI [*Library symbol*] [*Library of Congress*] (LCLS) ... MiGre
Greenville Public Library, Greenville, OH [*Library symbol Library of Congress*] (LCLS) ... OGr
Greenville, SC [*Location identifier FAA*] (FAAL) ... GMU
Greenville, SC [*Location identifier FAA*] (FAAL) ... GOX
Greenville, SC [*Location identifier FAA*] (FAAL) ... GYH
Greenville, SC [*FM radio station call letters*] ... WEPR
Greenville, SC [*AM radio station call letters*] ... WESC
Greenville, SC [*FM radio station call letters*] ... WESC-FM
Greenville, SC [*AM radio station call letters*] ... WFBC
Greenville, SC [*FM radio station call letters*] ... WFBC-FM
Greenville, SC [*Television station call letters*] ... WGGS
Greenville, SC [*AM radio station call letters*] (RBYB) ... WGVL-AM
Greenville, SC [*FM radio station call letters*] ... WLFJ
Greenville, SC [*AM radio station call letters*] ... WMUU
Greenville, SC [*FM radio station call letters*] ... WMUU-FM
Greenville, SC [*Television station call letters*] ... WNTV
Greenville, SC [*AM radio station call letters*] ... WPCI
Greenville, SC [*AM radio station call letters*] ... WPLS
Greenville, SC [*FM radio station call letters*] ... WTBI
Greenville, SC [*Television station call letters*] ... WYFF
Greenville/Sinoe [*Liberia*] [*ICAO location identifier*] (ICLI) ... GLGE
Greenville/Spartanburg [*South Carolina*] [*Airport symbol*] ... GSP
Greenville/Spartanburg [*South Carolina*] **Downtown** [*Airport symbol*] (OAG) ... SPA
Greenville Technical College, Greenville, SC [*Library symbol*] [*Library of Congress*] (LCLS) ... ScGTC
Greenville, TX [*Location identifier FAA*] (FAAL) ... GVT
Greenville, TX [*AM radio station call letters*] ... KGVL
Greenville, TX [*FM radio station call letters*] ... KIKT
Greenville, TX [*Location identifier FAA*] (FAAL) ... MJF
Greenwater Lake, SK [*Television station call letters*] ... CKBI-3
Greenway High School, Coleraine, MN [*Library symbol*] [*Library of Congress*] (LCLS) ... MnColH
Greenwell Resources Corp. [*Vancouver Stock Exchange symbol*] ... GNW
Greenwell Springs State Hospital, Greenwell Springs, LA [*Library symbol Library of Congress*] (LCLS) ... LGsSH
Greenwich [*United Kingdom*] [*Later, HAD*] [*Geomagnetic observatory code*] ... GRW
Greenwich Air Services 'A' [*NASDAQ symbol*] (TTSB) ... GASIA
Greenwich Air Services, Inc. [*NASDAQ symbol*] (SAG) ... GASI
Greenwich Air Services, Inc. [*Associated Press*] (SAG) ... GrnwAir
Greenwich Air Svcs'B' [*NASDAQ symbol*] (TTSB) ... GASIB
Greenwich & Johnsonville Railway Co. [*AAR code*] ... GJ
Greenwich Apparent Civil Time [*Astronomy*] (IAA) ... GACT
Greenwich Apparent Noon (ROG) ... GAN
Greenwich Apparent Sidereal Time (PDAA) ... GAST
Greenwich Apparent Time ... GAT
Greenwich Central Time [*Astronomy*] (IAA) ... GCT
Greenwich Civil Noon ... GCN
Greenwich Civil Time ... GCT
Greenwich Conservatory Time ... GCT
Greenwich, CT [*AM radio station call letters*] ... WGCH
Greenwich Date ... GD
Greenwich Hospital Pension [*British military*] (DMA) ... GHP
Greenwich Hour Angle ... GHA
Greenwich Hour Angle of Mean Sun ... GHAMS
Greenwich Hour Angle of True Sun ... GHATS
Greenwich Library, Greenwich, CT [*Library symbol Library of Congress*] (LCLS) ... CtGre
Greenwich Library, Greenwich, CT [*OCLC symbol*] (OCLC) ... GRN
Greenwich Mean Astronomical Time ... GMAT
Greenwich Mean Noon (ROG) ... GMN
Greenwich Mean Sidereal Time (WGA) ... GMST
Greenwich Mean [*or Meridian*] **Time** ... GMT
Greenwich Meridian [*Upper branch*] ... G
Greenwich Meridian [*Lower branch*] ... g
Greenwich Meridian ... GM
Greenwich Resources Ltd. [*Toronto Stock Exchange symbol Vancouver Stock Exchange symbol*] ... GRW
Greenwich Royal Observatory [*British*] (BARN) ... GRO
Greenwich Sidereal Noon (ROG) ... GSN
Greenwich Sidereal [*or Standard*] **Time** ... GST
Greenwich Street CA Muni Fd [*AMEX symbol*] (TTSB) ... GCM
Greenwich Street California Municipal Fund, Inc. [*AMEX symbol*] (SAG) ... GCM
Greenwich Street California Municipal Fund, Inc. [*Associated Press*] (SAG) ... GrnStCA
Greenwich Street California Municipal Fund, Inc. [*Associated Press*] (SAG) ... GrStCA
Greenwich Street Muni Fund [*NYSE symbol*] (TTSB) ... GSI
Greenwich Street Municipal Fund, Inc. [*Associated Press*] (SAG) ... GreenwSt
Greenwich Street Municipal Fund, Inc. [*NYSE symbol*] (SAG) ... GSI
Greenwich Time ... G
Greenwich Time ... GT
Greenwich Time Signal (DEN) ... GTS
Greenwich Zone Time ... GZT
Greenwood [*Mississippi*] [*Airport symbol*] (AD) ... GNL
Greenwood [*South Carolina*] [*Airport symbol*] (OAG) ... GRD
Greenwood [*Mississippi*] [*Airport symbol*] (OAG) ... GWO
Greenwood and Horwood's Conveyancing [*A publication*] (DLA) ... Green & H Conv
Greenwood and Martin's Magistrates' Police Guide [*A publication*] (DLA) ... Greenw & M Mag Pol
Greenwood, AR [*AM radio station call letters*] ... KPBI
Greenwood, AR [*FM radio station call letters*] ... KZKZ
Greenwood, Archer, and Pine [*Major streets in Tulsa, OK*] [*In musical group "The GAP Band"*] ... GAP
Greenwood Canadian Forces Base, NS [*ICAO location identifier*] (ICLI) ... CYZX
Greenwood Cotton Exchange (EA) ... GCE
Greenwood, IN [*FM radio station call letters*] ... WGGR
Greenwood Lake Public Library, Greenwood, NY [*Library symbol Library of Congress*] (LCLS) ... NGrl
Greenwood, MS [*Location identifier FAA*] (FAAL) ... GRW
Greenwood, MS [*AM radio station call letters*] ... WABG
Greenwood, MS [*Television station call letters*] ... WABG-TV
Greenwood, MS [*FM radio station call letters*] ... WGNL
Greenwood, MS [*AM radio station call letters*] ... WGRM
Greenwood, MS [*FM radio station call letters*] ... WGRM-FM
Greenwood, MS [*AM radio station call letters*] ... WKXG
Greenwood, MS [*FM radio station call letters*] ... WMAO
Greenwood, MS [*Television station call letters*] ... WMAO-TV
Greenwood, MS [*FM radio station call letters*] ... WYMX
Greenwood Museum, British Columbia [*Library symbol National Library of Canada*] (NLC) ... BGM
Greenwood Museum, Greenwood, BC, Canada [*Library symbol*] [*Library of Congress*] (LCLS) ... CaBGM
Greenwood on Courts [*A publication*] (DLA) ... Green Cts
Greenwood on Courts [*A publication*] (DLA) ... Greenw Cts
Greenwood Public Library, British Columbia [*Library symbol National Library of Canada*] (NLC) ... BGRE
Greenwood Public Library, Greenwood, IN [*Library symbol Library of Congress*] (LCLS) ... InGrew
Greenwood Public Library, Greenwood, WI [*Library symbol*] [*Library of Congress*] (LCLS) ... WGrw
Greenwood Publishing Corp., Westport, CT [*Library symbol Library of Congress*] (LCLS) ... GrP
Greenwood, SC [*Location identifier FAA*] (FAAL) ... GIW
Greenwood, SC [*AM radio station call letters*] ... WCRS
Greenwood, SC [*AM radio station call letters*] ... WLMA
Greenwood, SC [*AM radio station call letters*] ... WMTY

Greenwood, SC [*FM radio station call letters*] ... WMTY-FM
Greenwood, SC [*Television station call letters*] ... WNEH
Greenwood, SC [*FM radio station call letters*] ... WSCZ
Greenwood-Leflore [*Mississippi*] [*ICAO location identifier*] (ICLI) ... KGWO
Greenwood-Leflore Public Library, Greenwood, MS [*Library symbol Library of Congress*] (LCLS) ... MsGwL
Greenwood's Manual of Conveyancing [*9th ed.*] [*1897*] [*A publication*] (DLA) ... Green Conv
Greenwood's Manual of Conveyancing [*9th ed.*] [*1897*] [*A publication*] (DLA) ... Greenw Conv
Greer, SC [*Location identifier FAA*] (FAAL) ... GSP
Greer, SC [*Location identifier FAA*] (FAAL) ... LMJ
Greer, SC [*AM radio station call letters*] ... WCKI
Greer, SC [*FM radio station call letters*] (RBYB) ... WLOT-FM
Greer, SC [*AM radio station call letters*] ... WPJM
Greer, SC [*FM radio station call letters*] (RBYB) ... WXWZ
Greer's Irish Land Acts, Leading Cases [*1872-1903*] [*A publication*] (DLA) ... Greer
Greeting ... GRTG
Greeting Card and Calendar Association [*British*] ... GCCA
Greeting Card Association (EA) ... GCA
Greeting Letter Telegram (ADA) ... GLT
Greetings Telegram (IAA) ... GT
Grefrath/Niershorst [*Germany ICAO location identifier*] (ICLI) ... EDLF
Greg Manning Auctions [*NASDAQ symbol*] (TTSB) ... GMAI
Greg Manning Auctions, Inc. [*NASDAQ symbol*] (SAG) ... GMAI
Greg Manning Auctions, Inc. [*Associated Press*] (SAG) ... GMann
Greg Manning Auctions, Inc. [*Associated Press*] (SAG) ... GManning
Greg Manning Auctions Wrrt [*NASDAQ symbol*] (TTSB) ... GMAIW
Gregarious [*Biology*] ... G
Gregg and Pond's Railroad Laws of the New England States [*A publication*] (DLA) ... G & P RR Laws
Gregorian (ROG) ... GREG
Gregorian Institute of America [*Record label*] ... GIOA
Gregorowski's Reports of the High Court [*A publication*] (DLA) ... G
Gregorowski's Reports of the High Court [*A publication*] (DLA) ... Greg
Gregory Downs [*Australia Airport symbol Obsolete*] (OAG) ... GGD
Gregory Elementary School, Rockford, IL [*Library symbol*] [*Library of Congress*] (LCLS) ... IRoGrE
Gregory, SD [*FM radio station call letters*] ... KVCX
Greif Bros 'B' [*NASDAQ symbol*] (TTSB) ... GBCOB
Greif Brothers Corp. [*NASDAQ symbol*] (SAG) ... GBCO
Greif Brothers Corp. [*Associated Press*] (SAG) ... GreifBrA
Greif Brothers Corp. [*Associated Press*] (SAG) ... GreifBrB
Greig Cephalopolysyndactyly Syndrome [*Medicine*] ... GCPS
Greiner Engineering, Inc. [*NYSE symbol*] (SPSG) ... GII
Greiner Engineering, Inc. [*Associated Press*] (SAG) ... Greiner
Greiner's Louisiana Practice [*A publication*] (DLA) ... Grein Pr
Gremlin [*Refers to a person unskilled in skateboarding*] [*Slang British*] (DSUE) ... GREM
Grenada [*ANSI two-letter standard code*] (CNC) ... GD
Grenada [*MARC country of publication code Library of Congress*] (LCCP) ... gd
Grenada [*Windward Islands*] [*Airport symbol*] (OAG) ... GND
Grenada [*ANSI three-letter standard code*] (CNC) ... GRD
Grenada [*Seismograph station code, US Geological Survey*] (SEIS) ... GRE
Grenada [*Aircraft nationality and registration mark*] (FAAC) ... J3
Grenada [*MARC geographic area code Library of Congress*] (LCCP) ... nwgd
Grenada [*International vehicle registration*] (ODBW) ... WG
Grenada County Library, Grenada, MS [*Library symbol Library of Congress*] (LCLS) ... MsGren
Grenada Democratic Labour Party [*Political party*] (EY) ... GDLP
Grenada Democratic Movement [*Political party*] (EAIO) ... GDM
Grenada, MS [*Location identifier FAA*] (FAAL) ... SBQ
Grenada, MS [*FM radio station call letters*] ... WQXB
Grenada, MS [*AM radio station call letters*] ... WYKC
Grenada National Party [*Political party*] (PPW) ... GNP
Grenada Tourist Office (EA) ... GTO
Grenada United Labour Party [*Political party*] (PPW) ... GULP
Grenade (AABC) ... GREN
Grenade Launcher (AABC) ... GL
Grenade Launcher Attachment Development (MCD) ... GLAD
Grenade Machine Gun [*Military*] ... GMG
Grenade Safety Fuze ... GSF
Grenadier (AABC) ... GRENDR
Grenadier Guards [*Military British*] ... GG
Grenadines [*MARC geographic area code Library of Congress*] (LCCP) ... nwgs--
Grenchen [*Switzerland ICAO location identifier*] (ICLI) ... LSZG
Grenfell Association of America (EA) ... GAA
Grenier's Ceylon Reports [*A publication*] (DLA) ... Gren
Grenier's Ceylon Reports [*A publication*] (DLA) ... Grenier
Grenlock Energy, Inc. [*Vancouver Stock Exchange symbol*] ... GEI
Grenoble [*France*] [*Airport symbol*] (OAG) ... GNB
Grenoble [*France*] [*Seismograph station code, US Geological Survey*] (SEIS) ... GRN
Grenoble Energy [*Vancouver Stock Exchange symbol*] ... GRN
Grenoble/Le Versoud [*France ICAO location identifier*] (ICLI) ... LFLG
Grenoble/Saint-Geoirs [*France ICAO location identifier*] (ICLI) ... LFLS
Grenzpolizeihelfer [*Border Police Aide*] [*German*] ... GPH
Grenzschutzgruppe [*Border Protection Group*] [*German*] ... GSG
Grenzwache [*Frontier Guard*] [*German military - World War II*] ... GW
Gresham, OR [*FM radio station call letters*] ... KMHD
Gresham, OR [*AM radio station call letters*] (RBYB) ... KMUZ
Gresley's Equity Evidence [*A publication*] (DLA) ... GrEq
Gresley's Equity Evidence [*A publication*] (DLA) ... Gres EqEv
Gretna, FL [*FM radio station call letters*] ... WGWD
Gretna, LA [*AM radio station call letters*] ... KGLA
Gretna, LA [*AM radio station call letters*] ... KKNO
Gretna, VA [*AM radio station call letters*] ... WMNA
Gretna, VA [*FM radio station call letters*] ... WMNA-FM
Grey [*Unit of inpingent energy*] ... GY
Grey Advertising [*NASDAQ symbol*] (SAG) ... GREY
Grey Advertising [*NASDAQ symbol*] (TTSB) ... GREY
Grey Advertising, inc. [*Associated Press*] (SAG) ... GreyAd
Grey Eagle High School, Grey Eagle, MN [*Library symbol*] [*Library of Congress*] (LCLS) ... MnGeH
Grey Goose Corp. Ltd. [*Toronto Stock Exchange symbol*] ... GGC
Grey Nuns of the Sacred Heart [*Roman Catholic religious order*] ... GNSH
Grey Power [*Political party Australia*] ... GRY
Grey Power Movement [*Australia*] ... GPM
Grey Power News [*Australia A publication*] ... GPN
Greybull, WY [*Location identifier FAA*] (FAAL) ... GEY
Greybull, WY [*AM radio station call letters*] ... KZMQ
Greybull, WY [*FM radio station call letters*] ... KZMQ-FM
Greyhawk Resources Ltd. [*Vancouver Stock Exchange symbol*] ... GHK
Greyhound Club of America (EA) ... GCA
Greyhound Computer of Canada Ltd. [*Toronto Stock Exchange symbol*] ... GHC
Greyhound Food Management ... GFM
Greyhound Lines [*AMEX symbol*] (SPSG) ... BUS
Greyhound Lines [*Associated Press*] (SAG) ... GreyhndL
Greyhound Lines, Inc. [*Associated Press*] (SAG) ... GreyLne
Greyhound Lines of Canada Ltd. [*Toronto Stock Exchange symbol*] ... GHL
Greyhound Package Express ... GPX
Greyhound Racing ... GRY
Greying, Leisured, Affluent, and Married [*Lifestyle classification British*] ... GLAM
Greymouth [*New Zealand*] [*Seismograph station code, US Geological Survey Closed*] (SEIS) ... GRY
Grey's House of Commons Debates [*A publication*] (DLA) ... Grey Deb
Greystoke Exploration [*Vancouver Stock Exchange symbol*] ... GRY
Greytown [*South Africa*] [*ICAO location identifier*] (ICLI) ... FAGY
Greyvest Financial Services, Inc. [*Toronto Stock Exchange symbol*] ... GFI
Gribbin Elementary School, Glen Cove, NY [*Library symbol*] [*Library of Congress*] (LCLS) ... NGlcGE
Grid [*Electronics*] ... G
Grid (IDOE) ... g
Grid Base [*Electronics*] (EECA) ... GB
Grid Bearing [*Navigation*] ... GB
Grid Bias (DEN) ... GB
Grid Cathode Capacitance (IDOE) ... C_{GK}
Grid Cooperating Centre (EERA) ... GCC
Grid Course [*Navigation*] ... GC
Grid Dead Reckon [*Military*] (CAAL) ... GDR
Grid Driving Power ... GDP
Grid Heading [*Navigation*] ... GH
Grid Interval (IAA) ... GI
Grid Leak ... GDLK
Grid Leak ... GL
Grid Modulation ... GM
Grid Navigational Reference Beacon [*Navy*] (CAAL) ... GNRB
Grid Node Interface (PDAA) ... GNI
Grid North [*Army*] (ADDR) ... GN
Grid North Correction ... GNC
Grid Plate Capacitance (IDOE) ... C_{GP}
Grid Pool Tank ... GPT
Grid Procedure (SAA) ... GRDPRO
Grid Pulse (IAA) ... GP
Grid Reference Ship [*Navy*] (NVT) ... GRS
Grid Reference Unit [*Military*] (CAAL) ... GRU
Grid Resistance (IDOE) ... R_g
Grid Resistor ... GR
Grid Return ... GR
Grid Return (MSA) ... GRTN
Grid Space Relay ... GSR
Grid Sphere Drag [*DoD satellite*] ... GSD
Grid Spot Converter (NVT) ... GSC
Grid Test of Schizophrenic Thought Disorder [*Psychology*] ... GTSTD
Grid Variation [*Navigation*] ... GV
Grid-Controlled Electron Gun ... GCEG
Grid-Controlled Klystron ... GCK
Gridded Binary [*Data Format*] [*Marine science*] (OSRA) ... GRIB
Gridded Binary Form [*Computer science*] ... GRIB
Gridded Crossed Field Amplifier (IAA) ... GCFA
Gridded Line of Thrust (MCD) ... GLT
Gridded Traveling-Wave Tube (MCD) ... GTWT
Grid-Dip Meter (IAA) ... GDM
Grid-Dip Modulator ... GDM
Grid-Dip Oscillator ... GDO
Grid-Dip Oscillator (IDOE) ... gdo
Griddle (MSA) ... GRDL
Gridiron [*Typography*] [*Theater*] (WDMC) ... grid
Gridiron Club of Washington, DC (EA) ... GCW
Gridlays Bank International Zambia Ltd. ... GBI
Gridley, CA [*FM radio station call letters*] (RBYB) ... KMJE-FM
Gridley Public Library, Gridley, CA [*Library symbol Library of Congress*] (LCLS) ... CGrl
Grid-to-Magnetic Angle [*Navigation*] (INF) ... G-M
Griechische Geschichte [*A publication*] (OCD) ... Gr Gesch
Griechische Papyri im Museum des Oberhessischen Geschichtsvereins zu Giessen [*A publication*] (OCD) ... PGiess
Griechische und Lateinische Lehnwoerter im Talmud, Midrasch und Targum [*A publication*] (BJA) ... LW

Grief Bros CI'A' [*NASDAQ symbol*] (TTSB) .... GBCOA
Grievance and Employment Policy Board [*Army*] .... GEPB
Grievous Body Harm .... GBH
Griffin College, Tacoma, WA [*Library symbol*] [*Library of Congress*]
(LCLS) .... WaTGC
Griffin, GA [*AM radio station call letters*] .... WHIE
Griffin, GA [*AM radio station call letters*] .... WKEU
Griffin, GA (RBYB) .... WMVV
Griffin Gaming & Entertainment [*AMEX symbol*] (SAG) .... GGE
Griffin Gaming & Entertainment [*Associated Press*] (SAG) .... GrifGam
Griffin Technology, Inc. [*NASDAQ symbol*] (NQ) .... GRIF
Griffin Technology, Inc. [*Associated Press*] .... GrifTch
Griffin's Abstract of Patent Cases [*England*] [*A publication*] (DLA) .... Griffin PC
Griffin's London Poor Law Cases [*1821-31*] [*A publication*] (DLA) .... Grif PLC
Griffin's Nautical Series [*A publication*] .... GNS
Griffin's Patent Cases [*1866-87*] [*A publication*] (DLA) .... Grif Pat C
Griffin's Patent Cases [*1866-87*] [*A publication*] (DLA) .... Grif PC
Griffin's Patent Cases [*1866-87*] [*A publication*] (DLA) .... Griff Pat Cas
Griffin's Patent Cases [*1866-87*] [*A publication*] (DLA) .... Griffin Pat Cas
Griffiss Air Force Base [*New York*] .... GAFB
Griffith [*Australia Airport symbol*] (OAG) .... GFF
Griffith Observatory [*California*] [*Seismograph station code, US Geological
Survey*] (SEIS) .... GOC
Griffith on Arrangements with Creditors [*A publication*] (DLA) .... Grif Cr
Griffith on Military Law and Courts-Martial [*A publication*] (DLA) .... Grif Ct Mar
Griffith on Military Law and Courts-Martial [*A publication*] (DLA) .... Grif Mil Law
Griffith on the Judicature Acts [*A publication*] (DLA) .... Grif Jud Acts
Griffith University Faculty Staff Association [*Australia*] .... GUFSA
Griffith University, Nathan, QLD, Australia [*Library symbol Library of
Congress*] (LCLS) .... AuNaG
Griffiths & Bedell's [*System of stud tramways*] [*British*] (ROG) .... GB
Griffith's English Poor Rate Cases [*A publication*] (DLA) .... Grif PR Cas
Griffith's Institutes of Equity [*A publication*] (DLA) .... Grif Eq
Griffith's Institutes of Equity [*A publication*] (DLA) .... Grif Inst
Griffith's Law Register [*Burlington, NJ*] [*A publication*] (DLA) .... Grif L Reg
Griffith's London Poor Law Cases [*1821-31*] [*A publication*] (DLA) .... Grif PL Cas
Griffith's Married Women's Property Act [*A publication*] (DLA) .... Grif Mar Wom
Griffith's Poor Rate Cases [*A publication*] (DLA) .... Grif PRC
Griffith's Practice [*A publication*] (DLA) .... Grif Pr
Griffith's Reports [*1-5 Indiana Appeals and 117-132 Indiana*] [*A publication*]
(DLA) .... Griffith
Griffith's Stamp Duties [*A publication*] (DLA) .... Grif St
Griffon Corp. [*NYSE symbol*] (SAG) .... GFF
Griffon Corp. [*Associated Press*] (SAG) .... Griffon
Griffon Corp. 2nd Cv Pfd [*NYSE symbol*] (TTSB) .... GFFPrI
Grifora Umbellata Polysaccharide [*Antineoplastic drug*] .... GU-P
Grifton, NC [*FM radio station call letters*] .... WTND
Grifton, NC [*FM radio station call letters*] (RBYB) .... WXNR-FM
Grigna Settentrionale [*Italy ICAO location identifier*] (ICLI) .... LIMD
Grignard's Chemical Reaction .... GCR
Grigori Rasputin Society (EA) .... GRS
Grik [*Malaysia*] [*ICAO location identifier*] (ICLI) .... WMAH
Grill .... GRL
Grill Concepts [*NASDAQ symbol*] (TTSB) .... GRIL
Grill Concepts, Inc. [*NASDAQ symbol*] (SAG) .... GRIL
Grill Concepts, Inc. [*Associated Press*] (SAG) .... GrillCon
Grille .... GRL
Grille Opening Panel [*Automotive engineering*] .... GOP
Grille Opening Reinforcement [*Automotive engineering*] .... GOR
Grilled American Cheese Sandwich .... GAC
Grim File Reaper [*Computer hacker terminology*] (NHD) .... GFR
Grim Ruthless Upwardly Mobile Professional [*Lifestyle classification*] ..... Grumpie
Grimke on Executors and Administrators [*A publication*] (DLA) .... Grimke Ex
Grimke's Justice [*A publication*] (DLA) .... Grimke Jus
Grimke's Public Laws of South Carolina [*A publication*] (DLA) .... Grimke PL
Grimsby Museum, Ontario [*Library symbol National Library of Canada*]
(BIB) .... OGRM
Grimsby Public Library and Art Gallery, Grimsby, ON, Canada [*Library
symbol Library of Congress*] (LCLS) .... CaOGri
Grimsby Public Library and Art Gallery, Ontario [*Library symbol National
Library of Canada*] (NLC) .... OGR
Grimsey [*Iceland*] [*ICAO location identifier*] (ICLI) .... BIGR
Grimsey [*Iceland*] [*Airport symbol*] (OAG) .... GRY
Grimsey's Proceedings in Bankruptcy [*A publication*] (DLA) .... Grim Bank
Grimshaw Junior/Senior High School, Alberta [*Library symbol National
Library of Canada*] (BIB) .... AGWS
Grimshaw WI Municipal Library, Alberta [*Library symbol National Library of
Canada*] (NLC) .... AGWM
Grimshaw W.I. Municipal Library, Grimshaw, AB, Canada [*Library symbol*]
[*Library of Congress*] (LCLS) .... CaAGrWM
Grimsmoen [*Norway ICAO location identifier*] (ICLI) .... ENGN
Grind (ADA) .... GR
Grind (MSA) .... GRD
Grinder [*s*] [*Freight*] .... GRNDR
Grinder .... GRNDR
Grinding .... GRIND
Grinding Arbor .... GRAR
Grinding Fixture (MCD) .... GF
Grinding Fixture .... GRFX
Grinding Wheel Dresser .... GWD
Grinding Wheel Institute (EA) .... GWI
Grinnell College, Grinnell, IA [*Library symbol Library of Congress*] (LCLS) .... IaGG
Grinnell College, Grinnell, IA [*OCLC symbol*] (OCLC) .... IOG
Grinnell, IA [*Location identifier FAA*] (FAAL) .... GXL
Grinnell, IA [*FM radio station call letters*] .... KDIC

Grinnell, IA [*AM radio station call letters*] .... KGRN
Grinnell, IA [*FM radio station call letters*] .... KRTI
Grinning, Ducking, and Running (CDE) .... GD & R
Grip, Aim, Stance, and Posture [*Golf*] .... GASP
Grip Strength .... GS
Grip Strong and Equal [*Neurology*] (DAVI) .... GSE
Gripper Edge [*Bookbinding*] (DGA) .... GE
Grips Strong and Equal [*Medicine*] (MEDA) .... GES
Griqualand High Court Reports [*A publication*] (DLA) .... GWR
Griqualand High Court Reports [*A publication*] (DLA) .... HCG
Griqualand West Reports [*Cape Colony, South Africa*] [*A publication*]
(DLA) .... Kitchen
Grisaille (VRA) .... gris
Grise Fiord, NT [*ICAO location identifier*] (ICLI) .... CYGZ
Grisons [*Canton in Switzerland*] (ROG) .... GRIS
Grist Mill [*NASDAQ symbol*] (TTSB) .... GRST
Grist Mill Co. [*Associated Press*] (SAG) .... GristMil
Grist Mill Co. [*NASDAQ symbol*] (NQ) .... GRST
Griswold American, Griswold, IA [*Library symbol Library of Congress*]
(LCLS) .... IaGrisA
Griswold's Fire Underwriter's Text-Book [*A publication*] (DLA) .... Grisw Und
Griswold's Reports [*14-19 Ohio*] [*A publication*] (DLA) .... Grisw
Griswold's Reports [*14-19 Ohio*] [*A publication*] (DLA) .... Griswold
Grit Resources, Inc. [*Vancouver Stock Exchange symbol*] .... GIT
Gritman Memorial Hospital, Medical Library, Moscow, ID [*Library symbol*]
[*Library of Congress*] (LCLS) .... IdMGH
Gritty [*Quality of the bottom*] [*Nautical charts*] .... gty
Grivco International Ltd. [*Romania*] [*FAA designator*] (FAAC) .... GIV
Grivet Monkey Cell Line .... GMC
Grizzly Bear Club, San Francisco, CA [*Library symbol Library of Congress*]
(LCLS) .... CSfGB
Groblersdal [*South Africa*] [*ICAO location identifier*] (ICLI) .... FAGL
Grocery (WDAA) .... GROC
Grocery .... GROC
Grocery Manufacturers of America (EA) .... GMA
Grocery Manufacturers of Australia (EERA) .... GMA
Grocery Prices Index [*British*] .... GPI
Grocery Products Manufacturers of Canada [*See also FCPA*] .... GPMC
Grocery Store .... GS
Grocery Update and Billing .... GRUB
Grocka [*Yugoslavia*] [*Geomagnetic observatory code*] .... GCK
Grog [*i.e., entitled to draw a daily rum ration and doing so*] [*See also, T, UA*]
[*Obsolete*] [*Navy*] [*British*] .... G
Grog Money [*British military*] (DMA) .... GM
Grolier Club (EA) .... GC
Grolier Club, New York, NY [*Library symbol Library of Congress*] (LCLS) .... NNGr
Grolier Educational Corp. (AEBS) .... GEC
Grolier Electronic Publishing, Inc. [*Information service or system*] (IID) .... GEP
Grommet [*Automotive engineering*] .... GRMT
Grommet (KSC) .... GROM
Grondwet [*Constitution*] [*Netherlands*] (ILCA) .... G
Gronholt [*Denmark ICAO location identifier*] (ICLI) .... EKGH
Groningen [*Netherlands*] [*Airport symbol*] (OAG) .... GRQ
Groningen/Eelde [*Netherlands ICAO location identifier*] (ICLI) .... EHGG
Gronlandsfly [*ICAO designator*] (AD) .... GL
Gronlandsfly Ltd. [*Denmark ICAO designator*] (FAAC) .... GRL
Gronnedal [*Greenland*] [*ICAO location identifier*] (ICLI) .... BGGD
Gronningen. Siglum for Tablets [*Leiden*] [*A publication*] (BJA) .... Gron
Groom Lake Road [*Nevada*] [*Seismograph station code, US Geological
Survey*] (SEIS) .... GLR
Groom of the Stole [*British*] .... GR ST
Grooming .... GROOM
Groot Hertog von Luxemberg [*Grand Duke of Luxemburg*] [*Numismatics*]
(ROG) .... GHVL
Groote Eylandt Mining Co. [*Australia Commercial firm*] .... GEMCO
Groote Island [*Australia Airport symbol*] (OAG) .... GTE
Grootfontein [*Namibia*] [*ICAO location identifier*] (ICLI) .... FAGF
Grootfontein [*South-West Africa*] [*Airport symbol*] (OAG) .... GFY
Grootvlei Proprietary Mines Ltd. [*Associated Press*] (SAG) .... Grtv ADR
Grootvlei Proprietary Mines Ltd. [*NASDAQ symbol*] (SAG) .... GVPM
Groove (KSC) .... GRV
Groove between Parallel Folds .... GPF
Groove Gauge .... GG
Grooved .... GRVD
Grooved for Iron Tongues .... GIT
Grooved Roofing [*Lumber*] (DAC) .... G/Rfg
Grooved Roofing [*Lumber*] .... GR
Groover .... GRVR
Grooving .... GRVG
Gros [*Large*] [*French*] .... G
Groschen [*Monetary unit*] [*Austria*] .... G
Gross [*Leukemia antigen*] [*Immunochemistry*] .... GR
Gross .... GR
Gross (WDMC) .... gr
Gross (ODBW) .... gr
Gross (MSA) .... GRO
Gross Agricultural Product (WDAA) .... GAP
Gross and Microscopic [*Medicine*] (MEDA) .... GRS & MIC
Gross Annual Value [*Accounting*] (ODBW) .... GAV
Gross Asset [*Business term*] .... GA
Gross Available Capacity [*Electronics*] (IEEE) .... GAC
Gross Available Generation [*Electronics*] (IEEE) .... GAG
Gross Average Audience [*Nielsen rating*] [*Television*] (WDMC) .... GAA
Gross Average Tax Rate .... GATR
Gross Axle Weight Rating [*Auto safety*] .... GAWR

Gross Axle Weight Rating Front [*Auto safety*] .... GAWRF
Gross Axle Weight Rating Rear [*Auto safety*] .... GAWRR
Gross Brake Horsepower (MCD) .... GBHP
Gross Building Area (ADA) .... GBA
Gross Caloric Value .... GCV
Gross Capability Estimator [*Air Force*] .... GROCAP
Gross Capacity Factor (IEEE) .... GCF
Gross Cell-Surface Antigen [*Immunology*] .... GCSA
Gross Combination Test Weight [*Automotive engineering*] .... GCTW
Gross Combination Vehicle Weight [*Automotive engineering*] .... GCVW
Gross Combination Weight [*for tractor and loaded trailer*] .... GCW
Gross Combination Weight Rating [*Environmental Protection Agency*] .... GCWR
Gross Criminal Product .... GCP
Gross Cystic Disease Fluid Protein (DAVI) .... GCDFP
Gross Debt [*Business term*] .... GD
Gross Dependable Capacity [*Electronics*] (IEEE) .... GDC
Gross Domestic Expenditure (WDAA) .... GDE
Gross Domestic Fixed Capital Formation (EERA) .... GDFCF
Gross Domestic Output [*Economics*] .... GDO
Gross Domestic Product [*Economics*] .... GDP
Gross Domestic Product (Average) [*Economics*] .... GDP (A)
Gross Domestic Product (Expenditure) [*Economics*] .... GDP (E)
Gross Domestic Product (Income) [*Economics*] .... GDP (I)
Gross Domestic Product (Production) [*Economics*] .... GDP (P)
Gross Earnings [*Business term*] .... GE
Gross Earnings Deflator [*Economics*] (BARN) .... GED
Gross Ecosystem Exchange [*Biology*] .... GEE
Gross Energy Product .... GEP
Gross Error Test (PDAA) .... GET
Gross Expenditure on Research and Development/Gross Domestic Product [*Ratio*] .... GERD/GDP
Gross Expenditure on Research Development .... GERD
Gross External Area .... GEA
Gross Failed Fuel Detector [*Nuclear energy*] (NRCH) .... GFFD
Gross Fault Indicator Panel (SAA) .... GFIP
Gross Feasibility Estimator (MCD) .... GFE
Gross Fixed Capital Expenditure .... GFCE
Gross Fixed Capital Formation .... GFCF
Gross Floor Area (ADA) .... GFA
Gross Global Product .... GGP
Gross Gradability [*Truck specification*] .... GAG
Gross Heat Rate (DNAB) .... GHR
Gross Henle Chromoreaction [*Clinical chemistry*] .... GHCR
Gross Horsepower [*Engineering*] .... GHP
Gross' Illinois Compiled Statutes [*A publication*] (DLA) .... Gross St
Gross Impression [*Television ratings*] (NTCM) .... GI
Gross Impressions [*Advertising*] (WDMC) .... GIs
Gross Income .... GI
Gross Internal Area .... GIA
Gross Internal Product .... GIP
Gross Inventory (MHDB) .... GI
Gross Investment .... GI
Gross Lawyer Product [*Term for measurement of the income of attorneys*] .... GLP
Gross Leasable Area .... GLA
Gross Leukemia Virus .... GLV
Gross Lift-Off Mass [*NASA*] (KSC) .... GLOM
Gross Lift-Off Weight [*NASA*] .... GLOW
Gross Line [*Insurance*] .... GL
Gross Load Horsepower [*Automotive engineering*] .... HPGL
Gross Logical Design .... GLD
Gross Margin Return on Investment [*Air carrier designation symbol*] .... GMROI
Gross Maximum Capacity [*Electronics*] (IEEE) .... GMC
Gross Maximum Generation [*Electronics*] (IEEE) .... GMG
Gross Maximum Shipping Weight .... GMSW
Gross Motor .... GM
Gross Motor Activities (HGAA) .... GMA
Gross National Disposable Income [*Economics*] .... GNDI
Gross National Effluent .... GNE
Gross National Expenditure .... GNE
Gross National Income [*Economics*] .... GNI
Gross National Investment (EERA) .... GNI
Gross National Product [*Economics*] .... GNP
Gross National Recreation Experience [*Refers to cost of recreation in relation to gross national product*] .... GNRE
Gross National Sports Product [*Economics*] .... GNSP
Gross National Waste Product Forum [*Defunct*] (EA) .... GNWP
Gross Neutron Counter (PDAA) .... GNC
Gross Night Hour [*Advertising*] (WDMC) .... GNH
Gross Operating Surplus [*Economics*] .... GOS
Gross Performance Measuring System [*Air Force*] .... GPMS
Gross Premium [*Insurance*] (AIA) .... GP
Gross Primary Productivity .... GPP
Gross Processing Margin (MHDB) .... GPM
Gross Product Originating [*Department of Transportation*] .... GPO
Gross Profit [*Business term*] .... GP
Gross Profit Contribution .... GPC
Gross Profit Margin (WDAA) .... GPM
Gross Rate [*Insurance*] (AIA) .... GR
Gross Rating Point [*Television*] .... GRP
Gross Receipts [*Business term*] .... GR
Gross Redemption Yield (BARN) .... gry
Gross Reference List (DNAB) .... GRL
Gross Regional Product .... GRP
Gross Registered Tonnes (EERA) .... GRT
Gross Registered Tons [*Navigation*] .... GRT
Gross Rent Multiplier [*Business term*] (EMRF) .... GRM
Gross Replacement Cost (ADA) .... GRC
Gross Requirement (AABC) .... GR
Gross Reserve Generation [*Electronics*] (IEEE) .... GRG
Gross Revenue [*Business term*] .... GR
Gross Sales [*Business term*] .... GS
Gross Sarcoma Virus Antigen [*Immunology*] (MAE) .... GSA
Gross Seasonal Unavailable Generation [*Electronics*] (IEEE) .... GSUG
Gross' Select Cases Concerning the Law Merchant [*Selden Society*] [*A publication*] (DLA) .... Gro
Gross Social Product [*Economics*] .... GSP
Gross Soluble Antigen .... GSA
Gross Spread [*Business term*] .... GS
Gross State Product (OICC) .... GSP
Gross Subsidy Equivalent [*Tariffs*] [*Australia*] .... GSE
Gross Takeoff Weight [*of an aircraft*] [*Also, GTW*] .... GTOW
Gross Takeoff Weight [*of an aircraft*] [*Also, GTOW*] .... GTW
Gross Ton [*or Tonnage*] .... GT
Gross Ton-Mile (ADA) .... GRTM
Gross Tonne Kilometre (EERA) .... GTK
Gross Tons (ODBW) .... gro t
Gross Tons .... GRST
Gross Train Weight (DCTA) .... GTW
Gross Train Weight Rating .... GTWR
Gross Unit Unavailable Generation [*Electronics*] (IEEE) .... GUUG
Gross Universal Cash Heist [*Techno-economic term coined by Buckminster Fuller*] .... GRUNCH
Gross Value of Agricultural Output .... GVAO
Gross Value of Industrial and Agricultural Output .... GVIAO
Gross Value of Industrial Output .... GVIO
Gross Value of Output (MHDW) .... GVO
Gross Value of Production .... GVP
Gross Vehicle Mass Rating [*Load that a vehicle can carry*] .... GVMR
Gross Vehicle Test Weight [*Automotive engineering*] .... GVTW
Gross Vehicle Weight (MCD) .... GVW
Gross Vehicle Weight Rating .... GVWR
Gross Virus [*Leukemogenesis*] [*Immunochemistry*] .... GV
Gross Weight .... GRWT
Gross Weight (NG) .... GW
Gross Weight .... GWT
Gross Weight Category (DNAB) .... GWC
Gross Words per Minute [*Computer science*] (IAA) .... GWPM
Gross World Product .... GWP
Grossdeutsche Volkspartei [*Pan-German People's Party*] [*Austria Political party*] (PPE) .... GdVP
Grosse Ile Library, Magdalen Islands, Quebec [*Library symbol National Library of Canada*] (NLC) .... QGI
Grosse Ile Nature and Land Conservancy .... GINLC
Grosse Pointe Public Library, Grosse Pointe, MI [*Library symbol Library of Congress*] (LCLS) .... MiGp
Grosser Touren Kombiwagen [*Grand Touring Station Wagon*] [*German*] .... GTK
Grossesse Extra-Uterine [*Medicine*] .... GEU
Grosset & Dunlap [*Publisher*] .... G & D
Grosseto [*Italy*] [*Airport symbol*] (AD) .... GRS
Grosseto [*Italy ICAO location identifier*] (ICLI) .... LIRS
Grosshandelsgesellschaft [*Wholesale Business Establishment*] [*German*] .... GHG
Grosshandelskontor [*Wholesale Business Office*] [*German*] .... GHK
Grossly Bloody [*Biochemistry*] (DAVI) .... BLDY
Grossman's, Inc. [*NASDAQ symbol*] (NQ) .... GROS
Grossman's, Inc. [*Associated Press*] (SAG) .... Grosmn
Grossus [*Coarse*] [*Latin*] (MAE) .... gros
Grosswetterlage [*Meteorology*] .... GWL
Grosvenor Aviation Services [*British ICAO designator*] (FAAC) .... GRV
Grosvenor Barber and Associates (IID) .... GB & A
Grosvenor House Antiques Fair [*British*] (ITD) .... GHAF
Grosvenor Reference Division, Buffalo and Erie County Public Library, Buffalo, NY [*Library symbol Library of Congress*] (LCLS) .... NBuG
Groszy [*Monetary unit*] [*Poland*] .... G
Grote [*or Grotius*] [*Literature*] (ROG) .... GROT
Grotesque (ADA) .... GROT
Grotesque, Unbelievable, Bizarre, Unprecedented [*Term coined by an Irish politician to describe certain incidents in Irish politics*] .... GUBU
Grotius. De Jure Belli et Pacis [*A publication*] (DLA) .... Grot De JB
Grotius. De Jure Belli et Pacis [*A publication*] (DLA) .... Grot De JrB
Grotius. De Jure Belli et Pacis [*A publication*] (DLA) .... Grotius De Jure Belli
Grotius. Latin Law [*A publication*] (DLA) .... Grotius
Grotius' Rights of War and Peace [*Many eds.*] [*1625-1901*] [*A publication*] (DLA) .... Gro
Groton, CT [*Location identifier FAA*] (FAAL) .... TMU
Groton, CT [*FM radio station call letters*] .... WQGN
Groton, CT [*AM radio station call letters*] .... WSUB
Groton Minerals Ltd. [*Vancouver Stock Exchange symbol*] .... GTH
Groton Public Library, Groton, CT [*Library symbol Library of Congress*] (LCLS) .... CtGr
Groton School, Groton, MA [*Library symbol Library of Congress*] (LCLS) .... MGrS
Grottaglie [*Italy ICAO location identifier*] (ICLI) .... LIBG
Grottammare [*Italy ICAO location identifier*] (ICLI) .... LIBM
Grotto (ROG) .... GROT
Grouard Mission-High Prairie, AB [*Television station call letters*] CFRN-8
Grouard Northland School, Alberta [*Library symbol National Library of Canada*] (BIB) .... AGNS
Ground .... G
Ground .... GD
Ground (AAG) .... GND
Ground (IDOE) .... gnd

Ground ... Gr
Ground ... GRD
Ground (VRA) ... grd
Ground (ADA) ... GRND
Ground Acceptance [*or Article*] **Test Procedure** (MCD) ... GATP
Ground Accident Report (MCD) ... GAR
Ground Acquisition and Command Station (MCD) ... GA & CS
Ground Adjutant General Section [*World War II*] ... GNAGS
Ground Air Conditioning Unit (MCD) ... GACU
Ground/Air Defense Threat (MCD) ... GADT
Ground Air Transfer, Inc. [*ICAO designator*] (FAAC) ... SWG
Ground/Airborne Integrated Terminal [*Air Force*] (DOMA) ... G/AIT
Ground Anchor Placement Equipment ... GAPE
Ground and Amphibious Military Operations [*Army*] ... GAMO
Ground and Environmental (KSC) ... G & E
Ground Approach Radio Fuse (IAA) ... GARF
Ground Area Attainable ... GAA
Ground Attack [*Military*] ... GA
Ground Attack Night (MCD) ... GAN
Ground Attack Tactics [*for air delivery of weapons against a ground target*] ... GAT
Ground Attacker Aircraft ... GA
Ground Attitude Control (MCD) ... GAC
Ground Attitude Vertical Reference System [*Aviation*] ... GAVRS
Ground Aviation Radio Exchange System (MCD) ... GAREX
Ground Avionics Cooling Unit ... GACU
Ground Avoidance Simulation Program (MCD) ... GASP
Ground Backup (DNAB) ... GBU
Ground Backup Instrument (MUGU) ... GBI
Ground Based Common Sensor-Light/Heavy [*Military*] ... GBCS-L/H
Ground Based Free Electron LASER Proposal ... GBFEL
Ground Based RADAR-Experimental [*Army*] ... GBR-X
Ground Based Sensor [*Radar*] ... GBS
Ground Beacon [*Navigation*] (IAA) ... GB
Ground Beacon System (MCD) ... GBS
Ground Branch Exchange (DNAB) ... GBX
Ground Calcium Carbonate [*Inorganic chemistry*] ... GCC
Ground Check [*Aviation*] ... GNDCK
Ground Checkout [*NASA*] (NASA) ... GCO
Ground Checkout [*NASA*] (NASA) ... GND C/O
Ground Checkout and Test [*Aerospace*] ... GCT
Ground Checkout Display and Control [*NASA*] (NASA) ... GCDC
Ground Checkout Display and Control System (MCD) ... GCDCS
Ground Checkout Equipment [*Aerospace*] (AAG) ... GCE
Ground Checkout Unit [*Aerospace*] (MCD) ... GCU
Ground Claims Processing System ... GCPS
Ground Clearance Intercept [*System similar to US commercial RADAR for ground control of aircraft*] [*North Vietnam*] ... GCI
Ground Collision Avoidance System [*Army*] ... GCAS
Ground Combat Element [*Marine Corps*] (DOMA) ... GCE
Ground Combat Training Squadron ... GRCTS
Ground Combat-Readiness Evaluation Squadron ... GCRES
Ground Command Facility ... GCF
Ground Command Guidance ... GCG
Ground Command Post [*Army*] ... GNDCP
Ground Command System ... GCS
Ground Commanded [*or Controlled*] **Television Assembly** [*Apollo*] [*NASA*] ... GCTA
Ground Communication Activity (IAA) ... GCA
Ground Communications Controller ... GCC
Ground Communications Coordinator [*NASA*] (NASA) ... GCC
Ground Communications Equipment ... GCE
Ground Communications Facility [*NASA*] ... GCF
Ground Communications Facility - Communications Switcher [*NASA*] ... GCF-CS
Ground Communications Network ... GCN
Ground Communications System ... GCS
Ground Communications Tracking Systems ... GCTS
Ground Composite Signal Mixer ... GCSM
Ground Computer Controller ... GCC
Ground Computer Operating System [*NASA*] (NASA) ... GCOS
Ground Control [*Aviation*] (DA) ... G
Ground Control (AFM) ... GC
Ground Control ... GNDCON
Ground Control Interception Team (IAA) ... GCIT
Ground Control Point ... GCP
Ground Coolant Loop (MCD) ... GCL
Ground Cooling Heat Exchanger [*NASA*] (NASA) ... GCHX
Ground Cooling Unit [*NASA*] (NASA) ... GCU
Ground Cover [*Ecology*] ... GRCV
Ground Cruising Recreational Vehicle [*Owosso Motor Car Co.*] [*Owosso, MI*] ... GCRV
Ground Cutout ... GCO
Ground Data Acquisition System ... GDAS
Ground Data Equipment [*Electronics*] ... GDE
Ground Data Handling ... GDH
Ground Data Handling Centre [*Canada*] ... GDHC
Ground Data Handling System (MCD) ... GDHS
Ground Data Link Processor (GAVI) ... GDLP
Ground Data Management and Communications Network (MCD) ... GDMCN
Ground Data System ... GDS
Ground Data Systems Divsion [*NASA*] (NASA) ... GDSD
Ground Data Systems Manager (MCD) ... GDSM
Ground Data Systems Officer (MCD) ... GDSO
Ground Data Terminal ... GDT
Ground Decommutation Facility ... GDF
Ground Defense Forces ... GDF
Ground Delay Program [*Aviation*] (FAAC) ... GDPGM
Ground Delay Response [*Telecommunications*] (OA) ... GDR
Ground Delay Time (IAA) ... GDT
Ground Detector (MSA) ... GD
Ground Detector ... GRD
Ground Detector Indicator ... GDI
Ground Digit Control (IAA) ... GDC
Ground Directional (IAA) ... GD
Ground Display System ... GDS
Ground Distributed Control System (SSD) ... GDCS
Ground Diverted Force [*Military*] (CINC) ... GDF
Ground Earth Station [*Telecommunications*] ... GES
Ground Effect Machine (NG) ... GEM
Ground Effect Research Machine ... GERM
Ground Effect Takeoff and Landing ... GETOL
Ground Effect Vehicle ... GEV
Ground Effect Wing (PDAA) ... GEW
Ground Effects Phenomenon ... GEP
Ground Elapsed Time [*Aerospace*] ... GET
Ground Elapsed Time of Ignition [*Aerospace*] (KSC) ... GETI
Ground Elapsed Time of Landing ... GETIL
Ground Elapsed Time of Landing [*NASA*] (GFGA) ... GETL
Ground Electronic Maintenance Officer [*NASA*] (NG) ... GEMO
Ground Electronic System ... GES
Ground Electronics Engineering Installation Agency [*Air Force*] ... GEEIA
Ground Electronics Maintenance ... GEM
Ground Electro-Optic Unit ... GEU
Ground Elevation Meter (PDAA) ... GEM
Ground Emitter Location and Identification System [*Army*] ... GELIS
Ground Emitter Location and Identification System - High [*Army*] ... GELIS-H
Ground Emplaced Mine Scattering System [*Military*] (RDA) ... GEMMSS
Ground Emplaced Mine Scattering System [*Military*] (AABC) ... GEMS
Ground Emplaced Mine Scattering System [*Military*] (RDA) ... GEMSS
Ground Entry Point (NVT) ... GEP
Ground Entry Station (MCD) ... GES
Ground Entry Terminal (MCD) ... GET
Ground Environment and Navigational Aid (PDAA) ... GENA
Ground Environment Complex (MCD) ... GEC
Ground Environment Technical Installation System [*NATO*] (NATG) ... GETIS
Ground Environmental Control System (IAA) ... GECS
Ground Equipment ... GE
Ground Equipment Failure [*Air Force*] ... GEF
Ground Equipment Maintenance Squadron ... GEMS
Ground Equipment System ... GES
Ground Equipment Test Set ... GETS
Ground Equipment Turn Off (KSC) ... GETO
Ground Exploitation Module ... GEM
Ground Face [*Technical drawings*] ... GF
Ground Fault Circuit Breaker [*Electronics*] ... GFCB
Ground Fault Circuit Interrupter [*Electronics*] ... GFCI
Ground Fault Interrupter [*Electronics*] ... GFI
Ground Fault Protector (PDAA) ... GFP
Ground Fine Pitch (AIA) ... GFP
Ground Fire Locating System ... GFLS
Ground Fire Locator ... GFL
Ground/Flight Test ... G/F
Ground Fog [*Meteorology*] ... GF
Ground Foraging [*Ecology*] ... G
Ground Foraging [*Ecology*] ... GF
Ground Forces [*Military*] ... GF
Ground Forces Chief of Staff [*World War II*] ... GNGCS
Ground Forces Commanding General [*World War II*] ... GNDCG
Ground Forces Deputy Chief of Staff [*World War II*] ... GNGDC
Ground Forces Intelligence Study (MCD) ... GROFIS
Ground Forces Plans Section [*World War II*] ... GNGPS
Ground Forces Replacement Service [*World War II*] ... GFRS
Ground Forces Secretariat [*World War II*] ... GNGSE
Ground Forces Training Devices (Provisional) [*Army*] (RDA) ... GFD
Ground Forward Air Controller (MCD) ... GFAC
Ground Fuel Start Tank (AAG) ... GFST
Ground Fuel Ullage Tank (AAG) ... GFUT
Ground Gained Forward [*Aerial photography*] ... GGF
Ground Gained Sideways [*Aerial photography*] ... GGS
Ground, General [*JETDS nomenclature*] ... G
Ground Glass ... GGL
Ground Guidance [*Aerospace*] (AAG) ... GG
Ground Guidance Computer [*Aerospace*] ... GGC
Ground Guidance Equipment [*Aerospace*] ... GGE
Ground Guidance System [*Aerospace*] (AAG) ... GGS
Ground Gunner [*Air Force British*] ... GG
Ground Gunnery Range ... GGR
Ground Half Coupling (KSC) ... GHC
Ground Handling [*Aerospace*] ... GH
Ground Handling and Servicing Equipment [*Aerospace*] (IAA) ... GHSE
Ground Handling and Transportation [*Aerospace*] (KSC) ... GHAT
Ground Handling Equipment [*Aerospace*] ... GHE
Ground Handling System [*Aerospace*] (AAG) ... GHS
Ground Handling Test ... GHT
Ground Hazard Area (MUGU) ... GHA
Ground Heat Exchanger ... GHX
Ground Identification of Missions in Space ... GIMS
Ground Identification of Satellites (MCD) ... GISAT
Ground Information Processing System ... GIPS
Ground Instantaneous Field-of-View (MCD) ... GIFOV
Ground Instructor Pilot (DNAB) ... GIP

Ground Instrumentation and Communications System (IAA) ...... GICS
Ground Instrumentation Equipment ...... GIE
Ground Instrumentation System (IAA) ...... GIS
Ground Integration Requirements Document (MCD) ...... GIRD
Ground Integration Test Program (KSC) ...... GITP
Ground Interception (IAA) ...... GI
Ground Interface Technical Group [NASA] (NASA) ...... GITG
Ground Interface Working Group ...... GIWG
Ground Lamp (IAA) ...... GRLP
Ground LASER Designator Station (PDAA) ...... GLDS
Ground Launch Sequence [or Sequencer] (NASA) ...... GLS
Ground Level ...... GL
Ground Level Concentration (EG) ...... GLC
Ground Liaison Element (MCD) ...... GLE
Ground Liaison Officer [Military] ...... GLO
Ground Liaison Section [Military British] ...... GLSECT
Ground Lift-Off Weight [NASA] (NASA) ...... GLOW
Ground Line of Communications (AFM) ...... GLOC
Ground Logistics Operations [NASA] (KSC) ...... GLO
Ground Maintenance Support ...... GMS
Ground Malfunction ...... GM
Ground Map Pencil (DNAB) ...... GMP
Ground Mapping RADAR ...... GMR
Ground Mapping [or Marking] System ...... GMS
Ground Marker Release System [Army] (INF) ...... GMRS
Ground Master Measurements List ...... GMML
Ground Measurements Command List (MCD) ...... GMCL
Ground Meat/Analyzer [USDA] ...... GM/A
Ground Meteorological Detector [or Device] ...... GMD
Ground, Mobile [JETDS nomenclature] ...... M
Ground Mobile Cenetheodolite ...... GMC
Ground Mobile Command Center ...... GMCC
Ground Mobile Forces [Military] (RDA) ...... GMF
Ground Mobile Forces Satellite Communications (MCD) ...... GMFSC
Ground Mobile Forces/Tactical Satellite Communications (MCD) ..... GMF/TACSAT
Ground Mobile Forces/Tactical Satellite Communications Program ...... GMFS
Ground Mobile RADAR ...... GMR
Ground Mode ...... GM
Ground Monitor Facility (MCD) ...... GMF
Ground Movement Controller ...... GMC
Ground Movement Planner [Aviation] (OA) ...... GMP
Ground Movement RADAR [Military] ...... GMR
Ground Moving Target Indicator ...... GMTI
Ground Munitions Analysis Study (AABC) ...... GMAS
Ground Nester [Ornithology] ...... GN
Ground Network [Remote sensing] (EERA) ...... GN
Ground Network ...... GN
Ground Network Management System [Aviation] (DA) ...... GNMS
Ground Observation Reporting System ...... GORS
Ground Observer Aircraft Recognition [Army] ...... GOAR
Ground Observer Corps ...... GOC
Ground Observer Organization (NATG) ...... GOO
Ground Observer Post ...... GOP
Ground Observer RF [Radio Frequency] System [NASA] (NASA) ...... GORS
Ground Operation Order (NATG) ...... GOO
Ground Operational Equipment [NASA] ...... GOE
Ground Operational Equipment for the Orbiting Astronomical Observatory [NASA] (MUGU) ...... GOE for OAO
Ground Operational Equipment/Real Property Installed Equipment [NASA] (AFM) ...... GOE/RPIE
Ground Operational [or Operations] Requirements Plan [NASA] ...... GORP
Ground Operational [or Operations] Support System [NASA] ...... GOSS
Ground Operations Aerospace Language [Computer science NASA] ...... GOAL
Ground Operations and Material Management System (MCD) ...... GOMMS
Ground Operations Assembly Language [Computer science] ...... GOAL
Ground Operations Control Area [NASA] (NASA) ...... GOCA
Ground Operations Coordinator [NASA] (NASA) ...... GOC
Ground Operations Management System [NASA] (NASA) ...... GOMS
Ground Operations Manager ...... GOM
Ground Operations Panel [NASA] (NASA) ...... GOP
Ground Operations Planning Group [NASA] (NASA) ...... GOPG
Ground Operations Review (MCD) ...... GOR
Ground Operations Review Panel [NASA] (NASA) ...... GORP
Ground Operations System (MCD) ...... GOS
Ground Operations Working Group (MCD) ...... GOWG
Ground Optical Recorder for Intercept Determination ...... GORID
Ground Order of Battle (AFM) ...... GOB
Ground Out [Baseball] ...... GO
Ground Passive Electronic Reconnaissance Facility ...... GPERF
Ground Plane Antenna ...... GPA
Ground Plane Simulator ...... GPS
Ground Pneumatic (AAG) ...... GP
Ground Point of Impact ...... GPI
Ground Point of Intercept (AFM) ...... GPI
Ground Position Indicator [Dead-reckoning computer] ...... GPI
Ground Post (IAA) ...... GP
Ground Potential Model [Physics] ...... GPM
Ground Power Breaker [Electronics] (OA) ...... GPB
Ground Power Contactor ...... GPC
Ground Power Generator (DWSG) ...... GPG
Ground Power Generator System (DWSG) ...... GPGS
Ground Power Panel ...... GPP
Ground Power Supply [NASA] (NASA) ...... GPS
Ground Power Supply Unit [NASA] (AAG) ...... GPSU
Ground Power Unit ...... GPU

Ground Processing Simulation (MCD) ...... GPS
Ground Processing System [Aviation] ...... GPS
Ground Proximity Extraction System ...... GPES
Ground Proximity Sensor ...... GPS
Ground Proximity Warning System [FAA] ...... GPWS
Ground RADAR Aerial Delivery System (MCD) ...... GRADS
Ground RADAR Emitter for Training Aviators [Army] (RDA) ...... GRETA
Ground RADAR Equipment (IAA) ...... GRE
Ground Range ...... GR
Ground Reaction Force [Army] (INF) ...... GRF
Ground Reaction Vector (DMAA) ...... GRV
Ground Reconnaissance Equipment ...... GRE
Ground Reconnaissance Information Processing System (DNAB) ...... GRIPS
Ground Reconstruction Electronics [Used in photographing moon] [NASA] ...... GRE
Ground Reconstruction Equipment ...... GRE
Ground Reference Coverage Area (DOMA) ...... GRCA
Ground Relay Panel [Aerospace] (AAG) ...... GRP
Ground Rent (ROG) ...... GR
Ground Replay and Analysis Facility (GAVI) ...... GRAF
Ground Resistance Tester ...... GRT
Ground Resolved Distance [Satellite camera] ...... GRD
Ground Resonance Automatic Multi-Point Apparatus (PDAA) ...... GRAMPA
Ground Return Area Suppression (NATG) ...... GRAS
Ground Risks Only [Insurance] (AIA) ...... GRO
Ground Rods [JETDS nomenclature] [Military] (CET) ...... GP
Ground Roll Guidance System (MCD) ...... GRGS
Ground Round Rest [NASDAQ symbol] (TTSB) ...... GRXR
Ground Round Restaurants, Inc. [Associated Press] (SAG) ...... GrdRnd
Ground Round Restaurants, Inc. [NASDAQ symbol] (SAG) ...... GRXR
Ground Rule (MCD) ...... GR
Ground Rule Double [Baseball] ...... GRD
Ground Run-Up Enclosure [Aviation] (DA) ...... GRE
Ground Safety and Flight Safety Requirements (AAG) ...... GSFSR
Ground Safety Approval (MUGU) ...... GSA
Ground Safety Office [or Officer] [Air Force] ...... GSO
Ground Safety Plan (MUGU) ...... GSP
Ground Saucer Watch (EA) ...... GSW
Ground Self-Defense Force [Japan] ...... GSDF
Ground Self-Defense Force Japan ...... GSDFJ
Ground Sensor ...... GS
Ground Sensor Relay (IAA) ...... GSR
Ground Sensor Terminal (AABC) ...... GST
Ground Service [or Support] Cooling Unit (KSC) ...... GSCU
Ground Service Equipment [Air Force] ...... GSE
Ground Service Relay (MCD) ...... GSR
Ground Services Cart ...... GSC
Ground Shells [Quality of the bottom] [Nautical charts] ...... Grd
Ground Signal Mixer ...... GSM
Ground Software Development Laboratory [NASA] (NASA) ...... GSDL
Ground Sound Control, Inc. ...... GSCI
Ground Spacecraft Tracking and Data Network [Computer science] (MHDI) ...... GSTDN
Ground Special Security Forces ...... GSSF
Ground Speed [Aviation] ...... GS
Ground Squirrel Hepatitis Virus ...... GSHV
Ground Stabilized (MUGU) ...... GS
Ground Standard Interface Unit (MCD) ...... GSIU
Ground Standoff Minefield Detection System [Military] (RDA) ...... GSTAMIDS
Ground Station [Aerospace] (AAG) ...... GS
Ground Station Control (SSD) ...... GSC
Ground Station Data ...... GSD
Ground Station Modules [Communications] [Army] ...... GSM
Ground Stub-Up Connection [Aerospace] (AAG) ...... GSUC
Ground Studies Group [Military] (VNW) ...... GSG
Ground Subsystem Evaluation Facility [Army] (RDA) ...... GSEF
Ground Support Engineering Change Proposal [Aerospace] (AAG) ...... GSECP
Ground Support Equipment [Aviation] ...... GSE
Ground Support Equipment Division [Naval Air Engineering Center] ...... GSED
Ground Support Equipment End Item [Military] ...... GSEEI
Ground Support Equipment Illustration [Military] (MCD) ...... GSEI
Ground Support Equipment Illustration Data [Military] (MCD) ...... GSEID
Ground Support Equipment List [NASA] (NASA) ...... GSEL
Ground Support Equipment Recommendation Data [Military] (MCD) ...... GSERD
Ground Support Equipment Statistical Display (DNAB) ...... GSESD
Ground Support Equipment-Base Installation [Aviation] (SAA) ...... GSE-BI
Ground Support Equipment-Maintenance Equipment [Aviation] (SAA) .... GSE-ME
Ground Support Equipment-Maintenance Facility [Aviation] (SAA) ...... GSE-MF
Ground Support Equipment-Mechanical [Aviation] (SAA) ...... GSE-M
Ground Support Equipment-Strategic System [Aviation] (SAA) ...... GSE-SS
Ground Support Equipment-Structure [Aviation] (SAA) ...... GSE-S
Ground Support Equipment-System and Service [Aviation] (SAA) ...... GSE-SS
Ground Support Equipment-Systems Specification (IAA) ...... GSE-SS
Ground Support Equipment-Test Stand [Aviation] (SAA) ...... GSE-TS
Ground Support Equipment-Transportation and Handling [Aviation] (SAA) ...... GSE-T & H
Ground Support Equipment-Weapon System Requirement [Aviation] (SAA) ...... GSE-WSR
Ground Support Facilities [Later, MGE] [Aerospace] (AAG) ...... GSF
Ground Support Fighter (MCD) ...... GSF
Ground Support Maintenance (MCD) ...... GSM
Ground Support Maintenance Equipment [Aerospace] ...... GSME
Ground Support Office [or Officer] [Military] (AFIT) ...... GSO
Ground Support Operations [Aerospace] (MCD) ...... GSO
Ground Support Rocket System (DWSG) ...... GSRS

Ground Support Simulation Computer [*Aerospace*] (KSC) .... GSSC
Ground Support Software [*NASA*] (NASA) .... GSS
Ground Support System [*Aerospace*] (AAG) .... GSS
Ground Support System Integration (MCD) .... GSSI
Ground Support System Review [*Aerospace*] (AAG) .... GSSR
Ground Support System Specification [*Aerospace*] (AAG) .... GSSS
Ground Support Systems Activation [*NASA*] (NASA) .... GSSA
Ground Support Systems Contractor [*NASA*] (NASA) .... GSSC
Ground Support Verification Plan [*NASA*] (NASA) .... GSVP
Ground Surface (IAA) .... GS
Ground Surface Temperature .... GST
Ground Surveillance and Target Acquisition [*Military*] (MCD) .... GSTA
Ground Surveillance Qualification Course [*Army*] .... GSQC
Ground Surveillance RADAR .... GSR
Ground Surveillance RADAR System .... GSRS
Ground Swell .... G
Ground System (MCD) .... GS
Ground System Test [*NASA*] (NASA) .... GST
Ground System Test Procedure (IAA) .... GSTP
Ground System Validation Test (MCD) .... GSVT
Ground Systems Coordination Group .... GSCG
Ground Systems Group [*Hughes Aircraft Co.*] .... GSG
Ground Systems Laboratory .... GSL
Ground Systems Operations (MCD) .... GSO
Ground Systems Test Flow [*NASA*] (NASA) .... GSTF
Ground Takeoff and Landing (AAG) .... GTOL
Ground Target Detection .... GTD
Ground Target Marking System .... GTMS
Ground Team (MCD) .... GT
Ground Team Manager (MCD) .... GTM
Ground Telecommunication Equipment .... GTE
Ground Telemetry Subsystem .... GTS
Ground Terminal Operations Support (SSD) .... GTOS
Ground Terminal System .... GTS
Ground Test [*NASA*] (KSC) .... GNT
Ground Test [*NASA*] (NASA) .... GT
Ground Test Access (MCD) .... GTA
Ground Test and Acceptance [*NASA*] (NASA) .... GT & A
Ground Test Article [*NASA*] (NASA) .... GTA
Ground Test Conductor (MCD) .... GTC
Ground Test Equipment .... GTE
Ground Test Instrumentation (MCD) .... GTI
Ground Test Missile .... GTM
Ground Test Motor (MCD) .... GTM
Ground Test Plan (MCD) .... GTP
Ground Test Plan Summary Sheets (MCD) .... GTPSS
Ground Test Reactor [*Air Force*] .... GTR
Ground Test Station .... GTS
Ground Test Unit .... GTU
Ground Test Vehicle (KSC) .... GTV
Ground Thermal Conditioning Unit [*NASA*] (NASA) .... GTCU
Ground Tilt Isolation Platform .... GTIP
Ground Timing Generator (IAA) .... GTG
Ground to Slant (MCD) .... G/S
Ground Torquing Assembly (MCD) .... GTA
Ground Track .... GT
Ground Track Plotter .... GTP
Ground Tracking System (MCD) .... GRTS
Ground Tracking System (MCD) .... GTS
Ground Training Aid [*Aerospace*] (AAG) .... GTA
Ground Training Engine [*Military*] (AFIT) .... GTE
Ground Training System (MCD) .... GTS
Ground Transmit (AFM) .... GT
Ground Transport Equipment (KSC) .... GTE
Ground Transport Express [*Airport baggage computer*] .... GTX
Ground Transport Vehicle .... GTV
Ground Transportation Services [*MTMC*] (TAG) .... GTS
Ground Umbilical Carrier Plate (MCD) .... GUCP
Ground under Repair .... GUR
Ground Up-to-Space (MCD) .... GUTS
Ground/Vehicle Laser Locator Designation [*Homing device*] (NITA) .... G/VLLD
Ground Vehicle Mine Dispensing System [*Military*] .... GVMDS
Ground/Vehicular LASER Locator Designator (RDA) .... G/VLLD
Ground Vehicular LASER Locator Designator [*Military*] .... G/VLL-D
Ground Velocity (GAVI) .... VGND
Ground Vibration Survey [*Aerospace*] .... GVS
Ground Vibration Test [*Aerospace*] (MCD) .... GVT
Ground Vibration Test Article [*Aerospace*] (NASA) .... GVTA
Ground Visibility .... GV
Ground Water Council [*Defunct*] .... GWC
Ground Water for Windows [*Computer program*] .... GWW
Ground Water Institute [*Defunct*] (EA) .... GWI
Ground Water Management District .... GWMD
Ground Water Monitor [*A publication*] .... GWM
Ground Water Monitoring .... GWM
Ground Water Monitoring Review [*A publication*] .... GWMR
Ground Water Policy and Management Staff [*Environmental Protection Agency*] (GFGA) .... GWPMS
Ground Water Protection Standard [*Environmental Protection Agency*] (GFGA) .... GWPS
Ground Water Protection Strategy [*Environmental Protection Agency*] (GFGA) .... GPS
Ground Water Resources Institute [*Later, Ground Water Council*] .... GWRI
Ground Wave Emergency Network .... GWEN
Ground Wave Emergency Network .... GWEN

Ground Wave Over-the-Horizon RADAR (DNAB) .... GWOTH
Ground Waves (NATG) .... GW
Ground Wind Vortex Sensing System [*Aviation*] (DA) .... GWVSS
Ground Winds Data Reduction System [*NASA*] .... GWDRS
Ground Winds Tower [*NASA*] (NASA) .... GWT
Ground Wireless Station (IAA) .... GWSTN
Ground Zero [*Atomic detonation*] .... GZ
Ground Zero [*An association*] (EA) .... GZ
Ground Zero [*Nevada*] [*Seismograph station code, US Geological Survey Closed*] (SEIS) .... GZN
Ground Zero [*Nevada*] [*Seismograph station code, US Geological Survey Closed*] (SEIS) .... ZOX
Ground Zero Pairing Project (EA) .... GZPP
Ground Zero Resource Center [*Defunct*] (EA) .... GZRC
Ground Zero Tape Read (IAA) .... GZTPRD
Ground-Aided Acquisition .... GAA
Ground-Air Telerobotic Systems [*Marine Corps*] (DOMA) .... GATERS
Ground-Based Common Sensor .... GBCS
Ground-Based Computer .... GBC
Ground-Based Electronic Omnidirectional Satellite Communications Antenna .... GEOSCAN
Ground-based Electro-Optical Deep Space Surveillance (DICI) .... GEODES
Ground-Based Electro-Optical Deep Space Surveillance [*Satellite-tracking network*] .... GEODSS
Ground-Based Field .... GBF
Ground-Based Hypervelocity Rail Gun [*Military*] (SDI) .... GBHRG
Ground-Based Infrared Instrumentation .... GBII
Ground-Based Infrared Instrumentation System .... GBIIS
Ground-Based Interceptor [*Army*] (DOMA) .... GBI
Ground-Based Interceptor-Experiment [*US Army Strategic Defense Command*] (RDA) .... GBI-X
Ground-Based LASER (MCD) .... GBL
Ground-Based Measurement (MCD) .... GBM
Ground-Based Midcourse Interceptor [*Military*] (SDI) .... GBMI
Ground-Based RADAR [*Military*] .... GBR
Ground-Based RADAR Project Office [*Military*] (RDA) .... GBR-PO
Ground-Based RADAR Prototype [*Military*] .... GBR-P
Ground-Based Radiometer .... GBR
Ground-Based Scanner .... GBS
Ground-Based Scanning Antenna System (IAA) .... GBSAS
Ground-Based Software (MCD) .... GBS
Ground-Based Surface-to-Air .... GSA
Ground-Based Surveillance and Tracking System (MCD) .... GSTS
Ground-Based Telemetry .... GBT
Ground-Based Traffic Information System [*Aviation*] (DA) .... GTIS
Groundbirch Museum, British Columbia [*Library symbol National Library of Canada*] (NLC) .... BGRM
Groundbirch Museum, Groundbirch, BC, Canada [*Library symbol*] [*Library of Congress*] (LCLS) .... CaBGRM
Ground-Control Bombing System (NG) .... GCBS
Ground-Control Center .... GCC
Ground-Control Checkout (MCD) .... GCCO
Ground-Control Computer Center (MCD) .... GCCC
Ground-Control Equipment .... GCE
Ground-Control Intercept Squadron .... GCIS
Ground-Control Intercept Training [*Navy*] (ANA) .... GCITING
Ground-Control Intercept Training (NVT) .... GCITNG
Ground-Control Interface Logic (MCD) .... GCIL
Ground-Control Interface Logic Controller (MCD) .... GCILC
Ground-Control Interface Logic Unit (MCD) .... GCILU
Ground-Control Landing .... GCL
Ground-Control Message (MCD) .... GCM
Ground-Control Message Request (MCD) .... GCMR
Ground-Control Network [*NASA*] (NASA) .... GCN
Ground-Control Operational Equipment (IAA) .... GCOE
Ground-Control Station (MCD) .... GCS
Ground-Control Unit (AAG) .... GCU
Ground-Controlled Aircraft (AFM) .... GCA
Ground-Controlled Apparatus [*RADAR*] .... GCA
Ground-Controlled Approach [*for lateral and vertical guidance of landing aircraft through use of ground RADAR and radio communications*] .... GCA
Ground-Controlled Approach - Controller Training System (MCD) .... GCA-CTS
Ground-Controlled Intercept/Air Defense Center (DNAB) .... GCI/ADC
Ground-Controlled Interception [*RADAR*] .... GCI
Ground-Controlled RADAR .... GCR
Ground-Controlled Space System .... GCSS
Groundcrew Liquid Cooling System .... GCLCS
Ground-Detonated Flares [*Military*] (INF) .... GND
Grounded [*Electronics*] .... G
Grounded [*Electricity*] [*Electronics*] .... GND
Grounded Base .... GB
Grounded Cathode Amplifier .... GCA
Grounded Collector .... GC
Grounded Current Unity-Gain Amplifier .... GCUGA
Grounded Emitter .... GE
Grounded Grid [*Valve*] (DEN) .... GG
Grounded Grid Amplifier .... GGA
Grounded into Double Plays [*Baseball*] .... GDP
Grounded into Double Plays [*Baseball*] .... GIDP
Grounded Kathode Amplifier .... GKA
Grounded - Not Operationally Ready Maintenance (MCD) .... G-NORM
Grounded - Not Operationally Ready Supply (MCD) .... G-NORS
Grounded Plate Amplifier .... GPA
Grounded Surface Distribution Apparatus (IAA) .... GSDA
Grounded Unity Gain Amplifier (IAA) .... GUGA

Grounded Voltage Unity-Gain Amplifier (PDAA) .... GVUGA
Ground-Emplaced Seismic Intrusion Detector (NVT) .... GSID
Ground-Fault Interrupter (IDOE) .... gfi
Ground-Fault Warning (IEEE) .... GFW
Ground-LASER Attack Designator/Identification System (MCD) .... GLADIS
Ground-LASER Designators (RDA) .... GLD
Ground-LASER Locator Designator (MCD) .... GLLD
Ground-LASER Locator Designator/Vehicular LASER Locator Designator (MCD) .... GLLD/VLLD
Ground-LASER Locator Designator-Evaluator (MCD) .... GLLD-E
Ground-LASER Locator Designator-Thermal Night Sight (MCD) .... GLLD-TNS
Ground-LASER Tracking .... GLT
Ground-Launch Support System (MCD) .... GLSS
Ground-Launched Ballistic Missile .... GLBM
Ground-Launched Cruise Missile [*Pronounced "glick-em"*] .... GLCM
Ground-Launched HELLFIRE System (MCD) .... GLHS
Ground-Level Attack, Reconnaissance, and Electronic Countermeasures (MCD) .... GLARE
Ground-Level Event [*Geophysics*] .... GLE
Groundnut Chlorotic Spot Virus .... GCSV
Groundnut Eyespot Virus .... GEV
Groundnut Meal (PDAA) .... GN
Ground-Penetrating RADAR .... GPR
Ground-Protective [*Relay*] .... GP
Ground-Received Times [*Solar wind measurements*] .... GRT
Ground-Receiving and Analog Ranging Equipment [*AFSCF*] (MCD) .... GRARE
Grounds (DD) .... Grnds
Grounds and Maxims of English Law, by William Noye [*A publication*] (DLA) .... Noye
Ground-Speed Continuing [*Aviation*] .... GSC
Ground-Speed Drift Angle [*Aviation*] (NG) .... GSDA
Ground-Speed Indicator [*Aviation*] (MCD) .... GSI
Ground-Speed Oscillator [*Aviation*] .... GSO
Ground-Speed Returning [*Aviation*] .... GSR
Groundstar Resources Ltd. [*Vancouver Stock Exchange symbol*] .... GSA
Ground-to-Air [*Communications, weapons*] (MSA) .... G-A
Ground-to-Air Broadcast Network .... GABN
Ground-to-Air Communications (MCD) .... G/A COMM
Ground-to-Air Cycle .... GTAC
Ground-to-Air Data Link .... GADL
Ground-to-Air Missile (AAG) .... GAM
Ground-to-Air Missile (RDA) .... GTAM
Ground-to-Air Pilotless Aircraft [*Early US test missiles*] .... GAPA
Ground-to-Air Scanner Surveillance .... GRASS
Ground-to-Air Transmitter .... GAT
Ground-to-Air Transmitter Gate (MCD) .... GAT
Ground-to-Air Transmitter Terminal .... GATT
Ground-to-Air Transmitting-Receiving [*Station*] .... GATR
Ground-to-Air-to-Ground [*Aviation*] .... GAG
Ground-to-Air-to-Ground Data Terminal [*Air Force*] (MCD) .... GAGDT
Ground-to-Ground (IDOE) .... G/G
Ground-to-Ground [*Communications, weapons, etc.*] (MSA) .... G-G
Ground-to-Ground [*Communications, weapons, etc.*] .... GTG
Ground-to-Ground Missile .... GGM
Ground-to-Surface Vessel [*RADAR*] (NATG) .... GSV
Ground-Tree Foraging [*Ecology*] .... GT
Groundwater (EPA) .... GW
Groundwater Activated Carbon (EPA) .... GAC
Groundwater Database .... GWDB
Groundwater Level [*Hydrology*] (IAA) .... GWL
Groundwater Management Caucus (EA) .... GMC
Groundwater Management Districts Association (EA) .... GMDA
Groundwater Modeling Program [*US Army Engineer Waterways Experiment Station*] (RDA) .... GMP
Groundwater Modeling System .... GMS
Groundwater Pumping Incentives Scheme [*Victoria*] (EERA) .... GPIS
Groundwater Residue Guidance Level [*Environmental Protection Agency*] .... GRGL
Groundwater Supply Survey (GNE) .... GWSS
Groundwater Technology, Inc. [*Associated Press*] (SAG) .... Grdwtr
Groundwater Technology, Inc. [*NASDAQ symbol*] (NQ) .... GWTI
Groundwater Vistas [*Computer science*] .... GV
Groundwater Vistas .... GV
Groundwater Working Group [*Australia*] .... GWG
Groundwork for a Just World (EA) .... GW
Group .... G
Group (AFM) .... GP
Group (VRA) .... gp
Group .... GR
Group (WDMC) .... gr
Group (WGA) .... GRO
Group (KSC) .... GRP
Group (DD) .... grp
Group .... GRP
Group .... GRU
Group 1 Software [*NASDAQ symbol*] (TTSB) .... GSOF
Group 1 Software, Inc. [*Associated Press*] (SAG) .... Groupl
Group 1 Software, Inc. [*NASDAQ symbol*] (NQ) .... GSOF
Group A Beta-Hemolytic Streptococcus [*Pathology*] .... GABHS
Group A Streptococci [*Medicine*] .... GAS
Group Access Capabilities [*Library automation*] .... GAC
Group Action Request Lists .... GARL
Group Adjustment Therapy [*Psychology*] (DAVI) .... GAT
Group Against Smokers' Pollution (EA) .... GASP
Group and Pension Marketing Conference [*LIMRA*] .... GPMC
Group Announcement Bulletin [*Defense Documentation Center*] .... GAB
Group Armaments Officer [*British military*] (DMA) .... GArmO
Group Assembly Parts List (MCD) .... GAPL
Group Assembly Provisioning List (MCD) .... GAPL
Group Atmosphere (PDAA) .... GA
Group Attainment Program .... GAP
Group B Beta-Hemolytic Streptococcus [*Bacteriology*] (DAVI) .... GBBHS
Group B Beta-Hemolytic Streptococcus [*Medicine*] (MEDA) .... GBBS
Group B Streptococci [*Medicine*] .... GBS
Group Busy Hour [*Telecommunications*] (TEL) .... GBH
Group Capacity Analysis [*or Assessment*] .... GCA
Group Captain [*British military*] (DMA) .... G/Capt
Group Captain .... GC
Group Captain [*British military*] (DMA) .... Gp Capt
Group Captain [*British military*] (DMA) .... Gr Capt
Group Captain [*British military*] (DMA) .... Grp Capt
Group Carry Look-Ahead (MHDI) .... GCLA
Group Catering Officer [*British military*] (DMA) .... GCatO
Group Change Control .... GCC
Group Claims Processing System [*McAuto*] .... GCPS
Group Climate Questionnaire [*Occupational therapy*] .... GCQ
Group Code [*Dialog*] [*Searchable field*] [*Information service or system*] (NITA) .... GC
Group Code Recording [*Data storage method*] (NITA) .... GCR
Group Coded Recording [*Computer science*] (BUR) .... GCR
Group Cohesiveness [*Psychological testing*] .... GC
Group Commander [*Military*] (WDAA) .... GP CMDR
Group Commander .... GRUCOM
Group Conformity Rating (DMAA) .... GCR
Group Contribution Equation of State .... GCEOS
Group Control Center (MCD) .... GCC
Group D Nonenterococcal Streptococcus [*Bacteriology*] (DAVI) .... DNE
Group Delay Distortion (LAIN) .... GD
Group Delay Response (IAA) .... GDR
Group Dimensions Descriptions Questionnaire [*Psychology*] .... GDDQ
Group Display Device (MCD) .... GDD
Group Display Generator .... GDG
Group Distributing Frames .... GDF
Group Distribution Frame [*Telecommunications*] (NITA) .... GDF
Group Education Officer [*British military*] (DMA) .... GEdO
Group Embedded Figure Test [*Education*] .... GEFT
Group Employment Plan (MCD) .... GEP
Group Encoded Recording (NITA) .... GCR
Group Encounter Survey .... GES
Group Engineer .... GE
Group Environment Scale [*Personality development test*] [*Psychology*] .... GES
Group Equipment Staff Officer [*British military*] (DMA) .... GESO
Group European d'Echange d'Experience sur la Direction de la Recherche Textil e [*European Group for the Exchange of Information on Textile Research*] (PDAA) .... GEDRT
Group Feedback Analysis .... GFA
Group Final Selector (IAA) .... GFS
Group Finance Department .... GFD
Group Fire Distribution Center [*Army*] (AABC) .... GFDC
Group Flashing [*Navigation signal lights*] .... GPFL
Group Flashing Light [*Navigation*] (IAA) .... GPFLL
Group for Aquatic Primary Productivity [*ICSU*] .... GAP
Group for Environmental Education .... GEE
Group for Lunar Exploration and Planning (MCD) .... GLEP
Group for Technical Coordination [*Marine science*] (MSC) .... GTC
Group for the Advancement of Psychiatry (EA) .... GAP
Group for the European Unitarian Left [*EC*] (ECED) .... GUE
Group for the Standardization of Information Services (NITA) .... GSIS
Group for the Study of Irish Historic Settlement [*British*] .... GSIHS
Group for the Use of Psychology in History (EA) .... GUPH
Group Fore Golf Foundation (EA) .... GFGF
Group Fore - Women's Pro Golf Tour (EA) .... WPGT
Group Fuel Injection [*Automotive engineering*] .... GFI
Group Gross Assets (ADA) .... GGA
Group Health Association of America (EA) .... GHAA
Group Health Cooperative (DMAA) .... GHC
Group Health Cooperative of Puget Sound, Kathleen Hill Library, Seattle, WA [*Library symbol*] [*Library of Congress*] (LCLS) .... WaSGH-H
Group Health Cooperative of Puget Sound, Medical Library, Seattle, WA [*Library symbol Library of Congress*] (LCLS) .... WaSGH
Group Health, Inc., St. Paul, MN [*Library symbol Library of Congress*] (LCLS) .... MnSGH
Group Health Insurance [*British*] .... GHI
Group Health Service (GHCT) .... GHS
Group Inclusive Tour [*Airline fare*] .... GIT
Group Index (MCD) .... GRIND
Group Individual Retirement Account .... GIRA
Group Information Centre, Alcan Aluminum Ltd. [*Centre d'Information du Groupe, Alcan Aluminium Ltee*] **Montreal, Quebec** [*Library symbol National Library of Canada*] (NLC) .... QMA
Group Insurance .... GI
Group Intelligence Officer [*British military*] (DMA) .... GIO
Group Interaction Analysis .... GIA
Group Inventory for Finding Creative Talent [*Educational test*] .... GIFT
Group Inventory for Finding Interests [*Educational test*] .... GIFFI
Group Investment-Linked (ADA) .... GIL
Group Junction (MCD) .... GJ
Group Learning about Drugs .... GLAD
Group Legal Review [*A publication*] (DLA) .... Group Legal Rev
Group Life Assurance [*British*] .... GLA

Group Mark [*Computer science*] .... GM
Group Mark/Word Mark [*Computer science*] (OA) .... GM/WM
Group Medical Report .... GMR
Group Membership Scores [*Psychometrics*] .... GMS
Group Meteorological Officer [*British military*] (DMA) .... GMetO
Group Method of Data Handling [*Mathematical technique*] .... GMDH
Group Method of Determining Arguments [*Equation*] .... GMDA
Group Mobile (CINC) .... GM
Group MODEM (MCD) .... GM
Group Modulation Equipment (IAA) .... GME
Group Navigation Officer [*British military*] (DMA) .... GNavO
Group Number [*Dialog*] [*Searchable fields*] [*Information service or system*] (NITA) .... GN
Group Number No Count [*Military communication*] .... GRNC
Group Occulting Lights [*Navigation signal*] .... GPOCC
Group Occupancy Meter [*Telecommunications*] (NITA) .... GOM
Group of 24 [*A clearinghouse for monetary aid to Eastern Europe*] (ECON) G24
Group of 77 [*Coalition of environmentalists representing developing countries*] G-77
Group of Ancient Drama .... GOAD
Group of Association of Manufacturers of British Instrumentation, Control and Automation (ECII) .... GAMBICA
Group of Association of Manufacturers of British, Instruments, Control and Automation (ACII) .... GAMBICA
Group of Economic Experts (EERA) .... GEE
Group of Eight [*Nations*] (EERA) G-8
Group of European Metallurgical Thermodynamicists [*National Physical Laboratory*] [*Databank*] (NITA) .... GEMT
Group of Experts (NATG) .... GE
Group of Experts on Environmental Pollutants (EERA) .... GEEP
Group of Experts on Long-Term Scientific Policy and Planning [*UNESCO*] .... GELTSPAP
Group of Experts on Marine Information Management [*Marine science*] (OSRA) .... GEMIM
Group of Experts on Methods, Standards, and Intercalibration [*Oceanography*] (MSC) .... GEMSI
Group of Experts on Ocean Processes and Climate [*Marine science*] (OSRA) .... GE-OPC
Group of Experts on the Global Sea-Level Observing System [*Marine science*] (OSRA) .... GE-GLOSS
Group of Experts on the Scientific Aspects of Marine Environmental Protection [*Marine science*] (OSRA) .... GESAMP
Group of Experts on the Scientific Aspects of Marine Pollution [*ICSU*] (EAIO) .... GESAMP
Group of Five [*United States, Japan, West Germany, France, and Britain*] G5
Group of Fourteen [*NATO countries minus France*] (NATG) .... GF
Group of Latin American and Caribbean Sugar Exporting Countries [*See also GEPLACEA*] [*Mexico City, Mexico*] (EAIO) .... GLACSEC
Group of Mathematicians of Romance Languages [*See also GMEL*] [*Coimbra, Portugal*] (EAIO) .... GMRL
Group of National Travel Agents' Associations within the EEC (EAIO) .... ECTAA
Group of Negotiations on Services [*European Community*] .... GNS
Group of Officials on Biotechnology Regulation (EERA) .... GOBR
Group of Paths (SAA) .... GOP
Group of Pictures [*Computer science*] .... GOP
Group of Scientific Experts .... GSE
Group of Seven [*United States, Japan, West Germany, France, Britain, Italy, and Canada*] G-7
Group of Soviet Forces .... GSF
Group of Soviet Forces in Germany (MCD) .... GSF
Group of Soviet Forces in Germany (NATG) .... GSFG
Group of Specialists on Environmental Affairs and Conservation (EERA) .... GOSEAC
Group of Ten [*Nations*] (EERA) G-10
Group of Ten [*United States, Japan, West Germany, France, Britain, Italy, Canada, Sweden, Holland, Belgium, and Switzerland*] [*There are actually eleven member countries*] G10
Group of Thirty [*Financial think-tank*] (ECON) G30
Group of Units of Analysis [*Medicine*] (DMAA) .... GUA
Group Officer [*British military*] (DMA) .... GO
Group Officer [*British military*] (DMA) .... Gp Offr
Group on Electronic Devices .... GED
Group One, Inc. [*FAA designator*] (FAAC) .... TXT
Group Operating Services (NRCH) .... GOS
Group Operational Access Tester System [*AT & T*] .... GOATS
Group, Operations Analysis [*Air Force*] (MCD) .... GOA
Group Operations Center (NATG) .... GOC
Group Operations Instruction [*British military*] (DMA) .... GOI
Group Operations Order [*British military*] (DMA) .... GOO
Group Pacific .... GROPAC
Group per Message (IAA) .... GM
Group Personality Projective Test [*Psychology*] .... GPPT
Group Practice Association [*Medicine*] .... GPA
Group Practice Health Maintenance Organization [*Insurance*] (WYGK) .... GPHMO
Group Processing Logic (TEL) .... GPL
Group Project for Holocaust Survivors and Their Children (EA) .... GPHSC
Group Projective Test [*Psychology*] (BARN) .... GPT
Group Propogate / Zero Detect (MHDI) .... PG/ZD
Group Psychotherapy Suitability Evaluation Scale [*Psychology*] .... SES
Group Rapid Transit [*TRB*] (TAG) .... GRT
Group Reference Pilot [*Telecommunications*] (TEL) .... GRP
Group Regiment Officer [*British military*] (DMA) .... GRegO
Group Registration for Contributions to Periodicals [*US Copyright Office form*] .... GR/CP
Group Relations Ongoing Workshops .... GROW
Group Relations Training Association (AIE) .... GRTA
Group Repetition Frequency .... GRF
Group Repetition Interval (IEEE) .... GRI
Group Report .... GR
Group Room Availability Bank [*Sheraton Corp.*] .... GRAB
Group Routing and Charging Equipment [*British*] .... GRACE
Group Sail [*Navy*] (NVT) .... GRUSL
Group Sales Representative [*Health insurance*] (GHCT) .... GSR
Group Scout Master [*Scouting*] .... GSM
Group Select Panel (ECII) .... GSP
Group Selective Register .... GSR
Group Selector [*Telecommunications*] (TEL) .... GS
Group Selector Long Distance [*Telecommunications*] (IAA) .... GSLD
Group Selector of Secondary Long Distance [*Telecommunications*] (IAA) .... GSSLD
Group Separator [*Computer science*] .... GS
Group Shorr Imagery Test [*Personality development test*] [*Psychology*] .... GSIT
Group Signals Officer [*British military*] (DMA) .... GSigsO
Group Simplified Perturbed Hard Chain Theory [*Equation of state*] .... GSPHCT
Group Specific [*Antigen*] [*Immunology*] .... gs
Group Structured [*Counseling group*] .... GS
Group Study Course .... GSC
Group Support Equipment .... GSE
Group Support Equipment-Support Equipment [*Aviation*] (SAA) .... GSE-SE
Group Switching Center [*British Telecommunications*] (TEL) .... GSC
Group Switching Subsystem (ACRL) .... GSS
Group Talk Microphone .... GTM
Group Technologies [*NASDAQ symbol*] (TTSB) .... GRTK
Group Technologies Corp. [*Associated Press*] (SAG) .... GrpTech
Group Technologies Corp. [*NASDAQ symbol*] (SAG) .... GRTK
Group Technology .... GT
Group Technology Characterization Code (IAA) .... GTCC
Group Technology System (MCD) .... GTS
Group Teleconferencing System [*Telecommunications*] .... GTS
Group Tensions [*Medicine*] (DMAA) .... GT
Group Test Equipment Assembly .... GTEA
Group Therapy .... GpTh
Group Therapy .... GT
Group Timing Technique [*Industrial engineering*] .... GTT
Group to Establish Criteria for Certifying Munitions Systems to Electromagnetic Fields [*DoD*] (RDA) .... GECCMSEF
Group Training Association [*British*] (DCTA) .... GTA
Group Training Command [*Air Force British*] .... GTC
Group Training Company .... GTC
Group Transformation .... GT
Group Translating Equipment .... GTE
Group Unit Simulator (MCD) .... GUS
Group Universal Life Policy [*Insurance*] (DFIT) .... GULP
Group Universal Life Program .... GULP
Group Value Engineering .... GVE
Group Velocity [*Physics*] (IAA) .... GV
Group Velocity [*Symbol*] (DEN) .... u
Group View Display (MCD) .... GVD
Group Visionary Productions, Inc. [*Studio City, CA*] [*Telecommunications*] (TSSD) .... GVP
Group Weapons Staff Officer [*British military*] (DMA) .... GWpSO
Group Work (MAE) .... GW
Groupe AB SA [*NYSE symbol*] (SAG) .... ABG
Groupe AB SA [*Associated Press*] (SAG) .... Groupe
Groupe Consultatif International de Recherche sur le Colza [*International Consultative Research Group on Rape Seed*] (EAIO) .... GCIRC
Groupe d'Action Revolutionnaire Internationaliste [*International Revolutionary Action Group*] [*France Political party*] (PD) .... GARI
Groupe d'Analyse Macroeconomique Appliquee [*Group for Applied Macroeconomic Analysis*] [*University of Paris - Nanterre*] [*Information service or system*] (IID) .... GAMA
Groupe de Chasse [*French aircraft fighter unit*] [*World War II*] .... GC
Groupe de Contact Parlementaire et Scientifique [*European Parliamentary and Scientific Contact Group*] (EA) .... EPSCG
Groupe de Liaison de Docimologues en Milieu Scolaire [*Canada*] .... GLDMS
Groupe de Liberation Armee [*Armed Liberation Group*] [*Guadeloupe*] (PD) .... GLA
Groupe de Paris [*France*] (EAIO) .... GP
Groupe de Planification des Derives Urbaines [*Canada*] .... GPDU
Groupe de Recherche en Developpement de l'Est du Quebec [*Canada*] .... GRIDEQ
Groupe de Recherche en Enseignement Individualise [*Canada*] .... GREI
Groupe de Recherche en Semantique, Lexicologie, et Terminologie [*Universite de Montreal, Quebec*] [*Canada*] .... GRESLET
Groupe de Recherche et d'Echange Multidisciplinaires Feministes [*Universite Laval, Quebec*] [*Canada*] .... GREMF
Groupe de Recherche et d'Intervention en Ideologie [*Universite du Quebec a Montreal*] [*Canada*] .... GRI
Groupe de Recherche et d'Intervention Regionales [*Universite du Quebec a Chicoutimi*] [*Canada*] .... GRIR
Groupe de Recherche et d'Intervention sur les Systemes d'Activities Humaines [*University of Quebec at Rimouski*] [*Research center*] (RCD) .... GRISAH
Groupe de Recherche Interdisciplinaire en Sante [*Interdisciplinary Health Research Group - IHRG*] [*Universite de Montreal*] [*Canada*] [*Research center*] .... GRIS
Groupe de Recherche sur la Demographie Quebecoise [*Research Group on Quebec Demography*] [*Canada*] (IRC) .... GRDQ
Groupe de Recherche sur l'Efficacite Organisationnelle [*University of Quebec at Hull*] [*Research center*] (RCD) .... GREFICOR
Groupe de Recherche sur les Attitudes Envers la Criminalite [*Canada*] .... GRAC

Groupe de Recherche sur les Insectes Piqueurs [*University of Quebec at Trois-Rivieres*] [*Canada Research center*] (RCD) ..... GRIP
Groupe de Recherches Interdisciplinaires des Fertilisation des Forets [*Joint federal-provincial project*] [*Canada*] ..... GRIFF
Groupe de Recherches pour la Traduction Automatique [*Universite de Montreal*] [*Canada Research center*] ..... TAUM
Groupe de Recherches pour les Transports au Canada [*Canadian Transportation Research Forum*] ..... GRTC
Groupe de Travail Charge de la Mise en Oeuvre de l'Information et de la Statistique Juridique [*Implementation Work Group on Justice Information and Statistics - IWG*] [*Canada*] ..... GMO
Groupe de Travail Inter Agences sur l'Afrique Australe [*Inter-Agency Working Group on Southern Africa - IAWGSA*] [*Canadian Council for International Cooperation*] ..... GTAA
Groupe de Travail sur la Gestion de l'Energie dans les Etablissements d'Enseignement Post-Secondaire [*Postsecondary Education Task Force on Energy Management PETFEM*] [*Canada*] ..... GTGEEEPS
Groupe des Communications Informatiques [*Computer Communications Group*] [*Canada*] ..... GCI
Groupe des Democrates Patriotes [*Burkina Faso*] [*Political party*] (EY) ..... GDP
Groupe des Editeurs de Livres de la CEE [*Book Publishers Group of EEC*] (EAIO) ..... GELC
Groupe des Sept pour la Cooperation du Secteur Prive Europeen avec l'Afrique, les Caribes et le Pacific [*Group of Seven for European Private Sector Cooperation with Africa, the Caribbean, and the Pacific*] (EAIO) ..... ACP
Groupe d'Etude des Ressources Maritimes [*Universite du Quebec a Rimouski*] [*Canada Research center*] ..... GERMA
Groupe d'Etude en Regulation Metabolique [*University of Quebec at Rimouski*] [*Research center*] (RCD) ..... GERME
Groupe d'Etudes en Developpement International [*International Development Studies Group*] [*Canada*] ..... GEDI
Groupe d'Etudes en Developpement International [*International Development Studies Group*] [*Canada*] ..... GREDI
Groupe d'Etudes et d'Actions Urbaines [*Canada*] ..... GEAU
Groupe d'Etudes International pour l'Utilization de Profils Creux dans la Construction [*International Study Group on the Use of Hollow Sections in Construction*] [*Switzerland*] (PDAA) ..... GIPEC
Groupe d'Etudes Politiques Europeennes (EA) ..... GEPE
Groupe d'Etudes Sartriennes (EAIO) ..... GES
Groupe d'Information et de Soutien des Travailleurs Immigres [*Information and Support Group for Immigrant Workers*] [*France*] (EAIO) ..... GISTI
Groupe DMR, Inc., Montreal, Quebec [*Library symbol National Library of Canada*] (BIB) ..... QMDMR
Groupe d'Union Camerounaise [*Group for Cameroonian Union*] ..... GUC
Groupe Europeen d'Administration Publique [*European Group of Public Administration - EGPA*] [*Brussels, Belgium*] (EAIO) ..... GEAP
Groupe Europeen de Recherches Gazieres [*European Gas Research Group*] (EAIO) ..... GERG
Groupe Europeen des Femmes Diplomees des Universites [*University Women of Europe - UWE*] (EA) ..... GEFDU
Groupe Hygiene Naturelle [*European Natural Hygiene Society - ENHS*] (EAIO) ..... GHN
Groupe Interdisciplinaire de Recherche pour l'Amelioration des Situations de Travail [*University of Quebec at Rimouski*] [*Canada Research center*] (RCD) ..... GIRAST
Groupe Interdisciplinaire de Recherche Scientifique et Appliquee en Terminologie [*INFOTERM*] ..... GIRSTERM
Groupe International de Recherches sur la Preservation du Bois [*Sweden*] (EAIO) ..... GIRPB
Groupe International de Sociologie (EAIO) ..... CISC
Groupe International des Ressources Genetiques Vegetales [*International Board for Plant Genetic Resources - IBPGR*] (EA) ..... GIRGV
Groupe International Hachette [*France*] ..... GIH
Groupe International Laicat et Communaute Chretienne [*International Laity and Christian Community Group - ILCCG*] [*Defunct*] (EA) ..... LAECC
Groupe International Postal d'Echanges d'Information et d'Experience [*International Group for the Exchange of Information and Experience Among Postal Savings Institutions*] (EAIO) ..... GIE VI
Groupe International Postal d'Echanges d'Information et d'Experience [*International Group for the Exchange of Information and Experience among Postal Savings Institutions - IGEIEPSI*] (EAIO) ..... GIPEIE
Groupe Internationale des Importateur du Gaz Natural Liquefie ..... GIIGNL
Groupe Interuniversitaire des Recherches Oceanographiques du Quebec [*Interuniversity Group for Oceanographic Research of Quebec*] [*Laval University*] [*Canada*] [*Research center*] (RCD) ..... GIROQ
Groupe Liberal, Democratique, et Reformateur (EAIO) ..... GLDR
Groupe Regional pour la Coordination de la Production et du Transport de l'Energie Electrique entre l'Autriche, la Grece, l'Italie et la Yougoslavie (EA) ..... SUDEL
Groupe Revolutionnaire Socialiste [*Socialist Revolution Group*] [*France*] [*Political party*] ..... GRS
Groupe Revolutionnaire Socialiste [*Socialist Revolution Group*] [*Martinique*] [*Political party*] (PPW) ..... GRS
Groupe Socialiste du Parlement Europeen [*Socialist Group in the European Parliament - SGEP*] (EAIO) ..... GSPE
Groupe Speciale Mobile [*European digital cellular radio standard*] ..... GSM
Grouped Optimal Aggregation Technique (MCD) ..... GOAT
Groupement Belge des Banques d'Epargne [*Banking association*] [*Belgium*] (EY) ..... GBE
Groupement Canadien des Locataires des Logements Municipaux [*Canadian Organization of Public Housing Tenants*] ..... GCLLM
Groupement Carte a Memoire [*Group promoting use of 'smart' credit cards*] [*France*] (NITA) ..... GCM
Groupement Cinematographique International de Conciliation (EA) ..... GCIC
Groupement de la Caisse des Depots Automatisation pour le Management [*Bank Group for Automation in Management*] [*Information service or system*] (IID) ..... GCAM
Groupement des Acousticiens de Langue Francaise [*Group of French-Speaking Acousticians*] (EA) ..... GALF
Groupement des Allergologistes et Immunologistes de Langues Latines [*Latin Languages Speaking Allergists - LLSA*] (EAIO) ..... GAILL
Groupement des Associations de Librairies de la CEE [*Group of Booksellers Associations in the EEC*] (ECED) ..... GALC
Groupement des Associations Dentaires Francophones [*Group of Francophone Dentists' Associations*] [*Paris, France*] (EAIO) ..... GADEF
Groupement des Associations des Maisiers des Pays de la CEE [*Group of the Maize Processors Associations in the European Economic Community Countries*] [*Brussels, Belgium*] ..... EUROMAISIERS
Groupement des Associations des Maisiers des Pays de la CEE [*Group of Associations of Maize Processors of EEC Countries*] (EAIO) ..... EUROPMAISERS
Groupement des Associations Meunieres des Pays de la CEE [*Flour Milling Associations Group of the EEC Countries*] (EAIO) ..... GAM
Groupement des Caisses d'Epargne de la CEE [*Savings Bank Group of the European Economic Community*] ..... GCECEE
Groupement des Democrates Revolutionnaires [*Burkina Faso*] [*Political party*] (EY) ..... GDR
Groupement des Fabricants d'Appariels Sanitaires en Ceramique de la CEE [*Group of Manufacturers of Ceramic Sanitary Ware of the European Economic Community*] (PDAA) ..... GEFACS
Groupement des Mathematiciens d'Expression Latine [*Group of Mathematicians of Romance Languages - GMRL*] (EAIO) ..... GMEL
Groupement des Opticiens du Marche Commun [*Common Market Opticians' Group*] [*Paris, France*] ..... GOMAC
Groupement des Plastiques Renforces et Materiaux Composites [*Organization of Reinforced Plastics and Composite Materials*] (EAIO) ..... GPRMC
Groupement des Producteurs de Carreaux Ceramiques du Marche Commun [*Grouping of Ceramic Tile Producers of the Common Market*] (ECED) ..... CMC
Groupement d'Etudes et de Recherche pour le Developpement de l'Agronomie Tropicale [*Group for the Study and Research of Tropical Agronomy*] [*International Cooperation Center of Agricultural Research for Development*] [*Information service or system*] (IID) ..... GERDAT
Groupement Europeen de Lymphologie [*European Lymphology Group - ELG*] [*Brussels, Belgium*] (EAIO) ..... GEL
Groupement Europeen des Artistes des Ardennes et de l'Eifel [*European Group of Artists of the Ardennes and the Eifel*] (EAIO) ..... GEAAE
Groupement Europeen des Associations des Maisons de Reforme [*EC*] (ECED) ..... GEAMR
Groupement Europeen des Associations Nationales des Fabricants de Pesticides [*European Group of National Pesticide Manufacturer' Associations*] [*Common Market*] ..... GEFAP
Groupement Europeen des Caisses d'Epargne [*European Savings Bank Group*] [*EC*] (ECED) ..... GECE
Groupement Europeen des Enterprises de Distribution Integrees [*European Multiple Retailers Association*] [*Belgium EC*] (ECED) ..... GEDIS
Groupement Europeen des Fabricants de Pieces Techniques Plastiques [*European Group of Fabricators of Technical Plastics Parts*] (EAIO) ..... PLASTEUROTEC
Groupement Europeen des Maisons d'Alimentation et d'Approvisionnement a Succursales [*European Group of Food and Provision Chain Stores*] [*Common Market Brussels, Belgium*] ..... GEMAS
Groupement Europeen des Producteurs de Verre Plat [*European Group of Flat Glass Manufacturers*] (EAIO) ..... GEPVP
Groupement Europeen des Sources d'Eaux Minerales Naturelles [*European Group ofNatural Mineral Water Sources*] (EAIO) ..... GESEM
Groupement Francais des Fournisseurs d'Information en Ligne [*French Association of Online Information Providers*] [*Paris*] [*Information service or system*] (IID) ..... GFFIL
Groupement Francais des Producteurs de Bases et Banques de Donnees [*French Federation of Data Base Producers*] [*Information service or system*] (IID) ..... GFPBBD
Groupement Independant de Reflexion et d'Action [*Independent Grouping of Reflection and Action*] [*Central Africa*] (PD) ..... GIRA
Groupement International de l'Industrie Pharmaceutique des Pays de la CEE [*International Pharmaceutical Industry Group for the EEC Countries*] ..... GIIP
Groupement International d'Editeurs Scientifiques, Techniques, et Medicaux [*International Group of Scientific, Technical, and Medical Publishers*] (EAIO) ..... STM
Groupement International des Associations Nationales de Fabricants de Produits Agrochimiques [*International Group of National Associations of Manufacturers of Agrochemical Products*] (EAIO) ..... GIFAP
Groupement International d'Etiquetage pour l'Entretien des Textiles [*International Association for Textile Care Labelling*] [*Barcelona, Spain*] (EA) ..... GINETEX
Groupement International pour la Recherche Scientifique en Stomatologie et Odontologie [*International Group for Scientific Research on Stomato-Odontology*] (EA) ..... GIRSO
Groupement Latin et Mediterraneen de Medecine du Sport [*Latin and Mediterranean Group for Sport Medicine - LMGSM*] (EAIO) ..... GLMMS
Groupement Mobile 100 [*Elite French armed forces stationed in Vietnam*] (VNW) GM100
Groupement Pharmaceutique de la CE [*Pharmaceutical Group of the EC*] (ECED) ..... GPCE
Groupement pour l'Avancement des Methodes Spectroscopiques et Physio-Chimiques d'Analyse [*Group for the Advancement of Spectroscopic Methods and Physicochemical Analysis*] [*Information service or system*] (IID) ..... GAMS

Groupement Professionel des Pharmaciens de l'Industrie Pharmaceutique de la CEE [*Professional Grouping of Pharmacists of the Pharmaceuticals Industry of the EEC*] (ECED) .... GPPIPCEE
Groupement Technique de Assureurs du Canada [*Government Telecommunications Agency*] [*Canada*] .... GTA
Groupes Bibliques Universitaires [*University Biblical Groups*] [*Canada*] .... GBU
Groupes Evangile et Mission [*Institute of the Heart of Jesus - IHJ*] [*France*] (EA) .... GEM
Grouping Distance [*Industrial engineering*] .... GD
Group-Living Program (DAVI) .... GLP
Groupo Imsa Sa de CV [*Associated Press*] (SAG) .... GpoImsa
Groupo Imsa Sa de CV [*NYSE symbol*] (SAG) .... IMY
Groupo Mexicano Desarrollo [*NYSE symbol*] (SPSG) .... GMD
Group-Page-Line-Inserts (MCD) .... GPLI
Groups Against Sewage Pollution [*Australia*] .... GASP
Groups of Pulses per Second (DEN) .... GPS
Groups [*of code transmitted*] per Minute [*or Message*] [*Telecommunications*] .... GPM
Group-Specific Antigen [*Immunology*] .... GSA
Group-Specific Antigen Gene (DMAA) .... GAG
Group-Specific Component [*A serum group*] .... Gc
Group-Transfer Polymerization [*Du Pont process*] [*1983*] .... GTP
Grout [*Technical drawings*] .... GT
Grove (ADA) .... GR
Grove .... GRO
Grove [*Commonly used*] (OPSA) .... GROV
Grove [*Commonly used*] (OPSA) .... GROVE
Grove .... GRV
Grove .... GRV
Grove (ADA) .... GVE
Grove Bank for Savings [*NASDAQ symbol*] (NQ) .... GROV
Grove Bank for Savings [*Associated Press*] (SAG) .... GroveB
Grove Bank (MA) [*NASDAQ symbol*] (TTSB) .... GROV
Grove City College [*Pennsylvania*] .... GCC
Grove City College, Grove City, PA [*Library symbol Library of Congress*] (LCLS) .... PGcC
Grove City, OH [*FM radio station call letters*] .... WWCD
Grove City, PA [*FM radio station call letters*] .... WICT
Grove City, PA [*AM radio station call letters*] .... WSAJ
Grove City, PA [*FM radio station call letters*] .... WSAJ-FM
Grove City Public Library, Grove City, MN [*Library symbol*] [*Library of Congress*] (LCLS) .... MnGc
Grove City Public Library, Grove City, OH [*Library symbol Library of Congress*] (LCLS) .... OGc
Grove Dictionary of Music and Musicians [*A publication*] .... GD
Grove Explorations Ltd. [*Vancouver Stock Exchange symbol*] .... GVX
Grove, OK [*FM radio station call letters*] .... KGVE
Grove Real Estate Asset Trust [*AMEX symbol*] (SAG) .... GRE
Grove Real Estate Asset Trust [*Associated Press*] (SAG) .... GroveR
Grove Street College, Oakland, CA [*Library symbol Library of Congress*] (LCLS) .... COCiC
Groveland, CA [*FM radio station call letters*] .... KXSR
Grover City, CA [*FM radio station call letters*] .... KIXT-FM
Groves [*Commonly used*] (OPSA) .... GROVES
Groves [*Postal Service standard*] (OPSA) .... GRVS
Groves, TX [*FM radio station call letters*] .... KTFA
Grow Biz International [*NASDAQ symbol*] (TTSB) .... GBIZ
Grow Biz International, Inc. [*NASDAQ symbol*] (SAG) .... GBIZ
Grow Biz International, Inc. [*Associated Press*] (SAG) .... GrowBiz
Grow Victoria [*Mental health organisation*] [*Australia*] .... GV
Growing Degree Day [*Agriculture*] (PDAA) .... GDD
Growing Equity Mortgage .... GEM
Growing, Improving, Maturing - Puppy of the Year [*Canine award*] .... GIMPY
Growing Retired Active Monied Person in Excellent State [*Lifestyle classification*] .... GRAMPIES
Growing Up Born Again [*Pronounced "goobah"*] [*Book published by Fleming H. Revell Co.*] .... GUBA
Grown Diffused .... GD
Grown Junction (IEEE) .... GJ
Grown Offspring, Still Home [*Lifestyle classification*] .... GOSH
Grown-Up Mature Person [*Lifestyle classification*] .... Grumpie
Growth [*Business term*] .... G
Growth (SSD) .... GR
Growth [*A publication*] .... Grow
Growth .... GRTH
Growth [*Business term*] .... GW
Growth Analysis and Review (BUR) .... GAR
Growth and Development [*Pediatrics*] (DAVI) .... G & D
Growth and Differentiation Hormone [*Endocrinology*] .... GDH
Growth and Income [*Business term*] .... GI
Growth and Income Security [*Finance*] .... GAINS
Growth and Maturation Activity [*Biochemistry*] .... GMA
Growth Arrest-Specific Gene [*Medicine*] (DMAA) .... GAS
Growth at the Right Price .... GARP
Growth Differentiation Factor [*Embryology*] .... GDF
Growth, Economy, Management, and Customer Satisfaction [*Procedure for establishing management goals*] .... GEMS
Growth Environmental, Inc. [*NASDAQ symbol*] (SAG) .... GCER
Growth Environmental, Inc. [*Associated Press*] (SAG) .... GthEnvr
Growth Factor [*Endocrinology*] (DAVI) .... GF
Growth Financial Corp. [*NASDAQ symbol*] (SAG) .... GRFC
Growth Financial Corp. [*Associated Press*] (SAG) .... GthFn
Growth Fraction [*Endocrinology*] .... GF
Growth Fund of Spain [*NYSE symbol*] (SPSG) .... GSP
Growth Fund of Spain [*Associated Press*] (SAG) .... GthSpn

Growth Hormone [*Somatotrophin*] [*Also, SH, STH Endocrinology*] .... GH
Growth Hormone Binding Protein (DMAA) .... GHBP
Growth Hormone Deficiency [*Endocrinology*] .... GHD
Growth Hormone Insufficiency .... GHI
Growth Hormone Receptor [*Biochemistry*] .... GHR
Growth Hormone Release Inhibiting Factor [*Also, GH-RIH, GRIF, SRIF, SS*] [*Endocrinology*] .... GH-RIF
Growth Hormone Release Inhibiting Factor [*Also, GH-RIF, GH-RIH, SRIF, SS*] [*Endocrinology*] .... GRIF
Growth Hormone Release Inhibiting Hormone [*Also, GH-RIF, GRIF, SRIF, SS*] [*Endocrinology*] .... GH-RIH
Growth Hormone Releasing Factor [*Somatoliberin*] [*Also, GH-RH, GRF Endocrinology*] .... GH-RF
Growth Hormone Releasing Factor [*Somatoliberin*] [*Also, GH-RF, GH-RH Endocrinology*] .... GRF
Growth Hormone Releasing Hormone [*Somatoliberin*] [*Also, GH-RF, GRF Endocrinology*] .... GH-RH
Growth Hormone Releasing Hormone [*Somatoliberin*] [*Also, GH-RF, GRF Endocrinology*] (MAE) .... GRH
Growth Hormone Releasing Peptide [*Endocrinology*] .... GHRP
Growth Hormone Secretagogue [*Biochemistry*] .... GHS
Growth Hormone Transcription Factor [*Endocrinology*] .... GHF
Growth Hormone Variant [*Medicine*] (DMAA) .... GHV
Growth in Total Profit (MHDB) .... GP
Growth Index .... GI
Growth Inhibiting .... GI
Growth Inhibiting Factor [*Endocrinology*] (MAE) .... GIF
Growth Inhibiting Hormone [*Endocrinology*] (MAE) .... GIH
Growth Investment Corp. [*Toronto Stock Exchange symbol*] .... GRO
Growth Management Act .... GMA
Growth Monitoring, Oral Rehydration, Breastfeeding, and Immunization [*Program*] [*UNICEF plan to reduce child mortality in Third World countries*] .... GOBI
Growth of Strategic Materials in Space (MCD) .... GSMS
Growth of the American Family [*A study*] .... GAF
Growth Rate [*Biology*] .... GR
Growth Rate [*Botany*] .... GRATE
Growth Rate Adjustment [*Business term*] .... GRA
Growth Retardation, Alopecia, Pseudo-Anodontia, and Optic Atrophy Syndrome [*Medicine*] (DMAA) .... GAPO
Growth Space Station (KSC) .... GSS
Growth Stage .... GS
Growth Stock [*Investment term*] .... GS
Growth Stock Outlook Trust, Inc. (MHDW) .... GSO
Growth Test Vehicle (MCD) .... GTV
Growth Vessel .... GV
Growth with Equity in Mindano [*A USAID backed organization*] [*Philippines*] .... GEM
Growth-Adjusted Sonographic Age [*Obstetrics*] (DMAA) .... GASA
Growth-Associated Protein [*Cytochemistry*] .... GAP
Growth-Limiting Medium [*For microorganisms*] .... GLM
Growth-Rate-Controlling Factor [*Medicine*] (DMAA) .... GCF
Growth-Related Protein (DMAA) .... GRO
Growth-Stimulating Hormone [*Endocrinology*] (DAVI) .... GSH
Grozny [*Former USSR Seismograph station code, US Geological Survey*] (SEIS) .... GRO
Grubb & Ellis [*NYSE symbol*] (TTSB) .... GBE
Grubb & Ellis Co. [*NYSE symbol*] (SPSG) .... GBE
Grubb & Ellis Co. [*Associated Press*] (SAG) .... GrubbEL
Grube [*Germany ICAO location identifier*] (ICLI) .... EDHB
Gruene Aktion Zukunft [*Green Action for the Future*] [*Germany*] (PPW) .... GAZ
Gruene Liste Umweltschutz [*Green List Ecology*] [*Germany*] (PPE) .... GLU
Grumbalds [*England*] .... GRUMB
Grumman Aerospace Corp. [*of Grumman Corp.*] .... GAC
Grumman Aerospace Corp., Bethpage, NY [*Library symbol Library of Congress*] (LCLS) .... NBetG
Grumman Aerospace Engineering Language for Instructional Checkout .... GAELIC
Grumman Aircraft Engineering Corp. [*Later, Grumman Corp.*] .... GAEC
Grumman American Aviation [*ICAO aircraft manufacturer identifier*] (ICAO) .... G
Grumman Olson [*Grumman Corp.*] .... G-O
Grumman Submersible Vehicle .... GSV
Grumman-Alderson Research Dummy [*Aircraft ejection seats*] .... GARD
Grumpy Seven [*Facetious translation for the Group of Seven: United States, Japan West Germany, France, Britain, Italy, and Canada*] (ECON) G7
Grunberg Hydrofoil System .... GHS
Grundarfjordur [*Iceland*] [*Airport symbol*] (OAG) .... GUU
Grundbuch [*Land Register*] [*German*] (ILCA) .... GB
Grundbuchamt [*Land Registry*] [*German*] (ILCA) .... GBA
Grundrichtungslinie [*Base line, a gunnery term*] [*German military - World War II*] .... GRL
Grundrichtungspunkt [*Base point, a gunnery term*] [*German military - World War II*] .... GRP
Grundriss der Romischen Geschichte [*A publication*] (OCD) .... Rom Gesch
Grundriss der Vergleichenden Grammatik der Semitischen Sprachen [*A publication*] (BJA) .... GVG
Grundriss der Vergleichenden Grammatik der Semitischen Sprachen [*A publication*] (BJA) .... GVGSS
Grundriss der Vergleichenden Grammatik der Semitischen Sprachen [*A publication*] (BJA) .... VG
Grundy Center, IA [*FM radio station call letters*] (RBYB) .... KCRR
Grundy Center Public Library, Grundy Center, IA [*Library symbol Library of Congress*] (LCLS) .... IaGrc
Grundy Center Register, Grundy Center, IA [*Library symbol Library of Congress*] (LCLS) .... IaGrcR

Grundy County-Jewett Norris Library, Trenton, MO [*Library symbol Library of Congress*] (LCLS) .... MoTr
Grundy, VA [*Location identifier FAA*] (FAAL) .... GDY
Grundy, VA [*Television station call letters*] .... WLFG
Grundy, VA [*FM radio station call letters*] .... WMJD
Grundy, VA [*AM radio station call letters*] .... WNRG
Gruner & Jahr AG & Co. [*Magazine publisher*] [*Germany*] .... G & J
Gruner + Jahr [*A publisher*] [*Hamburg, Germany*] (WDMC) .... G+J
Grupo Andino - Junta del Acuerdo de Cartagena [*Andean Group - Cartagena Agreement Board - ANCOM*] (EAIO) .... JUNAC
Grupo Andino - Junta del Acuerdo de Cartagena [*Andean Group - Cartagena Agreement Board - ANCOM*] (EA) .... Junta del Acuer
Grupo Casa Autrey [*NYSE symbol*] (SPSG) .... ATY
Grupo Casa Autrey [*Associated Press*] (SAG) .... GCAutrey
Grupo Casa Autrey ADS [*NYSE symbol*] (TTSB) .... ATY
Grupo de Abogados Argentinos en el Exilio en Francia .... GAAEF
Grupo de Accion Revolucionaria Internacional [*International Revolutionary Action Group*] [*Spain Political party*] .... GARI
Grupo de Apoyo Mutuo [*Group for Mutual Support*] [*Mexico Political party*] .... GAM
Grupo de Artistas Latino Americanos [*An association*] .... GALA
Grupo de Auto-Defensa [*Self-Defense Group*] [*Uruguay*] [*Political party*] (PD) .... GAP
Grupo de Aviacion Ejecutiva, SA de CV [*Mexico*] [*FAA designator*] (FAAC) .... EJC
Grupo de Convergencia Democratica en Uruguay [*Group of Democratic Convergence in Uruguay*] (EA) .... GCDU
Grupo de Economistas y Asociados [*Provides economic analysis in Mexico and abroad*] (CROSS) .... GEA
Grupo de Informacion y Solidaridad Uruguay [*Switzerland*] .... GRISUR
Grupo de Oficiales Unidos [*Group of United Officers*] [*Argentina*] .... GOU
Grupo de Paises Latinoamericanos y del Caribe Exportadores de Azucar [*Group of Latin American and Caribbean Sugar Exporting Countries - GLACSEC*] (EAIO) .... GEPLACEA
Grupo de Solidariedade com America Latina [*Portugal*] .... GSAL
Grupo de Trabajo para los Pueblos Indigenas [*Indigenous Peoples Working Group*] [*Netherlands*] (EAIO) .... GTPI
Grupo Elektra GDS [*NYSE symbol*] (TTSB) .... EKT
Grupo Elektra SA de CV [*NYSE symbol*] (SAG) .... EKT
Grupo Elektra SA de CV [*Associated Press*] (SAG) .... GElektr
Grupo Embotellador de Mexico [*NYSE symbol*] (SAG) .... GEM
Grupo Embotellador de Mexico [*Associated Press*] (SAG) .... GEmbMx
Grupo Embotellador Mex GDS [*NYSE symbol*] (TTSB) .... GEM
Grupo Financiero Serfin [*NYSE symbol*] (SPSG) .... SFN
Grupo Financiero Serfin ADS [*NYSE symbol*] (TTSB) .... SFN
Grupo Fnanciero Serfin SA [*Associated Press*] (SAG) .... GFinSerf
Grupo Independente de Macau [*Independent Group of Macao*] [*Political party*] (PPW) .... Gima
Grupo Indl Durango ADS [*NYSE symbol*] (TTSB) .... GID
Grupo Indl Maseca ADS [*NYSE symbol*] (TTSB) .... MSK
Grupo Industrial Durango SA de CV [*Associated Press*] (SAG) .... GDurng
Grupo Industrial Durango SA de CV [*NYSE symbol*] (SAG) .... GID
Grupo Industrial Maseca SA de CV [*Associated Press*] (SAG) .... GMasec
Grupo Industrial Maseca SA de CV [*Associated Press*] (SAG) .... GMaseca
Grupo Industrial Maseca SA de CV [*NYSE symbol*] (SAG) .... MSK
Grupo Interamericano de Editores [*Interamerican publishers group*] (NITA) .... GIE
Grupo Iusacell SA de CV [*NYSE symbol*] (SAG) .... CEL
Grupo Iusacell SA de CV [*Associated Press*] (SAG) .... Gluscl IL
Grupo Iusacell SA de CV [*Associated Press*] (SAG) .... GlusclI
Grupo Iusacell S.A.'D'ADS [*NYSE symbol*] (TTSB) .... CEL.D
Grupo Iusacell S.A.'L ADS [*NYSE symbol*] (TTSB) .... CEL
Grupo Latinoamericano de Rehabilitacion Profesional [*Latin American Vocational Rehabilitation Group*] [*Bogata, Colombia*] (EAIO) .... GLARP
Grupo Marxista Revolucionario [*Marxist Revolutionary Group*] [*Portuguese Political party*] (PPE) .... GMR
Grupo Mex de Desarrollo 'L'ADS [*NYSE symbol*] (TTSB) .... GMD
Grupo Mexicano Desarrollo [*Associated Press*] (SAG) .... GMexDes
Grupo Mexicano Desarrollo [*NYSE symbol*] (SAG) .... GMD
Grupo Mexicano Desarrollo [*Associated Press*] (SAG) .... GMDesB
Grupo Radio Centro [*Associated Press*] (SAG) .... GpoRadio
Grupo Radio Centro [*NYSE symbol*] (SPSG) .... RC
Grupo Radio Centro ADS [*NYSE symbol*] (TTSB) .... RC
Grupo Sidek SA de CV [*Associated Press*] (SAG) .... GboSidek
Grupo Sidek SA de CV [*Associated Press*] (SAG) .... GSidekB
Grupo Sidek SA de CV [*NYSE symbol*] (SAG) .... SDK
Grupo Sidek S.A.'B' ADS [*NYSE symbol*] (TTSB) .... SDK.B
Grupo Sidek S.A.'L'ADS [*NYSE symbol*] (TTSB) .... SDK
Grupo Simec [*Commercial firm Associated Press*] (SAG) .... GrSimec
Grupo Simec [*AMEX symbol*] (SPSG) .... SIM
Grupo Simec ADS [*AMEX symbol*] (TTSB) .... SIM
Grupo Situr'B' [*ME symbol*] (TTSB) .... STRb M
Grupo Socialista [*Socialist Group*] [*Portugal Political party*] (PPE) .... GS
Grupo Televisa [*Associated Press*] (SAG) .... GTelevsa
Grupo Televisa S.A. [*NYSE symbol*] (SPSG) .... TV
Grupo Televisa S.A.GDS [*NYSE symbol*] (TTSB) .... TV
Grupo Tribasa S.A. ADS [*NYSE symbol*] (TTSB) .... GTR
Grupo Tribasa SA de CV [*NYSE symbol*] (SPSG) .... GTR
Grupo Tribasa SA de Cv [*Associated Press*] (SAG) .... GTribasa
Grupoaereo Monterrey, SA de CV [*Mexico*] [*FAA designator*] (FAAC) .... GMT
Grupos Armados Espanoles [*Armed Spanish Groups*] [*Political party*] (PD) .... GAE
Grupos Armados Libertarios [*Armed Libertarian Groups*] [*Spain Political party*] (PD) .... GAL
Grupos de Accion Unificadora [*Groups for Unified Action*] [*Uruguay*] (PD) .... GAU
Grupos de Resistencia Anti-Fascista Primero de Octubre [*October First Antifascist Resistance Groups*] [*Spain Political party*] (PPE) .... GRAPO
Gruppe Internationale Marxisten [*International Marxist Group*] [*Germany Political party*] (PPW) .... GIM
Gruppe Revolutionaerer Marxisten [*Group of Revolutionary Marxists*] [*Austria Political party*] (PPE) .... GRM
Gruppenfuehrer [*Squad Leader*] [*German military - World War II*] .... G
Gruppen-Hauptquartier [*Group Headquarters*] [*German military - World War II*] .... GRHQU
Gruppi Armati Radicali per il Comunismo [*Armed Radical Groups for Communism*] [*Italy*] (PD) .... GAR
Gruppo Esponenti Italiani (EA) .... GEI
Gruppo Finanziario Tessile [*Commercial firm*] .... GFT
Gruppo Italiano di Studio Tubercolosi e AIDS .... GISTA
Grus [*Constellation*] .... Gru
Gruver, TX [*Location identifier FAA*] (FAAL) .... GVX
Gruyeres [*Switzerland ICAO location identifier*] (ICLI) .... LSGT
Gryehound Racing Grounds Development Board [*Victoria, Australia*] .... GRGDB
Grygla Public School, Grygla, MN [*Library symbol*] [*Library of Congress*] (LCLS) .... MnGryS
Gryphon Holdings [*NASDAQ symbol*] (SAG) .... GRYP
Gryphon Holdings [*Associated Press*] (SAG) .... Gryphon
GS Financial Products [*Associated Press*] (SAG) .... GS Fin
GS Financial Products [*NYSE symbol*] (SAG) .... GSA
GSA Delegation of Procurement Authority (AAGC) .... GSA DPA
GSA [*General Services Administration*] **Procurement Regulations** .... GSPR
GSA [*General Services Administration*] **Stock Catalog** .... GSC
GSE Systems [*NASDAQ symbol*] (TTSB) .... GSES
GSE Systems, Inc. [*Associated Press*] (SAG) .... GSE Sy
GSE Systems, Inc. [*NASDAQ symbol*] (SAG) .... GSES
GSE [*Ground Support Equipment*] **Utilization List** [*NASA*] (NASA) .... GUL
GSR Goldsearch Resources [*Vancouver Stock Exchange symbol*] .... GSO
GST Telecommunications [*AMEX symbol*] (TTSB) .... GST
GST Telecommunications, Inc. [*AMEX symbol*] (SAG) .... GST
GST Telecommunications, Inc. [*Associated Press*] (SAG) .... GST Tele
Gstaad-Inn Grund [*Switzerland ICAO location identifier*] (ICLI) .... LSHA
GSW, Inc. [*Toronto Stock Exchange symbol*] .... GSW
GT Aviation [*British*] [*FAA designator*] (FAAC) .... GTA
GT Bicycles [*NASDAQ symbol*] (TTSB) .... GTBX
GT Bicycles, Inc. [*Associated Press*] (SAG) .... GTBicyc
GT Bicycles, Inc. [*NASDAQ symbol*] (SAG) .... GTBX
GT Global Developing Market Facts [*Associated Press*] (SAG) .... GTDvMk
GT Global Developing Market Fund [*NYSE symbol*] (SPSG) .... GTD
G.T. Global Dvlp Mkt Fund [*NYSE symbol*] (TTSB) .... GTD
G.T. Greater Europe Fd [*NYSE symbol*] (TTSB) .... GTF
GT Greater Europe Fund [*Associated Press*] (SAG) .... GT Euro
GT Greater Europe Fund [*NYSE symbol*] (SPSG) .... GTF
GT Interactive Software [*NASDAQ symbol*] (TTSB) .... GTIS
GTC Transcontinental Group Ltd. [*Toronto Stock Exchange symbol*] .... GRT
GTE Calif 5% cm Pfd [*NASDAQ symbol*] (TTSB) .... GTELN
GTE Calif 4.50% cm Pfd [*NASDAQ symbol*] (TTSB) .... GTELO
GTE Calif 4.50% cm Pfd [*NASDAQ symbol*] (TTSB) .... GTELP
GTE California, Inc. [*Associated Press*] (SAG) .... GTEC
GTE California, Inc. [*NASDAQ symbol*] (NQ) .... GTEL
GTE Corp. [*Formerly, General Telephone & Electronics Corp.*] [*NYSE symbol*] (SPSG) .... GTE
GTE Delaware Ltd. [*Associated Press*] (SAG) .... GTEDE
GTE Delaware LP [*NYSE symbol*] (SAG) .... GTE
GTE Fla $1.25 Pfd [*NYSE symbol*] (TTSB) .... GLFPrA
GTE Fla $1.30cm B Pfd [*NYSE symbol*] (TTSB) .... GLFPrB
GTE Fla 8.16% Pfd [*NYSE symbol*] (TTSB) .... GLFPrC
GTE Florida, Inc. [*NYSE symbol*] (SAG) .... GLF
GTE Florida, Inc. [*Associated Press*] (SAG) .... GTEF
GTE North, Inc., Westfield, IN [*Library symbol*] [*Library of Congress*] (LCLS) .... InWefG
GTE Service Corp., Library, Irving, TX [*Library symbol*] [*Library of Congress*] (LCLS) .... TxIrG
GTE Sylvania, Inc., Electronic Components Group, Seneca Falls, NY [*Library symbol Library of Congress*] (LCLS) .... NSnfG
GTECH Holdings [*NYSE symbol*] (TTSB) .... GTK
GTECH Holdings Corp. [*Associated Press*] (SAG) .... Gtech
GTECH Holdings Corp. [*NYSE symbol*] (SPSG) .... GTK
GTE-Sylvania, Electric Systems Group, Needham, MA [*Library symbol Library of Congress*] (LCLS) .... MNeeS
GThree Apparel Group Ltd. [*Associated Press*] (SAG) .... G-III
GTI Corp. [*NASDAQ symbol*] (SAG) .... GGTI
GTI Corp. [*Associated Press*] (SAG) .... GTI
GTO [*Gran Torismo Omologato*] **Association of America** (EA) .... GAA
GTS Duratek [*NASDAQ symbol*] (TTSB) .... DRTK
GTS Duratek [*Associated Press*] (SAG) .... GTS Drtk
GTS Duratek Corp. [*NASDAQ symbol*] (NQ) .... DRTK
Gua Musang [*Malaysia*] [*ICAO location identifier*] (ICLI) .... WMAI
Guacamayas [*Colombia*] [*Airport symbol*] (OAG) .... GCA
Guadalajara [*Mexico*] [*Airport symbol*] (OAG) .... GDL
Guadalajara [*Mexico*] [*Seismograph station code, US Geological Survey*] (SEIS) .... GUM
Guadalajara [*Bolivia*] [*ICAO location identifier*] (ICLI) .... SLGJ
Guadalajara/Miguel Hidalgo Y Costilla Internacional [*Mexico ICAO location identifier*] (ICLI) .... MMGL
Guadalupan Missionaries of the Holy Spirit (TOCD) .... MGSpS
Guadalupe, CA [*FM radio station call letters*] .... KIDI
Guadalupe Elementary School, Canejos School, Antonio, CO [*Library symbol*] [*Library of Congress*] (LCLS) .... CoAnG
Guadalupe Missioners (TOCD) .... mg
Guadalupe Pass, TX [*Location identifier FAA*] (FAAL) .... GDP
Guadeloupe [*ANSI three-letter standard code*] (CNC) .... GLP
Guadeloupe [*ANSI two-letter standard code*] (CNC) .... GP
Guadeloupe [*MARC country of publication code Library of Congress*] (LCCP) .... gp
Guadeloupe (ROG) .... GUAD

Guadeloupe [*MARC geographic area code Library of Congress*] (LCCP) ...... nwgp--
Guadeloupe Liberation Army ...... GLA
Guaiacol-Linoleic Acid Hydroperoxide Oxidoreductase [*An enzyme*] ...... GLO
Guaiacum [*Lignum Vitae*] [*Pharmacy*] (ROG) ...... GUIAC
Guaifenesin [*An expectorant*] [*Pharmacology*] (DAVI) ...... GG
Guaira [*Paraguay*] [*ICAO location identifier*] (ICLI) ...... SGGR
Guajara Mirim [*Brazil*] [*Airport symbol*] (AD) ...... GJM
Guajara-Mirim [*Brazil ICAO location identifier*] (ICLI) ...... SBGM
Gualala, CA [*FM radio station call letters*] ...... KWAN
Gualaquiza [*Ecuador*] [*ICAO location identifier*] (ICLI) ...... SEGZ
Gualcosius [*Flourished, 11th-12th century*] [*Authority cited in pre-1607 legal work*] (DSA) ...... Gal
Gualcosius [*Flourished, 11th-12th century*] [*Authority cited in pre-1607 legal work*] (DSA) ...... Gual
Gualcosius [*Flourished, 11th-12th century*] [*Authority cited in pre-1607 legal work*] (DSA) ...... Gualc
Guale [*Ecuador*] [*ICAO location identifier*] (ICLI) ...... SEGE
Gualeguaychu [*Argentina*] [*Airport symbol*] (OAG) ...... GHU
Gualeguaychu [*Argentina ICAO location identifier*] (ICLI) ...... SAAG
Guam [*IYRU nationality code*] (IYR) ...... GM
Guam [*MARC country of publication code Library of Congress*] (LCCP) ...... gu
Guam [*Postal code*] [*ANSI two-letter standard code*] (CNC) ...... GU
Guam [*Mariana Islands*] [*Seismograph station code, US Geological Survey*] ...... GUA
Guam [*ANSI three-letter standard code*] (CNC) ...... GUM
Guam [*Marianas*] [*Airport symbol*] (AD) ...... GUM
Guam [*Mariana Islands*] [*Seismograph station code, US Geological Survey*] (SEIS) ...... GUMO
Guam [*Mariana Islands*] [*ICAO location identifier*] (ICLI) ...... PGFW
Guam [*Mariana Islands*] [*ICAO location identifier*] (ICLI) ...... PGTW
Guam [*MARC geographic area code Library of Congress*] (LCCP) ...... pogu--
Guam Acoustic Range Facility [*Military*] (CAAL) ...... GARF
Guam Agricultural Experiment Station [*University of Guam*] [*Research center*] (RCD) ...... AES
Guam Civil Code [*A publication*] (DLA) ...... Guam Civ Code
Guam Code of Civil Procedure [*A publication*] (DLA) ...... Guam Code Civ Pro
Guam Government Code [*A publication*] (DLA) ...... Guam Gov't Code
Guam Probate Code [*A publication*] (DLA) ...... Guam Prob Code
Guam Reference Standards Laboratory (DNAB) ...... GRSL
Guam Stamp Club and Western Pacific Philatelic Collectors (EA) ...... GSCWPPC
Guam/Taguac [*Mariana Islands*] [*ICAO location identifier*] (ICLI) ...... PGAC
Guam Tracking Station [*NASA*] (MCD) ...... GTS
Guam Tracking Station [*NASA*] (KSC) ...... GWM
Guanacaste [*Costa Rica*] [*ICAO location identifier*] (ICLI) ...... MRGU
Guanaja [*Honduras*] [*ICAO location identifier*] (ICLI) ...... MHNJ
Guanajuato [*Mexico ICAO location identifier*] (ICLI) ...... MMGT
Guanambi [*Brazil*] [*Airport symbol*] (OAG) ...... GNM
Guanare [*Venezuela*] [*Airport symbol*] (OAG) ...... GUQ
Guanare, Portuguesa [*Venezuela ICAO location identifier*] (ICLI) ...... SVGU
Guanase [*An enzyme*] ...... GU
Guangshen Railway ADS [*NYSE symbol*] (TTSB) ...... GSH
Guangzhou [*China*] [*Airport symbol*] (OAG) ...... CAN
Guangzhou [*China*] [*ICAO location identifier*] (ICLI) ...... ZGZU
Guangzhou/Baiyun [*China*] [*ICAO location identifier*] (ICLI) ...... ZGGG
Guangzhou City [*China*] [*ICAO location identifier*] (ICLI) ...... ZGUA
Guangzhou Regional Administration of CAA of China [*ICAO designator*] (FAAC) ...... CSN
Guanidine [*Biochemistry*] (DAVI) ...... G
Guanidine [*Biochemistry*] ...... Gdn
Guanidine Aluminum Sulfate Hexahydrate [*Insecticide*] ...... GASH
Guanidine Aluminum Sulfate Hydrate [*Ferroelectrics*] ...... GASH
Guanidine Hydrochloride [*Organic chemistry*] ...... GHCl
Guanidinebenzimidazole [*Biochemistry*] ...... GBI
Guanidinium Chloride [*Biochemistry*] ...... GdmCl
Guanidinium Thiocyanate [*Biochemistry*] ...... GTC
Guanidinoethylmercaptosuccinic Acid [*Biochemistry*] ...... GEMSA
Guanidinosuccinic Acid (MAE) ...... GSA
Guanine [*Also, Gua*] [*Biochemistry*] ...... G
Guanine [*Also, G*] [*Biochemistry*] ...... Gua
Guanine, Cytosine [*Type*] [*Biochemistry*] ...... GC
Guanine Nucleotide [*Biochemistry*] ...... GN
Guanine Nucleotide Release Protein [*Biochemistry*] ...... GNRP
Guanine Phosphoribosyltransferase [*An enzyme*] ...... GPRT
Guanine-Nucleotide-Exchange Factor [*Biochemistry*] ...... GEF
Guanine-Nucleoxide Exchange Factor [*Biochemistry*] ...... GEF
Guanosine [*One-letter symbol; see Guo*] ...... G
Guanosine [*Also, G*] [*A nucleoside*] ...... Guo
Guanosine Diphosphate [*Biochemistry*] ...... GDP
Guanosine Diphosphomannose [*Biochemistry*] ...... GDPMan
Guanosine Dyphosphate [*Biochemistry*] ...... GDP
Guanosine Monophosphate [*Biochemistry*] ...... GMP
Guanosine Triphosphatase [*An enzyme*] ...... GTPase
Guanosine Triphosphatase Activating [*Biochemistry*] ...... GA
Guanosine Triphosphatase Activating Protein [*Biochemistry*] ...... GAP
Guanosine Triphosphate [*Biochemistry*] ...... GTP
Guantanamo [*Cuba*] [*Airport symbol*] (OAG) ...... GAO
Guantanamo [*Cuba ICAO location identifier*] (ICLI) ...... MUGT
Guantanamo Bay [*Cuba*] [*Seismograph station code, US Geological Survey Closed*] (SEIS) ...... GBC
Guantanamo Bay, Cuba ...... GTMO
Guantanamo, US Naval Air Base [*Cuba ICAO location identifier*] (ICLI) ...... MUGM
Guanylate Kinase [*An enzyme*] ...... GUK
Guanylate-Binding Protein [*Biochemistry*] ...... GBP
Guapi [*Colombia*] [*Airport symbol*] (OAG) ...... GPI
Guapi [*Colorado ICAO location identifier*] (ICLI) ...... SKGP
Guapiles [*Costa Rica*] [*Airport symbol*] (OAG) ...... GPL
Guapiles [*Costa Rica*] [*ICAO location identifier*] (ICLI) ...... MRGP
Guarani [*Monetary unit*] [*Paraguay*] ...... G
Guarani [*MARC language code Library of Congress*] (LCCP) ...... gua
Guarantee ...... GTEE
Guarantee ...... GU
Guarantee (MSA) ...... GUAR
Guarantee (ROG) ...... GUAREE
Guarantee (ABBR) ...... GUARTE
Guarantee (ABBR) ...... GURNT
Guarantee Life Companies, Inc. [*NASDAQ symbol*] (SAG) ...... GUAR
Guarantee Life Companies, Inc. [*Associated Press*] (SAG) ...... GuarLife
Guarantee Life Cos [*NASDAQ symbol*] (TTSB) ...... GUAR
Guarantee Material Inspection (MCD) ...... GMI
Guaranteed ...... GRD
Guaranteed ...... GRNTD
Guaranteed ...... GTD
Guaranteed (ABBR) ...... GUARTED
Guaranteed (ABBR) ...... GURNTD
Guaranteed Access Level [*Foreign Trade*] ...... GAL
Guaranteed Annual Income ...... GAI
Guaranteed Annual Income System ...... GAINS
Guaranteed Annual Minimum ...... GAM
Guaranteed Annual Wage ...... GAW
Guaranteed Assignment Retention Detailing [*Navy*] (NVT) ...... GUARD
Guaranteed Bond [*Business term*] ...... GB
Guaranteed Employment Level ...... GEL
Guaranteed Hourly Minimum ...... GHM
Guaranteed Hourly Wage ...... GHW
Guaranteed Income Contract ...... GIC
Guaranteed Income Stream [*UAW program included in the union's 1982 contract with General Motors Corp.*] ...... GIS
Guaranteed Income Supplement [*Program*] [*Canada*] ...... GIS
Guaranteed Insurability Option ...... GIO
Guaranteed Investment Contract ...... GIC
Guaranteed Market Index Investment [*Canada*] ...... GMII
Guaranteed Minimum Delivery Price (ADA) ...... GMDP
Guaranteed Minimum Income (ADA) ...... GMI
Guaranteed Minimum Pension [*British*] ...... GMP
Guaranteed Minimum Price ...... GMP
Guaranteed Minimum Value ...... GMV
Guaranteed Mortgage Certificate [*Federal Home Loan Mortgage Corp.*] ...... GMC
Guaranteed One Coat [*Brand of house paint*] ...... GOC
Guaranteed Overnight Delivery ...... GOD
Guaranteed Purchase Option [*Insurance*] ...... GPO
Guaranteed Recovery of Investment Principal [*Economics*] ...... GRIP
Guaranteed Retirement Income ...... GRI
Guaranteed Student Loan [*later, Stafford Loan*] [*Department of Education*] ...... GSL
Guaranteed Student Loan Program ...... GSLP
Guaranteed Supply Unit [*Telecommunications*] (OA) ...... GSU
Guaranteed Time Observer [*For telescope viewing*] ...... GTO
Guaranteed Underwriting Facilities (TDOB) ...... GUN
Guaranteed Voltage Breakdown ...... GVB
Guaranteed Weekly Minimum ...... GWM
Guaranteed Weekly Wage ...... GWW
Guaranteeing (ABBR) ...... GUARTEG
Guaranteeing (ABBR) ...... GURTG
Guarantor [*Legal term*] (ROG) ...... GUAROR
Guarantor (ABBR) ...... GUARTR
Guarantor (ABBR) ...... GURNTR
Guaranty (DLA) ...... Gty
Guaranty (ABBR) ...... GUART
Guaranty (ABBR) ...... GURNTY
Guaranty Federal Savings Bank [*NASDAQ symbol*] (SAG) ...... GFED
Guaranty Federal Savings Bank [*Associated Press*] (SAG) ...... GuarFS
Guaranty Fedl Svgs [*NASDAQ symbol*] (TTSB) ...... GFED
Guaranty Financial [*NASDAQ symbol*] (TTSB) ...... GSLC
Guaranty Financial Corp. [*NASDAQ symbol*] (SAG) ...... GSLC
Guaranty Financial Corp. [*Associated Press*] (SAG) ...... GuarFin
Guaranty National [*NYSE symbol*] (TTSB) ...... GNC
Guaranty National Corp. [*NYSE symbol*] (SPSG) ...... GNC
Guaranty National Corp. [*Associated Press*] (SAG) ...... GtyNtl
Guaranty Reserve Fund ...... GRF
Guaranty Savings & Loan FA [*NASDAQ symbol*] (SAG) ...... GSLC
Guaranty Savings & Loan FA [*Associated Press*] (SAG) ...... GuarSL
Guaranty Trust Co. of Canada [*Toronto Stock Exchange symbol*] ...... GY
Guaranty Trustco Ltd. [*Toronto Stock Exchange symbol*] ...... GTY
Guarantying (ABBR) ...... GURNTG
Guarapuava [*Brazil*] [*Airport symbol*] (AD) ...... GPP
Guaratingueta [*Brazil*] [*Airport symbol*] (OAG) ...... GUJ
Guaratingueta [*Brazil ICAO location identifier*] (ICLI) ...... SBGW
Guard [*Position in football, basketball, etc.*] ...... G
Guard (AABC) ...... GD
Guard ...... GRD
Guard ...... GRD
Guard Book (DGA) ...... GB
Guard Mail ...... GM
Guard of Tent [*Oddfellows*] (ROG) ...... GT
Guard Rail (AAG) ...... GDR
Guard Rail Common Sensor [*Army*] (DOMA) ...... GRCS
Guard Receiver (MCD) ...... GRCV
Guard Ring (BARN) ...... GR
Guard Ring Avalanche Photodiode (IAA) ...... GRAPD
Guard Ring Capacitor ...... GRC
Guard Ring Isolated Monolithic Integrated Circuit ...... GIMIC
Guard Society (EA) ...... GS

Guard Squadron ..... GS
Guard, Tomb of the Unknown Soldier Identification Badge [*Military decoration*] (AABC) ..... GTUSIdentBad
Guard Transmit/Receive (MCD) ..... GT/R
Guard Unit Armor Device Full-Crew Interaction Simulation Trainer ..... GUARD FIST
Guard Vessel [*Nuclear energy*] (NRCH) ..... GV
Guard Well Capacitor ..... GWC
Guardbridge Papers [*Manufacturer*] [*British*] ..... GB
Guard-Cell Mother Cell [*Botany*] ..... GMC
Guarded Relay Multiplexer ..... GRM
Guardhouse (AABC) ..... GDHSE
Guardhouse ..... GH
Guardhouse Lawyer [*Military slang*] ..... GHL
Guardia Republicana [*Peru*] ..... GRP
Guardian ..... G
Guardian (ROG) ..... GDIAN
Guardian ..... GDN
Guardian ..... GRDN
Guardian Ad Litem [*Social services*] (PAZ) ..... GAL
Guardian Angels (EA) ..... GA
Guardian Association (EA) ..... GA
Guardian Bancorp [*AMEX symbol*] (SPSG) ..... GB
Guardian Bancorp [*Associated Press*] (SAG) ..... GrdnB
Guardian Capital Group Ltd. [*Toronto Stock Exchange symbol*] ..... GCG
Guardian International Income Fund Units [*Toronto Stock Exchange symbol*] ..... GIF
Guardian Newspapers Ltd., Manchester, United Kingdom [*Library symbol Library of Congress*] (LCLS) ..... UkMaG
Guardian of Impressive Letters and Master of Excellent Replies ..... GILMER
Guardian Pacific Rim Corp. [*Toronto Stock Exchange symbol*] ..... GPF
Guardian Resources Corp. [*Vancouver Stock Exchange symbol*] ..... GUD
Guardian Royal Exchange Assurance [*British*] ..... GRE
Guardian Tech Intl Unit [*NASDAQ symbol*] (TTSB) ..... GRDNU
Guardian Technologies International, Inc. [*NASDAQ symbol*] (SAG) ..... GRDN
Guardian Technologies International, Inc. [*Associated Press*] (SAG) ..... GrdTch
Guardian Technologies International, Inc. [*Associated Press*] (SAG) ..... GuardTc
Guardian Weekly [*A publication*] (BRI) ..... GW
Guardian-Morton Shulman Precious Metals, Inc. [*Toronto Stock Exchange symbol Vancouver Stock Exchange symbol*] ..... GMS
Guardians of Hydrocephalus Research Foundation (EA) ..... GHRF
Guardianship and Administration Board [*Victoria, Australia*] ..... GAB
Guardianship Board [*Tasmania, Australia*] ..... GB
Guardianship for Senior Citizens ..... GSC
Guardiavecchia [*Italy ICAO location identifier*] (ICLI) ..... LIEG
Guarding [*Bookbinding*] (DGA) ..... GDG
Guardrail ..... GR
Guardrail/Common Sensor System [*Military*] ..... GR/CS
Guards [*British military*] (DMA) ..... Gds
Guards' Armoured Division [*Military unit*] [*British*] ..... GAD
Guards Artillery Division [*British*] ..... GAD
Guard's Expense in Returning Absentee [*Army*] ..... GERA
Guards Machine Gun Battalion [*British military*] (DMA) ..... GMGB
Guards Machine Gun Regiment [*British military*] (DMA) ..... GMGR
Guards Motorized Rifle Division (MCD) ..... GMRD
Guards Tank Division (MCD) ..... GTD
Guardship ..... GS
Guardsman [*Military*] ..... GDSM
Guardsman Products, Inc. [*NYSE symbol*] (SPSG) ..... GPI
Guardsman Products, Inc. [*Associated Press*] (SAG) ..... GrdPrd
Guari [*Papua New Guinea*] [*Airport symbol*] (OAG) ..... GUG
Guarnerius [*Irnerius*] [*Flourished, 1113-18*] [*Authority cited in pre-1607 legal work*] (DSA) ..... G
Guarnerius [*Irnerius*] [*Flourished, 1113-18*] [*Authority cited in pre-1607 legal work*] (DSA) ..... Guar
Guarumal [*Ecuador*] [*ICAO location identifier*] (ICLI) ..... SEGR
Guasdualito [*Venezuela*] [*Airport symbol*] (OAG) ..... GDO
Guasdualito, Apure [*Venezuela ICAO location identifier*] (ICLI) ..... SVGD
Guasipati, Bolivar [*Venezuela ICAO location identifier*] (ICLI) ..... SVGT
Guatemala [*ANSI two-letter standard code*] (CNC) ..... GT
Guatemala [*MARC country of publication code Library of Congress*] (LCCP) ..... gt
Guatemala [*ANSI three-letter standard code*] (CNC) ..... GTM
Guatemala [*IYRU nationality code*] (IYR) ..... GU
Guatemala (VRA) ..... GUAT
Guatemala (VRA) ..... Guat
Guatemala [*MARC geographic area code Library of Congress*] (LCCP) ..... ncgt--
Guatemala City [*Guatemala*] [*Seismograph station code, US Geological Survey Closed*] (SEIS) ..... GCG
Guatemala City [*Guatemala*] [*Airport symbol*] (OAG) ..... GUA
Guatemala Committee for Human Rights (EAIO) ..... GCHR
Guatemala/La Aurora [*Guatemala*] [*ICAO location identifier*] (ICLI) ..... MGGT
Guatemala News and Information Bureau (EA) ..... GNIB
Guatemalan Health Rights Support Project (EA) ..... GHRSP
Guatemalan Human Rights Commission/USA (EA) ..... GHR/USA
Guatemalan Solidarity Committee (EA) ..... GUASO
Guatuso [*Costa Rica*] [*ICAO location identifier*] (ICLI) ..... MRGT
Guayama, PR [*FM radio station call letters*] ..... WCRP
Guayama, PR [*AM radio station call letters*] ..... WIBS
Guayama, PR [*Television station call letters*] ..... WIDP
Guayama, PR [*FM radio station call letters*] ..... WMEG
Guayama, PR [*FM radio station call letters*] ..... WXRF
Guayana/Puerto Ordaz Internacional, Bolivar [*Venezuela ICAO location identifier*] (ICLI) ..... SVPR
Guayancourt [*France ICAO location identifier*] (ICLI) ..... LFPR
Guayanilla, PR [*AM radio station call letters*] ..... WOIZ

Guayaquil [*Ecuador*] [*Airport symbol*] (OAG) ..... GYE
Guayaquil/Simon Bolivar [*Ecuador*] [*ICAO location identifier*] (ICLI) ..... SEGU
Guayaramerin [*Bolivia*] [*Airport symbol*] (OAG) ..... GYA
Guayaramerin [*Bolivia*] [*ICAO location identifier*] (ICLI) ..... SLGY
Guaymas [*Mexico*] [*Seismograph station code, US Geological Survey*] (SEIS) ..... GYM
Guaymas [*Mexico*] [*Airport symbol*] (OAG) ..... GYM
Guaymas/General Jose Maria Yanez Internacional [*Mexico ICAO location identifier*] (ICLI) ..... MMGM
Guaymas, Mexico [*Remote site*] [*NASA*] (NASA) ..... GYM
Gubernatorial (ABBR) ..... GUBER
Gucci [*Designer*] ..... G
Gucci Group NV [*NYSE symbol*] (SAG) ..... GUC
Gucci Group NV [*Associated Press*] (SAG) ..... Gucci
Gudalupe Missioners (TOCD) ..... MG
Gude. Practice of the Crown Side of the Court of King's Bench [*1828*] [*A publication*] (DLA) ..... Gude Pr
Gudermannian Amplitude ..... GD
Guelph Collegiate Vocational Institute, Guelph, ON, Canada [*Library symbol*] [*Library of Congress*] (LCLS) ..... CaOGCV
Guelph Collegiate Vocational Institute, Ontario [*Library symbol National Library of Canada*] (NLC) ..... OGCV
Guelph, ON [*FM radio station call letters*] ..... CFRU
Guelph, ON [*FM radio station call letters*] ..... CIMJ
Guelph, ON [*AM radio station call letters*] ..... CJOY
Guelph Public Library, Guelph, ON, Canada [*Library symbol Library of Congress*] (LCLS) ..... CaOG
Guelph Public Library, Ontario [*Library symbol National Library of Canada*] (NLC) ..... OG
Gueret/Saint-Laurent [*France ICAO location identifier*] (ICLI) ..... LFCE
Guerilla ..... GUER
Guerilla (ABBR) ..... GUERL
Guerilla Urban Traffic System [*Refers to driving in Boston*] ..... GUTS
Guernsey [*International vehicle registration*] (ODBW) ..... GBG
Guernsey [*Channel Islands*] [*Airport symbol*] (OAG) ..... GCI
Guernsey Airlines [*ICAO designator*] (AD) ..... GE
Guernsey Airlines Ltd. [*British ICAO designator*] (FAAC) ..... GER
Guernsey, Channel Islands [*British ICAO location identifier*] (ICLI) ..... EGJB
Guernsey Freight Services [*British*] ..... GFS
Guernsey Growers Association [*British*] (DBA) ..... GGA
Guernsey on Questions of Insanity [*A publication*] (DLA) ..... Guern Ins
Guernsey, WY [*Location identifier FAA*] (FAAL) ..... GSZ
Guernsey's Key to Equity Jurisprudence [*A publication*] (DLA) ..... Guern Eq Jur
Guernsey's Mechanics' Lien Laws of New York [*A publication*] (DLA) ..... Guern Mech L
Guerra [*Dominican Republic*] [*ICAO location identifier*] (ICLI) ..... MDGA
Guerrero Negro [*Mexico*] [*Airport symbol*] ..... GUB
Guerrilla Art Action Group ..... GAAG
Guerrilla Warfare (AABC) ..... GW
Guerrilla Warfare Operational Area [*Army*] ..... GWOA
Guerrilleros de Cristo Rey [*Warriors of Christ and King*] [*Revolutionary Group Spain*] ..... GCR
Guertin Brothers Paint Library, Winnipeg, Manitoba [*Library symbol National Library of Canada*] (NLC) ..... MWGBP
Guertin Brothers Paint Library, Winnipeg, MB, Canada [*Library symbol Library of Congress*] (LCLS) ..... CaMWGBP
Guessed Average ..... GA
Guessed Mean [*Psychology*] (BARN) ..... GM
Guest Aerovias Mexico, SA ..... GAM
Guest House ..... GH
Guest Housing [*Army*] (AABC) ..... GHSG
Guest, Kean & Nettlefolds [*Steel-forging company*] [*British*] ..... GKN
Guest Name Record (IAA) ..... GNR
Guest Option [*Hotel plan, Hilton hotels*] ..... GO
Guest Supply [*NASDAQ symbol*] (TTSB) ..... GEST
Guest Supply, Inc. [*NASDAQ symbol*] (NQ) ..... GEST
Guest Supply, Inc. [*Associated Press*] (SAG) ..... GuestS
Guest-Host/Liquid Crystal Display [*Telecommunications*] (TEL) ..... GH/LCD
Gueterfernverkehr [*Carriage of Goods*] [*German Business term*] (ILCA) ..... GfV
Guetersloh [*Germany ICAO location identifier*] (ICLI) ..... EDUO
Guevara-McInteer-Wageman ..... GMW
Guggenheim Aeronautical Laboratory [*California Institute of Technology*] ..... GAL
Guggenheim Aeronautical Laboratory, California Institute of Technology (MCD) ..... GALCIT
Guggenheim Elementary School, Port Washington, NY [*Library symbol Library of Congress*] (LCLS) ..... NPtwGE
Guggenheim Foundation (BARN) ..... GF
Guggenheim Institute of Flight Structures (MUGU) ..... GIFS
GUI [*Graphical User Interface*] Programming Facility [*Computer science*] ..... GPF
Guiana (ROG) ..... GUI
Guiana Space Center (MCD) ..... GSC
Guias y Scouts de Europa [*Spain*] (EAIO) ..... GSE
Guidance (MSA) ..... GDNC
Guidance (AFM) ..... GDNCE
Guidance (ABBR) ..... GUDNC
Guidance (AAG) ..... GUID
Guidance (AABC) ..... GUIDN
Guidance ..... GUIDNC
Guidance Acceptance Test Set ..... GATS
Guidance Accuracy Study for SPRINT [*Missile*] [*Army*] (AABC) ..... GASS
Guidance Alignment and Checkout Console (IAA) ..... GACC
Guidance Amplifier (IAA) ..... GA
Guidance and Control [*Military*] (CAAL) ..... G & C
Guidance and Control [*Military*] (IAA) ..... GAC
Guidance and Control Analysis Team [*Space Flight Operations, NASA*] ..... GCAT

Guidance and Control Assembly (NG)	GCA
Guidance and Control Computer	GCC
Guidance and Control Coupler (KSC)	G & CC
Guidance and Control Coupler (IAA)	GACC
Guidance and Control Equipment Performance (KSC)	G & CEP
Guidance and Control Equipment Performance (IAA)	GACEP
Guidance and Control Flight Analysis Program [Aerospace]	GCFAP
Guidance and Control Information [DoD] (MCD)	GACIA
Guidance and Control Information Analysis Center [Chicago, IL DoD Also, an information service or system]	GACIAC
Guidance and Control Set Processor	GCSP
Guidance and Control System	G & CS
Guidance and Control Unit (NATG)	GCU
Guidance and Launch Operation [Aerospace] (IAA)	GLOP
Guidance and Learner Autonomy [Project] (AIE)	GALA
Guidance and Navigation [System] [Apollo] [NASA]	G & N
Guidance and Navigation	GAN
Guidance and Navigation Computer [NASA] (KSC)	GNC
Guidance and Navigation Development and Evaluation Routine (PDAA)	GANDER
Guidance and Navigation Electronics (KSC)	GNE
Guidance and Navigation Equipment	GNE
Guidance and Navigation Officer [NASA]	GUIDO
Guidance and Navigation System [Apollo] [NASA] (IAA)	GANS
Guidance and Navigation System	GNS
Guidance and Orbit Determination [NASA] (PDAA)	GOD
Guidance and Orbit Determination for Solar Electric Propulsion [NASA]	GODSEP
Guidance and Reporting System [Army]	G & RS
Guidance Attitude Space Position Indicator (MCD)	GASPI
Guidance Capsule Handling	GCH
Guidance Checkout Computer	GCC
Guidance Checkout Junction Box	GCJB
Guidance Checkout [or Control] Package (NG)	GCP
Guidance Command Test	GCT
Guidance Computer	GC
Guidance Computer Control Subsystem	GUCCO
Guidance Computer Test	GCT
Guidance Computer Test Equipment	GCTE
Guidance Control [NASA] (NASA)	GC
Guidance Control and Adapter Section (MCD)	GCA
Guidance, Control, and Airframe	GC & A
Guidance, Control, and Airframe (IAA)	GCAA
Guidance, Control, and Information Systems Division [NASA]	GCISD
Guidance Control and Navigation Subsystem	GSNS
Guidance, Control, and Ordnance	GC & O
Guidance Control and Sequencing Computer	GCSC
Guidance Control Group [Military]	GCG
Guidance Control Laboratory (AAG)	GCL
Guidance Control Launch Console (IAA)	GCLC
Guidance Control Officer (AAG)	GCO
Guidance Correction Input Panel	GCIP
Guidance Coupler Unit	GCU
Guidance Cutoff Signal [NASA] (NASA)	GCS
Guidance Data Converter [Aerospace] (AAG)	GDC
Guidance Design Manager (MCD)	GDM
Guidance Digital Evaluation Unit	GDEU
Guidance Digital Ground Station (IAA)	GDGS
Guidance Display Computer (DNAB)	GDC
Guidance Engine Cutoff [NASA] (KSC)	GECO
Guidance Error Analysis Vehicles [Air Force]	GEAV
Guidance Evaluation Missile	GEM
Guidance for Users of Integrated Data Processing Equipment	GUIDE
Guidance Heater Control	GHC
Guidance Inertial Data Analysis Program	GIDAP
Guidance Information System [Houghton Mifflin Co.] [Information service or system] (IID)	GIS
Guidance Integration Unit (MCD)	GIU
Guidance Inventory [Psychology]	GI
Guidance Monitor Set [Aerospace] (AAG)	GMS
Guidance, Navigation, and Control (MCD)	GN & C
Guidance, Navigation, and Control [Military] (IAA)	GNAC
Guidance, Navigation, and Control (NASA)	GNC
Guidance, Navigation, and Control Integration Simulator (NASA)	GNCIS
Guidance, Navigation, and Control System (MCD)	GNCS
Guidance Officer (KSC)	GDO
Guidance Optical Alignment Shelter (KSC)	GOAS
Guidance Optics and Sighting	GOST
Guidance Package	GP
Guidance Package Installation Dolly [Polaris missile]	GPID
Guidance Platform Assembly [Military] (AABC)	GPA
Guidance Position Tracking [Aerospace] (AAG)	GPT
Guidance Positioning Assembly	GPA
Guidance Power Supply	GPS
Guidance Power Temperature Regulator	GPTR
Guidance Rate Measurement	GRM
Guidance Reference Release (KSC)	GRR
Guidance Regulator Unit	GRU
Guidance Shipping Container	GSC
Guidance Signal Processor (KSC)	GSP
Guidance Signal Processor-Repeater (KSC)	GSP-R
Guidance Simulator	GS
Guidance Spare Power Supply	GSPS
Guidance Station [Aerospace] (AAG)	GS
Guidance Sustainer Cutoff [Aerospace] (AAG)	GSCO

Guidance Switching Unit [Aviation]	GSU
Guidance System [Aerospace] (AAG)	GS
Guidance System Analyst [Aerospace] (IAA)	GSA
Guidance System Console [Aerospace] (AAG)	GSC
Guidance System Evaluation [Military] (IAA)	GUISE
Guidance System Evaluation Laboratory [Military] (CAAL)	GSEL
Guidance System Simulator	GSS
Guidance System Test Equipment	GSTE
Guidance System Test Set	GSTS
Guidance System Test Unit	GSTU
Guidance Systems Operation Plan [NASA] (KSC)	GSOP
Guidance Test and Simulation Facility	GTSF
Guidance Test Equipment	GTE
Guidance Test Fixture	GTF
Guidance Test Set (AAG)	GTS
Guidance Test Unit	GTU
Guidance [or Guided] Test Vehicle	GTV
Guidance Transfer Container	GTC
Guidance Transmitter (AAG)	G/XMTR
Guidance Transmitter (NVT)	GT
Guidance Unit	GU
Guidance Unit Assembly	GUA
Guidance Using Stable Tuning Oscillations	GUSTO
Guidance Year [DoD]	GY
Guidant Corp. [NYSE symbol] (SAG)	GDT
Guidant Corp. [Associated Press] (SAG)	Guidant
Guide	G
Guide [or Guided] (MSA)	GDE
Guide (ABBR)	GUD
Guide	GUID
Guide Dog Foundation for the Blind [Also known as Second Sight Guiding Eyes - Guide Dog Foundation] (EA)	GDFB
Guide Dog Owners and Friends' Association [Australia]	GDOFA
Guide Dog Users (EA)	GDU
Guide Dogs for the Blind (EA)	GDB
Guide Dogs for the Blind Association [British] (EAIO)	GDBA
Guide Light (AAG)	GLT
Guide Line Identification Program for Antimissile Research [ARPA]	GLIPAR
Guide Line Paper [of Washington Standardization Officers] [Military]	GLP
Guide Ribonucleic Acid [Genetics]	gRNA
Guide Slope (MUGU)	GS
Guide to Air Pilots and Air Navigation [A publication]	GAPAN
Guide to American Directories [A publication]	GAD
Guide to Baseball Literature [A publication]	GBL
Guide to Computing Literature [A publication] (IT)	GCL
Guide to Football Literature [A publication]	GFL
Guide to International Education in the US [A publication]	GIEUS
Guide to International Scientific Publications and Associations [A publication]	GISPA
Guide to New Australian Books [A publication]	GNAB
Guide Tube Assembly (NRCH)	GTA
Guidebook	GB
Guidebook (ABBR)	GUDBK
Guided (ABBR)	GUDD
Guided Acoustic Wave Brillouin Scattering [Physics]	GAWBS
Guided Aerial Rocket	GAR
Guided Air Defense Rocket	GADR
Guided Air Missile (AAGC)	GAM
Guided Aircraft Missile [Obsolete]	GAM
Guided Aircraft Rocket	GAR
Guided Air-to-Surface Rocket (IAA)	GASR
Guided Antiaircraft Missile [Military] (IAA)	GAAM
Guided Antiarmor Mortar Projectile (INF)	GAMP
Guided Antiarmor Rocket	GAR
Guided Antiradiation Bomb	GARB
Guided Antitank Projectile (MCD)	GAP
Guided Atomic Warhead	GAW
Guided Bomb Unit (MCD)	GBU
Guided Fault Isolation	GFI
Guided Flight Test (MCD)	GFT
Guided Flight Vehicle	GFV
Guided Folding-Fin Aircraft Rocket	GFFAR
Guided Imagery [Psychology]	GI
Guided Intrusion Detection and Ranging (PDAA)	GUIDAR
Guided Missile	G/MSL
Guided Missile	GM
Guided Missile Aircraft Carrier [Navy symbol]	CVG
Guided Missile Aircraft Carrier [Navy symbol]	CVGH
Guided Missile Aircraft Carrier [Navy symbol]	CVHGN
Guided Missile Ammunition (AABC)	GMA
Guided Missile and Aerospace Intelligence Committee (AFM)	GMAIC
Guided Missile and Large Rocket	GMLR
Guided Missile Assembly Building (SAA)	GMAB
Guided Missile Aviation Destroyer [Navy symbol]	DDHG
Guided Missile Brigade [Army]	GMB
Guided Missile Capital Ship [Navy symbol Obsolete]	BBG
Guided Missile Coastal Escort [Ship symbol] (NATG)	PCG
Guided Missile Committee [Army]	GMC
Guided Missile Control (AAG)	GMC
Guided Missile Control Facility (AAG)	GMCF
Guided Missile Control Officer (AAG)	GMCO
Guided Missile Control Party (IAA)	GMCP
Guided Missile Countermeasure [NATO]	GMCM
Guided Missile Cruiser [Navy symbol]	CG
Guided Missile Cruiser (MCD)	CGX

Guided Missile Cruiser (Nuclear Propulsion) [*Navy symbol*] .... CGN
Guided Missile Data Exchange Program [*Navy*] .... GMDEP
Guided Missile Destroyer [*Navy symbol*] .... DDG
Guided Missile Destroyer .... DDGX
Guided Missile Destroyer [*Navy symbol*] .... DXG
Guided Missile Destroyer, Nuclear-Propulsion [*Navy symbol*] .... DXGN
Guided Missile Development Division [*NASA*] (KSC) .... GMDD
Guided Missile Escort Ship [*Navy symbol*] .... DEG
Guided Missile Evaluation Unit (MUGU) .... GMEVALU
Guided Missile Evaluator .... GME
Guided Missile Facilities (NG) .... GMF
Guided Missile Fast Patrol Boat [*Ship symbol*] (NATG) .... PBFG
Guided Missile Fire Control .... GMFC
Guided Missile Fire Control System (NG) .... GMFCS
Guided Missile Firing Panel .... GMFP
Guided Missile Frigate [*Navy symbol*] .... DLG
Guided Missile Frigate [*Navy symbol*] .... FFG
Guided Missile Frigate (Nuclear Propulsion) [*Navy symbol*] .... DLGN
Guided Missile General Support (MCD) .... GMGS
Guided Missile Group (MUGU) .... GMGRU
Guided Missile Heavy Cruiser (MCD) .... CAF
Guided Missile Heavy Cruiser [*Navy symbol Obsolete*] .... CAG
Guided Missile Heavy Cruiser (Nuclear Propulsion) [*Navy symbol*] .... CAG(N)
Guided Missile Launcher (NG) .... GML
Guided Missile Launching System .... GMLS
Guided Missile Launching System Control (DWSG) .... GMLSC
Guided Missile Light Aircraft Carrier (MCD) .... CVLG
Guided Missile Light Cruiser [*Navy symbol*] .... CLG
Guided Missile Light Cruiser (Nuclear Propulsion) [*Navy symbol Obsolete*] .... CLGN
Guided Missile Officer .... GMO
Guided Missile Operation and Control Unit .... GMOCU
Guided Missile Operations Officer (AAG) .... GMOO
Guided Missile Patrol Escort [*Ship symbol*] (NATG) .... PFGM
Guided Missile Range Division [*NASA*] (KSC) .... GMRD
Guided Missile Relay Working Group [*Navy*] .... GMRWG
Guided Missile School [*Dam Neck, VA*] .... GMS
Guided Missile Service Record .... GMSR
Guided Missile Service Report (NG) .... GMSER
Guided Missile Service Report (MCD) .... GMSR
Guided Missile Service Squadron (MUGU) .... GMSRON
Guided Missile Service Unit [*Air Force*] .... GMSU
Guided Missile Ship [*Navy symbol*] .... AVM
Guided Missile Simulator [*Military*] (CAAL) .... GMS
Guided Missile Squadron (MUGU) .... GMSQUAD
Guided Missile Strike Cruiser [*Navy symbol*] (NVT) .... CSG
Guided Missile Submarine [*Navy symbol*] .... SSG
Guided Missile Submarine (Nuclear Propulsion) [*Navy symbol*] .... SSGN
Guided Missile System .... GMS
Guided Missile System, Intercept-Aerial (MCD) .... GMSIA
Guided Missile System Test Set (NATG) .... GMSTS
Guided Missile Target (NG) .... GMT
Guided Missile Test Round [*Military*] (CAAL) .... GMTR
Guided Missile Test Set (AFM) .... GMTS
Guided Missile Test Unit (IAA) .... GMTU
Guided Missile Trainer .... GMT
Guided Missile Training Unit [*Navy*] .... GMTU
Guided Missile Unit .... GMU
Guided Missile Vertical Launch System [*Canadian Navy*] .... GMVLS
Guided Missile Weapon System [*Military*] (CAAL) .... GMWS
Guided Parafoil Aerial Delivery System .... GPADS
Guided Projectile [*Military*] (CAAL) .... GP
Guided Social Simulation .... GUSS
Guided Space Vehicle [*Air Force*] .... GSV
Guided Tactical Vehicle [*Army*] .... GTV
Guided Tour [*On a bus*] [*British*] .... G
Guided Unified S-Band (MCD) .... GUSB
Guided Warheads .... GWH
Guided Weapon [*Air Force*] .... GW
Guided Weapon Station (IAA) .... GWS
Guided Weapons Evaluation Facility (MCD) .... GWEF
Guided Wire [*British military*] (DMA) .... GW
Guided Writing Procedure [*Reading improvement method*] .... GWP
Guidelines and Rules for Data Systems Management (TEL) .... GUARDSMAN
Guidelines for Authority and Reference Entries [*Cataloguing*] [*Association for Library Collections and Technical Services*] .... GARE
Guidelines for Investigation, Planning, and Research .... GLIPAR
Guidelines for Review and Internal Development in Schools (AIE) .... GRIDS
Guidelines for the Use of Advisory and Assistance Services [*OMB Circular*] (AAGC) A-120
Guidelines Implementation Staff [*Environmental Protection Agency*] (GFGA) .... GIS
Guidelines Marketing Corp. .... GUIMARC
Guide-Number [*Photography*] .... GN
Guidepost (ABBR) .... GUDPST
Guiding (ABBR) .... GUDG
Guiding Eyes for the Blind (EA) .... GEB
Guiding Light Fan Club (EA) .... GLFC
Guido de Baysio [*Deceased, 1313*] [*Authority cited in pre-1607 legal work*] (DSA) .... G
Guido de Baysio [*Deceased, 1313*] [*Authority cited in pre-1607 legal work*] (DSA) .... G de Bay
Guido de Cumis [*Flourished, 13th century*] [*Authority cited in pre-1607 legal work*] (DSA) .... Gui
Guido de Suzaria [*Deceased, 1293*] [*Authority cited in pre-1607 legal work*] (DSA) .... G
Guido de Suzaria [*Deceased, 1293*] [*Authority cited in pre-1607 legal work*] (DSA) .... G de Suz
Guido de Suzaria [*Deceased, 1293*] [*Authority cited in pre-1607 legal work*] (DSA) .... Gi
Guido de Suzaria [*Deceased, 1293*] [*Authority cited in pre-1607 legal work*] (DSA) .... Gui
Guido de Suzaria [*Deceased, 1293*] [*Authority cited in pre-1607 legal work*] (DSA) .... Gui de Su
Guido de Suzaria [*Deceased, 1293*] [*Authority cited in pre-1607 legal work*] (DSA) .... Gui de Suz
Guido de Suzaria [*Deceased, 1293*] [*Authority cited in pre-1607 legal work*] (DSA) .... Gui de Suza
Guido Pancirolus [*Deceased, 1599*] [*Authority cited in pre-1607 legal work*] (DSA) .... Guid Pancir
Guido Pancirolus [*Deceased, 1599*] [*Authority cited in pre-1607 legal work*] (DSA) .... Guid Pancirol
Guido Papa [*Deceased, 1487*] [*Authority cited in pre-1607 legal work*] (DSA) .... Guid Pap
Guidonia [*Italy ICAO location identifier*] (ICLI) .... LIRG
Guidotti & C. [*Italy*] [*Research code symbol*] .... LG
Guierrezia Xylem Sap Potential [*Botany*] .... GXSP
Guiglo [*Ivory Coast*] [*ICAO location identifier*] (ICLI) .... DIGL
Guiglo [*Ivory Coast*] [*Airport symbol*] (OAG) .... GGO
Guild .... GLD
Guild .... GLD
Guild for Infant Survival [*Later, ICIS*] .... GIS
Guild for Religious Architecture [*Later, IFRAA*] .... GRA
Guild for the Promotion of Welsh Music (EAIO) .... GPWM
Guild Lawyer [*National Lawyers' Guild*] [*New York Chapter*] [*A publication*] (DLA) .... Guild Law
Guild Library [*Church of Scotland*] [*A publication*] .... GL
Guild of Agricultural Journalists .... GAJ
Guild of Air Pilots and Air Navigators (MCD) .... GAPAN
Guild of Air Traffic Control Officers [*British*] .... GATCO
Guild of All Saints [*British*] (ROG) .... GAS
Guild of All Souls [*British*] .... GAS
Guild of American Funeral Directors [*Defunct*] .... GAFD
Guild of American Luthiers (EA) .... GAL
Guild of Antique Dealers and Restorers [*British*] (DBA) .... GADAR
Guild of Architectural Ironmongers [*British*] (BI) .... GAI
Guild of Aviation Artists (DA) .... GAvA
Guild of Aviation Artists [*British*] (DBA) .... GAvA
Guild of Better Shoe Manufacturers .... GBSM
Guild of Book Workers (EA) .... GBW
Guild of Bricklayers [*British*] (BI) .... GB
Guild of British Butlers [*British*] (EAIO) .... GBB
Guild of British Camera Technicians (DBA) .... GBCT
Guild of British Dispensing Opticians (BI) .... GBDO
Guild of British Newspapers Editors (BI) .... GBNE
Guild of Business Travel Agents [*British*] (DBA) .... GBTA
Guild of Canadian Musical Theatre Writers [*Canada*] (WWLA) .... GCMTW
Guild of Carillonneurs in North America (EA) .... GCNA
Guild of Catholic Lawyers (EA) .... GCL
Guild of Catholic Psychiatrists [*Later, National Guild of Catholic Psychiatrists*] (EA) .... GCP
Guild of Church Musicians [*British*] (DBA) .... GCM
Guild of Cleaners and Launderers [*British*] (DBA) .... GCL
Guild of Computer Practitioners [*British*] (DBA) .... GCP
Guild of Dispensing Opticians (Australia) .... GDO(A)
Guild of Drama Adjudicators [*British*] (BI) .... GODA
Guild of Dyers and Cleaners [*British*] (BI) .... GDC
Guild of Ethical Funeral Practice (EA) .... GEFP
Guild of Experienced Motorists [*British*] (DBA) .... GEM
Guild of Guide Lecturers [*British*] .... GGL
Guild of Hospital Pharmacists [*British*] (DBA) .... GHP
Guild of Insurance Officials [*British*] (BI) .... GIO
Guild of International Butler Administrators and Personal Assistants [*British*] (EAIO) .... GIBAPA
Guild of Lady Drivers [*British*] (BI) .... GOLD
Guild of Memorial Craftsmen [*British*] (BI) .... GMC
Guild of Metal Perforators [*British*] (DBA) .... GMP
Guild of Natural Science Illustrators (EA) .... GNSI
Guild of New York Opera [*Record label*] .... GNYO
Guild of One Name Studies [*Organization to link people with a common surname for the study of family history*] [*British*] .... GOONS
Guild of Pastoral Psychology [*British*] (DBA) .... GPP
Guild of Prescription Opticians of America [*Later, OAA*] (EA) .... GPOA
Guild of Professional Launderers and Cleaners [*British*] (BI) .... GPLC
Guild of Public Pharmacists [*British*] (BI) .... GPP
Guild of Radio Service Engineers (BARN) .... GRSE
Guild of Saint Alban .... GSA
Guild of Saint Ives (EA) .... GSI
Guild of Saint Matthew .... GSM
Guild of Sorting Clerks and Telegraphists [*A union*] [*British*] .... GSCT
Guild of Surveyors [*Middlesex, England*] (EAIO) .... GS
Guild of Teachers of Backward Children [*British*] (BI) .... GTBC
Guild of Television Cameramen [*British*] (EA) .... GTC
Guild of Temple Musicians (EA) .... GTM
Guild of the Infant Saviour [*Defunct*] (EA) .... GIS
Guild of Traditional Butlers .... GTB
Guild of Travel Writers [*British*] .... GTW
Guild of Washington Incompetent Bureaucratic Idea Throatcutters [*An organizati on rumored to have been active in World War II*] .... GWIBIT

Guild of Young Printers (DGA) ... GYP
Guild Resource File [*Guild Products, Inc.*] [*Computer science*] (PCM) ... GRF
Guild to Revive Exhausted Nurses ... GREEN
Guild Vector Colorimeter ... GVC
Guilde Europeenne du Raid [*European Expedition Guild - EEG*] (EAIO) ... GER
Guilde International du Disque [*Record label*] [*France*] ... GID
Guilder [*Florin*] [*Monetary unit Netherlands*] ... FL
Guilder [*Modification of gulden*] [*Monetary unit*] [*Netherlands*] ... G
Guilder [*Modification of gulden*] [*Monetary unit*] [*Netherlands*] ... Gld
Guilder (ABBR) ... GUIL
Guilder [*Florin*] [*Monetary unit Netherlands Antilles*] ... NAF
Guildford [*City in England*] (ROG) ... GUILDF
Guildhall (ABBR) ... GUILDHL
Guildhall Library, Aldermanbury, London, United Kingdom [*Library symbol Library of Congress*] (LCLS) ... UkLG
Guildhall Museum [*London*] ... GMUS
Guildhall School of Music [*London*] ... GSM
Guildhall School of Music and Drama [*London*] (DI) ... GSMD
Guileful (ABBR) ... GUILFL
Guilefully (ABBR) ... GUILFY
Guileless (ABBR) ... GUILS
Guilelessly (ABBR) ... GUILSY
Guilford College, Greensboro, NC [*Library symbol Library of Congress*] (LCLS) ... NcGG
Guilford Courthouse National Military Park ... GUCO
Guilford, CT [*FM radio station call letters*] ... WGRS
Guilford High School, Rockford, IL [*Library symbol*] [*Library of Congress*] (LCLS) ... IRoGH
Guilford Mills [*NYSE symbol*] (SAG) ... GFD
Guilford Mills, Inc. [*Associated Press*] (SAG) ... Guilford
Guilford Pharmaceuticals [*NASDAQ symbol*] (TTSB) ... GLFD
Guilford Pharmaceuticals, Inc. [*NASDAQ symbol*] (SAG) ... GLFD
Guilford Pharmaceuticals, Inc. [*Associated Press*] (SAG) ... GuilfrdP
Guilford Technical Community College, Learning Resource Center, Greensboro, NC [*Library symbol Library of Congress*] (LCLS) ... NcGGT
Guilford Technical Institute, Jamestown, NC [*Library symbol Library of Congress*] (LCLS) ... NcJG
Guilford-Holley L Inventory [*Psychology*] ... GHLI
Guilford-Martin Personnel Inventory [*Psychology*] ... GMPI
Guilford-Zimmerman Aptitude Survey [*Test*] ... GZAS
Guilford-Zimmerman Aptitude Survey: General Reasoning [*Test*] ... GZAS:GR
Guilford-Zimmerman Aptitude Survey: Numerical Operations [*Test*] ... GZAS:NO
Guilford-Zimmerman Aptitude Survey: Perceptual Speed [*Test*] ... GZAS:PS
Guilford-Zimmerman Aptitude Survey: Spatial Orientation [*Test*] ... GZAS:SO
Guilford-Zimmerman Aptitude Survey: Spatial Visualization [*Test*] ... GZAS:SV
Guilford-Zimmerman Aptitude Survey: Verbal Comprehension [*Test*] ... GZAS:VC
Guilford-Zimmerman Interest Inventory [*Vocational guidance test*] ... GZII
Guilford-Zimmerman Personality Test [*Psychology*] (MAE) ... GZ
Guilford-Zimmerman Temperament Survey [*Psychology*] ... GZTS
Guilin [*China*] [*Airport symbol*] (OAG) ... KWL
Guilin [*China*] [*ICAO location identifier*] (ICLI) ... ZGKL
Guillain-Barre [*Syndrome*] [*Medicine*] ... GB
Guillain-Barre Syndrome [*Medicine*] ... GBS
Guillain-Barre Syndrome Foundation International (EA) ... GBSFI
Guillain-Barre Syndrome Support Group [*Later, GBSFI*] (EA) ... GBSSG
Guillain-Barre Syndrome Support Group International [*Later, GBSFI*] (EA) ... GBSSGI
Guillelmus de Accursio [*Deceased, 1314*] [*Authority cited in pre-1607 legal work*] (DSA) ... G Ac
Guillelmus de Accursio [*Deceased, 1314*] [*Authority cited in pre-1607 legal work*] (DSA) ... Gui
Guillelmus de Benedictis [*Flourished, 16th century*] [*Authority cited in pre-1607 legal work*] (DSA) ... Guil Bene
Guillelmus de Benedictis [*Flourished, 16th century*] [*Authority cited in pre-1607 legal work*] (DSA) ... Guillel Bened
Guillelmus de Cabriano [*Deceased, 1201*] [*Authority cited in pre-1607 legal work*] (DSA) ... G de Ca
Guillelmus de Cuneo [*Deceased, 1335*] [*Authority cited in pre-1607 legal work*] (DSA) ... G de Cu
Guillelmus de Cuneo [*Deceased, 1335*] [*Authority cited in pre-1607 legal work*] (DSA) ... Gui de Cu
Guillelmus de Cuneo [*Deceased, 1335*] [*Authority cited in pre-1607 legal work*] (DSA) ... Gul
Guillelmus de Ferreriis [*Deceased, 1295*] [*Authority cited in pre-1607 legal work*] (DSA) ... G de Fr
Guillelmus de Monte Lauduno [*Deceased, 1343*] [*Authority cited in pre-1607 legal work*] (DSA) ... G de Mon
Guillelmus de Monte Lauduno [*Deceased, 1343*] [*Authority cited in pre-1607 legal work*] (DSA) ... G de Mon Lau
Guillelmus de Monte Lauduno [*Deceased, 1343*] [*Authority cited in pre-1607 legal work*] (DSA) ... G de Mon Laud
Guillelmus de Monte Lauduno [*Deceased, 1343*] [*Authority cited in pre-1607 legal work*] (DSA) ... Guill de Montelaud
Guillelmus de Tocco [*Authority cited in pre-1607 legal work*] (DSA) ... G
Guillelmus de Tocco [*Authority cited in pre-1607 legal work*] (DSA) ... Gu
Guillelmus de Tocco [*Authority cited in pre-1607 legal work*] (DSA) ... Gui
Guillelmus Durandi [*Deceased, 1296*] [*Authority cited in pre-1607 legal work*] (DSA) ... G Dur
Guillelmus Durandi [*Deceased, 1296*] [*Authority cited in pre-1607 legal work*] (DSA) ... G Duran
Guillelmus Durandi [*Deceased, 1296*] [*Authority cited in pre-1607 legal work*] (DSA) ... Gil
Guillelmus Durandi [*Deceased, 1296*] [*Authority cited in pre-1607 legal work*] (DSA) ... Gil Dur
Guillelmus Durandi [*Deceased, 1296*] [*Authority cited in pre-1607 legal work*] (DSA) ... Guill
Guillelmus Naso [*Flourished, 1220-34*] [*Authority cited in pre-1607 legal work*] (DSA) ... G Nas
Guillelmus Naso [*Flourished, 1220-34*] [*Authority cited in pre-1607 legal work*] (DSA) ... Guil Na
Guillevin International, Inc. [*Toronto Stock Exchange symbol*] ... GII
Guillotine (MSA) ... GLTN
Guillotine [*Bookbinding*] (DGA) ... GULL
Guillotine (ABBR) ... GULTN
Guillotine Trimmed [*Bookbinding*] (DGA) ... GTE TMD
Guillotined (ABBR) ... GULTND
Guillotining (ABBR) ... GULTNG
Guilt Free Goodies [*Vancouver Stock Exchange symbol*] ... GTF
Guilty ... G
Guilty-but-Mentally-Ill [*Legal term*] ... GBMI
Guinea [*Aircraft nationality and registration mark*] (FAAC) ... 3X
Guinea [*MARC geographic area code Library of Congress*] (LCCP) ... f-gv--
Guinea [*Monetary unit*] [*Obsolete British*] ... G
Guinea [*ANSI three-letter standard code*] (CNC) ... GIN
Guinea [*ANSI two-letter standard code*] (CNC) ... GN
Guinea ... GU
Guinea [*Monetary unit*] [*Obsolete British*] (ROG) ... GUA
Guinea [*Monetary unit*] [*Obsolete British*] (ROG) ... GUIN
Guinea (VRA) ... Guin
Guinea [*MARC country of publication code Library of Congress*] (LCCP) ... gv
Guinea Airways Ltd. ... GAL
Guinea Gulf Line [*Steamship*] (MHDB) ... GG
Guinea Pig ... GP
Guinea Pig Albumin ... GPA
Guinea Pig Anti-Bovine Protection (OA) ... GPABP
Guinea Pig Anti-Insulin Serum [*Immunochemistry*] (MAE) ... GPAIS
Guinea Pig Complement [*Immunochemistry*] ... GPC
Guinea Pig Control Serum (OA) ... GPCS
Guinea Pig Embryo [*Medicine*] (DMAA) ... GPE
Guinea Pig Fibrinogen ... GPF
Guinea Pig Gamma Globulin [*Immunochemistry*] ... GPGG
Guinea Pig Herpes Virus (DMAA) ... GPHV
Guinea Pig Herpes-Like Virus [*Medicine*] (DMAA) ... GPHLV
Guinea Pig Ileum (DMAA) ... GPI
Guinea Pig Intestinal Mucosal Homogenate (MAE) ... GPIMH
Guinea Pig Intraperitoneal Infectious Dose [*Clinical chemistry*] (MAE) ... GPIPID
Guinea Pig Kidney Absorption (Test) [*Clinical chemistry*] ... GPKA
Guinea Pig Kidney Antigen [*Immunochemistry*] (MAE) ... GPK
Guinea Pig Myelin Basic Protein [*Immunochemistry*] ... GPBP
Guinea Pig Serum ... GPS
Guinea Pig Spinal Cord ... GPSC
Guinea Pig Spleen ... GPS
Guinea Pig Unit [*Endocrinology*] ... GPU
Guinea Pig Vascular Permeability Factor [*Biochemistry*] ... GVPF
Guinea-Bissau [*ANSI three-letter standard code*] (CNC) ... GNB
Guinea-Bissau [*ANSI two-letter standard code*] (CNC) ... GW
Guinea-Bissau [*International civil aircraft marking*] (ODBW) ... J5
Guinea-Bissau Peso [*Monetary unit*] ... GBP
Guinean Franc [*Monetary unit*] (ODBW) ... GF
Guinean Trawling Survey [*United Nations*] ... GTS
Guineas [*Monetary unit*] [*Obsolete British*] ... GNS
Guinee Air Lines SA [*Guinea*] [*ICAO designator*] (FAAC) ... GIF
Guinee Air Service [*Guinea*] [*ICAO designator*] (FAAC) ... GIS
Guinee Inter Air [*Guinea*] [*ICAO designator*] (FAAC) ... GIE
Guinness Overseas Ltd. [*British*] ... GOL
Guinness Peat Aviation [*Commercial firm British*] ... GPA
Guinness Peat Group [*British*] ... GPG
Guiratinga [*Brazil*] [*Airport symbol*] (AD) ... GUZ
Guiraudus Pargues [*Authority cited in pre-1607 legal work*] (DSA) ... Par
Guiraudus Pargues [*Authority cited in pre-1607 legal work*] (DSA) ... Pargs
Guiren [*China*] [*ICAO location identifier*] (ICLI) ... RCXY
Guiria [*Venezuela*] [*Airport symbol*] (OAG) ... GUI
Guiria, Sucre [*Venezuela ICAO location identifier*] (ICLI) ... SVGI
Guirsh [*Monetary unit*] [*Saudi Arabia*] ... G
Guiscriff-Scaer [*France ICAO location identifier*] (ICLI) ... LFES
Guitar [*Music*] ... G
Guitar [*Music*] ... GTR
Guitar [*Music*] ... GUI
Guitar [*Music*] ... Guit
Guitar and Accesories Music Marketing Association (EA) ... GAMMA
Guitar and Accessory Manufacturers Association [*Formerly, NAMMM*] ... GAMA
Guitar Foundation of America (EA) ... GFA
Guiuan, Eastern Samar [*Philippines*] [*ICAO location identifier*] (ICLI) ... RPVG
Guiyang [*China*] [*Airport symbol*] (OAG) ... KWE
Guiyang [*China*] [*ICAO location identifier*] (ICLI) ... ZUGY
Guizhon Airlines [*China*] [*FAA designator*] (FAAC) ... CGH
Guizot's History of Representative Government [*A publication*] (DLA) ... Guizot Rep Govt
Guizzardinus [*Deceased, 1222*] [*Authority cited in pre-1607 legal work*] (DSA) ... G
Guizzardinus [*Deceased, 1222*] [*Authority cited in pre-1607 legal work*] (DSA) ... Guiz
Guizzardinus [*Deceased, 1222*] [*Authority cited in pre-1607 legal work*] (DSA) ... Gz
Gujarat, India (ILCA) ... Guj Ind
Gujarat Law Reporter [*A publication*] (ILCA) ... Guj L Rep
Gujarati [*MARC language code Library of Congress*] (LCCP) ... guj
Gujrat [*Pakistan*] [*Airport symbol*] (AD) ... GRT
Gul [*Ecuador*] [*ICAO location identifier*] (ICLI) ... SEGL
Gulbarga [*India*] [*ICAO location identifier*] (ICLI) ... VOGB

Gulden [*Monetary unit*] [*Netherlands*] ... G
Gulderand Mining [*Vancouver Stock Exchange symbol*] ... GUM
Gules [*Heraldry*] ... G
Gules [*Heraldry*] ... GU
Gulf [*Maps and charts*] ... G
Gulf Air [*ICAO designator*] (AD) ... GF
Gulf Air [*United Arab Emirates*] [*ICAO designator*] (FAAC) ... GFA
Gulf Air, Inc. [*ICAO designator*] (FAAC) ... GAT
Gulf and Caribbean Fisheries Institute (EA) ... GCFI
Gulf & Mississippi Railroad ... G & M
Gulf & Ship Island Railroad Co. ... G & SI
Gulf & South American Steamship Co. (MHDB) ... GSA
Gulf & Western Industries, Inc. ... G & W
Gulf & Western Industries, Inc. ... G & WI
Gulf Atomic Mobile Assay System ... GAMAS
Gulf Breeze Environmental Research Laboratory [*Gulf Breeze, FL*] [*Environmental Protection Agency*] (GRD) ... ERL/GB
Gulf Breeze Environmental Research Laboratory [*Environmental Protection Agency*] (MSC) ... GBERL
Gulf Can ResAdjcm Ser 1 Pref [*NYSE symbol*] (TTSB) ... GOUPrA
Gulf Canada Ltd. [*UTLAS symbol*] ... GCL
Gulf Canada Ltd., Calgary, Alberta [*Library symbol National Library of Canada*] (NLC) ... ACGO
Gulf Canada Resources [*NYSE symbol*] (TTSB) ... GOU
Gulf Canada Resources Ltd. [*Associated Press*] (SAG) ... GlfCda
Gulf Canada Resources Ltd. [*AMEX symbol Toronto Stock Exchange symbol*] ... GOU
Gulf Central Airlines, Inc. [*ICAO designator*] (FAAC) ... GCN
Gulf Coast Base Service Unit ... GULFCOBASESERVUNIT
Gulf Coast Bible College, Houston, TX [*Library symbol Library of Congress*] (LCLS) ... TxHG
Gulf Coast Fisheries Center ... GCFC
Gulf Coast Hydroscience Center [*Department of the Interior*] [*National Space Technology Laboratories Station, MS*] (GRD) ... GCHC
Gulf Coast Low Water Datum ... GCLWD
Gulf Coast Research Laboratory [*Ocean Springs, MS*] ... GCRL
Gulf Coast Waste Disposal Authority [*Governmental industrial waste disposal system*] ... GCWDA
Gulf, Colorado & Santa Fe Railway Co. ... GC & SF
Gulf, Colorado & Santa Fe Railway Co. [*AAR code*] ... GCSF
Gulf Communications, Inc. [*Melbourne, FL*] [*Telecommunications service*] (TSSD) ... GCI
Gulf Control ... GULFCON
Gulf Cooperation Council [*Consists of Saudi Arabia, Bahrain, Kuwait, Oman, Qatar, and the United Arab Emirates*] ... GCC
Gulf Cooperative Council (EERA) ... GCC
Gulf Division Naval Facilities Engineering Command ... DIRGULFDOCKS
Gulf Division Naval Facilities Engineering Command ... GULFNAVFACENGCOM
Gulf Energy & Minerals Co. ... GEM
Gulf Environmental Measurements Program (MCD) ... GEP
Gulf Flite Center, Inc. [*ICAO designator*] (FAAC) ... SFY
Gulf Florida & Alabama Railway ... GF & A
Gulf General Atomic [*Commercial firm*] ... GGA
Gulf Intercoastal Conference ... GIC
Gulf International Bank [*Bahrain*] (EY) ... GIB
Gulf International Minerals [*Vancouver Stock Exchange symbol*] ... GIM
Gulf Intracoastal Waterway ... GIW
Gulf Intracoastal Waterway ... GIWW
Gulf Islands Secondary School, Ganges, BC, Canada [*Library symbol Library of Congress*] (LCLS) ... CaBGS
Gulf Islands Secondary School, Ganges, British Columbia [*Library symbol Library network*] (NLC) ... BGS
Gulf It to FORTRAN [*Translator*] [*Computer science*] ... GIF
Gulf Minerals Canada Ltd., Toronto, Ontario [*Library symbol National Library of Canada*] (NLC) ... OTGMC
Gulf Mobile & Northern Railroad ... GM & N
Gulf, Mobile & Ohio [*Railroad*] (MHDB) ... GFO
Gulf, Mobile & Ohio Railroad [*Later, Illinois Central Gulf Railroad*] (IIA) ... GFO
Gulf, Mobile & Ohio Railroad [*Later, Illinois Central Gulf Railroad*] ... GM & O
Gulf, Mobile & Ohio Railroad [*Later, Illinois Central Gulf Railroad*] [*AAR code*] ... GMO
Gulf of Alaska (FAAC) ... GLFALSK
Gulf of Alaska/Bering Sea, AK [*Location identifier FAA*] (FAAL) ... EZR
Gulf of Alaska Mesoscale Oceanographic Processes ... GAS-MOP
Gulf of Alaska SEASAT Experiment [*National Oceanic and Atmospheric Administration*] ... GOASEX
Gulf of California (FAAC) ... GLFCAL
Gulf of Mexico (FAAC) ... GLFMEX
Gulf of Mexico [*Also, GLFMEX*] ... GOM
Gulf of Mexico [*Project*] [*Marine science*] (OSRA) ... GUFMEX
Gulf of Mexico [*Project*] (USDC) ... GUFMEX
Gulf of Mexico [*MARC geographic area code Library of Congress*] (LCCP) ... nm----
Gulf of Mexico Estuarine Inventory (PDAA) ... GMEI
Gulf of Mexico Fishery Management Council (MSC) ... GMFMC
Gulf of Mexico, LA [*Location identifier FAA*] (FAAL) ... HQK
Gulf of St. Lawrence (FAAC) ... GLFSTLAWR
Gulf Offshore Weather Observing Network (USDC) ... GOWON
Gulf Offshore Weather Observing Network [*Marine science*] (OSRA) ... GOWON
Gulf Oil Canada Ltd., Calgary, AB, Canada [*Library symbol Library of Congress*] (LCLS) ... CaACGO
Gulf Oil Canada Ltd., Mississauga, ON, Canada [*Library symbol Library of Congress*] (LCLS) ... CaOMGO
Gulf Oil Chemicals Co. ... GOCHEM
Gulf Oil Co.-US, Central Reference Library, Houston, TX [*Library symbol Library of Congress*] (LCLS) ... TxHGO
Gulf Oil Real Estate Development Co. ... GOREDCO
Gulf Oil Trading Co. ... GOTCO
Gulf Oil Wholesale Marketers Association (EA) ... GOWMA
Gulf Organization for Development in Egypt ... GODE
Gulf Organization for Industrial Consulting [*Doha, Qatar*] (EAIO) ... GOIC
Gulf Permanent Assistance Committee [*Persian Gulf*] ... GUPAC
Gulf Publishing Co. ... GPC
Gulf Publishing Co., Houston, TX [*Library symbol Library of Congress*] (LCLS) ... TxHGP
Gulf Puerto Rico Lines [*Steamship*] (MHDB) ... GPRL
Gulf Range Drone Control Upgrade System ... GRDCUS
Gulf Regional Planning Commission ... GRPC
Gulf Research & Development Co., Pittsburgh, PA [*Library symbol Library of Congress*] (LCLS) ... PPiGulf
Gulf Rijad Bank [*Bahrain*] ... GR
Gulf Science Year [*1970*] ... GSY
Gulf Sea Frontier ... GSF
Gulf Sea Frontier ... GULFSEAFRON
Gulf Shelf [*Marine science*] (OSRA) ... GS
Gulf Shelf (USDC) ... GS
Gulf South Medical Supply [*NASDAQ symbol*] (TTSB) ... GSMS
Gulf South Medical Supply [*NASDAQ symbol*] (SAG) ... GSMS
Gulf South Medical Supply [*Associated Press*] (SAG) ... GulfSou
Gulf South Research Institute ... GSRI
Gulf South Research Institute, Baton Rouge, LA [*Library symbol Library of Congress*] (LCLS) ... LBrG
Gulf States Marine Fisheries Commission ... GSMFC
Gulf States Utilities Co. [*Associated Press*] (SAG) ... GlfSU
Gulf States Utilities Co. [*NYSE symbol*] (SPSG) ... GSU
Gulf States Utilities Co., Beaumont, TX [*OCLC symbol*] (OCLC) ... TGS
Gulf States Utilities Co., Beaumont, TX [*Library symbol Library of Congress*] (LCLS) ... TxBeaG
Gulf Titanium Ltd. [*Vancouver Stock Exchange symbol*] ... GUT
Gulf Transport [*AAR code*] ... GTC
Gulf Transportation Terminal Command ... GTTC
Gulf Underwater Flare Experiment [*Marine science*] (MSC) ... GUFEX
Gulf Universities Research Consortium (EA) ... GURC
Gulf Universities Research Corp. ... GURC
Gulf War Syndrome [*Medicine*] ... GWS
Gulfcoast Pulpwood Association (EA) ... GPA
Gulf-European Freight Association [*Defunct*] (EA) ... GEFA
Gulfmark International [*Associated Press*] (SAG) ... Glfmrk
Gulfmark International [*NASDAQ symbol*] (SPSG) ... GMRK
Gulfport/Biloxi [*Mississippi*] [*Airport symbol*] (OAG) ... GPT
Gulfport, MS [*AM radio station call letters*] ... WGCM
Gulfport, MS [*FM radio station call letters*] ... WGCM-FM
Gulfport, MS [*AM radio station call letters*] ... WQFX
Gulfport, MS [*AM radio station call letters*] ... WROA
Gulfport, MS [*FM radio station call letters*] ... WXLS
Gulfport, MS [*FM radio station call letters*] ... WXRG
Gulfport, MS [*Television station call letters*] ... WXXV
Gulfport-Carnegie-Harrison County Library, Gulfport, MS [*Library symbol Library of Congress*] (LCLS) ... MsGu
Gulfstream Aerospace Corp. [*ICAO designator*] (FAAC) ... GLF
Gulfstream Airlines, Inc. [*ICAO designator*] (FAAC) ... GFS
Gulfstream II [*Shuttle training aircraft*] [*NASA*] (NASA) ... G-II
Gulfstream International Airlines, Inc. [*ICAO designator*] (FAAC) ... GFT
Gulfstream Resources Canada Ltd. [*Toronto Stock Exchange symbol*] ... GUR
Gulfstream V ... G V
Gulfwest Oil [*NASDAQ symbol*] (TTSB) ... GULF
Gulfwest Oil Co. [*NASDAQ symbol*] (SAG) ... GFWO
Gulfwest Oil Co. [*Associated Press*] (SAG) ... Gulfwest
Gulielmus Rex [*King William*] ... GR
Gulistan [*Afghanistan*] [*ICAO location identifier*] (ICLI) ... OAGL
Gulkana [*Alaska*] [*Airport symbol*] (OAG) ... GKN
Gulkana [*Alaska*] [*ICAO location identifier*] (ICLI) ... PAGK
Gulkana, AK [*Location identifier FAA*] (FAAL) ... GKN
Gulkana, AK [*Location identifier FAA*] (FAAL) ... GLA
Gull Air [*ICAO designator*] (FAAC) ... GUL
Gull Air [*ICAO designator*] (AD) ... JI
Gull Laboratories [*AMEX symbol*] (TTSB) ... GUL
Gull Laboratories, Inc. [*AMEX symbol*] (SPSG) ... GUL
Gull Laboratories, Inc. [*Associated Press*] (SAG) ... GullLb
Gullet (ABBR) ... GULT
Gullibility (ABBR) ... GULBT
Gullible (ABBR) ... GULB
Gullibly (ABBR) ... GULBLY
Gulliver, MI [*FM radio station call letters*] ... WCMM
Gullwing Group (EA) ... GWG
Gullwing Group International (EA) ... GWGI
Gully (ADA) ... GLY
Gully (ABBR) ... GUL
Gullying (ABBR) ... GULYG
Gulmarg [*India*] [*Geomagnetic observatory code*] ... GUL
Gulp Valve [*Automotive engineering*] ... GV
Gulu [*Uganda*] [*Airport symbol*] (AD) ... GUU
Gulu [*Uganda*] [*ICAO location identifier*] (ICLI) ... HUGU
Gulu [*Uganda*] [*Airport symbol*] (OAG) ... ULU
Gum Print [*Gum bichromates*] (VRA) ... GMPT
Gum Skips [*Philately*] ... GS
Gummed All Edges [*Envelopes*] (DGA) ... GAE
Gummed All Over [*Envelopes*] (DGA) ... GAO
Gummed All Over Flap [*Envelopes*] ... GAOF

Gummed All Round [*Envelopes*] (DGA) ... GAR
Gummed Industries Association (EA) ... GIA
Gummed Long Edge [*Envelopes*] (DGA) ... GLE
Gummed Only [*Envelopes*] ... GO
Gummi Guttae Gambiae [*Gamboge*] [*Pharmacology*] (ROG) ... GGG
Gumminess (ABBR) ... GUMNS
GumTech International, Inc. [*NASDAQ symbol*] (SAG) ... GUMM
GumTech International, Inc. [*Associated Press*] (SAG) ... GumT
GumTech International, Inc. [*Associated Press*] (SAG) ... GumTch
GumTech Intl [*NASDAQ symbol*] (TTSB) ... GUMM
GumTech Intl Wrrt [*NASDAQ symbol*] (TTSB) ... GUMMW
Gun ... G
Gun [*s*] [*Freight*] ... GN
Gun Accessory System (MCD) ... GAS
Gun Aiming Sensor (MCD) ... GAS
Gun Air Defense Effectiveness Study (MCD) ... GADES
Gun Alignment and Control System (MCD) ... GACS
Gun Automatic (MCD) ... GAU
Gun Board [*British*] ... GB
Gun, Bomb, and Rocket ... GBR
Gun Branch [*Electronics*] (OA) ... GB
Gun Camera (MCD) ... GC
Gun Capital (DNAB) ... GC
Gun Captain ... GC
Gun Carriage ... GC
Gun Carriage ... GCRG
Gun Compatibility Test ... GCT
Gun Control ... GC
Gun Control Act [*1968*] ... GCA
Gun Control Australia ... GCA
Gun Control Console [*Military*] (CAAL) ... GCC
Gun Control Equipment (DNAB) ... GCE
Gun Control Officer [*Navy*] ... GCO
Gun Control Officer Console [*Military*] (CAAL) ... GCOC
Gun Control RADAR [*Military*] (CAAL) ... GR
Gun Control Tower [*British military*] (DMA) ... GCT
Gun Cruiser [*Navy symbol*] ... CA
Gun Damage Assessment (NVT) ... GDA
Gun Defence Position [*Navy British*] ... GDP
Gun Direction Computer ... GDC
Gun Direction Exercise [*British military*] (DMA) ... GDX
Gun Direction Officer (NATG) ... GDO
Gun Director Pointer [*Naval gunnery*] ... GDP
Gun Director Pointer (Cross Leveler) [*Naval gunnery*] ... GDP(CL)
Gun Director Pointer (Leveler) [*Naval gunnery*] ... GDP(L)
Gun Director Pointer (Pointer) [*Naval gunnery*] ... GDP(P)
Gun Director Pointer (Sight Setter) [*Naval gunnery*] ... GDP(SS)
Gun Director Pointer (Trainer) [*Naval gunnery*] ... GDP(T)
Gun Display System (MCD) ... GDS
Gun Effectiveness Model ... GEM
Gun Electron-Induced Semiconductor Hybrid Amplifier ... GEISHA
Gun Elevation Displacement Unit (DNAB) ... GEDU
Gun Evaluation Group [*Military*] (CAAL) ... GEG
Gun Feed Control (MCD) ... GFC
Gun Fire Control Computer [*Military*] (CAAL) ... GFCC
Gun Fire Control System Satellite Simulation [*Military*] (CAAL) ... GFCS SATSIM
Gun Group Commander [*British military*] (DMA) ... GGC
Gun Lay [*or Laying*] [*RADAR*] ... GL
Gun Laying RADAR ... GL RADAR
Gun Licence [*British*] (DAS) ... GL
Gun Line of Site [*Tank*] [*Army*] ... GLOS
Gun Low-Altitude Air Defense System (NASA) ... GLAADS
Gun Low-Altitude Air Defense System ... GLADS
Gun Metal ... GMET
Gun Motor Carriage ... GMC
Gun Mount [*Military*] (CAAL) ... GM
Gun Operations Room [*British military*] (DMA) ... GOR
Gun Owners Action Committee (EA) ... GOAC
Gun Owners, Inc. (EA) ... GOI
Gun Owners of America (EA) ... GOA
Gun Pointer [*Naval gunnery*] ... GP
Gun Position Officer (NATG) ... GPO
Gun Position Officer's Assistant [*British military*] (DMA) ... GPOA
Gun Program [*Military*] (MCD) ... GP
Gun Range-Finder Operator ... GRFO
Gun Safety Officer ... GSO
Gun Ship Qualification Trials (MCD) ... GSQT
Gun Sight Aiming Point ... GSAP
Gun Sound Ranging [*An acoustic device*] ... GSR
Gun Target (NVT) ... GT
Gun Target (AABC) ... GTGT
Gun/Target Line [*Navy*] (NVT) ... GTL
Gun Tractor [*British*] ... GT
Gun Trade Association Ltd. [*British*] (BI) ... GTA
Gun Turret ... GT
Gun Weapon System [*Military*] (CAAL) ... GWS
Gun Weapon System Improvement Program [*Military*] (CAAL) ... GWSIP
Gun Weapon System Replacement Program (NVT) ... GWSRP
Guna [*India*] [*ICAO location identifier*] (ICLI) ... VIGN
Gunboat [*Naval*] ... GB
Gunboat ... GBT
Gunboat (ABBR) ... GUNBT
Gunboat [*Coast Guard*] (NVT) ... WPB
Gun-Bus [*Gun-carrying plane*] [*Air Force British*] ... GB
Gunby's District Court Reports [*1885*] [*Louisiana*] [*A publication*] (DLA) ... Gunby
Gunby's District Court Reports [*1885*] [*Louisiana*] [*A publication*] (DLA) ... Gunby (LA)
Gunby's District Court Reports [*1805*] [*Louisiana*] [*A publication*] (DLA) ... Gunby's Dec
Guncotton (ABBR) ... GUN
Guncrete (ABBR) ... GUN
Gundeck ... GD
Gun-Defended Area ... GDA
Gundle Environmental Systems, Inc. [*AMEX symbol*] (SPSG) ... GUN
Gundle/SLT Environmental [*AMEX symbol*] (TTSB) ... GUN
Gundle-SLT Environmental Systems, Inc. [*Associated Press*] (SAG) ... Gundle
Gundry. Manuscripts in Lincoln's Inn Library [*A publication*] (DLA) ... Gundry
Gunes Ekspres Havacilik AS (Sunexpress) [*Turkey*] [*ICAO designator*] (FAAC) ... SXS
Gunfight (ABBR) ... GUNFIT
Gunfighter (ABBR) ... GUNFITR
Gunfire (ABBR) ... GUNFR
Gunfire Area ... GFA
Gunfire Control (DOMA) ... GFC
Gunfire Control Subsystem (DNAB) ... GFCSS
Gunfire Control System ... GFCS
Gunfire Control System-Backup (DNAB) ... GFCS-B
Gunfire Detection Device ... GFDD
Gunfire Support (NVT) ... GFS
Gunfire Support Ship ... GFSS
Gunflint Resources Ltd. [*Vancouver Stock Exchange symbol*] ... GUS
Gungywamp Society (EA) ... GS
Gunilla Hutton Fan Club (EA) ... GHFC
Gunite Contractors Association (EA) ... GCA
Gun-Launched/Rocket-Assisted (MCD) ... GLRA
Gunlayer Armourer [*British military*] (DMA) ... GA
Gun-Laying Mark I [*RADAR*] ... GM
Gun-Laying (Turret) (DEN) ... GL(T)
Gunman (ABBR) ... GUNMA
Gunmetal ... GM
Gunn Diode Oscillator [*Electronics*] (PDAA) ... GDO
Gunn Effect Device ... GED
Gunn Effect Material ... GEM
Gunn Hoffer & Associates Law Firm, Winnipeg, Manitoba [*Library symbol National Library of Canada*] (NLC) ... MWGHA
Gunn, Hoffer & Associates, Winnipeg, MB, Canada [*Library symbol Library of Congress*] (LCLS) ... CaMWGHA
Gunn Memorial Public Library, Yanceyville, NC [*Library symbol Library of Congress*] (LCLS) ... NcYG
Gunn Oscillator ... GO
Gunnar Gold, Inc. [*Toronto Stock Exchange symbol*] ... GGG
Gunnarn [*Sweden ICAO location identifier*] (ICLI) ... ESPD
Gunn-Diode X-Band Amplifier ... GXA
Gunned (ABBR) ... GUND
Gunnedah [*Australia Airport symbol*] (OAG) ... GUH
Gunner (AFM) ... GNR
Gunner ... GR
Gunner (ADA) ... GU
Gunner (ABBR) ... GUNR
Gunner Aiming Error (MCD) ... GAE
Gunner Instructor [*Navy British*] ... GI
Gunner Skills Test [*Army*] (INF) ... GST
Gunner (Torpedo) [*British military*] (DMA) ... Gr(T)
Gunner Tracking Evaluator (PDAA) ... GTE
Gunner-Assisted Autotracking ... GAAT
Gunner's Accuracy Control Panel (MCD) ... GACP
Gunner's Auxiliary Sight (MCD) ... GAS
Gunner's Control and Display Panel [*Military*] (RDA) ... GCDP
Gunner's Control Unit ... GCU
Gunner's Mate [*Navy rating*] ... GM
Gunner's Mate, Chief [*Navy rating*] ... GMC
Gunner's Mate, Construction Battalion [*Navy rating*] ... GMCB
Gunner's Mate, Construction Battalion, Armorer [*Navy rating*] ... GMCBA
Gunner's Mate, Construction Battalion, Powderman [*Navy rating*] ... GMCBP
Gunner's Mate, First Class [*Navy rating*] ... GM1
Gunner's Mate, Guns [*Navy rating*] ... GMG
Gunner's Mate, Guns, Chief [*Navy rating*] (DNAB) ... GMGC
Gunner's Mate, Guns, First Class [*Navy rating*] (DNAB) ... GMG1
Gunner's Mate, Guns, Seaman [*Navy rating*] (DNAB) ... GMGSN
Gunner's Mate, Guns, Seaman Apprentice [*Navy rating*] (DNAB) ... GMGSA
Gunner's Mate, Guns, Second Class [*Navy rating*] (DNAB) ... GMG2
Gunner's Mate, Guns, Third Class [*Navy rating*] (DNAB) ... GMG3
Gunner's Mate, Master Chief [*Navy rating*] ... GMCM
Gunner's Mate, Missile [*Navy rating*] ... GMM
Gunner's Mate, Missile, Chief [*Navy rating*] (DNAB) ... GMMC
Gunner's Mate, Missile, First Class [*Navy rating*] (DNAB) ... GMM1
Gunner's Mate, Missile, Seaman [*Navy rating*] (DNAB) ... GMMSN
Gunner's Mate, Missile, Seaman Apprentice [*Navy rating*] (DNAB) ... GMMSA
Gunner's Mate, Missile, Second Class [*Navy rating*] (DNAB) ... GMM2
Gunner's Mate, Missile, Third Class [*Navy rating*] (DNAB) ... GMM3
Gunner's Mate, Second Class [*Navy rating*] ... GM2
Gunner's Mate, Senior Chief [*Navy rating*] ... GMCS
Gunner's Mate, Ship Repair [*Navy rating Obsolete*] ... GMSR
Gunner's Mate, Ship Repair, Powderman [*Navy rating Obsolete*] ... GMSRP
Gunner's Mate, Technician [*Navy rating*] ... GMT
Gunner's Mate, Technician, First Class [*Navy rating*] (DNAB) ... GMT1
Gunner's Mate, Technician, Seaman [*Navy rating*] ... GMTSN
Gunner's Mate, Technician, Seaman Apprentice [*Navy rating*] ... GMTSA
Gunner's Mate, Technician, Second Class [*Navy rating*] (DNAB) ... GMT2
Gunner's Mate, Technician, Third Class [*Navy rating*] (DNAB) ... GMT3

Gunner's Mate, Third Class [*Navy rating*] ... GM3
Gunner's Primary Optics (MCD) ... GPO
Gunner's Primary Sight (MCD) ... GPS
Gunner's Primary Sight Extension ... GPSE
Gunnerudssatern [*Sweden*] [*Seismograph station code, US Geological Survey*] (SEIS) ... GNN
Gunnery [*Navy British*] ... g
Gunnery (AFM) ... GNRY
Gunnery (MSA) ... GUN
Gunnery (ABBR) ... GUNRY
Gunnery (ABBR) ... GY
Gunnery ... GY
Gunnery and Searchlight [*Control*] [*British World War II*] ... GS
Gunnery Division [*British military*] (DMA) ... GD
Gunnery Exercise [*Navy*] (NVT) ... GUNEX
Gunnery Flight ... GF
Gunnery Improvement Program [*Military*] (CAAL) ... GIP
Gunnery Liaison Officer [*Navy*] ... GLO
Gunnery Lieutenant [*British military*] (DMA) ... GL
Gunnery Lieutenant's Writer [*British military*] (DMA) ... GLW
Gunnery Officer [*Navy British*] ... GO
Gunnery Officer's Console [*Army*] (AABC) ... GOC
Gunnery Officers Ordnance School ... GOOS
Gunnery Officer's Writer [*Navy British*] ... GOW
Gunnery Prize Money [*British military*] (DMA) ... GPM
Gunnery Range ... GR
Gunnery School [*Air Force*] ... GS
Gunnery Schoolship [*Navy*] (NVT) ... GUNSS
Gunnery Sergeant [*Marine Corps*] ... E7
Gunnery Sergeant ... GS
Gunnery Sergeant (DNAB) ... GSGT
Gunnery Sergeant ... GUNSGT
Gunnery Sergeant ... GYSGT
Gunnery Support ... GS
Gunnery Training School [*British military*] (DMA) ... GTS
Gunnery Weapon Control Switchboard ... GWCSWBD
Gunning (ABBR) ... GUNG
Gunning on Tolls [*A publication*] (DLA) ... Gunn Tolls
Gunnison [*Colorado*] [*Airport symbol*] (OAG) ... GUC
Gunnison, CO [*FM radio station call letters*] ... KKYY
Gunnison, CO [*AM radio station call letters*] (RBYB) ... KPKE-AM
Gunnison, CO [*FM radio station call letters*] ... KVLE
Gunnison, CO [*FM radio station call letters*] ... KWSB
Gunnison County Public Library, Gunnison, CO [*Library symbol Library of Congress*] (LCLS) ... CoGu
Gunnison Valley School, Gunnison, CO [*Library symbol*] [*Library of Congress*] (LCLS) ... CoGuVS
Gunny (ABBR) ... GUN
Gunnybag (ABBR) ... GUNYBG
Gunpowder (ABBR) ... GUN
Gunpowder (ABBR) ... GUNPWDR
Guns and Magnetic Material Alarm [*Weapon-detecting device to prevent skyjacking*] ... GAMMA
Guns n' Roses [*Rock recording group*] ... G n R
Gunshot (ABBR) ... GUNSH
Gunshot Residue [*Forensics*] ... GSR
Gunshot Wound [*Medicine*] ... GSW
Gunshot Wound of the Abdomen [*Emergency medicine*] (DAVI) ... GWA
Gunshot Wound of the Throat [*Emergency medicine*] (DAVI) ... GWT
Gunshot Wound to the Abdomen ... GSWA
Gunsmith ... GNSMTH
Gunsmith (ABBR) ... GUNSM
Gunsteel Resources, Inc. [*Vancouver Stock Exchange symbol*] ... GUN
Gunstock (ABBR) ... GUNST
Gunston Hall Plantation Library, Lorton, VA [*Library symbol Library of Congress*] (LCLS) ... ViLoGH
Guntersville, AL [*AM radio station call letters*] ... WGSV
Guntersville, AL [*FM radio station call letters*] (RBYB) ... WJIA
Guntersville, AL [*FM radio station call letters*] ... WTWX
Guntersville Dam [*TVA*] ... GD
Gunther Elementary School, North Bellmore, NY [*Library symbol Library of Congress*] (LCLS) ... NNbeGE
Gunther International Ltd. [*Associated Press*] (SAG) ... GnthrInt
Gunther International, Ltd. [*NASDAQ symbol*] (SAG) ... SORT
Gunung Sitoli/Binaka [*Indonesia*] [*ICAO location identifier*] (ICLI) ... WIMB
Gunwhale (ABBR) ... GUNWHL
Gunzburg/Donauried [*Germany ICAO location identifier*] (ICLI) ... EDMG
Gunzenhausen [*Germany ICAO location identifier*] (ICLI) ... EDMH
Guppy (ABBR) ... GUP
Gupta Corp. [*NASDAQ symbol*] (SAG) ... GPTA
Gupta Corp. [*NASDAQ symbol*] (TTSB) ... GPTAE
Gupta Corp. [*Associated Press*] (SAG) ... Gupta
Gura [*Ethiopia*] [*ICAO location identifier*] (ICLI) ... HAGU
Gurayat [*Saudi Arabia*] [*Airport symbol*] (OAG) ... URY
Gurdon, AR [*FM radio station call letters*] ... KYXK
Gurgled (ABBR) ... GURGLD
Gurgling (ABBR) ... GURGLG
Gurgu (ABBR) ... GUR
Guri [*Venezuela*] [*Seismograph station code, US Geological Survey*] (SEIS) ... GUV
Guriat [*Saudi Arabia*] [*ICAO location identifier*] (ICLI) ... OEGT
Gurkha Army Service Corps [*British military*] (DMA) ... GASC
Gurkha Light Infantry [*British military*] (DMA) ... GLI
Gurkha Military Police [*British military*] (DMA) ... GMP
Gurkha Officer [*British military*] (DMA) ... GO
Gurkha Other Rank [*Military British*] ... GOR
Gurkha Rifles [*British military*] (DMA) ... GR
Gurkha Rifles Regimental Centre [*British military*] (DMA) ... GRRC
Gurkha Transport Regiment [*Military unit*] [*British*] ... GTR
Gusap [*Papua New Guinea*] [*Airport symbol Obsolete*] (OAG) ... GAP
Gusau [*Nigeria*] [*ICAO location identifier*] (ICLI) ... DNGU
Gusau [*Nigeria*] [*Airport symbol*] (AD) ... GSA
Gushier (ABBR) ... GUSHR
Gushiest (ABBR) ... GUSHST
Gushiness (ABBR) ... GUSHNS
Gushing (ABBR) ... GUSHG
Gusset (MSA) ... GUS
Gusset (ABBR) ... GUST
Gust Alleviation and Structural Dynamic Stability Augmentation [*Aviation*] ... GASDSAS
Gust Alleviation System [*Aviation*] (MCD) ... GAS
Gust Front Algorithm (USDC) ... GFA
Gust Front Detection Algorithm (USDC) ... GFDA
Gust Load Alleviation [*Aviation*] ... GLA
Gustatory Evoked Potential [*Medicine*] (DMAA) ... GEP
Gustatory Lacrimation [*Medicine*] (DMAA) ... GL
Gustavus [*Alaska*] [*Airport symbol*] (OAG) ... GST
Gustavus Adolphus College [*St. Peter, MN*] ... GAC
Gustavus Adolphus College, St. Peter, MN [*OCLC symbol*] (OCLC) ... MNG
Gustavus Adolphus College, St. Peter, MN [*Library symbol Library of Congress*] (LCLS) ... MnStpeG
Gustavus, AK [*Location identifier FAA*] (FAAL) ... GAV
Gustier (ABBR) ... GUSTR
Gustiest (ABBR) ... GUSTST
Gustily (ABBR) ... GUSTY
Gustiness (ABBR) ... GUSTNS
Gusts [*NWS*] (FAAC) ... GSTS
Gusty [*NWS*] (FAAC) ... GSTY
Gut-Associated [*Medicine*] ... GA
Gut-Associated Lymphoid Tissue [*Medicine*] ... GALT
Gutenberg Gesellschaft (EA) ... GG
Gutenkunst Public Library, State Center, IA [*Library symbol Library of Congress*] (LCLS) ... IaStc
Guterbock's Bracton [*A publication*] (DLA) ... Gut Brac
Guthrian, Guthrie Center, IA [*Library symbol Library of Congress*] (LCLS) ... IaGucG
Guthrie Bacterial Inhibition Assay [*Medicine*] (MAE) ... GBIA
Guthrie, C. B., Tariff Bureau Inc., Washington DC [*STAC*] ... GCB
Guthrie Center Times, Guthrie Center, IA [*Library symbol Library of Congress*] (LCLS) ... IaGucT
Guthrie County Vedette, Panora, IA [*Library symbol Library of Congress*] (LCLS) ... IaPanV
Guthrie, OK [*Location identifier FAA*] (FAAL) ... GOK
Guthrie, OK [*AM radio station call letters*] ... KOKC
Guthrie, OK [*Location identifier FAA*] (FAAL) ... LCY
Guthrie on Trade Unions [*A publication*] (DLA) ... Guth Tr Un
Guthrie, TX [*Location identifier FAA*] (FAAL) ... GTH
Guthrie's Landlord and Tenant [*A publication*] (DLA) ... Guth L & T
Guthrie's Principles of the Laws of England [*1843*] [*A publication*] (DLA) ... Guth Pr
Guthrie's Reports [*33-83 Missouri Appeals*] [*A publication*] (DLA) ... Guthrie
Guthrie's Sheriff Court Cases [*1861-92*] [*Scotland*] [*A publication*] (DLA) ... Guth Sh Cas
Guthrie's Sheriff Court Cases [*1861-92*] [*Scotland*] [*A publication*] (DLA) ... Guth Sher Cas
Guthrie's Sheriff Court Cases [*1861-92*] [*Scotland*] [*A publication*] (DLA) ... Guthrie
Guts and Determination (DSUE) ... G and D
Gutta [*Drop of Liquid*] [*Pharmacy*] ... GT
Gutta [*Drop of Liquid*] [*Pharmacy*] (ROG) ... GTA
Guttae [*Drops of liquid*] [*Pharmacy*] (CPH) ... G
Guttae [*Drops*] [*Pharmacy*] (DAVI) ... gts
Guttae [*Drops of Liquid*] [*Pharmacy*] ... GTT
Guttae [*Drops of Liquid*] [*Pharmacy*] ... GUTT
Gutta-Percha [*Dentistry*] (MAE) ... GP
Guttatim [*Drop by Drop*] [*Pharmacy*] (GPO) ... GUTTAT
Gutted (ABBR) ... GUTD
Guttenberg Press, Guttenberg, IA [*Library symbol Library of Congress*] (LCLS) ... IaGutP
Guttenberg Public Library, Guttenberg, IA [*Library symbol Library of Congress*] (LCLS) ... IaGut
Gutter (MSA) ... GUT
Gutter (ABBR) ... GUTR
Gutter Ball [*Bowling*] ... G
Gutter Pair [*Philately*] ... GP
Gutteral (ABBR) ... GUTRL
Gutterally (ABBR) ... GUTRY
Gutting (ABBR) ... GUTG
Guttis Quibusdam [*With Some Drops*] [*Pharmacy*] (ROG) ... GTT QUIBUSD
Guttis Quibusdam [*With a Few Drops*] [*Pharmacy*] ... GUTT QUIBUSD
Gutturi [*To the Throat*] [*Pharmacy*] ... GUTT
Guvercinlik [*Turkey ICAO location identifier*] (ICLI) ... LTAB
Guy in the Back [*Copilot*] [*Air Force slang*] ... GIB
Guy in the Backseat [*Copilot*] [*Air Force slang*] ... GIBS
Guy in the Front Seat [*Pilot*] [*Slang*] (DSUE) ... GIF
Guyana [*Aircraft nationality and registration mark*] (FAAC) ... 8R
Guyana [*ANSI three-letter standard code*] (CNC) ... GUY
Guyana [*MARC country of publication code Library of Congress*] (LCCP) ... gy
Guyana [*ANSI two-letter standard code*] (CNC) ... GY
Guyana [*MARC geographic area code Library of Congress*] (LCCP) ... s-gy--
Guyana Airways [*ICAO designator*] (AD) ... GY

Guyana Airways Corp. [*ICAO designator*] (FAAC) .... GYA
Guyana Labour Party [*Political party*] (EY) .... GLP
Guyana Republican Party [*Political party*] (EA) .... GRP
Guyane Air Transport [*Airline*] [*French Guiana*] .... GAT
Guyanese Defense Force .... GDF
Guymon City Library, Guymon, OK [*Library symbol Library of Congress*] (LCLS) .... OkGuy
Guymon, OK [*Location identifier FAA*] (FAAL) .... GUY
Guymon, OK [*AM radio station call letters*] .... KGYN
Guymon, OK [*FM radio station call letters*] .... KKBS
Guymon Public Library, Guymon, OK [*OCLC symbol*] (OCLC) .... GPL
Guyot's Instituts Feodales [*A publication*] (DLA) .... Guyot Inst Feod
Guy's Forensic Medicine [*7th ed.*] [*1895*] [*A publication*] (DLA) .... Guy For Med
Guy's Medical Jurisprudence [*A publication*] (DLA) .... Guy Med Jur
Guy's Repertoire de la Jurisprudence [*A publication*] (DLA) .... Guy Rep
Guzzle (ABBR) .... GUZL
Guzzle (ABBR) .... GZL
Guzzled (ABBR) .... GUZLD
Guzzled (ABBR) .... GZLD
Guzzler (ABBR) .... GUZLR
Guzzler (ABBR) .... GZLR
Guzzling (ABBR) .... GUZLG
Guzzling (ABBR) .... GZLG
GVN [*Government of Vietnam*] **Liaison Officer** .... GLO
Gwa [*Myanmar*] [*ICAO location identifier*] (ICLI) .... VBGW
Gwadar [*Pakistan*] [*Airport symbol*] (OAG) .... GWD
Gwadar [*Pakistan*] [*ICAO location identifier*] (ICLI) .... OPGD
Gwaka [*Zaire*] [*ICAO location identifier*] (ICLI) .... FZFW
Gwalior [*India*] [*Airport symbol*] (OAG) .... GWL
Gwalior [*India*] [*ICAO location identifier*] (ICLI) .... VIGR
GWE [*Global Weather Experiment*] **Operational Year** [*Marine science*] (MSC) .... GOY
Gwelo [*Zimbabwe*] [*Airport symbol*] (OAG) .... GWE
GWEN [*Ground Wave Emergency Network*] **Project** (EA) .... GP
Gweru/Gweru [*Zimbabwe*] [*ICAO location identifier*] (ICLI) .... FVGW
Gweru/Thornhill [*Zimbabwe*] [*ICAO location identifier*] (ICLI) .... FVTL
Gwil Industries, Inc. [*Toronto Stock Exchange symbol Vancouver Stock Exchange symbol*] .... GWS
Gwillim's Tithe Cases [*England*] [*1224-1824*] [*A publication*] (DLA) .... Gwil
Gwillim's Tithe Cases [*England*] [*A publication*] (DLA) .... Gwil Ti Cas
Gwillim's Tithe Cases [*England*] [*A publication*] (DLA) .... Gwill
Gwillim's Tithe Cases [*England*] [*A publication*] (DLA) .... Gwill Bac Abr
Gwillim's Tithe Cases [*England*] [*A publication*] (DLA) .... Gwill T Cas
Gwillim's Tithe Cases [*England*] [*A publication*] (DLA) .... Gwill Ti Cas
Gwilt's Encyclopedia of Architecture [*A publication*] (DLA) .... Enc Arch
Gwinn/K. I. Sawyer Air Force Base [*Michigan*] [*ICAO location identifier*] (ICLI) .... KSAW
Gwinn, MI [*Location identifier FAA*] (FAAL) .... SAW
Gwinner, ND [*Location identifier FAA*] (FAAL) .... GWR
Gwinnett County Law Library, Lawrenceville, GA [*Library symbol*] [*Library of Congress*] (LCLS) .... GLGL
Gwinnett County Public Schools, Lawrenceville, GA [*Library symbol*] [*Library of Congress*] (LCLS) .... GLGS
Gwinnett Technical Institute, Lawrenceville, GA [*Library symbol*] [*Library of Congress*] (LCLS) .... GLGT
GWR Resources [*Vancouver Stock Exchange symbol*] .... GWQ
Gwynedd [*County in Wales*] (WGA) .... GWYN
Gwynedd-Mercy College, Gwynedd, PA [*OCLC symbol*] (OCLC) .... GWY
Gwynedd-Mercy College, Gwynedd, PA [*Library symbol Library of Congress*] (LCLS) .... PGwvG
Gwynne on Sheriffs [*A publication*] (DLA) .... Gw Sh
Gyandoh and Griffiths. Sourcebook of the Constitutional Law of Ghana [*A publication*] (ILCA) .... G & G
[*The*] **Gymboree Corp.** [*NASDAQ symbol*] (SAG) .... GYMB
[*The*] **Gymboree Corp.** [*Associated Press*] (SAG) .... Gymbree
Gymnasium .... GYM
Gymnasium (VRA) .... gym
Gymnasium (ABBR) .... GYMN
Gymnast (ABBR) .... GYMNST
Gymnast (ABBR) .... GYMST
Gymnastic .... GYM
Gymnastic (ABBR) .... GYMSTC
Gymnastic [*Freight*] .... GYMSTIC
Gymnastic Equipment Manufacturers' Association [*British*] (BI) .... GEMA
Gymnastically (ABBR) .... GYMSTCY
Gymnastics (ADA) .... GYM
Gympie [*Australia Airport symbol*] .... GYP
Gympie Fruit Growers' Cooperative Association [*Australia*] .... GFGCA
Gynaecologist [*or Gynaecology*] [*British*] (ADA) .... GYNAEC
Gynaecology [*British*] .... GYNAE
Gynaecology [*British*] .... GYNAECOL
Gynecare [*NASDAQ symbol*] (SAG) .... GYNE
Gynecare Inc. [*NASDAQ symbol*] (TTSB) .... GYNE
Gynecare, Inc. [*Associated Press*] (SAG) .... Gynecre
Gynecologic (ABBR) .... GYNC
Gynecologic Oncology Group (EA) .... GOG
Gynecological (ABBR) .... GYNCL
Gynecologist .... GYN
Gynecologist (ABBR) .... GYNST
Gynecology .... GYN
Gynecology .... GYNCLGY
Gynecology .... GYNCLGY
Gynecology [*Medicine*] (DAVI) .... gyne
Gynecology .... Gynecol
Gynoecium [*Botany*] .... G
Gypped (ABBR) .... GYPD
Gypping (ABBR) .... GYPG
Gypsiologic (ABBR) .... GYPSIOL
Gypsum (KSC) .... GYP
Gypsum .... GYPS
Gypsum Association (EA) .... GA
Gypsum Community Library, Gypsum, CO [*Library symbol Library of Congress*] (LCLS) .... CoGy
Gypsum Dry Wall [*Technical drawings*] .... GPDW
Gypsum Drywall Contractors International [*Later, AWCI*] .... GDCI
Gypsum Lathe [*Technical drawings*] .... GPL
Gypsum Plaster [*Technical drawings*] .... GPPL
Gypsum Plasterboard Development Association [*British*] (BI) .... GPDA
Gypsum Products Development Association [*British*] (DBA) .... GPDA
Gypsum Requirement (OA) .... GR
Gypsum Roof Deck Foundation [*Later, NRDCA*] (EA) .... GRDF
Gypsum Sheathing Board [*Technical drawings*] .... GSB
Gypsum Tile [*Technical drawings*] .... GPT
Gypsum Wallboard [*Technical drawings*] .... GWB
Gypsum-Plaster Ceiling [*Technical drawings*] .... GPC
Gypsum-Plaster Wall [*Technical drawings*] .... GPW
Gypsy (ABBR) .... GYP
Gypsy Lore Society, North American Chapter (EA) .... GLS
Gypsy Moths [*An association*] (EA) .... GM
Gypsy Resources Ltd. [*Vancouver Stock Exchange symbol*] .... GPY
Gyrafrance [*France ICAO designator*] (FAAC) .... GYR
Gyrate (ABBR) .... GYRA
Gyrate Atrophy [*Medicine*] .... GA
Gyrated (ABBR) .... GYRAD
Gyrated (ABBR) .... GYRTD
Gyrating (ABBR) .... GYRAG
Gyration (ABBR) .... GYR
Gyration (ABBR) .... GYRAN
Gyrator (ABBR) .... GYRAR
Gyratory (ABBR) .... GYRARY
Gyro (ABBR) .... GY
Gyro Accelerometer Misalignment Erection Test .... GAMET
Gyro Assembly (NASA) .... GA
Gyro Compass .... GC
Gyro Compass .... GCMPS
Gyro Control .... GC
Gyro Control Assembly .... GCA
Gyro Control Gunsight .... GCG
Gyro Coupling Unit (KSC) .... GCU
Gyro Display Coupler (MCD) .... GDC
Gyro Drift Rate Compensation .... GDRC
Gyro Energy & Minerals Corp. [*Vancouver Stock Exchange symbol*] .... GEM
Gyro Erected Optical Navigation .... GEON
Gyro Error .... GE
Gyro Header Assembly .... GHA
Gyro International (EA) .... GI
Gyro Output Amplifier .... GOA
Gyro Package .... GP
Gyro Pitch Position .... GPP
Gyro Reference Assembly .... GRA
Gyro Reference System (AAG) .... GRS
Gyro Storage Oven .... GSO
Gyro Tilt Signal .... GTS
Gyro Torque (MCD) .... GT
Gyro Transfer Table System .... GTTS
Gyro Yaw Position .... GYP
Gyrocar (ABBR) .... GY
Gyrocompass (ABBR) .... GY
Gyrocompass (ABBR) .... GYRCMPS
Gyrocompass (ABBR) .... GYRO
Gyro-Compass Automatic Navigation [*System*] (RDA) .... GAN
Gyro-Compass, Desired Cluster Orientation (MCD) .... GCD
Gyro-Compass Trial (IAA) .... GCT
Gyrocopter (ABBR) .... GYROCOP
Gyrodynamic (ABBR) .... GYRODYN
Gyrodyne (ABBR) .... GY
Gyrodyne [*NASDAQ symbol*] (SAG) .... GYRO
Gyrodyne Co. Amer [*NASDAQ symbol*] (TTSB) .... GYRO
Gyrodyne Company of America, Inc. [*Associated Press*] (SAG) .... Gyrody
Gyroless Control System .... GCS
Gyromagnetic Kompass .... GMK
Gyromagnetic Ratio .... G
Gyrometer (ABBR) .... GYRMTR
Gyroplane (ABBR) .... GYRO
Gyroplane (ABBR) .... GYRPLN
Gyroscope (IAA) .... GS
Gyroscope .... GY
Gyroscope (AAG) .... GYRO
Gyroscope (ABBR) .... GYRSCP
Gyroscope Compassing .... GYROCOMP
Gyroscope Parameter Shift .... GPS
Gyroscope Pickoff Voltage .... GPV
Gyroscope Reference Unit (MCD) .... GRU
Gyroscope Vibration Absorber .... GVA
Gyroscopes-Rate Bomb-Direction System (AAG) .... GRBDS
Gyroscopic Heading and Altitude Reference System (SAA) .... GHARS
Gyroscopic Lower Power Control (IAA) .... GLOPC
Gyroscopic Low-Power Attitude Control .... GLOPAC
Gyrostabilizer .... GS
Gyrostabilizer (ABBR) .... GYRSTBR

Gyrus [*Brain anatomy*] .... Gy
Gyrus (ABBR) .... GYR
GZA GeoEnvironmental Tech [*NASDAQ symbol*] (TTSB) .... GZEA
GZA GeoEnvironmental Technologies [*NASDAQ symbol*] (SAG) .... GZEA
GZA GeoEnvironmental Technologies, Inc. [*Associated Press*] (SAG) .... GZA
GZA GeoEnvironmental Technologies, Inc. (NQ) .... GZEA

H
By Meaning

H. A. Simons Ltd., Vancouver, BC, Canada [*Library symbol Library of Congress*] (LCLS) .... CaBVaHS
H. A. Simons Ltd., Vancouver, British Columbia [*Library symbol National Library of Canada*] (NLC) .... BVAHS
H. Allen Smith Jet Propulsion Laboratory [*Former name, JPL, continues to be used as official name*] [*Name adopted in 1973 to honor retiring congressman*] .... HASJPL
H & D Aviation [*ICAO designator*] (FAAC) .... WVA
H & Q Healthcare Fund [*Associated Press*] (SAG) .... H & Q Hlt
H & Q Healthcare Investors [*NYSE symbol*] (SPSG) .... HQH
H & Q Life Sciences Investors [*Associated Press*] (SAG) .... H & Q Lfe
H & Q Life Sciences Investors [*NYSE symbol*] (SAG) .... HQL
H. Bergstrom International Ltd., Beaconsfield, Quebec [*Library symbol National Library of Canada*] (NLC) .... QBEHBI
H. D. Vest, Inc. [*Associated Press*] (SAG) .... HD Vest
H. Frank Carey High School, Franklin Square, NY [*Library symbol*] [*Library of Congress*] (LCLS) .... NFsCH
H. G. Wells Society (EA) .... HGWS
H. H. Franklin Club (EA) .... HHFC
H. J. Mulliner [*British coachbuilder*] .... HJM
H. J. Nugen Public Library, New London, IA [*Library symbol Library of Congress*] (LCLS) .... IaNl
H. Leslie Perry Memorial Library, Henderson, NC [*Library symbol Library of Congress*] (LCLS) .... NcHe
H. Lundbeck [*Denmark*] [*Research code symbol*] .... Lu
H. Lundbeck [*Denmark*] [*Research code symbol*] .... N
H. Mason [*Oregon*] [*Seismograph station code, US Geological Survey*] (SEIS) .... HMO
H. Pordes, Publisher and Bookseller, London, United Kingdom [*Library symbol Library of Congress*] (LCLS) .... UkLPo
H. W. Schroeder Junior/Senior High School Library, Webster, NY [*OCLC symbol*] (OCLC) .... RWL
H. W. Wilson Co. [*Publisher*] .... HWW
H. Ward Smith Library, Centre of Forensic Sciences, Toronto, Ontario [*Library symbol National Library of Canada*] (NLC) .... OTCF
Ha Ha Only Joking [*Computer hacker terminology*] (NHD) .... HHOJ
Ha Ha Only Kidding .... HHOK
Ha Ha Only Serious .... HHOS
Haadyai [*Thailand*] [*Airport symbol*] (OAG) .... HDY
Ha'Apai Lifuka [*Tonga*] [*ICAO location identifier*] (ICLI) .... NFTL
Haapavesi [*Finland ICAO location identifier*] (ICLI) .... EFHP
Haavara-Transfer (BJA) .... HT
Habacuc [*Old Testament book*] [*Douay version*] .... HAB
Habakkuk [*Old Testament book*] .... Hab
Habakkuk [*Old Testament book*] .... Hb
Habana [*Cuba ICAO location identifier*] (ICLI) .... MULB
Habana [*Cuba ICAO location identifier*] (ICLI) .... MULH
Habana/Jose Marti [*Cuba ICAO location identifier*] (ICLI) .... MUHA
Habana/Santa Fe [*Cuba ICAO location identifier*] (ICLI) .... MUSF
Habeas Corpus [*You Have the Body*] [*Legal*] [*Latin*] (ROG) .... HAB CORP
Habeas Corpus [*You Have the Body*] [*Legal term Latin*] (DLA) .... HC
Habeat [*Let Him Have*] [*Pharmacy*] .... HABT
Habeat [*Let Him Have*] [*Pharmacy*] (ROG) .... HBT
Habekacin [*Antibacterial*] .... HBK
Haberdashery (DSUE) .... HABY
Haberdashery .... HDASHY
Habere Facias Possessionem [*A writ to put the plaintiff in possession*] [*Legal term Latin*] .... Hab Fa Poss
Habere Facias Possessionem [*A writ to put the plaintiff in possession*] [*Latin Legal term*] (ROG) .... HAB FAC POSS
Habere Facias Seisenam [*A writ to put the plaintiff in actual possession*] [*Latin Legal term*] (ROG) .... HAB FA SEIS
Habere Facias Seisinam [*That You Cause to Have Seisin*] [*Latin Legal term*] (DLA) .... HAB FA SEIS
Habersham Bancorp [*NASDAQ symbol*] (SAG) .... HABC
Habersham Bancorp [*Associated Press*] (SAG) .... Habersh
Habilitation Center, Higginsville, MO [*Library symbol*] [*Library of Congress*] (LCLS) .... MoHigH
Habitability Assistance Team/Atlantic (DNAB) .... HAT/LANT
Habitability Assistance Team/Pacific (DNAB) .... HAT/PAC
Habitability/Crew Quarters (KSC) .... H/CQ
Habitability Improvement [*Navy*] (NVT) .... HI
Habitability Improvement Plan [*Navy*] .... HIP
Habitability Module Outfitting (SSD) .... HMO
Habitability Module Outfitting System (SSD) .... HMOS
Habitability Support System (MCD) .... HSS

Habitability System [*NASA*] (KSC) .... HS
Habitability Technology (SSD) .... HABT
Habitable (ABBR) .... HABTB
Habitable Zone [*Beyond the solar system*] .... HZ
Habitat [*Dwelling*] (ROG) .... HAB
Habitat (BARN) .... habit
Habitat and Human Settlements Foundation [*United Nations*] (EY) .... HHSF
Habitat Conservation Area .... HCA
Habitat Conservation Plan [*Ecology*] .... HCP
Habitat Evaluation Procedure [*Fishery science*] .... HEP
Habitat for Humanity (EA) .... HH
Habitat International Council [*The Hague, Netherlands*] (EAIO) .... HIC
Habitat Management Plan .... HMP
Habitation .... HAB
Habitation (ABBR) .... HABTAN
Habitation Module (SSD) .... HM
Habitation/Station Operations (SSD) .... HSO
Habitation/Station Operations Module (SSD) .... HSOM
Habitual [*FBI standardized term*] .... HAB
Habitual (ABBR) .... HABTL
Habitual Abortion [*Medicine*] .... HA
Habitual Criminal .... HC
Habitually (ABBR) .... HABTY
Habitualness (ABBR) .... HABTLNS
Habituate (ABBR) .... HABTA
Habituated (ABBR) .... HABTAD
Habituating (ABBR) .... HABTAG
Habituation (ABBR) .... HABTAN
Habituation Stimulus [*to light*] .... HS
Habitue (ABBR) .... HABTU
Habonim Dror North America (EA) .... HDNA
Haboro [*Japan*] [*Seismograph station code, US Geological Survey Closed*] (SEIS) .... HAB
Hac Nocte [*Tonight*] [*Pharmacy*] .... HAC NOCT
Hach Co. [*NASDAQ symbol*] (NQ) .... HACH
Hachette Filipacchi Magazines [*A publication*] .... HFM
Hachette Filipacchi Magazines .... HFM
Hachette-Filipacchi Telematique [*Information service or system*] (IID) .... HFT
Hachijojima [*Japan*] [*Seismograph station code, US Geological Survey*] (SEIS) .... HJJ
Hachijojima [*Japan ICAO location identifier*] (ICLI) .... RJTH
Hachijojima Island [*Japan*] [*Airport symbol*] (OAG) .... HAC
Hachinohe [*Japan*] [*Seismograph station code, US Geological Survey*] (SEIS) .... HAC
Hachinohe [*Japan ICAO location identifier*] (ICLI) .... RJSH
Hachtmann, J. I., Newark NJ [*STAC*] .... HJI
Hacia [*Around*] [*Spanish*] .... h
Hacienda (ABBR) .... HACN
Hacienda Jaco (Harbor Land) [*Costa Rica*] [*ICAO location identifier*] (ICLI) .... MRHJ
Hacienda La Suerte [*Costa Rica*] [*ICAO location identifier*] (ICLI) .... MRHS
Hacienda Platanar [*Costa Rica*] [*ICAO location identifier*] (ICLI) .... MRHP
Hacienda Rancho Grande [*Costa Rica*] [*ICAO location identifier*] (ICLI) .... MRHG
Hacienda Rio Cuarto [*Costa Rica*] [*ICAO location identifier*] (ICLI) .... MRHO
Hacienda Taura [*Ecuador*] [*ICAO location identifier*] (ICLI) .... SEHT
Hack and Band Saw Manufacturers Association of America .... HBSMA
Hack and Band Saw Manufacturers Association of America (EA) .... HBSMAA
Hackensack, MN [*Location identifier FAA*] (FAAL) .... HSK
Hackensack, NJ [*AM radio station call letters*] .... WWDJ
Hackers on Planet Earth [*An association*] .... HOPE
Hackett on the Geneva Award Acts [*A publication*] (DLA) .... Hack Gen Aw
Hackettstown, NJ [*FM radio station call letters*] .... WNTI
Hackettstown, NJ [*AM radio station call letters*] .... WRNJ
Hackley Public Library, Muskegon, MI [*Library symbol Library of Congress*] (LCLS) .... MiMu
Hackney [*Borough of London*] .... HACK
Hadag Air Seebaederflug [*ICAO designator*] (AD) .... GP
Hadamard Imaging Spectrometer (PDAA) .... HADIS
Hadamard-Transform [*Mathematics*] .... HT
Hadassah (BJA) .... HAD
Hadassah Israel Education Services [*Jerusalem*] .... HIES
Hadassah Medical Relief Association (EA) .... HMRA
Hadassah, The Women's Zionist Organization of America (EA) .... HWZOA
Hadassah Zionist Youth Commission (EA) .... HZYC
Hadco Corp. [*Associated Press*] (SAG) .... Hadco
Hadco Corp. [*NASDAQ symbol*] (NQ) .... HDCO

Haddam [*Connecticut*] [*Seismograph station code, US Geological Survey*] (SEIS) ... HDM
Haddam Neck Plant [*Nuclear energy*] (NRCH) ... HNP
Haddan's Administrative Jurisdiction of the Court of Chancery [*A publication*] (DLA) ... Had Chy Jur
Haddington's Manuscript Reports, Scotch Court of Session [*A publication*] (DLA) ... Had
Haddington's Manuscript Reports, Scotch Court of Session [*A publication*] (DLA) ... Hadd
Haddington's Manuscript Reports, Scotch Court of Session [*A publication*] (DLA) ... Haddington
Haddon Hall Library [*A publication*] ... HHL
Haddon Heights Public Library, Haddon Heights, NJ [*Library symbol Library of Congress*] (LCLS) ... NjHh
Haddon Township Free Library, Westmont, NJ [*Library symbol Library of Congress*] (LCLS) ... NjWem
Haddonfield Public Library, Haddonfield, NJ [*Library symbol Library of Congress*] (LCLS) ... NjH
Haderslev [*Denmark ICAO location identifier*] (ICLI) ... EKHV
Hadison Aviation [*Sudan*] [*ICAO designator*] (FAAC) ... FMS
Hadley Centre Climate Model ... HCCM
Hadley's Introduction to the Roman Law [*A publication*] (DLA) ... Hadl Rom Law
Hadley's Reports [*45-48 New Hampshire*] [*A publication*] (DLA) ... Had
Hadley's Reports [*45-48 New Hampshire*] [*A publication*] (DLA) ... Hadl
Hadley's Reports [*45-48 New Hampshire*] [*A publication*] (DLA) ... Hadley
Hadrian [*of Scriptores Historiae Augustae*] [*Classical studies*] (OCD) ... Hadr
Hadron-Elektron-Ring Anlage [*Hadron-Electron Ring Accelerator*] [*Germany*] ... HERA
Hadsund [*Denmark ICAO location identifier*] (ICLI) ... EKHS
Haem Oxygenase [*An enzyme*] ... HO
Haemaphysalis [*A genus of tick*] [*Entomology*] (DAVI) ... H
Haematocrit [*British*] ... HAEMAT
Haematology [*British*] ... HAEMATOL
Haematopoietic Cell Growth Factor [*Biochemistry*] ... HCGF
Haemolysis [*British*] ... HAEM
Haemonetics Corp. [*NYSE symbol*] (SPSG) ... HAE
Haemonetics Corp. [*Associated Press*] (SAG) ... Haemon
Haemophilia Foundation of Australia ... HFA
Haemophilia Society of New South Wales [*Australia*] ... HSNSW
Haemophilia society of Victoria [*Australia*] ... HSV
Haemophilus Influenzae, Type B ... HIB
Haemophilus Influenzae Type B (PAZ) ... Hib
Haemophilus Maintenance Broth [*Microbiology*] ... HMB
Haemorrhage [*British*] ... HAEMORRH
Haflinger Association of America (EA) ... HAA
Haflinger Registry of North America (EA) ... HRNA
Haflinger Society [*British*] (DBA) ... HSGB
Hafnium [*Chemical element*] ... Hf
Hafnium (IDOE) ... Hf
Hafnium Column Extractant [*Nuclear energy*] (NRCH) ... HAX
Hafnium Column Product [*Nuclear energy*] (NRCH) ... HAP
Hafnium Column Waste [*Nuclear energy*] (NRCH) ... HAW
Hafr Al-Batin Airport [*Saudi Arabia*] [*ICAO location identifier*] (ICLI) ... OEPA
Hafslund Nycomed ADS [*NYSE symbol*] (SPSG) ... HN
Hafslund Nycomed AS [*Associated Press*] (SAG) ... Hafslnd
Hafslund Nycomed AS [*Associated Press*] (SAG) ... Hafslnd
Haftarah (BJA) ... H
Haftentschaedigunsgesetz [*A publication*] (BJA) ... HEG
Haft-Gel [*Iran*] [*ICAO location identifier*] (ICLI) ... OIAK
Hafuf [*Saudi Arabia*] [*Airport symbol*] (OAG) ... HOF
Haga Comitum [*The Hague*] [*Imprint*] (ROG) ... HAG COM
Hagaman Memorial Library, East Haven, CT [*Library symbol Library of Congress*] (LCLS) ... CtEahav
Hagan's Reports [*West Virginia*] [*A publication*] (DLA) ... Hag
Hagan's Reports [*Utah*] [*A publication*] (DLA) ... Hag
Hagan's Reports [*Utah*] [*A publication*] (DLA) ... Hagan
Hagar Township Public Library, Markstay, Ontario [*Library symbol National Library of Canada*] (NLC) ... OMHT
Hagelkorn [*Hailstone*] [*Bomb*] [*German military - World War II*] ... H
Hageman Factor [*Factor XII*] [*Hematology*] ... HF
Hagensborg Resources Ltd. [*Vancouver Stock Exchange symbol*] ... HGS
Hagerman Public Library, Hagerman, ID [*Library symbol*] [*Library of Congress*] (LCLS) ... IdHg
Hagerman Township Public Library, Ontario [*Library symbol National Library of Canada*] (NLC) ... ODHT
Hagerstown [*Maryland*] [*Airport symbol*] (OAG) ... HGR
Hagerstown CATI [*Computer-Assisted Telephone Interviewing*] **Facility** [*Bureau of the Census*] (GFGA) ... HCF
Hagerstown Exponent, Hagerstown, IN [*Library symbol Library of Congress*] (LCLS) ... InHagE
Hagerstown, IN [*FM radio station call letters*] (RBYB) ... WBSH-FM
Hagerstown Junior College [*Maryland*] ... HJC
Hagerstown, MD [*AM radio station call letters*] ... WARK
Hagerstown, MD [*FM radio station call letters*] ... WARX
Hagerstown, MD [*FM radio station call letters*] ... WETH
Hagerstown, MD [*Television station call letters*] ... WHAG
Hagerstown, MD [*Television station call letters*] ... WJAL
Hagerstown, MD [*AM radio station call letters*] ... WJEJ
Hagerstown, MD [*FM radio station call letters*] ... WWMD
Hagerstown, MD [*Television station call letters*] ... WWPB
Hagerstown Public Library, Hagerstown, IN [*Library symbol Library of Congress*] (LCLS) ... InHag
Hagfors [*Sweden ICAO location identifier*] (ICLI) ... ESOH
Hagfors [*Sweden*] [*Seismograph station code, US Geological Survey*] (SEIS) ... HFS
Haggai [*Freemasonry*] ... H
Haggai [*Old Testament book*] ... Hag
Haggai [*Old Testament book*] ... Hg
Haggar Corp. [*Associated Press*] (SAG) ... Haggar
Haggar Corp. [*NASDAQ symbol*] (SAG) ... HGGR
Haggard's English Admiralty Reports [*A publication*] (DLA) ... Hag
Haggard's English Admiralty Reports [*A publication*] (DLA) ... Hag Adm
Haggard's English Admiralty Reports [*A publication*] (DLA) ... Hagg Adm
Haggard's English Admiralty Reports [*161 English Reprint*] [*A publication*] (DLA) ... Hagg Adm (Eng)
Haggard's English Consistory Reports [*161 English Reprint*] [*A publication*] (DLA) ... Hag Con
Haggard's English Consistory Reports [*161 English Reprint*] [*A publication*] (DLA) ... Hagg Con
Haggard's English Consistory Reports [*161 English Reprint*] [*A publication*] (DLA) ... Hagg Cons
Haggard's English Consistory Reports [*161 English Reprint*] [*A publication*] (DLA) ... Hagg Consist
Haggard's English Consistory Reports [*161 English Reprint*] [*A publication*] (DLA) ... Hagg Consist (Eng)
Haggard's English Ecclesiastical Reports [*162 English Reprint*] [*A publication*] (DLA) ... Hag Ecc
Haggard's English Ecclesiastical Reports [*162 English Reprint*] [*A publication*] (DLA) ... Hagg Ecc
Haggard's English Ecclesiastical Reports [*162 English Reprint*] [*1827-33*] [*A publication*] (DLA) ... Hagg Eccl
Haggard's English Ecclesiastical Reports [*162 English Reprint*] [*A publication*] (DLA) ... Hagg Eccl (Eng)
[*The*] **Haggin Museum, Stockton, CA** [*Library symbol*] [*Library of Congress*] (LCLS) ... CStoHM
Haggle (ABBR) ... HAGL
Haggled (ABBR) ... HAGLD
Haggler (ABBR) ... HAGLR
Haggling (ABBR) ... HAGLG
Hagigah (BJA) ... Hag
Hagiologist (ABBR) ... HAGLST
Hagiology (ABBR) ... HAGIOL
Hagley Museum and Library, Greenville, DE [*Library symbol*] [*Library of Congress*] (LCLS) ... DeGH
Haglund Industry International [*Vancouver Stock Exchange symbol*] ... HSN
Hagner and Miller's Reports [*2 Maryland Chancery*] [*A publication*] (DLA) ... Hagn & M
Hagner and Miller's Reports [*2 Maryland Chancery*] [*A publication*] (DLA) ... Hagn & Mill
Hagshult [*Sweden ICAO location identifier*] (ICLI) ... ESMV
[*The*] **Hague** [*Netherlands*] [*Airport symbol*] (AD) ... HAG
Hague Convention ... HC
Hague Court Reports [*A publication*] (DLA) ... Hague Ct Rep
Hague Resolutions ... HR
Haguenau [*France ICAO location identifier*] (ICLI) ... LFSH
Hahameinu Zikhronam Livrakha [*Our Sages of Blessed Memory*] [*Hebrew*] ... HAZAL
Ha-Hevra ha-Historit ha-Israelit [*Historical Society of Israel*] (EAIO) ... HHI
Hahira, GA [*AM radio station call letters*] (RBYB) ... WTHV
Hahn [*Germany ICAO location identifier*] (ICLI) ... EDAH
Hahn Automotive Warehouse [*NASDAQ symbol*] (TTSB) ... HAHN
Hahn Automotive Warehouse, Inc. [*NASDAQ symbol*] (SAG) ... HAHN
Hahn Automotive Warehouse, Inc. [*Associated Press*] (SAG) ... HahnAut
Hahnemann Elementary School Behavior Rating Scale [*Test*] ... HESB
Hahnemann High School Behavior Rating Scale [*Psychology*] ... HHSB
Hahnemann Medical College and Hospital, Philadelphia, PA [*OCLC symbol*] (OCLC) ... HHN
Hahnemann Medical College and Hospital, Philadelphia, PA [*Library symbol Library of Congress*] (LCLS) ... PPHa
Hahnemann University (GAGS) ... Hahnemann U
Hahnium [*Proposed name for chemical element 105*] ... Ha
Hahotoe [*Togo*] [*ICAO location identifier*] (ICLI) ... DXHO
Haibara [*Japan*] [*Seismograph station code, US Geological Survey*] (SEIS) ... HBR
Haida [*MARC language code Library of Congress*] (LCCP) ... hai
Haifa [*Israel*] [*Seismograph station code, US Geological Survey Closed*] (SEIS) ... HAF
Haifa [*Israel*] [*Airport symbol*] (OAG) ... HFA
Haifa On-line Bibliographic Text System [*University of Haifa Library*] [*Information service or system*] (IID) ... HOBITS
Haifa Symphony Orchestra (BJA) ... HSO
Haifa/U. Michaeli [*Israel*] [*ICAO location identifier*] (ICLI) ... LLHA
Haifa University (BJA) ... HU
Haight Elementary School, Rockford, IL [*Library symbol*] [*Library of Congress*] (LCLS) ... IRoHgE
Haikou [*China*] [*Airport symbol*] (OAG) ... HAK
Haikou [*China*] [*ICAO location identifier*] (ICLI) ... ZGHK
Haiku, HI [*AM radio station call letters*] ... KUAU
Haiku Society of America (EA) ... HSA
Hail [*Meteorological symbol*] ... A
Hail [*ICAO*] (FAAC) ... GR
Hail [*Meteorology*] ... H
Hail [*Saudi Arabia*] [*Airport symbol*] (OAG) ... HAS
Hail [*Saudi Arabia*] [*ICAO location identifier*] (ICLI) ... OEHL
Hail and Rain [*Meteorology*] (BARN) ... HR
Hail Detection Algorithm (USDC) ... HDA
Hail Detection Algorithm [*Marine science*] (OSRA) ... HDA
Hail Insurance Adjustment and Research Association [*Later, NCIA*] (EA) ... HIARA
Hailar [*China*] [*Airport symbol*] (OAG) ... HLD
Hailar [*China*] [*ICAO location identifier*] (ICLI) ... ZYLA

Hailes' Annals of Scotland [*A publication*] (DLA) ..... Hailes Ann
Hailes' Decisions, Scotch Court of Sessions [*A publication*] (DLA) ..... Hailes Dec
Hailey, ID [*Location identifier FAA*] (FAAL) ..... HLE
Hailey, ID [*Location identifier FAA*] (FAAL) ..... SUN
Hailey Public Library, Hailey, ID [*Library symbol*] [*Library of Congress*] (LCLS) ..... IdHl
Haileybury Public Library, Haileybury, ON, Canada [*Library symbol Library of Congress*] (LCLS) ..... CaOHai
Haileybury Public Library, Ontario [*Library symbol National Library of Canada*] (NLC) ..... OHAI
Haileybury School of Mines Campus, Northern College of Applied Arts and Technology, Ontario [*Library symbol National Library of Canada*] (BIB) ..... OHAINC
Hailstones [*NWS*] (FAAC) ..... HLSTO
Hailuoto [*Finland ICAO location identifier*] (ICLI) ..... EFHL
Haima [*Oman*] [*ICAO location identifier*] (ICLI) ..... OOHA
Hain Food Group [*NASDAQ symbol*] (TTSB) ..... NOSH
Hain Food Group, Inc. [*Associated Press*] (SAG) ..... HainFood
Hain Food Group, Inc. [*NASDAQ symbol*] (SAG) ..... NOSH
Hainan Airlines [*China*] [*FAA designator*] (FAAC) ..... CHH
Haines [*Alaska*] [*Airport symbol*] (OAG) ..... HNS
Haines, AK [*FM radio station call letters*] ..... KHNS
Haines Borough Public Library, Haines, AK [*Library symbol Library of Congress*] (LCLS) ..... AkH
Haines City, FL [*AM radio station call letters*] ..... WLVF
Haines City, FL [*FM radio station call letters*] ..... WLVF-FM
Haine's Illinois Justice of the Peace [*A publication*] (DLA) ..... Hain JP
Hair (VRA) ..... hr
Hair Cadmium Level [*Medicine*] ..... HCd
Hair Cell [*Otology*] ..... HC
Hair International/Associated Master Barbers and Beauticians of America (EA) ..... HI/AMBBA
Hair Replacement System ..... HRS
Hair Space [*Publishing*] (DGA) ..... HS
Hair Space between Letters [*Proofreader's mark*] ..... HR
Hair Tuning Bar ..... HTB
Haircutting ..... HAIRCTTNG
Hairdresser ..... HRDRSSR
Hairdressers and Cosmetologists Employers' Association [*Australia*] ..... HCEA
Hairdressers' Registration Council [*British*] (BI) ..... HRC
Hairdressing and Beauty Industry Association [*Australia*] ..... HBIA
Hairdressing Manufacturers' and Wholesalers' Association [*British*] (BI) ..... HMWA
Hairdressing Training Board (AIE) ..... HTB
Hairless Mouse [*Endocrinology*] (DMAA) ..... hr
Hairline (DAVI) ..... HL
Hair's Daily Requirement [*Brand of shampoo*] ..... HDR
Hairspace [*Printing*] (WDMC) ..... hr
Hairstyling ..... HRSTYLNG
Hairstylist ..... HRSTYLST
Hairy Anatomy Marine [*See also BAM*] [*Slang term for male marines*] [*Bowdlerized version*] ..... HAM
Hairy Cell Leukemia [*Medicine*] ..... HCL
Hairy Hill Public Library, Alberta [*Library symbol National Library of Canada*] (NLC) ..... AHH
Hairy Hill Public Library, Hairy Hill, AB, Canada [*Library symbol*] [*Library of Congress*] (LCLS) ..... CaAHh
Hairy Vetch as a Cover Crop [*Agriculture*] ..... HVCC
Hairy Woodpecker [*Ornithology*] ..... HW
Haiti [*or Haitian*] (WDAA) ..... HA
Haiti (ABBR) ..... HAI
Haiti ..... HAIT
Haiti [*ANSI two-letter standard code*] (CNC) ..... HT
Haiti [*MARC country of publication code Library of Congress*] (LCCP) ..... ht
Haiti [*ANSI three-letter standard code*] (CNC) ..... HTI
Haiti [*MARC geographic area code Library of Congress*] (LCCP) ..... nwht--
Haiti Air Freight [*ICAO designator*] (FAAC) ..... HLS
Haiti Air International [*ICAO designator*] (AD) ..... HC
Haiti International Air SA [*ICAO designator*] (FAAC) ..... HTI
Haiti National Airlines [*ICAO designator*] (FAAC) ..... HNR
Haiti North Airline [*ICAO designator*] (FAAC) ..... HTN
Haiti Trans Air [*ICAO designator*] (AD) ..... TV
Haiti Trans Air SA [*ICAO designator*] (FAAC) ..... HTC
Haitian Air Corps ..... HAC
Haitian Aviation Line SA [*ICAO designator*] (FAAC) ..... HBC
Haitian Campaign Medal ..... HCM
Haitian Coalition on AIDS (EA) ..... HCA
Haitian Development Fund [*Later, MH*] (EA) ..... HDF
Haitian Medical Association Abroad [*Later, AMHE*] (EA) ..... HMAA
Haitian Migrant Interdiction Operation [*Haitian-US agreement, allowing US Coast Guard to board Haitian vessels on high seas*] ..... HMIO
Haitian Philatelic Society (EA) ..... HPS
Haitian Refugee Center (EA) ..... HRC
Haitian Refugee Project [*Defunct*] (EA) ..... HRP
Haitian Unity Council, Inc. [*Defunct*] (EA) ..... HUCI
Haitian-American Association [*Defunct*] ..... HAA
Haitian-American Chamber of Commerce and Industry (EA) ..... HAMCHAM
Haitian-American Sugar Co. ..... HASCO
Haiwee [*California*] [*Seismograph station code, US Geological Survey Closed*] (SEIS) ..... HAI
Hajdu-Cheney Syndrome [*Medicine*] (DMAA) ..... HCS
Hajigak [*Afghanistan*] [*ICAO location identifier*] (ICLI) ..... OAHJ
Hajji Baba Club (EA) ..... HBC
Hajna-Damon Broth [*Medicine*] (DMAA) ..... HD
Hajvairy Airlines [*Pakistan*] [*ICAO designator*] (FAAC) ..... HAJ
Ha-Kibbuts ha-Me'uhad (BJA) ..... KM
Hakluyt Society (EA) ..... HS
Hakodate [*Japan*] [*Seismograph station code, US Geological Survey*] (SEIS) ..... HAK
Hakodate [*Japan*] [*Airport symbol*] (OAG) ..... HKD
Hakodate [*Japan ICAO location identifier*] (ICLI) ..... RJCH
Hal Roach Studios, Inc. ..... HRS
Halakha (BJA) ..... Hal
Halali [*Namibia*] [*ICAO location identifier*] (ICLI) ..... FAHI
Halberd ..... HLBRD
Halberton [*England*] ..... HALB
Halbfranzband [*Half-Calf Binding*] [*Publishing*] [*German*] ..... HFRZ
Halbkettenfahrzeug [*Half-Track Vehicle*] [*German military - World War II*] ..... HKF
Halbleinwand [*Half-Bound Cloth*] [*Bookbinding, publishing*] [*German*] ..... HLW
Halcomb's Mining Cases [*England*] [*A publication*] (DLA) ..... Halc
Halcomb's Mining Cases [*England*] [*A publication*] (DLA) ..... Halc Min Cas
Halcyon Resources Ltd. [*Vancouver Stock Exchange symbol*] ..... HYN
Halden Boiling Water Reactor [*Norway Nuclear energy*] ..... HBWR
Halden Reactor Project [*Norway*] ..... HPR
Haldimand County Museum Board, Cayuga, ON, Canada [*Library symbol Library of Congress*] (LCLS) ..... CaOCauHM
Haldimand County Museum Board, Cayuga, Ontario [*Library symbol National Library of Canada*] (NLC) ..... OCHM
Haldwani [*India*] [*Airport symbol*] (AD) ..... HWN
Hale Foundation (EA) ..... HF
Hale Observatories [*Formerly, Mount Palomar and Mount Wilson Observatories*] ..... HO
Hale Pohaku [*Hawaii*] [*Seismograph station code, US Geological Survey*] (SEIS) ..... HPU
Hale Resources Ltd. [*Toronto Stock Exchange symbol*] ..... HLE
Haleakala [*Hawaii*] [*Seismograph station code, US Geological Survey*] (SEIS) ..... HKL
Haleakala [*Hawaii*] [*Seismograph station code, US Geological Survey*] (SEIS) ..... HLK
Haleakala National Park ..... HALE
Haler [*Monetary unit*] [*Former Czechoslovakia*] ..... H
Hale's Analysis of the Law [*A publication*] (DLA) ..... Hal Anal
Hale's Analysis of the Law [*A publication*] (DLA) ..... Hale Anal
Hale's De Jure Maris, Appendix to Hall on the Sea Shore [*A publication*] (DLA) ..... De Jure Mar
Hale's De Jure Maris, Appendix to Hall on the Sea Shore [*A publication*] (DLA) ..... Hale De Jure Mar
Hale's De Portibus Maris [*A publication*] (DLA) ..... Hale De Port Mar
Hale's English Common Law [*A publication*] (DLA) ..... Hale
Hale's English Ecclesiastical Reports [*1583-1736*] [*A publication*] (DLA) ..... Hale Ecc
Hale's History of Parliament [*2nd ed.*] [*1745*] [*A publication*] (DLA) ..... Hale Parl
Hale's History of the Common Law [*A publication*] (DLA) ..... Hale C L
Hale's History of the Common Law [*A publication*] (DLA) ..... Hale Com Law
Hale's History of the Common Law [*A publication*] (DLA) ..... HHCL
Hale's History of the English Law [*A publication*] (DLA) ..... Hale Hist Eng Law
Hale's History of the Pleas of the Crown [*A publication*] (DLA) ..... HHPC
Hale's Jurisdiction of the House of Lords [*1796*] [*A publication*] (DLA) ..... Hale Jur HL
Hale's Pleas of the Crown [*England*] [*A publication*] (DLA) ..... Hale PC
Hale's Pleas of the Crown [*England*] [*A publication*] (DLA) ..... Hale PC (Eng)
Hale's Pleas of the Crown [*England*] [*A publication*] (DLA) ..... HPC
Hale's Precedents in (Ecclesiastical) Criminal Cases [*1475-1640*] [*A publication*] (DLA) ..... Hale Cr Prec
Hale's Precedents in (Ecclesiastical) Criminal Cases [*1475-1640*] [*A publication*] (DLA) ..... Hale Prec
Hale's Precedents in (Ecclesiastical) Criminal Cases [*1475-1640*] [*A publication*] (DLA) ..... Hale's
Hale's Reports [*33-37 California*] [*A publication*] (DLA) ..... Hale
Hale's Sheriff's Account [*A publication*] (DLA) ..... Sh Acc
Hale's Suggestion on Courts-Martial [*A publication*] (DLA) ..... Hale Sug CM
Hale's Summary of the Pleas of the Crown [*England*] [*A publication*] (DLA) ..... Hale Sum
Hale's Summary of the Pleas of the Crown [*England*] [*A publication*] (DLA) ..... Sum
Haley Industries Ltd. [*Toronto Stock Exchange symbol*] ..... HLY
Haleyville, AL [*AM radio station call letters*] ..... WJBB
Haleyville, AL [*FM radio station call letters*] ..... WJBB-FM
Half ..... H
Half (AAG) ..... HF
Half (WDMC) ..... hf
Half Adder [*Circuitry*] (MSA) ..... HA
Half Amplitude Duration [*Telecommunications*] (TEL) ..... HAD
Half Bandwidth [*Electronics*] ..... HBW
Half Bar Symbology ..... HBS
Half Bound [*Bibliography*] ..... HB
Half Bow [*Music*] (ROG) ..... HB
Half Breadth (AAG) ..... HB
Half Bridge Monorail [*Mobot Corp.*] [*Gantry robot*] (NITA) ..... HBM
Half Calf ..... HC
Half Chest ..... HC
Half Column [*Advertisement*] (DGA) ..... HF-COL
Half Covered [*Marine insurance*] (ROG) ..... HC
Half Double Crochet ..... HDC
Half Duplex [*Telecommunications*] (NITA) ..... HDX
Half Duplex (IAA) ..... HX
Half Duplex Teletype (KSC) ..... HDT
Half Duplex Transmission [*Data communication*] (CET) ..... HD
Half Duplex Transmission [*Data communication*] ..... HDX
Half Forward (ADA) ..... HF
Half Gross (DNAB) ..... HG

Half Hard [*Metallurgy*] ... HH
Half Hardy [*Horticulture*] ... HH
Half Height [*of an International Standards Organization container*] (DCTA) ... H/H
Half Hollow Hills Community Public Library, Dix Hills, NY [*Library symbol*] [*Library of Congress*] (LCLS) ... NDxhH
Half Hollow Hills Community Public Library, Huntington Station, NY [*Library symbol Library of Congress*] (LCLS) ... NHsH
Half Hollow Hills District Teacher's Center, Dix Hills, NY [*Library symbol Library of Congress*] (LCLS) ... NDxhHT
Half Hollow Hills High School East, Dix Hills, NY [*Library symbol Library of Congress*] (LCLS) ... NDxhHH-E
Half Hollow Hills High School West, Dix Hills, NY [*Library symbol Library of Congress*] (LCLS) ... NDxhHH-W
Half Inch Tape Cartridge [*Pressure group*] (NITA) ... HI/TC
Half Length [*Photography*] (DGA) ... HL
Half Line [*Illustration*] (DGA) ... HL
Half Moon Bay, CA [*Location identifier FAA*] (FAAL) ... HAF
Half Morocco ... HM
Half of 'O' Gauge [*Model railroading*] ... H-O
Half Page Printer ... HPP
Half Pay ... HP
Half Plate [*Photography*] ... HP
Half Power Point [*LASER technology*] ... HPP
Half Price (ROG) ... HP
Half Saddlebred Registry of America (EA) ... HSRA
Half Strength ... HS
Half Subtractor [*Circuitry*] ... HS
Half Symmetric Unstable Resonator (PDAA) ... HSUR
Half Symmetric Unstable Resonator with Intracavity Axicon (PDAA) ... HSURIA
Half Thickness Value (NRCH) ... HTV
Half Tone [*Printing*] (NITA) ... HT
Half Wave ... HW
Half Wave - Full Wave (EPA) ... HW-FW
Half Word (CET) ... HW
Halfback [*Football*] ... HB
Half-Bound [*or Binding*] (WDAA) ... HF BD
Half-Calf [*Bookbinding*] (DGA) ... HF-CF
Half-Caste (ADA) ... HC
Half-Changes [*Statistics*] ... HC
Half-Cloth [*Bookbinding*] (DGA) ... HF-CL
Half-Cycle Magnetizer (IDOE) ... HCM
Half-Duplex Transmission Module [*Telecommunications*] (ACRL) ... HDTM
Half-Hardy Annual [*Horticulture*] (ROG) ... HHA
Half-Hardy Biennial [*Horticulture*] (ROG) ... HHB
Half-Hardy Perennial [*Horticulture*] (ROG) ... HHP
Half-Life [*of radioactive elements*] ... HL
Half-Life of a Radioactive Substance (BARN) ... T
Half-Moon ... HLFM
Half-Morocco [*Bookbinding*] (DGA) ... HF-MOR
Half-Octave Bandwidth ... HOB
Halford-Robins-Godfrey [*British sports car maker*] ... HRG
Halfpenny Green [*British ICAO location identifier*] (ICLI) ... EGBO
Halfpennyworth [*British*] (ROG) ... HAPORTH
Half-plate (VRA) ... HALF
Half-Power Beamwidth [*or Bandwidth*] (IEEE) ... HPBW
Half-Quarter Horse Registry of America (EA) ... HQHRA
Half-Reversal [*Psychometrics*] ... HR
Half-Sample plus Complement [*Statistics*] ... HS + C
Half-Shade Plate ... HSP
Halfsheet [*Publishing*] (DGA) ... HS
Half-Tilt Containers (DCTA) ... HT
Half-timber (VRA) ... halftmb
Half-Time [*Survey*] [*Shipping*] ... HT
Half-Time Survey [*Shipping*] ... HTS
Half-Title [*Publishing*] ... HT
Halftone (VRA) ... HLFTN
Halftone [*Photoengraving*] ... HT
Halftone [*Photography*] [*Art*] (WDMC) ... ht
Half-Track [*A type of military vehicle*] (AABC) ... HTRAC
Half-Track [*A type of military vehicle*] ... HTRK
Half-Tracked [*Vehicle*] (NATG) ... HT
Half-Truck [*British*] ... H-T
Half-Value Depth (IAA) ... HVD
Half-Value Layer [*Radiology*] ... HVL
Half-Value Period ... HVP
Half-Value Thickness ... HVT
Half-Vellum [*Bookbinding*] (DGA) ... HF-VEL
Half-Wave Bridge Rectifier ... HWBR
Half-Wave Plate ... HWP
Half-Wave Rectifier ... HWR
Halfway, MD [*AM radio station call letters*] ... WHAG
Halfway, MD [*FM radio station call letters*] ... WQCM
Halfway, MO [*FM radio station call letters*] ... KYOO-FM
Half-Width at Half-Height (PDAA) ... HWHH
Half-Word Designator [*Computer science*] ... H
Half-Yearly Review ... HR
Halhed's Code of Gentoo Laws [*A publication*] (DLA) ... Halh Gent L
Haliburton County Public Library, Hastings, ON, Canada [*Library symbol Library of Congress*] (LCLS) ... CaOHaH
Haliburton County Public Library, Ontario [*Library symbol National Library of Canada*] (NLC) ... OHAL
Haliburton Highlands Museum, Haliburton, ON, Canada [*Library symbol*] [*Library of Congress*] (LCLS) ... CaOHalM
Haliburton Highlands Museum, Haliburton, Ontario [*Library symbol National Library of Canada*] (BIB) ... OHALM
Haliburton Public Library, Haliburton, ON, Canada [*Library symbol Library of Congress*] (LCLS) ... CaOHal
Halibut Association of North America (EA) ... HANA
Halic Havacilik, AS [*Turkey*] [*FAA designator*] (FAAC) ... GHC
Halieuticon Liber [*of Ovid*] [*Classical studies*] (OCD) ... Hal
Halifax [*Nova Scotia*] [*Seismograph station code, US Geological Survey*] (SEIS) ... HAL
Halifax [*Canada*] [*Airport symbol*] (OAG) ... YHZ
Halifax' Analysis of the Roman Civil Law [*A publication*] (DLA) ... Halifax Anal
Halifax and District Information Service [*British*] (NITA) ... HALDIS
Halifax City and Regional Library, Halifax, NS, Canada [*Library symbol Library of Congress*] (LCLS) ... CaNSH
Halifax City Regional Library [*UTLAS symbol*] ... HFX
Halifax City Regional Library, Nova Scotia [*Library symbol National Library of Canada*] (NLC) ... NSH
Halifax Conservatory of Music ... HCM
Halifax Corp. [*Associated Press*] (SAG) ... Halifax
Halifax Corp. [*AMEX symbol*] (SPSG) ... HX
Halifax County Library, Halifax, NC [*Library symbol Library of Congress*] (LCLS) ... NcHal
Halifax County Regional Library, Halifax, NS, Canada [*Library symbol Library of Congress*] (LCLS) ... CaNSHHC
Halifax County Regional Library, Lower Sackville, Nova Scotia [*Library symbol National Library of Canada*] (NLC) ... NSHHC
Halifax County Technical Institute, Weldon, NC [*Library symbol Library of Congress*] (LCLS) ... NcWelH
Halifax County-South Boston Regional Library, Halifax, VA [*Library symbol Library of Congress*] (LCLS) ... ViHal
Halifax Developments Ltd. [*Toronto Stock Exchange symbol*] ... HFD
Halifax Herald Ltd., Nova Scotia [*Library symbol National Library of Canada*] (NLC) ... NSHHE
Halifax Infirmary, Health Services Library, Halifax, NS, Canada [*Library symbol Library of Congress*] (LCLS) ... CaNSHHI
Halifax/International, NS [*ICAO location identifier*] (ICLI) ... CYHZ
Halifax, NS [*FM radio station call letters*] ... CBH
Halifax, NS [*FM radio station call letters*] ... CBHA
Halifax, NS [*Television station call letters*] ... CBHFT
Halifax, NS [*Television station call letters*] ... CBHT
Halifax, NS [*FM radio station call letters*] ... CHFX
Halifax, NS [*AM radio station call letters*] ... CHNS
Halifax, NS [*FM radio station call letters*] ... CIEZ
Halifax, NS [*Television station call letters*] ... CIHF
Halifax, NS [*FM radio station call letters*] ... CIOO
Halifax, NS [*AM radio station call letters*] ... CJCH
Halifax, NS [*Television station call letters*] ... CJCH-TV
Halifax, NS [*FM radio station call letters*] ... CKDU
Halifax Ocean Meeting Point ... HOMP
Halifax Regional Vocational School, Halifax, NS, Canada [*Library symbol Library of Congress*] (LCLS) ... CaNSHVH
Halifax Regional Vocational School, Nova Scotia [*Library symbol National Library of Canada*] (NLC) ... NSHVH
Halifax/Shearwater Canadian Forces Base, NS [*ICAO location identifier*] (ICLI) ... CYAW
Halite [*CIPW classification*] [*Geology*] ... hl
Halk Bankasi [*Peoples Bank of Turkey*] [*See also THB*] ... HB
Halkerston's Compendium of Scotch Faculty Decisions [*A publication*] (DLA) ... Halk
Halkerston's Compendium of Scotch Faculty Decisions [*A publication*] (DLA) ... Halk Comp
Halkerston's Digest of the Scotch Marriage Law [*A publication*] (DLA) ... Halk
Halkerston's Digest of the Scotch Marriage Law [*A publication*] (DLA) ... Halk Dig
Halkerston's Latin Maxims [*A publication*] (DLA) ... Halk
Halkerston's Latin Maxims [*A publication*] (DLA) ... Halk Lat Max
Halkerston's Latin Maxims [*A publication*] (DLA) ... Halk Max
Halkerston's Technical Terms of the Law [*A publication*] (DLA) ... Halk Tech Terms
Halkin Emek Partisi [*People's Labor Party*] [*Turkey Political party*] (EY) ... HEP
Hall ... H
Hall and Oates Fan Club (EA) ... HOFC
Hall and Twell's English Chancery Reports [*1849-50*] [*A publication*] (DLA) ... H & T
Hall and Twell's English Chancery Reports [*1849-50*] [*A publication*] (DLA) ... H & Tw
Hall and Twell's English Chancery Reports [*1849-50*] [*A publication*] (DLA) ... Ha & Tw
Hall and Twell's English Chancery Reports [*47 English Reprint*] [*A publication*] (DLA) ... Hal & Tw
Hall and Twell's English Chancery Reports [*47 English Reprint*] [*A publication*] (DLA) ... Hall & T
Hall and Twell's English Chancery Reports [*47 English Reprint*] [*A publication*] (DLA) ... Hall & Tw
Hall and Twell's English Chancery Reports [*47 English Reprint*] [*A publication*] (DLA) ... Hall & Tw (Eng)
Hall Beach [*Canada*] [*Airport symbol*] (OAG) ... YUX
Hall Beach, NT [*ICAO location identifier*] (ICLI) ... CYUX
Hall Effect [*Electromagnetism*] (OA) ... HE
Hall Effect Device ... HED
Hall Effect Function Generator ... HEFG
Hall Effect Generator ... HEG
Hall Effect Multiplier ... HEM
Hall Effect Probe ... HEP
Hall Effect Thruster [*Electric thruster type*] ... HET
Hall Effect Transducer ... HET
Hall Electrolytic Conductivity Detector [*Analytical instrumentation*] ... HECD
Hall of Fame (WDAA) ... H of F
Hall of Fame ... HOF

Hall of Fame for Great Americans (EA) .... HFGA
Hall of Records Commission, Annapolis, MD [*Library symbol Library of Congress*] (LCLS) .... MdAA
Hall on International Law [*A publication*] (DLA) .... Hall Int Law
Hall Township High School District 502, Spring Valley, IL [*Library symbol Library of Congress*] (LCLS) .... ISprvHSD
Hall Wardrobes [*Classified advertising*] (ADA) .... HR
Hallah (BJA) .... Ha
Hallah (BJA) .... Hal
Hallam Nuclear Power Facility [*Decommissioned*] [*AEC*] .... HNPF
Hallam's Constitutional History of England [*A publication*] (DLA) .... Const Hist
Hallam's Constitutional History of England [*A publication*] (DLA) .... Hal Const Hist
Hallam's Constitutional History of England [*A publication*] (DLA) .... Hall Const Hist
Hallam's Constitutional History of England [*A publication*] (DLA) .... Hall Hist
Hallam's Constitutional History of England [*A publication*] (DLA) .... Hallam
Halle [*German Democratic Republic*] [*Seismograph station code, US Geological Survey*] (SEIS) .... HLE
Halleck's International Law [*A publication*] (DLA) .... Hal Int Law
Halleck's International Law [*A publication*] (DLA) .... Hall Int Law
Halleck's International Law [*A publication*] (DLA) .... Halleck Int Law
Halleck's Law of War [*A publication*] (DLA) .... Hall Law of W
Halleck's Mining Laws of Spain and Mexico [*A publication*] (DLA) .... Hal Min Law
Hall-Effect Imaging [*Medical imaging*] .... HEI
Hallefors [*Sweden ICAO location identifier*] (ICLI) .... ESVH
Hallelujah Band .... HB
Hallervorden-Spatz Syndrome [*Medicine*] (AAMN) .... HSS
Hallett [*Antarctica*] [*Seismograph station code, US Geological Survey Closed*] (SEIS) .... HLL
Hallett [*Australia Seismograph station code, US Geological Survey*] (SEIS) .... HTT
Hallett's Reports [*1, 2 Colorado*] [*A publication*] (DLA) .... Hall
Hallett's Reports [*1, 2 Colorado*] [*A publication*] (DLA) .... Hall (Col)
Hallett's Reports [*1, 2 Colorado*] [*A publication*] (DLA) .... Hallett
Hallettsville, TX [*AM radio station call letters*] (RBYB) .... KHLT
Halley Bay [*Antarctica*] [*Seismograph station code, US Geological Survey Closed*] (SEIS) .... HBA
Halley Bay [*United Kingdom*] [*Geomagnetic observatory code*] .... HLY
Halley Multicolor Camera [*Instrumentation*] .... HMC
Halley Optical Probe Experiment .... HOPE
Halley Resources Ltd. [*Vancouver Stock Exchange symbol*] .... HLL
Halli [*Finland ICAO location identifier*] (ICLI) .... EFHA
Halliburton Co. [*NYSE symbol Toronto Stock Exchange symbol*] (SPSG) .... HAL
Halliburton Co. [*Associated Press*] (SAG) .... Halbtn
Hallicrafters Incremental Power Spectrum Analyzer .... HIPSA
Halliday's Elementary View of Chancery Proceedings [*A publication*] (DLA) .... Hall Ch Pr
Hallie, WI [*AM radio station call letters*] .... WOGO
Hallifax's Analysis of the Civil Law [*A publication*] (DLA) .... Hal Civ Law
Hallifax's Analysis of the Civil Law [*A publication*] (DLA) .... Hall Civ Law
Hallifax's Analysis of the Civil Law [*A publication*] (DLA) .... Hallif CL
Hallifax's Analysis of the Civil Law [*A publication*] (DLA) .... Hallifax Anal (of Civil Law)
Hallimaile, HI [*FM radio station call letters*] .... KPMW
Hallman, W. A., St. Paul MN [*STAC*] .... HWA
Hallmark [*Record label*] [*Canada*] .... Hall
Hallmark .... HLLMRK
Hallmark .... HM
Hallmark Capital [*NASDAQ symbol*] (TTSB) .... HALL
Hallmark Capital Corp. [*NASDAQ symbol*] (SAG) .... HALL
Hallmark Capital Corp. [*Associated Press*] (SAG) .... HallmkCa
Hallmark Cards, Inc., Kansas City, MO [*Library symbol*] [*Library of Congress*] (LCLS) .... MoKHC
Hallmark Financial Services [*AMEX symbol*] (SAG) .... HAF
Hallmark Resources [*Vancouver Stock Exchange symbol*] .... HKR
Hallock High School, Hallock, MN [*Library symbol*] [*Library of Congress*] (LCLS) .... MnHalH
Hallock Public Library, Hallock, MN [*Library symbol*] [*Library of Congress*] (LCLS) .... MnHal
Hall's Admiralty Practice and Jurisdiction [*A publication*] (DLA) .... Hall Adm
Hall's American Law Journal [*A publication*] (DLA) .... Hall ALJ
Hall's American Law Journal [*A publication*] (DLA) .... Hall Am LJ
Hall's American Law Journal [*A publication*] (DLA) .... Hall LJ
Hall's American Law Journal [*A publication*] (DLA) .... Hall's Am LJ
Hall's American Law Journal [*A publication*] (DLA) .... LJ
Halls Creek [*Australia ICAO location identifier*] (ICLI) .... APHC
Halls Creek [*Australia Airport symbol Obsolete*] (OAG) .... HCQ
Hall's Essay on Maritime Loans from the French of Emerigon [*A publication*] (DLA) .... Hall Emerig Mar Loans
Hall's Essay on Maritime Loans from the French of Emerigon [*A publication*] (DLA) .... Hall Marit Loans
Hall's Journal of Jurisprudence [*A publication*] (DLA) .... Jour Juris
Hall's Lagoon [*Australia Seismograph station code, US Geological Survey Closed*] (SEIS) .... HLA
Hall's Laws of Mexico Relating to Real Property, Etc. [*A publication*] (DLA) .... Hall Mex Law
Hall's Legal Forms [*A publication*] (DLA) .... HLF
Hall's New York Superior Court Reports [*A publication*] (DLA) .... Hall
Hall's New York Superior Court Reports [*A publication*] (DLA) .... Hall (NY)
Halls (Noncommercial) [*Public-performance tariff class*] [*British*] .... G
Hall's Reports [*56, 57 New Hampshire*] [*A publication*] (DLA) .... Hall
Hall's Reports [*56, 57 New Hampshire*] [*A publication*] (DLA) .... Hall NH
Hall's Rights and Duties of Neutrals [*1874*] [*A publication*] (DLA) .... Hall Neut
Hall's Rights in the Sea Shores [*A publication*] (DLA) .... Hall Shores
Hall's Tracts on Constitutional Law [*A publication*] (DLA) .... Hall Const L
Hall's Treatise on the Law Relating to Profits a Prendre, Etc. [*A publication*] (DLA) .... Hall Profits a Prendre
Hallstrom Elementary School, Rockford, IL [*Library symbol*] [*Library of Congress*] (LCLS) .... IRoHIE
Hallsville, MO [*Location identifier FAA*] (FAAL) .... HLV
Hallucination .... HALLUC
Hallux Abducto Valgus [*Orthopedics*] (DAVI) .... HAV
Hallux Abductus [*Orthopedics*] (DAVI) .... HA
Hallux Limitus [*Podiatry*] (DAVI) .... HL
Hallux Rigidus [*Orthopedics*] (DAVI) .... HR
Hallux Valgus [*Orthopedics*] (DAVI) .... HV
Hallviken [*Sweden ICAO location identifier*] (ICLI) .... ESNA
Hallwood Consolidated Res. [*NASDAQ symbol*] (TTSB) .... HCRC
Hallwood Consolidated Resources [*Associated Press*] (SAG) .... HallwdCon
Hallwood Consolidated Resources Corp. [*Associated Press*] (SAG) .... HalwdCn
Hallwood Consolidated Resources Corp. [*NASDAQ symbol*] (SAG) .... HCRC
Hallwood Energy Corp. [*Associated Press*] (SAG) .... HlwdE
Hallwood Energy Corp. [*NASDAQ symbol*] (NQ) .... HWEC
Hallwood Energy Partners Ltd. [*Associated Press*] (SAG) .... HalEP
Hallwood Energy Partners Ltd. [*AMEX symbol*] (SPSG) .... HEP
Hallwood Energy Ptnrs L.P. [*AMEX symbol*] (TTSB) .... HEP
Hallwood Energy Ptnrs L.P.'C' [*AMEX symbol*] (TTSB) .... HEP.C
Hallwood Group [*NYSE symbol*] (TTSB) .... HWG
Hallwood Group, Inc. [*Associated Press*] (SAG) .... Hallwd
Hallwood Group, Inc. [*NYSE symbol*] (SPSG) .... HWG
Hallwood Realty Partners [*Associated Press*] (SAG) .... HallRlty
Hallwood Realty Partners Ltd. [*Associated Press*] (SAG) .... HallRty
Hallwood Realty Partners Ltd. [*AMEX symbol*] (SPSG) .... HRY
Hallwood Rlty Ptnrs L.P. (New) [*AMEX symbol*] (TTSB) .... HRY
Halmark Financial Services [*Associated Press*] (SAG) .... HallmF
Halmstad [*Sweden ICAO location identifier*] (ICLI) .... ESMT
Halmstad [*Sweden*] [*Airport symbol*] (OAG) .... HAD
HA-LO [*NASDAQ symbol*] (SAG) .... HALO
HA-LO Industries [*NASDAQ symbol*] (TTSB) .... HALO
HA-LO Industries, Inc. [*Associated Press*] (SAG) .... HA-LO
Halo Orbit Space Station [*NASA*] .... HOSS
Haloacetic Acids [*Environmental chemistry*] .... HAA
Halocarbon Global-Warming Potential [*Meteorology*] .... HGWP
Halogen (WDAA) .... HAL
Halogen (IDOE) .... hal
Halogen Bulb .... HB
Halogen Interchangeable Light Source .... HILS
Halogen Occulation Experiment (MCD) .... HALOE
Halogen Quenched Tube .... HQT
Halogenated Cleaning Solvent Association (EA) .... HCSA
Halogenated Dibenzodioxin [*Organic chemistry*] .... HDD
Halogenated Dibenzofuran [*Organic chemistry*] .... HDF
Halogenated Hydrocarbon .... HALON
Halogenated Organic Carbons (GNE) .... HO
Halogenated Organic Compound [*Organic chemistry*] (FFDE) .... HOC
Halogenated Organic Compounds .... HOC
Halogenated Solvents Industry Alliance (EA) .... HSIA
Halogenated Volatile Organic Compound .... HVOC
HALON [*Halogenated Hydrocarbon*] (NFPA) .... H
HALON [*Halogenated Hydrocarbon*] **System** [*NFPA pre-fire planning symbol*] (NFPA) .... HL
Haloperidol [*A tranquilizer*] .... HAL
Haloperidol (DAVI) .... HL
Haloperidol [*Tranquilizer*] .... HPD
Haloperidol Decanoate [*Pharmacology*] (DAVI) .... HL-D
Halophilic Malate Dehydrogenase [*An enzyme*] .... hMDH
Halopredone Diacetate [*Endocrinology*] .... HDA
Halorhodopsin [*Biochemistry*] .... HR
Halothane [*Also, HAL*] [*An anesthetic*] .... H
Halothane [*Also, H*] [*An anesthetic*] .... HAL
Halothane Hepatitis [*Medicine*] (DMAA) .... HH
Halothane Hypoxia [*Medicine*] .... HH
Halothane, Oxygen, and Gas [*Nitrous oxide*] [*Anesthesiology*] (DAVI) .... HOG
Halothane-Caffeine Contracture Test [*Medical test*] (PAZ) .... CHCT
Halpern's AntiRADAR Point .... HARP
Halsbury's Statutes of England [*A publication*] (DLA) .... Halsbury
Halsbury's Statutes of England [*A publication*] (DLA) .... Halsbury's Statutes
Halsbury's Statutory Instruments [*A publication*] (DLA) .... Halsbury's S Is
Halsey Drug [*AMEX symbol*] (TTSB) .... HDG
Halsey Drug Co. [*Associated Press*] (SAG) .... Halsey
Halsey Drug Co. [*AMEX symbol*] (CTT) .... HDG
Halsgerichtsordnung [*German*] .... HGO
Halstead [*Urban district in England*] .... HALST
Halstead Energy [*NASDAQ symbol*] (TTSB) .... HSNR
Halstead Energy Corp. [*Associated Press*] (SAG) .... HalstdE
Halstead Energy Corp. [*Associated Press*] (SAG) .... HalstdEn
Halstead Energy Corp. [*NASDAQ symbol*] (SAG) .... HSNR
Halstead Neuropsychological Test Battery (EDAC) .... HNTB
Halstead-Reitan [*Neuropsychological battery*] (DAVI) .... HR
Halsted's Digest of the Law of Evidence [*A publication*] (DLA) .... Hal Ev
Halsted's Digest of the Law of Evidence [*A publication*] (DLA) .... Halst Ev
Halsted's New Jersey Chancery Reports [*A publication*] (DLA) .... Halst Ch
Halsted's New Jersey Chancery Reports [*A publication*] (DLA) .... Halsted (NJ)
Halsted's New Jersey Equity Reports [*A publication*] (DLA) .... Hals Ch
Halsted's New Jersey Equity Reports [*A publication*] (DLA) .... Hals Eq
Halsted's New Jersey Equity Reports [*A publication*] (DLA) .... Halst
Halsted's New Jersey Law Reports [*6-12 New Jersey*] [*A publication*] (DLA) .... Hal Law
Halsted's New Jersey Law Reports [*6-12 New Jersey*] [*A publication*] (DLA) .... Hals
Halsted's New Jersey Law Reports [*6-12 New Jersey*] [*A publication*] (DLA) .... Halst

Halt [*Computer science*] (MDG) ... H
Halt [*Computer science*] (MDG) ... HLT
Halt Acknowledge [*Computer science*] ... HLTA
Halt All Racist Tours [*British*] (DI) ... HART
HALT - An Organization of Americans for Legal Reform (EA) ... HALT-ALR
Halt and Catch Fire [*Computer hacker terminology*] (NHD) ... HCF
Halt and Jump [*Computer science*] (BUR) ... HJ
Halt and Proceed [*Computer science*] (SAA) ... HPR
Halt and Transfer ... HT
Halt and Transfer ... HTR
Halt Device (IAA) ... HDV
Halter Marine Group, Inc. [*Associated Press*] (SAG) ... HalterM
Halter Marine Group, Inc. [*AMEX symbol*] (SAG) ... HLX
Haltom City, TX [*FM radio station call letters*] (RBYB) ... KNBR-FM
Halton [*British ICAO location identifier*] (ICLI) ... EGWN
Halton Hills Public Libraries, Georgetown Branch, Georgetown, ON, Canada [*Library symbol*] [*Library of Congress*] (LCLS) ... CaOGEH
Halton Region Museum, Milton, Ontario [*Library symbol National Library of Canada*] (BIB) ... OMIHM
Halton Reinsurance Co. Ltd. [*Toronto Stock Exchange symbol*] ... HLN
Halton Rifles [*British military*] (DMA) ... HR
Halverson Project [*World War II plan to bomb Japan from China*] ... HALPRO
Ham Band Receiver (IAA) ... HBR
Hamada [*Japan*] [*Seismograph station code, US Geological Survey*] (SEIS) ... HMD
Hamadan [*Iran*] [*Airport symbol*] (AD) ... HDM
Hamadan [*Iran*] [*ICAO location identifier*] (ICLI) ... OIHH
Hamadan [*Iran*] [*ICAO location identifier*] (ICLI) ... OIHS
Hamadan [*Iran*] [*ICAO location identifier*] (ICLI) ... OIHT
Hamamatsu [*Japan*] [*Seismograph station code, US Geological Survey*] (SEIS) ... HMM
Hamamatsu [*Japan ICAO location identifier*] (ICLI) ... RJNH
Hamar/Stafsberg [*Norway ICAO location identifier*] (ICLI) ... ENHA
Hamarein Air [*United Arab Emirates*] [*ICAO designator*] (ICDA) ... HM
Hamarfly, AS [*Norway*] [*FAA designator*] (FAAC) ... HAM
Hamble [*British ICAO location identifier*] (ICLI) ... EGHM
Hambledon [*England*] ... HAMB
Hambrecht & Quist [*Investment banking firm*] ... H & Q
Hambro Resources, Inc. [*Vancouver Stock Exchange symbol*] ... HAN
Hamburg [*Germany ICAO location identifier*] (ICLI) ... EDDH
Hamburg [*Germany ICAO location identifier*] (ICLI) ... EDHA
Hamburg [*Germany Airport symbol*] (OAG) ... HAM
Hamburg [*Germany*] [*Seismograph station code, US Geological Survey*] (SEIS) ... HAM
Hamburg [*West Germany*] (ROG) ... HAMB
Hamburg [*New York*] [*Seismograph station code, US Geological Survey Closed*] (SEIS) ... HMB
Hamburg Airlines [*ICAO designator*] (AD) ... HX
Hamburg Airlines, GmbH [*Germany ICAO designator*] (FAAC) ... HAS
Hamburg, AR [*FM radio station call letters*] ... KHMB
Hamburg/Finkenwerder [*Germany ICAO location identifier*] (ICLI) ... EDHI
Hamburg Public Library, Hamburg, IA [*Library symbol Library of Congress*] (LCLS) ... IaHamb
Hamburg Rating Scale for Psychiatric Disorders [*Medicine*] (DMAA) ... HRPD
Hamburg Reporter, Hamburg, IA [*Library symbol Library of Congress*] (LCLS) ... IaHambR
Hamburg Township Library, Hamburg, MI [*Library symbol Library of Congress*] (LCLS) ... MiHamb
Hamburg-Amerika Linie [*Hamburg-America Steamship Co.*] ... HAL
Hamburg-Chicago Line [*Steamship*] (MHDB) ... HCL
Hamburger ... HAMBGR
Hamburger Hamlet Restaurants [*NASDAQ symbol*] (SPSG) ... HAMB
Hamburger Hamlet Restaurants, Inc. [*Associated Press*] (SAG) ... HmbHm
Hamburger University [*McDonald's Corp.*] ... HU
Hamburg-Sudamerikanische Dampschiffarts-Gesellschaft [*Hamburg-South American Steamship Co.*] [*Shipping*] (ROG) ... HSDG
Hamburg-Wechsler Intelligence Test [*Psychology*] ... HAWE
Hamburg-Wechsler-Intelligenztest fuer Kinder [*Hamburg-Wechsler Intelligence Test for Children*] [*Psychology*] ... HAWIK
Hamdard Foundation Pakistan (EAIO) ... HFP
Hamden, CT [*FM radio station call letters*] ... WKCI
Hamden, CT [*FM radio station call letters*] ... WQAQ
Hamden, CT [*AM radio station call letters*] (RBYB) ... WQUN-AM
Hamden, CT [*AM radio station call letters*] ... WXCT
Hamden Testing Services, Inc. ... HTS
Hameenkyro [*Finland ICAO location identifier*] (ICLI) ... EFHM
Hamel's International Law [*A publication*] (DLA) ... Ham Int
Hamel's Laws of the Customs [*A publication*] (DLA) ... Ham Cust
Hamel's Laws of the Customs [*A publication*] (DLA) ... Hamel Cust
Hamer Butte [*Idaho*] [*Seismograph station code, US Geological Survey*] (SEIS) ... HID
Hamer Elementary School, Hamer, ID [*Library symbol*] [*Library of Congress*] (LCLS) ... IdHamSD
Hamerton, Allen, and Otter's English Magistrates' Cases [*3 New Sessions Cases*] [*A publication*] (DLA) ... Ham A & O
Hamhung [*North Korea ICAO location identifier*] (ICLI) ... ZKHH
Hami [*China*] [*ICAO location identifier*] (ICLI) ... ZWHM
Hamilton [*Bermuda*] [*Airport symbol*] ... BDA
Hamilton [*Australia Airport symbol*] (OAG) ... HLT
Hamilton [*New Zealand*] [*Airport symbol*] (OAG) ... HLZ
Hamilton [*Ontario*] [*Seismograph station code, US Geological Survey Closed*] (SEIS) ... HML
Hamilton [*New York*] [*Seismograph station code, US Geological Survey*] (SEIS) ... HNY
Hamilton [*New Zealand*] [*ICAO location identifier*] (ICLI) ... NZHN
Hamilton [*Canada*] [*Airport symbol*] (OAG) ... YHM
Hamilton, AL [*Location identifier FAA*] (FAAL) ... HAB
Hamilton, AL [*AM radio station call letters*] ... WERH
Hamilton, AL [*FM radio station call letters*] ... WERH-FM
Hamilton & Kirkland Colleges, Clinton, NY [*Library symbol Library of Congress*] (LCLS) ... NCH
Hamilton Anxiety Scale [*Psychiatry*] (DMAA) ... HAMA
Hamilton Board of Education [*UTLAS symbol*] ... HBF
Hamilton Board of Education, Education Centre Library [*UTLAS symbol*] ... HBP
Hamilton Board of Education Schools [*UTLAS symbol*] ... HBE
Hamilton College, Clinton, NY [*OCLC symbol*] (OCLC) ... YHM
Hamilton Depression Rate Scale [*Psychiatry*] (DAVI) ... HDRS
Hamilton Education Centre, Hamilton, ON, Canada [*Library symbol Library of Congress*] (LCLS) ... CaOHEC
Hamilton Education Centre, Ontario [*Library symbol National Library of Canada*] (NLC) ... OHEC
Hamilton Financial Services Corp. [*Associated Press*] (SAG) ... HamlFn
Hamilton Financial Services Corp. [*NASDAQ symbol*] (SAG) ... HFSC
Hamilton Grange National Memorial ... HAGR
Hamilton Group Ltd. [*Toronto Stock Exchange symbol*] ... HGL
Hamilton Island [*Australia ICAO location identifier*] (ICLI) ... ABHM
Hamilton Island [*Australia Airport symbol*] (OAG) ... HTI
Hamilton, MT [*Location identifier FAA*] (FAAL) ... HMM
Hamilton, MT [*FM radio station call letters*] ... KBMG
Hamilton, MT [*AM radio station call letters*] ... KLYQ
Hamilton, MT [*FM radio station call letters*] (RBYB) ... KUFN-FM
Hamilton Normal School ... HNS
Hamilton, NY [*FM radio station call letters*] ... WRCU
(Hamilton of) Haddington's Manuscript Cases, Scotch Court of Session [*A publication*] (DLA) ... Ham
(Hamilton of) Haddington's Manuscript Cases, Scotch Court of Session [*A publication*] (DLA) ... Hamilton
Hamilton, OH [*Location identifier FAA*] (FAAL) ... HAO
Hamilton, OH [*FM radio station call letters*] ... WGRR
Hamilton, OH [*FM radio station call letters*] ... WHSS
Hamilton, OH [*AM radio station call letters*] ... WMOH
Hamilton, OH [*FM radio station call letters*] ... WYGY
Hamilton, ON [*FM radio station call letters*] ... CFMU
Hamilton, ON [*AM radio station call letters*] ... CHAM
Hamilton, ON [*Television station call letters*] ... CHCH
Hamilton, ON [*AM radio station call letters*] ... CHML
Hamilton, ON [*FM radio station call letters*] ... CJXY
Hamilton, ON [*FM radio station call letters*] ... CKLH
Hamilton, ON [*AM radio station call letters*] ... CKOC
Hamilton, ON [*ICAO location identifier*] (ICLI) ... CYHM
Hamilton on Company Law [*3 eds.*] [*1891-1910*] [*A publication*] (DLA) ... Hamilton
Hamilton Psychiatric Rating Scale for Depression ... HAM-D
Hamilton Public Library [*UTLAS symbol*] ... HPL
Hamilton Public Library, Hamilton, MO [*Library symbol*] [*Library of Congress*] (LCLS) ... MoHam
Hamilton Public Library, Hamilton, NY [*Library symbol Library of Congress*] (LCLS) ... NH
Hamilton Public Library, Hamilton, NY [*Library symbol*] [*Library of Congress*] (LCLS) ... NHL
Hamilton Public Library, Hamilton, ON, Canada [*Library symbol Library of Congress*] (LCLS) ... CaOH
Hamilton Public Library, Ontario [*Library symbol National Library of Canada*] (NLC) ... OH
Hamilton Ranch [*California*] [*Seismograph station code, US Geological Survey*] (SEIS) ... HMR
Hamilton Rating Scale (MAE) ... HRS
Hamilton Rating Scale for Deafness ... HRS-D
Hamilton Rating Scale for Depression [*Medicine*] (DMAA) ... HRS-D
Hamilton Spectator, Hamilton, ON, Canada [*Library symbol Library of Congress*] (LCLS) ... CaOHS
Hamilton Spectator, Ontario [*Library symbol National Library of Canada*] (NLC) ... OHS
Hamilton Standard (SAA) ... H-S
Hamilton Standard Carbon Dioxide Absorbent Material (NASA) ... HS-C
Hamilton Standard Division (NASA) ... HSD
Hamilton Technology, Inc. ... HTI
Hamilton, TX [*AM radio station call letters*] ... KCLW
Hamilton Watch Co., Lancaster, PA [*Library symbol Library of Congress Obsolete*] (LCLS) ... PLH
Hamiltonian Cycle Problem [*Computer science*] ... HCP
Hamiltonian Function [*Mathematics*] ... H
Hamiltonian Path Problem [*Mathematics*] ... HPP
Hamilton's American Negligence Cases [*A publication*] (DLA) ... Hamilton
Hamilton's Federalist [*A publication*] (DLA) ... Ham Fed
Hamish Hamilton [*Publisher*] [*British*] ... HH
Hamizrah Hehadash [*Jerusalem*] [*A publication*] (BJA) ... HH
Hamlet ... H
Hamlet [*Shakespearean work*] ... Ham
Hamlet [*Shakespearean work*] (BARN) ... Haml
Hamlet ... HMLT
Hamlet Evaluation Survey [*South Vietnam*] ... HES
Hamlet Evaluation System Monthly Report (MCD) ... HESRE
Hamlet, NC [*FM radio station call letters*] ... WJSG
Hamlet, NC [*AM radio station call letters*] ... WKDX
Hamlet Public Library, Hamlet, NC [*Library symbol Library of Congress*] (LCLS) ... NcHa
Hamlin Jet Ltd. [*British ICAO designator*] (FAAC) ... HJL
Hamlin, TX [*FM radio station call letters*] ... KCDD
Hamline University (GAGS) ... Hamline U
Hamline University, St. Paul, MN [*OCLC symbol*] (OCLC) ... MHA

Hamline University, St. Paul, MN [*Library symbol Library of Congress*] (LCLS) .... MnSH
Hamline University, School of Law, St. Paul, MN [*OCLC symbol*] (OCLC) .... MHL
Hamline University, School of Law, St. Paul, MN [*Library symbol Library of Congress*] (LCLS) .... MnSH-L
Hamlin's Reports [*81-93 Maine*] [*A publication*] (DLA) .... Hamlin
Hamlyn Publishing [*British*] .... H
Hamm/Lippewiesen [*Germany ICAO location identifier*] (ICLI) .... EDLH
Hammarskjold High School, Thunder Bay, Ontario [*Library symbol National Library of Canada*] (NLC) .... OTBHS
Hammel Green and Abrahamson, Inc. [*A national leader in innovative design*] .... HGA
Hammer (MSA) .... HMR
Hammer Form (MCD) .... HF
Hammer Head Crane (NASA) .... HHC
Hammer Makers' Society [*A union*] [*British*] .... HMS
Hammer Toe [*Orthopedics*] (DAVI) .... HT
Hammered (VRA) .... ham
Hammered Chainmakers' Society [*A union*] [*British*] .... HCS
Hammerfest [*Norway ICAO location identifier*] (ICLI) .... ENHF
Hammerfest [*Norway*] [*Airport symbol*] (OAG) .... HFT
Hammers Plastic Recycling [*NASDAQ symbol*] (TTSB) .... HAMRC
Hammersley Iron Proprietary Ltd. Railway [*Australia*] (DCTA) .... HIR
Hammerson Canada, Inc. [*Toronto Stock Exchange symbol*] .... HMC
Hammerson Properties Investment & Development Corp. Ltd. [*Toronto Stock Exchange symbol*] .... HPD
Hammick's Marriage Laws [*2nd ed.*] [*1887*] [*A publication*] (DLA) .... Ham Mar Laws
Hammon on Contracts [*A publication*] (DLA) .... Ham Cont
Hammond and Jackson's Reports [*45 Georgia*] [*A publication*] (DLA) .... Ham & J
Hammond and Jackson's Reports [*45 Georgia*] [*A publication*] (DLA) .... Hammond & Jackson
Hammond, IN [*AM radio station call letters*] .... WJOB
Hammond, IN [*Television station call letters*] .... WJYS
Hammond, IN [*FM radio station call letters*] .... WYCA
Hammond, LA [*Location identifier FAA*] (FAAL) .... HMU
Hammond, LA [*Location identifier FAA*] (FAAL) .... HPF
Hammond, LA [*FM radio station call letters*] .... KSLU
Hammond, LA [*Location identifier FAA*] (FAAL) .... TAO
Hammond, LA [*AM radio station call letters*] .... WFPR
Hammond, LA [*FM radio station call letters*] .... WHMD
Hammond, LA [*FM radio station call letters*] .... WKJN
Hammond Manufacturing Co. Ltd. [*Toronto Stock Exchange symbol*] .... HMM
Hammond Metallurgical Laboratory [*Yale*] (MCD) .... HML
Hammond on Fire Insurance [*A publication*] (DLA) .... Ham Ins
Hammond on Insanity [*A publication*] (DLA) .... Ham Ins
Hammond on Parties to Action [*A publication*] (DLA) .... Ham Part
Hammond on Parties to Action [*A publication*] (DLA) .... Ham Parties
Hammond Public Library, Hammond, IN [*OCLC symbol*] (OCLC) .... IHP
Hammond Public Library, Hammond, IN [*Library symbol Library of Congress*] (LCLS) .... InHam
Hammond Times, Hammond, IN [*Library symbol Library of Congress*] (LCLS) .... InHamT
Hammond's Air Service [*ICAO designator*] (AD) .... EM
Hammond's India and Burma Election Cases [*A publication*] (DLA) .... Ham
Hammond's Nisi Prius [*A publication*] (DLA) .... Ham NP
Hammond's Principles of Pleading [*1819*] [*A publication*] (DLA) .... Ham Pl
Hammond's Reports [*1-9 Ohio*] [*A publication*] (DLA) .... Ham
Hammond's Reports [*36-45 Georgia*] [*A publication*] (DLA) .... Hammond
Hammond's Reports [*1-9 Ohio*] [*A publication*] (DLA) .... Hammond
Hammons [*John Q.*] **Hotel, Inc.** [*Associated Press*] (SAG) .... JQHamm
Hammons [*John Q.*] **Hotels, Inc.** [*NYSE symbol*] (SAG) .... JQH
Hammons(John Q)Hotels'A' [*NYSE symbol*] (TTSB) .... JQR
Hammonton, NJ [*AM radio station call letters*] .... WONZ
Hammonton Public Library, Hammonton, NJ [*Library symbol Library of Congress*] (LCLS) .... NjHam
Hammurabi's Gesetz (BJA) .... HG
Ha-Mo'atsah ha-Hakla'it (BJA) .... MH
Hampden-Sydney College [*Virginia*] .... HSC
Hampden-Sydney College, Hampden-Sydney, VA [*OCLC symbol*] (OCLC) .... VHS
Hampden-Sydney College, Hampden-Sydney, VA [*Library symbol Library of Congress*] (LCLS) .... ViHdsC
Hampden-Sydney, VA [*FM radio station call letters*] .... WWHS
Hamper, Deritend, Birmingham [*Pseudonym used by William Hamper*] .... HDB
Hamper Industry Trade Association [*British*] (DBA) .... HITA
Hampshire [*County in England*] .... HAMPS
Hampshire [*County in England*] .... HANTS
Hampshire Aircraft Parks [*British military*] (DMA) .... HAP
Hampshire College, Amherst, MA [*OCLC symbol*] (OCLC) .... HAM
Hampshire College, Amherst, MA [*Library symbol Library of Congress*] (LCLS) .... MAH
Hampshire County Court Reports [*England*] [*A publication*] (DLA) .... Hamps Co Cas
Hampshire Group Ltd. [*NASDAQ symbol*] (SAG) .... HAMP
Hampshire Group Ltd. [*Associated Press*] (SAG) .... HampGp
Hampshire Group Ltd [*NASDAQ symbol*] (TTSB) .... HAMP
Hampshire Hunt [*British*] .... HH
Hampshire Imperial Yeomanry [*British military*] (DMA) .... HIY
Hampshire Inter-Library Center [*Library network*] .... HILC
Hampshire Inter-Library Center, Inc., Amherst, MA [*Library symbol Library of Congress Obsolete*] (LCLS) .... MHILC
Hampshire Local Militia [*British military*] (DMA) .... HLM
Hampshire Regiment [*Military unit*] [*British*] (ROG) .... HAMPS R
Hampshire Swine Registry (EA) .... HSR
Hampshire Technical Research Industrial and Commercial Service [*British*] (NITA) .... HATRICS
Hampshire Yeomanry Cavalry [*British military*] (DMA) .... HYC
Hampson. Trustees [*2nd ed.*] [*1830*] [*A publication*] (DLA) .... Hamp Tr
Hampstead [*Region of London*] .... HAMP
Hampstead Public Libraries, Central Library, London, United Kingdom [*Library symbol Library of Congress*] (LCLS) .... UkLH
Hampton & Branchville Railroad Co. [*AAR code*] .... HB
Hampton, AR [*FM radio station call letters*] .... KKOL
Hampton Bays, NY [*FM radio station call letters*] .... WWHB
Hampton Bays Public Library, Hampton Bays, NY [*Library symbol Library of Congress Obsolete*] (LCLS) .... NHamB
Hampton Bays Public Library, Hampton Bays, NY [*Library symbol Library of Congress*] (LCLS) .... NHampB
Hampton Chronicle, Hampton, IA [*Library symbol Library of Congress*] (LCLS) .... IaHampC
Hampton Elementary School, Mineola, NY [*Library symbol Library of Congress*] (LCLS) .... NMinHe
Hampton, IA [*Location identifier FAA*] (FAAL) .... HPT
Hampton, IA [*FM radio station call letters*] .... KLMJ
Hampton Indus [*AMEX symbol*] (TTSB) .... HAI
Hampton Industries, Inc. [*AMEX symbol*] (SPSG) .... HAI
Hampton Industries, Inc. [*Associated Press*] (SAG) .... HamptI
Hampton Institute, Hampton, VA [*Library symbol Library of Congress*] (LCLS) .... ViHaI
Hampton/Langley Air Force Base [*Virginia*] [*ICAO location identifier*] (ICLI) .... KLFI
Hampton Library, Bridgehampton, NY [*Library symbol Library of Congress*] (LCLS) .... NBrih
Hampton National Historic Site .... HAMP
Hampton, NH [*FM radio station call letters*] (RBYB) .... WSTG
Hampton One-Design Class Racing Association (EA) .... HODCRA
Hampton Roads Army Terminal .... HRART
Hampton Roads Army Terminal .... HRAT
Hampton, SC [*AM radio station call letters*] .... WBHC
Hampton, SC [*FM radio station call letters*] .... WBHC-FM
Hampton Times, Hampton, IA [*Library symbol Library of Congress*] (LCLS) .... IaHampT
[*The*] **Hampton University** (GAGS) .... Hampton U
Hampton Utilities Trust [*Associated Press*] (SAG) .... HmpU
Hampton, VA [*Location identifier FAA*] (FAAL) .... LFI
Hampton, VA [*FM radio station call letters*] .... WHOV
Hampton, VA [*AM radio station call letters*] .... WOJY
Hampton, VA [*Television station call letters*] .... WVEC
Hampton, VA [*FM radio station call letters*] .... WWDE
Hampton-Norfolk, VA [*Television station call letters*] .... WHRO
Hamster Embryo Fibroblast [*Medicine*] (DMAA) .... HEF
Hamster Embryonic Cell .... HEC
Hamster Leukemia Virus .... HaLV
Hamster Zona-Free Ovum [*Test*] [*Medicine*] (MEDA) .... HZFO
Hamstring-Quadriceps [*Anatomy*] .... H-Q
Hamtramck Public Library, Hamtramck, MI [*Library symbol Library of Congress*] (LCLS) .... MiHam
Hana [*Hawaii*] [*Airport symbol*] (OAG) .... HNM
Hana, Maui Island [*Hawaii*] [*ICAO location identifier*] (ICLI) .... PHHN
Hanahan, SC [*FM radio station call letters*] .... WAVF
Hanalei, HI [*FM radio station call letters*] (RBYB) .... KKCR-FM
Hanamaki [*Japan*] [*Airport symbol Obsolete*] (OAG) .... HNA
Hanamaki [*Japan ICAO location identifier*] (ICLI) .... RJSI
Hanapepe, HI [*Location identifier FAA*] (FAAL) .... PAK
Hanau [*Germany ICAO location identifier*] (ICLI) .... EDID
Hanbury-Jones on Uses [*A publication*] (DLA) .... Hanb Us
Hanbury's Judicial Error in the Law of Patents [*A publication*] (DLA) .... Hanb Pat
Hanceville, AL [*AM radio station call letters*] .... WRJL
Hancock [*Michigan*] [*Airport symbol*] (OAG) .... CMX
Hancock Airbase Library, Hancock Field, NY [*OCLC symbol*] (OCLC) .... ZUR
Hancock [*John*] **Bank & Thrift Opportunity Fund** [*NYSE symbol*] (SAG) .... BTO
Hancock [*John*] **Bank & Thrift Opportunity Fund** [*Associated Press*] (SAG) .... HancBT
Hancock Community Library, Hancock, MN [*Library symbol*] [*Library of Congress*] (LCLS) .... MnHan
Hancock Elementary School, Hancock, MN [*Library symbol*] [*Library of Congress*] (LCLS) .... MnHanE
Hancock Fabrics [*NYSE symbol*] (TTSB) .... HKF
Hancock Fabrics, Inc. [*Associated Press*] (SAG) .... HancFab
Hancock Fabrics, Inc. [*NYSE symbol*] (SPSG) .... HKF
Hancock High School, Hancock, MN [*Library symbol*] [*Library of Congress*] (LCLS) .... MnHanH
Hancock Holding [*NASDAQ symbol*] (TTSB) .... HBHC
Hancock Holding Co. [*Associated Press*] (SAG) .... HancHd
Hancock Holding Co. [*NASDAQ symbol*] (SAG) .... HBHC
Hancock, John, Income Securities Trust [*Associated Press*] (SAG) .... HanJS
Hancock, John, Income Securities Trust [*NYSE symbol*] (SAG) .... JHS
Hancock, John, Investors Trust [*Associated Press*] (SAG) .... HanJI
Hancock, John, Investors Trust [*NYSE symbol*] (SAG) .... JHI
Hancock, John, Patriot Preferred Dividend Fund [*Associated Press*] (SAG) .... HanPtPfd
Hancock, MI [*Location identifier FAA*] (FAAL) .... CMX
Hancock, MI [*Location identifier FAA*] (FAAL) .... CUT
Hancock, MI [*AM radio station call letters*] .... WMPL
Hancock, MI [*FM radio station call letters*] .... WZRK
Hancock, NY [*Location identifier FAA*] (FAAL) .... HNK
Hancock [*John*] **Patriot Global Dividend Fund** [*Associated Press*] (SAG) .... HanPtGlb
Hancock [*John*] **Patriot Global Dividend Fund** [*NYSE symbol*] (SPSG) .... PGD
Hancock [*John*] **Patriot Preferred Dividend Fund** [*NYSE symbol*] (SPSG) .... PPF
Hancock [*John*] **Patriot Premium Dividend Fund I** [*Associated Press*] (SAG) .... HanPtDiv
Hancock [*John*] **Patriot Premium Dividend Fund I** [*NYSE symbol*] (SAG) .... PDF

Hancock [*John*] **Patriot Premium Dividend Fund II** [*Associated Press*] (SAG) HanPtDv2
Hancock [*John*] **Patriot Premium Dividend, Inc. II** [*NYSE symbol*] (SPSG) ..... PDT
Hancock [*John*] **Patriot Prferred Dividend Fund** [*Associated Press*] (SAG) ..... HanPtPfd
Hancock [*John*] **Patriot Select Dividend Trust** [*NYSE symbol*] (SPSG) ..... DIV
Hancock [*John*] **Patriot Select Dividend Trust** [*Associated Press*] (SAG) ..... HanPtSel
Hancock Public-School Library, Hancock, MI [*Library symbol Library of Congress*] (LCLS) ..... MiHan
Hancock-Houghton [*Michigan*] [*Airport symbol*] (AD) ..... CMX
Hancock's System of Conveyancing [*Canada*] [*A publication*] (DLA) ..... Hanc Conv
Hand [*Music*] ..... H
Hand (ROG) ..... HD
Hand (WGA) ..... HND
Hand Actuated (IAA) ..... HA
Hand and Shoe Monitor [*Radiation detection*] ..... HSM
Hand/Automatic [*Nuclear energy*] (NRCH) ..... H/A
Hand Blood Flow [*Cardiology*] (DAVI) ..... HBF
Hand Brake [*Automotive engineering*] ..... H/BRK
Hand Carry (KSC) ..... H/C
Hand Carry ..... HC
Hand Colored (VRA) ..... HDCOL
Hand Control [*Technical drawings*] ..... HC
Hand Control Clutch (DNAB) ..... HCC
Hand Control Valve (NRCH) ..... HCV
Hand Controller Engage Driver (NASA) ..... HCED
Hand County Library, Miller, SD [*Library symbol Library of Congress*] (LCLS) ..... SdMi
Hand Crank ..... HC
Hand Cut [*Envelopes*] ..... HC
Hand, Foot, and Mouth [*Disease*] ..... HFM
Hand Form Block (MSA) ..... HFB
Hand Generator ..... HG
Hand Grip (DMAA) ..... HG
Hand Indicator Controller (NRCH) ..... HIC
Hand Jewel Pusher ..... HJP
Hand Knitting Association (EA) ..... HKA
Hand Lantern (AAG) ..... HL
Hand Microtelephone (IAA) ..... HMT
Hand Motion [*Vision*] [*Neurology*] (DAVI) ..... HM
Hand Motion and Light Perception [*Medicine*] (DAVI) ..... HM & LP
Hand Movement ..... HM
Hand Numerical Control (IAA) ..... HNC
Hand on Fines and Recoveries [*A publication*] (DLA) ..... Hand Fines
Hand on Patents [*A publication*] (DLA) ..... Hand Pat
Hand or Computer Universal Simulation [*PE Computer Services Ltd.*] [*Software package*] [*British*] ..... HOCUS
Hand Order Transmeter ..... HOSS
Hand Orthosis [*Medicine*] ..... HO
Hand Over (MCD) ..... HO
Hand Over Transmitter ..... HOT
Hand over Word ..... HOW
Hand RADAR (IAA) ..... HR
Hand Rail ..... HDR
Hand Rail ..... HNDRL
Hand Reach [*Automotive engineering*] ..... HR
Hand Receipt (AABC) ..... HR
Hand Receipt Holder (MCD) ..... HRH
Hand Reset ..... HR
Hand Surgery [*Medical specialty*] (DHSM) ..... HS
Hand Switch [*Nuclear energy*] (NRCH) ..... HS
Hand Target Designator ..... HTD
Hand Test [*Psychology*] ..... HT
Hand Tool Carrier [*NASA*] (KSC) ..... HTC
Hand Tools Institute (EA) ..... HTI
Hand Transceiver ..... HT
Hand Translation (MCD) ..... HT
Hand Valve [*Nuclear energy*] (NRCH) ..... HV
Handbag ..... HBAG
Handbag Supply Salesmen's Association (EA) ..... HSSA
Handbills (WDMC) ..... bills
Handbook (SAA) ..... H
Handbook ..... HANDB
Handbook (NASA) ..... HB
Handbook ..... HBK
Handbook (AFM) ..... HDBK
Handbook (WDMC) ..... hdbk
Handbook (WDAA) ..... HNBK
Handbook ..... HNDBK
Handbook Art ..... HBA
Handbook for Magistrates [*1853-55*] [*A publication*] (DLA) ..... Handb Mag
Handbook of Criminal Cases [*India*] [*A publication*] (DLA) ..... Desai
Handbook of Electronic Parts Reliability ..... HELPR
Handbook of Greek Mythology [*A publication*] (OCD) ..... Handb Gk Myth
Handbook of Information Technology Standards [*A publication*] ..... HITS
Handbook of Inspection Maintenance Requirements [*Navy*] (MCD) ..... HIMR
Handbook of Inspection Requirements [*Navy*] (MCD) ..... HIR
Handbook of Instructions for Aerospace Personnel Subsystem Designers ..... HIAPSD
Handbook of Instructions for Aerospace Systems Design ..... HIASD
Handbook of Instructions for Aerospace Vehicle Equipment Design ..... HIAVED
Handbook of Instructions for Air Force Subsystem Designers ..... HIAFSB
Handbook of Instructions for Aircraft Designers ..... HIAD
Handbook of Instructions for Aircraft Ground Support Equipment Designers ..... HIAGSE
Handbook of Instructions for Aircraft Ground Support Equipment Designers ..... HIAGSED
Handbook of Instructions for Aircraft Ground Support Equipment Designers ..... HIGSED
Handbook of Instructions for Ground Equipment Designers (MCD) ..... HIGED
Handbook of Instructions for Missile Designers ..... HIMD
Handbook of Instructions for Weapon Systems Designers ..... HIWSD
Handbook of Latin American Studies ..... HLAS
Handbook of Maintenance Instructions ..... HMI
Handbook of Military Forces (MCD) ..... HMF
Handbook of North-Semitic Inscriptions [*A publication*] (BJA) ..... NSI
Handbook of Occupational Groups and Series of Classes ..... HOGC
Handbook of Occupational Keywords [*For use in employment services*] [*Department of Labor*] ..... HOOK
Handbook of Operating Instructions [*Navy*] ..... HOI
Handbook of Operating Instructions [*Navy*] (MCD) ..... HOPI
Handbook of Operating Procedures ..... HOOP
Handbook of Overhaul Instructions [*Navy*] ..... HOHI
Handbook of Overhaul Instructions [*Navy*] (MCD) ..... HOI
Handbook of Overhaul Instructions [*Navy*] ..... HOVI
Handbook of Service Instructions ..... HOSI
Handbook of Service Instructions (MCD) ..... HSI
Handbook of Structural Repair (MCD) ..... HSR
Handbook of the Nations [*A publication*] ..... HON
Handbook on Emergency Measures (NATG) ..... HEM
Handbook Production ..... HBP
Handbooks for Bible Classes [*A publication*] ..... HBC
Handbooks for the Clergy [*A publication*] ..... HC
Handbooks of Archaeology and Antiquities [*A publication*] ..... HAA
Handbooks of English Literature [*A publication*] ..... HEL
Handbooks of Theology [*A publication*] ..... HTA
Handbuch der Altertumswissenschaft [*A publication*] (BJA) ..... HdAW
Handbuch der Altorientalischen Geisteskultur [*A publication*] (BJA) ..... HAOG
Handbuch der Literaturwissenschaft [*Potsdam*] [*A publication*] (BJA) ..... HLW
Handbuch der Orientalistik [*Leiden*] [*A publication*] (BJA) ..... HbOr
Handbuch der Orientalistik [*Leiden*] [*A publication*] (BJA) ..... HdO
Handbuch fuer Rundfunk und Fernsehen [*Handbook for Radio and Television*] [*NOMOS Datapool Database*] ..... HARU
Handbuch Theologischer Grundbegriffe [*Munich*] [*A publication*] (BJA) ..... HTG
Handbuch zum Alten Testament [*A publication*] (BJA) ..... HAT
Handbuch zum Neuen Testament [*A publication*] (BJA) ..... HNT
Handbuch zum Neuen Testament [*Lietzmann*] [*A publication*] (BJA) ..... HZNT
Handcarried (AABC) ..... HCD
Hand-Colored [*Photography*] ..... HC
Hand-Deboned Meat ..... HDM
Hand-Drawn ..... HD
Handel and Haydn Society, Boston, MA [*Library symbol Library of Congress*] (LCLS) ..... MBHH
Handel Society [*Record label*] ..... HDL
Handelsgesetzbuch [*Commercial Code*] [*German Legal term*] (DLA) ..... HGB
Handelskammer [*Chamber of Commerce*] [*German*] ..... HK
Hand-Emplaced Acoustic Intrusion Detector (NVT) ..... HAID
Hand-Emplaced Minefield Marking System (MCD) ..... HEMMS
Handes Amsorya [*Vienna*] (BJA) ..... HandAms
Handex Corp. [*NASDAQ symbol*] (TTSB) ..... HAND
Handex Environmental Recovery, Inc. [*NASDAQ symbol*] (NQ) ..... HAND
Handex Environmental Recovery, Inc. [*Associated Press*] (SAG) ..... Handex
Hand-Filled Capsules [*Pharmacy*] (DAVI) ..... HFC
Hand-Foot-and-Mouth Disease (PDAA) ..... HFMD
Hand-Foot-Uterus Syndrome [*Medicine*] (DMAA) ..... HFU
Handgun Control, Inc. (EA) ..... HCI
Handheld Computer ..... HHC
Handheld Computer Unit ..... HCU
Hand-Held Dental X-Ray (RDA) ..... HDX
Handheld Device Mark-up Language ..... HDML
Handheld Device Markup Language [*Computer science*] (PCM) ..... HDML
Hand-Held Encryption and Authentication Device (RDA) ..... HEAD
Hand-Held Equipment (DWSG) ..... HHE
Handheld Grenade-Launcher ..... HAGL
Hand-Held Information Processor ..... HHIP
Handheld Infrared Alarm (PDAA) ..... HIRA
Hand-Held Infrared Controller Overpopulation [*Computer science*] ..... HIROP
Hand-Held LASER Range-Finder [*Military*] (RDA) ..... HHLR
Hand-Held LASER Range-Finder [*Military British*] (INF) ..... HHLRF
Hand-Held LASER Range-Finder ..... HLR
Handheld Maneuvering Unit [*NASA*] ..... HHMU
Hand-Held Nebulizer [*Pharmacology*] (DAVI) ..... HHN
Handheld PC [*Personal Computer*] ..... HPC
Handheld Processor ..... HHP
Hand-Held Programmable Calculator (MCD) ..... HHPC
Handheld RADAR (AABC) ..... HHR
Hand-Held Self-Maneuvering Unit (SAA) ..... HHSMU
Handheld Standoff Minefield Detection System [*Military*] (RDA) ..... HSTAMIDS
Hand-Held Tactical RADAR (DNAB) ..... HHTR
Hand-Held Terminal [*Computer science*] (MHDB) ..... HT
Handheld Terminal Unit ..... HTU
Hand-Held Thermal Imager [*Navy British*] ..... HHTI
Handheld Thermal Unit ..... HTU
Handheld Thermal Viewer (RDA) ..... HHTV
Hand-Held Unit Chromatography ..... HC
Handheld Viewer ..... HHV
Handhole (AAG) ..... HH
Handicap ..... HANDICP

Handicap ... HCP
Handicap ... HNDP
Handicap International [*France*] (EAIO) ... ERAC
Handicap Introductions (EA) ... HI
Handicap Problems Inventory [*Psychology*] ... HPI
Handicap Race [*Horse racing*] ... HCP
Handicapped [*Medicine*] ... HC
Handicapped ... HCAP
Handicapped ... HNDCPD
Handicapped Action Committee ... HAC
Handicapped Adventure Playground Association [*British*] (DBA) ... HAPA
Handicapped Aid Program (DAVI) ... HAP
Handicapped Aid Program - USA [*Defunct*] (EA) ... HAP-USA
[*The*] **Handicapped and Elderly Travelers Association** [*Defunct*] (EA) ... THETA
Handicapped Artists of America (EA) ... HAA
Handicapped Assistance Loan ... HAL
Handicapped Boaters Association [*Defunct*] (EA) ... HBA
Handicapped Children's Early Education Programs ... HCEEP
Handicapped Children's Home Service [*Later, Easter Seal Home Service*] (EA) ... HCHS
Handicapped Children's Services ... HCS
Handicapped Driving Systems [*Burnsville, MN*] ... HDS
Handicapped Education Exchange [*Amateur Radio Research and Development Corp.*] [*Information service or system*] (IID) ... HEX
Handicapped Education Learner's Planning System [*Battelle Memorial Institute*] [*Information service or system*] (IID) ... HELPS
Handicapped Employee of the Year [*Award given to federal employees*] (RDA) ... HEOY
Handicapped Housing Society of Alberta, Edmonton, AB, Canada [*Library symbol*] [*Library of Congress*] (LCLS) ... CaAEHH
Handicapped Housing Society of Alberta, Edmonton, Alberta [*Library symbol National Library of Canada*] (NLC) ... AEHH
Handicapped Organized Women [*In association name, HOW, Inc.*] (EA) ... HOW
Handicapped Person ... HP
Handicapped Persons Research Unit (NITA) ... HPRU
Handicapped SCUBA Association (EA) ... HSA
Handicapped Travel Club (EA) ... HTC
Handicapped United in Brotherhood ... HUB
Handicapped Users' Database [*CompuServe Information Service*] [*Information service or system*] (CRD) ... HUD
Handicappers for Accountable Democracy (EA) ... HAD
Handicraft ... HNDCRFT
Handily [*Horse racing*] ... H
Handke Elementary School, Elk River, MN [*Library symbol*] [*Library of Congress*] (LCLS) ... MnErHE
Handkerchief ... HDKF
Handkerchief ... HKF
Handkerchief Industry Association [*Defunct*] (EA) ... HIA
Handkommentar zum Alten Testament [*Goettingen*] [*A publication*] (BJA) ... HK
Handkommentar zum Alten Testament [*Goettingen*] [*A publication*] (BJA) ... HkAT
Handkommentar zum Alten Testament (Goettingen) [*A publication*] (BJA) ... GHK
Handkommentar zum Neuen Testament [*A publication*] (BJA) ... HKNT
Handle (KSC) ... HDL
Handle Door Fastener ... HDF
Handlebar (ROG) ... HB
Handlebar Control [*Early automobiles*] (ROG) ... HBC
Handleman Co. [*Associated Press*] (SAG) ... Handlm
Handleman Co. [*NYSE symbol*] (SPSG) ... HDL
Handler (AABC) ... HDLR
Handler (NASA) ... HNDLER
Handler ... HNDLR
Handley Library, Winchester, VA [*Library symbol Library of Congress*] (LCLS) ... ViWn
Handley Page Association [*British*] (DBA) ... HPA
Handley-Page Ltd. ... H-P
Handling (AABC) ... HDLG
Handling ... HNLG
Handling and Checkout Requirements ... H & CR
Handling and Propulsion (AAG) ... HP
Handling and Transportation (KSC) ... H & T
Handling Capacity (DEN) ... HC
Handling Equipment ... HE
Handling Equipment Maintenance Facility [*Charleston Naval Shipyard*] ... HEMF
Handling Fee [*Coupon redemption*] ... H/F
Handling Fixture (MCD) ... HF
Handling Fixture - Hoist Tool (MCD) ... HFHT
Handling Fixture - Line Accessory (MCD) ... HFLA
Handling Fixture - Line Dolly (MCD) ... HFLD
Handling Fixture - Production (MCD) ... HFPR
Handling Fixture - Tow Bar (MCD) ... HFTB
Handling Ground Equipment ... HGE
Handling Instructions (MCD) ... HI
Handling of Alarms with Logic [*Nuclear reactors*] ... HALO
Handling Procedure (MCD) ... HP
Handling Qualities Rating [*Cooper-Harper*] ... HQR
Handling Qualities Rating Scale (MCD) ... HQRS
Handling Quality Criteria ... HQC
Handling Room ... HR
Handling Time ... HT
Handling Tool (AAG) ... HATO
Hand-Link Arm Safe Device ... HLASD
Handmade (VRA) ... handmd
Handmade ... HM
Handmade Loft-Dried Paper (DGA) ... HMLD
Handmade Paper ... HMP
Handmade Paper ... HP
Handmaids of Mary Immaculate [*Roman Catholic religious order*] ... AMI
Handmaids of the Most Holy Trinity (TOCD) ... HT
Handmaids of the Precious Blood [*Roman Catholic religious order*] ... HPB
Handmaids of the Sacred Heart of Jesus (TOCD) ... ACJ
Handmaids of the Sacred Heart of Jesus for Reparation (TOCD) ... AR
Handmaids of the Sacred Heart of Pohang (TOCD) ... HSH
Hand-Mirror Cell [*Oncology*] ... HMC
Hand-Mirror Cell Leukemia [*Oncology*] ... HMCL
Handoff Point [*Aviation*] (FAAC) ... HOP
Hand-Operated Positive Energy Control ... HOPEC
Handover ... H/O
Handover Coordinator (SAA) ... HOC
Handover Transfer and Receiver Accept Change [*SAGE*] ... HATRAC
Handover Transmitter (IAA) ... HAT
Handpainted (WGA) ... HP
Hand-Point Defense [*Military*] (IIA) ... HPD
Handprint ... HNDPRNT
Hand-Printed Books ... HPB
H&Q Healthcare Inv [*NYSE symbol*] (TTSB) ... HQH
H&Q Life Sciences Investors [*NYSE symbol*] (TTSB) ... HQL
Hand-Rearing [*of experimental animals*] (DMAA) ... h
Hands [*Units of measure, especially for the height of horses*] ... HH
Hands Across America [*Defunct*] (EA) ... HAA
Hand's Chancery Practice [*A publication*] (DLA) ... Hand Ch P
Hand's Crown Practice [*A publication*] (DLA) ... Hand Cr Pr
Hands of Mercy [*An association*] (EA) ... HM
Hands Off - Automatic (AAG) ... HOA
Hands Off Wildlife [*British*] (DI) ... HOWL
Hands on Throttle and Stick [*Aviation*] (MCD) ... HOTAS
Hand's Reports [*40-45 New York*] [*A publication*] (DLA) ... Hand
Hands to Knee [*Medicine*] ... H-K
Hand-Schueller-Christian [*Disease*] [*Medicine*] ... HSC
Hand-Schueller-Christian Disease (MEDA) ... HSCD
Handscroll (VRA) ... handscr
Handset ... HNDST
Handset ... HS
Handset, Wall Model (TEL) ... HW
Handshake [*Computers*] (MSA) ... HDSHK
Hands-On Annotated Recorded Search (NITA) ... HOARS
Hands-On Component ... HOC
Hands-On Training Exercise [*Military*] (ADDR) ... HOTX
Hands-On Training Simulator [*Vehicle*] ... HOTS
Hands-on Turret Trainer [*Military*] ... HOTT
Hands-on-Throttle-and-Stick [*Navy*] (DOMA) ... HOTAS
Hands-on-Training ... HOT
Hand-Starter ... HS
Hand-Tool Dexterity [*Motor performance test*] ... HTD
Handweavers Guild of America (EA) ... HGA
Handwheel ... HNDWL
Handwoerterbuch [*Pocket Dictionary*] [*German*] ... HWB
Handwoerterbuch der Sozialwissenschaft [*Dictionary of the Social Sciences*] [*A publication*] ... HDSW
Handwoerterbuch des Deutschen Aberglaubens [*A publication*] (BJA) ... HdA
Handwoerterbuch des Islam [*Leiden*] [*A publication*] (BJA) ... HWBI
Handwriting Analysts, International (EA) ... HAI
Handwriting Foundation ... HF
Handwritten (BJA) ... HW
Handwritten by Amanuensis (BJA) ... HWA
Handwritten Numeral Recognition (IAA) ... HNR
Handy ... HNDY
Handy & Harman [*Associated Press*] (SAG) ... HandH
Handy & Harman [*NYSE symbol*] (SPSG) ... HNH
Handy Dandy Orbital Computer (IEEE) ... HDOC
Handy Talky [*Radio*] ... HT
Handy-Cap Horizons [*Defunct*] (EA) ... H-CH
Handyman ... HNDYMN
Handy's Cincinnati Superior Court Reports [*Ohio*] [*A publication*] (DLA) ... Handy R
Handy's Ohio Reports [*12 Ohio Decisions*] [*A publication*] (DLA) ... H
Handy's Ohio Reports [*12 Ohio Decisions*] [*A publication*] (DLA) ... Han
Handy's Ohio Reports [*12 Ohio Decisions*] [*A publication*] (DLA) ... Hand
Handy's Ohio Reports [*12 Ohio Decisions*] [*A publication*] (DLA) ... Handy
Handy's Ohio Reports [*12 Ohio Decisions*] [*A publication*] (DLA) ... Handy (Ohio)
HANES [*Health and Nutrition Examination Survey*] **Data Index** [*Department of Health and Human Services*] (GFGA) ... HINDEX
Hanes' English Chancery [*A publication*] (DLA) ... Hanes
Hanes' United States Digest of Criminal Cases [*A publication*] (DLA) ... Hane Cr Dig
Haney [*British Columbia*] [*Seismograph station code, US Geological Survey*] (SEIS) ... HYC
Hanford [*Washington*] [*Seismograph station code, US Geological Survey*] (SEIS) ... HAN
Hanford [*Washington*] **Atomic Metal Trades Council** ... HAMTC
Hanford Atomic Products Operations [*General Electric Co.*] ... HAPO
Hanford, CA [*Television station call letters*] ... KFTV
Hanford, CA [*FM radio station call letters*] (RBYB) ... KGEN
Hanford, CA [*AM radio station call letters*] ... KIGS
Hanford, CA [*FM radio station call letters*] ... KMPH
Hanford, CA [*FM radio station call letters*] ... KRZR
Hanford Engineering and Development Laboratory [*Richland, WA*] [*Department of Energy*] ... HEDL
Hanford Engineering Service [*Nuclear energy*] (NRCH) ... HES
Hanford Engineering Works [*Nuclear energy*] ... HEW
Hanford Environmental Dose Reconstruction [*Radiobiology*] ... HEDR

Hanford Environmental Health Foundation [*Nuclear energy*] ... HEHF
Hanford Gable Butte [*Washington*] [*Seismograph station code, US Geological Survey*] (SEIS) ... HGB
Hanford Isotopes Plant [*Nuclear energy*] ... HIP
Hanford/Lemorre Naval Air Station [*California*] [*ICAO location identifier*] (ICLI) ... KNLC
Hanford Meteorology Surveys [*Nuclear energy*] (NRCH) ... HMS
Hanford Operations Office [*Nuclear energy*] (MCD) ... HOO
Hanford Plant Standard [*Formerly, HWS*] [*Nuclear energy*] (NRCH) ... HPS
Hanford Public Library, Hanford, CA [*Library symbol Library of Congress*] (LCLS) ... CHan
Hanford Remedial Action Environmental Impact Statement ... HRA EIS
Hanford School Library, Richland, WA [*Library symbol*] [*Library of Congress*] (LCLS) ... WaRiHS
Hanford Site [*Department of Energy*] [*Richland, WA*] (GAAI) ... HANFORD
Hanford Test Reactor (NRCH) ... HTR
Hanford Waste Vitrification Plant [*Department of Energy*] (GAAI) ... HWVP
Hanford Works Standard [*or Specification*] [*Later, HPS*] [*Nuclear energy*] (NRCH) ... HWS
Hanford's Entries [*1685*] [*A publication*] (DLA) ... Hanf
Hang Alle Laffe Landverraders Op [*Hang All Cowardly Traitors to Their Country*] [*Greeting for Dutch Nazis allegedly coined by the Netherlands people during World War II*] ... HALLO
Hang Alle Landverraders Op [*Hang all traitors*] [*Dutch*] [*WWII phrase*] ... HALLO
Hang Glider Association (EA) ... HGA
Hang Glider Manufacturers Association of America [*Defunct*] (EA) ... HGMAA
Hang Khong Viet Nam [*ICAO designator*] (FAAC) ... HVN
Hang Khong Vietnam [*ICAO designator*] (AD) ... VN
Hang Seng Index [*Hong Kong Futures Exchange Index*] ... HSI
Hangar (KSC) ... HGR
Hangar (KSC) ... HNGR
Hangar ... HNGR
Hangar 5 Air Services Norway [*FAA designator*] (FAAC) ... HAX
Hangar and Industrial Door Technical Council [*Defunct*] (MSA) ... HIDTC
Hangar and Support Facility [*NASA*] (NASA) ... HGR & SPTFAC
Hangar Control Officer [*Navy*] ... HCO
Hangar Control Position [*Navy*] ... HCP
Hangar Engineering Item ... HEI
Hangard Aviation Ltd. [*Mongolia*] [*ICAO designator*] (FAAC) ... HGD
Hangchow [*China*] [*Airport symbol*] (AD) ... HGH
Hanger ... HGR
Hanger Orthopedic Group, Inc. [*Associated Press*] (SAG) ... HangOr
Hanger Orthopedic Group, Inc. [*AMEX symbol*] (SPSG) ... HGR
Hanger Orthopedic Grp [*NASDAQ symbol*] (TTSB) ... HGR
Hanging (MSA) ... HNG
Hanging (VRA) ... hng
Hanging Ceiling (OA) ... HC
Hanging Handset [*Telecommunications*] (TEL) ... HH
Hanging Mercury Drop Electrode [*Electrochemistry*] ... HMDE
Hanging Scroll (VRA) ... hngscr
Hangup [*Telecommunications*] (TEL) ... HU
Hangup ... HUP
Hangzhou [*China*] [*Airport symbol*] (OAG) ... HGH
Hangzhou/Jianqiao [*China*] [*ICAO location identifier*] (ICLI) ... ZSHC
Hanhart on the Laws Relating to Married Women [*A publication*] (DLA) ... Han Mar Wom
Hanhart on the Laws Relating to Married Women [*A publication*] (DLA) ... Hanh Mar Wom
Hanimaadhoo [*Maldives*] [*ICAO location identifier*] (ICLI) ... VRHU
Hank [*Cotton*] (ROG) ... HK
Hank Snow Fan Club [*Defunct*] (EA) ... HSFC
Hank Williams Appreciation International Fan Club (EA) ... HWAIFC
Hank Williams Jr. Fan Club (EA) ... HWJFC
Hankes Foundation (EA) ... HF
Hanko [*Finland ICAO location identifier*] (ICLI) ... EFHN
Hanks Balanced Salt [*Solution*] [*Cell incubation medium*] ... HBS
Hanks Balanced Salt Solution [*Cell incubation medium*] ... HBSS
Hanksville, UT [*Location identifier FAA*] (FAAL) ... HVE
Hankyore Democratic Party [*South Korea Political party*] (EY) ... HDP
Hanmer Branch, Valley East Public Library [*Succursale Hanmer, Bibliotheque Publique de Valley-East*], Ontario [*Library symbol National Library of Canada*] (NLC) ... OHVE
Hanna [*M. A.*] **Co.** [*Associated Press*] (SAG) ... Hanna
Hanna [*M. A.*] **Co.** [*NYSE symbol*] (SPSG) ... MAH
Hanna Municipal Library, Alberta [*Library symbol National Library of Canada*] (NLC) ... AHM
Hanna Municipal Library, Hanna, AB, Canada [*Library symbol Library of Congress*] (LCLS) ... CaAHM
Hanna Pacific [*Vancouver Stock Exchange symbol*] ... HPS
Hannaford Bros [*NYSE symbol*] (TTSB) ... HRD
Hannaford Brothers, Inc. [*Associated Press*] (SAG) ... Hanfrd
Hannaford Brothers, Inc. [*NYSE symbol*] (SPSG) ... HRD
Hannah Dairy Research Institute [*British*] (BI) ... HDRI
Hannah Research Institute [*British*] (ARC) ... HRI
Hannay's New Brunswick Reports [*12, 13 New Brunswick*] [*A publication*] (DLA) ... Han
Hannay's New Brunswick Reports [*12, 13 New Brunswick*] [*A publication*] (DLA) ... Han (NB)
Hannay's New Brunswick Reports [*12, 13 New Brunswick*] [*A publication*] (DLA) ... Hann
Hannay's New Brunswick Reports [*12, 13 New Brunswick*] [*A publication*] (DLA) ... NBR Han
Hannibal Connecting R. R. [*AAR code*] ... HC
Hannibal Free Public Library, Hannibal, MO [*Library symbol Library of Congress*] (LCLS) ... MoH
Hannibal, MO [*Location identifier FAA*] (FAAL) ... HAE
Hannibal, MO [*FM radio station call letters*] ... KGRC
Hannibal, MO [*AM radio station call letters*] ... KHMO
Hannibal, MO [*Television station call letters*] ... KHQA
Hannibal-La Grange College [*Missouri*] ... HLGC
Hannover [*Germany ICAO location identifier*] (ICLI) ... EDDV
Hannover [*Germany ICAO location identifier*] (ICLI) ... EDVV
Hanoi [*Vietnam*] [*Airport symbol*] (OAG) ... HAN
Hanoi [*Viet Nam*] [*ICAO location identifier*] (ICLI) ... VVVV
Hanoi/Gialam [*Viet Nam*] [*ICAO location identifier*] (ICLI) ... VVGL
Hanoi/Noibai [*Viet Nam*] [*ICAO location identifier*] (ICLI) ... VVNB
Hanover [*Germany Airport symbol*] (OAG) ... HAJ
Hanover [*Former state in Germany*] ... HAN
Hanover [*New Hampshire*] [*Seismograph station code, US Geological Survey*] (SEIS) ... HNH
Hanover College, Hanover, IN [*OCLC symbol*] (OCLC) ... IHC
Hanover College, Hanover, IN [*Library symbol Library of Congress*] (LCLS) ... InHan
Hanover Direct [*Formerly, Horn & Hardart Co.*] [*AMEX symbol*] (SPSG) ... HNV
Hanover Direct, Inc. [*Associated Press*] (SAG) ... HanvDir
Hanover Gold [*NASDAQ symbol*] (TTSB) ... HVGO
Hanover Gold Company, Inc. [*Associated Press*] (SAG) ... HanovGld
Hanover Gold Company, Inc. [*NASDAQ symbol*] (SAG) ... HVGO
Hanover, NH [*AM radio station call letters*] ... WDCR
Hanover, NH [*FM radio station call letters*] ... WEVH
Hanover, NH [*FM radio station call letters*] ... WFRD
Hanover, NH [*FM radio station call letters*] ... WGXL
Hanover, NH [*AM radio station call letters*] ... WTSL
Hanover on the Law of Horses [*A publication*] (DLA) ... Han Hor
Hanover, PA [*AM radio station call letters*] ... WHVR
Hanover Public Library, Hanover, ON, Canada [*Library symbol Library of Congress*] (LCLS) ... CaOHan
Hanover Public Library, Ontario [*Library symbol National Library of Canada*] (NLC) ... OHAN
Hans Majestaet [*His Majesty*] [*Swedish*] ... H MAJ:T
Hansard (DCTA) ... HNSD
Hansard on Aliens [*A publication*] (DLA) ... Hans Al
Hansard Oral Questions [*Database*] [*House of Commons*] [*Canada*] [*Information service or system*] (CRD) ... HOQ
Hansard Questions Ecrites [*Hansard Written Question - HWQ*] [*Database House of Commons*] [*French*] [*Information service or system*] (CRD) ... HQE
Hansard Questions Orale [*Hansard Oral Questions - HOQ*] [*Database House of Commons*] [*French*] [*Information service or system*] (CRD) ... HQO
Hansard Society [*British*] (ILCA) ... HS
Hansard Written Questions [*Database*] [*House of Commons*] [*Canada*] [*Information service or system*] (CRD) ... HWQ
Hansard's Book of Entries [*1685*] [*A publication*] (DLA) ... Han
Hansard's Book of Entries [*1685*] [*A publication*] (DLA) ... Han Ent
Hansard's Book of Entries [*1685*] [*A publication*] (DLA) ... Hans Ent
Hansard's Parliamentary Debates [*A publication*] (DLA) ... Han Deb
Hansard's Parliamentary Debates [*A publication*] (DLA) ... Hans Deb
Hansard's Parliamentary Debates [*A publication*] (DLA) ... Hans Parl Deb
Hansard's Publishing Union (ROG) ... HPU
Hansbrough's Reports [*76-90 Virginia*] [*A publication*] (DLA) ... Hansb
Hanscom Air Force Base, Base Library, Hanscom AFB, MA [*OCLC symbol*] (OCLC) ... SCQ
Hanscom Electronic Request [*for Proposals*] **Bulletin Board** [*Air Force*] ... HERBB
Hansel Valley [*Utah*] [*Seismograph station code, US Geological Survey*] (SEIS) ... HVU
Hansell's Bankruptcy Reports [*1915-17*] [*A publication*] (DLA) ... HBR
Hansen Nat [*NASDAQ symbol*] (TTSB) ... HANS
Hansen Natural Corp. [*Associated Press*] (SAG) ... Hans
Hansen Natural Corp. [*NASDAQ symbol*] (SAG) ... HANS
Hansen Natural Corp. [*Associated Press*] (SAG) ... Hansen
Hansen Public Library, Hansen, ID [*Library symbol*] [*Library of Congress*] (LCLS) ... IdHn
Hansen's Disease [*Leprosy*] [*Medicine*] ... HD
Hansoms of John Clayton [*An association*] (EA) ... HJC
Hanson Ltd. [*AMEX symbol*] (SAG) ... HAN
Hanson on Probate Acts [*A publication*] (DLA) ... Hans Pr
Hanson on the Probate and Legacy Acts [*A publication*] (DLA) ... Han Prob
Hanson PLC [*Associated Press*] (SAG) ... Han
Hanson plc ADR [*NYSE symbol*] (TTSB) ... HAN
Hanson Trust Ltd. [*NYSE symbol*] (SPSG) ... HAN
Hanson Trust Ltd. [*Associated Press*] (SAG) ... Hanson
Hanson-McCook County Regional Library, Spencer, SD [*Library symbol Library of Congress*] (LCLS) ... SdSpen
Hanson's Bankruptcy Reports [*1915-17*] [*A publication*] (DLA) ... Han
Hanson-Street Nail (MEDA) ... HSN
Hantaan [*Virus*] ... HTN
Hantavirus Pulmonary Syndrome [*Medicine*] ... HPS
Hants Journal, Windsor, Nova Scotia [*Library symbol National Library of Canada*] (NLC) ... NSWHJ
Hants Journal, Windsor, NS, Canada [*Library symbol*] [*Library of Congress*] (LCLS) ... CaNSWiHJ
Hantsport and Area Historical Society, Hantsport, NS, Canada [*Library symbol*] [*Library of Congress*] (LCLS) ... CaNSHaHS
Hantsport and Area Historical Society, Nova Scotia [*Library symbol National Library of Canada*] (NLC) ... NSHHS
Hanukah Factor Serine Protease (DMAA) ... HFSP
Hanuman Foundation (EA) ... HF
Hanzhong [*China*] [*Airport symbol*] (OAG) ... HZG
Hao [*French Polynesia*] [*ICAO location identifier*] (ICLI) ... NTTO
Hao Island [*French Polynesia*] [*Airport symbol*] (OAG) ... HOI
Hapag Lloyd Fluggesellschaft GmbH [*Germany ICAO designator*] (FAAC) ... HLF

Haplequin Lake [Alaska] [Seismograph station code, US Geological Survey] (SEIS) .... HQN
Haploid Cell Line 1 .... H1
Haploid Chromosome Number (DOG) .... N
Haploid Generation [Biology] (BARN) X
Haploid Number [Genetics] .... N
Ha-Po'el ha-Mizrahi (BJA) .... PM
Happiness, Energy, and Longevity through Health [Title of 1979 film directed by Robert Altman] .... HEALTH
Happiness Express [NASDAQ symbol] (TTSB) .... HAPY
Happiness Express, Inc. [Associated Press] (SAG) .... Happiness
Happiness Express, Inc. [NASDAQ symbol] (SAG) .... HAPY
Happiness of Womanhood [Also known as LOH] [Defunct] .... HOW
Happy .... HAP
Happy Bay [Australia Airport symbol] (OAG) .... HAP
Happy Hours Brotherhood (EA) .... HHB
Happy Humpers (EA) .... HH
Happy Idiot News Team [Also, Happy Idiot News Talk] [Broadcasting] (WDMC) .... HINT
Happy Irish Celebration .... HIC
Happy New Year .... HNY
Happy Valley, AK [Location identifier FAA] (FAAL) .... HVY
Happy Valley, NF [FM radio station call letters] .... CFGB
Happy Valley Public Library, Happy Valley, NF, Canada [Library symbol Library of Congress] (LCLS) .... CaNfHV
Happy Valley Public Library, Newfoundland [Library symbol National Library of Canada] (NLC) .... NFHV
Haptic Intelligence Scale [Psychology] (AEBS) .... HIS
Haptoglobin [Hematology] (DAVI) .... HAPT
Haptoglobin [Hematology] .... Hp
Haptong Tongsin [Press agency] [South Korea] .... HAPTONG
Harare [Zimbabwe] [ICAO location identifier] (ICLI) .... FVHQ
Harare [Zimbabwe] [Airport symbol] (OAG) .... HRE
Harare/Charles Prince [Zimbabwe] [ICAO location identifier] (ICLI) .... FVCP
Harare/Harare [Zimbabwe] [ICAO location identifier] (ICLI) .... FVHA
Harari (BJA) .... Har
Harassing and Interdiction .... H & I
Harassing Fire [Military] (AABC) .... HF
Harassment and Interdiction Fires [Military] .... H and I
Harassment Vehicle (MCD) .... HARV
Harassment Vehicle [Military] .... HAS
Harassment Weapon System (MCD) .... HWS
Harbeck-Fruitdale, OR [FM radio station call letters] .... KLDR
Harbin [Manchuria] [Airport symbol] (OAG) .... HRB
Harbin/Yanjiagang [China] [ICAO location identifier] (ICLI) .... ZYHB
Harbinger Corp. [Associated Press] (SAG) .... Harbngr
Harbinger Corp. [Associated Press] (SAG) .... Harbrgr
Harbinger Corp. [NASDAQ symbol] (SAG) .... HRBC
Harbor [Maps and charts] .... H
Harbor (AFM) .... HAR
Harbor [Maps and charts] (ROG) .... HARB
Harbor [Commonly used] (OPSA) .... HARBOR
Harbor [Commonly used] (OPSA) .... HARBR
Harbor .... HBR
Harbor [Maps and charts] .... HBR
Harbor [Commonly used] (OPSA) .... HRBOR
Harbor Advisory RADAR .... HAR
Harbor Airlines [ICAO designator] (AD) .... HG
Harbor Airlines, Inc. [ICAO designator] (FAAC) .... HAR
Harbor Bay Telecommunications [Alameda, CA] (TSSD) .... HBT
Harbor Beach Public Library, Harbor Beach, MI [Library symbol Library of Congress] (LCLS) .... MiHb
Harbor Belt Line Railroad .... HBL
Harbor Belt Line Railroad (MHDB) .... HBLRR
Harbor Boat Service [Military] .... HBS
Harbor Branch Oceanographic Institution [Fort Pierce, FL] .... HBOI
Harbor Carriers of the Port of New York (EA) .... HCPNY
Harbor Clearance Unit [Navy] (NVT) .... HCU
Harbor Clearance Unit Detachment [Navy] (DNAB) .... HCUDET
Harbor Control Post .... HCP
Harbor Control Unit .... HCU
Harbor Craft .... HARCFT
Harbor Craft [Coast Guard symbol] (DNAB) .... WYTM
Harbor Defense [Military] .... HD
Harbor Defense Command [Army] .... HDC
Harbor Defense Exercise [Navy] (NG) .... HARDEX
Harbor Defense Motor Launch [NATO] (NATG) .... HDML
Harbor Defense SONARman [Navy] .... ESH
Harbor Echo Ranging and Listening Device .... HERALD
Harbor Elementary School, Baldwin, NY [Library symbol Library of Congress] (LCLS) .... NBaldHE
Harbor Entrance Control Post [Nautical charts] .... HECP
Harbor Entrance Control Vessel .... HECVES
Harbor Explosive Ordnance Disposal Team [Navy] (VNW) .... HEOD
Harbor Federal Bancorp [Associated Press] (SAG) .... HarbFed
Harbor Federal Bancorp [NASDAQ symbol] (SAG) .... HRBF
Harbor Federal Savings Bank [NASDAQ symbol] (SAG) .... HARB
Harbor Federal Savings Bank [Associated Press] (SAG) .... HarbrFd
Harbor Federal Svgs Bk [NASDAQ symbol] (TTSB) .... HARB
Harbor Hill Intermediate School, Greenvale, NY [Library symbol] [Library of Congress] (LCLS) .... NGvHI
Harbor Junior High School, Baldwin, NY [Library symbol Library of Congress] (LCLS) .... NBaldHJ
Harbor Launch [Coast Guard] (DNAB) .... AB
Harbor Maintenance Fee [Import/Export fee] .... HMF

Harbor Master .... Hbr Mr
Harbor Master .... HM
Harbor Minesweepers [Navy symbol] .... AMH
Harbor Motor Launch .... HML
Harbor Operations and Maintenance Support [Navy] (VNW) .... HOMS
Harbor Patrol Boat .... HPB
Harbor Patrol Element [Navy] (VNW) .... HPE
Harbor Patrol Fleet .... HPF
Harbor Springs, MI [FM radio station call letters] .... WCMW
Harbor Surveillance RADAR [Navigation] (IAA) .... HSR
Harbor Survey Assistance Program [Naval Oceanographic Office] .... HARSAP
Harbor Tug [Navy symbol] .... YT
Harbor Tug, Medium [Coast Guard symbol] (DNAB) .... WYTM
Harbor Tug, Small [Coast Guard symbol] (DNAB) .... WYTL
Harbor Utility Craft [Self-propelled] [Navy symbol] .... YFU
Harborfields High School, Greenlawn, NY [Library symbol] [Library of Congress] (LCLS) .... NGIHS
Harborfields High School, Greenlawn, NY [Library symbol Library of Congress] (LCLS) .... NGrIHS
Harborfields High School, Harborfields, NY [Library symbol] [Library of Congress] (LCLS) .... NHaHS
Harborfields Public Library, Greenlawn, NY [Library symbol] [Library of Congress] (LCLS) .... NGI
Harborfields Public Library, Greenlawn, NY [Library symbol Library of Congress] (LCLS) .... NGI
Harbors [Commonly used] (OPSA) .... HARBORS
Harbors [Postal Service standard] (OPSA) .... HBRS
Harbors .... HBRS
Harbors and Navigation Code [A publication] (DLA) .... Harb & Nav C
Harborside Healthcare Corp. [Associated Press] (SAG) .... HarborH
Harborside Healthcare Corp. [NYSE symbol] (SAG) .... HBR
Harbour Acceptance Trials [Missile] [British] .... HAT
Harbour Breton Public Library, Harbour Breton, NF, Canada [Library symbol Library of Congress] (LCLS) .... CaNfHB
Harbour Breton Public Library, Newfoundland [Library symbol National Library of Canada] (NLC) .... NFHB
Harbour Grace Public Library, Harbour Grace, NF, Canada [Library symbol Library of Congress] (LCLS) .... CaNfHG
Harbour Grace Public Library, Newfoundland [Library symbol National Library of Canada] (NLC) .... NFHG
Harbours Corp. of Queensland [Australia] .... HCQ
Harbourton Financial Services LP [Associated Press] (SAG) .... HarbourF
Harbourton Financial Services LP [NYSE symbol] (SAG) .... HBT
Harbourton Finl Svcs L.P. [NYSE symbol] (TTSB) .... HBT
Harcarse's Decisions, Scotch Court of Session [1681-91] [A publication] (DLA) .... Harc
Harco Air Services [Nigeria] [ICAO designator] (FAAC) .... HCO
Harcor Energy [NASDAQ symbol] (TTSB) .... HARC
HarCor Energy Co. [NASDAQ symbol] (NQ) .... HARC
HarCor Energy Co. [Associated Press] (SAG) .... HarcorE
Harcost Industries .... HI
Harcourt General [NYSE symbol] (TTSB) .... H
Harcourt General, Inc. [Formerly, General Cinema Corp.] [NYSE symbol] (SPSG) .... H
Harcourt General, Inc. [Associated Press] (SAG) .... HarcG
Harcourt General, Inc. [Associated Press] (SAG) .... HarcGn
Harcourt Genl'A'cm CvStk [NYSE symbol] (TTSB) .... HPrA
Harcum Junior College [Pennsylvania] .... HJC
Harcum, VA [Location identifier FAA] (FAAL) .... HCM
Hard [or Hardness] [Pencil leads] .... H
Hard (MSA) .... HD
Hard [Quality of the bottom] [Nautical charts] .... hrd
Hard and Soft Acids and Bases [Chemistry] .... HSAB
Hard Black [Pencil leads] .... HB
Hard Chromium .... HDCR
Hard Contact Lens [Ophthalmology] .... HCL
Hard Convex Body [Equation of state] .... HCB
Hard Copy [Computer science] .... HC
Hard Copy Module (NASA) .... HCM
Hard Copy Printer [Computer science] .... HCP
Hard Copy Response (SAA) .... HCR
Hard Copy System [Computer science] (MHDI) .... HCS
Hard Copy Unit .... HCU
Hard Core Monitor [Computer science] (IAA) .... HCM
Hard Disc Unit (NITA) .... HDU
Hard Disk [Computer science] .... HD
Hard Disk Drive [Computer science] .... HDD
Hard Disk Operating System .... HDOS
Hard Disk ToolKIT [Computer science] .... HDT
Hard Drives International (PCM) .... HDI
Hard Exudate [Ophthalmology] (DAVI) .... HE
Hard Failure .... HF
Hard Fibres Association (EA) .... HFA
Hard Filled [Capsules] [Pharmacy] .... HF
Hard Filled Capsules [Pharmacy] .... FC
Hard Firm [Pencil leads] .... HF
Hard Freeze [NWS] (FAAC) .... HDFRZ
Hard Gas-Permeable [Contact lenses] .... HGP
Hard Gelatin [Pharmacy] .... HG
Hard Kernel Bunch (IAA) .... HKB
Hard Labor .... HL
Hard Labor without Confinement .... HLW/OC
Hard Link Arm Safe Device (MCD) .... HILASD
Hard Lunar Landing [Aerospace engineering] (IAA) .... HLL
Hard Mobile Launcher [Boeing Aerospace-Loral Defense Systems] .... HML

Hard of Hearing ... HH
Hard of Hearing (MAE) ... HOH
Hard Over (KSC) ... H/O
Hard Plastic [*Doll collecting*] ... HP
Hard Point ... HP
Hard Point Decoys (MCD) ... HAPDEC
Hard Point Defense ... HPD
Hard Point Defense Intercept Missile (MCD) ... HPDIM
Hard Point Defense Interceptor ... HPDI
Hard Point Defense System ... HPDS
Hard Point Demonstration Array RADAR ... HAPDAR
Hard Processing Channel (IAA) ... HPC
Hard Red Spring [*Wheat*] ... HRS
Hard Red Winter [*Wheat*] ... HRW
Hard Replacement Assembly (MCD) ... HRA
Hard Rock International [*Restaurant chain*] ... HRI
Hard Rock Silo Development ... HRSD
Hard Rolled ... HR
Hard Sized Paper (DGA) ... HS
Hard/Soft [*Two tops for convertible automobile*] ... H/S
Hard/Soft Display (NITA) ... HSD
Hard Stability Augmentation System ... HSAS
Hard Stop (MCD) ... HSTP
Hard Stripping [*Agriculture*] (OA) ... HS
Hard Structure Module ... HSM
Hard Structure Munition ... HSM
Hard Structure Munition Weaponization Analysis (MCD) ... HSM-WA
Hard Tissue Replacement [*Dentistry*] ... HTR
Hard Top [*Automotive advertising*] ... HRD
Hard Top [*Automobile advertising*] ... HT
Hard Tube Modulator [*Electronics*] ... HTM
Hard Tube Monitor [*Electronics*] (IAA) ... HTM
Hard Upper Torso (MCD) ... HUT
Hard Valve (DEN) ... HV
Hard Wired (NITA) ... HW
Hard X-Ray Burst Spectrometer ... HXRBS
Hard X-Ray Imaging Spectrometer ... HXIS
Hard X-Ray Quanta ... HXQ
Hard X-Ray Telescope ... HXT
Hardanger Fiddle Association of America (EA) ... HFAA
Hardback [*Book cover*] (NTCM) ... HBK
Hardboard (VRA) ... hardbd
Hardboard (ADA) ... HB
Hardboard [*Technical drawings*] ... HBD
Hard-Boiled [*Egg*] ... HB
Hardcastle on Election Petitions [*A publication*] (DLA) ... Hard El Pet
Hardcastle on Statutory Law [*A publication*] (DLA) ... Hard St L
Hard-Clad Silica [*Materials science*] ... HCS
Hard-Coal Equivalents (BARN) ... hce
Hard-Copy Device [*Computer science*] (ECII) ... HCD
Hardcore ... HC
Hard-Covered Book (WDAA) ... HCB
Hard-Drawn [*Metallurgy*] ... HD
Hard-Drawn Wire [*Metallurgy*] (IAA) ... HDW
Hardeeville, SC [*FM radio station call letters*] ... WLVH
Hardeeville, SC [*Television station call letters*] ... WTGS
Harden (KSC) ... HDN
Harden and Grind [*Technical drawings*] ... H & G
Hardened Aircraft Shelter [*British military*] (DMA) ... HAS
Hardened Amplifier for Radiation Transients ... HART
Hardened and Dispersed (AFM) ... H & D
Hardened and Tempered [*Steel*] ... H & T
Hardened and Tempered (IAA) ... HAT
Hardened Array Solar Power System [*Military*] ... HASPS
Hardened Compact Fiber ... HCF
Hardened Digital Data Acquisition System [*US Army Waterways Experiment Station*] (RDA) ... HDAS
Hardened Electronic and Radiation Technology ... HEART
Hardened Electronic Component ... HEC
Hardened Electronics and Radiation Technology (MCD) ... HEART
Hardened Flexible Array ... HFA
Hardened Intersite Cable System (CET) ... HICS
Hardened Launch Control Facility (MUGU) ... HLCF
Hardened Memory System ... HMS
Hardened Operational Site Concept (AAG) ... HOSC
Hardened Power System ... HPS
Hardened Reentry Kill [*Air Force*] ... HARK
Hardened Silo Missile ... HSM
Hardened Site ... HS
Hardened Tactical Shelters ... HATS
Hardened Voice Channel [*NASA*] (KSC) ... HVC
Hardened Voice Channel (MSA) ... HVCH
Hardened Voice Circuit (CET) ... HVC
Hardening Design Responses ... HDR
Hardening Technology Studies Program (MCD) ... HARTS
Hardesty's Delaware Term Reports [*A publication*] (DLA) ... Hardes
Hard-Filled Capsules [*Pharmacy*] (DAVI) ... HFC
Hardin Bancorp [*NASDAQ symbol*] (TTSB) ... HFSA
Hardin Bancorp, Inc. [*Associated Press*] (SAG) ... Hardin
Hardin Bancorp, Inc. [*NASDAQ symbol*] (SAG) ... HFSA
Hardin County Historical Society, Eldora, IA [*Library symbol Library of Congress*] (LCLS) ... IaEldoHHi
Hardin County Historical Society, Eldora, IA [*Library symbol*] [*Library of Congress*] (LCLS) ... IaEldoHi
Hardin County Index, Eldora, IA [*Library symbol Library of Congress*] (LCLS) ... IaEldoI
Hardin County Times, Iowa Falls, IA [*Library symbol Library of Congress*] (LCLS) ... IaIfT
Hardin, MT [*FM radio station call letters*] ... KBMJ
Hardin, MT [*AM radio station call letters*] (RBYB) ... KHDN
Hardin, MT [*Television station call letters*] (RBYB) ... KHMT
Hardin, MT [*FM radio station call letters*] (RBYB) ... KMHK-FM
Hardin Reading Center, Hardin, IL [*Library symbol Library of Congress*] (LCLS) ... IHardR
Harding Carpets Ltd. [*Toronto Stock Exchange symbol*] ... HRD
Harding College, Searcy, AR [*OCLC symbol*] (OCLC) ... AHS
Harding College, Searcy, AR [*Library symbol Library of Congress*] (LCLS) ... ArSeH
Harding Elementary School, Pierz, MN [*Library symbol*] [*Library of Congress*] (LCLS) ... MnPiHE
Harding Graduate School of Religion, Memphis, TN [*Library symbol Library of Congress*] (LCLS) ... TMH
Harding Lake [*Alaska*] [*Seismograph station code, US Geological Survey*] (SEIS) ... HDA
Harding Lawson Assoc Grp [*NASDAQ symbol*] (TTSB) ... HRDG
Harding Lawson Associates Group, Inc. [*NASDAQ symbol*] (SAG) ... HRDG
Harding Lawson Associates Group, Inc. [*Associated Press*] (SAG) ... HrdgLaw
Harding on Ecclesiastical Law [*A publication*] (DLA) ... Hard Eccl L
Harding University (GAGS) ... Harding U
Hardinge, Inc. [*Associated Press*] (SAG) ... Hadng
Hardinge, Inc. [*NASDAQ symbol*] (SAG) ... HDNG
Hardingham on Trade Marks [*A publication*] (DLA) ... Hard Tr M
Harding-Passey Melanoma [*Oncology*] (AAMN) ... HPM
Hardin's Kentucky Reports [*A publication*] (DLA) ... Hard
Hardin's Kentucky Reports [*A publication*] (DLA) ... Hardin
Hardin's Kentucky Reports [*A publication*] (DLA) ... Hardin (KY)
Hardinsburg, KY [*AM radio station call letters*] ... WHIC
Hardinsburg, KY [*FM radio station call letters*] (RBYB) ... WULF
Hardinsburg, KY [*FM radio station call letters*] ... WXBC
Hardin-Simmons University (GAGS) ... Hardin-Simmons U
Hardin-Simmons University [*Texas*] ... HSU
Hardin-Simmons University, Abilene, TX [*Library symbol Library of Congress*] (LCLS) ... TxAbH
Hardin-Simmons University, Abilene, TX [*OCLC symbol*] (OCLC) ... TXS
Hardisty Public Library, Alberta [*Library symbol National Library of Canada*] (NLC) ... AHA
Hardline (MCD) ... HL
HARDMAN [*Hardware-Manpower Program*] **Comparability Methodology** [*Army*] ... HCM
Hardness [*Of precious stones*] ... H
Hardness (MSA) ... HDNS
Hardness Assessment Report ... HAR
Hardness Assurance (MSA) ... HA
Hardness Assurance Document ... HAD
Hardness Assurance Monitoring System (MCD) ... HAMS
Hardness Assurance Test ... HAT
Hardness Assurance Verification Testing (MCD) ... HAVT
Hardness Maintenance (MSA) ... HM
Hardness Rockwell C [*Materials testing*] ... HRC
Hardness Surveillance (MSA) ... HS
Hardness Test Plan [*Army*] (AABC) ... HTP
Hardness Test Program Plan ... HTPP
Hardness-Critical Item (MSA) ... HCI
Hardness-Critical Process (MSA) ... HCP
Hardover ... HDOV
Hardpoint Interceptor ... HARPI
Hardres' English Exchequer Reports [*145 English Reprint*] [*A publication*] (DLA) ... Hard
Hardres' English Exchequer Reports [*145 English Reprint*] [*1655-69*] [*A publication*] (DLA) ... Hardr
Hardres' English Exchequer Reports [*145 English Reprint*] [*A publication*] (DLA) ... Hardr (Eng)
Hardres' English Exchequer Reports [*145 English Reprint*] [*A publication*] (DLA) ... Hardres
Hardrock Extension, Inc. [*Toronto Stock Exchange symbol*] ... HRK
Hards Memorial Library, Central City, NE [*Library symbol Library of Congress*] (LCLS) ... NbCen
Hardship (AABC) ... HDSP
Hardship Relief Board [*Victoria, Australia*] ... HRB
Hardsite Data Processor [*Army*] (AABC) ... HSDP
Hardsite Defense [*Army*] (AABC) ... HSD
Hardsite Engagement Effectiveness Model (PDAA) ... HEEM
Hardsite Engagement Program ... HEP
Hardsite Missile Site RADAR [*Army*] (AABC) ... HSMSR
Hardstand ... HS
Hard-Target Kill [*Military*] (GFGA) ... HTK
Hard-Target Kill Potential [*Military*] (MCD) ... HTKP
Hardware [*Computer science*] (MDG) ... H
Hardware [*Computer science*] (EERA) ... H/W
Hardware [*Computer science*] (IAA) ... HA
Hardware (WDAA) ... HARD
Hardware [*Computer science*] ... HARDWR
Hardware [*Computer science*] (KSC) ... HDW
Hardware [*Computer science*] (IAA) ... HDWA
Hardware ... HDWE
Hardware (VRA) ... hdwe
Hardware ... HDWR
Hardware (WGA) ... HDWRE
Hardware (WGA) ... HRDWRE
Hardware [*Computer science*] (NASA) ... HW

Hardware Abstraction Layer [*Computer science*] (PCM) .... HAL
Hardware Action Officer [*Military*] (AABC) .... HAO
Hardware Affiliated Representatives [*Defunct*] (EA) .... HAR
Hardware Allocation Panel .... HAP
Hardware Associative Memory [*Computer science*] (DIT) .... HAM
Hardware Capability (NITA) .... HC
Hardware Capability Code [*Dialog*] [*Searchable field*] [*Information service or system*] (NITA) .... HCC
Hardware Capability Name (NITA) .... HN
Hardware Character Generator .... HCG
Hardware Check Routine .... HCR
Hardware Clipping, Rotation, Scaling, and Translation (MHDI) .... HCRST
Hardware Cloth .... HDWC
Hardware Compatibility Test [*Microsoft Corp.*] (PCM) .... HCT
Hardware Configuration Item .... HWCI
Hardware Correction Report .... HCR
Hardware Critical Design Review (MCD) .... HCDR
Hardware Description Language [*Computer science*] .... HDL
Hardware Description Language System (IAA) .... HDLS
Hardware Description Sheet (NASA) .... HDS
Hardware Design .... HD
Hardware Emulation [*Computer science*] .... HEL
Hardware Emulation Layer [*Computer science*] .... HEL
Hardware Error Recovery System [*Sperry UNIVAC*] .... HERS
Hardware Evaluator [*NASA*] .... HE
Hardware Executive .... HE
Hardware Federation of Australia .... HFA
Hardware Graphics Accelerator [*Computer science*] .... HGA
Hardware Implemented Fault Tolerance .... HIFT
Hardware in the Loop Simulation [*Computer science*] (MCD) .... HITLS
Hardware Indenture Code (KSC) .... HIC
Hardware Information System (MCD) .... HIS
Hardware Initiated Standalone Memory (NASA) .... HISAM
Hardware Installation Data (CAAL) .... HID
Hardware Interface Device (NASA) .... HID
Hardware Interface Module [*NASA*] (NASA) .... HIM
Hardware Interface Module Hierarchy of Interpretive Modules (MHDI) .... HIM
Hardware Interface Program (NASA) .... HIP
Hardware Interpreter .... HWI
Hardware Interrupt .... HI
Hardware Interrupt System (IAA) .... HIS
Hardware Logic Simulator [*Computer science*] (IEEE) .... HALSIM
Hardware Manufacturers' Association [*British*] (BI) .... HMA
Hardware Manufacturers Statistical Association [*Later, BHMA*] .... HMSA
Hardware Message Generator [*Telecommunications*] (TEL) .... HMG
Hardware Microcode Optimizer .... HMO
Hardware Mockup (NASA) .... HMU
Hardware Modelling Library [*Mentor Graphics*] (NITA) .... HML
Hardware Monitor [*Computer science*] (MHDI) .... HARDMON
Hardware Monitor Interface .... HMI
Hardware Multiple .... HM
Hardware Multiply Module .... HMM
Hardware Problem Report (MCD) .... HPR
[*A*] **Hardware Programming Language** [*1971*] [*Computer science*] (CSR) .... AHPL
Hardware Quality Engineer (MCD) .... HQE
Hardware Read-In Mode .... HRM
Hardware Reliability (MCD) .... HR
Hardware Requirements List .... HRL
Hardware Simulation Laboratory (NASA) .... HSL
Hardware/Software (MCD) .... HW/SW
Hardware/Software Coordination (NASA) .... HSC
Hardware/Software Integration Facility (SSD) .... HSIF
Hardware/Software Integration Review (MCD) .... H/SIR
Hardware/Software Interface (IAA) .... HSI
Hardware Specification Sheet (IAA) .... HSS
Hardware Status Register (MCD) .... HSR
Hardware Usage Report (MCD) .... HUR
Hardware Utilization List (NASA) .... HUL
Hardware Vector to Raster .... HVR
Hardware Verification Program (CAAL) .... HVP
Hardware Virtualizer [*Computer science*] (IEEE) .... HV
Hardware Wholesalers, Inc. .... HWI
Hardware Work Package (MCD) .... HWP
Hardware-Assisted Software Queue .... HASQ
Hardware-in-the-Loop .... HIL
Hardware-in-the-Loop .... HITL
Hardware-in-the-Loop .... HWIL
Hardware-Manpower Program [*Navy*] .... HARDMAN
Hardware-Software Configuration [*Computer science*] .... HSC
Hardwell FORTRAN [*Computer science*] (IEEE) .... HARTRAN
Hardwicke's Note Books [*A publication*] (DLA) .... Hardw NB
Hardwire Operating System (IAA) .... HOS
Hardwire Safing Panel .... HSP
Hardwood .... HDWD
Hardwood .... HW
Hardwood [*Technical drawings*] .... HWD
Hardwood Bleached Kraft [*Pulp and paper technology*] .... HBK
Hardwood Dimension Manufacturers Association [*Later, NDMA*] (EA) .... HDMA
Hardwood Distributors Association (EA) .... HDA
Hardwood Manufacturers Association (EA) .... HMA
Hardwood Plywood Institute [*Later, HPMA*] (EA) .... HPI
Hardwood Plywood Manufacturers Association [*Reston, VA*] (EA) .... HPMA
Hardwood Research Council (EA) .... HRC
Hardwood Weather Board (ADA) .... HWWB
Hardy [*Horticulture*] .... H
Hardy Annual [*Horticulture*] (ROG) .... HA
Hardy, AR [*FM radio station call letters*] .... KOOU
Hardy Associates, Calgary, Alberta [*Library symbol National Library of Canada*] (NLC) .... ACHA
Hardy Associates Ltd., Edmonton, AB, Canada [*Library symbol Library of Congress*] (LCLS) .... CaAEHA
Hardy Associates Ltd., Edmonton, Alberta [*Library symbol National Library of Canada*] (NLC) .... AEHA
Hardy Biennial [*Horticulture*] (ROG) .... HB
Hardy Perennial [*Horticulture*] (ROG) .... HP
Hardy Plant Society (EAIO) .... HPS
Hardy-Rand Rittler [*Test for color vision*] .... HRR
Hardy-Weinberg Equilibrium [*of genes*] [*Also, HWE*] .... HW
Hardy-Weinberg Equilibrium [*of genes*] [*Also, HW*] .... HWE
Hardy-Weinberg Expectation [*Genetics*] .... HWE
Hare and Wallace's American Leading Cases [*A publication*] (DLA) .... Hare & W
Hare Bay Public Library, Hare Bay, NF, Canada [*Library symbol Library of Congress*] (LCLS) .... CaNfHBa
Hare Bay Public Library, Newfoundland [*Library symbol National Library of Canada*] (NLC) .... NFHBA
Hare on Discovery of Evidence [*A publication*] (DLA) .... Hare Disc
Hare on Discovery of Evidence [*A publication*] (DLA) .... Hare Ev
Hare on Elections [*A publication*] (DLA) .... Hare Elec
Hare Tempore Wigram, Etc. [*1841-53*] [*A publication*] (DLA) .... H(Ha)
Harelip .... HL
Hare's American Constitutional Law [*A publication*] (DLA) .... Hare Const Law
Hare's English Chancery Reports [*A publication*] (DLA) .... H
Hare's English Chancery Reports, Appendix to Vol. X [*A publication*] (DLA) .... Har App
Hare's English Chancery Reports, Appendix to Vol. X [*A publication*] (DLA) .... Hare App
Hare's English Vice-Chancellors' Reports [*66-68 English Reprint*] [*1841-53*] [*A publication*] (DLA) .... Ha
Hare's English Vice-Chancellors' Reports [*66-68 English Reprint*] [*1841-53*] [*A publication*] (DLA) .... Hare
Hare's English Vice-Chancellors' Reports [*66-68 English Reprint*] [*1841-53*] [*A publication*] (DLA) .... Hare (Eng)
Harford Community College, Bel Air, MD [*OCLC symbol*] (OCLC) .... HAR
Harford Community College, Bel Air, MD [*Library symbol Library of Congress*] (LCLS) .... MdBaH
Harford County Library, Bel Air, MD [*Library symbol Library of Congress*] (LCLS) .... MdBaHC
Hargeisa [*Somalia*] [*ICAO location identifier*] (ICLI) .... HCMH
Hargeisa [*Somalia*] [*Airport symbol*] (OAG) .... HGA
Hargrave and Butler's Edition on Coke upon Littleton [*A publication*] (DLA) .... Harg & B Co Litt
Hargrave and Butler's Notes on Coke upon Littleton [*A publication*] (DLA) .... Hargrave & Butlers Notes on Co Litt
Hargrave on the Thellusson Act [*A publication*] (DLA) .... Harg Th
Hargrave's Collectanea Juridica [*1791-92*] [*A publication*] (DLA) .... Har Col Jur
Hargrave's Collectanea Juridica [*1791-92*] [*A publication*] (DLA) .... Harg Coll Jur
Hargrave's Francis-Jurisconsult Exercitations [*A publication*] (DLA) .... Jur Ex
Hargrave's Juridical Arguments and Collections [*A publication*] (DLA) .... Harg Jur Arg
Hargrave's Jurisconsult Exercitations [*A publication*] (DLA) .... Harg Exer
Hargrave's Law Tracts [*A publication*] (DLA) .... Harg Law Tracts
Hargrave's Law Tracts [*A publication*] (DLA) .... Harg LT
Hargrave's Notes to Coke on Littleton [*A publication*] (DLA) .... Harg Co Litt
Hargrave's Notes to Coke on Littleton [*A publication*] (DLA) .... Hargr Co Litt
Hargrave's State Trials [*A publication*] (DLA) .... Har St Tr
Hargrave's State Trials [*A publication*] (DLA) .... Harg
Hargrave's State Trials [*A publication*] (DLA) .... Harg St Tr
Hargrave's State Trials [*A publication*] (DLA) .... Harg State Tr
Hargrove's Reports [*68-75 North Carolina*] [*A publication*] (DLA) .... Harg
Hargrove's Reports [*68-75 North Carolina*] [*A publication*] (DLA) .... Hargrove
Hariana Lancers [*British military*] (DMA) .... HL
Haricots Verts [*Green Beans*] [*French*] .... HV
Hariston Corp. [*Associated Press*] (SAG) .... Haristn
Hariston Corp. [*NASDAQ symbol*] (SAG) .... HRSN
Hariston Corp. [*NASDAQ symbol*] (TTSB) .... HRSNF
Harka Air Services [*Nigeria*] [*FAA designator*] (FAAC) .... HAK
Harken Energy [*AMEX symbol*] (TTSB) .... HEC
Harken Energy Co. [*AMEX symbol*] (SPSG) .... HEC
Harken Energy Corp. [*Associated Press*] (SAG) .... Harken
Harken Technologies, Inc. [*Vancouver Stock Exchange symbol*] .... HKN
Harker Heights, TX [*FM radio station call letters*] .... KLTX
Harker Heights, TX [*FM radio station call letters*] (RBYB) .... KNRV-FM
Harker's Information Retrieval Systems [*Harker's Specialist Book Importers*] [*Information service or system*] (IID) .... HIRS
Harkers Island, NC [*FM radio station call letters*] .... WAED
Harkers Island, NC [*FM radio station call letters*] (RBYB) .... WLGP-FM
Harlan, IA [*Location identifier FAA*] (FAAL) .... HNR
Harlan, IA [*FM radio station call letters*] .... KNOD
Harlan, KY [*Television station call letters*] .... WAGV
Harlan, KY [*AM radio station call letters*] .... WFSR
Harlan, KY [*AM radio station call letters*] .... WHLN
Harlan, KY [*FM radio station call letters*] .... WTUK
Harlan News-Advertiser, Harlan, IA [*Library symbol Library of Congress*] (LCLS) .... IaHarNA
Harlan Public Library, Harlan, IA [*Library symbol Library of Congress*] (LCLS) .... IaHar
Harlan Tribune, Harlan, IA [*Library symbol Library of Congress*] (LCLS) .... IaHarT
Harland Bartholomew & Associates, Memphis, TN [*Library symbol Library of Congress*] (LCLS) .... TMHB
Harland [*John H.*] **Co.** [*Associated Press*] (SAG) .... Harlnd

Harland [*John H.*] **Co.** [*NYSE symbol*] (SPSG) .... JH
Harland (John H.) [*NYSE symbol*] (TTSB) .... JH
Harlech Television [*Wales*] .... HTV
Harleco Synthetic Resin (MAE) .... HSR
Harleian Collection, British Museum (DLA) .... HARL CBM
Harleian Manuscripts [*British*] (ROG) .... HARL MSS
Harleian Miscellany [*British*] (ROG) .... HARL MISC
Harlem Cultural Council (EA) .... HCC
Harlem Eastside Lifesaving Program [*Television program*] .... HELP
Harlem, GA [*FM radio station call letters*] .... WCHZ
Harlem Hospital Center, Health Sciences Library, New York, NY [*OCLC symbol*] (OCLC) .... VXA
Harlem Hospital Center, Medical Library, New York, NY [*Library symbol Library of Congress*] (LCLS) .... NNHH
Harlem Youth Opportunities Unlimited - Associated Community Teams [*A kind of Peace Corps for Harlem area of New York City*] .... HARYOU-ACT
Harlequin (WGA) .... HLQN
Harley Avenue Elementary School, East Northport, NY [*Library symbol Library of Congress*] (LCLS) .... NEanpHE
Harley Avenue Elementary School, Huntington, NY [*Library symbol*] [*Library of Congress*] (LCLS) .... NHuHAE
Harley Davidson, Inc. [*Associated Press*] (SAG) .... HarleyD
Harley Hummer Club (EA) .... HHC
Harley Owners' Group (EA) .... HOG
Harley-Davidson .... H-D
Harley-Davidson [*NYSE symbol*] (TTSB) .... HDI
Harley-Davidson, Inc. [*NYSE symbol*] (SPSG) .... HDI
Harleysville Group [*NASDAQ symbol*] (TTSB) .... HGIC
Harleysville Group, Inc. [*Associated Press*] (SAG) .... Harleys
Harleysville Group, Inc. [*NASDAQ symbol*] (NQ) .... HGIC
Harleysville National Corp. [*Associated Press*] (SAG) .... HarlyNat
Harleysville National Corp. [*NASDAQ symbol*] (SAG) .... HNBC
Harleysville Natl [*NASDAQ symbol*] (TTSB) .... HNBC
Harleysville Savings Association [*NASDAQ symbol*] (NQ) .... HARL
Harleysville Savings Association [*Associated Press*] (SAG) .... HarlySV
Harleysville Savings Bank [*NASDAQ symbol*] (TTSB) .... HARL
Harlin Resources [*Vancouver Stock Exchange symbol*] .... HRL
Harlingen [*Texas*] [*Airport symbol*] (OAG) .... HRL
Harlingen/Industrial Airpack [*Texas*] [*ICAO location identifier*] (ICLI) .... KHRL
Harlingen, TX [*FM radio station call letters*] .... KFRQ
Harlingen, TX [*FM radio station call letters*] .... KFRQ-FM
Harlingen, TX [*AM radio station call letters*] .... KGBT
Harlingen, TX [*Television station call letters*] .... KGBT-TV
Harlingen, TX [*FM radio station call letters*] .... KIWW
Harlingen, TX [*Television station call letters*] .... KLUJ
Harlingen, TX [*Television station call letters*] .... KMBH
Harlingen, TX [*FM radio station call letters*] .... KMBH-FM
Harlowton, MT [*Location identifier FAA*] (FAAL) .... HWQ
Harlyn Products [*AMEX symbol*] (TTSB) .... HRN
Harlyn Products, Inc. [*Associated Press*] (SAG) .... Harlyn
Harlyn Products, Inc. [*AMEX symbol*] (SPSG) .... HRN
Harman International [*NYSE symbol*] (TTSB) .... HAR
Harman International Industries, Inc. [*NYSE symbol*] (SPSG) .... HAR
Harman International Industries, Inc. [*Associated Press*] (SAG) .... Harman
Harmannus [*Authority cited in pre-1607 legal work*] (DSA) .... Harma
Harmelink Family Association (EA) .... HFA
Harmon Indus [*NASDAQ symbol*] (TTSB) .... HRMN
Harmon Industries, Inc. [*Associated Press*] (SAG) .... Harmon
Harmon Industries, Inc. [*NASDAQ symbol*] (NQ) .... HRMN
Harmona [*Record label*] [*Austria*] .... Hma
Harmonic (IDOE) .... H
Harmonic .... HAR
Harmonic (WDAA) .... HARM
Harmonic (MSA) .... HMNC
Harmonic and Spurious Totalizer .... HST
Harmonic Attenuation Table [*or Test*] (DAVI) .... HAT
Harmonic Distortion .... HD
Harmonic Distortion Meter (DEN) .... HDM
Harmonic Frequency Generator .... HFG
Harmonic Generator .... HG
Harmonic Identification Pitch Extraction (PDAA) .... HIPEX
Harmonic Lghtwaves, Inc. [*Associated Press*] (SAG) .... HarmLt
Harmonic Light Scattering [*Physics*] .... HLS
Harmonic Lightwaves [*NASDAQ symbol*] (TTSB) .... HLIT
Harmonic Lightwaves, Inc. [*Associated Press*] (SAG) .... HarmLgt
Harmonic Lightwaves, Inc. [*NASDAQ symbol*] (SAG) .... HLIT
Harmonic Mean [*Psychology*] .... H
Harmonic Mean [*Music*] .... HM
Harmonic Multiplier Source .... HMS
Harmonic Optimized Stabilization Technique (IAA) .... HOST
Harmonic Oscillator .... HO
Harmonic Progression .... HP
Harmonic Subcarrier Method (MCD) .... HSM
Harmonic Wire Projector (IAA) .... HWP
Harmonica [*of Ptolemy*] [*Classical studies*] (OCD) .... Harm
Harmonically Varying Field .... HVF
Harmonie Associates (EA) .... HA
Harmonisation of Environmental Measurement (EERA) .... HEM
Harmonised System [*Customs commodity coding and description*] [*British*] .... HS
Harmonized [*Apparent inconsistency explained and shown not to exist*] [*Used in Shepard's Citations*] [*Legal term*] (DLA) .... h
Harmonized System Code [*File indexing*] .... HSC
Harmonized Tariff Schedule of the United States [*Formerly, TSUS*] .... HTSUS
Harmon's Manual of United States Pension Laws [*A publication*] (DLA) .... Har Pen Man

Harmon's Manual of United States Pension Laws [*A publication*] (DLA) .... Harm Pens
Harmon's Reports [*13-15 California*] [*A publication*] (DLA) .... Harm
Harmon's Upper Canada Common Pleas Reports [*A publication*] (DLA) .... Harm
Harmon's Upper Canada Common Pleas Reports [*A publication*] (DLA) .... Harmon
Harmony [*South Africa*] [*ICAO location identifier*] (ICLI) .... FAHA
Harmony .... HARM
Harmony Brook [*NASDAQ symbol*] (TTSB) .... HBRK
Harmony Brook, Inc. [*Associated Press*] (SAG) .... HarmBrk
Harmony Brook, Inc. [*NASDAQ symbol*] (SAG) .... HBRK
Harmony Gold Mining Co. Ltd. [*NASDAQ symbol*] (SAG) .... HGMC
Harmony Gold Mining Co. Ltd. [*Associated Press*] (SAG) .... Hrm ADR
Harmony Heights [*Idaho*] [*Seismograph station code, US Geological Survey Closed*] (SEIS) .... HHI
Harmony Holdings [*NASDAQ symbol*] (TTSB) .... HAHO
Harmony Holdings, Inc. [*NASDAQ symbol*] (SAG) .... HAHO
Harmony Holdings, Inc. [*Associated Press*] (SAG) .... HrmHld
Harmony Products, Inc. [*Associated Press*] (SAG) .... HarmPd
Harmony Products, Inc. [*NASDAQ symbol*] (SAG) .... HRMY
Harmony-Emge-Ellis School District 175, Belleville, IL [*Library symbol Library of Congress*] (LCLS) .... IBelHSD
Harmsworth Public Library, Grand Falls, Newfoundland [*Library symbol National Library of Canada*] (NLC) .... NFGFHA
Harmsworth Public Library, Grand Falls, NF, Canada [*Library symbol Library of Congress*] (LCLS) .... CaNfGfHa
Harness (MSA) .... HARN
Harness .... HARN
Harness .... HRN
Harness and Cable Assembly .... HCA
Harness Assembly .... HA
Harness Horse Youth Foundation (EA) .... HHYF
Harness Horsemen International (EA) .... HHI
Harness or Saddlery .... HS
Harness Racing Authority of New South Wales [*Australia*] .... HRANSW
Harness Release Actuator (DNAB) .... HRA
Harness Tracks of America (EA) .... HTA
Harness Tracks Security [*Defunct*] (EA) .... HTS
Harnett County Public Library, Lillington, NC [*Library symbol Library of Congress*] (LCLS) .... NcLil
Harnischfeger Indus [*NYSE symbol*] (TTSB) .... HPH
Harnischfeger Industries [*NYSE symbol*] (SAG) .... HFH
Harnischfeger Industries [*NYSE symbol*] (SAG) .... HPH
Harnischfeger Industries, Inc. [*Associated Press*] (SAG) .... Harnish
Harnmoen [*Norway ICAO location identifier*] (ICLI) .... ENHN
Harnosand [*Sweden*] [*Airport symbol*] (AD) .... HSD
Harnosand/Myran [*Sweden ICAO location identifier*] (ICLI) .... ESUH
Harold Cohen Library [*University of Liverpool*] [*British*] (NITA) .... HCL
Harold D. Cooley Library, Nashville, NC [*Library symbol Library of Congress*] (LCLS) .... NcNv
Harold D. Fayette Elementary School, North Merrick, NY [*Library symbol*] [*Library of Congress*] (LCLS) .... NNmFE
Harold Institute [*Defunct*] (EA) .... HI
Harold, KY [*FM radio station call letters*] .... WXLR
Harold Washington Library Center [*Chicago Public Library*] .... HWLC
Harold's Stores [*AMEX symbol*] (TTSB) .... HLD
Harold's Stores, Inc. [*Associated Press*] (SAG) .... Harold
Harold's Stores, Inc. [*AMEX symbol*] (SPSG) .... HLD
Harp [*Music*] .... Hp
Harp Renaissance Society [*Defunct*] (EA) .... HRS
Harper & Row Publishers, Inc. .... H & R
Harper/Cape Palmas [*Liberia*] [*ICAO location identifier*] (ICLI) .... GLCP
Harper Group [*NASDAQ symbol*] (TTSB) .... HARG
Harper Group, Inc. [*NASDAQ symbol*] (NQ) .... HARG
Harper Group, Inc. [*Associated Press*] (SAG) .... HarpGp
Harper Hospital, Department of Libraries, Detroit, MI [*Library symbol Library of Congress*] (LCLS) .... MiDHH
Harper's Conspiracy Cases [*Maryland*] [*A publication*] (DLA) .... Harp Con Cas
Harper's Conspiracy Cases [*Maryland*] [*A publication*] (DLA) .... Harper
Harpers Ferry Center [*National Park Service*] (GRD) .... HFC
Harpers Ferry National Historical Park .... HAFE
Harper's Magazine [*A publication*] (BRI) .... HM
Harper's Magazine Press .... HMP
Harper's South Carolina Equity Reports [*A publication*] (DLA) .... Eq R
Harper's South Carolina Equity Reports [*A publication*] (DLA) .... Eq Rep
Harper's South Carolina Equity Reports [*A publication*] (DLA) .... Equity Rep
Harper's South Carolina Equity Reports [*A publication*] (DLA) .... Harp
Harper's South Carolina Equity Reports [*A publication*] (DLA) .... Harp Eq
Harper's South Carolina Equity Reports [*A publication*] (DLA) .... Harp Eq (SC)
Harper's South Carolina Equity Reports [*A publication*] (DLA) .... Harper
Harper's South Carolina Law Reports [*1823-30*] [*A publication*] (DLA) .... Harp L
Harper's South Carolina Law Reports [*1823-30*] [*A publication*] (DLA) .... Harp L
Harper's South Carolina Law Reports [*1823-30*] [*A publication*] (DLA) .... Harp L (SC)
Harper's South Carolina Law Reports [*1823-30*] [*A publication*] (DLA) .... Harper
Harpocration [*Classical studies*] (OCD) .... Harp
Harpoon (WDAA) .... HARP
Harpoon Aircraft Command and Launch Control Set [*Missiles*] (NVT) .... HACLCS
Harpoon Aircraft Command and Launch Subsystem [*Missiles*] (MCD) .... HACLS
Harpoon Asset Visibility System (MCD) .... HAVS
Harpoon Check List [*Missiles*] (MCD) .... HCL
Harpoon Data Processor [*Missiles*] (MCD) .... HDP
Harpoon Data System Cabinet [*Missiles*] (MCD) .... HDSC
Harpoon Environmental Correction Aid [*Navy*] (ANA) .... HECA
Harpoon Fire Control System [*Missiles*] (MCD) .... HFCS

Harpoon Firing Interlock Closed [*Missiles*] (MCD) .... HFIC
Harpoon Indicator Panel [*Missiles*] (MCD) .... HIP
Harpoon Interface Adapter Kit (DWSG) .... HIAK
Harpoon Logic Module [*Missiles*] (MCD) .... HLM
Harpoon Missile Select Relay Rack [*Missiles*] (MCD) .... HMSRR
Harpoon Shipboard Command and Launch Control Set [*Missiles*] (NVT) .... HSCLCS
Harpoon Shipboard Command and Launch Subsystem [*Missiles*] (MCD) .... HSCLS
Harpoon Standard Initiator (MCD) .... HSI
Harpoon Trainer Module [*Missiles*] (MCD) .... HTM
Harpoon Transfer Relay Rack [*Missiles*] (MCD) .... HTRR
Harpoon Weapon Control Console [*Missiles*] (MCD) .... HWCC
Harpoon Weapons System (NVT) .... HWS
Harpsichord (WDAA) .... HARP
Harpsichord [*Music*] .... HPCHD
Harpsichord [*Music*] .... HPSI
Harpsicord [*Music*] (WGA) .... HPS
Harpswell, ME [*FM radio station call letters*] .... WMSJ
Harradine Group [*Australia Political party*] .... Har
Harrah's Automobile Collection and Pony Express Museum, Reno, NV [*Library symbol Library of Congress*] (LCLS) .... NvRH
Harrah's Entertainment [*NYSE symbol*] (TTSB) .... HET
Harrahs Entertainment, Inc. [*Associated Press*] (SAG) .... HarrahE
Harrahs Entertainment, Inc. [*NYSE symbol*] (SAG) .... HET
Harrier (ROG) .... H
Harriette Person Memorial Library, Port Gibson, MS [*Library symbol Library of Congress*] (LCLS) .... MsPog
Harrigan and Thompson's Cases on the Law of Self-Defense [*A publication*] (DLA) .... H & T Self-Def
Harriman & Northeastern R. R. [*AAR code*] .... HNE
Harriman and Vance [*Code name for 1968 Paris peace talks on Vietnam, derived from the surnames of US negotiators W. Averell Harriman and Cyrus R. Vance*] .... HARVAN
Harriman College, Harriman, NY [*Library symbol Library of Congress*] (LCLS) .... NHarC
Harriman Public Library, Harriman, TN [*Library symbol Library of Congress*] (LCLS) .... TH
Harriman, TN [*FM radio station call letters*] .... WLIQ
Harrington Financial Group, Inc. [*NASDAQ symbol*] (SAG) .... HFGI
Harrington Financial Group, Inc. [*Associated Press*] (SAG) .... Hrringtn
Harrington Fin'l Grp [*NASDAQ symbol*] (TTSB) .... HFGI
Harrington Harbour [*Canada*] [*Airport symbol*] (OAG) .... YHR
Harrington Harbour, PQ [*FM radio station call letters*] .... CFTH
Harrington Institute of Interior Design, Chicago, IL [*Library symbol Library of Congress*] (LCLS) .... ICHID
Harrington Institute of Interior Design, Design Library, Chicago, IL [*OCLC symbol*] (OCLC) .... IEX
Harrington Public Library, Harrington, DE [*Library symbol*] [*Library of Congress*] (LCLS) .... DeHa
Harrington Public Library, Harrington, DE [*OCLC symbol*] (OCLC) .... HRG
Harrington Rod [*Orthopedics*] (DAVI) .... HR
Harrington Rod Instrumentation [*Orthopedics*] (DAVI) .... HRI
Harrington's Delaware Reports [*A publication*] (DLA) .... Har
Harrington's Delaware Reports [*1-5 Delaware*] [*A publication*] (DLA) .... Har Del
Harrington's Delaware Reports [*1-5 Delaware*] [*A publication*] (DLA) .... Harr
Harrington's Delaware Reports [*1-5 Delaware*] [*A publication*] (DLA) .... Harr (Del)
Harrington's Delaware Reports [*1-5 Delaware*] [*A publication*] (DLA) .... Harring
Harrington's Delaware Supreme Court Reports [*1832-55*] [*A publication*] (DLA) .... Harrington
Harrington's Michigan Chancery Reports [*A publication*] (DLA) .... Har
Harrington's Michigan Chancery Reports [*A publication*] (DLA) .... Har Ch
Harrington's Michigan Chancery Reports [*A publication*] (DLA) .... Har Chy
Harrington's Michigan Chancery Reports [*A publication*] (DLA) .... Harr
Harrington's Michigan Chancery Reports [*A publication*] (DLA) .... Harr Ch
Harrington's Michigan Chancery Reports [*A publication*] (DLA) .... Harr Ch (Mich)
Harrington's Michigan Chancery Reports [*A publication*] (DLA) .... Harr Ch R
Harrington's Michigan Chancery Reports [*A publication*] (DLA) .... Harr (Mich)
Harrington's Michigan Chancery Reports [*A publication*] (DLA) .... Harring
Harrington's Michigan Chancery Reports [*A publication*] (DLA) .... Harring Ch (Mich)
Harrington's Michigan Chancery Reports [*A publication*] (DLA) .... Harrington
Harris and Clarkson on Conveyancing, Etc. [*A publication*] (DLA) .... Harr & Cl Conv
Harris and Gill's Maryland Court of Appeals Reports [*1826-29*] [*A publication*] (DLA) .... H & G
Harris and Gill's Maryland Reports [*A publication*] (DLA) .... Har & G
Harris and Gill's Maryland Reports [*A publication*] (DLA) .... Har & G Rep
Harris and Gill's Maryland Reports [*A publication*] (DLA) .... Har & Gil
Harris and Gill's Maryland Reports [*A publication*] (DLA) .... Har & Gill
Harris and Gill's Maryland Reports [*A publication*] (DLA) .... Harr & G
Harris and Gill's Maryland Reports [*A publication*] (DLA) .... Harris & G
Harris and Gill's Maryland Reports [*A publication*] (DLA) .... Harris & Gill's MD R
Harris & Harris Group [*Associated Press*] (SAG) .... HarisHa
Harris & Harris Group [*NASDAQ symbol*] (TTSB) .... HHGP
Harris & Harris Group, Inc. [*NASDAQ symbol*] (NQ) .... HHGP
Harris and Johnson's Maryland Court of Appeals Reports [*1800-26*] [*A publication*] (DLA) .... H & J
Harris and Johnson's Maryland Court of Appeals Reports [*1800-26*] [*A publication*] (DLA) .... Har & John
Harris and Johnson's Maryland Reports [*A publication*] (DLA) .... H & John
Harris and Johnson's Maryland Reports [*A publication*] (DLA) .... Har & J
Harris and Johnson's Maryland Reports [*A publication*] (DLA) .... Har & J (MD)
Harris and Johnson's Maryland Reports [*A publication*] (DLA) .... Har & Johns MD Rep
Harris and Johnson's Maryland Reports [*A publication*] (DLA) .... Harr & J
Harris and Johnson's Maryland Reports [*A publication*] (DLA) .... Harr & J (MD)
Harris and Johnson's Maryland Reports [*A publication*] (DLA) .... Harris & J
Harris and McHenry's Maryland Court of Appeals Reports [*1785-99*] [*A publication*] (DLA) .... H & McH
Harris and McHenry's Maryland Reports [*A publication*] (DLA) .... H & McHenry
Harris and McHenry's Maryland Reports [*A publication*] (DLA) .... Har & McH
Harris and McHenry's Maryland Reports [*A publication*] (DLA) .... Har and M'Hen
Harris and McHenry's Maryland Reports [*A publication*] (DLA) .... Harr & M
Harris and McHenry's Maryland Reports [*A publication*] (DLA) .... Harr & McH
Harris and McHenry's Maryland Reports [*A publication*] (DLA) .... Harr & McH (MD)
Harris and McHenry's Maryland Reports [*A publication*] (DLA) .... Harr & McHen
Harris and McHenry's Maryland Reports [*A publication*] (DLA) .... Harr & M'H
Harris and Simrall's Reports [*49-52 Mississippi*] [*A publication*] (DLA) .... H & S
Harris and Simrall's Reports [*49-52 Mississippi*] [*A publication*] (DLA) .... Harr & Sim
Harris and Simrall's Reports [*49-52 Mississippi*] [*A publication*] (DLA) .... Harris & S
Harris and Simrall's Reports [*49-52 Mississippi*] [*A publication*] (DLA) .... Harris & Sim
Harris and Simrall's Reports [*49-52 Mississippi*] [*A publication*] (DLA) .... Harris & Simrall
Harris API [*Application Programming Interface*] [*Computer science*] .... HAPI
Harris Computer Systems [*NASDAQ symbol*] (TTSB) .... NHWK
Harris Computer Systems Corp. [*Associated Press*] (SAG) .... HarrisCS
Harris Computer Systems Corp. [*NASDAQ symbol*] (SAG) .... NHWK
Harris Consultive Services, Inc. [*Information service or system*] (IID) .... HCS
Harris Corp. [*Associated Press*] (SAG) .... Harris
Harris Corp. [*NYSE symbol*] (SPSG) .... HRS
Harris Daishowa Australia Ltd. [*Commercial*] (EERA) .... HDA
Harris Electronic News [*Service suspended*] [*Information service or system*] (IID) .... HEN
Harris' Elements of Roman Law [*A publication*] (DLA) .... Harr Rom Law
Harris Enhanced Language for Programmable Logic (NITA) .... HELP
Harris, GA [*Location identifier FAA*] (FAAL) .... HRS
Harris' Georgia Digest [*A publication*] (DLA) .... Har Dig
Harris' Georgia Digest [*A publication*] (DLA) .... Harr (GA)
Harris' Georgia Digest [*A publication*] (DLA) .... Harris Dig
Harris Government Systems Sector, Engineering Library, Melbourne, FL [*Library symbol*] [*Library of Congress*] (LCLS) .... FMeH
Harris' Hints on Advocacy [*18th ed.*] [*1943*] [*A publication*] (DLA) .... Harr Adv
Harris' Hints on Advocacy [*18th ed.*] [*1943*] [*A publication*] (DLA) .... Harr Hints
Harris Institute, Woonsocket, RI [*Library symbol Library of Congress*] (LCLS) .... RWoH
Harris' Justinian [*A publication*] (DLA) .... Har Just
Harris on Titles to Mines [*A publication*] (DLA) .... Harr Min
Harris' Principiae Primae Legum [*A publication*] (DLA) .... Harr Prin
Harris' Principles of the Criminal Law [*22nd ed.*] [*1973*] [*A publication*] (DLA) .... Harr Cr L
Harris Ranch [*California*] [*Seismograph station code, US Geological Survey Closed*] (SEIS) .... HRC
Harris' Reports [*A publication*] (DLA) .... Harr
Harris' Reports [*A publication*] (DLA) .... Harris
Harris Savings Bank [*Associated Press*] (SAG) .... HarisSvg
Harris Savings Bank [*NASDAQ symbol*] (SAG) .... HARS
Harris Savings Bank [*NASDAQ symbol*] (TTSB) .... HARS
Harris Steel Group, Inc. [*Toronto Stock Exchange symbol*] .... HSG
Harris [*Paul*] **Stores** [*NASDAQ symbol*] (SAG) .... PAUH
Harris Teachers College [*Missouri*] .... HTC
Harris Teachers College, St. Louis, MO [*Library symbol Library of Congress*] (LCLS) .... MoSHT
Harris Transducer Corp. (MCD) .... HTC
Harris' Translation of the Institute of Justinian [*A publication*] (DLA) .... Harr Just
Harris Trust and Savings Bank, Chicago, IL [*Library symbol Library of Congress*] (LCLS) .... ICHT
Harris Tweed Association [*British*] (DBA) .... HTA
Harrisburg [*Diocesan abbreviation*] [*Pennsylvania*] (TOCD) .... HBG
Harrisburg [*Pennsylvania*] [*Airport symbol*] (OAG) .... MDT
Harrisburg Area Community College, Harrisburg, PA [*Library symbol Library of Congress*] (LCLS) .... PHarC
Harrisburg/Capital City [*Pennsylvania*] [*ICAO location identifier*] (ICLI) .... KHAR
Harrisburg, IL [*Location identifier FAA*] (FAAL) .... HSB
Harrisburg, IL [*AM radio station call letters*] .... WEBQ
Harrisburg, IL [*FM radio station call letters*] .... WOOZ
Harrisburg, IL [*Television station call letters*] .... WSIL
Harrisburg International Airport (MCD) .... HIA
Harrisburg, NC [*FM radio station call letters*] (RBYB) .... WCCJ
Harrisburg, PA [*Location identifier FAA*] (FAAL) .... CXY
Harrisburg, PA [*Location identifier FAA*] (FAAL) .... HAR
Harrisburg, PA [*AM radio station call letters*] .... WCMB
Harrisburg, PA [*AM radio station call letters*] .... WHP
Harrisburg, PA [*Television station call letters*] .... WHP-TV
Harrisburg, PA [*Television station call letters*] .... WHTM
Harrisburg, PA [*FM radio station call letters*] .... WITF
Harrisburg, PA [*Television station call letters*] .... WITF-TV
Harrisburg, PA [*AM radio station call letters*] .... WKBO
Harrisburg, PA [*FM radio station call letters*] .... WNNK
Harrisburg, PA [*FM radio station call letters*] .... WRVV
Harrisburg, PA [*AM radio station call letters*] .... WTCY
Harrisburg, PA [*FM radio station call letters*] .... WWKL
Harrisburg, PA [*FM radio station call letters*] (RBYB) .... WXPH
Harrisburg, PA [*FM radio station call letters*] (RBYB) .... WYMJ
Harrisburg Polyclinic Hospital, Harrisburg, PA [*Library symbol Library of Congress*] (LCLS) .... PHarP
Harrisburg-Dayton [*Vancouver Stock Exchange symbol*] .... HRU
Harrisburg-New Cumberland [*Pennsylvania*] [*Airport symbol*] (AD) .... HAR

Harrismith [*South Africa*] [*ICAO location identifier*] (ICLI) ... FAHR
Harrison [*Arkansas*] [*Airport symbol*] (OAG) ... HRO
Harrison Air [*Canada ICAO designator*] (FAAC) ... HAA
Harrison and Hodgin's Upper Canada Municipal Reports [*1845-51*] [*A publication*] (DLA) ... H & H
Harrison and Hodgin's Upper Canada Municipal Reports [*1845-51*] [*A publication*] (DLA) ... Harr & H
Harrison and Hodgin's Upper Canada Municipal Reports [*1845-51*] [*A publication*] (DLA) ... Harr & Hodg
Harrison and Rutherford's English Common Pleas Reports [*1865-66*] [*A publication*] (DLA) ... Har & Ruth
Harrison and Rutherford's English Common Pleas Reports [*1865-66*] [*A publication*] (DLA) ... Harr & R
Harrison and Rutherford's English Common Pleas Reports [*1865-66*] [*A publication*] (DLA) ... Harr & Ruth
Harrison and Rutherfurd's English Common Pleas Reports [*1865-66*] [*A publication*] (DLA) ... H & R
Harrison and Wollaston's English King's Bench Reports [*A publication*] (DLA) ... H & W
Harrison and Wollaston's English King's Bench Reports [*A publication*] (DLA) ... Har & W
Harrison and Wollaston's English King's Bench Reports [*A publication*] (DLA) ... Har & Woll
Harrison and Wollaston's English King's Bench Reports [*A publication*] (DLA) ... Harr & W
Harrison and Wollaston's English King's Bench Reports [*A publication*] (DLA) ... Harr & W (Eng)
Harrison and Wollaston's English King's Bench Reports [*A publication*] (DLA) ... Harr & Woll
Harrison, AR [*FM radio station call letters*] ... KCWD
Harrison, AR [*AM radio station call letters*] ... KHOZ
Harrison, AR [*FM radio station call letters*] ... KHOZ-FM
Harrison Bay, AK [*Location identifier FAA*] (FAAL) ... HBA
Harrison/Boone County [*Arkansas*] [*ICAO location identifier*] (ICLI) ... KHRO
Harrison County Historical Society, Logan, IA [*Library symbol Library of Congress*] (LCLS) ... IaLoHi
Harrison County Historical Society, Persia, IA [*Library symbol Library of Congress*] (LCLS) ... IaPersHi
Harrison County Press, Corydon, IN [*Library symbol Library of Congress*] (LCLS) ... InCorCP
Harrison County Recorder's Office, Corydon, IN [*Library symbol Library of Congress*] (LCLS) ... InCorCR
Harrison Elementary School, Brainerd, MN [*Library symbol*] [*Library of Congress*] (LCLS) ... MnBrHE
Harrison Fisher Society (EA) ... HFS
Harrison Horncastle Holdings [*Investment firm*] [*British*] ... HHH
Harrison Memorial Hospital, Bremerton, WA [*Library symbol Library of Congress*] (LCLS) ... WaBrH
Harrison Memorial Library, Carmel, CA [*Library symbol Library of Congress*] (LCLS) ... CCarm
Harrison, MI [*FM radio station call letters*] ... WKKM
Harrison Narcotic Act ... HNA
Harrison, OH [*FM radio station call letters*] ... WNLT
Harrison on Probate and Divorce [*A publication*] (DLA) ... Har Prob
Harrison Public Library, Harrison, ID [*Library symbol*] [*Library of Congress*] (LCLS) ... IdHr
Harrison Public Library, Harrison, MI [*Library symbol Library of Congress*] (LCLS) ... MiHars
Harrison Public Library, Harrison, NY [*Library symbol Library of Congress*] (LCLS) ... NHarn
Harrison, Purchase, and North Castle [*Airport*] ... HPN
Harrison Township Historical Society, Mullica Hill, NJ [*Library symbol Library of Congress*] (LCLS) ... NjMuhHi
Harrisonburg [*Virginia*] [*Seismograph station code, US Geological Survey*] (SEIS) ... HBV
Harrisonburg, VA [*FM radio station call letters*] ... WEMC
Harrisonburg, VA [*AM radio station call letters*] ... WHBG
Harrisonburg, VA [*Television station call letters*] ... WHSV
Harrisonburg, VA [*AM radio station call letters*] ... WKCY
Harrisonburg, VA [*FM radio station call letters*] ... WKCY-FM
Harrisonburg, VA [*FM radio station call letters*] ... WMRA
Harrisonburg, VA [*FM radio station call letters*] ... WQPO
Harrisonburg, VA [*AM radio station call letters*] ... WSVA
Harrisonburg, VA [*FM radio station call letters*] ... WXJM
Harrison's Chancery Practice [*A publication*] (DLA) ... Har Ch Pr
Harrison's Chancery Practice [*A publication*] (DLA) ... Harrison Ch
Harrison's Common Law Procedure Act [*Canada A publication*] (DLA) ... Har Com Proc
Harrison's Common Law Procedure Act [*Canada*] [*A publication*] (DLA) ... Harr Proc
Harrison's Compilation of the Laws of New Jersey [*A publication*] (DLA) ... Har Com
Harrison's Condensed Louisiana Reports [*A publication*] (DLA) ... Har
Harrison's Condensed Louisiana Reports [*A publication*] (DLA) ... Harr Con LA R
Harrison's Digest of English Common Law Reports [*A publication*] (DLA) ... Har Dig
Harrison's Digest of English Common Law Reports [*A publication*] (DLA) ... Harr Dig
Harrison's Digest of English Common Law Reports [*A publication*] (DLA) ... Harrison Dig
Harrison's Law Reports [*16-19 New Jersey*] [*A publication*] (DLA) ... Harr
Harrison's Law Reports [*16-19 New Jersey*] [*A publication*] (DLA) ... Harr NJ
Harrison's Law Reports [*16-19 New Jersey*] [*A publication*] (DLA) ... Harrison
Harrison's Michigan Chancery Reports [*A publication*] (DLA) ... Har
Harrison's Municipal Law of Ontario [*A publication*] (DLA) ... Harr Mun Law
Harrison's Reports [*15-17, 23-29 Indiana*] [*A publication*] (DLA) ... Har
Harrison's Reports [*15-17, 23-29 Indiana*] [*A publication*] (DLA) ... Harr
Harrison's Reports [*15-17, 23-29 Indiana*] [*A publication*] (DLA) ... Harrison
Harrisonville, MO [*FM radio station call letters*] ... KCFX
Harris-Stowe State College Library, St. Louis, MO [*Library symbol*] [*Library of Congress*] (LCLS) ... MoSHS
Harrodsburg First Financial Bancorp, Inc. [*Associated Press*] (SAG) ... Harrod
Harrodsburg First Financial Bancorp, Inc. [*NASDAQ symbol*] (SAG) ... HFFB
Harrodsburg First Finl Bancorp [*NASDAQ symbol*] (TTSB) ... HFFB
Harrodsburg Historical Society, Harrodsburg, KY [*Library symbol Library of Congress*] (LCLS) ... KyHaHi
Harrodsburg, KY [*AM radio station call letters*] ... WHBN
Harrodsburg, KY [*FM radio station call letters*] ... WHBN-FM
Harrogate [*Postcode*] (ODBW) ... HG
Harrogate, TN [*FM radio station call letters*] ... WLMU
Harrogate, TN [*AM radio station call letters*] ... WRWB
Harrogate, TN [*FM radio station call letters*] ... WXJB
Harry [*Phonetic alphabet*] [*Royal Navy World War I Pre-World War II*] (DSUE) ... H
Harry Armenius Miller [*Automotive engineer*] ... HAM
Harry B. Thompson Junior High School, Syosset, NY [*Library symbol*] [*Library of Congress*] (LCLS) ... NSyoTJ
Harry Balfour School, Grande Prairie, Alberta [*Library symbol National Library of Canada*] (BIB) ... AGPHBS
Harry C. Stutz [*Designer of early automobile*] ... HCS
Harry Connick, Jr., Fan Club (EA) ... HCJFC
Harry Diamond Center [*Army*] ... HDC
Harry Diamond Laboratories [*Formerly, DOFL*] [*Adelphi, MD*] [*Army*] ... HDL
[*The*] **Harry Fox Agency** ... HFA
Harry Franco [*Pseudonym used by Charles F. Briggs*] ... HF
Harry James Appreciation Society (EAIO) ... HJAS
Harry S Truman [*US president, 1884-1972*] ... HST
Harry S Truman College, Chicago, IL [*OCLC symbol*] (OCLC) ... IEG
Harry S Truman Library ... HSTL
Harry S Truman Library, Independence, MO [*Library symbol Library of Congress*] (LCLS) ... MoIT
Harry S Truman Memorial Veterans Hospital, Columbia, MO [*Library symbol Library of Congress*] (LCLS) ... MoCoV
Harry S Truman Scholarship Foundation (EA) ... HSTSF
Harry's Farmers Market [*NASDAQ symbol*] (TTSB) ... HARY
Harry's Farmers Markets [*NASDAQ symbol*] (SAG) ... HARY
Harry's Farmers Markets [*Associated Press*] (SAG) ... HaryFar
Harrys Harbour Public Library, Harrys Harbour, NF, Canada [*Library symbol Library of Congress*] (LCLS) ... CaNfHH
Harrys Harbour Public Library, Newfoundland [*Library symbol National Library of Canada*] (NLC) ... NFHH
Hars Systems, Inc. [*Vancouver Stock Exchange symbol*] ... HSS
Harsco Corp. [*Associated Press*] (SAG) ... Harsco
Harsco Corp. [*NYSE symbol*] (SPSG) ... HSC
Harstad [*Norway*] [*Airport symbol*] (AD) ... HRD
Harston's California Practice and Pleading [*A publication*] (DLA) ... Hars Pr
Hart Brewing [*NASDAQ symbol*] (TTSB) ... HOPS
Hart Chemicals Ltd., Guelph, Ontario [*Library symbol National Library of Canada*] (NLC) ... OGHC
Hart Family Fan Club (EA) ... HFFC
Hart, MI [*FM radio station call letters*] ... WCXT
Hart Public Library, Hart, MI [*Library symbol Library of Congress*] (LCLS) ... MiHa
Hartco Enterprises, Inc. [*Toronto Stock Exchange symbol*] ... HTC
Harte Hanks Communications [*Associated Press*] (SAG) ... HartHnk
Hartebeespoortdam [*South Africa*] [*ICAO location identifier*] (ICLI) ... FAHB
Hartebeesthoek [*South Africa*] [*Geomagnetic observatory code*] ... HBK
Harte-Hanks Communications [*NYSE symbol*] (TTSB) ... HHS
Harte-Hanks Communications, Inc. [*NYSE symbol*] (SPSG) ... HHS
Hartenholm [*Germany ICAO location identifier*] (ICLI) ... EDHM
Hartford [*Connecticut*] [*Seismograph station code, US Geological Survey Closed*] (SEIS) ... HAR
Hartford [*Diocesan abbreviation*] [*Connecticut*] (TOCD) ... HRT
Hartford & New Haven Railroad ... H & NH
Hartford & Slocomb Railroad Co. [*AAR code*] ... HS
Hartford Bar Library Association, Hartford, CT [*Library symbol Library of Congress*] (LCLS) ... CtHB
Hartford/Brainard Field [*Connecticut*] [*ICAO location identifier*] (ICLI) ... KHFD
Hartford Cap I 7.70% 'QUIPS' [*NYSE symbol*] (TTSB) ... HIGPrQ
Hartford Capital I [*Associated Press*] (SAG) ... HartC
Hartford Capital I [*NYSE symbol*] (SAG) ... HIG
Hartford Capital II [*Associated Press*] (SAG) ... HartC
Hartford Capital II [*NYSE symbol*] (SAG) ... HIG
Hartford City, IN [*FM radio station call letters*] ... WWWO
Hartford City Public Library, Hartford City, IN [*Library symbol Library of Congress*] (LCLS) ... InHar
Hartford Conservatory, Hartford, CT [*Library symbol Library of Congress*] (LCLS) ... CtHHC
Hartford, CT [*Location identifier FAA*] (FAAL) ... AQD
Hartford, CT [*Location identifier FAA*] (FAAL) ... HFD
Hartford, CT [*AM radio station call letters*] ... WCCC
Hartford, CT [*FM radio station call letters*] ... WCCC-FM
Hartford, CT [*AM radio station call letters*] ... WDRC
Hartford, CT [*FM radio station call letters*] ... WDRC-FM
Hartford, CT [*Television station call letters*] ... WEDH
Hartford, CT [*Television station call letters*] ... WFSB
Hartford, CT [*FM radio station call letters*] ... WHCN
Hartford, CT [*Television station call letters*] ... WHCT
Hartford, CT [*FM radio station call letters*] ... WJMJ
Hartford, CT [*FM radio station call letters*] ... WKSS
Hartford, CT [*AM radio station call letters*] ... WPOP
Hartford, CT [*FM radio station call letters*] ... WQTQ

Hartford, CT [*FM radio station call letters*] ..... WRTC
Hartford, CT [*AM radio station call letters*] ..... WTIC
Hartford, CT [*FM radio station call letters*] ..... WTIC-FM
Hartford, CT [*Television station call letters*] ..... WTIC-TV
Hartford, CT [*FM radio station call letters*] ..... WZMX
Hartford Electric Light Co. ..... HELCO
Hartford, KY [*FM radio station call letters*] (RBYB) ..... WKHB-FM
Hartford, KY [*AM radio station call letters*] ..... WLLS
Hartford, KY [*FM radio station call letters*] ..... WLLS-FM
Hartford, KY [*AM radio station call letters*] (RBYB) ..... WSNR-AM
Hartford Medical Society, Hartford, CT [*Library symbol Library of Congress*] (LCLS) ..... CtHM
Hartford Memorial Hospital, Hartford, WI [*Library symbol Library of Congress*] (LCLS) ..... WHH
Hartford, MI [*FM radio station call letters*] (RBYB) ..... WZTY
Hartford Public Library, Hartford, CT [*Library symbol Library of Congress*] (LCLS) ..... CtH
Hartford Public Library, Hartford, CT [*OCLC symbol*] (OCLC) ..... HPL
Hartford Public Library, Hartford, IL [*Library symbol Library of Congress*] (LCLS) ..... IHart
Hartford Public Library, Hartford, MI [*Library symbol Library of Congress*] (LCLS) ..... MiHaf
Hartford Seminary Foundation [*Connecticut*] ..... HSF
Hartford Seminary Foundation, Hartford, CT [*Library symbol Library of Congress*] (LCLS) ..... CtHC
Hartford [*Connecticut*]/Springfield [*Massachusetts*] [*Derived from name of airport: Bradley Field*] [*Airport symbol*] ..... BDL
Hartford Steam Boiler & Inspection [*Associated Press*] (SAG) ..... HrtfdSt
Hartford Steam Boiler Inspection & Insurance Co. [*NYSE symbol*] (SPSG) ..... HSB
Hartford Stm Boiler Ins [*NYSE symbol*] (TTSB) ..... HSB
Hartford, VT [*FM radio station call letters*] ..... WGLV
Hartford, VT [*Television station call letters*] ..... WNNE
Hartford Whalers Booster Club (EA) ..... HWBC
Hartford, WI [*Location identifier FAA*] (FAAL) ..... HXF
Hartford, WI [*AM radio station call letters*] ..... WTKM
Hartford, WI [*FM radio station call letters*] ..... WTKM-FM
Hartington Branch, Frontenac County Library, Hartington, Ontario [*Library symbol National Library of Canada*] (BIB) ..... OHFC
Hartland [*United Kingdom*] [*Geomagnetic observatory code*] ..... HAD
Hartley and Hartley's Reports [*11-21 Texas*] [*A publication*] (DLA) ..... Hart & H
Hartley and Hartley's Reports [*11-21 Texas*] [*A publication*] (DLA) ..... Hartley & Hartley
Hartley and Hartley's Reports [*11-21 Texas*] [*A publication*] (DLA) ..... Hartley & Hartley Rep
Hartley Public Library, Hartley, IA [*Library symbol Library of Congress*] (LCLS) ..... IaHart
Hartley Public Library, Hartley, IA [*Library symbol*] [*Library of Congress*] (LCLS) ..... IaHartP
Hartley Sentinel, Hartley, IA [*Library symbol Library of Congress*] (LCLS) ..... IaHartS
Hartley's Digest of Texas Laws [*A publication*] (DLA) ..... Hart
Hartley's Digest of Texas Laws [*A publication*] (DLA) ..... Hart Dig
Hartley's Reports [*4-10 Texas*] [*A publication*] (DLA) ..... Hart
Hartley's Reports [*4-10 Texas*] [*A publication*] (DLA) ..... Hartley
Hartman Value Inventory [*Psychology*] ..... HVI
Hartman Value Profile [*Personality development test*] [*Psychology*] ..... HVP
Hartmann Dispersion Formula ..... HDF
Hartmann Number [*IUPAC*] ..... Ha
Hartmannus Hartmanni [*Deceased, 1586*] [*Authority cited in pre-1607 legal work*] (DSA) ..... Hart Hartm
Hartmannus Pistoris [*Deceased, 1601*] [*Authority cited in pre-1607 legal work*] (DSA) ..... Hart Pist
Hartmannus Pistoris [*Deceased, 1601*] [*Authority cited in pre-1607 legal work*] (DSA) ..... Hartm Pistor
Hartmannus Pistoris [*Deceased, 1601*] [*Authority cited in pre-1607 legal work*] (DSA) ..... Hartman Pist
Hartman's Solution [*Dentistry*] ..... HS
Hartmarx Corp. [*Associated Press*] (SAG) ..... Hartmx
Hartmarx Corp. [*NYSE symbol*] (SPSG) ..... HMX
Hartnell College, Salinas, CA [*Library symbol Library of Congress*] (LCLS) ..... CSalH
Hartree-Fock [*Orbitals*] [*Atomic structure*] ..... HF
Hartridge Smoke Unit [*Automotive engineering*] ..... HSU
Hart's Bankrupt Law and Practice [*A publication*] (DLA) ..... Hart Bank
Harts Bluff [*South Carolina*] [*Seismograph station code, US Geological Survey*] (SEIS) ..... HBF
Harts Range Meta-igneous Complex [*Geology*] ..... HRMC
Hart-Scott-Rodino Antitrust Improvements Act [*1976*] ..... HSR
Hartselle, AL [*FM radio station call letters*] ..... WTAK
Hartselle, AL [*AM radio station call letters*] ..... WYAM
Hartshorn Family Association (EA) ..... HFA
Hartsville Nuclear Plant (NRCH) ..... HNP
Hartsville, SC [*Location identifier FAA*] (FAAL) ..... HVS
Hartsville, SC [*AM radio station call letters*] ..... WHSC
Hartsville, SC [*FM radio station call letters*] ..... WHSC-FM
Hartsville, SC [*AM radio station call letters*] ..... WTNI
Hartsville, TN [*AM radio station call letters*] ..... WJKM
Hartwell, GA [*AM radio station call letters*] ..... WKLY
Hartwell Railway Co. [*AAR code*] ..... HRT
Hartwick College, Oneonta, NY [*Library symbol Library of Congress*] (LCLS) ..... NOneoC
Hartwick College, Oneonta, NY [*OCLC symbol*] (OCLC) ..... VZH
Harum [*Of These*] [*Pharmacy*] (ROG) ..... HAR
Harvard Air Cleaning Laboratory (NRCH) ..... HACL
Harvard Black Rock Forest, Cornwall, NY [*Library symbol Library of Congress*] (LCLS) ..... NCornB
Harvard Business Review [*A publication*] (BRI) ..... Har Bus R
Harvard Business Review-Online [*John Wiley & Son*] (NITA) ..... HBR-online
Harvard Business School ..... HBS
Harvard Business School, Boston, MA [*OCLC symbol*] (OCLC) ..... HBS
Harvard Business World (DLA) ..... Harv Bus World
Harvard Capital & Consulting [*An investment fund*] [*Czechoslovakia*] (ECON) ..... HC & C
Harvard Civil Rights - Civil Liberties Law Review [*A publication*] (ILCA) ..... Harv CR CL Law Rev
Harvard College Observatory ..... HCO
Harvard Community Health Plan (DMAA) ..... HCHP
Harvard Computer-Aided Legal Instruction Project (DLA) ..... HCLIP
Harvard Divinity School, Cambridge, MA [*OCLC symbol*] (OCLC) ..... BHA
Harvard Educational Review [*A publication*] (DLA) ..... Harv Ed Rev
Harvard Educational Review [*A publication*] (BRI) ..... HER
Harvard Environmental Law Review [*A publication*] (DLA) ..... Harv Env L Rev
Harvard Environmental Law Society (EA) ..... ELS
Harvard Expedition to Samaria (BJA) ..... HES
Harvard Gay & Lesbian Review [*A publication*] (BRI) ..... H G & L Rev
Harvard Graduate School of Education ..... HGSE
Harvard Group Scale of Hypnotic Susceptibility [*Psychology*] ..... HGSHS
Harvard, IL [*AM radio station call letters*] ..... WMCW
Harvard Industries [*NASDAQ symbol*] (TTSB) ..... HAVA
Harvard Industries, Inc. [*Associated Press*] (SAG) ..... HarvI
Harvard Industries, Inc. [*Associated Press*] (SAG) ..... HarvInd
Harvard Industries, Inc. [*NASDAQ symbol*] (NQ) ..... HAVA
Harvard Institute for International Development [*Harvard University*] [*Research center*] (RCD) ..... HIID
Harvard International Law Club. Bulletin [*A publication*] (DLA) ..... Harv Int'l L Club Bull
Harvard International Law Club. Journal [*A publication*] (DLA) ..... Harv Int'l L Club J
Harvard International Review [*A publication*] ..... HIR
Harvard Journal of Asiatic Studies [*A publication*] (BRI) ..... HJAS
Harvard Law Library. Information Bulletin [*A publication*] (DLA) ..... Harv L Lib Inf Bull
Harvard Law Review [*A publication*] (BRI) ..... HLR
Harvard Law School [*Massachusetts*] ..... HLS
Harvard Law School. Record [*A publication*] (DLA) ..... Harv LS Rec
Harvard Musical Association, Boston, MA [*Library symbol Library of Congress*] (LCLS) ..... MBHM
Harvard Negotiation Project ..... HNP
Harvard - Oak Ridge [*Massachusetts*] [*Seismograph station code, US Geological Survey*] (SEIS) ..... HRV
Harvard Pilgrim Health Care ..... HPHC
Harvard Pilgrim Healthcare ..... HPHC
Harvard Presentation Graphics [*Software Publishing Corp.*] [*Computer software*] ..... HPG
Harvard Project Physics ..... HPP
Harvard Radio Meteor Project ..... HRMP
Harvard Securities Group PLC (MHDW) ..... HARVY
Harvard Semitic Museum (BJA) ..... HSM
Harvard Step Test [*Physical tolerance test*] ..... HST
Harvard Student Agencies [*Inc.*] ..... HSA
Harvard Studies in Classical Philology [*A publication*] (OCD) ..... Harv Stud
Harvard Total Project Manager [*Computer software*] ..... HTPM
Harvard Ukrainian Research Institute ..... HURI
Harvard University [*Massachusetts*] ..... HARV
Harvard University (GAGS) ..... Harvard U
Harvard University [*Cambridge, MA*] ..... HU
Harvard University [*Cambridge, MA*] ..... HUX
Harvard University, Afro-American Studies, Lamont Undergraduate Library, Cambridge, MA [*Library symbol Library of Congress*] (LCLS) ..... MH-AA
Harvard University, Andover-Harvard Theological Library, Cambridge, MA [*Library symbol Library of Congress*] (LCLS) ..... MH-AH
Harvard University Archives, Cambridge, MA [*Library symbol Library of Congress*] (LCLS) ..... MH-Ar
Harvard University, Arnold Arboretum, Cambridge, MA [*Library symbol Library of Congress*] (LCLS) ..... MH-A
Harvard University, Arnold Arboretum, Horticultural Library, Jamaica Plain, MA [*Library symbol Library of Congress*] (LCLS) ..... MH-HJ
Harvard University, Biochemical Sciences Tutorial Library, Cambridge, MA [*Library symbol Library of Congress*] (LCLS) ..... MH-BS
Harvard University, Biological Laboratories, Cambridge, MA [*Library symbol Library of Congress*] (LCLS) ..... MH-BL
Harvard University, Blue Hill Meteorological Observatory, Cambridge, MA [*Library symbol Library of Congress*] (LCLS) ..... MH-BH
Harvard University, Busch-Reisinger Museum of Germanic Culture, Cambridge, MA [*Library symbol Library of Congress*] (LCLS) ..... MH-BR
Harvard University, Cabot Science Library, Cambridge, MA [*OCLC symbol*] (OCLC) ..... CLS
Harvard University, Cambridge, MA [*OCLC symbol*] (OCLC) ..... HLS
Harvard University, Cambridge, MA [*OCLC symbol*] (OCLC) ..... HUL
Harvard University, Cambridge, MA [*Library symbol Library of Congress*] (LCLS) ..... MH
Harvard University, Career Reference Library, Cambridge, MA [*Library symbol Library of Congress*] (LCLS) ..... MH-CL
Harvard University, Center for Analysis of Health Practices, Cambridge, MA [*Library symbol Library of Congress*] (LCLS) ..... MH-HP
Harvard University, Center for European Studies, Cambridge, MA [*Library symbol Library of Congress*] (LCLS) ..... MH-ES
Harvard University, Center for International Affairs, Semitic Museum, Cambridge,MA [*Library symbol Library of Congress*] (LCLS) ..... MH-CI
Harvard University, Center for Middle Eastern Studies, Cambridge, MA [*Library symbol Library of Congress*] (LCLS) ..... MH-ME

Harvard University, Center for Population Studies, Boston, MA [*Library symbol Library of Congress*] (LCLS) .... MH-CP
Harvard University Character Recognizer [*Computer science*] .... HUCR
Harvard University, Charles Warren Center for Studies in American History, Cambridge, MA [*Library symbol Library of Congress*] (LCLS) .... MH-WA
Harvard University, Chemistry Library, Cambridge, MA [*Library symbol Library of Congress*] (LCLS) .... MH-C
Harvard University, Child Memorial and English Tutorial Library, Cambridge, MA [*Library symbol Library of Congress*] (LCLS) .... MH-CM
Harvard University, Collection of Historic Scientific Instruments Collection, Cambridge, MA [*Library symbol*] [*Library of Congress*] (LCLS) .... MH-IC
Harvard University, Commission on Extension Courses, Cambridge, MA [*Library symbol Library of Congress*] (LCLS) .... MH-CE
Harvard University, Committee on Experimental Geology and Geophysics, Hoffman Laboratory, Cambridge, MA [*Library symbol Library of Congress*] (LCLS) .... MH-GG
Harvard University Division of Engineering and Applied Physics [*Cambridge, MA*] .... HU/DEAP
Harvard University, Documentation Center on Contemporary Japan, Cambridge, MA [*Library symbol Library of Congress*] (LCLS) .... MH-DJ
Harvard University, East Asian Research Center, Cambridge, MA [*Library symbol Library of Congress*] (LCLS) .... MH-EA
Harvard University, East Asian Studies Reading Room, Cambridge, MA [*Library symbol Library of Congress*] (LCLS) .... MH-ER
Harvard University, Farlow Reference Library, Cambridge, MA [*Library symbol Library of Congress*] (LCLS) .... MH-F
Harvard University, Fine Arts Library, Cambridge, MA [*Library symbol Library of Congress*] (LCLS) .... MH-FA
Harvard University, Frances Loeb Library, Cambridge, MA [*OCLC symbol*] (OCLC) .... FLL
Harvard University, Fred N. Robinson Celtic Seminar, Cambridge, MA [*Library symbol Library of Congress*] (LCLS) .... MH-RC
Harvard University, Geological Sciences Library, Cambridge, MA [*Library symbol Library of Congress*] (LCLS) .... MH-GS
Harvard University, George David Birkhoff Mathematics Library, Cambridge, MA [*Library symbol Library of Congress*] (LCLS) .... MH-BM
Harvard University, George R. Agassiz Station, Cambridge, MA [*Library symbol Library of Congress*] (LCLS) .... MH-AS
Harvard University, Godfrey Lowell Cabot Science Library, Cambridge, MA [*Library symbol Library of Congress*] (LCLS) .... MH-CS
Harvard University, Gordon McKay Library, Cambridge, MA [*Library symbol Library of Congress*] (LCLS) .... MH-GM
Harvard University, Graduate School of Business Administration, Boston, MA [*Library symbol Library of Congress*] (LCLS) .... MH-BA
Harvard University, Graduate School of Design, Cambridge, MA [*Library symbol Library of Congress*] (LCLS) .... MH-SD
Harvard University, Graduate School of Education, Cambridge, MA [*Library symbol Library of Congress*] (LCLS) .... MH-Ed
Harvard University, Gray Herbarium, Cambridge, MA [*Library symbol Library of Congress*] (LCLS) .... MH-G
Harvard University, Gutman Library, Cambridge, MA [*OCLC symbol*] (OCLC) .... HMG
Harvard University, Hamilton A. R. Gibb Islamic Seminar, Cambridge, MA [*Library symbol Library of Congress*] (LCLS) .... MH-GI
Harvard University, Harvard College Observatory, Cambridge, MA [*Library symbol Library of Congress*] (LCLS) .... MH-O
Harvard University, Harvard Forest Library, Petersham, MA [*Library symbol Library of Congress*] (LCLS) .... MH-HF
Harvard University, Harvard Institute for International Development, Cambridge, MA [*Library symbol*] [*Library of Congress*] (LCLS) ... MH-ID
Harvard University, Harvard Radio Astronomy Center, Fort Davis, TX [*Library symbol Library of Congress*] (LCLS) .... MH-RA
Harvard University, Harvard University Development Office, Cambridge, MA [*Library symbol*] [*Library of Congress*] (LCLS) .... MH-DO
Harvard University, Harvard-Yenching Institute [*Chinese-Japanese Library*],Cambridge, MA [*Library symbol Library of Congress*] (LCLS) ...... NH-HY
Harvard University, Harvard-Yenching Library, Cambridge, MA [*Library symbol Library of Congress*] (LCLS) .... MH-HY
Harvard University, Herbert Weir Smyth Classical Library, Cambridge, MA [*Library symbol Library of Congress*] (LCLS) .... MH-SC
Harvard University, Hilles Library of Radcliffe College, Cambridge, MA [*Library symbol Library of Congress*] (LCLS) .... MH-Hi
Harvard University, History Department Library, Cambridge, MA [*Library symbol Library of Congress*] (LCLS) .... MH-HD
Harvard University, History of Science Library, Cambridge, MA [*Library symbol Library of Congress*] (LCLS) .... MH-HS
Harvard University, Houghton Library, Cambridge, MA [*Library symbol Library of Congress*] (LCLS) .... MH-H
Harvard University, John Peabody Monks Library, Cambridge, MA [*Library symbol Library of Congress*] (LCLS) .... MH-MH
Harvard University, Kennedy Inter-Faculty Program in Medical Ethics, Cambridge, MA [*Library symbol Library of Congress*] (LCLS) .... MH-KM
Harvard University, Kennedy School for Government, Cambridge, MA [*OCLC symbol*] (OCLC) .... KSG
Harvard University, Kennedy School of Government, Cambridge, MA [*Library symbol Library of Congress*] (LCLS) .... MH-KG
Harvard University, Lamont Undergraduate Library, Cambridge, MA [*Library symbol Library of Congress*] (LCLS) .... MH-Lm
Harvard University, Law School, Cambridge, MA [*Library symbol Library of Congress*] (LCLS) .... MH-L
Harvard University, Linguistics Library, Cambridge, MA [*Library symbol Library of Congress*] (LCLS) .... MH-Li
Harvard University, Littauer Library of the Kennedy School of Government, Cambridge, MA [*Library symbol Library of Congress*] (LCLS) .... MH-PA

Harvard University, Lucien Howe Library of Ophthalmology, Boston, MA [*Library symbol Library of Congress*] (LCLS) .... MH-HO
Harvard University Medical School, Countway Library of Medicine, Boston, MA [*OCLC symbol*] (OCLC) .... HMS
Harvard University, Milman Parry Collection of Oral Literature, Cambridge, MA [*Library symbol Library of Congress*] (LCLS) .... MH-PL
Harvard University, Monographic Cataloging Support Service, Cambridge, MA [*OCLC symbol*] (OCLC) .... MCS
Harvard University, Museum of Comparative Zoology, Cambridge, MA [*Library symbol Library of Congress*] (LCLS) .... MH-Z
Harvard University, Music Library, Cambridge, MA [*Library symbol Library of Congress*] (LCLS) .... MH-Mu
Harvard University, Near Eastern Languages and Literatures Library, Cambridge, MA [*Library symbol Library of Congress*] (LCLS) .... MH-NE
Harvard University, Nieman Collection of Contemporary Journalism, Cambridge, MA [*Library symbol Library of Congress*] (LCLS) .... MH-NJ
Harvard University, Oakes Ames Library of Economic Botany, Cambridge, MA [*Library symbol Library of Congress*] (LCLS) .... MH-EB
Harvard University, Oakes Ames Orchid Library, Cambridge, MA [*Library symbol Library of Congress*] (LCLS) .... MH-AO
Harvard University, Palaeography Library, Cambridge, MA [*Library symbol Library of Congress*] (LCLS) .... MH-PC
Harvard University, Peabody Museum, Cambridge, MA [*Library symbol Library of Congress*] (LCLS) .... MH-P
Harvard University, Personnel Office Library, Cambridge, MA [*Library symbol Library of Congress*] (LCLS) .... MH-PO
Harvard University, Physics Research Library, Cambridge, MA [*Library symbol Library of Congress*] (LCLS) .... MH-PR
Harvard University, Preservation Center, Cambridge, MA [*Library symbol*] [*Library of Congress*] (LCLS) .... MH-Pv
Harvard University Press (DGA) .... HUP
Harvard University, Program for Science and International Affairs Library, Cambridge, MA [*Library symbol Library of Congress*] (LCLS) .... MH-SI
Harvard University, Psychology Research Library, Cambridge, MA [*Library symbol Library of Congress*] (LCLS) .... MH-Ps
Harvard University, Public Policy Program, Cambridge, MA [*Library symbol Library of Congress*] (LCLS) .... MH-PP
Harvard University, RISM-US Project Center, Cambridge, MA [*Library symbol*] [*Library of Congress*] (LCLS) .... MH-RI
Harvard University, Robbins Library of Philosophy, Cambridge, MA [*Library symbol Library of Congress*] (LCLS) .... MH-RP
Harvard University, Rubel Asiatic Research Bureau, Fogg Art Museum, Cambridge, MA [*Library symbol Library of Congress Obsolete*] (LCLS) .... MH-RB
Harvard University, Russian Research Center, Cambridge, MA [*Library symbol Library of Congress*] (LCLS) .... MH-R
Harvard University, Sanskrit Library, Cambridge, MA [*Library symbol Library of Congress*] (LCLS) .... MH-SL
Harvard University, Schering Foundation Library, Boston, MA [*Library symbol Library of Congress*] (LCLS) .... MH-SF
Harvard University, Science and Public Police Program Library, Cambridge, MA [*Library symbol Library of Congress*] (LCLS) .... MH-SP
Harvard University, Social Relations Library, Cambridge, MA [*Library symbol Library of Congress*] (LCLS) .... MH-SR
Harvard University, Statistics Library, Cambridge, MA [*Library symbol Library of Congress*] (LCLS) .... MH-S
Harvard University, Ticknor Library of Modern Languages, Cambridge, MA [*Library symbol Library of Congress*] (LCLS) .... MH-ML
Harvard University, Tozzer Library, Cambridge, MA [*OCLC symbol*] (OCLC) .... TOZ
Harvard University, Ukrainian Research Institute Reference Library, Cambridge, MA [*Library symbol Library of Congress*] (LCLS) .... MH-UR
Harvard Vocarium [*Record label*] .... Harv
Harvard Women's Law Journal [*A publication*] (DLA) .... Harv Women's LJ
Harvard World Tax Series [*A publication*] (DLA) .... Harv W Tax Ser
Harvard, Yale, and Princeton Universities .... HYP
Harvard-Smithsonian Reference Atmosphere .... HSRA
Harvest .... HARV
Harvest Aviation Ltd. [*British ICAO designator*] (FAAC) .... HAG
Harvest Financial Corp. [*Associated Press*] (SAG) .... HarvstFn
Harvest Financial Corp. [*NASDAQ symbol*] (SAG) .... HVEF
Harvest Help [*An association British*] (EAIO) .... HH
Harvest Home Financial Corp. [*Associated Press*] (SAG) .... HarvestH
Harvest Home Financial Corp. [*NASDAQ symbol*] (SAG) .... HHFC
Harvest Home Finl [*NASDAQ symbol*] (TTSB) .... HHFC
Harvest Index [*Agronomy*] .... HI
Harvey Cushing Society [*Later, AANS*] (EA) .... HCS
Harvey Entertainment [*NASDAQ symbol*] (TTSB) .... HRVY
Harvey Entertainment Co. [*Associated Press*] (SAG) .... HarveyE
Harvey Entertainment Co. [*NASDAQ symbol*] (SAG) .... HRVY
Harvey Gray & Associates .... HGA
Harvey, IL [*AM radio station call letters*] .... WBEE
Harvey Murine Sarcoma Virus [*Medicine*] (MEDA) .... HaMSV
Harvey Murine Sarcoma Virus .... HaMuSV
Harvey, ND [*AM radio station call letters*] .... KHND
Harvey Public Library, Harvey, IL [*Library symbol Library of Congress*] (LCLS) .... IHa
Harvey Public Library, Harvey, ND [*Library symbol Library of Congress*] (LCLS) .... NdHa
Harvey Ratner and Marvin Wolfenson [*Proprietors of Target Centre basketball arena*] (ECON) .... HARV and MARV
Harvey Society (EA) .... HS
Harvey Universal, Inc. [*NASDAQ symbol*] (SAG) .... HARV
Harvey Universal, Inc. [*Associated Press*] (SAG) .... HarveyU
Harvey Woods Ltd. [*Toronto Stock Exchange symbol*] .... HWL

Harveys Casinos Resorts [*Associated Press*] (SAG) .... HarvCas
Harveys Casinos Resorts [*NYSE symbol*] (SAG) .... HVY
Harwell Atomic Energy Establishment .... HAEE
Harwell Automated Loans [*Library circulation system*] .... HAL
Harwell Electro Osmosis Process [*British*] (NUCP) .... HELOS
Harwell Electrochemical Ion Exchange Process [*British*] (NUCP) .... HELIX
Harwich [*Municipal borough in England*] .... HARW
Harwich, MA [*FM radio station call letters*] .... WCCT
Harwich Port Library Association, Harwich Port, MA [*Library symbol*] [*Library of Congress*] (LCLS) .... MHp
Harwichport, MA [*FM radio station call letters*] (RBYB) .... WJCO-FM
Harwichport, MA [*FM radio station call letters*] (RBYB) .... WUNX
Harwin Exploration & Development, Inc. [*Vancouver Stock Exchange symbol*] .... HRN
Harwood Academic Publishers [*British*] .... HAP
Harwood Foundation, Taos, NM [*Library symbol Library of Congress*] (LCLS) .... NmTHF
Harwood's Practice of United States Naval Courts-Martial [*A publication*] (DLA) .... Har Ct Mar
Has .... H
Has Been Drinking [*Medical notation*] .... HBD
Has Been Reviewed (AAG) .... HBR
Has Been Reviewed and Concurred With (AAG) .... HBRACW
Has Not Voided [*Urology*] .... HNV
Has Voided [*Medicine*] (DAVI) .... HV
Hasbro, Inc. [*AMEX symbol*] (SPSG) .... HAS
Hasbro, Inc. [*Associated Press*] (SAG) .... Hasbro
Hasbrouck Heights Free Public Library, Hasbrouck Heights, NJ [*Library symbol Library of Congress*] (LCLS) .... NjHas
Hasbrouck's Reports [*Idaho*] [*A publication*] (DLA) .... Hasb
Hasenstrick [*Switzerland ICAO location identifier*] (ICLI) .... LSPK
Hash Algorithm Information Table .... HAIT
Hash Algorithm Library .... HAL
Hashed Index Sequential Access Method (PDAA) .... HAISAM
Hashemite Kingdom of Jordan (BARN) .... HKJ
Hashimoto's Thyroiditis [*Medicine*] (DMAA) .... HT
Hashomer Hatzair (EA) .... HH
Hashomer Hatzair Socialist Zionist Youth Movement (EA) .... HHSZYM
Hashomer Hatzair Zionist Youth Organization [*Later, HHSZYM*] (EA) .... HZYO
Hashtpar [*Iran*] [*ICAO location identifier*] (ICLI) .... OIGH
Haskel International, Inc. [*Associated Press*] (SAG) .... Haskel
Haskel International, Inc. [*NASDAQ symbol*] (SAG) .... HSKL
Haskel Intl 'A' [*NASDAQ symbol*] (TTSB) .... HSKL
Haskell Elementary School, Rockford, IL [*Library symbol*] [*Library of Congress*] (LCLS) .... IRoHaE
Haskell Free Library, Rock Island, Quebec [*Library symbol National Library of Canada*] (NLC) .... QRIB
Haskell, TX [*Location identifier FAA*] (FAAL) .... AKL
Haskell, TX [*FM radio station call letters*] .... KVRP
Haskell's Reports for United States Courts in Maine (Fox's Decisions) [*A publication*] (DLA) .... Hask
Haslam's Medical Jurisprudence [*A publication*] (DLA) .... Hasl Med Jur
Hassan Addakhil Dam [*Morocco*] [*Seismograph station code, US Geological Survey*] (SEIS) .... HAD
Hasselblad Data Camera (MCD) .... HDC
Hasselblad Electric Camera .... HEC
Hasselblad Electric Data Camera .... HEDC
Hasselblad Reflex Camera (MCD) .... HRC
Hasselt [*Belgium ICAO location identifier*] (ICLI) .... EBZH
Hassfurt/Mainwiesen [*Germany ICAO location identifier*] (ICLI) .... EDQT
Hassi Messaoud [*Algeria*] [*Airport symbol*] (OAG) .... HME
Hassi-Messaoud/Oued Irara [*Algeria*] [*ICAO location identifier*] (ICLI) .... DAUH
Hassium [*Proposed name and symbol for recently-discovered element*] .... Hs
Hassle [*Sweden*] [*Research code symbol*] .... H
Hasslosa [*Sweden ICAO location identifier*] (ICLI) .... ESFH
Hastech Users Group (EA) .... HUG
Hastings [*Sierra Leone*] [*ICAO location identifier*] (ICLI) .... GFHA
Hastings [*New Zealand*] [*Seismograph station code, US Geological Survey Closed*] (SEIS) .... HAS
Hastings [*Nebraska*] [*Airport symbol*] (OAG) .... HSI
Hastings and Prince Edward County Health Unit, Belleville, Ontario [*Library symbol National Library of Canada*] (BIB) .... OBEHP
Hastings and Prince Edward Regiment [*British military*] (DMA) .... HPER
Hastings Branch, Northumberland County Public Library, Ontario [*Library symbol National Library of Canada*] (BIB) .... OHN
Hastings Center (EA) .... HC
Hastings Center Report [*A publication*] (BRI) .... Hast Cen R
Hastings College, Hastings, NE [*OCLC symbol*] (OCLC) .... NBH
Hastings College, Hastings, NE [*Library symbol Library of Congress*] (LCLS) .... NbHC
Hastings County Historical Society, Belleville, Ontario [*Library symbol National Library of Canada*] (BIB) .... OBEH
Hastings' Encyclopaedia of Religion and Ethics [*A publication*] (BJA) .... HERE
Hastings Environment Council (EERA) .... HEC
Hastings' International and Comparative Law Review [*A publication*] (DLA) .... Hast Int & Comp L Rev
Hastings Manufacturing Co. [*Associated Press*] (SAG) .... Hasting
Hastings Manufacturing Co. [*AMEX symbol*] (SPSG) .... HMF
Hastings Mfg [*AMEX symbol*] (TTSB) .... HMF
Hastings, MI [*AM radio station call letters*] .... WBCH
Hastings, MI [*FM radio station call letters*] .... WBCH-FM
Hastings, MN [*AM radio station call letters*] .... KDWA
Hastings, NE [*FM radio station call letters*] .... KCNT
Hastings, NE [*FM radio station call letters*] .... KEZH
Hastings, NE [*FM radio station call letters*] (RBYB) .... KFKX-FM
Hastings, NE [*AM radio station call letters*] .... KHAS
Hastings, NE [*Television station call letters*] .... KHAS-TV
Hastings, NE [*FM radio station call letters*] .... KHNE
Hastings, NE [*Television station call letters*] .... KHNE-TV
Hastings, NE [*AM radio station call letters*] .... KICS
Hastings, NE [*Location identifier FAA*] (FAAL) .... PSS
Hastings Public Library, Hastings, MI [*Library symbol Library of Congress*] (LCLS) .... MiHas
Hastings Public Library, Hastings, NE [*Library symbol Library of Congress*] (LCLS) .... NbH
Hastings' Reports [*69, 70 Maine*] [*A publication*] (DLA) .... Hast
Hastings' Shorter Dictionary of the Bible [*A publication*] (BJA) .... HSDB
Hastings-On-Hudson Public Library, Hastings-On-Hudson, NY [*Library symbol Library of Congress*] (LCLS) .... NHas
Hasvik [*Norway ICAO location identifier*] (ICLI) .... ENHK
Hasvik [*Norway*] [*Airport symbol*] (OAG) .... HAA
Hat and Allied Feltmakers' Research Association [*British*] (BI) .... HAFRA
Hat Block and Die Makers Association (EA) .... HBDMA
Hat Institute (EA) .... HI
Hat Leather Association (EA) .... HLA
HAT [*Hypoxanthine-Aminopterin-Thymidine*] **with Ouabain** [*Growth medium*] [*Biochemistry*] .... HOT
Hatch [*Technical drawings*] .... H
Hatch Act [*1887*] .... HA
Hatch Associates Ltd., Toronto, ON, Canada [*Library symbol*] [*Library of Congress*] (LCLS) .... CaOTHA
Hatch Associates Ltd., Toronto, Ontario [*Library symbol National Library of Canada*] (NLC) .... OTHA
Hatch, NM [*FM radio station call letters*] (RBYB) .... KVLC
Hatch Public Library, Hatch, NM [*Library symbol Library of Congress*] (LCLS) .... NmHa
Hatchback [*Automotive advertising*] .... HB
Hatchback [*Automotive advertising*] .... HCHBK
Hatchback (BARN) .... Htbk
Hatched (ABBR) .... HACHD
Hatcher's Kansas Digest [*A publication*] (DLA) .... Hatcher's Kan Dig
Hatcher's Kansas Digest [*A publication*] (DLA) .... Kan Dig
Hatchery (ABBR) .... HACHY
Hatchery .... HTCHY
Hatching (ABBR) .... HACHG
Hatchlike Experiment Module [*NASA*] (NASA) .... HEM
Hatchway (DS) .... HA
Hatchway (ABBR) .... HACHWY
Hate Crimes Statistics Act .... HCSA
Hateruma [*Japan*] [*Airport symbol*] (OAG) .... HTR
Hateruma [*Ryukyu Islands*] [*ICAO location identifier*] (ICLI) .... RORH
Hatfield [*British ICAO location identifier*] (ICLI) .... EGTH
Hatfield BAE [*British ICAO designator*] (FAAC) .... HFD
Hatfield Consultants Ltd., West Vancouver, BC, Canada [*Library symbol Library of Congress*] (LCLS) .... CaBWvHC
Hatfield Consultants Ltd., West Vancouver, British Columbia [*Library symbol National Library of Canada*] (NLC) .... BWVHC
Hatfield Executive Aviation Ltd. [*British ICAO designator*] (FAAC) .... HEX
Hatfield Marine Science Center [*Marine science*] (OSRA) .... HMSC
Hatfield Marine Science Center (USDC) .... HMSC
Hatfield Peverel [*England*] .... HATFPEV
Hathaway Corp. [*NASDAQ symbol*] (NQ) .... HATH
Hathaway Corp. [*Associated Press*] (SAG) .... Hathwy
Hatia [*Bangladesh*] [*Airport symbol*] (AD) .... HAE
Hatillo, PR [*AM radio station call letters*] .... WMSW
Hatizyo [*Japan*] [*Geomagnetic observatory code*] .... HTY
Hato Corozal [*Colombia*] [*Airport symbol*] (OAG) .... HTZ
Hatran (BJA) .... Hat
Hatsell's Parliamentary Precedents [*1290-1818*] [*A publication*] (DLA) .... Hats
Hatsell's Parliamentary Precedents [*1290-1818*] [*A publication*] (DLA) .... Hats Pr
Hatsell's Parliamentary Precedents [*1290-1818*] [*A publication*] (DLA) .... Hats Prec
Hatteras Income Sec [*NYSE symbol*] (TTSB) .... HAT
Hatteras Income Securities, Inc. [*NYSE symbol*] (SPSG) .... HAT
Hatteras Income Securities, Inc. [*Associated Press*] (SAG) .... HattSe
Hatteras, NC [*Location identifier FAA*] (FAAL) .... HAT
Hatteras, NC [*FM radio station call letters*] .... WYND
Hatters' Fur Cutters Association of America [*Formerly, HFCAUS*] (EA) .... HFCAA
Hatters' Fur Cutters Association of the United States [*Later, HFCAA*] .... HFCAUS
Hatters Machinery and Equipment Association [*Defunct*] (EA) .... HMEA
Hattiesburg [*Mississippi*] [*Airport symbol*] (AD) .... HBG
Hattiesburg, Camp Shelby, MS [*Location identifier FAA*] (FAAL) .... HLW
Hattiesburg, MI [*FM radio station call letters*] (RBYB) .... WAII-FM
Hattiesburg, MS [*Location identifier FAA*] (FAAL) .... HBG
Hattiesburg, MS [*Location identifier FAA*] (FAAL) .... HHB
Hattiesburg, MS [*Location identifier FAA*] (FAAL) .... LBY
Hattiesburg, MS [*Location identifier FAA*] (FAAL) .... SLJ
Hattiesburg, MS [*AM radio station call letters*] .... WBKH
Hattiesburg, MS [*AM radio station call letters*] .... WFOR
Hattiesburg, MS [*FM radio station call letters*] .... WHER
Hattiesburg, MS [*Television station call letters*] .... WHLT
Hattiesburg, MS [*AM radio station call letters*] .... WHLV
Hattiesburg, MS [*AM radio station call letters*] .... WHSY
Hattiesburg, MS [*FM radio station call letters*] .... WJMG
Hattiesburg, MS [*AM radio station call letters*] .... WORV
Hattiesburg, MS [*FM radio station call letters*] .... WUSM
Hattiesburg, MS [*FM radio station call letters*] (RBYB) .... WXRR
Hattiesburg Public Library, Hattiesburg, MS [*Library symbol Library of Congress*] (LCLS) .... MsHa
Hatton Heritage Association (EA) .... HHA

Hattusilis (BJA) ... Hatt
Hatz Club (EA) ... HC
Haubitzgranate [*Howitzer Shell*] [*German military - World War II*] ... HGR
Hauch [*Antigen*] [*Immunology*] ... H
Haudompre [*France*] [*Seismograph station code, US Geological Survey*] (SEIS) ... HAU
Haugesund [*Norway*] [*Airport symbol*] (OAG) ... HAU
Haugesund/Karmoy [*Norway ICAO location identifier*] (ICLI) ... ENHD
Haughtier (ABBR) ... HAGTR
Haughtiest (ABBR) ... HAGTST
Haughtily (ABBR) ... HAGTY
Haughtiness (ABBR) ... HAGTNS
Haughton, LA [*FM radio station call letters*] ... KDKS-FM
Haul (MSA) ... HL
Haul Down and Handling System [*Canadian Navy*] ... HDHS
Hauling ... HLG
Hauling Class ... HC
Hauling Code ... HC
Haultain Resources Ltd. [*Vancouver Stock Exchange symbol*] ... HAU
Haunt Hunters (EA) ... HH
Hauppague Digital Wrrt'A' [*NASDAQ symbol*] (TTSB) ... HAUPW
Hauppauge Digital [*NASDAQ symbol*] (TTSB) ... HAUP
Hauppauge Digital, Inc. [*NASDAQ symbol*] (SAG) ... HAUP
Hauppauge Digital, Inc. [*Associated Press*] (SAG) ... HaupD
Hauppauge Digital, Inc. [*Associated Press*] (SAG) ... HaupgD
Hauptbahnhof [*Main Railroad Station*] [*German*] ... HBF
Hauptpunkte [*Crystallography*] ... HP
Hauptsatz [*Leading Theme*] [*Music*] ... HS
Hauptverband der Deutschen Holz und Kunststoffe Verarbeitenden Industrie und Verwandter Industriezweige eV [*Germany*] (EY) ... HDH
Hauptverbandplatz [*Clearing Station*] [*German military - World War II*] ... HVB
Hauptwachtmeister [*First Sergeant*] [*German military - World War II*] ... HW
Hauptwerk [*Masterpiece*] [*German*] ... HAUPTW
Hauptwerk [*Masterpiece*] [*German*] ... HK
Hauptwerk [*Masterpiece*] [*German*] ... HPTW
Hauptwerk [*Masterpiece*] [*German*] ... HW
Hauptwiderstandslinie [*Main line of resistance in a delaying action*] [*German military - World War II*] ... HWL
Hauptzollamt [*Chief Customs Office*] [*German*] (DLA) ... HZA
Haura [*South Arabia (Yemen)*] [*Airport symbol*] (AD) ... HRA
Hauriendus [*To Be Drunk*] [*Pharmacy*] (ROG) ... HAURIEND
Hausa [*MARC language code Library of Congress*] (LCCP) ... hau
Hausen Am Albis [*Switzerland ICAO location identifier*] (ICLI) ... LSZN
Hauser Chemical Research [*NASDAQ symbol*] (TTSB) ... HAUS
Hauser Chemical Research, Inc. [*NASDAQ symbol*] (SAG) ... HAUS
Hauser Chemical Research, Inc. [*Associated Press*] (SAG) ... HausCh
Hauser, Inc. [*NASDAQ symbol*] (SAG) ... HAUS
Hauser, Inc. [*Associated Press*] (SAG) ... Hauser
Haustus [*A Drink*] [*Pharmacy*] ... H
Haustus [*A Drink*] [*Pharmacy*] ... HAUST
Haustus [*A Drink*] [*Pharmacy*] ... HT
Haustus Purgans [*Purging Draught*] [*Pharmacy*] (ROG) ... HAUST PURG
Haustus Purgans [*Purging Draught*] [*Pharmacy*] (ROG) ... HP
Haustus Purgans Noster [*Purging Draught from the Doctor's Own Prescription*] [*Pharmacy*] (ROG) ... HPN
Haut Commissariat des Nations Unies pour les Refugies [*United Nations High Commission for Refugees - UNHCR*] [*Switzerland*] ... HCR
Haut Parleur [*Loudspeaker*] [*French*] ... HP
Hautboy [*Oboe*] ... HAUT
Haute Societe Protestante [*Protestant High Society*] (IIA) ... HSP
Haute-Contre [*Alto*] [*Music*] ... HC
Haut-Einheits-Dosis [*Unit Skin Dose*] [*Radiation therapy*] ... HED
Haut-Erythem-Dosis [*Skin erythema dose*] [*Radiation therapy*] (DAVI) ... HED
Hautes Etudes Commerciales (DD) ... HEC
Havana [*Cuba*] [*Airport symbol*] (OAG) ... HAV
Havana [*Cuba*] [*Geomagnetic observatory code*] ... HVN
Havana, FL [*FM radio station call letters*] ... WMLO
Havana, IL [*FM radio station call letters*] ... WDUK
Havana Rabbit Breeders Association (EA) ... HRBA
Havasu Airlines [*ICAO designator*] (AD) ... HW
Havasupai [*Arizona*] [*Airport symbol*] (OAG) ... HAE
Have (ROG) ... H
Have a Nice Day ... HAND
Have Alimony, Will Keep ... HAWK
Have Complied ... HAVCO
Have Not Yet Begun to Fight [*Simulated war game*] ... HOTBUN
Have Report [*Navy*] (ANA) ... HAVREP
Have You Stored Answers to Questions [*Computer science*] ... HAYSTAQ
Haveeru News Service [*Maldives*] (EY) ... HNS
Havelet Leasing Ltd. [*British ICAO designator*] (FAAC) ... HLL
Havelock, NC [*AM radio station call letters*] ... WCPQ
Havelock, NC [*FM radio station call letters*] ... WMSQ
Havelock North [*New Zealand*] [*Seismograph station code, US Geological Survey Closed*] (SEIS) ... HNZ
Havelock Public Library, Ontario [*Library symbol National Library of Canada*] (BIB) ... OHA
Havelock-Craven County Public Library, Havelock, NC [*Library symbol Library of Congress*] (LCLS) ... NcHav
Haven (ADA) ... H
Haven [*Commonly used*] (OPSA) ... HAVEN
Haven [*Commonly used*] (OPSA) ... HAVN
Haven [*Maps and charts*] ... Hn
Haven (MCD) ... HVN
Haven ... HVN
Haven Bancorp [*Associated Press*] (SAG) ... HavenB
Haven Bancorp [*NASDAQ symbol*] (SAG) ... HAVN
Haverfield Corp. [*Associated Press*] (SAG) ... Havrfld
Haverfield Corp. [*NASDAQ symbol*] (NQ) ... HVFD
Haverford College, Haverford, PA [*OCLC symbol*] (OCLC) ... HVC
Haverford College, Haverford, PA [*OCLC symbol*] (OCLC) ... HVF
Haverford College, Haverford, PA [*Library symbol Library of Congress*] (LCLS) ... PHC
Haverford State Hospital, Haverford, PA [*OCLC symbol*] (OCLC) ... PHH
Haverford Township Free Library, Havertown, PA [*Library symbol Library of Congress*] (LCLS) ... PHav
Haverfordwest [*British ICAO location identifier*] (ICLI) ... EGFE
Haverfordwest [*Wales*] [*Airport symbol*] (AD) ... HFW
Havergal Brian Society (EAIO) ... HBS
Haverhill, MA [*AM radio station call letters*] ... WHAV
Haverhill, MA [*FM radio station call letters*] ... WLYT
Haverhill, MA [*FM radio station call letters*] (RBYB) ... WXRV
Haverhill, NH [*FM radio station call letters*] ... WYKR
Haverhill Public Library, Haverhill, MA [*Library symbol Library of Congress*] (LCLS) ... MHa
Havering [*Borough in England*] ... HAV
Haverlift Systems Ltd., Calgary, AB, Canada [*Library symbol Library of Congress*] (LCLS) ... CaACHaS
Haverlift Systems Ltd., Calgary, Alberta [*Library symbol National Library of Canada*] (NLC) ... ACHAS
Haversine [*Mathematics*] ... HAV
Havertown, PA [*FM radio station call letters*] ... WHHS
Haverty Furniture [*NASDAQ symbol*] (TTSB) ... HAVT
Haverty Furniture Companies, Inc. [*Associated Press*] (SAG) ... Haverty
Haverty Furniture Companies, Inc. [*Associated Press*] (SAG) ... Havrty
Haverty Furniture Companies, Inc. [*NASDAQ symbol*] (NQ) ... HAVT
Haverty Furniture'A' [*NASDAQ symbol*] (TTSB) ... HAVTA
Haveth Childer Everywhere [*Key phrase in "Finnegan's Wake"*] ... HCE
Havilah [*California*] [*Seismograph station code, US Geological Survey Closed*] (SEIS) ... HAV
Haviland's Prince Edward Island Chancery Reports [*1850-72*] [*A publication*] (DLA) ... Hav Ch Rep
Haviland's Prince Edward Island Chancery Reports, by Peters [*1850-72*] [*Canada*] [*A publication*] (DLA) ... Hav
Haviland's Prince Edward Island Chancery Reports, by Peters [*1850-72*] [*Canada*] [*A publication*] (DLA) ... Peters
Haviland's Prince Edward Island Reports [*A publication*] (DLA) ... Hav PEI
Haviland's Prince Edward Island Reports [*A publication*] (DLA) ... Havil
Havildar [*British military*] (DMA) ... Hav
Havildar-Major [*British military*] (DMA) ... Hav-Maj
Hav-Info Computers, Inc. [*Vancouver Stock Exchange symbol*] ... HVC
Having (ROG) ... HG
Having Been Assigned to This Organization [*or Headquarters*] ... HBAT
Having Fun with Elvis [*Fan club*] (EA) ... HFWE
Havre [*Montana*] [*Airport symbol*] (OAG) ... HVR
Havre [*Montana*] [*ICAO location identifier*] (ICLI) ... KHVR
Havre, Antwerp, or Dunkirk [*Business term*] ... HA or D
Havre De Grace, MD [*AM radio station call letters*] ... WASA
Havre de Grace, MD [*FM radio station call letters*] ... WXCY
Havre Hill County Library, Havre, MT [*Library symbol*] [*Library of Congress*] (LCLS) ... MtHa
Havre, MT [*FM radio station call letters*] ... KNMC
Havre, MT [*AM radio station call letters*] ... KOJM
Havre, MT [*FM radio station call letters*] ... KPQX
Havre, MT [*FM radio station call letters*] ... KXEI
Havre, MT [*Location identifier FAA*] (FAAL) ... LDS
Havre Saint Pierre [*Canada*] [*Airport symbol*] (OAG) ... YGV
Havre to Hamburg [*Shipping*] ... H/H
Havre-Saint-Pierre, PQ [*FM radio station call letters*] (RBYB) ... CILE
Hawa-Air [*Belgium ICAO designator*] (FAAC) ... HWA
Hawaii [*or Hawaiian*] (WDAA) ... HA
Hawaii (KSC) ... HAW
Hawaii ... HAWA
Hawaii [*Postal code*] ... HI
Hawaii [*MARC country of publication code Library of Congress*] (LCCP) ... hiu
Hawaii [*MARC geographic area code Library of Congress*] (LCCP) ... n-us-hi
Hawaii Academy of Family Physicians (SRA) ... HAFP
Hawaii Agricultural Experiment Station [*Honolulu*] ... HAES
Hawaii Air Defense ... HAD
Hawaii Air Defense System ... HADS
Hawaii Army National Guard (CINC) ... HARNG
Hawaii Association of Nurserymen (SRA) ... HAN
Hawaii Attorney General Report [*A publication*] (DLA) ... Rep Hawaii Att'y Gen
Hawaii Bar News [*A publication*] (DLA) ... Hawaii BN
Hawaii Business Education Association (EDAC) ... HBEA
Hawaii Control Center [*Missiles*] (MUGU) ... HCC
Hawaii Council of Associations of Apartment Owners (SRA) ... HCAAO
Hawaii County Library, Hilo, HI [*Library symbol Library of Congress*] (LCLS) ... HHi
Hawaii Early Learning Profile [*Child development test*] [*Psychology*] ... HELP
Hawaii Educational Dissemination Diffusion System [*Hawaii State Department of Education*] [*Honolulu*] [*Information service or system*] (IID) ... HEDDS
Hawaii Federal [*Legal term*] (DLA) ... Haw Fed
Hawaii Flooring Association (SRA) ... HFA
Hawaii Foundation for American Freedoms (EA) ... HFAF
Hawaii Imaging Fabry-Perot Interferometer ... HIFI
Hawaii Institute of Geophysics [*University of Hawaii*] [*Seismograph station code, US Geological Survey Research center*] (SEIS) ... HIG
Hawaii Institute of Geophysics [*Marine science*] (OSRA) ... HIG

Hawaii Institute of Marine Biology [*University of Hawaii*] [*Research center*] (RCD) ... HIMB
Hawaii Institute of Tropical Agriculture and Human Resources [*University of Hawaii*] [*Research center*] (RCD) ... HITAHR
Hawaii International Services Agency ... HISA
Hawaii (Kauai) [*Spaceflight Tracking and Data Network*] [*NASA*] ... H2
Hawaii Medical Library, Inc., Honolulu, HI [*Library symbol Library of Congress*] (LCLS) ... HHH
Hawaii Medical Library, Inc., Honolulu, HI [*OCLC symbol*] (OCLC) ... HML
Hawaii Natural Energy Institute [*University of Hawaii at Manoa*] [*Research center*] (RCD) ... HNEI
Hawaii Ocean Science and Technology Park [*Research center*] (RCD) ... HOST
Hawaii Public Utilities Commission Decisions [*A publication*] (DLA) ... Hawaii PUC Dec
Hawaii Regional Library for the Blind and Physically Handicapped, Honolulu, HI [*Library symbol Library of Congress*] (LCLS) ... H-BPH
Hawaii Regional Tsunami Warning Network [*Marine science*] (OSRA) ... HRTWN
Hawaii Reports [*A publication*] (DLA) ... H
Hawaii Reports [*A publication*] (DLA) ... Haw Rep
Hawaii Reports [*A publication*] (DLA) ... Hawaii
Hawaii Reports [*A publication*] (DLA) ... Hawaii Rep
Hawaii Reports [*A publication*] (DLA) ... Hawaiian Rep
Hawaii Reports [*A publication*] (DLA) ... Hawn
Hawaii Reports [*A publication*] (DLA) ... HI
Hawaii Revised Statutes [*A publication*] (DLA) ... Haw Rev Stat
Hawaii Revised Statutes [*A publication*] (DLA) ... Hawaii Rev Stat
Hawaii Revised Statutes [*A publication*] ... HRS
Hawaii Revised Statutes Annotated [*A publication*] (AAGC) ... Haw Rev Stat Ann
Hawaii Rules and Regulations [*A publication*] (DLA) ... Hawaii Rules & Reg
Hawaii State Data Center [*Hawaii State Department of Planning and Economic Development*] [*Information service or system*] (IID) ... HSDC
Hawaii State Library System, Honolulu, HI [*Library symbol Library of Congress*] (LCLS) ... HH
Hawaii State Public Library System [*Hawaii State Department of Education*] [*Information service or system*] (IID) ... HSPLS
Hawaii Supreme Court Reports [*A publication*] (DLA) ... Haw
Hawaii Surfing Association (EA) ... HSA
Hawaii Tsunami Warning System [*Marine science*] (OSRA) ... HTWS
Hawaii Undersea Research Laboratory [*University of Hawaii*] [*Research center*] (RCD) ... HURL
Hawaii Volcanoes National Park ... HAVO
Hawaiian [*MARC language code Library of Congress*] (LCCP) ... haw
Hawaiian Air Defense Division ... HADD
Hawaiian Air Defense Identification Zone ... HADIZ
Hawaiian Air National Guard (FAAC) ... HANG
Hawaiian Airlines 'A' [*AMEX symbol*] (TTSB) ... HA
Hawaiian Airlines, Inc. [*AMEX symbol*] (SAG) ... HA
Hawaiian Airlines, Inc. [*ICAO designator*] (ICDA) ... HA
Hawaiian Airlines, Inc. [*ICAO designator*] (FAAC) ... HAL
Hawaiian Airlines, Inc. [*Associated Press*] (SAG) ... HawAir
Hawaiian Archives for Tsunamis ... HAT
Hawaiian Area Joint Committee [*Military*] (CINC) ... HAJC
Hawaiian Army and Air Force Exchange [*Military*] ... HAAFE
Hawaiian Defense Area ... HADA
Hawaiian Defense Command ... HDC
Hawaiian Department [*Army World War II*] ... HD
Hawaiian Development Irradiator [*AEC*] ... HDI
Hawaiian Elec Indus [*NYSE symbol*] (TTSB) ... HE
Hawaiian Electric Industries, Inc. [*Associated Press*] (SAG) ... HawEl
Hawaiian Electric Industries, Inc. [*NYSE symbol*] (SPSG) ... HE
Hawaiian Environmental Analysis and Prediction System (MUGU) ... HEAPS
Hawaiian Freight Tariff Bureau Inc., Maywood CA [*STAC*] ... HIB
Hawaiian Historical Society, Honolulu, HI [*Library symbol Library of Congress*] (LCLS) ... HHi
Hawaiian Integrated Air Defense System ... HIADS
Hawaiian International Billfish Association (EA) ... HIBA
Hawaiian Islands ... HI
Hawaiian Islands Reports [*A publication*] (DLA) ... HI Rep
Hawaiian Mission Children's Society, Honolulu, HI [*Library symbol Library of Congress*] (LCLS) ... HHMC
Hawaiian Ocean Time Series (USDC) ... HOT
Hawaiian Sea Frontier ... HAWSEAFRON
Hawaiian Sea Frontier ... HSF
Hawaiian Standard Time ... HST
Hawaiian Sugar Planters' Association (EA) ... HSPA
Hawaiian Sugar Planters' Association, Experiment Station, Honolulu, HI [*Library symbol Library of Congress*] (LCLS) ... HHS
Hawaiian Territory [*Prior to statehood*] ... HT
Hawaiian Theater [*Military*] ... HT
Hawaiian Time ... HT
Hawaiian Tracking Station ... HTS
Hawaiian Volcano Observatory [*Kilauea*] [*Hawaii*] [*Seismograph station code, US Geological Survey*] (SEIS) ... HVO
Hawaiian-Aleutian Standard Time ... HST
Hawarden [*British ICAO location identifier*] (ICLI) ... EGNR
Hawarden BAE [*British ICAO designator*] (FAAC) ... NEW
Hawarden Public Library, Hawarden, IA [*Library symbol Library of Congress*] (LCLS) ... IaHaw
Hawarde's Star Chamber Cases [*A publication*] (DLA) ... Haw
Hawarde's Star Chamber Cases [*A publication*] (DLA) ... Hawarde
Hawarde's Star Chamber Cases [*A publication*] (DLA) ... Hawarde St Ch
Hawes on Assignments [*A publication*] (DLA) ... Haw Ass
Hawes on Jurisdiction of Courts [*A publication*] (DLA) ... Hawes Jur
Hawes' Will Case [*A publication*] (DLA) ... Haw WC
Hawesville, KY [*AM radio station call letters*] ... WKCM
Hawi, HI [*Location identifier FAA*] (FAAL) ... UPP
Hawick Knitwear Manufacturers Association [*British*] (DBA) ... HKMA
HAWK [*Homing All the Way Killer*] **Assembly and Missile Checkout** (AAG) ... HAMCO
HAWK [*Homing All the Way Killer*] **Assembly System Checkout** (SAA) ... HASCO
HAWK [*Homing All the Way Killer*] **Equipment Logistics Program** [*Army*] ... HALP
HAWK [*Homing All-the-Way Killer*] **Equipment Logistics Program** [*Military*] (GFGA) ... HELP
HAWK [*Homing All the Way Killer*] **European Limited Improvement Program** [*NATO*] ... HELIP
HAWK [*Homing All the Way Killer*] **Improvement Program** ... HIP
HAWK [*Homing All the Way Killer*] **Improvement Program / Anti-Tactical Ballistic Missle** (SAA) ... HIP/ATBM
Hawk Inlet, AK [*Location identifier FAA*] (FAAL) ... HWI
HAWK [*Homing All the Way Killer*] **Institutional Training System** [*Military*] (RDA) ... HITS
HAWK [*Homing All the Way Killer*] **Intensified Management System Europe Program** [*Military*] ... HIMSEUR
HAWK [*Homing All the Way Killer*] **Logistics Complex** (MCD) ... HLC
HAWK [*Homing All the Way Killer*] **Logistics Group** (AABC) ... HLG
Hawk Migration Association of North America (EA) ... HMANA
HAWK [*Homing All the Way Killer*] **Missile Test Program System Device** (DWSG) ... HMTPSD
Hawk Mountain Sanctuary Association (EA) ... HMSA
HAWK [*Homing All the Way Killer*] **Project Field Facility - Europe** (MCD) ... HAPFF-EUR
Hawk Resources, Inc. [*Vancouver Stock Exchange symbol*] ... HWK
Hawker [*Australia Airport symbol*] (OAG) ... HWK
Hawker De Havilland [*Australia*] ... HDeH
Hawker De Havilland Australia Pty. Ltd., Kaman Aircraft Corp. [*ICAO aircraft manufacturer identifier*] (ICAO) ... HK
Hawker Siddeley Aviation Ltd. [*British ICAO aircraft manufacturer identifier*] (ICAO) ... AS
Hawker Siddeley Aviation Ltd. [*British ICAO aircraft manufacturer identifier*] (ICAO) ... AV
Hawker Siddeley Aviation Ltd. [*British ICAO aircraft manufacturer identifier*] (ICAO) ... BB
Hawker Siddeley Aviation Ltd. [*British ICAO aircraft manufacturer identifier*] (ICAO) ... HP
Hawker Siddeley Aviation Ltd. [*British ICAO designator*] (ICDA) ... HQ
Hawker Siddeley Aviation Ltd. [*British ICAO aircraft manufacturer identifier*] (ICAO) ... HS
Hawker Siddeley Aviation Ltd. [*British*] ... HSA
Hawker Siddeley Canada, Inc. [*Toronto Stock Exchange symbol Vancouver Stock Exchange symbol*] ... HSC
Hawker Siddeley Cda [*TS, exchange symbol*] (TTSB) ... HSC
Hawker-Siddeley Dynamics ... HSD
Hawker-Siddeley Electronics Ltd., Microform Division, Fairfield, V, Australia [*Library symbol Library of Congress*] (LCLS) ... HsE
Hawker-Siddeley Nuclear Power Co. Ltd. [*British*] ... HSNP
Hawkes Hospital of Mount Carmel, Mount Carmel Medical Center Library, Columbus, OH [*OCLC symbol*] (OCLC) ... HHM
Hawkesbury [*England*] ... HAWK
Hawkesbury General Hospital, Ontario [*Library symbol National Library of Canada*] (BIB) ... OHKGH
Hawkesbury Nepean Catchment Management Trust [*Resource management*] [*Australia*] ... HNCMT
Hawkesbury, ON [*FM radio station call letters*] ... CHPR
Hawkesbury Public Library, Hawkesbury, ON, Canada [*Library symbol Library of Congress*] (LCLS) ... CaOHk
Hawkesbury Public Library, Ontario [*Library symbol National Library of Canada*] (NLC) ... OHK
Hawkesville, KY [*FM radio station call letters*] ... WKCM-FM
Hawkeye and Libson Herald, Mount Vernon, IA [*Library symbol Library of Congress*] (LCLS) ... IaMvH
Hawkeye Bancorp [*Associated Press*] (SAG) ... HawkB
Hawkeye Bancorp [*NASDAQ symbol*] (NQ) ... HWKB
Hawkeye Institute of Technology, Area VII, Waterloo, IA [*Library symbol Library of Congress*] (LCLS) ... IaWH
Hawkeye Public Library, Hawkeye, IA [*Library symbol Library of Congress*] (LCLS) ... IaHweye
Hawkfarm One Design Association (EA) ... HODA
Hawkins' Abridgment of Coke upon Littleton [*A publication*] (DLA) ... Hawk Abr
Hawkins' Abridgment of Coke upon Littleton [*A publication*] (DLA) ... Hawk Coke Abr
Hawkins' Annual Reports [*19-24 Louisiana*] [*A publication*] (DLA) ... Haw
Hawkins' Annual Reports [*19-24 Louisiana*] [*A publication*] (DLA) ... Hawkins
Hawkins Chemical [*NASDAQ symbol*] (TTSB) ... HWKN
Hawkins Chemical, Inc. [*Associated Press*] (SAG) ... HawkC
Hawkins Chemical, Inc. [*NASDAQ symbol*] (NQ) ... HWKN
Hawkins' Coke upon Littleton [*A publication*] (DLA) ... Hawk Co Litt
Hawkins' Construction of Wills [*A publication*] (DLA) ... Hawk Wills
Hawkins Energy [*NASDAQ symbol*] (TTSB) ... HECI
Hawkins Energy Corp. [*NASDAQ symbol*] (SAG) ... HECI
Hawkins Energy Corp. [*Associated Press*] (SAG) ... HwkEn
Hawkins' Pleas of the Crown [*England*] [*A publication*] (DLA) ... Haw
Hawkins' Pleas of the Crown [*England*] [*A publication*] (DLA) ... Hawk
Hawkins' Pleas of the Crown [*England*] [*A publication*] (DLA) ... Hawk PC
Hawkins' Pleas of the Crown [*England*] [*A publication*] (DLA) ... Hawk Pl Cr
Hawkins' Pleas of the Crown [*England*] [*A publication*] (DLA) ... HPC
Hawkinsville, GA [*AM radio station call letters*] ... WCEH
Hawkinsville, GA [*FM radio station call letters*] ... WQSY
Hawkish (ABBR) ... HAK
Hawks Industries [*NASDAQ symbol*] (TTSB) ... HAWK
Hawks Industries, Inc. [*NASDAQ symbol*] (NQ) ... HAWK

Hawks Industries, Inc. [*Associated Press*] (SAG) .... Hawks
Hawks Nest Creek/Hawks Nest, Cat Island [*Bahamas*] [*ICAO location identifier*] (ICLI) .... MYCH
Hawks' North Carolina Reports [*A publication*] (DLA) .... Hawks
Hawks' North Carolina Reports [*A publication*] (DLA) .... Hawks (NC)
Hawksbill Resources, Inc. [*Vancouver Stock Exchange symbol*] .... HAW
Hawkshaw Ranch, Lasqueti Island Historical Society, British Columbia [*Library symbol National Library of Canada*] (NLC) .... BLIHS
Hawkwatch International (EA) .... HWI
Hawley Elementary School, Hawley, MN [*Library symbol*] [*Library of Congress*] (LCLS) .... MnHawE
Hawley High School, Hawley, MN [*Library symbol*] [*Library of Congress*] (LCLS) .... MnHawH
Hawley, PA [*FM radio station call letters*] .... WYCY
Hawley Public Library, Hawley, MN [*Library symbol*] [*Library of Congress*] (LCLS) .... MnHaw
Hawley's American Criminal Reports [*A publication*] (DLA) .... Haw Cr Rep
Hawley's American Criminal Reports [*A publication*] (DLA) .... Hawl Cr R
Hawley's American Criminal Reports [*A publication*] (DLA) .... Hawley
Hawley's American Criminal Reports [*A publication*] (DLA) .... Hawley's Crim Rep
Hawley's Reports [*10-20 Nevada*] [*A publication*] (DLA) .... Haw
Hawley's Reports [*10-20 Nevada*] [*A publication*] (DLA) .... Hawl
Hawley's Reports [*10-20 Nevada*] [*A publication*] (DLA) .... Hawley
Hawley-Smoot Act [*1930*] .... HSA
Hawser Laid .... HL
Hawthorn Elementary School, Massapequa, NY [*Library symbol Library of Congress*] (LCLS) .... NMassHE
Hawthorn Institute of Technology [*Australia*] .... HIT
Hawthorne [*Nevada*] [*Airport symbol Obsolete*] (OAG) .... HTH
Hawthorne Army Ammunition Plant (MCD) .... HAAP
Hawthorne Army Ammunition Plant (AABC) .... HWAAP
Hawthorne, CA [*Location identifier FAA*] (FAAL) .... HHR
Hawthorne Communications, Inc. .... HCI
Hawthorne Financial Corp. [*Associated Press*] (SAG) .... HawtFn
Hawthorne Financial Corp. [*NASDAQ symbol*] (NQ) .... HTHR
Hawthorne Finl [*NASDAQ symbol*] (TTSB) .... HTHR
Hawthorne Gold [*Vancouver Stock Exchange symbol*] .... HGD
Hawthorne Press, Inc., Hawthorne, NJ [*Library symbol Library of Congress*] (LCLS) .... NjHawP
Haxtun Public Library, Haxtun, CO [*Library symbol Library of Congress*] (LCLS) .... CoHa
Hay [*Australia Airport symbol*] (OAG) .... HXX
Hay and Marriott's English Admiralty Reports [*A publication*] (DLA) .... H & M
Hay and Marriott's English Admiralty Reports [*A publication*] (DLA) .... Hay & M
Hay and Marriott's English Admiralty Reports [*A publication*] (DLA) .... Hay & M (Eng)
Hay and Marriott's English Admiralty Reports [*A publication*] (DLA) .... Hay & Mar
Hay and Marriott's English Admiralty Reports [*A publication*] (DLA) .... Hay & Marr
Hay and Marriott's English Admiralty Reports [*A publication*] (DLA) .... Marr
Hay Fever [*Medicine*] .... HF
Hay Fever Prevention Society .... HFPS
Hay Lakes Public Library, Alberta [*Library symbol National Library of Canada*] (NLC) .... AHAL
Hay Management Consultants, Information Resources, Toronto, ON, Canada [*Library symbol*] [*Library of Congress*] (LCLS) .... CaOTHMC
Hay on Expatriation [*A publication*] (DLA) .... Hay Exp
Hay River [*Canada*] [*Airport symbol*] (OAG) .... YHY
Hay River, NT [*FM radio station call letters*] CJCD-1
Hay River, NT [*FM radio station call letters*] .... CKHR
Hay River, NT [*ICAO location identifier*] (ICLI) .... CYHY
Haycock, AK [*Location identifier FAA*] (FAAL) .... HAY
Hayden Analysis and Reporting Tool [*Computer science*] .... HART
Hayden, CO [*Location identifier FAA*] (FAAL) .... CHE
Hayden, CO [*Location identifier FAA*] (FAAL) .... HDN
Hayden, CO [*FM radio station call letters*] .... KIDN
Hayden, ID [*FM radio station call letters*] (RBYB) .... KHTQ
Hayden Lake Library, Hayden Lake, ID [*Library symbol*] [*Library of Congress*] (LCLS) .... IdHyl
Hayden Public Library, Hayden, AZ [*Library symbol Library of Congress*] (LCLS) .... AzHA
Hayden Public Library, Hayden, CO [*Library symbol Library of Congress*] (LCLS) .... CoHay
Hayden's Viburnum Compound [*Medicine*] .... HVC
Haydn Society [*Record label*] .... HS
Haydn Society [*Record label*] .... HSLP
Hayes and Jarman's Concise Forms of Wills [*18th ed.*] [*1952*] [*A publication*] (DLA) .... H & J Forms
Hayes and Jarman's Concise Forms of Wills [*18th ed.*] [*1952*] [*A publication*] (DLA) .... Hayes & J Wills
Hayes and Jones' Irish Exchequer Reports [*1832-34*] [*A publication*] (DLA) .... H & J
Hayes and Jones' Irish Exchequer Reports [*1832-34*] [*A publication*] (DLA) .... H & J Ir
Hayes and Jones' Irish Exchequer Reports [*A publication*] (DLA) .... Hay & J
Hayes and Jones' Irish Exchequer Reports [*1832-34*] [*A publication*] (DLA) .... Hay & Jo
Hayes and Jones' Irish Exchequer Reports [*1832-34*] [*A publication*] (DLA) .... Hayes & J
Hayes and Jones' Irish Exchequer Reports [*1832-34*] [*A publication*] (DLA) .... Hayes & J (Ir)
Hayes and Jones' Irish Exchequer Reports [*1832-34*] [*A publication*] (DLA) .... Hayes & Jo
Hayes and Jones' Irish Exchequer Reports [*1832-34*] [*A publication*] (DLA) .... Hayes & Jon
Hayes Center, NE [*Location identifier FAA*] (FAAL) .... HCT
Hayes Center, NE [*Television station call letters*] .... KWNB
Hayes' Concise Conveyancer [*A publication*] (DLA) .... Hayes Con Conv
Hayes' Dispositions to Heirs in Tail, Etc. [*A publication*] (DLA) .... Hayes Heirs
Hayes International Corp. .... HIC
Hayes' Introduction to Conveyancing [*A publication*] (DLA) .... Hayes Intr
Hayes' Irish Exchequer Reports [*1830-32*] [*A publication*] (DLA) .... Hay
Hayes' Irish Exchequer Reports [*1830-32*] [*A publication*] (DLA) .... Hay Exch
Hayes' Irish Exchequer Reports [*1830-32*] [*A publication*] (DLA) .... Hayes
Hayes' Irish Exchequer Reports [*1830-32*] [*A publication*] (DLA) .... Hayes Exch
Hayes' Irish Exchequer Reports [*1830-32*] [*A publication*] (DLA) .... Hayes Exch (Ir)
Hayes' Law of Uses, Devises, and Trust [*A publication*] (DLA) .... Hayes UD & T
Hayes on Conveyancing [*A publication*] (DLA) .... Hayes Conv
Hayes on Crimes and Punishments [*A publication*] (DLA) .... Hayes Cr & P
Hayes on Limitations as to Heirs of the Body, Etc. [*A publication*] (DLA) .... Hayes Lim
Hayes' Real Estate [*A publication*] (DLA) .... Hayes R Est
Hayes' Reports [*Calcutta*] [*A publication*] (DLA) .... Hay
Hayes Resources, Inc. [*Toronto Stock Exchange symbol*] .... HRI
Hayes Verification Protocol [*Computer science*] .... HVP
Hayes Wheels International [*NYSE symbol*] (SPSG) .... HAY
Hayes Wheels International [*Associated Press*] (SAG) .... Hayes
Hayes-Dana, Inc. [*Toronto Stock Exchange symbol*] .... HAY
Hayfield [*California*] [*Seismograph station code, US Geological Survey*] (SEIS) .... HAY
Hayfields [*Papua New Guinea*] [*Airport symbol*] (OAG) .... HYF
Hayl Kashish [*Elderly Army*] [*Israel*] .... HAKASH
Hayman Island [*Australia Airport symbol*] (OAG) .... HIS
Hayner Public Library, Alton, IL [*Library symbol Library of Congress*] (LCLS) .... IAl
Haynes' Chancery Practice [*1879*] [*A publication*] (DLA) .... Hayn Ch Pr
Haynes' Outlines of Equity [*5th ed.*] [*1880*] [*A publication*] (DLA) .... Hay Eq
Haynes' Outlines of Equity [*5th ed.*] [*1880*] [*A publication*] (DLA) .... Hayn Eq
Haynes' Outlines of Equity [*5th ed.*] [*1880*] [*A publication*] (DLA) .... Haynes Eq
Haynes' Students' Leading Cases [*A publication*] (DLA) .... Hayn Lead Cas
Haynes-Apperson Owners Club (EA) .... HAOC
Haynesville, LA [*AM radio station call letters*] .... KLVU
Haynesville, LA [*FM radio station call letters*] .... KWHN
Hay-Pasturage [*Agriculture*] .... HP
Hayridge [*England*] .... HAYR
Hays [*Kansas*] [*Airport symbol*] (OAG) .... HYS
Hays Army Ammunition Plant .... HYAPP
Hay's Decisions on Accidents and Negligence [*1860*] [*Scotland*] [*A publication*] (DLA) .... Hay Acc
Hay's Decisions on Accidents and Negligence [*1860*] [*Scotland*] [*A publication*] (DLA) .... Hay Dec
Hay's High Court Appeals Reports [*1862-63*] [*Bengal, India*] [*A publication*] (DLA) .... Hay
Hays, KS [*AM radio station call letters*] .... KAYS
Hays, KS [*Television station call letters*] .... KBSH
Hays, KS [*FM radio station call letters*] .... KHAZ
Hays, KS [*FM radio station call letters*] .... KJLS
Hays, KS [*Television station call letters*] .... KOOD
Hays, KS [*FM radio station call letters*] (RBYB) .... KPRD
Hay's Poor Law Decisions [*1711-1859*] [*Scotland*] [*A publication*] (DLA) .... Hay
Hay's Poor Law Decisions [*1711-1859*] [*Scotland*] [*A publication*] (DLA) .... Hay PL
Hay's Reports [*Calcutta*] [*A publication*] (DLA) .... Hay (Calc)
Hay's Scotch Decisions [*A publication*] (DLA) .... Hay
Haystack [*Washington*] [*Seismograph station code, US Geological Survey*] (SEIS) .... HTW
Haystack .... HYSTCK
Haysville Community Library, Haysville, KS [*Library symbol Library of Congress*] (LCLS) .... KHayv
Haysville, KS [*FM radio station call letters*] (RBYB) .... KWSJ-FM
Haysville, KS [*FM radio station call letters*] .... KXLK
Hayward [*Wisconsin*] [*Airport symbol*] (OAG) .... HYR
Hayward and Hazelton's United States Circuit Court Reports [*District of Columbia*] [*A publication*] (DLA) .... Hay & H
Hayward and Hazelton's United States Circuit Court Reports [*District of Columbia*] [*A publication*] (DLA) .... Hay & Haz
Hayward and Hazelton's United States Circuit Court Reports [*District of Columbia*] [*A publication*] (DLA) .... Hayw & H
Hayward and Hazelton's United States Circuit Court Reports [*District of Columbia*] [*A publication*] (DLA) .... Hayw & HDC
Hayward and Hazelton's United States Circuit Court Reports [*District of Columbia*] [*A publication*] (DLA) .... HH
Hayward and Hazelton's United States Circuit Court Reports [*District of Columbia*] [*A publication*] (DLA) .... US Cir Ct Rep DC
Hayward Area Historical Society, Hayward, CA [*Library symbol*] [*Library of Congress*] (LCLS) .... CHHi
Hayward, CA [*Location identifier FAA*] (FAAL) .... HWD
Hayward, CA [*FM radio station call letters*] .... KCRH
Hayward Map, CA [*Location identifier FAA*] (FAAL) .... MBU
Hayward Public Library, Hayward, CA [*Library symbol Library of Congress*] (LCLS) .... CH
Hayward, WI [*Location identifier FAA*] (FAAL) .... SLY
Hayward, WI [*AM radio station call letters*] .... WHSM
Hayward, WI [*FM radio station call letters*] .... WHSM-FM
Hayward, WI [*FM radio station call letters*] .... WRLS
Hayward's Law Register [*Boston*] [*A publication*] (DLA) .... Hayw LR
Haywood Bancshares, Inc. [*Associated Press*] (SAG) .... HaywdB
Haywood Bancshares, Inc. [*AMEX symbol*] (SAG) .... HBS
Haywood County Public Library, Canton Branch, Canton, NC [*Library symbol Library of Congress*] (LCLS) .... NcWayH-C
Haywood County Public Library, Waynesville, NC [*Library symbol Library of Congress*] (LCLS) .... NcWayH

Haywood Park General Hospital, Brownsville, TN [*Library symbol Library of Congress*] (LCLS) ...... TBroH
Haywood Technical Institute, Clyde, NC [*Library symbol Library of Congress*] (LCLS) ...... NcClIH
Haywood's Manual of the Statute Laws of North Carolina [*A publication*] (DLA) ...... Hayw Man
Haywood's North Carolina Reports [*A publication*] (DLA) ...... Hay
Haywood's North Carolina Reports [*A publication*] (DLA) ...... Hayw
Haywood's North Carolina Reports [*A publication*] (DLA) ...... Hayw NC
Haywood's Tennessee Reports [*A publication*] (DLA) ...... Hay
Haywood's Tennessee Reports [*A publication*] (DLA) ...... Hayw
Haywood's Tennessee Reports [*A publication*] (DLA) ...... Hayw Tenn
Haywood's Tennessee Reports [*A publication*] (DLA) ...... Haywood Tenn Rep
Hazara Mountain Battery [*British military*] (DMA) ...... HMB
Hazard [*or Hazardous*] (KSC) ...... HAZ
Hazard Action Report (MCD) ...... HAR
Hazard Analysis (NASA) ...... HA
Hazard Analysis ...... HAZAN
Hazard Analysis Critical Control Point [*Quality control*] ...... HACCP
Hazard Analysis Critical Control Points ...... HACCP
Hazard and Operability [*Chemical engineering*] ...... HAZOP
Hazard Assessment Computer System [*Coast Guard*] ...... HACS
Hazard Assessment of Rocket Propellants ...... HARP
Hazard Assessment System for Toxic Emissions [*Computer-based emergency management system*] [*Environmental Research & Technology*] ...... HASTE
Hazard Beacon (MSA) ...... HBCN
Hazard Beacon ...... HBN
Hazard Communication Standard [*OSHA*] ...... HCS
Hazard Community College, Hazard, KY [*Library symbol Library of Congress*] (LCLS) ...... KyHzC
Hazard Evaluation and Technical Assistance [*National Institute for Occupational Safety and Health*] ...... HETA
Hazard Evaluation Division [*Environmental Protection Agency*] ...... HED
Hazard Function ...... HF
Hazard Identification Capability Assessment and Multi-Year Development Plan [*Federal Emergency Management Agency*] (GFGA) ...... HICA/MYDP
Hazard Index (GNE) ...... HI
Hazard Information Transmission [*Chemical Manufacturers Association*] (FFDE) ...... HIT
Hazard Input Program (SAA) ...... HIP
Hazard, KY [*FM radio station call letters*] ...... WEKH
Hazard, KY [*FM radio station call letters*] ...... WJMD
Hazard, KY [*Television station call letters*] ...... WKHA
Hazard, KY [*AM radio station call letters*] ...... WKIC
Hazard, KY [*AM radio station call letters*] ...... WQXY
Hazard, KY [*FM radio station call letters*] ...... WSGS
Hazard, KY [*Television station call letters*] ...... WYMT
Hazard Prevention [*A publication*] (EAAP) ...... HP
Hazard Quotient [*Toxicology*] ...... HQ
Hazard Ranking and Allocation Methodology (MCD) ...... HRAM
Hazard Ranking System [*Environmental Protection Agency*] ...... HRS
Hazard Reduction Precedence Sequence (NASA) ...... HRPS
Hazard Report (MCD) ...... HR
Hazard Review Board ...... HRB
Hazard Warning Network ...... HWN
Hazardous [*Task classification*] [*NASA*] (NASA) ...... (H)
Hazardous Air Pollutant ...... HAP
Hazardous Air Pollutant Prioritization System [*Environmental Protection Agency*] (GFGA) ...... HAPPS
Hazardous Air Pollutants ...... HAPS
Hazardous Air Pollutants Enforcement Management System [*Environmental Protection Agency*] (GFGA) ...... HAPEMS
Hazardous Air Traffic Report ...... HATR
Hazardous and Noxious Substance ...... HNS
Hazardous and Solid Waste Amendments [*1984 amendments to RCRA*] ...... HSWA
Hazardous and Toxic Waste ...... HTW
Hazardous and Trace Emissions System [*Environmental Protection Agency*] ...... HATREMS
Hazardous Area ...... HA
Hazardous Area Reporting Service [*Aviation*] (FAAC) ...... HARS
Hazardous Atmospheric Release Model [*Marine science*] (OSRA) ...... HARM
Hazardous Atmospheric Release Model (USDC) ...... HARM
Hazardous Cargo [*Shipping*] ...... H
Hazardous Chemical ...... HAZCHEM
Hazardous Chemicals Advisory Committee [*New South Wales, Australia*] ...... HCAC
Hazardous Chemicals Information and Disposal [*University of Alberta*] [*Canada Information service or system*] (CRD) ...... HAZINF
Hazardous Chemicals Secretariat [*Victoria, Australia*] ...... HCS
Hazardous Communication Standards [*Occupational Safety and Health Administration*] (RDA) ...... HAZCOM
Hazardous Condition (NVT) ...... HAZCON
Hazardous Constituents (GNE) ...... HC
Hazardous Duty Incentive Pay [*Air Force*] (AFM) ...... HDIP
Hazardous Exposure Reduction and Safety Criteria Plan [*NASA*] (NASA) ...... HERSCP
Hazardous Gas Detection Systems (KSC) ...... HGDS
Hazardous Incident Report (MCD) ...... HIR
Hazardous Inflight Weather Advisory Service [*Aviation*] (FAAC) ...... HIWAS
Hazardous Liquid Pipeline Safety Act (GFGA) ...... HLPSA
Hazardous Material ...... HAZMAT
Hazardous Material (DNAB) ...... HM
Hazardous Material Incident [*Nuclear energy*] ...... HMI
Hazardous Material Response and Assessment Division [*Marine science*] (OSRA) ...... HAZMAT

Hazardous Materials Advisory Council (EA) ...... HMAC
Hazardous Materials Control Committee [*General Motors Corp.*] ...... HMCC
Hazardous Materials Control Research Institute (EA) ...... HMCRI
Hazardous Materials Identification System [*National Paint and Coating Association*] ...... HMIS
Hazardous Materials Information System (MCD) ...... HMIS
Hazardous Materials Management and Resource Recovery [*University of Alabama*] [*Research center*] (RCD) ...... HAMMARR
Hazardous Materials Regulation [*Department of Transportation*] ...... HMR
Hazardous Materials Regulation Board ...... HMRB
Hazardous Materials Release Response Policy [*Stanford University*] ...... HMRRP
Hazardous Materials Response and Assessment Division [*National Oceanic and Atmospheric Administration*] (USDC) ...... HAZMAT
Hazardous Materials Safety [*RSPA*] (TAG) ...... HMS
Hazardous Materials Systems [*A publication*] (EAAP) ...... HMS
Hazardous Materials Systems (Bureau of Explosives) (EA) ...... HMS(BOE)
Hazardous Materials Technical Center [*Rockville, MD*] [*DoD*] (GRD) ...... HMTC
Hazardous Materials Transportation Act [*1975*] ...... HMTA
Hazardous Materials Transportation and Uniform Safety Act ...... HMTUSA
Hazardous Organic NESHAP [*National Emission Standards for Hazardous Air Polluta nts*] (GNE) ...... HON
Hazardous Organic NESHAP (National Emission Standards for Hazardous Air Pollutants) [*Environmental Protection Agency*] ...... HON
Hazardous Organics [*Environmental science*] ...... HO
Hazardous Polluting Substances [*Shipping*] (DCTA) ...... HPS
Hazardous Processing Facility (SSD) ...... HPF
Hazardous Response Support Division [*Environmental Protection Agency*] ...... HRSD
Hazardous Site Control Division [*Environmental Protection Agency*] (GFGA) ...... HSCD
Hazardous Substance Incident Response Management Course [*Navy*] ...... HSIRMC
Hazardous Substance List [*Code of Federal Regulations*] (FFDE) ...... HSL
Hazardous Substances Act (DMAA) ...... HSA
Hazardous Substances Data Bank [*National Library of Medicine*] [*Information service or system*] ...... HADB
Hazardous Substances Data Bank [*National Library of Medicine*] [*Information service or system*] (IID) ...... HSDB
Hazardous, Toxic, and Radiological Waste [*US Army Corps of Engineers*] ...... HTRW
Hazardous Waste (GFGA) ...... HW
Hazardous Waste and Superfund Staff [*Environmental Protection Agency*] (GFGA) ...... HWSS
Hazardous Waste Data [*or Disposal*] Management System [*Environmental Protection Agency*] ...... HWDMS
Hazardous Waste Disposal ...... HWD
Hazardous Waste Enforcement Division [*Environmental Protection Agency*] (EPA) ...... HWED
Hazardous Waste Engineering Research Laboratory [*Cincinnati, OH*] [*Environmental Protection Agency*] (GRD) ...... HWERL
Hazardous Waste Federation (EA) ...... HWF
Hazardous Waste Groundwater Task Force [*Environmental Protection Agency*] (GFGA) ...... HWGTF
Hazardous Waste Indentification Rule [*Environmental Protection Agency*] ...... HWIR
Hazardous Waste Land Treatment (GNE) ...... HWLT
Hazardous Waste Management ...... HWM
Hazardous Waste Management Association ...... HWMA
Hazardous Waste Management Division [*Environmental Protection Agency*] (GFGA) ...... HWMD
Hazardous Waste Management Facility ...... HWMF
Hazardous Waste Management Plan ...... HWMP
Hazardous Waste Minimization ...... HAZMIN
Hazardous Waste Operations and Emergency Response Regulation ...... HAZWOPER
Hazardous Waste Remedial Action Program [*Oak Ridge National Laboratory*] ...... HAZWRAP
Hazardous Waste Research Center [*Louisiana State University*] [*Research center*] (RCD) ...... HWRC
Hazardous Waste Restrictions Task Force (GNE) ...... HWRTF
Hazardous Waste Services Association [*Defunct*] (EA) ...... HWSA
Hazardous Waste Treatment Council (EA) ...... HWTC
Hazards Analysis Board [*Air Force*] ...... HAB
Hazards Assessment Laboratory [*Colorado State University*] [*Research center*] (RCD) ...... HAL
Hazards File [*National Chemical Emergency Centre*] [*British*] (NITA) ...... HAZFILE
Hazards Monitoring System [*NASA*] (KSC) ...... HMS
Hazards of Electromagnetic Radiation to Fuel (TEL) ...... HERF
Hazards of Electromagnetic Radiation to Ordnance ...... HERO
Hazards of Electromagnetic Radiation to Personnel (TEL) ...... HERP
Hazard's Pennsylvania Register [*A publication*] (ILCA) ...... Haz P Reg
Hazard's Pennsylvania Register [*A publication*] (DLA) ...... Haz PA Reg
Hazard's Pennsylvania Register [*A publication*] (DLA) ...... Haz PA Reg (PA)
Hazard's Pennsylvania Register [*A publication*] (DLA) ...... Haz Reg
Hazard's United States Register [*A publication*] (DLA) ...... Haz US Reg
Haze [*Weather reports*] ...... H
Haze (WDAA) ...... HZ
Haze [*Meterology*] (BARN) ...... Z
Haze Filter [*Photography*] ...... HF
Hazel Green, AL [*AM radio station call letters*] ...... WBXR
Hazel M. Lewis Library (Powers Public Library), Powers, OR [*Library symbol*] [*Library of Congress*] (LCLS) ...... OrPoL
Hazeldean Branch, Kanata Public Library, Ontario [*Library symbol National Library of Canada*] (NLC) ...... OKAH
Hazelden Foundation (EA) ...... HF

Hazelden Foundation, Staff library, Center City, MN [*Library symbol*] [*Library of Congress*] (LCLS) .... MnCcH
Hazeltine Corp., Greenlawn, NY [*Library symbol*] [*Library of Congress*] (LCLS) .... NGIH
Hazeltine Corp., Greenlawn, NY [*Library symbol Library of Congress*] (LCLS) .... NGIH
Hazeltine Electronics Corp. (MCD) .... HEC
Hazelton Air Services [*ICAO designator*] (AD) .... ZL
Hazelton Airlines [*Australia ICAO designator*] (FAAC) .... HZL
Hazelton Airlines [*Airline code*] [*Australia*] .... ZL
Hazelton Public Library, British Columbia [*Library symbol National Library of Canada*] (NLC) .... BHA
Hazelton Public Library, Hazelton, BC, Canada [*Library symbol*] [*Library of Congress*] (LCLS) .... CaBHA
Hazelton Public Library, Hazelton, PA [*Library symbol Library of Congress*] (LCLS) .... PHa
Hazen, NV [*Location identifier FAAL*] (FAAL) .... HZN
Hazlehurst, GA [*Location identifier FAA*] (FAAL) .... AZE
Hazlehurst, GA [*AM radio station call letters*] .... WVOH
Hazlehurst, GA [*FM radio station call letters*] .... WVOH-FM
Hazlehurst, MS [*AM radio station call letters*] .... WMDC
Hazlehurst, MS [*FM radio station call letters*] .... WMDC-FM
Hazlet, NJ [*FM radio station call letters*] .... WCNJ
Hazleton [*Pennsylvania*] [*Airport symbol Obsolete*] (OAG) .... HZL
Hazleton Laboratories Europe Ltd. [*British*] (IRUK) .... HLE
Hazleton, PA [*Location identifier FAA*] (FAAL) .... HXM
Hazleton, PA [*AM radio station call letters*] .... WAZL
Hazleton, PA [*Television station call letters*] .... WWLF
Hazleton, PA [*FM radio station call letters*] .... WZMT
Hazlitt and Roche on Maritime Warfare [*A publication*] (DLA) .... Haz & R M War
Hazlitt and Roche's Bankruptcy Reports [*A publication*] (DLA) .... H & R Bank
Hazor (BJA) .... H
Hazrat Eman [*Afghanistan*] [*ICAO location identifier*] (ICLI) .... OAHE
HazTECH News [*A publication*] .... HTN
Hazy (ABBR) .... H
Hazy (WGA) .... HZY
Hazzard and Warburton's Prince Edward Island Reports [*A publication*] (DLA) .... H & W
H.B. Mattlin Middle School, Plainview, NY [*Library symbol*] [*Library of Congress*] (LCLS) .... NPIMM
HB [*Homeward Bound Ministries*] Tract Association (EA) .... HBTA
H-Beam [*Architecture*] .... H
HBO & Co. [*Associated Press*] (SAG) .... HBO
HBO & Co. [*NASDAQ symbol*] (NQ) .... HBOC
HCC Insurance Hldgs [*NYSE symbol*] (TTSB) .... HCC
HCC Insurance Holdings [*NYSE symbol*] (SAG) .... HCC
HCC Insurance Holdings [*Associated Press*] (SAG) .... HCC Ins
HCFA [*Health Care Financing Administration*] Common Procedures Coding System [*Department of Health and Human Services*] (GFGA) .... HCPCS
HCI Holdings Ltd. [*Toronto Stock Exchange symbol*] .... HCI
HCIA, Inc. [*NASDAQ symbol*] (SAG) .... HCIA
HCL Aviation, Inc. [*ICAO designator*] (FAAC) .... KYC
HDS Network Sys Wrrt [*NASDAQ symbol*] (TTSB) .... HDSXW
HDS Network Systems [*NASDAQ symbol*] (TTSB) .... HDSX
HDS Network Systems, Inc. [*Associated Press*] (SAG) .... HDS
HDS Network Systems, Inc. [*Associated Press*] (SAG) .... HDS Nt
HDS Network Systems, Inc. [*NASDAQ symbol*] (SAG) .... HDSX
H.D.Vest [*NASDAQ symbol*] (TTSB) .... HDVS
Head [*Anatomy*] (DAVI) .... H
Head [*Linguistics*] .... H
Head [*Horse racing*] .... H
Head (AAG) .... HD
Head (WDMC) .... hd
Head [*Anatomy*] (DAVI) .... he
Head Acceleration Device (PDAA) .... HAD
Head Access Area [*Nuclear energy*] (NRCH) .... HAA
Head and Cover (MSA) .... H & C
Head and Neck [*Medicine*] .... H & N
Head and Neck (DMAA) .... HN
Head and Neck Surgery [*Medical specialty*] (DHSM) .... HNS
Head and Shoulders [*Photography*] .... H & S
Head and Torso Simulator [*A dummy developed by British Telecommunications Ltd.*] .... HATS
Head Angulation Sighting Equipment [*British military*] (DMA) .... HASE
Head, Arms, and Trunk [*Anatomy*] (DAVI) .... HAT
Head Bar Address Register [*Computer science*] (MHDB) .... HBAR
Head Circumference [*Medicine*] .... HC
Head Compartment Support Structure [*Nuclear energy*] (NRCH) .... HCSS
Head Compression (AAMN) .... HC
Head Diameter .... HD
Head Disk Assembly .... HDA
Head Driven Phrase Structure Grammar [*Artificial intelligence*] .... HPSG
Head Driver (IAA) .... HD
Head, Ears, Eyes, Nose, Throat .... HEENT
Head End .... HE
Head End Off-Gas [*Nuclear energy*] (NRCH) .... HOG
Head End Steering .... HES
Head End Treatment Plant [*Nuclear energy British*] .... HETP
Head, Eyes, Ears, Nose, and Throat [*Medicine*] (HGAA) .... HENT
Head Gasket [*Automotive engineering*] .... HG
Head, Hand, and Chest Sets [*JETDS nomenclature*] [*Military*] (CET) .... H
Head, Head [*Coin-tossing possibility*] .... HH
Head, Heart, Hands, and Health [*As in 4H organizations*] 4H
Head, Heart, Hands, and Health [*As in 4H organizations*] .... HHHH
Head Injuries Rehabilitation Centre [*British*] (CB) .... HIRC

Head Injury [*Neurology*] (DAVI) .... HI
Head Injury Council of Australia .... HICOA
Head Injury Criteria [*Medicine*] .... HIC
Head Injury Routine [*Medicine*] (DMAA) .... HIR
Head Joint [*Technical drawings*] .... HJT
Head Linesman [*Football*] .... HL
Head Lining [*Automotive engineering*] .... H/LIN
Head Masters' Association (AIE) .... HMA
Head Masters' Conference [*British*] .... HMC
Head Military Figure in Charge .... HMFIC
Head Motion [*Gravity*] .... HM
Head, Neck, and Shaft [*of a bone*] [*Osteology*] .... HNS
Head Nigger in Charge [*Slang*] .... HNIC
Head Nurse .... HN
Head, Nut, and Washer [*Construction*] .... HNW
Head of a Procuring Activity [*Army*] (AABC) .... HPA
Head of Aircraft Department (Naval) [*British*] .... HAD(N)
Head of Bed [*Medicine*] .... HOB
Head of Bed Up for Shortness of Breath [*Medicine*] (DAVI) .... HOBUPSOB
Head of Bus (ACRL) .... HOB
Head of Contracting Activity [*Military*] (AABC) .... HCA
Head of Contracting Agency (DOMA) .... HCA
Head of Contracting Office (USDC) .... HCO
Head of Contracting Office [*Marine science*] (OSRA) .... HCO
Head of Defence Sales [*British*] (RDA) .... HDS
Head of Department .... HOD
Head of Faculty [*Education*] (AIE) .... HOF
Head of Form (IAA) .... HOF
Head of Government (ADA) .... HOG
Head of Household [*IRS*] .... HOH
Head of Household Program [*IRS*] .... HHP
Head of Units Group [*American Library Association*] .... HUG
Head Office .... HO
Head per Track .... H/T
Head per Track (BUR) .... HPT
Head Position Monitor .... HPM
Head Positioning Mechanism .... HPM
Head Post Assembly .... HPA
Head Post Office .... HPO
Head Postmaster [*British*] (DCTA) .... HP
Head Postmaster's Manual [*British*] (DCTA) .... HPM
Head Postmen's Association [*A union*] [*British*] .... HPA
Head Rice Yield .... HRY
Head Rotated Left [*Medicine*] .... HRL
Head Rotated Right [*Medicine*] .... HRR
Head Schoolmaster [*Navy British*] .... HdSchm
Head Set [*Telecommunications*] (TEL) .... HDS
Head Set [*Telecommunications*] (IAA) .... HS
Head Sling .... HS
Head Small Veins [*Anatomy*] .... HSV
Head Start Program [*Education*] .... HSP
Head Steward [*Navy British*] (ROG) .... H ST
Head Suppression (AAG) .... HS
Head Suppression Valve (AAG) .... HSV
Head, Tail [*Coin-tossing probability*] .... HT
Head to Abdomen (DMAA) .... H/A
Head to Come [*Publishing*] .... HTC
Head to Come [*A notation on copy that the headline will be written and set later*] (WDMC) .... HTK
Head to Kum [*Come*] [*Publishing*] .... HTK
Head, Track, and Selector .... HTS
Head Traumatic Syndrome [*Medicine*] (DMAA) .... HTS
Head Turn [*Industrial engineering*] .... HT
Head Wardmaster [*Navy British*] (ROG) .... HW
Head Width .... HW
Head Width Index .... HWI
Head Wind [*Navigation*] .... HW
Headache (DMAA) .... H/A
Headache .... HA
Headache (KSC) .... HDAC
Headache .... HDCH
Headache Assessment Questionnaire [*Neurology*] (DAVI) .... HAQ
Headache, Insomnia, Depression [*Syndrome*] .... HID
Headache Unit Index [*Medicine*] (DMAA) .... HUI
Head-Arm-Leg [*Medicine*] .... H-A-L
Headband (IAA) .... HB
Headcount .... HC
Head-Disc Interference [*Head crash*] (NITA) .... HDI
Head-Down Display [*Aviation*] .... HDD
Headed and Gutted [*Fish processing*] .... H & G
Headed Type .... HT
Header (NFPA) .... H
Header [*Computer science*] .... HDR
Header [*Automotive engineering*] .... HDR
Header Check Sequence [*Computer science*] .... HCS
Header Error Control [*Telecommunications*] (ACRL) .... HEC
Header Extension [*Telecommunications*] (ACRL) .... HE
Header Extension Length [*Telecommunications*] (ACRL) .... HEL
[*File*] Header Label [*Computer science*] (ECII) .... HDR
Header Label [*Computer science*] (IAA) .... HL
Headgear [*Mining engineering*] (IAA) .... HG
Headgear Receiver [*Mining engineering*] (IAA) .... HGR
Heading (AFM) .... HD
Heading (AFM) .... HDG
Heading Alignment Circle [*NASA*] (NASA) .... HAC

Heading Alignment Cone [*NASA*] (NASA) .... HAC
Heading Alignment Cylinder (MCD) .... HAC
Heading Altitude Sensor (IAA) .... HAS
Heading Altitude System .... HAS
Heading, Altitude, True Airspeed [*Aviation*] (CAAL) .... HATS
Heading Attitude Reference System (MCD) .... HARS
Heading Axis Perturbation .... HAP
Heading Marker Correction (SAA) .... HMC
Heading per Gyro Compass [*Navigation*] .... HPGC
Heading per Standard Compass [*Navigation*] .... HPSC
Heading per Steering Compass [*Navigation*] .... HPSTGC
Heading Reference System (AAG) .... HRS
Heading Reference Unit .... HRU
Heading Select (GAVI) .... HDG SEL
Heading to a Manual Termination (GAVI) .... VM
Heading to a Radial (GAVI) .... VR
Headlamp [*Automotive engineering*] .... H/LP
Headlamp [*Automotive engineering*] .... HL
Headlamp Housing [*Automotive engineering*] .... HH
Headland [*Maps and charts*] .... Hd
Headland (ADA) .... H-LAND
Headless (KSC) .... HDLS
Headline (WGA) .... HDL
Headline [*Advertising*] (DOAD) .... HED
Headline (WDMC) .... hed
Headline International Talent [*Commercial firm*] .... HIT
Headline News [*Cable television channel*] .... HN
Headliner .... HDLNR
Headlines (ABBR) .... H
Headlining .... HLNG
Headmaster [*or Headmistress*] .... HM
Headmaster Commander [*Navy British*] .... HC
Headmaster Lieutenant-Commander [*Navy British*] .... HLC
Headmaster-Lieutenant [*Navy British*] .... HL
Headmasters [*or Headmistresses*] **Association** (EA) .... HA
Head-Mounted Display [*Virtual reality technology*] (PS) .... HMD
Headnote .... HDNT
Head-of-Household Income (WDMC) .... HHI
Headphones [*Slang*] (WDMC) .... cans
Headquarters (ABBR) .... H
Headquarters [*Colorado*] [*Seismograph station code, US Geological Survey Closed*] (SEIS) .... HDQ
Headquarters .... HDQR
Headquarters .... HDQRS
Headquarters (NASA) .... HDQTRS
Headquarters .... HDQTRS
Headquarters (CINC) .... HED
Headquarters .... HQ
Headquarters .... HQS
Headquarters (KSC) .... HQTR
Headquarters Administration Division [*Coast Guard*] .... HA
Headquarters Administration Office [*British police*] .... HQ(A)
Headquarters Administrative Issuance Index System [*Military*] (DNAB) .... HAIIS
Headquarters, Air Force (AFM) .... HAF
Headquarters, Air Service Command [*Air Force*] .... HASC
Headquarters, Air Support Command [*NATO*] (NATG) .... HQASC
Headquarters, Allied Air Force, Central Europe [*NATO*] .... HAAFCE
Headquarters, Allied Forces .... HAF
Headquarters, Allied Forces, Mediterranean .... HAFMED
Headquarters, Allied Forces, Southern Europe (NATG) .... HAFSE
Headquarters, Allied Land Forces, Southeastern Europe .... HALFSEE
Headquarters and Headquarters Battery [*Army*] .... HHB
Headquarters and Headquarters Company [*Army*] .... H & HQ
Headquarters and Headquarters Company [*Army*] .... HHC
Headquarters and Headquarters Detachment [*Army*] (AABC) .... HHD
Headquarters and Headquarters Squadron [*Marine Corps*] .... H & HS
Headquarters and Headquarters Troop [*Army*] (AABC) .... HHT
Headquarters and Installation Support Activity [*Army*] (AABC) .... HISA
Headquarters and Maintenance Squad .... HAMS
Headquarters and Maintenance Squadron [*Marine Corps*] .... H & MS
Headquarters and Maintenance Squadron Detachment [*Marine Corps*] (DNAB) .... HAMSDET
Headquarters and Service [*Battery*] [*Army*] .... H & S
Headquarters and Service [*Marine Corps*] .... HQ & SERV
Headquarters and Service Squadron .... HS & SS
Headquarters and Service Troop [*Army*] .... H & STR
Headquarters and Supply Company [*Marine Corps*] (VNW) .... H & S
Headquarters Area Command [*Military*] .... HAC
Headquarters Area Command [*Military*] .... HACOM
Headquarters Base Area .... HQBA
Headquarters Battalion (DNAB) .... HQBN
Headquarters Battery [*Military*] (DNAB) .... HQBTRY
Headquarters, Bomber Command [*Later, HQSTC*] [*British*] (NATG) .... HQBC
Headquarters British Element Trieste Forces .... BETFOR
Headquarters Case Development Officer [*Environmental Protection Agency*] (GFGA) .... HQCDO
Headquarters Catalog Office .... HCO
Headquarters City [*Dialog*] [*Searchable field*] [*Information service or system*] (NITA) .... HC
Headquarters, Civil Air Patrol .... HQ-CAP
Headquarters, Coastal Command [*British*] (NATG) .... HQCC
Headquarters Command [*Military*] .... HC
Headquarters Command [*Military*] .... HEADCOM
Headquarters Command [*Military*] .... HEDCOM
Headquarters Command [*Air Force*] .... HQC
Headquarters Command [*Military*] .... HQCMD
Headquarters Command [*Military*] (KSC) .... HQCOM
Headquarters Command [*Air Force*] .... HQCOMD
Headquarters Command, United States Air Force .... HQCOMDUSAF
Headquarters Commandant (NATG) .... HQCOMDT
Headquarters Commitment Authorization [*Military*] (DNAB) .... HCA
Headquarters Companies [*San Francisco, CA*] (TSSD) .... HQ
Headquarters Company [*Military*] (DNAB) .... HQCO
Headquarters Data Manager (KSC) .... HQDM
Headquarters Defense Communications Agency, Washington, DC [*OCLC symbol*] (OCLC) .... DFC
Headquarters, Defense Supply Agency .... HQ DSA
Headquarters, Defense Traffic Management Service .... HQDTMS
Headquarters, Department of the Army .... HDA
Headquarters, Department of the Army .... HQDA
Headquarters, Department of the Pacific [*Marine Corps*] .... HQDP
Headquarters, Department of the Pacific [*Marine Corps*] .... MARPAC
Headquarters Engineering Economics Reference Centre, Bell Canada, Hull, Quebec [*Library symbol National Library of Canada*] (NLC) .... QHBEER
Headquarters, Equipment Authorization Review Center [*Army*] .... HQEARC
Headquarters Field Army (NATG) .... HFA
Headquarters, Fighter Command [*NATO*] (NATG) .... HQFC
Headquarters, Integrated Air Defense System [*Air Force*] .... HQIADS
Headquarters Integrated Office System [*Military*] (GFGA) .... HIOS
Headquarters, Joint Task Force (MCD) .... HQJTF
Headquarters Library, Energy, Mines and Resources Canada [*Bibliotheque Centrale, Energie, Mines et Ressources Canada*] **Ottawa, Ontario** [*Library symbol National Library of Canada*] (NLC) .... OOMR
Headquarters Library of the United Nations .... LIB (UN)
Headquarters Management Directive [*NASA*] .... HQMD
Headquarters, Marine Corps .... HQMC
Headquarters, Military Traffic Management Terminal Service (DNAB) .... HQMTMTS
Headquarters Mobile Command, Canada Department of National Defence [*Quartier-General du Commandement de la Defense Nationale*] **St-Hubert, Quebec** [*Library symbol National Library of Canada*] (NLC) .... QSTHUM
Headquarters Modification Request [*Military*] (CAAL) .... HMR
Headquarters Name [*Dialog*] [*Searchable field*] [*Information service or system*] (NITA) .... HN
Headquarters, Naval Material Command .... HQNAVMATCOM
Headquarters, Naval Material Command (AFIT) .... HQNMC
Headquarters, Navy-Marine Corps Military Affiliate Radio System Station (DNAB) .... HQNAVMARCORMARSTA
Headquarters Office Instruction .... HOI
Headquarters Operating Instruction .... HDI
Headquarters Operating Instructions [*Air Force*] (AFM) .... HOI
Headquarters Operational Command [*Australia*] .... HQOC
Headquarters Pamphlet [*Military*] (MCD) .... HP
Headquarters, Service Battalion [*Military*] (DNAB) .... HQSVCBN
Headquarters, Service Company [*Military*] (DNAB) .... HQSVCCO
Headquarters Signal Officer (NATG) .... HSO
Headquarters, Signals Command [*British*] (NATG) .... HQSC
Headquarters Squadron [*Obsolete*] .... HEDRON
Headquarters Squadron .... HQSQ
Headquarters Squadron [*Marine Corps*] .... HQSQN
Headquarters Squadron Fleet Air Wing .... HEDRONFAIRWING
Headquarters Squadron Personnel Group .... HDNPRSGR
Headquarters Staff [*British military*] (DMA) .... HQS
Headquarters Staff Instruction .... HSI
Headquarters Staff Instructor (AAGC) .... HSI
Headquarters Staff of the Royal Navy [*British*] .... HQSRN
Headquarters State (NITA) .... HS
Headquarters, Strike Command [*Formerly, HQBC*] [*British*] (NATG) .... HQSTC
Headquarters Support Activity .... HEDSUPPACT
Headquarters Support Activity .... HSA
Headquarters Support Activity - Saigon [*Obsolete Military*] (CINC) .... HSAS
Headquarters, Support Group [*Military*] .... HSG
Headquarters, Support Squadron [*Military*] (DNAB) .... HQSQDN
Headquarters Systems Replacement Program [*Military*] (GFGA) .... HSRP
Headquarters, Transport Command [*British*] (NATG) .... HQTC
Headquarters, United States Air Force (AFM) .... HQ USAF
Headquarters, U.S. Army Corps of Engineers .... HQUSACE
Headquarters, United States Army Forces, Central Pacific Area .... HUSAFICPA
Headquarters, United States Army Forces, Middle Pacific [*World War II*] .... HUSAFMIDPAC
Headquarters Zip Code [*Dialog*] [*Searchable field*] [*Information service or system*] (NITA) .... Hz
Heads [*Automotive engineering*] .... HDS
Heads of Commonwealth Operational Law Enforcement Agencies [*Australia*] .... HOCOLEA
Heads of Marine Agencies [*Commonwealth*] [*State*] (EERA) .... HOMA
Heads of Procuring Activities (MCD) .... HPA
Heads of Services and Offices [*Red Cross*] .... HS & O
Head's Tennessee Reports [*38-40 Tennessee*] [*A publication*] (DLA) .... Head (Tenn)
Head's Tennessee Supreme Court Reports [*1858-59*] [*A publication*] (DLA) .... Head
Headsdown Display .... HDD
Headseat Interface Unit (MCD) .... HIU
Headset (MCD) .... HDST
Headspace [*Above liquids*] .... HS
Headspace Sampler [*Instrumentation*] .... HS
Headspace Sampling-Gas Chromatography .... HS-GC
Headstart [*Education*] (OICC) .... HDST
Heads-Up Audio-Vision Logistics [*NASA*] .... HAL

Headsup Display ... HUD
Heads-Up Display Unit [*Aviation*] (RDA) ... HDU
Heads-Up Display Unit [*Aviation*] ... HUDU
Heads-Up Display Weapons Aiming Computer (IEEE) ... HUDWAC
Heads-Up Display Weapons Aiming System [*Air Force*] (MCD) ... HUDWAS
Head-to-Head [*Polymer structure*] ... HH
Head-to-Tail [*Polymer structure*] ... HT
Head-Up Display ... HUD
Head-Up Display Electronics (NASA) ... HUDE
Head-Up Guidance System [*Aviation*] ... HGS
Headwaiter ... HW
Headway Corporate Resources ... HDWY
Headway Corporate Resources, Inc. [*NASDAQ symbol*] (SAG) ... HDWY
Headway Corporate Resources, Inc. [*Associated Press*] (SAG) ... Headway
Headwear Institute of America (EA) ... HIA
Headwind (FAAC) ... HDWND
HEAF Emergency Service Tanks ... HEST
Heal the Children (EA) ... HC
Healdsburg, CA [*FM radio station call letters*] (RBYB) ... KFGY-FM
Healdsburg, CA [*FM radio station call letters*] (RBYB) ... KHBG
Healdsburg, CA [*FM radio station call letters*] ... KLCQ
Healdsburg Carnegie Public Library, Healdsburg, CA [*Library symbol Library of Congress*] (LCLS) ... CHe
Healdsburg Museum, Healdsburg, CA [*Library symbol*] [*Library of Congress*] (LCLS) ... CHeHM
Healdton, OK [*FM radio station call letters*] ... KICM
Healed Myocardial Infarction [*Cardiology*] (AAMN) ... HMI
Heale's Law of Church Pews [*A publication*] (DLA) ... Heal Pews
Healing Ministry Centre [*Australia*] ... HMC
Healing Our World [*An association*] ... HOW
Healing Well (DMAA) ... HW
Health ... HLTH
Health ... HLTH
Health Act (OICC) ... HA
Health Action International (EA) ... HAI
Health Activation Network [*Later, WHAN*] (EA) ... HAN
Health Advisory (GNE) ... HA
Health Advisory Council [*New South Wales, Australia*] ... HAC
Health Advisory Council [*Generic term*] (DHSM) ... HAC
Health Advocacy Services [*AARP*] ... HAS
Health Affairs [*Army*] (DOMA) ... HA
Health Alliance [*Consumer representation*] (ECON) ... HA
Health Alliance Plan ... HAP
Health and Accident [*Insurance*] ... H & A
Health and Accident Insurance (DAVI) ... H & A Ins
Health and Beauty Aid [*Retailing*] ... HBA
Health and Beauty Aids [*Retailing*] (AABC) ... HABA
Health and Beauty Aids [*Advertising*] (WDMC) ... haba
Health and Beauty Employers Federation [*British*] (DBA) ... HBEF
Health and Building Surveyors' Association of New South Wales [*Australia*] ... HBSANSW
Health and Community Services Research and Development Grants [*Australia*] ... HCSRDG
Health and Diet Survey [*Department of Health and Human Services*] (GFGA) ... HDS
Health and Drug Information Library ... HDIL
Health and Education Resources (EA) ... HER
Health and Energy Institute (EA) ... HEI
Health and Energy Learning Project (EA) ... HELP
Health and Environment (AABC) ... HEV
Health and Environmental Research Advisory Committee [*Department of Energy*] [*Washington, DC*] (EGAO) ... HERAC
Health and Environmental Review Division [*Environmental Protection Agency*] (GFGA) ... HERD
Health and Environmental Risk Analysis Program [*Department of Energy*] ... HERAP
Health and Environmental Studies Program [*Department of Energy*] (IID) ... HESP
Health and Healing Ministries (EA) ... HHM
Health and Human Relations Education Association [*Australia*] ... HHREA
Health and Human Services (DICI) ... HHS
[*Department of*] **Health and Human Services** ... HHS
Health and Human Services Acquisition Regulation (AAGC) ... HHSAR
Health and Human Services Procurement Regulations (AAGC) ... HHSPR
Health and Nutrition Examination Survey [*Public Health Service*] ... HANES
Health and Rehabilitative Library Services Division [*Later, ASCLA*] [*American Library Association*] ... HRLSD
Health and Research Employees' Association of Australia ... HREAA
Health & Retirement Prop Tr [*NYSE symbol*] (TTSB) ... HRP
Health & Retirement Properties Trust [*Formerly, Health/Rehabilitation Property*] [*NYSE symbol*] (SPSG) ... HRP
Health & Retirement Property Trust [*Associated Press*] (SAG) ... HltRet
Health and Safety at Work Act [*1974*] [*British*] (NUCP) ... HASAWA
Health and Safety at Work Act [*British*] ... HASWA
Health and Safety Code [*A publication*] (DLA) ... Health & SC
Health and Safety Commission [*Department of Employment*] [*British*] ... HSC
Health and Safety Executive [*Department of Employment*] [*Sheffield, England*] ... HSE
Health and Safety Executive Online [*Health and Safety Executive*] [*Bibliographic database*] [*British*] ... HSELINE
Health and Safety Guide [*Toxicology*] ... HSG
Health and Safety Laboratory [*ERDA*] ... HASL
Health and Safety Research and Test Center [*Bureau of Mines*] ... HSRTC
Health and Safety Research Division [*Oak Ridge National Laboratory*] ... HASRD
Health and Safety Science Abstracts [*Cambridge Scientific Abstracts*] [*Information service or system*] (CRD) ... HSSA
Health and Safety Technology Management (AIE) ... HASTAM
Health and Usage Monitoring (DA) ... HUM
Health and Welfare Canada ... HWC
Health and Welfare Canada, Environmental Health Directorate, Health Protection Branch, Ottawa, ON, Canada [*Library symbol*] [*Library of Congress*] (LCLS) ... CaOONHH
Health and Welfare Canada, Health Protection Branch, Library Services Division, Ottawa, ON, Canada [*Library symbol*] [*Library of Congress*] (LCLS) ... CaOONHHP
Health and Welfare Canada, Policy Planning and Information Library, Ottawa, ON, Canada [*Library symbol*] [*Library of Congress*] (LCLS) ... CaOONHPP
Health Appraisal Examination (DMAA) ... HAE
Health Aspects of Pesticides ... HAPS
Health Aspects of Pesticides [*Medicine*] (DMAA) ... HAsP
Health Aspects of Pesticides Abstract Bulletin [*Environmental Protection Agency*] ... HAPAB
Health Assessment Document [*Environmental Protection Agency*] (GFGA) ... HAD
Health Assessment Questionnaire (DMAA) ... HAQ
Health Associated Representatives [*Later, HIRA*] (EA) ... HEAR
Health Audiovisual On-Line Catalog [*Northeastern Ohio Universities*] [*Information service or system Defunct*] ... HAVC
Health Based Physical Education ... HBPE
Health Behavior Scale [*Psychiatry*] (DAVI) ... HBS
Health Belief Model (DMAA) ... HBM
Health Benefit ... HB
Health Benefit Advisor [*CHAMPUS*] ... HBA
Health Benefit Card (ADA) ... HBC
Health Benefits Organization [*Insurance*] ... HBO
Health Board [*Ireland*] ... HB
Health Care Administration ... HCA
Health Care Aide (DAVI) ... HCA
Health Care Alternatives Development (HCT) ... HAD
Health Care & Retirement [*NYSE symbol*] (TTSB) ... HCR
Health Care & Retirement Corp. [*NYSE symbol*] (SPSG) ... HCR
Health Care Assistant (MEDA) ... HCA
Health Care Association of Michigan (SRA) ... HCAM
Health Care Card (ADA) ... HCC
Health Care Complaints Commission [*Australia*] ... HCCC
Health Care Compliance Packaging Council (EA) ... HCPC
Health Care Consumers' Association of the Australian Capital Territory ... HCCAACT
Health Care Corp. [*Proposed*] (DHSM) ... HCC
Health Care Education ... HCE
Health Care Exhibitors Association (EA) ... HCEA
Health Care Financing Administration [*HHS*] ... HCFA
[*United States*] **Health Care Financing Administration** ... HCFA
Health Care Financing Administration Rulings [*A publication*] (DLA) ... HCFAR
Health Care Financing Review [*A publication*] (DLA) ... HCF Rev
Health Care Financing Review [*A publication*] (DLA) ... HCFR
Health Care Financing Study Group (EA) ... HCFSG
Health Care Finder ... HCF
Health Care for the Homeless (DMAA) ... HCH
Health Care for the Homeless Program [*Defunct*] (EA) ... HCHP
Health Care Information System (DMAA) ... HCIS
Health Care Insurance Commission, Edmonton, AB, Canada [*Library symbol Library of Congress*] (LCLS) ... CaAEHCI
Health Care Insurance Commission, Edmonton, Alberta [*Library symbol National Library of Canada*] (NLC) ... AEHCI
Health Care International [*British*] ... HCI
Health Care Item Name Directory [*A publication*] ... HIND
Health Care Labor Manual [*A publication*] (DLA) ... HCLM
Health Care Libraries Forum [*Association of Specialized and Cooperative Library Agencies*] ... HCLF
Health Care Literature Information Network [*Institut fuer Krankenhausbau*] [*Germany Information service or system*] (IID) ... HECLINET
Health Care Maintenance (DAVI) ... HCM
Health Care Material Management Society (EA) ... HCMMS
Health Care Opportunities Program [*Department of Health and Human Services*] ... HCOP
Health Care Organization (HCT) ... HCO
Health Care Plan Medical Center, West Seneca, NY [*Library symbol Library of Congress*] (LCLS) ... NWsHeaC
Health Care Practitioner Other Than Physician (MEDA) ... HCPOTP
Health Care Prepayment Plan ... HCPP
Health Care Products, Inc. [*Toronto Stock Exchange symbol*] ... HCP
Health Care Professionals Discussion Group [*American Occupational Therapy Association*] ... HCPDG
Health Care Professionals other than Physicians (HCT) ... HCPOTP
Health Care Prop Inv [*NYSE symbol*] (TTSB) ... HCP
Health Care Property Investors, Inc. [*NYSE symbol*] (SPSG) ... HCP
Health Care Property Investors, Inc. [*Associated Press*] (SAG) ... HlthCP
Health Care Purchasing Organization [*Insurance*] (WYGK) ... HPO
Health Care Quality Improvement Act [*1986*] (HCT) ... HCQIA
Health Care REIT [*NYSE symbol*] (SAG) ... HCN
Health Care REIT [*Associated Press*] (SAG) ... HlthCr
Health Care Research and Educational Foundation [*Later, AAMAREF*] (EA) ... HCREF
Health Care Research Division [*Brooke Army Medical Center*] ... HCRD
Health Care Research Foundation [*Australia*] ... HCRF
Health Care Research Institution [*Australia*] ... HCRI
Health Care Services Group [*NASDAQ symbol*] (SAG) ... HCSG
Health Care Services Group [*Associated Press*] (SAG) ... HlthCSv
Health Care Studies and Clinical Investigation Activity [*Fort Sam Houston, TX*] [*Army*] ... HCSCIA

Health Care Studies Division [*Academy of Health Sciences*] [*Army*] .... HCSD
Health Care Support [*System*] [*IBM Corp.*] .... HCS
Health Care Technology Study Section [*HEW*] (EGAO) .... HCTSS
Health Care Telecommunications Corp. [*Camp Hill, PA*] (TSSD) .... HTC
Health Care Unit [*DoD*] (GFGA) .... HCU
Health Certificate [*British*] (ADA) .... HC
Health Check Test (DMAA) .... HCT
Health Commons Institute .... HCI
Health Communications Network [*Medical University of South Carolina*] [*Charleston*] [*Telecommunications*] (TSSD) .... HCN
Health Computing Services [*Australia*] .... HCS
Health Conference for Business and Industry [*Defunct*] .... HCBI
Health Coordinating Council .... HCC
Health Data Policy Committee [*Department of Health and Human Services*] (GFGA) .... HDPC
Health Data Recorder [*Computer science*] (PDAA) .... HDR
Health Database Plus [*Information Access Co.*] [*Information service or system*] (PCM) .... HDB
Health Department of Western Australia .... HDWA
Health Development Services, Inc. [*Toronto Stock Exchange symbol*] .... HSI
Health Economics Research Center [*University of Wisconsin - Madison*] [*Research center*] (RCD) .... HERC
Health Economics Research Unit [*University of Aberdeen*] [*Scotland*] (IRC) .... HERU
Health, Education, and Human Services Division [*GAO*] (AAGC) .... HEHS
Health Education and Welfare [*Marine science*] (OSRA) .... HEW
Health, Education and Welfare (USDC) .... HEW
Health Education Assistance Loan [*Bureau of Health Professions*] .... HEAL
Health Education Authority [*British*] .... HEA
Health Education Council [*British*] (DAVI) .... HEC
Health Education Division, Newfoundland Department of Health, St. John's, Newfoundland [*Library symbol National Library of Canada*] (NLC) .... NFSHE
Health Education Foundation (EA) .... HEF
Health Education Library Program [*Library network*] .... HELP
Health Education Media Association [*Defunct*] (EA) .... HEMA
Health Education Research Service [*Department of Health and Human Services*] .... HERS
Health Education Resource Organization (EA) .... HERO
Health Education Technologies [*New York, NY*] (TSSD) .... HET
Health Effects Assessment Summary Tables .... HEAST
Health Effects Institute [*Research center*] (RCD) .... HEI
Health Effects Institute-Asbestos Research .... HEI-AR
Health Effects of Environmental Pollutants [*A publication*] .... HEEP
Health Effects of Environmental Pollution [*Database*] (NITA) .... HEEP
Health Effects of Ionizing Radiation [*Medicine*] (DAVI) .... HEIR
Health Effects Research Laboratory [*Research Triangle Park, NC*] [*Environmental Protection Agency*] (GRD) .... HERL
Health Emergency Loan Program [*Planned parenthood*] (DAVI) .... HELP
Health Environment Long-Range Planning Support [*A computer model*] .... HELPS
Health Equity and Access Reform Today [*Plan*] .... HEART
Health Evaluation and Learning Program .... HELP
Health Evaluation and Referral Service .... HERS
Health Evaluation and Risk Tabulation (MCD) .... HEART
Health Evaluation Center (DAVI) .... HEC
Health Evaluation through Logical Processing [*Computer science*] (DAVI) .... HELP
Health Examination Survey [*NCHS*] .... HES
Health Facilities Information File [*Australia*] .... HFI
Health Facilities Planning and Construction Service .... HFPCS
Health First International (EA) .... HFI
Health Fitness Physical Therapy [*NASDAQ symbol*] (SAG) .... HFPT
Health Fitness Physical Therapy [*Associated Press*] (SAG) .... HlthFit
Health Food Manufacturers Association [*British*] (DBA) .... HFMA
Health for Haiti Foundation (EA) .... HHF
Health Hazard Assessment [*Army*] .... HHA
Health Hazard Assessment Report [*Army*] .... HHAR
[*Department of*] **Health, Housing, Local Government and Community Services** (EERA) .... HHLGCS
Health Identification Number .... HIN
Health Illness Profile (DMAA) .... HIP
Health Images [*NYSE symbol*] (TTSB) .... HII
Health Images, Inc. [*NYSE symbol*] (SPSG) .... HII
Health Images, Inc. [*Associated Press*] (SAG) .... HltImg
Health Indication Test [*Engine system*] .... HIT
Health Industries Association [*Later, HIMA*] .... HIA
Health Industries Institute (EA) .... HII
Health Industry Advisory Committee [*Terminated, 1974*] (EGAO) .... HIAC
Health Industry Business Communications Council (EA) .... HIBCC
Health Industry Distributors Association (EA) .... HIDA
Health Industry Manufacturers Association (EA) .... HIMA
Health Industry Representatives Association (EA) .... HIRA
Health Industry Wage and Salary Committee [*Terminated, 1974*] (EGAO) .... HIWSC
Health Information Council [*An association*] (EA) .... HIC
Health Information Foundation .... HIF
Health Information Libraries of Westchester [*Library network*] .... HILOW
Health Information Library Network of Northeastern Pennsylvania [*Library network*] .... HILNNEP
Health Information Library Program [*Library network*] .... HILP
Health Information Network Services [*Database search service*] (OLDSS) .... HINS
Health Information Network Services, Everett, WA [*Library symbol*] [*Library of Congress*] (LCLS) .... WaEH
Health Information Policy Council [*Department of Health and Human Services*] (GFGA) .... HIPC
Health Information Series [*Federal government*] .... HIS
Health Information Services [*Australia*] .... HIS
Health Information Services [*Department of Health and Human Services*] .... HIS
Health Information System (DMAA) .... HIS
Health Information Technologies and Education Center [*University of Texas Health Science Center*] [*Houston, TX*] [*Computer science*] .... HITEC
Health Inspector [*British military*] (DMA) .... HI
Health Insurance .... HI
Health Insurance Advisory Committee [*Australia*] .... HIAC
Health Insurance Association of America [*Washington, DC*] (EA) .... HIAA
Health Insurance Benefits Advisory Council [*Department of Health and Human Services Inactive*] .... HIBAC
Health Insurance Claim Form .... HICF
Health Insurance Claim Number [*Medicare*] (DHSM) .... HIC
Health Insurance Council [*Later, Consumer and Professional Relations Division of HIAA*] (EA) .... HIC
Health Insurance/Employer Survey [*Department of Health and Human Services*] (GFGA) .... HIES
Health Insurance Institute (EA) .... HII
Health Insurance Manual .... HIM
Health Insurance Persistency Award [*Later, HIQA*] [*LIMRA*] .... HIPA
Health Insurance Plan .... HIP
Health Insurance Plans Survey [*Department of Health and Human Services*] (GFGA) .... HIPS
Health Insurance Purchasing Collective (DMAA) .... HIPC
Health Insurance Purchasing Cooperative (ECON) .... HIPC
Health Insurance Quality Award [*Formerly, HIPA*] [*LIMRA*] .... HIQA
Health Insurance Regional Office .... HIRO
Health Insurance Regulation .... HIR
Health Insurance Skeleton Eligibility Write-off File [*Department of Health and Human Services*] (GFGA) .... HISKEW
Health Insurance Standards Board .... HISB
Health Insurance Tax [*Social Security Administration*] (GFGA) .... HIT
Health Insurance Trust Fund .... HITF
Health Insuring Organization (DMAA) .... HIO
Health Interview Survey [*National Institutes of Health*] .... HIS
Health Issues for People with Developmental Disabilities .... DDHEALTH
Health Labour Relations Association [*Canada*] .... HLRA
Health Lawyers News Report [*A publication*] (DLA) .... HLNR
Health Learning Systems .... HLS
Health Maintenance Facility (MCD) .... HMF
Health Maintenance Organization .... HMO
Health Maintenance Organization Acts of 1973 and 1988 (WYGK) .... HMOA
Health Maintenance Organization Service [*Public Health Service*] .... HMOS
Health Management [*NASDAQ symbol*] (TTSB) .... HMIS
Health Management Associates, Inc. [*Associated Press*] (SAG) .... HltMgt
Health Management Associates, Inc. [*NYSE symbol*] (SPSG) .... HMA
Health Management, Inc. [*Associated Press*] (SAG) .... HltMInc
Health Management, Inc. [*NASDAQ symbol*] (SAG) .... HMIS
Health Management Resources [*Diet program*] .... HMR
Health Management Systems [*NASDAQ symbol*] (TTSB) .... HMSY
Health Management Systems, Inc. [*Associated Press*] (SAG) .... HlthMSys
Health Management Systems, Inc. [*Associated Press*] (SAG) .... HltMSys
Health Management Systems, Inc. [*NASDAQ symbol*] (SAG) .... HMSY
Health Manpower Advisory Council .... HMAC
Health Manpower Education Initiative Award .... HMEIA
Health Manpower Shortage Area .... HMSA
Health Manpower Shortage Area Placement Opportunity List [*Department of Health and Human Services*] (GFGA) .... HPOL
Health Media Education (EA) .... HME
Health Message Testing Services [*Department of Health and Human Services*] (GFGA) .... HMTS
Health Mgt Associates'A' [*NYSE symbol*] (TTSB) .... HMA
Health Ministers Council (EERA) .... HMC
Health Mobilization Series .... HMS
Health Mor, Inc. [*NASDAQ symbol*] (SAG) .... HMII
Health News Institute [*Defunct*] .... HNI
Health O Meter Products [*Associated Press*] (SAG) .... HltMetr
Health o meter Products [*NASDAQ symbol*] (TTSB) .... SCAL
Health O Meter Products, Inc. [*NASDAQ symbol*] (SAG) .... SCAL
Health Occupations Students of America (EA) .... HOSA
Health of Munition Workers Committee [*World War I*] [*British*] .... HMWC
Health of Naval Aviation (DOMA) .... HONA
Health of the Oceans [*Marine science*] (OSRA) .... HOTO
Health Officer Certificate (DAVI) .... HOC
Health Online Service [*Computer science*] [*Medicine*] .... HOS
Health Opportunity for People Everywhere [*Philanthropic project operating hospital ship*] .... HOPE
Health Optimizing Institute (EA) .... HOI
Health Organization to Preserve the Environment .... HOPE
Health, Physical Education, and Recreation .... HPER
Health, Physical Education, Recreation, and Dance (AEE) .... HPERD
Health Physics [*Nuclear energy*] (NRCH) .... HP
Health Physics Center [*Nuclear energy*] (NRCH) .... HPC
Health Physics Network [*Nuclear energy*] (NRCH) .... HPN
Health Physics Program (NRCH) .... HPP
Health Physics Research Reactor [*Oak Ridge, TN*] [*Oak Ridge National Laboratory*] [*Department of Energy*] .... HPRR
Health Physics Society (EA) .... HPS
Health Physics Station [*Nuclear energy*] (NRCH) .... HPS
Health Plan Employer Data and Information Set .... HEDIS
Health Plan Purchasing Cooperatives .... HPPC
Health Planning and Administration [*National Library of Medicine*] [*Database*] .... HEALTHLINE
Health Policy Advisory Center (EA) .... HPAC

Health Policy Agenda for the American People (HCT) .... HPA
Health Policy Council [*Defunct*] (EA) .... HPC
Health Power [*Associated Press*] (SAG) .... HlthPwr
Health Power [*NASDAQ symbol*] (SAG) .... HPWR
Health Practices Inventory (EDAC) .... HPI
Health Professional Shortage Area (DMAA) .... HPSA
Health Professionals [*Associated Press*] (SAG) .... HlthPro
Health Professionals [*AMEX symbol*] (TTSB) .... HPI
Health Professionals, Inc. [*AMEX symbol*] (SPSG) .... HPI
Health Professionals Loan Repayment Program [*Military*] .... HPLRP
Health Professions Scholarship Program [*Army*] .... HPSP
Health Professions Stress Inventory [*Medicine*] .... HPSI
Health Professions Student Loans .... HPSL
Health Programs Systems Center .... HPSC
Health Promotion and Disease Prevention Initiative [*Pronounced "hippy dippy"*] [*Department of Health and Human Services*] .... HPDPI
Health Promotion Pilot .... HPP
Health Promotion/Wellness Program [*Medicine*] (DMAA) .... HP/W
Health Protection Branch, Canada Department of National Health and Welfare [*Direction Generale de la Protection de la Sante, Ministere de la Sante Nationale et du Bien-Etre Social*] **Montreal, Quebec** [*Library symbol National Library of Canada*] (NLC) .... QMNHH
Health Protection Branch, Canada Department of National Health and Welfare [*Direction Generale de la Protection de la Sante, Ministere de la Sante Nationale et du Bien-Etre Social*] **Toronto, Ontario** [*Library symbol National Library of Canada*] (NLC) .... OTNHH
Health Protection Branch, Canada Department of National Health and Welfare [*Direction Generale de la Protection de la Sante, Ministere de la Sante Nationale et du Bien-Etre Social*] **Vancouver, British Columbia** [*Library symbol National Library of Canada*] (NLC) .... BVANH
Health Record .... HELREC
Health Record .... HREC
Health Related Fitness Test (EDAC) .... HRET
Health Related Quality of Life .... HRQOL
Health Research Group .... HRG
Health Research, Inc. [*New York State Department of Health*] [*Research center*] (RCD) .... HRI
Health Resources Administration [*Abolished, 1982, functions transferred to Health Resources and Services Administration*] [*HEW*] .... HRA
Health Resources and Services Administration [*Department of Health and Human Services*] .... HRSA
Health Risk Appraisal [*or Assessment*] [*Medicine*] .... HRA
Health Risk Management [*NASDAQ symbol*] (TTSB) .... HRMI
Health Risk Management, Inc. [*Associated Press*] (SAG) .... HlthRsk
Health Risk Management, Inc. [*NASDAQ symbol*] (SAG) .... HRMI
Health Risk Management Service [*Australian Capital Territory*] .... HRMS
Health Science Centre, Children's Centre, Winnipeg, MB, Canada [*Library symbol Library of Congress*] (LCLS) .... CaMWCCH
Health Science Cluster Program [*University of Connecticut*] [*Research center*] (RCD) .... HSCP
Health Science Libraries Information Cooperative [*Library network*] .... HSLIC
Health Science Libraries of Central Georgia [*Library network*] .... HSLCG
Health Sciences Advancement Award [*National Institutes of Health*] .... HSAA
Health Sciences Centre, General Centre, Winnipeg, MB, Canada [*Library symbol Library of Congress*] (LCLS) .... CaMWGCH
Health Sciences Centre, Medical Library, Winnipeg, MB, Canada [*Library symbol Library of Congress*] (LCLS) .... CaMWHM
Health Sciences Communications Association (EA) .... HESCA
Health Sciences Communications Association (DAVI) .... HSCA
Health Sciences Computing Facility [*UCLA*] .... HSCF
Health Sciences Consortium (EA) .... HSC
Health Sciences Education and Training Command [*Navy*] (DNAB) .... HSETC
Health Sciences Information Centre, Jewish Rehabilitation Hospital [*Centre d'Information sur les Sciences de la Sante, Hopital Juif de Readaptation*] **Chomedey, Quebec** [*Library symbol National Library of Canada*] (NLC) .... QCHJC
Health Sciences Library [*Library network*] .... MOHSLG
Health Sciences Library, Bloorview Children's Hospital, Willowdale, Ontario [*Library symbol National Library of Canada*] (BIB) .... OWBC
Health Sciences Library, Centracare Saint John, Inc., New Brunswick [*Library symbol National Library of Canada*] (NLC) .... NBSC
Health Sciences Library, General & Marine Hospital, Owen Sound, Ontario [*Library symbol National Library of Canada*] (NLC) .... OOWGM
Health Sciences Library, Grey Bruce Regional Health Centre, Owen Sound, Ontario [*Library symbol National Library of Canada*] (NLC) .... OOWGM
Health Sciences Library, Hotel-Dieu Hospital, Chatham, New Brunswick [*Library symbol National Library of Canada*] (BIB) .... NBCHD
Health Sciences Library, McMaster University, Hamilton, Ontario [*Library symbol National Library of Canada*] (NLC) .... OHMB
Health Sciences Library, Memorial University, St. John's, Newfoundland [*Library symbol National Library of Canada*] (NLC) .... NFSMM
Health Sciences Library, Miramichi Hospital, Newcastle, New Brunswick [*Library symbol National Library of Canada*] (NLC) .... NBNM
Health Sciences Library, Mississauga Hospital, Ontario [*Library symbol National Library of Canada*] (BIB) .... OMH
Health Sciences Library, Northwestern General Hospital, Toronto, Ontario [*Library symbol National Library of Canada*] (BIB) .... OTNGH
Health Sciences Library, Plains Health Centre, Regina, Saskatchewan [*Library symbol National Library of Canada*] (NLC) .... SRHS
Health Sciences Library, Saint John Regional Hospital [*Bibliotheque des Sciences de la Sante, Hopital Regional de Saint-Jean*], New Brunswick [*Library symbol National Library of Canada*] (NLC) .... NBSRH
Health Sciences Library, St. Paul's Hospital, Vancouver, British Columbia [*Library symbol National Library of Canada*] (NLC) .... BVASPH
Health Sciences Library, Sudbury Algoma Hospital, Sudbury, Ontario [*Library symbol National Library of Canada*] (NLC) .... OSAH
Health Sciences Library, The Moncton Hospital, New Brunswick [*Library symbol National Library of Canada*] (NLC) .... NBMMH
Health Sciences Library, Toronto Western Hospital, Ontario [*Library symbol National Library of Canada*] (NLC) .... OTTWH
Health Sciences Library, University of Ottawa [*Bibliotheque des Sciences de la Sante, Universite d'Ottawa*] **Ontario** [*Library symbol National Library of Canada*] (NLC) .... OOUH
Health Sciences Library, Victoria General Hospital, Halifax, Nova Scotia [*Library symbol National Library of Canada*] (NLC) .... NSHVGH
Health Screening Test (DAVI) .... HST
Health Security Action Council (EA) .... HSAC
Health Self Determination Index (MEDA) .... HSDI
Health Service Action [*Later, CNHS*] [*An association*] (EA) .... HSA
Health Service Agreement .... HSA
Health Service Area [*Military*] (AABC) .... HSA
Health Service Laboratory [*Army*] (AABC) .... HSL
Health Service Plan .... HSP
Health Service Region [*Army*] (AABC) .... HSR
Health Service Support [*Army*] (DOMA) .... HSS
Health Service Support Air Land Battle .... HSSALB
Health Services Administration [*Abolished, 1982, functions transferred to Health Resources and Services Administration*] .... HSA
Health Services and Mental Health Administration [*Later, ADAMHA*] [*Abolished, 1973*] [*HEW*] .... HSM
Health Services and Mental Health Administration [*Later, ADAMHA*] [*Abolished, 1973*] [*HEW*] .... HSMHA
Health Services and Promotion Branch, Department of National Health and Welfare [*Direction Generale des Services et de la Promotion de la Sante, Ministere dela Sante Nationale et du Bien-Etre Social*] **Ottawa, Ontario** [*Library symbol National Library of Canada*] (NLC) .... OONHHS
Health Services and Resources Administration (DAVI) .... HSRA
Health Services Association of New South Wales [*Australia*] .... HSANSW
Health Services Centre [*Institute of Organisation and Social Studies, Brunel University*] [*British*] (CB) .... HSC
Health Services Command [*Army*] .... HSC
Health Services Library, Halifax Infirmary, Nova Scotia [*Library symbol National Library of Canada*] (NLC) .... NSHHI
Health Services Research and Development [*Series*] [*A publication*] .... HSRD
Health Services Research and Development Service [*Washington, DC Veterans Administration*] (GRD) .... HSR & D
Health Services Research and Training Program [*Purdue University*] [*Research center*] (RCD) .... HSRTP
Health Services Research Center [*Georgia Institute of Technology*] [*Research center*] (RCD) .... HSRC
Health Services/Technology Assessment Text [*National Library of Medicine*] [*Information service or system*] .... HSTAT
Health Services Union of Australia .... HSUA
Health Services, Waterford Hospital, St. John's, Newfoundland [*Library symbol National Library of Canada*] (NLC) .... NFSWH
Health Stabilization Program [*NASA*] (NASA) .... HSP
Health Standards and Quality Bureau [*HEW*] .... HSQB
Health Standards Board .... HealSB
Health Surveillance System [*Shell Oil Co.*] .... HSS
Health Systems Agency [*New York, NY*] .... HSA
Health Systems Agency of Western New York, Inc., Buffalo, NY [*Library symbol Library of Congress*] (LCLS) .... NBuHSA
Health Systems Design [*NASDAQ symbol*] (TTSB) .... HSDC
Health Systems Design Corp. [*Associated Press*] (SAG) .... HlthSys
Health Systems Design Corp. [*NASDAQ symbol*] (SAG) .... HSDC
Health Systems International [*Associated Press*] (SAG) .... HlthSys
Health Systems International [*NYSE symbol*] (SAG) .... HQ
Health Systems Intl'A' [*NYSE symbol*] (TTSB) .... HQ
Health Systems Plan [*HEW*] .... HSP
Health Systems Research Institute .... HSRI
Health Systems Vendors Association [*San Francisco, CA*] (EA) .... HSVA
Health Underserved Rural Areas .... HURA
Health Visitor .... HV
Health Visitors' Association [*A union*] [*British*] (DCTA) .... HVA
Health Visitor's Certificate [*British*] .... HVC
Health Volunteers Overseas (EA) .... HVO
Health-Based Number [*Environmental science*] .... HBN
HealthCare and Retirement Corp. [*Associated Press*] (SAG) .... HCR
Healthcare Association of Hawaii (SRA) .... HAH
Healthcare Association of New York State (SRA) .... HANYS
HealthCare COMPARE [*NASDAQ symbol*] (TTSB) .... HCCC
HealthCare COMPARE Corp. [*NASDAQ symbol*] (NQ) .... HCCC
HealthCare COMPARE Corp. [*Associated Press*] (SAG) .... HltCmp
Healthcare Evaluation System [*National Planning Data Corp.*] [*Information service or system*] (CRD) .... HES
Healthcare Financial Management Association (EA) .... HFMA
HealthCare Financial Partners, Inc. [*NASDAQ symbol*] (SAG) .... HCFP
HealthCare Financial Partners, Inc. [*Associated Press*] (SAG) .... HlthCFP
Healthcare Financing Study Group (EA) .... HFSG
[*The*] **Healthcare Forum** (EA) .... HCF
Healthcare Imaging Services [*NASDAQ symbol*] (TTSB) .... HISS
HealthCare Imaging Services, Inc. [*Associated Press*] (SAG) .... HCIm
HealthCare Imaging Services, Inc. [*NASDAQ symbol*] (SAG) .... HISS
HealthCare Imaging Services, Inc. [*Associated Press*] (SAG) .... HltCrIm
Healthcare Imaging Sv Wrrt'B' [*NASDAQ symbol*] (TTSB) .... HISSZ
Healthcare Information and Management Systems Society (EA) .... HIMSS
Healthcare Information Systems Sharing Group (EA) .... HISSG
Health-Care Instruments and Devices Institute [*State University of New York at Buffalo*] [*Research center*] (RCD) .... HIDI

Healthcare International Audit Group (EA) .... HIAG
Healthcare Product .... HP
Healthcare Realty Tr [NYSE symbol] (TTSB) .... HR
Healthcare Realty Trust [Associated Press] (SAG) .... HltcrRty
Healthcare Realty Trust [NYSE symbol] (SPSG) .... HR
Healthcare Services Group, Inc. [NASDAQ symbol] (NQ) .... HCSG
Healthcare Svcs Group [NASDAQ symbol] (TTSB) .... HCSG
Healthcare Technologies Ltd. [NASDAQ symbol] (NQ) .... HCTL
Healthcare Technologies Ltd. [Associated Press] (SAG) .... HltcrTc
Healthcare Technologies Ltd [NASDAQ symbol] (TTSB) .... HCTLF
Health-Chem [AMEX symbol] (TTSB) .... HCH
Health-Chem Corp. [AMEX symbol] (SPSG) .... HCH
Health-Chem Corp. [Associated Press] (SAG) .... HlthCh
HealthCor Holdings, Inc. [NASDAQ symbol] (SAG) .... HCOR
HealthCor Holdings, Inc. [Associated Press] (SAG) .... HlthCor
Healthdyne, Inc. [NASDAQ symbol] (NQ) .... HDYN
Healthdyne, Inc. [Associated Press] (SAG) .... Hlthdyn
Healthdyne Info Enterprises [NASDAQ symbol] (TTSB) .... HDIE
Healthdyne Technologies [NASDAQ symbol] (SAG) .... HDTC
Healthdyne Technologies [Associated Press] (SAG) .... HlthdynT
Healthdyne Technologies [Associated Press] (SAG) .... HlthdyT
Health-Education Telecommunications [HEW] .... HET
Health-Oriented Libraries of San Antonio [Library network] .... HOLSA
Health-Oriented Physician Education .... HOPE
HealthPlan Services [NYSE symbol] (TTSB) .... HPS
Healthplan Services Corp. [Associated Press] (SAG) .... Hlthpln
Healthplan Services Corp. [Associated Press] (SAG) .... HlthplnSv
Healthplan Services Corp. [NYSE symbol] (SAG) .... HPS
Healthplex, Inc. [Associated Press] (SAG) .... Hltplx
Healthplex, Inc. [NASDAQ symbol] (NQ) .... HPLX
Health-Related Quality of Life .... HRQOL
Health-Related Quality-of-Life [Medicine] .... HRQL
HealthRite, Inc. [NASDAQ symbol] (SAG) .... HLRT
HealthRite, Inc. [Associated Press] (SAG) .... HlthRite
HealthRite, Inc. [NASDAQ symbol] (SAG) .... HURT
Health-Sickness Rating Scale (DMAA) .... HSRS
Healthsource, Inc. [Associated Press] (SAG) .... Hlthsrc
Healthsource, Inc. [Associated Press] (SAG) .... Hlthsrce
Healthsource, Inc. [NYSE symbol] (SPSG) .... HS
Healthsouth Corp. [Associated Press] (SAG) .... Hlthsth
HEALTHSOUTH Corp. [NYSE symbol] (TTSB) .... HRC
HEALTHSOUTH Rehabilitation Corp. [NYSE symbol] (SPSG) .... HRC
HealthTech International, Inc. [NASDAQ symbol] (SAG) .... CLUB
HealthTech International, Inc. [Associated Press] (SAG) .... HlthTc
HealthTech International, Inc. [Associated Press] (SAG) .... HlthTch
HealthTech International, Inc. [Associated Press] (SAG) .... HlthTech
HealthTech Intl [NASDAQ symbol] (TTSB) .... GYMM
HealthTech Intl Wrrt'A' [NASDAQ symbol] (TTSB) .... GYMMW
Healthwatch, Inc. [NASDAQ symbol] (NQ) .... HEAL
Healthwatch Inc. [NASDAQ symbol] (TTSB) .... HEALD
Healthwatch, Inc. [Associated Press] (SAG) .... Hlthwtch
Healthwise of America, Inc. [Associated Press] (SAG) .... HltwAm
Healthwise of America, Inc. [NASDAQ symbol] (SAG) .... HOAM
Healthy .... H
Healthy America [An association Defunct] (EA) .... HA
Healthy Cities Secretariat [Australia] .... HCS
Healthy Control [Medicine] (DMAA) .... HC
Healthy Hemophiliac [Medicine] (DMAA) .... HH
Healthy Male (ROG) .... HM
Healthy Mothers, Healthy Babies (EA) .... HMHB
Healthy Mothers, Healthy Babies National Coalition (PAZ) .... HMHB
Healthy Planet Prod [AMEX symbol] (TTSB) .... HPP
Healthy Planet Products, Inc. [Associated Press] (SAG) .... HltPlanet
Healthy Planet Products, Inc. [AMEX symbol] (SAG) .... HPP
Healthy Worker Effect (DMAA) .... HWE
Healthy Years Equivalent (DMAA) .... HYE
Healthy-Happy-Holy Organization 3HO
Heal-ᵧo-Shin [Test] [Neurology] (DAVI) .... HTS
Healy, AK [Location identifier FAA] (FAAL) .... HRR
Healy High School, Pierz, MN [Library symbol] [Library of Congress] (LCLS) .... MnPiH
Healy on Joint Stock Companies [A publication] (DLA) .... Heal JS Comp
Hear Now [An association] (EA) .... HN
Hear O Israel (EA) .... HOI
Hear What I Mean [Speech recognition system] .... HWIM
Hear You Are, Inc. [An association] (PAZ) .... HYAI
Heard (ROG) .... HD
Heard and McDonald Islands [ANSI two-letter standard code] (CNC) .... HM
Heard and McDonald Islands [MARC country of publication code Library of Congress] (LCCP) .... hm
Heard and McDonald Islands [MARC geographic area code Library of Congress] (LCCP) .... i-hm--
Heard Best at Left Lower Sternal Border [Cardiology] (DAVI) .... HBLLSB
Heard Best at Left Upper Sternal Border [Cardiology] (DAVI) .... HBLUSB
Heard Island [Region] (EERA) .... HI
Heard Island [Seismograph station code, US Geological Survey Closed] (SEIS) .... HII
Heard Island and McDonald Islands [ANSI three-letter standard code] (CNC) .... HMD
Heard Island Feasibility Test [Marine science] (OSRA) .... HIFT
Heard Island Feasibility Test [USDC) .... HIFT
Heard on Libel and Slander [A publication] (DLA) .... Heard Lib & Sl
Heard on the Hill [US Congress] .... HOH
Heard's Civil Pleading [A publication] (DLA) .... Heard Civ Pl
Heard's Criminal Pleading [A publication] (DLA) .... Heard Cr Pl

Heard's Curiosities of the Law Reporters [A publication] (DLA) .... Heard Cur Rep
Heard's Edition of Shortt on Extraordinary Legal Remedies [A publication] (DLA) .... Heard's Shortt Extr Rem
Heard's Equity Pleading [A publication] (DLA) .... Heard Eq Pl
Hearing .... HEAR
Hearing (ROG) .... HRG
Hearing .... HRNG
Hearing Aid .... HA
Hearing Aid Amplifier .... HAA
Hearing Aid Battery .... HAB
Hearing Aid Dispenser [Otorhinolaryngology] (DAVI) .... HAD
Hearing Aid Evaluation [Otorhinolaryngology] (DAVI) .... HAE
Hearing Aid Follow-Up and Orientation [Otorhinolaryngology] (DAVI) .... HAO
Hearing Aid Industry Association [British] (DBA) .... HAIA
Hearing Aid Industry Conference [Later, HIA] (EA) .... HAIC
Hearing Aid Manufacturers' and Suppliers' Association [British] (BI) ...... HAMSA
Hearing Aid Microphone .... HAM
Hearing Aid with Compression .... HAC
Hearing Aide of Minnesota (SRA) .... HAM
Hearing and Tinnitus Help Association [Later, AEAR] (EA) .... HTHA
Hearing Carry-Over [Hearing-impaired technology] .... HCO
Hearing Denied [Legal term] (HGAA) .... hg den
Hearing Distance [Medicine] .... HD
Hearing Distance with Watch [Medicine] .... HDW
Hearing Dog Project [Later, HDRC] (EA) .... HDP
Hearing Dog Resource Center (EA) .... HDRC
Hearing Ear Dog Program (EA) .... HEDP
Hearing Education and Awareness for Rockers [An association] .... HEAR
Hearing Education through Auditory Research [In association name, HEAR Center] (EA) .... HEAR
Hearing, Educational Aid and Research Foundation [Defunct] (EA) .... HEAR-FOUND
Hearing Examiner [Also, ALJ] .... HE
Hearing Examiner [Legal term] (DLA) .... Hear Exam
Hearing Impaired (OICC) .... HI
Hearing Impaired Consultants Creating Unique Partnerships [An association] .... HICCUP
Hearing Impaired Peer .... HIP
Hearing Industries Association (EA) .... HIA
Hearing Level .... HL
Hearing Loss .... HL
Hearing Office Systems Administrator [Computer science] .... HOSA
Hearing Office Tracking System [Computer science] .... HOTS
Hearing Performance Inventory for Children .... HPIC
Hearing Power (ROG) .... H
Hearing Protection Device .... HPD
Hearing Rehabilitation Research Center [Walt Disney] (BABM) .... HRRC
Hearing Test (CPH) .... HT
Hearing Threshold Level .... HTL
Hearing-for-Speech Test .... HFST
Hearing-Impaired Mentally Retarded .... HIMR
Hearing-Lookout Assist Device [Navigation] (OA) .... HLAD
Hearne, TX [FM radio station call letters] (RBYB) .... KHRN
Hearsay Evidence [Legal shorthand] (LWAP) .... HE
Hearsay Evidence Rule [Legal shorthand] (LWAP) .... HER
Hearst Free Library, Lead, SD [Library symbol Library of Congress] (LCLS) .... SdL
Hearst, ON [Television station call letters] CBLFT-5
Hearst, ON [AM radio station call letters] .... CHOH
Hearst, ON [FM radio station call letters] (RBYB) .... CINN-FM
Hearst Public Library, Hearst, ON, Canada [Library symbol Library of Congress] (LCLS) .... CaOHe
Hearst Public Library, Ontario [Library symbol National Library of Canada] (NLC) .... OHE
Heart [Freemasonry] (ROG) .... H
Heart (DMAA) .... He
Heart .... HRT
Heart .... HRT
Heart .... HT
Heart and Estrogen/Progestin Replacement Study [Medicine] .... HERS
Heart and Lung Foundation [Defunct] (EA) .... HLF
Heart and Lungs [Medicine] .... H & L
Heart Antibody [Medicine] (CPH) .... HAb
Heart Block [Medicine] .... HB
Heart Cell Aggregate [Cytology] .... HCA
Heart Cubic Content (DAC) .... HrtCC
Heart Cycle [Cardiology] (MAE) .... HC
Heart Disease [Medicine] .... HD
Heart Disease History [Medicine] (MAE) .... HDH
Heart Disease Research Foundation (EA) .... HDRF
Heart Facial Area (DAC) .... HrtFa
Heart Failure [Medicine] .... HF
Heart Fan Club (EA) .... HFC
Heart Girth (DAC) .... HrtG
Heart Information Center .... HIC
Heart Infusion Agar [Medicine] .... HIA
Heart Infusion Broth [Medicine] (DMAA) .... HIB
Heart Labs Amer [NASDAQ symbol] (TTSB) .... HLOAE
Heart Labs Amer Wrrt [NASDAQ symbol] (TTSB) .... HLOWE
Heart Labs of America [Associated Press] (SAG) .... HrtLabs
Heart Labs of America [Associated Press] (SAG) .... HrtLb
Heart Labs of America, Inc. [NASDAQ symbol] (SAG) .... HLOA
Heart, Liver, Kidney [Medicine] (MAE) .... HLK
Heart Minute Output [Cardiology] .... HMO
Heart Murmur [Cardiology] (MAE) .... HM
Heart Muscle Kinase [An enzyme] .... HMK

Heart of America Carnival Glass Association (EA) .... HOACGA
Heart of America Walking Horse Association (EA) .... HAWHA
Heart of England Tourist Board (DCTA) .... HETB
Heart of Texas Council of Governments .... HOTCOG
Heart Profile Recorder [*Medicine*] .... HPR
Heart Rate [*Medicine*] .... HR
Heart Rate [*Cardiology*] (DAVI) .... HRT
Heart Rate Acceleration .... HRA
Heart Rate Audiometry .... HRA
Heart Rate Range [*Medicine*] .... HRR
Heart Rate Retardation Index [*Medicine*] (DMAA) .... HRRI
Heart Research Institute [*Australia*] .... HRI
Heart Rhythm [*Cardiology*] .... HR
Heart Sounds [*Medicine*] .... HS
Heart Synchronized Evoked Potential [*Medicine*] (DMAA) .... HSEP
Heart Technology, Inc. [*Associated Press*] (SAG) .... HeartTc
Heart Technology, Inc. [*NASDAQ symbol*] (SAG) .... HRTT
Heart to Heart Foundation (EA) .... HTH
Heart Tones [*Medicine*] .... HT
Heart Transplantation .... HT
Heart Trouble [*Classification system used by doctors on Ellis Island to detain, re-examine, and possibly deny entry to certain immigrants*] .... H
Heart Valve Prostheses [*Medicine*] .... HVP
Heartbeat Period [*Medicine*] (DMAA) .... HBP
Heart-Circulation-Training [*Physical fitness*] .... HCT
Hearth Electric Furnace .... HEF
Heartland Express [*NASDAQ symbol*] (TTSB) .... HTLD
Heartland Express, Inc. [*Associated Press*] (SAG) .... HrtlndE
Heartland Express, Inc. [*NASDAQ symbol*] (NQ) .... HTLD
Heartland Institute [*Research center*] (RCD) .... HI
Heartland Partners Ltd. [*Associated Press*] (SAG) .... HeartInd
Heartland Partners Ltd. Class A [*AMEX symbol*] (SPSG) .... HTL
Heartland Partners L.P.'A' [*AMEX symbol*] (TTSB) .... HTL
Heartland Wireless Commun [*NASDAQ symbol*] (TTSB) .... HART
Heartland Wireless Communications, Inc. [*NASDAQ symbol*] (SAG) .... HART
Heartland Wireless Communications, Inc. [*Associated Press*] (SAG) .... HrtWire
Heartless Old Man [*Alternative sobriquet for William Gladstone, 1809-98, British statesman and prime minister, who was known to admirers as GOM, which see*] .... HOM
Heart-Lung Resuscitation [*or Resuscitator*] [*Medicine*] .... HLR
Heart-Lung Transplantation [*Medicine*] (DMAA) .... HLT
Heartport, Inc. [*Associated Press*] (SAG) .... Heartprt
Heartport, Inc. [*NASDAQ symbol*] (SAG) .... HPRT
Heartport Inc. [*NASDAQ symbol*] (TTSB) .... HPRT
Hearts (ADA) .... H
Heartsong Review [*A publication*] (BRI) .... Heartsong R
Heartstream, Inc. [*Associated Press*] (SAG) .... Heartst
Heartstream, Inc. [*NASDAQ symbol*] (SAG) .... HTST
Heartstream Inc. [*NASDAQ symbol*] (TTSB) .... HTST
Heartwood [*Forestry*] .... H
Heartwood [*Forestry*] (WGA) .... HRTWD
Heartworm Disease (DMAA) .... HWD
Hearx Ltd. [*AMEX symbol*] (SAG) .... EAR
HEARx Ltd. [*AMEX symbol*] (TTSB) .... EAR
Hearx Ltd. [*Associated Press*] (SAG) .... Hearx
Heaston Resources Ltd. [*Vancouver Stock Exchange symbol*] .... HNR
Heat [*or Heater*] .... H
Heat (AAG) .... HT
Heat [*or q*] [*Symbol IUPAC*] .... Q
Heat, Absence of Use, Redness, Pain, Pus, Swelling [*Medicine*] (MEDA) .... HARPPS
Heat and Flame Resistant, Armored (IAA) .... HFA
Heat and Frost Insulators and Asbestos Workers (MHDB) .... HFIA
Heat and Moisture Exchanger (MAE) .... HME
Heat Capacity [*Symbol*] [*IUPAC*] C
Heat Capacity [*Electronics*] (EECA) .... HC
Heat Capacity Map Mission [*NASA*] .... HCMM
Heat Capacity Mapping Mission [*Satellite*] (EERA) .... HCMM
Heat Capacity Mapping Radiometer [*NASA*] .... HCMR
Heat Control (IAA) .... HC
Heat Control Filter .... HCF
Heat Deflection Temperature [*of plastics*] .... HDT
Heat Detector [*NFPA pre-fire planning symbol*] (NFPA) .... HD
Heat Dissipation (DNAB) .... HD
Heat Distortion Temperature .... HDT
Heat Engine .... HE
Heat Engine/Battery Hybrid (PDAA) .... HEBAH
Heat Escape Lessening Posture [*First aid technique*] .... HELP
Heat Exchange [*or Exchanger*] .... HE
Heat Exchange Institute (EA) .... HEI
Heat Exchanger (KSC) .... HEX
Heat Exchanger (MCD) .... HTEXCH
Heat Exchanger (KSC) .... HTXGR
Heat Exchanger (MCD) .... HX
Heat Exchanger Computerized Aid for Technical Engineering (IAA) .... HECATE
Heat Exchanger Method (RDA) .... HEM
Heat Flow [*Physiology*] .... HF
Heat Flow and Convection (NASA) .... HFC
Heat Flux Sensing Unit .... HFSU
Heat Flux Sensor .... HFS
Heat Generator Assembly (KSC) .... HGA
Heat Index .... HI
Heat Infusion Agar [*Microbiology*] (DAVI) .... HIA
Heat Input Equivalent (PDAA) .... HIE
Heat Jacketed Proportioning Pump .... HJPP
Heat Jacketed Pump .... HJP
Heat Killed [*Medicine*] (MAE) .... HK
Heat Limiter Control Switch .... HLCS
Heat Loss Center (DMAA) .... HLC
Heat, Massage, Exercise [*Medicine*] .... HME
Heat, Massage, Exercise [*Medicine*] .... HMX
Heat of Combustion (ROG) .... HC
Heat of Combustion .... HOC
Heat of Combustion (of an Element under Constant Pressure) (ROG) .... HCp
Heat of Combustion (of an Element under Constant Volume) (ROG) .... HCv
Heat of Combustion of Fuel [*Aviation*] (DA) .... Hf
Heat of Detonation .... HOD
Heat of Formation .... HOF
Heat of Solution .... HOS
Heat of Vaporization .... HOV
Heat of Vaporization (ROG) .... HV
Heat Pipe Furnace .... HPF
Heat Pipe Reactor .... HPR
Heat Protection System .... HPS
Heat Pump Manufacturers' Association [*British*] .... HPMA
Heat Rate Variability .... HRV
Heat Recovery/Seed Recovery [*System*] .... HRSR
Heat Recovery Steam Generator [*Industrial engineering*] .... HRSG
Heat Recovery Ventilator .... HRV
Heat Reflector .... HR
Heat Rejection and Transport (SSD) .... HRT
Heat Rejection Loop .... HRL
Heat Rejection Radiator .... HRR
Heat Rejection System .... HRS
Heat Release Rate [*Engineering*] .... HRR
Heat Release Rate [*Flammability testing*] [*Fire safety*] .... HRR
Heat Resisting [*Technical drawings*] .... HR
Heat Shield [*Automotive engineering*] .... H/SHLD
Heat Shield [*Aerospace*] (AAG) .... HS
Heat Shield .... HTSHLD
Heat Shield Abort [*Aerospace*] (IAA) .... HSA
Heat Shield Entry [*Aerospace*] (IAA) .... HSE
Heat Shield Jettison [*Aerospace*] (IAA) .... HSJ
Heat Shield Recovery [*Aerospace*] (IAA) .... HSR
Heat Shock Activator Protein [*Biochemistry*] .... HAP
Heat Shock Protein [*Physiology*] .... HSP
Heat Shock Protein [*Gene*] (DMAA) .... hsp
Heat Shock Protein Synthesis .... HSPS
Heat Shrinkable Tubing .... HST
Heat Sink [*Automotive engineering*] .... H/SNK
Heat Sink (MSA) .... HTSK
Heat Sink Kit .... HSK
Heat Sink Welding [*Nuclear energy*] (NRCH) .... HSW
Heat Stable .... HS
Heat Sterilizable Potting Compound .... HSPC
Heat Sterilization Compound .... HSC
Heat Sterilization Test Program .... HSTP
Heat Stimulated Flow (PDAA) .... HSF
Heat Strain Decision [*Army*] (RDA) .... HSDA
Heat Stress Index .... HSI
Heat to Boiling Point [*Calorimetry*] .... HB
Heat Transfer (NASA) .... HT
Heat Transfer and Cryogenics .... HT & C
Heat Transfer and Fluid Flow Service [*British*] .... HTFFS
Heat Transfer and Fluid Flow Service [*Also, HTFFS*] [*British*] .... HTFS
Heat Transfer and Fluid Mechanics Institute (MCD) .... HTFMI
Heat Transfer Coefficient (BARN) .... U
Heat Transfer Efficiency Factor [*Engineering*] .... HTEF
Heat Transfer Fluid .... HTF
Heat Transfer Fluid Flow Thermodynamics (NRCH) .... HTFFT
Heat Transfer Instrument System [*Nuclear energy*] (NUCP) .... HTI
Heat Transfer Instrument System (NRCH) .... HTIS
Heat Transfer Laboratory [*MIT*] (MCD) .... HTL
Heat Transfer Loop (NRCH) .... HTL
Heat Transfer Medium [*Engineering*] .... HTM
Heat Transfer Meter .... HTM
Heat Transfer Module [*Furnace*] .... HTM
Heat Transfer Printing [*Textile technology*] .... HTP
Heat Transfer Reactor Experiment .... HTRE
Heat Transfer Research Institute (NRCH) .... HTRI
Heat Transfer Rotating Disc [*Engineering*] .... HTRD
Heat Transfer Section .... HTS
Heat Transfer Simulation Loop (IEEE) .... HTSL
Heat Transfer System .... HTS
Heat Transfer Unit .... HTU
Heat Transport Section [*Apollo*] [*NASA*] .... HTS
Heat Transport System [*NASA*] (NASA) .... HTS
Heat Treat .... HT
Heat Treat .... HTTR
Heat Treat Block (MCD) .... HTB
Heat Treat Fixture (MCD) .... HTF
Heat Treat Fixture .... HTFX
Heat Unit (MAE) .... HU
Heat Up Rate (IEEE) .... HUR
Heat-Activated Device (NRCH) .... HAD
Heat-Affected Zone .... HAZ
Heat-Aggregated Gamma Globulin [*Clinical chemistry*] .... HAGG
Heat-Aggregated Globulin (DMAA) .... HAG
Heat-Annealed Zone [*Metallurgy*] .... HAZ
Heat-Curing Epoxy Film .... HEF

Heated (MSA)	HTD
Heated Aerosol [*Pharmacology*] (DAVI)	ht aer
Heated Coil (NITA)	HC
Heated Effluents [*Cornell University*] [*Database*] (NITA)	HEF
Heated Exhaust Gas Oxygen [*Automotive engineering*]	HEGO
Heated Exhaust Gas Oxygen Ground [*Automotive engineering*]	HEGOG
Heated Experimental Carbon Thermal Oscillator Reactor [*British*]	HECTOR
Heated Flame Ionization Detection [*Analytical chemistry*]	HFID
Heated Oxygen Sensor [*Automotive engineering*]	HOS
Heated Rear Window [*Automotive accessory*]	HRW
Heated Serum Reagin [*Immunochemistry*] (DAVI)	HSR
Heated Window Control Unit	HWCU
Heated-Tube Reactor [*Chemical engineering*]	HTR
Heater (ABBR)	H
Heater (IAA)	HR
Heater (AAG)	HTR
Heater above Reheat Point (DNAB)	HARP
Heater Amplifier Assembly	HAA
Heater Center Tap [*Electronics*] (ECII)	HCT
Heater Center Top	HCT
Heater Cord	HC
Heater Kit	HK
Heater Middle (IAA)	HM
Heater Probe Unit (DMAA)	HPU
Heater Voltage	HV
Heater Voltage [*Electronics*] (OA)	Vh
Heaters, Vents, and Drains [*System*] [*Nuclear energy*] (NRCH)	HVD
Heat-Exchanger Network [*Chemical engineering*]	HEN
Heat-Flow Electronics	HFE
Heat-Flow Experiment	HFE
Heat-Flow [*or Flux*] Unit [*Nuclear energy*]	HFU
Heat-Generative Radioactive Wastes [*Nuclear energy*]	HGW
Heath Educational Robot [*Heath Co.*]	HERO
Heath, OH [*AM radio station call letters*]	WHTH
HEATH [*Higher Education and the Handicapped*] **Resource Center** (EA)	HRC
Heather Society (EA)	HS
Heathlands [*Australia Airport symbol Obsolete*] (OAG)	HAT
Heathrow Jet Charter Ltd. [*British ICAO designator*] (FAAC)	HJC
Heath's Maxims [*A publication*] (DLA)	Heath Max
Heath's Reports [*36-40 Maine*] [*A publication*] (DLA)	Heath
Heat-Inactivated Fetal Bovine Serum [*Immunology*]	HIFBS
Heat-Inactivated Muscle Extract	HIX
Heat-Inactivated Serum Pool [*Clinical chemistry*]	HISP
Heating (KSC)	HTG
Heating	HTG
Heating, Air Conditioning, Refrigeration, Plumbing (ADA)	HARP
Heating and Domestic Engineers' Union [*British*]	HDEU
Heating and Ventilating Contractors' Association [*British*]	HVCA
Heating and Ventilating Research Association [*British*]	HVRA
Heating and Ventilation (NATG)	H and V
Heating and Ventilation (AAG)	HV
Heating and Ventilation Estimating [*Tipdata Ltd.*] [*Software package*] (NCC)	HAVE
Heating Cabinet (AAG)	HC
Heating Coil (AAG)	HC
Heating Coils in Bunkers [*on a ship*] (DS)	HE Cls B
Heating Coils in Cargo Tanks [*on a ship*] (DS)	HE Cls C
Heating Degree Days [*Agriculture*]	HDD
Heating Plant (NATG)	HP
Heating, Refrigerating, and Air Conditioning Institute of Canada	HRAI
Heating Scow [*Navy symbol*]	YHT
Heating Seasonal Performance Factor	HSPF
Heating Seasonal Performance Factor	HSPF
Heating Surface	HS
Heating System	HS
Heating, Ventilating, and Air Conditioning	HVAC
Heating, Ventilating, and Air Conditioning Manufacturers Association Ltd. [*British*] (BI)	HEVAC
Heating, Ventilating, and Air-Conditioning Association [*Federation of Environmental Trade Associations*] [*British*]	HEVAC
Heating, Ventilating, and Cooling (AAG)	HV & C
Heating Ventilating Supply Unit (NRCH)	HVSU
Heating, Ventilation, Air Conditioning [*Marine science*] (OSRA)	HVAC
Heating Ventilation Unit (MCD)	HVU
Heat-Killed Listeria Monocytogene [*Medicine*] (MAE)	HKLM
Heat-Labile Citrororum Factor [*Biochemistry*]	HLCF
Heat-labile Enterotoxin [*Biochemistry*] (DAVI)	LT
Heat-Labile Factor	HLF
Heaton Mint [*British*]	H
Heat-Producing Element	HPE
Heat-Resistant Phenolic	HRP
Heat-Resisting Plastic	HRP
Heat-Sensing Device (DNAB)	HSD
Heat-Shield Boost [*Aerospace*]	HSB
Heat-Shield Qualification [*NASA*] (KSC)	HSQ
Heat-Shock Cognate [*Biochemistry*]	HSC
Heat-Shock Cognate Protein [*Biochemistry*]	HSCP
Heat-Shock Element [*Genetics*]	HSE
Heat-Shock Transcription Factor [*Genetics*]	HSF
Heat-Shock Transcription Factor [*Genetics*]	HSTF
Heat-Stable Alkaline Phosphatase [*An enzyme*]	HSAP
Heat-Stable Antigen [*Immunochemistry*]	HSA
Heat-Stable Esterase (PDAA)	HSE
Heat-Stable Fraction	HSF
Heat-Stable Lactic Dehydrogenase [*Clinical chemistry*]	HLDH

Heat-Treated Steel	HTS
Heat-Treatment Temperature	HTT
Heatup [*Nuclear energy*] (NRCH)	H/U
Heautontimorumenos [*of Terence*] [*Classical studies*] (OCD)	HT
Heaven Bone	Heaven B
Heavener, OK [*FM radio station call letters*]	KPRV
Heavier (WDAA)	HEVR
Heavier than Air	HTA
Heavier-than-Air Fighter/Attack/Experimental [*Aircraft*]	VFAX
Heaviest Duty Available [*Motor vehicle specifications*]	HDA
Heaviest Heavy Lift Helicopter (MCD)	HHLH
Heavily Armed Vessels	HAV
Heavily Included [*Colored gemstone grade*]	HI
Heavily Indebted Poor Country	HIPC
Heaviside [*Ionosphere*] (AAG)	HS
Heaviside-Campbell Bridge [*Electronics*]	HCB
Heavy (AAG)	H
Heavy [*Chain*] [*Biochemistry, immunochemistry*]	H
Heavy (AABC)	HV
Heavy (VRA)	hv
Heavy (AFM)	HVY
Heavy	HVY
Heavy [*Track condition*] [*Thoroughbred racing*]	HY
Heavy (NATG)	HY
Heavy [*ICAO*] (FAAC)	XX
Heavy Air Training Unit	HATU
Heavy Airborne Multipurpose System (MCD)	HAMPS
Heavy Aircraft Fuel (MSA)	HAF
Heavy & Specialized Carriers Tariff Bureau	H & SCTB
Heavy & Specialized Carriers Tariff Bureau, Washington DC [*STAC*]	HSC
Heavy Antiaircraft Artillery	HAA
Heavy Antiarmor Weapon	HAW
Heavy Antitank/Assault Weapon [*Army*]	HAAW
Heavy Antitank Convoy	HAC
Heavy Antitank Weapon (INF)	HAW
Heavy Artillery	HA
Heavy Artillery Tractor [*British military*] (DMA)	HAT
Heavy Assault Bridge	HAB
Heavy Assault Floating Bridge [*British military*] (DMA)	HAFB
Heavy Assault Rocket System (MCD)	HARS
Heavy Assault Weapon	HAW
Heavy Atmospheric Gas Oil [*Petroleum product*]	HAGO
Heavy Atom Method	HAM
Heavy Atomic Demolition Munition [*Military*] (AABC)	HADM
Heavy Atoms	HA
Heavy Attack Aircraft Commander (DNAB)	HAAC
Heavy Attack Aircraft Commander	HAC
Heavy Attack Aircraft Commander Training (DNAB)	HAACT
Heavy Attack Aircraft, Experimental	VAX
Heavy Attack Squadron (MUGU)	HATRON
Heavy Attack Squadron (DNAB)	HVATKRON
Heavy Attack Squadron [*Symbol*] (MCD)	VAH
Heavy Attack Training Unit	HATU
Heavy Attack Wing	HATWING
Heavy Attack Wing, Atlantic Fleet	HATWINGLANT
Heavy Attack Wing, Pacific Fleet	HATWINGPAC
Heavy Automotive Maintenance	HAM
Heavy Ballistic Missile	HBM
Heavy Barrel [*Rifles*]	HB
Heavy Barrel [*Rifles*]	H-BAR
Heavy Bombardment [*or Bomber*]	HB
Heavy Bomber (Night) [*British military*] (DMA)	HB(N)
Heavy Bomber Support	HBS
Heavy Capability Mapping Mission [*Satellite*]	HCMM
Heavy Chain [*Immunoglobulin*]	HC
Heavy Chain Disease [*Protein*]	HCD
Heavy Coker Gas Oil [*Petroleum technology*]	HCGO
Heavy Construction Contractors Association	HCCA
Heavy Conversion Unit [*British military*] (DMA)	HCU
Heavy Cruiser, Guided Missile [*Navy symbol*]	CAC
Heavy Current [*Electronics*] (IAA)	HC
Heavy Cycle Oil [*Petroleum technology*]	HCO
Heavy Distillate [*Fuel technology*]	HD
Heavy Drop [*Military*] (AABC)	HVDP
Heavy Dry Support Bridge [*Army*] (RDA)	HDSB
Heavy Duty Business Forum (EA)	HDBF
Heavy Duty Diesel Engine	HDDE
Heavy Duty Distribution [*A publication*]	HDD
Heavy Duty Engine [*Automotive engineering*]	HDE
Heavy Duty Engine	HDE
Heavy Duty Manufacturers' Association	HDMA
Heavy Duty Representatives Association (EA)	HDRA
Heavy Duty Transient Cycle	HDTC
Heavy Duty Truck [*Environmental Protection Agency*]	HDT
Heavy Duty Vehicle [*Environmental Protection Agency*]	HDV
Heavy Edge Tool Manufacturers' Association [*British*] (BI)	HETMA
Heavy Element and Radioactive Material Electromagnetic Separator [*British*]	HERMES
Heavy Element Facility [*Nuclear energy*] (NUCP)	HEF
Heavy Enamel (AAG)	HE
Heavy Enamel Bonded Cotton [*Wire insulation*]	HEBC
Heavy Enamel Bonded Double Cotton [*Wire insulation*] (AAG)	HEBDC
Heavy Enamel Bonded Double Paper [*Wire insulation*] (AAG)	HEBDP
Heavy Enamel Bonded Double Silk [*Wire insulation*] (AAG)	HEBDS
Heavy Enamel Bonded Paper [*Wire insulation*]	HEBP

Heavy Enamel Bonded Silk [*Wire insulation*] ... HEBS
Heavy Enamel Cotton Varnish [*Wire insulation*] ... HECV
Heavy Enamel Double Cotton [*Wire insulation*] ... HEDC
Heavy Enamel Double Cotton Varnish [*Wire insulation*] (AAG) ... HEDCV
Heavy Enamel Double Silk [*Wire insulation*] ... HEDS
Heavy Enamel Double Silk Varnish [*Wire insulation*] (AAG) ... HEDSV
Heavy Enamel Single Cellophane [*Wire insulation*] (IAA) ... HEC
Heavy Enamel Single Cellophane [*Wire insulation*] (AAG) ... HEK
Heavy Enamel Single Cotton [*Wire insulation*] (AAG) ... HEC
Heavy Enamel Single Glass [*Wire insulation*] (AAG) ... HEG
Heavy Enamel Single Silk [*Wire insulation*] (AAG) ... HES
Heavy Enamel Single Silk Varnish [*Wire insulation*] (AAG) ... HESV
Heavy End Aviation Fuel ... HEAF
Heavy Equipment (AFM) ... HE
Heavy Equipment Handling Package ... HEHP
Heavy Equipment Maintenance ... HEM
Heavy Equipment Test Chamber (MCD) ... HETC
Heavy Equipment Transporter ... HET
Heavy Equipment Transporter System [*Army*] (RDA) ... HETS
Heavy Expanded Mobility Ammunition Trailer [*Military*] ... HEMAT
Heavy Expanded Mobility Tactical Truck [*Army*] (RDA) ... HEMTT
Heavy Expanded Mobility Tactical Truck ... HEMTT
Heavy Field Artillery ... HFA
Heavy Fire Team [*Military*] ... HFT
Heavy Flushing Spray ... HFS
Heavy Force Modernization [*Army*] ... HFM
Heavy Force Modernization Survivability System ... HFMSS
Heavy Force Modernization System Safety Plan [*Army*] ... HFMSSP
Heavy Free Gas (IEEE) ... HFG
Heavy Freight Flight [*British military*] (DMA) ... HFF
Heavy Fuel [*Engine technology*] ... HF
Heavy Fuel Oil ... HFO
Heavy Fuel Oils [*Database*] [*Department of Energy*] ... HFO
Heavy Gas Oils [*Petroleum product*] ... HGO
Heavy Gauge Screwed Welded [*Conduit*] ... HGSW
Heavy Gauge Solid Drawn [*Conduit*] ... HGSD
Heavy Glider Conversion Unit [*British military*] (DMA) ... HGCU
Heavy Glider Maintenance Unit [*British military*] (DMA) ... HGMU
Heavy Goods Vehicles ... HGV
Heavy Handy Deadweight [*Scrap*] [*Shipping*] ... HHDW
Heavy Handy Deadweight Scrap Iron [*Shipping*] (DS) ... HHDWS
Heavy Heavy-Duty Diesel Engine [*Motor vehicle specifications*] ... HHDDE
Heavy Helicopter [*Military*] (VNW) ... HH
Heavy Helicopter Company [*Military*] (VNW) ... HHC
Heavy Helicopter Fire Team (DNAB) ... HHFT
Heavy Helo Fire Team [*Military*] (VNW) ... HHFT
Heavy Hinged [*Philately*] ... HH
Heavy Hydrogen ... HH
Heavy Industries Corp. of Malaysia (ECON) ... HICOM
Heavy Interdiction Missile ... HIM
Heavy Interdiction Missile System (MCD) ... HIMS
Heavy Ion Cloud [*Astrophysics*] ... HIC
Heavy Ion Fusion (PDAA) ... HIF
Heavy Ion Laboratory (PDAA) ... HILAB
Heavy Ion, Light Ion ... HILI
Heavy Ion Storage Ring for Atomic Physics ... HISTRAP
Heavy Ion-Induced Desorption [*Analytical chemistry*] ... HIID
Heavy Ion-Induced Satellite X-Ray Emission [*Analytical chemistry*] ... HISXE
Heavy Lift ... HL
Heavy Lift Cargo Airlines Ltd. [*British*] ... H
Heavy Lift Operability (PDAA) ... HELO
Heavy Lift Prepositioning Ship [*Navy*] ... HLPS
Heavy Lift Research Vehicle [*Military*] ... HLRV
Heavy/Light Corps (MCD) ... HLC
Heavy Loading (IAA) ... HL
Heavy Logistics System ... HLS
Heavy Machine Gun ... HMG
Heavy Machinery Repair Ship [*Navy symbol*] ... ARM
Heavy Maintenance [*Ordnance*] ... HM
Heavy Materiel Supply Units [*Military*] ... HMS
Heavy Meromyosin [*Biochemistry*] ... HMM
Heavy Metal [*Inorganic chemistry*] ... HM
Heavy Metal [*Rock music type*] ... HM
Heavy Metal Fluoride Glass ... HMFG
Heavy Military Electronic Equipment Division [*General Electric Co.*] (AAG) ... HMEED
Heavy Military Electronic System [*General Electric Co.*] (IAA) ... HMES
Heavy Military Electronics Department (SAA) ... HMED
Heavy Mobile ... HM
Heavy Mortar, Smart Munition ... HMSM
Heavy Narrow Gap [*Nuclear energy*] (NUCP) ... HNG
Heavy Observation Aircraft ... HOA
Heavy Oil Catalytic Cracking Unit [*Petroleum refining*] ... HOCCU
Heavy Oil Cracking [*Process*] [*Petroleum industry*] ... HOC
Heavy Oil Engine Tractor [*British*] ... HOET
Heavy Oil/Enhanced Recovery Index [*Alberta Oil Sands Technology and Research Authority*] [*Information service or system*] ... HERI
Heavy Operational Repair Squadron Engineer [*Air Force*] (AFM) ... HORSE
Heavy Ordnance Gunship (NVT) ... HOG
Heavy Photographic Squadron ... HEAVYPHOTORON
Heavy Photographic Squadron (DNAB) ... HVPHOTORON
Heavy Positive Ion ... HPI
Heavy Primary Nuclei ... HPN
Heavy Rail Transit (PDAA) ... HRT
Heavy Recovery Vehicle [*Marine Corps*] (VNW) ... HRV
Heavy Replaceable [*or Replacement*] **Assembly** ... HRA
Heavy Salvage Ship [*Navy symbol*] (VNW) ... LHC
Heavy Satellite (PDAA) ... H-SAT
Heavy Sea [*Navigation*] ... H
Heavy SEAL [*Sea-Air-Land*] **Support Craft** (NVT) ... HSSC
Heavy Section Machine Gun Corps [*British military*] (DMA) ... HSMGC
Heavy Section Steel Technology [*Nuclear Regulatory Commission*] ... HSST
Heavy Specialized Carriers Conference [*Later, SC & RA*] ... HSCC
Heavy Straight Run Naphtha [*Petroleum chemistry*] ... HSRN
Heavy, Stressed Platform ... HSP
Heavy Tactical Transport ... HTT
Heavy Tactical Vehicle (AAGC) ... FHTV
Heavy Tank ... HT
Heavy Teflon Coating ... HTC
Heavy Terminal [*AFSCF*] (MCD) ... HT
Heavy Terminal Complex (MCD) ... HTC
Heavy Thermoplastic (IAA) ... HT
Heavy Transport Aircraft [*Military*] ... HETAC
Heavy Truck Driver Trainer [*Army*] ... HTDT
Heavy Vacuum Gas Oil [*Petroleum product*] ... HVGO
Heavy Vehicle Electronic License Plate ... HELP
Heavy Wall ... HW
Heavy Water ... HW
Heavy Water Moderated Reactor [*Nuclear energy*] (NUCP) ... HWMR
Heavy Weapons [*British military*] (DMA) ... HW
Heavy Weapons Special Study Group [*Military*] (MCD) ... HWSSG
Heavy Weapons Testing Range [*Military*] (MCD) ... HWTR
Heavy Weather Patrol Boats (CINC) ... HWPB
Heavy-Aggregate Concrete (DEN) ... HAC
Heavy-Duty ... HD
Heavy-Duty ... HDY
Heavy-Duty Air Cylinder ... HDAC
Heavy-Duty Amplifier ... HDA
Heavy-Duty Automatic Press ... HDAP
Heavy-Duty Contractor (MCD) ... HDC
Heavy-Duty Detergent ... HDD
Heavy-Duty Diesel [*Vehicle*] ... HDD
Heavy-Duty Diesel Engine [*Motor vehicle specifications*] ... HDDE
Heavy-Duty Diesel Vehicle ... HDDV
Heavy-Duty Direct Injection [*Diesel engines*] ... HD-DI
Heavy-Duty Enzyme Detergent ... HDED
Heavy-Duty Gasoline [*Vehicle*] ... HDG
Heavy-Duty Industrial [*Internal combustion engines*] ... HDI
Heavy-Duty Industrial Filter ... HDIF
Heavy-Duty Industrial Relay ... HDIR
Heavy-Duty Liquid Detergent ... HDLD
Heavy-Duty Oil Classification Panel [*Automotive engineering*] ... HDOCP
Heavy-Duty Relay (IAA) ... HR
Heavy-Duty Thermoplastic Elastomer Insulation [*Automotive engineering*] ... HTE
Heavy-Duty Thermoplastic Insulation [*Automotive engineering*] ... HDT
Heavy-Duty Thermoset Elastomer Insulation [*Automotive engineering*] ... HTS
Heavy-Duty Truck Manufacturers Association (EA) ... HDTMA
Heavy-Duty Vehicle Inspection Program ... HDVIP
Heavy-Element Fission Tracer ... HEFT
Heavy-High-mobility [*Multipurpose Wheeled*] **Vehicle** [*See also HMMWV*] (DOMA) ... HHV
Heavy-Hull Repair Ship [*Navy symbol Obsolete*] ... ARH
Heavy-Ion Linear Accelerator [*Nuclear energy*] ... HILAC
Heavy-Ion Medical Accelerator in Chiba [*Japan*] ... HIMAC
Heavy-Ion Plasma Accelerator (IAA) ... HIPAC
Heavy-Ion Source ... HIS
Heavy-Lift Airship (MCD) ... HLA
Heavylift Cargo Airlines Ltd. [*British ICAO designator*] (FAAC) ... HLA
Heavy-Lift Helicopter ... HLH
Heavy-Lift Helicopter Advanced Technology Component [*Program*] [*Army*] (RDA) ... HLC-ATC
Heavy-Lift Helicopter, Experimental (SAA) ... HHX
Heavy-Lift Helicopter System ... HLHS
Heavy-Lift Launch Vehicle [*Rocketry*] (MCD) ... HLLV
Heavy-Lift Pontoon ... HLP
Heavy-Lift Preposition [*Ship*] (DOMA) ... HLP
Heavy-Lift System ... HLS
Heavy-Lift Vehicle ... HLV
Heavy-Media Separation [*Mining engineering*] (IAA) ... HMS
Heavy-Water Components Test Reactor [*Nuclear energy*] ... HWCTR
Heavy-Water Moderated Gas-Cooled Reactor [*Nuclear energy*] ... HWGCR
Heavy-Water Moderated Organic-Cooled Reactor [*Nuclear energy*] ... HWOCR
Heavy-Water Plant [*Nuclear energy*] ... HWP
Heavy-Water Reactor [*Nuclear energy*] ... HWR
Heavy-Water-Moderated, Boiling Light-Water-Cooled Reactor [*Nuclear energy*] (NRCH) ... HWLWR
Heavy-Weight Torpedo (DOMA) ... HWT
Hebbronville, TX [*Location identifier FAA*] (FAAL) ... HBV
Hebdomada [*A Week*] [*Pharmacy*] (ROG) ... HEBD
Hebdomada [*A Week*] [*Pharmacy*] ... HEBDOM
Heber City, UT [*AM radio station call letters*] ... KTMP
Heber Springs, AR [*Location identifier FAA*] (FAAL) ... HBZ
Heber Springs, AR [*AM radio station call letters*] ... KAWW
Heber Springs, AR [*FM radio station call letters*] ... KAWW-FM
Hebo [*Myanmar*] [*ICAO location identifier*] (ICLI) ... VBHH
Hebraeische Grammatik Voellig Umgearbeitet [*Gesenius and E. Kautzsch*] [*A publication*] (BJA) ... GK
Hebraeische Grammatik Voellig Umgearbeitet [*Gesenius and E. Kautzsch*] [*A publication*] (BJA) ... GKa

Hebraeisches und Aramaeisches Handwoerterbuch ueber das Alte Testament [*W. Gesenius and F. Buhl*] [*A publication*] (BJA) .... GesB
Hebraeisches und Aramaeisches Lexikon zum Alten Testament [*Leiden*] (BJA) .... HALAT
Hebraeisches und Aramaeisches Lexikon zum Alten Testament [*L. Koehler and W. Baumgarther*] [*A publication*] (BJA) .... KBL
Hebraic [*Language, etc.*] (ROG) .... HEB
Hebraic (BJA) .... Hebr
Hebrew (BJA) .... H
Hebrew (BJA) .... Hb
[*The*] **Hebrew** [*A publication*] (BJA) .... HE
Hebrew .... HEB
Hebrew [*MARC language code Library of Congress*] (LCCP) .... heb
Hebrew .... HEBR
Hebrew Actors Union (EA) .... HAU
[*A*] **Hebrew and English Lexicon of the Old Testament (Brown, Driver, and Briggs)** [*A publication*] (BJA) .... BDB
Hebrew Arts Foundation (EA) .... HAF
Hebrew Cabinet Makers' Union [*British*] .... HCMU
Hebrew Christian Alliance of America [*Later, MJAA*] .... HCAA
Hebrew Christian Fellowship (EA) .... HCF
Hebrew College (GAGS) .... Hebrew C
Hebrew College, Brookline, MA [*Library symbol*] [*Library of Congress*] (LCLS) .... MBrH
Hebrew Culture Foundation (EA) .... HCF
Hebrew Free Burial Association (EA) .... HFBA
Hebrew Grammar Gesenius, Kautzsch, Cowley [*A publication*] (BJA) .... GKC
Hebrew Immigrant Aid Society .... HIAS
Hebrew Jewellers' Society [*A union*] [*British*] .... HJS
Hebrew Language and Literature (BJA) .... HLL
Hebrew Leader (BJA) .... HL
Hebrew Letters (BJA) .... HL
Hebrew Literature (BJA) .... HL
Hebrew Master Bakers Association [*Defunct*] (EA) .... HMBA
Hebrew Order of David .... HOD
Hebrew Religious Protection Association of Greater New York (EA) .... HRPA
Hebrew School Headache (BJA) .... HSH
Hebrew Teachers College [*Massachusetts*] .... HTC
Hebrew Teachers College, Roxbury, MA [*Library symbol Library of Congress*] (LCLS) .... MRoxH
Hebrew Text (BJA) .... HT
Hebrew Theological College [*Skokie, IL*] (BJA) .... HTC
Hebrew Theological College, Skokie, IL [*Library symbol Library of Congress*] (LCLS) .... ISkH
Hebrew Union College [*Later, HUC-JIR*] .... HUC
Hebrew Union College - Jewish Institute of Religion [*Formerly, HUC*] [*Cincinnati, OH*] .... HUC-JIR
Hebrew Union College, Jewish Institute of Religion, Cincinnati, OH [*OCLC symbol*] (OCLC) .... HUC
Hebrew Union College - Jewish Institute of Religion, Cincinnati, OH [*Library symbol Library of Congress*] (LCLS) .... OCH
Hebrew Union College - Jewish Institute of Religion, Los Angeles, CA [*Library symbol Library of Congress*] (LCLS) .... CLHU
Hebrew Union College - Jewish Institute of Religion, New York, NY [*Library symbol Library of Congress*] (LCLS) .... NNHeb
Hebrew University [*Jerusalem*] (BJA) .... HU
Hebrew University [*Jerusalem*] (BJA) .... HUJ
Hebrew Veterans of the War with Spain (EA) .... HVWS
Hebrew Year [*Freemasonry*] (ROG) .... HY
Hebrew Young Men's Association .... HYMA
Hebrews [*Old Testament book*] .... HE
Hebrews [*New Testament book*] .... Heb
Hebron, NE [*Location identifier FAA*] (FAAL) .... HJH
Hebron Public Library, Hebron, IN [*Library symbol Library of Congress*] (LCLS) .... InHeb
Hecate [*A publication*] .... Hec
Hechalutz Organization of America [*Defunct*] (EA) .... HOA
Hechinger Co. [*Associated Press*] (SAG) .... Hchg
Hechinger Co. [*NASDAQ symbol*] (NQ) .... HECH
Hechinger Co. Cl'A' [*NASDAQ symbol*] (TTSB) .... HECHA
Hechinger Co. Cl'B' Cv [*NASDAQ symbol*] (TTSB) .... HECHB
Hecker's Cases on Warranty [*A publication*] (DLA) .... Heck Cas
Heckler and Koch [*Machine gun*] (MCD) .... HK
Heckscher-Ohlin-Samuelson [*Theorem*] .... HOS
Hecla Mining [*NYSE symbol*] (TTSB) .... HL
Hecla Mining Co. [*Associated Press*] (SAG) .... HeclaM
Hecla Mining Co. [*Associated Press*] (SAG) .... HeclM
Hecla Mining Co. [*NYSE symbol*] (SPSG) .... HL
Hecla Mining Co. Library, Couer d'Alene, ID [*Library symbol*] [*Library of Congress*] (LCLS) .... IdCHM
Hecla Mining Sr'B'Cv Pfd [*NYSE symbol*] (TTSB) .... HLPrB
Hectare (AAG) .... HA
Hectare .... ha
Hectare (DMAA) .... ha
Hectare (WDAA) .... HECT
Hecto [*A prefix meaning multiplied by 10^2*] [*SI symbol*] .... h
Hectocotylized Arm .... HA
Hectogram .... HECTOG
Hectogram .... HG
Hectogram (ROG) .... HGM
Hectograph .... HECTO
Hectoliter .... HECTOL
Hectoliter (GPO) .... HL
Hectometer [*100 meters*] .... HECTOM
Hectometer [*100 meters*] .... HM
Hectometric Emissions [*Radio astronomy*] .... HOM
Hectopascal [*ICAO designator*] (FAAC) .... HPA
Hector, CA [*Location identifier FAA*] (FAAL) .... HEC
Hector Communications [*NASDAQ symbol*] (TTSB) .... HCCO
Hector Communications Corp. [*NASDAQ symbol*] (SAG) .... HCCO
Hector Communications Corp. [*Associated Press*] (SAG) .... HectCm
Hector Public Library, Hector, MN [*Library symbol*] [*Library of Congress*] (LCLS) .... MnHe
Hector Public School, Hector, MN [*Library symbol*] [*Library of Congress*] (LCLS) .... MnHePS
Hector Resources, Inc. [*Vancouver Stock Exchange symbol*] .... HEC
Hecuba [*of Euripides*] [*Classical studies*] (OCD) .... Hec
Hed-Arzi [*Israel*] [*Record label*] .... Arzi
Hede/Hedlanda [*Sweden ICAO location identifier*] (ICLI) .... ESNC
Heden [*Sweden ICAO location identifier*] (ICLI) .... ESPJ
Hedges' Reports [*2-6 Montana*] [*A publication*] (DLA) .... Hedges
Hedge-to-Arrive [*Business term*] .... HTA
Hedingham [*England*] .... HEDING
HEDL [*Hanford Engineering Development Laboratory*] **Overpower** [*Nuclear energy*] (NRCH) .... HOP
HEDL [*Hanford Engineering Development Laboratory*] **Up Transient** [*Nuclear energy*] (NRCH) .... HUT
Hedley Pacific Mining [*Vancouver Stock Exchange symbol*] .... HED
Hedonism Limitation Talks [*British*] (DI) .... HELT
Hedrick Journal, Hedrick, IA [*Library symbol Library of Congress*] (LCLS) .... IaHeJ
Hedstrom Number [*Chemistry*] (DAVI) .... He
Heel [*Music*] .... H
Heel Breaster .... HLBR
Heel Line (MSA) .... HL
Heel Off Ground [*Medicine*] .... HO
Heel Sanding .... HLSD
Heel Spur [*Orthopedics*] (DAVI) .... HS
Heel Stick [*For blood samples*] [*Medicine*] (DAVI) .... HS
Heel Stick Blood Gas [*Medicine*] (DAVI) .... HSBG
Heel Strike [*Medicine*] .... HS
Heel to Buttock (DMAA) .... HB
Heel to Heel .... H to H
Heel to Knee .... H-K
Heel to Knee (DMAA) .... HTK
Heeling Force [*Sailing terminology*] .... F_H
Heel-Knee-Shin [*Test*] [*Neurology*] (DAVI) .... HKS
Heelstick [*Medicine*] (DAVI) .... H
Heel-to-Knee (DMAA) .... HK
Heel-to-Shin [*Test*] [*Neurology*] (DAVI) .... H-S
Heenan Petroleum Ltd. [*Toronto Stock Exchange symbol*] .... HP
Heenan Senlac Resources Ltd. [*Toronto Stock Exchange symbol*] .... HSL
Heeres-Atmer [*Service Oxygen Breathing Apparatus*] [*German military - World War II*] .... HA
Heeresbetriebsstofflager [*Army Gasoline-Supply Depot*] [*German military - World War II*] .... HBL
Heeresfahrzeug [*Army Vehicle*] [*German military - World War II*] .... HF
Heeres-Funkstelle [*Army Radio Station*] [*German military - World War II*] .... HFU
Heeresmunitionslager [*Army Ammunition Depot*] [*German military - World War II*] .... HML
Heeresnachrichtenwesen [*Army Communications System*] [*German military - World War II*] .... HNW
Heeres-Sauerstoffschutzgeraet [*Service Oxygen Breathing Apparatus*] [*German military - World War II*] .... HSS
Heeres-Sauerstoffschutzgeraet [*Service Oxygen Breathing Apparatus*] [*German military - World War II*] .... HSSG
Heeresverpflegungslager [*Army Ration Depot*] [*German military - World War II*] .... HVL
Heeresverwaltungsamt [*Army Administration Office*] [*German military - World War II*] .... HVA
Heereswaffenamt [*Army Ordnance Office*] [*German military - World War II*] .... HWAA
Heerlen [*Netherlands*] [*Seismograph station code, US Geological Survey*] (SEIS) .... HEE
Hees International Bancorp, Inc. [*Toronto Stock Exchange symbol*] .... HIL
Hefei [*China*] [*Airport symbol*] (OAG) .... HFE
Hefei/Luogang [*China*] [*ICAO location identifier*] (ICLI) .... ZSOF
Heflex Bioengineering Test [*NASA*] .... HBT
Heft [*Part*] [*German*] .... H
Heft (ROG) .... HFT
Hefte von Auschwitz (BJA) .... HA
Heftel Broadcasting Corp. [*NASDAQ symbol*] (SAG) .... HBCCA
Heftel Broadcasting Corp. [*Associated Press*] (SAG) .... Heftel
Heftel Broadcasting'A' [*NASDAQ symbol*] (TTSB) .... HBCCA
Hegel Society of America (EA) .... HSA
Heggebakken [*Norway ICAO location identifier*] (ICLI) .... ENHB
Heho [*Myanmar*] [*Airport symbol*] (OAG) .... HEH
HEI, Inc. [*Associated Press*] (SAG) .... HEI Mn
HEI, Inc. [*NASDAQ symbol*] (NQ) .... HEII
Heico Corp. [*AMEX symbol*] (SPSG) .... HEI
Heico Corp. [*Associated Press*] (SAG) .... Heico
Heide/Busum [*Germany ICAO location identifier*] (ICLI) .... EDXB
Heidelberg [*Germany ICAO location identifier*] (ICLI) .... EDIE
Heidelberg [*Germany ICAO location identifier*] (ICLI) .... EDIU
Heidelberg [*South Africa*] [*ICAO location identifier*] (ICLI) .... FAHG
Heidelberg [*Konigstuhl*] [*Federal Republic of Germany*] [*Seismograph station code, US Geological Survey*] (SEIS) .... HEI
Heidelberg [*City in Germany*] (ROG) .... HEIDELB
Heidelberg College, Tiffin, OH [*OCLC symbol*] (OCLC) .... HEI
Heidelberg College, Tiffin, OH [*Library symbol Library of Congress*] (LCLS) .... OTifH

Heidelberg, MS [*FM radio station call letters*] ... WEEZ
Heidelberg, United States Army [*Germany ICAO location identifier*] (ICLI) ... EDEE
Heidelberg, United States Army [*Germany ICAO location identifier*] (ICLI) ... EDOQ
Heidemij NV [*NASDAQ symbol*] (SAG) ... HEID
Heidemij NV [*Associated Press*] (SAG) ... Heidemj
Heidemij N.V. [*NASDAQ symbol*] (TTSB) ... HEIDF
Heifer Project International (EA) ... HPI
Height [*Symbol*] [*IUPAC*] ... h
Height ... H
Height (KSC) ... HGT
Height (AAG) ... HT
Height (VRA) ... ht
Height [*Also, h*] (WDMC) ... ht
Height above Airport (AFM) ... HAA
Height above Average Terrain ... HAAT
Height above Landing [*Area*] ... HAL
Height Above Plate [*Roofing*] ... HAP
Height above Runway Touchdown Zone Elevation [*Aviation*] ... HAT
Height above Spherical Earth ... HS
Height above Terrain ... HAT
Height Above Touchdown (PDAA) ... HAT
Height Adjustment Maneuver (MCD) ... HAM
Height Age (MAE) ... HA
Height Altimeter Set to 1013.2 Millibars Will Read on Landing [*Aviation code*] (AIA) ... QNE
Height and Plan Position Indicator (PDAA) ... HAPPI
Height Average (IAA) ... HAVE
Height by Width by Length (IEEE) ... HXWXL
Height Correction Factor ... HCF
Height Cross Range (MCD) ... HCR
Height Equivalent to a Theoretical Plate [*Chemical engineering*] ... HETP
Height Equivalent to a Theoretical Stage [*Chemical engineering*] (NRCH) ... HETS
Height Finder [*or Finding*] [*RADAR*] ... HF
Height Finder Operator (MUGU) ... HFO
Height Finder RADAR (CET) ... HFR
Height Finding (MSA) ... HTF
Height Indicator (NVT) ... HI
Height Integration Equipment ... HIE
Height Loss [*Aviation*] (DA) ... HL
Height of a Transfer Unit [*Distillation*] ... HTU
Height of Antenna Above Average Terrain [*Broadcasting*] (WDMC) ... HAAT
Height of Apogee ... HA
Height [*Depth*] **of Burst** ... HOB
Height [*Depth*] **of Burst, Altitude of Targets, Resources, Location, Objectives, and Time** [*Nuclear war games*] ... HARLOT
Height of Eye [*Navigation*] ... HE
Height of Eye [*Navigation*] ... HOE
Height of Fundus [*Obstetrics*] ... H of F
Height of Fundus [*Obstetrics*] ... HoF
Height of Fundus [*Obstetrics*] (DAVI) ... HofF
Height of Perigee ... HP
Height of Target ... HT
Height Overlap Coverage [*RADAR*] ... HOC
Height Range [*RADAR*] ... HR
Height Reply Analysis Processor (SAA) ... HTRAP
Height Root Mean Square (IAA) ... HRMS
Height Sensing Device ... HSD
Height/Size (DNAB) ... HT/SZ
Height Stimulator (IAA) ... HTSIM
Height Supervisor [*RADAR*] ... HTSUP
Height Technician [*Air Force*] ... HT
Height Telling [*RADAR*] ... HT
Height Tracking Console (MCD) ... HTC
Heightened (VRA) ... htnd
Height-Length ... HL
Height-Position Indicator (DEN) ... HPI
Height-Range Indicator [*Electronics*] ... HRI
Height-Range Indicator Operator [*Electronics*] ... HRIO
Height-Ranger Finder ... HRF
Heights [*Commonly used*] (OPSA) ... HEIGHT
Heights [*Commonly used*] (OPSA) ... HEIGHTS
Heights [*Commonly used*] (OPSA) ... HGTS
Heights [*Commonly used*] (OPSA) ... HT
Heights ... HTS
Heights (MCD) ... HTS
Heights (DD) ... Hts
Heights Primary School, Roslyn Heights, NY [*Library symbol*] [*Library of Congress*] (LCLS) ... NRoslhHP
Height-Telling Surveillance ... HTS
Height-to-Time Converter ... HTC
Height-Velocity ... H-V
Height-Velocity Diagram ... HVD
Heil Hitler [*Political organization*] [*British*] ... HH
Heilbrond [*South Africa*] [*ICAO location identifier*] (ICLI) ... FAHO
Heilbronn [*Germany ICAO location identifier*] (ICLI) ... EDIF
Heilig [*Holy, Saint*] [*German*] ... HL
Heilige Johannes [*Saint John*] [*Freemasonry*] [*German*] ... HJ
Heiliges Roemisches Reich [*Holy Roman Empire*] [*German*] (ROG) ... HRR
Heilig-Meyers [*NYSE symbol*] (TTSB) ... HMY
Heilig-Meyers Co. [*Associated Press*] (SAG) ... Heilig
Heilig-Meyers Co. [*NYSE symbol*] (SPSG) ... HMY
Heiltsuk Cultural Education Centre, Waglisla, British Columbia [*Library symbol National Library of Canada*] (NLC) ... BWHC
Heilungkiang Province [*China, Mainland*] [*MARC geographic area code Library of Congress*] (LCCP) ... a-cc-he
Heimlich-Armstrong-Rieveschl-Patrick [*Heart pump for aerospace use*] ... HARP
Heinemann, A. R., East Saint Louis IL [*STAC*] ... HAR
Heinemann Educational Books [*London, England*] ... HEB
Heinemann's Scientific Handbooks [*A publication*] ... HSH
Heiney Family Tree (EA) ... HFT
Heinkel [*German aircraft type*] [*World War II*] ... HE
Heinkel-Messerschmitt-Isetta Club [*Defunct*] (EA) ... HMIC
Heinsburg Public Library, Alberta [*Library symbol National Library of Canada*] (NLC) ... AHE
Heinsburg Public Library, Heinsburg, AB, Canada [*Library symbol*] [*Library of Congress*] (LCLS) ... CaAHe
Heintz, M. H., Chicago IL [*STAC*] ... HMH
Hein-Werner [*AMEX symbol*] (TTSB) ... HNW
Hein-Werner Corp. [*Associated Press*] (SAG) ... HeinWr
Hein-Werner Corp. [*AMEX symbol*] (SPSG) ... HNW
Heinz $1.70 cm Cv Pfd [*NYSE symbol*] (TTSB) ... HNZPr
Heinz [*H.J.*] **Co.** [*Associated Press*] (SAG) ... Heinz
Heinz [*H. J.*] **Co.** [*NYSE symbol*] (SPSG) ... HNZ
Heinz (H.J.) [*NYSE symbol*] (TTSB) ... HNZ
Heir ... H
Heir (ROG) ... HR
Heir Apparent (DAS) ... H App
Heir Apparent ... HA
Heir Presumptive ... HP
Heir-at-Law ... HL
Heiseman Memorial Library, West Union, IA [*Library symbol Library of Congress*] (LCLS) ... IaWu
Heisey Collectors of America (EA) ... HCA
Heiskell's Tennessee Reports [*48-59 Tennessee*] [*A publication*] (DLA) ... Heisk (Tenn)
Heiskell's Tennessee Supreme Court Reports [*1870-74*] [*A publication*] (DLA) ... Heisk
Heiss Island [*Former USSR Geomagnetic observatory code*] ... HIS
Heist [*C. H.*] **Corp.** [*Associated Press*] (SAG) ... HeistC
Heist [*C.H.*] **Corp.** [*AMEX symbol*] (SPSG) ... HST
Heitler-London-Slater-Pauling [*Method*] [*Physics*] ... HLSP
Hektoen Enteric Agar [*Medicine*] (DMAA) ... HE
Hel [*Poland*] [*Geomagnetic observatory code*] ... HLP
HeLa [*Helen Lake*]/Fibroblast [*Hybrid*] [*Cytology*] (DAVI) ... H/F
HeLa Tumor Suppression [*Medicine*] (DMAA) ... HTS
Held Back (DMAA) ... HB
Held by Civil Authorities ... HCA
Held by Manufacturer ... HBM
Held Covered [*Insurance*] ... HC
Held For (AAG) ... H/F
Held For [*Investment term*] (DFIT) ... H/F
Held for Blueprint (MCD) ... HBP
Held for Detail ... HFD
Held for Detail Available (MCD) ... HDA
Held for Manufacturing ... HFM
Held for Material ... HFM
Held for Perishable Tools ... HFPT
Held for Planning (MCD) ... HFP
Held for Tool Liaison ... HFTL
Held for Tooling ... HFT
Held [*or Hold*] **in Abeyance** [*Military*] (AFM) ... HIA
Held-Up Transient (IAA) ... HUT
Helen Baker Elementary School, Glencoe, MN [*Library symbol*] [*Library of Congress*] (LCLS) ... MnGBES
Helen Cornelius Fan Club (EA) ... HCFC
Helen Dwight Reid Educational Foundation ... HELDREF
Helen E. Taylor School, Wembley, Alberta [*Library symbol National Library of Canada*] (BIB) ... AWHT
Helen Forrest Fan Club (EA) ... HFFC
Helen, GA [*FM radio station call letters*] ... WHEL
Helen Hunt Jackson [*American novelist, 1830-1885*] [*Initials used as pseudonym*] ... HH
Helen Kate Furness Free Library, Wallingford, PA [*Library symbol Library of Congress*] (LCLS) ... PWal
Helen Keller International (EA) ... HKI
Helen Keller National Center for Deaf-Blind Youths and Adults (EA) ... HKNCDBYA
Helen Lake [*Tumour cells*] [*Medicine*] (BABM) ... HeLa
Helen M. Plum Memorial Library, Lombard, IL [*Library symbol*] [*Library of Congress*] (LCLS) ... ILo
Helen of Troy Corp. [*NASDAQ symbol*] (NQ) ... HELE
Helen of Troy Corp. [*Associated Press*] (SAG) ... HelenTr
Helen of Troy Ltd [*NASDAQ symbol*] (TTSB) ... HELE
Helen Thomas [*British author*] ... HT
Helena [*Diocesan abbreviation*] [*Montana*] (TOCD) ... HEL
Helena [*Montana*] [*Airport symbol*] (OAG) ... HLN
Helena, AR [*AM radio station call letters*] ... KFFA
Helena, AR [*FM radio station call letters*] (RBYB) ... KFFA-FM
Helena/Fort Harrison, MT [*Location identifier FAA*] (FAAL) ... ATN
Helena High School, Helena, MT [*Library symbol*] [*Library of Congress*] (LCLS) ... MtHHS
Helena, MT [*Location identifier FAA*] (FAAL) ... HAU
Helena, MT [*FM radio station call letters*] (RBYB) ... KAQR-FM
Helena, MT [*AM radio station call letters*] ... KBLL
Helena, MT [*FM radio station call letters*] ... KBLL-FM
Helena, MT [*AM radio station call letters*] ... KCAP
Helena, MT [*AM radio station call letters*] ... KMTX
Helena, MT [*FM radio station call letters*] ... KMTX-FM
Helena, MT [*Television station call letters*] ... KTVH
Helena, MT [*FM radio station call letters*] (RBYB) ... KUHM-FM

Helena, MT [*FM radio station call letters*] ..... KVCM
Helena, MT [*FM radio station call letters*] ..... KZMT
Helena Petrovna Blavatsky [*Famous 19th-century occultist*] ..... HPB
Helena Public Library, Helena, MT [*Library symbol Library of Congress*] (LCLS) ..... MtH
Helena Southwestern Railroad Co. [*AAR code*] ..... HSW
Helena Township Public Library, Alden, MI [*Library symbol Library of Congress*] (LCLS) ..... MiAld
Helena/West Helena, AR [*Location identifier FAA*] (FAAL) ..... HEE
Helene Curtis Industries, Inc. [*NYSE symbol*] (SPSG) ..... HC
Helene Curtis Industries, Inc. [*Associated Press*] (SAG) ..... HeleneC
Helenium Virus S [*Plant pathology*] ..... HEVS
Helgoland [*Germany Airport symbol*] (OAG) ..... HGL
Helgoland/Dune [*Germany ICAO location identifier*] (ICLI) ..... EDXH
Heli Air Services [*Bulgaria*] [*ICAO designator*] (FAAC) ..... HLR
Heli Europe [*Belgium ICAO designator*] (FAAC) ..... HEE
Heli France [*ICAO designator*] (FAAC) ..... HFR
Heli Inter [*France ICAO designator*] (FAAC) ..... HIN
Heli Services [*France ICAO designator*] (FAAC) ..... HES
Heli Transport [*France ICAO designator*] (FAAC) ..... HLT
Heli Union Heli Prestations [*France ICAO designator*] (FAAC) ..... HLU
Heli-Air-Monaco [*Monaco*] [*ICAO designator*] (ICDA) ..... EM
Heli-Air-Monaco [*ICAO designator*] (FAAC) ..... MCM
Heli-Air-Monaco [*ICAO designator*] (AD) ..... YO
Helian Health Group, Inc. [*Associated Press*] (SAG) ..... Helian
Helian Health Group, Inc. [*NASDAQ symbol*] (NQ) ..... HHGR
Heliarcos [*Spain*] [*FAA designator*] (FAAC) ..... ELI
Heliavia-Transporte Aereo Lda. [*Portugal ICAO designator*] (FAAC) ..... HEA
Heliax Coaxial Cable ..... HCC
Heliborne Emitter Location/Countermeasures ..... HEMLOC
Heliborne Illumination System (CINC) ..... HIS
Heliborne LASER Fire and Forget [*Missile system*] [*Army*] (RDA) ..... HELLFIRE
Helical ..... HLCL
Helical Antenna System ..... HAS
Helical Axial Rate Control (MCD) ..... HARC
Helical Compression ..... HLCPS
Helical Extension ..... HLEXT
Helical Flight Path ..... HFP
Helical Spring Lock Washer Institute ..... HSLWI
Helical Washer Institute [*Defunct*] (EA) ..... HWI
Helicap [*France ICAO designator*] (FAAC) ..... HLC
Helicocean [*France ICAO designator*] (FAAC) ..... OCE
Helicol Helicopteros Nacionales de Colombia [*ICAO designator*] (FAAC) ..... HEL
Helicopter [*When the second letter or only letter*] [*Designation for all US military aircraft*] ..... H
Helicopter (NATG) ..... H/C
Helicopter (CINC) ..... HCPTR
Helicopter (AABC) ..... HEL
Helicopter (AFM) ..... HELI
Helicopter (NG) ..... HELO
Helicopter (MSA) ..... HLCPTR
Helicopter ..... HLCPTR
Helicopter (NATG) ..... HP
Helicopter Acquisition Test (MCD) ..... HAT
Helicopter Action Group (NVT) ..... HAG
Helicopter Advanced Tactical System (MCD) ..... HATS
Helicopter Air Control [*Military*] (CAAL) ..... HAC
Helicopter Air Detachment [*Canadian Navy*] ..... HELAIRDET
Helicopter Air Service, Inc. [*ICAO designator*] (FAAC) ..... RCH
Helicopter Air Traffic Control [*ICAO designator*] (ICDA) ..... ZH
Helicopter Air Traffic Control [*FAA designator*] (FAAC) ..... ZHZ
Helicopter Aircraft Commander (NVT) ..... HAC
Helicopter Airline Association (EA) ..... HAA
Helicopter Air-to-Air Combat Simulation (MCD) ..... HATACS
Helicopter All-Weather Target Acquisition and Designation System ..... HAWTADS
Helicopter Ambulance Medical Detachment ..... HAMD
Helicopter Anti-Submarine ..... HAS
Helicopter Antisubmarine Squadron [*Navy*] ..... HELANTISUBRON
Helicopter Antisubmarine Squadron [*Navy*] ..... HELASRON
Helicopter Antisubmarine Squadron Detachment [*Navy*] (DNAB) ..... HELANTISUBRONDET
Helicopter Antisubmarine Squadron Light (NVT) ..... HSL
Helicopter Approach/Departure [*Military*] (CAAL) ..... HAD
Helicopter Approach Path Indicator (MCD) ..... HAPI
Helicopter Armored Experiment ..... HAX
Helicopter Assault Force (NVT) ..... HAF
Helicopter Assault Survivability in a Threat Environment (MCD) ..... HASTE
Helicopter Assault Wave ..... HAW
Helicopter Association International (EA) ..... HAI
Helicopter Association of America [*Later, HAI*] (EA) ..... HAA
Helicopter Association of Australia ..... HAA
Helicopter Attack Squadron [*Navy*] (DNAB) ..... HELATKRON
Helicopter Attack Squadron (Light) (CINC) ..... HA(L)
Helicopter Attack System ..... HATS
Helicopter Attack Warning RADAR (NVT) ..... HAWR
Helicopter Attitude Indicator ..... HAI
Helicopter Attitude Reference System (MCD) ..... HARS
Helicopter Avionics System [*Air Force*] ..... HAS
Helicopter Battle Damage Repair (RDA) ..... HBDR
Helicopter Blade Slap ..... HBS
Helicopter Club of America (EA) ..... HCA
Helicopter Collision Avoidance RADAR (NG) ..... HELCAR
Helicopter Combat (NVT) ..... HC
Helicopter Combat Support Squadron [*Navy*] (DNAB) ..... HC
Helicopter Combat Support Squadron [*Navy*] (DNAB) ..... HCRON
Helicopter Combat Support Squadron [*Navy*] (DNAB) ..... HELCOMBSUPPRON
Helicopter Combat Support Squadron [*Navy*] ..... HELSUPPRON
Helicopter Combat Support Squadron Detachment [*Navy*] (DNAB) ..... HELSUPPRONDET
Helicopter Command (NVT) ..... HC
Helicopter Command Instrumentation System (MCD) ..... HELCIS
Helicopter Control Center (NVT) ..... HCC
Helicopter Control Officer [*British military*] (DMA) ..... HCO
Helicopter Control Ship [*Navy*] (NVT) ..... HCS
Helicopter Control Unit (NVT) ..... HCU
Helicopter Coordination Center ..... HCC
Helicopter Coordinator [*Military*] (CAAL) ..... HC
Helicopter Coordinator (Airborne) (NVT) ..... HC(A)
Helicopter Council ..... HC
Helicopter Crash Crane (DNAB) ..... HCC
Helicopter Delivered ..... HD
Helicopter Depot Maintenance Center (MCD) ..... HDMC
Helicopter Direction (DNAB) ..... HD
Helicopter Direction Center ..... HDC
Helicopter Direction Inbound [*Military*] (CAAL) ..... HDI
Helicopter Direction Outbound [*Military*] (CAAL) ..... HDO
Helicopter Director [*Military*] (CAAL) ..... HD
Helicopter Electronic Landing Path [*Army*] ..... HELP
Helicopter Element Coordinator [*Navy*] (ANA) ..... HEC
Helicopter Employment and Assault Landing Table (NVT) ..... HEALT
Helicopter Escape and Personnel Survival System (MCD) ..... HEPSS
Helicopter Escort, Air Defense Suppression System ..... HEADSS
Helicopter Expendable Bathythermograph [*Naval Oceanographic Office*] ..... HXBT
Helicopter Experimental, Medium (MCD) ..... HXM
Helicopter Extended Area Platform ..... HEAP
Helicopter External Air Transport (MCD) ..... HEAT
Helicopter External Gondola System ..... HEGS
Helicopter Familiarization (MCD) ..... HFAM
Helicopter Foundation International (EA) ..... HFI
Helicopter Gravity-Measuring System [*Naval Oceanographic Office*] ..... HGMS
Helicopter Hauldown and Rapid Securing Device [*Military*] (CAAL) ..... HHRSD
Helicopter Hire Ltd. [*British ICAO designator*] (FAAC) ..... HHL
Helicopter Icing Spray System (RDA) ..... HISS
Helicopter In-Flight Monitoring System [*Army*] (RDA) ..... HIMS
Helicopter In-Flight Refueling (NVT) ..... HIFR
Helicopter Inflight Spray System (MCD) ..... HISS
Helicopter In-flight Validation System (PDAA) ..... HELIVALS
Helicopter Insecticide Dispersal Apparatus, Dry (NG) ..... HIDAD
Helicopter Insecticide Dispersal Apparatus, Fog (NG) ..... HIDAF
Helicopter Insecticide Dispersal Apparatus, Liquid (NG) ..... HIDAL
Helicopter Installed Television Monitor and Recorder (MCD) ..... HITMORE
Helicopter Instrument Rules ..... HIR
Helicopter Integrated Direction Equipment ..... HIDE
Helicopter Integrated Navigation System [*Canadian Navy*] ..... HINS
Helicopter Internal Cargo Handling System ..... HICHS
Helicopter Landing Area/Drop Zone [*Military*] (MCD) ..... HLA/DZ
Helicopter Landing Area/Drop Zone Study [*Military*] (MCD) ..... HLA/DZS
Helicopter Landing Exercise [*Amphibious*] [*Navy*] (NVT) ..... HELILEX
Helicopter Landing Site [*Military*] (INF) ..... HLS
Helicopter Landing Zone ..... HLZ
Helicopter Landing Zone Locator ..... HLZL
Helicopter LASER Range-Finder ..... HLR
Helicopter Lift Margin System (MCD) ..... HELMS
Helicopter Loggers Association (EA) ..... HLA
Helicopter Logistic Support Center (NVT) ..... HLSC
Helicopter Long-Range Acoustic Sensor [*Military*] (CAAL) ..... HELRAS
Helicopter Mounted LASER Weapon (MCD) ..... HEMLAW
Helicopter Multifunction System ..... HELMS
Helicopter Navigation System (RDA) ..... HELNAVS
Helicopter Night Vision System (PDAA) ..... HNVS
Helicopter Night-Landing System ..... HENILAS
Helicopter Noise Model [*OST*] (TAG) ..... HNM
Helicopter Operational Support Facility (DNAB) ..... HELOPSUPPFAC
Helicopter Operational Test and Evaluation Flight [*Canadian Navy*] ..... HOTEF
Helicopter Operations (DNAB) ..... HELOPS
Helicopter Operations (FAAC) ..... HOP
Helicopter Operations from Ships other than Aircraft Carriers [*Supplement*] (DOMA) ..... HOSTAC
Helicopter Operations in a Night Environment Against a Simulated Target [*Military*] (MCD) ..... HONEST
Helicopter Operations in Selected RADAR Environment (MCD) ..... HELORADE
Helicopter Optical Tracking and Control ..... HOTAC
Helicopter Outlying Field ..... HOLF
Helicopter Performance Computer (NG) ..... HPC
Helicopter Personnel Escape, Protection, and Survival (DNAB) ..... HEPS
Helicopter Pilot Control and Training ..... HEPCAT
Helicopter Plane Commander ..... HPC
Helicopter Position and Terrain Height ..... HELIPATH
Helicopter Protected Zone [*Military*] (DA) ..... HPZ
Helicopter Qualifications [*Navy*] (NVT) ..... HELOQUALS
Helicopter Remote Classification and Localization System (PDAA) ..... HERCULES
Helicopter Remote Wind Sensor ..... HRWS
Helicopter Request [*Military*] (NVT) ..... HR
Helicopter Safety Advisory Conference (EA) ..... HSAC
Helicopter Sea Control Wing (NVT) ..... HSCW
Helicopter Sensor Development Program ..... HESDEP
Helicopter Ship, Missile-Armed [*NATO*] ..... CHG
Helicopter SONAR Data Collection ..... HESODAC
Helicopter Squadron ..... HS
Helicopter Squadron, Antisubmarine (MCD) ..... HS

Helicopter Subcontrol Ship [*Navy*] (NVT) ... HSCS
Helicopter Subcontrol Unit (NVT) ... HSCU
Helicopter Support Team [*Navy*] (NVT) ... HST
Helicopter Surveillance and Target Acquisition RADAR ... HSTAR
Helicopter Survivability Assessment Model (MCD) ... HSAM
Helicopter System ... HS
Helicopter Tank Destroyer [*Military*] ... HELTAD
Helicopter Team ... HELITEAM
Helicopter Team Defense Missile ... HTDM
Helicopter Training (NVT) ... HELOTNG
Helicopter Training Squadron [*Navy*] ... HELTRARON
Helicopter Training Squadron [*Navy symbol*] (NVT) ... HT
Helicopter Transit Controller (MCD) ... HTC
Helicopter Transportable Launcher (MUGU) ... HTL
Helicopter Trap Weapon (SAA) ... HTW
Helicopter Utility (Piasecki) ... HUP
Helicopter Utility Squadron ... HUS
Helicopter Utility Squadron ... HUTRON
Helicopter Visual Rules ... HVR
Helicopter Weapons System ... HWS
Helicopter Wire Cutter System (MCD) ... HWCS
Helicopterborne Command and Control Communications Central ... HC4
Helicopter-Delivered Seismic Intrusion Detector (NVT) ... HELOSID
Helicopteros Andes [*Chile*] [*ICAO designator*] (FAAC) ... HAD
Helicopteros do Brasil SA [*Brazil ICAO aircraft manufacturer identifier*] (ICAO) ... H
Helicopteros Internacionales, SA de CV [*Mexico*] [*FAA designator*] (FAAC) ... HNT
Helicopteros Xel-Ha SA de CV [*Mexico ICAO designator*] (FAAC) ... XEL
Helicsa [*Spain*] [*FAA designator*] (FAAC) ... HHH
Heliflyg AG [*Sweden ICAO designator*] (FAAC) ... HFL
Heligoland [*Federal Republic of Germany*] [*Seismograph station code, US Geological Survey*] (SEIS) ... HLG
Heli-Holland BV [*Netherlands ICAO designator*] (FAAC) ... HHE
Heli-Home [*Recreational vehicle*] ... H-H
Heli-Iberica [*Spain ICAO designator*] (FAAC) ... HRA
Heli-Inter Guyane [*France ICAO designator*] (FAAC) ... HIG
Helijet [*Spain ICAO designator*] (FAAC) ... HJS
Helijet Airways [*Canada ICAO designator*] (FAAC) ... JBA
Helikopter Service AS [*Norway ICAO designator*] (FAAC) ... HKS
Helikoptertransport AB [*Sweden ICAO designator*] (FAAC) ... KTR
Heli-Link [*Switzerland ICAO designator*] (FAAC) ... HLK
Helio Aircraft Co. [*ICAO aircraft manufacturer identifier*] (ICAO) ... HE
Heliocentric Julian Day [*Astronomy*] ... HJD
Heliocentric Orbit Rendezvous (MCD) ... HOR
Heliodor [*Record label*] [*Great Britain*] ... Hel
Heliodor [*Record label*] [*Great Britain*] ... HP
Heliodorus [*Greek writer, c. 200AD*] (ROG) ... HELIOD
Heliogabalus [*of Scriptores Historiae Augustae*] [*Classical studies*] (OCD) ... Heliogab
Heliogram ... HG
Helionetics, Inc. [*Associated Press*] (SAG) ... Heliont
Helios - Joies de la Musique [*Record label*] [*France*] ... Helios
Helios Semiconductor (IAA) ... HS
Heliospheric Instrument for Spectra, Composition, and Anisotropy at Low Energies [*Astronomy*] ... HI-SCALE
Heliospheric Magnetic Field [*Solar physics*] ... HMF
Heliothis Zea [*Corn ear worm*] ... Hzea
Heliothis Zea Nuclear Polyhedrosis Virus ... HzNPV
Heliothis Zea Pheromone Biosynthesis Activating Neuropeptide ... Hez-PBAN
Heliotrope [*Philately*] ... hel
Heliotype [*Modified collotype*] (VRA) ... HTYP
Heliport [*ICAO designator*] (FAAC) ... HELI
Heliportugal-Trabalhos e Transporte Aereo, Representacoes, Importacao e Exportacao Lda. [*Portugal ICAO designator*] (FAAC) ... HPL
Helipotentiometer ... HPOT
Heliserv SA de CV [*Mexico ICAO designator*] (FAAC) ... HLV
Heliservicio Campeche SA de CV [*Mexico ICAO designator*] (FAAC) ... HEC
Heliservico-Sociedade Portuguesa de Exploracao de Meios Aeros Lda. [*Portugal ICAO designator*] (FAAC) ... HSV
Helisys, Inc. [*NASDAQ symbol*] (SAG) ... HELI
Helisys Inc. [*NASDAQ symbol*] (TTSB) ... HELI
Helisys, Inc. [*Associated Press*] (SAG) ... Helisys
Helitrans Air Service, Inc. [*ICAO designator*] (FAAC) ... HTS
Helium [*Chemical symbol is He*] (AAG) ... H
Helium [*Chemical element*] ... He
Helium Abundance Detector [*Instrumentation*] ... HAD
Helium Cadmium [*LASER*] (DGA) ... HECD
Helium Cadmium LASER ... HCL
Helium Charging Unit (AAG) ... HCU
Helium Check Valve (MCD) ... HECV
Helium Circulation [*System*] ... HC
Helium Circulator Seal (IEEE) ... HCS
Helium Component Test Facility [*Nuclear energy*] (NUCP) ... HCTF
Helium Emergency Supply ... HES
Helium Engineering Demonstration Loop [*Nuclear energy*] (NUCP) ... HENDEL
Helium Equilibration Time (MAE) ... HET
Helium Extraction ... HELEX
Helium Fill Line ... HFL
Helium Fill to Distribution Unit [*Aerospace*] (AAG) ... HFD
Helium Filled Bubble [*For study of air flow*] ... HFB
Helium Flow Control Valve (KSC) ... HFCV
Helium Fuel-Tank Pressurization (AAG) ... HFP
Helium Gauge (MCD) ... HEG
Helium Gauge Valve (MCD) ... HEGV
Helium Impurities Loop [*Nuclear energy*] (NRCH) ... HIL
Helium Ionization Detector [*Instrumentation*] ... HID
Helium Isolation Valve [*NASA*] (NASA) ... HIV
Helium Latching Solenoid Valve ... HLSV
Helium Leak Detector ... HLD
Helium Level ... HL
Helium Liquid Program [*NASA*] ... HELP
Helium Manual Valve (MCD) ... HEMV
Helium Neon [*LASER*] (DGA) ... HENE
Helium Neon [*LASER*] (DGA) ... HN
Helium Neon Gas LASER ... HNGL
Helium Neon LASER ... HNL
Helium Oxidizer-Tank Pressure (AAG) ... HOP
Helium Pressure Switch (MCD) ... HPS
Helium Pressure Vessel ... HPV
Helium Rebottled [*System*] ... HR
Helium, Refrigerated (AAG) ... HR
Helium Research Center ... HRC
Helium Selenium [*LASER*] (DGA) ... HESE
Helium Service Unit (MCD) ... HSU
Helium Speech Unscrambler [*Deep sea diving*] ... HSU
Helium to Heat Exchanger (AAG) ... HHE
Helium Underwater Speech Translating Equipment ... HUSTLE
Helium Vent Valve (MCD) ... HVV
Helium-Atom Diffraction (PDAA) ... HEAD
Helium-Neon (IDOE) ... He-Ne
Helix ... H
Helix ... HLX
Helix Angle ... HLXA
Helix Biotech [*Vancouver Stock Exchange symbol*] ... HXB
Helix Circuits, Inc. [*Toronto Stock Exchange symbol*] ... HLX
Helix Countercurrent Chromatography ... HCCC
Helix Linear Accelerator (PDAA) ... HELAC
Helix Pubic Library, Helix, OR [*Library symbol*] [*Library of Congress*] (LCLS) ... OrHx
Helix Systems Ltd. [*Vancouver Stock Exchange symbol*] ... HIX
Helix Technologies [*Associated Press*] (SAG) ... HelixTch
Helix Technology [*NASDAQ symbol*] (TTSB) ... HELX
Helix Technology Corp. [*NASDAQ symbol*] (NQ) ... HELX
Helix-Loop-Helix [*Genetics*] ... HLH
Helix-Span-Helix [*Protein structure*] ... HSH
Helix-Turn-Helix [*Protein structure*] ... HTH
Hella Electronics Corp. [*Automotive industry supplier*] ... HEC
Hellas Planitia [*A filamentary mark on Mars*] ... HP
Hellenic [*Classical studies*] (BARN) ... Hellen
Hellenic Advancement Council [*Australia*] ... HAC
Hellenic Aerospace Industry [*Greek*] ... HAI
Hellenic Affiliation Scale [*Psychology*] ... HAS
Hellenic Air Force [*Greece*] [*ICAO designator*] (FAAC) ... HAF
Hellenic Air SA [*Greece*] [*ICAO designator*] (FAAC) ... HLN
Hellenic Armed Forces (NATG) ... HAF
Hellenic Arms Industry [*Greek*] ... HAI
Hellenic Army (MCD) ... HA
Hellenic Chamber of Commerce in Australia ... HCCA
Hellenic College of Arts and Sciences and Holy Cross Greek Orthodox Theological School, Brookline, MA [*Library symbol Library of Congress*] (LCLS) ... MBrHC
Hellenic Marine Environment Protection Association ... HELMEPA
Hellenic Marine Environmental Protection Association (EERA) ... HELMEPA
Hellenic Philatelic Society of America (EA) ... HPSA
Hellenic Register [*Greek ship classification society*] (DS) ... HR
Hellenic Resources [*Vancouver Stock Exchange symbol*] ... HEL
Hellenica [*of Xenophon*] [*Classical studies*] (OCD) ... Hell
Hellenica Oxyrhynchia [*Classical studies*] (OCD) ... Hell Oxy
Hellenike Trapeza Biomechanikes Anaptyxeos ... ETBA
Hellenistic [*Period*] ... Hel
Hellenistische Dichtung in der Zeit des Kallimachos [*A publication*] (OCD) ... Hell Dicht
Heller, Erhman, White & McCauliffe, San Francisco, CA [*Library symbol*] [*Library of Congress*] (LCLS) ... CSfHE
Heller Financial [*Associated Press*] (SAG) ... HelrFn
Heller Financial [*NYSE symbol*] (SPSG) ... HLF
Heller Finl 8.125% Sr'A' Pfd [*NYSE symbol*] (TTSB) ... HLFPrA
HELLFIRE [*Heliborne LASER Fire and Forget*] **All-Weather Target Acquisition and Destruction System** (MCD) ... HAWTADS
HELLFIRE Fire and Forget Seeker [*Missile*] ... HFFS
HELLFIRE [*Heliborne LASER Fire and Forget*]/Ground LASER Designator [*Army*] (RDA) ... HELLFIRE/GLD
HELLFIRE Modular Missile System ... HMMS
Hellfire Optimized Missile System [*Army*] (DOMA) ... HOMS
Hellmann-Feynmann Electrostatic Theorem [*Physics*] ... HFET
Hellmuth, Obata & Kassabaum [*Architectural firm*] ... HOK
Hello Direct [*NASDAQ symbol*] (TTSB) ... HELO
Hello Direct, Inc. [*Associated Press*] (SAG) ... HelloD
Hello Direct, Inc. [*NASDAQ symbol*] (SAG) ... HELO
Helm Resources [*AMEX symbol*] (TTSB) ... HHH
Helm Resources, Inc [*AMEX symbol*] (SAG) ... HHH
Helm Resources, Inc. [*Associated Press*] (SAG) ... HelmRes
Helmerich & Payne [*NYSE symbol*] (TTSB) ... HP
Helmerich & Payne, Inc. [*Associated Press*] (SAG) ... HelmP
Helmerich & Payne, Inc. [*NYSE symbol*] (SPSG) ... HP
Helmet (NASA) ... HLMT
Helmet Airborne Display and Sight (MCD) ... HADAS
Helmet Cells [*Cytology*] (DAVI) ... HELM
Helmet Compatible Communications/Aural Protection System ... HCCAPS
Helmet Initiated Pointing System (MCD) ... HIPS

Helmet Integrated Tracking and Display System (MCD) .... HITADS
Helmet Shield .... HS
Helmet Sight Subsystem (RDA) .... HSS
Helmet Stowage Bag [NASA] (KSC) .... HSB
Helmet-Mounted Display .... HMD
Helmet-Mounted Display Device [Military] .... HMDD
Helmet-Mounted Optical Projection System .... HOPS
Helmet-Mounted Pick-Offs (MCD) .... HMP
Helmet-Mounted Sight [Aviation] .... HMS
Helmet-Mounted Sight Set .... HMSS
Helmet-Position Sensing System .... HELPS
Helmholtz Energy [Symbol] [IUPAC] .... A
Helmholtz Free Energy .... HFE
Helmholtz Function [Symbol] (DEN) .... F
Helmholtz Reciprocal Theorem [Physics] .... HRT
Helmholtz-Gemeinschaft Deutscher Forschungs-zentren [Helmholtz
  association of German research centres] .... HGF
Helminthosporium carbonum [A toxin-producing fungus] .... HC
Helminthosporium maydis race T [A toxin-producing fungus] ... HmT
Helminthosporium sacchari [A toxin-producing fungus] .... HS
Helminthosporium victoriae [A toxin-producing fungus] .... HV
Helms Athletic Foundation [Later, Citizens Savings Athletic Foundation]
  (EA) .... HAF
Helms, Mullis & Johnston Law Library, Charlotte, NC [Library symbol]
  [Library of Congress] (LCLS) .... NcCHM
Helm's Reports [2-9 Nevada] [A publication] (DLA) .... Helm
Helmstar Group [Associated Press] (SAG) .... Helmstr
Helmstar Group [AMEX symbol] (SPSG) .... HLM
Helmut Attitude Tracking System (MCD) .... HATS
Helmville [Montana] [Seismograph station code, US Geological Survey
  Closed] (SEIS) .... HLM
Helo Transportable Mulit-Mission Platform [Experimental military
  vehicle] .... HTMMP
Heloma Durum [A hard corn] [Orthopedics] (DAVI) .... HD
Help Abolish Legal Tyranny [In organization name HALT-ALR] (EA) .... HALT
Help Addicts Voluntarily End Narcotics .... HAVEN
Help Alopecia International Research [Defunct] (EA) .... HAIR
Help and Action Coordinating Committee [Defunct France] (EAIO) .... HACC
Help At Home [NASDAQ symbol] (TTSB) .... HAHI
Help At Home, Inc. [NASDAQ symbol] (SAG) .... HAHI
Help At Home, Inc. [Associated Press] (SAG) .... HlpHm
Help At Home, Inc. [Associated Press] (SAG) .... HlpHme
Help At Home Wrrt [NASDAQ symbol] (TTSB) .... HAHIW
Help Desk Services .... HDS
Help End Marijuana Prohibition [An association] .... HEMP
Help Establish Lasting Peace .... HELP
Help File [Computer science] .... HLP
Help for Incontinent People (EA) .... HIP
Help Hospitalized Veterans (EA) .... HHV
Help in Emergency (ADA) .... HIE
HELP, International [Defunct] (EA) .... HELP
Help Model for Windows .... HMfW
Help Obese People Everywhere .... HOPE
Help Other People [Scout motto] .... HOP
Help Our Headaches Group [Australia] .... HOH
Help Our Wolves Live .... HOWL
Help Our World .... HOW
Help Project [Computer science] (PCM) .... HPJ
Help Save America for Our Kids' Future (EA) .... HSAFOKF
Help the Aged [AAIA] [Superseded by] (EA) .... HTA
Help through Industry Retraining and Employment [Program] [Department of
  Labor] .... HIRE
Help To Run Our-Lines [Military] .... HTROL
Help Us Make a Nation (EA) .... HUMAN
Help Us Reach and Rehabilitate America's Handicapped [State-Federal
  rehabilitation program] .... HURRAH
Helpdesk Expert Automation Tool [Bendata Management Systems, Inc.] ..... HEAT
Helper .... HLP
Helper (BARN) .... HLPR
Helper (BARN) .... Hlpr
Helper Component [Biology] .... HC
Helper Factor [Immunology] .... HF
Helper/Suppressor [Cell ratio] .... H/S
Helper T-Lymphocyte [Immunology] .... HTL
Helpful Programs, Inc. [Computer science] .... HPI
Helping Other Parents in Normal Grieving (EA) .... HOPING
Helping Smokers Quit [American Cancer Society] (EA) .... HSQ
Helpmate Robotics [NASDAQ symbol] (TTSB) .... HELP
Helpmate Robotics, Inc. [NASDAQ symbol] (SAG) .... HELP
Helpmate Robotics, Inc. [Associated Press] (SAG) .... Helpmte
Helpmate Robotics, Inc. [Associated Press] (SAG) .... Hlpmte
Helpmate Robotics Unit [NASDAQ symbol] (TTSB) .... HELPU
Helpmate Robotics Wrrt [NASDAQ symbol] (TTSB) .... HELPW
Helps International Ministries (EA) .... HIM
Helsingborg/Harbour [Sweden ICAO location identifier] (ICLI) .... ESHH
Helsingen Juutalainen Seurakunta [Finland] [A publication] (BJA) .... HJS
Helsingfors [Helsinki] [Finland] [Seismograph station code, US Geological
  Survey] (SEIS) .... HEL
Helsingin Kauppakorkeakoulun Kirjasto [Helsinki School of Economics
  Library] [Finland] [Information service or system] (IID) .... HKKK
Helsingin Yliopisto [University of Helsinki], Helsinki, Finland [Library symbol
  Library of Congress] (LCLS) .... FiHU
Helsinki [Finland ICAO location identifier] (ICLI) .... EFKL
Helsinki [Finland] [Airport symbol] (OAG) .... HEL
Helsinki Guarantees for Ukraine Committee [Defunct] (EA) .... HGUC

Helsinki/Helsinki-Malmi [Finland ICAO location identifier] (ICLI) .... EFHF
Helsinki Stock Exchange [Finland] .... HSE
Helsinki University, Library of Agriculture, Viikki, Helsinki, Finland [Library
  symbol] [Library of Congress] (LCLS) .... FiHU-A
Helsinki University Library of Forestry [Helsingin Yliopiston Metsakirjaston],
  Helsinki, Finland [Library symbol] [Library of Congress] (LCLS) .... FiHU-F
Helsinki University of Technology .... HUT
Helsinki University of Technology Satellite .... HUTSAT
Helsinki/Vantaa [Finland ICAO location identifier] (ICLI) .... EFHK
Helston [Municipal borough in England] .... HELST
Helvetia [Switzerland] (ROG) .... HEL
Helvetia Association of North America [Defunct] (EA) .... HANA
Helvetica [Typography] (WDAA) .... HELV
Helwan [Egypt] [Seismograph station code, US Geological Survey] (SEIS) ...... HLW
HELWS-Integrated RADAR .... HIR
HELWS-Integrated Tracker .... HIT
HemaCare Corp. [NASDAQ symbol] (NQ) .... HEMA
HemaCare Corp. [Associated Press] (SAG) .... HemaC
Hemadsorption [Hematology] .... HA
Hemadsorption [Hematology] .... HAD
Hemadsorption [Virus], Type 1 [Hematology] (DAVI) HA1
Hemagen Diagnostics [Associated Press] (SAG) .... Hemagn
Hemagen Diagnostics [Associated Press] (SAG) .... Hemgn
Hemagen Diagnostics [NASDAQ symbol] (SAG) .... HMGN
Hemagglutinating [Virology] .... H
Hemagglutinating Activity [Hematology] (DAVI) .... HA
Hemagglutinating Antibody [Hematology] (DAVI) .... HA
Hemagglutinating Antigen [Hematology] (DAVI) .... HA
Hemagglutinating Anti-Penicillin Antibody [Virology] (MAE) .... HAPA
Hemagglutinating Encephalomyelitis [Neurology] (DAVI) .... HE
Hemagglutinating Encephalomyelitis Virus [Medicine] (DMAA) .... HEV
Hemagglutinating Unit [Immunochemistry] .... HU
Hemagglutinating Virus of Japan [Medicine] .... HVJ
Hemagglutination [Hematology] .... HA
Hemagglutination Inhibition [Immunochemistry] .... HAI
Hemagglutination Inhibition [Immunochemistry] .... HI
Hemagglutination Inhibition Antibody [Immunochemistry] .... HIA
Hemagglutination Inhibition Morphine Test [Immunochemistry] (DMAA) .... HIMT
Hemagglutination Inhibition Test [for pregnancy] [Medicine] .... HIT
Hemagglutination Titer [Medicine] .... HIT
Hemagglutination Treponemal Test for Syphilis [Medicine] (DMAA) .... HATTS
Hemagglutination Unit [Hematology] .... HAU
Hemagglutination-Inhibition Immunoassay [Immunochemistry] (DAVI) .... HII
Hemagglutinin-Neuraminidase [An enzyme] .... HN
Hemangioma-Thrombocytopenia Syndrome [Medicine] (MEDA) .... HTS
Hemasure, Inc. [Associated Press] (SAG) .... Hemasure
Hemasure, Inc. [NASDAQ symbol] (SAG) .... HMSR
HemaSure Inc. [NASDAQ symbol] (TTSB) .... HMSR
Hematemesis [Gastroenterology] (DAVI) .... hematem
Hematemesis Neonatorum [Medicine] (DMAA) .... HN
Hematite [A mineral] .... H
Hematite [A mineral] .... HEM
Hematite [CIPW classification] [Geology] .... hm
Hematocrit [Hematology] (DAVI) .... crit
Hematocrit [Medicine] .... H'CRIT
Hematocrit [Medicine] .... HCT
Hematocrit [Medicine] (DAVI) .... hemat
Hematoencephalic Barrier [or Blood brain barrier] [Medicine] (DAVI) .... HEB
Hematologic Abnormality [Medicine] .... hemat ab
Hematologist .... HEMATL
Hematology [Medicine] (DHSM) .... HEM
Hematology [Medicine] .... HEMAT
Hematology .... HEMATLGY
Hematology [or Hematologist] [Medicine] .... Hematol
Hematology and Oncology (DAVI) .... H/O
Hematology Profile [Medicine] (DAVI) .... HEMA
Hematopoietic Blood Stem Cell [Medicine] (DMAA) .... HBSC
Hematopoietic Cell [Hematology] .... HC
Hematopoietic Cell Kinase (DMAA) .... HCK
Hematopoietic Growth Factor [Biochemistry Medicine] .... HGF
Hematopoietic Progenitor Cell [Hematology] .... HPC
Hematopoietic Stem Cell [Hematology] .... HSC
Hematoporphyrin Derivative [Antineoplastic compound] .... HPD
Hematoxylin and Eosin [Biological stain] .... H & E
Hematoxylin and Eosin [Biological stain] .... HE
Hematoxylin-Phloxine-Saffron [Biochemistry] (MAE) .... HPS
Hematuria [Urology] .... hem
Hemavan [Sweden ICAO location identifier] (ICLI) .... ESUT
Hemdale Communications [NASDAQ symbol] (TTSB) .... HEMDE
Heme Oxygenase (DMAA) .... HMOX
Heme Synthetase [An enzyme] (AAMN) .... HS
Hemel Hempstead [Postcode] (ODBW) .... HP
Hemeroteca Nacional [Database] [Ministerio de Cultura] [Spanish] [Information
  service or system] (CRD) .... HENA
Hemet, CA [Location identifier FAA] (FAAL) .... HMT
Hemet, CA [AM radio station call letters] (RBYB) .... KSDT
Hemet, CA [FM radio station call letters] .... KXRS
Hemet Public Library, Hemet, CA [Library symbol Library of Congress]
  (LCLS) .... CHem
Hemgold Resources Ltd. [Vancouver Stock Exchange symbol] .... HEG
Hemibody Irradiation [Oncology] .... HBI
Hemic Subgroup [Magnetite, chromite, hematite] [CIPW classification
  Geology] .... H
Hemiconvulsion, Hemiplegia, and Epilepsy Syndrome [Neurology] (DAVI).... HEE
Hemiconvulsions, Hemiplegia, Epilepsy [Medicine] .... HHE

Hemicylindrical [*Leaf characteristic*] [*Botany*] ... HE
Hemidesmosome [*Cytology*] ... HD
Hemifacial Microsomia [*Medicine*] (DMAA) ... HFM
Hemifacial Spasm [*Medicine*] ... HFS
Hemigastrectomy and Vagotomy [*Medicine*] ... H & V
Hemihydrate-Dihydrate [*Chemical technology*] ... HDH
Hemihypertrophy, Intestinal Web, Preauricular Skin Tag, and Congenital Corneal Opacity Syndrome [*Medicine*] (DMAA) ... HIPO
Hemin [*Hematology*] ... H
Hemin Controlled Repressor [*Biochemistry*] ... HCR
Hemin Storage ... HMS
Hemingway, SC [*Location identifier FAA*] (FAAL) ... HEK
Hemingway, SC [*AM radio station call letters*] ... WKYB
Hemingway, SC [*FM radio station call letters*] ... WLGI
Hemingway Society (EA) ... HS
Hemingway's Mississippi Reports [*A publication*] (DLA) ... Heming
Hemingway's Mississippi Reports [*A publication*] (DLA) ... Heming (Miss)
Hemipalmitoylcarnitinium [*Biochemistry*] ... HPC
Hemiparalysis [*Medicine*] ... HEMI
Hemipelvectomy [*Medicine*] ... H/P
Hemiplegia [*Medicine*] ... HEMI
Hemiplegia [*Medicine*] ... Hp
Hemiplegic Migraine [*Neurology*] (DAVI) ... HPM
Hemisphere [*Anatomy*] (DAVI) ... H
Hemisphere ... HEM
Hemisphere [*Neurology*] (DAVI) ... Hemi
Hemisphere (AFM) ... HEMIS
Hemisphere Cylinder Body ... HCB
Hemisphere Development Corp. [*Vancouver Stock Exchange symbol*] ... HSD
Hemisphere Publishing Co. ... HPC
Hemispheric Activation Level [*Computer science*] (BYTE) ... HAL
Hemispheric Blood Flow [*Medicine*] (DMAA) ... HBF
Hemispheric Insurance Conference ... HIC
Hemispheric Thrombotic Infarction [*Medicine*] (DMAA) ... HTI
Hemispherical [*Automotive engineering*] ... HEMI
Hemispherical [*S-band antenna*] ... HEMI
Hemispherical Candlepower [*Optics*] (IAA) ... HCP
Hemispherical Candlepower Second [*Optics*] (IAA) ... HCPS
Hemispherical Reflective Antenna ... HRA
Hemispherical Resonating Gyro (PDAA) ... HRG
Hemispherical Search [*First frequency-scanning RADAR*] (MCD) ... HEMISEARCH
Hemispherx BioPharma, Inc. [*Associated Press*] (SAG) ... Hemis
Hemispherx BioPharma, Inc. [*Associated Press*] (SAG) ... Hemispx
Hemispherx BioPharma, Inc. [*NASDAQ symbol*] (SAG) ... HEMX
Hemispherx BioPharma, Inc. [*Associated Press*] (SAG) ... Hmisph
Hemispherx BioPharma Unit [*NASDAQ symbol*] (TTSB) ... HEMXU
Hemlo Explorations [*Vancouver Stock Exchange symbol*] ... HEX
Hemlo Gold Mines [*AMEX symbol*] (TTSB) ... HEM
Hemlo Gold Mines, Inc. [*Toronto Stock Exchange symbol AMEX symbol*] ... HEM
Hemlo Gold Mines, Inc. [*Associated Press*] (SAG) ... Hemlo
Hemlock Society (EA) ... HS
Hemmant's Select Cases in Exchequer Chamber [*Selden Society Publications, Vol. 51*] [*1377-1460*] [*A publication*] (DLA) ... Hemmant
Hemmeter Aviation, Inc. [*ICAO designator*] (FAAC) ... HEM
Hemmets Haerold [*Record label*] [*Sweden*] ... HH
Hemming and Miller's English Vice-Chancellors' Reports [*A publication*] (DLA) ... H & M
Hemming and Miller's English Vice-Chancellors' Reports [*A publication*] (DLA) ... H & M Ch
Hemming and Miller's English Vice-Chancellors' Reports [*A publication*] (DLA) ... Hem & M
Hemming and Miller's English Vice-Chancellors' Reports [*A publication*] (DLA) ... Hem & M (Eng)
Hemming and Miller's English Vice-Chancellors' Reports [*A publication*] (DLA) ... Hem & Mill
Hemmings Motor News [*A publication*] ... HMN
Hemochromatosis Research Foundation (EA) ... HRF
Hemocytometer (MAE) ... hemocyt
Hemodialysis [*Nephrology*] ... HD
Hemodialysis Unit [*Medicine*] ... HDU
Hemodilution ... HD
Hemodilution Combined with Hypotension ... HD-HT
Hemoglobin [*Biochemistry, medicine*] ... Hb
Hemoglobin [*Medicine*] (DMAA) ... HB
Hemoglobin [*Medicine*] (WDAA) ... HEM
Hemoglobin [*Medicine*] (DAVI) ... hemo
Hemoglobin [*Biochemistry, medicine*] ... HG
Hemoglobin [*Biochemistry, medicine*] ... HGB
Hemoglobin A and Hemoglobin S [*Medicine*] (MEDA) ... HbAS
Hemoglobin, Adult [*Medicine*] ... HbA
Hemoglobin and Hematocrit [*Clinical chemistry*] ... H & H
Hemoglobin and Hematocrit [*Hematology*] (DAVI) ... Hgb & Hct
Hemoglobin C [*An abnormal hemoglobin*] [*Hematology*] (DAVI) ... Hb C
Hemoglobin C Sickle Cell Disease [*Medicine*] ... HbSC
Hemoglobin, Carboxy [*Biochemistry, medicine*] ... HbCO
Hemoglobin Concentration [*Medicine*] (HGAA) ... HC
Hemoglobin Constant Spring [*An abnormal hemoglobin*] [*Hematology*] (DAVI) ... Hb CS
Hemoglobin D [*An abnormal hemoglobin*] [*Hematology*] (DAVI) ... Hb D
Hemoglobin Electrophoresis [*Medicine*] (AAMN) ... HE
Hemoglobin Electrophoresis [*Hematology*] (DAVI) ... HGB EL
Hemoglobin Electrophoresis [*Hematology*] (DAVI) ... HGB Elect
Hemoglobin, Fetal [*Also, HgF*] [*Medicine*] ... HbF
Hemoglobin Fetal [*Also, HbF, HgF*] [*Medicine*] (DAVI) ... Hgb F
Hemoglobin, Fetal [*Also, HbF*] [*Medicine*] ... HgF
Hemoglobin H [*An abnormal hemoglobin*] [*Hematology*] (DAVI) ... Hb H
Hemoglobin I [*Biochemistry, medicine*] ... HbI
Hemoglobin M [*Biochemistry*] (MAH) ... HbM
Hemoglobin, Oxy [*Biochemistry, medicine*] ... HbO_2
Hemoglobin Plasma [*Hematology*] (DAVI) ... HGB-PL
Hemoglobin, Reduced [*Biochemistry, medicine*] ... HHb
Hemoglobin, Sickle [*Medicine*] ... HbS
Hemoglobin Un-Ionized [*Hematology*] (DAVI) ... HHb
Hemoglobin Unit [*Of hydrolytic enzyme activity*] ... HU
Hemoglobinuric Bilious Fever [*Medicine*] (DMAA) ... HBF
Hemogram [*Hematology*] (DAVI) ... HGRM
Hemolysis [*Medicine*] ... HEM
Hemolysis [*or Hemolyze*] [*Medicine*] (DAVI) ... HEMO
Hemolysis, Elevated Liver Enzymes, and Low Platelet Count [*Clinical chemistry*] ... HELLP
Hemolysis Inhibition [*Medicine*] (AAMN) ... HLI
Hemolytic [*Hematology*] (DAVI) ... Hem
Hemolytic Anemia [*Hematology*] ... HA
Hemolytic Anemia Antigen [*Immunochemistry*] ... HAA
Hemolytic Disease of the Newborn [*Medicine*] ... HDN
Hemolytic Transfusion Reaction [*Medicine*] ... HTR
Hemolytic Unit [*Hematology*] ... HU
Hemolytic-Uremic Syndrome [*Nephrology*] ... HUS
Hemolyzed - Unable to Do Test [*laboratory science*] (DAVI) ... SHEM
Hemolyzing Dose [*Medicine*] ... HD
Hemophilia [*Medicine*] (DAVI) ... hemo
Hemophilia Research [*An association Defunct*] (EA) ... HR
Hemophilus [*Microbiology*] (MAE) ... H
Hemophilus, Actinobacillus, Cardiobacterium, Eikenella, and Kingella [*Gram-negative bacilli*] ... HACEK
Hemophilus Influenzae [*Bacteriology*] (DAVI) ... H flu
Hemophilus Influenzae Type B [*Medicine*] ... HIB
Hemophilus Pertussis Vaccine [*Medicine*] (MAE) ... HPV
Hemophilus Vaginalis [*Gynecology*] (DAVI) ... H vag
Hemopoietic Growth Factor [*Hematology*] ... HGF
Hemorrhage [*Medicine*] (WDAA) ... HEM
Hemorrhage [*Medicine*] ... HEMOR
Hemorrhage [*Medicine*] (DAVI) ... hemorr
Hemorrhage [*Medicine*] (ROG) ... HGE
Hemorrhage and Exudate [*Medicine*] ... H & E
Hemorrhage of Newborn [*Medicine*] (DMAA) ... HN
Hemorrhages, Exudates, and/or Nicking [*Ophthalmology*] (DAVI) ... HEN
Hemorrhagic Arteries [*Veterinary medicine*] ... HEA
Hemorrhagic Disease of Infants [*Medicine*] (DMAA) ... HDI
Hemorrhagic Encephalopathy of Rats (DMAA) ... HER
Hemorrhagic Erosive Gastritis [*Gastroenterology*] (DAVI) ... HEG
Hemorrhagic Factor [*Medicine*] ... HF
Hemorrhagic Fever [*Medicine*] (DAVI) ... HF
Hemorrhagic Fever of Deer [*Medicine*] (DMAA) ... HFD
Hemorrhagic Fever with Renal Syndrome [*Medicine*] ... HFRS
Hemorrhagic Retinopathy [*Ophthalmology*] ... HR
Hemorrhagic Shock [*Medicine*] ... HS
Hemorrhagic Shock and Encephalopathy [*Medicine*] (DMAA) ... HSE
Hemorrhagic Shock-Encephalopathy Syndrome [*Medicine*] (DMAA) ... HSES
Hemorrhagic Toxin Inhibitor [*Hematology*] ... HTI
Hemorrhoid [*Gastroenterology*] (DAVI) ... hem
Hemosiderin [*Hematology*] (DAVI) ... HEMSiD
Hemostatic Occlusive Leverage Device [*Cardiology*] (DAVI) ... HOLD
Hemostatic Screening Profile [*Medicine*] (DMAA) ... HSP
Hemphill, TX [*AM radio station call letters*] ... KAWS
Hempstead General Hospital, Medical Center, Hempstead, NY [*Library symbol Library of Congress*] (LCLS) ... NHemGH
Hempstead Middle School, Hempstead, NY [*Library symbol*] [*Library of Congress*] (LCLS) ... NHemMS
Hempstead, NY [*AM radio station call letters*] ... WHLI
Hempstead, NY [*FM radio station call letters*] ... WKJY
Hempstead, NY [*FM radio station call letters*] ... WRHU
Hempstead Public Library, Hempstead, NY [*Library symbol Library of Congress*] (LCLS) ... NHem
Hempstead Senior High School, Hempstead, NY [*Library symbol*] [*Library of Congress*] (LCLS) ... NHemSH
Hempstead, TX [*FM radio station call letters*] ... KEZB
Hempstead's Arkansas Reports [*A publication*] (DLA) ... Hemp
Hempstead's Arkansas Reports [*A publication*] (DLA) ... Hempst
Hempstead's United States Circuit Court Reports [*A publication*] (DLA) ... Hemp
Hempstead's United States Circuit Court Reports [*A publication*] (DLA) ... Hempst
Hempsted [*New York*] [*ICAO location identifier*] (ICLI) ... KJNT
Hemstitched ... HS
Hemus Air [*Bulgaria*] [*ICAO designator*] (FAAC) ... HMS
Hen Egg White Lysozyme [*Also, HEL*] [*An enzyme*] ... HEWL
Hen Packers Association [*British*] (DBA) ... HPA
Henbane Mosaic Virus [*Plant pathology*] ... HMV
Hence ... H
Henceforth (ROG) ... HEFTH
Henderson and Haggard [*Inhaler*] [*Medicine*] (DAVI) ... HH
Henderson & Pollard Ltd. [*New Zealand*] ... HP
Henderson County Junior College [*Texas*] ... HCJC
Henderson County Junior College, Athens, TX [*Library symbol Library of Congress*] (LCLS) ... TxAtH
Henderson County Public Library, Hendersonville, NC [*Library symbol Library of Congress*] (LCLS) ... NcHv
Henderson District Public Library, Henderson, NV [*Library symbol Library of Congress*] (LCLS) ... NvH

Henderson Free Library, Henderson, NY [*Library symbol Library of Congress*] (LCLS) .... NHen
Henderson, KY [*Location identifier FAA*] (FAAL) .... GVA
Henderson, KY [*FM radio station call letters*] .... WGBF
Henderson, KY [*FM radio station call letters*] .... WKDQ
Henderson, KY [*FM radio station call letters*] .... WKPB
Henderson, KY [*AM radio station call letters*] .... WSON
Henderson, NC [*AM radio station call letters*] .... WHNC
Henderson, NC [*AM radio station call letters*] .... WIZS
Henderson, NC [*FM radio station call letters*] .... WYFL
Henderson, NV [*AM radio station call letters*] .... KDOL
Henderson, NV [*FM radio station call letters*] (RBYB) .... KJMZ
Henderson, NV [*FM radio station call letters*] .... KMZQ
Henderson, NV [*Television station call letters*] .... KVVU
Henderson, NV [*FM radio station call letters*] .... KWNR
Henderson, NY [*FM radio station call letters*] .... WLKC
Henderson Regional Library, Winnipeg, Manitoba [*Library symbol National Library of Canada*] (NLC) .... MWHR
Henderson Regional Library, Winnipeg, MB, Canada [*Library symbol Library of Congress*] (LCLS) .... CaMWHR
Henderson State College [*Later, Henderson State University*] [*Arkansas*] .... HSC
Henderson State Teachers College [*Later, HSC*] [*Arkansas*] .... HSTC
Henderson State University (GAGS) .... Henderson St U
Henderson State University [*Arkadelphia, AR*] .... HSU
Henderson State University, Arkadelphia, AR [*OCLC symbol*] (OCLC) .... AKH
Henderson State University, Arkadelphia, AR [*Library symbol Library of Congress*] (LCLS) .... ArAT
Henderson, TN [*FM radio station call letters*] .... WFHC
Henderson, TN [*FM radio station call letters*] .... WFKX
Henderson, TN [*FM radio station call letters*] .... WHHM
Henderson, TX [*Location identifier FAA*] (FAAL) .... HNO
Henderson, TX [*FM radio station call letters*] .... KGRI
Henderson, TX [*AM radio station call letters*] .... KWRD
Henderson, WV [*Location identifier FAA*] (FAAL) .... HNN
Hendersonville, NC [*AM radio station call letters*] .... WHKP
Hendersonville, NC [*FM radio station call letters*] .... WMYI
Hendersonville, NC [*AM radio station call letters*] .... WTZQ
Hendersonville, TN [*Television station call letters*] .... WPGD
Hendersonville, TN [*FM radio station call letters*] .... WQQK
Hendircks Public School, Hendricks, MN [*Library symbol*] [*Library of Congress*] .... MnHendPS
Hendrick Hudson Free Library, Montrose, NY [*Library symbol Library of Congress*] (LCLS) .... NMontr
Hendricks Community Hospital, Hendricks, MN [*Library symbol*] [*Library of Congress*] (LCLS) .... MnHendH
Hendricks County Recorder's Office, Danville, IN [*Library symbol Library of Congress*] (LCLS) .... InDanCR
Hendrik Verwoerd Dam [*South Africa*] [*Seismograph station code, US Geological Survey*] (SEIS) .... HVD
Hendrik Verwoerddam [*South Africa*] [*ICAO location identifier*] (ICLI) .... FAHV
Hendrix College, Conway, AR [*OCLC symbol*] (OCLC) .... AKE
Hendrix College, Conway, AR [*Library symbol Library of Congress*] (LCLS).... ArCH
Henebery Aviation [*ICAO designator*] (AD) .... HZ
Henebury Aviation Co. [*Australia ICAO designator*] (FAAC) .... HAC
Hen-Egg White Lysozyme [*Also, HEWL*] [*An enzyme*] .... HEL
Hengam Island [*Iran*] [*ICAO location identifier*] (ICLI) .... OIKU
Hengchun [*Republic of China*] [*Seismograph station code, US Geological Survey*] (SEIS) .... HEN
Hengchun [*China*] [*ICAO location identifier*] (ICLI) .... RCKW
Hening and Munford's Reports [*11-14 Virginia*] [*A publication*] (DLA) .... H & M
Hening and Munford's Reports [*11-14 Virginia*] [*A publication*] (DLA) .... H & M (VA)
Hening and Munford's Reports [*11-14 Virginia*] [*A publication*] (DLA) .... Hen & Mun
Hening and Munford's Virginia Supreme Court Reports [*1806-10*] [*A publication*] (DLA) .... Hen & M
Hening's American Pleader [*A publication*] (DLA) .... Hen Am Pl
Hening's Maxims [*A publication*] (DLA) .... Hen Max
Hening's Statutes [*Virginia*] [*A publication*] (DLA) .... Hen St
Hening's Virginia Justice of the Peace [*A publication*] (DLA) .... Hen JP
Henkel Corp., Minneapolis, MN [*OCLC symbol*] (OCLC) .... HKC
Henkel Corp., Minneapolis, MN [*Library symbol Library of Congress*] (LCLS) .... MnMHen
Henley International, Inc. [*Later, MAXXIM Medical*] [*AMEX symbol*] (SPSG).... HEN
Henlow [*British ICAO location identifier*] (ICLI) .... EGWE
Henna [*Philately*] .... hn
Hennell's Forms [*A publication*] (DLA) .... Hen Forms
Hennen's Louisiana Digest [*A publication*] (DLA) .... Hen LA Dig
Hennepin Attendance Center, Hennepin, IL [*Library symbol Library of Congress*] (LCLS) .... IHennC
Hennepin County General Hospital, Minneapolis, MN [*Library symbol Library of Congress*] (LCLS) .... MnMHH
Hennepin County Law Library, Minneapolis, MN [*Library symbol Library of Congress*] (LCLS) .... MnMHLL
Hennepin County Library, Minneapolis, MN [*Library symbol Library of Congress*] (LCLS) .... MnMHCL
Hennepin County Medical Society, Minneapolis, MN [*Library symbol Library of Congress*] (LCLS) .... MnMH
Hennepin Lawyer [*A publication*] (DLA) .... Hen Law
Hennessey Public Library, Hennessey, OK [*Library symbol Library of Congress*] (LCLS) .... OkHenn
Hennessy Resource Corp. [*Vancouver Stock Exchange symbol*] .... HNY
Henniker, NH [*FM radio station call letters*] .... WNEC
Henniker, NH [*FM radio station call letters*] .... WNNH

Henning Public School, Henning, MN [*Library symbol*] [*Library of Congress*] (LCLS) .... MnHennS
Henoch-Schoenlein Purpura [*Medicine*] (AAMN) .... HSP
Henoch-Schoenlein Syndrome [*Medicine*] .... HS
Henrico County Public Library, Richmond, VA [*Library symbol Library of Congress*] (LCLS) .... ViRHC
Henricus Acconzaioco [*Flourished, 1374-82*] [*Authority cited in pre-1607 legal work*] (DSA) .... Her Aconza
Henricus Boich [*Flourished, 1320-30*] [*Authority cited in pre-1607 legal work*] (DSA) .... H Bo
Henricus Boich [*Flourished, 1320-30*] [*Authority cited in pre-1607 legal work*] (DSA) .... HB
Henricus Boich [*Flourished, 1320-30*] [*Authority cited in pre-1607 legal work*] (DSA) .... Hen
Henricus Boich [*Flourished, 1320-30*] [*Authority cited in pre-1607 legal work*] (DSA) .... Hen Bo
Henricus Boich [*Flourished, 1320-30*] [*Authority cited in pre-1607 legal work*] (DSA) .... Henric
Henricus de Baila [*Flourished, 1169-70*] [*Authority cited in pre-1607 legal work*] (DSA) .... Hn
Henricus de Baila [*Flourished, 1169-70*] [*Authority cited in pre-1607 legal work*] (DSA) .... Hr
Henricus Stephanus [*Imprint*] [*Latin*] (ROG) .... H STEPH
Henrietta Lacks [*Pseudonym, Helen Lake*] [*Line of tumor cells*] .... HeLa
Henrietta, NY [*FM radio station call letters*] .... WITR
Henry [*Symbol*] [*SI unit of inductance*] .... H
Henry .... HY
Henry [*Variation of the preferred H*] (IDOE) .... hy
Henry Adams, Inc. [*Baltimore, MD*] (TSSD) .... HA
Henry [*Jack*] & Associates, Inc. [*Associated Press*] (SAG) .... HenryJk
Henry Bradshaw Society [*British*] .... HBS
Henry Clay Memorial Foundation (EA) .... HCMF
Henry County Historical Society, Reference Room, New Castle, IN [*Library symbol Library of Congress*] (LCLS) .... InNcasHi
Henry County Library, Clinton, MO [*Library symbol*] [*Library of Congress*] (LCLS) .... MoCli
Henry County News-Republican, New Castle, IN [*Library symbol Library of Congress*] (LCLS) .... InNcasNR
Henry Doubleday Research Association [*Coventry, England*] (EAIO) .... HDRA
Henry Doubleday Research Association of Australia .... HDRAA
Henry Draper Catalogue [*Astronomy*] .... HD
Henry E. Huntington Library, San Marino, CA [*Library symbol Library of Congress*] (LCLS) .... CSmH
Henry, Edward, Mary, Philip, Elizabeth [*Bacon's prophecy*] .... HEMPE
Henry F. Schricker Library, Knox, IN [*Library symbol Library of Congress*] (LCLS) .... InKno
Henry Ford Community College [*Dearborn, MI*] .... HFCC
Henry Ford Hospital, Detroit, MI [*Library symbol Library of Congress*] (LCLS) .... MiDHF
Henry Ford Hospital, Medical Library, Detroit, MI [*OCLC symbol*] (OCLC) .... EYF
Henry Francis DuPont Winterthur Museum, Joseph Downs Manuscript and Microfilm Collection, Winterthur, DE [*Library symbol Library of Congress*] (LCLS) .... DeWint-M
Henry Francis DuPont Winterthur Museum, Winterthur, DE [*Library symbol Library of Congress*] (LCLS) .... DeWint
Henry Francis DuPont Winterthur Museum, Winterthur, DE [*OCLC symbol*] (OCLC) .... DLH
Henry George Foundation of America (EA) .... HGFA
Henry George Institute (EA) .... HGI
Henry H. Warren Memorial Library, Massena, NY [*Library symbol Library of Congress*] (LCLS) .... NMas
Henry, IL [*FM radio station call letters*] .... WRVY
Henry IV, Part I [*Shakespearean work*] 1H4
Henry IV, Part II [*Shakespearean work*] 2H4
Henry (Jack) & Assoc [*NASDAQ symbol*] (TTSB) .... JKHY
Henry, Jack Associates [*NASDAQ symbol*] (SAG) .... JKHY
Henry (King of England) (DLA) .... H
Henry (King of England) (DLA) .... Hen
Henry L. Stinson Junior High School, Huntington Station, NY [*Library symbol*] [*Library of Congress*] (LCLS) .... NHsSJH
Henry Louis Mencken [*American author/critic*] .... HLM
Henry M. Seymour Library, Indianola, MS [*Library symbol Library of Congress*] (LCLS) .... MsIn
Henry on Foreign Law [*A publication*] (DLA) .... Hen For L
Henry per Meter .... H/m
Henry Phipps Institute, Philadelphia, PA [*Library symbol Library of Congress Obsolete*] (LCLS) .... PPHPI
Henry Public Library, Henry, IL [*Library symbol Library of Congress*] (LCLS) .... IHen
Henry Public Library, Henry, IL [*OCLC symbol*] (OCLC) .... ISP
Henry Russell [*Astronomy*] .... HR
Henry Schein, Inc. [*Associated Press*] (SAG) .... HSchein
Henry Schein, Inc. [*NASDAQ symbol*] (SAG) .... HSIC
Henry Stephens Memorial Library, Almont, MI [*Library symbol Library of Congress*] (LCLS) .... MiAlmo
Henry V [*Shakespearean work*] H5
Henry VI, Part I [*Shakespearean work*] 1H6
Henry VI, Part II [*Shakespearean work*] 2H6
Henry VI, Part III [*Shakespearean work*] 3H6
Henry VIII [*Shakespearean work*] H8
Henry W. Grout Museum of History and Science, Waterlook, IA [*Library symbol Library of Congress*] (LCLS) .... IaWG
Henry Wadsworth Longfellow [*Initials used as pseudonym*] .... HWL
Henry Waldinger Memorial Library, Valley Stream, NY [*Library symbol Library of Congress*] (LCLS) .... NVs

Henry Wriothesley, Earl of Southampton; or Sir William Harvey; or William Hathaway; or William Herbert, Earl of Pembroke [*Possible identities of the W. H. to whom Shakespeare's sonnets were supposedly dedicated by publisher Thomas Thorpe in 1609*] .... WH
Henryetta, OK [*Location identifier FAA*] (FAAL) .... HET
Henryetta, OK [*FM radio station call letters*] .... KCKI
Henryetta, OK [*AM radio station call letters*] .... KDLB
Henryetta, OK [*FM radio station call letters*] .... KVAZ
Henry's Judgment in Ordwin V. Forbes [*A publication*] (DLA) .... Henry Judg
Henry's Law Constant .... H
Henry's Manumission Cases [*A publication*] (DLA) .... Hen Man Cas
Henryton State Hospital, Henryton, MD [*Library symbol Library of Congress*] (LCLS) .... MdHeH
Henson Associates [*Television production company*] .... HA
Henstridge [*British ICAO location identifier*] (ICLI) .... EGHS
Henties Bay [*Namibia*] [*ICAO location identifier*] (ICLI) .... FAHN
Hent's Forms and Use of Blanks in California [*A publication*] (DLA) .... Hent Forms
Hentsch & Compagnie [*Bank*] [*Switzerland*] .... H & Cie
Heongsung [*South Korea ICAO location identifier*] (ICLI) .... RKNH
HEP [*High Energy Physics*] Index (NITA) .... HEPI
Hepar Embryonis Bovis [*Embryonic bovine liver cells used in tissue culture studies of viruses*] [*Medicine*] .... HEB
Heparan Sulfate Proteoglycan [*Biochemistry*] .... HSPG
Heparin [*Pharmacology*] (DAVI) .... H
Heparin Assay Rapid Easy Method [*Medicine*] (DMAA) .... HAREM
Heparin Assay Rapid Method (DMAA) .... HARM
Heparin Induced Thrombocytopenia [*Hematology*] (DAVI) .... HIT
Heparin Lock [*Pharmacology*] (DAVI) .... HL
Heparin Neutralizing Activity [*Medicine*] .... HNA
Heparin Sulfate [*Biochemistry*] .... HS
Heparin Sulfate Proteoglycan [*Biochemistry*] .... HSP
Heparin Well [*Pharmacology*] (DAVI) .... HW
Heparin-Aspirin Reinfarction Trial [*Medicine*] (DMAA) .... HART
Heparin-Aspirin Reperfusion Trial [*Cardiology*] .... HART
Heparin-Associated Thrombocytopenia and Thrombosis [*Medicine*] (DMAA) .... HATT
Heparin-Binding Growth Factor [*Biochemistry*] .... HBGF
Heparin-Dependent Platelet-Associated Antibody [*Medicine*] (DMAA) .... HDPAA
Heparin-Induced Platelet Activation [*Medicine*] (DMAA) .... HIPA
Heparin-Induced Thrombosis-Thrombocytopenia Syndrome [*Medicine*] (DMAA) .... HITTS
Heparin-Precipitable Fraction (MAE) .... HPF
Hepatic [*Pertaining to the liver*] [*Pharmacy*] (ROG) .... HEP
Hepatic Arterial Perfusion Scintigraphy [*Cardiology*] (DAVI) .... HAPS
Hepatic Artery [*Anatomy*] (MAE) .... HA
Hepatic Artery Blood Flow .... HABF
Hepatic Artery Embolization [*Medicine*] (DAVI) .... HAE
Hepatic Artery Infusion [*Chemotherapy*] .... HAI
Hepatic Artery Ligation [*Medicine*] .... HAL
Hepatic Binding Protein [*Biochemistry*] .... HBP
Hepatic Blood Flow .... HBF
Hepatic Catalase [*An enzyme*] (MAE) .... HC
Hepatic Coma [*Medicine*] .... HC
Hepatic Distribution Volume [*Gastroenterology*] (DAVI) .... V_H
Hepatic Encephalography [*Medicine*] .... HE
Hepatic Encephalopathy [*Medicine*] .... HE
Hepatic Extraction [*Endocrinology*] .... HE
Hepatic Fat .... HF
Hepatic Glucose Output [*Physiology*] .... HGO
Hepatic Glucose Production [*Hematology*] (DMAA) .... HGP
Hepatic Hydroxymethylglutaryl Coenzyme A [*Organic chemistry*] (DAVI) .... HMG CoA
Hepatic Intramitochondrial Crystalloid [*Medicine*] (DMAA) .... HIMC
Hepatic Iron (Ferrum) Uptake [*Physiology*] .... HFeU
Hepatic Leukaemia Factor [*Medicine*] .... HLF
Hepatic Microcirculation [*Physiology*] .... HM
Hepatic Nonheme Iron Content [*Physiology*] .... HNHIC
Hepatic Outflow [*Medicine*] (DMAA) .... HOF
Hepatic Perfusion Index [*Medicine*] (DMAA) .... HPI
Hepatic Plasma Flow [*Medicine*] (DMAA) .... HPF
Hepatic Portal Venous Gas (MAE) .... HPVG
Hepatic Scintigraphy [*Medicine*] .... HS
Hepatic Stimulating Activity [*Physiology*] .... HSA
Hepatic Stimulator Substance .... HSS
Hepatic Triglyceride Lipase [*An enzyme*] .... HTGL
Hepatic Vascular Exclusion [*Medicine*] (MEDA) .... HVE
Hepatic Vein [*Anatomy*] .... HV
Hepatic Venous Pressure Gradient [*Medicine*] .... HVPG
Hepatic Volumetric Index .... HVI
Hepatitis [*Gastroenterology*] (DAVI) .... hep
Hepatitis A Antigen [*Immunology*] (DAVI) .... HAAg
Hepatitis A Virus .... HAV
Hepatitis A Virus Antigen [*Immunochemistry*] .... HAVAg
Hepatitis Associated [*Virus*] .... HA
Hepatitis Associated Antigen [*Clinical chemistry*] .... HAA
Hepatitis B [*Virus*] [*Infectious diseases*] (DAVI) .... HAB
Hepatitis B [*Medicine*] .... HB
Hepatitis B Antibody [*Immunology*] .... HBAb
Hepatitis B Antigen [*Immunology*] .... HBAg
Hepatitis B Core [*Immunology*] (MAE) .... HBc
Hepatitis B Core Antibody [*Immunology*] (MAE) .... HBcAb
Hepatitis B Core Antigen [*Immunology*] .... HBcAg
Hepatitis B Early [*Antibody or antigen*] [*Immunology*] (DAVI) .... HBe
Hepatitis B Early Antibody [*Immunology*] (DAVI) .... HB_eAb
Hepatitis B, Early Antigen [*or Antibody*] [*Immunology*] .... HBeAg

Hepatitis B Immune Globulin [*Immunology*] .... HBIG
Hepatitis B Surface [*Antibody or antigen*] [*Immunology*] (DAVI) .... HB_s
Hepatitis B Surface Antibody [*Immunology*] (PDAA) .... HBSAB
Hepatitis B Surface Antigen [*Immunology*] (DAVI) .... HB_sAg
Hepatitis B Vaccine [*Immunology*] .... HBV
Hepatitis B Virus .... HBV
Hepatitis B Virus Integration Site [*Medicine*] (DMAA) .... HBVS
Hepatitis B Virus Polymerase [*An enzyme*] .... HBVP
Hepatitis Battery-Acute [*Gastroenterology*] (DAVI) .... HEP-AC
Hepatitis C Virus .... HCV
Hepatitis Contagiosa Canis [*Virus*] .... HCC
Hepatitis D Virus [*Medicine*] (DMAA) .... HDV
Hepatitis Delta Antigen [*Immunology*] .... HDAg
Hepatitis Delta Virus .... HDV
Hepatitis G Virus .... HGV
Hepatitis Knowledge Base (NITA) .... HKB
Hepatobiliary [*Medicine*] (DMAA) .... HPB
Hepatobiliary Dysfunction [*Medicine*] .... HBD
Hepatobiliary Imaging [*Medicine*] (BABM) .... HI
Hepatoblastoma (DMAA) .... HBL
Hepatocatalase Peroxidase [*An enzyme*] (MAE) .... HCP
Hepatocellular Adenoma [*Medicine*] .... HCA
Hepatocellular Carcinoma [*Oncology*] .... HCC
Hepatocyte Growth Factor [*Biochemistry*] .... HGF
Hepatocyte Nuclear Factor [*Biochemistry*] .... HNF
Hepatocyte Nuclear Factor 1 [*Genetics*] HNF1
Hepatocyte Stimulating Factor [*Endocrinology*] .... HSF
Hepatoerythropoietic Porphyria [*Medicine*] .... HEP
Hepatoiminodiacetic Acid [*Scan*] [*Radiology*] (DAVI) .... HIDA
Hepatojugular [*Reflex*] [*Medicine*] .... HJ
Hepatojugular Reflex [*Medicine*] .... HJR
Hepatology [*Gastroenterology*] (DAVI) .... HEP
Hepatoma Cells [*Oncology*] .... HEC
Hepatoma Cells [*Cytology*] (DAVI) .... HTC
Hepatoma Tissue Culture [*Medicine*] .... HTC
Hepatoporphyrin Derivative-Phototherapy [*Medicine*] .... HpD-PT
Hepatorenal Syndrome [*Medicine*] .... HRS
Hepatosis Diaetetica [*Veterinary science*] (OA) .... HD
Hepatosplenic Schistosomiasis [*Medicine*] .... HS
Hepatosplenomegaly [*Gastroenterology*] (DAVI) .... HSM
Hepatotrophic Portal Blood Factor [*Medicine*] (DMAA) .... HPBF
Hepburn Library, Waddington, NY [*Library symbol Library of Congress*] (LCLS) .... NWadd
Hepburn's Reports [*California*] [*A publication*] (DLA) .... Hepb
Hepburn's Reports [*Pennsylvania*] [*A publication*] (DLA) .... Hepb
HEPES-Buffered EMEM .... HEM
HEPES-Saline-Albumin-Gelatin [*Medium*] [*Microbiology*] .... HSAG
Heplode [*Electronics*] (OA) .... h
Hepp [*Alaska*] [*Seismograph station code, US Geological Survey*] (SEIS) .... HPP
Heppner Public Library, Heppner, OR [*Library symbol Library of Congress*] (LCLS) .... OrHep
Hepsin (DMAA) .... HPN
Heptachlor Epoxide .... HPTE
Heptadecapeptide Gastrin [*Endocrinology*] .... HG
Heptafluorobutyrate [*or Heptafluorobutyric*] [*Organic chemistry*] .... HFB
Heptafluorobutyric Acid [*Organic chemistry*] .... HFBA
Heptafluorobutyrylimidazole [*Organic chemistry*] .... HFBI
Heptagonal Games Association (EA) .... HGA
Heptamethylnonane [*Fuel*] .... HMN
Heptaminol Adenosinemonophosphate Amidate [*Biochemistry*] .... HAA
Heptaploidy [*State of having seven sets of chromosomes*] [*Genetics*] (DAVI) 7n
Heptasaccharide Phytoalexin Elicitor [*Organic chemistry*] .... HPE
Heptode [*Electronics*] (IAA) .... HP
Heptyl [*Biochemistry*] .... Hp
Heptyl(hydroxy)quinoline N-Oxide [*Organic chemistry*] .... HOQNO
Heptyl(hydroxy)quinoline N-Oxide [*Organic chemistry*] .... HQNO
Heptyloxyazoxybenzene [*Organic chemistry*] .... HOAB
Hepworth Branch, Bruce County Public Library, Ontario [*Library symbol National Library of Canada*] (NLC) .... OHEP
Her Majesty's Australian Ship [*DOMA*] .... HMAS
Her Majesty's Customs and Excise [*British*] (BI) .... HMC
Her Majesty's Government Communications Centre [*British*] (PDAA) .... HMGCC
Her Majesty's Industrial Pollution Inspectorate (EERA) .... HMPIPI
Her [*or His*] Majesty's Inspector of Taxes [*British*] (ODBW) .... HMIT
Her Majesty's Nautical Almanac Office [*British*] (PDAA) .... HMNAO
Her Majesty's Nautical Almanac Office [*British*] (PDAA) .... NAO
Her [*or His*] Majesty's Prison [*British*] (BARN) .... HMP
Her Netherlands Majesty's Ship .... HNMS
Heracleum Latent Virus [*Plant pathology*] .... HLV
Heracleum Virus 6 [*Plant pathology*] HV6
Heraclidae [*of Euripides*] [*Classical studies*] (OCD) .... Heracl
Heraclides Ponticus [*Fourth century BC*] [*Classical studies*] (OCD) .... Heraclid Pont
Heraklion [*Greece*] [*Airport symbol*] (OAG) .... HER
Herald [*Record label*] [*Great Britain*] .... Her
Herald, Avalon, NJ [*Library symbol Library of Congress*] (LCLS) .... NjAvH
Herald International Mailings Ltd. [*British*] .... HIM
Herald (Melbourne) [*A publication*] .... Her (Mel)
Herald News, Passaic, NJ [*Library symbol Library of Congress*] (LCLS) .... NjPasH
Heraldic Quality Control System (AABC) .... HQCS
Heraldisk Selskab [*Denmark*] [*An association*] (EAIO) .... HS
Herald-Ledger, Eldora, IA [*Library symbol Library of Congress*] (LCLS) .... IaEldoHL
Herald-Mitchellville Index, Altoona, IA [*Library symbol Library of Congress*] (LCLS) .... IaAltoH
Herald-Register, Grinnell, IA [*Library symbol Library of Congress*] (LCLS) .... IaGHR
Heraldry .... HER

Heraldry (VRA) ... her
Heraldry Society (EA) ... HS
Heraldry Society of Australia ... HSA
Heraldry Society of Canada (EAIO) ... HSC
Heraldry Society of Canada [*Societe Heraldique du Canada*], Ottawa, Ontario [*Library symbol National Library of Canada*] (BIB) ... OOH
Heraldry Society of Ireland (EA) ... HSI
Heraldry Society of Scotland [*Edinburgh*] (EAIO) ... HSS
Heraldry Society of the United States of America (EA) ... HSUSA
Heralds' College [*British*] ... HC
Herat [*Afghanistan*] [*Airport symbol Obsolete*] (OAG) ... HEA
Herat [*Afghanistan*] [*ICAO location identifier*] (ICLI) ... OAHR
Herausgegeben [*Edited, Published*] [*German*] ... hrsg
Herb [*Botany*] ... H
Herb Growing and Marketing Network (EA) ... HGMN
Herb Research Foundation (EA) ... HRF
Herb Society of America (EA) ... HSA
Herb Trade Association (EA) ... HTA
Herba [*Herb*] [*Pharmacology*] (ROG) ... HB
Herbaceous (WDAA) ... HERB
Herbalife International, Inc. [*NASDAQ symbol*] (NQ) ... HERB
Herbalife International, Inc. [*Associated Press*] (SAG) ... Herblfe
Herbalife Intl. [*NASDAQ symbol*] (TTSB) ... HERB
Herbalist (ROG) ... HERB
Herbarium (WDAA) ... HERB
Herbarium Information Standards and Protocols for Interchange of Data [*Australia*] ... HISPID
Herbarium Recentium [*Of Fresh Herbs*] [*Pharmacy*] ... HERB RECENT
Herbert Clark Hoover [*US president, 1874-1964*] ... HCH
Herbert H. Lehman College of The City University of New York (GAGS) ... Lehman C (CUNY)
Herbert H. Lehman College of the City University of New York, New York, NY [*Library symbol Library of Congress*] (LCLS) ... NNL
Herbert Hoover National Historic Site ... HEHO
Herbert Hoover Presidential Library Association (EA) ... HHPLA
Herbert Hoover Presidential Library, West Branch, IA [*Library symbol Library of Congress*] (LCLS) ... IaWbH
Herbert Wescoat Memorial Library, McArthur, OH [*Library symbol Library of Congress*] (LCLS) ... OMc
Herbert Wescoat Memorial Library, McArthur, OH [*Library symbol*] [*Library of Congress*] (LCLS) ... OMcL
Herbert's Antiquities of the Inns of Court, Etc. [*A publication*] (DLA) ... Herb Ant
Herbicide ... HERBIC
Herbicide Assessment Commission ... HAC
Herbig-Haro [*Astronomy*] ... HH
Herbivore ... H
HERC Products [*NASDAQ symbol*] (SAG) ... HERC
H.E.R.C. Products [*NASDAQ symbol*] (TTSB) ... HERC
Hercegnovi [*Yugoslavia*] [*Airport symbol*] (AD) ... HNO
Hercules [*Constellation*] ... Her
Hercules [*Constellation*] ... Herc
Hercules Furens [*of Euripides*] [*Classical studies*] (OCD) ... HF
Hercules Graphics [*Computer science*] (CDE) ... HGC
Hercules Graphics Adapter (PCM) ... HGA
Hercules, Inc. [*Research code symbol*] ... AC
Hercules, Inc. [*Formerly, Hercules Power Co.*] [*Associated Press*] (SAG) ... Herculs
Hercules, Inc. [*Formerly, Hercules Powder Co.*] [*NYSE symbol*] (SPSG) ... HPC
Hercules, Inc., Wilmington, DE [*Library symbol Library of Congress*] (LCLS) ... DeWHI
Hercules Integrated Telecommunications System [*Telecommunications*] ... HITS
Hercules on Water [*Aircraft*] (MCD) ... HOW
Hercules Powder Co. [*Later, Hercules, Inc.*], Cellulose Products Division, Hopewell, VA [*Library symbol Library of Congress*] (LCLS) ... ViHopHC
Hercules Powder Co. [*Later, Hercules, Inc.*], Experiment Station, Wilmington,DE [*Library symbol Library of Congress*] (LCLS) ... DeWH
Hercules Powder Co. [*Later, Hercules, Inc.*], Virginia Cellulose Division, Hopewell, VA [*Library symbol Library of Congress*] (LCLS) ... ViHopHV
Hercules Ventures [*Vancouver Stock Exchange symbol*] ... HCV
Hercules-Baachus Resin Formulation ... HBRF
Herd Improvement Service of Western Australia [*Animal husbandry*] ... HISWA
Herd Test ... HT
Herder Correspondence [*London/New York*] [*A publication*] (BJA) ... HerdCor
Herder-Korrespondenz [*Freiburg Im Breisgau*] [*A publication*] (BJA) ... HerdKor
Herders Bibelkommentar [*A publication*] (BJA) ... HB
Herders Bibelkommentar [*A publication*] (BJA) ... HBk
Herders Theologischer Kommentar zum Neuen Testament [*Freiburg*] [*A publication*] (BJA) ... HTKNT
Herding Certified [*Purebred canine award*] ... HC
Herding Champion [*Prefix*] ... HCH
Herdis International Canada, Inc. [*Vancouver Stock Exchange symbol*] ... HDS
Herdwick Sheep Breeders Association [*British*] (DBA) ... HSBA
Here Comes Everybody [*Key phrase in "Finnegan's Wake"*] ... HCE
Here Our Love Lives and Never Dies [*Correspondence*] (DSUE) ... HOLLAND
Hereafter (ROG) ... HEAR
Hereafter ... HRAR
Hereat [*Legal*] [*British*] (ROG) ... HRAT
Hereby (ROG) ... HBY
Hereby Designated as a Student Naval Aviator (DNAB) ... HERDESNAVAV
Hereby Detached from Duty Assigned [*Military*] ... HERDET
Hereby Detached from Duty Assigned [*Military*] (DNAB) ... HEREDET
Hereby Detailed to Duty Involving Flying (DNAB) ... HERDUFLY
Hereditament [*Legal shorthand*] (LWAP) ... HDIT
Hereditaments (ROG) ... HEREDITS
Hereditaments [*Legal*] [*British*] (ROG) ... HRDITS
Hereditary (DMAA) ... hered
Hereditary Adenomatosis of the Colon and Rectum [*Medicine*] (DMAA) ... HACR
Hereditary Angioneurotic Edema [*Medicine*] ... HAE
Hereditary Angioneurotic Edema [*Medicine*] ... HANE
Hereditary Capillary Fragility [*Medicine*] (DMAA) ... HCF
Hereditary Cerebral Hemorrhage with Amyloidosis of the Dutch Type [*Medicine*] ... HCHWA-D
Hereditary Colon Cancer ... HCC
Hereditary Coproporphyria [*Medicine*] (MAE) ... HCP
Hereditary Cutaneous Malignant Melanoma [*Medicine*] (DMAA) ... HCMM
Hereditary Disease Foundation (EA) ... HDF
Hereditary Elliptocytosis [*Medicine*] ... HE
Hereditary Erythroblastic Multinuclearity Associated with a Positive Acidified-Serum Test [*Hematology*] ... HEMPAS
Hereditary Erythrocytic Multinuclearity with a Positive Acidified-Serum [*Test*] [*Hematology*] (DAVI) ... HEMPAS
Hereditary Expansile Polyostotic Dysplasia [*Medicine*] (DMAA) ... HEPOD
Hereditary Fructose Intolerance [*Medicine*] ... HFI
Hereditary Grand Almoner [*Freemasonry*] ... HGA
Hereditary Grand Master [*Freemasonry*] (ROG) ... HGM
Hereditary Grand Master Mason [*Freemasonry*] ... HGMM
Hereditary Haemochromatosis [*Medicine*] ... HH
Hereditary Hemolytic Anemia [*Medicine*] ... HHA
Hereditary Hemorrhagic Telangiectasia [*Medicine*] ... HHT
Hereditary Hypophosphatemic Rickets with Hypercalciuria [*Medicine*] (DMAA) ... HHRH
Hereditary Multifocal Relapsing Inflammation [*Medicine*] (DMAA) ... HEMRI
Hereditary Nephritis [*Medicine*] (MAE) ... HN
Hereditary Neuropathy with Liability to Pressure Palsies ... HNPP
Hereditary Nonpolyposis Colon Cancer [*Medicine*] ... HNPCC
Hereditary Nonspherocytic Hemolytic Anemia [*Medicine*] ... HNSHA
Hereditary Order of Armigerous Augustans (EA) ... OAA
Hereditary Order of the Descendants of Colonial Governors (EA) ... DCG
Hereditary Order of the First Families of Massachusetts (EA) ... HOFFM
Hereditary Osteo-Onychodysplasia [*Medicine*] ... HOOD
Hereditary Persistence of Fetal Hemoglobin [*Hematology*] ... HPFH
Hereditary Persistence of Hemoglobin F [*Genetics*] (DOG) ... HPHF
Hereditary Pyropoikilocytosis [*Medicine*] ... HPP
Hereditary Sensory Neuropathy [*Neurology*] ... HSN
Hereditary Sideroblastic Anemia [*Medicine*] (DMAA) ... HSA
Hereditary Spastic Paraplegia [*Medicine*] ... HSP
Hereditary Spherocytosis [*Medicine*] ... HS
Heredity ... HERED
Heredity ... HRDTY
Heredity and Environment ... H & E
Heredopathia Atactica Polyneuritiformis [*Medicine*] ... HAP
Hereford [*British depot code*] ... HFD
Hereford and Worcester [*County in Wales*] (WGA) ... Heref/Worcs
Hereford Otter Hounds ... HOH
Hereford, TX [*Location identifier FAA*] (FAAL) ... HRX
Hereford, TX [*AM radio station call letters*] ... KPAN
Hereford, TX [*FM radio station call letters*] ... KPAN-FM
Herefordshire [*County in England*] ... HERE
Herefordshire [*County in England*] ... HEREF
Herefordshire [*County in England*] (BARN) ... Hereford
Herefordshire [*County in England*] ... HEREFORDS
Herefordshire [*County in England*] ... HEREFS
Herefordshire [*County in England*] (ROG) ... HFD
Heregulin (DMAA) ... HGL
Herein [*Legal*] [*British*] (ROG) ... HRIN
Herein After Described [*Legal*] [*British*] (MHDI) ... HAD
Hereinafter [*Legal*] [*British*] (ROG) ... HRINAR
Hereinafter ... HRNAR
Hereinafter Mentioned [*Legal*] [*British*] (ROG) ... HNARMENTD
Hereinbefore [*Legal*] [*British*] (ROG) ... HRINBEFE
Hereinbefore [*Legal*] [*British*] (ROG) ... HRINBFR
Hereinbefore Mentioned [*Legal*] [*British*] (ROG) ... HNBEFMENTD
Herendeen Bay, AK [*Location identifier FAA*] (FAAL) ... HED
Herennius Modestinus [*Flourished, 3rd century*] [*Authority cited in pre-1607 legal work*] (DSA) ... Herenn Modest
Hereodox [*Commercial firm British*] ... HX
Hereon [*Legal*] [*British*] (ROG) ... HRON
Herero [*MARC language code Library of Congress*] (LCCP) ... her
Heres [*Heir*] [*Legal term Latin*] ... H
Heres [*Heir*] [*Legal term Latin*] ... HER
Here's Health [*Exhibition*] [*British*] ... HH
Hereto (ROG) ... HTO
Heretofore (ROG) ... HTFORE
Heretofore ... HTOFORE
Herewith [*Enclosures*] [*Navy*] ... HW
Herewith (ROG) ... HWTH
Herfindahl-Hirschman [*Economic indicator*] ... HH
Heringsdorf [*Germany ICAO location identifier*] (ICLI) ... ETHD
Herington, KS [*FM radio station call letters*] ... KDMM
Heritae Canada Foundation, Ottawa, ON, Canada [*Library symbol*] [*Library of Congress*] (LCLS) ... CaOOHC
Heritage ... HRTG
Heritage Association of Antigonish, Nova Scotia [*Library symbol National Library of Canada*] (NLC) ... NSAH
Heritage Australia Information System [*Computer science*] (EERA) ... HERA
Heritage Bancorp [*NASDAQ symbol*] (TTSB) ... HBCI
Heritage Bancorp, Inc. [*NASDAQ symbol*] (SAG) ... HBCI
Heritage Bancorp, Inc. [*Associated Press*] (SAG) ... HertgBc
Heritage Campus, CEGEP de l'Outaouais, Hull, Quebec [*Library symbol National Library of Canada*] (NLC) ... QHCH

Heritage Canada Foundation [*Fondation Canadienne pour la Protection du Patrimoine*] **Ottawa, Ontario** [*Library symbol National Library of Canada*] (NLC) ... OOHC
Heritage College, Toppenish, WA [*Library symbol*] [*Library of Congress*] (LCLS) ... WaToH
Heritage Committee [*Australian Capital Territory*] ... HC
Heritage Conservation Recreation Service [*Abolished, 1981, functions transferred to National Park Service*] [*Department of the Interior*] ... HCRS
Heritage Council of New South Wales [*Australia*] ... HCNSW
Heritage Education and Review Organization [*Defunct*] (EA) ... HERO
Heritage Financial Services [*Associated Press*] (SAG) ... HertgFS
Heritage Financial Services, Inc. [*NASDAQ symbol*] (NQ) ... HERS
Heritage Finl Svcs [*NASDAQ symbol*] (TTSB) ... HERS
Heritage Foundation [*Washington, DC*] (EA) ... HF
Heritage Hills Area Library Services Authority [*Library network*] ... HHALSA
Heritage Interpretation International ... HII
Heritage Manor (BJA) ... HM
Heritage Media [*Associated Press*] (SAG) ... HrtgMda
Heritage Media Corp. [*Associated Press*] (SAG) ... HrtgMd
Heritage Media Corp. [*AMEX symbol*] (CTT) ... HTG
Heritage Media'A' [*AMEX symbol*] (TTSB) ... HTG
Heritage Papers, Danielsville, GA [*Library symbol Library of Congress*] (LCLS) ... GDanH
Heritage Park, Fort McMurray, Alberta [*Library symbol National Library of Canada*] (BIB) ... AFMM
Heritage Petroleum [*Vancouver Stock Exchange symbol*] ... HER
Heritage Propane Partners LP [*Associated Press*] (SAG) ... HeritPpn
Heritage Propane Partners LP [*NYSE symbol*] (SAG) ... HPG
Heritage Roses Group (EA) ... HRG
Heritage Trails Fund (EA) ... HTF
Heritage U.S. Government Income Fund [*NYSE symbol*] (SPSG) ... HGA
Heritage U.S. Govt Income Fd [*NYSE symbol*] (TTSB) ... HGA
Heritage US Government [*Associated Press*] (SAG) ... HeritUS
Heritge Association of Antigonish, Antogonish, NS, Canada [*Library symbol*] [*Library of Congress*] (LCLS) ... CaNSAH
Herkimer County Community College, Herkimer, NY [*OCLC symbol*] (OCLC) ... VXH
Herkimer County Community College, Ilion, NY [*Library symbol Library of Congress*] (LCLS) ... NIIH
Herkimer County Historical Society, Herkimer, NY [*Library symbol Library of Congress*] (LCLS) ... NHerkCHi
Herkimer, NY [*AM radio station call letters*] ... WNRS
Herkimer, NY [*FM radio station call letters*] ... WVHC
Herkimer, NY [*FM radio station call letters*] ... WXUR
Herley Industries [*NASDAQ symbol*] (TTSB) ... HRLY
Herley Industries, Inc. [*Associated Press*] (SAG) ... Herley
Herley Industries, Inc. [*NASDAQ symbol*] (NQ) ... HRLY
Herlong, CA [*Location identifier FAA*] (FAAL) ... AHC
Herman Collegiate Institute, Windsor, ON, Canada [*Library symbol Library of Congress*] (LCLS) ... CaOWH
Herman Collegiate Institute, Windsor, Ontario [*Library symbol National Library of Canada*] (NLC) ... OWH
Herman Hospital [*Houston, TX*] ... HH
Herman Hospital, Houston, TX [*Library symbol Library of Congress*] (LCLS) ... TxHHH
Herman on Chattel Mortgages [*A publication*] (DLA) ... Her Chat
Herman on Chattel Mortgages [*A publication*] (DLA) ... Herm Chat Mortg
Herman on Mortgages of Real Estate [*A publication*] (DLA) ... Her Mort
Hermanas Catequistas Guadalupanas [*Sister Catechists of Guadeloupe*] [*Roman Catholic women's religious order*] ... HCG
Hermanas Contemplativas del Buen Pastor (TOCD) ... HBS
Hermanas del Buen Pastor (TOCD) ... SGS
Hermanas del Servico Social (TOCD) ... HSS
Hermanas Dominicanas de la Doctrine Cristiana (TOCD) ... OP
Hermanas Josefinas (TOCD) ... HJ
Hermand's Consistorial Decisions [*Scotland*] [*A publication*] (DLA) ... Herm
Hermand's Consistorial Decisions [*Scotland*] [*A publication*] (DLA) ... Hermand
Hermannus [*Authority cited in pre-1607 legal work*] (DSA) ... Her
Hermannus Schildis [*Deceased, 1357*] [*Authority cited in pre-1607 legal work*] (DSA) ... Herm Schil
Herman's Law of Estoppel [*A publication*] (DLA) ... Her Est
Herman's Law of Estoppel [*A publication*] (DLA) ... Herm Estop
Herman's Law of Executions [*A publication*] (DLA) ... Herm Ex'ns
Herman's Law of Executors [*A publication*] (DLA) ... Her Ex
Hermansky-Pudlak Syndrome [*Medicine*] ... HPS
Hermantown High School, Duluth, MN [*Library symbol*] [*Library of Congress*] (LCLS) ... MnDuHS
Hermantown, MN [*FM radio station call letters*] (RBYB) ... WWAX-FM
Hermanus [*South Africa*] [*ICAO location identifier*] (ICLI) ... FAHM
Hermanus [*South Africa*] [*Seismograph station code, US Geological Survey*] (SEIS) ... HER
Hermaphrodite-Specific Neuron [*Cytology*] ... HSN
Hermeneutische Untersuchungen zur Theologie [*Tuebingen*] [*A publication*] (BJA) ... HUzT
Hermens/Markair Express [*ICAO designator*] (FAAC) ... MRX
Hermes Data System [*Hermes Precisa International*] (NITA) ... HDS
Hermes Electronics Ltd., Dartmouth, Novia Scotia [*Library symbol National Library of Canada*] (NLC) ... NSDH
Hermes Electronics Ltd., Dartmouth, NS, Canada [*Library symbol Library of Congress*] (LCLS) ... CaNSDH
Hermes Global Orbiter [*NASA, proposed*] ... HGO
Hermes Ventures [*Vancouver Stock Exchange symbol*] ... HRM
Hermeter Master [*Freemasonry*] (ROG) ... HM
Hermetic Chip Carrier ... HCC
Hermetic Pivoting Seal ... HPS
Hermetic Rite [*Freemasonry*] (ROG) ... HR
Hermetically Sealed (IAA) ... HS
Hermetically Sealed Bushing ... HSB
Hermetically Sealed, Integrating Gyroscope ... HIG
Hermetically Sealed Zener Diode ... HSZD
Hermetic-Sealed Container (MSA) ... HSC
Hermiston [*Oregon*] [*Seismograph station code, US Geological Survey*] (SEIS) ... HRO
Hermiston, OR [*AM radio station call letters*] ... KOHU
Hermiston, OR [*FM radio station call letters*] ... KQFM
Hermiston Public Library, Hermiston, OR [*Library symbol Library of Congress*] (LCLS) ... OrHe
Hermit ... H
Hermit Sisters of Mary (TOCD) ... HSM
Hermit Sisters of Romuald (TOCD) ... HSSR
Hermitage ... HRMTG
Hermitage Public Library, Hermitage, NF, Canada [*Library symbol Library of Congress*] (LCLS) ... CaNfHe
Hermitage Public Library, Newfoundland [*Library symbol National Library of Canada*] (NLC) ... NFHE
Hermits of Mount Carmel (TOCD) ... HMC
Hermits of Our Lady of Mt. Carmel (TOCD) ... HOCarm
Hermogenianus [*Flourished, 4th century*] [*Authority cited in pre-1607 legal work*] (DSA) ... Herm
Hermogenianus [*Flourished, 4th century*] [*Authority cited in pre-1607 legal work*] (DSA) ... Hermo
Hermosillo [*Mexico*] [*Airport symbol*] (OAG) ... HMO
Hermosillo/Internacional [*Mexico ICAO location identifier*] (ICLI) ... MMHO
Hermotimus [*of Lucian*] [*Classical studies*] (OCD) ... Hermot
Hernandez Valley [*California*] [*Seismograph station code, US Geological Survey*] (SEIS) ... HVC
Hernando, FL [*AM radio station call letters*] ... WRZN
Herne's Law of Charitable Uses [*A publication*] (DLA) ... Her
Herne's Law of Charitable Uses [*A publication*] (DLA) ... Her Char U
Herne's Precedents [*A publication*] (DLA) ... Her Prec
Hernia [*Gastroenterology*] (DAVI) ... H
Hernia [*or Herniated*] [*Medicine*] ... HERN
Herniated Disc [*Medicine*] ... HD
Herniated Disc Syndrome [*Medicine*] ... HDS
Herniated Intervertebral Disc [*Medicine*] (DMAA) ... HID
Herniated Intervertebral Disc [*Medicine*] (DAVI) ... HIVD
Herniated Lumbar Disc [*Medicine*] ... HLD
Herniated Nucleus Pulposus [*Medicine*] ... HNP
Hernieuwde Progressieve Partij [*Renewed Progressive Party*] [*Surinam*] [*Political party*] (PPW) ... HPP
Herning/Skinderholm [*Denmark ICAO location identifier*] (ICLI) ... EKHG
He-Ro Group [*Associated Press*] (SAG) ... He-Ro
He-Ro Group [*NYSE symbol*] (SPSG) ... HRG
HERO Industries Ltd. [*Toronto Stock Exchange symbol Vancouver Stock Exchange symbol*] ... HRO
Hero of the Soviet Union [*Award*] (DOMA) ... HSU
Herodas [*Third century BC*] [*Classical studies*] (OCD) ... Herod
Herodian [*Period*] ... Her
Herodianus [*Greek scholar, c. 200AD*] [*Classical studies*] (OCD) ... Hdn
Herodianus [*Greek scholar, c. 200AD*] [*Classical studies*] (ROG) ... HERODIAN
Herodotus [*Greek historian, c. 484BC*] [*Classical studies*] (OCD) ... Hdt
Herodotus [*Greek historian, c. 484BC*] [*Classical studies*] (ROG) ... HEROD
Heroes of the Nations [*A publication*] ... HN
Heroes of the Reformation [*A publication*] ... HR
Heroides [*of Ovid*] [*Classical studies*] (OCD) ... Her
Heroin [*Slang*] ... H
Heroin and Cocaine (DSUE) ... H and C
Heroin Emergency Life Project ... HELP
Heroin, Morphine, and Cocaine [*Mixture*] [*Slang*] ... HMC
Heroin-Associated Nephropathy [*Medicine*] (DAVI) ... HAN
Heroin-Related Death [*Epidemiology*] ... HRD
Heron Lake Elementary School, Heron Lake, MN [*Library symbol*] [*Library of Congress*] (LCLS) ... MnHelES
Heron Lake Public Library, Heron Lake, MN [*Library symbol*] [*Library of Congress*] (LCLS) ... MnHel
Heron Park Campus, Algonquin College of Applied Arts and Technology, Ottawa, Ontario [*Library symbol National Library of Canada*] (BIB) ... OOACH
Heron Resources Ltd. [*Vancouver Stock Exchange symbol*] ... HRR
Heron's Jurisprudence [*1860*] [*A publication*] (DLA) ... Her Jur
Herpes Association [*British*] (DBA) ... HA
Herpes Genitalis [*Infectious disease*] (DAVI) ... HG
Herpes Gestationis [*Medicine*] ... HG
Herpes Help Support Group [*Australia*] ... HHSG
Herpes Network [*Defunct*] (EA) ... HN
Herpes Resource Center (EA) ... HRC
Herpes Simplex ... HS
Herpes Simplex Encephalitis [*Medicine*] ... HSE
Herpes Simplex Genitalis ... HSG
Herpes Simplex I [*Titer and virus*] [*Medicine*] (DAVI) ... HSI
Herpes Simplex Keratitis [*Medicine*] (DMAA) ... HSK
Herpes Simplex Labialis ... HSL
Herpes Simplex Thymidine Kinase [*An enzyme*] ... HSTK
Herpes Simplex Virus ... HSV
Herpes Simplex Virus [*Infectious disease*] (DAVI) ... HXV
Herpes Simplex Virus Encephalitis [*Medicine*] ... HSVE
Herpes Simplex Virus Glycoprotein D [*Biochemistry*] ... HSVgD
Herpes Simplex Virus Thymidine Kinase [*Medicine*] (DMAA) ... HSVtk
Herpes Stromal Keratitis [*Medicine*] ... HSK
Herpes Zoster [*Medicine*] ... HZ
Herpes Zoster Ophthalmicus [*Ophthalmology*] ... HZO

Herpes Zoster Virus .... HZV
Herpes-Dissociated Buffer [*Medicine*] .... HDB
Herpes-Like Virus .... HLV
Herpes-Type Virus .... HTV
Herpesvirus .... HV
Herpesvirus Ateles .... HVA
Herpesvirus Hominis .... HVH
Herpesvirus Hominis Membrane Antigen [*Medicine*] (MEDA) .... HVHMA
Herpesvirus of Saimiri .... HVS
Herpetic Eye Disease Study .... HEDS
Herpetics Engaged in Living Productively [*Later, Herpes Research Center*] (EA) .... HELP
Herpetological Information Search Systems .... HISS
Herpetologists' League (EA) .... HL
Herpetology [*or Herpetologist*] .... HERP
Herpetology (ADA) .... HERPET
Herr [*Sir, Mr.*] [*German*] .... HR
Herr, Regiere Mich durch Deinen Heiligen Geist [*Lord, Rule Me through Thy Holy Spirit*] [*Motto for a number of 16th and 17th century German and Bavarian rulers*] .... HRMDDHG
Herrera [*Dominican Republic*] [*ICAO location identifier*] (ICLI) .... MDHE
Herri Batazuna [*Union of the People*] [*Spain Political party*] (PPE) .... HB
Herrick Public Library, Holland, MI [*Library symbol Library of Congress*] (LCLS) .... MiHol
Herricks High School, New Hyde Park, NY [*Library symbol Library of Congress*] (LCLS) .... NNehpHH
Herricks High School, New Hyde Park, NY [*Library symbol*] [*Library of Congress*] (LCLS) .... NNhpHH
Herricks Middle School, Albertson, NY [*Library symbol*] [*Library of Congress*] (LCLS) .... NAlbHM
Herricks Senior High School, Herricks, NY [*Library symbol*] [*Library of Congress*] (LCLS) .... NHerrSH
Herrin, IL [*AM radio station call letters*] .... WJPF
Herrin, IL [*FM radio station call letters*] .... WVZA
Herring Buyers Association [*British*] (DBA) .... HBA
Herring Industries Board [*British*] .... HIB
Herringbone [*Electronics, engineering*] .... HGBN
Herringbone Strutting [*Construction*] .... HBS
Herringbone Twill .... HBT
Herringer-Hulster Effect .... HHE
Herrington, KS [*Location identifier FAA*] (FAAL) .... HRU
Herrljunga [*Sweden ICAO location identifier*] (ICLI) .... ESGH
Herrn [*Sirs, Gentlemen*] [*German*] (ROG) .... HRN
Herrold Hall Learning Resource Center, Zanesville, OH [*OCLC symbol*] (OCLC) .... OHH
Herrold's Egg Yolk Medium [*For growing microorganisms*] .... HEYM
Herron School of Art, Indianapolis, IN [*Library symbol Library of Congress*] (LCLS) .... InIJ
Herrschende Meinung [*Prevailing Opinion*] [*German*] (ILCA) .... hM
Herself .... HERS
Herself (DAVI) .... SE
Hersham & Walton Motors [*British specialty car maker*] .... HWM
Hershey Foods Corp. [*Associated Press*] (SAG) .... Hrshey
Hershey Foods Corp. [*NYSE symbol*] (SPSG) .... HSY
Hershey Foods Corp., Hershey, PA [*OCLC symbol*] (OCLC) .... HER
Hershey Medical Center, Hershey, PA [*Library symbol Library of Congress*] (LCLS) .... PHeM
Hershey, PA [*FM radio station call letters*] .... WRKZ
Herstigte Nasionale Party [*Reconstituted National Party*] [*South Africa*] [*Political party*] (PPW) .... HNP
Hertford [*City in England*] (ROG) .... HERTF
Hertford, NC [*FM radio station call letters*] .... WKJE
Hertfordshire [*County in England*] (EY) .... HERTS
Hertfordshire [*County in England*] (ODBW) .... Herts
Hertfordshire [*County in England*] (WGA) .... Hrt
Hertfordshire Association of Special Libraries [*British*] (NITA) .... HASL
Hertfordshire Hunt [*British*] (ROG) .... HH
Hertfordshire Imperial Yeomanry [*British military*] (DMA) .... HIY
Hertfordshire Light Horse [*British military*] (DMA) .... HLH
Hertfordshire Technical Library and Information Service [*British*] (NITA) .... HERTIS
Hertfordshire Yeomanry [*British military*] (DMA) .... HY
Hertfordshire Yeomanry Cavalry [*British military*] (DMA) .... HYC
HERTIS [*Hertfordshire Technical Library and Information Service*] **Subj ect Index** (NITA) .... HSI
Hertslet on Master and Servant [*A publication*] (DLA) .... Hert M & Serv
Hertslet's Map of Europe [*A publication*] (DLA) .... Hert Map Eur
Hertslet's Treaties [*A publication*] (DLA) .... Hert Treat
Hertz [*Symbol*] [*SI unit of frequency*] (AABC) .... Hz
Hertz (WDMC) .... Hz
Hertz Technology Group [*Associated Press*] (SAG) .... HertzTc
Hertz Technology Group [*NASDAQ symbol*] (SAG) .... HERZ
Hertzberg-New Method [*Standard periodical binding*] .... HNM
Hertzler Research Foundation, Halstead, KS [*Library symbol Library of Congress*] (LCLS) .... KHalH
Hertzog's High Court Reports [*South Africa*] [*A publication*] (DLA) .... H
Hertzog's Reports of Transvaal High Court [*A publication*] (DLA) .... Hertzog
Hertzsprung-Russell [*Diagram*] [*Astronomy*] .... H-R
Hertzsprung-Russell Diagram [*Astronomy*] .... HRD
Herut Zionists of America (EA) .... HZA
Hervey Bay [*Australia Airport symbol*] (OAG) .... HVB
Hervormde Teologiese Studies [*Pretoria, South Africa*] [*A publication*] (BJA) .... HervTS
Hervormde Teologiese Studies [*Pretoria, South Africa*] [*A publication*] (BJA) .... HervTST
Hervormde Teologiese Studies [*Pretoria, South Africa*] [*A publication*] (BJA) .... HTSt
Herzberg Continuum [*Spectral region*] .... HC
Herzfeld Caribbean Basin Fund [*NASDAQ symbol*] (SAG) .... CUBA
Herzfeld Caribbean Basin Fund [*Associated Press*] (SAG) .... HerzfldC
Herzlia [*Israel*] [*ICAO location identifier*] (ICLI) .... LLHZ
Herzo Base [*Germany ICAO location identifier*] (ICLI) .... EDIQ
Herzogenaurach [*Germany ICAO location identifier*] (ICLI) .... EDQH
Heschl's Gyrus [*Brain anatomy*] .... HG
Hesiod [*Greek poet, c. 800BC*] [*Classical studies*] (ROG) .... HES
Hesperia, CA [*AM radio station call letters*] .... KVVQ
Hesperia Fine Sandy Loam [*A soil type*] .... HFL
Hesperia Public Library, Hesperia, MI [*Library symbol Library of Congress*] (LCLS) .... MiHe
Hesperian Foundation (EA) .... HF
Hesperian Foundation (EA) .... HP
Hessische Bibliographie [*Database*] [*Arbeitsgemeinschaft Hessische Bibliographie*] [*German*] [*Information service or system*] (CRD) .... HESB
Hessische Landes- und Hochschulbibliothek, Darmstadt (Schloss), Germany [*Library symbol Library of Congress*] (LCLS) .... GyDaH
Hessischer Rundfunk [*Hessian Radio Network*] [*Germany*] .... HR
Hester Adrian Research Centre [*University of Manchester*] [*British*] (CB) .... HARC
Het Gilgamesj-Epos [*A publication*] (BJA) .... HGE
Hetastarch [*Biochemistry*] .... HES
Hetch Hetchy [*Railroad*] (MHDW) .... HH
Hetch Hetchy Railroad (IIA) .... HH
Hetero-Atom-in-Context .... HAIC
Heterocyclic Antidepressant [*Psychopharmaceutical*] .... HCA
Heterodera glycenes [*A nematode*] .... Hg
Heteroduplex Analysis (DMAA) .... HDA
Heteroduplex Mobility Analysis [*Genetics*] .... HMA
Heteroduplex Tracking Analysis [*Genetics*] .... HTA
Heterodyne (DEN) .... HET
Heterodyne (FAAC) .... HTN
Heterodyne Look-Thru [*Telecommunications*] (TEL) .... HLT
Heterodyne Matrix Detector .... HMD
Heterodyne Optical Correlation (IAA) .... HOC
Heterodyne Optical Optimization Communication System with Stops [*NASA*] .... HOPS
Heterodyne Vegetation Meter (IAA) .... HVM
Heterogeneous (ROG) .... HETEROG
Heterogeneous Element Processor [*Computer science*] (RDA) .... HEP
[*The*] **Heterogeneous Environment for Remote Execution** [*Computer science*] .... THERE
Heterogeneous LAN [*Local Area Network*] **Manager** (ACRL) .... HLM
Heterogeneous Nuclear [*Biochemistry*] .... hn
Heterogeneous Opposed Flow Diffusion .... HOFD
Heterojunction [*Electronics*] .... HJ
Heterojunction Bipolar Transistor [*Electronics*] .... HBT
Heterojunction Bipolar Transistor (MCD) .... HJBT
Heterojunction Device .... HJD
Heteronuclear Double Resonance (IAA) .... HNDR
Heteronuclear Multiple-Bond Correlation [*Physics*] .... HMBC
Heteronuclear Multiple-Quantum Coherence [*Physics*] .... HMQC
Heteronuclear Single Quantum Coherence [*Spectrum*] .... HSQC
Heteronuclear Single Quantum Correlation [*Spectrum*] .... HSQC
Heterophil Transplantation Antigen [*Medicine*] (DMAA) .... HTA
Heterophile Antibody [*Immunochemistry*] .... HA
Heterophile Beef [*Immunology*] (DAVI) .... HET-BE
Heterophile Guinea Pig [*Immunology*] (DAVI) .... HET-GP
Heterophile Presumptive [*Immunology*] (DAVI) .... HET-PR
Heterophyes [*A genus of trematode worms*] [*Gastroenterology*] (DAVI) .... H
Heteropoly Acid [*Inorganic chemistry*] .... HPA
Heteropowered Earth-Launched Inter-Orbital Spacecraft (KSC) .... HELIOS
Heterosexual (DSUE) .... HETERO
Heterosexual Attitudes toward Homosexuality [*Scale*] .... HATH
Heterosexual Relations [*Scale*] .... HR
Heterostructure Insulated Gate Field Effect Transistor (NITA) .... HIGFET
Heterothyrotropic Factor [*Medicine*] (MAE) .... HTF
Heterotopic Ossification [*Osteology*] .... HO
Heterotopic Ossification [*Orthopedics*] (DAVI) .... HTO
Heterotrophic Intestinal Nitrification [*Metabolism*] .... HIN
Heterozygosity [*Cytology*] .... H
Heterozygosity [*Cytology*] .... HET
Heterozygote [*Medicine*] (DMAA) .... Ht
Hethel [*British ICAO location identifier*] (ICLI) .... EGSK
Hethitisches Woerterbuch [*Heidelberg*] [*A publication*] (BJA) .... HW
Hetley's English Common Pleas Reports [*124 English Reprint*] [*A publication*] (DLA) .... Het
Hetley's English Common Pleas Reports [*124 English Reprint*] [*A publication*] (DLA) .... Het CP
Hetley's English Common Pleas Reports [*124 English Reprint*] [*A publication*] (DLA) .... Het (Eng)
Hetley's English Common Pleas Reports [*124 English Reprint*] [*A publication*] (DLA) .... Hetl
Hetrojunction Bipolar Mobility Transistor (NITA) .... HBT
Hettangian [*Geology*] .... H
Hettinger, ND [*Location identifier FAA*] (FAAL) .... HEI
Hettinger, ND [*AM radio station call letters*] .... KNDC
Heubach, Wurttemberg [*Germany ICAO location identifier*] (ICLI) .... EDTH
Heulandite [*A zeolite*] .... HEU
Heuristic Automated Transportation System (MCD) .... HATS
Heuristic Concepts (IEEE) .... HC
Heuristic Ideation Technique [*A procedure for generating ideas or solutions to a problem by analyzing a series of generalizations*] (WDMC) .... HIT

Heuristic Paper Trimming System (BUR) ... HUPATS
Heuristic Path Algorithm ... HPA
Heuristically-Programmed Algorithmic [*Name of computer in film, "2001: A Space Odyssey." Acronym is also considered to have been formed by combining the letters before IBM in the alphabet*] ... HAL
Heussler Air Service [*ICAO designator*] (AD) ... HQ
Heussler Air Service Corp. [*ICAO designator*] (FAAC) ... HUS
Hevra Kaddisha (BJA) ... HK
Hewett Elementary School, Rockville Centre, NY [*Library symbol Library of Congress*] (LCLS) ... NRockHE
Hewett-Packard, Boise Site Library, Boise, ID [*Library symbol*] [*Library of Congress*] (LCLS) ... IdBHP
Hewlett Elementary School, Hewlett, NY [*Library symbol Library of Congress*] (LCLS) ... NHewE
Hewlett Packard Engineering Graphics System (NITA) ... HP EGS
Hewlett Packard Interface Loop (NITA) ... HP IL
Hewlett Packard Personal Computer Instruments Bus (NITA) ... HP PCIB
Hewlett-Packard [*NYSE symbol*] (TTSB) ... HWP
Hewlett-Packard Co. [*Associated Press*] (SAG) ... HewlPk
Hewlett-Packard Co. ... HP
Hewlett-Packard Co. [*NYSE symbol*] (SPSG) ... HWP
Hewlett-Packard Co., Corporate Library, Palo Alto, CA [*Library symbol Library of Congress*] (LCLS) ... CPaHP
Hewlett-Packard Co., Fort Collins Division, Fort Collins, CO [*Library symbol Library of Congress*] (LCLS) ... CoFHP
Hewlett-Packard Co., Lake Stevens Instrument Division, Everett, WA [*Library symbol*] [*Library of Congress*] (LCLS) ... WaEHP
Hewlett-Packard Graphics Language ... HPGL
Hewlett-Packard Interface Bus [*Instrumentation*] ... HP-IB
Hewlett-Packard Printer Control Language ... HPPCL
Hewlett-Packard Printer Submodule (IAA) ... HPPS
Hewlett-Packard Visual User Environment [*Computer science*] ... HP VUE
Hewlett-Woodmere Public Library, Hewlett, NY [*Library symbol Library of Congress*] (LCLS) ... NHew
Hex Aluminum Nut ... HAN
Hex Head Electrical Squib ... HHES
Hex Head Squib ... HHS
Hex Head Steel (IAA) ... HHS
Hexaazaoctadecahydrocoronene [*Organic chemistry*] ... HAOC
Hexabromocyclododecane [*Flame retardant*] [*Organic chemistry*] ... HBCD
Hexachloroacetone [*Organic chemistry*] ... HCA
Hexachlorobenzene [*Organic chemistry*] ... HCB
Hexachlorobiphenyl [*Organic chemistry*] ... HCBP
Hexachlorobiphenyl [*Marine science*] (OSRA) ... HCBP
Hexachlorobutadiene [*Organic chemistry*] ... HCBD
Hexachlorocyclohexane [*Organic chemistry*] ... HCCH
Hexachlorocyclohexane [*Also, BHC, GBH*] [*Insecticide*] ... HCH
Hexachlorocyclopentadiene [*Also, HCP, HEX*] [*Organic chemistry*] ... HCCP
Hexachlorocyclopentadiene [*Also, HCCP, HEX*] [*Organic chemistry*] ... HCP
Hexachlorocyclopentadiene [*Also, HCCP, HCP*] [*Organic chemistry*] ... HEX
Hexachlorodibenzodioxin [*Organic chemistry*] ... HCDD
Hexachlorodibenzo-para-dioxin [*Organic chemistry*] ... HxCDD
Hexachloroepoxyoctahydro-exo-endo-dimethanonaphthalene [*Dieldrin*] [*Insecticide*] ... HEOD
Hexachloroethane [*Organic chemistry*] ... HC
Hexachlorohexahydrodimethanonaphthalene [*Insecticide, commonly called Aldrin*] ... HHDN
Hexachloronorbornadiene [*Organic chemistry*] (EPA) ... HEX-BCH
Hexachlorophene [*Germicide*] ... HCP
Hexachord [*Music*] (ADA) ... HEX
Hexadecadienyl Acetate [*Pheromone*] [*Organic chemistry*] ... HDDA
Hexadecanethiol [*Organic chemistry*] ... HDT
Hexadecenal [*Pheromone*] [*Organic chemistry*] ... HDAL
Hexadecenol [*Pheromone*] [*Organic chemistry*] ... HDOL
Hexadecenyl Acetate [*Pheromone*] [*Organic chemistry*] ... HDA
Hexadecimal (BUR) ... H
Hexadecimal [*System*] ... HEX
Hexadecimal [*Computer science*] (IAA) ... X
Hexadecimal Calculator [*Computer science*] (MHDI) ... HEXCALC
Hexadecimal Code [*Computer science*] (IAA) ... HD
Hexadecimal Digit [*Computer science*] (NHD) ... HEXIT
Hexadecimal Symbolic Loader [*Computer science*] (MHDI) ... HDLR
Hexadecimal-to-Binary [*Computer science*] (IEEE) ... H-B
Hexadecimal-to-Binary [*Computer science*] ... HTB
Hexadecimal-to-Decimal [*Computer science*] (IEEE) ... H-D
Hexadecyltrichlorosilane [*Organic chemistry*] ... HDTCS
Hexadecyltrimethylammonium ... HDTMA
Hexadecyltrimethylammonium Chloride [*Organic chemistry*] ... HTAC
Hexadecytrimethylammonium Bromide [*Organic chemistry*] ... HTAB
Hexaethyl Tetraphosphate [*Organic chemistry*] ... HETP
Hexaethylene Glycol [*Organic chemistry*] ... HEG
Hexafluoroacetone [*Organic chemistry*] ... HFA
Hexafluoroacetylacetone [*Organic chemistry*] ... HFA
Hexafluorodiethyl Ether [*Convulsant*] ... HFE
Hexafluoroisobutylene [*Organic chemistry*] ... HFIB
Hexafluoroisopropanol [*or Hexafluoroisopropyl*] [*Organic chemistry*] ... HFIP
Hexafluoropropylene [*Organic chemistry*] ... HFP
Hexafluoropropylene Oxide [*Organic chemistry*] ... HFPO
Hexafluorothioacetone [*Organic chemistry*] ... HFTA
Hexagon [*or Hexagonal*] ... HEX
Hexagon Tungsten Honeycomb ... HTH
Hexagonal [*Technical drawings*] ... HX
Hexagonal Close-Packed [*Crystallography*] ... HCP
Hexagonal Domain Structure ... HD
Hexagonal Field Effect Transistor (NITA) ... HEXFET
Hexagonal Head ... HEXHD
Hexagonal Mesoporous Silica [*Inorganic chemistry*] ... HMS
Hexagonal Nut ... HN
Hexahexylthiotriphenylene [*Organic chemistry*] ... HHTT
Hexahydrophthalic Anhydride [*Organic chemistry*] ... HHPA
Hex'air [*France ICAO designator*] (FAAC) ... HER
Hexamethonium [*Biochemistry*] (DAVI) ... C-6
Hexamethoxy(methyl)melamine ... HMM
Hexamethoxytriphenylene [*Organic chemistry*] ... HMT
Hexamethyl Hexacyclen [*Organic chemistry*] ... HMHCY
Hexamethylbenzene [*Organic chemistry*] ... HMB
Hexamethyldisilazane [*Organic chemistry*] ... HMDS
Hexamethyldisilazane [*Organic chemistry*] ... HMDZ
Hexamethyldisiloxane [*Organic chemistry*] ... HMDS
Hexamethyldisiloxane [*Organic chemistry*] ... HMDSO
Hexamethylene Bis(Acetamide) [*Organic chemistry*] ... HMBA
Hexamethylene Diisocyanate [*Organic chemistry*] ... HDI
Hexamethylene Diisocyanate [*Organic chemistry*] ... HMDI
Hexamethylene Tetramine [*Organic chemistry*] (WDAA) ... HEXA
Hexamethylenediamine [*Organic chemistry*] ... HMDA
Hexamethyleneimine [*Trademark*] [*Celanese Corp.*] ... HMI
Hexamethylenetetramine [*Also, HMTA*] [*Organic chemistry*] ... HMT
Hexamethylenetetramine [*Also, HMT*] [*Organic chemistry*] ... HMTA
Hexamethylenetetraselenafulvalenium [*Organic chemistry*] ... HMTSF
Hexamethylenetriamine [*Organic chemistry*] ... HMTA
Hexamethylmelamine [*Altretamine*] [*Also, HMM, HXM*] [*Antineoplastic drug*] ... HEX
Hexamethylmelamine [*Altretamine*] [*Also, HEX, HXM*] [*Antineoplastic drug*] ... HMM
Hexamethylmelamine [*Altretamine*] [*Also, HEX, HMM*] [*Antineoplastic drug*] ... HXM
Hexamethylmelamine [*Altretamine*], Adriamycin, Cyclophosphamide [*Antineoplastic drug regimen*] ... HAC
Hexamethylmelamine, Adriamycin, Diamminedichloroplatinum [*Cisplatin*] [*Antineoplastic drug regimen*] ... HAD
Hexamethylmelamine, Adriamycin, L-Phenylalanine Mustard [*Antineoplastic drug regimen*] (DAVI) ... HAM
Hexamethylmelamine, Adriamycin, Melphalan [*Antineoplastic drug regimen*] ... HAM
Hexamethylmelamine, Adriamycin, Methotrexate [*Antineoplastic drug regimen*] ... HAM
Hexamethylmelamine, Adriamycin, Methotrexate, Cisplatin [*Antineoplastic drug regimen*] (DAVI) ... HAMP
Hexamethylmelamine and Cisplatin [*Cisplatinum*] [*Antineoplastic drug*] (DAVI) ... HP
Hexamethylmelamine, Cyclophosphamide, Adriamycin, Platinol [*Cisplatin*] [*Antineoplastic drug regimen*] ... H-CAP
Hexamethylmelamine, Cyclophosphamide, Amethopterin [*Methotrexate*], Fluorouracil [*Antineoplastic drug regimen*] ... Hexa-CAF
Hexamethylmelamine, Oncovin [*Vincristine*], Methotrexate [*Antineoplastic drug regimen*] (DAVI) ... HOM
Hexamethylphosphoramide [*or Hexamethylphosphoric Triamide*] [*Also, HEMPA, HMPA, HMPT, HPT*] [*Organic chemistry*] ... HMP
Hexamethylphosphoramide [*or Hexamethylphosphoric Triamide*] [*Also, HEMPA, HMP, HMPT, HPT*] [*Organic chemistry*] ... HMPA
Hexamethylphosphoric Triamide [*Also, HMP, HMPA, HMPT, HPT*] [*Organic chemistry*] (MCD) ... HEMPA
Hexamethylphosphoric Triamide [*Also, HEMPA, HMP, HMPA, HPT*] [*Organic chemistry*] ... HMPT
Hexamethylphosphoric Triamide [*Also, HEMPA, HMP, HMPA, HMPT*] [*Organic chemistry*] ... HPT
Hexamethylpropylenamine Oxime [*Organic chemistry*] ... HMPAO
Hexamethyltrithiane [*Organic chemistry*] ... HMTT
Hexanediamine [*or Hexamethylenediamine*] [*Organic chemistry*] ... HDA
Hexanediol Diacrylate [*Also, HDODA*] [*Organic chemistry*] ... HDDA
Hexanediol Diacrylate [*Also, HDDA*] [*Organic chemistry*] ... HDODA
Hexanedione [*Organic chemistry*] ... HD
Hexane-Extractable Compound ... HE
Hexanitroazobenzene [*Organic chemistry*] ... HNAB
Hexanitrohexazaisowurtzitane [*An explosive*] ... HNIW
Hexanitromannite [*Organic chemistry*] ... HNM
Hexanitrostilbene [*High explosive*] ... HNS
Hexanitrostilbene [*High explosive*] (MCD) ... HNST
Hexaplaric Syriac (BJA) ... SyrH
Hexapole (OA) ... H
Hexasodium Metaphosphate [*Inorganic chemistry*] ... HMP
Hexateuch (ROG) ... HEX
Hexcel ... HXCL
Hexcel Corp. [*Associated Press*] (SAG) ... Hexcel
Hexcel Corp. [*NYSE symbol*] (SPSG) ... HXL
Hexcel Products, Technical Library, Berkeley, CA [*Library symbol Library of Congress*] (LCLS) ... CBH
Hexobarbital Sleeping Time [*In experimental animals*] ... HST
Hexode [*Electronics*] (OA) ... H
Hexode (DEN) ... Hx
Hexokinase [*An enzyme*] ... HK
Hexone-Extracted Acetone [*Chemistry*] (DAVI) ... HEA
Hexosaminidase-A ... HEX-A
Hexose Diphosphate [*Biochemistry*] ... HDP
Hexose Monophospate Shunt (PDAA) ... HMS
Hexose Monophosphate [*Biochemistry*] ... HMP
Hexose Monophosphate Pathway [*Biochemistry*] (DAVI) ... HMP
Hexose Monophosphate Pathway [*Biochemistry*] ... HMPP
Hexose Monophosphate Shunt [*Biochemistry*] ... HMPS
Hexosominidase-B ... HEX-B
Hexyl [*Biochemistry*] ... Hx
Hexylcarbonate of Salicylic Acid [*Analgesic*] ... HCSA

Hexylene Glycol [*Organic chemistry*] .... HG
Hexylresorcinol [*An antiseptic*] [*Pharmacology*] (DAVI) .... ST 37
Heyden Antibiotic [*Pharmacology*] .... HA
Heyl's United States Import Duties [*A publication*] (DLA) .... Heyl Imp D
Heywood and Massey's Court of Protection Practice [*9th ed.*] [*1971*] [*A publication*] (DLA) .... Heywood & Massey
Heywood on Elections [*A publication*] (DLA) .... Heyw Elec
Heywood Public Library, Heywood, Lancashire, United Kingdom [*Library symbol Library of Congress*] (LCLS) .... UkHe
Heywood's County Courts Practice [*4th ed.*] [*1876*] [*A publication*] (DLA) .... Heyw Co Ct
Heywood's Table of Cases [*Georgia*] [*A publication*] (DLA) .... Heyw Ca
Hezb Allah [*Party of God*] [*Arabic*] [*An Irananian terrorist organization*] .... HEZOBOLLAH
HF Bancorp [*NASDAQ symbol*] (TTSB) .... HEMT
HF Bancorp, Inc. [*NASDAQ symbol*] (SAG) .... HEMT
HF Bancorp, Inc. [*Associated Press*] (SAG) .... HFBcp
H.F. Carey High School, Sewanhaka, NY [*Library symbol*] [*Library of Congress*] (LCLS) .... NSewCH
HF Financial [*NASDAQ symbol*] (TTSB) .... HFFC
HF Financial Corp. [*Associated Press*] (SAG) .... HF Fnc
HF Financial Corp. [*NASDAQ symbol*] (SAG) .... HFFC
HF [*High Frequency*] **Modem Replacement** (DOMA) .... HFMR
HF [*High-Frequency*] **Recovery Antenna** .... HRA
HFIR [*High-Flux Isotope Reactor*] **Critical Experiment** [*Nuclear energy*] (NRCH) .... HFCE
HFIR [*High-Flux Isotope Reactor*] **Irradiation Facility Improvement** [*Nuclear energy*] .... HIFI
HFNC Financial [*NASDAQ symbol*] (TTSB) .... HFNC
HFNC Financial Corp. [*NASDAQ symbol*] (SAG) .... HFNC
HFNC Financial Corp. [*Associated Press*] (SAG) .... HFNCFn
HFS, Inc. [*Associated Press*] (SAG) .... HFS
HGI Realty [*NYSE symbol*] (TTSB) .... HGI
HGI Realty, Inc. [*Associated Press*] (SAG) .... HGI Rlty
H-Hour Coordinating Line [*Army*] (AABC) .... HHCL
Hi Rise Recycling Systems [*NASDAQ symbol*] (SAG) .... HIRI
Hi Rise Recycling Systems [*Associated Press*] (SAG) .... HiRise
Hi Shear Technology Corp. [*Associated Press*] (SAG) .... HiShearT
Hi Shear Technology Corp. [*Associated Press*] (SAG) .... HiShearTc
Hi Shear Technology Corp. [*AMEX symbol*] (SAG) .... HSR
Hi Tech Pharmacal Co. [*Associated Press*] (SAG) .... HiTcPhr
Hi Tech Pharmacal Co. [*NASDAQ symbol*] (SAG) .... HITK
Hi Tech Ventures, Inc. [*Vancouver Stock Exchange symbol*] .... HTV
Hialeah, FL [*AM radio station call letters*] (RBYB) .... WACC
Hialeah, FL [*FM radio station call letters*] .... WCMQ
Hiatal Hernia [*Medicine*] .... HH
Hiawatha, KS [*FM radio station call letters*] .... KNZA
Hibbard's Reports [*New Hampshire*] [*A publication*] (DLA) .... Hibb
Hibbard's Reports [*Opinions Attorneys-General*] [*A publication*] (DLA) .... Hibb
Hibbett Sporting Goods, Inc. [*NASDAQ symbol*] (SAG) .... HIBB
Hibbett Sporting Goods, Inc. [*Associated Press*] (SAG) .... Hibbett
Hibbing [*Minnesota*] [*Airport symbol*] (OAG) .... HIB
Hibbing/Chisholm-Hibbing [*Minnesota*] [*ICAO location identifier*] (ICLI) .... KHIB
Hibbing Community College, Hibbing, MN [*OCLC symbol*] (OCLC) .... HCC
Hibbing Community College, Hibbing, MN [*Library symbol Library of Congress*] (LCLS) .... MnHibC
Hibbing Junior College [*Later, Hibbing Community College*] [*Minnesota*] .... HJC
Hibbing, MN [*FM radio station call letters*] .... KADU
Hibbing, MN [*Television station call letters*] .... WIRT
Hibbing, MN [*AM radio station call letters*] .... WMFG
Hibbing, MN [*FM radio station call letters*] .... WMFG-FM
Hibbing, MN [*FM radio station call letters*] .... WTBX
Hibbing Public Library, Hibbing, MN [*Library symbol Library of Congress*] (LCLS) .... MnHib
Hibeh Papyri [*A publication*] (OCD) .... PHib
Hibernation Induction Trigger [*Biochemistry*] .... HIT
Hibernation Information Exchange [*Later, IHS*] .... HIE
Hibernation Trigger (BARN) .... HT
Hibernia [*Ancient name for Ireland*] (ROG) .... HIB
Hibernia Corp, Class A [*Associated Press*] (SAG) .... Hibern
Hibernia Corp. [*Associated Press*] (SAG) .... Hibern
Hibernia Corp. Cl'A' [*NYSE symbol*] (TTSB) .... HIB
Hibernia Corp. Class A [*NYSE symbol*] (SPSG) .... HIB
Hibernia Foods Ltd. [*NASDAQ symbol*] (SAG) .... HIBN
Hibernia Foods Ltd. [*Associated Press*] (SAG) .... HibrnFd
Hibernia Foods PLC [*NASDAQ symbol*] (SAG) .... HIBUF
Hibernia Foods PLC [*NASDAQ symbol*] (SAG) .... HIBW
Hibernia Foods PLC [*NASDAQ symbol*] (SAG) .... HIBZ
Hibernia Foods PLC [*Associated Press*] (SAG) .... HitFd
Hibernia Foods plc ADS [*NASDAQ symbol*] (TTSB) .... HIBNY
Hibernia Foods Unit [*NASDAQ symbol*] (TTSB) .... HIBUF
Hibernia Foods Wrrt'C' [*NASDAQ symbol*] (TTSB) .... HIBWF
Hibernia Foods Wrrt'D' [*NASDAQ symbol*] (TTSB) .... HIBZF
Hibernia Savings Bank [*Associated Press*] (SAG) .... HiberSv
Hibernia Savings Bank [*NASDAQ symbol*] (NQ) .... HSBK
Hibernia Savings Bk [*NASDAQ symbol*] (TTSB) .... HSBK
Hibiscus Air Services Ltd. [*New Zealand*] [*ICAO designator*] (FAAC) .... HIB
Hibiscus Chlorotic Ringspot Virus [*Plant pathology*] .... HCRSV
Hibiscus Latent Ringspot Virus [*Plant pathology*] .... HLRV
Hiburd Properties [*Vancouver Stock Exchange symbol*] .... HDP
Hiburnium [*Supposed chemical element, discovered 1922*] .... Hi
Hic [*Here*] [*Latin*] .... H
Hic Conditus Est [*Here Lies Buried*] [*Latin*] .... HCE
Hic Est [*Here Is, That is, or This is*] [*Latin*] .... HE
Hic Est Sepultus [*Here Is Buried*] [*Latin*] (ROG) .... HES
Hic Iacet [*Here Lies*] [*Latin*] .... HI
Hic Iacet Sepultus [*Here Lies Buried*] [*Latin*] .... HIS
Hic Jacet [*Here Lies*] [*Latin*] .... HJ
Hic Jacet Sepultus [*Here Lies Buried*] [*Latin*] .... HJS
Hic Pace Requiescat [*May He Here Rest in Peace*] [*Latin*] (ROG) .... HPR
Hic Requiescit in Pace [*Here Rests in Peace*] [*Latin*] .... HRIP
Hic Sepultus [*Here Is Buried*] [*Latin*] .... HS
Hic Sepultus Est [*Here Lies Buried*] [*Latin*] .... HSE
Hic Situs [*Here Lies*] [*Latin*] (GPO) .... HS
Hic Verbis [*In These Words*] [*Latin*] .... HV
Hickam Air Force Base, Hawaii [*NASA*] (NASA) .... HIC
Hickam United States Air Force Automatic Weather Switch, Oahu Island [*Hawaii*] [*ICAO location identifier*] (ICLI) .... PHWR
Hickman Catheter [*Medicine*] (DAVI) .... HC
Hickman Line [*Cardiology*] (DAVI) .... HL
Hickman on Naval Courts-Martial [*A publication*] (DLA) .... Hick Ct Mar
Hickok Electrical Instrument Co. [*NASDAQ symbol*] (SAG) .... HICK
Hickok, Inc. [*NASDAQ symbol*] (SAG) .... HICK
Hickok, Inc. [*Associated Press*] (SAG) .... Hickok
Hickok Inc. 'A' [*NASDAQ symbol*] (TTSB) .... HICKA
Hickory .... HCKRY
Hickory (VRA) .... hick
Hickory [*North Carolina*] [*Airport symbol*] (OAG) .... HKY
Hickory Handle Association (EA) .... HHA
Hickory Memorial Hospital Library, Hickory, NC [*Library symbol*] [*Library of Congress*] (LCLS) .... NcHyMH
Hickory/Municipal [*North Carolina*] [*ICAO location identifier*] (ICLI) .... KHKY
Hickory, NC [*Location identifier FAA*] (FAAL) .... BZM
Hickory, NC [*FM radio station call letters*] .... WEZC
Hickory, NC [*FM radio station call letters*] .... WFHE
Hickory, NC [*AM radio station call letters*] .... WHKY
Hickory, NC [*Television station call letters*] .... WHKY-TV
Hickory, NC [*AM radio station call letters*] .... WIRC
Hickory, NC [*FM radio station call letters*] .... WPAR
Hickory, NC [*FM radio station call letters*] .... WXRC
Hickory Tech [*NASDAQ symbol*] (TTSB) .... HTCO
Hickory Tech Corp. [*Associated Press*] (SAG) .... Hickory
Hickory Tech Corp. [*NASDAQ symbol*] (SAG) .... HTCO
Hicks & Greist [*Advertising agency*] .... H & G
Hicks on Materials and Methods of Legal Research [*A publication*] (DLA) .... Hicks Leg Research
Hicks on Men and Books Famous in the Law [*A publication*] (DLA) .... Hicks Men & Books
Hicks' Organization and Ethics of Bench and Bar [*A publication*] (DLA) .... Hicks Ethics
Hicksville Administration, Hicksville, NY [*Library symbol Library of Congress*] (LCLS) .... NHickAd
Hicksville Free Public Library, Hicksville, NY [*Library symbol Library of Congress*] (LCLS) .... NHick
Hicksville Junior High School, Hicksville, NY [*Library symbol*] [*Library of Congress*] (LCLS) .... HNickJS
Hicksville Senior High School, Hicksville, NY [*Library symbol Library of Congress*] (LCLS) .... NHickSH
Hidaka [*Japan*] [*Seismograph station code, US Geological Survey*] (SEIS) .... HDK
Hidalgo County Library System, McAllen, TX [*OCLC symbol*] (OCLC) .... HDL
Hidden Bay [*Alaska*] [*Seismograph station code, US Geological Survey*] (SEIS) AD4
Hidden Broad-Line Region [*Spectra*] .... HBLR
Hidden Frames Test [*Education*] (EDAC) .... HFT
Hidden Lake [*Pennsylvania*] [*Seismograph station code, US Geological Survey Closed*] (SEIS) .... HKP
Hidden Lake Formation [*Geology*] .... HLF
Hidden Lake Gold Mines [*Vancouver Stock Exchange symbol*] .... HIN
Hidden Markov Modeling [*Computer science*] .... HMM
Hidden Predictive Saccades [*Ophthalmology*] .... HPS
Hidden Variable Theory [*Physics*] .... HVT
Hideaway .... HDWY
Hideaways International [*Commercial firm*] (EA) .... HI
Hidelgo County Library System, McAllen, TX [*Library symbol Library of Congress*] (LCLS) .... TxMcaH
Hiding Power [*Paint technology*] .... HP
Hidradenitis Suppurative [*Medicine*] .... HS
Hidrotic Ectodermal Dysplasia [*Dermatology*] .... HED
Hienghene [*New Caledonia*] [*Airport symbol Obsolete*] (OAG) .... HNG
Hienghene/Henri Martinet [*New Caledonia*] [*ICAO location identifier*] (ICLI) .... NWWI
Hierachical Information Processor (PDAA) .... HIP
Hierarchial Lapped Transform [*Telecommunications*] .... HLT
Hierarchical Abstract Computer (MHDI) .... HAC
Hierarchical Access Method .... HAM
Hierarchical Classification [*Indexing*] .... HICLASS
Hierarchical Data Format [*Computer science*] .... HDF
Hierarchical Database Management System .... HDBMS
Hierarchical Development Method [*Computer science*] .... HDM
Hierarchical Direct .... HD
Hierarchical Direct Access Method [*Computer science*] (MCD) .... HDAM
Hierarchical Distributed Control [*Computer science*] .... HDC
Hierarchical Environmental Retrieval for Management Access and Networking [*Biological Information Service*] [*Database on biology*] (NITA) .... HERMAN
Hierarchical Environmental Retrieval for Management and Networking [*Biological Information Service*] [*Riverside, CA*] .... HERMAN
Hierarchical File Storage (ACRL) .... HFS
Hierarchical File System [*Computer science*] .... HFS
Hierarchical Identification .... HID

Hierarchical Indexed Direct Access Method [*Computer science*] (BUR) ..... HIDAM
Hierarchical Indexed Sequential Access Method [*Computer science*] (BUR) ..... HISAM
Hierarchical Indexed Sequential Direct Access Method [*Computer science*] ..... HISDAM
Hierarchical Information Control System [*Japanese*] ..... HICS
Hierarchical Input Process Output [*Diagram used in software assessment*] (NITA) ..... HIPO
Hierarchical Intensive Search [*of the literature*] ..... HIS
Hierarchical Memory Storage [*Computer science*] ..... HMS
Hierarchical Network Architecture ..... HNA
Hierarchical Object-Oriented Design [*Computer science*] (ODBW) ..... HOOD
Hierarchical Object-Oriented Picture System [*Computer science*] ..... HOOPS
Hierarchical Random Access Memory [*Computer science*] ..... HRAM
Hierarchical Richness Index [*Biodiversity*] (EERA) ..... HRI
Hierarchical Sequential Access Method [*Computer science*] ..... HSAM
Hierarchical Storage Controller (ACRL) ..... HSC
Hierarchical Storage Manager [*or Management*] ..... HSM
Hierarchical Structured Data Set (IAA) ..... HSD
Hierarchically Classified Index ..... HCI
Hierarchically Structured [*Indexing language*] (NITA) ..... HS
Hierarchy [*Computer science*] ..... HIR
Hierarchy plus Input-Process-Output [*Computer science*] ..... HIPO
Hierarchy Service System [*Toshiba Corp.*] ..... HSS
Hieratische Papyrus aus den Koeniglichen Museen zu Berlin [*A publication*] (BJA) ..... HPKMB
Hieroglyph (VRA) ..... hiergl
Hieroglyphics [*Freemasonry*] (ROG) ..... H
Hieroglyphics (WDAA) ..... HIER
Hieroglyphics ..... Hiero
Hieronymi Liber Interpretationis Hebraicorum Nominum (BJA) ..... LIHN
Hieronymus [*Jerome*] [*348-420AD*] (BJA) ..... Hier
Hieronymus [*Jerome*] [*348-420AD*] (OCD) ..... Hieron
Hieronymus Cagnolus [*Deceased, 1551*] [*Authority cited in pre-1607 legal work*] (DSA) ..... Hiero Cag
Hieronymus Cagnolus [*Deceased, 1551*] [*Authority cited in pre-1607 legal work*] (DSA) ..... Hiero Cagno
Hieronymus Cagnolus [*Deceased, 1551*] [*Authority cited in pre-1607 legal work*] (DSA) ..... Hieron Cagno
Hieronymus Gabrielius [*Deceased, 1587*] [*Authority cited in pre-1607 legal work*] (DSA) ..... Hier Gabr
Hieronymus Gabrielius [*Deceased, 1587*] [*Authority cited in pre-1607 legal work*] (DSA) ..... Hieron Gabriel
Hieronymus Gratus [*Deceased, 1544*] [*Authority cited in pre-1607 legal work*] (DSA) ..... Hieron Grat
Hieronymus Schurff [*Deceased, 1554*] [*Authority cited in pre-1607 legal work*] (DSA) ..... Hier Schurf
Hieronymus Torniellus [*Deceased, 1575*] [*Authority cited in pre-1607 legal work*] (DSA) ..... Hier Torniel
Hierro [*Canary Islands*] [*ICAO location identifier*] (ICLI) ..... GCHI
Hierusolymo [*Jerusalem*] (ROG) ..... HIER
Higgins' Digest of Patent Cases [*1890*] [*A publication*] (DLA) ..... Hig Pat Dig
Higgins' Pollution and Obstruction of Watercourses [*1877*] [*A publication*] (DLA) ..... Hig Waterc
Higgins' Tennessee Court of Civil Appeals Reports [*A publication*] (DLA) ..... Higgins
Higgins' Tennessee Court of Civil Appeals Reports [*A publication*] (DLA) ..... Tenn CCA (Higgins)
Higginsville, MO [*Location identifier FAA*] (FAAL) ..... HIG
Higginsville, MO [*Location identifier FAA*] (FAAL) LCX
High [*Standard & Poor's bond rating*] [*Investment term*] ..... AA
High [*Moody's bond rating*] [*Investment term*] ..... Aa
High ..... H
High [*Engineering*] ..... H
High [*Computer science*] (AAG) ..... HI
High Accuracy [*RADAR*] ..... HIAC
High Accuracy Reference Network [*Mathematics*] ..... HARN
High Accuracy Submersible Inertial Navigation System (PDAA) ..... HASINS
High Active Waste [*Nuclear energy*] ..... HAW
High Affinity-Low Capacity (DMAA) ..... HALC
High Air Flow with Oxygen Enrichment (PDAA) ..... HAFOE
High Air Pollution Potential ..... HAAP
High Air Pollution Potential ..... HAPP
High Alcohol Drinking [*Rat strain*] ..... HAD
High Altitude ..... HA
High Altitude (MCD) ..... HIALT
High Altitude Economic Carrier (PDAA) ..... HAEC
High Altitude/High Opening [*Army*] (ADDR) ..... HAHO
High Altitude Long Operation [*Airplane*] ..... HALO
High Altitude Radiation Environment Study [*FAA*] (PDAA) ..... HARES
High Altitude Route System [*FAA*] (TAG) ..... HARS
High Altitude Sampling Plane ..... HASP
High Altitude Temperature (PDAA) ..... HAT
High Amplitude (IAA) ..... HA
High and Very-High Frequency (IAA) ..... HVHF
High- and Very-High-Frequency Direction Finding ..... HVDF
High Angle ..... HA
High Angle of Attack [*Combat aircraft*] [*Navy*] ..... HAOA
High Anxiety (MAE) ..... HA
High Arcal Learning Objectives (AIE) ..... HALO
High Authority of the ECSC [*European Coal and Steel Community*] (ILCA) ..... HA
High Band (AAG) ..... HB
High Bay (KSC) ..... HB
High Beta Toroidal Experiment (PDAA) ..... HBTX
High Birth Weight [*Medicine*] (MAE) ..... HBW

High BIT [*Binary Digit*] Density Tape [*Skylab*] [*NASA*] ..... HBDT
High BIT [*Binary Digit*] Rate (KSC) ..... HBR
High Bit Rate Digital Subscriber Line [*Computer science*] (CDE) ..... HDSL
High Bleeding Frequency [*Medicine*] ..... HBF
High Blood Cholesterol ..... HBC
High Blood Pressure [*Medicine*] ..... HBP
High Blood Pressure Information Center [*Public Health Service*] (IID) ..... HBPIC
High Boilers ..... HB
High Breaking Capacity (IAA) ..... HBC
High Bridge Painting Co., High Bridge, NJ [*Library symbol Library of Congress*] (LCLS) ..... NjHibP
High Burst Rate (PDAA) ..... HBR
High Byte Enable ..... HBEN
High Byte Strobe [*Computer science*] (MHDI) ..... HBS
High Calorie (AAMN) ..... HC
High Calorie [*or Caloric*] [*Type of diet*] (DAVI) ..... hi-cal
High Calorific Value [*of a fuel*] ..... HCV
High Capability Buoy [*Marine science*] (MSC) ..... HCB
High Capacity Multiplexing [*Telecommunications*] (ACRL) ..... HCM
High Capacity Voice (ACRL) ..... HCV
High Carbohydrate Diet [*Medicine*] (DMAA) ..... HCD
High Carbohydrate, High Fiber [*Nutrition*] ..... HCF
High Carbohydrate, High Fiber [*Nutrition*] ..... HCHF
High Carbohydrate, Low Fiber [*Nutrition*] ..... HCLF
High Carbon [*Steel*] ..... HC
High Carbon, High Chrome ..... HCHC
High Charge Retention (PDAA) ..... HCR
High Chief Ranger [*Ancient Order of Foresters*] ..... HCR
High Church ..... HC
High Churchman [*British*] (ROG) ..... HC
High Circle Fatique ..... HCF
High Clad Silica (PDAA) ..... HCS
High Clouds Visible [*NWS*] (FAAC) ..... HCVIS
High Coefficient of Friction [*Engineering*] ..... HCF
High Color (CDE) ..... HC
High [*Altitude*] Combat Air Patrol (NVT) ..... HICAP
High Command ..... HICOM
High Command Secure Voice Network [*Navy*] (NVT) ..... HICOMSEVONET
High Commission [*or Commissioner*] ..... HICOM
High Commission Court [*1865*] [*England*] [*A publication*] (DLA) ..... Burn
High Commission Territories Corps [*Military unit*] [*British*] ..... HCT
High Commission Territories Reports [*Basutoland, Bechuanaland, and Swaziland*] [*A publication*] (DLA) ..... HCTLR
High Commissioner ..... HC
High Commissioner for Germany ..... HICOG
High Commissioner of Ryukyu Islands ..... HICOMRY
High Commissioner Trust Territory, Pacific Islands ..... HICOMTERPACIS
High, Common, Low [*Relay*] (IEEE) ..... HCL
High Compression ..... HC
High Conditioners [*Psychology*] ..... HC
High Conductivity [*Copper*] ..... HC
High Contrast [*Cinematography*] ..... hi-con
High Control/Low Nurturance [*Psychology*] ..... HC-LN
High Cost of Living ..... HC
High Cost of Living ..... HCL
High Court ..... H Ct
High Court ..... HC
High Court Junior Beadle [*Ancient Order of Foresters*] ..... HCJB
High Court Junior Woodward [*Ancient Order of Foresters*] ..... HCJW
High Court of Admiralty [*England*] (DLA) ..... Adm
High Court of Justice ..... HCJ
High Court of Lagos Law Reports [*Nigeria*] [*A publication*] (ILCA) ..... LLR
High Court Reports, India [*A publication*] (DLA) ..... HCR
High Court Reports, North West Frontier [*A publication*] (DLA) ..... HCRNWF
High Court Reports, Northwest Provinces [*India*] [*A publication*] (DLA) ..... HCRNWP
High Court Reports, Northwest Provinces [*India*] [*A publication*] (DLA) ..... High Ct
High Court Reports, Orange Free State [*A publication*] (DLA) ..... Gregorowski
High Court Reports, Orange Free State [*A publication*] (DLA) ..... OFC
High Court Secretary [*Ancient Order of Foresters*] ..... HCS
High Court Senior Beadle [*Ancient Order of Foresters*] ..... HCSB
High Court Senior Woodward [*Ancient Order of Foresters*] ..... HCSW
High Court Treasurer [*Ancient Order of Foresters*] ..... HCT
High Courts of Admiralty [*British*] ..... HCA
High Cross Range ..... HCR
High Cross-Range Orbiter (KSC) ..... HCR
High Current ..... HC
High Data Rate ..... HDR
High Data Rate Digital Subscriber Line [*Computer science*] ..... HDSL
High Data Register ..... HDR
High Definition Compatible Digital [*Compact-disc technology*] (PS) ..... HDCD
High Definition Electronic Production (NTCM) ..... HDEP
High Definition Imaging ..... HDI
High Definition RADAR ..... HDR
High Definition System for North America ..... HDS-NA
High Definition Video System ..... HDVS
High Density ..... HD
High Density (IAA) ..... HID
High Density Bipolar (NITA) ..... HDB
High Density Lipoprotein Fraction [*Biochemistry*] (DAVI) ..... HDL-C
High Density Recording (NITA) ..... HDR
High Dependency Unit [*Medicine*] (DMAA) ..... HDU
High Desert Racing Association ..... HDRA
High Detergent (WGA) ..... HD
High Detonation Pressure ..... HDP

High Dielectric Constant (IAA)	HIC
High Dirt Capacity [A type of filter] [Pall Trinity Micro Corp.]	HDC
High Dollar Group Sort (TDOB)	HDGS
High Dose [Medicine]	HD
High Dose Cytarabine [Medicine] (DMAA)	HDARAC
High Dose Methotrexate [Antineoplastic drug regimen]	HDMTX
High Dose Rate [Medicine] (DMAA)	HDR
High Drag [Navy] (NVT)	HD
High Dust	HD
High Duty Alloys Ltd.	HDA
High Duty Cycle (IAA)	HDC
High Dynamic	HD
High Dynamic User Equipment	HDUE
High Early Strength Cement [Technical drawings]	HES
High Earth Orbit (IEEE)	HEO
High Efficiency	HE
High Efficiency Linear Amplification by Parametic Synthesis (PDAA)	HELAPS
High Egg Passage [Rabies vaccine]	HEP
High Electroendosmosis [Analytical biochemistry]	HEEO
High Electron Mobility Transistor [Computer science]	HEMT
High Electron Mobility Transistor FET [Field Effect Transistor] [Honeywell] (NITA)	HEMT FET
High Elliptical Orbit Satellite	HEO
High Emission Cathode	HEC
High Endoatmospheric Defense Interceptor [Military] (RDA)	HEDI
High Endoatmospheric Defense System	HEDS
High Endothelial Venule [Cytology]	HEV
High Energy (MCD)	HE
High Energy Alpha-Proton Spectrometer (PDAA)	HEAPS
High Energy and Nuclear Physics Program [Department of Energy]	HENP
High Energy Density Facility [Proposed site for testing nuclear bombs]	HEDF
High Energy Forming	HEF
High Energy Physics Network [Computer science] (TNIG)	HEPnet
High Energy Prespark [Analytical chemistry]	HEPS
High Energy Radiation to Fuel	HERF
High Energy Shock Tunnel (IAA)	HEST
High Energy Transient Experiment [NASA]	HETE
High Energy Transient Explorer	HETE
High Energy X-Ray Experiment	HEXE
High Enthalpy Arc Tunnel [NASA]	HEAT
High Erucic Acid Development Effort	HEADE
High Erucic Acid Rapeseed [Agricultural chemistry]	HEAR
High Estimate Unconstrained	HEU
High Explosive (AAG)	HE
High Explosive (DNAB)	HEX
High Explosive - Improved Conventional Ammunition	HE-ICM
High Explosive, Rocket-Assisted	HERN
High Explosive, Tracer, Self-Destroying [Weaponry] (SAA)	HETSD
High Explosives Application Facility	HEAF
High Explosives Simulation Technique	HEST
High Fat [Type of diet]	HF
High Fibre Biscuits [British]	HIFI
High Fidelity Institute	HFI
High Fidelity Records [Record label]	HIFI
High Field (IAA)	HF
High Fill Rate [Valve] [Automotive engineering]	HFR
High Film Density Area (DMAA)	HFDA
High Flight Foundation (EA)	HFF
High Flow (MAE)	HF
High Flow Alarm (IEEE)	HFA
High Flow Shutoff Valve	HFSV
High Flux (IAA)	HF
High Flux Beam Research Reactor [Nuclear energy]	HFBR
High Flux Experimental Facility [Nuclear energy]	HFEF
High Flux Isotope Reactor	HFIR
High Flux Reactor [Netherlands] [Nuclear energy]	HFR
High Foliage Forager [Ecology]	HF
High Foliage Nester [Ecology]	HN
High Food Density [Ecology]	HF
High Force Actuator [Engineering]	HFA
High Forceps Delivery [Obstetrics] (DAVI)	HFD
High Fragmentation (MCD)	HIFRAG
High Freqency Wire Broadcasting (PDAA)	HFWB
High Frequency [Electronics]	HF
High Frequency (WDMC)	hf
High Frequency (WDMC)	v
High Frequency Broadcasting Schedule [Databank] (NITA)	HFBC
High Frequency Executive (NASA)	HFE
High Frequency Gas (WDAA)	HFG
High Frequency of Recombination [Medicine]	HFR
High Frequency Powder Air Conveyor (PDAA)	HFPAC
High Frequency Relay (NVT)	HEIFER
High Frontier (EA)	HF
High Functioning Autism	HFA
High Gain Antenna	HGA
High Gain Antenna Controller	HGAC
High Gain Antenna System (IEEE)	HGAS
High Gain Direction Finding System (PDAA)	HGDFS
High Gain Link	HGL
High Gelling Temperature [Analytical biochemistry]	HGT
High Geographic Aerospace Search RADAR	HIGH GASSER
High German [Language, etc.]	HG
High Glucose [Clinical chemistry]	HG
High Go Low Test	HGL
High Grade Dysplasia [Medicine]	HGD

High Grain (NASA)	HG
High Group Receiving	HGR
High Group Transmitting	HGT
High Harmonic Pitch Control (PDAA)	HHPC
High Heat [or Heating] Value	HHV
High Heparin Dose [Medicine] (DMAA)	HHD
High High Alarm (ECII)	HHA
High High-Altitude Clear Air Turbulence [Aviation]	HI-HICAT
High Holy Days (BJA)	HHD
High, Hot, and a Helluva Lot [Slang] (DAVI)	3H
High Impact	HI
High Impact	HIM
High Impact	HIMP
High Impact Incarceration Program [60-day paramilitary regimen for prisoners]	HIIP
High Impetus, Low Flame Temperature (MCD)	HILT
High Impulse Booster Experiment / Hardpoint Demonstration Array RADAR (SAA)	HIBEX/HAPDAR
High Impulsiveness (MAE)	HI
High Impulsiveness, High Anxiety [Psychology] (DAVI)	HIHA
High Impulsiveness, Low Anxiety (MAE)	HILA
High in Volatiles [Commercial grading]	HV
High Incidence Auto-Stabilizer (PDAA)	HIAS
High Incidence Target [Crime computer]	HIT
High Income Advantage [NYSE symbol] (TTSB)	YLD
High Income Advantage III [NYSE symbol] (TTSB)	YLH
High Income Advantage Trust [Associated Press] (SAG)	HiInco
High Income Advantage Trust [NYSE symbol] (SPSG)	YLD
High Income Advantage Trust II [Associated Press] (SAG)	HIncII
High Income Advantage Trust II [NYSE symbol] (CTT)	YLT
High Income Advantage Trust III [Associated Press] (SAG)	HiInIII
High Income Advantage Trust III [NYSE symbol] (SAG)	YLH
High Income Opp Fd [NYSE symbol] (TTSB)	HIO
High Income Opportunity Fund [Associated Press] (SAG)	HiIncoOp
High Income Opportunity Fund [NYSE symbol] (SAG)	HIO
High Income Trust Securities [Drexel Burnham Lambert, Inc.]	HITS
High Index of Suspicion [Medicine] (DMAA)	HIOS
High Information Delta Modulation [Computer science] (BUR)	HIDM
High Input, First Output [Computer science] (ECII)	HIFO
High Input Grant [Real estate] [Canada]	HIG
High Input Impedance	HII
High Input Shock Test	HIST
High Integrity Systems [Computer company] [British] (NITA)	HIS
High Integrity Trip Initiator (PDAA)	HITI
High Integrity Voting Equipment (PDAA)	HIVE
High Intensity	HI
High Intensity	HIN
High Intensity	HINT
High Intensity Drug Trafficking Area	HIDTA
High Intensity Lightweight Searchlight (PDAA)	HILS
High Intensity Radio Transmission Area [Army] (DOMA)	HIRTA
High Intensity Tutoring (EDAC)	HIT
High Interest Tracks	HIT
High Interest Unit [Navy] (ANA)	HIU
High Interference Signaling Environment	HISE
High Internal Phase [Emulsion chemistry]	HIP
High Internal Phase Ratio	HIPR
High Internal Pressure Producing Orifice (MCD)	HIPPO
High Iron Briquetting (DICI)	HIB
High Italian Technology [Automotive engineering]	HIT
High Jump	HJ
High Latitude Monitoring Station [Marine science] (OSRA)	HLMS
High Latitude Monitoring Station (USDC)	HLMS
High Latitude Particle (PDAA)	HILAP
High Latitude Rocket Campaign [A cooperative study by 7 laboratories in the UK] (PDAA)	HLRC
High Level	HL
High Level [Canada] [Airport symbol] (OAG)	YOJ
High Level, AB [ICAO location identifier] (ICLI)	CYOJ
High Level Ad Hoc Working Group [NATO] (NATG)	HLAHWG
High Level Analog Input System (NITA)	HLAIS
High Level Architecture [Department of Defense]	HLA
High Level Data Transistor Logic (NITA)	HLDTL
High Level Language Application Program Interface (NITA)	HLLAPI
High Level Municipal Library, Alberta [Library symbol National Library of Canada] (NLC)	AHL
High Level Public School, Alberta [Library symbol National Library of Canada] (BIB)	AHLPS
High Level Resources Ltd. [Vancouver Stock Exchange symbol]	HLR
High Level Scheduler (NITA)	HLS
High Level Waste Immobilisation Program [Nuclear energy] (NUCP)	HLWIP
High Light Intensity System (PDAA)	HILIS
High Liquid Level [Engineering]	HLL
High Loss Ferrite	HLF
High Low Alarm [Electronics] (ECII)	HLA
High Mach Flow	HMF
High Magnetic Field	HMF
High Magnification Viewer	HMV
High Mass Vehicle	HMV
High Medium [Moody's bond rating] [Investment term]	A
High Melt Strength [Plastic moldings]	HMS
High Melting (OA)	HM
High Melting Point	HMP
High Memory Area [Computer science] (PCM)	HMA
High Mileage (WDAA)	HI MI

High Mobility [*Vehicle analysis*] (MCD) ... HIMO
High Mobility Artillery Rocket System [*Army*] (DOMA) ... HIMARS
High Mobility Group [*of nonhistone proteins*] [*Biochemistry*] ... HMG
High Mobility Trailer ... HMT
High Modulus Glass Fiber ... HMGF
High Modulus Graphite [*Epoxy composite*] (MCD) ... HMG
High Modulus Yarn ... HMY
High Moisture Resistant ... HMR
High Moisture Shelled Corn (OA) ... HMC
High Molecular [*Weight*] [*Also, HMW*] [*Organic chemistry*] ... HM
High Molecular Weight [*Also, HM*] [*Organic chemistry*] ... HMW
High Molecular Weight ... HWM
High Molecular Weight Glycoprotein [*Medicine*] (DMAA) ... HMWGP
High Molecular Weight, High Density ... HMHD
High Molecular Weight Kallikrein [*Biochemistry*] ... HMWKa
High Molecular Weight Kininogen [*Biochemistry*] ... HMWK
High Museum of Art, Atlanta, GA [*Library symbol Library of Congress*] (LCLS) ... GAHM
High National Council ... HNC
High NATO Military Structure (NATG) ... HNMS
High Necrosis [*Medicine*] (DMAA) ... HN
High Needle Position [*on dial*] ... HNP
High Nickel Alloy ... HNA
High Nitrogen [*Clinical chemistry*] ... HN
High Noise-Level Margin ... HNLM
High Nutrient, Low Chlorophyll [*Biological oceanography*] ... HNLC
High Nutrition ... HN
High Oblique [*Aerospace*] ... HO
High Occupancy Vehicle [*Commuter routes*] [*Acronym usually followed by a number indicating the minimum number of people per vehicle*] ... HOV
High Old Genius [*Slang British*] ... HOG
High on Extraordinary Legal Remedies [*A publication*] (DLA) ... High Ex Rem
High on Extraordinary Legal Remedies [*A publication*] (DLA) ... High Extr Leg Rem
High on Injunctions [*A publication*] (DLA) ... High Inj
High on the Law of Receivers [*A publication*] (DLA) ... High Rec
High or Low ... H/L
High Order [*Computer science*] (OA) ... HO
High- [*or Higher-*] **Order Language** [*Computer science*] ... HOL
High- [*or Higher-*] **Order Language Working Group** [*Computer science*] (RDA) ... HOLWG
High Osmolar Contrast Agent [*Medicine*] ... HOCA
High Out of Range Alarm [*Electronics*] (ECII) ... HORA
High Output [*Automotive engineering*] ... HO
High Output Current ... HOC
High Oxygen (MAE) ... HO
High Oxygen Pressure ... HOP
High Oxygen-Pulping Enclosed System (PDAA) ... HOPES
High Pass [*Electronics*] ... HP
High Pass Filter ... HPF
High Pass Network ... HPN
High Pass Notch (IAA) ... HPN
High Penetration Resistant (PDAA) ... HPR
High Performance [*Automotive engineering*] ... HI-PERF
High Performance ... HP
High Performance Computing (EGAO) ... HPC
High Performance Computing Act (TNIG) ... HPCA
High Performance Computing and Communication [*Computer science*] ... HPCC
High Performance Computing and Communications (TNIG) ... HPPC
High Performance Computing and Communications Program and Information Technology (USDC) ... HPCC
High Performance Diesel Oil (PDAA) ... HPDO
High Performance FORTRAN [*Computer language*] ... HPF
High Performance Parallel Interface [*Computer science*] ... HIPPI
High Performance Work Organization ... HPWO
High Permittivity (DEN) ... HIK
High pH Anion Exchange Chromatography ... HPAEC
High Plains Agriculture Laboratory [*University of Nebraska - Lincoln*] [*Research center*] (RCD) ... HPAL
High Plains Corp. [*NASDAQ symbol*] (NQ) ... HIPC
High Plains Corp. [*Associated Press*] (SAG) ... HiPlains
High Plains Regional Climate Center [*NCPO*] ... HPRCC
High Point ... HPT
High Point College [*North Carolina*] ... HPC
High Point College, High Point, NC [*Library symbol Library of Congress*] (LCLS) ... NcHpC
High Point, NC [*Television station call letters*] ... WGHP
High Point, NC [*AM radio station call letters*] ... WGOS
High Point, NC [*FM radio station call letters*] ... WHPE
High Point, NC [*FM radio station call letters*] (RBYB) ... WHSL-FM
High Point, NC [*FM radio station call letters*] ... WMAG
High Point, NC [*AM radio station call letters*] ... WMFR
High Point, NC [*AM radio station call letters*] ... WOKX
High Point, NC [*FM radio station call letters*] ... WWIH
High Point Public Library, High Point, NC [*Library symbol Library of Congress*] (LCLS) ... NcHp
High Point Regional Hospital Medical Library, High Point, NC [*Library symbol*] [*Library of Congress*] (LCLS) ... NcHpH
High Point, Thomasville & Denton Railroad Co. [*AAR code*] ... HPTD
High Polar Latitude [*Geophysics*] ... HPL
High Position (MDG) ... H/P
High Potential (KSC) ... HIPOT
High Potential (IDOE) ... hipot
High Potential (IAA) ... HPOT
High Potential Iron Protein [*Biochemistry*] ... HIPIP
High Power ... HP
High Power [*Water boiler atomic reactor*] [*Dismantled*] ... HYPO
High Prairie, AB [*Television station call letters*] ... CBXAT-2
High Prairie, AB [*AM radio station call letters*] ... CKVH
High Prairie and District Centennial Museum, High Prairie, Alberta [*Library symbol National Library of Canada*] (BIB) ... AHPD
High Prairie Municipal Library, Alberta [*Library symbol National Library of Canada*] (NLC) ... AHPM
High Pressure (KSC) ... HIPR
High Pressure ... HIPRES
High Pressure ... HP
High Pressure Chamber ... HIPC
High Pressure Data Center [*National Institute of Standards and Technology Information service or system*] (IID) ... HPDC
High Pressure Fluid-Filled ... HPFF
High Pressure High Temperature [*Engineering*] ... HPHT
High Pressure Life Laboratory (PDAA) ... HPLL
High Pressure Partial Oxidation (PDAA) ... HPPO
High Pressure Technology Association [*British*] ... HPTA
High Priest ... HP
High Primary Sequence (IAA) ... HPS
High Priority (NG) ... HIPRI
High Priority ... HP
High Production Volume [*Manufacturing*] ... HPV
High Profile Terminal (IAA) ... HPT
High Protein [*Nutrition*] ... HP
High Pulse Recurrence Frequency (MCD) ... HPRF
High Purity ... H-P
High Purity Milled Carbon Fiber ... HPMCF
High Purity Quartz Yarn [*Materials science*] ... HPQY
High "Q" Circuit [*or Coil*] ... HQC
High "Q" Tuned Circuit ... HQTC
High Quality [*Home video system*] (IAA) ... HIQ
High Quality [*Home video systems*] ... HQ
High Quality Bonus Point [*Advancement system*] [*Navy*] (NVT) ... HQBP
High Quality Facsimile (DGA) ... HQF
High Rainfall Zone ... HRZ
High Random Access ... HIRAC
High Range-Resolution Monopulse (PDAA) ... HRRM
High Rate Bioreactor [*Chemical Engineering*] ... HRB
High Rate Forward ... HF
High Rate of Fire (NATG) ... HRF
High Reduction [*Microforms*] (NITA) ... HR
High Reflector (IAA) ... HR
High Refraction Layer ... HRL
High Reliability (IAA) ... HIREL
High Reserve Resources [*Vancouver Stock Exchange symbol*] ... HHR
High Resilience [*Plastics*] ... HR
High Resistance ... HR
High Resolution [*Computer science*] ... HI-RES
High Resolution (MCD) ... HR
High Resolution Imaging Spectrometer [*Instrument*] (EERA) ... HRIS
High Resolution Infrared Receiver (IAA) ... HRIR
High Resolution Infra-Red Spectroscopy ... HRIRS
High Resolution Microwave Survey [*Astronomy*] ... HRMS
High Resolution Scanning Radiometer [*Instrument*] (EERA) ... HRSR
High Resolution Spectrometer [*Marine science*] (OSRA) ... HRS
High Resolution Visible [*Imager*] ... HRV
High Reynolds Number Transonic Wind Tunnel ... HRNTWT
High Reynolds Number Tunnel ... HIRT
High Right Atrium [*Anatomy*] ... HRA
High Risk ... HR
High River, AB [*AM radio station call letters*] ... CHRB
High River Gold [*Vancouver Stock Exchange symbol*] ... HRG
High River Gold Mines Ltd. [*Toronto Stock Exchange symbol*] ... HRG
High River Municipal Library, Alberta [*Library symbol National Library of Canada*] (NLC) ... AHRM
High River Municipal Library, High River, AB, Canada [*Library symbol Library of Congress*] (LCLS) ... CaAHrM
High River Resources Ltd. [*Vancouver Stock Exchange symbol*] ... HGR
High Roughage Diet (PDAA) ... HRD
High Run ... HR
High Salinity Shelf Water [*Oceanography*] ... HSSW
High School ... HS
High School and Beyond Survey [*Department of Education*] (GFGA) ... HSB
High School Characteristics Index [*Research test*] [*Psychology*] ... HSCI
High School Completion (OICC) ... HSC
High School Diploma Graduate [*Military*] ... HSDG
High School Driver Education [*Department of Transportation*] ... HSDE
High School Education Program at University of Pennsylvania ... HEP-UP
High School Equivalency (OICC) ... HSE
High School Equivalency Index ... HSI
High School Equivalency Program ... HEP
High School Evangelism Fellowship (EA) ... HSEF
High School for Girls (ADA) ... HSG
High School for Health Professions ... HSHP
High School Geography Project [*Defunct*] ... HSGP
High School Graduate [*Classified advertising*] ... HSG
High School Interest Questionnaire [*Vocational guidance test*] ... HSIQ
High School Magazine [*A publication*] ... H Sch M
High School Magazine [*A publication*] (BRI) ... H Sch M
High School News Service [*Fleet Hometown News Center*] (DNAB) ... HSNS
High School Percentile Rank ... HSPR
High School Percentile Rank ... HSR
High School Personality Questionnaire [*Psychology*] ... HSPQ
High School Placement Test ... HSPT

High School Red Cross	HSRC
High School Size	HSS
High School Student Information Center (EA)	SIC
High School Students for Social Responsibility (EA)	HSSSR
High School Young Christian Students (EA)	YCS
High Sea State Container Transfer System [Army] (RDA)	HISEACOTS
High Seas Fleet [British military] (DMA)	HSF
High Seas Oil Recovery System	HSORS
High Season [Airline fare code]	H
High Sensitivity	HS
High Serum-Bound Iron [Biochemistry] (MAE)	HBI
High Shock Resistant (IAA)	HS
High Sierra Group [Nevada-based group proposing CD-ROM standards]	HSG
High Soap Suds Enema [Gastroenterology] (DAVI)	HSSE
High Solar Intensity	HSI
High Specific Activity [Radioisotope]	HSA
High Specific Output [Automotive engineering]	HSO
High Speed	HS
High Speed Boat (DOMA)	HSB
High Speed Bus Adaptor (NITA)	HSBA
High Speed Commercial Transport [MTMC] (TAG)	HSCT
High Speed Data Bus [Computer science] (DOMA)	HSDB
High Speed Fleet Broadcast (DOMA)	HSFB
High Speed Freight Vehicle (PDAA)	HSFV
High Speed Generation [Hybrid vehicles] [Automotive engineering]	HSG
High Speed Impact (SAA)	HSI
High Speed Line Adaptor (NITA)	HSLA
High Speed Local Area Network [Telecommunications] (ACRL)	HSLAN
High Speed Network	HSN
High Speed Optimized [General Tire Co.] [Automobile tires]	HSO
High Speed RAD [Rapid Access Data Dram] **Input/Output Processor** [Xerox] (NITA)	HSRIOP
High Speed Rail Association (EA)	HSRA
High Speed Rail/Maglev Association	HSR/MLA
High Speed Research Program [National Aeronautics and Space Administration] (USDC)	HSRP
High Speed Research Program [NASA] [Marine science] (OSRA)	HSRP
High Speed Steel Association [British] (BI)	HSSA
High Speed Strike System [Military]	HiSSS
High Speed Taxi-Way Turn Off [Aviation] (DA)	HST
High Spontaneous Activity	HS
High Spread Shears	HSS
High Springs, FL [Television station call letters]	WGFL
High Springs, FL [FM radio station call letters]	WYOC
High Stage (MCD)	HS
High Stocking Rate [Agriculture] (OA)	HSR
High Strand Intensity	HSI
High Strength [Steel] [Automotive engineering]	HS
High Strength Friction Grip (PDAA)	HSFG
High Strength Polyethylene [Organic chemistry]	HSPE
High Sub-Chief Ranger [Ancient Order of Foresters]	HSCR
High Sulphur Content (PDAA)	HSC
High Sulphur Fuel Oil	HSFO
High Survivability Test Vehicle, Lightweight [Military]	HSTVL
High Sustained G2 Acceleration [NASA] (NASA)	HSG
High Technology (WDAA)	HI TECH
High Technology (MCD)	HT
High Technology	HTEC
High Technology National Training (AIE)	HTNT
High Technology Professionals for Peace [Defunct] (EA)	HTPFP
High Technology Recruitment Index [A publication]	HTRI
High Technology Solution (DGA)	HTS
High Technology Transfer Co. [Czechoslovakia] (ECON)	HTT
High Temperature (WDAA)	HI-TEMP
High Temperature	HT
High Temperature (IEEE)	HTM
High Temperature Aerosol Decomposition [Chemistry]	HTAD
High Temperature and Pressure (GNE)	HTP
High Temperature Gas Reactor (EERA)	HTGR
High Temperature Gasdynamics Laboratory [Stanford University] [Research center] (RCD)	HTGL
High Temperature Materials Data Bank [Commission of the European Communities] [Information service or system] (IID)	HTM-DB
High Temperature Materials Information Analysis Center Information Analysis Center [Formerly, TEPIAC] [West Lafayette, IN] [DoD] (GRD)	HTMIAC
High Temperature Materials Laboratory [Oak Ridge, TN] [Oak Ridge National Laboratory] [Department of Energy] (GRD)	HTML
High Temperature Metals Recovery [For hazardous waste treatment]	HTMR
High Temperature Sodium Loop (PDAA)	HTSL
High Temperature Treatment [Materials science]	HTT
High Tensile	Hi Ten
High Tensile [Mechanics]	HTNSL
High Tensile Strength [Mechanics]	HTS
High Tension	HT
High Test Level Language (NASA)	HTLL
High Threshold Logic	HTL
High Threshold Mechanoreceptor [Neurophysiology]	HTMR
High Throughput Mission (SSD)	HTM
High Throughput Organic Synthesis [Chemistry]	HTOS
High Throughput Screening [Chemistry]	HTO
High Throughput Screening [For drug screening]	HTS
High Tibial Osteotomy [Orthopedics] (DAVI)	HTO
High Tide	HT
High Torque [Engineering] (IAA)	HIT

High Torque [Engineering] (IAA)	HT
High Torque, Low Rev	HTLR
High Toxic Hazard Material	HTHM
High Transform [Computer science]	HT
High Treason	HT
High Turbulence Level	HTL
High Twelve International (EA)	HI-12
High Vacuum (ADA)	HV
High Vacuum (IEEE)	HVAC
High Velocity	HV
High Velocity Armor-Piercing Projectile (SAA)	HIVAP
High Velocity Grenade Launcher [Projectile] (PDAA)	HVGL
High Velocity Metalworking (PDAA)	HVM
High Velocity Sheet Forming (PDAA)	HVSF
High Video Pass (NVT)	HVP
High Vinyl-Modified Epoxy (MCD)	HME
High Viscosity Index (IAA)	HVI
High Viscosity Index [Lubricants]	HVI
High Visibility (DS)	HV
High Vitamin [Pharmacology] (DAVI)	HiVit
High Vocal Center [Songbird anatomy]	HVC
High Voltage	HV
High Voltage CMOS [Complementary Metal Oxide Semiconductor] (NITA)	HVCMOS
High Voltage Engineering Corp.	HVEC
High Voltage Laboratory [MIT] (MCD)	HVL
High Voltage Research Laboratory [MIT] (MCD)	HVRL
High Volume	HV
High Water [Tides and currents]	HW
High Water Content Fluid [Hydraulics]	HWCF
High Water of Spring Tide	HWS
High Water Speed Technology Demonstrator [Marine Corps] (DOMA)	HWSTD
High Wet Modulus [Test for rayon]	HWM
High Wing [Aviation] (AIA)	HW
High Wycombe [British ICAO location identifier] (ICLI)	EGRH
High Wycombe [British ICAO location identifier] (ICLI)	EGUH
High Year of Tenure	HYT
High Yield [Material Strength] (DOMA)	HY
High Yield Catalyst Polypropylene (PDAA)	HYCPP
High Yield/High Stereospecificity Technology [for polypropylene] [Himont Corp.]	HY/HS
High Yield Income Fd [NYSE symbol] (TTSB)	HYI
High Yield Income Fund [Associated Press] (SAG)	HiYld
High Yield Income Fund [NYSE symbol] (SPSG)	HYI
High Yield Plus Fund [Associated Press] (SAG)	HiYdPl
High Yield Plus Fund [NYSE symbol] (SPSG)	HYP
High Yielding Variety [Agriculture]	HYV
High Z and E [Particles in outer space]	HZE
High-Abrasion Furnace (IEEE)	HAF
High-Abrasion Furnace Black (IAA)	HAFBLCK
High-Absorption Integrated Defense Electromagnetic Warfare System	HIDE
High-Acceleration Cockpit [Air Force]	HAC
High-Acceleration Rocket, Tactical (DNAB)	HART
High-Acceleration Rocket-Missile	HARM
High-Accuracy Airborne Location System (MCD)	HAALS
High-Accuracy Data [System] (MUGU)	HAD
High-Accuracy Data Transmission System (MUGU)	HADTS
High-Accuracy Instrumentation RADAR (DNAB)	HAIR
High-Accuracy RADAR Data Transmission System (MUGU)	HARDTS
High-Accuracy RADAR Data Transmission System (MUGU)	HAROTS
High-Accuracy Spacecraft Separation System (IAA)	HASSS
High-Accuracy Targeting Subsystem	HATS
High-Accuracy Voltmeter	HAV
High-Acid Column Product (NRCH)	HAP
High-Acid Waste [Nuclear energy] (NRCH)	HAW
High-Activity Mode (IAA)	HAM
High-Affinity Choline Transport	HAChT
High-Affinity Choline Transport	HACT
High-Altitude Abort [NASA] (KSC)	HAA
High-Altitude Air Pollution Program [FAA] (MCD)	HAAP
High-Altitude Air Traffic Control	HAATC
High-Altitude Airborne Observation	HAAO
High-Altitude Aircraft Detection	HAAD
High-Altitude Airdrop Resupply System	HAARS
High-Altitude Application	HAA
High-Altitude Auroral Research Project [Jointly operated by the Department of Defense and the Geophysical Institute at the University of Alaska]	HAARP
High-Altitude Balloon	HIBAL
High-Altitude Bombing [Military]	HAB
High-Altitude Bombsight (NATG)	HABS
High-Altitude Cerebral Edema [Medicine]	HACE
High-Altitude Clear Air Turbulence [Aviation]	HICAT
High-Altitude Compensation [Automotive engineering]	HAC
High-Altitude Delayed Opening Parachute Actuation Device (MCD)	HADOPAD
High-Altitude Density [Sounding rocket]	HAD
High-Altitude Diagnostic [Unit] [Rocket launcher]	HAD
High-Altitude Dive Bomb [Military]	HADB
High-Altitude Effects Simulation [Defense Nuclear Agency]	HAES
High-Altitude Electromagnetic Pulse	HAEMP
High-Altitude Electromagnetic Pulse (MCD)	HEMP
High-Altitude Fluorescence (IEEE)	HAF
High-Altitude Forecast Center	HAFC
High-Altitude Fuze [To activate weapons]	HAF
High-Altitude High-Speed Target [Formerly, HAST] (MCD)	HAHST
High-Altitude Infrared Detecting Set (MCD)	HAIRDS

High-Altitude Infrared Sensor System ..... HAISS
High-Altitude Large Area Surveillance Tactic [*Military*] (CAAL) ..... HILAST
High-Altitude Large Optics [*Air Force*] (MCD) ..... HALO
High-Altitude LASER Transmittance (MCD) ..... HALT
High-Altitude, Long-Endurance [*Proposed unmanned reconnaissance drone*] [*Military*] ..... HALE
High-Altitude Long-Focus Convergent Mapping System ..... HALCON
High-Altitude, Low-Opening Parachute Jump ..... HALO
High-Altitude Measurement Probe ..... HAMP
High-Altitude Missile (MCD) ..... HAM
High-Altitude Multiple Object Tracking System [*Air Force*] ..... HAMOTS
High-Altitude Navigation System ..... HANS
High-Altitude Nuclear Detection Studies [*National Institute of Standards and Technology*] ..... HANDS
High-Altitude Nuclear Effects [*Study*] ..... HANE
High-Altitude Nuclear Explosion ..... HANE
High-Altitude Observatory [*Boulder, CO*] [*National Center for Atmospheric Research*] ..... HAO
High-Altitude Orbital Space Station (IEEE) ..... HAOSS
High-Altitude Ozone Measuring and Educational Rocket [*NASA*] ..... HOMER
High-Altitude Particle Program Experiment [*NASA*] ..... HAPPE
High-Altitude Platform ..... HAP
High-Altitude Pollution Project [*FAA*] ..... HAPP
High-Altitude Powered Platforms (MCD) ..... HAPP
High-Altitude Probe (AAG) ..... HAP
High-Altitude Pulmonary Edema ..... HAPE
High-Altitude Pulmonary Oedema [*Medicine*] (DMAA) ..... HAPO
High-Altitude RADAR Altimeter [*NASA*] ..... HARA
High-Altitude RADAR Controller ..... HARC
High-Altitude Radiation Detection System (MCD) ..... HARDS
High-Altitude Radio Relay System (DNAB) ..... HARRS
High-Altitude Radiological Instrumentation System ..... HARIS
High-Altitude Ramjet Engine ..... HARE
High-Altitude Recombination Energy (IAA) ..... HAR
High-Altitude Recombination-Energy Propulsion (AAG) ..... HARE
High-Altitude Reconnaissance Platform ..... HARP
High-Altitude Relay Point ..... HARP
High-Altitude Research Probe (IAA) ..... HARP
High-Altitude Research Program [*or Project*] [*Military*] ..... HARP
High-Altitude Resonance Absorption Calculation (IEEE) ..... HARAC
High-Altitude Retinal Hemorrhage [*Medicine*] ..... HARH
High-Altitude Rocket Probe [*Army*] ..... HARP
High-Altitude Sampler ..... HAS
High-Altitude Sampling Program [*Air Force*] ..... HASP
High-Altitude Selection Test [*British military*] (DMA) ..... HAST
High-Altitude Solar Energy (PS) ..... HALSOL
High-Altitude Sounding Program (IAA) ..... HASP
High-Altitude Sounding Projectile ..... HASP
High-Altitude Sounding Rocket ..... HASR
High-Altitude Space Platform ..... HASP
High-Altitude Space Probe (IAA) ..... HASP
High-Altitude Space Velocity RADAR (AAG) ..... HASVR
High-Altitude Strike Indicator ..... HASTI
High-Altitude Superpressure Powered Aerostat [*Navy*] ..... HASPA
High-Altitude Supersonic Target [*Later, HAHST*] (MCD) ..... HAST
High-Altitude Surveillance Platform for Over-the-Horizon Targeting (MCD) ..... HISPOT
High-Altitude Synoptic Meteorological Observation (SAA) ..... HAMOS
High-Altitude Target ..... HAT
High-Altitude Target and Background [*Program*] (MUGU) ..... HITAB
High-Altitude Temperature Rocket ..... HAT
High-Altitude Terrain Contour Data Sensor (MSA) ..... HATCDS
High-Altitude Terrain Contour Data Sensor ..... HATS
High-Altitude Test and Evaluation of Infrared Sources (MCD) ..... HAIRS
High-Altitude Test Stand ..... HATS
High-Altitude Test Vehicle ..... HATV
High-Altitude Test Vehicle (MUGU) ..... HTV
High-Altitude Testing [*Sounding rocket*] ..... HAT
High-Altitude Transmitter ..... HAT
High-Alumina Basalt [*Geology*] ..... HAB
High-Aluminous Concrete ..... HAC
Highamerica Balloon Club (EA) ..... HBC
High-Angle Control System [*British military*] (DMA) ..... HACS
High-Angle Strafe ..... HAS
High-Angle Threat ..... HAT
High-Assault Risk Area [*DoD*] ..... HARA
High-Availability Manager (IAA) ..... HAM
High-Band Jammer (MCD) ..... HBJ
High-Band Warning Antenna (MCD) ..... HBWA
High-Band Warning Receiver (MCD) ..... HBWR
High-Beta Model (MCD) ..... HBM
High-Beta Stellarator (PDAA) ..... HBS
High-Brightness Relay [*Military*] (SDI) ..... HIBREL
Highbury College of Divinity [*British*] (ROG) ..... HIGHB
High-Calcium Pyroxene [*Mineralogy*] ..... HCP
High-Capacity ..... HC
High-Capacity (IAA) ..... HICAP
High-Capacity Active Control Suspension [*Automotive engineering*] ..... HICAS
High-Capacity Bomb ..... HCB
High-Capacity Communication System ..... HICAPCOM
High-Capacity Digital Transport Service [*Pacific Bell*] ..... Hicap
High-Capacity Fog Foam [*Navy*] (NVT) ..... HCFF
High-Capacity Fog Foam/Aqueous Film-Forming Foam (DNAB) ..... HCFF/AFFF
High-Capacity Heat Pipe (SSD) ..... HCHP
High-Capacity Mobile Telecommunications System (TEL) ..... HCMTS
High-Capacity Projectile (NVT) ..... HICAP
High-Capacity Satellite Digital Service [*AT & T*] (TSSD) ..... HCSDS
High-Capacity Signal Processor ..... HCSP
High-Capacity Storage System [*Novell, Inc.*] [*Computer science*] (PCM) ..... HCSS
High-Capacity Terrestrial Digital Service [*AT & T*] (TSSD) ..... HCTDS
High-Carbon Ferrochrome [*Metallurgy*] ..... HCF
High-Carbon Steel ..... HCS
High-Carbon Steel, Heat-Treated ..... HCSHT
High-Chromium White Iron ..... HCWI
High-Compression Swirl [*Automotive engineering*] ..... HCS
High-Conversion Critical Experiment (IEEE) ..... HI-C
High-Conversion Critical Experiment [*Nuclear energy*] (GFGA) ..... HI-CC
High-Current Density ..... HCD
High-Current Diode ..... HCD
High-Current Inductor ..... HCI
High-Cycle Fatigue [*Rocket engine*] ..... HCF
High-Data Rate Recorder ..... HDRR
High-Data Rate Switch (MCD) ..... HDRS
High-Data-Rate Assembly (MCD) ..... HDRA
High-Data-Rate Digital Subscriber Line [*Telecommunications*] (DOM) ..... HDSL
High-Data-Rate LASER (MCD) ..... HDRL
High-Data-Rate Multiplexer (MCD) ..... HDRM
High-Data-Rate Storage System [*or Subsystem*] [*NASA*] (MCD) ..... HDRSS
High-Definition Television [*Offers wider-screen pictures with high resolution that improves their depth, clarity, and detail*] ..... HDTV
High-Definition Video ..... HDV
High-Degree Helioseismometer ..... HOH
High-Density Acid ..... HDA
High-Density Air Navigation ..... HIDAN
High-Density Air Traffic Zone ..... HDATZ
High-Density Airspace Control Zone (MCD) ..... HIDACZ
High-Density Amorph [*Materials science*] ..... HDA
High-Density Binary (TEL) ..... HDB
High-Density Binary Three Level Signal (TEL) HDB3
High-Density Bipolar Code [*Telecommunications*] (TEL) ..... HDB
High-Density Bipolar-3 (IDOE) HDB-3
High-Density Data (KSC) ..... HDD
High-Density Data System [*Computer science*] ..... HDDS
High-Density Digital Recording ..... HDDR
High-Density Digital Tape ..... HDDT
High-Density Electronic Packaging ..... HDEP
High-Density Flexible ..... HDF
High-Density Helicopter Landing [*Army*] ..... HDHL
High-Density/High-Voltage Power Supply (DNAB) ..... HDHVPS
High-Density Interconnect ..... HDI
High-Density Lipoprotein [*Biochemistry*] ..... HDL
High-Density Lipoprotein [*Biochemistry*] (AAMN) ..... HDLP
High-Density Lipoprotein - Cell Surface Receptor [*Biochemistry*] ..... HDL-C
High-Density Lipoprotein Cholesterol [*Physiology*] ..... HDLC
High-Density/Low-Density Tariff ..... HiD/LoD
High-Density Mach Shock Wave ..... HDMSW
High-Density Memory System ..... HDMS
High-Density Microsome [*Cytology*] ..... HDM
High-Density MODEM System [*Microcom*] [*Norwood, MA*] [*Computer science*] ..... HDMS
High-Density Moderated Reactor (IEEE) ..... HDMR
High-Density Multichip Interconnect [*Semiconductor packaging*] ..... HDMI
High-Density Multi-Track ..... HDMT
High-Density Multitrack Recording (MCD) ..... HDMR
High-Density Nebulizer [*Medicine*] (MAE) ..... HDN
High-Density Nuclear Shock Wave ..... HDNSW
High-Density Plasma (SAA) ..... HDP
High-Density Polyethylene [*Plastics*] ..... HDPE
High-Density Power Supply ..... HDPS
High-Density Recorder [*Deep Space Instrumentation Facility, NASA*] ..... HDR
High-Density Shock Tube (IEEE) ..... HDST
High-Density Traffic Airport ..... HDTA
High-Discharge Pressure (IEEE) ..... HDP
High-Dollar Value ..... HDV
High-Dosage Depth [*Medicine*] (DMAA) ..... HDD
High-Dose Cyclophosphamide and Adriamycin [*Antineoplastic drug regimen*] (DAVI) ..... HDCCAMS
High-Dose Epinephrine [*Medicine*] ..... HDE
High-Dose Group [*Medicine*] (DMAA) ..... HDG
High-Dose Immunological Paralysis [*Medicine*] ..... HDIP
High-Dose Intravenous Methylprednisolone [*Medicine*] (DMAA) ..... HIMP
High-Dose Methotrexate, Leucovorin [*Antineoplastic drug regimen*] ..... HDMTX-LV
High-Dose Methotrexate-Citrovorum Factor [*Antineoplastic drug regimen*] ..... HDMTX-CF
High-Dose Urea in Invert Sugar (AAMN) ..... HUIS
High-Drag General-Purpose [*Navy*] (DNAB) ..... HDGP
High-Efficiency Antireflection [*Optics*] ..... HEA
High-Efficiency Particle Accumulator (NASA) ..... HEPA
High-Efficiency Particle Air Filter ..... HEPAF
High-Efficiency Particulate Air [*Filter*] ..... HEPA
High-Efficiency Radiator [*General Motors Corp.*] [*Automotive engineering*] ..... HER
High-Efficiency Solar Panel ..... HESP
High-Efficiency Transfer Solution [*CINNA/BIOTECX International, Inc.*] [*Analytical biochemistry*] ..... HETS
High-Endurance Coast Guard Cutter [*Later, WHEC*] (CINC) ..... WAPG
High-Endurance Coast Guard Cutter [*Formerly, WAPG*] (CINC) ..... WHEC
High-Energy Accelerator and Reactor for Thermonuclear Fusion with Ion Beams of Relativistic Energies ..... HEARTHFIRE
High-Energy Aim Point [*Weaponry*] (MCD) ..... HEAP
High-Energy Astronomy Observatory [*Pronounced "hee-oh"*] [*NASA*] ..... HEAO

High-Energy Astrophysics (NASA) ... HE
High-Energy Battery System ... HEBS
High-Energy Beam Transport [*For protons*] ... HEBT
High-Energy Benthic Boundary Layer Experiment [*Oceanography*] ... HEBBLE
High-Energy Chemistry ... HEC
High-Energy Cosmic Ray Experiment [*Balloon flight*] [*NASA*] ... HECRE
High-Energy Detector [*NASA*] ... HED
High-Energy Electrolyte Battery ... HEEB
High-Energy Electron Diffraction ... HEED
High-Energy Electronically Excited LASER ... HEEEL
High-Energy Firing Unit [*Army*] (AABC) ... HEFU
High-Energy Fuel [*Air Force*] ... HEF
High-Energy Gamma Ray ... HEGR
High-Energy Gas Fracturing [*For freeing natural gas from rock*] ... HEGF
High-Energy Ignition (KSC) ... HEI
High-Energy Impulse Pumpable Propellant (MCD) ... HIPP
High-Energy Intermediate [*Medicine*] (DAVI) ... HEI
High-Energy Ion Scattering Spectroscopy ... HEIS
High-Energy Ionizing Radiation [*Radiation therapy*] (DAVI) ... HEIR
High-Energy Isotope Experiment (SSD) ... HEIE
High-Energy Isotope Spectrometer Telescope (MCD) ... HEIST
High-Energy LASER ... HEL
High-Energy LASER Assessment Board (MCD) ... HELAB
High-Energy LASER Beam ... HELB
High-Energy LASER Component Servicing (MCD) ... HELCOS
High-Energy LASER Countermeasures (MCD) ... HELCM
High-Energy LASER Fire Control ... HFC
High-Energy LASER RADAR Acquisition and Tracking System (MCD) ... HELRATS
High-Energy LASER Review Group [*Terminated, 1977*] [*DoD*] ... HELRG
High-Energy LASER System ... HELS
High-Energy LASER System Test Facility (MCD) ... HELSTF
High-Energy LASER System Test Facility [*Army*] (DOMA) ... HELSTF
High-Energy LASER Tactical Air Defense System ... HELTADS
High-Energy LASER Technology Applications Study (MCD) ... HELTAS
High-Energy LASER Weapon System (MCD) ... HELWS
High-Energy Lightweight Propellant ... HELP
High-Energy Line Break [*Nuclear energy*] (NRCH) ... HELB
High-Energy Liquid Oxidizer ... HELO
High-Energy Microwave Laboratory [*Kirtland AFB*] [*Air Force*] (DOMA) ... HEML
High-Energy Neutron Reactions Experiment [*Nuclear energy*] ... HENRE
High-Energy Orbit [*NASA*] (NASA) ... HEO
High-Energy Organic Battery ... HEOB
High-Energy Organic Electrolyte Battery System ... HEOEBS
High-Energy Particle ... HEP
High-Energy Particle Physics Group [*Florida State University*] [*Research center*] (RCD) ... HEPP
High-Energy Particle Spectrometer (MCD) ... HEPS
High-Energy Phosphate [*Biochemistry*] ... HEP
High-Energy Physics ... HEP
High-Energy Physics Advisory Panel [*Department of Energy Washington, DC*] (EGAO) ... HEPAP
High-Energy Physics Laboratory [*Stanford University*] (MCD) ... HEPL
High-Energy Pipe Break [*Nuclear energy*] (NRCH) ... HEPB
High-Energy Propellant Safety (MCD) ... HEPS
High-Energy Proton and Alpha Detector ... HEPAD
High-Energy Proton Detection Experiment ... HEPDEX
High-Energy Pulse ... HEP
High-Energy Radiation Camera Using Light-Emitting Showers ... HERCULES
High-Energy Radiation Test Facility [*Military*] ... HERTF
High-Energy Radiation to Ordnance [*Army*] ... HERO
High-Energy Radiation to Personnel ... HERP
High-Energy Rate Forging [*Metalworking*] ... HERF
High-Energy Rate Forming ... HERF
High-Energy Ray ... HER
High-Energy Real-Time Inspections System (PDAA) ... HERTIS
High-Energy Recovery Pressure and Enthalpy Sensor (IAA) ... HERPES
High-Energy Rotor [*Helicopter*] [*Army*] ... HER
High-Energy Solid Oxidizer ... HESO
High-Energy Squib Simulator [*NASA*] (NASA) ... HESS
High-Energy Squib Simulators [*NASA*] (KSC) ... HESSES
High-Energy Symmetric Fission ... HESF
High-Energy Telescope [*Geophysics*] ... HET
High-Energy Telescope System [*Geophysics*] ... HETS
High-Energy Transfer Stage ... HETS
High-Energy Upper Stage [*NASA*] ... HEUS
High-Energy-Pulse LASER (PDAA) ... HEPL
High-Energy-Range Spectrometer [*Instrumentation*] ... HERS
High-Enthalpy Ablation Test ... HEAT
Higher ... HGHR
Higher (ROG) ... HR
Higher Anti-Submarine Detector [*British military*] (DMA) ... HSD
Higher Authority ... HA
Higher Award in Radiodiagnosis or Radiotherapy, College of Radiographers [*British*] (DBQ) ... HDCR(R) or (T)
Higher Certificate [*Academic degree*] (AIE) ... HC
Higher Clerical Officer [*Civil Service*] [*British*] ... HCO
Higher Dental Diploma [*British*] ... HDD
Higher Diploma in Education [*British*] ... H Dip E
Higher Diploma in Education [*Academic degree*] (AIE) ... HDipEd
Higher Diploma of Teaching ... HDipT
Higher Duties Allowance (ADA) ... HDA
Higher Education [*Educational Resources Information Center (ERIC) Clearinghouse*] [*George Washington University*] (PAZ) ... HE
Higher Education (ECON) ... HEC
Higher Education Accommodation Consortium [*British*] (DBA) ... HEAC
Higher Education Act [*1965*] ... HEA
Higher Education Act Amendment [*1992*] ... HEAA
Higher Education Action Research Team (AIE) ... HEART
Higher Education Administration Referral Service [*Defunct*] (EA) ... HEARS
Higher Education and the Handicapped [*An association*] (EA) ... HEATH
Higher Education Assistance Foundation ... HEAF
Higher Education Authority [*Ireland*] (AIE) ... HEA
Higher Education Authority (ACII) ... HEA
Higher Education Authority Network [*Irish*] [*Computer science*] (TNIG) ... HEANET
Higher Education Awards (ACII) ... HEA
Higher Education Business Enterprises Ltd. (AIE) ... HEBE
Higher Education Careers Service Unit (AIE) ... HECSU
Higher Education Consortium for Urban Affairs (EA) ... HECUA
Higher Education Consortium on Special Education (EDAC) ... HECSE
Higher Education Coordinating Council of Metropolitan St. Louis [*Library network*] ... HECC
Higher Education Data Base [*Information service or system*] (IID) ... HEIDI
Higher Education Data Sharing (EDAC) ... HEDS
Higher Education External Relations Association (AIE) ... HEERA
Higher Education Facilities Act of 1963 ... HEFA
Higher Education Facilities Commission ... HEFC
Higher Education Funding Act [*Australia*] ... HEFA
Higher Education Funding Council (AIE) ... HEFC
Higher Education Funding Council for England ... HEFCE
Higher Education General Information Survey [*Office of Education*] ... HEGIS
Higher Education Information Service (AIE) ... HEIS
Higher Education Institute [*Australia*] ... HEI
Higher Education Institution ... HEI
Higher Education Instructional Television [*West Virginia*] (EDAC) ... HEITV
Higher Education Learning Laboratory (EA) ... HELL
Higher Education Learning Programmes Information Service [*British Universities Film & Video Council*] [*Database*] ... HELPIS
Higher Education Learning Programmes Information Service (AIE) ... HELPIS
Higher Education Ministries Team/United Ministries in Higher Education (EA) ... HEMT/UMHE
Higher Education Opportunities Committee (EA) ... HEOC
Higher Education Panel (EA) ... HEP
Higher Education Policy and Administration Library and Information Service ... HEPALIS
Higher Education Price Index (EDAC) ... HEPI
Higher Education Research Institute [*University of California, Los Angeles*] [*Research center*] ... HERI
Higher Education Resource Services (EA) ... HERS
Higher Education Student Data Collection [*Australia*] ... HESDC
Higher Education Students Early Statistics (AIE) ... HESES
Higher Education Teachers of English (AIE) ... HETE
Higher Educational Test [*British military*] (DMA) ... HET
Higher Elementary School (ADA) ... HES
Higher Elongation (MCD) ... HE
Higher Equal Opportunity Program [*Education*] ... HEOP
Higher Executive Officer [*Civil service*] [*British*] ... HEO
Higher Executive Officer (Administration) [*Civil service*] [*British*] ... HEO(A)
Higher Executive Order ... HEO
Higher Fire Control [*British military*] (DMA) ... HFC
Higher Grade ... HG
Higher Harmonic Circulation Control [*Rotor*] [*Navy*] ... HHCC
Higher Harmonic Control (MCD) ... HHC
Higher High Water [*Tides and currents*] ... HHW
Higher High-Water Interval ... HHWI
Higher Integrative Functions [*Neurology*] ... HIF
Higher Introductory Technology and Engineering Conversion Courses [*Education*] [*British*] ... HITECC
Higher Layer Protocol Identifier [*Telecommunications*] (ACRL) ... HLPI
Higher Layers and Internetworking [*Computer science*] (ACRL) ... HILI
Higher Low Water ... HLW
Higher Low-Water Interval ... HLWI
Higher Military Command, Interior and Islands (MCD) ... HMCII
Higher National Certificate [*British*] ... HNC
Higher National Certificate/Diploma (ACII) ... HNC/D
Higher National Diploma [*British*] ... HND
Higher Order Language Development and Evaluation Tool [*Computer science*] (MHDB) ... HOLDET
Higher Order Laue Zone [*Crystal diffraction lines*] ... HOLZ
Higher Order Logic [*Computer science*] ... HOL
Higher Order Software, Inc. ... HOS
Higher Order Thinking Skills [*Education*] ... HOTS
Higher Rate ... HR
Higher School Certificate [*British*] ... HSC
Higher School Certificate Examination (ADA) ... HSCE
Higher Scientific Officer [*British*] ... HSO
Higher Telegraphist Detector [*British military*] (DMA) ... HTD
Higher Torque/Low-Speed (DNAB) ... HTLS
Higher Worth Control Rod [*Nuclear energy*] (NUCP) ... HWCR
Higher-Order Language Machine [*Computer science*] (KSC) ... HOLM
Highest [*Standard & Poor's bond rating*] ... AAA
Highest [*Price Quoted of a Stock*] [*Finance*] (BARN) ... H
Highest Astronomical Tide ... HAT
Highest Astronomical Tide of the Foreseeable Future (PDAA) ... HATOFF
Highest Astronomical Tide of the Month (PDAA) ... HATOM
Highest Astronomical Tide of the Year (PDAA) ... HATOY
Highest Asymptomatic [*Dose*] [*Medicine*] ... HAS
Highest Average Salary ... HAS
Highest Common Denominator ... HCD
Highest Common Factor [*Mathematics*] ... HCF

Highest Electroendosmosis [*Analytical biochemistry*] ... HE
Highest Equivalent Heart Rate [*Cardiology*] (DAVI) ... HEHR
Highest Hull [*Symbol*] [*American Bureau of Shipping*] (DS) ... A1
Highest In, First Out [*Accounting*] ... HIFO
Highest Low-Water Neap Tide (WDAA) ... HLWN
Highest Non-Toxic Dose (OA) ... HNTD
Highest Occupied Molecular Orbital [*Atomic physics*] ... HOMO
Highest Points Scored (ROG) ... HPS
Highest Possible (ROG) ... HP
Highest Possible [*or Probable*] **Frequency** [*Electronics*] ... HPF
Highest Possible Frequency (WDMC) ... hpf
Highest Score (ADA) ... HS
Highest Temperature [*NWS*] (FAAC) ... HITMP
Highest Temperature Equaled for All Time [*NWS*] (FAAC) ... HIEAT
Highest Temperature Equaled for the Month [*NWS*] (FAAC) ... HIEFM
Highest Temperature Equaled so Early [*NWS*] (FAAC) ... HIESE
Highest Temperature Equaled so Late [*NWS*] (FAAC) ... HIESL
Highest Temperature Exceeded for All Time [*NWS*] (FAAC) ... HIXAT
Highest Temperature Exceeded for the Month [*NWS*] (FAAC) ... HIXFM
Highest Temperature Exceeded so Early [*NWS*] (FAAC) ... HIXSE
Highest Temperature Exceeded so Late [*NWS*] (FAAC) ... HIXSL
Highest Useful Compression Ratio [*Aerospace*] ... HUCR
High-Expansion Foam ... HEF
High-Explosive, Antiaircraft [*Weaponry*] ... HEAA
High-Explosive, Antiarmor [*Weaponry*] (MCD) ... HEAA
High-Explosive Antiarmor Grenade [*Weaponry*] (MCD) ... HAG
High-Explosive, Antipersonnel [*Weaponry*] ... HEAP
High-Explosive, Antitank [*Weaponry*] ... HEAT
High-Explosive Anti-Tank Fin-Stabilized [*Military*] (PDAA) ... HEAFS
High-Explosive Antitank, Multipurpose [*Weaponry*] (MCD) ... HEAT-MP
High-Explosive Antitank, Multipurpose, Tracer [*Weaponry*] (MCD) ... HEAT-MP-T
High-Explosive Antitank, Target Practice, Tracer [*Weaponry*] (MCD) ... HEAT-TP-T
High-Explosive Antitank, Training Projectile [*Weaponry*] (MCD) ... HEAT-TP
High-Explosive Antitank-Tracer [*Weaponry*] (AABC) ... HEAT-T
High-Explosive Armor-Piercing [*Weaponry*] ... HEAP
High-Explosive Delay [*Weaponry*] (MCD) ... HED
High-Explosive, Discarding Sabot [*Weaponry*] (AAG) ... HEDS
High-Explosive Dual-Purpose [*Cartridge*] (RDA) ... HEDP
High-Explosive, Fragmentation [*Artillery*] (INF) ... HEFRAG
High-Explosive, Incendiary [*Weaponry*] ... HEI
High-Explosive, Incendiary Plug [*Weaponry*] (NATG) ... HEIP
High-Explosive, Incendiary Self-Destroying [*Weaponry*] (NATG) ... HEISD
High-Explosive, Incendiary [*Shell*] **Traced** [*i.e., fitted with tracer*] [*Weaponry*] ... HEIT
High-Explosive, Incendiary Tracer, Dark Ignition, Self-Destroying [*Weaponry*] (NATG) ... HEITDISD
High-Explosive, Incendiary Tracer, Self-Destroying [*Weaponry*] (NATG) ... HEITSD
High-Explosive Plastic [*Weaponry*] ... HEP
High-Explosive Plastic Antitank [*Weaponry*] (NATG) ... HEPAT
High-Explosive Plastic Tracer [*Weaponry*] (AABC) ... HEP-T
High-Explosive Plugged [*Weaponry*] ... HEP
High-Explosive - Point Detonating [*Weaponry*] (MCD) ... HE-PD
High-Explosive, Point Detonating Nose Plug [*Weaponry*] (NATG) ... HEPDNP
High-Explosive Proximity Fuse [*Weaponry*] (MCD) ... HE-PX
High-Explosive Ramjet [*Weaponry*] ... HERJ
High-Explosive Rocket Assisted [*Weaponry*] ... HERA
High-Explosive, Self-Destroying [*Weaponry*] (NATG) ... HESD
High-Explosive Spotting [*Weaponry*] ... HES
High-Explosive, Squash Head [*Weaponry*] (NATG) ... HESH
High-Explosive [*Shell*] **Traced** [*i.e., fitted with tracer*] [*Weaponry*] ... HET
High-Explosive, Tracer, Dark Ignition [*Weaponry*] (NATG) ... HETDI
High-Explosive Warhead [*Weaponry*] ... HEWH
High-Explosives Research and Development (MCD) ... HERD
High-Fiber Diet (DMAA) ... HFD
High-Fidelity [*Usually, in reference to home sound-reproducing equipment*] ... HI-FI
High-Fidelity [*Printing*] (WDMC) ... hi-fi
High-Fidelity Amplitude Modulation (DEN) ... HIFAM
High-Fidelity Mock-Up [*NASA*] (NASA) ... HFMU
High-Field Ignition Test Reactor [*Nuclear energy*] (MCD) ... HFITR
High-Field Magnetometer [*Instrumentation*] ... HFM
Highfield Property Investments Ltd. [*Toronto Stock Exchange symbol*] ... HFP
High-Field, Ultrathin Gel Electrophoresis [*Analytical biochemistry*] ... HUGE
High-Field-Strength Elements [*Geochemistry*] ... HFSE
High-Flux Beam Reactor (GAAI) ... HFBR
High-Flux Scram Trip [*Nuclear energy*] (IEEE) ... HFST
High-Flux Telescope ... HFT
High-Frequency Accelerometer (NASA) ... HFA
High-Frequency Airborne Antenna ... HFAA
High-Frequency Amplifier [*Electronics*] (IAA) ... HFA
High-Frequency Antenna (KSC) ... HFA
High-Frequency Antenna System (KSC) ... HFAS
High-Frequency Antijam (DWSG) ... HFAJ
High-Frequency Backup Program [*Military*] (CAAL) ... HFBUP
High-Frequency Band [*Electricity*] ... Hf-Bd
High-Frequency Choke ... HFC
High-Frequency Communications Replacement System Program (LAIN) ... HFCRSP
High-Frequency Correction ... HFC
High-Frequency Current ... HFC
High-Frequency Current ... HFCUR
High-Frequency Digital MODEM (LAIN) ... HFDM
High-Frequency Direction Finding [*Electronics*] ... HDF
High-Frequency Direction Finding [*Pronounced "huff duff"*] [*Electronics*] ... HFDF
High-Frequency Distribution Frame (IEEE) ... HFDF
High-Frequency Fixed Array RADAR ... HIFAR
High-Frequency Furnace ... HFF
High-Frequency Hearing Loss [*Otorhinolaryngology*] (DAVI) ... HFHL
High-Frequency Improvement Program (LAIN) ... HFIP
High-Frequency Induction Heating (PDAA) ... HFIH
High-Frequency Induction Welding [*Manufacturing term*] ... HFIW
High-Frequency Input (IAA) ... HFI
High-Frequency Instruments and Measurements (IEEE) ... HFIM
High-Frequency Intra-Task Force Communications (LAIN) ... HFIC
High-Frequency Jammer ... HFJ
High-Frequency Jet Ventilation [*Pulmonary ventilation*] ... HFJV
High-Frequency Mode (IAA) ... HFM
High-Frequency of Transduction [*Virology*] ... HFT
High-Frequency Oscillator ... HFO
High-Frequency Oscillatory Ventilation [*Medicine*] (DAVI) ... HFOV
High-Frequency Phase Shifter [*Telecommunications*] ... HFPS
High-Frequency Positive Pressure Ventilation [*Medicine*] ... HFPPV
High-Frequency Radio Direction Finding (IAA) ... HFRDF
High-Frequency Radio Group [*Military*] (CAAL) ... HFRG
High-Frequency Radio Transmitter ... HFRT
High-Frequency Recovery Antenna (KSC) ... HFRA
High-Frequency Repeater Distribution Frame (DEN) ... HFRDF
High-Frequency Resistance (IDOE) ... R_{HF}
High-Frequency Resistance Welding [*Manufacturing term*] ... HFRW
High-Frequency Resistor ... HFR
High-Frequency Single Sideband [*Telecommunications*] ... HFSSB
High-Frequency Sounder System (SSD) ... HFSS
High-Frequency Stimulation [*Physiology*] ... HFS
High-Frequency Swept Spectrum Communications ... HFSSC
High-Frequency Transceiver [*or Transducer*] ... HFX
High-Frequency Transfer (DMAA) ... HFT
High-Frequency Ventilation [*Medicine*] ... HFV
High-Frequency Wave Analyzer ... HFWA
High-Fructose Corn Sweetener [*or Syrup*] ... HFCS
High-Gain Emissive Display [*Technology*] ... HGED
High-Grade Plow Steel ... HGPS
High-Grade Squamous Intraepithelial Lesions [*OCLC symbol*] ... HSIL
Highgrade Ventures [*Vancouver Stock Exchange symbol*] ... HGV
High-Gradient Magnetic Filtration ... HGMF
High-Gradient Magnetic Separator (NRCH) ... HGMS
High-Grain/Low-Fiber [*Cereal*] (OA) ... HGLF
Highhams Railway [*Wales*] ... HR
High-Head Safety Injection [*Nuclear energy*] (NRCH) ... HHSI
High-Heat Waste (NRCH) ... HHW
High-Humidity Face Mask [*Medicine*] (MEDA) ... HHFM
High-Ignition-Temperature Propellant ... HITP
High-Ignition-Temperature Propellants Self-Extinguishing at Atmospheric Pressure [*Cartridge*] (RDA) ... HITP-SEAP
High-Impact Design (NRCH) ... HID
High-Impact Polystyrene [*Plastics technology*] ... HIPS
High-Impact Pressure ... HIP
High-Impedance Bridge ... HIB
High-Impedance Follower ... HIF
High-Impulse Booster Experiments [*DARPA/Army*] ... HIBEX
High-Impulse Gun Airborne Demonstrator (MCD) ... HIGAD
High-Impulse Retrorocket System ... HIRS
High-Incidence Research Model (MCD) ... HIRM
High-Income Advantage Trust III [*NYSE symbol*] (SPSG) ... YLH
High-Integrating Gyroscope (KSC) ... HIG
High-Integrity Containers (GAAI) ... HIC
High-Intensity Approach Lighting System [*Airport runways*] ... HIALS
High-Intensity Conflict [*Military*] ... HIC
High-Intensity Discharge [*Vapor lamp*] ... HID
High-Intensity Discharge ... HID
High-Intensity Food Irradiator ... HIFI
High-Intensity Language Training (AEBS) ... HILT
High-Intensity Learning Systems ... HILS
High-Intensity Light ... HIL
High-Intensity, Long-Duration, Continuous Aurora Event, Activity [*Astrophysics*] ... HILDCAA
High-Intensity Microphone ... HIM
High-Intensity Noise ... HIN
High-Intensity Noise Generator ... HING
High-Intensity Radiated Field [*Aviation*] ... HIRF
High-Intensity Radiation Development Laboratory [*Brookhaven National Laboratory*] [*Department of Energy*] ... HIRDL
High-Intensity Radiation Device ... HIRD
High-Intensity Reciprocity Failure ... HIRF
High-Intensity Runway Lights [*Aviation*] ... HIRL
High-Intensity Sound Simulator ... HISS
High-Intensity Sound System ... HISS
High-Intensity Spectrometer ... HIS
High-Intent Priority [*In the record business, a heavily promoted disk*] ... HIP
High-Interest Books for Teens [*A publication*] ... HIBT
High-Interest Shipping (MCD) ... HIS
High-Interest Tracker (MCD) ... HIT
High-Intermediate Level Cell [*Nuclear energy*] (NRCH) ... HILC
High-Iron Diamine ... HID
High-Iron Diamine-Alcian Blue [*A biological stain*] ... HID-AB
High-Isolation Transformer (IEEE) ... HIT
Highland ... HGLND
Highland Community Unit, School District 5, Highland, IL [*Library symbol Library of Congress*] (LCLS) ... IHigSD
Highland County District Library, Hillsboro, OH [*Library symbol Library of Congress*] (LCLS) ... OHilH

Highland Crow Resources Ltd. [*Toronto Stock Exchange symbol Vancouver Stock Exchange symbol*] ... HHC
Highland Cyclist Battalion [*British military*] (DMA) ... HCB
Highland Cyclists [*British military*] (DMA) ... HC
Highland Division [*British military*] (DMA) ... HD
Highland Elementary School, Crookston, MN [*Library symbol*] [*Library of Congress*] (LCLS) ... MnCrHE
Highland Express [*British ICAO designator*] (FAAC) ... TTN
Highland Federal Bank [*NASDAQ symbol*] (SAG) ... HBNK
Highland Federal Bank [*Associated Press*] (SAG) ... Hghland
Highland Free Library, Highland, NY [*Library symbol Library of Congress*] (LCLS) ... NHig
Highland Heights, KY [*FM radio station call letters*] ... WNKU
Highland Hospital, Medical Library, Asheville, NC [*Library symbol Library of Congress*] (LCLS) ... NcAHH
Highland Hospital, Portland, TN [*Library symbol Library of Congress*] (LCLS) ... TPorH
Highland Hospital, Williams Health Science Library, Rochester, NY [*OCLC symbol*] (OCLC) ... VQP
Highland, IL [*AM radio station call letters*] ... WINU
Highland Junior College [*Kansas*] ... HJC
Highland Light Infantry [*Military British*] (ROG) ... HIGH LI
Highland Light Infantry [*Military unit*] [*British*] ... HLI
Highland Light Infantry of Canada [*Military unit*] ... HLIC
Highland, NY [*FM radio station call letters*] ... WRWD
Highland Park, IL [*AM radio station call letters*] ... WEEF
Highland Park, IL [*FM radio station call letters*] ... WVVX
Highland Park Junior College [*Later, Highland Park College*] [*Michigan*] ... HPJC
Highland Park, MI [*FM radio station call letters*] ... WHPR
Highland Park News, Des Moines, IA [*Library symbol Library of Congress*] (LCLS) ... IaDmHN
Highland Park Public Library, Highland Park, IL [*Library symbol Library of Congress*] (LCLS) ... IHigp
Highland Park Public Library, Highland Park, IL [*OCLC symbol*] (OCLC) ... IHV
Highland Park, TX [*AM radio station call letters*] ... KDMM
Highland Park, TX [*FM radio station call letters*] ... KVIL-FM
Highland Queen Mines Ltd. [*Vancouver Stock Exchange symbol*] ... HQM
Highland Railway [*British*] (ROG) ... HIGH
Highland Railway [*Scotland*] ... HR
Highland Ranch [*Colorado*] [*Seismograph station code, US Geological Survey Closed*] (SEIS) ... HLR
Highland Regiment [*British military*] (DMA) ... HR
Highland Regional Council [*Scotland*] ... HRC
Highland Rim Regional Library Center, Murfreesboro, TN [*Library symbol Library of Congress*] (LCLS) ... TMurH
Highland Secondary School, Dundas, ON, Canada [*Library symbol Library of Congress*] (LCLS) ... CaODH
Highland Secondary School, Dundas, Ontario [*Library symbol National Library of Canada*] (NLC) ... ODH
Highland Springs, VA [*AM radio station call letters*] ... WCLM
Highland Springs, VA [*FM radio station call letters*] ... WHCE
Highland Valley Resources Ltd. [*Vancouver Stock Exchange symbol*] ... HVR
Highland, WI [*FM radio station call letters*] ... WHHI
Highlander Class International Association (EA) ... HCIA
Highlander Income Fund [*AMEX symbol*] (TTSB) ... HLA
Highlander Income Fund, Inc. [*Associated Press*] (SAG) ... HighldInc
Highlander Income Fund, Inc. [*AMEX symbol*] (SAG) ... HLA
Highlanders [*British*] ... HIGHRS
Highlands (DD) ... Hghlds
Highlands (MCD) ... HGLDS
Highlands [*Board on Geographic Names*] ... HLND
Highlands and Islands Development Board [*Scotland*] (ECON) ... HIDB
Highlands Insurance Group [*NYSE symbol*] (TTSB) ... HIC
Highlands, NC [*FM radio station call letters*] (RBYB) ... WHLC-FM
High-Latitude Mode ... HLM
High-Latitude Operation ... HLO
High-Latitude Research Satellite [*Defense Nuclear Agency*] ... HILAT
High-Level Air Defence [*Military British*] ... HLAD
High-Level Analog (MCD) ... HLA
High-Level Analog Input Subsystem [*Computer science*] (MHDI) ... HLAIS
High-Level Application Program Interface [*Computer science*] (PCM) ... HLLAPI
High-Level Arithmetic Function ... HLAF
High-Level Assembly Language (MCD) ... HLAL
High-Level Automatic Scheduling Program (BUR) ... HASP
High-Level Cell [*Nuclear energy*] (NRCH) ... HLC
High-Level Center (IAA) ... HLC
High-Level Compaction Station [*Nuclear energy*] (NRCH) ... HLCS
High-Level Compiler (IAA) ... HLC
High-Level Container Airdrop System [*Army*] (RDA) ... HLCADS
High-Level Control Station [*Hazardous materials control*] ... HLCS
High-Level Data Link Control [*International Standards Organization*] [*Data communication*] ... HDLC
High-Level Data Link Control (MCD) ... HLDC
High-Level Data Link Control [*Computer science*] (DOM) ... HLDLC
High-Level Data Link Control Adapter [*Data communication*] (MHDI) ... HDLA
High-Level Data Linkage Module [*Data communication*] (MHDB) ... HDLM
High-Level Diode Transistor Logic [*Computer science*] (MHDI) ... HLDTL
High-Level Flux Monitor ... HLFM
High-Level Forecast [*Meteorology*] ... HIFOR
High-Level Group [*NATO*] ... HLG
High-Level Heating [*Nuclear science*] (OA) ... HLH
High-Level Input Voltage ... HLIV
High-Level Interprocessor Transfer (DGA) ... HIT
High-Level Language [*Computer science*] ... HLL
High-Level Liquid Waste [*Nuclear energy*] ... HLLW

High-Level Liquid Waste Off-Gas [*Nuclear energy*] (NRCH) ... HLWOG
High-Level Liquid Waste Tank [*Nuclear energy*] (NRCH) ... HLLWT
High-Level Logic (IAA) ... HLL
High-Level Meeting (DCTA) ... HLM
High-Level Microprogramming Language ... HLML
High-Level Mixer ... HLM
High-Level Network Processing Language [*Computer science*] (MHDI) ... HNPL
High-Level Neutron Coincidence Counter [*Nuclear energy*] (NRCH) ... HLNCC
High-Level Nuclear Waste (BARN) ... HLNW
High-Level Output Voltage ... HLOV
High-Level Override [*Nuclear energy*] (NRCH) ... HLO
High-Level Programming Interface ... HLPI
High-Level Query Language ... HLQL
High-Level Question (DMAA) ... HLQ
High-Level Radio Modulator ... HLRM
High-Level Radioactive Waste (GNE) ... HLRW
High-Level Representation ... HLR
High-Level Service [*Computer science*] ... HLS
High-Level, Single-Ended ... HLSE
High-Level Solidified Waste [*Nuclear energy*] (NRCH) ... HLSW
High-Level Tactical ... HLT
High-Level Task Force (DOMA) ... HLTF
High-Level Terminal (CAAL) ... HLT
High-Level Test Language ... HLTL
High-Level Transistor Logic ... HLTL
High-Level Transistor Translator Logic ... HLTTL
High-Level Waste [*Nuclear energy*] ... HLW
High-Level Waste Calcination [*Nuclear energy*] (NRCH) ... HLWC
High-Level Waste Concentrate [*Nuclear energy*] (NRCH) ... HLWC
High-Level Waste Concentrator Distillate [*Nuclear energy*] (NRCH) ... HLWD
High-Level Waste Concentrator Feed [*Nuclear energy*] (NRCH) ... HLWF
High-Level Waste Surge [*Nuclear energy*] (NRCH) ... HLWS
Highlight (DGA) ... H/L
Highlights of Personal Experience in Agriculture Department ... HOPE
Highline (MSA) ... HL
High-Line Airways, Inc. [*Canada ICAO designator*] (FAAC) ... HLB
Highline Community College, Midway, WA [*Library symbol Library of Congress*] (LCLS) ... WaMiH
Highline Community Hospital Library, Seattle, WA [*Library symbol*] [*Library of Congress*] (LCLS) ... WaSHCH
High-Load Melt Index [*Plastics*] [*Automotive engineering*] ... HLMI
High-Low-Junction Emitter (PDAA) ... HLE
Highly Active Antiretroviral Therapy [*Medicine*] ... HAART
Highly Active Liquid [*Nuclear energy*] (NUCP) ... HAL
Highly Active Residues Vitrification and Engineered Storage [*Nuclear energy British*] (NUCP) ... HARVEST
Highly Active Residues Vitrification Engineering Studies [*Nuclear energy British*] (NUCP) ... HARVEST
Highly Active Waste ... HAW
Highly Advanced Laboratory for Communications and Astronomy [*Japanese satellite*] ... HALCA
Highly Aphid Transmissible [*Plant pathology*] ... HAT
Highly Automated Logic [*Computer science*] ... HAL
Highly Compensated Employee [*Human resources*] (WYGK) ... HCE
Highly Desirable (KSC) ... HD
Highly Eccentric Lunar Occultation Satellite ... HELOS
Highly Eccentric [*or Elliptical*] Orbit Satellite ... HEOS
Highly Enriched Reactor, Aldermaston [*British*] (DEN) ... HERALD
Highly Enriched Uranium [*Nuclear reactor technology*] ... HEU
Highly Enriched Waste Concentrate (PDAA) ... HEWC
Highly Extendable Language Processor [*Computer science*] ... HELP
Highly Extendable Language Processor (NITA) ... HELP
Highly Filled Materials Institute [*Stevens Institute of Technology*] ... HFMI
Highly Indebted Country ... HIC
Highly Instrumented Orbiting Primate Experiment ... HOPE
Highly Integrated Digital Engine Control (MCD) ... HIDEC
Highly Ionized Cloud [*Galactic science*] ... HIC
Highly Ionized Plasma ... HIP
Highly Leveraged Transaction [*Banking*] ... HLT
Highly Luminous QUASAR [*Astronomy*] ... HLQ
Highly Maneuverable Aircraft Technology Testbed [*Rockwell International Corp.*] (MCD) ... HIMAT
Highly Oriented Pyrolytic Graphite [*Engineering*] ... HOPG
Highly Polarized Quasar [*Galactic science*] ... HPQ
Highly Probably Drink [*Chemical depedency*] (DAVI) ... HPD
Highly Protected Risk [*Insurance*] ... HPR
Highly Purified ... HP
Highly Qualified (AFM) ... HQ
Highly Secure Database Management System [*Computer science*] (MHDI) ... HSDMS
Highly Selective Vagotomy [*Medicine*] ... HSV
Highly Sensitive Refractive Index ... HSRI
Highly Sensitive Ship Synthesis Model (DNAB) ... HSSSM
Highly Sensitive System (MCD) ... HS
Highly Siderophile Element [*Biology*] ... HSE
Highly Unusual Geophysical Operation [*A meteorological research vehicle*] ... HUGO
Highly Unusual Methods (ECON) ... HUM
Highly Variable Regions [*Of chromosomes*] [*Genetics*] ... HVR
Highly Variegated Maize ... HV
Highly Volatile Liquid (TAG) ... HVL
Highly-Chlorinated Oil (IAA) ... HCO
Highly-Indebted Middle-Income Country ... HIMIC
Highmark Resources [*Vancouver Stock Exchange symbol*] ... HMK
High-Mass X-Ray Binary [*Star system*] ... HMXB

High-Meaningfulness [*Psychology*] .... HM
High-Melting Explosive [*Proprietary name for cyclotetramethylene tetramintriamine*] .... HMX
High-Methoxy Pectin [*Food technology*] .... HMP
High-Mobility Artillery Rocket System [*Military*] .... HIMARS
High-Mobility Group [*Genetics*] .... HMG
High-Mobility Load Carrier [*British military*] (DMA) .... HMLC
High-Mobility Materiel Handling Equipment [*Army*] .... HMMHE
High-Mobility Multipurpose Wheeled Vehicle [*Nicknamed "hummer"*] [*Army*] (RDA) .... HMMWV
High-Mobility Multipurpose Wheeled Vehicle - Lightweight .... HMMWV-L
High-Mobility Tactical Trucks (MCD) .... HMTT
High-Mobility Weapons Carrier [*Army*] (MCD) .... HIMOWC
High-Mobility Weapons Carrier [*Army*] .... HMWC
High-Mobility Weapons Carrier/Combat Support Vehicle [*Army*] (MCD) .... HMWC/CSV
High-Mobility-Agility [*Test for combat vehicles*] (RDA) .... HIMAG
High-Molecular-Weight Polyethylene (MCD) .... HMWPE
High-Molecular-Weight Protein [*or Polypeptide*] [*Biochemistry*] .... HMWP
Highmore on Bail [*A publication*] (DLA) .... High Bail
Highmore on Lunacy [*A publication*] (DLA) .... High Lun
Highmore on Mortmain [*A publication*] (DLA) .... High Mort
High-Noise-Immunity Logic (MCD) .... HINIL
High-Noise-Immunity Logic .... HNIL
High-Orbital Bombardment System (KSC) .... HOBS
High-Order Algorithmic Language (SSD) .... HAL
High-Order Articulated Language [*Computer science*] (MCD) .... HAL
High-Order Assembly Language [*Computer science*] (NASA) .... HAL
High-Order Assembly Language for Shuttle Flight Computer (MCD) .... HAL/S
High-Order Assembly Language for Spacelab Usage [*NASA*] (NASA) .... HAL/S
High-Order Language Computer (NASA) .... HOLC
High-Order Multiplier (IAA) .... HOM
High-Order Position (AFIT) .... HOP
High-Order Software [*Computer science*] (NASA) .... HOS
High-Order Word (SSD) .... HOW
Highpass Filter (MSA) .... HPFL
High-Passage Virus .... HPV
High-Passage Virus [*Grown in*] Dog Kidney [*Cells*] .... HPV-DK
High-Passage Virus [*Grown in*] Duck Embryo [*Cells*] .... HPV-DE
High-Payoff Target [*Military*] (INF) .... HPT
High-Payoff Target List [*Military*] (INF) .... HPTL
High-Performance Adhesive System .... HPAS
High-Performance Advanced Attack Systems (MCD) .... HIPAAS
High-Performance Aerial Attack System (MCD) .... HPAAS
High-Performance Affinity Chromatography .... HPAC
High-Performance Aircraft Cannon (MCD) .... HIPAC
High-Performance Air-to-Ground .... HPAG
High-Performance Antenna Assembly (MHDI) .... HPAA
High-Performance Archiheater (MCD) .... HIPERARC
High-Performance Attack Aircraft System (MCD) .... HIPAAS
High-Performance Capillary Electrophoresis [*Analytical biochemistry*] .... HPCE
High-Performance Carbon Fiber [*Materials science*] .... HPCF
High-Performance Centrifugal Partition Chromatography .... HPCPC
High-Performance Common Channel Module [*Telecommunications*] .... HCCM
High-Performance Communications Adapter .... HPCA
High-Performance Computer and Research Center [*Department of Energy*] .... HPCRC
High-Performance Computing and Communications [*Computer science*] (EERA) .... HPCC
High-Performance Computing and Communications Program [*Department of Energy*] .... HPCC
High-Performance Control Center [*Aerospace*] (AAG) .... HPCC
High-Performance Demonstration Facility .... HPDF
High-Performance Demonstration Motor (MCD) .... HPDM
High-Performance Drone .... HPD
High-Performance Electrothermal Hydrazine Thruster (MCD) .... HIPEHT
High-Performance Estate Wagon [*Automobile model designation*] .... HPE
High-Performance External Gun .... HIPEG
High-Performance File System [*Computer science*] .... HPFS
High-Performance Forward-Looking Infrared (PDAA) .... HIPERFLIR
High-Performance Fuel Cell .... HPFC
High-Performance Fuels Laboratory .... HPFL
High-Performance Graphics System [*Computer science*] (MHDB) .... HPGS
High-Performance Hoist (MCD) .... HPH
High-Performance Immunoaffinity Chromatography .... HPIC
High-Performance Infiltrating Technique [*Materials science*] .... HPIT
High-Performance Insulation (MCD) .... HPI
High-Performance Insulation System .... HPIS
High-Performance Intercept .... HI-PI
High-Performance Ion Exchange Chromatography .... HPIEC
High-Performance Liquid Affinity Chromatography .... HPLAC
High-Performance [*or High-Pressure*] Liquid Chromatography .... HPLC
High-Performance Liquid Chromatography (USDC) .... HPLC
High-Performance, Low-Observable .... HPLO
High-Performance Low-Pressure Chromatography .... HPLPC
High-Performance Main Storage (IAA) .... HPMS
High-Performance Membrane [*Medicine*] (DMAA) .... HPM
High-Performance Membrane Chromatography .... HPMC
High-Performance Navigation System .... HIPERNAS
High-Performance Option (MCD) .... HPO
High-Performance Parallel Interface [*Computer science*] .... HPPI
High-Performance Plastic .... HPP
High-Performance Precision Approach Control RADAR (MCD) .... HIPAR
High-Performance Preparative Liquid Chromatography .... HPPLC
High-Performance Propulsion Module (MCD) .... HPPM

High-Performance Reporting Post (NATG) .... HPRP
High-Performance Reversed Phase Chromatography .... HPRPC
High-Performance Routing [*Computer science*] (CDE) .... HPR
High-Performance Size Exclusion Chromatography .... HPSEC
High-Performance Space Feed .... HIPSF
High-Performance Stand-Off Motor (MCD) .... HPSOM
High-Performance Thin-Layer Chromatography .... HPTLC
High-Performance Third Stage [*Rocket*] [*Army*] (AABC) .... HPTS
High-Performance Throttleable Injector (KSC) .... HIPERTHINO
High-Performance Train (ADA) .... HPT
High-Performance Turbine Engine [*Air Force*] .... HPTE
High-Performance Zone Electrophoresis .... HPZE
High-pH Anion-Exchange [*Analytical chemistry*] .... HPAE
High-Polymer Molecular [*Film*] .... HPM
High-Polymer Rheology .... HPR
High-Positive (MDG) .... HP
High-Potency [*Pharmacy*] .... HP
High-Potential Employee .... Hipo
High-Potential Iron Protein .... HIP
High-Potential Test (IEEE) .... HIPOTT
High-Potential Test [*or Tester*] .... HPT
High-Power Acquisition RADAR (AAG) .... HIPAR
High-Power Amplifier .... HPA
High-Power Broadband Vehicular Whip Antenna [*Army*] .... HPBVWA
High-Power Density .... HPD
High-Power Diffraction Limited Raman LASER .... HPDLRL
High-Power Effects [*Radio interference*] .... HPE
High-Power Field [*Microscopy*] .... HPF
High-Power Generator .... HPG
High-Power Ground (IAA) .... HPG
High-Power Group .... HPG
High-Power Illuminator (NATG) .... HPI
High-Power Illuminator RADAR [*Army*] (AABC) .... HIPIR
High-Power Illuminator RADAR [*Army*] (AABC) .... HIPIR
High-Power Illuminator Signal Source (MCD) .... HPISS
High-Power Jammer .... HPJ
High-Power Klystron .... HPK
High-Power Klystron Amplifier .... HPKA
High-Power LASER .... HPL
High-Power/Low-Power .... HP/LP
High-Power Microelectronic Noise Jammer .... HPMNJ
High-Power Microwave .... HPM
High-Power Microwave Assembly (AAG) .... HPMA
High-Power Multiplier (DNAB) .... HPM
High-Power Noise Jammer .... HPNJ
High-Power Self-Screening Noise Jammer [*Military*] (CAAL) .... HPSSNJ
High-Power Switching Device .... HPSD
High-Power Transistor-Transistor Logic (IEEE) .... HTTL
High-Power Transmitter Memory (DWSG) .... HPT
High-Power Veractor .... HPV
High-Powered Early Warning (NATG) .... HPEW
High-Powered, Nondirectional Radio Homing Beacon [*Navigation*] .... HH
High-Powered RADAR (NATG) .... HPR
High-Powered RADAR Post (NATG) .... HPRP
High-Powered Radio Range (Adcock) .... RA
High-Powered Transmit Set (DWSG) .... HPTS
High-Powered Vehicle .... HPV
High-Precision Parallax Collecting Satellite [*European Space Agency*] .... Hipparcos
High-Precision SHORAN (AAG) .... HIRAN
High-Precision SHORAN [*Short-Range Navigation*] .... HISRAN
High-Pressure (IDOE) .... h-p
High-Pressure Air .... HPA
High-Pressure Air Accumulator .... HPAA
High-Pressure Air Compressor (NVT) .... HPAC
High-Pressure Chamber .... HPCBR
High-Pressure Compressor (MCD) .... HPC
High-Pressure Constant (DNAB) .... HPC
High-Pressure Coolant Injection [*Nuclear energy*] (NRCH) .... HPCI
High-Pressure Coolant Injection System [*Nuclear energy*] (NRCH) .... HPCIS
High-Pressure Core Spray [*Nuclear energy*] (NRCH) .... HPCS
High-Pressure Cut-Off [*Air conditioning systems*] [*Automotive engineering*].... HPCO
High-Pressure Cylinder [*Especially, a locomotive cylinder*] .... HP
High-Pressure Cylinder (WDAA) .... HP CYL
High-Pressure Demineralized Water (NRCH) .... HDW
High-Pressure Drain (DNAB) .... HPD
High-Pressure Fire Protection (NRCH) .... HPFP
High-Pressure Fuel Pump (KSC) .... HPFP
High-Pressure Fuel Turbopump (MCD) .... HPFT
High-Pressure Fuel Turbopump (NASA) .... HPFTP
High-Pressure Gas (KSC) .... HPG
High-Pressure Gas System (NASA) .... HPGS
High-Pressure Gelatine (IAA) .... HPG
High-Pressure High-Density .... HPHD
High-Pressure Hose .... HPH
High-Pressure Impregnation Carbonization (MCD) .... HIPIC
High-Pressure Injection [*Nuclear energy*] (NRCH) .... HPI
High-Pressure Injection System [*Nuclear energy*] (NRCH) .... HPIS
High-Pressure Intensifier Pump .... HPIP
High-Pressure Ion Exchange Chromatography .... HPIEC
High-Pressure Jet .... HPJ
High-Pressure Liquid Jet .... HPLJ
High-Pressure Liquid-Affinity Chromatography (DMAA) .... HPLAC
High-Pressure Low-Flow .... HPLF
High-Pressure Low-Volume [*Automotive painting*] .... HPLV

High-Pressure Mercury Vapor ... HPMV
High-Pressure Nervous Syndrome [*Deep-sea diving*] ... HPNS
High-Pressure Oil-Filled [*Cable*] ... HPOF
High-Pressure Oxidizer Pump (NASA) ... HPOP
High-Pressure Oxidizer Turbopump (MCD) ... HPOT
High-Pressure Oxidizer Turbopump ... HPOTP
High-Pressure Oxygen [*Also, HBO, OHP*] ... HPO
High-Pressure Oxygen (AFM) ... HPOX
High-Pressure Recirculation System [*Nuclear energy*] (NRCH) ... HPRS
High-Pressure Relief Valve (KSC) ... HPRV
High-Pressure Safety Injection (NRCH) ... HPSI
High-Pressure Safety Injection Pump (NRCH) ... HPSIP
High-Pressure Safety Injection System (IEEE) ... HPSIS
High-Pressure Separator [*Chemical engineering*] ... HPS
High-Pressure Service Water [*Nuclear energy*] (NRCH) ... HPSW
High-Pressure Service Water System [*Nuclear energy*] (NRCH) ... HPSWS
High-Pressure Side Temperature Sensor [*Air conditioning systems*] [*Automotive engineering*] ... HSTS
High-Pressure Sintering [*Ceramic technology*] ... HPS
High-Pressure Size Exclusion Chromatography ... HPSEC
High-Pressure Sodium ... HPS
High-Pressure Solenoid Valve ... HPSV
High-Pressure Steam [*Technical drawings*] ... HPS
High-Pressure Stopped Flow [*Spectrometry*] ... HPSF
High-Pressure Tap ... HPT
High-Pressure Test ... HPT
High-Pressure Turbine (NRCH) ... HPT
High-Pressure Turbine [*on a ship*] (DS) ... HPTB
High-Pressure Unit ... HPU
High-Pressure Valve ... HPV
High-Pressure Zone ... HPZ
High-Priority Air Force Contract [*Generally in missile field*] (AAGC) ... HI-VALU
High-Priority Key [*IRS*] ... HK
High-Priority Mail (TSSD) ... HPM
High-Priority Mission Support Kit [*Military*] (AFIT) ... HPMSK
High-Priority Production Program [*NATO*] (NATG) ... HPPP
High-Priority Violator (GNE) ... HPV
High-Probability Behavior ... HPB
High-Probability-of-Intercept Receiver [*Telecommunications*] (IEEE) ... HPIR
High-Productivity Energy Crop ... HPEC
High-Protein (MEDA) ... HiPro
High-Protein Diet ... HPD
High-Protein Fraction [*Food technology*] ... HPF
High-Protein Supplement [*Nutrition*] ... HPS
High-Protein Wash Solution [*Clinical chemistry*] ... HPWSol
High-Purity Dual Hardness Armor (KSC) ... HP-DHA
High-Purity Water ... HPW
High-Quality Epitaxial Silicon ... HQES
High-Quality Life ... HQL
High-Quality Matrix [*Electronics*] ... HQM
High-Quality Silicon ... HQS
High-Quality Sound [*Home video system*] (IAA) ... HQS
High-Quality Television [*Home video system*] (IAA) ... HQTV
High-Radiation Area (DNAB) ... HRA
High-Range [*RADAR*] (DEN) ... HR
High-Range Juno [*Survey meter for radiation*] ... HRJ
High-Range Pressure Control ... HRPC
High-Rate Acquisition Assembly (MCD) ... HRAA
High-Rate Activated Sludge [*Waste treatment*] ... HRAS
High-Rate Data Assembly (MCD) ... HRDA
High-Rate Data Section (NASA) ... HRDS
High-Rate Demultiplexer (SSD) ... HRD
High-Rate Demultiplexer (MCD) ... HRDM
High-Rate Demultiplexer Instrument (SSD) ... HRDI
High-Rate Digital Recorder (MCD) ... HRDR
High-Rate Discharge (MCD) ... HRD
High-Rate Dosimeter (MCD) ... HRD
High-Rate Heat ... HRH
High-Rate Multiplexer (MCD) ... HRM
High-Rate Multiplexer Input/Output Test System (NASA) ... HITS
High-Rate Physical Vapor Deposition [*Metal*] ... HRPVD
High-Rate Reverse [*Ecology*] ... HR
High-Rate Station ... HRS
High-Rate Telemetry [*NASA*] ... HRT
High-Rate Telemetry System [*NASA*] ... HRTS
High-Ratio Compact Chamber [*Automotive engineering*] ... HRCC
High-Ratio Multiplier (NASA) ... HRM
High-Reliability Module (IAA) ... HRM
High-Reliability Relay ... HRR
High-Renin Essential Hypertension [*Medicine*] (DMAA) ... HREH
High-Repetition Illuminator System ... HRIS
High-Repetition LASER ... HRL
High-Repetition LASER Illuminating System ... HRLIS
High-Repetition LASER Illuminator ... HRLI
High-Repetition LASER System ... HRLS
High-Resolution Accelerometer Package (MCD) ... HIRAP
High-Resolution Bathymetry [*Instrumentation*] ... HRB
High-Resolution Capacitive Imaging Sensor [*Instrumentation*] ... HIRCIS
High-Resolution Display ... HRD
High-Resolution Doppler Imager (MCD) ... HRDI
High-Resolution Dynamic Imaging [*Electrophoresis*] ... HRDI
High-Resolution Echelle Spectrograph ... HIRES
High-Resolution Electrocardiography ... HRE
High-Resolution Electron Energy Loss Spectroscopy ... HREELS
High-Resolution Electron Microscopy ... HREM
High-Resolution Electronic System ... HRES
High-Resolution Electrophoresis [*Analytical biochemistry*] ... HRE
High-Resolution Energy-Loss Electron Spectroscopy ... HRELES
High-Resolution Energy-Loss Spectroscopy (MCD) ... HRELS
High-Resolution Facsimile [*Telecommunications*] ... HRF
High-Resolution Facsimile [*Telecommunications*] (TEL) ... HRFAX
High-Resolution Frequency Analysis [*of periodic phenomena*] ... HRFA
High-Resolution Gas Chromatography ... HRGC
High-Resolution Ground Map ... HRGM
High-Resolution Hemispherical Reflector Antenna Technique ... HIHAT
High-Resolution Image [*or Imager*] [*Astronomy*] ... HRI
High-Resolution Imaging Spectrometer ... HIRIS
High-Resolution Infared Sounder [*Marine science*] (OSRA) ... HIRS
High-Resolution Infrared Radiation Sounder ... HIRS
High-Resolution Infrared Radiation Sounder ... HRIRS
High-Resolution Infrared Radiometer ... HRIR
High-Resolution Interferometer Spectrometer ... HIS
High-Resolution Light Microscopy ... HRLM
High-Resolution Liquid Chromatography ... HRLC
High-Resolution LOFAR [*Military*] (CAAL) ... HRL
High-Resolution Mass Spectrometry ... HRMS
High-Resolution Monitor (MCD) ... HRM
High-Resolution/Moving Target Indicator (DNAB) ... HR/MTI
High-Resolution Multifrequency Microwave Radiometer (MCD) ... HMMR
High-Resolution Nuclear Magnetic Resonance ... HNMR
High-Resolution Permanent Magnet (MHDI) ... HRPM
High-Resolution Picture Transmission [*Service*] ... HRPT
High-Resolution Pointable Imager ... HRPI
High-Resolution Powder Diffractometer [*Crystallographic instrument*] ... HRPD
High-Resolution RADAR ... HRR
High-Resolution Scanning Electron Microscopy (OA) ... HRSEM
High-Resolution Solar Optical Telescope ... HIRSO
High-Resolution Spectrograph [*Hubble Space Telescope*] [*NASA*] ... HRS
High-Resolution Spin Scan Cloud Camera (NOAA) ... HRSSCC
High-Resolution Surface-Composition Mapping Radiometer (PDAA) ... HRSCMR
High-Resolution System ... HRS
High-Resolution Tangential Flow Filtration ... HRTF
High-Resolution Telescope and Spectrograph ... HRTS
High-Resolution Tracker ... HRT
High-Resolution Transmission Electron Microscope [*or Microscopy*] ... HRTEM
High-Resolution, Two-Dimensional [*Electrophoresis*] ... HR2D
High-Resolution Visible Range ... HVR
High-Resolution Wind Measurement Program (MUGU) ... HIREWIMP
High-Resolution X-Ray Spectroscopy ... HRXRS
Highridge Exploration Ltd. [*Toronto Stock Exchange symbol*] ... HRE
High-Rising Terminal Declarative [*Linguistics*] ... HRTD
High-Risk Hearing Register ... HRHR
High-Risk Patient [*Medicine*] (DMAA) ... HRP
High-Risk, People-Related Accident Syndrome (DICI) ... HRPRAS
High-Risk Test Site [*Later, Research Test Site*] ... HRTS
High-Risk Urban Problem [*Environmental Protection Agency*] (GFGA) ... HRUP
High-Rupturing Capacity ... HRC
High-Scope Educational Research Foundation (EA) ... H/serf
High-Similarity [*Psychology*] ... HS
High-Solid Waste Header [*Nuclear energy*] (NRCH) ... HSWH
High-Speed Accounting Machine (IAA) ... HSAM
High-Speed Adapter (IAA) ... HS
High-Speed Airdrop Container [*Military*] (RDA) ... HISAC
High-Speed Analog Computer (DEN) ... HSAC
High-Speed Anti-RADAR Missile ... HARM
High-Speed Arithmetic (IAA) ... HS
High-Speed Arithmetic and Logic Unit (IAA) ... HSALU
High-Speed Arithmetic Processing Unit Board ... HAPUB
High-Speed Automatic Monitor ... HAM
High-Speed Autoradiography ... HARG
High-Speed Bench Press ... HSBP
High-Speed Black and White [*Photography*] ... HBW
High-Speed Bombing RADAR ... HSBR
High-Speed Buffer ... HSB
High-Speed Bus [*Computer science*] ... HSB
High-Speed Card Punch [*Computer science*] (AABC) ... HSCP
High-Speed Card Reader [*Computer science*] (AABC) ... HSCR
High-Speed Card Teletypewriter Terminal [*Computer science*] (CET) ... HSCTT
High-Speed Carry ... HSC
High-Speed Channel [*Computer science*] ... HSC
High-Speed Civil Transport [*Supersonic plane*] ... HSCT
High-Speed Color Exterior ... HCEX
High-Speed Command Link ... HSCL
High-Speed Complementary Metal-Oxide Semiconductor (MCD) ... HCMOS
High-Speed Compound Terminal [*Computer science*] (MCD) ... HSCT
High-Speed Concentrator ... HSC
High-Speed Data ... HSD
High-Speed Data Acquisition [*Computer science*] ... HSDA
High-Speed Data Acquisition and Reduction System ... HS-DARS
High-Speed Data Assembly [*Ground Communications Facility, NASA*] ... HSDA
High-Speed Data Buffer ... HSDB
High-Speed Data Channel (IAA) ... HSDC
High-Speed Data Interface ... HSDI
High-Speed Data Line [*or Link*] ... HSDL
High-Speed Data Regeneration Assembly [*Ground Communications Facility, NASA*] ... HSRA
High-Speed Die Mounter ... HSDM
High-Speed Digital Filter ... HSDF
High-Speed Digital Subscriber Loop [*Computer science*] ... HDSL
High-Speed Direct Injection [*Diesel engines*] ... HSDI

High-Speed Displacement (IEEE) ... HSD
High-Speed Distributor Transmitter ... HSDT
High-Speed Draft [*Print quality*] ... HSD
High-Speed Electro-Drive Fan [*Automotive engineering*] ... HEDF
High-Speed Electrostatic Printer ... HSEP
High-Speed Encoder (IAA) ... HSE
High-Speed Flight Station [*NASA*] ... HSFS
High-Speed Force Feed ... HSFF
High-Speed Fuel Air Explosive ... HSFAE
High-Speed Gel Permeation Chromatography ... HSGPC
High-Speed Grinding (PDAA) ... HSG
High-Speed Ground Test Center [*Later, TTC*] [*Pueblo, CO*] ... HSGTC
High-Speed Ground Transportation ... HSGT
High-Speed Guided Ground Transportation [*TXDOT*] (TAG) ... HSSGT
High-Speed/High-Resolution Side Scan Sonar System [*National Oceanic and Atmospheric Administration*] ... HSHRSSS
High-Speed Integrated Injection Logic (IAA) ... HSIIL
High-Speed Integrated Space Transportation Evaluation Program (IAA) ... HISTEP
High-Speed Integrated Test System ... HITS
High-Speed Interface Message Processor (IAA) ... HSIMP
High-Speed Interferometer [*Measures chemical components of smog*] (KSC) ... HSI
High-Speed Launch [*Navy*] ... HSL
High-Speed Line Adapter (MHDI) ... HLA
High-Speed Liquid Chromatography ... HSLC
High-Speed Liquid-Liquid Chromatography ... HSLLC
High-Speed Local Network [*Telecommunications*] (OSI) ... HSLN
High-Speed Logic ... HSL
High-Speed, Low-Level Airdrop System [*Military*] (INF) ... HSLLADS
High-Speed Machining (MCD) ... HSM
High-Speed Measurement (IAA) ... HSM
High-Speed Membrane Osmometry (MCD) ... HSMO
High-Speed Memory [*Computer science*] ... HSM
High-Speed Metal-Oxide Semiconductor [*ROM*] ... HMOS
High-Speed Microwave Switch ... HSMS
High-Speed Minesweeper [*Navy symbol Obsolete*] ... DMS
High-Speed Modular Interface Message Processor ... HSMIMP
High-Speed Motor [*Electrical engineering*] ... HSM
High-Speed Multichannel Data Recorder [*Instrumentation*] ... HSMCDR
High-Speed Nonimpact Printer [*Acronym pronounced "hisnip"*] [*Computer science*] ... HSNP
High-Speed Packet Switched Data [*Computer science*] (ACRL) ... HSPSD
High-Speed Paper Tape Absolute Loader [*Computer science*] (MDG) ... HSPTAL
High-Speed Paper Tape Punch [*Computer science*] (AABC) ... HSPTP
High-Speed Paper Tape Reader [*Computer science*] (CET) ... HSPTR
High-Speed Parallel Adder ... HSPA
High-Speed Printer [*Computer science*] ... HSP
High-Speed Printer Interface (MCD) ... HSPI
High-Speed Pulse ... HSP
High-Speed Punch (IAA) ... HSP
High-Speed RADAR (MCD) ... HSR
High-Speed Radial [*Automotive tires*] ... HR
High-Speed Rail ... HSR
High-Speed Reader [*Computer science*] ... HSR
High-Speed Relay ... HSR
High-Speed Repetitive Operation ... HSRO
High-Speed Research Aircraft (PDAA) ... HRA
High-Speed Resin Transfer Molding [*Automotive engineering*] ... HSRTM
High-Speed Rotary Prism ... HSRP
High-Speed Scintillation Autoradiography ... HSARG
High-Speed Selector Channel ... HSEL
High-Speed Serial Data [*Automotive electronics*] ... HSSD
High-Speed Serial Data Buffer (MCD) ... HSSDB
High-Speed Serial Interface [*Telecommunications*] ... HSSI
High-Speed Serial Interface [*Computer science*] (CDE) ... HSSI
High-Speed Signal Control Equipment [*Data communication*] (MHDI) ... HSE
High-Speed Simultaneous [*Electric trip mechanism*] ... HSS
High-Speed Single Line Controller (MHDB) ... HSLC
High-Speed Storage [*Computer science*] (IEEE) ... HSS
High-Speed Supernatant [*Medicine*] (DAVI) ... HSS
High-Speed Surface Transport (MCD) ... HSST
High-Speed Switched Digital Service [*AT & T*] (TSSD) ... HSSDS
High-Speed Symbol Generator ... HSSG
High-Speed Synchronous Interface [*Computer science*] ... HSSI
High-Speed System [*Ground Communications Facility, NASA*] ... HSS
High-Speed Technology [*Computer science*] (BYTE) ... HST
High-Speed Telemetry ... HST
High-Speed Telemetry Link ... HSTL
High-Speed Test Track ... HSTT
High-Speed Train [*British*] ... HST
High-Speed Transistor-Transistor Logic ... HSTTL
High-Speed Transistor-Transistor Logic (IAA) ... HTTL
High-Speed Transport [*Navy symbol Obsolete*] ... APD
High-Speed Tunnel [*NASA*] ... HST
High-Speed Video [*Instrumentation*] ... HSV
High-Speed Wire Guidance ... HSWG
High-Stability Temperature-Compensated Crystal Oscillator [*Electronics*] (OA) ... HSTCO
High-Stability Temperature-Compensated Crystal Oscillator ... HSTCXO
High-Stage Valve (MCD) ... HSV
High-Starch Fraction [*Food technology*] ... HSF
High-Strength Adhesive ... HSA
High-Strength Cold-Rolled (PDAA) ... HSCR
High-Strength Low-Alloy [*or Light-Alloy*] [*Steel*] ... HSLA
High-Strength Quick Release (MCD) ... HSQR
High-Strength Sheet Molding Compound ... HMC
High-Strength Stainless Steel (PDAA) ... HSS
High-Strength, Steel ... HSS
High-Strength Thermal-Resistant Alloy ... HSTRA
High-Stress Strain (MCD) ... HSS
High-Subsonic Optically Teleguided [*Antitank system*] (INF) ... HOT
High-Sulfur Diesel Fuel [*Petroleum marketing*] ... HSD
High-Sulfur Residual Fuel Oil [*Petroleum technology*] ... HSRFO
High-Survivability Test Vehicle (MCD) ... HSTV
High-Swirl Combustion [*Engine*] ... HSC
High-Tar Content [*of cigarettes*] ... HTC
High-Technology Demonstrator Engine (MCD) ... HTDE
High-Technology Ejection Seat ... HTES
High-Technology Escape System (MCD) ... HTES
High-Technology Light Brigade [*Army*] (INF) ... HTLB
High-Technology Light Division [*DoD*] ... HTLD
High-Technology Motorized Division ... HTMD
High-Technology Test Bed [*Army*] ... HTTB
High-Temperature Adhesive ... HTA
High-Temperature Air Heat [*for magnetohydrodynamic power plants*] (MCD) ... HTAH
High-Temperature Alloy ... HTA
High-Temperature Ashing [*Analytical chemistry*] ... HTA
High-Temperature Burner-Duct Recuperator System ... HTBDR
High-Temperature Carbonization ... HTC
High-Temperature Catalyst ... HTC
High-Temperature Catalytic Oxidation [*Chemistry*] ... HTCD
High-Temperature Catalytic Oxidation [*Chemistry*] ... HTCO
High-Temperature Coil ... HTC
High-Temperature Conditioning ... HTC
High-Temperature Detection Lens ... HTDL
High-Temperature Distillation ... HTD
High-Temperature Electrolysis (MCD) ... HTE
High-Temperature Electrostatic Precipitator [*Anti-smoke pollution device*] ... HTESP
High-Temperature Fast-Flow Reactor [*See also HTFS*] ... HTFFR
High-Temperature Fluid-Wall [*Incineration process*] ... HTFW
High-Temperature Fuel Cell ... HTFC
High-Temperature Gas [*Reactor*] ... HTG
High-Temperature Gas-Cooled Reactor (BARN) ... HTGC
High-Temperature Gas-Cooled Reactor ... HTGCR
High-Temperature Gas-Cooled Reactor ... HTGR
High-Temperature Gas-Cooled-Reactor Critical Experiment ... HTGR-CX
High-Temperature Gas-Cooled-Reactor Experiment ... HTGRE
High-Temperature General-Purpose Furnace ... HTGPF
High-Temperature Heater ... HTH
High-Temperature Helium Turbine (PDAA) ... HHT
High-Temperature, High-Shear Viscometer ... HT-HS
High-Temperature, High-Shear-Rate [*Viscosity measurement*] ... HTHSR
High-Temperature Incinerator ... HTI
High-Temperature Isotropic ... HTI
High-Temperature Lacquer ... HTL
High-Temperature Lattice Test Reactor ... HTLTR
High-Temperature Mass Spectrometry ... HTMS
High-Temperature Materials ... HTM
High-Temperature Metallography ... HTM
High-Temperature Nitric Oxide Reduction [*Combustion technology*] ... HTNR
High-Temperature Operating Test (MCD) ... HTOT
High-Temperature Oxidation (IEEE) ... HTO
High-Temperature Photochemistry [*Aerochem Research Laboratories, Inc.*] [*Analytical chemistry*] ... HTP
High-Temperature Photolysis [*Physics*] ... HTP
High-Temperature Power and Voltage (IAA) ... HTPV
High-Temperature Reactor ... HTR
High-Temperature Reactor Development Associates ... HTRDA
High-Temperature Reactor Experiment [*Department of Energy*] (GAAI) ... HTRE
High-Temperature Resistor ... HTR
High-Temperature Reusable Surface Insulation [*Space shuttle*] [*NASA*] ... HRSI
High-Temperature Reverse Bias [*Electronics*] (IAA) ... HTRB
High-Temperature Semiconductor [*Electronics*] ... HTSC
High-Temperature Short-Time [*Pasteurization*] [*Food processing*] ... HTST
High-Temperature Size-Exclusion Chromatography ... HTSEC
High-Temperature Skim Milk (OA) ... HTSM
High-Temperature Sodium Facility [*Nuclear energy*] (NRCH) ... HTSF
High-Temperature Steam ... HTS
High-Temperature Strain Gauge ... HTSR
High-Temperature Superconductivity (ECON) ... HTS
High-Temperature Superconductivity [*Materials science*] ... HTSC
High-Temperature Superconductor [*Materials science*] ... HTS
High-Temperature Superconductor [*Materials science*] ... HTSC
High-Temperature Tetragonal [*Physics*] ... HTT
High-Temperature Thermomechanical Processing [*Alloy heat resistance*] ... HTMP
High-Temperature Thermomechanical Pulp [*Pulp and paper technology*] ... HTMP
High-Temperature Thermomechanical Treatment [*Steel forging*] ... HTT
High-Temperature Thermomechanical Treatment [*Steel forging*] ... HTTMT
High-Temperature Tunnel [*NASA*] ... HTT
High-Temperature Turbine Technology [*Power generation*] ... HTTT
High-Temperature Water ... HTW
High-Temperature Wire ... HTW
High-Temperature X-Ray Diffraction ... HTXRD
High-Temperature-Superconductivity Space Experiment [*Navy*] ... HTSSE
High-Tensile Cast Iron ... HTCI
High-Tensile Steel ... HTS

High-Tension Alternating Current (IAA) .... HTAC
High-Tension Battery .... H-TB
High-Tension Braided Sheath [*Automotive engineering*] .... HTB
High-Tension Direct Current (IAA) .... HTDC
High-Tension/High-Resistance [*Automotive engineering*] .... HTHR
High-Tension/Low-Resistance [*Automotive engineering*] .... HTLR
High-Tension Separation (IAA) .... HTS
High-Tension Supply (IAA) .... HTS
High-Tension Synthetic Insulation [*Automotive engineering*] .... HTS
High-Tension Thermoplastic Insulation [*Automotive engineering*] .... HTT
High-Test Hydrogen-Peroxide .... HTP
High-Test Hypochlorite (WGA) .... HTH
High-Test Recorder and Simulator System (IEEE) .... HYTRESS
High-Test Recorder and Simulator System .... HYTROSS
High-Titer, Low-Acidity [*Hematology*] .... HTLA
High-to-Medium-Altitude Air Defense (AABC) .... HIMAD
High-Torque Drive [*Engineering*] .... HTD
High-Trajectory Missiles (NRCH) .... HTM
Hight's Reports [*57-58 Iowa*] [*A publication*] (DLA) .... Hight
Hightstown Gazette, Hightstown, NJ [*Library symbol Library of Congress*] (LCLS) .... NjHigG
Hightstown Memorial Library, Hightstown, NJ [*Library symbol Library of Congress*] (LCLS) .... NjHig
High-Usage [*Telecommunications*] .... Hi-U
High-Usage [*Telecommunications*] (TEL) .... HU
High-Usage Intertoll Trunk [*Data communication*] (MHDI) .... HUT
High-Usage Load List (DNAB) .... HULL
High-Vacuum Calibration System (PDAA) .... HVCS
High-Vacuum Environment .... HVE
High-Vacuum Evaporation System .... HVES
High-Vacuum Evaporator .... HVE
High-Vacuum Flame Sterilization [*Food technology*] .... HVFS
High-Vacuum Orbital Simulator .... HIVOS
High-Vacuum Pump .... HVP
High-Vacuum Rectifier .... HVR
High-Value Accounting Control .... HIVAC
High-Value Airborne Assets (DOMA) .... HVAA
High-Value Asset Control .... HIVAC
High-Value Item (NATG) .... HVI
High-Value Product .... HVP
High-Value Target (NVT) .... HVT
High-Value Unit [*Torpedo defense system*] (MCD) .... HVU
High-Value Unit Combat Air Patrol [*Navy*] (DOMA) .... HVUCAP
High-Variation Medical Condition .... HVMC
Highveld Steel & Vanadium Corporation Ltd. [*Associated Press*] (SAG) .... Highvld
Highveld Steel & Vanadium Corp. Ltd. [*NASDAQ symbol*] (NQ) .... HSVL
Highveld Steel & VanadiumADR [*NASDAQ symbol*] (TTSB) .... HSVLY
High-Velocity Air Filter (EG) .... HVAF
High-Velocity Aircraft Rocket .... HVAR
High-Velocity Aircraft Rocket (High Explosive) (DNAB) .... HVAR(HE)
High-Velocity Anomaly [*Seismology*] .... HVA
High-Velocity Antitank [*Projectile*] .... HVAT
High-Velocity, Armor-Piercing [*Projectile*] .... HVAP
High-Velocity, Armor-Piercing, Discarding Sabot [*Projectile*] .... HVAPDS
High-Velocity, Armor-Piercing, Discarding Sabot, Fin Stabilized [*Projectile*] (MCD) .... HVAPDSFS
High-Velocity, Armor-Piercing, Fin Stabilized, Discarding Sabot [*Projectile*] (MCD) .... HVAPFSDS
High-Velocity Cloud [*Astronomy*] (OA) .... HVC
High-Velocity Detonation .... HVD
High-Velocity Fluidized Bed [*Chemical engineering*] .... HVFB
High-Velocity Grenade Launcher System [*Projectile*] (MCD) .... HVGLS
High-Velocity Hot-Air [*Oven*] .... HVHA
High-Velocity Hot-Air Impingement [*Organic chemistry*] .... HVHAI
High-Velocity, Low Penetration Paint .... HVLP
High-Velocity Missile [*Military*] (DAVI) .... HVM
High-Velocity Oxygen/Fuel [*Coating technology*] .... HVOF
High-Velocity, Target-Practice [*Projectile*] .... HVTP
High-Velocity, Target-Practice, Discarding Sabot [*Projectile*] .... HVTPDS
High-Viscosity Dispenser [*Packaging*] .... HVD
High-Viscosity Fuel .... H
High-Viscosity Fuel Oil (DCTA) .... HVF
High-Voltage Actuator [*Electronics*] (IEEE) .... HVAC
High-Voltage Alternating Current .... HVAC
High-Voltage Apparatus Coordinating Committee [*ANSI*] .... HVACC
High-Voltage Bias .... HVB
High-Voltage Capillary Electrophoresis .... HVCE
High-Voltage Connector .... HVC
High-Voltage Control .... HVC
High-Voltage Direct Current .... HVDC
High-Voltage Direct-Current Transmission [*Electronics*] .... HVDCT
High-Voltage Electrical Stimulation [*Meat treatment*] .... HVES
High-Voltage Electron Microscopy .... HVEM
High-Voltage Electrophoresis (AAMN) .... HVE
High-Voltage Generator .... HVG
High-Voltage Gradient .... HVG
High-Voltage Integrated Circuit [*Computer science*] .... HVIC
High-Voltage Mercury-Vapor Isolator .... HVMVI
High-Voltage Mode .... HVM
High-Voltage Paper Electrophoresis .... HVPE
High-Voltage Phase Retard .... HVPR
High-Voltage Photovoltaic Effect [*Physics*] .... HVPVE
High-Voltage Plasma Interaction (SSD) .... HVPI
High-Voltage Potential (IAA) .... HVP
High-Voltage Power Supply .... HVPS
High-Voltage Pump .... HVP
High-Voltage Rectifier .... HVR
High-Voltage Regulator (MSA) .... HVR
High-Voltage Relay .... HVR
High-Voltage Resistor .... HVR
High-Voltage Selenium Cartridge Rectifier .... HVSCR
High-Voltage Solar Array .... HVSA
High-Voltage Solar Experiment .... HVSE
High-Voltage Solar Panel .... HVSP
High-Voltage Switch .... HVS
High-Voltage Switching Transistor .... HVST
High-Voltage Termination .... HVT
High-Voltage Tester .... HVT
High-Voltage Thermal Battery (DNAB) .... HVTB
High-Voltage Threshold (IAA) .... HVT
High-Voltage Transformer .... HVT
High-Voltage Waveform .... HVW
High-Voltage Wire .... HVW
High-Voltage-Activated [*Neurochemistry*] .... HVA
High-Voltage-Hold-Down (PDAA) .... HVHD
High-Volume Air Sampler [*Environmental science*] (FFDE) .... hi-vol
High-Volume Electrostatic Sampler (MCD) .... HIVES
High-Volume Industrial Organics [*Environmental science*] (GFGA) .... HVIO
High-Volume Information Transfer .... HVIT
High-Volume Instrument [*Agricultural research*] .... HVI
High-Volume Low-Pressure [*Spray-painting process*] .... HVLP
High-Volume Printing System [*Computer science*] .... HVPS
High-Volume Time Sharing [*Computer science*] .... HVTS
High-Walled Endothelial Venule [*Anatomy*] .... HEV
High-Water Full and Change [*Tides and currents*] .... HWF & C
High-Water Interval .... HWI
High-Water Line [*Technical drawings*] .... HWL
High-Water Lunitidal Interval .... HWLI
High-Water Mark [*Maps and charts*] .... HWM
High-Water Neaps .... HWN
High-Water Ordinary Spring Tides [*Maps and charts*] .... HWOST
High-Water Quadrature .... HWQ
High-Water-Based Fluid [*Hydraulic and cutting fluids*] .... HWBF
High-Water-Content Fluid [*Nonpetroleum lubricant*] .... HWCF
Highway .... H/W
Highway (WGA) .... HGWY
Highway [*Commonly used*] (OPSA) .... HIGHWAY
Highway [*Commonly used*] (OPSA) .... HIGHWY
Highway [*Commonly used*] (OPSA) .... HIWAY
Highway [*Commonly used*] (OPSA) .... HIWY
Highway [*Commonly used*] (OPSA) .... HWAY
Highway .... HWY
Highway .... HWY
Highway (DD) .... Hwy
Highway .... Hy
Highway Action Coalition .... HAC
Highway Advisory Radio [*Vehicle communications*] .... HAR
Highway Advisory Radio [*Federal program*] .... HAR
Highway Aid by Radio Truck (IAA) .... HART
Highway and Traffic Technicians Association [*British*] (EAIO) .... HTTA
Highway Bridge Parapet (PDAA) .... HBP
Highway Bridge Replacement and Rehabilitation Program [*Department of Transportation*] .... HBRRP
Highway Capacity Manual [*FHWA*] (TAG) .... HCM
Highway Code [*A publication*] (DLA) .... HC
Highway Communications .... HY-COM
Highway Contract Route .... HCR
Highway Cost Allocation Study [*Also, FHCAS*] .... HCAS
Highway Driving Simulator [*MM*] (TAG) .... HYSIM
Highway Economic Requirements System [*FHWA*] (TAG) .... HERS
Highway Emergency Locating Paging Service [*For motorist assistance*] .... HELPS
Highway Emergency Locating Plan .... HELP
Highway Engineering Exchange Program (EA) .... HEEP
Highway Fleet Management System (MCD) .... HFMS
Highway Fuel Economy Test [*Environmental Protection Agency*] .... HFET
Highway Fuel Economy Test [*Environmental Protection Agency*] .... HWFET
Highway Holdings Ltd. [*Associated Press*] (SAG) .... HghwyH
Highway Holdings Ltd. [*Associated Press*] (SAG) .... HgwyH
Highway Holdings Ltd. [*NASDAQ symbol*] (SAG) .... HIHO
Highway Holdings Ltd. [*NASDAQ symbol*] (SAG) .... HIHW
Highway Innovation Technology .... HITEC
Highway Loss Data Institute (EA) .... HLDI
Highway Mobile Source [*Environmental Protection Agency*] (GFGA) .... HMS
Highway Performance-Monitoring System [*Department of Transportation*] (GFGA) .... HPMS
Highway Planning and Research [*MTMC*] (TAG) .... HP&R
Highway Post Office [*Bus or truck equipped with mail distribution facilities*] .... HIPO
Highway Post Office [*Bus or truck equipped with mail distribution facilities*] .... HPO
Highway Regulating Point (AABC) .... HRP
Highway Regulating Point Team [*MTMC*] (TAG) .... HRPT
Highway Research Board [*Later, TRB*] (EA) .... HRB
Highway Research in Progress [*British*] .... HRIP
Highway Research Information Service [*National Academy of Sciences*] [*Washington, DC*] .... HRIS
Highway Safety Act [*1970*] .... HSA
Highway Safety Information Service [*National Highway Safety Administration*] (IID) .... HSIS
Highway Safety Literature [*Database*] (NITA) .... HSL
Highway Safety Literature Service [*National Academy of Science*] [*Washington, DC*] .... HSL

Highway Safety Program Standard [*Department of Transportation*] ... HSPS
Highway Safety Research Center [*University of North Carolina, Chapel Hill*] [*Research center*] (RCD) ... HSRC
Highway Safety Research Institute [*University of Michigan*] ... HSRI
Highway Safety Statistical Indicator ... HSSI
Highway Speed Uniformity [*Automotive tire testing*] ... HSU
Highway Tariff Bureau [*Later, AMCTB*] ... HTB
Highway Traffic Act ... HTA
Highway Traffic Control ... HTC
Highway Traffic Control ... HWTC
Highway Traffic Point [*MTMC*] (TAG) ... HTP
Highway Traffic Regulation (AABC) ... HTR
Highway Traffic Safety Center [*Michigan State University*] ... HTSC
Highway Transportation Officer [*Army*] ... HTO
Highway Trust Fund ... HTF
Highway Users Federation for Safety and Mobility [*Later, ASF*] (EA) ... HUF
Highway Users Federation for Safety and Mobility [*FHWA*] (TAG) ... HUFSAM
Highway Users Federation for Safety and Mobility ... HUFSM
Highway Vehicle Object Simulation Model [*Computer-aided design*] [*Automotive engineering*] ... HVOSM
HighwayMaster Communic [*NASDAQ symbol*] (TTSB) ... HWYM
HighwayMaster Communications, Inc. [*Associated Press*] (SAG) ... Highwy
HighwayMaster Communications, Inc. [*Associated Press*] (SAG) ... Highwym
HighwayMaster Communications, Inc. [*NASDAQ symbol*] (SAG) ... HWYM
HighwayMaster Communications, Inc. [*NASDAQ symbol*] (SAG) ... HWYM
Highways Act [*British*] (ILCA) ... HA
Highways and Byways [*A publication*] ... HB
Highways for National Defense [*MTMC*] (TAG) ... AR 55-80
Highways for National Defense [*MTMC*] (TAG) ... HND
Highwood Res Ltd [*NASDAQ symbol*] (TTSB) ... HIWDF
Highwood Resources Ltd. [*Associated Press*] (SAG) ... Highwd
Highwood Resources Ltd. [*NASDAQ symbol*] (NQ) ... HIWD
Highwood Resources Ltd. [*Toronto Stock Exchange symbol*] ... HWD
Highwoods Properties [*NYSE symbol*] (TTSB) ... HIW
Highwoods Properties, Inc. [*Associated Press*] (SAG) ... Highwd
Highwoods Properties, Inc. [*NYSE symbol*] (SAG) ... HIW
High-Yield Fallout Trajectory (DNAB) ... HYFT
High-Yield Lithium Injection Fusion Energy (MCD) ... HYLIFE
High-Yield Tax-Exempt [*Finance*] (BARN) ... HYT
High-Yielding Wheat Variety (GNE) ... HYWV
Higuerote [*Venezuela*] [*Airport symbol*] (AD) ... HIU
Higuerote, Miranda [*Venezuela ICAO location identifier*] (ICLI) ... SVHG
Higuey [*Dominican Republic*] [*ICAO location identifier*] (ICLI) ... MDHY
Hikone [*Japan*] [*Seismograph station code, US Geological Survey*] (SEIS) ... HIK
Hikueru [*French Polynesia*] [*ICAO location identifier*] (ICLI) ... NTGH
Hilar High-Frequency Stimulation [*Neurophysiology*] ... HHFS
Hilar Node [*Medicine*] (MAE) ... HN
Hilary Sittings [*British Legal term*] (ROG) ... HILY SITTGS
Hilary Term [*England*] [*Legal term*] (DLA) ... H
Hilary Term [*England*] [*Legal term*] (DLA) ... Hil
Hilary Term [*England*] [*Legal term*] (DLA) ... Hil T
Hilary Term 4, William IV [*A publication*] (DLA) ... Hil Term 4 Will IV
Hilary Vacation [*British Legal term*] (DLA) ... HIL VAC
Hilb, Rogal & Hamilton [*NYSE symbol*] (TTSB) ... HRH
Hilb, Rogal & Hamilton Co. [*Associated Press*] (SAG) ... HilbRog
Hilbert College, Hamburg, NY [*Library symbol Library of Congress*] (LCLS) ... NHamH
Hilcoast Development [*NASDAQ symbol*] (TTSB) ... HCDV
Hilcoast Development Corp. [*NASDAQ symbol*] (SAG) ... HCDV
Hilcoast Development Corp. [*Associated Press*] (SAG) ... HilcstDv
Hilda Doolittle [*Initials used as pen name of American poet, 1886-1961*] ... HD
Hildesheim [*Germany ICAO location identifier*] (ICLI) ... EDUH
Hildon Mining [*Vancouver Stock Exchange symbol*] ... HDN
Hildyard on Insurance [*A publication*] (DLA) ... Hild Ins
Hildyard's Marine Insurance [*A publication*] (DLA) ... Hild Mar Ins
Hilevel Assembly Language Environment [*Hilever Technology Inc.*] [*Operating systems assembler*] (NITA) ... HALE
Hilf Du Heilige Dreifaltigkeit [*Help Thou Holy Trinity*] [*Motto of Johann Georg I, Prince of Anhalt-Dessau (1567-1618)*] [*German*] ... HDHD
Hilf Gott, Hilf Gott, Hilf Gott [*God Help, God Help, God Help*] [*Motto of Sophie Elisabeth, Countess of Schwarzenburg (1565-1621)*] ... HGHGHG
Hilf Gott zu Glueck [*May God Help Us to Fortune*] [*Motto of Magdalene, Princess of Anhalt (1585-1657)*] [*German*] ... HGZG
Hilf, Himmlischer Herr, Hoechster Hort [*Help, Heavenly Father, Highest Treasure*] [*Motto of Elisabeth, Duchess of Saxony-Coburg (1540-94)*] [*German*] ... HHHHH
Hilfsbuch des Pehlevi [*A publication*] (BJA) ... HbP
Hilfsfonds fuer die Opfer der Nuernberger Gesetze [*A publication*] (BJA) ... HNG
Hilfspolizei [*Auxiliary Police*] [*German*] ... HIPO
Hilina Pali [*Hawaii*] [*Seismograph station code, US Geological Survey*] (SEIS) ... HLP
Hilite Industries [*NASDAQ symbol*] (TTSB) ... HILI
Hilite Industries, Inc. [*NASDAQ symbol*] (SAG) ... HILI
Hilite Industries, Inc. [*Associated Press*] (SAG) ... Hilite
Hilkoth (BJA) ... H
Hill (ROG) ... H
Hill [*Commonly used*] (OPSA) ... HILL
Hill ... HL
Hill ... HL
Hill [*Board on Geographic Names*] ... HLL
Hill Air Force Base (SAA) ... HAFB
Hill and Denio's Lalor's Supplement [*New York*] [*A publication*] (DLA) ... Hill & D Supp
Hill & Knowlton, Inc. [*Public relations firm*] ... H & K
Hill and Redman's Law of Landlord and Tenant [*16th ed.*] [*1976*] [*A publication*] (DLA) ... Hill & Redman
Hill City, KS [*Location identifier FAA*] (FAAL) ... HLC
Hill City, KS [*FM radio station call letters*] ... KZNA
Hill City School, Hill City, MN [*Library symbol*] [*Library of Congress*] (LCLS) ... MnHcS
Hill Counselor Verbal Response Category System (EDAC) ... HCVRCS
Hill Elementary School, Pipestone, MN [*Library symbol*] [*Library of Congress*] (LCLS) ... MnPpHES
Hill Engineering Test Facility [*Air Force*] ... HETF
Hill Farming Research Organisation [*British*] ... HFRO
Hill Interaction Matrix [*Psychology*] ... HIM
Hill Interaction Matrix-A [*Personality development test*] [*Psychology*] ... HIM-A
Hill Junior College, Hillsboro, TX [*Library symbol Library of Congress*] (LCLS) ... TxHiC
Hill Monastic Manuscript Library [*Saint John's University, Collegeville, MN*] ... HMML
Hill on Trustees [*A publication*] (DLA) ... Hill Tr
Hill Radnor Flock Book Society [*British*] (DBA) ... HRFBS
Hill Samuel Investment Management [*British*] ... HSIM
Hill Staffers for the Hungry and Homeless (EA) ... HSHH
Hill Start Assist [*Transmission and braking systems*] [*Automotive engineering*] ... HSA
Hill State People's Democratic Party [*India*] [*Political party*] (PPW) ... HSPDP
Hill/Wendover/Dugway [*Ranges*] [*Military*] (MCD) ... HWD
Hill-Burton [*Federal grant and loan program for construction and modernization of medical facilities*] ... HB
HillCity, KS [*FM radio station call letters*] (RBYB) ... KKQY-FM
Hillcrest Academy, Fergus Falls, MN [*Library symbol*] [*Library of Congress*] (LCLS) ... MnFfHA
Hillcrest Community School, Fort Vermilion, Alberta [*Library symbol National Library of Canada*] (BIB) ... AFVHS
Hillcrest Resources Ltd. [*Toronto Stock Exchange symbol*] ... HRT
Hillenbrand Indus [*NYSE symbol*] (TTSB) ... HB
Hillenbrand Industries, Inc. [*NYSE symbol*] (SPSG) ... HB
Hillenbrand Industries, Inc. [*Associated Press*] (SAG) ... Hillenbd
Hillforest Historical Foundation, Inc., Aurora, IN [*Library symbol Library of Congress*] (LCLS) ... InAurHi
Hilliard on Bankruptcy and Insolvency [*A publication*] (DLA) ... Hill B & I
Hilliard on Bankruptcy and Insolvency [*A publication*] (DLA) ... Hill Bank
Hilliard on Contracts [*A publication*] (DLA) ... Hill Cont
Hilliard on New Trials [*A publication*] (DLA) ... Hill N Tr
Hilliard on New Trials [*A publication*] (DLA) ... Hill New Trials
Hilliard on Real Property [*A publication*] (DLA) ... Hill Real Prop
Hilliard on Real Property [*A publication*] (DLA) ... Hilliard RP
Hilliard on Remedies for Torts [*A publication*] (DLA) ... Hill Rem
Hilliard on Sales of Personal Property [*A publication*] (DLA) ... Hill Sales
Hilliard on the Law of Injunctions [*A publication*] (DLA) ... Hill Inj
Hilliard on the Law of Taxation [*A publication*] (DLA) ... Hill Tax
Hilliard on the Law of Torts [*A publication*] (DLA) ... Hil Torts
Hilliard on the Law of Torts [*A publication*] (DLA) ... Hill Torts
Hilliard on the Law of Vendors [*A publication*] (DLA) ... Hill Vend
Hilliard's Abridgment of Real Property Law [*A publication*] (DLA) ... Hill Abr
Hilliard's American Jurisprudence [*A publication*] (DLA) ... Hill Am Jur
Hilliard's American Law [*A publication*] (DLA) ... Hil Abr
Hilliard's American Law [*A publication*] (DLA) ... Hill Am Law
Hilliard's Elements of Law [*A publication*] (DLA) ... Hil Elem Law
Hilliard's Elements of Law [*A publication*] (DLA) ... Hill Elem Law
Hilliard's Law of Mortgages [*A publication*] (DLA) ... Hill Mor
Hilliard's Law of Mortgages [*A publication*] (DLA) ... Hill Mortg
Hillman Elementary School, Rockford, IL [*Library symbol*] [*Library of Congress*] (LCLS) ... IRoHiE
Hillman, MI [*FM radio station call letters*] ... WKJZ
Hillman Owners Club [*Lancing, Sussex, England*] (EAIO) ... HOC
Hillman Public Library, Hillman, MI [*Library symbol Library of Congress*] (LCLS) ... MiHilm
Hills [*Commonly used*] (OPSA) ... HILLS
Hills ... HLS
Hills (MCD) ... HLS
Hill's Annotated Codes and General Laws [*Oregon*] [*A publication*] (DLA) ... Hill's Ann Codes & Laws
Hill's Annotated Codes and General Laws [*Oregon*] [*A publication*] (DLA) ... Hill's Code
Hill's Annotated General Statutes and Codes [*Washington*] [*A publication*] (DLA) ... Hill's Ann St & Codes
Hill's Annotated General Statutes and Codes [*Washington*] [*A publication*] (DLA) ... Hill's Code
Hill's Chancery Practice [*A publication*] (DLA) ... Hill Ch Pr
Hills Christian School, Hills, MN [*Library symbol*] [*Library of Congress*] (LCLS) ... MnHilCS
Hills Department Stores, Inc. [*NYSE symbol*] (SPSG) ... HDS
Hill's Equity South Carolina Reports [*1833-37*] [*A publication*] (DLA) ... Hill Ch
Hill's Equity South Carolina Reports [*1833-37*] [*A publication*] (DLA) ... Hill Eq
Hill's Equity South Carolina Reports [*1833-37*] [*A publication*] (DLA) ... Hill Eq (SC)
Hill's Equity South Carolina Reports [*1833-37*] [*A publication*] (DLA) ... Hill SC
Hill's Illinois Chancery Practice [*A publication*] (DLA) ... Hill Ill Chy
Hill's Illinois Common Law Jurisdiction and Practice [*A publication*] (DLA) ... Hill Ill Com Law
Hill's Illinois Probate Jurisdiction and Practice [*A publication*] (DLA) ... Hill Prob
Hill's Law of Fixtures [*A publication*] (DLA) ... Hill Fixt
Hill's Liberty and Law [*A publication*] (DLA) ... Hill Lib & Law
Hill's New York Reports [*A publication*] (DLA) ... H
Hill's New York Reports [*A publication*] (DLA) ... Hill NY
Hill's New York Reports [*A publication*] (DLA) ... Hill NYR

Hill's New York Supreme Court Reports [*1841-44*] [*A publication*] (DLA) .... Hill
Hill's South Carolina Law Reports [*A publication*] (DLA) .... Hill
Hill's South Carolina Law Reports [*A publication*] (DLA) .... Hill SC
Hills Stores [*NYSE symbol*] (TTSB) .... HDS
Hills Stores Co. [*NYSE symbol*] (SAG) .... HDS
Hills Stores Co. [*Associated Press*] (SAG) .... HillsStrs
Hills Stores Co. [*Associated Press*] (SAG) .... HillStr
Hills Stores Sr'A' Cv Pfd [*NYSE symbol*] (TTSB) .... HDSPr
Hills-Beaver Creek Elementary School, Hills, MN [*Library symbol*] [*Library of Congress*] (LCLS) .... MnHilES
Hills-Beaver Creek High School, Hills, MN [*Library symbol*] [*Library of Congress*] (LCLS) .... MnHilHS
Hillsboro & North Eastern Railway Co. [*AAR code*] .... HLNE
Hillsboro Community Unit, School District 3, Hillsboro, IL [*Library symbol Library of Congress*] (LCLS) .... IHilbSD
Hillsboro, IL [*FM radio station call letters*] .... WXAJ
Hillsboro, NH [*FM radio station call letters*] .... WRCI
Hillsboro, OH [*Location identifier FAA*] (FAAL) .... HOC
Hillsboro, OH [*AM radio station call letters*] .... WSRW
Hillsboro, OH [*FM radio station call letters*] .... WSRW-FM
Hillsboro, OR [*Location identifier FAA*] (FAAL) .... HIO
Hillsboro, OR [*AM radio station call letters*] .... KUIK
Hillsboro Public Library, Hillsboro, IL [*Library symbol Library of Congress*] (LCLS) .... IHilb
Hillsboro Public Library, Hillsboro, OR [*Library symbol Library of Congress*] (LCLS) .... OrHil
Hillsboro, TX [*FM radio station call letters*] .... KBRQ
Hillsboro, TX [*AM radio station call letters*] .... KHBR
Hillsboro, WI [*Location identifier FAA*] (FAAL) .... HBW
Hillsborough Community College, Tampa, FL [*Library symbol*] [*Library of Congress*] (LCLS) .... FTHil
Hillsborough Public Library, Hillsborough, NJ [*Library symbol Library of Congress*] (LCLS) .... NjHb
Hillsdale College, Hillsdale, MI [*Library symbol Library of Congress*] (LCLS) .... MiHilC
Hillsdale College, Mossey Learning Center, Hillsdale, MI [*OCLC symbol*] (OCLC) .... EEI
Hillsdale County Railroad Co., Inc. [*AAR code*] .... HCRC
Hillsdale, MI [*AM radio station call letters*] .... WCSR
Hillsdale, MI [*FM radio station call letters*] .... WCSR-FM
Hillside Bedding [*NASDAQ symbol*] (TTSB) .... BEDSD
Hillside Bedding Corp. [*NASDAQ symbol*] (SAG) .... ATEC
Hillside Bedding Corp. [*Associated Press*] (SAG) .... HillBd
Hillside Bedding Corp. [*Associated Press*] (SAG) .... HillsBd
Hillside Energy [*Vancouver Stock Exchange symbol*] .... HFE
Hillside Free Public Library, Hillside, NJ [*Library symbol Library of Congress*] (LCLS) .... NjHil
Hillside Grade School, New Hyde Park, NY [*Library symbol*] [*Library of Congress*] (LCLS) .... NNhpHE
Hillside Hospital, Glen Oaks, NY [*Library symbol Library of Congress*] (LCLS) .... NGoH
Hillside Junior High School, Sauk Rapids, MN [*Library symbol*] [*Library of Congress*] (LCLS) .... MnSrHJ
Hillside Public Library, Hillside, IL [*Library symbol Library of Congress*] (LCLS) .... IHil
Hillside Public Library, New Hyde Park, NY [*Library symbol Library of Congress*] (LCLS) .... NNhpH
Hillside Times, Hillside, NJ [*Library symbol Library of Congress*] (LCLS) .... NjHilT
Hillsville, VA [*AM radio station call letters*] .... WHHV
Hilltop [*NWS*] (FAAC) .... HLTP
Hilltop .... HLTP
Hillyer College, Hartford, CT [*Library symbol Library of Congress*] (LCLS) .... CtHHy
Hillyer's Reports [*20-22 California*] [*A publication*] (DLA) .... Hillyer
Hilo [*Hawaii*] [*Seismograph station code, US Geological Survey*] (SEIS) .... HIL
Hilo [*Hawaii*] [*Airport symbol*] (OAG) .... ITO
Hi-Lo Automotive [*NYSE symbol*] (SPSG) .... HLO
Hi-Lo Automotive, Inc. [*Associated Press*] (SAG) .... HiLo
Hilo College, Hilo, HI [*Library symbol Library of Congress*] (LCLS) .... HHIC
Hilo/General Lyman Field, Hawaii Island [*Hawaii*] [*ICAO location identifier*] (ICLI) .... PHTO
Hilo, HI [*Location identifier FAA*] (FAAL) .... ITO
Hilo, HI [*AM radio station call letters*] .... KAHU
Hilo, HI [*FM radio station call letters*] .... KAOE
Hilo, HI [*Television station call letters*] .... KGMD
Hilo, HI [*Television station call letters*] .... KHAW
Hilo, HI [*Television station call letters*] .... KHBC
Hilo, HI [*AM radio station call letters*] .... KHLO
Hilo, HI [*Television station call letters*] .... KHVO
Hilo, HI [*FM radio station call letters*] .... KHWI
Hilo, HI [*AM radio station call letters*] .... KIPA
Hilo, HI [*FM radio station call letters*] .... KKBG
Hilo, HI [*FM radio station call letters*] (RBYB) .... KNWB
Hilo, HI [*AM radio station call letters*] .... KPUA
Hilo, HI [*FM radio station call letters*] .... KPVS
Hilo, HI [*Television station call letters*] .... KWHH
Hilo, HI [*FM radio station call letters*] .... KWXX
Hilongos, Leyte Del Norte [*Philippines*] [*ICAO location identifier*] (ICLI) .... RPVH
Hilprecht Anniversary Volume. Studies in Assyriology and Archaeology Dedicated to Hermann V. Hilprecht [*Leipzig*] [*A publication*] (BJA) .... HAV
Hilton Communications Network [*Hilton Hotels Corp.*] [*Beverly Hills, CA*] [*Telecommunications service*] (TSSD) .... HCN
Hilton Davis Chemical Co., Cincinnati, OH [*Library symbol Library of Congress*] (LCLS) .... OCHDC
Hilton Head Island [*South Carolina*] [*Airport symbol*] (OAG) .... HHH
Hilton Head Island, SC [*AM radio station call letters*] (RBYB) .... WFXH
Hilton Head Island, SC [*FM radio station call letters*] .... WFXH-FM
Hilton Head Island, SC [*FM radio station call letters*] .... WIJY
Hilton High School Library, Hilton, NY [*OCLC symbol*] (OCLC) .... RWM
Hilton Hotels [*NYSE symbol*] (TTSB) .... HLT
Hilton Hotels Corp. [*Associated Press*] (SAG) .... Hilton
Hilton Hotels Corp. [*NYSE symbol*] (SPSG) .... HLT
Hilton Resource Corp. [*Vancouver Stock Exchange symbol*] .... HIR
Hilton Union Public Library, Hilton Beach, Ontario [*Library symbol National Library of Canada*] (NLC) .... OHBHU
Hilton's New York Common Pleas Reports [*A publication*] (DLA) .... Hilt
Hilton's New York Common Pleas Reports [*A publication*] (DLA) .... Hilt (NY)
Hilversum [*Netherlands ICAO location identifier*] (ICLI) .... EHHV
HIM [*Hardware Interface Module*] **Configuration File** [*NASA*] (NASA) .... HCF
HIM [*Hardware Interface Module*] **Equipment Rack** [*NASA*] (NASA) .... HER
HIM [*Hardware Interface Module*] **Interface Distributor** (NASA) .... HID
Himac Resources Ltd. [*Vancouver Stock Exchange symbol*] .... HIM
Himachal Pradesh Tourist Development Corp. [*India*] .... HPTDC
Himachali [*MARC language code Library of Congress*] (LCCP) .... him
Himalaya Mountain Region [*MARC geographic area code Library of Congress*] (LCCP) .... ah----
Himeji [*Japan*] [*Seismograph station code, US Geological Survey*] (SEIS) .... HIM
Himself .... HIMS
Himself (DAVI) .... SE
Hincherton Hayfever Helmet [*Clear plastic head-enclosing device that allegedly relieves hayfever symptoms*] .... HHH
Hinchinbrook, AK [*Location identifier FAA*] (FAAL) .... HBK
Hinchinbrook Island [*Alaska*] [*Seismograph station code, US Geological Survey*] (SEIS) .... HIN
Hinchinbrook Island [*Australia Airport symbol*] .... HNK
Hinchinbrooke Public Library, Frontenac County Library, Parkham, Ontario [*Library symbol National Library of Canada*] (BIB) .... OPFC
Hinckley Elementary School, Hinckley, MN [*Library symbol*] [*Library of Congress*] (LCLS) .... MnHE
Hinckley High School, Hinckley, MN [*Library symbol*] [*Library of Congress*] (LCLS) .... MnHH
Hinckley Pilot 35 Association (EA) .... HPTA
Hincmari Epistolae [*A publication*] (DLA) .... Hincmar Epist
Hindenberg Society (EA) .... HS
Hindered Amine Light Stabilizers [*for plastics*] .... HALS
Hinde's Modern Practice of the High Court of Chancery [*A publication*] (DLA) .... Hinde Ch Pr
Hindi (WDAA) .... HI
Hindi [*MARC language code Library of Congress*] (LCCP) .... hin
Hindi (WDAA) .... HIND
Hindman, KY [*AM radio station call letters*] .... WKCB
Hindman, KY [*FM radio station call letters*] .... WKCB-FM
Hindmarch on Patents [*A publication*] (DLA) .... Hind Pat
Hindrance (ROG) .... HDRANCE
Hinds Junior College [*Raymond, MS*] .... HJC
Hinds Junior College, Raymond, MS [*OCLC symbol*] (OCLC) .... MRH
Hinds Junior College, Raymond, MS [*Library symbol Library of Congress*] (LCLS) .... MsRH
Hind's Practice [*A publication*] (DLA) .... Hind Pr
Hindu (ABBR) .... H
Hindu (WDAA) .... HIND
Hindu Law Journal [*A publication*] (DLA) .... Hind LJ
Hindu Law Journal [*A publication*] (DLA) .... HLJ
Hindu Law Quarterly [*A publication*] (DLA) .... Hind LQ
Hindu Meal [*Airline notation*] .... HNML
Hindustan .... Hind
Hindustan Aeronautics Ltd. .... HAL
Hindustan Bible Institute (EA) .... HBI
Hindustan-Aeronautics Ltd. [*India*] [*ICAO aircraft manufacturer identifier*] (ICAO) .... HN
Hindustani [*Language, etc.*] .... HIND
Hindustani Ghadar Party-Organization of Indian Marxist-Leninists Abroad .... HGP-OIMLA
Hine and Nicholas. Insurance Digest [*A publication*] (DLA) .... Hine & N Dig
Hine and Nicholas on Assignment of Life Policies [*A publication*] (DLA) .... Hine & N Ass
Hinekford [*England*] .... HINEKF
Hines Administrative Center [*Veterans Administration*] .... HAC
Hines Creek High School, Alberta [*Library symbol National Library of Canada*] (BIB) .... AHCS
Hines Creek Municipal Library, Alberta [*Library symbol National Library of Canada*] (NLC) .... AHCM
Hines Creek Municipal Library, Hines Creek, AB, Canada [*Library symbol*] [*Library of Congress*] (LCLS) .... CaAHcM
Hines' Reports [*83-96 Kentucky*] [*A publication*] (DLA) .... Hines
Hinesville, GA [*Location identifier FAA*] (FAAL) .... LHW
Hinesville, GA [*Location identifier FAA*] (FAAL) .... UTQ
Hinesville, GA [*AM radio station call letters*] .... WGML
Hinesville, GA [*FM radio station call letters*] (RBYB) .... WHVL
Hinesville, GA [*FM radio station call letters*] .... WSKX
Hinge [*Automotive engineering*] .... HGE
Hinge (MSA) .... HNG
Hinge Jaw (MSA) .... HJ
Hinge Line [*Technical drawings*] .... HL
Hinge Mount (MCD) .... HM
Hinge Pillar [*Technical drawings*] .... HPLR
Hinge Remnant [*Philately*] .... hr
Hinge Side .... HS
Hinged [*Philately*] .... H
Hinged Block [*British military*] (DMA) .... HB
Hinged Deoxyribonucleic Acid [*Biochemistry, genetics*] .... HDNA

Hinged Plotting Board ... HPB
Hinged Rotor Blade ... HRB
Hinged Seat (AAG) ... HS
Hingham Institution for Savings [*NASDAQ symbol*] (CTT) ... HIFS
Hingham Institution for Savings [*Associated Press*] (SAG) ... HingmS
Hingham Marine Museum, Hingham, MA [*Library symbol Library of Congress*] (LCLS) ... MHingM
Hino Fuel Economy Clean Air High-Durability [*Hino diesel engines*] ... HFCD
Hino Micro Mixing System [*Diesel engines*] ... HMMS
Hino Super Flow Turbine [*Diesel engine*] ... HSET
Hinojosa Del Duque [*Spain ICAO location identifier*] (ICLI) ... LEHI
Hinsdale Financial [*NASDAQ symbol*] (TTSB) ... HNFC
Hinsdale Financial Corp. [*Associated Press*] (SAG) ... Hinsdle
Hinsdale Financial Corp. [*NASDAQ symbol*] (SAG) ... HNFC
Hinsdale, IL [*FM radio station call letters*] ... WHSD
Hinsdale, NH [*FM radio station call letters*] ... WYRY
Hinsdale Public Library, Hinsdale, IL [*Library symbol Library of Congress*] (LCLS) ... IH
Hinton [*Test*] [*Medicine*] ... HINT
Hinton, AB [*AM radio station call letters*] ... CIYR
Hinton Public Library, Alberta [*Library symbol National Library of Canada*] (NLC) ... AH
Hinton, WV [*AM radio station call letters*] ... WMTD
Hinton, WV [*FM radio station call letters*] ... WMTD-FM
Hip Disarticulation [*Medicine*] ... HD
Hip Orthosis [*Medicine*] ... HO
Hip Osteoarthritis [*Medicine*] (DMAA) ... HOA
Hi-Peg Resources Ltd. [*Vancouver Stock Exchange symbol*] ... HEP
Hip-Knee Orthosis [*Medicine*] ... HKO
Hip-Knee-Ankle Orthosis [*Medicine*] ... HKAO
Hip-Knee-Ankle-Foot Orthosis [*Medicine*] ... HKAFO
Hi-Pot Dwell Time ... HDT
Hipparchus [*of Plato*] [*Classical studies*] (OCD) ... Hipparch
Hippeastrum Mosaic Virus [*Plant pathology*] ... HIMV
Hippelates [*A genus of insects*] [*Entomology*] (DAVI) ... H
Hippel-Lindau Syndrome [*Medicine*] (DMAA) ... HLS
Hippias Minor [*of Plato*] [*Classical studies*] (OCD) ... Hp Mi
Hippo Valley [*Zimbabwe*] [*Airport symbol*] (AD) ... HPO
Hippocampal ... HC
Hippocampal Fissure [*Neuroanatomy*] ... HF
Hippocampal Pyramidal Cell [*Neuroanatomy*] ... HP
Hippocampal Pyramidal Cell [*Neuroanatomy*] ... HPC
Hippocampus [*Brain anatomy*] ... HPC
Hippocrates [*Greek physician, 460 -377 BC*] ... HIPP
Hippocrates [*Greek physician, 460 -377 BC*] [*Classical studies*] (OCD) ... Hippoc
Hippodrome [*London*] (DSUE) ... HIPPO
Hippolytus [*of Euripides*] [*Classical studies*] (OCD) ... Hipp
Hippolytus Bonacossa [*Deceased, 1591*] [*Authority cited in pre-1607 legal work*] (DSA) ... Hipp Bonacoss
Hippolytus Marsilius [*Deceased, 1529*] [*Authority cited in pre-1607 legal work*] (DSA) ... Hipo
Hippolytus Riminaldus [*Deceased, 1589*] [*Authority cited in pre-1607 legal work*] (DSA) ... Hip Riminal
Hippopotamus (DSUE) ... HIPPO
Hirakud [*India*] [*ICAO location identifier*] (ICLI) ... VEHK
Hiram Abiff [*Freemasonry*] (ROG) ... HA
Hiram Abiff [*Freemasonry*] (ROG) ... HAB
Hiram College, Hiram, OH [*OCLC symbol*] (OCLC) ... HIR
Hiram College, Hiram, OH [*Library symbol Library of Congress*] (LCLS) ... OHirC
Hiram Halley Memorial Library, Pound Ridge, NY [*Library symbol*] [*Library of Congress*] (LCLS) ... NPour
Hiram, King of Tyre [*Freemasonry*] ... HKT
Hiram Scott College, Scottsbluff, NE [*Library symbol Library of Congress Obsolete*] (LCLS) ... NbSHS
Hiram Ulysses Grant [*US general and president, 1822-1885*] ... HUG
Hiram Walker - Gooderham & Worts [*Canada*] ... HWGW
Hiram Walker Historical Museum, Windsor, Ontario [*Library symbol National Library of Canada*] (BIB) ... OWHM
Hire and Rental Association of Australia ... HRAA
Hire Car (ADA) ... HC
Hire Purchase ... HP
Hire Purchase Trade Association [*British*] (BI) ... HPTA
Hired Farm Working Force ... HFWF
Hired Fishermen's Association [*A union*] [*British*] ... HFA
Hirel Holdings, Inc. [*Associated Press*] (SAG) ... HirelHld
Hirel Holdings, Inc. [*NASDAQ symbol*] (SAG) ... HIRL
Hiring (ROG) ... HIR
Hiring, Retention, and Tenure [*of college professors*] ... HRT
Hi-Rise Recycling Sys [*NASDAQ symbol*] (TTSB) ... HIRI
Hiroo [*Japan*] [*Seismograph station code, US Geological Survey*] (SEIS) ... HOO
Hiroshima [*Japan*] [*Airport symbol*] (OAG) ... HIJ
Hiroshima [*Japan*] [*Seismograph station code, US Geological Survey*] (SEIS) ... HIR
Hiroshima [*Japan ICAO location identifier*] (ICLI) ... RJOA
Hiroshima Peace Center Associates [*Defunct*] (EA) ... HPCA
Hirsch International Corp. [*Associated Press*] (SAG) ... Hirsch
Hirsch International Corp. [*NASDAQ symbol*] (SAG) ... HRSH
Hirsch Intl. Corp'A' [*NASDAQ symbol*] (TTSB) ... HRSH
Hirschsprung's Disease [*Medicine*] (DMAA) ... HD
Hirshhorn Museum and Sculpture Garden [*Smithsonian Institution*] ... HM & SG
Hirth KG [*Germany ICAO aircraft manufacturer identifier*] (ICAO) ... HI
Hirudo [*A Leech*] [*Pharmacy*] (ROG) ... HIRUD
His Beatitude [*or His Blessedness*] ... HB
His [*or Her*] **Britannic Majesty** ... HBM
His [*or Her*] **Britannic Majesty's Service** ... HBMS
His [*or Her*] **Britannic Majesty's Ship** (ROG) ... HBMS
His Bundle [*Cardiology*] ... HB
His Bundle Electrogram [*Cardiology*] ... HBE
His [*or Her*] **Catholic Majesty** ... HCM
His Eminence ... HE
His [*or Her*] **Exalted Highness** [*Term applied only to personages of British India*] ... HEH
His [*or Her*] **Excellency** ... HE
His [*or Her*] **Grace** ... HG
His [*or Her*] **Grand Ducal Highness** ... HGDH
His Hellenic Majesty's Ship ... HHMS
His [*or Her*] **Highness** ... HH
His Highness the Nizam's Cavalry [*British military*] (DMA) ... HHNC
His Holiness ... HH
His Honour [*British*] (ADA) ... HH
His [*or Her*] **Imperial and Royal Highness** ... HI and RH
His [*or Her*] **Imperial Highness** ... HIH
His Imperial Japanese Majesty's Ship ... HIJMS
His [*or Her*] **Imperial Majesty** ... HIM
His [*or Her*] **Majesty** ... HM
His [*or Her*] **Majesty's Aircraft Carrier** ... HMAC
His [*or Her*] **Majesty's Airship** ... HMA
His [*or Her*] **Majesty's Alkali and Clean Air Inspectorate** [*British*] (DCTA) ... HMACI
His [*or Her*] **Majesty's Armed Forces** ... HMAF
His [*or Her*] **Majesty's Army Vessel** [*British military*] (DMA) ... HMAV
His [*or Her*] **Majesty's Boom Defence Vessel** ... HMBDV
His [*or Her*] **Majesty's British Ship** ... HMBS
His [*or Her*] **Majesty's Canadian Navy** ... HMCN
His [*or Her*] **Majesty's Canadian Ship** ... HMCS
His [*or Her*] **Majesty's Civil Service** ... HMCS
His [*or Her*] **Majesty's Colonial Steamer** [*In use in 19th century*] ... HMCS
His [*or Her*] **Majesty's Council** (ROG) ... HMC
His [*or Her*] **Majesty's Customs** ... HMC
His [*or Her*] **Majesty's Customs and Excise** [*British*] (DCTA) ... HMC & E
His [*or Her*] **Majesty's Destroyer** [*British military*] (DMA) ... HMD
His [*or Her*] **Majesty's Dockyard** [*Navy British*] ... HMD
His [*or Her*] **Majesty's Drifter** ... HMD
His [*or Her*] **Majesty's Factory Inspectorate** [*Department of Employment*] [*British*] ... HMFI
His [*or Her*] **Majesty's Factory Inspectorate Headquarters** [*Department of Employment*] [*British*] ... HMFIHQ
His [*or Her*] **Majesty's Forces** ... HMF
His [*or Her*] **Majesty's Government** ... HMG
His [*or Her*] **Majesty's Gunboat** ... HMGB
His [*or Her*] **Majesty's Hospital Ship** ... HMHS
His [*or Her*] **Majesty's Household** ... HMH
His [*or Her*] **Majesty's Indian Military Forces** ... HMIMF
His [*or Her*] **Majesty's Indian Navy** ... HMIN
His [*or Her*] **Majesty's Indian Ship** [*British military*] (DMA) ... HMIS
His [*or Her*] **Majesty's Industrial Pollution Inspectorate for Scotland** (DCTA) ... HMIPI
His [*or Her*] **Majesty's Inspector** ... HMI
His [*or Her*] **Majesty's Inspector of Factories** (ROG) ... HMIF
His [*or Her*] **Majesty's Inspector of Schools** (ROG) ... HMIS
His [*or Her*] **Majesty's Inspectorate of Pollution** [*British*] ... HMIP
His [*or Her*] **Majesty's Land Registry** ... HMLR
His [*or Her*] **Majesty's Lieutenant** ... HML
His [*or Her*] **Majesty's Motor Launch** ... HMML
His [*or Her*] **Majesty's Motor Mine Sweeper** ... HMMMS
His [*or Her*] **Majesty's New Zealand Ship** ... HMNZS
His [*or Her*] **Majesty's Office of Works** (ROG) ... HMOW
His [*or Her*] **Majesty's Overseas Civil Service** ... HMOCS
His [*or Her*] **Majesty's Pollution Inspectorate** [*British*] (DCTA) ... HMPI
His [*or Her*] **Majesty's Procurator General and Treasury Solicitor** ... HMPGTS
His [*or Her*] **Majesty's Reserve Regiment** [*British military*] (DMA) ... HMRR
His [*or Her*] **Majesty's Royal Licence** (ROG) ... HMRL
His [*or Her*] **Majesty's Service** ... HMS
His [*or Her*] **Majesty's Ship** ... HMS
His [*or Her*] **Majesty's South African Ship** (DAS) ... HMSAS
His [*or Her*] **Majesty's Stationery Office** ... HMSO
His [*or Her*] **Majesty's Steamer** ... HMS
His [*or Her*] **Majesty's Submarine** ... HMS/M
His [*or Her*] **Majesty's Telegraph Ship** ... HMTS
His [*or Her*] **Majesty's Transport** ... HMT
His [*or Her*] **Majesty's Trawler** ... HMT
His [*or Her*] **Majesty's Troopship** [*British military*] (DMA) ... HMT
His [*or Her*] **Majesty's Tug** [*British military*] (DMA) ... HMT
His [*or Her*] **Majesty's Yacht** [*Navy British*] ... HMY
His Master's Voice [*Phonograph records*] ... HMV
His [*or Her*] **Royal and Imperial Highness** (ROG) ... HR & IH
His [*or Her*] **Royal Highness** ... HRH
His [*or Her*] **Royal Majesty** [*British*] ... HRM
His [*or Her*] **Serene Highness** [*Used for certain Continental European princes or princesses*] ... HSH
His [*or Her*] **Serene Majesty** ... HSM
Hi-Shear Indus [*NYSE symbol*] (TTSB) ... HSI
Hi-Shear Industries, Inc. [*Associated Press*] (SAG) ... HiShear
Hi-Shear Industries, Inc. [*NYSE symbol*] (SPSG) ... HSI
Hi-Shear Technology [*AMEX symbol*] (TTSB) ... HSR
Hiskey-Nebraska Test of Learning Aptitude (EDAC) ... H-NTLA
Hispania [*A publication*] (BRI) ... Hisp
Hispania Lineas Aereas SL [*Spain ICAO designator*] (FAAC) ... HSL
Hispanic ... H
Hispanic American Almanac [*A publication*] ... HAA

Hispanic American Historical Review [A publication] (BRI) .... HAHR
Hispanic American Ministries Task Force of JSAC [Joint Strategy and Action
  Committee] [Defunct] (EA) .... HAMTF
Hispanic Americans Information Directory [A publication] .... HAID
Hispanic Association of Colleges and Universities .... HACU
Hispanic Bar Association (EA) .... HBA
Hispanic Computing Association (EA) .... HCA
Hispanic Elected Local Officials (EA) .... HELO
Hispanic Employment Program [DoD] (MCD) .... HEP
Hispanic Employment Program Manager [DoD] .... HEPM
Hispanic Energy Forum [Defunct] (EA) .... HEF
Hispanic Health and Mental Health Data Base [National Institute of Mental
  Health] [Information service or system] (CRD) .... HHMHDB
Hispanic Health and Nutrition Examination Survey [Department of Health
  and Human Services] (GFGA) .... HHANES
Hispanic Higher Education Coalition [Defunct] (EA) .... HHEC
Hispanic Institute (EA) .... HI
Hispanic Institute for the Performing Arts [Defunct] (EA) .... HIFPA
Hispanic Institute in the United States [Later, HI] (EA) .... HIUS
Hispanic Literature Criticism [A publication] .... HLC
Hispanic Marketing Handbook [A publication] .... HMH
Hispanic National Bar Association (EA) .... HNBA
Hispanic Organization of Latin Actors (EA) .... HOLA
Hispanic Organization of Professionals and Executives [Silver Spring, MD]
  (EA) .... HOPE
Hispanic Policy Development Project (EA) .... HPDP
Hispanic Public Affairs Association (EA) .... HPAA
Hispanic Serving Institution .... HSI
Hispanic Society of America (EA) .... HSA
Hispanic Society of America, New York, NY [Library symbol Library of
  Congress] (LCLS) .... NNH
Hispanic Surname American .... HSA
Hispanic Urban Professional [Lifestyle classification] .... HUPPIE
Hispanic Writers [A publication] .... HW
Hispaniola [MARC geographic area code Library of Congress] (LCCP) .... nwhi--
Hispaniola Airways [Dominican Republic] [ICAO designator] (FAAC) .... HIS
Hispaniola Airways [ICAO designator] (AD) .... ZS
Hispano-Suiza Society (EA) .... HSS
Hispavox [Record label] [Spain] .... Hispa
Hissar [India] [ICAO location identifier] (ICLI) .... VIHR
Histadruth Ivrith of America .... HI
Histadruth Ivrith of America (EA) .... HIA
Histamine [Anesthesiology] .... H
Histamine Challenge Test [Biochemistry] (DAVI) .... HCT
Histamine Club [Later, HRSNA] (EA) .... HC
Histamine Equivalent Prick Unit [Immunology] .... HEP
Histamine Inhalation Test [Immunology] .... HIT
Histamine Methyltransferase [An enzyme] .... HMT
Histamine Phosphate Acid [Biochemistry] (DAVI) .... HAP
Histamine Release [Immunology] .... HR
Histamine Releasing Activity [Medicine] (DAVI) .... HRA
Histamine Releasing Factor [Immunology] .... HRF
Histamine Research Society of North America (EA) .... HRSNA
Histamine Sensitive [Immunology] .... HS
Histamine-Forming Capacity (DMAA) .... HFC
Histamine-Induced Suppressor Factor [Immunology] .... HSF
Histamine-Producing Cell-Stimulating Factor [Biochemistry] .... HCSF
Histamine-Release Inhibitory Factor [Antiinflammatory] .... HRIF
Histamine-Sensitizing Factor [Immunology] .... HSF
Histatin (DMAA) .... HIS
Histidine [One-letter symbol] .... H
Histidine [An amino acid] (MAE) .... Hi
Histidine [An amino acid] .... His
Histidine [An amino acid] (DOG) .... his
Histidine Decarboxylase [An enzyme] .... HDC
Histidine Protein Kinase [An enzyme] .... HPK
Histidinemia [Medicine] (AAMN) .... Hist
Histidine-Rich Glycoprotein [Biochemistry] .... HRG
Histidine-Rich Protein [Biochemistry, immunochemistry] .... HRP
Histidinol Dehydrogenase [An enzyme] .... HDH
Histiocytic Lymphoma [Oncology] .... HL
Histiocytosis X [or Histocytosis X] [Hematology] .... HX
Histioeosinophilic Granuloma [Medicine] .... HEG
Histochemical Society (EA) .... HCS
Histocompatibility Antigen Modifier [Genetics] .... HAM
Histocompatibility Locus [Immunology] .... HL
Histocompatibility Locus Antigens [System] [Immunology] .... HLA
Histocompatibility Y [Immunology] .... H-Y
Histocytic Medullary Reticulosis [Oncology] .... HMR
Histogram Average Ogive Calculator .... HAVOC
Histogram Scanning .... HIS
Histoire [History] [French] (ROG) .... HIST
Histoire Generale des Religions [A publication] (BJA) .... HGR
Histologic HCM [Hypertrophic Cardiomyopathy] Index .... HHI
Histologic Technician [or Technologist] (MAE) .... HT
Histologic Technician (American Society of Clinical Pathologists)
  (DMAA) .... HT(ASCP)
Histologic Technologist [Medicine] (MEDA) .... HTL
Histologic Transformation [Medicine] .... HT
Histology (ADA) .... HIST
Histology [Medicine] (DAVI) .... histo
Histology .... HISTOL
Histone Acetyltransferase [An enzyme] .... HAT
Histone Deacetylase [An enzyme] .... HD
Histoplasma [Biochemistry] (DAVI) .... H

Histoplasma [Medicine] (DAVI) .... histo
Histoplasmin [Skin test] [Medicine] (DAVI) .... histo
Histoplasmosis [Medicine] (DAVI) .... histo
Historia [A publication] (OCD) .... Hist
Historia Animalium [of Aristotle] [Classical studies] (OCD) .... HA
Historia Animalium [of Aristotle] [Classical studies] (OCD) .... Hist An
Historia Augusta [A publication] (OCD) .... Hist Aug
Historia Ecclesiastica [of Eusebius] [Classical studies] (OCD) .... HE
Historia Ecclesiastica [of Eusebius] [Classical studies] (OCD) .... Hist Eccl
Historia Numorum [A publication] (OCD) .... Hist Num
Historia Plantarum [of Theophrastus] [Classical studies] (OCD) .... Hist Pl
Historiae [of Sallust] [Classical studies] (OCD) .... H
Historiae [of Tacitus] [Classical studies] (OCD) .... Hist
Historiae Societatis Socius [Fellow of the Historical Society] [Latin] .... HSS
Historian [or History] (EY) .... HIS
Historian [or History] (AFM) .... HIST
Historian (AABC) .... HISTN
Historian's Microfilm Co., Cazenovia, NY [Library symbol Library of
  Congress] (LCLS) .... HmC
Historians of American Communism (EA) .... HAC
Historic Aircraft Association [British] .... HAA
Historic Aircraft Preservation Society Ltd. [British] (BI) .... HAPS
Historic Aircraft Restoration Society [Australia] .... HARS
Historic American Buildings [Survey] [Library of Congress] .... HAB
Historic American Buildings Survey [Library of Congress] .... HABS
Historic American Engineering Record [Department of the Interior] .... HAER
Historic Buildings and Ancient Monuments Act [Town planning]
  [British] .... HBAM
Historic Buildings Bureau [British] .... HBB
Historic Buildings Council [British] .... HBC
Historic Churches Preservation Trust [British] (BI) .... HCPT
Historic Commands of the American Revolution (EA) .... HCAR
Historic Commercial Vehicle Club [British] (DCTA) .... HCVC
Historic Commercial Vehicle Cooperative Society [Australia] .... HCVCS
Historic Control Trial [Medicine] (DMAA) .... HCT
Historic Cost Accounts [London Stock Exchange] .... HCA
Historic Deerfield (EA) .... HD
Historic Deerfield, Inc., Deerfield, MA [Library symbol Library of Congress]
  (LCLS) .... MDeeH
Historic Festivals of the United States [A publication] .... HFUS
Historic Fire Engine Association of Australia .... HFEAA
Historic House Association [British] .... HHA
Historic House Association of America (EA) .... HHAA
Historic Houses Trust of New South Wales [Australia] .... HHTNSW
Historic Landmarks of Irish America [A publication] .... HLIA
Historic Landscapes Group [British] (DBA) .... HLG
Historic Mobile Preservation Society Headquarters, Mobile, AL [Library
  symbol Library of Congress] (LCLS) .... AMobHi
Historic Motor Sports Association (EA) .... HMSA
Historic Naval Ships Association of North America (EA) .... HINAS
Historic Naval Ships of the World [Later, HINAS] (EA) .... HINASW
[The] Historic New Orleans Collection, New Orleans, LA [Library symbol
  Library of Congress] (LCLS) .... LNHiC
Historic Pensacola Preservation Board, Pensacola, FL [Library symbol]
  [Library of Congress] (LCLS) .... FPeHiP
Historic Photographic Collection, Vancouver Public Library, British
  Columbia [Library symbol National Library of Canada] (NLC) .... BVAHP
Historic Preservation Fund [National Trust for Historic Preservation] .... HPF
Historic Pullman Foundation (EA) .... HPF
Historic Record Society [Record label] .... HRS
Historic Rehabilitation Tax Credit .... HRTC
Historic Resources Conservation Subsection Office, Prairie Region
  Library, ParksCanada [Ressources et Conservation Historiques,
  Bibliotheque de la Region de s Pres, Parcs Canada] Winnipeg, Manitoba
  [Library symbol National Library of Canada] (NLC) .... MWPCPH
Historic Shipwrecks Advisory Committee [Victoria, Australia] .... HSAC
Historic Statistics of Black America [A publication] .... HSBA
Historic Stock Car Racing Group .... HSCRG
Historic Towns [A publication] .... HT
Historic Winslow House, Marshfield, MA [Library symbol Library of
  Congress] (LCLS) .... MMarsW
Historic World Leaders [A publication] .... HWL
Historic Yale Museum, British Columbia [Library symbol National Library of
  Canada] (NLC) .... BYM
Historical [Linguistics] .... HIST
Historical .... HISTL
Historical .... HISTRCL
Historical Artillery Corps [British] [An association] (DBA) .... HAC
Historical Association [British] (EAIO) .... HA
Historical Association of Southern Florida, Miami, FL [Library symbol Library
  of Congress] (LCLS) .... FMHiS
Historical Atlas of Canada [Project] .... HAC
Historical Automobile Society of Canada .... HASC
Historical Biographical Dictionaries Master Index [A publication] .... HBDMI
Historical Branch [Army] .... HB
Historical Breechloading Smallarms Association [British] (DBA) .... HBSA
Historical Climate Network .... HCN
Historical Commission .... HC
Historical Commission, Southern Baptist Convention (EA) .... HCSBC
Historical Committee of the Mennonite Church (EA) .... MHC
Historical Cost (ADA) .... HC
Historical Cost/Current Purchasing Power .... HC/CPP
Historical Cost Database .... HCDB
Historical Data Storage and Retrieval .... HDSR
Historical Data System [Air Force] (MCD) .... HDS

Historical Development .... HD
Historical Dictionary of American Slang [*Random House*] .... HDAS
Historical Division [*Air Force*] .... HD
Historical Earthquake Data (NRCH) .... HED
Historical English Dictionary [*A publication*] .... HED
Historical Evaluation and Research Organization (AEBS) .... HERO
Historical Farm Association (EA) .... HFA
Historical Foundation of the Presbyterian and Reformed Churches, Montreat, NC [*Library symbol Library of Congress*] (LCLS) .... NcMHi
Historical Handbook .... HH
Historical Intelligence Collection [*CIA*] .... HIC
Historical Labor Applications [*Military*] (AFIT) .... HLA
Historical Manuscripts Commission [*British*] .... HMC
Historical Metallurgy Society [*British*] (EAIO) .... HMS
Historical Model Railway Society [*British*] (BI) .... HMRS
Historical Motion Picture Milestones Association .... HMPMA
Historical Period [*Dialog*] [*Searchable field*] [*Information service or system*] (NITA) .... HP
Historical Period Ending Date [*Dialog*] [*Searchable field*] [*Information service or system*] (NITA) .... HE
Historical Period Starting Date [*Dialog*] [*Searchable field*] [*Information service or system*] (NITA) .... HS
Historical Preservation of America [*Publisher*] (EA) .... HPA
Historical Quotes [*Information retrieval*] .... HQ
Historical Radio Society of Australia .... HRSA
Historical Record (NASA) .... HR
Historical Record Log (SAA) .... HRL
Historical Records of Australian Science [*A publication*] .... H Rec A Sc
Historical Records of Victoria [*A publication*] .... HRV
Historical Re-Issue [*Record cataloging*] .... H
Historical Report - Korea Military Advisory Group .... HR-KMAG
Historical Review Press [*British*] .... HRP
Historical Sea Surface Temperature Data Project [*WMO*] (MSC) ... HSSTD
Historical Sea Surface Temperature Dataset [*Marine science*] (OSRA) ... HSSTD
Historical Society Nicholas Denis, Caraquet, NB, Canada [*Library symbol Library of Congress*] (LCLS) .... CaNBCH
Historical Society Nicolas Denys, Societe Historique Nicolas Denys, Caraquet, New Brunswick [*Library symbol National Library of Canada*] (NLC) .... NBCH
Historical Society of Berks County, Reading, PA [*Library symbol Library of Congress*] (LCLS) .... PRHi
Historical Society of Bloomfield, Bloomfield, NJ [*Library symbol Library of Congress*] (LCLS) .... NjBlHi
Historical Society of Cheshire County, Keene, NH [*Library symbol Library of Congress*] (LCLS) .... NhKeHi
Historical Society of Delaware, Wilmington, DE [*Library symbol Library of Congress*] (LCLS) .... DeHi
Historical Society of Early American Decoration [*Defunct*] (EA) ... HSEAD
Historical Society of Frankford, Philadelphia, PA [*Library symbol Library of Congress Obsolete*] (LCLS) .... PPFHi
[*The*] Historical Society of Frederick County, Inc., Frederick, MD [*Library symbol Library of Congress*] (LCLS) .... MdFreHi
Historical Society of Haddonfield, Haddonfield, NJ [*Library symbol Library of Congress*] (LCLS) .... NjHHi
Historical Society of Long Beach, Inc., Long Beach, CA [*Library symbol Library of Congress*] (LCLS) .... CLobHi
Historical Society of Montgomery County, Norristown, PA [*Library symbol Library of Congress Obsolete*] (LCLS) .... PNortHi
Historical Society of New Mexico, Santa Fe, NM [*Library symbol Library of Congress*] (LCLS) .... NmHi
Historical Society of Ottawa Library and the Bytown Historical Museum, Ontario [*Library symbol National Library of Canada*] (NLC) ... OOHi
Historical Society of Ottawa Library and the Bytown Historical Museum, Ottawa, ON, Canada [*Library symbol Library of Congress*] (LCLS) ... CaOOHi
Historical Society of Pennsylvania, Philadelphia, PA [*Library symbol Library of Congress*] (LCLS) .... PHi
Historical Society of Porter County, Valparaiso, IN [*Library symbol Library of Congress*] (LCLS) .... InValHi
Historical Society of Princeton, Princeton, NJ [*Library symbol Library of Congress*] (LCLS) .... NjPHi
Historical Society of Southern California, Los Angeles, CA [*Library symbol Library of Congress*] (LCLS) .... CLHi
Historical Society of the Episcopal Church (EA) .... HSEC
Historical Society of the Evangelical and Reformed Church [*Later, ERHS-UCC*] (EA) .... HSERC
Historical Society of the Evangelical United Brethren Church [*Later, General Commission on Archives and History of the United Methodist Church*] (EA) .... HSEUBC
Historical Society of the Northern Territory [*Australia*] .... HSNT
Historical Society of the Southern Convention, Congregation of Christian Churches, Elon College, NC [*Library symbol Library of Congress*] (LCLS) .... NcElonCH
Historical Society of the Tarrytowns, Tarrytown, NY [*Library symbol Library of Congress*] (LCLS) .... NTaHi
Historical Society of the Tonawandas, Tonawanda, NY [*Library symbol Library of Congress*] (LCLS) .... NTonHi
Historical Society of the United Methodist Church (EA) .... HS/UMC
Historical Society of Washington, DC (EA) .... HSWDC
Historical Society of Western Pennsylvania, Pittsburgh, PA [*Library symbol Library of Congress*] (LCLS) .... PPiHi
Historical Society of York County, York, PA [*Library symbol Library of Congress*] (LCLS) .... PYHi
Historical Sources Collection Program .... HSCP
Historical Survey .... HS
Historically Black Colleges and Universities .... HBCU

Historically Black Colleges, Universities, and Minority Institutions (RDA) .... HBCU/MI
Historically Socialist Economy (ECON) .... HSE
Historically Underutilized Business Zone (AAGC) .... HUBZone
Historicorum Romanorum Reliquiae [*A publication*] (OCD) .... HR Rel
Historische Burowelt [*A publication*] .... HBw
Historische Grammatik der Hebraeischen Sprache [*H. Bauer and P. Leander*] [*A publication*] (BJA) .... BLH
Historische Grammatik der Hebraeischen Sprache [*H. Bauer and P. Leander*] [*A publication*] (BJA) .... HGH
History [*Secondary school course*] [*British*] .... H
History (VRA) .... hist
History [*Medicine*] (DMAA) .... hs
History [*Medicine*] .... Hx
History [*Medicine*] .... Hy
History Abstracts [*Database*] (NITA) .... HA
History Advertising Trust [*British*] (DBA) .... HAT
History and Examination .... H & E
History and Jurisdiction of the Courts of Law [*1835*] [*A publication*] (DLA) .... Aldridge
History and Physical [*Examination*] [*Medicine*] .... H & P
History and Physical Examination [*Medicine*] .... HPE
History & Political Science (DD) .... Hist&PolSc
History and Theory [*A publication*] (BRI) .... Hist & T
History Behind the Headlines [*A publication*] .... HBH
[*The*] History Book Club .... HBC
History Institute Victoria [*Australia*] .... HIV
History Memory System (MCD) .... HMS
History Of [*Medicine*] .... H/O
[*A*] History of Ancient Geography [*A publication*] (OCD) .... Hist Anc Geog
History of Chief Complaint [*Medicine*] .... HCC
History of Coverage (MCD) .... HOC
History of Dermatology Society (EA) .... HDS
History of Earth Sciences Society (EA) .... HESS
History of Economics Society (EA) .... HES
History of Education Review [*A publication*] .... Hist Ed R
History of Education Society (EA) .... HES
History of English Law, Edited by W. Holdsworth [*A publication*] (DLA) ... HEL
History of Greece [*A publication*] (OCD) .... Hist G
History of Greek Mathematics [*A publication*] (OCD) .... Hist of Greek Maths
History of Greek Philosophy [*A publication*] (OCD) .... Hist Gk Phil
History of Medicine On-Line [*National Library of Medicine*] [*Bibliographic database*] (IID) .... HISTLINE
History of Present Illness [*Medicine*] (HGAA) .... HOPI
History of Present Illness .... HPI
History of Programming Languages .... HOPL
History of Science Cases .... HOSC
History of Science Society (EA) .... HSS
[*A*] History of the Athenian Constitution [*A publication*] (OCD) ... Hist Athen Const
[*A*] History of the Book in Australia [*Project*] .... HOBA
[*The*] History of the Destruction of Bel and the Dragon [*Apocrypha*] .... BEL AND DRAGON
[*A*] History of the Jewish People in the Time of Jesus Christ [*Emil Schurer*] [*A publication*] (BJA) .... SHJP
History Office (MCD) .... HO
History Record Folder (MCD) .... HRF
History Report (MCD) .... HR
History: Reviews of New Books [*A publication*] (BRI) .... HRNB
History Section [*Reference and Adult Services Division*] [*American Library Association*] .... HS
History Section, Metropolitan Toronto Library, Ontario [*Library symbol National Library of Canada*] (NLC) .... OTPH
History Teachers' Association of New South Wales [*Australia*] ... HTANSW
History Today [*A publication*] (BRI) .... HT
History Trust of South Australia .... HTSA
Histotechnologist (American Society of Clinical Pathologists) (DMAA) .... HTL(ASCP)
Hit and Miss (WDAA) .... H & M
Hit by Ball [*or Hit Batsman*] [*Baseball*] .... HB
Hit by Pitcher [*Baseball*] .... HBP
Hit by Pitcher [*Baseball*] .... HP
Hit Indicator System .... HIS
Hit Probability [*Military*] (MCD) .... HITPRO
Hit Rate (MUGU) .... HR
Hit Ratio .... HR
Hit Scoring Device .... HSD
Hit Wicket [*Cricket*] (BARN) .... ht wkt
Hit Wicket .... HW
Hitachi Arithmetic Processor [*Computer science*] (IEEE) .... HARP
Hitachi Bipolar CMOS [*Complementary Metal Oxide Semiconductor*] (NITA) .... HiBiCMOS
Hitachi Computer (DIT) .... HITAC
Hitachi Computer Services (NITA) .... HITAC
Hitachi Ltd. [*NYSE symbol*] (SPSG) .... HIT
Hitachi Ltd. [*Associated Press*] (SAG) .... Hitachi
Hitachi Network Architecture .... HNA
Hitachi Parametron Automatic Computer .... HIPAC
Hitachi Training Reactor [*Japan*] .... HTR
Hitachi,Ltd ADR [*NYSE symbol*] (TTSB) .... HIT
Hitchhike Experiment Module (MCD) .... HEM
Hitchhiker (Goddard Space Flight Center) [*NASA*] .... HH-G
Hitchhiker (Marshall Space Flight Center) [*NASA*] .... HH-M
Hitchhikers for America (EA) .... HFA
Hitching .... HTCHNG

Hitch's Practice and Procedure in the Probate Court of Massachusetts [*A publication*] (DLA) .... Hitch Pr & Proc
Hi-Tech Pharmacal [*NASDAQ symbol*] (TTSB) .... HITK
HITIL [*Hardware in-the-Loop*] **Encapsulation Methodology** .... HET
Hitler and Mussolini [*Slang*] (DSUE) .... HIT and MISS
Hitox Corp. [*NASDAQ symbol*] (TTSB) .... HTXA
Hitox Corporation of America [*Associated Press*] (SAG) .... Hitox
Hitox Corp. of America [*NASDAQ symbol*] (CTT) .... HTXA
Hits [*Baseball*] .... H
Hits per Gun per Minute (NVT) .... HPGPM
Hittell's California Codes [*A publication*] (DLA) .... Hitt Cod
Hittell's California General Laws [*A publication*] (DLA) .... Hittell's Laws
Hittite (BJA) .... Hit
Hittite .... HITT
Hittite Laws (BJA) .... HL
Hittite Texts in the Cuneiform Character from Tablets in the British Museum [*London*] (BJA) .... HT
Hittman Associates, Inc., Columbia, MD [*Library symbol Library of Congress*] (LCLS) .... MdCoH
HIV [*Human Immunodeficiency Virus*] **-Associated Dementia Complex** [*Medicine*] .... HADC
Hiva-Oa/Atuana [*French Polynesia*] [*ICAO location identifier*] (ICLI) .... NTMN
HIV-Suppressive Factors [*Medicine*] .... HIV-SF
Hiwange Town [*Zimbabwe*] [*ICAO location identifier*] (ICLI) .... FVWT
Hizb Dastur Mustaghil Somalia [*Somali Independent Constitution Party*] .... HDMS
Hizbia Dighill e Mirifle [*Somali political party*] .... HDM
Hizbul Muslimin [*Islamic Front*] [*Malaysia*] [*Political party*] (FEA) .... HAMIM
H.J.A. Brown Education Centre, J. A. Turner Professional Library, Mississauga, ON, Canada [*Library symbol*] [*Library of Congress*] (LCLS) .... CaOMJAT
Hjelms [*Jim*] **Private Collection** [*Associated Press*] (SAG) .... JHjelm
Hlinka Slovak National People's Party [*Political party*] .... HSNPP
Hlinkova Slovenska l'Udova Strana [*Hlinka's Slovak People's Party*] [*Also, SL'S*] [*Political party*] (PPE) .... HSL'S
Hlth Fitness Physl Therapy [*NASDAQ symbol*] (TTSB) .... HFPT
Hmawbi [*Myanmar*] [*ICAO location identifier*] (ICLI) .... VBHB
HMG/Courtland Prop [*AMEX symbol*] (TTSB) .... HMG
HMG Property Investors, Inc. [*Formerly, Hospital Mortgage Group*] [*AMEX symbol*] (SPSG) .... HMG
HMG Worldwide [*NASDAQ symbol*] (TTSB) .... HMGC
HMG Worldwide Corp. [*Associated Press*] (SAG) .... HMG Wd
HMG Worldwide Corp. [*NASDAQ symbol*] (SAG) .... HMGC
HMI Industries [*Associated Press*] (SAG) .... HMI Ind
HMI Industries [*NASDAQ symbol*] (SAG) .... HMII
HMMWV [*High-Mobility Multipurpose Wheeled Vehicle*] **Interchange Mount System** [*Military*] (INF) .... HIMS
HMN Financial [*NASDAQ symbol*] (TTSB) .... HMNF
HMN Financial, Inc. [*Associated Press*] (SAG) .... HMN Fn
HMN Financial, Inc. [*NASDAQ symbol*] (SAG) .... HMNF
HMOS [*High Speed Metal Oxide Semiconductor*] **Erasable** (NITA) .... HMOS-E
HMR World Enterprise [*Vancouver Stock Exchange symbol*] .... HMR
HMS King Alfred [*British military*] (DMA) .... KA
HMS King George V [*British military*] (DMA) KG5
HMT Technology [*NASDAQ symbol*] (TTSB) .... HMTT
HMT Technology Corp. [*NASDAQ symbol*] (SAG) .... HMTT
HMT Technology Corp. [*Associated Press*] (SAG) .... HMTTch
HMV [*His Master's Voice*], Gramophone Co. [*Record label*] [*Great Britain, Europe, etc.*] .... G
HN Engineering, Inc. [*Burnaby, BC*] [*Telecommunications*] (TSSD) .... HNE
HNC Software [*NASDAQ symbol*] (TTSB) .... HNCS
HNC Software, Inc. [*Associated Press*] (SAG) .... HNC Sft
HNC Software, Inc. [*NASDAQ symbol*] (SAG) .... HNCS
Ho [*Ghana*] [*ICAO location identifier*] (ICLI) .... DGAH
Ho Chi Minh [*Vietnam*] [*Airport symbol*] (OAG) .... SGN
Ho Chi Minh City [*Vietnam*] .... HCMC
Hoard Historical Museum, Fort Atkinson, WI [*Library symbol Library of Congress*] (LCLS) .... WFaH
Hoare Govett Small Companies Index [*British*] .... HGSC
Hobart [*Australia ICAO location identifier*] (ICLI) .... AMHB
Hobart [*Australia ICAO location identifier*] (ICLI) .... AMHF
Hobart [*Tasmania*] [*Airport symbol*] (OAG) .... HBA
Hobart [*Oklahoma*] [*ICAO location identifier*] (ICLI) .... KHBR
Hobart and William Smith Colleges, Geneva, NY [*Library symbol Library of Congress*] (LCLS) .... NGH
Hobart and William Smith Colleges, Geneva, NY [*OCLC symbol*] (OCLC) .... ZEM
Hobart Bay [*Alaska*] [*Airport symbol*] (OAG) .... HBH
Hobart Chamber of Commerce [*Australia*] .... HCC
Hobart Gazette, Hobart, IN [*Library symbol*] [*Library of Congress*] (LCLS) .... InHobG
Hobart Gazette, Hobart, IN [*Library symbol Library of Congress*] (LCLS) .... InHoG
Hobart Mills [*California*] [*Seismograph station code, US Geological Survey*] (SEIS) .... HBM
Hobart Mills [*California*] [*Seismograph station code, US Geological Survey*] (SEIS) .... HBT
Hobart, OK [*Location identifier FAA*] (FAAL) .... HBR
Hobart, OK [*FM radio station call letters*] .... KQTZ
Hobart, OK [*AM radio station call letters*] .... KTJS
Hobart Peace Centre [*Australia*] .... HPC
Hobart Town Gazette [*A publication*] .... HTG
Hobart's English Common Pleas Reports [*80 English Reprint*] [*1613-25*] [*A publication*] (DLA) .... Hob R
Hobart's English King's Bench Reports [*80 English Reprint*] [*A publication*] (DLA) .... Hob
Hobart's English King's Bench Reports [*80 English Reprint*] [*A publication*] (DLA) .... Hob R
Hobart's English King's Bench Reports [*80 English Reprint*] [*A publication*] (DLA) .... Hobart
Hobart's English King's Bench Reports [*80 English Reprint*] [*A publication*] (DLA) .... Hobart (Eng)
Hobbs [*New Mexico*] [*Airport symbol*] (OAG) .... HOB
Hobbs/Les County [*New Mexico*] [*ICAO location identifier*] (ICLI) .... KHOB
Hobbs, NM [*Location identifier FAA*] (FAAL) .... HBB
Hobbs, NM [*Television station call letters*] .... KHFT
Hobbs, NM [*AM radio station call letters*] .... KHOB
Hobbs, NM [*FM radio station call letters*] (RBYB) .... KIXN
Hobbs, NM [*AM radio station call letters*] .... KKEL
Hobbs, NM [*FM radio station call letters*] .... KLMA
Hobbs, NM [*FM radio station call letters*] .... KPER
Hobbs, NM [*AM radio station call letters*] (RBYB) .... KUCU-AM
Hobbs, NM [*AM radio station call letters*] .... KYKK
Hobbs, NM [*FM radio station call letters*] .... KZOR
Hobbs Public Library, Hobbs, NM [*OCLC symbol*] (OCLC) .... HOB
Hobbs Public Library, Hobbs, NM [*Library symbol Library of Congress*] (LCLS) .... NmHo
Hobby .... HOB
[*William P.*] **Hobby Airport** [*FAA*] (TAG) .... HOU
Hobby Clubs of America (EA) .... HCA
Hobby Eberly Telescope [*Texas*] .... HET
Hobby Eberly Telescope .... HET
Hobby Greenhouse Association (EA) .... HGA
Hobby Greenhouse Owners Association of America [*Defunct*] (EA) .... HGA
Hobby Guild of America (EA) .... HGA
Hobby Horse Brigade of the Legion of Guardsmen (EA) .... HHBLG
Hobby Industry Association of America .... HIA
Hobby Industry Association of America (EA) .... HIAA
Hobbyist's Interchange Tape Standard [*Data recording*] .... HITS
Hobbyists Sourcebook [*A publication*] .... HSB
Hobie Class Association (EA) .... HCA
Hoboken Free Public Library, Hoboken, NJ [*Library symbol Library of Congress*] (LCLS) .... NjHo
Hoboken Manufacturers [*AAR code*] .... HMR
Hoboken Shore Railroad [*AAR code*] .... HBS
Hobson City, AL [*AM radio station call letters*] .... WHOG
Hoc Anno [*This Year*] [*Latin*] .... HA
Hoc Est [*That Is or This Is*] [*Latin*] .... HE
Hoc Loco [*In This Place*] [*Latin*] .... HL
Hoc Loco Situs [*Laid in This Place*] [*Latin*] .... HLS
Hoc Mense [*In This Month*] [*Latin*] .... HM
Hoc Monumentum Fieri Fecit [*Caused This Monument to Be Made*] [*Latin*] .... HMFF
Hoc Monumentum Posuit [*He, or She, Erected This Monument*] [*Latin*] .... HMP
Hoc Nocte [*Tonight*] [*Pharmacy*] .... HN
Hoc Quaere [*Look For This or See This*] [*Latin*] .... HQ
Hoc Sensu [*In This Sense*] [*Latin*] (GPO) .... HS
Hoc Tempore [*At This Time*] [*Latin*] .... HT
Hoc Titulo [*In, or Under, This Title*] [*Latin*] .... HT
Hoc Verbum [*This Word*] [*Latin*] .... HV
Hoc Vespere [*Tonight*] [*Pharmacy*] .... HOC VESP
Hochiminh/Tansonnhat [*Viet Nam*] [*ICAO location identifier*] (ICLI) .... VVTS
Hocker Federation International (EA) .... HFI
Hocker International Federation (EA) .... HIF
Hockey Association [*British*] .... HA
Hockey Club .... HC
Hockey Night in Canada [*Television program*] .... HNIC
Hockey North America (EA) .... HNA
Hockey Rules Board [*Walton-On-Thames, Surrey, England*] (EAIO) .... HRB
Hockey Umpires' Association [*British*] .... HUA
Hocking Technical College, Nelsonville, OH [*OCLC symbol*] (OCLC) .... HTN
Hocking Technical College, Nelsonville, OH [*Library symbol Library of Congress*] (LCLS) .... ONeH
Hockley [*Texas*] [*Seismograph station code, US Geological Survey*] (SEIS) .... HKT
Hocutt-Ellington Memorial Library, Clayton, NC [*Library symbol Library of Congress*] (LCLS) .... NcCla
Hodayot. Hymns of Thanksgiving from Qumran. Cave One (BJA) 1QH
Hodeidah [*Yemen Arab Republic*] [*Airport symbol*] (OAG) .... HOD
Hodeidah [*Yemen*] [*ICAO location identifier*] (ICLI) .... OYHD
Hodenhagen [*Germany ICAO location identifier*] (ICLI) .... EDVH
Hodge on Presbyterian Law [*A publication*] (DLA) .... Hodge Presb Law
Hodgenville, KY [*FM radio station call letters*] .... WKMO
Hodges' English Common Pleas Reports [*1835-37*] [*A publication*] (DLA) .... Hod
Hodges' English Common Pleas Reports [*1835-37*] [*A publication*] (DLA) .... Hodg
Hodges' English Common Pleas Reports [*1835-37*] [*A publication*] (DLA) .... Hodges
Hodges' English Common Pleas Reports [*1835-37*] [*A publication*] (DLA) .... Hodges (Eng)
Hodges' Law of Railways [*A publication*] (DLA) .... Hodg Ry
Hodges-Lehmann Estimator [*Statistics*] .... HL
Hodgin's Canada Election Cases [*A publication*] (DLA) .... Hodg Can Elec Cas
Hodgin's Election Cases [*Ontario*] [*A publication*] (DLA) .... HEC
Hodgin's Election Cases [*Ontario*] [*A publication*] (DLA) .... Hodg
Hodgin's Election Cases [*Ontario*] [*A publication*] (DLA) .... Hodg El Cas
Hodgin's Election Cases [*Ontario*] [*A publication*] (DLA) .... Hodg El Cas (Ont)
Hodgin's Election Cases [*Ontario*] [*A publication*] (DLA) .... Hodg Ont Elect
Hodgins' Upper Canada Election Cases [*A publication*] (DLA) .... Hodg El
Hodgkin's Disease [*Medicine*] .... HD
Hodgkin's Disease [*Oncology*] (DAVI) .... HoD
Hodgkin's Disease Association [*British*] (DBA) .... HDA
Hodgkin's Lymphoma [*Medicine*] .... HL
Hodgkins Public Library District, Hodgkins, IL [*Library symbol Library of Congress*] (LCLS) .... IHod

Hodgson's Horse [*British military*] (DMA) ... HH
Hoechst Australia Ltd. [*Commercial firm*] ... HAL
Hoechst Canada, Inc, Medical Library, Montreal, PQ, Canada [*Library symbol*] [*Library of Congress*] (LCLS) ... CaQMHC
Hoechst Marion Roussel ... HMR
Hoechst-Roussel Pharmaceuticals, Inc. [*Research code symbol*] ... HOE
Hoechst-Roussel Pharmaceuticals, Inc. [*Research code symbol*] ... HR
Hoechst-Roussel Pharmaceuticals, Inc., Somerville, NJ [*Library symbol Library of Congress*] (LCLS) ... NjSoHR
Hoedspruit [*South Africa*] [*ICAO location identifier*] (ICLI) ... FAHS
Hoedspruit Civil/Burgerlike [*South Africa*] [*ICAO location identifier*] (ICLI) ... FAHT
Hoehere SS und Polizeifuehrer (BJA) ... HSSPF
Hoeheres Kommando [*Higher Command*] [*German military - World War II*] ... HK
Hoenig Group [*NASDAQ symbol*] (TTSB) ... HOEN
Hoenig Group, Inc. [*NASDAQ symbol*] (SPSG) ... HOEN
Hoenig Group, Inc. [*Associated Press*] (SAG) ... Hoenig
Hoerner [*Horns*] [*Music*] ... HR
Hoerner [*Horns*] [*Music*] ... HRN
Hoeven/Seppe [*Netherlands ICAO location identifier*] (ICLI) ... EHSE
Hoevenen [*Belgium ICAO location identifier*] (ICLI) ... EBHN
Hof [*Germany ICAO location identifier*] (ICLI) ... EDQM
Hof [*Federal Republic of Germany*] [*Seismograph station code, US Geological Survey*] (SEIS) ... HOF
Hof [*Germany Airport symbol*] (OAG) ... HOQ
Hofbibliothek, Aschaffenburg, Germany [*Library symbol Library of Congress*] (LCLS) ... GyAsH
Hofbibliothek, Aschaffenburg, Germany [*Library symbol*] [*Library of Congress*] (LCLS) ... GyAsH
Hoffer-Osmond Diagnostic Test [*Psychology*] ... HOD
Hoffman Core Driver ... HCD
Hoffman Military Products Division ... HMPD
Hoffman Modulation Contrast System ... HMCS
Hoffman, NC [*Location identifier FAA*] (FAAL) ... HFF
Hoffman on Referees [*A publication*] (DLA) ... Hoff Ref
Hoffman Public School, Hoffman, MN [*Library symbol*] [*Library of Congress*] (LCLS) ... MnHofS
Hoffman-La Roche Ltd., Etobicoke, Ontario [*Library symbol National Library of Canada*] (NLC) ... OEHL
Hoffman-La Roche Ltd., Vaudreuil, PQ, Canada [*Library symbol Library of Congress*] (LCLS) ... CaQVauH
Hoffman-Laroche Ltd., Etobicoke, ON, Canada [*Library symbol*] [*Library of Congress*] (LCLS) ... CaOEtHL
Hoffmann [*Reflex*] [*Neurology*] ... H
Hoffmann [*Reflex*] [*Medicine*] ... HOFF
Hoffmann & Campe [*Publisher*] [*Germany*] ... H & C
Hoffmann Evaluation Program and Procedure (IAA) ... HEPP
Hoffmann-La Roche, Inc. [*Research code symbol*] ... LA
Hoffmann-La Roche, Inc. [*Research code symbol*] ... NIH
Hoffmann-La Roche, Inc. [*Research code symbol*] ... NSC
Hoffmann-La Roche, Inc. [*Switzerland, USA*] [*Research code symbol*] ... Ro
Hoffmann-La Roche, Inc., Scientific Library, Nutley, NJ [*Library symbol Library of Congress*] (LCLS) ... NjNuH
Hoffman's Course of Legal Study [*A publication*] (DLA) ... Hoff Leg St
Hoffman's Decisions [*A publication*] (DLA) ... Hoff Dec
Hoffman's Decisions, United States District Court [*A publication*] (DLA) ... Hoffm Dec (F)
Hoffman's Ecclesiastical Law [*A publication*] (DLA) ... Hoff Ecc L
Hoffman's Land Cases, United States District Court [*A publication*] (DLA) ... Hoff
Hoffman's Land Cases, United States District Court [*A publication*] (DLA) ... Hoff L Cas
Hoffman's Land Cases, United States District Court [*A publication*] (DLA) ... Hoff Land
Hoffman's Land Cases, United States District Court [*A publication*] (DLA) ... Hoff Land Cas
Hoffman's Land Cases, United States District Court [*A publication*] (DLA) ... Hoff LC
Hoffman's Land Cases, United States District Court [*A publication*] (DLA) ... Hoffm
Hoffman's Land Cases, United States District Court [*A publication*] (DLA) ... Hoffm Ch
Hoffman's Land Cases, United States District Court [*A publication*] (DLA) ... Hoffm Land Cas (F)
Hoffman's Land Cases, United States District Court [*A publication*] (DLA) ... Hoffm Rep Land Cases
Hoffman's Leading Cases [*A publication*] (DLA) ... Hoff Lead Cas
Hoffman's Legal Outlines [*A publication*] (DLA) ... Hoff Out
Hoffman's Master in Chancery [*A publication*] (DLA) ... Hoff Mast
Hoffman's Master in Chancery [*A publication*] (DLA) ... Hoff Mast Ch
Hoffman's New York Chancery Reports [*A publication*] (DLA) ... Hoff
Hoffman's New York Chancery Reports [*A publication*] (DLA) ... Hoff Ch
Hoffman's New York Chancery Reports [*A publication*] (DLA) ... Hoff CR
Hoffman's New York Chancery Reports [*A publication*] (DLA) ... Hoff NY
Hoffman's New York Chancery Reports [*A publication*] (DLA) ... Hoffm
Hoffman's New York Chancery Reports [*A publication*] (DLA) ... Hoffm Ch
Hoffman's New York Chancery Reports [*A publication*] (DLA) ... Hoffm Ch (NY)
Hoffman's New York Chancery Reports [*A publication*] (DLA) ... Hoffman Ch R
Hoffman's New York Chancery Reports [*A publication*] (DLA) ... Hoffman's Ch R
Hoffman's Opinions [*A publication*] (DLA) ... Hoff Op
Hoffman's Opinions, United States District Court [*A publication*] (DLA) ... Hoffm Ops (F)
Hoffman's Provisional Remainders [*A publication*] (DLA) ... Hoff Pr Rem
Hoffman's Public Papers [*New York*] [*A publication*] (DLA) ... Hoff Pub P
Hofn [*Iceland*] [*Airport symbol*] (OAG) ... HFN
Hofn/Hornafjordur [*Iceland*] [*ICAO location identifier*] (ICLI) ... BIHN
Hofstra Labor Law Forum [*A publication*] (DLA) ... Hofstra Lab LF
Hofstra Labor Law Journal [*A publication*] (DLA) ... Hofstra Lab LJ
Hofstra University (GAGS) ... Hofstra U
Hofstra University, Hempstead, NY [*Library symbol Library of Congress*] (LCLS) ... NHemH
Hofstra University, Hempstead, NY [*OCLC symbol*] (OCLC) ... ZIH
Hofstra University, Law School, Library, Hempstead, NY [*OCLC symbol*] (OCLC) ... ZHL
Hofu [*Japan ICAO location identifier*] (ICLI) ... RJOF
Hog Cay, Exuma Island [*Bahamas*] [*ICAO location identifier*] (ICLI) ... MYEY
Hog Cholera Virus (DMAA) ... HCV
Hog Intrinsic Factor Concentrate ... HIFC
Hogan Air [*ICAO designator*] (FAAC) ... HGA
(Hogan of) Harcarse's Scotch Session Cases [*A publication*] (DLA) ... Hog
(Hogan of) Harcarse's Scotch Session Cases [*A publication*] (DLA) ... Hogan
Hogan Systems, Inc. [*Associated Press*] (SAG) ... Hogan
Hogan Systems, Inc. [*NASDAQ symbol*] (NQ) ... HOGN
Hoganas [*Sweden ICAO location identifier*] (ICLI) ... ESMH
Hogan's Irish Rolls Court Reports [*A publication*] (DLA) ... Hog
Hogan's Irish Rolls Court Reports [*A publication*] (DLA) ... Hogan
Hogan's Irish Rolls Court Reports [*A publication*] (DLA) ... Hogan (Ir)
Hogan's Pennsylvania State Trials [*A publication*] (DLA) ... Hog St Tr
Hogansville, GA [*AM radio station call letters*] ... WMXY
Hogansville, GA [*FM radio station call letters*] (RBYB) ... WZLG
Hogarth [*H.*] **and Sons** [*Steamship line*] (MHDW) ... HH
Hoge Raad [*Dutch Supreme Court*] (DLA) ... HR
Hogg Robinson & Gardner Mountain [*Insurance broker*] [*British*] ... HRGM
Hogshead ... HD
Hogshead ... HGD
Hogshead (DNAB) ... HH
Hogshead ... HHD
Hogskolan i Lulea [*Lulea University*], Lulea, Sweden [*Library symbol*] [*Library of Congress*] (LCLS) ... SwLuH
Hogue's Reports [*1-4 Florida*] [*A publication*] (DLA) ... Hogue
Hohenems-Dornbirn [*Austria ICAO location identifier*] (ICLI) ... LOIH
Hohenfels [*Germany ICAO location identifier*] (ICLI) ... EDIH
Hohenfels Training Area [*NATO*] ... HTA
Hohenheim [*Federal Republic of Germany*] [*Seismograph station code, US Geological Survey Closed*] (SEIS) ... HOH
Hohenwald, TN [*AM radio station call letters*] ... WMLR
Hohenzollern Society (EA) ... HS
Hohhot [*China*] [*Airport symbol*] (OAG) ... HET
Hohkeppel [*Federal Republic of Germany*] [*Seismograph station code, US Geological Survey*] (SEIS) ... HOK
Hohn [*Germany ICAO location identifier*] (ICLI) ... EDNQ
Hoisington, KS [*FM radio station call letters*] ... KHOK
Hoist ... HO
Hoist (MSA) ... HST
Hoist Manufacturers Association [*Later, HMI*] (EA) ... HMA
Hoist Manufacturers Institute (EA) ... HMI
Hoist Rotation Beam Assembly [*Military*] (CAAL) ... HRBA
Hoisting Tool (MCD) ... HT
Hojesteret [*Supreme Court*] [*Netherlands*] (ILCA) ... HR
Hoke County Public Library, Raeford, NC [*Library symbol Library of Congress*] (LCLS) ... NcRa
Hokhmah, Bimah, Daat [*Germinal, Developmental, and Conclusive Knowledge*] [*Hebrew*] ... HaBaD
Hokitika [*New Zealand*] [*Airport symbol*] (OAG) ... HKK
Hokitika [*New Zealand*] [*ICAO location identifier*] (ICLI) ... NZHK
Hokkai Gakuen University, Sapporo, Japan [*Library symbol Library of Congress*] (LCLS) ... JSHG
Hokkaido University [*Japan*] [*Seismograph station code, US Geological Survey*] (SEIS) ... HSS
Hokkaido University, Sapporo, Japan [*Library symbol Library of Congress*] (LCLS) ... JSU
Hokksund [*Norway ICAO location identifier*] (ICLI) ... ENHS
Hoko Exploration [*Vancouver Stock Exchange symbol*] ... HOK
Hola [*Kenya*] [*ICAO location identifier*] (ICLI) ... HKHO
Holbeach [*British ICAO location identifier*] (ICLI) ... EGYH
Holberg, BC [*ICAO location identifier*] (ICLI) ... CWHJ
Holbrook & Kellogg [*Publisher*] (AAGC) ... H & K
Holbrook, AZ [*AM radio station call letters*] ... KDJI
Holbrook, AZ [*FM radio station call letters*] ... KZUA
Holbrook High School Library, Holbrook, AZ [*Library symbol Library of Congress*] (LCLS) ... AzHH
Holbrook Research Institute, Oxford, MA [*Library symbol*] [*Library of Congress*] (LCLS) ... HrI
Holco Mortgage Acceptance Corp. [*AMEX symbol*] (SPSG) ... HOL
Holco Mortgage Acceptance Corp. [*Associated Press*] (SAG) ... Holco
Holcomb, KS [*AM radio station call letters*] ... KBUF
Holcomb Research Institute [*Butler University*] ... HRI
Holcombe's Equity Jurisdiction [*A publication*] (DLA) ... Holc Eq Jur
Holcombe's Law of Debtor and Creditor [*A publication*] (DLA) ... Holc Debt & Cr
Holcombe's Leading Cases of Commercial Law [*A publication*] (DLA) ... Holc L Cas
Hold ... HLD
Hold (WDMC) ... hld
Hold [*Shipping*] (DS) ... HO
Hold Acknowledge [*Computer science*] ... HLDA
Hold and Modify [*Computer display mode*] ... HAM
Hold Breakfast [*Medicine*] ... HB
Hold Breakfast for Blood Work [*Medicine*] ... HBBW
Hold Fire [*Military*] ... HF
Hold for Arrival of Goods ... HAG
Hold for Money [*Business term*] ... HFM
Hold for Release [*Advertising*] (BARN) ... HFR

Hold Harmless (OICC) ... HH
Hold in Abeyance [*Military*] ... HIA
Hold Off Generator (MSA) ... HOGEN
Hold Off Normal ... HON
Hold Request (IAA) ... HRQ
Hold Time Management Display [*NASA*] ... HTMD
Hold Up Tank (IEEE) ... HUT
Holddown (AAG) ... H/D
Holddown ... HD
Holddown ... HLDDN
Holddown (MSA) ... HLDN
Holddown Alignment Support (NASA) ... HAS
Holddown and Release (AAG) ... HDR
Holddown Arm (KSC) ... HDA
Holddown Post (NASA) ... HDP
Holden Arboretum, Mento, OH [*Library symbol*] [*Library of Congress*] (LCLS) ... OMeH
Holden Municipal Library, Alberta [*Library symbol National Library of Canada*] (BIB) ... AHOM
Holden's Air Transport Services [*Australia*] ... HATS
Holdenville, OK [*Location identifier FAA*] (FAAL) ... HDL
Holdenville, OK [*FM radio station call letters*] (RBYB) ... KCMA
Holdenville, OK [*AM radio station call letters*] ... KRAF
Holder ... HLDR
Holder (KSC) ... HLR
Holder in Due Course [*Owner or holder of a negotiable instrument at some future time*] ... H in DC
Holder in Due Course [*Owner or holder of a negotiable instrument at some future time*] ... HDC
Holder of Record [*Investment term*] ... HOR
Holderbank Management und Beratung AG [*Switzerland*] ... HMB
Holders of Public Office ... HOPO
Holding [*Electronics*] ... H
Holding (MSA) ... HLDG
Holding ... HLDNG
Holding Activity ... H/A
Holding and Approach-to-Land [*Procedure*] [*Aviation*] ... HAL
Holding and Positioning Aid (IEEE) ... HPA
Holding and Reconsignment [*Military*] ... H & R
Holding and Reconsignment Point [*Military*] ... H & RPO
Holding and Reconsignment Point (IAA) ... HARP
Holding and Reconsignment Point [*Military*] (AABC) ... HRP
Holding as Previously Instructed [*Aviation*] (FAAC) ... HAPI
Holding Coil (MSA) ... HC
Holding Company [*Business term*] ... HC
Holding Fixture (MSA) ... HF
Holding Out [*Cashier fraud*] ... HO
Holding Pattern [*Aviation*] ... HP
Holding Period Return (PDAA) ... HPR
Holding Pipette ... HP
Holding Potential [*Neurophysiology*] ... HP
Holding Procedures (SAA) ... HOP
Holding Register ... HR
Holding Time [*Telecommunications*] (TEL) ... HT
Holding under Promise of Payment ... HPP
Holdingford Elementary School, Holdingford, MN [*Library symbol*] [*Library of Congress*] (LCLS) ... MnHoE
Holdingford Jr./Sr. High School, Holdingford, MN [*Library symbol*] [*Library of Congress*] (LCLS) ... MnHoH
Holdings [*Online database field identifier*] ... HLD
Holdover [*Theater*] ... HO
Holdrege, NE [*Location identifier FAA*] (FAAL) ... HDE
Holdrege, NE [*FM radio station call letters*] (RBYB) ... KMTY-FM
Holdrege, NE [*AM radio station call letters*] ... KUVR
Holdrege, NE [*FM radio station call letters*] ... KUVR-FM
Holdrege-Phelps County Library, Holdrege, NE [*Library symbol Library of Congress*] (LCLS) ... NbHo
Holdup [*FBI standardized term*] ... HDLP
Holdup Alert - Local Transmission [*Bank robbery alarm system*] ... HALT
Hole Full of Water [*Drilling*] (DICI) ... HFW
Hole In The Wall Gang [*A sleep-away camp for kids with life-threatening illnesses*] (PCM) ... HITWG
Hole P-Type Semiconductor Material ... P
Hole-Accumulated Diode [*Sony Corp.*] ... HAD
Hole-Burning Spectroscopy ... HBS
Hole-Electron Pair ... HEP
Hole-in-Corner [*Paper*] (DSUE) ... HIC
Holes (ADA) ... HLS
Holesov [*Former Czechoslovakia*] [*ICAO location identifier*] (ICLI) ... LKHO
Holguin [*Cuba*] [*Airport symbol*] (OAG) ... HOG
Holguin [*Cuba ICAO location identifier*] (ICLI) ... MUHG
Holidair Airways [*Canada ICAO designator*] (FAAC) ... STP
Holiday ... HLDY
Holiday (AFM) ... HOL
Holiday Airlines (MHDW) ... HL
Holiday Airlines [*ICAO designator*] (AD) ... JO
Holiday Airlines Havacilik Ve Turizm Sanayi Ve Ticaret, AG [*Turkey*] [*FAA designator*] (FAAC) ... HLD
Holiday Airlines, Inc. [*ICAO designator*] (FAAC) ... HOL
Holiday Airlines, Inc. [*Air carrier designation symbol*] ... HOLX
Holiday and Leave [*Military*] (NVT) ... HOL
Holiday Camps [*Public-performance tariff class*] [*British*] ... HC
Holiday Caravan Parks [*Public-performance tariff class*] [*British*] ... HCP
Holiday, FL [*FM radio station call letters*] ... WLVU
Holiday Happenings Ornament Collectors Club (EA) ... HHOCC
Holiday Inn University, Olive Branch, MS [*Library symbol Library of Congress*] (LCLS) ... TMHI-U
Holiday Inns of America, Memphis, TN [*Library symbol Library of Congress*] (LCLS) ... TMHI
Holiday Institute of Yonkers (EA) ... HIY
Holiday Pay [*Army*] (AABC) ... HP
Holiday Project (EA) ... HP
Holiday Rambler Corp. ... HRC
Holiday Rambler Recreational Vehicle Club (EA) ... HRRVC
Holiday Route (CDAI) ... HR
Holiday RV Superstores [*NASDAQ symbol*] (TTSB) ... RVEE
Holiday RV Superstores, Inc. [*Associated Press*] (SAG) ... HldyRV
Holiday RV Superstores, Inc. [*NASDAQ symbol*] (NQ) ... RVEE
Holiday, Upkeep [*Military*] (NVT) ... HOLUPK
Holidays and Anniversaries of the World [*A publication*] ... HAW
Holidays for Humanity [*An association*] (EA) ... HH
Holidays, Vacation, and Sick Leave (NASA) ... HVSL
Holifield Heavy Ion Research Facility [*Department of Energy*] ... HHIRF
Holifield National Laboratory [*Later, Oak Ridge National Laboratory*] ... HNL
Holiness (BJA) ... H
Holiness ... HLNSS
Holiness Army (ROG) ... HA
Holiness Band ... HB
Holistic Dental Association (EA) ... HDA
Holistic Education Network (EDAC) ... HEN
Holistic Health [*Medicine*] (DAVI) ... HH
Holistic Health Havens (EA) ... HHH
Holistic Health Organizing Committee (EA) ... HHOC
Holistic Life Foundation [*Later, Feathered Pipe Foundation*] (EA) ... HLF
Holistic Nurses Association of Australia ... HNAA
Holistic Orthogonal Parameter Estimation [*Medicine*] (DMAA) ... HOPE
Holistic Resource Management (ECON) ... HRM
Holladay Park Hospital, Medical Library, Portland, OR [*Library symbol Library of Congress*] (LCLS) ... OrPHP
Holland [*IYRU nationality code*] (IYR) ... H
Holland ... HOLL
Holland (VRA) ... Holl
Holland America Cruises [*Formerly, Holland-America Line*] ... HAC
Holland & Barrett [*Grocery and health food shop chain*] [*British*] ... H & B
Holland & Holland [*Custom gun maker*] ... H & H
Holland Australia Club [*Australia*] ... HAC
Holland Australia Retirement Foundation of Victoria [*Australia*] ... HARF
Holland Automation International [*Software retailer*] (NITA) ... HAI
Holland Cheese Exporters Association [*Later, DDB*] (EA) ... HCEA
Holland College, Charlottetown, PE, Canada [*Library symbol Library of Congress*] (LCLS) ... CaPCHC
Holland College, Charlottetown, Prince Edward Island [*Library symbol National Library of Canada*] (NLC) ... PCHC
Holland Historical Trust (EA) ... HHT
Holland Lop Rabbit Specialty Club (EA) ... HLRSC
Holland, MI [*Location identifier FAA*] (FAAL) ... HLM
Holland, MI [*FM radio station call letters*] ... WAKX
Holland, MI [*AM radio station call letters*] ... WHTC
Holland, MI [*FM radio station call letters*] ... WKLQ
Holland, MI [*FM radio station call letters*] ... WTHS
Holland Mills [*Quebec*] [*Seismograph station code, US Geological Survey Closed*] (SEIS) ... HMC
Holland, OH [*FM radio station call letters*] ... WPOS
Holland on Composition Deeds [*A publication*] (DLA) ... Holl Comp Deeds
Holland Purchase Historical Society, Batavia, NY [*Library symbol Library of Congress*] (LCLS) ... NBatHHi
Holland Society of New York (EA) ... HSNY
Holland Society of New York, New York, NY [*Library symbol Library of Congress*] (LCLS) ... NNHol
Holland Vocational Preference Inventory [*Psychology*] ... HVPI
Holland West-Afrika Line [*Steamship*] (MHDB) ... HWAL
Holland-America Line [*Later, Holland America Cruises*] ... HAL
Holland's Elements of Jurisprudence [*A publication*] (DLA) ... Holl El Jur
Holland's Elements of Jurisprudence [*A publication*] (DLA) ... Holl Jur
Holland's Institutes of Justinian [*A publication*] (DLA) ... Holl Just
Hollandsche Bank-Unie [*Netherlands*] ... HBU
Hollandse Signaalapparaten [*Dutch*] ... HSA
Holland-Suco Color Co., Huntington, WV [*Library symbol Library of Congress*] (LCLS) ... WvHuH
Holleberg [*Germany ICAO location identifier*] (ICLI) ... EDVL
Holler Elementary School, South International Falls, MN [*Library symbol*] [*Library of Congress*] (LCLS) ... MnSifE
Hollerith Electronic Computer ... HEC
Hollidaysburg, PA [*FM radio station call letters*] ... WHPA
Hollinger Argus Ltd. [*Toronto Stock Exchange symbol*] ... HOL
Hollinger, Inc. [*Toronto Stock Exchange symbol Vancouver Stock Exchange symbol*] ... HLG
Hollinger Inc. [*NASDAQ symbol*] (TTSB) ... HLGRF
Hollinger, Inc. [*Associated Press*] (SAG) ... Holinger
Hollinger International, Inc. [*NYSE symbol*] (SAG) ... HLR
Hollinger International, Inc. [*NASDAQ symbol*] (SAG) ... HOLI
Hollinger International, Inc. [*Associated Press*] (SAG) ... Hollinger
Hollinger International, Inc. [*Associated Press*] (SAG) ... Hollng
Hollingworth Center for Highly Gifted Children (EA) ... HCHGC
Hollins College (GAGS) ... Hollins C
Hollins College, Hollins College, VA [*OCLC symbol*] (OCLC) ... VHC
Hollins College, Hollins College, VA [*Library symbol Library of Congress*] (LCLS) ... ViHo
Hollinshead's Reports [*1 Minnesota*] [*A publication*] (DLA) ... Holl
Hollinshead's Reports [*1 Minnesota*] [*A publication*] (DLA) ... Hollinshead

Hollis, AK [Location identifier FAA] (FAAL) .... HYL
Hollis & Eastern Railroad Co. [AAR code] .... HE
Hollister, CA [FM radio station call letters] (RBYB) .... KAXT
Hollister, CA [FM radio station call letters] (RBYB) .... KCDU-FM
Hollister, CA [AM radio station call letters] .... KMPG
Hollister Public Library, Hollister, CA [Library symbol Library of Congress]
    (LCLS) .... CHo
Holliston, MA [FM radio station call letters] .... WHHB
Holloman Air Development Center [Air Force] .... HADC
Holloman Air Force Base [New Mexico] .... HAFB
Holloman Air Force Test Base [New Mexico] (AAG) .... HAFTB
Holloman Development Research Report [Air Force] (MCD) .... HDRR
Holloman Infrared Target Simulator (OA) .... HITS
Hollow [Commonly used] (OPSA) .... HLLW
Hollow (MSA) .... HOL
Hollow [Commonly used] (OPSA) .... HOLLOW
Hollow [Commonly used] (OPSA) .... HOLLOWS
Hollow .... HOLW
Hollow .... HOLW
Hollow [Commonly used] (OPSA) .... HOLWS
Hollow Anistropic Beam Analysis (PDAA) .... HANBA
Hollow Back [Of lumber] (BARN) .... HBK
Hollow Cathode Discharge [Spectrometry] .... HCD
Hollow Cathode Lamp .... HCL
Hollow Cathode Tube .... HCT
Hollow Concrete Block .... HCB
Hollow Copper Conductor .... HCC
Hollow Core [Technical drawings] .... HC
Hollow Cylinder Apparatus [Nuclear energy] (NUCP) .... HCA
Hollow Electron Beam .... HEB
Hollow Enzyme [Medicine] (DMAA) .... HF
Hollow Fiber .... HF
Hollow Fiber Artificial Kidney [Medicine] (AAMN) .... HFAK
Hollow Fiber Membrane (NASA) .... HFM
Hollow Kathode Tube .... HKT
Hollow Metal [Technical drawings] .... HM
Hollow Metal Door and Buck Association (EA) .... HMDBA
Hollow Metal Door and Frame [Technical drawings] .... HMDF
Hollow Point Bullet .... HP
Hollow Shaft Rotary Actuator .... HSRA
Hollow Soft Point [Bullet] (DICI) .... HSP
Hollow Tile [Technical drawings] .... HT
Holloway White Allom [Building contractor] [British] .... HWA
Hollowback (DAC) .... HB
Hollow-Cathode Effect (IEEE) .... HCE
Hollow-Fiber Bioreactor [Chemical engineering] .... HFBR
Hollow-Metal Door (DAC) .... HMD
Holly Corp. [AMEX symbol] (SPSG) .... HOC
Holly Corp. [Associated Press] (SAG) .... HollyCp
Holly Hill, FL [FM radio station call letters] (RBYB) .... WANX
Holly Hill, FL [FM radio station call letters] .... WAPN
Holly Hill, FL [FM radio station call letters] (RBYB) .... WDXD-FM
Holly Hill, SC [AM radio station call letters] .... WJBS
Holly Holdings, Inc. [Associated Press] (SAG) .... HollyH
Holly Holdings, Inc. [Associated Press] (SAG) .... HollyHld
Holly Holdings, Inc. [Associated Press] (SAG) .... HollyP
Holly Holdings, Inc. [NASDAQ symbol] (SAG) .... HOPR
Holly Junior/Senior High School Library, Holly, NY [OCLC symbol]
    (OCLC) .... RWN
Holly Park Field Laboratory [University of Nevada - Reno] [Research center]
    (RCD) .... HPFL
Holly Products [Associated Press] (SAG) .... HlyPd
Holly Products [Associated Press] (SAG) .... HollyPd
Holly Products [NASDAQ symbol] (SAG) .... HOPR
Holly Products 10% Cv'D'Pfd [NASDAQ symbol] (TTSB) .... HOPRD
Holly Products Wrrt [NASDAQ symbol] (TTSB) .... HOPRW
Holly Society of America (EA) .... HSA
Holly Springs, MS [Location identifier FAA] (FAAL) .... HLI
Holly Springs, MS [Television station call letters] .... WBUY
Holly Springs, MS [AM radio station call letters] .... WKRA
Holly Springs, MS [FM radio station call letters] .... WKRA-FM
Holly Springs, MS [FM radio station call letters] .... WURC
Hollycroft Resource Corp. [Vancouver Stock Exchange symbol] .... HRC
Hollyfordair Travel Ltd. [New Zealand] [ICAO designator] (FAAC) .... HFT
Hollywood Casino Corp. [Associated Press] (SAG) .... HlywdCa
Hollywood Casino Corp. [NASDAQ symbol] (SAG) .... HWCC
Hollywood Casino'A' [NASDAQ symbol] (TTSB) .... HWCC
Hollywood Comedy Club (EA) .... HCC
Hollywood Entertainment [NASDAQ symbol] (TTSB) .... HLYW
Hollywood Entertainment Corp. [NASDAQ symbol] (SAG) .... HLYW
Hollywood Entertainment Corp. [Associated Press] (SAG) .... HlywdE
Hollywood, FL [Location identifier FAA] (FAAL) .... HWO
Hollywood, FL [AM radio station call letters] .... WLQY
Hollywood, FL [Television station call letters] .... WYHS
Hollywood Foreign Press Association (EA) .... HFPA
Hollywood Hotline [Information service or system] (IID) .... HHL
Hollywood Investments [Vancouver Stock Exchange symbol] .... HLD
Hollywood/North Perry [Florida] [ICAO location identifier] (ICLI) .... KHWO
Hollywood Overseas Committee (IIA) .... HOC
Hollywood Park [NASDAQ symbol] (TTSB) .... HPRK
Hollywood Park $0.70 Dep Cv Pfd [NASDAQ symbol] (TTSB) .... HPRKZ
Hollywood Park, Inc. [Associated Press] (SAG) .... HlwdP
Hollywood Park, Inc. [Associated Press] (SAG) .... HlwdPk
Hollywood Park, Inc. [NASDAQ symbol] (SAG) .... HPRK
Hollywood Productions, Inc. [NASDAQ symbol] (SAG) .... FILM

Hollywood Productions, Inc. [Associated Press] (SAG) .... HllywP
Hollywood Radio and Television Society (EA) .... HRTS
Hollywood Stock Exchange .... HSX
Hollywood Studio Collectors Club (EA) .... HSCC
Hollywood Women's Political Committee (EA) .... HWPC
Holm & Wonsild [Steamship] (MHDB) .... H & W
Holman/Holman Island, NT [ICAO location identifier] (ICLI) .... CYHI
Holman Island [Canada] [Airport symbol] (OAG) .... YHI
Holmavik [Iceland] [Airport symbol] (OAG) .... HVK
Holmen, WI [AM radio station call letters] .... WKBH
Holmes and Disbrow's Practice [A publication] (DLA) .... H & D Pr
Holmes and Narver, Inc. (NRCH) .... H & N
Holmes & Narver, Inc. (MCD) .... HNI
Holmes Beach, FL [FM radio station call letters] .... WISP
Holmes County Library, Durant, MS [Library symbol Library of Congress]
    (LCLS) .... MsD
Holmes County Public Library, Millersburg, OH [Library symbol Library of
    Congress] (LCLS) .... OMill
Holmes Junior College [Goodman, MS] .... HJC
Holmes Junior College, Goodman, MS [Library symbol Library of Congress]
    (LCLS) .... MsGoH
Holmes Library, Boonton, NJ [Library symbol Library of Congress]
    (LCLS) .... NjBoo
Holmes on the Common Law [A publication] (DLA) .... Holm Com Law
Holmes Protection Group [NASDAQ symbol] (TTSB) .... HLMS
Holmes Protection Group, Inc. [NASDAQ symbol] (SAG) .... HLMS
Holmes Protection Group, Inc. [Associated Press] (SAG) .... HolmPr
Holmes' Reports [15-17 Oregon] [A publication] (DLA) .... Holm
Holmes' Statesman [A publication] (DLA) .... Holm Statesman
Holmes' United States Circuit Court Reports [A publication] (DLA) .... Holm
Holmes' United States Circuit Court Reports [A publication] (DLA) .... Holmes
Holmium [Chemical element] .... Ho
Holmium LASER Illuminator .... HLI
Holmstrom Flyg AB [Sweden ICAO designator] (FAAC) .... ENT
Holocaust Curriculum Resources Material (BJA) .... HCRM
Holocaust Documentation and Education Center (EA) .... HDEC
Holocaust Information Network (EA) .... HIN
Holocaust Memorial Center, West Bloomfield, MI [Library symbol] [Library of
    Congress] (LCLS) .... MiWbH
Holocaust Oral History Project [An association] (EA) .... HOHP
Holocaust Remembrance Day (BJA) .... HRD
Holocaust Resource Center (EA) .... HRC
Holocaust Survivors and Friends in Pursuit of Justice (EA) .... HSFPJ
Holocaust Survivors Memorial Foundation (EA) .... HSMF
Holocaust Survivors of Auschwitz (EA) .... HSA
Hologic, Inc. [Associated Press] (SAG) .... Hologic
Hologic, Inc. [NASDAQ symbol] (SAG) .... HOLX
Hologic Inc. [NASDAQ symbol] (TTSB) .... HOLX
Hologram (VRA) .... holgr
Holograph (WDAA) .... HOLO
Holograph Assessment System .... HAS
Holograph Letter Signed .... HLS
Holograph Stress Strain Gauge .... HSSG
Holographic Data Storage System .... HDSS
Holographic Diffractive Structure [Advanced Environmental Research
    Group] .... HDS
Holographic Exposure Index (PDAA) .... HEI
Holographic Horizontal Situation Display .... HHSD
Holographic Ice Surveying System (PDAA) .... HISS
Holographic Lensless Fourier Transform (PDAA) .... HLFT
Holographic Nondestructive Testing .... HNDT
Holographic One-Tube [Goggles] (MCD) .... HOT
Holographic Optic Addressed Light Modulation (IAA) .... HOALM
Holographic Optical Element .... HOE
Holographic Stereogram (OA) .... HS
Holographic Visor Helmet-Mounted Display [Air Force] .... HVHMD
Holographic-One-Two (PDAA) .... HOT
HoloPak Technologies [NASDAQ symbol] (SPSG) .... HOLO
HoloPak Technologies [Associated Press] (SAG) .... HoLoPak
Holophane Corp. [NASDAQ symbol] (SAG) .... HLPH
Holophane Corp. [Associated Press] (SAG) .... Holophne
Holosystolic Murmur [Cardiology] (DAVI) .... HSM
Holotype .... HOLO
Holson Burnes Group, Inc. [NASDAQ symbol] (SAG) .... HBGI
Holson Burnes Group, Inc. [Associated Press] (SAG) .... HolsnB
Holstein Advance, Holstein, IA [Library symbol Library of Congress]
    (LCLS) .... IaHolA
Holstein Friesian Society of Great Britain and Ireland (DBA) .... HFS
Holstein-Friesian [Cattle breed] .... H-F
Holstein-Friesian Association of America (EA) .... HFAA
Holsteinsborg [Greenland] [ICAO location identifier] (ICLI) .... BGHB
Holstenair Lubeck, Luftverkehrsservice GmbH [Germany ICAO designator]
    (FAAC) .... HTR
Holston Army Ammunition Plant .... HAAP
Holston Army Ammunition Plant (AABC) .... HSAAP
Holston Defense Corp. (MCD) .... HDC
Holston Mountain, TN [Location identifier FAA] (FAAL) .... HMV
Holston Valley Community Hospital, Health Science Library, Kingsport, TN
    [Library symbol Library of Congress] (LCLS) .... TKiH
Holsworthy [Australia ICAO location identifier] (ICLI) .... ASHW
Holsworthy [England] .... HOLSW
Holt International Children's Services (EA) .... HICS
Holt on Libels [A publication] (DLA) .... Holt Lib
Holt on Navigation [A publication] (DLA) .... Holt Nav
Holt on Registration of Title [A publication] (DLA) .... Holt Reg

Holt on Shipping [*A publication*] (DLA) .... Holt Sh
Holt on Shipping [*A publication*] (DLA) .... Holt Shipp
Holt-Atherton Pacific Center for Western Studies [*University of the Pacific*]
    [*Research center*] (RCD) .... HAPCWS
Holter Monitoring [*Medicine*] (DMAA) .... HM
Holthouse's Law Dictionary [*A publication*] (DLA) .... Holt L Dic
Holthouse's Law Dictionary [*A publication*] (DLA) .... Holthouse
Holt-Jackson [*Commercial firm British*] .... HJ
Holton Inter-Urban Railway Co. [*AAR code*] .... HI
Holt's English Admiralty Cases (Rule of the Road) [*1863-67*]
    [*A publication*] (DLA) .... Holt Adm
Holt's English Admiralty Cases (Rule of the Road) [*1863-67*]
    [*A publication*] (DLA) .... Holt Adm Ca
Holt's English Admiralty Cases (Rule of the Road) [*1863-67*]
    [*A publication*] (DLA) .... Holt Adm Cas
Holt's English Admiralty Cases (Rule of the Road) [*A publication*]
    (DLA) .... Holt R of R
Holt's English Equity Reports [*1845*] [*A publication*] (DLA) ... Holt
Holt's English Equity Reports [*1845*] [*A publication*] (DLA) ... Holt Eq
Holt's English King's Bench Reports [*A publication*] (DLA) ..... Holt
Holt's English King's Bench Reports [*A publication*] (DLA) ..... Holt KB
Holt's English Nisi Prius Reports [*A publication*] (DLA) .... Holt
Holt's English Nisi Prius Reports [*A publication*] (DLA) .... Holt NP
Holtville, CA [*FM radio station call letters*] .... KGBA
Holtzman Inkblot Test [*Psychology*] .... HIT
Holtzman Sprague-Dawley Rat [*Medicine*] (DMAA) .... H(SD)
Holy .... H
[*The*] Holy Bible (1955) [*R.A. Knox*] [*A publication*] (BJA) .... KX
[*The*] Holy Bible from Ancient Eastern Manuscripts [*G. M. Lamsa*]
    [*A publication*] (BJA) .... La
[*The*] Holy Bible in Modern English (1903) [*Ferrar Fenton*] [*A publication*]
    (BJA) .... Fn
Holy Childhood Association (EA) .... HCA
Holy Communion .... HC
Holy Cross .... HC
Holy Cross [*California*] [*Seismograph station code, US Geological Survey*]
    (SEIS) .... HCC
Holy Cross [*Alaska*] [*Airport symbol*] (OAG) .... HCR
Holy Cross Foreign Mission Seminary, Washington, DC [*Library symbol
    Library of Congress*] (LCLS) .... DHCF
Holy Cross Foreign Mission Society (EA) .... HCFMS
Holy Cross Friary, Juniper Carol Library, New York, NY [*Library symbol
    Library of Congress*] (LCLS) .... NNHCF-C
Holy Cross Greek Orthodox School of Theology, Brookline, MA [*OCLC
    symbol*] (OCLC) .... BHC
Holy Cross Hospital, Calgary, Alberta [*Library symbol National Library of
    Canada*] (NLC) .... ACHC
Holy Cross School, Grande Prairie, Alberta [*Library symbol National Library
    of Canada*] (BIB) .... AGPHS
Holy Cross School, Kimball, MN [*Library symbol*] [*Library of Congress*]
    (LCLS) .... MnKHC
Holy Day of Obligation [*Roman Catholicism*] .... HO
Holy Days of Obligation [*Roman Catholicism*] (ROG) .... HDS
Holy Empire [*Freemasonry*] .... HE
Holy Eucharist .... HE
Holy Family Christian Association [*In 1983 movie "Zelig"*] .... HFCA
Holy Family College [*California, Pennsylvania, Wisconsin*] .... HFC
Holy Family College, Philadelphia, PA [*OCLC symbol*] (OCLC) ... HFC
Holy Family College, Philadelphia, PA [*Library symbol Library of Congress*]
    (LCLS) .... PPHFC
Holy Family Convent, Benet Lake, WI [*Library symbol Library of Congress*]
    (LCLS) .... WBelH
Holy Family Hospital, Manitowoc, WI [*Library symbol Library of Congress*]
    (LCLS) .... WManiH
Holy Family Hospital, Spokane, WA [*Library symbol Library of Congress*]
    (LCLS) .... WaSpH
Holy Family School, Albany, MN [*Library symbol*] [*Library of Congress*]
    (LCLS) .... MnAlH
Holy Family School, Grand Junction, CO [*Library symbol*] [*Library of
    Congress*] (LCLS) .... CoGjHF
Holy Family School, Grimshaw, Alberta [*Library symbol National Library of
    Canada*] (BIB) .... AGWHS
Holy Family School of Nursing, Manitowoc, WI [*Library symbol Library of
    Congress*] (LCLS) .... WManiHN
Holy Family School, Sauk Center, MN [*Library symbol*] [*Library of
    Congress*] (LCLS) .... MnScHF
Holy Family Seminary [*Connecticut*] .... HFS
Holy Father (ROG) .... HF
Holy Ghost .... HG
Holy Ghost Fathers (TOCD) .... CSSp
Holy Ghost Fathers, Congregation of the Holy Ghost (TOCD) ... cssp
Holy Innocents Reparation Committee (EA) .... HIRC
Holy Land Christian Mission (EA) .... HLCM
Holy Land Christian Mission International [*Later, HLCM*] (EA) ... HLCMI
Holy Land Conservation Fund (EA) .... HLCF
Holy Name Society [*Defunct*] (EA) .... HNS
Holy Names College (GAGS) .... Holy Names C
Holy of Holies [*Freemasonry*] (ROG) .... H of H
Holy Order of the Hospital of Jerusalem [*Freemasonry*] (ROG) ... HOH of J
Holy Orders (ROG) .... HO
Holy Redeemer College, Washington, DC [*Library symbol Library of
    Congress*] (LCLS) .... DHR
Holy Redeemer College, Waterford, WI [*Library symbol Library of Congress*]
    (LCLS) .... WWatfH
Holy Roman Church (WDAA) .... HRC

Holy Roman Emperor [*or Empire*] .... HRE
Holy Rosary Hospital, Weise-Biggs Memorial Medical Library, Ontario, OR
    [*Library symbol Library of Congress*] (LCLS) .... OrOnHR
[*The*] "Holy Scriptures" (1881) [*J. N. Darby*] [*A publication*] (BJA) ... Da
[*The*] Holy See .... HS
Holy Shroud Guild (EA) .... HSG
Holy Spirit Association for the Unification of World Christianity .... HSA-UWC
Holy Spirit School, St. Cloud, MN [*Library symbol*] [*Library of Congress*]
    (LCLS) .... MnStclHS
Holy Trinity .... HT
Holy Trinity .... HTRIN
Holy Trinity Diocesan High School, Hicksville, NY [*Library symbol*] [*Library
    of Congress*] (LCLS) .... NHickHT
Holy Trinity Hospital, Graceville, MN [*Library symbol*] [*Library of Congress*]
    (LCLS) .... MnGraH
Holy Trinity School, Winsted, MN [*Library symbol*] [*Library of Congress*]
    (LCLS) .... MnWsHT
Holyearth Foundation (EA) .... HF
Holyhead [*British ICAO location identifier*] (ICLI) .... EGCH
Holyoke, CO [*Location identifier FAA*] (FAAL) .... HEQ
Holyoke Community College [*Massachusetts*] .... HCC
Holyoke Community College, Holyoke, MA [*Library symbol Library of
    Congress*] (LCLS) .... MHolyC
Holyoke Junior College [*Later, Holyoke Community College*]
    [*Massachusetts*] .... HJC
Holyoke, MA [*FM radio station call letters*] .... WCCH
Holyoke Public Library, Holyoke, CO [*Library symbol Library of Congress*]
    (LCLS) .... CoHo
Holyoke Public Library, Holyoke, MA [*Library symbol Library of Congress*]
    (LCLS) .... MHoly
Holyrood Public Library, Newfoundland [*Library symbol National Library of
    Canada*] (BIB) .... NFH
Holzblaeser [*Woodwind Instrument*] [*Music*] .... HLZBL
Holzblaeser [*Woodwind Instrument*] [*Music*] .... HZBL
Holziken [*Switzerland ICAO location identifier*] (ICLI) .... LSXH
Holzknecht [*Unit*] .... H
Holzmacher, McLendon & Murrell, Inc., Melville, NY [*Library symbol Library
    of Congress*] (LCLS) .... NMelH
Homa Bay [*Kenya*] [*ICAO location identifier*] (ICLI) .... HKHB
Homach Gap Lathe .... HGL
Homalin [*Myanmar*] [*ICAO location identifier*] (ICLI) .... VBHL
Homatropine Methylbromide [*Anticholinergic*] .... HMB
Hombori [*Mali*] [*ICAO location identifier*] (ICLI) .... GAHB
Homcroft Elementary School, Duluth, MN [*Library symbol*] [*Library of
    Congress*] (LCLS) .... MnDuHE
Home .... H
Home (ROG) .... HM
Home Access Mortgage .... HAM
Home Accounting and Finance Office .... HAFO
Home Address .... HA
Home Address Block .... HAB
Home Address Gap [*Computer science*] (MHDB) .... HAG
Home Address Register .... HAR
Home All the Way [*Military*] (CAAL) .... HAW
Home Amateur [*Radio*] .... HAM
Home and Colonial School Society [*British*] .... HCSS
Home and Community-Based Services [*Department of Health and Human
    Services*] (GFGA) .... HCBS
Home and Community-Based Waiver for Aged [*Department of Health and
    Human Services*] (GFGA) .... HCBWAG
Home and Community-Based Waiver for Aged and Physically and
    Developmentally Disabled [*Department of Health and Human Services*]
    (GFGA) .... HCBWAGD
Home and Community-Based Waiver for Aged and Physically Disabled
    [*Department of Health and Human Services*] (GFGA) .... HCBWAGPD
Home and Community-Based Waiver for Mentally III [*Department of Health
    and Human Services*] (GFGA) .... HCBWMI
Home and Community-Based Waiver for Mentally Retarded and
    Developmentally Disabled [*Department of Health and Human Services*]
    (GFGA) .... HCBWMRDD
Home and Community-Based Waiver for Physically Disabled [*Department of
    Health and Human Services*] (GFGA) .... HCBWPDS
Home and Contract Furnishing Textiles Association [*British*] (DBA) ...... HCFTA
Home and Garden Bulletins [*A publication*] .... H & G
Home and Garden Show Executives International [*Defunct*] (EA) ...... HGSEI
Home & Garden Television .... HGTV
Home and Garden Television Network .... HGTV
Home and Law Publishers [*British*] .... HLP
Home and Office Banking Service [*Bank of Scotland*] (ECON) ...... HOBS
Home and School Institute (EA) .... HSI
Home and Store News, Ramsey, NJ [*Library symbol Library of Congress*]
    (LCLS) .... NjRamH
Home Area Toll [*Telecommunications*] (TEL) .... HAT
Home Automated Living .... HAL
Home Automation Association (EA) .... HAA
Home Baking Association (EA) .... HBA
Home Bancorp [*NASDAQ symbol*] (SAG) .... HBFW
Home Bancorp [*Associated Press*] (SAG) .... HmeBc
Home Bancorp of Elgin, Inc. [*NASDAQ symbol*] (SAG) .... HBEI
Home Bancorp of Elgin, Inc. [*Associated Press*] (SAG) .... HmBElg
Home Base [*Military*] (NVT) .... HBA
Home Base Development Committee [*Navy*] .... HBDC
Home Base, Ledger Office [*British military*] (DMA) .... HBLO
Home Beneficial Corp. [*NASDAQ symbol*] (NQ) .... HBEN
Home Beneficial Corp. [*Associated Press*] (SAG) .... HomBen

Home BeneficialCl'B' [*NASDAQ symbol*] (TTSB) ... HBENB
Home Birth Support Group [*Australia*] ... HBSG
Home Blood Glucose Monitoring [*Medicine*] ... HBGM
Home Blood Pressure Monitoring [*Medicine*] ... HBPM
Home Box Office [*Cable-television system*] ... HBO
Home Brewing and Winemaking Manufacturers Association [*British*] (DBA) ... HBWMA
Home Brewing and Winemaking Trade Association [*British*] (DBA) ... HBWTA
Home Builders Association of Maryland (SRA) ... HBAM
Home Builders Association of Massachusetts (SRA) ... HBAM
Home Building Bancorp [*NASDAQ symbol*] (SAG) ... HBBI
Home Building Bancorp [*Associated Press*] (SAG) ... HmBBc
Home Capital Group, Inc. [*Toronto Stock Exchange symbol*] ... HCG
Home Care ... HC
Home Care Aide [*Medicine*] (DMAA) ... HCA
Home Care Association of Washington (SRA) ... HCAW
Home Care Coordinator [*Medicine*] ... HCC
Home Care Program, Brockville, Ontario [*Library symbol National Library of Canada*] (BIB) ... OBRH
Home Care Service of New South Wales [*Australia*] ... HCSNSW
Home Center Institute (EA) ... HCI
Home Centers [*NASDAQ symbol*] (TTSB) ... HOMEF
Home Centers (DIY) Ltd. [*NASDAQ symbol*] (SAG) ... HOME
Home Centers (DIY) Ltd. [*Associated Press*] (SAG) ... HomeCnt
Home Cervical Traction Unit [*Medicine*] (DAVI) ... HCTU
Home Civil Servant [*British*] ... HCS
Home Civil Service [*British*] ... HCS
Home Computer (IAA) ... HC
Home Computing Weekly [*British*] (NITA) ... HCW
Home Consumption Price ... HCP
Home Conversion Loan Program [*Canada*] ... HCLP
Home Counties Master Printers' Alliance [*British*] (DGA) ... HCMPA
Home Counties Newspapers [*British*] (DGA) ... HCN
Home Counties Newspapers Ltd., Luton, United Kingdom [*Library symbol Library of Congress*] (LCLS) ... UkLuH
Home Counties Reserve Regiment [*British military*] (DMA) ... HCRR
Home Defence [*British World War II*] ... HD
Home Defence Security Executive [*British World War II*] ... HD(S)E
Home Defence Unit [*British military*] (DMA) ... HDU
Home Deposit Assistance Scheme [*Australia*] ... HDAS
Home Depot [*NYSE symbol*] (TTSB) ... HD
[*The*] **Home Depot, Inc.** [*NYSE symbol*] (SPSG) ... HD
[*The*] **Home Depot, Inc.** [*Associated Press*] (SAG) ... HmeDep
Home Dialysis [*Medicine*] (DMAA) ... HHD
Home Dockyard Regulations [*Navy*] (MCD) ... HDR
Home Drug Infusion Therapy [*Medicine*] ... HDIT
Home Economics [*Secondary school course*] [*British*] ... HE
Home Economics Association of Seventh-Day Adventists (EA) ... HEASDA
Home Economics Education Association (EA) ... HEEA
Home Economics Reading Service [*Recipe clipping service*] ... HERS
Home Economics Related Occupations ... HERO
Home Economics Research Institute [*Iowa State University*] [*Research center*] (RCD) ... HERI
Home Economics Research Reports ... HERR
Home Economics Resources in Education [*British*] (DBA) ... HERE
Home Economists in Business (EA) ... HEIB
Home Education Livelihood Program [*New Mexico*] ... HELP
Home Education Resource Center [*Defunct*] (EA) ... HERC
Home Emergency Ladies' Pal [*Book title*] ... HELP
Home Emergency Response System ... HERS
Home Energy Advisory Service [*Victoria, Australia*] ... HEAS
Home Energy Rating System [*Thermal technology*] (PS) ... HERS
Home Enteral Nutrition [*Medicine*] (DMAA) ... HEN
Home Entertainment Network [*Cable-television system*] ... HEN
Home Entertainment Service [*Cable-television system*] (IAA) ... HES
Home Entertainment System ... HES
Home Equity Conversion ... HEC
Home Equity Line of Credit (TDOB) ... HELOC
Home Equity Loan ... HEL
Home Executives National Networking Association ... HENNA
Home Fallout Protection Survey [*Formerly, EFPH*] [*Civil Defense*] ... HFPS
Home Fashions Products Association (EA) ... HFPA
Home Fed Bancorp [*NASDAQ symbol*] (TTSB) ... HOMF
Home Federal Bancorp [*Associated Press*] (SAG) ... HmFedIN
Home Federal Corp. [*NASDAQ symbol*] (NQ) ... HFMD
Home Federal Financial Corp. [*Associated Press*] (SAG) ... HFdSvF
Home Federal Financial Corp. [*NASDAQ symbol*] (SAG) ... HFSF
Home Federal (MD) [*NASDAQ symbol*] (TTSB) ... HFMD
Home Finance Contract ... HFC
Home Financial [*NASDAQ symbol*] (TTSB) ... HOFL
Home Financial Corp. Florida [*Associated Press*] (SAG) ... HmFnFL
Home Financial Corporation of Florida [*NASDAQ symbol*] (SAG) ... HOFL
Home Fleet [*Obsolete British*] ... HF
Home for Incurables [*Australia*] ... HFI
Home Forces [*Military British*] ... HF
Home Front ... HF
Home Furnishings Daily [*A publication*] [*Formerly HFD-Weekly Home Furnishings*] (WDMC) ... HFD
Home Furnishings Industry Committee [*Defunct*] (EA) ... HFIC
Home Furnishings International Association (EA) ... HFIA
Home Grown Cereals Authority (PDAA) ... HGCA
Home Grown Timber Marketing Corp. Ltd. [*British*] (BI) ... HGTMC
Home Guard [*British*] ... HG
Home Health [*Medicine*] (DAVI) ... HH
Home Health Agency ... HHA
Home Health Aid (DAVI) ... HHA
Home Health Care [*Medicine*] (DAVI) ... HHC
Home Health Corp. of Amer [*NASDAQ symbol*] (TTSB) ... HHCA
Home Health Corp. of America, Inc. [*NASDAQ symbol*] (SAG) ... HHCA
Home Health Corporation of America, Inc. [*Associated Press*] (SAG) ... HmeHlth
Home Health Services and Staffing Association (EA) ... HHSSA
Home Health Services Association [*Later, HHSSA*] (EA) ... HHSA
Home Help [*Medicine*] ... HH
Home Hill [*Australia Airport symbol*] ... HMH
Home Holdings [*NYSE symbol*] (SPSG) ... HHI
Home Holdings [*Associated Press*] (SAG) ... HomeHld
Home Improvement Dealers Association of America (EA) ... HIDA
Home Improvement Products Association [*Defunct*] (EA) ... HIPA
Home Improvement Research Institute (EA) ... HIRI
Home Information Technology Study [*Department of Education*] (GFGA) ... HITS
Home Instruction Program for Preschool Youngsters [*Israel*] ... HIPPY
Home Laundry Detergent ... HLD
Home Lines [*Steamship*] (MHDW) ... HL
Home Loan Bank Board [*Federal agency*] (GPO) ... HLBB
Home Location Register (ACRL) ... HLR
Home Location Register ... HLR
Home Maintenance and Modification Program [*Australia*] ... HM & M
Home Manufacturers Association [*Later, HMC*] (EA) ... HMA
Home Manufacturers Councils of NAHB [*National Association of Home Builders of the US*] (EA) ... HMC
Home Medical Advisor [*Schueler Corp.*] ... HMA
Home Medical Equipment ... HME
Home Mission ... HM
Home Mission Association [*Episcopalian*] ... HMA
Home Mission Board of the Southern Baptist Convention, Atlanta, GA [*Library symbol*] [*Library of Congress*] (LCLS) ... GAHoM
Home Mission Sisters of America (Glenmary) (TOCD) ... GHMS
Home Mortgage Access Corp. (EMRF) ... HOMAC
Home Mortgage Disclosure Act ... HMDA
Home News, New Brunswick, NJ [*Library symbol Library of Congress*] (LCLS) ... NjNbH
Home Numbering Plan Area [*AT & T*] ... HNPA
Home Nursing ... HN
Home Nursing Supervisor [*Red Cross*] ... HNS
Home Observation for Measurement of the Environment [*Child development test*] [*Psychology*] ... HOME
Home of Franklin D. Roosevelt and Vanderbilt Mansion National Historic Sites ... HOFR
Home of Peace Hospitals [*Australia*] ... HOPH
Home of Record ... HOR
Home of Selection and Completion of Travel within One Year Is Authorized [*Military*] ... HOSTWOY
Home Office [*British*] ... HO
Home Office Business Network [*Information service or system*] (IID) ... HOBN
Home Office Facility ... HOF
Home Office Forensic Science Laboratory [*British*] ... HOFSL
Home Office Large Major Enquiry System [*Computer system*] [*British*] ... HOLMES
Home Office Life Underwriters Association [*St. Louis, MO*] (EA) ... HOLUA
Home Office Quote (NITA) ... HOQ
Home Oil Co. Ltd. [*Associated Press*] (SAG) ... HmeOil
Home Oil Co. Ltd., Calgary, AB, Canada [*Library symbol Library of Congress*] (LCLS) ... CaACH
Home Oil Co. Ltd., Calgary, Alberta [*Library symbol National Library of Canada*] (NLC) ... ACH
Home on Decoy [*Military*] (CAAL) ... HOD
Home on Jamming ... HOJ
Home on Target [*Military*] (CAAL) ... HOT
Home Oncology Medical Extension [*A home treatment program*] ... HOME
Home Only [*British military*] (DMA) ... HO
Home Opportunity Loans Scheme [*Australia*] ... HOLS
Home Orchard Society (EA) ... HOS
Home Oriented Maternity Experience [*Defunct*] (EA) ... HOME
Home Owner Association ... HOA
Home Owners Assistance Program [*Military*] (AABC) ... HAP
Home Owners' Loan Act of 1933 ... HOLA
Home Owners' Loan Corp. [*Terminated, 1942*] ... HOLC
Home Owners' Loan Corporation Bonds (MHDB) ... HOKEYS
Home Owners Warranty [*National Association of Home Builders*] ... HOW
Home Ownership and Opportunity for People Everywhere [*Program*] [*HUD*] ... HOPE
Home Ownership Assistance Program [*Farmers Home Administration*] ... HOAP
Home Ownership Building Industry Scheme [*Australia*] ... HOBIS
Home Ownership Made Easy Association [*Defunct*] (EA) ... HOME
Home Parenteral Nutrition ... HPN
Home Peritoneal Dialysis [*Nephrology*] (DAVI) ... HPD
Home Plug and Play [*Technology*] ... HPnP
Home Policy Committee of War Cabinet [*British World War II*] ... HPC
Home Port [*Navy*] (NVT) ... HPO
Home Port [*Navy*] (NVT) ... HPT
Home Port/Area/City [*Code*] [*Navy*] (DNAB) ... HP/A/C
Home Port Bancorp [*NASDAQ symbol*] (TTSB) ... HPBC
Home Port Bancorp, Inc. [*Associated Press*] (SAG) ... HmPrt
Home Port Bancorp, Inc. [*NASDAQ symbol*] (CTT) ... HPBC
Home Products Safety Council (EA) ... HSC
Home Properties of New York [*NYSE symbol*] (SAG) ... HME
Home Properties of New York [*Associated Press*] (SAG) ... HmePrp
Home Quarters Warehouse, Inc. ... HQ
Home Recording Rights Coalition (EA) ... HRRC
Home Reunion Society [*British*] ... HRS
Home Rule ... HR

Home Run [*Baseball*] ... HR
Home Run Control System [*Computer science*] ... HCS
Home Satellite Dish (NTCM) ... HSD
Home School Legal Defense Association (PAZ) ... HSDLA
Home School Legal Defense Association (EA) ... HSLDA
Home Screening Questionnaire [*Test*] [*Psychology*] ... HSQ
Home Secretary [*British*] ... HS
Home Service Force [*British*] (BARN) ... HSF
Home Services Program [*Australia*] ... HSP
Home Shopper/Cable Value [*Cable television channel*] ... HS/CV
Home Shopping Club [*of the Home Shopping Network*] ... HSC
Home Shopping Network [*Cable-television system*] ... HSN
Home Shopping Network, Inc. [*Associated Press*] (SAG) ... HomeSh
Home Shopping Network, Inc. [*NYSE symbol*] (SPSG) ... HSN
Home Sports Entertainment [*Cable-television system*] ... HSE
Home Sports Entertainment Network [*Cable TV programming service*] ... HSEN
Home State Holdings [*NASDAQ symbol*] (TTSB) ... HOMS
Home State Holdings, Inc. [*Associated Press*] (SAG) ... HmeStat
Home State Holdings, Inc. [*NASDAQ symbol*] (SAG) ... HOMS
Home Station [*DoD*] ... HS
Home Study Exchange (EA) ... HOSTEX
Home Surgeon [*Medicine British*] ... HS
Home Team Sports [*Cable-television system*] ... HTS
Home Testing Institute, Inc. (NTCM) ... HTI
Home Theatre Network [*In network name "HTN Plus"*] [*Cable-television system*] ... HTN
Home Timber Merchants' Association of England and Wales (BI) ... HTMAEW
Home Total Parenteral Nutrition [*Medicine*] ... HTPN
Home Town Honey [*Slang*] ... HTH
Home Treatment [*Medicine*] ... HT
Home TRON [*The Real-Time Operating System Nucleus*] (NITA) ... H TRON
Home University Library [*A publication*] ... HUL
Home User Groups [*Computer science*] ... HUG's
Home Uterine Activity Assessment [*Medicine*] (DMAA) ... HUAA
Home Uterine Activity Monitoring ... HUAM
Home Ventilating Institute [*Later, HVIDAMCA*] (EA) ... HVI
Home Ventilating Institute Division of the Air Movement Control Association (EA) ... HVIDAMCA
Home Video [*Television*] ... HV
Home Video Recorder (NTCM) ... HVR
Home Video Tutorial ... HTV
Home Videotape Recorder (IAA) ... HVTR
Home View Network [*Cable-television system*] ... HVN
Home Wine and Beer Trade Association (EA) ... HWBTA
Home-Based Advanced Assignment Program [*Military*] ... HAAP
Home-Based Maintenance Allowance ... HBMA
Homebush Bay Ministerial Council [*New South Wales, Australia*] ... HBMC
Homecorp, Inc. [*NASDAQ symbol*] (SAG) ... HMCI
Homecorp, Inc. [*Associated Press*] (SAG) ... Hmecrp
Homedale Public Library, Homedale, ID [*Library symbol*] [*Library of Congress*] (LCLS) ... IdHm
Homegate Hospitality, Inc. [*NASDAQ symbol*] (SAG) ... HMGT
Homegate Hospitality, Inc. [*Associated Press*] (SAG) ... Homegte
Homeland Bankshares [*NASDAQ symbol*] (TTSB) ... HLND
Homeland Bankshares Corp. [*NASDAQ symbol*] (SAG) ... HLND
Homeland Bankshares Corp. [*Associated Press*] (SAG) ... HmlnBk
Homeland Park, SC [*AM radio station call letters*] ... WRIX
Home-Laundering Care Code [*British*] (DI) ... HLCC
Home-Laundering Consultative Council [*British*] (DI) ... HLCC
Homeless and At-Risk Population (DMAA) ... HARP
Homeless Chronically Mentally Ill [*Medicine*] ... HCMI
Homelessness Information Exchange (EA) ... HIE
Homemaker Home Health Aide (OICC) ... HHHA
Homemakers & Mothers Cooperatives, Inc. ... HOMOCO
Homemakers Equal Rights Association [*Defunct*] (EA) ... HERA
Homemaking and Volunteer Experience (DICI) ... HAVE
Homeobox [*Genetics*] ... HOX
Home-on-Burn ... HOB
Homeopath [*or Homeopathic*] (WDAA) ... HOMO
Homeopathic Council for Research and Education (EA) ... HCRE
Homeopathic Foundation [*Later, FHR*] (EA) ... HF
Homeopathic Medical Doctor [*Medicine*] ... HMD
Homeopathic Pharmacopoeia ... HP
Homeopathic Pharmacopoeia Convention of the United States ... HPCUS
Homeopathic Pharmacopoeia of the United States ... HPUS
Homeopathy (ADA) ... HOMEO
Homeopathy [*Medicine*] ... HOMEOP
Homeostatic Adaptive Control System ... HACS
Homeostatic Regulators [*British*] ... HR
Homeostatic Thymus Hormone [*Immunology*] ... HTH
Homeowner-Mortgage Eurosecurities [*Salomon Brothers*] [*Real estate*] ... HOMES
Homeowners' [*Insurance*] ... HO
Homeowners Assistance Fund, Defense [*DoD*] ... HOA
Homeowner's Association [*Computer science*] ... HOA
Homeowners Emergency Services, Inc. ... HES
Homeowners Group [*NASDAQ symbol*] (TTSB) ... HOMG
Homeowners Group, Inc. [*Associated Press*] (SAG) ... HmowG
Homeowners Group, Inc. [*NASDAQ symbol*] (NQ) ... HOMG
Homeowner's Land Corp. [*Federal agency formed in 1932*] [*Investment term*] ... HLC
Homeowners Using Savings and Energy Information to Negotiate Fair Offers [*Student legal action organization*] (EA) ... HOUSE-INFO
Homeplex Mortgage Investments [*Associated Press*] (SAG) ... Hmeplx
Homeplex Mortgage Investments [*NYSE symbol*] (SPSG) ... HPX
Homeplex Mtge Invmts [*NYSE symbol*] (TTSB) ... HPX
Homer (DA) ... Hmr
Homer [*Alaska*] [*Seismograph station code, US Geological Survey*] (SEIS) ... HOM
Homer [*Greek poet, c. 800BC*] [*Classical studies*] (ROG) ... HOM
Homer [*Alaska*] [*Airport symbol*] (OAG) ... HOM
Homer [*Alaska*] [*ICAO location identifier*] (ICLI) ... PAHO
Homer, AK [*Location identifier FAA*] (FAAL) ... ACE
Homer, AK [*AM radio station call letters*] ... KBBI
Homer, AK [*AM radio station call letters*] ... KGTL
Homer, AK [*FM radio station call letters*] ... KWVV
Homer City, PA [*AM radio station call letters*] ... WCCS
Homer Community Library, Homer, IL [*Library symbol Library of Congress*] (LCLS) ... IHom
Homer Hoyt Institute ... HHI
Homer, IL [*Location identifier FAA*] (FAAL) ... HMJ
Homer, LA [*Location identifier FAA*] (FAAL) ... HMQ
Homer, LA [*FM radio station call letters*] ... KZXB
Homer, NY [*FM radio station call letters*] ... WXHC
Homer Public Library, Homer, AK [*Library symbol Library of Congress*] (LCLS) ... AkHom
Homer Public Library, Homer, MI [*Library symbol Library of Congress*] (LCLS) ... MiHom
Homer Semana Dia (BJA) ... HSD
Homerville, GA [*Location identifier FAA*] (FAAL) ... HOE
Homerville, GA [*FM radio station call letters*] ... WBTY
Home's Manuscript Decisions, Scotch Court of Session [*A publication*] (DLA) ... Home
Home's Manuscript Decisions, Scotch Court of Session [*A publication*] (DLA) ... Home (Clk)
Home's Manuscript Decisions, Scotch Court of Session [*A publication*] (DLA) ... Home Ct of Sess
Home's Manuscript Decisions, Scotch Court of Session [*A publication*] (DLA) ... Home H Dec
Homes of Private Enterprise (EA) ... HOPE
Homes on Aboriginal Land [*Australia*] ... HOAL
Homes Per Rating Point [*Advertising*] (DOAD) ... HPRP
Homes Registration Office ... HRO
Homes Using Radio [*Ratings*] (NTCM) ... HUR
Homes Using Television [*Television ratings*] ... HUT
Home-School Liaison (AIE) ... HSL
Homestake Mining [*NYSE symbol*] (TTSB) ... HM
Homestake Mining Co. [*NYSE symbol*] (SPSG) ... HM
Homestake Mining Co. [*Associated Press*] (SAG) ... Hmstke
Home-Station Gunnery [*Military*] (INF) ... HSG
Homestead ... HMSTD
Homestead (WDAA) ... HMSTD
Homestead (DLA) ... HOMSTD
Homestead (ADA) ... HS
Homestead [*Florida*] [*Airport symbol*] (OAG) ... HST
Homestead Elementary School, Garden City, NY [*Library symbol*] [*Library of Congress*] (LCLS) ... NGcHE
Homestead, FL [*Location identifier FAA*] (FAAL) ... HST
Homestead, FL [*AM radio station call letters*] ... WOIR
Homestead, FL [*FM radio station call letters*] (RBYB) ... WRGP-FM
Homestead, FL [*FM radio station call letters*] ... WXDJ
Homestead/Homestead Air Force Base [*Florida*] [*ICAO location identifier*] (ICLI) ... KHST
Homestead National Monument ... HOME
Homestead Resources, Inc. [*Vancouver Stock Exchange symbol*] ... HSR
Homestead Village, Inc. [*Associated Press*] (SAG) ... HomeV
Homestead Village, Inc. [*Associated Press*] (SAG) ... HomeVil
Homestead Village, Inc. [*AMEX symbol*] (SAG) ... HSD
Homesteaders Association [*Defunct*] (EA) ... HA
Hometown Bancorp [*NASDAQ symbol*] (TTSB) ... HTWN
Hometown Bancorp, Inc. [*Associated Press*] (SAG) ... HmtwBc
Hometown Bancorp, Inc. [*NASDAQ symbol*] (NQ) ... HTWN
HomeTown Buffet [*NASDAQ symbol*] (TTSB) ... HTBB
Hometown Buffet, Inc. [*Associated Press*] (SAG) ... HomeTB
Hometown Buffet, Inc. [*NASDAQ symbol*] (SAG) ... HTBB
Hometown Public Library, Hometown, IL [*Library symbol Library of Congress*] (LCLS) ... IHot
HomeVideo [*Videocassette tape*] (NTCM) ... HV
Homewood Public Library, Homewood, IL [*Library symbol Library of Congress*] (LCLS) ... IHow
Homework ... HMWRK
Homeworkers Organized for More Employment (EA) ... HOME
Homfray Carpets Unit Trust [*Commercial firm*] [*British*] ... HCUT
Homicidal Ideation [*Psychiatry*] (DAVI) ... HI
Homicide (DLA) ... HOMI
Homicide [*Legal shorthand*] (LWAP) ... HOMIC
Homiletica en Biblica [*The Hague*] [*A publication*] (BJA) ... HomBib
Homily (ROG) ... HOM
Homing ... HOM
Homing All the Way Killer [*Small missile*] ... HAWK
Homing and Warning Computer (MCD) ... HAWC
Homing and Warning Programmer (MCD) ... HAWP
Homing Beacon [*Aviation*] ... HB
Homing Bomb System [*Air Force*] ... HOBOS
Homing Bomb System [*Air Force*] ... HOBS
Homing Comparator Unit (AAG) ... HCU
Homing Fixture (MCD) ... HOF
Homing Guidance (AAG) ... HG
Homing Instrumentation Unit (MCD) ... HIU
Homing Interceptor Technology [*Navigation*] (IEEE) ... HIT
Homing Level Gauge ... HLG
Homing on Offset Beacon ... HOB

Homing Optical Bomb (MCD) ... HOBO
Homing Optical Guidance ... HOG
Homing Optical Guidance System ... HOGS
Homing Optical System Study ... HOSS
Homing Overlay Equipment (MCD) ... HOE
Homing Overlay Experiment [*Ballistic missile defense*] (RDA) ... HOE
Homing Position Indicator (NATG) ... HPI
Homing Sequence (IAA) ... HS
Homing System Survey (MCD) ... HOSS
Homing Terrier [*Missile*] ... HT
Homing Terrier/Improved Tartar [*Missile*] (MCD) ... HT/IT
Homing Terrier Retrofit [*Missile*] (MCD) ... HTR
Homing Test Vehicle (NG) ... HTV
Homing Transponders ... HT
Homing Type (NATG) ... HT
Homing Weapons (NVT) ... HW
Hominid Corridor Research Project [*Palaeontology*] ... HCRP
Hominis Vis [*The Strength of Man*] [*Latin*] ... Hovis
Hommel AG [*Switzerland*] [*Research code symbol*] ... HH
Homo Dei. Przeglad Ascetyczno-Duszpasterski [*Warsaw/Wroclaw*] [*A publication*] (BJA) ... HomoD
Homo Sapiens (BARN) ... hom sap
Homo Sapiens [*Human species*] ... HSA
Homobonus de Cremona [*Deceased, 1272*] [*Authority cited in pre-1607 legal work*] (DSA) ... H
Homobonus de Cremona [*Deceased, 1272*] [*Authority cited in pre-1607 legal work*] (DSA) ... Ho
Homobonus de Cremona [*Deceased, 1272*] [*Authority cited in pre-1607 legal work*] (DSA) ... Hobonus
Homobonus de Cremona [*Deceased, 1272*] [*Authority cited in pre-1607 legal work*] (DSA) ... Hom
Homobonus de Cremona [*Deceased, 1272*] [*Authority cited in pre-1607 legal work*] (DSA) ... Homob
Homocysteate [*Biochemistry*] ... HCA
Homocysteine [*An amino acid*] ... Hcy
Homocystinuria [*Medicine*] ... HCU
Homocytotropic [*Medicine*] (MAE) ... HCT
Homoeodomain [*Genetics*] ... HD
Homoeopathy [*Medicine*] ... HOMOEO
Homofolic Acid [*Biochemistry*] ... HFA
Homogenate Survival Time ... HST
Homogeneity of Variance [*Statistics*] ... HOV
Homogeneous Aqueous Reactor [*Nuclear energy*] (NUCP) ... HAR
Homogeneous Assembly Zero Energy Level [*AERE*] ... HAZEL
Homogeneous Boundary Condition ... HBC
Homogeneous Computer System ... HCS
Homogeneous Continuous Stirred Tank Reactor [*Chemical engineering*] ... HCSTR
Homogeneous Differential Equation ... HDE
Homogeneous Enzyme Immunoassy [*Biochemistry*] (DAVI) ... HEI
Homogeneous Equilibrium Model (NRCH) ... HEM
Homogeneous Exposure Group [*Concept for acessing cancer risk*] ... HEG
Homogeneous Information Sets ... HIS
Homogeneous Reactor Experiments (NRCH) ... HRE
Homogeneous Reactor Test ... HRT
Homogeneous Thorium Reactor ... HTR
Homogeneous Time Resolved Fluorescence [*Analytical Chemistry*] ... HTRF
Homogeneously Staining Region [*Cytology*] ... HSR
Homogenization Medium ... HM
Homogenized Leaf Curing [*Tobacco industry*] ... HLC
Homogenous ... HOMO
Homogenous Element Processor (NITA) ... HEP
Homogenous Uniparental Embryo [*Embryology*] ... HUP
Homogentisate [*Biochemistry*] ... HGA
Homogentisic Acid [*Biochemistry*] (MAE) ... HGA
Homogentisic Acid [*In urine*] [*Genetics*] (DAVI) ... ALKAPT
Homograft Incus Prosthesis [*Medicine*] (DMAA) ... HIP
Homoharringtonine [*Antineoplastic drug*] ... HHT
Homolateral [*Medicine*] ... HOMOLAT
Homologous Canine Distemper [*Antiserum*] ... HCD
Homologous Leucocytic Antibodies ... HLA
Homologous Serum ... HS
Homologous Tetanus Immune Globulin [*Medicine*] (DMAA) ... HTIG
Homonuclear Polarization Transfer [*Physics*] ... HPT
Homonymous Hemianopsia [*Ophthalmology*] ... HH
Homophile Effort for Legal Protection [*An association Defunct*] (EA) ... HELP
Homopolar Disk Dynamo ... HDD
Homopolar Generator [*To power high-technology experiments*] ... HPG
Homopolar Inductor Alternator (PDAA) ... HIA
Homoptera [*Entomology*] ... Hom
Homoreactant [*Medicine*] ... HR
Homosassa Springs, FL [*FM radio station call letters*] ... WXCV
Homoserine Dehydrogenase [*An enzyme*] ... HD
Homoserine Kinase [*An enzyme*] ... HK
Homoserine Lactone [*An amino acid*] ... Hsl
Homosexual ... H
Homosexual ... HOMO
Homosexual Information Center (EA) ... HIC
Homosexual Law Reform Society [*British*] (BI) ... HLRS
Homosexual World Organization ... HWO
Homosexuals Anonymous Fellowship Services (EA) ... HAFS
Homothetic-Constant Differences of Elasticities of Substitution [*Statistics*] ... HCDE
Homovanillic Acid [*Biochemistry*] ... HVA
Homozygous Diabetes Insipidus [*A genetic variety of rat*] ... HODI
Homozygous Typing Cells [*Immunochemistry*] ... HTC
Hon [*Libya*] [*ICAO location identifier*] (ICLI) ... HLON
HON Indus [*NASDAQ symbol*] (TTSB) ... HONI
Hon Industries, Inc. [*NASDAQ symbol*] (NQ) ... HONI
Hon Industries, Inc. [*Associated Press*] (SAG) ... HonInd
Honan Province [*China, Mainland*] [*MARC geographic area code Library of Congress*] (LCCP) ... a-cc-ho
Honcho Gold Mines, Inc. [*Vancouver Stock Exchange symbol*] ... HNO
Honda [*Colombia*] [*Airport symbol*] (AD) ... HDA
Honda Car Club [*Defunct*] (EA) ... HCC
Honda Civic Club [*Later, H-I*] (EA) ... HCC
Honda Engineering ... HE
Honda Motor ADR [*NYSE symbol*] (TTSB) ... HMC
Honda Motor Co. Ltd. [*NYSE symbol*] (SPSG) ... HMC
Honda Motors Co. Ltd. [*Associated Press*] (SAG) ... Honda
Honda of America Manufacturing ... HAM
Honda Racing Corp. ... HRC
Honda Sport Touring Association (EA) ... HSTA
Hondacar International (EA) ... H-I
Honda-Mrkos-Pajdusakova [*Comet*] ... HMP
Hondo Oil & Gas [*AMEX symbol*] (TTSB) ... HOG
Hondo Oil & Gas Co. [*AMEX symbol*] (SPSG) ... HOG
Hondo Oil & Gas Co. [*Associated Press*] (SAG) ... Hondo
Hondo, TX [*Location identifier FAA*] (FAAL) ... HDO
Hondo, TX [*Location identifier FAA*] (FAAL) ... HMA
Hondo, TX [*AM radio station call letters*] (RBYB) ... KCWM
Hondo, TX [*FM radio station call letters*] (RBYB) ... KCWM-FM
Hondo, TX [*FM radio station call letters*] (RBYB) ... KRBH-FM
Honduran-American Association (EA) ... HAA
Honduran-American Chamber of Commerce [*See also CCHA*] (EA) ... HAMCHAM
Honduras [*ANSI two-letter standard code*] (CNC) ... HN
Honduras [*ANSI three-letter standard code*] (CNC) ... HND
Honduras [*MARC country of publication code Library of Congress*] (LCCP) ... ho
Honduras ... HON
Honduras ... HOND
Honduras (VRA) ... Hond
Honduras [*MARC geographic area code Library of Congress*] (LCCP) ... ncho--
Honduras Information Center (EA) ... HIC
Honea Path, SC [*FM radio station call letters*] ... WRIX
Hone-Finish Monolithic Floor [*Technical drawings*] ... HFMF
Honeoye Falls-Lima Senior High School Library, Honeoye Falls, NY [*OCLC symbol*] (OCLC) ... RWO
Honesdale, PA [*FM radio station call letters*] ... WDNH
Honesdale, PA [*AM radio station call letters*] ... WWCC
Honest Ballot Association (EA) ... HBA
Honest John [*A type of short range, unguided Army rocket*] ... HJ
Honest John Launcher [*See also HJ*] [*Army*] ... HJL
Honest John Rocket [*See also HJ*] [*Army*] ... HJR
Honestly Significant Difference ... HSD
Honest-to-God Cash Flow Yields [*Finance*] (EMRF) ... HTG
Honey (WGA) ... HNY
Honey (DSUE) ... HON
Honey Bee ... HB
Honey Bee Research and Development Council [*Australia*] ... HBRDC
Honey Bee Spiroplasma [*Bacteriology*] ... HBS
Honey Bee Venom [*Immunology*] ... HBV
Honey Industry Council of America [*Defunct*] (EA) ... HICA
Honey Packers and Marketers' Association of Australia ... HPMAA
Honey Research Council [*Australia*] ... HRC
Honeybee ... HNYB
Honeybee Research and Development Committee [*Australia*] ... HRDC
Honeycomb ... HNYCMB
Honeycomb Aluminum Panel ... HAP
Honeycomb Corrugated Construction ... HCC
Honeycomb Foundation (IIA) ... HCF
Honeycomb Propellant Matrix (SAA) ... HPM
Honeycomb Sandwich Aluminum Panel ... HSAP
Honeycombed Sandwich Joint ... HSJ
Honeycomb-Supported Screen ... HSS
Honeyoye Falls, NY [*FM radio station call letters*] ... WRCD
Honeysuckle Creek Tracking Station [*NASA*] (KSC) ... HSK
Honeywell Analog-Digital Input-Output Subsystem (IAA) ... HADIOS
Honeywell Associative Parallel Processing Ensemble ... HAPPE
Honeywell Automotive Accounting System (IAA) ... HAAS
Honeywell Business Computer [*or Compiler*] ... HBC
Honeywell Computer Users Association (HGAA) ... HCUA
Honeywell Distributed Manufacturing System (NITA) ... HDMS
Honeywell Electro-Optics Center Library, Lexington, MA [*OCLC symbol*] (OCLC) ... HON
[*The*] **Honeywell Engineering Status Information System** (SAA) ... THESIS
Honeywell Equipment Lease Plan ... HELP
Honeywell Error Analysis and Logging System ... HEALS
Honeywell File Access System ... HFAS
Honeywell Financial and Corporate Planning System (HGAA) ... HFCS
Honeywell, Inc. (NASA) ... HI
Honeywell, Inc. [*Formerly, MH, M-H*] [*NYSE symbol*] (SPSG) ... HON
Honeywell, Inc. [*Associated Press*] (SAG) ... Honywel
Honeywell Information Systems, Inc. (IEEE) ... HIS
Honeywell Information Systems, Inc. ... HISI
Honeywell Information Systems, Phoenix, AZ [*Library symbol Library of Congress*] (LCLS) ... AzPhH
Honeywell Institute for Information Science (IEEE) ... HIIS
Honeywell Integrating Gyro ... HIG
Honeywell Large Systems Users Association (EA) ... HLSUA

Honeywell Ltd., Advanced Technology Centre, Willowdale, ON, Canada [*Library symbol*] [*Library of Congress*] (LCLS) .... CaOTHL
Honeywell Sperry Inc., Defense System Division, Albuquerque, NM [*Library symbol*] [*Library of Congress*] (LCLS) .... NmAHS
Honeywell Time-Sharing System [*Computer science*] (IEEE) .... HTSS
Honeywell Users Group .... HUG
Honeywell Users Group - Small and Medium Systems [*Later, NAHU*] .... HUG-SMS
Honeywell Verification Simulation Facility (NASA) .... HVSF
Honeywell-Bull .... HB
Honeywell-NEC Supercomputers, Inc. .... HNSX
Honeywell's Manufacturing System [*Honeywell Information Systems Ltd.*] [*Software package*] (NCC) .... HMS
Hong Kong [*MARC geographic area code Library of Congress*] (LCCP) .... a-hk--
Hong Kong [*MARC country of publication code Library of Congress*] (LCCP) .... hk
Hong Kong [*ANSI two-letter standard code*] (CNC) .... HK
Hong Kong [*Seismograph station code, US Geological Survey*] (SEIS) .... HKC
Hong Kong [*Airport symbol*] (OAG) .... HKG
Hong Kong [*ANSI three-letter standard code*] (CNC) .... HKG
Hong Kong [*British Crown Colony*] [*Airport symbol*] (AD) .... HKG
Hong Kong [*IYRU nationality code*] (IYR) .... KH
Hong Kong [*Hong Kong*] [*ICAO location identifier*] (ICLI) .... VHHK
[*The*] **Hong Kong Academic and Research Network** [*Computer science*] (TNIG) .... HARNET
Hong Kong Airways Ltd. .... HKA
Hong Kong and Singapore Royal Artillery [*British military*] (DMA) .... HKSRA
Hong Kong and Singapore Royal Garrison Artillery [*British military*] (DMA) .... HKSRGA
Hong Kong Association of Banks (ECON) .... HKAB
Hong Kong Bank Australia .... HKBA
Hong Kong Bank of Canada (ECON) .... HBC
Hong Kong Bank of Canada .... HKBC
Hong Kong Cable Communications .... HKCC
Hong Kong Chemical Society .... HKCS
Hong Kong Commodities Exchange .... HKCE
Hong Kong Dragon Airlines (FEA) .... DRAGONAIR
Hong Kong Dragon Airlines Ltd. [*ICAO designator*] (FAAC) .... HDA
Hong Kong Futures Exchange .... HKFE
Hong Kong Interbank Offered Rate (DFIT) .... HIBOR
Hong Kong Inter-Bank Offered Rate (MHDW) .... HKIBOR
Hong Kong/International [*Hong Kong*] [*ICAO location identifier*] (ICLI) .... VHHH
Hong Kong Law Journal [*A publication*] (DLA) .... HKLJ
Hong Kong Law Journal [*A publication*] (DLA) .... Hong Kong LJ
Hong Kong Law Reports [*A publication*] (DLA) .... HKLR
Hong Kong Law Reports [*A publication*] (DLA) .... Hong Kong LR
Hong Kong Military Service Corps [*British military*] (DMA) .... HKMSC
Hong Kong Monetary Authority [*Banking*] .... HKMA
Hong Kong Regiment [*British military*] (DMA) .... HKR
Hong Kong Seamen's Union .... HKSU
Hong Kong Study Circle (EA) .... HKSC
Hong Kong Telecom ADR [*NYSE symbol*] (TTSB) .... HKT
Hong Kong Telecommunications Ltd. [*Associated Press*] (SAG) .... HK Tel
Hong Kong Telecommunications Ltd. [*NYSE symbol*] (CTT) .... HKT
Hong Kong Trade Advisory Group [*British Overseas Trade Board*] (DS) .... HKTAG
Hong Kong University .... HKU
Hong Kong University. Law Journal [*A publication*] (DLA) .... Hong Kong UL Jo
Hong Kong University of Science and Technology (ECON) .... HKUST
Hong Kong Volunteer Corps [*British military*] (DMA) .... HKVC
Hong Qi [*Red Flag*] [*China*] .... HQ
Hongjungri [*South Korea ICAO location identifier*] (ICLI) .... RKJO
Hongkong and Shanghai Banking Corp. .... HSBC
Hongo [*Japan*] [*Seismograph station code, US Geological Survey*] (SEIS) .... HGJ
Hongo [*Japan*] [*Seismograph station code, US Geological Survey Closed*] (SEIS) .... HNG
Honiara [*Solomon Islands*] [*ICAO location identifier*] (ICLI) .... AGGG
Honiara [*Guadalcanal*] [*Airport symbol*] (OAG) .... HIR
Honiara [*Solomon Islands*] [*Seismograph station code, US Geological Survey*] (SEIS) .... HNR
Honiara/Henderson, Guadalcanal Island [*Solomon Islands*] [*ICAO location identifier*] (ICLI) .... AGGH
Honington [*British ICAO location identifier*] (ICLI) .... EGXH
Honington FTU [*British ICAO designator*] (FAAC) .... HON
Honiton [*Municipal borough in England*] .... HON
Honningsvag [*Norway*] [*Airport symbol*] (OAG) .... HVG
Honningsvag/Valan [*Norway ICAO location identifier*] (ICLI) .... ENHV
Honnold Library, Claremont, CA [*Library symbol Library of Congress*] (LCLS) CCC
Honolulu [*Hawaii*] [*Airport symbol*] (OAG) .... HNL
Honolulu [*Hawaii*] [*Seismograph station code, US Geological Survey Closed*] (SEIS) .... HNL
Honolulu [*Hawaii*] [*Seismograph station code, US Geological Survey*] (SEIS) .... HON
Honolulu [*Hawaii*] (CINC) .... HONO
Honolulu Air Traffic Control Center [*Hawaii*] [*ICAO location identifier*] (ICLI) .... PHZH
Honolulu Community College, Honolulu, HI [*Library symbol Library of Congress*] (LCLS) .... HHC
Honolulu, HI [*Location identifier FAA*] (FAAL) .... EPC
Honolulu, HI [*Location identifier FAA*] (FAAL) .... HFO
Honolulu, HI [*Location identifier FAA*] (FAAL) .... HIK
Honolulu, HI [*Location identifier FAA*] (FAAL) .... HWN
Honolulu, HI [*Location identifier FAA*] (FAAL) .... IUM
Honolulu, HI [*AM radio station call letters*] .... KAIM
Honolulu, HI [*FM radio station call letters*] .... KAIM-FM
Honolulu, HI [*Television station call letters*] .... KBFD
Honolulu, HI [*AM radio station call letters*] .... KCCN
Honolulu, HI [*FM radio station call letters*] .... KCCN-FM
Honolulu, HI [*Television station call letters*] .... KFVE
Honolulu, HI [*Television station call letters*] .... KGMB
Honolulu, HI [*AM radio station call letters*] .... KGU
Honolulu, HI [*Television station call letters*] .... KHET
Honolulu, HI [*Television station call letters*] .... KHNL
Honolulu, HI [*AM radio station call letters*] .... KHNR
Honolulu, HI [*Television station call letters*] .... KHON
Honolulu, HI [*FM radio station call letters*] .... KHPR
Honolulu, HI [*AM radio station call letters*] .... KHVH
Honolulu, HI [*AM radio station call letters*] .... KIKI
Honolulu, HI [*FM radio station call letters*] .... KIKI-FM
Honolulu, HI [*Television station call letters*] .... KIKU
Honolulu, HI [*FM radio station call letters*] .... KINE
Honolulu, HI [*FM radio station call letters*] .... KIPO
Honolulu, HI [*AM radio station call letters*] .... KISA
Honolulu, HI [*Television station call letters*] .... KITV
Honolulu, HI [*FM radio station call letters*] .... KKLV
Honolulu, HI [*AM radio station call letters*] .... KLHT
Honolulu, HI [*AM radio station call letters*] .... KNDI
Honolulu, HI [*Television station call letters*] .... KOBN
Honolulu, HI [*AM radio station call letters*] .... KOHO
Honolulu, HI [*AM radio station call letters*] .... KORL
Honolulu, HI [*FM radio station call letters*] (RBYB) .... KORL-FM
Honolulu, HI [*FM radio station call letters*] .... KPOI
Honolulu, HI [*AM radio station call letters*] .... KQMQ
Honolulu, HI [*FM radio station call letters*] .... KQMQ-FM
Honolulu, HI [*AM radio station call letters*] .... KSSK
Honolulu, HI [*FM radio station call letters*] .... KTUH
Honolulu, HI [*AM radio station call letters*] .... KUMU
Honolulu, HI [*FM radio station call letters*] .... KUMU-FM
Honolulu, HI [*AM radio station call letters*] .... KWAI
Honolulu, HI [*Television station call letters*] .... KWHE
Honolulu, HI [*AM radio station call letters*] .... KZOO
Honolulu, HI [*Location identifier FAA*] (FAAL) .... NPS
Honolulu, HI [*Location identifier FAA*] (FAAL) .... ZHN
Honolulu/Hickam Air Force Base, Oahu Island [*Hawaii*] [*ICAO location identifier*] (ICLI) .... PHIK
Honolulu/International, Oahu Island [*Hawaii*] [*ICAO location identifier*] (ICLI) .... PHNL
Honolulu Japanese Chamber of Commerce (EA) .... HJCC
Honolulu Magnetic and Seismological Observatory .... HMSO
Honolulu Magnetic Observatory (CINC) .... HMO
Honolulu Star-Bulletin and Advertiser, Honolulu, HI [*Library symbol Library of Congress*] (LCLS) .... HHSA
Honolulu Stock Exchange [*Hawaii*] .... HSE
Honor .... H
Honor Contracts [*Insurance*] .... HC
Honorable .... HON
Honorable (DD) .... Hon
Honorable .... HON
Honorable .... HONBLE
Honorable Discharge [*Military*] .... HD
Honorable Discharge, Convenience of Government [*Military*] .... HDCG
Honorable Discharge, Convenience of Man [*Military*] .... HDCM
Honorable Discharge, Dependency Arising Since Enlistment [*Military*] .... HDDS
Honorable Discharge, Dependency Existing Prior to Enlistment [*Military*] .... HDDP
Honorable Discharge, Expiration of Enlistment [*Military*] .... HDEE
Honorable Discharge, Medical Survey [*Military*] .... HDMS
Honorable Discharge, Minors Enlisted without Consent, under Eighteen at Discharge [*Military*] .... HDMW
Honorable Discharge, under Age of Authorized Consent [*Military*] .... HDMU
Honorable Order of the Blue Goose, International [*West Bend, WI*] (EA) .... HOBGI
Honorary [*Academic degree*] .... H
Honorary (MSA) .... HON
Honorary (DD) .... honry
Honorary (WGA) .... HONY
Honorary Admiral of the Fleet [*Navy British*] (ROG) .... HON AF
Honorary Air Reserve [*Air Force*] .... HAR
Honorary Associate of the Royal Academy of Music [*British*] .... Hon ARAM
Honorary Associate of the Royal College of Music [*British*] (DI) .... HonARCM
Honorary Associate of the Royal College of Veterinary Surgeons [*British*] .... HARCVS
Honorary Associate of the Swimming Teachers' Association [*British*] (DBQ) .... HonASTA
Honorary Certified Claims Professional .... HCCP
Honorary Chaplain to the Forces [*British*] .... HCF
Honorary Colonel of the Corps [*Army*] .... HCOC
Honorary Colonel of the Regiment .... HCOR
Honorary Degree [*Freemasonry*] (ROG) .... HD
Honorary Doctor of Letters .... HonDLitt
Honorary Doctor of Science .... HonDSc
Honorary Doctorate of the Royal College of Art [*British*] (DBQ) .... HonDrRCA
Honorary Fellow of the British Institute of Interior Design (DBQ) .... HonFBID
Honorary Fellow of the British Institute of Non-Destructive Testing (DBQ) .... HonFInstNDT
Honorary Fellow of the Educational Institute of Scotland .... Hon FEIS
Honorary Fellow of the Hotel, Catering, and Institutional Management Association [*British*] (DBQ) .... HonFHCIMA
Honorary Fellow of the Institute of Energy [*British*] (DBQ) .... HonFInstE
Honorary Fellow of the Institute of Marine Engineers [*British*] (DBQ) .... HonFIMarE

Honorary Fellow of the Institute of Measurement [*British*] (DBQ) .... HonFInstMC
Honorary Fellow of the Institute of Printing [*British*] (DI) .... HonFIOP
Honorary Fellow of the Institute of Quality Assurance [*British*] (DBQ) .... HonFIQA
Honorary Fellow of the Institute of Training and Development [*British*] (DI) .... HonFITD
Honorary Fellow of the Institution of Gas Engineers [*British*] (DBQ) .... HonFIGasE
Honorary Fellow of the Institution of Industrial Managers [*British*] (DBQ) .... HonFIIM
Honorary Fellow of the Institution of Mechanical Engineers [*British*] (DBQ) .... HonFIMechE
Honorary Fellow of the Institution of Mining and Metallurgy [*British*] (DBQ) .... HonFIMM
Honorary Fellow of the Institution of Railway Signal Engineers [*British*] (DBQ) .... HonFIRSE
Honorary Fellow of the Institution of Works and Highways Technician Engineers [*British*] (DBQ) .... HonFIWHTE
Honorary Fellow of the Non-Destructive Testing Society of Great Britain .... Hon FNDTS
Honorary Fellow of the Royal Academy [*British*] .... HFRA
Honorary Fellow of the Royal Academy of Music [*British*] .... Hon FRAM
Honorary Fellow of the Royal College of Physicians and Surgeons [*Glasgow*] .... FRCPS(Hon)
Honorary Fellow of the Royal Photographic Society [*British*] .... Hon FRPS
Honorary Fellow of the Society of Certified Professionals [*British*] (DBQ) .... HonFSCP
Honorary Fellow of the Society of Engineers, Inc. [*British*] (DBQ) .... HonFSE
Honorary Fellow of the Society of Glass Technology [*British*] (DBQ) ..... HonFSGT
Honorary Fellow of the Society of Licensed Aircraft Engineers and Technologists [*British*] (DBQ) .... HonFSLAET
Honorary Fellow of the Welding Institute [*British*] (DBQ) .... HonFWeldI
Honorary Fellowship of the Institute of Wastes Management [*British*] (DBQ) .... FInstWM(Hon)
Honorary Foreign Associate of Royal Academy [*British*] .... HFARA
Honorary Foreign Member of the Royal Academy .... HFMRA
Honorary Lieutenant [*Navy British*] (ROG) .... HON L
Honorary Life Member of the Plastics and Rubber Institute [*British*] (DBQ) .... HonFPRI
Honorary Member [*Freemasonry*] (ROG) .... HM
Honorary Member (ROG) .... HON M
Honorary Member, American Institute of Architects (DAC) .... HAIA
Honorary Member of the British Institute of Non-Destructive Testing (DBQ) .... HonMInst NDT
Honorary Member of the Guildhall School of Music and Drama [*British*] (DBQ) .... HonGSM
Honorary Member of the Non-Destructive Testing Society of Great Britain .... Hon MNDTS
Honorary Member of the Royal Academy of Music [*British*] .... Hon RAM
Honorary Member of the Royal College of Music [*British*] (DBQ) .... HonRCM
Honorary Member of the Royal Hibernian Academy [*British*] .... HRHA
Honorary Member of the Royal Institute of Navigation [*British*] (DBQ) .... HonMRIN
Honorary Member of the Royal Institute of Oil Painters [*British*] .... HROI
Honorary Member of the Royal Institute of Painters in Water Colours [*British*] .... HRI
Honorary Member of the Royal Northern College of Music [*British*] (DBQ) .... HonRNCM
Honorary Member of the Royal School of Church Music [*British*] .... Hon RSCM
Honorary Member of the Royal Scottish Academy .... HRSA
Honorary Member of the Royal Scottish Water Colour Society .... HRSW
Honorary Member of the Women's Engineering Society [*British*] (DBQ) .... HonMWES
Honorary Naval Aide-de-Camp [*British*] .... HNADC
Honorary Order of Trumpeters Living in Possible Sin .... HOTLIPS
Honorary Physician to the King [*British*] .... HPK
Honorary Physician to the King [*British*] .... KHP
Honorary Reserve Section .... HRS
Honorary Royal Academician [*British*] .... HRA
Honorary Royal Cambrian Academician [*British*] .... HRCA
Honorary Secretary (ROG) .... HON SEC
Honorary Secretary .... HS
Honorary Sergeant Major of the Corps [*Marine Corps*] .... HSGMOC
Honorary Sergeant Major of the Regiment .... HSGM
Honorary Sergeant Major of the Regiment [*Army*] .... HSGMOR
Honorary Surgeon Lieutenant-Colonel [*Military British*] (ROG) .... HON SURG LIEUT COL
Honorary Surgeon of the King [*British*] .... HSK
Honorary Surgeon to the King [*British*] .... KHS
Honorary Surgeon to the Viceroy of India .... VHS
Honorary Vice-Admiral [*Navy British*] (ROG) .... HON VA
Honoree [*MARC relator code*] [*Library of Congress*] (LCCP) .... hnr
Honoris Causa [*For the Sake of Honor, Honorary*] [*Latin*] .... HC
Honoris Causa [*For the Sake of Honor, Honorary*] [*Latin*] (ADA) .... HONCAUS
Honorius de Kent [*Flourished, 1185-1208*] [*Authority cited in pre-1607 legal work*] (DSA) .... Hon
Honors (ADA) .... HNRS
Honors .... HONS
Honors (DD) .... Hons
Honors List (ADA) .... HL
Honors Program Student Association of the American Sociological Association (EA) .... HPSA
Honour School of Modern Languages [*British*] (ROG) .... HON SCH MOD LANG
Honourable Artillery Co. [*Military unit*] [*British*] .... HAC
Honourable East India Co. [*British*] .... HEIC
Honourable East India Co. Navy [*British military*] (DMA) .... HEICN
Honourable East India Company's Service [*British*] .... HEICS
Honourable Hudson's Bay Co. [*Canada*] .... HHBC
Honourable Society of the Inns of Court of Northern Ireland .... HSICNI
Honoured (ROG) .... HOND
Honours and Awards (ACII) .... H&A
Honours Bachelor of Arts in Business Administration (DD) .... HBA
Honours Graduate Teachers' Association [*British*] .... HGTA
Hood College (GAGS) .... Hood C
Hood College, Frederick, MD [*OCLC symbol*] (OCLC) .... HCF
Hood College, Frederick, MD [*Library symbol Library of Congress*] (LCLS) .... MdFreH
Hood Inflation System (DNAB) .... HIS
Hood on Executors [*A publication*] (DLA) .... Hood Ex
Hood River County Library, Hood River, OR [*Library symbol Library of Congress*] (LCLS) .... OrHr
Hood River, OR [*FM radio station call letters*] .... KCGB
Hood River, OR [*AM radio station call letters*] .... KIHR
Hood's Texas Brigade Association (EA) .... HTBA
Hoogeveen [*Netherlands ICAO location identifier*] (ICLI) .... EHHO
Hook .... HK
Hook Rail (MSA) .... HR
Hook Tongue Terminal .... HTT
Hook Up and Commissioning Conference [*Offshore Conference and Exhibitions Ltd.*] [*British*] .... HUC
Hook-Associated Protein [*Genetics*] .... HAP
Hook-Basal Body [*Genetics*] .... HBB
Hooker .... H
Hooker [*Ship's rigging*] (ROG) .... HKR
Hooker Chemical Corp. [*Later, Hooker Chemicals & Plastics Corp.*], Niagara Falls, NY [*Library symbol Library of Congress*] (LCLS) .... NNiaH
Hooker Chemicals & Plastics Corp., Business Library, Niagara Falls, NY [*Library symbol Library of Congress*] (LCLS) .... NNiaHC
Hooker Chemicals & Plastics Corp., Corporate Technical and Services Center Research Library, Grand Island, NY [*Library symbol Library of Congress*] (LCLS) .... NGiHC
Hooker Chemicals & Plastics Corp., Durez Division Library, North Tonawanda, NY [*Library symbol Library of Congress*] (LCLS) .... NNotHC
Hooker Creek [*Airport symbol*] .... HOK
Hooker Electro-Chemical Co. .... HECC
Hooker's Reports [*25-62 Connecticut*] [*A publication*] (DLA) .... Hook
Hooker's Reports [*25-62 Connecticut*] [*A publication*] (DLA) .... Hooker
Hooks, TX [*FM radio station call letters*] .... KLLI
Hookup (MSA) .... HKP
Hoonah [*Alaska*] [*Airport symbol*] (OAG) .... HNH
Hoonahan's Sind Reports [*India*] [*A publication*] (DLA) .... Hoon
Hoonahan's Sind Reports [*India*] [*A publication*] (DLA) .... Hoonahan
Hoop Quotient [*Basketball*] .... HQ
Hoopa, CA [*FM radio station call letters*] .... KIDE
Hooper Bay [*Alaska*] [*Airport symbol*] (OAG) .... HPB
Hooper Holmes [*AMEX symbol*] (TTSB) .... HH
Hooper Holmes, Inc. [*AMEX symbol*] (SPSG) .... HH
Hooper Holmes, Inc. [*Associated Press*] (SAG) .... HoopHl
Hooper Visual Organization Test [*Psychology*] .... HVOT
Hoopes Conductivity Bridge [*Electronics*] .... HCB
Hoopeston, IL [*FM radio station call letters*] .... WHPO
Hoopestown Community Memorial Hospital, Hoopestown, IL [*Library symbol Library of Congress*] (LCLS) .... IHoH
Hoopestown Public Library, Hoopestown, IL [*Library symbol Library of Congress*] (LCLS) .... IHo
Hoop-Iron Bond [*Construction*] .... HIB
Hooppole, Yorktown & Tampico Railroad (IIA) .... HY & T
Hoosac Tunnel & Wilmington R. R. [*AAR code*] .... HTW
Hoosick Falls, NY [*FM radio station call letters*] .... WNGN
Hooved Animal Humane Society (EA) .... HAHS
Hoover Co., Engineering Division, North Canton, OH [*Library symbol Library of Congress*] (LCLS) .... ONocHE
Hoover Historical Center (EA) .... HHC
Hoover Institution on War, Revolution, and Peace (EA) .... HIWRP
Hoover Institution Press (DGA) .... HIP
Hoover-Owens-Rentschler [*Engines*] .... HOR
Hop and Stamp [*Dance terminology*] .... HAMP
Hop Growers of America (EA) .... HGA
Hop Latent Virus [*Plant pathology*] .... HOLV
Hop Merchants Association [*British*] (BI) .... HMA
Hop Mosaic Virus [*Plant pathology*] .... HOMV
Hop Stunt Viroid [*Medicine*] (DMAA) .... HSV
Hop Trefoil Cryptic Virus [*Plant pathology*] .... HTCV
Hopantenate Calcium [*Cerebral activator*] .... HOPA
Hope [*Freemasonry*] (ROG) .... H
Hope [*Jamaica*] [*Seismograph station code, US Geological Survey*] (SEIS) .... HOJ
Hope [*Jamaica*] [*Seismograph station code, US Geological Survey Closed*] (SEIS) .... HOP
Hope, AR [*Location identifier FAA*] (FAAL) .... HPC
Hope, AR [*FM radio station call letters*] .... KHPA
Hope, AR [*AM radio station call letters*] .... KXAR
Hope, AR [*FM radio station call letters*] .... KXAR-FM
Hope, BC [*AM radio station call letters*] .... CKGO
Hope, BC [*ICAO location identifier*] (ICLI) .... CYHE
Hope Brook Gold, Inc. [*Toronto Stock Exchange symbol*] .... HBG
Hope College, Holland, MI [*OCLC symbol*] (OCLC) .... EXH
Hope College, Holland, MI [*Library symbol Library of Congress*] (LCLS) .... MiHolH
Hope Creek Generating Station (NRCH) .... HCGS
Hope Foundation Communicators [*Australia*] .... HFC
Hope Mills, NC [*FM radio station call letters*] .... WCCG
Hope Museum, British Columbia [*Library symbol National Library of Canada*] (NLC) .... BHM

Hope (of Kerse). Manuscript Decisions, Scotch Court of Session [*A publication*] (DLA) ... Hope
Hope (of Kerse). Manuscript Decisions, Scotch Court of Session [*A publication*] (DLA) ... Hope Dec
Hope Valley, RI [*AM radio station call letters*] ... WJJF
Hopedale, NF [*ICAO location identifier*] (ICLI) ... CYHO
Hopeh Province [*China, Mainland*] [*MARC geographic area code Library of Congress*] (LCCP) ... a-cc-hp
Hopen [*Norway ICAO location identifier*] (ICLI) ... ENHO
Hope's Compendium of the Commercial Law of the Pacific [*A publication*] (DLA) ... Hope Com Law
Hope's Major Practicks [*Scotland*] [*A publication*] (DLA) ... Hope Maj Pr
Hope's Minor Practicks [*Scotland*] [*A publication*] (DLA) ... Hop Min
Hope's Minor Practicks [*Scotland*] [*A publication*] (DLA) ... Hope Min Pr
Hopewell Museum, Hopewell, NJ [*Library symbol Library of Congress*] (LCLS) ... NjHopM
Hopewell Public Library, Hopewell, NJ [*Library symbol Library of Congress*] (LCLS) ... NjHop
Hopewell, VA [*Location identifier FAA*] (FAAL) ... HPW
Hopewell, VA [*AM radio station call letters*] ... WHAP
Hopewell Valley News, Hopewell, NJ [*Library symbol Library of Congress*] (LCLS) ... NjHopN
Hopewell Village National Historic Site ... HOVI
Hopital Charles Lemoyne, Bibliotheque Medical, Montreal, PQ, Canada [*Library symbol*] [*Library of Congress*] (LCLS) ... CaQMHCL
Hopital Communautaire du Pontiac [*Pontiac Community Hospital*], Shawville, Quebec [*Library symbol National Library of Canada*] (NLC) ... QSHCP
Hopital de Chicoutimi, Inc., Quebec [*Library symbol National Library of Canada*] (NLC) ... QCH
Hopital de l'Enfant-Jesus, Quebec, Quebec [*Library symbol National Library of Canada*] (NLC) ... QQHEJ
Hopital de Mont-Joli, Inc., Mont-Joli, PQ, Canada [*Library symbol Library of Congress*] (LCLS) ... CaQMjH
Hopital de Mont-Joli, Inc., Quebec [*Library symbol National Library of Canada*] (NLC) ... QMJH
Hopital des Sept-Iles, Quebec [*Library symbol National Library of Canada*] (NLC) ... QSIH
Hopital Docteur Georges - L. Dumont [*Docteur Georges - L. Dumont Hospital*]Moncton, New Brunswick [*Library symbol National Library of Canada*] (NLC) ... NBMHD
Hopital Docteur Georges-L. Dumont, Moncton, NB, Canada [*Library symbol*] [*Library of Congress*] (LCLS) ... CaNBMoHD
Hopital du Sacre-Coeur, Montreal, PQ, Canada [*Library symbol Library of Congress*] (LCLS) ... CaQMHSC
Hopital du Sacre-Coeur, Montreal, Quebec [*Library symbol National Library of Canada*] (NLC) ... QMHSC
Hopital du Saint-Sacrement, Quebec, PQ, Canada [*Library symbol Library of Congress*] (LCLS) ... CaQQHSS
Hopital du Saint-Sacrement, Quebec, Quebec [*Library symbol National Library of Canada*] (NLC) ... QQHSS
Hopital d'Youville de Sherbrooke, Centre de Documentation et d'Audio-Viseul, Sherbrooke, PQ, Canada [*Library symbol*] [*Library of Congress*] (LCLS) ... CaQSHERY
Hopital General de la Regie de l'Amiante, Inc., Thetford Mines, Quebec [*Library symbol National Library of Canada*] (BIB) ... QTMH
Hopital General Fleury, Montreal, PQ, Canada [*Library symbol Library of Congress*] (LCLS) ... CaQMHGF
Hopital General Fleury, Montreal, Quebec [*Library symbol National Library of Canada*] (NLC) ... QMHGF
Hopital Jean Talon, Montreal, PQ, Canada [*Library symbol Library of Congress*] (LCLS) ... CaQMHJT
Hopital Jean Talon, Montreal, Quebec [*Library symbol National Library of Canada*] (NLC) ... QMHJT
Hopital Laval, Ste.-Foy, Quebec [*Library symbol National Library of Canada*] (NLC) ... QSFHL
Hopital Louis H. LaFonataine, Montreal, Quebec [*Library symbol National Library of Canada*] (NLC) ... QMHSJ
Hopital Louis-H.-LaFontaine, Montreal, PQ, Canada [*Library symbol Library of Congress*] (LCLS) ... CaQMHSJ
Hopital Maisonneuve-Rosemont, Montreal, PQ, Canada [*Library symbol Library of Congress*] (LCLS) ... CaQMHMR
Hopital Maisonneuve-Rosemont, Montreal, Quebec [*Library symbol National Library of Canada*] (NLC) ... QMHMR
Hopital Marie-Enfant, Montreal, PQ, Canada [*Library symbol Library of Congress*] (LCLS) ... CaQMHME
Hopital Marie-Enfant, Montreal, Quebec [*Library symbol National Library of Canada*] (NLC) ... QMHME
Hopital Notre-Dame, Bibliotheque des Services Infirmiers, Montreal, PQ, Canada [*Library symbol Library of Congress*] (LCLS) ... CaQMHNDI
Hopital Notre-Dame, Montreal, Quebec [*Library symbol National Library of Canada*] (NLC) ... QMHND
Hopital Notre-Dame-De-L'Esperance-De-St-Laurent, Montreal, PQ, Canada [*Library symbol Library of Congress*] (LCLS) ... CaQMNDE
Hopital Notre-Dame-De-L'Esperance-De-St-Laurent, Montreal, Quebec [*Library symbol National Library of Canada*] (NLC) ... QMNDE
Hopital Riviere-Des-Prairies, Montreal, PQ, Canada [*Library symbol Library of Congress*] (LCLS) ... CaQMHRP
Hopital Riviere-Des-Prairies, Montreal, Quebec [*Library symbol National Library of Canada*] (NLC) ... QMHRP
Hopital Saint-Charles, Joliette, PQ, Canada [*Library symbol Library of Congress*] (LCLS) ... CaQJH
Hopital Sainte-Croix, Drummondville, PQ, Canada [*Library symbol*] [*Library of Congress*] (LCLS) ... CaQDHSC
Hopital Sainte-Croix, Drummondville, Quebec [*Library symbol National Library of Canada*] (NLC) ... QDHSC
Hopital Sainte-Justine, Centre d'Information sur la Sante de l'Enfant, Montreal,PQ, Canada [*Library symbol Library of Congress*] (LCLS) ... CaQMSTJ
Hopital Sainte-Justine, Centre d'Information sur l'Enfance et l'Adolescence Inadaptees, Montreal, PQ, Canada [*Library symbol Library of Congress Obsolete*] (LCLS) ... CaQMSTJC
Hopital Sainte-Justine, Departement de Sante Communautaire, Montreal, PQ, Canada [*Library symbol*] [*Library of Congress*] (LCLS) ... CaQMSTJS
Hopital Sainte-Marie, Trois-Rivieres, PQ, Canada [*Library symbol Library of Congress*] (LCLS) ... CaQTHSM
Hopital Sainte-Marie, Trois-Rivieres, Quebec [*Library symbol National Library of Canada*] (NLC) ... QTHSM
Hopital Saint-Joseph, Trois-Rivieres, PQ, Canada [*Library symbol Library of Congress*] (LCLS) ... CaQTHSJ
Hopital Saint-Joseph, Trois-Rivieres, Quebec [*Library symbol National Library of Canada*] (NLC) ... QTHSJ
Hopital Saint-Luc, Montreal, PQ, Canada [*Library symbol Library of Congress*] (LCLS) ... CaQMHSL
Hopital Saint-Luc, Montreal, Quebec [*Library symbol National Library of Canada*] (NLC) ... QMHSL
Hopital Santa Cabrini, Montreal, PQ, Canada [*Library symbol Library of Congress*] (LCLS) ... CaQMHSCA
Hopital Santa Cabrini, Montreal, Quebec [*Library symbol National Library of Canada*] (NLC) ... QMHSCA
Hopital Ste-Jeanne-D'Arc, Montreal, PQ, Canada [*Library symbol Library of Congress*] (LCLS) ... CaQMHSJA
Hopital Ste-Jeanne-D'Arc, Montreal, Quebec [*Library symbol National Library of Canada*] (NLC) ... QMHSJA
Hopital St-Francois d'Assise, Quebec, Quebec [*Library symbol National Library of Canada*] (NLC) ... QQHFA
Hopkins' Average [*4th ed.*] [*1884*] [*A publication*] (DLA) ... Hopk Av
Hopkins Elementary School, Granville, IL [*Library symbol Library of Congress*] (LCLS) ... IGranHS
Hopkins Marine Station, Pacific Grove, CA [*Library symbol Library of Congress*] (LCLS) ... CPgH
Hopkins, Mitchell & Carley, Law Library, San Jose, CA [*Library symbol*] [*Library of Congress*] (LCLS) ... CSjHMC
Hopkins' New York Chancery Reports [*A publication*] (DLA) ... Hopk
Hopkins' New York Chancery Reports [*A publication*] (DLA) ... Hopk CC
Hopkins' New York Chancery Reports [*A publication*] (DLA) ... Hopk Ch
Hopkins' New York Chancery Reports [*A publication*] (DLA) ... Hopk Chanc Rep
Hopkins' New York Chancery Reports [*A publication*] (DLA) ... Hopk Rep
Hopkins on Marine Insurance [*A publication*] (DLA) ... Hopk Mar Ins
Hopkins Psychiatric Rating Scale [*Personality development test*] [*Psychology*] ... HPRS
Hopkins Ultraviolet Telescope ... HUT
Hopkinson's Pennsylvania Admiralty Judgments [*A publication*] (DLA) ... Hopk Adm
Hopkinson's Pennsylvania Admiralty Judgments [*A publication*] (DLA) ... Hopk Judg
Hopkinson's Works [*Pennsylvania*] [*A publication*] (DLA) ... Hopk W
Hopkinson's Works [*Pennsylvania*] [*A publication*] (DLA) ... Hopk Wks
Hopkinson's Works [*Pennsylvania*] [*A publication*] (DLA) ... Hopk Works (PA)
Hopkinsville/Campbell Army Air Field [*Kentucky*] [*ICAO location identifier*] (ICLI) ... KHOP
Hopkinsville Community College, Hopkinsville, KY [*Library symbol*] [*Library of Congress*] (LCLS) ... KyHopC
Hopkinsville, KY [*Location identifier FAA*] (FAAL) ... FKP
Hopkinsville, KY [*Location identifier FAA*] (FAAL) ... HIX
Hopkinsville, KY [*Location identifier FAA*] (FAAL) ... HOP
Hopkinsville, KY [*Location identifier FAA*] (FAAL) ... HVC
Hopkinsville, KY [*Location identifier FAA*] (FAAL) ... HXW
Hopkinsville, KY [*AM radio station call letters*] ... WHOP
Hopkinsville, KY [*FM radio station call letters*] ... WHOP-FM
Hopkinsville, KY [*FM radio station call letters*] ... WNKJ
Hopkinsville, KY [*AM radio station call letters*] ... WQKS
Hopkinsville, KY [*FM radio station call letters*] ... WVVR
Hopper [*Freight*] ... HPR
Hopper Side Tanks [*on a ship*] (DS) ... HSDT
Hopper-Tainer [*A form of container*] [*British*] (DCTA) ... H
Hops Marketing Board [*British*] ... HMB
Hops Warehousing Association [*British*] (BI) ... HWA
Hopsten [*Germany ICAO location identifier*] (ICLI) ... EDNP
Hopwood and Coltman's English Registration Appeal Cases [*A publication*] (DLA) ... Hop & C
Hopwood and Coltman's English Registration Appeal Cases [*A publication*] (DLA) ... Hop & Colt
Hopwood and Coltman's English Registration Appeal Cases [*A publication*] (DLA) ... Hopw & C
Hopwood and Coltman's English Registration Appeal Cases [*A publication*] (DLA) ... Hopw & Colt
Hopwood and Philbrick's English Election Cases [*1863-67*] [*A publication*] (DLA) ... H & P
Hopwood and Philbrick's English Registration Appeal Cases [*A publication*] (DLA) ... Hop & Ph
Hopwood and Philbrick's English Registration Appeal Cases [*A publication*] (DLA) ... Hop & Phil
Hopwood and Philbrick's English Registration Appeal Cases [*A publication*] (DLA) ... Hopw & P
Hopwood and Philbrick's English Registration Appeal Cases [*A publication*] (DLA) ... Hopw & Phil
Hoquiam, WA [*Location identifier FAA*] (FAAL) ... HQM
Hoquiam, WA [*FM radio station call letters*] ... KGHO-FM
Hoquiam, WA [*AM radio station call letters*] (RBYB) ... KJET
Hora [*Hour*] [*Latin*] ... h
Hora Decubitus [*At Bedtime*] [*Pharmacy*] ... HD

Hora Decubitus [*At Bedtime*] [*Pharmacy*] .... HOR DECU
Hora Decubitus [*At Bedtime*] [*Pharmacy*] (ROG) ... HOR DECUB
Hora Locoque Consuetis [*At the Usual Time and Place*] [*Latin*] ...... HLQC
Hora Locoque Solitis [*At the Usual Time and Place*] [*Latin*] ...... HLQS
Hora Somni [*At Bedtime*] [*Pharmacy*] .... H SOM
Hora Somni [*At Bedtime*] [*Pharmacy*] .... HOR SOM
Hora Somni [*At Bedtime*] [*Latin*] (WDAA) .... HORA SOM
Hora Somni [*At Bedtime*] [*Pharmacy*] .... HS
Horace [*Roman poet, 65-8BC*] [*Classical studies*] (ROG) .... HOR
Horace Hardy Lestor Reactor .... HHLR
Horace Mann Bond Center for Equal Education [*Defunct*] (EA) ... HMBCEE
Horace Mann Educators [*NYSE symbol*] (TTSB) .... HMN
Horace Mann Educators Corp. [*NYSE symbol*] (SPSG) .... HMN
Horace Mann Educators Corp. [*Associated Press*] (SAG) .... HorMn
Horace Mann League of the USA (EA) .... HML
Horace Mann-Lincoln Institute of School Experimentation [*Columbia University*] (AEBS) .... HMLI
Horace May Elementary School, Bemidji, MN [*Library symbol*] [*Library of Congress*] (LCLS) .... MnBemHE
Horae Soederblomianae (BJA) .... HS
Horae Unius Spatio [*At the End of an Hour*] [*Pharmacy*] ...... HOR UN SPAT
Horae Unius Spatio [*At the End of an Hour*] [*Pharmacy*] (ROG) ..... HOR UN SPATIO
Horan, Wall & Walker [*Publisher*] (ADA) .... HWW
Horatio Alger Association of Distinguished Americans (EA) ...... HAADA
Horatio Alger Society (EA) .... HAS
Horatius Mandosius [*Deceased, 1594*] [*Authority cited in pre-1607 legal work*] (DSA) .... Horat Mand
Horayoth (BJA) .... Hor
Hordeum [*Barley*] [*Pharmacy*] (ROG) .... HORD
Hordeum Mosaic Virus [*Plant pathology*] .... HORMV
Horis Intermediis [*In the Intermediate Hours*] [*Pharmacy*] ... HOR INTERM
Horizon (ABBR) .... H
Horizon (KSC) .... HOR
Horizon (MSA) .... HORIZ
Horizon (MSA) .... HRZN
Horizon .... HRZN
Horizon Air [*ICAO designator*] (AD) .... QX
Horizon Airlines, Inc. [*ICAO designator*] (FAAC) .... QXE
Horizon Airlines Ltd. [*Nigeria*] [*FAA designator*] (FAAC) .... HZN
Horizon Air-Taxi Ltd. [*Switzerland ICAO designator*] (FAAC) .... HOR
Horizon Bancorp, Inc. (Texas) [*Associated Press*] (SAG) .... HrzBTX
Horizon Bancorp, Inc. (TX) [*Associated Press*] (SAG) .... HorzBcTx
Horizon Bancorp, Inc. (TX) [*NASDAQ symbol*] (SAG) .... LOAN
Horizon Bancorp (West Virginia) [*Associated Press*] (SAG) .... HrzBcWV
Horizon Bancorp West Virginia [*NASDAQ symbol*] (SAG) .... HZWV
Horizon Bancorp (WV) [*NASDAQ symbol*] (SAG) .... HZWV
Horizon Bancorp(TX) [*NASDAQ symbol*] (TTSB) .... LOAN
Horizon Bank [*NASDAQ symbol*] (NQ) .... HRZB
Horizon Cargo Transport, Inc. [*ICAO designator*] (FAAC) .... KOK
Horizon/CMS Healthcare [*NYSE symbol*] (TTSB) .... HHC
Horizon CMS Healthcare Corp. [*NYSE symbol*] (SAG) .... HHC
Horizon CMS Healthcare Corp. [*Associated Press*] (SAG) .... HrzHlt
Horizon Crossing Ascending .... HCA
Horizon Crossing Descending .... HCD
Horizon Definition Measurement Program (DNAB) .... HDMP
Horizon Financial [*NASDAQ symbol*] (TTSB) .... HRZB
Horizon Financial Corp. [*Associated Press*] (SAG) .... HorznFin
Horizon Financial Corp. [*NASDAQ symbol*] (SAG) .... HRZB
Horizon Financial Services Corp. [*Associated Press*] (SAG) .... HorizFS
Horizon Financial Services Corp. [*NASDAQ symbol*] (SAG) .... HZFS
Horizon Financial Svcs [*NASDAQ symbol*] (TTSB) .... HZFS
Horizon Flight Director [*Aircraft*] .... HFD
Horizon Group, Inc. [*NYSE symbol*] (SAG) .... HGI
Horizon Group, Inc. [*Associated Press*] (SAG) .... HoriznGp
Horizon Grow [*Astronomy*] (OA) .... HG
Horizon Gyroscope Unit [*Aviation*] (AIA) .... HGU
Horizon Healthcare Corp. [*NYSE symbol*] (SPSG) .... HHC
Horizon Healthcare Corp. [*Associated Press*] (SAG) .... HrzHlt
Horizon Mental Health Management [*AMEX symbol*] (SAG) .... HMH
Horizon Mental Health Management [*NASDAQ symbol*] (SAG) .... HMHM
Horizon Mental Health Management [*Associated Press*] (SAG) .... HorizMH
Horizon Mental Health Management [*Associated Press*] (SAG) .... HrzMH
Horizon Mental Health Mgmt [*NASDAQ symbol*] (TTSB) .... HMHM
Horizon Outlet Centers [*NYSE symbol*] (SPSG) .... HGI
Horizon Reference Indicator [*Aerospace*] (AAG) .... HRI
Horizon Reference Set (MCD) .... HRS
Horizon Scanner .... HS
Horizon Scanner (MSA) .... HSC
Horizon Sensor .... HS
Horizon Sensor Assembly .... HSA
Horizon Village [*Vancouver Stock Exchange symbol*] .... HVI
Horizonatal Flexible Mandrel (PDAA) .... HFM
Horizons Technology, Inc. .... HTI
Horizontal .... h
Horizontal (WDMC) .... h
Horizontal (WDMC) .... hor
Horizontal .... HOR
Horizontal (NITA) .... Horitz
Horizontal (AABC) .... HORIZ
Horizontal (IDOE) .... horiz
Horizontal .... HOZ
Horizontal Access Kit (NASA) .... HAK
Horizontal Acoustic Range Depiction (NVT) .... HARD
Horizontal Alidade Tie .... HAT
Horizontal Altitude Take-Off and Landing (PDAA) .... HATOL

Horizontal and Vertical (WDMC) .... H&V
Horizontal Arithmetic Unit .... HAU
Horizontal Arithmetic Unit [*Computer science*] (MHDI) .... HU
Horizontal Array of Dipoles .... HAD
Horizontal Assembly Building [*NASA*] (KSC) .... HAB
Horizontal Attenuated Total Reflection [*Spectroscopy*] .... HATR
Horizontal Axis Bearing .... HAB
Horizontal Axis Electrical Hairspring .... HAEH
Horizontal Axis Pivot .... HAP
Horizontal Axis Wind Turbine [*Generator*] [*Also, HAWTG*] (MCD) .... HAWT
Horizontal Axis Wind Turbine Generator [*Also, HAWT*] .... HAWTG
Horizontal Baffle (NRCH) .... HB
Horizontal Baffle Assembly [*Nuclear energy*] (NRCH) .... HBA
Horizontal Bands [*Navigation markers*] .... HB
Horizontal Blanking Interval (DOM) .... HBI
Horizontal Bomber .... HB
Horizontal Boring Mill .... HBM
Horizontal Bridgman [*Crystal growing technique*] .... HB
Horizontal Candlepower .... HCP
Horizontal Candlepower Seconds .... HCPS
Horizontal Cargo Integration Test Equipment (MCD) .... HCITE
Horizontal Cask Lifting Fixture [*Nuclear energy*] (NRCH) .... HCLF
Horizontal Cell [*Eye anatomy*] .... HC
Horizontal Center Line .... HCL
Horizontal Check (IAA) .... HC
Horizontal Clearance [*Nautical charts*] .... HOR CL
Horizontal Control Operator [*Military*] .... HCO
Horizontal Correlation Distance .... HCD
Horizontal Danger Angle [*Navigation*] .... HDA
Horizontal Data Processing .... HDP
Horizontal Deflection [*Symbol*] (DEN) X
Horizontal Dilution of Precision .... HDOP
Horizontal Display Indicator (NG) .... HDI
Horizontal Distance [*Photography*] (OA) .... HD
Horizontal Distributing Frame .... HDF
Horizontal Drain .... HD
Horizontal Drive .... HD
Horizontal Dynamic Balancing .... HDB
Horizontal Dynamic Balancing Adjustment .... HDBA
Horizontal Earth Rate .... HER
Horizontal Electrical Dipole (IEEE) .... HED
Horizontal Electrical Tunnel (NRCH) .... HET
Horizontal Enlarger [*Photography*] .... HOREN
Horizontal Equivalent .... HE
Horizontal Falling Film (PDAA) .... HFF
Horizontal Flight (NASA) .... HF
Horizontal Flight Simulator (MCD) .... HFS
Horizontal Flight Test Facility [*NASA*] (NASA) .... HFTF
Horizontal Flight Test Simulator [*NASA*] (NASA) .... HFTS
Horizontal Flight Testing [*NASA*] (KSC) .... HFT
Horizontal Flight Vector .... HFV
Horizontal Flow Barrier [*Computer science*] .... HFB
Horizontal Force of the Earth's Magnetism [*Amplitude of a tide*] .... H
Horizontal Function Checkout (KSC) .... HOFCO
Horizontal Gaze Nystagmus Test .... HGN
Horizontal Generator Mock-Up System [*NASA*] .... HGMUS
Horizontal Ground Plane [*Automotive engineering*] .... HGP
Horizontal Ground Vibration Test [*NASA*] (NASA) .... HGVT
Horizontal Impulse .... HIM
Horizontal Impulse (IEEE) .... HZMP
Horizontal Impulse Reaction (MSA) .... HIR
Horizontal Injection Press .... HIP
Horizontal Integral Float [*Automotive engineering*] .... HIF
Horizontal Interval .... HI
Horizontal Landing (KSC) .... HL
Horizontal Lights [*Navigation signal*] .... Hor
Horizontal Line .... HL
Horizontal Line Array (MCD) .... HLA
Horizontal Line Frequency .... HLF
Horizontal Liquid Spring .... HLS
Horizontal Location of Center of Gravity .... HCG
Horizontal Lockout .... HLO
Horizontal Marriage .... HM
Horizontal Mating Facility [*NASA*] (KSC) .... HMF
Horizontal Meridian [*Optics, eye anatomy*] .... HM
Horizontal Motion Carriage [*Engineering*] (OA) .... HMC
Horizontal Motion Index [*Printer technology*] .... HMI
Horizontal Null External Distance (OA) .... HNED
Horizontal Obstacle SONAR (IAA) .... HOS
Horizontal Opposed [*Aircraft engine*] .... O
Horizontal Oscillating Barrel (PDAA) .... HOB
Horizontal Output (IAA) .... HO
Horizontal Output Transformer .... HOT
Horizontal Output Tube .... HOT
Horizontal Panel Mount .... HPM
Horizontal Parallax [*Navigation*] .... HP
Horizontal Payloads Processing Facility .... HPDF
Horizontal Payloads Processing Facility (MCD) .... HPPF
Horizontal Planar Array (CAAL) .... HPA
Horizontal Planar Motion Mechanism (PDAA) .... HPMM
Horizontal Plot Table .... HPT
Horizontal Polar Diagram .... HPD
Horizontal Polarization .... HORIZ
Horizontal Polarization .... HP
Horizontal Position Finder (IAA) .... HPF

Horizontal Processing Facility [*Operation and Checkout*] [*NASA*] (NASA) .... HPF
Horizontal RADAR Display .... HORAD
Horizontal Radiation Pattern [*Electronics*] (DEN) .... HRP
Horizontal Reaction .... HZRN
Horizontal Recovery System .... HRS
Horizontal Redundancy Check (IEEE) .... HRC
Horizontal Reference Line [*Technical drawings*] .... HRL
Horizontal Resistance [*Plant pathology*] .... HR
Horizontal Retort .... HR
Horizontal Seismic Trigger (IEEE) .... HST
Horizontal Shear .... HS
Horizontal Side of an Intermediate Distribution Frame [*Telecommunications*] (TEL) .... HIDF
Horizontal Side of Main Distribution Frame (TEL) .... HMDF
Horizontal Situation Display .... HSD
Horizontal Situation Display System .... HSDS
Horizontal Situation Indicator [*Aviation*] .... HSI
Horizontal Situation Indicator / Course Deviation Indicator [*Aviation*] (PDAA) .... HSI/CDI
Horizontal Size Ratio [*Ophthalmology*] .... HSR
Horizontal Sling Kit [*NASA*] (NASA) .... HSK
Horizontal Sounding Balloon (IAA) .... HSB
Horizontal Stabilizer Trim Setting .... HSTS
Horizontal Static Balancing Adjustment .... HSBA
Horizontal Stripes [*On buoys, beacons*] .... HS
Horizontal Sweep Circuit Analyzer .... HSCA
Horizontal Sweep Generator [*Telecommunications*] (OA) .... HSG
Horizontal Synchronous [*Computer science*] .... HS
Horizontal Synchronous [*Computer science*] .... HSYNC
Horizontal System [*Government arrangement*] (OICC) .... HS
Horizontal Tab [*Computer science*] (DOM) .... HT
Horizontal Tabulate (NITA) .... HT
Horizontal Tabulation [*Computer science*] .... HT
Horizontal Tactical Display (NG) .... HTD
Horizontal Tactical Display Unit .... HTDU
Horizontal Tactics Indicator .... HTI
Horizontal Takeoff .... HTO
Horizontal Takeoff and Landing [*Name of proposed aircraft under development by the British government*] .... HOTOL
Horizontal Takeoff and Landing [*Proposed aircraft under development by the British government*] (IAA) .... HTOL
Horizontal Takeoff, Horizontal Landing (KSC) .... HTOHL
Horizontal Take-Off Vertical Landing [*Aviation*] (PDAA) .... HTOVL
Horizontal Technology Insertion .... HTI
Horizontal Technology Integration [*Business term*] (INF) .... HTI
Horizontal Trail Unit (MCD) .... HTU
Horizontal Unit Displacement [*Military*] (INF) .... HUD
Horizontal Vertex Error (OA) .... HVE
Horizontal Volute Spring Suspension [*Projectile*] .... HVSS
Horizontal Weather Depiction .... HWD
Horizontal-Axis Rotating-Wing Aeronautical System (PDAA) .... HARWAS
Horizontal-Branch [*Astronomy*] .... HB
Horizontal-Branch Oscillation [*Astronomy*] .... HBO
Horizontally Opposed [*Automotive engineering*] .... HO
Horizontally Polarized Shear Wave [*Physics*] .... HPSW
Horizontally Selective [*Medicine*] (DMAA) .... HS
Horizontal-Vertical Intersection [*Lighting*] [*Automotive engineering*] .... HV
Hormel [*George*] **& Co.** [*Associated Press*] (SAG) .... Hormel
Hormel [*Geo. A.*] **& Co.** [*NYSE symbol*] (SPSG) .... HRL
Hormel Foods [*NYSE symbol*] (TTSB) .... HRL
Hormel Institute, University of Minnesota, Austin, MN [*Library symbol Library of Congress*] (LCLS) .... MnAuH
Hormigueros, PR [*FM radio station call letters*] .... WEGM
Hormigueros, PR [*FM radio station call letters*] (RBYB) .... WRRH
Hormonal Growth Promotant .... HGP
Hormonal Response [*Medicine*] (DMAA) .... HR
Hormone [*Endocrinology*] .... H
Hormone Binding [*Endocrinology*] .... HB
Hormone Binding Domain [*Endocrinology*] .... HBD
Hormone Pregnancy Test .... HPT
Hormone Receptor Complex [*Endocrinology*] .... HR
Hormone Receptor Enzyme [*Endocrinology*] (DMAA) .... HRE
Hormone Receptor Site [*Endocrinology*] .... HRS
Hormone Regulatory Element [*Endocrinology*] .... HRE
Hormone Replacement Therapy [*Medicine*] .... HRT
Hormone-Responsive Element [*Endocrinology*] .... HRE
Hormone-Sensitive Lipase [*An enzyme*] .... HSL
Hormoz Island [*Iran*] [*ICAO location identifier*] (ICLI) .... OIKX
Horn .... H
Horn .... HN
Horn & Hardart Co. [*Later, Hanover Direct*] [*AMEX symbol*] (SPSG) .... HOR
Horn and Hurlstone's English Exchequer Reports [*1838-39*] [*A publication*] (DLA) .... H & H
Horn and Hurlstone's English Exchequer Reports [*1838-39*] [*A publication*] (DLA) .... Horn & H
Horn Book Guide [*A publication*] (BRI) .... HB Guide
Horn Book Magazine [*A publication*] (BRI) .... HB
Horn Fiber .... HNFBR
Horn Gap Switch .... HGSW
Horn Point Environmental Laboratories [*University of Maryland*] (PDAA) .... HPEL
Hornbeck Offshore Services, Inc. [*Associated Press*] (SAG) .... Hornbk
Hornbeck Offshore Services, Inc. [*NASDAQ symbol*] (NQ) .... HOSS
Hornblende Gneisses [*Geology*] .... HORN GN
Horne on Diplomacy [*A publication*] (DLA) .... Horne Dip
Hornell, NY [*FM radio station call letters*] .... WCKR
Hornell, NY [*AM radio station call letters*] .... WHHO
Hornell, NY [*FM radio station call letters*] .... WKPQ
Hornell, NY [*AM radio station call letters*] .... WLEA
Hornepayne [*Canada*] [*Airport symbol*] (OAG) .... YHN
Hornepayne Township Public Library, Ontario [*Library symbol National Library of Canada*] (NLC) .... OHT
Horner Syndrome [*Medicine*] (DMAA) .... HS
Horner's Annotated Revised Statutes [*Indiana*] [*A publication*] (DLA) .... Horner's Ann St
Horner's Annotated Revised Statutes [*Indiana*] [*A publication*] (DLA) .... Horner's Rev St
Horner's Reports [*11-23 South Dakota*] [*A publication*] (DLA) .... Horner
Horne's Mirror of Justice [*A publication*] (DLA) .... Horne Mir
Horne's Mirror of Justice [*A publication*] (DLA) .... Horne MJ
Horne's Mirror of Justice [*A publication*] (DLA) .... Mir
Horne's Mirror of Justice [*A publication*] (DLA) .... Mir Just
Horne's Mirror of Justice [*A publication*] (DLA) .... Mirr
Horn-Hellersberg Test [*Psychology*] .... HHT
Horniman Museum [*London*] .... HM
Hornsby, TX [*FM radio station call letters*] .... KOOP
Hornyhead Chub [*Ichthyology*] .... Hc
Horological Institute of America [*Later, AWI*] .... HIA
Horological Times [*A publication*] (EAAP) .... HT
Horologium [*Constellation*] .... Hor
Horologium [*Constellation*] .... Horo
Horology .... HOR
Horology .... HOROL
Horology Program [*Association of Independent Colleges and Schools specialization code*] .... HR
Horowitz-Eastman-Crane Symbol Array Governed by Orthodox Notation (NITA) .... HECSAGON
Horr and Bemis' Treatise on Municipal Police Ordinances [*A publication*] (DLA) .... Horr & B Mun Ord
Horrific [*Film certificate*] [*British*] .... H
Horrigan and Thompson's Cases on Self-Defense [*A publication*] (DLA) .... Cas Self Def
Horrigan and Thompson's Cases on Self-Defense [*A publication*] (DLA) .... Hor & Th Cas
Horrigan and Thompson's Cases on Self-Defense [*A publication*] (DLA) .... Horr & T Cas Self-Def
Horrigan and Thompson's Cases on Self-Defense [*A publication*] (DLA) .... Horr & Th
Horror Writers of America [*An association*] .... HWA
Horry County Memorial Library, Conway, SC [*Library symbol Library of Congress*] (LCLS) .... ScCon
Horry-Georgetown Technical College, Conway, SC [*Library symbol*] [*Library of Congress*] (LCLS) .... ScConH
Hors Concours [*Not Competing*] [*French*] .... HC
Horsching [*Austria ICAO location identifier*] (ICLI) .... LOXL
Horse [*Thoroughbred racing*] .... H
Horse (DMAA) .... Ho
Horse Anti-Human Thymocyte Globulin [*Immunology*] (AAMN) .... HATG
Horse Anti-Human Thymus Globulin [*Immunology*] (MAE) .... HAHTG
Horse Anti-Rhesus Lymphocyte Globulin [*Immunology*] .... HoaRhLG
Horse Antiserum to Rabbit Lymphocytes [*Immunology*] .... HARLS
Horse Anti-Tetanus Toxoid Globulin [*Immunology*] .... HoaTTG
Horse Artillery .... HA
Horse Canyon [*Utah*] [*Seismograph station code, US Geological Survey*] (SEIS) .... HCU
Horse Cave, KY [*FM radio station call letters*] (RBYB) .... WOVO-FM
Horse Cave, KY [*FM radio station call letters*] .... WXPC
Horse Guards [*British*] .... HG
Horse Hemolyzate Supernatant .... HHS
Horse Immunoglobulin [*Immunology*] .... Holg
Horse Immunoglobulin [*Immunology*] (DAVI) .... Holg
Horse Industry Branch, Alberta Agriculture, Calgary, Alberta [*Library symbol National Library of Canada*] (NLC) .... ACAH
Horse of the Americas Registry (EA) .... HAR
Horse Red Blood Cells [*Also, HRC*] .... HRBC
Horse Red Blood Cells [*Also, HRBC*] .... HRC
Horse Serum [*Immunology*] .... HoS
Horse Serum [*Immunology*] .... HS
Horse Serum Albumin [*Immunology*] .... HSA
Horseback Writers and Artists, International (EA) .... HWAI
Horsed Transport [*Military*] .... HT
Horse-Drawn .... HD
Horse-Drawn [*Obsolete Army*] .... H-Dr
Horse-Drawn Vehicle .... HDV
Horsehead Resource Development Company, Inc. [*Associated Press*] (SAG) .... Horshd
Horsehead Resource Dvlp [*NASDAQ symbol*] (TTSB) .... HHRD
Horseheads, NY [*AM radio station call letters*] .... WLNL
Horseheads, NY [*FM radio station call letters*] (RBYB) .... WPGI
Horseheads, NY [*FM radio station call letters*] .... WQIX
Horseheads, NY [*AM radio station call letters*] (RBYB) .... WQIX-AM
Horseless Carriage Club of America (EA) .... HCCA
Horse-Liver Alcohol Dehydrogenase [*Also, HLADH, HLALD*] [*An enzyme*] .... HLAD
Horse-Liver Alcohol Dehydrogenase [*Also, HLAD, HLALD*] [*An enzyme*] .... HLADH
Horse-Liver Alcohol Dehydrogenase [*Also, HLAD, HLADH*] [*An enzyme*] .... HLALD
Horsemanship Safety Association (EA) .... HSA
Horsemen's Benevolent and Protective Association (EA) .... HBPA
Horsepower .... HP
Horsepower (IDOE) .... hp

Horsepower ... HPR
Horsepower Nominal ... HPN
Horsepower Tonnage (DOMA) ... HPT
Horsepower-Hour ... HPH
Horsepower-Hour ... HP-HR
Horserace Betting Levy Board [*British*] ... HBLB
Horserace Totalisator [*Set up in 1926 to provide alternative form of betting and to generate income from improvement of racing*] [*British*] ... HT
Horseradish Latent Virus [*Plant pathology*] ... HLAV
Horseradish Peroxidase [*An enzyme*] ... HRP
Horseradish Peroxidase [*Also, HRP*] [*An enzyme*] ... HRPO
Horses' and Ponies' Protection Association [*British*] (DI) ... HPPA
Horseshoe (ROG) ... HSH
Horseshoe Bay [*British Columbia*] [*Seismograph station code, US Geological Survey Closed*] (SEIS) ... HBC
Horseshoe Bend District Library, Horseshoe Bend, ID [*Library symbol*] [*Library of Congress*] (LCLS) ... IdHb
Horseshoe Bend National Military Park ... HOBE
Horsham [*Australia Airport symbol Obsolete*] (OAG) ... HSM
Horsham Corp. [*Associated Press*] (SAG) ... Horsh
Horsham Corp. [*Toronto Stock Exchange symbol NYSE symbol*] ... HSM
Horta [*Azores*] [*Airport symbol*] (OAG) ... HOR
Horta [*Azores*] [*Seismograph station code, US Geological Survey*] (SEIS) ... HOR
Horta, Faial Island [*Portugal ICAO location identifier*] (ICLI) ... LPHR
Hortensis [*Of a Garden*] [*Latin*] ... hort
Horticultural ... HORTL
Horticultural Abstracts ... HA
Horticultural Advisory Council for England and Wales (BI) ... HAC
Horticultural Dealers Association (EA) ... HDA
Horticultural Education Association [*British*] ... HEA
Horticultural Enterprise [*A publication*] ... HE
Horticultural Market Access Committee [*Australia*] ... HMAC
Horticultural Marketing Council [*British*] (BI) ... HMC
Horticultural Marketing Inspectorate [*Ministry of Agriculture, Fisheries, and Food*] [*British*] ... HMI
Horticultural Policy Council (EERA) ... HPC
Horticultural Postharvest Group [*Queensland, Australia*] ... HPG
Horticultural Research Center [*University of Massachusetts*] (RCD) ... HRC
Horticultural Research Center [*Southern Illinois University at Carbondale*] (RCD) ... HRC
Horticultural Research Institute (EA) ... HRI
Horticultural Research Institute of Ontario [*Canada Research center*] (RCD) ... HRIO
Horticultural Research Institute of Ontario Ministry of Agriculture and Food, Vineland Station, Ontario [*Library symbol National Library of Canada*] (NLC) ... OVAG
Horticultural Society of New York, Inc., New York, NY [*Library symbol Library of Congress*] (LCLS) ... NNHor
Horticultural Trades Association [*British*] (BI) ... HTA
Horticulture ... HORT
Horticulture [*A publication*] (BRI) ... Hort
Horticulture ... HORT
Horticulture [*Freight*] ... HORTI
Horticulture ... HORTIC
Horticulture Awareness Association (EA) ... HAA
Horticulture Exhibitors Association [*British*] (DBA) ... HEA
Horton Hydrocarbons, Inc. [*Vancouver Stock Exchange symbol*] ... HHI
Horton [*D.R.*], Inc. [*NASDAQ symbol*] (SAG) ... DRHI
Horton, KS [*FM radio station call letters*] (RBYB) ... KAIR-FM
Horton, KS [*FM radio station call letters*] ... KERE-FM
Horwitz Information Services [*Information service or system*] (IID) ... HIS
Horwood's Year Books of Edward I [*A publication*] (DLA) ... Horw YB
Hosana [*Ethiopia*] [*Airport symbol*] (AD) ... HOS
Hosanna Army (ROG) ... HA
Hose (NFPA) ... H
Hose Bib (AAG) ... HB
Hose Cabinet [*or Connection*] [*NFPA pre-fire planning symbol*] (NFPA) ... HC
Hose Cart [*Early fire engines*] (ROG) ... HC
Hose Clamp (MSA) ... HC
Hose Connector ... HCONN
Hose Down Unit (DOMA) ... HDU
Hose Jacket (KSC) ... HJ
Hose Rack (AAG) ... HR
Hose Thread ... HSTH
Hosea [*Old Testament book*] (BJA) ... Ho
Hosea [*Old Testament book*] ... Hos
Hosea's Reports [*Ohio*] [*A publication*] (DLA) ... Hosea
Hosebe, SIC [*Ukraine*] [*FAA designator*] (FAAC) ... HOS
Hoshen Mishpat, Shulhan 'Arukh (BJA) ... HM
Hoshina [*Japan*] [*Seismograph station code, US Geological Survey*] (SEIS) ... HSJ
Hosiery ... HSY
Hosiery and Allied Trades Research Association [*British*] (BI) ... HATRA
Hosiery Wholesalers National Association (EA) ... HWNA
Hoskins [*Papua New Guinea*] [*Airport symbol*] (OAG) ... HKN
Hoskins' Reports [*2 North Dakota*] [*A publication*] (DLA) ... Hoskins
Hospice ... HSPC
Hospice Association (EA) ... HA
Hospice Education Institute (EA) ... HEI
Hospice Nurses Association (EA) ... HNA
Hospital (DAVI) ... H
Hospital [*Traffic sign*] [*British*] ... H
Hospital ... HOSP
Hospital (VRA) ... hosp
Hospital ... HOSP
Hospital Academy (EA) ... HA
Hospital Access and Response Terminal [*Health insurance*] (GHCT) ... HART
Hospital Activity Analysis [*British*] ... HAA
Hospital Adjustment Scale [*Psychology*] ... HAS
Hospital Administration [*or Administrator*] ... HAD
Hospital Administration [*A publication*] ... Hosp Admin
Hospital Administrative Services ... HAS
Hospital Admission ... HA
Hospital Admission and Surveillance Program (MEDA) ... HASP
Hospital Advisory Service [*British*] ... HAS
Hospital Aircraft [*ICAO designator*] (FAAC) ... HOSP
Hospital Alliance of Tennessee (SRA) ... HAT
Hospital and Community Psychiatry (DMAA) ... H&CP
Hospital and Health Care [*A publication*] ... Hosp Hlth Care
Hospital and Medial Care Association [*British*] (DBA) ... HMCA
Hospital and Specialist Services [*British*] ... HSS
Hospital Anxiety and Depression Scale [*Medicine*] (DMAA) ... HADS
Hospital Apprentice [*Navy rating*] ... HA
Hospital Apprentice, High School ... HA(HS)
Hospital Audiences (EA) ... HAI
Hospital Bed (DAVI) ... HB
Hospital Benefits Payment ... HBP
Hospital Blood Bank ... HBB
Hospital Bureau, Inc. [*Formerly, HBSS*] (EA) ... HBI
Hospital Bureau of Standards and Supplies [*Later, HBI*] ... HBSS
Hospital Bureau Research Institute [*Defunct*] (EA) ... HBRI
Hospital Car Service ... HCS
Hospital Care Evaluation Committee (MEDA) ... HCEC
Hospital Caterers Association [*British*] ... HCA
Hospital Charles Lemoyne, Department de Sante Communutaire, Montreal, PQ, Canada [*Library symbol*] [*Library of Congress*] (LCLS) ... CaQMHCLC
Hospital Communication and Information System [*McDonnell Douglas Automation Co.*] ... HCIS
Hospital Co. [*Marine Corps*] ... HOSPCO
Hospital Computer Sharing System (IEEE) ... HCSS
Hospital Consultants' and Specialists' Association [*British*] (DCTA) ... HCSA
Hospital Conveyance Corps [*British military*] (DMA) ... HCC
Hospital Corp. of America, Research/Information Services, Nashville, TN [*Library symbol Library of Congress*] (LCLS) ... TNHCA
Hospital Corps [*or Corpsman*] [*Navy*] ... HC
Hospital Corpsman [*Navy rating*] ... HM
Hospital Corpsman, Chief [*Navy rating*] ... HMC
Hospital Corpsman, First Class [*Navy rating*] ... HM1
Hospital Corpsman, Master Chief [*Navy rating*] ... HMCM
Hospital Corpsman, Second Class [*Navy rating*] ... HM2
Hospital Corpsman, Senior Chief [*Navy rating*] ... HMCS
Hospital Corpsman, Third Class [*Navy rating*] ... HM3
Hospital Cost and Utilization Project [*Department of Health and Human Services*] (GFGA) ... HCUP
Hospital Cost Report Information System (MEDA) ... HCRIS
Hospital Course (DAVI) ... HC
Hospital Data Center [*American Hospital Association*] [*Information service or system*] (IID) ... HDC
Hospital Day (DAVI) ... HD
Hospital Design/Hospital Equipment [*British*] ... HD/HE
Hospital Disaster Support Communications System ... HDSCS
Hospital Discharge Demonstration Project (EDAC) ... HDDP
Hospital Discharge Survey [*Public Health Service*] ... HDS
Hospital District Number 10, Virden, Manitoba [*Library symbol National Library of Canada*] (NLC) ... MVHD
Hospital Doctors Association [*British*] (DBA) ... HDA
Hospital Educational and Research Fund, Inc., Albany, NY [*Library symbol Library of Congress*] (LCLS) ... NAIH
Hospital Educational Services Officer [*Navy*] ... HESO
Hospital Emergency Ambulance Radio (LAIN) ... HEAR
Hospital Equipment and Supplies Directory [*A publication*] ... HESD
Hospital Equipment Loan Project ... HELP
Hospital Field Director [*Red Cross*] ... HFD
Hospital Finance Authority (GHCT) ... HFA
Hospital Financial Control [*McDonnell Douglas Automation Co.*] ... HFC
Hospital Financial Management Association [*Later, Healthcare Financial Management Association*] (EA) ... HFMA
Hospital Financial Support (DMAA) ... HFS
Hospital Food Directors Association ... HFDA
Hospital for Sick Children [*Toronto, ON*] [*Canada*] ... HSC
Hospital for Sick Children, Toronto, Ontario [*Library symbol National Library of Canada*] (NLC) ... OTHSC
Hospital for Special Surgery, New York, NY [*Library symbol Library of Congress*] (LCLS) ... NNHS
Hospital Health Plan ... HHP
Hospital Improvement Project ... HIP
Hospital Indicator for Physicians' Orders ... HIPO
Hospital Infection Society [*British*] (DBA) ... HIS
Hospital Information System [*Computer science*] ... HIS
Hospital In-Patient Enquiry [*British*] ... HIPE
Hospital In-Service Training ... HIST
Hospital, Institution, and Educational Food Service Society [*Later, Dietary Managers Association - DMA*] (EA) ... HIEFSS
Hospital Insurance ... HI
Hospital Insurance (DAVI) ... Hosp Ins
Hospital Insurance Program ... HIP
Hospital Journal [*A publication*] ... Hosp J
Hospital Journal of Australia [*A publication*] ... Hosp J Aust
Hospital Junior Staff Committee [*British*] (DI) ... HJSC
Hospital Library, York-Finch General Hospital, Downsview, Ontario [*Library symbol National Library of Canada*] (BIB) ... OTYF

Hospital Management, Hospital Problems [*British*] ... HMHP
Hospital Management Information System ... HMIS
Hospital Management Systems Society [*Later, HIMSS*] (EA) ... HMSS
Hospital Marketing Services, Inc. [*Commercial firm*] (DAVI) ... HMS
Hospital Medical Information System [*Medicine*] (DMAA) ... HMIS
Hospital Morbidity Data System ... HMDS
Hospital of the University of Pennsylvania ... HUP
Hospital Officers' Association of New South Wales [*Australia*] ... HOANSW
Hospital Onset of Infection [*Medicine*] (DMAA) ... HOI
Hospital Operating System - Structured Programming Language [*Computer science*] (CSR) ... HOS-STPL
Hospital Out-Patient Department (MEDA) ... HOPD
Hospital Participation [*Blood program*] [*Red Cross*] ... HP
Hospital Patient Accounting (PDAA) ... HOSPACT
Hospital Patient Transport Vehicle ... HTV
Hospital Physicians Association [*British*] ... HPA
Hospital Plane [*When suffixed to Navy plane designation*] ... H
Hospital Rations [*Navy*] ... HOSPRATS
Hospital Reading Society [*Defunct*] (EA) ... HRS
Hospital Record ... HR
Hospital Recruit ... HR
Hospital Recruit (High School) [*Navy*] (DNAB) ... HR(HS)
Hospital Report (MAE) ... HR
Hospital Research and Educational Trust (EA) ... HRET
Hospital Satellite Network [*Los Angeles, CA*] [*Cable-television system*] ... HSN
Hospital Saving Association [*British*] (BI) ... HSA
Hospital Savings Association (DAVI) ... HSA
Hospital Senior Medical Officer [*Australia*] ... HSMO
Hospital Sergeant (GFGA) ... Hosp Sgt
Hospital Service Plan [*British*] ... HSP
Hospital Services Commission, Edmonton, AB, Canada [*Library symbol Library of Congress*] (LCLS) ... CaAEHSC
Hospital Ship [*Navy symbol*] ... AH
Hospital Ship ... HS
Hospital Ship ... TAH
Hospital Sisters of the Third Order of St. Francis (TOCD) ... OSF
Hospital Staff ... HS
Hospital Staffing Services, Inc. [*Associated Press*] (SAG) ... HospSt
Hospital Staffing Services, Inc. [*NYSE symbol*] (SPSG) ... HSS
Hospital Staffing Svcs [*NYSE symbol*] (TTSB) ... HSS
Hospital Sterile Supply Department (DMAA) ... HSSD
Hospital Sterile Supply Unit (DMAA) ... HSSU
Hospital Surgeon [*British military*] (DMA) ... HS
Hospital Surgical Expansion Package [*Air Force*] (DOMA) ... HSEP
Hospital - Surgical - Medical ... HSM
Hospital Train ... HT
Hospital Transfer Order ... HTO
Hospital Unit (DOMA) ... HU
Hospital Utilization Project [*Western Pennsylvania*] ... HUP
Hospital Visit (AAMN) ... HV
Hospital-Acquired Infection [*Medicine*] ... HAI
Hospital-Acquired Penetration Contact [*Medicine*] (MAE) ... HAPC
Hospital-Based Home Care ... HBHC
Hospital-Based Practice (DMAA) ... HBP
Hospitality ... HOSPTY
Hospitality and Information Service (EA) ... HIS
[*The*] **Hospitality and Information Service** [*For diplomatic residents and families in Washington, DC*] ... THIS
Hospitality Association of South Carolina (SRA) ... HASC
Hospitality Committee for United Nations Delegations (EA) ... HCUND
Hospitality Franchise Sys Wrrt [*NASDAQ symbol*] (TTSB) ... HFSIW
Hospitality Franchise Systems [*NYSE symbol*] (SPSG) ... HFS
Hospitality Lodging and Travel Research Foundation [*Also known as Research Foundation*] (EA) ... HLTRF
Hospitality Properties Trust [*Associated Press*] (SAG) ... HospPT
Hospitality Properties Trust [*NYSE symbol*] (SAG) ... HPT
Hospitality Worldwide Services, Inc. [*Associated Press*] (SAG) ... HospWwde
Hospitality Worldwide Services, Inc. [*NASDAQ symbol*] (SAG) ... ROOM
Hospitalization (DAVI) ... Hx
Hospitalization and Treatment ... H & T
Hospitalization Proneness Scale [*Psychometrics*] ... HPS
Hospitalized Veterans Writing Project (EA) ... HVWP
Hospitaller Brothers of St. John of God (TOCD) ... OH
Hospitaller Brothers of St. John of God (TOCD) ... oh
Hospitaller Order of St. John of God [*Roman Catholic men's religious order*] ... OH
Hospitallers of Jerusalem [*Freemasonry*] (ROG) ... H of J
Hospitalman [*Nonrated enlisted man*] [*Navy*] ... HN
Hospitalman (Junior College) [*Navy*] (DNAB) ... HN(JC)
Hospitalman Recruit ... HR
Hospital-Oriented Programmed Environment ... HOPE
Hospitals Accreditation Committee [*Australia*] ... HAC
Hospitals, Administration, and Organizations [*British*] ... HAO
Hospitals Remuneration Tribunal [*Australia*] ... HRT
Hospitals Superannuation Board [*Victoria, Australia*] ... HSB
Hosposable Products [*NASDAQ symbol*] (TTSB) ... HOSP
Hosposable Products, Inc. [*NASDAQ symbol*] (NQ) ... HOSP
Hosposable Products, Inc. [*Associated Press*] (SAG) ... Hospos
Hosptial Peer Review (MEDA) ... HPR
Hossana [*Ethiopia*] [*ICAO location identifier*] (ICLI) ... HAHS
Host [*Freemasonry*] (ROG) ... H
Host Application Programming Interface ... HAPI
Host Bus Adapter [*Computer science*] ... HBA
Host Cell [*Parasitology*] ... HC
Host Command Facility ... HCF
Host Communications Processor ... HCP
Host Composition System [*Infograph Ltd.*] (NITA) ... HCS
Host Computer ... HC
Host Computer Basic Software (IAA) ... HCBS
Host Computer Interface ... HCI
Host Country (NATG) ... HC
Host Country Contributions [*Peace Corps*] ... HCC
Host Defensive Factor [*Immunology*] (AAMN) ... HDF
Host Digital Terminal [*Telecommunications*] (ACRL) ... HDT
Host Forms Description Language [*Xerox software*] (NITA) ... HFDL
Host Funding 'A' [*AMEX symbol*] (TTSB) ... HFD
Host Funding, Inc. [*AMEX symbol*] (SAG) ... HFD
Host Funding, Inc. [*Associated Press*] (SAG) ... HostFdg
Host Identifier (ACRL) ... HOSTID
Host Information Processor (NITA) ... HIP
Host Interface Manager (NITA) ... HIM
Host Interface Port [*Computer science*] ... HIP
Host Interface Processor [*Computer science*] (PDAA) ... HIP
Host Interface Unit ... HIU
Host Language ... HL
Host Language Interface ... HLI
Host Link Adapter Card [*Ideacomm Gateway*] ... HLAC
Host Marriot [*Formerly, Marriott Corp.*] [*NYSE symbol*] (SPSG) ... HMT
Host Marriott Corp. [*Associated Press*] (SAG) ... HostM
Host Marriott Corp. [*Associated Press*] (SAG) ... HostMar
Host Marriott Services [*NYSE symbol*] (TTSB) ... HMS
Host Marriott Services Corp. [*NYSE symbol*] (SAG) ... HMS
Host Marriott Services Corp. [*Associated Press*] (SAG) ... HostMS
Host Micro Interface [*CompuServe, Inc.*] [*Computer science*] (PCM) ... HMI
Host Nation (AABC) ... HN
Host Nation Support [*Military*] ... HNS
Host Nation Support Agreement [*Navy*] (ANA) ... HNSA
Host Packet Assembler/Disassembler (ACRL) ... HPAD
Host Preparation Facility (MHDI) ... HPF
Host Processor ... HP
Host Processor Adapter (IAA) ... HPA
Host Proximity Service [*Computer science*] ... HOPS
HOst Proximity Service [*Computer science*] ... HOPS
Host Remote Node Entry System ... HRNES
Host Resident Software ... HRS
Host Resident Software System ... HRSS
Host Software Testing Section [*Social Security Administration*] ... HSTS
Host to Network [*Computer science*] ... HN
Host Vehicle Pallet ... HVP
Host Versus Graft [*Medicine*] ... HVG
Hostage Bracelet Committee (EA) ... HBC
Hostage Negotiating Team (LAIN) ... HNT
Hostage Rescue Team [*Pronounced "hurt"*] [*FBI standardized term*] ... HRT
Hostage Rescue Unit (LAIN) ... HRU
Host-Associated Population [*Ecology*] ... HAP
Hosted Bus Controller Chip [*Electronics*] ... HBCC
Hosted Bus Controller Chip ... HBCC
Hosted Bus Controller Circuit [*Electronics*] ... HBCC
Hostel Care ... HC
Hostess (ROG) ... HOSTS
Hostiensis [*Deceased, 1271*] [*Authority cited in pre-1607 legal work*] (DSA) ... H
Hostiensis [*Deceased, 1271*] [*Authority cited in pre-1607 legal work*] (DSA) ... Ho
Hostiensis [*Deceased, 1271*] [*Authority cited in pre-1607 legal work*] (DSA) ... Hos
Hostiensis [*Deceased, 1271*] [*Authority cited in pre-1607 legal work*] (DSA) ... Host
Hostiensis [*Deceased, 1271*] [*Authority cited in pre-1607 legal work*] (DSA) ... Hosti
Hostile [*Military*] ... H
Hostile ... HOST
Hostile Aeroplane [*British military*] (DMA) ... HA
Hostile Aircraft Identification Equipment (DWSG) ... HAIDE
Hostile Artillery Positions (RDA) ... HATLS
Hostile Electromagnetic Emission (MCD) ... HEME
Hostile Environment Recovery Vehicle ... HERV
Hostile Environment Robotic Machine Intelligence Experiment Series [*Oak Ridge National Laboratory*] ... HERMIES
Hostile Fire Pay [*Special pay for hazardous duty*] [*Military*] (AABC) ... HFP
Hostile Fire Simulator [*Military*] (MCD) ... HFS
Hostile Intelligence Service [*Military*] (MCD) ... HOIS
Hostile, Unknown, Faker, and Big Photo [*Used in Semi-Automatic Ground Environment to designate certain tracks and raids*] (SAA) ... HUKB
Hostile, Unknown, Faker, and Pending [*Used in SAGE to designate certain tracks and raids*] ... HUKP
Hostile, Unknown, Faker, Pending Track Identities [*Used in Semi-Automatic Ground Environment to designate certain tracks and raids*] (SAA) ... HUKP
Hostile, Unknown, Faker, Special Track Identities [*Used in SAGE to designate certain tracks and raids*] (SAA) ... HUKS
Hostile Weapons Locating System (MCD) ... HWLS
Hostile Weapons Locator Study [*DARPA/Army*] (MCD) ... HOWLS
Hostilities Only [*Applied to men who joined for duration of war only*] [*Navy British World War II*] ... HO
Hostility Adjective Check List [*Psychology*] ... HACL
Hostility and Direction of Hostility Questionnaire [*Psychology*] ... HDHQ
Hostos Community College, New York, NY [*Library symbol Library of Congress*] (LCLS) ... NNHC
Host-Plant Resistance [*Entomology, phytochemistry*] ... HPR
Host-Tenant Support Agreement [*Military*] ... HTSA
Host-to-Satellite ... HTS
Hot ... H
Hot Air ... HA
Hot Air Balloon ... HAB
Hot Air Intake [*Automotive engineering*] ... HAI

Hot Air Vulcanization .... HAV
Hot and Cold (IAA) .... HAC
Hot and Cold (DMAA) .... H&C
Hot and Cold .... HC
Hot and Cold Running Water .... HCRW
Hot and Heavy [*In reference to a romance*] .... H^2
Hot Biquetted Iron .... HBI
Hot Blade Stripper .... HBS
Hot Boning [*Meat processing*] .... HB
Hot Bridgewire (KSC) .... HBW
Hot Carrier Quad .... HCQ
Hot Cathode Tube .... HCT
Hot Cranking Amperes [*Battery*] [*Automotive engineering*] .... HCA
Hot Critical Experiments [*Nuclear energy*] .... HOTCE
Hot Dark Matter [*Astronomy*] .... HDM
Hot Dip Galvanization .... HDG
Hot Dip Galvanizers Association [*British*] (BI) .... HDGA
Hot Dip Galvanizing After Fabrication [*Metallurgy*] .... HDGAF
Hot/Dry Clothing and Equipment System [*Army*] (INF) .... HDCES
Hot Dry Rock [*Geothermal science*] .... HDR
Hot Electron Amplifier .... HEA
Hot Experimental Reaction of O Power [*Nuclear energy*] .... HERO
Hot Filament Chemical Vapor Deposition [*Coating technology*] .... HFCVD
Hot Finished [*Drawing*] (DAC) .... HF
Hot Firing (MCD) .... HF
Hot Form Die .... HFD
Hot Fuel Examination Facility [*Nuclear energy*] .... HFEF
Hot Full Power [*Nuclear energy*] (NRCH) .... HFP
Hot Functional Testing [*Nuclear energy*] (NRCH) .... HFT
Hot Gas Bonder .... HGB
Hot Gas Generator .... HGG
Hot Gas Manifold (NASA) .... HGM
Hot Gas Radiating Facility .... HGRF
Hot Gas Reinjection (PDAA) .... HGR
Hot Gas Secondary Injection Thrust Vector Control (PDAA) .... HGSITVC
Hot Gas Soldering Equipment .... HGSE
Hot Gas System .... HGS
Hot Gas Thrust Vector Control .... HGTVC
Hot High Pressure Separator [*Chemical engineering*] .... HHPS
Hot Hydrogen Nozzle .... HHN
Hot Idle Compensation [*Automotive engineering*] .... HIC
Hot Ionized Medium [*Astrophysics*] .... HIM
Hot Isostatic Compaction .... HIC
Hot Isostatic Pressing of Waste [*Nuclear energy*] (NUCP) .... HIPOW
Hot Isostatically Pressed [*Materials processing*] .... HIP
Hot Issue [*Investment term*] .... HI
Hot Jet Exhaust .... HJE
Hot Jet Model .... HJM
Hot Kathode Tube .... HKT
Hot Leg [*Nuclear energy*] .... HLG
Hot Leg Check Valve [*Nuclear energy*] (NRCH) .... HLCV
Hot Leg Isolation Valve [*Nuclear energy*] (NRCH) .... HLIV
Hot Leg Temperature [*Nuclear energy*] (NRCH) .... TH
Hot Line [*Alert system*] (AAG) .... HL
Hot Line Alert System .... HLAS
Hot Line Gunsight System .... HLGS
Hot Melt Adhesive .... HMA
Hot Melt Applicator .... HMA
Hot Melt Equipment Manufacturers Association (EA) .... HEMA
Hot Melt Pressure Sensitive Adhesive .... HMPSA
Hot Metal Detector [*Electronics*] (IAA) .... HMD
Hot Moist Packs [*Medicine*] .... HMP
Hot Ore Briquetting (DICI) .... HOB
Hot Pack [*or Pad*] [*Physical therapy*] .... HP
Hot Particle Rolling (PDAA) .... HPR
Hot Photographic Report .... HOREP
Hot Photographic Report (MCD) .... HOTPHOTOREP
Hot Pilot [*An egotistic flying cadet*] [*Slang Air Force*] .... HP
Hot Pipe Chase [*Nuclear energy*] (NRCH) .... HPC
Hot Press Molding .... HPM
Hot Pressure Welding .... HPW
Hot Processing Plant [*Nuclear energy*] .... HPP
Hot Report .... HOREP
Hot Report (NATG) .... HT
Hot Resources Ltd. [*Vancouver Stock Exchange symbol*] .... HOR
Hot Rolled (MSA) .... HR
Hot Rolled, Pickled, and Oiled (MSA) .... HRPO
Hot Rolled Steel .... HRS
Hot Shop [*Nuclear energy*] (NRCH) .... HS
Hot Shot Tunnel .... HST
Hot Shutdown (IEEE) .... HSD
Hot Side .... HSD
Hot Situation (MCD) .... HOTSIT
Hot Soak [*Automotive engineering*] .... HS
Hot Spot [*Washington*] [*Seismograph station code, US Geological Survey Closed*] (SEIS) .... HSW
Hot Spot Tracking (DNAB) .... HOST
Hot Spraying .... HS
Hot Springs [*Arkansas*] [*Airport symbol*] (OAG) .... HOT
Hot Springs [*Virginia*] [*Airport symbol*] (AD) .... HSP
Hot Springs [*South Dakota*] [*Airport symbol*] (AD) .... HSR
Hot Springs, AR [*FM radio station call letters*] .... KALR
Hot Springs, AR [*AM radio station call letters*] .... KBHS
Hot Springs, AR [*FM radio station call letters*] .... KLAZ
Hot Springs, AR [*FM radio station call letters*] .... KLXQ
Hot Springs, AR [*FM radio station call letters*] .... KQUS
Hot Springs, AR [*FM radio station call letters*] .... KSBC
Hot Springs, AR [*Television station call letters*] (RBYB) .... KVTH
Hot Springs, AR [*AM radio station call letters*] .... KXOW
Hot Springs, AR [*AM radio station call letters*] .... KZNG
Hot Springs High School, Hot Springs, MT [*Library symbol*] [*Library of Congress*] (LCLS) .... MtHsHS
Hot Springs National Park .... HOSP
Hot Springs, NC [*Location identifier FAA*] (FAAL) .... HSS
Hot Springs Public Library, Hot Springs, MT [*Library symbol*] [*Library of Congress*] (LCLS) .... MtHs
Hot Springs, SD [*Location identifier FAA*] (FAAL) .... FTA
Hot Springs, SD [*Location identifier FAA*] (FAAL) .... HSR
Hot Springs, SD [*AM radio station call letters*] .... KZMX
Hot Springs, SD [*FM radio station call letters*] .... KZMX-FM
Hot Springs, VA [*Location identifier FAA*] (FAAL) .... HSP
Hot Springs, VA [*FM radio station call letters*] .... WBHA
Hot Springs Village, AR [*FM radio station call letters*] .... KVRE
Hot Stamping Press .... HSP
Hot Stove Club (EA) .... HSC
Hot Stuff [*Slang Bowdlerized version*] .... HS
Hot Tin (MSA) .... HT
Hot Topic, Inc. [*NASDAQ symbol*] (SAG) .... HOTT
Hot Topic, Inc. [*Associated Press*] (SAG) .... HotTopic
Hot Transient Exhaust Emissions [*Automotive engineering*] .... HT
Hot Tub Bath [*Medicine*] .... HTB
Hot Water .... HW
Hot Water Boiler [*on a ship*] (DS) .... HWB
Hot Water Bottle .... hwb
Hot Water Circulating [*Technical drawings*] .... HWC
Hot Water Extract (DMAA) .... HWE
Hot Water Heater (MSA) .... HWH
Hot Water Line (AAG) .... HWL
Hot Water Oxidizer (PDAA) .... HWO
Hot Water Return .... HWR
Hot Water Soluble .... HWS
Hot Water Temperature .... HWT
Hot Water-Insoluble Nitrogen [*Analytical chemistry*] .... HWIN
Hot Weather Battle Dress Uniform [*Army*] (INF) .... HWBDU
Hot Weather Boot [*Military*] (INF) .... HWB
Hot Wire (KSC) .... HW
Hot Wire Anemometer .... HWA
Hot Wire Detector [*Analytical instrumentation*] .... HWD
Hot Wire Emissive Probe .... HWEP
Hot Zero Power [*Nuclear energy*] (NRCH) .... HZP
Hot-Air Solder Leveling [*Materials science*] .... HASL
Hotan [*China*] [*Airport symbol*] (OAG) .... HTN
Hotan [*China*] [*ICAO location identifier*] (ICLI) .... ZWTN
Hot-Carrier Diode (IEEE) .... HCD
Hotchkiss Gunner [*British military*] (DMA) .... HG
Hotchkiss Public Library, Hotchkiss, CO [*Library symbol Library of Congress*] (LCLS) .... CoHotch
Hotel .... H
Hotel (ROG) .... HO
Hotel (WDAA) .... HTL
Hotel .... HTL
Hotel Accommodation Service [*British*] .... HOTAC
Hotel Accountants Association of New York City (EA) .... HAA
Hotel and Catering Industry Training Board [*British*] (BI) .... HCITB
Hotel and Catering Institute [*British*] (BI) .... HCI
Hotel and Catering Research Centre [*British*] (IRUK) .... HCRC
Hotel and Catering Trades Benevolent Association [*British*] (BI) .... HCTBA
Hotel and Catering Training Board [*British*] .... HCTB
Hotel and Catering Training Co. (AIE) .... HCTC
Hotel and Motel Brokers of America (EA) .... HMBA
Hotel and Restaurant Design and Interiors Exhibition [*British*] (ITD) .... HARDIS
Hotel and Restaurant Employees and Bartenders International Union [*Later, HERE*] (EA) .... HREBIU
Hotel and Restaurant Employees and Bartenders International Union [*Later, HERE*] .... HREU
Hotel & Restaurant Suppliers Association Inc. (AC) .... HRSA
Hotel Association of Washington, D.C. (SRA) .... HAWDC
Hotel Billing Information System [*Telecommunications*] (TEL) .... HOBIS
Hotel Call, Time, and Charges Mandatory [*Telecommunications*] (TEL) .... HTL
Hotel Catering and Institutional Management Association [*British*] (DI) .... HCIMA
Hotel, Catering, and Institutional Management Association [*British*] (DBA) .... HCIMA
Hotel Credit Managers Association [*Defunct*] (EA) .... HCMA
Hotel Dieu Hospital, Kingston, ON, Canada [*Library symbol*] [*Library of Congress*] (LCLS) .... CaOKHD
Hotel, Echo, November [*Russian submarine*] .... HEN
Hotel Employees and Restaurant Employees International Union (EA) .... HERE
Hotel Five [*Jordan*] [*ICAO location identifier*] (ICLI) .... OJHF
Hotel Four [*Jordan*] [*ICAO location identifier*] (ICLI) .... OJHR
Hotel Greeters of America [*Later, HMGI*] .... HGA
Hotel Institute Montreux [*Switzerland*] (ECON) .... HIM
Hotel, Motel, Resort Database [*American Database Corp.*] [*Santa Barbara, CA*] [*Information service or system*] (IID) .... HMR
Hotel Properties Ltd. [*Singapore*] (ECON) .... HPL
Hotel, Restaurant, and Institutional [*Business*] .... HRI
Hotel Sales and Marketing Association International (EA) .... HSMAI
Hotel Sales and Marketing Association International - European Office [*Utrecht, Netherlands*] (EAIO) .... HSMAI-EO
Hotel Sales Management Association [*Later, HSMAI*] (EA) .... HSMA
Hotel Sundry Fund [*Air Force*] .... HSF

Hotel-Dieu de Gaspe, Gaspe, PQ, Canada [Library symbol Library of Congress] (LCLS) .... CaQGaH
Hotel-Dieu de Gaspe, Quebec [Library symbol National Library of Canada] (NLC) .... QGAH
Hotel-Dieu de Levis, Levis, PQ, Canada [Library symbol] [Library of Congress] (LCLS) .... CaQLHD
Hotel-Dieu de Levis, Quebec [Library symbol National Library of Canada] (NLC) .... QLHD
Hotel-Dieu de Montreal, Quebec [Library symbol National Library of Canada] (NLC) .... QMHD
Hotel-Dieu de Quebec, Quebec [Library symbol National Library of Canada] (NLC) .... QQHD
Hotel-Dieu de Quebec, Quebec, PQ, Canada [Library symbol Library of Congress] (LCLS) .... CaQQHD
Hotel-Dieu de Roberval, Bibliotheque Medicale, Roberval, PQ, Canada [Library symbol] [Library of Congress] (LCLS) .... CaQRobHD
Hotel-Dieu de Saint-Jerome, Quebec [Library symbol National Library of Canada] (NLC) .... QSJHD
Hotel-Dieu du Sacre-Coeur, Quebec, PQ, Canada [Library symbol Library of Congress] (LCLS) .... CaQQHDS
Hotel-Dieu du Sacre-Coeur, Quebec, Quebec [Library symbol National Library of Canada] (NLC) .... QQHDS
Hotel-Dieu Hospital, Kingston, Ontario [Library symbol National Library of Canada] (NLC) .... OKHD
Hotel-Dieu Hospital, Montreal, PQ, Canada [Library symbol Library of Congress] (LCLS) .... CaQMHD
Hotel-Dieu Hospital, St. Catharines, Ontario [Library symbol National Library of Canada] (BIB) .... OSTCH
Hotel-Dieu Medical-Nursing Educational Media Center, El Paso, TX [Library symbol Library of Congress] (LCLS) .... TxEHD
Hoteles Dinamicos SA de CV [Mexico ICAO designator] (FAAC) .... HDI
Hotel-Motel Greeters International (EA) .... HMGI
Hotels and Restaurants [Public-performance tariff class] [British] .... E
Hotkey [Computer science] (PCM) .... HK
Hotot Rabbit Breeders International (EA) .... HRBI
Hot-Pressed [Paper] .... HP
Hot-Pressed Boron Nitride [Materials science and technology] .... HPBN
Hot-Pressed Ferrite (IAA) .... HPF
Hot-Pressed Silicon Nitride (RDA) .... HPSN
Hot-Wall Vacuum Evaporation [Photovoltaic energy systems] .... HWVE
Hot-Water Recirculation (DAC) .... HWRC
Hot-Water-Cure Mortar (PDAA) .... HWM
Hotwell [Nuclear energy] (NRCH) .... HW
Hotwell .... HWL
Hotwell Level Control [System] [Nuclear energy] (NRCH) .... HWLC
Houailou [New Caledonia] [Airport symbol] (OAG) .... HLU
Houailou/Nesson [New Caledonia] [ICAO location identifier] (ICLI) .... NWWH
Houard's Anglo-Saxon Laws [A publication] (DLA) .... Houard Anglo-Saxon Laws
Houard's Anglo-Saxon Laws, Etc. [A publication] (DLA) .... Hou Ang Sax Law
Houard's Dictionary of the Customs of Normandy [A publication] (DLA) .... Hou Dict
Houck on Mechanics' Lien Law [A publication] (DLA) .... Houck Mech Lien
Houck on the Law of Navigable Rivers [A publication] (DLA) .... Houck Riv
Houdini Historical Center (EA) .... HHC
Hough Development Corp. [Cleveland] .... HDC
Hough-Powell Digitizer .... H-PD
Hough's American Constitutions [A publication] (DLA) .... Hough Am Cons
Hough's Court-Martial Case Book [1821] [London] [A publication] (DLA) .... Hough C-M Cas
Hough's Military Law and Courts-Martial [A publication] (DLA) .... Hough CM
Houghton College, Buffalo Campus, West Seneca, NY [Library symbol Library of Congress] (LCLS) .... NWsH
Houghton College, Buffalo Campus, West Seneca, NY [OCLC symbol] (OCLC) .... YXO
Houghton College, Houghton, NY [OCLC symbol] (OCLC) .... VXO
Houghton Lake, MI [Location identifier FAA] (FAAL) .... HTL
Houghton Lake, MI [Location identifier FAA] (FAAL) .... ROQ
Houghton Lake, MI [AM radio station call letters] .... WHGR
Houghton Lake, MI [FM radio station call letters] .... WUPS
Houghton Lake Public Library, Houghton Lake, MI [Library symbol Library of Congress] (LCLS) .... MiHi
Houghton Lake/Roscommon [Michigan] [ICAO location identifier] (ICLI) .... KHTL
Houghton, MI [FM radio station call letters] .... WAAH
Houghton, MI [AM radio station call letters] .... WCCY
Houghton, MI [FM radio station call letters] .... WGGL
Houghton, MI [FM radio station call letters] .... WMTU
Houghton, MI [FM radio station call letters] .... WOLV
Houghton Mifflin [NYSE symbol] (TTSB) .... HTN
Houghton Mifflin Co. [Publisher] .... HM
Houghton Mifflin Co. [Associated Press] (SAG) .... HougM
Houghton Mifflin Co. [NYSE symbol] (SPSG) .... HTN
Houghton Mifflin Co., Boston, MA [OCLC symbol] (OCLC) .... HMC
Houghton Mifflin Co., Boston, MA [Library symbol Library of Congress] (LCLS) .... MBHoM
Houghton, NY [FM radio station call letters] .... WJSL
Houghton Pharmaceuticals [NASDAQ symbol] (TTSB) .... HPIP
Houghton Pharmaceuticals, Inc. [Associated Press] (SAG) .... Houghtn
Houghton Pharmaceuticals, Inc. [NASDAQ symbol] (SAG) .... HPIP
Houghton Poultry Research Station [British] (ARC) .... HPRS
Houghton's Reports [97 Alabama] [A publication] (DLA) .... Houghton
Houlihan Lokey Howard & Zukin [Financial advisors] (ECON) .... ALHZ
Houlton [Maine] [Airport symbol] (OAG) .... HUL
Houlton/International [Maine] [ICAO location identifier] (ICLI) .... KHUL
Houlton, ME [Location identifier FAA] (FAAL) .... HUL
Houlton, ME [FM radio station call letters] .... WHOU-FM

Houma [Louisiana] [Airport symbol] (OAG) .... HUM
Houma, LA [FM radio station call letters] .... KCIL
Houma, LA [FM radio station call letters] .... KHOM
Houma, LA [AM radio station call letters] .... KJIN
Houma-Thibodaux [Diocesan abbreviation] [Louisiana] (TOCD) .... HT
Houn [Libya] [Airport symbol] (OAG) .... HUQ
Hounde [Burkina Faso] [ICAO location identifier] (ICLI) .... DHOH
Hounsfield Unit [Medicine] (MAE) .... H
Hounsfield Unit [On computerized tomography] [Radiology] (DAVI) .... HA
Hour [Also, h] .... H
Hour (WDMC) .... h
Hour (WDMC) .... hr
Hour (ODBW) .... hr
Hour (AAG) .... HR
Hour .... hr
Hour Angle [Navigation] .... HA
Hour Angle of the Mean Sun [Navigation] .... HAMS
Hour Angle of the True Sun [Navigation] .... HATS
Hour Angle-Declination [Type of antenna mounting] .... HA-DEC
Hour Circle .... HC
Hour Hand [Clocks] (ROG) .... HH
Hour of Revival Association [British] .... HRA
Hourglass Contraction of Stomach [Gastroenterology] (DAVI) .... HCS
Hourglass Device [Military decoration] (AFM) .... HGD
Hourly Attendance and Absence Reporting System [Military] (MCD) .... HAARS
Hourly Difference [Navigation] .... HD
Hourly Earnings Index (OICC) .... HEI
Hourly Earnings Rate .... HERATES
Hourly Fetal Urine Production Rate [Medicine] (AAMN) .... HFUPR
Hourly Noise Level .... HNL
Hourly Postflight (MCD) .... HPO
Hourly Precipitation Data [A publication] .... HPD
Hourly Report (DNAB) .... HR
Hours (NATG) .... HRS
Hours (ODBW) .... hrs
Hours and Cost Detail Report .... HCDR
Hours/Minutes (HGAA) .... hh/mm
Hours, Minutes (ROG) .... HM
Hours, Minutes, Seconds .... HMS
Hours of Operation .... HO
Hours of Sleep [Medicine] .... HS
Hours per Patient Day [Medicine] (DMAA) .... HPPD
Hours per Week .... HPW
Hours Post Inoculation .... HPI
Hours Postprandial [Usually preceded by a numeral] [Pharmacology] (DAVI) .... hr pp
Hours to Run (ADA) .... HTR
Hours Waiting Parts (MCD) .... HWP
House .... H
House .... HO
House (VRA) .... hs
House .... HSE
House .... HSE
[A] House, a Tree, a Person [Psychological drawing test] .... H-T-P
House Account [Business term] .... HA
House Administration (DLA) .... HA
House Air Waybill [Shipping] (DS) .... HAWB
House Appropriations Committee [US Congress] (AAG) .... HAC
House Armed Services Committee [US Congress] (AABC) .... HASC
House Armed Services Investigation Subcommittee [US Congress] .... HASIS
House Armed Services Permanent Investigations Subcommittee [US Congress] (AAG) .... HASPID
House Bill [Legal term] (DLA) .... H
House Bill [In state legislatures] .... HB
House Boat [Navy symbol] .... YHB
House Budget Committee .... HBC
House Cable [Telecommunications] (TEL) .... HC
House Call [Medicine] .... HC
House Call Tax Service .... HCTS
House Committee on Internal Security [Formerly, HUAC] [Dissolved, 1975 US Congress] .... HCIS
House Committee on Space and Astronautics [US Congress] (AAG) .... HCSA
House Committee Substitute [US Congress] .... HCS
House Concurrent Resolution [US Congress] .... HCR
House Defense Appropriations Subcommittee [US Congress] (AAG) .... HDAS
House Democratic Research Organization (EA) .... DRO
House Democratic Research Organization [Defunct] (EA) .... HDRO
House Document .... HD
House Document .... HDOC
House Dress Institute (EA) .... HDI
House Dust (DMAA) .... HD
House Dust Mite .... HDM
House Ear Institute (EA) .... HEI
House Employees Position Classification Act [1964] .... HEPCA
House Energy and Commerce Committee (GFGA) .... HECC
House Error [Publishing] (WDMC) .... HE
House Exchange System [Telecommunications] (NITA) .... HES
House File (OICC) .... HF
House Formula [An in-house formula found in a particular hospital or clinic] (DAVI) .... HF
House Heating [Freight] .... HHTG
House Information Systems [House of Representatives] [Washington, DC] .... HIS
House Internal Security Committee .... HISC
House Joint Resolution (AAGC) .... H Joint Res
House Joint Resolution .... HJ Res

House Joint Resolution .... HJR
House Leadership Fund (EA) .... HLF
House Logic Unit .... HLU
House Magazine [*Australia A publication*] .... HM
House Magazine [*A publication*] .... House Mag
House Magazine Institute [*Later, NY/IABC*] .... HMI
House Merchant Marine and Fisheries Committee .... HMMFC
House Nigger [*Derogatory nickname for an obsequious black person*] .... HN
House of Assembly [*South Australia*] .... HOA
House of Commons [*British*] .... H of C
House of Commons [*British*] .... HC
House of Commons [*British*] .... HOC
House of Commons Bill [*British*] .... HCB
House of Commons Journals [*England*] [*A publication*] (DLA) .... Comm Journ
House of Commons Journals [*England*] [*A publication*] (DLA) .... HC Jour
House of Commons Weekly Information Bulletin [*A publication*] (DLA) .... HC Wkly Inf Bull
House of Correction .... HC
House of Fabrics, Inc. [*NYSE symbol*] (SPSG) .... HF
House of Fabrics, Inc. [*NASDAQ symbol*] (SAG) .... HFAB
House of Fabrics, Inc. [*Associated Press*] (SAG) .... HseFbr
House of Fabrics, Inc. [*Associated Press*] (SAG) .... HseFbrc
House of Fraser [*Department store conglomerate*] [*British*] .... HOF
House of Ill Fame .... H of IF
House of Issue [*Banking*] .... HOI
House of Keys [*Isle Of Man*] .... HK
House of Keys [*Isle Of Man*] .... HOK
House of Lords [*British*] .... HL
House of Lords [*British*] .... HOL
House of Lords Appeals, in Dunlop's Court of Session Cases, from Vol. 13 [*1851-62*] [*A publication*] (DLA) .... DHL
House of Lords' Appeals, in Macpherson's Court of Sessions Cases, Third Series [*1862-73*] [*Scotland*] [*A publication*] (DLA) .... M (HL)
House of Lords Cases [*A publication*] (DLA) .... HL Cas (Eng)
House of Lords Cases [*A publication*] (DLA) .... House of L
House of Lords Cases (Clark) [*England*] [*A publication*] (DLA) .... HL
House of Lords Cases (Clark) [*England*] [*A publication*] (DLA) .... HL Cas
House of Lords Cases (Clark) [*England*] [*A publication*] (DLA) .... HLC
House of Lords Journals [*England*] [*A publication*] (DLA) .... HL Jour
House of Lords Journals [*England*] [*A publication*] (DLA) .... LJ
House of Lords Record Office [*British*] (DLA) .... HLRO
House of Lords Weekly Information Bulletin [*A publication*] (DLA) .... HL Wkly Inf Bull
House of Representatives .... H
House of Representatives .... HR
House of Representatives Bill [*with Number*] .... HR
House of Representatives Bill .... HRB
House of Representatives Concurrent Resolution (DLA) .... H Con Res
House of Representatives Concurrent Resolution [*Legal term*] (DLA) .... HC Res
House of Representatives Concurrent Resolution [*Legal term*] (DLA) .... HR Con Res
House of Representatives Conference Report (BARN) .... H Conf Rept
House of Representatives Document (DLA) .... HR Doc
House of Representatives Information System .... HRIS
House of Representatives Joint Resolution [*Legal term*] (DLA) .... HRJ Res
House of Representatives Report (AAGC) .... H Rep
House of Representatives Reports [*A publication*] (DLA) .... HR Rep
House of Representatives Reports [*A publication*] (DLA) .... HR Rept
House of Representatives Reports [*A publication*] (DLA) .... HRept
House of Representatives Standing Committee on Environment and Conservation (EERA) .... HORSEC
House of Representatives Standing Committee on the Environment (EERA) .... HORSCERA
House of Representatives Ways and Means Committee (WDAA) .... HRWMC
House of Ruth (EA) .... HR
House of Solomon [*Freemasonry*] (ROG) .... H of S
House Office Building [*US Congress*] .... HOB
House Officer .... HO
House Operating Tape [*Telecommunications*] (TEL) .... HOP
House Painter (ROG) .... HP
House Permanent Select Committee on Intelligence (MCD) .... HPSCI
House Physician .... HP
House Plants Australia .... HPA
House Recedes .... HR
House Report .... HR
House Resolution .... HR
House Resolution, United States House of Representatives .... H Res
House Roll [*Legal term*] (DLA) .... HR
House Science and Astronautics Committee [*US Congress*] (AAG) .... HSAC
House Select Committee on the Outer Continental Shelf [*US Congress*] [*Marine science*] (MSC) .... HSCOCS
House Space Committee [*US Congress*] (AAG) .... HSC
House Spacecraft (KSC) .... HS/C
House Staff Check on Rounds [*Medicine*] .... HSCOR
House Supervisor .... HS
House Surgeon .... HS
House to House (ADA) .... H/H
House Trailer (AFM) .... HT
House Tube Feeding [*Medicine*] (DMAA) .... HTF
House Un-American Activities Committee [*Later, HCIS*] [*US Congress*] .... HUAC
House Veterans' Affairs Committee [*House of Representatives*] .... HVAC
House Ways and Means Committee .... HWMC
House Wednesday Group (EA) .... HWG
Houseboat Association of America (EA) .... HAA
Housebound (MAE) .... HB
Housebreaking .... HB
House-Breaking Implements [*British police term*] .... HBI
House-Builders Federation [*British*] (DBA) .... HBF
Housecall Medical Resources [*NASDAQ symbol*] (TTSB) .... HSCL
Housecall Medical Resources, Inc. [*Associated Press*] (SAG) .... HcllMed
Housecall Medical Resources, Inc. [*NASDAQ symbol*] (SAG) .... HSCL
Househld 9.50%'91 cm Dep Pfd [*NYSE symbol*] (TTSB) .... HIPrX
Househld Cap Tr 8.25% 'TOPrS' [*NYSE symbol*] (TTSB) .... HIPrT
Household .... HH
Household [*Marketing*] .... HHLD
Household [*Marketing*] (ROG) .... HOUSHD
Household .... HSEHLD
Household .... HSEHOLD
Household (MSA) .... HSHLD
Household 8.25% cm Dep Pfd [*NYSE symbol*] (TTSB) .... HIPrZ
Household and Industrial Chemical .... HIC
Household and Personal Products Industry [*A publication*] .... HAPPI
Household Battalion [*British military*] (DMA) .... HB
Household Capital Trust [*NYSE symbol*] (SAG) .... HI
Household Capital Trust [*Associated Press*] (SAG) .... HoCT
Household Capital Trust II [*NYSE symbol*] (SAG) .... HI
Household Capital Trust II [*Associated Press*] (SAG) .... HoCT
Household Cavalry [*British*] .... HC
Household Cavalry Regiment [*British military*] (DMA) .... HCR
Household Delivery Service [*British Post Office facility*] (DCTA) .... HDS
Household Disposable Income .... HDI
Household Earnings and Expenditure .... HEE
Household Economics Research Division [*of ARS, Department of Agriculture*] .... HHE
Household Effects [*Insurance*] .... HHE
Household Employment Association for Reevaluation and Training [*Later, Personnel Resources*] .... HEART
Household Expenditure Survey - Small Area Data [*Australian Bureau of Statistics*] .... HESSAD
Household Finance Corp., Chicago, IL [*Library symbol Library of Congress*] (LCLS) .... ICHFC
Household Financial Services [*Australia*] .... HFS
Household Financing Corp. (CDAI) .... HFC
Household Food Consumption .... HFC
Household Furniture [*Insurance*] .... HHF
Household Goods [*Insurance*] .... HHG
Household Goods/Baggage .... HB
Household Goods Carriers' Bureau (EA) .... HGCB
Household Goods Carriers Bureau .... HHGCB
Household Goods Carriers' Bureau Agent, Arlington VA [*STAC*] .... HGB
Household Goods Forwarders Association of America [*Washington, DC*] .... HGFA
Household Goods Forwarders Association of America (EA) .... HHGFAA
Household Goods Forwarders Tariff Bureau, Washington DC [*STAC*] .... HGF
Household Goods Military and Government Rate Tariff .... HGMGR
Household Goods Transportation Association, Washington DC [*STAC*] .... HGT
Household Hazardous Waste .... HHW
Household Hazardous Waste Project (EA) .... HHWP
Household International, Inc. [*NYSE symbol*] (SPSG) .... HI
Household International, Inc. [*Associated Press*] (SAG) .... HoInt
Household International, Inc. [*Associated Press*] (SAG) .... HoushInt
Household Intl [*NYSE symbol*] (TTSB) .... HI
Household Issuance Record [*Food Stamp Program*] (GFGA) .... HIR
Household Mortgage Corp. (ODBW) .... HMC
Household Pet (WGA) .... HHP
Household Textiles Association [*British*] (BI) .... HTA
Household Tracking Report [*Television ratings*] (NTCM) .... HTR
Householders for Safe Pesticide Use [*Australia*] .... HSPU
Households Using Television [*Television ratings*] .... HUT
Housekeeper (ROG) .... HSEKPR
Housekeeper (BARN) .... hskpr
Housekeeping .... HK
Housekeeping (SSD) .... HKG
Housekeeping (AFM) .... HSKPG
Housekeeping Data Acquisition (MCD) .... HDA
Housekeeping Element (TEL) .... HE
Houseman's Life Assurance [*9th ed.*] [*1977*] [*A publication*] (DLA) .... Hous Life Ass
Houses of Parliament [*British*] .... HP
Housewares .... HSWRS
Housewares and Home Entertainment Department, Canada General Electric Co. Ltd., Barrie, Ontario [*Library symbol National Library of Canada*] (NLC) .... OBCGEH
Housewares Industry News and Topics [*A publication*] (EAAP) .... HINT
Housewife .... HW
Housewife/Mother Career Concept (EDAC) .... HMCC
Housewives Association [*Australia*] .... HA
Housewives Elect Lower Prices [*New York women's lobby group*] .... HELP
Houshld 7.35% cm Dep Pfd [*NYSE symbol*] (TTSB) .... HIPrJ
Housing .... HOUS
Housing .... HOUSG
Housing (AABC) .... HSG
Housing .... HSNG
Housing .... HSNG
Housing Action Trust [*British*] (ECON) .... HAT
Housing Advisory Council [*South Australia*] .... HAC
Housing Aid & Advice Centre [*England*] .... HAAC
Housing Allowance [*Military*] .... HA
Housing and Community Development Act (GFGA) .... HCDA
Housing and Development Administration [*New York City*] .... HDA

Housing and Development Reporter [*Bureau of National Affairs*] [*A publication*] (DLA) .... Hous & Dev Rep
Housing and Development Reporter [*Bureau of National Affairs*] [*A publication*] (DLA) .... Housing & Devel Rep
Housing and Home Finance Agency [*Terminated 1965, functions taken over by HUD*] .... HHFA
Housing and Household Economic Statistics [*US Census Bureau*] .... HHES
Housing and Local Government [*A publication*] (DLA) .... HLG
Housing and Planning References [*A publication*] .... HPR
Housing and Urban Development Acquisition Regulations [*A publication*] (AAGC) .... HUDAR
Housing and Urban Development Act .... HUDA
Housing and Urban Development Association of Canada .... HUDAC
Housing and Urban Development Department [*More commonly, HUD*] (KSC) .... HUDD
Housing and Urban Development [*Department*] **Procurement Regulations** .... HUDPR
Housing and Urban-Rural Recovery Act of 1983 .... HURRA
Housing Assistance [*HUD*] .... HA
Housing Assistance Administration [*HUD*] .... HAA
Housing Assistance Council (EA) .... HAC
Housing Assistance Program .... HAP
Housing Association Grant [*British*] .... HAG
Housing Australia [*A publication*] .... Housing Aust
Housing Authority .... HA
Housing Authority of the City of Los Angeles .... HACLA
Housing Benefit [*British*] .... HB
Housing Census .... HC
Housing Commission [*Australia*] .... HC
Housing Construction and Land Development .... HCLD
Housing Corp. [*British*] (BI) .... HC
Housing Debtline [*Telephone service*] [*British*] .... HD
Housing Density .... HD
Housing Developers Association Ltd. [*British*] (BI) .... HDA
Housing Development Action Grant [*HUD*] .... HODAG
Housing Development and Public Participation Administration [*Turkey*] (ECON) .... HDPPA
Housing Development Corp. (EA) .... HDC
Housing Development Program .... HDP
Housing Division [*Census*] (OICC) .... HOUS
Housing Guaranty .... HG
Housing Improvement .... HI
Housing Improvement Program [*Federal government*] .... HIP
Housing Industry Association .... HIA
Housing Industry Development Council [*Australia*] .... HIDC
Housing Industry Dynamics [*Originator and databank*] (NITA) .... HID
Housing Information Management System .... HIMS
Housing Insurance Fund [*New Deal*] .... HIF
Housing Intelligence Quotient .... HIQ
Housing Investment Trust [*AFL-CIO*] .... HIT
Housing Library, Alberta Housing and Public Works, Edmonton, Alberta [*Library symbol National Library of Canada*] (NLC) .... AEHC
Housing Management [*HUD*] .... HM
Housing of Working Classes Act [*British*] (ROG) .... HWCA
Housing Operation with Training Opportunity [*Office of Economic Opportunity*] .... HOW-TO
Housing Operations Management System [*DoD*] .... HOMES
Housing Opportunity Assistance Program [*Federal Home Loan Bank Board*] .... HOAP
Housing Our People Economically .... HOPE
Housing Pressure Altitude Advance [*Automotive engineering*] .... HPAA
Housing Pressure Cold Advance [*Automotive engineering*] .... HPCA
Housing Production and Management Credit [*HUD*] .... HPMC
Housing Referral Office [*Military*] .... HRO
Housing Referral Service [*Military*] (AABC) .... HRS
Housing Referral Service Record System [*Military*] (DNAB) .... HSGREFSVCSYS
Housing Relocation Assistance Program [*US Army Corps of Engineers*] .... HRAP
Housing Revenue Account [*British*] .... HRA
Housing Scheme [*British*] .... HS
Housing Statistics .... HS
Housing Statistics Users Group (EA) .... HSUG
Housing Study Tours [*British*] .... HST
Housing Unit [*Bureau of the Census*] (GFGA) .... HU
Housing Victoria [*A publication*] .... Housing Vic
Housing Western Australia [*A publication*] .... Housing W Aust
Housman Society (EA) .... HS
Housman's Precedents in Conveyancing [*1861*] [*A publication*] (DLA) .... Hous Pr
Houston [*Texas*] [*Seismograph station code, US Geological Survey*] (SEIS) .... HOU
Houston [*Texas*] [*Airport symbol*] .... HOU
Houston Academy of Medicine for Texas Medical Center, Houston, TX [*OCLC symbol*] (OCLC) .... TMC
Houston Academy of Medicine for Texas Medical Center, Houston, TX [*Library symbol Library of Congress*] (LCLS) .... TxHAM
Houston Academy of Medicine, Houston, TX [*Library symbol Library of Congress*] (LCLS) .... TxHMC
Houston Advanced Research Center .... HARC
Houston Aerospace Language [*NASA*] (NASA) .... HAL
Houston, AK [*FM radio station call letters*] .... KADX
Houston, AK [*FM radio station call letters*] (RBYB) .... KCYT-FM
Houston [*Texas*] **Allen Center** [*Airport symbol*] (OAG) .... JLC
Houston Area League of PC [*Personal Computer*] **Users** .... HAL-PC
Houston Area Library System [*Library network*] .... HALS
Houston Area Oxidant Study [*Environmental Protection Agency*] (GFGA) .... HAOS
Houston [*Texas*] **Astrodome** [*Airport symbol*] (OAG) .... JMA
Houston Automatic Priority Spooling [*Computer science*] (NRCH) .... HAPS
Houston Automatic Spooling Priority System [*Computer science*] .... HASP
Houston Automatic Spooling Processor [*IBM equipment operating system*] (NITA) .... HASP
Houston Baptist University [*Texas*] .... HBU
Houston Baptist University, Houston, TX [*OCLC symbol*] (OCLC) .... TWH
Houston Baptist University, Houston, TX [*Library symbol Library of Congress*] (LCLS) .... TxHBC
Houston Belt & Terminal Railway Co. .... HB & T
Houston Belt & Terminal Railway Co. [*AAR code*] .... HBT
Houston Biotechnology [*AMEX symbol*] (TTSB) .... HBI
Houston Biotechnology, Inc. [*AMEX symbol*] (SPSG) .... HBI
Houston Biotechnology, Inc. [*Associated Press*] (SAG) .... HouB
Houston Biotechnology, Inc. [*Associated Press*] (SAG) .... HousBio
Houston Carnegie Public Library, Houston, MS [*Library symbol Library of Congress*] (LCLS) .... MsHou
Houston Chronicle, Houston, TX [*Library symbol Library of Congress*] (LCLS) .... TxHHC
Houston Community College System, Houston, TX [*Library symbol Library of Congress*] (LCLS) .... TxHC
Houston Community College System, Learning Resource Center, Houston, TX [*OCLC symbol*] (OCLC) .... THC
Houston Cotton Exchange and Board of Trade [*Defunct*] (EA) .... HCEBT
Houston County Court House, Dothan, AL [*Library symbol Library of Congress*] (LCLS) .... ADoC
Houston/Ellington Air Force Base [*Texas*] [*ICAO location identifier*] (ICLI) .... KEFD
Houston - ET [*Texas*] [*Seismograph station code, US Geological Survey Closed*] (SEIS) .... HET
Houston Exploration Co. (The) [*Associated Press*] (SAG) .... HoustEx
Houston Exploration Co. (The) [*NYSE symbol*] (SAG) .... THX
Houston [*Texas*] **Greenway** [*Airport symbol*] (OAG) .... JGP
Houston [*Texas*] **Guest Quarters** [*Airport symbol*] (OAG) .... JGQ
Houston Helicopters, Inc. [*ICAO designator*] (FAAC) .... HHO
Houston, Humble [*Texas*] [*ICAO location identifier*] (ICLI) .... KZHU
Houston Indus [*NYSE symbol*] (TTSB) .... HOU
Houston Industries, Inc. [*NYSE symbol*] (SPSG) .... HOU
Houston Industries, Inc. [*Associated Press*] (SAG) .... HouInd
Houston Industries, Inc. [*Associated Press*] (SAG) .... HoustInd
Houston [*Texas*] **Intercontinental** [*Airport symbol*] (OAG) .... IAH
Houston/Intercontinental [*Texas*] [*ICAO location identifier*] (ICLI) .... KIAH
Houston International Teleport [*Houston, TX*] [*Telecommunications*] (TSSD) .... HIT
Houston Law Review [*A publication*] (ILCA) .... HLR
Houston Lawyer [*A publication*] (DLA) .... Hous Law
Houston Lawyer [*A publication*] (DLA) .... Houston Law
Houston Lighting & Power Co., Houston, TX [*Library symbol Library of Congress*] (LCLS) .... TxHHL
Houston Metals Corp. [*Vancouver Stock Exchange symbol*] .... HML
Houston Mission Control Center [*NASA*] (KSC) .... HMCC
Houston, MO [*AM radio station call letters*] .... KBTC
Houston, MO [*FM radio station call letters*] .... KUNQ
Houston, MS [*AM radio station call letters*] .... WCPC
Houston, MS [*FM radio station call letters*] (RBYB) .... WJZB-FM
Houston, MS [*FM radio station call letters*] .... WSYE
Houston Network Controller [*NASA*] (KSC) .... HNET
Houston Oil and Mineral Corp., Corporate Library, Houston, TX [*Library symbol Library of Congress*] (LCLS) .... TxHHOM
Houston On Line Users Group (NITA) .... HOLUG
Houston [*Texas*] **Park-Ten** [*Airport symbol*] (OAG) .... JPT
Houston Post, Houston, TX [*Library symbol Library of Congress*] (LCLS) .... TxHHP
Houston Public Library, British Columbia [*Library symbol National Library of Canada*] (NLC) .... BH
Houston Public Library, Houston, BC, Canada [*Library symbol*] [*Library of Congress*] (LCLS) .... CaBH
Houston Public Library, Houston, TX [*Library symbol Library of Congress*] (LCLS) .... TxH
Houston Public Library, Houston, TX [*OCLC symbol*] (OCLC) .... TXN
Houston Research Institute, Houston, TX [*Library symbol Library of Congress*] (LCLS) .... TxHRI
Houston Test for Language Development [*Education*] .... HTLD
Houston [*Texas*] **Town/Country** [*Airport symbol*] (OAG) .... JTC
Houston, TX [*Location identifier FAA*] (FAAL) .... AAP
Houston, TX [*Location identifier FAA*] (FAAL) .... BOX
Houston, TX [*Location identifier FAA*] (FAAL) .... CDG
Houston, TX [*Location identifier FAA*] (FAAL) .... DWH
Houston, TX [*Location identifier FAA*] (FAAL) .... EFD
Houston, TX [*Location identifier FAA*] (FAAL) .... HEW
Houston, TX [*Location identifier FAA*] (FAAL) .... HSQ
Houston, TX [*Location identifier FAA*] (FAAL) .... HUB
Houston, TX [*Location identifier FAA*] (FAAL) .... JYV
Houston, TX [*FM radio station call letters*] .... KBXX
Houston, TX [*AM radio station call letters*] .... KCOH
Houston, TX [*Television station call letters*] .... KETH
Houston, TX [*AM radio station call letters*] .... KEYH
Houston, TX [*FM radio station call letters*] .... KHCB
Houston, TX [*FM radio station call letters*] .... KHMX
Houston, TX [*Television station call letters*] .... KHOU
Houston, TX [*Television station call letters*] .... KHTV
Houston, TX [*FM radio station call letters*] .... KIKK-FM
Houston, TX [*AM radio station call letters*] .... KILT
Houston, TX [*FM radio station call letters*] .... KILT-FM
Houston, TX [*AM radio station call letters*] .... KKBQ
Houston, TX [*FM radio station call letters*] .... KKRW
Houston, TX [*AM radio station call letters*] .... KLAT
Houston, TX [*FM radio station call letters*] .... KLDE
Houston, TX [*FM radio station call letters*] .... KLOL

Houston, TX [*FM radio station call letters*] ... KMJQ
Houston, TX [*AM radio station call letters*] ... KNUZ
Houston, TX [*Radio expansion station*] ... KNUZ Exp Stn
Houston, TX [*FM radio station call letters*] ... KODA
Houston, TX [*FM radio station call letters*] ... KPFT
Houston, TX [*AM radio station call letters*] ... KPRC
Houston, TX [*Television station call letters*] ... KPRC-TV
Houston, TX [*FM radio station call letters*] ... KQUE
Houston, TX [*FM radio station call letters*] ... KRBE
Houston, TX [*Television station call letters*] ... KRIV
Houston, TX [*AM radio station call letters*] ... KTRH
Houston, TX [*Television station call letters*] ... KTRK
Houston, TX [*FM radio station call letters*] ... KTRU
Houston, TX [*FM radio station call letters*] ... KTSU
Houston, TX [*Television station call letters*] ... KTXH
Houston, TX [*FM radio station call letters*] ... KUHF
Houston, TX [*Television station call letters*] ... KUHT
Houston, TX [*AM radio station call letters*] ... KXYZ
Houston, TX [*AM radio station call letters*] ... KYOK
Houston, TX [*Television station call letters*] ... KZJL
Houston, TX [*Location identifier FAA*] (FAAL) ... LPV
Houston, TX [*Location identifier FAA*] (FAAL) ... LYD
Houston, TX [*Location identifier FAA*] (FAAL) ... PRQ
Houston, TX [*Location identifier FAA*] (FAAL) ... SGR
Houston, TX [*Location identifier FAA*] (FAAL) ... TMZ
Houston, TX [*Location identifier FAA*] (FAAL) ... ZHU
Houston/William P. Hobby [*Texas*] [*ICAO location identifier*] (ICLI) ... KHOU
Houston-Galveston Area Council Library, Houston, TX [*Library symbol Library of Congress*] (LCLS) ... TxHHG
Houston's Delaware Criminal Cases [*A publication*] (DLA) ... HCr
Houston's Delaware Criminal Cases [*A publication*] (DLA) ... Houst Cr
Houston's Delaware Criminal Cases [*A publication*] (DLA) ... Houst Cr Cas
Houston's Delaware Criminal Cases [*A publication*] (DLA) ... Houst Crim (Del)
Houston's Delaware Reports [*A publication*] (DLA) ... Hou
Houston's Delaware Reports [*A publication*] (DLA) ... Hous
Houston's Delaware Reports [*A publication*] (DLA) ... Houst
Houston's Delaware Supreme Court Reports [*1855-93*] [*A publication*] (DLA) ... Houston
Houston's Law of Stoppage in Transitu [*A publication*] (DLA) ... Houst St Tr
Hoveden's Annals [*A publication*] (DLA) ... Hov Ann
Hoveden's Chronica [*A publication*] (DLA) ... Hoved
Hoven & Co., Bakersfield, CA [*Library symbol Library of Congress*] (LCLS) ... HoC
Hovenden on Frauds [*A publication*] (DLA) ... Hov
Hovenden on Frauds [*A publication*] (DLA) ... Hov Fr
Hovenden's Supplement to Vesey, Jr.'s, English Chancery Reports [*1789-1817*] [*A publication*] (DLA) ... Hov
Hovenden's Supplement to Vesey, Jr.'s, English Chancery Reports [*1789-1817*] [*A publication*] (DLA) ... Hov Sup
Hovenden's Supplement to Vesey, Jr.'s, English Chancery Reports [*1789-1817*] [*A publication*] (DLA) ... Hov Supp
Hovenweep National Monument ... HOVE
Hover (MCD) ... HVR
Hover Agility Rotor (RDA) ... HAR
Hover and Approach Coupler (MCD) ... HAC
Hover and Transition [*Simulator*] ... HOTRAN
Hover Augmentation System ... HAS
Hover Club [*British*] (DBA) ... HCGB
Hover Coupler System (DWSG) ... HCS
Hover Infrared Suppressor Subsystem ... HIRSS
Hover out of Ground Effect ... HOGE
Hoverclub of America (EA) ... HA
Hovercraft [*Military British*] ... HOV
Hovercraft-Helicopter Carrier ... HHC
Hovering ... HVRNG
Hovering in Ground Effect [*Army*] ... HIGE
Hovering Rocket Engine (MCD) ... HRE
Hovering Rocket System [*Army*] ... HRS
Hovering Vehicle Versatile Automatic Control ... HOVVAC
Hover-One-Engine-Inoperative (PDAA) ... HOEI
Hover-Out-of-Ground Environment ... HOGE
Hovik Medical [*Vancouver Stock Exchange symbol*] ... HVK
Hovnanian Enterpr Cl'A' [*AMEX symbol*] (TTSB) ... HOV
Hovnanian Enterprises, Inc. [*AMEX symbol*] (SPSG) ... HOV
Hovnanian Enterprises, Inc. [*Associated Press*] (SAG) ... HovnEn
How [*Phonetic alphabet*] [*World War II*] (DSUE) ... H
How (WGA) ... HW
How Do We Stand ... HDWS
How Do You Receive [*International telex abbreviation*] (WDMC) ... CRV
How I Feel Toward Others [*Psychology*] (EDAC) ... HIFTO
How I See Myself Scale [*Psychology*] (EDAC) ... HISM
How Products are Made [*A publication*] ... HPM
How to Fight/How to Support [*Military*] (MCD) ... HTF/S
How to Fight Manual [*Military*] (MCD) ... HTFM
How to Market to Women [*A publication*] ... HMW
How to Support [*Manuals*] [*Military*] (MCD) ... HTS
How Well Do You Know Yourself [*Psychological testing*] ... HWDYKY
How Will Arrival Report Be Filed Concerning [*Aviation*] (FAAC) ... HIRIV
How You Test is What You Get [*Education*] (AIE) ... HYTIWYG
Howard Aero Manufacturing [*ICAO aircraft manufacturer identifier*] (ICAO) ... HW
Howard Air Force Base [*Panama*] [*ICAO location identifier*] (ICLI) ... MPHO
Howard and Hutchinson's Mississippi Statutes [*A publication*] (DLA) ... How & H St
Howard County Courthouse, Cresco, IA [*Library symbol*] [*Library of Congress*] (LCLS) ... IaCreHC
Howard County Courthouse, Cresco, IA [*Library symbol Library of Congress*] (LCLS) ... IaCrescoCoC
Howard County Junior College [*Texas*] ... HCJC
Howard County Junior College, Big Spring, TX [*Library symbol Library of Congress*] (LCLS) ... TxBsH
Howard County Library, Big Spring, TX [*Library symbol Library of Congress*] (LCLS) ... TxBs
Howard County Library, Big Spring, TX [*Library symbol*] [*Library of Congress*] (LCLS) ... TxBsC
Howard County Library, Simpsonville, MD [*Library symbol Library of Congress*] (LCLS) ... MdSim
Howard County News, Greentown, IN [*Library symbol Library of Congress*] (LCLS) ... InGretN
Howard Hughes Medical Institute ... HHMI
Howard Ink Blot Test [*Psychology*] ... HIBT
Howard Johnson [*Restaurant chain*] [*Slang*] ... HOJO
Howard Journal [*A publication*] (DLA) ... How J
Howard Lake Public Library, Howard Lake, MN [*Library symbol*] [*Library of Congress*] (LCLS) ... MnHl
Howard Lake-Waverly Elementary School, Howard Lake, MN [*Library symbol*] [*Library of Congress*] (LCLS) ... MnHlE
Howard Lake-Waverly High School, Howard Lake, MN [*Library symbol*] [*Library of Congress*] (LCLS) ... MnHlH
Howard Law Review [*A publication*] (DLA) ... How L Rev
Howard League [*An association*] (EAIO) ... HL
Howard League for Penal Reform [*An association British*] (EAIO) ... HLPL
Howard Luke Junior-Senior High School, Fairbanks, AK [*Library symbol*] [*Library of Congress*] (LCLS) ... AkFLJS
Howard Mold Count [*Food quality measure*] ... HMC
Howard Payne College [*Texas*] ... HPC
Howard Payne College, Brownwood, TX [*Library symbol Library of Congress*] (LCLS) ... TxBrdH
Howard, Prim, Rice, Nemerovski, Canady & Pollak, San Francisco, CA [*Library symbol Library of Congress*] (LCLS) ... CSfHP
Howard Public Library, Howard, SD [*Library symbol Library of Congress*] (LCLS) ... SdHow
Howard Research Corp. ... HRC
Howard Robard Hughes [*1905-1976*] [*American businessman*] ... HRH
Howard Ross Library of Management, McGill University, Montreal, Quebec [*Library symbol National Library of Canada*] (NLC) ... QMMSC
Howard T. Herber Middle School, Malverne, NY [*Library symbol*] [*Library of Congress*] (LCLS) ... NMalvHM
Howard Terminal [*Later, HT*] [*AAR code*] ... HOWT
Howard Terminal [*AAR code*] ... HT
Howard University (GAGS) ... Howard U
Howard University, School of Law, Washington, DC [*Library symbol*] [*Library of Congress*] (LCLS) ... DHU-L
Howard University, Washington, DC [*Library symbol Library of Congress OCLC symbol*] (LCLS) ... DHU
Howard Young Medical Center, Woodruff, WI [*Library symbol Library of Congress*] (LCLS) ... WWooH
Howardite, Eucrite, Diogenite [*Meteorite composition*] ... HED
Howard's Irish Chancery Practice [*A publication*] (DLA) ... How C
Howard's Irish Chancery Practice [*A publication*] (DLA) ... How Ch
Howard's Irish Chancery Practice [*A publication*] (DLA) ... How Ch P
Howard's Irish Chancery Practice [*A publication*] (DLA) ... How Ch Pr
Howard's Irish Equity Exchequer Reports [*A publication*] (DLA) ... How EE
Howard's Irish Equity Exchequer Reports [*A publication*] (DLA) ... How Eq Exch
Howard's Irish Property Cases [*1720-73*] [*A publication*] (DLA) ... How Po Cas
Howard's Mississippi Supreme Court Reports [*1834-43*] [*A publication*] (DLA) ... Howard
Howard's New York Appeal Cases [*A publication*] (DLA) ... How A Cas
Howard's New York Appeal Cases [*A publication*] (DLA) ... How App
Howard's New York Court of Appeals Cases [*A publication*] (DLA) ... How App Cas
Howard's New York Court of Appeals Cases [*A publication*] (DLA) ... How App Cases
Howard's New York Court of Appeals Cases [*A publication*] (DLA) ... How Cas
Howard's New York Court of Appeals Cases [*A publication*] (DLA) ... How Ct App Cas
Howard's New York Practice Reports [*A publication*] (DLA) ... How
Howard's New York Practice Reports [*A publication*] (DLA) ... How (NY)
Howard's New York Practice Reports [*A publication*] (DLA) ... How Pr
Howard's New York Practice Reports [*A publication*] (DLA) ... How Pr Rep
Howard's New York Practice Reports [*A publication*] (DLA) ... How Pr Sup C
Howard's New York Practice Reports [*A publication*] (DLA) ... How Prac
Howard's New York Practice Reports [*A publication*] (DLA) ... How Prac (NY)
Howard's New York Practice Reports [*A publication*] (DLA) ... How Prac Rep
Howard's New York Practice Reports [*A publication*] (DLA) ... Howard Pr
Howard's New York Practice Reports [*A publication*] (DLA) ... Howard Pr Rep
Howard's New York Practice Reports [*A publication*] (DLA) ... Howard's Prac Reports
Howard's New York Practice Reports [*A publication*] (DLA) ... Howard's Practice
Howard's New York Practice Reports [*A publication*] (DLA) ... Howard's Spec Term Rep
Howard's New York Practice Reports [*A publication*] (DLA) ... HPR
Howard's New York Practice Reports [*A publication*] (DLA) ... NY Spec Term R
Howard's New York Practice Reports [*A publication*] (DLA) ... NY Spec Term Rep
Howard's New York Practice Reports, New Series [*A publication*] (DLA) ... How NS
Howard's New York Practice Reports, New Series [*A publication*] (DLA) ... How Pr NS
Howard's New York Practice Reports, New Series [*A publication*] (DLA) ... How Prac NS
Howard's New York Practice Reports, New Series [*A publication*] (DLA) ... HPr
Howard's Property Cases [*A publication*] (DLA) ... How Cas

Howard's Property Cases [*A publication*] (DLA) .... How Po Ca
Howard's Reports [*2-8 Mississippi*] [*A publication*] (DLA) .... How
Howard's United States Supreme Court Reports [*42-65 United States*] [*A publication*] (DLA) .... H
Howard's United States Supreme Court Reports [*42-65 United States*] [*A publication*] (DLA) .... How
Howard's United States Supreme Court Reports [*A publication*] (DLA) .... How SC
Howard's United States Supreme Court Reports [*A publication*] (DLA) .... How US
Howard's United States Supreme Court Reports [*A publication*] (DLA) .... Howard Rep
Howden [*D. H.*] **& Co. Ltd.** [*Toronto Stock Exchange symbol*] .... HDH
Howdy Doody Memorabilia Collectors Club (EA) .... HDMCC
Howe, IN [*FM radio station call letters*] .... WHWE
Howe, IN [*FM radio station call letters*] .... WQKO
Howe Memorial Library, Breckenridge, MI [*Library symbol Library of Congress*] (LCLS) .... MiBre
Howe Peak [*Idaho*] [*Seismograph station code, US Geological Survey*] (SEIS) .... HPI
Howe, TX [*FM radio station call letters*] .... KHYI
Howell and Beatty's Reports [*22 Nevada*] [*A publication*] (DLA) .... How & Beat
Howell and Norcross' Reports [*23, 24 Nevada*] [*A publication*] (DLA) .... How & N
Howell and Norcross' Reports [*23, 24 Nevada*] [*A publication*] (DLA) .... How & Nor
Howell Carnegie Library, Howell, MI [*Library symbol Library of Congress*] (LCLS) .... MiHow
Howell Corp. [*Associated Press*] (SAG) .... HowlC
Howell Corp. [*Associated Press*] (SAG) .... HowlCp
Howell Corp. [*NYSE symbol*] (SPSG) .... HWL
Howell Corp. [*NASDAQ symbol*] (SAG) .... HWLL
Howell Corp.$3.50 Cv'A'Pfd [*NASDAQ symbol*] (TTSB) .... HWLLP
Howell Henry Chaldecott Lury [*Advertising agency*] [*British*] .... HHCL
Howell Indus [*AMEX symbol*] (TTSB) .... HOW
Howell Industries, Inc. [*AMEX symbol*] (SPSG) .... HOW
Howell Industries, Inc. [*Associated Press*] (SAG) .... Howl In
Howell, MI [*AM radio station call letters*] .... WHMI
Howell, MI [*FM radio station call letters*] .... WHMI-FM
Howell Microfilms Co., College, MD [*Library symbol Library of Congress*] (LCLS) .... HoM
Howell Road School, Valley Stream, NY [*Library symbol*] [*Library of Congress*] (LCLS) .... NVsHE
Howell-Jolly [*Bodies*] [*Hematology*] .... HJ
Howell-Jolly Bodies [*Hematology*] (DAVI) .... HJB
Howell's Annotated Statutes [*Michigan*] [*A publication*] (DLA) .... How Ann St
Howell's Annotated Statutes [*Michigan*] [*A publication*] (DLA) .... How St
Howell's English State Trials [*1163-1820*] [*A publication*] (DLA) .... How St Tr
Howell's English State Trials [*1163-1820*] [*A publication*] (DLA) .... How State Tr
Howell's English State Trials [*1163-1820*] [*A publication*] (DLA) .... Howell St Tr
Howell's English State Trials [*1163-1820*] [*A publication*] (DLA) .... St Tr
Howell's Nisi Prius Reports [*Michigan*] [*A publication*] (DLA) .... How NP (Mich)
Howell's Nisi Prius Reports [*Michigan*] [*A publication*] (DLA) .... Howell NP
Howell's Probate Practice [*Ontario, Canada*] [*A publication*] (DLA) .... How Prob Pr
Howell's Reports [*22-26 Nevada*] [*A publication*] (DLA) .... How
Howe's Practice [*Massachusetts*] [*A publication*] (DLA) .... Howe Pr
However .... HOWR
However (FAAC) .... HWVR
Howison's Virginia Criminal Trials [*A publication*] (DLA) .... How Cr Tr
Howitt School, Farmingdale, NY [*Library symbol*] [*Library of Congress*] (LCLS) .... NFarHS
Howitzer (KSC) .... HOW
Howitzer [*British military*] (DMA) .... Howr
Howitzer Battery (DNAB) .... HOWBTRY
Howitzer Crew Trainer [*Military*] .... HCT
Howitzer Extended Life Program .... HELP
Howitzer Improvement Program .... HIP
Howitzer Motor Carriage .... HMC
Howitzer Strap-On Trainer [*Military*] (RDA) .... HSOT
Howitzer Test Bed (RDA) .... HTB
Howland, ME [*FM radio station call letters*] .... WSNV
Howler [*Communications; electronics*] .... HW
Howrah [*India*] [*Seismograph station code, US Geological Survey*] (SEIS) .... HOW
Howsoever (ROG) .... HOWSR
Howson on Patents [*A publication*] (DLA) .... How Pat
Howson on Patents [*A publication*] (DLA) .... Hows Pat
Howson on Reissued Patents [*A publication*] (DLA) .... Hows Reis Pat
Howson-Algraphy (DGA) .... H-A
Howtek, Inc. [*NASDAQ symbol*] (SAG) .... HOWT
Howtek Inc. [*NASDAQ symbol*] (TTSB) .... HOWT
Howtek, Inc. [*Associated Press*] (SAG) .... Howtek
How-to-Fight [*Manuals*] [*Military*] .... HTF
Hoxie, AR [*FM radio station call letters*] .... KHOX
Hoxie, AR [*FM radio station call letters*] (RBYB) .... KOCY-FM
Hoxter/Holzminden [*Germany ICAO location identifier*] (ICLI) .... EDVI
Hoy [*Ship's rigging*] (ROG) .... H
Hoy Island [*Scotland*] [*Airport symbol Obsolete*] (OAG) .... HOY
Hoya Society International (EA) .... HSI
Hoyle Resources Ltd. [*Vancouver Stock Exchange symbol*] .... HYL
Hoyre [*Conservative Party*] [*Norway Political party*] (PPE) .... H
Hoyrekvinners Landsforbund [*Women's Organization of the Conservative Party*] [*Norway Political party*] (EAIO) .... HKL
Hoyt Axton Fan Club (EA) .... HAFC
Hoyt Lakes Public Library, Hoyt Lakes, MN [*Library symbol*] [*Library of Congress*] (LCLS) .... MnHol
Hoyt Peak [*Utah*] [*Seismograph station code, US Geological Survey*] (SEIS) .... HTU
Hoyt's Compiled Laws of Arizona [*A publication*] (DLA) .... Hoyt Comp L
H-Plane Tee Junction .... HTJ
HPR, Inc. [*Associated Press*] (SAG) .... HPR
HPR Inc. [*NASDAQ symbol*] (SAG) .... HPRI
HPSC, Inc. [*NASDAQ symbol*] (NQ) .... HPSC
HPY Industry Ltd. [*Vancouver Stock Exchange symbol*] .... HPY
HQ Minerals Ltd. [*Vancouver Stock Exchange symbol*] .... HQ
HR Magazine [*A publication*] .... HR Mag
HR Magazine [*A publication*] (BRI) .... HR Mag
HRB-Singer, Inc., Science Park, State College, PA [*Library symbol Library of Congress*] (LCLS) .... PStcH
HRE Properties [*Formerly, Hubbard Real Estate Investments*] [*Associated Press*] (SAG) .... HRE
HRE Properties [*Formerly, Hubbard Real Estate Investments*] [*NYSE symbol*] (SPSG) .... HRE
HRIN [*Human Resource Information Network*] **Special Reports Library** [*Executive Telecom System, Inc.*] [*Information service or system*] (CRD) .... SRL
Hroswitha Club (EA) .... HC
Hrtz Technology Group [*Associated Press*] (SAG) .... HertzT
Hruska Meat Animal Research Center [*Department of Agriculture*] (GRD) .... MARC
Hrvatska Demokratska Zajednica [*Croatian Democratic Union*] [*Political party*] (EY) .... HDZ
Hrvatska Narodna Banka [*Croatian National Bank*] .... HNB
Hrvatska Narodna Stranka [*Croatian People's Party*] [*Political party*] .... HNS
Hrvatska Pucka Seljacka Stranka [*Croatian People's Peasant Party*] [*Former Yugoslavia*] [*Political party*] (PPE) .... HPSS
Hrvatska Republikanska Seljacka Stranka [*Croatian Republican Peasant Party*] [*Former Yugoslavia*] [*Political party*] (PPE) .... HRSS
Hrvatska Seljacka Stranka [*Croatian Peasant Party*] [*Former Yugoslavia*] [*Political party*] (PPE) .... HSS
Hrvatska Stranka Prava [*Croatian Party of Rights*] [*Former Yugoslavia*] [*Political party*] (PPE) .... HSP
Hrvatski Demokratski Stranka [*Croatian Democratic Party*] [*Political party*] (EY) .... HDS
Hrvatski Narodni Odbor [*Croatian National Resistance*] [*Former Yugoslavia*] (PD) .... HNO
HS Resources [*NYSE symbol*] (TTSB) .... HSE
HS Resources, Inc. [*Associated Press*] (SAG) .... HS Rsc
HS Resources, Inc. [*NYSE symbol*] (SAG) .... HSE
HSBC AmericasAdj Rt cm A Pfd [*NYSE symbol*] (TTSB) .... HSAPrA
HSIA [*Halogenated Solvent Industry Alliance*] **Water Work Group** [*Defunct*] (EA) .... WWG
Hsinchu [*Republic of China*] [*Seismograph station code, US Geological Survey*] (SEIS) .... HSN
Hsinchu Science-Based Industrial Park [*Taiwan*] (ECON) .... HSIP
Hsinking [*Sirkyo, Chang Chun*] [*Republic of China*] [*Seismograph station code, US Geological Survey*] (SEIS) .... HSK
Hsinkong [*Republic of China*] [*Also, SGK*] [*Seismograph station code, US Geological Survey*] (SEIS) .... HSI
Hsinkong [*Republic of China*] [*Also, HSI*] [*Seismograph station code, US Geological Survey*] (SEIS) .... SGK
Hsinying [*Republic of China*] [*Seismograph station code, US Geological Survey*] (SEIS) .... TWK
HSK Minerals Ltd. [*Toronto Stock Exchange symbol*] .... HSK
Htilin [*Myanmar*] [*ICAO location identifier*] (ICLI) .... VBHN
HTL Telemanagement Ltd. [*Burtonsville, MD*] (TSSD) .... HTLT
HTLV-1-Associated Myelopathy [*Medicine*] .... HAM
HTML [*Hypertext Markup Language*] [*Computer science*] [*Telecommunications*] .... h
HTR Industries, Inc. [*Vancouver Stock Exchange symbol*] .... HTR
Huacaraje [*Bolivia*] [*ICAO location identifier*] (ICLI) .... SLHJ
Huachi [*Bolivia*] [*ICAO location identifier*] (ICLI) .... SLHU
Huahine [*French Polynesia*] [*Airport symbol*] (OAG) .... HUH
Huahine/Fare [*French Polynesia*] [*ICAO location identifier*] (ICLI) .... NTTH
Hualalai [*Hawaii*] [*Seismograph station code, US Geological Survey*] (SEIS) .... HUH
Hualian [*China*] [*ICAO location identifier*] (ICLI) .... RCYU
Hualien [*Taiwan*] [*Airport symbol*] (OAG) .... HUN
Hualien [*Republic of China*] [*Seismograph station code, US Geological Survey*] (SEIS) .... TWD
Hualilan [*Argentina*] [*Seismograph station code, US Geological Survey*] (SEIS) .... HLN
Huamachuco [*Peru*] [*ICAO location identifier*] (ICLI) .... SPUC
Huambo [*Angola*] [*ICAO location identifier*] (ICLI) .... FNHU
Huambo [*Angola*] [*Airport symbol*] (OAG) .... NOV
Huanacopampa [*Peru*] [*ICAO location identifier*] (ICLI) .... SPPP
Huancabamba [*Peru*] [*ICAO location identifier*] (ICLI) .... SPAB
Huancayo [*Peru*] [*Seismograph station code, US Geological Survey*] (SEIS) .... HUA
Huancayo [*Peru*] [*ICAO location identifier*] (ICLI) .... SPHU
Huaneng Power International, Inc. [*NYSE symbol*] (SAG) .... HNP
Huaneng Power International, Inc. [*Associated Press*] (SAG) .... HuanPw
Huaneng Power Intl ADS [*NYSE symbol*] (TTSB) .... HNP
Huanuco [*Peru*] [*Airport symbol*] (OAG) .... HUU
Huanuco/Alferez FAP David Figuerao Fernandini [*Peru*] [*ICAO location identifier*] (ICLI) .... SPNC
Huanuco Viejo [*Peru*] [*ICAO location identifier*] (ICLI) .... SPHV
Huaraz [*Peru*] [*Seismograph station code, US Geological Survey*] (SEIS) .... HUZ
Hub Airlines, Inc. [*FAA designator*] (FAAC) .... HUB
Hub End (BARN) .... HE
Hub Group 'A' [*NASDAQ symbol*] (TTSB) .... HUBG
Hub Group, Inc. [*NASDAQ symbol*] (SAG) .... HUBG
Hub Group, Inc. [*Associated Press*] (SAG) .... HubGrp
Hub Management Interface [*Novell, Inc.*] (PCM) .... HMI
Hubback's Evidence of Succession [*A publication*] (DLA) .... Hub Ev
Hubback's Evidence of Succession [*A publication*] (DLA) .... Hub Suc
Hubback's Evidence of Succession [*A publication*] (DLA) .... Hubb Succ
Hubbard Brook Experimental Forest .... HBEF
Hubbard, OH [*Location identifier FAA*] (FAAL) .... HBD
Hubbard, OH [*FM radio station call letters*] .... WRBP

Hubbard Public Library, Hubbard, OH [Library symbol Library of Congress] (LCLS) .... OHu
Hubbard Tank [Medicine] .... HT
Hubbard's Reports [45-51 Maine] [A publication] (DLA) .... Hubb
Hubbard's Reports [45-51 Maine] [A publication] (DLA) .... Hubbard
Hubbel [Harvey], Inc. [Associated Press] (SAG) .... HubelB
Hubbell [Harvey] [NYSE symbol] (SAG) .... HUB
Hubbell, Harvey [Associated Press] (SAG) .... HubbelB
Hubbell [Harvey], Inc. [Associated Press] (SAG) .... HubelA
Hubbell Trading Post National Historic Site .... HUTR
Hubbell's Legal Directory [A publication] (DLA) .... Hub Leg Direc
Hubbert Unit [Petroleum technology] .... HU
Hubble Deep Field [Astronomy] .... HDF
Hubble Space Telescope [Great Observatory Program] [NASA] .... HST
Hubble's Constant [Astronomy] .... H_0
Hubcap Collector's Club (EA) .... HCC
HUBCO, Inc. [NASDAQ symbol] (SAG) .... HUBC
HUBCO, Inc. [Associated Press] (SAG) .... HUBCO
Huber's Praelectiones Juris Civilis [A publication] (DLA) .... Hub Prael JC
Hubert H. Humphrey Cancer Research Center [Boston University] [Research center] (RCD) .... HHH-CRC
Hubert Horatio Humphrey [American politician, 1911-1978] .... HHH
Hucknall [British ICAO location identifier] (ICLI) .... EGNA
HUD [Housing and Urban Development] Clearinghouse Service .... HCS
HUD [Department of Housing and Urban Development] Integrated Information Processing Service (GFGA) .... HIIPS
HUD [Department of Housing and Urban Development] Mortgage Accounting Project .... HUDMAP
HUD [Department of Housing and Urban Development] Teleprocessing Network .... HTN
Huddersfield [Postcode] (ODBW) .... HD
Huddersfield and District Information Service [British] (NITA) .... HADIS
Huddersfield/Crosland Moor [British ICAO location identifier] (ICLI) .... EGND
Huddersfield Healders and Twisters Trade and Friendly Society [A union] [British] (DCTA) .... HHTTFS
Huddersfield Public Libraries, Huddersfield, United Kingdom [Library symbol Library of Congress] (LCLS) .... UkHu
Hudiksvall [Sweden ICAO location identifier] (ICLI) .... ESNH
Hudiksvall [Sweden] [Airport symbol] (OAG) .... HUV
Hudson and Brooke's Irish King's Bench Reports [1827-31] [A publication] (DLA) .... H & B
Hudson and Brooke's Irish King's Bench Reports [1827-31] [A publication] (DLA) .... Hud & B
Hudson and Brooke's Irish King's Bench Reports [1827-31] [A publication] (DLA) .... Hud & Br
Hudson and Brooke's Irish King's Bench Reports [1827-31] [A publication] (DLA) .... Hud & Bro
Hudson & Manhattan [AAR code] .... HDM
Hudson Bay [AAR code] .... HUBA
Hudson Bay [MARC geographic area code Library of Congress] (LCCP) .... n-cnh-
Hudson Bay Mining & Smelting Co. Ltd. [Toronto Stock Exchange symbol] .... HBM
Hudson Bay Mining & Smelting Co. Ltd., Flin Flon, Manitoba [Library symbol National Library of Canada] (NLC) .... MFFHB
Hudson Bay Mining & Smelting Co. Ltd., Flin Flon, MB, Canada [Library symbol Library of Congress] (LCLS) .... CaMFFHB
Hudson Bay, SK [FM radio station call letters] .... CFMQ
Hudson Bay, SK [ICAO location identifier] (ICLI) .... CYHB
Hudson Chartered Bancorp [NASDAQ symbol] (TTSB) .... HCBK
Hudson Chartered Bancorp, Inc. [NASDAQ symbol] (SAG) .... HCBK
Hudson Chartered Bancorp, Inc. [Associated Press] (SAG) .... HudCB
Hudson Chartered Bancorp, Inc. [Associated Press] (SAG) .... HudsnCB
Hudson Falls, NY [FM radio station call letters] .... WENU
Hudson Falls, NY [FM radio station call letters] (RBYB) .... WHTR-FM
Hudson Falls, NY [FM radio station call letters] .... WMJR
Hudson Foods Cl'A' [NYSE symbol] (TTSB) .... HFI
Hudson Foods, Inc. [Associated Press] (SAG) .... HudsFd
Hudson Foods, Inc., Class A [NYSE symbol] (SPSG) .... HFI
Hudson General [AMEX symbol] (TTSB) .... HGC
Hudson General Corp. [AMEX symbol] (SPSG) .... HGC
Hudson General Corp. [Associated Press] (SAG) .... HudGn
Hudson Herald, Hudson, IA [Library symbol Library of Congress] (LCLS) .... IaHudH
Hudson Hope Museum, British Columbia [Library symbol National Library of Canada] (NLC) .... BHHM
Hudson Hope Public Library, British Columbia [Library symbol National Library of Canada] (NLC) .... BHH
Hudson Hotels Corp. [NASDAQ symbol] (SAG) .... HUDS
Hudson Hotels Corp. [Associated Press] (SAG) .... HudsHotl
Hudson, IA [FM radio station call letters] .... KZME
Hudson Institute (EA) .... HI
Hudson Institute, Croton-On-Hudson, NY [Library symbol Library of Congress] (LCLS) .... NCrohH
Hudson Institute, Indianapolis, IN [Library symbol] [Library of Congress] (LCLS) .... InIH
Hudson Library, Highlands, NC [Library symbol Library of Congress] (LCLS) .... NcHs
Hudson, MI [FM radio station call letters] (RBYB) .... WMXE
Hudson, NY [Location identifier FAA] (FAAL) .... PFH
Hudson, NY [AM radio station call letters] .... WHUC
Hudson, NY [FM radio station call letters] .... WHVP
Hudson, NY [FM radio station call letters] (RBYB) .... WTHK
Hudson on Building Contracts [A publication] (DLA) .... HCD
Hudson on Wills [A publication] (DLA) .... Hud Wills
Hudson Public Library, Hudson, CO [Library symbol Library of Congress] (LCLS) .... CoHud

Hudson Public Library, Hudson, IA [Library symbol Library of Congress] (LCLS) .... IaHud
Hudson Public Library, Hudson, MI [Library symbol Library of Congress] (LCLS) .... MiHu
Hudson Public Library, Hudson, NC [Library symbol Library of Congress] (LCLS) .... NcHu
Hudson Public Library, Hudson, WI [Library symbol Library of Congress] (LCLS) .... WHud
Hudson Resources Ltd. [Vancouver Stock Exchange symbol] .... HUD
Hudson Review [A publication] (BRI) .... HR
Hudson River Day Line [AAR code] .... HRDL
Hudson River Region Wine Council (EA) .... HRRWC
Hudson River Sloop Clearwater (EA) .... HRSC
Hudson Star-Observer, Hudson, WI [Library symbol Library of Congress] (LCLS) .... WHudSO
Hudson Technologies Inc. [NASDAQ symbol] (TTSB) .... HDSN
Hudson Technology, Inc. [NASDAQ symbol] (SAG) .... HDSN
Hudson Technology, Inc. [Associated Press] (SAG) .... HudsonTc
Hudson, TX [AM radio station call letters] .... KENR
Hudson Valley (FAAC) .... HDSVLY
Hudson Valley Community College, Troy, NY [Library symbol Library of Congress] (LCLS) .... NTH
Hudson Valley Community College, Troy, NY [OCLC symbol] (OCLC) VXV
Hudson, WI [AM radio station call letters] .... WMIN
Hudson-Essex-Terraplane Owners Club (EA) .... HETOC
Hudson's Bay Company [Facetious translations include "Here before Christ," "Here before Columbus," and "Hungry Belly Co.."] .... HBC
Hudson's Bay Co. [TS, exchange symbol] (TTSB) .... HBC
Hudson's Bay House, Winnipeg, Manitoba [Library symbol National Library of Canada] (NLC) .... MWHB
Hudson's Bay Oil & Gas Co. Ltd., Calgary, AB, Canada [Library symbol Library of Congress] (LCLS) .... CaACHB
Hudson's Executor's Guide [A publication] (DLA) .... Hud Exec
Hudsonville Public Library, Hudsonville, MI [Library symbol Library of Congress] (LCLS) .... MiHudv
Hudspeth, TX [Location identifier FAA] (FAAL) .... HUP
Hue [South Vietnam] [Airport symbol] (AD) .... HUI
Hue, Lightness, and Saturation [Color model] (BYTE) .... HLS
Hue/Phubai [Viet Nam] [ICAO location identifier] (ICLI) .... VVPB
Hue, Saturation, and Value [Color model] (BYTE) .... HSV
Hue/Saturation/Brightness [Color model] [Printer technology] (PCM) .... HSB
Hue, Saturation, Lightness [Color model] (PCM) .... HSL
Hue, Value, Saturation [Graphic arts] (WDMC) .... HVS
Hueckel Molecular Orbital [Atomic physics] .... HMO
Huehuetenango [Guatemala] [ICAO location identifier] (ICLI) .... MGHT
Huer Demokrat Parti [Free Democrat Party] [Turkish Cyprus] [Political party] (EY) .... HDP
Huerfano County Public Library, Walsenburg, CO [Library symbol Library of Congress] (LCLS) .... CoWa
Hue-Saturation-Intensity [Video monitor] (BYTE) .... HSI
Huesca [Spain ICAO location identifier] (ICLI) .... LEHC
Huffy Corp. [NYSE symbol] (SPSG) .... HUF
Huffy Corp. [Associated Press] (SAG) .... Huffy
Hug and Kiss (DAVI) .... X & O
Hug Club (EA) .... HC
Hug-a-Tree and Survive (EA) .... HAT
Hug-a-Tree and Survive (EA) .... HTAS
Hugh O'Brian Youth Foundation (EA) .... HOBY
Hugh O'Brian Youth Foundation Alumni Association (EA) .... HOBYAA
Hughenden [Australia Airport symbol] (OAG) .... HGD
Hughenden Public Library, Alberta [Library symbol National Library of Canada] (NLC) .... AHU
Hughes [Alaska] [Airport symbol] (OAG) .... HUS
Hughes' Abridgment [1663-65] [England] [A publication] (DLA) .... Hugh Abr
Hughes Active RADAR Augmentation System .... HARAS
Hughes Air Corp. [ICAO designator] (ICDA) .... RW
Hughes Air Defense RADAR [Military] .... HADR
Hughes Air West [ICAO designator] (AD) .... Hughes
Hughes Aircraft Co. .... HAC
Hughes Aircraft Co. (Aeronautical Operations) [ICAO designator] (FAAC) .... GMH
Hughes Aircraft Co., Communications Division Library, Airport Site, Inglewood, CA [Library symbol Library of Congress] (LCLS) .... CCuH-C
Hughes Aircraft Co., Culver City, CA [Library symbol Library of Congress] (LCLS) .... CCuH
Hughes Aircraft Co., Ground Systems Library, Fullerton, CA [Library symbol Library of Congress] (LCLS) .... CCuH-G
Hughes Aircraft Co., International Division .... HACI
Hughes Aircraft Co., Marketing Research Library, Airport Site, Inglewood, CA [Library symbol Library of Congress] (LCLS) .... CCuH-M
Hughes Aircraft Co., Research Laboratories Library, Malibu, CA [Library symbol Library of Congress] (LCLS) .... CCuH-R
Hughes Aircraft Co., Santa Barbara Research Center, Santa Barbara, CA [Library symbol Library of Congress] (LCLS) .... CCuH-RC
Hughes Aircraft Co., Semiconductor Division Library, Newport Beach, CA [Library symbol Library of Congress] (LCLS) .... CCuH-S
Hughes Artificial Intelligence Diagnostic Expert [Hughes Aircraft Co.] [Army] .... HAIDEX
Hughes Automated Lunar Observer [NASA] .... HALO
Hughes' Circuit Court Reports [A publication] (DLA) .... Hugh
Hughes' Circuit Court Reports [United States] [A publication] (DLA) .... Hughes (US)
Hughes Communications Division (SAA) .... HCD
Hughes Communications, Inc. [Hughes Aircraft Co.] [Los Angeles, CA] .... HCI
Hughes Communications Services, Inc. (NASA) .... HCSI
Hughes Dynamic Imagery Viewer .... HDIV

Hughes Earth Station [*Aerospace*] .... HES
Hughes' Edition of Van Heythuysen's Equity Draftsman [*A publication*] (DLA) .... Hugh Eq D
Hughes Emergency Locator Pack .... HELP
Hughes' Entries [*1659*] [*A publication*] (DLA) .... Hugh Ent
Hughes' Federal Practice [*A publication*] (DLA) .... Hughes Fed Prac
Hughes Hall Effect Function Generator .... HHEFG
Hughes Hall Effect Generator .... HHEG
Hughes Helicopter Co. .... HHC
Hughes Helicopter, Inc. .... HHI
Hughes Helicopters (MCD) .... HH
Hughes, Hubbard & Reed, New York, NY [*Library symbol*] [*Library of Congress*] (LCLS) .... NNHHR
Hughes Improved Terminal [*Aviation*] (MCD) .... HIT
Hughes, Induced Turbulence .... HIT
Hughes Integrated Classification System [*Hughes Aircraft Co.*] (NITA) .... HI CLASS
Hughes Integrated Synthetic Aperture Radar [*Hughes Electronics*] .... HISAR
Hughes' Kentucky Reports [*A publication*] (DLA) .... Hu
Hughes' Kentucky Reports [*A publication*] (DLA) .... Hugh
Hughes' Kentucky Supreme Court Reports [*1785-1801*] [*A publication*] (DLA) .... Hughes
Hughes Lockless Rifle/Machine Gun (MCD) .... LRMG
Hughes Mining Barge [*Support vessel for Glomar Explorer*] .... HMB
Hughes NADGE [*NATO Air Defense Ground Environment*] **Consortium** .... HUCO
Hughes Network Systems .... HNS
Hughes Night Vision System [*Aviation*] .... HNVS
Hughes on Insurance [*A publication*] (DLA) .... Hugh Ins
Hughes on Wills [*A publication*] (DLA) .... Hugh Wills
Hughes on Writs [*A publication*] (DLA) .... Hugh Wr
Hughes Photoelectric Reader .... HPR
Hughes Post Processor, Surveyor .... HPPS
Hughes' Precedents in Conveyancing [*2nd ed.*] [*1855-57*] [*A publication*] (DLA) .... Hugh Con
Hughes' Precedents in Conveyancing [*2nd ed.*] [*1855-57*] [*A publication*] (DLA) .... Hugh Conv
Hughes' Precedents in Conveyancing [*2nd ed.*] [*1855-57*] [*A publication*] (DLA) .... Hugh Prec
Hughes Research Laboratories [*Hughes Aircraft Co.*] .... HRL
Hughes Research Library, Malibu, CA [*Library symbol Library of Congress*] (LCLS) .... CMalH
Hughes Resources, Inc. [*Associated Press*] (SAG) .... Hughes
Hughes Resources, Inc. [*NASDAQ symbol*] (SAG) .... HURI
Hughes Satellite Communications Terminal .... HSCT
Hughes Satellite Earth Station .... HSES
Hughes Sports Network [*Formerly, SNI*] .... HSN
Hughes Supply [*NYSE symbol*] (TTSB) .... HUG
Hughes Supply, Inc. [*NYSE symbol*] (SPSG) .... HUG
Hughes Supply, Inc. [*Associated Press*] (SAG) .... HughSp
Hughes Technical Services Co. .... HTSC
Hughes Television Network [*New York, NY*] [*Cable-television system*] .... HTN
Hughes Tool Co. .... HTC
Hughes Tool Co. [*Aircraft Division*] [*ICAO aircraft manufacturer identifier*] (ICAO) .... HU
Hughes Tool Co., Houston, TX [*Library symbol Library of Congress*] (LCLS) .... TxHHT
Hughes Transportable Link Terminal .... HTLT
Hughes Unit Malfunction Isolation Detector .... HUMID
Hughes' United States Circuit Court Reports [*A publication*] (DLA) .... Hu
Hughes' United States Circuit Court Reports [*A publication*] (DLA) .... Hughes
Hughesville, PA [*AM radio station call letters*] (RBYB) .... WRKK-AM
Hug-Laf-Luv (EA) .... HUG
Hugo, CO [*Location identifier FAA*] (FAAL) .... HGO
Hugo de Alberico [*Flourished, 1168-71*] [*Authority cited in pre-1607 legal work*] (DSA) .... Hu
Hugo de Alberico [*Flourished, 12th century*] [*Authority cited in pre-1607 legal work*] (DSA) .... Hug
Hugo, OK [*AM radio station call letters*] .... KIHN
Hugo, OK [*FM radio station call letters*] .... KITX
Hugo Public Library, Hugo, CO [*Library symbol Library of Congress*] (LCLS) .... CoHu
Hugo Rizzuto [*ICAO designator*] (FAAC) .... KHX
Hugolinus [*Authority cited in pre-1607 legal work*] (DSA) .... Hugo
Hugolinus de Presbyteris [*Flourished, 1197-1238*] [*Authority cited in pre-1607 legal work*] (DSA) .... H
Hugolinus de Presbyteris [*Flourished, 1197-1238*] [*Authority cited in pre-1607 legal work*] (DSA) .... Hu
Hugolinus de Presbyteris [*Flourished, 1197-1238*] [*Authority cited in pre-1607 legal work*] (DSA) .... Hug
Hugolinus de Presbyteris [*Flourished, 1197-1238*] [*Authority cited in pre-1607 legal work*] (DSA) .... Hugol
Hugoniot Elastic Limit [*Thermodynamics*] .... HEL
Hugo's Histoire du Droit Romain [*A publication*] (DLA) .... Hugo Hist Dr Rom
Hugo's Histoire du Droit Romain [*A publication*] (DLA) .... Hugo Hist du Droit Rom
Hugoton Energy [*NASDAQ symbol*] (TTSB) .... HUGO
Hugoton Energy Corp. [*NASDAQ symbol*] (SAG) .... HUGO
Hugoton Energy Corp. [*Associated Press*] (SAG) .... HugotEn
Hugoton, KS [*Location identifier FAA*] (FAAL) .... HQG
Hugoton, KS [*FM radio station call letters*] .... KFXX
Huguccio [*Deceased, 1210*] [*Authority cited in pre-1607 legal work*] (DSA) .... H
Huguccio [*Deceased, 1210*] [*Authority cited in pre-1607 legal work*] (DSA) .... Hu
Huguccio [*Deceased, 1210*] [*Authority cited in pre-1607 legal work*] (DSA) .... Hug
Huguccio [*Deceased, 1210*] [*Authority cited in pre-1607 legal work*] (DSA) .... Hugu
Huguenot Historical Society (EA) .... HHS
Huguenot, NY [*Location identifier FAA*] (FAAL) .... HUO
Huguenot Society of Great Britain and Ireland (EAIO) .... HSGBI
Huguenot Society of the Founders of Manakin in the Colony of Virginia (EA) .... HSFMCV
Huguenot-Thomas Paine Historical Association (EA) .... HTPHA
Huhhot [*China*] [*ICAO location identifier*] (ICLI) .... ZBHH
Huhner Test [*Gynecology*] .... HT
Huius Anni [*This Year's*] [*Latin*] .... HA
Huius Loci [*Of This Place*] [*Latin*] .... HL
Huius Mensis [*This Month's*] [*Latin*] .... HM
Hukbong Mapagpalaya ng Bayan [*People's Liberation Army, Philippines*] (CINC) .... HUKS
Huldra Silver [*Vancouver Stock Exchange symbol*] .... HDA
Hulk [*Nautical charts*] .... Hk
Hull (ADA) .... H
Hull (DNAB) .... HU
Hull [*England*] [*Airport symbol*] (AD) .... HUY
Hull & Barnsley Railway [*British*] (ROG) .... H & BR
Hull Check Valve .... HCV
Hull Collector Tank .... HCT
Hull Construction Certificate .... HCC
Hull Electronics Unit [*Military*] (RDA) .... HEU
Hull Filter .... HF
Hull Gauge .... HG
Hull Identification Number [*USCG*] (TAG) .... HIN
Hull Maintenance Technician, Chief [*Navy*] (DNAB) .... HTC
Hull Maintenance Technician, Fireman [*Navy*] (DNAB) .... HTFN
Hull Maintenance Technician, Fireman Apprentice [*Navy*] (DNAB) .... HTFA
Hull Maintenance Technician, First Class [*Navy*] (DNAB) HT1
Hull Maintenance Technician, Second Class [*Navy*] (DNAB) HT2
Hull Maintenance Technician, Third Class [*Navy*] (DNAB) HT3
Hull, Mechanical, Electrical [*Ship equipment*] [*Navy*] .... HME
Hull Monitoring System (PDAA) .... HMS
Hull Moulding Release Note .... HMRN
Hull, PQ [*Television station call letters*] .... CFGS
Hull, PQ [*Television station call letters*] .... CHOT
Hull, PQ [*FM radio station call letters*] .... CIMF
Hull, PQ [*Television station call letters*] .... CIVO
Hull Pressure Switch .... HPS
Hull Product Improvement [*Navy*] (CAAL) .... HPI
Hull Propulsion and Auxiliaries [*Navy*] (DNAB) .... HP & A
Hull Seal Section .... HSS
Hull Solenoid Valve .... HSV
Hull Technical Interloan Scheme [*British*] (NITA) .... HULTIS
Hull Technician [*Navy*] .... HT
Hull Test Vehicle [*for submarines*] (MCD) .... HTV
Hull Urban Design Development Laboratory Enterprises, Inc. .... HUDDLE
Hull Vibration Information Retrieval System (PDAA) .... HVIRS
Hullavington [*British ICAO location identifier*] (ICLI) .... EGDV
Hullin (BJA) .... Hul
Hullock on Costs [*A publication*] (DLA) .... Hull Costs
Hull-to-Emitter Correlation [*Navy*] (CAAL) .... HULTEC
Hull-Turret Position Sensor [*Military*] (RDA) .... HTPS
Hulton's Convictions [*1835*] [*A publication*] (DLA) .... Hult Conv
Hultsfred [*Sweden ICAO location identifier*] (ICLI) .... ESSF
Hultsfred [*Sweden*] [*Airport symbol*] (OAG) .... HLF
Hum and Noise (DEN) .... H & N
Hum Modulation Factor (DEN) .... HMF
Humacao [*Puerto Rico*] [*Airport symbol*] (OAG) .... HUC
Humacao, PR [*AM radio station call letters*] .... WALO
Humacao-Palmas [*Puerto Rico*] [*Airport symbol*] (OAG) .... PPD
Humaita [*Brazil*] [*Airport symbol*] (AD) .... HYT
Human (DMAA) .... h
Human .... H
Human .... HMN
Human .... HMN
Human (ROG) .... HUM
Human Access Language [*Computer science*] .... HAL
Human Achaete-Scute Homologue [*Genetics*] .... haSH
Human Action Counselling and Training Unit [*British*] (DI) .... HACTU
Human Adaptability .... HA
Human Albumin Microsphere [*Clinical anesthesiology*] .... HAM
Human Albumin Solution [*Clinical chemistry*] .... HAS
Human Alveolar Macrophage [*Immunology*] .... HAM
Human Amnion (DMAA) .... HAm
Human and Organizational Errors [*Engineering*] .... HOE
Human Anti-Mouse Antibody [*Medicine*] .... HAMA
Human Anti-Murine Antibody [*Medicine*] (DMAA) .... HAMA
Human Antitumor Factor [*Biochemistry*] .... HAF
Human Aortic Endothelial Cell .... HAEC
Human Applications Standard Computer Interface [*Keyboard*] (MCD) .... HASCI
Human Argininosuccinate Lyase [*An enzyme*] .... HA
Human Artificial Chromosome [*Genetics*] .... HAC
Human Asset Accounting (ADA) .... HAA
Human Associative Memory .... HAM
Human Atrial Natriuretic Peptide [*Biochemistry*] .... hANP
Human Basophil Degranulation Test [*Medicine*] (DMAA) .... HBDT
Human Behavior [*National Science Foundation project*] .... HB
Human Behavior and Evolution Society [*An association*] .... HBES
Human Being [*Rorschach*] [*Psychology*] .... H
Human Being [*Slang*] .... HB
Human Being Detail [*Rorschach*] [*Psychology*] .... B
Human Being Movement [*Rorschach*] [*Psychology*] .... M
Human Beta-Globin [*Genetics*] .... HBB
Human Betterment Association for Voluntary Sterilization [*Later, AVS*] (EA) .... HBAVS

Human Biology Council (EA) .... HBC
Human BK Polyomavirus .... HuBKPV
Human B-Lymphotropic Virus .... HBLV
Human Body Counter (IAA) .... HBC
Human Brain Thromboplastin [Clinical chemistry] .... HBT
Human Breast Tumor [Type of cell line] .... HBT
Human Calcitonin [Endocrinology] .... hCt
Human Calcitonin Gene-Related Peptide [Biochemistry] ... hCGRP
Human Cervical Keratinocyte [Cytology] .... HCK
Human Chorionic Gonadotrophin [Endocrinology] .... HCG
Human Chorionic Gonadotropin [A hormone] (PAZ) .... hCG
Human Chorionic Somatomammotrophin [Also, CGP, hcs, HPL]
  [Endocrinology] .... HCS
Human Chorionic Somatomammotropin [Endocrinology] ...... HCSM
Human Chorionic Thyrotrophin [Endocrinology] .... HCT
Human Colony-Forming Unit [Genetics] .... hCFU
Human Component Analysis .... HCA
Human Cord Serum .... HCS
Human Coronavirus .... HCV
Human Cultured Lymphoblastoid [Cells] .... HCL
Human Cultured Lymphoblasts [Medicine] (DMAA) .... HCL
Human Cystic Fibrosis Transmembrane Conductance Regulator
  [Genetics] .... hCFTR
Human Cytomegalovirus .... HCMV
Human Cytomegalovirus .... HMCV
Human Dermal Microvascular Endothelial Cell [Biochemistry] ... HMVEC
Human Development .... HD
Human Development Index [Human Development Report] [United Nations
  Development Program] .... HDI
Human Development Index (EERA) .... HDI
Human Development Institute .... HDI
Human Dimension of Global Environmental Change Programme [The
  International Social Science Council] (ECON) .... HDP
Human Dimensions of Global Change Programme [Canada] (EAIO) ... HDGCP
Human Dimensions of Global Environmental Change (EERA) ... HDGEC
Human Dimensions of Global Environmental Change Program [Marine
  science] (OSRA) .... HDGECP
Human Diploid Cell [Cytology] (DAVI) .... HDC
Human Diploid Cell Strains [Immunology] .... HDCS
Human Diploid Cell Vaccine [For rabies] .... HDCV
Human Diploid Fibroblasts [Cytology] .... HDF
Human Diploid-Cell Rabies Vaccine .... HDRV
Human Disorientation Device .... HDD
Human/Dolphin Foundation (EA) .... H/DF
Human Ecology Action League (EA) .... HEAL
Human Ecology Fund (EA) .... HEF
Human Economy Center (EA) .... HEC
Human EGF [Epidermal Growth Factor] Receptor [Biochemistry] ... HER
Human Embryo Fibroblast [A cell line] .... HEF
Human Embryo Kinase [Medicine] (DMAA) .... HEK
Human Embryonic Intestine Cells [Medicine] (DMAA) ..... HEI
Human Embryonic Kidney [Type of cell line] .... HEK
Human Embryonic Lung [Type of cell line] .... HEL
Human Embryonic Lung Fibroblasts [Biochemistry] .... HELF
Human Embryonic Palatal Mesenchymal [Type of cell line] ... HEPM
Human Embryonic Retinoblast .... HER
Human Embryonic Skin [or Spleen] [Medicine] (DMAA) .... HES
Human Endogenous Retrovirus .... HERV
Human Endometrial Cancer [Oncology] .... HEC
Human Endothelial Cell [Cytology] .... HEC
Human Engineering .... HE
Human Engineering Computer-Aided Design [Air Force] .... HECAD
Human Engineering Criteria for Maintenance and Repair [GE, NASA] .... HECMAR
Human Engineering Criteria for Maintenance and Repair [GE, NASA] ..... HEMAR
Human Engineering Data .... HED
Human Engineering Discrepancy [Nuclear energy] (NRCH) ... HED
Human Engineering Information and Analysis Service [Tufts University] .... HEIAS
Human Engineering Institute .... HEI
Human Engineering Laboratories Battalion Artillery Test [Army] .... HELBAT
Human Engineering Laboratory [Aberdeen Proving Ground, MD] [Army] .... HEL
Human Engineering Laboratory Armor Systems Test [Army] (RDA) ... HELAST
Human Engineering Laboratory Counterair Program [Army] (RDA) ... HELCAP
Human Engineering Laboratory Field Office [Charlottesville, VA]
  [Military] .... HEL-FI
Human Engineering Laboratory Field Office [Charlottesville, VA]
  [Military] .... HEL-FIO
Human Engineering Laboratory Forward Area Supply and Transfer [Army]
  (RDA) .... HELFAST
Human Engineering Laboratory Helicopter Armament Test [Army]
  (RDA) .... HELHAT
Human Engineering Laboratory Infantry System Test [Army] (RDA) .... HELIST
Human Engineering Laboratory Logistics [Systems concept study]
  (MCD) .... HELLOG
Human Engineering Plan .... HEP
Human Engineering Program Plan .... HEPP
Human Engineering Systems Simulator [Air Force] .... HESS
Human Engineering Test Plan .... HETP
Human Enolase [An enzyme] .... HE
Human Enteric [Virology] .... HE
Human Enteric Coronavirus .... HEC
Human Enteric Coronavirus .... HECV
Human Enteric Virus .... HEV
Human Environment Center (EA) .... HEC
Human Epidermal Growth Factor [Biochemistry] .... HEGF
Human Epithelial [Cells] .... HEp

Human Epithelial Cell [Cytology] .... HEC
Human Error Action Report [NASA] (KSC) .... HEAR
Human Error Data Control Center [NASA] (KSC) .... HEDCC
Human Error Probability (IEEE) .... HEP
Human Error Rate .... HER
Human Error Research and Analysis Program (MCD) ...... HERAP
Human Erythrocyte Agglutination Test [Hematology] ...... HEAT
Human Erythrocyte Antigen [Hematology] (DAVI) .... HEA
Human Erythroleukemia [Type of cell line] .... HEL
Human Erythropoietin [Biochemistry] .... huEPO
Human Estrogen Receptor [Endocrinology] .... HER
Human Events [A publication] (BRI) .... HE
Human Exposure Assessment Location [Environmental Protection Agency]
  (GFGA) .... HEAL
Human Exposure Dose [Medicine] .... HE
Human Exposure Dose/Rodent Potency Dose [Toxicology] ... HERP
Human Exposure Modeling (GFGA) .... HEM
Human Factor Division [Air Research and Development Command] [Air
  Force] (AAG) .... HFD
Human Factor Evaluation Data for General Equipment ..... HEDGE
Human Factors .... HF
Human Factors and Operations Research [Army] (MCD) ... HF & OR
Human Factors and Organizational Systems Laboratory [Navy Personnel
  Research and Development Center] [San Diego, CA] ..... HFOSL
Human Factors and Personnel Resources (DNAB) .... HFPR
Human Factors and Safety Engineering (DNAB) .... HFSE
Human Factors Association of Canada .... HFAC
Human Factors Checklists [Navy] .... HFC
Human Factors Design [DMAA] .... HFD
Human Factors Engineering (AABC) .... HFE
Human Factors Engineering Analysis [or Assessment] [Army] (RDA) ... HFEA
Human Factors Engineering Data Guide for Evaluation .... HEDGE
Human Factors Engineering Testing (MCD) .... HFET
Human Factors Evaluation (MCD) .... HFE
Human Factors Group .... HFG
Human Factors in Electronics (MCD) .... HFE
Human Factors Information Center (SAA) .... HFIC
Human Factors Laboratory [University of South Dakota] [National Institute of
  Standards and Technology Research center] .... HFL
Human Factors, Manpower, Personnel, and Training [Military] (RDA) .... HMPT
Human Factors Measurement System .... HFMS
Human Factors Operation Research Laboratory [Air Force] ... HFORL
Human Factors Personnel Selection Inventory [Interpersonal skills and
  attitudes test] .... HFPSI
Human Factors Research .... HFR
Human Factors Society (EA) .... HFS
Human Factors Study .... HFS
Human Factors Test and Evaluation [Military] (MCD) ... HFTE
Human Factors Trade Studies [Navy] .... HFTS
Human Fertilization and Embryology Authority [British] ... HFEA
Human Fetal Diploid Kidney [Type of cell line] .... HFDK
Human Fetal Diploid Lung [Type of cell line] .... HFDL
Human Fetal Lung .... HFL
Human Fetal Spinal Cord .... HFSC
Human Fibroblast [Medicine] (DMAA) .... HF
Human Fibroblast Interferon [Medicine] (DMAA) .... HFI
Human Fibroblast Interferon [Cytology] .... HFIF
Human Fibronectin [Cytochemistry] .... HFN
Human Figures Drawing Test [Education] (EDAC) .... HFD
Human Foamy Virus .... HFV
Human Follicle Stimulating Hormone [Endocrinology] ..... HFSH
Human Follicular Fluid [Physiology] .... hFF
Human Foreskin [Anatomy] .... HF
Human Foreskin Epithelial Cell [Medicine] (DMAA) ..... HFEC
Human Foreskin Fibroblast [A cell line] .... HFF
Human Foreskin Keratinocyte [Cytology] .... HFK
Human Frontier Science Program [An international effort, proposed by Japan
  in 1987] .... HFSP
Human Gamma-Globulin [Endocrinology] .... HGG
Human Gene-Mapping .... HGM
Human Gene-Mapping Library [Database] .... HGML
Human Genetic Mutant Cell Repository .... HGMCR
Human Genome Analyzer [System for analysis of DNA] [Institute of Physical
  and Chemical Research, Japan Genetics] .... HUGA
Human Genome Diversity Project [Genetics] .... HGDP
Human Genome Organization [Genetics] .... HUGO
Human Genome Program [Genetics] .... HGP
Human Genome Sciences .... HGS
Human Genome Sciences [Commercial firm] .... HGS
Human Genome Sciences [NASDAQ symbol] (TTSB) .... HGSI
Human Genome Sciences, Inc. [NASDAQ symbol] (SAG) .... HGSI
Human Genome Sciences, Inc. [Associated Press] (SAG) ... HumGen
Human Glucocorticoid Receptor [Endocrinology] .... HGR
Human Glucose Output [Hematology] (DMAA) .... HGO
Human Gonadotrophin [Endocrinology] .... HG
Human Granulocyte, Colony Stimulation Factor [Hematology] ... HG-CSF
Human Granulocytic Ehrlichiosis [Medicine] .... HGE
Human Granulocytic Ehrlichiosis [Medicine] .... HGE
Human Granulocytic Ehrlichiosis .... HGE
Human Granulocytic Ehrlichiosis .... HGE
Human Growth [Factor] [Endocrinology] (DAVI) .... HG
Human Growth Foundation (EA) .... HGF
Human Growth Hormone [Also, hGH] [Endocrinology] .... HGH
Human Growth Hormone (DOG) .... hGH
Human Growth Hormone Receptor [Genetics] (DOG) .... hGHR

Human Growth-Hormone Releasing Factor [*Biochemistry*] .... HGRF
Human Hair [*Doll collecting*] .... HH
Human Health and the Environment (GNE) .... HHE
Human Health Assessment Group [*Environmental Protection Agency*] .... HHAG
Human Herpes Virus .... HHV
Human Humoral Hypercalcemic Factor [*Oncology*] .... hHCF
Human Hypoxanthine Phosphoribosyltransferase [*An enzyme*] .... HHPRT
Human Immune Deficiency [*Immunology*] .... HID
Human Immune Serum Globulin [*Immunochemistry*] .... HISG
Human Immunodeficiency Virus .... HIV
Human Immunodeficiency Virus Immunoglobulin [*Medicine*] .... HIVIG
Human Immunodeficiency Virus Information Exchange and Support Group (EA) .... HIVIES
Human Immunodeficiency Virus Vaccine [*Medicine*] .... HIVAC
Human Immunodeficiency Virus-1 Protease [*An enzyme*] .... HIV-1 PR
Human Immunodeficiency Virus-Associated Nephropathy [*Medicine*] (DMAA) .... HIVAN
Human Immunoglobulin [*Biochemistry*] (MAE) .... HIg
Human Immunoglobulin A (DOG) .... IgA
Human Individual Metamorphosis [*Flying saucer cult*] .... HIM
Human Infectious Dose [*Medicine*] (DMAA) .... HID
Human Information Processing Group [*Princeton University*] .... HIPG
Human Insulin Receptor [*Biochemistry*] .... HIR
Human Insulin-Degrading Enzyme [*An enzyme*] .... HIDE
Human Integrated Manufacturing .... HIM
Human Intelligence [*Spies, double agents, etc.*] [*CIA*] (AFM) .... HUMINT
Human Interaction .... HI
Human Interest .... HI
Human Interface [*Computer science*] (EERA) .... HI
Human Interferon [*Biochemistry*] .... HuIFN
Human Intestinal Epithelium [*Medicine*] (DMAA) .... HIE
Human Intracisternal A-Type Particle [*Cytology*] .... HIAP
Human Intracisternal Retrovirus [*Medicine*] .... HICRV
Human JC Polyomavirus .... HuJCPV
Human Kidney .... HK
Human Kidney Cell [*Medicine*] (DMAA) .... HKC
Human Lactation Center (EA) .... HLC
Human Lactoferrin [*Biochemistry*] .... HLF
Human Leucocyte Antigen [*Immunology*] .... HLA
Human Leucocyte Elastase [*An enzyme*] .... HLE
Human Leukocyte- [*or Lymphocyte-*] **Antigen** [*System for recognizing foreign tissue*] [*Immunology*] .... HL-A
Human Leukocyte Interferon [*Medicine*] (DMAA) .... HLI
Human Leukocyte Interferon Milieu [*Biochemistry*] (DAVI) .... HUIFM
Human Life Amendment .... HLA
Human Life and Natural Family Planning Foundation [*Defunct*] (EA) .... HLNFPF
Human Life Center (EA) .... HLC
Human Life Foundation (EA) .... HLF
Human Life International (EA) .... HLI
Human Life Protection Society [*Australia*] .... HLPS
Human Lipotropin [*Medicine*] (DMAA) .... HLT
Human Lung Fluid [*Medicine*] .... HLF
Human Luteinizing Hormone [*Endocrinology*] .... HLH
Human Lymphoblastoid Interferon [*Antineoplastic drug*] .... HLBI
Human Lymphocyte Transformation [*Immunology*] (MAE) .... hLT
Human Lymphocyte-Antigen Lymphocyte Defined [*Immunology*] .... HL-A LD
Human Lymphocyte-Antigen Serologically Defined [*Immunology*] .... HL-A SD
Human Lymphoid [*Immunology*] .... HL
Human Machine Interface .... HMI
Human Macrophage Inflammatory Protein [*Immunochemistry*] .... hMIP
Human Mammary Carcinoma Cell Membrane Proteinase [*Medicine*] (DMAA) .... HMCCMP
Human Mammary Epithelial Cell [*Cytology*] .... HMEC
Human Materials Resources Information System (DIT) .... HUMARIS
Human Menopausal Gonadotrophin [*Endocrinology*] .... HMG
Human Menopausal Gonadotropin [*Medicine*] (DMAA) .... hMG
Human Metallothioneine [*Biochemistry*] .... HMT
Human Milk [*Biochemistry*] (MAE) .... HM
Human Milk Lysozyme [*An enzyme*] .... HML
Human Milk Reverse Transcriptase Enzyme [*Medicine*] (DMAA) .... HMRTE
Human Milk Ribonuclease [*An enzyme*] .... HMR
Human Mineralocorticoid Receptor [*Endocrinology*] .... hMR
Human Molar Thyrotropin (MAE) .... hMT
Human Neutrophil Elastase [*An enzyme*] .... HNE
Human Normal Immunoglobulin [*Medicine*] (PDAA) .... HNIG
Human Nutrition [*Dietetics*] (DAVI) .... HN
Human Nutrition Center [*Oklahoma State University*] [*Research center*] (RCD) .... HNC
Human Nutrition Information Service [*Hyattsville, MD*] [*Department of Agriculture*] .... HNIS
Human Nutrition Research and Information Management System [*National Institute of Health*] .... HNRIM
Human Nutrition Research Division [*of ARS, Department of Agriculture*] .... HN
Human Old Tuberculin .... HOT
Human Operator (IAA) .... HO
Human Operator Response Analyser and Timer for Infrequent Occurrences (PDAA) .... HORATIO
Human Operator Simulator (MCD) .... HOS
Human Osteosarcoma [*Medicine*] .... HOS
Human Outreach and Advancement Institute .... HOAI
Human Ovarian Antitumor Serum [*Antineoplastic compound*] .... HOATS
Human Ovarian Cancer [*Cytology*] .... HOC
Human Pancreas Growth Hormone-Releasing Factor [*Immunochemistry*] .... hpGRF
Human Pancreatic Lipase [*An enzyme*] .... HPL
Human Pancreatic Polypeptide [*Endocrinology*] .... HPP
Human Papillomavirus [*or Parvovirus*] (MAE) .... HPA
Human Papillomavirus [*or Parvovirus*] .... HPV
Human Parotid Lysozyme [*An enzyme*] .... HPL
Human Performance Enhancement System [*Engineering*] .... HPES
Human Performance International, Motor Sport Research Group [*Research center*] (RCD) .... HPI-MSRG
Human Performance Laboratory [*Ball State University*] [*Research center*] (RCD) .... HPL
Human Performance Model [*Human Engineering Laboratory*] [*Aberdeen Proving Ground, MD*] (RDA) .... HPM
Human Performance Reliability .... HPR
Human Performance Research Laboratory [*University of Utah*] [*Research center*] (RCD) .... HPRL
Human Peripheral Blood Leukocyte .... HPBL
Human Peripheral Lymphocyte .... HPL
Human Peritoneal Macrophage [*Immunology*] .... HPM
Human Pituitary [*Endocrinology*] (MAE) .... HP
Human Pituitary Follicle-Stimulating Hormone [*Endocrinology*] (MAE) .... hPFSH
Human Pituitary Gonadotrophin [*Endocrinology*] .... HPG
Human Placenta Conditioned Medium .... HPCM
Human Placenta Thyrotrophin [*Endocrinology*] .... HPT
Human Placental Alkaline Phosphatase [*An enzyme*] .... HPAP
Human Placental Alkaline Phosphatase [*An enzyme*] .... HPLAP
Human Placental Lactogen [*Also, CGP, HCS*] [*Endocrinology*] .... HPL
Human Plasma [*Hematology*] .... HP
Human Platelet-Derived Growth Factor [*Biochemistry*] .... HPDGF
Human Platelet-Rich Plasma [*Medicine*] (DMAA) .... HPRP
Human Potential Movement [*Psychotherapy*] .... HPM
Human Potential Research Project [*University of Surrey*] [*British*] (AIE) .... HPRP
Human Powered Flight (DICI) .... HPF
Human Productivity Institute (EA) .... HPI
Human Proenkephalin [*Biochemistry*] .... HPE
Human Progesterone Receptor [*Endocrinology*] .... HPR
Human Prolactin [*Endocrinology*] .... HPR
Human Prolactin [*Endocrinology*] .... HPRL
Human Pronatriodilatin [*Endocrinology*] .... HPND
Human Rabies Immune Globulin [*Immunology*] .... HRIG
Human Read/Machine Read [*Microfilm memory system*] .... HRMR
Human Related Deaths .... HRD
Human Relations Area Files (EA) .... HRAF
Human Relations Area Files, New Haven, CT [*Library symbol Library of Congress*] (LCLS) .... CtNhH
Human Relations Committee [*Military*] (VNW) .... HRC
Human Relations Education (MCD) .... HRE
Human Relations Inventory [*Psychology*] .... HRI
Human Reliability .... HR
Human Reliability Analysis [*Engineering*] .... HRA
Human Reliability Program (AFM) .... HRP
Human Reovirus [*Medicine*] (DMAA) .... HRV
Human Reovirus-Like Agent [*Medicine*] (DMAA) .... HRLA
Human Reovirus-Like Agent (CPH) .... HRVLA
Human Research and Engineering Directorate [*Army*] (RDA) .... HRE
Human Research Facility (SSD) .... HRF
Human Research Need (RDA) .... HRN
Human Resource Accounting (ADA) .... HRA
Human Resource Development (EERA) .... HRD
Human Resource Development Staff .... HRDS
Human Resource Information Network [*Executive Telecom System, Inc.*] [*Information service or system*] (IID) .... HRIN
Human Resource Management Services, Inc. [*Database producer*] (IID) .... HRMS
Human Resource Management System .... HRMS
Human Resource Planning Society [*New York, NY*] (EA) .... HRPS
Human Resources .... HR
Human Resources [*Research*] **and Development Program** .... HRDP
Human Resources Availability (NVT) .... HRAV
Human Resources Center (EA) .... HRC
Human Resources Center, Albertson, NY [*Library symbol Library of Congress*] (LCLS) .... NAlbH
Human Resources Committee .... HRC
Human Resources Council (GNE) .... HRC
Human Resources Data .... HRD
Human Resources Department, Canadian Broadcasting Corp. [*Departement des Ressources Humaines, Societe Radio-Canada*], Ottawa, Ontario [*Library symbol National Library of Canada*] (BIB) .... OOCBH
Human Resources Development .... HRD
Human Resources Development Branch [*Environmental Protection Agency*] (EPA) .... HRDB
Human Resources Development Command [*Military*] (DNAB) .... HRDC
Human Resources Development Group [*British*] .... HRDG
Human Resources Development Institute (EA) .... HRDI
Human Resources Development Project Office [*Military*] (DNAB) .... HRDPO
Human Resources Division [*GAO*] (AAGC) .... HRD
Human Resources Information System (WYGK) .... HRIS
Human Resources Institute [*State University of New York at Buffalo*] [*Research center*] (RCD) .... HRI
Human Resources, Institutions, and Agrarian Reform Division [*FAO*] [*United Nations Italy Information service or system*] (IID) .... ESH
Human Resources Laboratory [*Air Force*] (MCD) .... HRL
Human Resources Management .... HRM
[*British Columbia*] **Human Resources Management Association** (AC) .... HRMA
Human Resources Management Center [*Navy*] .... HRMC
Human Resources Management Center/Detachment [*Navy*] (DNAB) .... HRMC/D
Human Resources Management Detachment [*Navy*] (DNAB) .... HRMD
Human Resources Management Detachment [*Navy*] (DNAB) .... HUMRESMANDET

Human Resources Management Instructor [*Navy*] (DNAB) ... HRMI
Human Resources Management School [*Navy*] (DNAB) ... HRMS
Human Resources Management School [*Navy*] (DNAB) ... HUMRESMANSCOL
Human Resources Management School Detachment [*Navy*] (DNAB) ... HUMRESMANSCOLDET
Human Resources Management Specialist [*Navy*] (NVT) ... HRMS
Human Resources Management Support System [*Navy*] (NVT) ... HRMSS
Human Resources Management Support Team [*Navy*] (DNAB) ... HRMST
Human Resources Need (MCD) ... HRN
Human Resources Network [*Information service or system*] (EA) ... HRN
Human Resources Research Center ... HRRC
Human Resources Research Development Program ... HRRD
Human Resources Research Institute ... HRRI
Human Resources Research Laboratory [*Air Force*] (MCD) ... HRRL
Human Resources Research Office [*NASA*] (AAG) ... HRRO
Human Resources Research Office [*George Washington University*] ... HumRRO
Human Resources Research Organization (EA) ... HumRRO
Human Resources System (MHDB) ... HRS
Human Resources Training ... HRT
Human Resources, Veterans, and Labor [*Office of Management and Budget*] ... HRVL
Human Response Element of DNA [*Endocrinology*] ... HRE
Human Rhinovirus [*Medicine*] ... HRV
Human Rights Advocates (EA) ... HRA
Human Rights Advocates International (EA) ... HRAI
Human Rights and Equal Opportunity Commission (EERA) ... HREOC
Human Rights Campaign Fund (EA) ... HRCF
Human Rights Commission ... HRC
Human Rights Committee ... HRC
Human Rights Committee (EA) ... HRC/CCPR
Human Rights Convention [*Council of Europe*] (DLA) ... HR
Human Rights for Women (EA) ... HRW
Human Rights Group [*Edinburgh, Scotland*] [*Defunct*] (EAIO) ... HRG
Human Rights in the Union of Soviet Socialist Republics [*A publication*] (DLA) ... Hum Rts USSR
Human Rights Information and Documentation System (EA) ... HURIDOCS
Human Rights International (EA) ... HRI
Human Rights International Documentation System (EA) ... HURIDOCS
Human Rights Internet (EA) ... HRI
Human Rights Journal [*A publication*] (DLA) ... Human Rts J
Human Rights Law Journal [*A publication*] (DLA) ... Hum Rts LJ
Human Rights Network [*British*] ... HRN
Human Rights Party [*Ann Arbor, MI*] ... HRP
Human Rights Political Action Committee (EA) ... HRPAC
Human Rights Program [*Harvard University*] [*Research center*] (RCD) ... HRP
Human Rights Protection Party [*Western Samoa*] [*Political party*] (PPW) ... HRPP
Human Rights Quarterly [*A publication*] (DLA) ... Hum Rts Q
Human Rights Resource Center (EAIO) ... HRRC
Human Rights Review [*A publication*] (DLA) ... Human Rts Rev
Human Rights Watch (EA) ... HRW
[*The*] **Human Role in Space** [*Study*] (SSD) ... THURIS
Human Rotaviruses ... HRV
Human Science Research [*Concept car*] [*Automotive engineering*] ... HSR
Human Sciences Advanced Technology Unit [*Longborough University*] [*British*] ... HUSAT
Human Sciences and Advanced Technology Research Centre [*University of Technology*] [*British*] (CB) ... HUSAT
Human Sciences Project [*National Science Foundation*] ... HSP
Human Sciences Research Council [*South Africa*] ... HSRC
Human Seminal Plasma Inhibitor [*Medicine*] (DMAA) ... HSI
Human Serum Albumin ... HSA
Human Serum Prealbumin ... HSP
Human Serum Thymus Factor [*Immunochemistry*] (DAVI) ... HSTF
Human SERVE [*Service Employees Registration and Voter Education*] **Campaign** (EA) ... HSC
Human Service Personnel Association [*Defunct*] (EA) ... HSPA
Human Services Division [*Air Force*] ... HSD
Human Services Forum [*Defunct*] (EA) ... HSF
Human Skeletal Growth Factor ... HSGF
Human Skin Collagen ... HSC
Human Spumaretrovirus ... HSRV
Human Standard Globulin [*Medicine*] ... HSG
Human Subjects Research Review Board [*Army*] (RDA) ... HSRRB
Human Superoxide Dismutase [*An enzyme*] ... HSOD
Human Systems Division [*Brooks Air Force Base, TX*] [*United States Air Force Systems Command*] (GRD) ... HSD
Human Systems Integration ... HSI
Human T-Cell Leukemia Virus Receptor [*Medicine*] (DMAA) ... HTLVR
Human T-Cell Lymphotrophic Virus-Type Three ... HTLV-III
Human T-Cell Lymphotropic [*formerly, Leukemia*] **Virus** ... HTLV
Human T-Cell Lymphotropic Virus Type Three/Lymphadenopathy-Associated Virus ... HTLV-III/LAV
Human Telomeric Repeat-Binding Factor [*Genetics*] ... HTRF
Human Teratocarcinoma [*A cell line*] ... HT
Human Tetanus Antitoxin [*Medicine*] (CPH) ... HTAT
Human Therapeutic Dose ... HTD
Human Thrombin [*Cytochemistry*] ... HT
Human Thymic Epithelial Medium [*Endocrinology*] ... HTEM
Human Thymic Leukemia [*Medicine*] ... HTL
Human Thymus Anti-Serum [*Medicine*] (MAE) ... HUTHAS
Human Thyroid Adenyl Cyclase Stimulator [*Endocrinology*] ... HTACS
Human Thyroid Peroxidase [*An enzyme*] ... HTPO
Human Thyroid Stimulating Hormone [*Also, htsh*] [*Endocrinology*] ... HTSH
Human Thyroid Stimulator [*Endocrinology*] ... HTS
Human Thyroid-Stimulating Immunoglobulin (PDAA) ... HTSI
Human T-Lymphocyte Antigen (DMAA) ... HTLA
Human Transferrin Receptor [*Biochemistry*] ... HTR
Human Transforming Growth Factor [*Biochemistry*] ... HTGF
Human Tumor [*Oncology*] ... HT
Human Tumor Bank [*Medicine*] (DMAA) ... HTB
Human Tumor Clonogenic Assay [*In-vitro testing system*] ... HTCA
Human Tumor Stem Cell Assay [*Oncology*] ... HTSCA
Human Umbilical Vein [*Medicine*] (DMAA) ... HUV
Human Umbilical Vein Endothelial ... HUVE
Human Umbilical Vein Endothelial Cell [*Cytology*] ... HUVEC
Human Upstream Binding Factor [*Genetics*] ... HUBF
Human Urinary Albumin [*Clinical chemistry*] ... HUA
Human Urinary Follicle-Stimulating Hormone [*Medicine*] (DMAA) ... HU-FSH
Human Urinary Kallikrein [*Medicine*] (DMAA) ... HUK
Human Urine [*Medicine*] (DMAA) ... HU
Human Use Review and Regulatory Affairs Office [*Army*] (RDA) ... HURRAO
Human Vaginal Swab [*Medicine*] ... HVS
Human Vascular Endothelial Cells ... HVEC
Human Vascular Permeability Factor [*Biochemistry*] ... HVPF
Human Vascular Smooth Muscle Cell [*Biology*] ... hVSMC
Human Visual System ... HVS
Human X Box Binding Protein [*Genetics*] ... hXBP
Humana, Inc. [*NYSE symbol*] (SPSG) ... HUM
Humana, Inc. [*Associated Press*] (SAG) ... Humana
Human-Aided Machine Translation ... HAMT
Human-Caused Error ... HCE
Human-Computer Interaction [*Computer science*] ... HCI
Human-Computer Interaction Laboratory [*University of Maryland*] (PCM) ... HCIL
Human-Computer Interface (RDA) ... HCI
Human-Controlled Repressor [*Genetics*] (DAVI) ... HCR
Humane Farming Association (EA) ... HFA
Humane Society (ROG) ... HS
Humane Society of Australia ... HSA
Humane Society of the United States (EA) ... HSUS
Humane Society of Tinplate Workers [*A union*] [*British*] ... HSTW
[*The*] **Human-Initiated Equipment Failures** ... THIEF
Human-Initiated Failure ... HIF
Human-Interface Equipment Catalog Item (TEL) ... HECI
Humanist [*A publication*] (BRI) ... Hum
Humanist Party [*Australia Political party*] ... HP
Humanist Student Union of North America ... HSUNA
Humanist Teachers' Association [*British*] ... HTA
Humanistic Organization for Personal Expansion ... HOPE
Humanistisch Instituut voor Ontwikkelings Samenwerking [*Humanistic Institute for Co-Operation with Developing Countries*] [*Hague, Netherlands*] (EAIO) ... HIVOS
[*The*] **Humanitarian** [*A publication*] (ROG) ... H
Humanitarian (ROG) ... HUM
Humanitarian and Civic Assistance (DOMA) ... HCA
Humanitarian Assistance [*Military*] (INF) ... HA
Humanitarian Assistance Group [*Iraq*] ... HAG
Humanitarian Assistance Project for Independent Agricultural Development in Nicaragua [*Defunct*] (EA) ... HAP-NICA
Humanitarian Civic Action ... HCA
Humanitarian Daily Ration [*Army*] (INF) ... HDR
Humanitarian Deferment [*Military*] ... HD
Humanitarian Emergency Evacuation [*Military*] (NVT) ... HUMEVAC
Humanitarian Reasons ... HUMS
Humanitarian Reassignment [*Military*] (AFM) ... HR
Humanitarian Service Medal (MCD) ... HSM
Humanitas International Human Rights Committee (EA) ... HIHRC
Humanite Society (EA) ... HS
Humanities ... HUM
Humanities Association of Canada [*See also ACH*] ... HAC
Humanities Center for Liberal Education ... HCLE
Humanities Research Center, University of Texas, Austin, TX [*Library symbol Library of Congress*] (LCLS) ... TxU-Hu
Humanities Research Council of Canada [*See also CCRH*] [*Later, SSHRCC*] ... HRCC
Humanities, Science, and Conservation [*Environment*] ... HUSICON
Humanization of Labor (IID) ... HOL
Human-Mannose Binding Protein-H ... H-MBP-H
Humanoid Catalog [*Mutual Unidentified Flying Object Network*] ... HUMCAT
Human-Piloted Alien Craft [*Flying saucer*] ... H-PAC
Human-Powered Vehicle ... HPV
Humans Against Rabbit Exploitation (EA) ... HARE
Humansdorp [*South Africa*] [*ICAO location identifier*] (ICLI) ... FAHD
Human-Subjects Review Committee [*Medicine*] (BABM) ... HSRC
HumaScan, Inc. [*Associated Press*] (SAG) ... HmaScn
HumaScan, Inc. [*NASDAQ symbol*] (SAG) ... HMSC
Humber Aviation Ltd. [*British ICAO designator*] (FAAC) ... HUA
Humber College of Applied Arts and Technology, Rexdale, Ontario [*Library symbol National Library of Canada*] (NLC) ... OTHC
Humber College of Applied Arts and Technology, Rexdale, Toronto, ON, Canada [*Library symbol Library of Congress*] (LCLS) ... CaOTHC
Humber Memorial Hospital, Weston, ON, Canada [*Library symbol Library of Congress*] (LCLS) ... CaOTHMH
Humber Memorial Hospital, Weston, Ontario [*Library symbol National Library of Canada*] (NLC) ... OTHMH
Humber Register [*St. Albans, Hertfordshire, England*] (EAIO) ... HR
Humberside [*British ICAO location identifier*] (ICLI) ... EGNJ
Humberside [*County in England*] (WGA) ... Humber
Humberside [*England*] [*Airport symbol*] (OAG) ... HUY
Humbert Humbert [*Character in Vladimir Nabokov's "Lolita"*] ... HH

Humbertus de Bouen [*Authority cited in pre-1607 legal work*]
(DSA) .... Humber de Bou
Humble (ROG) .... HUM
Humble .... Humb
Humble Oil & Refining Co. (MHDW) .... HO & RC
Humble Oil & Refining Co., Engineering Division Library, Baytown, TX
[*Library symbol Library of Congress*] (LCLS) .... TxByH-E
Humble Oil & Refining Co., General Services Library, Houston, TX [*Library
symbol Library of Congress*] (LCLS) .... TxHHO
Humble Oil & Refining Co., Marketing Research Library, Houston, TX
[*Library symbol Library of Congress*] (LCLS) .... TxHHO-E
Humble Oil & Refining Co., Mineral Department Library, Denver, CO
[*Library symbol Library of Congress*] (LCLS) .... CoDHO
Humble Oil & Refining Co., Technical Library, Baytown, TX [*Library symbol
Library of Congress*] (LCLS) .... TxByH
Humble, TX [*AM radio station call letters*] .... KGOL
Humble, TX [*FM radio station call letters*] .... KSBJ
Humbligny [*France*] [*Seismograph station code, US Geological Survey*]
(SEIS) .... HYF
Humboldt Bay Power Plant (NRCH) .... HBPP
Humboldt County Free Library, Eureka, CA [*Library symbol Library of
Congress*] (LCLS) .... CEH
Humboldt County Historical Society, Eureka, CA [*Library symbol*] [*Library of
Congress*] (LCLS) .... CEHi
Humboldt Energy [*Vancouver Stock Exchange symbol*] .... HUT
Humboldt, IA [*FM radio station call letters*] .... KHBT
Humboldt, NE [*Location identifier FAA*] (FAAL) .... HBO
Humboldt State College [*Later, Humboldt State University*] [*California*] .... HSC
Humboldt State College, Arcata, CA [*Library symbol Library of Congress*]
(LCLS) .... CArcHT
Humboldt State College, Arcata, CA [*OCLC symbol*] (OCLC) .... CHU
Humboldt State University (GAGS) .... Cal St U (Humboldt)
Humboldt State University [*Los Angeles, CA*] .... HSU
Humboldt, TN [*Location identifier FAA*] (FAAL) .... HDT
Humboldt, TN [*AM radio station call letters*] .... WHMT
Humboldt, TN [*AM radio station call letters*] (RBYB) .... WIRJ
Humboldt, TN [*FM radio station call letters*] .... WLSZ
Humboldt, TN [*FM radio station call letters*] .... WZDQ
Humbolt County Historical Association, Humbolt, IA [*Library symbol Library
of Congress*] (LCLS) .... IaHumHi
Humbolt Independent, Humbolt, IA [*Library symbol Library of Congress*]
(LCLS) .... IaHumI
Humbolt Public Library, Humbolt, IA [*Library symbol Library of Congress*]
(LCLS) .... IaHum
Humbolt Republican, Humbolt, IA [*Library symbol Library of Congress*]
(LCLS) .... IaHumR
Humbolt School, Humbolt, MN [*Library symbol*] [*Library of Congress*]
(LCLS) .... MnHumS
Hume Society (EA) .... HS
Humera [*Ethiopia*] [*ICAO location identifier*] (ICLI) .... HAHU
Humera [*Ethiopia*] [*Airport symbol*] (OAG) .... HUE
Humeral Plate [*Entomology*] .... HP
Hume's Commentaries on Crimes [*Scotland*] [*A publication*] (DLA) .... Hume Com
Hume's Court of Session Decisions [*1781-1822*] [*Scotland*] [*A publication*]
(DLA) .... Hume
Hume's History of England [*A publication*] (DLA) .... Hume Hist Eng
Humeston New Era, Humeston, IA [*Library symbol Library of Congress*]
(LCLS) .... IaHumeN
Humeston Public Library, Humeston, IA [*Library symbol Library of
Congress*] (LCLS) .... IaHume
Humic Acid [*Organic chemistry*] .... HA
Humic Degradation Matter (DICI) .... HDM
Humic Substances [*Biology*] .... HS
Humid (MSA) .... HMD
Humid Crepidations [*Medicine*] (ROG) .... HC
Humidity .... H
Humidity (NASA) .... HUM
Humidity Control .... HC
Humidity Index .... HI
Humidity Indicator Controller [*Aerospace*] .... HIC
Humidity Monitoring Panel .... HMP
Humidity, Relative .... HR
Humidity Test Procedure .... HTP
Humidity-Electronic Indicator .... HEI
Humidity-Temperature Chart (PDAA) .... HUTCH
Humility of Mary Service (EA) .... HMS
HUMINT [*Human Intelligence*] Information Management System .... HIMS
Hummel Collectors Club (EA) .... HCC
Hummingbird Communication Industries [*Associated Press*] (SAG) .... Humbird
Hummingbird Communication Industries [*NASDAQ symbol*] (SAG) .... HUMCF
Hummingbird Communications [*NASDAQ symbol*] (TTSB) .... HUMCF
Hummingbird Helicopters Maldives (Pvt) Ltd. [*ICAO designator*] (FAAC) ...... HUM
Hummocky Cross-Stratification [*Sedimentology*] .... HCS
Humm-Wadsworth Temperament Scale [*Psychology*] .... HWTS
Humnoke, AR [*FM radio station call letters*] (RBYB) .... KARN
Humor Association (EA) .... HA
Humor Correspondence Club (EA) .... HCC
Humor Stamp Club (EA) .... HSC
Humor Test of Personality [*Psychology*] .... HTP
Humoral Antibody Production [*Medicine*] (DMAA) .... HAP
Humoral Hypercalcemia of Malignancy [*Medicine*] .... HHM
Humorolics Anonymous (EA) .... HA
Humorous (ADA) .... HUM
Humper Dears (EA) .... HD
Humphrey Chimpden Earwicker [*Hero of "Finnegan's Wake"*] .... HCE

Humphrey Hospitality Tr Inc. [*NASDAQ symbol*] (TTSB) .... HUMP
Humphrey Hospitality Trust, Inc. [*NASDAQ symbol*] (SAG) .... HUMP
Humphrey Hospitality Trust, Inc. [*Associated Press*] (SAG) .... Humphry
Humphrey Township Public Library, Parry Sound, Ontario [*Library symbol
National Library of Canada*] (NLC) .... OPSHT
Humphreys College, Stockton, CA [*Library symbol Library of Congress*]
(LCLS) .... CStoH
Humphreys County Library, Belzoni, MS [*Library symbol Library of
Congress*] (LCLS) .... MsBel
Humphreys. District Registry Practice and Procedure [*1977*]
[*A publication*] (ILCA) .... Humph Dist Reg
Humphreys Engineering Center Support Activity (AAGC) .... HECSA
Humphrey's Tennessee Reports [*20-30 Tennessee*] [*A publication*]
(DLA) .... Humph
Humphrey's Tennessee Supreme Court Reports [*1839-51*] [*A publication*]
(DLA) .... Hum
Humphry's Common Precedents in Conveyancing [*2nd ed.*] [*1882*]
[*A publication*] (DLA) .... Humph Prec
Humungous Development Syndrome (EERA) .... HDS
Huna Forschunggesellschaft [*Huna Research Association - HRA*]
[*Switzerland*] (EAIO) .... HF
HUNA International (EA) .... OHI
Huna Research Association [*See also HF*] [*Switzerland*] (EAIO) .... HRA
Hunan Province [*China, Mainland*] [*MARC geographic area code Library of
Congress*] (LCCP) .... a-cc-hu
Hundersingen [*Federal Republic of Germany*] [*Seismograph station code, US
Geological Survey*] (SEIS) .... HUN
Hundred .... H
Hundred (WDMC) .... h
Hundred .... HD
Hundred (MUGU) .... HUN
Hundred .... HUND
Hundred Call Seconds [*Telecommunications*] .... HCS
Hundred Call Seconds Per Hour [*Telecommunications*] (ACRL) ...... HCSPR
Hundred Club of Massachusetts (EA) .... HCM
Hundred Feet .... HF
Hundred Million Club (EA) .... HMC
Hundred Pounds .... HP
Hundred Square Feet (DNAB) .... HS
Hundred Thousand (BARN) .... hunth
Hundred Woman Years [*of exposure*] [*Radiation*] .... HWY
Hundred Yards .... HY
Hundredsbarrow [*England*] .... HUNDREDSB
Hundredth Molar [*Solute concentration by volume*] [*Chemistry*] (DAVI) M/100
Hundredweight (AFM) .... CWT
Hundredweight .... Hdwt
Hungarian [*MARC language code Library of Congress*] (LCCP) .... hun
Hungarian .... HUNGN
Hungarian Association [*Australia*] .... HA
Hungarian Baptist Union of America (EA) .... HBUA
Hungarian Boy Scout Association (EA) .... HBSA
Hungarian Broadcasting [*NASDAQ symbol*] (TTSB) .... HBCO
Hungarian Broadcasting Corp. [*NASDAQ symbol*] (SAG) .... HBCO
Hungarian Broadcasting Corp. [*Associated Press*] (SAG) .... HungB
Hungarian Broadcasting Corp. [*Associated Press*] (SAG) .... HungBd
Hungarian Broadcasting Corp. [*Associated Press*] (SAG) .... HungBrd
Hungarian Broadcasting Wrrt [*NASDAQ symbol*] (TTSB) .... HBCOW
Hungarian Catholic League of America (EA) .... HCLA
Hungarian Catholic Priests' Association in America (EA) .... HCPAA
Hungarian Central Committee for Books and Education (EA) .... HCCBE
Hungarian Committee of Socialist Labor Party [*Defunct*] (EA) ...... HCSLP
Hungarian Congress (EA) .... HC
Hungarian Credit Bank .... HCB
Hungarian Cultural Foundation (EA) .... HCF
Hungarian Data Center [*Defunct*] (EA) .... HDC
Hungarian Democratic Forum [*Political party*] (EY) .... HDF
Hungarian Democratic Union of Romania [*Political party*] (EY) ..... HDUR
Hungarian Economic Information Service (IID) .... ECHO
Hungarian Freedom Fighters Federation USA (EA) .... HFFF
Hungarian Historical Society [*Australia*] .... HHS
Hungarian Horse Association (EA) .... HHA
Hungarian National Sports Federation (EA) .... HNSF
Hungarian Reformed Federation of America (EA) .... HRFA
Hungarian Social Democratic Party [*Political party*] (EY) .... HSDP
Hungarian Socialist Party [*Political party*] (EY) .... HSP
Hungarian Socialist Workers' Party [*Political party*] (PPW) .... HSWP
Hungarian Tel & Cable [*AMEX symbol*] (TTSB) .... HTC
Hungarian Teleconstruct [*NASDAQ symbol*] (SAG) .... HTEL
Hungarian Teleconstruction & Cable Corp. [*Associated Press*] (SAG) ..... HungTelc
Hungarian Telephone and Cable Corp. [*AMEX symbol*] (SAG) .... HTC
Hungarian Telephone & Cable Corp. [*NASDAQ symbol*] (SAG) ..... HTCC
Hungarian Telephone and Cable Corp. [*Associated Press*] (SAG) ... HungTel
Hungarian Tourist Board (EAIO) .... HTB
Hungarian Workers' Party [*Political party*] (PPW) .... HWP
Hungarian-Ukranian Heavy Lift Ltd. [*Hungary ICAO designator*] (FAAC) ...... HUK
Hungary [*MARC geographic area code Library of Congress*] (LCCP) .... e-hu--
Hungary .... H
Hungary [*MARC country of publication code Library of Congress*] (LCCP) .... hu
Hungary [*ANSI two-letter standard code*] (CNC) .... HU
Hungary [*ANSI three-letter standard code*] (CNC) .... HUN
Hungary .... HUNG
Hungary (VRA) .... Hung
Hungary [*License plate code assigned to foreign diplomats in the US*] .... KH
Hungary [*IYRU nationality code*] (IYR) .... M
Hunger Project (EA) .... HP

[*The*] **Hunger Project** (EA) ... THP
Hunger Relief and Development [*An association*] (EA) ... HRAD
Hungerford [*England*] ... HUNGF
Hungry ... HNGRY
Hungry Angry Lonely Tired [*Slogan used by Alcoholics Anonymous members to determine whether their emotions are so out of control that they may be tempted to take a drink*] ... HALT
Hungry Horse [*Montana*] [*Seismograph station code, US Geological Survey*] (SEIS) ... HHM
Hungry Mind Review [*A publication*] (BRI) ... HMR
Hun's New York Appellate Division Supreme Court Reports [*A publication*] (DLA) ... Hun
Hun-Stoffe [*Mustard gas*] [*Formerly, HS Also, HD, HT, M*] ... H
Hun-Stoffe [*US Chemical Corp. symbol for mustard gas*] [*Also, HD, HT, M Later, H*] ... HS
Hunt Clubs Association of Victoria [*Australia*] ... HCAV
Hunt Correctional Center (Louisiana Correctional Institute for Women), St. Gabriel, LA [*Library symbol Library of Congress*] (LCLS) ... LStgH
Hunt, Harold, Jr., Bala-Cynwyd PA [*STAC*] ... HHJ
Hunt High School Library, Wilson, NC [*Library symbol*] [*Library of Congress*] (LCLS) ... NcWilHS
Hunt Manufacturing Co. [*NYSE symbol*] (SPSG) ... HUN
Hunt Manufacturing Co. [*Associated Press*] (SAG) ... HuntMf
Hunt Mfg. [*NYSE symbol*] (TTSB) ... HUN
Hunt Saboteurs Association (EAIO) ... HSA
Hunt [*J.B.*] **Transport Services, Inc.** [*Associated Press*] (SAG) ... HuntJB
Hunt [*J. B.*] **Transport Services, Inc.** [*NASDAQ symbol*] (NQ) ... JBHT
Huntco Inc'A' [*NYSE symbol*] (TTSB) ... HCO
Huntco, Inc. [*NYSE symbol*] (SAG) ... HCO
Huntco, Inc. [*Associated Press*] (SAG) ... Huntco
Huntec Ltd., Toronto, ON, Canada [*Library symbol Library of Congress*] (LCLS) ... CaOTHu
Huntec Ltd., Toronto, Ontario [*Library symbol National Library of Canada*] (NLC) ... OTHU
Hunter ... HNTR
Hunter and Driffield [*System to indicate film emulsion speed*] (BARN) ... HD
Hunter Club of America (EA) ... HCA
Hunter College of The City University of New York (GAGS) ... Hunter C (CUNY)
Hunter College of the City University of New York, New York, NY [*Library symbol Library of Congress*] (LCLS) ... NNHuC
Hunter College of the City University of New York, New York, NY [*OCLC symbol*] (OCLC) ... ZHM
Hunter Development Board [*Australia*] ... HDB
Hunter Education Association (EA) ... HEA
Hunter Institute of Higher Education [*Australia*] ... HIHE
Hunter Institute of Technology [*Australia*] ... HIT
Hunter on Roman Law [*A publication*] (DLA) ... Hunt Rom L
Hunter on Roman Law [*A publication*] (DLA) ... Hunter Rom Law
Hunter Operational Fighter Training Unit [*India*] [*Air Force*] ... HOFTU
Hunter Personnel (United Kingdom) Ltd. ... HP(UK)
Hunter Postgraduate Medical Institute [*Australia*] ... HPGMI
Hunter Stockton Thompson ... HST
Hunter Transport [*Commercial firm British*] ... HT
Hunterdon County Clerk, Flemington, NJ [*Library symbol Library of Congress*] (LCLS) ... NjFICoC
Hunterdon County Democrat, Flemington, NJ [*Library symbol Library of Congress*] (LCLS) ... NjFID
Hunterdon County Historical Society, Flemington, NJ [*Library symbol Library of Congress*] (LCLS) ... NjFIHi
Hunterdon County Library, Flemington, NJ [*Library symbol Library of Congress*] (LCLS) ... NjFIH
Hunterdon Medical Center, Flemington, NJ [*Library symbol Library of Congress*] (LCLS) ... NjFIM
Hunterdon Review, Clinton, NJ [*Library symbol Library of Congress*] (LCLS) ... NjClinH
Hunterdon Review, Whitehouse Station, NJ [*Library symbol Library of Congress*] (LCLS) ... NjWhsH
Hunter-Killer [*Missile*] (MUGU) ... H-K
Hunter-Killer [*Operations against submarines*] [*Navy*] ... HUK
Hunter-Killer Antisubmarine Warfare Exercise [*Navy*] (NVT) ... HUKASWEX
Hunter-Killer Destroyer [*Navy ship symbol*] [*Navy Obsolete*] ... DDK
Hunter-Killer Forces [*Navy*] ... HUKFOR
Hunter-Killer Forces, Atlantic [*Navy*] ... HUKFORLANT
Hunter-Killer Forces, Pacific [*Navy*] ... HUKFORPAC
Hunter-Killer Ship [*Navy symbol Obsolete*] ... CLK
Hunter-Killer Submarine [*Navy*] ... HUKS
Hunter-Leggitt Military Reservation (AABC) ... HLMR
Hunters' Improvement Society [*British*] (BI) ... HIS
Hunter's Landlord and Tenant [*Scotland*] [*A publication*] (DLA) ... HL & T
Hunter's Landlord and Tenant [*Scotland*] [*A publication*] (DLA) ... Hunt L & T
Hunters Point Naval Shipyard ... HPNS
Hunter's Proceeding in a Suit in Equity [*A publication*] (DLA) ... Hunt Suit
Hunter's Proceeding in a Suit in Equity [*A publication*] (DLA) ... Hunter Suit Eq
Hunter's Torrens Cases [*Canada*] [*A publication*] (DLA) ... Hunt
Hunter's Torrens Cases [*Canada A publication*] (DLA) ... Hunt Torrens
Hunter-Schreger Bands [*Tooth structure*] ... HSB
Hunter-Wheel ... HW
Hunting (MSA) ... HNTG
Hunting and Angling With Kids ... HAWK
Hunting and Testing [*Apollo*] [*NASA*] ... HUNTEST
Hunting Aviation Services Ltd. [*British ICAO designator*] (FAAC) ... NVL
Hunting Business Aviation [*British ICAO designator*] (FAAC) ... HUN
Hunting Cargo Airlines Ltd. [*British ICAO designator*] (FAAC) ... ABR
Hunting Engineering Ltd. ... HEL
Hunting Oscillator (IAA) ... HO
Hunting Retriever Club (EA) ... HRC
Hunting Surveys & Consultants [*Commercial firm*] [*British*] ... HSC
Huntingburg, IN [*Location identifier FAA*] (FAAL) ... FNZ
Huntingburg, IN [*Location identifier FAA*] (FAAL) ... HNB
Huntingburg, IN [*FM radio station call letters*] ... WBDC
Huntingburg Public Library, Huntingburg, IN [*Library symbol Library of Congress*] (LCLS) ... InHub
Hunting-Clan Air Transport Ltd. ... HCA
Huntingdon & Broad Top Mountain Railroad & Coal Co. (IIA) ... H & BTM
Huntingdon & Broad Top Railroad ... H & BT
Huntingdon College, Montgomery, AL [*Library symbol Library of Congress*] (LCLS) ... AMH
Huntingdon Gleaner, Quebec [*Library symbol National Library of Canada*] (NLC) ... QSHERH
Huntingdon Gleaner, Sherbrooke, PQ, Canada [*Library symbol Library of Congress*] (LCLS) ... CaQSherH
Huntingdon International Holdings Ltd. [*Associated Press*] (SAG) ... HntgIn
Huntingdon International Holdings Ltd. [*NYSE symbol*] (CTT) ... HTD
Huntingdon Intl ADR [*NYSE symbol*] (TTSB) ... HTD
Huntingdon Militia [*British military*] (DMA) ... HM
Huntingdon, PA [*AM radio station call letters*] ... WHUN
Huntingdon, PA [*FM radio station call letters*] ... WKVR
Huntingdon, PA [*FM radio station call letters*] ... WLAK
Huntingdon, PA [*FM radio station call letters*] ... WQHG
Huntingdon Research Centre Ltd. [*British*] (IRUK) ... HRC
Huntingdon, TN [*AM radio station call letters*] (RBYB) ... WDAP
Huntingdon, TN [*FM radio station call letters*] ... WTKB
Huntingdon, TN [*FM radio station call letters*] ... WVHR
Huntingdon's Trial [*A publication*] (DLA) ... Hunt Tr
Huntingdonshire [*County in England*] ... HUNTS
Huntingtin-Associated Protein [*Biochemistry*] ... HAP
Huntington [*West Virginia*] [*Airport symbol*] (OAG) ... HTS
Huntington & Broad Top Mountain Railroad & Coal Co. (MHDB) ... H & BTM
Huntington Bancshares [*NASDAQ symbol*] (TTSB) ... HBAN
Huntington Bancshares, Inc. [*NASDAQ symbol*] (NQ) ... HBAN
Huntington Bankshares [*Associated Press*] (SAG) ... HuntBnk
Huntington Beach [*California*] ... HB
Huntington Beach, CA [*Television station call letters*] ... KOCE
Huntington Beach Development Engineering [*McDonnell Douglas Aircraft Corp.*] ... HBDE
Huntington Beach Public Library, Huntington Beach, CA [*Library symbol Library of Congress*] (LCLS) ... CHu
Huntington Beach Public Library, Huntington Beach, CA [*OCLC symbol*] (OCLC) ... HBL
Huntington College, Huntington, IN [*OCLC symbol*] (OCLC) ... IHH
Huntington College, Huntington, IN [*Library symbol Library of Congress*] (LCLS) ... InHuH
Huntington County Historical Society, Huntington, IN [*Library symbol Library of Congress*] (LCLS) ... InHuHi
Huntington County Recorder's Office, Huntington, IN [*Library symbol*] [*Library of Congress*] (LCLS) ... InHuCR
Huntington Elementary School, Huntington, NY [*Library symbol*] [*Library of Congress*] (LCLS) ... NHuHE
Huntington Galleries, Huntington, WV [*Library symbol Library of Congress*] (LCLS) ... WvHuG
Huntington Herald-Press, Huntington, IN [*Library symbol Library of Congress*] (LCLS) ... InHuHP
Huntington High School, Huntington, NY [*Library symbol Library of Congress*] (LCLS) ... NHuHS
Huntington Historical Society, Huntington, NY [*Library symbol Library of Congress*] (LCLS) ... NHuHi
Huntington Hospital, Huntington, NY [*Library symbol Library of Congress*] (LCLS) ... NHuH
Huntington, IN [*FM radio station call letters*] ... WEXI
Huntington, IN [*AM radio station call letters*] ... WPDJ
Huntington, IN [*FM radio station call letters*] ... WVSH
Huntington Medical Research Institutes [*Huntington Memorial Hospital*] [*Research center*] (RCD) ... HMRI
Huntington Memorial Hospital, Pasadena, CA [*Library symbol Library of Congress*] (LCLS) ... CPH
Huntington, NY [*AM radio station call letters*] ... WGSM
Huntington Public Library, Huntington, IN [*Library symbol Library of Congress*] (LCLS) ... InHu
Huntington Public Library, Huntington, NY [*Library symbol Library of Congress*] (LCLS) ... NHu
Huntington Public Library, Huntington, NY [*Library symbol*] [*Library of Congress*] (LCLS) ... NHuL
Huntington Resources, Inc. [*Vancouver Stock Exchange symbol*] ... HUN
Huntington Society of Canada ... HSC
Huntington, TX [*FM radio station call letters*] ... KAQU
Huntington, TX [*FM radio station call letters*] (RBYB) ... KYBI-FM
Huntington, WV [*Location identifier FAA*] (FAAL) ... TUU
Huntington, WV [*FM radio station call letters*] ... WEMM
Huntington, WV [*AM radio station call letters*] ... WHRD
Huntington, WV [*AM radio station call letters*] ... WKEE
Huntington, WV [*FM radio station call letters*] ... WKEE-FM
Huntington, WV [*FM radio station call letters*] ... WMUL
Huntington, WV [*Television station call letters*] ... WOWK
Huntington, WV [*Television station call letters*] ... WPBY
Huntington, WV [*AM radio station call letters*] ... WRVC
Huntington, WV [*Television station call letters*] ... WSAZ
Huntington, WV [*FM radio station call letters*] ... WTCR
Huntington, WV [*FM radio station call letters*] ... WVWV
Huntington's Chorea [*Medicine*] ... HC
Huntington's Disease [*Medicine*] ... HD

Huntington's Disease Association [*Australia*] ... HDA
Huntington's Disease Protein [*Biochemistry*] ... HDP
Huntington's Disease Society of America (EA) ... HDSA
Hunt(JB)Transport [*NASDAQ symbol*] (TTSB) ... JBHT
Hunt's Annuity Cases [*England*] [*A publication*] (DLA) ... Hunt
Hunt's Annuity Cases [*England*] [*A publication*] (DLA) ... Hunt Ann Cas
Hunt's Annuity Cases [*England*] [*A publication*] (DLA) ... Hunt Cas
Hunt's Annuity Cases [*England*] [*A publication*] (DLA) ... Hunt's AC
Hunt's Fraudulent Conveyances [*2nd ed.*] [*1897*] [*A publication*] (DLA) ... Hunt Fr Conv
Hunt's Law of Boundaries and Fences [*A publication*] (DLA) ... Hunt Bound
Hunt's Merchants' Magazine [*A publication*] (DLA) ... Hunt Mer Mag
Hunt's Suit in Equity [*A publication*] (DLA) ... Hunt Eq
Huntsman Marine Laboratory [*Canada*] (MSC) ... HML
Huntsville [*Alabama*] [*Airport symbol*] ... HSV
Huntsville, AL [*Location identifier FAA*] (FAAL) ... BFZ
Huntsville, AL [*Location identifier FAA*] (FAAL) ... CWH
Huntsville, AL [*Location identifier FAA*] (FAAL) ... ELL
Huntsville, AL [*Location identifier FAA*] (FAAL) ... HUA
Huntsville, AL [*Location identifier FAA*] (FAAL) ... RQZ
Huntsville, AL [*Television station call letters*] ... WAAY
Huntsville, AL [*Television station call letters*] ... WAFF
Huntsville, AL [*FM radio station call letters*] ... WAHR
Huntsville, AL [*AM radio station call letters*] ... WBHP
Huntsville, AL [*AM radio station call letters*] ... WDJL
Huntsville, AL [*AM radio station call letters*] ... WEUP
Huntsville, AL [*Television station call letters*] ... WHIQ
Huntsville, AL [*Television station call letters*] ... WHNT
Huntsville, AL [*FM radio station call letters*] ... WJAB
Huntsville, AL [*AM radio station call letters*] ... WLOR
Huntsville, AL [*FM radio station call letters*] ... WLRH
Huntsville, AL [*FM radio station call letters*] ... WNDA
Huntsville, AL [*FM radio station call letters*] ... WOCG
Huntsville, AL [*AM radio station call letters*] ... WTKI
Huntsville, AL [*Television station call letters*] ... WZDX
Huntsville, AR [*FM radio station call letters*] ... KREB
Huntsville Association of Technical Societies ... HATS
Huntsville, MO [*FM radio station call letters*] ... KAAM
Huntsville Nuclear Division [*Army Corps of Engineers*] (RDA) ... HND
Huntsville, ON [*FM radio station call letters*] ... CFBK
Huntsville Operations Support Center [*NASA*] (KSC) ... HOSC
Huntsville Public Library, Huntsville, AL [*Library symbol Library of Congress*] (LCLS) ... AH
Huntsville Public Library, Huntsville, MO [*Library symbol Library of Congress*] (LCLS) ... MoHu
Huntsville Public Library, Huntsville, ON, Canada [*Library symbol Library of Congress*] (LCLS) ... CaOHU
Huntsville Public Library, Ontario [*Library symbol National Library of Canada*] (NLC) ... OHU
Huntsville, TX [*FM radio station call letters*] ... KCEY
Huntsville, TX [*AM radio station call letters*] ... KSAM
Huntsville, TX [*FM radio station call letters*] ... KSAM-FM
Huntsville, TX [*FM radio station call letters*] ... KSHU
Huntsville, TX [*FM radio station call letters*] ... KVST
Huntsville, TX [*AM radio station call letters*] ... KYLR
Huntsville, TX [*Location identifier FAA*] (FAAL) ... UTS
Huntway Partners Ltd. [*Associated Press*] (SAG) ... Huntwy
Huntway Partners LP [*NYSE symbol*] (CTT) ... HWY
Hunza Research Society [*Defunct*] (EA) ... HRS
Hupa [*MARC language code Library of Congress*] (LCCP) ... hup
Hupeh Province [*China, Mainland*] [*MARC geographic area code Library of Congress*] (LCCP) ... a-cc-hh
Hupmobile Club (EA) ... HC
Hurbanovo [*Czechoslovakia*] [*Seismograph station code, US Geological Survey*] (SEIS) ... HRB
Hurco Companies [*NASDAQ symbol*] (TTSB) ... HURC
Hurco Companies, Inc. [*NASDAQ symbol*] (NQ) ... HURC
Hurco Companies, Inc. [*Associated Press*] (SAG) ... Hurco
Hurd on Personal Liberty [*A publication*] (DLA) ... Hurd Pers Lib
Hurd on the Laws of Freedom and Bondage in the United States [*A publication*] (DLA) ... Hurd F & B
Hurd on the Writ of Habeas Corpus [*A publication*] (DLA) ... Hurd Hab Cor
Hurdle ... HDLE
Hurd's Illinois Revised Statutes [*A publication*] (DLA) ... Hurd's Rev St
Hurd's Illinois Statutes [*A publication*] (DLA) ... Hurd St
Hurdy-Gurdy Society [*British*] (DBA) ... H-GS
Hurel Dubois [*Societe de Construction des Avions Hurel Dubois*] [*France ICAO aircraft manufacturer identifier*] (ICAO) ... HD
Hurghada [*Egypt*] [*ICAO location identifier*] (ICLI) ... HEGN
Hurghada [*Egypt*] [*Airport symbol*] (OAG) ... HRG
Hurler's Syndrome [*Medicine*] ... HS
Hurley, WI [*AM radio station call letters*] ... WHRY
Hurlingham Polo Association [*Midhurst, Sussex, England*] (EAIO) ... HPA
Hurlock, MD [*FM radio station call letters*] ... WAAI
Hurlstone and Coltman's English Exchequer Reports [*A publication*] (DLA) ... H & C
Hurlstone and Coltman's English Exchequer Reports [*A publication*] (DLA) ... Hurl & C
Hurlstone and Coltman's English Exchequer Reports [*A publication*] (DLA) ... Hurl & Colt
Hurlstone and Coltman's English Exchequer Reports [*A publication*] (DLA) ... Hurl Colt
Hurlstone and Coltman's English Exchequer Reports [*A publication*] (DLA) ... Hurlst & C
Hurlstone and Coltman's English Exchequer Reports [*A publication*] (DLA) ... Hurlst & C (Eng)
Hurlstone and Gordon's English Exchequer Reports [*A publication*] (DLA) ... H & G
Hurlstone and Gordon's English Exchequer Reports [*A publication*] (DLA) ... Hurl & G
Hurlstone and Gordon's English Exchequer Reports [*A publication*] (DLA) ... Hurl & Gord
Hurlstone and Gordon's English Exchequer Reports [*A publication*] (DLA) ... Hurlst & G
Hurlstone and Norman's English Exchequer Reports [*156, 158 English Reprint*] [*A publication*] (DLA) ... H & N
Hurlstone and Norman's English Exchequer Reports [*156, 158 English Reprint*] [*A publication*] (DLA) ... Hurl & N
Hurlstone and Norman's English Exchequer Reports [*156, 158 English Reprint*] [*A publication*] (DLA) ... Hurl & Nor
Hurlstone and Norman's English Exchequer Reports [*156, 158 English Reprint*] [*A publication*] (DLA) ... Hurlst & N (Eng)
Hurlstone and Walmsley's English Exchequer Reports [*1840-41*] [*A publication*] (DLA) ... H & W
Hurlstone and Walmsley's English Exchequer Reports [*1840-41*] [*A publication*] (DLA) ... Hurl & W
Hurlstone and Walmsley's English Exchequer Reports [*1840-41*] [*A publication*] (DLA) ... Hurl & Walm
Hurlstone and Walmsley's English Exchequer Reports [*1840-41*] [*A publication*] (DLA) ... Hurls & W (Eng)
Hurlstone and Walmsley's English Exchequer Reports [*1840-41*] [*A publication*] (DLA) ... Hurlst & W
Hurlstone on Bonds [*A publication*] (DLA) ... Hurl Bonds
Hurn [*England*] [*Airport symbol*] (AD) ... HUR
Huron [*South Dakota*] [*Airport symbol*] (OAG) ... HON
Huron College [*UTLAS symbol*] ... HCL
Huron College, Huron, SD [*Library symbol Library of Congress*] (LCLS) ... SdHuroC
Huron College, Huron, SD [*OCLC symbol*] (OCLC) ... SDU
Huron College, London, ON, Canada [*Library symbol Library of Congress*] (LCLS) ... CaOLH
Huron College, London, Ontario [*Library symbol National Library of Canada*] (NLC) ... OLH
Huron County Board of Education, Clinton, ON, Canada [*Library symbol*] [*Library of Congress*] (LCLS) ... CaOCHCB
Huron County Board of Education, Clinton, Ontario [*Library symbol National Library of Canada*] (NLC) ... OCHCB
Huron County Pioneer Museum, Goderich, Ontario [*Library symbol National Library of Canada*] (BIB) ... OGOHC
Huron County Public Library, Goderich, ON, Canada [*Library symbol Library of Congress*] (LCLS) ... CaOGoH
Huron County Public Library, Goderich, Ontario [*Library symbol National Library of Canada*] (NLC) ... OGOH
Huron Forest Products Joint Venture [*Commercial*] (EERA) ... HFP
Huron Lake-Okabena-Lakefield Junior High School, Okabena, MN [*Library symbol*] [*Library of Congress*] (LCLS) ... MnOkaHJH
Huron, OH [*FM radio station call letters*] (RBYB) ... WKFM
Huron, Ontario, Michigan, Erie, Superior [*Great Lakes*] ... HOMES
Huron Park Secondary School, Woodstock, Ontario [*Library symbol National Library of Canada*] (NLC) ... OWOH
Huron Public Library, Huron, OH [*Library symbol Library of Congress*] (LCLS) ... OHur
Huron Public Library, Huron, SD [*Library symbol Library of Congress*] (LCLS) ... SdHuro
Huron River Fishing Association [*Michigan*] ... HRFA
Huron, SD [*AM radio station call letters*] ... KIJV
Huron, SD [*AM radio station call letters*] ... KOKK
Huron, SD [*Television station call letters*] ... KTTM
Huron, SD [*FM radio station call letters*] ... KZKK
Huron, SD [*FM radio station call letters*] ... KZNC
Huron Valley Library System [*Library network*] ... HVLS
Huron Valley Library System, Ann Arbor, MI [*OCLC symbol*] (OCLC) ... EYH
Huronia Historical Park, Midland, ON, Canada [*Library symbol Library of Congress*] (LCLS) ... CaOMiH
Huronia Historical Park, Midland, Ontario [*Library symbol National Library of Canada*] (NLC) ... OMIH
Huronia Regional Centre, Orillia, ON, Canada [*Library symbol*] [*Library of Congress*] (LCLS) ... CaOOrHUR
Huronia Regional Centre, Orillia, Ontario [*Library symbol National Library of Canada*] (NLC) ... OOHUR
Hurrian (BJA) ... Hurr
Hurricane [*Alaska*] [*Seismograph station code, US Geological Survey*] (SEIS) ... HUR
Hurricane ... HURCN
Hurricane Analog ... HURRAN
Hurricane Deck ... HD
Hurricane Evacuation (NVT) ... HUREVAC
Hurricane Evacuation (DNAB) ... HURR-EVAC
Hurricane Hollow [*Tennessee*] [*Seismograph station code, US Geological Survey Closed*] (SEIS) ... HHT
Hurricane Microseismic Research Problem [*Aerology*] ... HMRP
Hurricane Operations Center (AFM) ... HOC
Hurricane Report ... HUREP
Hurricane Rescue Craft, Inc. [*Vancouver Stock Exchange symbol*] ... HCR
Hurricane Research Division [*Miami, FL*] [*National Oceanic and Atmospheric Administration*] (GRD) ... HRD
Hurricane Research Service [*Information service or system*] (IID) ... HRS
Hurricane Supersonic Research Site ... HSRS
Hurricane Warning Center [*Marine science*] (OSRA) ... HWC

Hurricane Warning Center (USDC) .... HWC
Hurricane Warning Office [*National Weather Service*] .... HWO
Hurricane Warning System (WDAA) .... HWS
Hurricane, WV [*AM radio station call letters*] (RBYB) .... WOKU-AM
Hurricane, WV [*AM radio station call letters*] .... WVKV
Hurst/Olds Club of America (EA) .... HOCA
Hurt on Duty .... HOD
Hurt, Richardson, Garner, Law Library, Atlanta, GA [*Library symbol*] [*Library of Congress*] (LCLS) .... GAHu
Hurter and Driffield [*Chemists for whom H & D Curve and H & D Speed System are named*] (DEN) .... H & D
Hurth [*Germany ICAO location identifier*] (ICLI) .... EDCH
Husavik [*Iceland*] [*ICAO location identifier*] (ICLI) .... BIHU
Husavik [*Iceland*] [*Airport symbol*] (OAG) .... HZK
Husband .... H
Husband [*Legal shorthand*] (LWAP) .... HUS
Husband .... husb
Husband (ROG) .... HUSBD
Husband [*Citizens band radio slang*] .... XYM
Husband and Wife (DLA) .... HUSB & W
Husband Doesn't Know (IIA) .... HDK
Husband on Married Women [*A publication*] (DLA) .... Husb Mar Wom
Husbandman .... HUSBN
Husbandry .... HUSB
Husband's Forensic Medicine [*A publication*] (DLA) .... Husb For Med
Husbands of Airline Pilots .... HALP
Hush House Tiedown .... HHT
Husiki [*Japan*] [*Seismograph station code, US Geological Survey*] (SEIS) .... HKI
Husky Oil Operation, Calgary, AB, Canada [*Library symbol Library of Congress*] (LCLS) .... CaACHO
Husky Oil Operations, Calgary, Alberta [*Library symbol National Library of Canada*] (NLC) .... ACHO
Huslia [*Alaska*] [*Airport symbol*] (OAG) .... HSL
Hussar [*British military*] (DMA) .... Hr
Hussar Municipal Library, Alberta [*Library symbol National Library of Canada*] (NLC) .... AHUM
Hussar Municipal Library, Hussar, AB, Canada [*Library symbol Library of Congress*] (LCLS) .... CaAHuM
Hussars [*Military unit*] [*British*] .... H
Hussars [*Military unit*] [*British*] .... HRS
Hussars [*Military unit*] [*British*] (ROG) .... HUSS
Husson College, Bangor, ME [*OCLC symbol*] (OCLC) .... HCL
Husson College, Bangor, ME [*Library symbol Library of Congress*] (LCLS) .... MeBaH
Hustings Court [*As in Virginia*] [*Legal term*] (DLA) .... Hust
Huston on Land Titles in Pennsylvania [*A publication*] (DLA) .... Hust L Tit
Huston-Tillotson College [*Austin, TX*] .... HTC
Huston-Tillotson College, Austin, TX [*OCLC symbol*] (OCLC) .... HTC
Huston-Tillotson College, Austin, TX [*Library symbol Library of Congress*] (LCLS) .... TxAuHT
Husum [*Germany ICAO location identifier*] (ICLI) .... EDNH
Hutch Apparel Ltd. [*Vancouver Stock Exchange symbol*] .... HAP
Hutcheson's Justice of the Peace [*A publication*] (DLA) .... Hutch JP
Hutcheson's Reports [*81-84 Alabama*] [*A publication*] (DLA) .... Hutch
Hutchinson [*Kansas*] [*Airport symbol*] (OAG) .... HUT
[*The*] **Hutchinson & Northern Railway Co.** [*AAR code*] .... HN
Hutchinson Board of Trade Association (EA) .... HBTA
Hutchinson Cablevision [*British*] .... HCV
Hutchinson Community Junior College, Hutchinson, KS [*Library symbol Library of Congress*] (LCLS) .... KHuC
Hutchinson County Library, Borger, TX [*Library symbol Library of Congress*] (LCLS) .... TxBor
Hutchinson Junior College [*Kansas*] .... HJC
Hutchinson, KS [*FM radio station call letters*] .... KHCC
Hutchinson, KS [*FM radio station call letters*] .... KHUT
Hutchinson, KS [*Television station call letters*] .... KPTS
Hutchinson, KS [*AM radio station call letters*] .... KWBW
Hutchinson, KS [*Television station call letters*] .... KWCH
Hutchinson, KS [*FM radio station call letters*] .... KZSN
Hutchinson Middle School, Hutchinson, MN [*Library symbol*] [*Library of Congress*] (LCLS) .... MnHuHMS
Hutchinson, MN [*Location identifier FAA*] (FAAL) .... HCD
Hutchinson, MN [*AM radio station call letters*] .... KDUZ
Hutchinson on Carriers [*A publication*] (DLA) .... Hutch Car
Hutchinson on Carriers [*A publication*] (DLA) .... Hutch Carr
Hutchinson Public Library, Hutchinson, KS [*Library symbol Library of Congress*] (LCLS) .... KHu
Hutchinson Public Library, Hutchinson, MN [*Library symbol*] [*Library of Congress*] (LCLS) .... MnHu
Hutchinson Senior High School, Hutchinson, MN [*Library symbol*] [*Library of Congress*] (LCLS) .... MnHuSH
Hutchinson Technology [*NASDAQ symbol*] (TTSB) .... HTCH
Hutchinson Technology, Inc. [*NASDAQ symbol*] (NQ) .... HTCH
Hutchinson Technology, Inc. [*Associated Press*] (SAG) .... HutchT
Hutchinson-Gilford Progeria Syndrome [*Medicine*] (DMAA) .... HGPS
Hutchinson's Code [*Mississippi*] [*A publication*] (DLA) .... Hutch Code
Hutchison House Museum, Peterborough Historical Society, Ontario [*Library symbol National Library of Canada*] (BIB) .... OPETHS
Hutchison, MN [*FM radio station call letters*] .... KKJR
Hutsonville Community Unit, School District 1, Hutsonville, IL [*Library symbol Library of Congress*] (LCLS) .... IHuSD
Hutt Adaptation of the Bender-Gestalt Test .... HABGT
Hutterian Brethren [*Hutterian Society of Brothers*] [*Acronym is based on former name,*] (EA) .... HSB
Hutto, TX [*FM radio station call letters*] (RBYB) .... KIKY
Hutto, TX [*FM radio station call letters*] (RBYB) .... KIKY-FM
Hutton Wood's Decrees in Tithe Cases [*England*] [*A publication*] (DLA) .... Wood H
Hutton's Courts of Requests [*A publication*] (DLA) .... Hut Ct Req
Hutton's Courts of Requests [*A publication*] (DLA) .... Hutt Ct Req
Hutton's English Common Pleas Reports [*1612-39*] [*A publication*] (DLA) .... Hut
Hutton's English Common Pleas Reports [*1612-39*] [*A publication*] (DLA) .... Hutt
Hutton's English Common Pleas Reports [*1612-39*] [*A publication*] (DLA) .... Hutton
Hutton's English Common Pleas Reports [*1612-39*] [*A publication*] (DLA) .... Hutton (Eng)
Huwei [*China*] [*ICAO location identifier*] (ICLI) .... RCSC
Huxley Institute for Biosocial Research (EA) .... HIBR
Huxley's Second Book of Judgments [*1675*] [*England*] [*A publication*] (DLA) .... Hux Judg
Hvide Marine Inc. [*NASDAQ symbol*] (SAG) .... HMAR
Hvide Marine, Inc. [*Associated Press*] (SAG) .... HvideM
H.W. Wilson Co., Bronx, NY [*Library symbol*] [*Library of Congress*] (LCLS) .... NNHWW
Hwalien [*Karenko*] [*Republic of China*] [*Seismograph station code, US Geological Survey*] (SEIS) .... HWA
Hwange/Hwange National Park [*Zimbabwe*] [*ICAO location identifier*] (ICLI) .... FVWN
Hwange National Park [*Zimbabwe*] [*Airport symbol*] (OAG) .... WKM
HWWA-Dossiers [*Society for Business Information*] [*Information service or system*] (IID) .... HADOSS
Hy & Zel's, Inc. [*Toronto Stock Exchange symbol*] .... HZI
Hyack Air Ltd. [*Canada ICAO designator*] (FAAC) .... HYA
Hyakuri [*Japan ICAO location identifier*] (ICLI) .... RJAH
Hyal Pharmaceutical [*NASDAQ symbol*] (TTSB) .... HYALF
Hyal Pharmaceutical Corp. [*NASDAQ symbol*] (SAG) .... HYAL
Hyal Pharmaceutical Corp. [*Associated Press*] (SAG) .... HyalPhr
Hyaline [*Cytology*] (DAVI) .... HYLO
Hyaline Casts [*Clinical chemistry*] .... HC
Hyaline Membrane Disease [*Later, RDS*] [*Medicine*] .... HMD
Hyaline-Vascular [*Oncology*] .... HV
Hyaluronic Acid [*Biochemistry*] .... HA
Hyaluronidase Unit for Semen (MAE) .... HUS
Hyannis [*Massachusetts*] [*Airport symbol*] (OAG) .... HYA
Hyannis Air Service, Inc. [*ICAO designator*] (FAAC) .... KAP
Hyannis Aviation [*ICAO designator*] (AD) .... YB
Hyannis, MA [*Location identifier FAA*] (FAAL) .... BCU
Hyannis, MA [*Location identifier FAA*] (FAAL) .... BZC
Hyannis, MA [*FM radio station call letters*] .... WCOD
Hyannis, MA [*FM radio station call letters*] .... WPXC
Hyannis Public Library, Hyannis, MA [*Library symbol Library of Congress*] (LCLS) .... MHy
Hyborean Legion (EA) .... HL
Hybrid (MSA) .... HYB
Hybrid Analog Logic Language (MCD) .... HYBALL
Hybrid Analog-Switching Attitude Control System for Space Vehicles .... HYACS
Hybrid Antibody [*Immunology*] .... HAB
Hybrid Arithmetic Unit .... HAU
Hybrid Assigned Nematic/Liquid Crystal Display (TEL) .... HAN/LCD
Hybrid AUTODIN Red Patch System (MCD) .... HARPS
Hybrid Automated Reliability Predictor .... HARP
Hybrid Circuit [*Electronics*] (IAA) .... HC
Hybrid Combustion Process (RDA) .... HCP
Hybrid Composit Structures for Crashworthy Body Shells and Safe Transportation Structures .... HYCOTRANS
Hybrid Computation and Simulation (SSD) .... HCS
Hybrid Computation and Simulation Laboratory .... HCSL
Hybrid Computational Science Laboratory .... HCSL
Hybrid Computer [*for processing both analog and digital data*] (NASA) .... HC
Hybrid Computer Block Oriented Compiler (IAA) .... HYBLOC
Hybrid Computer Interface (MHDB) .... HCI
Hybrid Computer Link .... HYCOL
Hybrid Computer Translator .... HYCOTRAN
Hybrid Data Acquisition System .... HDAS
Hybrid Development System .... HDS
Hybrid Device Controller (NASA) .... HDC
Hybrid Digital-Analog Computing [*System*] [*Satellite*] .... HYDAC
Hybrid Digital-Analog Pulse Time (MCD) .... HYDAP
Hybrid Digital-Analog Pulse Time .... HYDAPT
Hybrid Electromagnetic [*Wave*] .... HEM
Hybrid Electromagnetic Antenna Coupler .... HEMAC
Hybrid Electromagnetic Wave (MSA) .... HEMW
Hybrid Engineering Test Model (NASA) .... HETM
Hybrid Fabrication Procedure (MCD) .... HFP
Hybrid Fiber and Coax [*Cable technology*] (PCM) .... HFC
Hybrid Fiber/Coax (ACRL) .... HFC
Hybrid Fiber-Coax [*Telecommunications*] .... HFC
Hybrid Geotempered Envelope [*Architecture*] .... HGE
Hybrid Index [*Botany*] .... HI
Hybrid Infrared Source .... HIS
Hybrid Integrated Circuit .... HIC
Hybrid Integrated Network [*Bell System*] [*Telecommunications*] .... HIN
Hybrid Language Assembler .... HYLA
Hybrid Large Scale Integrated (PDAA) .... HLSI
Hybrid Lens Guide (PDAA) .... HLG
Hybrid LORAN .... HYLO
Hybrid Microcircuit (NASA) .... HMC
Hybrid Microelectronic Device (MSA) .... HYBMED
Hybrid Modular Redundancy .... HMR
Hybrid Mosaic on Stacked Silicon [*Materials science*] .... HYMOSS
Hybrid Multiplexer [*Telecommunications*] .... HMUX

Hybrid Operating Program [Computer science] (IEEE) .... HOP
Hybrid Orbital Rehybridization Method [Atomic physics] .... HORM
Hybrid Phase-Locked Loop (PDAA) .... HPLL
Hybrid Programmable Attitude Control Electronics [NASA] .... HYPACE
Hybrid Programming Language [Computer science] .... HPL
Hybrid Propulsion System .... HPS
Hybrid Pulse Code Modulation (PDAA) .... HPCM
Hybrid Receiver Circuit .... HRC
Hybrid Ring Control [Computer science] (TNIG) .... HRC
Hybrid Simulation System .... HSS
Hybrid Single Particle Lagrangian Integrated Trajectories [Model] [Marine science] (OSRA) .... HY-SPLIT
Hybrid Single Particle Lagrangian Integrated Trajectories [Model] (USDC) .... HY-SPLIT
Hybrid Superconducting Magnetic Bearing .... HSMB
Hybrid Switching [Telecommunications] .... HS
Hybrid Systems [Telecommunications] (NITA) .... HYB
Hybrid Tea [Roses] (ROG) .... HT
Hybrid Technology Computer .... HTC
Hybrid Test Set .... HTS
Hybrid Test Vehicle [Gasoline and electric motor] .... HTV
Hybrid Thermal Treatment System [Incinerator] [IT Corp.] (RDA) .... HTTS
Hybrid Translator (IAA) .... HYTRAN
Hybrid Unidigit Pulse Code Modulation (IAA) .... HUPCM
Hybrid with Advanced Yield for Surveillance [Strategic Defense Initiative] .... HYWAYS
Hybrid-Electric Vehicle .... HEV
Hybridization Protection Assay [Analytical biochemistry] .... HPA
Hybridoma [Cytology] .... HB
Hybridoma Bank (DMAA) .... HB
Hybridoma/Plasmacytome Growth Factor [Biochemistry] .... HPGF
Hybridon, Inc. [NASDAQ symbol] (SAG) .... HYBN
Hybridon Inc. [NASDAQ symbol] (TTSB) .... HYBN
Hybridon, Inc. [Associated Press] (SAG) .... Hybridon
Hyconeechee Regional Library, Yanceyville, NC [Library symbol Library of Congress] (LCLS) .... NcY
Hycor Biomedical [NASDAQ symbol] (TTSB) .... HYBD
Hycor Biomedical, Inc. [NASDAQ symbol] (NQ) .... HYBD
Hycor Biomedical, Inc. [Associated Press] (SAG) .... Hycor
Hycor Biomedical Wrrt [NASDAQ symbol] (TTSB) .... HYBDW
Hycroft Resources & Development Corp. [Vancouver Stock Exchange symbol] .... HYR
Hydaburg [Alaska] [Airport symbol] (OAG) .... HYG
Hydatid Disease [Medicine] (MAE) .... HD
Hydatidiform Mole [Gynecology] .... HM
Hyde Athletic Indus'A' [NASDAQ symbol] (TTSB) .... HYDEA
Hyde Athletic Indus'B' [NASDAQ symbol] (TTSB) .... HYDEB
Hyde Athletic Industries, Inc. [NASDAQ symbol] (NQ) .... HYDE
Hyde Athletic Industries, Inc. [Associated Press] (SAG) .... HydeAt
Hyde Athletic Industries, Inc. [Associated Press] (SAG) .... HydeAth
Hyde County Library, Highmore, SD [Library symbol Library of Congress] (LCLS) .... SdHig
Hyde Park [Utah] [Seismograph station code, US Geological Survey] (SEIS) .... HDU
Hyde Park, NY [FM radio station call letters] .... WCZX
Hyde Park, NY [AM radio station call letters] .... WHVW
Hyde Stud Bloodstock Investments Ltd. [British] .... HSBI
Hyden, KY [FM radio station call letters] .... WZQQ
Hyderabad [Pakistan] [Airport symbol] (OAG) .... HDD
Hyderabad [India] [Seismograph station code, US Geological Survey] (SEIS) .... HYB
Hyderabad [India] [Geomagnetic observatory code] .... HYB
Hyderabad [India] [Airport symbol] (OAG) .... HYD
Hyderabad [Pakistan] [ICAO location identifier] (ICLI) .... OPKD
Hyderabad [India] [ICAO location identifier] (ICLI) .... VOHY
Hyderabad Army Service Corps [British military] (DMA) .... HASC
Hyderabad Contingent [British military] (DMA) .... HC
Hyderabad Contingent Artillery [British military] (DMA) .... HCA
Hyderabad Contingent Cavalry [British military] (DMA) .... HCC
Hyderabad Contingent Infantry [India] [Army] .... HCI
Hyderabad Contingent Lancers [British military] (DMA) .... HCL
Hyderabad Imperial Service Troops [British military] (DMA) .... HIST
Hyderabad State Force [British military] (DMA) .... HSF
Hyderabad Volunteer Rifles [British military] (DMA) .... HVR
Hyde's Bengal Reports [India] [A publication] (DLA) .... Hyde
Hydra Explorations Ltd. [Toronto Stock Exchange symbol] .... HYX
Hydra Medium [Culture medium] .... HM
Hydragogue [Cathartic] [Pharmacy] (ROG) .... HYDR
Hydragyrum Mercury Medium Arc Length and Iodide [An arc lamp] (WDMC) .... HMI
Hydralazine [Antihypertensive drug] .... HD
Hydralazine [Antihypertensive agent] .... HZ
Hydralazine, Hydrochlorothiazide, and Reserpine (DMAA) .... HHR
Hydramatic [Automotive engineering] .... HYDRA
Hydranencephaly [Medicine] (AAMN) .... HC
Hydrangea Ringspot Virus [Plant pathology] .... HRSV
Hydrant .... H
Hydrant (ADA) .... HY
Hydrant (MSA) .... HYD
Hydrant (ADA) .... HYDT
Hydrant Refuelling System (IAA) .... HRS
Hydrargyrum [Mercury] [Chemical element] .... Hg
Hydrargyrum [Mercury] [Pharmacy] .... HYD
Hydrargyrum [Mercury] [Pharmacy] .... HYDRARG
Hydrated .... HYD
Hydrated (MSA) .... HYDTD

Hydrated Antimony Pentaoxide [Inorganic chemistry] .... HAP
Hydrated Textured Soy Flour .... HTSF
Hydraulic (AAG) .... HYD
Hydraulic (MSA) .... HYDR
Hydraulic .... HYDRLC
Hydraulic Actuation System (MCD) .... HAS
Hydraulic Actuator Assembly Container .... HAAC
Hydraulic Actuator Test Fixture .... HATF
Hydraulic Adjustable Speed .... HAS
Hydraulic [or Hydrologic] Analysis .... HYDRA
Hydraulic and Boatyard Association [A union] [British] .... HBA
Hydraulic and Optical Repair Vehicle (PDAA) .... HORV
Hydraulic Association of Great Britain (BI) .... HA
Hydraulic Bench Press .... HBP
Hydraulic Bore-Hole Mining [Coal] .... HBM
Hydraulic Brake Hose [Automotive engineering] .... HBH
Hydraulic Cement Concrete .... HCC
Hydraulic Charging Unit (NASA) .... HCU
Hydraulic Check Valve (GFGA) .... HCV
Hydraulic Clean (MSA) .... HC
Hydraulic Components Test .... HCT
Hydraulic Control Unit [Nuclear energy] (NRCH) .... HCU
Hydraulic Control Valve .... HCV
Hydraulic Core Mock-Up [Nuclear energy] (NRCH) .... HCM
Hydraulic Coupling (DCTA) .... HC
Hydraulic Coupling [of a ship] (DS) .... HYC
Hydraulic Coupling Unit [Automotive engineering] .... HCU
Hydraulic Cycling Unit (AFM) .... HCU
Hydraulic Cylinder .... HC
Hydraulic Electronic Unit Injector [Fuel system] [Automotive engineering] .... HEUI
Hydraulic End Design System [Computer-aided design] .... HEDS
Hydraulic, Engine, Fuel, Oxygen, Electrical (DNAB) .... HEFOE
Hydraulic Engineering Information Analysis Center [Army Corps of Engineers] (IID) .... HEIAC
Hydraulic Engineering Laboratory [University of California at Berkeley] .... HEL
Hydraulic Flight Control (NASA) .... HFC
Hydraulic Flight Control Test (NASA) .... HFCT
Hydraulic Fluid Filter .... HFF
Hydraulic Fluid Index (PDAA) .... HFI
Hydraulic Fluid Replenishment Equipment .... HFRE
Hydraulic Grade Elevations (NRCH) .... HGE
Hydraulic Hand Pump .... HHP
Hydraulic Horse Power .... HHP
Hydraulic Institute (EA) .... HI
Hydraulic Lash Adjuster [Automotive engine design] .... HLA
Hydraulic Maintenance Panel (AAG) .... HMP
Hydraulic Management Unit .... HMU
Hydraulic Mean Depth .... HMD
Hydraulic Mock-Up .... HMU
Hydraulic Multiplate Active Traction Intelligent Control [Automotive engineering] .... HYMATIC
Hydraulic Oil .... HYDO
Hydraulic Oil Power Module (DNAB) .... HOPM
Hydraulic Operator (NRCH) .... HO
Hydraulic Overspeed Control [Mechanical power transmission] .... HOC
Hydraulic Package Container .... HPC
Hydraulic Package Pressure Test Set .... HPPTS
Hydraulic Package Servovalve Actuator .... HPSA
Hydraulic Package Storage Container .... HPSC
Hydraulic Performance Analysis Facility (MCD) .... HPAF
Hydraulic Piston Corer .... HPC
Hydraulic Pneumatic Area (AAG) .... HPA
Hydraulic Pneumatic Panel (AAG) .... HPP
Hydraulic Power Control Relay Box .... HPCRB
Hydraulic Power Section [Later, HPU] (AAG) .... HPS
Hydraulic Power Supply .... HPS
Hydraulic Power Supply Kit .... HPSK
Hydraulic Power System (KSC) .... HPS
Hydraulic Power Transfer Panel .... HPTP
Hydraulic Power Transmission Fluid (MCD) .... HPTF
Hydraulic Power Unit (MCD) .... HPU
Hydraulic Pressure Indicator .... HPI
Hydraulic Propulsion Units [on a ship] (DS) .... HYD PRO UN
Hydraulic Pump Discharge (AAG) .... HPD
Hydraulic Pump Drive [Mechanical engineering] .... HPD
Hydraulic Pumping Unit (AABC) .... HPU
Hydraulic Punching Machine .... HPM
Hydraulic Quick Coupler .... HQC
Hydraulic Rate Damper .... HRD
Hydraulic Relief Valve .... HRV
Hydraulic Retention Time .... HRT
Hydraulic Rotary Actuator .... HRA
Hydraulic Selector Valve .... HSV
Hydraulic Steering and Diving [System] (DNAB) .... HSD
Hydraulic Subsystem Simulator (NASA) .... HSS
Hydraulic Subsystems Test Station (MCD) .... HSTS
Hydraulic Supply .... HS
Hydraulic Supply and Checkout Unit (NASA) .... HSCU
Hydraulic Supply Unit .... HSU
Hydraulic System .... HS
Hydraulic System Mineral Oil [Mechanical engineering] .... HSMO
Hydraulic System Module .... HSM
Hydraulic System Simulator (MCD) .... HSS
Hydraulic System Test and Repair Unit [Army] (MCD) .... HISTRU
Hydraulic System Test and Repair Unit [Army] (RDA) .... HSTRU

Hydraulic System Test and Repair Unit [*Army*] (MCD) ...... HYSTRU
Hydraulic Tachometer ...... HYTAC
Hydraulic Temperature Control (AAG) ...... HTC
Hydraulic Test Chamber (AAG) ...... HTC
Hydraulic Test Equipment ...... HTE
Hydraulic Test Set [*or Station*] ...... HTS
Hydraulic Tool Manufacturers Association [*Milwaukee, WI*] (EA) ...... HTMA
Hydraulic Valve Adjuster System [*Automotive engineering*] ...... HVAS
Hydraulic Valve Motor ...... HVM
Hydraulic Variable-Valve Train [*Automotive engine design*] ...... HVT
Hydraulically Extendable Dipperstick [*for tractors*] ...... HED
Hydraulically Operated Equipment ...... HOE
Hydraulics (ADA) ...... H
Hydraulics (ROG) ...... HYDRAUL
Hydraulics Engineer ...... HE
Hydraulics, External (DNAB) ...... HEX
Hydraulics Research Laboratory [*British*] ...... HRL
Hydraulics Research Ltd. [*British*] (IRUK) ...... HR
Hydraulics Research Station [*Research center British*] ...... HRS
Hydraulics, Turbine Throttle (DNAB) ...... HTT
Hydraulics-Resonance Changer (DNAB) ...... HRC
Hydrazine Auxiliary Rocket Engine ...... HARE
Hydrazine Catalytic Plenum ...... HCP
Hydrazine Electrolysis Plenum ...... HEP
Hydrazine Hand-Held Maneuvering Unit (MCD) ...... HHHMU
Hydrazine Monopropellant Thruster ...... HMT
Hydrazine Rocket Engine ...... HRE
Hydrazine Sulfate [*Toxic substance*] [*Inorganic chemistry*] ...... HS
Hydrazinobenzoic Acid [*Organic chemistry*] ...... HBA
Hydrazino(methyl)Benzothiazole [*Organic chemistry*] ...... HMBT
HydrazinomethylDOPA [*Biochemistry*] ...... HMD
Hydrazobenzene Derivative [*Organic chemistry*] ...... HABD
Hydride Generation Atomic Absorption [*Analytical chemistry*] ...... HGAA
Hydride Vapor Phase Epitaxy [*Crystallography*] ...... HVPE
Hydriodic Acid [*Inorganic chemistry*] ...... HI
Hydro Electricity Commission [*of Tasmania*] [*State*] (EERA) ...... HEC
Hydro Home Appliances Ltd. [*Formerly, Hemgold Resources Ltd.*] [*Vancouver Stock Exchange symbol*] ...... HHA
Hydro Reconnaissance Experimental [*British military*] (DMA) ...... HRE
Hydro-Air Library, Burbank, CA [*Library symbol Library of Congress*] (LCLS) ...... CBbH
Hydrobenzoate [*Organic chemistry*] ...... HBA
Hydrobromic Acid (MAE) ...... HBr
Hydrobromofluorocarbons [*Organic chemistry*] ...... HBCF
Hydrocarbon [*Organic chemistry*] ...... HC
Hydrocarbon Concentration [*Automotive engineering*] ...... HCC
Hydrocarbon Emission Index [*Automotive engineering*] ...... HCEI
Hydrocarbon Mass [*Automotive engineering*] ...... HCM
Hydrocarbon Pore Volume [*Petroleum technology*] ...... HCPV
Hydrocarbon Processing Industry ...... HPI
Hydrocarbon Solids Process [*Tosco Corp.*] [*Oil shale pyrolysis*] ...... HSP
Hydrocarbon-Induced Nephropathy [*Medicine*] ...... HIN
Hydrocarbons [*Chemical*] (EERA) ...... HC
Hydrochemical Form Die [*Tool*] (AAG) ...... HCFD
Hydrochloric Acid ...... HCl
Hydrochloric Acid [*Organic chemistry*] (DAVI) ...... HCR
Hydrochloride (CPH) ...... HCl
Hydrochlorofluorocarbon [*Organic chemistry*] ...... HCFC
Hydrochlorofluorocarbons (EERA) ...... HCFC
Hydrochlorothiazide [*Drug*] [*Also, HCTZ, HCZ*] [*Organic chemistry*] ...... HCT
Hydrochlorothiazide [*Drug*] [*Also, HCT, HCZ*] [*Organic chemistry*] ...... HCTZ
Hydrochlorothiazide [*Drug*] [*Also, HCT, HCTZ*] [*Organic chemistry*] ...... HCZ
Hydrocodone [*Medicine*] (MEDA) ...... HC
Hydrocollator Pack [*Physical therapy*] (DAVI) ...... HP
Hydrocollator [*Hot*] Pack [*Medicine*] ...... HY
Hydrocolloid (DMAA) ...... Hc
Hydrocolloid Dressing [*Dermatology*] ...... HCD
Hydrocolloid Impression [*Dentistry*] ...... HcIMP
Hydrocortisone [*Endocrinology*] ...... HC
Hydrocortisone [*Endocrinology*] ...... HCT
Hydrocortisone Acetate [*Pharmacology*] ...... HCA
Hydrocortisone Butyrate [*Glucocorticoid*] ...... HCB
Hydrocortisone(butyrate)propionate [*Endocrinology*] ...... HBP
Hydrocracking ...... HC
Hydrocracking-Distillation-Hydrotreatment (ECON) ...... HDH
Hydrocyanic Acid [*Inorganic chemistry*] ...... HCN
Hydrocylic Pressure Testing ...... HPT
Hydrodemetalation [*Petroleum refining*] ...... HDM
Hydrodenitrogenation [*of chemical compounds*] ...... HDN
Hydrodesulfurization ...... HDS
Hydrodevanadization [*Petroleum technology*] ...... HDV
Hydrodynamic Analysis Tool (DNAB) ...... HYDAT
Hydrodynamic Chromatography ...... HDC
Hydrodynamic Core Disruptive Accident [*Nuclear energy*] (NRCH) ...... HCDA
Hydrodynamic Elastic Magnets Plastic ...... HEMT
Hydrodynamic Equilibrium System [*For chromatography*] ...... HDES
Hydrodynamic Head ...... H
Hydrodynamic Interaction [*Chemistry*] ...... HI
Hydrodynamic Journal Bearing ...... HJB
Hydrodynamic Machining [*Manufacturing term*] ...... HDM
Hydrodynamic Modulation ...... HDM
Hydrodynamic Test System ...... HTS
Hydrodynamic Voltammogram [*Electrochemistry*] ...... HDV
Hydrodynamic Volume [*Physical chemistry*] ...... HDV
Hydrodynamic Welding ...... HDW

Hydrodynamically Modulated Voltammetry [*Analytical chemistry*] ...... HMV
Hydrodynamics ...... HYDRODYN
Hydrodynamics Laboratory [*MIT*] (MCD) ...... HL
Hydroelectric (IAA) ...... HE
Hydroelectric (MSA) ...... HYDRELC
Hydroelectric ...... HYDROELEC
Hydroelectric Plant ...... HEP
Hydroelectric Power ...... HEP
Hydroelectric Power [*Type of water project*] ...... HYD
Hydro-Electric Power Commission [*Canada*] (PDAA) ...... HEPC
Hydro-Electric Power Commission of Ontario, Toronto, ON, Canada [*Library symbol Library of Congress*] (LCLS) ...... CaOTH
Hydroelectric Unit ...... HEU
Hydrofluidic Stability Augmentation System ...... HYSAS
Hydrofluorether ...... HFE
Hydrofluoroalkane [*Organic chemistry*] ...... HFA
Hydrofluorocarbon ...... FC
Hydrofluorocarbon [*Organic chemistry*] ...... HFC
Hydrofluorsilicic Acid [*Inorganic chemistry*] ...... HFSA
Hydrofoil Advanced Research Study Program [*Navy*] ...... HARPY
Hydrofoil Air Cushion Ship ...... Hyacs
Hydrofoil Analysis and Design [*Computer science*] ...... HANDE
Hydrofoil Collision Avoidance and Tracking System [*Developed by Sperry*] ...... HYCATS
Hydrofoil Motor Torpedo Boat [*Ship symbol*] (NATG) ...... PTH
Hydrofoil Ocean Combatant ...... HOC
Hydrofoil Research Ship [*Navy symbol*] ...... AGEH
Hydrofoil Ship ...... HS
Hydrofoil Small Waterplane Area Ship ...... Hyswas
Hydrofoil Stabilization Device ...... HYSTAD
Hydrofoil Tactical Data System ...... HTDS
Hydrofoil Test Craft ...... HTC
Hydrofoil-Operated Rocket Submarine (NATG) ...... HORSE
Hydro-Form Die ...... HFD
Hydrogasification [*Gas from coal fuel*] ...... HYAS
Hydrogen [*Chemical element*] ...... H
Hydrogen [*Chemical*] (EERA) ...... H
Hydrogen H2
Hydrogen Actuation System (NASA) ...... HAS
Hydrogen Atmosphere Flame Ionization Detector ...... HAFID
Hydrogen Bomb ...... H (Bomb)
Hydrogen Bond Donor [*Solvent*] ...... HBD
Hydrogen Breath Test ...... H_2BT
Hydrogen Bubble Chamber ...... HBC
Hydrogen Burning (IEEE) ...... B
Hydrogen Chloride (AABC) ...... HC
Hydrogen Chloride [*Inorganic chemistry*] ...... HCl
Hydrogen Control System (NRCH) ...... HCS
Hydrogen Convection Zone ...... HCZ
Hydrogen Cyanide [*Also, HCN*] [*Poison gas Army symbol*] ...... AC
Hydrogen Cyanide [*Also, AC*] [*Inorganic chemistry*] ...... HCN
Hydrogen Dehydrogenase [*An enzyme*] ...... HDH
Hydrogen Depolarized Carbon Dioxide Concentrator (OA) ...... HDC
Hydrogen Detection System ...... HDS
Hydrogen Diffusion Anode [*Electrochemistry*] ...... HDA
Hydrogen Donor Diluents [*Petroleum chemistry*] ...... HDD
Hydrogen Drain (MCD) ...... HD
Hydrogen Embrittlement ...... HE
Hydrogen Embrittlement Cracking (PDAA) ...... HEC
Hydrogen Embrittlement Proof ...... HEP
Hydrogen Evolution Reaction [*Metallurgy*] ...... HER
Hydrogen Exchange (PDAA) ...... HX
Hydrogen Fill (MCD) ...... HF
Hydrogen Fluid Distribution System (MCD) ...... HFDS
Hydrogen Fluoride [*Inorganic chemistry*] (AFM) ...... HF
Hydrogen Fluoride/Deuterium Fluoride (MCD) ...... HF/DF
Hydrogen Gas [*System*] [*Nuclear energy*] (NRCH) ...... HG
Hydrogen Gas/Nitrogen Gas (NRCH) ...... HG/NG
Hydrogen Gas Saver (MCD) ...... HGS
Hydrogen Gas Valve (MCD) ...... HGV
Hydrogen Gasification ...... HYGAS
Hydrogen Generator ...... HG
Hydrogen Iodide [*Inorganic chemistry*] ...... HI
Hydrogen Ion Concentration [*Organic chemistry*] (DAVI) ...... cH
Hydrogen Ion Concentration (MAE) ...... pH
Hydrogen, Ions, Helium, Oxygen in the Exosphere (MUGU) ...... HIHOE
Hydrogen Leak Detection System (NASA) ...... HLDS
Hydrogen Line (MCD) ...... HL
Hydrogen Line Emission ...... HLE
Hydrogen Manual Valve (MCD) ...... HMV
Hydrogen MASER ...... HM
Hydrogen MASER for Navigation Satellite (MCD) ...... HYMNS
Hydrogen Organization for Progress, Education, and Cooperation [*Defunct*] (EA) ...... HOPEC
Hydrogen/Oxygen Second Stage (MCD) ...... HOSS
Hydrogen Peroxide [*Pharmacology*] (DAVI) ...... H_2O_2
Hydrogen Pressure Regulator (MCD) ...... HPR
Hydrogen Purge (MCD) ...... HP
Hydrogen Recombination and Purge System [*Nuclear energy*] (NRCH) ...... HRPS
Hydrogen Recombiner (NRCH) ...... HR
Hydrogen Relief (NASA) ...... HR
Hydrogen Saturated Vacancy [*Photovoltaic energy systems*] ...... HSV
Hydrogen Seal Oil [*System*] (NRCH) ...... HSO
Hydrogen Stress Cracking (PDAA) ...... HSC
Hydrogen Sulfide (GNE) ...... H_2S

Hydrogen Sulfide (GNE) .... HS
Hydrogen Swelling [*Chemistry*] .... HS
Hydrogen Technology Evaluation Center [*Upton, NY*] [*Brookhaven National Laboratory*] [*Department of Energy*] (GRD) .... HTEC
Hydrogen Thermal Electrochemical Converter .... HYTEC
Hydrogen to Carbon Atomic Ratio (EG) .... H/C
Hydrogen Transfer Catalysis [*Chemistry*] .... HTC
Hydrogen Uranyl Phosphate [*Inorganic chemistry*] .... HUP
Hydrogen Vent (MCD) .... HV
Hydrogen Vent Header [*Nuclear energy*] (NRCH) .... HVH
Hydrogen Ventilated Enclosure (PDAA) .... HYVE
Hydrogenated Amorphous Carbon [*Inorganic chemistry*] .... HAC
Hydrogenated Bisphenol A [*Organic chemistry*] .... HBPA
Hydrogenated Coconut Oil (PDAA) .... HCO
Hydrogenated Palm Oil .... HPO
Hydrogenation [*Chemistry*] .... HYD
Hydrogenation of Pyrolysis Naphtha [*Petroleum refining*] .... HPN
Hydrogen-Bond Acceptor [*Chemistry*] .... HBA
Hydrogen-Bond Network Rearrangement [*Physical chemistry*] .... HBNR
Hydrogen-Detected Ventricular Septal Defect [*Medicine*] (MAE) .... HVSD
Hydrogene Data [*National College of Chemistry of Paris*] [*France*] [*Information service or system*] (IID) .... HDATA
Hydrogen-Fueled Aircraft .... HFA
Hydrogen-Induced Blister Cracking [*Metallurgy*] .... HIBC
Hydrogen-Induced Cracking [*Metallurgy*] .... HIC
Hydrogenous Exponential Liquid Experiment [*British*] .... HELEN
Hydrogenous Polyethylene .... HPE
Hydrogen-Oxygen [*NASA*] (NASA) .... HO
Hydrogen-Oxygen [*Fuel system*] (DNAB) .... HYDROX
Hydrogen-Oxygen Fuel System [*NASA*] .... HOFS
Hydrogen-Oxygen Primary Extraterrestrial [*Fuel cell*] [*NASA*] .... HOPE
Hydrogen-Oxygen Reaction (SAA) .... HOR
Hydrogen-Oxygen Turbine: Super-High Operating Temperatures [*Hydrogen utilization technology*] .... HOT-SHOT
Hydrogen-Oxygen-Hydrogen [*Water*] (HGAA) .... HOH
Hydrogeochemical and Stream Sediment Reconnaissance (PDAA) .... HSSR
Hydrogeography .... Hydrog
Hydrographer [*British military*] (DMA) .... Hydr
Hydrographer of the Navy [*British*] .... H of N
Hydrographer of the Navy [*British*] .... Hydrog
Hydrographic .... HYD
Hydrographic .... HYDROG
Hydrographic Airborne LASER Sounder (PDAA) .... HALS
Hydrographic Automated Data Acquisitioning and Processing System (MCD) .... HADAPS
Hydrographic Center [*Defense Mapping Agency*] .... HC
Hydrographic Data Acquisition System .... HDAS
Hydrographic Data Acquisition System (PDAA) .... HYDAS
Hydrographic Data Logging and Plotting System (EERA) .... HYDLAPS
Hydrographic Digital Positioning and Depth Recording [*System*] [*NOO*] .... HYDRA
Hydrographic Information Committee [*NATO*] (NATG) .... HIC
Hydrographic Information for the Atlantic [*Navy*] (DNAB) .... HYDROLANT
Hydrographic Information for the Pacific [*Navy*] (DNAB) .... HYDROPAC
Hydrographic Oceanographic Data Sheets (NG) .... HODS
Hydrographic Office [*Terminated, 1963; later, NOO*] [*Navy*] .... HO
Hydrographic Office [*Terminated, 1963; later, NOO*] [*Navy*] .... HYDRO
Hydrographic Office Publications [*Obsolete Navy*] .... HOP
Hydrographic Office Scale [*Obsolete*] .... HOS
Hydrographic Office-Washington, DC [*Terminated, 1963; later, NOO*] [*Navy*] (MCD) .... HO-W
Hydrographic Personnel [*Navy*] .... HYPER
Hydrographic Precision Scanning Echo Sounder .... HYPSES
[*The*] **Hydrographic Society** [*Dagenham, Essex, England*] (EAIO) .... THS
Hydrographic Survey [*Navy British*] .... H
Hydrographic Survey Platform System (MCD) .... HSPS
Hydrographic Surveying and Charting [*System*] [*NOO*] .... HYSURCH
Hydrography .... HY
Hydrography .... HYDRO
Hydro-Hydrogen Pilot Project .... HHPP
Hydrologic .... HYDROL
Hydrologic Data Laboratory [*Agricultural Research Service*] (PDAA) .... HDL
Hydrologic Engineering Center [*Davis, CA*] [*Army*] (GRD) .... HEC
Hydrologic Evaluation of Landfill Performance [*Environmental Protection Agency*] .... HELP
Hydrologic Information Storage and Retrieval System [*North Carolina State University*] [*Raleigh, NC*] .... HISARS
Hydrologic Sensing Satellite (DNAB) .... HSS
Hydrologic Simulation Program Fortran .... HSPF
Hydrological and Meteorological Fixed Station [*ITU designation*] (CET) .... FXH
Hydrological and Meteorological Mobile Station [*ITU designation*] .... MOH
Hydrological Atmospheric Pilot Experiment [*Marine science*] (OSRA) .... HAPEX
Hydrological Atmospheric Pilot Experiments (EERA) .... HAPEX
Hydrological Database & Analysis .... HYDATA
Hydrological Institute and Belgrade University [*Marine science*] [*Yugoslavia*] (OSRA) .... HIBU
Hydrological Institute and Belgrade University (USDC) .... HIBU
Hydrological Operational Multipurpose Subprogramme [*World Meteorological Organization*] [*Information service or system*] (IID) .... HOMS
Hydrological Rainfall Runoff Model .... HYRROM
Hydrological Research Laboratory [*Silver Spring, MD*] [*National Weather Service*] (GRD) .... HRL
Hydrologist in Charge (NOAA) .... HIC
Hydrology Laboratory [*Department of Agriculture*] [*Information service or system*] (IID) .... HL
Hydrolysate Lactalbumin Earle's Glucose [*Medicine*] (DMAA) .... HLEG
Hydrolysis .... H
Hydrolytic Kinetic Resolution .... HKR
Hydrolyzable Tannin Level .... HT
Hydrolyzed Animal Protein [*Food technology*] .... HAP
Hydrolyzed Ethylene-Vinyl Acetate [*Plastics technology*] .... HEVA
Hydrolyzed Polar Lipid Fraction [*Biochemistry*] .... HPLF
Hydrolyzed Vegetable Protein [*Food additive*] .... HVP
Hydromagnetic Emission (IAA) .... HE
Hydromechanical Control System (KSC) .... HCS
Hydromechanical Unit .... HMU
Hydrometeorological .... HM
Hydrometer .... HYDM
Hydrometer Erosion and Recession Test (MCD) .... HEART
Hydron Technologies [*NASDAQ symbol*] (TTSB) .... HTEC
Hydron Technologies, Inc. [*NASDAQ symbol*] (SPSG) .... HTEC
Hydron Technologies, Inc. [*Associated Press*] (SAG) .... HydrTch
Hydronic Radiant Heating Association (EA) .... HRHA
Hydronics Institute (EA) .... HI
Hydronuclear Experiment .... HNE
Hydronuclear Experiments [*Nuclear physics*] .... HNE
Hydropathic (ADA) .... HYDRO
Hydroperoxide (DMAA) .... HPO
Hydroperoxyoctadecadienoic Acid [*Organic chemistry*] .... HPOD
Hydroperoxyoctadecatrienoic Acid [*Organic chemistry*] .... HPOT
Hydrophile/Lipophile [*Followed by a number*] .... H/L
Hydrophile-Lipophile Balance [*Surfactant technology*] .... HLB
Hydrophilic Group [*Surfactant technology*] .... HG
Hydrophilic Ointment [*Pharmacy*] (DAVI) .... HPO
Hydrophilic Petrolatum [*Pharmacology*] (DAVI) .... HP
Hydrophobic Alkali Soluble Emulsion [*Paint technology*] .... HASE
Hydrophobic Ethoxylated Urethane Resin [*Paint technology*] .... HEUR
Hydrophobic Interaction Chromatography .... HIC
Hydrophobic Microporous Hollow Fiber [*Membranes for chemical reactions*] .... HMHF
Hydrophobic Organic Chemical [*Physical chemistry*] .... HOC
Hydrophobic Organic Compound [*Marine science*] (OSRA) .... HOC
Hydrophobic Organic Compound (USDC) .... HOC
Hydrophobic Organic Contaminant [*Environmental science*] .... HOC
Hydrophobic Tail [*Surfactant technology*] .... HT
Hydrophobically-Modified Hydroxyethylcellulose [*Organic chemistry*] .... HMHEC
Hydrophobically-Modified Nonionic Polymers [*Organic chemistry*] .... HMNIP
Hydrophobically-Modified Polyacrylamide [*Organic chemistry*] .... HMPAA
Hydrophone .... HYPH
Hydrophone Allowance [*British military*] (DMA) .... HA
Hydrophone Effect [*Navy*] (NVT) .... HE
Hydropneumatic [*Freight*] .... HYDROPNEU
Hydropneumatic Suspension Device .... HSD
Hydropneumatic Suspension System (MCD) .... HSS
Hydropneumatic Trailer (MCD) .... HPT
Hydropneumatic Vehicle Suspension [*Automotive engineering*] .... HPVS
Hydroponic Society of America (EA) .... HSA
Hydropress Accessory [*Tool*] (AAG) .... HPAC
Hydropress Form [*Tool*] (AAG) .... HPFM
Hydro-Quebec [*Canada*] [*FAA designator*] (FAAC) .... APZ
Hydro-Quebec [*Institut de Recherche d'Hydro-Quebec*] [*Canada*] .... HQ
Hydro-Quebec, Bibliotheque [*UTLAS symbol*] .... HQM
Hydro-Quebec, Bibliotheque, Montreal, PQ, Canada [*Library symbol Library of Congress*] (LCLS) .... CaQMH
Hydro-Quebec, Montreal, Quebec [*Library symbol National Library of Canada*] (NLC) .... QMH
Hydroquench Thrust Termination System [*NASA*] (KSC) .... HTTS
Hydroquinone [*Organic chemistry*] .... HQ
Hydroquinone Cream [*Pharmacy*] (DAVI) .... HQC
Hydroquinone Monomethyl Ether [*Organic chemistry*] .... HQMME
Hydroshift Gun .... HSG
Hydrospace Information Report (MCD) .... HIR
Hydrospace Target Recognition, Evaluation, and Control .... HYTREC
Hydrostatic (KSC) .... HYDRO
Hydrostatic (MSA) .... HYDRST
Hydrostatic Equilibrium System [*For chromatography*] .... HSES
Hydrostatic Impact Rocket (NATG) .... HIR
Hydrostatic Indifference Point .... HIP
Hydrostatic Motor-Driven .... HMD
Hydrostatic Motor-Driven .... HMD
Hydrostatic Pressure .... HP
Hydrostatic Transmission [*Automotive engineering*] .... HST
Hydrostatic-Gauging Technology [*Engineering*] .... HGT
Hydrostatics .... HYD
Hydrostatics (ROG) .... HYDR
Hydrostatics (BARN) .... hydros
Hydrotalcite [*Mineralogy*] .... HT
Hydrotherapy [*Medicine*] .... HT
Hydrotherapy [*Medicine*] .... HYDRO
Hydrothermal Environment Research Observatory [*US-French Marine collaboration*] .... HERO
Hydrothermal Vent [*Geology*] .... HTV
Hydrothermally-Altered Granite [*Geology*] .... HAG
Hydrotreating [*or Hydrotreated*] [*Petroleum technology*] .... HDT
Hydrotreating [*Also, HDT*] [*Petroleum technology*] .... HT
Hydrotropic Electron-Donor [*Medicine*] (DMAA) .... HED
Hydrous .... HYD
Hydrous Titanium Oxide (PDAA) .... HTO
Hydroviscous Drive (DNAB) .... HVD
Hydroxide (IAA) .... HYDX

Hydroxocobalamin [*Pharmacology*] (DAVI) .... B₁₂b
Hydroxy [*As substituent on nucleoside*] [*Also, oh*] [*Biochemistry*] .... ho
Hydroxy [*As substituent on nucleoside*] [*Also, HO*] [*Biochemistry*] .... OH
Hydroxy Butyric Valeric Acid [*Polymer*] .... PHBV
Hydroxy (Ethyl) Methyl Furanone [*Organic chemistry*] .... HEMF
Hydroxy Fatty Acid [*Biochemistry*] (AAMN) .... OHFA
Hydroxy Polycyclic Aromatic Hydrocarbon [*Environmental chemistry*] .... HPAH
Hydroxy Polycyclic Aromatic Nitrogen Heterocycle [*Environmental chemistry*] .... HPANH
Hydroxy Polycyclic Aromatic Sulfur Heterocycle [*Environmental chemistry*] .... HPASH
Hydroxyacetophenone [*Organic chemistry*] .... HAP
Hydroxyacyl-Glutathione Hydrolase (DMAA) .... HAGH
Hydroxyalkylpropyl Sephadex [*Analytical biochemistry*] .... HAPS
Hydroxy-Aluminosilicate [*Inorganic chemistry*] .... HAS
Hydroxyaminoguanidine [*Biochemistry*] .... HAG
Hydroxyaminoquinoline Oxide [*Organic chemistry*] .... HAQO
Hydroxyandrostenedione [*Antineoplastic drug*] (CDI) .... OHA
Hydroxyapatite [*Also, HAP*] [*A mineral*] .... HA
Hydroxyapatite [*Also, HA*] [*A mineral*] .... HAP
Hydroxyapatite Deposition Disease [*Medicine*] (DAVI) .... HADD
(Hydroxyazobenzene)benzoic Acid [*Also, HBABA*] [*Organic chemistry*] .... HABA
(Hydroxyazobenzene)benzoic Acid [*Organic chemistry*] .... HABBA
(Hydroxybenzeneazo)benzoic Acid [*Also, HABA*] [*Organic chemistry*] .... HBABA
Hydroxybenzoic Acid Hydrazide [*Reagent*] .... HBAH
Hydroxybenzotriazole [*Organic chemistry*] .... HBT
Hydroxybenzotriazole .... HOBT
Hydroxybenzoylglycine [*Biochemistry*] .... HBG
Hydroxybenzyl Benzimidazole [*Clinical chemistry*] (MAE) .... HBB
Hydroxybenzylbutanediol [*Clinical chemistry*] .... HBBD
Hydroxybenzylbutyrolactone [*Clinical chemistry*] .... HBBL
Hydroxybenzylpindolol [*Neuropharmacology*] .... HYP
(Hydroxybutyl)guanine [*Biochemistry*] .... HBG
Hydroxybutylidene-p-aminobenzenesulfonic [*Organic chemistry*] .... HBPSA
Hydroxybutyrate Dehydrogenase [*Also, HBDH*] [*An enzyme*] .... HBD
Hydroxybutyrate Dehydrogenase [*Also, HBD*] [*An enzyme*] .... HBDH
Hydroxybutyric Dehydrogenase [*Organic chemistry*] (DAVI) .... FBH
Hydroxybutyric Dehydrogenase [*An enzyme*] (DAVI) .... HDBD
Hydroxybutyric Dehydrogenase [*Clinical chemistry*] (CPH) .... HDBH
Hydroxycalcium Phenoxide [*Organic chemistry*] .... HCP
Hydroxycamptothecin [*Antineoplastic drug*] .... HCPT
Hydroxychloroquine [*Disease modifying antirheumatic drug*] .... HCQ
Hydroxycholecalciferol [*Biochemistry*] .... HCC
Hydroxycholecalciferol [*A form of vitamin D*] (DAVI) .... OHC
Hydroxycobalamin [*Medicine*] (BABM) .... OH-Cbl
Hydroxycorticosteroid [*Endocrinology*] .... HOC
Hydroxycorticosteroid [*Endocrinology*] (DAVI) .... OH
Hydroxycorticosteroid [*Endocrinology*] (AAMN) .... OHCS
Hydroxycorticosteroids [*Pharmacology*] (DAVI) .... HCS
Hydroxycyclopentenone .... HCP
Hydroxydaunomycin [*See also ADR, Adriamycin*] [*Antineoplastic drug*] .... H
Hydroxydaunomycin [*Adriamycin*], Cytosine Arabinoside, Vincristine, Prednisone [*Antineoplastic drug regimen*] (DAVI) .... HOAP
Hydroxydaunomycin [*Adriamycin*], Oncovin , Prednisone [*Vincristine*] [*Antineoplastic drug regimen*] .... HOP
Hydroxydeoxycorticosterone [*Endocrinology*] (DAVI) .... OH-DOC
Hydroxydimethylpyrimidine [*Organic chemistry*] .... HDP
Hydroxydopamine [*Also, HDM, OHDA*] [*Biochemistry*] .... HDA
Hydroxydopamine [*Also, HDA, OHDA*] [*Biochemistry*] .... HDM
Hydroxydopamine [*Also, HDA, HDM*] [*Biochemistry*] .... OHDA
Hydroxyecdysone [*Endocrinology*] .... HE
Hydroxyeicosatetraenoic Acid [*Biochemistry*] .... HETE
Hydroxyergocalciferol [*Organic chemistry*] (MAE) .... HEC
Hydroxyethyl Acrylate [*Organic chemistry*] .... HEA
Hydroxyethyl Methacrylate [*Organic chemistry*] .... HEMA
Hydroxyethyl Methyl (Cellulose) [*Organic chemistry*] .... HEME
Hydroxyethyl Phosphonic Acid [*Organic chemistry*] .... HEPA
Hydroxyethyl Starch [*Plasma volume expander*] .... HES
Hydroxyethyl Terephthalate [*Organic chemistry*] .... HET
Hydroxyethylated Acid Modified Flour (OA) .... HEAMF
(Hydroxyethyl)cellulose [*Organic chemistry*] .... HEC
Hydroxyethylcysteine [*Organic chemistry*] .... HEC
Hydroxyethylenediaminetriacetic Acid [*Organic chemistry*] .... HEDTA
(Hydroxyethyl)ethylenediaminetetracetate [*or -tetracetic*] Acid [*Organic chemistry*] .... HEEDTA
(Hydroxyethyl)ethyleneimine [*Organic chemistry*] .... HEEI
Hydroxyethylflurazepam [*Sedative*] .... HEF
Hydroxyethylhomocysteine [*Organic chemistry*] .... HEHC
(Hydroxyethyl)hydrazine [*Organic chemistry*] .... HEH
(Hydroxyethylidene)diphosphonic Acid [*Also, EHDP*] [*Organic chemistry*] .... HEDP
(Hydroxyethyl)iminodiacetic Acid [*Organic chemistry*] .... HEIDA
Hydroxyethylmorpholine [*Organic chemistry*] .... HEM
(Hydroxyethyl)oxamic Acid [*Organic chemistry*] .... HOA
Hydroxyethylpiperazineethanesulfonic Acid [*A buffer*] .... HEPES
Hydroxyethylpiperazinepropanesulfonic Acid [*A buffer*] .... HEPPS
(Hydroxyethyl)trimethylammonium Chloride [*Organic chemistry*] .... HETMAC
Hydroxyheptadecatrienoic Acid [*Organic chemistry*] .... HHT
Hydroxyhexamide [*Organic chemistry*] (MAE) .... HH
Hydroxyhexenal [*Organic chemistry*] .... HH
Hydroxyindolacetic Acid [*Oncology*] (DAVI) .... OHIAA
Hydroxyindole [*Biochemistry*] (DAVI) .... HI
Hydroxyindole O-Methyltransferase [*Also, HOMT*] [*An enzyme*] .... HIOMT
Hydroxyindole O-Methyltransferase [*Also, HIOMT*] [*An enzyme*] .... HOMT
Hydroxyindoleacetic Acid [*Organic chemistry*] .... HIAA
Hydroxyinterlayered Smectite or Vermiculite .... HSV

Hydroxyisobutyric Acid [*Organic chemistry*] .... HIBA
Hydroxyisocaproic Acid (DMAA) .... HICA
Hydroxykynurenic Acid [*Organic chemistry*] .... HKYNA
Hydroxyl Ammonium Nitrate (MCD) .... HAN
Hydroxyl Concentration [*Organic chemistry*] (MAE) .... pOH
Hydroxyl Radical (AD) .... OH
Hydroxyl Terminated (MCD) .... HT
Hydroxyl Value [*Analytical chemistry*] .... HV
Hydroxylamine Acid Sulfate [*Inorganic chemistry*] .... HAS
Hydroxylamine Nitrate [*Organic chemistry*] (NUCP) .... HAN
Hydroxylamine Perchlorate [*Organic chemistry*] .... HAP
Hydroxylamine Phosphate Oxime [*Organic chemistry*] .... HPO
Hydroxylamine-ortho-sulfonic Acid [*Organic chemistry*] .... HAOS
Hydroxylammonium Nitrate [*Component of liquid propellants*] [*Inorganic chemistry*] .... HAN
Hydroxylammonium Sulfate [*Inorganic chemistry*] .... HAS
Hydroxylapatite [*Inorganic chemistry*] .... HA
Hydroxyl-Terminated Polybutadiene [*Organic chemistry*] .... HTPB
Hydroxyl-Terminated Polybutylene [*Organic chemistry*] (NASA) .... HTPB
Hydroxylysine [*Also, Hylys*] [*An amino acid*] .... Hyl
Hydroxylysine [*or (OH)Lys*] [*Also, Hyl An amino acid*] .... Hylys
Hydroxylysinonorleucine [*Biochemistry*] .... HLNL
Hydroxymethanesulfonate [*Organic chemistry*] .... HMSA
Hydroxy(methoxy)benzaldehyde [*Organic chemistry*] .... HMB
Hydroxymethoxybenzophenone [*Organic chemistry*] .... HMB
Hydroxymethoxymandelic Acid [*Also, VMA*] [*Biochemistry*] .... HMMA
Hydroxy(methoxy)phenylglycol [*Biochemistry*] (AAMN) .... HMPG
Hydroxymethyl [*As substituent on nucleoside*] [*Biochemistry*] .... hm
Hydroxymethyl Cytosine [*Biochemistry*] (DAVI) .... HMC
Hydroxymethyl Diacetone Acrylamide [*Organic chemistry*] .... HMDAA
Hydroxymethyl Hydroperoxide [*Organic chemistry*] .... HMP
Hydroxymethyl Phosphonic Acid [*Organic chemistry*] .... HMPA
Hydroxymethyl Uracil [*Organic chemistry*] (DAVI) .... hMT
Hydroxymethyladenine [*Biochemistry*] .... HMA
(Hydroxymethyl)carboline [*Biochemistry*] .... HMC
Hydroxymethylcystosine [*Organic chemistry*] .... HMC
Hydroxymethylenediphosphonate [*Organic chemistry*] .... HMDP
Hydroxymethylfuraldehyde [*Organic chemistry*] .... HMF
Hydroxymethylfurfural [*Organic chemistry*] (DAVI) .... HMF
Hydroxymethylglutaryl [*Biochemistry*] .... HMG
Hydroxymethylglutarylcoenzyme [*Organic chemistry*] .... HMGCO
Hydroxy-Methylglutaryl-Coenzyme A Reductase [*Medicine*] (MEDA) ...... HMG-CoA
Hydroxymethyl(methyl)benzanthracene [*Organic chemistry*] .... HMBA
Hydroxymethyl(methyl)propanediol [*Organic chemistry*] .... HMP
Hydroxymethyluracil [*Organic chemistry*] .... HMU
Hydroxynaphthoquinone [*Organic chemistry*] .... HNQ
Hydroxynitrobenzyl [*Organic chemistry*] .... HNB
Hydroxynitrobenzylbromide [*Organic chemistry*] (MAE) .... HNB
Hydroxynonenal [*Biochemistry*] .... HNE
Hydroxy(octylidene)bis(phosphonic Acid) [*Organic chemistry*] .... HOBP
Hydroxyoxo-L-norvaline [*Antibiotic*] .... HON
Hydroxyperoxyeicosatetraenoic Acid [*Biochemistry*] .... HPETE
Hydroxyphenyl Pyruvate [*Organic chemistry*] .... HPP
Hydroxyphenylacetic Acid [*Biochemistry*] (MAE) .... HPAA
Hydroxyphenylcinchoninic Acid [*Pharmacology*] .... HPC
(Hydroxyphenylisopropyl)adenosine .... HPIA
Hydroxyphenyllactic Acid [*Pharmacology*] (MAE) .... HPLA
(Hydroxyphenyl)phenylhydantoin [*Biochemistry*] (AAMN) .... HPPH
Hydroxyphenylpyruvic Acid [*Organic chemistry*] .... HPPA
Hydroxyphenylretinamide [*Biochemistry*] .... HPR
Hydroxypivalyl Hydroxypivalate [*Organic chemistry*] .... HPHP
Hydroxypregnanedione [*Endocrinology*] (DAVI) P-55
Hydroxyproline [*An amino acid*] .... HP
Hydroxyproline [*An amino acid*] (DAVI) .... HYD'PR
Hydroxyproline [*Also, Hypro*] [*An amino acid*] .... Hyp
Hydroxyproline [*or (OH)Pro*] [*Also, Hyp An amino acid*] .... Hypro
Hydroxyproline-Containing Protein .... HCP
Hydroxyproline-Rich Glycoprotein [*Biochemistry*] .... HRGP
Hydroxypropyl Acrylate [*Organic chemistry*] .... HPA
Hydroxypropyl Guar [*Organic chemistry*] .... HPG
Hydroxypropyl Methacrylate [*Organic chemistry*] .... HPMA
Hydroxypropyl Nitrate [*Organic chemistry*] .... HPN
Hydroxypropyl Starch [*Organic chemistry*] .... HPS
Hydroxypropylcellulose [*Organic chemistry*] .... HPC
Hydroxypropyl(methyl)cellulose [*Synthetic food gum*] [*Organic chemistry*] ... HMC
Hydroxypropyl(methyl)cellulose [*Synthetic food gum*] [*Organic chemistry*] .... HPMC
(Hydroxypropyl)xylan [*Organic chemistry*] .... HPX
Hydroxypyrazolopyrimidine Ribonucleoside [*Biochemistry*] .... HPPR
Hydroxypyrenetrisulfonic Acid [*Organic chemistry*] .... HPTS
Hydroxypyroline [*Biochemistry*] (AAMN) .... OHP
Hydroxyquinoline [*Organic chemistry*] .... HQ
Hydroxyquinoline Citrate [*Antiseptic*] .... HQC
Hydroxyquinolinesulfonic Acid [*Organic chemistry*] .... HQSA
Hydroxysteroid Dehydrogenase [*An enzyme*] .... HSD
Hydroxy(succinimidyl)azidobenzoate [*Organic chemistry*] .... HSAB
Hydroxy-Terminated Polybutadiene [*Organic chemistry*] .... HTPB
Hydroxy(tetramethyl)piperidineoxyl [*Organic chemistry*] .... HTMP
Hydroxytryptamine [*Biochemistry*] .... HT
Hydroxytryptamine [*Biochemistry*] (MAE) .... HTA
Hydroxytryptophan [*Biochemistry*] .... HTP
Hydroxytryptophol [*Laboratory*] (DAVI) .... HTOH
Hydroxyurea [*Also, HYD, HYDREA*] [*Antineoplastic drug*] .... HU
Hydroxyurea [*Antineoplastic drug*] (DAVI) .... HUR
Hydroxyurea [*Also, HU, HYDREA*] [*Antineoplastic drug*] .... HYD

Hydroxyurea [*Also, HU, HYD*] [*Antineoplastic drug*] .... HYDREA
Hydrozene Monopropellant (MCD) .... HMP
Hydrus [*Constellation*] .... Hya
Hydrus [*Constellation*] .... Hydi
Hyeres Aero Service [*France ICAO designator*] (FAAC) .... HYE
Hyeres/Le Palyvestre [*France ICAO location identifier*] (ICLI) .... LFTH
Hygiene [*Preventive and Industrial Medicine*] [*Medical Officer designation*] [*British*] .... H
Hygiene .... HYG
Hygiene .... HYGN
Hygiene Institute, La Salle, IN [*Library symbol Library of Congress*] (LCLS) .... InLasH
Hygiene Institute, Medical Library, LaSalle, IL [*Library symbol Library of Congress*] (LCLS) .... ILasH
Hygienic Community Network (EA) .... HCN
Hygienic Effect .... HE
Hygienic Electrician [*British*] (ROG) .... HE
Hygienic Laboratory [*US*] .... HL
Hygienist .... HYGNST
Hygienist (AABC) .... HYGST
Hygromycin Phosphotransferase .... HPT
Hygroscopic .... HYG
Hygroscopicity Potential (PDAA) .... HP
Hyland Laboratories, Los Angeles, CA [*Library symbol Library of Congress*] (LCLS) .... CLH
Hyman, TX [*Location identifier FAA*] (FAAL) .... HYM
Hymenolepis [*A genus of tapeworm*] [*Gastroenterology*] (DAVI) .... H
Hymenoptera [*Entomology*] .... Hym
Hymmus in Dianam [*of Callimachus*] [*Classical studies*] (OCD) .... Dian
Hymn Society in the United States and Canada (EA) .... HSUSC
Hymn Society of America [*Later, HSUSC*] (EA) .... HSA
Hymnal Prayer of Enheduanna (BJA) .... Enh
Hymnal-Epic Dialect (BJA) .... HED
Hymns Ancient and Modern .... HAM
Hymnus Homericus ad Apollinem [*Classical studies*] (OCD) .... Hymn Hom Ap
Hymnus Homericus ad Bacchum [*Classical studies*] (OCD) .... Hymn Hom Bacch
Hymnus Homericus ad Cererem [*Classical studies*] (OCD) .... Hymn Hom Cer
Hymnus Homericus ad Martem [*Classical studies*] (OCD) .... Hymn Hom Mart
Hymnus Homericus ad Mercurium [*Classical studies*] (OCD) .... Hymn Hom Merc
Hymnus Homericus ad Panem [*Classical studies*] (OCD) .... Hymn Hom Pan
Hymnus Homericus ad Venerem [*Classical studies*] (OCD) .... Hymn Hom Ven
Hymnus in Apollinem [*of Callimachus*] [*Classical studies*] (OCD) .... Ap
Hymnus in Cererem [*of Callimachus*] [*Classical studies*] (OCD) .... Cer
Hymnus in Delum [*of Callimachus*] [*Classical studies*] (OCD) .... Del
Hymnus in Jovem [*of Callimachus*] [*Classical studies*] (OCD) .... Jov
Hyoid Body (DMAA) .... HB
Hyoscine [*Organic chemistry*] .... H
Hyoscine, Morphine, and Cactine [*Tablets*] [*Medicine*] .... HMC
Hyoscyamus [*Henbane*] [*Pharmacology*] (ROG) .... HYOSCYAM
Hypanthium Pubescence [*Botany*] .... HYPUB
Hypatia Cluster [*Defunct*] (EA) .... HC
Hyper Active Children's Support Group [*British*] .... HACSG
Hyper Immunoglobulin Syndrome [*Medicine*] .... HIM
Hyperactive Child Syndrome .... HACS
Hyperactive Children's Association of Victoria [*Australia*] .... HCAV
Hyperactive Children's Support Group [*England*] .... HCSG
Hyperactive Help [*Australia*] .... HH
Hyperacute Experimental Autoimmune Encephalomyelitis [*Medicine*] (PDAA) .... HEAE
Hyperacute Rejection [*Medicine*] .... HAR
Hyperalimentation [*Intravenous feeding*] (DAVI) .... HA
Hyperalimentation [*Intravenous feeding*] (DAVI) .... HAL
Hyperalimentation [*Intravenous feeding*] [*Medicine*] (DAVI) .... hyperal
Hyperalimentation Solution [*Pharmacology*] (DAVI) .... HAS
Hyperandrogenism, Insulin Resistance, and Acanthosis Nigricans Syndrome [*Medicine*] (DMAA) .... HAIR-AN
Hyperbaric Chamber (SSD) .... HBC
Hyperbaric Oxygen [*Also, HPO, OHP*] [*Medicine*] .... HBO
Hyperbaric Oxygen [*Medicine*] .... HO
Hyperbaric Oxygen Drenching .... HOD
Hyperbaric Oxygen Therapy [*Medicine*] (DAVI) .... HBOT
Hyperbaric Oxygen Therapy [*Medicine*] (DAVI) .... HOT
Hyperbaric Oxygenation (DMAA) .... HBO
Hyperbola [*Mathematics*] .... HYPERB
Hyperbolic Area Control (IAA) .... HARCO
Hyperbolic Area Coverage [*Navigation*] .... HARCO
Hyperbolic Doppler .... HYPERDOP
Hyperbolic Fix .... HYFIX
Hyperbolic Grid System .... HGS
Hyperbolic Integer Programming [*Computer science*] (PDAA) .... HIP
Hyperbolic LOFAR Fix [*Military*] (CAAL) .... HLF
Hyperbolic Paraboloid Surface (MCD) .... HYPARS
Hyperbolic Secant (IDOE) .... sech
Hyperbolic Tangent (IDOE) .... tanh
Hyperbolic Type Gas Lens (IAA) .... HGL
Hyperbolic Zone Plate (PDAA) .... HZP
Hyperboloid Approximation Procedure .... HAP
Hypercalcemia of Malignancy [*Medicine*] .... HCM
Hyperemia Unit .... HU
Hyperenvironmental RADAR .... HER
Hyperenvironmental Test Station [*or System*] [*Air Force*] .... HETS
Hypereosinophilic Syndrome [*Medicine*] .... HES
Hyperextension Injury [*Orthopedics*] (DAVI) .... HE inj
Hyperfiltration (NASA) .... HF
Hyperfiltration Wash Water Recovery System [*NASA*] (NASA) .... HWWS

Hyperfine Coupling [*Spectroscopy*] .... HFC
Hyperfine Interaction .... HFI
Hyperfine Splitting Constant [*Spectroscopy*] .... HFSC
Hyperfine Structure .... HFS
Hypergeometric Group Testing [*Computer science*] (OA) .... HGT
Hyperglobulinemic Purpura [*Medicine*] (DMAA) .... HGP
Hyperglycemic Hyperosmolar Nonketotic Coma [*Endocrinology*] (CPH) .... HHNC
Hyperglycemic-Glycogenolytic [*Factor*] [*Endocrinology*] .... HG
Hyperglycemic-Glycogenolytic Factor [*Later, Glucagon*] [*Endocrinology*] .... HGF
Hypergol Maintenance Area (MCD) .... HMA
Hypergol Maintenance Facility [*NASA*] (NASA) .... HMF
Hypergol Servicing Facility [*NASA*] (NASA) .... HSF
Hypergolic (KSC) .... HYGL
Hypergolic .... HYP
Hypergolic Clean .... HGC
Hypergolic Ignition (KSC) .... HYPERIGN
Hypergolic Maintenance and Checkout (NASA) .... HMC
Hypergolic Maintenance and Checkout Cell (NASA) .... HMCC
Hypergolic Maintenance and Checkout Facility [*NASA*] (NASA) .... HMCF
Hypergolic Test Building (KSC) .... HTB
Hypergolic Vapor Detection System [*NASA*] (NASA) .... HVDS
Hypergraph-Based Data Structures .... HBDS
Hypergroup Reference Pilot [*Telecommunications*] (NITA) .... HRP
Hypergroup Translating Equipment (NITA) .... HTE
Hyper-High-Frequency (DEN) .... HHF
Hyperhydrated, Hyperventilating with Hyperpyrexia, Hyperexcitability, and Hyperrigidity [*Characteristics of drowning*] .... HYPER
Hyperimmune Antivariola Gamma Globulin .... HAGG
Hyperimmune Mice .... HM
Hyperimmune Mouse Ascite [*Medicine*] (DMAA) .... HMAS
Hyperimmune Serum [*Medicine*] (DMAA) .... HIS
Hyperimmunoglobulin M Syndrome [*Medicine*] .... HIM
Hyperintense Proximal Scanning .... HIPS
Hyperion 1997 Term Trust [*NYSE symbol*] (SPSG) .... HTA
Hyperion 1997 Term Trust [*Associated Press*] (SAG) HypT97
Hyperion 1999 Term Trust [*NYSE symbol*] (SPSG) .... HTT
Hyperion 1999 Term Trust [*Associated Press*] (SAG) HypT99
Hyperion 2002 Term Trust [*NYSE symbol*] (SPSG) .... HTB
Hyperion 2002 Term Trust [*Associated Press*] (SAG) HypT02
Hyperion 2005 Inv Grd Oppt Tr [*NYSE symbol*] (TTSB) .... HTO
Hyperion 2005 Investment Grade Opportunity Term Trust [*NYSE symbol*] (SPSG) .... HTO
Hyperion 2005 Investment Grade Opportunity Term Trust [*Associated Press*] (SAG) Hyp2005
Hyperion Energy Recovery System (GNE) .... HERS
Hyperion Resources [*Vancouver Stock Exchange symbol*] .... HPR
Hyperion Software [*NASDAQ symbol*] (TTSB) .... HYSW
Hyperion Software, Inc. [*Associated Press*] (SAG) .... HyprnSft
Hyperion Software, Inc. [*Associated Press*] (SAG) .... HyprSf
Hyperion Software, Inc. [*NASDAQ symbol*] (SAG) .... HYSW
Hyperion Total Return & Income Fund [*Associated Press*] (SAG) .... HyprnTR
Hyperion Total Return Fd [*NYSE symbol*] (TTSB) .... HTR
Hyperion Total Return Fund [*NYSE symbol*] (SPSG) .... HTR
Hyperkalemic Periodic Paralysis [*Medicine*] .... HYPP
Hyperkinesis Syndrome [*Medicine*] (DMAA) .... HKS
Hyperkinetic Behavior Syndrome [*Medicine*] .... HBS
Hyperkinetic Impulse Disorder [*Medicine*] .... HID
Hyperlipoproteinemia [*Medicine*] .... HLP
Hypermedia Communications [*NASDAQ symbol*] (SAG) .... HYPR
HyperMedia Communications [*NASDAQ symbol*] (TTSB) .... HYPR
Hypermedia Communications, Inc. [*Associated Press*] (SAG) .... HypmdCm
HyperMedia Management Protocol [*Computer science*] .... HMMP
Hyper-Media Management Schema [*Computer science*] .... HMMS
HyperMedia Object Manager [*Computer science*] .... HMOM
Hypermetropia [*Ophthalmology*] .... H
Hypermetropia [*Ophthalmology*] .... Hy
Hypermetropia, Absolute [*Ophthalmology*] .... HA
Hypermetropia, Latent [*Ophthalmology*] .... HL
Hypermetropia, Latent [*Medicine*] (DMAA) .... HI
Hypermetropia, Right [*Ophthalmology*] (DAVI) .... HTR
Hypermetropia, Total [*Ophthalmology*] .... Ht
Hypermetropic Keratomileusis [*Ophthalmology*] .... HKM
Hyperopia [*Ophthalmology*] (ROG) .... H
Hyperopia [*Ophthalmology*] (MAE) .... Hy
Hyperopia Latent [*Ophthalmology*] (DAVI) .... HI
Hyperopia Manifest [*Ophthalmology*] (DAVI) .... Hm
Hyperopia, Total [*Ophthalmology*] (AAMN) .... Ht
Hyperornithinemia, Hyperammonemia, Homocitrillinuria Syndrome [*Medicine*] (DMAA) .... HHH
Hyperornithinemia with Gyrate Atrophy [*Medicine*] (DMAA) .... HOGA
Hyperosmolar Hyperglycemic Nonketotic (Coma) [*Also, NKHHC*] [*Medicine*] .... HHNK
Hyper-Page-Mode [*Computer science*] (PCM) .... HPM
Hyperparathyroidism [*or Hyperthyroidism*] [*Endocrinology*] .... HP
Hyperparathyroidism [*or Hyperthyroidism*] [*Endocrinology*] .... HPT
Hyperparathyroidism [*Medicine*] (MEDA) .... HPTH
Hyperparathyroidism [*Medicine*] (DMAA) .... HRPT
Hyperparathyroidism [*Endocrinology*] (DAVI) .... hyperpara
Hyperphoria [*Ophthalmology*] (DAVI) .... H
Hyperphoria .... HP
Hyperplasia [*Medicine*] .... H
Hyperplasia Cystica Uteri [*Medicine*] (DMAA) .... HCU
Hyperplasia Interstitialis Uteri [*Medicine*] (DMAA) .... HIU
Hyperplastic Alveolar Nodules [*Precancerous lesions in mice*] .... HAN
Hyperplastic Liver Nodules [*Medicine*] .... HLN

Hyperpolarization ... HP
Hyperpolarizing Afterpotential [*Electrophysiology*] ... HAP
Hyperpolarizing Bipolar Cell [*In the retina*] ... HPBC
Hyperpure Germanium [*Also, HpGe*] [*Chemistry*] ... HPG
Hyperpure Germanium [*Also, HPG*] [*Chemistry*] ... HpGe
Hyperquasicenter ... HQC
Hyper-Quenched Glassy Water [*Material science*] ... HGW
Hyper-Rayleigh Scattering [*Physics*] ... HRS
Hyperresonance ... HYP
Hyperresponse Electric Motor ... HYPREM
Hypersegmented Neutrophil [*Hematology*] (DAVI) ... HYPP
Hypersensitive Response [*Biology*] ... HR
Hypersensitivity Lung Disease [*Medicine*] ... HLD
Hypersensitivity Pneumonitis [*Medicine*] ... HP
Hypersomnia-Sleep Apnea Syndrome [*Medicine*] (MAE) ... HSA
Hypersonic ... HS
Hypersonic Aerodynamic Weapon (DOMA) ... HAW
Hypersonic Aerothermal Dynamics (SAA) ... HAD
Hypersonic Aerothermaldynamic Facility ... HAF
Hypersonic Air Data Entry System ... HADES
Hypersonic Air Data Sensor (IEEE) ... HADS
Hypersonic Arbitrary Body Program [*NASA*] ... HABP
Hypersonic Arc-Heated Tunnel [*Langley Research Center*] [*NASA*] ... HAHT
Hypersonic Boost-Glide Missile ... HBGM
Hypersonic Commercial Transport [*Airplane*] ... HSCT
Hypersonic Flight Environmental Simulator ... HYFES
Hypersonic Flow ... HSF
Hypersonic In-Flight Refueling System ... HIRES
Hypersonic Interference Technique ... HIT
Hypersonic Local Pressure ... HLP
Hypersonic Propulsion Research Facility ... HPRF
Hypersonic Ramjet Engine ... HRE
Hypersonic Rarefied Flow ... HRF
Hypersonic Research Airplane [*NASA*] ... HRA
Hypersonic Research Engine [*NASA*] ... HRE
Hypersonic Research Facilities [*NASA*] ... HYFAC
Hypersonic Research Vehicle ... HRV
HyperSonic Sound ... HSS
Hypersonic Surface-to-Air Missile (MCD) ... HYSAM
Hypersonic Tactical Missile (MCD) ... HYTAM
Hypersonic Test Vehicle [*Air Force*] ... HTV
Hypersonic Transport [*Aircraft*] ... HST
Hypersonic Tunnel Facility [*NASA*] ... HTF
Hypersonic Vehicle Shield ... HVS
Hypersonic Wedge Nozzle (MCD) ... HYWN
Hypersonic Wide-Area Defense Missile (MCD) ... HWADM
Hypersonic Wind Tunnel ... HWT
Hyper-spectral Digital Imagery Collection Experiment [*National Oceanic and Atmospheric Administration*] ... HYDICE
Hypersthene [*CIPW classification*] [*Geology*] ... hy
Hyperstriatum Ventralis Pars Caudalis [*Bird brain anatomy*] ... HVc
Hypertension [*Medicine*] ... HPN
Hypertension [*Cardiology*] (DAVI) ... HT
Hypertension [*Medicine*] ... HTN
Hypertension ... HYPN
Hypertension (DMAA) ... hypn
Hypertension and Arteriosclerotic Heart Disease [*Medicine*] ... H & ASHD
Hypertension and Proteinuria [*Medicine*] ... HP
Hypertension Detection and Follow-Up Program [*NHLBI*] ... HDFP
Hypertension Optimal Treatment [*Antihypertensive medicine*] ... HOT
Hypertension Research Center [*Indiana University*] [*Research center*] (RCD) ... HRC
Hypertension Secondary to Renal Disease [*Medicine*] ... HSRD
Hypertensive Arteriosclerotic [*Cardiology*] ... HAS
Hypertensive Arteriosclerotic Cardiovascular Disease [*Cardiology*] (MAE) ... HASCVD
Hypertensive Cardiovascular Disease [*Medicine*] ... HCVD
Hypertensive Crisis [*Cardiology*] (DAVI) ... HTC
Hypertensive Encephalopathy [*Medicine*] (CPH) ... HTE
Hypertensive Group [*Cardiology*] ... HG
Hypertensive Heart Disease [*Medicine*] ... HHD
Hypertensive Heart Disease [*Medicine*] (MAE) ... HTHD
Hypertensive Intracerebral Hemorrhage [*Medicine*] (DMAA) ... HIH
Hypertensive Pulmonary Vascular Disease [*Medicine*] ... HPVD
Hypertensive Vascular Disease [*Cardiology*] (DAVI) ... HTVD
Hypertensive Vascular Disease [*Medicine*] ... HVD
Hypertext Editing System [*Computer science*] ... HES
Hypertext Markup Language [*Computer science*] ... HTML
Hypertext Markup Language [*Computer science*] ... html
Hypertext Markup Language [*Telecommunication*] ... HTML
Hypertext Reference [*Computer science*] (CDE) ... HREF
Hypertext Text Transfer Protocol [*Computer science*] (TNIG) ... HPPT
Hypertext Transfer Protocol [*Telecommunication*] ... HTTP
Hypertext Transfer Protocol [*Computer science*] ... HTTP
Hyperthyroidism [*Endocrinology*] (MAE) ... HT
Hypertonic Buffered Medium (DMAA) ... HBM
Hypertonic Saline Dextran [*Medicine*] ... HSD
Hypertonic Saline Solution ... HSS
Hypertransfused Polycythemic [*Medicine*] ... HP
Hypertrichosis Lanuginosa [*Medicine*] ... HL
Hypertriglyceridemia [*Medicine*] ... HT
Hypertriglyceridemia [*Medicine*] ... HTG
Hypertrophic Cardiomyopathy [*Cardiology*] ... HCM
Hypertrophic Hypersecretory Gastropathy [*Medicine*] (DMAA) ... HHG
Hypertrophic Infiltrative Tendinitis [*Medicine*] (MAE) ... HIT
Hypertrophic Muscular Subaortic Stenosis [*Cardiology*] (MAE) ... HMSAS
Hypertrophic Neuropathy [*Medicine*] (DMAA) ... HN
Hypertrophic Obstructive Cardiomyopathy [*Cardiology*] ... HOCM
Hypertrophic Osteoarthropathy [*Medicine*] (DMAA) ... HOA
Hypertrophic Pulmonary Osteoarthropathy [*Medicine*] (DAVI) ... HPO
Hypertrophic Pyloric Stenosis [*Medicine*] ... HPS
Hypertrophic Subaortic Stenosis [*Cardiology*] ... HSAS
Hypertrophic Subaortic Stenosis [*Cardiology*] ... HSS
Hypertrophy ... HYP
Hypertrophy of Tonsils and Adenoids [*Medicine*] (MAE) ... hyper T & A
Hypertropia [*Medicine*] ... HT
Hypertropy of Tonsils and Adenoids [*Otorhinolaryngology*] (DAVI) ... hyper T & A
Hypervariable ... HV
Hypervariable Region [*Genetics*] ... HVR
Hypervelocity (AABC) ... HV
Hypervelocity ... HVEL
Hypervelocity Aircraft Rocket, Tactical ... HART
Hypervelocity Antiradiation Missile (MCD) ... HARM
Hypervelocity, Armor-Piercing, Discarding Sabot, Fin Stabilized Projectile [*Army*] (SAA) ... HVAPDSFS
Hypervelocity, Armor-Piercing, Discarding Sabot Projectile [*Army*] (SAA) ... HVAPDS
Hypervelocity, Armor-Piercing - Tracer [*Projectile*] (AABC) ... HVAP-T
Hypervelocity Countermeasures Program ... HCP
Hypervelocity Flow Field ... HFF
Hypervelocity Free Flight Facility ... HFFF
Hypervelocity Gun [*Military*] (SDI) ... HVG
Hypervelocity Impulse Tunnel (MCD) ... HIT
Hypervelocity Intercept Guidance ... HIG
Hypervelocity Intercept Guidance Simulator Study ... HIGSS
Hypervelocity Interceptor Armament ... HYVIA
Hypervelocity Interceptor Guidance Simulation ... HIGS
Hypervelocity Kill Mechanism [*Air Force*] ... HKM
Hypervelocity Launcher [*Military*] (SDI) ... HVL
Hypervelocity, Medium Support ... HVMS
Hypervelocity Missile ... HVM
Hypervelocity Munition ... HVM
Hyper-Velocity Rocket-Assisted Projectile (PDAA) ... HVRAP
Hypervelocity Shock Tunnel (OA) ... HST
Hypervelocity, Target-Practice [*Projectile*] ... HVTP
Hypervelocity, Target-Practice - Tracer [*Projectile*] (AABC) ... HVTP-T
Hyperventilation ... HV
Hyphen Character [*Computer science*] ... HYP
Hyphenation and Justification [*Typography*] ... H & J
Hyphenation and Justification (CDE) ... H & J
Hypnosis ... HYP
Hypnosis ... HYPNO
Hypnosis ... HYPNS
Hypnotic Induction Profile ... HIP
Hypnotism ... HYPNOT
Hypo Eliminator [*Photography*] (DGA) ... HE
Hypoascorbemia-Kwashiorkor [*Orthomolecular medicine*] ... H-K
Hypobranchial [*Gland*] ... HY
Hypobranchial Gland ... HG
Hypocalcemic Vitamin D-Resistant Rickets [*Medicine*] ... HVDRR
Hypochoeris Mosaic Virus [*Plant pathology*] ... HYMV
Hypochondria (DSUE) ... HYPO
Hypochondria (DSUE) ... HYPOCON
Hypochondriasis [*Psychology*] ... Hs
Hypochromasia [*Hematology*] ... hypo
Hypochromasia [*Hematology*] (DAVI) ... HYPOC
Hypocomplementemic Glomerulonephritis [*Nephrology*] (DAVI) ... HCGN
Hypodermic ... H
Hypodermic (DMAA) ... h
Hypodermic (ROG) ... HYP
Hypodermic ... HYPO
Hypodermic (DMAA) ... Hypo
Hypodermic Tablet [*Medicine*] ... HT
Hypodermoclysis [*Medicine*] (DHSM) ... Clysis
Hypodermoclysis Infusion [*Medicine*] ... HINF
Hypofibrinogenic Plasma ... HFP
Hypogastric Artery Ligation [*Medicine*] ... HAL
Hypogastric Nerve [*Anatomy*] ... HGN
Hypoglycemia [*Medicine*] (DMAA) ... HG
Hypoglycemic Association [*Australia*] ... HA
Hypogonadism [*Endocrinology*] (DAVI) ... HH
Hypogonadotrophic [*Endocrinology*] (DAVI) ... HH
Hypogonadotrophic Eunuchoidism [*Medicine*] ... HE
Hypogonadotropic Hypogonadism [*Medicine*] ... HHG
Hypohidrotic Ectodermal Dysplasia [*Medicine*] ... HED
Hypohidrotic Ectodermal Dysplasia-Hypothyroidism [*Syndrome*] [*Medicine*] (DMAA) ... HEDH
Hypoiodism [*Medicine*] ... HIO
Hypomelanosis of Ito [*Medicine*] (DMAA) ... HI
Hypomelanosis of Ito [*Medicine*] (DMAA) ... HMI
Hypo-Osmotic Shock Treatment [*Analytical biochemistry*] ... HOST
Hypoparathyroidism [*Endocrinology*] ... HOPT
Hypoparathyroidism, Addison's Disease, and Musculocutaneous Candidiasis [*Medicine*] ... HAM
Hypophosphatemic Rickets [*Medicine*] (DMAA) ... HR
Hypophsrynx [*Qtorhinolaryngology*] (DAVI) ... HP
Hypophysectomized [*Medicine*] ... Hx
Hypophysectomy [*Medicine*] (DAVI) ... HE
Hypophysectomy [*Medicine*] ... HYPOX
Hypophysiotropic Area [*of hypothalamus*] [*Endocrinology*] ... HTA

Hypoplastic Left Atrium [*Cardiology*] (DAVI) .... HLA
Hypoplastic Left Heart [*Cardiology*] .... HLH
Hypoplastic Left Lung [*Medicine*] (DMAA) .... HLL
Hypoplastic Left Ventricle [*Cardiology*] (DAVI) .... HLV
Hypoplastic Left-Heart Syndrome [*Medicine*] .... HLHS
Hypoplastic Right Heart [*Cardiology*] .... HRH
Hypopressure Gas Chromatography .... HPGC
Hyporeninemic Hypoaldosteronism [*Endocrinology*] .... HH
Hypostyle (VRA) .... hypst
Hyposulfate [*Solium Thiosulphate*] [*A compound used in photography*] (WDMC) .... hypo
Hyposulfite of Sodium [*Photography*] (ROG) .... HYPO
Hypotension [*Medicine*] .... HT
Hypotenuse [*Mathematics*] .... HYP
Hypotenuse [*Mathematics*] (ROG) .... HYPOT
Hypothalamic Blood FLow [*Medicine*] (DMAA) .... HBF
Hypothalamic, Pituitary, Gonadal [*Endocrinology*] .... HPG
Hypothalamic Secretory Factor [*Endocrinology*] .... HSF
Hypothalamic-Pituitary-Adrenal [*Axis*] [*Endocrinology*] (DAVI) .... HPA
Hypothalamic-Pituitary-Adrenocortical [*Endocrinology*] .... HPA
Hypothalamo-Hypophyseal-Adrenal [*Endocrinology*] .... HHA
Hypothalamo-Neurohypophyseal Complex [*Endocrinology*] .... HNC
Hypothalamo-Pituitary-Adreno-Cortical [*Medicine*] (DMAA) .... HPAC
Hypothalamus [*Neurology*] .... HT
Hypothalamus [*Medicine*] (DMAA) .... HTH
Hypothalamus [*Neuroanatomy*] .... HYP
Hypothalmic Amenorrhea [*Medicine*] (DAVI) .... HA
Hypothalmic Secretory Factor for Adreno-Corticotropic Hormone (PDAA) .... HSF-ACTH
Hypothenar [*Anatomy*] .... Hy
Hypothenar Hammer Syndrome [*Medicine*] .... HHS
Hypothermal Coal Process (GNE) .... HCP
Hypothermally Treated (GNE) .... HT
Hypothesis .... H
Hypothesis .... HYP
Hypothesis (ADA) .... HYPOTH
Hypothesis Testing Model (IEEE) .... HTM
Hypothetical (WDAA) .... HYP
Hypothetical (MSA) .... HYPOTH
Hypothetical Core Disruptive Accident [*Nuclear energy*] .... HCDA
Hypothetical Future Samples [*Statistics*] .... HFS
Hypothetical Machine (MHDB) .... HM
Hypothetical Reference Circuit [*Telecommunications*] (TEL) .... HRC
Hypothetical Reference Connection [*Meteorology*] .... HRX
Hypothetical Reference Digital Path [*Meteorology*] .... HRDP
Hypothetical Syllogism [*Rule of inference*] [*Logic*] .... HS
Hypothetico-Deductive .... H-D
Hypotonia-Hypomentia-Hypogonadism-Obesity [*Medicine*] .... HHHO
Hypotonic Duodenogram [*Medicine*] .... HD
Hypotonic Lysis Buffer [*Analytical biochemistry*] .... HLB

Hypouricemia [*Medicine*] .... HUC
Hypovirulence-Associated Virus .... HAV
Hypoxanthine [*Also, Hyp, HYPX*] [*Biochemistry*] .... Hx
Hypoxanthine [*Also, Hx, HYPX*] [*Biochemistry*] .... Hyp
Hypoxanthine [*Also, Hx, Hyp*] [*Biochemistry*] .... HYPX
Hypoxanthine and Azaserine [*Medium*] .... HAS
Hypoxanthine Phosphoribosyltransferase [*Also, HGPRT*] [*An enzyme*] .... HPRT
Hypoxanthine-Aminopterin-Thymidine [*Medium*] [*Biochemistry*] .... HAT
Hypoxanthine-Guanine Phosphoribosyltransferase [*AO HPRT*] [*An enzyme*] .... HGPRT
Hypoxanthine-Guanine Phosphoribosyltransferase [*Also, HGPRT, HPRT*] [*An enzyme*] (DAVI) .... HG-PRTase
Hypoxanthine-Guanine-Phosphoribosyl Transferase (DOG) .... HPRT
Hypoxia-Inducible Factor [*Physiology*] .... HIF
Hypoxia-Responsive Element [*Molecular medicine*] .... HRE
Hypoxic Pulmonary Vascular Response [*Anesthesiology*] .... HPVR
Hypoxic Pulmonary Vasoconstriction [*Medicine*] .... HPV
Hypoxic Ventilatory Response [*Medicine*] .... HVR
Hypoxic-Ischemic Lesion [*Medicine*] (DAVI) .... HIL
Hypoxi-Ischemic Encephalopathy [*Neurology*] (DAVI) .... HIE
Hypsipyle [*of Euripides*] [*Classical studies*] (OCD) .... Hyps
Hysterectomy [*Medicine*] (AAMN) .... HYS
Hysterectomy [*Medicine*] .... hyst
Hysterectomy [*Gynecology*] (DAVI) .... hyster
Hysterectomy and Radiation [*Medicine*] .... H & R
Hysterectomy Educational Resources and Services Foundation (EA) .... HERS
Hysterectomy Produced and Artificially Reared (PDAA) .... HYPAR
Hysterectomy Support Group [*British*] (DBA) .... HSG
Hysteresis Comparator .... HC
Hysteresis Motor [*Electronics*] (IAA) .... HM
Hysteria [*Psychiatry*] (DAVI) .... hy
Hysteria .... HYS
Hysterical Conversion Reaction [*Psychiatry*] (DAVI) .... HCR
Hysterical Personality .... HP
Hysteroid-Obsessoid Questionnaire [*Psychology*] .... HOQ
Hysterosalpingogram [*Gynecology*] .... HSG
Hysterosalpingogram [*Gynecology*] (DHSM) .... HYSTERO
Hysterosalpingography [*Medicine*] (DMAA) .... HSG
Hysterosalpingography [*Gynecology*] (DAVI) .... HSGB
Hysterotomy and Sterilization [*Medicine*] .... H & S
Hythe Municipal Library, Alberta [*Library symbol National Library of Canada*] (NLC) .... AHYM
Hythe Municipal Library, Hythe, AB, Canada [*Library symbol*] [*Library of Congress*] (LCLS) .... CaAHyM
Hytone Film Lab, Inc., Des Moines, IA [*Library symbol Library of Congress*] (LCLS) .... HyF
Hytran Simulation Language [*Computer science*] (PDAA) .... HSL
Hyundai California Design [*Concept car*] .... HCD
Hyundai Motor America, Inc. .... HMA
Hyvinkaa [*Finland ICAO location identifier*] (ICLI) .... EFHV

I

By Meaning

I Am Chairman of Chrysler Corp. of America [*Acronym formed from name of Chrysler chairman Lee Iacocca*] .... IACOCCA
I Am Not a Doctor [*Internet*] .... IANAD
I Am Not a Lawyer [*Internet*] .... IANAL
I Baruch [*Apocrypha*] (BJA) .... I Bar
I Corps Tactical Zone [*Vietnamese designation for both a military zone and a political region*] .... ICTZ
I Dance Jazz [*Jazz music group*] (ECON) .... IDJ
I Got Mine [*Slang describing attitude of some nouveaux riches*] .... IGM
[*The*] I Hate Barney Secret Society (EA) .... TIHBSS
I Have a Dream Foundation (EA) .... IHAD
I Heard You (MHDI) .... IHY
I Kings [*Old Testament book*] .... 1 KG
I Love Dance [*Competition in US and Canada*] .... ILD
I Love You Very Much [*Correspondence*] (DSUE) .... ILUVM
I. N. McKinnon Memorial Library, Calgary, AB, Canada [*Library symbol Library of Congress*] (LCLS) .... CaACMM
I. N. McKinnon Memorial Library, Calgary, Alberta [*Library symbol National Library of Canada*] (NLC) .... ACMM
I/O [*Input/Output*] Privilege Level [*Computer science*] .... IOPL
I Owe You [*Slang*] .... IOU
I. P. Sharp Associates Ltd., Carleton Place, ON, Canada [*Library symbol Library of Congress*] (LCLS) .... CaOCpS
I. P. Sharp Associates Ltd., Carleton Place, Ontario [*Library symbol National Library of Canada*] (NLC) .... OCPS
I Pagliacci [*Opera*] (DSUE) .... PAG
I Quit [*Smoking*] .... IQ
I/S Datacentralen [*Information service or system*] (IID) .... DC
I Salmi [*Finland ICAO location identifier*] (ICLI) .... EFII
I Trust and Love You [*Correspondence*] (DSUE) .... ITALY
I V C Industries [*NASDAQ symbol*] (TTSB) .... IVCO
I V C Industries Wrrt [*NASDAQ symbol*] (TTSB) .... IVCOW
I Was There .... IWT
I Will Call You Again [*International telex abbreviation*] (WDMC) .... RAP
I Wish Everyone Would Stop Using Letters of the Alphabet to Designate Their Organizations [*Originated by Bea von Boeselager in "Line o' Type," Chicago Tribune*] .... IWEWSULOTATDTO
i2 Technologies [*NASDAQ symbol*] (TTSB) .... ITWO
Iacet Hic [*Here Lies*] [*Latin*] .... IH
IAEA [*International Atomic Energy Agency*] Marine Environment Laboratory [*Marine science*] (OSRA) .... IMEL
Iakutaviatrans [*Russian Federation*] [*ICAO designator*] (FAAC) .... IKT
IAL Consultancy Services [*Southall, England*] [*Telecommunications*] (TSSD) .... IACS
Iamalele [*Papua New Guinea*] [*Airport symbol*] (OAG) .... IMA
Iambic Verse (DSUE) .... IAMBI
IAPA [*Industrial Accident Prevention Association*] Library, Toronto, ON, Canada [*Library symbol Library of Congress*] (LCLS) .... CaOTIAP
IAPA [*Industrial Accident Prevention Association*] Library, Toronto, Ontario [*Library symbol National Library of Canada*] (NLC) .... OTIAP
Iasi [*Romania*] [*Airport symbol*] (OAG) .... IAS
Iasi [*Romania*] [*Seismograph station code, US Geological Survey*] (SEIS) .... IAS
Iasi [*Romania*] [*ICAO location identifier*] (ICLI) .... LRIA
IATA [*International Air Transport Association*] Containers [*Shipping*] (DCTA) .... IA
IATA [*International Air Transport Association*] Unit of Value [*International airline currency*] .... IUV
Iatros Health Network [*NASDAQ symbol*] (TTSB) .... IHNI
Iatros Health Network, Inc. [*Associated Press*] (SAG) .... IatrosHlt
Iatros Health Network, Inc. [*NASDAQ symbol*] (SAG) .... IHNI
Iatros Health Network Wrrt [*NASDAQ symbol*] (TTSB) .... IHNIW
Iauarete [*Brazil ICAO location identifier*] (ICLI) .... SBYA
Iba, Zambales [*Philippines*] [*ICAO location identifier*] (ICLI) .... RPUI
Ibadan [*Nigeria*] [*ICAO location identifier*] (ICLI) .... DNIB
Ibadan [*Nigeria*] [*Airport symbol*] (OAG) .... IBA
Ibadan [*Nigeria*] [*Geomagnetic observatory code*] .... IBD
Ibague [*Colombia*] [*Airport symbol*] (OAG) .... IBE
Ibague/Perales [*Colombia ICAO location identifier*] (ICLI) .... SKIB
IBAH, Inc. [*NASDAQ symbol*] (SAG) .... IBAH
Ibarra [*Ecuador*] [*ICAO location identifier*] (ICLI) .... SEIB
Ibbi-Sin (BJA) .... IS
I-Beam [*Structural metal shape*] I
I-Beam [*Lumber*] (DAC) .... IB
Ibeke [*Zaire ICAO location identifier*] (ICLI) .... FZBU
Iberia [*Peru*] [*ICAO location identifier*] (ICLI) .... SPBR
Iberia Air Lines of Spain [*ICAO designator*] (AD) .... IB
Iberia Air Lines of Spain (MCD) .... IBR

Iberia Parish Library, New Iberia, LA [*Library symbol Library of Congress*] (LCLS) .... LNil
Iberia-Lineas Aereas de Espana SA [*Spain ICAO designator*] (FAAC) .... IBE
Iberian Atlantic Area [*NATO*] (NATG) .... IBERLANT
Iberian Atlantic Planning Guidance (NATG) .... IAPG
Iberian Federation of Anarchist Groups [*Spain*] (PD) .... FIGA
Iberian Peninsula [*MARC geographic area code Library of Congress*] (LCCP) .... ei----
Iberian Peninsula Operating Committee [*World War II*] .... IPOC
Iberiotoxin [*Biochemistry*] .... IBX
Iberiotoxin [*Biochemistry*] .... ITX
Ibero Latin American College of Dermatology (EA) .... ILACD
Ibero-American Association of Chambers of Commerce [*See also AICO*] [*Bogota, Colombia*] (EAIO) .... IAACC
Ibero-American Bureau of Education [*See also OEI*] [*Madrid, Spain*] (EAIO) .... IABE
Iberoamerican Cultural Exchange Program [*An association*] (EA) .... ICEP
Ibero-American Institute of Agrarian Law and Agrarian Reform [*See also IIDARA*] [*Mexida, Venezuela*] (EAIO) .... IAIALAR
Ibero-American Organization of Pilots [*See also OIP*] [*Mexico City, Mexico*] (EAIO) .... IOP
Ibero-American Philosophical Society [*Madrid, Spain*] (EAIO) .... IPS
Ibero-American Society for Cell Biology [*See also SIABC*] (EAIO) .... IASCB
Ibero-Amerikanisches Institu Preussicher Kulturbesitz, Berlin, Germany [*Library symbol*] [*Library of Congress*] (LCLS) .... GyBIAI
Ibero-Armorican Arc [*A geological area of western Europe*] .... IAA
Iberville Parish Library, Plaquemine, LA [*Library symbol Library of Congress*] (LCLS) .... LPlaI
IBI Group, Toronto, Ontario [*Library symbol National Library of Canada*] (BIB) .... OTIBI
IBI [*Intergovernmental Bureau for Informatics*] International Computat ion Centre (NITA) .... IBI-ICC
IBIA News, Ames, IA [*Library symbol Library of Congress*] (LCLS) .... IaAIBI
Ibidem [*In the Same Place*] [*Latin*] .... IB
Ibidem [*Latin*] [*In the same place*] (WDMC) .... ib
Ibidem [*In the Same Place*] [*Latin*] .... IBID
Ibis [*of Ovid*] [*Classical studies*] (OCD) .... Ib
Ibis [*Belgium ICAO designator*] (FAAC) .... IBS
IBIS Information & Research Services, Vancouver, BC, Canada [*Library symbol*] [*Library of Congress*] (LCLS) .... CaBVaIB
IBIS Information & Research Services, Vancouver, British Columbia [*Library symbol National Library of Canada*] (NLC) .... BVAIB
Ibis Technology [*NASDAQ symbol*] (TTSB) .... IBIS
Ibis Technology Corp. [*NASDAQ symbol*] (SAG) .... IBIS
Ibis Technology Corp. [*Associated Press*] (SAG) .... IbisTc
Ibis Technology Corp. [*Associated Press*] (SAG) .... IbisTech
Ibis Technology Wrrt [*NASDAQ symbol*] (TTSB) .... IBISW
Ibiza [*Spain*] [*Airport symbol*] (OAG) .... IBZ
Ibiza [*Spain ICAO location identifier*] (ICLI) .... LEIB
IBM Canada Ltd., Don Mills, Ontario [*Library symbol National Library of Canada*] (NLC) .... ODMIBM
IBM Canada Ltd., Markham, Ontario [*Library symbol National Library of Canada*] (NLC) .... OMIBM
IBM Computer Users' Association (NITA) .... IBMCUA
IBM Corp., Library/15C, Charlotte, NC [*Library symbol Library of Congress*] (LCLS) .... NcCl
IBM Corp., Library Processing Center, White Plains, NY [*OCLC symbol*] (OCLC) .... XIB
IBM Corp., Office Products Division, Lexington, KY [*Library symbol Library of Congress*] (LCLS) .... KyLxl
IBM, Euroflight-Operations [*Switzerland ICAO designator*] (FAAC) .... BBL
IBM [*International Business Machines Corp.*] IGES Format [*Initial Graphics Exchange Specification*] .... IIF
IBM [*International Business Machines Corp.*] Information Network (HGAA) .... IIN
IBM [*International Business Machines Corp.*] Information Services (HGAA) .... IIS
IBM Library Processing Center, White Plains, NY [*Library symbol Library of Congress*] (LCLS) .... NWhpI
IBM Personal Dication System [*Computer science*] .... IPDS
IBM [*International Business Machines Corp.*] Recruitment Information System (IAA) .... IRIS
IBM Speech Server Series .... ISSS
IBM [*International Business Machines Corp.*] Standard Data (IAA) .... ISD
IBM Technical Information Retrieval Center [*International Business Machines Corp.*] [*Armonk, NY*] .... ITIRC
IBM Workers United (NITA) .... IBM WU
Ibori [*Bolivia*] [*ICAO location identifier*] (ICLI) .... SLIR

Ibotenic Acid [*Organic acid*] (DMAA) .... IA
Ibotenic Acid [*Organic acid*] .... IBO
IBP, Inc. [*NYSE symbol*] (SPSG) .... IBP
Ibra [*Oman*] [*ICAO location identifier*] (ICLI) .... OOIA
Ibri [*Oman*] [*ICAO location identifier*] (ICLI) .... OOII
IBS Financial [*NASDAQ symbol*] (TTSB) .... IBSF
IBS Financial Corp. [*Associated Press*] (SAG) .... IBS Fncl
IBS Financial Corp. [*NASDAQ symbol*] (SAG) .... IBSF
IBS Technologies Ltd. [*Vancouver Stock Exchange symbol*] .... IBT
Ibsen Society of America (EA) .... ISA
Ibukiyama [*Ibukisan*] [*Japan*] [*Seismograph station code, US Geological Survey*] [*Closed*] (SEIS) .... IBU
Ibuprofen [*A drug*] I
Ibycus [*Sixth century BC*] [*Classical studies*] (OCD) .... Ibyc
Ica [*Peru*] [*Seismograph station code, US Geological Survey*] (SEIS) .... ICA
Ica [*Peru*] [*ICAO location identifier*] (ICLI) .... SPIA
ICA [*International Co-Operative Alliance*] **Working Party on Co-Operative Communications** (EAIO) .... WPoCC
ICA [*International Co-Operative Alliance*] **Working Party on Co-Operative Press** [*Later, WPoCC*] (EAIO) .... WPoCP
Icabaru [*Venezuela*] [*Airport symbol*] (OAG) .... ICA
Icabaru [*Venezuela*] [*Airport symbol*] (AD) .... ICA
Icabaru, Bolivar [*Venezuela ICAO location identifier*] (ICLI) .... SVIC
ICAM [*Integrated Computer-Aided Manufacturing*] **Decision Support System** (IEEE) .... IDSS
ICAM Definition (MCD) .... IDEF
ICAN Minerals Ltd. [*Toronto Stock Exchange symbol*] .... IMI
Icana [*Brazil*] [*Airport symbol*] (AD) .... INA
ICAO [*International Civil Aviation Organization*] **Bird Strike Information System** [*Information service or system*] (IID) .... IBIS
Icar Airlines [*Ukraine*] [*FAA designator*] (FAAC) .... IPR
ICAR [*Interstate Cinderellans and Revenuers*] **Educational Club** (EA) .... ICAR
Icard Township, NC [*AM radio station call letters*] .... WUIV
Icaro [*Italy*] [*FAA designator*] (FAAC) .... ICA
ICBM [*Intercontinental Ballistic Missile*] **Blast Interference Test** (MCD) .... IBIT
ICBM [*Intercontinental Ballistic Missile*] **Code Processing System** (DWSG) .... ICPS
ICC [*International Chamber of Commerce*] **Counterfeiting Intelligence Bureau** (EA) .... CIB
ICC Technologies [*NASDAQ symbol*] (TTSB) .... ICGN
ICC Technologies, Inc. [*Associated Press*] (SAG) .... ICC Tch
ICC Technologies, Inc. [*NASDAQ symbol*] (SAG) .... ICGN
ICD [*Interface Control Document*] **Departure Authorization** [*NASA*] (NASA) .... DDA
Ice Age .... IA
Ice and Snow on Runway [*Aviation*] .... IASOR
Ice Breaker [*Freight*] .... I BKR
Ice Chest IC
Ice, Compression, Elevation (CPH) .... ICE
Ice, Compression, Elevation, Support [*Medicine*] (MEDA) .... ICES
Ice Condenser Instrumentation [*Nuclear energy*] (NRCH) ICI
Ice Cream [*Freight*] .... I CRM
Ice Cream Alliance Ltd. [*British*] (BI) .... ICA
Ice Cream Connoisseurs Club [*Defunct*] (EA) ICCC
Ice Cream Federation Ltd. [*British*] (BI) .... ICF
Ice Crystal Cloud ICC
Ice Crystals IC
Ice (Deposition) Nuclei [*Atmospheric science*] .... IN
Ice Fog .... IF
Ice Haulage .... IH
Ice Navigation Center [*Marine science*] (MSC) .... INC
Ice Nucleating Activity [*Biology*] [*Physics*] .... INA
Ice on Runway [*NWS*] (FAAC) .... IR
Ice on Runway - Patchy [*Aviation*] .... IRP
Ice Pellets [*Meteorology*] .... PE
Ice Plow [*Coast Guard*] (DNAB) .... IP
Ice Point .... IP
Ice Rinks [*Public-performance tariff class*] [*British*] .... IR
Ice Screamers (EA) .... IS
Ice Shelf Water [*Oceanography*] .... ISW
Ice Skating Institute of America (EA) .... ISIA
Ice Sounding RADAR .... ISR
Ice Station Resources [*Vancouver Stock Exchange symbol*] .... ICE
Ice Water Content .... IWC
Iceberg (ODBW) .... berg
Iceberg Athletic Club (EA) .... IAC
Iceberg Transport International Ltd. [*Saudi Arabia*] (PDAA) .... ITI
Ice-Binding Motif [*Biochemistry*] .... IBM
Icebird Airline Ltd. [*Iceland*] [*ICAO designator*] (FAAC) .... ICB
Icebreaker [*Navy ship symbol*] .... AGB
Ice-Cream Van [*Slang British*] ICV
Ice-Cuber .... ICBR
Ice-Cutter Semi-Submersible Drilling Vessel (PDAA) .... ICSDV
Icefield Ranges Research Project .... IRRP
Iceland [*MARC geographic area code Library of Congress*] (LCCP) .... e-ic--
Iceland [*MARC country of publication code Library of Congress*] (LCCP) ic
Iceland [*NATO*] IC
Iceland .... ICE
Iceland (VRA) .... Icel
Iceland [*IYRU nationality code*] IL
Iceland [*ANSI two-letter standard code*] (CNC) .... IS
Iceland [*ANSI three-letter standard code*] (CNC) .... ISL
Iceland [*International civil aircraft marking*] (ODBW) .... TF
Iceland Base Command [*Army World War II*] .... IBC
Iceland Communications and Control Enhancement .... ICCE
Iceland Defense Force .... ICEDEFOR
Iceland Ocean Meeting Point [*Navy*] .... ICOMP
Iceland Patrol [*Navy*] .... ICEPAT
Iceland Regional Operational Control Center [*Aircraft surveillance*] .... ICEROCC
Iceland Veterans [*Defunct*] (EA) IV
Icelandair [*ICAO designator*] (FAAC) .... ICE
Iceland-Canada Cable (NITA) .... ICECAN
Iceland-Canada Submarine Cable System [*Telecommunications*] (TEL) .... ICECAN
Icelandic [*MARC language code Library of Congress*] (LCCP) .... ice
Icelandic .... ICEL
Icelandic Air Defense Force (MUGU) .... IADF
Icelandic Coast Guard [*ICAO designator*] (FAAC) .... ICG
Icelandic Federation of Labor .... IFL
Icelandic Horse Adventure Society (EA) .... IHAS
Icelandic Horse Society [*British*] (DBA) .... IHSGB
Icelandic Horse Trekkers (EA) .... IHT
Icelandic Pony Trekkers [*Later, IHT*] (EA) .... IPT
Icelandic Research Drilling Project .... IRDP
Iceland-Scotland Overflow Water [*Oceanography*] .... ISOW
Ice-Penetrating Communications Buoy (DWSG) .... IPB
Ice-Rafted Debris [*Oceanography*] .... IRD
ICES [*Integrated Civil Engineering System*] **Users Group** [*Defunct*] (EA) .... IUG
ICF Kaiser International [*NYSE symbol*] (SPSG) .... ICF
ICF Kaiser International [*Associated Press*] (SAG) .... ICF Int
ICG Communications, Inc. [*AMEX symbol*] (SAG) .... ICG
ICG Communications, Inc. [*Associated Press*] (SAG) .... ICG Com
ICG Utilities (Ontario) Ltd. [*Toronto Stock Exchange symbol*] .... IUO
ICG Utility Investments Ltd. [*Toronto Stock Exchange symbol*] .... ICU
Ich Bau auf Gott [*I Build on God*] [*Motto of Heinrich Posthumus, Count Reuss (1572-1635)*] [*German*] .... IBAG
ICH Corp. [*Later, Southwestern Life*] [*AMEX symbol*] (SPSG) .... ICH
Ichigaya [*Japan ICAO location identifier*] (ICLI) .... RJAI
ICHOR Corp. [*Associated Press*] (SAG) .... ICHOR
ICHOR Corp. [*NASDAQ symbol*] (SAG) .... ICHR
Ichthyological Laboratory and Museum [*University of Miami*] .... IL & M
Ichthyology .... ICH
Ichthyology .... ICHTH
Ichthyology (BARN) .... ichthyol
Ichthyosis Bullosa of Siemens [*Medicine*] .... IBS
Ichthyosis Linearis Circumflex [*Medicine*] (DMAA) ILC
Ichud Habonim Labor Zionist Youth (EA) .... IHLZY
ICI America, Inc., Darco Experimental Laboratory Library, Marshall, TX [*Library symbol Library of Congress*] (LCLS) .... TxMalC
ICI Americas, Inc., Wilmington, DE [*OCLC symbol*] (OCLC) .... DLK
ICI Pharmaceuticals [*Great Britain*] [*Research code symbol*] ICI
Icing [*Aviation*] (FAAC) IC
Icing [*Meteorology*] (BARN) .... ICG
Icing in Clouds [*NWS*] (FAAC) .... ICGIC
Icing in Clouds and Precipitation [*NWS*] (FAAC) .... ICGICIP
Icing in Precipitation [*NWS*] (FAAC) .... ICGIP
Icing Research Tunnel [*Built at Lewis Research Center in 1944 by the National Advisory Committee for Aeronautics*] .... IRT
ICIS Management Group, Inc. [*NASDAQ symbol*] (SAG) .... ICIS
ICIS Management Group, Inc. [*Associated Press*] (SAG) .... ICIS Mgt
ICIS Mgmt Group [*NASDAQ symbol*] (TTSB) .... ICIS
ICN Pharmaceuticals [*NYSE symbol*] (TTSB) .... ICN
ICN Pharmaceuticals, Inc. [*Formerly, SPI Pharmaceuticals*] [*NYSE symbol*] (SPSG) .... ICN
ICN Pharmaceuticals, Inc. [*Formerly, International Chemical & Nuclear Corp.*] [*Associated Press*] (SAG) .... ICN Ph
ICO, Inc. [*Associated Press*] (SAG) .... ICO
ICO, Inc. [*Associated Press*] (SAG) .... ICO Inc
ICO, Inc. [*NASDAQ symbol*] (NQ) .... ICOC
ICO Inc. 6.75% Cv Dep Pfd [*NASDAQ symbol*] (TTSB) .... ICOCZ
ICOM [*International Council of Museums*] **Committee for Conservation** (EAIO) .... ICOM-CC
Icon [*Plate engraving*] IC
Icon (VRA) .... icn
Icon-Based Program Generators [*Software*] [*Computer science*] .... IBPG
Iconic Store, Central [*Psychophysiology*] .... ISc
Iconic Store, Peripheral [*Psychophysiology*] .... ISp
Iconized Flowchart Compilers [*Software*] [*Computer science*] .... IFCC
Iconoclasm (ADA) .... ICON
Iconography .... ICON
Iconography Classification [*Netherlands*] (NITA) .... ICONCLASS
Iconoscope (IAA) I
Iconoscope [*A television camera tube*] (WDMC) .... ike
Iconostasis (VRA) .... iconst
ICOR Oil & Gas Co. Ltd. [*Toronto Stock Exchange symbol*] .... IOO
ICOS Corp. [*NASDAQ symbol*] (SPSG) .... ICOS
ICOT Corp. [*NASDAQ symbol*] (NQ) .... ICOT
ICOT Corp. [*Associated Press*] (SAG) .... Icot
ICP [*International Computer Programs, Inc.*] **Software Information Database** [*Information service or system*] (CRD) .... SID
ICS [*Interpretive Computer Simulator*] **Control Program** [*Army*] .... ICP
ICSU [*International Council of Scientific Unions*] **Inter-Union Commission for Geodynamics** [*Marine science*] (MSC) .... IICG
ICT Group, Inc. [*Associated Press*] (SAG) .... ICT Grp
ICT Group, Inc. [*NASDAQ symbol*] (SAG) .... ICTG
Icteric [*Medicine*] (DAVI) IC
Icteric Serum Hepatitis [*Medicine*] .... ISH
Icterus [*Jaundice*] [*Medicine*] .... ICT
Icterus Index [*Liver function test*] [*Medicine*] (AAMN) .... ict ind
Icterus Neonatorum [*Medicine*] .... IN
Icterus Precox [*Medicine*] .... IP
ICU Medical [*NASDAQ symbol*] (TTSB) .... ICUI
ICU Medical, Inc. [*Associated Press*] (SAG) .... ICU Med

ICU Medical, Inc. [*NASDAQ symbol*] (SAG) .... ICUI

Icy Grain Halo [*Model of comet structure*] .... IGH

Id [*That*] [*Latin*] (GPO) I

ID Biomedical [*NASDAQ symbol*] (TTSB) .... IDBEF

ID Biomedical Corp. [*Associated Press*] (SAG) .... ID Bio

ID Biomedical Corp. [*Associated Press*] (SAG) .... ID Biom

ID Biomedical Corp. [*NASDAQ symbol*] (SAG) .... IDBE

Id, Ego, Superego [*Test*] [*Psychology*] .... IES

Id Est [*That Is*] [*Latin*] .... IE

Id Quod Erat Demonstrandum [*That Which Was to Be Proved*] [*Latin*] .... IQED

ID Table Entry [*Galaxy*] [*Computer science*] .... IDTE

Ida County Historical Society, Battle Creek, IA [*Library symbol Library of Congress*] (LCLS) .... IaBclHi

Ida County Historical Society, Ida Grove, IA [*Library symbol Library of Congress*] (LCLS) .... IaldglHi

Ida County Pioneer-Record, Ida Grove, IA [*Library symbol Library of Congress*] (LCLS) .... laldgPR

Ida Grove, IA [*Location identifier FAA*] (FAAL) .... IDG

Ida Grove, IA [*FM radio station call letters*] .... KIDA

Ida Public Library, Belvidere, IL [*Library symbol Library of Congress*] (LCLS) .... IBelv

Idabel, OK [*Location identifier FAA*] (FAAL) .... IBO

Idabel, OK [*AM radio station call letters*] .... KBEL

Idabel, OK [*FM radio station call letters*] .... KBEL-FM

Idaho I

Idaho [*Postal code*] .... ID

Idaho .... IDA

Idaho [*MARC country of publication code Library of Congress*] (LCCP) .... idu

Idaho [*MARC geographic area code Library of Congress*] (LCCP) .... n-us-id

Idaho Administrative Code [*A publication*] (AAGC) .... Idaho Adm Code

Idaho Administrative Code [*A publication*] (AAGC) .... IDAPA

Idaho Array [*Idaho*] [*Seismograph station code, US Geological Survey Closed*] (SEIS) .... IDA

Idaho Association of Public Accountants (SRA) .... IAPA

Idaho Association of School Administrators (SRA) .... IASA

Idaho Association of Soil Conservation Districts (SRA) .... IASCD

Idaho Automobile Dealers Association (SRA) .... IADA

Idaho Bean Commission (SRA) .... IBC

Idaho Beer and Wine Distributors Association (SRA) .... IBWDA

Idaho Building Contractors Association (SRA) .... IBCA

Idaho Cattle Association (SRA) .... ICA

Idaho Chemical Processing Plant [*AEC*] .... ICPP

Idaho Cooperative Fishery Research Unit [*University of Idaho*] [*Research center*] (RCD) .... ICFRU

Idaho Department of Health and Welfare [*Division of Environmental Quality*] (DOGT) .... DEQ

Idaho Drug Information Service [*Information service or system*] (IID) .... IDIS

Idaho Education Association (SRA) .... IEA

Idaho Elks Rehabilitation Hospital, Medical Library, Boise, ID [*Library symbol*] [*Library of Congress*] (LCLS) .... IdBEH

Idaho Falls [*Idaho*] [*Airport symbol*] (OAG) .... IDA

Idaho Falls, ID [*FM radio station call letters*] .... KFTZ

Idaho Falls, ID [*AM radio station call letters*] .... KICN

Idaho Falls, ID [*AM radio station call letters*] .... KID

Idaho Falls, ID [*FM radio station call letters*] .... KID-FM

Idaho Falls, ID [*Television station call letters*] .... KIDK

Idaho Falls, ID [*Television station call letters*] .... KIFI

Idaho Falls, ID [*FM radio station call letters*] .... KOSZ-FM

Idaho Falls, ID [*AM radio station call letters*] .... KUPI

Idaho Falls, ID [*FM radio station call letters*] .... KUPI-FM

Idaho Falls, ID [*Location identifier FAA*] (FAAL) .... SWU

Idaho Falls Public Library, Idaho Falls, ID [*Library symbol Library of Congress*] (LCLS) .... IdIf

Idaho Genealogical Society, Boise, ID [*Library symbol Library of Congress*] (LCLS) .... IdHi-G

Idaho Health Libraries Network [*Library network*] .... IDA-HEAL-NET

Idaho Hospital Association (SRA) .... IHA

Idaho Industrial Accident Board Reports [*A publication*] (DLA) .... Ida IAB

Idaho Laboratory Facility [*Later, IRC*] [*Idaho Falls, ID*] [*Department of Energy*] (GRD) .... ILF

Idaho Law Journal [*A publication*] (DLA) .... ID LJ

Idaho Law Journal [*A publication*] (DLA) .... Idaho LJ

Idaho Legislative Council, Legislative Library, Boise, ID [*Library symbol*] [*Library of Congress*] (LCLS) .... IdBL

Idaho Medical Association (SRA) .... IMA

Idaho Mining and Minerals Resources Research Institute [*University of Idaho*] [*Research center*] (RCD) .... IMMRRI

Idaho Mining Association (SRA) .... IMA

Idaho Motor Tariff Bureau, Boise ID [*STAC*] .... IMT

Idaho Museum of Natural History [*Idaho State University*] [*Research center*] (RCD) .... IMNH

Idaho National Engineering Laboratory [*Idaho Falls, ID*] [*Department of Energy*] .... INEL

Idaho Nuclear (MCD) .... IN

Idaho Nuclear Code Automation [*AEC*] .... INCA

Idaho Nuclear Corp. .... INC

Idaho Oil Marketers Association (SRA) .... IOMA

Idaho Operations Office [*Energy Research and Development Administration*] .... ID

Idaho Operations Office [*Energy Research and Development Administration*] (MCD) .... IDO

Idaho Operations Office [*Energy Research and Development Administration*] .... IOO

Idaho Potato Commission (EA) .... IPC

Idaho Power [*NYSE symbol*] (TTSB) .... IDA

Idaho Power Co. [*NYSE symbol*] (SPSG) .... IDA

Idaho Power Co. [*Associated Press*] (SAG) .... IdahoP

Idaho Power Co. .... IPCO

Idaho Reports [*A publication*] (DLA) .... ID

Idaho Reports [*A publication*] (DLA) .... Ida

Idaho Reports, New Series [*A publication*] (DLA) .... Idaho NS

Idaho Springs Public Library, Idaho Springs, CO [*Library symbol Library of Congress*] (LCLS) .... CoIs

Idaho State College [*Later, Idaho State University*] (AEBS) .... ISC

Idaho State Grange (SRA) .... ISG

Idaho State Historical Society, Boise, ID [*Library symbol Library of Congress*] (LCLS) .... IdHi

Idaho State Library, Blind and Physically Handicapped Services, Boise, ID [*Library symbol Library of Congress*] (LCLS) .... Id-BPH

Idaho State Library, Boise, ID [*Library symbol Library of Congress*] (LCLS) .... Id

Idaho State School & Hospital, Medical Library, Nampa, ID [*Library symbol*] [*Library of Congress*] (LCLS) .... IdNI

Idaho State School for the Deaf and Blind, Gooding, ID [*Library symbol*] [*Library of Congress*] (LCLS) .... IdGoS

Idaho State University (GAGS) .... Idaho St U

Idaho State University, Pocatello, ID [*Library symbol Library of Congress*] (LCLS) .... IdPI

Idaho Statesman Library, Boise, ID [*Library symbol*] [*Library of Congress*] (LCLS) .... IdBS

Idaho Sugarbeet Growers Association (SRA) .... ISGA

Idaho Supplement [*A publication*] (DLA) .... Ida Supp

Idaho Supreme Court, Idaho State Law Library, Boise, ID [*Library symbol Library of Congress*] (LCLS) .... Id-L

Idaho Supreme Court Reports [*A publication*] (DLA) .... Idaho

Idaho Territory .... ID TER

Idaho Territory [*Obsolete*] (ROG) .... IT

Idaho Test Station [*Nuclear energy*] (NRCH) .... ITS

Idaho Thoroughbred Breeders Association (SRA) .... ITBA

Idaho Veterinary Medical Association (SRA) .... IVMA

Idaho Water and Energy Resources Research Institute [*University of Idaho*] [*Research center*] (RCD) .... IWERRI

Idaho White Pine [*Lumber*] .... IWP

Idalou, TX [*FM radio station call letters*] (RBYB) .... KRBL

Ida-May Resources Ltd. [*Vancouver Stock Exchange symbol*] .... IMY

Idan Software Ind ISI [*NASDAQ symbol*] (TTSB) .... IDANF

Idan Software Industries ISI Ltd. [*NASDAQ symbol*] (NQ) .... IDAN

Idan Software Industries ISI Ltd. [*Associated Press*] (SAG) .... IdanSft

Idar-Oberstein [*Germany ICAO location identifier*] (ICLI) .... EDZJ

IDD Information Services, Inc. (IID) .... IDDIS

Iddin-Dagan (BJA) .... ID

Iddings' Dayton Term Reports [*Ohio*] [*A publication*] (DLA) .... IDD TR

Iddings' Dayton Term Reports [*Ohio*] [*A publication*] (DLA) .... Iddings DRB

Iddings' Dayton Term Reports [*Ohio*] [*A publication*] (DLA) .... Iddings TRD

Iddings' Dayton Term Reports [*Ohio*] [*A publication*] (DLA) .... Idings TRD

IDE Engineering Co., Winnipeg, Manitoba [*Library symbol National Library of Canada*] (NLC) .... MWIDE

IDE Engineering Co., Winnipeg, MB, Canada [*Library symbol Library of Congress*] (LCLS) .... CaMWIDE

Idea [*Slang*] .... ID

Idea Corp., Toronto, ON, Canada [*Library symbol*] [*Library of Congress*] (LCLS) .... CaOTIC

Idea Corp., Toronto, Ontario [*Library symbol National Library of Canada*] (NLC) .... OTIC

Ideal .... IDL

Ideal Adsorbed Solution [*Physical chemistry*] .... IAS

Ideal Body Weight [*Medicine*] .... IBW

Ideal Cement Co. Research Library, Fort Collins, CO [*Library symbol Library of Congress*] (LCLS) .... CoFI

Ideal Current Negative Immittance Converter .... INIC

Ideal Design of Effective and Logical Systems .... IDEALS

Ideal Effort Multiplier .... IEM

Ideal Gas Law .... IGL

Ideal Group of Companies, Inc. [*Toronto Stock Exchange symbol*] .... IDL

Ideal Liquidus Structures (IEEE) .... ILS

Ideal Low Pass Filter .... ILPF

Ideal Man Helicopter Engineering Project .... IMHEP

Ideal Modulation (IAA) .... IM

Ideal One-Dimensional Device (IAA) .... IODD

Ideal Quota [*Vitamin supplement*] [*British*] .... IQ

Ideal Solidus Structures (IEEE) .... ISS

Idealist International, Inc. (EA) III

Idealization to Frustration to Demoralization .... IFD

Ideas in the Teaching of Mathematics and Science (AIE) .... ITeMS

Ideas, Resources, Exchange [*Computer*] [*British*] .... IREX

IDEAssociates, Inc. [*Telecommunications*] (TSSD) .... IDEA

Ideational Fluency [*Research test*] .... IF

IDEC Pharmaceuticals [*NASDAQ symbol*] (TTSB) .... IDPH

IDEC Pharmaceuticals Corp. [*Associated Press*] (SAG) .... IDEC

IDEC Pharmaceuticals Corp. [*NASDAQ symbol*] (SPSG) .... IDPH

Idees pour l'Europe [*Paris, France*] (EAIO) .... IE

Idem [*The Same*] [*Latin*] .... ID

Idem Ac [*The Same As*] [*Latin*] .... ID AC

Idem Quod [*The Same As*] [*Latin*] .... IQ

Identa-Band (DAVI) .... IAB

Identical (MSA) .... IDENT

Identical by State [*Genetics*] .... IBS

Identical Location of Accelerometer and Force [*NASA*] .... ILAF

Identical-By-Descent [*Genetics*] .... IBD

Identification I

Identification [*Computer science*] .... ID

Identification (AFM) .... IDENT

Identification Accuracy [*Rate*] (MCD) .... IAC
Identification and Compliance Record (MCD) .... ICR
Identification and Exposition [*Also, ident-and-expo*] (WDMC) .... i&e
Identification and Reference Sheets (MCD) .... IRS
Identification and Traceability (IAA) .... IT
Identification Beacon [*Aviation*] (IAA) .... IB
Identification Beacon .... IBN
Identification Code IC
Identification Data .... ID
Identification Data Accessory (NTCM) .... IDA
Identification Date .... ID
Identification Dissector (MCD) .... ID
Identification, Distribution, and Exchange for Action [*Project*] .... IDEA
Identification, Friend or Foe [*Military*] .... IFF
Identification Friend or Foe/Air-Traffic Control RADAR Beacon System [*Military*] .... IFF/ATCRBS
Identification, Friend or Foe or Neutral (MCD) .... IFFN
Identification, Friend or Foe/Selective Identification Feature [*Military*] .... IFF/SIF
Identification, Friend or Foe, Switching Circuit [*Military*] (MSA) .... IFFS
Identification, Friend or Foe, Switching Circuit [*Military*] .... IFS
Identification, Friend or Foe Unit (MCD) .... IFFU
Identification Light .... IDLT
Identification Line [*Photojournalism*] (WDMC) .... i-line
Identification List IL
Identification List .... ILS
Identification Mark (IAA) .... IMK
Identification Number (DNAB) .... ID NO
Identification of Aircraft .... INDAIR
Identification of Position .... IP
Identification Officer [*Military*] .... IDO
Identification Peculiarity .... IP
Identification Point .... IP
Identification Record [*Computer science*] (MCD) .... IDR
Identification Safety Range [*Military*] (NVT) .... ISR
Identification Section .... IDS
Identification Supervisor [*Military*] .... IDS
Identification System for Questioned Documents [*Book title*] .... ISQD
Identification Transponder (MCD) .... IT
Identification Unit (MSA) .... IU
Identification-Acknowledge (MCD) .... ID-ACK
Identified (ROG) .... IDENTIFD
Identified Aerial Vehicle .... IAV
Identified Camouflaged Objects [*Hunting*] .... ICO
Identified Flying Object [*Air Force*] .... IFO
Identified Friendly [*Military*] .... IDFR
Identified Friendly Prior to Interception [*Military*] .... IPI
Identified Outward Dialing [*Telecommunications*] (TEL) .... IOD
Identified Parts List .... IPL
Identifier [*Online database field identifier*] .... ID
Identifier [*Dialog*] [*Searchable field*] (NITA) .... ID
Identifier (IAA) .... IDF
Identifier Block .... IB
Identify [*or Identification*] (DAVI) .... ID
Identify (ECII) .... IDENT
Identifying Criteria for Success [*Software package*] [*Development Dimensions Inc.*] .... ICS
Identity .... ID
Identity Card (BARN) IC
Identity Correct, Location Correct [*Psychology*] IcLc
Identity Correct, Location Incorrect [*Psychology*] IcLi
Identity Incorrect, Location Correct [*Psychology*] IiLc
Identity Incorrect, Location Incorrect [*Psychology*] IiLi
Identity Preserved [*Wheat*] [*Department of Agriculture*] .... IP
Identity-By-Descent Affected-Pedigree-Member [*Genetics*] .... IBD-APM
Identix, Inc. [*Associated Press*] (SAG) .... Identix
Identix, Inc. [*AMEX symbol*] (SPSG) .... IDX
Ideological .... Ideo
Ideological Survey [*Psychology*] .... IS
Ideon Group, Inc. [*Associated Press*] (SAG) .... Ideon
Ideon Group, Inc. [*NYSE symbol*] (SAG) .... IQ
[*The*] Ides .... ID
IDEX Corp. [*Associated Press*] (SAG) .... Idex
IDEX Corp. [*NYSE symbol*] (SPSG) .... IEX
IDEXX Laboratories [*NASDAQ symbol*] (SPSG) .... IDXX
IDEXX Laboratories, Inc. [*Associated Press*] (SAG) .... IdexxLb
IDG Conference Management Group [*Framingham, MA*] (TSSD) .... IDG/CMG
Idiana Council of Community Mental Health Centers (SRA) .... ICCMHC
Idiofa [*Zaire*] [*ICAO location identifier*] (ICLI) .... FZCB
Idiopathic Acquired Hemolytic Disease [*Medicine*] (MAE) .... IAHD
Idiopathic Acquired Refractory Sideroblastic Anemia [*Medicine*] (DMAA) .... IARSA
Idiopathic Adrenal Hyperplasia [*Medicine*] .... IAH
Idiopathic Alveolar Fibrosis [*Medicine*] (DMAA) .... IAF
Idiopathic Arterial Calcification of Infancy [*Medicine*] (DMAA) .... IACI
Idiopathic Aseptic Necrosis [*Medicine*] (DMAA) .... IAN
Idiopathic Calcification of Basal Ganglia [*Medicine*] (DMAA) .... ICBG
Idiopathic Carpal Tunnel Syndrome [*Medicine*] (DMAA) .... ICTS
Idiopathic CD4-Lymphocytopenia [*Medicine*] ILC
Idiopathic Cerebral Dysfunction [*Medicine*] (CPH) .... ICD
Idiopathic Congestive Cardiomyopathy [*Medicine*] .... ICCM
Idiopathic Cortical Hyperostosis [*Medicine*] (DMAA) .... ICH
Idiopathic Cyclic Oedema [*Medicine*] (DMAA) .... ICO
Idiopathic Dilated Cardiomyopathy [*Cardiology*] .... IDC
Idiopathic Disease of the Myocardium [*Cardiology*] (MAE) .... IDM
Idiopathic Fibroplasia [*Medicine*] (DMAA) .... IF

Idiopathic Fibrosing Alveolitis [*Medicine*] (DMAA) .... IFA
Idiopathic Flushing [*Medicine*] (DMAA) .... IF
Idiopathic Growth Hormone [*Medicine*] (MAE) .... IGH
Idiopathic Headache Score [*Neurology*] (DAVI) .... IHS
Idiopathic Hemachromatosis [*Medicine*] .... IHC
Idiopathic Hemochromatosis [*Medicine*] (CPH) .... IHC
Idiopathic Hyperaldosteronism [*Medicine*] (DMAA) .... IHA
Idiopathic Hypercalcemia [*Medicine*] .... IHC
Idiopathic Hypercalciuria [*Medicine*] .... IH
Idiopathic Hypereosinophilic Syndrome [*Medicine*] (DMAA) .... IHES
Idiopathic Hyperkinetic Heart Syndrome [*Medicine*] (DMAA) .... IHHS
Idiopathic Hyperplastic Aldosteronism [*Endocrinology*] .... IHA
Idiopathic Hypertrophic Aortic Stenosis [*Cardiology*] (DAVI) .... IHAS
Idiopathic Hypertrophic Cardiomyopathy [*Cardiology*] .... IHCM
Idiopathic Hypertrophic Osteoarthopathy [*Medicine*] .... IHO
Idiopathic Hypertrophic Subaortic Stenosis [*Medicine*] .... IHSS
Idiopathic Hypogonadotropic Hypogonadism [*Endocrinology*] .... IHH
Idiopathic Hypoparathyroidism [*Medicine*] .... IHP
Idiopathic Hypopituitarism [*Medicine*] (AAMN) .... IHP
Idiopathic Ineffective Erythropoiesis [*Hematology*] (AAMN) .... IIE
Idiopathic Juvenile Periodontitis [*Dentistry*] (PDAA) .... IJP
Idiopathic Membranous Nephropathy [*Nephrology*] .... IMN
Idiopathic Midline Destructive Disease [*Dentistry*] .... IMDD
Idiopathic Myeloid Proliferation [*Medicine*] (DMAA) .... IMP
Idiopathic Myocardial Hypertrophy [*Cardiology*] .... IMH
Idiopathic Nephrotic Syndrome .... INS
Idiopathic Orthostatic Hypotension [*Medicine*] .... IOH
Idiopathic Pain Syndrome [*Medicine*] (DMAA) .... IPS
Idiopathic Parkinson's Disease [*Medicine*] (CPH) .... IPD
Idiopathic Portal Hypertension [*Medicine*] .... IPH
Idiopathic Postprandial Syndrome [*Medicine*] (DMAA) .... IPS
Idiopathic Pulmonary Fibrosis [*Medicine*] .... IPF
Idiopathic Pulmonary Hemosiderosis [*Medicine*] .... IDPH
Idiopathic Pulmonary Hemosiderosis [*Medicine*] .... IPH
Idiopathic Refractory Sideroblastic Anemia [*Medicine*] (MAE) .... IRSA
Idiopathic Respiratory Distress Syndrome [*Pediatrics*] .... IRDS
Idiopathic Retroperitoneal Fibrosis [*Medicine*] (DMAA) .... IRF
Idiopathic Short Stature [*Medicine*] (DMAA) .... ISS
Idiopathic Thrombocytopenic Purpura [*Hematology*] (DAVI) .... ITCP
Idiopathic Thrombocytopenic Purpura [*Medicine*] .... ITP
Idiopathic Torsion Dystonia [*Medicine*] .... ITD
Idiopathic Torsion Dystonia [*Medicine*] .... ITD
Idiopathic Torsion Dytonia [*Medicine*] .... ITD
Idiopathic Ulcerative Colitis [*Medicine*] .... IUC
Idioventricular Rhythm [*Cardiology*] (DMAA) .... IVR
Idirect Fluorescence [*Medicine*] (DMAA) .... IF
Iditol Dehydrogenase (MAE) .... ID
Idle (BUR) IL
Idle Air Bleed [*Fuel system*] [*Automotive engineering*] .... IAB
Idle Air Bypass Control [*Fuel system*] [*Automotive engineering*] .... IABC
Idle Air Control [*Automotive engineering*] .... IAC
Idle Air Control Valve [*Fuel system*] [*Automotive engineering*] .... IACV
Idle Air Jet [*Fuel system*] [*Automotive engineering*] .... IAJ
Idle Channel Noise (IAA) .... ICN
Idle Line Network .... ILN
Idle Load Compensator [*Automotive engineering*] ILC
Idle Matrix Search [*Computer science*] .... IMS
Idle Money [*Business term*] (MHDB) .... IM
Idle Other Reasons [*Vessel status*] [*Navy*] .... IDREA
Idle Signal Unit [*Electronics*] (EECA) .... IDU
Idle Speed Actuator [*Automotive engineering*] .... ISA
Idle Speed Control [*Automotive engineering*] .... ISC
Idle Speed Control Actuator [*Automotive engineering*] .... ISCA
Idle Speed Control Valve [*Exhaust emissions*] [*Automotive engineering*] .... ISCV
Idle Tracking Switch [*Automotive engineering*] .... ITS
Idle Used for Storage [*Shipping*] .... IDSTO
Idle Vacuum Valve [*Exhaust emissions*] [*Automotive engineering*] IVV
Idle Validation Switch [*Automotive electronics*] .... IVS
Idle Waiting Convoy Forward [*Vessel status*] [*Navy*] .... IDFOR
Idle Waiting to Load [*Shipping*] .... IDLOD
Idler .... IDL
Idlewild Public Library, Idlewild, MI [*Library symbol*] [*Library of Congress*] (LCLS) .... Mild
IDM Environmental [*NASDAQ symbol*] (TTSB) .... IDMC
IDM Environmental Corp. [*Associated Press*] (SAG) .... IDM
IDM Environmental Corp. [*Associated Press*] (SAG) .... IDM Env
IDM Environmental Corp. [*NASDAQ symbol*] (SAG) .... IDMC
IDM Environmental Wrrt'A' [*NASDAQ symbol*] (TTSB) .... IDMCW
Idol of My Heart Elvis Presley Fan Club (EA) .... IMHEPFC
Idoneo-Vehiculo [*In a Suitable Vehicle*] [*Pharmacy*] .... IDON VEHIC
Idongus [*Proper*] [*Pharmacy*] (ROG) .... IDON
Idoxuridine [*or Iododeoxyuridine*] [*Also, IDUR, IdUrd, IUDR*] [*Pharmacology*] .... IDU
Idoxuridine [*or Iododeoxyuridine*] [*Also, IDU, IdUrd, IUDR*] .... IDUR
IDPS/Large File (NITA) .... IDPS/LF
Idre [*Sweden ICAO location identifier*] (ICLI) .... ESUE
IDS Aircraft Ltd. [*British ICAO designator*] (ICDA) .... IS
IDS Aircraft Lt. [*British*] [*FAA designator*] (FAAC) .... IDS
IDT Corp. [*NASDAQ symbol*] (TTSB) .... IDTC
IDT Corp. [*NASDAQ symbol*] (SAG) .... IDTC
IDT Corp. [*Associated Press*] (SAG) .... IDTCorp
Idumbe [*Zaire*] [*ICAO location identifier*] (ICLI) .... FZVU
Iduronate Sulfatase [*An enzyme*] .... IdS
Iduronic Acid .... IdUA
Idus [*The Ides*] [*Latin*] I
IDX Systems Corp. [*NASDAQ symbol*] (SAG) .... IDXC

IDX Systems Corp. [*Associated Press*] (SAG) .... IDXSys
IDX Systmes [*NASDAQ symbol*] (TTSB) .... IDXC
Idylls [*of Theocritus*] [*Classical studies*] (OCD) .... Id
Idyllwild, CA [*FM radio station call letters*] .... KATY
Idyllwild School of Music and the Arts [*California*] .... ISOMATA
IE Industries, Inc. (MHDW) .... IEL
IEC Electronics [*NASDAQ symbol*] (TTSB) .... IECE
IEC Electronics Corp. [*Associated Press*] (SAG) .... IEC Elc
IEC Electronics Corp. [*NASDAQ symbol*] (NQ) .... IECE
IEEE Acoustics, Speech, and Signal Processing Society (EA) .... ASSPC
IEEE Aerospace and Electronics Systems Society (EA) .... AESS
IEEE Antennas and Propagation Society (EA) .... APS
IEEE [*Institute of Electrical and Electronics Engineers*] **Automatic Control** (IAA) .... IEAC
IEEE Broadcast Technology Society (EA) .... BTS
IEEE [*Institute of Electrical and Electronics Engineers*] **Circuit Theory** (IAA) .... IECT
IEEE Circuits and Systems Society (EA) .... CSS
IEEE Communications Society (EA) .... CS
IEEE Components, Hybrids, and Manufacturing Technology Society (EA) .... CHMTS
IEEE Computer Society (EA) .... CS
IEEE Consumer Electronics Society (EA) .... CES
IEEE Control Systems Society (EA) .... CSS
IEEE Dielectrics and Electrical Insulation Society (EA) .... DEIS
IEEE Education Society (EA) .... ES
IEEE [*Institute of Electrical and Electronics Engineers*] **Electrical Insulation** (IAA) .... IEEI
IEEE Electromagnetic Compatability Society (EA) .... ECS
IEEE [*Institute of Electrical and Electronics Engineers*] **Electromagnetic Compatibility Society** (IAA) .... IEMC
IEEE Electron Devices Society (EA) .... EDS
IEEE [*Institute of Electrical and Electronics Engineers*] **Electronic Computer** (IAA) .... IEEC
IEEE Engineering in Medicine and Biology Society (EA) .... EMBS
IEEE Engineering Management Society (EA) .... EMS
IEEE Expert: Intelligent Systems and Their Applications [*A publication*] (BRI) .... IEEE Exp
IEEE Geoscience and Remote Sensing Society (EA) .... GRSS
IEEE [*Institute of Electrical and Electronics Engineers*] **Geoscience Electronics** (IAA) .... IEGE
IEEE Industrial Electronics Society (EA) .... IES
IEEE [*Institute of Electrical and Electronics Engineers*] **Industry and General Applications** (IAA) .... IIGA
IEEE Industry Applications Society (EA) .... IAS
IEEE [*Institute of Electrical and Electronics Engineers*] **Information Theory Society** (IAA) .... IEIT
IEEE Information Theory Society (EA) .... ITS
IEEE [*Institute of Electrical and Electronics Engineers*] **Instrumentation and Measurement Society** (IAA) .... IEIM
IEEE Instrumentation and Measurement Society (EA) .... IMS
IEEE [*Institute of Electrical and Electronics Engineers*] **LASERS and Electro-Optics Society** (EA) .... LEOS
IEEE [*Institute of Electrical and Electronics Engineers*] **Magnetics** (IAA) .... IMAG
IEEE Magnetics Society (EA) .... MS
IEEE Medical Imaging Committee (EA) .... MIC
IEEE Microwave Theory and Techniques Society (EA) .... MTTS
IEEE Nuclear and Plasma Sciences Society (EA) .... NPSS
IEEE Oceanic Engineering Society (EA) .... OES
IEEE [*Institute of Electrical and Electronics Engineers*] **Parts, Materials and Packaging** (IAA) .... IPMP
IEEE Power Electronics Council (EA) .... PEC
IEEE Power Engineering Society (EA) .... PES
IEEE Professional Communication Society (EA) .... PCS
IEEE [*Institute of Electrical and Electronics Engineers*] **Quantum Electronics** (IAA) .... IEQE
IEEE Reliability Society (EA) .... RS
IEEE Robotics and Automation Council (EA) .... RAC
IEEE Social Implications of Technology Society (EA) .... SITS
IEEE [*Institute of Electrical and Electronics Engineers*] **Sonics and Ultrasonics** (IAA) .... IESU
IEEE Systems, Man, and Cybernetics Society (EA) .... SMCS
IEEE Ultrasonics, Ferroelectrics, and Frequency Control Society (EA) .... UFFCS
IEEE Vehicular Technology Society (EA) .... VTS
Iejima [*Ryukyu Islands*] [*ICAO location identifier*] (ICLI) .... RORE
Iejima United States Air Force Base [*Ryukyu Islands*] [*ICAO location identifier*] (ICLI) .... RODE
IES [*Information Exchange System*] **Data Collections** [*Commission of the European Communities*] [*Information service or system*] (CRD) .... IES-DC
IES Industries [*NYSE symbol*] (SPSG) .... IES
IES Util 7.875%JrSubDebs [*NYSE symbol*] (TTSB) .... IEU
IES Utilities [*Associated Press*] (SAG) .... IES Ut25
IES Utilities [*NYSE symbol*] (SAG) .... IEU
Iesous Hemeteros Soter [*Jesus, Our Savior*] [*Greek*] .... IHS
Iesu Christo Duce [*With Jesus Christ as Leader*] [*Latin*] .... ICD
Iesu Christo Tutore [*With Jesus Christ as Protector*] [*Latin*] .... ICT
Iesus Christus [*Jesus Christ*] [*Latin*] IC
Iesus Christus [*Jesus Christ*] [*Latin*] IX
Iesus Heiland Seligmacher [*Jesus, Savior, Sanctifier*] [*German*] .... IHS
Iesus Hominum Salvator [*Jesus, Savior of Mankind*] [*Latin*] (ADA) .... IHS
Iesus Nazarenus Rex Iudaeorum [*Jesus of Nazareth, King of the Jews*] [*Latin*] .... INRI
Iesus Salvator Mundi [*Jesus, Savior of the World*] [*Latin*] .... ISM
If and Only If (IEEE) .... IFF
If Approach Missed Proceed [*Aviation*] (FAAC) .... IFAMP
If Clause .... IFC
If Flight Visibility Becomes Less Than [*Aviation*] (FAAC) .... IFVLS
If Holding [*Aviation*] (FAAC) .... IFHOL
If I Tell You, Will You Buy Me a Drink [*Tavern sign*] .... IITYWYBMAD
If Incorrect Advise [*Aviation*] .... IIA
If Incorrect Service Direct (FAAC) .... IISD
If Instrument Conditions Encountered [*Aviation*] (FAAC) .... IFINS
If Not Already Processed, Orders Cancelled [*Military*] .... NOPROCAN
If Not Available Notify This Office at Once .... INOAVNOT
If Not Available Your Command, Obtain Accounting Data from Administrative Command [*Army*] (AABC) .... NACOA
If Not Off (FAAC) .... INOF
If Not Possible (FAAC) .... INP
If Signal Source (MCD) .... IFSS
If Unable [*Aviation*] (FAAC) .... IFUN
If Visibility Remains [*Aviation*] (FAAC) .... IFVR
If You See What I Mean (PDAA) .... ISWIM
Iferouane [*Niger*] [*ICAO location identifier*] (ICLI) .... DRZI
IFF Reply Evaluator .... IRE
Iffley [*Australia Airport symbol Obsolete*] (OAG) .... IFF
IFIP [*International Federation for Information Processing*] **Committee for International Liaison** ICIL
IFlow Corp. [*NASDAQ symbol*] (SAG) .... IFLO
I-Flow Corp. [*NASDAQ symbol*] (TTSB) .... IFLO
IFlow Corp. [*Associated Press*] (SAG) .... I-Flow
Ifni [*MARC geographic area code Library of Congress*] (LCCP) .... f-if--
Ifosfamide, Mesna, Adriamycin, Cisplatin [*Antineoplastic drug*] (CDI) .... IMAC
Ifosfamide, Methotrexate, Fluorouracil (CDI) .... IMF
Ifostamide, Doxorubicin [*Antineoplastic drug*] (CDI) .... ID
Ifostamide, Methotrexate, VePesid (CDI) .... IMVP
IFR Systems [*NASDAQ symbol*] (TTSB) .... IFRS
IFR Systems, Inc. [*Associated Press*] (SAG) .... IFR
IFR Systems, Inc. [*NASDAQ symbol*] (NQ) .... IFRS
Ifrane [*Morocco*] [*ICAO location identifier*] (ICLI) .... GMFI
Ifrane [*Morocco*] [*Seismograph station code, US Geological Survey*] (SEIS) .... IFR
Igap [*Former USSR*] [*FAA designator*] (FAAC) .... IGP
IGEN, Inc. [*NASDAQ symbol*] (SAG) .... IGEN
IGF Metals, Inc. [*Vancouver Stock Exchange symbol*] .... IGF
IGI, Inc. [*AMEX symbol*] (SPSG) .... IG
IGI, Inc. [*Associated Press*] (SAG) .... IGI
Igitur [*Therefore*] [*Latin*] (ADA) .... IGR
Igiugig [*Alaska*] [*Airport symbol*] (OAG) .... IGG
Iglesia Ni Cristo [*Religious organization*] .... INC
Igloo [*Spacelab Pallet Missions*] .... IG
Igloo Environment Control Subsystem (MCD) .... IECS
Igloo Internal Thermal Control Section [*Aerospace*] (MCD) .... IITCS
Igloo Pallet [*Spacelab*] [*NASA*] (NASA) .... IP
Igloo Passive Thermal Control Section [*Aerospace*] (MCD) .... IPTCS
Igloo Thermal Control [*Aerospace*] (MCD) .... ITC
Igloo Vertical Access Kit [*Aerospace*] (NASA) .... IVAK
Iglooklik, NT [*ICAO location identifier*] (ICLI) .... CYGT
Igloolik [*Northwest Territories*] [*Seismograph station code, US Geological Survey*] (SEIS) .... IGL
Ignace Public Library, Ignace, ON, Canada [*Library symbol Library of Congress*] (LCLS) .... CaOIg
Ignace Public Library, Ontario [*Library symbol National Library of Canada*] (NLC) .... OIG
Ignacio, CO [*FM radio station call letters*] .... KSUT
Ignacio Public Library, Ignacio, CO [*Library symbol Library of Congress*] (LCLS) .... CoIg
Igneous & Geothermal Processes [*Marine science*] (OSRA) .... IGP
Igneous & Geothermal Processes (USDC) .... IGP
Ignitability Corrosivity, Reactivity, Extraction (GNE) .... ICRE
Igniter .... IGNR
Igniter (MSA) .... IGNTR
Igniter Booster Assembly [*Aerospace*] .... IBA
Igniter Circuit Test (IAA) .... ICT
Igniter Initiator II
Igniter Initiator Cartridge [*or Container*] IIC
Igniter Initiator Test Set .... IITS
Igniter Nozzle Closure .... INC
Igniter-Fuel Assembly .... IFA
Igniter-Fuel Valve (KSC) .... IFV
Ignition (KSC) .... IGN
Ignition .... IGN
Ignition Ackowledge Module [*Diesel engine controls*] [*Automotive engineering*] .... IAM
Ignition and Separation (IAA) .... IS
Ignition and Separation Assembly .... ISA
Ignition Control Additive (IAA) .... ICA
Ignition Control Programmer (MCD) .... ICP
Ignition Detector .... IGNDET
Ignition Diagnostic Monitor [*Automotive engineering*] .... IDM
Ignition Energetics Characterization Device (MCD) .... IECD
Ignition Manufacturers Institute [*Later, TMI*] (EA) .... IMI
Ignition Module Signal [*Automotive engineering*] .... IMS
Ignition Point [*Chemistry*] (IAA) .... IP
Ignition Pressure Switch [*Automotive engineering*] .... IPS
Ignition Shielding System .... ISS
Ignition Test Reactor (MCD) .... ITR
Ignition Test Simulator .... ITS
Ignition Timing Vacuum Switch [*Automotive engineering*] .... ITVS
Ignition Transmission Line .... ITL
Ignitor [*Electron device*] (MSA) .... IG
Ignitron [*Electronics*] .... IGN
Ignorant .... IGN

Ignorant Bloody Aircrafthand [British Royal Air Force slang] .... IBA
Ignotus [Unknown] [Latin] .... IGN
Igor-Patrick Air Force Base (KSC) .... IGPA
IGOSS [Integrated Global Ocean Station System] Basic Observation Network Design [Marine science] (MSC) .... IBOND
IGOSS [Integrated Global Ocean Station System] Data Processing and Services System (MSC) .... IDPSS
IGOSS [Integrated Global Ocean Station System] Observing System [Marine science] (MSC) .... IOS
IGOSS [Integrated Global Ocean Services System] Pilot Project on AlimetricSea-Surface Topography Data [Marine science] (OSRA) .... IPAST
IGOSS [Integrated Global Ocean Services System] Scientific Advisory Group [Marine science] (OSRA) .... ISAG
IGOSS [Integrated Global Ocean Services System] Sea Level Project [Marine science] (OSRA) .... ISLP
IGOSS [Integrated Global Ocean Services System] Sea Level Project in the Pacific [Marine science] (OSRA) .... ISLP-Pac
Iguassu Falls [Brazil] [Airport symbol] (OAG) .... IGU
Iguatu [Brazil] [Airport symbol] (AD) .... IGZ
Iguazu [Argentina] [Airport symbol] (OAG) .... IGR
Iguazu/Cataratas Del Iguazu [Argentina ICAO location identifier] (ICLI) .... SARI
Iguela [Gabon] [ICAO location identifier] (ICLI) .... FOOI
Iguela [Gabon] [Airport symbol Obsolete] (OAG) .... IGE
IHOP Corp. [NASDAQ symbol] (SAG) .... IHOP
IHOP Corp. [Associated Press] (SAG) .... IHOPCp
Ihosy [Madagascar] [ICAO location identifier] (ICLI) .... FMSI
Ihr [Your] [German] I
Ihre Koenigliche Hoheit [His (or Her) Royal Highness] [German] .... IKH
IHS [Information Handling Services] Product/Subject Index [Information service or system] (CRD) .... IHPI
Ihu [Papua New Guinea] [Airport symbol] (OAG) .... IHU
Ihud ha-Kibbutsim (BJA) .... IK
II Baruch [Pseudepigrapha] (BJA) .... II Bar
II Kings [Old Testament book] .... 2 KG
IIC Industries [NASDAQ symbol] (TTSB) .... IICR
IIC Industries, Inc. [Associated Press] (SAG) .... IIC Ind
IIC Industries, Inc. [NASDAQ symbol] (SAG) .... IICR
Iida [Japan] [Seismograph station code, US Geological Survey] (SEIS) .... IID
III Baruch [Pseudepigrapha] (BJA) .... III Bar
Iinan [Japan] [Seismograph station code, US Geological Survey] (SEIS) .... INA
IIS Intelligent Information Systems [Associated Press] (SAG) .... IIS
I.I.S. Intellig't Info [NASDAQ symbol] (TTSB) .... IISLF
IIS [Intelligent Information Systems] Ltd. [NASDAQ symbol] .... IISL
IIT Chicago-Kent College of Law, Chicago, IL [OCLC symbol] (OCLC) .... ILK
IITC Holdings [NASDAQ symbol] (TTSB) .... IITCF
IITC Holdings Ltd. [NASDAQ symbol] (SAG) .... IITC
IITC Holdings Ltd. [Associated Press] (SAG) .... IITCHld
II-VI, Inc. [NASDAQ symbol] (NQ) IIVI
Iizuka [Japan] [Seismograph station code, US Geological Survey Closed] (SEIS) .... IZK
Ijui [Brazil] [Airport symbol] (OAG) .... IJU
Ikaros DK [Denmark ICAO designator] (FAAC) .... IKR
Ikatan Buruh Kendaaran Bermotor [Motor Transport Workers' Union] [Indonesia] .... IBKB
Ikatan Buruh Kereta Api [Railroad Workers' Union] [Indonesia] .... IBKA
Ikatan Buruh Umum [General Workers' Union] [Indonesia] .... IBU
Ike and Tina Turner [Singers] .... I & TT
Ikebana International [Japan] II
Ikela [Zaire] [ICAO location identifier] (ICLI) .... FZGV
Ikela [Zaire] [Airport symbol] (AD) .... IKL
Iki [Japan] [Airport symbol] (OAG) .... IKI
Iki [Japan ICAO location identifier] (ICLI) .... RJDB
IKOS Systems [NASDAQ symbol] (TTSB) .... IKOS
Ikos Systems, Inc. [NASDAQ symbol] (SAG) .... IKOS
Ikusaka [Japan] [Seismograph station code, US Geological Survey] (SEIS) .... IKJ
Il Papiro Vaticano Greco II [A publication] (OCD) .... PVat II
ILA [Instruction Look Ahead] Associative Memory [Computer science] .... IAM
ILA [Instruction Look Ahead] Interrupt Address [Computer science] .... IIA
I-Labeled Iodoamphetamine .... I-IMP
Ilaga [Indonesia] [ICAO location identifier] (ICLI) .... WABL
Ilaka-Est [Madagascar] [ICAO location identifier] (ICLI) .... FMMQ
Ilam [Iran] [ICAO location identifier] (ICLI) .... OICI
Ilan [Giran] [Republic of China] [Seismograph station code, US Geological Survey] (SEIS) .... ILA
Ilan [China] [ICAO location identifier] (ICLI) .... RCMS
ILC Technology [NASDAQ symbol] (TTSB) .... ILCT
ILC Technology, Inc. [Associated Press] (SAG) .... ILC Tc
ILC Technology, Inc. [NASDAQ symbol] (NQ) .... ILCT
Ile a la Crosse Public Library, Ile a la Crosse, SK, Canada [Library symbol] [Library of Congress] (LCLS) .... CaSIL
Ile a la Crosse Public Library, Saskatchewan [Library symbol National Library of Canada] (NLC) .... SIL
Ile Art/Wala, Iles Belep [New Caledonia] [ICAO location identifier] (ICLI) ..... NWWC
Ile Des Pins [New Caledonia] [Airport symbol] (OAG) .... ILP
Ile Des Pins/Moue [New Caledonia] [ICAO location identifier] (ICLI) .... NWWE
Ile Ouen/Edmond-Cane [New Caledonia] [ICAO location identifier] (ICLI) .... NWWO
Ilebo [Zaire] [ICAO location identifier] (ICLI) .... FZVS
Ile-D'Yeu/Le Grand Phare [France ICAO location identifier] (ICLI) .... LFEY
Ilejejunal [Gastroenterology] (DAVI) .... IJ
Ileocecal [Gastroenterology] (DAVI) IC
Ileocecal Junction [Anatomy] (DAVI) .... ICJ
Ileocecal Sphincter [Medicine] (DMAA) .... ICS
Ileocolonic Junction [Anatomy] .... ICJ
Ileorectal Anastomosis [Medicine] .... IRA
Ileostomy Association of Great Britain and Ireland .... IA

Ileostomy Association of New South Wales [Australia] .... IANSW
Ileostomy Association of South Australia .... IASA
Ileostomy Association (Victoria) [Australia] .... IA(V)
Iles De La Madeleine [Canada] [Airport symbol] (OAG) .... YGR
Iles De La Madeleine, PQ [FM radio station call letters] CBGA-1
Iles De La Madeleine, PQ [Television station call letters] .... CBIMT
Iles De La Madeleine, PQ [ICAO location identifier] (ICLI) .... CYGR
Iles-de-la-Madeline, PQ [FM radio station call letters] .... CFIM
Ileum [Anatomy] .... ILE
Ilha do Sal [Cape Verde Islands] [Airport symbol] (AD) .... SID
Ilheus [Brazil] [Airport symbol] (OAG) .... IOS
Ilheus [Brazil ICAO location identifier] (ICLI) .... SBIL
Ili [Former USSR Seismograph station code, US Geological Survey Closed] (SEIS) ILI
Iliac Chamber [Anatomy] (IAA) IC
Iliac Crest [Anatomy] .... ICR
Iliad [of Homer] [Classical studies] (OCD) II
Iliamna [Alaska] [Airport symbol] (OAG) ILI
Iliamna [Alaska] [Seismograph station code, US Geological Survey] (SEIS) ...... ILM
Iliamna [Alaska] [ICAO location identifier] (ICLI) .... PAIL
Iliamna Air Taxi, Inc. [ICAO designator] (FAAC) .... IAR
Iliamna, AK [Location identifier FAA] (FAAL) ILI
Iliff School of Theology, Denver, CO [Library symbol Library of Congress] (LCLS) .... CoDI
Iliff School of Theology, Denver, CO [OCLC symbol] (OCLC) .... COI
Iligan [Philippines] [Airport symbol] (OAG) .... IGN
Iligan, Lanao Del Norte [Philippines] [ICAO location identifier] (ICLI) .... RPWX
Iliococcygeal [Muscle] [Anatomy] (DAVI) IC
Iliocostal [Muscle] [Anatomy] (DAVI) IC
Ilioinguinal Nerve [Anatomy] .... IN
Iliopsoas [Muscle] [Anatomy] (DAVI) .... IP
Iliotibial [Anatomy] (DAVI) .... IT
Iliotibial Band [Anatomy] .... ITB
Iliotibial Tract [Medicine] (DMAA) .... ILT
Iliotibial Tract [Orthopedics] (DAVI) .... ITT
Iliaga [Indonesia] [Airport symbol] (OAG) .... ILA
Illankai Tamil Arasu Kadchi [Federal Party] [Sri Lanka] [Political party] (PPW) .... ITAK
Illawarra Greens [Political party Australia] .... IG
Illawarra Workers Party [Political party Australia] .... IWP
Illegal Immigrant .... I-I
Illegal Immigrant II
Illegal Jewish Immigrant [British occupation of Palestine, 1945-48] (DI) .... IJI
Illegal Possession of Government Property .... IPGP
Illegal Support Officer [CIA] (LAIN) .... ISO
Illegal Wearing of Uniform .... IWU
Illegitimate (WDAA) .... ILLEGIT
Illertissen [Germany ICAO location identifier] (ICLI) .... EDMI
Illesheim [Germany ICAO location identifier] (ICLI) .... EDIK
Illicit Diamond Buyer [or Buying] .... IDB
Illicit Diamond Dealing (ROG) .... IDD
Illicit Gold Buyer [or Buying] .... IGB
Illicit Gold Dealer .... IGD
Illico Lagena Obturatur [Stopper the Bottle at Once] [Pharmacy] .... ILLIC LAG OBTURAT
Illinantur [Anoint] [Pharmacy] (ROG) .... ILLIN
Illinendus [To Be Smeared] [Pharmacy] .... ILLINEND
ILLINET [Illinois Library Information Network], Springfield, IL [OCLC symbol] (OCLC) .... TQA
ILLINET [Illinois Library Information Network], Springfield, IL [OCLC symbol] (OCLC) .... TQB
Illinium [or Promethium] [Cardiology] (DAVI) II
Illinium (MAE) IL
Illinois [Postal code] IL
Illinois (AFM) ILL
Illinois (ROG) .... ILLS
Illinois [MARC country of publication code Library of Congress] (LCCP) .... ilu
Illinois [MARC geographic area code Library of Congress] (LCCP) .... n-us-il
Illinois Academy of Physician Assistants (SRA) .... IAPA
Illinois Administrative Code [A publication] (AAGC) .... III Adm Code
Illinois Administrative Code [A publication] (AAGC) .... III Admin Code
Illinois Agricultural Association (SRA) .... IAA
Illinois Agricultural Association & Affiliated Co., Bloomington, IL [OCLC symbol] (OCLC) .... JAE
Illinois Agricultural Association, Bloomington, IL [Library symbol Library of Congress] (LCLS) .... IBloA
Illinois Agricultural Aviation Association (SRA) .... IAAA
Illinois Algorithmic Decoder [Southern Illinois University] (SAA) .... ILLIAC
Illinois Appellate Court Reports [A publication] (DLA) .... App
Illinois Appellate Court Reports [A publication] (DLA) .... IL A
Illinois Appellate Court Reports [A publication] (DLA) .... III A
Illinois Appellate Court Reports [A publication] (DLA) .... III Ap
Illinois Appellate Court Reports [A publication] (DLA) .... III App Ct Rep
Illinois Appellate Court Reports [A publication] (DLA) .... III Apps
Illinois Appellate Court Reports [A publication] (DLA) .... IIIs App
Illinois Appellate Court Reports, Second Series [A publication] (DLA) ...... IL A 2d
Illinois Appellate Court Reports, Second Series [A publication] (DLA) ... III App 2d
Illinois Appellate Court Reports, Third Series [A publication] (DLA) ...... IL A 3d
Illinois Appellate Court Reports, Third Series [A publication] (DLA) ... III App 3d
Illinois Asphalt Pavement Association (SRA) .... IAPA
Illinois Association for Educational Data Systems (EDAC) .... ILAEDS
Illinois Association for Supervision and Curriculum Development (SRA) .... IASCD
Illinois Association of Biology Teachers (EDAC) .... IABT

Illinois Association of Collegiate Registrars and Admissions Officers (SRA) .... IACRAO
Illinois Association of Community College Biologists (EDAC) .... IACCB
Illinois Association of Community Mental Health Agencies (SRA) .... IACMHA
Illinois Association of County Officials (SRA) .... IACO
Illinois Association of Groundwater Professionals (SRA) .... IAGP
Illinois Association of School Administrators (SRA) .... IASA
Illinois Association of School Boards (EDAC) .... IASB
Illinois Attorney General's Opinion [*A publication*] (DLA) .... Ill Op Att'y Gen
Illinois Attorney General's Opinion [*A publication*] (DLA) .... Op Ill Att'y Gen
Illinois Automobile Dealer Association (SRA) .... IADA
Illinois Baptist Historical Library, Springfield, IL [*Library symbol Library of Congress*] (LCLS) .... ISB
Illinois Benedictine College, Lisle, IL [*OCLC symbol*] (OCLC) .... ICG
Illinois Benedictine College, Lisle, IL [*Library symbol Library of Congress*] (LCLS) .... ILS
Illinois Bulk Carriers Association (SRA) .... IBCA
Illinois Cancer Council Comprehensive Cancer Center [*Research center*] (RCD) ICC
Illinois Central [*Illinois Central Gulf Railroad Co.*] [*AAR code*] IC
Illinois Central College, East Peoria, IL [*OCLC symbol*] (OCLC) .... IDB
Illinois Central College, East Peoria, IL [*Library symbol Library of Congress*] (LCLS) .... IEpI
Illinois Central Corp. [*NYSE symbol*] (SPSG) IC
Illinois Central Corp. [*Associated Press*] (SAG) .... IlliCtr
Illinois Central Gulf Railroad Co. [*AAR code*] .... ICG
Illinois Central Railroad .... ICR
Illinois Central Railroad Historical Society (EA) .... ICRHS
Illinois Certified Public Accountants Society (SRA) .... ICPAS
Illinois Chiropractic Society (SRA) .... ICS
Illinois Circuit Court (DLA) .... Ill Cir
Illinois Circuit Court Reports [*A publication*] (DLA) .... Ill Cir Ct
Illinois Coal Association (SRA) .... ICA
Illinois College, Jacksonville, IL [*OCLC symbol*] (OCLC) .... ICH
Illinois College, Jacksonville, IL [*Library symbol Library of Congress*] (LCLS) .... IJI
Illinois College of Optometry [*Chicago*] .... ICO
Illinois College of Optometry, Chicago, IL [*Library symbol Library of Congress*] (LCLS) .... ICICO
Illinois College of Podiatric Medicine, Chicago, IL [*Library symbol Library of Congress*] (LCLS) .... ICPM
Illinois Commerce Commission Opinions and Orders [*A publication*] (DLA) .... Ill CC
Illinois Continuing Legal Education [*A publication*] (DLA) .... Ill Cont L Ed
Illinois Corn Growers Association (SRA) .... ICGA
Illinois Cosmetology Association (SRA) .... ICA
Illinois Council for the Gifted (EDAC) .... ICG
Illinois Council on Health System Pharmacists (SRA) .... ICHP
Illinois Council on Long Term Care (SRA) .... ICLTC
Illinois Court of Claims (AAGC) .... Ill Ct Cl
Illinois Court of Claims Reports [*A publication*] (DLA) .... IIC Cl
Illinois Decisions [*A publication*] (DLA) .... Ill Dec
Illinois Department of Mental Health and Developmental Disabilities, Herman M. Adler Center Library, Champaign, IL [*Library symbol Library of Congress*] (LCLS) .... IChamMH
Illinois Department of Nuclear Safety .... IDNS
Illinois Department of Nuclear Safety (DOGT) .... IDNS
Illinois Education Association (SRA) .... IEA
Illinois Environmental Council (SRA) .... IEC
Illinois Environmental Protection Agency (DOGT) .... IEPA
Illinois Environmental Protection Agency .... IEPA
Illinois Functional Programming Language [*Computer science*] .... IFP
Illinois Health Libraries Consortium [*Library network*] .... IHL
Illinois Hearing Aid Society (SRA) .... IHAS
Illinois Historical Survey, University of Illinois, Urbana, IL [*Library symbol Library of Congress*] (LCLS) .... IU-HS
Illinois Home Care Council (SRA) .... IHCC
Illinois Hospital and Health Systems Association (SRA) .... IHA
Illinois, Indiana, Iowa (IIA) III
Illinois Institute for Advanced Computing .... ILLIAC
Illinois Institute for Environmental Quality (PDAA) .... IIEQ
Illinois Institute for Environmental Quality, Chicago, IL [*Library symbol Library of Congress*] (LCLS) .... ICIEQ
Illinois Institute of Technology (IID) .... IIT
Illinois Institute of Technology (GAGS) .... Ill Inst Tech
Illinois Institute of Technology, Armour Research Foundation, Chicago, IL [*Library symbol Library of Congress*] (LCLS) .... ICI-A
Illinois Institute of Technology, Chicago, IL [*OCLC symbol*] (OCLC) .... IAH
Illinois Institute of Technology, Chicago, IL [*Library symbol Library of Congress*] (LCLS) ICI
Illinois Institute of Technology, Chicago-Kent College of Law, Chicago, IL [*Library symbol Library of Congress*] (LCLS) .... ICI-K
Illinois Institute of Technology, Institute of Design, Chicago, IL [*Library symbol Library of Congress*] (LCLS) .... ICI-D
Illinois Institute of Technology, Institute of Gas Technology, Chicago, IL [*Library symbol Library of Congress*] (LCLS) .... ICI-G
Illinois Institute of Technology Research Institute (MCD) .... IIT RES IN
Illinois Institute of Technology Research Institute [*Information service or system*] (IID) .... IITRI
Illinois Integrator and Automatic Computer [*University of Illinois*] (BUR) .... ILLIAC
Illinois Intrastate Motor Carrier Rate & Tariff Bureau, Springfield IL [*STAC*] .... IIB
Illinois Inventory of Parent Opinion .... IIPO
Illinois Law and Practice [*A publication*] (DLA) .... ILP
Illinois Law Bulletin [*A publication*] (DLA) .... Ill LB
Illinois Law Forum (DLA) .... IL LF
Illinois Law Quarterly [*A publication*] (DLA) .... Ill LQ
Illinois Law Record [*A publication*] (DLA) .... Ill L Rec
Illinois League for Nursing (SRA) .... ILN
Illinois Legislative Service (West) [*A publication*] (DLA) .... Ill Legis Serv
Illinois Library and Information Network [*Library network*] .... ILLINET
Illinois Manufacturers Association (SRA) .... IMA
Illinois Masonic Medical Center, Chicago, IL [*Library symbol Library of Congress*] (LCLS) .... ICMM
Illinois Mathematics and Science Academy .... IMSA
Illinois Microfilm Automated Cataloging [*Illinois State Library*] (NITA) .... IMAC
Illinois Motor Truck Operators Association, Chicago IL [*STAC*] .... ITA
Illinois Natural History Survey [*Illinois Institute of Natural Resources*] [*Research center*] (RCD) .... INHS
Illinois Northern Railway [*AAR code*] .... IN
Illinois Optometric Association (SRA) .... IOA
Illinois Park and Recreation Association (SRA) .... IPRA
Illinois Pharmacists Association (SRA) .... IphA
Illinois Power Capital Ltd. [*Associated Press*] (SAG) .... ILLPC
Illinois Power Co. [*Associated Press*] (SAG) .... IIIP
Illinois Power Co. [*Associated Press*] (SAG) .... IlPow
Illinois Power Co. [*NYSE symbol*] (SPSG) .... IPC
Illinois Power Financing I [*Associated Press*] (SAG) .... IIIPF
Illinois Power Financing I [*NYSE symbol*] (SAG) .... IPC
Illinois Prairie District Public Library, Metamora, IL [*OCLC symbol*] (OCLC) .... IEQ
Illinois Propane Gas Association (SRA) .... IPGA
Illinois Psychiatric Society (SRA) .... IPS
Illinois Public Health Association (SRA) .... IPHA
Illinois Public Utilities Commission Opinions and Orders [*A publication*] (DLA) .... Ill PUC Ops
Illinois Pwr 4.08% Pfd [*NYSE symbol*] (TTSB) .... IPCPrA
Illinois Pwr 4.20% Pfd [*NYSE symbol*] (TTSB) .... IPCPrB
Illinois Pwr 4.26% Pfd [*NYSE symbol*] (TTSB) .... IPCPrC
Illinois Pwr 4.42% Pfd [*NYSE symbol*] (TTSB) .... IPCPrD
Illinois Pwr 4.70% Pfd [*NYSE symbol*] (TTSB) .... IPCPrE
Illinois Pwr Adj Rt A Pfd [*NYSE symbol*] (TTSB) .... IPCPrL
Illinois Pwr Cap 9.45%'MIPS' [*NYSE symbol*] (TTSB) .... IPCPrM
Illinois Pwr Fin I 8%'TOPrS' [*NYSE symbol*] (TTSB) .... IPCPrT
Illinois Railroad and Warehouse Commission Decisions [*A publication*] (DLA) .... Ill R & WCD
Illinois Railroad and Warehouse Commission Reports [*A publication*] (DLA) .... Ill R & WC
Illinois Railway Museum (EA) .... IRM
Illinois Regional Library Council [*Library network*] .... IRLC
Illinois Regional Library for the Blind and Physically Handicapped, Chicago Public Library, Chicago, IL [*Library symbol Library of Congress*] (LCLS) .... IC-BPH
Illinois Register [*A publication*] (DLA) .... Ill Admin Reg
Illinois Register [*A publication*] (AAGC) .... Ill Reg
Illinois Reports [*A publication*] (AAGC) Ill
Illinois Reports [*A publication*] (DLA) Ill
Illinois Reports [*A publication*] (DLA) .... Ill R
Illinois Reports [*A publication*] (DLA) .... Ill Rep
Illinois Reports [*A publication*] (DLA) .... Illinois Rep
Illinois Reports [*A publication*] (DLA) .... Ills
Illinois Reports [*A publication*] (DLA) .... Ills R
Illinois Reports [*A publication*] (DLA) .... Ills Rep
Illinois Reports, Second Series [*A publication*] (DLA) .... Ill 2d
Illinois Research and Reference Center Libraries .... IRRN
Illinois Resource and Dissemination Network [*Illinois State Board of Education*] [*No longer in operation*] [*Information service or system*] (IID) .... IRDN
Illinois Resource Network [*University of Illinois*] [*Urbana*] [*Information service or system*] (IID) .... IRN
Illinois Revised Statutes [*A publication*] (DLA) .... Ill Rev Stat
Illinois Revised Statutes [*A publication*] (AAGC) .... Ill Rev Stat
Illinois School Library Media Association (SRA) .... ISLMA
Illinois School Transportation Association (SRA) .... ISTA
Illinois Seed Trade Association (SRA) .... ISTA
Illinois Sheriffs Association (SRA) .... ISA
Illinois Sign Association (SRA) .... ISA
Illinois Society of Allergy, Asthma, and Immunology (SRA) .... ISAAI
Illinois Soybean Association (SRA) .... ISA
Illinois Specialty Growers' Association (SRA) .... ISGA
Illinois State Academy of Science (PDAA) .... ISAS
Illinois State Bar Association. Quarterly Bulletin [*A publication*] (DLA) .... Ill BA Bull
Illinois State Bar Association. Quarterly Bulletin [*A publication*] (DLA) .... Ill SBAQB
Illinois State Bar Association. Reports [*A publication*] (DLA) .... Ill SBA
Illinois State Bowling Proprietors Association (SRA) .... IBPA
Illinois State Data Center Cooperative [*Illinois State Bureau of the Budget*] [*Springfield*] [*Information service or system*] (IID) .... ISDCC
Illinois State Department of Conservation, Division of Parks and Memorials, Galena, IL [*Library symbol Library of Congress*] (LCLS) .... IGaDC
Illinois State Geological Survey [*Champaign*] [*Information service or system*] (IID) .... ISGS
Illinois State Geological Survey, Champaign,IL [*Library symbol*] [*Library of Congress*] (LCLS) .... IChamIG
Illinois State Geological Survey, Urbana, IL [*Library symbol Library of Congress*] (LCLS) .... IUrG
Illinois State Historical Library, Springfield, IL [*Library symbol Library of Congress*] (LCLS) .... IHi
Illinois State Library, Archives Division, Springfield, IL [*Library symbol Library of Congress*] (LCLS) .... I-Ar
Illinois State Library Microfilm Automated Catalog (PDAA) .... IMAC

Illinois State Library, Springfield, IL [*Library symbol Library of Congress*] I
    (LCLS)
Illinois State Library, Springfield, IL [*OCLC symbol*] (OCLC) .... SPI
Illinois State Medical Society (SRA) .... ISMS
Illinois State Normal University .... ISNU
Illinois State Psychiatric Institute .... ISPI
Illinois State Psychiatric Institute, Chicago, IL [*Library symbol Library of Congress*] (LCLS) .... ICSP
Illinois State Society of Radiologic Technologists (SRA) .... ISSRT
Illinois State University (GAGS) .... Ill St U
Illinois State University, Normal, IL [*OCLC symbol*] (OCLC) .... IAI
Illinois State University, Normal, IL [*Library symbol Library of Congress*] (LCLS) .... INS
Illinois State Water Survey [*Illinois Department of Energy and Natural Resources*] [*Research center*] (RCD) .... ISWS
Illinois State Water Survey, Urbana, IL [*Library symbol Library of Congress*] (LCLS) .... IUrW
Illinois Statewide Curriculum Study Center in the Preparation of Secondary School English Teachers .... ISCPET
Illinois Superconductor [*NASDAQ symbol*] (TTSB) .... ISCO
Illinois Superconductor Corp. [*Associated Press*] (SAG) .... IlliniSup
Illinois Superconductor Corp. [*NASDAQ symbol*] (SAG) .... ISCO
Illinois Supreme Court Reports [*A publication*] (DLA) IL
Illinois Supreme Court Reports, Second Series [*A publication*] (DLA) .... IL 2d
Illinois Supreme Court, Springfield, IL [*Library symbol Library of Congress*] (LCLS) .... I-SC
Illinois Terminal Railroad Co. .... ILLT
Illinois Terminal Railroad Co. [*AAR code*] .... ITC
Illinois Test of Psycholinguistic Abilities .... ITPA
Illinois Thoroughbred Breeders and Owners Foundation (SRA) .... ITBOF
Illinois Tool Works [*NYSE symbol*] (TTSB) .... ITW
Illinois Tool Works, Inc. [*NYSE symbol*] (SPSG) .... ITW
Illinois University (IEEE) .... ILU
Illinois University Logical Design by Implicit Enumeration Using the All-Interconnection Inequality Formulation (PDAA) .... ILLODIE-AIF
Illinois Valley Community College, Oglesby, IL [*Library symbol Library of Congress*] (LCLS) .... IOglV
Illinois Valley Community Hospital, Peru, IL [*Library symbol Library of Congress*] (LCLS) .... IPerlH
Illinois Valley Library System [*Library network*] .... IVLS
Illinois Valley Library System, Pekin, IL [*OCLC symbol*] (OCLC) .... IDM
Illinois Valley Library System, Peoria, IL [*Library symbol Library of Congress*] (LCLS) .... IPIV
Illinois Veterans Home, Quincy, IL [*Library symbol*] [*Library of Congress*] (LCLS) .... IQV
Illinois Vocational Association (SRA) .... IVA
Illinois Vocational Curriculum Center (EDAC) IVCC
Illinois Wesleyan University [*Bloomington*] .... IWU
Illinois Wesleyan University, Bloomington, IL [*Library symbol Library of Congress*] (LCLS) .... IBloW
Illinois Wesleyan University, Bloomington, IL [*OCLC symbol*] (OCLC) .... ICO
Illinois Workmen's Compensation Cases [*A publication*] (DLA) .... Ill WCC
Illinova Corp Holding Co. [*Formerly, Illinois Power*] [*Associated Press*] (SAG) .... Illinova
Illinova Corp. [*NYSE symbol*] (TTSB) .... ILN
Illinova Corp. Holding Co. [*Formerly, Illinois Power*] [*NYSE symbol*] (SAG) .... ILN
Illionois Inventory of Educational Progress (EDAC) .... IIEP
Illite [*A mineral*] I
Illite [*A mineral*] IL
Illiteracy Rate .... ILL rate
Illiterate .... ILLIT
Illium [*Anatomy*] (IAA) IL
Illizi [*Algeria*] [*ICAO location identifier*] (ICLI) .... DAAP
Illness Adaptation Scale (EDAC) .... IAS
Illness and Injuries (DMAA) .... I&I
Illness-Correctional Environments .... ICE
Illogical Sequence Error (IAA) .... ISE
Illuminate (KSC) .... ILLUM
Illuminated (WDMC) I
Illuminated (WDMC) ill
Illuminated (NTCM) ILL
Illuminated (VRA) .... illum
Illuminated Internal Graticule .... IIG
Illuminated Manuscript (VRA) .... mss
Illuminated Push Button (NASA) .... IPB
Illuminated Runway Distance Marker (PDAA) .... IRDM
Illuminating [*Ammunition*] (NATG) ILL
Illuminating and Allied Glassware Manufacturers Association [*Defunct*] (EA) .... IAGMA
Illuminating Engineering Research Institute (EA) .... IERI
Illuminating Engineering Society .... IES
Illuminating Engineering Society of North America (EA) .... IESNA
Illumination (IAA) I
Illumination Industries, Inc. III
Illumination per Minute .... IPM
Illumination Rate (CAAL) .... IR
Illumination Unit (MCD) .... LUU
Illuminator [*MARC relator code*] [*Library of Congress*] (LCCP) .... ilu
Illuminator RADAR (NATG) .... IR
Illusion ILL
Illusion Theater (EA) .... IT
Illustrate [*or Illustration*] .... ILLUS
Illustrated [*or Illustrator*] il
Illustrated (BJA) ill
Illustrated (ROG) .... ILLD

Illustrated (WDMC) .... illus
Illustrated Australian News [*A publication*] .... IAN
Illustrated Handbooks of Art History [*A publication*] .... IHAH
Illustrated Legal News [*India*] [*A publication*] (DLA) .... Ill Leg N
Illustrated London News [*A publication*] (BRI) .... ILN
Illustrated Maintenance Parts List .... IMPL
Illustrated Melbourne Post [*A publication*] .... IMP
Illustrated Parts Book (IAA) .... IPB
Illustrated Parts Breakdown (AFIT) .... IPB
Illustrated Parts Catalog (AAG) .... IPC
Illustrated Parts List (NATG) .... IPL
Illustrated Pocket Library [*A publication*] .... IPL
Illustrated Provisioning Document (MCD) .... IPD
Illustrated Shipboard Shopping Guide [*Navy*] .... ISSG
Illustrated World Encyclopedia [*A publication*] .... IWE
Illustration IL
Illustration ILL
Illustration (WDMC) ill
Illustration .... ILLSTN
Illustration (VRA) .... illus
Illustration (WDMC) .... illus
Illustration .... ILLUSTN
Illustration Change Request .... ICR
Illustration Makeup Data Sheet .... IMUDS
Illustration Request .... IR
Illustrative Evaluation Scenario (DOMA) .... IES
Illustrative Material (VRA) .... illus mat
Illustrative Planning Scenario [*DoD*] .... IPS
Illustrator [*MARC relator code*] [*Library of Congress*] (LCCP) ill
Illustrator (WDMC) .... illus
Illustrator (ROG) .... ILLUSTR
Illustrator Draftsman [*Navy rating*] .... DM
Illustrator Draftsman, Seaman [*Navy rating*] .... DMSN
Illustrator Draftsman, Seaman Apprentice [*Navy rating*] .... DMSA
Illustrators Guild [*Later, GA*] (EA) .... IG
Illustrissimo [*Most Illustrious*] [*Latin*] .... ILLMO
Illustrissimo [*Most Illustrious*] [*Latin*] (WGA) .... ILMO
Illustrissimus [*Most Illustrious*] [*Latin*] ILL
Ilmajoki [*Finland ICAO location identifier*] (ICLI) .... EFIL
Ilmenite [*Also, ILM*] [*CIPW classification Geology*] il
Ilmenite [*Also, il*] [*Geology*] .... ILM
Ilo [*Peru*] [*ICAO location identifier*] (ICLI) .... SPLO
I-Load Data Tape (NASA) .... IDT
Ilocano [*MARC language code Library of Congress*] (LCCP) .... ilo
Iloilo [*Philippines*] [*Airport symbol*] (OAG) .... ILO
Iloilo [*Philippines*] [*Seismograph station code, US Geological Survey Closed*] (SEIS) .... ILO
Iloilo, Iloilo [*Philippines*] [*ICAO location identifier*] (ICLI) .... RPVI
Ilorin [*Nigeria*] [*ICAO location identifier*] (ICLI) .... DNIL
Ilorin [*Nigeria*] [*Airport symbol*] (OAG) .... ILR
Ilpo Aruba Cargo NV [*ICAO designator*] (FAAC) .... ILP
ILX, Inc. [*NASDAQ symbol*] (SAG) .... ILEX
ILX, Inc. [*Associated Press*] (SAG) .... ILX Inc
Ilyushin [*Former USSR ICAO aircraft manufacturer identifier*] (ICAO) IL
Im Auftrage [*By Order Of*] [*German*] .... IA
Im Deutschen Reich. Zeitschrift des Central-Vereins Deutscher Staatsbuerger Juedischen Glaubens [*Berlin*] [*A publication*] (BJA) .... IDR
Im Jahre [*In the Year*] [*German*] .... IJ
Im Jahre der Welt [*In the Year of the World*] [*German*] .... IJDW
Im Lande der Bibel [*Berlin-Dahlem*] [*A publication*] (BJA) .... LBibel
I'm Leavin' Elvis Photos, Exclusive (EA) IL
Im Mittel [*On an Average*] [*German*] .... IM
I'm So Optimistic [*Dance company*] .... ISO
I'm Sorry, I'll Read That Again [*BBC radio comedy program*] .... ISIRTA
Im Yirtseh Hashem (BJA) .... IY'H
Image [*File*] [*Computer science*] [*Telecommunications*] I
Image .... IMG
Image .... IMG
Image Acquisition [*Computer graphics*] .... IA
Image Amplification [*Radiology*] (DAVI) .... IA
Image Analysing Computers, Inc. .... IMANCO
Image Analysis Facility [*Computer science*] (PDAA) .... IAF
Image Analyzing Microscope (PDAA) .... IAM
Image and Document Management System [*Aquidneck Data Corp.*] (NITA) .... IDMS
Image Array Processor (NITA) IA-1
Image Array Processor .... IAP
Image Auto Tracker .... IAT
Image Capture Board [*Video monitor*] [*AT & T*] (BYTE) .... ICB
Image Chamber (IAA) IC
Image Check (IAA) IC
Image Communications [*Computer graphics*] IC
Image Control Table (MCD) .... ICTL
Image Converter Camera ICC
Image Converter Tube .... ICT
Image Creation Terminal (NITA) .... ICT
Image Data Processing System .... IDAPS
Image Data Processor .... IDP
Image Data System Simulation [*NASA*] .... IDSS
Image Definition Device .... IDD
Image Description File .... IDF
Image Digitizer [*Computer science*] .... ID
Image Discrimination, Enhancement, and Combination System [*Electronic optical system*] .... IDECS
Image Display and Analysis (MAE) .... IDA

Image Display and Manipulation System [*NASA*] .... IDAMS
Image Display System .... IDS
Image Dissector (KSC) .... ID
Image Dissector Camera .... IDC
Image Dissector Camera System .... IDCS
Image Dissector Echelle Spectrograph [*Instrumentation*] .... IDES
Image Dissector Photomultiplier Tube .... IDPT
Image Dissector Scanner [*Instrumentation*] .... IDS
Image Dissector Tube .... IDT
Image Edge Profile [*Photography*] (OA) .... IEP
Image Entertainment [*NASDAQ symbol*] (TTSB) .... DISK
Image Entertainment, Inc. [*NASDAQ symbol*] (NQ) .... DISK
Image Entertainment, Inc. [*Associated Press*] (SAG) .... ImagEn
Image Feature Extraction [*Air Force*] .... IFE
Image Feature Extraction System [*Air Force*] .... IFES
Image File Directory [*Computer science*] .... IFD
Image Frequency (IAA) .... IF
Image Generation Facility (MCD) .... IGF
Image Generator (MCD) .... IG
Image Guided Surgery .... IGS
Image Guided Surgery .... IGS
Image Guided Technologies, Inc. [*NASDAQ symbol*] (SAG) .... IGTI
Image Guided Technologies, Inc. [*Associated Press*] (SAG) .... ImgeGud
Image Industries [*NASDAQ symbol*] (SAG) .... IMAG
Image Industries [*Associated Press*] (SAG) .... ImageInd
Image Input to Automatic Computers .... IMITAC
Image Intensification I2
Image Intensification Tube (MCD) .... ITT
Image Intensified System .... IIS
Image Intensifier II
Image Intensifier Assembly .... IIA
Image Intensifier Device .... IID
Image Intensifier Night Sight .... IINS
Image Intensifier Orthicon .... IIO
Image Intensifier Plumbicon Camera .... IIPC
Image Intensifier Tube .... IIT
Image Intensifier Viewer IIV
Image Intensifier Viewing Device .... IIVD
Image Interpretation Cell IIC
Image Interpreter Response .... IIR
Image Management System [*Filenet*] (NITA) .... IMS
Image Mapping and Display (NOAA) .... IM & D
Image Motion Compensation [*or Compensator*] .... IMC
Image Motion Compensation and Calibration .... IMCC
Image Motion Configuration .... IMC
Image Motion Simulator .... IMS
Image 'N Transfer [*Developed by 3M Co.*] (WDMC) .... INT
Image Navigation and Registration (GAVI) .... INR
Image Network (DMAA) .... INET
Image Object Content Architecture (CDE) .... IOCA
Image of Vocational Education [*ERIC*] .... IVE
Image Optical Scanner .... IOS
Image Orthicon .... IO
Image Orthicon Camera .... IOC
Image Orthicon Control .... IOC
Image Orthicon System .... IOS
Image Output Terminal [*Computer science*] (HGAA) .... IOT
Image Photon Counting System [*Instrumentation*] .... IPCS
Image Power Amplifier (IAA) .... IPA
Image Previewer (DGA) .... IP
Image Process .... IP
Image Processing and Color Transmission [*Time, Inc. photograph transmission center*] .... IMPACT
Image Processing Applications [*Computer graphics*] .... IPA
Image Processing Center [*Drexel University*] [*Research center*] (RCD) .... IPC
Image Processing Interface [*Computer science*] (PCM) .... IPI
Image Processing Laboratory [*University of Houston*] [*Research center*] (RCD) .... IPL
Image Processing Program [*Computer program*] .... IMP
Image Processing System (MCD) .... IPS
Image Processing Technology [*Computer graphics*] .... IPT
Image Products Co. .... IPC
Image Quality Indicator .... IQI
Image Quality Merit Function [*Color image*] .... IQMF
Image Readout [*Computer graphics*] .... IR
Image Recording System, Low Light .... IRSLL
Image Rejection .... IR
Image Rejection Mixer [*Electronics*] (OA) .... IRM
Image Rejection Technology [*RADAR detection*] .... IRT
Image Resources, Inc. [*Winter Park, FL*] [*Telecommunications*] (TSSD) .... IRI
Image Sensing Systems [*NASDAQ symbol*] (TTSB) .... ISNS
Image Sensing Systems, Inc. [*Associated Press*] (SAG) .... ImageS
Image Sensing Systems, Inc. [*NASDAQ symbol*] (SAG) .... ISNS
Image Sensor System .... ISS
Image Sharpness Scale [*Photography*] (OA) .... ISS
IMAGE Software [*NASDAQ symbol*] (TTSB) .... ISOL
Image Software, Inc. [*Associated Press*] (SAG) .... ImageSft
Image Software, Inc. [*NASDAQ symbol*] (SAG) .... ISOL
Image Stabilization [*Technology from Canon*] .... IS
Image Stabilization Program [*Photography*] .... ISP
Image Stabilizer [*Canon's technology for binoculars*] .... IS
Image Storage Panel [*Computer science*] (PDAA) .... ISP
Image Storage Retrieval .... ISR
Image Storage Translation and Reproduction .... ISTAR
Image Store Management System .... ISMS
Image Store Processor [*Computer science*] .... ISP
Image Synthesis Processor [*Computer science*] .... ISP
Image Technology Patent Information System [*Printing technology*] [*Rochester Institute of Technology Rochester, NY*] .... ITPAIS
Image Understanding Architecture [*Computer science*] .... IUA
Image Velocity Detector .... IVD
Image West Entertainment Corp. [*Vancouver Stock Exchange symbol*] .... IGW
Image-Intensified Television (MCD) .... IITV
Image-Matched Filter (IAA) .... IMF
ImageMatrix Corp. [*NASDAQ symbol*] (SAG) .... IMCX
ImageMatrix Corp. [*Associated Press*] (SAG) .... ImgeM
ImageMatrix Corp. [*Associated Press*] (SAG) .... ImgeMat
Image-Maximum [*Photography*] .... IMAX
Imagery Acquisition and Management Plan .... IAMP
Imagery Analysis Memorandum (MCD) .... IAM
Imagery Analysis Notice (MCD) .... IAN
Imagery Analysis Report (MCD) .... IAR
Imagery Analyst (MCD) .... IA
Imagery Collection Requirements Subcommittee [*Military*] .... ICRS
Imagery Communications and Operations Node (DOMA) .... ICON
Imagery Exploitation Group .... IEG
Imagery Exploitation System (DOMA) .... IES
Imagery Intelligence Group [*Military*] (MCD) .... IIG
Imagery Interpretation II
Imagery Interpretation Center IIC
Imagery Interpretation Key .... IIK
Imagery Interpretation System (MCD) .... IIS
Imagery Processing and Dissemination System (DOMA) .... IPDS
Imagery Related Data Handling System (MCD) .... IRDHS
Imagery Requirement Objectives File (MCD) .... IROF
Imagery Requirements Objectives List (MCD) .... IROL
Imagery Requirements Objectives Plan (MCD) .... IROP
Image-Selected in Vivo Spectroscopy .... ISIS
Image-to-Frame Ratio (MUGU) .... I/F
Image-to-Frame Ratio .... IFR
Imaginary (IAA) I
Imaginary [*Mathematics*] .... Im
Imaginary Basketball Federation (EA) .... IBF
Imaginary Part [*of a complex number*] (DEN) .... IP
Imaginary Transition Structure [*Organic chemistry*] .... ITS
Imaginary Unit (WGA) i
Imagination .... IMGNTN
ImagiNation Network [*Entertainment*] .... INN
Imaginative Educational Cooperation Project (EDAC) .... IEC
Imagine [*or Imaginary*] (MSA) .... IMAG
Imagines [*of Philostratus*] [*Classical studies*] (OCD) .... Imag
Imaging .... IMGNG
Imaging Infrared [*Pronounced "eye-squared ar"*] .... I²R
Imaging Infrared [*Air Force*] (MCD) .... IIR
Imaging Intelligence [*RADAR, photos, etc.*] .... IMINT
Imaging Kernel System [*Computer science*] (BTTJ) .... IKS
Imaging Management Associates [*NASDAQ symbol*] (SAG) .... IMAI
Imaging Management Associates [*Associated Press*] (SAG) .... ImgMgt
Imaging Mgmt Assoc [*NASDAQ symbol*] (TTSB) .... IMAI
Imaging Optics Assembly (MCD) .... IOA
Imaging Polarimeter [*or Photopolarimetry*] [*NASA*] .... IPP
Imaging Proportional Counter [*Astronomy*] .... IPC
Imaging RADAR (MCD) .... IR
Imaging Science Subsystem .... ISS
Imaging Seeker Surface-to-Surface Missile (PDAA) .... ISSSM
Imaging Soft X-Ray LASER Microscope .... IXRALM
Imaging Spectrometer (SSD) .... IS
Imaging Spectrometric Observatory (MCD) .... ISO
Imaging Workstation in X-Ray Microanalysis .... IMIX
Imagyn Medical [*NASDAQ symbol*] (TTSB) .... IGYN
Imagyn Medical, Inc. [*NASDAQ symbol*] (SAG) .... IGYN
Imagyn Medical, Inc. [*Associated Press*] (SAG) .... Imagyn
Imasco Financial Corp. [*Vancouver Stock Exchange symbol Toronto Stock Exchange symbol*] .... IFC
Imasco Foods Ltd., Montreal, Quebec [*Library symbol National Library of Canada*] (NLC) .... QMIF
Imasco Ltd. [*Toronto Stock Exchange symbol Vancouver Stock Exchange symbol*] .... IMS
Imasse [*Zaire*] [*ICAO location identifier*] (ICLI) .... FZFB
Imatec Ltd. [*Associated Press*] (SAG) .... Imatec
Imatec Ltd. [*NASDAQ symbol*] (SAG) .... IMEC
Imatron, Inc. [*NASDAQ symbol*] (NQ) .... IMAT
Imatron, Inc. [*Associated Press*] (SAG) .... Imatrn
Imax Corp. [*Associated Press*] (SAG) .... Imax Cp
Imax Corp. [*NASDAQ symbol*] (SAG) .... IMAXF
Imbaimadai [*Guyana*] [*Airport symbol*] (OAG) .... IMB
Imbaimadai [*Guyana*] [*ICAO location identifier*] (ICLI) .... SYIB
Imbedded Drive Electronics [*Computer science*] .... IDE
Imbedded Error [*Factor analysis*] .... IE
Imbibition Printing [*Cinematography*] (WDMC) .... IB
IMBLMS [*Integrated Medical Behavioral Measurement System*] **Digital Computer** (MCD) .... IDC
Imbokodvo National Movement [*Swaziland*] [*Political party*] (PPW) .... INM
Imbricated Program for Information Transfer [*Computer science*] .... IMPRINT
IMC Chemical Group, Inc., Technical Library, Terre Haute, IN [*Library symbol Library of Congress*] (LCLS) .... InTIMC
IMC Global [*NYSE symbol*] (TTSB) .... IGL
IMC Global, Inc. [*Formerly, IMC Fertilizer Group*] [*NYSE symbol*] (SAG) .... IGL
IMC Global, Inc. [*Formerly, IMC Fertilizer Group*] [*Associated Press*] (SAG) .... IMC Glob

IMC Mortgage Co. [*Associated Press*] (SAG) ... IMC Mt
IMC Mortgage Co. [*NASDAQ symbol*] (SAG) ... IMCC
ImClone Systems [*NASDAQ symbol*] (TTSB) ... IMCL
ImClone Systems, Inc. [*NASDAQ symbol*] (SPSG) ... IMCL
ImClone Systems, Inc. [*Associated Press*] (SAG) ... Imclne
IMCO Recycling [*NYSE symbol*] (TTSB) ... IMR
IMCO Recycling, Inc. [*Associated Press*] (SAG) ... IMCO
IMCO Recycling, Inc. [*NYSE symbol*] (NQ) ... IMR
Imco Resources Ltd. [*Vancouver Stock Exchange symbol*] ... IMC
Imero Fiorentino Associates, Inc. [*New York, NY*] [*Telecommunications*] (TSSD) ... IFA
Imex Medical Systems [*NASDAQ symbol*] (TTSB) ... IMEX
Imex Medical Systems, Inc. [*NASDAQ symbol*] (NQ) ... IMEX
IMI of Philadelphia, Camp Hill, PA [*Library symbol Library of Congress*] (LCLS) ... Iml
Imidazole Buffered Saline [*Clinical chemistry*] ... IBS
Imidazole (Carbonic Acid) Dinitroanilide [*Organic chemistry*] ... ICDNA
Imidazole Glycerol Phosphate [*Biochemistry*] ... IGP
Imidazoleacetic Acid [*Also, I-AC, IMAA*] [*Biochemistry*] ... IAA
Imidazoleacetic Acid [*Biochemistry*] (AAMN) ... I-Ac
Imidazoleacetic Acid [*Biochemistry*] ... IMAA
Imidazoleacetic Acid Ribonucleotide (DMAA) ... IAAR
Imidazoleglycerol-phosphate Dehydratase [*An enzyme*] ... IGPD
Imidazolelactic Acid [*Medicine*] (MEDA) ... I-Lac
Imidazolyl-Thioguanine Chemotherapy [*Medicine*] (MAE) ... ITC
Iminobispropylamine [*Organic chemistry*] ... IBPA
Imino(cyanomorpholinyl)deaminoadriamycin [*Antineoplastic drug*] ... ICMA
Iminodaunorubicin [*Antineoplastic drug*] ... IDR
Iminodiacetic Acid [*Organic chemistry*] ... IDA
Iminodipropionitrile [*Biochemistry*] ... IDPN
Imipramine [*Antidepressant*] ... IMI
Imitate [*or Imitative*] (WDAA) ... IMIT
Imitation (MSA) ... IMIT
Imitation Art Paper (DGA) ... IA
Imitation Art Paper (DGA) ... IAP
Imitation Greaseproof Parchment (DGA) ... IGP
Imitation Handmade Deckle Edges Paper (DGA) ... IHMDE
Imitation Handmade Paper (DGA) ... IHM
Imitation Kraft [*Paper*] (DGA) ... IK
Imitation Russia [*Bookbinding*] (DGA) ... IR
Imitation Vegetable Parchment [*Paper*] (DGA) ... IVP
Imitative Communication Deception [*Military*] ... ICD
IML Air Services Ltd. [*British ICAO designator*] (ICDA) ... JB
Immaculata College, Immaculata, PA [*OCLC symbol*] (OCLC) ... IMM
Immaculata College, Immaculata, PA [*Library symbol Library of Congress*] (LCLS) ... PIm
Immaculate ... IMMAC
Immaculate ... IMMCLT
Immaculate Conception Junior College [*New Jersey*] ... ICJC
Immaculate Conception Seminary, College of Philosophy, Troy, NY [*Library symbol Library of Congress*] (LCLS) ... NTIC
Immaculate Conception Seminary, Huntington, NY [*Library symbol Library of Congress*] (LCLS) ... NHuI
Immaculate Conception Theological Seminary, Ramsey, NJ [*Library symbol Library of Congress*] (LCLS) ... NjRamI
Immaculate Heart College [*California*] ... IHC
Immaculate Heart College, Los Angeles, CA [*Inactive*] [*OCLC symbol*] (OCLC) ... CLI
Immaculate Mary Fan Club (EA) ... IMFC
Immanuel Lutheran College, Eau Claire, WI [*Library symbol Library of Congress*] (LCLS) ... WEI
Immanuel Lutheran School, Willmar, MN [*Library symbol*] [*Library of Congress*] (LCLS) ... MnWilIL
Immaterial (AABC) ... IMMAT
Immature ... IM
Immature ... IMMAT
Immature Brown-Fat [*Cells*] ... IBF
Immature Dead Female Child [*Neonatology*] (DAVI) ... IDFC
Immature Dead Male Child [*Neonatology*] (DAVI) ... IDMC
Immature Granule (DMAA) ... IG
Immature Living Female Child [*Neonatology*] (DAVI) ... ILFC
Immature Living Male Child [*Neonatology*] (DAVI) ... ILMC
Immature Lymphocytes [*Hematology*] (DAVI) ... IMTLYM
Immediate ... IMM
Immediate ... IMMDT
Immediate (AFM) ... IMMED
Immediate ... IMT
Immediate Access (IAA) ... IA
Immediate Access Storage (AFM) ... IAS
Immediate Action [*Military*] ... IA
Immediate Action Authority (AAG) ... IAA
Immediate Action Directive ... IAD
Immediate Action Drill [*Military*] (LAIN) ... IAD
Immediate Action Letter (NASA) ... IAL
Immediate Annuity ... IA
Immediate Business Systems [*Commercial firm British*] ... IBS
Immediate Cable Equalizer (IAA) ... ICE
Immediate Commanding Officer ... ICO
Immediate Constituent ... IC
Immediate Constituent Analyzer [*Computer science*] (DIT) ... ICA
Immediate Damage Assessment ... IDA
Immediate Delivery [*Shipping*] ... ID
Immediate Delivery Required (DNAB) ... IMMDELREQ
Immediate Free Recall (PDAA) ... IFR
Immediate Hypersensitivity [*Immunology*] ... IH
Immediate Identifiable Emergency Action [*Red Cross*] ... IIEA
Immediate Impact Point (SAA) ... IIP
Immediate Information for Merchant and Customer (PDAA) ... INFORMAC
Immediate Knowledge of Results ... IKOR
Immediate Material Requirement List ... IMRL
Immediate Money Transfer (DCTA) ... IMT
Immediate Network-In Dial/Network-Out Dial (DNAB) ... INID/NOD
Immediate Operation Use ... IOU
Immediate Operational Requirement (MCD) ... IOR
Immediate Oxygen Demand [*Marine science*] (MSC) ... IOD
Immediate Participation Guarantee Plan [*Insurance*] ... IPG
Immediate Past Master [*Freemasonry*] ... IPM
Immediate Past President (ADA) ... IPP
Immediate Permanent Incapacitation [*Radiation casualty criterion*] [*Army*] ... IP
Immediate Photograph Intelligence Report [*Military*] (AFM) ... IPIR
Immediate Pick-Up (DNAB) ... IPU
Immediate Pigment Darkening [*Dermatology*] ... IPD
Immediate Postprandial Upper Abdominal Distress ... IPPUAD
Immediate Psychiatric Aid and Referral Center ... IMPAC
Immediate Reaction Company [*Military*] (INF) ... IRC
Immediate Reaction Force [*Military*] (AABC) ... IRF
Immediate Ready Element [*Military*] (AABC) ... IRE
Immediate Ready Reserve [*Army*] ... IRR
Immediate Replacement Support Requirement (MCD) ... IRSR
Immediate Reserve [*Air Force British*] ... IR
Immediate Response Unit [*Police*] [*British*] (DI) ... IRU
Immediate Superior in Command [*Military*] ... ISIC
Immediate Superior in Command [*Military*] ... ISINC
Immediate Track Control [*Automotive engineering*] ... ITC
Immediate Transient Incapacitation [*Radiation casualty criterion*] [*Army*] ... IT
Immediate Transient Incapacitation [*Radiation casualty criterion*] [*Army*] (AABC) ... ITI
Immediate Transportation ... IT
Immediate Unit Commander [*Navy*] (NVT) ... IUC
Immediate-Early [*Genetics*] ... IE
Immediately (BARN) ... imdt
Immediately (WGA) ... IMDTLY
Immediately ... IMMY
Immediately after Onset [*Medicine*] ... IAO
Immediately After Passing [*Aviation*] (FAAC) ... IMAP
Immediately Available ... IA
Immediately Dangerous to Life and Health ... IDLH
Immediately Dangerous to Life or Health Concentration [*Toxicology*] ... IDLHC
Immediately Early Gene [*Genetics*] ... IEG
Immediately Report ... IMREP
Immediate-or-Cancel Order [*Stock exchange term*] ... IOC
Immersed Deflection Vidicon Device (IAA) ... IDVID
Immersion (ECII) ... IMM
Immersion (MSA) ... IMRS
Immersion Fixation [*Microbiology*] ... IF
Immersion Foot [*Medicine*] (DMAA) ... IF
Immigrant Genealogical Society (EA) ... IGS
Immigrant Inspector [*Immigration and Naturalization Service*] ... II
Immigrants in the Labour Force [*British*] ... ILF
Immigration ... IMG
Immigration ... IMMGRTN
Immigration ... IMMIG
Immigration Act of 1990 (WYGK) ... IMAC 90
Immigration and Nationality Act (GFGA) ... INA
Immigration and Nationality Department Electronic Computer System (BARN) ... INDECS
Immigration and Nationality Laws Administrative Decisions [*Department of Justice*] [*A publication*] (DLA) ... I & N
Immigration and Nationality Laws Administrative Decisions [*A publication*] (DLA) ... I & N Dec
Immigration and Naturalization [*Service*] [*Department of Justice*] ... I & N
Immigration and Naturalization Service [*Department of Justice*] ... INS
Immigration and Refugee Board [*Commission d'Immigration et du Status de Refugie*], Ottawa, Ontario [*Library symbol National Library of Canada*] (BIB) ... OOIRB
Immigration Appeal Board [*Canada*] ... IAB
Immigration Appeal Board, Ottawa, ON, Canada [*Library symbol*] [*Library of Congress*] (LCLS) ... CaOOIAB
Immigration Appeal Cases [*Canada*] [*A publication*] (DLA) ... IAC
Immigration Appeal Reports [*A publication*] (DLA) ... Imm AR
Immigration Bar Bulletin [*A publication*] (DLA) ... Immig B Bull
Immigration History Research Center [*University of Minnesota*] [*Research center*] (RCD) ... IHRC
Immigration History Society (EA) ... IHS
Immigration Law Enforcement Monitoring Project [*American Friends Service Committee*] (CROSS) ... ILEMP
Immigration Marriage Fraud Amendments Act of 1986 ... IMFA
Immigration Newsletter [*A publication*] (DLA) ... Immig Newsl
Immigration Nursing Relief Advisory Committee [*Department of Labor*] (EGAO) ... INRAC
Immigration Patrol Inspector [*Immigration and Naturalization Service*] ... IPI
[*The*] **Immigration Reform and Control Act** [*1986*] (ECON) ... IRCA
Immigration Reform and Control Act of 1986 ... IRCA
Immigration Restriction League ... IRL
Imminent Peril to the Public (MHDB) ... IPP
Immiscible Lattice-Gas Automata [*Fluid mechanics*] ... ILGA
Immobile Suspension Feeders on Soft Substrata [*Oceanography*] ... ISOSS
Immobilization Hypercalcemia [*Medicine*] (DAVI) ... IHC
Immobilize [*Medicine*] ... IMMOB
Immobilize (BABM) ... IMMOBIL

Immobilized (NVT) .... IMO
Immobilized Artificial Membranes [*Chemistry*] .... IAM
Immobilized Enzyme [*Physiology*] .... IE
Immobilized Enzyme .... IME
Immobilized Histamine [*Biochemistry*] .... IH
Immobilized Knee [*Orthopedics*] .... IK
Immobilized Metal Affinity [*Protein chromatography*] .... IMA
Immobilized Metal Affinity Chromatography .... IMAC
Immobilized pH Gradient Isoelectric Focusing [*Analytical biochemistry*] .... IPGF
Immobilized pH Gradients [*Chemistry*] .... IPG
Immobilized-Enzyme Reactor .... IMER
Immobilized-Liquid Membrane [*Chemical engineering*] .... ILM
Immobilizing Accelerating Factor (PDAA) .... IAF
Immokalee, FL [*Location identifier FAA*] (FAAL) .... IMM
Immokalee, FL [*AM radio station call letters*] (RBYB) .... WAFZ
Immokalee, FL [*FM radio station call letters*] (RBYB) .... WGCQ
Immola [*Finland ICAO location identifier*] (ICLI) .... EFIM
Immortalis [*Immortal*] [*Latin*] (GPO) i
Immortalis Dei Auspicio [*With the Help of God*] [*Latin*] .... IDA
Immortalist Society (EA) .... IS
Immotile Cilia Syndrome [*Medicine*] (DMAA) .... ICS
ImmuCell Corp. [*NASDAQ symbol*] (NQ) ICCC
ImmuCell Corp. [*Associated Press*] (SAG) .... ImmuCell
Immucor, Inc. [*NASDAQ symbol*] (NQ) .... BLUD
Immucor, Inc. [*Associated Press*] (SAG) .... Imucor
Immudyne, Inc. [*Vancouver Stock Exchange symbol*] .... IMU
ImmuLogic Pharmaceutical [*NASDAQ symbol*] (TTSB) .... IMUL
ImmuLogic Pharmaceutical Corp. [*NASDAQ symbol*] (SPSG) .... IMUL
ImmuLogic Pharmaceutical Corp. [*Associated Press*] (SAG) .... ImuLog
Immuncogen, Inc. [*NASDAQ symbol*] (SAG) .... IMGN
Immuncogen, Inc. [*Associated Press*] (SAG) .... Imungn
Immune [*or Immunization*] (AFM) .... IMM
Immune Adherence [*Immunology*] .... IA
Immune Adherence Haemagglutination [*Immunochemistry*] (PDAA) .... IAH
Immune Adherence Hemagglutination [*Immunochemistry*] .... IAHA
Immune Body .... IB
Immune Complex [*Immunology*] IC
Immune Complex Disease .... ICD
Immune Cytotoxicity [*Immunochemistry*] (DAVI) IC
Immune Defense Mechanism [*Medicine*] (DMAA) .... IDM
Immune Deficiency Associated Virus .... IDAV
Immune Deficiency Foundation (EA) .... IDF
Immune Deficiency State .... IDS
Immune Deficiency Syndrome "Innocently" Acquired (ADA) .... IDSIA
Immune Diffusion Test [*Medicine*] (DMAA) .... IDT
Immune Electron Microscopy .... IEM
Immune Globulin .... IG
Immune Globulin, Intravenous (CPH) .... IGIV
Immune Hemolytic Anemia [*Medicine*] .... IHA
Immune Interferon (DMAA) .... IFI
Immune Interferon [*Cell biology*] .... IIF
Immune Lysis [*Medicine*] (DMAA) .... ImLy
Immune Precipitate [*Immunology*] .... IP
Immune Region Associated Antigen [*Immunology*] .... Ia
Immune Renal Disease [*Medicine*] .... IRD
Immune Response [*Also, Ir*] [*Genetics*] .... IR
Immune Response Corp. [*NASDAQ symbol*] (SAG) .... IMNR
Immune Response Corp. [*Associated Press*] (SAG) .... ImunRsp
Immune Response Gene-Associated Antigen [*Immunology*] (DAVI) .... Ia
Immune Serum [*Also, IS*] .... ImS
Immune Serum [*Also, ImS*] .... IS
Immune Serum Globulin .... ISG
Immune Spleen Cell .... ISC
Immune Thrombocytopenic Purpura [*Medicine*] .... ITP
Immunekoerper [*Immune Bodies*] [*Medicine*] .... IK
Immunex Corp. [*NASDAQ symbol*] (NQ) .... IMNX
Immunex Corp. [*Associated Press*] (SAG) .... Imunex
Immunitaetseinheit [*Immunizing Unit*] [*Medicine*] .... IE
Immunity .... IMMUN
Immunity Test .... IT
Immunization (WDAA) .... IMMUN
Immunization Against Leprosy Program [*World Health Organization*] .... IMMLEP
Immunization Rate (AFM) .... IR
Immunization Readiness Training Exercises [*Army*] .... IMRETES
Immunizing Unit [*Medicine*] (MEDA) .... ImmU
Immunizing Unit [*Medicine*] .... IU
Immunoassay [*Marine science*] (OSRA) .... IM
Immunoassay (USDC) .... IM
Immunoaugmentative Therapy [*Oncology*] .... IAT
Immunobead Binding Test [*Biochemistry*] .... IBT
Immunobiologic Activity [*Immunology*] (AAMN) .... IA
Immunobiology Research Institute [*Annandale, NJ*] .... IRI
Immunoblastic Lymphadenopathy [*Medicine*] (CPH) .... IBL
Immunoblastic Sarcoma [*Medicine*] (DMAA) .... IBS
Immunoblastic T-Cell [*Lymphadenopathy*] .... IBT
Immunochemiluminometric Assay [*Analytical biochemistry*] .... ILMA
Immunochemistry System [*Medicine*] .... ICS
Immunocompetent Cell [*Medicine*] (MAE) ICC
Immunoconglutinin (MAE) .... IK
Immunocytochemical Analysis .... ICA
Immunocytochemistry [*Immunochemstry*] (DAVI) IC
Immunocytochemistry [*Immunology*] ICC
Immunocytochemistry, ELISA [*Enzyme-Linked Immunosorbent Assay*], and Immunoblotting .... IEI
Immunodeficiency [*Immunology*] .... ID
Immunodeficiency Cancer Registry .... ICR
Immunodeficiency-Virus-Suppressing Lymphokine [*Virology*] .... ISL
Immunodiffusion [*Immunology*] .... ID
Immunodiffusion Complement Fix [*Immunochemistry*] (DAVI) .... IDCF
Immunodiffusion in Gel (PDAA) .... IDG
Immunodiffusion Procedure [*Immunochemistry*] .... IDP
Immuno-Electroadsorption [*Medicine*] (DMAA) .... IEA
Immunoelectroosmophoresis [*Analytical biochemistry*] .... IEOP
Immunoelectrophoresis [*Analytical biochemistry*] .... IE
Immunoelectrophoresis [*Analytical biochemistry*] .... IEP
Immunoenzyme Assay [*Biochemistry*] (DAVI) .... IEA
Immunoenzymometric Assay [*Clinical chemistry*] .... IEMA
Immunofixation [*Clinical chemistry*] .... IFX
Immunofixation [*Analytical biochemistry*] .... IMF
Immunofixation Electrophoresis [*Clinical chemistry*] .... IFE
Immunofluorescence [*Immunochemistry*] .... IF
Immunofluorescence [*or Immunofluorometric*] **Assay** [*Also, IFMA*] [*Analytical biochemistry*] .... IFA
Immunofluorescence [*or Immunofluorometric*] **Assay** [*Also, IFA*] [*Analytical biochemistry*] .... IFMA
Immunofluorescence Test [*Immunology*] .... IFT
Immunofluorescence-Viral Capsid Antigen [*Clinical chemistry*] .... IF-VCA
Immunofluorescent [*Immunology*] .... IMF
Immunofluorescent Antibody [*Immunochemistry*] .... IFA
Immunofluorometric Assay [*Analytical biochemistry*] .... IFMA
ImmunoGen, Inc. [*NASDAQ symbol*] (NQ) .... IMGN
Immunogenetics .... ImG
Immunoglobulin [*Immunology*] .... Ig
Immunoglobulin [*Immunology*] (DAVI) .... IMMUNO
Immunoglobulin A [*Immunology*] .... IgA
Immunoglobulin A Immune Complex [*Immunochemistry*] .... IgAIC
Immunoglobulin A Nephropathy [*Nephrology*] .... IgAN
Immunoglobulin D [*Immunology*] .... IgD
Immunoglobulin Deficiency [*Immunology*] (AAMN) .... ID
Immunoglobulin E [*Immunology*] .... IgE
Immunoglobulin G [*Immunology*] .... IgG
Immunoglobulin G Immune Complex [*Immunochemistry*] .... IgGIC
Immunoglobulin Heavy Chain [*Biochemistry*] .... IgH
Immunoglobulin M [*Immunology*] .... IgM
Immunoglobulin M Immune Complex [*Immunochemistry*] .... IgMIC
Immunoglobulin M - Rheumatoid Factor [*Medicine*] .... IgM-RF
Immunoglobulin Macro [*Also known as RF*] [*Immunology*] .... IgM
Immunoglobulin ND [*Immunology, provisional class*] .... IgND
Immunoglobulin Reference Preparation [*Clinical chemistry*] .... IRP
Immunoglobulin Superfamily [*Immunology*] .... IgSF
Immunoglobulin-Binding Factor [*Immunology*] (MAE) .... IBF
Immunogold Silver Staining [*Cytochemistry*] .... IGSS
Immunogold Stain [*Cytochemistry*] .... IGS
Immunohematology .... IMMUNHMTLGY
Immunohistochemical .... IHC
Immunohistochemistry .... IHC
Immunologic Contact Urticaria [*Medicine*] (DMAA) .... ICU
Immunological Chromatographic Analysis .... ICA
Immunological Distance [*in primate phylogeny*] .... ID
Immunological Distance Unit [*Genetics*] .... IDU
Immunological Similarity .... IS
Immunologically Detectable Insulin [*Medicine*] (DMAA) .... IDI
Immunologically Measurable Insulin [*Medicine*] (AAMN) .... IMI
Immunologically Mediated Disease [*Medicine*] .... IMD
Immunology [*Medical specialty*] (DHSM) .... IG
Immunology (ADA) .... IMMUN
Immunology .... IMMUNOL
Immunomedics, Inc. [*NASDAQ symbol*] (NQ) .... IMMU
Immunomedics, Inc. [*Associated Press*] (SAG) .... Imunmd
Immunonephelometric Assay [*Clinical chemistry*] .... INA
Immunoperoxidase [*An enzyme*] .... IMP
Immunoperoxidase Antibody Assay [*Clinical chemistry*] .... IPA
Immunoperoxidase (Technique) [*Clinical chemistry*] .... IP
Immunopotentiating Reconstituted Influenza Virosome [*Immunochemistry*] .... IRIV
Immunoprecipitation Technique [*Clinical chemistry*] .... IPT
Immunoproliferative Small Intestinal Disease (MAE) .... IPSID
Immunoradioassayable Human Chorionic Somatomammotropin [*Medicine*] (MAE) .... IRHCS
Immunoradiometric Assay [*Immunology*] .... IRMA
Immunoreactive .... IR
Immunoreactive Adrenocorticotropic Hormone [*Medicine*] (DMAA) .... IR-ACTH
Immunoreactive Atrial Natriuretic Factor .... IRANF
Immunoreactive Beta-Endomorphin [*Immunochemistry*] (DMAA) .... IB-EP
Immunoreactive Bovine Serum Albumin [*Immunochemistry*] .... IBSA
Immunoreactive Calcitonin [*Endocrinology*] .... ICT
Immunoreactive Gastric Inhibitory Peptide [*Biochemistry*] .... IR-GIP
Immunoreactive Gastrin [*Medicine*] (MEDA) .... iG
Immunoreactive Gastrin [*Medicine*] (DMAA) .... IRG
Immunoreactive Glucagon [*Immunochemistry*] .... IRG
Immunoreactive Glucagon [*Immunochemistry*] .... IRGI
Immunoreactive Growth Hormone [*Immunology*] (MAE) .... IGH
Immunoreactive Growth Hormone [*Immunology*] .... IRGH
Immunoreactive Human Growth Hormone [*Immunology*] (AAMN) .... IRHGH
Immunoreactive Insulin .... IRI
Immunoreactive Luteinizing Hormone (DMAA) .... ILH
Immunoreactive Parathyroid Hormone [*Endocrinology*] .... IPTH
Immunoreactive Peptides [*Biochemistry*] .... IRP
Immunoreactive Plasma [*Immunochemistry*] (DMAA) .... IRP
Immunoreactive Proinsulin [*Immunochemistry*] .... IRP

Immunoreactive Secretin [*Endocrinology*] .... IRS
Immunoreactive Somatomedin [*Endocrinology*] .... IRSM
Immunoreactive Somatostatin [*Endocrinology*] .... IRS
Immunoreactive Substance P [*Immunology*] .... ISP
Immunoreactive Tag [*Clinical chemistry*] .... IT
Immunoreactive Trypsin .... IRT
Immunoreceptor Tyrosine Activation Motif [*Biochemistry*] .... ITAM
Immunoreceptor Tyrosine-Based Activation Motif [*Immunology*] .... ITAM
Immunoregulatory alpha-Globulin [*Immunology*] .... IRA
Immunosorbent Electron Microscopy .... ISEM
Immunostimulating Reconstituted Influenza Virosome [*Immunochemistry*] .... IRIV
Immunostimulatory Complex [*Immunochemistry*] .... ISCOM
Immuno-Suppression Method [*For increasing fertility*] .... IM
Immunosuppressive [*Immunochemistry*] .... IS
Immunosuppressive Acidic Protein [*Immunochemistry*] (DMAA) .... IAP
Immunosuppressive Drug [*Medicine*] (DMAA) .... ISD
Immunotherapy [*Medicine*] .... IT
Immunotoxin .... IT
Immunotoxin with A-Chain .... IT-A
Immunotoxin with Ricin .... IT-R
Immunoturbidimetry [*Analytical biochemistry*] .... IT
IMNET Systems [*NASDAQ symbol*] (TTSB) .... IMNT
Imnet Systems, Inc. [*Associated Press*] (SAG) .... Imnet
Imnet Systems, Inc. [*NASDAQ symbol*] (SAG) .... IMNT
Imo Industries [*NYSE symbol*] (TTSB) .... IMD
Imo Industries, Inc. [*NYSE symbol*] (SPSG) .... IMD
Imo Industries, Inc. [*Associated Press*] (SAG) .... ImoInd
Imonda [*Papua New Guinea*] [*Airport symbol*] (OAG) .... IMD
IMP Aviation Services Ltd. [*Canada ICAO designator*] (FAAC) .... BLU
IMP Group Ltd. Aviation Services [*Canada ICAO designator*] (FAAC) .... XGG
IMP, Inc. [*Associated Press*] (SAG) .... IMP
IMP, Inc. [*NASDAQ symbol*] (SAG) .... IMPX
Impact (KSC) .... IMP
Impact .... IMP
Impact and Capabilities [*Study*] [*DoD*] .... I & C
Impact Assessment Sheet (NASA) .... IAS
Impact Assessment Study .... IAS
Impact Bag (SAA) .... IB
Impact Copolymer Polypropylene [*Plastics*] [*Automotive engineering*] .... ICP
Impact Data Pulse Generator (IAA) .... IDPG
Impact Energy Density .... IED
Impact Excited Transmitter .... IET
Impact Force Measuring System .... IFMS
Impact Hand Tool .... IHT
Impact Ionization Avalanche Transit Time [*Solid state diodes*] [*Transistor technology*] .... IMPATT
Impact Ionization Diode .... IID
Impact Isolation Class [*Noise rating of insulation*] IIC
Impact Limit Lines (MUGU) ILL
Impact Mechanical Fuse (MCD) .... IMF
Impact Memorandum (MCD) .... IM
Impact Message Inventory (EDAC) .... IMI
Impact Noise Rating [*of insulation*] .... INR
Impact of Hypertension Information Study [*Department of Health and Human Services*] (GFGA) .... IHI
Impact on Hunger (EA) .... IH
Impact Point (AFM) .... IP
Impact Prediction Data (AFM) .... IPD
Impact Prediction Point [*NASA*] .... IPP
Impact Predictor [*NASA*] (MUGU) .... IMP
Impact Predictor [*NASA*] .... IP
Impact Predictor Monitor Set [*NASA*] (AAG) .... IPMS
Impact Predictor System [*NASA*] .... IPS
Impact Pressure [*Symbol*] (WDAA) .... QC
Impact Printer [*Computer science*] .... IP
Impact Prognosticator [*Aerospace*] (AAG) .... IP
Impact Ratio (AAGC) .... IRA
Impact Shock Isolation System [*Tennis-racket technology*] [*Dunlop Slazenger Corp.*] .... ISIS
Impact Short Delay Fuze (MCD) .... ISDF
Impact Signature Training Practice Warhead [*Army*] .... ISTPW
Impact/Static Pressure Ratio (WDAA) .... QC/PS
Impact Switch (SAA) .... IS
Impact Systems [*NASDAQ symbol*] (TTSB) .... MPAC
Impact Systems, Inc. [*Associated Press*] (SAG) .... ImpctSy
Impact Systems, Inc. [*NASDAQ symbol*] (NQ) .... MPAC
Impact Transition Temperature (MCD) .... ITT
Impact Warning System .... IWS
Impact-Collision Ion Scattering Spectroscopy .... ICISS
Impacted [*Medicine*] (DMAA) .... Impx
Impaction [*Medicine*] (DMAA) .... imp
Impaction [*or Impacted*] [*Medicine*] (DAVI) .... IMP
Impaction [*Dentistry*] .... IMPX
Impacts on the Australian Economy [*A publication*] .... Impacts Aust Econ
Impaired .... IMP
Impaired .... IMPRD
Impaired Gas Exchange (DMAA) .... IGE
Impaired Glucose Tolerance [*Physiology*] .... IGT
Impaired Physician Program (EA) .... IPP
Impairing the Morals of a Minor [*Police terminology*] (IIA) .... IMM
Impala Resources [*Vancouver Stock Exchange symbol*] .... IMR
Impartial Hearing Officer .... IHO
Impasse (DD) .... imp
Impasto (VRA) .... impst
Impath, Inc. [*Associated Press*] (SAG) .... Impath
Impath, Inc. [*NASDAQ symbol*] (SAG) .... IMPH
Impath Inc. [*NASDAQ symbol*] (TTSB) .... IMPH
Impatiens Latent Virus [*Plant pathology*] ILV
Impedance (KSC) .... IMP
Impedance [*Electricity*] .... IMPD
Impedance [*Symbol*] [*IUPAC*] .... Z
Impedance and Admittance (IAA) .... IMMITTANCE
Impedance Angle .... IA
Impedance Cardiac Output [*Medicine*] (DMAA) .... ICO
Impedance Cardiogram [*Medicine*] (DMAA) .... ICG
Impedance Cardiogram (NASA) .... ZCG
Impedance Matching Attenuator .... IMA
Impedance Matching Unit (MCD) .... IMU
Impedance Measuring Devices [*JETDS nomenclature*] [*Military*] (CET) .... ZM
Impedance Plethysmography [*Medicine*] .... IPG
Impedance Pneumograph [*Apollo*] [*NASA*] .... ZPN
Impedance Probe .... IP
Impedance Unit (MCD) .... IU
Impedance-Reduction Factor (IAA) .... IRF
Impeded Harmonic Operation .... IHO
Impediment .... IMPDMNT
Impedor .... IMPR
Impeller .... IMP
Impeller [*Mechanical engineering*] .... IMPLR
Imperative .... IMP
Imperative (WDMC) .... imp
Imperative .... IMPER
Imperative .... IMPV
Imperative (WGA) .... IPV
Imperator [*or Imperatrix*] [*Emperor or Empress*] [*Latin*] I
Imperator [*or Imperatrix*] [*Emperor or Empress*] [*Latin*] .... IMP
Imperator Napoleon Rex Italiae [*Emperor Napoleon, King of Italy*] [*Latin*] .... INRI
Imperatrix [*Empress*] [*Latin*] .... IMPX
Imperatriz [*Brazil*] [*Airport symbol*] (OAG) .... IMP
Imperatriz [*Brazil ICAO location identifier*] (ICLI) .... SBIZ
Imperfect .... IMP
Imperfect (WDMC) .... imp
Imperfect .... IMPER
Imperfect .... IMPERF
Imperfect (MSA) .... IMPF
Imperfect (ADA) .... IMPFT
Imperfect Single Stamp [*Philately*] .... ISS
Imperfect Time [*Represents an incomplete circle and refers to 4/4 time*] [*Music*] C
Imperforate [*Philately*] .... IMPERF
Imperial I
Imperial (AFM) .... IMP
Imperial [*Record label*] .... Imp
Imperial [*British military*] (DMA) .... Impl
Imperial (MSA) .... IMPRL
Imperial .... IMPRL
Imperial Air [*Peru*] [*ICAO designator*] (FAAC) .... IMP
Imperial Airlines [*ICAO designator*] (AD) II
Imperial Airlines [*British*] [*FAA designator*] (FAAC) .... REJ
Imperial Airways, Inc. [*ICAO designator*] (FAAC) .... PNX
Imperial Airways Ltd. [*British*] (ADA) .... IA
Imperial Airways Ltd. [*British*] .... IAL
Imperial and Foreign Money Orders .... IFMO
Imperial and Foreign Parcel Post (IAA) .... IFPP
Imperial and Foreign Post (IAA) .... IFP
Imperial Aramaic (BJA) .... ImprAr
Imperial Art League [*British*] (BI) .... IAL
Imperial Ballet of Canada, Ottawa, ON, Canada [*Library symbol Library of Congress*] (LCLS) .... CaOOIB
Imperial Ballet of Canada, Ottawa, Ontario [*Library symbol National Library of Canada*] (NLC) .... OOIB
Imperial Bancorp [*NASDAQ symbol*] (NQ) .... IBAN
Imperial Bancorp [*Associated Press*] (SAG) .... ImprBc
Imperial Beach, CA [*Location identifier FAA*] (FAAL) .... NRS
Imperial British Conservative Party [*Political party*] (ADA) .... IBCP
Imperial Bushel (WDAA) .... IBU
Imperial Bushmen Contingent [*British military*] (DMA) .... IBC
Imperial, CA [*Location identifier FAA*] (FAAL) .... IPL
Imperial, CA [*FM radio station call letters*] .... KMXX
Imperial Camel Corps [*British military*] (DMA) ICC
Imperial Cancer Research Fund [*British*] .... ICRF
Imperial Cancer Research Fund 159 [*Razoxane*] [*Antineoplastic drug*] .... ICRF 159
Imperial Cargo Airlines Ltd. [*Ghana*] [*ICAO designator*] (FAAC) .... IMG
Imperial Chemical Industries [*Great Britain*] [*Research code symbol*] .... M
Imperial Chemical Industries [*British*] .... UCI
Imperial Chemical Industries Ltd. [*NYSE symbol*] (SPSG) ICI
Imperial College Computing Center (PDAA) ICCC
Imperial College - London Hospital [*British*] (DI) .... ICLH
Imperial College of Science [*British*] .... ICS
Imperial College of Science and Technology (PDAA) .... ICST
Imperial College of Science and Technology Centre for Environmental Technology [*British*] (IRUK) .... ICCET
Imperial College of Science and Technology Centre for Fusion Studies [*British*] (IRUK) .... ICCFS
Imperial College of Tropical Agriculture Association [*British*] (BI) .... ICTAA
Imperial College Reactor Centre [*Imperial College of Science and Technology*] [*British*] (WND) .... ICRC
Imperial College Thermophysical Properties Data Centre [*British*] (CB) .... ICTPDC
Imperial Communications [*World War II*] ICC

Imperial Council of the Ancient Arabic Order of the Nobles of the Mystic Shrine for North America [*Freemasonry*] (EA) .... AAONMS
Imperial County Free Library, El Centro, CA [*Library symbol Library of Congress*] (LCLS) .... CEcl
Imperial Court, Daughters of Isis (EA) .... ICDI
Imperial Credit [*NASDAQ symbol*] (TTSB) ICII
Imperial Credit Industries, Inc. [*NASDAQ symbol*] (SAG) ICII
Imperial Credit Industries, Inc. [*Associated Press*] (SAG) .... ImpCrd
Imperial Credit Mortagage Holdings, Inc. [*AMEX symbol*] (SAG) .... IMH
Imperial Credit Mortgage Holdings, Inc. [*Associated Press*] (SAG) .... ImpCM
Imperial Credit Mortgage Holdings, Inc. [*Associated Press*] (SAG) .... ImpCMtg
Imperial Credit Mtge Hldgs [*AMEX symbol*] (TTSB) .... IMH
Imperial Defence College [*British*] .... IDC
Imperial Dictionary [*A publication*] .... IMP DICT
Imperial Direct West India Mail Service Co. (ROG) .... IDWI
Imperial Ethiopian Air Force .... IEAF
Imperial Ethiopian Government (CINC) .... IEG
Imperial Fascist League [*British*] .... IFL
Imperial Father [*of the Chapel*] [*Unions*] [*British*] (DGA) .... IF
Imperial Forestry Institute [*British*] (BI) .... IFI
Imperial Gallon .... IG
Imperial Gallons per Minute .... IGPM
Imperial General Staff .... IGS
Imperial German Military Collector's Association (EA) .... IGMCA
Imperial Ginseng Prod [*NASDAQ symbol*] (TTSB) .... IGPFF
Imperial Ginseng Products Ltd. [*NASDAQ symbol*] (SAG) .... IGPF
Imperial Glass Collectors Society (EA) .... IGCS
Imperial Group Ltd. .... IMPG
Imperial Holly Corp. [*AMEX symbol*] (SPSG) .... IHK
Imperial Holly Corp. [*Associated Press*] (SAG) .... ImpHly
Imperial/Imperial County [*California*] [*ICAO location identifier*] (ICLI) .... KIPL
Imperial Institute [*British*] (DAS) II
Imperial Institute of Entomology [*British*] .... IIE
Imperial Iranian Air Force .... IIAF
Imperial Iranian Ground Forces .... IIGF
Imperial Japanese Army [*World War II*] .... IJA
Imperial Japanese Navy [*World War II*] .... IJN
Imperial Life Assurance Co. of Canada [*Toronto Stock Exchange symbol*] IL
Imperial Light Horse [*Military British*] (ROG) .... IHL
Imperial Light Horse [*Military British*] (ROG) .... ILH
Imperial Measure .... IM
Imperial Merchant Service Guild [*A union*] [*British*] .... IMSG
[*The*] Imperial Merchant Service Guild [*British*] .... MSG
Imperial Metal Industries Ltd. [*British*] .... IMI
Imperial Metals Corp. [*Toronto Stock Exchange symbol Vancouver Stock Exchange symbol*] .... IPM
Imperial Military Foul-Up [*Bowdlerized version*] (DSUE) .... IMFU
Imperial Military Nursing Service [*British*] .... IMNS
Imperial Military Railways [*British military*] (DMA) .... IMR
Imperial, NE [*Location identifier FAA*] (FAAL) .... IML
Imperial Oil Enterprises Ltd., Engineering Division, Sarnia, ON, Canada [*Library symbol Library of Congress Obsolete*] (LCLS) .... CaOSIE
Imperial Oil Enterprises Ltd., Sarnia, ON, Canada [*Library symbol Library of Congress*] (LCLS) .... CaOSI
Imperial Oil Ltd. [*AMEX symbol Toronto Stock Exchange symbol Vancouver Stock Exchange symbol*] (SPSG) .... IMO
Imperial Oil Ltd. [*Associated Press*] (SAG) .... ImpOil
Imperial Oil Ltd., Calgary, AB, Canada [*Library symbol Library of Congress*] (LCLS) .... CaACI
Imperial Oil Ltd., Toronto, ON, Canada [*Library symbol Library of Congress*] (LCLS) .... CaOTIOL
Imperial Oil Ltd., Toronto, Ontario [*Library symbol National Library of Canada*] (NLC) .... OTIOL
Imperial Order of Daughters of the Empire [*Canada*] .... IODE
Imperial Order of the Crown of India [*British*] CI
Imperial Order of the Crown of India [*British*] (ROG) .... IOCI
Imperial Order of the Dragon (EA) .... IOD
Imperial Owners Club, International (EA) .... IOC
Imperial Pale Ale .... IPA
Imperial Paper (DGA) I
Imperial Parliament Series [*A publication*] .... IPS
Imperial Preference (ADA) .... IP
Imperial Public Library, Imperial, CA [*Library symbol Library of Congress*] (LCLS) .... CImp
Imperial Service College [*British*] .... ISC
Imperial Service Medal [*British*] .... ISM
Imperial Service Order [*British*] .... ISO
Imperial Service Sappers [*British military*] (DMA) .... ISS
Imperial Smelting Furnace [*Zinc and lead*] .... ISF
Imperial Smelting Process .... ISP
Imperial Society of Teachers of Dancing .... ISTD
Imperial Standard Gallon .... ISG
Imperial Standard Wire Gauge .... ISWG
Imperial Thrift & Loan [*NASDAQ symbol*] (TTSB) .... ITLA
Imperial Thrift & Loan Association [*Associated Press*] (SAG) .... ImpThft
Imperial Thrift & Loan Association [*NASDAQ symbol*] (SAG) .... ITLA
Imperial Tobacco Co. [*of Great Britain and Ireland*] Ltd. .... ITC
Imperial Tobacco Co. of Canada Ltd., Montreal, PQ, Canada [*Library symbol Library of Congress*] (LCLS) .... CaQMIT
Imperial Tobacco Co. of Canada Ltd., Montreal, Quebec [*Library symbol National Library of Canada*] (NLC) .... QMIT
Imperial Tobacco Co. of Canada Ltd., Research Library, Montreal, PQ, Canada [*Library symbol Library of Congress*] (LCLS) .... CaQMITR
Imperial Tobacco Co. Shares [*Stock exchange term British*] (DSUE) .... IMPS
Imperial Valley College [*California*] IVC

Imperial Valley College, Imperial, CA [*OCLC symbol*] (OCLC) IVX
Imperial Valley Dune Buggy Association .... IVDBA
Imperial War Cabinet [*British military*] (DMA) .... IWC
Imperial War Graves Commission [*British*] .... IWGC
Imperial War Museum [*England*] .... IWM
Imperial Wire Gauge (ROG) .... IWG
Imperial Yeomanry [*British*] .... IY
Imperial Yeomanry Bearer Corps [*British military*] (DMA) .... IYB
Imperial Yeomanry Hospitals [*Military British*] (ROG) .... IYH
Imperio [*Costa Rica*] [*ICAO location identifier*] (ICLI) .... MRIP
Imperious [*Grammar*] (ROG) .... IMP
Imperium [*Empire*] [*Latin*] .... IMP
Impersonal .... IMP
Impersonal (ROG) .... IMPER
Impersonal .... IMPERS
Impersonating [*FBI standardized term*] .... IMP
Impetigo Neonatorum [*Medicine*] (DMAA) .... IN
Impetus [*A publication*] .... IMP
Impey's Law and Practice of Mandamus [*1826*] [*A publication*] (DLA) .... Imp Man
Impey's Modern Pleader [*2nd ed.*] [*1814*] [*A publication*] (DLA) .... Imp Pl
Impey's Office of Sheriff [*6th ed.*] [*1835*] [*A publication*] (DLA) .... Imp Sh
Impey's Practice, Common Pleas [*A publication*] (DLA) .... Imp Pr CP
Impey's Practice, King's Bench [*A publication*] (DLA) .... Imp Pr KB
Impfondo [*Congo*] [*ICAO location identifier*] (ICLI) .... FCOI
Impfondo [*Congo*] [*Airport symbol*] (OAG) .... ION
Imphal [*India*] [*Airport symbol*] (OAG) .... IMF
Imphal [*India*] [*ICAO location identifier*] (ICLI) .... VEIM
Impingement [*Engineering*] .... IGMT
Impingement Point .... IP
Implantable Artificial Heart .... IAH
Implantable Artificial Heart Energy System .... IAHES
Implantable Beacon Transmitter [*Oceanography*] .... IBT
Implantable Cardioverter-Defibrillator [*Medical device for heart patients*] .... ICD
Implantable Drug Delivery System [*Pharmacology*] (DAVI) .... IDDS
Implantable Insulin Pump .... IIP
Implantable Micro-Identification Device [*for laboratory animals*] .... IMI
Implantable Programmable Infusion Pump [*Medicine*] .... IPIP
Implantation Doping Technique .... IDT
Implantation Test [*Medicine*] (MAE) .... IT
Implanted Advanced Composed Technology [*Texas Instruments, Inc.*] .... IMPACT
Implanted Electrode Technique .... IET
Implanted Zener Diode (MCD) .... IZD
Implement (AFM) .... IMP
Implement (AABC) .... IMPL
Implement .... IMPL
Implementation .... IMPLNTN
Implementation and Conversion (MCD) IC
Implementation Delay Report [*Social Security Administration*] .... IDR
Implementation Field Microfilm/Micrographics Information System .... IFMIS
Implementation/Installation Plan [*Telecommunications*] (TEL) .... IIP
Implementation Instructions (MCD) II
Implementation Language [*Edinburgh multiaccess system*] (CSR) .... IMP
Implementation Language (NITA) .... IMPL
Implementation Monitoring (HCT) .... IM
Implementation of Change IC
Implementation of New Carrier Arrangements [*Telecommunications*] .... INCA
Implementation of Plan (NG) .... IP
Implementation Period .... IP
Implementation Planning and Control Technique [*Computer science*] .... IMPACT
Implementation Planning Program [*Environmental Protection Agency*] (GFGA) .... IPP
Implementation Special Interest Group [*Association for the Development of Computer-Based Instructional Systems*] (EDAC) .... ISIG
Implementation Support Package [*Army*] .... ISP
Implementation Under Test [*Telecommunications*] (OSI) .... IUT
Implementation Work Group [*DoD*] .... IWG
Implementation Work Group on Justice Information and Statistics [*See also GMO*] [*Canada*] .... IWG
Implementing Agency (KSC) .... IA
Implementing New Concepts of the Library for Urban Disadvantaged Ethnics [*Cleveland Public Library*] (NITA) .... INCLUDE
Implementing Primary Science Education (AIE) .... IPSE
Implicit I
Implicit Continuous-Fluid Eulerian .... ICE
Implicit Pressure, Explicit Saturation [*Petroleum reservoir simulation*] .... IMPES
Implicit Price Deflator .... IPD
Implicit Price Deflator Index [*Economics*] .... IPDI
Implicit Price Index (MHDW) .... IPI
Implicit Transport (PDAA) .... IMTRAN
Implied Valve Position (ACII) .... IVP
Implosive Therapy [*Type of behavior therapy*] .... IT
Import (WDMC) .... IMPRT
Import .... IMPRT
Import [*Economics*] .... Mp
Import Annual Data [*Department of Commerce*] (GFGA) .... IA
Import Car of the Year [*Automotive promotion*] .... ICOTY
Import Cargo Electronic System .... ICES
Import Certificate Delivery Verification [*Military*] .... ICDV
Import Duty [*Customs*] (DS) .... ID
Import Duty Act [*British*] (DS) .... IDA
Import Entitlement Agreement [*United Arab Republic*] .... IEA
Import Executive [*British*] .... IE
Import License .... I/L
Import Monthly Data [*Department of Commerce*] (GFGA) .... IM
Import Parity Pricing (ADA) .... IPP

Import Penetration ... IP
Import Release Note (DS) ... IRN
Import Tabulation System [*United Nations*] (PDAA) ... ITS
Importance ... IMPCE
Importance Factor [*Statistics*] ... IF
Important ... IMP
Important (WDMC) ... imp
Important (BARN) ... impt
Important Risk Data Notice [*Insurance*] ... IRDN
Importation ... IMPN
Imported ... IMP
Imported ... IMPRTD
Imported Content ... IC
Imported Crude Oil Processing ... ICOP
Imported Food Regulations [*British*] ... IFR
Imported Food Risks Advisory Committee [*Australia*] ... IFRAC
Imported Tobacco Products Advisory Council [*British*] (DBA) ... ITPAC
Importer (WDAA) ... IMP
Importer ... IMPRTR
Importer (ADA) ... IMPTR
Importers' Association of South Australia ... IASA
Importing ... IMPRTNG
Impose (MSA) ... IMPS
Imposition (DSUE) ... IMPO
Imposition (ROG) ... IMPOSN
Imposition (DSUE) ... IMPOT
Impossible (ADA) ... IMPOSS
Impossible Mission Force [*Fictitious group of undercover agents in TV series, "Mission: Impossible"*] ... IMF
Imposta sul Valore Aggiunto [*Value-Added Tax*] [*Italian*] ... IVA
Imposter Pass Rate (MHDI) ... IPR
Impostor Phenomenon [*Subject of book "If I'm So Successful, Why Do I Feel Like a Fake - The Impostor Phenomenon" by Joan C. Harvey*] [*Psychology*] ... IP
Impotence Institute of America (EA) ... IIA
Impotent Grain Boundary Dislocation ... IGBD
Impotents Anonymous (EA) ... IA
Impoverished Conditions ... IC
Impracticable (FAAC) ... IMP
Impracticable (DSUE) ... IMPRAC
Impractical (AABC) ... IMPR
Impregnable (ADA) ... IMPREG
Impregnate (IAA) ... IMPE
Impregnate (KSC) ... IMPG
Impregnate (AABC) ... IMPRG
Impregnated (TEL) ... IMPREG
Impressed Current Corrosion Protection ... ICCP
Impression (DAVI) ... I
Impression ... IMP
Impression (ROG) ... IMPR
Impression ... IMPRESS
Impression (MSA) ... IMPRSN
Impression Cylinder [*Typography*] (DGA) ... IC
Impression Cylinder [*Publishing*] (DGA) ... IMP CYL
Impressionism (VRA) ... Impr
Impressions per Hour [*Printing*] ... IPH
Imprest Fund (MCD) ... IF
Imprial Chem Ind ADR [*NYSE symbol*] (TTSB) ... ICI
Imprial Ginseng Products Ltd. [*Associated Press*] (SAG) ... IGinseng
Imprimatur [*Latin for let it be printed*] (WDMC) ... imp
Imprimatur [*Let It Be Printed*] [*Latin*] ... IMP
Imprimatura (VRA) ... imprm
Imprime [*Printed*] [*French*] (ILCA) ... Imp
Imprimerie Centrale d'Afrique [*Publisher*] [*Gabon*] (EY) ... IMPRIGA
Imprimerie Nationale du Burundi [*Government publishing house*] [*Burundi*] (EY) ... INABU
Imprimes Historiques, Universite du Quebec, Trois-Rivieres, Quebec [*Library symbol National Library of Canada*] (NLC) ... QTUIH
Imprimeur [*Printer*] [*French*] (ILCA) ... Imp
Imprimis [*In the First Place*] [*Latin*] (WGA) ... IMP
Imprint ... IMP
Imprint [*Online database field identifier*] ... IMPR
Imprint Immuno-Fixation [*Immunochemistry*] ... IIF
Imprint Records, Inc. [*NASDAQ symbol*] (SAG) ... IMPR
Imprint Records, Inc. [*Associated Press*] (SAG) ... Imprint
Imprint Records, Inc. [*Associated Press*] (SAG) ... ImprintR
Imprisonment [*British military*] (DMA) ... Impt
Improbatur [*Latin*] ... i
Improper (ADA) ... IMPROP
Improper Order ... IMO
Improper Use of Adjective [*Used in correcting manuscripts, etc.*] ... ADJ
Improper Use of Adverb [*Used in correcting manuscripts, etc.*] ... ADV
Impropriator (ROG) ... IMP
Improve [*Real estate*] (ROG) ... IMPVE
Improved ... IMP
Improved [*Real estate*] (ROG) ... IMPD
Improved ... IMPR
Improved [*Real estate*] (ROG) ... IMPVD
Improved Accuracy Program (MCD) ... IAP
Improved Aerial Refueling System Program ... IARS
Improved Amphibious Reconnaissance Equipment [*Military*] (MCD) ... IARE
Improved Anode Catalyst ... IAC
Improved Antimateriel Warhead ... IAMW
Improved Antimateriel Warhead ... IAMWH
Improved Antimateriel Warhead ... IAW
Improved Antimateriel Warhead ... IAWH
Improved Army Tactical Communications System (DOMA) ... IATACS
Improved Army Tactical Missile System (RDA) ... IMP-ATACMS
Improved Assault Fire Units [*Military*] (MCD) ... IAFU
Improved Basic Point Defense Surface Missile System (DNAB) ... IBPDSMS
Improved Benevolent Protective Order of Elks of the World (EA) ... IBPOEW
Improved Biological Detection System [*Military*] (MCD) ... IBDS
Improved Bradley Acquisition Subsystem [*Army*] (RDA) ... IBAS
Improved Bradley Acquisition System [*Army*] (INF) ... IBAS
Improved Brilliant Anti-Armor [*Army*] (RDA) ... IBAT
Improved Capability [*for aircraft*] (MCD) ... IC
Improved Capability [*for aircraft*] (MCD) ... ICAP
Improved Capability Minuteman (SAA) ... ICM
Improved Capability Missile [*Air Force*] ... ICM
Improved Capability Missile [*Air Force*] (IAA) ... IMCPM
Improved Capability Missile [*Air Force*] (MCD) ... IMPCM
Improved Capital Value [*Business term*] (ADA) ... ICV
Improved Chaparral [*Military*] (MCD) ... ICHAP
Improved Cobra Agility and Maneuverability [*Military*] (MCD) ... ICAM
Improved Cobra Armament Program [*Military*] (MCD) ... ICAP
Improved Cobra Armament System [*Military*] (MCD) ... ICAS
Improved Combustion ... IMCO
Improved Commander's Weapon Station ... ICWS
Improved Complex Terrain Dispersion Model (USDC) ... CTDMPLUS
Improved Computer-Controlled Dwell [*Automotive engineering*] ... ICCD
Improved Continuous-Wave Acquisition RADAR [*Army*] (AABC) ... ICWAR
Improved Conventional Dive System (DOMA) ... ICDS
Improved Conventional Mine System [*Military*] (MCD) ... ICOM
Improved Conventional Munitions ... ICM
Improved Cost Estimate (RDA) ... ICE
Improved Crew Optical Sight (NASA) ... ICOS
Improved Data Display System ... IDDS
Improved Data Effectiveness and Availability ... IDEA
Improved Data Interchange ... IDI
Improved Data Modem ... IDM
Improved Data Modem [*Air Force*] (DOMA) ... IDM
Improved Deep Moored Sweep [*Military*] (MCD) ... IDMS
Improved Definition Television (NTCM) ... IDT
Improved Definition Television ... IDTV
Improved Doppler Tracking System ... IDTS
Improved Effectiveness Nuclear Depth Bomb ... IMPEND
Improved Efficiency of Learning [*Project*] (AIE) ... IEL
Improved Emergency Message Automatic Transmission System (MCD) ... IEMATS
Improved Erector-Launcher (SAA) ... IEL
Improved Explosive Device ... IED
Improved Fiber Optics ... IFO
Improved Fiber Optics Bundle ... IFOB
Improved Fire Control System [*Military*] (MCD) ... IFCS
Improved Fleet Ballistic Missile ... IFBM
Improved Flotation Chamber ... IFC
Improved Frequency Modulation (MCD) ... IFM
Improved Gas Turbine (MCD) ... IGT
Improved Gray Scale ... IGS
Improved Ground Reconnaissance Equipment [*Military*] (MCD) ... IGRE
Improved Ground Rents (ROG) ... IGR
Improved Guard Rail V [*Army*] (DOMA) ... IGRV
Improved Guidance and Control (MCD) ... IMPGAC
Improved Gunner's Sight Unit [*Military*] (MCD) ... IGSU
Improved HAWK Simulator [*Military*] ... IHS
Improved HAWK Training Detachment ... IHTD
Improved HAWK-Tracking Adjunct System [*Military*] (MCD) ... IH-TAS
Improved High Speed Rail (PDAA) ... IHSR
Improved High-Frequency Radio (INF) ... IHFR
Improved High-Power Illuminator (CAAL) ... IHPI
Improved High-Power Illuminator RADAR [*IHAWK Missile*] (MCD) ... IHIPIR
Improved High-Speed Bombing RADAR ... IHSBR
Improved Holographic Image ... IHI
Improved Homing All the Way Killer [*Missile*] ... IHAWK
Improved Industrial Standard Process (MCD) ... IISP
Improved Infrared Missile ... IIRM
Improved Infrared Source ... IIS
Improved Inter-Range Vector (MCD) ... IIRV
Improved Launcher Mechanical System [*Military*] ... ILMS
Improved Life Blower Bearing ... ILBB
Improved Light Antiarmor [*or Antitank*] **Weapon** (RDA) ... I-LAW
Improved Lighting System for Army Aircraft (RDA) ... ILSAA
Improved Light-Scattering Dust Monitor (PDAA) ... ILSOM
Improved Limb Atmospheric Spectrometer [*Matsushita Electronics*] ... ILAS
Improved Line Charge (DOMA) ... ILC
Improved Main Rotor Blade (RDA) ... IMRB
Improved Maintenance Guidance Information ... IMGI
Improved Maintenance Program [*Air Force*] (AFM) ... IMP
Improved Management Procurement and Contracting Technique (AABC) ... IMPACT
Improved Manned Interceptor [*Proposed plane*] [*Air Force*] ... IMI
Improved Manpower Production and Controller Technique [*Navy*] ... IMPACT
Improved Manufacturing Procedure [*Computer science*] (PDAA) ... IMP
Improved Many-on-Many [*Computer science*] ... IMOM
Improved Massed Intercept (MCD) ... IMI
Improved Medical Programs and Readiness Immediately, Not Tomorrow [*TROA*] ... IMPRINT
Improved Meteorological Conditions (MCD) ... IMC
Improved Military Parts Availability and Selection Working Group [*Army*] (RDA) ... IMPAS-WG

Improved Military Rifle (PDAA) .... IMR
Improved Minimum Essential Medium [*Microbiology*] .... IMEM
Improved Mobile Telephone Service [*Telecommunications*] .... IMTS
Improved Mobility Package [*Wheelchair system*] .... IMP
Improved Modern Pricing and Costing Techniques [*Air Force*] (MCD) .... IMPACT
Improved Multi-Band Encoding [*Telecommunications*] (ACRL) .... IMBE
Improved Navigational Satellite .... INS
Improved Night Sight .... INS
Improved Nike Hercules [*Missile*] .... INH
Improved Nonnuclear LANCE .... INNL
Improved Operational Test, Training, and Evaluation [*Military*] .... IOTT & E
Improved Order of Red Men .... IORM
Improved Performance Space Motor (MCD) .... IPSM
Improved Plow Steel (PDAA) .... IPS
Improved Point Defense .... IPD
Improved Point Defense Missile System [*Sea Sparrow*] (DOMA) .... IBPDMS
Improved Point Defense Missile System [*Navy*] (DOMA) .... IPDS
Improved Point Defense Surface Missile System .... IPDSMS
Improved Position Locator (PDAA) .... IPL
Improved Pregnancy Outcome [*Medicine*] (DMAA) .... IPO
Improved Processing Inspection [*Food Safety and Inspection Service*] [*Department of Agriculture*] .... IPI
Improved Processing System (MCD) .... IPPS
Improved Processing System .... IPS
Improved Programmer Test Station (IEEE) .... IMPTS
Improved Programmer Test Station / Power Station (SAA) .... IPTS/PS
Improved Programming Technologies (BUR) .... IPT
Improved Protective Entrance/Tent [*Army*] .... IPE/T
Improved Pulse Acquisition RADAR (AABC) .... IPAR
Improved RADAR Data Correlator (DWSG) .... IRDC
Improved RADAR Simulation (DWSG) .... IRS
Improved Radiator Standards Association (EA) .... IRSA
Improved Random Access Memory [*Computer science*] .... IRAM
Improved Range-Only RADAR (MCD) .... IROR
Improved Rearming Rate Program [*Military*] (NVT) .... IRRP
Improved Rearming Rates [*Military*] (NG) .... IRR
Improved Recovery Vehicle [*Army*] (RDA) .... IRV
Improved Reliability and Maintainability .... IRAM
Improved Reliability Operational System (MCD) .... IROS
Improved Remote-Area Armor Mine (MCD) .... IRAAM
Improved Remotely Monitored Battlefield Sensor System .... IREM-BASS
Improved Repairables Asset Management (DNAB) .... IRAM
Improved Replenishment-at-Sea Program (MCD) .... IRP
Improved Retrofit (CAAL) .... IR
Improved Ribbon-Type Bridge [*Military*] (RDA) .... IRB
Improved Risk Mutuals (EA) .... IRM
Improved Rotor Blade [*Rotorcraft*] .... IRB
Improved SAGE [*Semiautomatic Ground Environment*] **Manned Intercept System** (IAA) .... ISMIS
Improved Saturn Launch Facility .... ISLF
Improved Secure Voice Conferencing System [*Military*] (MCD) .... ISVCS
Improved Sensing Munitions (RDA) .... ISM
Improved Side-Lobe Supression (PDAA) .... ISLS
Improved SONAR Processing Equipment [*Military*] (CAAL) .... ISPE
Improved Space Manned Interceptor (IAA) .... ISMI
Improved Spartan Homing Sensor [*Missiles*] .... ISHS
Improved SPRINT [*Solid-Propellant Rocket Intercept*] **Missile Subsystem** [*Army*] .... ISMS
Improved SPRINT [*Solid-Propellant Rocket Intercept*] **Missile Subsystem - Derated** [*Army*] .... ISMS-D
Improved Standard Electronic Module (MHDB) .... ISEM
Improved State-of-the-Art (PDAA) .... ISOA
Improved Stratospheric and Mesospheric Sounder (MCD) .... ISAMS
Improved Submarine Communication (MCD) .... ISC
Improved Suspension (MCD) .... IS
Improved Symbolic Optimizing Assembly Routine .... ISOPAR
Improved System Technology (NITA) .... IST
Improved Tactical Air-Launched Decoy (DWSG) .... ITALD
Improved Tactical Attack System .... ITAS
Improved Target Acquisition System [*Army*] .... ITAS
Improved Tartar .... IT
Improved Tartar Retrofit [*Missile*] (MCD) .... ITR
Improved Thayer-Martin [*Medium*] (DMAA) .... ITM
Improved Third Stage [*of Minuteman rocket*] .... ITS
Improved TIROS [*Television Infrared Observation Satellite*] **Operational Satellite** [*or System*] [*National Oceanic and Atmospheric Administration*] .... ITOS
Improved Touring [*Class of racing cars*] .... IT
Improved TOW [*Tube-Launched, Optically Tracked, Wire-Guided (Weapon)*] **Vehicle** .... ITV
Improved TOW [*Tube-Launched, Optically Tracked, Wire-Guided (Weapon)*] **Vehicle Evasive Target Simulator** [*Military*] (MCD) .... ITVETS
Improved Transtage Injector Program (MCD) .... ITIP
Improved Tube-Launched, Optically Tracked, Wire-Guided [*Weapon*] (RDA) .... ITOW
Improved United Kingdom Air Defense Ground Environment .... IUKADGE
Improved Value (ADA) IV
Improved Virtual Orbitals [*Atomic physics*] .... IVO
Improved Visible Marker .... IVM
Improved Water Analysis Kit .... IWAK
Improved Weather Reconnaissance .... IWR
Improved-Cycle Boiling-Water Reactor [*Nuclear energy*] .... ICBWR
Improvement [*Real estate*] .... IMP
Improvement (MSA) .... IMPROV
Improvement (AABC) .... IMPRV
Improvement .... IMPRVMNT
Improvement .... IMPRVMT
Improvement [*Real estate*] (ROG) .... IMPT
Improvement and Betterments [*Real estate*] .... I & B
Improvement and Modernization (AABC) .... I & M
Improvement Data Plan (MCD) .... IDP
Improvement Data Plan Sheet (MCD) .... IDPS
Improvement Data System (MCD) .... IDS
Improvement District No. 9/Banff Municipal Library, Alberta [*Library symbol National Library of Canada*] (NLC) .... ABIDM
Improvement Maintenance Program (MCD) .... IMP
Improvement Program (AFM) .... IP
Improvement Purchase (ADA) .... IP
Improving Career Education (OICC) .... ICE
Improving the Definition of the Objective Force [*Military*] .... IDOFOR
Improvised Explosive Device .... IED
Improvised Explosive Device Disposal (PDAA) .... IED
Improvised Nuclear Device .... IND
Impulse (KSC) .... IMP
Impulse (FAAC) .... IMPL
Impulse (MSA) .... IMPLS
Impulse Amplitude Modulation (IAA) .... IAM
Impulse Balance System .... IBS
Impulse Bandwidth (MCD) .... IBW
Impulse Base Flow Facility [*NASA*] .... IBFF
Impulse Conducting System [*Physiology*] .... ICS
Impulse Conductor (MSA) IC
Impulse Duplexer Study .... IDS
Impulse Fast Reactor [*Former USSR*] .... IFR
Impulse Generator (IAA) .... IG
Impulse Generator .... IMP
Impulse Generator (IAA) .... IMPGEN
Impulse International Auto Club [*Defunct*] (EA) .... IIAC
Impulse Modulation .... IM
Impulse Noise .... IPN
Impulse P Wave [*Earthquakes*] [*Exclamation point signifies a very sharp earthquake*] .... iP
Impulse Resistance Bridge .... IRB
Impulse Response Area Ratio .... IRAR
Impulse Sequencing Relay .... ISR
Impulse, Specific (KSC) .... ISP
Impulse Transfer Function (KSC) .... ITF
Impulse Transfer Orbit .... ITO
Impulse Weight (IAA) .... IW
Impulse-Aero [*Russian Federation*] [*ICAO designator*] (FAAC) .... IMR
Impulse-Modulated Telemetry (IAA) .... IMT
Impulses, Ego, and Superego Test [*Psychology*] (AEBS) .... IEST
Impulses per Minute [*Telecommunications*] .... IPM
Impulses per Second [*Telecommunications*] (TEL) .... IPS
Impulsive Classroom Behavior Scale (EDAC) .... ICBS
Impulsive Ergodic Collision Theory [*Mathematics*] .... IECT
Impulsive Stimulated Raman Scattering [*Physics*] .... ISRS
Impurity Monitoring and Analysis System [*Nuclear energy*] (NRCH) .... IMAS
Impurity Photoconductivity (PDAA) .... IPC
Impurity Removal Subsystem (MCD) .... IR
Impurity Removal System .... IRS
Impurity Study Experiment [*Oak Ridge National Laboratory*] .... ISX
Imputation .... IMPTN
Imputation .... IMPUTN
IMRE Corp. [*NASDAQ symbol*] (NQ) .... IMRE
IMS-Data Communications (NITA) .... IMS-DC
IMS-Database (NITA) .... IMS-DB
Imtec, Inc. [*NASDAQ symbol*] (NQ) .... IMTC
Imtec, Inc. [*Associated Press*] (SAG) .... Imtec
Imutec Corp. [*NASDAQ symbol*] (SAG) .... IMUT
Imutec Corp. [*Associated Press*] (SAG) .... Imutec
IMUTEC Corp. [*NASDAQ symbol*] (TTSB) .... IMUTF
In Absentia [*In Absence*] [*Latin*] .... IA
In Accordance With .... IAW
In Accordance with Contract .... IAWC
In Addition to Other Duties [*Military*] .... IAOD
In Addition to Other Duties [*Military*] .... IATOD
In Amenas [*Algeria*] [*Airport symbol*] (OAG) .... IAM
In Amguel [*Issek Toufreg*] [*Algeria*] [*Seismograph station code, US Geological Survey*] [*Closed*] (SEIS) .... IAA
In and Out (MAE) .... I & O
In and Out of Clouds [*ICAO*] (FAAC) .... IAO
In and Out Processing [*Computer science*] (AFM) .... I & OP
In Any Event [*Internet language*] [*Computer science*] .... IAE
In Appreciation of the Hollies (EA) .... IAOH
In Auri [*To the Ear*] [*Pharmacy*] .... IN AUR
In Bankruptcy or Receivership [*Investment term*] (DFIT) VI
In Black and White [*A publication*] .... IBW
In Bond [*Wines and Spirits*] .... IB
In Bonis [*In the Goods Of*] [*Latin*] (ADA) .... IN B
In Bono [*In Good Order*] .... INB
In Bulk (IAA) .... IB
In Case Of .... ICO
In Casu [*In This Case*] [*Latin*] ic
In Catilinam [*of Cicero*] [*Classical studies*] (OCD) .... Cat
In Charge Of IC
In Charge of Room [*Military*] (DNAB) .... ICOR
In Christi Nomine [*In the Name of Christ*] [*Latin*] .... ICN
In Christo [*In Christ*] [*Latin*] IX
In Circuit Test [*Electronics*] (EECA) .... ICT
In Clouds [*ICAO*] (FAAC) .... INC

In Command (ADA) IC
In Commission, Active [Vessel status] [Navy] (DNAB) .... ICAT
In Commission, In Reserve [Vessel status] [Navy] .... ICIR
In Commission, Special [Vessel status] [Navy] (DNAB) .... ICSP
In Compliance [FDA] IC
In Compliance With (MUGU) .... ICW
In Conjunction With (ADA) .... CONJ
In Conjunction With (AAGC) .... ICW
In Connection With .... ICW
In Control, Inc. [NASDAQ symbol] (SAG) .... INCL
In Defense of Animals (EA) .... IDA
In Dei Nomine [In God's Name] [Latin] .... IDN
In dem Herrn Ist das Heil [In the Lord Is Salvation] [Motto of Dorothee, Princess of Anhalt (1580-1618)] [German] .... IDHIDH
In Deo Faciemus Virtutem [Through God We Shall Do Valiantly] [(Ps., IX. 12) Motto of August, Prince of Anhalt-Plotzkau (1575-1653)] [Latin] .... IDFV
In Dies [Daily] [Pharmacy] .... IN D
In Domino Fiducia Nostra [In the Lord Is Our Trust] [Motto of August, Prince of Anhalt-Plotzkau (1575-1653)] [Latin] .... IDFN
In Excess .... IE
In Extenso [At Full Length] [Latin] (ROG) .... IN EX
In Fine [Finally] [Latin] .... IN F
In Flaccum [of Philo Judaeus] (BJA) .... Flac
In Flaccum [of Philo Judaeus] [Classical studies] (OCD) .... In Flacc
In Flagrante Delicto [Caught in the Act] [Latin] .... IFD
In Focus System, Inc. [Associated Press] (SAG) .... InFocu
In Focus System, Inc. [NASDAQ symbol] (SAG) .... INFS
In Focus Systems [NASDAQ symbol] (TTSB) .... INFS
In Folio (DGA) .... INF
In Folio Argenti Volvendae [To Be Silvered] [Pharmacy] .... IN FOL ARG VOLVEND
In Forma Pauperis [As a Pauper] [Latin] .... IFP
In Front Of (WDAA) .... IFO
In Full .... IF
In Hands of Civil Authorities [Military] .... IHCA
In His Name .... IHN
In Hoc Signo (Vinces) [In This Sign (You Will Conquer)] [Latin] .... IHS
In Home [Men's lacrosse position] .... IH
In Home Health, inc. [Associated Press] (SAG) .... InHome
In Home Health, Inc. [NASDAQ symbol] (NQ) .... IHHI
In Honor Of .... IHO
In Initio [In the Beginning] [Latin] .... IN INIT
In Kind Matching (OICC) .... IKM
In Ladestreifen [Loaded in Clips] [German military - World War II] IL
In Liebe Vereint bis in dem Tod [United in Love until Death] [German] .... ILVBIDT
In Lieu Of .... ILO
In Lieu Of .... INLO
In Lieu of Until Exhausted [Military] .... ILOUE
In Lieu Thereof [Military] .... ILT
In Limine [At the Outset] [Latin] .... IN LIM
In Litteris [In Correspondence] [Latin] .... IN LITT
In Loco [In the Place Of] [Latin] .... IN LOC
In Loco Citato [In the Place Mentioned] [Latin] (ROG) .... IN LOC CIT
In Maintenance .... IM
In Margine [On the Margin] [Latin] .... im
In Medio Currere Metuo [I Fear to Go in the Middle] [Motto of Julius, Duke of Braunschweig-Wolfenbuttel (1529-89)] [Latin] .... IMCM
In Memoriam [In Memory Of] [Latin] (ROG) .... IN MEM
In My Arrogant Opinion [Computer hacker terminology] (NHD) .... IMAO
In My Honest Opinion .... IMHO
In My Humble Opinion [Internet language] [Computer science] .... IMHO
In My Humble Opinion (BARN) .... INMHO
In My Not-So-Humble Opinion [Computer hacker terminology] (NHD) .... IMNSHO
In My Opinion [Internet language] [Computer science] .... IMO
In Nomine Christi [In the Name of Christ] [Latin] .... INC
In Nomine Dei [In the Name of God] [Latin] .... IND
In Nomine Iesu [In the Name of Jesus] [Latin] .... INI
In Nomine Jesu [In the Name of Jesus] [Latin] .... INJ
In Nomine Sanctae Trinitatis [In the Name of the Holy Trinity] [Latin] .... INST
In Oedibus [In the House Of] [Latin] (ROG) .... IN OEDIB
In Operation (IAA) .... IOPN
In Order .... IO
In Other Words .... IOW
In Our Culture .... IOC
In Our Own Way (EA) .... IOOW
In Pace [In Peace] [Latin] .... INP
In Partibus Infidelium [In the Countries, Lands, or Regions of Unbelievers] [Latin] .... IPI
In Phase/Quadrature (MCD) .... I/Q
In Pisonem [of Cicero] [Classical studies] (OCD) .... Pis
In Place (DOG) .... in situ
In Place [Dancing] .... IP
In Plaster [Medicine] (DAVI) .... IP
In Port [Navy] (NVT) .... INPT
In Port [Navy] (NVT) .... IPT
In Praesentia Dominorum [In the Presence of the Lords of Session] [Latin] .... IPD
In Principio [In the Beginning] [Latin] (ROG) .... IN PR
In Process .... IP
In Progress (MCD) .... I/P
In Progress .... INPR
In Propria Persona [In Person] [Latin Legal term] (DLA) .... IPP
In Pulmento [In Gruel] [Pharmacy] .... IN PULM
In Pulse to Register [Telecommunications] (TEL) .... IPR
In Pulse to Sender [Telecommunications] (TEL) .... IPS
In Quires [Publishing] (DGA) .... IN QRS
In Reference To .... IN REF

In Reference To (NVT) .... IRT
In Regard To .... IN RE
In Regard To (MCD) .... IRT
In Reply To (NVT) .... IRT
In Response To (NVT) .... IRT
In Salah [Algeria] [ICAO location identifier] (ICLI) .... DAUI
In Salah [Algeria] [Airport symbol] (OAG) .... INZ
In Search Of [Classified advertising] .... ISO
In Service [Military] (CAAL) .... INSERV
In Service [Telecommunications] (TEL) .... IS
In Service, Active [Vessel status] [Navy] (DNAB) .... ISAC
In Service, In Reserve [Vessel status] [Navy] .... ISIR
In Shop (MCD) .... IS
In Silentio et Spe [In Silence and in Hope] [Motto of Bernhard, Prince of Anhalt (1572-96)] [Latin] .... ISES
In Situ [In Place] [Latin] (ADA) .... INS
In Situ [In Place] [Latin] .... IS
In Situ Combustion [Engineering] .... ISC
In Situ Hybridization [Biology] .... ISH
In Situ Hybridization Histochemistry .... ISHH
In Situ Leaching (GAAI) .... ISL
In Situ Vapro Stripping [Environmental science] .... ISVS
In Situ Vitrification [Radioactive waste cleanup] .... ISV
In Statu Pupillari [Subject to the Rule of the Institution] [Latin] (BARN) .... in stat pup
In Status Quo .... ISQ
In System Evaluator [National Semiconductor Company] (NITA) .... ISE
In the Business [Refers to television and film industries] .... ITB
In the Ear [Hearing aid] .... ITE
In the Left Arm While Reclining [Diastolic] [or Recumbent] [Cardiology] (DAVI) .... BP 120/80 Lar
In the Manner Directed [Abbreviation from the Latin] [Pharmacy] (ROG) .... MOD DICT
In the Name of the Great Architect of the Universe [Freemasonry] (ROG) .... ITNOTGAOTU
In the Overcast [Aviation] .... IOVC
In the Place Cited [Loco citato] [Latin] (WDMC) .... loc cit
in the Right Arm While Reclining [Diastolic] [or recumbent] [Cardiology] (DAVI) .... BP 120/80 Rar
In the Vicinity Of (FAAC) .... INVOF
In Touch Networks (EA) .... ITN
In Transit .... INTNS
In Transitu [In Transit] [Latin] (ROG) .... IN TRANS
In Transitu [In Transit] [Latin] .... IT
In Trust For [Banking] .... ITF
In Utero [Gynecology] .... IU
In Vapour (ROG) IV
In Verbo [Under the Word] [Latin] IV
In Verrem [of Cicero] [Classical studies] (OCD) .... Verr
In View IV
In Vitro [Medicine] (MAE) IV
In Vitro Diagnostics [Clinical chemistry] .... IVD
In Vitro Expression Cloning [Analytical biochemistry] .... IVEC
In Vitro Fertilization [Gynecology] .... IVF
In Vitro Fertilization with Embryo Transfer [Gynecology] .... IVFET
In Vitro Protein Digestibility [Nutrition] .... IVPD
In Vitro Rumen Digestibility [Nutrition] .... IVRD
In Vitro Synthesized Protein [Biochemistry] .... IVSP
In Vivo [Medicine] (MAE) IV
In Vivo Adhesive Platelet [Medicine] (MAE) .... IVAP
In Vivo Expression Technology [Genetics] .... IVET
In Vivo Neutron Activation Analysis [Analytical chemistry] .... IVNAA
INA Investment Sec [NYSE symbol] (TTSB) .... IIS
INA Investment Securities, Inc. [NYSE symbol] (SPSG) .... IIS
INA Investment Securities, Inc. [Associated Press] (SAG) .... INAIn
Inaccessible Pore Volume [Petroleum technology] .... IPV
Inacom Corp. [NASDAQ symbol] (SAG) .... INAC
Inacom Corp. [Associated Press] (SAG) .... Inacom
Inactivate [or Inactive] (MSA) (MSA) .... INACTV
Inactivated Fetal Calf Serum [Medicine] (DMAA) .... IFCS
Inactivated Fetal-Calf Serum [Immunology] .... IFS
Inactivated Horse Serum [Immunology] .... IHS
Inactivated Polio Vaccine [Also, Salk vaccine] (PAZ) .... IPV
Inactivated Poliovirus Vaccine .... IPV
Inactivating Dose [Medicine] (DMAA) .... IAD
Inactivator Accelerator [Immunology] .... INA
Inactive [Chemistry] i
Inactive .... inac
Inactive (AABC) .... INACT
Inactive Account [Banking] .... IA
Inactive Aerospace Vehicle [or Aircraft] .... IA
Inactive Aerospace Vehicle [or Aircraft] Authorization .... IAA
Inactive Aerospace Vehicle [or Aircraft] Inventory .... IAI
Inactive Air Reserve .... IAR
Inactive Duty Training [Military] (AABC) .... IDT
Inactive Duty Training [Air Force] (AFM) .... INACDUTRA
Inactive Equipment Maintenance (DNAB) .... IEM
Inactive Fleet, Atlantic Fleet (DNAB) .... INACTFLTLANT
Inactive Fleet, Atlantic Fleet .... INACTLANT
Inactive Fleet, Pacific Fleet .... INACTFLTPAC
Inactive Fleet, Pacific Fleet .... INACTPAC
Inactive - In Commission, In Reserve [Vessel status] [Navy] .... INA/IC
Inactive - In Service, In Reserve [Vessel status] [Navy] .... INA/IS
Inactive Insurance (DLA) .... I/Ins
Inactive Item Review Card [Military] (AFIT) .... IIRC
Inactive Materiel Request History and Status File [Army] .... IMRHS

Inactive National Guard ... ING
Inactive National Guard (DOMA) ... ING
Inactive Nondisability Retirement Branch [*BUPERS*] ... INDRB
Inactive - Out of Commission, In Reserve [*Vessel status*] [*Navy*] ... INA/OC
Inactive - Out of Service, In Reserve [*Vessel status*] [*Navy*] ... INA/OS
Inactive Renin Activity [*Medicine*] (DMAA) ... IRA
Inactive Reserve Officer Status Branch [*BUPERS*] ... IROSB
Inactive Reserve Section [*Military*] ... IRS
Inactive Service Craft Facility [*Military*] (DNAB) ... INACTSERVCRAFAC
Inactive Ship Maintenance Facility [*Navy*] ... INACTSHIPFAC
Inactive Ship Maintenance Facility ... ISMF
Inactive Ship Supply Overhaul Team ... ISSOT
Inactive Ships Navy Custody (NVT) ... ISNAC
Inactive Specific Transcriptase (BARN) ... XIST
Inactive Status List (MUGU) ... ISL
Inactive Status List Reserve Section ... ISLRS
Inactive-Officer Master File (DNAB) ... IOMF
Inadequate (AFM) ... INAD
Inadequate (FAAC) ... INADQT
Inadequate Core Cooling [*Nuclear energy*] (NRCH) ... ICC
Inadequate Core Cooling Monitor [*Nuclear energy*] (NUCP) ... ICCM
Inadvertent ... INAD
Inadvertent Destruct [*Aerospace*] (AAG) ... IDS
Inadvertent Ignition Panel ... IIP
Inadvertent Missile Ignition Detection ... IMID
Inadvertent Modification of the Stratosphere [*Interagency government task force*] ... IMOS
Inadvertent Opening of a Safety Relief Valve [*Nuclear energy*] (NRCH) ... IORV
Inadvertent Separation and Destruct System [*Aerospace*] ... ISDS
Inagua [*Bahamas*] [*Airport symbol*] (OAG) ... IGA
Inamed Corp. [*NASDAQ symbol*] (NQ) ... IMDC
Inamed Corp. [*Associated Press*] (SAG) ... Inamed
Inanities per Page [*Facetious criterion for determining insignificance of Supreme Court Justices*] [*Proposed by University of Chicago professor David P. Currie*] ... IPP
Inanna's Descent (BJA) ... ID
Inanna's Descent to the Netherworld (BJA) ... IDN
Inanwatan [*West Irian, Indonesia*] [*Airport symbol*] (AD) ... INX
Inanwatan [*Indonesia*] [*ICAO location identifier*] (ICLI) ... WASI
Inappropriate Antidiuretic Hormone [*Endocrinology*] (MAE) ... IADH
Inappropriate Antidiuretic Hormone Syndrome [*Endocrinology*] ... IADHS
Inappropriate Gonadotrophin Secretion [*Endocrinology*] ... IGS
Inappropriate Secretion of Antidiuretic Hormone [*Endocrinology*] (MAE) ... ISADH
In-Arm Suspension Unit [*Tank Technology*] ... ISU
Inaugural Dissertation (BJA) ... ID
Inaugurated (ADA) ... INAUG
In-Band Framing System [*Simulation Laboratories, Inc.*] ... IFS
Inboard (DS) ... I
Inboard (NASA) ... IB
Inboard (KSC) ... INBD
Inboard (ADA) ... INBRD
Inboard Booster Engine Cutoff (MCD) ... IBECO
Inboard Engine Cutoff ... IECO
Inboard/Outboard Profile (NASA) ... I/OP
Inboard Rotating Shield ... IRS
Inboard-Outboard [*Boating*] ... I/O
Inborn Error of Metabolism [*Medicine*] ... IEM
Inbound ... IB
Inbound ... INBD
Inbound/Outbound Traffic Analysis [*Military*] (AABC) ... IOTA
Inbound Tourism Organisation of Australia ... IOTA
Inbound Tourism Organisation of Australia ... ITOA
In-Branch Operator Training [*British*] (DCTA) ... IBOT
Inbrand Corp. [*NASDAQ symbol*] (SAG) ... INBR
Inbrand Corp. [*Associated Press*] (SAG) ... Inbrand
Inbred Livestock Registry Association (EA) ... ILRA
Inbreeding Coefficient [*Genetics*] (DAVI) ... F
INCA [*International Newspaper Color Association*]-FIEJ Research Association [*Federation Internationale des Editeurs de Journaux*] [*Research center Germany*] (IRC) ... IFRA
Inca Pacific Resources [*VS, exchange symbol*] (TTSB) ... IP
Inca Resources, Inc. [*Toronto Stock Exchange symbol Vancouver Stock Exchange symbol*] ... IRI
Incalzando [*Music*] ... Incalz
In-Can Melter [*Nuclear energy*] (NUCP) ... ICM
Incan Superior Ltd. [*AAR code*] ... NCAN
In-Can System [*Device that improves quality of beer and ale*] [*British*] ... ICS
Incandescent (WDMC) ... incan
Incandescent (MSA) ... INCAND
Incandescent ... INCD
Incandescent Lamp Manufacturers Association [*Defunct*] (EA) ... ILMA
Incandescent Liquid Spheroidal Formation [*Combustion technology*] ... ILSF
Incapacitated Emergency Egress Practice [*NASA*] (KSC) ... IEEP
Incapacitated Passengers' Handling Advice [*British*] ... INCAD
In-Car Entertainment [*Automotive audio system*] ... ICE
In-Car Temperature Sensor [*Automotive engineering*] ... ICTS
Incarcerated Innocent ... II
Incarnate Word College (GAGS) ... Incarnate Word C
Incarnate Word College [*Texas*] ... IWC
Incarnate Word College, San Antonio, TX [*Library symbol Library of Congress*] (LCLS) ... TxSaI
Incarnation ... INCRNTN
Incarnational Consecration (TOCD) ... IC
Incendiary [*Bomb*] ... I
Incendiary ... INC
Incendiary (AABC) ... INCD
Incendiary (MSA) ... INCND
Incendiary Bomb ... IB
Incendiary Bomb (DSUE) ... INCY
Incendiary Bomb with Explosive Nose ... IBEN
Incendiary Fragmentation Bomb ... IFB
Incendiary Munitions Evaluation ... IME
Incendiary Torch Remote Opening Device (MCD) ... ITROD
Incense Cedar [*Botany*] ... IC
In-Center Hemodialysis [*Medicine*] (DMAA) ... IHD
Incentive Award [*Military*] ... IA
Incentive Awards Program [*of the federal government, administered by CSC*] ... IAP
Incentive Bonus Scheme [*British*] ... IBS
Incentive Compensation (MCD) ... IC
Incentive Compensation Plan (MCD) ... ICP
Incentive Cost plus Fixed Fee [*Contracts*] ... ICPFF
Incentive Manufacturers Representatives Association [*Naperville, IL*] (EA) ... IMRA
Incentive Pay ... IP
Incentive PERT [*Program Evaluation and Review Technique*] **Events** ... IPE
Incentive Spirometer [*or Spirometry*] [*Medicine*] (DMAA) ... IS
Incentive Spirometry Breathing [*Medicine*] (DAVI) ... ISB
Incentive Stock Option ... ISO
Incentive Travel [*Travel industry*] ... IT
Incentive Travel and Meeting Executives Show [*Trade show*] ... IT & ME
Incentive Travel and Meeting Executives Show [*Trade show*] (ITD) ... IT/ME
Incentive-Based Policy [*for environmental improvement*] ... IB
Incentives Management Index [*Test*] ... IMI
Inception (ROG) ... INCEPT
Inception-to-Date ... ITD
Incertae Sedis [*Uncertain Position*] [*Biology, taxonomy*] ... inc sed
Incest Survivors' Association [*Australia*] ... ISA
Incest Survivors Resource Network, International (EA) ... ISRNI
Inch (EY) ... IN
Inch ... in
Inch (VRA) ... in
Inch (IDOE) ... in
Inch Trim Moment [*Nautical*] ... ITM
Inches (VRA) ... in
Inches (EY) ... INS
Inches (ODBW) ... ins
Inches Penetration per Month (IAA) ... IPM
Inches per Foot (IAA) ... IPF
Inches per Hour ... IN/H
Inches per Hour (TEL) ... IPH
Inches per Minute ... IPM
Inches per Minute (IDOE) ... ipm
Inches per Pound ... IN/LB
Inches per Revolution ... IPR
Inches per Second ... IN/S
Inches per Second (WDAA) ... IN/SEC
Inches per Second ... IPS
Inches per Second (DOM) ... ips
Inches per Second (IDOE) ... ips
Inches per Tooth (IAA) ... IPT
Inches per Year ... IPY
Inchoate (ADA) ... INCHO
Inchoative (WGA) ... INCH
Inchon [*Tyosen, Zinsen*] [*South Korea*] [*Seismograph station code, US Geological Survey*] [*Closed*] (SEIS) ... INC
Inch-Ounce ... IN-OZ
Inch-Pound ... IN-LB
Incide [*Cut*] [*Pharmacy*] ... INCID
Incidence Rate (WDAA) ... IR
Incidence Rate Ratio [*Mathematics*] ... IRR
Incident (AABC) ... ICDT
Incident (MSA) ... INCDT
Incident at Sea [*Navy*] (NVT) ... INCSEA
Incident Command System [*Regional emergency response system*] (DHSM) ... ICS
Incident Energy Density ... IED
Incident Investigation Review Committee [*Nuclear Regulatory Commission*] (NRCH) ... IIRC
Incident Management Center [*Nuclear Regulatory Commission*] (NRCH) ... IMC
Incident Power Flux Density (NITA) ... IPFD
Incident Power Monitor [*Military*] (CAAL) ... IPM
Incident Ray (IDOE) ... I
Incident Report [*Military*] (CINC) ... INCREP
Incident Report ... IR
Incident Reporting System [*IAEA*] (NUCP) ... IRS
Incident Resource and Information System [*Police*] [*British*] (NITA) ... IRIS
Incident Response Action Coordination Team [*Nuclear energy*] (NRCH) ... IRACT
Incident Response Center [*Nuclear Regulatory Commission*] (NRCH) ... IRC
Incident Tracking System ... ITS
Incidental Amplitude Modulation ... IAM
Incidental Appendectomy [*Medicine*] ... IA
Incidental Campaign Expense [*Ticket scalping*] ... ICE
Incidental Phase [*or Pulse*] **Modulation** ... IPM
Incident-Shock Equilibrium Expansion ... ISEE
Incident-Shock Frozen Expansion ... ISFE
Incidit [*Engraved*] [*Latin*] (ROG) ... INC
Incinerator ... INC
Incinerator (MSA) ... INCIN
Incinerator Institute of America [*Later, NSWMA*] (EA) ... IIA
Incipient Failure Everywhere [*Hypothesis descending forces in a sand-pile*] ... IFE

Incipient Fire Detection ... IFD
Incipient Heavies [*Slang for rising young bureaucrats in the foreign policy field*] ... IH
Incipient Lethal Concentration ... ILC
Incipient Nonequilibrium Index ... INI
In-Circuit Emulator [*A trademark*] ... ICE
In-Circuit Program Generator [*Computer science*] (PDAA) ... IPG
Incisal [*Dentistry*] (DAVI) ... I
Incisal Mandibular Plane Angle [*Dentistry*] ... IMPA
Incisal Opening [*Medicine*] (MAE) ... IO
Incised (VRA) ... inc
Incised Wound [*On Autopsy*] [*Pathology*] (DAVI) ... REW
Incision ... inc
Incision and Curettage [*Medicine*] (CPH) ... I & C
Incision and Drainage [*Medicine*] ... I & D
Incisional Surgical Wound Infection [*Medicine*] (DMAA) ... ISWI
Incisolabial [*Dentistry*] ... ILa
Incisolingual [*Dentistry*] ... IL
Incisoproximal [*Dentistry*] ... IP
Incisopulpal [*Dentistry*] ... IP
Incisor (Deciduous) [*Dentistry*] ... i
Incisor (Permanent) [*Dentistry*] ... I
Incisors, Canines, Premolars, Molars [*Dentistry*] ... ICPMM
Incisus [*Being Cut*] [*Pharmacy*] (ROG) ... INC
Incisus [*Being Cut*] [*Pharmacy*] (ROG) ... INCIS
Inclinable Indexing Table ... IIT
Inclination ... I
Inclination [*Angular distance from equator in degrees*] ... INCL
Inclination of a Plane to the Plane of the Earth's Equator [*Aerospace*] ... IPEE
Inclination of the Ascending Return [*Aviation*] (NASA) ... IR
Inclination Removal Ionospheric Beacon Satellite (PDAA) ... IRIBS
Incline Village, NV [*FM radio station call letters*] ... KZAK
Inclined (MSA) ... INCLN
Inclined Bottom Tank [*Fermenter*] ... IBT
Inclined Cleated Belt Conveyor ... ICBC
Inclined Drive Shaft (DA) ... IDS
Inclined Heterolithic Stratification [*Geology*] ... IHS
Inclined Ladder (AAG) ... IL
Inclosure ... INC
Inclosure (AFM) ... INCL
Inclosure (MSA) ... INCLS
Include [*or Including*] (EY) ... INCL
Include Accounting Data ... CLUDACTDAT
Include This Headquarters Information Addressee [*Army*] (AABC) ... IHIA
Includes Extra [*Investment term*] (DFIT) ... A
Including ... INC
Including (WDMC) ... incl
Including [*Freight*] ... INCLD
Including Air ... INCAIR
Including Loading ... IL
Including Particular Average [*Insurance*] ... IPA
Including Sheeting ... IS
Inclusion ... INCLN
Inclusion Body [*Cytology*] ... IB
Inclusion Body [*Cytology*] ... IncB
Inclusion Body Myositis ... IBM
Inclusion Conjunctivitis Neonate [*Ophthalmology*] ... ICN
Inclusion Disease [*Medicine*] ... ID
Inclusive ... INC
Inclusive ... INCL
Inclusive (WDMC) ... incl
Inclusive (ROG) ... INCLU
Inclusive (FAAC) ... INCLV
Inclusive (MSA) ... INCV
Inclusive Depth [*Typography*] (DGA) ... ID
Inclusive Tour (MCD) ... IT
Inclusive Tour Charter ... ITC
Inclusive Tour Excursion [*Airline fare*] ... ITX
Inclusive Tour Service (ADA) ... ITS
Inco Homes [*NASDAQ symbol*] (TTSB) ... INHM
Inco Homes Corp. [*Associated Press*] (SAG) ... IncoHm
Inco Homes Corp. [*NASDAQ symbol*] (SAG) ... INHM
INCO Ltd. [*Formerly, International Nickel Co. of Canada*] [*Associated Press*] (SAG) ... INCO
INCO Ltd. [*Formerly, International Nickel Co. of Canada Ltd.*] [*NYSE symbol Toronto Stock Exchange symbol*] (SPSG) ... N
Inco Ltd. [*NYSE symbol*] (SAG) ... NVB
Inco Ltd., Mississauga, Ontario [*Library symbol National Library of Canada*] (NLC) ... OMIN
Inco Ltd., Process Technology Department, Copper Cliff, ON, Canada [*Library symbol*] [*Library of Congress*] (LCLS) ... CaOCCIN
Incognito [*Unknown*] [*Latin*] ... incog
Incoherent (MSA) ... INCOH
Incoherent Electronic Oscillator ... IEO
Incoherent Inelastic Neutron Scattering [*Physics*] ... IINS
Incoherent Scatter ... IS
Incoherent Scatter RADAR [*Instrumentation*] ... ISR
INCOLSA [*Indiana Cooperative Library Services Authority*] **Processing Center, Indianapolis, IN** [*OCLC symbol*] (OCLC) ... ICP
Income ... I
Income ... In
Income (ROG) ... INC
Income (WDMC) ... inc
Income ... INCM
Income and Expense Statement (MHDW) ... IES
Income and Price Index (DICI) ... IPI
Income Approach to Value (MHDB) ... IATV
Income Averaging (MHDB) ... IA
Income Before Taxes (AAGC) ... IBT
Income Capital Certificate ... ICC
Income Contingent Loan ... ICL
Income Data Service [*Research firm*] [*British*] ... IDS
Income Debenture [*Type of bond*] [*Investment term*] ... ID
Income Distribution Survey ... IDS
Income Eligibility Determination [*Food and Nutrition Service*] [*Department of Agriculture*] (GFGA) ... IED
Income Eligibility Verification Systems (BARN) ... IEVS
Income Equalization Deposit (ADA) ... IED
Income Equalization Deposits Scheme ... IEDS
Income in Respect of a Decedent [*Banking*] ... IRD
Income Maintenance (OICC) ... IM
Income Maintenance Unit [*Work Incentive Program*] [*Department of Labor*] ... IMU
Income Matching System ... IMS
Income Monitoring Kit ... IMK
Income Not Paying Interest [*Standard & Poor's bond rating*] ... C
Income Opportunities Fd 1999 [*NYSE symbol*] (TTSB) ... IOF
Income Opportunities Fd 2000 [*NYSE symbol*] (TTSB) ... IFT
Income Opportunities Fund [*NYSE symbol*] (SPSG) ... IOF
Income Opportunities Fund 2000 [*NYSE symbol*] (SPSG) ... IFT
Income Opportunities Fund 2000 [*Associated Press*] (SAG) ... IncOp2000
Income Opportunities Fund II, Inc. [*Associated Press*] (SAG) ... IncOp2
Income Opportunity Realty [*AMEX symbol*] (SPSG) ... IOT
Income Opportunity Realty Trust [*Associated Press*] (SAG) ... IncOpRT
Income Opportunity Rlty [*AMEX symbol*] (TTSB) ... IOT
Income Over Feed Cost [*Livestock*] (OA) ... IOFC
Income Statement [*Business term*] ... IS
Income Survey Development Program [*Department of Health and Human Services*] (GFGA) ... ISDP
Income Tax ... IT
Income Tax Act Regulations [*Commerce Clearing House Canadian Ltd.*] [*Information service or system*] (CRD) ... ITA
Income Tax Information Release (DLA) ... IT Info
Income Tax Law Journal [*India*] [*A publication*] (DLA) ... Inc Tax LJ
Income Tax Law Journal [*India*] [*A publication*] (DLA) ... ITLJ
Income Tax Office (DAS) ... ITO
Income Tax Order ... ITO
Income Tax Payers' Society [*British*] (BI) ... ITPS
Income Tax Professional (ADA) ... ITP
Income Tax Reports [*India*] [*A publication*] (DLA) ... Inc Tax R
Income Tax Reports [*India*] [*A publication*] (DLA) ... ITR
Income Tax Rulings [*A publication*] ... IT Rulings
Income Tax Unit ... ITU
Income Tax Unit Rulings [*US Internal Revenue Service*] ... IT
Incoming [*Telecommunications*] (TEL) ... I/C
Incoming [*Telecommunications*] (KSC) ... INC
Incoming (MSA) ... INCM
Incoming ... INCMG
Incoming Call Barred [*Telecommunications*] (TEL) ... ICB
Incoming Call Identification [*Telecommunications*] ... ICI
Incoming Caller Identification [*Telecommunications*] ... ICLID
Incoming Capital Property Record ... ICPR
Incoming Correspondence Log (AAG) ... ICL
Incoming Data (MCD) ... INDAT
Incoming Echo Suppressor [*Telecommunications*] (TEL) ... IES
Incoming Junction [*Telecommunications*] (TEL) ... ICJ
Incoming Letter ... IL
Incoming Line ... ICL
Incoming Line (IAA) ... INCL
Incoming Matching Loss [*Telecommunications*] (TEL) ... IML
Incoming Message [*Telecommunications*] ... ICM
Incoming Orders ... IO
Incoming [*Message*] **Process** [*Telecommunications*] (TEL) ... ICP
Incoming Procurement Authorization Document [*Air Force*] (AFM) ... IPAD
Incoming Replacement [*Army*] (AABC) ... INREPL
Incoming Teletype ... ITT
Incoming Transaction Listing (AFM) ... ITL
Incoming Trunk [*Telecommunications*] (BUR) ... ICT
Incoming Trunk [*Telecommunications*] (TEL) ... INC
Incoming Trunk Message Junction [*Telecommunications*] (OA) ... ITMJ
Incoming Trunk Terminal [*Telecommunications*] (IAA) ... ITT
In-Commission (MCD) ... IC
In-Commission Rate ... ICR
INCOMNET, Inc. [*Formerly, Intelligent Commercial Net*] [*NASDAQ symbol*] (NQ) ... ICNT
INCOMNET, Inc. [*Associated Press*] (SAG) ... Incomnt
Incompatible ... I
Incompatible [*Medicine*] ... INCOMPAT
Incompatible Blood Transfusion (PDAA) ... IBT
Incompatible Hemolytic Blood Transfusion ... IHBT
Incompatible Hemolytic Blood Transfusion Disease (MAE) ... IHBTD
Incompatible Simultaneous Transfer (IAA) ... IST
Incompatible Time-sharing System (NHD) ... ITS
Incomplete ... I
Incomplete (DAVI) ... IC
Incomplete ... INC
Incomplete (WDMC) ... inc
Incomplete (AABC) ... INCOM
Incomplete (MSA) ... INCOMP
Incomplete ... INCOMPL
Incomplete (WDMC) ... incompl

Incomplete Abortion [*Obstetrics*] (DAVI) .... Inc Ab
Incomplete Block Design (MCD) .... IBD
Incomplete Correlation Matrix Memory (PDAA) .... ICMM
Incomplete Data Base [*Statistics*] (DAVI) .... IDB
Incomplete Freund's Adjuvant .... IFA
Incomplete Heart Block [*Cardiology*] (DAVI) .... IHB
Incomplete Lower Motor Neuron [*Lesion*] [*Neurology*] (DAVI) .... ILMN
Incomplete Male Pseudohermaphroditism [*Medicine*] (AAMN) .... IMP
Incomplete Resolution, Scan to Follow [*Radiology*] (DAVI) .... INCS
Incomplete Right Bundle Branch Block [*Cardiology*] .... IRBBB
Incomplete Sequence (MSA) .... IS
Incomplete Task Log (AAG) .... ITL
Incomplete Testicular Feminization Syndrome [*Medicine*] (AAMN) .... ITFS
Incomplete Translation [*Telecommunications*] (TEL) .... IT
Incompletely Specified Sequential Machine (PDAA) .... ISSM
Incompletely-Specified Finite State Machine (MHDB) .... ISFSM
Incompressible Turbulent Boundary Layer .... ITBL
Inconclusive .... INC
Inconclusive .... INCL
In-Containment Chilled Water [*Nuclear energy*] (NRCH) .... ICCW
Incontinent [*Medicine*] I
Incontinent [*Medicine*] .... INC
Incontinent [*Medicine*] (DAVI) .... incont
InControl, Inc. [*Associated Press*] (SAG) .... InControl
InControl, Inc. [*Associated Press*] (SAG) .... InControl
In-Core Analysis [*Nuclear energy*] (NRCH) .... INCA
In-Core Fuel Management (PDAA) .... ICFM
In-Core Instrument Test Facility [*Nuclear energy*] (IAA) .... IITF
In-Core Monitoring System [*Nuclear energy*] (NRCH) .... IMS
In-Core Nuclear Detection System [*Nuclear energy*] (IEEE) .... INDS
In-Core Shim Assembly [*Nuclear energy*] (NRCH) .... ICSA
In-Core Temperature Monitoring System [*Nuclear energy*] (NRCH) .... ITMS
In-Core Test Facility [*Nuclear energy*] (NRCH) .... INCOT
In-Core Thermionic Reactor [*Nuclear energy*] .... ITR
Incorporate Engineer (ACII) .... IEng
Incorporated (WDMC) .... inc
Incorporated .... INC
Incorporated (EY) .... INC
Incorporated [*Legal term*] (EY) .... INCD
Incorporated [*Legal term*] .... INCOR
Incorporated [*Legal term*] (EY) .... INCORP
Incorporated Accountant .... IA
Incorporated Accountant [*British*] (ROG) .... INCPD ACCT
Incorporated Accountants and Auditors [*British*] (DAS) .... IAA
Incorporated Advertising Managers' Association [*British*] (BI) .... IAMA
Incorporated Association of Architects and Surveyors [*British*] (DBA) .... IAAS
Incorporated Association of Assistant Masters [*British*] .... IAAM
Incorporated Association of Head Masters [*British*] .... IAHM
Incorporated Association of Organists [*British*] .... IAO
Incorporated Association of Preparatory Schools [*British*] (DCTA) .... IAPS
Incorporated Brewers' Guild [*British*] (EAIO) .... IBG
Incorporated British Institute of Certified Carpenters (BI) .... IBICC
Incorporated Bronte Society [*Keighley, West Yorkshire, England*] (EAIO) .... IBS
Incorporated Church Building Society [*British*] .... ICBS
Incorporated Council of Law Reporting for England and Wales [*Established in 1866*] .... ICLREW
Incorporated Council of Law Reporting for the State of Queensland [*Australia*] .... ICLRSQ
Incorporated Institute of British Decorators (DAS) .... IIBD
Incorporated Institute of British Decorators and Interior Designers (BI) .... IBD
Incorporated Institute of British Decorators and Interior Designers (BI) .... IIBDID
Incorporated Land Society of Northern Ireland .... ILSNI
Incorporated Law Society [*British*] .... ILS
Incorporated Phonographic Society [*British*] (BI) .... IPS
Incorporated Practitioners in Radio and Electronics Ltd. [*British*] (BI) .... IPRE
Incorporated Research Institutions for Seismology .... IRIS
Incorporated Society of Auctioneers and Landed Property Agents [*British*] (ILCA) .... ISALPA
Incorporated Society of Authors, Playwrights, and Composers (BARN) .... ISAPC
Incorporated Society of British Advertisers [*British*] .... ISBA
Incorporated Society of Chiropodists [*British*] (DI) .... ISCh
Incorporated Society of Irish/American Lawyers (EA) .... ISIAL
Incorporated Society of Licensed Trade Stocktakers [*British*] (DBA) .... ISLTS
Incorporated Society of London Fashion Designers .... ISLFD
Incorporated Society of Musicians [*British*] .... ISM
Incorporated Society of Organ Builders [*British*] (BI) .... ISOB
Incorporated Society of Registered Naturopaths [*British*] .... ISRN
Incorporated Society of Valuers and Auctioneers (EAIO) .... ISVA
Incorporated Staff Sight-Singing College [*London*] .... ISC
Incorporation [*Legal term*] (ROG) .... INCORPN
Incorporation .... INCTN
Incorporation of Readiness into Effectivenss Modeling (MCD) .... IREM
Incorporeal Personal Agency [*Parapsychology*] .... IPA
Incorrect (MSA) .... INCOR
Incorrect (ADA) .... INCORR
Incorrect Negative Expectancy [*Psychometrics*] .... INE
Incoterm Data Entry Software [*Incoterm*] (NITA) .... IDES
INCOTERM [*International Commerce Term*] **Transaction Entry Management System** .... ITEMS
Increase (IAA) IC
Increase (AABC) .... INC
Increase (WDMC) .... inc
Increase (WDMC) .... incr
Increase (AFM) .... INCR
Increase and Replacement of Armor, Armament, and Ammunition [*Naval budget appropriation title*] .... IRAA & A
Increase and Replacement of Construction and Machinery [*Naval budget appropriation title*] .... IRC & M
Increase and Replacement of Emergency Construction [*Ships*] [*Naval budget appropriation title*] .... IREC
Increase and Replacement of Naval Vessels [*Naval budget appropriation title*] .... IRNV
Increase Feedback .... IncFB
Increase in Life-Span .... ILS
Increase (Relative) (AAMN) .... inc(r)
Increase Reliability of Operational Systems (AFM) .... IROS
Increased Capacity Drum Feed System (MCD) .... ICDFS
Increased Chromosomal Breakage Rate [*Medicine*] (DMAA) .... ICBR
Increased Combat Effectiveness (AFM) .... ICE
Increased Deployability [*Posture*] (DOMA) .... ID
Increased Forward Stocking [*Military*] (DNAB) .... IFS
Increased Growth Response [*Botany*] .... IGR
Increased Hazard Rate .... IHR
Increased Intracranial Pressure (CPH) .... IICP
Increased Maneuverability Kit .... IMK
Increased Readiness Information System .... IRIS
Increased Take-Home Pay .... ITHP
Increased Value IV
Increasing Failure Rate .... IFR
Increasing Failure Rate Average [*Statistics*] .... IFRA
Increasing Hazard Rate Average .... IHRA
Increasing Intracranial Pressure [*Medicine*] .... IIP
Incredibly Small Transistor (IAA) .... IST
Increment .... INC
Increment (AFM) .... INCR
Increment .... INCRE
Increment and Skip on Zero [*Computer science*] .... ISZ
Increment Memory Unit .... IMU
Increment Number (DOMA) .... INCNR
Increment of Response [*Psychology*] .... DR
Incremental .... INCREM
Incremental Analysis [*Statistics*] .... IA
Incremental Capital Output Ratio .... ICOR
Incremental Cost (KSC) IC
Incremental Cost Effectiveness Model .... ICEM
Incremental Critical Design Review (NASA) .... ICDR
Incremental Differential Pressure System (AAG) .... IDPS
Incremental Digital Recorder .... IDR
Incremental Dividend Preferred [*Share*] [*Investment term*] .... IDP
Incremental Financial Rate of Return .... IFR
Incremental Frequency Control .... IFC
Incremental Growth Vehicle (MCD) .... IGV
Incremental Life Support Operations .... ILSO
Incremental Microwave Power Spectrum Analyzer [*Air Force*] .... IPSA
Incremental Multiple Development (PDAA) .... IMD
Incremental Preliminary Design Review (MCD) .... IPDR
Incremental Proof Testing .... IPT
Incremental Provisioning Parts Breakdown (SAA) .... IPPB
Incremental Purchasing System (SAA) .... IPS
Incremental Range Summary .... IRS
Incremental Stock Number Sequence List [*Military*] (CAAL) .... ISNSL
Incremental Stretch Forming .... ISF
Incremental System Programming Language [*Computer science*] .... ISPL
Incremental System Test .... IST
Incremental Tactical Communications Capability Study [*Military*] (MCD) .... ITACC
Incremental Tape Recorder .... ITR
Incremental Velocity Indicator [*NASA*] IVI
Increment-Decrement Life Table [*Statistics*] .... IDLT
Incremented Dynamic Scanning (DAVI) .... IDS
Incstar Corp. [*Associated Press*] (SAG) .... Incstar
Incstar Corp. [*AMEX symbol*] (SPSG) .... ISR
Incstar Corp. [*NASDAQ symbol*] (TTSB) .... ISTR
Incubation Period [*Medicine*] .... IP
Incubator (MSA) .... INCBR
Incue [*News broadcasting*] (NTCM) IC
Incumbent (ROG) I
Incumbent (ROG) .... INC
Incumbent (ROG) .... INCT
Incumbent .... INCUMB
Incumbent Come Home [*Political humor*] [*Pronounced "itch"*] .... ICH
Incumbered (ROG) .... INCUMBD
Incumbrance (ROG) .... INCUMBCE
Incunable Short Title Catalogue [*British Library*] [*Information service or system*] (IID) .... ISTC
Incunabula (ADA) .... INCUN
Incurable [*Medicine*] .... INCUR
Incurably Ill for Animal Research (EA) .... IIAR
Incurably Ill for Animal Research (EA) .... IIFAR
Incurred .... inc
Incurred Accidentally [*Medicine*] (MEDA) .... IA
Incurred but Not Reported [*Insurance*] .... IBNR
Incurred but Unreported Claims [*Health insurance*] (GHCT) .... IUC
Incurred in Military Service [*Medicine*] (MAE) .... IMS
Incurred Loss Ratio [*Insurance*] .... ILR
Incurved Cactus [*Horticulture*] IC
Incus Replacement Prosthesis [*Medicine*] (DMAA) .... IRP
INCYTE Pharmaceuticals [*NASDAQ symbol*] (TTSB) .... INCY
Incyte Pharmaceuticals, Inc. [*Associated Press*] (SAG) .... Incyte
INCYTE Pharmaceuticals, Inc. [*AMEX symbol*] (SPSG) .... IPI

Ind Coope Burton Brewery [British] .... ICBB
INDA, Association of the Nonwoven Fabrics Industry [Formerly, International Nonwovens and Disposables Association .... INDA
Indagen [Papua New Guinea] [Airport symbol] (OAG) .... IDN
Indal Ltd. [Toronto Stock Exchange symbol] ICL
Indebtedness [Legal term] (DLA) .... Indebt
Indecent [FBI standardized term] .... IND
Indecent Displays (Control) Act [British] .... ID(C)A
Indeclinable (BJA) .... indec
Indeclinable [Grammar] .... INDECL
Indefeasible Right of User [Telecommunications] (TEL) .... IRU
Indefinite (AABC) .... INDEF
Indefinite Admittance Matrix [Network analysis] (IEEE) .... IAM
Indefinite Ceiling [Meteorology] (BARN) .... W
Indefinite Delivery [Shipping] .... ID
Indefinite Delivery/Indefinite Quantity [Military] (RDA) .... IDIQ
Indefinite Delivery, Indefinite Quantity [Type of contract] (AAGC) .... IDIQ
Indefinite Delivery Type Contract [DoD] .... IDTC
Indefinite Operations (NVT) .... INDEFOPS
Indefinite Quantity (AFM) .... IQ
[An] Indefinite Quantity [Mathematics] (ROG) .... n
Indefinite Substitute Temporary Mail Handler [US Postal Service employee classification] .... ISTMH
Indefinite-Quantity Contract (AAGC) .... IQC
Indemnify [Legal shorthand] (LWAP) .... INDEMFY
Indemnity [Legal term] (DLA) .... Indem
Indemnity [Legal shorthand] (LWAP) .... INDEMTY
Indemnity (ROG) .... INDEMY
Indemnity [Legal term] .... INDM
Indemnity .... INDMNTY
Indemnity [Legal term] (DLA) .... Indty
IndeNet, Inc. [NASDAQ symbol] (SAG) .... INDE
IndeNet Inc. [NASDAQ symbol] (TTSB) .... INDE
IndeNet, Inc. [Associated Press] (SAG) .... IndeNet
Indent (MSA) .... INDT
Indent Both (WDMC) .... ib
Indent Hanging [Graphic arts] (DGA) .... IH
Indent Left [Typography] (DGA) IL
Indent Left (WDMC) il
Indent Load Deflection [Measure of hardness] .... ILD
Indent Right [Typography] (DGA) .... IR
Indent Right (WDMC) .... ir
Indent Tab Character [Computer science] .... IT
Indentation Force Deflection [Automotive seat testing] .... IFD
Indentation Residual Gauge Level [Automotive engineering] .... IRGL
Indenture (ROG) .... INDENT
Indenture .... INDRE
Indenture Part List (KSC) .... IDP
Indentured Drawing List .... IDL
Indentured Parts List .... IPL
Indentured Parts Price List (MCD) .... IPPL
Indeo Video Interactive [Computer science] IVI
Independants et Paysans d'Action Sociale [Independents and Peasants of Social Action] [French] (PPE) .... IPAS
Independence [Kansas] [Airport symbol] (AD) .... IDP
Independence [Belize] [Airport symbol] (OAG) .... INB
Independence .... INDPDNC
Independence Banc 9% Cv Pfd [NASDAQ symbol] (TTSB) .... IBNJP
Independence Bancorp, Inc. [NASDAQ symbol] (SAG) .... IBNJ
Independence Bancorp, Inc. [Associated Press] (SAG) .... IndBc
Independence Bancorp, Inc. [Associated Press] (SAG) .... IndepBc
Independence Bancorp NJ [NASDAQ symbol] (TTSB) .... IBNJ
Independence Bulletin-Journal, Independence, IA [Library symbol] [Library of Congress] (LCLS) .... IaIndpB
Independence, CA [FM radio station call letters] .... KDAY
Independence Community Junior College, Independence, KS [Library symbol Library of Congress] (LCLS) .... KIJ
Independence Conservative, Independence, IA [Library symbol Library of Congress] (LCLS) .... IaIndpC
Independence Dogs [An association] (EA) .... ID
Independence Fed Svgs Bk [NASDAQ symbol] (TTSB) .... IFSB
Independence Federal Savings Bank [NASDAQ symbol] (NQ) .... IFSB
Independence Federal Savings Bank [Associated Press] (SAG) .... IndFdl
Independence Hldg [NASDAQ symbol] (TTSB) .... INHO
Independence Holding Co. [Associated Press] (SAG) .... IndepHld
Independence Holding Co. [NASDAQ symbol] (NQ) .... INHO
Independence, IA [Location identifier FAA] (FAAL) .... IIB
Independence, IA [AM radio station call letters] .... KQMG
Independence, IA [FM radio station call letters] .... KQMG-FM
Independence, KS [Location identifier FAA] (FAAL) .... IDP
Independence, KS [AM radio station call letters] .... KIND
Independence, KS [FM radio station call letters] .... KIND-FM
Independence Medical Center, Independence, MO [Library symbol Library of Congress] (LCLS) .... MoIMC
Independence, MO [AM radio station call letters] .... KCTE
Independence National Historical Park .... INDE
Independence National Historical Park, Philadelphia, PA [Library symbol Library of Congress] (LCLS) .... PPIn
Independence Petroleums [Vancouver Stock Exchange symbol] .... IDP
Independence Plan for Neighborhood Councils (EA) .... IPNC
Independence Public Library, Independence, OR [Library symbol Library of Congress] (LCLS) .... OrI
Independence Public School District, Independence, MO [Library symbol [Library of Congress] (LCLS) .... MoIPS

Independence Sanitarium and Hospital, Independence, MO [Library symbol Library of Congress] (LCLS) .... MoIS
Independence Square Income Securities [Associated Press] (SAG) .... IndSqS
Independence Square Income Securities [NASDAQ symbol] (SAG) .... ISIS
Independence Square Income Securities, Inc. [Associated Press] (SAG) .... IndSqS
Independence Square Income Securities, Inc. [NASDAQ symbol] (NQ) .... ISIS
Independent I
Independent .... IND
Independent (WDMC) .... ind
Independent (AFM) .... INDEP
Independent [Filmmaking] [Slang] (WDMC) .... indie
Independent .... INDPNDNT
Independent Accountants Association of Michigan (SRA) .... IAAM
Independent Accountants International (EAIO) .... IAI
Independent Action (EA) .... IA
Independent Activities Questionnaire [Psychology] .... IAQ
Independent Administrators Association of California (SRA) .... IAA
Independent Aeronautical Dealers Association [Defunct] (EA) .... IADA
Independent Agricultural Merchants' Association [Australia] .... IAMA
Independent Air Carriers Association [Defunct] (EA) .... IACA
Independent Air Force [British military] (DMA) .... IAF
Independent Air Revitalization System (NASA) .... IARS
Independent Airlines Association (EA) .... IAA
Independent Aluminum Residential Fabricators Association (EA) .... IARFA
Independent American Whiskey Association [Later, ABAA] (EA) .... IAWA
Independent Americans (EA) .... IA
Independent Appeals Authority for School Examinations (AIE) .... IAASE
Independent Armored Car Operators Association (EA) .... IACOA
Independent Assessment and Research Centre [British] (CB) .... IARC
Independent Association of Builders' Labourers [A union] [British] .... IABL
Independent Association of Preparatory Schools .... IAPS
Independent Association of Publishers' Employees (EA) .... IAPE
Independent Association of Questioned Document Examiners (EA) .... IAQDE
Independent Association of Stocking Manufacturers [Defunct] .... IASM
Independent Association of Victorian Registered Teachers [Australia] .... IAVRT
Independent Associaton of Accredited Registrars [For quality control] .... IAAR
Independent Auto Dealers Association - Utah (SRA) .... IADA-UT
Independent Automotive Damage Appraisers Association [Milwaukee, WI] (EA) .... IADA
Independent Automotive Service Association (EA) .... IASA
Independent Aviation Operators .... IAO
Independent Bakers Association (EA) .... IBA
Independent Bakers' Cooperative [W. E. Long Co.] (EA) .... IBC
Independent Bakery Employees Union .... BEU
Independent Bakery Employees Union (EA) .... IBEU
Independent Bank [NASDAQ symbol] (TTSB) .... IBCP
Independent Bank Corp. [NASDAQ symbol] (NQ) .... IBCP
Independent Bank Corp. [NASDAQ symbol] (NQ) .... INDB
Independent Bank Corp. Massachusetts [Associated Press] (SAG) .... IndBkMA
Independent Bank Corp. Michigan [Associated Press] (SAG) .... IndBkMI
Independent Bankers Association of America (EA) .... IBAA
Independent Bankers Association of Texas (SRA) .... IBAT
Independent Bank(MA) [NASDAQ symbol] (TTSB) .... INDB
Independent Banks of South Carolina (SRA) .... IBSC
Independent Bankshares [AMEX symbol] (TTSB) .... IBK
Independent Bankshares, Inc. [AMEX symbol] (SAG) .... IBK
Independent Bankshares, Inc. [Associated Press] (SAG) .... IndBnk
Independent Bar Association .... IBA
Independent Battery Manufacturers Association (EA) .... IBMA
Independent Black Institution .... IBI
Independent Board Authority [Board granting franchises to new companies] [British] .... IBA
Independent Board for Presbyterian Foreign Missions (EA) .... IBPFM
Independent Bread Manufacturers of New South Wales [Australia] .... IBMNSW
Independent Broadcast Institute [British] .... IBI
Independent Broadcasting Authority [Formerly, ITA] [British] .... IBA
Independent Business Unit .... IBU
Independent Cabinet Makers' Association [A union] [British] .... ICMA
Independent Cable Makers' Association [British] (BI) .... ICMA
Independent Canadian Steelworkers' Union .... ICSU
Independent Canadian Transit Union .... ICTU
Independent Carbon-Dioxide Manufacturers Association (EA) .... ICDMA
Independent Carpenters' and Joiners' Society [A union] [British] .... ICJS
Independent Carrier Military Traffic Office [MTMC] (TAG) .... ICMTO
Independent Cash Register Dealers Association (EA) .... ICRDA
Independent Cattlemen's Association of Texas (SRA) .... ICA
Independent Channel Handler (IAA) .... INCH
Independent Chemical Information Services Ltd. [Information service or system] (IID) .... ICIS
Independent Cinema Artists and Producers (EA) .... ICAP
Independent Citizens' Movement [US Virgin Islands] (PPW) .... ICM
Independent Citizens Research Foundation for the Study of Degenerative Diseases (EA) .... ICRFSDD
Independent Cluster Emission Model [Atomic physics] .... ICEM
Independent Cold Extruders Institute .... ICEI
Independent College Assistance Center (EA) .... ICAC
Independent College Funds of America [Later, FIHE] (EA) .... ICFA
Independent Colleges and Universities of Texas (SRA) .... ICUT
Independent Colleges of Arkansas (SRA) .... ICA
Independent Colleges of Further Education [British] .... ICFE
Independent Colleges of Indiana Foundation (SRA) .... ICIF
Independent Collision Avoidance System .... ICAS
Independent Color Matching [Computer science] .... ICM
Independent Commercial Importer [Automotive retailing] ICI

Independent Commission on International Development Issues [Also known as the Brandt Commission] [Studies problems arising from the inequity between more developed Northern nations and less developed Southern countries] .... ICIDI
Independent Community Consultants (EA) ICC
Independent Component Release [Computer science] (IBMDP) .... ICR
Independent Computer Consultants Association (EA) .... ICCA
Independent Computer Peripheral Equipment Manufacturers .... ICPEM
Independent Conducting Officer .... ICO
Independent Contractor IC
Independent Contractor (DLA) .... INDEP CONTR
Independent Corps Tactical Operations Center .... ICTOC
Independent Cosmetic Manufacturers and Distributors (EA) .... ICMAD
Independent Cost Analysis (AAGC) .... ICA
Independent Cost Assessment (MCD) .... ICA
Independent Cost Estimate .... ICE
Independent Curators, Inc. (EA) ICI
Independent Data Communications Manufacturers Association (EA) .... IDCMA
Independent Database Application Program Interface (PCM) .... IDAPI
Independent Dealer [Automobile sales] .... ID
Independent Dealer Committee Dedicated to Action (EA) .... IDCDA
Independent Democratic Party [Gibraltar] [Political party] .... IDP
Independent Democratic Party [Liberia] [Political party] (EY) .... IDP
Independent Democratic Union of Cape Verde [Political party] (PD) .... UCID
Independent Deployable Unit Detachment (MCD) .... IDUD
Independent Design Review (NRCH) .... IDR
Independent Design Verification Program (NRCH) .... IDVP
Independent Development Environment [Computer science] (PCM) .... IDE
Independent Distributor .... ID
Independent Division Tactical Operations Center [Army] (AABC) .... IDTOC
Independent Double Sideband .... IDSB
Independent Education Union [Australia] .... IEU
Independent Educational Consultants Association (EA) .... IECA
Independent Educational Services (EA) .... IES
Independent Election Corp. of America (WDMC) .... IECA
Independent Electrical Contractors (EA) .... IEC
Independent Electrical Manufacturers Association (EA) .... IEMA
Independent Electron Pair Approximation [Physics] .... IEPA
Independent Electronic Music Center [Defunct] .... IEMC
Independent Energy Consultants Group [British] .... IECG
Independent Estimate [Army] .... IE
Independent European Program Group [NATO] .... IEPG
Independent Evaluation (MCD) .... IE
Independent Evaluation Group (SDI) .... IEG
Independent Evaluation Plan .... IEP
Independent Evaluation Report .... IER
Independent Evaluation Teams [Army Systems Acquisitions Review Council] (MCD) .... IET
Independent Exchange Plan .... IEP
Independent Expenditure [Campaign-finance law provision] .... IE
Independent Exploratory Development [Navy] (NG) .... IED
Independent Fabric Retailers Association [Defunct] (EA) .... IFRA
Independent Family Schools Resource Center (EA) .... IFSRC
Independent Feature Project (EA) .... IFP
Independent Federation of Chinese Students and Scholars (EA) .... IFCSS
Independent Federation of Flight Attendants (EA) .... IFFA
Independent Fee Appraiser/Counselor [National Association of Independent Fee Appraisers, Inc.] [Designation awarded by] .... IFAC
Independent Fee Appraiser, Member [National Association of Independent Fee Appraisers, Inc.] [Designation awarded by] .... IFA
Independent Fee Appraiser, Senior [National Association of Independent Fee Appraisers, Inc.] [Designation awarded by] .... IFAS
Independent Film and Video Makers' Association [British] .... IFVA
Independent Film Channel .... IFC
Independent Film Distributors' Association [British] .... IFDA
Independent Film Importers and Distributors of America [Defunct] (EA) .... IFIDA
Independent Film Producers Export Corp. [Defunct] .... IFPEC
Independent Film Producers of America (NTCM) .... IFPA
Independent Film, Video, and Photographers Association [British] (DBA) .... IFVPA
Independent Financial Adviser [British] (ECON) .... IFA
Independent Financial Analysis (ADA) .... IFA
Independent Fire Control [Area] (NATG) .... IFC
Independent Fission Yield .... IFY
Independent Fluorspar Producers Association (EA) .... IFPA
Independent Footwear Retailers Association [British] (DBA) .... IFRA
Independent Force [British military] (DMA) .... IF
Independent Forward Bloc [Mauritian political party] .... IFB
Independent Foundation .... IF
Independent Free Papers of America (EA) .... IFPA
Independent Front Suspension [Automotive engineering] .... IFS
Independent Fuel Oil Marketers of America [Defunct] (EA) .... IFOMA
Independent Fuel Terminal Operators' Association .... IFTOA
Independent Fundamental Churches of America (EA) .... IFCA
Independent Furniture Manufacturers' Associaiton [British] (DBA) .... IFMA
Independent Garage Owners of America [Later, Automotive Service Councils] (EA) .... IGOA
Independent Gasoline Marketers Council [Defunct] (EA) .... IGMC
Independent Government Cost Estimate [Army] .... IGCE
Independent Government Estimate (MCD) .... IGE
Independent Grocers Alliance Distributing Co. [Facetious translation: "I Get Attention"] .... IGA
Independent Hardware Vendor [Computer science] (CDE) .... IHV
Independent Health Insurance Institute [Inactive] (EA) .... IHII
Independent High Frequency (IAA) .... IHF

Independent Hospital Workers Union (EA) .... IHWU
Independent Hospitals Association [British] (DBA) .... IHA
Independent Hungarian Democratic Party [Political party Hungary] (EAIO) .... IHDP
Independent Identically Distributed [Statistics] (IEEE) .... IID
Independent Infantry Battalion .... IIB
Independent Innkeepers Association (EA) .... IIA
Independent Inspection Agency [RSPA] (TAG) .... IIA
Independent Inspector (AIE) II
[The] Independent Institute [An association] (EA) .... TII
Independent Institute, NAD, Dublin, OH [OCLC symbol] (OCLC) .... OTH
Independent Insurance Agents Association of New York (SRA) .... IIAANY
Independent Insurance Agents of America [New York, NY] (EA) .... IIAA
Independent Insurance Agents of Connecticut (SRA) .... IIAC
Independent Insurance Agents of Delaware (SRA) .... IIAD
Independent Insurance Agents of New Hampshire (SRA) .... IIANH
Independent Insurance Agents of New Jersey (SRA) .... IIANJ
Independent Insurance Agents of New Mexico (SRA) .... IIANM
Independent Insurance Agents of North Carolina (SRA) .... IIANC
Independent Insurance Agents of Oregon (SRA) .... IIAO
Independent Insurance Agents of Pennsylvania (SRA) .... IIAP
Independent Insurance Agents of Rhode Island (SRA) .... IIARI
Independent Insurance Agents of South Carolina (SRA) .... IIASC
Independent Insurance Agents of Utah (SRA) .... IIAU
Independent Insurance Agents of Vermont (SRA) .... IIAV
Independent Insurance Conference IIC
Independent Insurance Group, Inc. [NASDAQ symbol] (NQ) .... INDH
Independent Insurance Group, Inc. [Associated Press] (SAG) .... IndInsr
Independent Investment Co. [British] IIC
Independent Investor Protective League (EA) .... IIPL
Independent Investors Forum [Information service or system] (IID) .... IIF
Independent Jewelers Organization (EA) .... IJO
Independent Label Association (EA) .... ILA
Independent Labor Congress [Nigeria] ILC
Independent Labour Party [British] .... ILP
Independent Landing Monitor [RADAR-TV landing guidance] [NASA] .... ILM
Independent Lateral Band (IAA) .... ILB
Independent Learning Modules (ACII) .... ILM
Independent Liberal (WDAA) .... IND L
Independent Liberal Party [Israel] [Political party] (BJA) .... ILP
Independent Librarians Exchange Round Table [American Library Association] .... ILERT
Independent Liquid Terminals Association (EA) .... ILTA
Independent Literary Agents Association (EA) .... ILAA
Independent Living [An association Defunct] (EA) IL
Independent Living Research Utilization Program (PAZ) .... ILRU
Independent Living Skills [Needed by the handicapped] .... ILS
Independent Local Radio [British] .... ILR
Independent Lubricant Manufacturers Association (EA) .... ILMA
Independent Manned Manipulator [NASA] (KSC) .... IMM
Independent Manufacturers Representatives Forum (EA) .... IMRF
Independent Manufacturing Assessment (MCD) .... IMA
Independent Meat Buyers Ltd. [British] (BI) .... IMBL
Independent Media Producers Association [Later, IMPC] (EA) .... IMPA
Independent Media Producers Council (EA) .... IMPC
Independent Medical Distributors Association (EA) .... IMDA
Independent Medical Examination [British] .... IME
Independent Medical Examiner (HGAA) .... IME
Independent Medical Insurance Consultants Ltd. [British] .... IMIC
Independent Methodist (WDAA) .... I METH
Independent Methodist (WDAA) .... IND METH
Independent Microelectronics Applications [British] (NITA) .... INMAP
Independent Midwives Association [British] (DBA) .... IMA
Independent Military Air Transport Association [Later, Independent Airlines Association] .... IMATA
Independent Mixed Brigade [Military] .... IMB
Independent Model Triangulation (PDAA) .... IMT
Independent Modification Review [Military] (AFIT) .... IMR
Independent Module Development (PDAA) .... IMD
Independent Monthly [A publication] .... Ind M
Independent Mortar Battery [British military] (DMA) .... IMB
Independent Motion Picture Co. .... IMP
Independent Motion Picture Distributors Association of America .... IMPDAA
Independent Motion Picture Producers Association [Defunct] (EA) .... IMPPA
Independent Motorcycle Retailers of America [Defunct] (EA) .... IMRA
Independent Munitions Maintenance Unit .... IMMU
Independent Music Association (EA) .... IMA
Independent National Patriotic Front of Liberia [Political party] (EY) .... INPFL
Independent Network News [Television] .... INN
Independent News Service [In TV series "The Night Stalker"] .... INS
Independent Newsletter Association .... INA
Independent Nuclear Disarmament Election Committee [British] (DI) .... INDEC
Independent Oil and Gas Association of West Virginia (SRA) .... IOGAWV
Independent Oil Compounders Association [Later, ILMA] (EA) .... IOCA
Independent Oil Marketer's Association of New England (SRA) .... IOMA
Independent Operational Test and Evaluation [Military] .... IOT & E
Independent Order Ladies of Vikings (EA) .... IOLV
Independent Order of B'nai B'rith [Later, BBI] .... IOBB
Independent Order of Engineers and Machinists Trade and Friendly Society [A union] [British] .... IOEMTFS
Independent Order of Foresters [Buffalo, NY] (EA) .... IOF
Independent Order of Odd Fellows (EA) .... IOOF
Independent Order of Rechabites .... IOR
Independent Order of St. Luke [Defunct] (EA) .... IOSL
Independent Order of Sons of Malta .... IOSM
Independent Order of Svithiod (EA) .... IOS

Independent Order of the Free Sons of Israel [*Freemasonry*] (ROG) .... IOFSI
Independent Order of Vikings [*Des Plaines, IL*] (EA) .... IOV
Independent Order Sons of Hermann .... IOSH
Independent Parametric Cost Analysis (MCD) .... IPCA
Independent Parametric Cost Estimate (AABC) .... IPCE
Independent People's Party [*Political party Germany*] (EAIO) .... IPP
Independent Pet and Animal Transportation Association (EA) .... IPATA
Independent Petroleum Association of America (EA) .... IPAA
Independent Petroleum Association of Canada .... IPAC
Independent Petroleum Association of Mountain States .... IPAMS
Independent Physician Association (HCT) .... IPA
Independent Police Complaints Authority [*British*] .... IPCA
Independent Political Entity [*Board on Geographic Names*] .... PCLI
Independent Postal System of America [*Alternative to US Postal Service*] .... IPSA
Independent Poster Exchanges of America (EA) .... IPEA
Independent Power Generation Conference and Exhibition [*British*]
(ITD) .... INPOWER
Independent Power Producer .... IPP
Independent Power Projects (AAGC) .... IPP
Independent Press, Bloomfield, NJ [*Library symbol Library of Congress*]
(LCLS) .... NjBll
Independent Press, New Providence, NJ [*Library symbol Library of
Congress*] (LCLS) .... NjNpl
Independent Primary Inspection Agency [*Department of Housing and Urban
Development*] (GFGA) .... IPIA
Independent Product Assurance (SSD) .... IPA
Independent Professional Electronic Technicians .... IPET
Independent Professional Painting Contractors Association of America
(EA) .... IPPCA
Independent Professional Representatives Organization (EA) .... I-PRO
Independent Professional Review [*Medicaid*] (DHSM) .... IPR
Independent Professional Typists Network (EA) .... IPTN
Independent Programme Producers' Association [*British*] .... IPPA
Independent Public Accountant .... IPA
Independent Publishers' Association [*Canada*] .... IPA
Independent Publishers Group .... IPG
Independent Publishers' Guild [*British*] .... IPG
Independent Publishers League [*Defunct*] (EA) .... IPL
Independent Pump [*Liquid gas carriers*] i
Independent Rabbinate of America .... IROA
Independent Racing Pigeon Federation [*Australia*] .... IRPF
Independent Rear Suspension [*Automotive engineering*] .... IRS
Independent Record Charts (EA) .... IRC
Independent Refiners Association of America [*Later, AIRA*] (EA) .... IRAA
Independent Regulatory Agency [*US Government*] .... IRA
Independent Reinol Distributors Association [*British*] (DBA) .... IRDA
Independent Research (NG) .... IR
Independent Research and Development .... IR & D
Independent Research and Development .... IRAD
Independent Research and Development (AAGC) .... IR&D
Independent Research and Development/Bid and Proposal ..../...... IR & D/B & P
Independent Research/Independent Exploratory Development .... IR/IED
Independent Research/Independent Objectives Document [*Military*]
(DNAB) .... IR/IOD
Independent Research Libraries Association (EA) .... IRLA
Independent Research Service [*Defunct*] .... IRS
Independent Reservation System [*Hotels and motels*] .... INRES
Independent Retail Lumber Dealers Association .... IRLDA
Independent Retail Tobacconists Association of America [*Defunct*] (EA).... IRTA
Independent Retailer Organisation (EAIO) .... IRO
Independent Review [*London*] [*A publication*] (ROG) .... INDEP R
Independent Road Service Association (EA) .... IRSA
Independent Routing Processor [*Telecommunications*] (ACRL) .... IRP
Independent Safety Board Act of 1974 .... ISBA
Independent Safety Consultants Association (DBA) .... ISCA
Independent Safety Engineering Group [*Nuclear energy*] (NRCH) .... ISEG
Independent Sales Organization (HGAA) .... ISO
Independent Scheduled Exercises .... ISE
Independent Scholars of Asia (EA) .... ISA
Independent Scholarship National Program [*Defunct*] (EA) .... ISNP
Independent School [*British*] I
Independent School (BARN) .... IS
Independent School District No. 1, Curriculum Resource Center, Lewiston,
ID [*Library symbol*] [*Library of Congress*] (LCLS) .... IdLI-C
Independent School District No. 1, Lewiston, ID [*Library symbol*] [*Library of
Congress*] (LCLS) .... IdLl
Independent Schools Association [*British*] (AEBS) .... ISA
Independent Schools Association [*British*] .... ISAI
Independent Schools Association Inc. (AIE) .... ISAI
Independent Schools Association of the Central States (AEBS) .... ISACS
Independent Schools Bursars' Association [*British*] .... ISBA
Independent Schools Careers Organisation [*British*] .... ISCO
Independent Schools Education Board [*Later, National Association of
IndependentSchools*] (AEBS) .... ISEB
Independent Schools Information Service [*British*] .... ISIS
Independent Schools Joint Action Committee (AIE) .... ISJAC
Independent Schools Joint Council [*British*] .... ISJC
Independent Schools Microelectronics Centre [*British*] .... ISMC
Independent Schools Physical Education Conference (AIE) .... ISPEC
Independent Schools Section [*American Association of School Libraries*]
[*American Library Association*] .... ISS
Independent Schools Talent Search Program [*Later, A Better Chance*]
(EA) .... ISTSP
Independent Schools Working Group (AIE) .... ISWG
Independent Scientific Committee on Smoking and Health [*British*] .... ISCSH

Independent Search Consultants (EA) .... ISC
Independent Secretarial Training Association [*British*] .... ISTA
Independent Sector (EA) .... IS
Independent Sector Coordinating Committee on Environment and
Development (GNE) .... ISCCED
Independent Service Provider [*Telecommunications*] .... ISP
Independent Sewing Machine Dealers Association (EA) .... ISMDA
Independent Ship Exercise [*Navy*] .... ISE
Independent Ship, Riverside, and General Labourers' Union [*British*] ..... ISRGLU
Independent Shoemen of America [*Defunct*] (EA) .... IS
Independent Shoemen of America [*Defunct*] .... ISA
Independent Sideband .... ISB
Independent Signal Unit [*Telecommunications*] (TEL) .... ISU
Independent Signcrafters of America (EA) .... ISA
Independent Small Business Employers of America (EA) .... ISBE
Independent Small Business Employers of America [*Later, ISBE*] (EA) ..... ISBEA
Independent Smallholders' Party [*Hungary Political party*] (EY) .... ISP
Independent Snowmobile Medical Research [*An association*] (EA) .... ISMR
Independent Social Democratic Party of Germany [*Political party*]
(EAIO) .... ISDPG
Independent Society of Bricklayers [*A union*] [*British*] .... ISB
Independent Society of Stick Makers [*A union*] [*British*] .... ISSM
Independent Software Vendor [*Computer science*] .... ISV
Independent Space Research Group (EA) .... ISRG
Independent Spent Fuel Storage Facility [*Department of Energy*] [*Nuclear
energy*] .... ISFSF
Independent Spent Fuel Storage Installation [*Nuclear energy*] (NRCH) .... ISFSI
Independent Spherical Aluminum Tank [*on a ship*] (DS) .... IS
Independent Stores Association Ltd. [*British*] (BI) .... ISA
Independent Studies Project [*Navy*] .... ISP
Independent Study Program [*IBM Corp.*] .... ISP
Independent Subcarrier Method (PDAA) .... ISM
Independent Sweep System .... ISS
Independent Tank (DS) .... IT
Independent Tank Center [*of a ship*] (DS) .... ITC
Independent Tank Common [*of a ship*] (DS) .... ITX
Independent Tank Wing [*of a ship*] (DS) .... ITW
Independent Tanker Owners Association (DS) .... ITOA
Independent Taxation with Transferable Allowance [*British*] (DI) .... ITTA
Independent Telecommunication Network (ACRL) .... ITN
Independent Telecommunications Analysts [*Boulder, CO*] (TSSD) .... ITA
Independent TeleMedia Group [*NASDAQ symbol*] (SAG) .... INDE
Independent Telephone Co. [*Telecommunications*] IC
Independent Telephone Pioneer Association (EA) .... ITPA
Independent Television .... ITV
Independent Television Association [*British*] (DBA) .... ITA
Independent Television Authority [*Later, IBA*] [*British*] .... ITA
Independent Television Commission [*British*] (ECON) .... ITC
Independent Television Companies Association [*British*] .... ITCA
Independent Television for Wales and the West of England .... TWW
Independent Television News [*British*] .... ITN
Independent Television News Association [*News service*] .... ITNA
Independent Television Organization (NTCM) .... ITO
Independent Television Publications [*British*] (ECON) .... ITP
Independent Television Service .... ITVS
Independent Television Service Dealers' Association .... ITVSDA
Independent Terminal Operators Association (EA) .... ITOA
Independent Trade Union Association [*Turkey*] .... ITUA
Independent Travel Agencies of America Association (EA) .... ITAA
Independent Triggering System .... ITS
Independent Truck Owner/Operator Association (EA) .... I-TOO
Independent Truck Owner-Operators Association .... ITOO
Independent Truckers and Drivers Association (EA) .... ITDA
Independent True Whig Party [*Liberia*] [*Political party*] .... ITW
Independent Union of Plant Protection Employees (EA) .... IUPPE
Independent Union of Plant Protection Employees in the Electrical and
Machine Industry .... PPE
Independent United Australia Party [*Political party*] .... InduAP
Independent United Labor Congress [*Nigeria*] .... IULC
Independent United Order of Mechanics - Western Hemisphere
(EA) .... IUOMWH
Independent US Tanker Owners Committee [*Defunct*] (EA) .... IUSTOC
Independent Validation and Verification (CAAL) .... IV & V
Independent Variable (IAA) IV
Independent Variable Depth SONAR .... IVDS
Independent Variable Hull [*Statistics*] .... IVH
Independent Verification and Test .... IV & T
Independent Vertical System .... IVS
Independent Video Programmers Association [*Defunct*] (EA) .... IVPA
Independent Viewing Console IVC
Independent Visually Impaired Enterprisers (EA) .... IVIE
Independent Voters Association [*Political organization in North Dakota, 1918-
1932*] .... IVA
Independent Waste Paper Processors Association [*British*] (DBA) .... IWPPA
Independent Watchmen's Association (EA) .... IWA
Independent Watchmen's Association .... WA
Independent Wire Drawers Association [*Later, AWPA*] .... IWDA
Independent Wire Producers Association [*Later, AWPA*] (EA) .... IWPA
Independent Wire Rope Center [*or Core*] .... IWRC
Independent Wire Rope Manufacturers Association (EA) .... IWRMA
Independent Zinc Alloyers Association (EA) .... IZAA
Independently (ROG) .... INDEPTY
Independently Targeted Vehicle [*Military*] (DA) .... ITV
Independent-Practice Association [*Medical insurance*] .... IPA
Independents [*Pakistan*] [*Political party*] .... Ind

Indermaur and Thwaites' Principles of the Common Law [*12th ed.*] [*1914*] [*A publication*] (DLA) ... Ind Com Law
Indermaur's Leading Cases in Common Law [*10th ed.*] [*1921*] [*A publication*] (DLA) ... Ind LC Com Law
Indermaur's Leading Cases in Conveyancing and Equity [*A publication*] (DLA) ... Ind LC Eq
Indermaur's Practice of the Supreme Court of Judicature [*12th ed.*] [*1919*] [*A publication*] (DLA) ... Ind Jud Pr
Indermaur's Practice of the Supreme Court of Judicature [*12th ed.*] [*1919*] [*A publication*] (DLA) ... Ind Jur Pr
Inderwick on Wills [*1866*] [*A publication*] (DLA) ... Ind Wills
Inderwick's Divorce and Matrimonial Causes Acts [*1862*] [*A publication*] (DLA) ... Ind Div
Indescor Hydrodynamics, Inc. [*Vancouver Stock Exchange symbol*] ... IHS
Indeterminate (MSA) ... INDET
Indeterminate Engineering Items ... IEI
Indeterminate Mass Particle ... IMP
Indeterminative (BJA) ... indeterm
Index ... I
Index (MSA) ... IDX
Index ... IND
Index (WDMC) ... ind
Index [*Computer science*] (BUR) ... IX
Index [*Computer science*] ... X
Index Array (IAA) ... IA
Index Catalogue ... IC
Index Character [*Computer science*] ... INX
Index Chemicals Registry System [*Databank*] (NITA) ... ICRS
Index Chemicus [*See also ICRS*] ... IC
Index Chemicus Registry System [*Information service or system A publication*] ... ICRS
Index Concordance [*International Serials Catalogue*] [*A publication*] ... I/C
Index Correction [*on a sextant*] [*Navigation*] ... IC
Index Correletion (WDAA) ... IC
Index Error [*Navigation*] ... IE
Index for Design Engineering Applications [*Data retrieval service*] [*Product engineering*] ... IDEA
Index Guided LASER (IAA) ... IGL
Index Linked [*Government bonds*] [*British*] ... IL
Index Lists [*DoD*] ... IL
Index Management System (PDAA) ... IMS
Index Manager (MHDI) ... IXM
Index Marker (MHDB) ... IM
Index of Adjustment and Values (AEBS) ... IAV
Index of Axis Deficiency [*Embryology*] ... IAD
Index of Body Build [*Anatomy*] ... IB
Index of Childhood Memory and Imagination ... ICMI
Index of Codes for Research Drugs [*A publication*] ... ICRD
Index of Coincidence (MHDB) ... IC
Index of Combat Effectiveness (CINC) ... ICE
Index of Community Noise ... ICN
Index of Competitive Ability (PDAA) ... ICA
Index of Conservation and Analytical Records: Unified System [*Computer science*] ... ICARUS
Index of Continuing Education Attitudes ... ICEATT
Index of Continuing Education Participation ... ICEPART
Index of Cooperation ... IOC
Index of Cranial Capacity [*Cladistics*] ... ICC
Index of Discrimination ... ID
Index of Dissimilarity ... ID
Index of Economic Activity (ADA) ... IEA
Index of Enrichment ... IE
Index of Environmental Quality (WDAA) ... IEQ
Index of Federal Specifications and Standards ... IFSS
Index of Gravity [*Engineering*] ... IG
Index of Homogeneity [*Botany*] ... IH
Index of Industrial Production ... IIP
Index of Limited Distribution Reports [*A publication*] ... ILDR
Index of Medical Underservice (DMAA) ... IMU
Index of National Enervation and Related Trends [*Department of Commerce*] ... INERT
Index of Nutritional Quality ... INQ
Index of Performance ... IP
Index of Preprogramming [*Computer science*] (PDAA) ... IP
Index of Prices Paid [*Economics*] ... IPP
Index of Prices Received [*Economics*] ... IPR
Index of Production Industries [*Department of Employment*] [*British*] ... IPI
Index of Refraction (MCD) ... IOR
Index of Relative Worth (MCD) ... IRW
Index of Response [*Medicine*] (DMAA) ... IOR
Index of Response [*Medicine*] (MAE) ... IR
Index of Social Position [*Advertising*] (DOAD) ... ISP
Index of Specifications and Standards (MCD) ... ISS
Index of Spouse Abuse ... ISA
Index of Stability of Relative Magnitudes [*Statistics*] ... ISRM
Index of Status Characteristics ... ISC
Index of Submarine Technical Repair Standards [*Military*] (DNAB) ... ISTRS
Index of Sustainable Economic Welfare (PS) ... ISEW
Index of Technical Manuals [*Military*] (DNAB) ... ITM
Index of Technical Publications [*Military*] (DNAB) ... ITP
Index of Vertical Transmission [*Cultural evolution*] ... IVT
Index Preparation System [*Foxon-Maddocks Associates*] [*Information service or system*] (IID) ... IPS
Index Register (WDAA) ... IR
Index Register ... XR
Index Retrieval Language [*Computer science*] (PDAA) ... IRL
Index Return Character [*Computer science*] ... IRT
Index Sequential Access Method [*Telecommunications*] (ACRL) ... ISAM
Index Sequential Module (IAA) ... ISMOD
Index Term [*Computer science*] ... IT
Index to Australian Book Reviews [*A publication*] ... IABR
Index to Book Reviews in the Sciences [*A publication*] ... IBRS
Index to Canadian Legal Periodical Literature [*A publication*] (DLA) ... Ind Can L P Lit
Index to Current Legal Research in Canada [*A publication*] (DLA) ... ICLR Can
Index to Current Urban Documents [*Information service or system*] (IID) ... ICUD
Index to Indian Legal Periodicals [*A publication*] (DLA) ... IILP
Index to Indian Legal Periodicals [*A publication*] (DLA) ... Ind Ind LP
Index to International Statistics [*A publication*] ... IIS
Index to Legal Periodical Literature [*1887-1937*] [*A publication*] (DLA) ... ILPL
Index to Maritime Publications [*A publication*] ... IMP
Index to Periodical Articles Related to Law [*A publication*] (DLA) ... IPAL
Index to Proceedings [*Information service or system United Nations*] (DUND) ... ITP
Index to Religious Periodical Literature [*Database*] ... IRPL
Index to Reviews of Australian Books [*A publication*] ... IRAB
Index to Scientific and Technical Proceedings and Books [*Institute for Scientific Information*] [*Database*] ... ISTP & B
Index to Speeches [*Information service or system United Nations*] (DUND) ... ITS
Index Translation Unit [*Computer science*] (MHDB) ... IXU
Index Translationum [*UNESCO*] ... IT
Index Word [*Online database field identifier*] ... IW
Indexation Information Statement [*Accounting*] ... IIS
Index-Digest Quarterly System ... DQS
Indexed and Paged ... I & P
Indexed by Name (IAA) ... IBN
Indexed Currency Option Note [*Student Loan Marketing Association*] ... ICON
Indexed Currency Option Notes (TDOB) ... ICON
Indexed Direct Access Method ... IDAM
Indexed, Folioed, and Titled [*Publishing*] (DGA) ... IFT
Indexed, Paged, and Titled (ADA) ... IPT
Indexed Random Access Memory (NITA) ... IRAM
Indexed References to Biomedical Engineering Literature [*A publication*] (IID) ... IRBEL
Indexed Repayment Loan ... IRL
Indexed Security Investment Plan [*Canada*] ... ISIP
Indexed Sequential [*Computer science*] ... IS
Indexed Sequential Access Method [*Pronounced "i-sam"*] [*Computer science*] ... ISAM
Indexed Sequential File Management System [*Computer science*] (BUR) ... ISFMS
Indexed Sequential File Manager [*Computer science*] ... ISFM
Indexed Sequential Processor ... ISP
Indexed Sequential Table Retrieval ... ISTR
Indexes of Firepower Potential ... IFP
Indexible Address Tag (SAA) ... IAT
Indexing and Abstracting (NITA) ... I & A
Indexing and Abstracting Services ... INAS
Indexing and Abstracting Society of Canada [*Toronto, ON*] ... IASC
Indexing by Statistical Analysis Techniques (PDAA) ... IBSAT
Indexing in Source ... IS
Indexing Slide Table ... IST
Index-Linked Mortgage and Investment (DI) ... ILMI
India [*MARC geographic area code Library of Congress*] (LCCP) ... a-ii--
India [*Phonetic alphabet*] [*International*] (DSUE) ... I
India [*MARC country of publication code Library of Congress*] (LCCP) ... ii
India [*ANSI two-letter standard code*] (CNC) ... IN
India [*IYRU nationality code*] [*ANSI three-letter standard code*] (CNC) ... IND
India Alert [*An association*] (EA) ... IA
India America Trade Council ... IATC
India Chemists and Chemical Engineers Club (EA) ... ICCEC
India Development Service (EA) ... IDS
India Docks Joint Committee (ROG) ... IDJC
India Engineering Export Promotion Council (EA) ... EEPC
India Fund [*NYSE symbol*] (TTSB) ... IFN
India Fund, Inc. [*NYSE symbol*] (SAG) ... IFN
India Fund, Inc. [*Associated Press*] (SAG) ... IndiaFd
India Growth Fund [*NYSE symbol*] (TTSB) ... IGF
India Growth Fund, Inc. [*NYSE symbol*] (CTT) ... IGF
India Growth Fund, Inc. [*Associated Press*] (SAG) ... IndiaG
India High Commission, Ottawa, Ontario [*Library symbol National Library of Canada*] (BIB) ... OOIHC
India Ink (VRA) ... ind i
India International Airways (P) Ltd. [*ICAO designator*] (FAAC) ... IIL
India International Philatelic Exhibition ... INDIPEX
India Office [*British*] ... IO
India Office Library and Records [*British*] ... IOL
India Office Library and Records, Foreign and Commonwealth Office, London, United Kingdom [*Library symbol Library of Congress*] (LCLS) ... UkLIO
India, Pakistan, and Bangladesh Association (PDAA) ... IPBA
India, Pakistan, Bangladesh Conference (DS) ... IPBC
India Pale Ale ... IPA
India Paper ... IP
India Paper Proofs ... IPP
India Press Agency ... IPA
India Satellite [*Telecommunications*] (NITA) ... INSAT
India Study Circle for Philately (EA) ... ISCP
India Supreme Court Reports [*A publication*] (DLA) ... India S Ct
India Weekly Reporter, Miscellaneous Appeals [*A publication*] (DLA) ... Suth Mis
India-America Chamber of Commerce (EA) ... IACC

India-America Society ... IAS
India-Burma [*World War II*] ... IB
India-Burma Theater [*World War II*] ... I-BT
India-China Wing [*World War II*] ... ICW
Indiae Imperator [*Emperor of India*] [*Latin*] ... IND IMP
Indiai Kommunista Part [*Communist Party of India*] [*Political party*] ... IKP
Indian (WGA) ... I
Indian (WDAA) ... IN
Indian (AABC) ... IND
Indian ... INDN
Indian Administrative Service [*British*] ... IAS
Indian Advanced Field Veterinary Hospital [*British military*] (DMA) ... IAFVH
Indian Advocate [*A publication*] (DLA) ... Ind Advocate
Indian Affairs (DLA) ... IA
Indian Agricultural Research Institute ... IARI
Indian Air Force ... IAF
Indian Air Force ... InAF
Indian Airlines (PDAA) ... IA
Indian Airlines (PDAA) ... IAL
Indian Airlines [*ICAO designator*] (AD) ... IC
Indian Airlines Corp. [*ICAO designator*] (FAAC) ... IAC
Indian American Forum for Political Education (EA) ... IAFPE
Indian and Metis Brotherhood Organization ... IMBO
Indian and Native American Employment and Training Program [*Department of Labor*] ... INAETP
Indian and Northern Affairs, B.C. Region, Resource Center Information Services, Vancouver, BC, Canada [*Library symbol*] [*Library of Congress*] (LCLS) ... CaBVaINA
Indian and Northern Affairs Canada [*Affaires Indiennes et du Nord Canada*],Amherst, Nova Scotia [*Library symbol National Library of Canada*] (BIB) ... NSAIN
Indian and Northern Affairs Canada, Amherst, NS, Canada [*Library symbol*] [*Library of Congress*] (LCLS) ... CaNSAIN
Indian and Northern Affairs Canada, Eastern Artic Reserch Laboratory, Igloolik, NT, Canada [*Library symbol*] [*Library of Congress*] (LCLS) ... CaNWIIE
Indian and Northern Affairs Canada, Engineering and Architecture, Edmonton, AB, Canada [*Library symbol*] [*Library of Congress*] (LCLS) ... CaAEINE
Indian and Northern Affairs Canada, Northern Program, Whitehorse, YT, Canada [*Library symbol*] [*Library of Congress*] (LCLS) ... CaYWIN
Indian and Northern Affairs Canada [*Affaires Indiennes et du Nord Canada*] **Ottawa, Ontario** [*Library symbol National Library of Canada*] (NLC) ... OORD
Indian and Northern Affairs Canada [*Affaires Indiennes et du Nord Canada*] **Prince Albert, Saskatchewan** [*Library symbol National Library of Canada*] (NLC) ... SPAIN
Indian and Northern Affairs Canada [*Affaires Indiennes et du Nord Canada*],Quebec [*Library symbol National Library of Canada*] (BIB) ... QQIN
Indian and Northern Affairs Canada, Quebec, PQ, Canada [*Library symbol*] [*Library of Congress*] (LCLS) ... CaQQIN
Indian and Northern Affairs Canada [*Affaires Indiennes et du Nord Canada*],Regina, Saskatchewan [*Library symbol National Library of Canada*] (BIB) ... SRIN
Indian and Northern Affairs Canada, Regina, SK, Canada [*Library symbol*] [*Library of Congress*] (LCLS) ... CaSRIN
Indian and Northern Affairs Canada [*Affaires Indiennes et du Nord Canada*],Winnipeg, Manitoba [*Library symbol National Library of Canada*] (BIB) ... MWIN
Indian and Northern Affairs Canada, Winnipeg, MB, Canada [*Library symbol*] [*Library of Congress*] (LCLS) ... CaMWIN
Indian and Northern Affairs Canada [*Affaires Indiennes et du Nord Canada*] **Yellowknife, Northwest Territories** [*Library symbol National Library of Canada*] (NLC) ... NWYIN
Indian and Northern Affairs Department [*Canada*] ... INA
Indian Army ... IA
Indian Army Act [*British military*] (DMA) ... IAA
Indian Army Circular [*British military*] (DMA) ... IAC
Indian Army Form [*British military*] (DMA) ... IAF
Indian Army Medical Corps ... IAMC
Indian Army Ordnance Control [*British*] ... IAOC
Indian Army Reserve of Officers ... IARO
Indian Army Service Corps [*British military*] (DMA) ... IASC
Indian Army Veterinary Corps [*British military*] (DMA) ... IAVC
Indian Artillery [*British military*] (DMA) ... IA
Indian Arts and Crafts Association (EA) ... IACA
Indian Arts and Crafts Board [*Department of the Interior*] ... IACB
Indian Association for Special Libraries and Information Centres (NITA) ... IASLIC
Indian Association of America (EA) ... IAA
Indian Astronautical Society ... IAS
Indian Australian Association of South Australia ... IAASA
Indian Auxiliary Force [*British*] ... IAF
Indian Banks Association (PDAA) ... IBA
Indian Base Depot Veterinary Stores [*British military*] (DMA) ... IBDVS
Indian Campaign Medal ... ICM
Indian Cases [*India*] [*A publication*] (DLA) ... IC
Indian Cases [*India*] [*A publication*] (DLA) ... Ind Cas
Indian Chamber of Commerce in Great Britain (DS) ... ICCGB
Indian Child Welfare Act [*1978*] ... ICWA
Indian Childhood Cirrhosis [*Medicine*] (MAE) ... ICC
Indian Church Aid [*British*] (BI) ... ICAA
Indian Church Quarterly Review [*A publication*] (ROG) ... IN CH Q
Indian Civil Rights Act [*1968*] ... ICRA
Indian Civil Service [*British*] ... ICS
Indian Claims Commission [*Terminated, 1976*] ... ICC
Indian Claims Commission, Ottawa, ON, Canada [*Library symbol Library of Congress*] (LCLS) ... CaOOICC
Indian Claims Commission [*Commission d'Etude des Revendications des Indiens*] **Ottawa, Ontario** [*Library symbol National Library of Canada*] (NLC) ... OOICC
Indian Code of Criminal Procedure, Curries' Edition [*A publication*] (DLA) ... Cur Cr Proc
Indian Commissioned Officer [*British military*] (DMA) ... ICO
Indian Communications Project ... ICP
Indian Communist Party [*Political party*] ... IKP
Indian Community Action ... ICA
Indian Community Action Program (OICC) ... ICAP
Indian Council for Agricultural Research ... ICAR
Indian Council of Arbitration. Quarterly [*A publication*] (DLA) ... IC Arb Q
Indian Council of Historical Research ... ICHR
Indian Council of Medical Research ... ICMR
Indian Council of South America [*See also CISA*] [*Lima, Peru*] (EAIO) ... ICSA
Indian Cultural Center [*Defunct*] (EA) ... ICC
Indian Defense Rules ... IDR
Indian Dental Association (USA) (EA) ... IDA (USA)
Indian Diamond and Colorstone Association (EA) ... IDCA
Indian Distinguished Service Medal [*British*] ... IDSM
Indian Educational Service [*British*] ... IES
Indian Evidence Act (ROG) ... IEA
Indian Expeditionary Force [*British military*] (DMA) ... IEF
Indian Federation of Working Journalists ... IFWJ
Indian Field Depot Veterinary Stores [*British military*] (DMA) ... IFDVS
Indian Field Veterinary Hospital [*British military*] (DMA) ... IFVH
Indian Financial Questions [*British*] ... IF
Indian Foodgrain Requirements [*British*] ... IFR
Indian Forest Service [*British*] ... IFS
Indian Gaming Regulatory Act ... IGRA
Indian General Service Medal [*British*] ... IGSM
Indian Geostationary Satellite [*Marine science*] (OSRA) ... INSAT
Indian Gold Resources Ltd. [*Vancouver Stock Exchange symbol*] ... IGD
Indian Head, MD [*AM radio station call letters*] ... WNTL
Indian Head, PA [*Location identifier FAA*] (FAAL) ... IHD
Indian Head [*Maryland*] **- Quality Assurance Department** [*Naval ordnance station*] ... IH/QAS
Indian Head Research and Development Department [*Naval Ordnance Station*] [*Maryland*] ... IH/RE
Indian Health Service ... IHS
Indian Heritage Council (EA) ... IHC
Indian Hollow Elementary School, Commack, NY [*Library symbol*] [*Library of Congress*] (LCLS) ... NCoIE
Indian Hospital Corps [*British military*] (DMA) ... IHC
Indian Housing Authorities (USGC) ... IHA
Indian Housing Authority [*Department of Housing and Urban Development*] (GFGA) ... IHA
Indian Income Tax Decisions [*A publication*] (DLA) ... Hari Rao
Indian Jurist [*Calcutta or Madras*] [*A publication*] (DLA) ... Ind Jur
Indian Jurist, New Series [*A publication*] (DLA) ... Ind Jur NS
Indian Jurist, Old Series [*A publication*] (DLA) ... IJ
Indian Jurist, Old Series [*A publication*] (DLA) ... Ind Jur OS
Indian Land Consolidation Act [*1983*] ... ILCA
Indian Law Herald [*A publication*] (DLA) ... Ind LH
Indian Law Journal [*A publication*] (DLA) ... Indian LJ
Indian Law Magazine [*A publication*] (DLA) ... Ind L Mag
Indian Law Quarterly [*A publication*] (DLA) ... ILQ
Indian Law Quarterly [*A publication*] (DLA) ... Ind LQ
Indian Law Quarterly Review [*A publication*] (DLA) ... ILQR
Indian Law Quarterly Review [*A publication*] (DLA) ... Ind LQ Rev
Indian Law Reporter [*A publication*] (DLA) ... Ind L Rep
Indian Law Reports [*A publication*] (DLA) ... ILR
Indian Law Reports [*A publication*] (DLA) ... Indian LR
Indian Law Reports, Allahabad Series [*A publication*] (DLA) ... Al Ser
Indian Law Reports, Allahabad Series [*A publication*] (DLA) ... All
Indian Law Reports, Allahabad Series [*A publication*] (DLA) ... ILR All
Indian Law Reports, Allahabad Series [*A publication*] (DLA) ... Ind LR All
Indian Law Reports, Allahabad Series [*A publication*] (DLA) ... Ind LR Alla
Indian Law Reports, Andhra Series [*A publication*] (DLA) ... ILR And
Indian Law Reports, Andhra Series [*A publication*] (DLA) ... Ind LR And
Indian Law Reports, Assam Series [*A publication*] (DLA) ... ILR Assam
Indian Law Reports, Assam Series [*A publication*] (DLA) ... Ind LR Assam
Indian Law Reports, Bombay Series [*A publication*] (DLA) ... B
Indian Law Reports, Bombay Series [*A publication*] (DLA) ... Bomb
Indian Law Reports, Bombay Series [*A publication*] (DLA) ... Bomb Ser
Indian Law Reports, Bombay Series [*A publication*] (DLA) ... ILR Bom
Indian Law Reports, Bombay Series [*A publication*] (DLA) ... Ind LR Bomb
Indian Law Reports, Calcutta Series [*A publication*] (DLA) ... C
Indian Law Reports, Calcutta Series [*A publication*] (DLA) ... Calc
Indian Law Reports, Calcutta Series [*A publication*] (DLA) ... ILR Cal
Indian Law Reports, Calcutta Series [*A publication*] (DLA) ... ILR Calc
Indian Law Reports, Calcutta Series [*A publication*] (DLA) ... ILRC
Indian Law Reports, Calcutta Series [*A publication*] (DLA) ... Ind LR Calc
Indian Law Reports, Calcutta Series [*A publication*] (DLA) ... Indian L R Calc
Indian Law Reports (East) [*A publication*] (DLA) ... Ind LR
Indian Law Reports, Hyderabad Series [*A publication*] (DLA) ... Hyderabad
Indian Law Reports, Hyderabad Series [*A publication*] (DLA) ... ILR Hyderabad
Indian Law Reports, Hyderabad Series [*A publication*] (DLA) ... Ind LR Hyderabad
Indian Law Reports, Karachi Series [*A publication*] (DLA) ... ILR Kar
Indian Law Reports, Karachi Series [*A publication*] (DLA) ... Ind LR Kar
Indian Law Reports, Karachi Series [*A publication*] (DLA) ... Kar
Indian Law Reports, Kerala Series [*A publication*] (DLA) ... ILR Ker
Indian Law Reports, Kerala Series [*A publication*] (DLA) ... ILR Trav-Cochin

Indian Law Reports, Kerala Series [*A publication*] (DLA) ... Ind LR Ker
Indian Law Reports, Kerala Series [*A publication*] (DLA) ... Ker
Indian Law Reports, Kerala Series [*A publication*] (DLA) ... Trav-Cochin
Indian Law Reports, Lahore Series [*A publication*] (DLA) ... ILR Lah
Indian Law Reports, Lahore Series [*A publication*] (DLA) ... Ind LR Lah
Indian Law Reports, Lahore Series [*A publication*] (DLA) ... Lah
Indian Law Reports, Lucknow Series [*A publication*] (DLA) ... ILR Luck
Indian Law Reports, Lucknow Series [*A publication*] (DLA) ... Ind LR Luck
Indian Law Reports, Lucknow Series [*A publication*] (DLA) ... Luck
Indian Law Reports, Lucknow Series [*A publication*] (DLA) ... Luck Ser
Indian Law Reports, Madhya Bharat Series [*A publication*] (DLA) ... ILR Madhya Bharat
Indian Law Reports, Madhya Bharat Series [*A publication*] (DLA) ... Ind LR Madhya Bharat
Indian Law Reports, Madras Series [*A publication*] (DLA) ... ILR Mad
Indian Law Reports, Madras Series [*A publication*] (DLA) ... Ind LR Mad
Indian Law Reports, Madras Series [*A publication*] (DLA) ... Indian LR Mad
Indian Law Reports, Madras Series [*A publication*] (DLA) ... LR Mad
Indian Law Reports, Madras Series [*A publication*] (DLA) ... M
Indian Law Reports, Madras Series [*A publication*] (DLA) ... Mad
Indian Law Reports, Madras Series [*A publication*] (DLA) ... Mad Ser
Indian Law Reports, Mysore Series [*A publication*] (DLA) ... ILR Mysore
Indian Law Reports, Mysore Series [*A publication*] (DLA) ... Ind LR Mysore
Indian Law Reports, Nagpur Series [*A publication*] (DLA) ... ILR Nag
Indian Law Reports, Nagpur Series [*A publication*] (DLA) ... Ind LR Nag
Indian Law Reports, Nagpur Series [*A publication*] (DLA) ... Nag
Indian Law Reports, Orissa Series [*A publication*] (DLA) ... Cut
Indian Law Reports, Orissa Series [*A publication*] (DLA) ... ILR Cut
Indian Law Reports, Orissa Series [*A publication*] (DLA) ... ILR Or
Indian Law Reports, Orissa Series [*A publication*] (DLA) ... Ind LR Or
Indian Law Reports, Orissa Series [*A publication*] (DLA) ... Or
Indian Law Reports, Patiala Series [*A publication*] (DLA) ... ILR Patiala
Indian Law Reports, Patiala Series [*A publication*] (DLA) ... Ind LR Patiala
Indian Law Reports, Patiala Series [*A publication*] (DLA) ... Patiala
Indian Law Reports, Patna Series [*A publication*] (DLA) ... ILR Pat
Indian Law Reports, Patna Series [*A publication*] (DLA) ... ILRP
Indian Law Reports, Patna Series [*A publication*] (DLA) ... Ind LR Pat
Indian Law Reports, Patna Series [*A publication*] (DLA) ... P
Indian Law Reports, Patna Series [*A publication*] (DLA) ... Pat
Indian Law Reports, Patna Series [*A publication*] (DLA) ... Pat Ser
Indian Law Reports, Punjab Series [*A publication*] (DLA) ... ILR Pun
Indian Law Reports, Punjab Series [*A publication*] (DLA) ... Ind LR Pun
Indian Law Reports, Punjab Series [*A publication*] (DLA) ... Pun
Indian Law Reports, Rajasthan Series [*A publication*] (DLA) ... ILR Rajasthan
Indian Law Reports, Rajasthan Series [*A publication*] (DLA) ... Ind LR Rajasthan
Indian Law Reports, Rajasthan Series [*A publication*] (DLA) ... Rajasthan
Indian Law Reports, Rangoon Series [*A publication*] (DLA) ... ILR Ran
Indian Law Reports, Rangoon Series [*A publication*] (DLA) ... Ind LR Ran
Indian Law Resource Center (EA) ... ILRC
Indian Law Times [*A publication*] (DLA) ... Ind LT
Indian Legal Information Development Service (EA) ... I-LIDS
Indian Limitation Act [*British*] (ROG) ... ILA
Indian Local Forces [*Military British*] ... ILF
Indian Major Crimes Act [*1909*] ... IMCA
Indian Medical Department [*British military*] (DMA) ... IMD
Indian Medical Service [*British*] ... IMS
Indian Mercantile Marine Training Ship [*British*] ... IMMTS
Indian Military Academy ... IMA
Indian Military Veterinary Hospital [*British military*] (DMA) ... IMVH
Indian Mineral Development Act of 1982 ... IMDA
Indian Mobile Veterinary Stores [*British military*] (DMA) ... IMVS
Indian Motorcycle Club of America (EA) ... IMCA
Indian Mountain [*Alaska*] [*Seismograph station code, US Geological Survey*] (SEIS) ... IMA
Indian Mountain Air Force Station [*Alaska*] [*ICAO location identifier*] (ICLI) ... PAIM
Indian Mountain, AK [*Location identifier FAA*] (FAAL) ... UTO
Indian Mountain Battery [*British military*] (DMA) ... IMB
Indian Nation Restoration Committee ... INRC
Indian National Airways ... INA
Indian National Army [*World War II*] ... INA
Indian National Cement Workers' Federation ... INCWF
Indian National Congress ... INC
Indian National Democratic Congress (BARN) ... INDC
Indian National Electricity Workers' Federation ... INEWF
Indian National Iron and Steel Workers' Federation ... INISWF
Indian National Mine Workers' Federation ... INMWF
Indian National Oceanographic Data Centre [*Information service or system*] (IID) ... INODC
Indian National Satellite System [*Bangalore, India*] [*Telecommunications*] ... INSAT
Indian National Scientific Documentation Center, Hillside Road, New Delhi, India [*Library symbol*] [*Library of Congress*] (LCLS) ... IiNI
Indian National Scientific Documentation Centre [*New Delhi*] ... INSDC
Indian National Scientific Documentation Centre [*Council of Scientific and Industrial Research*] ... INSDOC
Indian National Scientific Documentation Centre, New Delhi, India [*Library symbol Library of Congress*] ... IiNI
Indian National Textile Workers' Federation ... INTWF
Indian National Trades Union Congress ... INTUC
Indian Nations Council of Governments ... INCOG
Indian Navy ... IN
Indian Ocean [*MARC geographic area code Library of Congress*] (LCCP) ... i-----
Indian Ocean ... IndO
Indian Ocean ... IO
Indian Ocean Airlines [*Australia ICAO designator*] (FAAC) ... CCX
Indian Ocean and Southern Hemisphere Analysis Center (BARN) ... INOSHAC
Indian Ocean Area (MCD) ... IOA
Indian Ocean Arts Association [*Australia*] ... IOA
Indian Ocean Biological Center (BARN) ... IOBC
Indian Ocean Commission [*Port Louis, Mauritius*] (EAIO) ... IOC
Indian Ocean Conventional Target List (MCD) ... IOCTL
Indian Ocean Experiment ... INDEX
Indian Ocean Fishery Commission [*FAO*] [*Italy United Nations*] ... IOFC
Indian Ocean Geochemistry [*France*] [*Marine science*] (OSRA) ... INDIGO
Indian Ocean GEOSECS Program (MSC) ... INDOCHEM
Indian Ocean Marine Affairs Cooperation Conference ... IOMACI
Indian Ocean/Persian Gulf ... IO/PG
Indian Ocean Region [*INTELSAT*] ... IOR
Indian Ocean Ship ... IOS
Indian Ocean Standard Net ... IOSN
Indian Ocean Station (MCD) ... IOS
Indian Ocean Station Support ... IOSS
Indian Ocean Zone of Peace ... IOZP
Indian Order of Merit ... IOM
Indian Other Rank [*British military*] (DMA) ... IOR
Indian Overseas Airways ... IOA
Indian Overseas Communication Project ... IOCP
Indian Pattern [*British military*] (DMA) ... IP
Indian Peace-Keeping Force [*Army*] ... IPKF
Indian Peanut Clump Virus [*Plant pathology*] ... IPCV
Indian Penal Code [*A publication*] (DLA) ... India Pen Code
Indian Pension [*Army British*] (ROG) ... IND PENS
Indian People's Association in North America (EA) ... IPANA
Indian Pharmacopoeia [*A publication*] (ROG) ... IN PH
Indian Pharmacopoeia (ROG) ... IND PH
Indian Point Station [*Nuclear energy*] (NRCH) ... IPS
Indian Police Service [*British*] ... IPS
Indian Political Service [*British*] ... IPS
Indian Preference [*Civil Service*] ... IP
Indian Print and Paper [*A publication*] (DGA) ... IPP
Indian Privy Council Decisions [*A publication*] (DLA) ... Priv CDl
Indian Registration Act [*British*] (ROG) ... IRA
Indian Remote-Sensing Satellite ... IRS
Indian Remount and Veterinary Corps [*British military*] (DMA) ... IRVC
Indian Reorganization Act (OICC) ... IRA
Indian Reports [*A publication*] (DLA) ... In
Indian Reports, Allahabad Series [*A publication*] (DLA) ... A
Indian Reservation Roads System [*Bureau of Indian Affairs*] ... IRR
Indian Revenue Decisions [*A publication*] (DLA) ... RD
Indian Ridge Treatment Center, Resident Library, Arlington, WA [*Library symbol Library of Congress*] (LCLS) ... WaArl-R
Indian Ridge Treatment Center, Resident Library, Arlington, WA [*Library symbol Library of Congress*] (LCLS) ... WArl-R
Indian Ridge Treatment Center, Staff Library, Arlington, WA [*Library symbol Library of Congress*] (LCLS) ... WaArl
Indian Rights Association (EA) ... IRA
Indian River Community College, Fort Pierce, FL [*Library symbol Library of Congress*] (LCLS) ... FFpI
Indian River Public Library, Indian River, MI [*Library symbol Library of Congress*] (LCLS) ... MiInr
Indian River Resources, Inc. [*Vancouver Stock Exchange symbol*] ... IRR
Indian River Shores, FL [*FM radio station call letters*] (RBYB) ... WOSN-FM
Indian Rocks Beach, FL [*AM radio station call letters*] ... WXYB
Indian Rulings [*A publication*] (DLA) ... Indian Rul
Indian Rulings [*A publication*] (DLA) ... IR
Indian Rulings, Allahabad Series [*A publication*] (DLA) ... IR All
Indian Rulings, Bombay Series [*A publication*] (DLA) ... IR Bom
Indian Rulings, Calcutta Series [*A publication*] (DLA) ... IR Cal
Indian Rulings, Federal Court [*A publication*] (DLA) ... Fed Ct
Indian Rulings, Federal Court [*A publication*] (DLA) ... IR Fed Ct
Indian Rulings, Journal Section [*A publication*] (DLA) ... IR Jour
Indian Rulings, Lahore Series [*A publication*] (DLA) ... IR Lah
Indian Rulings, Lahore Series [*A publication*] (DLA) ... Lah
Indian Rulings, Madras Series [*A publication*] (DLA) ... IR Mad
Indian Rulings, Madras Series [*A publication*] (DLA) ... Mad
Indian Rulings, Nagpur Series [*A publication*] (DLA) ... IR Nag
Indian Rulings, Nagpur Series [*A publication*] (DLA) ... Nag
Indian Rulings, Oudh Series [*A publication*] (DLA) ... IR Oudh
Indian Rulings, Patna Series [*A publication*] (DLA) ... IR Pat
Indian Rulings, Patna Series [*A publication*] (DLA) ... Pat
Indian Rulings, Peshawar Series [*1933-47*] [*A publication*] (DLA) ... IR Pesh
Indian Rulings, Peshawar Series [*1933-47*] [*A publication*] (DLA) ... IR Peshawar
Indian Rulings, Peshawar Series [*1933-47*] [*A publication*] (DLA) ... Peshawar
Indian Rulings, Privy Council [*1929-47*] [*A publication*] (DLA) ... IR Pr C
Indian Rulings, Privy Council [*1929-47*] [*A publication*] (DLA) ... IRPC
Indian Rulings, Privy Council [*1929-47*] [*A publication*] (DLA) ... PC
Indian Rulings, Rangoon Series [*A publication*] (DLA) ... IR Ran
Indian Rulings, Sind Series [*A publication*] (DLA) ... IR Sind
Indian Rulings, Sind Series [*A publication*] (DLA) ... Sind
Indian Satellite (USDC) ... INSAT
Indian School of International Studies [*Delhi*] ... ISIS
Indian Scientific Satellite ... INDASAT
Indian Self-Determination Act [*1975*] ... ISDA
Indian Self-Determination Memorandum [*Indian Health Service*] [*Department of Health and Human Services*] (GFGA) ... ISDM
Indian Self-Identified Certified Staff (EDAC) ... ISICS
Indian Service of Engineers [*British*] ... ISE
Indian Society of Human Genetics ... ISHG
Indian Space Research Organization ... ISRO
Indian Spring Low Water [*Tides and currents*] ... ISLW

Indian Springs/Indian Springs Army Air Field [*Nevada*] [*ICAO location identifier*] (ICLI) .... KINS
Indian Springs, NV [*Location identifier FAA*] (FAAL) .... INS
Indian Springs, NV [*FM radio station call letters*] .... KPXC
Indian Staff Corps [*British*] (ROG) .... ISC
Indian Standard (IAA) .... IS
Indian Standard Time (IAA) .... IST
Indian Standards Institution .... ISI
Indian State Railway (ROG) .... ISR
Indian States Force [*British military*] (DMA) .... ISF
Indian Statistical Institute .... ISI
Indian Steel Training and Education Program [*India*] .... INSTEP
Indian Stores Depot [*British military*] (DMA) .... ISD
Indian Subordinate Medical Department [*British military*] (DMA) .... ISMD
Indian Supply Mission [*World War II*] .... ISM
Indian Tax Journal [*A publication*] (DLA) .... ITJ
Indian Tax Reports [*A publication*] (ILCA) .... ITR
Indian Telephone Industries (NITA) .... ITI
Indian Territorial Force [*British military*] (DMA) .... ITF
Indian Territorial Force Medical Corps [*British military*] (DMA) .... ITFMC
Indian Territory (ROG) .... IND T
Indian Territory .... IND TER
Indian Territory (DLA) .... Ind Terr
Indian Territory [*in United States*] .... IT
Indian Territory Annotated Statutes [*A publication*] (DLA) .... Ind T Ann St
Indian Territory Reports [*A publication*] (DLA) .... Ind Ter
Indian Territory Reports [*A publication*] (DLA) .... Indian Terr
Indian Trails Public Library District, Wheeling, IL [*Library symbol Library of Congress*] (LCLS) .... IWhI
Indian Trails Public Library District, Wheeling, IL [*OCLC symbol*] (OCLC) .... JAG
Indian Transcontinental Airways .... ITCA
Indian Tribal Organization (GFGA) .... ITO
Indian Unattached List [*British military*] (DMA) .... IUL
Indian University Association for Continuing Education .... IUACE
Indian Valley College, Novato, CA [*Library symbol Library of Congress*] (LCLS) .... CNovI
Indian Valley Colleges Library, Novato, CA [*OCLC symbol*] (OCLC) CIV
Indian Valley Public Library, Telford, PA [*Library symbol Library of Congress*] (LCLS) .... PTe
Indian Veterinary Convalescent Depot [*British military*] (DMA) .... IVCD
Indian Veterinary Hospital [*British military*] (DMA) .... IVH
Indian Yearbook of International Affairs [*A publication*] (DLA) .... Ind YB Int'l Aff
Indian Youth of America (EA) .... IYA
Indiana [*Obsolete*] (ROG) .... IA
Indiana [*Postal code*] .... IN
Indiana .... IND
Indiana .... INDI
Indiana [*MARC country of publication code Library of Congress*] (LCCP) .... inu
Indiana [*MARC geographic area code Library of Congress*] (LCCP) .... n-us-in
Indiana Academy of Science, Indianapolis, IN [*Library symbol Library of Congress*] (LCLS) .... InIA
Indiana Administrative Code [*A publication*] (AAGC) .... IAC
Indiana Airways [*ICAO designator*] (AD) .... WY
Indiana & Michigan Power [*NYSE symbol*] (SAG) .... IME
Indiana & Michigan Power [*NYSE symbol*] (SAG) .... IMJ
Indiana & Michigan Power [*Associated Press*] (SAG) .... IndiM
Indiana Appellate Court Reports [*A publication*] (DLA) .... InA
Indiana Appellate Court Reports [*A publication*] (DLA) .... Ind App Ct
Indiana Army Ammunition Plant (AABC) .... INAAP
Indiana Association of Homes for the Aging (SRA) .... IAHA
Indiana Association of Osteopathic Physicians and Surgeons (SRA) .... IAOPS
Indiana Attorney General Reports [*A publication*] (DLA) .... Rep & Ops Atty Gen Ind
Indiana Beef Cattle Association (SRA) .... IBCA
Indiana Bowling Proprietors Association (SRA) .... IBPA
Indiana Business Research Center [*Indiana University*] [*Bloomington, IN*] [*Information service or system*] (IID) .... IBRC
Indiana Cases [*A publication*] (DLA) .... Indian Cas
Indiana Central University, Indianapolis, IN [*OCLC symbol*] (OCLC) III
Indiana Central University, Indianapolis, IN [*Library symbol Library of Congress*] (LCLS) .... InICC
Indiana Certified Public Accountants Society (SRA) .... ICPAS
Indiana City Press, Indiana City, IN [*Library symbol Library of Congress*] (LCLS) .... InEcIP
Indiana Cmnty Bk SB [*NASDAQ symbol*] (TTSB) .... INCB
Indiana Community Bank A Savings Bank [*NASDAQ symbol*] (SAG) .... INCB
Indiana Community Bank a Savings Bank [*Associated Press*] (SAG) .... IndiCBk
Indiana Computer Educators (EDAC) .... ICE
Indiana Cooperative Library Service Authority (INCOLSA), Indianapolis, IN [*Library symbol Library of Congress*] (LCLS) .... InII
Indiana Cooperative Library Services Authority [*Indianapolis, IN*] [*Library network*] .... INCOLSA
Indiana Cooperative Library Services Authority, Indianapolis, IN [*OCLC symbol*] (OCLC) .... INC
Indiana Cooperative Library Services Authority, Indianapolis, IN [*OCLC symbol*] (OCLC) .... TQC
Indiana Cooperative Library Services Authority, Indianapolis, IN [*OCLC symbol*] (OCLC) .... TQD
Indiana Court of Appeals Reports [*A publication*] (DLA) .... Ind App
Indiana Decisions [*A publication*] (DLA) .... Ind Dec
Indiana Decisions and Law Reporter [*A publication*] (DLA) .... Ind Dec
Indiana Energy [*NYSE symbol*] (TTSB) .... IEI
Indiana Energy, Inc. [*NYSE symbol*] (SPSG) .... IEI
Indiana Energy, Inc. [*Associated Press*] (SAG) .... IndiEngy
Indiana Exchange, Inc. .... INDEX
Indiana Federal [*NASDAQ symbol*] (TTSB) .... IFSL

Indiana Federal Corp. [*NASDAQ symbol*] (NQ) .... IFSL
Indiana Federal Corp. [*Associated Press*] (SAG) .... IndiFdl
Indiana Federal Corp. [*Associated Press*] (SAG) .... IndiFedl
Indiana Harbor Belt Railroad Co. [*AAR code*] .... IHB
Indiana Higher Education Telecommunication System [*Indianapolis*] [*Telecommunications*] (TSSD) .... IHETS
Indiana Historical Society, Indianapolis, IN [*Library symbol Library of Congress*] (LCLS) .... InHi
Indiana Historical Society, Indianapolis, IN [*OCLC symbol*] (OCLC) .... XHS
Indiana Hospital and Health Association (SRA) .... IHHA
Indiana Hotel and Motel Association (SRA) .... IHMA
Indiana, Illinois, Iowa [*Old baseball league*] 3-I
Indiana Information Retrieval System [*Library network*] .... INDIRS
Indiana Institute of Technology, Fort Wayne, IN [*Library symbol Library of Congress*] (LCLS) .... InFwI
Indiana Institute of Technology, McMillen Library, Fort Wayne, IN [*OCLC symbol*] (OCLC) .... IMX
Indiana Interstate Railroad Co., Inc. [*AAR code*] .... IIRC
Indiana Journal of International Law [*A publication*] (DLA) .... Ind J Int'l L
Indiana Land Improvement Contractors Association (SRA) .... INLICA
Indiana Law Encyclopedia [*A publication*] (DLA) .... ILE
Indiana Law Reporter [*1881*] [*A publication*] (DLA) .... Ind L Rep
Indiana Law Reporter [*1881*] [*A publication*] (DLA) .... Ind LR
Indiana Law Student [*A publication*] (DLA) .... Ind L Stud
Indiana Law Student [*A publication*] (DLA) .... Ind LS
Indiana Legal Register [*A publication*] (DLA) .... Ind L Reg
Indiana Legal Register [*A publication*] (DLA) .... Ind LR
Indiana Legislative Council, State House, Indianapolis, IN [*Library symbol Library of Congress*] (LCLS) .... In-LB
Indiana Limestone Institute of America (EA) ILI
Indiana Limestone Institute of America .... ILIA
Indiana Manufacturers Association (SRA) .... IMA
Indiana Masonic Library and Museum, Indianapolis, IN [*Library symbol Library of Congress*] (LCLS) .... InIMa
Indiana Mich Pwr 8%JrSubDebs [*NYSE symbol*] (TTSB) .... IMJ
Indiana Motor Rate and Tariff Bureau Inc., Indianapolis IN [*STAC*] .... INB
Indiana Optometric Association (SRA) .... IOA
Indiana, PA [*Location identifier FAA*] (FAAL) .... IDI
Indiana, PA [*Location identifier FAA*] (FAAL) .... INP
Indiana, PA [*AM radio station call letters*] .... WDAD
Indiana, PA [*FM radio station call letters*] .... WIUP
Indiana, PA [*FM radio station call letters*] .... WQMU
Indiana Propane Gas Association (SRA) .... IPGA
Indiana Railroad System .... IR
Indiana Register [*A publication*] (AAGC) .... IR
Indiana Reports [*A publication*] (DLA) .... Ind R
Indiana Reports [*A publication*] (DLA) .... Ind Rep
Indiana Reports [*A publication*] (DLA) .... Indiana
Indiana Reports [*A publication*] (DLA) .... Indiana Sup Ct Rep
Indiana Sheriffs' Association (SRA) .... ISA
Indiana Soybean Growers Association (SRA) .... ISGA
Indiana State Bar Association Reports [*A publication*] (DLA) .... Ind SBA
Indiana State Data Center [*Indiana State Library*] [*Indianapolis*] [*Information service or system*] (IID) .... ISDC
Indiana State Grange (SRA) .... ISG
Indiana State Library, Blind and Physically Handicapped Division, Indianapolis, IN [*Library symbol Library of Congress*] (LCLS) .... In-BPH
Indiana State Library, Indianapolis, IN [*Library symbol Library of Congress*] (LCLS) .... In
Indiana State Library, Indianapolis, IN [*OCLC symbol*] (OCLC) .... ISL
Indiana State Medical Association (SRA) .... ISMA
Indiana State Supreme Court, Law Library, Indianapolis, IN [*Library symbol Library of Congress*] (LCLS) .... In-SC
Indiana State Techers Association (SRA) .... ISTA
Indiana State University (GAGS) .... Ind St U
Indiana State University [*Terre Haute*] .... ISU
Indiana State University, Evansville Campus, Evansville, IN [*Library symbol Library of Congress*] (LCLS) .... InES
Indiana State University, Evansville Campus, Evansville, IN [*OCLC symbol*] (OCLC) .... ISE
Indiana State University Remote Sensing Laboratory [*Research center*] (RCD) .... ISURSL
Indiana State University, Terre Haute, IN [*Library symbol Library of Congress*] (LCLS) .... InTI
Indiana State University, Terre Haute, IN [*OCLC symbol*] (OCLC) .... ISU
Indiana Supreme Court Law Library, Indianapolis, IN [*Library symbol Library of Congress*] (LCLS) .... InISC
Indiana Supreme Court Reports [*A publication*] (DLA) .... Ind
Indiana Unemployment Compensation Division, Selected Appeal Tribunal Decisions [*A publication*] (DLA) .... Ind UCD
Indiana Union List of Serials .... IULS
Indiana Union List of Serials, Indianapolis, IN [*OCLC symbol*] (OCLC) .... ILS
Indiana United Bancorp [*Associated Press*] (SAG) .... IndUtd
Indiana United Bancorp [*NASDAQ symbol*] (SAG) .... IUBC
Indiana University (GAGS) .... Ind U
Indiana University .... IU
Indiana University, Anatomy-Physiology Laboratory, Bloomington, IN [*Library symbol Library of Congress*] (LCLS) .... InU-A
Indiana University, Archive of Traditional Music, Bloomington, IN [*Library symbol*] [*Library of Congress*] (LCLS) .... InU-AT
Indiana University at Bloomington, Lilly Rare Books, Bloomington, IN [*Library symbol Library of Congress*] (LCLS) .... InU-R
Indiana University at Bloomington, Music Library, Bloomington, IN [*Library symbol*] [*Library of Congress*] (LCLS) .... InU-Mu
Indiana University at South Bend .... IUSB

Indiana University at South Bend, South Bend, IN [*Library symbol Library of Congress*] (LCLS) .... InSU
Indiana University, Biology Library, Bloomington, IN [*Library symbol Library of Congress*] (LCLS) .... InU-B
Indiana University, Bloomington, IN [*Library symbol Library of Congress*] (LCLS) .... InU
Indiana University, Bloomington, IN [*OCLC symbol*] (OCLC) .... IUL
Indiana University Cyclotron Facility [*Research center*] (RCD) .... IUCF
Indiana University, Fort Wayne Regional Campus, Fort Wayne, IN [*Library symbol Library of Congress*] (LCLS) .... InU-Fw
Indiana University, Indianapolis Regional Campus, Indianapolis, IN [*Library symbol Library of Congress*] (LCLS) .... InU-I
Indiana University, Institute for Sex Research, Bloomington, IN [*Library symbol Library of Congress*] (LCLS) .... InU-ISR
Indiana University, Kokomo Regional Campus, Kokomo, IN [*Library symbol Library of Congress*] (LCLS) .... InU-K
Indiana University, Law Library, Indianapolis, IN [*Library symbol Library of Congress*] (LCLS) .... InU-L
Indiana University, Lilly Library, Bloomington, IN [*Library symbol Library of Congress*] (LCLS) .... InU-Li
Indiana University, Northwest Regional Campus, Gary, IN [*Library symbol Library of Congress*] (LCLS) .... InU-N
Indiana University of Pennsylvania (GAGS) .... Ind U Penn
Indiana University of Pennsylvania .... IUP
Indiana University of Pennsylvania, Indiana, PA [*Library symbol Library of Congress*] (LCLS) .... PInU
Indiana University of Pennsylvania, Indiana, PA [*OCLC symbol*] (OCLC) .... PZI
Indiana University, Optometry Library, Bloomington, IN [*Library symbol Library of Congress*] (LCLS) .... InU-O
Indiana University Press (DGA) .... IND U PR
Indiana University Press .... IUP
Indiana University - Purdue University at Fort Wayne .... IPFW
Indiana University - Purdue University at Indianapolis .... IUPUI
Indiana University - Purdue University at Indianapolis, Downtown Campus, Indianapolis, IN [*Library symbol Library of Congress*] (LCLS) .... InIU
Indiana University - Purdue University at Indianapolis, Indianapolis, IN [*OCLC symbol*] (OCLC) .... IUP
Indiana University - Purdue University at Indianapolis, School of Law, Indianapolis, IN [*Library symbol Library of Congress*] (LCLS) .... InIU-L
Indiana University - Purdue University at Indianapolis, School of Physical Education, Indianapolis, IN [*Library symbol Library of Congress*] (LCLS) .... InIPE
Indiana University, School of Business Administration, Bloomington, IN [*Library symbol Library of Congress*] (LCLS) .... InU-BA
Indiana University, School of Dentistry, Indianapolis, IN [*Library symbol Library of Congress*] (LCLS) .... InU-D
Indiana University, School of Dentistry, Indianapolis, IN [*OCLC symbol*] (OCLC) .... IUD
Indiana University, School of Law Library, Bloomington, IN [*OCLC symbol*] (OCLC) .... IUB
Indiana University, School of Law Library, Indianapolis, IN [*OCLC symbol*] (OCLC) ILI
Indiana University, School of Medicine, Health Library Cooperative, Indianapolis, IN [*OCLC symbol*] (OCLC) .... IUH
Indiana University, School of Medicine, Indianapolis, IN [*Library symbol Library of Congress*] (LCLS) .... InU-M
Indiana University, School of Medicine, Indianapolis, IN [*OCLC symbol*] (OCLC) .... IUM
Indiana University, School of Medicine, Medical Education Resources Program, Indianapolis, IN [*OCLC symbol*] (OCLC) XLC
Indiana University, South Bend Regional Campus, South Bend, IN [*Library symbol Library of Congress*] (LCLS) .... InU-Sb
Indiana University Southeast, New Albany, IN [*Library symbol Library of Congress*] (LCLS) .... InU-Nea
Indiana University, Southeastern Regional Campus, Jeffersonville, IN [*Library symbol Library of Congress*] (LCLS) .... InU-Se
Indiana Veal Association (SRA) .... IVA
Indiana Veterinary Medical Association (SRA) .... IVMA
Indiana Youth Institute, Indianapolis, IN [*Library symbol*] [*Library of Congress*] (LCLS) .... InIY
Indianapolis [*Indiana*] [*Airport symbol*] (OAG) .... IND
Indianapolis [*Indiana*] [*ICAO location identifier*] (ICLI) .... KZID
Indianapolis Ballet Theatre .... IBT
Indianapolis Center for Advanced Research [*Indiana University - Purdue University at Indianapolis*] [*Research center*] (RCD) .... ICFAR
Indianapolis Commercial, Indianapolis, IN [*Library symbol Library of Congress*] (LCLS) .... InIC
Indianapolis, IN [*Location identifier FAA*] (FAAL) .... BJP
Indianapolis, IN [*Location identifier FAA*] (FAAL) .... COA
Indianapolis, IN [*Location identifier FAA*] (FAAL) .... EYE
Indianapolis, IN [*Location identifier FAA*] (FAAL) .... MQJ
Indianapolis, IN [*Location identifier FAA*] (FAAL) .... TYQ
Indianapolis, IN [*Location identifier FAA*] (FAAL) .... UZK
Indianapolis, IN [*FM radio station call letters*] .... WBDG
Indianapolis, IN [*AM radio station call letters*] .... WBRI
Indianapolis, IN [*FM radio station call letters*] .... WEDM
Indianapolis, IN [*FM radio station call letters*] .... WFBQ
Indianapolis, IN [*FM radio station call letters*] .... WFMS
Indianapolis, IN [*FM radio station call letters*] .... WFYI
Indianapolis, IN [*Television station call letters*] .... WFYI-TV
Indianapolis, IN [*FM radio station call letters*] .... WGRL
Indianapolis, IN [*FM radio station call letters*] .... WHHH
Indianapolis, IN [*Television station call letters*] .... WHMB
Indianapolis, IN [*AM radio station call letters*] .... WIBC
Indianapolis, IN [*FM radio station call letters*] .... WICR

Indianapolis, IN [*Television station call letters*] .... WISH
Indianapolis, IN [*FM radio station call letters*] .... WJEL
Indianapolis, IN [*AM radio station call letters*] .... WMYS
Indianapolis, IN [*FM radio station call letters*] .... WNAP
Indianapolis, IN [*AM radio station call letters*] .... WNDE
Indianapolis, IN [*FM radio station call letters*] .... WRFT
Indianapolis, IN [*Television station call letters*] .... WRTV
Indianapolis, IN [*FM radio station call letters*] .... WRZX
Indianapolis, IN [*AM radio station call letters*] .... WSYW
Indianapolis, IN [*Television station call letters*] .... WTBU
Indianapolis, IN [*Television station call letters*] .... WTHR
Indianapolis, IN [*AM radio station call letters*] .... WTLC
Indianapolis, IN [*FM radio station call letters*] .... WTLC-FM
Indianapolis, IN [*FM radio station call letters*] .... WTPI
Indianapolis, IN [*Television station call letters*] .... WXIN
Indianapolis, IN [*AM radio station call letters*] .... WXLW
Indianapolis, IN [*Location identifier FAA*] (FAAL) .... ZID
Indianapolis/International [*Indiana*] [*ICAO location identifier*] (ICLI) .... KIND
Indianapolis Law Catalog Consortium, Indiana University School of Law Library, Indianapolis, IN [*OCLC symbol*] (OCLC) IIL
Indianapolis Law School, Indianapolis, IN [*Library symbol Library of Congress*] (LCLS) .... InILS
Indianapolis Motor Speedway [*Auto racing venue*] .... IMS
Indianapolis Museum of Art, Indianapolis, IN [*OCLC symbol*] (OCLC) .... IMO
Indianapolis Museum of Art, Reference Library, Indianapolis, IN [*Library symbol Library of Congress*] (LCLS) .... InIMu
Indianapolis Public Schools, Indianapolis, IN [*OCLC symbol*] (OCLC) .... IPP
Indianapolis Raceway Park [*Auto racing venue*] .... IRP
Indianapolis Star and News, Indianapolis, IN [*Library symbol*] [*Library of Congress*] (LCLS) .... InSIN
Indianapolis Union [*AAR code*] .... IU
Indianapolis, Zoological Society, Inc., Indianapolis, IN [*Library symbol*] [*Library of Congress*] (LCLS) .... InIZ
Indianapolis-Marion County Public Library, Indianapolis, IN [*OCLC symbol*] (OCLC) .... IMD
Indianapolis-Marion County Public Library, Indianapolis, IN [*Library symbol Library of Congress*] (LCLS) .... InI
Indiana-Purdue University, Fort Wayne, IN [*Library symbol Library of Congress*] (LCLS) .... InFwIP
Indian-Eskimo Association of Canada [*Later, CASNP*] (EA) .... IEA
Indianfields Public Library, Caro, MI [*Library symbol Library of Congress*] (LCLS) .... MiCa
Indianola, IA [*FM radio station call letters*] .... KSTM
Indianola, IA [*AM radio station call letters*] (RBYB) .... KXLQ
Indianola, MS [*Location identifier FAA*] (FAAL) .... IDL
Indianola, MS [*FM radio station call letters*] .... WDLJ
Indianola, MS [*AM radio station call letters*] .... WNLA
Indianola, MS [*FM radio station call letters*] .... WNLA-FM
Indianola Public Library, Indianola, IA [*Library symbol*] [*Library of Congress*] (LCLS) .... IaInd
Indians into Communications Association (EA) .... IICA
Indians into Medicine (EA) .... INMED
Indiantown, FL [*FM radio station call letters*] .... WPBZ
Indiantown Gap, PA [*Location identifier FAA*] (FAAL) .... BZJ
India-Rubber (DEN) .... IR
India-Rubber Vulcanized, Braided [*Wire insulation*] (IAA) .... IRVB
India-US Foundation (EA) .... IUSF
Indic [*MARC language code Library of Congress*] (LCCP) .... inc
Indicate [*or Indicator*] (KSC) .... IND
Indicate (FAAC) .... INDC
Indicate .... INDI
Indicate (AABC) .... INDIC
Indicated [*or Indicative*] I
Indicated Air Speed .... IAS
Indicated Air Temperature (AFM) .... IAT
Indicated Altitude [*Navigation*] .... IA
Indicated Angle-of-Attack (GAVI) .... IAOA
Indicated Boiling Point [*Physics*] .... IBP
Indicated Final Cost (SAA) .... IFC
Indicated Horsepower I
Indicated Horsepower .... IHP
Indicated Horsepower-Hour .... IHPH
Indicated Horsepower-Hour .... IHP-HR
Indicated Kilowatts per Hour [*Engine emissions testing*] .... IKW
Indicated Mach Number (AFM) .... IMN
Indicated Main Engine I
Indicated Mean Effective Pressure [*Aerospace*] .... IMEP
Indicated Pressure Altitude .... IPA
Indicated Specific Carbon Monoxide .... ISCO
Indicated Specific Fuel Consumption .... ISFC
Indicated Specific Hydrocarbon [*Automotive exhaust emission testing*] .... ISHC
Indicated Specific Oxides of Nitrogen [*Automotive exhaust emission testing*] .... ISNOX
Indicated Terminal Efficiency (DNAB) .... ITE
Indicated Thermal Efficiency [*Automotive engineering*] .... ITE
Indicated True Air Speed [*Aviation*] (AFM) .... ITAS
Indicateur Electronique de Pilotage [*Electronic Pilotage Indicator*] [*Aviation*] .... IEP
Indicating Controller (NRCH) IC
Indicating Device .... ID
Indicating Direction Finder (IAA) .... IDF
Indicating Light IL
Indicating Light Relay .... ILR
Indicating Recorder [*Electronics*] (ECII) .... IR
Indicating Recording Controller [*Electronics*] (ECII) .... IRC
Indicating Round Technique [*British*] .... IRT

Indicating Switch (NRCH) ... IS
Indication ... INDICN
Indication (WGA) ... INDN
Indication Cycle (IAA) ... IC
Indication of Hostilities [*Military*] ... IOH
Indication of Interest [*Business term*] (MHDW) ... IOI
Indication Report (MCD) ... INDIC
Indications and Warning [*Subsystems*] [*Military*] (MCD) ... IW
Indications and Warning Training System [*Military*] (MCD) ... IWTS
Indications Center Watch Officer [*Military*] (MCD) ... ICWO
Indications Communications (MCD) ... INDICOM
Indications Review Committee [*Military*] (CINC) ... IRC
Indicative (ROG) ... IND
Indicative [*Grammar*] ... INDIC
Indicative Planning Figure ... IPF
Indicative World Plan for Agricultural Development [*United Nations*] ... IWP
Indicator ... I
Indicator (IDOE) ... ind
Indicator ... INDCTR
Indicator (WDAA) ... INDIC
Indicator (IAA) ... INDR
Indicator and Control ... IC
Indicator Co. [*Hungary*] [*FAA designator*] (FAAC) ... IDR
Indicator Compiler (IAA) ... INCOM
Indicator Control Panel ... ICP
Indicator Control Unit ... ICU
Indicator Coupling Network (IAA) ... ICN
Indicator Digest Average [*Stock exchange term*] (SPSG) ... IDA
Indicator Drive Screw ... IDS
Indicator Drive Unit (IAA) ... IDU
Indicator Driver (MSA) ... ID
Indicator Equipment (IAA) ... IE
Indicator Group (MCD) ... IG
Indicator Group Speed ... IGS
Indicator Kit ... IK
Indicator of Authoritativeness [*Library symbol*] ... IA
Indicator Panel ... IP
Indicator Reading (IAA) ... IR
Indicator Register (IAA) ... IR
Indicator Time Test [*Chemistry*] ... ITT
Indicator-Transmitter ... INDTR
Indices of General Industrial Worth ... IGIW
Indictione [*In the Indiction*] [*Latin*] (ROG) ... IDNE
Indies ... IND
Indifference Curve [*Economics*] ... IC
Indigenous (AABC) ... INDIG
Indigenous Communications Association (EA) ... ICA
Indigenous Defense Fighter [*Military*] ... IDF
Indigenous Minorities Research Council [*British*] ... IMRC
Indigenous People's Network (EA) ... IPN
Indigenous Women's Network (EA) ... IWN
Indigent Medical Care (HCT) ... IMC
Indigo ... IND
Indigo (WDMC) ... ind
Indigo NV [*NASDAQ symbol*] (SAG) ... INDGF
Indigo NV [*Associated Press*] (SAG) ... IndigoNV
Indigo Technologies, Inc. [*Vancouver Stock Exchange symbol*] ... IDG
Indio, CA [*FM radio station call letters*] ... KCMJ
Indio, CA [*FM radio station call letters*] ... KCRY
Indio, CA [*FM radio station call letters*] (RBYB) ... KLCX
Indio, CA [*AM radio station call letters*] ... KUNA
Indio Public Library, Indio, CA [*Library symbol Library of Congress*] (LCLS) ... CInd
Indiopahtic Nephrotic Syndrome [*Nephrology*] (DAVI) ... INS
Indirect ... IND
Indirect Address (NITA) ... IA
Indirect Address Buffer ... IAB
Indirect Address Register ... IAR
Indirect Addressing ... IA
Indirect Antiglobulin Test [*Clinical chemistry*] ... IAT
Indirect Bilirubin [*Biochemistry*] (DAVI) ... IDBR
Indirect Blood Pressure Measuring System ... IBPMS
Indirect Bomb-Damage Assessment ... IBDA
Indirect by Direct (MCD) ... IDD
Indirect Calorimetry [*Physiology*] (DAVI) ... IC
Indirect Centrifugal Flotation ... ICF
Indirect Command File [*Computer science*] (WDAA) ... IDCF
Indirect Component Improvement Program ... ICIP
Indirect Control Register [*Computer science*] ... ICR
Indirect Coombs' Test [*Immunochemistry*] ... ICT
Indirect Coombs Test [*Hematology*] (DAVI) ... INDIR
Indirect Cost Management System (NASA) ... ICMS
Indirect Cost Monitoring Office (AAGC) ... ICMO
Indirect Costs ... IDC
Indirect Coulometric Titration [*Analytical chemistry*] ... ICT
Indirect Damage [*Insurance*] ... ID
Indirect Data Address List [*Computer science*] (ECII) ... IDAL
Indirect Departmental (DGA) ... ID
Indirect Environmental Warming Impact ... IEWI
Indirect Enzyme-Linked Immunosorbent Assay ... INDELISA
Indirect Fire Casualty Assessment/Suppression System [*Military*] (MCD) ... IFCAS
Indirect Fluorescent ... IF
Indirect Fluorescent Antibody [*Immunochemistry*] ... IFA
Indirect Fluorescent Antibody Test [*Immunology*] ... IFAT
Indirect Fluorescent Rabies Antibody Test [*Immunology*] (MAE) ... IFRA
Indirect Hemagglutination [*Hematology*] (DAVI) ... IH
Indirect Hemagglutination [*Clinical chemistry*] ... IHA
Indirect Hemagglutination Antibody [*Medicine*] (DMAA) ... IHA
Indirect Hire [*Military*] ... INDH
Indirect Identification System [*Military*] (MCD) ... IIS
Indirect Immunofluorescence [*Immunochemistry*] ... IIF
Indirect Immunofluorescence Assay [*AIDS confirmation test*] (CPH) ... IIA
Indirect Immunofluorescence Technique [*Immunochemistry*] ... IIFT
Indirect Immunofluorescent Antibody Test [*Clinical chemistry*] ... IFAT
Indirect Injection Engine [*Engineering*] ... IDI
Indirect Labor (AAG) ... I/D
Indirect Maintenance Man-Hour ... IMMH
Indirect Manufacturing Expense ... IME
Indirect Material Purchasing Information Standards ... IMPIS
Indirect Maximum Breathing Capacity [*Medicine*] ... IMBC
Indirect Measuring System ... IMS
Indirect Medical Education [*Department of Health and Human Services*] (GFGA) ... IME
Indirect Medical Education Adjustment ... IMEA
Indirect Method ... IDM
Indirect Microhemagglutination Test [*Medicine*] (DMAA) ... IMH
Indirect Operating Costs ... IOC
Indirect Photometric Chromatography ... IPC
Indirect Plaque-Forming Cell [*Immunology*] ... iPFC
Indirect Productive Time Factors (MCD) ... IDPTF
Indirect Proof [*Method in logic*] ... IP
Indirect Pulp Capping [*Dentistry*] ... IPC
Indirect Reading Measuring Instruments (DICI) ... IRMI
Indirect Reading Pocket Chamber ... IRPC
Indirect Reference Word (BUR) ... IRW
Indirect Representative Supplement [*British*] ... IRS
Indirect Source Model for Air Pollution [*Environmental Protection Agency*] (GFGA) ... ISMAP
Indirect Source Review [*Environmental Protection Agency*] (FFDE) ... ISR
Indirect Strike Control ... ISC
Indirect Tag Memory ... ITM
Indirect Target Damage Assessment (AAG) ... ITDA
Indirect to Job Costs (DGA) ... IJ
Indirect Video Display (MCD) ... IVD
Indirect Waste ... IW
Indirect Work Breakdown Structure (NASA) ... IWBS
Indirectly ... IDRTY
Indirectly Heated (DEN) ... IH
Indirectly Heated Cathode ... IHC
Indium [*Chemical element*] ... In
Indium Aluminum Gallium Phophide [*Organic chemistry*] ... InAlGaP
Indium Antimode Varactor ... IAV
Indium Arsenide Filter ... IAF
Indium Arsenide Infrared Detector ... IAID
Indium Gallium Arsenide ... INGA
Indium Gallium Arsenide Avalanche Photodiode ... InGaAs APD
Indium Phosphide [*Inorganic chemistry*] (IAA) ... INP
Indium Phosphide [*Materials science*] ... IP
Indium Tin Oxide ... ITO
Indium-Gallium-Aluminum Phosphide [*Light-emitting diode construction*] ... INGAALP
Individual [*Missile launch environment symbol*] ... F
Individual (AFM) ... INDIV
Individual [*Freight*] ... INDIVL
Individual Acceptance Tests ... IAT
Individual Accession and Training System (MCD) ... IATS
Individual Account Number File [*IRS*] ... IANF
Individual Action Report ... IAR
Individual Aerial Mobility System [*Military*] (MCD) ... IAMS
Individual Aircraft Tracking Program (MCD) ... IAT
Individual Aircraft Tracking Program (MCD) ... IATP
Individual and Collective Training Development (MCD) ... ICTD
Individual and Marriage Counseling Inventory [*Psychology*] ... IMCI
Individual Battle Shooting Range (PDAA) ... IBSR
Individual Bias ... IB
Individual Career Exploration [*Vocational guidance test*] ... ICE
Individual Case Basis (TEL) ... ICB
Individual Case Management (WYGK) ... ICM
Individual Cell Voltmeter (DNAB) ... ICV
Individual Census Report (GFGA) ... ICR
Individual Circuit Analysis [*Telecommunications*] (TEL) ... ICAN
Individual Circuit Usage and Peg Count [*Telecommunications*] (TEL) ... ICUP
Individual Cleared for Access to Classified Material (AAG) ... ICFATCM
Individual Cleared for Access to Classified Material Up to and Including ... ICFATCMUTAI
Individual Clutch Modulation [*Automotive engineering*] ... ICM
Individual/Collective (MCD) ... IC
Individual/Collective Integration ... ICI
Individual Collective Training [*Army*] ... ICT
Individual/Collective Training Plan [*Army*] ... ICTP
Individual Combat Actions [*Army*] ... ICA
Individual Commitment to Excellence [*DoD*] ... ICE
Individual Compass Error (IAA) ... ICE
Individual Component Repair List [*DoD*] ... ICRL
Individual Concealment Cover ... ICC
Individual Counsel (DNAB) ... IC
Individual Counseling [*Psychology*] (DAVI) ... IC
Individual Criterion-Referenced Test [*Education*] ... ICRT
Individual Data Record ... IDR

Individual Defense Counsel .... IDC
Individual Development .... ID
Individual Development Plan (RDA) .... IDP
Individual Development Program [*Civil Service Commission*] .... IDP
Individual Differences Scaling (PDAA) .... INDSCAL
Individual Documented Quality Assurance .... IDQA
Individual Dose [*Radioactivity calculations*] .... ID
Individual Drill Attendance and Retirement Transaction [*Military*] (DNAB) .... IDART
Individual Drinking Water Flavors [*Developed by Natick Research and Development Center to encourage soldiers to drink more fluids to prevent dehydration*] (INF) .... IDWF
Individual Drop Glider .... IDG
Individual DSS [*Direct Support System*] **Activity Performance Report** .... IDAPR
Individual Education Plan .... IEP
Individual Education Record .... IER
Individual Effective Dose (IEEE) .... IED
Individual Employment Rights Manual [*A publication*] .... IERM
Individual Engagement Model (MCD) .... IEM
Individual Evaluation Plan [*Army*] .... IEP
Individual Evaluation Report .... IER
Individual Field of View .... IFOV
Individual Flexible Barrier Shelter Systems (MCD) .... IFBSS
Individual Flight Activity Reporting System [*Navy*] .... IFARS
Individual Flight Plans from This Point [*Aviation*] (FAAC) .... IFPFP
Individual Flying Time Report System [*Military*] (DNAB) .... IFTRS
Individual Freedom Federation (EA) .... IFF
Individual/Group (ACRL) .... I/G
Individual Health Care Account (HCT) .... IHCA
Individual Housing Account .... IHA
Individual Implementation Plan [*For the education of a handicapped person*] .... IIP
Individual Inclusive Tour [*Air fare plan*] .... IIT
Individual, Inc. [*Associated Press*] (SAG) .... Individul
Individual, Inc. [*NASDAQ symbol*] (SAG) .... INDV
Individual Inc. [*NASDAQ symbol*] (TTSB) .... INDV
Individual Index File [*Computer science*] (PCM) .... IDX
Individual Investor Group [*NASDAQ symbol*] (SAG) .... INDI
Individual Investor Group [*Associated Press*] (SAG) .... Indvl
Individual Investor Group [*Associated Press*] (SAG) .... IndvInv
Individual Job Order .... IJO
Individual Knowledge Evaluation Test (AFM) .... IKET
Individual Learning Disabilities Classroom Screening Instruments .... ILDCSI
Individual Learning Laboratory (OICC) ILL
Individual Learning Package (OICC) .... ILP
Individual Learning Programme (AIE) .... ILP
Individual Ledger [*Business term*] (MHDW) .... Ind Led
Individual Level Cost Method [*Insurance*] .... ILCM
Individual Line (IAA) IL
Individual Load Operation .... ILO
Individual Maintenance Material Readiness List (MCD) .... IMMRL
Individual Maintenance Readiness List .... IMRL
Individual Master File .... IMF
Individual Material Readiness List [*DoD*] .... IMRL
Individual Medical Record .... IMR
Individual Medley [*Swimming*] .... IM
Individual Merit Promotion .... IMP
Individual Microclimate Cooling System [*Army*] (INF) .... IMCS
Individual Mobilization Augmentation [*or Augmentees*] [*DoD*] .... IMA
Individual Mobilization Augmentee (AAGC) .... IMA
Individual Motor Behavior Survey [*Test*] .... IMBS
Individual Movement Technique [*Military*] (INF) .... IMT
Individual Multipurpose Shelter [*Army*] (INF) .... IMPS
Individual Name and Address File [*IRS*] .... INAF
Individual Name and Address Key Index File [*IRS*] .... IKIF
Individual Needs Test (DNAB) .... INT
Individual Nonrecurrence Action (KSC) .... INA
Individual Nonrecurrence Action (SAA) .... INRA
Individual Operation Test .... IOT
Individual Operator Training Equipment (MCD) .... IOTE
Individual Package Delivery [*Shipping*] .... IPD
Individual Parameter Perturbation .... IPP
Individual Patient Usage .... IPU
Individual Pay Record [*Military*] .... IPR
Individual Perception Threshold (PDAA) .... IPT
Individual Personal Hygiene Equipment (KSC) .... IPHE
Individual Personal Hygiene Module (KSC) .... IPHM
Individual Plan of Care .... IPC
Individual Practice Association [*Medicine*] .... IPA
Individual Program Plan .... IPP
Individual Protection Laboratory [*Natick, MA*] [*Army*] (RDA) .... IPL
Individual Protective Device [*Toxicology*] .... IPD
Individual Protective Equipment .... IPE
Individual Psychology Association of New York .... IPANY
Individual Quick Blanching (DICI) .... IQB
Individual Ready Reserve [*Army*] .... IRR
Individual Ready Reserve - Alternative Preassignment System Test (MCD) .... IRRAPST
Individual Ready Reserve System [*Military*] .... IRRS
Individual Recorder [*Sports*] .... IR
Individual Records Brief [*Military*] (AABC) .... IRB
Individual Referral (OICC) .... IR
Individual Reliability Test .... IRT
Individual Repair Parts Ordering Data [*Program*] [*DoD*] .... IRPOD
Individual Resource Protection Sensor .... IRPS
Individual Responsibility Program [*Medicine*] (DHSM) .... IRP
Individual Retirement Account .... IRA
Individual Retirement Account File [*IRS*] .... IRAF
Individual Retirement Account Register [*IRS*] .... IRAR
Individual Retirement Annuity [*Insurance*] .... IRA
Individual Retirement Mortgage Account .... IRMA
Individual Retirement Record [*Air Force*] (AFM) .... IRR
Individual Reverse Mortgage Account [*American Homestead, Inc.*] .... IRMA
Individual Rights and Responsibilities Newsletter [*A publication*] (DLA) .... IRR Newsl
Individual Risk Premium Modification [*Insurance*] .... IRPM
Individual Rod Position Indicator [*Nuclear energy*] (NRCH) .... IRPI
Individual Sales Transaction .... IST
Individual Savings Account [*Proposed*] .... ISA
Individual Scale for Indian South Africans [*Intelligence test*] .... ISISA
Individual Seal Packaging [*Food technology*] .... ISP
Individual Service Plan .... ISP
Individual Ship Exercises [*Navy*] .... ISE
Individual Soldier Energy [*Military*] (RDA) .... ISE
Individual Soldier Radio [*Military*] (INF) .... ISR
Individual Soldier's Computer [*Army*] (RDA) .... ISC
Individual Soldier's Computer/Radio [*Military*] .... ICS/R
Individual Soldier's Computer/Radio [*Army*] (INF) .... ISC/R
Individual Soldier's Report .... ISR
Individual Store and Forward .... ISF
Individual Survival Vest for Aircrew [*Army*] (RDA) .... ISVESTA
Individual System Automation Plans [*Military*] .... ISAP
Individual System Operation .... ISO
Individual System/Organization Cost (MHDB) .... ISOC
Individual Tactical Air Vehicle .... ITAV
Individual Tactical Load Bearing Vest [*Army*] (INF) .... ITLBV
Individual Tactical Technical Training [*Military*] (MCD) .... ITTT
Individual Task Authorization .... ITA
Individual Taxpayer Identification Number .... ITIN
Individual Taxpayer Information File [*IRS*] .... ITIF
Individual Technical Training [*Military*] .... ITT
Individual Therapy .... IT
Individual Tour Basing [*Fares*] .... ITB
Individual Training [*Navy*] (NVT) .... INDTNG
Individual Training [*Army*] .... IT
Individual Training Analysis and Design (MCD) .... ITAD
Individual Training and Evaluation Program [*Army*] (INF) .... ITEP
Individual Training and Performance Research Laboratory [*Army*] (RDA) .... ITPRL
Individual Training Evaluation (MCD) .... ITE
Individual Training Evaluation Group (MCD) .... ITEG
Individual Training Plan [*Army*] .... ITP
Individual Training Plan Proposal [*Army*] .... ITPP
Individual Training Program (MCD) .... ITP
Individual Training Record [*Military*] (INF) .... ITR
Individual Transferable Quota .... ITQ
Individual Transportation [*Urban planning*] .... IT
Individual Travel Order [*Military*] (CINC) .... ITO
Individual Treatment Plan [*For the medical care and the education of a handicapped person*] .... ITP
Individual Unit Action Model .... IUA
Individual Vessel Quota [*Fisheries management*] .... IVQ
Individual Viable Cells [*Metabolic studies*] IVC
Individual Weapon (MCD) .... IW
Individual Weapon Thermal Sight [*Army*] (INF) .... IWTS
Individual Weapons Captured .... IWC
Individual Whole of Life and Endowment [*Insurance*] (ADA) .... IWLE
Individual Yield Coverage Program [*Department of Agriculture*] .... IYC
Individual-Based Model [*Marine science*] (OSRA) .... IBM
Individual-Based Model (USDC) .... IBM
Individualized Bilingual Instruction (EDAC) .... IBI
Individualized Classroom Environment Questionnaire (EDAC) .... ICEQ
Individualized Computer Literacy Education Plan (EDAC) .... ICLEP
Individualized Dementia Questionnaire [*Medicine*] (DMAA) .... IDQ
Individualized Education and Training Plan (OICC) .... IETP
Individualized Education Plan [*Special education*] (PAZ) .... IEP
Individualized Education Program [*For the education of a handicapped person*] .... IEP
Individualized Family Service Plan [*Required under the Individuals with Disabilities Education Act (IDEA)*] (PAZ) .... IFSP
Individualized Functional Assessment [*Social Security Administration*] .... IFA
Individualized Habilitation Plan .... IHP
Individualized Instruction II
Individualized Learning (OICC) IL
Individualized Learning System (DNAB) .... INLS
Individualized Manpower Training System (OICC) .... IMTS
Individualized Mathematics System [*Education*] .... IMS
Individualized Reading Program [*Education*] .... IRP
Individualized Science Instructional System [*National Science Foundation project*] .... ISIS
Individualized Study by Telecommunications [*Alaska*] (EDAC) .... IST
Individualized Written Rehabilitation Program [*Department of Education*] .... IWRP
Individually (MSA) .... INDV
Individually Carried Records [*Military*] .... ICR
Individually Controlled Ventilation ICV
Individually Guided Education [*for upgrading students' skills*] .... IGE
Individually Planned [*or Prescribed*] **Instruction** [*Education*] .... IPI
Individually Planned Instruction/Management and Information System .... IPI/MIS
Individually Polymerized Grass [*Organic chemistry*] (DAVI) .... IPG
Individually Prescribed Instructional Systems (OICC) .... IPIS

Individually Presented Instruction (NITA) .... IPI
Individually Quick-Frozen [*Food technology*] .... IQF
Individual'naya Trudovaya Deyatel'nost' [*Individual Labor Activity*] [*Government program designed to foster private enterprise*] [*Russian*] .... ITD
Individuals .... idv
Individuals for a Rational Society [*Defunct*] (EA) .... IFRS
Individuals with Disabilities Education Act [*Formerly, The Education for All Handicapped Children Act*] (PAZ) .... IDEA
Individuelle Quantitative Wert [*Mean Total Ridge Count*] [*Anatomy*] .... IQW
Indivisualized Instruction for Data Access [*Drexel University and Franklin Institute*] [*Education package*] (NITA) .... IIDA
Indo-Africa, Inc. (ECON) .... IAI
Indo-American Chamber of Commerce (PDAA) .... IACC
Indo-American Sports Association [*Later, FIA-USC*] .... IASA
Indo-Aryan [*Linguistics*] .... IA
Indo-British Cultural Exchange .... IBCE
Indochina [*MARC geographic area code Library of Congress*] (LCCP) .... ai----
Indochina IC
Indochina [*or Indochinese*] (WDAA) .... INDOC
Indochina Curriculum Group [*Defunct*] (EA) .... ICG
Indochina Ethnic Chinese Association of Victoria [*Australia*] .... ICECA
Indochina Institute (EA) II
Indochina Postwar Reconstruction .... IPR
Indochina Project [*An association*] (EA) .... IP
Indochina Resource Action Center (EA) .... IRAC
Indo-Chinese Australian Women's Association [*Australia*] .... ICAWA
Indo-Chinese Communist Party [*Vietnam*] [*Political party*] (VNW) .... ICP
Indo-Chinese Elderly Refugee Association of Victoria [*Australia*] .... ICERA-VIC
Indo-Chinese Refugee Association (Victoria) [*Australia*] .... ICRA(V)
Indoctrinate (AABC) .... INDOC
Indoctrination Naval Regional Reporting Center (DNAB) .... INDOCNREGREPCEN
Indocyanine Green [*Liver function test*] [*Medicine*] .... ICG
Indo-European .... IE
Indo-European .... Ind-Eur
Indo-European (ROG) .... INDO-EUR
Indo-European [*MARC language code Library of Congress*] (LCCP) .... ine
Indo-Germanic [*Language, etc.*] .... IG
Indo-Germanic [*Language, etc.*] (ROG) .... INDO-GER
Indogermanische Forschungen [*A publication*] (OCD) .... Indo-Germ Forsch
Indo-Hittite (BJA) .... IH
Indol Glycerophosphate [*Biochemistry*] .... InGP
Indol, Methyl Red, Voges-Proskauer, Citrate Reactions [*Bacteriology*] [*Medicine*] (BABM) .... IMViC
Indolaminergic-Accumulating [*Cytology*] (DAVI) .... IA
Indole, Methyl Red, Voges-Proskauer, Citrate [*Reaction and test*] [*Biochemistry*] (DAVI) .... IMViC
Indole, Methyl-Red, Voges-Proskauer, Citrate Test [*Bacteriology*] .... IMVCi
Indoleacetic Acid [*Plant growth promoter*] .... IAA
Indolebutyric Acid [*Plant growth regulator*] .... IBA
Indoleethanol [*Organic chemistry*] .... IEA
Indoleglycerolphosphate Synthase [*Biochemistry*] .... InGPS
Indomethacin [*An analgesic*] .... IM
Indomethacin [*An analgesic*] .... IND
Indomethacin [*An analgesic*] .... INDO
Indomethacin-Treated Platelet Microsomes .... IPM
Indonesia [*a-pt (Portuguese Timor) used in records cataloged before April 1980*] [*MARC geographic area code Library of Congress*] (LCCP) .... a-io--
Indonesia [*ANSI two-letter standard code*] (CNC) .... ID
Indonesia [*ANSI three-letter standard code*] (CNC) .... IDN
Indonesia .... INDO
Indonesia (BARN) .... Indon
Indonesia [*pt (Portuguese Timor) used in records cataloged before January 1978*] [*MARC country of publication code Library of Congress*] (LCCP) .... io
Indonesia [*IYRU nationality code*] (IYR) .... RI
Indonesia Air Transport PT [*ICAO designator*] (FAAC) .... IDA
Indonesia Fund [*NYSE symbol*] (SPSG) .... IF
Indonesia Fund [*Associated Press*] (SAG) .... Indones
Indonesian [*MARC language code Library of Congress*] (LCCP) .... ind
Indonesian Air Force .... IAF
Indonesian Aquatic Sciences Fisheries Information System [*Marine science*] (OSRA) .... INFIS
Indonesian Commodity Exchange Board [*Badan Pelaksana Bursa Komoditi*] [*Indonesia*] (FEA) .... ICEB
Indonesian Communist Party [*Political party*] .... IKP
Indonesian Documentation and Information Centre [*Leiden, Netherlands*] (EAIO) .... INDOC
Indonesian Institute of Sciences [*Marine science*] (OSRA) .... LIPI
Indonesian Muslim Intellectuals Association [*Political party*] (EY) .... ICMI
Indonesian Satellite Corp. [*NYSE symbol*] (SAG) .... IIT
Indonesian Satellite Corp. [*Associated Press*] (SAG) .... IndoSatel
Indonesian Students Association in the United States (EA) .... ISAUS
Indonesian Telekomunikas [*Associated Press*] (SAG) .... IndoTel
Indonesian Telekomunikas [*NYSE symbol*] (SAG) .... TLK
Indonesian Wildlife Forum [*Indonesia*] (EERA) .... WAHLI
Indonesian-British Association (DS) .... IBA
Indoor Air Pollution .... IAP
Indoor Air Quality .... IAQ
Indoor Citrus and Rare Fruit Society [*Defunct*] (EA) .... IC & RFS
Indoor Cricket Victoria [*Australia An association*] ICV
Indoor Gardening Society of America (EA) .... IGSA
Indoor Light Gardening Society of America (EA) .... ILGSA
Indoor Simulated Marksmanship Trainer [*Military*] .... ISMT
Indoor Sports Club (EA) .... ISC
Indoor Tennis Association [*Later, NTA*] (EA) .... ITA
Indoor Testing Range [*Golf*] (PS) .... ITR
Indoors (ROG) .... IND
Indo-Pacific Council of the International Committee of Scientific Management .... IPCCIOS
Indo-Pacific Fisheries Commission [*or Council*] [*FAO ICSU Bangkok, Thailand*] [*United Nations*] (ASF) .... IPFC
Indo-Pacific Fishery Commission (EAIO) .... IPFC
Indo-Pacific International [*ICAO designator*] (AD) .... JP
Indo-Pacific Sea Level Network [*Marine science*] (OSRA) .... IPSLN
Indo-Pacific Sea Level Network (USDC) .... IPSLN
Indo-Pacific Theosophical Federation (EAIO) .... IPTF
Indophenol Oxidase [*An enzyme*] .... IPO
Indore [*India*] [*Airport symbol*] (OAG) .... IDR
Indore [*India*] [*Airport symbol*] (AD) .... IDR
Indore [*India*] [*ICAO location identifier*] (ICLI) .... VAID
Indore Mill Mazdoor Sangh [*Indore Textile Labour Association*] [*India*] .... IMMS
Indorse [*Legal term*] (AABC) .... IND
Indorsement Irregular [*Banking*] .... I/I
Indo-West Pacific [*Biogeographic region*] .... IWP
Indstrie Natuzzi ADS [*NYSE symbol*] (TTSB) .... NTZ
Induced Circular Dichroism [*Physics*] .... ICD
Induced Contamination Experimental Monitor (MCD) .... ICEM
Induced Course Load Matrix (PDAA) .... ICLM
Induced Dipole Moment .... IDM
Induced Directional FM .... IDFM
Induced Draft .... ID
Induced Electrical Effect .... IEE
Induced Electromagnetic Pulse (RDA) .... IEMP
Induced Electron Emission .... IEE
Induced Environmental Contamination Monitor (MCD) .... IECM
Induced Fluid Flow .... IFF
Induced Magnetization .... IM
Induced Muscular Tension [*Physiology*] .... IMT
Induced Nuclear Disintegration .... IND
Induced Polarization [*Geophysical prospecting*] .... IP
Induced Protein [*Biochemistry*] (DAVI) .... IP
Induced Psycho-Intellectual Activity (PDAA) .... IPIA
Induced Pulse Transient (PDAA) .... INPUT
Induced Radiation Flux .... IRF
Induced Remanent Magnetization .... IRM
Induced Spatial Incoherence [*Physics*] .... ISI
Induced Sputum [*Otorhinolaryngology*] (DAVI) .... IS
Induced Surface Effect .... ISE
Induced-Air Flotation [*Chemical engineering*] .... IAF
Inducible Cell Adhesion Molecule [*Immunochemistry*] .... INCAM
Inducing Resistance Factor [*Plant pathology*] .... IRF
Induct Vent IV
Inductance [*Electromagnetism*] (IAA) .... ID
Inductance .... IND
Inductance (IDOE) .... ind
Inductance [*Symbol*] (AAG) L
Inductance/Capacitance (AAG) .... L/C
Inductance Decade Box .... IDB
Inductance Regulator (IEEE) .... INDREG
Inductance, Resistance, Capacitance [*Electronics*] (BARN) .... IRC
Inductance-Capacitance IC
Inductance-Capacitance-Resistance .... ICR
Inductance-Capacitance-Resistance (CET) .... LCR
Inducted [*Army*] .... Indctd
Inductee Special Assignment .... ISA
Induction I
Induction (MSA) .... IND
Induction .... INDN
Induction (DNAB) .... INDT
Induction (AABC) .... INDUC
Induction and Recruiting Station [*Marine Corps*] .... IRS
Induction Balance (ADA) .... IB
Induction Brazing .... IB
Induction Certificate Examination [*British Institute of Innkeeping*] .... ICE
Induction Communications System .... ICS
Induction Compass .... ICMPS
Induction Field Locator (IAA) .... IFL
Induction Heating Stress Improvement [*Nuclear energy*] (NUCP) .... IHSI
Induction Ion LASER IIL
Induction Loop Communications System .... ILCS
Induction Neutralizing Transformer [*Computer science*] .... INT
Induction of Labor [*Obstetrics*] (DMAA) .... IOL
Induction of Psychoneuroses by Conditioned Reflex under Stress [*In book and film "The Ipcress File"*] .... IPCRESS
Induction Output Tube .... IOT
Induction Period [*Medicine*] .... IP
Induction Plasma Gun .... IPG
Induction Plasma Torch .... IPT
Induction Soldering .... IS
Induction System Deposit .... ISD
Induction Tube Modulation .... ITM
Induction Welding .... IW
Induction-Conduction Heating .... ICH
Induction-Delivery Interval [*Medicine*] .... IDI
Inductive Coupling IC
Inductive Data Exploration and Analysis [*Computer science*] .... IDEA
Inductive Energy Storage .... IES
Inductive Energy Storage Modulator .... IESM
Inductive Loop Detector .... ILD
Inductive Loss Factor (IEEE) .... ILF
Inductive Null Voltage .... INV

Inductive Potential Divider [Electronics] (ECII) .... IPOT
Inductive Potentiometer (MDG) .... IPOT
Inductive Reactance (IDOE) .... X_L
Inductive Recording Head .... IRH
Inductive Storage Switch .... ISS
Inductive Voltage Divider [Electromagnetism] (IAA) .... IVD
Inductively Coupled Argon Plasma [Spectrometry] .... ICAP
Inductively Coupled Plasma [Spectrometry] .... ICP
Inductively Coupled Plasma [Chemical analysis] .... ICP
Inductively Coupled Plasma - Atomic Emission Spectrometry [See also ICPES] .... ICP-AES
Inductively Coupled Plasma Emission Spectrometry [See also ICP-AES] .... ICPES
Inductively Coupled Plasma - Mass Spectrometry .... ICP-MS
Inductively Coupled Plasma - Optical Emission Spectrometry .... ICP-OES
Inductor (MSA) .... IDCTR
Inductor (IDOE) .... ind
Inducto-Ratio Bridge .... IRB
Inductosyn .... ISYN
Inductosyn Angle Position Simulator .... IAPS
Inductosyn Linearity Checkout Kit .... ILCK
Indulin Agar [Microbiology] .... IA
Indus [Constellation] .... Ind
Indus [Constellation] .... Indi
Indus Electronic, Winnipeg, Manitoba [Library symbol National Library of Canada] (NLC) .... MWIE
Indus Electronic, Winnipeg, MB, Canada [Library symbol Library of Congress] (LCLS) .... CaMWIE
Indus Group [NASDAQ symbol] (TTSB) .... IGRP
Indus Group, Inc. (The) [NASDAQ symbol] (SAG) .... IGRP
Indus Group, Inc. (The) [Associated Press] (SAG) .... IndusG
Indus School, Birchdale, MN [Library symbol] [Library of Congress] (LCLS) .... MnBirIS
Indus Tsangpo Suture [Paleogeography] .... ITS
Indusmin Ltd. [Toronto Stock Exchange symbol] .... IML
Industir-Matematik International Corp. [NASDAQ symbol] (SAG) .... IMIC
Industir-Matematik International Corp. [Associated Press] (SAG) .... IndusMt
Industri Pesawat Terbang Nusantara PT [Indonesia] [ICAO designator] (FAAC) .... IPN
Industria Brasileira de Produtos Eletronicos e Electricos, SA .... IBRAPE
Industria del Hierro [Part of a large Mexican industrial complex] .... I/H
Industria Machine Electroniche [Computer manufacturer] [Italy] (NITA) .... IME
Industrial I
Industrial .... IND
Industrial (DD) .... ind
Industrial (WDMC) .... ind
Industrial .... IND
Industrial (MSA) .... INDL
Industrial (WGA) .... INDSL
Industrial [or Industry] .... INDUST
Industrial .... INDUSTL
Industrial (ROG) .... INDUSTR
Industrial Accident Board .... IAB
Industrial Accident Commission Decisions [A publication] (DLA) .... IAC
Industrial Accident Prevention Association [Canada] (HGAA) .... IAPA
Industrial Accountable Property Officer [Air Force] .... IAPO
Industrial Acoustics Co., Inc. [NASDAQ symbol] (NQ) .... IACI
Industrial Acoustics Co., Inc. [Associated Press] (SAG) .... InAcous
Industrial Administration (DD) .... IndAdmin
Industrial Advertising Research Institute [Later, CMC] (EA) .... IARI
Industrial Advisers to the Blind Ltd. [British] (BI) .... IAB
Industrial Advisory Board [World War II] .... IAB
Industrial Aerodynamics Information Service [British] (IID) .... IAIS
Industrial Air Filtration .... IAF
Industrial Air Pollution Inspectorate (PDAA) .... IAPI
Industrial Analysis and Control Council .... IACC
Industrial Analytical Instrumentation Group (ACII) .... IAIG
Industrial and Commercial Bank [China] .... ICB
Industrial and Commercial Company ICC
Industrial and Commercial Development Corp. [Kenya] .... ICDC
Industrial and Commercial Finance Corp. [British] .... ICFC
Industrial and Commercial Power Systems (MCD) .... ICPS
Industrial and Construction Equipment Division (EA) .... ICED
Industrial and Entertainment Funds [Correctional institutions] .... I & E
Industrial and Extractive Processes Division [Environmental Protection Agency] (EPA) .... IEPD
Industrial and Institutional [Business term] .... I & I
Industrial and Institutional [Waste] (GAAI) .... I/I
Industrial and Intellectual Property in Australia [A publication] (DLA) .... Ind & Intell Prop Aust
Industrial and Labor Relations .... ILR
Industrial and Labor Relations Review [A publication] (DLA) .... ILR Rev
Industrial and Labor Relations Review [A publication] (BRI) .... ILRR
Industrial and Labor Relations Review [A publication] (AAGC) .... Indus & Lab Rel Rev
Industrial & Materials Technologies (ACII) .... IMT
Industrial and Mining Standard [A publication] .... Ind Mining Stand
Industrial and Occupational Knowledge (AIE) .... IOK
Industrial and Operations Engineer (PGP) .... IOE
Industrial and Pastoral Holdings (ADA) .... IPH
Industrial and Performance Technology [Human performance analysis] .... IPT
Industrial and Technological Information Bank [UNIDO] (IID) .... INTIB
Industrial and Trade Fairs Ltd. [Solihull, West Midlands, England] (TSSD) .... ITF
Industrial Appointment Full Time [Chiropody] [British] .... IF
Industrial Arbitration Board [British] .... IAB

Industrial Arbitration Registrars' Association [Australia] .... IARA
Industrial Arbitration Reports, New South Wales (Australia) [A publication] (ILCA) .... AR Austrl
Industrial Areas Foundation (EA) .... IAF
Industrial Arts (OICC) .... IA
Industrial Arts and Vocational Education (AEBS) .... IAVE
Industrial Arts Curriculum Project [Education] (AEE) .... IACP
Industrial Association of Juvenile Apparel Manufacturers (EA) .... IAJAM
Industrial Audio-Visual Association [Later, AVMA] (EA) .... IAVA
Industrial Australian and Mining Standard [A publication] .... Indust Austn & Mining Std
Industrial Awards Recommendations [New Zealand] [A publication] (DLA) .... Ind Awards
Industrial Bancorp [NASDAQ symbol] (TTSB) .... INBI
Industrial Bancorp, Inc. [NASDAQ symbol] (SAG) .... INBI
Industrial Bancorp, Inc. [Associated Press] (SAG) .... IndsBc
Industrial Bank of Japan .... IBJ
Industrial Bank of Japan Database [Originator and databank on trade and economics] [Japan] (NITA) .... IBJ Data
Industrial Bank of Japan International Ltd. (ECON) .... IBJI
[The] Industrial Bank of Kuwait .... IBK
Industrial Bankers' Association [British] (BI) .... IBA
Industrial Base Engineering Activity (RDA) .... IBEA
Industrial Base Program .... IBP
Industrial Biotechnology Association (EA) .... IBA
Industrial Bio-Test Laboratories, Inc. .... IBT
Industrial Bulletin [A publication] (DLA) .... Indust Bull
Industrial Business [Insurance term] [British] .... IB
Industrial Capacity Committee of the Production Council [British World War II] ICC
Industrial Cases Reports [Law reports] [British] (DCTA) .... ICR
Industrial Cases Reports [Law reports] [British] (DLA) .... Indus Cas R
Industrial Catering Association [British] .... ICA
Industrial Central Atmosphere Monitoring System [Perkin Elmer Corp.] [Computer controlled chemical detection system] (NITA) .... ICAMS
Industrial Chemical Research Association (EA) .... ICRA
Industrial Christian Fellowship [British] (DBA) .... ICF
Industrial Civil Defence Association [British] (BI) .... ICDA
Industrial Civil Defense Management .... ICDM
Industrial Cleaning Machine Manufacturers Association [British] (DBA) .... ICMMA
Industrial College of the Armed Forces (DOMA) .... ICAF
[The] Industrial College of the Armed Forces [Later, UND] .... ICAF
[The] Industrial College of the Armed Forces [Later, UND] .... TICAF
Industrial Combustion Emissions Model [Environmental Protection Agency] (GFGA) .... ICE
Industrial/Commercial .... I/C
Industrial, Commercial, and Institutional Accountant (DD) .... ICIA
Industrial Common Ownership Finance [An association British] .... ICOF
Industrial Common Ownership Movement [British] .... ICOM
Industrial Communication Council ICC
Industrial Communications Association (HGAA) .... ICA
Industrial Compressor Distributors Association (EA) .... ICDA
Industrial Computer Enclosure (IAA) .... ICE
Industrial Concentration (MHDB) IC
Industrial Control (IAA) .... ICTL
Industrial Control Center (NITA) ICC
Industrial Control Products (MCD) .... ICP
Industrial Control System .... ICS
Industrial Control Unit (IAA) .... ICU
Industrial Cooperation Division [Navy] .... ICD
Industrial Cooperative Association (EA) .... ICA
Industrial Copyright Reform Association [British] (DBA) .... ICRA
Industrial Cost and Performance Report (NG) .... ICPR
Industrial Cost Exclusion [Amendment to Federal Clean Water Act which limits use of federal money] .... ICE
Industrial Cost Recovery [Environmental Protection Agency] .... ICR
Industrial Council for Educational Training Technology [British] (DS) .... ICETT
Industrial Coupling Program [Refers to university-industry interaction] .... ICP
Industrial Court (DLA) IC
Industrial Court Awards [England] [A publication] (DLA) .... Ind C Aw
Industrial Court Awards [England] [A publication] (DLA) .... Ind Court Aw
Industrial Court Awards [England] [A publication] (DLA) .... Ind Ct Awards
Industrial Court Awards [England] [A publication] (DLA) .... Indust C Aw
Industrial Court Awards [England] [A publication] (DLA) .... Indust Ct Aw
Industrial Court Reports [England] [A publication] (DLA) .... ICR
Industrial Credit & Investment Corp. of India Ltd. ICICI
Industrial Damage Reports [Formerly, ITR] [British World War II] .... IDR
Industrial Data Acquisition and Control [Computer science] (MHDI) .... INDAC
Industrial Data Acquisition Control (IAA) .... IDAC
Industrial Data Acquisition System (IAA) .... IDAS
Industrial Data Bank Department [Gulf Organization for Industrial Consulting] [Qatar] [Information service or system] (IID) .... IDB
Industrial Data Processing .... IDP
Industrial Data Reduction (MUGU) .... IDR
Industrial Data Terminal .... IDT
Industrial Data Terminals Corporation (NITA) .... IDT
Industrial Democracy .... ID
Industrial Democracy and Personnel Development .... ID & PD
Industrial Design (WGA) .... ID
Industrial Design Assistance Program [National Design Council, Canada] .... IDAP
Industrial Design Award .... IDA
Industrial Design Certificate [British] .... IDC
Industrial Design Corp., Portland, OR [Library symbol] [Library of Congress] (LCLS) .... OrIPID
Industrial Design Excellence Award .... IDEA

Industrial Designers' Institute [*Later, IDSA*] (EA) .... IDI
Industrial Designers' Society of America (EA) .... IDSA
Industrial Development .... ID
Industrial Development Abstracts [*Database*] [*UNIDO*] (CRD) .... IDA
Industrial Development Advisory Board [*British*] .... IDAB
Industrial Development Authority [*Ireland*] .... IDA
Industrial Development Bank [*Jordan*] .... IDB
Industrial Development Bank [*Kenya*] (IMH) .... IDB
Industrial Development Bank of India (ECON) .... IDBI
Industrial Development Bank of Israel (IMH) .... IDBI
Industrial Development Bank of Turkey (PDAA) .... IDBT
Industrial Development Board [*Northern Ireland*] (GEA) .... IDB
Industrial Development Bond .... IDB
Industrial Development Center for Arab States [*Later, AIDO*] .... IDCAS
Industrial Development Certificate [*Department of Industry*] [*British*] .... IDC
Industrial Development Corp. .... IDC
Industrial Development Department, Alberta Research Council, Calgary, Alberta [*Library symbol National Library of Canada*] (BIB) .... ACRI
Industrial Development Division [*Vietnam*] .... IDD
Industrial Development Group (MCD) .... IDG
Industrial Development Institute [*France*] .... IDI
Industrial Development Office, National Research Council Canada [*Bureau du Developpement Industriel, Conseil National de Recherches Canada*], Scarborough, Ontario [*Library symbol National Library of Canada*] (NLC) .... OTNI
Industrial Development Organization [*United Nations*] .... IDO
Industrial Development Quotient .... IDQ
Industrial Development Research Council (EA) .... IDRC
Industrial Development Revenue Bond [*Investment term*] .... IDR
Industrial Development Unit (IEEE) .... IDU
Industrial Diamond Association of America (EA) .... IDA
Industrial Diamond Association of America .... IDAA
Industrial Diamond Information Bureau [*British*] (BI) .... IDIB
Industrial Diesel Fuel .... IDF
Industrial Diesel Oil (ADA) .... IDO
Industrial Disease Standards Panel, Toronto, Ontario [*Library symbol National Library of Canada*] (BIB) .... OTID
Industrial Disputers Tribunal [*British*] .... IDT
Industrial Disputes Investigation Act [*Canada*] .... IDIA
Industrial Documentation and Information Department [*Industrial Development Center for Arab States*] [*Information service or system*] (IID) .... IDID
Industrial Dynamics [*Management analysis*] .... ID
Industrial Editors Association .... IEA
Industrial Education Institute .... IEI
Industrial Electrification Council [*Later, TEC*] (EA) .... IEC
Industrial Electronic Engineer (IAA) .... IEE
Industrial Electronic Security (AABC) .... INDELSEC
Industrial Electronic System (EA) .... IES
Industrial Electronics (MCD) .... IE
Industrial Electronics and Control Instrumentation (MCD) .... IECI
Industrial Electronics Group [*of General Motors Corp.*] .... IEG
Industrial Energy Conservation (ODBW) .... IEC
Industrial Energy Conservation Abstracts [*UNIDO*] [*United Nations*] (DUND) .... INECA
Industrial Engineer [*or Engineering*] .... IE
Industrial Engineer .... Ind E
Industrial Engineer for Management .... IEM
Industrial Engineering (DD) .... IndEng
Industrial Engineering 1922-1931 (New York) [*A publication*] .... Ind Eng 1922-1931 (NY)
Industrial Engineering Activity [*Army*] (AAGC) .... IEA
Industrial Engineering Institute .... IEI
Industrial Engineering Services .... IES
Industrial Engineering Standard (MCD) .... IES
Industrial Environmental Research Laboratory [*Environmental Protection Agency*] .... IERL
Industrial Equipment Manufacturers Council [*Later, ICED*] (EA) .... IEMC
Industrial Equipment Reserve .... IER
Industrial Equipment Reserve Committee (SAA) .... IERC
Industrial Evaluation Board [*BDSA*] .... IEB
Industrial Fabrics Association International (EA) .... IFAI
Industrial Facilities and Material Information System .... IFMIS
Industrial Facilities Handbook [*A publication*] (AAGC) .... IFH
Industrial Facilities Protection Program [*DoD*] .... IFPP
Industrial Fasteners Institute (EA) .... IFI
Industrial Field Trip (DOMA) .... IFT
Industrial Finance and Investment Corp. [*British*] .... IFICO
Industrial Finishing Equipment Manufacturers Association (EA) .... IFEMA
Industrial Fire Protection Association of Great Britain .... IFPA
Industrial Fire Safety Library [*National Fire Protection Association*] .... IFSL
Industrial Forecast Requirements (DNAB) .... IFREQ
Industrial Forestry Association [*Later, NFA*] (EA) .... IFA
Industrial Frequency Changer .... IFC
Industrial Fuel Choice Analysis Model [*Environmental Protection Agency*] (GFGA) .... IFCAM
Industrial Fugitive Process Particulate (GNE) .... IFPP
Industrial Fund (AFM) .... IF
Industrial Funding Corp. [*NASDAQ symbol*] (NQ) .... IFDC
Industrial Funding Corp. [*Associated Press*] (SAG) .... IndFdg
Industrial Funding Fee (AAGC) .... IFF
Industrial Gas Cleaning Institute (EA) .... IGCI
Industrial Grade .... IG
Industrial Grain Products Ltd., Montreal, PQ, Canada [*Library symbol Library of Congress*] (LCLS) .... CaQMIG

Industrial Grain Products Ltd., Montreal, Quebec [*Library symbol National Library of Canada*] (NLC) .... QMIG
Industrial Graphics International [*Later, IG*] [*An association*] (EA) .... IGI
Industrial Guest Investigator [*NASA*] .... IGI
Industrial Health (DD) .... IndHealth
Industrial Health Advisory Council [*British*] .... IHAC
Industrial Health and Hazards Update [*Merton Allen Associates*] [*Information service or system*] (CRD) .... IH & HU
Industrial Health Foundation (EA) .... IHF
Industrial Health Research Board [*British*] .... IHRB
Industrial Heating Equipment Association (EA) .... IHEA
Industrial Hldgs Wrrt'B' [*NASDAQ symbol*] (TTSB) .... IHIIZ
Industrial Holdgs Wrrt'A' [*NASDAQ symbol*] (TTSB) .... IHIIW
Industrial Holdings [*NASDAQ symbol*] (TTSB) .... IHII
Industrial Holdings, Inc. [*NASDAQ symbol*] (SAG) .... IHII
Industrial Holdings, Inc. [*Associated Press*] (SAG) .... IndH
Industrial Holdings, Inc. [*Associated Press*] (SAG) .... IndusHld
Industrial Holdings, Inc. [*Associated Press*] (SAG) .... InHld
Industrial House (ROG) .... IH
Industrial Hygiene Foundation of America .... IHF
Industrial Hygienist [*Occupational Safety and Health Administration*] .... IH
Industrial Incentive Plan [*NAVFAC*] (DNAB) .... IIP
Industrial Indemnity Co., San Francisco, CA [*Library symbol Library of Congress*] (LCLS) .... CSfII
Industrial Information, Alberta Research Council, Edmonton, Alberta [*Library symbol National Library of Canada*] (NLC) .... AERIS
Industrial Information and Advisory Services [*UNIDO*] (IID) .... INDIS
Industrial Information Bulletin [*A publication*] .... IIB
Industrial Information Services [*Southern Methodist University*] [*Dallas, TX*] .... IIS
Industrial Information System [*UN Industrial Development Organization*] (NITA) .... INDIS
Industrial Information Transfer (NITA) .... IIT
Industrial Information's Record Management System [*Computer science*] .... IIRMS
Industrial Injuries Advisory Council [*British*] (DCTA) .... IIAC
Industrial Intelligence Centre [*British World War II*] IIC
Industrial Jacks Product Section of the Material Handling Institute [*Defunct*] (EA) .... IJPSMHI
Industrial Labor Relations Office [*DoD*] .... ILRO
Industrial Land Development Subcommittee [*New South Wales, Australia*] .... ILDSC
Industrial Lands Development Authority [*Australia*] .... ILDA
Industrial Language Training Service [*British*] .... ILTS
Industrial Launch Vehicle ILV
Industrial Law Review [*A publication*] (ILCA) .... ILR
Industrial Law Review [*A publication*] (ILCA) .... Ind LR
Industrial Law Review [*A publication*] (DLA) .... Indus L Rev
Industrial Law Review [*A publication*] (DLA) .... Indust L Rev
Industrial Law Review [*A publication*] (DLA) .... Indust Law Rev
Industrial Learning Modules (ACII) .... ILM
Industrial Leathers Federation [*British*] (BI) .... ILF
Industrial Liaison Centre [*British*] ILC
Industrial Liaison Organization [*MIT*] .... ILO
Industrial Liaison Program [*Refers to university-industry interaction*] .... ILP
Industrial Liaison Technical Officer [*British*] (DI) .... ILTO
Industrial Life Offices Association [*British*] (BI) .... ILOA
Industrial Lift and Loading Ramp Institute [*Defunct*] (EA) .... ILLRI
Industrial Light Magic [*Electronics Commercial firm*] .... ILM
Industrial Lighting Distributors of America (EA) .... ILDA
Industrial Local Area Network [*Telecommunications*] (OSI) .... ILAN
Industrial Local Area Network (NITA) .... ILAN
Industrial Location Planning System [*Department of Commerce*] (GFGA) ..... ILPS
Industrial Locomotive Society [*British*] .... ILS
Industrial Management Assistance Survey [*Air Force*] .... IMAS
Industrial Management Improvement Program (NG) .... IMIP
Industrial Management Program .... IMP
Industrial Management Qualification .... IMQ
Industrial Management Society (EA) .... IMS
Industrial Manager .... IM
Industrial Manager .... INDMAN
Industrial Manager .... INDMGR
Industrial Marketing Associates (EA) .... IMA
Industrial Marketing Research Association [*British*] .... IMRA
Industrial Materials Handling Equipment .... IMHE
Industrial Mathematics Society (EA) .... IMS
Industrial Measurement Systems/ Institute of Manpower Studies [*British*]..... IMS
Industrial Medical Administrators' Association [*Later, OMAA*] (EA) .... IMAA
Industrial Medical Association [*Later, AOMA*] (EA) .... IMA
Industrial Medicine (DAVI) .... IM
Industrial Medicine (DMAA) .... IND
Industrial Membrane Processing [*Chemical engineering*] .... IMP
Industrial Metal Containers Section of the Material Handling Institute (EA) .... IMC
Industrial Metal Containers Section of the Material Handling Institute (EA) .... IMCSMHI
Industrial Methylated Spirit .... IMS
Industrial Microcomputer .... IMC
Industrial Microfilm Co., Detroit, MI [*Library symbol Library of Congress*] (LCLS) .... ImC
Industrial Mineral Insulation Manufacturers Institute [*Later, TIMA*] .... IMIMI
Industrial Mineral Service [*Midland, ON*] .... INDUSMIN
Industrial Mobilization Planning .... IMP
Industrial Mobilization Production Planning [*DoD*] .... IMPP
Industrial Mobilization Training Program .... IMTP
Industrial Model Vocational Training Systems (EDAC) .... IMVTS

Industrial Models and Patterns [A publication] (EAAP) .... IMP
Industrial Modernization Improvement Plan [DoD] (RDA) .... IMIP
Industrial Modernization Incentive Program [DoD] .... IMIP
Industrial Multilevel Process Analysis and Control (IAA) .... IMPAC
Industrial Naval Air Stations (NG) .... INAS
Industrial Networking, Inc. [Joint venture of Ungermann-Bass, Inc. and
  General Electric Corp.] .... INI
Industrial Oil Consumers Group (EA) .... IOCG
Industrial Operations (MCD) .... IO
Industrial Order of Battle (MCD) .... IOB
Industrial Painters Group [British] (BI) .... IPG
Industrial Participation [Civil Defense] .... IP
Industrial Participation Association [British] .... IPA
Industrial Partnering Program [Department of Energy] .... IPP
Industrial Perforators Association (EA) .... IPA
Industrial Personal Computer (NITA) .... IPC
Industrial Pest Control Association [British] (BI) .... IPCA
Industrial Photographers Association of America [Later, Industrial
  Photographers of New Jersey] (EA) .... IPAA
Industrial Photographers of New Jersey (EA) .... IPNJ
Industrial Physics Group [University of Essex] [British] (IRUK) .... IPG
Industrial Planning .... IP
Industrial Planning Committee [NATO] (NATG) .... IPC
Industrial Planning Specification .... IPS
Industrial Plant [or Production] Equipment .... IPE
Industrial Plant Equipment Reutilization System [DoD] .... IPERS
Industrial Plant Modernization Program [Air Force] .... IPMP
Industrial Platinum Resistance Thermometer (PDAA) .... IPRT
Industrial Police .... IP
Industrial Police and Security Association [British] (BI) .... IPSA
Industrial Policy .... IP
Industrial Policy Council [Washington, DC] (EA) .... IPC
Industrial Power Tube .... IPT
Industrial Premises [Public-performance tariff] [British] I
Industrial Preparedness Measures .... IPM
Industrial Preparedness Planning [DoD] .... IPP
Industrial Preparedness Planning List .... IPPL
Industrial Preparedness Production Planning [DOD] (AAGC) .... IPPP
Industrial Preparedness Program [DOD] (AAGC) .... IPP
Industrial Process Control [by computers] .... IPC
Industrial Process Heat .... IPH
Industrial Production .... IP
Industrial Production Equipment Reserve (NG) .... IPER
Industrial Production Index (PDAA) .... IPI
Industrial Production Performance Reporting .... IPPR
Industrial Programmable Controller (IAA) .... IPC
Industrial Progress and Development [A publication] .... Ind Prog Dev
Industrial Property [Legal term] (DLA) .... Ind Prop
Industrial Property [Legal term] (DLA) .... Indust Prop
Industrial Property Administration .... IPA
Industrial Property Committee [US Military Government, Germany] .... IPC
Industrial Property Organization for English-Speaking Africa [Nairobi,
  Kenya] (EAIO) .... ESARIPO
Industrial Property Policy Program [Insurance] .... IPPP
Industrial Property Quarterly [A publication] (DLA) .... Ind Prop Q
Industrial Property Quarterly [A publication] (DLA) .... Indust Prop Q
Industrial Property Quarterly [A publication] (DLA) .... Industr Prop'y Q
Industrial Property Yearbook [A publication] (DLA) .... Indust Prop'y Yb
Industrial Publicity Association (EA) .... IPA
Industrial Publishing Co. .... IPC
Industrial Quality Control .... IQC
Industrial Quality, Inc. .... IQI
Industrial Quality Management Science [Quality control] .... IQMS
Industrial Raw Materials Planning Committee [NATO] (NATG) ...... IRMPC
Industrial Rayon Corp., Covington, VA [Library symbol Library of Congress]
  (LCLS) .... ViCovI
Industrial Reactor Laboratories [New Jersey] .... IRL
Industrial Readiness and Mobilization Production Planning [Military] .... IRMP
Industrial Readiness Planning [Military] (NG) .... IRP
Industrial Readiness Planning Program .... IRPP
Industrial Reading Test .... IRT
Industrial Readjustment Branch .... IRB
Industrial Regional Development Program [Canada] .... IRDP
Industrial Registry [New South Wales, Australia] .... IR
Industrial Rehabilitation Units [British] .... IRU
Industrial Relations .... IR
Industrial Relations Act [1971] [British] (DCTA) .... IRA
Industrial Relations Advisory Council [Australia] .... IRAC
Industrial Relations, American Labor Arbitration (Prentice-Hall, Inc.)
  [A publication] (DLA) .... P-H Ind Rel Lab Arb
Industrial Relations and Labor Studies Center [University of Maryland]
  [Research center] (RCD) .... IRLSC
Industrial Relations and Personnel Development [A publication] .... IRPD
Industrial Relations Board [Navy] .... IRB
Industrial Relations Bulletin [A publication] (AAG) .... IRB
Industrial Relations Center [University of Minnesota] [Research center]
  (RCD) .... IRC
Industrial Relations Certificate (ODBW) .... IRCert
Industrial Relations Commission of New South Wales [Australia] .... IRCNSW
Industrial Relations Commission of Queensland [Australia] .... IRCQ
Industrial Relations Commission of Victoria [Australia] .... IRCV
Industrial Relations Council for the Plumbing and Pipe Fitting Industry
  [Chicago, IL] (EA) .... IRC
Industrial Relations Council for the Plumbing and Pipe Fitting Industry
  (EA) .... IRCPPFI

Industrial Relations Counselors [New York, NY] (EA) .... IRC
Industrial Relations Counselors, New York, NY [Library symbol Library of
  Congress] (LCLS) .... NNIR
Industrial Relations Guide [A publication] (DLA) .... Indus Rel Guide
Industrial Relations Information Service [Labour Canada] .... IRIS
Industrial Relations: Journal of Economy and Society [A publication]
  (DLA) .... Ind Rel J Econ & Soc
Industrial Relations Law Reports [British] (DCTA) .... IRLR
Industrial Relations Office [Army] .... IRO
Industrial Relations Personnel Record [Military] (DNAB) .... IR-PERS-REC
Industrial Relations Policy Committee [General Council of British Shipping]
  (DS) .... IRPC
Industrial Relations Reform Act [Australia] .... IRRA
Industrial Relations Research Association (EA) .... IRRA
Industrial Relations Research Institute [University of Wisconsin - Madison]
  [Research center] (RCD) .... IRRI
Industrial Relations Review and Report [A publication] .... IRRR
Industrial Relations Section [Princeton University] [Research center] (RCD) .... IRS
Industrial Relations Services [Eclipse Group Ltd.] [British] (ECON) ...... IRS
Industrial Relations, Union Contracts, and Collective Bargaining (Prentice-
  Hall,Inc.) [A publication] (DLA) .... P-H Ind Rel Union Conts
Industrial Reports [Australia A publication] .... IR
Industrial Reprocessing Group (SAA) .... IRG
Industrial Research .... I-R
Industrial Research and Development .... IR & D
Industrial Research and Development Advisory Committee [European
  Union] .... IRDAC
Industrial Research and Development Center [University of Virginia]
  (PDAA) .... IRDC
Industrial Research and Development Investment Assistance [Department
  of Industry] [Canada] (PDAA) .... IRDIA
Industrial Research and Service Institute .... IRSI
Industrial Research Assistance Program [Canada] .... IRAP
Industrial Research Institute [Canada Research center] (RCD) .... IRI
Industrial Research Laboratories [A publication] .... IRL
Industrial Restructuring and Education Network Europe .... IRENE
Industrial Retaining Ring Co. .... IRR
Industrial Revenue Bond .... IRB
Industrial Risk Insurers (EA) .... IRI
Industrial Rope Access Trade Association [British] (DBA) .... IRATA
Industrial Safety Advisory Council [British] .... ISAC
Industrial Safety Equipment Association [Arlington, VA] (EA) .... ISEA
Industrial Safety Office .... ISO
Industrial School [British] (ROG) .... IS
Industrial Scientific [NASDAQ symbol] (TTSB) .... ISCX
Industrial, Scientific, and Medical (IAA) .... ISM
Industrial, Scientific and Medical Applications .... ISM
Industrial Scientific Corp. [Associated Press] (SAG) .... IndSci
Industrial Scientific Corp. [NASDAQ symbol] (SAG) .... ISCX
Industrial Security Acquisition (MCD) .... ISA
Industrial Security Association of Canada .... ISAC
Industrial Security Clearance Review Office [DoD] .... ISCRO
Industrial Security International .... ISI
Industrial Security Letter [DoD] .... ISL
Industrial Security Manual (MCD) .... ISM
Industrial Security Plan [Nuclear energy] (NRCH) .... ISP
Industrial Security Program [Air Force, Army] .... ISP
Industrial Security Regulations [DoD] .... ISR
Industrial Security Section [NATO] (NATG) .... ISS
Industrial Sentence Completion Form [Psychology] .... ISCF
Industrial Service [Equipment specifications] .... IS
Industrial Services of America, Inc. [NASDAQ symbol] (SAG) .... IDSA
Industrial Services of America, Inc. [Associated Press] (SAG) ...... InSrvAm
Industrial Silencer Manufacturers Association (EA) .... ISMA
Industrial Social Welfare Center [Columbia University] [Research center]
  (RCD) .... ISWC
Industrial Society (AIE) .... IS
Industrial Source (GNE) .... IS
Industrial Source Complex [Environmental science] (GFGA) .... ISC
Industrial Source Complex Long-Term Model [Environmental Protection
  Agency] (GFGA) .... ISCLT
Industrial Source Complex Short-Term Model [Environmental Protection
  Agency] (GFGA) .... ISCST
Industrial Source Complex Short-Term Model Version 2 .... ISCST2
Industrial Space Facility [Space Industries, Inc.] .... ISF
Industrial Specialist .... IS
Industrial Specialty Chemical Association (EA) .... ISCA
Industrial Sports Clubs Secretaries' Association [British] (BI) .... ISCSA
Industrial Staffing Plan Occupations (MCD) .... ISPO
Industrial Standards and Military Specifications [Information Handling
  Services] [Information service or system] (CRD) .... ISMS
Industrial Stapling and Nailing Technical Association (EA) .... I-SANTA
Industrial Static Inverter .... ISI
Industrial Support Contractor (KSC) .... ISC
Industrial Systems (DS) .... IS
Industrial Tachometer Generator .... ITG
Industrial Target Report [Later, IDR] [British World War II] .... ITR
Industrial Technical Information Service [Singapore] (IID) .... ITIS
Industrial Technol Wrrt'A' [NASDAQ symbol] (TTSB) .... INTIW
Industrial Technol Wrrt'B' [NASDAQ symbol] (TTSB) .... INTIZ
Industrial Technological Associates, Inc. [Information service or system] .... ITA
Industrial Technologies [NASDAQ symbol] (TTSB) .... INTI
Industrial Technologies, Inc. [Associated Press] (SAG) .... IndTc
Industrial Technologies, Inc. [Associated Press] (SAG) .... IndTech
Industrial Technologies, Inc. [NASDAQ symbol] (SAG) .... INTI

Industrial Technology .... IT
Industrial Technology and Machine Intelligence (NITA) ... ITMI
Industrial Technology Centre [*Manitoba Research Council*] [*Canada Research center*] (RCD) ... ITC
Industrial Technology Division [*Environmental Protection Agency*] (GFGA) ..... ITD
Industrial Technology Fund [*British*] ... ITF
Industrial Technology Institute [*Research center*] (RCD) ... ITI
Industrial Technology Research Institute [*Integrated Circuit Design Centre*] [*Taiwan*] (NITA) ... ITRI
Industrial Technology Securities [*Investment firm*] [*British*] ... ITS
Industrial Television ... ITV
Industrial Television Society [*Later, ITVA*] (EA) ... ITS
Industrial Test Laboratory [*Philadelphia Navy Yard*] [*Navy*] ... ITL
Industrial Therapy Organisation [*British*] ... ITO
Industrial Training ... IT
Industrial Training [*NASDAQ symbol*] (TTSB) ... ITCC
Industrial Training and Research Unit (ACII) ... ITRU
Industrial Training Board [*British*] ... ITB
Industrial Training Corp. [*Associated Press*] (SAG) ... IndTrn
Industrial Training Corp. [*NASDAQ symbol*] (NQ) ... ITCC
Industrial Training Council ... ITC
Industrial Training Opportunities Exhibition (ITD) ... INTO
Industrial Training School [*British*] (ROG) ... I
Industrial Training Service (AIE) ... ITS
Industrial Transistor Value Automatic Computer ... ITVAC
Industrial Tribunal [*British*] (DCTA) ... IT
Industrial Tribunal Reports (DCTA) ... ITR
Industrial TRON (NITA) ... ITRON
Industrial Truck Association [*Washington, DC*] (EA) ... ITA
Industrial Union Department [*of AFL-CIO*] (EA) ... IUD
Industrial Union of Marine and Shipbuilding Workers of America (EA) ... IUMSWA
Industrial Union Party (EA) ... IUP
Industrial Unit of Tribology [*University of Leeds*] [*An association Research center British*] (EA) ... IUT
Industrial Unit, University of Ulster [*British*] (IRUK) ... IUUU
Industrial User (ERG) ... IU
Industrial Vegetation Management Association [*Defunct*] (EA) ... IVMA
Industrial Veterinarians' Association [*Later, AAIV*] (EA) ... IVA
Industrial View Camera ... IVC
Industrial Warm Air Heater Manufacturers ... IWAHMA
Industrial Waste Elimination Research Center [*Illinois Institute of Technology*] [*Research center*] (RCD) ... IWERC
Industrial Waste Filter System (IEEE) ... IWFS
Industrial Waste Management (MCD) ... IWM
Industrial Waste Reduction Program [*Environmental science*] ... IWRP
Industrial Waste Treatment Management (MCD) ... IWT
Industrial Waste Treatment System (NRCH) ... IWTS
Industrial Wastewater Treatment Plant ... IWTT
Industrial Water Conditioning Institute (EA) ... IWCI
Industrial Water Society [*British*] (DBA) ... IWS
Industrial Water Supply ... IWS
Industrial Water System (KSC) ... IWS
Industrial Welfare Society [*British*] (ILCA) ... IWS
Industrial Wire Cloth Institute [*Later, AWCI*] (EA) ... IWCI
Industrial Workers of the World (EA) ... IWW
Industrial X-Ray Film ... IXF
Industrial-Development Revenue Bond [*Issued by a state or local government to finance construction by a private company, which then becomes responsible for repaying the debt*] [*Investment term*] ... IDRB
Industrialist ... Indus
Industrialized Building (PDAA) ... IB
Industrialized Building Systems and Components (IEEE) ... IBSAC
Industrialized Housing Manufacturer's Association (EA) ... IHMA
Industrialk Base Information System (AAGC) ... IBIS
Industrias Titan SA [*Spain ICAO designator*] (FAAC) ... ITN
Industrie Air Charter [*France ICAO designator*] (FAAC) ... IAZ
Industrie Gewerkschaft Chemie, Papier, und Keramik [*West German union*] ... IGCPK
Industrie Natuzzi [*NYSE symbol*] (SPSG) ... NTZ
Industrie Natuzzi SA [*Associated Press*] (SAG) ... IndNatuz
Industriegewerkschaft [*Industrial Trade Union*] [*Germany*] ... IG
Industrielle-Services Techniques Inc. [*Industrial Life-Technical Services Inc.*] [*Information service or system*] (IID) ... IST
Industries & Science Department (ACII) ... I&S
Industries Assistance Commission (EERA) ... IAC
Industries Development Committee ... IDC
Industries Development Strategy ... IDS
Industrija Motornih Vozil [*Yugoslav automaker*] ... IMV
Industrija Nafta [*State-owned company*] [*Yugoslavia*] ... INA
Industriradets Industriregister [*Federation of Danish Industries' Register of Industries*] (EY) ... IREG
Industry (AFM) ... IND
Industry ... INDUS
Industry ... INDUST
Industry Advisory Committee [*World War II*] ... IAC
Industry Advisory Committee on Survey and Mapping [*Queensland*] [*State*] (EERA) ... IAC
Industry Advisory Conference [*Underwriters Laboratories*] [*Telecommunications*] ... IAC
Industry Advisory Council [*Formerly, DIAC*] ... IAC
Industry Advisory Group [*Underwriters Laboratories*] [*Telecommunications*] ... IAG
Industry Advisory Group for Air Logistics ... IAGAL
Industry and Commerce Association of South Dakota (SRA) ... ICA
Industry and Environment Office (GNE) ... IEO

Industry and General Applications (MCD) ... IGA
Industry and Teacher Education Liaison (AIE) ... INDTEL
Industry and Trade Administration [*Later, International Trade Administration*] [*Department of Commerce*] ... ITA
Industry Application (IAA) ... IA
Industry Applications Programs [*Computer science*] (IBMDP) ... IAP
Industry Bar Code Alliance (EA) ... IBCA
Industry Capacity Utilization [*Engineering economics*] ... ICU
Industry Center for Trade Negotiations [*Defunct*] ... ICTN
Industry Coalition for Fire Safety [*Defunct*] (EA) ... ICFS
Industry Coalition on Technology Transfer (EA) ... ICOTT
Industry Committee for Packaging and the Environment [*British*] (DI) ..... INCPEN
Industry Competitive (AFIT) ... IC
Industry Composites and Polymer Processing Program [*Massachusetts Institute of Technology*] [*Research center*] (RCD) ... P3
Industry Cooperative for Ozone Layer Protection ... ICOLP
Industry Cooperative Program [*United Nations*] ... ICP
Industry Council for Tangible Assets [*Washington, DC*] (EA) ... ICTA
Industry Crew Escape Systems Committee ... ICESC
Industry Data Exchange Program ... IDEP
Industry Data Sources [*Information Access Co.*] [*Information service or system*] (CRD) ... IDS
Industry Degraded Core Rulemaking Program [*Nuclear industry sponsored group*] ... IDCOR
Industry Development Arrangement ... IDA
Industry Direct Purchase Manufacturer (AFIT) ... IDPM
Industry Division [*Census*] (OICC) ... IND
Industry, Education Councils of America (OICC) ... IECA
Industry Education Liaison (AIE) ... INDEL
Industry Energy Research and Development Program [*Canada*] ... IERD
Industry File Index System [*Chemical Information Systems, Inc.*] [*Information service or system*] (CRD) ... IFIS
Industry/Government Open Systems Specification (ACRL) ... IGOSS
Industry Large Structures Assembly (SSD) ... ILSA
Industry Launch Service (Cryogenic) (SSD) ... ILS(C)
Industry Launch Services - Storable (SSD) ... ILSS
Industry Manufacturers [*FCC*] (MCD) ... IX
Industry Market Potential [*Business term*] (MHDW) ... IMP
Industry Media Publishing System [*Omni Industry Corp.*] [*Information service or system*] (IID) ... IMPS
Industry Missile and Space Conference ... IMSC
Industry Motion Picture [*FCC*] (MCD) ... IM
Industry Network for Social, Urban, and Rural Efforts ... INSURE
Industry News [*A publication*] ... Ind News
Industry/Occupation (OICC) ... I/O
Industry Planning Council (EA) ... IPC
Industry Planning Representative [*DoD*] ... IPR
Industry Program [*Defense Systems Management College*] (DOMA) ... IP
Industry Recognition Program (MCD) ... IRP
Industry Remarketer (CDE) ... IR
Industry Restructuring Task Force ... IRTF
Industry Satellite Services Facility (SSD) ... ISSF
Industry, Science, and Technology ... IS & T
Industry, Science, and Technology Canada [*Government agency*] ... ISTC
Industry Sector Advisory Committee [*Established by Trade Reform Act for industry-to-government advice*] ... ISAC
Industry Service Bureaus ... ISB
Industry Service Package ... ISP
Industry Sole Source (AFIT) ... ISS
Industry Standard Architecture [*Computer hardware*] (PCM) ... ISA
Industry Standard Item (AAG) ... ISI
Industry Standard Specifications (AAG) ... ISS
Industry Superannuation Property Trust ... ISPT
Industry Technology Group [*Air Force*] (MCD) ... ITG
Industry Telephone Maintenance [*FCC*] (IEEE) ... IT
Industry Test Group [*Air Force*] ... ITG
Industry Training Fund for Women [*Australia*] ... ITFW
Industry Training Support ... ITS
Industry Transistor [*Electronics*] (IAA) ... IT
Industry, TX [*Location identifier FAA*] (FAAL) ... IDU
Industry/University Cooperation Research Center [*National Science Foundation*] ... IUCRC
Industry/University Cooperative Research Center for Software Engineering [*University of Florida, Purdue University*] [*Research center*] (RCD) ... SERC
Industry Working Group ... IWG
Industry-Developed Equipment (AAG) ... IDE
Industry-Labor Council (EA) ... ILC
Industry-Organized Government-Approved ... IOGA
Industry-Wide Bargaining (MHDB) ... IWB
Indwelling Transcutaneous Vascular Access Device [*Pharmacology*] (DAVI) ... ITVAD
Indwelling Venous Catheter [*Medicine*] ... IDVC
Indy Racing League [*Automobile racing*] ... IRL
Ine [*Marshall Islands*] [*Airport symbol*] (OAG) ... IMI
Inedible ... INED
Inedites [*Unpublished*] [*French*] (ROG) ... INED
Ineditus [*Not Made Known*] [*Latin*] ... INED
Ineffective Airway Clearance [*Medicine*] (DMAA) ... IAC
Ineffective Iron Turnover (DMAA) ... IIT
Inefficiency ... INEFFCY
Inefficiency (AABC) ... INEFFY
[*The*] Inefficient-Market Fund [*AMEX symbol*] (SPSG) ... IMF
[*The*] Inefficient-Market Fund [*Associated Press*] (SAG) ... InefMkt
INEL [*Idaho National Engineering Laboratory*] Research Center [*Idaho Falls, ID*] [*Department of Energy*] (GRD) ... IRC

Inel Resources Ltd. [*Vancouver Stock Exchange symbol*] ... ILE
Inelastic Atom Scattering (PDAA) ... IAS
Inelastic Demand (MHDB) ... ID
Inelastic Electron Tunneling Spectroscopy ... IETS
Inelastic Incoherent Neutron Scattering [*Spectrometry*] ... IINS
Inelastic Low-Energy Electron Diffraction (IAA) ... ILEED
Inelastic Mean Free [*or Face*] **Path** [*Surface analysis*] ... IMFP
Inelastic Neutron Scattering ... INS
Inelastic Tunnelling Electron Spectroscopy ... ITES
INELEC Library Project, Menomonie, WI [*Inactive*] [*OCLC symbol*] (OCLC) ... WIN
Ineligible Reserve Section ... IRS
Inequality Constrained Least-Squares [*Statistics*] ... ICLS
Inert Building [*NASA*] (KSC) ... IB
Inert Components Parts Building ... ICPB
Inert Filler ... INRTFLR
Inert Fluid Fill (AAG) ... IFF
Inert Gas ... INRTG
Inert Gas Generator ... IGG
Inert Gas Receiving and Processing (NRCH) ... IGR & P
Inert Gas Receiving and Processing (IAA) ... IGRAP
Inert Gas Receiving and Processing System (NRCH) ... IGRPS
Inert Gas Storage ... IGS
Inert Gas System [*Engineering*] ... IGS
Inert Gas Wire Enamel Stripper (PDAA) ... IGWES
Inert Nitrogen Protection (IEEE) ... INP
Inert Operational Missile (NG) ... IOM
Inert Ordnance Warehouse ... IOW
Inert Processing Building ... IPB
Inertia (AAG) ... I
Inertia (KSC) ... INRT
Inertia Compensated Balance ... ICB
Inertia Fuel Shutoff Switch [*Automotive engineering*] ... IFSS
Inertia Resonance Induction System [*Automotive engineering*] ... IRIS
Inertia Test Weight [*Exhaust emissions*] [*Automotive engineering*] ... ITW
Inertia Weight [*Exhaust emissions*] [*Automotive engineering*] ... IW
Inertial (MCD) ... IN
Inertial (KSC) ... INER
Inertial (MSA) ... INRTL
Inertial Attitude Control System [*Aerospace*] ... IACS
Inertial Component ... IC
Inertial Component Test Equipment ... ICTE
Inertial Components Temperature Controller (KSC) ... ICTC
Inertial Confinement Fusion [*Nuclear physics*] ... ICF
Inertial Confinement Fusion Advisory Committee [*Department of Energy*] ... ICFAC
Inertial Confinement Fusion Reactor [*Nuclear energy*] (MCD) ... ICR
Inertial Coupling Data Unit (NASA) ... ICDU
Inertial Coupling Display Unit (KSC) ... ICDU
Inertial Dampened Servomotor ... IDSM
Inertial Data Box (KSC) ... IDB
Inertial Data System ... IDS
Inertial Doppler Navigation Equipment (DNAB) ... IDNE
Inertial Doppler System ... IDS
Inertial Flight Data System (KSC) ... IFDS
Inertial Guidance ... IG
Inertial Guidance and Calibration Group [*Air Force*] ... IGCG
Inertial Guidance Maintenance Facility (IAA) ... IGMF
Inertial Guidance Mode ... IGM
Inertial Guidance Package ... IGP
Inertial Guidance Platform ... IGP
Inertial Guidance System [*NASA*] ... IGS
Inertial Guidance System Maintenance Area [*Aerospace*] (AAG) ... IGSMA
Inertial Guidance System Simulator [*NASA*] (IAA) ... IGSS
Inertial Guidance Test Center [*Aerospace*] (IAA) ... IGTC
Inertial Gyroscope ... IG
Inertial Height Sensing Device ... IHSD
Inertial Instrument Assembly ... IIA
Inertial Interchange True Polar Wander [*Geophysics*] ... IITPW
Inertial Laboratory [*NASA*] (KSC) ... IL
Inertial Lead Vertical Speed Indicator (IAA) ... IVSI
Inertial Measurement Group (KSC) ... IMG
Inertial Measurement Unit ... IMU
Inertial Measurement Unit Ground Support Equipment (SAA) ... IMUGSE
Inertial Measuring Set [*or System*] (NVT) ... IMS
Inertial Navigation (IAA) ... IN
Inertial Navigation and Attack System (MCD) ... INAS
Inertial Navigation and Guidance [*Aerospace*] (AAG) ... ING
Inertial Navigation and Weapons Attack System (MCD) ... INWAS
Inertial Navigation Computer (MCD) ... INC
Inertial Navigation Equipment (MCD) ... INE
Inertial Navigation Gyro ... ING
Inertial Navigation Measurement Unit (MCD) ... INMU
Inertial Navigation Sensor (IAA) ... INS
Inertial Navigation System [*Aviation*] ... INS
Inertial Navigation Unit ... INU
Inertial Platform ... IP
Inertial Positioning System (PDAA) ... IPS
Inertial Processing (MCD) ... IP
Inertial Quality Attitude ... IQA
Inertial Range Atmospheric Turbulence Entrainment (PDAA) ... IRATE
Inertial Rate Gyro (KSC) ... IRG
Inertial Rate Integrating Gyro (NASA) ... IRIG
Inertial Rate of Descent Sensor (MCD) ... IRODS
Inertial Reactor with Internal Separation [*Coal furnace*] [*Tecogen, Inc.*] ... IRIS
Inertial Reference (MCD) ... INR
Inertial Reference and Control System [*Aerospace*] (AAG) ... IRCS
Inertial Reference Integrating Gyro [*NASA*] (NASA) ... IRIG
Inertial Reference Navigational System ... IRNS
Inertial Reference Package (MCD) ... IRP
Inertial Reference Sensor ... IRS
Inertial Reference Stabilization System ... IRSS
Inertial Reference System [*Aviation*] ... IRS
Inertial Reference Unit ... IRU
Inertial Referenced Flight Inspection System [*Aviation*] (PDAA) ... IRFIS
Inertial Retical System ... IRS
Inertial Sensing Unit ... ISU
Inertial Sensor Assembly [*Military*] (CAAL) ... ISA
Inertial Sensor System (KSC) ... ISS
Inertial Sensor System Breadboard ... ISSBB
Inertial Start Command ... ISC
Inertial Subsystem (MCD) ... ISS
Inertial Systems (AFIT) ... IS
Inertial Systems Laboratory [*NASA*] (GFGA) ... ISL
Inertial Timing Switch (IAA) ... ITS
Inertial Unit Assembly ... IUA
Inertial [*formerly, Interim*] **Upper Stage** [*Air Force*] ... IUS
Inertial Velocity (MCD) ... INRTLVEL
Inertial Velocity ... VI
Inertial Velocity Measurement Unit (IEEE) ... IVMU
Inertial Vertical Speed (GAVI) ... HDOT
Inertial-Command Off-Set System (MCD) ... ICOSS
Inertialess Scanning, Tracking, and Ranging ... INSTAR
Inertialess Steerable Communications Antenna ... ISCAN
Inertia-Measuring Device [*Mechanical engineering*] ... IMD
Inerting and Preheating [*Nuclear energy*] (NRCH) ... I & P
Inerting and Preheating (IAA) ... IAP
Inert-Ion Beam Etching ... IBE
Inex Adria Aviopromet [*Yugoslavia*] [*ICAO designator*] (FAAC) ... IAA
Inexco Oil Co. [*Toronto Stock Exchange symbol*] ... INX
Inexpensive In-Circuit Emulator (NITA) ... INICE
Inexperienced (DAVI) ... INEX
Infamous [*FBI standardized term*] ... INF
Infancy (ROG) ... INFCY
Infancy [*Legal shorthand*] (LWAP) ... INFY
Infant ... INF
Infant ... INFNT
Infant (ROG) ... INFT
Infant and Dietetic Foods Association [*British*] (DBA) ... IDFA
Infant and Juvenile Manufacturers Association (EA) ... IJMA
Infant Care Review Committee [*Medicine*] (DMAA) ... ICRC
Infant Care Unit [*Medicine*] (DMAA) ... ICU
Infant Death (MAE) ... ID
Infant Development Distress Syndrome [*Medicine*] (ADA) ... IDD
Infant Formula Action Coalition (EA) ... INFACT
Infant Formula Council (EA) ... IFC
Infant Health and Development Program ... IHDP
Infant Hypercalcemia [*Medicine*] ... IHC
Infant Intensive Care Unit [*of a hospital*] ... IICU
Infant, Low Birth Weight [*Medicine*] (DMAA) ... ILB
Infant, Low Birth Weight ... ILBW
Infant Mortality (ROG) ... IM
Infant Mortality Rate ... IMR
Infant Mortality Review Team [*Department of Health and Human Services*] (GFGA) ... IMRT
Infant Mortality Risk [*Medicine*] (DMAA) ... IMR
Infant of Diabetic Mother [*Medicine*] ... IDM
Infant of Diabetic Mother [*Neonatology*] (DAVI) ... IODM
Infant of Gestational Diabetic Mother [*Obstetrics*] ... IGDM
Infant of Nondiabetic Mother [*Obstetrics*] ... INDM
Infant of Substance-Abusing Mother [*Pediatrics*] ... ISAM
Infant of Very Low Birth Weight [*Neonatology*] (DAVI) ... IVLBW
Infant Orphan [*British*] (ROG) ... IO
Infant Rating Scale [*Child development test*] ... IRS
Infant Respiratory Distress Syndrome [*Medicine*] ... IRDS
Infant Soy Formula ... ISF
Infant Temperament Questionnaire ... ITQ
Infant Water Loss [*Medicine*] (CPH) ... IWL
Infanterie-Ersatzbataillon [*Infantry Replacement Training Battalion*] [*German military - World War II*] ... IEB
Infanterie-Ersatzregiment [*Infantry Replacement Training Regiment*] [*German military - World War II*] ... IER
Infanteriegeschuetz - Kompanie [*Infantry Howitzer Co.*] [*German military - World War II*] ... IGK
Infanteriegranate [*Infantry Howitzer Shell*] [*German military - World War II*] ... IGR
Infanteriekolonne [*Infantry Supply Column*] [*German military - World War II*] ... IK
Infanterie-Lehrregiment [*Infantry Demonstration Regiment*] [*German military - World War II*] ... ILR
Infantile (CPH) ... INF
Infantile (DMAA) ... inf
Infantile Amaurotic Family Idiocy [*Medicine*] ... IAFI
Infantile Bilateral Striatal Necrosis [*Ophthalmology*] ... IBSN
Infantile Gastroenteritis Virus [*Medicine*] (PDAA) ... IGU
Infantile Genetic Agranulocytosis [*Medicine*] (DMAA) ... IGA
Infantile Myofibromatosus [*Medicine*] ... IM
Infantile Necrotizing Encephalomyelopathy [*Medicine*] (MAE) ... INE
Infantile Neuroaxonal Dystrophy [*Medicine*] (DMAA) ... INAD
Infantile Neuronal Ceroid Lipofuscinoses [*Medicine*] ... INCL
Infantile Nuclear Cerebral Degeneration [*Medicine*] (DMAA) ... INCD
Infantile Periarteritis Nodosa [*Cardiology*] (DAVI) ... IPN
Infantile Polycistic Disease (DAVI) ... IPCD

Infantile Spinal Muscular Atrophy [*Medicine*] (DAVI) .... ISMA
Infantry I
Infantry [*Army*] .... IN
Infantry (AFM) .... INF
Infantry [*British military*] (DMA) .... Infty
Infantry [*British military*] (DMA) .... Infy
Infantry Antiarmor Weapon Systems [*Military*] (INF) .... IAAWS
Infantry Armored Fighting Vehicle (NATG) .... IAFV
Infantry Battalion [*Army*] .... IB
Infantry Battalion [*Army*] .... INFBAT
Infantry Battalion as a Combat System [*Study*] (MCD) .... INBACS
Infantry Brigade [*British military*] (DMA) .... IB
Infantry Combat Developments Agency [*Pronounced "ick-da"*] [*Army*] .... ICDA
Infantry Combat Vehicle (MCD) ICV
Infantry Direct-Fire Simulation System (MCD) .... IDFSS
Infantry Division .... ID
Infantry Division - 1986 .... ID-86
Infantry Division (Light) [*Army*] (INF) .... ID(L)
Infantry Drill Regulations .... IDR
Infantry Fighting Vehicle .... IFV
Infantry Issues and Lessons Learned Analysis System [*Software*] (INF) .... I²L²AS
Infantry LASER Weapon (MCD) .... INLAW
Infantry Leader Course [*Army*] (INF) ILC
Infantry Liaison Team (INF) .... ILT
Infantry Manportable Antiarmor Weapon System .... IMAAWS
Infantry Mortar Leader's Course [*Army*] (INF) .... IMLC
Infantry Mortar Plan (MCD) .... IMP
Infantry Mortar Platoon Course (INF) .... IMPC
Infantry Mortar Program (MCD) .... IMOP
Infantry Moving Target Carrier [*Army*] .... IMTC
Infantry Officer [*British military*] (DMA) .... IO
Infantry Officer Advanced Correspondence Course/Reserve Component
(INF) .... IOAC/RC
Infantry Officer Advanced Course [*Army*] (INF) .... IOAC
Infantry Officer Basic Course [*Army*] .... IOBC
Infantry Officer Basic Course-Reserve Component (INF) .... IOBC-RC
Infantry Officer Career Course [*Army*] .... IOCC
Infantry Officers Training Camp .... IOTC
Infantry Precommand Course [*Army*] (INF) .... IPCC
Infantry Reinforcement Training Depot [*British military*] (DMA) .... IRTD
Infantry Remote Targeting System [*Army*] (RDA) .... IRETS
Infantry Replacement Training Center .... IRTC
Infantry Research and Development Liaison Office [*Army*] (RDA) .... IRDLO
Infantry Reserve Corps (WDAA) .... IRC
Infantry Rifle Unit Study [*Army*] .... IRUS
Infantry Sailing Association [*British*] .... ISA
[*The*] Infantry School [*Army*] (MCD) .... IS
[*The*] Infantry School [*Army*] .... TIS
Infantry Squad Battle Course [*Army*] .... ISBC
Infantry Systems Program Review [*Army*] (AABC) .... ISPR
Infantry Target Mechanism [*Army*] .... ITM
Infantry Training Center [*Army*] .... ITC
Infantry Training Replacement .... ITR
Infantry Trials and Development Unit [*British military*] (DMA) .... ITDU
Infants' and Children's Coat Association [*Later, ICGSCA*] (EA) .... ICCA
Infants' and Children's Novelties Association (EA) .... ICNA
Infants' and Children's Wear Salesmen's Guild (EA) .... ICWSG
Infants', Children's, and Girls' Sportswear and Coat Association (EA) .... ICGSCA
Infants', Children's, and Teens' Wear Buyers Association (EA) .... ICTBA
Infarct Size Index [*Cardiology*] .... ISI
Infared Diving Binoculors (MCD) .... IDB
Infaunal Trophic Index [*Marine pollution*] .... ITI
Infected (CPH) .... inf
Infected Area .... IA
Infection [*Medicine*] .... INF
Infection [*or Infectious*] (DAVI) .... infect
Infection Control (HCT) IC
Infection Efficiency [*Pathology*] .... IE
Infection Potentiating Factor (AAMN) .... IPF
Infection Prevention .... IP
Infection Structure [*Plant pathology*] .... IS
Infection Surveillance and Control Program [*Medicine*] (DMAA) .... ISCP
Infection Type [*Pathology*] .... IT
Infection-Control Practitioner [*Medicine*] .... ICP
Infectious Bovine Keratoconjunctivitis [*Veterinary medicine*] .... IBK
Infectious Bovine Keratoconjunctivitis (PDAA) .... IBKC
Infectious Bovine Rhinotracheitis [*Also, IBRV*] [*Virus*] .... IBR
Infectious Bovine Rhinotracheitis Virus [*Also, IBR*] .... IBRV
Infectious Bronchitis [*Medicine*] .... IB
Infectious Bronchitis Vaccine [*Pharmacology*] (DAVI) .... IBV
Infectious Bronchitis Virus [*Avian*] .... IBV
Infectious Bursal Disease [*Avian pathology*] .... IBD
Infectious Bursal Disease Virus .... IBDV
Infectious Canine Hepatitis [*Veterinary medicine*] .... ICH
Infectious Cell Protein [*Genetics*] .... ICP
Infectious Disease [*Medicine*] .... ID
Infectious Disease (MEDA) .... inf dis
Infectious Disease [*Medicine*] (CPH) .... infec dis
Infectious Disease Service (DAVI) .... IDS
Infectious Diseases Society of America (EA) .... IDSA
Infectious Equine Anemia [*Veterinary medicine*] (DMAA) .... IEA
Infectious Hematopoietic Necrosis [*Fish pathology*] .... IHN
Infectious Hepatitis [*Medicine*] .... IH
Infectious Human Hepatitis [*Medicine*] (DMAA) .... IHH

Infectious Hypodermal and Hematopoietic Necrosis Virus
[*Aquaculture*] .... IHHNV
Infectious Laryngo-Tracheitis [*Medicine*] (ADA) .... ILT
Infectious Mononucleosis [*Medicine*] .... IM
Infectious Mononucleosis [*Medicine*] (MAE) .... inf mono
Infectious Mononucleosis [*Medicine*] (DAVI) .... INFM
Infectious Mononucleosis Receptor [*Biochemistry*] (AAMN) .... IMR
Infectious Nucleic Acid (DMAA) .... INA
Infectious Pancreatic Necrosis [*Medicine*] .... IPN
Infectious Pancreatic Necrosis Virus .... IPNV
Infectious Porcine Encephalomyelitis [*Medicine*] (DMAA) .... IPE
Infectious Pustular Vaginitis [*Medicine*] .... IPV
Infectious Pustular Vulvovaginitis [*Veterinary medicine*] .... IPV
Infectious Unit .... IU
Infectious Waste / Chemotherapeutic Waste .... IW/CW
Infective Dose .... ID
Infective Dose, Median .... ID₅₀
Infective Endocarditis [*Cardiology*] .... IE
Infective Toxic Shock [*Medicine*] (DMAA) .... ITS
Inference (MSA) .... INFRN
Inference Corp. [*Associated Press*] (SAG) .... Infernce
Inference Corp. [*NASDAQ symbol*] (SAG) .... INFR
Inference Corp.'A' [*NASDAQ symbol*] (TTSB) .... INFR
Inference Execution Language .... INFEREX
Inferential Value Testing (KSC) .... IVT
Inferior .... INF
Inferior (WDMC) .... inf
Inferior (ROG) .... INFR
Inferior Angle [*Anatomy*] .... IA
Inferior Colliculus [*Also, ICC*] [*Brain anatomy*] IC
Inferior Colliculus [*Also, IC*] [*Brain anatomy*] ICC
Inferior Colliculus ICX
Inferior Division [*Medicine*] (DAVI) .... ID
Inferior Frontal Gyrus [*Brain anatomy*] .... IFG
Inferior Mesenteric Artery [*Anatomy*] .... IMA
Inferior Mesenteric Ganglia [*Anatomy*] .... IMG
Inferior Mesenteric Vein [*Anatomy*] .... IMV
Inferior Myocardial Infarction [*Cardiology*] .... IMI
Inferior Myocardial Infarction [*Cardiology*] .... Inf MI
Inferior Nasal Artery [*Medicine*] (DMAA) .... INA
Inferior Oblique [*Muscle*] [*Anatomy*] .... IO
Inferior Olivary Nucleus [*Neuroanatomy*] .... ION
Inferior Olive [*Neuroanatomy*] .... IO
Inferior Orbitomeatal Line [*Brain anatomy*] .... IOM
Inferior Parietal Lobule [*Anatomy*] .... IPL
Inferior Point [*of the*] Pubic [*Bone*] [*Anatomy*] (DAVI) .... IPP
Inferior Rectus [*Muscle*] [*Anatomy*] .... IR
Inferior Temporal [*Anatomy*] .... IT
Inferior Temporal Artery [*Medicine*] (DMAA) .... ITA
Inferior Temporal Quadrant [*Medicine*] (DMAA) .... ITQ
Inferior Temporal Vein [*Medicine*] (DMAA) .... ITV
Inferior Thalamic Peduncle [*Anatomy*] .... ITP
Inferior Turbinate [*Otorhinolaryngology*] (DAVI) .... IT
Inferior Tympanic Artery [*Anatomy*] .... ITA
Inferior Vena Cava [*Anatomy*] IVC
Inferior Vena Cava Pressure [*Medicine*] .... IVCP
Inferior Vena Cava Reconstruction [*Medicine*] (DMAA) .... IVCR
Inferior Vena Cava Thrombosis [*Medicine*] (DMAA) .... IVCT
Inferior Venacavogram [*Cardiology*] (DAVI) IVC
Inferior Venacavography [*Medicine*] IVCV
Inferior Wall Myocardial Infarction [*Cardiology*] .... IWMI
Inferolateral Myocardial Infarct [*or Infarction*] [*Cardiology*] (DAVI) .... ILMI
Inferolateral Trunk [*Neuroanatomy*] .... ILT
Inferoposterior Myocardial Infarct [*or Infarction*] [*Cardiology*] (DAVI) .... IPMI
Infertility Associates International [*Commercial firm*] (EA) .... IAI
Infield I
Infield (WGA) .... INF
Infielder [*Position in baseball*] .... IF
Infiltrate [*or Infiltrated*] (DAVI) .... infil
Infiltration and Exfiltration (DOMA) .... INFIL/EXFIL
Infiltration and Inflow [*Environmental science*] (FFDE) .... I & I
Infiltration Surveillance Center (CINC) .... ISC
Infinite (MSA) .... INF
Infinite .... INFINT
Infinite Capitalism [*Book title*] IC
Infinite Impulse Response [*Electronics*] .... IIR
Infinite Machines [*NASDAQ symbol*] (TTSB) .... IMCI
Infinite Machines Corp. [*NASDAQ symbol*] (SAG) .... IMCI
Infinite Machines Corp. [*Associated Press*] (SAG) .... InfMach
Infinite Machines Corp. [*Associated Press*] (SAG) .... InfMch
Infinite Machines Wrrt [*NASDAQ symbol*] (TTSB) .... IMCIW
Infinite Periodic Minimal Surface .... IPMS
Infinite Position Indicator (PDAA) .... IPI
Infinite Resources, Inc. [*Vancouver Stock Exchange symbol*] .... INF
Infinite Time Span .... ITS
Infinite-Duration Impulse (IAA) .... IDR
Infinite-Duration Impulse-Response (IEEE) .... IIR
Infinitely Rigid Beam [*Engineering*] (OA) .... IRB
Infinitely Rigid System [*Engineering*] (OA) .... IRS
Infinitely Variable Transmission [*Automotive engineering*] (PS) .... IVT
Infinite-Resolution Trimmer .... IRT
Infiniti Personalized Protection System .... IPPS
Infinitive (WDMC) .... inf
Infinitive .... INF
Infinitive [*Grammar*] .... INFIN

Infinity	INF
Infinity Broadcasting Corp. [NYSE symbol] (SAG)	INF
Infinity Broadcasting Corp. [Associated Press] (SAG)	InfinBr
Infinity Broadcasting Corp. [Associated Press] (SAG)	InfinBrd
Infinity Broadcasting'A' [NYSE symbol] (TTSB)	INF
Infinity Color-Corrected System [Optics]	ICC
Infinity Color-Corrected System [Optics]	ICS
Infinity Financial Technology, Inc. [Associated Press] (SAG)	InfFincl
Infinity Financial Technology, Inc. [NASDAQ symbol] (SAG)	INFN
Infinity, Inc. [NASDAQ symbol] (SAG)	IFNY
Infinity, Inc. [Associated Press] (SAG)	Infinity
Infirm	INFRM
Infirmary	INF
Infirmary	INFIRM
Infirmary	INFMRY
Infirmary	INFRMRY
Infisy Systems, Inc. [Vancouver Stock Exchange symbol]	IFI
Infite Ltd. [British ICAO designator] (FAAC)	IEJ
Inflammable	INFL
Inflammable	INFLAM
Inflammation [or Inflammatory] (DAVI)	inflam
Inflammation of Connective Tissue [Medicine]	ICT
Inflammatory Abdominal Aortic Aneurysm [Medicine] (DMAA)	IAAA
Inflammatory Bowel Disease [Medicine]	IBD
Inflammatory Fibroid Polyp [Gastroenterology]	IFP
Inflammatory Joint Disease [Medicine] (DMAA)	IJD
Inflammatory Osteoarthritis [Medicine]	IOA
Inflammatory Papillary Hyperplasia [Dentistry]	IPH
Inflammatory Pelvic Disease [Medicine] (MAE)	IPD
Inflatable (MSA)	IFL
Inflatable Boat Association (EA)	IBA
Inflatable Boat, Small (NVT)	IBS
Inflatable Boat, Small/Silent Propulsion System (MCD)	IBS/SPS
Inflatable Body and Head Restraint System [Aviation] (RDA)	IBAHRS
Inflatable Body and Head Restraint System (DOMA)	IBAHRS
Inflatable Exit Cone (MCD)	IEC
Inflatable Micrometeoroid Paraglide	IMP
Inflatable Occupant Restraint System	IORS
Inflatable Penile Prosthesis [Urology] (DAVI)	IPP
Inflatable Rescue Boat	IRB
Inflatable Restraint System [Automotive engineering]	IRS
Inflatable Ward Unit (SAA)	IFU
Inflated (ADA)	INFL
Inflating-Deflating	IFL-DFL
Inflation Accounting Steering Group (MHDB)	IASG
Inflation from an Energy Perspective [Economic theory]	IFEP
Inflation Pressure Retention [Tire technology]	IPR
Inflation Protected Income (DICI)	IPI
Inflation Quotient	IQ
Inflationary Impact Statement [Economics]	IIS
Inflation-Indexed Charge [Medicare] (GFGA)	IIC
In-Flight (AAG)	IF
In-Flight Abort (MCD)	IFA
In-Flight Aeromedical Evacuation Team	IAET
In-Flight Alignment (PDAA)	IFA
In-Flight Analysis	IFA
Inflight Blood Collection System [On space flights]	IBCS
In-Flight Calibration (KSC)	IFC
Inflight Calibration Lamp [Instrumentation]	ICL
In-Flight Checkout System (IEEE)	IFCS
In-Flight Coverall Garment [Apollo] [NASA]	ICG
In-Flight Deployment	IFD
In-Flight Diverted Force (CINC)	IDF
In-Flight Emergency (MCD)	IFE
In-Flight Emergency Assistance [FAA] (TAG)	IFEA
Inflight Engine Condition Monitoring System [Military] (CAAL)	IECMS
In-Flight Engine Monitor (MCD)	IFEM
In-Flight Entertainment	IFE
In-Flight Experiments Panel	IFEP
Inflight Food Service Association (EA)	IFFSA
In-Flight Helium	IFH
In-Flight Helmet Stowage Bag (KSC)	IHSB
In-Flight Insertion (NG)	IFI
In-Flight Interceptor Communications System [Military]	IFICS
In-Flight Maintenance	IFM
In-Flight Management System	IFMS
In-Flight Management System	IMS
In-Flight Medical Support System [Skylab] [NASA]	IMSS
In-Flight Operable Bomb Rack Lock (MCD)	IFOBRL
In-Flight Operational Evaluation of a Space System	INFOES
In-Flight Operations and Training (MCD)	IFOT
In-Flight Performance	IFP
In-Flight Performance Monitor	IFPM
In-Flight Performance Signal [Aviation] (IAA)	IFPS
In-Flight Power Loss (MCD)	IFPL
In-Flight Power Loss/Shutdown (MCD)	IFPL/SD
In-Flight Refueling	IFR
Inflight Refueling Operator	IRO
In-Flight Replaceable Unit (KSC)	IFRU
In-Flight Safety	IFS
In-Flight Safety Inhibit Test	IFSIT
Inflight Shutdown (MCD)	IFSD
Inflight Survey [USTTA] (TAG)	IFS
In-Flight Test [Air Force]	IFT
In-Flight Test and Maintenance (KSC)	IFTM
In-Flight Test System	IFTS
In-Flight Test System Scan Select (IAA)	IFTSSS
In-Flight Thrust Augmentation	IFTA
In-Flight Training Aid	IFTA
Inflorescence [Botany]	infl
Influence (WDAA)	INF
Influence (ROG)	INFCE
Influence	INFL
Influence Coefficient Tests (MCD)	ICT
Influenza [Medicine] (DAVI)	flu
Influenza [Medicine]	INF
Influenza Virus Hemagglutinin [Immunology]	InfHA
Influenza-C [Medicine]	INF-C
Influenza-Like Illness [Medicine]	ILI
Influx	INFL
InfoColor Conversion Unit (DGA)	ICU
Infocon Information Services Ltd., Calgary, AB, Canada [Library symbol] [Library of Congress] (LCLS)	CaACIS
Infocon Information Services Ltd., Calgary, Alberta [Library symbol National Library of Canada] (NLC)	ACIS
Infodata Systems [NASDAQ symbol] (TTSB)	INFD
Infodata Systems, Inc. [NASDAQ symbol] (NQ)	INFD
Infodata Systems, Inc. [Associated Press] (SAG)	Infodat
Infodata Systems, Inc. [Information service or system] (IID)	ISI
INFO-DOC [ACCORD] [UTLAS symbol]	USA
Infogrow Communications Information Exchange [Database directory] (NITA)	ICIE
Infomart, Toronto, Ontario [Library symbol National Library of Canada] (NLC)	OTINF
Infomed Holdings, Inc. [NASDAQ symbol] (SAG)	IMHI
Infomed Holdings, Inc. [Associated Press] (SAG)	Infomed
Infonautics, Inc. [NASDAQ symbol] (SAG)	INFO
Infonautics, Inc. [Associated Press] (SAG)	Infonau
Infonautics Inc.'A' [NASDAQ symbol] (TTSB)	INFO
Inform	INF
Inform (ROG)	INFM
Informaatiopalvelulaitos [Information Service] [Technical Research Center of Finland Espoo] [Information service or system] (IID)	INF
Informal [FCC special temporary authorization] (NTCM)	I
Informal	INF
Informal Clearance Document [Customs]	ICD
Informal Communication	IC
Informal Composite Negotiating Text [United Nations Conference on the Law of the Sea]	ICNT
Informal Decorative [Horticulture]	ID
Informal Memorandum (MCD)	IM
Informal Memorandum Report	IMR
Informal Policy Committee for Germany	IPCOG
Informal Progress Report	IPR
Informal Reading Inventory [Education]	IRI
Informal Report	IR
Informal Routing Slip	IRS
Informal Single Negotiating Text [Marine science] (MSC)	ISNT
Informal Spelling Inventory [Education]	ISI
Informal Training (NASA)	INFT
Informal World Recognition Inventory [Education] (EDAC)	IWRI
Informant (WGA)	INF
Informant Questionnaire on Cognitive Decline in the Elderly	IQCODE
Informart Resources Center, Dallas, TX [Library symbol] [Library of Congress] (LCLS)	TxDal
Informart, Toronto, ON, Canada [Library symbol Library of Congress] (LCLS)	CaOTINF
Informatech France-Quebec, Montreal, PQ, Canada [Library symbol Library of Congress] (LCLS)	CaQMIFQ
Informatech France-Quebec, Montreal, Quebec [Library symbol National Library of Canada] (NLC)	QMIFQ
Informatheque des Affaires Sociales du Quebec, Montreal, PQ, Canada [Library symbol Library of Congress] (LCLS)	CaQMASIN
Informatheque des Affaires Sociales du Quebec, Quebec, PQ, Canada [Library symbol Library of Congress] (LCLS)	CaQQIAS
Informatheque IRSST [Institut de Recherche en Sante et Securite au Travail], Montreal, PQ, Canada [Library symbol] [Library of Congress] (LCLS)	CaQMIRS
Informatheque IRSST [Institut de Recherche en Sante et Securite au Travail] Montreal, Quebec [Library symbol National Library of Canada] (NLC)	QMIRS
Informatica Bulgarien Corp. [Bulgaria] [ICAO designator] (FAAC)	IBC
Informatics Services [Oakville, ON] [Telecommunications service] (TSSD)	ISL
Informatie en Communicatie Unie [Information and Communication United] [Dutch publishing house]	ICU
Information [Computer science]	I
Information [Computer science] (MDG)	IFN
Information [Computer science]	INF
Information (WDMC)	inf
Information (ROG)	INFN
Information (AFM)	INFO
Information (DD)	info
Information	INFO
Information (DSUE)	INFOR
Information	INFORM
Information	INFORMN
Information Access Co. [Information service or system] (IID)	IAC
Information Acquisition System (MCD)	IAS
Information Activities Office [or Officer]	IAO
Information Agency	IA
Information America [Information service or system] (IID)	IA

Information Analysis and Retrieval [*Computer science*] (ECII) .... IAR
Information Analysis and Retrieval Division [*American Institute of Physics*] (PDAA) .... IARD
Information Analysis Center [*DoD*] .... IAC
Information and Action (MUGU) .... I & A
Information and Censorship [*Allied Forces*] [*World War II*] .... INC
Information and Communication .... IAC
Information and Communication Technology .... ICT
Information and Communication Technology ICI
Information & Communications, Inc. ICI
Information and Communications Technology Exposition (ITD) .... INFOCOMM
Information and Computing Services Association (ACII) .... ICSA
Information and Coordination (ADA) .... I & C
Information and Coordination Central ICC
Information and Data Base Publishing Report [*A publication*] .... IDP
Information and Data Exchange Experimental Activities .... IDEEA
Information and Data Exchange System (IAA) .... IDES
Information and Data Management (SSD) .... IDM
Information and Data Management System (SSD) .... IDMS
Information and Direction Center .... IDC
Information and Documentation (NITA) .... I and D
Information and Documentation [*British Film Institute*] .... IAD
Information and Documentation [*Royal Tropical Institute*] [*Information service or system*] (IID) .... ID
Information and Documentation Center [*Royal Institute of Technology Library*] [*Information service or system*] (IID) .... IDC
Information and Documentation on Science and Technology (NITA) .... IDST
Information and Editorial [*Career program*] .... I & E
Information and Education [*Military*] .... I & E
Information and Education .... IAE
Information and Education (IAA) .... IAE
Information and Education (AAGC) .... IE
Information and Forwarding (MUGU) .... IAF
Information and Historical [*Military*] .... I & H
Information & Library Services [*Information service or system*] (IID) .... ILS
Information and Manufacturing Technologies Division [*British*] .... IMT
Information and Office Systems Division [*Exxon Research and Engineering Co.*] [*Information service or system*] (IID) .... IOSD
Information and Records Management .... IRM
Information and Referral [*Services*] [*Used to assist the handicapped*] .... I & R
Information and Referral Service, Boise, ID [*Library symbol*] [*Library of Congress*] (LCLS) .... IdBI
Information and Regulatory Systems Division [*Environmental Protection Agency*] (GFGA) .... IRSD
Information and Research Utilization Center in Physical Education and Recreationfor the Handicapped [*American Association for Health, Physical Education, and Recreation*] .... IRUC
Information and Technology [*Educational Resources Information Center (ERIC) Clearinghouse*] [*Syracuse University*] (PAZ) .... IR
Information and Technology for the Disabled .... ITD
Information and Technology Transfer Database [*International Research and Evaluation*] .... ITTD
Information and Telecommunications Technologies Group [*Electronic Industries Association*] [*Washington, DC*] (TSSD) .... ITG
Information Assessment Team (NRCH) .... IAT
Information Asset Management (SSD) .... IAM
Information Associates of Ithaca [*Information service or system*] (IID) .... IAI
Information Bank (I and II) (NITA) .... IB (I and II)
Information Bearing Radiation .... IBR
Information Bit [*Computer science*] (BARN) .... infobit
Information Builders, Inc. [*New York*] [*Commercial firm*] (CDE) .... IBI
Information Bulletin .... IB
Information Bulletin of Australian Criminology [*A publication*] .... IBAC
Information Bureau [*Telecommunications*] (TEL) .... IB
Information Bus (IAA) .... IB
Information Calling Services [*Telecommunications*] .... ICS
Information Canada .... InfoCan
Information Canada, Publishing Division, Ottawa, ON, Canada [*Library symbol Library of Congress Obsolete*] (LCLS) .... CaOOQP
Information Center IC
Information Center (MCD) .... INFOCEN
Information Center Complex [*ORNL*] (GRD) ICC
Information Center for Individuals with Disabilities (EA) .... ICID
Information Center for Internal Exposure [*Department of Energy*] [*Defunct*] (IID) .... ICIE
Information Center Management System [*Cullinet*] (NITA) .... ICMS
Information Center of Science and Technology for National Defense [*Chinese library*] .... ICSTND
Information Center of the Ministry of Agriculture and Food [*Ministry of Agriculture and Food*] [*Information service or system*] (IID) .... AGROINFORM
Information Center on Children's Cultures [*Defunct*] (EA) ICCC
Information Center on Crime and Delinquency [*National Council on Crime and Delinquency*] (IID) .... ICCD
Information Center on Education [*New York State Education Department*] [*Albany*] [*Information service or system*] (IID) .... ICE
Information Center on Instructional Technology .... ICIT
Information Center on Nuclear Standards [*American Nuclear Society*] [*Information service or system*] .... ICNS
Information Center on Nuclear Standards [*American Nuclear Society*] [*La Grange Park, IL*] [*Information service or system*] .... ICONS
Information Center - Recreation for the Handicapped .... ICRH
Information Centers Service [*United States Information Agency*] (IID) .... ICS
Information Centre, Canadian Security Intelligence Service [*Centre d'Information, Service Canadien du Renseignement de Securite*], Montreal, Quebec [*Library symbol National Library of Canada*] (BIB) .... QMRS
Information Centre Exchange [*Canada*] (EAIO) .... ICE

Information Centre, Falconbridge Nickel Mines Ltd., Toronto, Ontario [*Library symbol National Library of Canada*] (NLC) .... OTFN
Information Centre for Polish Affairs (EAIO) .... ICPA
Information Centre, Giffels Associates Ltd., Rexdale, Ontario [*Library symbol National Library of Canada*] (NLC) .... OTGA
Information Centre, Glaxo Canada, Inc., Toronto, Ontario [*Library symbol National Library of Canada*] (BIB) .... OTG
Information Centre International [*Telecommunications service*] (TSSD) ICI
Information Centre, Investment Canada [*Centre d'Information, Investissement Canada*] Ottawa, Ontario [*Library symbol National Library of Canada*] (NLC) .... OOIC
Information Centre, J. Walter Thompson Co. Ltd., Toronto, Ontario [*Library symbol National Library of Canada*] (NLC) .... OTJWT
Information Centre, Manalta Coal Ltd., Calgary, Alberta [*Library symbol National Library of Canada*] (NLC) .... ACMC
Information Centre, Molson Breweries of Canada Ltd., Mississauga, Ontario [*Library symbol National Library of Canada*] (NLC) .... OMMB
Information Centre of the European Railways .... ICER
Information Centre, Prince Edward Island Food Technology Centre, Charlottetown [*Library symbol National Library of Canada*] (BIB) .... PCFT
Information Centre, Programme in Gerontology, University of Toronto, Ontario [*Library symbol National Library of Canada*] (NLC) .... OTUPG
Information Centre, SUNCOR Inc. Resources Group, Fort McMurray, Alberta [*Library symbol National Library of Canada*] (NLC) .... AFMSI
Information Circular IC
Information Clearing House, Inc. .... ICH
Information Codes (NITA) IC
Information Collection and Evaluation System (DMAA) .... ICES
Information Collection and Exchange [*Peace Corps*] .... ICE
Information Collection Budget [*Office of Management and Budget*] (GFGA) .... ICB
Information Collection Request [*Paperwork Reduction Act*] (GFGA) .... ICR
Information Collection Rule (ACII) .... ICR
Information Collection Rule [*Environmental Protection Agency*] .... ICR
Information Collection Rule [*Environmental Protection Agency*] .... ICR
Information Collection System (MHDI) .... ICS
Information Collector (SAA) .... IF
Information Committee [*International Organization for Standardization*] (IEEE) .... INFCO
Information Committee of the International Standards Organization (NITA) .... INFCO
Information, Computer and Communications Policy (MHDI) .... ICCP
Information Computer System (IAA) .... ICS
Information Concepts, Inc. ICI
Information Consultants, Inc. [*Information service or system*] (IID) ICI
Information Content (DEN) IC
Information Content Natural Unit [*Information theory*] .... NAT
Information Control Center [*Military*] (IAA) ICC
Information Control Console (DNAB) ICC
Information Control System [*Military*] .... ICS
Information Coordination Control [*Computer*] (MCD) ICC
Information Council of the Americas (EA) .... INCA
Information Data Handling System .... IDHS
Information Data Processing .... IDP
Information Data Search, Inc. [*Information service or system*] (IID) .... IDS
Information, Decision, Action .... IDA
Information Decision Support System (MCD) .... IDSS
Information Definition Requirements Document (NASA) .... IDRD
Information Delivery Service [*Telecommunications*] .... IDS
Information Delivery System Inc. [*Information service or system*] (NITA) .... INDESYS
Information Description Language .... IDL
Information Descriptor Record (MHDB) .... IDR
Information Design Change (NG) .... IDC
Information Design Change List (MCD) .... IDCL
Information Design Journal [*A publication*] (DGA) .... IDJ
Information Dimensions, Inc. [*Information service or system*] (IID) .... IDI
Information Display System .... IDS
Information Displays Automatic Drafting System (IEEE) .... IDAS
Information Displays, Incorporated, Input-Output Machine .... IDIIOM
Information Dissemination and Retrieval [*System*] [*Reuters Ltd.*] .... IDR
Information Dissemination System (OICC) .... IDS
Information Distributor .... ID
Information Document Matching Program [*IRS*] .... IDM
Information/Documentation [*Information service or system*] (IID) .... INFO/DOC
Information Dynamics Corp. .... IDC
Information Dynamics Corp., Reading, MA [*Library symbol Library of Congress*] (LCLS) .... MRI
Information Element (ACRL) .... IE
Information Engineering (CDE) .... IE
Information Engineering Advanced Technology Programme [*British*] .... IEATP
Information Engineering Facility (CDE) .... IEF
Information Engineering Workbench (CDE) .... IEW
Information Enterprises [*Chesterfield, MO*] [*Telecommunications service*] (TSSD) .... IE
Information Environment .... IE
Information Exchange [*Advanced photo system*] IX
[*The*] Information Exchange (EA) .... TIE
Information Exchange Center .... IEC
Information Exchange Group [*National Institutes of Health*] .... IEG
Information Exchange, Inc. [*Telecommunications service*] (TSSD) .... INFOEX
Information Exchange List [*Military*] (AABC) .... IEL
[*The*] Information Exchange on Young Adult Chronic Patients (EA) .... TIE
[*The*] Information Exchange on Young Adult Chronic Patients (EA) .... TIEYACP
Information Exchange Program [*or Project*] [*Military*] .... IEP
Information Exchange Protocol [*Telecommunications*] (NTCM) .... IXP

Information Exchange System [or Subsystem] [Military] (DNAB) ...... IXES
Information Exchange System [or Subsystem] [Military] (CAAL) ...... IXS
Information Exchange Systems [British] ...... IES
Information Expert Environment [Software] [Market research organization]
  (NITA) ...... IEE
Information Facility for Indigenous Resources for Australia ...... IFIRA
Information Feedback ...... IF
Information Field (NITA) ...... I (field)
Information Film Producers of America [Later, Association of Visual
  Communicators] (EA) ...... IFPA
Information Flow Analysis (MHDB) ...... IFA
Information Flow Standards (KSC) ...... IFS
Information for Avionics Laboratory ...... INFORMAL
Information for Decision-Makers System (MCD) ...... IDMS
Information for Industry Inc. (NITA) ...... IFI
Information for Industry Office [Air Force] (MCD) ...... IFIO
Information for Latin American Countries Project (NITA) ...... INFOLAC
Information for Management Planning Analysis and Coordination
  (PDAA) ...... IMPAC
Information for Optimum Resource Management (MCD) ...... INFORM
Information for Public Affairs, Inc. [Information service or system] (IID) ...... IPA
Information for the Contracting Officer (MCD) ...... ICO
Information Gained per Unit Cost [Computer science] ...... IGUC
Information Gatekeepers, Inc. [Telecommunications Information service or
  system] (IID) ...... IGI
Information General, Inc. [Information service or system] (IID) ...... IGI
Information Group Separator ...... IGS
Information Group West Corp., Calgary, Alberta [Library symbol National
  Library of Canada] (BIB) ...... ACIG
Information Group West Corp., Calgary, Alberta [National Library of Canad
  a] [Library symbol] (IID) ...... IGW
Information Grouping Logic [Computer science] ...... IGL
Information Handling Project (DIT) ...... IHP
Information Handling Services [Englewood, CO] ...... IHS
Information Handling Services, Englewood, CO [OCLC symbol] (OCLC) ...... CIH
Information in Science Extension [INTERBRIGHT database] [Budapest,
  Hungary] [Information service or system] (IID) ...... ISE
Information Index [LIMRA] II
Information Indicator (ACRL) II
Information Industries Committee [Information service or system] (IID) IIC
Information Industries Education and Training Foundation [Australia] ...... IIETF
Information Industry Association (EA) ...... IIA
Information Industry Bulletin [Digital Information Group] [Information service
  or system] (IID) ...... IIB
Information Industry Directory [A publication] ...... IID
Information Infrastructure Task Force [Marine science] (OSRA) ...... IITF
Information Infrastructure Task Force (USDC) ...... IITF
Information Infrastructure Technology Applications (USDC) ...... IITA
Information Infrastructure Technology Applications [Marine science]
  (OSRA) ...... IITA
Information Intelligence, Inc. [Information service or system] (IID) III
Information International, Inc. [Phoenix, AZ] [Information broker] (MCD) III
Information International, Inc. [NASDAQ symbol] (NQ) ...... IINT
Information International, Inc. [Associated Press] (SAG) ...... InfoIntl
Information Item Only ...... IIO
Information Labeling IL
Information Lead Distance ...... ILD
Information Library, British High Commission, Ottawa, Ontario [Library
  symbol National Library of Canada] (BIB) ...... OOBH
Information Logic Machine (IEEE) ...... ILM
Information Luxembourg (NITA) ...... INFORMALUX
Information Management (AAGC) ...... IM
Information Management and Compliance Division [Department of
  Education] (GFGA) ...... IMCD
Information Management and Consulting Association [Information service or
  system] (IID) ...... IMCA
Information Management & Engineering Ltd. [Information service or
  system] (IID) ...... IME
Information Management and Processing Association [Defunct] (EA) ...... IMPA
Information Management and Services Division [Environmental Protection
  Agency] (GFGA) ...... IMSD
Information Management and Technology Division (AAGC) ...... IMTED
Information Management and Telecommunications Pentagon Renovation
  (RDA) ...... IM & TPR
Information Management, Archiving, and Communication (DMAA) ...... IMAC
Information Management by Application Generation (IAA) ...... IMAGE
Information Management Consultants [Database producer] (IID) ...... IMC
Information Management / Data Management (HGAA) ...... IM/DM
Information Management Division [Environmental Protection Agency]
  (GFGA) ...... IMD
Information Management / Information Processing Family (HGAA) ...... IM/IPF
Information Management Master Plan [DoD] ...... IMMP
Information Management Plan [DoD] ...... IMP
Information Management Process Reporting System (HGAA) ...... IMPRS
Information Management Processor (NITA) ...... IMP
Information Management Program [Army] ...... IMP
Information Management Resources, Inc. [NASDAQ symbol] (SAG) ...... IMRS
Information Management Resources, Inc. [Associated Press] (SAG) ...... InfMgeR
Information Management, Retrieval, and Dissemination System (DIT) ...... IMRADS
Information Management Review [A publication] (NITA) ...... IMR
Information Management Simulation (KSC) ...... IMSIM
Information Management Specialists, Denver, CO [OCLC symbol] (OCLC) ...... DVI
Information Management Specialists, Inc. [Denver, CO] [Information service
  or system] (IID) ...... IMS
Information Management Staff [Environmental Protection Agency] (GFGA) ...... IMS

Information Management System [IBM Corp.] [Computer science] ...... IMS
Information Management System Inquiry ...... IMS/INQ
Information Management System Interface ...... IMSI
Information Management System/Virtual Storage (MCD) ...... IMS/VS
Information Management Technology [NASDAQ symbol] (SAG) ...... IMTAC
Information Management Technology [NASDAQ symbol] (SAG) ...... IMTK
Information Management Technology [NASDAQ symbol] (SAG) ...... IMTWC
Information Management Technology [Associated Press] (SAG) ...... InfMgt
Information Management Unit (NITA) ...... IMU
Information Management / Virtual Environment (HGAA) ...... IM/VE
Information Management / Zero Effort User System (HGAA) ...... IM/ZEUS
Information Manager [A publication] ...... IM
Information Manipulation Language ...... IML
Information Market [Commission of the European Communities] [Information
  service or system] ...... IM
Information Market [Exhibition and conference centre] [Dallas] (NITA) ...... INFOMART
Information Market News [Database] [EC] (ECED) ...... INFOMARK
Information Marketing Achievement Award [Information Industry
  Association] ...... IMMY
Information Marketing International [Information service or system] (IID) ...... IMI
Information Medicale Automatisee [Automated Medical Information]
  [INSERM] [Information service or system] (IID) ...... IMA
Information Memory (MCD) ...... IM
Information Mgmt Tech Wrrt'A' [NASDAQ symbol] (TTSB) ...... IMTKW
Information Mgmt Tech'A' [NASDAQ symbol] (TTSB) ...... IMTKA
Information Mission Area ...... IMA
Information Mission Area Modernization [Army] (RDA) ...... IMA MOD
Information Mission Area Training Center of Excellence [Army] (RDA) ...... IMATCE
Information Mission Management Plan ...... IMMP
Information Necessary for Optimum Resource Management and
  Protection (PDAA) ...... INFORMAP
Information Network [British Telecommunications] (TEL) ...... INFONET
Information Network and File Organization [Computer science] (BUR) ...... INFO
Information Network and File Organization (MHDB) ...... INFOR
Information Network for Freight Overhead Billing, Rating, and Message
  Switching ...... INFORM
Information Network for Official Statistics [Department of Statistics]
  [Information service or system] (IID) ...... INFOS
Information Network for Ontario [Canada] ...... INFO
Information Network for Operations [Computer science] ...... INFO
Information Network for Public Health Officials [CDC] ...... INPHO
Information Network on New and Renewable Energy Resources and
  Technologies for Asia and the Pacific [UNESCO] (DUND) ...... INNERTAP
Information Network System [Japan] ...... INS
Information Not Available (OICC) ...... INA
Information Not Provided by Manufacturer ...... INPBM
Information Officer ...... IO
Information Officer, Basic [DoD Information School] (DNAB) ...... IOB
Information Officers Working in Voluntary Organisations (AIE) ...... INVOG
Information on Demand, Inc. [Information service or system] (IID) ...... IOD
Information on Hosts (NITA) ...... INFOHOST
Information on Nuclear Site Data System [Nuclear Regulatory Commission]
  (GFGA) ...... INSITE
Information on Request (MCD) ...... INREQ
Information on Research in Baden-Wurttemberg [Fachinformationszentrum
  Karlsruhe GmbH] [Germany Information service or system] (CRD) ...... INFORBW
Information on Technology in Manufacturing Engineering [Society of
  Manufacturing Engineers] [Dearborn, MI] ...... Intime
Information Operation [Military] (RDA) ...... IO
Information Organization Reporting and Management System (IAA) ...... INFORMS
Information Oriented Language [Information retrieval] ...... INFOL
Information Overload ...... IO
Information Overload Testing Aid [or Apparatus] ...... IOTA
Information Overload Testing Apparatus (NITA) ...... IOTA
Information Packets [or Packages] (GNE) ...... IP
Information Paper ...... IP
[The] Information Partnership [Information service or system] (IID) ...... TIP
Information Parts Breakdown (MCD) ...... IPB
[The] Information Place [Information service or system] (IID) ...... TIP
Information Planning Group (SSD) ...... IPG
Information Plus Library, Toronto, Ontario [Library symbol National Library of
  Canada] (BIB) ...... OTINP
Information Policy Group (NITA) ...... IPG
Information Pool (IAA) ...... IP
Information Presentation Technologies, Inc. ...... IPT
Information Privacy Principle ...... IPP
Information Privacy Research Center [Purdue University] (PDAA) ...... IPRC
Information Process Analysis (BUR) ...... IPA
Information Processing (BUR) ...... IP
Information Processing and Control [Systems Laboratory] [Northwestern
  University] ...... IPAC
Information Processing Architecture (IAA) ...... IPA
Information Processing Association [Israel] ...... IPA
Information Processing Center [of General Motors Corp.] ...... IPC
Information Processing Code (DIT) ...... IPC
Information Processing Division [NASA] (NASA) ...... IPD
Information Processing Equipment ...... IPE
Information Processing Facility (MHDI) ...... IPF
Information Processing Improvement Program ...... IPIP
Information Processing in Command and Control [Air Force] ...... IPCC
Information Processing in Command and Control Systems [Air Force] ...... IPCCS
Information Processing in the Central Nervous System ...... INPRONS
Information Processing Language [Computer science] ...... IPL
Information Processing Language Five ...... IPLV
Information Processing Network ...... IPN

Information Processing Professional .... IPP
Information Processing Society of Canada .... IPSOC
Information Processing Society of Japan (NITA) .... IPSJ
Information Processing Standards for Computers .... IPSC
Information Processing Supplies Council [Defunct] (EA) .... IPSC
Information Processing System .... IPS
Information Processing System Simulator [Computer science] (MHDI) .... IPSS
Information Processing Systems Standards Board [Later, Board of Standards Review of ANSI] [American Standards Association] .... IPSSB
Information Processing Technology .... IPT
Information Processing Utility .... IPU
Information Professionals Institute (IID) .... IPI
Information Provider .... IP
Information Publication [HUD] .... IP
Information Publications [Singapore, Hong Kong, Australia] .... IP
Information Publications International [Publisher] [British] .... IPI
Information Publishing .... IP
Information Publishing Corp. [Telecommunications service] (TSSD) .... IPC
Information Publishing Group [The Thomson Corp.] .... IPG
Information Query Language (NITA) .... IQL
Information Quick (PDAA) .... IQ
Information Recovery Capsule .... IRC
Information Recovery [or Retrieval] System [or Subsystem] .... IRS
Information Reduction Research [Information service or system] (IID) .... IRR
Information Referral Manual .... IRMA
Information Referral System for Technical Co-operation among Developing Countries [United Nations Development Programme] [Information service or system] (IID) .... TCDC/INRES
Information Relayed Instantly from the Source [Project] .... IRIS
Information Release (DLA) .... IR
Information Report (CINC) .... INFOREP
Information Report .... IR
Information Reporting Program [IRS] (EGAO) .... IRP
Information Request (AAG) .... IR
Information Requested [or Required] .... INFOREQ
Information Requested .... INREQ
Information Requested in Above Referenced Message [Army] (AABC) .... IRRM
Information Requests [Army] (AABC) .... INREQS
Information Requirement [Military intelligence] (INF) .... IR
Information Requirement [Military] .... IRQR
Information Requirements Control Automated System [Defense Supply Service/Pentagon] (AABC) .... IRCAS
Information Requirements Description [or Document] (KSC) .... IRD
Information Requirements List (KSC) .... IRL
Information Requirements of the Social Sciences [British] (DIT) .... INFROSS
Information Res Engineering [NASDAQ symbol] (TTSB) .... IREG
Information Research Analysts [Database producer] (IID) .... INFRA
Information Research and Analysis [Oak Ridge National Laboratory] [Oak Ridge, TN] [Department of Energy] (GRD) .... IR & A
Information Research Center (DIT) .... IRC
Information Research Ltd. [Information service or system] (IID) .... IRL
Information Research Management (MCD) .... IRM
Information Research Services [Information service or system] (IID) .... IRS
Information Researchers, Inc. [Information service or system] (IID) .... IRI
Information Resource Administration .... IRA
Information Resource Centre, Bell Canada [Centre d'Information Specialisee, Bell Canada], Montreal, Quebec [Library symbol National Library of Canada] (NLC) .... QMB
Information Resource Centre, Consumers Gas, Scarborough, Ontario [Library symbol National Library of Canada] (NLC) .... OSCG
Information Resource Centre, Maritime Tel & Tel, Halifax, Nova Scotia [Library symbol National Library of Canada] (NLC) .... NSHMTT
Information Resource Centre, Ontario Municipal Employees Retirement Board, Toronto [Library symbol National Library of Canada] (BIB) .... OTOME
Information Resource Centre, Systems Development [Centre d'Information Specialise, Systemes-Applications Pratiques], Montreal, Quebec [Library symbol National Library of Canada] (BIB) .... QMSD
Information Resource Consultants [Information service or system] (IID) .... IRC
Information Resource Engineering, Inc. [Associated Press] (SAG) .... InfRsc
Information Resource Engineering, Inc. [NASDAQ symbol] (SAG) .... IREG
Information Resource Group [Information service or system] (IID) .... IRG
Information Resource Management [Computer science] .... IRM
Information Resource Management Association of Canada (EAIO) .... IRMAC
Information Resource Management Council [DoD] .... IRMC
Information Resource Management Service [Veterans Administration Medical Center] [Information service or system] (IID) .... IRMS
Information Resource Repository .... IRR
Information Resources [NASDAQ symbol] (TTSB) .... IRIC
Information Resources Administration Councils [General Services Administration] [Washington, DC] (EGAO) .... IRAC
Information Resources Center [of Mental Health Materials Center] .... IRC
Information Resources Center, Manitoba Health, Winnipeg, Manitoba [Library symbol National Library of Canada] (NLC) .... MWHP
Information Resources Dictionary System (SSD) .... IRDS
Information Resources, Hay Management Consultants, Toronto, Ontario [Library symbol National Library of Canada] (NLC) .... OTHMC
Information Resources, Inc. [Associated Press] (SAG) .... InfoRes
Information Resources, Inc. [Information service or system] (IID) .... IRI
Information Resources, Inc. [NASDAQ symbol] (NQ) .... IRIC
Information Resources Information System [Library of Congress] .... IRIS
Information Resources Management [Marine science] (OSRA) .... IRM
Information Resources Management (USDC) .... IRM
Information Resources Management College (USGC) .... IRMC
Information Resources Management Office [Army Corps of Engineers] .... IRMO
Information Resources Press [Washington, DC] .... IRP

Information Resources Procurement and Management Review (AAGC) .... IRPMR
Information Resources, Royal Bank of Canada, Toronto, Ontario [Library symbol National Library of Canada] (NLC) .... OTRBI
Information Resources Specialists [Information service or system] (IID) .... IRS
Information Retrieval [Computer science] .... IR
Information Retrieval Advisory Services Limited [British] (NITA) .... IRAS
Information Retrieval and Display Language [Computer science] (AABC) ..... IRDL
Information Retrieval & Library Automation [A publication] (BRI) .... IRLA
Information Retrieval and Management System (IAA) .... IRMS
Information Retrieval Automatic Language [Computer science] .... INFRAL
Information Retrieval Center [BBDO International] [Information service or system] (IID) .... IRC
Information Retrieval Center on the Disadvantaged [ERIC] .... IRCD
Information Retrieval Databank (IEEE) .... IRDB
Information Retrieval Group of the Museums Association [British] (NITA) .... IRGMA
Information Retrieval, Inc. .... IRI
Information Retrieval Language [Computer science] .... IRL
Information Retrieval Ltd. [Database originator] [British Information service or system] .... IRL
Information Retrieval Research Laboratory [University of Illinois] [Urbana] [Information service or system] (IID) .... IRRL
Information Retrieval Service [Memphis State University Libraries] (OLDSS) .... IRS
Information Retrieval Service [European Space Agency] (IID) .... IRS
Information Retrieval Specialist Group [British Computer Society] (NITA) ..... IRSG
Information Retrieval System (OICC) .... IRS
Information Retrieval System for the Sociology of Leisure and Sport [University of Waterloo] [Information service or system] (IID) .... SIRLS
Information Retrieval Technique (AAG) .... IRT
Information Retrieval Television [Tele-education project] (NITA) .... IRTV
Information Retrieval Unit (NITA) .... IRU
Information Return Program [IRS] .... IRP
Information Returns Processing [Computer science] .... IRP
Information Revision and Manuscript Assembly .... IRMA
Information Science (IEEE) .... IS
Information Science and Automation Division [Later, LITA] [American Library Association] .... ISAD
Information Science and Scientometrics Research Unit [Hungarian Academy of Sciences Library] [Budapest] [Information service or system] (IID) .... ISSRU
Information Science and Technology (BUR) .... IST
Information Science and Technology Office [Arlington, VA] [DoD] (TSSD) .... ISTO
Information Science Center (MCD) .... ISC
Information Science Corporation (NITA) .... ISC
Information Science Discussion Group [British] (NITA) .... ISDG
Information Science, Inc. [Information service or system] (IID) .... INSCI
Information Science, Inc. .... ISI
Information Science Index Language Text (NITA) .... ISILT
Information Science Technology Assessment for Research [Army] .... ISTAR
Information Sciences and Systems Planning (SAA) .... ISSP
Information Sciences Institute [University of Southern California, Marina Del Rey] .... ISI
Information Search and Processing [Database search service] (OLDSS) .... ISP
Information Search and Recording System [of UMREL] .... ISRS
Information Search Language .... ISL
Information Section, Ontario Ministry of Natural Resources, Toronto, Ontario [Library symbol National Library of Canada] (NLC) .... OTLC
Information Security Oversight Office [National Archives and Records Service] .... ISOO
Information Security Program Regulation (MCD) .... ISPR
Information Seekers .... IS
Information Separation (NITA) .... IS
Information Separator [Control character] [Computer science] .... IS
Information Service .... IS
Information Service Computer System (DIT) .... ISCS
Information Service Data Network [Telecommunications] .... ISDN
Information Service in Mechanical Engineering [Cambridge Scientific Abstracts] [British Information service or system] (IID) .... ISMEC
Information Service of India .... ISI
Information Service on Technological Alternatives for Development [ILO] [United Nations] (DUND) .... INSTEAD
Information Service on Toxicity and Biodegradability [Water Pollution Research Laboratory] [British] (IID) .... INSTAB
Information Service: Physics, Electrical and Electronics, and Computers and Con trol [Information service] [British] (NITA) .... INSPEC
Information Service Representative [Veterans Administration] .... ISR
Information Service Unit [International Potato Center] [Information service or system] (IID) .... ISU
Information Services [Portion of InterNIC General Atomics Corporation] .... IS
Information Services, Asia Pacific Foundation of Canada, Vancouver, British Columbia [Library symbol National Library of Canada] (NLC) ...... BVAAP
Information Services Branch [Chalk River Nuclear Laboratories] [Atomic Energy of Canada Ltd.] [Information service or system] (IID) .... ISB
Information Services Branch [SHAPE Technical Center] [The Hague, Netherlands] .... ISB
Information Services Control Branch [Control Commission for Germany] [World War II] .... ISC
Information Services Department [Ohio State University Libraries] [Columbus] [Information service or system] .... ISD
Information Services Division [Mississippi State Research and Development Center] [Information service or system] (IID) .... ISD
Information Services Division [Scottish Health Service] [Research center] ...... ISD
Information Services in Physics, Electronics, and Computers [Information service or system] .... INSPEC
Information Services, Inc. [Information service or system] (IID) .... ISI

Information Services International [*Information service or system*] (IID) .... ISI
Information Services Ltd. [*Publisher*] [*British*] .... ISL
Information Services of Cranston [*Information service or system*] (IID) .... ISC
Information Services of Warwick [*Rhode Island*] [*Information retrieval*] (IID) .... ISW
Information Services Officer .... ISO
Information Services on Latin America (EA) .... ISLA
Information Services, Ontario Centre for Microelectronics, Nepean, Ontario [*Library symbol National Library of Canada*] (NLC) .... OOOCM
Information Services to Education [*American Society for Information Science*] .... ISE
Information Sharing System (NITA) .... ISS
Information Society of Canada (MCD) .... ISC
Information Sort and Predict .... ISAP
Information Sources [*Information service or system*] (IID) .... INFOSOR
Information Specialists Ltd. [*Information service or system*] (IID) .... Infospecs
Information Specialties Corp. (IID) .... ISC
Information Storage and Retrieval [*Computer science*] (DIT) .... ISAR
Information Storage and Retrieval [*Computer science*] .... ISR
Information Storage and Retrieval System [*Computer science*] .... INSTARS
Information Storage Devices [*NASDAQ symbol*] (TTSB) .... ISDI
Information Storage Devices, Inc. [*Associated Press*] (SAG) .... InfoStor
Information Storage Devices, Inc. [*NASDAQ symbol*] (SAG) .... ISDI
Information Storage, Inc. .... ISI
Information Storage Retrieval and Dissemination (NITA) .... ISRD
Information Storage, Selection, and Retrieval [*Computer science*] .... ISSR
Information Storage System (IEEE) .... ISS
Information Structure Design .... ISD
Information Superhighway [*Telecommunications*] (PCM) .... ISH
Information Superhighway (CDE) .... i-way
Information Support System [*Nondestructive Testing Information Analysis Center - NTIAC*] [*Southwest Research Institute*] [*Information service or system*] (CRD) .... ISS
Information Switching Exchange (IAA) .... ISX
Information System .... IS
Information System Access Lines [*Computer science*] .... ISAL
Information System Base Language .... ISBL
Information System Development [*Telecommunications*] (TEL) .... ISD
Information System Electronic Command [*Army*] .... ISEC
Information System for Adaptive, Assistive, and Rehabilitation Equipment [*For the handicapped*] .... ISAARE
Information System for Advanced Academic Computing (IID) .... ISAAC
Information System for Coffee and Other Product Economics [*International Coffee Organization*] (NITA) .... INSCOPE
Information System for Hazardous Organics in Water [*Database*] [*Environmental Protection Agency Information service or system*] (CRD) .... ISHOW
Information System for Improved Plant Protection [*FAO*] [*United Nations*] (DUND) .... ISIPP
Information System for Vocational Decisions Program .... ISVD
Information System Indexing System [*Federal Judicial Center*] [*Database*] .... ISIS
Information System Language [*Computer science*] (IEEE) .... ISL
Information System Management Board [*NATO*] (NATG) .... ISMB
Information System Manager (NATG) .... ISM
Information System Plan (MCD) .... ISP
Information System Security Evaluation Method (IAA) .... ISSEM
Information System Service Request (DNAB) .... ISSR
Information System Software Update Environment .... ISSUE
Information System Theory Project (IAA) .... ISTP
Information Systems (KSC) .... INS
Information Systems [*Ori, Inc.*] [*Information service or system*] (IID) .... IS
Information Systems Advisory Committee .... ISAC
Information Systems and Communications Group (HGAA) .... IS & CG
Information Systems and Media Services [*Eastern Illinois University*] [*Information service or system*] (IID) .... ISMS
Information Systems and Services Division [*Department of Commerce*] (IID) .... ISSD
Information Systems Architecture [*AT & T*] .... ISA
Information Systems Association (EA) .... ISA
Information Systems Branch [*National Institutes of Health*] (IID) .... ISB
Information Systems Command [*DoD*] .... ISC
Information Systems Command [*Army*] (AAGC) .... USAISC
Information Systems Committee [*Universities Funding Council*] (AIE) .... ISC
Information Systems Consultants, Inc. [*Information service or system*] (IID) .... ISCI
Information Systems Department [*Franklin Research Center, Inc.*] [*Information service or system*] (IID) .... ISD
Information Systems Design Optimization System .... ISDOS
Information Systems Development Division (SAA) .... ISDD
Information Systems Directorate [*Kennedy Space Center*] [*NASA*] (NASA) .... IN
Information Systems Division [*Ori, Inc.*] [*Bethesda, MD*] .... ISD
Information Systems Engineering Command (SSD) .... ISEC
Information Systems Factory (NITA) .... ISF
Information Systems Flight [*Military*] .... ISF
Information Systems for Management (IEEE) .... ISM
Information Systems Laboratories, Inc. .... ISL
Information Systems Marketing, Inc. [*Information service or system*] (IID) ...... ISM
Information Systems Network [*AT & T*] [*Telecommunications*] .... ISN
Information Systems Office [*NASA*] (NASA) .... IFO
Information Systems Office [*Library of Congress*] .... ISO
Information Systems Plan [*USAID*] (ECON) .... ISP
Information Systems Professional (DD) .... ISP
Information Systems Program [*University of Oklahoma*] [*Norman, OK*] .... ISP
Information Systems Resource Manager .... ISRM

Information Systems Section [*Battelle Memorial Institute*] [*Information service or system*] (IID) .... ISS
Information Systems Security (AAGC) .... INFOSEC
Information Systems Security .... ISS
Information Systems Security Association (EA) .... ISSA
Information Systems Selection and Acquisition Agency (AAGC) .... ISSAA
Information Systems Services [*Brigham Young University*] [*Research center*] (RCD) .... ISS
Information Systems Software Center [*Fort Belvoir, VA*] [*Army*] (RDA) .... ISSC
Information Systems Specialists Office [*Library of Congress*] (NITA) .... ISS
Information Systems Standards Board [*American National Standards Institute*] [*Telecommunications*] .... ISSB
Information Systems Standards Management Board .... ISSMB
Information Systems Subdivision (MCD) .... ISS
Information Systems Support Group (AAGC) .... ISSG
Information Systems Technical Integration Panel (SSD) .... ISTIP
Information Technology [*Computer science*] (ECON) .... IT
Information Technology 1995 [*Marine science*] (OSRA) IT-95
Information Technology 1995 (USDC) IT-95
Information Technology Acquisition and Marketing Association [*Defunct*] (EA) .... ITAMA
Information Technology Advisory Board [*British*] .... ITAB
Information Technology Advisory Committee [*Office of Management and Budget*] (GFGA) .... ITAC
Information Technology Advisory Panel [*British*] .... ITAP
Information Technology and Communications Bureau [*United Nations*] (ECON) .... ITCOM
Information Technology and Libraries [*A publication*] .... ITAL
Information Technology Association of America [*Arlington, VA*] (CDE) .... ITAA
Information Technology Centre [*Training centres*] [*British*] (NITA) .... ITEC
Information Technology Centre Consultancy Unit [*British*] (AIE) .... ITCCU
Information Technology Consultancy Unit (NITA) .... ITCU
Information Technology Co-Ordinating Group [*International Electrotechnical Commission*] [*ISO*] (DS) .... ITCG
Information Technology Development [*Project*] [*DoD*] (RDA) .... ITD
Information Technology Directorate [*British*] .... ITD
Information Technology Division [*Naval Research Laboratory*] .... ITD
Information Technology Electronics and Computers [*A publication*] .... ITEC
Information Technology Exchange Exhibition [*British*] (ITD) .... ITEX
Information Technology for Libraries [*Formerly, JOLA*] [*A publication*] (NITA) .... ITAL
Information Technology Fund (AAGC) .... ITF
Information Technology in Engineering [*British*] .... ITE
Information Technology Industry Council (AAGC) .... ITIC
Information Technology Information Services Network [*British*] (NITA) .... ITISN
Information Technology Laboratory [*Army Corps of Engineers*] .... ITL
Information Technology Ltd. [*British*] (NITA) .... ITC
Information Technology Ltd. [*British*] (NITA) .... ITL
Information Technology Management Reform Act of 1996 (AAGC) .... ITMRA
Information Technology Research [*Waltham, MA*] [*Telecommunications*] (TSSD) .... ITR
Information Technology Services [*California State University, Long Beach*] [*Research center*] (RCD) .... ITS
Information Technology Services [*National Library of Canada*] (TSSD) .... ITS
Information Technology Services [*Stanford University*] [*Information service or system*] (IID) .... ITS
Information Technology Services, National Library of Canada [*Services de Technologie de l'Information, Bibliotheque Nationale de Canada*], Ottawa, Ontario [*Library symbol National Library of Canada*] (NLC) .... OONLD
Information Technology Skills Agency (NITA) .... ITSA
Information Technology Standards Unit [*British*] .... ITSEC
Information Technology Standards Unit (NITA) .... ITSU
Information Technology Strategic Alliances Database (IID) .... ITSA
Information Technology Systems .... ITS
Information Technology Training Accreditation Council [*British*] (NITA) .... ITTAC
Information Technology Users Group [*Exxon Corp.*] .... ITUG
Information Technology Users' Standards Association [*British*] .... ITUSA
Information Technology Year [*1982*] .... ITY
Information Theory (MCD) .... IT
Information Trade Directory [*Gale Research Co.*] (NITA) .... ITD
Information, Training and Agricultural Development [*British consultancy and training service*] (ECON) .... ITAD
Information Transfer Exchange [*Library science*] .... INTREX
Information Transfer Exchange (PDAA) .... ITX
Information Transfer Experiment [*Massachusetts Institute of Technology*] (DIT) .... INTREX
Information Transfer Module [*Telecommunications*] (NITA) .... ITM
Information Transfer Satellite (KSC) .... ITS
Information Transfer [*or Transmission*] System .... ITS
Information Transform [*Information service or system*] (IID) .... IT
Information Transform, Inc. [*Information service or system*] (IID) .... ITI
Information Type (ACRL) .... IT
Information Unit .... IU
Information Unit Separator [*Computer science*] .... IUS
Information Unlimited [*Information service or system*] (IID) .... IU
Information Unltd., Berkeley, CA [*Library symbol Library of Congress*] (LCLS) .... CBI
Information Utilization Laboratory [*University of Pittsburgh*] (NITA) .... IUL
Information via Telex [*Telecommunications*] (TEL) .... INFOTEX
Information Victoria [*Australia An association*] IV
Information Viewing Device .... IVD
Information Warfare Squadron [*Air Force*] .... IWS
Information World [*A publication*] .... IW
Information World Review [*A publication Information service or system*] (IID) .... IWR

Informational	INFMTL
Informational Acquisition and Interpretation	IAI
Informational Media Guaranty	IMG
Information-Based Complexity [*Mathematics*]	IBC
Information-Based School Development	IBSD
Information-Documentation and Communication (PDAA)	INDOC
Information-Memory-Concentration (DMAA)	IMC
Information-Need-Product [*Sales technique*]	INP
Informations- und Dokumentationssystem Umwelt [*Environmental Information and Documentation System*] [*Berlin*] [*Information retrieval*]	UMPLIS
Informationsdienst-AUSTAUSCH [*Information Service-EXCHANGE*] [*NOMOS Datapool Database*] (IID)	HIZA
Informationsstelle Lateinamerika [*Germany*]	ILA
Informationssystem Beliebiger Andwendungssystem [*Germany*] (NITA)	IBAS
Informationssystem Karlsruhe [*Karlsruhe Information System*] [*Information service or system Germany*]	INKA
Informationssystem Karlsruhe - Conference [*Database*]	INKA-CONF
Informationssystem Karlsruhe - Corporates in Energy [*Database*] [*Defunct*]	INKA-CORP
Informationssystem Karlsruhe - Data Compilations in Energy and Physics [*Database*]	INKA-DATACOMP
Informationssystem Karlsruhe - Mathematical Education [*Database*]	INKA-MATHDI
Informationssystem Karlsruhe - Mathematics [*Database*]	INKA-MATH
Informationssystem Karlsruhe - Nuclear Database Part: Conference Papers: NuclearResearch, Nuclear Technology [*Database*]	INKA-NUCLEAR PART KKK
Informationssystem Karlsruhe - Nuclear Database Part: International Nuclear Information System [*Database*]	INKA-NUCLEAR PART INIS
Informationssystem Karlsruhe - Nuclear Database Part: Nuclear Science Abstracts [*Database*]	INKA-NUCLEAR PART NSA
Informationssystem Karlsruhe - Physics [*Database*]	INKA-PHYS
Informationsverbundzentrum Raum und Bau [*Germany*] (NITA)	IRB
Informationszentrum fuer Schnittwerte [*Cutting Data Information Center*] [*Germany Information service or system*] (IID)	INFOS
Informationszentrum Raum und Bau [*Information Center for Regional Planning and Building Construction*] [*Germany Information service or system*] (IID)	IRB
Informationszentrum Sozialwissenschaften [*Social Sciences Information Center*] [*Information service or system*] (IID)	IZ
Informationszentrum und Bibliotheken [*Information retrieval*]	INF
Information-technology Promotion Agency [*Japan*] (NITA)	IPA
Informatsionnoye Agentstvo Novosti [*Novosti Press Agency*] [*Russian Federation*]	IAN
Informed	INF
Informed	INFD
Informed (ROG)	IAMA
Informed Americans Monitor (EA)	IBP
Informed Birth and Parenting [*Later, IH/IBP*] (EA)	IH
Informed Homebirth [*Later, IH/IBP*] (EA)	IH/IBP
Informed Homebirth/Informed Birth and Parenting (EA)	INM
Informed Notaries of Maine (SRA)	IMED
Informedics, Inc. [*NASDAQ symbol*] (SAG)	IMED
Informedics, Inc. [*Associated Press*] (SAG)	Informed
Informetrica Ltd., Ottawa, Ontario [*Library symbol National Library of Canada*] (NLC)	OOI
Informix Corp. [*NASDAQ symbol*] (NQ)	IFMX
Informix Corp. [*Associated Press*] (SAG)	Informx
Inforonics Inc., Littleton, MA [*Library symbol Library of Congress*] (LCLS)	MLitl
Infortiatum [*A publication*] (DSA)	Inf
Infosafe Sys Units'99 [*NASDAQ symbol*] (TTSB)	ISFEU
Infosafe Sys Wrrt'A' [*NASDAQ symbol*] (TTSB)	ISFEW
Infosafe Sys Wrrt'B' [*NASDAQ symbol*] (TTSB)	ISFEZ
Infosafe Systems, Inc. [*Associated Press*] (SAG)	Infosafe
Infosafe Systems, Inc. [*Associated Press*] (SAG)	Infosf
Infosafe Systems, Inc. [*Associated Press*] (SAG)	Infosfe
Infosafe Systems, Inc. [*NASDAQ symbol*] (SAG)	ISFEA
Infosafe Systems'A' [*NASDAQ symbol*] (TTSB)	ISFEA
Info-Search/NW, Bothell, WA [*Library symbol*] [*Library of Congress*] (LCLS)	WaBolS
Infoseek Corp. [*Associated Press*] (SAG)	Infoseek
Infoseek Corp. [*NASDAQ symbol*] (SAG)	SEEK
InfoSoft International, Inc. [*NASDAQ symbol*] (SAG)	INSO
Info-Stop Communications [*Vancouver Stock Exchange symbol*]	IFO
Infra (IAA)	I
Infra [*Beneath or Below*] [*Latin*]	INF
Infra Dignitatem [*Undignified*] [*Latin*]	INFRA DIG
Infra Low-Frequency [*Telecommunications*] (TEL)	ILF
Infra-Audible [*Sound*]	IA
Infrablack Region	IBR
Infracostal Margin [*Anatomy*] (DAVI)	ICM
Infraed Data Association (PS)	IRDA
Infraestructura Teatral [*Ministerio de Cultura*] [*Spain Information service or system*] (CRD)	ITEA
Infrahepatic Interruption of the Inferior Vena Cava [*Medicine*] (AAMN)	IIIVC
In-Frame Response [*Automotive engineering Electronics*]	IFR
Infraorbitomeatal Line [*Anatomy*] (DAVI)	IOML
Infrapatellar Contracture Syndrome [*Sports medicine*]	IPCS
Infrared (MCD)	IF
Infrared	IFR
Infrared (VRA)	infra
Infrared	IR
Infrared Acquisition and Designation System (DOMA)	IRADS
Infrared Acquisition RADAR (MSA)	IRACOR
Infrared Acquisition RADAR	IRACQ

Infrared Active Homing (MCD)	IRAH
Infrared Advisory Center	IRAC
Infrared Aiming Light [*Military*] (INF)	IAL
Infrared Air Defense Detection System	IRADDS
Infrared Airborne RADAR (PDAA)	IRAR
Infrared Alternate Head	IRAH
Infrared Ambush Device	IRAD
Infrared Amplification by Stimulated Emission of Radiation	IRASER
Infrared Array Camera	IRAC
Infrared Astronomical Satellite [*NASA*] (MCD)	IRAS
Infrared Attack System	IRAS
Infrared Attack Weapon System	IRAWS
Infrared Augmentation Reliability (MCD)	IRAR
Infrared Auroral Emission	IAE
Infrared Automatic Mass Screening [*Electronics*]	IRAMS
Infrared Automatic System (DNAB)	IRAS
Infrared Background Imaging Seeker (MCD)	IBIS
Infrared Background Signature Survey [*Military*] (SDI)	IBSS
Infrared Binocular [*Military*] (VNW)	IRB
Infrared Brazing	IRB
Infrared Brightness Temperature	IRBT
Infrared Calibration System	ICS
Infrared Camera System	ICS
Infrared Cell, Electronically Refrigerated	ICER
Infrared Charge-Coupled Device	IRCCD
Infrared Chemistry Experiments Coordinated Auroral Program [*Defense Nuclear Agency*] (PDAA)	ICECAP
Infrared Coagulator [*Hematology*] (DAVI)	IRC
Infrared Command Unit	ICU
Infrared Communications System	ICS
Infrared Communications System	IRCS
Infrared Counter-Countermeasures [*Military electronics*]	IRCCM
Infrared Countermeasures [*Military electronics*]	IRC
Infrared Countermeasures [*Military electronics*] (NVT)	IRCM
Infrared Countermeasures Equipment [*Military Electronics*] (CAAL)	ICE
Infrared Countermeasures System [*Military Electronics*]	ICS
Infrared Data Association (PCM)	IrDA
Infrared Decoy Evaluator	IDE
Infrared Detecting Set [*or System*] (MCD)	IRDS
Infrared Detection Array	IDA
Infrared Detection Array	IRDA
Infrared Detection Set	IDS
Infrared Detection Unit	IDU
Infrared Detection Unit	IRDU
Infrared Detector	IFD
Infrared Detector	IRD
Infrared Detector Cryostat	IDC
Infrared Developers Association (PCM)	IRDA
Infrared Discrimination System	IDS
Infrared Display	IRD
Infrared Drying Oven	IDO
Infrared Drying Oven	IRDO
Infrared Early Warning System	IREWS
Infrared Electronic Warfare	IREW
Infrared Emission	IE
Infrared Emission	IRE
Infrared Emission	IRER
Infrared Extra Rapid (ADA)	IRER
Infrared Fault Isolation Test System	IRFITS
Infrared Filter	IF
Infrared Filter Radiometer	IFR
Infrared Fire Control	IFC
Infrared Fire Control System	IFCS
Infrared Flight Inspection System (IAA)	IFIS
Infrared Focal Plane Array [*DoD*]	IRFPA
Infrared Frequency Synthesis	IFS
Infrared Gas Analyzer	IRGA
Infrared Gas Radiation	IRGAR
Infrared Generator	IRG
Infrared Guided Bomb [*DoD*]	IRGB
Infrared Guided Projectile (MCD)	IRGP
Infrared Gunfire Locator	IGL
Infrared Gunfire Locator	IRGL
Infrared Heater	IRH
Infrared Heterodyne Radiometer	IHR
Infrared Homing Bomb (IEEE)	IRBO
Infrared Homing System (AAG)	IHS
Infrared Horizon Sensor	IHS
Infrared Image Converter	IRIC
Infrared Image Scanner	IRIS
Infrared Imagery	IRI
Infrared Imaging Seeker	IRIS
Infrared Imaging Seeker Head (MCD)	IRISH
Infrared Imaging System	IIS
Infrared Imaging System	IRIS
Infrared Information and Analysis Center [*University of Michigan*] (MCD)	IIAC
Infrared Information and Analysis Center [*University of Michigan*]	IRIA
Infrared Information and Analysis Center [*University of Michigan*]	IRIAC
Infrared Information Exchange	IRIE
Infrared Information System [*Sadtler Research Laboratories, Inc.*] [*Philadelphia, PA Database*]	IRIS
Infrared Instrumentation	IRI
Infrared Instrumentation System	IIS
Infrared Interferometer Spectrometer	IRIS
Infrared Interferometer Spectrometer - Michelson	IRIS-M
Infrared Intruder System	IRIS

Infrared Intrusion Detection (NVT) ... IID
Infrared Jammer ... IRJ
Infrared Jammer Equipment ... IRJE
Infrared Kit ... IRK
Infrared Lamp [*or Light*] ... IRL
Infrared LASER ... IRLAS
Infrared LASER Atmospheric Monitoring System ... ILAMS
Infrared LASER Ranger (MCD) ... IRLR
Infrared LASER Spectrometer ... IRLS
Infrared Lens ... IRL
Infrared Light Emitting Diode (PDAA) ... IRLED
Infrared Line Scanner (MCD) ... IRLS
Infrared Live Scanner [*Medicine*] (DMAA) ... ILS
Infrared Mapper ... IRM
Infrared Mapping System ... IRMS
Infrared MASER (CET) ... IRASER
Infrared Measurement ... IRM
Infrared Measurement Instrument ... IMI
Infrared Measurement Program ... IRMP
Infrared Measuring System ... IMS
Infrared Milk Analyzer (PDAA) ... IRMA
Infrared Miniaturized Intrusion Detector (PDAA) ... IMID
Infrared Miniaturized Jammer ... IMJ
Infrared Miniaturized Jammer ... IRMJ
Infrared Miss-Distance Approximator ... IRMA
Infrared Mobile Optical Radiation Laboratory [*Navy*] (PDAA) ... IMORL
Infrared Monochromatic Radiation ... IMRA
Infrared Monochromatic Radiation (MSA) ... IRMRA
Infrared Multiple-Photon [*Physics*] ... IRMP
Infrared Multiple-Photon Dissociation [*Physics*] ... IRMPD
Infrared Nondestructive Testing [*Electrical technique*] ... INT
Infrared Nondestructive Testing [*Electrical technique*] ... IRNDT
Infrared on Target ... IROT
Infrared Operational Satellite (NOAA) ... IROS
Infrared Optical Film ... IOF
Infrared Optical Intelligence (MCD) ... IROP
Infrared Optical Noise (IAA) ... IRON
Infrared Oven ... IRO
Infrared Physical Measurement ... IRPM
Infrared Plume Target ... IPT
Infrared Pointer Package ... IPP
Infrared Pointer Package ... IRPP
Infrared Preamplifier ... IRP
Infrared Projector (MCD) ... IRP
Infrared Projector Energy Monitor (MCD) ... IEM
Infrared Proximity Warning Indicator ... IPWI
Infrared Quantum Counter ... IRQC
Infrared RADAR Measurement Program ... IRRMP
Infrared RADAR Suppressor (MCD) ... IRS
Infrared Radiation ... IR
Infrared Radiation Profile ... IRP
Infrared Radiation Thermometer (NOAA) ... IRT
Infrared Radiometer ... IR
Infrared Radiometer ... IRR
Infrared Radiometer Clear Air Turbulence [*Instrument*] ... IRCAT
Infrared Range and Detection ... IRRAD
Infrared Receiver ... IRR
Infrared Reconnaissance ... IR
Infrared Reconnaissance Set ... IRRS
Infrared Reconnaissance Set (MCD) ... IRS
Infrared Reconnaissance System (MCD) ... IRRS
Infrared Reflectance (IAA) ... IR
Infrared Reflection Absorption Spectroscopy [*Also, IRRAS, RAIR, RAIRS, RAIS*] ... IRAS
Infrared Reflection Absorption Spectroscopy [*Also, IRAS, RAIR, RAIRS, RAIS*] ... IRRAS
Infrared Reflection Spectroscopy ... IRRS
Infrared Reflective Spectra ... IRS
Infrared Research Information Symposium (AAG) ... IRIS
Infrared Resolution Target System (MCD) ... IRRTS
Infrared Responsive Phosphor ... IRP
Infrared Scanner ... IRSCAN
Infrared Scanning Radiometer (KSC) ... ISR
Infrared Search and Track ... IRST
Infrared Search and Track System ... IRSTS
Infrared Search Set ... IRSS
Infrared Search Set Operator ... IRSSO
Infrared Search System [*Database*] [*Environmental Protection Agency Information service or system*] (CRD) ... IRSS
Infrared Search System [*Institut za Nuklearne Nauke Boris Kidric*] [*Former Yugoslavia*] [*Information service or system*] (CRD) ... IRSS
Infrared Sensitive Element Evaluation Program ... ISEEP
Infrared Sensor System ... IRSS
Infrared Sensor System ... ISS
Infrared Sightline Control ... ISC
Infrared Small Astronomical Spacecraft ... ISAS
Infrared Smoke Simulator (MCD) ... IRSS
Infrared Solder Oven ... IRSO
Infrared Soldering ... IRS
Infrared Source ... IRS
Infrared Space Observatory ... ISO
Infrared Spectral Hygrometer (PDAA) ... IRSH
Infrared Spectral Measurement System (MCD) ... ISMS
Infrared Spectrometer [*or Spectroscopy*] ... IRS
Infrared Spectrometer [*or Spectroscopy*] ... IRSP
Infrared Spectrometer [*or Spectroscopy*] (MCD) ... IRSPECT
Infrared Spectrometer [*or Spectroscopy*] (IAA) ... IS
Infrared Spectrophotometer ... ISP
Infrared Star (BARN) ... IRS
Infrared Structural Correlation Tables [*A publication*] ... IRSCOT
Infrared Suppression Device ... ISD
Infrared Surveillance and Target Designation System (PDAA) ... IRSTDS
Infrared Surveillance of Surface Targets [*Military*] (CAAL) ... ISST
Infrared Surveillance Set ... ISS
Infrared Surveillance Subsystem ... IRSS
Infrared Systems and Guidance Heads Laboratory ... IRSGHL
Infrared Systems Engineering ... IRSE
Infrared Systems Manufacturing ... IRSM
Infrared Systems Manufacturing ... ISM
Infrared Tail Warning Set (MCD) ... IRTWS
Infrared Target Detector ... IRTD
Infrared Target Detector ... ITD
Infrared Target Pointer/Illuminator/Aiming Laser [*Military*] (INF) ... ITPIAL
Infrared Target Seeker (MSA) ... IRTS
Infrared Telescope ... IRT
Infrared Telescope Facility ... IRTF
Infrared Temperature ... IRT
Infrared Temperature Profile Radiometer ... ITPR
Infrared Temperature Sounder (PDAA) ... IRTS
Infrared Terminally-Guided Submunition ... IRTGSM
Infrared Thermal Mapper [*NASA*] ... IRTM
Infrared Thermography ... IRT
Infrared Thermometer ... IRT
Infrared Tracker ... IRT
Infrared Tracking Display Unit ... ITDU
Infrared Tracking System ... ITS
Infrared Transmission ... IRTRN
Infrared Transmission through the Diffusion (PDAA) ... IRTTD
Infrared Transmitting ... INTRAN
Infrared Transmitting ... IRTRAN
Infrared Tube ... IRT
Infrared/Ultraviolet Line Scanner (PDAA) ... IR/UV-LS
Infrared Vertical Sounding System [*Oceanography*] (MSC) ... IRVSS
Infrared Video Automatic Tracking (PDAA) ... IRVAT
Infrared Video-Auto Tracker (DWSG) ... IRVAT
Infrared Vidicon Tube ... IRICON
Infrared Viewing Set ... IVS
Infrared Warning Receiver [*Aviation*] (MCD) ... IRWR
Infrared Warning Receiver [*Aviation*] (DNAB) ... IWR
Infrared Window ... IRW
Infrared-Emitting Diode (IEEE) ... IRED
Infrascriptum [*Written Below*] [*Latin*] (ROG) ... INFRAPTUM
Infrasonic ... IS
Infrasonic Frequency ... ISF
Infrasonics, Inc. [*NASDAQ symbol*] (NQ) ... IFRA
Infrasonics, Inc. [*Associated Press*] (SAG) ... Infrasnc
Infrastructural, Logistics, Council Operations [*NATO*] ... ILCO
Infrastructure Account Unit (NATG) ... IAU
Infrastructure Committee of the North Atlantic Council [*NATO*] ... IC
Infrastructure Payments and Progress Committee [*NATO*] (NATG) ... IPPC
Infrastructure Special Committee [*NATO*] (NATG) ... ISC
Infricetur [*Let It Be Rubbed In*] [*Pharmacy*] ... INFRIC
Infunde [*Pour In*] [*Pharmacy*] ... INF
Infunde [*Pour In*] [*Pharmacy*] ... INFUND
Infundibular Process [*Medicine*] (DMAA) ... IP
Infundibular Pulmonic Stenosis [*Medicine*] (DAVI) ... IPS
Infundibulopelvic [*Ligament*] [*Anatomy*] (DAVI) ... IP
Infused Emitter Coupling ... IEC
Infusible Platelet Membrane [*Substitute for blood tranfusion*] ... IPM
Infusion [*Medicine*] ... INF
Infusion Hepatic Angiography [*Medicine*] ... IHA
Infusion Urogram [*Medicine*] (DMAA) ... IUG
Infusion-Forming Units [*Medicine*] ... IFU
Infusoria Killing [*Unit*] [*Medicine*] ... IK
Infusum [*Infusion*] [*Pharmacy*] (ROG) ... INF
Infusum [*Infusion*] [*Pharmacy*] (ROG) ... INFUS
Infusum Rhei [*Infusion of Rhubarb*] [*Pharmacy*] (ROG) ... INF RHEI
Infu-Tech, Inc. [*NASDAQ symbol*] (SAG) ... INFU
Infu-Tech, Inc. [*Associated Press*] (SAG) ... InfuTech
Inga [*Zaire*] [*ICAO location identifier*] (ICLI) ... FZAN
Ingalls Memorial Hospital, Harvey, IL [*Library symbol Library of Congress*] (LCLS) ... IHal
Ingatestone [*Village in England*] ... INGAT
Inge Lehmann [*Greenland*] [*Seismograph station code, US Geological Survey Closed*] (SEIS) ... ILG
Ingende [*Zaire*] [*ICAO location identifier*] (ICLI) ... FZEI
Ingenieur [*Engineer*] [*French*] (EY) ... ING
Ingenieur (DD) ... ing
Ingenieur [*Engineer*] [*French*] ... Ir
Ingenieur Constructeur [*Academic degree*] ... IC
Ingenium Baccalaureus [*Bachelor of Engineering*] ... Ing B
Ingenium Doctor [*Doctor of Engineering*] ... Ing D
Ingenium Magister [*Master of Engineering*] ... Ing M
Ingersoll on Habeas Corpus [*A publication*] (DLA) ... Ing Hab Corp
Ingersoll Public Library, Ingersoll, ON, Canada [*Library symbol Library of Congress*] (LCLS) ... CaOI
Ingersoll Public Library, Ontario [*Library symbol National Library of Canada*] (NLC) ... OI
Ingersoll Rand [*Associated Press*] (SAG) ... IngerRd
Ingersoll-Rand [*NYSE symbol*] (TTSB) ... IR

Ingersoll-Rand Co. [*NYSE symbol*] (SPSG) ... IR
Ingersoll's Digest of the Laws of the United States [*A publication*] (DLA) ... Ing Dig
Ingersoll's Edition of Roccus' Maritime Law [*A publication*] (DLA) ... Ing Roc
Ingestible Thermal Monitoring System ... ITMS
Ingestion Exposure Pathway [*Nuclear emergency planning*] ... IEP
Ingglish Speling 3soesiaesh3n [*An organization to reform spelling*] [*See also IS3*] (EA) ... IS
Ingglish Speling 3soesiaesh3n [*English Spelling Association*] (EA) ... IS3
Ingham [*Australia Airport symbol*] ... IGH
Ingham County Library, Mason, MI [*Library symbol Library of Congress*] (LCLS) ... MiMas
Ingham Medical Center, John W. Chi Memorial Library, Lansing, MI [*Library symbol*] [*Library of Congress*] (LCLS) ... MiLIM
Inglaterra [*Bolivia*] [*ICAO location identifier*] (ICLI) ... SLIG
Ingles Markets, Inc. [*NASDAQ symbol*] (NQ) ... IMKT
Ingles Markets, Inc. [*Associated Press*] (SAG) ... InglMkt
Ingles Markets'A' [*NASDAQ symbol*] (TTSB) ... IMKTA
Ingleside Branch, Stormont, Dundas, and Glengarry County Library, Ontario [*Library symbol National Library of Canada*] (BIB) ... OISDG
Ingleside, TX [*FM radio station call letters*] (RBYB) ... KAHX-FM
Inglewood, CA [*FM radio station call letters*] ... KACE
Inglewood, CA [*AM radio station call letters*] ... KTYM
Inglewood Public Library, Inglewood, CA [*Library symbol Library of Congress*] (LCLS) ... CIng
Inglewood [*Forest*] **Rifle Volunteers** [*British military*] (DMA) ... IRV
Inglis, FL [*FM radio station call letters*] ... WAVQ
Inglis Ltd. [*Toronto Stock Exchange symbol*] ... ING
Ingmarso [*Sweden ICAO location identifier*] (ICLI) ... ESHI
Ingoldstadt [*Germany ICAO location identifier*] (ICLI) ... EDSI
Ingot (DNAB) ... IG
Ingot (MSA) ... IGT
Ingot Iron ... II
Ingot Metallurgy ... IM
Ingot Resources Ltd. [*Vancouver Stock Exchange symbol*] ... IGT
Ingraham on Insolvency [*Pennsylvania*] [*A publication*] (DLA) ... Ing Insolv
Ingram Micro, Inc. [*NYSE symbol*] (SAG) ... IM
Ingram Micro, Inc. [*Associated Press*] (SAG) ... IngrmM
Ingram Ranch [*California*] [*Seismograph station code, US Geological Survey*] (SEIS) ... ING
Ingram-Rude Information Researchers [*Information service or system*] (IID) ... IR
Ingram's Compensation for Interest in Lands [*2nd ed.*] [*1869*] [*A publication*] (DLA) ... Ing Comp
Ingredient ... INGRD
Ingredient ... INGRDNT
Ingreee Router (ACRL) ... IR
Ingress/Egress ... I/E
Ingress Node (ACRL) ... IN
In-Ground (ADA) ... IG
In-Ground Effect [*Aviation*] (NG) ... IGE
Inguinal [*Anatomy*] ... ING
Inguinal Hernia [*Gastroenterology*] (DAVI) ... IH
Ingvar Kamprad, Elmtaryd, Agunnaryd [*Initialism is company name derived from the names of its founder, the farm on which he grew up, and a Swedish village*] ... IKEA
Inhabitant ... INHAB
Inhabited (ROG) ... INHABD
Inhabited Building Distance [*Army*] (AABC) ... IBD
Inhaca [*Mozambique*] [*ICAO location identifier*] (ICLI) ... FQIA
Inhalable Particulate Matter (GNE) ... IPM
Inhalatio [*Inhalation*] [*Pharmacy*] ... INHAL
Inhalation (DMAA) ... I
Inhalation ... INH
Inhalation Anesthesia ... IH-ANES
Inhalation Cycle Histogram [*Biometrics*] ... ICH
Inhalation Test [*Clinical medicine*] (MAE) ... IT
Inhalation Therapy [*or Therapist*] [*Medicine*] ... IT
Inhalation Toxicology Division [*Environmental Protection Agency*] (GFGA) ... ITD
Inhalation Toxicology Research Institute [*Albuquerque, NM*] [*Department of Energy*] ... ITRI
Inhale Therapeutic Sys [*NASDAQ symbol*] (TTSB) ... INHL
Inhale Therapeutic Systems [*Associated Press*] (SAG) ... InhalTh
Inhale Therapeutic Systems [*NASDAQ symbol*] (SAG) ... INHL
Inhaled Gas Analyzer ... IGA
Inhaled Particles [*or Particulates*] [*Environmental chemistry*] ... IP
Inhambane [*Mozambique*] [*ICAO location identifier*] (ICLI) ... FQIN
Inhambane [*Mozambique*] [*Airport symbol*] (AD) ... INH
Inherent Availability (AAGC) ... Ai
Inherent Availability ... AI
Inherent Corrective Maintenance Workload ... ICMW
Inherent Equipment Reliability ... IER
Inherent Explosion Clause [*Insurance*] ... IEC
Inherent Mobile Availability ... AIM
Inherent Mobile Availability [*Military*] ... IMA
Inherent Secondary Shutdown System (PDAA) ... ISSS
Inherently Low-Emissions Vehicle ... ILEV
Inherently Safe Mining Systems (PDAA) ... ISMS
Inheritance [*Legal shorthand*] (LWAP) ... INH
Inheritance [*Legal term*] (ROG) ... INHCE
Inheritance [*Legal term*] (DLA) ... Inher
Inheritance, Estate, and Gift Tax Reports (Commerce Clearing House) [*A publication*] (DLA) ... Inher Est & Gift Tax Rep (CCH)
Inheritance of Acquired Characteristics ... IAC
Inheritance Tax [*British*] ... IHT
Inherited Epidermal Dysplasia [*Medicine*] (DMAA) ... IED
Inherited Releasing Mechanism [*Psychiatry*] ... IRM
Inherited Rights Filter [*Computer science*] ... IRF
Inherited Rights Mask (ACRL) ... IRM
Inhibin [*Biochemistry*] ... IHB
Inhibin Alpha (DMAA) ... INHA
Inhibin Beta (DMAA) ... INHB
Inhibit ... IH
Inhibit (NASA) ... INH
Inhibit (MSA) ... INHB
Inhibit Halt Flip-Flop [*Computer science*] ... IHF
Inhibit Halt Flip-Flop [*Computer science*] (MSA) ... IHFF
Inhibit Momentum Dump ... IMD
Inhibit/Override Summary Snapshot Display (NASA) ... ISS
Inhibit Simultaneity (IAA) ... ISIM
Inhibited ... INHBD
Inhibited Maximum Density Fuming Nitric Acid (MCD) ... IMDFNA
Inhibited Nitrogen Tetroxide ... INTO
Inhibited Red Fuming Nitric Acid [*Rocket fuel*] ... IRFNA
Inhibited Red Fuming Nitric Acid and Unsymmetrical Dimethylhydrazine [*Rocket fuel*] ... IRFN/UDMH
Inhibited Sexual Desire [*Sex therapy*] ... ISD
Inhibited Sexual Excitement [*Medicine*] (DMAA) ... ISE
Inhibited Sporozoite Invasion [*Immunology*] ... ISI
Inhibited White Fuming Nitric Acid (PDAA) ... IWES
Inhibited White Fuming Nitric Acid [*Rocket fuel*] (SAA) ... IWFA
Inhibited White Fuming Nitric Acid [*Rocket fuel*] (IAA) ... IWFNA
Inhibiting Factor ... IF
Inhibiting Hormone ... IH
Inhibition ... INHIB
Inhibition Concentration [*Biochemistry*] ... IC
Inhibition of Protein Content, 50% [*Biochemistry*] ... IC50
Inhibitor (DMAA) ... I
Inhibitor of Apoptosis Protein [*Cytology*] ... IAP
Inhibitor of DNA Synthesis [*Immunochemistry*] ... IDS
Inhibitor of Mevalonate Incorporation to Cholesterol [*Food science*] ... IMIC
Inhibitor Substance [*Medicine*] (DMAA) ... I-Sub
Inhibitor-Containing Minimal Medium [*Microbiology*] ... IMM
Inhibitory ... I
Inhibitory Concentration [*Toxicology*] ... IC
Inhibitory Dose [*Medicine*] ... ID
Inhibitory Junction Potential [*Neurophysiology*] ... IJP
Inhibitory Postsynaptic Current [*Neurophysiology*] ... IPSC
Inhibitory Postsynaptic Potential [*Neurophysiology*] ... IPSP
In-Home Respite Care ... IHRC
In-Home Support Services [*Medicine*] (MEDA) ... IHSS
Inhomogeneous Big Bang Nucleosynthesis [*Cosmology*] ... IBBN
Inhomogeneous Channel Field-Effect Transistor (PDAA) ... ICFET
Inhomogeneously Broadened Absorber [*Optics*] ... IBA
In-House ... IH
In-House Laboratories Independent Research Program [*Army*] (RDA) ... ILIR
Inhouse Publishing (IAA) ... IP
In-House Systems Developer [*Personal computer*] (PCM) ... IHSD
Iniciativa Canaria [*Spain Political party*] (EY) ... ICAN
Iniciativia per Catalunya [*Spain Political party*] (EY) ... IC
Iniguazu [*Bolivia*] [*ICAO location identifier*] (ICLI) ... SLIJ
Initial ... I
Initial (AFM) ... INIT
Initial ... INIT
Initial (IAA) ... INT
Initial Active Duty for Training [*Military*] (AABC) ... IADT
Initial Address Designator ... IAD
Initial Address Information [*Telecommunications*] (TEL) ... IAI
Initial Address Message (TEL) ... IAM
Initial Address Register [*Computer science*] (HGAA) ... IAR
Initial/Advanced Defense Communications Satellite Program (SAA) ... I/ADCSP
Initial Aiming Point [*Gunnery*] ... IAP
Initial Airborne Target Acquisition Designation System (MCD) ... IATADS
Initial Alignment Unit ... IAU
Initial Allowance Equipage List [*Military*] (CAAL) ... IAEL
Initial Allowance Parts List [*Military*] (CAAL) ... IAPL
Initial and Final Terminal Arrival Date [*Army*] (AABC) ... IFTAD
Initial and Key Personnel ... I & KP
Initial Appearance [*RADAR*] ... IA
Initial Approach [*Aviation*] ... IAP
Initial Approach Course [*Aviation*] ... IAC
Initial Approach Fix [*Aviation*] (AFM) ... IAF
Initial Approved Program ... IAP
Initial Attack Management System [*Weather system*] ... IAMS
Initial Authorization ... IA
Initial Beachhead [*Military*] ... IBH
Initial Beachhead [*Military*] ... IBHD
Initial Boiling Point (MCD) ... IBP
Initial Boiling-Point Temperature ... IBT
Initial Bomb Release Line ... IBRL
Initial Brake Temperature [*Automotive engineering*] ... IBT
Initial Calibration ... IC
Initial Calibration Verification ... ICV
Initial Capabilities Inspection [*Military*] (AFM) ... ICI
Initial Case Design (MCD) ... ICD
Initial Cash Clothing Allowance [*Military*] ... ICCA
Initial Cash Clothing Allowance [*Military*] (DNAB) ... INITCCA
Initial Chaining Value [*Computer science*] ... ICV
Initial Civilian Cash Clothing Allowance [*Military*] (DNAB) ... INITCCCA
Initial Clothing Monetary Allowance [*Military*] ... ICMA

Initial COHORT [*Cohesion, Operational Readiness Training*] **Unit Training** [*Military*] (GFGA) ... ICUT
Initial Combat Employment [*of new munitions*] ... ICE
Initial Communications Connectivity [*DoD*] ... ICC
Initial Condition Evaluation [*Orbit identification*] ... ICEV
Initial Condition Word [*Computer science*] ... ICW
Initial Conditions ... IC
Initial Connection Protocol [*Computer science Telecommunications*] ... ICP
Initial Contact Control Time [*Aerospace*] (AAG) ... ICCT
Initial Contingency Capability (MCD) ... ICC
Initial Control Program Load [*Computer science*] (IAA) ... ICPL
Initial Cooling Experiment [*Nuclear physics research*] ... ICE
Initial Course [*Navigation*] ... IC
Initial Cruise Altitude ... ICA
Initial Defense Communications Satellite (MCD) ... IDCS
Initial Defense Communications Satellite Program [*or Project*] ... IDCSP
Initial Defense Communications Satellite Program / Advanced Defense Communications Satellite Program (SAA) ... IDCSP/ADCSP
Initial Defense Communications Satellite Program-Augmented (CET) ... IDCSP-A
Initial Defense Communications Satellite System (NATG) ... IDCSS
Initial Defense Experiment (IEEE) ... IDEX
Initial Defense Satellite Communication (KSC) ... IDSCM
Initial Defense Satellite Communication System (KSC) ... IDSCS
Initial Defense Satellite Communications Project [*Telecommunications*] (TEL) ... IDSCP
Initial Delay Position [*Military*] (AABC) ... IDP
Initial Denial Authority (AAGC) ... ID
Initial Denial Authority (AABC) ... IDA
Initial Design Evaluation (MCD) ... IDE
Initial Design Review ... IDR
Initial Development Ltd. [*Vancouver Stock Exchange symbol*] ... IDV
Initial Diagnosis [*Medicine*] (CPH) ... ID
Initial Distribution ... ID
Initial Domain Identifier [*Computer science*] (TNIG) ... IDI
Initial Domain Part [*Telecommunications*] (OSI) ... IDI
Initial Domain Part [*Telecommunications*] (OSI) ... IDP
Initial Dose [*Medicine*] (CPH) ... ID
Initial Dose [*Medicine*] ... IN
Initial Dose Period [*Medicine*] (MAE) ... IDP
Initial Draft Presidential Memorandum ... IDPM
Initial dyskinesia [*Medicine*] (DMAA) ... ID
Initial Education and Training Committee (ACII) ... IETC
Initial Effective Data (IAA) ... IED
Initial Engagement Range (MCD) ... IER
Initial Engine Development [*Air Force*] ... IED
Initial Engine Test ... IET
Initial Engine Test Facility ... IETF
Initial Engine Test Firing (IAA) ... IETF
Initial Enrollment Period [*Insurance*] ... IEP
Initial Entry Rotary Wing [*Student*] (MCD) ... IERW
Initial Entry Training ... IET
Initial Equipment [*Navy aircraft*] ... IE
Initial Establishment [*British military*] (DMA) ... IE
Initial File Generation Language ... IFGL
Initial Fill Date [*Army*] (AABC) ... IFD
Initial Fleet Command Center [*Navy*] (CAAL) ... IFCC
Initial Flight Level ... IFL
Initial Floristic Composition [*Theory of plant succession*] ... IFC
Initial Full-Scale Engineering Development ... IFSED
Initial Graphics Exchange Specification [*or System*] [*National Standards Institute*] ... IGES
Initial Graphics Exchange Specification/Product Definition Exchange Specification ... IGES/PDES
Initial Gross Depot Maintenance Requirement [*Military*] ... IGDMR
Initial Heading ... IH
Initial Hydrocarbon Pore Volume [*Petroleum technology*] ... IHCPV
Initial Image Generating Subsystem [*ERTS*] (MCD) ... IIGS
Initial Ion Event ... IIE
Initial Issue ... II
Initial Issue Provisioning [*Marine Corps*] (DOMA) ... IIP
Initial Issue Quantities [*Military*] ... IIQ
Initial Launch Capability [*Aerospace*] ... ILC
Initial Launch Capability (IEEE) ... INLC
Initial Launch Capability Complex [*Aerospace*] ... ILCC
Initial Light Off Procedure (MCD) ... ILOP
Initial Load Block ... ILB
Initial Lung Burden [*Medicine*] (DMAA) ... ILB
Initial Lung Deposit (PDAA) ... ILD
Initial Machine Load [*Computer science*] (IBMDP) ... IML
Initial Maritime Satellite Consortium [*Six United States and two British oil companies and tanker operators*] (PDAA) ... IMSCO
Initial Marks [*Held*] **Constant** [*Psychology*] ... IMC
Initial Mass [*Agronomy*] ... IM
Initial Mass Function [*Galactic science*] ... IMF
Initial Mass in Earth Orbit [*NASA*] ... IMEO
Initial Materiel Support Office [*Army*] (AABC) ... IMSO
Initial Measurement List (KSC) ... IML
Initial Measurement System [*Nuclear missiles*] ... IMS
Initial Memory Protection (MCD) ... IMP
Initial Microprogram Load [*Also, IMPL*] [*Computer science*] (IBMDP) ... IML
Initial Microprogram Load [*Also, IML*] [*Computer science*] ... IMPL
Initial Military Assistance (CINC) ... IMA
Initial Military Program (NATG) ... IMP
Initial Missile Report (CINC) ... IMR
Initial Moisture Content (IAA) ... IMC
Initial Mortality Rate ... IMR
Initial Navigation System (AABC) ... INS
Initial Notification of an Aircraft Accident [*Aviation code*] ... ACCID
Initial Office Visit [*Medicine*] (DAVI) ... IOV
Initial Only (AFM) ... IO
Initial Opening [*Pressure*] [*Measurement*] (DAVI) ... IO
Initial Operating Capability ... IOC
Initial Operating Production (MCD) ... IOP
Initial Operating Test and Evaluation (MCD) ... IOT & E
Initial Operating Test and Evaluation (IAA) ... IOTAE
Initial Operating Test and Evaluation Period [*Navy*] ... IOTEP
Initial Operation Capability Date [*Military*] (AABC) ... IOCD
Initial Operational Capability [*Military*] ... IOC
Initial Operational Capability - Force Development Testing and Experimentation ... IOC-FDTE
Initial Operational Capacity ... IOC
Initial Operational Flight (MCD) ... IOF
Initial Operational Nuclear Detection System ... IONDS
Initial Operational Support Date (MCD) ... IOSD
Initial Operational Test [*Army*] ... IOT
Initial Operational Test and Evaluation [*Army*] (DOMA) ... IOT & E
Initial Orbit Time [*Aerospace*] ... IOT
Initial Orbital Configuration (MCD) ... IOC
Initial Order Condition (MCD) ... IOC
Initial Outfitting Allowance [*Navy*] ... IOA
Initial Outfitting List [*for advanced naval bases*] ... IOL
Initial Outfitting List / Complete Repair, Parts, and Tools (SAA) ... IOL/CR
Initial Outfitting Technical Evaluation (MCD) ... IOTE
Initial Performance Data ... IPD
Initial Phase (IEEE) ... IP
Initial Photographic Interpretation Report [*Air Force*] ... IPIR
Initial Planning Conference [*Military*] (INF) ... IPC
Initial Planning Option [*Medicine*] (DAVI) ... IPO
Initial Point [*Military*] ... IP
Initial Point/H-Hour Control Line [*Aviation*] ... IP/HHCL
Initial Portable Equipment ... IPE
Initial Position ... IP
Initial Post [*Military*] ... IP
Initial Pre-planned Supply Support (DOMA) ... IPSS
Initial Pressure [*On lumbar puncture*] [*Neurosurgery*] (DAVI) ... IP
Initial Pressure Regulator [*Nuclear energy*] (NRCH) ... IPR
Initial Priority Number [*Computer science*] (OA) ... IPN
Initial Processing Number (NITA) ... IPN
Initial Product Inspection ... IPI
Initial Production ... IP
Initial Production and Information Control System [*Computer science*] (PDAA) ... IPICS
Initial Production Facilities (AABC) ... IPF
Initial Production Test [*Army*] (AABC) ... IPT
Initial Production Unit ... IPU
Initial Prognostic Score [*Medicine*] (MAE) ... IPS
Initial Program and Budget Estimate [*Army*] ... IP & BE
Initial Program Load [*Computer science*] ... INP
Initial Program Load [*Computer science*] ... IPL
Initial Program Specification (SAA) ... IPS
Initial Project Design Description (NRCH) ... IPDD
Initial Propulsion Test Vehicle ... IPTV
Initial Protective Force ... IPF
Initial Protocol Identifier [*Computer science*] (TNIG) ... IPI
Initial Provisioning (MCD) ... IP
Initial Provisioning List (MCD) ... IPL
Initial Psychiatric Evaluation (DAVI) ... IPE
Initial Public Offering [*Business term*] ... IPO
Initial Public Offering [*Stock exchange term*] ... IPO
Initial Qualification Training ... IQT
Initial Quality Survey ... IQS
Initial Quantity Order (NG) ... IQO
Initial Rate of Return [*Finance*] (MCD) ... IRR
Initial Reactive Results ... IR
Initial Receiving Point ... IRP
Initial Recruiting and Training Plan [*Military*] ... IRTP
Initial Regulatory Flexibility Analysis (AAGC) ... IRFA
Initial Release (MCD) ... IR
Initial Release Memorandum ... IRM
Initial Reliability Review ... IRR
Initial Repair Parts Requirements List (MCD) ... IRPRL
Initial Reserve ... IR
Initial Review Group [*National Institutes of Health*] ... IRG
Initial Sample Inspection Report ... ISIR
Initial Sample Laboratory Report ... ISLR
Initial Sample Report ... ISR
Initial Satellite Command and Control Center (MCD) ... ISACC
Initial Satellite Communications Control Center (MCD) ... ISACCC
Initial Satisfactory Performance Test (AAG) ... ISPT
Initial Screening Training Effectiveness Analysis ... ISTEA
Initial Search Depth ... ISD
Initial Segment Membrane ... ISM
Initial Selection Done ... ISD
Initial Sequence Number (IAA) ... ISN
Initial Service Test (AABC) ... IST
Initial Ship Design ... ISD
Initial Shipping Instructions (MCD) ... ISI
Initial Shortage (AFM) ... IS
Initial Shut-In Drill Pipe Pressure ... ISIDPP
Initial Signal Unit [*Telecommunications*] (TEL) ... ISU

Initial Slope Circuit [*Telecommunications*] (OA) .... ISC
Initial Software Configuration Map (MCD) .... ISC
Initial Space Station (KSC) .... ISS
Initial Spare Parts List (IAA) .... ISL
Initial Spare Parts List (IAA) .... ISPL
Initial Spares and Repair Parts .... ISRP
Initial Spares Support List (AFM) .... ISSL
Initial Specialty [*Military*] (INF) .... INSPEC
Initial Specific Impulse (MCD) .... ISP
Initial Staging Base [*Army*] (DOMA) .... ISB
Initial Status Word (IAA) .... ISW
Initial Stocks List .... ISL
Initial Student Characteristics .... ISC
Initial Subordinate Dominates Bystander [*Sociology*] .... ISDB
Initial Support Element (MCD) .... ISE
Initial Support Increments [*Army*] (AABC) .... ISI
Initial Support Item .... ISI
Initial Support Package (MCD) .... ISP
Initial Support Team [*Military*] (AFM) .... IST
Initial Surface Absorption Test .... ISAT
Initial System Evaluation Experiment [*Photovoltaic energy systems*] .... ISEE
Initial System Loading .... ISL
Initial System Release (MCD) .... ISR
Initial Systems Checkout .... ISCO
Initial Systems Installation (NASA) .... ISI
Initial [*or Interim*] Tactical Flag Command Center (MCD) .... ITFCC
Initial Task Assignment List .... ITAL
Initial Task Index (AAG) .... ITI
Initial Teacher Education and New Technology [*Project*] (AIE) .... INTENT
Initial Teacher Training (AIE) .... ITT
Initial Teaching Alphabet [*A 44-symbol alphabet planned to simplify beginning reading by representing sounds more precisely*] .... i/t/a
Initial Temperature Difference (IAA) .... ITD
Initial Track (MCD) .... I/T
Initial Training [*Aviation*] (FAAC) .... INIT
Initial Training Requirement .... ITR
Initial Training School [*British military*] (DMA) .... ITS
Initial Training Wing [*British military*] (DMA) .... ITW
Initial Trial Phase (NG) .... ITP
Initial Trouble Report (IAA) .... ITR
Initial Uniform Allowance [*Military*] .... INITUNIFALW
Initial Upper Stage [*NASA*] .... IUS
Initial Upper State (IEEE) .... IUS
Initial User Capability (SSD) .... IUC
Initial Value IV
Initial Vapor Pressure .... IVP
Initial Vector Display Point (IAA) .... IVDP
Initial Velocity [*Ballistics*] IV
Initial Velocity .... Vo
Initial Ventricular Impulse IVI
Initial Virtual Memory .... IVM
Initial Voice Switched Network [*NATO integrated communications system*] (NATG) .... IVSN
Initial Voluntary Indefinite [*Status*] [*Army*] (INF) IVI
Initial-Final Address Message [*Telecommunications*] (TEL) .... IFAM
Initialization (KSC) .... INIT
Initialization Load (MCD) .... ILOAD
Initialize Reset Tape .... IRT
Initialized Moore Probabilistic Automation (IAA) .... IMPA
Initialized Stochastic Sequential Machine (IAA) .... ISSM
Initiate (NASA) .... INIT
Initiated BIT (MCD) .... IBIT
Initiating Event (NRCH) .... IE
Initiating Production by Sales Order (PDAA) .... IPSO
Initiating Reference Document (MCD) .... IRD
Initiating Reference Letter (MCD) .... IRL
Initiation (MSA) .... INIT
Initiation and Development .... I & D
Initiation Area Discriminator [*RADAR*] .... IAD
Initiation Factor [*Protein biosynthesis*] .... IF
Initiation for Bid .... IFB
Initiation of Contraction IC
Initiation Supervisor .... IS
Initiation Technician (SAA) .... IT
Initiative America (EA) .... IA
Initiative America Foundation (EA) .... IAF
Initiative and Referendum .... I & R
Initiative and Referendum [*Legal term*] (DLA) .... INIT & REF
Initiative Committee for National Economic Planning .... ICNEP
Initiative Communications Deception (PDAA) .... ICD
Initiative d'Un Mouvement d'Animation Jeunesse pour l'Annee Internationale de laJeunesse en 1985 [*Canada*] .... IMAJ
Initiative Electronic Deception (ADDR) .... IED
Initiative in Biomolecular Structures [*University of New South Wales*] [*Australia*] .... IBiS
Initiative on Communication Arts for Children (AIE) .... ICAL
Initiative Resource Center [*Defunct*] (EA) .... IRC
Initiatives for Not-for-Profit Entrepreneurship [*Research center*] (RCD) .... INE
Initiator Command Module .... ICM
Initiator Resistance Measuring Equipment (NASA) .... IRME
Initio [*In the Beginning*] [*Latin*] (ROG) .... INIT
Initio, Inc. [*Associated Press*] (SAG) .... Initio
Initio, Inc. [*NASDAQ symbol*] (SAG) .... INTO
Injae [*South Korea ICAO location identifier*] (ICLI) .... RKNI
Inject .... INJ

Injectable Polio Vaccine [*Medicine*] .... IPV
Injected Beam Cross Field Amplifier (IAA) .... IBCFA
Injected Dose .... ID
Injected Electric Current Perturbation .... IECP
Injected Minimum Detectable Quantity [*Analytical chemistry*] .... IMDQ
Injecting Drug User .... IDU
Injectio [*An Injection*] [*Pharmacy*] .... INJ
Injectio Hypodermica [*Hypodermic Injection*] [*Pharmacy*] .... INJ HYP
Injection .... INJCTN
Injection [*Medicine*] .... INJECT
Injection Assistee par Air Comprise [*Pneumatic Direct Fuel Injection*] [*French*] .... IAPAC
Injection Compression System .... ICS
Injection Coupled Synchronous Logic (IAA) .... ISL
Injection Electrode Catheter .... IEC
Injection Facilities (DNAB) .... INJFACS
Injection LASER Diode (TEL) .... ILD
Injection LASER Illuminator ILI
Injection Locked Amplifier (PDAA) .... ILA
Injection Long Wheelbase [*Automotive engineering*] IL
Injection Luminescence Device .... ILD
Injection Microwave Plasma [*Oak Ridge National Laboratory*] .... IMP
Injection Mold (MCD) .... IM
Injection Molding Kit .... IMK
Injection of Fuel Containing Dissolved Gas [*Diesel engines*] .... IFCDG
Injection-Coupled Acoustic Stability Evaluation (MCD) .... ICASE
Injection-Locked Oscillator (IEEE) .... ILO
Injection-Molded Thermoplastic [*Materials science*] .... IMTP
Injector (KSC) .... INJ
Injector Face Acoustic Resonator (MCD) .... IFAR
Injector Orifice .... IO
Injiciatur [*Let It Be Given*] [*Pharmacy*] (ROG) .... INJIC
Injiciatur [*Let It Be Given*] [*Pharmacy*] (ROG) .... INJICIAT
Injiciatur Enema [*Let an Enema Be Injected*] [*Pharmacy*] .... INJ ENEM
Injunction [*Legal term*] .... Inj
Injunction [*Legal term*] .... INJCT
Injunction [*Legal term*] (ROG) .... INJN
Injunction [*Legal term*] (ROG) .... INJON
Injure (AABC) .... INJ
Injured as Result of Hostile Action [*Military*] (NVT) .... IRHA
Injured on Duty .... IOD
Injury (CPH) .... INJ
Injury Control Center [*An association*] (EA) ICC
Injury Control Research Laboratory [*HEW*] .... ICRL
Injury Control Research Laboratory Research Report [*HEW*] .... ICRL-RR
Injury Prevention Program .... IPP
Injury Severity Index (MCD) .... ISI
Injury Severity Score [*Auto safety research*] .... ISS
Injury-Prone Behavior [*Medicine*] (DMAA) .... IPB
Ink (VRA) i
Ink [*Phonetic alphabet*] [*Royal Navy World War I Pre-World War II*] (DSUE) I
Ink Blot Test [*Rorschach test*] [*Psychology*] (DAVI) .... IBT
Ink Jet Printing .... IJP
Ink Receptivity .... IR
INKA Nuclear Science and Technology [*Database*] (NITA) .... INKA-NUCLEAR
INKA Patent Documentation (NITA) .... INPADOC
Inkatha Freedom Party [*Afrikaans Political party*] (ECON) .... IFP
Inkisi [*Zaire*] [*ICAO location identifier*] (ICLI) .... FZAS
Inkopah [*California*] [*Seismograph station code, US Geological Survey*] (SEIS) .... IKP
Inkster, MI [*AM radio station call letters*] .... WMKM
Inland .... INLND
Inland [*Aviation code*] .... LAN
Inland Airlines .... IAL
Inland Architect [*A publication*] (ROG) .... IN ARCH
Inland Auto Dismantlers Association (SRA) .... IADA
Inland Bird Banding Association (EA) .... IBBA
Inland Buoy Tender [*USCG*] (TAG) .... WLI
Inland Casino [*NASDAQ symbol*] (TTSB) .... INLD
Inland Casino Corp. [*NASDAQ symbol*] (SAG) .... INLD
Inland Casino Corp. [*Associated Press*] (SAG) .... InldCas
Inland Clearance Depot [*Shipping*] .... ICD
Inland Commercial Fisheries Association (EA) .... ICFA
Inland Computer Service (IEEE) .... ICS
Inland Construction Buoy Tender [*USCG*] (TAG) .... WLIC
Inland Container [*Shipping*] (DCTA) IC
Inland Daily Press Association .... IDPA
Inland Empire Airlines [*ICAO designator*] (AD) .... LQ
Inland Fish Farming Association of Australia .... IFFAA
Inland Fisher Guide [*General Motors Corp.*] .... IFG
Inland Fisheries Trust, Inc. [*Republic of Ireland*] (BI) .... IFT
Inland Forest Resource Council (EA) .... IFRC
Inland International Trade Association [*Sacramento, CA*] (EA) .... IITA
Inland Lake Yachting Association (EA) .... ILYA
Inland Library System [*Library network*] .... ILS
Inland Library System, Redlands, CA [*Library symbol Library of Congress*] (LCLS) .... CRedll
Inland Library System, Redlands, CA [*OCLC symbol*] (OCLC) .... LNI
Inland Marine [*Insurance*] .... IM
Inland Marine Insurance Bureau [*Later, ISO*] (EA) .... IMIB
Inland Marine Underwriters Association [*New York, NY*] (EA) .... IMUA
Inland Natural Gas Co. Ltd. [*Toronto Stock Exchange symbol Vancouver Stock Exchange symbol*] .... INL
Inland Navigation Facility .... INF
Inland Navigational Rules Act of 1980 .... INRA

Inland Postage (IAA) ..... IP
Inland Printer / American Lithographer [*A publication*] (DGA) ..... IP/AL
Inland Rail Depot (DCTA) ..... IRD
Inland Recovery Group [*Vancouver Stock Exchange symbol*] ..... ILD
Inland Resources [*Associated Press*] (SAG) ..... InldRs
Inland Resources [*NASDAQ symbol*] (SAG) ..... INLN
Inland Revenue [*British*] ..... IR
Inland Revenue Commissioners [*England*] (DLA) ..... IR Comrs
Inland Revenue Commissioners [*British*] ..... IRC
Inland Revenue Office [*or Officer*] [*British*] ..... IRO
Inland Revenue Staff Federation [*A union*] [*British*] (DCTA) ..... IRSF
Inland Rivers Ports and Terminals (EA) ..... IRPT
Inland Seas Education Association ..... ISEA
Inland Shipping Group [*British*] ..... ISG
Inland Steel Indus [*NYSE symbol*] (TTSB) ..... IAD
Inland Steel Industries, Inc. [*NYSE symbol*] (SPSG) ..... IAD
Inland Steel Industries, Inc. [*Associated Press*] (SAG) ..... IldStl
Inland Transport Committee [*United Nations*] ..... ITC
Inland Transport War Council [*World War II*] ..... ITWC
Inland Water Transport [*British*] ..... IWT
Inland Waters Directorate [*Canada*] ..... IWD
Inland Waters Directorate, Environment Canada [*Direction Generale des Eaux Interieures, Environnement Canada*] **Regina, Saskatchewan** [*Library symbol National Library of Canada*] (NLC) ..... SREIW
Inland Waterway (AABC) ..... IWW
Inland Waterway Service ..... IWS
Inland Waterways [*Organization that administered British canals during World War II*] [*Facetious translation: "Idle Women," due to high female workforce*] ..... IW
Inland Waterways Amenity Advisory Council [*British*] (DCTA) ..... IWAAC
Inland Waterways Association [*British*] (DCTA) ..... IWA
Inland Waterways Common Carriers Association [*Defunct*] (EA) ..... IWCCA
Inland Waterways Corp. [*Later, Federal Barge Lines, Inc.; liquidated, 1963*] ..... IWC
In-Law ..... I-L
Inlay (MAE) ..... inl
Inlay (VRA) ..... inl
Inlet [*Rotary piston meter*] I
Inlet [*Maps and charts*] ..... IN
Inlet (KSC) ..... INL
Inlet [*Commonly used*] (OPSA) ..... INLET
Inlet ..... INLT
Inlet [*Board on Geographic Names*] (MCD) ..... INLT
Inlet Absolute Pressure ..... IAP
Inlet and Outlet (MSA) ..... I & O
Inlet and Outlet ..... IXO
Inlet and Outlet Head (MSA) ..... I & OH
Inlet and Outlet Head ..... IXOH
Inlet Contact IC
Inlet Cubic Feet per Minute (PDAA) ..... ICFM
Inlet Gear Box (MCD) ..... IGB
Inlet Guide Valve (MCD) ..... IGV
Inlet Guide Vane ..... IGV
Inlet Manhole [*Technical drawings*] ..... IMH
Inlet Over Exhaust [*Automotive engineering*] ..... IOE
Inlet Particle Separator (MCD) ..... IPS
Inlet Resources Ltd. [*Vancouver Stock Exchange symbol*] ..... INS
Inlet Temperature Rise ..... ITR
Inlet Valve (MCD) ..... I/V
Inlet Vane Actuator ..... IVA
In-Line Filter Degasser ..... IFD
In-Line Infinity Optical System ..... ILIOS
In-Line Instrument Package [*Nuclear energy*] (NRCH) ..... ILIP
In-Line Integrated Circuit ILIC
In-Line Needle Valve ..... INV
In-Line Printer ..... ILP
In-Line Reciprocator ..... ILR
In-Line Relief Valve ..... ILRV
In-Lock IL
In-Lock Detector ..... ILD
INLOGOV [*Institute of Local Government*] **Local Authority Game** ..... ILAG
Inmac Corp. [*Associated Press*] (SAG) ..... Inmac
Inmac Corp. [*NASDAQ symbol*] (NQ) ..... INMC
Inmark Enterprises, Inc. [*NASDAQ symbol*] (SAG) ..... IMKE
Inmark Enterprises, Inc. [*Associated Press*] (SAG) ..... InEnt
Inmark Enterprises, Inc. [*Associated Press*] (SAG) ..... InmkEnt
Inmate Information System [*Bureau of Prisons*] (GFGA) ..... IIS
In-Mold Coating [*Organic chemistry*] ..... IMC
In-Mold Compounding ..... IMC
In-Mold Surfacing [*Plastics technology*] ..... IMS
Innamincka [*South Australia*] [*Airport symbol*] (AD) ..... INM
Innate Release Mechanism [*Endocrinology*] ..... IRM
Innateness Hypothesis [*Linguistics*] ..... IH
Innenstadt von Babylon [*A publication*] (BJA) ..... IvB
Inner I
Inner ..... INNR
Inner (MSA) ..... INR
Inner Approach Channel ..... IAC
Inner Artillery Zone ..... IAZ
Inner Back End (MSA) ..... IBE
Inner [*Edge of*] **Basal Piece** ..... IBP
Inner Blanket Assembly [*Nuclear energy*] (NRCH) ..... IBA
Inner Border Zone ..... IBZ
Inner Bottom [*Technical drawings*] ..... IB
Inner Cabin IC
Inner Canthal Distance [*Medicine*] (DMAA) IC
Inner Cell Mass [*Embryology*] ..... ICM
Inner Circle [*Numismatics*] IC
Inner Circle [*An association*] (EA) IC
Inner Circle of Advocates [*Tucson, AZ*] (EA) ..... ICA
Inner Circle of American Revenuers (EA) ..... ICAR
Inner City Business Improvement Forum ..... ICBIF
Inner City Enterprises [*British*] ..... ICE
Inner City Partnership [*EEC and British program to regenerate blighted areas*] ..... ICP
Inner Continental Shelf Sediments and Structure Program [*Army Corps of Engineers*] (GFGA) ..... ICONS
Inner Core [*Geology*] IC
Inner Cortical Blood Flow [*Medicine*] (DMAA) ..... ICBF
Inner Dead-Center (DNAB) ..... IDC
Inner Defense Zone ..... IDZ
Inner Diameter ..... ID
Inner Enamel Epithelium [*Dentistry*] ..... IEE
Inner Forme [*Imposition*] (DGA) ..... IF
Inner Front End (MSA) ..... IFE
Inner Gimbal ..... IG
Inner Gimbal Angle (NASA) ..... IGA
Inner Gimbal Assembly ..... IGA
Inner Gimbal Axis ..... IGA
Inner Gimbal Axis (NASA) ..... IGAX
Inner Glide Slope [*Aviation*] (NASA) ..... IGS
Inner Grid Injection ..... IGI
[*The*] **Inner Group Corp.** [*Associated Press*] (SAG) ..... Intgrp
Inner Guard [*Freemasonry*] ..... IG
Inner Gulf Shelf [*Marine science*] (OSRA) ..... IGS
Inner Gulf Shelf (USDC) ..... IGS
Inner Hair Cells [*of cochlea*] [*Anatomy*] ..... IHC
Inner Half (MAE) ..... IH
Inner Heel Wedge [*Orthopedics*] (DAVI) ..... IHW
Inner Helmholtz Plane (IAA) ..... IHP
Inner Integument [*Botany*] ..... INI
Inner Keel ..... IK
Inner Lead Bond [*Integrated circuit technology*] ..... ILB
Inner Lindblad Resonance [*Galactic science*] ..... ILR
Inner London Education Authority [*British*] ..... ILEA
Inner London Tertiary Education Board [*British*] (AIE) ..... ILTEB
Inner Marker [*Part of an instrument landing system*] [*Aviation*] ..... IM
Inner Marker [*Part of an instrument landing system*] [*Aviation*] ..... IMKR
Inner Medullary Collecting Ducts [*Kidney anatomy*] ..... IMCD
Inner Metropolitan Region (ADA) ..... IMR
Inner Mitochondrial Membrane [*Cytology*] ..... IMiM
Inner Mitochondrial Membrane [*Cytology*] ..... IMM
Inner Mongolia Autonomous Region [*China, Mainland*] [*MARC geographic area code Library of Congress*] (LCCP) ..... a-cc-im
Inner Nuclear Layer ..... INL
Inner Peace Movement (EA) ..... IPM
Inner Pilot Valve ..... IPV
Inner Plexiform Layer [*Retina*] ..... IPL
Inner Polar Site [*Cytology*] ..... IPS
Inner Quantum Number ..... IQN
Inner Radiation Belt ..... IRB
Inner Radiation Zone ..... IRZ
Inner Roll Gimbal (NASA) ..... IR
Inner Roll Gimbal (MCD) ..... IRG
Inner Scapular Line [*Medicine*] (DMAA) ..... ISL
Inner Seal Collar Tool [*Nuclear energy*] (NRCH) ..... ISCT
Inner Self-Helper [*Mulitple personality*] [*Psychology*] ..... ISH
Inner Sheath [*Botany*] ..... IS
Inner Shelf Transfer and Recycling [*Marine science*] (OSRA) ..... ISHTAR
Inner Temple ..... IT
Inner Transport Area ..... ITA
Inner Vertical Resonance [*Physics*] ..... IVR
Inner Wall [*Medicine*] (DMAA) ..... IW
Inner-City Simulation Laboratory [*Teacher training game*] ..... ICSL
Inner-City Ventures Fund [*National Trust for Historical Preservation*] ..... ICVF
Inner-Core Boundary [*Geology*] ..... ICB
Innerdyne, Inc. [*NASDAQ symbol*] (SAG) ..... IDYN
Innerdyne, Inc. [*Associated Press*] (SAG) ..... Innerdyn
Inner-Shell Photoelectron Spectroscopy ..... ISPES
Innervation [*Medicine*] ..... INNERV
Innes Clan Society (EA) ..... ICS
Innes on Easements [*8th ed.*] [*1911*] [*A publication*] (DLA) ..... Inn Eas
Innes on Easements [*8th ed.*] [*1911*] [*A publication*] (DLA) ..... Inn Ease
Innes' Registration of Title [*A publication*] (ILCA) ..... Innes
Innes' Scotch Legal Antiquities [*A publication*] (DLA) ..... Inn Sc Leg Ant
Inning (WGA) ..... INN
Innings Pitched [*Baseball*] ..... IP
Innings Played [*Baseball*] ..... Ip
Innis College, University of Toronto, Ontario [*Library symbol National Library of Canada*] (NLC) ..... OTUINC
Innisfail [*Australia Airport symbol*] ..... IFL
Innisfail Canegrower [*A publication*] ..... Innisfail Canegr
Innisfail Public Library, Alberta [*Library symbol National Library of Canada*] (NLC) ..... AIN
Inniskilling Dragoon Guards [*British military*] (DMA) ..... IDG
Inniskilling Dragoons [*Military British*] ..... ID
Innkeeper ..... INNKPR
Innkeepers Society of America [*Defunct*] (EA) ..... ISA
Innkeepers USA Trust [*Associated Press*] (SAG) ..... Innkeepr
Innkeepers USA Trust [*NYSE symbol*] (SAG) ..... KPA
Innkeepers USA Trust [*NASDAQ symbol*] (SAG) ..... NKPR

Innocent ... INNCNT
Innocent Civilian [*Military*] ... IC
Innocente [*Innocently*] [*Music*] (ROG) ... INNO
Innocenzo Gasparini Institute for Economic Research ... IGIER
Innodata Corp. [*Associated Press*] (SAG) ... Innodata
Innodata Corp. [*NASDAQ symbol*] (SAG) ... INOD
Innodata Corp. [*Associated Press*] (SAG) ... Inodta
Innodata Corp.Wrrt [*NASDAQ symbol*] (TTSB) ... INODW
Innopac, Inc. [*Toronto Stock Exchange symbol*] ... INA
InnoPet Brands Corp. [*NASDAQ symbol*] (SAG) ... INBC
InnoPet Brands Corp. [*Associated Press*] (SAG) ... InnoPet
InnoServ Technologies [*NASDAQ symbol*] (TTSB) ... ISER
InnoServe Technologies, Inc. [*Associated Press*] (SAG) ... InnoServe
InnoServe Technologies, Inc. [*NASDAQ symbol*] (SAG) ... ISER
Innotech Aviation Enterprises Ltd. [*Toronto Stock Exchange symbol*] ... IAV
Innotech Aviation Ltd. [*Canada ICAO designator*] (FAAC) ... IVA
Innotech, Inc. [*NASDAQ symbol*] (SAG) ... IIII
Innotech Inc. [*NASDAQ symbol*] (TTSB) ... IIII
Innotech, Inc. [*Associated Press*] (SAG) ... Innotech
Innovasive Devices, Inc. [*NASDAQ symbol*] (SAG) ... IDEA
Innovasive Devices, Inc. [*Associated Press*] (SAG) ... InnoDev
Innovation ... INNVTN
Innovation Access Method [*Computer science*] (MHDI) ... IAM
Innovation and Entrepreneurship ... I & E
Innovation Information Center [*George Washington University*] (PDAA) ... IIC
Innovation Ontario Corp., Toronto, Ontario [*Library symbol National Library of Canada*] (NLC) ... OTIC
Innovation through Creative Analysis (PDAA) ... INCA
Innovations [*Record label*] ... Inno
Innovations Deserving Exploratory Analysis Program [*FHWA*] (TAG) ... IDEAS
Innovations et Reseaux pour le Developpement [*Development Innovations and Networks*] [*Geneva, Switzerland*] (EAIO) ... IRED
Innovations in Land Use Management Symposium ... ILUMS
Innovations in Medical Education Grant (DMAA) ... IMEG
Innovationstechnik GmbH & Co. [*Database producer*] (IID) ... ITG
Innovative ... INNVTV
Innovative/Alternative [*Recycling technologies*] ... I/A
Innovative Design Fund, Inc. (EA) ... IDF
Innovative Feasibility Test ... IFT
Innovative Gaming Corp. [*NASDAQ symbol*] (SAG) ... IGCA
Innovative Gaming Corp. [*Associated Press*] (SAG) ... InovGme
Innovative Gaming Corp. Amer [*NASDAQ symbol*] (TTSB) ... IGCA
Innovative Interfaces, Inc. [*Information service or system*] (IID) ... III
Innovative Medical Services [*Associated Press*] (SAG) ... InnoM
Innovative Medical Services [*Associated Press*] (SAG) ... InnoMed
Innovative Medical Services [*NASDAQ symbol*] (SAG) ... PURE
Innovative Naval Reserve Concept (DOMA) ... INRC
Innovative Photovoltaics Applications for Residences ... IPAR
Innovative Project ... IP
Innovative Resources, Inc. ... IRI
Innovative Rural Education and Training Program ... IRETP
Innovative Science and Technology (DOMA) ... IS & T
Innovative Science and Technology [*DoD*] ... IST
Innovative Software Design [*South Africa ICAO designator*] (FAAC) ... ISD
Innovative Strategic Aircraft Design Studies (IEEE) ... ISADS
Innovative Systems Research (NITA) ... ISR
Innovative Tech Sys Wrrt'A' [*NASDAQ symbol*] (TTSB) ... ITSYW
Innovative Tech Systems, Inc. [*Associated Press*] (SAG) ... InnovT
Innovative Tech Systems, Inc. [*Associated Press*] (SAG) ... InnoVTch
Innovative Tech Systems, Inc. [*NASDAQ symbol*] (SAG) ... ITSY
Innovative Test ... IT
Innovative Training Project ... ITP
Innovative Training Projects - National Skills Shortage ... ITP-NSS
Innovative Vehicle Electronic Control System [*Motor vehicles*] ... INVECS
Innovator Multiple Source Drug Product ... IMSDP
Innovator of the Month ... IOM
Innovator's Digest [*The Infoteam, Inc.*] [*Information service or system*] (IID) ... ID
Innovators International [*Defunct*] (EA) ... II
Innovex, Inc. [*Associated Press*] (SAG) ... Innovex
Innovex, Inc. [*NASDAQ symbol*] (NQ) ... INVX
Innovir Laboratories [*NASDAQ symbol*] (TTSB) ... INVR
Innovir Laboratories, Inc. [*Associated Press*] (SAG) ... InnovirL
Innovir Laboratories, Inc. [*Associated Press*] (SAG) ... Innvr
Innovir Laboratories, Inc. [*NASDAQ symbol*] (SAG) ... INVR
Innovir Laboratories Wrrt'A' [*NASDAQ symbol*] (TTSB) ... INVRW
Innovir Laboratories Wrrt'B' [*NASDAQ symbol*] (TTSB) ... INVRZ
Innovo Group [*NASDAQ symbol*] (TTSB) ... INNO
Innovo Group, Inc. [*NASDAQ symbol*] (SAG) ... INNO
Innovo Group, Inc. [*Associated Press*] (SAG) ... Innovo
Innovus Corp. [*Associated Press*] (SAG) ... Innovus
Innovus Corp. [*NASDAQ symbol*] (SAG) ... INUS
Innovus Corp. [*NASDAQ symbol*] (TTSB) ... INUS
Inns of Court and City Yeomanry [*Military unit*] [*British*] ... IC & CY
Inns of Court Rifle Volunteers [*Military British*] (ROG) ... ICRV
Inns of Court School of Law [*British*] (DI) ... ICSL
Inns of Court Volunteer Decoration [*Military British*] (ROG) ... ICVD
Innsbruck [*Austria*] [*Seismograph station code, US Geological Survey*] (SEIS) ... IBK
Innsbruck [*Austria*] [*Airport symbol*] (OAG) ... INN
Innsbruck [*Austria*] [*Seismograph station code, US Geological Survey Closed*] (SEIS) ... INN
Innsbruck [*Austria ICAO location identifier*] (ICLI) ... LOWI
Inocan Technologies Ltd. [*Vancouver Stock Exchange symbol*] ... ICN
Inoculation (AABC) ... INOC
Inoculum Density ... ID
Inoffizielle Mitarbeiter [*Unofficial Collaborators*] [*German*] ... IM
Inolex Pharmaceutical Co., Park Forest South, IL [*Library symbol Library of Congress*] (LCLS) ... IPfsI
Inomeni Parataksis Ethnikofronon [*United Front of Nationalists*] [*Political party*] (PPE) ... HPE
Inongo [*Zaire*] [*ICAO location identifier*] (ICLI) ... FZBA
Inongo [*Zaire*] [*Airport symbol*] (OAG) ... INO
Inoperative ... INOP
In-Orbit Plane (KSC) ... IOP
Inorganic ... INORG
Inorganic Ablative Insulative Plastic ... IAIP
Inorganic Ablative Plastic ... IAP
Inorganic Carbon ... IC
Inorganic Chemical [*Environmental science*] ... IOC
Inorganic Crystal Structure Database [*University of Bonn*] [*Germany*] ... ICSD
Inorganic Halogen Oxidizer ... IHO
Inorganic Insulative Plastic ... IIP
Inorganic Phosphate [*Chemistry*] (DAVI) ... P_1
Inorganic Phosphorus [*Biochemistry*] (DAVI) ... inor phos
Inorganic Phosphorus [*Medicine*] (MEDA) ... Inorg phos
Inorganic Phosphorus (OA) ... IP
Inorganic Resin System [*Fire-resistant cement*] ... IRS
Inorganic Sampling and Analysis ... ISA
Inosine [*One-letter symbol; see Ino*] ... I
Inosine [*Also, I*] [*A nucleoside*] ... Ino
Inosine (DMAA) ... INO
Inosine Diphosphate [*Biochemistry*] ... IDP
Inosine Monophosphate [*Biochemistry*] ... IMP
Inosine Monophosphate Dehydrogenase [*An enzyme*] ... IMPDH
Inosine Phosphorylase [*An enzyme*] (MAE) ... IP
Inosine Triphosphate [*Biochemistry*] ... ITP
Inosinic Acid [*Biochemistry*] (DAVI) ... IMP
Inositol [*Biochemistry*] ... Ins
Inositol Hexaphosphate [*Biochemistry*] ... IHP
Inositol-Phosphoglycan [*Biochemistry*] ... IPG
Inotek Technologies [*NASDAQ symbol*] (TTSB) ... INTK
Inotek Technologies, Inc. [*Associated Press*] (SAG) ... Inotek
Inotek Technologies, Inc. [*NASDAQ symbol*] (SAG) ... INTK
In-Out Converter ... IOC
Inova Optics, Inc. [*Vancouver Stock Exchange symbol*] ... IVO
INPADOC [*International Patent Documentation Center*] **Data Base** [*Information service or system*] (CRD) ... IDB
INPADOC Patent Gazette (NITA) ... IPG
Inpatient [*Medicine*] (DAVI) ... IN-PT
Inpatient [*Medicine*] ... IP
Inpatient Ambulatory Activity Questionnaire [*Medicine*] ... IAA
Inpatient Data Administration (PDAA) ... IDA
Inpatient Exercise Center [*Rehabilitation*] (DAVI) ... IEC
Inpatient, Hospital ... IH
Inpatient Multidimensional Psychiatric Scale ... IMP
Inpatient Multidimensional Psychiatric Scale ... IMPS
Inpatient Non-Availability Statement [*DoD*] ... INAS
Inpatient Unit [*Medicine*] ... IPU
Inpatient Ward [*Medicine*] (DMAA) ... IW
In-Pavement System ... IPS
In-Phase [*Gynecology*] ... IP
Inphase/Midphase (MHDI) ... IP/MP
Inphynet Medical Management [*NASDAQ symbol*] (SAG) ... IMMI
Inphynet Medical Management [*Associated Press*] (SAG) ... Inphynet
InPhyNet Medical Mgmt [*NASDAQ symbol*] (TTSB) ... IMMU
INPI Database 1 [*Database on French patents*] (NITA) ... INPI 1
INPI Database 2 [*Database on European patents*] (NITA) ... INPI 2
In-Place Cleanable Oilfilter ... IPCO
In-Place Repair ... IPR
In-Place Repairable Assembly (MCD) ... IPRA
In-Plant Management Association (EA) ... IPMA
In-Plant Powder Metallurgy Association (EA) ... IPPMA
In-Plant Printing Management Association ... IPMA
In-Plant Printing Management Association ... IPPMA
In-Plant Quality Evaluation Program (AAGC) ... IQUE
In-Plant Support (MCD) ... IPS
In-Plant Test (KSC) ... IPT
In-Plant Test Program (IAA) ... IPTP
In-Plant Training ... IPT
In-Plant Transporter (MCD) ... IPT
In-Plant Verification (AFIT) ... IPV
In-Port Damage Control Training [*Navy*] (NVT) ... DCLPT
In-Port Operations [*USCG*] (TAG) ... I/O
In-Principle Agreement ... IPA
In-Process Factor ... IPF
In-Process Quality Control ... IPQC
In-Process Report ... IPR
In-Process Review ... IPR
In-Process Self Test (MCD) ... IPST
In-Process Testing ... IPT
In-Progress Review (DOMA) ... IPR
Input ... I
Input [*Computer science*] ... I/P
Input (MDG) ... IN
Input (IDOE) ... in
Input (MSA) ... INP
Input Acknowledge (MCD) ... IA
Input and Compare Register ... ICR
Input and Output Driven Selt-Timing Repeater (PDAA) ... IODSTR
Input Axis (KSC) ... IA

Input Bias Current	IBC
Input BIT [*Binary Digit*] [*Computer science*] (NASA)	INBIT
Input Blocking Factor [*Computer science*] (IBMDP)	BI
Input Buffer [*Telecommunications*] (TEL)	IB
Input Buffer Full [*Computer science*] (MHDB)	IBF
Input Bus [*Computer science*]	IB
Input Capacitance (IDOE)	circ
Input Channel Buffer Register [*Computer science*] (IAA)	ICBR
Input Circuit	IC
Input Code (IAA)	IC
Input Collection Reports Data [*IRS*]	ICRD
Input Command Word	ICW
Input Compiler (IAA)	INCOM
Input Contactor Switch	ICS
Input Control Element (MCD)	ICE
Input Control Register [*Computer science*]	ICR
Input Control Subsystem	ICS
Input Control System [*Military*]	INC
Input Control Word [*Computer science*] (MCD)	ICW
Input Controller (MCD)	I/C
Input Current	IC
Input Current Offset [*Computer science*]	ICO
Input Data Assembler	IDA
Input Data Buffer	IDB
Input Data Buffer Register [*Computer science*] (MHDB)	IDBR
Input Data Processor (CET)	IDP
Input Data Request	IDR
Input Data Strobe	IDS
Input Data Word	IDW
Input Data Word (MCD)	IDWD
Input Destination Message Handler	IDMH
Input Display [*Computer science*] (IAA)	ID
Input Display Console [*Computer science*]	IDC
Input Expansion Unit	IEU
Input Frequency Tolerance [*Computer science*]	IFT
Input Impedance	II
Input Interface Unit [*Computer science*]	IIU
Input Language Converter [*Computer science*] (IAA)	ILC
Input Logic Level	ILL
Input Marginal Checking and Distribution	IMCD
Input Memory Buffer [*Computer science*]	IMB
Input Message Acknowledgment [*Computer science*]	IMA
Input Message Processor	IMP
Input Offset Current	IOC
Input Offset Voltage	IOV
Input/Output [*Computer science*]	I/O
Input/Output [*Computer science*]	I/O
Input/Output Access Unit [*Computer science*]	IOAU
Input/Output and Transfer (NITA)	IOT
Input/Output Arithmetic Unit [*Computer science*] (IAA)	IOAU
Input/Output Block [*Computer science*] (CMD)	IOB
Input/Output Buffer (NITA)	IOBFR
Input/Output Buffering System [*Computer science*]	IOBS
Input/Output Bus [*Computer science*] (NASA)	I/OB
Input/Output Computer Service (IAA)	IOCS
Input/Output Connector (NITA)	IOC
Input/Output Console [*Computer science*] (CAAL)	I/OC
Input/Output Control (NITA)	IOC
Input/Output Control Console [*Computer science*] (CAAL)	I/OCC
Input/Output Control Element [*Computer science*] (MCD)	I/OCE
Input/Output Control Processor [*Computer science*]	IOCP
Input/Output Control Program [*Computer science*]	IOCP
Input/Output Control Routine [*Computer science*] (IAA)	IOCR
Input/Output Controller (NITA)	I/OC
Input/Output Controller (NITA)	IOCTR
Input/Output Device [*Telecommunications*] (TEL)	IOD
Input/Output Dump Program [*Computer science*] (IAA)	IOD
Input/Output Front End [*Computer science*]	IOF
Input Output, Inc. [*Associated Press*] (SAG)	InputOut
Input Output, Inc. [*NYSE symbol*] (SAG)	IO
Input/Output Inc. [*NYSE symbol*] (TTSB)	IO
Input/Output Interface Element [*Computer science*] (NITA)	IP/OP
Input/Output Interrupt Handler [*Computer science*]	IOIH
Input/Output Label System [*Computer science*] (OA)	IOLS
Input/Output Line Adaptor (NITA)	IOLA
Input/Output Link Adapter [*Computer science*]	IOLA
Input/Output Link Control [*Computer science*]	IOLC
Input/Output Link Controller (NITA)	IOLC
Input/Output Message Processor [*Computer science*] (IAA)	IOMP
Input/Output Microprocessor (NITA)	IOMP
Input Output of a Record and Transfer [*Computer science*] (SAA)	IORT
Input/Output Operation (HGAA)	IOO
Input/Output Operation [*Computer science*]	IOOP
Input/Output Package [*IBM Corp.*] [*Computer science*]	IOPKG
Input/Output Processor Group (NITA)	IOPG
Input/Output Record Block [*Computer science*]	IORB
Input/Output Register (IAA)	IOREG
Input/Output Request [*Computer science*]	IOREQ
Input Output Requirements Language [*Teledyne Braun Engineering*] (NITA)	IORL
Input/Output Subsystem (NITA)	IOS
Input/Output Subsystem [*NCR Corp.*]	IOSS
Input/Output System [*General Automation*] [*Computer science*]	IOS
Input/Output Systems Association [*Defunct*] (EA)	IOSA
Input/Output Task Group [*CODASYL*]	IOTG
Input/Output Test [*Computer science*] (NASA)	I/OT
Input/Output Trunk (NITA)	IOT
Input Output under Count Control and Disconnect [*Computer science*] (SAA)	IOCD
Input/Output under Count Control and Proceed [*Computer science*] (IAA)	IOCP
Input/Output under Signal and Proceed [*Computer science*] (IAA)	IOSP
Input/Output under Signal and Transfer [*Computer science*] (IAA)	IOST
Input Position Map [*Computer science*] (OA)	IPM
Input Power [*Computer science*]	IP
Input Preparation Unit [*Computer science*] (WDAA)	IPU
Input, Process, and Output (MHDB)	IPO
Input Processor [*Computer science*]	IP
Input Processor Programs [*Computer science*]	IPP
Input Queue Manager (NITA)	IQM
Input Queue Message Handler [*Computer science*]	IQMH
Input Read Submodule	IRS
Input Reference Axis (IEEE)	IRA
Input Register Full	IRF
Input Resistance (IDOE)	R_i
Input Resistance (IDOE)	R_{in}
Input Revision Typewriter	IRT
Input Secondary [*Electronics*]	IS
Input Select and Reset (IAA)	ISR
Input Shift Register	ISR
Input Signal Voltage	ISV
Input Simulator	IS
Input Source Message Handler	ISMH
Input Stack Tape (IAA)	IST
Input Subsystem	ISS
Input System for Operator Connected Calls (PDAA)	ISOCC
Input Terminal	IT
Input Terminal Unit (SSD)	ITU
Input Test Equipment	ITE
Input Translator [*IBM Corp.*] [*Computer science*]	INTRAN
Input Translator [*IBM Corp.*] [*Computer science*] (MSA)	INXLTR
Input Translator [*IBM Corp.*] [*Computer science*]	IT
Input Translator Program [*Computer science*]	ITP
Input Unit	IU
Input Value Table [*Computer science*] (ECII)	IVT
Input Voltage	IV
Input Voltage (IDOE)	V_i
Input Voltage (IDOE)	V_{in}
Input Voltage Offset	IVO
Input Voltage Supply	IVS
Input-Checking Equipment	ICE
Input-Output Adapter [*Computer science*] (NASA)	IOA
Input-Output Address [*Computer science*] (KSC)	IOA
Input-Output Analysis [*Economics*]	IOA
Input-Output Assembly [*Computer science*] (MCD)	IOA
Input-Output Box [*Computer science*] (MCD)	IOB
Input-Output Box and Peripheral Simulator [*Computer science*] (MCD)	IOBPS
Input-Output Buffer [*Computer science*]	IOB
Input-Output Channel [*Computer science*] (DIT)	IOC
Input-Output Comparator [*Computer science*]	IOC
Input-Output Control Center [*or Command*] [*Computer science*]	IOCC
Input-Output Control System [*Computer science*]	IOCS
Input-Output Control Unit [*Computer science*]	IOCU
Input-Output Controller [*Computer science*]	IOC
Input-Output Converter [*Computer science*]	IOC
Input-Output Data Channel [*Computer science*]	IODC
Input-Output Data Document [*Computer science*] (MCD)	IODD
Input-Output Delay Counter [*Computer science*]	IODC
Input-Output Error Log Table [*Computer science*] (MCD)	IOE
Input-Output Executive [*Computer science*] (MHDI)	IOX
Input-Output Gate [*Computer science*]	IOG
Input-Output Generation [*Computer science*]	IOGEN
Input-Output Management System [*Computer science*] (MHDI)	IOMS
Input-Output Module [*Computer science*] (MCD)	IOM
Input-Output Multiplexer [*Computer science*]	I/OM
Input-Output Package [*IBM Corp.*] [*Computer science*]	IOP
Input-Output Port [*Computer science*] (MCD)	IOP
Input-Output Processor [*Computer science*]	IOP
Input-Output Programming System [*Computer science*]	IOPS
Input-Output Pulse [*Computer science*]	IOP
Input-Output Queue [*Computer science*] (IBMDP)	IOQ
Input-Output Queue Element [*Computer science*] (MCD)	IOQE
Input-Output Read Control [*Computer science*] (MHDI)	IORC
Input-Output Register [*SAGE*]	IOR
Input-Output Remote Terminal [*Computer science*] (MHDI)	IORT
Input-Output Request Subroutine [*Computer science*] (MHDI)	IORS
Input-Output Selector [*Computer science*] (IEEE)	IOS
Input-Output Sense [*Computer science*] (KSC)	IOS
Input-Output Skip [*Computer science*]	IOS
Input-Output Supervision [*Computer science*] (NASA)	IOS
Input-Output Switch [*Computer science*]	IOS
Input-Output Termination [*Computer science*]	IOT
Input-Output Transfer [*Computer science*]	IOT
Input-Output Trap [*Computer science*] (MHDI)	IOT
Input-Output Unit [*Computer chip*]	IOU
Input-Output Utility [*Computer science*]	IOU
Input-Output Wait Queue [*Computer science*] (MHDI)	IOWQ
Input-Output Write [*Computer science*] (MHDI)	IOW
Inquest (ROG)	INQT
Inquire (ECII)	INQ

Inquired (ROG) ... INQD
Inquiry (AFM) ... INQ
Inquiry (WDMC) ... inq
Inquiry (ROG) ... INQY
Inquiry and Reporting System ... IRS
Inquiry Data Entry Access System (IAA) ... IDEAS
Inquiry Message Exchange ... IMX
Inquiry/Response [*Automotive engineering Electronics*] ... I/R
Inquisitio Post-Mortem [*Latin*] (ROG) ... INQ PM
Inquisitive ... INQSTV
Inquix Consulting Ltd. [*Information service or system*] (IID) ... IQ
In-Reactor Thimble (IEEE) ... IRT
Inrealistic Neutron Scattering [*Physics*] ... INS
Inroads [*Database*] [*Australia*] ... ROAD
INS Insurance [*Vancouver Stock Exchange symbol*] ... IN
Insan Haklari Merkezi, Siyasal Bilgiler Fakueltesi [*Turkey*] ... IHM-SBF
Insane (ROG) ... INS
Insanity Defense Reform Act of 1984 ... IDRA
Inschrift (BJA) ... Inschr
Insci Corp. [*Associated Press*] (SAG) ... Insci
INSCI Corp. [*NASDAQ symbol*] (TTSB) ... INSI
Insci Corp. [*NASDAQ symbol*] (SAG) ... INSIU
INSCI Corp.Wrrt [*NASDAQ symbol*] (TTSB) ... INSIW
INSCOM [*Intelligence and Security Command*] **Automated Systems Support Activity** [*Army*] (MCD) ... IASA
Inscribed ... INS
Inscribed [*or Inscription*] (MSA) ... INSC
Inscribed Circle (IAA) ... IC
Inscriber [*MARC relator code*] [*Library of Congress*] (LCCP) ... ins
Inscription (ADA) ... INS
Inscription ... INSCR
Inscription (VRA) ... inscr
Inscription ... INSCRPTN
Inscriptiones Graecae [*Epigraphic notation*] ... IG
Inscriptiones Graecae ad Res Romanas Pertinentes [*A publication*] (OCD) ... IG Rom
Inscriptiones Graecae ad Res Romanas Pertinentes [*A publication*] (BJA) ... IGR
Inscriptiones Graecae Antiquissimae (BJA) ... IGA
Inscriptiones Latinae Christianae Veteres ... ILCV
Inscriptiones Latinae Liberae Rei Publicae [*A publication*] (OCD) ... ILLRP
Inscriptiones Mithriacae Duranae (BJA) ... IMDur
Inscriptiones Orae Septentrionalis Ponti Euxini [*A publication*] (OCD) ... IPE
Inscriptions Antiques du Maroc (BJA) ... IAM
Inscriptions Cuneiformes du Kultepe (BJA) ... ICK
Inscriptions Latines des Trois Gaules [*A publication*] (OCD) ... I L de Gaule
[*The*] **Inscriptions of Roman Tripolitania** (BJA) ... IRT
Inscriptions of the Reigns of Evil-Merodach, Neriglissar, and Laborosoarchod (BJA) ... EvM
Insearch Institute of Commerce [*University of Technology, Sydney, Australia*] ... IIC
Insect ... INS
Insect Balanced Salt Solution [*Cytology*] ... IBSS
Insect Biotech Canada [*Queen's University*] [*Research center*] (RCD) ... IBC
Insect Carrier Toxicant ... ICT
Insect Growth Regulator ... IGR
Insect Populations Management Research Unit [*Department of Agriculture*] (GRD) ... IPM
Insect Screen (AAG) ... IS
Insect Screening Weavers Association (EA) ... ISWA
Insect Visual System ... IVS
Insect Wire Screening Bureau [*Later, Insect Screening Weavers Association*] (EA) ... IWSB
Insecta Research [*Vancouver Stock Exchange symbol*] ... ISA
Insecticidal Crystal Protein [*Agrochemistry*] ... ICP
Insecticidal Viral Product [*Agricultural chemistry*] ... IVP
Insecticide (MSA) ... ICTCD
Insecticide(s) [*Freight*] ... INSECTI
Insectivorous Cyprinids [*Pisciculture*] ... INC
Insecure ... INSCR
Insemination ... INSEM
Insensible Water Loss [*Medicine*] ... IWL
Insensible Weight Loss (MEDA) ... IL
Insensitive High Explosive (MCD) ... IHE
Insensitive High Explosives and Propellants [*DoD/DOE program*] (RDA) ... IHEP
Insensitive Munitions (MCD) ... IM
Insensitive Nuclei Enhanced by Polarization Transfer [*Spectroscopy*] ... INEPT
Inseparable (MSA) ... INSEP
Insert (NVT) ... INS
Insert (MSA) ... INSR
Insert Bit String [*Computer science*] (PCM) ... IBTS
Insert Card Section ... ICS
Insert Exon [*Genetics*] ... IE
Insert Extract (IAA) ... IE
Insert Screw Thread ... INST
Insert Shot [*Film production*] (NTCM) ... INS
Insert Storage Key (IEEE) ... ISK
Insert Subcaliber Device [*Weaponry*] (INF) ... ISD
Insertable Nuclear Components (MCD) ... INC
Inserted Connection Loss [*Telecommunications*] ... ICL
Insertion Approval (NRCH) ... IA
Insertion Burn [*Orbital Maneuvering Subsystem 1*] [*NASA*] (NASA) ... INS
Insertion Device [*Series of magnets*] [*Physics*] ... ID
Insertion/Extraction Device [*Aviation*] ... IED
Insertion Loss ... IL
Insertion Mutation [*Genetics*] ... INS
Insertion Phase Delay ... IPD
Insertion Sequence [*Genetics*] ... IS
Insertion Test Signal [*Telecommunications*] (TEL) ... ITS
Insertion Velocity Adjust Routine [*NASA*] ... IVAR
Insertion-Deletion Loop-Type [*Genetics*] ... IDL
In-Service Education (ADA) ... ISE
In-service Education for Teachers [*Australia*] ... INSET
In-Service Engineering [*Navy*] ... ISE
Inservice Engineering Agent [*Military*] (CAAL) ... ISEA
In-Service Inspection (NRCH) ... ISI
In-Service Inspection, Testing, Evaluation, and Monitoring Service ... ITEMS
In-Service Inspections and In-Service Testing ... ISI/IST
In-Service Institute [*National Science Foundation*] ... ISI
In-Service Planned Derated Hours [*Electronics*] (IEEE) ... IPDH
In-Service Recruiter [*Army*] ... ISR
In-Service Training (PDAA) ... INSET
In-Service Training and Education Panel (AIE) ... INSTEP
In-Service Training of Teachers [*Scottish National Committee*] ... ISTT
In-Service Unit Derated Hours [*Electronics*] (IEEE) ... IUNDH
In-Service Unplanned Derated Hours [*Electronics*] (IEEE) ... IUDH
Inshore Fire Support Ship [*Later, LFR*] ... IFS
Inshore Fire Support Ship [*Navy symbol*] ... LFR
Inshore Life Boat (PDAA) ... ILB
Inshore Minesweeper [*Navy British*] ... IMS
Inshore Patrol ... INSHOREPAT
Inshore Patrol ... INSPAT
Inshore Patrol Cutter [*Coast Guard symbol*] (DNAB) ... WYTM
Inshore Undersea Warfare [*Navy*] ... IUW
Inshore Undersea Warfare Control Center [*Navy*] (NVT) ... IUWCC
Inshore Undersea Warfare Craft [*Navy*] ... IUWC
Inshore Undersea Warfare Group [*Navy*] ... INSHORUNSEAWARGRU
Inshore Undersea Warfare Group [*Navy*] ... INSUWG
Inshore Undersea Warfare Group [*Navy*] ... IUWG
Inshore Undersea Warfare Surveillance Unit [*Navy*] (DNAB) ... IUWSU
Inside ... I
Inside [*Automotive engineering*] ... I/S
Inside (MSA) ... INS
Inside Air Temperature ... IAT
Inside Back Cover ... IBC
Inside Battery Limits [*Chemical engineering*] ... ISBL
Inside Cloud Lightning [*Meteorology*] ... IC
Inside Continental United States [*Military*] ... ICUS
Inside Diameter ... ID
Inside Diameter of Outer Conductor ... IDOC
Inside Diameter/Outside Diameter ... ID/OD
Inside Dimensions ... ID
Inside Edge [*Skating*] ... I
Inside Edge ... IE
Inside Face (DAC) ... IF
Inside Front Cover [*Publishing*] (NTCM) ... IFC
Inside Frosted ... IF
Inside Guardian [*Freemasonry*] (ROG) ... IG
Inside Height ... IH
Inside Home [*Baseball*] ... IH
Inside Layer [*Technical drawings*] ... IL
Inside Left [*Soccer position*] ... IL
Inside Leg (ADA) ... IL
Inside Length [*Technical drawings*] ... IL
Inside Mold Line [*Technical drawings*] ... IML
Inside Nazi Germany [*A publication*] ... ING
Inside of Metal (MSA) ... I/M
Inside of Metal ... ISM
Inside of the Battery Limits [*Engineering Economics*] ... IBL
Inside Pipe Size (DAC) ... IPS
Inside Radius [*Technical drawings*] ... IR
Inside Reactor Building (NRCH) ... IRB
Inside Right [*Soccer position*] ... IR
Inside Sentinel [*Freemasonry*] ... IS
Inside Skin (MCD) ... ISS
Inside Surface (MCD) ... ISS
Inside the United States ... INUS
Inside Trim (DAC) ... IST
Inside Trim Template (MSA) ... ITT
Inside Vapor Phase Oxidation [*Glass technology*] ... IVPO
Inside Wheel Turning Angle [*Automotive engineering*] ... ITA
Inside Width ... IW
Inside Wire [*Telecommunications*] (TEL) ... IW
Inside Wiring Cable [*Telecommunications*] (TEL) ... IWCA
Inside-Out [*Biochemistry*] ... ISO
Inside-Out Helmholtz ... IOH
Inside-Out Vesicle [*Biochemistry*] ... IOV
Insider Network Market Report [*Information service or system*] (IID) ... INMR
Insider Trading Sanctions Act of 1984 ... ITSA
Inside-the-Needle Catheter [*Cardiology*] (DAVI) ... INC
Insight Enterprises, Inc. [*Associated Press*] (SAG) ... Insight
Insight Enterprises, Inc. [*NASDAQ symbol*] (SAG) ... NSIT
Insight Entertainment Corp. [*Associated Press*] (SAG) ... InsgtEnt
Insight Entertainment Corp. [*NASDAQ symbol*] (SAG) ... ISTV
InSight Health Services Corp. [*NASDAQ symbol*] (SAG) ... IHSC
InSight Health Services Corp. [*Associated Press*] (SAG) ... InSghtH
Insignia (MSA) ... ISGN
Insignia Financial Group [*NYSE symbol*] (SAG) ... IFS
Insignia Financial Group [*Associated Press*] (SAG) ... InsgFn
Insignia Financial Grp'A' [*NYSE symbol*] (TTSB) ... IFS
Insignia Solutions [*Associated Press*] (SAG) ... InsgSol

Insignia Solutions [*NASDAQ symbol*] (SAG) .... INSGY
Insignia Solutions ADS [*NASDAQ symbol*] (TTSB) .... INSGY
Insignia Sys [*NASDAQ symbol*] (TTSB) .... ISIG
Insignia Systems, Inc. [*Associated Press*] (SAG) .... Insignia
Insignia Systems, Inc. [*NASDAQ symbol*] (SAG) .... ISIG
Insiht Enterprises [*NASDAQ symbol*] (TTSB) .... NSIT
Insilco Corp. [*Associated Press*] (SAG) .... Insilco
Insilco Crop. [*NASDAQ symbol*] (SAG) .... INSL
InSite Vision [*NASDAQ symbol*] (TTSB) .... INSV
InSite Vision, Inc. [*Associated Press*] (SAG) .... InSiteVis
InSite Vision, Inc. [*NASDAQ symbol*] (SAG) .... INSV
In-Situ Heat Transfer Experiment [*Nuclear energy*] (NUCP) .... ISHTE
Insituform East [*NASDAQ symbol*] (TTSB) .... INEI
Insituform East, Inc. [*NASDAQ symbol*] (NQ) .... INEI
Insituform East, Inc. [*Associated Press*] (SAG) .... InsitE
Insituform Mid-America, Inc. [*NASDAQ symbol*] (NQ) .... INSM
Insituform Technol'A' [*NASDAQ symbol*] (TTSB) .... INSUA
Insituform Technology [*Associated Press*] (SAG) .... InsitTc
Insituform Technology [*NASDAQ symbol*] (SPSG) .... INSU
Inslee Family Association (EA) .... IFA
INSO Corp. [*Associated Press*] (SAG) .... INSO
INSO Corp. [*NASDAQ symbol*] (SAG) .... INSO
Insol International (EA) II
Insolated Platform .... IP
Insoluble I
Insoluble (MSA) .... INSOL
Insoluble Bone Gelatin [*Cardiology*] (DMAA) .... IBG
Insoluble Collagen [*Biochemistry*] .... ISC
Insoluble Metaphosphate [*Inorganic chemistry*] .... IMP
Insoluble Organic Material [*or Matter*] [*Analytical chemistry*] .... IOM
Insoluble Residue .... IR
Insolvency [*Legal term*] (DLA) .... Ins
Insolvency [*Legal term*] (DLA) .... Insolv
Insolvency Practitioners Association [*British*] (EAIO) .... IPA
Insolvent [*Legal term*] (ADA) .... INSOLV
Insolvent (ROG) .... INSOLVT
Insoplanar Integrated Injection Logic (NITA) 13L
In-Space Ground Support Equipment [*NASA*] (NASA) .... IGSE
Inspect [*or Inspector*] (AFM) .... INSP
Inspect and Repair as Necessary [*Aviation*] .... IRAN
Inspect and Repair Only as Necessary [*or Needed*] [*Military*] .... IROAN
Inspect [*and Repair*] **Only as Needed** [*MTMC*] (TAG) .... IOAN
Inspect, Supervise, Generally Superintend Recruitment Methods .... INSUPGENCRUIT
Inspect, Test, and Correct as Necessary (MCD) .... ITCAN
Inspected and Condemned [*Military*] (AAG) .... I & C
Inspected and Condemned [*Military*] IC
Inspected Variety Purity [*Agriculture*] .... IVP
Inspecteur General des Institutions Financieres, Quebec, Quebec [*Library symbol National Library of Canada*] (NLC) .... QQIF
Inspecting Chief Officer [*Military British*] (ROG) .... ICO
Inspecting Commander [*Military British*] (ROG) IC
Inspecting Ordnance Officer .... IOO
Inspecting Torpedo Officer [*Navy*] .... ITO
Inspection .... INSPCTN
Inspection .... INSPEC
Inspection (ROG) .... INSPON
Inspection Acceptance Record (SAA) .... IAR
Inspection Administration [*Navy*] .... IA
Inspection Analysis Review Board (MCD) .... IARB
Inspection and Acceptance .... I & A
Inspection and Enforcement (NRCH) .... IE
Inspection and Maintenance .... I & M
Inspection and Maintenance (ERG) .... I/M
Inspection and Safety Center [*Military*] .... ISC
Inspection and Security .... I & S
Inspection and Survey Board [*Navy*] .... PRESINSURV
Inspection and Survey Board Sub Board [*Navy*] .... SUBINSURV
Inspection and Test (NRCH) .... I & T
Inspection and Test (IAA) .... IT
Inspection and Test Instruction (NASA) .... ITI
Inspection and Test (Planning) (MCD) .... I & T(P)
Inspection Apply Template (MCD) .... IAT
Inspection Authorization (GAVI) .... IA
Inspection Bulletin .... IB
Inspection by Attribute .... IBA
Inspection by Variables .... IBV
Inspection Card IC
Inspection Chamber IC
Inspection Check Fixture (MSA) .... ICF
Inspection Check Template (MSA) .... ICT
Inspection Committee IC
Inspection Control Test (SAA) .... ICT
Inspection Data Bulletin .... IDB
Inspection Data Card (MCD) .... IDC
Inspection Departmental Instruction (AAG) .... IDI
Inspection Discrepancy Report (MCD) .... IDR
Inspection Discrepancy Tag (KSC) .... IDT
Inspection Division [*Coast Guard*] .... INS
Inspection Due Notice [*Military*] .... IDN
Inspection Equipment .... IE
Inspection Equipment Drawing .... IED
Inspection Error (KSC) .... IE
Inspection Fixture .... INFX
Inspection Gauge (MCD) .... IG
Inspection Gauge .... INGA
Inspection Gauges Production (MCD) .... IGP
Inspection Generale des Affaires Sociales [*General Inspection of Social Affairs*] [*France*] .... IGAS
Inspection Generale des Affaires Sociales [*France*] .... IGAS
Inspection Hold Tag .... IHT
Inspection Holding Fixture (MCD) .... IHF
Inspection Instruction Sheet .... IIS
Inspection Item Change Request (MCD) .... IICR
Inspection Item Sheet (MCD) .... IIS
Inspection Laws (DLA) .... INSP L
Inspection Lot Size .... ILS
Inspection Manual (MCD) .... IM
Inspection Memorandum .... IM
Inspection Method Control .... IMC
Inspection Opening (ADA) .... IO
Inspection Operation Procedure (MCD) .... IOP
Inspection Operation Sheet (AAG) .... IOS
Inspection Operation System (AAG) .... IOS
Inspection Operation Tag .... IOT
Inspection Order (NATG) .... IO
Inspection Outline .... IO
Inspection, Palpation, Percussion, Auscultation [*Medicine*] .... IPPA
Inspection Pit [*Motor garage*] (ROG) .... IP
Inspection Planning and Reliability (SAA) .... IPR
Inspection Planning Document [*Military*] (MCD) .... IPD
Inspection Planning Order .... IPO
Inspection Procedure [*Nuclear energy*] (NRCH) .... IP
Inspection Progress Notification .... IPN
Inspection Quality Assurance .... IQA
Inspection Record (MCD) .... IR
Inspection Record Card [*Navy*] (NG) .... IRC
Inspection Record Sheet .... IRS
Inspection Rejection .... IR
Inspection Rejection Report [*NASA*] (KSC) .... IRR
Inspection Release .... IR
Inspection, Repair, Overhaul, and Rebuild .... IROR
Inspection [*or Inspector's*] **Report** .... IR
Inspection Request (IAA) .... IR
Inspection Requirements Handbook [*Navy*] (NG) .... IRH
Inspection Requirements Manual (AAG) .... IRM
Inspection Review Board (KSC) .... IRB
Inspection Services, Inc. (EA) .... IS
Inspection Shell .... INSH
Inspection Tag .... IT
Inspection Test and Analysis Plan (NRCH) .... IT & AP
Inspection Test and Analysis Plan (IAA) .... ITAAP
Inspection Test Assembly (MCD) .... ITA
Inspection Test Procedure .... ITP
Inspection Test Report .... ITR
Inspection Test Work Order (SAA) .... ITWO
Inspection Validation Center [*Nuclear energy*] (NUCP) IVC
Inspection Verification Tag .... IVT
Inspection Visual Aid (AAG) .... IVA
Inspection Zone .... IZ
Inspections and Investigations Staff [*Vietnam*] .... IIS
Inspector I
Inspector .... INS
Inspector .... INSPCTR
Inspector .... INSPR
Inspector and Instructor [*For reserve units*] [*Marine Corps*] (DOMA) .... I & I
Inspector General [*Air Force, Army, Marine Corps*] .... IG
[*Office of the*] **Inspector General** .... IG
Inspector General [*Navy*] .... INSGEN
Inspector General (WGA) .... Insp Gen
[*The*] **Inspector General** [*Army*] .... TIG
Inspector General, Atlantic Fleet [*Navy*] .... INSGENLANTFLT
Inspector General, Department of Defense (USGC) .... IGDOD
Inspector General Division [*Environmental Protection Agency*] (GFGA) .... IGD
Inspector General Field Office [*Military*] .... IGFO
Inspector General, Foreign Assistance [*Department of State*] .... IGFA
Inspector General Network [*Military*] (GFGA) .... IGNET
Inspector General, Pacific Fleet and Pacific Ocean Areas [*Navy*] .... INSGENPAC
Inspector General Reports (AAGC) .... Inspector Gen Rep
Inspector General, Supply Corps .... IGSC
Inspector General's Department .... IGD
Inspector General's Office [*Air Force*] .... IGO
Inspector/Killer .... I/K
Inspector of Army Schools [*British military*] (DMA) .... IAS
Inspector of Degaussing [*Navy*] .... IDG
Inspector of Dental Activities .... INSDEN
Inspector of Machinery .... IM
Inspector of Naval Aircraft .... INA
Inspector of Naval Aircraft .... INSAIR
Inspector of Naval Engineering .... INSENG
Inspector of Naval Machinery .... INM
Inspector of Naval Machinery .... INSMACH
Inspector of Naval Material .... INM
Inspector of Naval Material .... INSMAT
Inspector of Naval Material, Petroleum .... INSMAT PET
Inspector of Naval Ordnance [*British*] .... INO
Inspector of Navigational Material .... INSNAVMAT
Inspector of Navy Recruiting and Naval Officer Procurement .... INSCRUIT
Inspector of Ordnance .... INSORD
Inspector of Ordnance in Charge .... INSORDINC

Inspector of Ordnance Machinery [*British military*] (DMA) ... IOM
Inspector of Petroleum Reserves ... INSPETRES
Inspector of Radio Material ... INSRADMAT
Inspector of Radio Services [*Military*] (IAA) ... IRS
Inspector of Schools [*British*] (DAS) ... IOS
Inspector of the Royal Artillery [*British*] ... IRA
Inspector of Torpedoes and Mines [*Navy*] ... ITM
Inspector of Training Corps and Cadets [*Military British*] ... ITCA
Inspector of Weights and Measures [*British*] (ROG) ... INSP W & M
Inspector of Works ... IW
Inspectorate of Armaments (PDAA) ... IARM
Inspectorate of Electrical and Mechanical Engineering [*Military*] (IAA) ... IEME
Inspectorate of Fighting Vehicles and Mechanical Equipment [*Military*] ... IFVME
Inspector-General of Communications [*British military*] (DMA) ... IGC
Inspector-General of Fortifications [*British*] ... IGF
Inspector-General of Hospitals and Fleets [*Navy British*] (ROG) ... IH
Inspector-General of the Royal Air Force [*British*] ... IGRAF
Inspector-General of Transportation [*British military*] (DMA) ... IGT
Inspector-General to the Forces for Training [*British military*] ... IGT
Inspector-Instruction [*Marine Corps*] ... INSP-INSTR
Inspector-Instructor [*Marine Corps*] ... I-I
Inspector-Instructor, Naval Reserve ... INSINSTR
Inspector-Instructor Staff [*Military*] (DNAB) ... INSPINSTF
Inspectors Based in Schools [*British*] (AIE) ... IBIS
Inspectors of Naval Material (AAGC) ... INSMATS
Inspector's Report Addendum (AAG) ... IRA
Inspekteur der Artillerie [*Inspector of Artillery*] [*German military - World War II*] ... IDA
Inspekteur der Ordnungspolizei [*Inspector of Uniformed Police*] [*German military - World War II*] ... IDO
Inspiration ... INSP
Inspiration [*or Inspiratory*] (CPH) ... inspir
Inspiration-Phase Gas (DMAA) ... IPG
Inspiratory Capacity [*Physiology*] ... IC
Inspiratory Center [*Physiology*] ... IC
Inspiratory Flow Rate [*Physiology*] ... IFR
Inspiratory Muscle Training [*Medicine*] (DMAA) ... IMT
Inspiratory Positive Airway Pressure [*Medicine*] (DMAA) ... IPAP
Inspiratory Reserve Capacity [*Physiology*] (MAE) ... IRC
Inspiratory Reserve Volume [*Physiology*] ... IRV
Inspiratory Time [*Medicine*] (DAVI) ... IT
Inspiratory-Expiratory (Ratio) [*Physiology*] ... I/E
Inspired [*Medicine*] (DAVI) ... I
Inspired Humidity [*Anesthesiology*] ... IH
Inspired Partial Pressure [*Physiology*] ... IPP
Inspired Vital Capacity (AAMN) ... IVC
Inspired Volume per Minute [*Medicine*] (DAVI) ... V_I
Inspiretur [*Let It Be Inspired*] [*Pharmacy*] ... INSPIR
Instability (FAAC) ... INSTBY
Instalbud [*Poland ICAO designator*] (FAAC) ... INB
Install and Dismantle [*Expositions and exhibitions*] ... I & D
Installable Compression, Manager [*Computer science*] ... ICM
Installable File System [*Computer science*] ... IFS
Installation ... INSTAL
Installation ... INSTALLN
Installation (AFM) ... INSTL
Installation (VRA) ... instl
Installation ... INSTLN
Installation ... INSTLTN
Installation, Administrative Use, and Command Design Motor Vehicle Management System [*Army*] ... IAUMS
Installation Aircraft Inventory Reporting System [*Army*] ... IAIRS
Installation and Calibration (SAA) ... I & C
Installation and Checkout [*Military*] (AFM) ... I & C
Installation and Checkout (NASA) ... I & C/O
Installation and Checkout (IAA) ... IAC
Installation and Checkout [*Military*] (CAAL) ... INCO
Installation and Checkout (NASA) ... INSTL & C/O
Installation and Construction [*Military*] ... I & C
Installation and Logistics (IAA) ... IAL
Installation and Maintenance ... I & M
Installation and Maintenance Guide ... IMG
Installation and Maintenance Instruction ... IMI
Installation and Materiel District Office [*FAA*] ... IMDO
Installation and Operational Checkout ... IOC
Installation and Removal Record [*NASA*] (KSC) ... IRR
Installation and Service Engineering (IEEE) ... I & SE
Installation and Services ... I & S
Installation and Test [*Army*] (AABC) ... I & T
Installation and Test Support Associate Contractor [*Air Force*] ... ITSA
Installation, Assembly or Detail (AAG) ... IAD
Installation Automated Budget System [*Army*] ... IABS
Installation Automated Manpower Utilization System [*Army*] ... IAMUS
Installation Aviation Standardization Board (MCD) ... IASB
Installation Calibration and Checkout (KSC) ... IC & C
Installation Calibration and Checkout (KSC) ... ICC
Installation Completion Date (CET) ... ICD
Installation Confinement Facility [*Army*] (AABC) ... ICF
Installation Console (MCD) ... INCON
Installation Control [*Computer science*] (PCM) ... INCTRL
Installation Control Drawing [*DoD*] ... ICD
Installation CONUS FORSTAT System [*Military*] ... ICFS
Installation Damage Report [*Air Force*] ... INREP
Installation Data ... ID
Installation Data Record ... IDR
Installation Engineers Office (SAA) ... IEO
Installation Enhancement Release [*Computer science*] ... IER
Installation Environmental Impact Assessment (PDAA) ... IEIA
Installation Equipment [*Army*] (AABC) ... IE
Installation Equipment Management Office [*Military*] (AFIT) ... IEMO
Installation Equipment Management System (MCD) ... IEM
Installation Equipment Management System ... IEMS
Installation Fixtures (MCD) ... IF
Installation Handbook ... IH
Installation Identification Element (MCD) ... IIE
Installation Input Change Package (MCD) ... ICP
Installation Inspection Procedure Report ... IIPR
Installation Instruction ... II
Installation Lead Time ... ILT
Installation, Logistics and Financial Management (AAGC) ... IL&FM
Installation Maintenance Activity (MCD) ... IMA
Installation Maintenance Management System (MCD) ... IMMS
Installation Maintenance Officer [*Military*] (AABC) ... IMO
Installation Management Information System [*Army*] ... IMIS
Installation Master File (MCD) ... IMF
Installation Master Planning [*Military*] ... IMP
Installation Material (AAGC) ... IM
Installation Materiel Condition Status Reporting System [*Army*] ... IMCSRS
Installation Materiel Readiness Reporting System [*Army*] ... IMRRS
Installation, Modification, Maintenance, and Repair (AAG) ... IMMR
Installation Notice Card (KSC) ... INC
Installation Notification Certification (MCD) ... INC
Installation of Systems (IAA) ... IS
Installation Operating Program (AABC) ... IOP
Installation Operation Budget (AABC) ... IOB
Installation Parts List (AAG) ... IPL
Installation Performance Specification [*Computer science*] (IBMDP) ... IPS
Installation Planning Order ... IPO
Installation Preflight Test ... IPT
Installation Procedure ... IP
Installation Production Order ... IPO
Installation Productivity Option [*IBM Corp.*] ... IPO
Installation Productivity Option/Extended [*IBM Corp.*] ... IPO/E
Installation Property Book [*Military*] (AABC) ... IPB
Installation Qualification (ACII) ... IQ
Installation Readiness System [*Army*] ... IRS
Installation Report ... IR
Installation Restoration (MCD) ... IR
Installation Restoration Program [*Army*] (RDA) ... IRP
Installation Restoration Technology Coordinating Group [*Army*] (RDA) ... IRTCG
Installation Service Supply Support ... ISSS
Installation Shipping and Receiving Capability [*Army*] (AABC) ... ISARC
Installation Site Survey (MCD) ... ISS
Installation Specification Drawing (MCD) ... ISD
Installation Spill Contingency Plan [*DoD*] (AFIT) ... ISCP
Installation Squadron ... INS
Installation Standard Command Automated Data Processing Management System [*Army*] ... ISCAMS
Installation Start [*Telecommunications*] (TEL) ... IS
Installation Start Date (CET) ... ISD
Installation Supply Accounting ... ISA
Installation Supply Activity ... ISA
Installation Supply Division [*Military*] (AABC) ... ISD
Installation Supply Officer [*Military*] ... ISO
Installation Support (KSC) ... IS
Installation Support and Evaluation (AAG) ... ISE
Installation Support School [*Army*] ... ISS
Installation Support Services (NASA) ... ISS
Installation Test (NASA) ... IT
Installation Test Program ... ITP
Installation Test Requirements Outline (MCD) ... ITRO
Installation, Testing, and Firing Apparatus [*Military*] (INF) ... ITFA
Installation the Army Authorization Document System ... ITAADS
Installation Training/Coordination Section [*Social Security Administration*] ... ITCS
Installation Transportation Office [*or Officer*] [*Air Force*] (AFM) ... ITO
Installation Verification Procedure (MCD) ... IVP
Installation Volunteer Coordinator ... IVC
Installation Worldwide Ammunition Reporting System [*Army*] ... IWARS
Installational and Operational Qualifications [*Manufacturing*] ... IOQ
Installations and Logistics ... I & L
Installations and Services Agency [*Army Materiel Command*] ... ISA
Installations Fragenkommission [*Later, International Commission on Rules for the Approval of Electrical Equipment*] [*CEE*] ... IFK
Installations Planning and Review Board [*DoD*] ... IPRB
Installed ... INST
Installed Capacity [*Electronics*] (IEEE) ... IC
Installed First Cost (ACRL) ... IFC
Installed Maximum Operating Time ... IMOT
Installed User Program [*Computer science*] ... IUP
Installed User System [*Computer science*] (IAA) ... IUS
Installer ... INSTLLR
Installer ... INSTLR
Installer Point of Purchase ... IPOP
Installment [*Business term*] ... INST
Installment ... INSTL
Installment Agreement ... I/A
Installment Mortgage (WDAA) ... IM
Installment Paid [*Business term*] ... IP
Installment Sales Revision Act of 1980 ... ISRA
Instans [*The Current Month*] [*Latin*] ... INST

Instant (VRA) .... ins
Instant .... INST
Instant (ODBW) .... inst
Instant .... INSTNT
Instant Big Mouth [*Martini*] [*Slang*] .... IBM
Instant Computer Arbitration Search [*Database*] [*Labor Relations Press*] [*Information service or system*] (CRD) .... ICAS
Instant Computer Public Employment Relations Search [*Database*] [*Labor Relations Press*] [*Information service or system*] (CRD) .... ICPERS
Instant Control Point [*British police*] .... ICP
Instant Corn-Soya-Milk .... ICSM
Instant Data Access Control [*National Design Center, Inc.*] [*Information service or system*] (IID) .... IDAC
Instant Dimmer Memory (IAA) .... IDM
Instant Drug Index [*A publication*] (DAVI) .... IDI
Instant Language [*Trademark*] [*Computer science*] .... INLAN
Instant Lead Vertical Speed Indicator (MCD) .... ILVSI
Instant Lunar Ionosphere ILI
Instant Messaging [*Computer science*] .... IM
Instant Mini/Micro Computer Accessories and Cables [*Manufacturer/distributor*] [*British*] (NITA) .... INMAC
Instant Ocean Culture System .... IOCS
Instant Oxide Thickness Analyzer (IAA) .... IOTA
Instant Potato Products Association [*Defunct*] (EA) .... IPPA
Instant Private Network .... IPN
Instant Publisher [*NASDAQ symbol*] (TTSB) .... TIPIF
[*The*] **Instant Publisher, Inc.** [*NASDAQ symbol*] (SAG) .... TIPIF
[*The*] **Instant Publishers, Inc.** [*Associated Press*] (SAG) .... InstPubl
Instant Purchase Excursion Fares [*Aviation*] .... IPEX
Instant Release [*Typography*] (DGA) .... IR
Instant Response Information System (IEEE) .... IRIS
Instant Response Ordering System [*Teleordering system*] [*Information service or system*] (IID) .... IROS
Instant Sales Indicator System (IAA) .... ISIS
Instant Thin-Layer Chromatography .... ITLC
Instant Transaction (IAA) .... IT
Instant Transference .... ITF
Instant Update [*Professional Farmers of America*] [*Information service or system*] (TSSD) .... IU
Instant Video Receiver [*Electronics*] .... IVR
Instant Visual Index IVI
Instant Yellow Pages [*Information service or system*] .... IYP
Instantaneous I
Instantaneous (MSA) .... INST
Instantaneous Airborne Count (MCD) .... IAC
Instantaneous Audience Measurement System .... IAMS
Instantaneous Automatic Frequency Control .... IAFC
Instantaneous Automatic Gain Control [*or Circuit*] [*RADAR*] .... IAGC
Instantaneous Automatic Level Control (IDOE) .... IALC
Instantaneous Automatic Video Control (IEEE) .... IAVC
Instantaneous Automatic Volume Control [*Electronics*] .... IAVC
Instantaneous Broadcast Audience Counting (IAA) .... IBAC
Instantaneous Cardiac Death [*Cardiology*] (DAVI) .... ICD
Instantaneous Center of Motion .... ICM
Instantaneous Center of Rotation .... ICR
Instantaneous Compressor Performance Analysis Computer .... ICPAC
Instantaneous Current (IDOE) I
Instantaneous Diastolic Pressure (MAE) .... IDP
Instantaneous Direction Finding (MCD) .... IDF
Instantaneous Drilling Evaluation Log (PDAA) .... IDEEA
Instantaneous Effective Photo .... IEP
Instantaneous Effective Photocathodes (MCD) .... IEPC
Instantaneous Field of View .... IFOV
Instantaneous Field of View (DNAB) .... IFV
Instantaneous Field Tube [*Astrophysics*] .... IFT
Instantaneous Flow [*Medicine*] (DMAA) .... IF
Instantaneous Fourier Transform [*Computer science*] .... IFT
Instantaneous Frequency Correlation .... IFC
Instantaneous Frequency Correlation (NG) .... IFRC
Instantaneous Frequency Discriminator (IEEE) .... IFD
Instantaneous Frequency Measurement .... IFM
Instantaneous Frequency [*Indicating*] **Receivers** (IEEE) .... IFR
Instantaneous Geometric Field of View .... IGFOV
Instantaneous Grid (IAA) .... IG
Instantaneous Impact Points (KSC) .... IIP
Instantaneous Impact Prediction System (DNAB) .... IIPS
Instantaneous Impact Predictor .... IIP
Instantaneous Launch Control Officer [*Aerospace*] (AAG) .... ILCO
Instantaneous Lead Computing Optical Sight [*Gunsight*] [*Navy*] (DOMA) .... ILCOS
Instantaneous Overload .... IOL
Instantaneous Panoramic Display Unit .... IPDU
Instantaneous Power Output .... IPO
Instantaneous Pressure [*Medicine*] (MAE) .... IP
Instantaneous Readout Detector [*Satellite instrument*] .... IROD
Instantaneous Relay .... IR
Instantaneous Release (IAA) .... IR
Instantaneous Sound Pressure .... ISP
Instantaneous Spatial Transference .... IST
Instantaneous Speed Variation [*Tape recorders*] .... ISV
Instantaneous Systems Display [*Computer science*] (MHDB) .... INSYD
Instantaneous Trip Block [*Computer science*] (IAA) .... ITB
Instantaneous Unit Hydrograph (PDAA) .... IHU
Instantaneous Unit Hydrograph .... IUH
Instantaneous Value (IDOE) I
Instantaneous Vertical Speed Indicator [*NASA*] .... IVSI
Instantaneous Vertical Velocity IVV
Instantaneous Vertical Velocity Indicator IVVI
Instantaneous Vertical Velocity Sensor (NATG) .... IVVS
Instantaneous Word Encoder (IAA) .... IWE
Instant-Set Polymer (PDAA) .... ISP
Instead (ROG) .... INSTD
Insteel Industries [*NYSE symbol*] (SAG) III
Insteel Industries Inc. [*NYSE symbol*] (TTSB) III
Insteel Industries, Inc. [*Associated Press*] (SAG) .... Insteel
InStent Inc. [*NASDAQ symbol*] (TTSB) .... ININ
Instent, Inc. [*Associated Press*] (SAG) .... InStent
InStent, Inc. [*NASDAQ symbol*] (SAG) .... INTN
Instillandus [*To Be Dropped In*] [*Pharmacy*] .... INSTILL
Instillation Delivery Time [*Medicine*] (DMAA) .... IDT
Institue of Arable Crop Research [*British*] .... IACR
Institut Africain de Developpement Economique et de Planification [*African Institute for Economic Development and Planning*] [*Dakar, Senegal*] (AF) .... IDEP
Institut Agricole d'Oka, LaTrappe, PQ, Canada [*Library symbol Library of Congress Obsolete*] (LCLS) .... CaQTO
Institut Albert Prevost, Montreal, PQ, Canada [*Library symbol Library of Congress*] (LCLS) .... CaQMIAP
Institut Albert Tessier, Trois-Rivieres, PQ, Canada [*Library symbol Library of Congress*] (LCLS) .... CaQTI
Institut Albert Tessier, Trois-Rivieres, Quebec [*Library symbol National Library of Canada*] (NLC) .... QTI
Institut Armand-Frappier [*University of Quebec*] [*Formerly, Institute of Microbiology and Hygiene of Montreal*] [*Research center*] (RCD) .... IAF
Institut Armand-Frappier, Universite du Quebc, Laval, Quebec [*Library symbol National Library of Canada*] (NLC) .... QMIM
Institut Belge de Normalisation [*Belgian Institute for Standardization*] [*Information service or system*] (IID) .... IBN
Institut Canadien d'Acupuncture [*Canadian Acupuncture Institute*] .... ICA
Institut Canadien d'Administration de la Justice (AC) .... ICAJ
Institut Canadien de Conservation [*Canadian Conservation Institute - CCI*] ICC
Institut Canadien de la Construction en Acier [*Canadian Institute of Steel Construction*] .... ICCA
Institut Canadien de la Mediterranee [*Canadian Mediterranean Institute*] .... ICM
Institut Canadien de la Sante Infantile [*Canadian Institute of Child Health*] .... ICSI
Institut Canadien de l'Information Scientifique et Technique [*Canadian Institute for Scientific and Technical Information - CISTI*] .... ICIST
Institut Canadien de Microreproductions Historiques [*Canadian Institute for Historical Microreproductions - CIHM*] .... ICMH
Institut Canadien de Recherches en Telecommunications (AC) .... ICTR
Institut Canadien de Recherches pour l'Avancement de la Femme [*Canadian Research Institute for the Advancement of Women*] .... ICRAF
Institut Canadien de Recherches sur les Femmes (AC) .... ICREF
Institut Canadien de Tole d'Acier en Batiment [*Canadian Sheet Steel Building Institute*] .... ICTAB
Institut Canadien d'Education des Adultes [*Canadian Institute of Adult Education*] .... ICEA
Institut Canadien d'Enseignement Personnalise Inc. (AC) .... ICEP
Institut Canadien des Actuaires [*Canadian Institute of Actuaries*] .... ICA
Institut Canadien des Affaires Africaines [*Canadian Institute of African Affairs*] .... ICAA
Institut Canadien des Affaires Internationales [*Canadian Institute of International Affairs*] .... ICAI
Institut Canadien des Comptables Agrees [*Canadian Institute of Chartered Accountants*] .... ICCA
Institut Canadien des Ingenieurs [*Engineering Institute of Canada*] ICI
Institut Canadien des Mines et de la Metallurgie [*Canadian Institute of Mining and Metallurgy*] (EAIO) .... ICM
Institut Canadien des Oceans [*Oceans Institute of Canada*] (IRC) .... ICO
Institut Canadien des Textiles [*Canadian Textiles Institute*] (EAIO) .... ICT
Institut Canadien du Film [*Canadian Film Institute - CFI*] .... ICF
Institut Canadien pour la Deficience Mentale [*Canadian Institute on Mental Retardation*] [*Canada*] .... ICDM
Institut Culturel Africain [*African Cultural Institute*] (EAIO) .... ICA
Institut Culturel Avataq, Montreal, Quebec [*Library symbol National Library of Canada*] (BIB) .... QMICAV
Institut d'Administration des Entreprises [*Institute of Company Management*] [*Information service or system*] (IID) .... IAE
Institut d'Amenagement et d'Urbanisme de la Region de l'Ile de France (NITA) .... IAURIF
Institut de Cardiologie de Montreal, Montreal, PQ, Canada [*Library symbol Library of Congress*] (LCLS) .... CaQMICM
Institut de Cardiologie de Montreal, Quebec [*Library symbol National Library of Canada*] (NLC) .... QMICM
Institut de Developpement International et de Cooperation [*Institute for International Development and Cooperation IIDC*] [*University of Ottawa*] [*Canada*] .... IDIC
Institut de Droit International [*Institute of International Law*] .... IDI
Institut de Formation et de Recherche Demographiques [*Institute for Training and Demographic Research - ITDR*] (EAIO) .... IFORD
Institut de Genie des Materiaux, Longueuil, PQ, Canada [*Library symbol Library of Congress*] (LCLS) .... CaQLoGM
Institut de Geographie, Universite Laval, Quebec, Quebec [*Library symbol National Library of Canada*] (NLC) .... QQLAG
Institut de la Medecine du Travail et de l'Environnement [*Institute of Occupational and Environmental Health*] [*Canada*] .... IMTE
Institut de la Medecine du Travail et des Ambiances [*Institute of Occupational and Environmental Health*] [*Canada*] .... IMTA
Institut de l'Amiante [*Asbestos Institute - AI*] (EA) .... IA
Institut de Mecanique des Fluides [*Originator and database on fluid mechanics*] [*France*] (NITA) .... IMF

Institut de Microbiologie et d'Hygiene de Montreal, Montreal, PQ, Canada [*Library symbol Library of Congress*] (LCLS) .... CaQMIM
Institut de Physique du Globe [*France*] .... IPG
Institut de Police du Quebec, Nicolet, PQ, Canada [*Library symbol Library of Congress*] (LCLS) .... CaQNIP
Institut de Police du Quebec, Nicolet, Quebec [*Library symbol National Library of Canada*] (NLC) .... QNIP
Institut de Radio-Telediffusion pour Enfants [*Children's Broadcast Institute*] [*Canada*] .... IRTE
Institut de Recherche Appliquee sur le Travail [*Canada*] .... IRAT
Institut de Recherche Appliquee sur le Travail, Centre de Documentation, Montreal, PQ, Canada [*Library symbol Library of Congress*] (LCLS) .... CaQMRAD
Institut de Recherche des Nations Unies pour le Developpement Social [*United Nations Research Institute for Social Development*] .... IRNU
Institut de Recherche d'Hydro-Quebec [*Canada*] .... IREQ
Institut de Recherche d'Hydro-Quebec, Varennes, PQ, Canada [*Library symbol Library of Congress*] (LCLS) .... CaQVaH
Institut de Recherche d'Hydro-Quebec, Varennes, Quebec [*Library symbol National Library of Canada*] (NLC) .... QVAH
Institut de Recherche d'Informatique et d'Automatique [*French Research center*] .... IRIA
Institut de Recherche en Exploration Minerale [*Mineral Exploration Research Institute*] [*Canada Research center*] (RCD) .... IREM
Institut de Recherche et de Formation aux Relations Humaines [*Institute for Research and Training in Human Relations*] [*Research center France*] (IRC) .... IRFRH
Institut de Recherche sur le Profil d'Apprentissage [*Canada*] .... IRPA
Institut de Recherches Agronomiques Tropicales et des Cultures Vivrieres [*Food and agricultural research foundation supported by France and several African states*] .... IRAT
Institut de Recherches Cliniques, Montreal, PQ, Canada [*Library symbol Library of Congress*] (LCLS) .... CaQMIRC
Institut de Recherches Cliniques, Montreal, Quebec [*Library symbol National Library of Canada*] (NLC) .... QMIRC
Institut de Recherches et d'Applications des Methodes de Developpement [*Institute of Research and Application of Development Methods - IRAM*] (EAIO) .... IRAM
Institut de Recherches et de Normalisation Economiques en Scientifiques [*Canada*] .... IRNES
Institut de Recherches et d'Etudes Europeennes [*Institute of European Research and Studies*] (EAIO) .... IREE
Institut de Recherches et d'Etudes pour le Traitement de l'Information Juridique [*Institute of Research and Study for the Treatment of Legal Information*] [*University of Montpellier*] [*Information service or system*] (IID) .... IRETIJ
Institut de Recherches et d'Etudes sur le Monde Arabe et Musulman [*Institute for Research and Studies on the Arab and Muslim World*] [*France Information service or system*] (IID) .... IREMAM
Institut de Recherches Scientifiques au Congo .... IRSC
Institut de Recherches sur les Fruits et Agrumes [*Institute of Research on Fruits and Citrus Fruits*] [*International Cooperation Center of Agricultural Research for Development Database producer*] .... IRFA
Institut de Reescompte et de Garantie [*Development bank*] [*Belgium*] (EY).... IRG
Institut de Technologie Agricole et Alimentaire de St.-Hyacinthe, Quebec [*Library symbol National Library of Canada*] (NLC) .... QSTHTA
Institut de Technologie Agricole, Kamouraska, PQ, Canada [*Library symbol Library of Congress*] (LCLS) .... CaQKITA
Institut de Technologie Agricole, Kamouraska, Quebec [*Library symbol National Library of Canada*] (NLC) .... QKITA
Institut de Technologie Agricole, La Pocatiere, PQ, Canada [*Library symbol Library of Congress*] (LCLS) .... CaQPES
Institut de Tourisme et d'Hotellerie du Quebec, Montreal, PQ, Canada [*Library symbol Library of Congress*] (LCLS) .... CaQMTH
Institut de Tourisme et d'Hotellerie du Quebec, Montreal, Quebec [*Library symbol National Library of Canada*] (NLC) .... QMTH
Institut d'Elevage et de Medecine Veterinaire des Pays Tropicaux [*Institute of Stockraising and Veterinary Medicine in Tropical Countries*] [*France*].... IEMVT
Institut des Arts Appliques, Montreal, PQ, Canada [*Library symbol Library of Congress*] (LCLS) .... CaQMIAA
Institut des Arts Appliques, Montreal, Quebec [*Library symbol National Library of Canada*] (NLC) .... QMIAA
Institut des Arts Graphiques, Montreal, PQ, Canada [*Library symbol Library of Congress*] (LCLS) .... CaQMIAG
Institut des Arts Graphiques, Montreal, Quebec [*Library symbol National Library of Canada*] (NLC) .... QMIAG
Institut des Etudes Medievales, Universite de Montreal, Montreal, PQ, Canada [*Library symbol Library of Congress*] (LCLS) .... CaQMUE
Institut des Hautes Etudes Cinematographiques [*French institute for the study of the motion picture*] .... IDHEC
Institut des Hautes Etudes de l'Amerique Latine, Universite de Paris, Paris, France [*Library symbol Library of Congress*] (LCLS) .... FrPU-AL
Institut des Ingenieurs des Transports [*Institute of Transportation Engineers*] [*Canada*] .... IIT
Institut des Moeurs Humaines [*Institute of Human Values - IHV*] [*Canada*] ..... IMH
Institut des Producteurs de Ferro-Alliages d'Europe Occidentale [*Institute of Ferro-Alloy Producers in Western Europe - IFAPWE*] [*Defunct*] (EA) .... IPFEO
Institut d'Etudes Congolaises [*Congolese Institute of Studies*] .... IEC
Institut d'Etudes Juridiques Europeennes [*Benelux*] .... IEJE
Institut d'Histoire de l'Amerique Francaise [*Institute of French America History*] [*Canada*] .... IHAF
Institut du Cancer de Montreal, Quebec [*Library symbol National Library of Canada*] (NLC) .... QMINC
Institut du Textile [*Textile Institute*] (EAIO) .... IT
Institut du Transport Aerien [*Institute of Air Transport*] [*Research center France*] (IRC) .... ITA
Institut d'Urbanisme du Canada [*Town Planning Institute of Canada*] .... ICU
Institut Europeen d'Administration des Affaires [*European Business Management Institute*] [*France*] (PDAA) .... INSEAD
Institut Europeen d'Administration Publique [*European Institute of Public Administration - EIPA*] (EAIO) .... IEAP
Institut Europeen de la Communication [*European Institute for the Media - EIM*] (EAIO) .... IEC
Institut Europeen de Recherches et d'Etudes Superieures en Management [*European Institute for Advanced Studies in Management - EIASM*] [*Brussels, Belgium*] (EA) .... IERESM
Institut Europeen d'Ecologie et de Cancerologie [*European Institute of Ecology and Cancer - EIEC*] (EA) .... INEC
Institut Europeen des Armes de Chasse et de Sport [*European Institute of Hunting and Sporting Weapons - EIHSW*] (EAIO) .... IEACS
Institut Europeen des Industries de la Gomme de Caroube [*European Institute of Carob Gum Industries*] [*EC*] (ECED) .... INEC
Institut Europeen des Industries de la Pectine [*European Institute of the Pectin Industries*] .... IEIP
Institut Europeen du Jouet [*European Toy Institute - ETI*] (EAIO) .... IEJ
Institut Europeen du Zinc [*European Zinc Institute - EZI*] (EA) .... IEZ
Institut Europeen Interuniversitaire de l'Action Sociale [*Inter-University European Institute on Social Welfare - IEISW*] (EAIO) .... IEIAS
Institut Europeen pour la Promotion des Entreprises .... IEP
Institut Federatif de Recherche [*Federal Research Institute*] [*France*] .... IFR
Institut Forestier du Canada [*Formerly, Canadian Society of Forest Engineers*] (AC) .... IFC
Institut Francais d'Afrique Noire [*French Institute of Black Africa*] .... IFAN
Institut Francais d'Archeologie Orientale du Caire. Bibliotheque d'Etude [*A publication*] (BJA) .... IFAO Bibl d'Et
Institut Francais de l'Energie [*French Institute of Energy*] [*Paris*] [*Information service or system*] (IID) .... IFE
Institut Francais de l'Environnement [*Marine science*] [*France*] (OSRA) .... IFEN
Institut Francais de Recherche et de Technologie Polaires [*Public interest group*] [*French Southern and Antarctic Territories*] (EY) .... IFRIP
Institut Francais de Recherche pour l'Exploitation de la Mer [*French Research Institute for Ocean Utilization*] [*Research center*] (IID) .... IFREMER
Institut Francais d'Opinion Publique [*French Institute of Public Opinion*] .... IFOP
Institut Francais du Petroles [*French Institute of Petroleum*] [*Paris*] .... IFP
Institut fuer Arbeitsmarkt- und Berufsforschung [*Institute for Employment Research*] [*Federal Employment Institute*] [*Germany*] (IID) .... IAB
Institut fuer Auslandsbeziehungen, Stuttgart, Germany [*Library symbol Library of Congress*] (LCLS) .... GySIA
Institut fuer Deutsche Sprache [*Institute for German Language*] [*Information service or system*] (IID) .... IDS
Institut fuer Dokumentation, Information, und Statistik [*Institute for Documentation, Information, and Statistics*] [*Information service or system*] (IID) .... IDIS
Institut fuer Dokumentation und Information ueber Sozialmedizin und Oeffentliches Gesundheitswesen [*Institute for Documentation and Information in Social Medicine and Public Health*] [*Information retrieval Germany*] .... IDIS
Institut fuer Dokumentationswesen [*Germany*] .... IDW
Institut fuer Europaeische Politik [*Institute of European Politics*] (EAIO) .... IEP
Institut fuer Europaeische Umweltpolitik [*Institute for European Environmental Policy - IEEP*] (EAIO) .... IEUP
Institut fuer Seeverkehrwirtschaft und Logistik [*Institute of Shipping Economics and Logistics - ISEL*] [*Bremen, Federal Republic of Germany*] (EAIO) .... ISL
Institut fur Maschinelle Dokumentation (NITA) .... IMD
Institut fur Organische Chemie der Universitat Basel, Basel, Switzerland [*Library symbol Library of Congress*] (LCLS) .... SzBaU-IO
Institut fur Zeitgeschichte [*Institute of Modern History*], Munchen, Federal Republic of Germany [*Library symbol Library of Congress*] (LCLS) .... GyMIZ
Institut fur Zeitungsforschung, Dortmund, Germany [*Library symbol Library of Congress*] (LCLS) .... GyDIZ
Institut Genealogique Drouin, Montreal, PQ, Canada [*Library symbol Library of Congress*] (LCLS) .... CaQMD
Institut Genealogique Drouin, Montreal, Quebec [*Library symbol National Library of Canada*] (NLC) .... QMD
Institut Henry-Dunant [*Henry Dunant Institute*] [*Geneva, Switzerland*] (EAIO) .... IHD
Institut Interafricain du Travail .... IIT
Institut International Catholique de Recherches Socio-Ecclesiales [*International Catholic Institute for Socio-Religious Research*] [*Later, FERES*] .... ICARES
Institut International d'Aluminium Primaire [*International Primary Aluminum Institute*] (EAIO) .... IIAP
Institut International d'Anthropologie [*International Institute of Anthropology*] (EAIO) .... IIA
Institut International de Bibliographie .... IIB
Institut International de Droit d'Expression Francaise [*International Institute of Law of the French Speaking Countries - IILFSC*] [*Paris, France*] (EAIO) .... IDEF
Institut International de Droit Humanitaire [*International Institute of Humanitarian Law - IIHL*] (EAIO) .... IIDH
Institut International de Droit Linguistique Compare [*International Institute of Comparative Linguistic Law*] (EAIO) .... IIDLC
Institut International de Finances Publiques [*International Institute of Public Finance*] (EAIO) .... IIFP
Institut International de la Potasse [*International Potash Institute*] (EAIO) .... IIP
Institut International de la Presse [*International Press Institute*] .... IIP
Institut International de la Soudure [*International Institute of Welding - IIW*] (EAIO) .... IIS

Institut International de l'Epargne ... IIE
Institut International de Philosophie [*International Institute of Philosophy*] (EAIO) ... IIP
Institut International de Planification de l'Education [*International Institute for Educational Planning*] ... IIPE
Institut International de Recherches Betteravieres [*International Institute for Sugar Beet Research*] [*Brussels, Belgium*] (EA) ... IIRB
Institut International de Recherches Graphologiques ... IIRG
Institut International de Statistique [*International Statistical Institute*] ... IIS
Institut International des Brevets [*International Patent Institute*] ... IIB
Institut International des Caisses d'Epargne [*International Savings Banks Institute - ISBI*] [*Geneva, Switzerland*] (EAIO) ... IICE
Institut International des Civilisations Differentes [*International Institute of Differing Civilizations*] ... INCIDI
Institut International des Communications [*International Institute of Communications*] (EA) ... IIC
Institut International des Meteorologists [*International Institute of Forecasters*] (EAIO) ... IIM
Institut International des Sciences Administratives [*International Institute for Administrative Sciences*] ... IISA
Institut International des Sciences Humaines Integrales [*International Institute of Integral Human Sciences - IIIHS*] (EAIO) ... IISHI
Institut International d'Etude et de Documentation en Matiere de Concurrence Commerciale [*International Institute for Commercial Competition*] [*Belgium*] (EA) ... IICC
Institut International d'Etudes Ligures [*International Institute for Ligurian Studies - IILS*] (EAIO) ... IIEL
Institut International d'Etudes sur l'Education [*International Institute for Education Studies*] ... IIEE
Institut International du Froid [*International Institute of Refrigeration*] ... IIF
Institut International du Froid [*International Institute of Refrigeration*] [*France*] (EA) ... IIR
Institut International du Manganese [*International Insitute of Manganese*] [*France*] (EAIO) ... IIM
Institut International du Travail Temporaire - International Institute for Temporary Work (EAIO) ... IITT-IITW
Institut International Jacques Maritain [*International Jacques Maritain Institute - IJMI*] (EAIO) ... IIJM
Institut International pour l'Unification du Droit Prive [*International Institute for the Unification of Private Law*] (EAIO) ... UNIDROIT
Institut Internationale du Theatre [*International Theatre Institute - ITI*] (EAIO) ... IIT
Institut Kimia Malaysia ... IKM
Institut Laue-Langevin [*Grenoble, France*] (ECON) ... ILL
Institut Maritime, CEGEP de Rimouski, PQ, Canada [*Library symbol Library of Congress*] (LCLS) ... CaQRIM
Institut Maritime, CEGEP de Rimouski, Quebec [*Library symbol National Library of Canada*] (NLC) ... QRIM
Institut Maritime du Quebec, CEGEP de Rimouski, Quebec, PQ, Canada [*Library symbol Library of Congress*] (LCLS) ... CaQQIM
Institut Metapsychique International [*International Metaphysics Institute*] [*France*] (EAIO) ... IMI
Institut Mondial d'Ecologie et de Cancerologie [*World Institute of Ecology and Cancer - WIEC*] (EAIO) ... IMEC
Institut National Canadien pour les Aveugles, Montreal, PQ, Canada [*Library symbol*] [*Library of Congress*] (LCLS) ... CaQMINCA
Institut National Canadien pour les Aveugles, Montreal, Quebec [*Library symbol National Library of Canada*] (NLC) ... QMINCA
Institut National de la Communication Audiovisuelle [*France*] (NITA) ... INA
Institut National de la Propriete Industrielle [*National Institute for Industrial Property*] [*France Information service or system*] (IID) ... INPI
Institut National de la Propriete Industrielle, Centre Regional, Marseilles, France [*Library symbol Library of Congress*] (LCLS) ... FrMC
Institut National de la Recherche Agronomique (NITA) ... INRA
Institut National de la Recherche Scientifique [*National Institute for Scientific Research*] [*Canada Research center*] ... INRS
Institut National de la Recherche Scientifique (Energie), Varennes, PQ, Canada [*Library symbol*] [*Library of Congress*] (LCLS) ... CaQVal
Institut National de la Recherche Scientifique-Georessources, Ste. Foy, PQ, Canada [*Library symbol*] [*Library of Congress*] (LCLS) ... CaQSFIG
Institut National de la Sante et de la Recherche Medicale [*National Institute for Health and Medical Research*] [*France Information service or system*] (IID) ... INSERM
Institut National de la Statistique et des Etudes Economiques [*National Institute of Statistics and Economic Research*] [*Paris, France*] ... INSEE
Institut National de Productivite, Montreal, Montreal, PQ, Canada [*Library symbol Library of Congress*] (LCLS) ... CaQMIMM
Institut National de Productivite, Montreal, Quebec [*Library symbol National Library of Canada*] (NLC) ... QMINP
Institut National de Radiodiffusion [*Belgium*] ... INR
Institut National de Recherche en Informatique et en Automatique [*National Institute for Research in Informatics and Automation*] [*Research center and database originator*] [*France Information service or system*] (IID) ... INRIA
Institut National de Recherches en Hydrologie [*National Hydrology Research Institute*] [*Canada*] ... INRH
Institut National de Systematique Appliquee [*Canada*] ... INSA
Institut National des Appellations d'Origine [*Semigovernmental organization that fixes the appellations on all French wines*] ... INAO
Institut National des Techniques de la Documentation [*National Institute for Information Science*] [*France Information service or system*] (IID) ... INTD
Institut National d'Etudes Demographiques, Paris, France [*Library symbol Library of Congress*] (LCLS) ... FrPED
Institut National d'Optique, Ste.-Foy, Quebec [*Library symbol National Library of Canada*] (BIB) ... QSFIO
Institut National du Cancer du Canada [*National Cancer Institute of Canada*] (EAIO) ... INCC
Institut National pour l'Etude Agronomique du Congo [*National Institute for the Study of Agronomy in the Congo*] ... INEAC
Institut Nauchnoi Informatsii po Obshchestvennym Naukam, Akademiia Nauk SSSR [*Institute of Scientific Information on Social Sciences, Academy of Sciences of the USSR*], Moscow, Soviet Union [*Library symbol Library of Congress*] (LCLS) ... RuMIN
Institut Nazareth et Louis-Braille, Longueuil, PQ, Canada [*Library symbol*] [*Library of Congress*] (LCLS) ... CaQLoNLB
Institut Nazareth et Louis-Braille, Longueuil, Quebec [*Library symbol National Library of Canada*] (NLC) ... QLNLB
Institut Oecumenique pour le Developpement des Peuples [*Ecumenical Institute for the Development of Peoples*] [*Paris, France*] (EAIO) ... INODEP
Institut Panafricain pour le Developpement, Afrique Centrale [*Pan African Institute for Development, Central Africa*] [*Cameroun*] (PDAA) ... IPD/AC
Institut Pasteur [*France*] [*Research code symbol*] ... C
Institut Philippe Pinel de Montreal, Montreal, PQ, Canada [*Library symbol Library of Congress*] (LCLS) ... CaQMIPP
Institut Philippe Pinel de Montreal, Quebec [*Library symbol National Library of Canada*] (NLC) ... QMIPP
Institut pour la Recherche Scientifique en Afrique Centrale [*Brussels*] ... IRSAC
Institut pour la Repression des Ravageurs Forestiers [*Forest Pest Management Institute*] [*Canada*] ... IRRF
Institut pour une Synthese Planetaire [*Institute for Planetary Synthesis - IPS*] [*Geneva, Switzerland*] (EAIO) ... ISP
Institut Professionnel de la Fonction Publique du Canada [*Professional Institute of the Public Service of Canada - PIPS*] ... IPFP
Institut Quebecois de la Recherche sur la Culture [*Database producer*] ... IQRC
Institut Quebecois de Recherche sur la Culture, Quebec, PQ, Canada [*Library symbol Library of Congress*] (LCLS) ... CaQQIQRC
Institut Quebecois de Recherche sur la Culture, Quebec, Quebec [*Library symbol National Library of Canada*] (NLC) ... QQIQRC
Institut Romand de Recherche Numerique en Physique des Materiaux ... IRRMA
Institut Royal d'Architecture du Canada [*Royal Architectural Institute of Canada*] (EAIO) ... IRAC
Institut Superieur des Affaires [*Chamber de Commerce et d'Industrie de Paris*] (ECON) ... ISA
Institut Technique du Batiment [*Technical Institute for Building*] [*France Information service or system*] (IID) ... ITB
Institut Technique du Batiment et des Travaux Publics [*Technical Institute for Building and Public Works*] [*Information service or system*] (IID) ... ITBTP
Institut Textile de France [*French Textile Institute*] [*Boulogne-Billancourt*] [*Information service or system*] (IID) ... ITF
Institut TNO voor Toegepaste Informatica [*TNO Institute of Applied Computer Science*] [*Information service or system*] (IID) ... ITI
Institut Voluntas Dei (EA) ... iv Dei
Institute [*or Institution*] ... I
Institute [*or Institution*] (AFM) ... INST
Institute ... INST
Institute Against Prejudice and Violence (EA) ... IAPV
Institute and Society of Practictioners in Electrolysis Ltd. [*British*] (BI) ... ISPE
Institute Centrale Catalogo Unico delle Bibliotheche Italiane e per le Informazioni Bibliografiche, Rome, Italy [*Library symbol*] [*Library of Congress*] (LCLS) ... ItRI
Institute Circumpolaire Canadien [*Canadian Circumpolar Institute, University of Alberta*] (IRC) ... ICC
Institute de l'Information Scientifique et Technique [*Institute of Scientific and Technical Information*] [*Information service or system*] (IID) ... INIST
Institute for 21st Century Studies [*Defunct*] (EA) ... ITCS
Institute for a Drug-Free Workplace (EA) ... IDFW
Institute for a New Middle East Policy (EA) ... INMEP
Institute for Academic Technology ... IAT
Institute for Administrative Justice [*University of the Pacific*] [*Research center*] (RCD) ... IAJ
Institute for Advanced Concepts [*In 1980 film "Simon"*] ... IAC
Institute for Advanced Interdisciplinary Engineering Studies [*Purdue University*] (MCD) ... IAIES
Institute for Advanced Materials, Mechanics, and Design [*Army Materiel Command*] ... IAMM & D
Institute for Advanced Pastoral Studies (EA) ... IAPS
Institute for Advanced Research in Asian Science and Medicine (EA) ... IARASM
Institute for Advanced Russian Studies [*Smithsonian Institution*] ... IARS
Institute for Advanced Studies [*Army*] ... IAS
Institute for Advanced Studies in the Theatre Arts (EA) ... IASTA
Institute for Advanced Studies of World Religions (EA) ... IASWR
Institute for Advanced Study in Human Sexuality (DAVI) ... IASHS
Institute for Advanced Study of the Communication Processes [*University of Florida*] [*Research center*] (RCD) ... IASCP
Institute for Advanced Study, Princeton, NJ [*Library symbol Library of Congress*] (LCLS) ... NjPI
Institute for Advanced Talmudic Studies [*Beth Medrash Govoha*] [*Canada*] (IRC) ... IATS
Institute for Advanced Technology [*Control Data Corp.*] [*Bloomington, MN*] [*Telecommunications*] ... IAT
Institute for Advancement of Medical Communication [*Defunct*] (EA) ... IAMC
Institute for Aerobics Research (EA) ... IAR
Institute for Aerospace Studies, University of Toronto, Ontario [*Library symbol National Library of Canada*] (NLC) ... OTUA
Institute for Air Research (WDAA) ... IAR
Institute for Alternative Agriculture (EA) ... IAA
Institute for Alternative Futures [*Defunct*] (EA) ... IAF
Institute for American Church Growth (EA) ... IACG
Institute for American Democracy (EA) ... IAD
Institute for American Strategy [*Later, ASCF*] ... IAS

Institute for American Universities (EA) ... IAU
Institute for American Values (EA) ... IAV
Institute for Animal Disease Research [*Research center British*] (IRC) ... IADR
Institute for Animal Health [*Agricultural and Food Research Council*] [*British*] (IRC) ... IAH
Institute for Anthropology [*State University of New York at Albany*] [*Research center*] (RCD) ... INA
Institute for Antiquity and Christianity [*Claremont University*] [*Research center*] (RCD) ... IAC
Institute for Applied Technology [*Superseded by NEL*] [*National Institute of Standards and Technology*] ... IAT
Institute for Archaeo-Metallurgical Studies [*British*] (IRUK) ... IAMS
Institute for Art and Urban Resources (EA) ... IAUR
Institute for Arthritis and Autoimmunity [*Nile Research Center*] [*West Haven, CT*] ... IAA
Institute for Astrophysics and Planetary Exploration [*University of Florida*] [*Research center*] (RCD) ... APEX
Institute for Atmospheric Sciences [*South Dakota School of Mines*] [*Research center Environmental Science Services Administration*] ... IAS
Institute for Atomic Sciences in Agriculture ... IASA
Institute for Australasian Geodynamics [*Flinders University*] [*Australia*] ... IAG
[*The*] **Institute for Automated Systems Network** (TNIG) ... IASnet
Institute for Basic Research [*National Institute of Standards and Technology*] ... IBR
Institute for Basic Research on Mental Retardation ... IBRMR
Institute for Basic Standards [*Later, NSL*] [*National Institute of Standards and Technology*] ... IBS
Institute for Behavioral Genetics [*University of Colorado - Boulder*] [*Research center*] (RCD) ... IBG
Institute for Behavioral Research [*York University*] [*Canada Research center*] (IID) ... IBR
Institute for Behavioral Research in Creativity [*Research center*] (RCD) ... IBRIC
Institute for Better Packaging [*Later, PPC*] (EA) ... IBP
Institute for Biblical Research (EA) ... IBR
Institute for Bioenergetic Analysis [*Later, IIBA*] (EA) ... IBA
Institute for Biomedical Communication [*South African Medical Research Council*] [*Information service or system*] (IID) ... IBC
Institute for Biomedical Engineering Research [*University of Akron*] [*Research center*] (RCD) ... IBER
Institute for Biophysical Research and Macromolecular Assemblies [*Johns Hopkins University*] ... IBRMA
Institute for Biotechnological Studies [*University of Kent*] [*British*] (IRUK) ... IBS
Institute for Biotechnology Research [*University of Waterloo*] [*Research center*] (RCD) ... IBR
Institute for Briquetting and Agglomeration (EA) ... IBA
Institute for Bronx Regional and Community History Studies [*Lehman College of City University of New York*] [*Research center*] (RCD) ... BRACHS
Institute for Business Planning ... IBP
Institute for Canadian Futures ... ICF
Institute for Cancer Research (EA) ... ICR
Institute for Cancer Research, Philadelphia, PA [*Library symbol Library of Congress*] (LCLS) ... PPICR
Institute for Cardiovascular Studies [*University of Houston*] [*Research center*] (RCD) ... ICSC
Institute for Cell Analysis [*University of Miami*] [*Research center*] (RCD) ... ICA
Institute for Central European Research (EA) ... ICER
Institute for Certification of Computer Professionals (EA) ... ICCP
Institute for Certification of Tax Professionals (EA) ... ICTP
Institute for Certified Park Operators (EA) ... ICPO
Institute for Chemical Education (EA) ... ICE
Institute for Chemical Science and Technology [*Canada*] ... ICST
Institute for Chemical Studies (GNE) ... ICS
Institute for Chemical Waste Management (GNE) ... ICWM
Institute for Child Behavior Research (IID) ... ICBR
Institute for Childhood Resources (EA) ... INICR
Institute for Children, Youth, and Families [*Michigan State University*] [*Research center*] (RCD) ... ICYF
Institute for Christian Education [*Australia*] ... ICE
Institute for Christian Studies ... ICS
Institute for Circadian Physiology [*Boston, MA*] ... ICP
Institute for Clinical Systems Integration (DMAA) ... ICSI
Institute for Cognitive Science [*University of California, San Diego*] [*Research center*] (RCD) ... ICS
Institute for College and University Administrators [*Later, CPAA*] (EA) ... ICUA
Institute for Communications Research [*Texas Tech University*] [*Research center*] (RCD) ... ICR
Institute for Community Design Analysis (EA) ... ICDA
Institute for Community Economics (EA) ... ICE
Institute for Community Education Development [*Ball State University*] [*Research center*] (RCD) ... ICED
Institute for Community Resource Development [*Australia*] ... ICRDD
Institute for Comparative and Environmental Toxicology [*Cornell University*] [*Research center*] (RCD) ... ICET
Institute for Complementary Medicine [*An association*] (EAIO) ... ICM
Institute for Composite Materials [*Defunct*] (EA) ... ICM
Institute for Comprehensive Planning [*Defunct*] (EA) ... ICP
Institute for Computational Mathematics and Applications [*University of Pittsburgh*] [*Research center*] (RCD) ... ICMA
Institute for Computer Applications in Science and Engineering [*Universities Space Research Association*] [*Research center*] (RCD) ... ICASE
Institute for Computer Integrated Manufacturing [*Strathclyde University*] [*British*] ... ICIM
Institute for Computer Research [*University of Waterloo*] [*Canada Research center*] (RCD) ... ICR
Institute for Computer Research in the Humanities [*New York University*] ... ICRH
Institute for Computer Sciences (HGAA) ... ICS
Institute [*formerly, Center*] **for Computer Sciences and Technology** [*Gaithersburg, MD*] [*NIST*] ... ICST
Institute for Computers in Jewish Life (EA) ... ICJL
Institute for Computing Science and Computer Applications [*University of Texas at Austin*] [*Research center*] (RCD) ... ICSCA
Institute for Conflict Analysis and Resolution [*George Mason University*] [*Research center*] (RCD) ... ICAR
Institute for Congress ... IC
Institute for Constitutional Research (EA) ... ICR
Institute for Consumer Ergonomics [*British*] (IRUK) ... ICE
Institute for Consumer Financial Education (EA) ... ICFE
Institute for Contemporary Studies (EA) ... ICS
Institute for Continuing Education (AIE) ... ICE
Institute for Continuing Legal Education, New Jersey (DLA) ... NJCLE
Institute for Continuing Studies in Design, Management and Communication [*University of Cincinnati*] [*Research center*] (RCD) ... ICS/DMC
Institute for Cooperative Research ... ICR
Institute for Court Management of the National Center for State Courts (EA) ... ICM
Institute for Creation Research (EA) ... ICR
Institute for Criminal Justice, University of Richmond (DLA) ... ICJR
Institute for Crippled and Disabled (DAVI) ... ICD
Institute for Cultural Exchange thru Photography (EA) ... ICEP
Institute for Cultural Policy Studies [*Griffith University*] [*Australia*] ... ICPS
Institute for Cultural Research [*Research center British*] (IRC) ... ICR
Institute for Cultural Studies [*Defunct*] (EA) ... ICS
Institute for Defense Analyses (EA) ... IDA
Institute for Defense Analysis Gaming Model (MCD) ... IDAGAM
Institute for Defense Analysis-Communications Research Division ... IDA-CRD
Institute for Defense and Disarmament Studies (EA) ... IDDS
Institute for Delphinid Research (EA) ... IDR
Institute for Democracy in Eastern Europe (EA) ... IDEE
Institute for Democratic Education [*Absorbed by Anti-Defamation League of B'nai B'rith*] (EA) ... IDE
Institute for Democratic Socialism (EA) ... IDS
Institute for Demographic and Economic Studies [*Research center*] (RCD) ... IDES
Institute for Development Anthropology (EA) ... IDA
Institute for Development of Educational Activities (EA) ... I/D/E/A
Institute for Development Policy and Management [*University of Manchester*] [*British*] (ECON) ... IDPM
Institute for Drafting and Design [*Australia*] ... IDD
Institute for Earth Education (EA) ... IEE
Institute for Earth Sciences [*Environmental Science Services Administration*] ... IES
Institute for Ecological Policies [*Defunct*] (EA) ... IEP
Institute for Econometric Research (EA) ... IER
Institute for Economic Analysis (EA) ... IEA
Institute for Economic and Business Research [*University of Kansas*] [*Research center*] (RCD) ... IEBR
Institute for Education by Radio [*Defunct*] (NTCM) ... IER
Institute for Education by Radio-Television (NTCM) ... IERT
Institute for Educational Affairs (EA) ... IEA
Institute for Educational Development [*Defunct*] ... IED
Institute for Educational Innovation [*Later, Education Development Center*] ... IEI
Institute for Educational Leadership (EA) ... IEL
Institute for Encyclopedia of Human Ideas on Ultimate Reality and Meaning (EA) ... IEHIURM
Institute for Engineering Research in the Oceans [*Marine science*] (MSC) ... IERO
Institute for Environmental Awareness (EA) ... IEA
Institute for Environmental Education (EA) ... IEE
Institute for Environmental Research [*Environmental Science Services Administration*] ... IER
Institute for Environmental Research Technical Memorandum ... IERTM
Institute for Environmental Studies [*University of Wisconsin, Madison*] [*Research center*] (RCD) ... IES
Institute for Environmental Studies [*University of Washington*] [*Research center*] (RCD) ... IES
Institute for Environmental Studies [*University of Toronto*] [*Research center*] (RCD) ... IES
Institute for Epidemiologic Studies of Violence (EA) ... IESV
Institute for Esperanto in Commerce and Industry (EA) ... IECI
Institute for European Environmental Policy [*Germany*] (EAIO) ... IEEP
Institute for Experimental Psychiatry ... IEP
Institute for Expressive Analysis (EA) ... IEA
Institute for Family and Child Study [*Michigan State University*] [*Research center*] (RCD) ... IFCS
Institute for Family Research and Education [*Defunct*] (EA) ... IFRE
Institute for Financial Crime Prevention [*Later, NACFE*] (EA) ... IFCP
Institute for Fiscal Studies [*British*] ... IFS
Institute for Fluitronics Education (EA) ... IFE
Institute for Folklore Studies in Britain and Canada ... IFSBAC
Institute for Food and Development Policy (EA) ... IFDP
Institute for Foreign Policy Analysis, Inc. [*Tufts University*] [*Research center*] (RCD) ... IFPA
Institute for Friendship through Learning (EA) ... IFTL
Institute for Genome Research for Developing Countries [*Tunisia*] [*Proposed for 1996*] ... IGRDC
Institute for Global Communications (EA) ... IGC
Institute for Global Communications [*Internet*] ... IGC
Institute for Graphic Communication [*Defunct*] (EA) ... IGC
Institute for Grassland and Animal Production [*Research center British*] (IRC) ... IGAP

Institute for Gravitational Strain Pathology (EA) .... IGSP
Institute for Guided Ground Transport [Canada] (PDAA) .... IGGT
Institute for Health Services Research [Tulane University] [Research center] (RCD) .... IHSR
Institute for Healthcare Improvement (DMAA) .... IHI
Institute for High-Energy Physics [China] .... IHEP
Institute for Higher Defense Studies [National Defense University] .... IHDS
Institute for Historical Review (EA) .... IHR
Institute for Housing Management Innovations (EA) .... IHMI
Institute for Housing Urban Development Studies [Netherlands] .... IHS
Institute for Human Progress [Defunct] .... IHP
Institute for Human Rights Research (EA) .... IHRR
Institute for Humane Studies, Inc. [Research center] (RCD) .... IHS
Institute for Hydrogen Systems [UTLAS symbol] .... IHS
Institute for Hydrogen Systems, Mississauga, ON, Canada [Library symbol] [Library of Congress] (LCLS) .... CaOMIHS
Institute for Hydrogen Systems, Mississauga, Ontario [Library symbol National Library of Canada] (NLC) .... OMIHS
Institute for Independent Education (EA) .... IIE
Institute for Independent Social Journalism (EA) .... IISJ
Institute for Information Industry [Information service or system] (IID) III
Institute for Information Management (EA) .... IIM
Institute for Information Retrieval and Computational Linguistics [Bar Ilam University] [Israel] (NITA) .... IRCOL
Institute for Information Storage Technology [University of Santa Clara] [Research center] (RCD) .... IIST
Institute for Information Studies [Inactive] [Research center] (RCD) .... IIS
Institute for Integral Development (EA) .... IID
Institute for Interconnecting and Packaging Electronic Circuits (EA) .... IIPEC
Institute for Interconnecting and Packaging Electronic Circuits [Formerly, Institute of Printed Circuits] (EA) .... IPC
Institute for Intercultural Studies (EA) .... IIS
Institute for Internal Combustion Engines (MCD) .... IICE
Institute for International Development and Cooperation [University of Ottawa] [See also IDIC] [Canada] .... IIDC
Institute for International Economics .... IIE
Institute for International Health and Development (EA) .... IIHD
Institute for International Information Programs [University of Maryland] (NITA) .... IIIP
Institute for International Order [Later, IWO] .... IIO
Institute for International Youth Affairs .... IIYA
Institute for Jewish Policy Planning and Research [Defunct] (EA) .... IJPPR
Institute for Jewish-Christian Relations (EA) .... IJCR
Institute for Justice Research [American University] [Research center] (RCD) .... IJR
Institute for Juvenile Research [Illinois Department of Mental Health-University of Illinois at Chicago] [Research center] (RCD) .... IJR
Institute for Juvenile Research, Chicago, IL [Library symbol Library of Congress] (LCLS) .... ICIJ
Institute for Labor and Mental Health (EA) .... ILMH
Institute for Labor Relations. Bulletin [A publication] (DLA) .... Inst Lab Rel Bull
Institute for Labor Studies, Appalachian Center, Morgantown, WV [Library symbol Library of Congress] (LCLS) .... WvMIL
Institute for Land Information [Research center Information service or system] ILI
Institute for Latin American and Iberian Studies [Columbia University] [Research center] (RCD) .... ILAIS
Institute for Law and Social Research (IID) .... INSLAW
Institute for Liberty and Community (EA) ILC
Institute for Local Self-Reliance (EA) .... ILSR
Institute for Manpower Management (EA) .... IMM
Institute for Marine Biochemistry [British] .... IMB
Institute for Marine Dynamics [Canada] (PDAA) .... IMD
Institute for Marine Environmental Research [British] (ARC) .... IMER
Institute for Marine Information [Defunct] (EA) .... IMI
Institute for Materials Research [Later, NSL] [National Institute of Standards and Technology] .... IMR
Institute for Mathematical Studies in the Social Sciences [Stanford University] [Research center] (RCD) .... IMSSS
Institute for Mathematics and Its Applications [University of Minnesota] [Research center] (RCD) .... IMA
Institute for Media Analysis (EA) .... IMA
Institute for Mediation and Conflict Resolution (EA) .... IMCR
Institute for Medical Record Economics (EA) .... IMRE
Institute for Medical Research [Camden, New Jersey] .... IMR
Institute for Mediterranean Affairs (EA) .... IMA
Institute for Mediterranean Art and Archaeology [Defunct] (EA) .... IMAA
Institute for Mental Health Initiatives (EA) .... IMHI
Institute for Mesoamerican Studies [State University of New York, Albany] [Research center] (RCD) .... IMS
Institute for Metal Forming [Lehigh University] [Research center] (RCD) .... IMF
Institute for Military Assistance [Army] .... IMA
Institute for Mining and Mineral Research [University of Kentucky] [Research center] (RCD) .... IMMR
Institute for Mining and Minerals Research, Lexington, KY [Library symbol Library of Congress] (LCLS) .... KyLxIMM
Institute for Minority Business Education [Defunct] (EA) .... IMBE
Institute for Molecular and Agricultural Genetic Engineering [University of Idaho] [Research center] .... IMAGE
Institute for Molecular and Cellular Evolution [University of Miami] [Research center] (RCD) .... IMCE
Institute for Molecular Manufacturing .... IMM
Institute for Monetary Freedom (EA) .... IMF
Institute for Municipal Engineering .... IME
Institute for Muscle Disease [Defunct] (EA) .... IMD

Institute for Muscle Disease, New York, NY [Library symbol Library of Congress Obsolete] (LCLS) .... NNIMD
Institute for Natural Products Research [University of Georgia] [Research center] (RCD) .... INPR
Institute for Naval Oceanography [Bay St. Louis, MS] [Navy] .... INO
Institute for Naval Studies .... INS
Institute for New Antibiotics [Former USSR] .... INA
Institute for New Enterprise Development .... INED
Institute for Non-Destructive Testing [Milwaukee School of Engineering] (PDAA) .... INDT
Institute for Nonprofit Organizations .... INPO
Institute for Nuclear Study [Japan] .... INS
Institute for Numerical Computation and Analysis (MCD) .... INCA
Institute for Objectivist Studies (EA) .... IOS
Institute for Oceanography [Environmental Science Services Administration] .... IO
Institute for Optimum Nutrition [British] .... ION
Institute for Palestine Studies (EA) .... IPS
Institute for Paralegal Training [Later, Philadelphia Institute] [Commercial firm] (EA) .... IPT
Institute for Peace and International Security (EA) .... IPIS
Institute for Peace and Justice (EA) .... IPJ
Institute for Personal Computing (EA) .... IPC
Institute for Personality and Ability Testing [Champaign, IL] .... IPAT
Institute for Personality and Ability Testing, Children's Personality Questionnaire [Psychology] (AEBS) .... IPAT CPQ
Institute for Personality and Ability Testing, Neurotic Personality Factor Test [Psychology] (AEBS) .... IPAT NPFT
Institute for Philosophy and Public Policy (EA) .... IPPP
Institute for Physical Science and Technology [University of Maryland] [Research center] (RCD) .... IPST
Institute for Physics of the Atmosphere .... IPA
Institute for Policy Analysis [University of Toronto] [Canada] (IRC) .... IPA
Institute for Policy Research [University of Wyoming] [Research center] (RCD) .... IPR
Institute for Policy Research [University of Cincinnati] [Research center] (RCD) .... IPR
Institute for Policy Studies (EA) .... IPS
Institute for Polyacrylate Absorbents (EA) .... IPA
Institute for Practical Idealism (EA) .... IPI
Institute for Problems of Materials Science [Ukraine] .... IPMS
Institute for Professional Development (EA) .... IPD
Institute for Program Evaluation (AAGC) .... IPE
Institute for Protection and Nuclear Safety (NUCP) .... IPSN
Institute for Psychiatry and Foreign Affairs [Defunct] (EA) .... IPFA
Institute for Psychoanalysis, Chicago, IL [Library symbol Library of Congress] (LCLS) .... ICIP
Institute for Psychoanalytic Training and Research .... IPTAR
Institute for Psychohistory (EA) .... IP
Institute for Psychological Study of the Arts [University of Florida] [Research center] (RCD) .... IPSA
Institute for Psychosomatic and Psychiatric Research and Training [Research center] (RCD) .... PPI
Institute for Public Information .... IPI
Institute for Public Interest Representation [Later, CCCIPR] [Georgetown University] .... INSPIRE
Institute for Public Interest Representation [Later, CCCIPR] [Georgetown University] .... IPIR
Institute for Public Policy and Administration [Later, CPPUI] (EA) .... IPPA
Institute for Public Policy Research [British] (ECON) .... IPPR
Institute for Public Research (AAGC) .... IPR
Institute for Public Understanding (EA) .... IPU
Institute for Puerto Rican Policy (EA) .... IPRP
Institute for Puerto Rican Policy, Inc. [Research center] (RCD) .... IPR
Institute for Radiological Technologists .... IRT
Institute for Rapid Transit [Later, APTA] (EA) .... IRT
Institute for Rational Living [Absorbed by IRET] .... IRL
Institute for Rational-Emotive Therapy (EA) .... IRET
Institute for Reactor Research [Switzerland] .... IRR
Institute for Reality Therapy (EA) .... IRT
Institute for Regional and International Studies (EA) .... IRIS
Institute for Regional, Rural, and Community Studies [Western Illinois University] [Research center] (RCD) .... IRRCS
Institute for Rehabilitation and Research [Baylor College of Medicine] [Research center] (RCD) .... IRR
[The] Institute for Rehabilitation and Research [Houston, TX] .... TIRR
Institute for Religious and Social Studies (EA) .... IRSS
Institute for Reproductive Health (EA) .... IRH
Institute for Research and Development in Occupational Education [City University of New York] [Research center] (RCD) .... IRDOE
Institute for Research and Education on Human Rights [Defunct] (EA) ..... IREHR
Institute for Research in Construction [National Research Council of Canada] [Database producer] (IID) .... IRC
Institute for Research in History .... IRH
Institute for Research in Human Relations (MCD) .... IRHR
Institute for Research in Hypnosis [Later, IRHP] (EA) .... IRH
Institute for Research in Hypnosis and Psychotherapy (EA) .... IRHP
Institute for Research in Information and Scholarship [Brown University] [Research center] (RCD) .... IRIS
Institute for Research in Public Safety [Indiana University] [Research center] (RCD) .... IRPS
Institute for Research in Social Behavior [Research center] (RCD) .... IRSB
Institute for Research in Social Science [University of North Carolina at Chapel Hill] [Research center] (RCD) .... IRSS
Institute for Research in the Social Sciences [University of York] [British] (IRC) .... IRISS

Institute for Research into Mental and Multiple Handicap [*British*] .... IRMMH
Institute for Research into Mental Retardation .... IRMR
Institute for Research of Rheumatic Diseases [*Defunct*] (EA) .... IRRD
Institute for Research on Animal Diseases [*British*] .... IRAD
Institute for Research on Educational Finance and Governance [*Department of Education*] (GRD) .... IFG
Institute for Research on Interactive Systems [*Research center*] (TSSD) .... IRIS
Institute for Research on Land and Water Resources [*Pennsylvania State University*] (PDAA) .... IRLWR
Institute for Research on Learning Disabilities [*University of Minnesota*] [*Research center*] (RCD) .... IRLD
Institute for Research on Poverty [*University of Wisconsin - Madison*] [*Research center*] (RCD) .... IRP
Institute for Research on Public Policy [*Canada*] .... IRPP
Institute for Research on Public Policy [*Institut de Recherches Politiques*] Montreal, Quebec [*Library symbol National Library of Canada*] (NLC) .... QMIRP
Institute for Research on Public Policy, Ottawa, ON, Canada [*Library symbol*] [*Library of Congress*] (LCLS) .... CaOOIRP
Institute for Research on Public Policy [*Institut de Recherches Politiques*], Ottawa, Ontario [*Library symbol National Library of Canada*] (NLC) .... OOIRP
Institute for Research on Teaching [*East Lansing, MI*] [*Department of Education*] (GRD) .... IRT
Institute for Research on the Economics of Taxation [*Research center*] (RCD) .... IRET
Institute for Resource and Environmental Studies [*Dalhousie University*] [*Canada Research center*] (RCD) .... IRES
Institute for Resource and Security Studies (EA) .... IRSS
Institute for Resource Management (EA) .... IRM
Institute for Responsive Education (EA) .... IRE
Institute for Retired Professionals (EA) .... IRP
Institute for Risk Research [*University of Waterloo*] [*Canada Research center*] (RCD) .... IRR
Institute for Robotics and Intelligent Systems [*Research center*] (RCD) .... IRIS
Institute for Rural Environmental Health [*Colorado State University*] [*Research center*] (RCD) .... IREH
Institute for Rural Water (EA) .... IRW
Institute for Scientific Analysis (EA) .... ISA
Institute for Scientific Humanism [*Later, WISH*] .... ISH
Institute for Scientific Information [*Philadelphia, PA*] [*Database producer*] .... ISI
Institute for Security and Cooperation in Outer Space (EA) .... ISCOS
Institute for Security Design (EA) .... ISD
Institute for Sex Research, Inc. [*National Institute of Mental Health*] (IID) .... ISR
Institute for Sex Research Library Records [*Database*] [*Kinsey Institute for Research in Sex, Gender, and Reproduction*] [*Information service or system*] (CRD) .... ISRREC
Institute for Simulation and Training [*University of Central Florida*] [*Research center*] (RCD) .... IST
Institute for Social Dance Studies [*Defunct*] (EA) .... ISDS
Institute for Social Economic Change .... ISEC
Institute for Social Evaluation and Design .... ISED
Institute for Social Inquiry [*University of Connecticut*] [*Storrs*] [*Information service or system*] (IID) .... ISI
Institute for Social Justice (EA) .... ISJ
Institute for Social Research [*University of Michigan*] (EA) .... ISR
Institute for Social Research [*York University*] [*Information service or system*] (IID) .... ISR
Institute for Social Research and Development [*University of New Mexico*] .... ISRAD
Institute for Social Science Research [*Research center*] (RCD) .... ISSR
Institute for Socioeconomic Studies (EA) .... ISES
Institute for Socioeconomic Studies (EA) .... ISS
Institute for Software Engineering (EA) .... ISE
Institute for Solid Wastes .... ISW
Institute for Southern Studies (EA) .... ISS
Institute for Soviet-American Relations (EA) .... ISAR
Institute for Space and Security Studies (EA) .... ISSS
Institute for Space and Terrestrial Science [*Research center Canada*] (RCD) .... ISTS
Institute for Space Science and Technology, Inc. [*Research center*] (RCD) .... ISST
Institute for Space Studies [*NASA*] .... ISS
Institute for Storm Research (MCD) .... ISR
Institute for Strategic Studies [*Later, IISS*] [*Obsolete*] .... ISS
Institute for Studies in American Music (EA) .... ISAM
Institute for Studies in Pragmaticism [*Texas Tech University*] [*Research center*] (RCD) .... ISP
Institute for Studies in Psychological Testing .... ISPT
Institute for Studies of Destructive Behaviors and the Suicide Prevention Centerof Los Angeles [*California*] (EA) .... SPC
Institute for Study of Regulation [*Defunct*] (EA) .... ISR
Institute for Sustainable Agriculture [*Australia*] .... ISA
Institute for Systems Design and Optimization .... ISDO
Institute for Telecommunication Sciences [*Formerly, ITSA*] [*Boulder, CO*] [*Department of Commerce*] .... ITS
Institute for Telecommunication Sciences and Aeronomy [*Later, ITS*] [*National Oceanic and Atmospheric Administration*] .... ITSA
Institute for Telecommunications and Aeronomy [*ESSA*] (MCD) .... ITA
Institute for the Advanced Study of Black Family Life and Culture (EA) .... IASBFLC
Institute for the Advancement of Engineering (EA) .... IAE
Institute for the Advancement of Hawaiian Affairs .... IAHA
Institute for the Advancement of Health [*Defunct*] (EA) .... IAH
Institute for the Advancement of Human Behavior (EA) .... IAHB
Institute for the Advancement of Notary Public Education (EA) .... IANPE
Institute for the Advancement of Philosophy for Children (EA) .... IAPC
Institute for the Advancement of Sailing [*Commercial firm*] (EA) .... IAS
Institute for the Certification of Engineering Technicians [*Later, National Institute for Certification in Engineering Technologies*] .... ICET
Institute for the Community as Extended Family (EA) .... ICEF
Institute for the Comparative Study of History, Philosophy, and the Sciences Ltd. [*British*] (BI) .... ICS
Institute for the Comparative Study of Political Systems .... ICOPS
Institute for the Development of Emotional and Life Skills (EA) .... IDEALS
Institute for the Development of Indian Law (EA) .... IN-DEV-IL
Institute for the Development of the Harmonious Human Being (EA) .... IDHHB
Institute for the Editing of Historical Documents .... IEHD
Institute for the Future .... IFF
Institute for the Future [*Research center Telecommunications*] (RCD) .... IFTF
Institute for the History and Philosophy of Science and Technology [*University of Toronto*] [*Canada*] (IRC) .... IHPST
Institute for the Human Environment (EA) .... IHE
Institute for the Integration of Latin America .... IILA
Institute for the Officialization of Esperanto .... IOE
Institute for the Protection of Lesbian and Gay Youth (EA) .... IPLGY
Institute for the Study and Treatment of Delinquency [*British*] .... ISTD
Institute for the Study of American Cultures (EA) .... ISAC
Institute for the Study of Animal Behavior (BARN) .... ISAB
Institute for the Study of Animal Problems [*Defunct*] (EA) .... ISAP
Institute for the Study of Business Markets [*Pennsylvania State University*] [*Research center*] (RCD) .... ISBM
Institute for the Study of Conflict [*British*] .... ISC
Institute for the Study of Conscious Evolution [*Defunct*] (EA) .... ISCE
Institute for the Study of Defects in Solids [*State University of New York at Albany*] [*Research center*] (RCD) .... ISDS
Institute for the Study of Developing Nations (EA) .... ISDN
Institute for the Study of Drug Addiction [*Later, ISDM*] (EA) .... ISDA
Institute for the Study of Drug Dependence [*London*] .... ISDD
Institute for the Study of Drug Misuse [*Formerly, ISDA*] (EA) .... ISDM
Institute for the Study of Earth and Man [*Southern Methodist University*] [*Research center*] (RCD) .... ISEM
Institute for the Study of Fatigue Fracture and Structural Reliability [*George Washington University*] .... ISFFSR
Institute for the Study of Genocide (EA) .... ISG
Institute for the Study of Human Issues (EA) .... ISHI
Institute for the Study of Human Knowledge (EA) .... ISHK
Institute for the Study of Inquiring Systems .... ISIS
Institute for the Study of Intellectual Behavior [*University of Colorado*] (PDAA) .... ISIB
Institute for the Study of Labor and Economic Crisis (EA) .... ISLEC
Institute for the Study of Learning Difficulties [*Flinders University*] [*Australia*] .... ISLD
Institute for the Study of Man (EA) .... ISM
Institute for the Study of Matrimonial Laws (EA) .... ISML
Institute for the Study of Natural Systems (EA) .... ISNS
Institute for the Study of Nonviolence [*Defunct*] (EA) .... ISNV
Institute for the Study of Sexual Assault [*Defunct*] (EA) .... ISSA
Institute for the Study of Sport and Society .... ISSS
Institute for the Study of Traditional American Indian Arts (EA) .... ISTAIA
Institute for the Study of Universal History through Arts and Artifacts [*Defunct*] (EA) .... ISUH
Institute for the Technology and Industrialization of Tropical Agricultural Products [*Ivory Coast*] .... ITIPAT
Institute for the Transfer of Technology to Education (EA) .... ITTE
Institute for Theological and Philosophical Studies (EA) .... ITPS
Institute for Theological Encounter with Science and Technology (EA) .... ITEST
Institute for Training and Demographic Research (EA) .... ITDR
Institute for Training and Development .... INSTAD
Institute for Training in Municipal Administration (EA) .... ITMA
Institute for TransPacific Networking [*Oakland, CA*] [*Telecommunications service*] (TSSD) .... ITN
Institute for Transportation and Development Policy (EA) .... ITDP
Institute for Transportation Research and Education [*University of North Carolina*] [*Research center*] (RCD) .... ITRE
Institute for Transportation Studies [*University of Calgary*] [*Canada Research center*] (RCD) .... ITS
Institute for Twenty-First Century Studies (EA) .... ITFCS
Institute for Urban Affairs and Research [*Howard University*] [*Research center*] (RCD) .... IUAR
Institute for Urban and Public Policy Research [*University of Colorado - Denver*] [*Research center*] (RCD) .... IUPPR
Institute for Urban Design (EA) .... IUD
Institute for Urban Development .... IUD
Institute for Ventures in New Technology .... INVENT
Institute for Victims of Trauma (EA) .... IVT
Institute for Water Resources [*Fort Belvoir, VA*] [*Army*] (MSC) .... IWR
Institute for Wholistic Education [*Later, SCIWE*] (EA) .... IWE
Institute for Wildlife Research [*Defunct*] (EA) .... IWR
Institute for Women's Studies in the Arab World [*Beirut, Lebanon*] (EAIO) .... IWSAW
Institute for Workers' Control .... IWC
Institute for World Order (EA) .... IWO
Institute in Basic Youth Conflicts (EA) .... IBYC
Institute of Aboriginal and Torres Strait Islander Studies [*Australia*] .... IATSIS
Institute of Acoustics [*British*] (DBA) .... IOA
Institute of Actuaries [*British*] .... IA
Institute of Actuaries [*British*] .... InstAct
Institute of Administration [*University of New South Wales*] [*Australia*] .... IoA
Institute of Administrative Accountants [*Sevenoaks, Kent, England*] (EAIO) .... IAA

Institute of Administrative Accounting and Data Processing Limited [British] (NITA) ..... IAA

Institute of Administrative Management [British] (DCTA) ..... IAM

Institute of Administrative Management / Telecommunications Managers Division (HGAA) ..... IAM/TMD

Institute of Advanced Legal Studies. Annals [A publication] (DLA) ..... Inst Ad Legal Stud Ann

Institute of Advanced Machine Tool and Control Technology [British] ..... IAMTACT

Institute of Advanced Machine Tool and Control Technology (MCD) ..... IAMTCT

Institute of Advanced Manufacturing Sciences [University of Cincinnati] ..... IAMS

Institute of Advanced Marketing Studies - American Marketing Association (EA) ..... IAMS

Institute of Advanced Motorists [British] ..... IAM

Institute of Advanced Philosophic Research (EA) ..... IAPR

Institute of Advanced Studies [Australian National University] ..... IAS

Institute of Advanced Studies of World Religions, Stony Brook, NY [Library symbol Library of Congress] (LCLS) ..... NSbIA

Institute of Advertising Practitioners in Ireland (BI) ..... IAPI

Institute of Aeronautical Engineers ..... IAeE

Institute of Aerospace Safety and Management [University of Southern California] ..... IASM

Institute of Aerospace [formerly, Aeronautical] Sciences ..... IAES

Institute of Aerospace [formerly, Aeronautical] Sciences [Later, AIAA] ..... IAS

Institute of African Studies. Research Review [A publication] ..... IASRR

Institute of Afro-American Affairs [New York University] [Research center] (RCD) ..... IAAA

Institute of Agricultural Market Management & Administration [India] ..... IAMMA

Institute of Agricultural Secretaries (DBA) ..... IAgS

Institute of Agricultural Secretaries of Australasia ..... IASA

Institute of Agriculture Remote Sensing Laboratory [University of Minnesota] ..... IARSL

Institute of Air Weapons Research [Air Force] ..... IAWR

Institute of Alcohol Studies [British] (DBA) ..... IAS

Institute of Allegheny Life and Culture (EA) ..... IALC

Institute of Amateur Cinematographers [British] (BI) ..... IAC

Institute of Ambulance Officers [Australia] ..... IAO

Institute of American Indian and Alaska Native Culture and Arts Development (EA) ..... IAIA

Institute of American Poultry Industries [Later, PEIA] (EA) ..... IAPI

Institute of American Relations [Defunct] (EA) ..... IAR

Institute of Andean Research (EA) ..... IAR

Institute of Andean Studies (EA) ..... IAS

Institute of Animal Behavior [Rutgers University] [Research center] (RCD) ..... IAB

Institute of Animal Physiology [British] ..... IAP

Institute of Animal Physiology and Genetics Research [Research center British] (IRC) ..... IAPGR

Institute of Animal Resource Ecology [University of British Columbia] [Research center] (RCD) ..... IARE

Institute of Animal Sciences (ASF) ..... IAS

Institute of Animal Technology [London] ..... IAT

Institute of Antarctic and Southern Ocean Studies (EERA) ..... IASOS

Institute of Apostolic Oblates (EA) ..... IAO

Institute of Appliance Manufacturers [Later, GAMA] (EA) ..... IAM

Institute of Applied Clicheology ..... IAC

Institute of Applied Economic and Social Research (EERA) ..... IAESR

Institute of Applied Economic Research [Concordia University] [Canada Research center] (RCD) ..... IAER

Institute of Applied Economics [University of Montreal] [Canada] (IRC) ..... IEA

Institute of Applied Language Studies [Edith Cowan University] [Australia] ..... IALS

Institute of Applied Mathematics [University of British Columbia] [Canada Research center] (RCD) ..... IAM

Institute of Applied Mathematics and Statistics [University of British Columbia] [Research center] (RCD) ..... IAMS

Institute of Applied Natural Science (EA) ..... IANS

Institute of Applied Physiology and Medicine [Formerly, Institute of Environmenta l Medicine and Physiology] [Research center] (RCD) ..... IAPM

Institute of Arbitrators [British] (DI) ..... IArb

Institute of Arbitrators Australia ..... IAA

Institute of Archeology and Anthropology [University of South Carolina at Columbia] [Research center] (RCD) ..... IAA

Institute of Architects [Australia] ..... IA

Institute of Arctic and Alpine Research [University of Colorado] ..... INSTAAR

Institute of Arctic Biology [Research center] (RCD) ..... IAB

Institute of Arctic Mineral Resources [University of Alaska] ..... IAMR

Institute of Arthropodology and Parasitology [Georgia Southern University] [Research center] (RCD) ..... IAP

Institute of Asian Research [Canada] (IRC) ..... IAR

Institute of Asian Studies (EA) ..... IAS

Institute of Asphalt Technology [British] ..... IAT

Institute of Association Management Companies (EA) ..... IAMC

Institute of Atmospheric Physics [University of Arizona] [Research center] ..... IAP

Institute of Atomic Energy [Academy of Sciences, USSR] ..... IAE

Institute of Auctioneers and Appraisers in Scotland (EAIO) ..... IAAS

Institute of Automobile Assessors [British] (BI) ..... IAA

Institute of Automobile Engineers ..... IAE

Institute of Automotive and Aeronautical Engineers (WDAA) ..... IAAE

Institute of Automotive Engineer Assessors [British] (EAIO) ..... IAEA

Institute of Aviation Medicine [Royal Canadian Air Force] ..... IAM

Institute of Aviation Studies [University of Newcastle] [Australia] ..... IAS

Institute of Bankers [Later, CIB] [British] (DI) ..... IB

Institute of Bankers [Later, CIB] [British] (EAIO) ..... IOB

Institute of Bankers in Scotland (ODBW) ..... IB(Scot)

Institute of Bankers in Scotland (DI) ..... IOBS

Institute of Baths and Recreation Management [British] ..... IBRM

Institute of Baths Management [British] (BI) ..... IBM

Institute of Behavioral Science [University of Colorado - Boulder] [Research center] (RCD) ..... IBS

Institute of Behavioural Studies [University of Newcastle] [Australia] ..... IBS

Institute of Biology [British] ..... IB

Institute of Biology [British] (DI) ..... IBiol

Institute of Biomedical Engineering [University of Toronto] [Research center] (RCD) ..... IBME

Institute of Black Studies [Defunct] (EA) ..... IBS

Institute of Boiler and Radiator Manufacturers [Later, Hydronics Institute] (EA) ..... IBR

Institute of Boiler and Radiator Manufacturers [Later, Hydronics Institute] ..... IBRM

Institute of Bookkeepers [British] (DAS) ..... IBK

Institute of Brewing [Also, IOB] [British] ..... IB

Institute of Brewing [Also, IB] [British] ..... IOB

Institute of British Architects ..... IBA

Institute of British Bakers (BI) ..... IBB

Institute of British Carriage and Automobile Manufacturers (BI) ..... IBCAM

Institute of British Engineers (DAS) ..... IBE

Institute of British Engineers ..... IBritishE

Institute of British Foundrymen (EAIO) ..... IBF

Institute of British Geographers (BI) ..... IBG

Institute of British Geographers (DBA) ..... IBG

Institute of British Industrial Art ..... IBIA

Institute of British Oil Paintings ..... IBOP

Institute of British Photographers (DGA) ..... IBP

Institute of British Surgical Technicians (BI) ..... IBST

Institute of Broadcast Engineers [Later, SBE] (NTCM) ..... IBE

Institute of Broadcasting Financial Management [Later, BCFMA] ..... IBFM

Institute of Builders Merchants [British] (DBA) ..... IBM

Institute of Building [British] ..... IB

Institute of Building [or Builders] [British] ..... IOB

Institute of Building Control [British] (DBA) ..... IBC

Institute of Building Estimators Ltd. [British] (BI) ..... IBE

Institute of Building Quality Australia ..... IBQA

Institute of Building Site Management [British] (BI) ..... IBSM

Institute of Burial and Cremation Administration [British] ..... IBCA

Institute of Business Appraisers (EA) ..... IBA

Institute of Business Designers (EA) ..... IBD

Institute of Careers Officers [British] ..... ICO

Institute of Care-Home Managers [British] (DBA) ..... ICHM

Institute of Carpenters [British] (DBA) ..... IOC

Institute of Caster Manufacturers (EA) ..... ICM

Institute of Ceramic Engineers (NUCP) ..... ICE

Institute of Ceramics [Stoke-On-Trent, Staffordshire, England] (EAIO) IC

Institute of Certified Ambulance Personnel [British] (BI) ..... ICAP

Institute of Certified Business Counselors (EA) ..... ICBC

Institute of Certified Business Counselors (EA) ..... ISBC

Institute of Certified Financial Planners (EA) ..... ICFP

Institute of Certified Management Accountants [Montvale, NJ] (EA) ..... ICMA

Institute of Certified Professional Business Consultants [Chicago, IL] (EA) ..... ICPBC

Institute of Certified Professional Managers [Harrisonburg, VA] (EA) ..... ICPM

Institute of Certified Records Managers (EA) ..... ICRM

Institute of Certified Travel Agents (EA) ..... ICTA

Institute of Charity [Rosminians] [Roman Catholic religious order] IC

Institute of Charity (TOCD) ic

Institute of Charity Fundraising Managers [British] (DBA) ..... ICFM

Institute of Chart Foresters [British] (DBA) ..... ICF

Institute of Chartered Accountants in England and Wales (BI) ..... ICA

Institute of Chartered Accountants in England and Wales ..... ICAEW

Institute of Chartered Accountants in Ireland (EAIO) ..... ICAI

Institute of Chartered Accountants of Newfoundland, St. John's, Newfoundland [Library symbol National Library of Canada] (NLC) ..... NFSICA

Institute of Chartered Accountants of Newfoundland, St. John's, NF, Canada [Library symbol Library of Congress] (LCLS) ..... CaNfSICA

Institute of Chartered Accountants of Ontario, Toronto, ON, Canada [Library symbol Library of Congress] (LCLS) ..... CaOTICA

Institute of Chartered Accountants of Ontario, Toronto, Ontario [Library symbol National Library of Canada] (NLC) ..... OTICA

Institute of Chartered Accountants of Quebec, Montreal, PQ, Canada [Library symbol Library of Congress] (LCLS) ..... CaQMICA

Institute of Chartered Accountants of Quebec [Institut Canadien des Comptables Agrees du Quebec] Montreal, Quebec [Library symbol National Library of Canada] (NLC) ..... QMICA

Institute of Chartered Accountants of Scotland (AIE) ..... ICAS

Institute of Chartered Financial Analysts [Later, AIMR] (EA) ..... ICFA

Institute of Chartered Foresters [British] ..... IFGB

Institute of Chartered Life Underwriters of Canada ..... CLU

Institute of Chartered Secretaries and Administrators (AIE) ..... ICSA

Institute of Chartered Shipbrokers [British] ..... ICS

Institute of Chemical Analysis, Applications, and Forensic Science [Northeastern University] [Research center] (RCD) ..... CAAFS

Institute of Chemistry [British] IC

Institute of Chemistry [British] (DAS) ..... IOC

Institute of Chemistry of Ireland (BI) ICI

Institute of Chemists-Opticians [British] (DAS) ..... ICO

Institute of Child Study [University of Toronto] [Research center] (RCD) ..... ICS

Institute of Child Study Security Test [Psychology] ..... ICSST

Institute of Child Study, University of Toronto, Ontario [Library symbol National Library of Canada] (NLC) ..... OTUCS

Institute of Chinese Culture (EA) ICC

Institute of Chocolate and Confectionery Distributors [British] (BI) ..... ICCD

Institute of Circuit Technology [Oxford, England] [Defunct] (EAIO) ..... ICT

Institute of Circuit Technology Ltd. (NITA) .... ICT
Institute of Cistercian Studies, Western Michigan University, Kalamazoo, MI [Library symbol Library of Congress] (LCLS) .... MiKCS
Institute of Civil Defence [British] (EAIO) .... ICD
Institute of Civil Defence and Disaster Studies [British] (EAIO) .... ICDDS
Institute of Civil War Studies (EA) .... ICWS
Institute of Clay Technology [British] .... ICT
Institute of Clay Workers [British] (BI) .... ICW
Institute of Clerks of Work (PDAA) .... ICW
Institute of Clinical Analysis .... ICA
[Myasnikov] Institute of Clinical Cardiology [Russian] ICC
Institute of Clinical Molecular Biology [British] (DBA) .... IMM
Institute of Clinical Pharmacology PLC (MHDW) .... ICPYY
Institute of Club Managers and Secretaries [Australia] .... ICMS
Institute of Coal Research [University of Newcastle] [Australia] .... ICR
Institute of Coastal Oceanography and Tides [British] .... ICOT
Institute of Cognitive Science [University of Colorado, Boulder] [Research center] (RCD) .... ICS
Institute of Collective Bargaining and Group Relations (EA) .... ICB
Institute of Combined Arms and Support [Fort Leavenworth, KS] [Army] ..... ICAS
Institute of Commerce [British] (DBA) .... IOC
Institute of Commercial and Technical Representatives Ltd. [British] (BI) .... ICTR
Institute of Commonwealth Studies [British] .... ICS
Institute of Commonwealth Studies, London, United Kingdom [Library symbol Library of Congress] (LCLS) .... UkLCS
Institute of Community and Family Psychiatry, Jewish General Hospital, Montreal,Quebec [Library symbol National Library of Canada] (NLC) ...... QMJGI
Institute of Community Development [British] (DBA) .... ICD
Institute of Company Accountants [British] (DAS) .... ICA
Institute of Company Accountants [British] (EAIO) .... IComA
Institute of Comparative Biology (BARN) .... ICB
Institute of Complementary Sciences [Defunct] (EA) .... ICS
Institute of Computational Mechanics [University of Cincinnati] [Research center] (RCD) .... ICOM
Institute of Computer Aided Engineering and Management [University of Dundee] [British] (IRUK) .... ICEAM
Institute of Computer Science, University of Toronto, Ontario [Library symbol National Library of Canada] (NLC) .... OTUCC
Institute of Computer Technology .... ICT
Institute of Concrete Technology [British] .... ICT
Institute of Construction Management [British] .... ICM
Institute of Consumer Advisers [British] (DBA) .... ICA
Institute of Contemporary Arts [British] .... ICA
Institute of Contemporary Asian Studies [Monash University] [Australia] ...... ICAS
Institute of Contemporary Russian Studies [Fordham University] .... ICRS
Institute of Continuing Legal Education [Research center] (RCD) .... ICLE
Institute of Continuing Legal Education in Georgia [University of Georgia School of Law] (DLA) .... GICLE
Institute of Continuing Legal Education, Louisiana State University Law Center (DLA) .... LSU
Institute of Continuing Legal Education, University of Michigan (DLA) ..... MICLE
Institute of Cooperative Directors (ODBW) .... ICD
Institute of Corn and Agricultural Merchants Ltd. [British] (BI) .... ICAM
Institute of Cornish Studies [British] .... ICS
Institute of Corporate Managers, Secretaries and Administrators [Australia] .... ICMSA
Institute of Cost Analysis [Later, SCEA] (EA) .... ICA
Institute of Cost and Management Accountants [British] .... ICMA
Institute of Cost and Works Accountants [British] (BI) .... ICWA
Institute of Credit Management [British] .... ICM
Institute of Critical Care Medicine [University of Southern California] [Research center] (RCD) .... ICCM
Institute of Cultural Affairs (EA) .... ICA
Institute of Cultural Affairs International (EA) .... ICAI
Institute of Cultural Affairs International [Information service or system] (IID) .... ICIA
Institute of Current World Affairs (EA) .... ICWA
Institute of Data Processing [Later, IDPM] .... IDP
Institute of Data Processing Management [DPMA and Institute of Data Processing - IDP] [Formed by a merger of] (EAIO) .... IDPM
Institute of Defense Analysis Compiler (SAA) .... IDABEE
Institute of Developing Economics, Tokyo [UTLAS symbol] .... IDE
Institute of Development Studies [University of Sussex] [British] .... IDS
Institute of Directors [British] .... InstD
Institute of Directors [British] (DCTA) .... IOD
Institute of Directors [British] (ODBW) .... IoD
Institute of Distribution [Defunct] .... ID
Institute of Diving (EA) .... IOD
Institute of Donations and Public Affairs Research [Canada] .... IDPAR
Institute of Donations and Public Affairs Research [Former name of Canadian Centre for Business in the Community] (NFD) .... IDPAR
Institute of Drug Technology Australia .... IDTA
Institute of Early American History and Culture (EA) .... IEAHC
Institute of Early American History and Culture, Williamsburg, VA [Library symbol Library of Congress] (LCLS) .... ViWI
Institute of Early Childhood [Macquarie University] [Australia] .... IEC
Institute of Earth and Planetary Physics [University of Alberta] [Research center] (RCD) .... IEPP
Institute of East Asian Studies [University of California, Berkeley] [Research center] (RCD) .... IEAS
Institute of Ecology [Research center] (RCD) .... IOE
[The] Institute of Ecology [Defunct] .... TIE
Institute of Economic Affairs [British] .... IEA
Institute of Economic Botany [New York Botanical Garden] .... IEB
Institute of Ecosystem Studies .... IES

Institute of Educational Cinematography [British] .... IEC
Institute of Educational Research [Defunct] (EA) .... IER
Institute of Educational Technology [British] .... IET
Institute of Electrical and Electronics Engineering (USDC) .... IEEE
Institute of Electrical and Electronics Engineering (NITA) .... IEEE
Institute of Electrical and Electronics Engineers (EA) .... IEEE
Institute of Electrical and Electronics Engineers - Computer Society ..... IEEE-CS
Institute of Electrical and Electronics Engineers, Piscataway, NJ [Library symbol Library of Congress] (LCLS) .... NjPwIE
Institute of Electrical Engineering [Hitchin, Herts., England] (NATG) .... IEE
Institute of Electrology Educators (EA) .... IEE
Institute of Electrolysis [British] (DBA) .... IofE
Institute of Electronic Communications Engineers of Japan .... IECEJ
Institute of Electronics and Radio Engineers [British] .... IERE
Institute of Electronics & Telecommunications Engineers of Japan (NITA) .... IETEJ
Institute of Employment Consultants Ltd. [British] .... IEC
Institute of Energy [An association] (EAIO) .... IE
Institute of Engineering Research [Research center British] (IRC) .... IER
Institute of Engineering Research [University of California] [Research center] (MCD) .... IER
Institute of Engineers and Technicians [British] .... IE
Institute of Engineers and Technicians [British] (EAIO) .... IET
Institute of Engineers of Chile .... IEC
Institute of English Studies (DBA) .... IES
Institute of Environment Studies, University of Toronto, Ontario [Library symbol National Library of Canada] (NLC) .... OTF
Institute of Environmental Action (EA) .... IEA
Institute of Environmental Engineers [Later, IES] .... IEE
Institute of Environmental Health Officers [British] .... IEHO
Institute of Environmental Medicine and Physiology .... IEMP
Institute of Environmental Sciences (EA) .... IES
Institute of Epidemiology and Behavioral Medicine [Medical Research Institute of San Francisco] [Research center] (RCD) .... IEBM
Institute of Estate Planning, University of Miami Law Center (DLA) .... UMLC
Institute of European Defence and Strategic Studies [British] (DBA) .... IEDSS
Institute of European Studies (EA) .... IES
Institute of Evolutionary Morphology and Animal Ecology [Commonwealth of Independent States] .... IEMAE
Institute of Experimental Meteorology [Former USSR] .... IEM
Institute of Expertology (EA) .... IE
Institute of Exploratory Research [Army] .... IER
Institute of Explosive Engineers (PDAA) .... IEXPE
Institute of Export [British] .... IE
Institute of Family History and Genealogy (EA) .... IFHG
Institute of Family Therapy [British] (DBA) .... IFT
Institute of Fence Engineers [British] (DBA) .... IFenE
Institute of Ferro-Alloy Producers in Western Europe [Defunct] (EA) .... IFAPWE
Institute of Field Archaeologists [British] (DBA) .... IFA
Institute of Financial Accountants (EAIO) .... IFA
Institute of Financial Education [Chicago, IL] (EA) .... IFE
Institute of Financial Services [Australia] .... IFS
Institute of Fire Engineers .... IFE
Institute of Fire Engineers in Australia .... IFEA
Institute of Fire Prevention Officers [British] (DBA) .... IFPO
Institute of Fireplace Equipment Manufacturers (EA) .... IFEM
Institute of Fiscal and Political Education [Defunct] (EA) .... IFPE
Institute of Fisheries Management [British] .... IFM
Institute of Fisheries Research [University of North Carolina] .... IFR
Institute of Flight Structures [Columbia University] .... IFS
Institute of Fluid Power .... IFP
Institute of Food Research [British] .... IFR
Institute of Food Science and Technology of the United Kingdom .... IFST
Institute of Food Technologists (EA) .... IFT
Institute of Foreign Bankers [New York, NY] (EA) .... IFB
Institute of Freight Forwarders [British] .... IFF
Institute of Fuel [British] .... IF
Institute of Fuel [British] .... InstF
Institute of Fuel [British] (BI) .... IOF
Institute of Gas Technology (EA) .... IGT
Institute of Gas Technology, Chicago, IL [OCLC symbol] (OCLC) .... IHF
Institute of General Semantics (EA) .... IGS
[The] Institute of Genomic Research .... TIGR
Institute of Geological Sciences [British] .... IGS
Institute of Geological Sciences [British] [Marine science] (OSRA) .... IGS
Institute of Geomantic Research (EAIO) .... IGR
Institute of Geophysics [Later, IGPP] [University of California] (MCD) .... IG
Institute of Geophysics and Planetary Physics [Livermore, CA] [Department of Energy] (MCD) .... IGPP
Institute of Geriatric Medicine and Gerontology [British] .... IGMG
Institute of Government Studies [University of California at Berkeley] .... IGS
Institute of Grassland and Environmental Research [British] .... IGER
Institute of Grocery Distribution Ltd. [British] .... IGD
Institute of Groundsmanship (EA) .... IG
Institute of Groundsmanship [British] (ITD) .... IOG
Institute of Health Education [British] .... IHE
Institute of Health Food Retailing [British] (DBA) .... IHFR
Institute of Health Services Management (DBA) .... IHSM
Institute of Heat Technology .... IHT
Institute of Heating and Air-Conditioning Industries .... IHAI
Institute of Heraldic and Genealogical Studies [British] .... IHGS
[The] Institute of Heraldry [Military] .... IOH
[The] Institute of Heraldry [Military] .... TIOH
Institute of High Energy Physics [Former USSR] .... IHEP
Institute of High Fidelity [Formerly, IHFM] [Later, EIA] (EA) .... IHF

Institute of High Fidelity Manufacturers [*Later, IHF*] ... IHFM
Institute of Higher Education ... IHE
Institute of Higher Education Research and Services [*University of Alabama*] [*Research center*] (RCD) ... IHERS
Institute of Highway Engineers [*British*] ... IHE
Institute of Highway Incorporated Engineers [*British*] (EAIO) ... IHIE
Institute of Home Economics [*of ARS, Department of Agriculture*] ... IHE
Institute of Home Economics [*British*] (DBA) ... IHEc
Institute of Home Help Organisers [*British*] ... IHHO
Institute of Home Office Underwriters [*Louisville, KY*] (EA) ... IHOU
Institute of Home Safety [*British*] (DBA) ... IHS
Institute of Horticultural Research [*Research center British*] (IRC) ... IHR
Institute of Hospital Administrators [*British*] (BI) ... IHA
Institute of Hospital Catering [*Australia*] ... IHC
Institute of Hospital Engineering (EAIO) ... IHE
Institute of Hospital Engineering (PDAA) ... IHOSPE
Institute of Housing [*British*] ... IH
Institute of Housing [*British*] (DBA) ... IOH
Institute of Housing Managers [*British*] (BI) ... IHM
Institute of Human Development [*University of California, Berkeley*] [*Research center*] (RCD) ... IHD
Institute of Human Origins (EA) ... IHO
Institute of Human Science and Services [*University of Rhode Island*] [*Research center*] (RCD) ... IHSS
Institute of Human Values [*See also IMH*] [*Canada*] ... IHV
Institute of Human Virology [*University of Maryland*] ... IHV
Institute of Hydrology [*Research center British*] ... IH
Institute of Hypertension Studies - Institute of Hypertension School of Research[*Later, NIHS*] (EA) ... IHS
Institute of Incorporated Photographers [*British*] ... IIP
Institute of Incorporated Practitioners in Advertising [*British*] (BI) ... IIPA
Institute of Industrial Economics [*University of Newcastle*] [*Australia*] ... IIE
Institute of Industrial Engineers (EA) ... IIE
Institute of Industrial Launderers (EA) ... IIL
Institute of Industrial Race Relations ... IIRR
Institute of Industrial Relations [*Loyola University of Chicago*] [*Research center*] (RCD) ... IIR
Institute of Industrial Research and Standards [*Ireland*] [*Research center Database producer*] (IID) ... IIRS
Institute of Information Scientists [*British*] (DLA) ... I Inf Sc
Institute of Information Scientists [*British*] (EAIO) ... IIS
Institute of Insurance Consultants [*British*] (DBA) ... IIC
Institute of Inter-American Affairs [*Washington, DC*] ... IIA
Institute of Inter-American Affairs [*United Nations*] ... IIAA
Institute of Interamerican Studies [*University of Miami*] [*Research center*] (RCD) ... IIAS
Institute of Intermodal Repairers (EA) ... IIR
Institute of Internal Affairs ... IIA
Institute of Internal Auditors [*Altamonte Springs, FL*] (EA) ... IIA
Institute of International Affairs ... IIA
Institute of International Container Lessors (EA) ... IICL
Institute of International Cooperation, University of Ottawa [*Institut de Cooperation Internationale, Universite d'Ottawa*] **Ontario** [*Library symbol National Library of Canada*] (NLC) ... OOUIC
Institute of International Education (EA) ... IIE
Institute of International Education, New York, NY [*Library symbol Library of Congress*] (LCLS) ... NNIIE
Institute of International Finance [*Washington, DC*] (EA) ... IIF
Institute of International Labor Research (EA) ... IILR
Institute of International Law [*Geneva, Switzerland*] (EA) ... IIL
Institute of International Licensing Practitioners (EAIO) ... IILP
Institute of International Medical Education ... IIME
Institute of International Studies (EA) ... IIS
Institute of International Trade and Development (EA) ... IITD
Institute of Inventors [*British*] (BI) ... II
Institute of Iron and Steel Wire Manufacturers (MHDB) ... IISWM
Institute of Islamic and Arabic Sciences in America (EA) ... IIASA
Institute of Islamic Understanding [*Think-tank*] [*Malaysia*] (ECON) ... IKIM
Institute of Jamaica, National Library of Jamaica, Kingston, Jamaica [*Library symbol*] [*Library of Congress*] (LCLS) ... JamKI-L
Institute of Jazz Studies [*Rutgers University, University of New Jersey*] [*Research center*] (EA) ... IJS
Institute of Jazz Studies, Rutgers, the State University, Newark, NJ [*Library symbol*] [*Library of Congress*] (LCLS) ... NjNIJS
Institute of Jewish Affairs (EA) ... IJA
Institute of Jewish Education [*British*] (DBA) ... IJE
Institute of Jewish Life Media Project [*Later, JMS*] ... IJL
Institute of Journalists [*British*] (NTCM) ... IJ
Institute of Journalists [*British*] ... IOJ
Institute of Judicial Administration (EA) ... IJA
Institute of Labor and Industrial Relations [*University of Illinois*] [*Research center*] (RCD) ... ILIR
Institute of Labor and Industrial Relations [*University of Michigan*] [*Research center*] (RCD) ... ILIR
Institute of Laboratory Animal Resources (EA) ... ILAR
Institute of Labour Management ... ILM
Institute of Land Combat [*Army*] ... ILC
Institute of Land Warfare [*Military*] ... ILW
Institute of Land Warfare [*Association of the US Army*] (DOMA) ... ILW
Institute of Landscape Architects [*British*] ... ILA
Institute of Languages and Linguistics (DIT) ... ILL
Institute of Latin American Studies [*China*] (IRC) ... ILAS
Institute of Legal Executives [*Australia*] ... ILE
Institute of Legal Executives (AIE) ... ILEx
Institute of Legal Executives [*British*] (DBA) ... ILEX
Institute of Legal Executives (Victoria) [*Australia*] ... ILE(V)
Institute of Leisure and Amenity Management (EAIO) ... ILAM
Institute of Library Research [*University of California*] (DIT) ... ILR
Institute of Life Insurance [*Later, ACLI*] (EA) ... ILI
Institute of Life Sciences [*British*] (DBA) ... ILS
Institute of Lifetime Learning (EA) ... ILL
Institute of Linguists [*British*] (BI) ... IL
Institute of Lithuanian Studies (EA) ... ILS
Institute of Local Government [*University of Birmingham*] [*British*] (AIE) ... INLOGOV
Institute of Local Government Administration [*British*] ... ILGA
Institute of Local Government Studies [*British*] ... INLOGOV
Institute of Logistics and Distribution Management [*British*] (DBA) ... ILDM
Institute of Logistics Research [*Army*] (RDA) ... ILR
Institute of Logopedics, Wichita, KS [*Library symbol Library of Congress*] (LCLS) ... KWiIL
Institute of London Underwriters (ECON) ... ILU
Institute of Machine Woodworking Technology [*British*] (BI) ... IMWoodT
Institute of Maintenance and Building Management [*British*] (DBA) ... IMBM
Institute of Makers of Explosives (EA) ... IME
Institute of Male Masseurs [*British*] (DBA) ... IMM
Institute of Man and Resources ... IMR
Institute of Man and Resources, Charlottetown, PE, Canada [*Library symbol Library of Congress*] (LCLS) ... CaPCIMR
Institute of Management Accounting (EA) ... IMA
Institute of Management Consultants [*New York, NY*] (EA) ... IMC
[*The*] **Institute of Management Sciences** ... IMS
[*The*] **Institute of Management Sciences** [*Providence, RI*] (EA) ... TIMS
Institute of Management Services [*British*] ... IMS
Institute of Management Specialists [*Royal Leamington Spa, Warwickshire, England*] (EAIO) ... IMS
Institute of Manpower Studies [*Department of Employment*] [*British*] ... IMS
Institute of Manufacturing [*Royal Leamington Spa, Warwickshire, England*] (EAIO) ... IMANF
Institute of Marine and Terrestrial Ecology [*Research center*] (RCD) ... IMTEC
Institute of Marine Biomedical Research [*University of North Carolina at Wilmington*] [*Research center*] (RCD) ... IMBR
Institute of Marine Engineers [*British Database producer*] ... IMarE
Institute of Marine Engineers [*British*] ... IME
Institute of Marine Geology and Geophysics [*Russian Federation*] [*Marine science*] (OSRA) ... IMGG
Institute of Marine Research, Helsinki, Finland [*Library symbol*] [*Library of Congress*] (LCLS) ... FiHMR
Institute of Marine Resources [*University of California*] [*Research center*] (RCD) ... IMR
Institute of Marine Science [*University of Alaska*] [*Research center*] ... IMS
Institute of Marine Science, University of Texas, Port Aransas, TX [*Library symbol Library of Congress*] (LCLS) ... TxPaIMS
Institute of Marine Sciences and Technology ... IMST
Institute of Marine Scientific and Technological Information [*China*] [*Marine science*] (OSRA) ... IMSTI
Institute of Market and Reward Regional Surveys [*British*] ... IMRRS
Institute of Market Officers [*British*] ... IMO
Institute of Marketing (EAIO) ... IM
Institute of Marketing and Sales Management [*British*] (BI) ... IMSM
Institute of Marriage and Family Relations (EA) ... IMFR
Institute of Masonry Research [*Defunct*] (EA) ... IMR
Institute of Master Tutors of Driving [*British*] (BI) ... IMTD
Institute of Masters of Wine (BARN) ... IMW
Institute of Materials [*British*] (EAIO) ... IOM
Institute of Materials and Advanced Processes [*University of Idaho*] [*Research center*] (RCD) ... IMAP
Institute of Materials Handling [*British*] (BI) ... IMH
Institute of Materials Management [*British*] (DBA) ... IMM
Institute of Materials Science (KSC) ... IMS
Institute of Mathematical Statistics (EA) ... IMS
Institute of Mathematics and Its Applications [*South-End-On-Sea, England*] (CSR) ... IMA
Institute of Mathematics and Its Applications [*South-End-On-Sea, England*] ... IMIA
Institute of Mathematics Education [*La Trobe University*] [*Australia*] ... IME
Institute of Measurement and Control [*British*] ... IMC
Institute of Measurement and Control [*British*] (EAIO) ... INSTMC
Institute of Meat [*British*] (DBA) ... IOM
Institute of Mechanical Engineers [*British*] ... IME
Institute of Mechanical Engineers [*British*] (WDAA) ... INST ME
Institute of Media Executives [*British*] ... Inst M E
Institute of Medical and Biological Illustration [*British*] ... IMBI
Institute of Medical Laboratory Sciences [*British*] ... IMLS
Institute of Medical Laboratory Technology [*British*] (DI) ... IMLT
Institute of Medical Social Workers [*British*] (BI) ... IMSW
Institute of Medicine [*National Academy of Sciences*] ... IM
Institute of Medicine [*National Academy of Sciences*] (EA) ... IOM
Institute of Medicine ... IoM
Institute of Mental Subnormality [*British*] ... IMS
[*The*] **Institute of Metal Finishing** [*British*] ... IMF
Institute of Metal Repair (EA) ... IMR
Institute of Metals [*British*] ... InstMet
Institute of Metals [*Institution of Metallurgists - IM and Metals Society - MS*] [*Formed by a merger of*] (EAIO) ... IOM
Institute of Microbiology ... IMB
Institute of Microbiology (of the Academy of Sciences, USSR) ... INMI
Institute of Microbiology, Rutgers University [*New Jersey*] ... IMRU
Institute of Mining Engineers [*British*] ... IME
Institute of Modern Languages ... IML

Institute of Modern Procedures [*Defunct*] (EA) ... IMP
Institute of Molecular & Cell Biology [*Singapore*] ... IMCB
Institute of Molecular Biology and Biochemistry [*Simon Fraser University*] [*Canada*] ... IMBB
Institute of Molecular Biology and Biotechnology [*Greece*] ... IMBB
Institute of Molecular Biophysics [*Florida State University*] [*Research center*] (RCD) ... IMB
Institute of Molecular Biotechnology [*Germany*] ... IMB
Institute of Molecular Pathology [*Austria*] ... IMP
Institute of Motorcycling [*British*] (DBA) ... IMC
Institute of Municipal Building Management [*British*] ... IMBM
Institute of Municipal Maintenance Engineers [*British*] (BI) ... IMME
Institute of Municipal Transport [*British*] (DBA) ... IMT
Institute of Municipal Treasurers and Accountants [*Later, CIPFA*] [*British*] ... IMTA
Institute of Museum Services [*National Foundation of the Arts and the Humanities*] (GRD) ... IMS
Institute of Musical Instrument Technology [*British*] (BI) ... IMIT
Institute of Muslim Minority Affairs (EAIO) ... IMMA
Institute of Natural Resources [*University of Georgia*] [*Research center*] (RCD) ... INR
Institute of Natural Resources [*Montana State University*] [*Research center*] (RCD) ... INR
Institute of Natural Resources, Chicago, IL [*Library symbol Library of Congress*] (LCLS) ... ICINR
Institute of Natural Resources, Springfield, IL [*OCLC symbol*] (OCLC) ... IFF
Institute of Nautical Archaeology (EA) ... INA
Institute of Naval Medicine [*British*] (DMA) ... INM
Institute of Naval Medicine [*British*] ... MedSch(N)
Institute of Navigation [*US and British*] ... IN
Institute of Navigation (EA) ... ION
Institute of Navigation ... ION
Institute of Neurological Science [*University of Pennsylvania*] ... INS
Institute of Neuroscience [*University of Oregon*] [*Research center*] (RCD) ... ION
Institute of Neurotoxicology [*Yeshiva University*] [*Research center*] (RCD) ... ION
Institute of New Generation Computer Technology [*Japan*] ... ICOT
Institute of Newspaper Controllers and Finance Officers [*Later, INFE*] (EA) ... INCFO
Institute of Noetic Sciences (EA) ... IONS
Institute of Noise Control Engineering (EA) ... INCE
Institute of Non-Numerical Information Processing [*Switzerland*] [*Information service or system*] (IID) ... INIP
Institute of Nuclear Materials Management (EA) ... INMM
Institute of Nuclear Power Operations (EA) ... INPO
Institute of Nuclear Research [*Poland*] ... INR
Institute of Nuclear Studies [*Oak Ridge, TN*] ... INS
Institute of Occupational and Environmental Health [*See also IMTA, IMTE*] ... IOEH
Institute of Occupational Medicine [*British*] (IRUK) ... IOM
Institute of Ocean Sciences [*Canadian Department of Fisheries and Oceans*] [*Research center*] (RCD) ... IOS
Institute of Ocean Sciences, Fisheries and Oceans Canada [*Institut des Sciences Oceanographiques, Peches et Oceans Canada*] **Sidney, British Columbia** [*Library symbol National Library of Canada*] (NLC) ... BVIEM
Institute of Oceanographic Sciences [*British Research center*] (IRC) ... IOS
Institute of Oceanographic Sciences Deacon Laboratory [*Natural Environment Research Council*] [*British*] (IRC) ... IOSDL
Institute of Oceanography Nova Scotia [*Canada*] [*Marine science*] (OSRA) ... IONS
Institute of Oceanography, University of British Columbia ... IOUBC
Institute of Office Management [*British*] (BI) ... IOM
Institute of Offshore Engineering [*Heriot-Watt University*] [*Information service or system*] (IID) ... IOE
Institute of Operating Theatre Technicians [*British*] ... IOT
Institute of Ophthalmology, Presbyterian Hospital, New York, NY [*Library symbol Library of Congress*] (LCLS) ... NNPH-O
Institute of Optimization and Systems Theory [*Stockholm*] ... IOS
Institute of Outdoor Advertising [*New York, NY*] (EA) ... IOA
Institute of Outdoor Drama (EA) ... IOD
Institute of Pacific Islands Forestry [*Honolulu, HI*] [*Department of Agriculture*] (GRD) ... IPIF
Institute of Pacific Relations ... IPR
Institute of Packaging [*British*] (BI) ... IOP
Institute of Packaging Professionals (EA) ... IoPP
Institute of Painters in Oil Colours [*British*] ... IOP
Institute of Paper Chemistry [*Lawrence University*] [*Research center*] (EA) ... IPC
Institute of Paper Chemistry, Appleton, WI [*Library symbol Library of Congress*] (LCLS) ... WAP
Institute of Paper Conservation (EA) ... IOPC
Institute of Paper Conservation [*Formerly, International Institute for Conservation of Historic and Artistic Works Paper Group*] (EA) ... IPC
Institute of Parasitoloy, Macdonald College, Ste-Anne-De-Bellevue, Quebec [*Library symbol National Library of Canada*] (NLC) ... QMIP
Institute of Park and Recreation Administration [*British*] (BI) ... IPRA
Institute of Pastoral Care (EA) ... IPC
Institute of Patentees and Inventors [*British*] (ILCA) ... IPI
Institute of Peace Research [*La Trobe University*] [*Australia*] ... IPR
Institute of Personal Image Consultants (EA) ... IPIC
Institute of Personality Assessment and Research [*University of California*] [*Research center*] ... IPAR
Institute of Personnel Management [*British*] (DCTA) ... IPM
Institute of Petroleum [*British*] (BI) ... IOP
Institute of Petroleum [*British*] ... IP
Institute of Petroleum Technologists ... IPT
Institute of Physical Distribution Management [*British*] ... IPDM
Institute of Physical High Technology [*Germany*] ... IPHT
Institute of Physical Medicine and Rehabilitation, Peoria, IL [*Library symbol Library of Congress*] (LCLS) ... IPI
Institute of Physical Problems [*Former USSR*] (MCD) ... IFP
Institute of Physical Sciences in Medicine [*British*] (DBA) ... IPSM
Institute of Physics [*British*] (WDAA) ... INST P
Institute of Physics [*British*] (EAIO) ... IOP
Institute of Physics [*British*] (EAIO) ... IP
Institute of Physics and the Physical Society [*British*] (DI) ... IPPS
Institute of Planetary and Space Science (MCD) ... IPSS
Institute of Plant Science [*Australia*] ... IPS
Institute of Plant Science Research [*Research center British*] (IRC) ... IPSR
Institute of Plasma and Fusion Research [*University of California, Los Angeles*] [*Research center*] (RCD) ... IPFR
Institute of Plasma Physics, Japan ... IPPJ
Institute of Plumbing (EAIO) ... IOP
Institute of Polar Studies [*Ohio State University*] [*Later, BPRC*] ... IPS
Institute of Polarology [*British*] ... IPOL
Institute of Policy Analysis and Research [*Nairobi, Kenya*] [*Research center*] (ECON) ... IPAR
Institute of Population Registration [*British*] ... IPR
Institute of Population Studies (BARN) ... IPS
Institute of Post Office Electrical Engineers [*British*] ... IPOEE
Institute of Poultry Industries ... IPI
Institute of Practical Mathematics [*Germany*] ... IPM
Institute of Practitioners in Advertising ... IPA
Institute of Practitioners in Work Study, Organisation, and Management (AIE) ... IPWSOM
Institute of Precious Metals [*China*] ... IPM
Institute of Print Purchasing (DGA) ... IPP
Institute of Printed Circuits (MCD) ... IPC
Institute of Printing [*British*] ... IOP
Institute of Printing [*British*] ... IP
Institute of Printing Management [*British*] ... IPM
Institute of Private Clinical Psychologists of Australia ... IPCPA
Institute of Private Practicing Psychologists [*Australia*] ... IPPP
Institute of Production Control [*British*] ... IPC
Institute of Production Engineers [*British*] ... IPE
Institute of Production Engineers [*British*] (DI) ... IProdE
Institute of Professional Businesswomen (EA) ... IPB
Institute of Professional Civil Servants [*British*] ... IPCS
Institute of Professional Designers ... IPD
Institute of Professional Goldsmiths [*British*] (DBA) ... IPG
Institute of Professional Investigators (EA) ... IPI
Institute of Professional Librarians [*Canada*] ... IPL
Institute of Profit Improvement Executives [*British*] (DBA) ... IPIE
Institute of Property Taxation (EA) ... IPT
Institute of Psychophysical Research [*British*] ... IPR
Institute of Public Administration (EA) ... IPA
Institute of Public Administration, New York, NY [*Library symbol Library of Congress*] (LCLS) ... NNIP
Institute of Public Administration of Canada ... IPAC
Institute of Public Administration of Canada, Toronto, ON, Canada [*Library symbol Library of Congress*] (LCLS) ... CaOTPA
Institute of Public Administration of Canada [*Institut d'Administration Publique du Canada*] **Toronto, Ontario** [*Library symbol National Library of Canada*] (NLC) ... OTPA
Institute of Public Affairs [*Dalhousie University*] [*Canada Research center*] ... IPA
Institute of Public Affairs, Dalhousie University, Halifax, Nova Scotia, [*Library symbol National Library of Canada*] (NLC) ... NSHDIP
Institute of Public Finance [*British*] (ECON) ... IPF
Institute of Public Health Engineers [*British*] ... IPHE
Institute of Public Loss Assessors [*British*] (DBA) ... IPLA
Institute of Public Relations [*British*] ... IPR
Institute of Public Utilities (EA) ... IPU
Institute of Purchasing and Supply [*British*] ... InstPS
Institute of Purchasing and Supply [*British*] ... IPS
Institute of Pure Chiropractic [*British*] (DBA) ... IPC
Institute of Pyramidology [*Harpenden, Hertfordshire, England*] (EA) ... IOP
Institute of Qualified Private Secretaries Ltd. [*British*] (BI) ... IQPS
Institute of Quality Assurance [*British*] ... IQA
Institute of Quantity Surveyors [*Later, RICS*] ... IQS
Institute of Quarrying [*British*] ... IOQ
Institute of Quarrying [*British*] ... IQ
Institute of Race Relations [*British*] (EAIO) ... IRR
Institute of Radio Engineers [*Later, IEEE*] (IAA) ... INSTRE
Institute of Radio Engineers [*Later, IEEE*] ... IRE
Institute of Real Estate Management [*Chicago, IL*] (EA) ... IREM
Institute of Reconstructive Plastic Surgery [*New York University*] [*Research center*] (RCD) ... IRPS
Institute of Refractories Engineers [*British*] (DBA) ... IRE
Institute of Refrigeration [*British*] ... IR
Institute of Registered Architects [*British*] ... IRA
Institute of Rehabilitation Medicine (DAVI) ... IRM
Institute of Religion and Medicine [*British*] (DBA) ... IRM
Institute of Religion, Texas Medical Center, Houston, TX [*Library symbol Library of Congress*] (LCLS) ... TxHIR
Institute of Religious Studies [*Australia*] ... IRS
Institute of Rent Officers [*British*] (DBA) ... IRO
Institute of Reprographic Technology ... IRT
Institute of Resource Recovery (GNE) ... IRR
Institute of Revenues, Rating, and Valuation [*British*] ... IRRV
Institute of Risk Management (EAIO) ... IRM
Institute of Risk Management Consultants [*Later, SRMC*] (EA) ... IRMC
Institute of Road Safety Officers [*British*] ... IRSO

Institute of Road Transport Engineers (EAIO) ... IRTE
Institute of Roofing [*British*] (DBA) ... IoR
Institute of Rubber Research (MCD) ... IRR
Institute of Rural Business Administration of Australasia ... IRBAA
Institute of Rural Life at Home and Overseas [*British*] (BI) ... IRL
Institute of Sales and Marketing Management [*British*] ... Inst SMM
Institute of Sales Promotion [*ICSU*] [*British*] ... ISP
Institute of Salesian Studies ... ISS
Institute of Sanitary Engineers [*British*] (DAS) ... ISE
Institute of Sanitation Management [*Later, EMA*] (EA) ... ISM
Institute of School and College Governors [*British*] (EAIO) ... ISCG
Institute of Science and Technology [*University of Michigan*] [*Research center*] (RCD) ... IST
Institute of Scientific and Technical Communicators [*British*] ... ISTC
Institute of Scientific and Technical Information of China [*INFOTERM*] [*Beijing*] ... ISTIC
Institute of Scientific Business [*British*] ... ISB
Institute of Scrap Iron and Steel [*Later, ISRI*] (EA) ... ISIS
Institute of Seaweed Research [*British*] ... ISR
Institute of Sedimentary and Petroleum Geology [*Geological Survey of Canada*] [*Research center*] (RCD) ... ISPG
Institute of Sedimentary and Petroleum Geology, Calgary, AB, Canada [*Library symbol Library of Congress*] (LCLS) ... CaACSP
Institute of Sedimentary and Petroleum Geology, Calgary, Alberta [*Library symbol National Library of Canada*] (NLC) ... ACSP
Institute of Semiconductor Research [*Former USSR*] ... ISR
Institute of Senior Educational Administrators of New South Wales [*Australia*] ... ISEANSW
Institute of Sex Education and Research [*British*] (DBA) ... ISER
Institute of Sheet Metal Engineering [*British*] ... ISME
Institute of Shipping Economics and Logistics [*See also ISL*] [*Bremen, Federal Republic of Germany*] (EAIO) ... ISEL
Institute of Shops Acts Administration [*British*] (BI) ... ISAA
Institute of Shortening and Edible Oils (EA) ... ISEO
Institute of Single Dynamics (EA) ... ISD
Institute of Sisters of Mercy of Australia ... ISMA
Institute of Small Business [*British*] ... ISB
Institute of Social and Economic Research [*Formerly, ISEGR*] [*University of Alaska*] ... ISER
Institute of Social and Economic Research [*Memorial University of Newfoundland*] [*Research center Canada*] (RCD) ... ISER
Institute of Social, Economic, and Governmental Research [*Later, ISER*] [*University of Alaska*] ... ISEGR
Institute of Social Ethics (EA) ... ISE
Institute of Social Order of the Society of Jesus [*Later, JCSS*] (EA) ... ISOSJ
Institute of Social Research [*Indiana University*] [*Information service or system*] (IID) ... ISR
Institute of Social Services Alternatives [*Defunct*] (EA) ... ISSA
Institute of Social Studies [*Netherlands*] ... ISS
Institute of Social Welfare [*British*] (BI) ... ISW
Institute of Society, Ethics, and Life Sciences [*Later, HC*] (EA) ... ISELS
Institute of Society, Ethics, and Life Sciences, The Hastings Center, Hastings- On-Hudson, NY [*Library symbol Library of Congress*] (LCLS) ... NHasI
Institute of Solid Waste Management [*British*] (DCTA) ... ISWM
Institute of Sound and Vibration (MCD) ... ISAV
Institute of Sound and Vibration Research [*Southampton University, England*] ... ISVR
Institute of Southeast Asian Studies ... ISEAS
Institute of Space and Aeronautical Science [*Japan*] ... ISAS
Institute of Space Law ... ISL
Institute of Space Research [*Former USSR Acronym is based on foreign phrase*] ... IKI
Institute of Special Studies [*Army*] ... ISS
Institute of Spiritualist Mediums [*British*] (DBA) ... ISM
Institute of Sports Medicine [*British*] ... ISM
Institute of Sports Sponsorship [*British*] (DBA) ... ISS
Institute of Statisticians [*British*] (DBA) ... IOS
Institute of Statisticians [*British*] ... IS
Institute of Sterile Services Management [*British*] (DBA) ... ISSM
Institute of Store Planners (EA) ... ISP
Institute of Strata Title Management [*Australia*] ... ISTM
Institute of Strategic and International Studies [*Malaysia*] (ECON) ... ISIS
Institute of Strategic and Stability Operations [*Army*] ... ISSO
Institute of Supervisory Management [*British*] ... ISM
Institute of Surgical Research [*San Antonio, TX*] [*Army*] ... ISR
Institute of Surplus Dealers (EA) ... ISD
Institute of Swimming Pool Engineers [*British*] (DBA) ... ISPE
Institute of Systems Analysis [*Army*] ... ISA
Institute of Tape Learning [*British*] (DBA) ... ITL
Institute of Tax Consultants (EA) ... ITC
Institute of Technical Communicators of Southern Africa (EAIO) ... ITCSA
Institute of Technical Publicity and Publications [*British*] (BI) ... ITPP
Institute of Technology [*Air Force*] ... IT
Institute of Technology, United States Air Force [*Wright-Patterson Air Force Base, Dayton, OH*] (AAG) ... ITUSAF
Institute of Telecommunications Engineers ... ITE
Institute of Telecommunications Services (MSC) ... ITS
Institute of Temporary Services [*Later, National Association of Temporary Services*] (EA) ... ITS
Institute of Terrestrial Ecology [*Research center British*] (IRC) ... ITE
Institute of Textile Technology (EA) ... ITT
Institute of Textile Technology, Charlottesville, VA [*Library symbol Library of Congress*] (LCLS) ... ViCT
Institute of the American Musical (EA) ... IAM
Institute of the American West [*Later, INAW*] (EA) ... IAW
Institute of the Arts [*Australian National University*] ... ITA
Institute of the Black World [*Defunct*] (EA) ... IBW
Institute of the Blessed Virgin Mary [*Sisters of Loretto*] [*Roman Catholic religious order*] ... IBVM
Institute of the Brothers of the Sacred Heart [*See also IFSC*] [*Rome, Italy*] (EAIO) ... IBSH
[*The*] **Institute of the Franciscan Sisters of the Eucharist** (TOCD) ... FSE
Institute of the Furniture Warehousing and Removing Industry (EAIO) ... IFWRI
Institute of the Great Plains (EA) ... IGP
Institute of the Ironworking Industry (EA) ... III
Institute of the Motor Industry, Inc. [*British*] (BI) ... IMI
Institute of the Northamerican West (EA) ... INAW
Institute of the Pennsylvania Hospital, Philadelphia, PA [*Library symbol Library of Congress*] (LCLS) ... PPPH-I
Institute of the Sisters of Our Lady of Mt. Carmel (TOCD) ... OCarm
Institute of the Sisters of St. Dorothy [*Roman Catholic religious order*] ... SSD
Institute of Theoretical Astronomy [*University of Cambridge*] ... IOTA
Institute of Theoretical Astronomy [*Leningrad, USSR*] ... ITA
Institute of Theoretical Science [*University of Oregon*] [*Research center*] (RCD) ... ITS
Institute of Thread Machiners [*Defunct*] ... ITM
Institute of Totally Useless Skills [*An association*] (EA) ... ITUS
Institute of Trade Mark Agents [*British*] (DI) ... ITMA
Institute of Trading Standards Administration [*British*] ... ITSA
Institute of Traditional Science, Cambridge, MA [*Library symbol Library of Congress*] (LCLS) ... MCIT
Institute of Traffic Administration [*British*] ... ITA
Institute of Traffic Engineers (EA) ... ITE
Institute of Training and Development (EAIO) ... ITD
Institute of Transactional Analysis [*British*] (DBA) ... ITA
Institute of Translation and Interpreting [*British*] (DBA) ... ITI
Institute of Transport Administration [*British*] (DCTA) ... IOTA
Institute of Transport Administration [*Later, IoTA*] (EAIO) ... ITA
Institute of Transport Aviation (KSC) ... ITA
Institute of Transport of Great Britain ... ITGB
Institute of Transportation and Regional Planning (EA) ... ITRP
Institute of Transportation and Traffic Engineering [*UCLA*] ... ITTE
Institute of Transportation Engineers [*District 7*] [*Canada*] ... CITE
Institute of Transportation Engineers (EA) ... ITE
Institute of Transportation Studies [*University of California*] [*Research center*] (RCD) ... ITS
Institute of Transportation Studies Library, University of California, Berkeley,CA [*OCLC symbol*] (OCLC) ... CBT
Institute of Transportation, Travel, and Tourism ... ITTT
Institute of Travel Agents [*British*] (BI) ... ITA
Institute of Travel and Tourism [*British*] (DBA) ... ITT
Institute of Travel Management [*British*] (DBA) ... TM
Institute of Trichologists (EAIO) ... IT
Institute of Tropical Forestry [*Rio Piedras, PR*] [*Department of Agriculture*] [*Research center*] ... ITF
Institute of Turkish Studies (EA) ... ITS
Institute of University Safety Officers [*British*] (DBA) ... IUSO
Institute of Urban and Environmental Studies [*Brock University*] [*Canada Research center*] (RCD) ... UEST
Institute of Urban and Regional Development [*University of California, Berkeley*] [*Research center*] (RCD) ... IURD
Institute of Urban and Regional Studies [*Washington University*] [*Research center*] (RCD) ... IURS
Institute of Urban Life (EA) ... IUL
Institute of Urban Studies, University of Winnipeg [*UTLAS symbol*] ... IUS
Institute of Value Management [*British*] ... IVM
Institute of Vertebrate Palaeontology and Palaeoanthropology [*China*] ... IVPP
Institute of Virology [*British*] (ARC) ... IOV
Institute of Vitreous Enamellers [*British*] ... IVE
Institute of Volcanic Geology and Geochemistry [*Commonwealth of Independent States*] ... IVGG
Institute of Wastes Management [*British*] ... IWM
Institute of Water Engineers [*British*] ... IWE
Institute of Water Pollution Control [*Later, IWEM*] (EAIO) ... IWPC
Institute of Water Research [*Michigan State University*] ... IWR
Institute of Weights and Measures Administration [*Wales*] ... IWMA
Institute of Women Today (EA) ... IWT
Institute of Wood Science [*British*] (BI) ... IWS
Institute of Wood Science Ltd. [*British*] ... IWSc
Institute of Work Study Practitioners [*British*] (BI) ... IWSP
Institute of Works and Highways Superintendents [*British*] ... IWHS
Institute of World Affairs [*Later, UFSI-IWA*] (EA) ... IWA
Institute of World Economics and International Affairs [*Russian*] (BARN) ... IMEMO
Institute on Aging [*Portland State University*] [*Research center*] (RCD) ... IOA
Institute on Aging [*University of Wisconsin - Madison*] [*Research center*] (RCD) ... IOA
Institute on American Freedoms [*Defunct*] ... IAF
Institute on East Central Europe [*Columbia University*] [*Research center*] (RCD) ... IECE
Institute on Federal Taxation (DLA) ... Inst Fed Tax
Institute on Global Conflict and Cooperation [*University of California, Berkeley*] ... IGCC
Institute on Hospital and Community Psychiatry (EA) ... IHCP
Institute on Man and Science [*Formerly, Council on World Tensions*] ... IMS
Institute on Money and Inflation (EA) ... IMI
Institute on Planning, Zoning, and Eminent Domain. Proceedings [*Southwestern Legal Foundation*] (DLA) ... Inst on Plan Zoning & Eminent Domain

Institute on Planning, Zoning, and Eminent Domain. Proceedings [*A publication*] (DLA) .... Inst Plan & Zoning
Institute on Planning, Zoning, and Eminent Domain. Proceedings [*A publication*] (DLA) .... Inst Plan Zoning & ED
Institute on Pluralism and Group Identity (EA) .... IPGI
Institute on Private Investments and Investors Abroad. Proceedings [*A publication*] (DLA) .... Inst on Priv Inv & Inv Abroad
Institute on Religion and Democracy (EA) .... IRD
Institute on Religion in an Age of Science (EA) .... IRAS
Institute on Religious Life (EA) .... IRL
Institute on Securities Regulation [*A publication*] (DLA) .... Inst Sec Reg
Institute on the Church in Urban-Industrial Society [*Defunct*] .... ICUIS
Institute on the Federal Theatre Project and New Deal Culture [*George Mason University*] [*Research center*] (RCD) .... IFTPNDC
Institute on the Military and the Economy (EA) .... IME
Institute on United States Taxation of Foreign Income [*Later, ITI*] (EA) .... IUSTFI
Institute Technical Group .... ITG
Institute Warranty Limits [*Shipping*] (DS) .... IWL
Institutes and Research Divisions [*National Institutes of Health*] .... I/RD
Institutes for Behavior Resources (EA) .... IBR
Institutes for Oceanography [*Marine science*] (MSC) .... IOC
Institutes for the Achievement of Human Potential (EA) .... IAHP
Institutes of England, in Two Parts, or A Commentary upon Littleton by Sir Edward Coke [*A publication*] (DLA) .... Inst
Institutes of Justinian [*Roman law*] [*A publication*] (DSA) .... Insti
Institutes of Justinian [*Roman law*] [*A publication*] (DLA) .... Institutes
Institutes of Justinian [*Roman law*] [*A publication*] (DLA) .... J
Institutes of Justinian [*Roman law*] [*A publication*] (DLA) .... Jus Inst
Institutes of Religion and Health (EA) .... IRH
Institutio Oratoria [*of Quintilian*] [*Classical studies*] (OCD) .... Inst
Institution [*Online database field identifier*] .... IN
Institution (VRA) .... inst
Institution .... INSTN
Institution .... INSTN
Institution des Sourds de Montreal, Centre de Ressources Multimedia, Montreal, PQ, Canada [*Library symbol Library of Congress*] (LCLS) .... CaQMISM
Institution for Mentally Retarded [*Generic term*] (DHSM) .... IMR
Institution of Agricultural Engineers (EAIO) .... IAgrE
Institution of Agricultural Engineers [*British*] (DBA) .... IAgrE
Institution of Analysis and Programmers (WDAA) .... IAP
Institution of Biomedical Engineering (Australia) .... IBE(A)
Institution of Body Engineers [*British*] (BI) .... IBE
Institution of British Engineers .... Inst BE
Institution of Business Agents [*British*] .... IBA
Institution of Chemical Engineers [*British*] .... I Ch E
Institution of Chemical Engineers [*British*] .... I Chem E
Institution of Chemical Engineers [*British*] (EAIO) .... ICE
Institution of Chemical Engineers in Australia .... ICEA
Institution of Civil Engineering Surveyors [*British*] (DBA) .... ICES
Institution of Civil Engineering Surveyors (DAC) .... InstCES
Institution of Civil Engineers [*British*] .... ICE
Institution of Civil Engineers of Ireland (BI) .... ICEI
Institution of Computer Sciences [*British*] (DIT) .... ICS
Institution of Corrosion Science and Technology (PDAA) .... ICORRST
Institution of Corrosion Science and Technology (PDAA) .... ICST
Institution of Corrosion Technology (PDAA) .... ICORRT
Institution of Corrosion Technology (PDAA) .... ICT
Institution of Economic Development Officers [*British*] (DBA) .... IEDO
Institution of Electrical and Electronics Inc. Engineers (DS) .... IEEIE
Institution of Electrical and Electronics Technician Engineers (MCD) .... IEETE
Institution of Electrical Engineers [*London, England*] [*Database producer*] .... IEE
Institution of Electrical Engineers (IAA) .... INSTEE
Institution of Electrical Engineers New South Wales [*Australia*] .... IEENSW
Institution of Electrical Engineers Victoria [*Australia*] .... IEEV
Institution of Electronics and Telecommunications Engineers [*Information service or system*] (TSSD) .... IETE
Institution of Engineering Designers [*British*] (BI) .... IED
Institution of Engineering Inspection [*British*] (BI) .... IEI
Institution of Engineers and Shipbuilders [*Scotland*] (DI) .... IES
Institution of Engineers of Ireland (ACII) .... IEI
Institution of Engineers-in-Charge [*British*] (BI) .... IEIC
Institution of Environmental Sciences [*British*] (DBA) .... IEnvSc
Institution of Environmental Sciences (EAIO) .... IES
Institution of Gas Engineers [*British*] (DAS) .... IGE
Institution of Geologists (EAIO) .... IG
Institution of Heating and Ventilating Engineers [*Later, CIBSE*] .... IHVE
Institution of Highways and Transportation [*British*] (DBA) .... IHT
Institution of Incorporated Executive Engineers [*British*] (DBA) .... IIExE
Institution of Industrial Managers [*British*] .... IIM
Institution of Lighting Engineers (EAIO) .... ILE
Institution of Mechanical Engineers [*British*] .... I Mech E
Institution of Mechanical Engineers (Australian Branch) .... IME(AB)
Institution of Mechanical General Technician Engineers [*British*] .... IMGTechE
Institution of Mechanical Incorporated Engineers [*British*] (EAIO) .... IMECHIE
Institution of Metallurgists [*British*] .... IM
Institution of Mining and Metallurgy [*London, England*] .... IMM
Institution of Mining and Metallurgy (BARN) .... Inst MM
Institution of Mining Electrical and Mining Mechanical Engineers (EAIO) .... IMEMME
Institution of Mining Engineers [*British*] .... IMIE
Institution of Mining Engineers [*British*] .... IMinE
Institution of Municipal Engineers [*British*] .... IMunE
Institution of Naval Architects [*British*] .... INA
Institution of Naval Architects (BARN) .... Inst NA
Institution of Nuclear Engineers (PDAA) .... INE
Institution of Nuclear Engineers [*British*] .... INucE
Institution of Occupational Safety and Health [*British*] (DBA) .... IOSH
Institution of Plant Engineers [*British*] .... IPE
Institution of Plant Engineers [*British*] (EAIO) .... IPlantE
Institution of Production Engineers [*British*] .... I Prod E
Institution of Professional Civil Servants [*British*] (BI) .... IPCS
Institution of Professionals, Managers, and Specialists [*British*] .... IPMS
Institution of Public Lighting Engineers [*British*] .... IPLE
Institution of Railway Signal Engineers [*British*] .... IRSE
Institution of Sales Engineers [*British*] (BI) .... ISE
Institution of Structural Engineers [*British*] (EAIO) .... ISE
Institution of Structural Engineers [*British*] .... ISTRUCTE
Institution of Surveyors in Civil Engineering [*British*] .... ICES
Institution of Technician Engineers in Mechanical Engineering [*British*] .... ITEME
Institution of the Rubber Industry [*British*] .... IRI
Institution of Training Officers [*British*] .... ITO
Institution of Water and Environmental Management (EAIO) .... IWEM
Institution of Water Engineers [*British*] (BI) .... IWE
Institution of Works and Highways Management [*British*] (DBA) .... IWHM
Institution of Works Managers [*British*] .... IWM
Institution on Farm Training .... IOFT
Institutional (WDMC) I
Institutional .... INSTNL
Institutional .... INSTNL
Institutional and Municipal Parking Congress (EA) .... IMPC
Institutional and Service Textile Distributors Association (EA) .... ISTDA
Institutional Animal Care and Use Committee [*Department of Agriculture*] .... IACUC
Institutional Biosafety Committee [*National Institutes of Health*] .... IBC
Institutional Bond Quote Service [*Database*] [*Chase Econometrics Interactive Data*] [*Information service or system*] (CRD) .... IBQ
Institutional Brokers Estimate System [*Lynch, Jones & Ryan*] [*Database*] [*New York, NY Information service or system*] (IID) .... IBES
Institutional Care [*British*] IC
Institutional Characteristics [*of the Integrated Postsecondary Education Data System*] [*Department of Education*] (GFGA) IC
Institutional Child Protection Project [*Ohio State University*] (EDAC) .... ICPP
Institutional Conduct of Fire Trainer [*Army*] .... I-COFT
Institutional Conservation Program (GNE) .... ICP
Institutional Data System Division [*Johnson Space Center*] [*NASA*] (NASA) .... IDSD
Institutional Development and Economic Affairs Service [*Defunct*] (EA) .... IDEAS
Institutional Food Distributors of America [*Later, NAWGA*] (EA) .... IFDA
Institutional Goals Inventory [*Test*] .... IGI
Institutional Investor [*Business term*] II
Institutional Management in Higher Education (AIE) .... IMHE
Institutional Meat Purchase Specification [*Department of Agriculture*] .... IMPS
Institutional Networks Corp. .... INSTINET
Institutional Patent Agreements [*General Services Administration*] .... IPA
Institutional Payment Summary [*Pell Grant Program*] [*Department of Education*] (GFGA) .... IPS
Institutional Population Component [*National Medical Expenditure Survey*] [*Department of Health and Human Services*] (GFGA) .... IPC
Institutional Quality Control [*Department of Education*] (GFGA) .... IQC
Institutional Quality Control Pilot Project [*Department of Education*] (GFGA) .... IQCPP
Institutional Research and Development Office [*Kirksville College of Osteopathic Medicine*] [*Research center*] (RCD) .... IRAD
Institutional Research Council [*Defunct*] (EA) .... IRC
Institutional Review Board .... IRB
Institutional Review Committee [*Generic term*] .... IRC
Institutional Revolutionary Party [*Mexico Political party*] .... IRP
Institutional Revolutionary Party [*Mexico*] [*Political party*] .... PRI
Institutional Sector Investment Services [*Chase Manhattan Securities*] [*British*] .... ISIS
Institutional Skill Training (OICC) .... IST
Institutional Space Inventory Technique [*Computer science*] .... INSITE
Institutional Support Planning Group [*NASA*] (NASA) .... ISPG
Institutional Training (OICC) .... IT
Institutionendokumentation zur Arbeitsmarkt- und Berufsforschung [*Database*] [*Institut fuer Arbeitsmarkt- und Berufsforschung der Bundesanstalt fuer Arbeit*] [*German*] [*Information service or system*] (CRD) .... InstDokAB
Institutionenverzeichnis Auslaendischer Gesellschaften [*NOMOS Database*] [*Information service or system*] .... IVAG
Institutionenverzeichnis fuer Internationale Zusammenarbeit [*Institutions for International Cooperation*] [*NOMOS Datapool Database*] (IID) .... IVIZ
Institutiones Iustiniani [*Classical studies*] (OCD) .... Inst Iust
Institutiones Juris Anglicani, by Cowell [*A publication*] (DLA) .... Inst Jur Angl
Institutions (ROG) .... INSTNS
Institutions for Mental Diseases [*Department of Health and Human Services*] (GFGA) .... IMD
Instituto Argentine de Oceanografia [*Marine science*] (OSRA) .... IADO
Instituto Brasileiro de Informacao em Ciencia e Tecnologia [*Brazilian Institute for Information in Science and Technology*] [*National Council of Scientific and Technological Development*] [*Information service or system*] (IID) .... IBICT
Instituto Cartografico de Cataluna [*Spain ICAO designator*] (FAAC) ICC
Instituto Centro Americano de Investigacion y Tecnologia Industrial, Guatemala City, Guatemala [*Library symbol*] [*Library of Congress*] (LCLS) .... GuGIN
Instituto Centroamericano de Administracion de Empresas [*Central American Institute of Business Administration*] [*Nicaragua*] .... INCAE

Instituto Centroamericano de Administracion Publica [*Central American Institute of Public Administration*] [*Costa Rica*] .... ICAP

Instituto Centroamericano de Documentacion y Investigacion Social (EA) .... ICADIS

Instituto Centroamericano de Investigacion y Tecnologia Industrial [*Central American Institute of Research and Industrial Technology*] [*Guatemala*] [*Research center*] (IRC) .... ICAITI

Instituto Centroamericano de Investigacion y Tecnologia Industrial, Guatemala City, Guatemala [*Library symbol Library of Congress*] .... GuGIN

Instituto Cubao de Higrafia [*Cuba*] [*Marine science*] (OSRA) .... ICH

Instituto de Biologia Marina, San Antonia [*Argentina*] [*Marine science*] (OSRA) .... IBM

Instituto de Ciencias del Mar [*Barcelona, Spain*] [*Marine science*] (OSRA) .... ICM

Instituto de Estudios de Estados Unidos [*Studies Mexico/US relations, US domestic politics, US economy, and US foreign policy*] [*Mexico*] (CROSS) .... IEEU

Instituto de Estudios Politicos para America Latina y Africa [*Spain*] .... IEPALA

Instituto de Estudios Superiores de Administracion [*Institute of Higher Studies of Administration*] [*Venezuela*] .... IESA

Instituto de Fomento Nacional [*Industrial promotion agency*] [*Nicaragua*] .... INFONAC

Instituto de Geociencias Universidade Federal de Minas Gerais .... IG-CUFMG

Instituto de Informacion y Documentacion en Ciencia y Tecnologia [*Institute for Information and Documentation in Science and Technology*] [*Database originator and host*] [*Information service or system*] [*Spain*] (IID) .... ICYT

Instituto de Informacion y Documentacion en Ciencias Sociales y Humanidades [*Institute for Information and Documentation in the Social Sciences and Humanities*] [*Higher Council for Scientific Research*] [*Information service or system*] (IID) .... ISOC

Instituto de Nutricion de Centro America y Panama [*Institute of Nutrition of Central America and Panama*] [*Guatemala, Guatemala*] (EAIO) .... INCAP

Instituto de Nutricion de Centro America y Panama, Guatemala City, Guatemala [*Library symbol Library of Congress*] (LCLS) .... GuGIC

Instituto de Promocao Turistica [*Portugal*] (EY) .... IPT

Instituto de Seguros de Portugal [*Insurance regulatory agency*] [*Portugal*] (EY) .... ISP

Instituto de Sistemas Audio-Visuales [*Institute of Audio-Visual Media*] [*Colombia*] .... ISAV

Instituto del Mar de Peru [*Marine science*] (OSRA) .... IMARPE

Instituto do Comercio Externo (Lisbon, Portugal) [*Institute of Commercial Exports*] (EY) .... ICEP

Instituto Geofisico del Peru [*Marine science*] (OSRA) .... IGP

Instituto Iberoamericano de Derecho Agrario y Reforma Agraria [*Ibero-American Institute of Agrarian Law and Agrarian Reform - IAIALAR*] (EAIO) .... IIDARA

Instituto Interamericano (EA) II

Instituto Interamericano de Derechos Humanos [*Inter-American Institute of Human Rights - IIHR*] (EA) .... IIDH

Instituto Interamericano de Direito de Autor [*Interamerican Copyright Institute*] (EAIO) .... IIDA

Instituto Interamericano de Estadistica [*Inter-American Statistical Institute - IASI*] [*Washington, DC*] .... IIE

Instituto Interamericano del Nino [*Inter-American Children's Institute*] [*Uruguay*] (EA) .... IIN

Instituto Internacional de Andragogia [*International Institute of Andragogy - IIA*] (EAIO) .... INSTIA

Instituto Internacional de Ciencias Administrativas [*International Institute of Administrative Sciences*] .... IICA

Instituto Internacional de Literatura Iberoamericana [*International Institute of Iberoamerican Literature*] (EA) IILI

Instituto Italiano di Cultura, Montreal, PQ, Canada [*Library symbol Library of Congress*] (LCLS) .... CaQMII

Instituto Italo Latino Americano [*Italo-Latin American Institute*] (EAIO) .... IILA

Instituto Latinoamericano de Cooperacion y Desarrollo [*Latin American Institute for Cooperation and Development*] (EAIO) .... ILACDE

Instituto Latinoamericano de Derecho Tributario [*Latin American Tax Law Institute*] (EAIO) .... ILADT

Instituto Latinoamericano de Doctrina y Estudios Sociales [*Latin American Institute of Social Doctrine and Social Studies*] [*Chile*] (EAIO) .... ILADES

Instituto Latinoamericano de Estudios Transnacionales [*Latin American Institute for Transnational Studies - LAITS*] (EAIO) .... ILET

Instituto Latinoamericano de Planificacion Economica y Social [*Latin American Institute for Economic and Social Planning*] [*Santiago, Chile*] [*United Nations*] .... ILPES

Instituto Latinoamericano del Fierro y el Acero [*Latin American Iron and Steel Institute*] (EAIO) .... ILAFA

Instituto Magdalena Aulina [*Magdalena Aulina Institute*] [*Barcelona, Spain*] (EAIO) .... IMA

Instituto Nacional de Estadistica, Geografia e Informatica [*Main government clearinghouse for statistical information*] [*Mexico*] (CROSS) .... INEGI

Instituto Nacional de Fomento de la Exportacion [*National Institute of Export Development*] [*Spain*] (EY) .... INFE

Instituto Nacional de Industria [*National Institute for Industry*] [*Spain*] .... INI

Instituto Nacional de Metrologia, Normalizacao e Qualidade Industrial [*Government advisory body*] [*Brazil*] (EY) .... INMETRO

Instituto Nacional de Tecnica Aeroespacial Satellite [*Spain*] .... INTASAT

Instituto Nacional del Libro Espanol .... INLE

Instituto Nicaraguense de Turismo (EY) .... INTURISMO

Instituto Panamericano de Alta Direccion de Empresa [*Panamerican Institute for Business Management*] [*Mexico*] (PDAA) .... IPADE

Instituto Panamericano de Geografia e Historia [*Panamerican Institute of Geography and History*] [*Peru*] .... IPGH

Instituto Panamericano de Ingenieria Naval [*Pan American Institute of Naval Engineering*] (EAIO) .... IPIN

Instituto para la Integracion de America Latina [*Institute for Latin American Integration*] (EAIO) .... INTAL

Instituto Pastoral Latinoamericano .... IPLA

Instituto per le Opere di Religione [*Institute for Religious Works*] [*The Vatican bank*] .... IOR

Instituto Profesional para el Desarrollo [*Professional Development Institute*] [*Colombia*] .... INPRODE

Instituto Sudamericano del Petroleo [*South American Petroleum Institute*] .... ISAP

Instituto Tecnologico Autonomo de Mexico [*Economic research*] [*Mexico*] (CROSS) .... ITAM

Instituto Tecnologico Centroamericano [*El Salvador*] .... ITCA

Instituto Tecnologico de Estudios Superiores de Monterrey [*Research institute onMexico/US relations*] [*Mexico*] (CROSS) .... ITESM

Instituto Tecnologico y de Estudios Superiores de Monterrey, Monterrey, Mexico [*Library symbol Library of Congress*] (LCLS) .... MxMoT

Instituto Zimotecnico, Piracicaba, Brazil [*Library symbol Library of Congress*] (LCLS) .... BrPI

Instituts Federatifs de Recherche [*France*] .... IFR

Institutul National de Informare si Documentare [*National Institute for Information and Documentation*] [*National Council for Science and Technology*] [*Information service or system*] (IID) .... INID

Institutum Judaicum Delitzschianum (BJA) .... IJD

Instituut voor Mechanistie Arbeid en Gebouwen [*Netherlands*] (NITA) .... IMAG

Instock Footwear Suppliers Association [*British*] (DBA) .... IFSA

In-Store Promotions [*Marketing events for US goods held by retail establishments in foreign countries*] [*Department of Commerce*] .... ISP

Instream Flow Service Group [*United States Fish and Wildlife Service*] .... IFG

In-Stream Waste Concentration [*Environmental science*] (GFGA) .... IWC

Instron Corp. [*Associated Press*] (SAG) .... Instron

Instron Corp. [*AMEX symbol*] (SPSG) .... ISN

Instruct [*or Instructor*] (AABC) .... INSTR

Instructed (ROG) .... INSTRD

Instruction I

Instruction [*or Instructor*] (AFM) .... INST

Instruction [*Computer science*] (TEL) .... INSTN

Instruction .... INSTR

Instruction .... INSTRN

Instruction .... INSTRUC

Instruction Address [*Computer science*] .... IA

Instruction Address Generation [*Computer science*] .... IAG

Instruction Address Register [*Computer science*] (MDG) .... IAR

Instruction Address Register [*Computer science*] .... INSAR

Instruction and Further Assignment by Commander, Naval Military Personnel Command (DNAB) .... INSTFURASPERS

Instruction and Inspection (IAA) .... I & II

Instruction and Research [*Individually-guided education*] (AEE) .... I & R

Instruction and Research Computer Center [*Ohio State University*] [*Research center*] (RCD) .... IRCC

Instruction and Research Information Systems [*Computer science*] .... IRIS

Instruction Bank [*Computer science*] .... I (Bank)

Instruction Bank [*Computer science*] .... IB

Instruction Book .... IB

Instruction Buffer Unit [*Computer science*] (IAA) .... IBU

Instruction Bus [*Computer science*] .... IB

Instruction by Objective .... IBO

Instruction Cache Unit [*Computer science*] .... ICU

Instruction Card (MSA) IC

Instruction Cell IC

Instruction Change Request (NASA) .... ICR

Instruction Code (AAG) IC

Instruction Control Memory .... ICM

Instruction Control Memory Update Processor (MHDB) .... ICMUP

Instruction Control Unit .... ICU

Instruction Counter [*Computer science*] IC

Instruction Cycle [*Computer science*] (IAA) IC

Instruction Cycle [*Computer science*] (IAA) .... ICY

Instruction Cycle (NITA) .... I-cycle

Instruction/Data (IEEE) .... I/D

Instruction Definition Language .... IDL

Instruction Execution (IAA) .... IE

Instruction Execution [*Computer science*] (IAA) .... IEX

Instruction Execution Function (NITA) .... IEF

Instruction Execution Unit [*Computer science*] (IAA) .... IEU

Instruction Fetch Pipeline [*Computer science*] .... IFP

Instruction Fetch Unit [*Computer science*] .... IFU

Instruction Field .... IF

Instruction Folder (MSA) .... IF

Instruction [*or Instructor*] Guide .... IG

Instruction in Motivation Achievement and General Education [*YMCA program*] .... IMAGE

Instruction Input Unit .... IIU

Instruction Leaflet (MSA) IL

Instruction Length Code [*Computer science*] (BUR) ILC

Instruction Length Counter [*Computer science*] (IAA) ILC

Instruction List IL

Instruction Location Counter ILC

Instruction Location Register (NITA) .... ILR

Instruction Look-Ahead [*Unit*] [*Computer science*] .... ILA

Instruction Manual .... IM

Instruction Memory .... IM

Instruction Memory Unit .... IMU

Instruction Pamphlet .... IP

Instruction Plate (MSA) .... IP

Instruction Pointer [*Computer science*] .... IP

Instruction Preprocessing Function .... IPPF

Instruction Processing Unit (BUR) .... IPU
Instruction Processor [*Computer science*] .... IP
Instruction Pulse (MSA) .... IP
Instruction Register [*Computer science*] .... IR
Instruction Register, Address Portion [*Computer science*] (MHDI) .... IRA
Instruction Section [*Association of College and Research Libraries*] [*American Library Association*] .... IS
Instruction Set Architecture [*Computer science Army*] (RDA) .... ISA
Instruction Set Design System (PDAA) .... ISDS
Instruction Set Process (ECII) .... IDS
Instruction Set Processor [*Computer science*] (ECII) .... ISP
Instruction Set Processor [*1971*] [*Computer science*] .... ISP
Instruction Set Processor Language [*Computer science*] .... ISPL
Instruction Set Processor Specification [*1977*] [*Computer science*] (CSR) .... ISPS
Instruction Sheet .... IS
Instruction Space Key .... ISK
Instruction Staticizing Control (IEEE) .... ISC
Instruction Storage Unit .... ISU
Instruction Stream Unit (IAA) .... ISU
Instruction Summary Sheet (NASA) .... ISS
Instruction Tag (MSA) .... IT
Instruction to Proceed (NATG) .... ITP
Instruction Translation Lookaside Buffer [*Computer science*] (PCM) .... ITLB
Instruction Unit [*Computer science*] .... IU
Instruction Update Command System .... IUCS
Instruction Used BIT [*Binary Digit*] [*Computer science*] (MHDI) .... IUB
Instruction Word [*Computer science*] (IAA) .... IW
Instruction Word Buffer (NITA) .... IWB
Instruction Work Stack (MHDB) .... IWS
Instructional .... INSTRL
Instructional .... INSTRNL
Instructional Advance Directive .... IAD
Instructional Allowance [*British military*] (DMA) .... IA
Instructional Center Library ICL
Instructional Communications Systems [*University of Wisconsin*] [*Telecommunications service*] (TSSD) .... ICS
Instructional Developer (MCD) .... ID
Instructional Development Laboratory [*University of Minnesota of Minneapolis Saint Paul*] [*Research center*] (RCD) .... IDL
Instructional Dialogue Facility (IAA) .... IDF
Instructional Dynamics, Inc. (AEBS) .... IDI
Instructional Improvement Committee [*Individually-guided education*] (AEE) IIC
Instructional Logic Diagram (IAA) .... ILD
Instructional Management System (IEEE) .... IMS
Instructional Material Adequacy Guide and Evaluation Standard (RDA) .... IMAGES
Instructional Materials Center .... IMC
Instructional Materials Centers/Regional Media Centers .... IMC/RMC
Instructional Materials Information System [*Database*] .... IMIS
Instructional Materials Reference Center [*American Printing House for the Blind - APH*] [*Absorbed by*] (EA) .... IMRC
Instructional Media Distribution Center [*University of Wisconsin - Madison*] [*Research center*] (RCD) .... IMDC
Instructional Media Laboratory .... IML
Instructional Objectives Preference List (AEBS) .... IOPL
Instructional Procedures Preference Inventory .... IPPI
Instructional Program (NTCM) I
Instructional Program Development (NVT) .... IPD
Instructional Programming Model [*Individually-guided education*] (AEE) .... IPM
Instructional Psychologist (MCD) .... IP
Instructional Quality Inventory .... IQI
Instructional Resource Package (ACII) .... IRP
Instructional Resources Information System [*Ohio State University*] [*Information service or system*] .... IRIS
Instructional Review System .... IRS
Instructional Scientific Equipment Program [*National Science Foundation*] .... ISEP
Instructional System Design Model .... ISD
Instructional System in Mathematics Program (EDAC) .... ISM
Instructional System Package (MCD) .... ISP
Instructional System Review .... ISR
Instructional Systems Association (EA) .... ISA
Instructional Systems Design (DOM) .... ISD
Instructional Systems Development (AFM) .... ISD
Instructional Systems Development Squadron .... ISDS
Instructional Systems Development Team [*Air Force*] .... ISDT
Instructional Systems Language [*Computer science*] (IEEE) .... ISL
Instructional Technologist (EDAC) .... IT
Instructional Technologist Unit .... ITU
Instructional Technology .... IT
Instructional Telecommunications Consortium (EA) .... ITC
Instructional Television .... ITV
Instructional Television, Fixed [*FCC*] (NTCM) .... IF
Instructional Television Fixed Service [*Educational TV*] .... ITFS
Instructional Television Funding Cooperative (NTCM) .... ITBC
Instructional-Based Appraisal System [*Education*] .... IBAS
Instruction-Level Parallelism [*Computer science*] .... ILP
Instructions .... INSTNS
Instructions (ROG) .... INSTRONS
Instructions for Commodores of Convoys [*Navy Obsolete*] .... ICOC
Instructions for Mailers [*A publication*] .... IFOMA
Instructions for Service .... IFS
Instructions per Second [*Computer science*] .... IPS
Instructions to Ship (AAG) .... IS
Instruction-Set Translator [*IBM Corp.*] .... IST
Instructor [*Army skill qualification identifier*] (INF) .... H
Instructor (WDAA) I
Instructor [*Navy British*] .... In
Instructor [*A publication*] (BRI) .... Inst
Instructor .... INSTRCTR
Instructor Aid System (MCD) .... IAS
Instructor and Course Evaluation System (EDAC) .... ICES
Instructor and Key Personnel .... IKP
Instructor and Key Personnel Training .... IKPT
Instructor Clericalis (DLA) .... Inst Cler
Instructor Clericalis (DLA) .... Instr Cler
Instructor Contact Hours (MCD) .... ICH
Instructor Control Panel .... ICP
Instructor Display Panel .... IDP
Instructor/Equipment Operator .... I/EO
Instructor in Cookery [*Navy British*] (ROG) IC
Instructor in Gunnery [*Military British*] .... IG
Instructor Lieutenant-Commander [*Navy British*] ILC
Instructor Model Characteristics for Automated Speech Technology (MCD) .... IMCAST
Instructor Navigator (AFM) .... IN
Instructor of Artillery [*British*] .... I of A
Instructor of Musketry [*British*] .... I of M
Instructor Operation Station [*Army*] (NASA) .... IOS
Instructor/Operator .... I/O
Instructor Pilot [*Air Force*] .... INSTRPIT
Instructor Pilot [*Air Force*] (AFM) .... IP
Instructor Squadron .... IS
Instructor Trainer [*Red Cross*] .... IT
Instructor Training Course .... ITC
Instructor Under Training [*Navy*] (NVT) .... IUT
Instructor Utilization Course (MCD) .... IUC
Instructor Weapons System Officer [*Military*] .... IWSO
Instructor-Flown Advisory Target .... IFT
Instructor-Lieutenant [*Navy British*] IL
Instructor-Patient [*Medicine*] .... IP
Instructors Basic Training Unit .... IBTU
Instructor's Computer Utility Programming Language for Interactive Teaching (IAA) .... ICUPLANT
Instructor's Journal [*Air Force*] .... IJ
In-Structure Shock [*Army*] (RDA) .... ISS
Instrument (AAG) .... INST
Instrument (WGA) .... INSTMT
Instrument .... INSTR
Instrument (VRA) .... instr
Instrument .... INSTR
Instrument .... INSTRMT
Instrument (IAA) .... IS
Instrument Abstracts .... IA
Instrument Air [*System*] [*Nuclear energy*] (NRCH) .... IA
Instrument Air Filter .... IAF
Instrument Air Receiver (AAG) .... IAR
Instrument Air System [*Nuclear energy*] (NRCH) .... IAS
Instrument and Controls .... I & C
Instrument and Electrical Technician (MCD) .... IET
Instrument Approach and Landing Chart [*Aviation*] .... IAL
Instrument Approach and Landing Chart [*Aviation*] .... IALC
Instrument Approach Chart (AAG) .... IAC
Instrument Approach Fix .... IAF
Instrument Approach Procedure [*Aviation*] (AFM) .... IAP
Instrument Approach Procedure Chart [*Aviation*] (NOAA) .... IAPC
Instrument Approach Procedures Automation [*FAA*] (TAG) .... IAPA
Instrument Approach System .... IAS
Instrument Array Cable .... IAC
Instrument Bearing Jewel .... IBJ
Instrument Bus Computer .... IBC
Instrument Bus Control Language [*National Instruments Corp.*] [*Austin, TX*] .... IBCL
Instrument Calibration and Maintenance Record (MCD) .... ICMR
Instrument Calibration and Maintenance Schedule .... ICMS
Instrument Calibration and Recall System [*Nuclear energy*] (NRCH) .... ICRS
Instrument Calibration Laboratory ICL
Instrument Calibration Procedure .... ICP
Instrument Carrier Landing System [*Navy*] (DOMA) .... ICLS
Instrument Checkout Equipment [*NASA*] (KSC) .... ICE
Instrument Communication .... ICE
Instrument Compressed Air (AAG) .... ICA
Instrument Contracting and Engineering Association (EA) .... ICEA
Instrument Control and Automation .... ICA
Instrument Control Center (KSC) ICC
Instrument Control Computer ICC
Instrument Control Language [*Computer science*] ICL
Instrument Correction I
Instrument Correction IC
Instrument Correlation (WDAA) IC
Instrument Data Acquisition System .... IDAS
Instrument Data Processing System .... IDPS
Instrument Data System .... IDS
Instrument Definition Team .... IDT
Instrument Detection Level [*Analytical chemistry*] .... IDL
Instrument Development Laboratories .... IDL
Instrument Development Section .... IDS
Instrument Development Set .... IDS
Instrument Engineering .... IE
Instrument Field of View .... IFOV

Instrument Flag Motor ... IFM
Instrument Flight (IAA) ... IF
Instrument Flight Center [*Air Force*] ... IFC
Instrument Flight Instructors School [*Navy*] ... IFIS
Instrument Flight Recovery [*NASA*] ... IFR
Instrument Flight Rules [*Aviation*] ... IFR
Instrument Flight Safety System (MUGU) ... IFSS
Instrument Flight Simulator (MCD) ... IFS
Instrument Flight Trainer (MCD) ... IFT
Instrument Flight Training (NVT) ... INSTFLTNG
Instrument Flying [*Aviation*] ... IF
Instrument for Evaluation of Photographs ... IEP
Instrument for the Analysis of Science Teaching (EDAC) ... IAST
Instrument Formation Flight System for Helicopters ... IFFSH
Instrument Ground (NASA) ... IG
Instrument Ground Optical Recording ... IGOR
Instrument Ground Support Equipment (MCD) ... IGSE
Instrument Guidance System [*Aviation*] (DA) ... IGS
Instrument Guide Tube [*Nuclear energy*] (NRCH) ... IGT
Instrument Head ... IH
Instrument Landing (IAA) ... IL
Instrument Landing Aid ... ILA
Instrument Landing Approach ... ILA
Instrument Landing Approach System [*Aviation*] (IAA) ... ILAS
Instrument Landing Guidance ... ILG
Instrument Landing System [*Aviation*] ... ILS
Instrument Landing System and TACAN ... ILSTAC
Instrument Landing System Approach [*Aviation*] ... ILSAP
Instrument Landing System / VHF [*Very-High-Frequency*] **Omnidirectional Range** [*Aviation*] (SAA) ... ILS/VOR
Instrument Loop Diagram (ACII) ... ILD
Instrument Low Approach [*Aircraft landing method*] ... ILA
Instrument Low-Approach System [*Aircraft landing method*] ... ILAS
Instrument Maintenance Procedure [*Nuclear energy*] (NRCH) ... IMP
Instrument Marking Kit ... IMK
Instrument Material Bulletin (MCD) ... IMB
Instrument [*Flight*] **Meteorological Conditions** [*Aviation*] ... IMC
Instrument [*Flight*] **Meteorological Conditions - Instrument Flight Rules** [*Aviation*] (DNAB) ... IMC-IFR
Instrument Myopia (PDAA) ... IM
Instrument Note ... IN
Instrument Operating Assembly ... IOA
Instrument Operating System ... IOS
Instrument or on-Top-of-Clouds Authorized ... INSTOP
Instrument Panel [*Automotive engineering*] ... I/PNL
Instrument Panel ... INSTPN
Instrument Panel [*Automotive engineering*] ... IP
Instrument Panel [*Automotive engineering*] ... PNL
Instrument Panel Cluster [*Automotive engineering*] ... IPC
Instrument Panel Lighting (MCD) ... IPL
Instrument Performance Assessment ... IPA
Instrument Pilot Instructor [*Air Force*] ... INSTRPI
Instrument Pilot Instructor School [*Air Force*] ... IPIS
Instrument Pointing System (MCD) ... IPS
Instrument Pool Laboratory (IAA) ... IPL
Instrument Quality (IAA) ... IQ
Instrument Rating [*Aviation*] (AIA) ... I/R
Instrument Rating Examiner [*Aviation*] (DA) ... IRE
Instrument Reading (AFM) ... IR
Instrument Reference (IAA) ... INSTREF
Instrument Register (IAA) ... IR
Instrument Reliability Factor (PDAA) ... IRF
Instrument Response Function ... IRF
Instrument Restricted Controlled Airspace (DA) ... IR
Instrument Retrieval Containers [*Medicine*] (DAVI) ... IRT
Instrument Retrieval System [*Containers*] [*Medicine*] (DAVI) ... IRS
Instrument Servo System ... ISS
Instrument Society of America (EA) ... ISA
Instrument Standards Foundation (ACII) ... ISF
Instrument Standards Laboratory [*Space Flight Operations Facility, NASA*] ... ISL
Instrument Subassembly (IEEE) ... ISA
Instrument Systems Corp. [*NYSE symbol*] (SAG) ... ISY
Instrument Takeoff ... ITO
Instrument Technician ... IT
Instrument Technician Service Organization ... ITSO
Instrument Technician Training Program (ACII) ... ITTP
Instrument Technicians Labor-Management Cooperation Fund (EA) ... ITLMCF
Instrument Technology-Journal of ISA (ACII) ... INTECH
Instrument Test [*or Tree*] [*Nuclear energy*] (NRCH) ... IT
Instrument Test Repair Laboratory (AAG) ... ITRL
Instrument Test Rig [*Liquid Metal Engineering Center*] [*Energy Research and Development Administration*] (IEEE) ... ITR
Instrument Time (Actual) ... ITA
Instrument Time (Simulated) ... ITS
Instrument Transformer ... IT
Instrument Tree Flow and Temperature Removal Instrument Assembly [*Nuclear energy*] (NRCH) ... ITFTRIA
Instrument Tree Removable Instrument Assembly [*Nuclear energy*] (NRCH) ... ITRIA
Instrument Tree/Spool Piece [*Nuclear energy*] (NRCH) ... IT/SP
Instrument Unit [*NASA*] ... IU
Instrument/Visual Controlled Airspace (DA) ... I/V
Instrument Voltage Regulator [*Automotive engineering*] ... IVR
Instrumental [*or Instrumentation*] ... I
Instrumental [*Grammar*] ... instr
Instrumental Activation Analysis ... IAA
Instrumental Activities of Daily Living Survey [*Department of Health and Human Services*] (GFGA) ... IADL
Instrumental Delivery [*Obstetrics*] (DAVI) ... INST
Instrumental Engineering Division [*National Weather Service*] ... IED
Instrumental Laboratory SpA [*NASDAQ symbol*] (SAG) ... ILAB
Instrumental Magnitude [*Earthquakes*] ... M
Instrumental Manual Adequacy Guide and Evaluation Standard ... IMAGES
Instrumental Neutron Activation Analysis ... INAA
Instrumental Photon Activation Analysis [*National Institute of Standards and Technology*] ... IPAA
Instrumental Test Vehicle ... ITV
Instrumental Variable-Approximate Maximum Likelihood (PDAA) ... IVAML
Instrumentarium 'B' ADR [*NASDAQ symbol*] (TTSB) ... INMRY
Instrumentarium Corp. [*NASDAQ symbol*] (NQ) ... INMR
Instrumentarium Corp. [*Associated Press*] (SAG) ... InstruCp
Instrumentation (MDG) ... IM
Instrumentation (ECII) ... IM
Instrumentation (MSA) ... INSTM
Instrumentation ... INSTMN
Instrumentation (MUGU) ... INSTN
Instrumentation ... INSTRMNTN
Instrumentation ... INSTRU
Instrumentation Amplifier (IEEE) ... IA
Instrumentation Analysis Branch (SAA) ... IAB
Instrumentation and Calibration Network (AAG) ... ICN
Instrumentation and Communication ... I and C
Instrumentation and Communication (MCD) ... INST/COMM
Instrumentation and Communication Subsystem [*NASA*] (KSC) ... ICS
Instrumentation and Communication (System) ... I & C(S)
Instrumentation and Communications [*Cable system*] (KSC) ... I & C
Instrumentation and Communications Monitor ... ICM
Instrumentation and Communications Officer [*NASA*] ... INCO
Instrumentation and Control [*Aerospace*] (AAG) ... I & C
Instrumentation and Control (IAA) ... IAC
Instrumentation and Control [*Aerospace*] (IAA) ... INSTCTL
Instrumentation and Control in Scotland [*A publication*] ... I & C in Scot
Instrumentation and Control Subsystem ... ICS
Instrumentation and Electronic Systems Division [*NASA*] (MCD) ... IESD
Instrumentation and Measurement (MCD) ... IM
Instrumentation and Range Safety [*NASA*] (KSC) ... I & RS
Instrumentation and Range Safety System [*NASA*] (KSC) ... IRSS
Instrumentation Calibration and Checkout (SAA) ... IC & C
Instrumentation Calibration and Checkout (IAA) ... ICAC
Instrumentation Calibration Incident Repair Service ... INSCAIRS
Instrumentation Checkout Complex (MCD) ... ICC
Instrumentation Checkout Station (AAG) ... ICS
Instrumentation Communication Equipment (NASA) ... ICE
Instrumentation Configuration Log (IAA) ... ICL
Instrumentation Control and Automation [*Water industry*] [*British*] ... ICA
Instrumentation Control Center (AAG) ... ICC
Instrumentation Control Document (KSC) ... ICD
Instrumentation Control Officer (AAG) ... ICO
Instrumentation Control Racks (AAG) ... ICR
Instrumentation Controller (KSC) ... IC
Instrumentation/Data Collection System ... IDCS
Instrumentation Data Distribution System (MUGU) ... IDDS
Instrumentation Data Items (NASA) ... IDI
Instrumentation Data Test Station ... IDTS
Instrumentation Data Transmission System ... IDTS
Instrumentation Data Transmission System Controller ... IDTSC
Instrumentation Development Laboratory Report (MCD) ... IDLR
Instrumentation Development Plan (MCD) ... IDP
Instrumentation Development Request (MCD) ... IDR
Instrumentation Digital On-Line Transcriber [*Computer science*] ... IDIOT
Instrumentation Directorate [*White Sands Missile Range*] [*Army*] ... ID
Instrumentation/Displays and Controls [*Subsystem*] (MCD) ... I/D & C
Instrumentation Equipment Configuration Log (SAA) ... IECL
Instrumentation Ground Equipment (MCD) ... IGE
Instrumentation Ground System ... IGS
Instrumentation Group ... IG
Instrumentation Habitability Power (MCD) ... IHP
Instrumentation in Aerospace Simulation Facilities ... IASF
Instrumentation Inertial Reference Set [*Aviation*] ... IIRS
Instrumentation Laboratory (MCD) ... IL
Instrumentation Laboratory SpA [*Associated Press*] (SAG) ... InstrLab
Instrumentation Manager [*NASA*] (KSC) ... IM
Instrumentation Notice (AAG) ... IN
Instrumentation Online Transcriber (IDOE) ... IDOT
Instrumentation Operating Area ... IOA
Instrumentation Operation Station ... IOS
Instrumentation Operations Engineer (MCD) ... IOE
Instrumentation Package Container ... IPC
Instrumentation Papers [*Air Force*] (MCD) ... IP
Instrumentation Payload (NASA) ... IP
Instrumentation PCM [*Power Control Mission*] [*NASA*] ... IP
Instrumentation Plan (MUGU) ... IP
Instrumentation Plan Number (MUGU) ... IPN
Instrumentation Power (MCD) ... IP
Instrumentation Power Supply ... IPS
Instrumentation Power System [*or Subsystem*] [*NASA*] (NASA) ... IPS
Instrumentation Program and Component (KSC) ... IP & C
Instrumentation Program and Component List (NASA) ... IPCL
Instrumentation Program List ... IPL
Instrumentation RADAR and Acquisition ... IRACQ

Instrumentation RADAR Set ... IRS
Instrumentation Report ... IR
Instrumentation Requirements (MUGU) ... IR
Instrumentation Revision Record (IAA) ... IRR
Instrumentation Section Test and Monitor Console (SAA) ... ISTMC
Instrumentation Ships Project [*Navy*] ... IS
Instrumentation Ships Project Office [*Navy*] ... ISPO
Instrumentation Specialties Co. ... ISCO
Instrumentation Squadron [*Military*] ... INSTMNS
Instrumentation Status Report (MUGU) ... ISR
Instrumentation Subsystem [*NASA*] (NASA) ... INSTRUM
Instrumentation Suitability Evaluation (MCD) ... ISE
Instrumentation Summary (MUGU) ... IS
Instrumentation Support Instruction (KSC) ... ISI
Instrumentation Support Plan (MCD) ... ISP
Instrumentation Support Service ... ISS
Instrumentation Support Team (KSC) ... IST
Instrumentation System (MCD) ... INSTSYS
Instrumentation System (KSC) ... IS
Instrumentation System Assessment Center (MCD) ... ISAC
Instrumentation System Corp. (MCD) ... ISC
Instrumentation Systems Center [*University of Wisconsin - Madison*] [*Research center*] (RCD) ... ISC
Instrumentation Tape Recorder ... ITR
Instrumentation, Target, and Threat Simulator [*Army*] (RDA) ... ITTS
Instrumentation Technology Associates, Inc. ... ITA
Instrumentation Telemetry Station [*NASA*] (NASA) ... ITS
Instrumentation Telemetry System [*NASA*] (IAA) ... ITS
Instrumentation Television (AFM) ... INTV
Instrumentation Test Equipment (KSC) ... ITE
Instrumentation to Follow the Course of an Accident [*Nuclear energy*] (NRCH) ... IFCA
Instrumentation Tracking Controller ... ITC
Instrumentation Unit Update Command System [*NASA*] (NASA) ... IUCS
Instrument-Controlled Landing [*Aviation*] (IAA) ... ICL
Instrumented ... INSTRM
Instrumented Architectural Level Emulation ... IALE
Instrumented Bend Test ... IBT
Instrumented Factory for Gears [*Illinois Institute of Technology Research Institute*] [*Research center*] (RCD) ... INFAC
Instrumented Fuel Assembly (PDAA) ... IFA
Instrumented Laboratory Training ... IT
Instrumented Measuring System ... IMS
Instrumented Monkey Pod ... IMP
Instrumented Range Acquisition (KSC) ... IRACQ
Instrumented Runway Visual Range [*Aviation*] (DA) ... IRVR
Instrumented Sensor Technologies ... IST
Instrumented Team Learning (ADA) ... ITL
Instrumented Test Range [*Fort Huachuca, AZ*] [*United States Army Electronic Proving Ground*] (GRD) ... ITR
Instrumented Vibration Measuring System ... IVMS
Instrumented Visual Range (IAA) ... IVR
Instrumentman [*Navy rating*] ... IM
Instrumentman, First Class [*Navy rating*] ... IM1
Instrumentman, Second Class [*Navy rating*] ... IM2
Instrumentman, Third Class [*Navy rating*] ... IM3
Instruments Authorized (FAAC) ... INSTA
Instruments, Electronics, and Automation [*Exhibit*] ... IEA
Instruments, Systems and Automation (ACII) ... ISA
Instytut Informacji Naukowej, Technicznej, i Ekonomicznej [*Institute of Scientific, Technical, and Economic Information*] [*Information service or system*] (IID) ... IINTE
Instytut Informacji Naukowej, Technicznej, i Ekonomicznej, Warsaw, Poland [*Library symbol Library of Congress*] (LCLS) ... PoWC
Insufficient (AABC) ... INSUF
Insufficient Data For Reporting (WDMC) ... IFR
Insufficient Funds ... IF
Insufficient Scheduled Time Available [*Aviation*] (FAAC) ... INSUF
Insufficient Therapeutic Effect [*Medicine*] (DAVI) ... ITE
Insufficiently Stamped [*Post office*] [*British*] (ROG) ... IS
Insufflatio [*An Insufflation*] [*Pharmacy*] ... INSUFF
In-Suit Drink Bag [*Aerospace*] (MCD) ... IDB
Insular ... INS
Insular Force ... IF
Insular Force - Additional Initial Clothing Monetary Allowance [*Military*] (DNAB) ... IF-ADD ICMA
Insular Force - Special Initial Clothing Monetary Allowance [*Military*] (DNAB) ... IF-SICMA
Insular Segment of Middle Cerebral Artery [*Cardiology*] (DAVI) ... M_2
Insulate ... INS
Insulate ... INSL
Insulated (DS) ... I
Insulated [*Shipping*] (DCTA) ... IN
Insulated ... INSLTD
Insulated [*or Insulation*] ... INSUL
Insulated Binding Post ... IBP
Insulated Building Distribution Network [*Northern Telecom*] ... IBDN
Insulated Cable Engineers Association (EA) ... ICEA
Insulated Case Circuit Breaker (DWSG) ... ICCB
Insulated Conductors (MCD) ... IC
Insulated Core Reactor ... ICR
Insulated [*or Insulating*] **Core Transformer** ... ICT
Insulated Food Container [*Military*] (INF) ... IFC
Insulated Gate (DEN) ... IG
Insulated Platform (MCD) ... IP
Insulated Power Cable Engineers Association [*Later, ICEA*] (EA) ... IPCEA
Insulated Signal Coupler (IAA) ... ISC
Insulated Steel Door Systems Institute (EA) ... ISDSI
Insulated Tank [*Liquid gas carriers*] ... I
Insulated Tank Container [*Shipping*] (DCTA) ... IT
Insulated-Gate Field-Effect Transistor [*Electronics*] ... IGFET
Insulated-Gate Tetrode (IAA) ... IGT
Insulating ... INSLUG
Insulating Compound (IAA) ... IC
Insulating Concrete [*Technical drawings*] ... INSC
Insulating Fill [*Technical drawings*] ... INSF
Insulating Glass Certification Council (EA) ... IGCC
Insulating Siding Association [*Defunct*] (EA) ... ISA
Insulating Siding Core Board Association [*Defunct*] (EA) ... ISCBA
Insulating Sleeve ... IS
Insulating Transformer (KSC) ... IT
Insulation ... INSLTN
Insulation Board Institute [*Later, ABPA*] (EA) ... IBI
Insulation Breakdown Tester ... IBDT
Insulation Breakdown Tester ... IBT
Insulation, Building, and Hard Board Association [*British*] (BI) ... IBHA
Insulation Contractors Association of America (EA) ... ICAA
Insulation Displacement ... ID
Insulation Displacement Connector [*Electronics*] ... IDC
Insulation Distributor Contractors National Association [*Later, NICA*] (EA) ... IDCNA
Insulation Fabricators Association [*Defunct*] (EA) ... IFA
Insulation Level (IAA) ... IL
Insulation Materials Corp. of America ... IMCOA
Insulation Resistance ... IR
Insulation Specification (MSA) ... ISPEC
Insulation System Module [*Engineering*] (OA) ... ISM
Insulation Test Specification (MSA) ... ITS
Insulator ... INSULR
Insulator Nose Projection [*Automotive spark plugs*] ... INP
Insulators [*JETDS nomenclature*] [*Military*] (CET) ... IL
Insulin ... In
Insulin [*Endocrinology*] (DAVI) ... Ins
Insulin and Glucose [*Medicine*] (DMAA) ... IG
Insulin Antibody [*Immunology*] ... IA
Insulin Antibody [*Endocrinology*] (DAVI) ... INS AB
Insulin Autoantibody [*Immunology*] ... IAA
Insulin Autoimmune Syndrome [*Medicine*] (DMAA) ... IAIS
Insulin Clearance [*Medicine*] (MAE) ... Cin
Insulin Coma Therapy [*Medicine*] ... ICT
Insulin Convulsive Therapy [*Medicine*] (MAH) ... ICT
Insulin Dialysance [*Endocrinology*] (DAVI) ... D_I
Insulin Gene Family ... IGF
Insulin Hypoglycemia Test [*Endocrinology*] (DAVI) ... IHT
Insulin Production Rate [*Medicine*] (DMAA) ... IPR
Insulin Promoter Factor [*Biochemistry*] ... IPF
Insulin Protamine Zinc (DMAA) ... IPZ
Insulin Radioimmunoassay ... IRI
Insulin Receptor [*Medicine*] (DMAA) ... INSR
Insulin Receptor Kinase [*An enzyme*] ... IRK
Insulin Receptor Species [*Medicine*] (DMAA) ... IRS
Insulin Receptor Substrate [*Biochemistry*] ... IRS
Insulin Resistance Index [*Medicine*] (DMAA) ... IRI
Insulin Secretion Rate [*Medicine*] (DMAA) ... ISR
Insulin Sensitivity Test ... IST
Insulin Shock Therapy [*Psychiatry*] ... IST
Insulin Tolerance Test [*Physiology*] ... ITT
Insulin Zinc Suspension ... IZS
Insulin-Degrading Enzyme [*Biochemistry*] ... IDE
Insulin-Dependent Diabetes ... IDD
Insulin-Dependent Diabetes [*Mellitus*] [*Endocrinology*] (DAVI) ... IID
Insulin-Dependent Diabetes Mellitus ... IDDM
Insulin-Independent Diabetes Mellitus (MAE) ... IID
Insulin-Like Activity ... ILA
Insulin-Like Growth Factor ... IGF
Insulin-Like Growth Factor ... ILGF
Insulin-Like Growth Factor Binding Protein [*Biochemistry*] ... IGFBP
Insulin-Like Growth Factor Receptor (DMAA) ... IGFR
Insulin-Like Growth Factor-1 ... IGF-1
Insulin-Like Material ... ILM
Insulin-Reactive Immunoglobulin [*Endocrinology*] (DAVI) ... IRIg
Insulin-Regulatable Glucose Transporter [*Biochemistry*] ... IRGT
Insulin-Releasing Polypeptide [*Medicine*] (DMAA) ... IRP
Insulin-Stimulated Protein Kinase [*An enzyme*] ... ISPK
Insurance ... IN
Insurance ... INCE
Insurance (AFM) ... INS
Insurance ... INS
Insurance (ODBW) ... ins
Insurance ... INSCE
Insurance ... Insur
Insurance Accountants Association [*Later, SIA*] ... IAA
Insurance Accounting and Statistical Association [*Later, Insurance Accounting and Systems Association*] (EA) ... IASA
Insurance Accounting and Statistical Society ... IASS
Insurance Accounting and Systems Association [*Durham, NC*] (EA) ... IASA
Insurance Accounting Principles ... IAP
Insurance Adjustment ... IA
Insurance Advertising Conference [*Later, IMCA*] (EA) ... IAC
Insurance Agents International Union ... IAIU

Insurance and Liability Law Bulletin [*A publication*] ..... ILLB
Insurance Auditor ..... I/A
Insurance Auto Auctions [*NASDAQ symbol*] (SPSG) ..... IAAI
Insurance Auto Auctions [*Associated Press*] (SAG) ..... InsAut
Insurance Bureau of Canada ..... IBC
Insurance Code [*A publication*] (DLA) ..... Ins C
Insurance Communication Service [*IBM Information Network*] [*Tampa, FL*] [*Telecommunications*] (TSSD) ..... ICS
Insurance Company and Bank Purchasing Agents Association ..... ICBPA
Insurance Company Education Directors Society (EA) ..... ICEDS
Insurance Co. of North America ..... INA
Insurance Co., of North America, Corporate Archives, Philadelphia, PA [*Library symbol Library of Congress*] (LCLS) ..... PPINA
Insurance Conference Planners (EA) ..... ICP
Insurance Corp. of British Columbia, North Vancouver [*Library symbol National Library of Canada*] (BIB) ..... BNVIC
Insurance Counsel Journal [*A publication*] (DLA) ..... Ins Couns J
Insurance Crime Prevention Institute [*Westport, CT*] (EA) ..... ICPI
Insurance Development Bureau [*Guelph, ON*] (EAIO) ..... IDB
Insurance Economics Society of America [*Defunct*] (EA) ..... IESA
Insurance Employers' Industrial Association [*Australia*] ..... IEIA
Insurance Industry Meetings Association [*St. Louis, MO*] (EA) ..... IIMA
Insurance Industry Training Council (PDAA) ..... IITC
Insurance Information Institute [*New York, NY*] (EA) III
Insurance Institute for Asia and the Pacific (DS) ..... IIAP
Insurance Institute for Highway Safety (EA) ..... IIHS
Insurance Institute of America (EA) ..... IIA
Insurance Institute of Canada IIC
Insurance Institute of the Province of Quebec, Montreal, PQ, Canada [*Library symbol Library of Congress*] (LCLS) ..... CaQMI
Insurance Institute of the Province of Quebec [*Insitut d'Assurance du Quebec*] **Montreal, Quebec** [*Library symbol National Library of Canada*] (NLC) ..... QMI
Insurance Institute of Winnipeg, Manitoba [*Library symbol National Library of Canada*] (NLC) ..... MWI
Insurance Institute of Winnipeg, Winnipeg, MB, Canada [*Library symbol Library of Congress*] (LCLS) ..... CaMWI
Insurance Law Bulletin [*Australia A publication*] ..... ILB
Insurance Law Reporter [*A publication*] (DLA) ..... ILR
Insurance Law Reporter [*A publication*] (DLA) ..... Ins L Rep
Insurance Law Reporter [*A publication*] (DLA) ..... Ins LR
Insurance Law Reporter [*A publication*] (DLA) ..... Insur L Rep
Insurance Liability Reports [*A publication*] (DLA) ..... Ins Liability Rep
Insurance Library Association of Boston, Boston, MA [*Library symbol Library of Congress*] (LCLS) ..... MBI
Insurance Logistics Automated (PDAA) ..... ILA
Insurance Loss Control Association [*Indianapolis, IN*] (EA) ..... ILCA
Insurance Management Decision Game ..... IMDEG
Insurance Management Performance Evaluation Life (MHDB) ..... IMPEL
Insurance Market Risk Assessment ..... IMRA
Insurance Marketing Communications Association (EA) ..... IMCA
Insurance Monitor [*A publication*] (DLA) ..... Ins Mon
Insurance Ombudsman Bureau (PDAA) ..... IOB
Insurance Patient [*Medicine*] ..... IP
Insurance Periodicals Index [*Nils Publishing Co.*] [*Chatsworth, CA*] [*Information service or system*] (IID) ..... IPI
Insurance Premium Finance Association (EA) ..... IPFA
Insurance Rating Board [*Later, ISO*] ..... IRB
Insurance Record of Australia and New Zealand [*A publication*] ..... Insur Rec Aust NZ
Insurance Regulatory Information System [*National Association of Insurance Commissioners*] ..... IRIS
Insurance Reporter [*A publication*] (DLA) ..... Ins Rep
Insurance Research Council (EA) ..... IRC
Insurance Service Associates [*Later, Assurex International*] ..... ISA
Insurance Service Association of America [*Later, Assurex International*] (EA) ..... ISAA
Insurance Services Group ..... ISG
Insurance Services Office [*An association*] (EA) ..... ISO
Insurance Society of New York [*New York, NY*] (EA) ..... ISNY
Insurance Society of New York, New York, NY [*Library symbol Library of Congress*] (LCLS) ..... NNInS
Insurance Society of Philadelphia, Philadelphia, PA [*Library symbol Library of Congress Obsolete*] (LCLS) ..... PPPI
Insurance, Surety, and Fidelity (MHDB) ..... ISF
Insurance Testing Institute [*Malvern, PA*] (EA) ..... ITI
Insurance Underwriters Association of the Pacific, San Francisco, CA [*Library symbol Library of Congress*] (LCLS) ..... CSfFU
Insurance Value (IAA) IV
Insurance Value-Added Network Services [*Insurance Institute for Research*] (TSSD) ..... IVANS
Insurance Workers International Union ..... IWIU
Insurance Year-Book [*A publication*] (DLA) ..... Enc Ins US
Insure ..... INS
Insured ..... INSD
Insured Locksmiths and Safemen of America [*Defunct*] (EA) ..... ILSA
Insured Muni Income Fd [*NYSE symbol*] (TTSB) ..... PIF
Insured Municipal Income Fund [*Associated Press*] (SAG) ..... InsMuni
Insured Municipals-Income Trust [*Investment term*] ..... IM-IT
Insured Unemployment Rate (OICC) ..... IUR
Insured Value [*Business term*] (MHDB) ..... Insd Val
Insurers' Advisory Organization of Canada ..... IAO
Insurgency (AABC) ..... INSGCY
Insurgent Incident Data ..... IID
Insurrection (DLA) ..... INSURR
In-Tabulation [*Broadcasting*] (WDMC) ..... in-tab
Intacapsular Lens Extraction [*Ophthalmology*] (DAVI) ..... ICLE
Intact (DAVI) I
Intact (DAVI) ..... IT
INTACT [*Infants Need to Avoid Circumcision Trauma*] **Educational Foundation** [*Later, NO-CIRC*] (EA) ..... IEF
Intact Months of Patient Survival [*Medicine*] (DMAA) ..... IMPS
Intact Reentry Heat Source (OA) ..... IRHS
Intact Rock Strength [*Mining*] ..... IRS
Intact Ventricular System [*Cardiology*] ..... IVS
Intag [*Ecuador*] [*ICAO location identifier*] (ICLI) ..... SEIG
Intaglio [*Engraving*] (ROG) ..... INTAG
Intaglio (VRA) ..... intg
Intair, Inc. [*Canada ICAO designator*] (FAAC) ..... INT
Intake (AAMN) I
Intake ..... IN
Intake ..... INT
Intake (MSA) ..... INTK
Intake Air Temperature [*Automotive engineering*] ..... IAT
Intake Air Temperature Sensor [*Automotive engineering*] ..... IATS
Intake and Exhaust [*Automotive engineering*] ..... I & E
Intake and Output [*Medicine*] ..... I & O
Intake Closes [*Valve position*] IC
Intake Cooling Water (IEEE) ..... ICW
Intake Manifold Absolute Pressure Sensor [*Automotive engineering*] ..... IMAPS
Intake Manifold Charge Temperature Sensor [*Automotive engineering*] ..... IMCTS
Intake (of a Unit of Food) Energy [*Nutrition*] ..... IE
Intake Opens [*Valve position*] ..... IO
Intake Opposite Exhaust (IAA) ..... IOE
Intake Restriction [*Automotive engineering*] ..... IR
Intake Valve Closing [*Automotive engineering*] IVC
Intake Valve Detergent [*Automotive fuels*] ..... IVD
Intake Valve Open [*Automotive engineering*] ..... IVO
Intaken Piled Fathom [*Shipping*] (DS) ..... IPF
Intangible Asset [*i.e., Patented rights*] ..... IA
Intangible Drilling Costs [*Petroleum industry*] ..... IDC
In-Tank Solidification ..... ITS
Intarsia (VRA) ..... intr
Intasys Corp. [*NASDAQ symbol*] (SAG) ..... INTA
Intasys Corp. [*Associated Press*] (SAG) ..... Intasys
Intavia Ltd. [*British*] [*FAA designator*] (FAAC) ..... FFL
Integ Inc. [*Associated Press*] (SAG) ..... Integ
Integ Inc. [*NASDAQ symbol*] (SAG) ..... NTEG
Integer (IAA) I
Integer ..... INT
Integer Extraction (PDAA) ..... INTEX
Integer Function Language [*Computer science*] (PDAA) ..... IFL
Integer Linear Programming Model [*Statistics*] ..... ILP
Integer Non-Linear Programming [*Computer science*] (PDAA) ..... INLP
Integer Quantum Hall Effect [*Solid state physics*] ..... IQHE
Integer Unit [*Computer science*] ..... IU
Integon Corp. [*NYSE symbol*] (SAG) ..... IN
Integon Corp. [*Associated Press*] (SAG) ..... Integn
Integon Corp. [*Associated Press*] (SAG) ..... Integon
Integon Cp $3.875 Cv Pfd [*NYSE symbol*] (TTSB) ..... INPr
Integra Financial Corp. [*Associated Press*] (SAG) ..... IntegFn
Integra Financial Corp. [*NYSE symbol*] (SPSG) ..... ITG
Integra Life Sciences [*NASDAQ symbol*] (TTSB) ..... IART
Integra LifeSciences Corp. [*NASDAQ symbol*] (SAG) ..... IART
Integra LifeSciences Corp. [*Associated Press*] (SAG) ..... ItgLfSci
Integra Systems, Inc. [*Toronto Stock Exchange symbol Vancouver Stock Exchange symbol*] ..... ISI
Integral (IAA) I
Integral (MSA) ..... INT
Integral (KSC) ..... INTGL
Integral and Differential Monitoring [*Telecommunications*] (OA) ..... IDM
Integral Boiling and Superheat Reactor ..... IBSHR
Integral Boiling Reactor ..... IBR
Integral Carrier ASW [*Antisubmarine Warfare*] **Prediction System** [*Marine science*] (MSC) ..... ICAPS
Integral Cesium Reservoir ..... ICR
Integral Charge-Control Model [*Electronics*] (OA) ..... ICM
Integral Circuit Package ..... ICP
Integral Components of End Items (MCD) ..... ICOEI
Integral Derivative (IAA) ..... ID
Integral Direct Station Selection (PDAA) ..... IDS
Integral Driver Coil on Plug ..... IDCOP
Integral Dryway Route [*Nuclear energy*] (NUCP) ..... IDR
Integral Economizer Once-Through Steam Generator (NRCH) ..... IEOTSG
Integral Equation Formulation (PDAA) ..... IEF
Integral Error Squared (PDAA) ..... IEA
Integral Error Squared (IEEE) ..... IES
Integral Fast Reactor [*Nuclear energy*] ..... IFR
Integral Fire Control Equipment (AAG) ..... IFCE
Integral Frequency Scan Approach and Landing ..... IFSAL
Integral Green Fluorescence (DMAA) ..... IGFL
Integral [*or Integrated*] **Launch and Recovery Vehicle** [*or Reentry*] [*NASA*] ..... ILRV
Integral [*or Integrated*] **Launch and Recovery Vehicle System** [*or Reentry*] [*NASA*] ..... ILRVS
Integral Lift Fan [*Aviation*] ..... ILF
Integral Linear Error (IAA) ..... ILE
Integral Membrane Protein [*Cytology*] ..... IMP
Integral of Absolute Delay Error (IAA) ..... IADE
Integral of Absolute Error ..... IAE

Integral of Absolute Ideal Error (IAA) .... IAIE
Integral of Absolute Linear Error (IAA) .... IALE
Integral of Time Squared Error [*Statistics*] (PDAA) .... ITSE
Integral Plate Chamber .... IPC
Integral Pulse Frequency Modulation (IEEE) .... IPFM
Integral Quantum Hall Effect [*Solid-state physics*] .... IQHE
Integral Radiative Heat Flux .... IRHF
Integral Reactor Flow Model [*Nuclear energy*] (NRCH) .... IRFM
Integral Red Fluorescence (DMAA) .... IRFL
Integral Rocket Ramjet [*Navy*] .... IRR
Integral Rocket Ramjet Surface-to-Air Missile (MCD) .... IRRSAM
Integral Rocket Ramjet Surface-to-Surface Missile (MCD) .... IRRSSM
Integral Rocket Ramjet Torpedo Tube Missile (MCD) .... IRRTTM
Integral Service Information System (IAA) .... ISIS
Integral Simulation Test [*Nuclear energy*] (NRCH) .... IST
Integral Skinned Polyurethane Foam (PDAA) .... ISPF
Integral Spar Inspection System .... ISIS
Integral Square Delay Error (IAA) .... ISDE
Integral Square Ideal Error (IAA) .... ISIE
Integral Square Linear Error (IAA) .... ISLE
Integral Squared Error .... ISE
Integral Superheat Reactor .... ISR
Integral Sys MD [*NASDAQ symbol*] (TTSB) .... ISYS
Integral Systems Experimental Requirements (NRCH) .... ISER
Integral Systems, Inc. [*Associated Press*] (SAG) .... Integral
Integral Systems, Inc. [*NASDAQ symbol*] (SAG) .... ISYS
Integral Telemetry .... ITM
Integral Terminal Block .... ITB
Integral Throat/Exit Cone (MCD) .... ITEC
Integral Trap Door [*Technical drawings*] .... ITD
Integral Tube Component (IAA) .... ITC
Integral Weight and Balance System [*Aviation*] .... IWBS
Integrally Molded Insulation .... IMI
Integrally Stiffened .... IS
IntegraMed America, Inc. [*NASDAQ symbol*] (SAG) .... INMD
IntegraMed America, Inc. [*Associated Press*] (SAG) .... IntegMed
Integrase [*Biochemistry*] .... INT
Integrate [*or Integrating*] (MSA) .... INTEG
Integrate [*or Integration*] (NASA) .... INTEGR
Integrate (AABC) .... INTGR
Integrate (AFIT) .... INTRG
Integrate and Dump Detection [*Telecommunications*] (TEL) .... I & D
Integrate Sample and Dump [*Telecommunications*] (IAA) .... ISAD
Integrated (MCD) .... INT
Integrated .... INTGRD
Integrated .... INTGRTD
Integrated Academic Information Management System [*Georgetown University Medical Center*] .... IAIMS
Integrated Access and Crossconnect System (ACRL) .... IACS
Integrated Access Device [*BBN Communications Corp.*] .... IAD
Integrated Access Network [*Computer science*] (MHDB) .... IANET
Integrated Acoustic Communication System [*Military*] (NVT) .... IACS
Integrated Acoustic Communication System - Low Data Rate (MCD) .... IACS-LDR
Integrated Action Plan .... IAP
Integrated Adapter .... IA
Integrated Advance Avionics for Aircraft .... IAAA
Integrated Aeronautic Program [*Military*] (AFIT) .... IAP
Integrated Air Cancer Project [*Environmental Protection Agency*] .... IACP
Integrated Air Defense System (MCD) .... IADS
Integrated Air/Fuel System [*Automotive engine design*] .... IAFS
Integrated Air Warfare Training Complex [*Military*] (CAAL) .... IAWTC
Integrated Airbase Defense .... IAD
Integrated Aircraft Armament System (MCD) .... INTAAS
Integrated Aircraft Instrumentation .... IAI
Integrated Air-Fuel Module .... IAFM
Integrated Air-Fuel System [*Automotive engineering*] .... IAFS
Integrated Alternator Regulator [*Automotive engineering*] .... IAR
Integrated Analytical System (IAA) .... IAS
Integrated Anchor Leg Mooring [*Naval engineering*] .... IALM
Integrated Antiairborne Defense System .... IAADS
Integrated Armament Control System (MCD) .... IACS
Integrated Assembly and Checkout (SSD) .... IACO
Integrated Assessment of Security Assistance [*Military*] .... IASA
Integrated Attack Sensor Package .... IASP
Integrated AUTODIN [*Automatic Digital Information Network*] System [*DoD*] .... IAS
Integrated AUTODIN [*Automatic Digital Information Network*] System Architecture (MCD) .... IASA
Integrated Automated Fingerprint Identification System [*FBI standardized term*] .... IAFIS
Integrated Automated Intelligence Processing System (MCD) .... IAIPS
Integrated Automatic Detection and Tracking [*Military*] (CAAL) .... IADT
Integrated Automatic Documentation [*System*] .... IAD
Integrated Automation Systems .... IAS
Integrated Avionic System Trainer [*Military*] (CAAL) .... IAST
Integrated Avionics Control System (RDA) .... IACS
Integrated Avionics Fault Tree Analyzer (MCD) .... IAFTA
Integrated Avionics System (MCD) .... IAS
Integrated Avionics Test (MCD) .... IAT
Integrated Basic Research [*of ASRA*] [*National Science Foundation*] .... IBP
Integrated Battlefield Casualty Manikin [*Medical training*] [*Navy*] .... IBCM
Integrated Battlefield Communications Systems / Triple Capability-Armoured, Infantry and Air Cavalry [*Military*] (PDAA) .... IBCS/TRICAP
Integrated Battlefield Control System [*Army*] .... IBCS
Integrated Battlefield Control System (MCD) .... INCS

Integrated Block Channel (MHDB) .... IBC
Integrated Block Controller (NITA) .... IBC
Integrated Book Manufacturing Machine .... IBMM
Integrated Booking System [*Army*] (RDA) .... IBS
Integrated Border Environment Plan [*Mexico/US border policy*] (CROSS) .... IBEP
Integrated Botanical Information System [*Computer database*] .... IBIS
Integrated Brands [*NASDAQ symbol*] (SAG) .... IBIN
Integrated Brands [*Associated Press*] (SAG) .... IntgrBr
Integrated Brands 'A' [*NASDAQ symbol*] (TTSB) .... IBIN
Integrated Bridge Rectifier (IEEE) .... IBR
Integrated Bridge System (MCD) .... IBS
Integrated Broadband Communication Network [*Telecommunications*] .... IBCN
Integrated Broadband Communications (MHDB) .... IBC
Integrated Broadband Fiber Optic Network [*Telecommunications*] .... IBFN
Integrated Building and Construction Solutions .... IBACOS
Integrated Building Industry System (PDAA) .... IBIS
Integrated Business Communications [*British*] (NITA) .... IBC
Integrated Business Computers [*Manufacturer*] (NITA) .... IBC
Integrated Business Exchange (MCD) .... IBX
Integrated Business Systems [*Trifid Software*] (NITA) .... IBS
Integrated Business Terminal [*Computer science*] (PDAA) .... IBT
Integrated Business-Oriented Language Support (IAA) .... IBOLS
Integrated Carrier Acoustic Prediction System [*Navy*] (NVT) .... ICAPS
Integrated Carrier [*or Command*] ASW Prediction System .... ICARDS
Integrated Carrier Catapult Station (MCD) .... ICCS
Integrated Carrier Catapult System (DNAB) .... ICCS
Integrated Carrier Landing System [*Military*] (MCD) .... ICLS
Integrated Case Study [*Medicine*] (DMAA) .... ICS
Integrated Catalog Algorithm (MCD) .... INCA
Integrated Catalog Facility (HGAA) .... ICF
Integrated Catapult Control Station (MCD) .... ICCS
Integrated Catchment Management [*Water resources*] .... ICM
Integrated Change Control Board [*NASA*] (NASA) .... ICCB
Integrated Chassis Control System [*Automotive*] .... ICCS
Integrated Checkout (NASA) .... ICO
Integrated Checkout (NASA) .... INTC/O
Integrated Checkout System (KSC) .... ICOS
Integrated Checkout System (KSC) .... ICS
Integrated Chemical Information System [*Information Consultants, Inc.*] [*Information service or system*] (IID) .... ICIS
Integrated Chemical Retrieval System [*Pergamon InfoLine*] [*Computer science*] .... ICRS
Integrated Chemists of the Philippines .... ICP
Integrated Child Development Scheme (DMAA) .... ICDS
Integrated Chip Circuit ICC
Integrated Chopper .... INCH
Integrated Chromatography IC
Integrated Circuit [*Electronics*] IC
Integrated Circuit Analysis [*Computer science*] .... ICAN
Integrated Circuit and Message Switch .... ICMS
Integrated Circuit Array .... ICA
Integrated Circuit Breadboard [*Electronics*] (IAA) .... ICB
Integrated Circuit Communications Data Processor (MHDI) .... ICCDP
Integrated Circuit Description Language .... ICDL
Integrated Circuit Failure Analysis Expert System .... ICFAX
Integrated Circuit Keyset Central Multiplexer (CAAL) .... ICKCMX
Integrated Circuit Logic ICL
Integrated Circuit Mask .... ICM
Integrated Circuit Operational Amplifier [*Electronics*] (IAA) .... ICOPAMP
Integrated Circuit Parameter Retrieval [*Information Handling Services*] [*Database*] .... ICPR
Integrated Circuit Sys [*NASDAQ symbol*] (TTSB) .... ICST
Integrated Circuit System (IMH) .... ICS
Integrated Circuit Systems [*NASDAQ symbol*] (SPSG) .... ICST
Integrated Circuit Systems [*Associated Press*] (SAG) .... IntegCirc
Integrated Circuit Test Set .... ICTS
Integrated Circuit Tester .... ICT
Integrated Circuits Demonstration Plant [*Taiwan*] (NITA) .... ICDP
Integrated Circuits Engineering Corp. .... ICE
Integrated Civil Engineering Executive (MHDI) .... ICEX
Integrated Civil Engineering System [*Programming language*] [*Computer science*] .... ICES
Integrated Clinical Encounters .... ICE
Integrated Closed-Loop Environmental Control System (PDAA) .... ICECS
Integrated Cluster Controller ICC
Integrated Coastal Zone Management [*Marine science*] (OSRA) .... ICZM
Integrated Coil Electronic [*Automotive engineering*] .... ICE
Integrated Collection System [*IRS*] .... ICS
Integrated Color Removal [*Printing technology*] .... ICR
Integrated Combat Group [*Air Force*] .... ICG
Integrated Combat Ship .... ICS
Integrated Combat System .... ICS
Integrated Combat Systems Test Facility (NVT) .... ICSTF
Integrated Combined System Test .... ICST
Integrated Command Accounting and Reporting .... ICAR
Integrated Command ASW [*Antisubmarine Warfare*] Prediction System [*Navy*] (CAAL) .... ICAPS
Integrated Command Support Center [*Military*] (MCD) .... ICSC
Integrated Command System .... ICS
Integrated Command System Management Plan [*Military*] (DNAB) .... ICSMP
Integrated Commercial Intrusion Detection System [*Army*] .... ICIDS
Integrated Commun Ntwk [*NASDAQ symbol*] (TTSB) .... ICNI
Integrated Communication Control Panel (MCD) .... ICCP
Integrated Communication, Navigation, and Identification Avionics [*Air Force*] .... ICNIA

Integrated Communication, Navigation, Identification [*System*] ... ICNI
Integrated Communication/Navigation/Identification Control Panel (MCD) ... ICNICP
Integrated Communication/Navigation/Identification Control Set (MCD) ... ICNICS
Integrated Communication Systems, Inc. [*Roswell, GA*] [*Telecommunications*] (IEEE) ... ICS
Integrated Communications (MCD) ... IC
Integrated Communications Access Method [*Computer science*] ... ICAM
Integrated Communications Adapter (MCD) ... ICA
Integrated Communications Adapter Extended (BUR) ... ICAE
Integrated Communications Agency [*Air Force*] ... INCA
Integrated Communications and Navigation System ... ICNS
Integrated Communications Architecture [*Navy*] (DOMA) ... ICA
Integrated Communications Center (MCD) ... ICC
Integrated Communications Collection System [*Military*] (MCD) ... ICCS
Integrated Communications Control (MCD) ... ICC
Integrated Communications Environment [*Computer architecture*] (NITA) ... ICE
Integrated Communications Network, Inc. [*NASDAQ symbol*] (SAG) ... ICNI
Integrated Communications Network, Inc. [*Associated Press*] (SAG) ... ItgCom
Integrated Communications System, Alaska [*Air Force, FAA*] ... ICSAL
Integrated Communications System South-East Asia [*Australia*] ... ICSSEA
Integrated Compact Mill [*Steel manufacture*] ... ICM
Integrated Compatible Use Zone [*Army*] (RDA) ... ICUZ
Integrated Composite Spinning (PDAA) ... ICS
Integrated Computer Network ... ICN
Integrated Computer Solutions ... ICS
Integrated Computer Systems [*Culver City, CA*] [*Telecommunications service*] (TSSD) ... ICS
Integrated Computer Telemetry ... ICT
Integrated Computer-Aided Manufacturing (IEEE) ... ICAM
Integrated Computer-Aided Software Engineering ... I-CASE
Integrated Computerized Management Information System (PDAA) ... ICMIS
Integrated Computerized Test Set ... ICTS
Integrated Computer-Reactor Monitoring System (PDAA) ... ICRMS
Integrated COMSEC [*Communications Security*] [*Army*] (DOMA) ... ICON
Integrated Concept Team [*Army*] (INF) ... ICT
Integrated Conceptual Environment [*Computer science*] ... ICE
Integrated Configuration List (NG) ... ICL
Integrated Configuration Management Office [*NASA*] (NASA) ... ICMO
Integrated Configuration Summary (AAG) ... ICS
Integrated Conformal Array ... ICA
Integrated Conning System (PDAA) ... ICS
Integrated Continuous Controlled Color System (DGA) ... ICCCS
Integrated Control ... ICON
Integrated Control and Avionics for Air Superiority (MCD) ... ICAAS
Integrated Control and Display ... ICAD
Integrated Control and Display System (MCD) ... ICDS
Integrated Control Facility [*Sperry UNIVAC*] ... ICF
Integrated Control Storage [*Computer science*] ... ICS
Integrated Control System (NRCH) ... ICS
Integrated Control System [*Navy*] (NVT) ... INCOS
Integrated Control Unit ... ICU
Integrated Control Unit (NITA) ... ICU
Integrated Controller Module [*Automotive engineering*] ... ICM
Integrated CONUS [*Continental United States*] **Medical Mobilization Pla n** (DOMA) ... ICMMP
Integrated Conventional Ammunition Maintenance Plan [*DoD*] (RDA) ... ICAMP
Integrated Conventional Ammunition Procurement Plan ... ICAPP
Integrated Conventional Stores Management System [*DoD*] (DWSG) ... ICSMS
Integrated Cooling for Electronics ... ICE
Integrated Corporate Database ... ICDB
Integrated Correction Action Plan [*Military*] (MCD) ... ICAP
Integrated Correlation and Display System [*Air Force*] (DOMA) ... ICADS
Integrated Cost Accounting ... ICA
Integrated Cost Accounting Application ... ICAA
Integrated Cost Operation System (IAA) ... ICOS
Integrated Cover and Deception Systems [*Military*] (MCD) ... ICADS
Integrated Crew and Aircraft Planning (PDAA) ... INCRAPLAN
Integrated Criminal Apprehension Program ... ICAP
Integrated Crop Management [*Agriculture*] ... ICM
Integrated Cryogenic Isotope Cooling Equipment ... ICICLE
Integrated Crystal Filter (IAA) ... ICF
Integrated Curriculum Environment [*Army*] ... ICE
Integrated Daily Cycle Test (MCD) ... IDCT
Integrated Data Access (NITA) ... IDA
Integrated Data Acquisition and Control [*Jet Propulsion Laboratory, NASA*] ... IDAC
Integrated Data Acquisition System (MCD) ... IDAS
Integrated Data Base [*Computer science*] ... IDB
Integrated Data Coding System (NG) ... IDCS
Integrated Data Communications Controller ... IDCC
Integrated Data Dictionary ... IDD
Integrated Data Display System ... IDDS
Integrated Data File ... IDF
Integrated Data for Enforcement Analysis System [*Environmental science*] ... IDEA
Integrated Data Generation Implementation Technique ... IDGIT
Integrated Data Handling System ... IDHS
Integrated Data Presentation (MCD) ... IDP
Integrated Data Processing ... IDP
Integrated Data Processing Center ... IDPC
Integrated Data Processing System ... IDPS
Integrated Data Retrieval System [*Department of the Treasury*] ... IDRS
Integrated Data Storage (NITA) ... IDS
Integrated Data Store [*or System*] [*Honeywell, Inc.*] [*Computer science*] ... IDS
Integrated Data Transmittal Package ... IDTP
Integrated Database Management System ... IDBMS
Integrated Database Management System ... IDMS
Integrated Debugging Aid (IAA) ... IDA
Integrated Decoy Launching System [*Navy*] (CAAL) ... IDLS
Integrated Defense Avionics System [*Air Force*] (DOMA) ... IDAS
Integrated Defense System ... IDES
Integrated Defensive Avionics Program [*Navy*] (DOMA) ... IDAP
Integrated Defensive System ... IDS
Integrated Delivery Networks [*Health care provider*] ... IHN
Integrated Delta Modulation (IAA) ... IDM
Integrated Departmental Instructions Manual ... IDIM
Integrated Design Analysis System [*Space shuttle*] [*NASA*] ... IDEAS
Integrated Design and Engineering Automated System (IEEE) ... IDEAS
Integrated Design Automation System (MCD) ... IDAS
Integrated Design Engineering Aid [*Computer science*] (RDA) ... IDEA
Integrated Design Engineering and Logistics (PDAA) ... IDEAL
Integrated Design Inspection (NRCH) ... IDI
Integrated Design Methodology [*Electrical engineering*] ... IDM
Integrated Detection and Classification Station ... IDACS
Integrated Development and Debugging Environment [*Symantec Corp.*] [*Computer science*] (PCM) ... IDDE
Integrated Development Environment ... IDE
Integrated Development Test Matrix [*Army*] ... IDTM
Integrated Development Test Schedule ... IDTS
Integrated Device Controller ... IDC
Integrated Device Electronics ... IDE
Integrated Device Tech [*NASDAQ symbol*] (TTSB) ... IDTI
Integrated Device Technology [*NASDAQ symbol*] (SAG) ... IDTI
Integrated Device Technology, Inc. (PS) ... IDT
Integrated Device Technology, Inc. (NQ) ... IDTI
Integrated Device Technology, Inc. [*Associated Press*] (SAG) ... IntgDv
Integrated Diagnostics (AAGC) ... ID
Integrated Digital Access [*Telecommunications*] ... IDA
Integrated Digital Avionics (MCD) ... IDA
Integrated Digital Avionics for Medium STOL Transport (MCD) ... IDAMST
Integrated Digital Backbone Network [*Telecommunications*] ... IDBN
Integrated Digital Electric Aircraft (PDAA) ... IDEA
Integrated Digital Electronic Automatic (PDAA) ... IDEA
Integrated Digital Enhanced Network [*Telecommunications*] ... iDEN
Integrated Digital Logic Circuit ... IDLC
Integrated Digital Loop Carrier [*Telecommunications*] (ACRL) ... IDLC
Integrated Digital Network [*Telecommunications*] ... IDN
Integrated Digital Network Exchange [*Telecommunications*] (ACRL) ... IDNX
Integrated Digital Photogrammetric Facility [*National Oceanic and Atmospheric Administration*] ... IDPF
Integrated Digital-Analog Converter (MCD) ... IDAC
Integrated Direct Ignition [*Automotive engineering*] ... IDI
Integrated Direct Numerical Control [*Burroughs Machines Ltd.*] [*Software package*] (NCC) ... IDNC
Integrated Direct Support Maintenance (MCD) ... IDSM
Integrated Disbursing and Accounting (MCD) ... IDA
Integrated Disbursing and Accounting Financial Information Processing System [*DoD*] ... IDAFIPS
Integrated Disbursing and Accounting Financial Management System (DNAB) ... IDAFMS
Integrated Disk Adapter [*Sperry UNIVAC*] ... IDA
Integrated Disk Control [*NCR Corp.*] ... IDC
Integrated Display Development Station (MCD) ... IDDS
Integrated Display Set ... IDS
Integrated Display Situation ... IDS
Integrated Displays and Controls (MCD) ... IDC
Integrated Disposal Management System [*DoD*] ... IDMS
Integrated Dose Environment Analysis ... IDEA
Integrated Drive Electronics [*Hard disk interface*] [*Computer science*] (PCM) ... IDE
Integrated Drive Generator (MCD) ... IDG
Integrated Drug Abuse Management Information Systems ... IDAMIS
Integrated Drug Abuse Reporting Process [*National Institutes of Health*] ... IDARP
Integrated Dry Route (PDAA) ... IDR
Integrated Dual-Use Commercial Companies ... IDCC
Integrated Dynamic Tester ... IDT
Integrated Educational Information System (PDAA) ... IEIA
Integrated Electric Drive [*Navy*] (DOMA) ... IED
Integrated Electromyogram [*Medicine*] ... IEMG
Integrated Electronic Assembly [*NASA*] ... IEA
Integrated Electronic Components (BUR) ... IEC
Integrated Electronic Control ... IEC
Integrated Electronic Filing System [*Computer science*] (DGA) ... IEFS
Integrated Electronic Office (NITA) ... IEO
Integrated Electronic Office System (IAA) ... IEOS
Integrated Electronic Signal Processor ... IESP
Integrated Electronic System ... IES
Integrated Electronic Vertical Display ... IEVD
Integrated Electronic Warfare System ... IEWS
Integrated Electronic Warfare System ... INEWS
Integrated Electronics Engineering Center [*State University of New York, Binghamton*] [*Research center*] (RCD) ... IEEC
Integrated Electronics Unit (MCD) ... IEU
Integrated Emergency Management Information System [*Federal Emergency Management Agency*] (GFGA) ... IEMIS
Integrated Engine Control ... IEC
Integrated Engine Instrument System (MCD) ... IEIS
Integrated Engine Pressure Ratio (GAVI) ... IEPR

Integrated Engineering Design Service (PDAA) .... IED
Integrated Engineering Planning Parts List .... IEPPL
Integrated Engineering Program .... IEP
Integrated Environmental Control (AAG) .... IEC
Integrated Environmental Design (PDAA) .... IED
Integrated Environmental Management Division [*Environmental Protection Agency*] (EPA) .... IEMD
Integrated Environmental Management Project [*Environmental Protection Agency*] (GFGA) .... IEMP
Integrated Equipment Component .... IEC
Integrated Equipment Test [*Nuclear energy*] .... IET
Integrated Equipment Test Facility [*Department of Energy*] .... IETF
Integrated Expert System [*Computer science*] .... IEXS
Integrated Extravehicular Mobility Unit (SSD) .... IEMU
Integrated Facilities Design Criteria (SAA) .... IFDC
Integrated Facilities Management Information System .... IFMIS
Integrated Facilities System [*Army*] .... IFS
Integrated Facility for Avionics System Test [*Air Force*] .... IFAST
Integrated Family of Test Equipment [*Army*] (RDA) .... IFTE
Integrated Farm Management Program Option [*Department of Agriculture*] .... IFMPO
Integrated Farm Management System .... IFMS
Integrated Feed Antenna .... IFA
Integrated File Adapter [*Computer science*] (BUR) .... IFA
Integrated File Processor .... IFP
Integrated Financial Management System (AABC) .... IFMS
Integrated Fire Control [*RADAR*] .... IFC
Integrated Fire Direction System for the Artillery Battery [*German*] .... IFAB
Integrated Flagship Data System [*Navy*] (NG) .... IFDS
Integrated Fleet Operations .... INFO
Integrated Flight and Fire Control .... IFFC
Integrated Flight and Propulsion Control (MCD) .... IFPC
Integrated Flight Control/Navigation Computer (MCD) .... IFNC
Integrated Flight Control System .... IFCS
Integrated Flight Data Processing System [*Air Force*] .... IFDAPS
Integrated Flight Director [*Aviation*] .... IFD
Integrated Flight Instrument System .... IFIS
Integrated Flight Optimization (PDAA) .... INFLO
Integrated Flight Prediction System [*Aviation*] (DA) .... IFLIPS
Integrated Flight System .... IFS
Integrated Flight/Weapons Controls (MCD) .... IFWC
Integrated Flood Observing and Warning System [*National Oceanic and Atmospheric Administration*] .... IFLOWS
Integrated Fluorescence Unit [*Image formation*] .... IFU
Integrated Force Administration System [*Bell System*] .... IFAMS
Integrated Forcing Contribution [*Environmental science*] .... IFC
Integrated Foreign Exchange and Banking System (PDAA) .... IFEBS
[*The*] Integrated FORSTAT [*Force Status and Identity Reporting System*] File .... TIFF
Integrated Front End Processor (NITA) .... IFEP
Integrated Fuel Cycle Facilities [*Nuclear energy*] (NRCH) .... IFCF
Integrated Fuel/Engine Display (MCD) .... IFED
Integrated Fuel/Engine Instrument (MCD) .... IFEI
Integrated Functions Assessment Steering Committee [*NASA*] (NASA) .... IFASC
Integrated Fuse Logic (NITA) .... IFL
Integrated Gasification Humid Air Turbine [*Chemical engineering*] .... IGHAT
Integrated Gasification-Combined Cycle [*Chemical engineering*] .... IGCC
Integrated Genetics .... IG
Integrated Global Ocean Monitoring [*Marine science*] (OSRA) .... IGOM
Integrated Global Ocean Services System [*Marine science*] (OSRA) .... IGOSS
Integrated Global Ocean Station System [*Surrey, England*] [*See also IGOSS UNESCO*] .... IGLOSS
Integrated Global Ocean Station System [*See also IGLOSS*] [*UNESCO*] [*British*] .... IGOSS
Integrated Graduate Development Scheme [*British*] .... IGDS
Integrated Grant Administration .... IGA
Integrated Graphics System [*Computer science*] (BUR) .... IGS
Integrated Ground/Airborne Avionics System (MCD) .... IGAAS
Integrated Ground Test .... IGT
Integrated Ground Water Information System .... IGWIS
Integrated GUARDRAIL V .... IGRV
Integrated Guidance and Control System [*Aerospace*] .... IGACS
Integrated Guidance and Control System [*Aerospace*] (AAG) .... IGCS
Integrated Hazard Function .... IHF
Integrated Headgear Subsystem [*Army*] (RDA) .... IHS
Integrated Health Services, Inc. [*NYSE symbol*] (SPSG) .... IHS
Integrated Health Services, Inc. [*Associated Press*] (SAG) .... IntgHS
Integrated Health Svcs [*NYSE symbol*] (TTSB) .... IHS
Integrated Healthcare Network [*Health care provider*] .... IDN
Integrated Heat Sink (PDAA) .... IHS
Integrated Helicopter Avionics System [*Navy*] (NG) .... IHAS
Integrated Helicopter Avionics System / Integrated Light Attack Avionics System [*Navy*] (SAA) .... IHAS/ILAAS
Integrated Helmet and Display Sight System .... IHADSS
Integrated Helmet Display System .... IHDS
Integrated High Payoff Rocket Propulsion Technology .... IHPRPT
Integrated High-Frequency Antenna System .... IHFAS
Integrated High-Performance Turbine Engine Technology Initiative [*NASA and DOD*] .... IHPTET
Integrated Hit Indicator .... IHI
Integrated Hit Indicator System .... IHIS
Integrated Hospital Information System (DMAA) .... IHIS
Integrated Hybrid Transistor Switch (PDAA) .... IHTS
Integrated Hydrographic Survey System (PDAA) .... IHSS

Integrated Individual Fighting System [*US Army Natick Research, Development, and Engineering Center*] (INF) .... IIFS
Integrated Individual Fighting System Program [*Army*] (INF) .... IIFSP
Integrated Inertial Navigation System (MCD) .... IINS
Integrated Inertial Reference Assembly (PDAA) .... IIRA
Integrated Inertial Sensor Assembly (MCD) .... IISA
Integrated Information Centre of the Ministry of Foreign Affairs [*Saudi Arabia*] (NITA) .... IICMFA
Integrated Information Display (MCD) .... IID
Integrated Information Display System (MCD) .... IIDS
Integrated Information Presentation and Control System [*Aviation*] .... IIPACS
Integrated Information Processing .... INTIP
Integrated Information Processing System [*Air Development Center, Rome, NY*] .... INTIPS
Integrated Information Support System [*Computer science*] .... IISS
Integrated Information System [*Marine Corps*] I2S
Integrated Information System .... IIS
Integrated Information System (Financial) [*Marine Corps*] .... I2S(FIN)
Integrated Information System (Logistics) [*Marine Corps*] .... I2S(LOG)
Integrated Information System (Manpower) [*Marine Corps*] .... I2S(MPR)
Integrated Information System (Manpower and Functional Area Manpower Management System) [*Marine Corps*] .... I2S(MPR/MMS)
Integrated Information System (Operational) [*Marine Corps*] .... I2S(OPS)
Integrated Information Technology Conference and Exposition [*National Trade Productions*] (TSPED) .... INTECH
Integrated Information Transport (ACRL) .... IIT
Integrated Initial Flight Plan Processing System [*Aviation*] (DA) .... IFPS
Integrated Injection Logic [*Microprocessing*] .... I²L
Integrated Injection Logic (NITA) .... I²L
Integrated Injection Logic [*Microprocessing*] (BUR) IIL
Integrated Input/Output Processor .... IIOP
Integrated Installation Requirement Plan (MCD) .... IIRP
Integrated Instructional Information Resource [*Educational Products Information Exchange Institute*] [*Information service or system*] (CRD) .... IIIR
Integrated Instrument Development .... IID
Integrated Instrument Development Program .... IIDP
Integrated Instrument Sheet (MCD) .... IIS
Integrated Instrumentation Display System .... IIDS
Integrated Instrumentation RADAR .... IIR
Integrated Instruments System .... IIS
Integrated Insulation System .... IIS
Integrated Intelligence Development Plan (MCD) .... IIDP
Integrated Interface Circuit (IAA) IIC
Integrated Joint Broadband System [*Army*] (AABC) .... IJBS
Integrated Joint Communication System [*Military*] (AABC) .... IJCS
Integrated Joint Communication System - Pacific [*Military*] .... IJCS-PAC
Integrated Key Set [*Computer science*] .... IKS
Integrated Knowledge Based Modelling (NITA) .... IKBM
Integrated Laboratory Automation .... ILA
Integrated Laboratory Sequence [*A system of teaching chemistry devised by Mary L. Good at Louisiana State University in New Orleans*] .... ILS
Integrated Lake-Watershed Acidification Study .... ILWAS
Integrated LASER Optical Sight Set .... ILOSS
Integrated LASER System [*Salford Engineering*] .... ILS
Integrated LASER Systems [*Software*] [*British*] .... ILS
Integrated Launch and Recovery Television System (MCD) .... ILARTS
Integrated Launch Complex (MCD) ILC
Integrated Launch Control and Checkout (KSC) ILCC
Integrated Launch Control and Checkout System .... ILCCS
Integrated Leak Rate Test [*Nuclear energy*] (NRCH) .... ILRT
Integrated Learning System (AIE) .... ILS
Integrated Library Administration and Cataloguing System (PDAA) .... ILACS
Integrated Library System [*National Library of Medicine*] [*Information service or system*] (IID) .... ILS
Integrated Library System Users Society [*Defunct*] (EA) .... ILSUS
Integrated Life Science Shuttle Experiments (MCD) .... ILSSE
Integrated Life Support System [*NASA*] .... ILSS
Integrated Light Attack Aircraft [*or Attack Avionics*] System .... ILAAS
Integrated Light Attack Avionics System [*Navy*] (NVT) .... ILASS
Integrated Living Communities, Inc. [*NASDAQ symbol*] (SAG) ILCC
Integrated Living Communities, Inc. [*Associated Press*] (SAG) .... IntLivC
Integrated Local Area Planning .... ILAP
Integrated Logic Circuit ILC
Integrated Logistic Management (DNAB) .... ILM
Integrated Logistic Management Program (NG) .... ILMP
Integrated Logistic Support Analysis Paper (MCD) .... ILSA
Integrated Logistic Support - Detail Specification .... ILS-DS
Integrated Logistic Support Maintenance [*or Management*] Plan (MCD) .... ILSMP
Integrated Logistic Support Management Review Team .... ILSMRT
Integrated Logistic Support Management Team .... ILSMT
Integrated Logistic Support Office [*DoD*] .... ILSO
Integrated Logistic Support Plan [*or Program*] .... ILSP
Integrated Logistics Data System .... ILDS
Integrated Logistics Management Team .... ILMT
Integrated Logistics Panel (NASA) .... ILP
Integrated Logistics Subgroup [*Military*] (MCD) .... ILSG
Integrated Logistics Support [*DoD*] .... ILS
Integrated Logistics Support (AAGC) .... ILS
Integrated Logistics Support Cadre (AFIT) .... ILSC
Integrated Logistics Support Control Manual (MCD) .... ILSCM
Integrated Logistics Support Coordination Meeting (MCD) .... ILSCM
Integrated Logistics Support Data File .... ILSDF
Integrated Logistics Support/Information System/Dictionary .... ILS/IS/D
Integrated Logistics Support Manager [*Military*] (MCD) .... ILSM

Integrated Logistics Support Milestone Reporting System [*Military*] (MCD) .... ILSMRS
Integrated Logistics Support Model [*Military*] (MCD) .... ILSM
Integrated Logistics Support Performance Evaluation Report [*Military*] (MCD) .... ILSPER
Integrated Logistics Support Plan .... ILSP
Integrated Logistics Support Review [*Military*] (MCD) .... ILSR
Integrated Logistics Support System (SSD) .... ILSS
Integrated Logistics Support Working Group (SSD) .... ILSWG
Integrated Logistics System [*Army*] (RDA) .... ILOGS
Integrated Logistics System .... ILS
Integrated Logistics System and Logistics Assessment Review (MCD) .... ILS/LAR
Integrated Logistics System and Logistics Assessment Review .... ISL/LAR
Integrated Low-Light-Level Television .... ILLLTV
Integrated Magnetic Memory (IAA) .... IMM
Integrated Mail Preparation System .... IMPS
Integrated Maintenance Chart [*or Concept*] .... IMC
Integrated Maintenance Database (MCD) .... IMDB
Integrated Maintenance Facility .... IMF
Integrated Maintenance Management .... IMM
Integrated Maintenance Management Information Retrieval System [*DoD*] .... IMMIRS
Integrated Maintenance Management Plan .... IMMP
Integrated Maintenance Management System [*Army*] .... IMMS
Integrated Maintenance Management Team .... IMMT
Integrated Maintenance Manual .... IMM
Integrated Maintenance Plan [*or Procedure*] .... IMP
Integrated Maintenance Program Operation (MCD) .... IMPOP
Integrated Maintenance Schedule .... IMS
Integrated Maintenance System .... IMS
Integrated Maintenance Test Plan .... IMTP
Integrated Maintenance Test Requirement Outline .... IMTRO
Integrated Management and Economic Analysis Model [*Federal Emergency Management Agency*] (GFGA) .... IMEASY
Integrated Management Development Program [*Australia*] .... IMDP
Integrated Management Information System [*Air Force*] .... IMIS
Integrated Management Planning and Control Technique [*British*] .... IMPACT
Integrated Management Planning Information Systems [*Computer science*] .... IMPIS
Integrated Managerial Programming Analysis Control Technique [*Air Force*] .... IMPACT
Integrated Maneuvering and Life Support System [*NASA*] .... IMLSS
Integrated Manufacturing Exposition [*Penton/IPC*] (TSPED) .... IMEX
Integrated Manufacturing Information System .... IMIS
Integrated Manufacturing Plan (IAA) .... IMP
Integrated Manufacturing Program Information and Control System (PDAA) .... IMPICS
Integrated Manufacturing System (MHDI) .... IMS
Integrated Mapping System .... IMS
Integrated Marketing Communications [*Advertising*] [*Public relations*] (WDMC) .... IMC
Integrated Mass Storage Processor .... IMSP
Integrated Master (NRCH) .... IM
Integrated Master Plan [*Business term*] (RDA) .... IMP
Integrated Master Programming and Scheduling .... IMPS
Integrated Master Schedule [*Business term*] (RDA) .... IMS
Integrated Materials Handling Production and Control Technology .... IMPACT
Integrated Materials Research Laboratory [*Sandia National Laboratories*] .... IMRL
Integrated Materiel Management [*Military*] IM2
Integrated Materiel Management [*or Manager*] .... IMM
Integrated Mathematics Project (AIE) .... IMP
Integrated Mean Square Error [*Statistics*] .... IMSE
Integrated Measurement Sys [*NASDAQ symbol*] (TTSB) .... IMSC
Integrated Measurement Systems [*NASDAQ symbol*] (SAG) .... IMSC
Integrated Medical and Behavioral Laboratory Management (DNAB) .... IMBLM
Integrated Medical and Behavioral Laboratory Measurement System .... IMBLMS
Integrated Medical Resources, Inc. [*NASDAQ symbol*] (SAG) .... IMRI
Integrated Medical Resources, Inc. [*Associated Press*] (SAG) .... IntgMed
Integrated Medical Services .... IMS
Integrated Memory Processor .... IMP
Integrated Message Processor (NITA) .... IMP
Integrated Meteorological System [*Army*] (RDA) .... IMETS
Integrated Meteorological System [*Army*] (IEEE) .... IMS
Integrated Micro Products [*British*] (NITA) .... IMP
Integrated Micro Products [*NASDAQ symbol*] (SAG) .... IMPT
Integrated Micro Products [*Associated Press*] (SAG) .... IntgMic
Integrated Microcomputer Processing System [*Bureau of the Census*] (GFGA) .... IMPS
Integrated Microcomputer Systems, Inc. .... IMS
Integrated Microelectronic Circuitry (AAG) .... IMC
Integrated Microform Parts Cataloging (PDAA) .... IMPACT
Integrated Microimage Terminal [*Kodak*] (NITA) .... IMT
Integrated Microprocessor [*National Semiconductor*] .... IMP
Integrated Microwave Amplifier Converter .... IMAC
Integrated Microwave Circuit .... IMC
Integrated Microwave Package (IAA) .... IMP
Integrated Microwave Products (IEEE) .... IMP
Integrated MIDI [*Musical Instrument Digital Interface*] **Processor** .... IMP
Integrated Missile Electronics Set .... IMES
Integrated Missile Flight Safety System .... IMFSS
Integrated Missile Ground Control Network .... IMGCN
Integrated Mission Control Center [*NASA*] .... IMCC
Integrated Model of Plumes and Atmosphere in Complex Terrain [*Environmental Protection Agency*] (GFGA) .... IMPACT
Integrated MODEM .... IM
Integrated, Modification and Trial .... IMAT
Integrated Modular Avionics [*Honeywell, Inc.*] .... IMA
Integrated Modular Panel System .... IMPS
Integrated Modular Personnel Software [*Percom*] (NITA) .... IMP
Integrated Monitor and Control Panel (MCD) .... IMCP
Integrated Monitoring Panel .... IMP
Integrated Monolithic Circuit .... IMC
Integrated Motorists' Information System [*Computerized guidance system to speed traffic and avoid tie-ups*] .... IMIS
Integrated Multifrequency RADAR (MCD) .... IMFRAD
Integrated Multifunction Keyboard (MCD) .... IMFK
Integrated Multiplexer Channel .... IMC
Integrated Multiport Repeater [*Computer science*] (PCM) .... IMR
Integrated Multisensor Airborne Display .... IMAD
Integrated Municipal Information System (IAA) .... IMIS
Integrated Navigation and Collision Avoidance System (PDAA) .... INCAS
Integrated Navigation and Communications, Automatic .... INCA
Integrated Navigation System .... INS
Integrated Network and Premise Management [*MUX Lab*] .... INPM
Integrated Network Architecture .... INA
Integrated Network Communication Architecture (OSI) .... INCA
Integrated Network Corp. (PCM) .... INC
Integrated Network Fiber Optics (MCD) .... INFO
Integrated Network Management [*for Companies*] .... INM
Integrated Network Management System [*Telecommunications*] (ACRL) .... INMS
Integrated Network Processor .... INP
Integrated Network Systems, Inc. .... INS
Integrated Neutron Activation Prediction [*Code system*] .... INAP
Integrated News Gathering .... ING
Integrated Nitrogen System (SSD) .... INS
Integrated Nondestructive Evaluation (MCD) .... INDE
[*The*] **Integrated Nozzle Assembly** (MCD) .... TINA
Integrated Nuclear and Chemical Analysis .... INCA
Integrated Nuclear Communications Assessment .... INCA
Integrated Numerical Control Approach .... INCA
Integrated Observation Device (MCD) .... IOD
Integrated Observation System (MCD) .... IOS
Integrated Obstacle Plan [*Military*] .... IOP
Integrated Ocean Surveillance System [*Navy*] (NG) .... IOSS
Integrated Office System [*JSB Computer Systems/Olivetti*] (NITA) .... IOS
Integrated Online Library Systems .... IOLS
Integrated On-Line Non-Stop Manufacturing [*Safe Computing Ltd.*] [*Software package*] (NCC) .... ION-M
Integrated On-Line Text Arrangement .... IOTA
Integrated Open Problem List (NASA) .... IOPL
Integrated Operation Plan [*NASA*] (NASA) .... IOP
Integrated Operational Ground Equipment .... IOGE
Integrated Operational Hydrological System [*Marine science*] (MSC) .... IOHS
Integrated Operational Intelligence Center .... IOIC
Integrated Operational Intelligence Center System [*Military*] (DNAB) .... IOICS
Integrated Operational Intelligence System (MCD) .... IOIS
Integrated Operational Nuclear Detonation Detection System .... IONDS
Integrated Operational Support Study (MCD) .... IOSS
Integrated Operations Support Center [*NASA*] (NASA) .... IOSC
Integrated Operator System [*Telecommunications*] .... IOS
Integrated Optical Circuit [*or Component*] .... IOC
Integrated Optical Density [*Instrumentation*] .... IOD
Integrated Optical Logic Circuit .... IOLC
Integrated Optical Spectrum Analyzer (CAAL) .... IOSA
Integrated Optics and Optical Fiber Communications (MCD) .... IOOC
Integrated Optimization Control [*Engineering*] .... IOC
Integrated Optoelectronic Circuit .... IOC
Integrated Orbital Operations Simulation Facility .... IOOSF
Integrated Ordnance Package (MCD) .... IOP
Integrated Packaging Assembly [*NASDAQ symbol*] (TTSB) .... IPAC
Integrated Packaging Assembly Corp. [*Associated Press*] (SAG) .... IntPack
Integrated Packaging Assembly Corp. [*NASDAQ symbol*] (SAG) .... IPAC
Integrated Packet Network [*Hughes Network Systems, Inc.*] .... IPN
Integrated Pancreatic Polypeptide Response [*Medicine*] (DMAA) .... IPPR
Integrated Passive Action Detection Acquisition Equipment .... IPADAE
Integrated Pathology Audio-Visual Learning System (PDAA) .... IPALS
Integrated Payload [*NASA*] .... IPL
Integrated Perceived Level [*Acoustics*] .... IPL
Integrated Perceived Noise Level [*Acoustics*] .... IPNL
Integrated Performance Evaluation Program .... IPEP
Integrated Peripheral Adapter .... IPA
Integrated Peripheral Channel .... IPC
Integrated Peripheral Controller [*Computer chip*] .... IPC
Integrated Personnel Information Report (AAG) .... IPIR
Integrated Personnel Planning and Budgeting System .... IPPBS
Integrated Personnel Requirement Report (AAG) .... IPRR
Integrated Pest Control .... IPC
Integrated Pest Management [*Agronomy*] .... IPM
Integrated Pest Management and Program Coordination Staff [*Environmental Protection Agency*] (GFGA) .... IPMPCS
Integrated Photodetection Assemblies (IEEE) .... IPA
Integrated Photogrammetric Instrument Network (PDAA) .... IPIN
Integrated Physiological Unit .... IPU
Integrated Pin Diode .... IPD
Integrated Plan of Action (MCD) .... IPA
Integrated Planning Parts List (MCD) .... IPPL
Integrated Planning Summary (MCD) .... IPS
Integrated Plant Control and Information System [*Nuclear energy*] (NUCP) .... IPCIS

Integrated Plant Safety Assessment Report [*Nuclear energy*] (NRCH) .... IPSAR
Integrated Plotting Package (NRCH) ..... IPP
Integrated Pneumatic Air System (MCD) ..... IPAS
Integrated Point Defense Missile System [*Military*] (CAAL) .... IPDMS
Integrated Pollution Control ..... IPC
Integrated Pollution Prevention and Control [*Environmental science*] .... IPPC
Integrated Polygenerator Fertilizer System ..... IPFS
Integrated Position Indicator ..... IPI
Integrated Postsecondary Education Data System [*National Center for Education Statistics*] (OICC) ..... IPEDS
Integrated Power and Attitude-Control System [*NASA*] ..... IPACS
Integrated Power and Environmental Control System (MCD) ..... IPECS
Integrated Power Semiconductors Ltd. [*British*] (NITA) ..... IPS
Integrated Power System ..... IPS
Integrated Powertrain Control System [*Automotive engineering*] ..... IPCS
Integrated Powertrain Test System ..... IPTS
Integrated Pressurized Water Reactor (PDAA) ..... IPWR
Integrated Printer Adapter ..... IPA
Integrated Printing Collating Processing (DGA) ..... IPCP
Integrated Priority List [*DoD*] ..... IPL
Integrated Procedures Control ..... IPC
Integrated Process Control (IAA) ..... IPC
Integrated Process Demonstration [*Nuclear energy*] ..... IPD
Integrated Process Equipment [*NASDAQ symbol*] (SAG) ..... IPEC
Integrated Process Equipment [*Associated Press*] (SAG) ..... ItgPrc
Integrated Process Team [*Business term*] ..... IPT
Integrated Processing Facility [*DoD*] ..... IPF
Integrated Processor [*Computer science*] ..... IP
Integrated Processor Board ..... IPB
Integrated Procurement System [*Army*] ..... IPS
Integrated Product and Process Development [*Business term*] (RDA) ..... IPPD
Integrated Product and Process Development Team [*Military*] (RDA) ..... IPPDT
Integrated Product Development [*Business term*] (RDA) ..... IPD
Integrated Product Development System [*FAA*] (TAG) ..... IPDS
Integrated Product Team [*Business term*] ..... IPT
Integrated Product Team [*Business term*] (RDA) ..... IPT
Integrated Program Aircraft Design ..... IPAD
Integrated Program, Budget, Manpower [*System*] [*Defense Supply Agency*] ..... IPBM
Integrated Program Development Support System [*Allen Bradley*] (NITA) ..... IPDS
Integrated Program Management System [*Navy*] ..... IPMS
Integrated Program Study (MCD) ..... IPS
Integrated Program Summary [*Military*] (CAAL) ..... IPS
Integrated Programme for Commodities [*UNCTAD*] (EY) ..... IPC
Integrated Programmed Operational and Functional Appraisals ..... IPOFA
Integrated Programming Support Environment [*BIS Applied Systems*] [*British*] ..... IPSE
Integrated Programs for Aerospace-Vehicle Design ..... IPAD
Integrated Project Support (IAA) ..... IPS
Integrated Project Support Environment (NITA) ..... IPSE
Integrated Propulsion Control System [*Air Force*] ..... IPCS
Integrated Propulsion System (MCD) ..... IPS
Integrated Quality Control [*Department of Health and Human Services*] (GFGA) ..... IQC
Integrated Quality Control Data Processing System [*Department of Health and Human Services*] (GFGA) ..... IQCDPS
Integrated Radio and Intercommunications System [*Canada*] ..... IRIS
Integrated Radio Control (NVT) ..... IRC
Integrated Radio Management System (MCD) ..... IRMS
Integrated Radio Room (MCD) ..... IRR
Integrated RADOME [*RADAR Dome*] Antenna ..... IRA
Integrated RADOME [*RADAR Dome*] Antenna Structure ..... IRAS
Integrated Random Access Channel (PDAA) ..... IRAC
Integrated Random-Access Memory [*Computer science*] ..... IRAM
Integrated Range Instrumentation ..... IRI
Integrated Range Missile (MCD) ..... IRM
Integrated Range Mission [*Military*] ..... IRM
Integrated Range Safety System (IAA) ..... IRSS
Integrated Rate System ..... IRS
Integrated Reactor Vessel Head [*Nuclear energy*] (NRCH) ..... IRVH
Integrated Readiness Testing ..... IRT
Integrated Real-Time Contamination Monitor [*Module*] ..... IRTCM
Integrated Receiver Decoder [*Telecommunications*] ..... IRD
Integrated Reconnaissance Intelligence System (IEEE) ..... IRIS
Integrated Record System (KSC) ..... IRS
Integrated Refractive Effects Prediction System [*Military*] (CAAL) ..... IREPS
Integrated Regional Development Planning (GNE) ..... IRDP
Integrated Regional Environmental Management Project (EA) ..... IREM
Integrated Relay Controller Module [*Ford Motor Co.*] [*Automotive engineering*] ..... IRCM
Integrated Reliability Data System (AAG) ..... IRDS
Integrated Reliability Evaluation Program [*Nuclear energy*] (NRCH) ..... IREP
Integrated Reliability Test Program ..... IRTP
Integrated Research Aircraft Control Technology (MCD) ..... INTERACT
Integrated Research Volkswagen [*Automotive engineering*] ..... IRVW
Integrated Review Model ..... IRM
Integrated Review Schedule [*Department of Health and Human Services*] (GFGA) ..... IRS
Integrated Revolutionary Organizations [*Cuba*] (PPW) ..... OCI
Integrated Risk Information System [*Environmental Protection Agency*] ..... IRIS
Integrated Sachs-Wolfe [*Effect in cosmic microwave background*] ..... ISW
Integrated Safeguard Information System (NRCH) ..... ISIS
Integrated Safeguards Experiment ..... ISE
Integrated Safety Assessment Program [*Nuclear energy*] (NRCH) ..... ISAP
Integrated Sander Machine [*Disk controller*] [*Apple Computer, Inc.*] (BYTE) ..... ISM

Integrated Satellite [*Military spacecraft*] ..... IS
Integrated Satellite System ..... ISS
Integrated Schottky Logic (IEEE) ..... ISL
Integrated Scientific Information System ..... ISIS
Integrated Scientific Processor [*Sperry*] (NITA) ..... ISP
Integrated Sealift Study [*Army*] (AABC) ..... ISS
Integrated Sec Sys Wrrt [*NASDAQ symbol*] (TTSB) ..... IZZIW
Integrated Secondary Propulsion System (MCD) ..... ISPS
Integrated Secretory Response [*Biochemistry*] (DAVI) ..... ISR
Integrated Secure Voice System ..... ISVS
Integrated Security Sys [*NASDAQ symbol*] (TTSB) ..... IZZI
Integrated Security Systems [*Associated Press*] (SAG) ..... IntgSc
Integrated Security Systems [*Associated Press*] (SAG) ..... IntgSec
Integrated Security Systems [*NASDAQ symbol*] (SAG) ..... IZZI
Integrated Sensor Interpretation Techniques ..... INSITE
Integrated Separation Systems [*Electrophoresis*] ..... ISS
Integrated Services Branch Exchange [*Telecommunications*] (OSI) ..... ISBX
Integrated Services Digital Exchange [*British*] ..... ISDX
Integrated Services Digital Network [*Telecommunications*] ..... ISDN
Integrated Services Local Area Network [*Telecommunications*] (ACRL) ..... ISLAN
Integrated Services PBX [*Telecommunications*] (NITA) ..... ISPBX
Integrated Services Satellite Digital Network (MCD) ..... ISSDN
Integrated Services User Part ..... ISUP
Integrated Servicing and Test Facilities [*Canada*] ..... ISTF
Integrated Set of Information Systems (IAA) ..... ISIS
Integrated Shear Plate ..... ISP
Integrated Ship Design System (IEEE) ..... ISDS
Integrated Ship Instrumentation System (IAA) ..... ISIS
Integrated Side-Impact System [*Automotive safety*] ..... ISIS
Integrated Side-Lobe Ratio ..... ISLR
Integrated Sight Unit [*Weaponry*] (INF) ..... ISU
Integrated Silicon Solution [*NASDAQ symbol*] (TTSB) ..... ISSI
Integrated Silicon Solution, Inc. [*NASDAQ symbol*] (SAG) ..... ISSI
Integrated Silicon Systems [*Associated Press*] (SAG) ..... IntSilSy
Integrated Silicon Systems [*NASDAQ symbol*] (SAG) ..... ISSS
Integrated Simulation Evaluation Model ..... ISEM
Integrated Simulation Language Environment [*Computer science*] ..... ISLE
Integrated Site Facilities and Equipment (MCD) ..... ISFE
Integrated Skills Method [*Education*] ..... ISM
Integrated Small Business Software (NITA) ..... ISBS
Integrated Smart Artillery Synthesis (RDA) ..... ISAS
Integrated Software ..... ISW
Integrated Software Development System ..... ISDS
Integrated Software Functional Design ..... ISFD
Integrated Software Invocation System [*Computer science*] (MHDI) ..... ISIS
Integrated Software Maintenance System ..... ISMS
Integrated Software Research and Development Program (MCD) ..... ISRAD
Integrated Software Systems Corp. ..... ISSCO
Integrated SONAR System for Surface Ships (SAA) ..... ISSSS
Integrated Sounding System [*Marine science*] (OSRA) ..... ISS
Integrated Sounding System (USDC) ..... ISS
Integrated Space Experiment (MCD) ..... ISE
Integrated Spacecraft Avionics System (IAA) ..... ISAS
Integrated Spacecraft Operations Plan [*NASA*] ..... ISOP
Integrated Stage Concept (MCD) ..... ISC
Integrated Start System (AAG) ..... ISS
Integrated Statistical Information Service (WDAA) ..... ISIS
Integrated Status Reporting System (MCD) ..... ISRS
Integrated Stock Listing ..... ISL
Integrated Storage Control ..... ISC
Integrated Storage Element [*Computer science*] ..... ISE
Integrated Storage System (NITA) ..... ISS
Integrated Stores Monitor and Management System [*Later, Armament Control Panel*] (MCD) ..... ISMMS
Integrated Strike and Interceptor System ..... ISIS
Integrated Structural Seat [*Automotive engineering*] ..... ISS
Integrated Subject File ..... ISF
Integrated Submarine Automated Broadcast Processing System [*Navy*] (CAAL) ..... ISABS
Integrated Submarine Automated Broadcasting Processing System (MCD) ..... ISABPS
Integrated Submarine Communications Antenna System [*Navy*] (CAAL) ..... ISCAS
Integrated Submarine Communications System (MCD) ..... ISCS
Integrated Submarine SONAR System Technician ..... ISSST
Integrated Subrate Data Multiplexer (TEL) ..... ISMX
Integrated Subsystem Calibration Plan (SAA) ..... ISCP
Integrated Subsystem Test Bed (NASA) ..... ISTB
Integrated Support Area (NVT) ..... ISA
Integrated Support Facility (DWSG) ..... ISF
Integrated Support Parts Requirement (KSC) ..... ISPR
Integrated Support Plan (MCD) ..... ISP
Integrated Support Requirements (AAG) ..... ISR
Integrated Support Services Management Information System (AABC) ..... ISSMIS
Integrated Support System Sort [*Computer science*] (MHDB) ..... ISSS
Integrated Support Working Group (SDI) ..... ISWG
Integrated Surface Irradiance Study [*Marine science*] (OSRA) ..... ISIS
Integrated Surface Irradiance Study (USDC) ..... ISIS
Integrated Surface Search and Attack Coordinate ..... ISSAC
Integrated Surgical Systems, Inc. [*Associated Press*] (SAG) ..... IntgSrg
Integrated Surgical Systems, Inc. [*Associated Press*] (SAG) ..... IntgSrg
Integrated Surgical Systems, Inc. [*NASDAQ symbol*] (SAG) ..... RDOC
Integrated Survey Grid ..... ISG
Integrated Surveys Processing Network [*Bureau of the Census*] (GFGA) ..... ISPN
Integrated Sustainment Maintenance ..... ISM
Integrated Switch Stick (IAA) ..... ISS

Integrated Switched Data Service [*Telecommunications*] (TEL) ...... ISDS
Integrated Switching and Multiplexing [*IBM Corp.*] ...... ISAM
Integrated Switching and Transmission [*Telecommunications*] (TEL) ...... IST
Integrated Switching and Transmission Network [*Telecommunications*] (TEL) ...... ISTN
Integrated Symbolic Debugger [*Computer science*] (IID) ...... ISD
Integrated Synthesis Logic [*Computer science*] ...... ISL
Integrated Sys Consulting Gp [*NASDAQ symbol*] (TTSB) ...... ISCG
Integrated System (NITA) ...... IST
Integrated System Control [*Military*] ...... ISYSCON
Integrated System Definition Language [*Computer science*] (IEEE) ...... IDEF
Integrated System for Automated Acquisition and Control ...... ISAAC
Integrated System for Improved Separations [*Membrane filtration*] ...... ISIS
Integrated System Maintenance Trainer (MCD) ...... ISMT
Integrated System of Pipework Estimating, Detailing, and Control (PDAA) ...... ISOPEDAC
Integrated System Peripheral [*Computer science*] ...... ISP
Integrated System Safety Engineering Plan ...... ISSEP
Integrated System Safety Program Plan [*DoD*] ...... ISSPP
Integrated System Schematic (NASA) ...... ISS
Integrated System Test Flow (NASA) ...... ISTF
Integrated System Trainer (MCD) ...... IST
Integrated System Transformer (IEEE) ...... IST
Integrated Systems Consulting Group, Inc. [*Associated Press*] (SAG) ...... IntSysC
Integrated Systems Consulting Group, Inc. [*NASDAQ symbol*] (SAG) ...... ISCG
Integrated Systems Demonstrator (MCD) ...... ISD
Integrated Systems, Inc. [*NASDAQ symbol*] (SAG) ...... INTS
Integrated Systems, Inc. [*Associated Press*] (SAG) ...... ItgSys
Integrated Systems Planning, Inc. [*Baltimore, MD*] (TSSD) ...... ISP
Integrated Systems Technology (IAA) ...... IST
Integrated Systems Test [*NASA*] (KSC) ...... IST
Integrated Tactical Air Control System ...... ITACS
Integrated Tactical Aircraft Control [*Air Force*] (DOMA) ...... ITAC
Integrated Tactical Amphibious Warfare Data System [*Navy*] (NVT) ...... ITAWDS
Integrated Tactical Attack System (MCD) ...... ITAS
Integrated Tactical Communications Study [*or System*] [*Army*] (AABC) ...... INTACS
Integrated Tactical Countermeasures [*Army*] ...... ITCM
Integrated Tactical Electronic Warfare System ...... ITEWS
Integrated Tactical Intelligence Support System (MCD) ...... ITISS
Integrated Tactical Navigation System [*Navy*] ...... ITNS
Integrated Tactical Navigation System/Doppler - Altitude Heading Reference System ...... ITNS/D-AHRS
Integrated Tactical Surveillance System ...... ITSS
Integrated Tactical-Strategic Data Network (DOMA) ...... ITDN
Integrated Tank Insulation System ...... ITIS
Integrated Target Central System [*Military*] (CAAL) ...... ITCS
Integrated Target Command [*or Control*] System (IAA) ...... ITCS
Integrated Target Control System (MCD) ...... ITCS
Integrated Target Sensor Suite (MCD) ...... ITSS
Integrated Target System (AAG) ...... ITS
Integrated Task Index (AAG) ...... ITI
Integrated Technical Assessment Panel [*NASA*] (NASA) ...... ITAP
Integrated Technical Data System (PDAA) ...... ITDS
Integrated Technical Documentation and Training ...... ITDT
Integrated Technical Information System [*Department of Energy Information service or system*] (IID) ...... ITIS
Integrated Technical Processing System (NITA) ...... ITPS
Integrated Technology Demonstration ...... ITD
Integrated Technology Rotor ...... ITR
Integrated Technology USA, Inc. [*Associated Press*] (SAG) ...... IntegTc
Integrated Technology USA, Inc. [*AMEX symbol*] (SAG) ...... ITH
Integrated Technology Validation ...... ITV
Integrated Telemetry Complex ...... ITC
Integrated Telephone Customer Information System [*Telecommunications*] (IAA) ...... ITCIS
Integrated Telephone Recorder [*Telecommunications*] (TEL) ...... ITR
Integrated Teleprocessing Network ...... ITN
Integrated Teleprocessing System (IEEE) ...... ITPS
Integrated Terminal Controller (NITA) ...... ITC
Integrated Terminal Guidance ...... ITG
Integrated Terminal Weather System [*Marine science*] (OSRA) ...... ITWS
Integrated Terminal Weather System (USDC) ...... ITWS
Integrated Termination System (IAA) ...... ITS
Integrated Terminology Document Management System (IAA) ...... INTERDOC
Integrated Terrain Access and Retrieval System [*Hughes Aircraft*] [*Digital mapping project*] (NITA) ...... ITARS
Integrated Terrain Retrieval System (MCD) ...... ITARS
Integrated Test (NASA) ...... INT
Integrated Test and Alignment System ...... ITAS
Integrated Test and Checkout Procedures (MCD) ...... ITCP
Integrated Test and Maintenance (PDAA) ...... ITEM
Integrated Test Area (MCD) ...... ITA
Integrated Test Block ...... ITB
Integrated Test Document (MCD) ...... ITD
Integrated Test Equipment Facility (MCD) ...... ITEF
Integrated Test/Evaluation Program (AABC) ...... ITEP
Integrated Test Facility [*Computer science*] ...... ITF
Integrated Test Operate Panel ...... ITOP
Integrated Test Package (CAAL) ...... ITP
Integrated Test Plan (AAGC) ...... ITP
Integrated Test Program ...... ITP
Integrated Test Program Board ...... ITPB
Integrated Test Requirements ...... ITR
Integrated Test Requirements Analysis (CAAL) ...... ITRA
Integrated Test Requirements Documents (MCD) ...... ITRD

Integrated Test Requirements Documents (MCD) ...... ITRDS
Integrated Test Requirements Outline ...... ITRO
Integrated Test Schedule [*Army*] ...... ITS
Integrated Test Software (CAAL) ...... ITS
Integrated Testing (NASA) ...... INT
Integrated Testing, Analysis, and Verification System ...... ITAVS
Integrated Theater Engagement Model ...... ITEM
Integrated Thermal Flux (AAG) ...... ITF
Integrated Thermal Micrometeoroid Garment [*Spacesuit*] ...... ITMG
Integrated Thruster Assembly (KSC) ...... ITA
Integrated Thyristor Rectifier (IAA) ...... ITR
Integrated Time and Absolute Error ...... ITAE
Integrated Toolkit for Operating System Security [*Computer security system*] ...... ITOSS
Integrated Torso Limb Suit Assembly [*NASA*] (KSC) ...... ITLSA
Integrated Tour Operating Digital Network Service (MHDI) ...... ITDNS
Integrated Tourism Resort ...... ITR
Integrated Tracking System [*ARTRAC*] [*Obsolete*] (MCD) ...... ITS
Integrated Training Area Management [*Military*] (INF) ...... ITAM
Integrated Training Brigade [*Navy*] ...... ITB
Integrated Training Management System [*DoD*] ...... ITMS
Integrated Training System Plan [*Army*] ...... ITSP
Integrated Trajectory Computations ...... ITC
Integrated Trajectory Error Display [*Aviation*] ...... ITED
Integrated Trajectory System ...... ITS
Integrated Transaction Processor (MHDI) ...... ITP
Integrated Transfer Launch Complex (IAA) ...... ITLC
Integrated Transportation Management Information System [*Army*] ...... ITMIS
Integrated Tsunami Research Information System [*Marine science*] (OSRA) ...... ITRIS
Integrated Tug Barge (DS) ...... ITB
Integrated Tunnel Diode Amplifier ...... ITDA
Integrated Tunnel Diode Device (IAA) ...... ITDD
Integrated Two-Step Liquefaction [*Chemical engineering*] ...... ITSL
Integrated Undersea-Surveillance System [*Oceanography*] (ECON) ...... IUSS
Integrated Underwater Surveillance System [*Navy*] [*Marine science*] (OSRA) ...... IUSS
Integrated Underwater Surveillance System [*Navy*] (USDC) ...... IUSS
Integrated Unit Record Processor ...... IURP
Integrated Vacuum Circuit IVC
Integrated Vector Management [*Insect control*] ...... IVM
Integrated Vehicle (MCD) IV
Integrated Vehicle Baseline Configuration (MCD) ...... IVBC
Integrated Vehicle Management Subsystem (MCD) ...... IVMS
Integrated Vehicle System Technology (MCD) ...... INVEST
Integrated Vehicular Communication System (MCD) ...... IVCS
Integrated Vehicular Information System [*Army*] (RDA) ...... IVIS
Integrated Versaplot Software (PDAA) ...... IVS
Integrated Video Terminal ...... IVT
Integrated Visual Approach and Landing Aid [*System*] [*RADAR*] ...... IVALA
Integrated Visual Testing Device ...... IVTD
Integrated Visualization Environment [*Computer science*] (BTTJ) ...... IVE
Integrated Voice and Data Telecommunications System (AAGC) ...... IVDTS
Integrated [*or Interior*] Voice Communications System (MCD) ...... IVCS
Integrated Voice Data Multiplexer [*Telecommunications*] (ACRL) ...... IVDM
Integrated [*or Interactive*] Voice Data Terminal [*Telecommunications*] ...... IVDT
Integrated Voice Messaging System [*Commterm, Inc.*] [*Atlanta, GA*] (TSSD) ...... IVMS
Integrated Voltage Regulator (IEEE) ...... IVR
Integrated Vulnerability Assessment [*Military*] ...... IVA
Integrated Warfare Requirements Methodology ...... IWRM
Integrated Waste Fluid System (SSD) ...... IWFS
Integrated Waste Services, Inc. [*Associated Press*] (SAG) ...... IntgWst
Integrated Waste Services, Inc. [*NASDAQ symbol*] (SAG) ...... IWSI
Integrated Waste Svcs [*NASDAQ symbol*] (TTSB) ...... IWSI
Integrated Waste Water Treatment ...... IWT
Integrated Water System (SSD) ...... IWS
Integrated Weapon Secret Panel (MCD) ...... IWSP
Integrated Weapon Support Management (AFM) ...... IWSM
Integrated Weapon System ...... IWS
Integrated Weapon System Representative [*or Review*] (MCD) ...... IWSR
Integrated Weapon System Training [*Air Force*] ...... IWST
Integrated Weapons Control System ...... IWCS
Integrated Weapons Display ...... IWD
Integrated Weed Management System [*Agriculture*] ...... IWMS
Integrated Wideband Communications System [*Military*] ...... IWCS
Integrated Wideband Communications System/Southeast Asia (IEEE) ...... IWCS/SEA
Integrated Wire Termination System (IAA) ...... IWTS
Integrated Work Sequence/Inspection Traveler (NRCH) ...... IWS/IT
Integrated Work Statement (MCD) ...... IWS
Integrated Worldwide Topographic System (PDAA) ...... IWTS
Integrated Woz Machine [*Apple Computer, Inc.*] ...... IWM
Integrated X-Ray Reflection ...... IXR
Integrate-Transfer-Launch [*Complex*] [*NASA*] ...... ITL
Integrating Assembly and Checkout Contractor ...... IACC
Integrating Assembly Contractor ...... IAC
Integrating Associate Contractor ...... IAC
Integrating Center IC
Integrating Contractor (AAG) IC
Integrating Digital Voltmeter ...... IDV
Integrating Digital Voltmeter ...... IDVM
Integrating Fluctuation Meter ...... IFM
Integrating Graduate Education and Research Training [*National Science Foundation*] ...... IGERT

Integrating Gyro Accelerometer .... IGA
Integrating Light Detector (PDAA) .... ILD
Integrating Motor Pneumotachograph .... IMP
Integrating Regulatory Transcription Units [*Genetics*] .... IRTU
Integrating Support .... IS
Integrating Waveguide Technology (PDAA) .... INWATE
Integration (NASA) .... INTG
Integration Acceptance Test [*Military*] (CAAL) .... IAT
Integration Analog-to-Digital Converter (IEEE) .... IADIC
Integration and Checkout (KSC) .... I & C
Integration and Test .... I & T
Integration and Test Order (MCD) .... ITO
Integration, Assembly, and Checkout .... IAC
Integration, Assembly, and Test .... IA & T
Integration Building and Equipment Scheduling (PDAA) .... IBES
Integration Change Allowance (MCD) .... ICA
Integration Change Board [*NASA*] .... ICB
Integration Control (MCD) IC
Integration Facility (MCD) .... IF
Integration Hardware and Software Review (MCD) .... IH/SR
Integration Host Factor [*Genetics*] .... IHF
Integration Level Test Series [*Psychology*] .... ILTS
Integration Modified .... IM
Integration of Cellular Responses [*Research initiative*] [*bbswrc - Biotechnology and Biological Sciences Research Council*] [*British*] .... ICR
Integration of Intelligence from All Sources (MCD) .... IIFAS
Integration/Operations and Maintenance Instruction [*NASA*] (NASA) .... I/OMI
Integration Review Section [*Social Security Administration*] .... IRS
Integration Shop/Laboratory Manager (MCD) .... ISLM
Integration Support Service .... ISS
Integration Test and Demonstration (SDI) .... ITD
Integration Test Equipment (MCD) .... ITE
Integration Trade and Analysis-Cycle O (SSD) .... ITACO
Integration Unit .... INU
Integration with Britain Party [*Gibraltar*] (PPE) .... IWBP
Integration with Controlled Error (MCD) .... ICE
Integrative Decision Making (MCD) .... IDM
Integrative Master of Business Administration (PGP) .... IMBA
Integrator Card (IAA) IC
Integrator Cutoff .... ICO
Integrator Register Address Register (PDAA) .... IRAR
Integrator Register Control Register (PDAA) .... IRCR
Integrator Register Counter (PDAA) .... IRC
Integriertes Statistisches Informationssystem [*Integrated Statistical Information System*] [*Central Statistical Office Vienna, Austria*] [*Information service or system*] (IID) .... ISIS
Integrin (DMAA) .... ITG
Integrin Alpha (DMAA) .... ITGA
Integrin Beta (DMAA) .... ITGB
Integrin-Binding Sialoprotein (DMAA) .... IBSP
Integrin-Linked Kinase [*An enzyme*] .... ILK
Integrity and Reliability [*Military*] (AFIT) .... I & R
Integrity and Reliability [*Military*] (AFIT) .... IAR
Integrity, Inc. [*Associated Press*] (SAG) .... Integrity
Integrity, Inc. [*NASDAQ symbol*] (SAG) .... ITGR
Integrity Loss Factor .... ILF
Integrity Music, Inc. [*Associated Press*] (SAG) .... IntgMus
Integrity Music, Inc. [*NASDAQ symbol*] (SAG) .... ITGR
Integrity Music'A' [*NASDAQ symbol*] (TTSB) .... ITGR
Integro-Differential Analyzer .... IDA
Integument [*Dermatology*] (DAVI) .... INTEG
INTEK Diversified [*NASDAQ symbol*] (TTSB) .... IDCC
INTEK Diversified Corp. [*NASDAQ symbol*] (NQ) .... IDCC
INTEK Diversified Corp. [*Associated Press*] (SAG) .... Intek
Intel Communications Amplifications Specification [*Interface*] .... ICAS
Intel Comparative Microprocessor Performance Index (PCM) .... iCOMP
Intel Corp. [*NASDAQ symbol*] (NQ) .... INTC
Intel Corp. [*Associated Press*] (SAG) .... Intel
Intel Corp., Santa Clara, CA [*Library symbol Library of Congress*] (LCLS) .... CStcII
Intel Corp.Wrrt [*NASDAQ symbol*] (TTSB) .... INTCW
Intel Mobile Module .... IMM
Intel Mobile Module [*Computer science*] .... MMO
Intel Power Monitor (PCM) .... IPM
Intel Smart Video Recorder III ISVR3
Intelcom Group [*Associated Press*] (SAG) .... Intelcm
Intelcom Group [*AMEX symbol*] (SPSG) .... ITR
Intelcom Radiation Technology, Inc. .... IRT
Intelect Communications [*NASDAQ symbol*] (TTSB) .... ICOMF
Intelect Communications Systems Ltd. [*NASDAQ symbol*] (SAG) .... ICOM
Intelect Communications Systems Ltd. [*Associated Press*] (SAG) .... Intelect
InteliData Technologies Corp. [*NASDAQ symbol*] (SAG) .... INTD
InteliData Technologies Corp. [*Associated Press*] (SAG) .... InteliDta
Intellectual Achievement Responsibility Questionnaire [*Psychology*] (EDAC) .... IARQ
Intellectual Digest [*A publication*] .... ID
Intellectual Disability Review Panel .... IDRP
Intellectual Disability Rights Service .... IDRS
Intellectual Disability Services [*Australian Capital Territory, Queensland*] .... IDS
Intellectual Framework .... IF
Intellectual Freedom .... IF
Intellectual Freedom Committee [*American Library Association*] .... IFC
Intellectual Freedom Round Table [*American Library Association*] .... IFRT
Intellectual Property (MCD) .... IP
Intellectual Property and Technology .... IP & T
Intellectual Property Forum [*A publication*] .... IPF
Intellectual Property Journal [*A publication*] .... IPJ
Intellectual Property Law Review [*A publication*] (DLA) .... Intellectual Property L Rev
Intellectual Property Network, Ltd. [*Information service or system*] (IID) .... IPN
Intellectual Property Owners (EA) .... IPO
Intellectual Property Rights .... IPR
Intellectual Property Transfer .... IPT
Intellectually Gifted Children .... IGC
Intelli Corp., Inc. [*Associated Press*] (SAG) .... Intelli
Intellicall, Inc. [*NYSE symbol*] (SPSG) ICL
Intellicall, Inc. [*Associated Press*] (SAG) .... Intelcal
Intellicell Corp. [*NASDAQ symbol*] (SAG) .... FONE
Intellicell Corp. [*Associated Press*] (SAG) .... Intllcll
IntelliCorp, Inc. [*NASDAQ symbol*] (NQ) .... INAI
Intelligence I
Intelligence .... IN
Intelligence .... INT
Intelligence (AABC) .... INTEL
Intelligence (ROG) .... INTELL
Intelligence .... INTLLGNC
Intelligence Advisory Committee .... IAC
Intelligence Analysis .... IA
Intelligence Analysis Center [*Marine Corps*] (MCD) .... IAC
Intelligence Analysis Group [*Military*] .... IAG
Intelligence Analysis Squadron .... IAS
Intelligence Analysts Associates [*Air Force*] .... IAA
Intelligence and Counterespionage [*Fictitious organization in the Matt Helm series of books and movies*] .... ICE
Intelligence and Criminal Justice Academy [*Defunct*] (EA) .... ICJA
Intelligence and Electronic Warfare [*System*] [*Military*] (RDA) .... IEW
Intelligence and Interdiction [*Military*] (VNW) .... I & I
Intelligence and Law Enforcement Division [*Coast Guard*] .... INT
Intelligence and Reconnaissance .... I & R
Intelligence and Reconnaissance (IAA) .... IAR
Intelligence and Research (DNAB) .... INR
Intelligence and Security Board [*Army*] (RDA) .... INSB
Intelligence and Security Board [*Military*] (MCD) .... ISB
Intelligence and Security Command [*Army*] (RDA) .... INSCOM
Intelligence and Threat Analysis Center .... ITAC
Intelligence and Threat Analysis Center [*Air Force*] (DOMA) .... ITAC
Intelligence Assessment (DOMA) .... IA
Intelligence Automatic Data Processing Group (CINC) .... IADPG
Intelligence Bandwidth .... IBW
Intelligence Branch .... IB
Intelligence Broadcast (DOMA) .... INTELCAST
Intelligence Bulletin (CINC) .... INTBUL
Intelligence Career Development Program (AFM) .... ICDP
Intelligence Case Control and Time Reporting System [*IRS*] .... ICCTR
Intelligence Center (CAAL) IC
Intelligence Center .... INTELCEN
Intelligence Center and School [*Army*] (RDA) .... ICS
Intelligence Center, Pacific [*Military*] (MCD) .... IPAC
Intelligence Center, Pacific Ocean Areas [*Obsolete*] .... ICPOA
Intelligence Center, Pacific Ocean Areas [*Obsolete*] .... INTELCENPAC
Intelligence Civic Actions Program [*Army*] (VNW) .... ICAPS
Intelligence Civilian Career Program [*Army*] (AABC) .... ICCP
Intelligence Collator [*British police term*] IC
Intelligence Collect Program .... ICOP
Intelligence Collection [*Military*] (MCD) IC
Intelligence Collection [*Military*] (NVT) .... INTCOL
Intelligence Collection Area [*Military*] (NATG) .... ICA
Intelligence Collection Plan [*Military*] (AFM) .... ICP
Intelligence Collection Reporting System [*Military*] (MCD) .... ICRS
Intelligence Collection Requirement [*Army*] (RDA) .... ICR
Intelligence Committee [*NATO*] (NATG) IC
Intelligence Communications Architecture .... INCA
Intelligence Community [*Military*] (MCD) IC
Intelligence Community Staff [*Military*] (MCD) .... ICS
Intelligence Contingency Funds (CINC) .... ICF
Intelligence Coordination [*Program*] [*Department of State*] .... INC
Intelligence Coordination and Exploitation [*Joint CIA-MACV program*] .... ICEX
Intelligence Corps [*Military unit*] [*British*] IC
Intelligence Corps [*Army*] (RDA) .... IN
Intelligence Corps [*Army*] .... INTC
Intelligence Cutoff Date [*Military*] (MCD) .... ICOD
Intelligence Cycle (LAIN) IC
Intelligence Cycle Time (MCD) .... ICT
Intelligence Data Element Authorization Standards [*Military*] (MCD) .... IDEAS
Intelligence Data Handling Division [*United States European Command*] .... IDD
Intelligence Data Handling System (AFM) .... IDHS
Intelligence Data Handling System Communications (MCD) .... IDHSC
Intelligence Data Input Package (MCD) .... IDIP
Intelligence Data Processing (MCD) .... IDP
Intelligence Data System .... IDS
Intelligence Defector Source File [*Military*] (MCD) .... IDSF
Intelligence Department [*Army*] (MCD) .... ID
Intelligence Division [*NATO*] (NATG) .... ID
Intelligence Division Gaming Operations .... INDIGO
Intelligence Division Indications Center [*Military*] (MCD) .... IDIC
Intelligence Duties .... ID
Intelligence Duty Officer .... IDO
Intelligence/Electronic Warfare Family of Systems Study [*Military*] (MCD) .... I/EW FOSS
Intelligence Electronic Warfare Support Element (ADDR) .... IEWSE
Intelligence/Electronic Warfare Unmanned Aerial Vehicle [*Army*] .... IEW-UAV
Intelligence Estimate for Planning .... IEP

Intelligence Evaluation Center [*Saigon*] [*Obsolete*] (CINC) ... IECS
Intelligence Evaluation Committee [*Department of Justice*] ... IEC
Intelligence Evaluation Staff ... IES
Intelligence Exploitation Squadron [*Air Force*] ... IES
Intelligence Exploitation Squadron [*Air Force*] ... IESq
Intelligence Family of Systems Study [*Military*] (MCD) ... IFOSS
Intelligence Field Unit [*Navy*] ... IFU
Intelligence Finished Reports Information Subsystem [*Computer science*] ... IFRIS
Intelligence for which the Source Reliability Cannot be Judged ... F
Intelligence Fusion [*Army*] (RDA) ... IF
Intelligence Gathering Vessel [*Military*] ... AGI
Intelligence Generator ... IG
Intelligence Graphics Controller [*Computer science*] ... IGC
Intelligence Guidance for COMINT [*Communications Intelligence*] **Programming** (MCD) ... IGCP
Intelligence Handling Committee [*Military*] ... IHC
Intelligence in the Sky [*An extraterrestrial intelligence with whom Dr. Andrija Puharich and psychic Uri Geller claim to have communicated*] ... IS
Intelligence Industries Association (EA) ... IIA
Intelligence Information Center [*Military*] (MCD) ... IIC
Intelligence Information Report (NVT) ... IIR
Intelligence Information Report Photo Index [*Military*] (MCD) ... IRPIA
Intelligence Information Subsystem [*Military*] ... I2S2
Intelligence Information Subsystem [*Military*] (MCD) ... IISS
Intelligence Information System [*Military*] (DNAB) ... IIS
Intelligence Interactive Test Terminal ... I2T2
Intelligence Interface and Warning [*Military*] (MCD) ... II & W
Intelligence Liaison [*Program*] [*Department of State*] ... IL
Intelligence Management Information System [*Military*] (MCD) ... IMIS
Intelligence Material Development Office [*Military*] (MCD) ... IMDO
Intelligence Materiel Development and Support Office [*Army*] (RDA) ... IMDSO
Intelligence Memorandum ... IM
Intelligence Mission Area Analysis [*Military*] (MCD) ... IMAA
Intelligence Network (DOMA) ... INTELNET
Intelligence Office [*or Officer*] ... IO
Intelligence Officer [*Military*] ... INTELO
Intelligence Officer [*Army*] ... INTO
Intelligence Operations Center [*Air Force*] (DOMA) ... IOC
Intelligence Operations Specialist [*Military*] (MCD) ... IOS
Intelligence Organization Stationing Study [*Army*] (MCD) ... IOSS
Intelligence Oversight (DOMA) ... IO
Intelligence Oversight ... IOS
Intelligence Oversight Board [*Federal government*] ... IOB
Intelligence, Pacific Area Command (MCD) ... IPAC
Intelligence Planning Document [*Military*] (MCD) ... IPD
Intelligence Preparation of the Battlefield [*Army*] (RDA) ... IPB
Intelligence Preparatory Brief [*Army*] (DOMA) ... IPB
Intelligence Priorities Committee [*British World War II*] ... IPC
Intelligence Priorities for Strategic Planning [*Military*] ... IPSP
Intelligence Production Activity [*Military*] (MCD) ... IPA
Intelligence Production Database [*Military*] (MCD) ... IPDB
Intelligence Production Requests ... IPR
Intelligence Production Requirement (AFIT) ... IPR
Intelligence Property Book [*Army*] (ADDR) ... IPB
Intelligence Publications (MCD) ... IP
Intelligence Publications Index [*Published January, 1953, through February, 1968, by the Defense Intelligence Agency*] ... IPI
Intelligence Quotient [*Psychological and educational testing*] ... IQ
Intelligence RADAR Reporting ... IRR
Intelligence Ratio ... IR
Intelligence Related Activities [*Military*] (MCD) ... IRA
Intelligence Report (NATG) ... INTREP
Intelligence Report ... INTREPT
Intelligence Report ... IR
Intelligence Report Index Summary ... IRIS
Intelligence Report Plan (NATG) ... IRP
Intelligence Reports Information Subsystem [*Computer science*] ... IRIS
Intelligence Request (DOMA) ... IR
Intelligence Requirement [*Military*] (INF) ... IR
Intelligence Research and Development Council (MCD) ... IRDC
Intelligence Research Specialist [*Military*] (MCD) ... IRS
Intelligence Resources [*Program*] [*Department of State*] ... IRE
Intelligence Resources Advisory Committee [*To supervise US intelligence budget*] ... IRAC
Intelligence Review ... IR
Intelligence Review and Assessment Task Element [*Study of the effectiveness of the air war in Southeast Asia*] ... IRATE
Intelligence School, United States Army Intelligence Center ... ISUSAIC
Intelligence Score (MCD) ... ISCORE
Intelligence Section [*of an air staff; also, officer in charge of this section*] [*Air Force*] ... A-2
Intelligence Section [*of a joint military staff; also, the officer in charge of this section*] ... J-2
Intelligence Section [*in Army brigades or smaller units, and in Marine Corps units smaller than a brigade; also, the officer in charge of this section*] ... S-2
Intelligence Section, Operations [*Control Commission for Germany*] [*World War II*] ... IS(O)
Intelligence Section, Operations [*Joint Intelligence Subcommittee of Chiefs of Staff*] [*World War II*] ... IS(Ops)
Intelligence, Security, and Electronic Warfare [*DoD*] ... ISEW
Intelligence Service (IAA) ... IS
Intelligence Specialist [*Navy*] ... IS
Intelligence Specialist, First Class [*Navy*] (DNAB) ... IS1
Intelligence Specialist, Seaman [*Navy*] (DNAB) ... ISSN
Intelligence Specialist, Seaman Apprentice [*Navy*] (DNAB) ... ISSA
Intelligence Specialist, Second Class [*Navy*] (DNAB) ... IS2
Intelligence Specialist, Third Class [*Navy*] (DNAB) ... IS3
Intelligence Subject Code ... ISC
Intelligence Summary ... INTSUM
Intelligence Summary ... ISUM
Intelligence Support [*Program*] [*Department of State*] ... IS
Intelligence Support Activity [*Military*] ... ISA
Intelligence Support and Indications Center [*Military*] (MCD) ... ISIC
Intelligence Support Center ... ISC
Intelligence Support Display System [*Military*] (MCD) ... ISDS
Intelligence Support Element [*Military*] (MCD) ... ISE
Intelligence Support Interface Program ... ISIP
Intelligence Support System ... ISS
Intelligence, Surveillance, and Target Acquisition [*Military*] ... ISTA
Intelligence Systems [*Military*] (MCD) ... IS
Intelligence Systems Branch [*Military*] (IAA) ... ISB
Intelligence Systems Program Review [*Military*] (MCD) ... INSPR
Intelligence Task Force (DOMA) ... ITF
Intelligence Terminal Family [*Military*] (MCD) ... ITF
Intelligence Threat Analysis Detachment [*Army*] (RDA) ... ITAD
Intelligence Threat Analysis Group [*Military*] (DNAB) ... ITAG
Intelligence Threat Evaluation Model [*Military*] (MCD) ... ITEM
Intelligence Town Plan ... ITP
Intelligence Tracking Analysis and Correlation (MCD) ... ITAC
Intelligence Training [*Military*] (NVT) ... INTELTNG
Intelligence Users' Guide (MCD) ... IUG
Intelligence Watch Condition [*NATO*] (NATG) ... AIWC
Intelligence Watch Officer [*Military*] (MCD) ... IWO
Intelligence Working Group [*Military*] (CINC) ... IWG
Intelligent Actuation & Measurement (ACII) ... IAM
Intelligent Actuators & Transmitters (ACII) ... IAT
Intelligent Actuatot (ACII) ... IA
Intelligent Agent ... IA
Intelligent and Innovative Vehicle Electronic Control System ... INVECS
Intelligent Array Subsystem Core ... IAS
Intelligent Assistant [*Computer science*] ... IA
Intelligent Asynchronous Controller [*Computer terminal connector*] (NITA) ... IAC
Intelligent Authoring Systems (EDAC) ... IAS
Intelligent Body Assembly System [*Robotics*] [*Nissan Motor Co. Ltd.*] ... IBAS
Intelligent Broadband Controller (NITA) ... IBC
Intelligent Buildings Corp. [*Broomfield, CO*] [*Telecommunications service*] (TSSD) ... IBC
Intelligent Buildings Institute (EA) ... IBI
Intelligent Business Information System (NITA) ... IBIS
Intelligent Character Recognition [*Computer science*] ... ICR
Intelligent Communication Subsystem Two Board [*Controls input from computer terminals to mainframe*] [*Prime Computer, Inc.*] ... ICS2
Intelligent Communications Adapter [*Computer hardware*] (PCM) ... ICA
Intelligent Communications Interface (IEEE) ... ICI
Intelligent Communications Processor ... ICP
Intelligent Computer Systems Research Institute [*University of Miami*] [*Research center*] (RCD) ... ICSRI
Intelligent Computer-Aided Design ... ICAD
Intelligent Computer-Aided Troubleshooting ... I-CAT
Intelligent Computer-Assisted Instruction ... ICAI
Intelligent Concept Extraction [*Technology*] [*Computer science*] ... ICE
Intelligent Configuration Identification System [*NASA*] ... ICIS
Intelligent Connector Unit [*Telecommunications*] (TSSD) ... ICU
Intelligent Console Architecture (PCM) ... ICA
Intelligent Content Recognition Technology [*Computer science*] ... iCRT
Intelligent Controls, Inc. [*Associated Press*] (SAG) ... IntlgC
Intelligent Controls, Inc. [*AMEX symbol*] (SAG) ... ITC
Intelligent Copier [*Electrophotography*] (DGA) ... IC
Intelligent Copier-Printer [*Electrophotography*] ... IC-P
Intelligent Cruise Control [*Automotive engineering*] ... ICC
Intelligent Data Access ... IDA
Intelligent Data Acquisition System ... IDAS
Intelligent Data Network ... IDN
Intelligent Data Terminal ... IDT
Intelligent Database Assistant ... IDA
Intelligent Database Machine [*Computer science*] ... IDM
Intelligent Digital Exchange (NITA) ... IDX
Intelligent Digitizer ... ID
Intelligent Disaster Recovery [*Computer science*] ... IDR
Intelligent Disk Subsystem [*Northgate Computer Systems*] [*Computer science*] (PCM) ... IDS
Intelligent Display System [*Computer science*] ... IDS
Intelligent Distributed Editor (HGAA) ... IDE
Intelligent Document Management [*Computer science*] ... IDM
Intelligent Documentation [*Computer science*] ... ID
Intelligent Drive Array [*COMPAQ Computer Corp.*] [*Computer science*] ... IDA
Intelligent Drive Electronics ... IDE
Intelligent Dual Interface ... IDI
Intelligent Dummy Data Acquisition System [*Crash testing*] [*Automotive engineering*] ... IDDAS
Intelligent Electroncs [*NASDAQ symbol*] (TTSB) ... INEL
Intelligent Electronic Warfare Common Sensor (DWSG) ... IEWCS
Intelligent Electronics Europa (NITA) ... IEE
Intelligent Electronics, Inc. [*NASDAQ symbol*] (NQ) ... INEL
Intelligent Electronics, Inc. [*NASDAQ symbol*] (SAG) ... INEL
Intelligent Fault Locator [*McDonnell Douglas Helicopter Co.*] [*Army*] ... IFL
Intelligent Field Device (ACII) ... IFD
Intelligent File Store [*British*] ... IFS
Intelligent Forces [*Army*] (RDA) ... IFOR

Intelligent Forms Language [*Delrina Corp.*] [*Computer science*] (PCM) .... IFL
Intelligent Front End (NITA) .... IFE
Intelligent Gateway Processor [*Computer science*] .... IGP
Intelligent Geographic System [*Computer science*] .... IGIS
Intelligent Graphics Processor [*Computer science*] (PCM) .... IGP
Intelligent Graphics Terminal [*Tektronix*] (NITA) .... IGT
Intelligent Image Caching Software [*Courtland Group, Inc.*] (PCM) .... IICS
Intelligent Input Output Channel (NITA) .... IIOC
Intelligent Input/Output Processor [*Disk Controller*] .... IIOP
Intelligent Keyboard Device .... IKBD
Intelligent Knowledge-Based System [*Artificial intelligence*] .... IKBS
Intelligent Life Elsewhere .... ILE
Intelligent Line Adapter .... ILA
Intelligent Machine Research (NITA) .... IMR
Intelligent Manufacturing Systems [*Japan*] [*Agreement for conducting cooperative global research*] .... IMS
Intelligent Mark Document Reader (MHDI) .... IMDR
Intelligent Matrix Control [*T-Bar, Inc.*] .... IMC
Intelligent Measurement [*Function*] (ACII) .... IM
Intelligent Medical Imaging, Inc. [*NASDAQ symbol*] (SAG) .... IMII
Intelligent Medical Imaging, Inc. [*Associated Press*] (SAG) .... IntMedI
Intelligent Med'l Imaging [*NASDAQ symbol*] (TTSB) .... IMII
Intelligent Memory Manager [*Computer science*] .... IMM
Intelligent Message Processor [*Delta Data Systems*] (NITA) .... IMP
Intelligent Microimage Terminal [*Kodak*] .... IMT
Intelligent Motion Control System [PDAA] .... IMCS
Intelligent Multiplexer [*Telecommunications*] (ACRL) .... IMUX
Intelligent Multiport Cards [*Computer hardware*] (PCM) .... IMP
Intelligent Naval Structures Assistant .... INSTRUCTA
Intelligent Network [*Telecommunications*] .... IN
Intelligent Network [*Telecom Canada*] [*Database*] .... INET
Intelligent Network Processor .... INP
Intelligent Peripheral [*Computer science*] (ACRL) .... IP
Intelligent Peripheral Controller [*Computer science*] .... IPC
Intelligent Peripheral Interface [*Computer science*] .... IPI
Intelligent Plant Operating Manual [*Combustion Engineering Simcon, Inc.*] .... IPOM
Intelligent Power Integrated Circuit [*Electronics*] .... IPIC
Intelligent Power Management [*Laptop computers*] (BYTE) .... IPM
Intelligent Power Management System [*Laptop computers*] (BYTE) .... IPS
Intelligent Power Switch [*Electronics*] .... IPS
Intelligent Printer Data Systems .... IPDS
Intelligent Printer Interface .... IPI
Intelligent Printing System [*Dataroyal, Inc.*] .... IPS
Intelligent Processing of Materials [*Computer science*] .... IPM
Intelligent Processing Unit [*Canon, Inc.*] [*Computer science*] (PCM) .... IPU
Intelligent Program Editor (PDAA) .... IPE
Intelligent Protection Device [*American Solenoid Co.*] [*Somerset, NJ*] .... IPD
Intelligent Query .... IQ
Intelligent Quisine [*Campbell Soup Co.*] .... IQ
Intelligent Remote Batch Terminal [*Computer science*] (IAA) .... IRBT
Intelligent Remote Input Stand [*Computer science*] .... IRIS
Intelligent Remote Multiplexer [*Computer science*] (MHDI) .... IRM
Intelligent Remote Terminal Unit .... IRTU
Intelligent Serial Interface [*Computer science*] .... ISI
Intelligent Support System .... ISS
Intelligent Surgical LASERs, Inc. [*Associated Press*] (SAG) .... IntlSrgL
Intelligent Surgical Lasers, Inc. [*Associated Press*] (SAG) .... IntSr
Intelligent Surgical Lasers, Inc. [*NASDAQ symbol*] (SAG) .... ISLS
Intelligent Synchronous Controller [*Computer science*] (NITA) .... ISC
Intelligent Systems Corp. [*AMEX symbol*] (SPSG) .... INS
Intelligent Systems Corp. [*Associated Press*] (SAG) .... IntlgSys
Intelligent Systems Corp. .... ISC
Intelligent Tape Controller (PDAA) .... ITC
Intelligent Telecommunication Controller (IAA) .... ITC
Intelligent Television [*Home video game*] [*Mattel, Inc.*] .... INTELLIVISION
Intelligent Terminal [*Computer science*] .... IT
Intelligent Terminal System [*IBM Corp.*] .... ITS
Intelligent Time-Division Multiplexer .... ITDM
Intelligent Transaction Controller (MHDB) .... ITC
Intelligent Transaction Router [*Telecommunications*] .... IT
Intelligent Transmitter (ACII) .... IT
Intelligent Transport System [*Traffic management*] (ECON) .... ITS
Intelligent Transportation Infrastructure .... ITI
Intelligent Transportation Society [*formerly, IVHS, Intelligent Vehicle-Highway Society*] .... ITS
Intelligent Transportation System [*FTA*] [*NHTSA*] (TAG) .... ITS
Intelligent Tutoring Media [*Artificial intelligence*] .... ITM
Intelligent Tutoring System (RDA) .... ITS
Intelligent Vehicle/Highway System .... IVHS
Intelligent Vehicle Highway System (USGC) .... IVHS
Intelligent Vehicle Highway Systems .... IHVS
Intelligenzalter [*Mental Age*] [*Psychology*] .... IA
Intelligible Crosstalk Ratio .... IXTR
Intellignet Electronics, Inc. [*Associated Press*] (SAG) .... IntelEl
Intelligroup, Inc. [*Associated Press*] (SAG) .... IntIgrp
Intelligroup, Inc. [*NASDAQ symbol*] (SAG) .... ITIG
IntelliQuest Information Group, Inc. [*Associated Press*] (SAG) .... IntQuest
IntelliQuest Information Group, Inc. [*NASDAQ symbol*] (SAG) .... IQST
Intellisoft Accounting Series [*Computer science*] (PCM) .... IAS
INTELSAT Assistance and Development Program .... IADP
INTELSAT Business Service [*MCI Communications Corp.*] .... IBS
INTELSAT Operations Center .... IOC
Intemperate to Alcohol [*An alcoholic*] [*Slang*] .... IA
Intend (FAAC) .... INTD

Intendant-General .... IG
Intended .... INTDD
Intenist .... INTERNST
Intense [*Philately*] .... int
Intense .... INTS
Intense Bunched Ion Source (IEEE) .... IBIS
Intense Ion Beam .... IIB
Intense Irregular Field .... IIF
Intense Islet Stimulation Test [*Endocrinology*] .... IIST
Intense Magnetic Field .... IMF
Intense Neutron Generator .... ING
Intense Product Inspection .... IPI
Intense Pulsed Neutron Source .... IPNS
Intense Relativistic Electron Beams [*Physics*] .... IREB
Intense Sample Data Collection System (MCD) .... ISDC
Intense Thermal Radiation .... ITR
Intensely Transfused Dialysis [*Medicine*] (DMAA) .... ITD
Intensified Charge Injection Device [*For television camera used in astronomy*] .... ICID
Intensified Charge-Coupled Device [*Electronics*] .... ICCD
Intensified Combat Training Program .... ICTP
Intensified Confirmatory Troop Test (AABC) .... ICTT
Intensified Conventional Insulin Therapy [*Medicine*] .... ICIT
Intensified Drug Inspection Program [*FDA*] .... IDIP
Intensified Silicon Intensifier Target (MCD) .... ISIT
Intensifier [*Linguistics*] .... INT
Intensifier Vidicon IV
Intensify .... INTSF
Intensify (DNAB) .... INTSY
Intensity I
Intensity .... IN
Intensity .... INT
Intensity (MSA) .... INTEN
Intensity .... INTST
Intensity Duration (Curve) .... I-D
Intensity Factor .... IF
Intensity Fluctuation Factor [*Telecommunications*] (TEL) .... IFF
Intensity Level [*Physics*] (IAA) IL
Intensity Measuring Devices [*JETDS nomenclature*] [*Military*] (CET) .... IM
Intensity Millicurie [*Nucleonics*] (IAA) .... IMC
Intensity Millicurie [*Nucleonics*] (IAA) .... IMCU
Intensity Modulated / Frequency Modulated (WDAA) .... IM/FM
Intensity Modulation .... IM
Intensity of Magnetization [*Symbol*] (DEN) .... M
Intensity of Operational Employment [*Army*] (RDA) .... IOE
Intensity of Telephone Interference (IAA) .... IT
Intensity Probability Density Function (PDAA) .... IPDF
Intensity Resources Ltd. [*Toronto Stock Exchange symbol*] .... ITY
Intensity, Severity, and Discharge [*Medicine*] (DHSM) .... ISD
Intensity-Maximizing Multidither (PDAA) .... IMMD
Intensiva HealthCare Corp. [*NASDAQ symbol*] (SAG) .... IHCC
Intensiva Healthcare Corp. [*Associated Press*] (SAG) .... Intensva
Intensive .... INTENS
Intensive (WGA) .... INTSV
Intensive Biometric Intertidal Survey [*Botany*] .... IBIS
Intensive Care [*Medicine*] IC
Intensive Care Certificate [*Medicine*] ICC
Intensive Care Facility [*Medicine*] .... ICF
Intensive Care Nursery [*Medicine*] .... ICN
Intensive Care Observation Unit [*Medicine*] (DMAA) .... IOU
Intensive Care Room [*Medicine*] (DAVI) .... ICR
Intensive Care Society [*British*] (EAIO) .... ICS
Intensive Care, Surgical [*Medicine*] .... ICS
Intensive Caring Unlimited [*An association*] (EA) .... ICU
Intensive Conventional Therapy [*Medicine*] (DAVI) .... ICT
Intensive Coronary Care [*Medicine*] ICC
Intensive Coronary Care Unit [*of a hospital*] .... ICCU
Intensive Employability Services [*Work Incentive Program*] .... IES
Intensive Flux Array [*Marine science*] (OSRA) .... IFA
Intensive Flux Array (USDC) .... IFA
Intensive Immunosuppression [*Medicine*] (DMAA) .... IIS
Intensive Intravenous Treatment [*Medicine*] .... IIVT
Intensive Item Management System (AABC) .... IIMS
Intensive Management Items (MCD) .... IMI
Intensive Manpower Services (OICC) .... IMS
Intensive Matched Probation and After-Care Treatment (PDAA) .... IMPACT
Intensive Military Training Area (DA) .... IMTA
Intensive Neurosurgery Unit (DAVI) .... INSU
Intensive Observation Period [*Marine science*] (OSRA) .... IOP
Intensive Observing Period (USDC) .... IOP
Intensive Pig Producers of Australia .... IPPA
Intensive Reading .... IR
Intensive Student Jet Training Area .... ISJTA
Intensive Therapy [*Medicine*] (MAE) .... IT
Intensive Therapy Observation Unit (MAE) .... IOU
Intensive Therapy Observation Unit [*Medicine*] (DMAA) .... ITOU
Intensive Therapy Unit [*Medicine*] (MAE) .... ITU
Intensive Training Program .... ITP
Intensive-Care Unit [*of a hospital*] .... ICU
Intensively Supervised Probation [*Legal term*] (BARN) .... ISP
Intent [*FBI standardized term*] .... INT
Intent to Change .... ITC
Intent to Launch (NG) .... ITL
Intention (ROG) .... INTENTN
Intention .... INTN

Intentional ... INTNTNL
Intentional Bases on Balls [*Baseball*] ... IBB
Intentional Jitter Antijam [*Military*] ... IJAJ
Intentional Jitter Jamming Unit [*Military*] ... IJJU
Intentions (FAAC) ... INTNS
Inter Action Council of Former Heads of Government (EA) ... IACFHG
Inter Air AB [*Sweden ICAO designator*] (FAAC) ... INR
Inter Alia [*Among Other Things*] [*Latin*] ... IA
Inter Alia [*Among Other Things*] [*Latin*] (WDAA) ... IN AL
Inter Alia [*Among Other Things*] [*Latin*] ... INT AL
Inter American University (GAGS) ... Inter American U
Inter Block Gap ... IBG
Inter Cable Communications, Inc. [*Toronto Stock Exchange symbol*] ... ICT
Inter Canadian Development [*Vancouver Stock Exchange symbol*] ... ICD
Inter Cibos [*Between Meals*] [*Pharmacy*] ... IC
Inter Cibos [*Between Meals*] [*Pharmacy*] ... INT CIB
Inter City Airlines [*British*] ... ICA
Inter City Express [*Electric train*] [*Germany*] ... ICE
Inter Documentation Co. AG, Zug, Switzerland [*Library symbol Library of Congress*] (LCLS) ... IDC
Inter Laboratory Data Acceptance (PDAA) ... ILDA
Inter Mirifica [*Decree on the Instruments of Social Communication*] [*Vatican II document*] ... IM
Inter Mountain Development, Inc. [*Vancouver Stock Exchange symbol*] ... IND
Inter Noctem [*During the Night*] [*Pharmacy*] ... INT NOCT
Inter Noctem [*During the Night*] [*Pharmacy*] ... INTER NOCT
Inter/Press Service - Third World News Agency (EA) ... IPS
Inter RCA [*Central African Republic*] [*ICAO designator*] (FAAC) ... CAR
Inter Research Council Coordinating Committee on Biotechnology (NITA) ... IRCCCOB
Inter System Emulator (NITA) ... ISE
Intera Information Technologies Corp. [*NASDAQ symbol*] (SAG) ... IITC
Intera Information Technologies Corp. [*Associated Press*] (SAG) ... Intera
Interact Ministries [*An association*] (EA) ... IM
Interacting Boson Model [*Of nuclear structure*] ... IBM
Interacting Correlated Fragment [*Physical chemistry*] ... ICF
Interacting Equipment Documents (MCD) ... IED
Interacting Protein A [*Biochemistry*] ... DIPA
Inter-Action (MCD) ... IA
Interaction ... INRCTN
Interaction/American Council for Voluntary International Action (EA) ... I/ACVIA
Interaction Computing and Control Facility (NITA) ... ICCF
Interaction Control Table [*Computer science*] (OA) ... ICT
Interaction Cross Talk [*Telecommunications*] (TEL) ... IXT
Interaction Database ... IDB
Interaction Graphics Display ... IGD
Interaction Handler [*Computer science*] (OA) ... IH
Interaction Mean Free Path [*Astrophysics*] ... IMFP
InterAction Media Corp. [*NASDAQ symbol*] (SAG) ... IKEC
InterAction Media Corp. [*Associated Press*] (SAG) ... InterAct
InterAction Media Corp. [*Associated Press*] (SAG) ... IntrAct
Interaction Place Map (EDAC) ... IPM
Interaction Resistance [*Plant pathology*] ... IR
Interaction Resources Ltd. [*Toronto Stock Exchange symbol*] ... INR
Interactive ... INTRCTV
Interactive Algebraic Manipulation [*Computer science*] ... IAM
Interactive Alphanumeric Television ... IATV
Interactive Analysis System [*Computer science*] (PCM) ... IAS
Interactive Application Generator (HGAA) ... IAG
Interactive Application System (IAA) ... IAS
Interactive Applications Supervisor ... IAS
Interactive Applicon Graphics Language [*Automotive engineering*] ... IAGL
Interactive Array Computer ... IAC
Interactive Audio Teletraining System [*Valencia Community College*] [*Orlando, FL*] (TSSD) ... IAT
Interactive Balancing through Simulation (PDAA) ... IBALS
Interactive Bibliographic Search and Retrieval (NITA) ... IBSR
Interactive Brain Wave Analyzer [*IBVA Technology*] [*Computer science*] (PCM) ... IBVA
Interactive Business-Oriented Language ... IBOL
Interactive Cable Television ... ICTV
Interactive Careers Guidance System (AIE) ... ICGS
Interactive Cash and Credit Register [*Datacap Systems, Inc.*] ... ICCR
Interactive Chart Utility [*IBM Corp.*] ... ICU
Interactive COBOL Operating System ... ICOS
Interactive Command Test [*Computer science*] ... ICT
Interactive Communications Feature [*IBM Corp.*] ... ICF
Interactive Communications Software ... ICS
Interactive Compatibility Software [*Gateway Communications, Inc.*] [*Computer science*] (PCM) ... ICS
Interactive Composition and Editing Facility [*IBM Corp.*] ... ICEF
Interactive Computer Facility (NITA) ... ICF
Interactive Computer Graphics ... ICG
Interactive Computer Learning ... ICL
Interactive Computer Presentation Panel [*To display computer-generated information for military use*] ... ICPP
Interactive Computer System [*Information science*] ... IACS
Interactive Computer Systems Ltd. (NITA) ... ICSL
Interactive Computer Worded Forecast (USDC) ... ICWF
Interactive Computer Worded Forecast [*Marine science*] (OSRA) ... ICWF
Interactive Computer-Aided Design Evaluation ... ICADE
Interactive Computer-Based Office Support System [*Military*] (MCD) ... ICBOSS
Interactive Computing and Control Facility [*IBM Corp. program product*] ... ICCF
Interactive Concurrent Engineering [*Software*] ... ICE
Interactive Conflict Resolution (PDAA) ... ICR
Interactive Construction Industry System [*NCR Ltd.*] [*Software package*] (NCC) ... ICIS
Interactive Continuous Process Dynamic Simulation (PDAA) ... ICPDS
Interactive Continuous Simulation Language [*Computer science*] (PDAA) ... ICSL
Interactive Continuous Systems Modeling Program ... ICSMP
Interactive Counting System (IAA) ... ICS
Interactive Courseware [*Air Force*] ... ICW
Interactive Data Class [*Telecommunications*] ... IDC
Interactive Data Corporation (NITA) ... IDC
Interactive Data Entry ... IDE
Interactive Data Entry Access [*Data General Corp.*] ... IDEA
Interactive Data Entry Network [*Computer science*] (MHDB) ... IDEN
Interactive Data Entry System [*Computer science*] (MHDI) ... IDES
Interactive Data Language [*Marine science*] (OSRA) ... IDL
Interactive Data Language (USDC) ... IDL
Interactive Data Machines [*British*] (NITA) ... IDM
Interactive Data on Accidents [*Engineering*] ... IDA
Interactive Data Services, Inc. [*Database producer*] [*Information service or system*] (IID) ... IDSI
Interactive Data System [*Computer science*] ... IDS
Interactive Database Design Laboratory [*Computer science*] (MHDB) ... IDDL
Interactive Database Manipulator and Summarizer ... IDMAS
Interactive Database Processor [*Xerox Corp.*] (MCD) ... IDP
Interactive Debugging (IEEE) ... ID
Interactive Debugging Aid ... IDA
Interactive Design of Control Systems (DI) ... INDECS
Interactive Design Software (NITA) ... IDS
Interactive Development and Debugging Environment (PCM) ... IDDE
Interactive Dialogue Facility [*Programming language*] (CSR) ... IDF
Interactive Differential Analyzer ... IDA
Interactive Digital Electronic Appliance [*Computer science*] ... IDEA
Interactive Digital Electronic Appliances ... IDEA
Interactive Digital Image Display and Analysis System [*Marine science*] (OSRA) ... IDIDAS
Interactive Digital Image Display and Analysis System (USDC) ... IDIDAS
Interactive Digital Image Manipulation System [*Minicomputer*] ... IDIMS
Interactive Direct Processing System [*NCR Corp.*] ... IDPS
Interactive Disk Operating System [*Computer Associates, Inc.*] ... IDOS
Interactive Display and Control Component (MCD) ... IDCC
Interactive Display and Update Facility (SSD) ... IDUF
Interactive Display Panel (MCD) ... IDP
Interactive Display System ... IDS
Interactive Display Terminal (MCD) ... IDT
Interactive Drafting and Digitizing System (MCD) ... IDADS
Interactive Drawing Editing Station (MCD) ... IDES
Interactive Duct Sizing [*Facet Ltd.*] [*Software package*] (NCC) ... INDUS
Interactive Electronic Technical Manual [*Military*] (RDA) ... IETM
[*The*] **Interactive Encyclopedia System** [*University of Maryland research project*] (PCM) ... TIES
Interactive Estimating [*Camic Ltd.*] [*Software package*] (NCC) ... INTEREST
Interactive Executive (HGAA) ... ix
Interactive Facility [*Control Data Corp.*] ... IAF
Interactive File Manager [*Computer science*] ... IFM
Interactive File Sharing ... IFS
Interactive Financial Planning System [*Harris Systems Ltd.*] [*Software package*] (NCC) ... IFPS
Interactive Finite Element Analysis and Design [*Software*] [*Automotive engineering*] ... IFAD
Interactive Flash Flood Analyzer ... IFFA
Interactive Flight Tech Unit [*NASDAQ symbol*] (TTSB) ... FLYTU
Interactive Flight Tech'A' [*NASDAQ symbol*] (TTSB) ... FLYT
Interactive Flight Technologies, Inc. [*NASDAQ symbol*] (SAG) ... FLYT
Interactive Flight Technologies, Inc. [*Associated Press*] (SAG) ... IntrFlt
Interactive Flight Technologies, Inc. Cl.A [*NASDAQ symbol*] (SAG) ... FLYT
Interactive Flight Technologies, Inc. Cl.A [*Associated Press*] (SAG) ... InFlt
Interactive Flight Technologies, Inc. Cl.A [*Associated Press*] (SAG) ... IntrFlt
Interactive Flight Wrrt'A' [*NASDAQ symbol*] (TTSB) ... FLYTW
Interactive Flight Wrrt'B' [*NASDAQ symbol*] (TTSB) ... FLYTZ
Interactive Flow Simulator (TEL) ... IFS
Interactive Forecasting Model (GFGA) ... IFMOD
Interactive FORTRAN [*Formula Translating System*] [*Computer science*] (IAA) ... IFOR
Interactive FORTRAN [*Formula Translating System*] [*Computer science*] (IAA) ... INFOR
Interactive General Accounting System (MHDB) ... IGAS
Interactive Generalized Modeling System (PDAA) ... IGEMS
Interactive Grafics Digitizer [*Computer science*] ... IGD
Interactive Graphic and Retrieval System ... INGRES
Interactive Graphic Transit Design System (PDAA) ... IGTDS
Interactive Graphic Transit Simulator (PDAA) ... IGTS
Interactive Graphics Analysis ... INGA
Interactive Graphics Design System (MCD) ... IGDS
Interactive Graphics Display Systems [*Computer monitor*] [*Military*] ... IGDS
Interactive Graphics Finite Element System (RDA) ... IGFES
Interactive Graphics Language ... IGL
Interactive Graphics Network System (MCD) ... IGNS
Interactive Graphics Packaging Program [*Computer science*] ... IGPP
Interactive Graphics System [*Computer science*] ... IGS
Interactive Graphics Terminal [*Computer science*] ... IGT
Interactive Group [*NASDAQ symbol*] (TTSB) ... INTE
Interactive Group, Inc. [*NASDAQ symbol*] (SAG) ... INTE
Interactive Group, Inc. [*Associated Press*] (SAG) ... Interact
Interactive Guidance Mode (NASA) ... IGM
Interactive Guidance on Routes [*FHWA*] (TAG) ... IGOR
Interactive Home System (PDAA) ... IHS

Interactive Instructional Presentation System [*IBM*] (NITA) .... IIPS
Interactive Instructional System [*IBM Corp.*] .... IIS
Interactive Instructional Systems-Presentation and Authoring Special Interest Group [*Association for the Development of Computer-Based Instructional Systems*] (EDAC) .... IISPA
Interactive International Banking System [*NCR Corp.*] .... IIBS
Interactive Job Submission [*Computer science*] .... IJS
Interactive Keyboard and Terminal [*Computer science*] (MCD) .... IKAT
Interactive Laboratory System (NITA) .... ILS
Interactive Learning International Corp. .... ILINC
Interactive Mainframe Facility (HGAA) .... IMF
Interactive Maintenance Language [*Denelcor*] (NITA) .... IML
Interactive Man/Computer Augmentation System .... IMCAS
Interactive Manpower Alternatives Processor (DNAB) .... IMAP
Interactive Manufacturing Control System [*NCR Ltd.*] [*Software package*] (NCC) .... IMCS
Interactive Map Definition (IAA) .... IMD
Interactive Market Systems [*New York, NY Information service or system*] (IID) .... IMS
Interactive Mathematics Program [*High school curriculum*] .... IMP
Interactive Med Tech Ltd [*NASDAQ symbol*] (TTSB) .... ITAM
Interactive Media Systems [*Information service or system*] (IID) .... IMS
Interactive Media Technologies, Inc. (NQ) .... IMTX
Interactive Microprogrammable Control (MCD) .... IMP
Interactive Modal Analysis and Gain Estimation for Eigensystem [*NASA digital computer program*] .... IMAGES
Interactive Mode (IAA) .... IM
Interactive Module Controller .... IMC
Interactive Multimedia .... IMM
Interactive Multimedia Association [*Database producer*] (IID) .... IMA
Interactive Multi-Media Exercises [*A Windows-based program*] .... IMMEX
Interactive Multimedia System (MCD) .... IMMS
Interactive Multiple Regression System (MCD) .... IMUR
Interactive Multiprogramming Operating System [*NCR Corp.*] .... IMOS
Interactive Multi-Programming Operating System (PDAA) .... IMPOS
Interactive Network .... IN
Interactive Networks Functioning on Adaptive Neural Topographies [*Robot*] .... INFANT
Interactive Operating System [*Computer science*] .... IOS
Interactive Operations Facility [*Honeywell, Inc.*] .... IOF
Interactive Pattern Analysis and Classification System (PDAA) .... IPACS
Interactive Photorealistic Rendering [*Computer-assisted design*] .... IPR
Interactive Pictures Systems [*In IPS Dance, a computer program for choreographers*] .... IPS
Interactive Planetary Image Processing System .... IPIPS
Interactive Planning System (MHDI) .... IPSY
Interactive Policy Analysis Simulation System [*Department of Agriculture*] .... IPASS
Interactive Population Statistical System [*Computer science*] .... IPSS
Interactive Presentation Graphics [*IBM Corp.*] .... IPG
Interactive Press Kit [*Public relations*] (WDMC) .... IPK
Interactive Problem-Control System [*IBM Corp.*] .... IPCS
Interactive Processing (IAA) .... IP
Interactive Processing and Display System (MCD) .... IPADS
Interactive Productivity Facility (HGAA) .... IPF
Interactive Profiles [*Computer science*] .... I/Pro
Interactive Programming [*Computer science*] .... IAP
Interactive Query and Report Processor [*IBM Corp.*] [*Computer science*] .... IQRP
Interactive Query Facility [*Computer science*] .... IQF
Interactive Query Language [*Digital Equipment Corp.*] [*Computer science*] .... IQL
Interactive Query Pre-Processor (NITA) .... IQPP
Interactive Query System [*Computer science*] (IAA) .... IQS
Interactive Reader Language [*Computer science*] .... IRL
Interactive Real-Time Advanced Display .... INRAD
Interactive Real-Time Information System [*Marine science*] (MSC) .... IRIS
Interactive Real-Time Music Assembler (PDAA) .... IRMA
Interactive Recorded Information Service [*British Telecommunications*] (TEL) .... IRIS
Interactive Remote Job Entry .... IRJE
Interactive Report Definition Facility (MCD) .... IRDF
Interactive Request Modification (IAA) .... IRM
Interactive Resource Executive [*NCR Corp.*] .... IRX
Interactive Retrieval and Text Editor [*Computer science*] (PDAA) .... IRATE
Interactive Root Locus (PDAA) .... IRL
Interactive Route Development and Analysis (CAAL) .... IRDA
Interactive Satellite Education Network [*IBM Corp.*] [*New York, NY*] (TSSD) .... ISEN
Interactive Sciences Corp. [*Information service or system*] (IID) .... ISC
Interactive Screen Definition (IAA) .... ISD
Interactive Search of Bibliographic Files .... ISBF
Interactive Simulation Language [*Computer science*] (IEEE) .... ISL
Interactive Simulation Program with Integrated Circuit Emphasis [*Computer science*] (MHDI) .... ISPICE
Interactive Single Isomorphous Replacement [*Crystallographic procedure*] .... ISIR
Interactive Siting Method (PDAA) .... ISM
Interactive Software Engineering .... ISE
Interactive Solids Modeling System [*Gould Electronics Ltd. Computer Systems*] [*Software package*] (NCC) .... ISMS
Interactive SQL [*Computer science*] .... ISQL
Interactive Structural Layout and Design [*Module*] .... ISLADE
Interactive Structural Sizing and Analysis System [*Computer science*] .... ISSAS
Interactive Survey Analysis (IAA) .... ISA
Interactive Survey Analysis Package (IAA) .... ISAP
Interactive Synthesizer of Letterforms .... ITSYLF
Interactive System for Investigation by Graphics of Hydrological Trends (PDAA) .... INSIGHT
Interactive System for Pattern Analysis, Classification, and Enhancement (PDAA) .... INTERSPACE
Interactive System Productivity Facility [*Computer science*] .... ISPF
Interactive System Productivity Facility/Program Development Facility [*Computer science*] .... ISPF/PDF
Interactive Tech [*NASDAQ symbol*] (TTSB) .... ITNL
Interactive Technologies Corp. [*NASDAQ symbol*] (SAG) .... ITNL
Interactive Technologies Corp., Inc. [*Associated Press*] (SAG) .... InteracT
Interactive Technology Laboratory [*New York Institute of Technology*] [*Research center*] (RCD) .... ITL
Interactive Teleprocessing System (NITA) .... ITPS
Interactive Television .... IT
Interactive Television .... ITV
Interactive Television Association .... ITA
Interactive Television Network [*Dartmouth-Hitchcock Medical Center*] [*Hanover, NH*] [*Telecommunications*] (TSSD) .... INTERACT
Interactive Terminal Display [*Computer science*] (DGA) .... ITD
Interactive Terminal Facility .... ITF
Interactive Terminal Interface [*Computer science*] (IEEE) .... ITI
Interactive Terminal Operating System (NITA) .... ITOS
Interactive Terminal Protocol [*Computer science*] .... ITP
Interactive Terminal Service (NITA) .... ITS
Interactive Terminal Support [*Computer science*] .... ITS
Interactive Test Controller (MHDI) .... INTERTEST
Interactive Test Preparation System [*Computer science*] (MHDI) .... ITPS
Interactive Text Processing System (NITA) .... ITPS
Interactive Textual Information Management Experiment (PDAA) .... INTIME
Interactive Transaction .... ITX
Interactive Transaction Dump Facility [*Computer science*] (MHDB) .... ITDF
Interactive Tsunami Modeling System [*Marine science*] (OSRA) .... ITMS
Interactive Typographic Display [*Computer science*] (DGA) .... ITD
Interactive Vehicle Scheduling System (MHDI) .... IVESS
Interactive Video (PDAA) IV
Interactive Video and Data Service .... IVDS
Interactive Video Association (EA) .... IVA
Interactive Video Enterprises [*US West, Inc.*] (PCM) .... IVE
Interactive Video in Education [*National Interactive Video Centre*] (AIE) .... IVIE
Interactive Video Industry Association (EA) .... IVIA
Interactive Video Service (LAIN) .... IVS
Interactive Video Technology [*Database*] [*Heartland Communications*] [*Information service or system*] (CRD) .... IVT
Interactive Videodisc [*Army*] (INF) .... IAVD
Interactive Videodisc (INF) .... IVD
Interactive Videodisc Consortium [*Defunct*] (EA) IVC
Interactive Videodisc for Special Education Technology (EDAC) .... IVSET
Interactive Voice Response .... IVR
Interactive Voice Response System [*Military*] (INF) .... IVRS
Interactive Voice System [*Electronics*] .... IVS
Interactive Wholesale Distribution System (MHDI) .... IWDS
Interactive Work Station (MHDB) .... IWS
Inter-African Advisory Committee on Epizootic Diseases .... IACED
Inter-African and Malagasy States Organization (NATG) .... IAMSO
Inter-African Bureau for Animal Health and Protection .... IBAHP
Inter-African Bureau for Epizootic Diseases [*Later, IBAR*] .... IBED
Inter-African Bureau of Animal Resources [*Kenya*] .... IBAR
Inter-African Coffee Organization (EAIO) .... IACO
Inter-African Committee for Hydraulic Studies [*See also CIEH*] [*Ouagadougou, Burkina Faso*] (EAIO) .... ICHS
Inter-African Labour Institute ILI
Inter-African Phytosanitary Commission .... IAPSC
Inter-African Phytosanitary Commission .... IPC
Interagency .... INTAGCY
Interagency Advanced Power Group .... IAPG
Interagency Advisory Committee on Security Equipment .... IACSE
Interagency Advisory Group [*Civil Service Commission*] .... IAG
Interagency Agreement (GNE) .... IA
Interagency Agreement .... IAG
Inter-Agency Air Cartographic Committee .... IACC
Interagency Arctic Policy Group [*Marine science*] (OSRA) .... IAPG
Interagency Arctic Policy Group (USDC) .... IAPG
Interagency Arctic Research Coordinating Committee [*Terminated, 1978*] [*National Science Foundation*] .... IARCC
Interagency Assessment Advisory Committee (GNE) .... IAAC
Interagency Board of Examiners [*Civil Service Commission*] .... IAB
Interagency Career Education Committee (OICC) .... ICEC
Interagency Checklist [*United States Employment Service*] (OICC) ICL
Interagency Chemical Rocket Propulsion Group .... ICRPG
Interagency Classification Review Committee [*Abolished, 1978*] [*DoD*] .... ICRC
Interagency Clean Car Advisory Committee [*HEW Terminated*] (EGAO) .... ICCAC
Interagency Collaborative Group on Environmental Carcinogenesis [*Bethesda , MD*] [*National Institutes of Health*] (EGAO) .... ICGEC
Interagency [*or Interdepartmental*] **Committee for Applied Meteorological Research** .... ICAMR
Interagency Committee for Computer Support of Handicapped Employees [*General Services Administration*] (EGAO) .... ICCSHE
Interagency Committee for International Athletics [*Defunct*] .... IACIA
Interagency Committee for Outdoor Recreation [*Department of the Interior*] .... IAC
Interagency Committee for World Weather Programs [*Department of Commerce*] (NOAA) .... ICWWP
Interagency Committee on Automatic Data Processing [*Office of Management and Budget*] .... IAC/ADP
Interagency Committee on Back Contamination [*Aerospace*] .... ICBC

Interagency Committee on Climate Services and Research ... ICCSR
Interagency Committee on Dam Safety [*Federal Emergency Management Agency*] [*Washington, DC*] (EGAO) ... ICODS
Interagency Committee on Environment and Development (EERA) ... IACED
Interagency Committee on Excavation Technology [*Federal Council for Science and Technology*] [*Terminated, 1976*] ... ICET
Interagency Committee on Intelligence ... ICI
Interagency Committee on Intermodal Cargo ... ICIC
Interagency Committee on International Aviation Policy [*Department of State*] (AFM) ... ICIAP
Interagency Committee on Marine Environmental Prediction [*Marine science*] (OSRA) ... ICMAREP
Interagency Committee on Marine Environmental Prediction (USDC) ... ICMAREP
Interagency Committee on Marine Science and Engineering [*Federal Council for Science and Technology*] ... ICMSE
Interagency Committee on Marine Science, Research, Engineering, and Facilities ... ICMREF
Interagency Committee on Medical Records (AAGC) ... ICMR
Interagency Committee on Ocean Exploration and Environmental Services [*Terminated, 1971*] (NOAA) ... ICOEES
Interagency Committee on Ocean Exploration and Environmental Services [*Terminated, 1971*] (EGAO) ... OEES
Interagency Committee on Oceanography [*Later, ICMSE*] ... ICO
Interagency Committee on Product Information (EA) ... ICPI
Interagency Committee on Radiological Assistance ... ICRA
Interagency Committee on the Transportation of Radioactive Materials ... ICTRM
Interagency Committee on Transportation Security [*Department of Transportation*] ... ICOTS
Interagency Committee on Water Resources ... ICWR
Interagency Communications System [*Military*] ... ICS
Interagency Conference (MCD) ... IAC
Inter-Agency Consultative Board (EY) ... IACB
Interagency Contingency Options Plan [*Military*] ... ICOP
Interagency Cooperative Issuances (OICC) ... ICI
Interagency Coordinating Committee for Astronomy [*Federal Council for Science and Technology*] [*Terminated, 1976*] ... ICCA
Interagency Coordinating Committee for Earth Resource Survey Programs [*National Aeronautics and Space Council*] ... ICCERSP
Interagency Coordinating Committee on the Validation of Alternative Methods [*To amend for biological testing*] ... ICCVAM
Interagency Coordinating Committee on US-Soviet Affairs [*Department of State*] ... ICCUSA
Interagency Council on Library Resources for Nursing (EA) ... ICLRN
Interagency Crisis Task Force ... ICTF
Interagency Data Exchange Program [*Later, GIDEP*] (RDA) ... IDEP
Interagency Data Processing Committee ... IADPC
Inter-Agency Data Systems Facility [*General Services Administration*] (MCD) ... IDSF
Interagency Defector Committee ... IDC
Interagency Dialing System [*Telephones*] ... IDS
Interagency Economic Growth Project [*Department of Transportation*] ... IEGP
Interagency Emergency Coordinating Group [*Federal disaster planning*] ... IECG
Interagency Emergency Planning Board [*Federal disaster planning*] ... IEPB
Interagency Emergency Planning Committee ... IEPC
Interagency Emergency Transportation Committee ... IETC
Interagency Energy/Environment Program [*Environmental Protection Agency*] ... IEEP
Interagency Fleet Management System (AAGC) ... IFMS
Interagency Fleet Management System [*GSA*] (TAG) ... IFMS
Interagency Geothermal Coordinating Council ... IGCC
Interagency Grizzly Bear Committee [*Forest Service*] [*Missoula, MT*] (EGAO) ... IGBC
Interagency Grizzly Bear Study Team [*Montana State University*] [*Bozeman, MT*] (EGAO) ... IGBST
Interagency Group [*Federal government*] ... IG
Interagency Group for Computer-Based Training [*Later, IGITT*] (EA) ... IGCBT
Interagency Group for Interactive Training Technologies (EA) ... IGITT
Interagency Group on International Aviation ... IGIA
Interagency Group on International Programs in Atmospheric Science ... IGIPAS
Interagency Integrated Pest Management Coordinating Committee [*Terminated, 1980*] [*Council on Environmental Quality*] (EGAO) ... IMP
Interagency Intelligence Memorandum (MCD) ... IIM
Interagency Interim National Research and Education Network (TNIG) ... IINREN
Interagency Life Sciences Supporting Space Research and Technology Exchange ... ILSE
Interagency Map and Publications Acquisitions Committee [*Department of State*] [*Washington, DC*] ... IMPAC
Interagency Materials Sciences Exchange ... IMSE
Interagency Mechanical Operations Group [*Lawrence Livermore Laboratory*] ... IMOG
Inter-Agency Meeting on Language Arrangements, Documentation, and Publications [*United Nations*] ... IAMLADP
Interagency Monitoring of Protected Visual Environments [*Marine science*] (OSRA) ... IMPROVE
Interagency Monitoring of Protected Visual Environments (USDC) ... IMPROVE
Inter-Agency Motor Pool (WDAA) ... IAMP
Inter-Agency Network Safety Review Panel [*NASA*] (NASA) ... INSRP
Interagency Noise Abatement Program ... IANAP
Interagency Nuclear Safety Review Pane (USDC) ... INSRP
Interagency Nuclear Safety Review Panel ... INSRP
Interagency Oil Policy Committee ... IOPC
Interagency Placement Assistance Program [*Office of Personnel Management*] ... IPAP
Interagency Primate Steering Committee [*National Institutes of Health*] ... IPSC
Interagency Radiological Assistance Program [*Nuclear Regulatory Commission*] (NRCH) ... IRAP
Interagency Rate (AFM) ... IAR
Interagency Regulatory Group ... IRG
Interagency Regulatory Liaison Group [*Comprising several federal agencies*] [*Terminated, 1981*] ... IRLG
Interagency Rehabilitation Research Information System [*National Institute on Disability and Rehabilitation Research*] [*Washington, DC Information service or system*] (IID) ... IRRI
Interagency Report (PDAA) ... IR
Interagency Report Control Number ... IRCN
Interagency Research Animal Committee [*Department of Health and Human Services*] (GFGA) ... IRAC
Interagency Review Group [*Nuclear Regulatory Commission*] (NRCH) ... IRG
Interagency Risk Management Council [*Environmental Protection Agency*] (EPA) ... IRMC
Interagency Solar Terrestrial Programme [*European Space Agency*] ... ISTP
Interagency Source Register [*Intelligence*] (MCD) ... ISR
Interagency Staff Committee on Public Law 480 [*Department of Agriculture*] (EGAO) ... ISC
Interagency Task Force [*for Indochina*] [*South Vietnam refugee relief*] ... IATF
Interagency Task Force (AAGC) ... ITF
Interagency Taxonomy Information System [*A database of all the flora and fauna in North America*] [*Created by the EPA and other agencies*] ... ITIS
Interagency Testing Committee [*Toxicology*] ... ITC
Interagency Textile Administrative Committee ... ITAC
Interagency Toxic Substances Data Committee [*Washington, DC*] [*Environmental Protection Agency*] (EGAO) ... ITSDC
Interagency Trade Data Advisory Committee [*Department of Commerce*] (EGAO) ... ITDAC
Interagency Working Group (MCD) ... IAWG
Inter-Agency Working Group on Southern Africa [*Canadian Council for International Cooperation*] ... IAWGSA
Interagency Zero-Based Budgeting [*Federal government*] ... IZBB
Interair Aviation Ltd. [*British ICAO designator*] (FAAC) ... INA
Inter-Air, Inc. [*ICAO designator*] (FAAC) ... ITA
Inter-Allied Aeronautical Commission of Control ... IAACC
Inter-Allied Committee on Post-War Requirements [*World War II*] ... IACPWR
Interallied Confederation of Reserve Officers [*See also CIOR*] (EAIO) ... ICRO
Interallied Force [*NATO*] (NATG) ... IAF
Inter-Allied Insurance Organization [*NATO*] (NATG) ... IIO
Inter-Allied Nuclear Force (AABC) ... IANF
Inter-Allied Personnel Board [*World War II*] ... IAPB
Inter-Allied Postwar Requirements Bureau [*World War II*] ... IPRB
Inter-Allied Reparations Agency [*Brussels*] ... IARA
Interallied Staff Communications Board [*World War II*] ... ISCB
Interallied Tactical Study Group [*NATO*] (NATG) ... INTASGRO
Inter-Alpha-Trypsin Inhibitor (DMAA) ... IATI
Inter-America Bank (WDAA) ... IAB
Interamerican Accounting Association [*Mexico City, Mexico*] (EA) ... IAA
Inter-American Accounting Association ... IAAA
Inter-American Air Force Academy [*Operated by US Air Force to provide training for Latin American countries*] ... IAAFA
Inter-American Association for Democracy and Freedom (EA) ... IADF
Inter-American Association of Broadcasters [*Later, IAB-AIR*] ... IAAB
Inter-American Association of Gastroenterology (EA) ... IAAG
Inter-American Association of Industrial Property [*See also ASIPA*] [*Buenos Aires, Argentina*] (EAIO) ... IAAIP
Inter-American Association of Sanitary Engineering [*Later, Inter-American Association of Sanitary and Environmental Engineering*] (EA) ... IAASE
Inter-American Association of Sanitary Engineering and Environmental Sciences (EAIO) ... IAASEES
Inter-American Bank Bond (MHDW) ... IABB
Inter-American Bank for Latin America (WDAA) ... IABLA
Inter-American Bar Association (EA) ... IABA
Inter-American Bar Foundation (EA) ... IABF
Inter-American Bibliographical and Library Association (EA) ... IBLA
Inter-American Cement Federation [*Colombia*] (EAIO) ... IACF
Inter-American Center for Agricultural Documentation and Information (NITA) ... ICADI
Inter-American Center for Integral Development [*OAS*] ... IACID
Inter-American Center for Regional Development (EAIO) ... IACRD
Inter-American Centre for Research and Documentation on Vocational Training [*See also CINTERFOR*] [*Montevideo, Uruguay*] (EAIO) ... IACRDVT
Inter-American Children's Institute [*Uruguay*] [*Research center*] (IRC) ... IACI
Inter-American Children's Institute [*OAS*] ... ICI
Inter-American College Association (EA) ... IACA
Interamerican College of Physicians and Surgeons (EA) ... ICPS
Inter-American Commercial Arbitration Commission (EA) ... I-ACAC
Inter-American Commission of Women [*Organization of American States*] [*Washington, DC*] ... IACW
Inter-American Commission of Women [*OAS*] ... ICW
Inter-American Commission on Human Rights (EA) ... IACHR
Inter-American Commission on Human Rights [*OAS*] (PD) ... ICHR
Inter-American Committee for Science and Technology ... IACST
Inter-American Committee for the Alliance for Progress [*Superseded by Permanent Executive Committee of the Inter-American Economic and Social Council*] ... ICAP
Inter-American Committee of Presidential Representatives ... IACPR
Inter-American Committee on Peaceful Settlement [*Defunct Defunct*] (EA) ... IACPS
Inter-American Committee on Science and Technology [*Organization of American States*] (ASF) ... CICYT

Inter-American Confederation for Catholic Education [*Bogota, Colombia*] (EAIO) .... IACCE
Interamerican Confederation of Cattlemen (EA) .... IACC
Inter-American Conference on Social Security [*See also CISS*] [*Mexico City, Mexico*] (EAIO) .... IACSS
Inter-American Congress of Radiology .... IACR
Inter-American Cooperative Institute ICI
Inter-American Council .... IAC
Inter-American Council for Education, Science, and Culture .... IACESC
Inter-American Council of Commerce and Production .... IACCP
Inter-American Council of Jurists [*Organization of American States*] [*Washington, DC*] .... IACJ
Inter-American Council of Psychiatric Associations (DAVI) .... IACPA
Inter-American Cultural Association (EA) .... IACA
Inter-American Cultural Council (EA) .... IACC
Inter-American Cultural Council ICC
Inter-American Defense Board (EA) .... IADB
Inter-American Defense Board (EA) .... IDB
Inter-American Defense Board Medal [*Military decoration*] .... IADB-MED
Inter-American Defense College [*Washington, DC*] .... IADC
Inter-American Defense College, Fort McNair, Washington, DC [*Library symbol Library of Congress*] (LCLS) .... DIAD
Inter-American Development Bank [*Also, IDB*] .... IADB
Inter-American Development Bank [*Also, IADB*] .... IDB
Inter-American Development Bank, Washington, DC [*OCLC symbol*] (OCLC) .... BID
Inter-American Development Bank, Washington, DC [*Library symbol Library of Congress*] (LCLS) .... DIDB
Inter-American Development Bank's Wives Association (EA) .... IADBWA
Inter-American Development Commission .... IADC
Inter-American Driving Permit .... IADP
Inter-American Economic and Social Council [*United Nations*] .... IAECOSOC
Inter-American Economic and Social Council [*United Nations*] .... IAESC
Inter-American Education Association (EA) .... IAEA
Inter-American Emergency Advisory Committee for Political Defense .... IAEACPD
Inter-American Federation for Adult Education .... IAFAE
Inter-American Federation of Entertainment Workers .... IFEW
Interamerican Federation of Public Relations Associations .... IFPRA
Inter-American Federation of the Construction Industry [*See also FIIC*] [*Mexico City, Mexico*] (EAIO) .... IAFCI
Inter-American Federation of Touring and Automobile Clubs [*See also FITAC*] (EAIO) .... IFTAC
Inter-American Federation of Working Newspapermen's Organizations .... IAFWNO
Inter-American Foundation (MCD) .... IAF
Inter-American Foundation for the Arts [*Defunct*] .... IAFA
Inter-American Freight Conference - Section C (EA) .... IAFC
Inter-American Geodetic Survey .... IAGS
Inter-American Hospital Association [*Defunct*] .... IAHA
Inter-American Hotel Association .... IAHA
Inter-American Human Rights Commission .... IAHRC
Inter-American Indian Institute [*OAS*] [*Mexico City, Mexico*] (EA) .... IAII
Inter-American Indian Institute [*OAS*] III
Inter-American Institute (USDC) .... IAI
Interamerican Institute for Cooperation on Agriculture [*Formerly, IAIAS*] (EA) .... IICA
Inter-American Institute for Global Change Research [*Marine science*] (OSRA) .... IAI
Inter-American Institute for Global Change Research (USDC) .... IAI
Inter-American Institute of Agricultural Sciences [*Later, IICA*] [*OAS*] .... IAIAS
Inter-American Institute of Ecology [*Ecological Society of America*] .... IAIE
Inter-American Institute of Ecology [*Ecological Society of America*] .... IIE
Inter-American Institute of Human Rights [*See also IIDS*] [*San Jose, Costa Rica*] (EAIO) .... IIHR
Inter-American Juridical Committee .... IAJC
Interamerican Labour Institute ILI
Inter-American Legal Services Association (EA) .... ILSA
Inter-American Literacy Foundation (EA) .... IALF
Inter-American Markets Corp. [*Latin America*] .... IAMC
Interamerican Medical and Health Association (EA) .... IMHA
Inter-American Municipal Organization .... IMO
Inter-American Music Council (EAIO) .... IAMC
Interamerican Naval Coordinating Authority (CINC) .... IANCA
Inter-American Naval Telecommunications Network (MCD) .... IANTN
Inter-American Nuclear Energy Commission [*Organization of American States*] (NRCH) .... IANEC
Inter-American Organization for Higher Education [*See also OUI*] .... IOHE
Inter-American Parliamentary Group on Population and Development (EA) .... IAPGPD
Inter-American Peace Committee [*Later, Inter-American Committee on Peaceful Settlement*] [*OAS*] .... IAPC
Inter-American Peacekeeping Force .... IAPF
Inter-American Police Academy (AABC) .... IAPA
Inter-American Press Association (EA) .... IAPA
Interamerican Press Association .... IPA
Interamerican Program for Linguistics and Language Teaching (EA) .... IAPLLT
Inter-American Program for Social Progress [*AID*] .... IAPSP
Interamerican Regional Organization of the International Federation of Commercial, Clerical, Professional, and Technical Employees [*Willemstad, Netherlands Antilles*] (EAIO) .... IRO-FIET
Inter-American Safety Council (EA) .... IASC
Inter-American Scout Committee [*See also CIE*] [*San Jose, Costa Rica*] (EAIO) .... IASC
Inter-American Social Development Institute [*Later, IAF*] .... IASDI

Inter-American Society of Cardiology [*Mexico City, Mexico*] (EAIO) .... ISC
Interamerican Society of Psychology (EA) .... ISP
Inter-American Statistical Institute (EA) .... IASI
Inter-American Statistical Institute .... IASI
Inter-American Statistical Teaching Center .... IASC
Inter-American System .... IAS
Inter-American Technical Council on Archives (DIT) .... ITCA
Inter-American Telecommunications Commission .... IATC
Inter-American Telecommunications Union [*US*] .... IATU
Interamerican Textile, Leather, Garment, and Shoe Workers Federation (EA) .... ITLGSWF
Inter-American Translators Association [*Defunct*] (EA) .... AIT
Inter-American Travel Agents Society (EA) .... ITAS
Inter-American Travel Congresses (EA) .... CIT
Inter-American Travel Congresses .... IATC
Inter-American Travel Congresses .... ITC
Inter-American Tropical Tuna Commission (EA) .... IATTC
Inter-American Tropical Tuna Commission [*Scripps Institution of Oceanography*] .... ITTC
Interamerican Underwater Festival .... IAUF
Interamerican Underwater Festival .... IUF
Inter-American University Association .... IUA
Inter-American University Council for Economic and Social Development (EA) .... IUCESD
Inter-American University of Puerto Rico, San Juan Campus, San Juan, PR [*Library symbol Library of Congress*] (LCLS) .... PrIAU-SJ
Inter-American War Game (MCD) .... IAWG
Interamericana de Aviacion Ltda. [*Colombia*] [*ICAO designator*] (FAAC) .... IIA
InterAmericas Communications Corp. [*NASDAQ symbol*] (SAG) .... ICCA
InterAmericas Communications Corp. [*Associated Press*] (SAG) .... IntACom
Interapplication Communication [*Apple Computer, Inc.*] .... IAC
Interapplication Communication Architecture [*Computer science*] (BTTJ) .... ICA
InterApplication Communications [*Computer science*] (CDE) .... IAC
Inter-Applications Communication [*Computer science*] (EERA) .... IAC
Interarray Communications (NVT) .... IAC
Interarray Processor (NVT) .... IAP
Inter-Asia Equities [*Vancouver Stock Exchange symbol*] .... IAE
Inter-Association Commission on Tsunami [*Brussels, Belgium*] (EAIO) .... IACT
Inter-Association Committee on Health .... IACH
Inter-Association Group .... IAG
Inter-Association Task Force on Alcohol Issues (EA) .... IATFAI
Interatrial Septal Aneurysm [*Medicine*] (DMAA) .... IASA
Interatrial Septal Defect [*Cardiology*] .... IASD
Interatrial Septum [*Cardiology*] (MAE) .... IAS
Interatrial Shunting [*Medicine*] (DMAA) .... IAS
Interaural Amplitude Modulation [*Audiology*] .... IAM
Interaural Intensity Disparity [*Audiology*] .... IID
Interaural Phase Disparity [*Audiology*] .... IPD
Interaural Phase Modulation [*Audiology*] .... IPM
Interaural Time Difference [*Andiology*] .... ITD
Interavia Aerospace Review [*Interavia Publications*] [*Information service or system*] (CRD) .... IAR
Interavia Space Markets [*Interavia Publications*] [*Information service or system*] (CRD) .... ISM
Interband Magneto-Optic [*Effect*] (DEN) .... IMO
Interbank [*Credit cards*] I
Interbank (ADA) .... IK
Interbank Card Association [*Mastercard International*] (EA) .... ICA
Interbank Merchants Association [*Pigeon Forge, TN*] (EA) .... IMA
Interbank National Authorization System .... INAS
Interbank Network for Electronic Transfer .... INET
Interbed-Storage Package [*Geological program*] .... IBS
Interbev Packaging Corp. [*Vancouver Stock Exchange symbol*] .... INB
Interblock Communication Word (IAA) .... ICW
Interboard Committee for Christian Work in Japan [*Later, JNAC*] (EA) .... IBC
Interbomb Spacing (DNAB) .... IBS
Interboro Rapid Transit [*A New York City subway line*] .... IRT
Inter-Borough Nomination Scheme [*British*] (DI) .... IBNS
Interbrasil Star, SA [*Brazil*] [*FAA designator*] (FAAC) .... ITB
Inter-Bureau Citation of Funds [*Navy*] .... ICF
Interbureau Insurance Advisory Group .... IIAG
Interburst Interval [*Electrophysiology*] .... IBI
Inter-Byte Separation [*Automotive engineering Electronics*] .... IBS
Inter-Byte Spacing [*Computer science*] .... IBS
Intercalated Polymer-Derived Carbon [*Chemistry*] .... IPC
Inter-California Line in Mexico R. R. [*AAR code*] .... ICLM
Intercampus Committee for Handicapped Students (EA) .... ICCHS
Intercan Leasing, Inc. [*Toronto Stock Exchange symbol*] ILI
Inter-Canadian [*ICAO designator*] (FAAC) .... ICN
Intercanthal Distance [*Anatomy*] .... ICD
Intercapillary Glomerulosclerosis (PDAA) .... IGS
InterCapital Cal Ins Muni Inc. [*NYSE symbol*] (TTSB) IIC
InterCapital Cal Qual Muni Sec [*NYSE symbol*] (TTSB) .... IQC
InterCapital California Insurance Municipal Income Fund [*NYSE symbol*] (SPSG) IIC
Intercapital California Insured Municipal Income Trust [*Associated Press*] (SAG) .... IntrCal
InterCapital California Quality Municipal Securities [*NYSE symbol*] (SPSG) .... IQC
Intercapital California Quality Municipal Security Trust [*Associated Press*] (SAG) .... IntCAQI
InterCapital Income Securities, Inc. [*NYSE symbol*] (SPSG) .... ICB
Intercapital Income Securities, Inc. [*Associated Press*] (SAG) .... ItcpSe
InterCapital Inc. Sec [*NYSE symbol*] (TTSB) .... ICB
InterCapital Ins Cal Muni Sec [*NYSE symbol*] (TTSB) .... ICS

InterCapital Ins Muni Bd Fd [*NYSE symbol*] (TTSB) .... IMB
InterCapital Ins Muni Income [*NYSE symbol*] (TTSB) .... IIM
InterCapital Ins Muni Sec [*NYSE symbol*] (TTSB) .... IMS
InterCapital Ins Muni Tr [*NYSE symbol*] (TTSB) .... IMT
InterCapital Insurance Municipal Bond Fund [*NYSE symbol*] (SPSG) .... IMB
Intercapital Insurance Municipal Bond Fund [*Associated Press*] (SAG) .... IntcapIn
InterCapital Insurance Municipal Income Fund [*NYSE symbol*] (SPSG) .... IIM
InterCapital Insured California Municipal Securities [*NYSE symbol*] (SAG) .... ICS
InterCapital Insured California Municipal Securities [*Associated Press*] (SAG) .... IntIns CA
Intercapital Insured Municipal Income Trust [*Associated Press*] (SAG) ..... IntcpIM
InterCapital Insured Municipal Securities [*NYSE symbol*] (SAG) .... IMS
InterCapital Insured Municipal Securities [*Associated Press*] (SAG) .... IntcapIns
InterCapital Insured Municipal Trust [*NYSE symbol*] (SAG) .... IMT
Intercapital Insured Municipal Trust [*Associated Press*] (SAG) .... IntIMT
Intercapital New York Quality Municipal Securities [*NYSE symbol*] (SAG) ..... IQN
Intercapital New York Quality Municipal Security Trust [*Associated Press*] (SAG) .... IntNYQ
InterCapital N.Y.Qual Muni Sec [*NYSE symbol*] (TTSB) .... IQN
InterCapital Qual Muni Income [*NYSE symbol*] (TTSB) .... IQI
InterCapital Qual Muni Inv [*NYSE symbol*] (TTSB) .... IQT
InterCapital Qual Muni Sec [*NYSE symbol*] (TTSB) .... IQM
InterCapital Quality Municipal Income [*NYSE symbol*] (SPSG) .... IQI
Intercapital Quality Municipal Income Trust [*Associated Press*] (SAG) ...... IQMInc
Intercapital Quality Municipal Investment Trust [*Associated Press*] (SAG) .... IQMInv
Intercapital Quality Municipal Investment Trust [*NYSE symbol*] (SPSG) .... IQT
InterCapital Quality Municipal Securities [*NYSE symbol*] (SPSG) .... IQM
InterCapital Quality Municipal Securities [*Associated Press*] (SAG) .... IQMSec
Intercardia, Inc. [*Associated Press*] (SAG) .... Intcardia
Intercardia, Inc. [*NASDAQ symbol*] (SAG) .... ITRC
Intercardia Inc. [*NASDAQ symbol*] (TTSB) .... ITRC
Intercargo Corp. [*NASDAQ symbol*] (NQ) .... ICAR
Intercargo Corp. [*Associated Press*] (SAG) .... Intrcrgo
Intercarrier Interface (ACRL) ICI
Intercarrier Sound (IAA) .... ICS
Intercel, Inc. [*NASDAQ symbol*] (SAG) .... ICEL
Intercel, Inc. [*Associated Press*] (SAG) .... Intercel
Intercellular Adhesion Molecule [*Biochemistry*] .... ICAM
Intercellular Space (DMAA) .... ICS
Inter-Celtic Society (EAIO) .... ICS
Inter-Center Data Link (MCD) .... ICDL
Inter-Center Vector (MCD) ICV
Intercept .... INCPT
Intercept [*or Interceptor*] (CINC) .... INT
Intercept (GAVI) .... INTC
Intercept (AFM) .... INTCP
Intercept [*Telecommunications*] (TEL) .... ITC
Intercept Arm (MUGU) .... IA
Intercept Controller IC
Intercept Deployment Plan [*National Security Agency*] .... IDP
Intercept Direction (SAA) .... ID
Intercept Director [*Military*] .... IND
Intercept Distance Aid (SAA) .... IDA
Intercept During Boost [*Aerospace*] .... IDB
Intercept During Reentry [*Aerospace*] (IAA) .... IDR
Intercept During Unpowered Rise [*Aerospace*] (IAA) .... IDUR
Intercept Ground Optical Recorder [*NASA*] .... IGOR
Intercept Ground Optical Recorder Tracking Telescope [*NASA*] .... IGORTT
Intercept Monitoring Display .... IMD
Intercept Officer .... IO
Intercept Point [*Air Force*] .... IP
Intercept Priorities Board [*Armed Forces Security Agency*] .... IPB
Intercept Range .... INTCP RNG
Intercept System Environment [*Army*] (AABC) .... ISE
Intercept Target Optical Reader .... ITOR
Intercept Tracking and Control Group .... INTAC
Intercept-Aerial [*Missile mission symbol*] I
Intercepted Photosynthetically Active Radiation [*Photosynthesis*] .... IPAR
Interception [*Football*] .... IN
Interception [*Football*] .... INTER
Interception Mission [*Air Force*] .... INM
Interception with Satellite Tracking .... INSATRAC
Interceptor [*Aircraft*] .... F
Interceptor I
Interceptor .... INCEP
Interceptor Aim Points .... IAP
Interceptor Command IC
Interceptor Computer (IAA) IC
Interceptor Day Fighter (NATG) .... IDF
Interceptor Director Technician (SAA) .... INDT
Interceptor Distance Computer .... IDC
Interceptor Generation and Umpiring Program (SAA) .... IGAUP
Interceptor Identification Capability IIC
Interceptor Improvement Program .... IIP
Interceptor Launch Module [*Military*] .... ILM
Interceptor Missile .... IM
Interceptor Missile (IAA) .... IMS
Interceptor Missile Direction Center .... IMDC
Interceptor Missile Interrogation RADAR .... IMIR
Interceptor Missile Squadron and Supervisory Control Equipment .... IMSSCE
Interceptor Missile Squadron Operations Center [*Air Force*] .... IMSOC
Interceptor Missile Squadron Supervisory Station .... IMSSS
Interceptor Missile, Surface-to-Air-Missile (MCD) .... IMSAM
Interceptor Mission Sheet (SAA) .... IMS
Interceptor Monitor and Controller .... IMC
Interceptor Night Fighter (NATG) .... INF
Interceptor Operator Simulator (IAA) .... IOS
Interceptor Pilot Research Laboratory (SAA) .... IPRL
Interceptor Pilot Simulator [*SSTM*] .... IPS
Interceptor Reaction Control System .... IRCS
Interceptor Simulator (SAA) .... INS
Interceptor Subsystem Controller .... ISC
Interceptor Tactical Missile [*Air Force*] .... ITM
Interceptor Technology Integration .... ITI
Interceptor Technology Program .... ITP
Interceptor/Transporter/Loader .... ITL
Interceptor Trap .... IT
Interceptor Vehicle IV
Interceptor Weapon Control System .... IWCS
Interceptor Weapons Instructor School [*Air Force*] .... IWIS
Intercessors for America (EA) .... IA
Intercessors for America (EA) .... IFA
Interchange .... I/C
Interchange .... ICH
Interchange .... INT
Interchange .... INTRCHNG
Interchange Address (NITA) .... IA
Interchange Center IC
Interchange Data Element [*Telecommunications*] (OSI) .... IDE
Interchange File Format [*Computer science*] .... IFF
Interchange File Separator [*Computer science*] (BUR) .... IFS
Interchange Financial Services Corp. [*Associated Press*] (SAG) .... InFinSv
Interchange Financial Services Corp. [*Formerly, Interchange State Bank*] [*AMEX symbol*] (SPSG) .... ISB
Interchange Finl Svcs [*AMEX symbol*] (TTSB) .... ISB
Interchange Group Separator [*Computer science*] (BUR) .... IGS
Interchange of Scientific and Technical Information in Machine Language [*Office of Science and Technology*] .... ISTIM
Interchange: Papers on Biblical and Current Questions [*A publication*] (APTA) .... Int
Interchange Record Separator [*Computer science*] (BUR) .... IRS
Interchange Resource Center (EA) .... IRC
Interchange Unit Selector (NITA) .... IUS
Interchange Unit Separator [*Computer science*] (BUR) .... IUS
Interchange Units Separation (ECII) .... IVS
Interchangeability (AAG) I
Interchangeability .... Ity
Interchangeability and Replaceability [*or Replacement*] (AAG) .... I & R
Interchangeability and Substitutability (AFM) .... I & S
Interchangeability and Substitutability Item Subgroup (MCD) .... ISIS
Interchangeability and Substitution .... IS
Interchangeability Control Tool (MCD) .... ICT
Interchangeability Document Change Notice (KSC) .... IDCN
Interchangeability Document Change Request (MCD) .... IDCR
Interchangeability Survey Board .... ISB
Interchangeability Test (MCD) .... ICT
Interchangeable (MSA) .... INTCHG
Interchangeable Alternate .... IA
Interchangeable and Substitute Group [*Military*] (AFIT) .... ISG
Interchangeable at Attachment Point Only (AAG) .... IAPO
Interchangeable Control Media (MCD) .... ICM
Interchangeable Cycle Check (MCD) ICC
Interchangeable Solid and Screen Panels [*Technical drawings*] .... IP
Interchangeable With (AAG) .... I/W
Interchangeable-Substitute Items (AAG) .... INS
Interchanger (NASA) .... ICH
Interchanger (NASA) .... INTCHGR
Interchannel Communicator (MCD) ICC
Inter-Channel Comparison Unit [*Nuclear energy*] (NRCH) .... ICCU
Interchannel Master Pulse .... ICMP
Interchannel Time Base Error (IAA) .... ITBE
Inter-Channel Time Displacement .... ICTD
Interchannel Time Displacement [*Magnetic recording*] .... ITD
Interchannel Time Displacement Error [*Magnetic recording*] .... ITDE
Interchemical Printing Inks .... IPI
Interchromatin Granular Cluster [*Cytology*] .... IGS
[*The*] **Interchurch Center** (EA) .... TIC
Inter-Church Committee on Human Rights in Latin America [*Canada*] (EAIO) .... ICCHRLA
Interchurch Medical Assistance (EA) .... IMA
Interchurch Response for the Horn of Africa (EA) .... IRHA
Interchurch Transportation Council [*Defunct*] (EA) .... ITC
Interciencia Association [*Caracas, Venezuela*] (EAIO) .... IA
Intercistronic Spacer [*Genetics*] .... ICS
Intercity [*ICAO designator*] (AD) .... YI
Intercity Airways [*Australia*] .... IA
Inter-City Products [*AMEX symbol*] (TTSB) .... IPR
Inter-City Products Corp. [*Associated Press*] (SAG) .... InCtPd
Inter-City Products Corp. [*AMEX symbol*] (SPSG) .... IPR
Intercity Relay [*Broadcasting*] (NTCM) .... ICR
Inter-City Short Takeoff and Landing [*Aviation*] .... INTERSTOL
Intercity Transportation Efficiency (OA) .... ITE
Intercity Voice Network [*FTS*] (DNAB) .... IVN
Interclick Interval [*Entomology*] ICI
Interco, Inc. [*Formerly, International Shoe Co.*] [*Associated Press*] (SAG) .... Interco
INTERCO, Inc. [*Formerly, International Shoe Co.*] [*NYSE symbol*] (SPSG) .... ISS
Intercoastal Steamship Freight Association (EA) .... ISFA
Intercoastal Steamship Freight Association, New York NY [*STAC*] .... ISA
Intercoastal Waterway .... ICW

Intercockpit Communications System [*Navy*] (DOMA) ... ICS
Intercoiffure America (EA) ... IA
Intercollegiate Association for Study of the Alcohol Problem (EA) ... IASAP
Intercollegiate Association of Amateur Athletes of America (EA) ... IAAAA
Intercollegiate Association of Amateur Athletes of America [*Also, IAAAA, ICAAAA*] ... IC4A
Intercollegiate Association of Amateur Athletes of America [*Also, IAAAA, IC4A*] (EA) ... ICAAAA
Intercollegiate Association of Women Students (AEBS) ... IAWS
Intercollegiate Broadcasting System (EA) ... IBS
Intercollegiate Conference of Faculty Representatives (EA) ... ICFR
Intercollegiate Dramatic Association [*Defunct*] (EA) ... IDA
Intercollegiate Fencing Association (EA) ... IFA
Intercollegiate Horse Show Association (EA) ... IHSA
Intercollegiate Ice Hockey Association [*Later, ECHA*] (EA) ... IIHA
Intercollegiate Knights [*An association*] (EA) ... IK
Intercollegiate Men's Chorus, a National Association of Male Choruses (EA) ... IMC
Intercollegiate Opera Group [*Defunct*] (EA) ... IOG
Intercollegiate Outing Club Association (EA) ... IOCA
Intercollegiate Program of Graduate Studies ... IPGS
Intercollegiate Rowing Association (EA) ... IRA
Intercollegiate Soccer Association of America (EA) ... ISAA
Intercollegiate Soccer-Football Association of America [*Later, ISAA*] (EA) ... ISFAA
Intercollegiate Studies Institute (EA) ... ISI
Intercollegiate Tennis Coaches Association (EA) ... ITCA
Intercollegiate Women's Fencing Association [*Later, NIWFA*] ... IWFA
Inter-Collegiate Yacht Racing Association [*of North America*] [*Later, ICYRA/NA*] ... ICYRA
Inter-Collegiate Yacht Racing Association of North America (EA) ... ICYRA/NA
Intercolonial (ADA) ... INTERCOL
Intercolonial Railway [*1858-1923*] [*Canada*] ... ICR
Intercom (KSC) ... I/C
Intercom Information Resources, Inc. [*Information service or system*] (IID) ... IIR
Intercomm Users' Group (EA) ... IUG
Intercommunication (MSA) ... ICM
Intercommunication Control Station (KSC) ... ICS
Intercommunication Devices (MCD) ... ID
Intercommunication Drum (MSA) ... IC DRUM
Intercommunication Flip-Flop [*Computer science*] ... ICF
Intercommunication Logic ... ICL
Intercommunication Service System Inc. [*Information service or system*] (IID) ... ISS
Intercommunication System ... INTERCOM
Intercommunication Teleprocessing Monitor (IAA) ... ITM
Intercommunication-Communication Control Group [*Navy*] (NVT) ... ICCG
Intercommunications ... IC
Intercommunications (NASA) ... ICOM
Intercommunications/Emergency Station (MCD) ... IC/ES
Intercommunications System ... ICS
Intercommunicator ... I/C
Inter-Community Memorial Hospital, Newfane, NY [*Library symbol Library of Congress*] (LCLS) ... NNefH
Intercomp Design, Inc. [*Neshanic Station, NJ*] [*Telecommunications*] (TSSD) ... IDI
Intercompany Agreement (IAA) ... ICA
Inter-Company Correspondence ... ICC
Intercompany Data Requirements List (MCD) ... IDRL
Intercompany Services Coordination [*Telecommunications*] (TEL) ... ISC
Intercompany Services Coordination/Universal Service Order [*Telecommunications*] (TEL) ... ISC/USO
Intercomplex Radio Communications System (IAA) ... IRCS
Intercomponent Subcontractor (MCD) ... ISC
Intercomponent Work Order ... ICWO
Inter-Component Work Transmitted (MCD) ... ICWT
Intercomputer (MCD) ... IC
Intercomputer Adapter ... ICA
Intercomputer Channel (KSC) ... IC
Intercomputer Channel (NASA) ... ICC
Intercomputer Communication (MCD) ... ICC
Intercomputer Communication Logic (NITA) ... ICL
Intercomputer Communication System ... ICCS
Intercomputer Communication Unit (IAA) ... ICCU
Intercomputer Compatibility Unit [*Computer science*] ... ICCU
Intercomputer Coupler (IAA) ... ICC
Intercomputer Electronics (IAA) ... ICE
Intercon Petroleum, Inc. [*Vancouver Stock Exchange symbol*] ... ITP
Interconexion Electrica, Sociedad Anonima ... ISA
Interconnect Backplane Capability ... IBC
Interconnect Carrier [*Telecommunications*] ... IC
Interconnect Device Arrangement (HGAA) ... IDA
Interconnect Facility ... ICF
Interconnect Group (CAAL) ... IG
Interconnected Business System ... ICBS
Interconnected Porosity Level ... IPL
Interconnected Systems Group ... ISG
Interconnecting Digital-Analog Converter (NG) ... IDAC
Interconnecting Network (MHDI) ... IN
Interconnecting Station (MCD) ... IS
Interconnection (IAA) ... IC
Interconnection (MSA) ... INTCON
Interconnection (KSC) ... INTERCON
Interconnection and Program Bay (IAA) ... IPB
Interconnection Device (MCD) ... ID
Interconnection Diagram (IAA) ... ID
Interconnection Equipment ... IE
Interconnection Unit [*Computer science*] ... ICU
Interconnections Packaging Circuitry (MCD) ... IPC
Intercontinental ... INTCNTL
Intercontinental ... INTERCON
Inter-Continental Aerospacecraft-Range Unlimited System ... ICARUS
Intercontinental Airlines Ltd. [*Nigeria*] [*ICAO designator*] (FAAC) ... VVV
Intercontinental Areas (Eastern Hemisphere) [*MARC geographic area code Library of Congress*] (LCCP) ... m-----
Intercontinental Areas (Western Hemisphere) [*MARC geographic area code Library of Congress*] (LCCP) ... c-----
Intercontinental Ballistic Missile ... IBM
Intercontinental Ballistic Missile ... ICBM
Intercontinental Ballistic Missile Operational Capability (AAG) ... IBMOC
Intercontinental Ballistic Missile System ... ICBMS
Intercontinental Ballistic Missile Test Maintenance Squadron ... ICBMTMS
Intercontinental Ballistic Transport ... ICBT
Intercontinental Bank [*NASDAQ symbol*] (SAG) ... ICBK
Intercontinental Bank [*Associated Press*] (SAG) ... IntctlBk
Intercontinental Church Society [*British*] (EAIO) ... ICS
Intercontinental Cruise Missile (IAA) ... ICCM
Intercontinental Data [*Vancouver Stock Exchange symbol*] ... ITD
Intercontinental Data Control Corp. Ltd. [*Ottawa, ON*] [*Telecommunications*] (TSSD) ... INTERDACO
Intercontinental de Aviacion Ltd. [*Colombia*] [*ICAO designator*] (FAAC) ... ICT
Inter-Continental Energy [*Vancouver Stock Exchange symbol*] ... ITG
Intercontinental Glide Bomber [*Unmanned*] ... IGB
Intercontinental Glide [*or Guided*] **Missile** (KSC) ... ICGM
Intercontinental Jet Unmanned Bomber ... ICJUB
Intercontinental Life Corp. [*NASDAQ symbol*] (NQ) ... ILCO
Intercontinental Life Corp. [*Associated Press*] (SAG) ... IntLfe
Intercontinental Medical Book Corp. ... IMB
Intercontinental Missile (IAA) ... ICM
Intercontinental Missile / Multiple Independently-Fuided Reentry Vehicle (PDAA) ... ICM/MIRV
Intercontinental Press Publishing Association [*Defunct*] (EA) ... IPPA
Intercontinental Reconnaissance Missile (DNAB) ... ICRM
Intercontinental Shipping Corp. (MHDW) ... INSCO
Intercontinental Trailsea Corp. ... ITC
Intercontinental UFO Galactic Spacecraft Research and Analytic Network (EA) ... ICUFON
Intercontinental Venture [*Vancouver Stock Exchange symbol*] ... INQ
Intercontl Life [*NASDAQ symbol*] (TTSB) ... ILCO
Intercontract Material Transfer ... ICMT
Intercooled [*Automotive engineering*] ... I
Intercooled Recuperative [*Engine*] (DOMA) ... ICR
Intercooled Steam-Injected Gas Turbine ... ISTIG
Intercooler ... INCLR
Intercooler ... INCOLR
Inter-Corporate Ownership [*Canada Systems Group*] [*Information service or system*] (IID) ... CLRA
Intercostal [*Between the ribs*] [*Medicine*] ... IC
Intercostal Margin [*Anatomy*] ... ICM
Intercostal Space [*Medicine*] ... ICS
Intercostal Space [*Medicine*] ... IS
Intercostobronchial Trunk [*Medicine*] (DAVI) ... ICBT
Intercristo [*An association*] (EA) ... ICO
Intercrystalline Corrosion [*Metallurgy*] ... IC
Intercultural Action Learning Program ... INTERALP
Intercultural Awareness ... IA
Intercultural Development Research Association (EA) ... IDRA
Intercultural Relations (DNAB) ... ICR
Intercylinder ... INTCYL
Interdata Telecommunications Access Method [*Computer science*] (MHDB) ... ITAM
Interdata Transaction Controller [*Perkin-Elmer*] ... ITC
Inter-Dealer Broker [*British*] ... IDB
Interdecadal Climate Variability [*Marine science*] (OSRA) ... ICV
Interdenominational ... INTER
Interdenominational Church Ushers Association ... ICUA
Interdenominational Foreign Mission Association of North America (EA) ... IFMA
Interdenominational Theological Center, Atlanta, GA [*Library symbol Library of Congress*] (LCLS) ... GAITh
Inter-Dentale Inferius [*Medicine*] (DMAA) ... IDI
Interdepartment Council on Radio Propagation and Standards (NTCM) ... ICAS
Interdepartment Courier Service ... IDCS
Inter-Department Data Exchange Program [*Air Force*] (AFM) ... IDEP
Interdepartment Radio Advisory Committee [*Department of Commerce*] (EGAO) ... IRAC
Interdepartmental ... INTDEPT
Interdepartmental (KSC) ... INTERDEPT
Interdepartmental Advisory and Development Committee (EERA) ... IADC
Interdepartmental Advisory Committee [*World War II*] ... IAC
Interdepartmental Air Traffic Control Board ... IATCB
Interdepartmental Committee ... IDC
Interdepartmental Committee ... INDEC
Interdepartmental Committee for Applied Meteorological Research (USDC) ... ICAMR
Interdepartmental Committee for Atmospheric Sciences [*Terminated, 1976*] ... ICAS
Interdepartmental Committee for Meteorological Services [*National Weather Service*] ... ICMS
Interdepartmental Committee of External Relations [*Canada*] ... ICER
Interdepartmental Committee on Air Pollution Research [*British*] ... ICAPR

Interdepartmental Committee on Internal Security [Washington, DC] ICIS
Interdepartmental Committee on Labour Requirements [British World War II] ICLR
Interdepartmental Committee on Land [Canada] ICL
Interdepartmental Committee on Manpower Requirements [British World War II] MRC
Interdepartmental Committee on Nuclear Energy [Netherlands] (EY) ICK
Interdepartmental Committee on Nutrition for National Defense ICNND
Interdepartmental Committee on Software Engineering [British] ICSE
Interdepartmental Committee on the Status of Women [Terminated, 1978] ICSW
Interdepartmental Committee on Weather Modification [Military] ICWM
Interdepartmental Communication IDC
Inter-Departmental Consultative Committee IDCC
Interdepartmental Dial Service [or System] [Telephones] IDS
Interdepartmental Group [DoD] IG
Interdepartmental Intelligence Conference [Interagency conference of the National Security Council] (EGAO) IIC
Interdepartmental Memorandum (AAG) IM
Interdepartmental Planning Committee on Germany [US] IPCOG
Interdepartmental Procurement Request IPR
Interdepartmental Purchase Request [DoD] (AFIT) IPR
Interdepartmental Regional Group [Army] (AABC) IRG
Interdepartmental Savings Bond Committee [Military] (AABC) ISBC
Interdepartmental Screw Thread Committee [Departments of Commerce and Defense] ISTC
Interdepartmental Work Release Order IWRO
Interdepartmental Workers' Compensation Task Force [Department of Labor] [Terminated, 1976] (EGAO) IWCTF
Interdiction Executive Board (MCD) IEB
Interdiction Mission [Air Force] IDM
Interdiction of Lines of Communication (PDAA) INTLOC
Interdiction Operations [Navy] (NVT) INTOPS
Interdiction Reconnaissance Attack System (PDAA) IRAS
Interdiction Target Graphic (MCD) ITG
Interdictor Strike IDS
Interdigestive Migrating Contractions [Medicine] (DMAA) IMC
Interdigestive Migrating Motor Complex [Medicine] (DMAA) IMMC
Interdigestive Motility Complex [Gastroenterology] IDMC
Interdigestive Myoelectric Complex [Gastroenterology] IMC
Interdigit Pause [Telecommunications] (TEL) IDP
Interdigital [Telecommunications] (IEEE) ID
Interdigital Band-Pass Filter [Electronics] (IAA) IDBPF
Interdigital Communications [AMEX symbol] (SPSG) IDC
Interdigital Communications Corp. [Associated Press] (SAG) IntCm
Interdigital Communications Corp. [Associated Press] (SAG) InterDig
Interdigital Pause [Telecommunications] (TEL) IP
Interdigital Transducer [Physics] IDT
Interdigitated Array [Electronics] IDA
Interdigitating Cell [Medicine] (DMAA) IDC
Inter-Director Designation (NG) IDD
Interdisciplinary ID
Interdisciplinary INTDISP
Interdisciplinary Biblical Research Institute (EA) IBRI
Interdisciplinary Care Plan [Information service or system] (HCT) ICP
Interdisciplinary Center for Creative Studies [State University College at Buffalo] [Research center] (RCD) ICCS
Interdisciplinary Committee on Institutes and Conferences ICIC
Interdisciplinary Communications Program ICP
Interdisciplinary Engineering, Winnipeg, Manitoba [Library symbol National Library of Canada] (NLC) MWTE
Interdisciplinary Enquiry [Education] (AIE) IDE
Interdisciplinary Health Research Group [See also GRIS] [Universite de Montreal] [Canada] [Research center] IHRG
Interdisciplinary Machine Processing for Research and Education in Social Sciences [Dartmouth College, Hanover, NH] [Data processing system] IMPRESS
Interdisciplinary Master of Arts (PGP) IMA
Interdisciplinary Materials Laboratory [Various universities] IDL
Interdisciplinary Model Programs in the Arts for Children and Teachers IMPACT
Interdisciplinary Patient Care Plan (HCT) IPCP
Interdisciplinary Programs in Health [Harvard University] IPH
Interdisciplinary Research Center on Suicide [Italy] (EAIO) IRCS
Interdisciplinary Research Centre [British] IRC
Interdisciplinary Research Equipment Program IREP
Interdisciplinary Research Relevant to Problems of Our Society [Later, RANN] [National Science Foundation] IRPOS
Interdisciplinary Research Relevant to Problems of Our Society [Later, RANN] [National Science Foundation] IRRPOS
Interdisciplinary Scientific Commission [COSPAR] ISC
Interdisciplinary Student-Originated Research Training [National Science Foundation] ISORT
Inter-Disciplinary Studies [Education] (AIE) IDS
Interdisciplinary Team [Education] IDT
Interdisciplinary Team Training in Geriatrics [Veterans Administration] (GFGA) ITTG
Interdistrict Settlement Fund [Banking] ISF
Interdivision Invoice (AAG) IDI
Interdivision Time [Cytology] IDT
Interdivision Transfer (AAG) IDT
Inter-Division Work Order IDWO
Inter-Divisional Agreement IDA
Interdivisional Information Unit [Department of Justice intelligence unit] IDIU
Interdivisional Operations [NASA] (NASA) IDO

Interdivisional Order IDO
Interdivisional Sales Order [NASA] (NASA) IDSO
Interdivisional Technical Agreement [NASA] (NASA) IDTA
Interdivisional Transfer Register IDTR
Interdivisional Work Authorization IDWA
Interdivisional Work Authorization (AAGC) IWA
Interdivisional Work Order (AAGC) IWO
Interdomain Routing Protocol [Computer science] (TNIG) IDRP
Inter-Dynamic Balance IDB
Intereact Ltd. [British] IL
Interelement Protection (IAA) IP
Inter-Entity Boundary Line [Military] (INF) IEBL
Interessen Gemeinschaft der Farbenindustrie Aktiengesellschaft [A dye trust] [Germany] IGFA
[With] Interest [Commerce] (BARN) cum int
Interest [Economics] I
Interest [Finance, Law] (ADA) IN
Interest [Finance, Law] (AFM) INT
Interest (WDMC) int
Interest INTRST
Interest [Finance, Law] (ROG) INTST
Interest [Finance, Law] (ROG) INTT
Interest Assessment Scales IAS
Interest Bearing Deposit [Banking] (ADA) IBD
Interest by Member of Congress CONGINT
Interest Checklist [US Employment Service] [Department of Labor] ICL
Interest Coverage Ratio ICR
Interest Deductible [Banking] (ADA) ID
Interest Determination and Assessment System [Vocational guidance test] IDEAS
Interest During Construction IDC
Interest Equalization Tax IET
Interest Group IG
Interest Inventory for Elementary Grades [Psychology] IIEG
Interest on Investment (AFIT) IOI
Interest on Lawyers' Trust Accounts IOLTA
Interest on Trust Accounts Program IOTA
Interest Only [Finance] IO
Interest Only Strip [Mortgage security] IO
Interest Questionnaire for Indian South Africans [Vocational guidance test] IQISA
Interest Rate of Return [Finance] IROR
Interest Rate Reduction Refinancing [Veterans Administration] IRRR
Interest Standby Credit Arrangement ISCA
Interestatal de Aviacion SA de CV [Mexico ICAO designator] (FAAC) ITE
Interest-Bearing Eligible Liabilities IBEL
Interest-Bearing Liability IBL
Interest-Bearing Transaction Account (DICI) IBTA
Interested Future Attorneys Negotiating for Tot Safety [Student legal action organization] INFANTS
Interested Parties List IPL
Interesting Transcript [genetics] IT
Interest-Only/Principal-Only [Stock exchange term] IOPO
Intereuropean Airways Ltd. [British ICAO designator] (FAAC) IEA
Inter-Exchange [Telecommunications] (NITA) IX
Interexchange Carrier [Telecommunications] IC
Interexchange Carrier [Telecommunications] IEC
Interexchange Carrier [Telecommunications] (PCM) IXC
Interexchange Carrier and Carrier Forum [Exchange Carriers Standards Association] [Telecommunications] ICCF
Interexchange Carrier Interface [Telecommunications] (ACRL) ICI
Interexchange Channel [Telecommunications] IXC
Interexchange Channel [Computer science] (TNIG) IXT
Interexchange Circuit [Telecommunications] (TSSD) IXC
Inter-Exchange Control (NITA) IXC
Interexchange Mileage (CET) IXC
Interface [Computer science] (KSC) I/F
Interface (KSC) INF
Interface INT
Interface (NASA) INTF
Interface (MSA) INTFC
Interface Adapter (NASA) I/A
Interface Adapter Unit [Computer science] (MCD) IAU
Interface Agreement Document (KSC) IAD
Interface Amplifier IA
Interface Analysis Document (KSC) IAD
Interface and Display Electronics Assembly IDEA
Interface and Priority Unit IPU
Interface Assurance Contractor IAC
Interface Bus [Computer science] IB
Interface Bus Control Language [Computer science] IBCL
Interface Bus Interactive Control [Computer science] IBIC
Interface Cancellation Equipment [Telecommunications] (EECA) ICE
Interface Change Notice (MCD) ICN
Interface Change Proposal ICP
Interface Clear (IAA) IFC
Interface Compatibility Record (NASA) ICR
Interface Configuration Control System (DNAB) ICCS
Interface Connecting Device [Air Force] (DOMA) ICD
Interface Control [or Controller] IC
Interface Control Action Request (NRCH) ICAR
Interface Control Action Sheet (DNAB) ICAS
Interface Control Agreement ICA
Interface Control Board (NRCH) ICB
Interface Control Chart (NASA) ICC

Interface Control Configuration List	ICCL
Interface Control Diagram (NRCH)	ICD
Interface Control Dimension (IAA)	ICD
Interface Control Document [Apollo] [NASA]	ICD
Interface Control Document	ICD
Interface Control Documentation Log (KSC)	ICDL
Interface Control Drawings (NRCH)	ICD
Interface Control Drawings Change Proposal (IAA)	ICDCP
Interface Control Envelope Drawings (KSC)	ICED
Interface Control Environment Drawing (IAA)	ICED
Interface Control Function (MCD)	ICF
Interface Control Panel (MCD)	ICP
Interface Control Register (IAA)	ICR
Interface Control Register (IAA)	IFCR
Interface Control Specification (MCD)	ICS
Interface Control Tooling (NASA)	ICT
Interface Control Unit [Army]	ICU
Interface Control Unit (NITA)	ICU
Interface Control Unit [Army] (IAA)	IFCU
Interface Control/Weapon Delivery	ICWD
Interface Control Word [Computer science]	ICW
Interface Control Working Group [NASA] (KSC)	ICWG
Interface Control Working Group Action [NASA] (KSC)	ICWGA
Interface Coordination and Control Procedure (NASA)	ICCP
Interface Coordination Memorandum (MCD)	ICM
Interface Coordinator (MCD)	IC
Interface Data Register (IAA)	IFDR
Interface Data Report (NRCH)	IDR
Interface Data Sheet (NASA)	IDS
Interface Definition Document (MCD)	IDD
Interface Definition Language [Computer science]	IDL
Interface Definition Object [Computer science]	IDO
Interface Demonstration Unit (NASA)	IDU
Interface Design Definition Paper [Military] (CAAL)	IDDP
Interface Design Document (DOMA)	IDD
Interface Design Plan [Air Force]	IDP
Interface Design Specification (CAAL)	IDS
Interface Designation Drawing	IDD
Interface Device (MCD)	ID
Interface Digital Processor (MCD)	IDPS
Interface Display Assembly [NASA] (NASA)	IDA
Interface Document (NASA)	ID
Interface Document Control (MCD)	IDC
Interface Document Master Index (DNAB)	IDMI
Interface Efficiency Council [Computer science]	IEC
Interface Electronics Assembly	IEA
Interface Electronics Unit [NASA]	IEU
Interface Element (NITA)	IFACE
Interface Engineering Change Procedure	IECP
Interface Evaluation Report (KSC)	IER
Interface File (NITA)	IFILE
Interface Functional Analysis (NASA)	IFA
Interface Group, Inc. [ICAO designator] (FAAC)	FIV
Interface Identification Data Document (DNAB)	IIDD
Interface, Inc. [NASDAQ symbol] (NQ)	IFSI
Interface, Inc. [Associated Press] (SAG)	Intrfcln
Interface Inc.'A' [NASDAQ symbol] (TTSB)	IFSIA
Interface Keying Unit [Computer science] (KSC)	IKU
Interface Latching Element	ILE
Interface Management Agent (MCD)	IMA
Interface Management Office	IMO
Interface Management Plan [Air Force]	IMP
Interface Message Processor [Computer science]	IMP
Interface Message Processors [Computer science] (NITA)	IMPS
Interface Module (MCD)	IM
Interface Noise Inverter	INI
Interface Peripheral Standard Olivetti (NITA)	IPSO
Interface Problem Sheet (NASA)	IPS
Interface Problem Status Log (NASA)	IPSL
Interface Processor [Computer science]	IP
Interface Program [Computer science] (IAA)	IP
Interface Program Plan (MCD)	IPP
Interface Register	IFR
Interface Requirement List (NASA)	IRL
Interface Requirements Document	IRD
Interface Requirements Document [DoD]	IRS
Interface Requirements Review (SSD)	IRR
Interface Requirements Specification (MCD)	IRS
Interface Requirements Working Group (SSD)	IRWG
Interface Revision Notice [NASA] (KSC)	IRN
Interface Sharing Unit	ISU
Interface Signal Chart	ISC
Interface Signal Simulator (SAA)	ISS
Interface Simulation System (CAAL)	ISS
Interface Specification	IFS
Interface Specification Control Document (KSC)	ISCD
Interface Supply Support (SAA)	ISS
Interface Surveillance Unit (SAA)	ISU
Interface Switching Assembly	ISA
Interface Switching Unit (BUR)	ISU
Interface Systems [NASDAQ symbol] (TTSB)	INTF
Interface Systems, Inc. [Associated Press] (SAG)	Interf
Interface Systems, Inc. [Associated Press] (SAG)	Interfc
Interface Systems, Inc. [NASDAQ symbol] (NQ)	INTF
Interface Technical Working Group	ITWG

Interface Technology [British] (NITA)	INTEC
Interface Test Adapters (MCD)	ITA
Interface Timing Diagram	ITD
Interface Tool (MCD)	IFT
Interface Transformation Unit (SAA)	ITU
Interface Unit [Computer science] (NASA)	I/FU
Interface Unit [Computer science]	INTFU
Interface Unit [Computer science] (MCD)	IU
Interface Unit Adapter [Computer science] (MCD)	IUA
Interface Unit Error Count Table (MCD)	IUE
Interface Verification Equipment (NASA)	IVE
Interface Verification Procedure [NASA] (IAA)	IVP
Interface Virtual Machine [Computer science]	IVM
Interface Volume (MCD)	IV
Interface/Weapon Aiming Computer (MCD)	I/WAC
Interface Working Group [NASA] (SSD)	IFWG
Interface Working Group [NASA] (NASA)	IWG
Interfaced between Two Immiscible Electrolyte Solutions [Physical chemistry]	ITIES
Interfacial Communications (MCD)	IC
Interfacial Surface Generation [Instrumentation]	ISG
Interfacial Tension [Physical chemistry]	IFT
Interfacial Tension [Physical chemistry] (IAA)	IT
Interfacial Test	IFT
Interfacial Zone	IZ
Interfacial-Force Microscope	IFM
Interfacility Communication Network	IFCN
Interfacility Data (FAAC)	IDAT
Interfacility Data Link [FAA] (TAG)	IDL
Inter-Facility Flow Control Network [FAA] (TAG)	IFCN
Interfacility Link (LAIN)	IFL
Interfaith	INTRFTH
Interfaith Action for Economic Justice (EA)	IAEJ
Interfaith Center on Corporate Responsibility (EA)	ICCR
Interfaith Center to Reverse the Arms Race (EA)	ICRAR
Interfaith Coalition on Energy (EA)	ICE
Interfaith Committee on Social Responsibility in Investments [Later, ICCR] (EA)	ICSRI
Inter-Faith Compassionists (EA)	IFC
Interfaith Council for Human Rights (EA)	ICHR
Interfaith Council for the Protection of Animals and Nature (EA)	ICPAN
Interfaith Forum on Religion, Art, and Architecture (EA)	IFRAA
Interfaith Hunger Appeal (EA)	IHA
Interfaith Movement [Defunct] (EA)	IM
Interfaith Office on Accompaniment (EA)	IOA
Inter-Faith Task Force (EA)	IFTF
Interference [Broadcasting]	I
Interference (KSC)	INF
Interference [Telecommunications] (MDG)	INTEC
Interference (IAA)	INTERF
Interference	INTERFER
Interference (FAAC)	INTFC
Interference (AABC)	INTFER
Interference (KSC)	INTFR
Interference [Telecommunications] (MSA)	INTRF
Interference Accommodation Zone [Geology]	INAZ
Interference Blanker Set	IBS
Interference Blanking Unit	IBU
Interference Cancellation Equipment [Telecommunications]	ICE
Interference Check Sample [Spectroscopy]	ICS
Interference Compliance Test (SAA)	ICT
Interference Control (IAA)	IC
Interference Control Monitor (AAG)	ICM
Interference Detection and Interdiction Countermeasures Team [Electromagnetic compatibility programs]	INTERDICT
Interference Filter	IF
Interference Frequency Rejection Unit [Military]	IFRU
Interference Guard Bands	IGB
Interference Mockup (IAA)	IMU
Interference Pattern (CAAL)	IP
Interference Prediction Model	IPM
Interference Reflection Microscopy	IRM
Interference Reporting Point (NATG)	IRP
Interference Suppression Unit (IAA)	ISU
Interference Suppressor (IEEE)	IS
Interference Technology Engineer's Master (IEEE)	ITEM
Interference Unit [Military]	IU
Interference-to-Noise Ratio (IEEE)	IN
Interference-to-Noise Ratio	INR
Interfering Transmitter (IAA)	IT
Interferometer	INTERF
Interferometer and Doppler	ID
Interferometer Direction Finding System [Military] (CAAL)	IDFS
Interferometric Fiber Optic Gyroscope	IFOG
Interferometric Landmark Tracker (PDAA)	ILT
Interferometric LASER Source	ILS
Interferometric Synthetic Aperture RADAR (RDA)	IFSAR
Interferon [Also, IFN] [Biochemistry]	IF
Interferon [Also, IF] [Biochemistry]	IFN
Interferon (DOG)	IFN
Interferon (DMAA)	ITF
Interferon Foundation [Defunct] (EA)	IF
Interferon Gamma [Medicine] (DMAA)	IFNG
Interferon Gamma-Inducing Factor [Biochemistry]	IGIF
Interferon Reference Unit	IRU

Interferon Regulatory Element [*Biochemistry*] ..... IRE
Interferon Regulatory Factor [*Biochemistry*] ..... IRF
Interferon Response Sequence [*Genetics*] ..... IRS
Interferon Sciences [*NASDAQ symbol*] (TTSB) ..... IFSC
Interferon Sciences, Inc. [*NASDAQ symbol*] (NQ) ..... IFSC
Interferon Sciences, Inc. [*Associated Press*] (SAG) ..... Intfrn
Interferon Unit [*Medicine*] (DMAA) ..... IFU
Interferons [*Biology*] (DOG) ..... IFNs
Interferon-Stimulated Gene Factor [*Biochemistry*] ..... ISGF
Interferon-Stimulated Response Element [*Medicine*] ..... ISRE
Interfiber Distance ..... IFD
Inter-Fighter Director ..... IFD
Inter-Financial Association (EA) ..... IFA
Interfirm Accounting Project (IAA) ..... IFAC
Interfirm Comparison (ADA) ..... IFC
Interflight [*British ICAO designator*] (FAAC) ..... IFT
Interflight, Inc. [*ICAO designator*] (FAAC) ..... DEX
Interflight (Learjet) Ltd. [*British ICAO designator*] (FAAC) ..... IJT
Interflora Australia ..... IA
Interflug [*ICAO designator*] (AD) ..... IF
Interfraternity Research and Advisory Council [*Defunct*] (EA) ..... IRAC
Interfreight Forwarding Ltd. [*Sudan*] [*ICAO designator*] (FAAC) ..... IFF
Inter-Freight International [*Steamship*] (MHDB) ..... IFI
Interfruitlet Corking [*of pineapple*] ..... IFC
Interfunk & Co. [*Yugoslavia*] [*ICAO designator*] (FAAC) ..... IFK
Interfurnishings USA (TSPED) ..... IF/USA
Interfuture (EA) ..... IF
Intergalactic Infrared Radiation Field ..... IIRF
Intergalactic Magnetic Fields ..... IGMF
Intergalactic Medium ..... IGM
Intergalactic SYSOP [*System Operator*] **Alliance** (EA) ..... ISA
Intergalactic World Brain [*Underground press service*] (IIA) ..... IWB
Inter-Gas System ..... IG
Intergency Global Positioning System Executive Board ..... IGEB
Intergenic Repeat Unit [*Genetics*] ..... IRU
Intergenic Spacer [*Genetics*] ..... IGS
Intergeniculate Leaflet [*Anatomy*] ..... IGL
Inter-German Border (MCD) ..... IGB
Inter-Globe Resources Ltd. [*Vancouver Stock Exchange symbol*] ..... IGR
Intergovernmental ..... INTERGOVT
Intergovernmental Advisory Council on Education (AEE) ..... IACE
Intergovernmental Affairs Fellowship Program (RDA) ..... IAFP
Intergovernmental Affairs Fellowship Program [*Military*] (MCD) ..... IGAF
Intergovernmental Agreement on the Environment [*Commonwealth*] [*State*] (EERA) ..... IAG
Intergovernmental Agreement on the Environment [*Australia*] ..... IGAE
Intergovernmental Authority on Drought and Development [*Djibouti*] (EY) ..... IGADD
Intergovernmental Bureau for Informatics [*Telecommunications*] (EA) ..... IBI
Intergovernmental Bureau for Informatics - International Computation Center (CSR) ..... IBI-ICC
Intergovernmental Commission for Chagas Disease (ECON) ..... ICCD
Intergovernmental Commission on Oceanography (NUCP) ..... ICO
Intergovernmental Committee for European Migration [*Later, ICM*] ..... ICEM
Intergovernmental Committee for Ocean Science and Living Resources [*Marine science*] (OSRA) ..... OSLR
Intergovernmental Committee for Physical Education and Sport [*United Nations France*] (EY) ..... ICPES
Intergovernmental Committee for Promoting the Return of Cultural Property to ItsCountries of Origin or Its Restitution in Case of Illicit Appropriation (EA) ..... ICPRCPCO
Intergovernmental Committee on Refugees [*Post-World War II*] (DLA) ..... IGC
Intergovernmental Committee on Refugees [*Post-World War II*] ..... IGCR
Intergovernmental Committee on Science and Technology (BARN) ..... IGST
Intergovernmental Committee on Urban and Regional Research [*Canada*] ..... ICURR
Inter-Governmental Conference [*European Union*] (ECON) ..... IGC
Inter-Governmental Conference ..... IGC
Intergovernmental Conference on Oceanic Research ..... ICOR
Intergovernmental Conference on Oceanographic Research (MCD) ..... INCOR
Inter-Governmental Conferences [*European Community*] ..... IGC
Intergovernmental Copyright Committee [*See also CIDA*] [*Paris, France*] (EAIO) ..... IGC
Intergovernmental Copyright Committee [*See also CIDA*] ..... IGCC
Intergovernmental Council for ADP [*Automatic Data Processing*] ..... ICA
Intergovernmental Council for the International Hydrological Programme (EA) ..... IHP
Intergovernmental Forum on Chemical Safety ..... IFCS
Intergovernmental Geographic Commission Voluntary Cooperation Program [*Marine science*] (OSRA) ..... IOC-VCP
Inter-Governmental Group for Indonesia [*Defunct*] ..... IGGI
Intergovernmental Health Policy Project (EA) ..... IHPP
Intergovernmental Informatics Programme [*UNESCO*] ..... IIP
Intergovernmental Liaison Staff [*Environmental Protection Agency*] (GFGA) ..... ILS
Intergovernmental Maritime Consultative Organization ..... IMCO
Intergovernmental Oceanographic Commission [*See also COI*] [*ICSU Paris, France*] (EAIO) ..... IOC
Intergovernmental Oceanographic Commission - Bureau and Consultative Council [*UNESCO*] ..... IOC/B & CC
Intergovernmental Oceanographic Commission/Executive Council (MSC) ..... IOC/EC
Intergovernmental Oceanographic Commission/Voluntary Assistance Program (MSC) ..... IOC/VAP
Intergovernmental Organization [*Generic term*] ..... IGO
Intergovernmental Panel on Climate Change [*World Meteorological Organization*] ..... IGCC
Intergovernmental Panel on Climate Change [*World Meteorological Organization*] ..... IPCC
Intergovernmental Personnel Act [*1970*] ..... IPA
Inter-Governmental Philatelic Corp. (EA) ..... IGPC
Intergovernmental Policy Advisory Committee on Trade ..... IGPAC
Intergovernmental Refugee Committee [*London*] [*World War II*] ..... IRC
Intergovernmental Relations (OICC) ..... IR
Intergovernmental Review System (OICC) ..... IGR
Intergovernmental Science and Public Technology [*of ASRA*] [*National Science Foundation*] ..... ISPT
Intergovernmental Science and Research Utilization [*National Science Foundation*] ..... ISRU
Intergovernmental Science, Engineering, and Technology Advisory Panel [*National Science Foundation*] ..... ISETAP
Intergovernmental Science Programs ..... ISP
Intergovernmental Steering Committee on World Food Day (EA) ..... ISCWFD
Intergovernmental Working Group [*United Nations*] ..... IWG
Intergovernmental Working Group on Marine Pollution [*Inter-Governmental Maritime Consultative Organization*] ..... IWGMP
Intergovernmental Working Group on Monitoring or Surveillance [*United Nations*] (ASF) ..... IWGM
Intergovernmental Working Group on Monitoring or Surveillance [*United Nations*] (MSC) ..... IWGMS
Intergranular [*Metallurgy*] ..... IG
Inter-Granular (MCD) ..... IG
Intergranular Attack [*Nuclear energy*] (NRCH) ..... IGA
Intergranular Corrosion (PDAA) ..... IGC
Intergranular Cyclic Crack Growth Rate [*Nuclear energy*] (NUCP) ..... ICCGR
Intergranular Hydrogen Embrittlement [*Metallurgy*] ..... IHE
Intergranular Stress-Corrosion Cracking [*Plant engineering*] ..... IGSCC
Intergraph Corp. [*NASDAQ symbol*] (NQ) ..... INGR
Intergraph Corp. [*Associated Press*] (SAG) ..... Intgph
Intergraph Corp./Engineering Modeling System ..... I/EMS
Intergrated Avionics Computer (DA) ..... IAC
Intergroup Corp. [*NASDAQ symbol*] (TTSB) ..... INTG
Intergroup Ewing Sarcoma Study [*Medicine*] (DMAA) ..... IESS
Intergroup Rhabdomyosarcoma Study [*Oncology*] ..... IRS
Inter-Hemispheric Education Resource Center (EA) ..... IHERC
Interim [*FCC*] (NTCM) I
Interim (MSA) ..... INT
Interim Acceptance Criteria (NRCH) ..... IAC
Interim Access Authorization ..... IAA
Interim Accessory Bulletin (DNAB) ..... IAYB
Interim Accessory Change (MCD) ..... IAYC
Interim Action Committee [*British*] ..... IAC
Interim Admission Note [*Medical records*] (DAVI) ..... IAN
Interim/Advanced Defense Communications Satellite Program (DNAB) ..... I/ADCSP
Interim Air Defense Weapon System [*Army*] ..... IADWS
Interim Air Toxics Data Base (GNE) ..... IATDB
Interim Airframe Bulletin (MCD) ..... IAB
Interim Airframe Bulletin ..... IAFB
Interim Airframe Change (NG) ..... IAFC
Interim Amphibious Refresher Training [*Navy*] (NVT) ..... INTPHIBRFT
Interim Antenna Pointing Subsystem [*Deep Space Instrumentation Facility, NASA*] ..... IAPS
Interim Antiradiation Missile (MCD) ..... IARM
Interim Aquanaut Equipment System (PDAA) ..... IAES
Interim Armament Bulletin (MCD) ..... IAB
Interim Availability (DNAB) ..... INTAV
Interim Aviation Airframe Bulletin (DNAB) ..... IAAB
Interim Ballistic Instrumentation ..... IBI
Interim Billing and Follow-Up System [*Social Security Administration*] (GFGA) ..... IBFS
Interim Bomber Defense Missile ..... IBDM
Interim Brigade Afloat Force [*Prepositioning force*] [*Army*] (DOMA) ..... IBAF
Interim Cargo Integration Operations (MCD) ..... ICIO
Interim Cargo Integrator (MCD) ICI
Interim Catalog Module [*MEDLARS*] ..... ICM
Interim Change (AFM) IC
Interim Change Bulletin (NASA) ..... ICB
Interim Change Notice (AFM) ..... ICN
Interim Charging [*Electric vehicle technology*] ..... INCH
Interim Checkout Device ..... ICD
Interim Circuit Order Control System [*Bell System*] ..... ICOCS
Interim Command and Control System (MCD) ..... ICCS
Interim Command Switchboard [*Navy*] (NVT) ..... ICSB
Interim Commission IC
Interim Commission for the International Trade Organization ..... ICITO
Interim Commission of the International Refugee Organization ..... ICIRO
Interim Commission on Satellite Communication (NITA) ..... ICSC
Interim Committee IC
Interim Committee for Coordination of Investigations of the Lower Mekong Basi n [*of the United Nations Economic and Social Commission for Asia and the Pacific*] [*Thailand*] (EAIO) ..... CCILMB
Interim Committee for Coordination of Investigations of the Lower Mekong Basin (EA) ..... ICCILMB
Interim Communications Satellite Committee ..... ICSC
Interim Conservation Order ..... ICO
Interim Contractor Depot Support [*DoD*] ..... ICDS
Interim Contractor Depot Support Plan [*DoD*] ..... ICDSP
Interim Contractor Support (MCD) ..... ICS
Interim Contractor Support Plan ..... ICSP

Interim Co-ordinating Committee for International Commodity Arrangements .... ICCICA
Interim Daily System Operational Test [*Navy*] (NG) .... IDSOT
Interim Data Communications Collection Center .... IDCCC
Interim Data Element [*Army*] (AABC) .... IDE
Interim Data Switching Facility (ADA) .... IDSF
Interim Decay Storage [*Nuclear energy*] (NRCH) .... IDS
Interim Decisions of the Department of Justice .... IDDJ
Interim Defense Communications Satellite Program [*DoD*] .... IDCSP
Interim Depot Repair .... IDR
Interim Design and Workmanship Rules (PDAA) .... IDWR
Interim Design Review (MCD) .... IDR
Interim Development Order (ADA) .... IDO
Interim Development Report .... IDR
Interim Digital-Analog Converter .... IDAC
Interim Discrepancy Report .... IDR
Interim Dividend [*Investment term*] .... ID
Interim Drydocking [*Navy*] (NVT) .... IDD
Interim Electronic Maintenance Support (AFIT) .... IEMS
Interim Employment Services Regulatory Authority .... IESRA
Interim Engineering Order (AAG) .... IEO
Interim Engineering Report .... IER
Interim Equipment Order Control System [*Bell System*] .... IEOCS
Interim Escort Towed Array System (MCD) .... IETAS
Interim European Telecommunication Standard (OSI) .... I-ETS
Interim Examination and Maintenance [*Nuclear energy*] (NRCH) .... IEM
Interim Examination and Maintenance Training Facility [*Nuclear energy*] (NRCH) .... IEMTF
Interim Expendable Emitter (NVT) .... IEE
Interim [*Contact*] **File** (MCD) .... ITF
Interim Final Rule [*RSPA*] (TAG) .... IFR
Interim Fire Support Automation System [*Army*] (DOMA) .... IFSAS
Interim Fleet Command Center [*Navy*] (MCD) .... IFCC
Interim Functional Alternate .... IFA
Interim Fund for Science and Technology for Development [*International Council of Scientific Unions*] .... IFSTD
Interim Geophysical Data Record [*From spacecraft data*] .... IGDR
Interim Ground Station Module [*Joint Surveillance/Target Attack RADAR Syste m*] (DOMA) .... IGSM
Interim High-Data Rate Terminal (CAAL) .... IHDRT
Interim High-Level Container Airdrop System .... IHLCADS
Interim Housing Allowance [*Military*] (AFM) .... IHA
Interim Hypersonics Test Vehicle [*NASA*] (NASA) .... IHTV
Interim Hypersonics Test Vehicle .... IHX
Interim Impact Predictor (AAG) .... IIP
Interim Infantry Fighting Vehicle [*Military*] (MCD) .... IIFV
Interim Integrated Aircraft Instrumentation and Letdown System .... IIAILS
Interim International Information Service [*World War II*] .... IIIS
Interim Interswitch Signaling Protocol [*Telecommunications*] (ACRL) .... IISP
Interim JTIDS [*Joint Tactical Information Distribution System*] **Message Standard** .... IJMS
Interim Logistics Support Guide (NVT) .... ILSG
Interim Low-Altitude Air Defense System .... ILAADS
Interim Maintenance Assistance Team (MCD) .... IMAT
Interim Maintenance Engineering Order (AAG) .... IMEO
Interim Maneuver Identification System (IAA) .... IMIS
Interim Manned Interceptor (PDAA) .... IMI
Interim Manpower Maintenance System .... IMMS
Interim Maximum Operating Time .... IMOT
Interim Measures .... IM
Interim Memorandum .... IM
Interim Message Change .... IMC
Interim Meteorological Satellite .... IMS
Interim Military Microwave Landing System (RDA) .... IMMLS
Interim Minesweeping Force [*Military*] .... IMF
Interim Missile Guidance Test (MCD) .... IMGT
Interim Mobile Independent Target System [*Military*] (INF) .... IMITS
Interim Mobile Logistic Support Group [*Military*] (CAAL) .... IMLSG
Interim Monitoring Program .... IMP
Interim Motorized Infantry Division Capability Analysis [*Military*] .... IMIDCA
Interim Narrow-Band Secure Voice (NVT) .... INBSV
Interim National Coordinating Committee [*Ghana*] (PPW) .... INCC
Interim National Space Surveillance Control Center .... INSSCC
Interim Operating Instructions .... IOI
Interim Operating Procedure (NVT) .... IOP
Interim Operation Meteorological System .... IOMS
Interim Operational Capability .... IOC
Interim Operational System .... IOS
Interim Pacific Oceanographic Support System (DNAB) .... IPOSS
Interim Paris Commission [*British*] .... IPARCOM
Interim Parts List [*Navy*] .... IPL
Interim Point Defense Target Acquisition System [*Military*] (IAA) .... IPDTAS
Interim Policy Letter [*Air Force*] (AAGC) .... IPL
Interim Policy Statement (NRCH) .... IPS
Interim POMSEE [*Performance, Operating, and Maintenance Standards for Electronic Equipment*] **Sheet** .... IPS
Interim Problem Report (NASA) .... IPR
Interim Progress Report .... IPR
Interim Range Operations (MUGU) .... IRO
Interim Rapid Action Change (MCD) .... IRAC
Interim Recovery Technical Specification (IEEE) .... IRTS
Interim Refresher Training [*Navy*] .... INTRFT
Interim Refresher Training [*Navy*] (NVT) .... IRFT
Interim Release Request (MCD) .... IRR
Interim Reliability Evaluation Program [*Nuclear energy*] .... IREP
Interim Remedial Measure (EPA) .... IRM
Interim Remote Area Terminal Equipment [*Air Force*] .... IRATE
Interim Remote Terminals (MCD) .... IRT
Interim Repair Parts List .... IRPL
Interim Report .... IR
Interim Research Memo .... IRM
Interim Response Actions [*Army*] (DOMA) .... IRA
Interim Revision Notice (SAA) .... IRN
Interim Scientific Report .... ISR
Interim Scout Helicopter (MCD) .... ISH
Interim Sea Control Ship (MCD) .... ISCS
Interim Services [*NASDAQ symbol*] (TTSB) .... INTM
Interim Services, Inc. [*Associated Press*] (SAG) .... Interim
Interim Shipboard Availability (MCD) .... INSAV
Interim Simulation Display [*FAA*] (TAG) .... ISD
Interim Spare Parts List (AAG) .... ISPL
Interim Standard (ACRL) .... IS
Interim Standard Airborne Digital Computer (MCD) .... ISADC
Interim Standard Microwave Landing System [*Aviation*] .... ISMLS
Interim Standard Set .... ISS
Interim Status (GNE) .... IS
Interim Status Compliance Letter [*Environmental Protection Agency*] (GFGA) .... ISCL
Interim Status Document [*Environmental Protection Agency*] (GFGA) .... ISD
Interim Status Standards (GNE) .... ISS
Interim Stowage Assembly .... ISA
Interim Stowage Shelf (KSC) .... ISS
Interim Support Equipment Bulletin (MCD) .... ISEB
Interim Support Item (MCD) .... ISI
Interim Support Items List (NASA) .... ISIL
Interim Support Period .... ISP
Interim Support Plan (MCD) .... ISP
Interim Surface Missile (PDAA) .... ISM
Interim Surface-to-Surface Missile [*Military*] (CAAL) .... ISSM
Interim Surface-to-Surface Missile Capability [*Military*] (CAAL) .... ISSMC
Interim Surface-to-Surface Missile System [*Military*] (NVT) .... ISSMS
Interim System Review (SSD) .... ISR
Interim Table Simulation (SAA) .... ITS
Interim Tactical ELINT [*Electronic Intelligence*] **Processor** .... ITEP
Interim Tactical Information Processing and Interpretation .... ITIPI
Interim Target Acquisition and Designation System .... ITAADS
Interim Technical Directive (MCD) .... ITD
Interim Technical Memorandum .... ITM
Interim Technical Note .... ITN
Interim Technical Order (AFM) .... ITO
Interim Technical Order Field Change Notice [*Air Force*] (MCD) .... ITOFCN
Interim Technical Report .... ITR
Interim Teleprinter System .... ITS
Interim Terminal Test Environment [*FAA*] .... ITTE
Interim Test Procedure (MCD) .... ITP
Interim Test Report .... ITR
Interim Towed Array Surveillance System [*Military*] (NVT) .... ITASS
Interim Training Program [*Army*] (INF) .... ITP
Interim Upper Stage [*Missile*] .... IUS
Interim Use Item (MCD) .... IUI
Interim Use Material (MCD) .... IUM
Interim Use Material Authorization (MCD) .... IUMA
Interim Use Sheet (NASA) .... IUS
Interim Water Velocity Meter Test Set .... IWVMTS
Interim Wideband Communications (MCD) .... IWBC
Interim Wilderness Committee [*Australia*] .... IWC
Interim Wool Industry Policy Council [*Australia*] .... IWIPC
Inter-Image Amplifying Chemistry [*Color film technology*] .... IIAC
Inter-Industry Conference on Auto Collision Repair (EA) .... I-CAR
Inter-Industry Emission Control [*Program*] (EA) .... IIEC
Inter-Industry Highway Safety Committee [*Later, DSMC*] (EA) .... IIHSC
Inter-Industry Management Program (IAA) .... IMP
Inter-Institutional Committee on Nutrition .... ICON
Inter-Institutional Integrated Services Information System .... INSIS
Inter-Integrated Circuit [*Philips*] (NITA) .... I^2C
Interionic Attraction Theory .... IAT
Interior (KSC) .... INT
Interior (VRA) .... int
Interior (WDMC) .... int
Interior .... INTR
Interior (KSC) .... INTR
Interior and Insular Affairs .... I & IA
Interior Ballistic Division [*Ballistic Research Laboratory*] [*Army*] (RDA) .... IBD
Interior Ballistics Laboratory [*Aberdeen, MD*] [*Army*] .... IBL
Interior Board of Contract Appeals (in United States Interior Decisions) [*A publication*] (DLA) .... IBCA
Interior Board of Indian Affairs (in United States Interior Decisions) [*A publication*] (DLA) .... IBIA
Interior Board of Land Appeals [*Department of the Interior*] .... IBLA
Interior Board of Mine Operations Appeals (in United States Interior Decisions) [*A publication*] (DLA) .... IBMA
Interior Board of Surface Mine Appeals (in United States Interior Decisions) [*A publication*] (DLA) .... IBSMA
Interior Committee on Research and Development .... ICRD
Interior Communication IC
Interior Communication and Fire Control Distribution (MSA) .... IC & FCD
Interior Communication Switching Center (DNAB) .... ICSC
Interior Communications Electrician [*Navy rating*] IC
Interior Communications Electrician, Chief [*Navy rating*] ICC
Interior Communications Electrician, First Class [*Navy rating*] IC1

Interior Communications Electrician, Second Class [Navy rating] IC2
Interior Communications Electrician, Third Class [Navy rating] IC3
Interior Communications Switchboard .... ICSWBD
Interior Contractor Support .... ICS
Interior Control Board .... ICB
Interior Decorators and Designers Association [British] (EAIO) .... IDDA
Interior Department .... ID
Interior Department Decisions [United States] [A publication] (DLA) .... ILT
Interior Design Educators Council (EA) .... IDEC
Interior Design Society (EA) .... IDS
Interior Designers of Canada [See also DIC] .... IDC
Interior Electromagnetic Pulse (MCD) .... IEMP
Interior Facet [Medicine] (DMAA) .... IF
Interior Gateway Protocol [Computer science] (TNIG) .... IGP
Interior Gateway Routing Protocol [Cisco Systems, Inc.] .... IGRP
Interior Insulating Window Institute [Defunct] (EA) .... IIWI
Interior Landscape Division of ALCA [Later, ALCA/IPD] (EA) .... ALCA/ILD
Interior Length IL
Interior Ministerial Real Estate Committee [Vietnam] .... IMREC
Interior Nasal Quadrant [Medicine] (DMAA) .... INQ
Interior Plantscape Association [Later, ALCA/IPD] (EA) .... IPA
Interior Plantscape Division of ALCA (EA) .... ALCA/IPD
Interior Procurement Regulations [Department of the Interior] .... IPR
Interior Surface .... IS
Interior Upper Stage (NASA) .... IUS
Interior Width (IAA) .... IW
Interiors Engineering and Industrial Design (MCD) .... IE & ID
Interiors, Inc. [Associated Press] (SAG) .... Inter
Interiors, Inc. [Associated Press] (SAG) .... Interiors
Interiors, Inc. [Associated Press] (SAG) .... Intrirs
Interiors, Inc. [NASDAQ symbol] (SAG) .... INTXA
Interiors Inc.'A' [NASDAQ symbol] (TTSB) .... INTXA
Interiors Inc.Cv'A'Pfd [NASDAQ symbol] (TTSB) .... INTXP
Interiors Inc. Wrrt [NASDAQ symbol] (TTSB) .... INTXL
Interiors Inc. Wrrt'A' [NASDAQ symbol] (TTSB) .... INTXW
Interiors Inc.Wrrt'B' [NASDAQ symbol] (TTSB) .... INTXZ
Inter-Island Air, Inc. [ICAO designator] (FAAC) .... UGL
Inter-Island Air Services Ltd. [Grenada] [ICAO designator] (FAAC) .... IES
Interjection .... INT
Interjection .... INTERJ
Interjection (WDMC) .... interj
Interjet [Greece] [FAA designator] (FAAC) .... INJ
Interjob Communications (MHDB) .... IJC
Interkernal Communication (NITA) .... IKC
Interkinase Domain [Genetics] .... IK
Interlaboratory Air-to-Air Missile Technology (MCD) .... ILAAT
Inter-Laboratory Committee (SAA) .... ILABC
Inter-Laboratory Committee on Editing and Publishing [Navy] (MCD) .... ILCEP
Inter-Laboratory Committee on Facilities [Navy] (MCD) .... ILCF
Inter-Laboratory Method Detection Limit [Environmental Protection Agency] .... IMDL
Interlaboratory Working Group for Data Exchange [Computer science] (MHDI) .... IWGDE
Interlace Airlines Ltd. [Gambia] [FAA designator] (FAAC) .... ITG
Interlaced .... INTRLCD
[The] Interlake Corp. [NYSE symbol] (SPSG) .... IK
Interlake Corp. [NYSE symbol] (TTSB) .... IK
[The] Interlake Corp. [Associated Press] (SAG) .... Intrlke
Interlake Development [Vancouver Stock Exchange symbol] .... IRK
Interlake Sailing Class Association (EA) .... ISCA
Interlake School, Staff Library, Medical Lake, WA [Library symbol Library of Congress] (LCLS) .... WaMel
Inter-Lake Yachting Association (EA) .... I-LYA
Interlaminar Adhesive Layer .... IAL
Interlaminar Shear Strength (MCD) .... ILSS
Interlayer Tunneling [Model for superconductivity] .... ILT
Interleaf, Inc. [Associated Press] (SAG) .... Intrleaf
Interleaf, Inc. [Cambridge, MA] [NASDAQ symbol] (NQ) .... LEAF
Interleave (DGA) .... INTER
Interleaved (WGA) .... INT
Interleaver (MCD) .... INTLVR
Interleaver (NASA) .... INTRLVR
Interleukin [Biochemistry] IL
Interleukin Receptor [Medicine] (DMAA) .... ILR
Interleukin Receptor Antagonist Protein [Biochemistry] .... IRAP
Interleukin Regulation of Immune System [Medicine] (DMAA) .... IRIS
Interleukin-Converting Enzyme [Biochemistry] .... ICE
Interlibrary Cooperation & Networking [Association of Specialized and Cooperative Library Agencies] [American Library Association] .... ICAN
Interlibrary Delivery Service of Pennsylvania [Library network] .... IDS
Inter-Library Electronic Mail (NITA) .... ILEM
Interlibrary Loan ILL
Interlibrary Network of Baltimore County [Library network] .... INBC
Interlibrary Users Association [University of Maryland] [College Park, MD] [Library network] .... IUA
Interline IL
Interline Resources [Exchange symbol] (TTSB) .... IRC.EC
Interline Resources Corp. [Associated Press] (SAG) .... Intrlne
Interline Resources Corp. [AMEX symbol] (SAG) .... IRC
Interlineation (ROG) .... INLINON
INTERLING Software Corp. [NASDAQ symbol] (SAG) .... INLQ
Interlingua [MARC language code Library of Congress] (LCCP) .... int
Interlingua Institute (EA) II
Interlingue Union .... IU

Interlink Business and Communications Services [British telecommunications service company] (IBCS) .... IBCS
Interlink Electronics [NASDAQ symbol] (TTSB) .... LINK
Interlink Electronics, Inc. [Associated Press] (SAG) .... Interlink
Interlink Electronics, Inc. [Associated Press] (SAG) .... Intrlk
Interlink Electronics, Inc. [NASDAQ symbol] (SAG) .... LINK
Interlink Electrs Wrrt [NASDAQ symbol] (TTSB) .... LINKW
Interlink Press Service (EA) .... IPS
Interlinked Computerized Storage and Processing System of Food and Agricultural Data [Databank] [United Nations Information service or system] (IID) .... ICS
Interlinq Software [NASDAQ symbol] (SAG) .... INLQ
INTERLINQ Software [NASDAQ symbol] (TTSB) .... INLQ
INTERLINQ Software Corp. [Associated Press] (SAG) .... Interlinq
Interlochen Center for the Arts (EA) .... ICA
Interlochen, MI [FM radio station call letters] .... WIAA
Interlock [Technical drawings] .... ILK
Interlock (MSA) .... INTLK
Interlocked .... INTRLKD
Interlocked Grain Index [Botany] .... IGI
Interlocked Metallic Armor [Technical drawings] I
Interlocking Concrete Pavement Institute .... ICPI
Interlocking Directorate [Business term] .... ID
Interlocking Paving Manufacturers Association [Defunct] (EA) .... IPMA
Interlook Dormant Period (NVT) .... ILDP
Interloop Heat Exchanger [NASA] (NASA) .... IHX
Interlovhen Public Library, Interlochen, MI [Library symbol] [Library of Congress] (LCLS) .... MiInt
Interlutheran Theological Seminary and Bible School, Minneapolis, MN [Library symbol Library of Congress] (LCLS) .... MnMI
Intermachine Trunk [Telecommunications] (TEL) .... IMT
Intermagnetics General Corp. .... IGC
Intermagnetics General Corp. [AMEX symbol] (SPSG) .... IMG
Intermagnetics General Corp. [Associated Press] (SAG) .... Intrmagn
INTERMARC [International Machine-Readable Cataloging] [French National Library Source file] [UTLAS symbol] .... IMC
INTERMARC [International Machine-Readable Cataloging] [French National Library] [UTLAS symbol] .... INT
Intermarket Association of Advertising Agencies [Dayton, OH] (EA) .... IAAA
Intermarket Surveillance Information System (DFIT) .... ISIS
Intermarket Trading System (IEEE) .... ITS
Intermaxillary Fixation (MAE) .... IMF
Intermeccanica-Puch [Italian-Austrian specialty car maker] .... IMP
Inter-media (VRA) .... intr-md
Intermedia Communications [NASDAQ symbol] (TTSB) ICIX
Intermedia Communications, Inc. [NASDAQ symbol] (SAG) ICIX
Intermedia Communications of Florida, Inc. [Associated Press] (SAG) .... IntrCm
Intermedia Priority Pollutant (GNE) .... IPP
Intermediary Letter IL
Intermediary Music Language (NITA) .... IML
Intermediary Musical Language (PDAA) .... IML
Intermediary Organization [Physiology] .... IO
Intermediate [Vessel load line mark] I
Intermediate (NASA) .... IMD
Intermediate (MCD) .... INT
Intermediate (AAG) .... INTER
Intermediate (WDMC) .... inter
Intermediate .... INTER
Intermediate (ADA) .... INTERMED
Intermediate (KSC) .... INTM
Intermediate (MSA) .... INTMD
Intermediate (AFM) .... INTMED
Intermediate Access Memory (NITA) .... IAM
Intermediate Air [Combustion] .... IA
Intermediate Air Command [Air Force] (AFM) .... IAC
Intermediate Altitude Communication Satellite (IAA) .... IACS
Intermediate Altitude Sounding Rocket (MUGU) .... IASR
Intermediate Amplifier .... IA
Intermediate Amplifier (IAA) .... INTAMP
Intermediate and Depot Maintenance Manual (NASA) .... IDMM
Intermediate and Medial Part of the Hyperstriatum Ventrale [Bird brain anatomy] .... IMHV
Intermediate and Organizational Maintenance (MCD) .... I & OM
Intermediate Automatic Test Equipment .... IATE
Intermediate Bachelor of Arts [British] (ROG) .... INTER BA
Intermediate Behavioral Language (SAA) .... IBL
Intermediate Block Diagram (IAA) .... IBD
Intermediate BTU [British Thermal Unit] Gas .... IBG
Intermediate Bulk Containers [Shipping] .... IBC
Intermediate Cable Equalizers (IEEE) .... ICE
Intermediate Capacity Automated Telecommunications System [Air Force] (CET) .... ICATS
Intermediate Capacity Transit System .... ICTS
Intermediate Care [Medicine] IC
Intermediate Care Facility [Medicine] .... ICF
Intermediate Care Facility for the Mentally Retarded .... ICFMR
Intermediate Care Facility for the Mentally Retarded/Developmentally Disabled .... ICF-MR/DD
Intermediate Care Unit [of a hospital] .... ICU
Intermediate Chain [Biochemistry] IC
Intermediate Chain Home (IAA) .... ICH
Intermediate Change Control Board .... ICCB
Intermediate Circuit (IAA) IC
Intermediate Circulating Reflux [Chemical engineering] .... ICR
Intermediate Cold-Wet Boot [Military] (INF) .... ICWB

Intermediate Command IC
Intermediate Communication Associative Processor [Computer science] .... ICAP
Intermediate Configuration Control Board [Western Electric] (AABC) .... ICCB
Intermediate Coronary Care Unit [Medicine] .... ICCU
Intermediate Cryptanalysis Course [Military] (DNAB) ICC
Intermediate Current Stability Experiment (DEN) .... ICSE
Intermediate Decay Storage [Nuclear energy] (NRCH) .... IDS
Intermediate Defense Communications Satellite System (IAA) .... IDCSS
Intermediate Density Lipoprotein [Biochemistry] .... IDL
Intermediate Description (IEEE) .... ID
Intermediate Design Review (NASA) .... IDR
Intermediate Dialing Center on a Toll Ticket [Telecommunications] (TEL) .... D
Intermediate Digital Distribution Frame [Telecommunications] (TEL) .... IDDF
Intermediate Direct Support [DoD] .... IDS
Intermediate Direct Support/Intermediate General Support [Army] .... IDS/IGS
Intermediate Direct Support Maintenance (MCD) .... IDSM
Intermediate Distributing Frame [Telecommunications] .... IDF
Intermediate Distribution Frame (ACRL) .... IDF
Intermediate Drum Storage (CET) .... IDS
Intermediate Early [Genetics] .... IE
Intermediate Earth Orbit (SSD) .... IEO
Intermediate Education Unit .... IEU
Intermediate Emergency Medical Technician [Also, EMT-I] (DHSM) .... IEMT
Intermediate Erection .... IE
Intermediate Examiner Training School [Federal Home Loan Bank Board] .... IETS
Intermediate Filament [Anatomy] .... IF
Intermediate Filament Protein (DMAA) .... IFP
Intermediate Fix [FAA] (TAG) .... IF
Intermediate Flush and Fill (AAG) .... IF & F
Intermediate Focal Length Optical Tracker .... IFLOT
Intermediate Focal Length Tracking Telescope (MUGU) .... IFLTT
Intermediate Force Beachhead [Military] (DNAB) .... IFBH
Intermediate Forward [Army] .... IF
Intermediate Forward Test Equipment .... IFTE
Intermediate Frame Memory [Computer science] .... IFM
Intermediate Frequency [Electronics] .... IF
Intermediate Frequency Amplifier [or Attenuator] .... IFA
Intermediate Frequency Crystal Filter .... IFCF
Intermediate Frequency/Medium Frequency (NATG) .... IF/MF
Intermediate Frequency Range (MCD) .... IFR
Intermediate Frequency Strip .... IFS
Intermediate Frequency Time Averaged Clutter Coherent Airborne [RADAR] (DNAB) .... IF TACCA
Intermediate Frequency Time Averaged Clutter Coherent Airborne RADAR (NG) .... IF TACCAR
Intermediate Frequency Transformer .... IFT
Intermediate Frequency Video Microwave (MCD) .... IFVM
Intermediate Future Forecasting System [Department of Energy] (GFGA) .... IFFS
Intermediate Gearbox (DA) .... IGB
Intermediate General Support [Army] .... IGS
Intermediate Heat Exchanger [Nuclear energy] .... IHE
Intermediate Heat Exchanger [Nuclear energy] .... IHX
Intermediate Heat Exchanger Guard Vessel [Nuclear energy] (NRCH) .... IHXGV
Intermediate Heat Transport System [Nuclear energy] (NRCH) .... IHTS
Intermediate High Frequency (IIA) .... IHF
Intermediate Infrared .... IIR
Intermediate Intensive Care Unit [Medicine] .... IICU
Intermediate Intercontinental Ballistic Missile .... IICBM
Intermediate Land (DNAB) IL
Intermediate Language [Computer science] (BUR) IL
Intermediate Language [Computer science] (TEL) .... IML
Intermediate Language Machine [Computer science] .... ILM
Intermediate Language Processor [Computer science] (BUR) .... ILP
Intermediate Language Program [Computer science] .... ILP
Intermediate Lay-Up Tool [Plastics technology] .... ILT
Intermediate Level (MCD) IL
Intermediate Level Amplifier (MHDB) .... ILA
Intermediate Level Avionics Support System (MCD) .... ILASS
Intermediate Level Reactor Test (IEEE) .... ILRT
Intermediate Level Sample Flow (IEEE) .... ILSF
Intermediate Level Test Station (MCD) .... ILTS
Intermediate Long-Range Interceptor System .... ILRIS
Intermediate Loop IL
Intermediate Lymphocytic Lymphoma [Medicine] ILL
Intermediate Machine Instruction .... IMI
Intermediate Maintenance (MCD) .... IM
Intermediate Maintenance Activity .... IMA
Intermediate Maintenance Availability .... IMAV
Intermediate Maintenance Costs (MCD) .... IMC
Intermediate Maintenance Facility .... IMF
Intermediate Maintenance Level .... IML
Intermediate Maintenance Manual [Military] (CAAL) .... IMM
Intermediate Maintenance Repair Level (MCD) .... IMRL
Intermediate Maintenance Requirements List .... IMRL
Intermediate Maintenance Squadron (MCD) .... IMS
Intermediate Maintenance Support Equipment [Army] .... IMSE
Intermediate Maintenance Trainer [Army] .... IMT
Intermediate Manned Interceptor (MUGU) .... IMI
Intermediate Message Change (AAGC) .... IMC
Intermediate Metal Conduit .... IMC
Intermediate Minimum Property Standards [Department of Housing and Urban Development] (GFGA) .... IMPS
Intermediate Missile (MSA) .... IM
Intermediate Modeling [Marine science] (OSRA) .... IM
Intermediate Modeling (USDC) .... IM

Intermediate Modulation .... IM
Intermediate Moisture (KSC) .... IM
Intermediate Moisture Food .... IMF
Intermediate Naval Nuclear Forces (DOMA) .... INNF
Intermediate Neglect of Differential Overlap [Quantum mechanics] .... INDO
Intermediate Network Node (IAA) .... INN
Intermediate Object Code File [Computer science] .... OBJ
Intermediate Objective Lens .... IOL
Intermediate of Arts [British] (ROG) .... INTER ARTS
Intermediate Pallet (NASA) .... IP
Intermediate Payload Launch Vehicle .... IPLV
Intermediate Peritoneal Dialysis [Medicine] (BARN) .... IPD
Intermediate Personality Questionnaire for Indian Pupils [Personality development test] [Psychology] .... IPQI
Intermediate Phase Training (DOMA) .... IPT
Intermediate Plot File .... IPF
Intermediate Plutonium Storage System [Nuclear energy] (NUCP) .... IPSS
Intermediate Postsurgical Fitting [Medicine] .... IPSF
Intermediate Power Amplifier [Electronics] .... IPA
Intermediate Pressure .... IP
Intermediate Processing Centers .... IPC
Intermediate Processor (SSD) .... IP
Intermediate Query Language [Computer science] .... IQL
Intermediate Range (MCD) .... IR
Intermediate Range Construction Program [Military] .... IRCP
Intermediate Range Cruise Missile [Military] (CAAL) .... IRCM
Intermediate Range Monitor (NRCH) .... IRM
Intermediate Rated Power (MCD) .... IRP
Intermediate Rated Thrust [Military] (CAAL) .... IRT
Intermediate Reference Structure .... IRS
Intermediate Register [Telecommunications] (OA) .... IR
Intermediate Related Power .... IRP
Intermediate Remedial Measures (GNE) .... IRM
Intermediate Resource Usage Condition (MHDI) .... IRUC
Intermediate Restorative Material [Dentistry] .... IRM
Intermediate Retention of Differential Overlap [Physics] .... IRDO
Intermediate Review (NATG) .... IR
Intermediate Rotating Plug (NRCH) .... IRP
Intermediate Scale Facility [Department of Energy] .... ISF
Intermediate Scale Homogeneous Reactor .... ISHR
Intermediate Scale Warfare .... ISW
Intermediate School .... IS
Intermediate School District (AEE) .... ISD
Intermediate School District 101, Professional Materials Library, Spokane, WA [Library symbol Library of Congress] (LCLS) .... WaSpln
Intermediate School District 113, Instructional Materials Center, Galvin, WA [Library symbol Library of Congress] (LCLS) .... WaGal
Intermediate Science Curriculum Study .... ISCS
Intermediate Section .... INTERSEC
Intermediate Service School [Military] (AFM) .... ISS
Intermediate Session Routing (ACRL) .... ISR
(Intermediate) Shaft Horsepower .... (I)SHP
Intermediate Sideband (NATG) .... ISB
Intermediate Slope [Skiing] I
Intermediate Sodium Characterization Package [Nuclear energy] (NRCH) .... ISCP
Intermediate Sodium Disposal Facility [Nuclear energy] (NRCH) .... ISDF
Intermediate Sodium Removal [Nuclear energy] (NRCH) .... ISR
Intermediate Specific Activity [Radioisotope] .... ISA
Intermediate Staging Base .... ISB
Intermediate Station .... INTERMSTA
Intermediate Station Operation (IAA) .... ISO
Intermediate Storage Device .... ISD
Intermediate Super-Abrasion Furnace .... ISAF
Intermediate Supply Activity [Marine Corps] (DOMA) .... ISA
Intermediate Support Base [Military] (NVT) .... ISB
Intermediate Suppression (MCD) .... IS
Intermediate System [Computer science] (TNIG) .... IS
Intermediate System Hello [Computer science] (TNIG) .... ISH
Intermediate System Mock-Up Loop (IEEE) .... ISML
Intermediate System-to-Intermediate System [Telecommunications] .... IS-IS
Intermediate Tape [Telecommunications] (TEL) .... IMT
Intermediate Tape Store (CET) .... ITS
Intermediate Teachers Association .... ITA
Intermediate Technology [An association] (EA) .... IT
Intermediate Technology Development Group [Rugby, Warwickshire, England] (EAIO) .... ITDG
Intermediate Technology Development Group of North America (EA) .... ITDG/NA
Intermediate Technology Industrial Services [ITDG] [British] .... IT-IS
Intermediate Test Facility (MCD) .... ITF
Intermediate Test Vessel (NRCH) .... ITV
Intermediate Text Block .... ITB
Intermediate Text Language (NITA) .... ITL
Intermediate Thermal Infrared Radiometer (SSD) .... ITIR
Intermediate Thermomechanical Treatment (MCD) .... ITMT
Intermediate Thrust Arc .... ITA
Intermediate Toll Center [Telecommunications] (TEL) .... ITC
Intermediate Training [Naval Air] .... INTERMTRA
Intermediate Training Assessment (DOMA) .... ITA
Intermediate Training Objective [Army] (INF) .... ITO
Intermediate Transfer Language .... ITL
Intermediate Transmission Block [Computer science] (BUR) .... ITB
Intermediate Treatment [Special provision of British law for juvenile offenders] .... IT
Intermediate Vector Boson [Physics] .... IVB
Intermediate Velocity Cloud [Astronomy] (OA) IVC
Intermediate Volitility Agents (MCD) .... IVA

Intermediate Voltage (MSA) ... IV
Intermediate Water Depth (MCD) ... IWD
Intermediate Water Depth Mine (MCD) ... IWDM
Intermediate Zone ... IZ
Intermediate Zone Yaw ... IZY
Intermediate-Dose Methotrexate [*Medicine*] (DMAA) ... IDM
Intermediate-Level Automatic Test Equipment (PDAA) ... IATE
Intermediate-Level Cell [*Nuclear energy*] (NRCH) ... ILC
Intermediate-Level Diagram (IAA) ... ILD
Intermediate-Level Maintenance Training ... ILMT
Intermediate-Level Support Equipment (MCD) ... ILSE
Intermediate-Level Waste Concentrate [*Nuclear energy*] (NRCH) ... ILWC
Intermediate-Level Waste Distillate [*Nuclear energy*] (NRCH) ... ILWD
Intermediate-Level Waste Feed [*Nuclear energy*] (NRCH) ... ILWF
Intermediate-Level Waste Storage [*Nuclear energy*] (GFGA) ... ILWS
Intermediate-Level Wastes (IEEE) ... ILW
Intermediate-Range Ballistic Missile ... IRBM
Intermediate-Range Function Test (IAA) ... IRFC
Intermediate-Range Intercontinental Ballistic Missile ... IRICBM
Intermediate-Range/Medium-Range Ballistic Missile (NG) ... IR/MRBM
Intermediate-Range Nuclear Forces ... INF
Intermediate-Range Task Force ... IRTF
Intermediate-Range Technology ... IRT
Intermediate-Size Cargo Container ... INTERCON
Intermediate-Term Standby [*Business term*] (EMRF) ... ITS
Intermembrane Space [*Biochemistry*] ... IMS
Intermenstrual Bleeding [*Medicine*] ... IMB
Interment (AABC) ... INTRMT
Interment Association of America [*Later, PIAA*] (EA) ... IAA
Interment Exchange of America ... IEA
Interment Is Authorized for the Remains Of [*Military*] ... IAR
Intermessage Processor (IAA) ... IMP
Inter-Message Separation [*Communications*] ... IMS
Intermet Corp. [*NASDAQ symbol*] (NQ) ... INMT
Intermet Corp. [*Associated Press*] (SAG) ... IntmetC
Intermetallic Compound [*Materials science*] ... IMC
Intermetallic Matrix Composite [*Materials science*] ... IMC
Intermetatarsal [*Anatomy*] (DAVI) ... IM
Intermetco Ltd. [*Toronto Stock Exchange symbol*] ... INT
Intermin Treatment Plan [*Medicine*] (DAVI) ... ITP
Intermittent (DMAA) ... I
Intermittent ... INT
Intermittent ... INTER
Intermittent (MSA) ... INTMT
Intermittent (AFM) ... INTR
Intermittent Abdominal Compression ... IAC
Intermittent Abdominal Pressure Ventilation [*Medicine*] (DMAA) ... IAPV
Intermittent Acute Porphyria [*Medicine*] ... IAP
Intermittent Aortic Occlusion [*Cardiology*] ... IAO
Intermittent Assisted Ventilation [*Medicine*] (MEDA) ... IAV
Intermittent Bladder Irrigation [*Medicine*] ... IBI
Intermittent Catheter Routine [*Medicine*] (DMAA) ... ICR
Intermittent Catheterization [*Urology*] (DAVI) ... IC
Intermittent Cervical Traction [*Orthopedics*] (DAVI) ... ICT
Intermittent Cervical Traction [*Medicine*] (DMAA) ... ICTX
Intermittent Claudication [*Medicine*] (MAE) ... IC
Intermittent Commercial and Amateur Service [*Radio*] ... ICAS
Intermittent Control Strategy [*Environmental Protection Agency*] (GFGA) ... ICS
Intermittent Control System [*Environmental Protection Agency*] ... ICS
Intermittent Demand Ventilation [*Medicine*] ... IDV
Intermittent Drive Unit ... IDU
Intermittent Dual-Fluid Exhaust Burner ... IDEB
Intermittent Duty (IAA) ... ID
Intermittent Duty (MSA) ... IDTY
Intermittent Electrical Contact (IAA) ... IEC
Intermittent Esotropia [*Ophthalmology*] (DAVI) ... E(T)
Intermittent Exotropia [*Ophthalmology*] (DAVI) ... X(T)
Intermittent Explosive Disorder ... IED
Intermittent Mandatory Ventilation [*Respiratory therapy*] [*Medicine*] ... IMV
Intermittent Mechanical Ventilation [*Respiratory therapy*] [*Medicine*] (DAVI) ... IMV
Intermittent Motion Driver ... IMD
Intermittent Negative-Pressure Ventilation [*Medicine*] ... INPV
Intermittent Noise ... IN
Intermittent Operating Life (IAA) ... IOPL
Intermittent Operation during the Time Indicated [*Broadcasting*] ... I
Intermittent Pelvic Traction (DAVI) ... IPT
Intermittent Pelvic Traction [*Medicine*] (DMAA) ... IPTX
Intermittent Peritoneal Dialysis [*Medicine*] ... IPD
Intermittent Positive Control [*Aviation*] ... IPC
Intermittent Positive Control - Automatic Seperation [*Aviation*] (PDAA) ... IPC-ASA
Intermittent Positive Pressure [*Medicine*] ... IPP
Intermittent Positive Pressure Breathing [*Medicine*] ... IPPB
Intermittent Positive Pressure Breathing/Inspiratory ... IPPB/I
Intermittent Positive Pressure Respiration ... IPPR
Intermittent Positive Pressure Ventilation ... IPPV
Intermittent Positive Pressure with Oxygen [*Medicine*] ... IPPO
Intermittent Positive-Pressure Breathing Apparatus [*Medicine*] (MEDA) ... IPPBA
Intermittent Reinforcement [*Psychology*] ... IRF
Intermittent Trouble Indication [*Telecommunications*] (TEL) ... ITI
Intermittent-Duty Rating ... IDR
Intermittent-Integrated Doppler (OA) ... IID
Intermodal Association of North America ... IANA
Intermodal Automated Transfer (PDAA) ... IMAT
Intermodal Management System [*VDOT*] (TAG) ... IMS
Intermodal Marketing Company [*A third-party shipping broker*] (ECON) ... IMC
Intermodal Surface Transportation Efficiency Act [*1990*] ... ISTEA
Intermodal Transportation Association (EA) ... ITA
Intermodulation ... IM
Intermodulation Distortion ... ID
Intermodulation Distortion (NTCM) ... IM
Intermodulation Distortion (MSA) ... IMD
Intermodulation Distortion Percentage ... IDP
Intermodulation Product ... IMP
Inter-Module Bus (NITA) ... IMB
Intermodule Connector (SSD) ... IMC
Intermolecular Energy Transfer [*Chemistry*] ... IET
Intermolecular Pair Potential Surface [*Physical chemistry*] ... IPS
Intermolecular Potential (Energy) Surface [*Spectroscopy*] ... IPS
Inter-Mountain Airways [*ICAO designator*] (FAAC) ... IMA
Intermountain Automated Clearing House Association (MHDW) ... IMACHA
Intermountain Aviation, Inc. [*Air carrier designation symbol*] ... ITAX
Intermountain College Association (AEBS) ... ICA
Intermountain Electrical Association (SRA) ... IEA
Intermountain Field Operations Center [*Bureau of Mines*] [*Denver, CO*] (GRD) ... IFOC
Intermountain Forest Industry Association (EA) ... IFIA
Intermountain Graphic Arts Association (DGA) ... IGAA
Inter-Mountain Region (FAAC) ... INTRMTRGN
Intermountain Regional Medical Program (BABM) ... IRMP
Intermountain Respiratory Intensive Care Unit [*Medicine*] (BABM) ... IRICU
Intermountain Stock Exchange [*Salt Lake City, UT*] ... ISE
Intermountain Tariff Bureau, Inc. ... ITB
Intermountain Tariff Bureau, Inc., Salt Lake City UT [*STAC*] ... IMB
Intermountain Veterinary Medical Association (EA) ... IVMA
Intermuscular [*Anatomy*] (DAVI) ... IM
Intermuseum Conservation Association (EA) ... ICA
Intern ... I
Intern Admission Note [*Medical records*] (DAVI) ... IAN
Intern on Call (HGAA) ... IOC
Intern Training Center [*DARCOM*] ... ITC
Internacia Asocio de Bibliistoj kaj Orientalistoj [*International Association of Biblicists and Orientalists - IABO*] (EA) ... IABO
Internacia Asocio de Esperantistaj Matematikistoj [*International Association of Esperantist Mathematicians*] (EAIO) ... IAdEM
Internacia Asocio Monda Turismo [*International Association for World Tourism*] (EAIO) ... MT
Internacia Centro de la Neutrala Esperanto-Movado [*International Center of the Neutral Esperanto Movement*] [*Defunct*] (EAIO) ... ICNEM
Internacia Ekologia-Ekonomia Akademio [*International Ecological-Economic Academy*] [*Bulgaria*] (EAIO) ... EKO
Internacia Esperanto - Asocio de Juristoj [*International Esperanto - Association of Jurists*] [*Graz, Austria*] (EAIO) ... IEAJ
Internacia Esperanto Klubo Automobilista [*International Automobile Esperanto Club*] (EAIO) ... IEKA
Internacia Esperanto-Amikaro de Rotarianoj [*International Esperanto Fellowship of Rotarians*] [*British*] (EAIO) ... IEAR
Internacia Esperanto-Asocio de Bibliotekistoj [*International Association of Esperanto-Speaking Librarians*] [*Later, IAEL*] (EA) ... IEAB
Internacia Fervojista Esperanto Federacio [*International Federation of Esperantist Railwaymen*] (EAIO) ... IFEF
Internacia Katolica Unuigo Esperantista [*International Catholic Esperanto Association*] (EA) ... IKUE
Internacia Komitato por Etnaj Liberecoj [*International Committee for Ethnic Liberty - ICEL*] [*Eschweiler, Federal Republic of Germany*] (EAIO) ... IKEL
Internacia Libro-Klubo Esperantista (EA) ... ILKE
Internacia Ligo de Agrikulturaj Specialistoj-Esperantistoj [*International League of Agricultural Specialists-Esperantists - ILASE*] (EAIO) ... ILASE
Internacia Ligo de Esperantistaj Foto-Kino-Magnetofon-Amatoroj [*International League of Esperantist Amateur Photographers, Cinephotographers, and Tape-Recording*] (EAIO) ... ILEF
Internacia Ligo de Esperantistaj Instruistoj [*International League of Esperantist Teachers*] (EAIO) ... ILEI
Internacia Naturista Organizo Esperantista [*International Esperantist Organization of Naturists - IEON*] (EAIO) ... INOE
Internacia Postista kaj Telekomunikista Esperanto-Asocio [*International Esperanto Association of Post and Telecommunication Workers*] (EAIO) ... IPTEA
Internacia Scienca Asocio Esperantista [*International Association of Esperanto-Speaking Scientists*] [*Oslo, Norway*] (EA) ... ISAE
Internacia Scienca Kolegio [*International College of Scientists - ICS*] [*Paderborn, Federal Republic of Germany*] (EAIO) ... ISK
Internacia Socio de Juristoj-Esperantistoj [*International Association of Esperantist Lawyers*] ... IAJE
Internacia Unuigo de la Esperantistoj-Filologoj [*International Union of Esperantist-Philologists - IUEP*] [*Sofia, Bulgaria*] (EAIO) ... IUEF
Internacia Unuigo de la Esperantistoj-Filologoj [*International Union of Esperantist-Philologists - IUEP*] [*Sofia, Bulgaria*] (EA) ... IUEFI
Internacional De Ceramica ADS [*NYSE symbol*] (TTSB) ... ICM
Internacional de Ceramica SA de CV [*NYSE symbol*] (SAG) ... ICM
Internacional de Ceramica SA de CV [*Associated Press*] (SAG) ... IntlCer
Internacional de Ingenieria y Estudios Tecnicos SA [*Spain*] (PDAA) ... INTESCA
Internal ... I
Internal (AAG) ... INT
Internal (WDMC) ... int
Internal (KSC) ... INTER
Internal ... INTERN
Internal ... INTERNL
Internal ... INTL
Internal (KSC) ... INTR

Internal (ECII) ... ITNL
Internal Absorbed Dose ... IAD
Internal Acoustic Meatus [*Medicine*] (MAE) ... IAM
Internal Air Portability ... IAP
Internal Air Transportability (MCD) ... IAT
Internal Airlift/Helicopter Slingable Container Unit [*MTMC*] (TAG) ... ISU
Internal Alignment Sensor (MCD) ... IAS
Internal Array Processor [*Data General Corp.*] ... IAP
Internal Audit ... IA
Internal Audit Division [*Environmental Protection Agency*] (GFGA) ... IAD
Internal Auditory Canal [*Anatomy*] ... IAC
Internal Auditory (Ear) ... IA
Internal Auditory Meatus [*Anatomy*] ... IAM
Internal Automation Operation ... IAO
Internal Bean Bacterial Infusion Test [*Plant pathology*] ... IBBIT
Internal Bearing Stabilized Sighting Unit (MCD) ... IBSSU
Internal Bond [*Pulp and paper technology*] ... IB
Internal Bore Weld [*Nuclear energy*] (NUCP) ... IBW
Internal Browning [*of Fruits and Vegetables*] (BARN) ... IB
Internal Bus [*Computer science*] ... IB
Internal Capsule [*Neuroanatomy*] ... IC
Internal Carotid [*Artery*] [*Cardiology*] (DAVI) ... IC
Internal Carotid Artery [*Anatomy*] ... ICA
Internal Carotid Artery Occlusion [*Medicine*] (MAE) ... ICAO
Internal Cerebral [*Neurology*] (DAVI) ... IC
Internal Change Identifier (MCD) ... ICI
Internal Chemical Shift ... ICS
Internal Cholecystectomy [*Gastroenterology*] (DAVI) ... IC
Internal Combustion ... IC
Internal Combustion [*Freight*] ... INTL COMB
Internal Combustion Engine ... ICE
Internal Combustion Engine Institute [*Later, EMA*] (EA) ... ICEI
Internal Combustion Engine Powered Material (MCD) ... ICEPM
Internal Combustion Engine Repair Ship [*Navy symbol*] ... ARG
Internal Combustion Engine Repair Shop ... ICERP
Internal Combustion Engine Vehicle ... ICEV
Internal Combustion Piston Engine (PDAA) ... ICPE
Internal Combustion Powered (ADA) ... ICP
Internal Common Bus [*Computer science*] ... ICB
Internal Communication System [*Space Flight Operations Facility, NASA*] ... ICS
Internal Communications (CAAL) ... IC
Internal COMPOOL [*Communications Pool*] **Table** (SAA) ... ICT
Internal Conjugate [*Diameter*] [*Gynecology*] (DAVI) ... IC
Internal Connection [*Electronics*] ... IC
Internal Connection Protocol [*Telecommunications*] ... ICP
Internal Connectionless Protocol [*Telecommunications*] ... ICLP
Internal Control Audit Planning Summary (AAGC) ... ICAPS
Internal Control Description Database ... ICDDB
Internal Control Description Language ... ICDL
Internal Control Description Language Analyzer [*Computer science*] (MHDI) ... ICDLA
Internal Control Loop [*Chemical engineering*] ... ICL
Internal Control Questionnaire (ADA) ... ICQ
Internal Control Region [*Genetics*] ... ICR
Internal Control Review [*DoD*] ... ICR
Internal Control Review Program [*Air Force*] (DOMA) ... ICRP
Internal Conversion [*Nuclear science*] (OA) ... IC
Internal Conversion Coefficient [*Radiology*] ... ICC
Internal Coordination Control Drawing ... ICCD
Internal Correction Voltage ... ICV
Internal Countermeasures Set (MCD) ... ICS
Internal Data Channel ... IDC
Internal Data Manipulation Language [*Computer science*] (PDAA) ... IDML
Internal Data Processing (IAA) ... IDP
Internal Data Requirement Description (MCD) ... IDRD
Internal Defense and Development [*Army*] (AABC) ... IDAD
Internal Defense Identification Area (SAA) ... IDIA
Internal Defense Plans (CINC) ... IDP
Internal Delay Factor [*Computer science*] ... IDF
Internal Derangement of Knee [*Medicine*] (DMAA) ... IDK
Internal Derangement of Knee Joint ... IDK
Internal Design Pressure (PDAA) ... IDP
Internal Development and Assistance Program (AFM) ... IDAP
Internal Development and Production Program ... IDP
Internal Development Report ... IDR
Internal Diameter (MSA) ... ID
Internal Diameter to External Diameter [*Ratio for cardiac valve replacement*] [*Cardiology*] (DAVI) ... ID/ED
Internal Distribution Frame [*Television*] (IAA) ... IDF
Internal Distribution Only (SAA) ... IDO
Internal Distribution Publication [*Navy*] (MCD) ... IDP
Internal Distribution System [*Television*] ... IDS
Internal Document Control ... IDC
Internal Dose Information Center [*ORNL*] ... IDIC
Internal Drive Generator ... IDG
Internal Economic Problems [*British*] ... IEP
Internal Economic Rate of Return ... IER
Internal Elastic Lamina [*Medicine*] (DMAA) ... IEL
Internal Elastica [*Artery anatomy*] ... IE
Internal Electromagnetic Pulse ... IEMP
Internal Electronic Countermeasure ... IECM
Internal Energy (DAVI) ... E
Internal Energy [*Symbol*] [*Thermodynamics*] ... U
Internal Engine Generator (PDAA) ... IEG
Internal Environment ... IE
Internal Environment Monitoring ... IEM
Internal Environment Simulator ... IES
Internal Feed Rate Override ... IFRO
Internal Fetal Monitor [*Medicine*] (DMAA) ... IFM
Internal Field Emission ... IFE
Internal Fixation [*Orthopedics*] (DAVI) ... IF
Internal Floating Roof Tank [*Engineering*] ... IFRT
Internal Focus Sensor (PDAA) ... IFS
Internal Format Object Report (MCD) ... IFOR
Internal Friction Damping (PDAA) ... IFD
Internal Frosted (IAA) ... INTF
Internal Function [*Electronics*] (ECII) ... IF
Internal Function Register ... IFR
Internal Gain Control (IAA) ... IGC
Internal Gamma Flux Monitor ... IGFM
Internal Granule Layer [*Cytology*] ... IGL
Internal Gravity Wave [*in the atmosphere*] ... IGW
Internal Guidance (NASA) ... IG
Internal Guide Sequence [*Genetics*] ... IGS
Internal Job Processing (IAA) ... IJP
Internal Jugular [*Anatomy*] ... IJ
Internal Jugular Pressure [*Medicine*] (MAE) ... IJP
Internal Jugular Vein [*Medicine*] (DMAA) ... IJV
Internal Junctor [*Electronics*] (IAA) ... IJ
Internal Limiting Membrane [*Medicine*] (DMAA) ... ILM
Internal Load Deflection [*Automotive seating*] ... ILD
Internal Locus of Control [*Psychology*] ... ILC
Internal Macedonian Revolutionary Organization [*Bulgaria*] [*Political party*] (PPE) ... IMRO
Internal Macedonian Revolutionary Organization - Democratic Party for Macedonian[*Bulgaria*] **National Unity** [*Political party*] (EY) ... IMRO-DPMNU
Internal Macedonian Revolutionary Organization - Democratic Party for MacedonianNational Unity [*Political party*] ... VMRO-DPMNE
Internal Magnetic Focus ... IMF
Internal Mammary Artery Bypass [*Medicine*] (DMAA) ... IMAB
Internal Mammary Artery Graft [*Cardiology*] (DAVI) ... IMAG
Internal Mammary Artery (Implant) [*Medicine*] ... IMA
Internal Mammary Artery Implant [*Medicine*] (DMAA) ... IMAI
Internal Mammary Chain [*Medicine*] (DAVI) ... IMC
Internal Mammary Coronary Artery Bypass [*Cardiology*] ... IMCAB
Internal Mammary [*Lymph*] **Node** [*Medicine*] (DAVI) ... IMN
Internal Management Control (DOMA) ... IMC
Internal Management System [*Military*] (AFIT) ... IMS
Internal Measurement System ... IMS
Internal Measurement Unit (NASA) ... IMU
Internal Measuring Unit System (MCD) ... IMUS
Internal Medial Malleolus [*Medicine*] (DMAA) ... IMM
Internal Medicine (AAMN) ... I
Internal Medicine ... IM
Internal Medicine (AABC) ... INTMED
Internal Medicine Group [*Group practice*] (DAVI) ... IMG
Internal Medullary Lamina [*Neuroanatomy*] ... IML
Internal Memorandum ... IM
Internal Message Distribution Center (NATG) ... IMDC
Internal Messenger Service [*Hotels*] ... INTMS
Internal Model Control [*Chemical engineering*] [*Computer science*] ... IMC
Internal Mold Release [*Plastics technology*] ... IMR
Internal Motor Vehicle [*Type of tugboat*] (DS) ... IMV
Internal Navigation System ... INS
Internal Noise Level (IEEE) ... INL
Internal Note ... IN
Internal Operating Budget ... IOB
Internal Operating Instruction ... IOI
Internal Operating Procedure ... IOP
Internal Os [*or Orifice*] [*Medicine*] (DAVI) ... IO
Internal Packet Protocol [*Telecommunications*] ... IPP
Internal Phloem [*Botany*] ... IP
Internal Pipe Thread ... IPT
Internal Plate Screen (IAA) ... IPS
Internal Podalic Version [*Obstetrics*] ... IPV
Internal Polarization Modulation (IEEE) ... IPM
Internal Positive Control [*Genetics*] ... IPC
Internal Power Supply [*Computer science*] ... IPS
Internal Problem Generator (IAA) ... IPG
Internal Procedures Instruction ... IPI
Internal Progress Report ... IPR
Internal Protocol (SSD) ... IP
Internal Quality ... IQ
Internal Rate of Return [*Telecommunications*] (TEL) ... IROR
Internal Rate of Return [*Finance*] ... IRR
Internal Reference Number ... IRN
Internal Reflection Element [*Spectroscopy*] ... IRE
Internal Reflection Plate ... IRP
Internal Reflection Spectroscopy ... IRS
Internal Reflection Technique ... IRT
Internal Regenerative (KSC) ... INTEREGEN
Internal Register (IAA) ... IR
Internal Release Agent ... IRA
Internal Reliability ... IR
Internal REM [*Roentgen-Equivalent-Man*] [*Radiation dose*] ... INREM
Internal Repeat [*Genetics*] ... IR
Internal Report ... IR
Internal Representation (MHDB) ... IREP
Internal Research and Development [*Army*] ... IR & D
Internal Resistance ... IR

Internal Revenue (ROG) ... INT REV
Internal Revenue ... IR
Internal Revenue Act ... IRA
Internal Revenue Bulletin [*A publication*] (DLA) ... Int Rev Bull
Internal Revenue Bulletin ... IRB
Internal Revenue Bureau Committee on Appeals and Review, Memorandum [*United States*] [*A publication*] (DLA) ... ARM
Internal Revenue Bureau Committee on Appeals and Review, Recommendation [*United States*] [*A publication*] (DLA) ... ARR
Internal Revenue Bureau Miscellaneous Tax Ruling [*United States*] [*A publication*] (DLA) ... MT
Internal Revenue Code ... IRC
Internal Revenue Decisions [*Department of the Treasury*] [*A publication*] (DLA) ... IR
Internal Revenue Department ... IRD
Internal Revenue Looseleaf Regulations System ... IRR
Internal Revenue Office [*or Officer*] ... IRO
Internal Revenue Service [*Department of the Treasury*] [*Washington, DC*] ... IRS
Internal Revenue Service Centers ... IRSC
Internal Revenue Service Library, Washington, DC [*OCLC symbol*] (OCLC) ... IRS
Internal Revenue (Service) Manual [*A publication*] (AAGC) ... IRM
Internal Revenue Service Mimeographed Ruling (AAGC) ... IR Mim
Internal Review [*Army*] (AABC) ... IR
Internal Review and Audit Compliance [*Army*] ... IR & AC
Internal Review and System Improvement [*Army*] ... IRASI
Internal Ribosomal Entry Site [*Genetics*] ... IRES
Internal Ribosome Entry Sequence [*To 21st site sequence*] ... IRES
Internal Rotation [*Orthopedics*] (DAVI) ... int rot
Internal Rotation [*Myology*] ... IR
Internal Rotation in Extension [*Orthopedics*] (DAVI) ... IRE
Internal Rotation in Flexion [*Orthopedics*] (DAVI) ... IRF
Internal Routing Network ... IRN
Internal Scientific Report ... ISR
Internal Security ... INSEC
Internal Security [*Military British*] ... IS
Internal Security Division [*Abolished 1973; functions transferred to Criminal Division*] [*Department of Justice*] ... ISD
Internal Security Plan (CINC) ... ISP
Internal Shape Components (CINC) ... INSC
Internal Shield [*Electronics*] ... IS
Internal Shutter Grid ... ISG
Internal Spectral Shifter and Energy Converter (MCD) ... ISSEC
Internal Standard [*Chemistry*] ... IS
Internal Standard Line ... ISL
Internal Standard Operating Procedure [*Military*] (MCD) ... ISOP
Internal Standard Organization Code (CMD) ... ISO
Internal Statement Number (IAA) ... ISN
Internal Status Word (IAA) ... ISW
Internal Storage Area [*Computer science*] (BYTE) ... ISA
Internal Surface (AAG) ... IS
Internal Surface Area of Lung at Volume of 5 Liters [*Medicine*] (MAE) ... ISA_5
Internal Surface Reverse Phase [*Chromatography column*] ... ISRP
Internal Switching System ... ISS
Internal Symbol Dictionary [*Computer science*] (OA) ... ISD
Internal System Organization (ECII) ... ISO
Internal Technical Memorandum ... ITM
Internal Technical Report ... ITR
Internal Teleprocessing System (CMD) ... ITPS
Internal Test Directive (KSC) ... ITD
Internal Thoracic Artery [*Medicine*] (DMAA) ... I&T
Internal Thread ... IT
Internal Tibial Torsion [*Orthopedics*] (DAVI) ... ITT
Internal Tide Experiment [*Marine science*] (MSC) ... ITEX
Internal Time Sharing (IAA) ... ITS
Internal Transcribed Spacer [*Genetics*] ... ITS
Internal Transfer Bus ... ITB
Internal Translation Information Subsystem [*Computer science*] ... ITIS
Internal Translator [*Carnegie Institute*] [*IBM Corp.*] ... IT
Internal Transmittance [*Symbol*] [*IUPAC*] ... T
Internal Triangular Hinge Ligament [*of scallops*] ... ITHL
Internal Tympaniform Membrane [*Zoology*] ... ITM
Internal Unstable Damper (MCD) ... IUD
Internal Vapor Deposition (ACRL) ... IVD
Internal Variable (NASA) ... IVAR
Internal Velocity ... IV
Internal Velocity (SSD) ... VI
Internal Vibration Isolator ... IVI
Internal Visual Reference [*Motion sickness*] ... IVR
Internal Waste Manifest [*Stanford University*] ... IWM
Internal Wave Experiment (NOAA) ... IWEX
Internal Web Channel Bus (IAA) ... IWCB
Internal Working Paper ... IWP
Internally and Externally (NRCH) ... I & E
Internally Blown Flap [*Aviation*] ... IBF
Internally Flawless [*Diamond clarity grade*] ... IF
Internally Linked Operation ... ILO
Internally Matched FETs [*Field Effect Transistor*] [*Avantek*] (NITA) ... IMFET
Internally Specified Index ... ISI
Internally Stored Program (AAG) ... ISP
Internally Switched Interface System [*Tymnet, Inc.*] ... ISIS
Internally-Silvered Lamp [*Light bulb*] (DI) ... ISL
Internal-Mix Nozzle ... IMN
Internal-Mix Spray Nozzle ... IMSN
Internals Indexing Fixture (NRCH) ... IIF
Internal-to-Internal Interface (MCD) ... ITII
Intern-Architect Development Program (DICI) ... IDP
Inter-NASA Data Exchange (IEEE) ... INDEX
Internatioal Internet Association ... IIA
Internation Nuclear Information Service [*International Atomic Energy Authority*] (NITA) ... INIS
Inter-Nation Simulation [*Simulation of international relations*] ... I-NS
Internationaal Belasting Documentatie Bureau [*International Bureau of Fiscal Documentation*] (EAIO) ... IBDB
Internationaal Instituut voor Lucht-en Ruimtekaartering an Aardkunde [*International Institute for Aerospace Survey and Earth Sciences*] [*Netherlands*] (EAIO) ... ITC
Internationaal Instituut voor Sociale Geschiedenis [*International Institute for Social History*] (EA) ... IISG
Internationaal Juridisch Instituut [*International Juridical Institute*] [*BENELUX*] ... IJI
Internationaal Ontmoetings Centrum [*International Network for Self-Reliance - INS*] (EA) ... IOC
Internationaal Watertribunaal [*International Water Tribunal*] [*Netherlands*] (EAIO) ... IWT
International ... I
International (EY) ... INT
International (WDMC) ... int
International ... INTERN
International ... INTERNAT
International ... INTERNATL
International (AFM) ... INTL
International (VRA) ... intl
International (WDMC) ... intl
International ... INTN'L
International ... INTRNTL
International 210 Association (EA) ... ITA
International Abolitionist Federation [*India*] ... IAF
International Absorbents [*NASDAQ symbol*] (SAG) ... IABS
International Absorbents [*Associated Press*] (SAG) ... IntAbs
International Abstaining Motorists' Association [*Hagersten, Sweden*] (EAIO) ... IAMA
International Abstracting Board [*Also, ICSU AB*] [*International Council of Scientific Unions*] ... IAB
International Academic Union (EA) ... IAU
International Academy at Santa Barbara (EA) ... IASB
International Academy for Child Brain Development (EA) ... IACBD
International Academy for Environmental Safety ... IAES
International Academy for Quality [*Grobenzell, Federal Republic of Germany*] (EAIO) ... IAQ
International Academy of Aquatic Art (EA) ... IAAA
International Academy of Astronautics [*Paris, France*] (EA) ... IAA
International Academy of Aviation and Space Medicine (EAIO) ... IAASM
International Academy of Biological Medicine [*Defunct*] (EA) ... IABM
International Academy of Ceramics [*See also AIC*] [*Geneva, Switzerland*] (EAIO) ... IAC
International Academy of Chest Physicians and Surgeons (EA) ... IACPS
International Academy of Cosmetic Surgery [*Rome, Italy*] (EA) ... IACS
International Academy of Cytology [*Quebec, PQ*] (EA) ... IAC
International Academy of Eclectic Psychotherapists [*St. Ives, NSW, Australia*] (EAIO) ... IAEP
International Academy of Gnathology - American Section (EA) ... IAG
International Academy of Health Care Professionals (EA) ... IAHCP
International Academy of Indian Culture (EAIO) ... IAIC
International Academy of Law & Mental Health (AC) ... IALMH
International Academy of Management [*Knoxville, TN*] (EA) ... IAM
International Academy of Medicine and Psychology [*Australia*] (EA) ... IAMP
International Academy of Metabology (EA) ... IAM
International Academy of Myodontics (EA) ... IAM
International Academy of Myodontics, Asian Chapter [*Tokyo, Japan*] (EAIO) ... IAMA
International Academy of Myodontics, Oceanic Chapter [*Sydney, NSW, Australia*] (EAIO) ... IAM
International Academy of Nutrition and Preventive Medicine (EA) ... IANPM
International Academy of Nutritional Consultants [*AANC*] [*Absorbed by*] (EA) ... IANC
International Academy of Optimum Dentistry [*Defunct*] (EA) ... IAOD
International Academy of Oral Medicine and Toxicology ... IAOMT
International Academy of Pathology (EA) ... IAP
International Academy of Pediatric Transdisciplinary Education [*British*] (EAIO) ... IAPTE
International Academy of Preventive Medicine (EA) ... IAPM
International Academy of Proctology [*Defunct*] (EA) ... IAP
International Academy of Sciences (EAIO) ... IAS
International Academy of Sports Vision [*Formerly, National Academy of Sports Vision*] (EAIO) ... NASV
International Academy of the History of Medicine [*Defunct*] (EA) ... IAHM
International Academy of the History of Science [*Paris, France*] (EA) ... IAHS
International Academy of Toxicological Risk Assessment (EA) ... IATRA
International Academy of Trial Lawyers (EA) ... IATL
International Academy of Twirling Teachers (EA) ... IATT
International Accidental War Information Sharing Project [*Nuclear Age Peace Foundation*] (EA) ... IAWISP
International Accountants Society ... IAS
International Accounting and Traffic Analysis Equipment [*Telecommunications*] (NITA) ... IATAE
International Accounting and Traffic Analysis Equipment [*Telecommunications*] (TEL) ... IATE
International Accounting Standards ... IAS

International Accounting Standards Committee [*of the International Federation of Accountants*] [*British*] (EAIO) .... IASC
International Accreditation Forum [*For quality control*] .... IAF
International Acetylene Association [*Later, CGA*] .... IAA
International Acronyms, Initialisms, and Abbreviations Dictionary [*A publication*] .... IAIAD
International Action Against Hunger (EAIO) .... IAAH
International Action for the Rights of the Child [*See also AIDE*] [*Paris, France*] (EAIO) .... IARC
International Active Sun Years .... IASY
International Activities Committee [*American Chemical Society*] .... IAC
International Activities Fund [*Canadian Labour Congress*] [*See also FAI*] .... IAF
International Activities Program [*US Army Western Command*] .... IAP
International Ad Hoc Committee (PCM) .... IAHC
International Administrative Aeronautical Radio Conference [*Also known as WARC*] .... IAARC
International Advanced Life Information System (BUR) .... INTERALIS
International Advanced Microlithography Society [*Defunct*] (EA) .... IAMS
International Advertising Association [*Later, AAF*] (EA) .... IAA
International Advertising Executives' Association (NTCM) .... IAEA
International Advisory Committee [*ANSI*] .... IAC
International Advisory Committee of the International Teletraffic Congress (EAIO) .... IACITC
International Advisory Committee on Bibliography, Documentation and Terminology (NITA) .... IACBDT
International Advisory Committee on Bibliography [*UNESCO*] (WDAA) .... IACB
International Advisory Committee on Documentation, Libraries, and Archives [*UNESCO*] (DIT) .... IACDLA
International Advisory Committee on Marine Sciences [*UNESCO*] (ASF) .... IACOMS
International Advisory Council for Homosexual Men and Women in Alcoholics Anonymous (EA) .... IAC
International Advisory Group on Technology Management [*Information broker and consultancy*] (NITA) .... INTAG
International Aeradio Caribbean Ltd. .... IACL
International Aeradio Ltd. [*British*] .... IAL
International Aeradio Ltd. [*British ICAO designator*] (ICDA) XI
International Aeradio PLC [*British ICAO designator*] (FAAC) .... IAL
International Aero Press .... IAP
International Aerobatic Club (EA) .... IAC
International Aeronautical Federation .... IAF
International Aeronautical Telecommunications Switching Center .... IATSC
International Aerosol Association [*Zurich, Switzerland*] (EAIO) .... IAA
International Aerospace Abstracts [*American Institute of Aeronautics and Astronautics*] [*A publication*] (AEBS) .... IAA
International Affairs (DD) .... IntlAffairs
International Affairs (London) [*A publication*] .... IAL
International Affiliation of Independent Accounting Firms [*Later, Independent Accountants International*] (EA) .... IA
International Affiliation of Independent Accounting Firms (EA) .... IAIAF
International African Institute [*British*] .... IAI
International African Law Association .... IALA
International African Migratory Locust Organization [*See also OICMA*] (EA) .... IAMLO
International Afro-American Museum [*Later, AAM*] (EA) .... IAM
International Afroid Science Conference (MCD) .... IASC
International Agency for Research on Cancer [*World Health Organization*] [*Lyon, France*] [*Research center*] (EAIO) .... IARC
International Agency for Research on Cancer (EERA) .... IARC
International Agency for the Prevention of Blindness (EA) .... IAPB
International Agreement Competitive Restrictions (AAGC) .... IACR
International Agreement Regarding the Maintenance of Certain Lights in the Red Sea (EA) .... IARMCLRS
International Agricultural Aviation Centre [*Defunct*] (EA) .... IAAC
International Agricultural Aviation Foundation (EA) .... IAAF
International Agricultural Club (EA) .... IAC
International Agricultural Development Service [*Later, WIIAD*] [*Department of Agriculture*] .... IADS
International Agricultural Exchange Association [*British*] (EA) .... IAEA
International Agricultural Research Center .... IARC
International Agricultural Research Centre (EERA) .... IARC
International Agricultural Students Association of the Americas (EA) .... IASAA
International AIDS Prospective Epidemiology Network (EA) .... INAPEN
International AIDS Society (EAIO) .... IAS
International AIDS Vaccine Initiative .... IAVI
International Aikido Federation [*Tokyo, Japan*] (EAIO) .... IAF
International Air Bahama [*ICAO designator*] (AD) .... IW
International Air Cadet Exchange .... IACE
International Air Cargo Corp. [*Egypt*] [*ICAO designator*] (FAAC) .... IACC
International Air Cargo Corp. [*Egypt*] [*ICAO designator*] (FAAC) .... IAK
International Air Carrier Association [*Zaventhem, Belgium*] (EAIO) .... IACA
International Air Carrier Association [*ICAO designator*] (FAAC) .... ITC
International Air Convention .... IAC
International Air Corp. [*FAA designator*] (FAAC) .... EXX
International Air Freight Forwarder (AABC) .... IAFF
International Air Line Stewards and Stewardesses Association .... IALSSA
International Air Navigation Convention .... IANC
International Air Safety Association (EA) .... IASA
International Air Safety Seminar .... IASS
International Air Service Co. [*ICAO designator*] (FAAC) .... IAS
International Air Traffic Communications .... IATC
International Air Traffic Communications Receiver Station .... IATCR
International Air Traffic Communications Station .... IATCS
International Air Traffic Communications System (MCD) .... IATCS
International Air Traffic Communications Transmitter Station .... IATCT

International Air Transport Association [*ICAO designator*] (FAAC) .... IAT
International Air Transport [*formerly, Traffic*] Association [*Canada*] .... IATA
International Air Transport Association (IATA) [*ICAO designator*] (ICDA) .... XB
International Air Transport Association, Montreal, PQ, Canada [*Library symbol Library of Congress*] (LCLS) .... CaQMIA
International Air Transport Association [*Association du Transport Aerien International*] Montreal, Quebec [*Library symbol National Library of Canada*] (NLC) .... QMIA
International Air Transportation Competition Act of 1979 .... IATCA
International Aircraft Leasing Co. .... IALCO
International Airforwarders and Agents Association (EA) .... IAAA
International Airline Navigators Council [*Defunct*] .... IANC
International Airline Passengers Association .... APA
International Airline Passengers Association (EA) .... IAPA
International Airlines Technical Pool (PDAA) .... IATP
International Airport .... IAP
International Airports Authority of India [*ICAO designator*] (FAAC) .... ATY
International Al Jolson Society (EA) .... IAJS
International Alban Berg Society (EA) .... IABS
International Alert (EA) .... IA
International Algebraic Compiler .... IAC
International Algebraic Language [*Programming language*] [*Replaced by ALGOL*] .... IAL
International Algorithmic Language [*Computer science*] (BUR) .... IAL
[*The*] International Alliance, an Association of Executive and ProfessionalWomen [*Baltimore, MD*] (EA) .... TIA
International Alliance for Distribution by Cable [*Formerly, International Alliancefor Distribution by Wire*] (EA) .... IADC
International Alliance for Sustainable Agriculture (EA) .... IASA
International Alliance for Sustainable Agriculture (GNE) .... IASA
International Alliance of Bill Posters, Billers, and Distributors of US and Canada [*Defunct*] (EA) .... BPBD
International Alliance of Bill Posters, Billers, and Distributors of US and Canada [*Defunct*] .... IABPBD
International Alliance of Catholic Churches (EA) .... IACC
International Alliance of Film Producers [*Later, IAIP*] (EA) .... IAFP
International Alliance of Messianic Congregations and Synagogues (EA) .... IAMCS
International Alliance of Nutrimedical Associations (EA) .... IANA
International Alliance of Theatrical Stage Employees (NTCM) .... IA
International Alliance of Theatrical Stage Employees and Moving Picture Machine Operators of the United States and Canada .... IA
International Alliance of Theatrical Stage Employees and Moving Picture Machine Operators of the US and Canada (EA) .... IATSE
International Alliance of Theatrical Stage Employes [*An AFL-CIO union*] [*New York, NY*] (WDMC) .... IATSE
International Alliance of Women [*See also AIF*] [*Valetta, Malta*] (EAIO) .... IAW
International Alliance Services, Inc. [*NASDAQ symbol*] (SAG) .... IASI
International Alliance Services, Inc. [*Associated Press*] (SAG) .... IntlAllSv
International Allied Printing Trades Association (EA) .... IAPTA
International Aloe Science Council (EA) .... IASC
International Alphabet .... IA
International Alphabet .... ITA
International Alphabet 5 (NITA) IA-5
International Alphabet-2 [*Standard telegraphy code*] (NITA) IA-2
International Aluminum Corp. [*NYSE symbol*] (SPSG) .... IAL
International Aluminum Corp. [*Associated Press*] (SAG) .... IntAlu
International Amateur Athletic Federation [*See also FIAA*] [*British*] (EAIO) .... IAAF
International Amateur Boat Building Society [*Defunct*] .... IABBS
International Amateur Boxing Association .... IABA
International Amateur Cycling Federation (EA) .... IACF
International Amateur Karate Federation (EA) .... IAKF
International Amateur Racquetball Federation (EA) .... IARF
International Amateur Radio Network .... IARN
International Amateur Radio Union (EA) .... IARU
International Amateur Snowshoe Racing Federation (EA) .... IASSRF
International Amateur Surfing Federation (EA) .... IASF
International Amateur Swimming Federation (EA) .... IASF
International Amateur Theatre Association [*Denmark*] .... IATA
International Amateur-Professional Photoelectric Photometry [*An association*] .... IAPPP
International Amco Corp. [*Toronto Stock Exchange symbol*] .... IAM
International American Saddlebred Pleasure Horse Association (EA) .... IASPHA
International Americas Cup Class [*Yachting*] .... IACC
International Analysis Code [*Meteorology*] .... IAC
International Anatomical Nomenclature Committee [*British*] (EAIO) .... IANC
International and Comparative Law Bulletin [*A publication*] (DLA) .... Int'l & Comp L Bull
International Anesthesia Research Society (EA) .... IARS
International Angstrom .... IA
International Animal Rights Alliance [*Defunct*] (EA) .... IARA
International Animated Film Society (EA) .... IAFS
International Annealed Copper Standard .... IACS
International Antarctic Glaciological Project [*Defunct*] (EA) .... IAGP
International Antarctic Meteorological Research Center (PDAA) .... IAMRC
International Antarctic Meteorological Research Centre (PDAA) .... IAMRC
International Anti-Counterfeiting Coalition (EA) .... IAC
International Anticounterfeiting Coalition (EA) .... IACC
International Anti-Euthanasia Task Force (EA) .... IAETF
International Antituberculosis Association (DAVI) .... IAA
International Apparel Federation [*Berlin, Federal Republic of Germany*] (EAIO) .... IAF
International Apple Association [*Later, IAI*] (EA) .... IAA
International Apple Institute (EA) .... IAI
International Applications Group [*IFIP*] .... IAG

International Applied Systems (NITA) ... IAS
International Appropriate Technology Association [*Defunct*] (EA) ... IATA
International Aquaculture Foundation (EA) ... IAF
International Arab Federation ... IAF
International Arabian Horse Association (EA) ... IAHA
International Arabian Horse Registry of North America (EA) ... IAHRONA
International Arbitration Journal [*A publication*] (DLA) ... Int Arb J
International Arbitration Journal [*A publication*] (DLA) ... Int'l Arb J
International Archery Federation (EA) ... IAF
International Arctic Buoy Program [*Marine science*] (OSRA) ... IABP
International Arctic Science Committee ... IASC
International Arctic Seas Assessment Project [*Marine science*] (OSRA) ... IASAP
International Arid Lands Consortium (EERA) ... IALC
International Armaments Cooperative Opportunities Plan ... IACOP
International Arms-Control Symposium ... IACS
International Army Staff (MCD) ... IAS
International Aroid Society (EA) ... IAS
International Art Cinemas Confederation (EAIO) ... IACC
International Art Guild (EA) ... IAG
International Art Register ... IAR
International Arthroscopy Association (EA) ... IAA
International Arthur Schnitzler Research Association (EA) ... IASRA
International Arthurian Society/North American Branch [*Canada*] (EAIO) ... IAS/NAB
International Artist Network (EA) ... IAN
International Artists' Cooperation (EAIO) ... IAC
International Artists' Cooperation Audio Art Center [*Defunct*] (EA) ... IACAAC
International Arts and Sciences Press ... IASP
International Arts Medicine Association [*Philadelphia, PA*] ... IAMA
International Arts Relations ... INTAR
International Assembly of Grocery Manufacturers Associations (EAIO) ... IAGMA
International Assets Hldg Wrrt [*NASDAQ symbol*] (TTSB) ... IAACW
International Assets Holding Corp. [*NASDAQ symbol*] (SAG) ... IAAC
International Assets Holding Corp. [*Associated Press*] (SAG) ... IntlAsst
International Assets Holding Corp. [*Associated Press*] (SAG) ... IntlAst
[*The*] **International Assets Valuation Standards Committee** [*of the American Institute of Real Estate Appraisers*] [*British*] (EAIO) ... TIAVSC
International Association Against Painful Experiments on Animals (EA) ... IAAPEA
International Association Against Torture (EAIO) ... IAAT
International Association Auto Theft Investigators (EA) ... IAATI
International Association for a Union of Democracies [*Defunct*] (EA) ... IAUD
International Association for Accident and Traffic Medicine (EA) ... IAATM
International Association for Advancement of Appropriate Technology for Developing Countries (EA) ... IAAATDC
International Association for Analytical Psychology (EA) ... IAAP
International Association for Aquatic Animal Medicine (EA) ... IAAAM
International Association for Bear Research and Management (EA) ... IABRM
International Association for Better Basic Education (EA) ... IABBE
International Association for Biological Oceanography [*Aberdeen, Scotland*] (EAIO) ... IABO
International Association for Bridge and Structural Engineering [*ICSU*] [*Zurich, Switzerland*] [*Research center*] (EA) ... IABSE
International Association for Business Organizations [*Baltimore, MD*] (EA) ... INAFBO
International Association for Business Research and Corporate Development [*West Wickham, Kent, England*] (EAIO) ... EVAF
International Association for Byzantine Studies [*See also AIEB*] [*Thessaloniki, Greece*] (EAIO) ... IABS
International Association for Cereal Science and Technology [*Formerly, International Association of Cereal Chemists*] [*Acronym represents association's former name*] [*Austria*] ... ICC
International Association for Child and Adolescent Psychiatry and Allied Professions [*Copenhagen, Denmark*] (EA) ... IACAPAP
International Association for Child Psychiatry and Allied Professions [*Later, IACAPAP*] ... IACP
International Association for Child Psychiatry and Allied Professions [*Later, IACAPAP*] ... IACPAP
International Association for Classical Archaeology [*See also AIAC*] [*Rome, Italy*] (EAIO) ... IACA
International Association for Clear Thinking (EA) ... IACT
International Association for Commodity Science and Technology (EAIO) ... IACST
International Association for Comparative Research on Leukemia and Related Diseases (EA) ... IACRLRD
International Association for Computational Mechanics [*International Council of Scientific Unions*] ... IACM
International Association for Computer Systems Security (EA) ... IACSS
International Association for Computing in Education [*Also, an information service or system*] (EA) ... IACE
International Association for Conservation of Natural Resources and Energy ... IACNRE
International Association for Continuing Education and Training (EA) ... IACET
International Association for Crosscultural Communication [*State University of Ghent*] [*Research center Belgium*] (IRC) ... AIMAV
International Association for Cross-Cultural Psychology [*Canada*] (EA) ... IACCP
International Association for Cryptologic Research (EA) ... IACR
International Association for Cultural Freedom [*Defunct*] (EA) ... IACF
International Association for Cybernetics [*See also AIC*] [*Namur, Belgium*] (EAIO) ... IAC
International Association for Dance Medicine and Science ... IADMS
International Association for Dental Research (EA) ... IADR
International Association for Earthquake Engineering [*ICSU*] [*Tokyo, Japan*] (EAIO) ... IAEE
International Association for Ecology [*University of Georgia*] [*Athens, GA*] (EAIO) ... INTECOL
International Association for Educational and Vocational Guidance [*See also AIOSP*] [*Belfast, Northern Ireland*] (EAIO) ... IAEVG
International Association for Educational and Vocational Information [*See also AIISUP*] [*Paris, France*] (EAIO) ... IAEVI
International Association for Educational Assessment (EA) ... IAEA
International Association for Energy Economics (EERA) ... IAEE
International Association for Enterostomal Therapy (EA) ... IAET
International Association for Esperanto in Libraries [*See also TEBA*] (EAIO) ... IAEL
International Association for Falconry and Conservation of Birds of Prey (EAIO) ... IAF
International Association for Financial Planning (EA) ... IAFP
International Association for Food Self-Sufficiency (EA) ... IAFS
International Association for Gerda Alexander Eutony [*See also AIEGA*] [*Switzerland*] (EAIO) ... IAGAE
International Association for Germanic Studies (EAIO) ... IAGS
International Association for Great Lakes Research (EA) ... IAGLR
International Association for Healthcare Security and Safety (EA) ... IAHSS
International Association for Hospital Security [*Later, IAHSS*] (EA) ... IAHS
International Association for Housing Science (EA) ... IAHS
International Association for Hydraulic Research [*ICSU*] [*Delft, Netherlands*] (EA) ... IAHR
International Association for Hydrogen Energy (EA) ... IAHE
International Association for Identification (EA) ... IAI
International Association for Impact Assessment (EA) ... IAIA
International Association for Information and Documentation in Public Administration (EAIO) ... IAIDPA
International Association for Integrative Education [*Versoix, Switzerland*] (EAIO) ... IAIE
International Association for Iranian Art and Archaeology (EA) ... IAIAA
International Association for Learning Laboratories (EA) ... IALL
International Association for Machine Translation ... IAMT
International Association for Marriage and Family Counselors (EA) ... IAMFC
International Association for Mass Communication Research [*British*] ... IAMCR
International Association for Maternal and Neonatal Health [*Zurich, Switzerland*] (EAIO) ... IAMANEH
International Association for Mathematical Geology (EA) ... IAMG
International Association for Mathematics and Computers in Simulation ... IAMACS
International Association for Mathematics and Computers in Simulation (EA) ... IMACS
International Association for Maxillo-Facial Surgery (EA) ... IAMFS
International Association for Medical Assistance to Travellers (EA) ... IAMAT
International Association for Medical Research and Cultural Exchange ... IAMR
International Association for Metropolitan Research and Development ... INTERMET
International Association for Mission Studies [*Hamburg, Federal Republic of Germany*] (EAIO) ... IAMS
International Association for Mobilization of Creativity ... IAMC
International Association for Modular Exhibitry (EA) ... IAME
International Association for Near-Death Studies [*See also AEEPM*] (EA) ... IANDS
International Association for Neo-Latin Studies [*St. Andrews, Scotland*] (EAIO) ... IANLS
International Association for Neuro-Linguistic Programming (EAIO) ... IA/NLP
International Association for Non-Violent Sport [*See also AICVS*] [*Monte Carlo, Monaco*] (EAIO) ... IANVS
International Association for Official Statistics [*International Statistical Institute*] [*Voorburg, Netherlands*] (EAIO) ... IAOS
International Association for Oxygen Therapy ... IAOT
International Association for Past and Present History of the Art of Printing (EA) ... IAPPHAP
International Association for Pattern Recognition [*British*] (EA) ... IAPR
International Association for Personnel Women (EA) ... IAPW
International Association for Philosophy and Literature (EA) ... IAPL
International Association for Philosophy of Law and Social Philosophy [*See also AIPDPS*] ... IAPLSP
International Association for Philosophy of Law and Social Philosophy, American Section (EA) ... AMINTAPHIL
International Association for Plant Physiology [*Australia*] (EAIO) ... IAPP
International Association for Plant Taxonomy [*Utrecht, Netherlands*] (EA) ... IAPT
International Association for Pollution Control [*Defunct*] (EA) ... IAPC
International Association for Preventive Pediatrics (DAVI) ... IAPP
International Association for Psychotronic Research [*Prague, Czechoslovakia*] (EA) ... IAPR
International Association for Radiation Research [*Rijswijk, Netherlands*] (EAIO) ... IARR
International Association for Regional and Urban Statistics [*Voorburg, Netherlands*] (EA) ... IARUS
International Association for Religion and Parapsychology [*Tokyo, Japan*] (EA) ... IARP
International Association for Religious Freedom [*Germany*] (EY) ... IARF
International Association for Research in Income and Wealth (EA) ... IARIW
International Association for Research in Learning Disabilities ... IARLD
International Association for Research on Income and Wealth (EERA) ... IARIW
International Association for Rural Development (AIE) ... IARD
International Association for Rural Development Overseas (AIE) ... AIDR
International Association for Scandinavian Studies [*Norwich, England*] (EAIO) ... IASS
International Association for Seminar Management (EA) ... IASM
International Association for Shell and Spatial Structures [*Madrid, Spain*] (EA) ... IASS
International Association for Shopping Center Security (EA) ... IASCS

International Association for Social Progress ... IASP
International Association for Social Science Information Service and Technology (EA) ... IASSIST
International Association for Social Science Information Services and Technology (NITA) ... IASSIST
International Association for Social Tourism and Workers' Leisure (EAIO) ... IASTWL
International Association for Sports Information [*The Hague, Netherlands*] (EA) ... IASI
International Association for Statistical Computing (EA) ... IASC
International Association for Statistics in Physical Sciences ... IASPS
International Association for Structural Mechanics in Reactor Technology (EAIO) ... IASMIRT
International Association for Suicide Prevention (EA) ... IASP
International Association for Television Editors ... IATE
International Association for Temperance Education [*Later, IVES*] (EA) ... IATE
International Association for Testing Materials (IEEE) ... IATM
International Association for Textile Care Labelling (EA) ... IATCL
International Association for the Advancement of Earth and Environmental Sciences (EA) ... IAAEES
International Association for the Advancement of Educational Research ... IAAER
International Association for the Advancement of Teaching and Research in Intellectual Property (EA) ... ATRIP
International Association for the Child's Right to Play (EAIO) ... IACRP
International Association for the Child's Right to Play [*International Pl ayground Association*] [*Acronym is based on former name,*] (EA) ... IPA
International Association for the Development and Management of Existing and NewTowns (EAIO) ... INTA
International Association for the Development of International and World Universities [*See also AIDUIM*] [*Aulnay-Sous-Bois, France*] (EAIO) ... IADIWU
International Association for the Economics of Self-Management [*Belgrade, Yugoslavia*] (EAIO) ... IAFES
International Association for the Evaluation of Educational Achievement [*See also AIERS*] [*University of Stockholm*] [*Sweden*] (EAIO) ... IEA
International Association for the Exchange of Students for Technical Experience [*Lisbon, Portugal*] (EAIO) ... IAESTE
International Association for the Exchange of Students for Technical Experience - United States [*Later, AIPT*] ... IAESTE/US
International Association for the Fantastic in the Arts (EA) ... IAFA
International Association for the History of Physical Education and Sport [*Belgium*] ... HISPA
International Association for the History of Religions [*Marburg, Federal Republic of Germany*] (EAIO) ... IAHR
International Association for the Physical Sciences of the Ocean (EA) ... IAPSO
International Association for the Prevention of Blindness [*Later, InternationalAgency for the Prevention of Blindness*] (EA) ... IAPB
International Association for the Promotion and Protection of Private Foreign Investments ... APPI
International Association for the Properties of Steam [*Later, IAPWS*] (EA) ... IAPS
International Association for the Properties of Water and Steam (EA) ... IAPWS
International Association for the Protection of Industrial Property ... IAPIP
International Association for the Protection of Monuments and Restoration of Buildings (EAIO) ... IAMB
International Association for the Rhine Vessels Register [*Netherlands*] (EY) ... IVR
International Association for the Scientific Study of Mental Deficiency [*Dublin, Republic of Ireland*] (EA) ... IASSMD
International Association for the Study of Anglo-Irish Literature [*Maynooth, Republic of Ireland*] (EAIO) ... IASAIL
International Association for the Study of Common Property (EA) ... IASCP
International Association for the Study of Cooperation in Education (EA) ... IASCE
International Association for the Study of Lung Cancer (EA) ... IASLC
International Association for the Study of Organized Crime (EA) ... IASOC
International Association for the Study of Pain (EA) ... IASP
International Association for the Study of Popular Music [*Berlin, German Democratic Republic*] (EAIO) ... IASPM
International Association for the Study of the Italian Language and Literature [*See also AISLLI*] [*Padua, Italy*] (EAIO) ... IASILL
International Association for the Study of the Liver [*Gottingen, Federal Republic of Germany*] (EAIO) ... IASL
International Association for Training and Education in Distribution ... TED
International Association for Vegetation Science [*See also IVV*] [*Gottingen, Federal Republic of Germany*] (EAIO) ... IAVS
International Association for Vehicle Systems Dynamics [*ICSU*] [*Delft, Netherlands*] (EAIO) ... IAVSD
International Association for Vocational Guidance ... IAVG
International Association for Volunteer Education (EA) ... IAVE
International Association for Water Law [*See also AIDA*] [*Rome, Italy*] (EAIO) ... IAWL
Inter-National Association for Widowed People (EA) ... IAWP
International Association for Wind Engineering [*Aachen, Federal Republic of Germany*] (EAIO) ... IAWE
International Association of Accident and Health Underwriters [*Later, NAHU*] ... IAAHU
International Association of Accident Boards and Commissions. Newsletter [*A publication*] (DLA) ... ABC Newsl
International Association of Addictions and Offender Counseling (EA) ... IAAOC
International Association of African and American Black Business People [*Detroit, MI*] (EA) ... IAAABBP
International Association of Agricultural Economists (EA) ... IAAE
International Association of Agricultural Librarians and Documentalists (EA) ... IAALD
International Association of Agricultural Medicine and Rural Health (EAIO) ... AAMRH
International Association of Agricultural Medicine and Rural Health (EA) ... IAAMRH
International Association of Agricultural Students [*See also AIEA*] [*Uppsala, Sweden*] (EAIO) ... IAAS
International Association of Airborne Veterans (EA) ... IAAV
International Association of Aircraft Brokers and Agents [*Norway*] (EAIO) ... IABA
International Association of Aircraft Owners and Pilots Association (BARN) ... IAAOPA
International Association of Airport and Seaport Police [*Canada*] (EAIO) ... IAASP
International Association of Airport Duty Free Stores (EA) ... IAADFS
International Association of Allergology [*Later, IAACI*] ... IAA
International Association of Allergology and Clinical Immunology (EA) ... IAACI
International Association of Amateur Boat Builders (EA) ... IAABB
International Association of Amusement and Park Owners ... IAAPO
International Association of Amusement Parks [*Later, IAAPA*] ... IAAP
International Association of Amusement Parks and Attractions (EA) ... IAAPA
International Association of Applied Linguistics (EA) ... IAAL
International Association of Applied Psychology [*Nijmegen, Netherlands*] (EA) ... IAAP
International Association of Applied Social Scientists [*Later, CCI*] ... IAASS
International Association of Approved Basketball Officials (EA) ... IAABO
International Association of Aquaculture Economics and Management ... IAAEM
International Association of Aquatic and Marine Science Libraries & Information Centers [*Marine science*] (OSRA) ... IAMSLIC
International Association of Arson Investigators (EA) ... IAAI
International Association of Art [*See also AIAP*] (EA) ... IAA
International Association of Art Critics [*Australia*] ... IAAC
International Association of Art for the Future [*Indonesia*] (EAIO) ... IAAF
International Association of Assessing Officers (EA) ... IAAO
International Association of Assessing Officers, Chicago, IL [*Library symbol*] [*Library of Congress*] (LCLS) ... ICIAO
International Association of Assessing Officers, Chicago, IL [*OCLC symbol*] (OCLC) ... ILW
International Association of Astacology (EA) ... IAA
International Association of Asthmology [*Lisbon, Portugal*] (EAIO) ... INTERASMA
International Association of Audio-Visual Media in Historical Research and Education [*Bologna, Italy*] (EAIO) ... IAMHIST
International Association of Auditorium Managers (EA) ... IAAM
International Association of Automotive Modelers [*Defunct*] (EA) ... IAAM
International Association of Bibliophiles [*See also AIB*] [*Paris, France*] (EAIO) ... IAB
International Association of Biological Standardization [*See also AISB*] [*ICSU Geneva, Switzerland*] (EAIO) ... IABS
International Association of Black and White Men Together [*Later, NABWMT*] (EA) ... IABWMT
International Association of Black Business Educators [*Defunct*] (EA) ... IABBE
International Association of Black Professional Fire Fighters (EA) ... IABPFF
International Association of Blue Print and Allied Industries [*Later, IRGBA, IRA*] (EA) ... IABPAI
International Association of Boards of Examiners in Optometry (EA) ... IAB
International Association of Bomb Technicians and Investigators (EA) ... IABTI
International Association of Book Publishing Consultants [*Inactive*] (EA) ... IABPC
International Association of Bookkeepers [*British*] (EAIO) ... IAB
International Association of Book-Keepers [*Sevenoaks, Kent, England*] (EA) ... IABK
International Association of Botanic Gardens [*Australia*] (EA) ... IABG
International Association of Bridge, Structural, and Ornamental Iron Workers ... BSOIW
International Association of Bridge, Structural, and Ornamental Iron Workers (BARN) ... IABSIW
International Association of Bridge, Structural, and Ornamental Iron Workers (EA) ... IABSOIW
International Association of Broadcast Monitors (EA) ... IABM
International Association of Broadcasting (NTCM) ... IAB
International Association of Broadcasting - Asociacion Internacional de Radiodifusion [*Formerly, Inter-American Association of Broadcasters*] (EA) ... IAB-AIR
International Association of Broadcasting Manufacturers [*Hayes, Middlesex, England*] (EAIO) ... IABM
International Association of Buddhist Studies (EA) ... IABS
International Association of Building Companions [*See also IBO*] [*Marche-En-Famenne, Belgium*] (EAIO) ... IABC
International Association of Business (EA) ... IAB
International Association of Business Communicators (EA) ... IABC
International Association of Business Forecasting (EA) ... IABF
International Association of Businessmen and Professionals (EA) ... IABP
International Association of Buying Groups [*See also IVE*] (EAIO) ... IABG
International Association of Campus Law Enforcement Administrators (EA) ... IACLEA
International Association of Cancer Registries [*Lyon, France*] (EAIO) ... IACR
International Association of Cancer Victors and Friends (EA) ... IACVF
International Association of Certified Duncan Teachers (EA) ... IACDT
International Association of Charities [*See also AIC*] (EAIO) ... IAC
International Association of Chiefs of Police (EA) ... IACP
International Association of Circulation Managers ... IACM
International Association of Civil Aviation Chaplains (EA) ... IACAC
International Association of Classification Societies (EAIO) ... IACS
International Association of Cleaning and Dye House Workers ... CDHW
International Association of Clerks, Recorders, Election Officials, and Treasurers (EA) ... IACREOT

International Association of Clinical Laser Acupuncturists (EA) .... IACLA
International Association of Clothing Designers (EA) .... IACD
International Association of Computer Crime Investigators [*Defunct*] (EA) .... IACCI
International Association of Computer Programmers .... IACP
International Association of Computer Service Managers .... IACSM
International Association of Computer Users Groups (EA) .... IACUG
International Association of Concert and Festival Managers [*Later, ISPAA*] (EA) .... IACFM
International Association of Concert Managers [*Later, ISPAA*] (EA) .... IACM
International Association of Concrete Repair Specialists (EA) .... IACRS
International Association of Conference Centers (EA) .... IACC
International Association of Constitutional Law [*See also AIDC*] [*Belgrade, Yugoslavia*] (EAIO) .... IACL
International Association of Consulting Actuaries (MHDB) .... IACA
International Association of Contact Lens Educators .... IACLE
International Association of Convention and Visitor Bureaus (EA) .... IACVB
International Association of Convention Bureaus [*Later, IACVB*] (EA) .... IACB
International Association of Cooking Professionals (EA) .... IACP
International Association of Cooking Schools (EA) .... IACS
International Association of Coroners and Medical Examiners (EA) .... IACME
International Association of Corporate Real Estate Executives (EA) .... IACREE
International Association of Correctional Officers (EA) .... IACO
International Association of Counseling Services (EA) .... IACS
International Association of Counselors and Therapists (EA) .... IACT
International Association of Counterterrorism and Security Professionals .... IACSP
International Association of Crafts and Small- and Medium-Sized Enterprises [*Switzerland*] (EY) .... IACME
International Association of Credit Card Investigators (EA) .... IACCI
International Association of Crime Prevention Practitioners (EA) .... IACPP
International Association of Crime Writers (EAIO) .... IACW
International Association of Cross-Reference Directory Publishers (EA) .... IACRDP
International Association of Cylindrical Hydraulic Engineers (EA) .... IACHE
International Association of Defense Counsel (EA) .... IADC
International Association of Democratic Lawyers [*Brussels, Belgium*] (EA) .... IADL
International Association of Dental Students [*British*] .... IADS
International Association of Dentistry for Children [*British*] (EAIO) .... IADC
International Association of Dentistry for the Handicapped [*Toronto, ON*] (EAIO) .... IADH
International Association of Dento-Maxillo-Facial Radiology (EAIO) .... IADMFR
International Association of Department Stores [*See also AIGM*] (EAIO) .... IADS
International Association of Dive Rescue Specialists (EA) .... IADRS
International Association of Documentalists and Information Officers [*France*] (EY) .... IAD
International Association of Dollbaby Parents [*Defunct*] (EA) .... IADP
International Association of Dredging Companies [*The Hague, Netherlands*] (EA) .... IADC
International Association of Drilling Contractors .... IADC
International Association of Dry Cargo Shipowners (EAIO) .... INTERCARGO
International Association of Eating Disorders Professionals (EA) .... IAEDP
International Association of Educational Peace Officers (EA) .... IAEPO
International Association of Educators for World Peace (EA) .... IAEWP
International Association of Electrical Contractors [*See also AIE*] (EAIO) .... IAEC
International Association of Electrical Inspectors (EA) .... IAEI
International Association of Electrical Leagues [*Later, ILEA*] (EA) .... IAEL
International Association of Electrotypers and Stereotypers [*Later, Printing Platemakers Association*] .... IAES
International Association of Empirical Aesthetics [*Paris, France*] (EAIO) .... IAEA
International Association of Energy Economists (EA) .... IAEE
International Association of Engineering Geology [*International Union of Geological Sciences*] [*ICSU Paris, France*] (EA) .... IAEG
International Association of Entertainment Lawyers [*Amsterdam, Netherlands*] (EAIO) .... IAEL
International Association of Environmental Analytical Chemistry [*Therwil, Switzerland*] (EAIO) .... IAEAC
International Association of Environmental Coordinators [*Belgium*] (DCTA) .... IAEC
International Association of Environmental Mutagen Societies [*Helsinki, Finland*] (EAIO) .... IAEMS
International Association of Environmental Testing Laboratories (EA) .... IAETL
International Association of Equine Dental Technicians (EA) .... IAEDT
International Association of Ethicists (EA) .... IAE
International Association of Evening Student Councils [*Later, USAES*] (EA) .... IAESC
International Association of Exchange Dealers [*British*] (EA) .... IAED
International Association of Fairs and Expositions (EA) .... IAFE
International Association of Family Sociology (EA) .... IAFS
International Association of Filipino Patriots (EA) .... IAFP
International Association of Financial Consultants (BARN) .... IAFC
International Association of Fire Chiefs (EA) .... IAFC
International Association of Fire Chiefs Foundation (EA) .... IAFCF
International Association of Fire Fighters (EA) .... IAFF
International Association of Fish and Wildlife Agencies (EA) .... IAFWA
International Association of Fish Ethologists [*Normal, IL*] (ASF) .... IAFE
International Association of Fish Meal Manufacturers [*Potters Bar, Hertfordshire, England*] (EAIO) .... IAFMM
International Association of Forensic Sciences [*Defunct*] (EA) .... IAFS
[*The*] **International Association of Forensic Toxicologists** [*Newmarket, Suffolk, England*] (EAIO) .... TIAFT
International Association of Former Soviet Political Prisoners and Victims of Communist Regime .... IASPPV
International Association of French-Language University Presses [*Defunct*] (EA) .... IAFLUP
International Association of French-Speaking Aircrews (EAIO) .... IAFSA
International Association of French-Speaking Congress Towns [*See also AIVFC*] [*France*] (EAIO) .... IAFCT
International Association of French-Speaking Directors of Educational Institutions (EAIO) .... IAFSDEI
International Association of Friends of Angkor Wat (EAIO) .... IAFAW
International Association of Game, Fish, and Conservation Commissioners [*Later,IAFWA*] (EA) .... IAGFCC
International Association of Garment Manufacturers [*Absorbed by NOSA*] (EA) .... IAGM
International Association of Genito-Urinary Surgeons (DAVI) .... IAGUS
International Association of Geochemistry and Cosmochemistry [*Edmonton, AB*] (EA) .... IAGC
International Association of Geodesy [*ICSU*] [*Paris, France*] (EAIO) .... IAG
International Association of Geographic Pathology (DAVI) .... IAGP
International Association of Geomagnetism and Aeronomy [*ICSU*] [*Scotland*] (ASF) .... IAGA
International Association of Geophysical Contractors (EA) .... IAGC
International Association of Germanic Languages and Literatures [*See also IVG*] (EAIO) .... IAGLL
International Association of Gerontology (EA) .... IAG
International Association of Golf Administrators (EA) .... IAGA
International Association of Governmental Fair Agencies (EA) .... IAGFA
International Association of Governmental Labor Officials [*Later, NAGLO*] (EA) .... IAGLO
International Association of Great Lakes Ports (EA) .... IAGLP
International Association of Greeting Card Workers .... IAGCW
International Association of Group Psychotherapy (EA) .... IAGP
International Association of Hail Insurers (EA) .... IAHI
International Association of Hand Papermakers and Paper Artists (EAIO) .... IAPMA
International Association of Health and Therapy Instruments [*Japan*] (EAIO) .... IHT
International Association of Health Underwriters [*Later, NAHU*] (EA) .... IAHU
International Association of Healthcare Central Service Materials Management (EA) .... IAHCSM
International Association of Heart Patients [*Formerly, IAPP*] (EA) .... IAHP
International Association of Heat and Frost Insulators and Asbestos Workers (EA) .... HFIAW
International Association of Heat and Frost Insulators and Asbestos Workers .... IAHFIAW
International Association of Hillel Directors (EA) .... IAHD
International Association of Historians of Asia [*Quezon City, Philippines*] (EA) .... IAHA
International Association of Holiday Inns (EA) .... IAHI
International Association of Holistic Health Practitioners (EA) .... IAHHP
International Association of Home Improvement Councils [*Defunct*] (EA) .... IAHIC
International Association of Home Safety and Security Professionals (EA) .... IAHSSP
International Association of Horticultural Producers [*The Hague, Netherlands*] (EA) .... AIPH
International Association of Horticultural Producers .... IAHP
International Association of Hospitality Accountants [*Austin, TX*] (EA) .... IAHA
International Association of Hotel Management Schools (EA) .... IAHMS
International Association of Human Biologists [*ICSU*] [*Newcastle-Upon-Tyne, England*] (EAIO) .... IAHB
International Association of Human-Animal Interaction Organizations (EA) .... IAHAIO
International Association of Hydrogeologists [*Arnhem, Netherlands*] (EA) .... IAH
International Association of Hydrological Sciences [*See also AISH*] [*British*] .... AHS
International Association of Hydrological Sciences .... IAHS
International Association of Hydrology .... IAH
International Association of Ice Cream Manufacturers [*Later, IICA*] (EA) .... IAICM
International Association of Incubators (EA) .... IAI
International Association of Independent Colleges and Universities (EA) .... IAICU
International Association of Independent Producers (EA) .... IAIP
International Association of Independent Scholars (EA) .... IAIS
International Association of Independent Tanker Owners .... IAITO
International Association of Independent Tanker Owners [*Oslo, Norway*] (EAIO) .... INTERTANKO
International Association of Individual Psychology (EA) .... IAIP
International Association of Industrial Accident Boards and Commissions (EA) .... IAIABC
International Association of Industrial Radiation [*France*] (PDAA) .... IAIR
International Association of Institutes of Navigation [*British*] (EAIO) .... IAIN
International Association of Insurance and Reinsurance Intermediaries [*See also BIPAR*] [*Paris, France*] (EAIO) .... IAIRI
International Association of Insurance Counsel [*Later, IADC*] (EA) .... IAIC
International Association of Intermodal Equipment Surveyors [*Defunct*] (EA) .... IAIES
International Association of Islamic Banks .... IAIB
International Association of Jai Alai Players (EA) .... IAJAP
International Association of Jazz Appreciation (EA) .... IAJA
International Association of Jazz Educators (EA) .... IAJE
International Association of Jazz Record Collectors (EA) .... IAJRC
International Association of Jim Beam Bottle and Specialties Clubs (EA) .... IAJBBSC
International Association of Judges [*Rome, Italy*] (EAIO) .... IAJ
International Association of Justice Volunteerism (EA) .... IAJV

International Association of Juvenile and Family Court Magistrates [*Paris, France*] (EA) ... IAJFCM
International Association of Knowledge Engineers (EA) ... IAKE
International Association of Labour History Institutions [*Zurich, Switzerland*] (EAIO) ... IALHI
International Association of Laryngectomees (EA) ... IAL
International Association of Latin American Air Carriers [*ICAO designator*] (FAAC) ... ALA
International Association of Latin American and Caribbean Studies (EAIO) ... IALACS
International Association of Law Enforcement Firearms Instructors (EA) ... IALEFI
International Association of Law Enforcement Intelligence Analysts (EA) ... IALEIA
International Association of Law Firms [*Defunct*] (EA) ... IALF
International Association of Law Libraries (EAIO) ... IALL
International Association of Law Libraries. Bulletin [*A publication*] (DLA) ... Int'l Assoc L Lib Bull
International Association of Legal Science [*See also AISJ*] [*Paris, France*] (EAIO) ... IALS
International Association of Liberal Religious Women (EA) ... IALRW
International Association of Lighthouse Authorities [*Paris, France*] (EA) ... IALA
International Association of Lighting Designers (EA) ... IALD
International Association of Lighting Maintenance Contractors [*Later, NALMCO*] (EA) ... IALMC
International Association of Lighting Management Companies (EA) ... NALMCO
International Association of Limnology (PDAA) ... IAL
International Association of Linguistics (DIT) ... IAL
International Association of Lions Clubs ... IALC
International Association of Logopedics and Phoniatrics [*Dublin, Republic of Ireland*] (EA) ... IALP
International Association of Lyceum Clubs ... IALC
International Association of Machinists and Aerospace Workers (EA) ... IAM
International Association of Machinists and Aerospace Workers (MCD) ... IAMAW
International Association of Marble, Slate and Stone Polishers, Rubbers and Sawyers, Tile and Marble Setters' Helpers, and Marble Mosaic and Terrazzo Workers' Helpers [*Later, Tile, Marble, Terrazzo Finishers, Shopworkers, and Granite Cutters International Union*] (EA) ... MSSP
International Association of Margaret Morris Method [*Glasgow, Scotland*] (EAIO) ... IAMMM
International Association of Marine Science Libraries and Information Centers (EA) ... IAMSLIC
International Association of Master Penmen and Teachers of Handwriting (EA) ... IAMPTH
International Association of Mathematical Physics (EA) ... IAMP
International Association of Meat Processors (EA) ... IAMP
International Association of Medical Esperantists (EA) ... IAME
International Association of Medical Laboratory Technologists [*Bootle, Merseyside, England*] (EA) ... IAMLT
International Association of Medical Museums [*Later, IAP*] ... IAMM
International Association of Medicine and Biology of Environment [*See also AIMBE*] [*Paris, France*] (EAIO) ... IAMBE
International Association of Mercury Producers [*Spain, Italy, Turkey, Yugoslavia, Peru, Algeria*] ... IAMP
International Association of Merger and Acquisition Consultants (EA) ... INTERMAC
International Association of Metaphysicians ... IAM
International Association of Meteorology and Atmospheric Physics (EA) ... IAMAP
International Association of Meteorology and Atmospheric Sciences (EERA) ... IAMAS
International Association of Metropolitan City Libraries [*The Hague, Netherlands*] (EA) ... INTAMEL
International Association of Microbiological Societies [*ICSU*] [*Later, IUMS*] ... IAMS
International Association of Milk Control Agencies (EA) ... IAMCA
International Association of Milk, Food, and Environmental Sanitarians (EA) ... IAMFES
International Association of Ministers' Wives and Ministers' Widows (EAIO) ... IAMWMW
International Association of Model and Talent Scouts (EAIO) ... IAMTS
International Association of Mouth and Foot Painting Artists (EA) ... IAMFPA
International Association of Municipal Statisticians [*Later, IARUS*] ... IAMS
International Association of Museums of Arms and Military History [*Ingolstadt, Federal Republic of Germany*] (EA) ... IAMAM
International Association of Music Libraries (NITA) ... IAML
International Association of Music Libraries, Archives, and Documentation Centers (EA) ... IAML
International Association of Mutual Insurance Companies [*See also AISAM*] (EAIO) ... IAMIC
International Association of Natural Resource Pilots (EA) ... IANRP
International Association of Nitrox and Technical Divers ... IANTD
International Association of Nitrox Divers ... IAND
International Association of Ocular Surgeons (EA) ... IAOS
International Association of Official Human Rights Agencies (EA) ... IAOHRA
International Association of Olympic Medical Officers [*Rugby, Warwickshire, England*] (EAIO) ... IAOMO
International Association of Opera Directors [*Sweden*] (EAIO) ... AIDO
International Association of Opera Directors (EAIO) ... IAOD
International Association of Optometric Executives (EA) ... IAOE
International Association of Oral and Maxillofacial Surgeons (EA) ... IAOMS
International Association of Oral Myology (DMAA) ... IAOM
International Association of Oral Pathologists (EA) ... IAOP
International Association of Oral Surgeons (EAIO) ... IAOS
International Association of Organ Teachers USA [*Later, KTA*] (EA) ... IAOT
International Association of Orientalist Librarians (EA) ... IAOL
International Association of Original Art Diffusors (EAIO) ... IAOAD
International Association of Orthodontics (EA) ... IAO
International Association of Pacemaker Patients [*Later, IAHP*] (EA) ... IAPP
International Association of Packaging Research Institutes [*British*] (EAIO) ... IAPRI
International Association of Paediatric Dentistry [*British*] (EAIO) ... IAPD
International Association of Paper Historians (DGA) ... IAPH
International Association of Paper Historians (EA) ... IPH
International Association of Parapsychologists (EA) ... IAP
International Association of Parents and Professionals for Safe Alternatives in Childbirth (EA) ... IAPSAC
International Association of Parents and Professionals for Safe Alternatives in Childbirth [*Association retains acronym of its former name*] (EA) ... NAPSAC
International Association of Parents of the Deaf [*Later, ASDC*] (EA) ... IAPD
International Association of Penal Law [*Freiburg, Federal Republic of Germany*] (EAIO) ... IAPL
International Association of Personnel in Employment Security (EA) ... IAPES
International Association of Pet Cemeteries (EA) ... IAPC
International Association of Photoplate Makers (DGA) ... IAPM
International Association of Photoplatemakers (EA) ... IAP
International Association of Physical Education and Sport for Girls and Women (EA) ... IAPESGW
International Association of Physical Geography (BARN) ... IAPG
International Association of Physical Oceanography [*Later, IAPSO*] ... IAPO
International Association of Physicians in Audiology (EAIO) ... IAPA
International Association of Piano Builders and Technicians (EA) ... IAPBT
International Association of Pipe Smokers Clubs (EA) ... IAPSC
International Association of Planetology [*Brussels, Belgium*] (EA) ... IAP
International Association of Plant Breeders for the Protection of Plant Varieties (EAIO) ... IAPBPPV
International Association of Plant Taxonomists (EERA) ... IAPT
International Association of Plumbing and Mechanical Officials (EA) ... IAPMO
International Association of Police Professors [*Later, ACJS*] ... IAPP
International Association of Political Consultants (EA) ... IAPC
International Association of Ports and Harbors [*Japan*] ... IAPH
International Association of Printers' Overseers (DGA) ... IAPO
International Association of Printing House Craftsmen (EA) ... IAPHC
International Association of Professional Bureaucrats (EA) ... INATAPROBU
International Association of Professional Congress Organizers [*Brussels, Belgium*] (EAIO) ... IAPCO
International Association of Professional Natural Hygienists (EA) ... IAPNH
International Association of Professional Numismatists [*See also AINP*] [*Zurich, Switzerland*] (EAIO) ... IAPN
International Association of Professional Security Consultants (EA) ... IAPSC
International Association of Psychoanalytic Gerontology [*Paris, France*] (EAIO) ... IAPG
International Association of Psycho-Social Rehabilitation Services (EA) ... IAPSRS
International Association of Pteridologists (EERA) ... IAP
International Association of Public Cleansing [*Later, ISWA*] ... INTAPUC
International Association of Public Pawnbroking Institutions [*Milan, Italy*] (EA) ... IAPPI
International Association of Pupil Personnel Workers (EA) ... IAPPW
International Association of Quality Circles (EA) ... IAQC
International Association of Radiopharmacology (EA) ... IAR
International Association of Railway Employees (EA) ... IARE
International Association of Railway Employees ... IRE
International Association of Railway Operating Officers (EA) ... IAROO
International Association of Rattan Manufacturers and Importers [*Defunct*] (EA) ... IARMI
International Association of Rebekah Assemblies, IOOF [*Independent Order of Odd Fellows*] (EA) ... IARA
International Association of Refrigerated Warehouses (EA) ... IARW
International Association of Registered Financial Planners (EA) ... IARFP
International Association of Religious Science Churches [*Later, RSI*] (EA) ... IARSC
International Association of Research Institutes for the Graphic Arts Industry [*St. Gallen, Switzerland*] ... IARIGAI
International Association of Retired Persons [*Superseded by IFA*] (EA) ... IARP
International Association of Rolling Stock Builders [*See also AICMR*] (EAIO) ... IARSB
International Association of Rural and Isolated Libraries [*Australia*] ... IARIL
International Association of Sand Castle Builders (EA) ... IASCB
International Association of Sanskrit Studies (EA) ... IASS
International Association of Satellite Users [*Later, IASUS*] (EA) ... IASU
International Association of Satellite Users and Suppliers (EA) ... IASUS
International Association of Scholarly Publishers [*Norway*] ... IASP
International Association of School Librarianship (PDAA) ... IASL
International Association of School Security Directors [*Later, NASSD*] (EA) ... IASSD
International Association of Schools in Advertising ... IASA
International Association of Schools of Social Work [*Austria*] ... IASSW
International Association of Science and Technology for Development [*Calgary, AB*] (EAIO) ... IASTED
International Association of Scientific Hydrology [*Later, International Association of Hydrological Sciences*] [*of International Union of Geodesy and Geophysics*] ... IASH
International Association of Scuba Technicians ... IAST
International Association of Security Service (EA) ... IASS
International Association of Sedimentologists [*Liege, Belgium*] (EA) ... IAS
International Association of Seed Crushers [*British*] (EAIO) ... IASC

International Association of Seismology and Physics of the Earth's Interior [*ICSU*] [*Newbury, Berkshire, England*] (EAIO) ... IASPEI
International Association of Semiotic Studies [*Palermo, Italy*] (EA) ... IASS
International Association of Service Companies [*NACSA*] [*Absorbed by*] (EA) ... IASCO
International Association of Sheet Metal Workers (BARN) ... IASMW
International Association of Siderographers (EA) ... IAS
International Association of Silver Art Collectors (EA) ... IASAC
International Association of Skal Clubs [*Spain*] (EAIO) ... IASC
International Association of Soil Science ... IASS
International Association of Sound Archives [*Milton, Keynes, England*] (EAIO) ... IASA
International Association of South-East European Studies [*See also AIESEE*] [*Bucharest, Romania*] (EAIO) ... IASEES
International Association of Space Philatelists (EA) ... IASP
International Association of Sports Museums and Halls of Fame (EA) ... IASMHF
International Association of Sports Physicians [*Defunct*] (EA) ... IASP
International Association of State Trading Organizations of Developing Countries [*Ljubljana, Yugoslavia*] (EAIO) ... ASTRO
International Association of Strategic Planning Consultants [*Defunct*] (EA) ... IASPC
International Association of Structural Movers (EA) ... IASM
International Association of Sublimation Printers (EA) ... IASP
International Association of Supreme Administration Jurisdictions GG2 [*See also AIHJA*] (EAIO) ... IASAJ
International Association of Survey Statisticians [*See also AISE*] [*France*] (EA) ... IASS
International Association of Teachers of English as a Foreign Language [*Whitstable, Kent, England*] (EAIO) ... IATEFL
International Association of Teachers of German [*See also IDV*] [*Copenhagen, Denmark*] (EAIO) ... IATG
International Association of Teachers of Italian [*Belgium*] (EAIO) ... IATI
International Association of Technological University Libraries [*Goteborg, Sweden*] ... IATUL
International Association of Telecomputer Networks (EA) ... IATN
International Association of Textile Dyers and Printers [*See also AITIT*] (EAIO) ... IATDP
International Association of the Genesis of Ore Deposits [*ICSU*] [*Prague, Czechoslovakia*] (EAIO) ... IAGOD
International Association of Theological Libraries ... IATL
International Association of Theoretical and Applied Limnology [*ICSU*] (EA) ... IAL
International Association of Theoretical and Applied Limnology [*See also SILTA*] (EA) ... IATAL
International Association of Tool Craftsmen (EA) ... IATC
International Association of Torch Clubs (EA) ... IATC
International Association of Tour Managers (DI) ... IATM
International Association of Tour Managers - North American Region (EA) ... IATM-NAR
International Association of Trade Exchanges [*Later, IRTA*] (EA) ... IATE
International Association of Traffic and Safety Sciences [*Tokyo, Japan*] (EAIO) ... IATSS
International Association of Transport Museums [*See also AIMT*] [*Berne, Switzerland*] (EAIO) ... IATM
International Association of Travel Exhibitors (EA) ... IATE
International Association of Travel Journalists (EA) ... IATJ
International Association of Triathlon Clubs (EA) ... IATC
International Association of Trichologists (EA) ... IAT
International Association of Tungsten Producers ... IATP
International Association of Universities [*France*] ... IAU
International Association of University Presidents ... IAUP
International Association of University Professors and Lecturers (EAIO) ... IAUPL
International Association of University Professors of English [*British*] ... IAUPE
International Association of Veterinary Food Hygienists ... IAVFH
International Association of Visual Communications Management [*Formerly, SRE*] ... IAVCM
International Association of Voice Identification [*Later, IAI*] (EA) ... IAVI
International Association of Volcanology and Chemistry of the Earth's Interior [*Germany*] ... IAVCEI
International Association of Volunteer Effort (EA) ... IAVE
International Association of Wall and Ceiling Contractors [*Later, AWCI*] (EA) ... IAWCC
International Association of Wall and Ceiling Contractors - Gypsum Drywall Contractors International [*Later, AWCI*] (EA) ... IAWCC/GD
International Association of Water Polo Referees (EA) ... IAWPR
International Association of Waterworks in the Rhine Basin Area (EAIO) ... IAWRBA
International Association of Wholesalers [*Defunct*] ... IAW
International Association of Wiping Cloth Manufacturers (EA) ... IAWCM
International Association of Women and Home Page Journalists (EA) ... IAWHPJ
International Association of Women in Radio and Television (NTCM) ... IAWRT
International Association of Women Ministers (EA) ... IAWM
International Association of Women Philosophers [*Zurich, Switzerland*] (EAIO) ... IAWP
International Association of Women Police (EA) ... IAWP
International Association of Wood Anatomists [*Utrecht, Netherlands*] (EA) ... IAWA
International Association of Wool and Textile Laboratories (EAIO) ... INTERWOOLABS
International Association of Word Processing Specialists [*Formerly, NAWPS*] (EA) ... WPS
International Association of Workers for Troubled Children and Youth [*See also AIEJI*] (EAIO) ... IAWMC
International Association of Workshop Way Educators (EA) ... IAWWE
International Association of Youth Magistrates [*Later, IAJFCM*] ... IAYM
International Association of Y's Men's Clubs [*Geneva, Switzerland*] (EA) ... IAYMC
International Association of Zoo Educators (EA) ... IZE
International Association on Food Distribution ... IAFD
International Association on Mechanization of Field Experiments [*Aas, Norway*] (EA) ... IAMFE
International Association on the Political Use of Psychiatry [*Amsterdam, Netherlands*] (EAIO) ... IAPUP
International Association on Water Pollution Research [*Later, IAWPRC*] ... IAWPR
International Association on Water Pollution Research and Control [*British*] (EA) ... IAWPRC
International Association Residential and Community Alternatives (EAIO) ... IARCA
International Association to Combat Terrorism [*Defunct*] (EA) ... IACT
International Astrological Association ... IAA
International Astronautical Congress ... IAC
International Astronautical Federation [*ICSU*] [*Research center France*] ... IAF
International Astronomical Union [*ICSU*] [*Paris, France*] [*Research center*] (IRC) ... IAU
International Astrophysical Decade ... IAD
International Atherosclerosis Society (EA) ... IAS
International Athletic Footwear and Apparel Manufacturers Association [*Zurich, Switzerland Defunct*] (EAIO) ... IAF
International Atlantic Salmon Foundation [*Canada*] (EA) ... IASF
International Atomic Energy Accord (DOMA) ... IAEA
International Atomic Energy Agency [*Database originator and operator*] [*United Nations*] [*Austria*] ... IAEA
International Atomic Energy Agency (USDC) ... IAEM
International Atomic Energy Agency Marine Environmental Laboratory [*Marine science*] (OSRA) ... IAEA-MEL
International Atomic Energy Committee ... IAEC
International Atomic Time ... IAT
International Atomic-Development Authority [*Proposed by Bernard M. Baruch, 1946, but never created*] ... IADA
International Audiovisual Society (EA) ... IAS
International Audio-Visual Technical Centre [*Netherlands*] ... IAVTC
International Auditing Guideline ... IAG
International Auditing Practices Committee ... IAPC
International Auto Show Producers Association (EA) ... IASPA
International Auto Sound Challenge Association (EA) ... IASCA
International Automatic Time ... IAT
International Automotive Design ... IAD
International Automotive Hall of Shame (EA) ... IAHS
International Automotive Parts and Accessories Trade Show [*British*] (ITD) ... AUTOPARTAC
International Autumn Fair [*British*] (ITD) ... IAF
International Auxiliary Language Association [*Later, UMI*] ... IALA
International Aviation Affairs [*FAA*] (MCD) ... IAA
International Aviation Association ... INTAVA
International Aviation Facilities Act [*1948*] ... IAFA
International Aviation Service [*FAA*] ... IAS
International Aviation Services [*Belgium*] ... IAS
International Aviation Theft Bureau [*ACPI*] [*Superseded by*] (EA) ... IATB
International B & B [*Bed and Breakfast*] **Fly-Inn Club** (EA) ... IBBFIC
International B-24 Liberator Club (EA) ... IBLC
International Baby Food Action Network (EA) ... IBFAN
International Baccalaureate ... IB
International Baccalaureate Office [*See also OBI*] [*Later, International Baccalaureate Organization Grand-Saconnex, Switzerland*] (EAIO) ... IBO
International Bach Society [*Defunct*] (EA) ... IBS
International Backgammon Association (EA) ... IBA
International Backpackers Association [*Later, AHS*] (EA) ... IBA
International Badminton Federation [*Cheltenham, Gloustershire, England*] (EAIO) ... IBF
International Balance Disorder Association [*Defunct*] (EA) ... IBDA
International Balance of Payments [*Economics simulation game*] ... BALPAY
International Balance of Payments (AAGC) ... IBOP
International Balance of Payments (AFM) ... IBP
International Balance of Payments Reporting System ... IBOP
International Balint Federation [*Brussels, Belgium*] (EAIO) ... IBF
International Ballet Competition ... IBC
International Ballet Council ... IBC
International Balloon Association (EA) ... IBA
International Baltic Sea Fishery Commission [*Warsaw, Poland*] (ASF) ... IBSFC
International Balut Federation [*Bangkok, Thailand*] (EAIO) ... IBF
International Banana Association (EA) ... IBA
International Banana Club (EA) ... IBC
International Bandy Federation [*Lulea, Sweden*] (EAIO) ... IBF
International Bank Bond (MHDB) ... IBB
International Bank for Economic Cooperation [*Moscow, USSR*] (EY) ... IBEC
International Bank for Reconstruction and Development [*Also known as World Bank*] ... IB
International Bank for Reconstruction and Development [*Also known as World Bank*] ... IBRD
International Bank for Settlements (MHDW) ... IBS
International Bank for West Africa Ltd. ... IBWA
International Bank Information System ... IBIS
International Bank Note Society (EA) ... IBNS
International Bank of Yemen ... IBY
International Banker Association (EA) ... IBA

International Bankers, Inc. .... IBI
International Banking Act [*1978*] .... IBA
International Banking Campaign Against South Africa [*Later, ICABA*] (EAIO) .... IBCASA
International Banking Centre [*British*] .... IBC
International Banking Facility .... IBF
International Banking Facility (TDOB) .... IBF
International Bar Association [*British*] (EA) .... IBA
International Bar Association (DLA) .... Internat Bar Assoc
International Bar Association. Bulletin [*A publication*] (DLA) .... Int'l BA Bull
International Bar Fly [*Sign in Harry's New York Bar, Paris*] .... IBF
International Bar Journal [*A publication*] (DLA) .... Int Bar J
International Bar Journal [*A publication*] (DLA) .... Int'l Bar J
International Bar Journal [*A publication*] (DLA) .... Int'l BJ
International Barbed Wire Collectors Association (EA) .... IBWCA
International Barber Schools Association (EA) .... IBSA
International Barbie Doll Collectors Club (EA) .... IBDCC
International Baron Resources [*Vancouver Stock Exchange symbol*] .... IBQ
International Bartenders Association [*Paris, France*] (EAIO) .... IBA
International Baseball Association (EA) .... IBA
International Basic Economic Cooperation [*Investment term*] (DS) .... IBEC
International Basic Res [*NASDAQ symbol*] (TTSB) .... IBRM
International Basic Resources, Inc. [*NASDAQ symbol*] (NQ) .... IBRM
International Basic Resources, Inc. [*Associated Press*] (SAG) .... IntBas
International Basketball Association [*Defunct*] (EA) .... IBA
International Bathymetric Chart [*Marine science*] (OSRA) .... IBC
International Bathymetric Chart of the Caribbean Sea and Gulf of Mexico [*Marine science*] (OSRA) .... IBBCA
International Bathymetric Chart of the Central Eastern Atlantic [*Marine science*] (OSRA) .... IBCEA
International Bathymetric Chart of the Red Sea and Gulf of Aden [*Proposed*] [*Marine science*] (OSRA) .... IBCRSGA
International Bathymetric Chart of the Western Indian Ocean [*Marine science*] (OSRA) .... IBCWIO
International Bathymetric Chart of the Western Pacific [*Marine science*] (OSRA) .... IBCWP
International Baton Twirling Association of America and Abroad [*Defunct*] (EA) .... IBTA
International Battery Data Base [*Robert Morey Associates*] [*Information service or system*] (IID) .... IBDB
International Bauxite Association [*Kingston, Jamaica*] .... IBA
International Bee Research Association [*Cardiff, Wales*] (EA) .... IBRA
International Beefalo Breeders' Registry (EA) .... IBBR
International Beer Tasting Society (EA) .... IBTS
International Bellevue Ventures Ltd. [*Vancouver Stock Exchange symbol*] .... IBV
International Benchrest Shooters (EA) .... IBS
International Benevolent Society (EA) .... IBS
International Benjamin Franklin Society [*Defunct*] (EA) .... IBFS
International Bentham Society (EAIO) .... IBS
International Benzoate Unit [*Pharmacology*] .... IBU
International Betta Congress (EA) .... IBC
International Beverage Co. [*Vancouver Stock Exchange symbol*] .... IBE
International Beverage Industry Exhibition and Congress [*National Soft Drink Association*] .... INTERBEV
International Bible Reading Association [*Redhill, Surrey, England*] (EAIO) .... IBRA
International Bible Society (EA) .... IBS
International Bible Students Association (EA) .... IBSA
International Bibliographical Description .... IBID
International Bibliography of the History of Religions [*A publication*] (BJA) .... IBHR
International Bibliography of the Social Sciences, Economics, and Sociology [*International Committee for Social Science Information and Documentation*] [*Information service or system*] (CRD) .... IBS
International Bicycle Fund (EA) .... IBF
International Bicycle Touring Society (EA) .... IBTS
International Biliary Association [*Later, IHBPA*] (EAIO) .... IBA
International Binding Center at Elat [*Israel*] .... IBCE
International Biodeterioration Bulletin. Reference Index [*A publication*] .... IBBRIS
International Biodeterioration Research Group (EA) .... IBRG
International Bio-Environmental Foundation (EA) .... IBEF
International Biographical Centre [*British*] (CB) .... IBC
International Biological Program [*Concluded, 1974*] [*National Academy of Sciences*] .... IBP
International Biological Programme/Conservation of Terrestrial Biological Communities [*London, England*] .... IBP/CT
International Biological Year .... IBY
International Biomass Institute (EA) .... IBI
International Biometric Association (EA) .... IBA
International Biophysical Center .... IBC
International Biosciences Network .... IBN
International Biotechnologies, Inc. .... IBI
International Biotoxicological Center [*World Life Research Institute*] [*US*] (ASF) .... IBC
International Bird Rescue Research Center (EA) .... IBRRC
International Black Peoples' Foundation [*Defunct*] (EA) .... IBPF
International Black Toy Manufacturers Association (EA) .... IBTMA
International Black Women's Congress (EA) .... IBWC
International Black Writers (EA) .... IBW
International Black Writers and Artists (EA) .... IBWA
International Black Writers Conference [*Later, IBW*] (EA) .... IBWC
International Blind Sports Association [*See also AISA*] [*Farsta, Sweden*] (EAIO) .... IBSA
International Blue Jay Class Association (EA) .... IBJCA
International Bluegrass Music Association (EA) .... IBMA
International Board for Plant Genetic Resources [*FAO*] [*Italy*] .... IBPGR
International Board for Soil Research and Management [*Thailand*] .... IBSRAM
International Board of Auditors (NATG) .... IBA
International Board of Cytopathology [*International Academy of Cytology*] [*Quebec, PQ*] (EAIO) .... IBC
International Board of Environmental Medicine (EA) .... IBEM
International Board of Jewish Missions (EA) .... IBJM
International Board of Medicine and Psychology [*Later, IAMP*] (EA) .... IBMP
International Board of Standards and Practices for Certified Financial Planners (EA) .... IBCFP
International Board on Books for Young People [*Basel, Switzerland*] (EA) .... IBBY
International Bobsled Federation .... IBF
International Bocce Association (EA) .... IBA
International Bodyguard Association (EA) .... IBA
International Bone Marrow Transplant Registry .... IBMTR
International Book Bank (EA) .... IBB
International Book Export Group .... IBEG
International Book Fair of Radical Black and Third World Books .... IBFRBTWB
International Book Information Service .... IBIS
International Book Printers Association [*Later, NABM*] (EA) .... IBPA
International Book Project (EA) .... IBP
International Book Service, Inc. .... IBS
International Book Year [*1972*] [*UNESCO*] .... IBY
International Bookbinders Secretariat (DGA) .... IBS
International Books in Print [*A publication*] .... IBIP
International Booksellers Federation [*Formerly, ICBA*] [*Austria*] (EA) .... IBF
International Boot and Shoe Workers' Union .... IBSWU
International Border Area .... IBA
International Border Fancy Canary Club (EA) .... IBFCC
International Borzoi Council (EA) .... IBC
International Bottled Water Association (EA) .... IBWA
International Boundary and Water Commission .... IBWC
International Boundary Study [*A publication*] .... IBS
International Bowhunting Organization .... IBO
International Bowling Board (EA) .... IBB
International Boxing Federation (EA) .... IBF
International Boxing Guild .... IBG
International Boxing Hall of Fame (EA) .... IBHF
International Boxing Writers Association (EA) .... IBWA
International Brace Resources [*Vancouver Stock Exchange symbol*] .... IBI
International Braford Association (EA) .... IBA
International Braille Chess Association [*Abcoude, Netherlands*] (EA) .... IBCA
International Brain Research Organization [*Paris, France*] (EA) .... IBRO
International Brancusi Society (EA) .... IBS
International Brands and Their Companies [*Formerly, ITND*] [*A publication*] .... IBTC
International Brangus Breeders Association (EA) .... IBBA
International BRCA [*Breast Cancer*] **Consortium** .... IBC
International Brecht Society [*See also IBG*] (EA) .... IBS
International Breeding Consortium for St. Vincent Parrot (EAIO) .... IBCSVP
International Brick Collectors' Association (EA) .... IBCA
International Bridge Academy [*The Hague, Netherlands*] (EA) .... IBA
[*The*] **International Bridge & Terminal Co.** [*AAR code*] .... IBT
International Bridge Press Association (EA) .... IBPA
International Bridge, Tunnel, and Turnpike Association (EA) .... IBTTA
International Brightness Coefficient .... IBC
International Broadcast Institute [*Later, IIC*] .... IBI
International Broadcasting .... IB
International Broadcasting and Television Organization (NTCM) .... IBTO
International Broadcasting Convention [*Legal term*] (DLA) .... IBC
International Broadcasting Corp. [*Vancouver Stock Exchange symbol*] .... IBC
International Broadcasting Organization .... IBO
International Broadcasting Station [*ITU designation*] (DEN) .... BCI
International Broadcasting Trust [*British*] .... IBT
International Broadcasting Union [*Defunct*] (NTCM) .... IBU
International Bronchoesophagological Society (EA) .... IBES
International Bronchoesophagological Society (EA) .... IBS
International Broom and Whisk Makers' Union of America [*Defunct*] (EA) .... BWM
International Brotherhood of Boilermakers, Iron Shipbuilders, Blacksmiths, Forgers, and Helpers .... BBF
International Brotherhood of Bookbinders [*Later, Graphic Arts International Union*] .... IBB
International Brotherhood of Du Pont Workers (EA) .... IBDPW
International Brotherhood of Electrical Workers (EA) .... IBEW
International Brotherhood of Firemen and Oilers (EA) .... IBFO
International Brotherhood of Live Steamers (EA) .... IBLS
International Brotherhood of Locomotive Engineers (EA) .... IBLE
International Brotherhood of Longshoremen .... IBL
International Brotherhood of Magicians (EA) .... IBM
International Brotherhood of Motorcycle Campers (EA) .... IBMC
International Brotherhood of Old Bastards (EA) .... IBOB
International Brotherhood of Operative Potters [*Later, IBPAW*] (EA) .... IBOP
International Brotherhood of Painters and Allied Trades (EA) .... IBPAT
International Brotherhood of Painters and Allied Trades .... PAT
International Brotherhood of Papermakers [*Later, United Paperworkers International Union*] .... IBPM
International Brotherhood of Police Officers (EA) .... IBPO
International Brotherhood of Pottery and Allied Workers [*Formerly, IBOP*] (EA) .... IBPAW
International Brotherhood of Pulp, Sulphite, and Paper Mill Workers [*Later, UPIU*] .... PSPMW
International Brotherhood of Teamsters [*Union*] .... IBT
International Brotherhood of Teamsters, Chauffeurs, Warehousemen, and Helpers ofAmerica .... IB of TCWHA

International Brotherhood of Teamsters, Chauffeurs, Warehousemen, and Helpers of America (EA) .... IBT

International Bryozoology Association [See also AIB] [Paris, France] (EAIO) .... IBA

International Buckskin Horse Association (EA) .... IBHA

International Buddhist Meditation Center (EA) .... IBMC

International Builders Exchange Executives (EA) .... IBEE

International Building Classification Committee [Netherlands] .... IBCC

International Building Exposition .... IBEX

International Building Services Index [Database] [BSRIA] [Information service or system] (CRD) .... IBSEDEX

International Bulb Society (EAIO) .... IBS

International Bulk Chemical .... IBC

International Bulletin of Bibliography on Education [A publication] (AIE) .... BIBE

International Bulletin of Industrial Property [A publication] (DLA) .... Int Bull Indust Prop

International Bundle Branch Block Association (EA) .... IBBBA

International Bureau for Epilepsy [Alderley Edge, Cheshire, England] (EAIO) .... IBE

International Bureau for Informatics (CSR) .... IBI

International Bureau for the Suppression of Traffic in Persons (DI) .... IBSTP

International Bureau of Documentation and Information on Sport (NITA) .... IBDI

International Bureau of Education [See also BIE] [UNESCO] (EAIO) .... IBE

International Bureau of Education Documentation and Information System (NITA) .... IBEDOC

International Bureau of Fiscal Documentation (EAIO) .... IBFD

International Bureau of Legal Metrology .... IBLM

International Bureau of Social Tourism [See also BITS] [Brussels, Belgium] (EAIO) .... IBST

International Bureau of Software Test .... IBST

International Bureau of Strata Mechanics [See also IBG] (EAIO) .... IBSM

International Bureau of the Federations of Master Printers .... IBFMP

International Bureau of the Permanent Court of Arbitration (EAIO) .... IBPCA

International Bureau of Weights and Measures (IDOE) .... BIPM

International Bureau of Weights and Measures .... IBWM

International Bureau of Weights and Measures (ECII) .... IBWN

International Burgers Now Ltd. [Vancouver Stock Exchange symbol] .... IBU

International Bus Collectors Club (EA) .... IBC

International Business Air [Sweden ICAO designator] (FAAC) .... IBZ

International Business Aircraft Association (DA) .... IBAA

International Business Aircraft, Inc. [FAA designator] (FAAC) .... IBY

International Business Aviation Council (EA) .... IBAC

International Business Brokers Association [Defunct] (EA) .... IBBA

International Business Communications [Commercial firm British] .... IBC

International Business Communications Council [Japan] (ECON) .... IBBC

International Business Communications Council (ECON) .... IBCC

International Business Consultants [Commercial firm] .... IBC

International Business Contact Club .... IBCC

International Business Contacts .... IBC

International Business Corp. .... IBC

International Business Council (EA) .... IBC

International Business Council Midamerica (EA) .... IBCM

International Business Database [Information service or system] (IID) .... IBD

International Business Development Program [Northwestern University] [Research center] (RCD) .... IBD

International Business Earth Stations [Communications Satellite Corp.] .... IBES

International Business Education and Research Program [University of Southern California] [Research center] (RCD) .... IBEAR

International Business Forms Industries (EA) .... IBFI

International Business Intelligence [A publication] .... iBi

International Business Lawyer [A publication] (DLA) .... Int Bus Lawy

International Business Lawyer [London, England] [A publication] (DLA) .... Int'l Bus Lawyer

International Business Machines [Associated Press] (SAG) .... IBM

International Business Machines Corp. [Facetious translations: I Buil t a Macintosh; I Buy Money; Inferior But Marketable; Insidious Black Magic; It's Been Malfunctioning; Incontinent Bowel Movement] [NYSE symbol Toronto Stock Exchange symbol] (SPSG) .... IBM

International Business Machines Corp., Components Division Library, Hopewell Junction, NY [Library symbol Library of Congress] (LCLS) .... NHjI

International Business Machines Corporation, Corporation Library, Houston, TX [Library symbol Library of Congress] (LCLS) .... TxHI

International Business Machines Corp., IBM CPD Library, Durham, NC [Library symbol Library of Congress] (LCLS) .... NcDurIBM

International Business Machines Corp., Kingston, NY [Library symbol Library of Congress] (LCLS) .... NKiI

International Business Machines Corp., Oswego, NY [Library symbol Library of Congress] (LCLS) .... NOsI

International Business Machines Corp., San Jose, CA [Library symbol Library of Congress] (LCLS) .... CSjIBM

International Business Machines Corp., Systems Development Division, Poughkeepsie, NY [Library symbol Library of Congress] (LCLS) .... NPI

International Business Machines Corp., Systems Development Library, Endicott, NY [Library symbol Library of Congress] (LCLS) .... NEnI

International Business Machines Corp., Systems Manufacturing Division, Boulder, CO [Library symbol Library of Congress] (LCLS) .... CoBIBM

International Business Machines Corp., Thomas J. Watson Research Center, Yorktown Heights, NY [Library symbol Library of Congress] (LCLS) .... NYhI

International Business Machines System .... IBSYS

International Business Machine's Timesharing System (TEL) .... IBM TSS

International Business Opportunities Service [World Bank] [United Nations] (DUND) .... IBOS

International Business Press Associates (PDAA) .... IBPA

International Business Reply [Post Office] [British] .... IBR

International Business Schools [NASDAQ symbol] (SAG) .... IBSDF

International Business Schools [Associated Press] (SAG) .... IntBusSch

International Business Schools, Inc. [Associated Press] (SAG) .... IntlBus

International Business Series [A publication] (DLA) .... Int'l Bus Ser

International Business Services [Switzerland] (ECON) .... IBS

International Business Services [Telecommunications] (TSSD) .... IBS

International Business Unit [British Information service or system] (IID) .... IBU

International Business Week .... IBW

International Businessmen of Jeddah [Saudi Arabia] (EAIO) .... ABJ

International Butec Industry [Vancouver Stock Exchange symbol] .... IB

International C Class Catamaran Association of America (EA) .... ICCCA

International Cable Protection Committee [British] (EAIO) .... ICPC

International Cablecasting Technologies [Vancouver Stock Exchange symbol] ICC

International Cablecasting Technologies, Inc. [Associated Press] (SAG) .... IntCabl

International Cabletel, Inc. [NASDAQ symbol] (SAG) .... ICTL

International Cabletel, Inc. [Associated Press] (SAG) .... IntCble

International Cabletel, Inc. [Associated Press] (SAG) .... IntlCable

International Call for Tenders (NATG) .... ICT

International Camaro Club (EA) ICC

International Camellia Society [Worcester, England] (EAIO) .... ICS

International Camero Resources [Vancouver Stock Exchange symbol] .... ISM

International Camp Counselor Program (EA) .... ICCP

International Campaign Against Banking on Apartheid (EAIO) .... ICABA

International Campaign for Tibet (EA) .... ICT

International Cancer Information Center [Public Health Service] [Information service or system] (IID) ICIC

International Cancer League [Defunct] (EA) ICL

International Cancer Patient Data Exchange System .... ICPDES

International Cancer Research Data Bank [National Cancer Institute] [Database producer] (IID) .... ICRDB

International Cancer Research Technology Transfer [Program] .... ICRETT

International Cancer Research Workshop .... ICREW

International Candle .... ICD

International Cannabis Alliance Reform (DI) .... ICAR

International Canoe Federation [See also FIC] [Florence, Italy] (EAIO) .... ICF

International Capri Resources [Vancouver Stock Exchange symbol] .... ICQ

International Car Wash Institute (EA) .... ICWI

International Carbohydrate Organization [Aberdeen, Scotland] (EAIO) .... ICO

International Cardero Resources [Vancouver Stock Exchange symbol] .... ICO

International Cardiac Doppler Society (DMAA) .... ICDS

International Cardiology Foundation (EA) .... ICF

International Cardiovascular Society .... ICS

International Cardiovascular Society (EA) .... ICVS

International Cargo Advisory Bureau .... ICAB

International Cargo Gear Bureau (EA) .... ICGB

International Cargo Handling Coordination Association [London, England] (EA) .... ICHCA

International Carnival Glass Association (EA) .... ICGA

International Carnivorous Plant Society (EA) .... ICPS

International Carpet and Rug Market (ITD) .... ICRM

International Carpet Classification Organization [Brussels, Belgium] (EAIO) .... ICCO

International Carpet Fair .... ICF

International Cartographic Association [Australia] (EA) .... ICA

International Cartridge Recycling Association (EA) .... ICRA

International Carwash Association (EA) .... ICA

International Carwash Association .... ICWA

International Carwash Association/National Carwash Council [Later, ICA] (EA) .... ICA/NCC

International Casting Federation (EAIO) .... ICF

International Castles Institute (EA) ICI

International Castor Oil Association (EA) .... ICOA

[The] International Cat Association (EA) .... TICA

International Catacomb Society (EA) .... ICS

International Caterers Association [Defunct] (EA) .... ICA

International Catholic Association for Radio, Television and Audiovisuals [Belgium] (EAIO) .... UNDA

International Catholic Auxiliaries (EA) .... ICA

International Catholic Child Bureau [Geneva, Switzerland] (EA) .... ICCB

International Catholic Confederation of Hospitals [Later, IHF] (EA) .... ICCH

International Catholic Conference of Guiding (EAIO) .... ICCG

International Catholic Deaf Association (EA) .... ICDA

International Catholic Girls' Society .... ICGS

International Catholic Library [A publication] ICL

International Catholic Migration Commission [See also CICM] [Geneva, Switzerland] (EAIO) .... ICMC

International Catholic Organizations .... ICO

International Catholic Press Union [Later, UCIP] .... ICPU

International Catholic Rural Association .... ICRA

International Catholic Truth Society (EA) .... ICTS

International Catholic Union of the Press (EA) .... ICUP

International Catholic Youth Federation [Later, WFCY] .... ICYF

International CBX Owners Association (EA) .... ICOA

International Cell Research Organization [ICSU] [Paris, France] (EAIO) .... ICRO

International Cello Centre [Duns, Scotland] (EAIO) ICC

International Cellulose Research Ltd., Hawkesbury, ON, Canada [Library symbol Library of Congress] (LCLS) .... CaOHkC

International Cemetery Supply Association (EA) .... ICSA

International Center for Advanced Mediterranean Agronomic Studies [FAO] .... ICAMAS

International Center for Agricultural Research in Dry Areas [Syria] .... ICARDA

International Center for Aquaculture [Auburn University] [Research center] (RCD) .... ICA

International Center for Arid and Semi-Arid Land Studies [*Texas Technological University*] .... ICASALS
International Center for Athletic and Educational Opportunities (EA) .. ICAEO
International Center for Biological Control [*University of California, Berkeley and Riverside*] .... ICBC
International Center for Communication Arts and Sciences ..... ICCAS
International Center for Companies of the Food Trade and Industry [*Formerly, International Association of Chain Stores*] (EAIO) .... CIES
International Center for Companies of the Food Trade and Industry (EA) .... ICCFTI
International Center for Comparative Criminology (EA) ICCC
International Center for Computer-Aided Design (MHDB) .... ICCAD
International Center for Control of Nutritional Anemia [*University of Kansas*] [*Research center*] (RCD) .... ICCNA
International Center for Cooperation in BioInformatics [*UNESCO*] .... ICCB
International Center for Coordination of Legal Assistance [*Switzerland*] (PDAA) .... ICCLA
International Center for Criminological Studies (BARN) .... ICCS
International Center for Development Policy (EA) .... ICDP
International Center for Diarrhoeal Diseases Research (PDAA) .... ICDDR
International Center for Dynamics of Development (EA) .... ICDD
International Center for Energy and Economic Development .... ICEED
International Center for High Quality Scrap [*Scrap salvage*] .... INCH
International Center for Holocaust Studies (EA) .... ICHS
International Center for Industry and the Environment (DCTA) ..... ICIE
International Center for Interdisciplinary Studies of Immunology at Georgetown [*Georgetown University*] [*Research center*] (RCD) .... ICISI
International Center for Law in Development (EA) .... ICLD
International Center for Living Aquatic Resources Management (EAIO) .... CLARM
International Center for Living Aquatic Resources Management [*Makati, Metro Manila, Philippines*] (EAIO) .... ICLARM
International Center for Living Aquatic Resources Management .... ICLARM
International Center for Marine Resources Development (ASF) ...... ICMARD
International Center for Marine Resources Development [*University of Rhode Island*] .... ICMRD
International Center for Medicine and Law (EA) .... ICML
International Center for Monetary and Banking Studies [*Switzerland*] (ECON) .... ICMB
International Center for Orthopaedic Education .... ICOE
International Center for Peace in the Middle East (EA) .... ICPME
International Center for Public Enterprises in Developing Countries [*Ljubljana, Yugoslavia*] (EAIO) .... ICPE
International Center for Research on Bilingualism [*Universite Laval*] [*Canada*] .... ICRB
International Center for Research on Language Planning (AC) ..... CRIP
International Center for Research on Language Planning [*Laval University*] (IRC) .... ICRLP
International Center for Research on Women (EA) .... ICRW
International Center for Science Information Services in Phytovirology .... ICSISP
International Center for Scientific and Technical Information [*Moscow, USSR*] (EAIO) .... ICSTI
International Center for Social Gerontology [*Later, TCSG*] [*Defunct*] (EA) .... ICSG
International Center for the Advancement of Management Education [*Stanford University*] .... ICAME
International Center for the Disabled (EA) .... ICD
International Center for the Environment .... ICE
International Center for the Solution of Environmental Problems (EA) ..... ICSEP
International Center for the Typographic Arts .... ICTA
International Center for Theoretical Physics [*Trieste, Italy*] (EA) .... ICTP
International Center in New York (EA) .... ICNY
International Center of Free Trade Unionists in Exile [*France Defunct*] ..... ICFTUE
International Center of Genetic Epistemology [*Geneva, Switzerland*] .... ICGE
International Center of Information on Antibiotics (EAIO) .... ICIA
International Center of Medical and Psychological Hypnosis [*Milan, Italy*] (EA) .... ICMPH
International Center of Medieval Art (EA) .... ICMA
International Center of Photography (EA) .... ICP
International Center of Studies on Early Music .... ICSEM
International Center of the International Serials Data System [*UNESCO*] (PDAA) .... ISDS/IC
International Center of Theatre Research (EA) .... ICTR
International Centre for Advanced Technical and Vocational Training [*British*] .... ICATVT
International Centre for Art Education (EAIO) .... ICAE
International Centre for Chemical Studies [*See also CIEC*] (EAIO) .... ICCS
International Centre for Computer Aided Design (PDAA) .... ICCAD
International Centre for Diarrhoeal Disease Research [*Bangladesh*] .... ICDDR
International Centre for Diarrhoeal Disease Research, Bangladesh (ECON) .... CDDRB
International Centre for Diarrhoeal Disease Research, Bangladesh (ECON) .... ICDDRB
International Centre for Distance Learning [*United Nations University*] (DUND) .... ICDL
International Centre for Earth Tides [*See also CIMT*] [*Belgium*] (EAIO) .... ICET
International Centre for Economics [*British*] .... ICE
International Centre for Ethnic Studies (EA) .... ICES
International Centre for Genetic Engineering and Biotechnology [*United Nations Development Organization*] (EAIO) .... ICGEB
International Centre for Genetic Engineering and Biotechnology Network [*United Nations Development Organization*] (DUND) .... ICGEBNET
International Centre for Heat and Mass Transfer (EAIO) .... ICHMT
International Centre for Industrial Studies [*United Nations*] .... ICIS

International Centre for Integrated Mountain Development [*Kathmandu*] (ECON) .... ICIMOD
International Centre for Local Credit [*The Hague, Netherlands*] (EAIO) ICLC
International Centre for Mathematical Sciences [*Heriot-Watt University*] (ECON) .... ICMS
International Centre for Migration Policy Development [*Austria*] (ECON) .... ICMPD
International Centre for Ocean Development [*See also CIEO*] [*Canada*] ...... ICOD
International Centre for Ocean Development, Halifax, Nova Scotia [*Library symbol National Library of Canada*] (BIB) .... NSHIC
International Centre for Pure and Applied Mathematics [*United Nations*] (EA) .... ICPAM
International Centre for Research in Accounting [*University of Lancaster*] [*British*] (CB) .... ICRA
International Centre for Settlement of Investment Disputes (EA) .... ICSID
International Centre for Studies in Religious Education [*Brussels, Belgium*] (EAIO) .... ICSRE
International Centre for the Application of Pesticides [*British*] (IRUK) .... ICAP
International Centre for the Study of the Preservation and the Restoration of Cultural Property [*Rome, Italy*] (EAIO) .... ICCROM
International Centre for the Terminology of the Social Sciences [*Grand-Saconnex, Switzerland*] (EA) .... INTERCENTRE
International Centre of Ancient and Modern Tapestry .... ICAMT
International Centre of Films for Children .... ICFC
International Centre of Films for Children and Young People [*France*] (EY) .... ICFCYP
International Centre of Insect Physiology and Ecology [*ICSU*] [*Nairobi, Kenya*] (EAIO) .... ICIPE
International Centre of Research and Information on Collective Economy .... ICRICE
International Centrum voor Beurzen en Kongressen [*Belgium*] (EAIO) .... ICBK
International Ceramic Association (EA) .... ICA
International Cerebral Palsy Society [*British*] (EAIO) .... ICPS
International Cesarean Awareness Network [*Formerly Cesarean Prevention Movement (CPM)*] (PAZ) .... ICAN
International Chain of Industrial and Technical Advertising Agencies (EA) .... ICITA
International Chain Salon Association (EA) .... ICSA
International Chain Saw Wood Sculptors Association (EA) .... ICSWSA
International Chamber of Commerce [*See also CCI*] [*Paris, France*] (EAIO)..... ICC
International Chamber of Commerce (IEEE) .... INCO
International Chamber of Shipping [*British*] (EAIO) .... ICS
International Champlain-Richelieu Engineering Board [*Canada*] ..... ICREB
International Chaplain's Ministry (EA) .... ICM
International Charter Xpress Limited Liability Co. [*ICAO designator*] (FAAC) ICX
International Cheerleading Foundation (EA) .... ICF
International Cheese and Deli Association [*Later, IDDA*] (EA) .... ICDA
International Chefs' Association (EA) .... ICA
International Chemalloy Corp. [*Toronto Stock Exchange symbol*] .... ITC
International Chemical Congress of Pacific Basin Societies (EA) .... ICCPBS
International Chemical Society [*Proposed*] .... ICS
International Chemical Workers Union .... ICW
International Chemical Workers Union (EA) .... ICWU
International Chemistry Olympiad [*For high school students*] .... IChO
International Chemometrics Internet Conference .... InCINC
International Chemometrics Society [*Brussels, Belgium*] (EAIO) .... ICS
International Cherokee [*Vancouver Stock Exchange symbol*] .... ICK
International Chessology Club (EA) ICC
International Chianina Association (EAIO) .... ICA
International Child Abduction Remedies Act [*1988*] .... ICARA
International Child Care (USA) (EA) .... ICCUSA
International Child Health Foundation (EA) .... ICHF
International Child Resource Institute (EA) .... ICRI
International Childbirth Education Association (EA) .... ICEA
International Children's Book Day [*Australia*] .... ICBD
International Children's Centre [*Paris, France*] ICC
International Children's Emergency Fund [*United Nations*] (DLA) .... ICEF
International Chili Society (EA) .... ICS
International China Painting Teachers Organization [*Later, International Porcelain Artist Teachers*] .... ICPTO
International Chinese Snuff Bottle Society (EA) .... ICSBS
International Chiropractors Association (EA) .... ICA
International Christian Accrediting Association (EA) .... ICAA
International Christian Aid Relief Enterprises [*Australia*] .... ICARE
International Christian Broadcasters [*Defunct*] (EA) .... ICB
International Christian Classic Motorcyclists (EA) .... ICCM
International Christian Dance Fellowship (EAIO) .... ICDF
International Christian Education Association (EA) .... ICEA
International Christian Esperanto Association (EA) .... ICEA
International Christian Graduate University, San Bernardino, CA [*Library symbol*] [*Library of Congress*] (LCLS) .... CSbIC
International Christian Leadership (EA) ICL
International Christian Leprosy Mission (EA) .... ICLM
International Christian Maritime Association [*Felixstone, Suffolk, England*] (EAIO) .... ICMA
International Christian Media Commission (EA) .... ICMC
International Christian Studies Association (EA) .... ICSA
International Christian University [*Tokyo*] .... ICU
International Christian University Library [*UTLAS symbol*] .... ICU
International Christian Youth (EA) .... ICY
International Christian Youth Exchange (EA) .... ICYE
International Christians for Unity in Social Action (EA) .... ICUSA
International Church of Metaphysics (EA) .... ICOM
International Churchill Society (EA) .... ICS

International Cigar Band Society [*Defunct*] (EA) ICBS
International Cigarette Makers' Association [*A union*] ICMA
International Circle for Research in Philosophy [*Research center*] (RCD) ICRIP
International Circuit Technology [*Electronics*] (IAA) ICT
International Circulation Distributors, Inc. ICD
International Circulation Managers Association (EA) ICMA
International Cirrus Experiment [*Funded by West Germany, Britain, France, Sweden, and the European Communities Commission*] [*Climatology*] ICE
International City Management Association [*Later, ICMA-The Professional Local Government Management Association*] (EA) ICMA
International Civil Airports Association [*Orly, France*] (EAIO) ICAA
International Civil Aviation Authority [*Database originator*] [*Canada*] (NITA) ICAA
International Civil Aviation Message Routing System ICAMRS
International Civil Aviation Organization [*Montreal, PQ*] [*United Nations*] ICAO
International Civil Aviation Organization [*ICAO designator*] (FAAC) ICO
International Civil Aviation Organization, Montreal, PQ, Canada [*Library symbol Library of Congress*] (LCLS) CaQMIC
International Civil Aviation Organization [*Organisation de l'Aviation Civile Internationale*] **Montreal, Quebec** [*Library symbol National Library of Canada*] (NLC) QMIC
International Civil Defence Organization [*Switzerland*] ICDO
International Civil Service Advisory Board ICSAB
International Civil Service Commission (EA) ICSC
International Civil Service Training Organization ICSTO
International Claim Association [*Rock Island, IL*] (EA) ICA
International Claims Commission of the United States [*Abolished, 1954*] [*Department of State*] ICCUS
International Claims Settlement Act of 1949 ICSA
International Clarinet Society [*Later, ICS/CI*] (EA) ICS
International Clarinet Society/Clarinetwork International (EA) ICS/CI
International Classification (DAVI) IC
International Classification of Clinical Services (HCT) ICCS
International Classification of Diseases [*A publication*] ICD
International Classification of Diseases. 9th Revision [*A publication*] (DHSM) ICD-9
International Classification of Diseases. 9th Revision. Clinical Modification [*A publication*] (DHSM) ICD-9-CM
International Classification of Diseases - Adopted Code for Hospitals H-ICDA
International Classification of Diseases, Adopted for Use in the United States ICDA
International Classification of Diseases, Adopted for Use in the United States. 8th Revision [*A publication*] (DHSM) ICDA-8
International Classification of Impairments, Disabilities, and Handicaps [*Occupational therapy*] ICIDH
International Classification of Nursing Practice (DMAA) ICNP
International Classification of Patents [*Council of Europe*] (PDAA) ICP
International Cleaner Production Information Clearinghouse (GNE) ICPIC
International Clearinghouse on the Military and the Environment (EA) ICME
International Clergy Council (EA) ICC
International Cliff Richard Movement (EAIO) ICRM
International Climate Zone ICZ
International Climatic Decades ICD
International Climatic Research Program ICRP
International Clinical Laboratories, Inc. ICL
International CLIVAR [*Climate Variability and Prediction*] **Project Office** [*Marine science*] (OSRA) ICPO
International Club for Collectors of Hatpins and Hatpin Holders (EA) ICC of H & HH
International Clubroot Working Group (EAIO) ICWG
International CMOS Technology [*Computer science*] ICT
International Coal Trade Model [*Department of Energy*] (GFGA) ICTM
International Coalition Against Violent Entertainment (EA) ICAVE
International Coalition for Development Action [*See also CIAD*] (EAIO) ICDA
International Coalition on Energy for Development ICED
International Coalition to End Domestics' Exploitation INTERCEDE
International Coast Minerals Corp. [*Vancouver Stock Exchange symbol*] INK
International Cocoa Organization [*London, England*] (EAIO) ICCO
International Cocoa Trades Federation [*British*] ICTF
International Code Designator [*Telecommunications*] (OSI) ICD
International Code of Advertising Practice (DI) ICAP
International Code of Botanical Nomenclature ICBN
International Code of Medical Ethics ICME
International Code of Signals (IAA) ICS
International Code of Signals INTCO
International Code of Signals (PDAA) INTERCO
International Code Use (BARN) ICU
International CODEN Service [*Chemical Abstracts Service*] [*Information service or system*] (IID) INTERCODE
International Coffee Agreement [*Signed September, 1962*] ICA
International Coffee Organization (EAIO) ICO
International Cogeneration Society (EA) ICS
International Coil Winding Association (EA) ICWA
International Cold Storage ICS
International Colin Energy [*Associated Press*] (SAG) IntColng
International Collaboration in Infectious Diseases Research [*Tulane University*] [*Research center*] (RCD) ICIDR
International College Art Program [*Red Cross Youth*] ICAP
International College in Copenhagen [*Denmark*] ICC
International College of Angiology (EA) ICA
International College of Applied Kinesiology (EA) ICAK
International College of Applied Nutrition (EA) ICAN
International College of Chiropractors (EA) ICC
International College of Dentists (EA) ICD
International College of Hotel Management ICHM
International College of Officers [*Salvation Army*] ICO
International College of Podiatric Laser Surgery (EA) ICPLS
International College of Real Estate Consulting Professionals (EAIO) RECP
International College of Scientists [*See also ISK*] [*International Academy of Sciences*] [*Paderborn, Federal Republic of Germany*] (EAIO) ICS
International College of Surgeons (EA) ICS
International College of Surgeons, Chicago, IL [*Library symbol Library of Congress*] (LCLS) ICICS
International Collegiate Sports Foundation (EA) ICSF
International Colloquium about Gas Marketing (EA) ICGM
International Color Computer Club (EA) ICCC
International Color Consortium ICC
International Colour Management [*Commercial firm British*] ICM
International Columbian Quincentenary Alliance (EA) ICQA
International Coma Recovery Institute (EA) ICRI
International Cometary Explorer [*Formerly, International Sun-Ea rth Explorer*] [*NASA*] ICE
International Comfort Products ICP
International Commerce Term [*International Chamber of Commerce*] INCOTERM
International Commercial Arbitration (BARN) ICA
International Commercial Bank of China [*Taiwan*] ICBC
International Commercial Business Establishment [*Saudi Arabia*] CBE
International Commercial Exchange [*Defunct*] (EA) ICE
International Commission Against Concentration Camp Practices [*Brussels, Belgium*] [*Defunct*] (EAIO) ICACCP
International Commission for Agricultural Industries ICAI
International Commission for Air Navigation ICAN
International Commission for Bee Botany [*Later, ICPBR*] (EA) ICBB
International Commission for Central American Recovery and Development ICCARD
International Commission for Environmental Assessment (GNE) ICEA
International Commission for Microbial Genetics [*International Council of Scientific Unions*] ICMG
International Commission for Optics [*See also CIO*] [*ICSU Delft, Netherlands*] (EAIO) ICO
International Commission for Orders of Chivalry (EA) ICOC
International Commission for Plant-Bee Relationships (EAIO) ICPBR
International Commission for Protection Against Environmental Mutagens and Carcinogens [*Rijswljk, Netherlands*] (EAIO) ICPEMC
International Commission for Small Scale Vegetation Maps [*Pondicherry, India*] (EAIO) ICSSVM
International Commission for Supervision and Control [*Composed of delegates from Canada, India and Poland established by the 1954 Geneva Accords*] (VNW) ICSC
International Commission for the Conservation of Atlantic Tunas [*Spain*] ICCAT
International Commission for the Co-ordination of Solidarity among Sugar Workers [*Canada*] ICCSASW
International Commission for the Eriksson Prize Fund (EAIO) ICEPF
International Commission for the History of Representative and Parliamentary Institutions [*Rome, Italy*] (EAIO) ICHRPI
International Commission for the History of Social Movements and Social Structures [*Paris, France*] (EAIO) ICHSMSS
International Commission for the Nomenclature of Cultivated Plants [*Wageningen, Netherlands*] (EA) ICNCP
International Commission for the Northwest Atlantic Fisheries [*Superseded by NAFO*] ICNAF
International Commission for the Preservation of Islamic Cultural Heritage (EA) ICPICH
International Commission for the Prevention of Alcoholism [*Later, InternationalCommission for the Prevention of Alcoholism and Drug Dependency*] ICPA
International Commission for the Prevention of Alcoholism and Drug Dependency (EA) ICPADD
International Commission for the Protection of the Moselle Against Pollution (EA) ICPMP
International Commission for the Protection of the Rhine Against Pollution [*See also ICPRP, IKSR*] [*Germany*] (EAIO) ICPRAP
International Commission for the Scientific Exploration of the Mediterranean Sea (EAIO) ICSEM
International Commission for the Scientific Exploration of the Mediterranean Sea (NOAA) ICSEMS
International Commission for the Southeast Atlantic Fisheries [*See also CIPASE*] (EAIO) ICSAF
International Commission for the Southeast Atlantic Fisheries ICSEAF
International Commission for the Teaching of History [*Brussels, Belgium*] (EA) ICTH
International Commission for Uniform Methods of Sugar Analysis [*Mackay, QLD, Australia*] (EAIO) ICUMSA
International Commission of Agricultural Engineering ICAE
International Commission of Catholic Prison Chaplains (EA) ICPC
International Commission of Control and Supervision [*Composed of representatives of Canada, Hungary, Indonesia, and Poland, and charged with supervising the ceasefire in Vietnam, 1973*] ICCS
International Commission of Health Professionals for Health and Human Rights (EA) ICHP
International Commission of Jurists [*Switzerland*] ICJ
International Commission of Jurists Australian Section ICJAS
International Commission of Military History ICMH
International Commission of Occupational Health (EA) ICOH
International Commission on Acoustics [*Aachen, Federal Republic of Germany*] (EAIO) ICA
International Commission on Atmospheric Chemistry and Global Pollution (USDC) ICACGP

International Commission on Atmospheric Chemistry Global Pollution [*Marine science*] (OSRA) .... ICACGP
International Commission on Atmospheric Electricity (EA) .... ICAE
International Commission on Civil Status [*See also CIEC*] [*Strasbourg, France*] (EAIO) .... ICCS
International Commission on Commercial Activities (EAIO) .... ICCA
International Commission on Erosion Sedimentation (NUCP) .... ICES
International Commission on Fungal Genetics [*International Council of Scientific Unions*] .... ICFG
International Commission on Glass [*See also CIV*] [*Prague, Czechoslovakia*] (EAIO) .... ICG
International Commission on Human Ecology (EA) .... ICHE
International Commission on Illumination [*Since 1951, has been known exclusively as CIE, which see*] ICI
International Commission on Irrigation and Drainage [*See also CIID*] [*ICSU New Delhi, India*] (EAIO) .... ICID
International Commission on Large Dams [*See also CIGB*] [*ICSU Paris, France*] (EAIO) .... ICOLD
International Commission on Mathematical Instruction [*British*] ...... ICMI
International Commission on Microbiological Specifications for Foods (EA) .... ICMSF
International Commission on Mushroom Science [*Later, ISMS*] (EA) .... ICMS
International Commission on Mycotoxicology [*International Council of Scientific Unions*] .... ICMT
International Commission on National Parks [*Later, CNPAA*] (EA) .... ICNP
International Commission on Physics Education [*See also CIEP*] (EA) ...... ICPE
International Commission on Radiation Units and Measurements (EA) ...... ICRU
International Commission on Radiation Units and Measurements .... ICRUM
International Commission on Radiological Education (DMAA) .... ICRE
International Commission on Radiological Protection [*International Society of Radiology*] [*British*] .... ICRP
International Commission on Rules for the Approval of Electrical Equipment [*Later, CEE*] .... ICRAEE
International Commission on Signs and Symbols .... ICSS
International Commission on Snow and Ice .... ICSI
International Commission on the Biological Effects of Noise (GNE) .... ICBN
International Commission on the History of the Geological Sciences [*ICSU*] [*Paris, France*] (EAIO) .... INHIGEO
International Commission on the Meteorology of the Upper Atmosphere .... ICMUA
International Commission on the Taxonomy of Fungi .... ICTF
International Commission on Trichinellosis (EA) .... ICT
International Commission on Yeasts and Yeast-Like Microorganisms [*ICSU*] [*France*] (EAIO) .... ICY
International Commission on Zoological Nomenclature [*British*] (EAIO) ...... ICZN
International Committee Against Apartheid, Racism, and Colonialism in Southern Africa [*British Defunct*] (EAIO) .... ICSA
International Committee Against Involuntary Exile (EA) .... ICAIE
International Committee Against Mental Illness (EA) .... ICAMI
International Committee Against Racism (EA) .... INCAR
International Committee for Accounting Co-Operation .... ICAC
International Committee for Amateur-Built Aircraft (EA) .... CIACA
International Committee for Automobile Documentation .... ICAD
International Committee for Breaking the Language Barrier .... ICBLB
International Committee for Coal Petrology [*Liege, Belgium*] (EAIO) .... ICCP
International Committee for Coal Research [*Brussels, Belgium*] (EAIO) .... ICCR
International Committee for Contraceptive Research .... ICCR
International Committee for Ethnic Liberty [*See also IKEL*] (EAIO) .... ICEL
International Committee for European Security and Co-Operation [*See also CISCE*] (EAIO) .... ICESC
International Committee for Historical Sciences [*Paris, France*] (EA) ...... ICHS
International Committee for Horticultural Congresses .... ICHC
International Committee for Human Rights in Taiwan (EA) .... ICHRT
International Committee for Life Assurance Medicine [*Zurich, Switzerland*] (EAIO) .... ICLAM
International Committee for Lift Regulations [*See also CIRA*] [*Saint-Yvelines, France*] (EAIO) .... ICLR
International Committee for Microbiological and Immunological Documentation [*International Council of Scientific Unions*] .... ICMID
International Committee for Outer Space Onomastics .... ICOSO
International Committee for Recording the Productivity of Milk Animals [*See also CICPLB*] [*Rome, Italy*] (EAIO) .... ICRPMA
International Committee for Research and Study on Environmental Factors .... ICEF
International Committee for Social Science Information and Documentation [*Information service or system*] (IID) .... ICSSD
International Committee for Social Science Information and Documentation [*Paris, France Information service or system*] (IID) .... ICSSID
International Committee for Social Sciences Documentation and Information (NITA) .... ICSSD
International Committee for Soviet and East European Studies (EAIO) .... ICSEES
International Committee for Standardization in Haematology [*Louvain, Belgium*] [*Research center*] (EAIO) .... ICSH
International Committee for Standardization in Human Biology .... ICSHB
International Committee for the Anthropology of Food and Food Habits [*Defunct*] (EA) .... ICAFFH
International Committee for the Centennial of Light ICCL
International Committee for the Check-List of the Fishes of the North-Eastern Atlantic and Mediterranean .... CLOFNAM
International Committee for the Conservation of Mosaics [*Hungerford, Berkshire, England*] (EAIO) .... ICCM
International Committee for the Conservation of Mud-Brick (EAIO) ...... ICCMB
[*The*] International Committee for the Conservation of the Industrial Heritage (EA) .... TICCIH
International Committee for the Cooperation of Journalists (NATG) .... ICCJ

International Committee for the Coordination of Clinical Application and Teaching of Autogenic Therapy [*North Vancouver, BC*] (EAIO) .... ICAT
International Committee for the Defense of Salman Rushdie and His Publishers (EAIO) .... ICDSRHP
International Committee for the Defense of the Breton Language [*See also CISLB*] [*Brussels, Belgium*] (EAIO) .... ICDBL
International Committee for the History of Technology (EA) .... ICOHTEC
International Committee for the History of the Second World War (EAIO) .... ICHSWW
International Committee for the Indians of the Americas [*Kaiseraugst, Switzerland*] (EAIO) .... INCOMINDIOS
International Committee for the Release of Anatoly Scharansky [*Defunct*] (EA) .... ICRAS
International Committee for the Sociology of Sport .... ICSS
International Committee for the Study and Conservation of Earthen Architecture (EAIO) .... ICCEA
International Committee for Training and Education of Co-Operators (EAIO) .... INCOTEC
International Committee for World Day of Prayer (EA) .... ICWDP
International Committee of Acquired Immunodeficiency Syndrome Service Organisations (DMAA) .... ICASO
International Committee of Architectural Photogrammetry .... ICAP
International Committee of Automation of Mines and Quarries [*Budapest, Hungary*] (EAIO) .... ICAMQ
International Committee of Catholic Nurses [*See also CICIAMS*] [*Vatican City, Vatican City State*] (EAIO) .... ICCN
International Committee of Children's and Adolescents' Movements .... ICCAM
International Committee of Creole Studies [*Aix-En-Provence, France*] (EAIO) .... ICCS
International Committee of Electrochemical Thermodynamics and Kinetics (IEEE) .... ICETK
International Committee of Enamelling Creators (EAIO) .... ICEC
International Committee of French-Speaking Historians and Geographers (EAIO) .... ICFSHG
International Committee of Hard of Hearing Young People [*Frederiksberg, Denmark*] (EAIO) .... ICHOHYP
International Committee of ICOM [*International Council of Museums*] for Conservation [*Later, ICOM-CC*] (EAIO) ICC
International Committee of Lawyers for Tibet .... ICLT
International Committee of Medical Journal Editors [*An association*] .... ICMJE
International Committee of Military Medicine [*Belgium*] (EAIO) .... ICMM
International Committee of Military Medicine and Pharmacy [*Belgium*] .... ICMMP
International Committee of North American Federation .... ICNAF
International Committee of Onomastic Sciences [*Belgium*] .... ICOS
International Committee of Paper and Board Converters in the Common Market (ECED) .... CITPA
International Committee of Passenger Lines (PDAA) .... ICPL
International Committee of Plant Nutrition (EA) .... ICPN
International Committee of Slavists [*Sofia, Bulgaria*] (EAIO) .... ICS
International Committee of Toy Industries (EA) .... ICTI
International Committee of Youth Organizations (EAIO) .... ICYO
International Committee on Aeronautical Fatigue [*Delft University of Technology*] [*Netherlands*] (EAIO) .... ICAF
International Committee on Alcohol, Drugs, and Traffic Safety [*Linkoping, Sweden*] (EA) .... ICADTS
International Committee on Arctic Arboviruses .... ICAA
International Committee on Chemical Warfare .... CCW
International Committee on Chemical Warfare, Crop Destruction .... CCW(CD)
International Committee on Clinical Sociology [*See also CISC*] [*Later, International Group on Clinical Sociology*] (EAIO) .... ICCS
International Committee on Economic and Applied Microbiology [*ICSU*] (EAIO) .... ICEAM
International Committee on English in the Liturgy (EA) .... ICEL
International Committee on Food Microbiology and Hygiene [*ICSU*] [*Frederiksberg, Denmark*] (EAIO) .... ICFMH
International Committee on Future Accelerators [*International Union of Pure and Applied Physics*] .... ICFA
International Committee on Laboratory Animals .... ICLA
International Committee on Microbial Ecology [*ICSU*] (EAIO) .... ICOME
International Committee on NDT [*Nondestructive Testing*] [*Brazil*] (EAIO) ..... ICNDT
International Committee on Nomenclature of Viruses [*Later, ICTV*] .... ICNV
International Committee on Ocean Exploration and Environmental Services [*Defunct*] (USDC) .... ICOEES
International Committee on Polar Viruses .... ICPV
International Committee on Refugees [*World War II*] .... ICR
International Committee on Remote Sensing and Data Transmission [*Marine science*] (OSRA) .... ICRSDT
International Committee on Sarcoidosis [*British*] (EAIO) .... ICS
International Committee on Seafarer's Welfare Office (EAIO) .... ICSW
International Committee on Smoking Issues [*Brussels, Belgium*] (EAIO) ...... ICOSI
International Committee on Social Psychological Research in Developing Countries (EA) .... ICSPRDC
International Committee on Systematic Bacteriology [*London, ON*] (EA) ..... ICSB
International Committee on Taxonomy of Viruses [*ICSU*] [*Rennes, France*] (EAIO) .... ICTV
International Committee on the Organisation of Traffic at Sea [*British*] (DS) .... ICOTAS
International Committee on the Standardization of Physical Fitness Tests .... ICSPFT
International Committee on the University Emergency (EA) .... ICUE
International Committee on Thrombosis and Hemostasis .... ICTH
International Committee on Urgent Anthropological and Ethnological Research [*Vienna, Austria*] (EAIO) .... ICUAER
International Committee on Urgent Surgery [*Milan, Italy*] (EAIO) .... ICUS

International Committee on Veterinary Anatomical Nomenclature [See also CINAV] [Zurich, Switzerland] (EAIO) .... ICVAN
International Committee on Veterinary Gross Anatomical Nomenclature [Cornell University] [Ithaca, NY] (EY) .... ICVGAN
International Committee on Weights and Measures .... ICWM
International Committee to Coordinate Activities of Technical Groups in CoatingsIndustry [Paris, France] (EAIO) .... ICCATCI
International Committee to the Red Cross [Geneva, Switzerland] (EAIO) ...... ICRC
International Commodities Clearing House [British Business term] .... ICCH
International Commodity Agreement .... ICA
International Commodity Production Data [United Nations Statistical Office] (NITA) .... ICPDATA
International Common Law Exchange Society (EA) .... ICLES
International Communes Network (EAIO) .... ICN
International Communication Agency [Also, USICA] [Formerly called BECA and USIA, it later became known again as USIA] .... ICA
International Communication and Negotiation Simulation .... ICONS
International Communication Association (EA) .... ICA
International Communication Information Retrieval System [University of Florida] (PDAA) .... INCIRS
International Communication of Orthodox Nations .... ICON
International [or Internal] Communication Unit [Telecommunications] (TEL) .... ICU
International Communications Agency Procurement Regulation [A publication] (AAGC) .... ICAPR
International Communications Association (EA) .... ICA
International Communications Corp. [Miami, FL] (CSR) ICC
International Communications Industries Association (EA) .... ICIA
International Communications Ltd. [Fayville, MA] [Telecommunications service] (TSSD) ICL
International Communications Satellite Consortium (MCD) .... ICSC
International Communications Sciences .... ICS
International Communications System .... ICS
International Communications Systems Consultants [British] (NITA) .... ICSC
International Community for the Relief of Starvation and Suffering (EA) .... ICROSS
International Community of Booksellers' Associations [Later, IBF] .... ICBA
International Companies and Their Brands [A publication] .... ICTB
International Company for Finance and Investment [Russian bank] .... ICFM
International Comparative Literature Association (EA) .... ICLA
International Comparative Political Parties Project [Northwestern University] [Inactive] (IID) .... ICPP
International Competitive Bid (NATG) .... ICB
International Computaprint Corp. [Fort Washington, PA] ICC
International Computation Center [Sponsored by UNESCO] [Rome, Italy] ICC
International Computer and Telecommunications Conference [International Conference Management, Inc.] [Dallas, TX] [Telecommunications] (TSSD) .... COMTEL
International Computer Association .... ICA
International Computer Bibliography [A publication of National Computing Center] .... ICB
International Computer Casting [Information service or system] (IID) ICC
International Computer Center (HGAA) ICC
International Computer Chess Association .... ICCA
International Computer Component Exchange .... ICE
International Computer Exchange (IAA) ICX
International Computer Exhibition .... INCOMEX
International Computer Facsimile Association (PS) .... ICFA
International Computer Forum and Exposition (MHDB) .... COMFOR
International Computer Orphanage (EA) .... ICO
International Computer Programs, Inc. [Indianapolis, IN] [Information service or system] .... ICP
International Computer Resources, Inc. [Information service or system] (IID) .... ICR
International Computer Security Association .... ICSA
International Computer System (IAA) .... ICS
International Computer Training Association (PCM) .... ICTA
International Computer Users Groups Association [Defunct] (EA) .... ICUGA
International Computer-Assisted Instruction Facility (AEBS) .... ICAIF
International Computers and Tabulators Ltd. [Later, ICL] .... ICT
International Computers Ltd. [Great Britain] [Computer manufacturer] ICL
International Computing Center's Preparatory Committee .... ICCPC
International Computing Centre [United Nations] (ECON) ICC
International Concatenated Order of Hoo-Hoo [Later, International Order of Hoo-Hoo] (EA) .... ICOHH
International Concentration Camp Committee [Vienna, Austria] (EAIO) ICCC
International Concept Study Team [for bridges] [US, Great Britain, Germany] (RDA) .... ICST
International Concerns Committee for Children (EA) ICCC
International Concrete and Aggregates Show (ITD) .... CON/AGG
International Confederation for Disarmament and Peace [British] .... ICDP
International Confederation for Electroacoustic Music (EA) .... ICEM
International Confederation for Plastic and Reconstructive Surgery [Montreal, PQ] (EAIO) .... IPRS
International Confederation for Plastic Surgery .... IPS
International Confederation for Thermal Analysis [Jerusalem, Israel] (EA) .... ICTA
International Confederation of Accordionists [Vienna, Austria] (EA) .... ICA
International Confederation of Arab Labour Unions .... ICALU
International Confederation of Arab Trade Unions .... ICATU
International Confederation of Architectural Museums [Montreal, PQ] (EAIO) .... ICAM
International Confederation of Associations of Experts and Consultants [Paris, France] (EA) .... ICAEC
International Confederation of Book Actors (EA) .... ICOBA

International Confederation of Catholic Organizations for Charitable and Social Action [Vatican] [Acronym is based on foreign phrase] .... CARITAS
International Confederation of Christian Family Movements (EAIO) .... ICCFM
International Confederation of Former Prisoners of War .... ICFPW
International Confederation of Free Trade Unions [Belgium] .... ICFTU
International Confederation of Free Trade Unions-Asian Regional Organisation [India] .... ICFTU-ARO
International Confederation of Genealogy and Heraldry [See also CIGH] [Paris, France] (EAIO) .... ICGH
International Confederation of Midwives [British] (EAIO) .... ICM
International Confederation of Music Publishers [British] (EAIO) .... ICMP
International Confederation of Paper and Board Converters in the European Commuity [Germany] (EA) .... CITPA
International Confederation of Popular Credit [See also CICP] [Paris, France] (EAIO) .... ICPC
International Confederation of Societies of Authors and Composers .... ICSAC
International Confederation of Societies of Music (EA) .... ICSM
International Conference IC
International Conference for Promoting Technical Uniformity on Railways [Berne, Switzerland] (EAIO) .... ICPTUR
International Conference Group [Commercial firm] (EA) .... ICG
International Conference Harmonization .... ICH
International Conference Industry Association [Defunct] (EA) .... ICIA
International Conference Management, Inc. [Telecommunications service] (TSSD) .... IMC
International Conference of Administrators of Residential Centers for Youth [Defunct] (EA) .... ICA
International Conference of African States on Insurance Supervision [See also CICA] [Gabon] (EAIO) .... ICASIS
International Conference of Agricultural Economists [Later, IAAE] .... ICAE
International Conference of Building Officials (EA) .... ICBO
International Conference of Catholic Charities ICCC
International Conference of Coordination Chemistry ICCC
International Conference of Historians of the Labour Movement [Vienna, Austria] (EAIO) .... ICHLM
International Conference of Jewish Communal Service [Later, WCJCS] (EA) .... ICJCS
International Conference of Police Associations [Defunct] .... ICPA
International Conference of Police Chaplains (EA) .... ICPC
International Conference of Raman Spectroscopy .... ICORS
International Conference of Social Work .... ICSW
International Conference of Symphony and Opera Musicians (EA) .... ICSOM
International Conference of Women Engineers and Scientists .... ICWES
International Conference on Acoustics, Speech, and Signal Processing (MCD) .... ICASSP
International Conference on Assistance for Refugees in Africa [See also CIARA] [United Nations Geneva, Switzerland] (EAIO) .... ICARA
International Conference on Automatic Control of Mines and Collieries .... ICAMC
International Conference on Cataloging Principles .... ICCP
International Conference on Circuits and Computers (MCD) ICCC
International Conference on Communications [IEEE] ICC
International Conference on Composite Structures [Paisley, Scotland] (EAIO) .... ICCS
International Conference on Computer Applications [in developing countries] [1977] .... ICCA
International Conference on Computers and the Humanities .... ICCH
International Conference on Cryogenics - International Steering Committee (EAIO) .... INCONCRYO-ISC
International Conference on Crystal Growth (PDAA) .... ICCG
International Conference on Education in Chemistry .... ICEC
International Conference on Energy Use Management .... ICEUM
International Conference on Environmental Sensing and Assessment ..... ICESA
International Conference on Genetic Algorithms .... ICGA
International Conference on High Energy Physics and Nuclear Structure .... ICOHEPANS
International Conference on Information Processing [Paris, 1959] .... ICIP
International Conference on Integrated Optics and Optical Fiber Communication (PDAA) .... IOOC
International Conference on Large Chemical Plants [Antwerp, Belgium] (EAIO) .... ICLCP
International Conference on Large Electrical Systems .... ICLES
International Conference on Machine Searching and Translation .... ICMST
International Conference on Magnetics (MCD) .... INTERMAG
International Conference on Marine Pollution (ILCA) .... ICMP
International Conference on Marine Simulation (PDAA) .... MARSIM
International Conference on Mechanics in Medicine and Biology (EA)..... ICMMB
International Conference on Medical Electronics .... ICME
International Conference on Medical Electronics (ECII) .... ICME
International Conference on Non-Destructive Testing (PDAA) .... ICNDT
International Conference on Numerical Methods in Geomechanics ...... ICONMIG
International Conference on Nutrition [United Nations] .... ICN
International Conference on Organometallic Chemistry .... ICOMC
International Conference on Phenomena in Ionised Gases (PDAA) .... ICPIC
International Conference on Phenomena in Ionised Gases (PDAA) .... ICPIG
International Conference on Public Education [International Bureau of Education] [Switzerland] .... ICPE
International Conference on Quality Control (PDAA) .... ICQC
International Conference on Scientific Information .... ICSI
International Conference on Solid State Transducers (EA) .... ICSST
International Conference on Solid Surfaces .... ICSS
International Conference on Superlattices, Microstructures, and Microdevices .... ICSMM
International Conference on Teaching Statistics .... ICOTS
International Conference on the Applications of the Mossbauer Effect .... ICAME

International Conference on the Holocaust and Genocide (EAIO) ... ICHG
International Conference on the Hydraulic Transport of Solids in Pipes (PDAA) ... ICHTSP
International Conference on the Peaceful Uses of Atomic Energy ... ICPUAE
International Conference on the Performance of Computer Installations (PDAA) ... ICPCI
International Conference on the Physics of Electronic and Atomic Collisions ... ICPEAC
International Conference on the Properties of Steam ... ICPS
International Conference on the Unity of the Sciences ... ICUS
International Conference on Thin Films (PDAA) ... ICTF
International Conference on Tribo-Terotechnology and Maintenance Engineering (PDAA) ... ICTME
International Conference on University Education for Public Relations ... ICUEPR
International Conference on Waste Oil Recovery and Reuse ... ICWORR
International Congregational Council ... ICC
International Congregational Fellowship (EA) ... ICF
International Congress and Convention Association [*Amsterdam, Netherlands*] (EA) ... ICCA
International Congress for Data Processing ... ICD
International Congress for Measurement and Automation (IEEE) ... INTERMAMA
International Congress of Acarology ... ICA
International Congress of Accountants ... ICA
International Congress of African Studies (EAIO) ... ICA
International Congress of Africanists [*Lagos, Nigeria*] (EAIO) ... ICA
International Congress of Americanists [*Manchester, England*] (EA) ... ICA
International Congress of Applied Psychology (PDAA) ... ICAP
International Congress of Dealers Associations (EA) ... ICDA
International Congress of Dealers Associations (EA) ... InCODA
International Congress of Electrical and Electronic Communications ... ICEEC
International Congress of Entomology [*Later, CICE*] (EA) ... ICE
International Congress of Genetics ... ICG
International Congress of Heterocyclic Chemistry ... ICHC
International Congress of Industrial Waste Water and Wastes ... ICIWWW
International Congress of Maritime Museums (EA) ... ICMM
International Congress of Mathematicians ... ICM
International Congress of Medical Laboratory Technologists ... ICMLT
International Congress of Oral Implantologists (EA) ... ICOI
International Congress of Photographic Science ... ICPS
International Congress of Physical Medicine (PDAA) ... ICPM
International Congress of Publishers (DIT) ... ICP
International Congress of Radiology ... ICR
International Congress of Supreme Audit Institutions (PDAA) ... INCOSAI
International Congress of the Transplantation Society ... ICTS
International Congress of Theoretical and Applied Mechanics (PDAA) ... ICTAM
International Congress of University Adult Education [*Fredericton, NB*] (EAIO) ... ICUAE
International Congress on Applications of Lasers and Electro-Optics [*Laser Institute of America*] ... ICALEO
International Congress on Bauxite-Alumina-Aluminium (PDAA) ... ICSOBA
International Congress on Combustion Engines ... ICCE
International Congress on Fracture [*ICSU*] [*Sendai, Japan*] (EAIO) ... ICF
International Congress on High-Speed Photography and Photonics (EA) ... ICHSPP
International Congress on Instrumentation in Aerospace Simulation Facilities ... ICIASF
International Congress on Lightweight Concrete (PDAA) ... ICLC
International Congress on Mathematical Education [*International Council of Scientific Unions*] ... ICME
International Congress on Mathematical Education (AIE) ... ICME
International Congress on Mechanical Behaviour of Materials (EAIO) ... ICM
International Congress on the Education of the Deaf ... ICED
International Congress on Women in Music [*Defunct*] (EA) ... ICWM
International Congresses on Tropical Medicine and Malaria ... ICTMM
International Connecting Set (IAA) ... ICS
International Connoisseurs of Green and Red Chile (EA) ... ICGRC
International Conrad Society (EA) ... ICS
International Consommateurs Organization des Unions [*International Organization of Consumers Unions*] ... ICOU
International Construction Database [*Information Centre for Regional Planning and Building Construction of the Fraunhofer-Society*] [*Database*] ... ICONDA
International Construction Equipment Exhibition (ITD) ... ICE
International Consultants Foundation (EA) ... ICF
International Consultative Council of Travel Agents ... ICCTA
International Consultative Research Group on Rape [*See also GCIRC*] (EAIO) ... ICRGR
International Consulting Economists Association [*British*] (DBA) ... ICEA
International Consumer Credit Association [*Later, ICA*] (EA) ... ICCA
International Consumer Reports [*Consumers' Association*] [*British Information service or system*] (IID) ... ICR
International Container Bureau [*Paris*] ... ICB
International Container Terminal Services, Inc. [*Philippines*] [*Commercial firm*] ... ICTSI
International Contemporary Art Fair [*London, England*] ... ICAF
International Contemporary Furniture Fair (ITD) ... ICFF
International Contemporary Music Exchange (EA) ... ICME
International Continental Scientific Drilling Program [*Originated by the US, China, and Germany*] ... ICDP
International Contraception, Abortion, and Sterilization Campaign [*Later, WGNRR*] (EAIO) ... ICASC
International Contract Flooring Exhibition [*British*] (ITD) ... ICFE
International Contracting Terms (AAGC) ... INCOTERMS
International Control ... IC
International Control Centre [*Telecommunications*] (NITA) ... ICC
International Control Commission [*Representatives of Canada, India, and Poland charged with supervising thecease-fire in Laos established at Geneva Conference of 1962*] ... ICC
International Control Mechanism ... ICM
International Control Plan (MCD) ... ICP
International Controlled Industry [*Vancouver Stock Exchange symbol*] ... ICS
International Controls Corp. ... ICC
International Convention ... INTERCON
International Convention Center [*British*] (ECON) ... ICC
International Convention for Safe Containers ... CSC
International Convention for Safety of Life at Sea (BARN) ... ICSLS
International Convention for the Prevention of Pollution from Ships [*1973*] ... MARPOL
International Convention for the Regulation of Whaling (ASF) ... ICRW
International Convention for the Safety of Life at Sea (EERA) ... SOLAS
International Convention of Faith, Churches, and Ministers (EA) ... ICFCM
International Convention of Faith Ministries (EA) ... ICFM
International Convention of the Northwest Atlantic Fisheries (USDC) ... ICNAF
International Convention on the Continental Shelf (NOAA) ... ICCS
International Convention on Transistors and Semiconductor Devices ... ICTASD
International Conventions and Congresses Association [*Australia*] ... ICCA
International Cooperation ... IC
International Cooperation Administration [*Later, Agency for International Development*] ... ICA
International Cooperation Council [*Later, UDC*] ... ICC
International Cooperation for Development [*Commercial firm British*] (ECON) ... ICD
International Cooperation in Information Retrieval among Examining Patent Offices ... ICIREPAT
International Cooperation in the Field of Transport Economics Documentation [*European Conference of Ministers of Transport*] [*Information service or system*] (IID) ... ICTED
International Cooperation Year [*1965*] [*20th anniversary of UN*] ... ICY
International Co-Operative Alliance [*Grand-Saconnex, Switzerland*] (EA) ... ICA
International Co-operative Bulletin [*A publication*] ... ICB
International Cooperative Development Association [*Later, ACDI*] ... ICDA
International Cooperative Fracture Institute ... ICFI
International Cooperative Housing Development Association ... ICHDA
International Cooperative Insurance Federation [*Manchester, England*] (EAIO) ... ICIF
International Cooperative Investigations of the Tropical Atlantic [*Navy*] ... ICITA
International Cooperative Logistics (AFIT) ... ICL
International Cooperative Petroleum Association (EA) ... ICPA
International Co-Operative Reinsurance Bureau [*Manchester, England*] (EAIO) ... ICRB
International Cooperative Training Center ... ICTC
International Co-operative Women's Guild ... ICWG
International Coordinating Committee for the Presentation of Science and the Development of Out-of-School Scientific Activities [*See also CIC*] (EAIO) ... ICC
International Coordinating Committee on Solid State Sensors and Actuators Research (EA) ... ICCSSSAR
International Coordinating Committee on Solid State Transducers Research (EA) ... ICCSTR
International Coordinating Council of Aerospace Industries Associations (EA) ... ICCAIA
International Coordination Committee for Immunology of Reproduction [*Bulg aria*] [*Research center*] (IRC) ... ICCIR
International Coordination Committee for the Accounting Profession ... ICCAP
International Coordination Council of Societies of Mineral Deposits Geology ... CCSMDG
International Coordination Group (USDC) ... ICG
International Coordination Group for the Tsunami Warning System in the Pacific [*Marine science*] (OSRA) ... ICG-ITSU
International Coordination Group for the Tsunami Warning System in the Pacific [*Marine science*] (OSRA) ... ITSU
International Coordination Working Group [*Marine science*] (OSRA) ... ICWG
International Coordination Working Group (USDC) ... ICWG
International Copper Association [*British*] (IRC) ... ICA
International Copper Research Association [*Research center British*] (IRC) ... INCRA
International Copyright Information Center (EA) ... INCINC
International Copyright Information Centre [*UNESCO*] (PDAA) ... ICIC
International Copyrights Information Center (WDAA) ... ICIC
International Cork Cutters' Society [*A union*] ... ICCS
International Cornish Bantam Breeders' Association (EA) ... ICBBA
International Corona Resources Ltd. [*Vancouver Stock Exchange symbol*] ... ICR
International Coronelli Society [*See also ICGGI*] (EAIO) ... ICS
International Corp. [*Generic term*] ... IC
International Correspondence Chess Federation ... ICCF
International Correspondence of Corkscrew Addicts (EA) ... ICCA
International Correspondence School ... ICS
International Correspondence Society of Allergists (EA) ... ICSA
International Correspondence Society of Obstetricians and Gynecologists (EA) ... ICSOG
International Corrosion Council [*Orsay, France*] (EAIO) ... ICC
International Corrugated Case Association [*Paris, France*] (EAIO) ... ICCA
International Cost Engineering Council (EA) ... ICEC
International Cotton Advisory Committee (EA) ... ICAC
International Council Against Bullfighting (EA) ... ICAB
International Council for Adult Education [*Toronto, ON*] (EAIO) ... ICAE
International Council for Adult Education, Toronto, Ontario [*Library symbol National Library of Canada*] (BIB) ... OTNC
International Council for Bird Preservation [*Cambridge, England*] (EAIO) ... ICBP

International Council for Bird Preservation (GNE) .... ICBP
International Council for Bird Protection (Australian Section) .... ICBP(AS)
International Council for Building Research, Studies, and Documentation (DIT) .... ICBRSD
International Council for Canadian Studies [*See also CIEC*] .... ICCS
International Council for Canadian Studies [*Conseil International d'Etudes Canadiennes*], Ottawa, Ontario [*Library symbol National Library of Canada*] (BIB) .... OOICCS
International Council for Children's Play [*Groningen, Netherlands*] (EAIO) .... ICCP
International Council for Christian Leadership (EA) ICL
International Council for Commercial Arbitration [*Vienna, Austria*] (EAIO) .... ICCA
International Council for Computer Communication (EA) ICCC
International Council for Computers in Education (EA) .... ICCE
International Council for Correspondence Education [*Later, ICDE*] .... ICCE
International Council for Dispute Resolution (EA) .... ICDR
International Council for Distance Education [*Australia*] (EAIO) .... ICDE
International Council for Education of the Visually Handicapped [*Bensheim, Federal Republic of Germany*] (EAIO) .... ICEVH
International Council for Educational Development (EA) .... ICED
International Council for Educational Films [*Later, ICEM*] .... ICEF
International Council for Educational Media [*Formerly, ICEF*] .... ICEM
International Council for Elementary and Secondary School Philosophy (EA) .... ICESSP
International Council for Exceptional Children [*Later, CEC*] .... ICEC
International Council for Health, Physical Education, and Recreation (EA) .... ICHPER
International Council for Infant Survival [*Later, NCGIS*] (EA) .... ICIS
International Council for Local Environmental Initiatives [*Marine science*] (OSRA) .... ICLEI
International Council for Local Environmental Initiatives (USDC) .... ICLEI
International Council for Pastoral Care and Counselling (EAIO) .... ICPCC
International Council for Philosophical Inquiry with Children [*Iceland*] (EAIO) .... ICPIC
International Council for Philosophical Inquiry with Children (EA) .... ICPIWC
International Council for Philosophy and Humanistic Studies [*Paris, France*] .... ICPHS
International Council for Physical Fitness Research [*Research center Canada*] (IRC) .... ICPFR
International Council for Pressure Vessel Technology (EA) .... ICPVT
International Council for Reprography .... ICR
International Council for Research in Agroforestry [*See also ICRAF*] [*Kenya*] (EAIO) .... ICRAF
International Council for Research in the Sociology of Co-operation .... ICRSC
International Council for Scientific and Technical Information [*Information service or system*] (IID) .... ICSTI
International Council for Small Business (EA) .... ICSB
International Council for the Exploration of the Sea [*Denmark*] .... ICES
International Council for the Social Studies (DIT) .... ICSS
International Council for Traditional Music (EA) .... ICTM
International Council - National Academy of Television Arts and Sciences (EA) .... IC/NATAS
International Council of Accrediting Agencies [*Australia*] (EAIO) .... ICAA
International Council of Air Shows (EA) .... ICAS
International Council of Aircraft Owner and Pilot Associations (EA) .... IAOPA
International Council of Aircraft Owner and Pilot Associations (DI) .... ICAOPA
International Council of Associations for Science Education [*See also FIAPS*] (EAIO) .... ICASE
International Council of Associations of Surfing (EA) .... ICAS
International Council of Associations of Theological Libraries (EA) .... ICATL
International Council of Ballroom Dancing [*British*] (EAIO) .... ICBD
International Council of Catholic Men [*See also FIHC*] [*Vatican City, Vatican City State*] (EAIO) .... ICCM
International Council of Chemical Associations .... ICCA
International Council of Christian Churches (EA) ICCC
International Council of Christians and Jews [*Heppenheim, Federal Republic of Germany*] (EAIO) .... ICCJ
International Council of Commerce Employers .... ICCE
International Council of Community Churches (EA) ICCC
International Council of Containership Operators [*British*] (DCTA) .... ICCO
International Council of Employers of Bricklayers and Allied Craftsmen (EA) .... ICEBAC
International Council of Environmental Law [*Bonn, Federal Republic of Germany*] (EA) .... ICEL
International Council of Fan Clubs [*Defunct*] (EA) .... ICFC
International Council of Fine Arts Deans (EA) .... ICFAD
International Council of Folklore Festival Organizations and Folk Art (EA) .... ICFFO
International Council of French-Speaking Radio and Television (EAIO) .... ICFSRT
International Council of Goodwill Industries (EA) .... ICGI
International Council of Graphic Design Associations [*British*] (EA) .... ICOGRADA
International Council of Health Fitness and Sports Therapists [*British*] .... ICHFST
International Council of Hindoo Youth (EAIO) .... ICHY
International Council of Holistic Therapists [*British*] .... ICHT
International Council of Homehelp Services [*See also CISAF*] [*Driebergen-Rijsenburg, Netherlands*] (EAIO) .... ICHS
International Council of Industrial Editors [*Later, IABC*] .... ICIE
International Council of Industrial Engineers .... ICIE
International Council of Infant Food Industries .... ICIFI
International Council of Jewish Women (EA) .... ICJW
International Council of Jews from Czechoslovakia [*British Defunct*] (EAIO) .... ICJC
International Council of Kinetography Laban (EA) .... ICKL
International Council of Library Association Executives (EA) .... ICLAE
International Council of Marine Industry Associations [*Weybridge, Surrey, England*] (EA) .... ICOMIA
International Council of Masonry Engineering for Developing Countries [*Formerly, International Symposium on Reinforced and Prestressed Masonry*] (EA) .... ICMEDC
International Council of Monuments and Sites [*France*] (EA) .... ICOMOS
International Council of Museums [*France*] .... ICOM
International Council of Museums Committee of the American Association of Museums (EA) .... AAM/ICOM
International Council of Nurses [*Switzerland*] (EY) .... ICN
International Council of Ophthalmology (EA) .... ICO
International Council of Perfusion Societies [*Defunct*] (EA) .... ICPS
International Council of Plant Nutrition [*Australia*] (EAIO) .... IPNC
International Council of Prison Medical Services [*Vancouver, BC*] (EAIO) .... ICPMS
International Council of Psychologists (EA) .... ICP
International Council of Scientific Unions [*Research center France*] .... ICSU
International Council of Scientific Unions Abstracting Board [*Also, IAB*] [*Later, ICSTI*] (EA) .... ICSU AB
International Council of Seamen's Agencies (EA) .... ICOSA
International Council of Sex Education and Parenthood (EA) .... ICSEP
International Council of Shopping Centers (EA) .... ICSC
International Council of Shopping Centres [*Australia*] .... ICSC
International Council of Social Democratic Women [*Later, SIW*] (EA) .... ICSDW
International Council of Societies of Industrial Design [*Helsinki, Finland*] (EA) .... ICSID
International Council of Societies of Pathology (EA) .... ICSP
International Council of Sport and Physical Education .... ICSPE
International Council of Sport Science and Physical Education (EA) .... ICSSPE
International Council of Tanners [*See also CIT*] [*Lewes, East Sussex, England*] (EAIO) .... ICT
International Council of the Aeronautical Sciences .... ICAS
International Council of the Architects of Historical Monuments .... ICARMO
International Council of the French Language [*See also CILF*] [*Paris, France*] (EAIO) .... ICFL
International Council of the National Academy of Television Arts and Sciences (EA) .... IC/NATVAS
International Council of Voluntary Agencies (GNE) .... ICVA
International Council of Women [*France*] .... ICW
International Council of Women Psychologists [*Later, ICP*] .... ICWP
International Council on Alcohol and Addictions [*Switzerland*] .... ICAA
International Council on Archives [*UNESCO*] (EA) .... ICA
International Council on Disability (EA) .... ICOD
International Council on Education for Teaching (EA) .... ICET
International Council on Electrocardiology [*Glasgow, Scotland*] (EAIO) .... ICE
International Council on Jewish Social and Welfare Services [*Geneva, Switzerland*] (EAIO) .... INTERCO
International Council on Management of Population Programmes [*Kuala Lumpur, Malaysia*] (EAIO) .... ICOMP
International Council on Metals and the Environment .... ICME
International Council on Social Welfare (EA) .... ICSW
International Council on the Future of the University [*Defunct*] .... ICFU
International Council on United Fund Raising (EA) .... ICUFR
International Council to Combat Lethal Yellowing .... ICCLY
International Councils on Higher Education [*Defunct*] .... ICHE
International Counseling Center (EA) ICC
International Country and Western Music Association (EA) .... ICWMA
International Court of Justice [*United Nations*] .... ICJ
International Courtly Literature Society (EA) .... ICLS
International Crane Foundation (EA) .... ICF
International Craniofacial Foundations (EA) .... ICF
International Craniopathic Society [*SORSI*] [*Absorbed by*] (EA) .... ICS
International Creative Management [*Commercial firm*] .... ICM
International Creative Writers League (EA) .... ICWL
International Credit Association [*St. Louis, MO*] (EA) .... ICA
International Credit Insurance Association [*Zurich, Switzerland*] (EAIO) .... ICIA
International Cremation Federation (EAIO) .... ICF
International Cricket Conference (EA) ICC
International Criminal Investigative Training Assistance Program [*Department of Justice*] .... ICITAP
International Criminal Justice Association (EA) .... ICJA
International Criminal Justice Clearinghouse [*Law Enforcement Ass istance Administration*] [*Information service or system*] .... ICJC
International Criminal Law Commission (EA) ICLC
International Criminal Police Commission [*Later, INTERPOL*] .... ICPC
International Criminal Police Organization [*France*] .... ICPO
International Criminal Police Organization .... INTERPOL
International Criminal Police Review [*A publication*] (DLA) .... Int'l Crim Pol Rev
[*The*] **International Critical Commentary on the Holy Scriptures of the Old and New Testament** [*Edinburgh*] [*A publication*] (BJA) ICC
International Critical Tables .... ICT
International Crocodilian Society [*Defunct*] (EA) .... ICS
International Crop Improvement Association [*Later, AOSCA*] (EA) .... ICIA
International Crops Research Institute for the Semi-Arid Tropics [*India*] .... ICRISAT
International Cross-Country Union (EA) .... ICCU
International Cruise Passengers Association (EA) .... ICPA
International Cruiser/Race Class [*Yachting*] .... IC/R
International Cruiseships [*Vancouver Stock Exchange symbol*] .... ISC
International Cryogenic Engineering Committee (EAIO) .... ICEC
International Cryogenic Materials Conference (EA) .... ICMC
International Cultural Centers for Youth (EA) .... ICCY
International Cultural Exchange [*An association*] (EA) .... ICE
International Cultural Exchange ICX
International Cultural Exchange Service .... ICES

International Cultural Society of Korea [*Seoul, Republic of Korea*] (EAIO) .... ICSK
International Culture Institute [*Japan*] (EAIO) ICII
International Curator Resources [*Vancouver Stock Exchange symbol*] IC
International Curling Federation (EAIO) .... ICF
International Curling Federation - Ladies Committee [*Defunct*] (EA) .... ICFLC
International Customer Service Association [*Chicago, IL*] (EA) .... ICSA
International Customs Tariffs Bureau [*International Bureau for the Publi cation of Customs Tariffs*] [*Acronym is based on former name,*] (EA) .... IBPCT
International Customs Tariffs Bureau (DLA) .... ICTB
International Cutlery Ltd. [*NASDAQ symbol*] (SAG) .... ICUT
International Cutlery Ltd. [*Associated Press*] (SAG) .... IntlCt
International Cutlery Ltd. [*Associated Press*] (SAG) .... IntlCut
International Cycling Union (EA) .... ICU
International Cystic Fibrosis Mucoviscidosis Association (EA) .... ICFMA
International Dairy Committee .... IDC
International Dairy Development Programme [*FAO/DANIDA Dairy Development P rogramme and International Scheme for the Coordination of Dairy Development*] [*Formed by a merger of United Nations*] (EAIO) .... IDDP
International Dairy Development Scheme .... IDDS
International Dairy Federation [*See also FIL*] [*Brussels, Belgium*] (EAIO) .... IDF
International Dairy Foods Association (EA) .... IDFA
International Dairy Queen [*Associated Press*] (SAG) .... InDairA
International Dairy Queen [*Associated Press*] (SAG) .... InDairB
International Dairy Queen, Inc. [*Associated Press*] (SAG) .... InDair
International Dairy Queen, Inc. [*NASDAQ symbol*] (NQ) .... INDQ
International Dairy-Deli Association (EA) .... IDDA
International Daleco Technology [*Vancouver Stock Exchange symbol*] .... ID
International Dalkon Shield Victims Education Association (EA) .... IDEA
International Damascus Resources [*Vancouver Stock Exchange symbol*] .... IDR
International Dance Alliance (EA) .... IDA
International Dance Council [*See also CIDD*] (EAIO) .... IDC
International Dance-Exercise Association (EA) .... IDEA
International Dancing Masters Association (BARN) .... IDMA
International Dark-Sky Association (EA) .... IDSA
International Data and Analysis [*Bureau of Mines*] .... IDA
International Data Base [*Bureau of Census*] [*Database*] .... IDB
International Data Base Management Association (EA) .... IDBMA
International Data Collecting Platform (TEL) .... IDCP
International Data Connector .... IDC
International Data Consultants [*Market research organization*] (NITA) .... IDC
International Data Corp. [*Information service or system*] (IID) .... IDC
International Data Encryption Algorithm [*Telecommunications*] .... IDEA
International Data Exchange for Aviation Safety [*ICAO*] (DA) .... IDEAS
International Data Exchange Program (NITA) .... IDEP
International Data Group [*Publisher of computer magazines*] [*Framingham, MA*] .... IDG
International Data Library and Reference Service .... IDL & RS
International Data Processing Institute (MCD) .... IDPI
International Data Services Corp. [*Vancouver Stock Exchange symbol*] .... IDS
International Database Access Service [*Bahrain Telecommunications Co.*] [*Information service or system*] (IID) .... IDAS
International Database Association [*Defunct*] (EA) .... IDA
International Date Line (MCD) .... IDL
International David Cassidy Fan Club (EAIO) .... IDCFC
International Decade for Natural Disaster Reduction [*1990's*] [*United Nations*] .... IDNDR
International Decade of Cetacean Research .... IDCR
International Decade of Exploration and Assessment of the Seas [*Inactive*] [*Marine science*] (OSRA) .... IDEAS
International Decade of Exploration and Assessment of the Seas [*Defunct*] (USDC) .... IDEAS
International Decade of Ocean Exploration [*1970's*] .... IDOE
International Decorative Accessories Center (EA) .... IDAC
International Deep Drawing Research Group [*British*] .... IDDRG
International Deep Profiling of Tibet and the Himalaya [*Geology*] [*China*] .... INDEPTH
International Defence and Aid Fund for Southern Africa [*British*] (EAIO) .... IDAF
International Defenders of Animals (EA) .... IDA
International Defense and Aid Fund for Southern Africa, US Committee (EA) .... D & A
International Defense and Aid Fund for Southern Africa, US Committee [*Defunct*] (EA) .... IDAF
International Defense Directory [*A publication*] .... IDD
International Defense Equipment Exhibitors Association (EA) .... IDEEA
International Defense Review [*Interavia Publications*] [*Information service or system A publication*] (CRD) .... IDR
International Deli-Bakery Association [*Defunct*] (EA) .... IDBA
International Delta Resources [*Vancouver Stock Exchange symbol*] .... IDQ
International Democrat Union (EA) .... IDU
International Democratic Fellowship .... IDF
International Demographic Data Center [*Bureau of the Census*] [*Database*] [*Information service or system*] (IID) .... IDDC
International Demographic Data Directory [*Agency for International Development*] (IID) .... IDDD
International Dendrology Union .... IDU
International Dental Federation [*British*] .... IDF
International Dental Health Foundation (EA) .... IDHF
International Deployment of Accelerometers [*Project*] [*Seismography*] .... IDA
International Depositary Receipt [*Investment term*] .... IDR
International Desalination and Environmental Association [*Later, IDA*] (EA) .... IDEA
International Desalination Association (EA) .... IDA
International Desert Locust Information Service .... IDLIS
International Desert Racing Association [*Automobile racing*] .... IDRA
International Design Center, New York .... IDCNY
International Design Conference in Aspen (EA) .... IDCA
International Destination Management Association (EAIO) .... IDMA
International Destron Technologies, Inc. [*Vancouver Stock Exchange symbol*] .... IDN
International Development Agency [*United Nations*] (NUCP) .... IDA
International Development and Assistance Program (KSC) .... IDAP
International Development and Refugee Foundation .... IDRF
International Development Association (EA) .... IDA
International Development Conference (EA) .... IDC
International Development Cooperation Act of 1979 .... IDCA
[*United States*] **International Development Cooperation Agency** (USGC) .... IDCA
International Development Corp. [*Proposed corporation to combine Alliance for Progress and Agency for International Development*] .... IDC
International Development Data Center [*Georgia Institute of Technology*] .... IDDC
International Development - Economics Awareness System .... IDEAS
International Development Education Documentation Service [*University of Pittsburgh*] (IID) .... IDEDS
International Development Education Resources Association .... IDERA
International Development Foundation (EA) .... IDF
International Development Institute [*Agency for International Development program*] .... IDI
International Development Research Centre [*ICSU*] [*Research center Canada*] .... IDRC
International Development Research Centre (GNE) .... IRDC
International Development Research Centre, Ottawa, ON, Canada [*Library symbol Library of Congress*] (LCLS) .... CaOOID
International Development Research Centre [*Centre de Recherches pour le Developpement International*] **Ottawa, Ontario** [*Library symbol National Library of Canada*] (NLC) .... OOID
International Development Services .... IDS
International Development Strategy [*United Nations*] .... IDS
International Development Studies Group .... IDSEG
International Development Support Services Pty. Ltd. [*Australia*] (ECON) .... IDSS
International Diabetes Federation [*See also FID*] (EAIO) .... IDF
International Diabetes Institute [*Australia*] (IRC) .... IDI
International Diabetic Athletes Association (EA) .... IDAA
International Diagnostic Technology [*Medicine*] .... IDT
International Dialect Institute .... IDI
International Diamond Council [*Antwerp, Belgium*] (EAIO) .... IDC
International Diamond Security Organization (BARN) .... IDSO
International Diastema Club (EA) .... IDC
International Dictionary of Architects and Architecture [*A publication*] .... IDAA
International Dictionary of Medicine and Biology [*A publication*] .... IDMB
International Die Sinkers' Conference .... DSC
International Die Sinkers' Conference (EA) .... IDSC
International Differential Treatment Association .... IDTA
International Digest of Health Legislation [*A publication*] (DLA) .... Int'l Dig Health Leg
International Digital Channel Service [*Federal Trade Commission*] .... IDCS
International Digital Data Service [*Western Union Corp.*] [*Data transmission service*] .... IDDS
International Direct Dialing [*Telecommunications*] .... IDD
International Direct Distance Dialing [*AT & T*] .... IDDD
International Direct Mail [*British*] .... IDM
International Directories in Print [*A publication*] .... IDIP
International Directory Network (USDC) .... IDN
International Directory of Astronomical Associations and Societies [*A publication*] .... IDAAS
International Directory of Company Histories [*A publication*] .... IDCH
International Directory of Directories [*A publication*] .... IDOD
International Directory of Marine Scientists [*Marine science*] (OSRA) .... IDMS
International Directory of Non-Official Statistical Sources [*A publication*] .... IDNSS
International Directory of Professional Astronomical Institutions [*A publication*] .... IDPAI
International Directory of Research and Development Scientists [*A publication*] .... IDR & DS
International Disarmament Organization .... IDO
International Disaster Advisory Committee .... IDAC
International Disaster Institute [*British*] .... IDI
International Disaster Recovery Association (EA) .... IDRA
International Discotheque Association [*Defunct*] (EA) .... IDA
International Discount Telecommunications (ECON) .... IDT
International Dispensary Association [*Acronym is used as association name*] (EAIO) .... IDA
International Display Corp. [*Vancouver Stock Exchange symbol*] .... IDC
International Distillers & Vintners [*British*] .... IDV
International Distress Frequency (MUGU) .... IDF
International District Heating and Cooling Association (EA) .... IDHCA
International District Heating Association [*Later, IDHCA*] (EA) .... IDHA
International District Office .... IDO
International Diving Educators Association .... IDEA
International Diving Schools Association (EA) .... IDSA
International Division [*Army Service Forces*] [*World War II*] .... ID
International DN [*Detroit News*] **Ice Yacht Racing Association** (EA) .... IDNIYRA
International Doctors in Alcoholics Anonymous (EA) .... IDAA
International Doctor's Society (EA) .... IDS
International Documentary Association (EA) .... IDA
International Documentation and Communication Center [*Formerly, Council for Development of Religious Information and Documentation - IDOC International*] [*Rome, Italy*] (SLS) .... IDOC
International Documentation and Information Centre .... INTERDOK
International Documentation Center .... IDC
International Documentation in Chemistry (DIT) .... IDC

International Documentation on the Contemporary Church [*Later, International Documentation and Communication Center*] (EA) .... IDOC
International Documents Service [*Defunct*] (EA) .... IDS
International Documents Task Force [*Government Documents Round Table*] [*American Library Association*] .... IDTF
International Doll Association [*Defunct*] (EA) .... IDA
International Doll Makers Association (EA) .... IDMA
International Dolphin Conservation Act [*1993*] .... IDCA
International Domesticated Furs Ltd. [*Vancouver Stock Exchange symbol*] .... IDF
International Donkey Protection Trust (EAIO) .... IDPT
International Dorado Resources [*Vancouver Stock Exchange symbol*] .... IDD
International Dostoevsky Society (EA) .... IDS
International Double Reed Society (EA) .... IDRS
International Dove Society [*Defunct*] (EA) .... IDS
International Downtown Association (EA) .... IDA
International Downtown Executives Association [*Later, IDA*] (EA) .... IDEA
International Dragon Class Association (EAIO) .... IDCA
International Drapery Association (EA) .... IDA
International Drawing Rights .... IDR
International Dredging Association .... IDA
International Dredging Conference Coordinating Committee (EAIO) .... IDCCC
International Drilling Federation (EA) .... IDF
International Drilling Fluids [*Singapore*] .... IDF
International Drivers' Behaviour Research Association [*Paris, France*] (EAIO) .... IDBRA
International Driving Permit .... IDP
International Drought Information Center .... IDIC
International Drug Enforcement Conference .... IDEC
International Drycleaners Congress (EA) .... IDC
International Dull Folks Unlimited [*Defunct*] (EA) .... IDFUN
International Dull Men's Club (EA) .... IDMC
International Dun's Market Identifiers [*Dun & Bradstreet International*] [*Information service or system*] (IID) .... IDMI
International Dwarf Fruit Trees Association (EA) .... IDFTA
International E-22 Class Association (EA) .... IETCA
International Earth Rotation Services .... IERS
International Ecology Society (EA) .... IES
International Economic Appraisal Service [*The Economist Publications Ltd.*] [*British Information service or system*] .... IEAS
International Economic Association [*See also AISE*] [*Paris, France*] (EAIO) .... IEA
International Economic Consultative Organization for Korea [*Ten-nation consortium*] .... IECOK
International Economic Conversion Campaign [*Defunct*] (EA) .... IECC
International Economic History Association [*Paris, France*] (EA) .... IEHA
International Economic Indicators Database [*Columbia Business School*] [*Information service or system*] (CRD) .... IEIDATA
International Economic Policy .... IEP
International Economic Policy Act of 1972 .... IEPA
International Economic Policy Association (EA) .... IEPA
International Edsel Club (EA) .... IEC
International Education Act .... IEA
International Education and Resource Network [*Information service or system*] (IID) .... IEARN
International Education Assembly [*World War II*] .... IEA
International Education Association .... IEA
International Education Exchange Liaison Group (EA) .... IEELG
International Education Exchange Service [*Department of State*] .... IEES
International Education Exchange Service [*Department of State*] .... IES
International Education Information Program .... IEIP
International Education Office [*World War II*] .... IEO
International Education Project [*American Council on Education*] (PDAA) .... IEP
International Education Research Foundation (EA) .... IERF
International Education Series [*A publication*] .... IES
International Education Year [*UN designation*] .... IEY
International Educational and Cultural Exchange .... IEC
International Educational Reporting Service [*International Bureau of Education*] [*United Nations*] (EY) .... IERS
International Educator's Institute (EA) .... IEI
International Egg Commission [*British*] (EAIO) .... IEC
International Electrical and Electronic Engineering Exhibition [*Interfama Pte. Ltd.*] .... ENEX-ASIA
International Electrical Testing Association (EAIO) .... IETA
International Electrical Testing Association (EA) .... NETA
International Electrochemical Commission .... IEL
International Electron Devices Meeting (PDAA) .... IED
International Electronic Devices [*Conference*] (MCD) .... IED
International Electronic Facsimile Users Association (EA) .... IEFUA
International Electronic Packaging Symposium (MCD) .... IECPS
International Electronic Post [*Postal Service*] .... INTELPOST
International Electronic Publishing Research Centre [*British*] (IRC) .... IEPRC
International Electronic Research Corp. (MCD) .... IERC
International Electronics Corp. (MUGU) .... IEC
International Electronics Engineering, Inc. (AAG) .... IEEI
International Electronics, Inc. [*NASDAQ symbol*] (NQ) .... IEIB
International Electronics, Inc. [*Associated Press*] (SAG) .... IntlElec
International Electronics Manufacturing Co. (AAG) .... IEMC
International Electronics Packaging Society (EA) .... IEPS
International Electrotechnical Commission [*See also CEI*] [*Standards body Geneva, Switzerland*] (EAIO) .... IEC
International Electrotechnical Commission [*Geneva*] .... IEC
International Electrotechnical Commission Quality Assessment (PDAA) .... IECQU
International Electrotechnical Commission System for Conformity Testing to Standards for Safety of Electrical Equipment [*Switzerland*] (EA) .... IECEE
International Electrotechnical Exhibition [*British Electrical and Allied Manufacturers Association*] .... ELECTREX
International Electrotechnical Vocabulary (IEEE) .... IEV
International Electrs [*NASDAQ symbol*] (TTSB) .... IEIE
International Elvis Presley Fan Club, Hong Kong (EAIO) .... IEPFCHK
International Embryo Transfer Society (EA) .... IETS
International Emergency Action [*See also AUI*] [*Paris, France*] (EAIO) .... IEA
International Emergency Economic Powers Act [*1977*] .... IEEPA
International Emergency Food Council [*Post-World War II*] .... IEFC
International Enamellers Institute [*Derby, England*] (EAIO) .... IEI
International Encyclopedia of Comparative Law [*A publication*] (DLA) .... Int Enc Comp Law
International Encyclopedia of Comparative Law [*A publication*] (DLA) .... Int'l Encycl Comp L
International Encyclopedia of the Social Sciences [*A publication*] .... IESS
International Energy Agency [*OECD*] [*Research center France*] (IRC) .... IEA
International Energy Bank Ltd. [*British*] .... IEB
International Energy Program .... IEP
International Engineering and Construction Industries Council (PDAA) .... IECIC
International Engineering Task Force [*Computer science*] .... IETF
International English Shepherd Registry (EA) .... IESR
International Entrepreneurs Association [*Later, AEA*] (EA) .... IEA
International Environment and Development Service (GNE) .... IEDS
International Environment Protection Act of 1983 .... IEPA
International Environmental Bureau for the Non-Ferrous Metals Industry .... IEB
International Environmental Data Service [*European Commodities Exchange*] [*United Nations*] (DUND) .... IEDS
International Environmental Technology Centre [*United Nations*] (ECON) .... IETC
International Environmental Technology Transfer Advisory Board [*Environmental Protection Agency*] (EGAO) .... IETTAB
International Epidemiological Association (EA) .... IEA
International Epitek, Inc. [*Toronto Stock Exchange symbol*] .... IEI
International Equestrian Federation (EAIO) .... IEF
International Ergonomics Association (EA) .... IEA
International Erosion Control Association (EA) .... IECA
International Esperantist Chess League [*See also ESLI*] (EAIO) .... IECL
International Esperantist League for Go (EA) .... IELG
International Esperantist Organization of Naturists [*See also INOE*] [*Frankfurt, Federal Republic of Germany*] (EAIO) .... IEON
International Esperanto Fellowship of Rotarians [*See also IEAR*] (EAIO) .... IEFR
International Evaluations, Inc. .... IEI
International Exchange Association (EA) .... IEA
International Exchange of Authenticated Electronic Component Performance Tests Data (PDAA) .... EXACT
International Exchange Office (AFM) .... IEO
International Exchange Service [*For publications*] [*Smithsonian Institution*] .... IES
International Exchangors Association (EA) .... INTEREX
International Executive Board [*UAW*] .... IEB
International Executive Masters of Business Administration (PGP) .... IEMBA
International Executive Masters Programme [*London Business School*] .... IEMP
International Executive Service Corps [*Stamford, CT*] (EA) .... IESC
International Executives Association (EA) .... IEA
International Exhibition (IMH) .... IE
International Exhibition for Agricultural Mechanization and Breeding Stock .... AGROMEK
International Exhibition for the Hotel and Restaurant Trades Communities .... HORECOM
International Exhibition Logistics Associates [*Geneva, Switzerland*] (EAIO) .... IELA
International Exhibition of Foodstuffs, Fast Food, and Traditional and Mass Catering .... INTERFOOD
International Exhibition of Industrial Electronics (MCD) .... INEI
International Exhibition of Inventions and Novel Features (TSPED) .... INVEX
International Exhibitions Bureau .... IEB
International Exhibitions Foundation (EA) .... IEF
International Exhibitors Association (EA) .... IEA
International Explorers Society .... IES
International Exposition for Food Processors (ITD) .... IEFP
International Eye Foundation (EA) .... IEF
International Fabricare Institute (EA) .... IFI
International Facilitating Committee [*World Resources Institute*] .... IFC
International Facility for Food Irradiation Technology [*Netherlands*] (WND) .... IFFIT
International Facility Management Association (EA) .... IFMA
International Facsimile Association (EA) .... IFAXA
International Facsimile Service [*Telecommunications*] (TEL) .... IFAX
International Fair of Furniture, Decoration, Lighting Fixtures, Machinery, and Equipment [*Hellexpo*] .... FURNIDEC
International Falcon Movement .... IFM
International Falcon Movement - Socialist Educational International .... IFM-SEI
International Falcon Resources Ltd. [*Vancouver Stock Exchange symbol*] .... ILF
International Fallout Warning Exercise (NATG) .... INTEX
International Falls [*Minnesota*] [*Airport symbol*] (OAG) .... INL
International Falls [*Minnesota*] [*ICAO location identifier*] (ICLI) .... KINL
International Falls Elementary School, International Falls, MN [*Library symbol*] [*Library of Congress*] (LCLS) .... MnIfE
International Falls High School, International Falls, MN [*Library symbol*] [*Library of Congress*] (LCLS) .... MnIfH
International Falls, MN [*Location identifier FAA*] (FAAL) .... INL
International Falls, MN [*FM radio station call letters*] .... KBHW
International Falls, MN [*AM radio station call letters*] .... KGHS
International Falls, MN [*FM radio station call letters*] .... KSDM
International Falls Public Library, International Falls, MN [*Library symbol Library of Congress*] (LCLS) .... MnIf
International Family Entertainment .... IFE

International Family Entertainment [*Associated Press*] (SAG) ... IntFam
International Family Entertainment, Inc. [*NYSE symbol*] (SPSG) ... FAM
International Family Planning Research Association [*Later, ISRM*] (EA) ... IFPRA
International Family Recreation Association (EA) ... IFRA
International Fan Club Association [*Formerly, FCA*] (EA) ... IFCA
International Fan Club Organization (EA) ... IFCO
International Fancy Food and Confection Show (ITD) ... IFFCS
International Fancy Guppy Association (EA) ... IFGA
International Fantasy Gaming Society (EA) ... IFGS
International Farm Management Association [*Reading, Berkshire, England*] (EAIO) ... IFMA
International Farm Youth Exchange ... IFYE
International Farmers Association for Education [*Defunct*] (EA) ... IFAE
International Fashion and Boutique Show (ITD) ... IFBS
International Fashion Group [*Later, Fashion Group International*] (EA) ... IFG
International Fast Food Corp. [*NASDAQ symbol*] (SAG) ... FOOD
International Fast Food Corp. [*Associated Press*] (SAG) ... IntFast
International Fasteners Exposition (ITD) ... IFE
International Federal Film [*Fictitious organization of agents in TV series "Scarecrow and Mrs. King"*] ... IFF
International Federation for Choral Music (EA) ... IFCM
International Federation for Documentation [*Also, FID*] [*Later, IFID*] ... IFD
International Federation for Enteric Phage Typing [*International Council of Scientific Unions*] ... IFEPT
International Federation for Family Health [*Bandung, Indonesia*] (EA) ... IFFH
International Federation for Family Life Promotion (EA) ... IFFLP
International Federation for Gerda Alexander Eutony [*Belgium*] (EAIO) ... IFGAE
International Federation for Home Economics [*See also FIEF*] [*Paris, France*] (EAIO) ... IFHE
International Federation for Housing and Planning [*Netherlands*] ... IFHP
International Federation for Housing and Town Planning ... IFHTP
International Federation for Hygiene, Preventive, and Social Medicine [*France*] (EAIO) ... IFHPSM
International Federation for Information and Documentation [*See also FIID*] (EAIO) ... IFID
International Federation for Information Processing [*Formerly, IFIPS*] (EA) ... IFIP
International Federation for Internal Freedom [*Later, Castalia Foundation*] (EA) ... IFIF
International Federation for Medical and Biological Engineering [*ICSU*] [*Ottawa, ON*] (EA) ... IFMBE
International Federation for Medical Electronics ... IFME
International Federation for Medical Psychotherapy [*See also IGAP*] [*Oslo, Norway*] (EAIO) ... IFMP
International Federation for Narcotic Education ... IFNE
International Federation for Parent Education [*See also FIEP*] [*Sevres, France*] (EAIO) ... IFPE
International Federation for Preventive and Social Medicine (EAIO) ... IFPSM
International Federation for Secular Humanistic Judaism (EA) ... IFSHJ
International Federation for Systems Research (EAIO) ... IFSR
International Federation for the Application of Standards (PDAA) ... IFAS
International Federation for the Heat Treatment of Materials (PDAA) ... IFHTM
International Federation for the Theory of Machines and Mechanisms [*Warsaw, Poland*] (EAIO) ... IFToMM
International Federation for Theatre Research [*British*] (EAIO) ... IFTR
International Federation for Victory over Communism ... IFVC
International Federation for Weeks of Art ... IFWA
International Federation of Accountants (ADA) ... IFA
International Federation of Accountants [*New York, NY*] (EA) ... IFAC
International Federation of Actors ... IFA
International Federation of Advertising Agencies [*Sarasota, FL*] (EA) ... IFAA
International Federation of Aestheticians [*Brussels, Belgium*] (EAIO) ... INFA
International Federation of Agricultural Producers (BARN) ... IFAP
International Federation of Agricultural Research Systems for Development [*Netherlands*] ... IFARD
International Federation of Air Line Pilots Associations [*Egham, England*] (EAIO) ... IFALPA
International Federation of Air Traffic Controllers' Associations [*Dublin, Republic of Ireland*] (EAIO) ... IFATCA
International Federation of Air Traffic Safety Electronic Associations [*British*] (EAIO) ... IFATSEA
International Federation of Airworthiness [*Middlesex, England*] (EAIO) ... IFA
International Federation of Airworthiness Technology and Engineering [*Later, IFA*] ... IFATE
International Federation of American Homing Pigeon Fanciers (EA) ... IF
International Federation of American Homing Pigeon Fanciers (EA) ... IFAHPF
International Federation of Aquarium Societies ... IFAS
International Federation of Asian and Pacific Associations of Optometrists [*Australia*] (EAIO) ... IFAPAO
International Federation of Asian and Western Pacific Contractors' Associations [*Pasig, Metro Manila, Philippines*] (EAIO) ... IFAWPCA
International Federation of Associations of Anatomists (EA) ... IFAA
International Federation of Associations of Computer Users in Engineering Architecture and Related Fields (EAIO) ... FACE
International Federation of Associations of Pharmaceutical Physicians [*Italy*] (EAIO) ... IFAPP
International Federation of Audio-Visual Workers Unions [*See also FISTA*] (EAIO) ... IFAVWU
International Federation of Audit Bureaux of Circulations (EAIO) ... IFABC
International Federation of Automatic Control [*Laxenburg, Austria*] ... IFAC
International Federation of Blood Donor Organizations [*See also FIODS*] [*Dole, France*] (EAIO) ... IFBDO
International Federation of Boat Show Organisers (EA) ... IFBSO
International Federation of Bodybuilders [*Montreal, PQ*] (EA) ... IFBB
International Federation of Building and Wood Workers [*Sweden*] ... IFBWW
International Federation of Business and Professional Women (EA) ... IFBPW
International Federation of Camping and Caravanning ... IFCC
International Federation of Catholic Alumnae (EA) ... IFCA
International Federation of Catholic Journalists ... IFCJ
International Federation of Catholic Pharmacists ... IFCP
International Federation of Catholic Rural Movements (EAIO) ... IFCRM
International Federation of Catholic Universities [*See also FIUC*] [*Paris, France*] (EAIO) ... IFCU
International Federation of Cell Biology [*Toronto, ON*] (EAIO) ... IFCB
International Federation of Cervical Pathology and Colposcopy [*Dundee, Scotland*] (EAIO) ... IFCPC
International Federation of Chemical and General Workers Union ... ICF
International Federation of Chemical and General Workers Union ... IFCGWU
International Federation of Chemical Workers' Unions ... IFCWU
International Federation of Children of Mary Immaculate [*Paris, France*] (EAIO) ... IFCMI
International Federation of Children's Communities [*Later, FICE*] ... IFCC
International Federation of Christian Metalworkers Unions ... IFCM
International Federation of Christian Miners' Unions ... IFCMU
International Federation of Christian Trade Unions [*Often uses initialism CISC, based on name in French, to avoid confusion with ICFTU*] ... IFCTU
International Federation of Christian Trade Unions of Building and Wood Workers ... IFCTUBWW
International Federation of Christian Trade Unions of Graphical and Paper Industries ... IFCTUGP
International Federation of Christian Unions of Agricultural Workers ... IFCUAW
International Federation of Clinical Chemistry [*Vienna, Austria*] (EA) ... IFCC
International Federation of Clinical Neurophysiology (EAIO) ... IFCN
International Federation of Commercial, Clerical, and Technical Employees ... IFCCTE
International Federation of Commercial Travelers Insurance Organizations [*Later, CTIF*] (EA) ... IFCTIO
International Federation of Community Centre Associations ... IFCCA
International Federation of Computer Sciences ... IFCS
International Federation of Consulting Engineers (NUCP) ... IFCE
International Federation of Cotton and Allied Textile Industries [*Later, ITMF*] ... IFCATI
International Federation of Dalit Organizations (EA) ... IFDO
International Federation of Data Organizations for the Social Sciences [*Amsterdam, Netherlands*] (EAIO) ... IFDO
International Federation of Dental Anesthesiology Societies [*British*] (EAIO) ... IFDAS
International Federation of Electron Microscope Societies ... IFEMS
International Federation of Elvis Presley Fan Clubs [*Defunct*] (EA) ... IFEPFC
International Federation of Employees in Public Service [*Brussels, Belgium*] (EAIO) ... INFEDOP
International Federation of Engine Reconditioners [*See also FIRM*] [*Paris, France*] (EAIO) ... IFER
International Federation of Essential Oils and Aroma Trades [*British*] (EAIO) ... IFEAT
International Federation of Europe Houses [*See also FIME*] (EAIO) ... IFEH
International Federation of Falerists (EA) ... IFF
International Federation of Fertility Societies (EAIO) ... IFFS
International Federation of Film Archives ... IFFA
International Federation of Film Producers' Associations ... IFFPA
International Federation of Film Societies ... IFFS
International Federation of Free Evangelical Churches (EA) ... IFFEC
International Federation of Free Journalists [*British*] ... IFFJ
International Federation of Free Teachers' Unions [*See also SPIE*] [*Amsterdam, Netherlands*] (EAIO) ... IFFTU
International Federation of Fruit Juice Producers [*See also FIJU*] [*Paris, France*] (EAIO) ... IFFJP
International Federation of Gastronomical and Vinicultural Press ... IFGVP
International Federation of Grocers' Associations [*See also IVLD*] [*Bern, Switzerland*] (EAIO) ... IFGA
International Federation of Grocery Manufacturers Associations (EA) ... IFGMA
International Federation of Gynecology and Obstetrics ... IFGO
International Federation of Health and Beauty Therapists ... IFHBT
International Federation of Health Professionals (EA) ... IFHP
International Federation of Health Records Organizations [*Munich, Federal Republic of Germany*] (EAIO) ... IFHRO
International Federation of Hospital Engineering (PDAA) ... IFHE
International Federation of Hydraulic Platform Manufacturers [*Later, IPAF*] (EAIO) ... IFHPM
International Federation of Importers and Wholesale Grocers Associations [*The Hague, Netherlands*] (EAIO) ... IFIWA
International Federation of Independent Air Transport ... IFIAT
International Federation of Industrial Energy Consumers [*Geneva, Switzerland*] (EA) ... IFIEC
International Federation of Industrial Organizations and General Workers' Unions ... IFIF
International Federation of Infantile and Juvenile Gynecology [*See also FIGIJ*] [*Sierre, Switzerland*] (EAIO) ... IFIJG
International Federation of Information Processing Societies [*Later, IFIP*] ... IFIPS
International Federation of Institutes for Advanced Study [*ICSU*] [*Toronto, ON*] (EAIO) ... IFIAS
International Federation of Institutes for Socio-Religious Research [*Louvain, Belgium*] (EA) ... IFISRR
International Federation of Interior Architects/Interior Designers [*Amsterdam, Netherlands*] (EAIO) ... IFI
International Federation of International Furniture Removers [*See also FIDI*] [*Brussels, Belgium*] (EAIO) ... IFIFR
International Federation of Inventors' Associations [*Stockholm, Sweden*] (EAIO) ... IFIA

International Federation of Ironmongers and Iron Merchants Associations [*See also FIDAQ*] [*Zurich, Switzerland*] (EAIO) ... IFIA
International Federation of Journalists [*See also FIJ*] [*Brussels, Belgium*] (EAIO) ... IFJ
International Federation of Kennel Clubs [*Belgium*] (EAIO) ... FCI
International Federation of Kennel Clubs (EA) ... IFKC
International Federation of Knitting Technologists [*See also FITB*] [*Frauenfeld, Switzerland*] (EAIO) ... IFKT
International Federation of Landscape Architects [*Versailles, France*] (EAIO) ... IFLA
International Federation of Latin American Study Centers [*Mexico City, Mexico*] (EAIO) ... IFLASC
International Federation of Law Students (DLA) ... IFLS
International Federation of Leather Guilds (EA) ... IFLG
International Federation of Liberal and Radical Youth (EAIO) ... IFLRY
International Federation of Library Associations (NITA) ... IFLA
International Federation of Library Associations and Institutions ... IFLA
International Federation of Little Singers (EAIO) ... IFLS
International Federation of Magical Societies [*See also FISM*] (EAIO) ... IFMS
International Federation of Manual Medicine (EA) ... IFMM
International Federation of Margarine Associations [*Brussels, Belgium*] (EAIO) ... IFMA
International Federation of Maritime Philately [*Livorno, Italy*] (EAIO) ... IFMP
International Federation of Married Priests (EAIO) ... IFMP
International Federation of Master-Craftsmen [*See also IFH*] (EAIO) ... IFC
International Federation of Master-Craftsmen (EA) ... IFMC
International Federation of Medical Students Associations [*See also FIAEM*] [*Vienna, Austria*] (EAIO) ... IFMSA
International Federation of Motorhome Clubs [*Belgium*] (EAIO) ... IFMC
International Federation of Multiple Sclerosis Societies [*British*] (EAIO) ... IFMSS
International Federation of Municipal Engineers [*See also FIIM*] [*British*] (EAIO) ... IFME
International Federation of Netball Associations [*Glasgow, Scotland*] (EAIO) ... IFNA
International Federation of Newspaper Publishers (NTCM) ... IFNP
International Federation of Operation Research Societies (BARN) ... IFOR
International Federation of Operational Research Societies [*ICSU*] [*Lyngby, Denmark*] (EAIO) ... IFORS
International Federation of Ophthalmological Societies [*Nijmegen, Netherlands*] (EA) ... IFOS
International Federation of Organic Agriculture Movements [*Witzenhausen, Federal Republic of Germany*] (EA) ... IFOAM
International Federation of Original Art Diffusors [*France*] (EAIO) ... IFOAD
International Federation of Oto-Rhino-Laryngological Societies [*Berchem, Belgium*] (EAIO) ... IFOS
International Federation of Palynological Societies (EAIO) ... IFPS
International Federation of Park and Recreation Administration [*Reading, England*] (EAIO) ... IFPRA
International Federation of Pedestrians (EA) ... IFP
International Federation of Pelota Vasca (EA) ... IFPV
International Federation of Petroleum and Chemical Workers (EA) ... IFPCW
International Federation of Petroleum Workers ... IFPW
International Federation of Pharmaceutical Manufacturers Associations [*See also FIIM*] [*Geneva, Switzerland*] (EAIO) ... IFPMA
International Federation of Philosophical Societies [*See also FISP*] [*Fribourg, Switzerland*] (EAIO) ... IFPS
International Federation of Phonogram and Videogram Producers (EA) ... IFPVP
International Federation of Photographic Art ... IFPA
International Federation of Physical Medicine ... IFPM
International Federation of Physical Medicine and Rehabilitation (EA) ... IFPMR
International Federation of Plantation, Agricultural, and Allied Workers [*Switzerland*] ... IFPAAW
International Federation of Popular Sports [*See also IVV*] (EAIO) ... IFPS
International Federation of Popular Travel Organisations [*Paris, France*] (EAIO) ... IFPTO
International Federation of Postcard Dealers (EA) ... IFPD
International Federation of Practitioners of Natural Therapeutics [*British*] ... IFPNT
International Federation of Press Cutting Agencies (EA) ... IFPCA
International Federation of Professional and Technical Engineers (EA) ... IFPTE
International Federation of Professional and Technical Engineers ... PTE
International Federation of Protestant Workers' Associations ... IFPWA
International Federation of Psoriasis Associations [*Stockholm, Sweden*] (EAIO) ... IFPA
International Federation of Psychoanalytic Societies (EA) ... IFPS
International Federation of Psychological-Medical Organizations [*See also FIOPM*] [*Lausanne, Switzerland*] (EAIO) ... IFPMO
International Federation of Public Warehouse Keepers Associations [*Later, IFPWA*] (EAIO) ... IFPWKA
International Federation of Public Warehousing Associations [*Formerly, IFPWKA*] (EAIO) ... IFPWA
International Federation of Purchasing ... IFP
International Federation of Purchasing and Materials Management [*Aarau, Switzerland*] (EAIO) ... IFPMM
International Federation of Railway Advertising Companies [*British*] (EA) ... IFRAC
International Federation of Railwaymen's Travel Associations (EA) ... IFRTA
International Federation of Recreational Vehicle Users [*Later, FOR*] (EA) ... IFORVU
International Federation of Reproductive Rights Organisations (AIE) ... IFRRO
International Federation of Resistance Fighters (BJA) ... IFRF
International Federation of Resistance Movements [*Vienna, Austria*] (EA) ... IFRM
International Federation of Retail Distributors (EAIO) ... IFRD
International Federation of Roofing Contractors [*See also IFD*] (EAIO) ... IFRC
International Federation of Sanitarians Organizations [*Defunct*] (EA) ... IFSO
International Federation of Scientific Editors' Associations (EA) ... IFSEA
International Federation of Scoliosis Associations (EA) ... IFSA
International Federation of Senior Police Officers (EA) ... IFSPO
International Federation of Settlements and Neighbourhood Centers (EAIO) ... IFS
International Federation of Settlements and Neighbourhood Centres [*Defunct*] ... IFSNC
International Federation of Sewing Thread Manufacturers (EA) ... IFSTM
International Federation of Shipmasters Associations [*See also FIAPN*] (EAIO) ... IFSMA
International Federation of Shorthand and Typewriting ... IFST
International Federation of Sleddog Sports (EA) ... IFSS
International Federation of Social Science Organizations [*See also FIOSS*] [*Copenhagen, Denmark*] (EAIO) ... IFSSO
International Federation of Social Workers [*Switzerland*] ... IFSW
International Federation of Societies for Electroencephalography and Clinical Neurophysiology [*Amsterdam, Netherlands*] (EA) ... IFSECN
International Federation of Societies for Electron Microscopy (EA) ... IFSEM
International Federation of Societies for Histochemistry and Cytochemistry (EAIO) ... IFSHC
International Federation of Societies for Surgery of the Hand (EA) ... IFSSH
International Federation of Societies of Cosmetic Chemists [*Luton, England*] (EAIO) ... IFSCC
International Federation of Societies of Philosophy ... IFSP
International Federation of Sound Hunters (EA) ... IFSH
International Federation of Sports Acrobatics [*Sofia, Bulgaria*] (EAIO) ... IFSA
International Federation of Sports Medicine (EA) ... FISM
International Federation of Sports Medicine (EA) ... IFSM
International Federation of Stamp Dealers' Associations (EA) ... IFSDA
International Federation of Students in Political Sciences ... IFSPS
International Federation of Surgical Colleges [*Dublin, Republic of Ireland*] (EAIO) ... IFSC
International Federation of Surveyors [*See also FIG*] (EAIO) ... IFS
International Federation of Teachers' Associations [*Later, WCOTP*] (EAIO) ... IFTA
International Federation of Teachers of French [*See also FIPF*] [*Sevres, France*] (EAIO) ... IFTF
International Federation of Teachers of Rhythmics (EA) ... IFTR
International Federation of Teachers' Unions ... IFTU
International Federation of Telephonic Emergency Services [*Jorn, Sweden*] (EA) ... IFOTES
International Federation of Television Archives [*See also FIAT*] [*Madrid, Spain*] (EAIO) ... IFTA
International Federation of Teratology Societies (EA) ... IFTS
International Federation of Textile Workers' Associations ... IFTWA
International Federation of Thanatologists Associations [*Saint-Ouen, France*] (EA) ... IFTA
International Federation of the Blind [*Later, WBU*] ... IFB
International Federation of the Blue Cross [*Formerly, International Federation of the Temperance Blue Cross Societies*] (EA) ... IBC
International Federation of the Blue Cross (EA) ... IFBC
International Federation of the Cinematographic Press [*See also FIPRESCI*] (EAIO) ... IFCP
International Federation of the Hard of Hearing [*Kampen, Netherlands*] (EAIO) ... IFHOH
International Federation of the Little Brothers of the Poor [*See also FIPFP*] (EAIO) ... IFLBP
International Federation of the Phonographic Industry (EAIO) ... IFPI
International Federation of the Photographic Industry ... IFPI
International Federation of the Rights of Man ... IFRM
International Federation of the Socialist and Democratic Press [*Milan, Italy*] (EAIO) ... IFSDP
International Federation of the Societies of Classical Studies (EA) ... IFSCS
International Federation of the Technical and Periodical Press (DIT) ... IFTPP
International Federation of the Temperance Blue Cross Societies [*Later, IBC*] (EA) ... IFTBCS
International Federation of Thermalism and Climatism [*Bad Ragaz, Switzerland*] (EA) ... IFTC
International Federation of Tiddlywinks Associations (EA) ... IFTwA
International Federation of Tobacco Workers ... IFTW
International Federation of Tour Operators [*Lewes, East Sussex, England*] (EAIO) ... IFTO
International Federation of Trade Unions ... IFTU
International Federation of Trade Unions of Transport Workers [*See also FIOST*] [*Brussels, Belgium*] (EAIO) ... IFTUTW
International Federation of Training and Development Organizations (EA) ... IFTDO
International Federation of Translators [*See also FIT*] [*Ghent, Belgium*] (EAIO) ... IFT
International Federation of Unions of Employees in Public and Civil Services ... IFPCS
International Federation of University Women (EA) ... IFUW
International Federation of Wargaming [*Defunct*] (EA) ... IFW
International Federation of Wines and Spirits [*See also FIVS*] (EAIO) ... IFWS
International Federation of Wines and Spirits, Trade, and Industry (EA) ... IFWSTI
International Federation of Women Lawyers (EA) ... IFWL
International Federation of Women's Hockey Associations ... IFWHA
International Federation of Women's Travel Organizations (EA) ... IFWTO
International Federation of Workers' Educational Associations [*See also IVB*] [*Tel Aviv, Israel*] (EAIO) ... IFWEA
International Federation of Young Cooperators ... IFYC
International Federation on Ageing [*Formerly, IARP*] (EA) ... IFA

International Feedstuffs Institute [*Utah State University*] [*Research center Defunct*] (RCD) ... IFI
International Fellowship of Evangelical Students (EA) ... IFES
International Fellowship of Evangelical Students Link Group (EA) ... IFESLG
International Fellowship of Former Scouts and Guides [*Brussels, Belgium*] ... IFOFSAG
International Fellowship of Reconciliation [*Alkmaar, Netherlands*] (EA) ... IFOR
International Feminist Network ... IFN
International Fence Industry Association (EA) ... IFIA
International Fencing Federation [*Paris, France*] (EA) ... IFF
International Ferret Association (EA) ... IFA
International Ferro-Alloys Congress ... INFACON
International Ferrocement Information Center [*Asian Institute of Technology*] (IID) ... IFIC
International Fertility Association [*Defunct*] ... IFA
International Fertility Research Program [*Later, FHI*] ... IFRP
International Fertility Research Program, Durham, NC [*Library symbol Library of Congress*] (LCLS) ... NcDurIF
International Fertilizer Development Center (EA) ... IFDC
International Fertilizer Development Center, Muscle Shoals, AB, Canada [*Library symbol*] [*Library of Congress*] (LCLS) ... CaAMsIF
International Fertilizer Development Center, Muscle Shoals, AL [*Library symbol Library of Congress*] (LCLS) ... AMuI
International Fertilizer Development Center, Muscle Shoals, Alberta [*Library symbol National Library of Canada*] (NLC) ... AMSIF
International Fertilizer Industry Association [*Paris, France*] (EAIO) ... IFA
International Fertilizer Supply Scheme [*FAO*] [*United Nations*] ... IFSS
International Festivals Association (EA) ... IFA
International Fiber Optics and Communications Exposition and Show on Local Area Networks ... FOC/LAN
International Fibercom, Inc. [*NASDAQ symbol*] (SAG) ... IFCI
International Fibercom, Inc. [*Associated Press*] (SAG) ... IntFib
International Fibercom, Inc. [*Associated Press*] (SAG) ... IntFibcm
International Fibercom Wrrt [*NASDAQ symbol*] (TTSB) ... IFCIW
International Fibrodysplasia Ossificans Progressiva Association (EA) ... IFOPA
International Fiction Association (EAIO) ... IFA
International FidoNet Association [*Defunct*] (EA) ... IFNA
International Field Year for the Great Lakes ... IFYGL
International Fighter Aircraft ... IFA
International Fighter Pilots Academy [*Slovak Air Force*] ... IFPA
International Fighter RADAR ... IFR
International Fight'n Rooster Cutlery Club (EA) ... IFRCC
International Figure Skating Writers Association [*Defunct*] ... IFSWA
International Filariasis Association (EA) ... IFA
International Film and Television Council [*Rome, Italy*] ... IFTC
International Film Completion Corp. ... IFC
International Film Foundation ... IFF
International Film Institute ... IFI
International Film Management Ltd. [*Australia*] ... IFML
International Film Representatives [*Division of International Film Completion Corp.*] ... IFR
International Film Seminars (EA) ... IFS
International Finance Alert [*Financial Times Business Information*] [*British Information service or system*] (CRD) ... IFA
International Finance and Leasing Association (MHDB) ... IFLA
International Finance Corp. [*AMEX symbol*] (SAG) ... GYW
International Finance Corp. [*Affiliate of International Bank for Reconstruction and Development*] ... IFC
International Finance Corp. [*Associated Press*] (SAG) ... InFnDM
International Finance Corp. [*Associated Press*] (SAG) ... InFnDY
International Finance Corp. [*Associated Press*] (SAG) ... InFnYB
International Finance Corp. [*Associated Press*] (SAG) ... IntF
International Finance Corp. [*NYSE symbol*] (SAG) ... OPT
International Finance Corp. [*AMEX symbol*] (SAG) ... YNW
International Finance Corp. [*AMEX symbol*] (SAG) ... YPW
International Finance Investment and Commerce Bank Ltd. [*Bangladesh*] (EY) ... IFICB
International Finance Managers Study [*Database*] [*Research Services Ltd.*] [*Information service or system*] (CRD) ... IFM
International Financial Institution ... IFI
International Financial Institutions Act [*1977*] ... IFIA
International Financial Intelligence Service (NITA) ... IFIS
International Financial Law Review [*A publication*] (DLA) ... IFL Rev
International Financial Law Review [*A publication*] (DLA) ... Int'l Fin L Rev
International Financial Markets Trading Ltd. ... IFM
International Financial Networks ... INFINET
International Financial Services and Technology Exhibition [*British*] ... IFSAT
International Financial Services Research Center [*Massachusetts Institute of Technology*] [*Research center*] (RCD) ... IFSRC
International Financing Review [*A publication*] ... IFR
International Fine Particle Research Institute ... IFPRI
International Fine Print Dealers Association ... IFPDA
International Finn Association [*Madrid, Spain*] (EAIO) ... IFA
International Fire Administration Institute ... IFAI
International Fire and Security Exhibition and Conference [*British*] (ITD) ... IFSEC
International Fire Buff Associates (EA) ... IFBA
International Fire Chiefs' Association of Asia (EAIO) ... IFCAA
International Fire Photographers Association (EA) ... IFPA
International Fire, Security and Safety Exhibition and Conference (PDAA) ... IFSSEC
International Fire Service Training Association (EA) ... IFSTA
International Fiscal Association [*Rotterdam, Netherlands*] (EAIO) ... IFA
International Fiscal Association, Australian Branch ... IFAAB
International Fisheries Commission [*Later, IPHC*] [*US and Canada*] ... IFC
International Fisheries Commission, Seattle, WA [*Library symbol Library of Congress*] (LCLS) ... WaSIF
International Fisheries Cooperative Organization (BARN) ... IFCO
International Fishing Equipment Exposition [*Canada*] (ITD) ... IFEEX
International Fixed Public ... IFP
International FJ Class Organization (EA) ... FJUS
International Flat Earth Research Society (EA) ... IFERS
International Flavors & Fragrances, Inc. [*NYSE symbol*] (SPSG) ... IFF
International Flavors & Fragrances, Inc. [*Associated Press*] (SAG) ... IntFlav
International Flavors & Fragrances, Inc., Union Beach, NJ [*Library symbol Library of Congress*] (LCLS) ... NjUbI
International Flight Attendants Association (EA) ... IFAA
International Flight Information Manual ... IFIM
International Flight Service Station [*FAA*] ... IFSS
International Florists Association [*Later, National Florists Association*] (EA) ... IFA
International Flow Aids Association (EA) ... IFAA
International Flower Trades Exhibition [*British*] (ITD) ... IFTEX
International Fly Fishing Association (EAIO) ... IFFA
International Flyer Resources Ltd. [*Vancouver Stock Exchange symbol*] ... IFR
International Flying Dutchman Class Association of the US (EA) ... IFDCAUS
International Flying Dutchmen Class Organization [*Berlin, Federal Republic of Germany*] (EAIO) ... IFDCO
International Flying Farmers (EA) ... IFF
International Flying Nurses Association (EA) ... IFNA
International Flying Saucer Bureau [*Defunct*] ... IFSB
International Flying Services SRL [*Italy ICAO designator*] (FAAC) ... IFS
International Focus Resources, Inc. [*Vancouver Stock Exchange symbol*] ... IFS
International Folk Music Council [*Later, ICTM*] ... IFMC
International Food Additives Council (EA) ... IFAC
International Food Aid Information System [*World Food Program*] [*United Nations*] (DUND) ... INTERFAIS
International Food and Drink Exhibition [*British*] (ITD) ... IFE
International Food Information Council (EA) ... IFIC
International Food Information Service [*Database producer*] [*Germany*] ... IFIS
International Food Irradiation Project [*Food and Agricultural Organization*] (PDAA) ... IFIP
International Food Policy Research Institute (EA) ... IFPRI
International Food Policy Research Institute, Washington, DC [*Library symbol Library of Congress*] (LCLS) ... DIFP
International Food Processing and Packaging Technology Exhibition and Conferencefor South East Asia ... PROPAKASIA
International Food Service Executive's Association (EA) ... IFSEA
International Food, Wine, and Travel Writers Association (EAIO) ... IFWTWA
International Foodservice Distributors Association (EA) ... IFDA
International Foodservice Editorial Council (EA) ... IFEC
International Foodservice Manufacturers Association (EA) ... IFMA
International Footprint Association (EA) ... IFA
International Footwear Association (EA) ... IFA
International Ford Retractable Club (EA) ... IFRC
International Forest Products Ltd. [*Toronto Stock Exchange symbol Vancouver Stock Exchange symbol*] ... IFP
International Fortean Organization (EA) ... INFO
International Fortran Organization (NITA) ... IFO
International Forum (EA) ... IF
International Forum for AIDS Research [*Institute of Medicine*] ... IFAR
International Forum Foundation ... IFF
International Foundation (EAIO) ... IF
[*The*] International Foundation (EA) ... TIF
International Foundation Directory [*A publication*] ... IFD
International Foundation for Agricultural Development [*Defunct*] (EA) ... IFAD
International Foundation for Airline Passengers (EAIO) ... IFAP
International Foundation for Art Research (EA) ... IFAR
International Foundation for Cancer Research (EA) ... IFCR
International Foundation for Development Alternatives [*See also FIPAD*] [*Nyon, Switzerland*] (EAIO) ... IFDA
International Foundation for Electoral Systems (EA) ... IFES
International Foundation for Ethical Research (EA) ... IFER
International Foundation for Gender Education (EA) ... IFGE
International Foundation for Homeopathy (EA) ... IFH
International Foundation for Hygiene, Preventative Medicine, Social Medicine (BABM) ... IFHPMSM
International Foundation for Independence (EA) ... IFI
International Foundation for Protection Officers (EA) ... IFPO
International Foundation for Research in the Field of Advertising ... IFRA
International Foundation for Science [*See also FIS*] [*ICSU Stockholm, Sweden*] (EAIO) ... IFS
International Foundation for Stutterers (EA) ... IFS
International Foundation for Telemetering (EA) ... IFT
International Foundation for Theatrical Research (EA) ... IFTR
International Foundation for Timesharing (EA) ... IFT
International Foundation of Airline Passengers Associations (EAIO) ... IFAPA
International Foundation of Doll Makers (EA) ... IFDM
International Foundation of Employee Benefit Plans (EA) ... IFEBP
International Foundation of Employee Benefit Plans, Information Center, Brookfield, WI [*Library symbol Library of Congress*] (LCLS) ... WBrI
International Foundry Exhibition ... FOUNDEX
International Fox-Tango Club [*Defunct*] (EA) ... IFTC
International Fragrance Association [*Geneva, Switzerland*] (EAIO) ... IFRA
International Franchise Association (EA) ... IFA
International Franchised Dealers Association [*Later, SFDA*] (EA) ... IFDA
International Frankenstein Society (EA) ... IFS
International Frederic Chopin Foundation [*Poland*] (EAIO) ... IFCF
International Free Academy of New Cosmology (EA) ... IFANC
International Free Trade Area ... IFTA
International Freedom Foundation (EA) ... IFF

International Freedom Foundation - United Kingdom Branch (EAIO) .... IFF-UK
International Freelance Photographers Organization .... IFPO
International Freeze-Dry Floral Association (EA) .... IFDFA
International Freight Apron .... IFA
International Frequency List (NATG) .... IFL
International Frequency List Committee .... IFLC
International Frequency Registration Board [*ITU*] [*United Nations*] .... IFRB
International Frequency Tables .... IFT
International Friendly Circle of the Blind (EA) .... IFCB
International Friends of Nature [*See also NFI*] [*Zurich, Switzerland*] (EAIO) .... IFN
International Friendship League [*Defunct*] (EA) .... IFL
International Frisbee Association [*Later, IFDA*] .... IFA
International Frisbee Disc Association [*Formerly, IFA*] (EA) .... IFDA
International Frozen Food Association (EA) .... IFFA
International Frozen Food Exhibition and Congress .... IFFEX
International Fuel Tax Agreement [*FHWA*] (TAG) .... IFTA
International Fund for Agricultural Development [*United Nations*] .... IFAD
International Fund for Animal Welfare (EA) .... IFAW
International Fund for Concerned Photography [*Later, ICP*] .... IFCP
International Fund for Ireland [*United States, Canada, and New Zealand*] .... IFI
International Fund for Monuments .... IFM
International Fund-Raising Association (EA) .... IFRA
International Fund-Raising Institute [*Later, IFRA*] .... IFRI
International Fur and Leather Workers Union (MHDB) .... IFLWU
International Fur and Leather Workers Union of United States and Canada .... FLW
International Fur Trade Federation [*British*] (EAIO) .... IFTF
International Furnishings and Design Association (EA) .... IFDA
International Furniture and Accessory Association (EA) .... IFAA
International Fusion Superconducting Magnet Test Facility [*Oak Ridge National Laboratory*] .... IFSMTF
International Futures Research Conference (PDAA) .... IFRC
International Fuzzy Systems Association (EA) .... IFSA
International G. G. Drayton Association (EA) .... IGGDA
International Galdos Association (EA) .... IGA
International Gallery Invitational (ITD) .... IGI
International Galvanizing Conference (MCD) .... INTERGALVA
International Game Fish Association (EA) .... IGFA
International Game Technology (MHDW) .... IGAM
International Game Technology [*NYSE symbol*] (SPSG) .... IGT
International Game Technology [*Associated Press*] (SAG) .... IntGame
International Gamers Association (EA) .... IGA
International Garden Club (EA) .... IGC
International Garden Horticultural Industry Association (EA) .... IGHIA
International Garment Processors .... IGP
International Garment Workers' Federation .... IGWF
International Gas Bearings Symposium (PDAA) .... IGBS
International Gas Turbine Institute [*Later, ASMEIGTI*] (EA) .... IGTI
International Gas Union [*See also UIIG*] (EAIO) .... IGU
International Gay and Lesbian Human Rights Commission (EA) .... IGLHRC
International Gay Association - International Association of Lesbians/Gay Women and Gay Men (EAIO) .... IGA
International Gay Information Center [*Defunct*] (EA) .... IGIC
International Gay Travel Association (EA) .... IGTA
International Gem Finders Society .... IGFS
International Genealogical Fellowship of Rotarians (EA) .... IGFR
International Genealogical Index [*A publication Australia*] .... IGI
International Genealogy Consumer Organization (EA) .... IGCO
International General (EA) .... IG
International General Assembly of Spiritualists [*Later, LDTF*] (EA) .... IGAS
International General Aviation .... IGA
International General Certificate of Secondary Education (AIE) .... IGCSE
International Genetic Resources Programme [*Later, RAFI-USA*] (EA) .... IGRP
International Genetics Federation [*See also FIG*] [*England*] (EA) .... IGF
International Geneva Association (EA) .... IGA
International Geodynamics Project .... IGP
International Geographic Information Foundation .... IGIF
International Geographical Association [*Esperantist*] .... IGA
International Geographical Union [*ICSU*] [*Edmonton, AB*] (EA) .... IGU
International Geographical Union Commission on Climatology [*Switzerland*] (EAIO) .... IGUCC
International Geographics [*Vancouver Stock Exchange symbol*] .... IGE
International Geological Congress .... IGC
International Geological Correlation Programme [*See also PICG*] [*ICSU Paris, France*] (EAIO) .... IGCP
International Geological-Geophysical Cruise Inventory [*Marine science*] (OSRA) .... IG-GCI
International Geomagnetic Reference Field .... IGRF
International Geophysical Committee [*Also, CIG*] .... IGC
International Geophysical Cooperation [*World Meteorological Organization*] .... IGC
International Geophysical Extension .... IGE
International Geophysical Union .... IGU
International Geophysical Year [*1958-1959*] [*ICSU*] .... IGY
International Geophysical Year, World Data Center .... IGY-WDC
International Geoscience and Remote Sensing Symposium (MCD) .... IGARSS
International Geosphere-Biosphere Program [*ICSU*] [*Proposed for 1992*] .... IGBP
International Geosphere-Biosphere Programme [*Australia*] .... IGBP
International Geranium Society (EA) .... IGS
International Glaciological Society [*Cambridge, England*] .... IGS
International Glaucoma Association (EAIO) .... IGA
International Glaucoma Congress (EA) .... IGC
International Global Atmospheric Chemistry [*Project*] (USDC) .... IGAC
International Global Atmospheric Chemistry Program [*Marine science*] (OSRA) .... IGAC
International Glove Workers' Union of America [*Later, ACTWU*] .... GWU
International Glove Workers' Union of America [*Later, ACTWU*] .... IGWU
International Glove Workers Union of America (MHDB) .... IGWUA
International Glutamate Technical Committee (EA) .... IGTC
International Gold and Silver Plate Society (EA) .... IGSPS
International Gold Bullion Exchange [*Bankrupt investment firm*] .... IGBE
International Golf Association (EA) .... IGA
International Golf Sponsors' Association [*Later, AGS*] .... IGSA
International Good Neighbor Council [*See also CIBV*] [*Monterrey, Mexico*] (EAIO) .... IGNC
International Good Templar Youth Federation [*Oslo, Norway*] (EAIO) .... IGTYF
International Graduate Achievement [*Defunct*] (EA) .... IGA
International Graduate School of Management .... IGSM
International Graduate School, St. Louis, MO [*OCLC symbol*] (OCLC) .... JNS
International Graduate School, St. Louis, MO [*Library symbol Library of Congress*] (LCLS) .... MoSIG
International Grail Movement (EA) .... IGM
International Grains Arrangement .... IGA
International Graphic Arts Education Association (EA) .... IGAEA
International Graphic Arts Society (EA) .... IGAS
International Graphical Federation [*See also FGI*] [*Berne, Switzerland*] (EAIO) .... IGF
International Graphics [*Formerly, IGI*] (EA) .... IG
International Graphics Exchange Specification [*Computer science*] .... IGES
International Graphics Exchange Standard (NITA) .... IGES
International Graphics, Inc. [*Defunct*] (EA) .... IGI
International Graphoanalysis Society (EA) .... IGAS
International Graphological Society (EA) .... IGS
International Grassland Congress .... IGC
International Gravimetric Bureau [*Marine science*] (OSRA) .... BGI
International Gravimetric Bureau [*Toulouse, France*] (EAIO) .... IGB
International Gravis Computer Technology, Inc. [*Formerly, Gravis Computer Peripherals, Inc.*] [*Vancouver Stock Exchange symbol*] .... IGV
International Gravity Standardization Net (PDAA) .... IGSN
International Great Lakes Datum .... IGLD
International Green Alliance (EA) .... IGA
International Green Party - Ecologism USA (EA) .... IGP
International Greenland Sea Project (USDC) .... IGSP
International Grooving and Grinding Association (EA) .... IG & GA
International Grotius Foundation for the Propagation of International Law .... IGFPIL
International Ground Environment Subcommittee [*NATO*] .... IGESUCO
International Ground Source Heat Pump Association (EA) .... IGSHPA
International Ground Water Modeling Center [*Butler University*] .... IGWMC
[*The*] **International Group for Historic Aircraft Recovery** [*Wilmington, DE*] .... TIGHAR
International Group for Studies in National Planning .... INTERPLAN
International Group for the Advancement of Physics Teaching (AIE) .... GIREP
International Group for the Exchange of Information and Experience Among Postal Savings Institutions [*Geneva, Switzerland*] (EAIO) .... IGEIEPSI
International Group of Agents and Bureaus (EA) .... IGAB
International Group of Scientific, Technical, and Medical Publishers (EAIO) .... STM
International Group of Women Pilots (EA) .... IGWP
International Group on Clinical Sociology [*Formerly, International Committee on Clinical Sociology*] (EA) .... ICCS
International Group on Soil Sampling .... IGOSS
International Grouping of Pharmaceuticals Distributors in the EEC (ECED) .... GRIP
International Guards Union of America .... GUA
International Guards Union of America (EA) .... IGUA
International Guides' Club (EAIO) .... IG
International Guides' Club (EAIO) .... IGC
International Guiding Eyes (EA) .... IGE
International Guild of Candle Artisans (EA) .... IGCA
International Guild of Craft Journalists, Authors, and Photographers [*Inactive*] (EA) .... IGCJAP
International Guild of Hypnotists (EA) .... IGH
International Guild of Miniature Artisans (EA) .... IGMA
International Guild of Opticians [*International Guild of Dispensing Optic ians*] [*Acronym is based on former name,*] (EAIO) .... IGDO
International Guild of Prestidigitators [*Defunct*] (EA) .... IGP
International Guild of Professional Electrologists (EA) .... IGPE
International Guild of Symphony, Opera, and Ballet Musicians (EA) .... IGSOBM
International Guild of Vatican Philatelists [*Defunct*] (EA) .... IGVP
International Gymnastic Federation [*See also FIG*] (EAIO) .... IGF
International H Boat Class Association (EA) .... IHBCA
International Hahnemannian Association [*Defunct*] .... IHA
International Hajji Baba Society (EA) .... IHBS
International Halfway House Association (EA) .... IHHA
International Halley Watch [*Defunct*] (EA) .... IHW
International Handball Federation [*Basel, Switzerland*] (EA) .... IHF
International Handgun Metallic Silhouette Association (EA) .... IHMSA
International Handicappers' Net (EA) .... IHN
International Hard Suits [*Vancouver Stock Exchange symbol*] .... IHD
International Hardwood Products Association (EA) .... IHPA
International Harvester Co. .... IH
International Harvester Co. .... IHC
International Harvester Co., Memphis, TN [*Library symbol Library of Congress*] (LCLS) .... TMI
International Harvester Credit Corp. (ADA) .... IHCC
International Headquarters (DNAB) .... IHQ
International Headquarters of the Salvation Army (EA) .... IHSA
International Health and Beauty Council [*British*] .... IHBC
International Health and Temperance Association (EA) .... IHTA
International Health Center .... IHC

International Health Centre of Socio-Economics Researches and Studies [*See also CIERSES*] [*Lailly En Val, France*] (EAIO) .... IHCSERS
International Health Consultants (EA) .... IHC
International Health Council (EA) .... IHC
International Health Economics and Management Institute (EA) .... IHEMI
International Health Evaluation Association (EA) .... IHEA
International Health Foundation [*Brussels, Belgium*] (EAIO) .... IHF
International Health Industries Association (EA) .... IHIA
International Health Physics Data Base [*Creative Information Systems, Inc.*] [*Information service or system*] (CRD) .... IHPD
International Health Policy and Management Institute (EAIO) .... IHPMI
International Health Program Office [*Atlanta, GA*] [*Department of Health and Human Services*] (GRD) .... IHPO
International Health Society (EA) .... IHS
International Healthcare Safety Professional Certification Board (EA) .... IHSPCB
International Hearing Dog, Inc. (EA) .... IHDI
International Hearing Society (PAZ) .... IHS
International Hearts Air Supply Fan Club [*Defunct*] (EA) .... IHASFC
International Heat Stress Research Center [*Sudan*] (IRC) .... IHSRC
International Hebrew Christian Alliance [*Ramsgate, Kent, England*] (EA) .... IHCA
International Heinrich Schutz Society [*See also IHSG*] [*Germany*] (EA) .... IHSS
International Helicopter Foundation [*Later, HFI*] (EA) .... IHF
International Helicopter Technology and Operations Conference and Exhibition [*British*] (ITD) .... HELITECH
International Help for Children .... IHC
International Helsinki Federation for Human Rights [*Austria*] (EAIO) .... HIF
International Helsinki Federation for Human Rights (ECON) .... IHF
International Helsinki Federation for Human Rights (EA) .... IHFHR
International Hepato-Biliary-Pancreatic Association (EA) .... IHBPA
International Herb Growers and Marketers Association [*Defunct*] (EA) .... IHGMA
International Heritage Site [*UNESCO*] .... IHS
International Heroines of Jericho [*Later, General Conference of Grand Courts Heroines of Jericho, Prince Hall Affiliation, USA*] (EA) .... IHJ
International Herring Larvae Survey .... IHLS
International Hibernation Society (EA) .... IHS
International Hide and Allied Trades Improvement Society .... IHATIS
International High-Technology Training Association (EA) .... IHTTA
International Historic Enterprises .... IHE
International Hobie Class Association (EA) .... IHCA
International Hockey Federation (BARN) .... IHF
International Hockey League (EA) .... IHL
International Hod Carriers', Building and Common Laborers' Union of America [*Later, Laborers' International Union of North America*] .... HCL
International Home and Private Poker Players Association (EA) IH3PA
International Home Furnishings Marketing Association (EA) .... IHFMA
International Home Furnishings Representatives Association (EA) .... IHFRA
International Homeopathic League .... IHL
International Homestock Resources Ltd. [*Vancouver Stock Exchange symbol*] .... IHK
International Hop Growers Convention [*See also CICH*] [*Zalec, Yugoslavia*] (EAIO) .... IHGC
International Hopkins Association .... IHA
International Horn Society (EA) .... IHS
International Horticultural Advisory Board .... IHAB
International Hospital Federation (EA) .... IHF
International Hot Rod Association (EA) .... IHRA
International Hotel and Motel Educational Exposition [*Later, IHM & RS*] (EA) .... IH & MEE
International Hotel Association [*Paris, France*] (EA) .... IHA
International Hotel/Motel and Restaurant Show (EA) .... IHM & RS
International House Association [*Defunct*] .... IHA
International House, Cunningham Library, New Orleans, LA [*Library symbol Library of Congress*] (LCLS) .... LNTC
International House of Pancakes [*Restaurant chain*] [*Pronounced "eye-hop"*] .... IHOP
International House - World Trade Center [*Later, WTC*] (EA) .... IN
International Hug Center [*Defunct*] (EA) .... IHC
International Human Assistance Programs (EA) .... IHAP
International Human Powered Vehicle Association (EA) .... IHPVA
International Human Resources, Business, and Legal Research Association (EA) .... IHRBLR
International Human Rights Advisory Group [*Switzerland*] .... HRAG
International Human Rights Law Group (EA) .... IHRLG
International Humanist and Ethical Union [*Utrecht, Netherlands*] (EA) .... IHEU
International Humic Substances Society .... IHSS
International Hurling Society .... IHS
International Husserl and Phenomenological Research Society (EA) .... IHPRS
International Hydrofoil Society (EAIO) .... IHS
International Hydrographic Bureau [*Later, IHO*] [*Monaco*] .... IHB
International Hydrographic Organization [*See also BHI*] [*Monaco*] .... IHO
International Hydrographic Program .... IHP
International Hydrological Decade [*UNESCO*] [*Later, IHP*] .... IHD
International Hydrological Program [*UNESCO*] [*France*] .... IHP
International Hydrolyzed Protein Council (EA) .... IHPC
International Ice Cream Association (EA) .... IICA
International Ice Hockey Federation (EAIO) .... IIHF
International Ice Patrol [*Coast Guard*] IIC
International Ice Patrol [*Coast Guard*] .... IIP
International Ice Racing Association .... IIRA
International Icelandic Pony Association (EA) .... IIPA
International Illawarra Association [*Defunct*] (EA) .... IIA
International Imagery Association (EA) .... IIA
International Imaging Materials, Inc. [*NASDAQ symbol*] (SAG) .... IMAK
International Imaging Materials, Inc. [*Associated Press*] (SAG) .... IntImag
International Impala Resources [*Vancouver Stock Exchange symbol*] .... IIR
International Independent Christian Youth [*See also JICI*] [*Paris, France*] (EAIO) .... IICY
International Indian Ocean Expedition [*Navy*] .... IIOE
International Indian Treaty Council (EA) .... IITC
International Industrial Information Ltd. [*Information service or system*] (IID) III
International Industrial Marketing Club [*Formerly, MMEC*] [*Defunct*] (EA) .... IIMC
International Industrial Relations Association [*Geneva, Switzerland*] (EA) .... IIRA
International Industrial Relations Institute .... IRI
International Industrial Television Association (NTCM) .... ITVA
International Industry Working Group [*of the Air Transport Association of America*] (EAIO) .... IIWG
International Information Administration [*Transferred to U SIS, 1953*] [*Department of State*] .... IIA
International Information Centre for Standards in Information and Documentation (ADA) .... ISODOC
International Information Centre for Terminology [*UNESCO*] (IID) .... INFOTERM
International Information Management Congress (EA) .... IMC
International Information Office of the Democratic Revolutionary Front of El Salvador [*See also OIIFDRES*] [*San Jose, Costa Rica*] (EAIO) .... IIODRFES
International Information on Peace-Keeping Operations .... IPKO
International Information Service Ltd. [*Information service or system*] (IID) .... IIS
International Information Service via a Computer-Oriented Network (TSSD) .... IRICON
International Information Services for the Physics and Engineering Communities .... INSPEC
International Information System for the Agricultural Sciences and Technology [*Food and Agriculture Organization*] [*United Nations Information service or system*] (IID) .... AGRIS
International Information System on Research in Documentation [*International Federation for Documentation*] [*UNESCO*] (IID) .... ISORID
International Information/Word Processing Association [*Formerly, IWPA*] [*Later, IWP*] (EA) .... IIWPA
International Information/Word Processing Association [*Formerly, IWPA*] (EA) .... IWP
International Institute for Adult Literacy Methods [*Tehran, Iran*] (EAIO) .... IIALM
International Institute for Advanced Studies (EA) .... IIAS
International Institute for Applied Systems Analysis .... IIASA
International Institute for Arab-American Relations [*Defunct*] (EA) .... IIAAR
International Institute for Bioenergetic Analysis (EA) .... IIBA
International Institute for Children's Literature and Reading Research [*Vienna, Austria*] (EA) .... IICLRR
International Institute for Comparative Music Studies and Documentation [*Berlin, Federal Republic of Germany*] (EA) .... IICMSD
International Institute for Conservation of Historic and Artistic Works [*British*] (EAIO) IIC
International Institute for Conservation of Historic and Artistic Works .... IICHAW
International Institute for Cotton [*Belgium*] (FEA) IIC
International Institute for Economic Research (EA) .... IIER
International Institute for Educational Planning [*Paris, France*] [*United Nations*] (EA) .... IIEP
International Institute for Energy Conservation (EA) .... IIEC
International Institute for Environment and Development [*Research center British*] (IRC) .... IIED
International Institute for Environment and Development [*British*] .... iied
International Institute for Environmental Affairs [*Later, IIED*] .... IIEA
International Institute for Environmental Studies (ASF) .... IIES
International Institute for Home Literature [*See also MIKK*] [*Belgrade, Yugoslavia*] (EAIO) .... IIHL
International Institute for Hydraulic and Environmental Engineering [*Netherlands*] (IRC) .... IEE
International Institute for Hydraulic and Environmental Engineering [*Netherlands Universities Foundation for International Cooperation*] [*Research center*] .... IHE
International Institute for Labor Studies [*Switzerland*] .... IILS
International Institute for Lath and Plaster (EA) .... IILP
International Institute for Ligurian Studies (EA) .... IILS
International Institute for Management Development .... IMD
International Institute for Music, Dance, and Theatre in the Audio-Visual Media [*Later, Mediacult International Institute for Audio-Visual Communication and Cultural Development*] .... IMDT
International Institute for Peace [*Vienna, Austria*] (EA) .... IIP
International Institute for Production Engineering Research (EAIO) .... IIPER
International Institute for Promotion and Prestige [*Geneva, Switzerland*] (EAIO) .... IIPP
International Institute for Resource Economics [*Defunct*] (EA) .... IIRE
International Institute for Robotics (EA) .... IIR
International Institute for Safety in Transportation [*Formerly, IST*] (EA) .... IIST
International Institute for Safety in Transportation [*Later, IIST*] (EA) .... IST
International Institute for Strategic Studies (EA) .... IISS
International Institute for Study and Research in the Field of Commercial Competition IICC
International Institute for Sugar Beet Research (EA) .... IISBR
International Institute for the Conservation of Museum Objects IIC
International Institute for the Management of Technology [*Defunct*] (EA) .... IIMT
International Institute for the Science of Sintering [*Belgrade, Yugoslavia*] (EAIO) .... IISS
International Institute for the Study of Death (EA) .... IISD
International Institute for the Study of Death and Immortality [*Later, IISD*] (EA) .... IISDI
International Institute for the Unification of Private Law. Yearbook [*Rome, Italy*] [*A publication*] (DLA) .... Unidroit Yb
International Institute for Traditional Music [*Germany*] (EAIO) .... IITM
International Institute for Visually Impaired, Zero-7 (EA) .... IIVI 0-7
International Institute for Women's Political Leadership [*Defunct*] (EA) .... IIWPL
International Institute of African Languages and Culture (BARN) .... IIAL

International Institute of Agriculture ... IIA
International Institute of American Ideals (EA) ... IIAI
International Institute of Ammonia Refrigeration (EA) ... IIAR
International Institute of Andragogy [*See also INSTIA*] (EAIO) ... IIA
[*The*] **International Institute of Applied Linguistics** ... TIIAL
International Institute of Arts and Letters ... IIAL
International Institute of Biological Control [*CAB International*] [*British*] (IRC) ... IIBC
International Institute of Biological Husbandry [*Ipswich, Suffolk, England*] [*Defunct*] (EAIO) ... IIBH
International Institute of Biotechnology [*University of Kent at Canterbury*] [*British*] (IRC) ... IIB
International Institute of Carpet and Upholstery Certification (EA) ... IICUC
International Institute of Cellular and Molecular Pathology [*Belgium*] (IRC) ... ICP
International Institute of Children's Nature and Their Rights (EA) ... IICNTR
International Institute of Communications [*Formerly, IBI*] (EA) ... IIC
International Institute of Communications ... IIC
International Institute of Dental Ergonomics and Technology [*Germany*] (EAIO) ... IIDET
International Institute of Embryology [*Later, ISDB*] ... IIE
International Institute of Films on Art ... IIFA
International Institute of Fisheries Economics and Trade (EA) ... IIFET
International Institute of Foods and Family Living (EA) ... IIFFL
International Institute of Forecasters [*See also IIM*] (EA) ... IIF
International Institute of Genetics and Biophysics [*Italy*] ... IIGB
International Institute of Health and Holistic Therapies [*British*] ... IIHHT
International Institute of Human Rights (EA) ... IIHR
International Institute of Humanitarian Law [*See also IIDH*] [*San Remo, Italy*] (EAIO) ... IIHL
International Institute of Iberoamerican Literature (EA) ... IIIL
International Institute of Instructional Technology [*British*] ... IIIT
International Institute of Integral Human Sciences [*See also IISHI*] (EAIO) ... IIIHS
International Institute of Intellectual Cooperation of the League of Nations [*Obsolete*] ... IIIC (LN)
International Institute of Interpreters [*United Nations*] (BARN) ... III
International Institute of Investment and Merchant Banking [*Washington, DC*] (EA) ... IIIMB
International Institute of Islamic Thought (EA) ... IIIT
International Institute of Law of the French Speaking Countries [*See also IDEF*] [*Paris, France*] (EAIO) ... IILFSC
International Institute of Maritime Culture (EA) ... IIMC
International Institute of Municipal Clerks (EA) ... IIMC
International Institute of Novel Computing [*Japan*] ... IINC
International Institute of Nuclear Science and Engineering ... IINSE
International Institute of Philosophy (AEBS) ... IIP
International Institute of Practical Geomancy [*Formerly, Society for Symbolic Studies*] (EA) ... IIPG
International Institute of Public Finance [*Saarbrucken, Federal Republic of Germany*] (EAIO) ... IIPF
International Institute of Rehabilitation [*Defunct*] (EA) ... IIR
International Institute of Rural Reconstruction (EA) ... IIRR
International Institute of Seismology and Earthquake Engineering [*Japan*] [*Seismograph station code, US Geological Survey*] (SEIS) ... IIS
International Institute of Site Planning (EA) ... IISP
International Institute of Social Economics [*Hull, England*] (EAIO) ... IISE
International Institute of Sociology ... IIS
International Institute of Space Law [*Baarn, Netherlands*] (EAIO) ... IISL
International Institute of Sports Therapy [*British*] ... IIST
International Institute of Stress (EA) ... IIS
International Institute of Stress [*Institut International du Stress*] **Montreal, Quebec** [*Library symbol Obsolete National Library of Canada*] (NLC) ... QMIIST
International Institute of Synthetic Rubber Producers (EA) ... IISRP
International Institute of Tropical Agriculture [*Ibadan, Nigeria*] [*Research center*] (EAIO) ... IITA
International Institute of Valuers (EA) ... IIV
International Institute of Welding [*See also IIS*] [*British*] (EAIO) ... IIW
International Institutional Services (EA) ... IIS
International Insurance Advisory Council [*Later, IIC*] (EA) ... IIAC
International Insurance Council (EA) ... IIC
International Insurance Intelligence ... III
International Insurance Seminars [*University, AL*] (EA) ... IIS
International Insurance Society (EAIO) ... IIS
International Intellectual Property Association (EA) ... IIPA
International Intelligence, Inc. ... INTERTEL
International Intelligent Buildings Association [*Washington, DC*] (EA) ... IIBA
International Interactive Communications Society [*San Francisco, CA*] [*Telecommunications service*] (TSSD) ... IICS
International Interchangeability ... I2
International Inter-Church Film Center [*Hilversum, Netherlands*] (EAIO) ... INTERFILM
International Interdependent Research and Development (AABC) ... IIRD
International Interest and Exchange Rate Database [*Citicorp Database Services*] [*Information service or system*] (IID) ... FXBASE
International Intersociety Committee on Pathology ... IICP
International Intertrade Index [*No longer available online*] [*Information service or system*] (IID) ... III
International Inter-Visitation Program in Educational Administration [*UniverstiyCouncil for Educational Administration*] (AEE) ... IIP
International Intra-Ocular Implant Club (EAIO) ... IIOIC
International Inventor's Association [*Defunct*] (EA) ... IIA
International Inventors Registry (NITA) ... IIR
International Investment Bank [*Moscow, USSR*] ... IIB
International Investment Monitor [*Global Analysis Systems*] [*Information service or system*] (CRD) ... IIM
International Investment Trust ... IIT
International Investors Association (EA) ... IIA
International Ionarc, Inc. [*Vancouver Stock Exchange symbol*] ... IIC
International Iron and Steel Institute [*Brussels, Belgium*] [*Research center*] (EA) ... IISI
International Irrigation Information Center (IID) ... IIIC
International Irrigation Management Institute [*Sri Lanka*] [*Research center*] (IRC) ... IIMI
International Irrigation Management Institute (GNE) ... IMMI
International Irwin Allen Fan Club (EA) ... IIAFC
International Islamic Federation of Student Organizations [*Salimiyan, Kuwait*] (EAIO) ... IIFSO
International Islamic News Agency [*Jeddah, Saudi Arabia*] (EAIO) ... IINA
International Isotope Society (EA) ... IIS
International Jacques Brel Foundation (EA) ... IJBF
International Jacques Maritain Institute [*See also IIJM*] (EAIO) ... IJMI
International Jazz Federation (EA) ... IJF
International Jelly and Preserve Association (EA) ... IJPA
International Jensen, Inc. [*NASDAQ symbol*] (SAG) ... IJIN
International Jensen, Inc. [*Associated Press*] (SAG) ... IntJen
International Jet Ski Boating Association (EA) ... IJSBA
International Jewelry Workers Union [*Later, Service Employees International Union*] (EA) ... IJWU
International Jewelry Workers Union [*Later, Service Employees International Union*] ... JWU
International Jewish Committee on Interreligious Consultations (EA) ... IJCIC
International Jewish Labor Bund (EA) ... IJLB
International Jewish Sports Hall of Fame ... IJSHOF
International Jewish Vegetarian Society [*Formerly, Jewish Vegetarian Society*] (EA) ... IVJS
International John Steinbeck Society (EA) ... IJSS
International Joint Commission (EA) ... IJC
International Joint Commission, Ottawa, ON, Canada [*Library symbol*] [*Library of Congress*] (LCLS) ... CaOOIJC
International Joint Commission [*Commission Mixte Internationale*], Ottawa, Ontario [*Library symbol National Library of Canada*] (NLC) ... OOIJC
International Joint Commission, Windsor, ON, Canada [*Library symbol Library of Congress*] (LCLS) ... CaOWIJC
International Joint Commission [*Commission Mixte Internationale*] **Windsor, Ontario** [*Library symbol National Library of Canada*] (NLC) ... OWIJC
International Joint Conference on Artificial Intelligence ... IJCAI
International Joint Conference on Neural Networks ... IJCNN
International Joint Rules Committee on Softball [*Later, ASA*] (EA) ... IJRCS
International Joseph Diseases Association (EA) ... IJDA
International Joseph Diseases Foundation (EA) ... IJDF
International Journal of African Historical Studies [*A publication*] ... IJAHS
International Journal of Criminology and Penology [*A publication*] (DLA) ... Int J Criminol
International Journal of Criminology and Penology [*A publication*] (DLA) ... Int'l J Crim & Pen
International Journal of Criminology and Penology [*A publication*] (DLA) ... Int'l J Crimin & Penol
International Journal of Impotence Research [*A publication*] ... IJIR
International Journal of Legal Research [*A publication*] (DLA) ... Internat J of Leg Res
International Journal of Legal Research [*A publication*] (DLA) ... Int'l J Legal Res
International Journal of Leprosy [*A publication*] ... IJL
International Journal of Micrographics and Video Technology [*A publication*] ... IJMVT
International Journal of Offender Therapy and Comparative Criminology [*A publication*] (DLA) ... Int'l J Off Ther & Comp Crim
International Journal of Osteoarchaeology [*A publication*] ... IJO
International Journal of Politics [*A publication*] (DLA) ... Int J Pol
International Jugglers Association (EA) ... IJA
International Junior Brangus Breeders Association (EA) ... IJBBA
International Juridical Association. Bulletin [*A publication*] (DLA) ... Int Jurid Assn Bull
International Juridical Association. Bulletin [*A publication*] (DLA) ... Int'l Jurid Ass'n Bull
International Juridical Organization [*Later, IJOED*] (EAIO) ... IJO
International Juridical Organization for Environment and Development (EAIO) ... IJOED
International Justice Network [*Defunct*] (EA) ... IJN
International Juvenile Officers' Association (EA) ... IJOA
International Juvenile Publications ... IJP
International Kart Federation (EA) ... IKF
International Kenergy Resource Corp. [*Vancouver Stock Exchange symbol*] ... INE
International Kennel Club of Chicago (EA) ... IKC
International Kids Fashion Show (ITD) ... IKFS
International Kirlian Research Association (EA) ... IKRA
International Kitefliers Association [*Defunct*] (EA) ... IKA
International Klaus Tennstedt Society [*Defunct*] (EA) ... IKTS
International Klein Blue [*Color named after French painter Yves Klein*] ... IKB
International Knife and Fork Clubs (EA) ... IKFC
International Kodak Historical Society (EA) ... IKHS
International Kodaly Society (EAIO) ... IKS
International Kolping Society [*See also IKW*] [*Cologne, Federal Republic of Germany*] (EAIO) ... IKS
International Korfball Federation (EA) ... IKF
International Kraft Federation (EA) ... IKF
International Labelling Centre [*Defunct*] (EA) ... ILC
International Labor and Working Class History Study Group (EA) ... ILWCHSG

International Labor Communications Association (EA) .... ILCA
International Labor Conference [*A section of the International Labor Organization*] [*United Nations*] ILC
International Labor Defense [*An association*] .... ILD
International Labor History Association .... ILHA
International Labor Office [*A section of the International Labor Organization*] [*United Nations*] .... ILO
International Labor Organization, Bureau of Statistics Database (GFGA) .... LABORSTAT
International Labor Organization Staff Union [*Geneva, Switzerland*] (EAIO) .... ILOSU
International Labor Press Association (EA) .... ILPA
International Labor Rights Education and Research Fund (EA) .... ILRERF
International Labor Rights Working Group (EA) .... ILRWG
International Laboratory Accreditation Conference [*Gaithersburg, MD*] [*National Institute of Standards and Technology*] (EGAO) .... ILAC
International Laboratory for Research on Animal Diseases [*Nairobi, Kenya*] .... ILRAD
International Laboratory of Genetics and Biophysics .... ILGB
International Labour Documentation [*International Labour Office*] [*Geneva, Switzerland Bibliographic database*] .... LABORDOC
International Labour Film Institute [*Defunct*] .... ILFI
International Labour Office, Montreal, PQ, Canada [*Library symbol Library of Congress*] (LCLS) .... CaQMILO
International Labour Office [*Bureau International du Travail*] **Montreal, Quebec** [*Library symbol National Library of Canada*] (NLC) .... QMILO
International Labour Organisation [*Geneva, Switzerland*] [*United Nations*] (EA) .... ILO
International Labour Reports [*A publication*] (DLA) .... Int'l Lab Reports
International Labour Review [*A publication*] (BRI) .... ILR
International Laco Resources [*Vancouver Stock Exchange symbol*] .... ILR
International Lacrosse Federation (EA) .... ILF
International Lactation Consultant Association (EA) .... ILCA
International Ladies' Garment Workers' Union (EA) .... ILGWU
International Laity and Christian Community Group [*See also LAEEC*] [*Sion, Switzerland*] [*Defunct*] (EAIO) .... ILCCG
International Land Development Consultants Ltd. .... ILACO
International Landworkers' Federation [*Later, IFPAAW*] .... ILF
International Language for Aviation .... ILA
International Language for Servicing and Maintenance (PDAA) .... ILSAM
International Language Society of Great Britain .... ILSGB
International Larder Minerals, Inc. [*Toronto Stock Exchange symbol*] ILL
International Laser Acupuncture Society (EA) .... ILAS
International LASER Display Association (EA) .... ILDA
International LASER RADAR Conference (PDAA) .... ILRC
International Laser Tech, Inc. [*Vancouver Stock Exchange symbol*] ILV
International Latex Corp. ILC
International Latitude Service .... ILS
International Laughter Society [*Commercial firm*] (EA) .... ILS
International Laundry Association .... ILA
International Law [*A publication*] (DLA) .... Int'l Law
International Law Association [*British*] (EA) .... ILA
International Law Bulletin [*A publication*] (DLA) .... Int L Bull
International Law Commission [*United Nations*] ILC
International Law Commission (USDC) ILC
International Law Commission [*United Nations*] (DLA) .... Int'l L Comm'n
International Law Commission of the United Nations .... ILC (UN)
International Law Documents [*A publication*] (DLA) .... Int'l L Doc
International Law Enforcement Officers Association (EA) .... ILEOA
International Law Enforcement Stress Association (EA) .... ILESA
International Law Institute (EA) ILI
International Law News [*A publication*] .... ILN
International Law Notes [*England*] [*A publication*] (DLA) .... Int L Notes
International Law Notes [*A publication*] (DLA) .... Int LN
International Law Notes [*London*] [*A publication*] (DLA) .... Interna LN
International Law Notes [*A publication*] (DLA) .... Internat LN
International Law Perspective [*A publication*] (DLA) .... Int'l L Persp
International Law Quarterly [*A publication*] (AAGC) .... ILQ
International Law Reports [*A publication*] .... ILR
International Law Reports [*A publication*] (DLA) .... Int'l L Rep
International Law Reports [*A publication*] .... Int'l LR
International Law Reports [*A publication*] (DI) .... IntLR
International Law Students Association (EAIO) .... ILSA
International Law Studies [*Naval War College*] [*A publication*] (DLA) .... Int'l L Stud
International Law Tracts [*A publication*] (DLA) .... Int Law Tr
International Lawn Hockey Federation .... IHF
International Lawn Tennis Federation [*Later, ITF*] .... ILTF
International Lawyers in Alcoholics Anonymous (EA) .... ILAA
International Lead and Zinc Study Group [*British*] (EA) .... ILZSG
International Lead Zinc Research Organization (EA) .... ILZRO
International Leadership Center [*Defunct*] (EA) ILC
International Leadership Training Conference .... ILTC
International League [*Baseball*] IL
International League Against Epilepsy (EA) .... ILAE
International League Against Rheumatism (EA) .... ILAR
International League for Animal Rights (EA) .... ILAR
International League for Bolivarian Action (EA) .... ILBA
International League for Human Rights (EA) .... ILHR
International League for the Protection of Horses (DI) .... ILPH
International League for the Repatriation of Russian Jews (EA) .... ILRRJ
International League for the Rights and Liberation of Peoples [*Rome, Italy*] (EAIO) .... ILRLP
International League for the Rights of Man [*Later, ILHR*] .... ILRM
International League of Antiquarian Booksellers [*See also LILA*] [*Bonn, Federal Republic of Germany*] (EAIO) .... ILAB
International League of Blind Esperantists [*See also LIBE*] [*Belgrade, Yugoslavia*] (EAIO) .... ILBE
International League of Commercial Travelers and Agents (EA) .... ILCTA
International League of Dermatological Societies [*Vancouver, BC*] (EAIO) .... ILDS
International League of Electrical Associations (EA) .... ILEA
International League of Esperantist Radio Amateurs (EA) .... ILERA
International League of New York .... ILNY
International League of Professional Baseball Clubs (EA) .... ILPBC
International League of Religious Socialists [*Aerdenhout, Netherlands*] (EAIO) .... ILRS
International League of Societies for Persons with Mental Handicap [*Brussels, Belgium*] (EA) .... ILSMH
International League of Women Composers (EA) .... ILWC
International Learning Systems .... ILS
International Leased Telegraph Message Switching Service [*British Telecom*] [*Telecommunications*] (TEL) .... ILTMS
International Leather Goods, Plastic, and Novelty Workers' Union (EA) .... ILGPNWU
International Leather Goods, Plastic, and Novelty Workers' Union (EA) .... LGPN
International Lecithin and Phospholipid Society .... ILPS
International Legal Aid Association [*Defunct*] .... ILAA
International Legal Center [*Formerly, SAILER*] [*Later, International Center for Law and Development*] (EA) ILC
International Legal Center. Newsletter [*A publication*] (DLA) .... ILC Newl
International Legal Defense Counsel (EA) .... ILDC
International Legal Education Newsletter [*A publication*] (DLA) .... Int'l Legal Ed Newsl
International Legal Materials [*A publication*] (DLA) .... Int Legal Materials
International Legal Services Advisory Committee .... ILSAC
International Legion of Intelligence [*Acronym is used as official name of association*] (EA) .... INTERTEL
International Legume Database and Information Service .... ILDIS
International Leisure Group [*Commercial firm British*] .... ILG
International Leisure Hosts Ltd. [*NASDAQ symbol*] (NQ) .... ILHL
International Leisure Hosts Ltd. [*Associated Press*] (SAG) .... IntLeisr
International Lelio Basso Foundation for the Rights and Liberation of Peoples (EA) .... ILBFRLP
International Lending Supervision Act of 1983 .... ILSA
International Leprosy Association [*India*] .... ILA
International Lesbian and Gay Association [*Formerly, International Gay Association*] (EA) .... ILGA
International Liaison Center of Schools of Cinema and Television .... ILOST
International Liaison Committee for Research on Korea .... ILCORK
International Liaison Committee for Reunification and Peace in Korea (EAIO) .... ILCRPK
International Liaison Committee of Organizations for Peace .... ILCOP
International Liaison Committee on Co-Operative Thrift and Credit [*Paris, France*] (EA) .... ILCCTC
International Liaison Forum of Peace Forces [*See also FILFP*] [*Moscow, USSR*] (EAIO) .... ILF
International Library [*A publication*] IL
International Library, Archives, and Museum of Optometry, St. Louis, MO [*Library symbol Library of Congress*] (LCLS) .... MoSIO
International Library Information Center (EA) ILIC
International Library of Philosophy, Psychology, and Scientific Method [*Book publishing*] [*British*] .... ILPPSM
International Library of Sports and Pastimes [*A publication*] .... ILSP
International Licensed Carrier [*Telecommunications*] ILC
International Licensing and Merchandisers' Association [*Later, ILIMA*] (EA) .... ILMA
International Licensing Industry and Merchandisers' Association (EA) .... ILIMA
International Life Sciences Institute [*Later, ILSI-NF*] (EA) .... ILSI
International Life Sciences Institute - Nutrition Foundation (EA) .... ILSI-NF
International Life Services, Inc. (EA) .... ILSI
International Lifeboat Federation [*England*] (EAIO) .... ILF
International Life-Saving Appliance Manufacturers Association (PDAA) .... ILAMA
International Lifesaving Museum and Water Safety Center [*Defunct*] (EA) .... ILMWSC
International Light Tackle Tournament Association (EA) .... ILTTA
International Lightning Class Association (EA) .... ILCA
International Lilac Society (EA) .... ILS
International Limnological Society [*See also SIL*] (ASF) .... ILS
International Line Selector .... ILS
International Linen Promotion Commission (EA) .... ILPC
International Lines of Communication (MCD) ILC
International Links Program [*Overseas aid*] [*Australia*] .... ILP
International List IL
International Listening Association (EA) .... ILA
International Literacy Year .... ILY
International Literary and Information Centre in Science Extension (IID) .... INTERBRIGHT
International Literary Market Place [*A publication*] .... ILMP
International Livestock Brand and Theft Conference (EA) .... ILBTC
International Livestock Brand Conference (EA) .... ILBC
International Livestock Centre for Africa [*Addis Ababa, Ethiopia*] .... ILCA
International Livestock Investigators Association (EA) .... ILIA
International Llama Association (EA) .... ILA
International Log Rolling Association .... ILRA
International Logistics (AABC) IL
International Logistics Center [*Army*] ILC
International Logistics Control Office .... ILCO
International Logistics Control Office (AAGC) .... ILCO
International Logistics Field Office [*Army*] (AABC) .... ILFO
International Logistics Functional Coordinating Group (MCD) .... ILFCG

International Logistics Information File (MCD) ... ILIF
International Logistics Negotiations [*Military export sales*] ... ILN
International Logistics Program ... ILP
International Logistics Supply Delivery Plan (MCD) ... ILSDP
International Logistics Supply Performance Improvement Program (NG) ... ILSPIP
International Logistics Training ... ILT
International Long-Range Reconnaissance Patrol ... ILRRP
International Longshoremen's and Warehousemen's Union (EA) ... ILWU
International Longshoremen's and Warehousemen's Union, San Francisco, CA [*Library symbol Library of Congress*] (LCLS) ... CSfIL
International Longshoremen's Association (EA) ... ILA
International Lottery & Totalizator Systems [*Associated Press*] (SAG) ... IntLotTot
International Lottery & Totalizator Systems [*NASDAQ symbol*] (SAG) ... ITSI
International Lottery, Inc. [*AMEX symbol*] (SAG) ... ILI
International Lottery, Inc. [*Associated Press*] (SAG) ... IntLotry
International Lotto Fund ... ILF
International Low Water ... ILW
International Lubricant Standardization and Approval Committee [*Automotive engine oils*] ... ILSAC
International Luge Federation [*Austria*] ... ILF
International Luggage Registry [*Computer system for recovery of airline luggage*] ... ILR
International Lunar Society [*Spain*] ... ILS
International Lutheran Deaf Association (EA) ... ILDA
International Lutheran Laymen's League (EA) ... ILLL
International Lutheran Laymen's League (EA) ... Int'l LLL
International Lutheran Women's Missionary League (EA) ... ILWML
International M [*formerly, Mensa*] **Philatelists Society** (EA) ... IMPS
International Machine Readable Catalogue ... INTERMARC
International Machine Tool Show (ITD) ... IMTS
International Machinery Insurers Association [*Munich, Federal Republic of Germany*] (EAIO) ... IMIA
International Magazine Collection [*JA Micropublishing, Inc.*] [*Eastchester, NY*] [*Information service or system*] (IID) ... IMC
International Maggie Mines Ltd. [*Vancouver Stock Exchange symbol*] ... IMM
International Magic Dealers Association (EA) ... IMDA
International Magnesium Association (EA) ... IMA
International Magnetospheric Explorer [*NASA/ESRO*] ... IME
International Magnetospheric Study [*1976-78*] [*National Science Foundation*] ... IMS
International Magnetospheric Study / Satellite Situation Committee [*NASA*] (PDAA) ... IMS/SSC
International Mahogany Corp. [*Toronto Stock Exchange symbol Vancouver Stock Exchange symbol*] ... IMY
International Mail [*A publication*] ... INTMA
International Mail Art Network (EA) ... IMAN
International Mail Dealers Association (EA) ... IMDA
International Mail Gram (MHDB) ... IMG
International Mailbag Club (EA) ... IMC
International Mailers Union [*Later, International Typographical Union*] (EA) ... IMU
International Maintenance Agency ... IMA
International Maintenance Control [*Telecommunications*] ... IMC
International Maintenance Group [*FAA*] (TAG) ... IMG
International Maintenance Institute (EA) ... IMI
International Majestic Holdings Ltd. [*Formerly, Majestic Resources Corp.*] [*Vancouver Stock Exchange symbol*] ... IMH
International Makaoo [*Vancouver Stock Exchange symbol*] ... IMK
International Maledicta Society (EA) ... IMS
International Management and Development Institute ... IMDI
International Management and Engineering Group [*British*] ... IMEG
International Management Association [*Later, AMA/I*] (EA) ... IMA
International Management Center [*Hungary*] (ECON) ... IMC
International Management Communications, Inc. [*Database producer*] ... IMC
International Management Council (EA) ... IMC
International Management Group ... IMG
International Management Institute [*Switzerland*] ... IMI
International Management Services, Inc. [*Framingham, MA*] [*Information service or system*] (IID) ... IMS
International Management Services, Inc. [*Franklyn, MA*] (TSSD) ... IMS INC
International Management Systems Association [*Later, Internet-International Management Systems Association*] (EA) ... IMSA
International Manganese Institute [*France*] (EAIO) ... IMI
International Manufacturers Representatives Association [*Tulsa, OK*] (EA) ... IMRA
International Map Collectors' Society (EAIO) ... IMCoS
International Map Dealers Association (EA) ... IMDA
International Map of the World ... IMW
International Maple Institute ... IMI
International Maple Leaf Resource Corp. [*Vancouver Stock Exchange symbol*] ... IMP
International Maple Syrup Institute (EA) ... IMSI
International Marian Research Institute [*University of Dayton*] [*Research center*] (RCD) ... IMRI
International Marine and Shipping Conference (NOAA) ... IMAS
International Marine Biotechnology Conference ... IMBC
International Marine Environment Award [*Marine science*] (OSRA) ... GPIEM
International Marine Global Change Study [*Research programs*] ... IMAGES
International Marine Radio Aids to Navigation ... IMRAN
International Marine Sciences Affairs Panel [*Defunct*] (USDC) ... IMSAP
International Marine Trades Exhibit and Convention [*National Marine Manufacturers Association*] ... IMTEC
International Marine Transit Association (EA) ... IMTA
International Maritime Bureau [*Research center British*] (IRC) ... IMB
International Maritime Committee ... IMC
International Maritime Consultive Organization ... IMCO
International Maritime Dangerous Goods ... IMDG
International Maritime Dangerous Goods Code (MCD) ... IMDGC
International Maritime Industries Forum [*British*] (EAIO) ... IMIF
International Maritime Mobile [*Telecommunications*] ... IMM
International Maritime Organization [*See also OMI*] [*ICSU London, England*] (EAIO) ... IMO
International Maritime Pilots Association (EAIO) ... IMPA
International Maritime Satellite [*Satellite communications organization*] (NITA) ... INMARSAT
International Maritime Satellite [*Organization*] (DOMA) ... INSMARSAT
International Maritime Satellite Organization ... INMARSAT
International Markatech [*Vancouver Stock Exchange symbol*] ... IMT
International Market Development Program [*Department of Energy*] ... IMD
International Market Intelligence [*Databank originator*] [*Norway*] (NITA) ... IMI
International Market Letter: East Europe [*A publication*] (DLA) ... East Europe
International Marketing Audit Association (EA) ... IMAA
International Marketing Commission [*See also CIM*] [*Brixham, Devonshire, England*] (EAIO) ... IMC
International Marketing Federation [*Paris, France*] (EAIO) ... IMF
International Marketing Handbook [*A publication*] ... IMH
International Marketing Institute (EA) ... IMI
International Marketing Program for Agricultural Commodities and Trade Center [*Washington State University*] [*Research center*] (RCD) ... IMPACT
International Marketing Services ... IMS
International MarketNet [*System of broker work stations created by IBM Corp. and Merrill Lynch & Co.*] [*New York, NY*] ... IMNET
International Martial Arts Federation (EAIO) ... IMAF
International Martial Arts Pen Pal Association [*Defunct*] (EA) ... IMAPPA
International Marxist Group [*British*] (PPW) ... IMG
International Masonry Institute (EA) ... IMI
International Masonry Institute Apprenticeship and Training (EA) ... IMIAT
International Mass Education Movement (EA) ... IMEM
International Mass Media Institute (EA) ... IMMI
International Mass Transit Association (EA) ... IMTA
International Master of Busness Administration [*University of South Carolina*] ... IMBA
International Master Printers Association [*Brussels, Belgium*] ... IMPA
International Match Point [*Game of bridge*] ... IMP
International Material Management Society (EA) ... IMMS
International Materials Conference (DCTA) ... IMC
International Materials Organization (NATG) ... IMO
International Materiel Evaluation Program [*Army*] (RDA) ... IME
International Materiel Evaluation Program [*Army*] (RDA) ... IMEP
International Mathematical and Statistical Libraries, Inc. ... IMSL
International Mathematical Olympiad (RDA) ... IMO
International Mathematical Union [*See also UMI*] [*ICSU Helsinki, Finland*] (EAIO) ... IMU
International Mathematics and Statistics Library [*Marine science*] (OSRA) ... IMSL
International Mathematics and Statistics Library (USDC) ... IMSL
International MC Class Sailboat Racing Association (EA) ... IMCCSRA
International Measurement and Inspection Technology Exposition ... INSPEX
International Measurement System [*Sailing*] ... IMS
International Meat Development Scheme [*United Nations Defunct*] (EAIO) ... IMDS
International Meat Processors Association (EA) ... IMPA
International Mechanism for Appropriate Technology ... IMAT
International Media Buyers Association [*Defunct*] (EA) ... IMBA
International Medical and Research Foundation [*Later, AMREF*] (EA) ... IMRF
International Medical Assistance [*Society*] ... IMA
International Medical Association for Radio and Television [*Brussels, Belgium*] (EAIO) ... IMART
International Medical Centers ... IMC
International Medical Commission for Health and Human Rights [*Switzerland*] ... IMC
International Medical Corps (EA) ... IMC
International Medical Exchange [*Defunct*] (EA) ... IME
International Medical Imagery [*Vancouver Stock Exchange symbol*] ... IIS
International Medical Informatics Association [*IFIP special interest group*] [*Richmond Hill, ON*] (EAIO) ... IMIA
International Medical Information Center, Inc. [*Tokyo, Japan*] ... IMIC
International Medical Research ... IMR
International Medication Systems [*Pharmacology*] (DAVI) ... IMS
International Meditation Society ... IMS
International Meeting Center [*Germany*] (EAIO) ... IMC
International Meeting in Community Service [*Germany*] (EAIO) ... IMCS
International Meeting of Cataloging Experts ... IMCE
International Meeting on Radiation Processing (EA) ... IMRP
International Men's and Boys' Wear Exhibition ... IMBEX
International Merchant Purchases Authorization Care [*Visa*] (RDA) ... IMPAC
International Mercury Owners Association (EA) ... IMOA
International Meridian Resources [*Vancouver Stock Exchange symbol*] ... IRL
International Message Centre [*Vancouver Stock Exchange symbol*] ... IMA
International Messaging Associates [*Commercial firm*] ... IMA
International Messianic Jewish Hebrew Christian Alliance [*British*] (EAIO) ... IMJHCA
International Messianic Outreach (EA) ... IMO
International Metallic Silhouette Association (DICI) ... IMSA
International Metallographic Society (EA) ... IMS
International Metals Acquisition Corp. [*NASDAQ symbol*] (SAG) ... IMAC
International Metals Acquisition Corp. [*Associated Press*] (SAG) ... IntMet
International Metalworkers Federation [*See also FIOM*] [*Geneva, Switzerland*] (EAIO) ... IMF
International Metaphysical Association [*Defunct*] (EA) ... IMA
International Meteorological Committee ... IMC

International Meteorological Institute [*Marine science*] (OSRA) ...... IMI
International Meteorological Organization [*Later, World Meteorological
   Organization*] ...... IMO
International Meteorological Teletype Network Europe (NATG) ...... IMTNE
International Metered Communications ...... IMCO
International Methanol Producers and Consumers Association
   [*British*] ...... IMPCA
International Metric System ...... IMS
International Mexican Bank Ltd. [*British*] (EY) ...... Intermex
International Microcircuit Card Association [*Paris, France*] [*Defunct*]
   (EAIO) ...... INTAMIC
International Microcomputer Exhibition (NITA) ...... IME
International Microcomputer Exposition ...... IME
[*The*] International Microcomputer Information Exchange (EA) ...... TIMIX
International Microcomputer Software, Inc. [*NASDAQ symbol*] (SAG) ...... IMSI
International Microcomputer Software, Inc. [*Associated Press*] (SAG) ...... IntMicr
International Microelectronic Products, Inc. [*Associated Press*] (SAG) ...... IMP
International Microfiche Parts Access Catalogue [*Auto parts*]
   [*A publication*] ...... IMPAC
International Microfilm Journal of Legal Medicine, New York, NY [*Library
   symbol Library of Congress*] (LCLS) ...... IntMJ
International Microform Distribution Service (NITA) ...... IMDS
International Micrographic Congress (EA) ...... IMC
International Microgravity Laboratory ...... IML
International Micro-Print Preservation, Inc. ...... IMP
International Micro-Print Preservation, Inc., New York, NY [*Library symbol
   Library of Congress*] (LCLS) ...... IntMP
International Microprogrammers' Society ...... IMPS
International Microwave Power Institute (EA) ...... IMPI
International Microwave Power Institute (PDAA) ...... IMPL
International Middle East Association (EA) ...... IMEA
International MIDI [*Musical Instrument Digital Interface*] Association (EA) ...... IMA
International Military and Defense Encyclopedia [*A publication*] ...... IMADE
International Military Archives (EA) ...... IMA
International Military Assistance Office ...... IMAO
International Military Club Executives Association (EA) ...... IMCEA
International Military Education and Training [*Program of grant military
   training in the United States for foreign military and civilian personnel*] ...... IMET
International Military Education and Training Program [*DoD*] ...... IMETP
International Military Headquarters (CINC) ...... IMHQ
International Military Police [*NATO*] ...... INTERMILPOL
International Military Rationalization, Standardization, and Interoperability
   (RDA) ...... IM-RSI
International Military Recreation Association [*Defunct*] (EA) ...... IMRA
International Military Services Ltd. [*Ministry of Defence*] [*British*] ...... IMS
International Military Staff [*NATO*] ...... IMS
International Military Staff Communication [*NATO*] (NATG) ...... IMSCOM
International Military Staff Memorandum [*NATO*] (NATG) ...... IMSM
International Military Staff Memorandum [*NATO*] (NATG) ...... MILSTAM
International Military Staff Summary [*NATO*] (NATG) ...... IMSUM
International Military Staff Working Memorandum [*NATO*] (NATG) ...... IMSWM
International Military Tribunal [*Post-World War II*] ...... IMT
International Military Tribunal for Europe [*Post-World War II*] ...... IMTE
International Military Tribunal for Japan [*Post-World War II*] ...... IMTFJ
International Milling Association [*See also AIM*] [*Brussels, Belgium*]
   (EAIO) ...... IMA
International Milliunit ...... IMU
International Mimes and Pantomimists [*Defunct*] ...... IMP
International Mine Water Association [*Madrid, Spain*] (EAIO) ...... IMWA
International Mineralogical Association [*ICSU*] [*Marburg, Federal Republic of
   Germany*] (EA) ...... IMA
International Minerals & Chemical Corp. ...... IMC
International Miniature Horse Registry (EA) ...... IMHR
International Minilab Association (EA) ...... IMA
International Ministerial Federation [*Defunct*] (EA) ...... IMF
International Ministers' and Widows' Association (EA) ...... IMWA
International Ministries to Israel (EA) ...... IMI
International Mirtone, Inc. [*Toronto Stock Exchange symbol*] ...... IME
International Mission Board ...... IMB
International Mission Radio Association (EA) ...... IMRA
International Missionary Council [*Later, CWME*] ...... IMC
International Missions [*An association*] (EA) ...... IM
International Missions (EA) ...... IMI
International Mobile Air Conditioning Association (EA) ...... IMACA
International Mobile Telecommunications for the Year 2000 ...... IMT-2000
International Mobjack Association (EA) ...... IMA
International Model Managers Association (EA) ...... IMMA
International Model Power Boat Association (EA) ...... IMPBA
International Mohair Association (EAIO) ...... IMA
International Molders' and Allied Workers' Union [*AFL-CIO*] (EA) ...... IM & AWU
International Molders' and Allied Workers' Union [*AFL-CIO*] ...... IMAW
International Molders' and Foundry Workers' Union of North America
   [*Later, IM &AWU*] ...... IMFWUNA
[*The*] International Molinological Society (EA) ...... TIMS
International Monetary Conference (ECON) ...... IMC
International Monetary Fund [*United Nations*] (EA) ...... IMF
International Monetary Fund and International Bank for Reconstruction
   and Development ...... IMF/IBRD
International Monetary Fund and International Bank for Reconstruction
   and Development, Joint Bank-Fund Library, Washington, DC [*Library
   symbol*] [*Library of Congress*] (LCLS) ...... DJBF
International Monetary Market [*Chicago Mercantile Exchange*] ...... IMM
International Money Management [*Business term*] ...... IMM
International Money Order [*Business term*] (DS) ...... IMO
International Monitor for Auroral Geomagnetic Effects ...... IMAGE

International Monitoring System [*For nuclear tests*] ...... IMS
International Montessori Society ...... IMS
International Morab Breeders Association (EA) ...... IMBA
International Morse Code (ADDR) ...... IMC
International Moth Class Association - US (EA) ...... IMCA-US
International Motion Picture and Lecturers Association (EA) ...... IMPALA
International Motor Contest Association (EA) ...... IMCA
International Motor Press Association (EA) ...... IMPA
International Motor Sports Association (EA) ...... IMSA
International Motor Sports Hall of Fame [*Automotive racing history*] ...... IMHOF
International Motor Vehicle Inspection Committee [*Belgium*] (EAIO) ...... IMVIC
International Motor Vehicle Program [*MIT*] ...... IMVP
International Motorcycle Manufacturers Association (EAIO) ...... IMMA
International Mountain Bicycling Association (EA) ...... IMBA
International Mountain Society (EA) ...... IMS
International Movement ATD Fourth World [*France*] (EAIO) ...... IMATDFW
International Movement for Atlantic Union ...... IMAU
International Movement for Therapeutic Free Choice [*France*] (EAIO) ...... IMTFC
International Movement of Apostolate of Children [*Paris, France*] (EA) ...... IMAC
International Movement of Catholic Agricultural and Rural Youth [*See also
   MIJARC*] [*Louvain, Belgium*] (EAIO) ...... IMCARY
International Movement of Catholic Agricultural and Rural Youth G2 [*See
   also MIJARC*] ...... IMCAR
International Movement of Catholic Jurists (EAIO) ...... IMCJ
International Movement of Catholic Lawyers [*France*] ...... IMCL
International Movement of Catholic Students [*France*] ...... IMCS
International Movement of Catholic Students [*France*] ...... INTL
International Movement of Catholic Students - African Secretariat [*An
   association*] (EAIO) ...... IMCSAC
International Movement of Conscientious War Resisters [*Tel Aviv, Israel*]
   (EAIO) ...... IMCWR
International Movement of Esperantist Bicyclists [*See also BEMI*] [*The
   Hague, Netherlands*] (EAIO) ...... IMEB
International Movements toward Educational Change [*Later, IMTEC-The
   International Learning Cooperative*] (EAIO) ...... IMTEC
International Movie Group, Inc. [*Vancouver Stock Exchange symbol*] ...... IMV
International MTM [*Methods-Time-Measurement*] Directorate (EA) ...... IMD
International Multicenter Angina Exercise (DMAA) ...... IMAGE
International Multifoods Corp. [*NYSE symbol*] (SPSG) ...... IMC
International Multifoods Corp. [*Associated Press*] (SAG) ...... IntMult
International Multihull Society [*Formerly, International Hydrofoil and Multihull
   Society*] [*Defunct*] ...... IMS
International Multimedia Teleconferencing Consortium ...... IMTC
International Municipal Signal Association (EA) ...... IMSA
International Murex Technologies [*Associated Press*] (SAG) ...... IntMur
International Murex Technologies [*NASDAQ symbol*] (SAG) ...... MURXF
International Musa Testing Program [*United Nations*] (ECON) ...... IMTP
International Museum of Photography, Eastman House, Rochester, NY
   [*OCLC symbol*] (OCLC) ...... VZZ
International Museum Photographers Association (EA) ...... IMPA
International Mushroom Society for the Tropics (EAIO) ...... IMST
International Music Association ...... IMA
International Music Conference (AEBS) ...... IMC
International Music Council [*Paris, France*] (EA) ...... IMC
International Music Guide [*A publication*] ...... IMG
International Music Industry Conference ...... IMIC
International Musician, Newark, NJ [*Library symbol Library of Congress*]
   (LCLS) ...... NjNIM
International Musicological Society [*Basel, Switzerland*] (EA) ...... IMS
International Muslim Students Union (EA) ...... IMSU
International Mycological Association [*See also AIM*] [*England*] (EAIO) ...... IMA
International Mycophagist Association (EA) ...... IMA
International Myomassethics Federation (EA) ...... IMF
International Myopia Prevention Association (EA) ...... IMPA
International Myopia Prevention Centre (DAVI) ...... IMPC
International Nanny Association (EA) ...... INA
International Naples Sabot Association (EA) ...... INSA
International Narcotic Enforcement Officers Association (EA) ...... INEOA
International Narcotics Control Act ...... INCA
International Narcotics Control Board (DMAA) ...... INCB
International Narcotics Control Strategy Report [*Department of State*] ...... INCSR
International Narcotics Matters [*Department of State*] ...... INM
International Natural Rubber Organization [*Kuala Lumpur, Malaysia*]
   (EAIO) ...... INRO
International Natural Sausage Casing Association (EA) ...... INSCA
International Naturist Federation [*Antwerp, Belgium*] (EA) ...... INF
International Naturopathic Association [*Later, IAHHP*] (EA) ...... INA
International Nautical Mile ...... INM
International Naval Research Organization (EA) ...... INRO
International Navigation System ...... INS
International Negotiating Committee [*World Resources Institute*] ...... INC
International Netsuke Collectors Society [*Commercial firm*] (EA) ...... INCS
International Network Controlling Center [*Telecommunications*] (TEL) ...... INCC
International Network for Chemical Education [*Samoa*] (EAIO) ...... INCE
International Network for Educational Information (EAIO) ...... INED
International Network for Mutual Help Centers (EA) ...... INMHC
International Network for Religion and Animals (EA) ...... INRA
International Network for Self-Reliance (EA) ...... INS
International Network for Social Network Analysis [*University of Toronto*]
   [*Toronto, ON*] (EAIO) ...... INSNA
International Network for Terminology [*INFOTERM*] [*Vienna, Austria*] ...... TERMNET
International Network for the Improvement of Banana and Plantain [*Affilia
   ted with the Consultative Group on International Agricultural Research*]
   [*France*] ...... INIBAP
International Network Management Center [*Telecommunications*] (TEL) ...... INMC

International Network of Centres for Documentation and Communication Research and Policies (EAIO) .... COMNET
International Network of Children of Jewish Holocaust Survivors (EA) .... INCJHS
International Network of Communication Documentation Centres [*Formerly, International Network of Centers for Documentation and Communication Research and Policies*] [*France*] (EAIO) .... COMNET
International Network of Feed Information Centers (EA) .... INFIC
International Network of Food Data Systems [*Massachusets Institute of Technology*] [*Cambridge*] [*Information service or system*] (IID) .... INFOODS
International Network of Women Liberals (EAIO) .... INWL
International Network on Genetic Evaluation in Rice (ECON) .... INGER
International Network Services [*NASDAQ symbol*] (SAG) .... INSS
International Network Services [*Associated Press*] (SAG) .... IntlNtwk
International Network Working Group [*International Federation for Information Processing*] .... INWG
International Neural Network Society (EA) .... INNS
International Neuroblastoma Staging System [*Medicine*] (DMAA) .... INSS
International Neurological Association (DAVI) .... INA
International Neurotoxicology Association .... INA
International New Thought Alliance (EA) .... INTA
International News [*Database*] (IT) .... INTNEW
International News Photo .... INP
International News Service [*Later, UPI*] .... INS
International Newsletter of Special Libraries [*A publication*] .... INSPEL
International Newspaper Advertising and Marketing Executives (EA) .... INAME
International Newspaper Advertising Executives [*Later, INAME*] (EA) .... INAE
International Newspaper and Colour Association [*Later, IFRA*] (EA) .... INCA
International Newspaper Collector's Club (EA) .... INCC
International Newspaper Financial Executives (EA) .... INFE
International Newspaper Group (EA) .... ING
International Newspaper Marketing Association (EA) .... INMA
International Newspaper Promotion Association (EA) .... INPA
International Newsreel and News Film Association [*Later, INANEWS*] (EAIO) .... INA
International Newsreel and News Film Association [*Belgium*] (EAIO) .... INNA
International Newsreel Association (EAIO) .... INANEWS
International Nick Tate Club (EAIO) .... INTC
International Nickel Co. .... INCO
International Nickel Co. of Canada Ltd., Toronto, Ontario [*Library symbol National Library of Canada*] (NLC) .... OTIN
International Nickel Co. of Canada, Mississauga, ON, Canada [*Library symbol Library of Congress*] (LCLS) .... CaOMIN
International Nickel Co. of Canada, Toronto, ON, Canada [*Library symbol Library of Congress*] (LCLS) .... CaOTIN
International Nickel Co., Technical Library, New York, NY [*Library symbol Library of Congress*] (LCLS) .... NNIND
International Nippon Collectors Club (EA) .... INCC
International Non-Governmental Organization .... INGO
International Nongovernmental Youth Organization (PDAA) .... INGYO
International Nonproprietary Names [*World Health Organization*] .... INN
International Nonviolent Initiatives (EA) .... INI
International Normal Atmosphere .... INA
International Normalized Ratio [*Hematology*] .... INR
International North American Resources, Inc. [*Vancouver Stock Exchange symbol*] .... INJ
International North Pacific Fisheries Commission (EA) .... INPFC
International North Pacific Fisheries Commission, United States Section .... INPFC-US
International North Pacific Fisheries, Vancouver, BC, Canada [*Library symbol Library of Congress*] (LCLS) .... CaBVal
International North Pacific Fisheries, Vancouver, British Columbia [*Library symbol National Library of Canada*] (NLC) .... BVAI
International Norton Owners' Association (EA) .... INOA
International NOTAM Office [*ICAO designator*] (ICDA) .... YN
International Nubian Breeders Association (EA) .... INBA
International Nuclear and Energy Association [*Defunct*] (EA) .... IN & EA
International Nuclear Corp., Denver, CO [*Library symbol Library of Congress*] (LCLS) .... CoDIN
International Nuclear Credit Bank (NRCH) .... INCB
International Nuclear Data Committee [*of International Atomic Energy Agency*] .... INDC
International Nuclear Event Scale .... INES
International Nuclear Forces (NATG) .... INF
International Nuclear Fuel Authority .... INFA
International Nuclear Fuel Cycle Evaluation .... INFCE
International Nuclear Information System [*International Atomic Energy Agency*] (IID) .... INIS
International Nuclear Information System [*International Atomic Energy Agency*] [*Vienna, Austria Bibliographic database*] .... INIS ATOMINDEX
International Nuclear Law Association [*See also AIDN*] [*Brussels, Belgium*] (EAIO) .... INLA
International Nuclear Model [*Department of Energy*] (GFGA) .... INM
International Nuclear Safety Advisory Group [*United Nations*] (EY) .... INSAG
International Number Dialing [*Telecommunications*] (TEL) .... IND
International Numbering System for Tides (MSC) .... INST
International Numismatic Commission .... INC
International Numismatic Society (EAIO) .... INS
International Numismatic Society Authentication Bureau (EA) .... INSAB
International Nurse Education Program .... INEP
International Nurses Anonymous (EA) .... INA
International Nursing Services, Inc. [*Associated Press*] (SAG) .... IntlNurs
International Nursing Services, Inc. [*Associated Press*] (SAG) .... IntNur
International Nursing Services, Inc. [*NASDAQ symbol*] (SAG) .... NURS
International Nursing Svcs [*NASDAQ symbol*] (TTSB) .... NURS
International Nursing Wrrt [*NASDAQ symbol*] (TTSB) .... NURSW
International Nut Council (EAIO) .... INC
International Nutrition & Genetics Corp. [*Vancouver Stock Exchange symbol*] .... INU
International Nutrition Research Foundation (EA) .... INRF
International Nutritional Immunology Group (EA) .... INIG
International Observations (DNAB) .... INTEROBS
International Occultation Timing Association (EA) .... IOTA
International Ocean Disposal Symposium (EA) .... IODS
International Ocean Institute [*Valetta, Malta*] (EAIO) .... IOI
International Oceanographic Commission [*NASA*] .... IOC
International Oceanographic Data and Information Exchange [*Marine science*] (OSRA) .... IODE
International Oceanographic Data Exchange .... IODE
International Oceanographic Foundation (EA) .... IOF
International Octal (IAA) .... IO
International Oculoplastic Society, Inc. (EA) .... IOSI
International Office for Audiophonology (EA) .... IOA
International Office for Water Education [*Utah State University*] .... IOWE
International Office of Cocoa and Chocolate [*Later, IOCCSC*] (EAIO) .... IOCC
International Office of Cocoa, Chocolate, and Sugar Confectionary [*Belgium*] (EAIO) .... IOCCC
International Office of Cocoa, Chocolate, and Sugar Confectionary [*IOCC a nd International Sugar Confectionary Manufacturers Association*] [*Formed by a merger of*] (EAIO) .... IOCCSC
International Office of Documentation on Military Medicine (EA) .... IODMM
International Office of Epizootics .... IOE
International Officer School [*Military*] .... IOS
International Offshore Rule [*Yachting*] .... IOR
International Oil Compensation Fund .... IOCF
International Oil Industry TBA Group (EA) .... IOITBAG
International Oil Pollution Compensation [*In association name IOPC Fund*] [*See also FIPOL*] .... IOPC
International Oil Pollution Exhibition and Conference (PDAA) .... IOPEC
International Oil Pollution Prevention .... IOPP
International Oil Scouts Association (EA) .... IOSA
International Oil Tanker Terminal Safety Group (PDAA) .... IOTTSG
International Old Lacers (EA) .... IOL
International Old Lacers, Inc. (EA) .... IOLI
International Oleander Society (EA) .... IOS
International Olive Oil Council [*See also COI*] [*Madrid, Spain*] (EAIO) .... IOOC
International Olympic Academy .... IOA
International Olympic Committee .... IOC
International Ombudsman Institute [*University of Alberta*] [*Edmonton, AB*] [*Research center*] (EAIO) .... IOI
International Omega Association (EA) .... IOA
International Online Data Base [*The WEFA Group*] [*Information service or system*] .... INTLINE
International Online Information Meeting .... IOLIM
International Online Information Retrieval Service [*Institute of Scientific and Technical Information of China*] [*Beijing*] [*Information service or system*] (IID) .... IOIRS
International Operations Simulation (IEEE) .... INTOP
International Optical Telecommunications, Inc. [*Information service or system*] (IID) .... IOT
International Options Market [*Australian Options Market, European Options Exchange in Amsterdam, Montreal Exchange, and Vancouver Stock Exchange*] .... IOM
International Optometric and Optical League [*British*] (EAIO) .... IOOL
International Order of Hoo-Hoo (EA) .... IOHH
International Order of Job's Daughters (EA) .... IOJD
International Order of Kabbalists (EA) .... IOK
International Order of Runeberg (EA) .... IOR
International Order of Saint Luke the Physician (EA) .... OSL
International Order of the Armadillo (EA) .... IOA
International Order of the Golden Rule [*Springfield, IL*] (EA) .... IOGR
International Order of the King's Daughters and Sons (EA) .... IOKDS
International Organ Festival Society (EA) .... IOFS
International Organisation for Science and Technology Education (AIE) .... IOSTE
International Organisation for the Elimination of All Forms of Racial Discrimin ation [*Geneva, Switzerland*] (EAIO) .... EAFORD
International Organization Against Trachoma [*Creteil, France*] (EA) .... IOAT
International Organization for Biological Control of Noxious Animals and Plants [*See also OILB*] [*ICSU Montpellier, France*] [*Research center*] (EAIO) .... IOBC
International Organization for Chemical Sciences in Development [*Brussels, Belgium*] (EA) .... IOCD
International Organization for Consumer Co-Operative Distributive Trade (EAIO) .... INTERCOOP
International Organization for Cooperation in Health Care [*See also MMI*] [*Nijmegen, Netherlands*] (EAIO) .... IOCHC
International Organization for Cultivating Human Spirit [*Later, OISCA*] .... IOCHS
International Organization for Forensic Odonto-Stomatology [*Formerly, International Society of Forensic Odonto-Stomatology*] (EA) .... IOFOS
International Organization for Housing Finance Institutions (EA) .... IOHFI
International Organization for Human Ecology (EAIO) .... IOHE
International Organization for Justice and Development (EAIO) .... IOJD
International Organization for Legal Metrology .... IOLM
International Organization for Marine Geology [*Council for Mutual Economic Assistance*] [*Riga, Union of Soviet Socialist Republics Defunct*] (EAIO) .... INTERMORGEO
International Organization for Masoretic Studies .... IOMS
International Organization for Medical Cooperation .... IOMC
International Organization for Medical Physics (DAVI) .... IOMP

International Organization for Migration (EAIO) .... IOM
International Organization for Motor Trades and Repairs [*Rijswljk, Netherlands*] (EAIO) .... IOMTR
International Organization for Mycoplasmology (EA) .... IOM
International Organization for Plant Information .... IOPI
International Organization for Pure and Applied Biophysics .... IOPAB
International Organization for Rural Development .... IORD
International Organization for Septuagint and Cognate Studies (EA) .... IOSCS
International Organization for Standardization [*Official initialism is ISO*] .... IOS
International Organization for Standardization [*Geneva, Switzerland*] [*United Nations*] .... ISO
International Organization for Standardization Draft International Standard (IAA) .... ISODIS
International Organization for Standardization Information Network [*United Nations*] [*Geneva, Switzerland*] (IID) .... ISONET
International Organization for Standardization Open Systems Interconnection Model .... IOS/OSI
International Organization for Technical Cooperation in Geology (EAIO) .... IOTCG
International Organization for the Defense of Human Rights in Iraq (EA) .... IODHRI
International Organization for the Education of the Hearing Impaired (EA) .... IOEHI
International Organization for the Study of Group Tensions (EA) .... IOSGT
International Organization for the Study of Human Development [*Defunct*] (EA) .... IOSHD
International Organization for the Study of the Endurance of Wire Ropes [*Paris, France*] (EAIO) .... IOSEWR
International Organization for the Study of the Old Testament [*British*] .... IOSOT
International Organization for the Transition of Professionals Dancers [*Switzerland*] .... IOTPD
International Organization for Vacuum Science and Technology .... IOVST
International Organization of Biotechnology and Bioengineering [*Guatemala, Guatemala*] .... IOBB
International Organization of Citrus Virologists (EA) .... IOCV
International Organization of Consumers Unions [*The Hague, Netherlands*] (EA) .... IOCU
International Organization of Employers [*Geneva, Switzerland*] .... IOE
International Organization of Experts (EAIO) .... IOE
International Organization of Good Templars [*Oslo, Norway*] (EAIO) .... IOGT
International Organization of Journalists [*See also OIJ*] [*Prague, Czechoslovakia*] (EAIO) .... IOJ
International Organization of Masters, Mates, and Pilots .... IOMMP
International Organization of Masters, Mates, and Pilots (EA) .... MMP
International Organization of Motor Vehicle Manufacturers (EAIO) .... IOMVM
International Organization of Nerds (EA) .... ION
International Organization of Old Testament Scholars .... IOOTS
International Organization of Palaeobotany [*British*] .... IOP
International Organization of Plant Biosystematists [*St. Anne De Bellevue, PQ*] (EA) .... IOPB
International Organization of Psychophysiology [*See also IPO*] [*Montreal, PQ*] (EAIO) .... IOP
International Organization of Space Communications [*Moscow, USSR*] (EAIO) .... INTERSPUTNIK
International Organization of Supreme Audit Institutions [*Vienna, Austria*] (EA) .... INTOSAI
International Organization of the Flavor Industry [*Geneva, Switzerland*] (EAIO) .... IOFI
International Organization of Women Executives [*Defunct*] (EA) .... IOWE
International Organization of Women in Telecommunications [*Defunct*] (TSSD) .... IOWIT
International Organization of Women in Telecommunications [*Defunct*] (EA) .... IOWT
International Organization of Wooden Money Collectors (EA) .... IOWMC
International Organizations [*A publication*] .... IO
International Organizations Procurement Act of 1947 .... IOPA
International Orienteering Federation, Scientific Group [*See also IOFWA*] (EAIO) .... IOFSG
International Originating Toll Center [*Bell System*] .... IOTC
International Ornithological Congress [*New Zealand*] .... IOC
International Orphans, Inc. (EA) .... IOI
International Orthokeratology Society (EA) .... IOS
International Orthoptic Association [*British*] (EAIO) .... IOA
[*The*] **International Osprey Foundation** (EA) .... TIOF
International Osteopathic Association (EA) .... IOA
International Outboard Grand Prix .... IOGP
International Oxygen Manufacturers Association (EA) .... IOMA
International Ozone Association (EA) .... IOA
International Ozone Commission [*IAMAP*] (NOAA) .... IOC
International Ozone Institute [*Later, IOA*] (EA) .... IOI
International Pacific Cypress Minerals Ltd. [*Vancouver Stock Exchange symbol*] .... IPC
International Pacific Halibut Commission (EA) .... IPHC
International Pacific Salmon Fisheries Commission [*Marine science*] (OSRA) .... IPFSC
International Pacific Salmon Fisheries Commission (USDC) .... IPFSC
International Pacific Salmon Fisheries Commission [*Canada*] (EA) .... IPSFC
International Packaging Exhibition [*British*] (ITD) .... PAKEX
International Packaging Material Suppliers (DGA) .... IPACK
International Packaging Material Suppliers Association (PDAA) .... IPACK
International Packet Switch Stream [*Computer science*] .... IPSS
International Packet Switched Service [*Telecommunications system*] (NITA) .... IPSS
International Packet Switching Service [*British Telecom International, Inc.*] [*Telecommunications service*] (TSSD) .... IPSS
International Packet-Switching Service [*MCI International, Inc.*] [*Rye Brook, NY*] [*Telecommunications*] (TSSD) .... IMPACS
International Pact Organization .... IPO
International Paddle Racket Association [*Later, AARA*] .... IPRA
International Paddleball Association [*Later, AARA*] (EA) .... IPA
International PAF User's Group (EA) .... IPAFUG
International Pagurian Corp. Ltd. [*Toronto Stock Exchange symbol Vancouver Stock Exchange symbol*] .... IPG
International Pain Foundation (EA) .... IPF
International Paintball Players Association (EA) .... IPPA
International Palaeontological Association (EA) .... IPA
International Paleoclimatic Data Network .... IPDN
International Paleontological Union .... IPU
International Pallet Recycling Organization (PDAA) .... IPRO
International Palm Society (EA) .... IPS
International Paper Co. [*Associated Press*] (SAG) .... IntPap
International Paper Co. [*NYSE symbol*] (SPSG) .... IP
International Paper Co. (WDMC) .... IPCO
International Paper Co., Corporate Research and Development Division, Technical Information Center, Tuxedo Park, NY [*Library symbol Library of Congress*] (LCLS) .... NTuxpI
International Paracelsus Society [*Salzburg, Austria*] (EA) .... IPS
International Parents' Organization [*Later, PS*] (EA) .... IPO
International Parliamentary Group for Human Rights in the Soviet Union (EA) .... IPG
International Partners Facility .... IPE
International Partners in Prayer (EA) .... IPP
International Passenger Airline Reservations System .... IPARS
International Passenger Ship Association [*Merger of Atlantic Passenger St eamship Conference, Trans-Atlantic Passenger Steamship Conference, Caribbean Cruise Association*] [*Defunct*] .... IPSA
International Patent Agreement .... IPA
International Patent and Trademark Association [*Later, IIPA*] (EA) .... IPTA
International Patent Classification .... IPC
International Patent Documentation Center [*Information service or system*] (IID) .... INPADOC
International Patent Institute [*Later, EPO*] .... IPI
International Patent Research Office (IAA) .... IPRO
International Pathfinder, Inc. [*Toronto Stock Exchange symbol*] .... IPB
International Patient Education Council (EAIO) .... IPEC
International Payment Order (DCTA) .... IPO
International Payments Group (NATG) .... IPG
International PBX [*Private Branch Exchange*]/Telecommunicators (EA) .... IPC
International Peace Academy .... IPA
International Peace Bureau [*Geneva, Switzerland*] (EA) .... IPB
International Peace Campaign .... IPC
International Peace, Communication, and Coordination Center [*The Hague, Netherlands*] (EAIO) .... IPCCC
International Peace, Economy, and Ecology (EA) .... IPEE
International Peace Information Service [*Belgium*] .... IPIS
International Peace Research Association (EA) .... IPRA
International Peace Research Institution, Oslo [*Norway*] .... PRIO
International Peace Walk [*An association*] (EA) .... IPW
International Peasant Union .... IPU
International Peat Society [*See also IMTG*] [*Helsinki, Finland*] (EAIO) .... IPS
International Pectin Producers Association [*Switzerland*] (EAIO) .... IPPA
International Pediatric Association [*See also AIP*] [*Paris, France*] (EAIO) .... IPA
International Pediatric Nephrology (EA) .... IPNA
International PEN [*Official name; PEN, never spelled out in use, is said to stand for poets, playwrights, editors, essayists, novelists*] (EAIO) .... PEN
International PEN - Centre of German-Speaking Writers Abroad (EAIO) .... GSWA
International PEN [*Poets, Playwrights, Editors, Essayists, Novelists*]-Estonian Center (EAIO) .... IPENEB
International Pen Friend Service (EA) .... IPFS
International PEN - Guatemalan Writers Abroad (EA) .... GWA
International PEN - Hong Kong English (EAIO) .... IPENHKE
International PEN - Ireland (EAIO) .... IPENI
International PEN - Scotland (EAIO) .... IPENS
International PEN - United States [*Later, PCUSAW*] (EA) .... IPENUS
International PEN [*Poets, Playwrights, Editors, Essayists, Novelists*]-Writers inExile [*British*] (EAIO) .... IPENWIE
International PEN - Yiddish (EA) .... IPENY
International Penal and Penitentiary Commission [*Later, IPPF*] .... IPPC
International Penal and Penitentiary Foundation [*See also FIPP*] [*Bonn, Federal Republic of Germany*] (EAIO) .... IPPF
International Penguin Class Dinghy Association (EA) .... IPCDA
International Penpal Club (EAIO) .... IPC
International Pen-Pals Association [*Cross River State Pen-Pals Associatio n*] [*Acronym is based on former name,*] (EAIO) .... CRSPPA
International Pentecostal Press Association (EA) .... IPPA
International Pepper Community [*Indonesia*] [*Research center*] (IRC) .... IPC
International Percy Grainger Society (EA) .... IPGS
International Perimetric Society (EA) .... IPS
International Periodical Distributors Association (EA) .... IPDA
International Permanent Bureau of Motor Manufacturers (BARN) .... IPBMM
International Personnel Management Association (EA) .... IPMA
International Peruvian Paso Horse Association (EA) .... IPPHA
International Pesticide Application Research Centre [*Imperial College at Silwood Park*] [*British*] (CB) .... IPARC
International Pesticide Applicators Association (EA) .... IPAA
International Pesticide Institute .... IPI
International Pet Trade Organization [*Defunct*] (EAIO) .... IPTO
International Peter Noone Fan Club (EA) .... IPNFC
International Petroleum Annual [*Department of Energy*] [*Database*] .... IPA
International Petroleum Cartel .... IPC

International Petroleum Co. ... INTERPET
International Petroleum Corp. [*Associated Press*] (SAG) ... IntPtr
International Petroleum Corp. [*Vancouver Stock Exchange symbol Toronto Stock Exchange symbol*] ... IRP
International Petroleum Corp. [*NASDAQ symbol*] (SAG) ... IRPP
International Petroleum Exchange [*British*] ... IPE
International Petroleum Industry Environmental Conservation Association [*British*] (EAIO) ... IPIECA
International Petula Clark Society (EAIO) ... IPCS
International Pharmaceutical Cosmetics, Toiletry, and Allied Industries Exhibition [*England*] ... INTERPHES
International Pharmaceutical Excipients Council (EA) ... IPEC
International Pharmaceutical Federation [*Netherlands*] (EAIO) ... IPF
International Pharmaceutical Students' Federation [*Jerusalem, Israel*] (EAIO) ... IPSF
International Pharmacopoeia [*A publication*] ... Int P
International Pharmacopoeia ... IP
International Pharmacopoeia ... Phl
International Pharmadyne Ltd. [*Vancouver Stock Exchange symbol*] ... IPH
International Phasor Telecom [*Vancouver Stock Exchange symbol*] ... IPX
International Phenomenological Society (EA) ... IPS
International Philatelic Exhibition [*American Stamp Dealers Association*] ... INTERPEX
International Philatelic Press Club (EA) ... IPPC
International Philippine Philatelic Society (EAIO) ... IPPS
International Philosophers for the Prevention of Nuclear Omnicide (EA) ... IPPNO
International Philosophical Quarterly [*A publication*] (BRI) ... IPQ
International Phoenix Energy [*Vancouver Stock Exchange symbol*] ... IPY
International Phonetic Alphabet ... IPA
International Phonetic Association [*University College*] [*Leeds, England*] (EA) ... IPA
International Photo Optical Show Association [*Defunct*] (EA) ... IPOSA
International Photo-Engravers Union [*Later, GAIU*] (EA) ... IPEU
International Photographic Historical Organization (EA) ... InPHO
International Photosynthesis Committee [*Stockholm, Sweden*] (EAIO) ... IPC
International Phototelegraph Position [*Telecommunications*] (TEL) ... IPP
International Phototherapy Association (EA) ... IPA
International Phototherapy Institute [*Defunct*] (EA) ... IPI
International Phycological Society (EA) ... IPS
International Physical Fitness Association (EA) ... IPFA
International Physicians Commission for the Protection of Prisoners (EA) ... IPCPP
International Physicians for the Prevention of Nuclear War (EA) ... IPPNW
International Piano Archives at Maryland, University of Maryland, College Park, MD [*Library symbol Library of Congress*] (LCLS) ... MdU-I
International Piano Guild (EA) ... IPG
International Piano Teachers Association [*Defunct*] ... IPTA
International Pietenpol Association (EA) ... IPA
International Pig Veterinary Society [*Amer, Spain*] (EAIO) ... IPVS
International Pigeon Federation [*See also FCI*] (EAIO) ... IPF
International Pilot Study of Schizophrenia [*WHO*] ... IPSS
International Pin Collectors Club (EA) ... IPCC
International Pinball Association (EA) ... IPA
International Pipe Association [*Later, TPF*] (EA) ... IPA
International Pipe Line and Offshore Contractors Association [*Belgium*] (EAIO) ... IPLOCA
International Pipe Line and Offshore Contractors Association [*Belgium*] (EAIO) ... IPOCA
International Pipe Line Contractors Association [*Later, IPOCA*] (EA) ... IPLCA
International Pipe Standard ... IPS
International Pipe Thread (NASA) ... IPT
International Pizza Co. [*Associated Press*] (SAG) ... IntlPizza
International Planetarium Society (EA) ... IPS
International Planned Music Association (EA) ... IPMA
International Planned Parenthood Federation (EA) ... IPPF
International Planned Parenthood Federation, Documentation and Publications Center, New York, NY [*Library symbol Library of Congress*] (LCLS) ... NNIPF
International Planned Parenthood Federation, Western Hemisphere Region (EA) ... IPPF/WHR
International Planning Corp. ... IPC
International Planning Group [*Belgium, Germany, Netherlands*] (AABC) ... IPG
International Planning Team [*NATO*] (NATG) ... IPT
International Plant Biotech Network (EA) ... IPBNet
International Plant Genetic Resources Institute [*Italy*] ... IPGRI
International Plant Index [*A publication*] ... IPlx
International Plant Propagators Society, Eastern Region (EA) ... IPPS
International Plant Protection Center [*Oregon State University*] [*Research center*] (RCD) ... IPPC
International Plant Research Institute (PDAA) ... IPRI
International Plasma Corp. ... IPC
International Plastic Modelers Society (EA) ... IPMS
International Plastic Modelers Society/US Branch (EA) ... IPMS/USA
International Plastics and Rubber Exhibition [*British Plastics Federation*] (TSPED) ... INTERPLAS
International Plastics Association Directors ... IPAD
International Plastics Exhibition ... PLASMEX
International Plastics Selector, Inc. [*Information service or system*] (IID) ... IPS
International Plate Collectors Association (EA) ... IPCA
International Plate Collectors Guild (EA) ... IPCG
International Plate Printers, Die Stampers, and Engravers' Union of North America (EA) ... IPPDSEU
International Plate Printers, Die Stampers, and Engravers' Union of North America ... PPDSE
International Platform Association (EA) ... IPA
International Platinum Corp. [*Associated Press*] (SAG) ... IntlPlatin
International Platinum Corp. [*Toronto Stock Exchange symbol*] ... IPN
International Playing-Card Society (EA) ... IPCS
International Podrabinek Fund [*Defunct*] (EA) ... IPF
International Poetry Forum (EA) ... IPF
International Poetry Forum, Pittsburgh, PA [*Library symbol Library of Congress*] (LCLS) ... PPiI
International Polar Motion Service ... IPMS
International Polar Transportation Conference ... IPTC
International Polar Year ... IPY
International Polaris Energy Corp. [*Toronto Stock Exchange symbol*] ... IPS
International Polar-Orbiting Meteorological Satellite ... IPOMS
International Police Academy [*Formerly, Inter-American Police Academy*] ... IPA
International Police and Fire Athletic Association [*Defunct*] (EA) ... IPFAA
International Police Association [*Maidstone, Kent, England*] (EAIO) ... IPA
International Police Dogs (EA) ... IPD
International Police Exhibition and Conference [*British*] (ITD) ... IPEC
International Police Services ... INPOLSE
International Polio Network (EA) ... IPN
International Poliomyelitis Congress ... IPC
International Political Science Association (EA) ... IPSA
International Polka Association (EA) ... IPA
International Poplar Commission [*FAO*] [*Rome, Italy*] [*United Nations*] (EA) ... IPC
International Population Institute [*Defunct*] (EA) ... IPI
International Population Research Center [*University of California*] [*Defunct*] ... IPOR
International Porcelain Art Teachers [*Later, IPA*] (EA) ... IPAT
International Porcelain Artist (EA) ... IPA
International Portrait Gallery ... IPG
International Post Ltd. [*Associated Press*] (SAG) ... IntlPost
International Post Ltd. [*NASDAQ symbol*] (SAG) ... POST
International Postage Stamp Exhibition ... INPEX
International Postal Collectors League [*Commercial firm*] (EA) ... IPCL
International Postcard Collectors Association (EA) ... IPCA
International Post-Partum Mental Health Network (EA) ... IPPMHN
International Pot and Kettle Clubs (EA) ... IPKC
International Potash Institute [*See also IIP*] (EAIO) ... IPI
International Potential [*Vancouver Stock Exchange symbol*] ... IEP
International Potter Distilling Corp. [*Toronto Stock Exchange symbol Vancouver Stock Exchange symbol*] ... IOP
International Powder and Bulk Solids Technology Exhibition and Conference ... POWTECH
International Power and Engineering Consultants ... IPEC
International Powered Access Federation (EAIO) ... IPAF
International Powerlifting Federation [*Hagersten, Sweden*] (EAIO) ... IPF
International Powertech Systems, Inc. [*Vancouver Stock Exchange symbol*] ... IPW
International Practical Scale of Temperature (PDAA) ... IPST
International Practical Temperature Scale [*National Institute of Standards and Technology*] ... IPTS
International Praxis Resources [*Vancouver Stock Exchange symbol*] ... IPQ
International Prayer Fellowship (EA) ... IPF
International Precious Metals [*Associated Press*] (SAG) ... IntlPrec
International Precious Metals [*Associated Press*] (SAG) ... IntlPrecM
International Precious Metals [*NASDAQ symbol*] (SAG) ... IPMCF
International Precious Metals Institute (EA) ... IPMI
International Prepress Association (EA) ... IPA
International Presort Airmail [*US Postal Service*] ... IPSAM
International Press Association [*Defunct*] (EA) ... IPA
International Press Institute [*British*] ... IPI
International Press Institute [*Switzerland*] (PDAA) ... IPI
International Press Institute, American Committee (EA) ... IPI
International Press Institute/Management and Information System [*Switzerland*] ... IPI/MIS
International Press Telecommunications Council [*See also CIPT*] [*Telecommunications An association Defunct*] (EA) ... IPTC
International Preview Society (EA) ... IPS
International Price Program [*Bureau of Labor Statistics*] (GFGA) ... IPP
International Primary Aluminium Institute [*British*] (EAIO) ... IPAI
International Primary Market Association (EAIO) ... IPMA
International Primate Protection League (EA) ... IPPL
International Primatological Society (EA) ... IPS
International Prime Tech [*Vancouver Stock Exchange symbol*] ... IPV
International Primitive Money Society (EA) ... IPMS
International Printers Supply Salesmen's Guild (EA) ... IPSSG
International Printing and Graphic Communications Union ... IPGCU
International Printing and Graphic Communications Union ... PGCU
International Printing Exhibition ... IPEX
International Printing Pressmen and Assistants' Union of North America [*Later, IPGCU*] ... IPPA
International Printing Pressmen and Assistants' Union of North America [*Later, IPGCU*] (EA) ... IPPAU
International Priority Paid (ADA) ... IPP
International Prism Exploration Ltd. [*Vancouver Stock Exchange symbol*] ... IPE
International Prison Ministry (EA) ... IPM
International Prisoners Aid Association (EA) ... IPAA
International Private Investment Advisory Council on Foreign Aid [*Agency for International Development*] (EGAO) ... IPIACFA
International Private Leased Circuits [*British Telecom International*] (NITA) ... IPLC
International Probation Organization (EA) ... INTERPRO
International Processes Simulation [*Game*] ... IPS
International Procurement Committee [*ABA*] (AAGC) ... IPC

International Procurement Committee Report [*ABA*] [*A publication*] (AAGC) ... IPC Rept
International Production, Service, and Sales Union ... PSS
International Production Technology (IAA) ... IPT
International Productions and Safety Research [*Auto accident reconstruction*] ... INTERSEARCH
International Professional Association for Environmental Affairs (EA) ... IPRE
International Professional Rodeo Association (EA) ... IPRA
International Professional Security Association [*Paignton, Devonshire, England*] (EAIO) ... IPSA
International Professional Ski Racers Association (EA) ... IPSRA
International Professional Surrogates Association (EA) ... IPSA
International Professional Tennis Players Association (BARN) ... IPTPA
International Professional Vinyl Repair Association (EA) ... IPVRA
International Program for Antarctic Buoys [*Marine science*] (OSRA) ... IPAB
International Program for Human Resource Development [*Defunct*] (EA) ... IPHRD
International Program for Population Analysis ... IPPA
International Program for the Development of Communications [*UNESCO*] ... IPDC
International Program in Environmental Management Education ... IPEME
International Program of Laboratories for Population Statistics ... POPLAB
International Program of Ocean Drilling [*Formerly, DSDP*] [*National Science Foundation*] ... IPOD
International Program on Chemical Safety (GNE) ... IPCS
International Programme on Chemical Safety (EA) ... IPCS
International Programme on Conflict Resolution and Ethnicity ... INCORE
International Programming (IAA) ... IP
International Programs and Studies Office [*Later, DIA*] (EA) ... IPSO
International Programs Steering Group [*DoD*] ... IPSG
International Progress Organization [*Vienna, Austria*] (EAIO) ... IPO
International Project for Soft Energy Paths [*Defunct*] (EA) ... IPSEP
[*The*] **International Project Management Group, Inc.** [*Glyndon, MD*] [*Telecommunications*] (TSSD) ... TIPMG
International Project of the Association for Voluntary Sterilization ... IPAVS
International Property Investment Journal [*A publication*] (DLA) ... Int'l Prop Inv J
International Prototype Kilogram ... IPK
International Prototype Meter ... IPM
International PSI Committee of Magicians [*See also CIEPP*] (EAIO) ... IPSICM
International Psycho-Analytical Association [*British*] (EAIO) ... IPA
International Psychogeriatric Association (EA) ... IPA
International Psychohistorical Association (EA) ... IPA
International Psychosomatics Institute (EA) ... IPI
International Public Policy Institute ... IPPI
International Public Relations (ADA) ... IPR
International Public Relations Association ... INPRA
International Public Relations Association [*London, England*] (WDMC) ... IPRA
International Public Relations Association, US Section (EA) ... IPRA
International Public Television [*An association*] (NTCM) ... INPUT
International Public Works Federation (EA) ... IPWF
International Publishers Advertising Representatives Association ... IPARA
International Publishers Association [*See also UIE*] [*Geneva, Switzerland*] (EAIO) ... IPA
International Publishing Corp. [*England*] ... IPC
International Publishing Newsletter (NITA) ... IPN
International Pulse Trade and Industry Confederation [*FAO*] ... IPTIC
International Pumpkin Association (EA) ... IPA
International Pursuit Corp. [*Toronto Stock Exchange symbol*] ... IPJ
International "Q" Signal ... IQS
International Quail Foundation [*Defunct*] (EA) ... IQF
International Quality Award [*LIMRA*] ... IQA
International Quality Centre ... IQC
International Quick Printing Foundation [*Defunct*] (EA) ... IQPF
International Quiet Sun Year [*1964-65*] [*Also, IQSY, IYQS*] (IAA) ... IQSU
International Quiet Sun Year [*1964-65*] [*Also, IYQS*] ... IQSY
International Quorum of Film and Video Producers (EA) ... IQ
International Rabbinic Committee for the Safety of Israel (EA) ... IRCSI
International Race of Champions [*Auto racing*] ... IROC
International Racquet Sports Association [*Later, IRSAAQC*] (EA) ... IRSA
International Racquetball Association [*Later, AARA*] (EA) ... IRA
International Racquetball Federation (EAIO) ... IRF
International Radiation Commission [*of the International Association of Meteorology and Atmospheric Physics*] (EAIO) ... IRC
International Radiation Detectors [*Marine science*] (OSRA) ... IRD
International Radiation Detectors (USDC) ... IRD
International Radiation Investigation Satellite [*NASA*] ... IRIS
International Radiation Protection Association [*Vienna, Austria*] (EAIO) ... IRPA
International Radio Air Safety Association ... IRASA
International Radio and Electrical Distributors Association (MHDB) ... IREDA
International Radio and Television Foundation, Inc. [*International Radio and Television Society*] (NTCM) ... IRTF
International Radio and Television Society (EA) ... IRTS
International Radio Call Sign ... IRCS
International Radio Carrier (NTCM) ... IRC
International Radio Club of America (EA) ... IRCA
International Radio Consultative Committee ... CCIR
International Radio Consultative Committee ... IRCC
International Radio Frequency Board ... IRFB
International Radio Interferometric Surveying [*International Association of Geodesy*] ... IRIS
International Radio Scientific Union (DEN) ... IRSU
International Radio Silence ... IRS
International Radium Unit ... IRU
International Ragdoll Cat Association (EA) ... IRCA
International Raiffeisen Union (EA) ... IRU
International Railway Congress Association [*Belgium*] ... IRCA
International Railway Temperance Union ... IRTU
International Railway-Owned Company for Refrigerated Transport (EAIO) ... INTERFRIGO
International Rainwear Council ... IRC
International Randonneurs [*An association*] (EA) ... IR
International Raod Research Documentation (NITA) ... IRRD
International Rate of Return [*Finance*] ... IRR
International Rating Class [*Yachting*] ... IRC
International Rationalization, Standardization, and Interoperability Office (MCD) ... IRSIO
International Ray Price Fan Club (EA) ... IRPFC
International Rayon and Synthetic Fibres Committee [*See also CIRFS*] [*Paris, France*] (EAIO) ... IRSFC
International Reading Association (EA) ... IRA
International Ready-to-Assemble Furniture Show (ITD) ... IRTAFS
International Real Estate Directory [*Real estate computer site*] ... IRED
International Real Estate Federation ... IREF
International Real Estate Federation Australian Chapter ... IREFAC
International Real Estate Institute (EA) ... IREI
International Reception Operators [*Defunct*] (EA) ... IRO
International Reciprocal Trade Association (EA) ... IRTA
International Record Carrier [*Telecommunication companies providing international service*] (TSSD) ... IRC
International Record Collectors' Club [*Record label*] ... IRCC
International Records Syndicate, Inc. ... IRS
International Recreation Association [*Later, WLRA*] ... IRA
International Recruitment Investigation in the Subarctic [*Marine science*] (OSRA) ... IRIS
International Recruitment Investigations in the Subarctic (USDC) ... IRIS
International Rectifier Corp. [*Associated Press*] (SAG) ... IntRect
International Rectifier Corp. [*NYSE symbol*] (SPSG) ... IRF
International Red Cross and Red Crescent Movement (EAIO) ... IRC
International Red Cross Committee [*World War II*] ... IRCC
International Red Locust Control Organization for Central and Southern Africa (EAIO) ... IRLCO-CSA
International Red Locust Control Service ... IRLCS
International Reference Center for Abortion Research (IID) ... IRCAR
International Reference Centre [*Community water supply and sanitation*] (NITA) ... IRC
International Reference Collection of Soybean Arthropods [*INTSOY*] ... IRCSA
International Reference Ionosphere ... IRI
International Reference Organization in Forensic Medicine and Sciences (EA) ... INFORM
International Reference Preparation [*World Health Organization*] ... IRP
International Reference Version (OSI) ... IRV
International Reference Zero [*Level for pure-tone audiometers*] ... IRZ
International Referral Center for Information Handling Equipment [*Former Yugoslavia*] [*UNESCO*] (IID) ... IRCIHE
International Referral System [*United Nations Environment Programme*] ... IRS
International Referral System for Sources of Environmental Information [*Formerly, IRS*] [*United Nations Environment Program*] (ASF) ... INFOTERRA
International Reform Federation (EA) ... IRF
International Refugee Integration Resource Centre [*Later, CDR*] (EAIO) ... IRIRC
International Refugee Organization [*Later, UNHCR*] ... IRO
International Register (IAA) ... IRG
International Register for the White Eared Pheasant (EAIO) ... IRWEP
International Register of Manipulative Therapists ... IRMT
International Register of Potentially Toxic Chemicals [*United Nations Environment Program*] [*Geneva, Switzerland*] ... IRPTC
International Registration (BARN) ... IR
International Registration Authority [*Botany*] (PDAA) ... IRA
International Registry of Early Corvettes (EA) ... IREC
International Registry of Organization Development Professionals (EA) ... IRODP
International Registry of World Citizens ... IRWC
International Regulations for Preventing Collisions at Sea [*1972*] ... COLREGS
International Rehabilitation Medicine Association (EA) ... IRMA
International Rehabilitation Research Information System [*National Institute of Handicapped Research*] [*Database*] ... IRRIS
International Rehabilitation Week [*Trade show*] ... IRW
International Relations and Foreign Policy [*Army British*] ... IRFP
International Relations and Peace Research Institute [*Guatemala*] (EAIO) ... IRPRI
International Relations Committee [*American Library Association*] ... IRC
International Relations Committee [*Library Association of Australia*] ... IRC
International Relations Exercise (DNAB) ... IRE
International Relations Information System [*Forschungsinstitut fuer Internationale Politik und Sicherheit*] [*Germany*] (IID) ... IRIS
International Relations Office [*American Library Association*] ... IRO
International Relations Round Table [*American Library Association*] ... IRRT
International Relay, Inc. [*New York, NY*] [*Telecommunications*] (TSSD) ... IRI
International Relief and Rescue Committee [*Post-World War II*] ... IRRC
International Relief Organization [*Post-World War II*] ... IRO
International Relief Service of Caritas Catholica [*Belgium*] (EAIO) ... IRSCC
International Relief Union ... IRU
International Religious Fellowship (EA) ... IRF
International Religious Fine Art Program (EA) ... IRFAP
International Religious Liberty Association (EA) ... IRLA
International Religious Studies Unit [*American Topical Association*] (EA) ... IRSU
International Remodeling Contractors Association (EA) ... IRCA
International Remote Imaging Systems, Inc. [*AMEX symbol*] (SPSG) ... IRI
International Remote Imaging Systems, Inc. [*Associated Press*] (SAG) ... IRIS
International Remote Sensing Institute (MCD) ... IRSI
International Rendezvous (MCD) ... IR

International Rendezvous and Docking Mission [*Aerospace*] ... IRDM
International Repeater Station [*Telecommunications*] (TEL) ... IRS
International Reply Coupon ... IRC
International Reporting and Information Services [*International Private Intelligence Service*] [*Terminated, 1983*] ... IRIS
International Reporting Information Systems ... IRIS
International Repro Graphic Blueprint Association [*Later, IRA*] (EA) ... IRGBA
International Reprographics Association (EA) ... IRA
International Reprographics Association (EA) ... IRgA
International Republican Institute (ECON) ... IRI
International Rescue and Emergency Care Association (EA) ... IRECA
International Rescue and First Aid Association [*Later, IRECA*] (EA) ... IRFAA
International Rescue Committee (EA) ... IRC
International Research and Development ... IRD
International Research & Development Co. Ltd. [*Northern Engineering Industries*] [*British*] (IRUK) ... IRD
International Research and Evaluation [*Research Center*] [*Also, an information service or system*] (IID) ... IRE
International Research and Evaluation - Information and Technology Transfer Database [*International Research and Evaluation*] [*Information service or system*] (CRD) ... IRE-ITTD
International Research and Exchanges Board (EA) ... IREX
International Research and Technology, Inc. ... IRT
International Research and Training Center on Erosion and Sedimentation [*China*] (EAIO) ... IRTCES
International Research and Training Institute for the Advancement of Women [*Dominican Republic*] [*United Nations Research center*] (IRC) ... INSTRAW
International Research Career Development Program [*Public Health Service*] ... IRCDP
International Research Center for Energy and Economic Development [*University of Colorado*] [*Research center*] ... ICEED
International Research Centers Directory [*A publication*] ... IRCD
International Research Centre on Lindane [*See also CIEL*] [*Brussels, Belgium*] (EAIO) ... IRCL
International Research Committee on the Biokinetics of Impacts [*Later, International Research Council on the Biokinetics of Impacts*] (EAIO) ... IRCOBI
International Research Communications System [*Electronic journal publisher*] [*British*] ... IRCS
International Research Council [*Later, ICSU*] ... IRC
International Research Council of Neuromuscular Disorders (EA) ... IRCND
International Research Council on Pure and Applied Linguistics (EA) ... IRCPAL
International Research, Development, and Standardization [*Division*] [*Army*] (RDA) ... IRD & S
International Research Fellowship Program [*Department of Health and Human Services*] (GFGA) ... IRF
International Research Group on Colour Vision Deficiencies [*Ghent, Belgium*] (EAIO) ... IRGCVD
International Research Group on Refuse Disposal [*Later, ISWA*] ... IRGRD
International Research Group on Wear of Engineering Materials (PDAA) ... IRG
International Research Group on Wood Preservation [*Stockholm, Sweden*] (EAIO) ... IRG
International Research Information Service [*American Foundation for the Blind*] ... IRIS
International Research Institute for Climate Prediction [*Marine science*] (OSRA) ... IRICP
International Research Institute for Climate Prediction (USDC) ... IRICP
International Research on Communist Techniques ... IRCT
International Research on the Interior of the Sun ... IRIS
International Research Society for Children's Literature [*Cadaujac, France*] (EA) ... IRSCL
International Resistance Co. (AAG) ... IRC
International Resistor Center ... IRC
International Resource Development, Inc. [*Norwalk, CT*] [*Telecommunications Information service or system*] (IID) ... IRD
International Resources Bank ... IRB
International REST [*Restricted Environmental Stimulation Techniques*] **Investigators Society** (EA) ... IRIS
International Retail Systems, Inc. [*Toronto Stock Exchange symbol Vancouver Stock Exchange symbol*] ... IRE
International Rett Syndrome Association (EA) ... IRSA
International Revenue Record [*New York City*] [*A publication*] (DLA) ... IRR
International Review of Administrative Sciences [*A publication*] (DLA) ... Int'l Rev Ad Sci
International Review of Criminal Policy [*United Nations*] (DLA) ... Int Rev Crim Pol
International Review of Criminal Policy [*United Nations*] (DLA) ... Int'l Rev Crim Policy
International Review of Publications in Sociology [*Sociological Abstracts, Inc.*] [*Information service or system*] (CRD) ... IRPS
International Rex Ventures, Inc. [*Vancouver Stock Exchange symbol*] ... IRV
International Rhinologic Society (EA) ... IRS
International Rhodes Resources [*Vancouver Stock Exchange symbol*] ... IRH
International Rhythm and Blues Association (EA) ... IRBA
International Rice (IIA) ... IR
International Rice Bran Industries Ltd. [*Vancouver Stock Exchange symbol*] ... IRB
International Rice Commission [*See also CIR*] (EAIO) ... IRC
International Rice Research Institute [*Philippines*] ... IRRI
International Right of Way Association (EA) ... IRWA
International Rights Information Service ... IRIS
International Risk Management Institute [*Dallas, TX*] (EA) ... IRMI
International Rivers Network (EA) ... IRN
International Road Documentation Center ... IRDC
International Road Documentation Scheme (NITA) ... IRDS
International Road Federation (EA) ... IRF
International Road Transport Union [*Geneva, Switzerland*] (EAIO) ... IRU
International Robert Musil Society [*See also SIRM*] [*Saarbrucken, Federal Republic of Germany*] (EAIO) ... IRMS
International Robotmotion Intelligence (NITA) ... IRI
International Rock 'n' Roll Music Association (EA) ... IRMA
International Rocket Week ... IRW
International Rodeo Association (EA) ... IRA
International Rodeo Writers Association [*Later, RMA*] (EA) ... IRWA
International Roleo Association [*Later, International Log Rolling Association*] (EA) ... IRA
International Roller Skating Federation (EA) ... IRSF
International Romani Union (EA) ... IRU
International Rope Skipping Organization ... IRSO
International Rorschach Society [*Strasbourg, France*] (EA) ... IRS
International Rose O'Neill Club (EA) ... IROC
International Rostrum of Young Performers [*See also TIJE*] (EAIO) ... IRP
International Rotary Engine Club [*Later, RX-7 Club of America*] (EA) ... IREC
International Roughness Index [*BTS*] [*FHWA*] (TAG) ... IRI
International Round Table for the Advancement of Counseling [*British*] ... IRTAC
International Routing and Reporting Activity (DNAB) ... IRRA
International Routing Plan [*Telecommunications*] (TEL) ... IRP
International Rowing Federation ... IRF
International Royal Enterprises (EA) ... IRE
International Royalon Minerals, Inc. [*Vancouver Stock Exchange symbol*] ... IRM
International Rubber Association [*Kuala Lumpur, Malaysia*] (EAIO) ... IRA
International Rubber Conference Organization (EAIO) ... IRCO
International Rubber Development Committee ... IRDC
International Rubber Hardness Degree ... IRHD
International Rubber Regulation Committee [*World War II*] ... IRRC
International Rubber Research and Development Board [*Brickendonbury, Hertford, England*] (EAIO) ... IRRDB
International Rubber Research Board ... IRRB
International Rubber Study Group [*London, England*] (EAIO) ... IRSG
International Rugby Board [*Australia*] ... IRB
International Rural Sociology Association (EA) ... IRSA
International Sacerdotal Society Saint Pius X [*Switzerland*] (EAIO) ... FSSPX
International Sacerdotal Society Saint Pius X (EA) ... ISSSP
International Sacred Recordings, Christian Artists' Record Corp. [*Record label*] ... ISR
International Safety Academy ... ISA
International Safety and Health Exhibition [*British*] (ITD) ... ISHE
International Safety Guide for Oil Tankers and Terminals (DS) ... ISGOTT
International Safety Institute [*Defunct*] (EA) ... ISI
International Sailing Craft Association [*Exeter, Devonshire, England*] (EAIO) ... ISCA
International Sailing Schools Association (EA) ... ISSA
International Salmonella Center ... ISC
International Salon of Cartoons (EA) ... ISC
International Salvage Union (PDAA) ... ISU
International Sand Collectors Society (EA) ... ISCS
International Sanitary Convention for Air Navigation ... ISCAN
International Sanitary Regulations [*World Health Organization*] ... ISR
International Sanitary Supply Association (EA) ... ISSA
International Satellite Cloud Climatology Project ... ISCCP
International Satellite for Ionospheric Research [*NASA Canada*] (IAA) ... ISIR
International Satellite for Ionospheric Studies [*NASA-Canada*] (NOAA) ... ISI
International Satellite for Ionospheric Studies [*NASA-Canada*] ... ISIS
International Satellite Geodesy Experiment ... ISAGEX
International Satellite, Inc. [*Telecommunications*] ... ISI
International Satellite Land Surface Climatology Project [*Federal government*] ... ISLSCP
International Satellite Verification Agency ... ISVA
International Satellites for Ionosphere Studies - Experimental [*NASA/Canada*] (SAA) ... ISIS-X
International Savant Society (EA) ... ISS
International Save the Pun Foundation (EA) ... ISPF
International Savings Banks Institute [*See also IICE*] [*Geneva, Switzerland*] (EAIO) ... ISBI
International Saw and Knife Association (EA) ... ISKA
International Scale of Nuclear Events ... ISNE
International Scheme for the Coordination of Dairy Development (EAIO) ... ISCDD
International School Art Program [*Defunct*] ... ISAP
International School for Nuclear Science and Engineering ... ISNSE
International School of Disarmament and Research on Conflicts ... ISODARCO
[*The*] **International School of Inforamtion Management, Inc.** [*Denver, CO*] (ECON) ... ISIM
[*The*] **International School of Information Management, Inc.** [*Denver, CO*] (ECON) ... ISIM
International School of Sailing ... ISS
International School Sport Federation (EAIO) ... ISF
International Schools Association [*Geneva, Switzerland*] (EA) ... ISA
International Schools Services (EA) ... ISS
International Science and Engineering Fair ... ISEF
International Science and Technology Advisory Committee [*Australia*] ... ISTAC
International Science & Technology Center ... ISTC
International Science Foundation (EA) ... ISF
International Science Information Services [*Earth sciences data center*] [*Dallas, TX*] ... ISIS
International Science Organization ... ISO
International Science Policy Foundation (EAIO) ... ISPF
International Science Writers Association ... ISWA
International Scientific and Technical Information System (EAIO) ... ISTIS
International Scientific Collectors Association (EA) ... ISCA
International Scientific Film Association ... ISFA

International Scientific Film Library ISFL
International Scientific Management Group [GARP] (NOAA) ISMG
International Scientific Publications [Tel Aviv, Israel] ISC
International Scientific Radio Union [Also, URSI] ISRU
International Scientific Series [A publication] ISS
International Scientific Union ISU
International Scientific Vocabulary ISV
International Scleroderma Federation [Later, SF] (EA) ISF
International Scotist Society [See also SIS] [Rome, Italy] (EAIO) ISS
International Screen Advertising Producer's Association [Defunct] (EA) ISAPA
International Screen Publicity Association ISPA
International Sculpteurs et Designers Associes [Paris, France] (EAIO) ISDA
International Seabed Authority ISA
International Sea-Bed Authority [Marine science] [United Nations] (OSRA) ISBA
International Seabed Research Authority ISRA
International Seal, Label, and Cigar Band Society (EA) ISLCBS
International Seaman's Union ISU
International Seaway Trading Corp. (MHDW) INS
International Seaweed Association (EAIO) ISS
International Seaweed Symposium [Trondheim, Norway] (MSC) ISS
International Secretariat for Research on the History of Agricultural Implements [Lyngby, Denmark] (EAIO) ISRHAI
International Secretariat for the University Study of Education ISUSE
International Secretariat for Volunteer Service [Defunct] ISVS
International Secretariat of Arts, Communications Media, and Entertainment TradeUnions (EAIO) ISACMETU
International Secretariat of Entertainment Trade Unions [Geneva, Switzerland] ISETU
International Secretariat of Jurists for an Amnesty and Democracy in Paraguay [Paris, France] (EAIO) SIJADEP
International Secretariat of the Knitting Industries [Paris, France] (EAIO) ISKI
International Section of ISSA [International Social Security Association] on the Prevention of Occupational Risks in the Construction Industry [Boulogne-Billancourt, France] (EAIO) ISISSAPORCI
International Securities Market Association [Switzerland] (EAIO) AIBD
International Securities Regulatory Organisation [London, England] [Business term] ISRO
International Security Affairs [DoD] ISA
International Security Affairs Committee ISAC
International Security Agency ISA
International Security and Detective Alliance (EA) ISDA
International Security Conference and Exposition (ITD) ISC
International Security Council (EA) ISC
International Security Management Association [Boston, MA] (EA) ISMA
International Security Officer's Police and Guard Union (EA) ISOPGU
International Security Technics [Organization in TV series "The Gemini Man"] INTERSECT
International Seebeck Study Society (EA) ISSS
International Seed Testing Association [Switzerland] ISTA
International Seismic Data Exchange [Geology] ISDE
International Seismological Centre [ICSU] [Newbury, Berkshire, England] (EAIO) ISC
International Self-Service Organization ISO
International Self-Service Organization [Cologne, Federal Republic of Germany] (EAIO) ISS
International Seminars Support Scheme ISSS
International Semi-Tech Microelectronics, Inc. [Toronto Stock Exchange symbol] ISE
International Senior Citizens Association (EA) ISCA
International Sensitivity Index [Hematology] ISI
International Serials Catalogue [A publication] ISC
International Serials Data System [Database] (EA) ISDS
International Sericultural Commission [See also CSI] [La Mulatiere, France] (EAIO) ISC
International Service Agencies ISA
International Service Coordination Center [Communications] ISCC
International Service for National Agricultural Research [The Hague, Netherlands] ISNAR
International Service for the Acquisition of Agri-Biotech Applications ISAAA
International Service Robot Congress ISRC
International Services [Red Cross] IS
International Shade Tree Conference [Later, ISA] (EA) ISTC
International Shadow Project (EA) ISP
International Shakespeare Association (EA) ISA
International Shasta Resources [Vancouver Stock Exchange symbol] ISR
International Sheep and Goat Institute [Utah State University] [Research center] (RCD) ISGI
International Sheep Dog Society [Bedford, England] (EAIO) ISDS
International Ship Electric Service Association [British] (EAIO) ISES
International Ship Structures Congress (NOAA) ISSC
International Ship Suppliers Association [Wimbledon, England] (EA) ISSA
International Shipholding Corp. [Associated Press] (SAG) IntShip
International Shipholding Corp. [NYSE symbol] (NQ) ISH
International Shipmasters Association (EA) ISMA
International Shipmasters Association of the Great Lakes (EA) ISA
International Shipmasters Association of the Great Lakes ISAGL
International Shipowners' Association [See also MAS] [Gdynia, Poland] (EAIO) INSA
International Shipping Federation [British] (EAIO) ISF
International Shipping Information Service (DS) ISIS
International Ships-in-Bottles Association (EA) ISBA
International Shoe and Leather Workers' Federation ISLWF
International Shooter Development Fund [National Rifle Association] ISDF
International Shooting Coaches Association (EA) ISCA
International Shooting Union ISU
International Shopfitting Organization [Zurich, Switzerland] (EAIO) ISO
International Short Film Conference (EAIO) ISFC
International Show Car Association (EA) ISCA
International Shuffleboard Association (EA) ISA
International Siberian Husky Club ISHC
International Side-Saddle Organization (EA) ISSO
International Sight and Sound Exposition ISSE
International Sightseeing and Tours Association [Defunct] (EA) ISTA
International Sigma Security, Inc. [Vancouver Stock Exchange symbol] ISU
International Sign Association [NESA] [Absorbed by] (EA) ISA
International Signal and Control [Army] ISC
International Sikh Organization (EA) ISO
International Silk Association - USA (EA) ISA
International Silo Association (EA) ISA
International Silver Co. [Acronym now used as firm's name] INSILCO
International Simulation and Gaming Association (EA) ISAGA
International Simultaneous Translation Service ISTS
International Sinabarb [Vancouver Stock Exchange symbol] ISB
International Sinatra Society (EA) ISS
International Single Comb Black Minorca Club (EA) ISCBMC
International Sivananda Yoga Vedanta Center (EAIO) ISYVC
International Sivananda Yoga Vedanta Organization [Val Morin, PQ] (EAIO) ISYVO
International Six Days Enduro [Motorcycle racing] ISDE
International Six Days Trial [Motorcycling] ISDT
International Skateboard Association (EA) ISA
International Skating Union [See also UIP] [Davos-Platz, Switzerland] (EAIO) ISU
International Skeeter Association ISA
International Skeletal Society (EA) ISS
International Ski Club of Journalists (EAIO) ISCJ
International Ski Federation ISF
International Ski Instructors' Association (ECON) ISIA
International Ski Racers Association [Later, WPS-RA] ISRA
International Ski Writers Association [Riehen, Switzerland] (EA) ISWA
International Skilled Trades Advisory Committee [UAW] ISTAC
International Sled Dog Racing Association (EA) ISDRA
International Slurry Seal Association (EA) ISSA
International Slurry Surfacing Association (EAIO) ISSA
International Smart Shoppers Club (EA) ISSC
International Snow Leopard Trust (EA) ISLT
International Snowmobile Industry Association (EA) ISIA
International Snowshoe Council [Defunct] (EA) ISSC
International Snowshoe Federation (EA) ISF
International Soap Box Derby, Inc. (EA) ISBD
International Soccer League ISL
International Social Affiliation of Women Airline Pilots [Later, ISWAP] (EA) ISA + 21
International Social Development Institute ISDI
International Social Science Council [See also CISS] [Paris, France] [Research center] (EAIO) ISSC
International Social Science Institute [Later, International Academy at Santa Barbara] (EA) ISSI
International Social Security Association [Geneva, Switzerland] (EA) ISSA
International Social Service [See also SSI] [Geneva, Switzerland] (EAIO) ISS
International Social Service, American Branch (EA) ISS/AB
International Social Service, Australian Branch [An association] ISSAB
International Social Travel Federation [See also FITS] [Brussels, Belgium] (EAIO) ISTF
International Socialist Organization (EA) ISO
International Socialists IS
International Society Against Breast Cancer (EAIO) ISABC
International Society and Federation of Cardiology [International Cardiol ogy Federation and International Society of Cardiology - ISC] [Formed by a merger of] (EAIO) ISFC
International Society Biomedical Research on Alcoholism (EAIO) ISBRA
International Society for a Complete Earth (EA) ISCE
International Society for Aerosols in Medicine [See also IGAeM] (EAIO) ISAeM
International Society for Aerosols in Medicine (EAIO) ISAM
International Society for AIDS Education (EA) ISAE
International Society for Alternative and Augmentative Communication (EA) ISAAC
International Society for Analytical Cytology (EAIO) ISAC
International Society for Animal Blood Group Research [Australia] (EAIO) ISABR
International Society for Animal Genetics [Australia] (EAIO) ISABR
International Society for Animal Rights (EA) ISAR
International Society for Artificial Organs (EA) ISAO
International Society for Astrological Research (EA) ISAR
International Society for Autistic Children [Defunct] (EA) ISAC
International Society for Biochemical Pharmacology ISBP
International Society for Boundary Elements (EAIO) ISBE
International Society for British Genealogy and Family History (EA) ISBGFH
International Society for Burn Injuries (EAIO) ISBI
International Society for Business Education, US Chapter [Reston, VA] (EA) ISBE
International Society for Cardiovascular Surgery (EA) ICVS
International Society for Cardiovascular Surgery (DAVI) ISCS
International Society for Cell Biology [Later, IFCB] (ASF) ISCB
International Society for Chinese Philosophy (EA) ISCP
International Society for Chronobiology (EA) ISC
International Society for Classical Bibliography [Paris, France] (EAIO) ISCB
International Society for Clinical and Experimental Hypnosis [Charles University] (EA) ISCEH

International Society for Clinical Biostatistics (EAIO) .... ISCB
International Society for Clinical Electroretinography .... ISCERG
International Society for Clinical Enzymology [*Hanover, Federal Republic of Germany*] (EAIO) .... ISCE
International Society for Clinical Laboratory Technology (EA) .... ISCLT
International Society for Community Development (EA) .... ISCD
International Society for Comparative Psychology (EA) .... ISCP
International Society for Computational Methods in Engineering (EAIO) .... ISCME
International Society for Contemporary Music (EA) .... ISCM
International Society for Developmental Neuroscience (EA) .... ISDN
International Society for Developmental Psychobiology (EA) .... ISDP
International Society for Disaster Medicine (EA) .... ISDM
International Society for Diseases of the Esophagus [*Tokyo, Japan*] (EAIO) .... ISDE
International Society for Ecological Modelling [*Vaerloese, Denmark*] (EAIO) .... ISEM
International Society for Economic Evaluation of Medicines .... ISEEM
International Society for Education through Art [*Corsham, England*] .... INSEA
International Society for Educational Planning (EA) .... ISEP
International Society for Eighteenth-Century Studies [*See also SIEDS*] [*Oxford, England*] (EAIO) .... ISECS
International Society for Electrostimulation (EA) .... ISE
International Society for Engineering Education [*Austria*] (EAIO) .... ISEE
International Society for Environmental Toxicology and Cancer (EAIO) .... ISETC
International Society for Evolutionary Protistology (EA) .... ISEP
International Society for Fat Research .... ISF
International Society for Fluoride Research .... ISFR
International Society for Folk-Narrative Research [*Turku, Finland*] (EA) .... ISFNR
International Society for General Semantics (EA) .... ISGS
International Society for Geothermal Engineering [*Defunct*] (EA) .... ISGE
International Society for Heart and Lung Transplantation (EAIO) .... ISHLT
International Society for Heart Research [*Winnipeg, MB*] (EA) .... ISHR
International Society for Heart Transplantation (EA) .... ISHT
International Society for Hildegard Von Bingen Studies (EA) .... ISHVBS
International Society for Historical Linguistics (EAIO) .... ISHL
International Society for Horticultural Science [*See also SISH*] [*ICSU Wageningen, Netherlands*] (EAIO) .... ISHS
International Society for Human and Animal Mycology [*London School of Hygiene and Tropical Medicine*] [*British*] .... ISHAM
International Society for Human Ethology (EA) .... ISHE
International Society for Human Rights [*See also IGM*] [*Frankfurt, Federal Republic of Germany*] (EAIO) .... ISHR
International Society for Humor Studies (EA) .... ISHS
International Society for Hybrid Microelectronics (EA) .... ISHM
International Society for Individual Liberty (EAIO) .... ISIL
International Society for Individualized Instruction (AIE) .... ISII
International Society for Intercultural Education, Training, and Research (EA) .... SIETAR/INTL
International Society for Japanese Philately (EA) .... ISJP
International Society for Knowledge Organization [*Germany*] (EAIO) .... ISKO
International Society for Krishna Consciousness (EA) .... ISKCON
International Society for Labor Law and Social Legislation [*Later, International Society for Labor Law and Social Security United States National Branch*] (EA) .... ISLLSL
International Society for Labor Law and Social Security [*International Co ngresses of Labour Law and International Society for Social Law*] [*Formed by a merger of*] (EAIO) .... ISLLSS
International Society for Medical and Psychological Hypnosis (EA) .... ISMPH
International Society for Mental Imagery Techniques [*France*] (EAIO) .... ISMIT
International Society for Metaphysics (EA) .... ISM
International Society for Mushroom Science [*Braunschweig, Federal Republic of Germany*] (EA) .... ISMS
International Society for Music Education (EA) .... ISME
International Society for Music in Medicine (EAIO) .... ISMM
International Society for Neoplatonic Studies (EA) .... ISNS
International Society for Neurochemistry [*Kjeller, Norway*] (EA) .... ISN
International Society for New Atlantis (EA) .... ISNA
International Society for Ocular Fluorophotometry (EAIO) .... ISOF
International Society for Ophthalmic Ultrasound (EA) .... ISOU
International Society for Optical Engineering (EA) .... ISOE
International Society for Orbital Disorders (EAIO) .... ISOD
International Society for Organ History and Preservation (EA) .... ISOHP
International Society for Pediatric Neurosurgery (EA) .... ISPN
International Society for Peritoneal Dialysis (EA) .... ISPD
International Society for Phenomenology and Human Sciences (EA) .... ISPHS
International Society for Phenomenology and Literature (EA) .... ISPL
International Society for Philosophical Enquiry (EA) .... ISPE
International Society for Photogrammetry [*Later, ISPRS*] .... ISP
International Society for Photogrammetry and Remote Sensing [*Royal Institute of Technology*] [*Research center Sweden*] (IRC) .... ISPRS
International Society for Plant Pathology (EAIO) .... ISPP
International Society for Plastination (EA) .... ISP
International Society for Portuguese Philately (EA) .... ISPP
International Society for Prevention of Child Abuse and Neglect (EA).... ISPCAN
International Society for Prevention of Infertility (EAIO) .... ISPI
International Society for Preventive Oncology (EA) .... ISPO
International Society for Professional Hypnosis (EA) .... ISPH
International Society for Prosthetics and Orthotics - US Committee [*Later, ISPO*] (EA) .... ISPOUSC
International Society for Prosthetics and Orthotics - US National Member Society (EA) .... ISPO
International Society for Range Management (EA) .... ISRM
International Society for Rehabilitation of the Disabled [*Later, RehabilitationInternational*] .... ISRD
International Society for Research on Aggression (EA) .... ISRA
International Society for Research on Civilization Diseases and Vital Substances (PDAA) .... ISRCDVS
International Society for Respiratory Protection (EA) .... ISRP
International Society for Retirement Planning [*Later, ISRP*] (EA) .... ISPP
International Society for Retirement Planning (EA) .... ISRP
International Society for Rock Mechanics [*Lisbon, Portugal*] (EA) .... ISRM
International Society for Sandwich Construction and Bonding .... ISSCB
International Society for Social Defence [*See also SIDS*] [*Paris, France*] (EAIO) .... ISSD
International Society for Socialist Studies .... ISSS
International Society for Soil Mechanics and Foundation Engineering [*See also SIMSTF*] (EA) .... ISSMFE
International Society for Soilless Culture [*Wageningen, Netherlands*] (EAIO) .... ISOSC
International Society for STD [*Sexually Transmitted Diseases*] **Research** (EA) .... ISSTDR
International Society for Stereology (EA) .... ISS
International Society for Strategic Studies (Africa) [*Formerly, Africa Society forStrategic Studies*] (EA) .... ISSSA
International Society for Technology in Education (EAIO) .... ISTE
International Society for Terrain-Vehicle Systems (EA) .... ISTVS
International Society for Testing and Failure Analysis (MCD) .... ISTFA
International Society for Testing Materials .... ISTM
International Society for the Abolition of Data Processing Machines (EA) .... ISADPM
International Society for the Advancement of Humanistic Studies in Gynecology (EA) .... ISFAHSIG
International Society for the Arts, Sciences, and Technology (EA) .... ISAST
International Society for the Comparative Study of Civilizations (EA) .... ISCSC
International Society for the History of Ideas (EA) .... ISHI
International Society for the History of Physical Education and Sport [*Belgium*] (EAIO) .... ISHPES
International Society for the History of Rhetoric (EA) .... ISHR
International Society for the Immunology of Reproduction (EA) .... ISIR
International Society for the Interaction of Mechanics and Mathematics (EA) .... ISIMM
International Society for the Prevention of Water Pollution [*Alton, Hampshire, England*] (EAIO) .... ISPWP
International Society for the Protection of Animals [*Later, WSPA*] [*British*] (EA) .... ISPA
International Society for the Protection of Horses (DI) .... ISPH
International Society for the Protection of Mustangs and Burros (EA) .... ISPMB
International Society for the Psychology of Writing (EA) .... ISPW
International Society for the Sociology of Knowledge [*St. John's, NF*] [*Defunct*] (EAIO) .... ISSK
International Society for the Sociology of Religion [*Italy*] (EAIO) .... ISSR
International Society for the Study of Behavioural Development [*Nijmegen, Netherlands*] (EAIO) .... ISSBD
International Society for the Study of Church Monuments [*Later, CMS*] (EA) .... ISSCM
International Society for the Study of Dendrobatid Frogs (EA) .... ISSDF
International Society for the Study of Expressionism [*Formerly, ETMS*] (EA) .... ISSE
International Society for the Study of Expressionism - Ernst Toller Memorial Society (EA) .... ISSE-ETMS
International Society for the Study of Ghosts and Apparitions .... ISSGA
International Society for the Study of Individual Differences (EAIO) .... ISSID
International Society for the Study of Multiple Personality and Dissociation (EA) .... ISSMPD
International Society for the Study of Prenatal Psychology (EAIO) .... ISPP
International Society for the Study of Symbols .... ISSS
International Society for the Study of the Human-Companion Animal Bond [*Later, IAHAIO*] (EA) .... ISSHCAB
International Society for the Study of the Origin of Life (EA) .... ISSOL
International Society for the Study of Time (EA) .... ISST
International Society for the Study of Vulvar Disease (DAVI) .... ISSVD
International Society for the Study of Xenobiotics .... ISSX
International Society for the Welfare of Cripples [*Later, Rehabilitation International*] .... ISWC
International Society for Third-Sector Research (NFD) .... ISTR
International Society for Training and Culture .... ISTC
International Society for Trenchless Technology (EAIO) .... ISTT
International Society for Tropical Ecology (EA) .... ISTE
International Society for Twin Studies [*Rome, Italy*] (EA) .... ISTS
International Society for Utilitarian Studies [*British*] (EAIO) .... ISUS
International Society for Vaccines [*Gaithersburg, MD*] .... ISV
International Society for Vehicle Preservation (EA) .... ISVP
International Society for Vibroacoustics (EAIO) .... ISVA
International Society of African Scientists (EA) .... ISAS
International Society of Air Safety Investigators (EA) .... ISASI
International Society of Analytical Trilogy [*See also SITA*] [*Sao Paulo, Brazil*] (EAIO) .... ISAT
International Society of Animal License Collectors (EA) .... ISALC
International Society of Antique Scale Collectors (EA) .... ISASC
International Society of Appraisers [*Hoffman Estates, IL*] (EA) .... ISA
International Society of Arboriculture (EA) .... ISA
International Society of Art and Psychopathology [*Paris, France*] (EA) .... ISAP
International Society of Aviation Writers .... ISAW
International Society of Barristers (EA) .... ISOB
International Society of Barristers. Quarterly [*A publication*] (DLA) .... Int'l Soc'y of Barr Q
International Society of Bassists (EA) .... ISB
International Society of Bible Collectors (EA) .... ISBC
International Society of Bioclimatology and Biometeorology (IEEE) .... ISBB

International Society of Biometeorology [*See also SIB*] [*Zurich, Switzerland*] (EAIO) ... ISB
International Society of Biophysical Medicine [*British*] (IRUK) ... ISBM
International Society of Biorheology [*Germany*] (EAIO) ... ISB
International Society of Blood Transfusion (EA) ... ISBT
International Society of Cardiology [*Later, ISFC*] ... ISC
International Society of Cardiovascular Surgeons ... ISCVS
International Society of Certified Electronics Technicians (EA) ... ISCET
International Society of Certified Employee Benefit Specialists [*Brookfield, WI*] (EA) ... ISCEBS
International Society of Chemical Ecology (EA) ... ISCE
International Society of Chemotherapy [*Bad Heilbrunn, Federal Republic of Germany*] (EAIO) ... ISC
International Society of Christian Endeavor ... CE
International Society of Christian Endeavor (EA) ... ISCE
International Society of Citriculture (EA) ... ISC
International Society of City and Regional Planners [*See also AIU*] ... ISCRP
International Society of City and Regional Planners [*See also AIU*] [*The Hague, Netherlands*] (EAIO) ... ISoCaRP
International Society of Clinical Pathology [*Later, WASP*] ... ISCP
International Society of Communications Specialists (EA) ... ISCS
International Society of Comparative Pathology (DMAA) ... ISCP
International Society of Continuing Education in Dentistry [*See also SIECD*] [*Brussels, Belgium*] (EAIO) ... ISCED
International Society of Copier Artists (EA) ... ISCA
International Society of Copoclephologists [*British*] (EAIO) ... ISC
International Society of Corvette Owners ... ISCO
International Society of Crime Prevention Practitioners (EAIO) ... ISCPP
International Society of Cryosurgery [*Turin, Italy*] (EAIO) ... ISC
International Society of Cryptozoology (EA) ... ISC
International Society of Cybernetic Medicine (EA) ... ISCM
International Society of Dermatologic Surgery (EA) ... ISDS
International Society of Dermatology: Tropical, Geographic, and Ecologic (EA) ... ISD
International Society of Development Biologists [*Formerly, IIE*] [*Nogent-Sur-Marne, France*] ... ISDB
International Society of Developmental and Comparative Immunology (EA) ... ISDCI
International Society of Dietetic Including All Infant and Young Children Food Industries (EAIO) ... ISDI
International Society of Differentiation (EA) ... ISD
International Society of Dramatists (EA) ... ISD
International Society of Electrochemistry [*Graz, Austria*] (EA) ... ISE
International Society of Electromyographic Kinesiology (EA) ... ISEK
International Society of Electrophysiological Kinesiology [*Montreal, PQ*] (EA) ... ISEK
International Society of Emergency Medical Services (EA) ... ISEMS
International Society of Endocrinology (EA) ... ISE
International Society of Endoscopy ... ISE
International Society of Esperantist-Philologists [*See also IUEFI*] (EAIO) ... ISEP
International Society of Explosives Specialists (EA) ... ISES
International Society of Family Law [*Cambridge, England*] (EAIO) ... ISFL
International Society of Financiers (EA) ... ISF
International Society of Fine Arts Appraisers (EA) ... ISFAA
International Society of Fire Service Instructors (EA) ... FSI
International Society of Fire Service Instructors (EA) ... ISFSI
International Society of Flying Engineers [*Defunct*] (EA) ... ISFE
International Society of Folk Harpers and Craftsmen (EA) ... ISFHC
International Society of Food Service Consultants [*Later, FCSI*] (EA) ... ISFSC
International Society of Free Space Colonizers [*Superseded by Political Action Caucus*] (EA) ... ISFSC
International Society of Friendship and Good Will (EA) ... ISFGW
International Society of Gastroenterology ... ISGE
International Society of General Practice [*Germany*] (PDAA) ... ISGP
International Society of Geographic Ophthalmology [*Montreal, PQ*] (EAIO) ... ISGO
International Society of Geographical Pathology [*Australia*] (EY) ... ISGP
International Society of Guatemala Collectors (EA) ... ISGC
International Society of Healthcare Executives (EA) ... ISHE
International Society of Hematology (DAVI) ... ISH
International Society of Hotel Association Executives (EA) ... ISHAE
International Society of Hypertension (EA) ... ISH
International Society of India Chemists and Chemical Engineers (EA) ... ISICCE
International Society of Industrial Fabric Manufacturers (EA) ... ISIFM
International Society of Industrial Yarn Manufacturers [*Later, ISIFM*] (EA) ... ISIYM
International Society of Interior Designers (EA) ... ISID
International Society of Internal Medicine [*Langenthal, Switzerland*] (EA) ... ISIM
International Society of Introduction Services (EA) ... ISIS
International Society of Invertebrate Reproduction (EA) ... ISIR
International Society of Jewish Librarians (EA) ... ISJL
International Society of Literature [*Ilkley, Yorkshire, England*] (EAIO) ... ISL
International Society of Lymphology (EA) ... ISL
International Society of Magnetic Resonance ... ISMAR
International Society of Marine Engineers ... ISME
International Society of Mathematical Biology [*See also SIBM*] [*Antony, France*] (EAIO) ... ISMB
International Society of Mechanical Engineers ... ISME
International Society of Medical Hydrology and Climatology ... ISMH
International Society of Medical Hydrology and Climatology (EA) ... ISMHC
International Society of Microbiologists (DAVI) ... ISM
International Society of Mini- and Micro-Computers [*Calgary, AB*] (EAIO) ... ISMM
International Society of Naturopathic Physicians ... ISNP
International Society of Nephrology ... ISN
International Society of Offshore and Polar Engineers ... ISOPE
International Society of Organbuilders [*Levallois-Perret, France*] (EAIO) ... ISO
International Society of Parametric Analysts (EA) ... ISPA
International Society of Performing Arts Administrators (EA) ... ISPAA
International Society of Pharmaceutical Engineers (EA) ... ISPE
International Society of Philology ... SP
International Society of Phonetic Sciences (EA) ... ISPhS
International Society of Phonetic Sciences (EA) ... ISPS
International Society of Plant Molecular Biology (EA) ... ISPMB
International Society of Plant Morphologists [*Delhi, India*] (EAIO) ... ISPM
International Society of Plastic and Audio-Visual Art ... ISPAA
International Society of Political Psychology (EA) ... ISPP
International Society of Postmasters [*Montreal, PQ*] (EAIO) ... ISP
International Society of Prenatal and Perinatal Psychology and Medicine (EAIO) ... ISPP
International Society of Psychology of Handwriting [*Milan, Italy*] (EA) ... ISPH
International Society of Psychosomatic Obstetrics and Gynaecology (PDAA) ... ISPOG
International Society of Radiographers and Radiological Technicians [*Don Mills, ON*] (EA) ... ISRRT
International Society of Radiology [*Berne, Switzerland*] (EA) ... ISR
International Society of Radiology Congress ... ISRC
International Society of Reply Coupon Collectors (EA) ... RCC
International Society of Reproductive Medicine (EA) ... ISRM
International Society of Sculptors, Painters, and Gravers ... IS
International Society of Shropshires (EA) ... ISS
International Society of Soil Science [*See also AISS*] [*ICSU Wageningen, Netherlands*] (EAIO) ... ISSS
International Society of Sport Sponsors (EA) ... ISSS
International Society of Sports Psychology (EA) ... ISSP
International Society of Statistical Science in Economics (EA) ... ISSSE
International Society of Stress Analysts (EA) ... ISSA
International Society of Sugar Cane Technologists [*Piracicaoa, Brazil*] (EA) ... ISSCT
International Society of Surgery (DAVI) ... ISS
International Society of the Knee (EA) ... ISK
International Society of Transport Aircraft Trading (EA) ... ISTAT
International Society of Tropical Dermatology [*Later, International Society of Dermatology: Tropical, Geographic, and Ecologic - ISD*] ... ISTD
International Society of Tropical Dermatology (DAVI) ... ISTD
International Society of Tropical Foresters [*See also SIIFT*] (EA) ... ISTF
International Society of Tropical Pediatrics [*Philippines*] (EAIO) ... ISTP
International Society of Urology [*See also SIU*] [*Lille, France*] (EAIO) ... ISU
International Society of Videographers (EA) ... ISV
International Society of Violin and Bow Makers [*Basel, Switzerland*] (EAIO) ... ISVBM
International Society of Wang Users (EA) ... ISWU
International Society of Weekly Newspaper Editors (EA) ... ISWNE
International Society of Weighing and Measurement (EA) ... ISWM
International Society of Wine Tasters [*Defunct*] (EA) ... ISWT
International Society of Women Airline Pilots (EA) ... ISA
International Society of Women Airline Pilots (EA) ... ISWAP
International Society of Worldwide Stamp Collectors [*Formerly, Worldwide Collectors' Club - WCC*] ... ISWSC
International Society on Infectious Diseases and Human Infertility (EA) ... ISIDHI
International Society on Metabolic Eye Disease (EA) ... ISMED
International Society on Thrombosis and Hemostasis (EA) ... ISTH
International Society on Toxicology (EA) ... IST
International Sociological Association [*Research center Spain*] (IRC) ... ISA
International Softball Congress (EA) ... ISC
International Softball Federation (EA) ... ISF
International Softbill Society (EA) ... ISS
International Software AG Users Group (EA) ... ISAGUG
International Software Marketing (HGAA) ... ISM
International Soil Museum ... ISM
International Soil Reference and Information Centre [*Research center Netherlands*] (IRC) ... ISRIC
International Soil Tillage Research Organization [*Netherlands*] (EAIO) ... ISTRO
International Solar Energy Society [*Australia*] (EAIO) ... ISES
International Solar Polar [*Mission*] [*NASA*] ... ISP
International Solar Polar Mission [*NASA*] ... ISPM
International Solar Terrestrial Physics [*Proposed NASA mission*] ... ISTP
International Solid State Circuits Conference (MCD) ... ISSCC
International Solidarity Committee with Algerian Youth ... ISCAY
International Soling Association [*Bordon, Hampshire, England*] (EAIO) ... ISA
International Solvent Extraction Conference [*Toronto, ON, 1977*] [*Canada*] ... ISEC
International Somali Cat Club ... ISCC
International Songwriters' Association (EAIO) ... ISA
International Sorghum and Millet Research ... INTSORMIL
International Soros Science Education Program [*Privately-funded program for former Soviet Republics*] ... ISSEP
International Sorption Information Retrieval System [*Nuclear Energy Agency*] (EY) ... ISIRS
International Sound Programming Center [*Telecommunications*] ... ISPC
International Soundex Reunion Registry (EA) ... ISRR
International Sourdough Reunion (EA) ... ISR
International South Atlantic Buoy Program [*Marine science*] (OSRA) ... ISABP
International Southern Ocean Study [*National Science Foundation*] ... ISOS
International Soybean Program ... INTSOY
International Spa and Fitness Association ... I/SPA
International Spa and Tub Council [*Defunct*] (EA) ... ISTC
International Spa and Tub Institute (EA) ... ISTI
International Space: 1999 Alliance (EA) ... ISNA

International Space Congress ... ISC
International Space Corp. ... ISC
International Space Exploration and Colonization Company [*An association*] (EA) ... ISECCo
International Space Information System [*United Nations*] (DUND) ... ISIS
International Space Station ... ISS
International Space University [*Strasbourg, France*] ... ISU
International Space Year [*1992*] ... ISY
International Special Commission on Radio Interference (MCD) ... ISPR
International Special Dietary Foods Industries [*France*] (EAIO) ... ISDI
International Special Events Society (EA) ... ISES
International Special Librarians Day ... ISLD
International Special Tooling Association [*Frankfurt, Federal Republic of Germany*] (EA) ... ISTA
International Specialized Books Services [*Book distributor*] ... ISBS
International Specialty Products [*Associated Press*] (SAG) ... IntSpclty
International Specialty Products [*NYSE symbol*] (SPSG) ... ISP
International Species Information System (IID) ... ISIS
International Species Inventory System [*Data processing for animal mating*] [*Minnesota Zoological Gardens Apple Valley, MN*] ... ISIS
International Speedway Corp. [*Associated Press*] (SAG) ... IntlSpdw
International Speedway Corp. [*NASDAQ symbol*] (SAG) ... ISCA
International Spinal Research Trust [*British*] ... ISRT
International Spiritualist Federation [*British*] ... ISF
International Sport Show Producers Association (EA) ... ISSPA
International Sporting and Leisure Club ... ISLC
International Sporting Press Association ... ISPA
International Sports Equipment Fair [*Germany*] ... ISPO
International Sports Exchange (EA) ... ISE
International Sports Massage Federation (EA) ... ISMF
International Sports Organization for the Disabled [*Farstn, Sweden*] (EA) ... ISOD
International Sports Union of Post, Telephone, and Telecommunications Service (EA) ... ISUPTTS
International Sports Wagering, Inc. [*Associated Press*] (SAG) ... IntlSpr
International Sports Wagering, Inc. [*NASDAQ symbol*] (SAG) ... ISWI
International Spotted Pony Club [*Defunct*] (EA) ... ISPC
International Spring Fair [*British*] (ITD) ... ISF
International Squash Players Association [*Cardiff, Wales*] (EAIO) ... ISPA
International Squash Rackets Federation [*Cardiff, Wales*] (EAIO) ... ISRF
International Staff (NATG) ... IS
International Staff Disaster Assistance Information Coordinator [*NATO*] (NATG) ... ISDAIC
International Staff Duty Officer [*NATO*] (NATG) ... ISDO
International Staff Planners Memo [*NATO*] (NATG) ... ISPMEMO
International Staff Planners Message [*NATO*] (NATG) ... ISPM
International Stained Glass Association (EA) ... ISGA
International Stamp Collectors Society (EA) ... ISCS
International Stamp Exchange Association ... ISEA
International Standard ... IS
International Standard [*Vancouver Stock Exchange symbol*] ... IST
International Standard Atmosphere ... ISA
International Standard Atmosphere [*ICAO*] (FAAC) ... ISA
International Standard Bible Encyclopaedia [*A publication*] (BJA) ... ISBE
International Standard Bibliographic Description [*Library of Congress*] ... ISBD
International Standard Bibliographic Description - Antiquarian ... ISBD(A)
International Standard Bibliographic Description (Component Parts) ... ISBD(CP)
International Standard Bibliographic Description for Cartographic Materials [*Library of Congress*] ... ISBD(CM)
International Standard Bibliographic Description for Monographs [*Library of Congress*] ... ISBD(M)
International Standard Bibliographic Description for Non-Book Materials ... ISBD(NBM)
International Standard Bibliographic Description for Printed Music ... ISBD(PM)
International Standard Bibliographic Description for Serials [*Library of Congress*] ... ISBD(S)
International Standard Bibliographic Description - General ... ISBD(G)
International Standard Book Number [*Library of Congress*] ... ISBN
International Standard Book Number [*Online database field identifier*] ... SB
International Standard Classification of Education (MCD) ... ISCED
International Standard Classification of Occupations (WDAA) ... ISCO
International Standard Code for Information Interchange (NATG) ... ISCII
International Standard Commodity Classification of All Goods and Services ... ISCC
International Standard Data Network (NITA) ... ISDN
International Standard Density Unit (DGA) ... ISDU
International Standard Electric Corp. (NATG) ... ISEC
International Standard Engineering, Inc. (NATG) ... ISEI
International Standard Equipment Practice (MHDB) ... ISEP
International Standard Industrial Classification (EY) ... ISIC
International Standard Orthopaedic Measurements [*Medicine*] ... ISOM
International Standard Paper Sizes ... ISPS
International Standard Program Number [*Numbering system for software*] ... ISPN
International Standard Serial Number [*Library of Congress*] ... ISSN
International Standard Statistical Classification of Aquatic Animals and Plants ... ISSCAAP
International Standard Thread (MCD) ... INTSTDTHD
International Standard Thread (MSA) ... IST
International Standards Association ... ISA
International Standards Group Ltd. [*Associated Press*] (SAG) ... IntStand
International Standards Group Ltd. [*NASDAQ symbol*] (SAG) ... ISGI
International Standards Method (IAA) ... ISM
International Standards Organization [*Communications*] (PCM) ... ISO
International Standards Organization/Open System Interface [*Motorola, Inc.*] ... ISO/OSI
International Standards Organization-Authorized Alphabetic Characters (MCD) ... ISO-ALPHABET
International Standing Committee on Distribution Problems [*International Water Supply Association*] ... ISCDP
International Standing Committee on Water Quality and Treatment [*International Water Supply Association*] ... ISCWQT
International Standing Conference for the History of Education (AIE) ... ISCHE
International Standing Conference on Philanthropy [*Yalding, Kent, England*] (EAIO) ... INTERPHIL
International Staple, Nail, and Tool Association (EA) ... ISANTA
International Star Class Yacht Racing Association (EA) ... ISCYRA
International Star Registry ... ISR
International Stationary Steam Engine Society (EAIO) ... ISSES
International Statistical Classification ... ISC
International Statistical Education Centre [*India*] ... ISEC
International Statistical Institute [*ICSU*] [*Voorburg, Netherlands*] (EA) ... ISI
International Statistical Institute Research Center [*Research center Netherlands*] (IRC) ... ISIRC
International Statistical Programs Center [*Department of Commerce*] (IID) ... ISPC
International Statistical Programs Office [*Department of Commerce*] (IEEE) ... ISPO
International Steam Table Calorie (IIA) ... IT
International Steamboat Society (EA) ... ISS
International Steel Guitar Convention (EA) ... ISGC
International Stereoscopic Union (PDAA) ... ISU
International Stereotypers and Electrotypers Union [*Later, IPGCU*] ... ISEU
International Sterling [*Vancouver Stock Exchange symbol*] ... ISH
International Stiltwalkers Association (EA) ... ISA
International Stock [*Business term*] ... IS
International Stock Exchange ... ISE
International Stock Exchange of the United Kingdom and the Republic of Ireland (DFIT) ... ISE
International Stoke Mandeville Games Federation [*Aylesbury, Buckinghamshire, England*] (EA) ... ISMGF
International Stop Continental Drift Society [*Defunct*] (EA) ... ISCDS
International Strabismological Association (EAIO) ... ISA
International Strategic Studies Association (EA) ... ISSA
International Streptomyces Project ... ISP
International Stress and Tension Control Association (EA) ... ISTC
International Student Conference ... ISC
International Student Exchange Program [*United States Information Agency*] ... ISEP
International Student Identity Card (BARN) ... ISIC
International Student Information Service ... ISIS
International Student Pugwash [*Formerly, USSPC*] [*Later, Student Pugwash (USA)*] (EA) ... ISP
International Student Relief [*Later, WUS*] ... ISR
International Student, Trade, Environment and Development Program (CROSS) ... INSTEAD
International Student Travel Confederation [*Switzerland*] (EAIO) ... ISTC
International Students, Inc. (EA) ... ISI
International Students Peace Network (EA) ... ISPN
International Students Society [*Defunct*] (EA) ... ISS
International Studies Association (EA) ... ISA
International Study Commission for Traffic Police ... ISCTP
International Study Group for Aerogrammes ... ISGA
International Study Group for Mathematics Learning [*British*] ... ISGML
International Study Group for Steroid Hormones [*Rome, Italy*] (EAIO) ... ISGSH
International Study Group for Waterworks in the Rhine Catchment Area [*See also IAWR*] (EAIO) ... ISGWRCA
International Study Group of Diabetes in Children and Adolescents [*Linkoping, Sweden*] (EAIO) ... ISGD
International Study Group on Risk Analysis ... ISGRA
International Study Institution of the Middle Classes [*Brussels, Belgium*] (EAIO) ... ISIMC
International Study of Infarct Survival [*Medicine*] ... ISIS
International Study of Kidney Disease in Children ... ISKDC
International Study Program ... ISP
International Subcommittee on Lactobacilli and Closely Related Organisms ... ISL
International Subscriber Dialing [*Later, IDD*] [*Telecommunications*] ... ISD
International Sugar Agreement [*1958*] ... ISA
International Sugar Council [*London*] [*Later, ISO*] ... ISC
International Sugar Organization [*See also OIA*] [*British*] (EAIO) ... ISO
International Sugar Research Foundation [*Later, WSRO*] (EA) ... ISRF
International Sun-Earth Explorer [*NASA/ESRO satellite*] ... ISEE
International Sun-Earth Explorer [*Marine science*] (OSRA) ... ISEE
International Sun-Earth Physics Satellite ... ISEPS
International Suneva Resources [*Vancouver Stock Exchange symbol*] ... ISN
International Sunfish Class Association (EA) ... ISCA
International Sunshine Society (EA) ... ISS
International Superconductivity Industry Summit [*Conference*] ... ISIS
International Superconductivity Technology Center [*Japan*] ... ISTEC
International Superphosphate Manufacturers' Association [*Later, IFA*] ... ISMA
International Supply Committee [*World War II*] ... ISC
International Supreme Council of World Masons (EA) ... ISC
International Surfing Association [*Swansea, England*] (EAIO) ... ISA
International Survey Libraries Association [*University of Connecticut*] (NITA) ... ISLA
International Survey Library Association (EA) ... ISLA
International Survey of Legal Decisions on Labour Law [*1925-38*] [*A publication*] (DLA) ... Int'l Surv LDLL
International Survey of Legal Decisions on Labour Law [*1925-38*] [*A publication*] (DLA) ... ISLL

International Survey Research [*London consultancy firm*] ... ISR
International Survey Research Corp. ... ISRC
International Swap Dealers' Association ... ISDA
International Swaps and Derivatives Association (ECON) ... ISDA
International Sweets Market [*Trade fair*] [*Cologne, West Germany 1982*] ... ISM
International Swift Association (EA) ... ISA
International Swimming Hall of Fame (EA) ... ISHOF
International Switching and Testing Center [*Communications*] ... ISTC
International Switching Center [*Communications*] ... ISC
International Switching Maintenance Center [*Communications*] ... ISMC
International Swizzle Stick Collectors Association (EA) ... ISSCA
International Symbol of Access [*Department of Transportation*] (EGAO) ... ISA
International Symposium for Testing and Failure Analysis [*Annual electronics symposium*] (NITA) ... ISTFA
International Symposium on Aerospace Nuclear Propulsion (MCD) ... ISASNP
International Symposium on Antarctic Glaciological Exploration ... ISAGE
International Symposium on Biomembranes ... ISB
International Symposium on Chemical Reaction Engineering ... ISCRE
International Symposium on Chemiluminescence ... ISC
International Symposium on Circuits and Systems [*IEEE*] (MCD) ... ISCAS
International Symposium on Column Liquid Chromatography [*1986*] [*San Francisco, CA*] ... ISCLC
International Symposium on Comparative Law [*A publication*] (DLA) ... Int'l Sym Comp L
International Symposium on Cooling Systems (PDAA) ... ISCS
International Symposium on Dredging Technology (PDAA) ... ISDT
International Symposium on Fluorine Chemistry ... ISFC
International Symposium on HLtd. of Proteins, Peptides, and Polynucleotides ... ISPPP
International Symposium on Homogeneous Catalysis ... ISHC
International Symposium on Identification and Measurement of Environmental Pollutants (PDAA) ... ISIMEP
International Symposium on Industrial Robots (PDAA) ... ISIR
International Symposium on Jet Cutting Technology (PDAA) ... ISJCT
International Symposium on Laboratory Automation and Robotics ... ISLAR
International Symposium on Laboratory Robotics ... ISLR
International Symposium on Microchemistry ... ISM
International Symposium on Microtechniques ... ISM
International Symposium on Novel Aromatic Compounds ... ISNA
International Symposium on Olfaction and Taste ... ISOT
International Symposium on Purine Metabolism in Man ... ISPMM
International Symposium on Rocket and Satellite Meteorology ... ISRSM
International Symposium on Space Electronics (MCD) ... ISSET
International Symposium on Space Technology and Science (MCD) ... ISTS
International Symposium on Subscribers' Loops and Services [*Telecommunications*] (TEL) ... ISSLS
International Symposium on the Aerodynamics and Ventilation of Vehicle Tunnels (PDAA) ... ISAVVT
International Symposium on the Application of Computers and Operations Research in the Mineral Industries ... APCOM
International Symposium on the Chemistry of the Organic Solid State ... ISCOSS
International Symposium on the Industrial Applications of the Mossbauer Effect ... ISIAME
International Symposium on Ultrasonic Diagnostics in Ophthalmology [*Later, ISO U*] (EA) ... ISUDO
International Symposium on Wave and Tidal Energy (PDAA) ... WTE
International Synthetic Rubber Co. [*United Kingdom*] ... ISR
International Sysmposium on Marine Engineering (PDAA) ... ISME
International SYSOP [*System Operator*] **Guild** ... ISG
International System [*FHWA*] (TAG) ... SI
International System for Human Cytogenetic Nomenclature ... ISCN
International System of Units ... ISU
International System of Units (ACII) ... SI
International Systems Meeting [*Computer science*] ... ISM
International Table Calorie [*Dietetics*] (DAVI) ... ITc
International Table Calorie ... ITCAL
International Table Tennis Federation [*British*] ... ITTF
International Table Tennis League (EA) ... ITTL
International Tandem Users' Group (EA) ... ITUG
International Tanker Nominal Freight Scale Association ... ITNFSA
International Tanker Owners Pollution Federation ... ITOPF
International Tanker Safety Conference (DS) ... INTASAFCON
International Tanning Manufacturers Association [*Defunct*] (EA) ... ITMA
International Tap Association (EA) ... ITA
International Tape Association (NITA) ... ITA
International Tape/Disc Association (EA) ... ITA
International Tar Conference [*See also CIG*] [*Paris, France*] (EAIO) ... ITC
International Target Audience Code [*International Federation of Library Associations*] ... ITAC
International Taurus Resources [*Vancouver Stock Exchange symbol*] ... ITU
International Tax and Business Lawyer [*A publication*] (DLA) ... Int'l Tax & Bus Law
International Tax Institute (EA) ... ITI
International Tax Journal [*A publication*] (DLA) ... Int Tax Jour
International Tax Management System [*Price Waterhouse & Co.*] ... ITMS
International Taxicab Association (EA) ... ITA
International Tea Committee (EAIO) ... ITC
International Tea Promotion Association [*Defunct*] (EAIO) ... ITPA
International Teachers Temperance Association [*Denmark*] (EAIO) ... IVES
International Technical Caramel Association (EA) ... ITCA
International Technical Communications Conference [*Society for Technical Communication*] ... ITCC
International Technical Institute of Flight Engineers ... ITI
International Technical Integration Panel ... ITIP
International Technical Tropical Timber Association ... ITTTA
International Technogeographical Society ... ITS
International Technologies & Systems [*Computer science*] ... ITS
International Technology Corp. [*Associated Press*] (SAG) ... IT
International Technology Corp. [*Associated Press*] (SAG) ... IT Corp
International Technology Corp. [*NYSE symbol*] (SPSG) ... ITX
International Technology Council [*Defunct*] (EA) ... ITC
International Technology Education Association (EA) ... ITEA
International Technology Institute (EA) ... ITI
International Technology Underwriters [*Consortium, Washington*] (NITA) ... INTEC
International Tele/Conferencing Association (EA) ... IT/CA
International Telecom Systems, Inc. [*Madison, WI*] [*Telecommunications*] (TSSD) ... ITS
International Telecommunication Advisory Committee-Telecommunications (ACRL) ... ITAC-T
International Telecommunication Data Systems, Inc. [*Associated Press*] (SAG) ... IntlTDS
International Telecommunication Data Systems, Inc. [*NASDAQ symbol*] (SAG) ... ITDS
International Telecommunication Union [*Formerly, International Telegraphic Union*] [*A specialized agency of the United Nations*] [*Switzerland Research center*] ... ITU
International Telecommunication Union-Radio Communication Sector (ACRL) ... ITU-R
International Telecommunication Union-Telecommunication Development Sector (ACRL) ... ITU-D
International Telecommunication Union-Telecommunication Standardization Sector (ACRL) ... ITU-T
International Telecommunications Post [*Facsimile transmission service*] (NITA) ... INTELPOST
International Telecommunications Satellite Consortium [*Later, International Telecommunications Satellite Organization*] (IAA) ... INTELSA
International Telecommunications Satellite Consortium (NITA) ... INTELSAT
International Telecommunications Satellite Consortium [*Superseded by International Telecommunications Satellite Organization*] ... ITSC
International Telecommunications Satellite Organization (EA) ... INTELSAT
International Telecommunications Satellite Organization [*Washington, D.C.*] (WDMC) ... Intelsat
International Telecommunications Society (EA) ... ITS
International Telecommunications Union [*An association*] (PCM) ... ITU
International Telecommunications Union - Telecommunications Switching System (PCM) ... ITU-TSS
International Telecommunications Users Group [*Telecommunications Information service or system*] (IID) ... INTUG
International Telecommunictaions Standards Technical Council (OSI) ... ITSTC
International Telegraph Alphabet (NATG) ... ITA
International Telegraph and Telephonic Advisory Committee (AABC) ... ITTAC
International Telemetering Conference ... ITC
International Telephone and Telegraph Communication System ... ITTCS
International Telephone & Telegraph Corp. [*New York, NY*] [*Facetious translation: International Travel and Talk*] ... IT and T
International Telephone & Telegraph Corp., Gilfillan Division, Engineering Library, Van Nuys, CA [*Library symbol Library of Congress*] (LCLS) ... CVnITT
International Telephone and Telegraph Federal Laboratories ... ITTF
International Telephone and Telegraph Federal Laboratories ... ITTFL
International Telephone and Telegraph Laboratories (SAA) ... ITTL
International Telephone & Telegraph World Communications, Inc. ... ITTCOM
International Telephone Credit Union Association (EA) ... ITCUA
International Telephone Exchange [*Telecommunications*] (TEL) ... ITE
International Telephone Services Center [*Telecommunications*] (TEL) ... ITSC
International Telepresence Corp. (ECON) ... ITC
International Teleproduction Society (EA) ... ITS
International Telesis Industries Corp. [*Vancouver Stock Exchange symbol*] ... ITI
International Teletraffic Congress [*Telecommunications*] ... ITC
International Televent (EA) ... INTELEVENT
International Television (IAA) ... INTERVISION
International Television Association (EA) ... ITVA
International Television Broadcasting ... ITVB
International Television Center [*Communications*] ... ITC
International Television News [*A publication*] (EAAP) ... ITN
International Television Program Center [*Telecommunications*] (TEL) ... ITPC
International Television Service [*Turner Teleport, Inc.*] [*Atlanta, GA*] [*Telecommunications service*] (TSSD) ... ITS
International Telex Subscriber Dialling (NITA) ... IXSD
International Temperance Association [*Later, IHTA*] (EA) ... ITA
International Temperance Union ... ITU
International Temperature Scale (MUGU) ... ITS
International Tennis Federation [*Formerly, ILTF*] (EA) ... ITF
International Tennis Hall of Fame (EA) ... ITHOF
International Terminal Accounting and Banking Service [*Computer science*] (MHDB) ... INTABS
International Tesla Society (EA) ... ITS
International Test and Evaluation Association (EA) ... ITEA
International Test Operations Procedure [*DoD*] ... ITOP
International Test Pilot School [*British ICAO designator*] (FAAC) ... ITP
International Testing Services Inc. [*Associated Press*] (SAG) ... IntTest
International Texcan Tech [*Vancouver Stock Exchange symbol*] ... ITA
International Textbook Co. ... INTEXT
International Textile and Fabrics Trade Fair ... INTERTEX
International Textile and Garment Workers' Federation [*Later, ITGLWF*] ... ITGWF
International Textile, Garment, and Leather Workers' Federation [*See also FITTHC*] [*Brussels, Belgium*] (EAIO) ... ITGLWF
International Textile Manufacturers Federation [*Zurich, Switzerland*] (EA) ... ITMF
International Theatre Institute [*Paris, France*] (EAIO) ... ITI

International Theatre Institute of the United States (EA) .... ITI/US
International Theatrical Agencies Association (EA) .... ITAA
International Theological Library [*A publication*] .... ITL
International Thermal Storage Advisory Council (EAIO) .... ITSAC
International Thermographers Association (EA) .... ITA
International Thermonuclear Experimental Reactor .... ITER
International Thesaurus of Quotations [*A publication*] .... ITQ
International Thespian Society (EA) .... ITS
International Third World Legal Studies Association (EA) .... INTWORLSA
International Thomson Books .... ITB
International Thomson Books - International Division .... ITB-ID
International Thomson Business Press, Inc. [*Publisher*] .... ITBP
International Thomson Holdings, Inc. .... ITHI
International Thomson Industrial Press .... ITIP
International Thomson Information, Inc. [*Later, ITLS*] .... ITII
International Thomson Library Services .... ITLS
International Thomson Organisation [*Later, The Thomson Corp.*] .... ITO
International Thomson Organisation, Inc. .... ITOI
International Thomson Organisation Ltd. [*Later, TTC*] .... ITOL
International Thomson Organisation Public Limited Co. .... ITOPLC
International Thomson Professional Publishing .... ITPP
International Thomson Publishing [*Also, ITPI*] .... ITP
International Thomson Publishing, Inc. [*Also, ITP*] .... ITPI
International Thomson Publishing - International Division .... ITP-ID
International Thomson Publishing Services .... ITPS
International Thoroughbred Breeders, Inc. [*Associated Press*] (SAG) .... InThr
International Thoroughbred Breeders, Inc. [*Associated Press*] (SAG) .... IntThr
International Thoroughbred Breeders, Inc. [*AMEX symbol*] (SPSG) .... ITB
International Thoroughbred Exposition and Conference [*Kentucky Thoroughbred Association, Inc.*] (TSPED) .... ITEC
International Thrift Institute .... ITI
International through Government Bill of Lading .... ITGBL
International Throughbred Breeders, Inc. [*Associated Press*] (SAG) .... IntThrgh
International Thunderbird Class Association (EA) .... ITCA
International Thunderwood Explorations Ltd. [*Vancouver Stock Exchange symbol Toronto Stock Exchange symbol*] .... IUE
International Tillex Enterprises Ltd. [*Vancouver Stock Exchange symbol*] .... ITX
International Time Bureau .... ITB
International Time-Sharing Corporation [*Telecommunications*] (NITA) .... ITS
International Tin Agreement .... ITA
International Tin Council [*See also CIE*] [*Defunct*] (EAIO) .... ITC
International Tin Research Council [*Middlesex, England*] (EAIO) .... ITRC
International Tin Research Institute (EAIO) .... ITRI
International Tire Association (EA) .... ITA
International Toastmistress Clubs (EA) .... ITC
International TOGA [*Tropical Ocean Global Atmosphere*] **Project Office** [*Geneva, Switzerland*] (EAIO) .... ITPO
International TOKAMAK Reactor [*Thermonuclear-fusion system*] .... INTOR
International Tolerance .... IT
International Toll Free [*Telecommunications*] .... ITF
International Tornado Association [*Germany*] (EAIO) .... ITA
International Torus Design [*Nuclear energy*] (NUCP) .... INTOR
International Totalizator Systems, Inc. [*NASDAQ symbol*] (NQ) .... ITSI
International Touring Alliance [*Belgium*] (EAIO) .... ITA
International Tourism Management [*Australia*] .... ITM
International Tourist Entertainment Corp. [*Associated Press*] (SAG) .... InTour
International Tourist Entertainment Corp. [*Associated Press*] (SAG) .... IntTourE
International Tourist Entertainment Corp. [*NASDAQ symbol*] (SAG) .... ITEC
International Tourist Year .... ITY
International Toxicity Equivalency Factor [*Toxicology*] .... I-TEF
International Toy Buff's Association (EA) .... ITBA
International Tracing Service [*Arolsen, Germany*] (EAIO) .... ITS
International Track and Field Coaches Association [*Athens, Greece*] (EAIO) .... ITFCA
International Track Association [*Defunct*] .... ITA
International Trade Administration [*Washington, DC Department of Commerce*] .... ITA
International Trade and Arms Regulations .... ITAR
International Trade and Investment Act [*1984*] .... ITIA
International Trade and Resource Information System [*University of Alaska at Anchorage*] [*Information service or system*] (CRD) .... ITRIS
International Trade Association [*BTS*] (TAG) .... ITA
International Trade Centre [*Switzerland United Nations*] (MCD) .... ITC
International Trade Club of Chicago [*Later, IBCM*] (EA) .... ITC
International Trade Commission [*Databank originator*] .... ITC
International Trade Commission, Washington, DC [*Library symbol Library of Congress*] (LCLS) .... DTC
International Trade Council (EA) .... ITC
International Trade Enhancement Program .... ITEP
International Trade Exhibitions in France (EA) .... ITEF
International Trade Fair [*New Zealand*] .... ITF
International Trade Fairs Office [*Department of Commerce*] .... ITFO
International Trade in Textiles [*Textile trade agreement*] .... ITT
International Trade Information Service .... ITIS
International Trade Law Branch [*United Nations*] (DUND) .... ITLB
International Trade Law Journal [*A publication*] (DLA) .... Int Trade LJ
International Trade Names Dictionary [*Later, IBTC*] [*A publication*] .... ITND
International Trade Organization .... ITO
International Trade Secretariats [*ICFTU*] .... ITS
International Trade Unions Committee of Social Tourism and Leisure [*See also CSITSL*] [*Prague, Czechoslovakia*] (EAIO) .... ITUCSTL
International Traders Association (EA) .... IT
International Traders Club (EA) .... ITC
International Trading Certificate (DS) .... ITC
International Traditional Karate Federation (EA) .... ITKF
International Traffic in Arms Regulation [*US*] .... ITAR
International [*Passenger*] **Traffic Management System** [*MTMC*] (TAG) .... ITRAM
International Training Branch [*Office of Education*] .... ITB
International Training College [*Salvation Army*] .... ITC
International Training in Communication (EA) .... ITC
International Training Institute .... ITI
International Training School .... ITS
International Trans Asia [*Vancouver Stock Exchange symbol*] .... ITC
International Transactional Analysis Association (EA) .... ITAA
International Transboundary Resource Center [*University of New Mexico Law School*] (CROSS) .... CIRT
International Transfer Printing Institute (EA) .... ITPI
International Translations Centre [*Formerly, ETC*] (EA) .... ITC
International Translator (IAA) .... ITSL
International Transmission Maintenance Center [*Communications*] .... ITMC
International Transplant Nurses Society (EA) .... ITNS
International Transport Exhibition .... ITEC
International Transport Workers' Federation [*London, England*] (EAIO) .... ITF
International Transport Workers' Federation .... ITWF
International Transportation Advisory Board [*BTS*] (TAG) .... ITAB
International Transportation Tracking System [*Department of Transportation*] .... INTRANST
International Trauma Anesthesia and Critical Care Society (EA) .... ITACCS
International Travel (MCD) .... INTRA
International Travel and Trailer Club (EA) .... ITTC
International Travel Host Exchange .... ITHE
International Travel Market Research Council .... ITMRC
International Travel Orders .... ITO
International Travel Show (ITD) .... ITS
International Travel-Adventure Film Guild [*Defunct*] (EA) .... INTRAFILM
International Travelers Health Institute (EA) .... ITHI
International Travellers [*YWCA*] .... IT
International Tree Crops Institute USA (EA) .... ITCI
International Tree Disease Register [*US Forest Service*] (NITA) .... INTREDIS
International Tree Disease Register System for Literature Retrieval in Forest Pathology [*National Agricultural Library*] .... INTREDIS
International Tree-Ring Data Bank [*University of Arizona*] (IID) .... ITRDB
International Tremor Foundation (EA) .... ITF
International Triathlon Union (EAIO) .... ITU
International Trojan Development Corp. [*Vancouver Stock Exchange symbol*] .... ITJ
International Trombone Association (EA) .... ITA
International Tropical Fern Society [*Defunct*] (EA) .... ITFS
International Tropical Timber Agreement (ECON) .... ITTA
International Tropical Timber Council [*Australia*] .... ITTC
International Tropical Timber Organization [*Yokohama, Japan*] [*United Nations*] .... ITTO
International Trotting and Pacing Association (EA) .... ITPA
International Truck of the Year .... ITOY
International Truck of the Year .... ITOY
International Truck Parts Association (EA) .... ITPA
International Truck Restorers Association (EA) .... ITRA
International Trucking Show (ITD) .... ITS
International Trumpet Guild (EA) .... ITG
International Trypanotolerance Centre [*Gambia*] .... ITC
International Tsunami Information Center (EA) .... ITIC
International Tube Association [*Leamington Spa, Warwickshire, England*] (EAIO) .... ITA
International Tuberculosis Association (DAVI) .... ITA
International Tuberculosis Campaign .... ITC
International Tug-of-War Association (EA) .... ITWA
International Tungsten Industry Association (EAIO) .... ITIA
International Tunnelling Association (EA) .... ITA
International Turbine Tech [*Vancouver Stock Exchange symbol*] .... ITN
International Turfgrass Society (EA) .... ITS
International Turquoise Association (EA) .... ITA
International Turtle and Tortoise Society (EA) .... IT & TS
International Twelve-Star Admiral and Deputy Custodian of the Fountain of Inexhaustible Knowledge [*Rank in Junior Woodchucks organization mentioned in Donald Duck comic by Carl Barks*] .... ITSAADCOTFOIK
International Twin Study [*University of Southern California*] [*Research center*] (RCD) .... ITS
International Twins Association [*Defunct*] (EA) .... ITA
International Typeface Corp. .... ITC
International Typographic Association (MCD) .... ITA
International Typographic Composition Association [*Later, TIA*] (EA) .... ITCA
International Typographical Union (EA) .... ITU
International Typographical Union Ruling Machine .... ITURM
International Tyre, Rubber, and Plastic Federation (EAIO) .... ITRPF
International Ultraviolet Explorer [*NASA*] .... IUE
International Underwater Contractors, Inc. .... IUC
International Underwater Research Corp. .... IURC
International Underwater Spearfishing Association (EA) .... IUSA
International Unicycling Federation (EA) .... IUF
International Union Against Cancer [*An association*] (CDI) .... IUAC
International Union Against Tuberculosis [*Later, IUATLD*] (EAIO) .... IUAT
International Union Against Tuberculosis (DAVI) .... IUTM
International Union Against Tuberculosis and Lung Disease [*See also UICTMR*] (EAIO) .... IUATLD
International Union Against Venereal Diseases and Treponematoses (EAIO) .... IUVDT
International Union, Allied Industrial Workers of America (EA) .... AIW
International Union for Child Welfare [*Geneva, Switzerland*] [*Defunct*] .... IUCW
International Union for Conservation of Nature [*World Conservation Union*] (USDC) .... IUCN

International Union for Conservation of Nature and Natural Resources [*Research Center*] [*ICSU*] [*Switzerland*] (EA) .... IUCN
International Union for Conservation of Nature and Natural Resources [*ICS U*] [*Research center Switzerland*] .... IUCNNR
International Union for Electroheat [*Also, IUE-H*] .... IUE
International Union for Electroheat [*Also, IUE*] .... IUE-H
International Union for Inland Navigation [*Strasbourg, France*] (EA) .... IUIN
International Union for Land Value Taxation and Free Trade [*British*] (EAIO) .... IULVTFT
International Union for Moral and Social Action .... IUMS
International Union for Physical and Engineering Sciences in Medicine [*ICSU*] [*Ottawa, ON*] (EAIO) .... IUPESM
International Union for Protecting Public Morality [*Later, International Union for Moral and Social Action*] .... IUPM
International Union for Quaternary Research [*Research center France*] (IRC) .... INQUA
International Union for Research of Communication [*Berne, Switzerland*] (EAIO) .... IURC
International Union for Surface Finishing (EAIO) .... IUSF
International Union for the Conservation of Nature's Primate Specialist Group (EA) .... IUCNPSG
International Union for the Protection of Literary and Artistic Works .... IUPLAW
International Union for the Protection of Nature [*Later, IUCN*] .... IUPN
International Union for the Protection of New Varieties of Plants (GNE) .... IUPOV
International Union for the Protection of New Varieties of Plants (EERA) .... UPOV
International Union for the Scientific Study of Population [*Liege, Belgium*] .... IUSSP
International Union for the Study of Social Insects [*Utrecht, Netherlands*] .... IUSSI
International Union for Toxicology .... IUTOX
International Union for Vacuum Science, Technique, and Applications [*See also UISTAV*] (EAIO) .... IUVSTA
International Union of Academies (EA) .... IUA
International Union of Advertisers Associations [*Later, WFA*] (EAIO) .... IUAA
International Union of Agricultural Journalists .... IUAJ
International Union of Air Pollution Prevention Associations [*See also UIAPPA*] [*England*] (EAIO) .... IUAPPA
International Union of Allied Novelty and Production Workers (EA) .... IUANPW
International Union of Allied Novelty and Production Workers .... NPW
International Union of Alpine Associations .... IUAA
International Union of Anthropological and Ethnological Sciences [*See also UISAE*] [*ICSU Gwynedd, Wales*] (EAIO) .... IUAES
International Union of Architects .... IUA
International Union of Associations of Doctor-Motorists .... IUADM
International Union of Aviation Insurers [*British*] (EAIO) .... IUAI
International Union of Bakery, Confectionery, and Tobacco Workers (BARN) .... IUBCTW
International Union of Biochemistry (EA) .... IUB
International Union of Biological Sciences [*Paris, France*] .... IUBS
International Union of Bricklayers and Allied Craftsmen (EA) .... BAC
International Union of Building Societies and Savings Associations [*Later, IOHFI*] [*Chicago, IL*] (EA) .... IUBSSA
International Union of Commercial Agents and Brokers [*EC*] (ECED) .... IUCAB
International Union of Co-operative and Associated Tourism (EAIO) .... UITCA
International Union of Crystallography [*See also UIC*] (EA) .... IU Cr
International Union of Crystallography .... IUC
International Union of Directors of Zoological Gardens [*Canada*] (EAIO) .... IUDZG
International Union of Doll and Toy Workers of the US and Canada [*Later, IUANPW*] (EA) .... IDTW
International Union of Electrical, Radio, and Machine Workers .... IUE
International Union of Electrical, Radio, and Machine Workers (IAA) .... IUERMW
International Union of Electrical Workers .... IUEW
International Union of Electronic [*Electrical, technical, salaried and machine workers*] (NITA) .... IUE
International Union of Electronic, Electrical, Technical, Salaried, Machine, andFurniture Workers (EA) .... IUE
International Union of Elevator Constructors (EA) .... IUEC
International Union of Esperantist-Philologists [*Sofia, Bulgaria*] (EAIO) .... IUEP
International Union of European Guides and Scouts [*See also UIGSE*] [*Chateau Landon, France*] (EAIO) .... IUEGS
International Union of Family Organizations [*Paris, France*] .... IUFO
International Union of Food and Allied Workers' Associations [*See also IUL*] [*Petit-Lancy, Switzerland*] (EAIO) .... IUF
International Union of Food, Drink, and Tobacco Workers' Associations .... IUFDT
International Union of Food Science and Technology [*ICSU*] [*Dublin, Republic of Ireland*] (EAIO) .... IUFoST
International Union of Forestry Research Organizations [*Vienna, Austria*] [*Research center*] (EAIO) .... IUFRO
International Union of French-Language Journalists and Press [*See also UIJPLF*] [*Paris, France*] (EAIO) .... IUFLJP
International Union of Game Biologists [*Canada*] (EAIO) .... IUGB
International Union of Geodesy and Geophysics [*Brussels, Belgium*] .... IUGG
International Union of Geodesy and Geophysics Tsunami Commission [*Marine science*] (OSRA) .... IUGGTC
International Union of Geological Sciences [*ICSU*] [*Trondheim, Norway*] (EA) .... IUGS
International Union of Gospel Missions (EA) .... IUGM
International Union of Graphic Reproduction Industries [*Later, IUI*] (EAIO) .... IUGRI
International Union of Health Education [*See also UIES*] [*Paris, France*] (EAIO) .... IUHE
International Union of Hotel, Restaurant, and Bar Workers .... IUHR
International Union of Housing Finance Institutions (EAIO) .... IUHFI
International Union of Immunological Societies (EA) .... IUIS
International Union of Journeymen Horseshoers of the United States and Canada (EA) .... IUJHUSC
International Union of Journeymen Horseshoers of the United States and Canada .... UJH
International Union of Leather Chemists Societies .... IULCS
International Union of Liberal Christian Women .... IULCW
International Union of Life Insurance Agents [*Milwaukee, WI*] (EA) .... IULIA
International Union of Life Insurance Agents .... LIA
International Union of Local Authorities [*The Hague, Netherlands*] (EA) .... IULA
International Union of Lorry Drivers [*See also UICR*] [*Munich, Germany*] (EAIO) .... IULD
International Union of Marine Insurance [*Basel, Switzerland*] .... IUMI
International Union of Master Painters [*See also UNIEP*] [*Brussels, Belgium*] (EAIO) .... IUMP
International Union of Microbiological Societies [*University of Newcastle*] (EA) .... IUMS
International Union of Microbiological Societies Bacteriology Division [*B eckenham, Kent, England*] (EAIO) .... IUMSBD
International Union of Mine, Mill, and Smelter Workers [*Later, USWA*] .... IUMMSW
International Union of Mine, Mill, and Smelter Workers [*Later, USWA*] .... MMSW
International Union of Nutritional Sciences [*Wageningen, Netherlands*] .... IUNS
International Union of Official Travel Organisations [*Later, WTO*] .... IUOTO
International Union of Operating Engineers (EA) .... IUOE
International Union of Petroleum and Industrial Workers (EA) .... IUPIW
International Union of Petroleum Workers [*Later, IUPIW*] (EA) .... IUPW
International Union of Pharmacology [*ICSU*] [*Buckingham, England*] (MSC) .... IUPHAR
International Union of Phlebology [*Paris, France*] (EA) .... IUP
International Union of Physiological Sciences [*ICSU*] [*Gif-sur-Yvette, France*] (ASF) .... IUPS
International Union of Police Associations (EA) .... IUPA
International Union of Practitioners in Advertising .... IUPA
International Union of Prehistoric and Protohistoric Sciences [*Ghent, Belgium*] (EAIO) .... IUPPS
International Union of Psychological Science (EA) .... IUPS
International Union of Psychological Science (EA) .... IUPsyS
International Union of Public Transportation .... IUPT
International Union of Pure and Applied Biophysics [*ICSU*] [*Pecs, Hungary*] [*Research center*] (EA) .... IUPAB
International Union of Pure and Applied Chemistry [*Research center British*] (IRC) .... IUPAC
International Union of Pure and Applied Physics [*ICSU*] [*Goteborg, Sweden*] (EA) .... IUPAP
International Union of Radio Science (MSC) .... IURS
International Union of Radioecologists (EA) .... IUR
International Union of Railway Medical Services (EA) .... IURMS
International Union of Railways [*Paris*] .... IUR
International Union of Reticuloendothelial Societies (EA) .... IURES
International Union of Roofing and Plumbing (EAIO) .... IURP
International Union of School and University Health and Medicine [*See also UIHMSU*] [*Brussels, Belgium*] (EAIO) .... IUSUHM
International Union of Security Officers (EA) .... IUSO
International Union of Socialist Democratic Teachers (EAIO) .... IUSDT
International Union of Socialist Youth .... IUSY
International Union of Societies for the Aid of Mental Health [*Bordeaux, France*] (EAIO) .... IUSAMH
International Union of Societies of Foresters [*See also UISIF*] [*Ottawa, ON*] (EAIO) .... IUSF
International Union of Speleology [*See also UIS*] [*Vienna, Austria*] (EAIO) .... IUS
International Union of Students [*See also UIE*] [*Prague, Czechoslovakia*] (EAIO) .... IUS
International Union of Technical Associations and Organizations [*France*] (EAIO) .... IUTAO
International Union of Technical Cinematograph Associations [*See also UNIATEC*] [*Paris, France*] (EAIO) .... IUTCA
International Union of Tenants [*Stockholm, Sweden*] (EAIO) .... IUT
International Union of the History and Philosophy of Science [*ICSU*] [*Uppsala, Sweden*] (EAIO) .... IUHPS
International Union of the Medical Press (DIT) .... IUMP
International Union of Theoretical and Applied Mechanics [*Germany*] .... IUTAM
International Union of Tool, Die, and Mold Makers (EA) .... IUTDM
International Union of Tool, Die, and Mold Makers (EA) .... IUTDMM
International Union of Tool, Die, and Mold Makers .... TDMM
International Union of United Brewery, Flour, Cereal, Soft Drink, and DistilleryWorkers of America [*Later, Brewery and Soft Drink Workers Conference - USA and Canada*] .... BFCSD
International Union of Women Architects [*See also UIFA*] [*Paris, France*] (EAIO) .... IUWA
International Union of Wood, Wire, and Metal Lathers (MHDB) .... IUWWML
International Union of Young Christian Democrats [*Rome, Italy*] .... IUYCD
International Union Resources, Inc. [*Vancouver Stock Exchange symbol*] .... IUR
International Union, United Automobile, Aerospace, and Agricultural Implement Workers of America [*Also known as United Auto Workers*] (EA) .... UAW
International Union, United Cement, Lime and Gypsum Workers (MHDB) .... IUUCLGW
International Union, United Mine Workers of America [*Also known as UMW*] (EA) .... UMWA
International Union, United Plant Guard Workers of America (EA) .... UPGWA
International Union, United Welders [*Later, IUOE*] .... IUUW
International Unit .... IU

International Unit [*of enzyme activity*] (DAVI) ... U
International Units per Liter ... IU/L
International Universal Time [*Telecommunications*] (TEL) ... UTI
International Universities Bureau ... IUB
International Universities' Sports Board [*Defunct*] (EA) ... IUSB
International University Consortium for Telecommunications in Learning [*Later, IUC*] (EA) ... IUC
International University Contact for Management Education ... IUC
International University Contact for Management Education ... IUCME
International University Foundation (EA) ... IUF
International University of America [*San Francisco, CA*] (ECON) ... IUA
International University of Communication [*Washington, DC*] ... IUC
International University of Japan (ECON) ... IUJ
International Uranium Resources Evaluation Project ... IUREP
International Urgency Signal ... XXX
International URSI [*Union Radio Scientifique Internationale*]-gram and World Day Service ... IUWDS
International Users Resource Allocation Panel ... IURAP
International Vaccine Institute [*Korea*] ... IVI
International Vegetarian Union [*Stockport, Cheshire, England*] ... IVU
International Vending Technologies Corp. [*Vancouver Stock Exchange symbol*] ... IVD
International Venture Capital Institute (EA) ... IVCI
International Verifact, Inc. [*Associated Press*] (SAG) ... IntVer
International Verifact, Inc. [*Associated Press*] (SAG) ... IntVerif
International Verifact, Inc. [*Toronto Stock Exchange symbol*] ... IVI
International Verifact, Inc. [*NASDAQ symbol*] (SAG) ... IVIAF
International Verifact Wrrt [*NASDAQ symbol*] (TTSB) ... IVIAW
International Verticillium Research Group (EAIO) ... IVRG
International Vestor Resources [*Vancouver Stock Exchange symbol*] ... IVS
International Veteran Boxers Association (EA) ... IVBA
International Veterinary Acupuncture Society (EA) ... IVAS
International Veterinary Association for Animal Production [*See also AIVPA*] [*Brussels, Belgium*] [*Research center*] (EAIO) ... IVAAP
International Veterinary Federation of Zootechnics [*Later, IVAAP*] ... IVFZ
International Veterinary Students Association [*Utrecht, Netherlands*] (EAIO) ... IVSA
International Veterinary Students Union [*Later, IVSA*] ... IVSU
International Video and Communications Exhibition [*British*] (ITD) ... IVAC
International Video and Communications Exhibition (NITA) ... IVCE
International Video Contest for Amateurs and Professionals [*British*] ... IVCAP
International Video Entertainment ... IVE
International Videotex Industry Association ... IVIA
International Videotex Information Providers' Association [*British Information service or system*] (IID) ... IVIPA
International Vine and Wine Office ... IVWO
International Violin and Guitar Makers Association (EA) ... IVGMA
International Visitors Information Service (EA) ... IVIS
International Visual Literacy Association (EA) ... IVLA
International Vitamin A Consultative Group (EA) ... IVACG
International Vitamin Corp. [*Associated Press*] (SAG) ... IntlVit
International Vitamin Corp. [*NASDAQ symbol*] (SAG) ... IVCO
International Vocational Education and Training Association (EA) ... IVETA
International Volleyball Association [*Defunct*] (EA) ... IVA
International Volleyball Association [*Defunct*] ... IVBA
International Volleyball Federation (EA) ... IVBF
International Voluntary Action and Voluntary Association Research Organization [*Defunct*] (EA) ... IVAR
International Voluntary Historical Enlightenment Society Memorial (EAIO) ... IVHESM
International Voluntary Services (EA) ... IVS
International Voyage Alliance (EA) ... IVA
International Wallcovering Manufacturers Association [*Belgium*] (EAIO) ... IGI
International Walther League (EA) ... IWL
International War Crimes Tribunal ... IWCT
International War Veterans' Alliance (EA) ... IWVA
International Watch Fob Association, Inc. (EA) ... IWFAI
International Water Quality Association [*British*] (EAIO) ... UKNCIAWPRC
International Water Resources Association (EA) ... IWRA
International Water Resources Institute [*George Washington University*] [*Research center*] (RCD) ... WRI
International Water Supply Association [*British*] (EAIO) ... IWSA
International Water Tribunal Foundation [*Netherlands*] (EAIO) ... IWTF
International Waterfowl and Wetlands Research Bureau (EAIO) ... IWRB
International Waterfowl and Wetlands Research Bureau (EAIO) ... IWWRB
International Waterproofing Association [*See also AIE*] [*Brussels, Belgium*] (EAIO) ... IWA
International Wattier [*Process*] [*A method of making transparencies for rotogravure plates*] ... IW
International Waxes Ltd., Agincourt, Ontario [*Library symbol National Library of Canada*] (NLC) ... OAIW
International Weddell Sea Oceanographic Expedition ... IWSOE
International Weed Science Society (EA) ... IWSS
International Weightlifting Federation [*See also FHI*] [*Budapest, Hungary*] (EAIO) ... IWF
International Werner Tech [*Vancouver Stock Exchange symbol*] ... IWI
International Westward Development Corp. [*Vancouver Stock Exchange symbol*] ... IWW
International Whaling Commission [*Cambridge, England*] ... IWC
International Wheat Agreement [*London*] ... IWA
International Wheat Council [*See also CIB*] [*British*] (EAIO) ... IWC
International Wheat Gluten Association (EA) ... IWGA
International Wheelchair Road Racers Club (EA) ... IWRRC
International Who's Who [*A publication*] ... IWW
International Who's Who in Community Service [*A publication*] ... IWWCS
International Who's Who in Music and Musicians Directory [*A publication*] ... IWWM
International Who's Who in Poetry [*A publication*] ... IWWP
International Wild Rice Association (EA) ... IWRA
International Wild Waterfowl Association (EA) ... IWWA
International Wildcat Resources [*Vancouver Stock Exchange symbol*] ... IWC
International Wilderness Leadership Foundation ... IWLF
International Wildlife Coalition (EA) ... IWC
International Wildlife Rehabilitation Council (EA) ... IWRC
International Wildrose Resources, Inc. [*Vancouver Stock Exchange symbol*] ... IWS
International Willow Collectors [*An association*] (EA) ... IWC
International Window Film Association (EA) ... IWFA
International Windsurfer Class Association (EA) ... IWCA
International Wine and Food Society [*British*] (EAIO) ... IWFS
International Wine and Spirit Record ... IWSR
International Wine Society (EA) ... IWS
International Wire and Machinery Association [*Leamington Spa, Warwickshire, England*] (EAIO) ... IWMA
International Wizard of Oz Club (EA) ... IWOC
International Woman Lawyer [*A publication*] (DLA) ... Int Woman L
International Woman Lawyer [*A publication*] (DLA) ... Int'l Woman Law
International Women's Anthropology Conference (EA) ... IWAC
International Women's Auxiliary to the Veterinary Profession ... IWA
International Women's Cricket Council [*Australia*] (EAIO) ... IWCC
International Women's Day ... IWD
International Women's Decade ... IWD
International Women's Film Project (EA) ... IWFP
International Women's Fishing Association (EA) ... IWFA
International Women's Forum [*National Women's Forum*] [*Acronym is based on former name,*] (EA) ... NWF
International Women's Health Coalition (EA) ... IWHC
International Women's Media Project [*Defunct*] (EA) ... IWMP
International Women's Network on Pharmaceuticals [*Amsterdam, Netherlands*] (EAIO) ... WEMOS
International Women's Rights Action Watch (EAIO) ... IWRAW
International Women's Tribune Centre (EA) ... IWTC
International Women's Writing Guild (EA) ... IWWG
International Women's Year [*1975*] ... IWY
International Wood Collectors Society (EA) ... IWCS
International Woodworkers of America (EA) ... IWA
International Woodworking Machinery and Furniture Supply Fair (ITD) ... IWF
International Wool Secretariat [*British*] ... IWS
International Wool Study Group [*British Defunct*] (EAIO) ... IWSG
International Wool Study Group [*Defunct*] ... WSG
International Wool Testing Organisation [*Australia*] ... IWTO
International Wool Textile Organization [*See also FLI*] [*Brussels, Belgium*] (EAIO) ... IWTO
International Word Processing Association (NITA) ... IWP
International Word Processing Association [*Later, IIWPA, IWP*] ... IWPA
International Work Group for Indigenous Affairs [*Copenhagen, Denmark*] (EAIO) ... IWGIA
International Workers Sport Association ... IWSA
International Working Group [*NATO*] (NATG) ... IWG
International Working Group in Clinical Sociology (EAIO) ... IWGCS
International Working Group on Fast Reactors (NRCH) ... IWGFR
International Working Group on Graminaceous Downy Mildews [*Defunct*] (EAIO) ... IWGGDM
International Working Party ... IWP
International Working Team [*NATO*] (NATG) ... IWT
International Working-Group of Soilless Culture ... IWOSC
International World Calendar Association (EA) ... IWCA
International World Day Service ... IWDS
International World Games Association (EA) ... IWGA
International Writers Guild ... IWG
International Wrought Copper Council [*British*] (EAIO) ... IWCC
International X-Ray and Extreme Ultraviolet Explorer ... IXEE
International X-Ray Astrophysics Explorer ... IXAE
International Yacht Racing Union [*British*] ... IYRU
International Year for the Preparation of Disarmament [*Pugwash Conference*] ... IYPD
International Year of Canadian Music [*1986*] ... IYCM
International Year of Shelter for the Homeless [*1987*] ... IYSH
International Year of the Child [*United Nations*] (AEE) ... IYC
International Year of the Disabled Person [*1981*] ... IYDP
International Year of the Family ... IYF
International Year of the Quiet Sun [*1964-65*] [*Also, IQSY*] (KSC) ... IYQS
International Year of the World's Indigenous People ... IYWIP
International Yoga Teachers Association (ADA) ... IYTA
International Yogurt Co. [*Associated Press*] (SAG) ... IntYog
International Yogurt Co. [*NASDAQ symbol*] (NQ) ... YOCM
International Young Christian Workers [*See also JOCI*] (EAIO) ... IYCW
International Young Christian Workers [*Acronym is based on foreign phrase Belgium*] ... YOW
International Young Democratic Union [*Defunct*] (EAIO) ... IYDU
International Young Fish Survey [*Denmark, Great Britain, Norway, West Germany*] [*1987-88 Oceanography*] ... IYFS
International Young Friends Society [*Pakistan*] (EAIO) ... IYFS
International Youth and Student Movement for the United Nations [*Geneva, Switzerland*] (EA) ... ISMUN
International Youth Congress ... IYC
International Youth Council (EA) ... IYC
International Youth Federation for Environmental Studies and Conservation (EAIO) ... IYF

International Youth Hostel Federation [*See also FAIJ*] [*Welwyn Garden City, Hertfordshire, England*] (EAIO) .... IYHF
International Youth Library [*See also IJB*] [*Munich, Federal Republic of Germany*] (EAIO) .... IYL
International Youth Year [*1985*] (AIE) .... IYY
International Youth Year Commission [*Defunct*] (EA) .... IYYC
International Zebu Breeders Association (EA) .... IZBA
International Zen Association [*Formerly, European Zen Association*] (EA) .... IZA
International Zeolite Association .... IZA
International Zetcentrum [*International Typesetting Center, The Netherlands*] .... IZC
International Zoo Yearbook [*A publication*] .... IZY
International Zuma Class Association (EA) .... IZCA
Internationale Akademie fuer Bader-, Sport-, und Freizeitheitbau [*International Board for Aquatic, Sports, and Recreation Facilities*] [*Bad Neustadt/Saale, Federal Republic of Germany*] (EAIO) .... IAB
Internationale Arbeitsgemeinschaft der Archiv-, Bibliotheks-, und Graphikrestauratoren [*International Association for Conservation of Books, Paper, and Archival Material*] (EAIO) .... IADA
Internationale Arbeitsgemeinschaft der Wasserwerke im Rheineinzugsgebiet [*International Association of Waterworks in the Rhine Basin Area - IAWRBA*] (EAIO) .... IAWR
Internationale Arbeitsgemeinschaft Donauforschung [*International Working Association for Danube Research*] (EAIO) .... IAD
Internationale Arbeitsgemeinschaft von Sortimentsbuchhaendler Vereinigungen [*International Community of Booksellers' Associations*] .... IASV
Internationale Armbrustschutzen Union [*International Crossbow Shooting Union*] (EAIO) .... IAU
Internationale Atomreactorbau [*German*] .... INTERATOM
Internationale Begegnung in Gemeinschaftsdiensten [*Germany*] (EAIO) .... IBG
Internationale Bildungs- und Informations- Datenbank [*International Education and Information Data Bank*] [*Thiede & Thiede Mittelstandische Systemberatung GmbH*] [*Information service or system*] (IID) .... IBD
Internationale Bouworde [*International Association of Building Companions - IABC*] [*Marche-En-Famenne, Belgium*] (EAIO) .... IBO
Internationale Brecht Gesellschaft [*International Brecht Society*] (EAIO) .... IBG
Internationale Bruckner Gesellschaft [*Vienna, Austria*] (EAIO) .... IBG
Internationale Buchhandler-Vereinigung [*International Booksellers Federation - IBF*] (EAIO) .... IBV
Internationale Chretienne Professionelle pour les Industries Graphiques et Papetieres [*International Federation of Christian Trade Unions of Graphical and Paper Industries*] .... ICPIGP
Internationale Coronelli-Gesellschaft fuer Globen- und Instrumentkunde [*International Coronelli Society - ICS*] (EAIO) .... ICGGI
Internationale de la Resistance [*Resistance International - RI*] (EAIO) .... IR
Internationale de Services Industriels and Scientifiques .... ISIS
Internationale Democrate Chretienne [*Christian Democrat International*] [*Belgium*] (EAIO) .... IDC
Internationale Demokratische Frauenfoederation [*Women's International Democratic Federation*] .... IDFF
Internationale des Amis de la Nature [*International Federation of Friends of Nature*] .... IAN
Internationale des Resistants a la Guerre [*War Resisters International - WRI*] [*British*] (EA) .... IRG
Internationale des Services Publics [*Public Service International - PSI*] [*Ferney Voltaire, France*] (EAIO) .... ISP
Internationale Dokumentationsgesellschaft fuer Chemie [*International Company for Documentation in Chemistry*] [*Frankfurt, West Germany*] .... IDC
Internationale du Personnel des Postes, Telegraphes, et Telephones [*Postal, Telegraph, and Telephone International - PTTI*] [*Geneva, Switzerland*] (EAIO) .... IPTT
Internationale Eisenbahn-Kongress-Vereinigung [*International Railway Congress Association*] .... IEKV
Internationale Foderation der Ausschusse Normenpraxis [*International Federation for the Application of Standards*] (EAIO) .... IFAN
Internationale Foderation der Vereine der Textilchemiker und Coloristen [*International Federation of Associations of Textile Chemists and Colorists*] (EAIO) .... IFVTCC
Internationale Foderation des Dachdeckerhandwerks [*International Federation of Roofing Contractors*] (EAIO) .... IFD
Internationale Foderation des Handwerks [*International Federation of Master-Craftsmen - IFMC*] [*Vienna, Austria*] (EAIO) .... IFH
Internationale Foederation der Eisenbahn-Reklame-Gesellschaften [*International Federation of Railway Advertising Companies*] [*British*] (EA) .... IFER
Internationale Foederation fuer Kurzschrift und Maschinenschreiben [*International Federation of Shorthand and Typewriting*] .... IFKM
Internationale Frauenliga fuer Frieden und Freiheit [*Women's International League for Peace and Freedom*] .... IFFF
Internationale Gemeinschaft fuer Holz-technologie-Transfer [*International Community for Wood-Technology Transfer*] (EAIO) .... COMBOIS
Internationale Gesellschaft der Schriftpsychologie [*International Society for the Psychology of Writing*] .... IGSP
Internationale Gesellschaft fuer Aerosole in der Medizin [*International Society for Aerosols in Medicine - ISAeM*] (EAIO) .... IGAeM
Internationale Gesellschaft fuer Allgemeinmedizin [*International Society of General Medicine*] .... IGAM
Internationale Gesellschaft fuer Arztliche Psychotherapie [*International Federation for Medical Psychotherapy - IFMP*] [*Oslo, Norway*] (EAIO) .... IGAP
Internationale Gesellschaft fuer Geschichtsdidaktik [*International Society for History Didactics*] (EAIO) .... IGG
Internationale Gesellschaft fuer Ingenieurpaedagogik [*International Society for Engineering Education*] (EAIO) .... IGIP
Internationale Gesellschaft fuer Kiefer- und Gesichtschirurgie [*International Association for Maxillo-Facial Surgery*] (EAIO) .... IGKG
Internationale Gesellschaft fuer Lymphologie [*International Society of Lymphology*] (EAIO) .... IGL
Internationale Gesellschaft fuer Menschenrechte [*International Society for Human Rights - ISHR*] (EA) .... IGFM
Internationale Gesellschaft fuer Menschenrechte [*International Society for Human Rights - ISHR*] (EAIO) .... IGM
Internationale Gesellschaft fuer Stereologie [*International Society for Stereology*] (EAIO) .... ISS
Internationale Gesellschaft fuer Urheberrecht [*International Copyright Society*] (EAIO) .... INTERGU
Internationale Gesellschaft fuer Warenkunde und Technologie [*International Association for Commodity Science and Technology*] (EA) .... IGWT
Internationale Gewasserschutz Kommission fur den Bodensee [*International Commission for the Protection of Lake Constance*] (EA) .... IGKB
Internationale Gewerbeunion [*International Association of Crafts and Small and Medium Sized Enterprises - IACME*] [*Berne, Switzerland*] (EAIO) .... IGU
Internationale Gustav Mahler Gesellschaft [*International Gustav Mahler Society*] (EA) .... IGMG
Internationale Hegel Gesellschaft (EA) .... IHG
Internationale Hegel-Vereinigung [*Munich, Federal Republic of Germany*] (EAIO) .... IHV
Internationale Heinrich Schutz-Gesellschaft [*International Heinrich Schutz Society*] (EAIO) .... IHSG
Internationale Hoptrenbaubuero [*International Hop Growers Convention*] .... IHB
Internationale Horngesellschaft [*International Horn Society*] (EAIO) .... IH
Internationale Hugo Wolf Gesellschaft [*Vienna, Austria*] (EAIO) .... IHWG
Internationale Judo Foederation [*International Judo Federation*] [*Germany*] (EA) .... IJF
Internationale Jugendbibliothek [*International Youth Library - IYL*] [*Munich, Federal Republic of Germany*] (EAIO) .... IJB
Internationale Juristen-Kommission [*International Commission of Jurists*] .... IJK
Internationale Katholische Mittelstandsbewegung [*International Catholic Union of the Middle Class*] .... IKMB
Internationale Katholische Vereinigung fuer Soziale Arbeit [*Catholic International Union for Social Service*] .... IKVSA
Internationale Kommission fuer Alpines Rettungswesen [*International Commission for Alpine Rescue*] [*Birchwil, Switzerland*] (EAIO) .... IKAR
Internationale Kommission fuer Glas [*International Commission on Glass*] .... IKG
Internationale Kommission fuer Numismatik [*International Numismatic Commission*] .... IKN
Internationale Kommission zum Schutze des Rheins Gegen Verunreinigung [*International Commission for the Protection of the Rhine Against Pollution - ICPRAP*] (EAIO) .... IKSR
Internationale Kommunistenbond [*International Communist League*] [*Netherlands*] (PPW) .... IKB
Internationale Kriminalpolizeiliche Organisation [*International Criminal Police Organization*] .... IKPO
Internationale Kunstgilde [*International Art Guild - IAG*] (EAIO) .... IG
Internationale Messtechnische Konfoderation [*International Measurement Confederation*] [*ICSU Budapest, Hungary*] (EAIO) .... IMEKO
Internationale Metall Union [*International Metal Union*] (EA) .... IMU
Internationale Moor und Torf-Gesellschaft [*International Peat Society - IPS*] (EAIO) .... IMTG
Internationale Nederlanden Groep [*Netherlands*] (ECON) .... ING
Internationale Organisation fuer Sukkulentenforschung [*International Organization for Succulent Plant Study - IOS*] (EAIO) .... IOS
Internationale Orientierungslauf Foderation [*International Orienteering Federation*] (EA) .... IOF
Internationale Orientierungslauf Foderation, Wissenschaftliche Arbeitsgruppe [*International Orienteering Federation, Scientific Group - IOFSG*] (EAIO) .... IOFWA
Internationale Paracelsus-Gesellschaft zu Salzburg (EAIO) .... IPGS
Internationale Paracelsus-Gesellschaft zu Salzburg [*International Paracelsus Society*] (EA) .... IPS
Internationale Raiffeisen-Union [*International Raiffeisen Union*] (EAIO) .... IRU
Internationale Rat fuer Vogelschutz [*International Council for Bird Preservation*] .... IRV
Internationale Richard Strauss Gesellschaft [*An association*] (EAIO) .... IRSG
Internationale Schulsport Foderation [*International School Sport Federation*] (EAIO) .... ISF
Internationale Schutzenunion [*International Shooting Union*] (EAIO) .... IS
Internationale Seidenbau Kommission [*International Sericultural Commission*] .... ISK
Internationale Studiengemeinschaft fuer Pranatale Psychologie [*International Society for the Study of Prenatal Psychology - ISPP*] (EAIO) .... ISPP
Internationale Tieraerztliche Vereinigung fuer Tierproduktion [*International Veterinary Association for Animal Production*] .... ITVTP
Internationale Union der Lebens- und Genussmittelarbeiter-Gewerkschaften [*International Union of Food and Allied Workers Associations - IUF*] [*Petit-Lancy, Switzerland*] (EAIO) .... IUL
Internationale Union Junger Christlicher Demokraten [*International Union of Young Christian Democrats*] .... IUJCD
Internationale Vereinigung der Anschlussgeleise-Benuetzer [*International Association of Users of Private Sidings*] .... IVA
Internationale Vereinigung der Eisenwaren- und Eisenhaendlerverbaende [*International Federation of Ironmongers and Iron Merchants Association*] .... IVE
Internationale Vereinigung der Klein- und Mittelbetriebe des Handels [*International Federation of Small and Medium-Sized Commercial Enterprises*] .... IVKMH
Internationale Vereinigung der Lehrerverbaende [*International Federation of Teachers' Associations*] IVL
Internationale Vereinigung der Musikbibliotheken, Musikarchive, und Dokumentationszentren [*International Association of Music Libraries, Archives, and Documentation Centers*] .... IVMB

Internationale Vereinigung der Organisationen von Lebensmittel-Detail-Listen [*International Federation of Grocers' Associations - IFGA*] (EAIO) ..... IVLD
Internationale Vereinigung der Textileinkaufsverbande [*International Association of Textile Purchasing Societies*] ..... IVT
Internationale Vereinigung fuer Brueckenbau und Hochbau [*International Association for Bridge and Structural Engineering*] ..... IVBH
Internationale Vereinigung fuer Germanische Sprach - und Literaturwissenschaft [*International Association of Germanic Studies - IAGS*] [*Tokyo, Japan*] (EAIO) ..... IVG
Internationale Vereinigung fuer Geschichte und Gegenwart der Druckkunst [*International Association for Past and Present History of the Art of Printing*] (EAIO) ..... IVGGD
Internationale Vereinigung fuer Gewerblichen Rechtsschultz [*International Association for the Protection of Industrial Property*] ..... IVFGR
Internationale Vereinigung fuer Individualpsychologie [*International Association of Individual Psychology*] ..... IVIP
Internationale Vereinigung fuer Jugendhilfe [*International Union for Child Welfare*] ..... IVJH
Internationale Vereinigung fuer Rechts- und Sozialphilosophie [*International Association for Philosophy of Law and Social Philosophy*] (EAIO) ..... IVR
Internationale Vereinigung fuer Soziale Sicherheit [*International Social Security Association*] ..... IVSS
Internationale Vereinigung fuer Theoretische und Angewandte Limnologie [*International Association of Theoretical and Applied Limnology*] IVL
Internationale Vereinigung fuer Vegetationskunde [*International Association for Vegetation Science - IAVS*] (EAIO) IVV
Internationale Vereinigung von Einkaufsverbanden [*International Association of Buying Groups - IABG*] (EAIO) ..... IVE
Internationale Vereniging voor Neerlandistiek [*International Association of Dutch Studies*] (EAIO) ..... IVN
Internationale Viola Forschunggesellschaft [*International Viola Society*] [*Germany*] (EAIO) ..... IVF
Internationale Warenhaus-Vereinigung [*International Association of Department Stores*] ..... IWV
Internationale Weltfriedens Partei [*International World Peace Party*] [*Germany Political party*] (PPW) ..... IWP
Internationalen Union fuer Angewandte Ornithologie [*International Union for Applied Ornithology*] (EAIO) ..... IUAO
Internationaler Arbeitskreis Sport- und Freizeiteninrichtungen [*International Working Group for the Construction of Sports and Leisure Facilities*] (EAIO) ..... IAKS
Internationaler Bund der Bau-Haolzarbeiter [*International Federation of Building and Woodworkers*] ..... IBBH
Internationaler Bund Freier Evangelischer Gemeinden [*International Federation of Free Evangelical Churches - IFFEC*] (EA) ..... IBFEG
Internationaler Bund Freier Gewerkschaften [*International Confederation of Free Trade Unions*] ..... IBFG
Internationaler Deutschlehrerverband [*International Association of Teachers of German - IATG*] [*Copenhagen, Denmark*] (EAIO) ..... IDV
Internationaler Elektronik-Arbeitskreis [*International Electronics Association*] ..... INEA
Internationaler Faustball-Verband (EAIO) ..... IFV
Internationaler Frauenrat [*International Council of Women*] ..... IFR
Internationaler Genossenschaftsbund [*International Cooperative Alliance*] ..... IGB
Internationaler Jugendaustausch und Besucherdienst der Bundesrepublik Deutschland [*International Youth Exchange and Visitor Service of the Federal Republic of Germany*] ..... IJAB
Internationaler Kranckenhausverbaund [*International Hospital Federation*] ..... IKV
Internationaler Metalarbeiterbund [*International Metalworkers' Federation*] ..... IMB
Internationaler Metzgermeisterverband [*International Federation of Meat Traders' Associations*] (EAIO) ..... IMV
Internationaler Milchwirtschaftverband [*International Dairy Federation*] ..... IMV
Internationaler Rat der Hauspflegedienste [*International Council of Home-Help Services*] ..... IRHD
Internationaler Ring fuer Landarbeit [*International Committee of Scientific Management in Agriculture*] ..... IRL
Internationaler Staendiger Verband fuer Schiffahrt-Kongresse [*Permanent International Association of Navigation Congresses*] ..... ISVSK
Internationaler Studentenbund [*International Union of Students*] ..... ISB
Internationaler Suchdienst [*International Tracing Service*] (EAIO) ..... IS
Internationaler Turnerbund [*International Gymnastic Federation*] ..... ITB
Internationaler Verband der Gastronomie- und Weinbuau-Presse [*International Federation of Gastronomical and Vinicultural Press*] ..... IVGWP
Internationaler Verband der Pektinproduzenten [*International Pectin Producers Association*] [*Switzerland*] (EAIO) ..... IVP
Internationaler Verband der Petroleum- und Chemiearbeiter [*International Federation of Petroleum and Chemical Workers*] ..... IVPC
Internationaler Verband der Stadt-, Sport-, und Mehrzweckhallen [*International Federation of City, Sport, and Multi-Purpose Halls*] (EAIO) ..... VDSM
Internationaler Verband fuer Arbeiterbildung [*International Federation of Workers' Educational Associations - IFWEA*] (EAIO) ..... IVA
Internationaler Verband fuer Arbeiterbildung [*International Federation of Workers' Educational Associations - IFWEA*] (EAIO) ..... IVB
Internationaler Verband fuer Erziehung zu Suchtmittelfreiem Leben [*International Association for Education to a Life without Drugs*] (EAIO) ..... IVES
Internationaler Verband fuer Hauswirtschaft [*International Federation for Home Economics*] ..... IVHW
Internationaler Verband fuer Wohnungswesen, Staedtebau und Raumordnung [*International Federation for Housing and Planning*] ..... IVWSR
Internationaler Volkssportverband [*International Federation of Popular Sports - IFPS*] (EAIO) IVV
Internationaler Zivildienst [*International Voluntary Service*] ..... IZD
Internationales Arbeiter-Hilfswerk [*International Workers Aid*] [*Bonn, Federal Republic of Germany*] (EAIO) ..... IAH
Internationales Auschwitz-Komitee [*International Auschwitz Committee*] [*Warsaw, Poland*] (EAIO) ..... IAK
Internationales Begegnungszentrum Friedenshaus [*Germany*] (EAIO) ..... IBF
Internationales Burgen-Institut [*International Castles Institute*] [*Rozendaal, Netherlands*] (EA) ..... IBI
Internationales Buro fuer Gebirgsmechanik [*International Bureau of Strato-Mechanics - IBSM*] (EAIO) ..... IBG
Internationales Daunen- und Federn-Bureau [*International Down and Feather Bure au*] (EAIO) ..... IDFB
Internationales Federn-Bureau [*International Feather Bureau - IFB*] (EAIO) ..... IFB
Internationales Gewerkschafts Buro [*International Trades Union Office*] ..... IGB
Internationales Institut der Sparkassen [*International Savings Banks Institute*] ..... IIS
Internationales Institut fuer Nationalitatenrecht und Regionalismus [*International Institute for Ethnic Group Rights and Regionalism*] (EA) ..... INTEREG
Internationales Institut fuer Verwaltungswissenschaften [*International Institute of Administrative Sciences*] ..... IIVW
Internationales Katholisches Missionswerk [*Pontifical Mission Society*] [*Aachen, Federal Republic of Germany*] (EAIO) ..... MISSIO
Internationales Kolpingwerk [*International Kolping Society - IKS*] [*Cologne, Federal Republic of Germany*] (EAIO) ..... IKW
Internationales Komittee vom Roten Kreuz [*International Committee of the Red Cross*] ..... IKRK
Internationales Kuratorium fuer das Jugendbuch [*International Board on Books for Young People*] ..... IKJ
Internationales Musikzentrum [*International Music Center*] [*Vienna, Austria*] (EAIO) ..... IMZ
International-Great Northern [*AAR code*] ..... IGN
Internationality Alphabet ffi2 (MCD) ITAffi2
Internationalization [*The 18 replaces the eighteen letters between I and N*] [*C omputer hacker terminology*] (NHD) I18N
Internationally Protected Person (ADA) ..... IPP
Internationally Syndicated Information Services [*Information service or system Defunct*] (IID) ..... ISIS
Internationella Forsurningssekretariatet [*International Secretariat on Acid Rain*] [*Sweden*] (EAIO) ..... IFS
Internatl Fetal Heart Rate [*Medicine*] (MEDA) ..... Int FHR
Interne [*Medicine British*] ..... INT
Interned (AABC) ..... INT
Internegative [*Photography*] (WDMC) ..... IN
Internegative [*Photography*] (NTCM) ..... ITN
Internet Ad Hoc Coalition [*Computer science*] ..... IAHC
Internet Ad Hoc Committee ..... IAHC
[*The*] **Internet Adapter** [*Intermind Corp.*] ..... TIA
Internet Address Naming Authority [*Computer science*] (ACRL) ..... IANA
Internet & Web Services Corp. ..... IWSC
Internet Architecture Board ..... IAB
Internet Assigned Numbers Authority (PCM) ..... IANA
Internet Assigned Numbers Authority ..... IANA
Internet Business Center [*Information service or system*] (IID) ..... IBC
Internet Commerce Exchange ..... ICE
Internet Communications [*NASDAQ symbol*] (SAG) ..... INCC
Internet Communications [*Associated Press*] (SAG) ..... Internt
Internet Connection Services [*Computer science*] (PCM) ..... ICSAPI
Internet Connection Wizard [*Computer science*] ..... ICW
Internet Connections for Engineering ..... ICE
Internet Connectivity Option [*Galacticomm, Inc.*] [*Telecommunications*] ..... ICO
Internet Content Coalition [*Computer science*] ICC
Internet Content Provider [*Computer science*] ..... ICP
Internet Control and Configuration Board [*Computer science*] (ACRL) ..... ICCB
Internet Control and Message Protocol [*Telecommunications*] ..... ICMP
Internet Control Protocol [*Telecommunications*] (PCM) ..... ICP
Internet Database Connector [*Computer science*] (PCM) ..... IDC
Internet Datagram Protocol [*Computer science*] (ACRL) ..... IDP
Internet Department of Motor Vehicles ..... I-DMV
Internet Domain Registrars ..... IDR
Internet Engineering Planning Group ..... IEPG
Internet Engineering Steering Group [*Computer science*] (ACRL) ..... IESG
Internet Engineering Task Force ..... IETF
Internet Entertainment Group, Inc. ..... IEG
Internet Etiquette [*Computer science*] ..... Netiquette
Internet Explorer [*Microsoft Corp.*] ..... IE
Internet Group Management Protocol [*Computer science*] ..... IGMP
Internet Group Management Protocol [*Computer science*] (PCM) ..... IGMP
Internet Header Length [*Computer science*] (ACRL) ..... IHL
Internet Information Server [*Computer science*] (PCM) ..... IIS
Internet Information Server (PCM) ..... IIS
Internet Inter-ORG [*Object Request Broker*] **Protocol** [*Computer science*] ..... IIOP
Internet Mail Access Protocol [*Computer science*] ..... IMAP
Internet Message Access Protocol 4 [*Electronic mail*] IMAP4
Internet Message Center ..... IMC
Internet Multicasting Service [*Non-profit information service*] ..... IMS
Internet Name Server Protocol (TNIG) ..... INSP
Internet Network Information Center ..... InterNIC
Internet Network Information Center [*Computer science*] ..... InterNIC
Internet Nodal Processor [*Computer science*] (ACRL) ..... INP
Internet Packet Exchange / Sequenced Packet [*Computer science*] (PCM) ..... IPX/SPX
Inter-Net Predicts (MCD) ..... INP
Internet Printing System [*Computer science*] ..... IPS
Internet Profiles Corp. ..... I/PRO
Internet Protection Module [*Computer science*] ..... IPM
Internet Protocol [*Computer science*] (PCM) ..... IP
Internet Protocol Next Generation (CDE) ..... IPng

Internet Query [*Computer science*] ... IQY
Internet Reach and Involvement Scale [*Advertising value of an Internet site*] ... IRIS
Internet Relay Chat [*Computer science*] ... IRC
Internet Research Steering Group [*Computer science*] (ACRL) ... IRSG
Internet Research Task Force ... IRTF
Internet Routing and Access Service [*Computer science*] (ACRL) ... IRAS
Internet Server API [*All-Purpose Interface*] [*Microsoft and Process Software Corp.*] [*Computer science*] ... ISAPI
Internet Service Provider ... ISP
Internet Service Provider Association ... ISPA
Internet Service Providers [*Telecommunications*] ... ISP
Internet Services API [*Computer science*] ... ISAPI
Internet Society ... ISOC
[*The*] **Internet Society** (TNIG) ... ISOC
Internet Transaction Broker [*Computer science*] ... ITB
Internet Underground Music Archive ... IUMA
Internet University [*Computer science*] ... IU
Internet Value-Added Service (PCM) ... IVAS
Internet World ... INW
Internet3D Space Builder ... ISB
Internetwork Packet Exchange ... IPX
Internetwork Protocol Exchange [*Novell, Inc.*] [*Computer science*] (PCM) ... IPX
Internetwork Routing Service [*Telecommunications*] (OSI) ... IRS
Internetworking Function [*Computer science*] (ACRL) ... IWF
Interneuron [*Neurology*] (DAVI) ... IN
Interneuron Pharmaceuticals [*NASDAQ symbol*] (TTSB) ... IPIC
Interneuron Pharmaceuticals, Inc. [*Associated Press*] (SAG) ... Interneur
Interneuron Pharmaceuticals, Inc. [*Associated Press*] (SAG) ... Intrn
Interneuron Pharmaceuticals, Inc. [*Associated Press*] (SAG) ... Intrnu
Interneuron Pharmaceuticals, Inc. [*NASDAQ symbol*] (SAG) ... IPIC
Internist [*Medicine*] ... I
Internist [*Medicine*] ... INT
Internment Camp ... IC
Internment Serial Number ... ISN
Internodal Link (ACRL) ... INL
Internordic Investment Bank [*Scandinavia*] ... IIB
Inter-Nordic Standardization ... INSTA
Interns for Peace (EA) ... IFP
Intern's Progress Note [*Medical records*] (DAVI) ... IPN
Internship (DAVI) ... INT
Interntional Greenland Sea Project [*Marine science*] (OSRA) ... IGSP
Interntional Nursing Services, Inc. [*Associated Press*] (SAG) ... IntNur
Internuclear Bridging (DMAA) ... INB
Internuclear Company ... IC
Internuclear Double Resonance ... INDOR
Internuclear Ophthalmoplegia ... INO
Internus [*Internal*] [*Latin*] ... int
Inter-Ocean Canal Study Commission (PDAA) ... ICSC
Interoceanic Canal Project [*National Oceanic and Atmospheric Administration*] (NOAA) ... ICP
Inter-Oceanic Resources Ltd. [*Formerly, Inter-Oceanic Oil & Gas*] [*Vancouver Stock Exchange symbol*] ... INO
Interocular Asynchrony [*Ophthalmology*] ... IOA
Interocular Transfer [*Ophthalmology*] ... IOT
Inter-Office Channel [*Telecommunications*] (TSSD) ... IOC
Interoffice Comment Sheet (NATG) ... IOCS
Interoffice Correspondence ... IOC
Interoffice Memorandum ... IOM
Interoffice Trunk (IAA) ... IOT
Interoperability [*The 14 replaces the fourteen letters between I and Y*] [*Computer hacker terminology*] (NHD) ... I14Y
Interoperability ... INTEROP
Interoperability Configuration Manager ... ICM
Interoperable Systems Project [*Computer science*] ... ISP
Interoperatbility Technology Association for Information Technology (OSI) ... INTAP
Interorbital Distance [*Ophthalmology*] (DAVI) ... IOD
Interorbital Space Vehicle (MCD) ... IOSV
Interorbital Space Vehicle ... ISV
Interorbital Vehicle Assembly Mode ... IVAM
Inter-Organization Board for Information Systems [*United Nations*] (IID) ... IOB
Inter-Organization Board for Information Systems and Related Activities (NITA) ... IOB
Interorganizational Transfer (AAGC) ... IOT
Interorganizational Work Authorization (KSC) ... IOWA
Interot Air Service [*Germany ICAO designator*] (FAAC) ... IRT
Inter-Pacific Resource Corp. [*Vancouver Stock Exchange symbol*] ... IPA
Inter-Parliamentary Consultative Council of Benelux (EA) ... IPCCB
Inter-Parliamentary Union [*See also UI*] [*Switzerland*] ... IPU
Interpeduncular Nucleus [*Cytology*] ... IPN
Interpenduncular Cistern [*Medicine*] (DAVI) ... IPC
Interpenetrating Elastomeric Networks [*Organic chemistry*] ... IEN
Interpenetrating Networks of Samples [*Statistics*] ... IPNS
Interpenetrating Polymer Network [*Organic chemistry*] ... IPN
Inter-Person Perception Test [*Personality development test*] [*Psychology*] ... IPPT
Interpersonal Behavior Inventory [*Veterans Administration*] ... IBI
Interpersonal Behavior Survey [*Psychology*] ... IBS
Interpersonal Check List [*Psychology*] ... ICL
Interpersonal Cognitive Problem-Solving Program (EDAC) ... ICPS
Interpersonal Communication Behavior Analysis Method (PDAA) ... ICBAM
Interpersonal Communication Inventory [*Interpersonal skills and attitudes test*] ... ICI
Interpersonal Diagnosis of Personality [*Psychology*] ... IDP
Interpersonal Mail System [*Computer science*] (TNIG) ... IPM
Interpersonal Messaging [*Telecommunications*] (OSI) ... IPM
Interpersonal Messaging Service ... IPM
Interpersonal Orientation (BARN) ... IO
Interpersonal Perception Method [*Psychology*] ... IPM
Interpersonal Process Recall [*Psychology*] ... IPR
Interpersonal Reaction Test [*Medicine*] (MAE) ... IPRT
Interpersonal Relations Questionnaire [*Personality development test*] [*Psychology*] ... IRQ
Interpersonal Relationship Scale (EDAC) ... IRS
Interpersonal Style Inventory [*Personality development test*] [*Psychology*] ... ISI
Interpersonal Therapy [*Mental health treatment technique*] ... IPT
Interphalangeal [*Anatomy*] ... IP
Interphalangeal [*Anatomy*] ... IPH
Interphalangeal Joint [*Anatomy*] (DAVI) ... IPJ
Interphalangeal Keratosis [*Orthopedics*] (DAVI) ... IPK
Interphase Chromosome Volume ... ICV
Interphase Corp. [*NASDAQ symbol*] (SAG) ... INPH
Interphase Corp. [*Associated Press*] (SAG) ... Intphse
Interphase Transformer [*Electronics*] ... INTPHTR
Interphase Transformer [*Electronics*] (IAA) ... IPT
Interphase Unit ... IPU
Interphone (IAA) ... I
Interphone ... INPH
Interphone (MDG) ... INT
Interphone (MCD) ... INTER
Interphone ... INTPH
Interphone Control Station ... ICS
Interphone Control System ... ICS
Interphone (Service F) Resumed Operation [*Aviation*] (FAAC) ... IFORO
Interphotoreceptor Matrix [*Ophthalmology*] ... IPM
Interphotoreceptor Retinoid-Binding Protein [*Biochemistry*] ... IRBP
Inter-Plan Data Reporting System [*Health insurance*] (GHCT) ... IPDR
Interplanetare Sonnensonde ... ISOS
Interplanetary ... IP
Interplanetary Ballistic Missile [*Air Force*] ... IPBM
Interplanetary Communications (AAG) ... IPC
Interplanetary Craft for Advanced Research in Vicinity of Sun ... ICARVS
Interplanetary Dust Particle ... IDP
Interplanetary Global Model [*Marine science*] (OSRA) ... IGM
Interplanetary Global Model (USDC) ... IGM
Interplanetary Magnetic Field ... IMF
Interplanetary Magnetometer Probe ... IMP
Interplanetary Measurement Probe ... IMP
Interplanetary Measurement Satellite (IAA) ... IMS
Interplanetary Medium ... IPM
Interplanetary Meteoroid Experiment [*NASA*] ... IME
Interplanetary Mission Support ... IMS
Interplanetary Mission Support Requirements ... IMSR
Interplanetary Monitor Satellite (IAA) ... IMS
Interplanetary Monitoring Platform [*A spacecraft*] ... IMP
Interplanetary Monitoring Probe [*A spacecraft*] ... IMP
Interplanetary Network [*Astronomy*] ... IPN
Interplanetary Scintillation ... IPS
Interplanetary Shock Propagation Model [*Marine science*] (OSRA) ... ISPM
Interplanetary Shock Propagation Model (USDC) ... ISPM
Interplanetary Space Travel Research Association ... ISTRA
Interplanetary Travel (AAG) ... IPT
Interplant Job Ticket ... IPJT
Interplant Material Requisition Order ... IMRO
Interplant Shipping Authority ... ISA
Interplant Shipping Notice ... ISN
Interplant Shipping Order ... ISO
Interplant Work Order (MCD) ... IPWO
Interplate Shear Zone [*Geology*] ... ISZ
Interplatform Alignment System (MCD) ... IPAS
Interplead [*Legal shorthand*] (LWAP) ... INTERPL
Interpleader [*Legal*] [*British*] (ROG) ... INTPLDR
Interpoint [*NASDAQ symbol*] (SAG) ... INTP
Interpoint Corp. [*NASDAQ symbol*] (TTSB) ... INTP
Interpoint Corp. [*Associated Press*] (SAG) ... Intpnt
Interpolated Data and Speech Transmission [*Computer science*] ... IDAST
Interpolated Learning [*Psychology*] ... IL
Interpolated Voice Data (IAA) ... IVD
Interpolated Water Elevation (PDAA) ... IWE
Interpolating Delta Modulator ... IDM
Interpolation (MSA) ... INTRPL
Interpole (IAA) ... I
Interpole [*Electromagnetics*] ... INTPO
Interpole Winding [*Wiring*] (DNAB) ... IPW
Interpool, Inc. [*Associated Press*] (SAG) ... Interpol
Interpool, Inc. [*Associated Press*] (SAG) ... Intrpol
Interpool, Inc. [*NYSE symbol*] (SPSG) ... IPX
Interpool Inc. 5.75% Cv Pfd [*NYSE symbol*] (TTSB) ... IPXPrA
Interpore International [*NASDAQ symbol*] (SAG) ... BONZ
Interpore International [*Associated Press*] (SAG) ... Intpore
Interpore Intl. [*NASDAQ symbol*] (TTSB) ... BONZ
Interport Corp. [*ICAO designator*] (FAAC) ... IPT
Interport Trucking [*MTMC*] (TAG) ... INTP
Interposed Abdominal Compression - Cardiopulmonary Resuscitation ... IAC-CPR
Interposed Abdominal Counterpulsation [*Medicine*] ... IAC
Interpositive [*Photography*] (WDMC) ... IP
Interpositive/Internegative [*Photography*] (WDMC) ... IP/IN
Interpost Junction Panel ... IPJP
Interpret (AFM) ... INTPR

Interpret Parity Error	IPE
Interpret Sign Error	ISE
Interpretation (AFM)	INTPN
Interpretation: A Journal of Bible and Theology [A publication] (BRI)	Intpr
Interpretation Canada [Federal agency]	IC
Interpretation Canada. Ontario Section [A publication]	ICOS
Interpretation Division, Environment Canada - Parks [Direction de l'Interpretation, Environnement Canada - Parcs], Ottawa, Ontario [Library symbol National Library of Canada] (NLC)	OOEIB
Interpretation Report	IR
Interpretative Opinion [Legal term] (DLA)	Interp Op
Interpretative Trace and Trap Program (SAA)	ITT
Interpretative Trace and Trap Program Plus Modifications (SAA)	ITT/PMD
Interpreter	I
Interpreter	INT
Interpreter	INTERP
Interpreter (WGA)	INTERPR
Interpreter Generator	INTGEN
Interpreter Officer [Military British]	IO
Interpreter, Second Class [British]	AI
Interpreter's Bible	IB
Interpreter's Dictionary of the Bible	IDB
Interpretive Coding Language	ICL
Interpretive Computer Simulator	ICS
Interpretive Computer System	ICS
Interpretive Debugger [Computer science] (ECII)	IDB
Interpretive Language (PDAA)	IL
Interpretive Operation	IO
Interpretive Programming System	IPS
Interpretive Structural Modeling [A computer-assisted learning process for structuring information]	ISM
Inter-Process Communication (NITA)	IPC
Interprocess Communication Facility [Digital Equipment Corp.]	IPCF
Interprocess Controller	IPC
Inter-Process Coupler (NITA)	IPC
Interprocessor Buffer	IPB
Interprocessor Channel (IAA)	IPC
Interprocessor Communication (BUR)	IPC
Interprocessor Communication and Control Routine (MCD)	ICC
Inter-Processor/Multiplexer (MCD)	IPM
Interprocessor Process [Telecommunications] (TEL)	IPP
Interprocessor Signal Bus	IPSB
Interprocessor Signaling System [Telecommunications] (TEL)	IPSS
Interprocessor Unit	IPU
Inter-Professional Ad Hoc Group for Environmental Information Sharing	IPAHGEIS
Interprofessional Council on Environmental Design (EA)	ICED
Interprofessional Fostering of Ophthalmic Care for Underserved Sectors [An association] (EA)	IFOCUS
Interprofessional Research Commission on Pupil Personnel Services [Defunct]	IRCOPPS
Interprogram Communication Facility [Prime Computer, Inc.]	IPCF
Interproject Control Station (IAA)	IPCS
Interproject Group	IPG
Interprovincial Advisory Council on Energy [Canada]	IPACE
Inter-Provincial Diversified Holding Ltd. [Toronto Stock Exchange symbol]	IPD
Interprovincial Pipe Line Ltd. [Toronto Stock Exchange symbol]	IPL
Interprovincial Steel & Pipe Corp. Ltd., (IPSCO), Regina, Saskatchewan [Library symbol National Library of Canada] (NLC)	SRISP
Interprovincial Steel & Pipe Corp. Ltd., Regina, SK, Canada [Library symbol Library of Congress] (LCLS)	CaSRISP
[The] Interpublic Group of Companies, Inc. [Associated Press] (SAG)	IntpbGp
[The] Interpublic Group of Companies, Inc. [NYSE symbol] (SPSG)	IPG
Interpublic Grp Cos. [NYSE symbol] (TTSB)	IPG
Interpulse Interval	IPI
Interpupillary	INTRPLRY
Interpupillary Distance	IPD
Interpupillary Distance	PD
Interquartile Range	IQR
Interquest Resources Corp. [Toronto Stock Exchange symbol]	IQT
Interracial Council for Business Opportunity [New York, NY] (EA)	ICBO
Interracial Family Alliance (EA)	IFA
Interracial Family Circle [An association]	IFC
Interracial-Intercultural Pride (EA)	I-PRIDE
Inter-Range and Global Planning Group [White Sands Missile Range] (MUGU)	IRGPG
Interrange Communications Planning Committee	ICPC
Inter-Range Documentation Group [White Sands Missile Range]	IRDG
Inter-Range Instrumentation Group [White Sands Missile Range]	IRIG
Inter-Range Instrumentation Group B [NASA] (GFGA)	IRIG-B
Inter-Range Instrumentation Group - Meteorological Working Group [White Sands Missile Range]	IRIG-MWG
Inter-Range Missile Flight Safety Group [White Sands Missile Range]	IRMFSG
Inter-Range Missile Ground Safety Group [White Sands Missile Range] (KSC)	IRMGSG
Inter-Range Operations Planning Group [White Sands Missile Range]	IROPG
Interrange Telemetry Working Group	IRTWG
Inter-Range Vector [NASA] (KSC)	IRV
Interrecord Gap (IAA)	IRG
Inter-Record Gap [Computer science Telecommunications] (MCD)	IRG
Interrectal Spike Discharge [Neurophysiology]	ID
Inter-Regional Capital Account [Inter-American Development Bank]	IRC
Inter-Regional Fin. Gr. [NYSE symbol] (TTSB)	IFG
Inter-Regional Financial Group, Inc. [NYSE symbol] (SPSG)	IFG
Inter-Regional Insurance Conference [Later, ISO]	IRIC

Inter-Regional Subject Coverage Scheme [Libraries cooperative scheme] [British] (NITA)	IRSC
Inter-Regional Training Information System [International Labor Organization] [United Nations] (DUND)	IRTIS
Interrelated Flow Simulation	IFS
Interrelated Logic Accumulating Scanner	ILAS
Interrelationship Graph (PDAA)	IRG
Interreligious Committee of General Secretaries (EA)	ICGS
Interreligious Emergency Campaign for Economic Justice (EA)	IECEJ
Interreligious Foundation for Community Organization (EA)	IFCO
Inter-Religious Task Force on Central America [Defunct] (EA)	IRTF
Interreligious Taskforce on US Food Policy (EA)	ITUSFP
InterRent [Car rental group]	IR
Inter-Research Council Committee on Pollution Research [British]	IRCCOPR
Interresponse Time [Psychometrics]	IRT
Interrogate (MDG)	INT
Interrogate (NASA)	INTEROG
Interrogate (AABC)	INTG
Interrogate (MSA)	INTRG
Interrogation [British naval signaling]	INT
Interrogation (ADA)	INTER
Interrogation	INTERROG
Interrogation and Information Reception Circuit [Telecommunications] (OA)	IIRC
Interrogation and Locating	IRL
Interrogation Entry Register (IAA)	IE
Interrogation Prisoner of War	IPW
Interrogation, Recording, and Locating System [Naval Oceanographic Office]	IRLS
Interrogation Repetition Frequency [RADAR beacon]	IRF
Interrogation Report	IR
Interrogation Requirements Information System [DoD] (AFIT)	IRIS
Interrogation Side-Lobe Suppression	ISLS
Interrogation-Translation Team [Military] (CINC)	ITT
Interrogative	INTER
Interrogative (BJA)	interr
Interrogative [Linguistics]	Wh
Interrogatories (ROG)	INTERROGS
Interrogator-Responder	IR
Interrogator-Responder-Transducer	IRT
Interrogator-Transponder (KSC)	IT
Interrogatory (ROG)	INTERROGY
Interrupt [Computer science Telecommunications]	I
Interrupt	INT
Interrupt	INTER
Interrupt [Computer science Telecommunications]	INTR
Interrupt	INTRP
Interrupt (MSA)	INTRPT
Interrupt (NASA)	RUPT
Interrupt Acknowledge [Computer science]	INTA
Interrupt Acknowledgment Latency [Computer science]	IACKL
Interrupt Address Register	IAR
Interrupt Address to Bus [Computer science]	IAB
Interrupt and Timing [Telecommunications] (TEL)	INTIM
Interrupt Control Block (NASA)	ICB
Interrupt Control Register [Computer science]	ICR
Interrupt Control Register [Computer science] (MSA)	INCR
Interrupt Control Unit [Computer science] (IAA)	ICU
Interrupt Disk Operating System	IDOS
Interrupt Enable [Computer science]	IE
Interrupt Enable [Computer science]	INTE
Interrupt Feedback Line [Computer science] (IAA)	IFB
Interrupt Flag [Computer science]	IF
Interrupt Flag Register [Computer science] (IAA)	IFR
Interrupt Handler [Computer science] (IAA)	IH
Interrupt Inhibit	II
Interrupt Jet Sensor	IJS
Interrupt Level Status Word	ILSW
Interrupt Level Subroutine (CMD)	ILS
Interrupt Mask	IM
Interrupt Priority Level	IPL
Interrupt Processor (IAA)	IRP
Interrupt Register (IAA)	IR
Interrupt Request [Computer science] (MHDI)	INTRQ
Interrupt Request [Computer science] (MHDB)	IR
Interrupt Request [Computer science]	IRQ
Interrupt Request Block (CMD)	IRB
Interrupt Request Line [Computer science]	IRQ
Interrupt Request Vector	IRV
Interrupt Return [PC instruction] (PCM)	IRET
Interrupt Return Register	IRR
Interrupt Service Routine (IEEE)	ISR
Interrupt Service Subroutine (CMD)	ISS
Interrupt Status Register (IAA)	ISR
Interrupt Storage Area	ISA
Interrupt Storage Area Table [Computer science] (OA)	ISAT
Interrupt System Enable	ISE
Interrupt Vector Generator	IVG
Interrupt-Descriptor Table [Computer science]	IDT
Interrupted Continuous Wave [Electronics]	ICW
Interrupted Continuous Wave Telegraphy (IAA)	ICWT
Interrupted Feedback [Wireless earphone] (NTCM)	IFB
Interrupted Quick Flashing Light [Navigation signal]	I Qk Fl
Interrupted Quick Flashing Light [Navigation signal]	INTQKFL
Interrupted Quick [Flashing] Light [Navigation signal]	I Qk

Interrupted Quick [*Flashing*] **Light** [*Navigation signal*] ... Int Qk
Interrupted Quick [*Flashing*] **Light** [*Navigation signal*] ... IQ
Interrupted Ring Tone [*Telecommunications*] (TEL) ... IRT
Interrupted Task Paradigm [*Psychometrics*] ... ITP
Interrupted Ultraquick [*Flashing*] **Light** [*Navigation signal*] ... IUQ
Interrupted Very Quick [*Flashing*] **Light** [*Navigation signal*] ... IVQ
Interrupter (MSA) ... INT
Interrupting Capacity (IAA) ... IC
Interruption Address Storage Register (NITA) ... IASR
Interruption Code (IAA) ... IC
Interruption of Air Traffic Services (FAAC) ... INATS
Interruption of Pregnancy for Psychiatric Indication ... IPPI
Interruption of the Aortic Arch [*Medicine*] (DMAA) ... IAA
Interruption Queue Element [*Computer science*] (MHDI) ... IQE
Interruptions per Minute ... IPM
Interruptions per Minute/Second (DEN) ... IPM/S
Interruptions per Second ... IPS
Interrupt-Mask Register [*Computer science*] ... IMR
Intersatellite Link ... ISL
Inter-School Christian Fellowship [*British*] (BI) ... ISCF
Interscience Computer [*NASDAQ symbol*] (TTSB) ... INTR
Interscience Computer Wrrt [*NASDAQ symbol*] (TTSB) ... INTRW
Interscience Conference on Antimicrobial Agents and Chemotherapy ... ICAAC
Interscience Publishers ... IP
Interscience Technological Forecasting Methodology Study Group ... ITFMSG
Intersciences Computer Corp. [*Associated Press*] (SAG) ... IntCpt
Intersciences Computer Corp. [*NASDAQ symbol*] (SAG) ... INTR
Intersciences Computer Corp. [*Associated Press*] (SAG) ... IntscCpt
Inter-Seamount Acoustic Range ... ISAR
Inter-Secretariat Committee on Scientific Problems Relating to Oceanography [*United Nations*] ... ICSPRO
Intersect (MSA) ... INTSCT
Intersecting Storage Accelerator [*In name of atomic reactor, Isabelle*] ... ISA
Intersecting Storage Ring [*High-energy physics*] ... ISR
Intersection Loop Detection (MHDI) ... ILD
Intersection Midblock Model [*Environmental Protection Agency*] (GFGA) ... IMM
Intersection of Air Routes [*Aviation*] ... IAR
Intersection of Range Legs ... IRL
Intersection of Runways [*Aviation*] ... IXR
Intersection of the Shift Fringes (PDAA) ... ISF
Intersection Point Generator (PDAA) ... IPGEN
Intersection With (WDAA) ... INTER/W
Intersectional Transportation Service ... ITS
Intersegmental ... IS
Intersegmental Muscles [*Anatomy*] (DAVI) ... ISM
Intersegmental Travel Time [*Zoology*] ... ISTT
Interserve/USA [*An association*] (EA) ... IUSA
Interservice ... IS
Inter-Service Agency Automated Message Processing Exchange ... IS/A AMPE
Interservice Agreement [*DoD*] ... ISA
Interservice Balkan Intelligence Committee [*World War II*] ... ISBIC
Interservice Committee on Technical Facilities [*Aerospace*] (AAG) ... ISCTF
Inter-Service Communication [*British World War II*] ... ISC
Interservice/Cross Service [*Support*] ... ISCS
Interservice Data Exchange Program (AFIT) ... IDEP
Interservice Depot Maintenance Interrogation Systems ... ISMIS
Interservice Experiments Program ... ISEP
Interservice Group [*Military*] ... ISG
Interservice Group for Flight Vehicle Power [*Military*] ... IGFVP
Interservice Home Exchange [*Commercial firm*] (EA) ... IHE
Interservice Hovercraft Trials Unit [*Military*] ... IHTU
Interservice Hovercraft Unit [*Military*] ... IHU
Interservice/Industry Training Equipment Conference [*Military*] ... I/ITEC
Interservice/Industry Training Systems Conference [*Military*] ... I/ITSC
Interservice/Interagency Support Agreement (MCD) ... IISA
Inter-Service Ionosphere Bureau [*Military*] ... ISIB
Interservice Liaison Office [*Military*] (CAAL) ... ILO
Interservice Materiel Utilization Agency [*Military*] (AABC) ... IMUA
Inter-Service Metallurgical Research Council [*British*] (MCD) ... ISMET
Interservice Occupational Task Analysis Program [*Military*] (NVT) ... ISOTAP
Interservice Procedures for Instructional Systems Development ... IPISD
Interservice Procedures for Systems Development [*Military*] ... IPSD
Interservice Radiation Measurement Program ... IRMP
Interservice Radio Frequency Management School (DOMA) ... IRFMS
Inter-Service Radio Measurements [*British World War II*] ... ISRM
Interservice Radio Propagation Laboratory (MCD) ... IRPL
Interservice Recruiting Committee [*Military*] (DNAB) ... IRC
Inter-Service Research Bureau [*British*] ... ISRB
Interservice Security Board [*World War II*] ... ISSB
Inter-Service Sports Council [*Military*] ... ISC
Interservice Sports Council [*Later, ISC*] ... ISSC
Interservice Supply Support [*Military*] (AABC) ... ISS
Interservice Supply Support Agreements [*Military*] ... ISSA
Interservice Supply Support Committee [*or Coordinator*] [*Military*] (AABC) ... ISSC
Interservice Supply Support Program [*Military*] (AABC) ... ISSP
Interservice Supply Support Records Office [*Military*] (AABC) ... ISSRO
Interservice Supply Support Subcommittee [*Military*] (CINC) ... ISSSC
Interservice Support Agreement [*Military*] ... ISA
Interservice Support Code [*Military*] ... ISC
Interservice Technical Information Exchange System [*Military*] (AFIT) ... ITIES
Inter-Service Topographical Department [*British*] ... ISTD
Interservice Training Review Board (MCD) ... ITRB
Interservice Training Review Organization [*Military*] (NVT) ... ITRO
Interservice Undergraduate Navigator Training ... IUNT
Interservice Warehousing Support Services Agreement ... IWSSA
Inter-Service Working Group for Cooperation and Standardization of Foto Interpretation Procedures, Equipment, and Related Matters ... IWGCSFIPERM
Inter-Services Liaison Department [*World War II*] ... ISLD
Inter-Services Metallurgical Research Council [*British*] ... ISMRC
Inter-Services Signals Unit [*British military*] (DMA) ... ISSU
Inter-Shift Coordination [*Medicine*] (DMAA) ... ISC
Intership ... INTSHP
Intership [*Freight forwarding company*] [*British*] ... IS
Intersite Radio Communications System (MCD) ... IRCS
Intersite Transmission Subsystem [*Ground Communications Facility, NASA*] ... ISTS
Intersite Transportation Equipment [*NASA*] (NASA) ... ITE
Inter-Society Color Council (EA) ... ISCC
Inter-Society Commission for Heart Disease Resources (EA) ... ICHD
Intersociety Commission for Heart Disease Resources [*American Heart Assoc iation - AHA*] [*Absorbed by*] ... ICHDR
Inter-Society Commission for Heart Disease Resources ... ISCHDR
Intersociety Committee on Methods for Air Sampling and Analysis (EA) ... ICMASA
Intersociety Committee on Methods for Air Sampling and Analysis ... ISC
Intersociety Committee on Pathology Information (EA) ... ICPI
Intersociety Council on Laboratory Medicine of Canada ... ICLMC
Inter-Society Cytology Council [*Later, American Society of Cytology - ASC*] ... ISCC
Intersociety Energy Conversion Engineering Conference ... IECEC
[*An*] **Intersociety Liaison Committee on the Environment** ... AISLE
INTERSOLV [*NASDAQ symbol*] (TTSB) ... ISLI
Intersolv, Inc. [*Associated Press*] (SAG) ... Interslv
Intersolv, Inc. [*NASDAQ symbol*] (SAG) ... ISLI
Inter-Sound Interval (EDAC) ... ISI
Interspace ... IS
Interspace (MAE) ... ISP
Interspecies Communication [*An association*] (EA) ... IC
Interspecies Ovum Penetration Test [*Medicine*] (BABM) ... ISPT
Interspersed Repetitive Sequence [*Genetics*] ... IRS
Interspike Interval [*Neurophysiology*] ... ISI
Interspike Interval Histogram [*Neurophysiology*] ... ISIH
Interspinal [*Anatomy*] (DAVI) ... ISP
Interspinous Ligament [*Medicine*] (DMAA) ... ISL
Interstage ... I/S
Interstage (KSC) ... INTRSTG
Interstage ... INTSTG
Interstage Section Container ... ISC
Interstage Section Shell ... ISS
Interstate [*Highways*] ... I
Interstate (FAAC) ... INSTA
Interstate [*Railroad*] (MHDW) ... INT
Interstate [*Legal shorthand*] (LWAP) ... INTERST
Interstate ... INTSTE
Interstate ... IS
Interstate Agreement on Detainers Act [*1970*] ... IADA
Interstate Air Quality Agencies /Commissions [*Environmental Protection Agency*] ... IAQA/C
Interstate Airlines Ltd. [*Nigeria*] [*ICAO designator*] (FAAC) ... IAE
Interstate Airways Communications (IAA) ... INSAC
Interstate Airways Communications Station (IAA) ... INACS
Interstate Airways Communications Station ... INSACS
Interstate and Foreign Commerce (DLA) ... IFC
Interstate Association of Commissions on the Status of Women ... IACSW
Interstate Bakeries [*NYSE symbol*] (TTSB) ... IBC
Interstate Bakeries Corp. [*NYSE symbol*] (SPSG) ... IBC
Interstate Bakeries Corp. [*Formerly, Interstate Brands Corp.*] [*Associated Press*] (SAG) ... IntstBak
Interstate Carriers Conference (EA) ... ICC
Interstate Clearing House on Mental Health [*Defunct*] ... ICHMH
Interstate Club (EA) ... IC
Interstate Commerce ... ISC
Interstate Commerce Act [*1887*] ... ICA
Interstate Commerce Commission [*Independent government agency*] ... ICC
Interstate Commerce Commission [*Independent government agency*] (DLA) ... Int Com Commn
Interstate Commerce Commission Reports [*A publication*] (DLA) ... IC Rep
Interstate Commerce Commission Reports [*A publication*] (DLA) ... ICC Rep
Interstate Commerce Commission Reports [*A publication*] (DLA) ... ICCR
Interstate Commerce Commission Reports [*A publication*] (DLA) ... Inst Com Com
Interstate Commerce Commission. Reports [*A publication*] (DLA) ... Int Com Com
Interstate Commerce Commission Reports [*A publication*] (DLA) ... Int Com Rep
Interstate Commerce Commission Reports [*A publication*] (DLA) ... Inters Com Rep
Interstate Commerce Commission Reports [*A publication*] (DLA) ... Interst Com R
Interstate Commerce Commission Transport Mobilization [*Federal emergency order*] ... ICC-TM
Interstate Commerce Commission Valuation Reports [*A publication*] (DLA) ... ICC Valuation Rep
Interstate Commerce Reports [*A publication*] (DLA) ... IC
Interstate Commerce Reports [*A publication*] (DLA) ... Interstate Com R
Interstate Commission on the Delaware River Basin ... INCODEL
Interstate Commission on the Potomac River Basin ... ICPRB
Interstate Conference of Employment Security Agencies (EA) ... ICESA
Interstate Conference on Water Policy (EA) ... ICWP
Interstate Congress for Equal Rights and Responsibilities (EA) ... ICERR
Interstate Cost Estimate [*Federal Highway Administration*] ... ICE
Interstate Council of State Boards of Cosmetology [*Later, NIC*] ... ICSBC
Interstate Distributive Education Curriculum Consortium (EDAC) ... IDECC
Interstate Electronics Corp. (MCD) ... IEC

Interstate Electronics Corp., Anaheim, CA [*Library symbol Library of Congress*] (LCLS) .... CAnaI
Interstate Energy [*Vancouver Stock Exchange symbol*] .... ITS
Interstate Fisheries Management Program (GNE) .... ISFMP
Interstate Freeze Lobbying Network (EA) .... IFLN
Interstate Gambling Activities .... IGA
Interstate General Ltd. [*AMEX symbol*] (SPSG) .... IGC
Interstate General Ltd. [*Associated Press*] (SAG) .... IntstGC
Interstate Genl L.P. [*AMEX symbol*] (TTSB) .... IGC
Interstate Identification Index [*NCIC*] III
Interstate Job Bank .... IJB
Interstate/Johnson Lane [*NYSE symbol*] (TTSB) .... IJL
Interstate/Johnson Lane [*Formerly, Interstate Securities, Inc.*] [*NYSE symbol*] (SPSG) .... IS
Interstate Johnson Lane, Inc. [*NYSE symbol*] (SAG) .... IJL
Interstate/Johnson Lane, Inc. [*Formerly, Interstate Securities, Inc.*] [*Associated Press*] (SAG) .... IntJhn
Interstate Land Sales [*HUD*] .... ILS
Interstate Land Sales Registration Office [*HUD*] (IAA) .... ILSRO
Interstate Loan Library [*Council of State Governments*] (IID) ILL
Interstate Migrant Education Council (EA) .... IMEC
Interstate Mining Compact Commission (EA) .... IMCC
Interstate National Dealer Services, Inc. [*Associated Press*] (SAG) .... IntNDS
Interstate National Dealer Services, Inc. [*Associated Press*] (SAG) .... IntstNDS
Interstate National Dealer Services, Inc. [*NASDAQ symbol*] (SAG) .... ISTN
Interstate Natl Dealer Svcs [*NASDAQ symbol*] (TTSB) .... ISTN
Interstate Natl Dealer Wrrt [*NASDAQ symbol*] (TTSB) .... ISTNW
Interstate Natural Gas Association of America (EA) .... INGAA
Interstate Oil Compact .... IOC
Interstate Oil Compact Commission (EA) .... IOCC
Interstate Oil Compact Commission. Bulletin [*A publication*] (DLA) .... IOCC Bull
Interstate Organized Crime Index [*Computer databank*] .... IOCI
Interstate Postgraduate Medical Association of North America (EA) .... IPMANA
Interstate Power [*NYSE symbol*] (TTSB) .... IPW
Interstate Power Co. [*Associated Press*] (SAG) .... IntstPw
Interstate Power Co. [*NYSE symbol*] (SPSG) .... IPW
Interstate Processing Center [*Department of Labor*] .... IPC
Interstate Producers Livestock Association (EA) .... IPLA
Interstate Railroad Co. [*AAR code*] .... INT
Interstate Settlement Information System [*AT & T*] .... ISIS
Interstate Shellfish Sanitation Conference .... ISSC
Interstate Solar Coordination Council (EA) .... ISCC
Interstate Substitute Cost Estimate [*Federal Highway Administration*] .... ISCE
Interstate Tariff Bureau, Inc. .... ISTB
Interstate Tariff Bureau, Inc., Lakewood OH [*STAC*] .... ISB
Interstate Theft .... IT
Interstate Towing Auxiliary (EA) .... ITA
Interstate Transmission of Wagering Information .... ITWI
Interstate Transport Region .... ITR
Interstate Transport Region Commission .... ITRC
Interstate Transportation in Aid of Racketeering .... ITAR
Interstate Transportation of Fireworks .... ITF
Interstate Transportation of Gambling Devices .... ITGD
Interstate Transportation of Lottery Tickets .... ITLT
Interstate Transportation of Obscene Matter .... ITOM
Interstate Transportation of Prison-Made Goods .... ITPMG
Interstate Transportation of Prize Fight Films .... ITPFF
Interstate Transportation of Stolen Aircraft .... ITSA
Interstate Transportation of Stolen Cattle .... ITSC
Interstate Transportation of Stolen Motor Vehicle .... ITSMV
Interstate Transportation of Stolen Property .... ITSP
Interstate Transportation of Strikebreakers .... ITSB
Interstate Transportation of Unsafe Refrigerators .... ITUR
Interstate Transportation of Wagering Paraphernalia .... ITWP
Interstate Truckers Association .... ITA
Interstate Truckload Carriers Conference .... ITCC
Interstation Noise Suppression .... INS
Interstation Supersonic Track Conferences (MCD) .... ISTRACON
Interstation Transmission (KSC) .... IST
Interstellar Communications (AAG) .... ISC
Interstellar Medium [*Planetary science*] .... ISM
Interstellar Scattering [*of radio waves in the galaxy*] .... ISS
Interstellar [*Phase*] **Scintillation** [*Galactic science*] .... ISS
Interstellar Travel (AAG) .... IST
Interstimulus Interval .... ISI
Interstitial Cell Fluid (DMAA) .... ISCF
Interstitial Cell Stimulating Hormone [*Also, LH, LSH*] [*Endocrinology*] .... ICSH
Interstitial Cell-Conditioned Medium [*Clinical chemistry*] .... ICCM
Interstitial Cells [*Histology*] IC
Interstitial Cells [*Histology*] .... ISC
Interstitial Cyst [*Pulmonary medicine*] IC
Interstitial Cystitis [*Nephrology*] IC
Interstitial Cystitis Association (EA) .... ICA
Interstitial Fluid [*Physiology*] .... IF
Interstitial Fluid [*Physiology*] .... ISF
Interstitial Fluid Space [*Medicine*] (DMAA) .... IFS
Interstitial Fluid Volume [*Medicine*] (DMAA) .... ISFV
Interstitial Hyperthermia [*Medicine*] (DMAA) .... ITH
Interstitial Keratitis [*Ophthalmology*] .... IK
Interstitial Lung Disease .... ILD
Interstitial Nephritis [*Medicine*] (DMAA) .... IN
Interstitial Nuclei of the Anterior Hypothalamus [*Brain anatomy*] .... INAH
Interstitial Nucleus of Cajal [*Brain anatomy*] .... INC
Interstitial Pulmonary Emphysema [*Medicine*] (AAMN) .... IPE
Interstitial Pulmonary Fibrosis [*Medicine*] (DMAA) .... IPF
Interstitial Radiation Pneumonitis [*Medicine*] (DMAA) .... IRP
Interstitial Radiotherapy (DMAA) .... IRT
Interstitial Retinol-Binding Protein [*Biochemistry*] .... IRBP
Interstitial Transfer Facility [*Nuclear energy*] (NRCH) .... ITF
Interstitial Water [*Physiology*] .... ISW
Interstitial-Free [*Metallurgical engineering*] .... IF
Interstrat Resources, Inc. [*Vancouver Stock Exchange symbol*] .... ITE
Interstudy, Minneapolis, MN [*Library symbol Library of Congress*] (LCLS) .... MnMIn
Intersubblock Gap .... ISG
Intersun Havacilik Anonim Sirketi [*Turkey*] [*FAA designator*] (FAAC) .... SWW
Interswitching System Interface [*Telecommunications*] (ACRL) .... ISSI
Interswitching System Interface Protocol [*Telecommunications*] (ACRL) .... ISSIP
Intersymbol Interference .... ISI
Intersymbol Interference Corrector .... ISIC
Inter-System Communication (NITA) .... ISC
Inter-System Crossing [*Chemical Kinetics*] .... ISC
Intersystem Crossing [*Physics*] .... ISC
Intersystem Designation (CAAL) .... ISD
Intersystem Link .... ISL
Intersystems, Inc. [*Formerly, Bamberger Polymers, Inc.*] [*AMEX symbol*] (SPSG) II
Intersystems, Inc. [*Associated Press*] (SAG) .... Intrsy
Intersystems, Inc. [*Associated Press*] (SAG) .... Intrsystm
Intersystems Inc. Wrrt [*AMEX symbol*] (TTSB) .... IIWS
Intertan, Inc. [*Associated Press*] (SAG) .... Intrtan
InterTan, Inc. [*NYSE symbol*] (CTT) .... ITN
Intertank (NASA) .... I/T
Intertank (KSC) .... INTK
Intertank Structural Test Assembly [*NASA*] (NASA) .... ISTA
Intertape Polymer Group [*Associated Press*] (SAG) .... IntPly
Intertape Polymer Group [*Associated Press*] (SAG) .... IntPoly
Intertape Polymer Group [*AMEX symbol*] (SAG) .... ITP
Intertechnique .... IN
Inter-Tel, Inc. [*NASDAQ symbol*] (NQ) .... INTL
Inter-Tel Inc. [*NASDAQ symbol*] (TTSB) .... INTL
Inter-Tel, Inc. [*Associated Press*] (SAG) .... IntrTel
Inter-Territorial Catholic Bishops' Conference (EAIO) .... ITCABIC
Inter-Theater Transfer [*Army*] (AABC) .... ITT
Interthecal [*Anesthesiology*] .... ITh
Intertime Switch [*Connection or Call*] [*Telecommunications*] (TEL) .... ITS
Intertoll [*Trunk*] [*Telecommunications*] (TEL) .... IT
Intertoll Trunk [*Telecommunications*] .... ITT
Intertrack Time Displacement Error (IAA) .... ITDE
Intertrial Interval [*Psychology*] .... ITI
Intertribal Christian Communications .... INTERCOM
Inter-Tribal Indian Ceremonial Association (EA) .... ITIC
Intertriginous Xanthoma [*Medicine*] (AAMN) .... ITX
Intertrochanteric Femoral Fracture [*Medicine*] (MEDA) .... ITFF
Intertropical Convergence [*Trade winds*] [*Meteorology*] .... ITC
Intertropical Convergence Zone [*Trade winds*] [*Meteorology*] .... ICZ
Intertropical Convergence Zone [*Trade winds*] [*Meteorology*] .... ITCZ
Inter-Tropical Convergence Zone .... ITZ
Intertropical Discontinuity [*Meteorology*] .... ITD
Intertropical Front [*Meteorology*] (BARN) .... ITF
Intertuberous [*Diameter*] [*Medicine*] .... IT
Inter-Turbine Temperature (ADA) .... ITT
Intertype (DGA) .... INTER
Intertype Fototronic Photographic System (DIT) .... IFPTS
Intertype Training [*Navy*] (NVT) .... ITT
Inter-Union Commission of Advice to Developing Countries [*of the International Union of Geodesy and Geophysics*] [*Mississauga, ON*] (EAIO) .... IUCADC
Inter-Union Commission of European Dehydrators [*See also CIDE*] [*Paris, France*] (EAIO) .... IUCED
Inter-Union Commission on Frequency Allocations for Radio Astronomy and Space Science (EA) .... IUCAF
Inter-Union Commission on Frequency Allocations for Radio Astronomy and Space Science (EA) .... IUCFA
Inter-Union Commission on Radio Meteorology [*International Council of Scientific Unions*] [*Research center*] .... IUCRM
Inter-Union Commission on Solar-Terrestrial Physics (MCD) .... IUCSTP
Inter-Union Commission on Spectroscopy [*International Council of Scientific Unions*] .... IUCS
Interunion Commission on the Application of Science to Agriculture, Forestry, and Aquaculture [*ICSU*] [*Ottawa, ON*] (EAIO) .... CASAFA
Inter-Union Commission on the Lithosphere [*NASA*] ICL
Inter-Union Geodynamics Commission [*Also, ICG*] (MSC) .... IGC
Inter-University Case Program .... ICP
Inter-University Center for Astronomy and Astrophysic [*India*] .... IUCAA
Interuniversity Centre for European Studies [*Canada*] (IRC) .... ICES
Interuniversity Centre for the Study of Religion [*Canada*] .... ICSR
Inter-University Committee for Debate on Foreign Policy [*Defunct*] .... IUC
Inter-University Committee for Research on Consumer Behavior (EA) .... IUCRCB
Inter-University Committee on Israel [*Later, America-Israel Cultural Foundation*] (EA) .... IUCI
Inter-University Committee on the Superior Student [*Defunct*] (EA) .... ICSS
Inter-University Committee on Travel Grants .... IUCTG
Interuniversity Communications Council (EA) .... EDUCOM
Interuniversity Consortium for Educational Computing [*Database*] .... ICEC
Inter-University Consortium for Political and Social Research (EA) .... ICPSR
Inter-University Consortium for Political and Social Research, Ann Arbor, MI [*Library symbol*] [*Library of Congress*] (LCLS) .... MiAaI
Inter-University Consortium for Political Research [*Later, ICPSR*] (EA) .... ICPR
Inter-University Cooperation Program [*EC*] (ECED) .... ICP
Inter-University Council .... IUC

Interuniversity Council for Higher Education Overseas [*British*] (DI) .... ICHEO
Inter-University European Institute on Social Welfare (EA) .... IEISW
Inter-University Institute of Engineering Control (PDAA) .... IUIEC
Inter-University Labor Education Committee .... IULEC
Interuniversity Library Council: Reference and Interlibrary Loan Service [*Library network*] .... IULC-RAILS
Inter-University Seminar on Armed Forces and Society (EA) .... IUS
Inter-University Software Committee [*Inter-University Committee on Computing*] (AIE) .... IUSC
Interuniversity Southeast Asia Committee [*of the Association for Asia*] .... ISAC
Inter-University Transit System [*Interlibrary loan service*] [*Canada*] (NITA) .... IUTS
Inter-Urban Microwave-Powered Air-Cushion Vehicle (PDAA) .... IMPAV
Inter-User Reliability .... IUR
Interval .... INT
Interval (WDMC) .... int
Interval .... INTERV
Interval (MSA) .... INTVL
Interval (IAA) IV
Interval Availability .... IA
Interval Between Eruptions [*of Geyser*] .... IBE
Interval Embossed Tube .... IET
Interval International (EA) II
Interval Modulation Information Coding (PDAA) .... IMIC
Interval of Uncertainty [*Psychology*] .... IU
Interval Pulse Time Modulation .... IPTM
Interval Rate [*Army*] (AABC) .... IR
Interval Selection Circuit .... ISC
Interval Service Value (BUR) .... ISV
Interval Signal .... IS
Interval Time Control [*Computer science*] (OA) .... ITC
Interval Timer [*Computer science*] .... IT
Interval Training [*Physical fitness program*] .... IT
Intervalence Charge-Transfer [*Phyical chemistry*] .... IVCT
Intervalometer [*Military ordnance*] .... INTVLM
Intervalometer (KSC) IVL
Intervals Between Aircraft in Stream Type Formation [*Aviation*] (FAAC) .... IBASF
Intervals of Pulsations of Diminishing Period .... IPDP
Intervalve Coupling (DEN) IC
Intervalve Transformer (IAA) .... IVT
Inter-Varsity Christian Fellowship of the United States of America (EA) ..... IVCF
Inter-Varsity Fellowship of Evangelical Unions [*British*] (BI) .... IVF
Inter-Varsity Missions Fellowship (EA) .... IVMF
Inter-Varsity Press [*British*] .... IVP
Intervega - Movement for Compassionate Living the Vegan Way (EAIO) ..... MCL
Inter-Vehicle Power Transfer (MCD) .... IVPT
Intervehicular Communication (KSC) IVC
Intervehicular Information System [*Army*] (RDA) .... IVIS
Intervehicular Transfer (KSC) .... IVT
Intervening Sequence [*Genetics*] .... IVS
Intervention Board for Agricultural Products [*Government body*] [*British*] .... IBAP
Intervention Moves Parents and Children Together [*Drug abuse treatment program sponsored by Phoenix House Foundation*] .... IMPACT
Interventional Cardiac Catheterization [*Medicine*] ICC
Interventional Fluoroscopy [*Medicine*] (DMAA) .... IF
Interventional Radiography [*Medicine*] .... IVR
Interventricular [*Medicine*] IV
Interventricular Foramen [*Medicine*] (DMAA) .... IVF
Interventricular Septal Defect [*Cardiology*] .... IVSD
Interventricular Septum [*Cardiology*] .... IVS
Intervertebral [*or Intravertebral*] [*Medicine*] IV
Intervertebral Disc [*Medicine*] .... IVD
Intervertebral Joint Complex [*Medicine*] .... IVJC
Intervideo Network, Inc. [*Beverly Hills, CA*] [*Telecommunications*] (TSSD) .... INI
Interview .... INT
Interview .... INTERV
Interview (CINC) .... INTV
Interview (AFM) .... INTVW
Interview Schedule for Children .... ISC
Interview-after-Combat .... IAC
Interviewer .... int
Interviewer .... INTERV
Interviewer Card Scheme [*Business term*] .... ICS
Interviewer's Classification Guide .... ICG
Interviewing, Assessment, and Referral or Counseling (ADA) .... IAR/C
Interview-Oriented Background Investigation (MCD) .... IBI
Intervisual Books, Inc. [*Associated Press*] (SAG) .... IntvisB
Intervisual Books, Inc. [*NASDAQ symbol*] (SAG) .... IVBK
Intervisual Books'A' [*NASDAQ symbol*] (TTSB) .... IVBK
InterVoice [*NASDAQ symbol*] (TTSB) .... INTV
InterVoice, Inc. [*NASDAQ symbol*] (NQ) .... INTV
InterVoice, Inc. [*Associated Press*] (SAG) .... Intvoice
Intervuelo SA [*Mexico ICAO designator*] (FAAC) .... ITV
InterWest Bancorp [*Associated Press*] (SAG) .... IntrWBcp
InterWest Bancorp [*NASDAQ symbol*] (TTSB) .... IWBK
Interwest Home Medical [*NASDAQ symbol*] (TTSB) .... IWHM
Interwest Home Medical, Inc. [*NASDAQ symbol*] (SAG) .... IWHM
Interwest Home Medical, Inc. [*Associated Press*] (SAG) .... IwstHM
InterWest Savings Bank [*NASDAQ symbol*] (SAG) .... IWBK
Interworking Unit [*Computer science*] (TNIG) .... IWU
Interzonal Trade Office [*NATO*] (NATG) .... IZTO
Intestacy [*Legal shorthand*] (LWAP) .... INTSTY
Intestacy [*Legal*] (ROG) .... INTY
Intestinal (AAMN) .... Int
Intestinal .... INTEST
Intestinal Brush Border [*Medicine*] (MAE) .... IBB
Intestinal Distress .... ID
Intestinal Glycoprotein [*Biochemistry*] (MAE) .... IGP
Intestinal Groove .... IG
Intestinal Iron (Ferrum) Transport [*Physiology*] .... IFeT
Intestinal Mast Cells [*Anatomy*] .... IMC
Intestinal Metaplasia [*Medicine*] .... IM
Intestinal Mutagenicity Test [*Clinical chemistry*] .... IMT
Intestinal Obstruction [*Medicine*] (MAE) .... int obst
Intestinal Obstruction [*Medicine*] .... IO
Intestinal Trefoil Factor [*Biochemistry*] .... ITF
Intestinal Type [*of epithelium*] .... IT
Intestinal Type Adenocarcinoma [*Oncology*] .... ITAC
Intestine I
Intetnational Colin Energy [*NYSE symbol*] (SAG) .... KCN
Intevac, Inc. [*Associated Press*] (SAG) .... Intevac
Intevac, Inc. [*NASDAQ symbol*] (SAG) .... IVAC
Intext Educational Publishers .... IEP
Intimacy Potential Quotient .... IPQ
Intimal Thickening [*Medicine*] (MEDA) .... IT
Intimate Apparel Associates [*Defunct*] (EA) .... IAA
Intimate Apparel Manufacturers Association (EA) .... IAMA
Intimate Apparel Square Club (EA) .... IASC
Intimate Brands 'A' [*NYSE symbol*] (TTSB) .... IBI
Intimate Brands, Inc. [*NYSE symbol*] (SAG) .... IBI
Intimate Brands, Inc. [*Associated Press*] (SAG) .... Intimte
Intimate Relationship Questionnaire .... IRQ
Intime Sys Intl Wrrt [*NASDAQ symbol*] (TTSB) .... TAMSW
Intime Systems International, Inc. [*Associated Press*] (SAG) .... Intime
Intime Systems International, Inc. [*NASDAQ symbol*] (SAG) .... TAMS
Intime Systems Intl Unit [*NASDAQ symbol*] (TTSB) .... TAMSU
Intime Systems Intl'A' [*NASDAQ symbol*] (TTSB) .... TAMSA
Intl Absorbents [*NASDAQ symbol*] (TTSB) .... IABSF
Intl Aluminum [*NYSE symbol*] (TTSB) .... IAL
Intl Asset Holding [*NASDAQ symbol*] (TTSB) .... IAAC
Intl Bus. Mach 7 1/2% Dep Pfd [*NYSE symbol*] (TTSB) .... IBMPrA
Intl Bus. Machines [*NYSE symbol*] (TTSB) .... IBM
Intl Business Schs [*NASDAQ symbol*] (TTSB) .... IBSDF
Intl Cabletel [*NASDAQ symbol*] (TTSB) .... ICTL
Intl Colin Energy [*NYSE symbol*] (TTSB) .... KCN
Intl Cutlery [*NASDAQ symbol*] (TTSB) .... ICUT
Intl Cutlery Wrrt'A' [*NASDAQ symbol*] (TTSB) .... ICUTW
Intl Cutlery Wrrt'B' [*NASDAQ symbol*] (TTSB) .... ICUTZ
Intl Dairy Queen 'A' [*NASDAQ symbol*] (TTSB) .... INDQA
Intl Dairy Queen 'B' [*NASDAQ symbol*] (TTSB) .... INDQB
Intl Family Entert'nt 'B' [*NYSE symbol*] (TTSB) .... FAM
Intl Fibercom Inc. [*NASDAQ symbol*] (TTSB) .... IFCI
Intl Flavors/Fragr [*NYSE symbol*] (TTSB) .... IFE
Intl Game Technology [*NYSE symbol*] (TTSB) .... IGT
Intl Imaging Materials [*NASDAQ symbol*] (TTSB) .... IMAK
Intl Leisure Hosts [*NASDAQ symbol*] (TTSB) .... ILHL
Intl Lottery [*AMEX symbol*] (TTSB) ILL
Intl Lottery & Totalizator [*NASDAQ symbol*] (TTSB) .... ITSI
Intl Microcomputer Software [*NASDAQ symbol*] (TTSB) .... IMSI
Intl Multifoods [*NYSE symbol*] (TTSB) .... IMC
Intl Murex Technologies [*NASDAQ symbol*] (TTSB) .... MURXF
Intl Paper [*NYSE symbol*] (TTSB) .... IP
Intl Petroleum [*NASDAQ symbol*] (TTSB) .... IRPPF
Intl Post Ltd [*NASDAQ symbol*] (TTSB) .... POST
Intl Precious Metals [*NASDAQ symbol*] (TTSB) .... IPMLF
Intl Rectifier [*NYSE symbol*] (TTSB) .... IRF
Intl Remote Imaging [*AMEX symbol*] (TTSB) .... IRI
Intl Shipholding [*NYSE symbol*] (TTSB) .... ISH
Intl Specialty Products [*NYSE symbol*] (TTSB) .... ISP
Intl Standards Group Ltd [*NASDAQ symbol*] (TTSB) .... ISGI
Intl Technology [*NYSE symbol*] (TTSB) .... ITX
Intl ThoroughBred [*AMEX symbol*] (TTSB) .... ITB
Intl ThoroughBred A Pfd [*AMEX symbol*] (TTSB) .... ITBPrA
Intl Thunderbird Gaming [*Exchange symbol*] (TTSB) .... INB
Intl Verifact [*NASDAQ symbol*] (TTSB) .... IVIAF
Intl Yogurt [*NASDAQ symbol*] (TTSB) .... YOCM
IntlCom Group [*AMEX symbol*] (TTSB) .... ICG
IntlJensen [*NASDAQ symbol*] (TTSB) .... IJIN
Intolerance and Toxicity [*Medicine*] (DMAA) .... I&T
Intoxicated [*Airline notation*] .... AL
Intoxicated Driver Testing Unit [*Criminology*] (LAIN) .... IDTU
Intoxicating Liquor [*Legal term*] (DLA) .... INTOX L
Intoxication .... INTOX
Intoxication and Intercourse .... I & I
Intra Aortic [*Cardiology*] (MAE) .... IA
Intra-Abdominal [*Artery*] .... IAB
Intra-Abdominal Infection [*Gastroenterology*] (DAVI) .... IAI
Intra-Abdominal Pressure .... IAP
Intra-Alaska Facsimile [*National Weather Service*] .... IAF
Intra-Amniotic [*Medicine*] (AAMN) .... i amniot
Intra-Amniotic [*Medicine*] (AAMN) .... IA
Intra-Amniotic Saline [*Infusion*] [*Medicine*] .... IAS
Intra-Aortic Ballon Pumping [*Cardiology*] (DMAA) .... IBP
Intra-Aortic Balloon [*Cardiology*] .... IAB
Intra-Aortic Balloon Assist [*Cardiology*] .... IABA
Intra-Aortic Balloon Catheter [*Cardiology*] (DAVI) .... IABC
Intra-Aortic Balloon Counterpulsation [*Cardiology*] .... IABC
Intra-Aortic Balloon Pump [*Cardiology*] .... IABP
Intra-Aortic Balloon Pumping Assistance [*Cardiology*] (AAMN) .... IABPA
Intra-Aortic Counterpulsation [*Cardiology*] (DAVI) .... IACP
Intra-Aortic Counterpulsation Balloon [*Cardiology*] (DAVI) .... IACB

Intra-Application Communication Area [*Computer science*] (PCM) ... IACA
Intra-Arterial [*Cardiology*] (AAMN) ... i arter
Intra-Arterial [*Cardiology*] ... IA
Intra-Arterial Chemotherapy [*Medicine*] ... IAC
Intra-Arterial Digital Subtraction Arteriography [*Cardiology*] (DAVI) ... IA DSA
Intra-Arterial Pressure ... IAP
Intra-Arterial Vasopressin [*Cardiology*] ... IAV
Intra-Articular [*Medicine*] ... IA
Intra-Articular Steroid [*Physiology*] ... IAS
Intraaterial Digital Subtraction Angiography [*Medicine*] ... IADSA
Intra-Atrial [*Cardiology*] ... IA
Intra-Atrial Electrocardiogram [*Cardiology*] (MAE) ... IAE
Intra-Auricular [*Cardiology*] (DAVI) ... IA
Intra-Bureau Change Committee ... IBCC
Intracapillary Space [*In bioreactor*] ... ICS
Intracapsular (CPH) ... IC
Intracapsular Cataract Extraction [*Ophthalmology*] ... ICCE
Intracapsular Cataract Extraction with Peripheral Iridectomy [*Ophthalmology*] ... ICCEcPI
Intracarcass Pressure [*Tire technology*] ... ICP
Intracardiac [*Medicine*] ... IC
Intracardiac Catheter Recording [*Medicine*] (DMAA) ... ICR
Intracardiac Infection [*Medicine*] (DMAA) ... ICI
Intracarotid [*Medicine*] (MAE) ... IC
Intracavitary [*Medicine*] ... IC
Intracavity [*or Intracavitary*] [*Medicine*] ... ICAV
Intracavity LASER Absorption Spectroscopy ... ICLAS
Intracellular ... IC
Intracellular Enveloped Virus ... IEV
Intracellular Fluid [*Physiology*] ... ICF
Intracellular Fluid Volume [*Physiology*] ... IFV
Intracellular Mature Virus ... IMV
Intracellular Virus [*Medicine*] (PDAA) ... ICV
Intracellular Water [*Physiology*] ... ICW
Intracellular-Binding Proteins [*Medicine*] ... ICBP
Intracellular-Like Solution [*Cardioplegic solution*] [*Pharmacology*] (DAVI) ... ICS
Intracerebral [*Medicine*] ... IC
Intracerebral Hemorrhage [*Medicine*] ... ICH
Intracerebroventricular [*Also, ICTV, ICV*] [*Brain anatomy*] ... ic
Intracerebroventricular [*Also, ic, ICV*] [*Brain anatomy*] ... ICTV
Intracerebroventricular [*Also, ic, ICTV*] [*Brain anatomy*] ... ICV
Intracisternal [*Neruology*] (DAVI) ... IC
Intracisternal (DMAA) ... ICi
Intracisternal A-Particle [*Biochemistry*] ... IAP
In-Track Contiguous ... ITC
In-Track Noncontiguous ... ITNC
Intra-Class Correlation Coefficient ... ICC
Intracloud [*Climatology*] ... IC
Intracluster Medium [*Galactic science*] ... ICM
Intracoastal Waterway ... IWW
Intra-Collisional Field Effect (IAA) ... ICFE
Intracommunication System ... ICS
Intracommunity Directive [*Meat-shipping plants*] [*European Community*] ... ICD
Intracompany Correspondence (AAG) ... ICC
Intracompany Memorandum ... ICM
Intracoronary [*Cardiology*] ... IC
Intracoronary Nitroglycerine [*Pharmacology*] ... ICNTG
Intracoronary Streptokinase [*An enzyme*] ... ICSK
Intracoronary Streptokinase [*An enzyme*] ... ICSTK
Intracortical Microstimulation [*For study of brain function*] ... ICMS
Intracranial ... IC
Intracranial Aneurysm [*Medicine*] ... ICA
Intracranial Hemorrhage [*Medicine*] ... ICH
Intracranial Pressure [*Medicine*] ... ICP
Intracranial Pressure Catheter [*Neurology*] (DAVI) ... ICPC
Intracranial Reinforcement ... ICR
Intracranial Self-Administration [*Neurophysiology*] ... ICSA
Intracranial Self-Stimulation [*Also, ICSS*] [*Neurophysiology*] ... ICS
Intracranial Self-Stimulation [*Also, ICS*] [*Neurophysiology*] ... ICSS
Intracranial Stimulation [*Neurophysiology*] ... ICS
Intractable Diarrhea of Infancy [*Pediatrics*] ... IDI
Intractable Pain Society of Great Britain and Ireland ... IPS
Intractable Plantar Keratosis [*Orthopedics*] (DAVI) ... IPK
Intracuff Pressure [*In mechanical ventilation*] [*Medicine*] ... ICP
Intracutaneous [*Medicine*] ... IC
Intracytoplasmic Immunoglobulin ... ICIg
Intracytoplasmic Sperm Injection [*In vitro fertilization*] ... ICSI
Intracytoplasmic Sperm Injection ... ICSI
Intradermal [*Medicine*] (AAMN) ... i derm
Intradermal [*Medicine*] ... ID
Intradermal Cancer Test [*Oncology*] ... ICT
Intradermal Reaction [*Medicine*] (MAE) ... IDR
Intradermal Skin Test Score [*Immunology*] ... ISTS
Intradermal Test [*Medicine*] (MAE) ... IT
Intradermal Typhoid [*Medicine*] (DMAA) ... IDT
Intradiplochromatid Interchange (PDAA) ... IDCI
Intraductal [*Anatomy*] ... ID
Intraductal [*Medicine*] ... IN
Intraductal and Infiltrating Duct Carcinoma [*Oncology*] ... IFDC
Intraductal Carcinoma [*Medicine*] (MEDA) ... IC
Intraductal Carcinoma [*Oncology*] ... IDC
Intraductal Mammary Pressure ... IDMP
Intraduodenal [*Medicine*] (MAE) ... ID
Intraepithelial Carcinoma [*Medicine*] ... IEC
Intraepithelial Lymphocyte [*Hematology*] ... IEL
Intra-European Payments Agreement ... IEPA
Intra-Fleet Supply Support Operations Program [*Navy*] (DNAB) ... ISSOP
Intra-Fleet Supply Support Operations Team [*Navy*] (DNAB) ... ISSOT
Intrafusal Muscle [*Anatomy*] ... IFM
Intragastric ... IG
Intragastric Titration [*Gastroenterology*] ... IGT
Intra-Governmental Professional Advisory Council on Drugs and Devices [*Inactive*] [*FDA*] (EGAO) ... IPADD
Intrahepatic Arteriovenous Shunt [*Medicine*] ... IHS
Intrahepatic Cholestasis [*Medicine*] (DMAA) ... IHPC
Intrahepatic Duct [*or Ductule*] [*Gastroenterology*] (DAVI) ... IHD
Intrahepatic Portal Hypertension [*Medicine*] (MAE) ... IHPH
Intrahepatic Portosystemic Shunt [*Medicine*] ... TIPS
Intrahepatic Resistance [*Medicine*] (MAE) ... IHR
Intra-Industry Management Program [*Small Business Administration*] ... IMP
Intra-Industry Trade ... IIT
Intralaunch Facility and Launch Control Facility Cabling Subsystem (IAA) ... ILLCS
Intralesional [*Medicine*] (MEDA) ... i-lesion
Intralipid [*Pharmacology*] (DAVI) ... IL
Intra-List Stimulus Similarity (PDAA) ... ISS
Intramedullary [*Medicine*] ... IM
Intramedullary Metatarsal Decompression [*Medicine*] (DMAA) ... IMDC
Intramembranous Particle [*Cytology*] ... IMP
Intramolecular Charge Transfer [*Physical chemistry*] ... ICT
Intramolecular Vibrational Redistribution [*Chemistry*] ... IVR
Intramolecular Vibrational Relaxation [*Organic chemistry*] ... IVR
Intramolecular Vibration-Rotation Energy Transfer [*Chemistry*] ... IVRET
Intramural ... IM
Intramural (DLA) ... Intra
Intramural Law Journal [*A publication*] (DLA) ... Intramural LJ
Intramural Law Review [*A publication*] (DLA) ... Intramural L Rev
Intramural Law Review (St. Louis University) [*A publication*] (DLA) ... Intra L Rev (St LU)
Intramural Left Anterior Artery [*Medicine*] (DMAA) ... IMLA
Intramural Research Training Award [*National Institutes of Health*] ... IRTA
Intramuscular [*Injection*] [*Medicine*] ... IM
Intramuscular Compartment Pressure [*Medicine*] (DMAA) ... IMP
Intramuscular Gammaglobulin [*Medicine*] (DMAA) ... IMGG
Intramuscular Immunoglobulin [*Immunology*] (DAVI) ... IMIG
Intramuscular Injection [*Medicine*] (MAE) ... IMI
Intranasal ... IN
Intranet Business Information System (PDAA) ... IBIS
Intranet Solutions, Inc. [*NASDAQ symbol*] (SAG) ... INRS
Intranet Solutions, Inc. [*Associated Press*] (SAG) ... IntnetS
Intranet Solutions, Inc. [*Associated Press*] (SAG) ... IntnetSol
Intranet Visability [*Army*] ... ITV
Intransit Asset Visibility (MCD) ... IAV
In-Transit Control System (PDAA) ... INTRACONS
Intransit Data Card (AFM) ... IDC
Intransit Inventory (AFM) ... II
Intransit Item Visibility System (MCD) ... IIVS
In-Transit Rendezvous ... ITR
Intransitive ... I
Intransitive ... INT
Intransitive ... INTR
Intransitive (ROG) ... INTRANS
Intranuclear Inclusion ... INI
Intranuclear Ophthalmolplegia [*Ophthalmology*] (DAVI) ... INO
Intraocular ... IO
Intraocular Fluid [*Ophthalomology*] (DAVI) ... IOF
Intraocular Foreign Body [*Ophthalmology*] ... IOFB
Intraocular Lens [*Ophthalmology*] (DAVI) ... IL
Intraocular Lens [*Ophthalmology*] ... IOL
Intraocular Lens Manufacturers Association [*Defunct*] (EA) ... ILMA
Intraocular Pressure [*Ophthalmology*] ... IOP
Intraocular Tension [*Ophthalmology*] (DAVI) ... IOT
Intraocular Tension [*Ophthalmology*] (DAVI) ... Tn
Intraocular Tension Recorder ... ITR
Intraocular Transfer [*Ophthalmology*] (DAVI) ... IOT
Intraoperative Autologous Transfusion [*Medicine*] ... IAT
Intraoperative Autotransfusion [*Medicine*] ... IOA
Intraoperative Cholangiogram [*Radiology*] (DAVI) ... IOC
Intraoperative Cholecystogram [*Radiology*] (DAVI) ... IOCG
Intraoperative Electron Beam Therapy [*Medicine*] (DAVI) ... IOEBT
Intraoperative Localization Device [*Medicine*] (DMAA) ... ILD
Intraoperative Myocardial Ischemia [*Cardiology*] ... IMI
Intraoperative Neurosonography [*Radiology*] ... IONS
Intraoperative Radiation Therapy [*Medicine*] ... IORT
Intraoperative Sonography [*Radiology*] (DAVI) ... IOS
Intraoperative Spinal Sonography [*Radiology*] ... IOSS
Intraoperative Vascular Angiography [*Cardiology*] ... IVA
Intraoral Recurrent Herpes Simplex [*Medicine*] ... IRHS
Intrapair Interval ... IPI
Intraparenchymal Hemorrhage [*Medicine*] ... IPH
Intrapartum Fetal Distress [*Obstetrics*] (DAVI) ... IPFD
Intrapartum Stillbirth [*Medicine*] (DMAA) ... IPS
Intrapatellar Fat Pad (DMAA) ... IFP
Intra-Penile Device [*Contraceptive*] (DI) ... IPD
Intraperitoneal [*Medicine*] ... IP
Intraperitoneal [*Medicine*] (MEDA) ... i-periton
Intraperitoneal Shock [*Psychology*] ... IPS
Intrapictures [*Electronics*] (ACRL) ... I
Intrapleural ... IPL
Intrapleural Catheter [*Medicine*] (DAVI) ... IC

Intrapleural Pressure [*Biology*] .... IPP
Intrapleural Pressure [*Medicine*] (DAVI) .... Ppl
Intrapulmonary Interstitial Emphysema [*Medicine*] (DMAA) .... ITE
Intrapulse Demodulation Analysis .... IPDA
Intrarenal Reflux [*Medicine*] (AAMN) .... IRR
Intraretinal Microangiopathy [*Ophthalmology*] .... IRMA
Intraretinal Microvascular Abnormality [*Ophthalmology*] .... IRMA
Intraseasonal Atmospheric Oscillation (USDC) .... ISO
Intrasite Cabling (CET) .... ISC
Intraspecific Antigenic Typing (PDAA) .... IST
Intraspecific Brood Parasitism [*Biology*] .... IBP
Intraspinal [*Injection*] .... IS
Intraspinal .... ISP
Intrastate [*Legal shorthand*] (LWAP) .... INTRAST
Intrasynovial [*Medicine*] .... ISY
Intrasystem Electromagnetic Compatibility Analysis Program [*Computer science Air Force*] .... IEMCAP
Intratheater Imagery Transmission System [*Air Force*] .... IITS
Intrathecal [*Medicine*] (AAMN) .... i thec
Intrathecal [*Medicine*] .... INTH
Intrathecal [*Medicine*] .... IT
Intrathecal [*Medicine*] (CPH) .... Ith
Intrathoracic [*Medicine*] .... IT
Intrathoracic [*Anatomy*] .... ITh
Intrathoracic Gas Volume [*Medicine*] (MAE) .... IGV
Intrathoracic Pressure [*Medicine*] .... ITP
Intrationum Liber [*A publication*] (DSA) .... Int Lib
Intratrabecular Osteoclastic Tunneling Resorption [*Medicine*] .... IOTR
Intratracheal [*Medicine*] (AAMN) .... i trach
Intratracheal [*Medicine*] .... IT
Intratracheal [*Medicine*] .... ITR
Intratracheal Tube [*Medicine*] .... IT
Intratumoral [*Medicine*] (MAE) .... IT
Intrauterine [*Medicine*] .... IU
Intrauterine Adhesion [*Medicine*] (DMAA) .... IUA
Intrauterine Contraceptive Device [*Medicine*] .... ICD
Intrauterine Contraceptive Device [*Medicine*] .... IUCD
Intrauterine Death [*Medicine*] .... IUD
Intrauterine Device [*A contraceptive*] [*Medicine*] .... IUD
Intrauterine Fetal Death [*or Demise*] [*Obstetrics*] (DAVI) ... IUFD
Intrauterine Fetal Growth Retardation [*Obstetrics*] (DAVI) ..... IUFGR
Intrauterine Fetally Malnourished [*Medicine*] (MAE) .... IUM
Intrauterine Foreign Body [*Gynecology*] .... IUFB
Intrauterine Gestation [*Obstetrics*] (DAVI) .... IUG
Intrauterine Growth Rate [*Medicine*] (MAE) .... IUGR
Intrauterine Growth Retardation [*Neonatology*] (DAVI) .... IGR
Intrauterine Growth Retardation [*Medicine*] .... IUGR
Intrauterine Insemination [*Medicine*] (DMAA) .... IUI
Intrauterine Pregnancy (CPH) .... IUP
Intrauterine Pressure [*Gynecology*] .... IUP
Intrauterine Progesterone Contraceptive System [*Gynecology*] ... IPCS
Intrauterine Transfusion [*Gynecology*] .... IUT
Intrauterne Pregnancy, Delivered [*Obstetrics*] (DAVI) .... IUPD
Intrav, Inc. [*Associated Press*] (SAG) .... Intrav
Intrav, Inc. [*NASDAQ symbol*] (SAG) .... TRAV
Intravaginal [*Medicine*] (MAE) .... IVag
Intravaginal Culture [*Alternative to traditional in-vitro fertilization (IVF)*] (PAZ) IVC
Intravascular [*Medicine*] IV
Intravascular Blood Coagulation [*Medicine*] (DMAA) .... IVBC
Intravascular Bronchoalveolar Tumor [*Medicine*] (DMAA) .... IBAT
Intravascular Bronchoalveolar Tumor [*Oncology*] .... IVBAT
Intravascular Coagulation and Fibrinolysis Syndrome [*Medicine*] ... ICF
Intravascular Consumption Coagulopathy [*Medicine*] IVCC
Intravascular Erythrocyte Aggregation [*Hematology*] .... IEA
Intravascular Fluid [*Medicine*] .... IVF
Intravascular Mass (MAE) .... IVM
Intravascular Oxygenator [*Artificial lung*] [*Medicine*] .... IVOX
Intravascular Papillary Endothelial Hyperplasia [*Medicine*] .. IPEH
Intravascular Red Cell Aggregation [*Medicine*] (DMAA) .... IRCA
Intravascular Ultrasound [*Medicine*] .... IVUS
Intravehicular (MCD) IV
Intravehicular Activity .... IVA
Intravehicular Referenced Information [*NASA*] .... IRI
Intravehicular Umbilical [*NASA*] (KSC) .... IVU
Intravenous [*Medicine*] .... INTRN
Intravenous [*Medicine*] IV
Intravenous Accurate Control [*Pharmacology*] (DAVI) .... IVAC
Intravenous Anesthetic [*Medicine*] .... IV-ANES
Intravenous Cholangiography [*Medicine*] IVC
Intravenous Cholangiography [*or Cholangiogram*] [*Medicine*] (DAVI) .. IVCh
Intravenous Cholangiography [*Medicine*] (DMAA) .... IVCH
Intravenous Digital Subtraction Angiography .... IVDSA
Intravenous Drip [*Pharmacology*] (DAVI) .... IVD
Intravenous Drug Abuser .... IVDA
Intravenous Drug User .... IVDU
Intravenous Fat Emulsion [*Pharmacology*] (DAVI) .... IVFE
Intravenous Fluid [*Pharmacology*] (DAVI) .... IVF
Intravenous Glucose Tolerance Test [*Clinical medicine*] ...... IGTT
Intravenous Glucose Tolerance Test [*Clinical medicine*] ...... IVGTT
Intravenous Histamine Test [*Clinical Medicine*] (MAE) .... IHT
Intravenous Hyperalimentation [*Medicine*] .... IVH
Intravenous Immunoglobulin [*Medicine*] (CPH) .... IVIG
Intravenous Methylprednisolone [*Medicine*] .... IVMP
Intravenous Nitroglycerin [*Medication order*] (CPH) .... IVNTG
Intravenous Nurses Society (EA) .... INS

Intravenous Nutrition [*Medicine*] .... IVN
Intravenous Piggyback [*Method of drug administration*] [*Pharmacology*] ... IVPB
Intravenous Pitocin [*Pharmacology*] (DAVI) .... IVP
Intravenous Push [*Medicine*] .... IVP
Intravenous Pyelogram [*Radiology*] .... IVP
Intravenous Solu-Set [*Medicine*] (MEDA) .... IVSS
Intravenous Streptokinase [*An enzyme*] .... IVSK
Intravenous Streptokinase in Acute Myocardial Infarction [*Cardiology study*] .... ISAM
Intravenous Tolbutamide Tolerance Test [*Clinical medicine*] (MAE) ... IVTTT
Intravenous Transfusion [*Medicine*] .... IVT
Intravenous Urogram [*or Urography*] [*Medicine*] .... IVU
Intravenous Vasopressin [*Endocrinology*] IVV
Intravenous Volume [*Pharmacology*] (DAVI) .... IV vol
Intravenous-Patient-Controlled-Analgesia .... IV-PCA
Intraventricular [*Cardiology*] IV
Intraventricular [*Cardiology*] .... IVT
Intraventricular Block [*Medicine*] (DMAA) .... IVB
Intraventricular Cannula [*Medicine*] IVC
Intraventricular Catheter [*Cardiology*] (DAVI) IVC
Intraventricular Conduction Defect [*Cardiology*] .... IVCD
Intraventricular Conduction Delay [*Cardiology*] (AAMN) ..... IVCD
Intraventricular Hemorrhage [*Cardiology*] .... IVH
Intraventricular Hemorrhage Parents (EA) .... IVHP
Intraventricular Pressure [*Cardiology*] (AAMN) .... IVP
Intraventricular Septum [*Cardiology*] (AAMN) .... IS
Intravertebral [*Anatomy*] (DAVI) IV
Intravoxel Incoherent Motion [*Imaging technique*] .... IVIM
INTREC, Inc., Santa Monica, CA [*Library symbol Library of Congress*] (LCLS) .... CStmol
Intrenet, Inc. [*NASDAQ symbol*] (SAG) .... INET
Intrenet, Inc. [*Associated Press*] (SAG) .... Intrnt
Intricate (MSA) .... INTRC
Intrinsic Clearance [*Physiology*] .... Clint
Intrinsic Coercive Force .... ICF
Intrinsic Electric Strength (IEEE) .... IES
Intrinsic Electron Conduction (IAA) .... IEC
Intrinsic Energy [*Symbol*] [*Physics*] .... U
Intrinsic Factor [*Biochemistry*] .... IF
Intrinsic Factor Cobalamin (Complex) [*Biochemistry*] .... IFCbl
Intrinsic Factor Concentrate [*Biochemistry*] .... IFC
Intrinsic Heart Rate [*Cardiology*] .... IHR
Intrinsic Infrared Detector .... IID
Intrinsic Monomer Stress [*Physical chemistry*] .... IMS
Intrinsic Multiprocessing (IEEE) .... IMP
Intrinsic Payload Value .... IPV
Intrinsic Peroxidase Inhibition Solution [*Clinical chemistry*] ... IPXI
Intrinsic Reaction Coordinate [*Physical chemistry*] .... IRC
Intrinsic Rectifying Factor [*Biochemistry*] .... IRF
Intrinsic Semiconductor (IDOE) I
Intrinsic Sympathomimetic Activity [*Biochemistry*] .... ISA
Intrinsically Conductive Plastic [*Organic chemistry*] .... ICP
Intrinsicoid Deflection [*Cardiology*] .... ID
Intrinsic-Type, Semiconductor Material I
Intrnational Coordination Group for the Tsunami Warning System in the Pacific (USDC) .... ICG/ITSU
Introduced [*Ecology*] I
Introducing Broker (MHDB) .... IB
Introducing the World [*An association Canada*] .... ITW
Introduction (WDMC) .... ID
Introduction (DLA) .... Int
Introduction .... INTR
Introduction (MSA) .... INTRO
Introduction (WDMC) .... intro
Introduction .... INTROD
Introduction, Methodology, Results, and Discussion (WDMC) ... IMRAD
Introduction, Methods, Results, and Discussion [*Scientific writing*] ... IMRAD
[*An*] Introduction to the Apocrypha [*B. Metzger*] [*A publication*] (BJA) ... MIA
Introduction to the Books of the Old Testament [*A publication*] (BJA) ... IBOT
Introduction to the Federal Supply Catalog System .... IFSC
[*An*] Introduction to the Literature of the Old Testament [*S. R. Driver*] [*A publication*] (BJA) .... DILOT
Introductory (WDMC) .... intro
Introductory Physical Science [*Project*] [*Education*] .... IPS
Introductory Science Text-Books [*A publication*] .... ISTB
Introductory Trials Allowance List [*Military*] (AFIT) .... ITAL
Introduzione [*Introductory Movement*] [*Music*] (ROG) .... INTROD
Introit .... INT
Intromission and Ejaculatory Mechanism [*Physiology*] .... IEM
Intromogenous Computer Network .... ICN
Intron Binding Site [*Genetics*] .... IBS
Intropulmonary Shunt Ratio [*Medicine*] (DAVI) .... Qs/Qt
Introscripta [*Written Within*] [*Latin*] (ROG) .... INTROPTA
Introversion/Extroversion [*Psychology*] (AEE) .... I/E
Introverted, Intuitive, a Feeler, and Perceiver [*Keirsey Temperament Test Result*] [*Psychology*] .... INFP
Intruder .... INTR
Intruder Monitoring and Guidance Equipment (MCD) .... IMAGE
Intrusion Alarm System .... IAS
Intrusion Detection Alarm (CINC) .... IDA
Intrusion Detection Alarm System .... IDAS
Intrusion Detection and Identification System (PDAA) .... IDIS
Intrusion Detection and Sensor Laboratory [*Army*] (RDA) ... IDSL
Intrusion Detection Equipment .... IDE

Intrusion Detection Optical Communications System [*Computer system security*] .... IDOCS
Intrusion Detection System (MCD) .... IDS
Intrusion Resistant Communications Cable System (DNAB) .... IRCCS
Intubated Continuous Positive Pressure [*Medicine*] (DAVI) .... ICPP
Intuit, Inc. [*NASDAQ symbol*] (SAG) .... INTU
Intuit, Inc. [*Associated Press*] (SAG) .... Intuit
Intuit Services Corp. .... ISC
Intuitive Network Total Office [*Benchmark Associates*] [*Computer science*] .... INTO
Intumescent Fire Seals Association [*British*] (DBA) .... IFSA
Intuto [*Peru*] [*ICAO location identifier*] .... SPNT
Inuit Circumpolar Conference [*Godthaab, Greenland, Denmark*] (EAIO) ICC
Inuit Cultural Institute [*Canada*] ICI
Inuit Tapirisat of Canada, Ottawa, ON, Canada [*Library symbol*] [*Library of Congress*] (LCLS) .... CaOOIT
Inuit Tapirisat of Canada, Ottawa, Ontario [*Library symbol National Library of Canada*] (NLC) .... OOIT
Inukjuak, PQ [*ICAO location identifier*] (ICLI) .... CYPH
Inulin [*Biochemistry*] (DAVI) .... In
Inulin Dialysance [*Medicine*] (MAE) .... Di
In-Use Maintenance Test .... IM
Inuvik [*Northwest Territories*] [*Seismograph station code, US Geological Survey*] (SEIS) .... INK
Inuvik [*Canada*] [*Airport symbol*] (OAG) .... YEV
Inuvik, NT [*AM radio station call letters*] .... CHAK
Inuvik, NT [*Television station call letters*] .... CHAK-TV
Inuvik, NT [*ICAO location identifier*] (ICLI) .... CYEV
Inuvik Scientific Resource Centre, Indian and Northern Affairs Canada [*CentreScientifique de Ressources d'Inuvik, Affaires Indiennes et du Nord Canada*], Northwest Territories [*Library symbol National Library of Canada*] (NLC) .... NWII
Inuyama [*Japan*] [*Seismograph station code, US Geological Survey*] (SEIS) .... INU
Invacare Corp. [*Associated Press*] (SAG) .... Invcare
Invacare Corp. [*NASDAQ symbol*] (NQ) .... IVCR
Invader Resources Ltd. [*Vancouver Stock Exchange symbol*] IVL
Invalid (IAA) .... INV
Invalid (IAA) .... INVAL
Invalid Care Allowance [*British*] .... ICA
Invalid Children's Aid Association [*London*] .... ICAA
Invalid Children's Aid Nationwide [*British*] (EAIO) .... ICAN
Invalid Decimal (IAA) .... IVD
Invalid Memory Address [*Computer science*] .... IMA
Invalid Pension .... IP
Invalid Tricycle Action Group [*British*] (DI) .... ITAG
Invalidate Data [*Cache*] [*Computer instruction*] (PCM) .... INVD
Invalided from Service [*Medicine Navy*] .... IS
Invariant .... INVAR
Invariant-Azimuth States (PDAA) .... IAS
Invariant-Ellipticity States (PDAA) .... IES
Invasion .... INV
Invasive I
Invasive (MAE) IV
Invasive Activity Test [*Oncology*] .... IAT
Invasive Cancer of the Cervix [*Oncology*] ICC
Invasive Meningococcal Disease .... IMD
Invasive Mole .... IM
Invasive Pulmonary Aspergillosis [*Medicine*] (DAVI) .... IPA
Invective .... INV
In-Vehicle Communications Device [*Highway safety research*] .... IVCD
In-Vehicle Route Guidance System [*FHWA*] (TAG) .... IVRG
In-Vehicle Safety Advisory and Warning System [*FHWA*] (TAG) .... IVSAWS
In-Vehicle Safety Advisory and Warning System .... IVSAWS
In-Vehicle Unit [*Electronic system for charging for road usage*] [*Singapore*] (ECON) .... IVU
Invenit [*He, or She, Designed It*] [*Latin*] .... INV
Invenit [*He, or She, Designed It*] [*Latin*] (ROG) .... INVT
Invent (AABC) .... INV
Inventaire Bibliographique des Isiaca (BJA) .... IBIS
Inventaire des Tablettes de Tello. Mission Francaise en Chaldee [*Paris*] [*A publication*] (BJA) .... ITT
Inventario del Patrimonio Arquitectonico [*Database*] [*Ministerio de Cultura*] [*Spanish*] [*Information service or system*] (CRD) .... IPAA
Inventario del Patrimonio Historico Artistico Espanol [*Ministerio de Cultura*] [*Spain Information service or system*] (CRD) .... IPAT
Inventario Musical [*Database*] [*Ministerio de Cultura*] [*Spanish*] [*Information service or system*] (CRD) .... IMUS
Invented-File-Search System (DICI) .... INFIRS
Inventing and Patenting Sourcebook [*A publication*] .... IPS
Invention Industry Association of America .... IIA
Invention Marketing, Inc. [*Information service or system*] (IID) .... IMI
Invention Marketing Institute (EA) .... IMI
Invention Report .... IR
Invention Submission Corp. [*Information service or system*] (IID) .... ISC
Inventions and Inventors [*A publication*] II
Inventors [*Pergamon-Infoline*] (NITA) .... IN
Inventors Association of America (EA) .... IAA
Inventors Clubs of America (EA) .... ICA
Inventor's Desktop Companion [*A publication*] .... IDC
Inventors' Workshop International [*Later, IWIEF*] (EA) .... IWI
Inventors Workshop International Education Foundation (EA) .... IWIEF
Inventory I
Inventory (AFM) .... INV
Inventory (MSA) .... INVN
Inventory (AABC) .... INVT
Inventory .... INVTY

Inventory (ROG) .... INVY
Inventory Accounting Cost Control Number System (MCD) .... IACCN
Inventory Adjustment (MCD) .... INVADJ
Inventory Adjustment Document .... IAD
Inventory Adjustment Rate .... IAR
Inventory Adjustment Report [*Military*] .... IAR
Inventory Adjustment Voucher [*Military*] (AFM) .... IAV
Inventory and Inspection Report [*Army*] II
Inventory and Inspection Report [*Army*] (MUGU) .... IIR
Inventory and Management Analysis (AFM) .... I & MA
Inventory and Requirements Planning (MHDI) .... IRP
Inventory Available Date (TEL) .... IAD
Inventory by Exception (MHDB) .... IBE
Inventory Change Report .... ICR
Inventory Control and Analysis (MHDB) .... INCA
Inventory Control and Requirements Review Board [*CNO*] .... IC & RR
Inventory Control Center [*of Field Army Support Command*] ICC
Inventory Control Company ICC
Inventory Control Effectiveness .... ICE
Inventory Control Manager (MCD) .... ICM
Inventory Control Officer .... ICO
Inventory Control Point .... ICOP
Inventory Control Point .... ICP
Inventory Control Point Europe .... ICPE
Inventory Control System [*Computer science*] .... ICS
Inventory Control System With Varying Reorders (MHDB) .... Q-SYSTEM
Inventory Difference [*Formerly, MUF*] [*NRC/ERDA*] .... ID
Inventory Equipment Requirement .... IER
Inventory Equipment Requirement Specification .... IERS
Inventory Equipment Sheet .... IES
Inventory Forecasting and Replenishment Modules [*IBM Corp.*] .... INFOREM
Inventory in Motion .... IIM
Inventory Index (MCD) IVI
Inventory Locator Service [*Database*] [*Inventory Locator Service, Inc.*] [*Information service or system*] (CRD) .... ILS
Inventory Management [*Business term*] .... I/M
Inventory Management (MCD) .... INV MGT
Inventory Management Activity .... IMA
Inventory Management and Material Control (IAA) .... IMMAC
Inventory Management and Production Control [*ISTEL*] [*Software package*] (NCC) .... IMPCON
Inventory Management and Simulator .... IMS
Inventory Management Center (MCD) .... IMC
Inventory Management Plan [*Military*] (AFIT) .... IMP
Inventory Management, Product Replenishment and Order Validity Evaluation (MHDB) .... IMPROVE
Inventory Management Program and Control Technique [*IBM Corp.*] [*Computer science*] .... IMPACT
Inventory Management Record [*Military*] (AFM) .... IMR
Inventory [*or Item*] Management Responsibility Code .... IMRC
Inventory Management Review .... IMR
Inventory Management System (NASA) .... IMS
Inventory Manager [*Military*] .... IM
Inventory Manager Stock Control and Distribution [*Military*] (AFM) .... IMSC & D
Inventory Manager Stock Control and Distribution System [*Military*] .... IMSC & DS
Inventory Master File (NASA) .... IMF
Inventory Modified Round .... IMR
Inventory Nonrecurring (MCD) .... IN
Inventory Objective .... IO
Inventory of Affective Tolerance [*Psychology*] .... IAT
Inventory of American Sculpture .... IAS
Inventory of Anger Communication [*Personality development test*] [*Psychology*] .... IAC
Inventory of Canadian Agri-Food Research [*Canandian Agricultural Research Council*] [*Information service or system*] .... ICAR
Inventory of Contaminants in Aquatic Organisms [*Databank*] (NITA) .... ICAQUO
Inventory of General Hospital Mental Health Services [*Department of Health and Human Services*] (GFGA) .... IGHMHS
Inventory of Job Attitudes [*LIMRA*] .... IJA
Inventory of Job Openings [*State Employee Security Agency*] (OICC) .... IJO
Inventory of Land Use (BARN) .... ILU
Inventory of Long-Term Care Places [*Department of Health and Human Services*] (GFGA) .... ILTCP
Inventory of Marriage and Family Literature [*Sage Publications, Inc.*] (IID) .... IMFL
Inventory of Mental Health Organizations [*Department of Health and Human Services*] (GFGA) .... IMHO
Inventory of Mental Health Organizations and General Hospital Mental Health Services [*Department of Health and Human Services*] (GFGA) .... IMHO/GHMHS
Inventory of Mental Health Services in State Adult Correctional Facilites [*Department of Health and Human Services*] (GFGA) .... IMHSSACE
Inventory of Perceptual Skills [*Visual and auditory test*] .... IPS
Inventory of Psychosocial Development .... IPD
Inventory of Sources for History of Twentieth Century Physics [*University of California, Berkeley*] [*Information service or system*] (IID) .... ISHTCP
Inventory on Hand .... IOH
Inventory Policy Model (MHDI) .... IPM
Inventory, Print, and Index [*System*] .... IPI
Inventory Record (MCD) .... INVREC
Inventory Research Office [*Army*] .... IRO
Inventory Schedule .... IS
Inventory Service System (AFIT) .... ISS
Inventory Simulation (IAA) .... ISIM

Inventory Status Report ... ISR
Inventory Stock Cataloging Program ... ISCP
Inventory Temporarily in Use [*Army*] (AABC) ... ITIU
Inventory Temporarily in Use [*Army*] (AFIT) ... ITU
Inventory to Diagnose Depression [*Psychology*] ... IDD
Inventory to Sales Ratio [*Business term*] ... I/S
Inventory Transfer ... IT
Inventory Transfer Receipt ... IT/R
Inventory Trial Allowance List ... ITAL
Inventory Update Rule [*Environmental Protection Agency*] ... IUR
Inventory Validation Listing [*Computer science*] ... IVL
Inventory Valuation Adjustment [*Business term*] ... IVA
Inventory Verification Manual ... IVM
Inventrepreneurs' Forum (EA) ... IF
Inver Hills State Junior College, Inver Grove Heights, MN [*Library symbol Library of Congress*] (LCLS) ... MnIgS
Inveralochy [*Australia Seismograph station code, US Geological Survey*] (SEIS) ... INV
Invercargill [*New Zealand*] [*Airport symbol*] (OAG) ... IVC
Invercargill [*New Zealand*] [*ICAO location identifier*] (ICLI) ... NZNV
Inverell [*Australia Airport symbol*] (OAG) ... IVR
Inveresk Research International Ltd. [*British*] (IRUK) ... IRI
Invermay Resources [*Vancouver Stock Exchange symbol*] ... INC
Invermere, BC [*AM radio station call letters*] ... CKIR
Invermere Public Library, British Columbia [*Library symbol National Library of Canada*] (NLC) ... BIN
Inverness [*Scotland*] [*Airport symbol*] (OAG) ... INV
Inverness [*County in Scotland*] ... INVERN
Inverness/Dalcross [*British ICAO location identifier*] (ICLI) ... EGPE
Inverness, FL [*Television station call letters*] ... WGOX
Inverness, FL [*AM radio station call letters*] ... WINV
Inverness, FL [*FM radio station call letters*] (RBYB) ... WJUF
Inverness, NS [*Television station call letters*] ... CJCB-1
Inverness Petroleum Ltd. [*Toronto Stock Exchange symbol*] ... IES
Inverni & Della Beffa [*Italy*] [*Research code symbol*] ... IDB
Inverse [*or Invert*] ... INV
Inverse (IDOE) ... inv
Inverse (MSA) ... INVS
Inverse Address Resolution Protocol [*Telecommunications*] (ACRL) ... InARP
Inverse Boresight Ranging (MCD) ... IBSR
Inverse Check ... IC
Inverse Conical Scan (DNAB) ... ICS
Inverse Cosecant [*Mathematics*] ... ARCCSE
Inverse Cosine [*Mathematics*] ... ARCCOS
Inverse Cotangent [*Mathematics*] ... ARCCOT
Inverse Current [*Electronics*] (IAA) ... INVCURR
Inverse Discrete Cosine Transform [*Mathematics*] ... ICDT
Inverse Discrete Cosine Transform [*Electronics*] (ACRL) ... IDCT
Inverse Discrete Fourier Transform [*Electronics*] (IEEE) ... IDFT
Inverse Document Frequency (NITA) ... IDF
Inverse Electrode Current ... IEC
Inverse Fast Fourier Transform (IAA) ... IFFT
Inverse Fourier Transform Module [*An enzyme*] (MCD) ... IFTM
Inverse Free Electron LASER [*Plasma physics*] ... IFEL
Inverse Gain (NVT) ... IG
Inverse Gas Chromatography ... IGC
Inverse Gaussian [*Statistics*] ... IG
Inverse Hyperbolic Function ... IHF
Inverse Joule Effect ... IJE
Inverse Kinematics [*Computer science*] ... IK
Inverse Kinetics Rod Drop [*Nuclear energy*] (NRCH) ... IKRD
Inverse Kinetics Simulator ... IKS
Inverse Negative Impedance Converter (IAA) ... INIC
Inverse Photoelectric Effect ... IPE
Inverse Photoemission [*Spectroscopy*] ... IP
Inverse Photoemission Spectroscopy ... IPES
Inverse Photoemission Spectroscopy ... IPS
Inverse Polarity Protection ... IPP
Inverse Polymerase Chain Reaction [*Genetics*] ... IPCR
Inverse Raman Scattering [*Spectroscopy*] ... IRS
Inverse Reflex Tetrode [*Physics*] ... IRT
Inverse Sampling Procedure ... ISP
Inverse Secant [*Mathematics*] ... ARCSEC
Inverse Sine [*Mathematics*] ... ARCSIN
Inverse Standard Deviation of Nucleolar Area [*Oncology*] ... ISDNA
Inverse Synthetic Aperture RADAR [*Navy*] (ANA) ... ISAR
Inverse Tangent [*Mathematics*] ... ARCTAN
Inverse Taper Lens ... ITL
Inverse Thermoremanent Magnetization ... ITRM
Inverse Time Element (MUGU) ... ITE
Inverse Time Limit (MSA) ... ITL
Inverse Time Relay (KSC) ... ITR
Inverse Trigonometric Function ... ITF
Inverse Voltage [*Electronics*] (IAA) ... INVV
Inverse Wulff Plot (PDAA) ... IWP
Inversed Ratio of Ventilation ... IRV
Inversia [*Latvia*] [*ICAO designator*] (FAAC) ... INV
Inversion (DAVI) ... inv
Inversion (DAVI) ... inver
Inversion [*NWS*] (FAAC) ... INVRN
Inversion Recovery [*NMR imaging*] ... IR
Inversiones Ayacucho, SA, "Jet Privado" [*Peru*] [*FAA designator*] (FAAC) ... JPR
Invert (MSA) ... INVT
Invert Indicator from Accumulator (SAA) ... IIA
Invert Indicator From Storage (SAA) ... IIS
Invert Indicator of the Left Half (IAA) ... IIL
Invert Indicator of the Right Half (SAA) ... IIR
Invert Sugar [*10%*] **in Saline** [*Medicine*] ... I-10/S
Invert Sugar [*5%*] **in Water** [*Medicine*] ... I5/W
Invertebrate (WGA) ... INVERT
Invertebrate ... INVERTEB
Inverted Bowl Centrifuge ... IBC
Inverted Coaxial Magnetron (MCD) ... ICEM
Inverted Echo Sounder ... IES
Inverted Energy Population ... IEP
Inverted File (NITA) ... IF
Inverted File Access Method ... IFAM
Inverted File Information Retrieval System [*UK Chemical Information Service*] (NITA) ... INFIRS
Inverted Groundplane (PDAA) ... IGP
Inverted Hand Position [*Neuropsychology*] ... IHP
Inverted Index (NITA) ... IX
Inverted Microscope [*Instrumentation*] ... IM
Inverted Polypoid Hamartoma of the Rectum [*Medicine*] (DMAA) ... IPHR
Inverted Repeat [*Genetics*] ... IR
Inverted Rib Waveguide (NITA) ... IRW
Inverted Roof Membrane Assembly [*Construction*] ... IRMA
Inverted Sentence [*Used in correcting manuscripts, etc.*] ... I
Inverted Socket Process Architecture [*Computer science*] ... ISPA
Inverted Terminal Repeat [*Genetics*] ... ITR
Inverted Vertical [*Aircraft engine*] ... IV
Inverted Y-Suspensor [*Medicine*] ... IYS
Inverter ... I
Inverter (KSC) ... INV
Inverter ... INVTR
Inverter ... IV
Inverter Assembly ... IA
Inverter/ATCS [*Active Thermal Control Subsystem*] **Support Structure** (MCD) ... IASS
Inverter Distribution and Control Assembly (MCD) ... ID & CA
Inverter Light Control Assembly (MCD) ... ILCA
Inverter Power Supply (NASA) ... IPS
Invesco Funding [*Associated Press*] (SAG) ... InvescoF
Invesco PLC [*Associated Press*] (SAG) ... Invesco
Invesco PLC [*NYSE symbol*] (SAG) ... IVC
INVESCO PLC ADS [*NYSE symbol*] (TTSB) ... IVC
In-Vessel Handling Machine [*Nuclear energy*] (NRCH) ... IVHM
In-Vessel Handling Machine-Engineering Model [*Nuclear energy*] (NRCH) ... IVHM-EM
In-Vessel Heat Exchanger [*Nuclear energy*] (NRCH) ... IVHX
In-Vessel Storage [*Nuclear energy*] (NRCH) ... IVS
In-Vessel Storage Module [*Nuclear energy*] (NRCH) ... IVSM
In-Vessel Transfer Machine [*Nuclear energy*] (NRCH) ... IVTM
Invest ... INVST
Invest in Britain Bureau ... IBB
Invest to Compete Alliance [*Washington, DC*] (EA) ... ITCA
Invested ... INVSTD
Investext [*Business Research Corp.*] ... INVT
Investigate [*or Investigation*] (AFM) ... INVES
Investigate and Report (FAAC) ... INVSTAR
Investigating Officer ... IO
Investigation ... INV
Investigation ... INVEST
Investigation ... INVESTIG
Investigation ... INVSTGTN
Investigation [*Dialog*] [*Searchable field*] [*Information service or system*] (NITA) ... IV
Investigation and Censure Review Branch [*BUPERS*] ... I & CRB
Investigation and Corrective Action Report (KSC) ... ICAR
Investigation and Security Service Field Representative [*Veterans Administration*] ... I & SSFR
Investigation and Suspension ... I & S
Investigation Branch [*British Australia*] (DCTA) ... IB
Investigation into Information Requirements of Social Sciences [*1970s study*] [*British*] (NITA) ... INFROSS
Investigation on Teaching Using Microcomputers as an Aid ... ITMA
Investigation Record ... IR
Investigational Device Exemption [*Food and Drug Administration*] ... IDE
Investigational New Animal Drug [*Food and Drug Administration*] ... INAD
Investigational New Drug [*Application*] [*FDA*] ... IND
Investigational New Drug [*Medicine*] (DMAA) ... IND
Investigations of Marine Shallow Water Ecosystems (NOAA) ... IMSWE
Investigations of Marine Shallow-Water Ecosystems Program [*Smithsonian Institution*] (GFGA) ... IMSWEP
Investigative ... INVSTGTV
Investigative and Corrective Action (KSC) ... ICA
Investigative Dermatological Society (DAVI) ... IDS
Investigative Group International ... IGI
Investigative Reporters and Editors (EA) ... IRE
Investigative Support Information System [*Federal Bureau of Investigation*] ... ISIS
Investigator ... IN
Investigator ... INVSTR
Investigator Name [*Dialog*] [*Searchable field*] (NITA) ... IN
Investigator's Working Group [*Spacelab mission*] ... IWG
Invest-in-America National Council [*Later, RA*] (EA) ... IANC
Investing Builders Association ... IBA
Investment ... I
Investment ... INV
Investment ... INVEST

Investment (DD) ... invest
Investment ... INVSTMNT
Investment Account [*Postal Service*] [*British*] ... INVAC
Investment Advisers Act [*1940*] ... IAA
Investment Analysis Language [*Computer science*] (BUR) ... IAL
Investment Bank for Trade and Finance [*United Arab Emirates*] ... IBTF
Investment Bankers Association of America [*Later, SIA*] (EA) ... IBA
Investment Canada Act ... ICA
Investment Canada, Information Centre, Ottawa, ON, Canada [*Library symbol*] [*Library of Congress*] (LCLS) ... CaOOIC
Investment Casting Institute (EA) ... ICI
Investment Casting Mold (MCD) ... ICM
Investment Company ... IC
Investment Company Act [*1940*] ... ICA
Investment Company Data, Inc. [*Database producer*] (IID) ... ICD
Investment Company Institute (EA) ... ICI
Investment Co-Operative Programme Office [*UNIDO*] ... ICPO
Investment Counsel Association of America (EA) ... ICAA
Investment Counselor (MHDB) ... IC
Investment Dealers Association of Canada ... IDA
Investment Dollar Premium (ADA) ... IDP
Investment Education Institute (EA) ... IEI
Investment Equipment (MCD) ... IVE
Investment Feasibility Studies (TEL) ... IFS
Investment Feasibility Study Facility [*United Nations Development Programme*] [*Ghana*] ... IFSF
Investment Finance Bank Ltd. [*Malta*] ... IFB
Investment Grade Muni Inc. [*NYSE symbol*] (TTSB) ... PPM
Investment Grade Municipal Income Fund [*Associated Press*] (SAG) ... InvGrMu
Investment Grade Municipal Income Fund [*NYSE symbol*] (SAG) ... PPM
Investment Grant [*British*] ... IG
Investment Grant Office [*British*] ... IGO
Investment Guaranty Program [*AID*] ... IGP
Investment in Default [*Business term*] ... IID
Investment Income Surcharge [*Finance*] (MHDW) ... IIS
Investment Laws of the World [*A publication*] (DLA) ... ILW
Investment Management Consultants Association (EA) ... IMCA
Investment Management Institute [*Information service or system*] (IID) ... IMI
Investment Managers Regulatory Organisation [*British*] (ECON) ... IMRO
Investment Partnership Association (EA) ... IPA
Investment Performance Monitoring Service [*British*] ... IPMS
Investment Promotion Centre [*Tanzania*] ... IPC
Investment Promotion Information System [*UNIDO*] [*United Nations*] (DUND) ... INPRIS
Investment Promotion Program ... IPP
Investment Promotion Zone ... IPZ
Investment Property Databank [*London, England*] ... IPD
Investment Quotient ... IQ
Investment Recovery Association (EA) ... IRA
Investment Recurring (MCD) ... IR
Investment Savings Account (ADA) ... ISA
Investment Strategy [*Game*] ... INSTRAT
Investment Tax Credit ... IC
Investment Tax Credit ... ITC
Investment Tech Group [*NASDAQ symbol*] (TTSB) ... ITGI
Investment Technology Group [*Associated Press*] (SAG) ... InvTech
Investment Technology Group [*NASDAQ symbol*] (SAG) ... ITGI
Investment Trust Funds under Management ... ITM
Investment Trust Savings Scheme [*British*] ... ITSS
Investment Trust Unit [*British*] ... ITU
Investment-Return Assumption [*Finance*] (PDAA) ... IRA
Investment-Savings [*Economics*] ... IS
Investment-Savings Curve [*Economics*] ... I-S
Investment-Savings, Liquidity-Money [*Economics*] (ODBW) ... ISLM
Investor Relations ... IR
Investor Responsibility Research Center (EA) ... IRRC
Investor-Owned Utilities (BARN) ... IOU
Investors Bank Corp. [*Associated Press*] (SAG) ... InvBank
Investor's Business Daily [*A publication*] ... IBD
Investors Chronicle/Hillier Parker [*British A publication*] ... ICHP
Investors Daily [*JA Micropublishing, Inc.*] ... IVDA
Investors Diversified Services, Inc. [*Mutual funds*] ... IDS
Investors Financial Services Corp. [*NASDAQ symbol*] (SAG) ... IFIN
Investors Financial Services Corp. [*Associated Press*] (SAG) ... InvFnSv
Investors Finl Svcs [*NASDAQ symbol*] (TTSB) ... IFIN
Investors Group, Inc. [*Toronto Stock Exchange symbol*] ... IGI
Investors in Industry [*British*] ... III
Investors in Industry International BV ... 3I
Investors Ins Group [*AMEX symbol*] (TTSB) ... IIG
Investors Insurance Group [*Formerly, Gemco National, Inc.*] [*AMEX symbol*] (SPSG) ... IIG
Investors Insurance Group [*Associated Press*] (SAG) ... InvIns
Investors Overseas Services Ltd. [*Firm which sells mutual funds in foreign countries*] ... IOS
Investors Planning Corp. ... IPC
Investors Protection Scheme (DCTA) ... IPS
Investors Service Bureau [*Investment term*] ... ISB
Investors Title Co. [*NASDAQ symbol*] (TTSB) ... ITIC
Investors Title Insurance Co. [*Associated Press*] (SAG) ... InvTitl
Investors Title Insurance Co. [*NASDAQ symbol*] (SAG) ... ITIC
Invisible Empire Knights of the Ku Klux Klan (EA) ... IEKKK
Invisible Empire Knights of the Ku Klux Klan (EA) ... KKK
Invisible Ministry (EA) ... IM
Invisible Panel Warming Association [*British*] (BI) ... IPWA
Invisible Trade Balance [*Business term*] (MHDW) ... ITB
InVision Technologies [*NASDAQ symbol*] (TTSB) ... INVN
InVision Technologies, Inc. [*Associated Press*] (SAG) ... InVision
InVision Technologies, Inc. [*NASDAQ symbol*] (SAG) ... INVN
Invitation ... INV
Invitation (KSC) ... INVIT
Invitation for Bid ... IFB
Invitation for Bid [*Marine science*] (OSRA) ... IFB
Invitation for Bid (DOMA) ... IFB
Invitation for Proposal (NOAA) ... IFP
Invitation for Quote (MCD) ... IFQ
Invitation of Member Only ... IOMO
Invitation to Bid ... ITB
Invitation to Quote (MCD) ... ITQ
Invitation to Register (ADA) ... ITR
Invitation to Register Interest ... ITRI
Invitation to Send [*Western Union*] [*Data communications*] ... ITS
Invitation to Tender (SSD) ... ITT
Invitational ... INVTNL
Invitational Computer Conference ... ICC
Invitational Race [*Harness racing*] ... INV
Invitational Travel Order [*Army*] (AABC) ... ITO
Invite, Show, and Test [*Military*] (SDI) ... ISAT
Invited Contractor ... IC
Invitro International [*Formerly, Ropak Laboratories*] [*NASDAQ symbol*] (SPSG) ... INVI
Invitro International [*Associated Press*] (SAG) ... Invitr
Invivo Corp. [*Associated Press*] (SAG) ... Invivo
Invivo Corp. [*NASDAQ symbol*] (SAG) ... SAFE
Invoice ... INV
Invoice [*Billing*] (ODBW) ... inv
Invoice [*Billing*] (AFM) ... INV
Invoice [*Billing*] (ROG) ... INVCE
Invoice Book [*Business term*] ... IB
Invoice Book Inward [*Business term*] ... IBI
Invoice Book Outbound [*Business term*] ... IBO
Invoice Cost and Charges [*Business term*] ... IC & C
Invoice Discrepancy Report [*Business term*] ... IDR
Invoice Distribution ... ID
Invoice Register Number [*Business term*] (MCD) ... IRN
Invoice Shipping Documentation [*Business term*] ... ISD
Invoice Value [*Business term*] ... IV
Invoice Value (ODBW) ... iv
Invoice with Documents Attached [*Billing*] (ROG) ... INV DOC ATTACH
Involucrin (DMAA) ... IVL
Involuntary ... INV
Involuntary ... INVOL
Involuntary Extension ... INVOLEX
Involuntary Second SEA [*Southeast Asia*] **Tour** [*Air Force*] ... ISST
Involuntary Servitude and Slavery ... ISS
Involute ... INVLT
Involve [*Coat*] [*Pharmacy*] ... INVOLV
Involved Field [*Medicine*] ... IF
Involved Field Radiotherapy [*Medicine*] (DMAA) ... IFRT
Involvement Limited to Bone [*Oncology*] ... ILB
Inward (MSA) ... INWD
Inward Call Detail Recording [*Telecommunications*] (TEL) ... ICDR
Inward Grade of Service (DNAB) ... IGOS
Inward Processing Relief (DCTA) ... IPR
Inward Wide Area Telephone Service [*Bell System*] ... INWATS
INX Insearch Group of Companies Ltd. [*Vancouver Stock Exchange symbol*] ... IIN
Inyo County Free Library, Bishop, CA [*Library symbol Library of Congress*] (LCLS) ... CBisI
Inyo County Free Library, Independence, CA [*Library symbol Library of Congress*] (LCLS) ... CInI
Inyokern [*California*] [*Airport symbol*] (OAG) ... IYK
Inyokern, CA [*Location identifier FAA*] (FAAL) ... IYK
Inyokern, CA [*Location identifier FAA*] (FAAL) ... NID
Io Flux Tube [*Cosmology*] ... IFT
Io Plasma Torus [*Cosmology*] ... IPT
Ioannina [*Greece*] [*Airport symbol*] (OAG) ... IOA
Ioannina [*Greece*] [*ICAO location identifier*] (ICLI) ... LGIO
IOC [*Intergovernmental Oceanographic Commission*] **Group of Experts on Oceanographic Research as It Relates to IGOSS** [*Marine science*] (MSC) ... IRES
IOC [*Intergovernmental Oceanographic Commission*] **Sub-commission for the Caribbean and Adjacent Region** [*Marine science*] (OSRA) ... IOCARIBE
Iodinated Bovine Serum Albumin (DMAA) ... IBSA
Iodinated Human Serum Albumin ... IHSA
Iodinated Macroaggregated Albumin [*Medicine*] (MAE) ... IMAA
Iodinated Rat Serum Albumin (DMAA) ... IRSA
Iodinated Serum Albumin [*Medicine*] ... ISA
Iodine [*Chemical element*] ... I
Iodine [*Chemical element*] (DAVI) ... I_2
Iodine Azide Test [*Medicine*] ... IAT
Iodine Binding Capacity [*of starch*] ... IBC
Iodine Deficiency Disorders [*Medicine*] ... IDD
Iodine Dextrin Color ... IDC
Iodine Generating and Dispensing System (NASA) ... IGDS
Iodine Lotion [*Medicine*] ... ILo
Iodine Protection Factor [*Nuclear energy*] (GFGA) ... IPF
Iodine Radiation Monitor (IEEE) ... IRM
Iodine Removal System [*Nuclear energy*] (NRCH) ... IRS
Iodine Value [*Analytical biochemistry*] ... IV
Iodine-129 ... I-129

Iodinium [*Iodine*] [*Symbol is I*] [*Chemical element Pharmacy*] (ROG) — JODIN
Iodo [*As substituent on nucleoside*] [*Biochemistry*] — io
Iodoacetamide [*Organic chemistry*] — IAA
(Iodoacetamido)fluorescein [*Biochemical label*] — IAF
Iodoantipyrine [*Biochemistry*] — IAP
Iodocyanopindolol [*Biochemistry*] — ICYP
Iododacetic Acid [*Organic chemistry*] — IAA
Iododeoxyuridine (DMAA) — IDU
Iododeoxyuridine [*Also, IDU, IDUR, IUDR*] [*Pharmacology*] — IdUrd
Iodohydroxybenzylpindolol [*Organic chemistry*] — IHYP
Iodomercuri-Hydroxypropane [*Chemistry*] (DAVI) — IMHP
Iodonaphthyl Azide [*Organic chemistry*] — INA
Iodonitrotetrazolium Violet — INT
Iodophenyl(piperidinoacetyl)piperazine [*Biochemistry*] — IPAP
Iodopropynyl Butyl Carbamate [*Wood preservative*] — IPBC
Iodosobenzoic Acid [*Organic chemistry*] (RDA) — IBA
Iodosuccinyl CAMP Tyrosine Methyl Ester [*Biochemistry*] — ISCAMPME
Iodouracildeoxyriboside [*Biochemistry*] — IUdR
Iodovinylmethoprenol Analog [*Organic chemistry*] — IVMA
Iokea [*Papua New Guinea*] [*Airport symbol*] (OAG) — IOK
Iola Free Public Library, Iola, KS [*Library symbol Library of Congress*] (LCLS) — KIo
Iola, KS [*AM radio station call letters*] — KALN
Iola, KS [*FM radio station call letters*] — KIKS
Iola, KS [*Location identifier FAA*] (FAAL) — MSB
Iolani Place Irregulars (EA) — IPI
Ioma [*Papua New Guinea*] [*Airport symbol*] (OAG) — IOP
IOMEC Users Association [*Formerly, DUA*] [*Defunct*] (EA) — IUA
Iomega Corp. [*Associated Press*] (SAG) — Iomega
Iomega Corp. [*NASDAQ symbol*] (NQ) — IOMG
Ion Acoustic Instability Enterprises (PDAA) — IAI
Ion Acoustic Plasma Pulse — IAPP
Ion Atom Interaction — IAI
Ion Auxiliary Propulsion System [*for satellites*] — IAPS
Ion Beam Activated Deposition [*Coating technology*] — IAD
Ion Beam Analysis — IBA
Ion Beam Deposition [*Coating technology*] — IBD
Ion Beam Mass Spectrometer — IBMS
Ion Beam Projector — IBP
Ion Beam Scanning — IBS
Ion Beam Spectrochemical Analysis (PDAA) — IBSCA
Ion Beam Sputtering — IBS
Ion Beam Technology — IBT
Ion Beam Weapon — IBW
Ion Chamber [*Nucleonics*] — IC
Ion Chromatography — IC
Ion Chromatography Exclusion — ICE
Ion Chromatography Module — ICM
Ion Composition Instrument [*Cometary physics*] — ICI
Ion Conductance Modulator [*Cytochemistry*] — ICM
Ion Convection Electrodynamics (MCD) — ICE
Ion Coupled Plasma [*Oil analysis*] — ICP
Ion Cyclotron Double Resonance — ICDR
Ion Cyclotron Radiation — ICR
Ion Cyclotron Radio Frequency — ICRF
Ion Cyclotron Resonance [*Spectrometry*] — ICR
Ion Cyclotron Resonance Frequency [*Nuclear energy*] — ICRF
Ion Cyclotron Resonance Heating (MCD) — ICRH
Ion Cyclotron Resonance Photodissociation [*Spectrometry*] — ICRPDS
Ion Density Electronics Package — IDEP
Ion Dip Spectroscopy — IDS
Ion Dipole Interaction — IDI
Ion Doping Technique — IDT
Ion Drift Meter [*Instrumentation*] — IDM
Ion Drift Semiconductor — IDS
Ion Energy Selector — IES
Ion Engine (AAG) — IO
Ion Engine Simulator — IES
Ion Engine System — IES
Ion Engine System Section — IESS
Ion Exchange (WDAA) — IE
Ion Exchange (NRCH) — INX
Ion Exchange Chromatography — IEC
Ion Exchange Desalination — IED
Ion Exchange Evaporation Filter (PDAA) — IEEF
Ion Exchange Membrane — IEM
Ion Exchange Resin — IER
Ion Exchange Unit — IEU
Ion Exchanger — IEX
Ion Exchanger (NRCH) — IX
Ion Focusing Technique — IFT
Ion Formation from Organic Solids [*International conference*] — IFOS
Ion Gun Assembly — IGA
Ion Gun Collector — IGC
Ion Implantation Doping — IID
Ion Implantation Doping Technique — IIDT
Ion Implantation Manufacturing System — IIMS
Ion Implantation, Oxide Isolation with Scaling (NITA) — IMOX-S
Ion Implantation Study — IIS
Ion Kinetic Energy — IKE
Ion Kinetic Energy Spectrometry — IKES
Ion Laser Technology [*AMEX symbol*] (TTSB) — ILT
Ion Laser Technology [*Associated Press*] (SAG) — IonLaser
Ion Laser Technology, Inc. [*AMEX symbol*] (SAG) — ILT
Ion Laser Technology, Inc. [*Associated Press*] (SAG) — IonLsr
Ion Mass Spectrometer — IMS
Ion Microprobe [*Surface analysis*] — IMP
Ion Microprobe Analysis — IMPA
Ion Microprobe Analyzer — IMA
Ion Microprobe Mass Analyzer — IMMA
Ion Microtomography [*High-resolution imaging technique*] — IMT
Ion Microwelding Instrument — IMI
Ion Mobility Detector [*Instrumentation*] — IMD
Ion Mobility Spectrometry — IMS
Ion Moderated Partition [*Chromatography*] — IMP
Ion Pair Yield — IPY
Ion Plating Supply — IPS
Ion Production Rate — IPR
Ion Pump Vacuum System — IPVS
Ion Recombination Chamber — IRC
Ion Release Module [*Spacecraft*] [*Germany*] — IRM
Ion Scattering Analysis — ISA
Ion Selective Microelectrodes [*Instrumentation*] — ISM
Ion Silicon System (IAA) — ISS
Ion Source [*Spectroscopy*] — IS
Ion Source Injector — ISI
Ion Source Kit — ISK
Ion Spectroscopy Scattering [*Surface analysis*] — ISS
Ion Switch (IAA) — ISW
Ion Temperature Gradient [*Physics*] — ITG
Ion Thrust System — ITS
Ion Thruster Beam — ITB
Ion Time of Flight — ITOF
Ion Trap [*Instrumentation*] — IT
Ion Trap Detector [*Spectroscopy*] — ITD
Ion Trap Mass Spectrometer — ITMS
Ion Trap System — ITS
Ion Vacuum Pump — IVP
Ion Vapor Deposition [*Coating technology*] — IVD
Iona Appliances [*NASDAQ symbol*] (TTSB) — IAAPF
Iona Appliances, Inc. [*NASDAQ symbol*] (SAG) — IAAFF
Iona Appliances, Inc. [*Toronto Stock Exchange symbol*] — IAP
Iona Appliances, Inc. [*Associated Press*] (SAG) — IonaApp
Iona College (GAGS) — Iona C
Iona College, New Rochelle, NY [*Library symbol Library of Congress*] (LCLS) — NNerI
Iona College, New Rochelle, NY [*OCLC symbol*] (OCLC) — VXI
Iona Industries, Inc. [*Vancouver Stock Exchange symbol*] — IOA
Iona National Airways Ltd. [*Republic of Ireland*] [*ICAO designator*] (FAAC) — IND
Ion-Assisted Deposition [*Coating technology*] — IAD
Ion-Backscattering Analysis (IAA) — IBA
Ion-Beam-Assisted Deposition [*Organic chemistry*] — IBAD
Ion-Binding/Ion-Bouncing Model [*Physical chemistry*] — IBBM
Ion-Channel Switch [*Biochemistry*] — ICS
Ion-Controlled Diode [*Electronics*] (IAA) — ICD
Ione, WA [*Location identifier FAA*] (FAAL) — ION
Ion-Excited X-Ray Analysis — IXA
Ion-Getter-Pumping [*Electron microscopy*] — IGP
Ionia, MI [*AM radio station call letters*] — WION
Ionic — ION
Ionic Charge Number [*Chemistry*] (DAVI) — Z
Ionic Drive — IDRV
Ionic Fuel Technology [*NASDAQ symbol*] (TTSB) — IFTI
Ionic Fuel Technology, Inc. [*NASDAQ symbol*] (SAG) — IFTI
Ionic Fuel Technology, Inc. [*Associated Press*] (SAG) — Ionic
Ionic Fuel Technology, Inc. [*Associated Press*] (SAG) — IonicFuel
Ionic Fuel Technology Wrrt'A' [*NASDAQ symbol*] (TTSB) — IFTIW
Ionic Fuel Technology Wrrt'B' [*NASDAQ symbol*] (TTSB) — IFTIZ
Ionic Heated Cathode — IHC
Ionic Heated Kathode — IHK
Ionic Propulsion (IAA) — IPROP
Ionic Strength — I
Ionic Thermoconductivity [*or Thermocurrent*] — ITC
Ionics, Inc. [*NYSE symbol*] (SPSG) — ION
Ionics, Inc. [*Associated Press*] (SAG) — Ionics
Ion-Implanted Base Transistor — IBT
Ion-Implanted Base Transistor Technology (IAA) — IIBTT
Ion-Implanted Metal-Oxide Semiconductor — IMOS
Ion-Induced Light Emission (MCD) — IILE
Ion-Ion Collision — IIC
Ionium [*Th^{230}, radioactive isotope of thorium*] — Io
Ionization and Momentum Sensor — IMS
Ionization Chamber — IC
Ionization Chamber Smoke Detector [*Nuclear energy*] (NRCH) — ICSD
Ionization Constant [*Symbol*] [*Chemistry*] — K
Ionization Current Source (PDAA) — ICS
Ionization Energy [*Chemistry*] — IE
Ionization Front Accelerator [*Physics*] — IFA
Ionization Gauge Tube — IGT
Ionization Potential — IP
Ionization Test Apparatus — ITA
Ionization-Detected Stimulated Raman Spectroscopy — IDSRS
Ionized Calcium Analyzer — ICA
Ionized Cluster Beam Deposition [*Coating technology*] — ICBD
Ionized Flow Field — IFF
Ionized Gas LASER — IGL
Ionized Vacuum Deposit (MCD) — IVD
Ionized Yeast — IY
Ionizer, Slab Fabrication — ISF
Ionizing Wet Scrubber [*Environmental science*] (GFGA) — IWS

Ion-Neutralization Spectroscopy ... INS
Ionosphere (MSA) ... IONO
Ionosphere and Aural Phenomena Advisory Committee [*European Space Research Organization*] (IEEE) ... ION
Ionosphere Research Committee (MCD) ... IRC
Ionosphere Research Laboratory [*Pennsylvania State University*] (PDAA) ... IRL
Ionospheric Beacon Satellite (PDAA) ... IBS
Ionospheric Dispersion Analysis [*Air Force*] ... IDA
Ionospheric Electron Density ... IED
Ionospheric Explorer [*NASA/National Bureau of Standards*] ... IE
Ionospheric Forward Scatter (TEL) ... IFS
Ionospheric Ion Density ... IID
Ionospheric Prediction Service [*Telecommunications*] (TEL) ... IPS
Ionospheric Propagation Path ... IPP
Ionospheric Radio Signal ... IRS
Ionospheric Sounding Satellite [*Japan*] ... ISS
Ion-Pair [*Physical chemistry*] ... IP
Ion-Pair Comonomers [*Organic chemistry*] ... IPC
Ion-Pair High-Performance Liquid Chromatography [*Medicine*] ... IP-HPLC
Ion-Pair-Reversed-Phase Liquid Chromatography ... IP-RPLC
Ion-Scattering Spectrometer [*or Spectrometry*] ... ISS
Ion-Selective Electrode [*Instrumentation*] ... ISE
Ion-Selective Field Effect Transistor ... ISFET
Ion-Selective Material [*Chemistry*] ... ISM
Ion-Sensitive Electrode [*Instrumentation*] (IAA) ... ISE
Ion-Sieve-Type Manganese Oxide [*Inorganic chemistry*] ... ISMO
Iori Enterprises, Inc. [*Vancouver Stock Exchange symbol*] ... IOI
Iosco-Arenac Regional Library, AuGres Branch Library, AuGres, MI [*Library symbol Library of Congress*] (LCLS) ... MiTc-A
Iosco-Arenac Regional Library, East Tawas Branch Library, East Tawas, MI [*Library symbol Library of Congress*] (LCLS) ... MiTc-E
Iosco-Arenac Regional Library, Oscoda Township Branch Library, Oscoda, MI [*Library symbol Library of Congress*] (LCLS) ... MiTc-O
Iosco-Arenac Regional Library, Plainfield Township Branch Library, Hale, MI [*Library symbol Library of Congress*] (LCLS) ... MiTc-P
Iosco-Arenac Regional Library, Standish Branch Library, Standish, MI [*Library symbol Library of Congress*] (LCLS) ... MiTc-S
Iosco-Arenac Regional Library, Tawas City Branch Library, Tawas City, MI [*Library symbol Library of Congress*] (LCLS) ... MiTc-T
Iosco-Arenac Regional Library, Tawas City, MI [*Library symbol Library of Congress*] (LCLS) ... MiTc
Iosco-Arenac Regional Library, Whittemore Branch Library, Whittemore, MI [*Library symbol Library of Congress*] (LCLS) ... MiTc-W
Iota [*Ninth letter of the Greek alphabet*] (DAVI) ... I
Iota Beta Sigma [*An association*] (WDMC) ... IBS
Iota Exploration Ltd. [*Vancouver Stock Exchange symbol*] ... IEL
Iota Phi Lambda Sorority (AEBS) ... IPL
Iota-Cam Fiberscope [*Also, ICFS*] ... ICF
Iota-Cam Fiberscope [*Also, ICF*] ... ICFS
Iota-Cam Fiberscope Instrument ... ICFI
Iowa [*Postal code*] ... IA
Iowa [*MARC country of publication code Library of Congress*] (LCCP) ... iau
Iowa ... IO
Iowa [*MARC geographic area code Library of Congress*] (LCCP) ... n-us-ia
Iowa Academy of General Dentistry (SRA) ... IAGD
Iowa Achievement Test [*Psychology*] (DAVI) ... IAT
Iowa Administrative Bulletin [*A publication*] (AAGC) ... IAB
Iowa Administrative Bulletin [*A publication*] (DLA) ... Iowa Admin Bull
Iowa Administrative Code [*A publication*] (AAGC) ... IAC
Iowa Administrative Code [*A publication*] (DLA) ... Iowa Admin Code
Iowa Agriculture and Home Economics Experiment Station [*Iowa State University*] [*Research center*] (RCD) ... IAHEES
Iowa Airlines and Horizon Airways [*ICAO designator*] (AD) ... BF
Iowa Airways [*ICAO designator*] (AD) ... JT
Iowa Airways, Inc. [*ICAO designator*] (FAAC) ... IOA
Iowa Army Ammunition Plant (AABC) ... IAAP
Iowa Association of Homes for the Aging (SRA) ... IAHA
Iowa Association of School Boards (SRA) ... IASB
Iowa Auctioneers Association (SRA) ... IAA
Iowa Automated Clearing House Association ... IACHA
Iowa Automobile Dealers Association (SRA) ... IADA
Iowa Bancorporation, Inc. [*NASDAQ symbol*] (SAG) ... IOWA
Iowa Bancorporation, Inc. [*Associated Press*] (SAG) ... IowaBcp
Iowa Bar Review [*A publication*] (DLA) ... IA B Rev
Iowa Bar Review [*A publication*] (DLA) ... IA Bar Rev
Iowa Bar Review [*A publication*] (DLA) ... Iowa B Rev
Iowa Bar Review [*A publication*] (DLA) ... Iowa Bar Rev
Iowa Business Council (SRA) ... IBC
Iowa Cattlemen's Association (SRA) ... ICA
Iowa Central Community College, Fort Dodge, IA [*Library symbol Library of Congress*] (LCLS) ... IaFdIC
Iowa Chiropractic Society (SRA) ... ICS
Iowa City [*Iowa*] [*Airport symbol*] (AD) ... IOW
Iowa City, IA [*Location identifier FAA*] (FAAL) ... IOW
Iowa City, IA [*AM radio station call letters*] ... KCJJ
Iowa City, IA [*Television station call letters*] ... KIIN
Iowa City, IA [*FM radio station call letters*] ... KKRQ
Iowa City, IA [*FM radio station call letters*] ... KRNA
Iowa City, IA [*FM radio station call letters*] ... KRUI
Iowa City, IA [*FM radio station call letters*] ... KSUI
Iowa City, IA [*TV station call letters*] (RBYB) ... KWKB-TV
Iowa City, IA [*AM radio station call letters*] ... KXIC
Iowa City, IA [*AM radio station call letters*] ... WSUI
Iowa City Press-Citizen, Iowa City, IA [*Library symbol Library of Congress*] (LCLS) ... IaIaP
Iowa City Public Library [*Iowa*] ... ICPL
Iowa City Public Library, Iowa City, IA [*Library symbol Library of Congress*] (LCLS) ... IaIa
Iowa Code, Annotated [*A publication*] (DLA) ... ICA
Iowa Commission for the Blind, Des Moines, IA [*Library symbol Library of Congress*] (LCLS) ... IaDmB
Iowa Community College Telenetwork [*Marshalltown*] (TSSD) ... ICCT
Iowa Computer-Assisted Network [*Iowa State Library*] [*Des Moines*] [*Information service or system*] (IID) ... ICAN
Iowa Corn Growers Association (SRA) ... ICGA
Iowa County Farmer, Williamsburg, IA [*Library symbol Library of Congress*] (LCLS) ... IaWmbgI
Iowa County Historical Society, Parnell, IA [*Library symbol Library of Congress*] (LCLS) ... IaParnHi
Iowa Court Reporters Association (SRA) ... ICRA
Iowa Drug Information Service [*University of Iowa*] [*Information service or system*] (IID) ... IDIS
Iowa Egg Council (SRA) ... IEC
Iowa Emergency Medical Services Association (SRA) ... IEMSA
Iowa Falls Citizen, Iowa Falls, Iowa [*Library symbol Library of Congress*] (LCLS) ... IaIfC
Iowa Falls, IA [*Location identifier FAA*] (FAAL) ... IFA
Iowa Falls, IA [*AM radio station call letters*] ... KIFG
Iowa Falls, IA [*FM radio station call letters*] ... KIFG-FM
Iowa Farm Bureau Spokesman, Grundy Center, IA [*Library symbol Library of Congress*] (LCLS) ... IaGrcI
Iowa Farm-to-Market Carriers Tariff Bureau, Ottumwa IA [*STAC*] ... IFM
Iowa Hearing Aid Society (SRA) ... IHAS
Iowa Hospitality Association (SRA) ... IHA
Iowa Institute of Hydraulic Research [*University of Iowa*] [*Research center*] (MCD) ... IIHR
Iowa Law Bulletin [*A publication*] (DLA) ... IA L Bull
Iowa Law Bulletin [*A publication*] (DLA) ... Iowa L Bull
Iowa Law Bulletin [*A publication*] (DLA) ... Iowa LB
Iowa Legionnaire, Des Moines, IA [*Library symbol Library of Congress*] (LCLS) ... IaDmL
Iowa Legislative Service (West) [*A publication*] (DLA) ... Iowa Legis Serv
Iowa Library Information Teletype Exchange [*Des Moines, IA*] [*Telecommunications Library network*] ... I-LITE
Iowa Limestone Producers Association (SRA) ... ILPA
Iowa Masonic Library, Cedar Rapids, IA [*Library symbol Library of Congress*] (LCLS) ... IaCrM
Iowa Mountaineers (EA) ... IM
Iowa Natural Areas Inventory [*Iowa State Conservation Commission*] [*Des Moines*] [*Information service or system*] (IID) ... INAI
Iowa Nursery and Landscape Association (SRA) ... INLA
Iowa Park and Recreation Association (SRA) ... IPRA
Iowa Pressure Articulation Test (DMAA) ... IPAT
Iowa Quality [*of pigs*] ... IQ
Iowa Railroad Commissioners Reports [*A publication*] (DLA) ... Iowa RC
Iowa Reports [*A publication*] (DLA) ... IA
Iowa Reports [*A publication*] (DLA) ... Iow
Iowa Safety Council (SRA) ... ISC
Iowa Silent Reading Tests [*Education*] ... ISRT
Iowa Southern Utilities [*Southern Industrial Railroad, Inc.*] [*AAR code*] ... ISU
Iowa Soybean Association (SRA) ... ISA
Iowa Starter, Iowa State University, Ames, IA [*Library symbol Library of Congress*] (LCLS) ... IaAIS
Iowa State Bar Association. Proceedings [*A publication*] (DLA) ... Iowa SBA
Iowa State Bar Association. Quarterly [*A publication*] (DLA) ... Iowa St BAQ
Iowa State College of Agriculture and Mechanic Arts [*Later, Iowa State University*] (MCD) ... ISC
Iowa State Commerce Commission, Records and Information Center, Des Moines, IA [*Library symbol Library of Congress*] (LCLS) ... IaDmC
Iowa State Department of History and Archives, Des Moines, IA [*Library symbol Library of Congress*] (LCLS) ... Ia-HA
Iowa State Education Association, Des Moines, IA [*Library symbol Library of Congress*] (LCLS) ... IaDmE
Iowa State Genealogical Society, Genealogical Library, Des Moines, IA [*Library symbol Library of Congress*] (LCLS) ... IaGen
Iowa State Historical Society, Iowa City, IA [*OCLC symbol*] (OCLC) ... IOQ
Iowa State Law Library, Des Moines, IA [*Library symbol Library of Congress*] (LCLS) ... Ia-L
Iowa State Library Commission, Des Moines, IA [*Library symbol Library of Congress*] (LCLS) ... Ia
Iowa State Medical Library, Des Moines, IA [*Library symbol Library of Congress*] (LCLS) ... Ia-M
Iowa State Mining and Mineral Resources Research Institute [*Iowa State University*] [*Research center*] (RCD) ... ISMMRRI
Iowa State University [*Ames*] ... ISU
Iowa State University / Cyclone Computer Laboratory (PDAA) ... ISU/CCL
Iowa State University - Engineering Research Institute (PDAA) ... ISU-ERI
Iowa State University of Science and Technology (GAGS) ... Iowa St U
Iowa State University of Science and Technology, Ames, IA [*Library symbol Library of Congress*] (LCLS) ... IaAS
Iowa State University of Science and Technology, Ames, IA [*OCLC symbol*] (OCLC) ... IWA
Iowa State University of Science and Technology, School of Veterinary Medicine, Ames, IA [*Library symbol Library of Congress*] (LCLS) ... IaAS-V
Iowa State University Press (DGA) ... ISUP
Iowa State Water Resources Research Institute [*Iowa State University*] [*Department of the Interior Research center*] (RCD) ... ISWRRI
Iowa Supreme Court Reports [*A publication*] (DLA) ... Iowa
Iowa Terminal Railroad Co. [*AAR code*] ... IAT
Iowa Tests of Basic Skills ... ITBS

Iowa Tests of Educational Development .... ITED
Iowa Transfer System .... ITS
Iowa University. Law Bulletin [*A publication*] (DLA) .... Iowa Univ L Bull
Iowa Veterinary Medical Association (SRA) .... IVMA
Iowa Water Resources Data System [*Iowa State Geological Survey*] [*Iowa City*] [*Information service or system*] (IID) .... IWARDS
Iowa Wesleyan College .... IWC
Iowa Wesleyan College, Mount Pleasant, IA [*Library symbol Library of Congress*] (LCLS) .... IaMpI
Iowa Wesleyan College, Mount Pleasant, IA [*OCLC symbol*] (OCLC) .... IOI
Iowegian & Citizen, Centerville, IA [*Library symbol Library of Congress*] (LCLS) .... IaCenvI
IP Timberlands Cl'A' [*NYSE symbol*] (TTSB) .... IPT
IP Timberlands Ltd. [*Associated Press*] (SAG) .... IP Timb
IP Timberlands Ltd. [*NYSE symbol*] (SAG) .... IPT
IP Timberlands Ltd. [*NYSE symbol*] (SPSG) .... IPT
IP Timberlands Ltd. [*Associated Press*] (SAG) .... IPTimb
IPAC [*Intelligence, Pacific Area Command*] **Special Report** .... ISPER
IPALCO Enterprises [*NYSE symbol*] (TTSB) .... IPL
IPALCO Enterprises, Inc. [*Associated Press*] (SAG) .... Ipalco
IPALCO Enterprises, Inc. [*NYSE symbol*] (SPSG) .... IPL
Ipatinga [*Brazil*] [*Airport symbol*] (OAG) .... IPN
Ipatinga/Usiminas [*Brazil ICAO location identifier*] (ICLI) .... SBIP
Ipatropium [*Pharmacology*] .... IP
IPC Holdings [*NASDAQ symbol*] (TTSB) .... IPCRF
IPC Holdings Ltd. [*Associated Press*] (SAG) .... IPCHold
IPC Holdings Ltd. [*NASDAQ symbol*] (SAG) .... IPCR
IPC Information Systems [*NASDAQ symbol*] (TTSB) .... IPCI
IPC Information Systems, Inc. [*Associated Press*] (SAG) .... IPC Info
IPC Information Systems, Inc. [*NASDAQ symbol*] (SAG) .... IPCI
IPC International Prospector [*Vancouver Stock Exchange symbol*] .... IPZ
IPC Newspapers Ltd., London, United Kingdom [*Library symbol Library of Congress*] (LCLS) .... UkLIP
Ipec Aviation Pty Ltd. [*Australia ICAO designator*] (FAAC) .... IPA
Ipecacuanha [*Pharmacy*] (ROG) .... IPECAC
Iphigenia Aulidensis [*of Euripides*] [*Classical studies*] (OCD) .... IA
Iphigenia Taurica [*of Euripides*] [*Classical studies*] (OCD) .... IT
IPI, Inc. [*NASDAQ symbol*] (SAG) .... INST
IPI, Inc. [*NASDAQ symbol*] (SAG) .... INST
IPI, Inc. [*Associated Press*] (SAG) .... IPI Inc
IPI, Inc. [*Associated Press*] (SAG) .... IPI Inc
Ipiales [*Colombia*] [*Airport symbol*] (OAG) .... IPI
Ipiales/San Luis [*Colorado ICAO location identifier*] (ICLI) .... SKIP
IPL Energy [*NASDAQ symbol*] (TTSB) .... IPPIF
IPL Energy, Inc. [*Associated Press*] (SAG) .... IPL En
IPL Energy, Inc. [*NASDAQ symbol*] (SAG) .... IPPIF
IPL Systems Cl'A' [*NASDAQ symbol*] (TTSB) .... IPLS
IPL Systems, Inc. [*Associated Press*] (SAG) .... IPL Sy
IPL Systems, Inc. [*NASDAQ symbol*] (NQ) .... IPLS
Ipoh [*Malaysia*] [*Airport symbol*] (OAG) .... IPH
Ipoh [*Malaysia*] [*ICAO location identifier*] (ICLI) .... WMKI
Ipora [*Brazil*] [*Airport symbol*] (AD) .... IPO
Ipota [*Vanuatu*] [*Airport symbol*] (OAG) .... IPA
Ipota [*Vanuatu*] [*ICAO location identifier*] (ICLI) .... NVVI
Ipplepen [*England*] .... IPP
Iproniazid Phosphate [*Organic chemistry*] .... INPH
Ipsco, Inc. [*NASDAQ symbol*] (SAG) .... IPSC
IPSCO Inc. [*NASDAQ symbol*] (TTSB) .... IPSCF
Ipsco, Inc. [*Associated Press*] (SAG) .... Ipsco
Ipsco, Inc. [*Toronto Stock Exchange symbol*] .... ISP
Ipse Fecit [*He Did It Himself*] [*Latin*] .... IF
Ipsilateral Associational-Commissural [*Anatomy*] .... IAC
Ipsilateral Instinctive Grasp Reaction [*Medicine*] (DMAA) .... IIGR
Ipsilateral Optic Tectum [*Medicine*] .... IOT
Ipsilateral Routing of Signal .... IROS
Ipso Facto [*By the Fact Itself*] [*Latin*] .... IF
Ipswich [*British ICAO location identifier*] (ICLI) .... EGSE
Ipswich [*City in England*] (ROG) .... IPSW
Ipswich [*England*] [*Airport symbol*] (AD) .... IPW
Ipswich Savings Bank [*NASDAQ symbol*] (SAG) .... IPSW
Ipswich Savings Bank [*Associated Press*] (SAG) .... IpswchSv
Ipswich Savings Bank [*Associated Press*] (SAG) .... IpswichSv
Ipswich Svgs Bk Mass [*NASDAQ symbol*] (TTSB) .... IPSW
IQ Software [*NASDAQ symbol*] (TTSB) .... IQSW
IQ Software Corp. [*Associated Press*] (SAG) .... IQSoft
IQ Software Corp. [*NASDAQ symbol*] (SAG) .... IQSW
Iqaluit, NT [*AM radio station call letters*] .... CFFB
Iquique [*Chile*] [*Airport symbol*] (OAG) .... IQQ
Iquique [*Chile*] [*Seismograph station code, US Geological Survey*] (SEIS) .... IQQ
Iquique/Gral Diego Aracena [*Chile*] [*ICAO location identifier*] (ICLI) .... SCDA
Iquique/Los Condores [*Chile*] [*ICAO location identifier*] (ICLI) .... SCCD
Iquitos [*Peru*] [*Airport symbol*] (OAG) .... IQT
Iquitos/Coronel FAP Francisco Secada Vignetta [*Peru*] [*ICAO location identifier*] (ICLI) .... SPQT
Iraklion [*Greece*] [*ICAO location identifier*] (ICLI) .... LGIR
Irakskaia Kommunisticheskaia Partiia [*Iraqi Communist Party*] [*Political party*] .... IKP
Iran [*MARC geographic area code Library of Congress*] (LCCP) .... a-ir--
Iran [*License plate code assigned to foreign diplomats in the US*] .... DM
Iran [*MARC country of publication code Library of Congress*] (LCCP) .... ir
Iran [*ANSI two-letter standard code*] (CNC) .... IR
Iran [*ANSI three-letter standard code*] (CNC) .... IRN
Iran Air [*ICAO designator*] (AD) .... IR
Iran Air [*Airline flight code*] (ODBW) .... IR
Iran Aircraft Industries (MCD) .... IACI
Iran American Chamber of Commerce (EA) .... IACC
Iran Asseman Airline [*ICAO designator*] (FAAC) .... IRC
Iran Electronics Industries .... IEI
Iran Freedom Foundation (EA) .... IFF
Iran Long-Period Array [*Iran*] [*Seismograph station code, US Geological Survey*] (SEIS) IR1
Iran Long-Period Array [*Iran*] [*Seismograph station code, US Geological Survey*] (SEIS) IR2
Iran Long-Period Array [*Iran*] [*Seismograph station code, US Geological Survey*] (SEIS) IR3
Iran Long-Period Array [*Iran*] [*Seismograph station code, US Geological Survey*] (SEIS) IR4
Iran Long-Period Array [*Iran*] [*Seismograph station code, US Geological Survey*] (SEIS) IR5
Iran Long-Period Array [*Iran*] [*Seismograph station code, US Geological Survey*] (SEIS) IR6
Iran Long-Period Array [*Iran*] [*Seismograph station code, US Geological Survey*] (SEIS) IR7
Iran National Airlines [*ICAO designator*] (AD) .... IR
Iran National Airlines Corp. [*ICAO designator*] (FAAC) .... IRA
Iran National Tourist Organization .... INTO
Iran Shahr [*Iran*] [*ICAO location identifier*] (ICLI) .... OIZI
Iranair Tours Co. [*Iran*] [*ICAO designator*] (FAAC) .... IRB
Iranian [*MARC language code Library of Congress*] (LCCP) .... ira
Iranian [*Language, etc.*] (ROG) .... IRAN
Iranian Aircraft Program [*Military*] (MCD) .... IAP
Iranian Airways Co. .... IRA
Iranian B'nei Torah Movement (EA) .... IBTOM
Iranian Communist Party [*Political party*] .... IKP
Iranian Democratic Committee (EA) .... IDC
Iranian Documentation Centre [*Ministry of Culture and Higher Education*] [*Tehran*] .... IRANDOC
Iranian Documentation Centre, Tehran, Iran [*Library symbol Library of Congress*] (LCLS) .... IrTD
Iranian Government Communications Satellite [*NASA*] (NASA) .... IRANSAT
Iranian Marine International Oil Co. .... IMINICO
Iranian National Front (PPW) .... INF
Iranian [*or Islamic Republic*] **News Agency** .... IRNA
Iranian Oil Operating Companies .... IOOC
Iranian Oil Participants Ltd. .... IOP
Iranian Peace Zebra Program [*Military*] (MCD) .... IPZP
Iranian Research and Publication Group .... IRPG
Iranian Students Association in the United States .... ISAUS
Iranian Students Counseling Center (EA) .... ISCC
Iraq [*MARC geographic area code Library of Congress*] (LCCP) .... a-iq--
Iraq [*Formerly, TS*] [*License plate code assigned to foreign diplomats in the US*] .... BZ
Iraq [*MARC country of publication code Library of Congress*] (LCCP) .... iq
Iraq [*ANSI two-letter standard code*] (CNC) .... IQ
Iraq [*ANSI three-letter standard code*] (CNC) .... IRQ
Iraq [*Later, BZ*] [*License plate code assigned to foreign diplomats in the US*] .... TS
Iraq Federation of Trade Unions .... IFTU
Iraqi I
Iraqi Air Force .... IqAF
Iraqi Airways [*ICAO designator*] .... IA
Iraqi Airways [*ICAO designator*] (FAAC) .... IAW
Iraqi Communist Party [*Political party*] (PPW) .... ICP
Iraqi Communist Party [*Political party*] .... IKP
Iraqi Communist Party [*Also, ICP*] [*Political party*] (MENA) .... IRC
Iraqi Confederation of Trade Unions .... ICTU
Iraqi Dinar [*Monetary unit*] (BJA) .... ID
Iraqi Intelligence Service .... ISS
Iraqi National Congress [*Political party*] (ECON) .... INC
Iraqi National Oil Co. [*Government company*] .... INOC
Iraqi News Agency .... INA
Iraqi Petroleum Co. .... IPC
Iraq-Saudi Arabia Neutral Zone [*MARC geographic area code Library of Congress*] (LCCP) .... awiy--
Iraq-Saudi Arabia Neutral Zone [*MARC country of publication code Library of Congress*] (LCCP) .... iy
Iraq-Saudi Arabia Neutral Zone [*ANSI two-letter standard code*] (CNC) .... NT
Iraq-Saudi Arabia Neutral Zone [*ANSI three-letter standard code*] (CNC) .... NTZ
Irata, Inc. [*NASDAQ symbol*] (SAG) .... IRATA
Irata Inc.'A' [*NASDAQ symbol*] (TTSB) .... IRATA
Irata Inc.Wrrt [*NASDAQ symbol*] (TTSB) .... IRATW
Irate Parent (ADA) .... IP
Irbid [*Jordan*] [*ICAO location identifier*] (ICLI) .... OJBD
IRC International Water and Sanitation Centre [*International Reference Ce ntre for Community Water Supply and Sanitation*] [*Acronym is based on former name,*] (EAIO) .... IRC
IRC [*Institute for Research in Construction*] **Library, National Research Council Canada Ottawa, Ontario** [*Bibliotheque IRC (Institut de Recherche en Construction), Conseil National de Recherches Canada*] [*Library symbol National Library of Canada*] (NLC) .... OONBR
Iredell Memorial Hospital, Statesville, NC [*Library symbol*] [*Library of Congress*] (LCLS) .... NcStH
Iredell Public Library, Statesville, NC [*Library symbol Library of Congress*] (LCLS) .... NcSt
Iredell's North Carolina Digest [*A publication*] (DLA) .... Ired Dig
Iredell's North Carolina Equity Reports [*A publication*] (DLA) .... Ir
Iredell's North Carolina Equity Reports [*36-43 North Carolina*] [*A publication*] (DLA) .... Ired
Iredell's North Carolina Equity Reports [*36-43 North Carolina*] [*A publication*] (DLA) .... Ired Eq

Iredell's North Carolina Equity Reports [36-43 North Carolina] [A publication] (DLA) .... Ired Eq (NC)
Iredell's North Carolina Equity Reports [36-43 North Carolina] [A publication] (DLA) .... Ired L
Iredell's North Carolina Law Reports [A publication] (DLA) .... Ir
Iredell's North Carolina Law Reports [A publication] (DLA) .... Ired L (NC)
Ireland [MARC geographic area code Library of Congress] (LCCP) .... e-ie--
Ireland I
Ireland [MARC country of publication code Library of Congress] (LCCP) .... ie
Ireland [ANSI two-letter standard code] (CNC) .... IE
Ireland [IYRU nationality code] (ROG) .... IR
Ireland .... IRE
Ireland (VRA) .... Ire
Ireland [ANSI three-letter standard code] (CNC) .... IRL
Ireland Fund (EA) .... IF
Irene [South Africa] [ICAO location identifier] (ICLI) .... FAIR
Irgun Olej Merkas Europa (BJA) .... IOME
Irgun Zeva'i Le'umi (BJA) .... IZL
Iridescent (WGA) .... IRID
Iridex Corp. [Associated Press] (SAG) .... Iridex
Iridex Corp. [NASDAQ symbol] (SAG) .... IRIX
IRIDEX Corp. [NASDAQ symbol] (TTSB) .... IRIX
Iridium [Chemical element] .... Ir
Irina Dunn Environment Independents [Political party Australia] .... EI
Iringa [Tanzania] [ICAO location identifier] (ICLI) .... HTIR
Iringa [Tanzania] [Airport symbol] (OAG) .... IRI
Iris Diaphragm [Photography] .... ID
Iris Epithelium Cell [Cytology] .... IEC
Iris Guide (PDAA) .... IG
Iris Hamartoma [Oncology] (DAVI) .... IHs
Iris Mild Mosaic Virus .... IMMV
Iris Neovascularization [Opthalmology] .... INV
Iris Severe Mosaic Virus .... ISMV
Iris-Clip Lens (DMAA) ICL
Irish .... IR
Irish [MARC language code Library of Congress] (LCCP) .... iri
Irish Academy of Letters (BI) .... IAL
Irish Agricultural Officers Organisation (BI) .... IAOO
Irish Agricultural Organisation Society Ltd. (BI) .... IAOS
Irish Agricultural Wholesale Society Ltd. (BI) .... IAWS
Irish Air Corps [ICAO designator] (FAAC) .... IRL
Irish Air Tours [ICAO designator] (FAAC) .... RDK
Irish Amateur Boxing Association (BI) .... IABA
Irish Amateur Gymnastics Association (EAIO) .... IAGA
Irish Amateur Open Championship [Golf] (ROG) .... IAOC
Irish Amateur Rowing Union [British] (EAIO) .... IARU
Irish Amateur Swimming Association (EAIO) .... IASA
Irish Amateur Weightlifting Association (EAIO) .... IAWA
Irish Amateur Wrestling Association (EAIO) .... IAWA
Irish American Cultural Association (EA) .... IACA
Irish American Cultural Institute (EA) .... IACI
Irish American Defense Fund [Defunct] (EA) .... IADF
Irish American Sports Foundation (EA) .... IASF
Irish American Unity Conference (EA) .... IAUC
Irish Anti-Apartheid Movement (EAIO) .... IAAM
Irish Assessment & Guidance Service (ACII) .... IAGS
Irish Association for Curriculum Development (AIE) .... IACD
Irish Association for Documentation and Information Services (NITA) .... IADIS
Irish Association for the Blind (BI) .... IAB
Irish Association of Master Bakers (BI) .... IAMB
Irish Astronomical Association (EAIO) .... IAA
Irish Bank Officials' Association [Northern Ireland] .... IBOA
Irish Baron (ROG) .... IB
Irish Basketball Association (DBA) .... IBBA
Irish Broadcasting Revenue .... IBR
Irish Business Equipment Trade Association (ACII) .... IBETA
Irish Business Equipment Trade Association (DBA) .... IBETA
Irish Campaign for Nuclear Disarmament (EAIO) .... ICND
Irish Central Library for Students (BI) ICL
Irish Chancery Reports [A publication] (DLA) .... Ch R
Irish Chancery Reports [A publication] (DLA) .... Ch Rep
Irish Chancery Reports [A publication] (DLA) .... Ch Rep Ir
Irish Chancery Reports [A publication] (DLA) .... Ch Repts
Irish Chancery Reports [A publication] (DLA) .... I Ch R
Irish Chancery Reports [A publication] (DLA) .... ICR
Irish Chancery Reports [A publication] (DLA) .... Ir Ch
Irish Chancery Reports [A publication] (DLA) .... Ir Ch Rep
Irish Chancery Reports [A publication] (DLA) .... Ir R Ch
Irish Chancery Reports [A publication] (DLA) .... Ir Rep Ch
Irish Christian Study Centre [New University of Ulster] [British] (CB) .... ICSC
Irish Church Missions .... ICM
Irish Circuit Cases [A publication] (DLA) .... Ir Circ Cas
Irish Circuit Reports [1841-43] [A publication] (DLA) .... ICR
Irish Circuit Reports [1841-43] [A publication] (DLA) .... Ir Cir
Irish Circuit Reports [1841-43] [A publication] (DLA) .... Ir Circ Rep
Irish Commission for Justice and Peace [An association] (EAIO) .... ICJP
Irish Common Law and Chancery Reports, New Series [1850-53] [A publication] (DLA) .... Ir Law & Ch
Irish Common Law Reports [A publication] (DLA) CL
Irish Common Law Reports [A publication] (DLA) .... ICLR
Irish Common Law Reports [A publication] (DLA) .... Ir CL
Irish Common Law Reports [A publication] (DLA) .... Ir Com L Rep
Irish Common Law Reports [A publication] (DLA) .... Ir Com Law Rep
Irish Common Law Reports, New Series [A publication] (DLA) .... Ir L NS
Irish Common Law Reports, New Series [A publication] (DLA) .... Ir Law Rep NS

Irish Common Law Reports, New Series [A publication] (DLA) .... Ir Rep NS
Irish Communist Party [Political party] .... IKP
Irish Company Profiles [Institute of Industrial Research and Standards - IIRS] [Dublin, Ireland] [Information service or system] (IID) .... ICP
Irish Computer Exhibition [SDL Exhibitions Ltd.] (TSPED) .... COMPUTEX
Irish Computer Society .... ICS
Irish Congress of Trade Unions .... ICTU
Irish Constitution (ADA) IC
Irish Council European Movement .... ICEM
Irish Council for Civil Liberties (EAIO) ICCL
Irish Council for Overseas Students .... ICOS
Irish Council of Churches ICC
Irish Countrywomen's Association (BI) .... ICA
Irish Creamery Milk Suppliers' Association (BI) .... ICMSA
Irish Dental Association (BI) .... IDA
Irish Dinghy Racing Association (BI) .... IDRA
Irish Distributive and Administrative Trade Union (EAIO) .... IDATU
Irish Drug Association (BI) .... IDA
Irish Duke (ROG) .... ID
Irish Earl (ROG) .... IE
Irish Ecclesiastical Reports, by Milward [1819-43] [A publication] (DLA) .... Ir Eccl
Irish El Salvador Support Committee (EAIO) .... IESSC
Irish Emigrant Society (EA) .... IES
Irish Equity Reports [A publication] (DLA) .... I Eq R
Irish Equity Reports [A publication] (DLA) .... IER
Irish Equity Reports [A publication] (DLA) .... Ir Eq Rep
Irish Evangelistic Band .... IEB
Irish Export Board .... IEB
Irish Exporters Association (EAIO) .... IEA
Irish Family History Society (EA) .... IFHS
Irish Family Names Society (EA) .... IFNS
Irish Features Agency [News agency] .... IFA
Irish Flour Millers Association (BI) .... IFMA
Irish Football Association (BI) .... IFA
Irish Free State [Later, Republic of Ireland] .... IFS
Irish Fusiliers [British military] (DMA) .... IF
Irish Gas Association (BI) .... IGA
Irish Genealogical Foundation (EA) .... IGF
Irish Genealogical Research Society (EAIO) .... IGRS
Irish Genealogical Society (EA) .... IGS
Irish Georgian Society (EA) .... IGS
Irish Goods Council (ACII) .... IGC
Irish Graphical Society (BI) .... IGS
Irish Guards [Military unit] .... IG
Irish Health Services Development Corp. .... IHSDC
Irish Heritage Foundation (EA) .... IHF
Irish Horse [British military] (DMA) .... IH
Irish Hotel and Restaurant Managers' Association (BI) .... IHRMA
Irish Hotels Federation (EAIO) .... IHF
Irish Immigration Reform Movement (EA) .... IIRM
Irish Independence Party [Political party] (PPW) .... IIP
Irish Institute (EA) II
Irish Institute of Secretaries Ltd. (BI) .... IIS
Irish Intercontinental Bank Ltd. .... IIB
Irish International Peace Movement (EAIO) .... IIPM
Irish Investment Fund [Associated Press] (SAG) .... IrishIn
Irish Investment Fund [NYSE symbol] (SAG) .... IRL
Irish Joint Fiction Reserve Scheme (AIE) .... IJFRS
Irish Jurist Reports [1849-66] [A publication] (DLA) .... Ir Jur
Irish Jurist Reports [1849-66] [A publication] (DLA) .... Ir Jur Rep
Irish Laboratory Accreditation Board [Now the Irish National Accreditation Board] (ACII) .... ILAB
Irish Labour Party [Political party] (ROG) .... ILP
Irish Land Purchase Cases [1904-11] [A publication] (DLA) .... Maxwell
Irish Land Reports (Fitzgibbon) [A publication] (DLA) IL
Irish Law and Equity Reports [1838-50] [A publication] (DLA) .... Ir Law & Eq
Irish Law and Equity Reports [1838-50] [A publication] (DLA) .... IrL & Eq
Irish Law Journal [1895-1902] [A publication] (DLA) .... Ir LJ
Irish Law Recorder [1827-38] [A publication] (DLA) .... Ir Law Rec
Irish Law Recorder [1827-38] [A publication] (ILCA) .... Law Rec
Irish Law Recorder, First Series [1827-31] [A publication] (DLA) .... Ir L Rec
Irish Law Recorder, New Series [1833-38] [A publication] (DLA) .... Ir Law Rec NS
Irish Law Reports [A publication] (DLA) .... ILR
Irish Law Reports [A publication] (DLA) .... IR
Irish Law Reports [A publication] (DLA) .... Ir Law Rep
Irish Law Reports [A publication] (DLA) .... Ir LR
Irish Law Reports [A publication] (DLA) .... Ir R
Irish Law Reports [A publication] (DLA) .... IrL
Irish Law Times, County Courts [A publication] (DLA) .... Co Ct ILT
Irish Law Times Journal [A publication] (DLA) .... ILT Jo
Irish Law Times Journal [A publication] (DLA) .... Ir LT Jour
Irish Law Times Journal [A publication] (DLA) .... Ir LTJ
Irish Law Times Reports [A publication] (DLA) .... ILTR
Irish Law Times Reports [A publication] (DLA) .... Ir LT Rep
Irish Law Times Reports [A publication] (DLA) .... Ir LTR
Irish Linen Guild [Defunct] (EA) .... ILG
Irish Literary Supplement [A publication] (BRI) .... ILS
Irish Management Institute (EAIO) .... IMI
Irish Marquis (ROG) .... IM
Irish Mathematics Society .... IMS
Irish Medical Association .... IMA
Irish Microforms Ltd., Dublin, Ireland [Library symbol Library of Congress] (LCLS) .... ImL
Irish Missionary Union (EAIO) .... IMU
[The] Irish National Accreditation Board (ACII) .... INAB

Irish National Association of Australasia ... INAA
Irish National Caucus (EA) ... INC
Irish National Group of International Federation of the Phonographic Industry (EAIO) ... INGIFPI
Irish National Hunt Steeplechase (ROG) ... INHS
Irish National Liberation Army ... INLA
Irish National Petroleum Corp. ... INPC
Irish National Pipe Band ... INPB
Irish National Productivity Committee (BI) ... INPC
Irish National Teachers' Organisation ... INTO
Irish National Union of Woodworkers (BI) ... INUW
Irish Nationalist (ROG) ... IN
Irish Northern Aid ... INA
Irish Northern Aid Committee (EA) ... NORAID
Irish Nurses Organisation (BI) ... INO
Irish Nutrition and Dietetics Institute (EAIO) ... INDI
Irish Office ... IO
Irish Offshore Services Association (EAIO) ... IOSA
Irish Orienteering Association (EAIO) ... IOA
Irish Paper Box Association (BI) ... IPBA
Irish Party (ROG) ... IP
Irish Peace Council (EAIO) ... IPC
Irish Peat Board (EAIO) ... IPB
Irish Petty Sessions Journal [*A publication*] (DLA) ... Ir Pet SJ
Irish Postal Union ... IPU
Irish Presbyterian Church (ROG) ... IPC
Irish Print Union (DGA) ... IPU
Irish Printing Federation (BI) ... IPF
Irish Productivity Council (ACII) ... IPC
Irish Quality Association (ACII) ... IQA
Irish Railway Record Society ... IRRS
Irish Reports, Common Law Series [*A publication*] (DLA) ... Ir RCL
Irish Reports, Common Law Series [*A publication*] (DLA) ... Ir Rep CL
Irish Reports, Common Law Series [*A publication*] (DLA) ... IRCL
Irish Reports, Equity Series [*A publication*] (DLA) ... IR Eq
Irish Reports, Equity Series [*A publication*] (DLA) ... Ir R Eq
Irish Reports, Equity Series [*A publication*] (DLA) ... Ir Rep Eq
Irish Reports, Registration Appeals [*1868-76*] [*A publication*] (DLA) ... Ir R Reg App
Irish Reports, Registry and Land Cases [*A publication*] (DLA) ... Ir R Reg & L
Irish Reports, Registry and Land Cases [*A publication*] (DLA) ... IRR & L
Irish Reports, Verbatim Reprint [*A publication*] (DLA) ... Ir Rep VR
Irish Republican Army ... IRA
Irish Republican Brotherhood ... IRB
Irish Republican Socialist Party [*Pairti Poblachtach Soisialach na h-Eireann*] (PPW) ... IRSP
Irish Research Scientists Association ... IRSA
Irish Royal Rifles [*Military British*] (ROG) ... IRR
Irish Rugby Football Union (EAIO) ... IRFU
Irish School of Ecumenics ... ISE
Irish School of Music (ROG) ... ISM
Irish Schools Swimming Association (EAIO) ... ISSA
[*The*] **Irish Science and Technology Agency** [*Information service or system*] (IID) ... EOLAS
Irish Setter Club of America (EA) ... ISCA
Irish Society ... IS
Irish Society for the Prevention of Cruelty to Animals (DBA) ... ISPCA
Irish Society for the Prevention of Cruelty to Children (DI) ... ISPCC
Irish Special Interest Group of American Mensa (EA) ... ISIG
Irish Squash Rackets Association (EAIO) ... ISRA
Irish Standard (IAA) ... IRS
Irish Standard (IAA) ... IS
Irish State Trials (Ridgeway's) [*A publication*] (DLA) ... Ir St Tr
Irish Statutes [*A publication*] (DLA) ... Ir Stat
Irish Ten Pin Bowling Association (EAIO) ... ITBA
Irish Term Reports, by Ridgeway, Lapp, and Schoales [*A publication*] (DLA) ... Ir Term Rep
Irish Term Reports, by Ridgeway, Lapp, and Schoales [*A publication*] (DLA) ... Ir TR
Irish Term Reports, by Ridgeway, Lapp, and Schoales [*A publication*] (DLA) ... ITR
Irish Terrier Club of America (EA) ... ITCA
Irish Texts Society (EAIO) ... ITS
Irish Times Eurolex Legal Information Service [*Database*] (NITA) ... ITELIS
Irish Tourist Board (EA) ... ITB
Irish Tourist Office (BI) ... ITO
Irish Trade Protection Association (DBA) ... ITPA
Irish Trade Union Congress ... ITUC
Irish Transport and General Workers' Union (DCTA) ... ITGWU
Irish Union of Distributive Workers and Clerks (BI) ... IUDWC
Irish United Nations Association (EAIO) ... IUNA
Irish University Press ... IUP
Irish Ursuline Union (TOCD) ... OSU
Irish Viscount (ROG) ... IV
Irish Volunteers [*British military*] (DMA) ... IV
Irish War Hospital Supply Depot [*British military*] (DMA) ... IWHSD
Irish Water Polo Association (EAIO) ... IWPA
Irish Water Spaniel Club of America (EA) ... IWSCA
Irish Waterski Federation (EAIO) ... IWSF
Irish Weekly Law Reports [*1895-1902*] [*A publication*] (DLA) ... Ir WLR
Irish Wholesale Ryegrass Machiners Association (BI) ... IWRMA
Irish Wolfhound Club of America (EA) ... IWCA
Irish Women's Squash Rackets Association (EAIO) ... IWSRA
Irish Work Study Institute Ltd. (BI) ... IWSI
Irish Workers' Party [*Political party*] (PPW) ... IWP
Irish Workmen's Compensation Cases [*A publication*] (DLA) ... Ir WCC
Irish Yachting Association (EAIO) ... IYA
Irish Youth Hostel Association (EAIO) ... IYHA
Irish-American Labor Coalition [*Later, ALCHRNI*] (EA) ... IALC
Irkutsk [*Former USSR Airport symbol*] (OAG) ... IKT
Irkutsk [*Former USSR Seismograph station code, US Geological Survey*] (SEIS) ... IRK
Irkutsk [*Former USSR ICAO location identifier*] (ICLI) ... UIII
Irma Community Library, Alberta [*Library symbol National Library of Canada*] (NLC) ... AIRC
Irma Community Library, Irma, AB, Canada [*Library symbol*] [*Library of Congress*] (LCLS) ... CaAIrmC
Irma Graphics for DOS [*Digital Operation System*] [*DCA, Inc.*] ... IGD
Irma Graphics for Macintosh [*DCA, Inc.*] ... IGM
Irma Graphics for Windows [*DCA, Inc.*] ... IGW
Irnerius [*Flourished, 1113-18*] [*Authority cited in pre-1607 legal work*] (DSA) ... I
Irnerius [*Flourished, 1113-18*] [*Authority cited in pre-1607 legal work*] (DSA) ... Ir
Irogo [*Congo*] [*ICAO location identifier*] (ICLI) ... FCMI
Iron (VRA) ... fe
Iron (IDOE) ... Fe
Iron [*Chemical*] (EERA) ... Fe
Iron [*Symbol is Fe*] [*Chemical element*] (ROG) ... I
Iron [*CIPW classification*] [*Geology*] ... ir
Iron [*Chemical element*] (DAVI) ... IRN
Iron Age ... IA
Iron and Steel ... I & S
Iron and Steel Dressers Trade Society [*A union*] [*British*] ... ISDTS
Iron and Steel Holdings and Realisation Agency [*British*] ... ISHRA
Iron and Steel Industry Training Board [*British*] (BI) ... ISITB
Iron and Steel Institute (MCD) ... ISI
Iron and Steel Institute of Japan ... ISIJ
Iron and Steel Society - of AIME (EA) ... ISS
Iron and Steel Trades Confederation [*British*] ... ISTC
Iron and Steel Trades Employers' Association [*British*] (BI) ... ISTEA
Iron and Steel Workers' Union [*India*] ... ISWU
Iron & Steelmaker [*A publication*] (EAAP) ... I & SM
Iron and Total Iron Binding Capacity [*Hematology*] (DAVI) ... IRONS
Iron Bay Trust [*Toronto Stock Exchange symbol*] ... IRY
Iron Body Bronze-Mounted ... IBBM
Iron Bolts ... IB
Iron Bridge Public Library, Ontario [*Library symbol National Library of Canada*] (NLC) ... OIB
Iron Butterfly Fan Club [*Later, IBIN*] (EA) ... IBFC
Iron Butterfly Information Network (EA) ... IBIN
Iron Canyon [*California*] [*Seismograph station code, US Geological Survey*] (SEIS) ... IRC
Iron Casting Research Institute (EA) ... ICRI
Iron Castings Society (EA) ... ICS
Iron Caulkers' Association [*A union*] [*British*] ... ICA
Iron City [*Pittsburgh, PA*] ... IC
Iron Deficiency Anemia [*Medicine*] ... IDA
Iron Dragon-Fly Ltd. [*Russian Federation*] [*ICAO designator*] (FAAC) ... IDF
Iron Dressers Trade Society [*A union*] [*British*] ... IDTS
Iron Fortified Common Salt [*Nutrition*] ... IFS
Iron Hematoxylin [*A dye*] ... IH
Iron Horse Resources, Inc. [*Vancouver Stock Exchange symbol*] ... IHN
Iron in Urine [*Biochemistry*] (DAVI) ... FE-UR
Iron Inclusion Bodies [*Hematology*] (DAVI) ... FE INC
Iron Information Center [*Battelle Memorial Institute*] [*Information service or system*] (IID) ... IIC
Iron Lady Resources [*Vancouver Stock Exchange symbol*] ... IRD
Iron Maiden Fan Club [*British*] (EAIO) ... IMFC
Iron Masters Board of Trade ... IMBT
Iron Mining Association of Minnesota (SRA) ... IMA
Iron Mountain [*Michigan*] [*Airport symbol*] (OAG) ... IMT
Iron Mountain [*NASDAQ symbol*] (TTSB) ... IMTN
Iron Mountain, Inc. [*NASDAQ symbol*] (SAG) ... IMTN
Iron Mountain, Inc. [*Associated Press*] (SAG) ... IronMnt
Iron Mountain/Kingsford, MI [*Location identifier FAA*] (FAAL) ... IMT
Iron Mountain, MI [*Television station call letters*] ... WDHS
Iron Mountain, MI [*FM radio station call letters*] ... WIMK
Iron Mountain, MI [*FM radio station call letters*] ... WJNR
Iron Mountain, MI [*AM radio station call letters*] ... WMIQ
Iron Nickel Alloy ... INA
Iron Nickel System ... INS
Iron or Steel [*Freight*] ... IRN
Iron or Wood [*Freight*] ... IWD
Iron Ore Co., Mineralogy Laboratory, Sept-Iles, PQ, Canada [*Library symbol Library of Congress*] (LCLS) ... CaQSiIOM
Iron Ore Co. of Canada Ltd. ... IOC
Iron Ore Co. of Canada, Training Department, Labrador City, NF, Canada [*Library symbol Library of Congress*] (LCLS) ... CaNfLIO
Iron Ore Transport [*Steamship*] (MHDW) ... IOT
Iron Overload Diseases Association (EA) ... IOD
Iron Overload Diseases Association (EA) ... IODA
Iron Phosphate Coating ... IPC
Iron Pipe ... IP
Iron Pipe Size (WGA) ... IPS
Iron Pipe Thread (MSA) ... IPT
Iron Plate Workers' Society [*A union*] [*British*] ... IPWS
Iron, Quinine, and Strychnine [*Elixir*] ... IQ & S
Iron Range [*Queensland*] [*Airport symbol*] (AD) ... IRG
Iron Range Historical Society, Gilbert MN [*Library symbol*] [*Library of Congress*] (LCLS) ... MnGiHi
Iron Range Research Center, Chisholm, MN [*OCLC symbol*] (OCLC) ... IRR

Iron Range Research Library, Chisholm, MN [*Library symbol Library of Congress*] (LCLS) ... MnChil
Iron Regulatory Protein [*Biochemistry*] ... IRP
Iron Replacement Element [*Biosynthesis*] ... IRE
Iron River, MI [*AM radio station call letters*] ... WIKB
Iron River, MI [*FM radio station call letters*] ... WIKB-FM
Iron River Public Library, Alberta [*Library symbol National Library of Canada*] (NLC) ... AIR
Iron River Public Library, Iron River, AB, Canada [*Library symbol Library of Congress*] (LCLS) ... CaAIr
Iron River Resources [*Vancouver Stock Exchange symbol*] ... IRN
Iron River, WI [*FM radio station call letters*] (RBYB) ... WNXR
Iron Rotating Band ... IRB
Iron Safe Engineers' Society [*A union*] [*British*] ... ISES
Iron Soldering ... INS
Iron, Steel and Heavy Transporters Association, Cleveland OH [*STAC*] ... IST
Iron, Steel, and Wood Barge Builders' and Helpers' Association [*A union*] [*British*] ... ISWBBHA
Iron, Steel, Metal Dressers, and Kindred Trades Society [*A union*] [*British*] ... ISMDKTS
Iron Wire Gauge ... IWG
Iron Wire Rope Core [*Nuclear energy*] (NRCH) ... IWRC
Iron-Binding Capacity [*Clinical chemistry*] ... IBC
Iron-Binding Protein ... IBP
Ironbound Crier, Newark, NJ [*Library symbol Library of Congress*] (LCLS) ... NjNI
Ironclad ... IRC
Iron-Core Reactor (MSA) ... ICR
Irondale, AL [*AM radio station call letters*] ... WLPH
Irondequoit, NY [*FM radio station call letters*] ... WMAX
Ironfounders' National Confederation [*British*] (BI) ... INC
Ironical (ROG) ... Iron
Ironing Board (MSA) ... IB
Iron-Regulated Membrane Protein [*Biochemistry*] ... IRMP
Iron-Responsive Element [*Genetics*] ... IRE
Iron-Responsive Element - Binding Protein ... IRE-BP
Irons on Police Law [*A publication*] (DLA) ... Irons Pol Law
Irons on Public Houses [*A publication*] (DLA) ... Irons Pub H
Iron-Solution Value (PDAA) ... ISV
Ironton, OH [*AM radio station call letters*] ... WIRO
Ironton, OH [*FM radio station call letters*] ... WMLV
Ironton, OH [*FM radio station call letters*] ... WOUL
[*The*] **Ironton Railroad Co.** [*Absorbed into Consolidated Rail Corp.*] [*AAR code*] ... IRN
Ironwood (VRA) ... fewd
Ironwood [*Michigan*] [*Airport symbol*] (OAG) ... IWD
Ironwood Carnegie Library, Ironwood, MI [*Library symbol Library of Congress*] (LCLS) ... MiIrw
Ironwood, MI [*Location identifier FAA*] (FAAL) ... IWD
Ironwood, MI [*FM radio station call letters*] ... WIMI
Ironwood, MI [*AM radio station call letters*] ... WJMS
Ironwood, MI [*FM radio station call letters*] ... WUPM
Ironwork ... IRNWRK
Iron-Wustite [*Geology*] ... IW
Iroquios Bancorp [*Associated Press*] (SAG) ... IroquoisB
Iroquoian [*MARC language code Library of Congress*] (LCCP) ... iro
Iroquois Bancorp [*NASDAQ symbol*] (TTSB) ... IROQ
Iroquois Bancorp, Inc. [*NASDAQ symbol*] (SAG) ... IROQ
Iroquois Bancorp, Inc. [*Associated Press*] (SAG) ... Iroquoi
Iroquois County Film Library, Watseka, IL [*Library symbol*] [*Library of Congress*] (LCLS) ... IWatF
Iroquois Falls Public Library, Iroquois Falls, ON, Canada [*Library symbol Library of Congress*] (LCLS) ... CaOIf
Iroquois Falls Public Library, Ontario [*Library symbol National Library of Canada*] (NLC) ... OIF
Iroquois Memorial Hospital, Watseka, IL [*Library symbol Library of Congress*] (LCLS) ... IWatH
Iroquois Night Fighter and Night Tracker [*Military*] (MCD) ... INFANT
Iroquois Night Fighter and Night Tracker [*Military*] (DNAB) ... INFNT
Iroquois Public Library, Iroquois, ON, Canada [*Library symbol*] [*Library of Congress*] (LCLS) ... CaOIR
Iroquois Public Library, Ontario [*Library symbol National Library of Canada*] (BIB) ... OIR
Irradiance [*Symbol*] [*IUPAC*] ... E
Irradiance [*Electromagnetism*] (IAA) ... IR
Irradiance (BARN) ... W
Irradiance Measuring System ... IMS
Irradiated (NASA) ... I
Irradiated Fuel Processing Plant (DEN) ... IFPP
Irradiated Fuel Transfer System [*Nuclear energy*] (NRCH) ... IFTS
Irradiated Fuels Storage Facility [*National Reactor Testing Station*] ... IFSF
Irradiated Fused Silica Open Tubular [*Column for chromatography*] ... IFSOT
Irradiated Materials Laboratory ... IML
Irradiated Silicon Vidicon ... ISV
Irradiation ... irr
Irradiation ... IRRADN
Irradiation Correction ... J
Irradiation Effects (NRCH) ... IE
Irradiation Effects Simulation (NRCH) ... IES
Irradiation Special Purchase Order (SAA) ... ISPO
Irradiation Test Management Activity (NRCH) ... ITMA
Irrational Beliefs Test [*Psychology*] ... IBT
Irredeemable [*Banking*] ... IRR
Irredeemable (ROG) ... IRRED
Irredundant Conjunctive Normal Formula ... ICNF
Irredundant Disjunctive Normal Formula ... IDNF
Irredundant Normal Formula ... INF
Irregular (ROG) ... I
Irregular (WGA) ... IRR
Irregular (KSC) ... IRREG
Irregular (WDMC) ... irreg
Irregular Cavalry [*British military*] (DMA) ... IC
Irregular Force [*Military*] (CINC) ... IF
Irregular Input Process [*Telecommunications*] (TEL) ... I/P
Irregular Light [*Navigation signal*] ... Irreg
Irregular Outer Edge [*Army*] (ADDR) ... IOE
Irregular Route Carrier ... IRC
Irregular Route Motor Carriers Bureau, Oklahoma City OK [*STAC*] ... IRB
Irregular Serials and Annuals [*A publication*] ... ISA
Irregular Spiking Activity [*Electrophysiology*] ... ISA
Irregularly (WDMC) ... irreg
Irrelevancy [*Used in correcting manuscripts, etc.*] ... IR
Irrelevant Talk [*Slang*] ... IT
Irreversible Loss Rate (DMAA) ... ILR
Irreversible Warmup Indicator [*To detect whether frozen foods have risen above an acceptable temperature level*] [*Pronounced "ee-wee"*] ... IWI
Irreversibly Sickled Cell [*Hematology*] ... ISC
Irrevocable ... IRREV
Irrevocable Letter of Credit [*Business term*] ... ILC
Irrevocable Letter of Credit [*Business term*] (DS) ... ILOC
Irricana Municipal Library, Alberta [*Library symbol National Library of Canada*] (NLC) ... AI
Irridescent (VRA) ... irid
Irridescent Color Exchange [*Heat-sensitive clothing*] ... ICE
Irrigate [*or Irrigated*] (DAVI) ... irr
Irrigate ... IRRIG
Irrigated Agriculture Research and Extension Center [*Washington State University*] [*Research center*] (RCD) ... IAREC
Irrigated, Conventionally Tilled [*Agriculture*] ... ICT
Irrigated, Double Cropped [*Agriculture*] ... IDC
Irrigated, No Tillage [*Agriculture*] ... INT
Irrigation [*Medicine*] ... I
Irrigation [*Type of water project*] ... IRR
Irrigation ... IRRG
Irrigation ... IRRGTN
Irrigation and Aspiration [*Ophthalmology*] (DAVI) ... I & A
Irrigation and Debridement [*Surgery*] (DAVI) ... I & D
Irrigation and Drainage [*Surgery*] (DAVI) ... I & D
Irrigation Area (ADA) ... IA
Irrigation Association (EA) ... IA
Irrigation Canal [*Board on Geographic Names*] ... CNLI
Irrigation Division, Alberta Agriculture, Lethbridge, Alberta [*Library symbol National Library of Canada*] (NLC) ... ALAI
Irrigators and Water Users' League [*Australia*] ... IWUL
Irritable Bowel Disease [*Medicine*] (DMAA) ... IBD
Irritable Bowel Syndrome [*Medicine*] ... IBS
Irritable Colon [*Medicine*] ... IC
Irritable Colon Syndrome [*Medicine*] (DMAA) ... ICS
Irritable Gut [*Medicine*] (DMAA) ... IG
Irritant ... IRR
Irritation (DAVI) ... IRR
Irritation of Nociceptors [*Medicine*] (DMAA) ... IN
Irrotationally Bound Water [*Biophysics*] ... IBW
IRSA Inversiones y Rep GDS [*NYSE symbol*] (TTSB) ... IRS
IRSA Inversiones y Representaciones SA [*Associated Press*] (SAG) ... IRSA
IRSA Inversions y Representaciones SA [*NYSE symbol*] (SAG) ... IRS
IRSA [*International Racquet Sports Association*], the Association of Quality Clubs (EA) ... IRSAAQC
IRT Properities [*Formerly, Investors Realty Trust*] [*Associated Press*] (SAG) ... IRT
IRT Property [*NYSE symbol*] (TTSB) ... IRT
IRT Property Co. [*Formerly, Investors Realty Trust*] [*NYSE symbol*] (SPSG) ... IRT
Iruma [*Japan ICAO location identifier*] (ICLI) ... RJTJ
Irvco Resources [*Vancouver Stock Exchange symbol*] ... IVR
Irvine Apartment Communities [*NYSE symbol*] (SAG) ... IAC
Irvine Apartment Communities [*Associated Press*] (SAG) ... IrvineApt
Irvine, CA [*FM radio station call letters*] ... KUCI
Irvine Computer Sciences Corporation (NITA) ... ICSC
Irvine Group [*An association*] (EA) ... IG
Irvine, KY [*FM radio station call letters*] ... WCYO
Irvine, KY [*AM radio station call letters*] ... WIRV
Irvine, KY [*Location identifier FAA*] (FAAL) ... XYC
Irvine/Michigan/Brookhaven [*Experiment on proton decay*] ... IMB
Irvine Municipal Library, Alberta [*Library symbol National Library of Canada*] (NLC) ... AIM
Irvine Research Unit [*University of California, Irvine*] ... IRU
Irvine Sensors [*NASDAQ symbol*] (TTSB) ... IRSN
Irvine Sensors Corp. [*NASDAQ symbol*] (NQ) ... IRSN
Irvine Sensors Corp. [*Associated Press*] (SAG) ... Irvine
Irvine's Justiciary Cases [*England*] [*A publication*] (DLA) ... IJ Cas
Irvine's Justiciary Cases [*England*] [*A publication*] (DLA) ... IJC
Irvine's Justiciary Cases [*England*] [*A publication*] (DLA) ... Irv Just
Irvine's Justiciary Cases [*England*] [*A publication*] (DLA) ... Irvine Just Cas
Irvine's Scotch Justiciary Reports [*1851-68*] [*A publication*] (DLA) ... Irv
Irving Independent School District, Irving, TX [*OCLC symbol*] (OCLC) ... IJA
Irving Independent School District, Irving, TX [*Library symbol Library of Congress*] (LCLS) ... TxIrS
Irving Langmuir Laboratory [*New Mexico Institute of Mining and Technology*] [*Research center*] (RCD) ... ILL
Irving Municipal Library, Irving, TX [*Library symbol Library of Congress*] (LCLS) ... TxIr
Irving Oil Ltd. [*Canada ICAO designator*] (FAAC) ... XIA

Irving Public Library System, Irving, TX [*OCLC symbol*] (OCLC) .... IJC
Irving R. Silver Associates Library [*IRSA*], Ottawa, Ontario [*Library symbol National Library of Canada*] (NLC) .... OOIRS
Irving, TX [*Television station call letters*] .... KHSX
Irving's Civil Law [*A publication*] (DLA) .... Irv Civ Law
Irving's Civil Law [*A publication*] (DLA) .... Irving Civ Law
Irvington Public Library, Irvington, NY [*Library symbol Library of Congress*] (LCLS) .... NIr
Irwin Allen Fan Club [*Defunct*] (EA) .... IAFC
Irwin, Australia [*Spaceflight Tracking and Data Network*] [*NASA*] .... WIN
Irwin Financial Corp. [*Associated Press*] (SAG) .... IrwinFin
Irwin Financial Corp. [*NASDAQ symbol*] (SAG) .... IRWN
Irwin Financial Corp. [*Associated Press*] (SAG) .... IrwnFn
Irwin Stone Foundation for Ascorbate Capability and Therapy .... IS-FACT
Irwin Toy Ltd. [*Toronto Stock Exchange symbol*] .... IWT
Irwinton, GA [*FM radio station call letters*] .... WVKX
Is Amended to Add .... IATA
Is Amended to Delete .... IATD
Is Amended to Read .... IATR
Is Between (MHDB) .... IB
ISA [*Instruments, Systems and Automation*] **International** (ACII) .... ISAI
Isaac Garrison Family Association (EA) .... IGFA
Isaac Garrison Family Association (EA) .... ISFA
Isaac Newton Optical Telescope .... INT
Isaac Pitblado's Lectures on Continuing Legal Education [*A publication*] (DLA) .... Pitblado Lect
Isabela, PR [*AM radio station call letters*] .... WISA
Isabela, PR [*FM radio station call letters*] .... WKSA
Isabella [*California*] [*Seismograph station code, US Geological Survey*] (SEIS) .... ISA
Isabella [*Cuba ICAO location identifier*] (ICLI) .... MUIS
Isaenmaallinen Kansanliike [*Patriotic People's Movement*] [*Finland Political party*] (PPE) .... IKL
Isaeus [*Fourth century BC*] [*Classical studies*] (OCD) .... Isae
Isafjordur [*Iceland*] [*ICAO location identifier*] (ICLI) .... BIIS
Isafjordur [*Iceland*] [*Airport symbol*] (OAG) .... Is
Isaiah [*Old Testament book*] .... Is
Isaiah [*Old Testament book*] .... Isa
Isaias [*Old Testament book*] [*Douay version*] .... ISA
Isangel [*New Hebrides*] [*Seismograph station code, US Geological Survey*] (SEIS) .... INH
Isanti County Historical Society, Cambridge, MN [*Library symbol*] [*Library of Congress*] (LCLS) .... MnCaHi
Isanti Elementary School, Isanti, MN [*Library symbol*] [*Library of Congress*] (LCLS) .... MnIsE
Isatin-beta-thiosemicarbazone [*Organic chemistry*] .... IBT
ISB Financial [*NASDAQ symbol*] (TTSB) .... ISBF
ISB Financial Corp. [*Associated Press*] (SAG) .... ISB Fn
ISB Financial Corp. [*NASDAQ symbol*] (SAG) .... ISBF
Ischemia Research and Education Foundation .... IREF
Ischemic Bowel Disease [*Medicine*] (DAVI) .... IBD
Ischemic Brain Infarction [*Medicine*] (DMAA) .... IBI
Ischemic Cardiac Pain [*Cardiology*] .... ICP
Ischemic Cardiomyopathy [*Cardiology*] IC
Ischemic Cardiomyopathy [*Also, IC*] [*Cardiology*] .... ICM
Ischemic Cerebrovascular Headache [*Medicine*] (DAVI) .... ICVH
Ischemic Contracture [*Hematology*] IC
Ischemic Coronary Disease [*Medicine*] .... ICD
Ischemic Heart Disease .... IHD
Ischemic Leg Disease [*Medicine*] .... ILD
Ischemic Limb Disease [*Medicine*] .... ILD
Ischemic Necrosis of Femoral Head [*Orthopedics*] (DAVI) .... INFH
Ischemic Optic Neuropathy [*Medicine*] .... ION
Ischemic Optic Neuropathy Decompression Trial .... IONDT
Ischial Tuberosity [*Medicine*] .... IT
Isco, Inc. [*Associated Press*] (SAG) .... Isco
Isco, Inc. [*NASDAQ symbol*] (NQ) .... ISKO
Iscove's Modified Dulbecco's Medium [*For nematode culture*] .... IMDM
Iscozacin [*Peru*] [*ICAO location identifier*] (ICLI) .... SPEN
Iscrizioni Antico-Ebraici Palestinesi (BJA) .... IAE
ISDN [*Integrated Services Digital Network*] **Gateway Module** [*Telecommunications*] .... IGM
ISDN [*Integrated Services Digital Network*] **Link Controller** [*Telecommunications*] ILC
ISDN [*Integrated Services Digital Network*] **Numbering Forum** (OSI) .... INF
ISDN [*Integrated Services Digital Network*] **Ordering Code** (PCM) .... IOC
ISDN [*Integrated Services Digital Network*] **Remote Subscriber Unit** [*Telecommunications*] .... IRSU
ISDN [*Integrated Services Digital Network*] **Subscriber Module** [*Telecommunications*] .... ISM
ISDN [*Integrated Services Digital Network*] **Trunk Module** [*Telecommunications*] .... ITM
ISDN [*Integrated Services Digital Network*] **User Part** [*Telecommunications*] .... ISUP
ISDS Canada, National Library of Canada [*ISDS Canada, Bibliotheque Nationale du Canada*], Ottawa, Ontario [*Library symbol National Library of Canada*] (BIB) .... OONLI
Ise [*Japan*] [*Seismograph station code, US Geological Survey*] (SEIS) .... ISE
Isethionyl Acetimidate [*Biochemistry*] .... IAI
Isfahan [*Iran*] [*Airport symbol*] (OAG) .... IFN
Isfjord [*Norway*] [*Seismograph station code, US Geological Survey Closed*] (SEIS) .... ISF
ISG International Software Group [*Associated Press*] (SAG) .... ISG Intl
ISG International Software Group [*NASDAQ symbol*] (SAG) .... SISG
ISG Intl Software Group [*NASDAQ symbol*] (TTSB) .... SISGF
I.S.G. Technologies [*NASDAQ symbol*] (TTSB) .... ISGTF

ISG Technologies, Inc. [*Associated Press*] (SAG) .... ISG Tech
ISG Technologies, Inc. [*NASDAQ symbol*] (SAG) .... ISGT
ISG Technologies, Inc. [*Toronto Stock Exchange symbol*] .... ISO
Isham, Lincoln & Beale, Chicago, IL [*OCLC symbol*] (OCLC) .... ILZ
Isham-Lincoln-Beale, Chicago, IL [*Library symbol*] [*Library of Congress*] (LCLS) .... ICILB
Ishasha [*Zaire*] [*ICAO location identifier*] (ICLI) .... FZNI
Ishigaki [*Japan*] [*Airport symbol*] (OAG) .... ISG
Ishigaki Jima [*Ryukyu Islands*] [*ICAO location identifier*] (ICLI) .... ROIG
Ishigakijima [*Ryukyu Islands*] [*Seismograph station code, US Geological Survey*] (SEIS) .... ISI
Ishihara [*Japan*] [*Seismograph station code, US Geological Survey Closed*] (SEIS) .... IHR
Ishikawajima-Harima Heavy Industries [*Japan*] (ECON) .... IHI
Ishikawajima-Harima Heavy Industries Co. Ltd. [*Japan*] .... IHI
Ishinomaki [*Japan*] [*Seismograph station code, US Geological Survey*] (SEIS) .... ISN
Ishpeming Carnegie Library, Ishpeming, MI [*Library symbol Library of Congress*] (LCLS) .... Mils
Ishpeming, MI [*AM radio station call letters*] .... WIAN
Ishpeming, MI [*FM radio station call letters*] .... WJPD
Ishpeming, MI [*FM radio station call letters*] .... WMQT
Ishpeming, MI [*AM radio station call letters*] .... WMVN
Ishpeming, MI [*AM radio station call letters*] (RBYB) .... WZAM-AM
Ishtion [*Former USSR Seismograph station code, US Geological Survey*] (SEIS) .... ISH
Ishurdi [*Bangladesh*] [*Airport symbol*] (OAG) .... IRD
Ishurdi [*Bangladesh*] [*ICAO location identifier*] (ICLI) .... VGIS
ISI/Index to Scientific and Technical Proceedings and Books [*Institute for Scientific Information*] [*Philadelphia, PA Bibliographic database*] .... ISI/ISTP & B
ISI Infosearch, Port Coquitlam, BC, Canada [*Library symbol*] [*Library of Congress*] (LCLS) .... CaBPcl
ISI Infosearch, Port Coquitlam, British Columbia [*Library symbol National Library of Canada*] (NLC) .... BPCI
Isidis Planitia [*A filamentary mark on Mars*] .... IP
Isidore [*Authority cited in pre-1607 legal work*] (DSA) .... Is
Isiolo [*Kenya*] [*ICAO location identifier*] (ICLI) .... HKIS
Isiro [*Zaire*] [*ICAO location identifier*] (ICLI) .... FZJA
Isiro [*Zaire*] [*Airport symbol*] (OAG) .... IRP
Isiro/Matari [*Zaire*] [*ICAO location identifier*] (ICLI) .... FZJH
Isis Pharmaceuticals [*NASDAQ symbol*] (SPSG) .... ISIP
Isis Pharmaceuticals, Inc. [*Associated Press*] (SAG) .... Isis
ISIS [*Women's International Information Communication Service*] - **Women's International Cross-Cultural Exchange** (EAIO) .... ISIS-WICCE
Isis-Chemie KG [*Germany*] [*Research code symbol*] .... S
Isisford [*Australia Airport symbol*] (OAG) .... ISI
Isithebe [*South Africa*] [*ICAO location identifier*] (ICLI) .... FAIS
Iskenderon [*Turkey*] [*Airport symbol*] (AD) .... ISK
Iskenderun [*Turkey ICAO location identifier*] (ICLI) .... LTAK
Iskra Associated Enterprise [*Yugoslavia*] [*Telecommunications*] .... IAE
Iskustvennyi Sputnik Zemil [*Former USSR*] .... ISZ
Iskut Gold Corp. [*Vancouver Stock Exchange symbol*] .... ISK
Isla De Coche, Nueva Esparta [*Venezuela ICAO location identifier*] (ICLI) .... SVIE
Isla De Culebra, PR [*Location identifier FAA*] (FAAL) .... CPX
Isla De Pascua [*Easter Island*] [*Seismograph station code, US Geological Survey Closed*] (SEIS) .... PSC
Isla De Pascua [*Easter Island*] [*Chile*] [*ICAO location identifier*] (ICLI) .... SCIZ
Isla De Pascua/Mataveri [*Easter Island*] [*Chile*] [*ICAO location identifier*] (ICLI) .... SCIP
Isla De Vieques, PR [*Location identifier FAA*] (FAAL) .... VQS
Isla Desecheo [*Puerto Rico*] [*Seismograph station code, US Geological Survey*] (SEIS) .... IDE
Isla Grande Flying School [*Puerto Rico*] [*ICAO designator*] (FAAC) .... IGS
Isla Mona [*Puerto Rico*] [*Seismograph station code, US Geological Survey*] (SEIS) .... IMO
Isla Mona [*Puerto Rico*] [*Seismograph station code, US Geological Survey Closed*] (SEIS) .... IMR
Isla Mujeres [*Mexico ICAO location identifier*] (ICLI) .... MMIM
Isla Rey Jorge/Base Aerea Teniente R. Marsh Martin [*Chile*] [*ICAO location identifier*] (ICLI) .... SCRM
Isla Rey Jorge/Centro Meteorologico Antartico Presidente Frei [*Chile*] [*ICAO location identifier*] (ICLI) .... SCEF
Isla San Miguel [*Ecuador*] [*ICAO location identifier*] (ICLI) .... SEIM
Isla Verde [*Bolivia*] [*ICAO location identifier*] (ICLI) .... SLIV
Islahat Refah Partisi [*Reformation and Welfare Party*] [*Turkish Cypriot*] (PPE) .... Is
Islam (BJA) .... Is
Islam Abad [*Iran*] [*ICAO location identifier*] (ICLI) .... OICH
Islam Qala [*Afghanistan*] [*ICAO location identifier*] (ICLI) .... OAEQ
Islamabad/Chaklala [*Pakistan*] [*ICAO location identifier*] (ICLI) .... OPRN
Islamabad/Rawalpindi [*Pakistan*] [*Airport symbol*] (OAG) .... ISB
Islamic Action Front [*Political party*] [*Jordan*] .... IAF
Islamic Alliance for the Liberation of Afghanistan (PD) .... IALA
Islamic Bank International .... IBI
Islamic Bank of Bangladesh [*Commercial bank*] (EY) .... IBBL
Islamic Center of New York (EA) .... ICNY
Islamic Centre for Development of Trade [*See also CIDC*] [*Casablanca, Morocco*] (EAIO) .... ICDT
Islamic Chamber of Commerce, Industry and Commodity Exchange [*See also CICIEM*] [*Karachi, Pakistan*] (EAIO) .... ICCICE
Islamic Committee for Human Rights in Iraq [*Later, IODHRI*] (EA) .... ICHRI
Islamic Congress IC
Islamic Correctional Reunion Association (EA) .... ICRA
Islamic Council of Europe .... ICE
Islamic Democratic Alliance [*Pakistan*] [*Political party*] .... IDA

Islamic Development Bank [*Saudi Arabia*] ... IDB
Islamic Dinar [*Monetary unit*] (EY) ... ID
Islamic Educational, Scientific, and Cultural Organization [*United Nations*] ... ISESCO
Islamic Foundation for Science, Technology, and Development (BARN) ... IFSTAD
Islamic Foundation for Science, Technology and Development [*Saudi Arabia*] (PDAA) ... IFSTD
Islamic Front for Liberation of Oromo [*Ethiopia*] [*Political party*] (EY) ... IFLO
Islamic Front for the Liberation of Bahrain [*Political party*] (PD) ... IFLB
Islamic Information Center of America (EA) ... IICA
Islamic Jamhoori Ittedad [*Islamic Democratic Alliance*] [*Pakistan*] [*Political party*] ... IJI
Islamic Jurisprudence Academy [*See also IFA*] (EAIO) ... IJA
Islamic Liberation Organization ... ILO
Islamic Liberation Party [*Tunisia*] [*Political party*] (MENA) ... ILP
Islamic Medical Association (EA) ... IMA
Islamic Mission of America (EA) ... IMA
Islamic Missionaries Guild of the Caribbean and South America (EAIO) ... IMGCSA
Islamic Renaissance Party [*Commonwealth of Independent States*] (ECON) ... IRP
Islamic Republican Party [*Iran*] [*Political party*] (PPW) ... IRP
Islamic Research Foundation (EA) ... IRF
Islamic Salvation Front [*Algeria*] [*Political party*] (ECON) ... FIS
Islamic Society for International Unity and Peace [*Pakistan*] (EAIO) ... ISIUP
Islamic States Broadcasting Organization [*Jeddah, Saudi Arabia*] (EAIO) ... ISBO
Islamic Studies Library, McGill University, Montreal, Quebec [*Library symbol National Library of Canada*] (NLC) ... QMIIS
Islamic Texts Society [*British*] (DBA) ... ITS
Islamic Unity of Afghan Mujahadeen [*Afghanistan*] [*Political party*] ... IUAM
Island [*Maps and charts*] ... I
Island (ADA) ... ID
Island (DA) ... IS
Island ... IS
Island [*Board on Geographic Names*] ... ISL
Island [*Commonly used*] (OPSA) ... ISLAND
Island [*Commonly used*] (OPSA) ... ISLND
Island Air [*ICAO designator*] (AD) ... IL
Island Air Charters, Inc. [*ICAO designator*] (FAAC) ... ISC
Island Air Ltd. [*Fiji*] [*ICAO designator*] (FAAC) ... IML
Island Airlines [*ICAO designator*] (FAAC) ... XYZ
Island Airlines, Inc. [*ICAO designator*] (FAAC) ... ISA
Island Arc Basalt [*Geology*] ... IAB
Island Arts and Crafts Club, Victoria [*1910, IACS from 1922*] (NGC) ... IACC
Island Arts and Crafts Society, Victoria [*1922, founded 1910 as IACC*] (NGC) ... IACS
Island Aviation & Travel Ltd. [*British ICAO designator*] (FAAC) ... IOM
Island Base Section [*Navy*] ... IBS
Island Canyon Mines, Inc. [*Vancouver Stock Exchange symbol*] ... IAY
Island Commander ... ISCOM
Island Commander Azores ... ISCOMAZORES
Island Commander Bermuda ... ISCOMBERMUDA
Island Commander Faroes ... ISCOMFAROES
Island Commander Greenland ... ISCOMGREENLAND
Island Commander Iceland ... ISCOMICELAND
Island Commander Madeira (AABC) ... ISCOMADEIRA
Island Games Foundation [*Canada*] (EAIO) ... IGF
Island Helicopters, Inc. [*ICAO designator*] (FAAC) ... MTP
Island Hospital, Anacortes, WA [*Library symbol*] [*Library of Congress*] (LCLS) ... WaAnH
Island Lagoon [*Australia Seismograph station code, US Geological Survey Closed*] (SEIS) ... ILN
Island Lake [*Canada*] [*Airport symbol*] (OAG) ... YIV
Island Lake/Garden Hill, MB [*ICAO location identifier*] (ICLI) ... CYIV
Island Magazine [*A publication*] ... Is Mag
Island Manager (FAAC) ... ISMGR
Island Mining [*Vancouver Stock Exchange symbol*] ... IMX
Island Missionary Society (EA) ... IMS
Island of Calleja [*Neuroanatomy*] ... IC
Island Park Geothermal Area ... IPGA
Island Park Public Library, Island Park, NY [*Library symbol Library of Congress*] (LCLS) ... NIp
Island Resources Foundation (EA) ... IRF
Island Technologies Corp. [*Vancouver Stock Exchange symbol*] ... ITH
Island Telephone Co. Ltd. [*Toronto Stock Exchange symbol*] ... IT
Island Trees High School, Levittown, NY [*Library symbol Library of Congress*] (LCLS) ... NLevIH
Island Trees Memorial Junior High School, Levittown, NY [*Library symbol Library of Congress*] (LCLS) ... NLevIJ
Island Trees Public Library, Levittown, NY [*Library symbol Library of Congress*] (LCLS) ... NLevI
Island Tug & Barge [*AAR code*] ... ITB
Island-Arc Volcanic [*Geology*] ... IAV
Islander ... ISLER
Islands [*Maps and charts*] ... Is
Islands [*Commonly used*] (OPSA) ... ISLANDS
Islands [*Commonly used*] (OPSA) ... ISLNDS
Islands [*Board on Geographic Names*] ... ISLS
Islands [*Postal Service standard*] (OPSA) ... ISS
Islands ... ISS
Islands Museum and Tourist Bureau, Tiverton, Nova Scotia [*Library symbol National Library of Canada*] (NLC) ... NSTIM
Islands Museum and Tourist Bureau, Tiverton, NS, Canada [*Library symbol*] [*Library of Congress*] (LCLS) ... CaNSTiIM
Islands of Cartilage Pattern [*Anatomy*] ... ICP
Islands Research Foundation [*Inactive*] (EA) ... IRF
Islas Del Cisne O Santanilla [*Honduras*] [*ICAO location identifier*] (ICLI) ... MHIC
Islay [*Scotland*] [*Airport symbol*] (OAG) ... ILY
Islay/Port Ellen [*British ICAO location identifier*] (ICLI) ... EGPI
Isle ... I
Isle (EY) ... IS
Isle ... ISL
Isle [*Postal Service standard*] (OPSA) ... ISLE
Isle [*Commonly used*] (OPSA) ... ISLES
Isle des Pins [*New Caledonia*] [*Airport symbol*] (AD) ... ILP
Isle High School/Elementary School, Isle, MN [*Library symbol*] [*Library of Congress*] (LCLS) ... MnIH
Isle Of Angelsey [*Wales*] (ROG) ... I/A
Isle Of Aran ... IA
Isle of Man [*England*] ... I of M
Isle of Man [*England*] ... IM
Isle of Man [*England*] [*Airport symbol*] (OAG) ... IOM
Isle of Man Family History Society [*British*] (EAIO) ... IMFHS
Isle Of Man (Great Britain) ... GBM
Isle Of Man Railways [*British*] (ROG) ... IOMR
Isle Of Man/Ronaldsway [*British ICAO location identifier*] (ICLI) ... EGNS
Isle Of Man Steam Packet Co. [*British*] (ROG) ... IOMSPCo
Isle Of Man Tourist Board (DCTA) ... IMTB
Isle Of Skye [*Scotland*] (ROG) ... I/S
Isle Of Skye [*Scotland*] ... IOS
Isle Of Skye [*Scotland*] [*Airport symbol*] (OAG) ... SKL
Isle of Wight ... I of W
Isle Of Wight ... IOW
Isle of Wight ... IW
Isle Of Wight Railway [*British*] ... IWR
Isle Of Wight Rifles [*British military*] (DMA) ... IWR
Isle Royale National Park ... ISRO
Islena de Inversiones SA [*Honduras*] [*ICAO designator*] (FAAC) ... ISV
Isles Of Scilly [*England*] [*Airport symbol*] (OAG) ... ISC
Isles of Scilly Skybus [*ICAO designator*] (AD) ... FW
Isles of Scilly Skybus Ltd. [*British ICAO designator*] (FAAC) ... IOS
Isles Of Scilly-Tresco [*Airport symbol*] (OAG) ... TSO
Islet [*Maps and charts*] ... It
Islet Amyloid Polypeptide [*Biochemistry*] ... IAPP
Islet Cell Antibody [*Immunology*] ... ICA
Islet Cell Surface Antibody [*Immunology*] ... ICSA
Islet Cells [*of the pancreas*] [*Endocrinology*] ... IC
Islet-Activating Protein [*Biochemistry*] ... IAP
Islet-Infiltrating T ... IIT
Islets of Langerhans [*Anatomy*] ... IS of LANG
Isle-Wahkon Elementary School, Wahkon, MN [*Library symbol*] [*Library of Congress*] (LCLS) ... MnWE
Islington (ROG) ... ISL
Islip/MacArthur Field [*New York*] [*ICAO location identifier*] (ICLI) ... KISP
Islip, NY [*Location identifier FAA*] (FAAL) ... ISP
Islip, NY [*Location identifier FAA*] (FAAL) ... RXN
Islip, NY [*AM radio station call letters*] (RBYB) ... WLUX
Islip Public Library, Islip, NY [*Library symbol Library of Congress*] (LCLS) ... NIs
Isme-Dagan Hymn (BJA) ... IH
Isnati Middle School, Isanti, MN [*Library symbol*] [*Library of Congress*] (LCLS) ... MnIsM
Iso and Bizzarrini Owners Club (EA) ... IBOC
ISO [*International Organization for Standardization*] **Status Accumulating Binaries Extraordinary Logic** [*Using*] ... ISABEL
Iso Ventures, Inc. [*Vancouver Stock Exchange symbol*] ... ISV
Isobaric Analog Resonance [*Nuclear structure*] ... IAR
Isobaric Analog State ... IAS
Isobaric Cooling [*Geology*] ... IBC
Isobaric Multiplet Mass Equation ... IMME
Isobaric Solution (DMAA) ... IBS
Isobutene-Isoprene Rubber ... IIR
Isobutoxycarbonylation [*Organic chemistry*] ... IBOC
Isobutoxymethyl Acrylamide [*Organic chemistry*] ... IBMA
Isobutyl Cyanoacrylate [*Organic chemistry*] ... IBCA
Isobutyl Isobutyrate [*Organic chemistry*] ... IBIB
Isobutyl Methyl Ketone [*Organic chemistry*] ... IBMK
Isobutyl Vinyl Ether [*Organic chemistry*] ... IBVE
Isobutyl Vinyl Ether [*Organic chemistry*] ... IVE
Isobutylamine [*Organic chemistry*] ... IBA
Isobutylbenzene [*Organic chemistry*] ... IBB
Isobutylidenediurea [*Organic chemistry*] ... IBDU
Isobutyl(methoxy)pyrazine [*Organic chemistry*] ... IBMP
Isobutylmethylxanthine [*Also, MIX*] [*Biochemistry*] ... IBMX
Isobutylphenylpropionic Acid (BARN) ... ibuprofen
Isocapnic Hyperventilation with Cold Air [*Medicine*] (DMAA) ... IHCA
Isochromatic (ROG) ... ISO
Isochromic Color Perception Plates [*Ophthalmology*] (DAVI) ... ICPP
Isochromosome (MAE) ... i
Isochronous Ethernet [*Computer science*] (CDE) ... IsoENET
Isochronous Maintenance Channel [*Electronics*] ... IMC
Isocitrate Dehydrogenase [*Also, ICDH, IDH*] [*An enzyme*] ... ICD
Isocitrate Dehydrogenase [*Also, ICD, IDH*] [*An enzyme*] ... ICDH
Isocitrate Dehydrogenase [*Also, ICD, ICDH*] [*An enzyme*] ... IDH
Isocitrate Lyase [*An enzyme*] ... ICL
Isocitrate Lyase (DMAA) ... ICL
Isocrates [*436-338BC*] [*Classical studies*] (OCD) ... Isoc
Isodecyl Diphenyl Phosphate [*Organic chemistry*] ... IDDP
Isodensitracer ... IDT
Iso-Echo Contour ... IEC
Isoelectric Focusing [*Analytical chemistry*] ... IEF

Isoelectric Focusing Facility	IFF
Isoelectric Focusing in Polyacrylamide [Gel] [Analytical chemistry]	IFPA
Isoelectric Interval (DMAA)	IEI
Isoelectric Point [Also, IP, PH1, pI] [Chemistry]	IEP
Isoelectric Point [Also, IEP, PH1, pI] [Chemistry]	IP
Isoelectric Point [Chemistry] (DAVI)	pH_1
Isoelectric Point (MAE)	pI
Isoenzyme (AAMN)	isoenz
Isoenzyme of Creatine Kinase with Brain Subunits [Medicine] (MEDA)	CK-BB
Isoenzyme of Creatine Kinase with Muscle and Brain Subunits [Medicine] (MEDA)	CK-MB
Isoenzyme of Creatine Kinase with Muscle Subunits [Medicine] (MEDA)	CK-MM
Isoetharine [Medicine]	I
Isoflurane [An anesthetic]	ISO
Isoflurane [An anesthetic]	ISO
Isoform of Nitric Oxide Synthase [An enzyme]	INOS
Isogrid Payload Fairing (MCD)	IPLF
Isoimmune Hydrops [Medicine]	IIH
Isoka [Zambia] [ICAO location identifier] (ICLI)	FLIK
Isola [France] [Seismograph station code, US Geological Survey] (SEIS)	ISO
Isolate [or Isolated] (DAVI)	isol
Isolated [Slang] (WDMC)	iso
Isolated Adrenal Cell [Endocrinology] (DAVI)	IAC
Isolated Asymmetric Septal Hypertrophy [Medicine] (DMAA)	ISO
Isolated Camera (NTCM)	IC
Isolated Children's Assistance Scheme	ICAS
Isolated Flow Responder [Physiology]	IFR
Isolated Fully Recessed Complementary Metal-Oxide Semiconductor (TEL)	ISO-CMOS
Isolated Gate Bipolar Transistor [Electronics]	IGBT
Isolated Growth Hormone Deficiency [Medicine]	IGHD
Isolated Lactase Deficiency [Medicine] (DMAA)	ILD
Isolated Neutron Star [Astrophysics]	INS
Isolated Pentagon Rule [Physical chemistry]	IPR
Isolated Perfused Porcine Skip Flap [Clinical chemistry]	IPPSF
Isolated Rat Hepatocyte Complex	IRHC
Isolated Safflower Protein [Food technology]	ISP
Isolated Signal Line (IAA)	ISL
Isolated Single Wheel Load (AIA)	ISWL
Isolated Soy Protein [Food technology]	ISP
Isolated Spontaneous Psychokinesis [Parapsychology]	ISPK
Isolated Step	IS
Isolated Systolic Hypertension [Cardiology] (DAVI)	ISH
Isolated Ultrafiltration [Organic chemistry] (DAVI)	IUF
Isolated Volume Responders [Physiology]	IVR
Isolated Word Recognition (MCD)	IWR
Isolated-Gate Field-Effect Transistor [Electronics]	IGFET
Isolateral Human Growth Deficiency [Medicine] (DMAA)	IHGD
Isolation	IS
Isolation (MSA)	ISLN
Isolation	ISO
Isolation	ISO
Isolation (KSC)	ISOL
Isolation	ISOLN
Isolation Accommodation Zone [Geology]	ISAZ
Isolation Amplifier	IA
Isolation Bed [Infectious disease] (DAVI)	IB
Isolation Condenser (NRCH)	IC
Isolation Configuration and Monitor Unit (MCD)	ICMU
Isolation Containment Spray [Nuclear energy] (IEEE)	ICS
Isolation, Control, and Monitoring [Pollution control]	ICM
Isolation Functional Testing (PDAA)	IFT
Isolation Mode Rejection (IAA)	IMR
Isolation Mode Rejection Ratio (IAA)	IMRR
Isolation Network (PDAA)	ISON
Isolation of Dimensions and Elimination of Alternatives	IDEA
Isolation Pulse	IP
Isolation Test Routine (IAA)	ITR
Isolation Working Unit [Telecommunications] (TEL)	IWU
Isolation Zone [Nuclear energy] (NRCH)	IZ
Isolationer	ISOLR
Isolation-Physiological Characterization [Microbiology]	IPC
Isolator (MSA)	ISLR
Isoleucine [One-letter symbol; see Ile] [An amino acid]	I
Isoleucine [or iLeu, Ileu] [Also, I An amino acid]	Ile
Isoleucine [An amino acid] (DOG)	ile
Isoleucine [or iLeu, Ile] [Also, I An amino acid]	Ileu
Isoleucyl-tRNA Synthetase [An enzyme]	IRS
Isolyser Co. [NASDAQ symbol] (TTSB)	OREX
Isolyser Co., Inc. [Associated Press] (SAG)	Isolyser
Isolyser Company, Inc. [NASDAQ symbol] (SAG)	OREX
Isomedix, Inc. [NYSE symbol] (SAG)	ISO
Isomedix Inc. [NYSE symbol] (TTSB)	ISO
Isomedix, Inc. [Associated Press] (SAG)	Isomdx
Isomeric Shift (OA)	IS
Isomeric Transition [Radioactivity]	IT
Isomeric Transition Level [Radioactivity]	ITL
Isomet Corp. [NASDAQ symbol] (NQ)	IOMT
Isomet, Corp. [Associated Press] (SAG)	Isomet
Isometric [Botany]	I
Isometric (MSA)	ISO
Isometric (VRA)	iso
Isometric (KSC)	ISOM
Isometric Contraction Time [Medicine] (DAVI)	ICT

Isometric Piping Efficiency Program	ISOPEP
Isometric Relaxation Time [Medicine] (DAVI)	IRT
Isometric Strength Testing Unit [Medicine] (DMAA)	ISTU
Isomorphously Doped Ammonium Perchlorate	IDAP
Isoniazid [Pharmacology] (DAVI)	FSR-3
Isoniazid (DMAA)	INH
Isoniazid [An Antibacterial] [Pharmacology] (DAVI)	TB-Vis
Isonicotinic Acid [Organic chemistry]	INA
Isonicotinic Acid Hydrazide [See also INH, ISONIAZID] [Antituberculous agent]	INAH
Isonicotinic Acid Hydrazide [or Isonicotinylhydrazine] [See also INAH, ISONIAZID] [Antituberculous agent]	INH
Isonicotinic Acid Hydrazide [See also INAH, INH] [Antituberculous agent]	ISONIAZID
Isonicotinoyloxycarbonyl [Medicine] (DMAA)	INOC
Isooctyl Thioglycolate [Organic chemistry]	IOTG
Isopenicillin N Synthase [An enzyme]	IPNS
Isopentenyl [As substituent on nucleoside] [Biochemistry]	i
Isopentenyl Pyrophosphate [Organic chemistry]	IPP
Isopentenyl Transferase [An enzyme]	IPT
Isopentenyladenosine [Biochemistry]	IPA
Isophase	Iso
Isophorone Diamine [Organic chemistry]	IPD
Isophorone Diisocyanate [Organic chemistry]	IPDI
Isophosphamide, Hydroxydaunomycin [Adriamycn], Oncovin , Prednisone [Vincristine] [Antineoplastic drug regimen] (DAVI)	IHOP
Isophosphamide, Methotrexate, and Vincristine [Medicine] (DMAA)	IMV
Isophosphamide, Methotrexate, Vesposide [Antineoplastic drug regimen] (DAVI)	IMVP-16
Isophthalic Acid [Organic chemistry]	IA
Isophthalic Acid [Organic chemistry]	IPA
Isophthalic Glass Reinforced Plastic [Materials science]	IGRP
Isophthalonitrile [Organic chemistry]	IPN
Isopin (WDAA)	I
Isoplanar Integrated Injection Logic	I^3L
Isoplanar Integrated Injection Logic (MCD)	IIIL
Isoprene Rubber	IR
Isopropane [Organic chemistry]	IPA
Isopropenyloxytrimethylsilane [Organic chemistry]	IPOTMS
Isopropyl Alcohol [Organic chemistry]	IPA
Isopropyl Carbanilate [Also, INPC, IPPC] [Herbicide]	IPC
Isopropyl Chlorophenyl [Medicine] (MAE)	IPC
Isopropyl Ether [Organic chemistry]	IPE
Isopropyl Methyl Pyrimidinone [Organic chemistry]	IMHP
Isopropyl Myristate [Pharmacology]	IPM
Isopropyl N-phenylcarbamate [Also, INPC, IPC] [Herbicide]	IPPC
Isopropyl Oxalyl Hydroxamate [Organic chemistry]	IpOHA
Isopropyl Percarbonate [or Diisopropyl Peroxydicarbonate] [Organic chemistry]	IPP
Isopropyl Phenylcarbamate [Also, IPC, IPPC] [Herbicide]	INPC
(Isopropylamino)ethanol [Organic chemistry]	IPAE
Isopropylantipyrine [Biochemistry]	IAP
Isopropylidene Glycerol [Biochemistry]	IPG
Isopropyl(methoxy)pyrazine [Organic chemistry]	IPMP
Isopropyl(methyl)nitrobenzene [Organic chemistry]	IMNB
Isopropylnoradrenaline	IPNA
Isopropylphenyl Acetate [Organic chemistry]	IPPA
Isopropylphenyl(diphenyl)phosphate [Fire-resistant hydraulic fluid]	IPDP
Isopropyl(phenyl)para-phenylene Diamine [Organic chemistry]	IPPD
Isopropylthiogalactoside [Also, IPTG] [Organic chemistry]	IPG
Isopropylthiogalactoside [Also, IPG] [Organic chemistry]	IPTG
Isoproterenol [An adrenergic]	IP
Isoproterenol [An adrenergic]	IPR
Isoproterenol [An adrenergic]	ISO
Isoproterenol [An adrenergic]	ISP
Isoproterenol (DMAA)	IPV
Isopycnic Potential Vorticity [Oceanography]	IPV
Isopycnic Potential Vorticity Gradient [Oceanography]	IPVG
Isortoq [Greenland] [ICAO location identifier] (ICLI)	BGIS
Isosceles [Triangle]	ISOS
Isosorbide Dinitrate [Also, ISDN] [Coronary vasodilator]	ISDIN
Isosorbide Dinitrate [Also, ISDIN] [Coronary vasodilator]	ISDN
Isosorbide Dinitrite [Coronary vasodilator]	ISD
Isosorbide Mononitrate [Coronary vasodilator]	ISMN
Isostatic Hot Pressing (PDAA)	IHP
Isotachophoresis [Analytical biochemistry]	ITP
Isotactic Polypropylene [Organic chemistry]	IPP
Isothermal (KSC)	ISOTH
Isothermal Chemical Vapor Infiltration [Materials science]	ICVI
Isothermal Community College, Polk Campus, Tryon, NC [Library symbol Library of Congress] (LCLS)	NcTyl
Isothermal Community College, Spindale, NC [Library symbol Library of Congress] (LCLS)	NcSpil
Isothermal Controlled Electrophoresis	ICE
Isothermal Gas Chromatography	IGC
Isothermal Heating Furnace	IHF
Isothermal Luminescence (PDAA)	ITL
Isothermal Pressure Profile	IPP
Isothermal Remanent Magnetization	IRM
Isothermal Storage Test [For hazardous chemicals]	IST
Isothermal Titration Calorimetry [Analytical chemistry]	ITC
Isothermal Transformation [Metallurgy]	IT
Isothermogravimetric Analysis	ITGA
Isotocin [Endocrinology]	IT
Isotope (DMAA)	I

Isotope ... ISO
Isotope ... ISTP
Isotope Cisternography (DMAA) ... ICG
Isotope Detection System [*Nuclear energy*] (NRCH) ... IDS
Isotope Development Ltd. ... IDL
Isotope Development Program [*AEC*] (MCD) ... IDP
Isotope Dilution ... ID
Isotope Dilution Alpha Spectrometry ... IDAS
Isotope Dilution Analysis ... IDA
Isotope Dilution Analysis Mass Spectrometry ... IDAMS
Isotope Dilution Mass Spectrometry ... IDMS
Isotope Dilution Thermal Ionization Mass Spectrometry ... IDTIMS
Isotope Exciter Light Source ... IELS
Isotope Heat Source ... IHS
Isotope Miniature Thermionic Electric (IAA) ... ISOMITE
Isotope Nephrogram (DMAA) ... ING
Isotope Power Generator ... IPG
Isotope Power Unit ... IPU
Isotope Production Facility ... IPF
Isotope Radiography System ... IRS
Isotope Ratio Mass Spectrometry ... IRMS
Isotope Ratio Tracer (PDAA) ... IRT
Isotope Reactor [*Former USSR*] ... IR
Isotope Reentry Vehicle [*NASA*] (NASA) ... IRV
Isotope Removal Service (IEEE) ... IRS
Isotope Separation Factor (MCD) ... ISF
Isotope Separation Power ... ISP
Isotope Thermoelectric Converter ... ISOTEC
Isotope-Heated Catalytic Oxidizer System (KSC) ... IHCOS
Isotope-Powered Device ... IPD
Isotope-Powered Thermoelectric Generator (PDAA) ... ITEG
Isotopes and Radiation Division [*American Nuclear Society*] ... IRD
Isotopes and Radiation Technology [*A publication*] ... ISRT
Isotopes Information Center [*ORNL*] ... IIC
Isotopes of Carbon, Oxygen, Nitrogen, and Sulfur [*AEC project*] ... ICONS
Isotopes Process Development Laboratory [*AEC*] ... IPDL
Isotope-Shift, Zeeman-Effect Atomic Absorption ... IZAA
Isotope-Voiding Cystourethrogram [*Urology*] (DAVI) ... IVCU
Isotopic Atomic Weight ... IAW
Isotopic Chemical Vapor Deposition (PDAA) ... ICVD
Isotopic Dilution Analysis ... IDA
Isotopic Low-Weight Device (IAA) ... ISOLDE
Isotopic Separation [*Subsystem*] (MCD) ... IS
Isotopic Separation Subsystem ... ISS
Isotopic Source Adjustable Fissometer [*Nuclear energy*] (NRCH) ... ISAF
Isotopic Source Assay System ... ISAS
Isotopic Ventriculogram [*Cardiology*] (DAVI) ... IVG
Isotopic Weight ... IW
Isotropic (KSC) ... ISO
Isotropic Distribution Function ... IDF
Isotta Fraschini Owner's Association [*Defunct*] (EA) ... IFOA
Isotta-Fraschini [*Italian luxury auto maker*] ... IF
Isotype ... ISO
Isovaleric Acid (DMAA) ... IVA
Isove's Modified Dulbrecco's Medium [*Oncology*] ... IMD
Isovolume Pressure Flow Curve [*Cardiology*] (MAE) ... IVPF
Isovolumic Confraction [*Cardiology*] ... IVC
Isovolumic Contraction [*Medicine*] (DMAA) ... IC
Isovolumic Contraction Time [*Cardiology*] ... ICT
Isovolumic Relaxation [*Time*] [*Cardiology*] (DAVI) ... IVR
Isovolumic Relaxation Time [*Cardiology*] ... IRT
Isovolumic Relaxation Time (DMAA) ... IVRT
Isparta [*Turkey ICAO location identifier*] (ICLI) ... LTBM
Israel [*Aircraft nationality and registration mark*] (FAAC) ... 4X
Israel [*MARC geographic area code Library of Congress*] (LCCP) ... a-is--
Israel [*ANSI two-letter standard code*] (CNC) ... IL
Israel [*MARC country of publication code Library of Congress*] (LCCP) ... is
Israel [*IYRU nationality code*] (BJA) ... Is
Israel [*ANSI three-letter standard code*] (CNC) ... ISR
Israel (VRA) ... Isr
Israel Air Force (BJA) ... IAF
Israel Aircraft Industries Ltd. [*ICAO designator*] (FAAC) ... IAI
Israel Aircraft Industries Ltd. [*ICAO aircraft manufacturer identifier*] (ICAO) ... RV
Israel Aircraft Industries Ltd. [*ICAO aircraft manufacturer identifier*] (ICAO) ... WW
Israel Airports Authority Headquarters [*Israel*] [*ICAO location identifier*] (ICLI) ... LLAA
Israel Aliyah Center (EA) ... IAC
Israel Antiquities Authority ... IAA
Israel Atomic Energy Commission, Soreq Nuclear Research Centre, Yavne, Israel [*Library symbol Library of Congress*] (LCLS) ... IsYAEC
Israel Book World [*A publication*] ... IBW
Israel Chemical Ltd. [*NYSE symbol*] (SAG) ... ICH
Israel Chemical Ltd. [*Associated Press*] (SAG) ... Israel Ch
[*The*] **Israel Commercial Economic Newsletter** [*A publication Also, an information service or system*] (IID) ... ICEN
Israel Discount Bank ... IDB
Israel Economic Conference ... IEC
Israel Education Fund ... IEF
Israel Folk Dance Institute (EA) ... IFDI
Israel Folktale Archive (BJA) ... IFA
Israel General Security Service [*Acronym represents Hebrew phrase*] ... SHIN BET
Israel Histadrut Foundation (EA) ... IHF
Israel Institute of Technology (KSC) ... IIT
Israel Jewish Press (BJA) ... IJP
Israel Labor Party [*Political party*] ... ILP
Israel Land & Development Co. [*NASDAQ symbol*] (SAG) ... ILDC
Israel Land & Development Co. [*Associated Press*] (SAG) ... IsrlLd
Israel Ld Dev Ltd [*NASDAQ symbol*] (TTSB) ... ILDCY
Israel Lira (BJA) ... IL
Israel Music Foundation (EA) ... IMF
Israel National Committee on the Biosphere and Environment ... INCBE
Israel Naval Ship (BJA) ... INS
Israel News Agency ... INA
Israel News Service (BJA) ... INS
Israel Plate Block Society (EA) ... IPBS
Israel Program for Scientific Translations [*An agency of the Government of Israel*] ... IPST
Israel Society of Special Libraries and Information Centers ... ISLIC
Israel South Control Area Control Center Unit [*Israel*] [*ICAO location identifier*] (ICLI) ... LLSC
Israel Space Agency [*Israel*] ... ISA
Israel Student Tourist Association ... ISSTA
Israel Students Organization ... ISO
Israel Studies in Criminology [*Jerusalem, Israel*] [*A publication*] (DLA) ... Israel Stud Criminol
Israel Television (BJA) ... ITV
Israel Trade Commission ... ITC
Israel Universities Press ... IUP
Israel-America Chamber of Commerce and Industry (EAIO) ... IACC
Israeli ... I
[*The*] **Israeli Academic Network** [*Computer science*] (TNIG) ... ILAN
Israeli Academy of Sciences and Humanities ... IASH
Israeli Air Force ... IsAF
Israeli Air Services (MCD) ... IAS
Israeli Air-Force [*ICAO designator*] (FAAC) ... IAF
Israeli Communist Party [*Political party*] ... IKP
Israeli Defense Forces ... IDF
Israeli Pound (BJA) ... IP
Israeli Research Reactor ... IRR
Israeli Society for the Application of Mathematics (MCD) ... ISAM
Israelitische Kultusgemeinde [*Vienna*] [*A publication*] (BJA) ... IKG
Israelitisches Gemeindeblatt [*Muelheim/Koeln*] [*A publication*] (BJA) ... IGB
Israel-Jordan Demilitarized Zones [*MARC geographic area code Library of Congress*] (LCCP) ... awiw--
Israel-Jordan Demilitarized Zones [*is (Israel) used in records cataloged after January 1978*] [*MARC country of publication code Library of Congress*] (LCCP) ... iw
Israel-Palestine Philatelic Society of America [*Later, SIP*] ... IPPSA
Israel's Herald [*A publication*] (BJA) ... IH
Israel-Syria Demilitarized Zones [*MARC geographic area code Library of Congress*] (LCCP) ... awiu--
Israel-Syria Demilitarized Zones [*is (Israel) used in records cataloged after January 1978*] [*MARC country of publication code Library of Congress*] (LCCP) ... iu
Isramco, Inc. [*Associated Press*] (SAG) ... Isramc
Isramco, Inc. [*NASDAQ symbol*] (NQ) ... ISRL
Isramco, Inc. [*Associated Press*] (SAG) ... Isrm
Isramco Inc.Wrrt'A' [*NASDAQ symbol*] (TTSB) ... ISRLW
Isramco Inc.Wrrt'B' [*NASDAQ symbol*] (TTSB) ... ISRLZ
ISS International Service Systems AS [*NYSE symbol*] (SAG) ... ISG
ISS International Service Systems AS [*Associated Press*] (SAG) ... ISS Int
ISS-Intl Service Sys ADS [*NYSE symbol*] (TTSB) ... ISG
ISSN [*International Standard Serial Number*] [*Online database field identifier*] ... IS
Issoire/Le Broc [*France ICAO location identifier*] (ICLI) ... LFHA
Issoudun/Le Fay [*France ICAO location identifier*] (ICLI) ... LFEK
Issue (ROG) ... I
Issue (AABC) ... ISS
Issue Authority Voucher ... IAV
Issue Book [*DoD*] ... IB
Issue Book (DOMA) ... IB
Issue by Issue Tally ... IBIT
Issue Category Code (NITA) ... ICC
Issue Code [*Online database field identifier*] ... IS
Issue Date ... ID
Issue Definition Memorandum [*Jimmy Carter Administration*] ... IDM
Issue Exception Code [*Air Force*] (AFIT) ... IEX
[*The*] **Issue Exchange** (EA) ... TIE
Issue Necessary Orders ... INO
Issue Number [*Dialog*] [*Searchable field*] (NITA) ... IS
Issue of Data ... IOD
Issue on Request [*or Requisition*] ... IOR
Issue Paper ... IP
Issue Price [*Business term*] ... IP
Issue Priority Designator ... IPD
Issue Priority Designators (AFIT) ... IP's
Issue Priority Group [*Army*] ... IPG
Issue Restriction Code (MCD) ... IRC
Issue, Rule, Application, Conclusions (AAGC) ... IRAC
Issue Time Check [*Aviation*] (FAAC) ... ITCK
Issue While in Stock ... IWISTK
Issue-Based Information System [*Computer science*] ... IBIS
Issued Capital Stock ... ICS
Issue-Position-Argument [*Computer science*] (BYTE) ... IPA
Issues and Criteria ... I & C
Issues & Observations [*A publication*] (EAAP) ... I & O
Issues in Bank Regulation [*Bank Administration Institute*] [*A publication*] ... IBR
Issues Management Association (EA) ... IMA
Issuing Agency (AFM) ... IA
Issuing Houses Association [*British Defunct*] (DI) ... IHA
Issuing Office ... IO

Issuing Point ... IP
Issy-Les Moulineaux Airport [*France*] ... ISS
Istanbul [*Turkey*] [*Airport symbol*] (OAG) ... IST
Istanbul [*Turkey*] [*Seismograph station code, US Geological Survey*] (SEIS) ... IST
Istanbul [*Turkey ICAO location identifier*] (ICLI) ... LTBB
Istanbul [*Trabzon*] [*Turkey*] [*Seismograph station code, US Geological Survey*] (SEIS) ... TBZ
Istanbul Airlines [*Turkey*] [*ICAO designator*] (FAAC) ... IST
Istanbul Arkeoloji Muzelerinde Bulunan Bogazkoy Tableteri I and II [*Istanbul*] [*A publication*] (BJA) ... IBoT
Istanbul Asariatica Muzeleri Nesriyati (BJA) ... IAMN
Istanbul/Yesilkoy [*Turkey ICAO location identifier*] (ICLI) ... LTBA
Istanbuler Mitteilungen [*A publication*] (BJA) ... IM
Istanbul-Kandilli [*Turkey*] [*Seismograph station code, US Geological Survey*] (SEIS) ... ISK
i-STAT [*NASDAQ symbol*] (TTSB) ... STAT
I-STAT Corp. [*Associated Press*] (SAG) ... I-STAT
I-Stat Corp. [*NASDAQ symbol*] (SAG) ... STAT
Istec-Industries Technologies [*NASDAQ symbol*] (SAG) ... ISTDF
Istec-Industries Technologies [*Associated Press*] (SAG) ... IstecIn
Istel Network Monitoring System (NITA) ... INM
Istesso Tempo [*Same Time*] [*Music*] (ROG) ... ISTES TEMP
Isthmian (ROG) ... ISTHM
Isthmian Canal Zone ... ICZ
Isthmian Odes [*of Pindar*] [*Classical studies*] (OCD) ... Isthm
Isthmo-Optic Nucleus [*or Nuclei*] [*In midbrain of chick*] ... ION
Isthmus [*Board on Geographic Names*] ... ISTH
Istituto Affairi Internazionali [*Institute for International Affairs*] [*Italy*] ... IAI
Istituto Chemioterapico Italiano [*Italy*] [*Research code symbol*] ... ICI
Istituto de Angeli [*Italy*] [*Research code symbol*] ... DA
Istituto delle Suore Maestre di Santa Dorotea [*Rome, Italy*] (EAIO) ... ISMSD
Istituto di Fisica Cosmica [*Italy*] ... IFC
Istituto di Fisica dell'Atmosfera [*Institute of Atmospheric Physics*] [*Italy*] ... IFA
Istituto di Studi per lo Sviluppo Economico [*Institute for the Study of Economic Development*] [*Italy*] ... ISVE
Istituto di Studi sulla Ricerca e Documentazione Scientifica [*Institute for Study of Scientific Research and Documentation*] [*National Research Council*] [*Information service or system*] (IID) ... ISRDS
Istituto Internazionale di Psicologia della Reliosita' [*International Institute for the Psychology of Religion*] [*Italy*] (IRC) ... IIPR
Istituto Internazionale di Studi Liguri [*International Institute for Ligurian Studies*] ... IISL
Istituto Internazionale Suore di Santa Marcellina [*Milan, Italy*] (EAIO) ... IISSM
Istituto Internazionale Suore di Santa Marcellina [*Also, Instituto Marcelline*] [*Italy*] (EAIO) ... ISM
Istituto Italiano Di Cultura Biblioteca, New York, NY [*Library symbol*] [*Library of Congress*] (LCLS) ... NNIIC
Istituto Italiano di Cultura, Montreal, Quebec [*Library symbol National Library of Canada*] (NLC) ... QMII
Istituto Italo-Latino-Americano [*Italian-Latin American Institute*] [*Rome, Italy*] ... IILA
Istituto Mobilaire Italiano [*NYSE symbol*] (SAG) ... IMI
Istituto Mobilaire Italiano [*Associated Press*] (SAG) ... IstMobl
Istituto Mobiliare Ital ADS [*NYSE symbol*] (TTSB) ... IMI
Istituto Mobiliare Italiana [*Italian state-owned bank*] (ECON) ... IMI
Istituto Nazionale ADS [*NYSE symbol*] (TTSB) ... INZ
Istituto Nazionale della Previdenza Sociale [*Italy*] (ECON) ... INPS
Istituto Nazionale Delle Assicorazionо SPA [*Associated Press*] (SAG) ... INAsicrz
Istituto Nazionale Delle Assicorazionо SPA [*NYSE symbol*] (SAG) ... INZ
Istituto Nazionale Fisica Nucleare Network [*National Institute for Nuclear Physics Network*] [*Italian*] [*Computer science*] (TNIG) ... INFNET
Istituto Nazionale per lo Studio della Congiuntura [*Data Resources, Inc.*] [*Database*] ... ISCO
Istituto per la Ricostruzione Industriale [*Institute for Industrial Reconstruction*] [*Government holding company Italy*] ... IRI
Istituto per l'Assistenza allo Sviluppo del Mezzogiorno [*Italy*] (EY) ... IASM
Istituto Sindacale per la Cooperazione con i Paesi in Via di Sviluppo [*Trade Union Institute for Cooperation with Developing Countries*] [*Italy*] (EAIO) ... ISCPVS
Istituto Superiore di Sanita [*Italy*] [*Research code symbol*] ... IS
Istituto Superiore Internazionale di Scienze Criminali [*Italy*] ... ISISC
Istra Air [*Slovakia*] [*ICAO designator*] (FAAC) ... ISR
Istres/Le Tube [*France ICAO location identifier*] (ICLI) ... LFMI
It Scale for Children [*Psychology*] ... ITSC
It Still Does Nothing [*Facetious translation for ISDN - Integrated Services Digital Network*] ... ISDN
It Would Be Nice If [*Computer hacker terminology*] (NHD) ... IWBNI
ITA [*Itapemirim Transportes Aereos SA*] [*Brazil*] [*ICAO designator*] (FAAC) ... ITM
Itabuna [*Brazil*] [*Airport symbol*] (OAG) ... ITN
Itacoatiara [*Brazil*] [*Airport symbol*] (AD) ... ITA
Itaconic Acid [*Organic chemistry*] ... ITA
Itaguazurenda [*Bolivia*] [*ICAO location identifier*] (ICLI) ... SLIT
Itaipu [*Paraguay*] [*ICAO location identifier*] (ICLI) ... SGIB
Itajai [*Brazil*] [*Airport symbol*] (AD) ... ITJ
Italfarmaco [*Italy*] [*Research code symbol*] ... ITF
[*The*] **Italia Philatelic Society** (EA) ... TIPS
Italian ... IT
Italian [*MARC language code Library of Congress*] (LCCP) ... ita
Italian ... ITAL
Italian ... ITAL
Italian (BARN) ... Itl
Italian Actors Union (EA) ... IAU
Italian Agency for Air Navigation Services [*Italy ICAO location identifier*] (ICLI) ... LIIR
Italian Air Force (NATG) ... IAF
Italian Aircraft Corp. ... IAC
Italian American Business [*American Chamber of Commerce in Italy*] [*A publication*] ... IAB
Italian American Forum [*Defunct*] (EA) ... IAF
Italian American Librarians Caucus (EA) ... IALC
Italian American Stamp Club (EA) ... IASC
Italian American War Veterans of the United States [*Defunct*] (EA) ... ITAM VETS
Italian Army (NATG) ... IA
Italian Baptist Association of America [*Later, AEIM*] (EA) ... IBAA
Italian Catholic Federation Central Council (EA) ... ICF
Italian Chamber of Commerce (EA) ... ICC
Italian Chamber of Commerce and Industry in Australia ... ICCIA
Italian Chamber of Commerce in Great Britain (DS) ... ICCGB
Italian Charities of America (EA) ... ICA
Italian Communist Party ... ICP
Italian Communist Party [*Political party*] ... IKP
Italian Cultural Exchange in the United States (EA) ... ICE
Italian Cultural Institute (EA) ... ICI
Italian Culture Council (EA) ... ICC
Italian Expeditionary Force ... IEF
Italian Folk Art Federation of America (EA) ... IFAFA
Italian for Idiots [*Facetious travel terminology*] ... IFI
Italian Greyhound Club of America (EA) ... IGCA
Italian Historical Society of America (EA) ... IHS
Italian Instrument Society (ACII) ... AIS
Italian International Bank ... IIB
Italian Language and Culture Center [*Australia*] ... ILCC
Italian Liberal Youth [*Political party*] (EAIO) ... ILY
Italian Lira [*Monetary unit*] ... IL
Italian MGM [*Record label*] ... ItMGM
Italian Navy (NATG) ... IN
Italian Oven [*NASDAQ symbol*] (TTSB) ... OVEN
[*The*] **Italian Oven, Inc.** [*Associated Press*] (SAG) ... ItlOven
[*The*] **Italian Oven, Inc.** [*NASDAQ symbol*] (SAG) ... OVEN
Italian Patent (IAA) ... IP
Italian Patent (IAA) ... ITP
Italian Pharmacopoeia [*A publication*] ... It P
Italian Polydor Variable Microgroove [*Record label*] ... IPV
Italian RCA [*Victor*] [*Record label*] ... ItV
Italian Red Cross Society ... IRCS
Italian Research Interim Stage (NASA) ... IRIS
Italian Service Unit [*Italian prisoners of war who became volunteers in the Allied war effort*] ... ISU
Italian Society of Physics ... ISP
Italian Space Commission ... ISC
Italian Tile Center (EA) ... ITC
Italian Trade Commission (EA) ... ITC
Italian Tribune, Newark, NJ [*Library symbol Library of Congress*] (LCLS) ... NjNIT
Italian Vox [*Record label*] ... ItVox
Italian Welfare League (EA) ... IWL
Italian Wine and Food Institute (EA) ... IWFI
Italian Yearbook of International Law [*A publication*] (DLA) ... Italian Yb of Int'l L
Italian-American Chamber of Commerce (EA) ... IACC
Italian-American Civil Rights League ... IACRL
Italian-American Cultural Society (EA) ... IACS
Italians in Service of the US [*World War II*] ... ITIS
Italic (IAA) ... IT
Italic [*or Italics*] ... ITAL
Italic (WDMC) ... ital
Italic Dialects [*A publication*] (OCD) ... Ital Dial
Italic Studies Institute (EA) ... ISI
Italics ... ITAX
Italo American National Union (EA) ... IANU
Italo Svevo International Association [*Defunct*] (EA) ... ISIA
Italo-Latin American Institute (EA) ... ILAI
Italy [*MARC geographic area code Library of Congress*] (LCCP) ... e-it--
Italy [*IYRU nationality code*] ... I
Italy [*ANSI two-letter standard code*] (CNC) ... IT
Italy [*MARC country of publication code Library of Congress*] (LCCP) ... it
Italy (VRA) ... It
Italy [*ANSI three-letter standard code*] (CNC) ... ITA
Italy and Colonies Study Circle (EA) ... ICSC
Italy Fund [*NYSE symbol*] (TTSB) ... ITA
Italy Fund, Inc. [*NYSE symbol*] (SPSG) ... ITA
Italy Fund, Inc. [*Associated Press*] (SAG) ... Italy
Italy International NOTAM Office [*Italy ICAO location identifier*] (ICLI) ... LIIA
Italy Military International NOTAM Office [*Italy ICAO location identifier*] (ICLI) ... LIIC
Italy-America Chamber of Commerce (EA) ... IACC
Itambacuri [*Brazil*] [*Airport symbol*] (AD) ... IBU
Itapemirim Transportes Aereos SA [*Brazil*] [*ICAO designator*] (FAAC) ... ITA
Itapetinga [*Brazil*] [*Airport symbol*] (AD) ... ITI
Itaqui [*Brazil*] [*Airport symbol*] (AD) ... ITQ
Itasca Community College, Grand Rapids, MN [*OCLC symbol*] (OCLC) ... MIC
Itasca Community College, Grand Rapids, MN [*Library symbol Library of Congress*] (LCLS) ... MnGrI
Itasca Junior College [*Later, Itasca Community College*] [*Minnesota*] ... IJC
Itavia [*ICAO designator*] (AD) ... IH
Itawamba Junior College [*Fulton, MS*] ... IJC
Itawamba Junior College, Tupelo Campus, Tupelo, MS [*Library symbol Library of Congress*] (LCLS) ... MsTI
Itbayat, Batanes [*Philippines*] [*ICAO location identifier*] (ICLI) ... RPXI
ITC [*International Trade Commission*] **Trial Lawyers Association** (EA) ... ITCTLA
Itek Positive Plate [*Publishing*] (DGA) ... IPP
ItelliQuest Info Group [*NASDAQ symbol*] (TTSB) ... IQST

Item [*Phonetic alphabet*] [*World War II*] (DSUE) I
Item (MCD) .... IT
Item [*Online database field identifier*] .... ITM
Item Accounting (MCD) .... I/A
Item Acquisition/Production Trade-Off Model .... IA/PT
Item Analysis Program, General (PDAA) .... IAPG
Item Category Code ICC
Item Change Analysis (KSC) .... ICA
Item Change Request (AFIT) .... ICR
Item Characteristic Curve [*Statistics*] ICC
Item Control Area (NRCH) .... ICA
Item Control Point (AFM) .... ICP
Item Data File (MCD) .... IDF
Item Description .... ID
Item Description Sheet (NASA) .... IDS
Item Design Change .... IDC
Item Detail Card [*Military*] (AABC) .... IDC
Item Documentation (IEEE) .... ID
Item Entry Control (AFM) .... IEC
Item Identification (MSA) II
Item Identification Code IIC
Item Identification File .... ITMID
Item Identification Guide .... IIG
Item Identification Number (AFM) .... IIN
Item Intelligence File [*DoD*] .... IFF
Item Intelligence Maintenance [*DoD*] .... IIM
Item List (AFIT) IL
Item Logistics Data Transmittal .... ILDT
Item Logistics Data Transmittal Form (NATG) .... ILDTF
Item Logistics Management Data [*DoD*] .... ILMD
Item Management .... IM
Item Management Coding [*Military*] (AABC) .... IMC
Item Management Coding Program [*Military*] (AFM) .... IMCP
Item Management Concept .... IMC
Item Management Control Code (AABC) .... IMCC
Item Management Data Element Standardization [*or System*] [*Military*] .... IMDES
Item Management Data Reply (MCD) .... IMDR
Item Management Plan (AAGC) .... IMP
Item Management Statistical Series .... IMSS
Item Manager (AAGC) .... IM
Item Manager [*DoD*] .... IMA
Item Mark (BUR) .... IM
Item Master Card [*Military*] (AABC) .... IMC
Item Master File (MCD) .... IMF
Item Mission Essentially Code (MCD) .... IMEC
Item Name [*Military*] .... IN
Item Name Code [*Military*] (AFM) .... INC
Item Name Policy Review Committee [*DoD Washington, DC*] (EGAO) .... INPRC
Item No Longer Required .... INLR
Item Number (WDAA) .... I/N
Item Number (IAA) .... IN
Item Number .... INO
Item [*or Items*] **on Hand** .... IOH
Item Operation Trouble Report (AAG) .... IOTR
Item Processing .... IP
Item Processing Card .... IPC
Item Processing System (BUR) .... IPS
Item Rating Value (DNAB) .... IRV
Item Record (AFIT) .... IR
Item Reduction Studies (MSA) .... IRS
Item Removal Notice [*Nuclear energy*] (NRCH) .... IRN
Item Repair Level Analysis [*DoD*] .... IRLA
Item Response Theory (GFGA) .... IRT
Item Responsibility Code .... IRC
Item Selection List .... ISL
Item Selection Working Group [*NATO*] (NATG) .... ISWG
Item Sequence Number (MCD) .... ISN
Item Standardization Information System [*DoD*] .... ISIS
Item Station and Indenture (AAG) .... ISI
Item Status Code (NATG) .... ISC
Item Study Listings .... ISL
Item Support Plan Policies Statement (AFIT) .... ISPPS
Item Survey List (DNAB) .... ISL
Item Transfer .... IT
Item Urgently Required [*Army*] (AFIT) .... IURGRQR
Items for Negotiation .... IFN
Items Not Available through Cannibalization, Fabrication, or Local Procurement or Replacement from Maintenance Float Stock .... ICFLPRMFS
Items Troop Installed or Authorized List (MCD) .... ITIAL
Iterated Deferred Correction (PDAA) .... IDC
Iterated Function System [*Computer science*] (BYTE) .... IFS
Iterated Function System-Image Synthesizer [*Computer science*] (BYTE) .... IFSIS
Iterated Ordinary Least Squares [*Statistics*] .... IOLS
Iterated Prisoner's Dilemma [*Psychology*] .... IPD
Iterated Proportional Fitting Procedure [*Statistics*] .... IPFP
Iterative Differential Analyzer (IAA) .... IDA
Iterative Differential Analyzer Control .... IDACON
Iterative Differential Analyzer Pinboard .... IDAP
Iterative Differential Analyzer Slave .... IDAS
Iterative Guidance Mode [*NASA*] .... IGM
Iterative Least-Squares Fitting [*Mathematics*] .... ILSF
Iterative Logic Array (MCD) .... ILA
Iterative Natural Orbital [*Atomic physics*] .... INO
Iterative Operation .... IO
Iterative Orbit Calculator .... IOC
Iterative Scheme Using a Direct Solution .... ISUDS
Iterative Self-Organizing Data Analysis Technique A [*Computer science*] .... ISODATA
Iterative Single Isomorphous Replacement [*Crystallography*] .... ISIR
Iterative Single Wavelength Anomalous Scattering [*Crystallography*] .... ISAS
Iterative Target Transformation Factor Analysis [*Computer science*] .... ITTFA
Iterative Time Optimal System .... ITOS
Iterative Weighted Least Squares [*Statistics*] .... IWLS
Itex Corp. [*NASDAQ symbol*] (SAG) .... ITEX
Itex Corp. [*Associated Press*] (SAG) .... ItexCp
Ithaca [*New York*] [*Seismograph station code, US Geological Survey*] (SEIS) .... INY
Ithaca [*New York*] [*Airport symbol*] (OAG) .... ITH
Ithaca [*New York*] [*Seismograph station code, US Geological Survey Closed*] (SEIS) .... ITH
Ithaca College (GAGS) .... Ithaca C
Ithaca College, Ithaca, NY [*Library symbol Library of Congress*] (LCLS) .... NIIC
Ithaca College, Ithaca, NY [*OCLC symbol*] (OCLC) .... XIM
Ithaca, NY [*Location identifier FAA*] (FAAL) .... ITH
Ithaca, NY [*AM radio station call letters*] .... WHCU
Ithaca, NY [*FM radio station call letters*] .... WICB
Ithaca, NY [*FM radio station call letters*] .... WQNY
Ithaca, NY [*FM radio station call letters*] .... WSQG
Ithaca, NY [*AM radio station call letters*] .... WTKO
Ithaca, NY [*FM radio station call letters*] .... WVBR
Ithaca, NY [*FM radio station call letters*] .... WYXL
Ithaca Railroad Association [*Defunct*] (EA) .... IRA
Ithomi [*Greece*] [*Seismograph station code, US Geological Survey*] (SEIS) .... ITM
ITI Technologies [*NASDAQ symbol*] (TTSB) .... ITII
ITI Technologies, Inc. [*Associated Press*] (SAG) .... ITI Tech
ITI Technologies, Inc. [*NASDAQ symbol*] (SAG) .... ITII
Itim Mizrah News Agency. Teleprinter Service (BJA) .... IMTP
Itinerant (FAAC) .... ITNRNT
Itinerant Recruiting Detail .... IRD
Itinerary (AFM) .... ITIN
Itinerary (FAAC) .... ITRY
Itinerating (ROG) .... ITIN
ITL Industries Ltd. [*Toronto Stock Exchange symbol*] .... ITL
Ito [*Zaire*] [*ICAO location identifier*] (ICLI) .... FZCU
Ito [*Japan*] [*Seismograph station code, US Geological Survey Closed*] (SEIS) .... ITO
Ito System Color Television [*Japan*] .... ISCT
Ito Yokado Ltd ADR [*NASDAQ symbol*] (TTSB) .... IYCOY
Itoh [*C.*] **Electronics** [*British*] (NITA) .... CIE
Itokama [*Papua New Guinea*] [*Airport symbol*] (OAG) .... ITK
Itonut Yisrael Meugedet [*ITIM News Agency of the Associated Israel Press Ltd.*] .... ITIM
Ito-Reenstierna [*Reaction*] [*Medicine*] .... I-R
Ito-Yokado Co. Ltd. [*Associated Press*] (SAG) .... ItoYokd
Ito-Yokado Co. Ltd. [*NASDAQ symbol*] (NQ) .... IYCO
Itron, Inc. [*NASDAQ symbol*] (SAG) .... ITRI
Itron, Inc. [*Associated Press*] (SAG) .... Itron
It's Close Enough .... ICE
It's Life, I Can't, I Must [*Element of psychotherapist Joseph Bird's self-help theory*] .... IL-IC-IM
It's That Man Again [*Long-running English radio comedy, 1939-1949*] .... ITMA
ITT [*Institute of Textile Technology*] **Austria** (NITA) .... ITTA
ITT Canada Ltd. [*Toronto Stock Exchange symbol*] .... ITT
ITT [*Institute of Textile Technology*] **Communications and Information Services Inc.** (NITA) .... ITTCOINS
ITT Corporate Communications Services, Inc. .... ITTCCS
ITT Corp. [*Formerly, International Telephone & Telegraph Corp.*] [*Wall Street slang name: "It Girl," the sobriquet for early movie star Clara Bow*] [*NYSE symbol*] (SPSG) .... ITT
ITT Corp. [*Associated Press*] (SAG) .... ITT Corp
ITT Corp. [*Formerly, International Telephone & Telegraph Corp.*] [*Wall Street slang name: "It Girl," the sobriquet for early movie star Clara Bow*] [*Associated Press*] (SAG) .... ITT Cp
ITT Educational Services, Inc. [*NYSE symbol*] (SAG) .... ESI
ITT Educational Services, Inc. [*Associated Press*] (SAG) .... ITT Ed
ITT Educational Svcs [*NYSE symbol*] (TTSB) .... ESI
ITT Employment & Training Systems, Inc. [*Telecommunications service*] (TSSD) .... ITTETS
ITT [*Institute of Textile Technology*] **Gallium Arsenide Technology Cen ter** (NITA) .... ITTGATC
ITT Hartford Group [*NYSE symbol*] (TTSB) .... HIG
ITT Industries [*NYSE symbol*] (TTSB) .... IIN
ITT Industries, Inc. Indiana [*NYSE symbol*] (SAG) .... IIN
ITT Industries, Inc. Indiana [*Associated Press*] (SAG) .... ITT Inds
ITT Rayonier, Inc., Olympic Research Center, Shelton, WA [*Library symbol Library of Congress*] (LCLS) .... WaShIR
ITT [*International Telephone & Telegraph Corp.*] **Secure Ranging and Communications System** .... ISRAC
ITT [*Institute of Textile Technology*] **Testability Analysis Program** (NITA) .... ITTAP
ITT United States Transmission Systems, Inc. [*Telecommunications service*] (TSSD) .... ITT-USTS
Itta Bena, MS [*FM radio station call letters*] .... WVSD
Itumbiara/Hidroelectrica [*Brazil ICAO location identifier*] (ICLI) .... SBIT
Ituzaingo [*Argentina ICAO location identifier*] (ICLI) .... SARO
Itxassou [*France ICAO location identifier*] (ICLI) .... LFIX
Itzehoe Hungriger Wolf [*Germany ICAO location identifier*] (ICLI) .... EDCI
IUBS Commission on Biological Education (AIE) .... IUBS-CBE
IUD Claims Information Source (EA) .... ICIS
IUGG Tsunami Commission (USDC) .... IUGG/TC
Iuka, MS [*FM radio station call letters*] .... WFXO
Iuka, MS [*AM radio station call letters*] .... WVOM
Iuliu Maniu American Romanian Relief Foundation (EA) .... IMF

Iultin [*Former USSR Seismograph station code, US Geological Survey*] (SEIS) .... ILT
IUME/ERIC [*Institute for Urban and Minority Education/Educational Resources Information Center*] **Clearinghouse on Urban Education** [*Columbia University*] [*Research center*] (RCD) .... CUE
Iuppiter Tragoedus [*of Lucian*] [*Classical studies*] (OCD) .... Iupp Trag
IUS [*Interior Upper Stage*] **Assembly Building** [*NASA*] (MCD) .... IAB
IUS Processing Facility [*NASA*] (NASA) .... IPF
Ius Romanum Medii Aevi [*Latin*] .... IRMAE
IVA [*Intravehicular Activity*] **Replacement Unit** (SSD) .... IRU
Ivac [*Intravenous monitor*] [*Medicine*] (DHSM) .... IVA
Ivaco, Inc. [*Toronto Stock Exchange symbol*] .... IVA
Ivaco Industries [*Associated Press*] (SAG) .... IvaxCp
Ivalo [*Finland ICAO location identifier*] (ICLI) .... EFIV
Ivalo [*Finland*] [*Airport symbol*] (OAG) IVL
Ivan Franko Museum & Library, Winnipeg, Manitoba [*Library symbol National Library of Canada*] (NLC) .... MWIF
Ivanhoe Lake Fault Zone [*Geology*] [*Canada*] .... ILFZ
Ivanhoe Public Library, Ivanhoe, MN [*Library symbol*] [*Library of Congress*] (LCLS) .... MnIv
Ivanof Bay, AK [*Location identifier FAA*] (FAAL) .... KIB
IVAX Corp. [*AMEX symbol*] (SAG) IVX
Ivdel [*Former USSR ICAO location identifier*] (ICLI) .... USSI
I've Never Seen One Like That [*Antiques market*] .... INSOLT
Iveco Trucks of North America, Inc. .... ITONA
Iventronics Ltd. [*Toronto Stock Exchange symbol*] .... IVT
Ives Laboratories [*Research code symbol*] IL
Ives on Military Law [*A publication*] (DLA) .... Ives Mil Law
Ivex Packaging Corp. [*Associated Press*] (SAG) .... IvexPkg
Ivex Packaging Corp. [*AMEX symbol*] (SAG) .... IXP
IVF America [*NASDAQ symbol*] (TTSB) .... IVFA
IVF America, Inc. [*Associated Press*] (SAG) .... IVF
IVF America, Inc. [*Associated Press*] (SAG) .... IVF Am
IVF America, Inc. [*NASDAQ symbol*] (SAG) .... IVFA
IVI Publishing [*NASDAQ symbol*] (TTSB) .... IVIP
IVI Publishing, Inc. [*Associated Press*] (SAG) .... IVI Pub
IVI Publishing, Inc. [*NASDAQ symbol*] (SAG) .... IVIP
Ivigtut [*Greenland*] [*ICAO location identifier*] (ICLI) .... BGIT
Ivigtut [*Greenland*] [*Seismograph station code, US Geological Survey Closed*] (SEIS) IVI
Ivinghoe [*England*] .... IVING
Ivishak, AK [*Location identifier FAA*] (FAAL) .... IVH
Ivory (VRA) iv
Ivory and Bone Brushmakers' Trade Protection Society [*A union*] [*British*] .... IBBTPS
Ivory Coast [*ANSI two-letter standard code*] (CNC) CI
Ivory Coast [*ANSI three-letter standard code*] (CNC) CIV
Ivory Coast [*MARC geographic area code Library of Congress*] (LCCP) .... f-iv--
Ivory Coast [*MARC country of publication code Library of Congress*] (LCCP) iv
Ivory Coast (VRA) .... Iv Co
Ivory Coast .... Iv Cst

Ivory Coast Basin [*Geology*] .... ICB
Ivory Coast - Ghana Ridge [*Geology*] .... ICGR
Ivory. Notes on Erskine's Institutes [*A publication*] (ILCA) .... Iv Ersk
Ivory Oil & Minerals [*Vancouver Stock Exchange symbol*] .... IVY
Ivugivik [*Canada*] [*Airport symbol*] (OAG) .... YIK
Ivy League (EA) IL
Ivy Vein Clearing Virus [*Plant pathology*] IVCV
Ivybridge [*England*] .... IVYBR
Iwakuni [*Japan*] [*Airport symbol*] (AD) .... IWA
Iwakuni [*Japan ICAO location identifier*] (ICLI) .... RJOI
IWC Resources Corp. [*Associated Press*] (SAG) .... IWC
IWC Resources Corp. [*NASDAQ symbol*] (NQ) .... IWCR
Iwerks Entertainment [*NASDAQ symbol*] (TTSB) .... IWRK
Iwerks Entertainment, Inc. [*Associated Press*] (SAG) .... Iwerks
Iwerks Entertainment, Inc. [*NASDAQ symbol*] (SAG) .... IWRK
IWI Holding Ltd. [*Associated Press*] (SAG) .... IWI Hold
IWI Holding Ltd. [*NASDAQ symbol*] (SAG) .... JEWLF
Iwo Jima [*Japan ICAO location identifier*] (ICLI) .... RJAW
Ixiamas [*Bolivia*] [*ICAO location identifier*] (ICLI) .... SLIX
Ixora Communications System [*Vancouver Stock Exchange symbol*] IXC
Ixtapalapa [*Mexico*] [*Seismograph station code, US Geological Survey Closed*] (SEIS) .... IXT
Ixtepec [*Mexico*] [*Airport symbol*] (AD) .... IZT
Izaak Walton Killam Hospital for Children, Halifax, Nova Scotia [*Library symbol National Library of Canada*] (NLC) .... NSHKH
Izaak Walton Killam Hospital for Children, Halifax, NS, Canada [*Library symbol Library of Congress*] (LCLS) .... CaNSHKH
Izaak Walton League of America (EA) .... IWLA
Izaak Walton League of America Endowment (EA) .... IWLAE
Izki [*Oman*] [*ICAO location identifier*] (ICLI) .... OOIZ
Izmenyaemaya Geometriya [*Variable Geometry*] [*Suffix letters on Soviet combat aircraft*] .... IG
Izmir [*Turkey*] [*Airport symbol*] (OAG) .... IZM
Izmir [*Turkey*] [*Seismograph station code, US Geological Survey*] (SEIS) .... IZM
Izmir/Cigli [*Turkey ICAO location identifier*] (ICLI) .... LTBL
Izmir [*Turkey*] **Cigli Airport** [*Airport symbol*] (OAG) .... IGL
Izmir/Cumaovasi [*Turkey ICAO location identifier*] (ICLI) .... LTBJ
Izmir/Gaziemir [*Turkey ICAO location identifier*] (ICLI) .... LTBK
Izone International Ltd. [*Vancouver Stock Exchange symbol*] .... IZN
Izozog [*Bolivia*] [*ICAO location identifier*] (ICLI) .... SLIZ
Izquierda Cristiana [*Christian Left*] [*Chile*] [*Political party*] (EY) IC
Izquierda de los Pueblos [*Spain*] [*Political party*] (ECED) .... IP
Izquierda Democratica [*Democratic Left*] [*Ecuador*] [*Political party*] (PPW) .... ID
Izquierda Republicana [*Republican Left*] [*Spain Political party*] (PPE) .... IR
Izquierda Unida [*United Left*] [*Peru*] [*Political party*] .... IU
Izquierda Unida [*United Left*] [*Spain*] [*Political party*] (ECED) .... IU
Izquierda Unida [*United Left*] [*Bolivia*] [*Political party*] (EY) .... IU
Iztepec [*Mexico ICAO location identifier*] (ICLI) .... MMIT
Izuhara [*Japan*] [*Seismograph station code, US Geological Survey*] (SEIS) .... IZU
Izumo [*Japan*] [*Airport symbol*] (OAG) .... IZO
Izumo [*Japan ICAO location identifier*] (ICLI) .... RJOC

J
By Meaning

J A Micropublishing, Inc., Eastchester, NY [*Library symbol Library of Congress*] (LCLS) .... JaM
J. A. Prestwick [*British auto and motorcycle engine maker*] .... JAP
J. A. Turner Professional Library, H. J. A. Brown Education Centre, Mississauga,Ontario [*Library symbol National Library of Canada*] (NLC) .... OMJAT
J & J Air Charters Ltd. [*British ICAO designator*] (FAAC) .... JAY
J & J Snack Foods Corp. [*Associated Press*] (SAG) .... J & J Sn
J & J Snack Foods Corp. [*NASDAQ symbol*] (NQ) .... JJSF
J & L Specialty Steel [*Associated Press*] (SAG) .... J & L SpSt
J & L Specialty Steel [*NYSE symbol*] (SPSG) .... JL
J. Arthur Rank [*Motion picture company in England*] .... JAR
J. C. Bamford Excavators [*British*] .... JCB
J. C. Penney Communications, Inc. [*J. C. Penney Co., Inc.*] [*Telecommunications service*] (TSSD) .... JCPC
J. C. Smith Marketing Corp. [*Vancouver Stock Exchange symbol*] .... JC
J. C. Sproule & Associates Ltd., Calgary, AB, Canada [*Library symbol Library of Congress*] (LCLS) .... CaACS
J. C. Sproule & Associates Ltd., Calgary, Alberta [*Library symbol National Library of Canada*] (NLC) .... ACS
J. F. Kennedy Consolidated Community School District 129, Cedar Point, IL [*Library symbol Library of Congress*] (LCLS) .... ICpKSD
J. F. Macfarlan & Co. [*Scotland*] [*Research code symbol*] .... M
J. Fred Sparke Elementary School, Levittown, NY [*Library symbol*] [*Library of Congress*] (LCLS) .... NLevJSE
J. H. Morgan Consultants [*Morristown, NJ*] [*Information service or system Telecommunications*] (TSSD) .... JHMCO
J. Inglis Wright [*Advertising agency*] [*New Zealand*] .... JIW
J. J. Hands Library, Lohrville, IA [*Library symbol Library of Congress*] (LCLS) .... IaLohr
J. L. Richard & Associates Ltd., Ottawa, Ontario [*Library symbol National Library of Canada*] (NLC) .... OORIA
J. Lewis Ames Junior High School, Massapequa, NY [*Library symbol*] [*Library of Congress*] (LCLS) .... NMassAJ
J. Lewis Crozer [*Chester Public*] Library, Chester, PA [*Library symbol Library of Congress*] (LCLS) .... PC
J. N. Adam Developmental Center, Perrysburg, NY [*Library symbol Library of Congress*] (LCLS) .... NPerbA
J. P. Morgan Securities .... JPMS
J. Paul Getty Center, Arts Archives, Santa Monica, CA [*Library symbol*] [*Library of Congress*] (LCLS) .... CMalG-A
J. Paul Getty Center, Conservation Institute, Santa Monica, CA [*Library symbol*] [*Library of Congress*] (LCLS) .... CMalG-CI
J. Paul Getty Center for the History of Art & the Humanities, Vocabulary Coordination Group, Santa Monica, CA [*Library symbol*] [*Library of Congress*] (LCLS) .... CMalG-V
J. Paul Getty Center for the History of Arts and the Humanities, Photo Archives,Santa Monica, CA [*Library symbol*] [*Library of Congress*] (LCLS) .... CMalG-P
J. Paul Getty Museum, Malibu, CA [*Library symbol Library of Congress*] (LCLS) .... CMalG
J. S. Canner & Co., Boston, MA [*Library symbol Library of Congress*] (LCLS) .... Mcan
J. S. Woodsworth Secondary School, Nepean, Ontario [*Library symbol National Library of Canada*] (NLC) .... ONJSW
J. Sargeant Reynolds Community College, Downtown Campus, Richmond, VA [*Library symbol Library of Congress*] (LCLS) .... ViRRC
J. V. Fletcher Library, Westford, MA [*Library symbol Library of Congress*] (LCLS) .... MWfo
J. William Horsey Library, Ontario Bible College, Ontario Theological College, Willowdale, Ontario [*Library symbol National Library of Canada*] (NLC) .... OWOBC
J2 Communications [*NASDAQ symbol*] (TTSB) .... JTWO
J2 Communications Wrrt'A' [*NASDAQ symbol*] (TTSB) .... JTWOW
J.A. Hughes Elementary School, Red Lake Falls, MN [*Library symbol*] [*Library of Congress*] (LCLS) .... MnRlfHE
Ja Niin Edespain [*And So On*] [*Finnish*] .... JNE
Jaakko Poyry, Inc., Raleigh, NC [*Library symbol*] [*Library of Congress*] (LCLS) .... NcRJP
Jaarboek [*Yearbook*] [*Netherlands*] (BJA) .... Jb
Jabalpur [*India*] [*Airport symbol*] (OAG) .... JLR
Jabalpur [*India*] [*ICAO location identifier*] (ICLI) .... VAJB
Jabara Award for Airmanship [*Military decoration*] .... JAAA
Jabat [*Marshall Islands*] [*Airport symbol*] (OAG) .... JAT
Jabil Circuit [*NASDAQ symbol*] (TTSB) .... JBIL
Jabil Circuit, Inc. [*Associated Press*] (SAG) .... Jabil

Jabil Circuit, Inc. [*NASDAQ symbol*] (SAG) .... JBIL
Jabul Saraj [*Afghanistan*] [*ICAO location identifier*] (ICAO) ...... OAJS
Jacare-Acanga [*Brazil ICAO location identifier*] (ICLI) .... SBEK
Jachal [*Argentina ICAO location identifier*] (ICLI) .... SAMJ
Jack [*In card game*] .... J
Jack [*Technical drawings*] .... J
Jack (MSA) .... JK
Jack Adapter .... JA
Jack and Jill of America (EA) .... JJA
Jack and Jill of America Foundation (EA) .... JJAF
Jack Carl 312 Futures [*NASDAQ symbol*] (SAG) .... FUTR
Jack Carl 312 Futures Inc. [*NASDAQ symbol*] (TTSB) .... FUTR
Jack Carl/312 Futures, Inc. [*Associated Press*] (SAG) .... JCarlFut
Jack Connection [*Electronics*] (IAA) .... JC
Jack Cover .... JC
Jack Criswell Resources [*Vancouver Stock Exchange symbol*] .... JCR
Jack Daniels [*A brand name of whiskey*] .... JD
Jack Field .... JF
Jack Jones Music Appreciation Society [*Defunct*] (EAIO) .... JJMAS
Jack Knight Air Mail Society (EA) .... JKMS
Jack Knight Airmail Society (EA) .... JKAS
Jack L. Ahr [*Designer's mark on US bicentennial quarter*] .... JLA
Jack London Research Center (EA) .... JLRC
Jack Lynn Memorial Museum, Horsefly, British Columbia [*Library symbol National Library of Canada*] (NLC) .... BHJL
Jack Morton Productions, Inc. [*New York, NY*] [*Telecommunications*] (TSSD) .... JMP
Jack O'Dwyer's Newsletter [*A publication*] [*New York, NY*] (WDMC) ...... O'Dwyer
Jack Panel .... JP
Jack Panel Assembly .... JPA
Jack Patch Cord .... JPC
Jack Point Preservation Society (EA) .... JPPS
Jack Russell Terrier Club of America (EA) .... JRTCA
Jack Scalia Fan Club (EA) .... JSFC
Jack Screw .... JS
Jackal (ABBR) .... JKL
Jackass (ABBR) .... JKAS
Jackboot (ABBR) .... JKBT
Jacked (ABBR) .... JKD
Jacket (ROG) .... JCT
Jacket (ABBR) .... JKET
Jacket (KSC) .... JKT
Jacket Card [*A printed card inside the box holding a cassette tape or compact disc*] (WDMC) .... J card
Jacket Decladding Waste (PDAA) .... JDW
Jacket Water .... JW
Jacketed (ABBR) .... JKTD
Jacketed Hollow-Point [*Ammunition*] .... JHP
Jacketed Soft-Point [*Ammunition*] .... JSP
Jacketing (ABBR) .... JKTG
Jacketted (ABBR) .... JKETD
Jackhammer (ABBR) .... JKMR
Jackie Robinson Foundation (EA) .... JRF
Jacking (ABBR) .... JKG
Jack-in-the-Box Dummy [*CIA*] .... JIB
Jackknife (ABBR) .... JKNIF
Jackpot (ABBR) .... JKPT
Jackpot Enterprises [*NYSE symbol*] (TTSB) .... Jackpt
Jackpot Enterprises [*Associated Press*] (SAG) .... Jackpt
Jackpot Enterprises [*NASDAQ symbol*] (SAG) .... JKPT
Jackpot Enterprises, Inc. [*NYSE symbol*] (CTT) .... J
Jackpot Enterprises, Inc. [*Associated Press*] (SAG) .... Jackpot
Jackpot Enterprises Wrrt [*NASDAQ symbol*] (TTSB) .... JKPTW
Jacks (ABBR) .... JKS
Jacks Creek, TN [*Location identifier FAA*] (FAAL) .... JKS
Jacksboro, TN [*Location identifier FAA*] (FAAL) .... JAU
Jacksboro, TX [*FM radio station call letters*] (RBYB) .... KAIH
Jacksboro, TX [*FM radio station call letters*] (RBYB) .... KJKB-FM
Jackscrew [*Mechanical engineering*] .... JKSCR
Jackson [*Wyoming*] [*Airport symbol*] (OAG) .... JAC
Jackson [*Mississippi*] [*Airport symbol*] (OAG) .... JAN
Jackson [*Diocesan abbreviation*] [*Mississippi*] (TOCD) .... JKS
Jackson [*Michigan*] [*Airport symbol*] (AD) .... JNX
Jackson [*Michigan*] [*Airport symbol*] (OAG) .... JXN
Jackson [*Tennessee*] [*Airport symbol*] (OAG) .... MKL
Jackson Air Services Ltd. [*Canada ICAO designator*] (FAAC) .... JCK

Jackson, AL [*AM radio station call letters*] ... WHOD
Jackson, AL [*FM radio station call letters*] ... WHOD-FM
Jackson/Allen C. Thompson Field [*Mississippi*] [*ICAO location identifier*] (ICLI) ... KJAN
Jackson and Gross' Treatise on the Law of Landlord and Tenant in Pennsylvania [*A publication*] (DLA) ... Jack & G Landl & Ten
Jackson and Lumpkin's Reports [*59-64 Georgia*] [*A publication*] (DLA) ... Jack & L
Jackson and Lumpkin's Reports [*59-64 Georgia*] [*A publication*] (DLA) ... Jackson & Lumpkin
Jackson & Moreland, Inc. (MCD) ... JMI
Jackson Avenue Elementary School, Mineola, NY [*Library symbol Library of Congress*] (LCLS) ... NMinJE
Jackson, CA [*FM radio station call letters*] ... KNGT
Jackson Clinic, Madison, WI [*Library symbol Library of Congress*] (LCLS) ... WMaJ
Jackson Community College, Jackson, MI [*Library symbol Library of Congress*] (LCLS) ... MiJaCc
Jackson County Historical Society, Brownstown, IN [*Library symbol Library of Congress*] (LCLS) ... InBrtHi
Jackson County Historical Society, Maquoketa, IA [*Library symbol Library of Congress*] (LCLS) ... IaMaqHi
Jackson County Library, Jackson, MI [*Library symbol Library of Congress*] (LCLS) ... MiJaC
Jackson County Library System, Jackson, MN [*Library symbol*] [*Library of Congress*] (LCLS) ... MnJ
Jackson County Library System, Medford, OR [*OCLC symbol*] (OCLC) ... JCL
Jackson County Library System, Medford, OR [*Library symbol Library of Congress*] (LCLS) ... OrMeJ
Jackson County Medical Society, Kansas City, MO [*Library symbol Library of Congress*] (LCLS) ... MoKJ
Jackson County - Pascagoula City Library, Pascagoula, MS [*Library symbol Library of Congress*] (LCLS) ... MsP
Jackson County Public Hospital, Kansas City, MO [*Library symbol Library of Congress*] (LCLS) ... MoKCoH
Jackson County Public Library, Marianna, FL [*Library symbol Library of Congress*] (LCLS) ... FMaJ
Jackson County Public Library, Sylva, NC [*Library symbol Library of Congress*] (LCLS) ... NcSy
Jackson County Public Library, Walden, CO [*Library symbol Library of Congress*] (LCLS) ... CoW
Jackson Elementary School, Hempstead, NY [*Library symbol*] [*Library of Congress*] (LCLS) ... NHemJE
Jackson Elementary School, Jackson, MN [*Library symbol*] [*Library of Congress*] (LCLS) ... MnJES
Jackson Elementary School, Rockford, IL [*Library symbol*] [*Library of Congress*] (LCLS) ... IRoJaE
Jackson Estuarine Laboratory [*University of New Hampshire*] [*Research center*] (RCD) ... JEL
Jackson, GA [*FM radio station call letters*] ... WJGA
Jackson Hewitt [*Associated Press*] (SAG) ... JackHwt
Jackson Hewitt [*NASDAQ symbol*] (SAG) ... JTAX
Jackson Hole Preserve (EA) ... JHP
Jackson Intermediate School, Pasadena, TX [*Library symbol*] [*Library of Congress*] (LCLS) ... TxPJI
Jackson Junior College [*Florida; Michigan*] ... JJC
Jackson, KY [*Location identifier FAA*] (FAAL) ... JKL
Jackson, KY [*AM radio station call letters*] ... WEKG
Jackson, KY [*FM radio station call letters*] ... WJSN
Jackson, LA [*FM radio station call letters*] (RBYB) ... WBJJ-FM
Jackson Laboratory, Bar Harbor, ME [*Library symbol Library of Congress*] (LCLS) ... MeBarhJ
Jackson Metropolitan Library System, Jackson, MS [*OCLC symbol*] (OCLC) ... MJP
Jackson, MI [*FM radio station call letters*] (RBYB) ... WBHR
Jackson, MI [*FM radio station call letters*] ... WIBM
Jackson, MI [*AM radio station call letters*] (RBYB) ... WJKN
Jackson, MI [*FM radio station call letters*] ... WJXQ
Jackson, MI [*AM radio station call letters*] ... WKHM
Jackson, MN [*AM radio station call letters*] ... KKOJ
Jackson, MN [*FM radio station call letters*] ... KRAQ
Jackson, MN [*Location identifier FAA*] (FAAL) ... MJQ
Jackson, MO [*AM radio station call letters*] ... KUGT
Jackson, MS [*Location identifier FAA*] (FAAL) ... FRL
Jackson, MS [*Location identifier FAA*] (FAAL) ... HKS
Jackson, MS [*Location identifier FAA*] (FAAL) ... JAN
Jackson, MS [*Location identifier FAA*] (FAAL) ... JHF
Jackson, MS [*Television station call letters*] ... WAPT
Jackson, MS [*Television station call letters*] ... WDBD
Jackson, MS [*AM radio station call letters*] ... WJDS
Jackson, MS [*FM radio station call letters*] ... WJDX
Jackson, MS [*FM radio station call letters*] ... WJMI
Jackson, MS [*FM radio station call letters*] ... WJSU
Jackson, MS [*Television station call letters*] ... WJTV
Jackson, MS [*AM radio station call letters*] ... WJXN
Jackson, MS [*FM radio station call letters*] ... WKTF
Jackson, MS [*AM radio station call letters*] ... WKXI
Jackson, MS [*Television station call letters*] ... WLBT
Jackson, MS [*FM radio station call letters*] ... WMPN
Jackson, MS [*Television station call letters*] ... WMPN-TV
Jackson, MS [*FM radio station call letters*] ... WMPR
Jackson, MS [*FM radio station call letters*] ... WMSI
Jackson, MS [*AM radio station call letters*] ... WOAD
Jackson, MS [*AM radio station call letters*] ... WSLI
Jackson, MS [*FM radio station call letters*] ... WTYX
Jackson, MS [*AM radio station call letters*] ... WZRX
Jackson Municipal Library, Jackson, MS [*Library symbol Library of Congress*] (LCLS) ... MsJ
Jackson News, Jackson, NJ [*Library symbol Library of Congress*] (LCLS) ... NjJacN
Jackson, NH [*FM radio station call letters*] ... WZJN
Jackson, OH [*FM radio station call letters*] ... WCJO
Jackson on Pleadings [*1933*] [*A publication*] (DLA) ... Jack Pl
Jackson Parish Library, Jonesboro, LA [*Library symbol Library of Congress*] (LCLS) ... LJo
Jackson Personality Inventory [*Personality development test*] [*Psychology*] ... JPI
Jackson Public Library, Jackson, MI [*Library symbol Library of Congress*] (LCLS) ... MiJa
Jackson Public Library, Jackson, OH [*Library symbol Library of Congress*] (LCLS) ... OJ
Jackson Public Schools, Jackson, MN [*Library symbol*] [*Library of Congress*] (LCLS) ... MnJPS
Jackson Resources Ltd. [*Vancouver Stock Exchange symbol*] ... JSR
Jackson Sentinel, Maquoketa, IA [*Library symbol Library of Congress*] (LCLS) ... IaMaqS
Jackson State College [*Later, Jackson State University*] [*Mississippi*] ... JSC
Jackson State College [*Later, Jackson State University*], Jackson, MS [*Library symbol Library of Congress*] (LCLS) ... MsJS
Jackson State Community College, Jackson, TN [*Library symbol*] [*Library of Congress*] (LCLS) ... TJaC
Jackson State University (GAGS) ... Jackson St U
Jackson State University, Jackson, MS [*OCLC symbol*] (OCLC) ... MJU
Jackson Structured Programming [*Program design tool*] (NITA) ... JSP
Jackson System Development [*Systems development methodology*] (NITA) ... JSD
Jackson, TN [*Location identifier FAA*] (FAAL) ... MKL
Jackson, TN [*FM radio station call letters*] (RBYB) ... WAMP
Jackson, TN [*Television station call letters*] ... WBBJ
Jackson, TN [*AM radio station call letters*] ... WDXI
Jackson, TN [*AM radio station call letters*] (RBYB) ... WJAK-AM
Jackson, TN [*FM radio station call letters*] ... WKNP
Jackson, TN [*Television station call letters*] ... WMTU
Jackson, TN [*FM radio station call letters*] ... WMXX
Jackson, TN [*FM radio station call letters*] ... WNWS
Jackson, TN [*AM radio station call letters*] ... WQCR
Jackson, TN [*AM radio station call letters*] ... WTJS
Jackson, TN [*FM radio station call letters*] ... WTNV
Jackson Township, PA [*FM radio station call letters*] ... WRTY
Jackson Township Publishing Co., Jackson, NJ [*Library symbol Library of Congress*] (LCLS) ... NjJacP
Jackson Turbidity Unit [*Water pollution*] ... JTU
Jackson Vocational Interest Survey [*Vocational guidance test*] ... JVIS
Jackson, WI [*AM radio station call letters*] (RBYB) ... WZER
Jackson, WY [*Location identifier FAA*] (FAAL) ... JAC
Jackson, WY [*Television station call letters*] ... KJVI
Jackson, WY [*TV station call letters*] (RBYB) ... KJWY-TV
Jackson, WY [*FM radio station call letters*] ... KMTN
Jackson, WY [*AM radio station call letters*] ... KSGT
Jackson, WY [*FM radio station call letters*] ... KUWJ
Jackson, WY [*FM radio station call letters*] ... KZJH
Jackson-Madison County General Hospital, Learning Center, Jackson, TN [*Library symbol Library of Congress*] (LCLS) ... TJaGH
Jackson-Pratt [*Drain*] [*Surgery*] (DAVI) ... JP
Jackson's Index to the Georgia Reports [*A publication*] (DLA) ... Jack Geo Ind
Jackson's Reports [*A publication*] (DLA) ... Jack Tex App
Jackson's Reports [*1-29 Texas Court of Appeals*] [*A publication*] (DLA) ... Jackson
Jackson's Reports [*46-58 Georgia*] [*A publication*] (DLA) ... Jackson
Jacksonville [*Florida*] [*Seismograph station code, US Geological Survey Closed*] (SEIS) ... JAC
Jacksonville [*Illinois*] [*Airport symbol*] (AD) ... JAE
Jacksonville [*Florida*] [*Airport symbol*] (OAG) ... JAX
Jacksonville [*North Carolina*] [*Airport symbol*] (OAG) ... OAJ
Jacksonville, AL [*AM radio station call letters*] (RBYB) ... WJXL
Jacksonville, AL [*FM radio station call letters*] ... WLJS
Jacksonville, AL [*AM radio station call letters*] (RBYB) ... WNSI-AM
Jacksonville, AR [*FM radio station call letters*] ... KDDK
Jacksonville, AR [*Location identifier FAA*] (FAAL) ... LRF
Jacksonville Bancorp, Inc. [*Associated Press*] (SAG) ... Jksnvll
Jacksonville Bancorp, Inc. [*NASDAQ symbol*] (SAG) ... JXVL
Jacksonville Beach, FL [*AM radio station call letters*] ... WXTL
Jacksonville College, Jacksonville, TX [*Library symbol Library of Congress*] (LCLS) ... TxJaC
Jacksonville, FL [*Location identifier FAA*] (FAAL) ... CRG
Jacksonville, FL [*Location identifier FAA*] (FAAL) ... CZH
Jacksonville, FL [*Location identifier FAA*] (FAAL) ... HEG
Jacksonville, FL [*Location identifier FAA*] (FAAL) ... NFF
Jacksonville, FL [*Location identifier FAA*] (FAAL) ... NHI
Jacksonville, FL [*Location identifier FAA*] (FAAL) ... NIP
Jacksonville, FL [*Location identifier FAA*] (FAAL) ... NZC
Jacksonville, FL [*Location identifier FAA*] (FAAL) ... PEK
Jacksonville, FL [*Location identifier FAA*] (FAAL) ... RRW
Jacksonville, FL [*FM radio station call letters*] ... WAPE
Jacksonville, FL [*Television station call letters*] ... WAWS
Jacksonville, FL [*AM radio station call letters*] ... WCGL
Jacksonville, FL [*AM radio station call letters*] ... WCRJ
Jacksonville, FL [*FM radio station call letters*] ... WEJZ
Jacksonville, FL [*FM radio station call letters*] ... WIVY
Jacksonville, FL [*AM radio station call letters*] ... WJAX
Jacksonville, FL [*FM radio station call letters*] ... WJCT
Jacksonville, FL [*Television station call letters*] ... WJCT-TV
Jacksonville, FL [*Television station call letters*] ... WJEB
Jacksonville, FL [*FM radio station call letters*] ... WJFR
Jacksonville, FL [*AM radio station call letters*] ... WJGR

Jacksonville, FL [*Television station call letters*] .... WJKS
Jacksonville, FL [*Television station call letters*] .... WJXT
Jacksonville, FL [*FM radio station call letters*] .... WKQL
Jacksonville, FL [*FM radio station call letters*] .... WKTZ
Jacksonville, FL [*FM radio station call letters*] .... WNCM
Jacksonville, FL [*Television station call letters*] .... WNFT
Jacksonville, FL [*AM radio station call letters*] .... WNZS
Jacksonville, FL [*AM radio station call letters*] (RBYB) .... WOBS-AM
Jacksonville, FL [*AM radio station call letters*] .... WOKV
Jacksonville, FL [*AM radio station call letters*] .... WPDQ
Jacksonville, FL [*AM radio station call letters*] .... WQIK
Jacksonville, FL [*FM radio station call letters*] .... WROO
Jacksonville, FL [*AM radio station call letters*] .... WROS
Jacksonville, FL [*AM radio station call letters*] .... WSVE
Jacksonville, FL [*TV station call letters*] (RBYB) .... WTEV-TV
Jacksonville, FL [*Television station call letters*] .... WTLV
Jacksonville, FL [*AM radio station call letters*] .... WVOJ
Jacksonville, FL [*AM radio station call letters*] .... WZAZ
Jacksonville, FL [*AM radio station call letters*] .... WZNZ
Jacksonville, FL [*Location identifier FAA*] (FAAL) .... ZJX
Jacksonville Hillard [*Florida*] [*ICAO location identifier*] (ICLI) .... KZJX
Jacksonville, IL [*Location identifier FAA*] (FAAL) .... IJX
Jacksonville, IL [*AM radio station call letters*] .... WJIL
Jacksonville, IL [*AM radio station call letters*] .... WLDS
Jacksonville, IL [*Television station call letters*] .... WSEC
Jacksonville, IL [*FM radio station call letters*] .... WYMG
Jacksonville/International [*Florida*] [*ICAO location identifier*] (ICLI) .... KJAX
Jacksonville/Jacksonville Naval Air Station [*Florida*] [*ICAO location identifier*] (ICLI) .... KNIP
Jacksonville/Little Rock Air Force Base [*Arkansas*] [*ICAO location identifier*] (ICLI) .... KLRF
Jacksonville Museum, Jacksonville, OR [*Library symbol Library of Congress*] (LCLS) .... OrJM
Jacksonville, NC [*Location identifier FAA*] (FAAL) .... HAH
Jacksonville, NC [*Location identifier FAA*] (FAAL) .... NCA
Jacksonville, NC [*Location identifier FAA*] (FAAL) .... NTL
Jacksonville, NC [*Location identifier FAA*] (FAAL) .... OAJ
Jacksonville, NC [*TV station call letters*] (RBYB) .... WFXZ-TV
Jacksonville, NC [*AM radio station call letters*] .... WJCV
Jacksonville, NC [*AM radio station call letters*] .... WJNC
Jacksonville, NC [*FM radio station call letters*] .... WKOO
Jacksonville, NC [*AM radio station call letters*] .... WLAS
Jacksonville, NC [*FM radio station call letters*] .... WQSL
Jacksonville, NC [*Television station call letters*] .... WUNM
Jacksonville, NC [*FM radio station call letters*] .... WXQR
Jacksonville/New River Marine Corps Air Station [*North Carolina*] [*ICAO location identifier*] (ICLI) .... KNCA
Jacksonville Public Library, Jacksonville, IL [*Library symbol Library of Congress*] (LCLS) .... IJ
Jacksonville Public Library System, Jacksonville, FL [*Library symbol Library of Congress*] (LCLS) .... FJ
Jacksonville Public Library System, Jacksonville, FL [*OCLC symbol*] (OCLC) .... JPL
Jacksonville Savings & Loan Association [*Texas*] [*Associated Press*] (SAG) .... JksnvlSL
Jacksonville Savings & Loan Association [*Texas*] [*NASDAQ symbol*] (SAG) .... JXVL
Jacksonville Savings Bank (Illinois) [*Associated Press*] (SAG) .... JksnvSB
Jacksonville Savings Bank (Illinois) [*NASDAQ symbol*] (SAG) .... JXSB
Jacksonville State University (GAGS) .... Jacksonville St U
Jacksonville State University [*Jacksonville, AL*] .... JSU
Jacksonville State University, Jacksonville, AL [*Library symbol Library of Congress*] (LCLS) .... AJacT
Jacksonville State University, Jacksonville, AL [*OCLC symbol*] (OCLC) .... AJB
Jacksonville Terminal Co. [*AAR code*] .... JTCO
Jacksonville, TX [*Location identifier FAA*] (FAAL) .... JSO
Jacksonville, TX [*FM radio station call letters*] .... KBJS
Jacksonville, TX [*AM radio station call letters*] .... KEBE
Jacksonville, TX [*Television station call letters*] .... KETK
Jacksonville, TX [*FM radio station call letters*] .... KOOI
Jacksonville, TX [*FM radio station call letters*] .... KSIZ
Jacksonville University (GAGS) .... Jacksonville U
Jacksonville University, Jacksonville, FL [*Library symbol Library of Congress OCLC symbol*] (LCLS) .... FJU
Jackson-Washabaugh County Library, Kadoka, SD [*Library symbol Library of Congress*] (LCLS) .... SdKJ
Jackstone Froster Ltd. [*Commercial firm British*] .... JF
Jacky Ward Fan Club [*Defunct*] (EA) .... JWFC
Jaclyn, Inc. [*Associated Press*] (SAG) .... Jaclyn
Jaclyn, Inc. [*AMEX symbol*] (SPSG) .... JLN
Jacmel [*Haiti*] [*ICAO location identifier*] (ICLI) .... MTJA
Jaco Electronics [*NASDAQ symbol*] (TTSB) .... JACO
Jaco Electronics, Inc. [*NASDAQ symbol*] (NQ) .... JACO
Jaco Electronics, Inc. [*Associated Press*] (SAG) .... JacoEl
Jaco Electronics, Inc. [*Associated Press*] (SAG) .... JacoElec
Jacob and Walker's English Chancery Reports [*A publication*] (DLA) .... J & W
Jacob and Walker's English Chancery Reports [*37 English Reprint*] [*A publication*] (DLA) .... Jac & W
Jacob and Walker's English Chancery Reports [*37 English Reprint*] [*A publication*] (DLA) .... Jac & W (Eng)
Jacob and Walker's English Chancery Reports [*37 English Reprint*] [*A publication*] (DLA) .... Jac & Walk
Jacob Blaustein Institute for the Advancement of Human Rights (EA) .... JBI
Jacob Gold Corp. [*Vancouver Stock Exchange symbol*] .... JGC
Jacob More Society (EA) .... JMS
Jacob S. Mauney Memorial Library, Kings Mountain, NC [*Library symbol Library of Congress*] (LCLS) .... NcKm
Jacob Sheep Society [*British*] (DBA) .... JSS
Jacob Simpson Payton Library, Alexandria, VA [*Library symbol Library of Congress*] (LCLS) .... ViAlP
Jacobabad [*Pakistan*] [*ICAO location identifier*] (ICLI) .... OPJA
Jacobabad [*Pakistan*] [*ICAO location identifier*] (ICLI) .... OPJC
Jacobean (WDAA) .... JAC
Jacobean (VRA) .... Jacbn
Jacobeian Determinant (ROG) .... J
Jacobi Elliptic Function [*Mathematics*] .... JEF
Jacobi Matrix Method [*Mathematics*] .... JMM
Jacobi Polynomial [*Mathematics*] .... JP
Jacobina [*Brazil*] [*Airport symbol*] (OAG) .... JCM
Jacob's American Edition of Fisher's English Digest [*A publication*] (DLA) .... Jac Fish Dig
Jacobs Engineering Group, Inc. [*Associated Press*] (SAG) .... Jacobs
Jacobs Engineering Group, Inc. [*NYSE symbol*] (SPSG) .... JEC
Jacob's English Chancery Reports [*1821-22*] [*A publication*] (DLA) .... Jac
Jacob's English Chancery Reports [*1821-22*] [*A publication*] (DLA) .... Jacob
Jacobs Engr Group [*NYSE symbol*] (TTSB) .... JEC
Jacob's Horse [*British military*] (DMA) .... JH
Jacobs [*Jay*], **Inc.** (MHDW) .... JAYT
Jacob's Introduction to the Common, Civil, and Canon Law [*A publication*] (DLA) .... Jac Int
Jacob's Law Dictionary [*A publication*] (DLA) .... Jac
Jacob's Law Dictionary [*A publication*] (DLA) .... Jac Dict
Jacob's Law Dictionary [*A publication*] (DLA) .... Jac L Dict
Jacob's Law Dictionary [*A publication*] (DLA) .... Jac Law Dict
Jacob's Law Dictionary [*A publication*] (DLA) .... Jac LD
Jacob's Law Dictionary [*A publication*] (DLA) .... Jacob
Jacob's Law Grammar [*A publication*] (DLA) .... Jac LG
Jacob's Lex Mercatoria [*A publication*] (DLA) .... Jac Lex Mer
Jacobs Library, Clinton, SC [*Library symbol Library of Congress Obsolete*] (LCLS) .... ScCliJ
Jacob's Prevocational Skills Assessment .... JPSA
Jacobsen's Law of the Sea [*A publication*] (DLA) .... Jac Sea Laws
Jacobson Stores, Inc. [*Associated Press*] (SAG) .... Jacbsn
Jacobson Stores, Inc. [*NASDAQ symbol*] (NQ) .... JCBS
Jacobus [*James*] [*King of England*] (DLA) .... Jac
Jacobus Balduini [*Deceased, 1235*] [*Authority cited in pre-1607 legal work*] (DSA) .... Ja
Jacobus Balduini [*Deceased, 1235*] [*Authority cited in pre-1607 legal work*] (DSA) .... Jac
Jacobus de Albenga [*Flourished, 13th century*] [*Authority cited in pre-1607 legal work*] (DSA) .... Ja
Jacobus de Ardizone [*Flourished, 1213-50*] [*Authority cited in pre-1607 legal work*] (DSA) .... Jacob Ardiz
Jacobus de Arena [*Deceased, 1297*] [*Authority cited in pre-1607 legal work*] (DSA) .... Ja Are
Jacobus de Porta Ravennate [*Deceased, 1178*] [*Authority cited in pre-1607 legal work*] (DSA) .... J
Jacobus de Porta Ravennate [*Deceased, 1178*] [*Authority cited in pre-1607 legal work*] (DSA) .... Jus
Jacobus de Ravanis [*Deceased, 1296*] [*Authority cited in pre-1607 legal work*] (DSA) .... Ja
Jacobus Guaraguilia [*Authority cited in pre-1607 legal work*] (DSA) .... Ja Guara
Jacobus Rex [*King James*] .... JR
Jacor Communications [*NASDAQ symbol*] (TTSB) .... JCOR
Jacor Communications, Inc. [*Associated Press*] (SAG) .... JacorC
Jacor Communications, Inc. [*Associated Press*] (SAG) .... JacorCm
Jacor Communications, Inc. [*Associated Press*] (SAG) .... JacrCm
Jacor Communications, Inc. [*NASDAQ symbol*] (NQ) .... JCOR
Jacor Communications Wrrt [*NASDAQ symbol*] (TTSB) .... JCORW
Jacqueline Gold [*Vancouver Stock Exchange symbol*] .... JCQ
Jacques Timothe Boucher Sieur de Montbrun Heritage Society (EA) .... JTBSMHS
Jacques-Yves Cousteau [*French marine explorer*] [*Initialism pronounced "Jheek" when used as nickname*] .... JYC
Jacquinot Bay [*Papua New Guinea*] [*Airport symbol*] (OAG) .... JAQ
Jactitation of Marriage [*Legal*] [*British*] (ROG) .... JM
Jadassohn-Lewandowsky [*Syndrome*] [*Thickening of the nails*] [*Medicine*] (DAVI) .... JL
Jade (VRA) .... ja
Jadeite (VRA) .... jadt
Jaegdtiger [*Tank-destroyer*] [*German military - World War II*] .... JAEG
Jaeger Test Type One [*Ophthalmology*] J-1
Jaeger's Cases and Statutes on Labor Law [*A publication*] (DLA) .... Jaeger Labor Law
Jaffa [*Israel*] [*Airport symbol*] (AD) .... JFA
Jaffe-Lichtenstein [*Syndrome*] [*or Fibrous dysplasia Orthopedics*] (DAVI) .... JL
Jaffna [*Ceylon*] [*Airport symbol*] (AD) .... JAF
Jaffna/Kankesanturai [*Sri Lanka*] [*ICAO location identifier*] (ICLI) .... VCCJ
Jaffrey, NH [*Location identifier FAA*] (FAAL) .... AFN
JAG Listing [*Military*] .... JL
Jagdverband [*German aircraft fighter unit*] [*World War II*] .... JV
Jagersfontein [*South Africa*] [*ICAO location identifier*] (ICLI) .... FAJF
Jaggard on Torts [*A publication*] (DLA) .... Jagg Torts
Jaguar [*Automobile*] .... JAG
Jaguar Clubs of North America (EA) .... JCNA
Jaguar Diagnostic System [*Automotive engineering*] .... JDS
Jaguar Equity, Inc. [*Vancouver Stock Exchange symbol*] .... JGE
Jaguar PLC (MHDW) .... JAGRY
Jaguar-Daimler Heritage Trust Collection .... JDHTC
Jaguar-Rover-Triumph .... JRT

Jahrbuch [*Yearbook*] [*German*] ... JB
Jahrbuch fuer Internationales und Auslaendisches Oeffentliches Recht [*1948-*] [*A publication German*] (ILCA) ... Jb Int R
Jahrbucher fuer Classische Philologie. Supplementband [*A publication*] (OCD) ... Jahrb f Cl Phil Suppl
Jahresbericht [*Journal, Annual Report*] [*German*] (BJA) ... Jber
Jahresberichte ueber die Fortschritte der Altertumswissenschaft [*1873-*] [*A publication*] (OCD) ... Jahresb
Jahreshefte des Oesterreichischen Archaeologischen Instituts in Wien [*A publication*] (OCD) ... JO AI
Jahresverzeichnis der Deutschen Hochschulschriften [*A bibliographic publication*] [*Germany*] ... JVDHS
Jahrgang [*Year of Publication/Volume*] [*German*] ... JG
Jahrom [*Iran*] [*ICAO location identifier*] (ICLI) ... OISJ
JAI Press [*Division of Johnson Associates, Inc.*] ... JAI
Jaicos [*Brazil*] [*Airport symbol*] (AD) ... JCS
Jail Accounting Microcomputer System ... JAM
Jail Release Information ... JRI
Jailbird (ABBR) ... JLBD
Jailbreak (ABBR) ... JLBRK
Jailer (ABBR) ... JLR
Jailer ... JLR
Jailolo/Kuripasai [*Indonesia*] [*ICAO location identifier*] (ICLI) ... WAMD
Jainamosa [*Dominican Republic*] [*ICAO location identifier*] (ICLI) ... MDJM
Jaipur [*India*] [*Airport symbol*] (OAG) ... JAI
Jaipur [*India*] [*Geomagnetic observatory code*] ... JAI
Jaipur [*India*] [*ICAO location identifier*] (ICLI) ... VIJP
Jaipur Law Journal [*India*] [*A publication*] (DLA) ... Jaipur LJ
Jaiselmer [*India*] [*ICAO location identifier*] (ICLI) ... VIJR
Jakalapaa [*Finland ICAO location identifier*] (ICLI) ... EFJP
Jakarta [*Indonesia*] [*Airport symbol*] (OAG) ... HLP
Jakarta [*Indonesia*] (ABBR) ... JKA
Jakarta [*Indonesia*] [*Airport symbol*] (OAG) ... JKT
Jakarta [*Indonesia*] [*ICAO location identifier*] (ICLI) ... WIIX
Jakarta [*Indonesia*] [*ICAO location identifier*] (ICLI) ... WIIZ
Jakarta/Cengkareng [*Indonesia*] [*ICAO location identifier*] (ICLI) ... WIII
Jakarta Growth Fund [*Associated Press*] (SAG) ... Jakarta
Jakarta Growth Fund [*NYSE symbol*] (SPSG) ... JGF
Jakarta/Halim Perdanakusuma [*Indonesia*] [*ICAO location identifier*] (ICLI) ... WIIH
Jakarta/Kemayoran [*Indonesia*] [*ICAO location identifier*] (ICLI) ... WIID
Jakarta/Pondok Cabe [*Indonesia*] [*ICAO location identifier*] (ICLI) ... WIIP
Jakarta/Pulau Panjang [*Indonesia*] [*ICAO location identifier*] (ICLI) ... WIIG
Jakes Pizza International [*NASDAQ symbol*] (SAG) ... JAKE
Jakes Pizza International [*Associated Press*] (SAG) ... JakePza
Jakes Pizza Intl [*NASDAQ symbol*] (TTSB) ... JAKE
JAKKS Pacific [*NASDAQ symbol*] (TTSB) ... JAKK
Jakks Pacific, Inc. [*NASDAQ symbol*] (SAG) ... JAKK
Jakks Pacific, Inc. [*Associated Press*] (SAG) ... JkksPac
Jakob-Creutzfeldt [*Disease or syndrome*] [*Neurology*] (DAVI) ... JC
Jakobshavn [*Greenland*] [*ICAO location identifier*] (ICLI) ... BGJN
Jal Public Library, Jal, NM [*Library symbol Library of Congress*] (LCLS) ... NmJ
Jalagh [*Iran*] [*ICAO location identifier*] (ICLI) ... OIZA
Jalalabad [*Afghanistan*] [*ICAO location identifier*] (ICLI) ... OAJL
Jalapa [*Mexico ICAO location identifier*] (ICLI) ... MMJA
Jalapae [*Jalap*] [*Pharmacology*] (ROG) ... JALAP
Jalate, Inc. [*Associated Press*] (SAG) ... Jalate
Jalate, Inc. [*AMEX symbol*] (SAG) ... JLT
Jalate Ltd [*AMEX symbol*] (TTSB) ... JLT
Jalkeen Puolenpaiuan [*Afternoon*] [*Finland*] ... JPP
Jalna Resources [*Vancouver Stock Exchange symbol*] ... JLA
Jaluit [*Marshall Islands*] [*Airport symbol*] (OAG) ... UIT
Jam Angle Tracking ... JAT
Jam Exceeds Threshold ... JET
Jam Frequency Hopper ... JFH
Jam, Jute, and Journalism [*3 major industries of Dundee, Scotland*] ... 3J's
Jam on Target ... JOT
Jam Resistant ... JR
Jam Strobe (IEEE) ... JS
Jam Strobe Extractor ... JSE
Jam to Signal Ratio ... J/S
Jam to Signal Ratio (MCD) ... JSR
Jama'at Ahmadiyyah [*Ahmadiyya Muslim Association*] (EAIO) ... JA
Jamaat-i-Islami [*Pakistan*] [*Political party*] (FEA) ... JI
Jamahiriya Airways [*Libya*] [*ICAO designator*] (FAAC) ... JAW
Jamahiriya Libyan Arab Airlines [*ICAO designator*] (FAAC) ... LAA
Jamahiriyah News Agency [*Libya*] ... JANA
Jamaica [*Aircraft nationality and registration mark*] (FAAC) ... 6Y
Jamaica ... JA
Jamaica [*ANSI three-letter standard code*] (CNC) ... JAM
Jamaica (VRA) ... Jama
Jamaica [*ANSI two-letter standard code*] (CNC) ... JM
Jamaica [*MARC country of publication code Library of Congress*] (LCCP) ... jm
Jamaica [*IYRU nationality code*] (IYR) ... KJ
Jamaica [*MARC geographic area code Library of Congress*] (LCCP) ... nwjm
Jamaica Association of Villas and Apartments [*Later, JRJ*] ... JAVA
Jamaica Broadcasting Corp. ... JBC
Jamaica (BWI) Study Group [*Defunct*] (EA) ... JSG
Jamaica Community Unit School District, Sidell, IL [*Library symbol*] [*Library of Congress*] (LCLS) ... ISidSD
Jamaica Elementary School, Plainview, NY [*Library symbol Library of Congress*] (LCLS) ... NPlJE
Jamaica Freight and Shipping Co. Ltd. (EY) ... JFS
Jamaica International Telecommunications Ltd. [*Kingston*] [*Telecommunications service*] ... JAMINTEL
Jamaica Labour Party [*Political party*] (PPW) ... JLP
Jamaica Law Journal [*A publication*] (DLA) ... Jam LJ
Jamaica Law Reports [*1953-55*] [*A publication*] (DLA) ... JLR
Jamaica Law Reports (Braithwaite) [*A publication*] (DLA) ... Braith
Jamaica Library Service, Kingston, Jamaica [*Library symbol Library of Congress*] (LCLS) ... JamKLS
Jamaica Merchant Marine (EY) ... JMM
Jamaica Statutes [*A publication*] (DLA) ... Jam St
Jamaica Supreme Court Judgment Books [*A publication*] (DLA) ... SCJB
Jamaican Defense Forces ... JDF
Jamaican Workers' Party [*Political party*] (PPW) ... JWP
Jamaire [*ICAO designator*] (AD) ... IM
Jamb (ABBR) ... JMB
Jambi [*Indonesia*] [*Airport symbol*] (OAG) ... DJB
Jambi/Dusun Aro [*Indonesia*] [*ICAO location identifier*] (ICLI) ... WIPJ
Jambi/Sultan Taha [*Indonesia*] [*ICAO location identifier*] (ICLI) ... WIPA
Jamboree (ABBR) ... JMBRE
Jamboree on the Air [*Boy Scouts of America*] ... JOTA
James [*New Testament Book*] (WDAA) ... JAM
James [*New Testament book*] ... Jas
James [*New Testament book*] (BJA) ... Jm
James A. Fitzpatrick [*Nuclear power plant*] (NRCH) ... JAF
James A. FitzPatrick Nuclear Power Plant (NRCH) ... JFNPP
James A. Ryder Transportation [*Acronym is trade name of truck-rental firm*] ... JARTRAN
James Abram Garfield [*US president, 1831-1881*] ... JAG
James Allen Fan Club (EA) ... JAFC
James B. Lansing Sound, Inc. ... JBL
James' Bankrupt Law PB (DLA) ... James Bk L
James Beard Foundation (EA) ... JBF
James Blackstone Memorial Library, Branford, CT [*Library symbol*] [*Library of Congress*] (LCLS) ... CtBrJ
James Bond 007 Fan Club [*Defunct*] (EA) ... JBDFC
James Bond 007 Fan Club [*British*] (EAIO) ... JBFC
James Bond British Fan Club (EAIO) ... JBBFC
James Bond Journalism [*Term coined by leader Sinnathamby Bajaratman of Singapore and referring to Western journalism*] ... JBJ
James Boswell [*Initials used as pseudonym*] ... JB
James Brake [*Aviation*] (DA) ... JBD
James Branch Cabell Society (EA) ... JBCS
James Broadwell [*Custom-built racing car*] ... JABRO
James Buchanan [*US president, 1791-1868*] ... JB
James Buchanan Foundation (EA) ... JBF
James Carson Breckinridge Library, Quantico, VA [*OCLC symbol*] (OCLC) ... QMC
James Clerk Maxwell Telescope [*Mauna Kea, HI*] [*Operated by the Royal Observatory in Edinburgh, Scotland*] ... JCMT
James Cook University of North Queensland, Townsville, QLD, Australia [*Library symbol Library of Congress*] (LCLS) ... AuTJC
James Crowe Traders International [*Commercial firm British*] ... JCTI
James Darren Fan Club [*Defunct*] (EA) ... JDFC
James Dean Memory Club (EA) ... JDMC
James E. Rush Associates, Inc. [*Also, an information service or system*] (IID) ... JERA
James E. Wickson Memorial Library, Frankenmuth, MI [*Library symbol Library of Congress*] (LCLS) ... MiFram
James Ewell Brown Stuart [*American Confederate general known as Jeb Stuart, 1833-1864*] ... JEB
James F. MacLaren Ltd., Willowdale, Ontario [*Library symbol National Library of Canada*] (NLC) ... OTJFM
James F. MacLaren Ltd., Willowdale, Toronto, ON, Canada [*Library symbol Library of Congress*] (LCLS) ... CaOTJFM
James Forrestal Research Center [*Princeton University*] (MCD) ... JFRC
James Franck Institute [*University of Chicago*] [*Research center*] (RCD) ... JFI
James Griffiths & Sons [*AAR code*] ... JGS
James' Guide to Friendly Societies [*A publication*] (DLA) ... James Fr Soc
James House, Bridgetown, Nova Scotia [*Library symbol National Library of Canada*] (NLC) ... NSBJH
James House, Bridgetown, NS, Canada [*Library symbol*] [*Library of Congress*] (LCLS) ... CaNSBrJH
James Industries [*Vancouver Stock Exchange symbol*] ... JME
James J. Hill Reference Library, St. Paul, MN [*OCLC symbol*] (OCLC) ... MNR
James J. Hill Reference Library, St. Paul, MN [*Library symbol Library of Congress*] (LCLS) ... MnSJ
James J. Johnston [*FAA designator*] (FAAC) ... JMJ
James Joyce Society (EA) ... JJS
James K. Polk Memorial Association (EA) ... JKPMA
James Knox Polk [*US president, 1795-1849*] ... JKP
James' Law of Joint Stock Companies [*A publication*] (DLA) ... James JS
James Logan Morgan, Jr., Newport, AR [*Library symbol Library of Congress*] (LCLS) ... ArNeJM
James M. Peed [*Designer's mark when appearing on US coins*] ... JP
James Madison [*US president, 1751-1836*] ... JM
James Madison Elementary School, Virginia, MN [*Library symbol*] [*Library of Congress*] (LCLS) ... MnVME
James Madison Foundation (EA) ... JMF
James Madison High School Library, Rochester, NY [*OCLC symbol*] (OCLC) ... RWP
James Madison University (GAGS) ... James Madison U
James Madison University [*Virginia*] ... JMU
James Madison University, Harrisonburg, VA [*Library symbol Library of Congress*] (LCLS) ... ViHarT
James Madison University, Harrisonburg, VA [*OCLC symbol*] (OCLC) ... VMC
James Madison's Papers [*A publication*] (DLA) ... Mad Papers
James Martin Associates [*Database consulting group*] [*British*] ... JMA
James McNeill Whistler [*Nineteenth-century American painter and etcher*] ... JMW

James Memorial Library, Williston, ND [*Library symbol Library of Congress*] (LCLS) .... NdWi
James' Merchant Shipping [*1866*] [*A publication*] (DLA) .... James Sh
James Millikin University, Decatur, IL [*Library symbol Library of Congress*] (LCLS) .... IDecJ
James Monroe [*US president, 1758-1831*] .... JM
James Monroe High School Library, Rochester, NY [*OCLC symbol*] (OCLC) .... RWQ
James Monroe Memorial Foundation (EA) .... JMMF
James Monroe Memorial Foundation, Fredericksburg, VA [*Library symbol Library of Congress*] (LCLS) .... ViFreJM
James on Courts-Martial [*A publication*] (DLA) .... James Ct Mar
James on Salvage [*1867*] [*A publication*] (DLA) .... James Salv
James' Opinions, Charges, Etc. [*A publication*] (DLA) .... James Op
James Paton Memorial Hospital, Gander, Newfoundland [*Library symbol National Library of Canada*] (NLC) .... NFGJPH
James Paton Memorial Hospital, Gander, NF, Canada [*Library symbol Library of Congress*] (LCLS) .... CaNfGJPH
James Prendergast Free Library, Jamestown, NY [*Library symbol Library of Congress*] (LCLS) .... NJam
James R. Hay & Associates, Pointe Claire, Quebec [*Library symbol National Library of Canada*] (BIB) .... QMJRH
James "Rebel" O'Leary and Jammie Ann Tape Club [*Defunct*] (EA) .... JROJATC
James "Rebel" O'Leary Fan Club (EA) .... JROFC
James' Reports [*2 Nova Scotia*] [*A publication*] (DLA) .... James
James' Reports [*2 Nova Scotia*] [*A publication*] (DLA) .... James (N Sc)
James River 9% 'DECS' [*NYSE symbol*] (TTSB) .... JRPrP
James River 8.25% Dep Pfd [*NYSE symbol*] (TTSB) .... JRPrO
James River Bankshares [*NASDAQ symbol*] (TTSB) .... JRBK
James River Bankshares, Inc. [*NASDAQ symbol*] (SAG) .... JRBK
James River Bankshares, Inc. [*Associated Press*] (SAG) .... JRivBsh
James River Corp. [*NYSE symbol*] (TTSB) .... JR
James River Corp. of Virginia [*NYSE symbol*] (SPSG) .... JR
James River Corp. of Virginia [*Associated Press*] (SAG) .... JRiver
James River Corp. of Virginia [*Associated Press*] (SAG) .... JRvr
James River Dep Cv Ex Pfd [*NYSE symbol*] (TTSB) .... JRPrL
James River$3.375Cv Ex K Pfd [*NYSE symbol*] (TTSB) .... JRPrK
James Robison Evangelistic Association (EA) .... JREA
James Roosevelt Library, Hyde Park, NY [*Library symbol Library of Congress Obsolete*] (LCLS) .... NHpJR
James' Select Cases [*1835-55*] [*Nova Scotia*] [*A publication*] (DLA) .... James Sel Cas
James' Select Cases [*1835-55*] [*Nova Scotia*] [*A publication*] (DLA) .... James Sel Cases
James Sperry High School Library, Henrietta, NY [*OCLC symbol*] (OCLC) .... RWR
James Sprunt Technical Institute, Kenansville, NC [*Library symbol Library of Congress*] (LCLS) .... NcKeS
James Taylor [*Singer*] .... JT
James V. Brown Library of Williamsport and Lycoming County, Williamsport, PA [*OCLC symbol*] (OCLC) .... JVB
James V. Brown Library of Williamsport and Lycoming County, Williamsport, PA [*Library symbol Library of Congress*] (LCLS) .... PWmP
James Vernon Middle School, East Norwich, NY [*Library symbol*] [*Library of Congress*] (LCLS) .... NEnoVM
James Whitcomb Riley Home, Indianapolis, IN [*Library symbol Library of Congress*] (LCLS) .... InIR
James Willard Schultz Society (EA) .... JWSS
Jameson and Montagu's English Bankruptcy Reports [*Vol. 2 of Glyn and Jameson*] [*1821-28*] [*A publication*] (DLA) .... James & Mont
Jameson Inns [*NASDAQ symbol*] (TTSB) .... JAMS
Jameson Inns, Inc. [*Associated Press*] (SAG) .... JamesnIn
Jameson Inns, Inc. [*NASDAQ symbol*] (SAG) .... JAMS
Jameson's Constitutional Convention [*A publication*] (DLA) .... James Const Con
Jamestown [*California*] [*Seismograph station code, US Geological Survey*] (SEIS) .... JAS
Jamestown [*New York*] [*Airport symbol*] (OAG) .... JHW
Jamestown [*North Dakota*] [*Airport symbol*] (OAG) .... JMS
Jamestown Area Furniture Haulers Association, Inc., Buffalo NY [*STAC*] .... JAF
Jamestown Canyon Virus [*Medicine*] (DMAA) .... JCV
Jamestown College, Jamestown, ND [*OCLC symbol*] (OCLC) .... NDJ
Jamestown College, Jamestown, ND [*Library symbol Library of Congress*] (LCLS) .... NdJC
Jamestown Community College [*New York*] .... JCC
Jamestown Community College, Jamestown, NY [*Library symbol Library of Congress*] (LCLS) .... NJamCC
Jamestown Foundation (EA) .... JF
Jamestown General Hospital, Jamestown, NY [*Library symbol Library of Congress*] (LCLS) .... NJamH
Jamestown, KY [*AM radio station call letters*] .... WJKY
Jamestown, KY [*FM radio station call letters*] .... WJRS
Jamestown, ND [*Location identifier FAA*] (FAAL) .... JMS
Jamestown, ND [*Television station call letters*] .... KJRR
Jamestown, ND [*FM radio station call letters*] .... KPRJ
Jamestown, ND [*AM radio station call letters*] .... KQDJ
Jamestown, ND [*AM radio station call letters*] .... KSJB
Jamestown, ND [*FM radio station call letters*] .... KSJZ
Jamestown, ND [*FM radio station call letters*] (RBYB) .... KXGT-FM
Jamestown, ND [*FM radio station call letters*] .... KYNU
Jamestown, NY [*Location identifier FAA*] (FAAL) .... JHW
Jamestown, NY [*FM radio station call letters*] .... WCOT
Jamestown, NY [*FM radio station call letters*] .... WHUG
Jamestown, NY [*AM radio station call letters*] .... WJTN
Jamestown, NY [*AM radio station call letters*] .... WKSN
Jamestown, NY [*FM radio station call letters*] .... WNJA
Jamestown, NY [*Television station call letters*] .... WTJA
Jamestown, NY [*FM radio station call letters*] .... WUBJ
Jamestown, NY [*FM radio station call letters*] .... WWSE
Jamestown Paint & Varnish Co. .... JAPCO
Jamestown Press, Jamestown, IN [*Library symbol Library of Congress*] (LCLS) .... InJamP
Jamestown Public Library, Jamestown, NC [*Library symbol*] [*Library of Congress*] (LCLS) .... NcJ
Jamestown, TN [*AM radio station call letters*] .... WCLC
Jamestown, TN [*FM radio station call letters*] .... WCLC-FM
Jamestown, TN [*AM radio station call letters*] .... WDEB
Jamestown, TN [*FM radio station call letters*] .... WDEB-FM
Jamestown Township Library, Jamestown, MI [*Library symbol Library of Congress*] (LCLS) .... MiJam
Jamestown, Westfield & Northwestern Railroad (IIA) .... JW & NW
Jamestowne Society (EA) .... JS
Jamestown-Williamsburg-Yorktown Celebration Committee .... JWYCC
Jamiat Adduwal Alarabia [*League of Arab States - LAS*] (EAIO) .... JAA
Jami'at Al Islan [*Defunct*] (EA) .... JAI
Jamiat-i-Talaba [*Pakistan*] [*Political party*] (PD) .... JIT
Jamiatul Ulama-i-Islam [*Pakistan*] [*Political party*] (FEA) .... JUI
Jamiatul Ulama-i-Pakistan [*Political party*] (FEA) .... JUP
Jamie Frontier Resources, Inc. [*Toronto Stock Exchange symbol*] .... JFR
Jamieson Scotch Dictionary [*A publication*] (ROG) .... JAM
Jamijarvi [*Finland ICAO location identifier*] (ICLI) .... EFJM
Jamin Effect [*Electronics*] .... JE
Jammer System Analysis .... JSA
Jammer System Analysis Simulator .... JSAS
Jammers Tracked by Azimuth Crossings [*RADAR*] .... JAMTRAC
Jammie Ann Fan Club (EA) .... JAFC
Jamming [*Military*] (NVT) .... JAM
Jamming .... JAMG
Jamming Amplitude Versus Azimuth (NVT) .... JAVA
Jamming and Warning System (MCD) .... JAWS
Jamming Avoidance Response .... JAR
Jamming Control Authority (NATG) .... JCA
Jamming Direction Finder [*Military*] (CAAL) .... JDF
Jamming Equipment .... JE
Jamming Exercise [*Military*] (NVT) .... JAMEX
Jamming Guarded Radio - VHF [*Very High Frequency*] (PDAA) .... JAGUAR-V
Jamming Modulation Analysis .... JMA
Jamming of Beacons and Blind Landing [*Aviation*] (IAA) .... JBBL
Jamming Package [*Air Force*] .... JAMPAC
Jamming Package [*Air Force*] (MCD) .... JAMPACK
Jamming RADAR Coverage Indicator (MSA) .... JRCI
Jamming Report .... JAMREP
Jamming Station (IAA) .... JST
Jamming Tactics Evaluation .... JTE
Jamming to Signal .... J/S
Jammu [*India*] [*Airport symbol*] (OAG) .... IXJ
Jammu [*India*] [*ICAO location identifier*] (ICLI) .... VIJU
Jammu and Kashmir Force [*British military*] (DMA) .... JAKFORCE
Jammu and Kashmir Liberation Front [*India*] [*Political party*] (ECON) .... JKLF
Jammu and Kashmir National Conference [*India*] [*Political party*] (PPW) .... JKNC
Jamnagar [*India*] [*Airport symbol*] (OAG) .... JGA
Jamnagar [*India*] [*ICAO location identifier*] (ICLI) .... VAJM
Jam-Resistant Antenna .... JRA
Jam-Resistant Secure Communications .... JRSC
Jam-Resistant Secure Voice Communications (MCD) .... JRSVC
Jamshedpur [*India*] [*Airport symbol*] (AD) .... IXW
Jamshedpur [*India*] [*ICAO location identifier*] (ICLI) .... VEJS
Jamshedpur Mazdoor Union [*India*] .... JMU
Jan Bell Marketing [*AMEX symbol*] (TTSB) .... JBM
Jan Bell Marketing, Inc. [*Associated Press*] (SAG) .... JanBell
Jan Bell Marketing, Inc. [*AMEX symbol*] (SPSG) .... JBM
Jan Berry and the Alohas Fan Club (EA) .... JBAFC
Jan Howard Friends Club (EA) .... JHFC
Jan Mayen [*Norway ICAO location identifier*] (ICLI) .... ENJA
Jan Mayen [*MARC country of publication code Library of Congress*] (LCCP) .... jn
Jan Mayen [*MARC geographic area code Library of Congress*] (LCCP) .... lnjn--
Jan Mayen Island [*Seismograph station code, US Geological Survey*] (SEIS) .... JMI
Jan Voet's Commentarius ad Pandectas [*A publication*] (DLA) .... J Voet Com ad Pand
Jana Jae Fan Club (EA) .... JJFC
JanAir, Inc. [*ICAO designator*] (FAAC) .... JAX
Janak-Botkin-Wallis [*Data processing program regarding forest growth; named for three men involved in program*] .... JABOWA
Janakpur [*Nepal*] [*Airport symbol*] (OAG) .... JKR
Janakpur [*Nepal*] [*ICAO location identifier*] (ICLI) .... VNJP
Janat Abad [*Iran*] [*ICAO location identifier*] (ICLI) .... OIML
Janata Party [*India*] [*Political party*] (PPW) .... JP
Janatha Vimukhti Peramuna [*People's Liberation Front*] [*Sri Lanka*] [*Political party*] (PPW) .... JVP
Jandel Video Analysis System .... JAVA
Jandel Video Analysis System .... JVAS
J&J Snack Foods [*NASDAQ symbol*] (TTSB) .... JJSF
Jane Addams Peace Association (EA) .... JAPA
Jane Austen Society [*Basingstoke, Hampshire, England*] (EAIO) .... JAS
Jane Austen Society of North America (EA) .... JASNA
Jane Badler Society (EA) .... JBS
Jane Powell Fan Club (EA) .... JPFC
Janes Aviation 748 Ltd. [*British ICAO designator*] (FAAC) .... JAN
Janes Aviation Ltd. [*British ICAO designator*] (FAAC) .... JAV
Janesbury Valve [*Aerospace*] (KSC) .... JV

Janesville Public Library, Janesville, WI [*Library symbol Library of Congress*] (LCLS) .... WJa
Janesville, WI [*Location identifier FAA*] (FAAL) .... JVL
Janesville, WI [*AM radio station call letters*] .... WCLO
Janesville, WI [*Television station call letters*] .... WJNW
Janesville, WI [*FM radio station call letters*] .... WJVL
Janex International, Inc. [*Associated Press*] (SAG) .... Janex
Janex International, Inc. [*NASDAQ symbol*] (SAG) .... JANX
Janex Intl. [*NASDAQ symbol*] (TTSB) .... JANX
Janex Intl. Wrrt [*NASDAQ symbol*] (TTSB) .... JANXW
Jani Anglorum Facies Nova [*1680*] [*A publication*] (DLA) .... Jan Angl
Janina [*Greece*] [*Seismograph station code, US Geological Survey*] (SEIS) ...... JAN
Janis Ian Fan Club (EA) .... JIFC
Janitor .... JAN
Janitor (ABBR) .... JNTR
Janitor Closet (MSA) .... JC
Janitorial .... JANTRL
Janitorial (ABBR) .... JTRL
Janlen Enterprises, West Allis, WI [*Library symbol Library of Congress*] (LCLS) .... WWeaJ
Janna Contact Personal [*Janna Systems*] [*Computer interface*] (PCM) .... JCP
Jannasch-Zafirion-Farrington [*Marine sediment trap*] (JZF) .... JZF
Janney Cylinder Co. .... JCC
Jannock Ltd. [*NASDAQ symbol*] (SAG) .... JANNF
Jannock Ltd. [*Associated Press*] (SAG) .... Jannock
Jannock Ltd. [*Toronto Stock Exchange symbol*] .... JN
Jansky [*A unit of electromagnetic flux density*] .... Jy
Jansky Screening Index [*Psychology*] (DAVI) .... JSI
Janssen [*Belgium*] [*Research code symbol*] .... R
Jantar Resources Corp. [*Vancouver Stock Exchange symbol*] .... JAN
Januaria [*Brazil*] [*Airport symbol*] (AD) .... JNA
January .... J
January .... JA
January (EY) .... JAN
January (ODBW) .... Jan
January (ROG) .... JANY
January (ABBR) .... JNY
January and July [*Denotes semiannual payments of interest or dividends in these months*] [*Business term*] .... J & J
January, April, July, and October [*Denotes quarterly payments of interest or dividends in these months*] [*Business term*] .... JAJO
January Assumption Budget [*Budget based on economic forecasts available as of January*] .... JAB
Janus Information Facility [*Later, J2CP Information Services*] (EA) .... JIF
Janvier [*January*] [*French*] .... JANV
Japan [*MARC geographic area code Library of Congress*] (LCCP) .... a-ja--
Japan [*IYRU nationality code*] .... J
Japan [*ry (Ryukyu Islands, Southern) used in records cataloged before January 1978*] [*MARC country of publication code Library of Congress*] (LCCP) .... ja
Japan (KSC) .... JAP
Japan (VRA) .... Jap
Japan [*ANSI two-letter standard code*] (CNC) .... JP
Japan [*ANSI three-letter standard code*] (CNC) .... JPN
Japan Air Charter Co. Ltd. [*ICAO designator*] (FAAC) .... JAZ
Japan Air Commuter Co. Ltd. [*ICAO designator*] (FAAC) .... JAC
Japan Air Defense Force .... JADF
Japan Air Lines .... JAL
Japan Air Lines [*ICAO designator*] (OAG) .... JL
Japan Air Lines Co. Ltd. [*NASDAQ symbol*] (NQ) .... JAPN
Japan Air Lines Ltd. [*ICAO designator*] (FAAC) .... JAL
Japan Air System Co. Ltd. [*ICAO designator*] (FAAC) .... JAS
Japan Airlines [*Associated Press*] (SAG) .... JapnAr
Japan Airlines Co. Ltd. [*Associated Press*] (SAG) .... JapnAr
Japan Airlines Co. Ltd ADR [*NASDAQ symbol*] (TTSB) .... JAPNY
Japan Airlines Development Co. .... JDC
Japan Amateur Satellite-1 .... JAS-1
Japan and East China Seas Study [*Marine science*] (OSRA) .... JECSS
Japan Animal Welfare Society [*London, England*] .... JAWS
Japan Annual of Law and Politics [*A publication*] (DLA) .... Japan Ann L & Pol
Japan Area .... JAPA
Japan Area Defense Environment .... JADE
Japan Asia Airways .... JAA
Japan Asia Airways Co. Ltd. [*ICAO designator*] (FAAC) .... JAA
Japan Asia Sea Cable .... JASC
Japan Asian Dance Event .... JADE
Japan Association for Radiation Research on Polymers .... JARRP
Japan Atomic Energy Commission .... JAEC
Japan Atomic Energy Insurance Pool .... JAEIP
Japan Atomic Energy Research Institute [*Tokyo*] .... JAERI
Japan Atomic Fuel Corp. .... JAFC
Japan Atomic Industrial Forum .... JAIF
Japan Atomic Power Co. .... JAPCO
Japan Australia Venture Capital Fund .... JAVCF
Japan Auto Parts Industries Association .... JAPIA
Japan Automatic Transmission Co. .... JATCO
Japan Automobile Federation .... JAF
Japan Automobile Importers Association .... JAIA
Japan Automobile Manufacturers Association, Washington Office (EA) .... JAMA
Japan Automobile Research Institute .... JARI
Japan Automobile Tire Manufacturers Association .... JATMA
Japan Automotive Research Institute .... JARI
Japan Aviation Electronics Industry Ltd. .... JAE
Japan Center for International Exchange (EA) .... JCIE/USA
Japan Chamber of Commerce and Industry, Sydney [*Australia*] .... JCCIS
Japan Civil Aviation Bureau (MCD) .... JCAB

Japan Club of Sydney [*Australia*] .... JCS
Japan Communist Party [*Nikon Kyosanto*] [*Political party*] (PPW) .... JCP
Japan Convention Bureau (EA) .... JCB
Japan Database Industry Association [*Tokyo*] [*Information service or system*] (IID) .... DINA
Japan Development Bank (PDAA) .... JDB
Japan Directory of Professional Associations [*Japan Publications Guide Service*] [*Information service or system*] (CRD) .... JDPA
Japan Documentation Center [*Columbia University*] .... JDC
Japan Domestic Airlines (PDAA) .... JDA
Japan Earth Remote Sensing Satellite .... JERS
Japan Earth Resources Satellite [*Marine science*] (OSRA) .... JERS-I
Japan Economic Daily [*Database*] [*Kyodo News International, Inc.*] [*Information service or system*] (CRD) .... JED
Japan Economic Institute of America (EA) .... JEI
Japan Economic Newswire [*Kyodo News International, Inc.*] [*Information service or system*] (CRD) .... JEN
Japan Economic Review [*A publication*] (WDAA) .... JER
Japan Electric Computer Corporation [*Japan*] (NITA) .... JECC
[*The*] Japan Electrical Measurements Manufacturers' Association (ACII) .... JEMIMA
Japan Electronic Parts Industry Association .... JEPIA
Japan Electronics Show .... JES
Japan Engineering Test Reactor .... JETR
Japan English Publications in Print [*Japan Publications Guide Service*] [*Japan Information service or system*] (CRD) .... JEPP
Japan Environmental Systems .... JES
Japan Equity Fund [*NYSE symbol*] (SPSG) (SAG) .... JEQ
[*The*] Japan Equity Fund, Inc. [*Associated Press*] (SAG) .... JapnEq
Japan External Trade Organization [*New York, NY*] (EA) .... JETRO
Japan Federation of Employers Association .... JFEA
Japan Foundation [*Also, Kokusai Koryu*] (EA) .... JF
Japan High Tech Review [*Database*] [*Kyodo News International, Inc.*] [*Information service or system*] (CRD) .... JHTR
Japan Hour Association [*Later, JHB*] (EA) .... JHA
Japan Hour Broadcasting (EA) .... JHB
Japan Information and Communication Association [*Information service or system*] (IID) .... JICOA
Japan Information Center for Science and Technology .... JICST
Japan Information Center of Science and Technology [*Tokyo*] (IID) .... JICST
Japan Information Center of Science and Technology, Tokyo, Japan [*Library symbol Library of Congress*] (LCLS) .... JTJ
Japan Information Exchange [*Comtex Scientific Corp.*] [*Information service or system Defunct*] (CRD) .... JIE
Japan Information Processing Development Center (NITA) .... JIPDEC
Japan Institute [*Defunct*] (EA) .... JI
Japan Institute for International Studies and Training .... JIIST
Japan International Center of Science and Technology (USGC) .... JICST
Japan International Christian University Foundation (EA) .... JICUF
Japan International Cooperation Agency .... JICA
Japan International Measuring and Control Industry Show .... JAPANMEC
Japan International Science and Technology Exchange Center .... JISTEC
Japan Investment Service [*Reuters Holdings Ltd.*] [*British Information service or system*] (CRD) .... JIS
Japan Karate Association of Australia .... JKAA
Japan Light Machinery Information Center (EA) .... JLMIC
Japan Marine Safety Agency [*Marine science*] (OSRA) .... JMSA
Japan Marine Science and Technology Center .... JAMSTEC
Japan Meteorological Agency .... JMA
Japan Microfilm Service Center Co. Ltd., Tokyo, Japan [*Library symbol Library of Congress*] (LCLS) .... JmSC
Japan Microphotography Association .... JMA
Japan National Assembly of Disabled Peoples' International (EAIO) .... JNADPI
Japan National Tourist Organization (EA) .... JNTO
Japan Nuclear Codes Group .... JNCG
Japan Oceanographic Data Center [*Information service or system*] (IID) .... JODC
Japan Online Information System [*Database*] .... JOIS
Japan OTC Equity Fund [*NYSE symbol*] (TTSB) .... JOF
Japan OTC Equity Fund, Inc. [*NYSE symbol*] (SPSG) .... JOF
Japan OTC Equity Fund, Inc. [*Associated Press*] (SAG) .... JpOTC
Japan Paper .... JP
Japan Paper Proofs .... JPP
Japan Patent Information Organization [*Database producer*] .... JAPIO
Japan Patient Information Center [*Information service or system*] (IID) .... JAPATIC
Japan Petroleum Development Co. .... JPDC
Japan Pharmaceutical Information Center [*Tokyo*] [*Information service or system*] (IID) .... JAPIC
Japan Photo [*Norway*] [*FAA designator*] (FAAC) .... JAP
Japan Power Demonstration Reactor .... JPDR
Japan Press Service .... JPS
Japan Procurement Agency .... JPA
Japan Publications Guide Service [*Information service or system*] (IID) .... JPGS
Japan Publishers Directory [*Japan Publications Guide Service*] [*Japan Information service or system*] (CRD) .... JPD
Japan Racing Association (ECON) .... JRA
Japan Satellite Systems [*Commercial firm*] .... JSAT
Japan Scholarship Foundation (EA) .... JSF
Japan Science Review [*A publication*] .... JSR
Japan Self-Defense Force (CINC) .... JSDF
Japan Silk Association (EA) .... JSA
Japan Socialist Party [*Nikon Shakaito*] [*Political party*] (PPW) .... JSP
Japan Society (EA) .... JS
Japan Society for the Promotion of Science .... JSPS
Japan Society Library, New York, NY [*Library symbol*] [*Library of Congress*] (LCLS) .... NNJS

Japan Society of Library Science (NITA) .... JSLS
Japan Society of Mechanical Engineers .... JSME
Japan Sports Prototype Championship [Auto racing] .... JSPC
Japan Synthetic Rubber Co. Ltd. .... JSR
Japan Techno-Economics Society (EA) .... JATES
Japan Technology Information and Evaluation Service (IID) .... J-TIES
Japan Telecommunications Engineering and Consultancy .... JTEC
Japan Textile Federation .... JTF
Japan Times [A publication] (BARN) .... JT
Japan Trade Advisory Group [British Overseas Trade Board] (DS) .... JTAG
Japan Transocean Air Co. Ltd. [ICAO designator] (FAAC) .... JTA
Japan Tropical Rainforest Action Network .... JATAN
Japan Troposcatter Systems .... JTS
Japan Union of Scientists and Engineers (BARN) .... JUSE
Japan Universal System Transport Co. Ltd. [ICAO designator] (FAAC) .... JST
Japan UNIX Network [Japan] [Computer science] (TNIG) .... JUNET
Japan Victor Co. .... JVC
Japan-America Institute [Defunct] (EA) .... JAI
Japan-America Society of Southern California .... JASSC
Japan-America Society of Washington (EA) .... JASW
Japan-America Student Conference (EA) .... JASC
Japan-American Cultural Society (EAIO) .... JACS
Japan-American Institute of Management Science .... JAIMS
Japan-Australia Foundation .... JAF
Japanesae National Railways (BARN) .... JNR
Japanese (ROG) .... JAP
Japanese (ODBW) .... Jap
Japanese [MARC language code Library of Congress] (LCCP) .... jpn
Japanese Accepted Name (DMAA) .... JAN
Japanese Air Defense Environment .... JADE
Japanese Air Self-Defense Force .... JASDF
Japanese Airborne Early Warning .... JAEW
Japanese American Citizens League (EA) .... JACL
Japanese American Curriculum Project (EA) .... JACP
Japanese American Philatelic Society [Later, JASP] .... JAPS
Japanese American Society for Legal Studies (EA) .... JASLS
Japanese American Society for Philately (EA) .... JASP
Japanese Animation Network (EA) .... JAN
Japanese Antarctic Research Expedition [1956-] .... JapARE
Japanese Antarctic Research Expedition [1956-] .... JARE
Japanese, Arabic, Chinese, Korean, Persian, Hebrew, Yiddish [Nonroman languages] [Library of Congress] .... JACKPHY
Japanese Army Air Force .... JAAF
Japanese Association for International Chemical Information [Tokyo] .... JAICI
Japanese Association for the Promotion of International Trade (EY) .... JAPIT
Japanese B Encephalitis [Medicine] .... JBE
Japanese Canadian Citizens' Association .... JCCA
Japanese Canadian Citizens' Council .... JCCC
Japanese Canadian Citizens' League .... JCCL
Japanese Canadian Committee for Democracy .... JCCD
Japanese Chamber of Commerce and Industry in the United Kingdom (DS) .... JCCIUK
Japanese Chamber of Commerce of New York [Later, JCCINY] (EA) .... JCC
Japanese Chin Club of America (EA) .... JCCA
Japanese COARE [Coupled Ocean-Atmosphere Response Experiment] (USDC) .... J-COARE
Japanese Columbia [Record label] .... JpC
Japanese Coupled Ocean-Atmosphere Response Experiment [Marine science] (OSRA) .... JCOARE
Japanese Defense Agency (MCD) .... JDA
Japanese Digital Road Mapping Association .... JDRMA
Japanese Earthquake Prediction Plan .... JEPP
Japanese El Nino Experiment [Marine science] (OSRA) .... JENEX
Japanese Electronic Computer Co. .... JECC
Japanese Electronic Industries Association .... JEIA
Japanese Electronic Industry Development Association (CDE) .... JEIDA
Japanese Electrotechnical Committee .... JEC
Japanese Encephalitis [Medicine] .... JE
Japanese Encephalitis Virus [Medicine] .... JEV
Japanese Equine Encephalitis [Medicine] .... JEE
Japanese Erection Ring [Medicine] (BABM) .... JER
Japanese Expeditions to the Deep Sea .... JEDS
Japanese Experiment Module .... JEM
Japanese Export Standard .... JES
Japanese Federation of Economic Organizations .... JFEO
Japanese Fermentation Institute .... JFI
Japanese Fiscal Year (CINC) .... JFY
Japanese Government and Public Research in Progress [International database] .... JGRIP
Japanese Government Bond (ECON) .... JGB
Japanese Ground Self-Defense Forces (AABC) .... JGSDF
Japanese Industrial Standards .... JIS
Japanese Industrial Standards Committee [Agency of Industrial Science and Technology, Ministry of International Trade and Industry] .... JISC
Japanese Industrial Technology Association .... JITA
Japanese Institute of Electrical Engineers .... JIEE
Japanese International Protein Information Database .... JIPID
Japanese International Satellite Organization [Cable-television system] .... JISO
Japanese Keyword Indexing Simulator .... JAKIS
Japanese Land-Based Test Site (MCD) .... JLBTS
Japanese Linear Collider [High energy physics] .... JLC
Japanese Maritime Self-Defense Force .... JMSDF
Japanese Medical Abstract Scanning System [International Medical Information Center] [Japan] (NITA) .... JAMASS
Japanese Military Administration .... JMA

Japanese National Committee of the International Music Council (EAIO) .... JNCIMC
Japanese National Laboratory .... JNL
Japanese Navy Air Force .... JNAF
Japanese Pacific Climate Study [Marine science] (OSRA) .... JAPACS
Japanese Pacific Ocean Climate Studies (USDC) .... JAPACS
Japanese Patent (IAA) .... JAPP
Japanese Phonograph Record Association [An association] (NITA) .... JPRA
Japanese Plating Supplier's Association [Environmetal science] .... JPSA
Japanese Polydor Variable Microgroove [Record label] .... JpPV
Japanese Polydor-Deutsche Grammophon [Record label] .... JpPol
Japanese Proficiency Test [Educational test] .... JPT
Japanese Racing Association .... JRA
Japanese Research Reactor .... JRR
Japanese Rocket Society .... JRS
Japanese Science and Technology Agency (USDC) .... STA
Japanese Securities Dealers Association (ECON) .... JSDA
Japanese Self-Defense Agency .... JSDA
Japanese Society for Alternatives to Animal Experiments .... JSAAE
Japanese Society in Brisbane [Australia] .... JSB
Japanese Society of Sydney [Australia] .... JSS
Japanese Software Support Environment .... JSSE
Japanese Space Shuttle Utilization Program (MCD) .... JSSUP
Japanese Spaniel Club of America [Later, JCCA] (EA) .... JSCA
Japanese Standard Time .... JST
Japanese Standards Association (NTCM) .... JSA
Japanese Studies Center [Monash University] [Australia] .... JSC
Japanese Sword Society of the United States (EA) .... JSS/US
Japanese Technical Abstracts [A publication] .... JTA
Japanese Technical Information Service [University Microfilms International] [Information service or system] (IID) .... JTIS
Japanese Tourist Board .... JTB
Japanese Union of Scientists and Engineers (ACII) .... JUSE
Japanese Union of Scientists and Engineers [Databank originator] (NITA) .... JUSE
Japanese University Network (ACRL) .... JUNET
Japanese Urban Professional [Lifestyle classification] .... JUPPIE
Japanese Vellum .... JV
Japanese Vellum Proofs .... JVP
Japanese Victor [Record label] .... JpV
Japanese Weekend School .... JWS
Japanese Yen [Monetary unit] .... JY
Japanese-Soviet Fisheries Commission for the Northwest Pacific .... JSFC
Japanned [Finished with a hard, glossy varnish] (BARN) .... jap
Japan-North American Commission on Cooperative Mission .... JNAC
Japan-Republic of Korea Joint Fisheries Commission [Marine science] (OSRA) .... JKFC
JAPOS Study Group [Defunct] (EA) .... JAPOS
Jaque [Panama] [Airport symbol] (OAG) .... JQE
Jaque [Panama] [ICAO location identifier] (ICLI) .... MPJE
Jaqui [Peru] [ICAO location identifier] (ICLI) .... SPQJ
Jar (MCD) .... JR
Jaramillo [Ecuador] [ICAO location identifier] (ICLI) .... SEJA
Jardin Botanique de Montreal, Montreal, PQ, Canada [Library symbol Library of Congress] (LCLS) .... CaQMJB
Jardin Botanique, Montreal, Quebec [Library symbol National Library of Canada] (NLC) .... QMJB
Jardin Zoologique de Quebec, Charlesbourg, Quebec [Library symbol National Library of Canada] (NLC) .... QQZ
Jardin Zoologique de Quebec, Quebec, PQ, Canada [Library symbol Library of Congress] (LCLS) .... CaQQZ
Jardine Fleming China Reg Fd [NYSE symbol] (TTSB) .... JFC
Jardine Fleming China Region [Associated Press] (SAG) .... JardFlCh
Jardine Fleming China Regular Fund [NYSE symbol] (SPSG) .... JFC
Jardine Fleming India Fund [NYSE symbol] (SAG) .... JFI
Jardine Fleming India Fund [Associated Press] (SAG) .... JFIndia
Jardines .... JARD
Jardine's Criminal Trials [A publication] (DLA) .... Jar Cr Tr
Jardine's Index to Howell's State Trials [A publication] (DLA) .... Jard Ind
Jared Martin Fan Club [Defunct] (EA) .... JMFC
Jaref/Sirte [ICAO location identifier] (ICLI) .... HLRF
Jarf North [Oman] [ICAO location identifier] (ICLI) .... OOJN
Jarful (ABBR) .... JRFL
Jargon [Used in correcting manuscripts, etc.] .... J
Jargon (WDAA) .... JAR
Jargon (ABBR) .... JRGN
Jargon Society (EA) .... JS
Jarisch-Herxheimer Reaction [Immunology] (DAVI) .... JHR
Jarlsberg [Norway ICAO location identifier] (ICLI) .... ENJB
Jarman and Bythewood's Conveyancing [A publication] (DLA) .... Jar & By Conv
Jarman on Wills [8 eds.] [1841-51] [A publication] (DLA) .... Jar Wills
Jarman's Chancery Practice [A publication] (DLA) .... Jar Chy Pr
Jarman's Edition of Powell on Devises [A publication] (DLA) .... Jar Pow Dev
Jaro International SA [Romania] [ICAO designator] (FAAC) .... MDJ
Jarred (ABBR) .... JRD
Jarring (ABBR) .... JRG
Jarrow Press, Inc. .... JP
Jarvie Public Library, Alberta [Library symbol National Library of Canada] (NLC) .... AJA
Jarvis Branch, City of Nanticoke Public Library, Ontario [Library symbol National Library of Canada] (BIB) .... OJCN
Jarvis Christian College [Hawkins, TX] .... JCC
Jarvis Christian College, Hawkins, TX [OCLC symbol] (OCLC) .... JCC
Jarvis Christian College, Hawkins, TX [Library symbol Library of Congress] (LCLS) .... TxHaJ

Jarvis Island [*Line Islands*] [*ICAO location identifier*] (ICLI) ... PLUR
Jarvis Resources [*Vancouver Stock Exchange symbol*] ... JRL
Jascan Resources, Inc. [*Toronto Stock Exchange symbol*] ... JSC
Jask [*Iran*] [*ICAO location identifier*] (ICLI) ... OIZJ
Jasmine (ABBR) ... JSMIN
Jason, Inc. [*NASDAQ symbol*] (NQ) ... JASN
Jason, Inc. [*Associated Press*] (SAG) ... Jason
Jasonville Leader, Jasonville, IN [*Library symbol Library of Congress*] (LCLS) ... InJaL
Jasonville Public Library, Jasonville, IN [*Library symbol*] [*Library of Congress*] (LCLS) ... InJa
Jasper [*Gem*] (ROG) ... JASPR
Jasper (VRA) ... jsp
Jasper, AB [*AM radio station call letters*] ... CKYR
Jasper, AB [*ICAO location identifier*] (ICLI) ... CYJA
Jasper, AL [*AM radio station call letters*] ... WARF
Jasper, AL [*FM radio station call letters*] ... WOWC
Jasper, AL [*AM radio station call letters*] ... WZPQ
Jasper County Courthouse, Newton, IA [*Library symbol Library of Congress*] (LCLS) ... IaNewtCoC
Jasper County Courthouse, Newton, IA [*Library symbol*] [*Library of Congress*] (LCLS) ... IaNewtJC
Jasper County Public Library, Rensselaer, IN [*Library symbol Library of Congress*] (LCLS) ... InRen
Jasper County Tribune, Colfax, IA [*Library symbol Library of Congress*] (LCLS) ... IaColJ
Jasper, GA [*AM radio station call letters*] (RBYB) ... WYYZ
Jasper Herald, Jasper, IN [*Library symbol Library of Congress*] (LCLS) ... InJH
Jasper, IN [*AM radio station call letters*] ... WITZ
Jasper, IN [*FM radio station call letters*] ... WITZ-FM
Jasper National Park [*Alberta*] [*Airport symbol*] (AD) ... JNP
Jasper Public Library, Alberta [*Library symbol National Library of Canada*] (NLC) ... AJ
Jasper Public Library, Jasper, AB, Canada [*Library symbol Library of Congress*] (LCLS) ... CaAJ
Jasper Public Library, Jasper, IN [*Library symbol Library of Congress*] (LCLS) ... InJ
Jasper Public Library, Jasper, IN [*OCLC symbol*] (OCLC) ... XJP
Jasper Public Schools, Jasper, MN [*Library symbol*] [*Library of Congress*] (LCLS) ... MnJaPS
Jasper, TN [*Location identifier FAA*] (FAAL) ... APT
Jasper, TN [*AM radio station call letters*] ... WWAM
Jasper, TX [*Location identifier FAA*] (FAAL) ... JAS
Jasper, TX [*FM radio station call letters*] (RBYB) ... KJAS-FM
Jasper, TX [*FM radio station call letters*] ... KMIA
Jasper, TX [*FM radio station call letters*] ... KNKE
Jasper, TX [*AM radio station call letters*] ... KTXJ
Jasper, TX [*FM radio station call letters*] ... KWYX
Jasper, TX [*Location identifier FAA*] (FAAL) ... PIN
Jaspers Society of North America (EA) ... JSNA
Jaswant Singh and Bhattacharji [*Staining method for blood cells, named for its discoverers*] [*Medicine*] ... JSB
Jatai [*Brazil*] [*Airport symbol*] (AD) ... JTI
Jatiya Janata Party [*National People's Party*] [*Bangladesh*] [*Political party*] (PPW) ... JJP
Jatiya Party [*Bangladesh*] [*Political party*] ... JP
Jatiya Samajtantrik Dal [*National Socialist Party*] [*Bangladesh*] [*Political party*] (PPW) ... JSD
Jauja [*Peru*] [*ICAO location identifier*] (ICLI) ... SPJJ
Jaundice [*Medicine*] (DMAA) ... j
Jaundice [*Medicine*] ... JAUN
Jaundice [*Medicine*] ... JAUND
Jaunt (ABBR) ... JNT
Jauntier (ABBR) ... JNTIR
Jauntiest (ABBR) ... JNTST
Jauntily (ABBR) ... JNTLY
Jauntiness (ABBR) ... JNTINS
Jaunty (ABBR) ... JNTY
Java ... JAV
Java Centrale [*NASDAQ symbol*] (TTSB) ... JAVC
Java Centrale, Inc. [*Associated Press*] (SAG) ... JavaCt
Java Centrale, Inc. [*Associated Press*] (SAG) ... JavaCtrl
Java Centrale, Inc. [*NASDAQ symbol*] (SAG) ... JAVC
Java Database Connect [*Computer science*] ... JDBC
Java Developer's Kit (PCM) ... JDK
Java Media Framework [*Computer science*] ... JMF
Java Native Interface [*Computer science*] ... JNI
JAVA [*Jamaica Association of Villas and Apartments*] **Reservations Jamaica** (EA) ... JRJ
Java Virtual Machine [*Computer science*] ... JVM
Java Virtual Machine [*Computer science*] ... JVM
Javan LASER ... JL
Javanese [*MARC language code Library of Congress*] (LCCP) ... jav
JavaSoft Java Archive [*Computer science*] ... JAR
Javelin Class Association (EA) ... JCA
Javelin Rocket Vehicle ... JRV
Javelin Systems, Inc. [*Associated Press*] (SAG) ... Javelin
Javelin Systems, Inc. [*NASDAQ symbol*] (SAG) ... JVLN
Javits-Wagner-O'Day Act ... JWOD
Javolenus Priscus [*Flourished, 60-120*] [*Authority cited in pre-1607 legal work*] (DSA) ... Jav
Javolenus Priscus [*Flourished, 60-120*] [*Authority cited in pre-1607 legal work*] (DSA) ... Javole
Jaw Jerk [*Medicine*] ... JJ
Jaw Joints and Allied Musculo-Skeletal Disorders Foundation (EA) ... JJAMD
Jawahrlal Institute of Postgraduate Medical Education and Research [*India*] ... JIPMER
Jawand [*Afghanistan*] [*ICAO location identifier*] (ICLI) ... OAJW
Jay County Commercial Review, Portland, IN [*Library symbol Library of Congress*] (LCLS) ... InPtlC
Jay County Recorder's Office, Portland, IN [*Library symbol Library of Congress*] (LCLS) ... InPtlCR
Jay Jacobs [*NASDAQ symbol*] (TTSB) ... JAYJ
Jay Jacobs, Inc. [*NASDAQ symbol*] (NQ) ... JAYJ
Jayapura [*Indonesia*] [*Airport symbol*] (OAG) ... DJJ
Jayapura [*Indonesia*] [*Seismograph station code, US Geological Survey*] (SEIS) ... JAY
Jayapura Sector [*Indonesia*] [*ICAO location identifier*] (ICLI) ... WAJZ
Jayapura/Sentani [*Indonesia*] [*ICAO location identifier*] (ICLI) ... WAJJ
Jayark Corp. [*NASDAQ symbol*] (NQ) ... JAYA
Jayark Corp. [*Associated Press*] (SAG) ... Jayark
Jaycees Community Foundation [*Australia*] ... JCF
Jaycees International (EA) ... JCI
Jayco Jafari International Travel Club (EA) ... JJITC
Jayhawk Acceptance [*NASDAQ symbol*] (TTSB) ... JACC
Jayhawk Acceptance Corp. [*NASDAQ symbol*] (SAG) ... JACC
Jayhawk Acceptance Corp. [*Associated Press*] (SAG) ... Jayhwk
Jayne Mansfield Fan Club (EA) ... JMFC
Jazz [*A radio station format*] (WDMC) ... JZ
Jazz Action Society of Tasmania ... JAST
Jazz Arts Society (EA) ... JAS
Jazz at the Philharmonic ... JATP
Jazz Centre Society [*British*] ... JCS
Jazz Composers Orchestra Association (EA) ... JCOA
Jazz Dance World Congress ... JDWC
Jazz for Life Project [*Defunct*] (EA) ... JLP
Jazz Interactions (EA) ... JI
Jazz International ... JI
Jazz World Society (EA) ... JWS
Jazz-Lift [*Provides jazz records to persons in Iron Curtain countries*] [*Defunct*] (EA) ... JL
Jazzman Resources, Inc. [*Vancouver Stock Exchange symbol*] ... JZM
JB Oxford Holdings [*Associated Press*] (SAG) ... JB Oxfrd
J-Band Detector ... JD
JCP & L Capital LP [*Associated Press*] (SAG) ... JCPCap
JCP & L Capital LP [*NYSE symbol*] (SAG) ... JYP
JCP&L Cap L.P.8.56%'MIPS' [*NYSE symbol*] (TTSB) ... JYPPrZ
JCS [*Joint Chiefs of Staff*] **Support** (MCD) ... JS
JDA Software Group [*NASDAQ symbol*] (TTSB) ... JDAS
JDA Software Group, Inc. [*NASDAQ symbol*] (SAG) ... JDAS
JDA Software Group, Inc. [*Associated Press*] (SAG) ... JDASoft
JDN Realty [*NYSE symbol*] (TTSB) ... JDN
JDN Realty Corp. [*NYSE symbol*] (SAG) ... JDN
JDS Capital Ltd. [*Toronto Stock Exchange symbol*] ... JDS
JDS Investments Ltd. [*Toronto Stock Exchange symbol*] ... JDI
J.E. Pearson Elementary School, Wheaton, MN [*Library symbol*] [*Library of Congress*] (LCLS) ... MnWhePE
Je Vous Salue par les Noms Maconniques que Nous Seul Connoissons [*I Salute You by the Masonic Names, Which We Only Know*] [*Freemasonry*] [*French*] ... JVSPLNMQNSC
Jeaffreson's Book about Lawyers [*A publication*] (DLA) ... Jeaf
Jealous (ABBR) ... JELOS
Jealous (ABBR) ... JLUS
Jealously (ABBR) ... JLUSLY
Jealousness (ABBR) ... JLUSNS
Jealousy (ABBR) ... JELOSY
Jealousy (ABBR) ... JLUSY
[*The*] **Jean and Dorothy Newman Industrial Relations Library, Center for Industrial Relations, University of Toronto, Ontario** [*Library symbol National Library of Canada*] (NLC) ... OTUIRN
Jean Coutu Group (PJC), Inc. [*Toronto Stock Exchange symbol*] ... PJC
Jean Philippe Fragrances [*NASDAQ symbol*] (TTSB) ... JEAN
Jean Philippe Fragrances, Inc. [*NASDAQ symbol*] (NQ) ... JEAN
Jean Philippe Fragrances, Inc. [*Associated Press*] (SAG) ... JeanPhl
Jean Piaget Society [*Later, JPSSSKD*] (EA) ... JPS
Jean Piaget Society: Society for the Study of Knowledge and Development (EA) ... JPSSSKD
Jean Pierre Cosmetiques, Inc. [*Vancouver Stock Exchange symbol*] ... JP
Jeanes Hospital, Philadelphia, PA [*Library symbol Library of Congress Obsolete*] (LCLS) ... PPJea
Jeanette MacDonald International Fan Club (EA) ... JMIFC
Jeanette, PA [*AM radio station call letters*] ... WBCW
Jean-Jacques Servan-Schreiber [*French publisher*] ... J-J S-S
Jeanne Pruett Fan Club (EA) ... JPFC
Jeannie C. Riley Fan Club (EA) ... JCRFC
Jeans Viscosity Equation [*Physics*] ... JVE
Jeanswear Communication (EA) ... JC
Jebb and Bourke's Irish Queen's Bench Reports [*1841-42*] [*A publication*] (DLA) ... Jebb & B
Jebb and Bourke's Irish Queen's Bench Reports [*1841-42*] [*A publication*] (DLA) ... Jebb & B (Ir)
Jebb and Symes' Irish Queen's Bench Reports [*A publication*] (DLA) ... J & S
Jebb and Symes' Irish Queen's Bench Reports [*A publication*] (DLA) ... Jebb & S
Jebb and Symes' Irish Queen's Bench Reports [*A publication*] (DLA) ... Jebb & S (Ir)
Jebb and Symes' Irish Queen's Bench Reports [*A publication*] (DLA) ... Jebb & Sym
Jebb's Irish Crown and Presentment Cases [*A publication*] (DLA) ... Jebb Cr & Pr Cas
Jebb's Irish Crown Cases [*1822-40*] [*A publication*] (DLA) ... Jebb

Jebb's Irish Crown Cases [*1822-40*] [*A publication*] (DLA) .... Jebb CC
Jebb's Irish Crown Cases [*1822-40*] [*A publication*] (DLA) .... Jebb CC (Ir)
Jebel Dhana [*United Arab Emirates*] [*ICAO location identifier*] (ICLI) .... OMAJ
Jeberos/Bellavista [*Peru*] [*ICAO location identifier*] (ICLI) .... SPBS
Jedburgh Teams [*Allied intelligence-gathering units in Europe*] [*World War II*] .... JEDS
Jeddah [*Saudi Arabia*] [*Airport symbol*] (OAG) .... JED
Jeddah [*Saudi Arabia*] [*ICAO location identifier*] (ICLI) .... OEJD
Jeddah/King Abdul Aziz International [*Saudi Arabia*] [*ICAO location identifier*] (ICLI) .... OEJN
Jedediah (BJA) .... Jed
Jedlicka Junior High School, Proctor, MN [*Library symbol*] [*Library of Congress*] (LCLS) .... MnProJ
Jeep Junior [*Automobile model designation*] .... JJ
Jeep-Truck Engine Controller .... JTEC
Jeff Healey Fan Club (EA) .... JHFC
JeffBanks, Inc. [*NASDAQ symbol*] (SAG) .... JEFF
JeffBanks, Inc. [*Associated Press*] (SAG) .... JeffBanks
Jefferies Group [*NYSE symbol*] (TTSB) .... JEF
Jefferies Group, Inc. [*Associated Press*] (SAG) .... JeffrGp
Jefferies Group, Inc. [*NASDAQ symbol*] (NQ) .... JEFG
Jeffersn-Pilot 7.25% 'ACES' [*NYSE symbol*] (TTSB) .... NBX
Jefferson Bancorp (FL) [*NASDAQ symbol*] (TTSB) .... JBNC
Jefferson Bancorp, Inc. [*NASDAQ symbol*] (NQ) .... JBNC
Jefferson Bancorp, Inc. [*Los Angles*] [*Associated Press*] (SAG) .... JeffBcLA
Jefferson Bancorp, Inc. [*Associated Press*] (SAG) .... JeffBcp
Jefferson Bancorp, Inc. (Los Angeles) [*NASDAQ symbol*] (SAG) .... JEBC
Jefferson Bancorp(LA) [*NASDAQ symbol*] (TTSB) .... JEBC
Jefferson Bankshares, Inc. [*NASDAQ symbol*] (NQ) .... JBNK
Jefferson Bankshares, Inc. [*Associated Press*] (SAG) .... JefBsh
Jefferson Bee, Jefferson, IA [*Library symbol Library of Congress*] (LCLS) .... IaJB
Jefferson City [*Diocesan abbreviation*] [*Missouri*] (TOCD) .... JC
Jefferson City [*Missouri*] [*Airport symbol*] (OAG) .... JEF
Jefferson City Junior College [*Discontinued operation, 1958*] [*Missouri*] .... JCJC
Jefferson City, MO [*Location identifier FAA*] (FAAL) .... JCQ
Jefferson City, MO [*Location identifier FAA*] (FAAL) .... JEF
Jefferson City, MO [*FM radio station call letters*] .... KJLU
Jefferson City, MO [*FM radio station call letters*] .... KJMO
Jefferson City, MO [*AM radio station call letters*] .... KLIK
Jefferson City, MO [*Television station call letters*] .... KNLJ
Jefferson City, MO [*Television station call letters*] .... KRCG
Jefferson City, MO [*FM radio station call letters*] .... KTXY
Jefferson City, MO [*AM radio station call letters*] .... KWOS
Jefferson City, MO [*Location identifier FAA*] (FAAL) .... MEO
Jefferson City, TN [*FM radio station call letters*] .... WEZG
Jefferson City, TN [*AM radio station call letters*] .... WJFC
Jefferson College, Washington, MS [*Library symbol Library of Congress Obsolete*] (LCLS) .... MsWJ
Jefferson Community College, Library, Watertown, NY [*OCLC symbol*] (OCLC) .... VND
Jefferson Community College, Louisville, KY [*OCLC symbol*] (OCLC) .... KJC
Jefferson Community College, Louisville, KY [*Library symbol Library of Congress*] (LCLS) .... KyLoJ
Jefferson Community College, Watertown, NY [*Library symbol Library of Congress*] (LCLS) .... NWattJ
Jefferson County Court House, Birmingham, AL [*Library symbol Library of Congress*] (LCLS) .... ABC
Jefferson County District Library, Hamer Branch, Hamer, ID [*Library symbol*] [*Library of Congress*] (LCLS) .... IdMen-H
Jefferson County District Library, Heart of the Valley Branch, Terreton, ID [*Library symbol*] [*Library of Congress*] (LCLS) .... IdMen-HV
Jefferson County District Library, Menan Branch, Menan, ID [*Library symbol*] [*Library of Congress*] (LCLS) .... IdMen
Jefferson County Historical Society, Watertown, NY [*Library symbol Library of Congress*] (LCLS) .... NWattJHi
Jefferson County Law Library, Birmingham, AL [*Library symbol Library of Congress*] (LCLS) .... ABJ
Jefferson County Library, Fayette, MS [*Library symbol Library of Congress*] (LCLS) .... MsFa
Jefferson County Library, Golden, CO [*Library symbol Library of Congress*] (LCLS) .... CoGJ
Jefferson County Library, Golden, CO [*Library symbol*] [*Library of Congress*] (LCLS) .... CoGJCL
Jefferson County Library, Madras, OR [*Library symbol Library of Congress*] (LCLS) .... OrMad
Jefferson County Rural Library District, Hadlock, WA [*Library symbol*] [*Library of Congress*] (LCLS) .... WaHJ
Jefferson County School District R-1, Library Media Processing, Lakewood, CO [*Library symbol Library of Congress*] (LCLS) .... CoLakJ
Jefferson County Youth Center, Golden, CO [*Library symbol Library of Congress*] (LCLS) .... CoGJY
Jefferson Davis Association (EA) .... JDA
Jefferson Davis County Library, Prentiss, MS [*Library symbol Library of Congress*] (LCLS) .... MsPr
Jefferson Davis Parish Library, Jennings, LA [*Library symbol Library of Congress*] (LCLS) .... LJJ
Jefferson Educational Foundation (EA) .... JEF
Jefferson Elementary School, Huntington, NY [*Library symbol*] [*Library of Congress*] (LCLS) .... NHuJE
Jefferson Elementary School, LaSalle, IL [*Library symbol Library of Congress*] (LCLS) .... ILasJ
Jefferson Elementary School, Princeton, IL [*Library symbol Library of Congress*] (LCLS) .... IPriJS
Jefferson Elementary School, St. Cloud, MN [*Library symbol*] [*Library of Congress*] (LCLS) .... MnStclJ
Jefferson Elementary School, Willmar, MN [*Library symbol*] [*Library of Congress*] (LCLS) .... MnWilJES
Jefferson Foundation (EA) .... JF
Jefferson, GA [*AM radio station call letters*] .... WBKZ
Jefferson Herald, Jefferson, IA [*Library symbol Library of Congress*] (LCLS) .... IaJH
Jefferson High School, Alexandria, MN [*Library symbol*] [*Library of Congress*] (LCLS) .... MnAleJH
Jefferson High School, Rockford, IL [*Library symbol*] [*Library of Congress*] (LCLS) .... IRoJH
Jefferson, IA [*Location identifier FAA*] (FAAL) .... EFW
Jefferson, IA [*FM radio station call letters*] .... KGRA
Jefferson Lyons [*Commercial firm British*] .... JL
Jefferson Medical College of Philadelphia .... JMCP
Jefferson National Expansion Memorial National Historic Site .... JEFF
Jefferson, OH [*Location identifier FAA*] (FAAL) .... JFN
Jefferson, OH [*FM radio station call letters*] .... WCVJ
Jefferson Parish Library, Metairie, LA [*Library symbol Library of Congress*] (LCLS) .... LMetJ
Jefferson Parish Public Library, Gretna, LA [*Library symbol Library of Congress*] (LCLS) .... LGrJ
Jefferson Parish Recreation Department, Metairie, LA [*Library symbol Library of Congress*] (LCLS) .... LMetR
Jefferson Pilot [*Associated Press*] (SAG) .... JeffPlt
Jefferson Pilot [*Associated Press*] (SAG) .... JeffPOO
Jefferson Pilot [*NYSE symbol*] (SAG) .... JP
Jefferson Pilot [*NYSE symbol*] (SAG) .... NBX
Jefferson Proving Ground [*Madison, IN*] [*Army*] (AABC) .... JPG
Jefferson Public Library, Jefferson, IA [*Library symbol Library of Congress*] (LCLS) .... IaJ
Jefferson Public Library, Jefferson, OR [*Library symbol Library of Congress*] (LCLS) .... OrJe
Jefferson Savings Bancorp [*Associated Press*] (SAG) .... JeffSvg
Jefferson Savings Bancorp [*NASDAQ symbol*] (SAG) .... JSBA
Jefferson School of Social Science, New York, NY [*Library symbol Library of Congress Obsolete*] (LCLS) .... NNJef
Jefferson Smurfit [*NASDAQ symbol*] (TTSB) .... JJSC
Jefferson Smurfit Corp. [*Associated Press*] (SAG) .... JefSmrf
Jefferson Smurfit Corp. [*NASDAQ symbol*] (SAG) .... JJSC
Jefferson Smurfit Group PLC [*NYSE symbol*] (SAG) .... JS
Jefferson Smurfit Group PLC [*Associated Press*] (SAG) .... JSmrfG
Jefferson Smurfit Grp ADS [*NYSE symbol*] (TTSB) .... JS
Jefferson State Junior College, Birmingham, AL [*Library symbol Library of Congress*] (LCLS) .... ABJS
Jefferson, TX [*FM radio station call letters*] .... KJTX
Jefferson-Pilot [*NYSE symbol*] (TTSB) .... JP
Jefferson-Pilot Corp. [*Associated Press*] (SAG) .... JeffPilot
Jefferson-Pilot Corp. [*NYSE symbol*] (SPSG) .... JP
Jefferson's Manual of Parliamentary Law [*A publication*] (DLA) .... Jeff Man
Jefferson's Virginia General Court Reports [*A publication*] (DLA) .... Jeff
Jefferson's Virginia General Court Reports [*A publication*] (DLA) .... Jeff (VA)
Jeffersontown, KY [*FM radio station call letters*] .... WLSY
Jeffersontown, KY [*FM radio station call letters*] (RBYB) .... WMJM-FM
Jeffersonville, GA [*FM radio station call letters*] .... WMGB
Jeffersonville, IN [*Location identifier FAA*] (FAAL) .... JVY
Jeffersonville, IN [*FM radio station call letters*] .... WQMF
Jeffersonville, IN [*AM radio station call letters*] .... WXVW
Jeffersonville, NY [*FM radio station call letters*] .... WJFF
Jeffersonville, NY [*FM radio station call letters*] .... WPDA
Jeffersonville Township Public Library, Jeffersonville, IN [*OCLC symbol*] (OCLC) .... IJV
Jeffersonville Township Public Library, Jeffersonville, IN [*Library symbol Library of Congress*] (LCLS) .... InJe
Jefjen Capital [*Vancouver Stock Exchange symbol*] .... JEF
Jehosaphat [*Biblical*] (ROG) .... JEHO
Jehovah (ROG) .... JHVA
Jehovah (ABBR) .... JHVH
Jehovah's Witnesses (ADA) .... JW
Jehovah's Witnesses for Animal Rights [*An association*] (EA) .... JWAR
Jehovistic and Elohistic [*Theology*] .... J & E
Jehuda [*On Hebrew coins of the fourth century*] .... JHD
Jejunal Diverticulitis [*Gastroenterology*] (DAVI) .... JD
Jejunal Segment [*Gastroenterology*] (DAVI) .... JS
Jejunectomy (ABBR) .... JEJUN
Jejunitis (ABBR) .... JEJUN
Jejunogastric Intussusception [*Gastroenterology*] (DAVI) .... JGI
Jejunoileal [*Medicine*] (MEDA) .... JI
Jejunoileal Bypass [*Gastroenterology*] (DAVI) .... JIB
Jejunoileitis [*Gastroenterology*] (DAVI) .... JI
Jejunoileostomy [*Gastroenterology*] (DAVI) .... JI
Jejunojejunostomy [*Gastroenterology*] (DAVI) .... JJ
Jejunostomy Tube [*Medicine*] (DMAA) .... JT
Jejunum [*Medicine*] .... JEJ
Jellico, TN [*FM radio station call letters*] .... WEKX
Jellico, TN [*AM radio station call letters*] .... WJJT
Jellico, TN [*Television station call letters*] .... WPMC
Jellied (ABBR) .... JLYD
Jelly (ABBR) .... JLY
Jellybean (ABBR) .... JLYBN
Jellyfish (ABBR) .... JLYFSH
Jellylike (ABBR) .... JLYLK
Jem Group Products [*Vancouver Stock Exchange symbol*] .... JGP
Jen Min Piao [*or Yuan*] [*Peoples money of China*] (BARN) .... JMP
Jena [*German Democratic Republic*] [*Seismograph station code, US Geological Survey Closed*] (SEIS) .... JEN

Jena, LA [*Location identifier FAA*] (FAAL) .... JLY
Jena, LA [*AM radio station call letters*] .... KJNA
Jena, LA [*FM radio station call letters*] .... KJNA-FM
Jena Nomina Anatomic a [*Also, INA*] [*Anatomy*] (DAVI) .... INA
Jena Nomina Anatomica [*Also, INA*] [*Anatomy*] .... JNA
Jenair Ltd. [*Cyprus*] [*ICAO designator*] (FAAC) .... JEN
Jencken's Bills of Exchange [*1880*] [*A publication*] (DLA) .... Jenck Bills
Jencken's Negotiable Securities [*1880*] [*A publication*] (DLA) .... Jenck Neg S
Jendarata [*Malaysia*] [*ICAO location identifier*] (ICLI) .... WMAJ
Jendouba [*Tunisia*] [*ICAO location identifier*] (ICLI) .... DTTN
Jenkins Activity Survey [*Personality development test*] [*Psychology*] .... JAS
Jenkins' Eight Centuries of Reports, English Exchequer [*145 English Reprint*] [*1220-1623*] [*A publication*] (DLA) .... Jenk
Jenkins' Eight Centuries of Reports, English Exchequer [*145 English Reprint*] [*1220-1623*] [*A publication*] (DLA) .... Jenk Cent
Jenkins' Eight Centuries of Reports, English Exchequer [*145 English Reprint*] [*1220-1623*] [*A publication*] (DLA) .... Jenkins (Eng)
Jenkins, KY [*FM radio station call letters*] .... WIFX
Jenkins, KY [*AM radio station call letters*] .... WKVG
Jenkinson and Formoy's Select Cases in the Exchequer of Pleas [*Selden Society Publication, Vol. 48*] [*A publication*] (DLA) .... Jenk & Formoy
Jenkinsville [*South Carolina*] [*Seismograph station code, US Geological Survey*] (SEIS) .... JSC
Jenkintown, PA [*FM radio station call letters*] .... WIBF
Jenks, OK [*Location identifier FAA*] (FAAL) .... JEX
Jenks' Reports [*58 New Hampshire*] [*A publication*] (DLA) .... Jenks
Jenner and Block, Chicago, IL [*Library symbol Library of Congress*] (LCLS) .... ICJB
Jenner & Block, Chicago, IL [*OCLC symbol*] (OCLC) .... IPB
Jennett's Sugden Acts [*A publication*] (DLA) .... Jenn Sug A
Jenney Beechcraft, Inc. [*ICAO designator*] (FAAC) .... JNY
Jennie Belle Stephens Smith Library, New Albany, MS [*Library symbol Library of Congress*] (LCLS) .... MsNa
Jennifer Bassey Fan Club (EA) .... JBFC
Jennifer Burnett Fan Club (EA) .... JBFC
Jennifer Convertibles, Inc. [*Associated Press*] (SAG) .... JenfCv
Jennifer Jo [*In TV series "The Governor and JJ"*] .... JJ
Jennings County Public Library, North Vernon, IN [*Library symbol Library of Congress*] (LCLS) .... InNovJ
Jennings County Recorder's Office, Vernon, IN [*Library symbol Library of Congress*] (LCLS) .... InVnCR
Jennings, LA [*Location identifier FAA*] (FAAL) .... JNZ
Jennings, LA [*AM radio station call letters*] .... KJEF
Jennings, LA [*FM radio station call letters*] .... KJEF-FM
Jennings Public Library, Jennings, LA [*Library symbol Library of Congress*] (LCLS) .... LJ
Jennings, Strouss, Salmon, Phoenix, AZ [*Library symbol*] [*Library of Congress*] (LCLS) .... AzPhJ
Jennison's Reports [*14-18 Michigan*] [*A publication*] (DLA) .... Jenn
Jenny Craig [*NYSE symbol*] (SPSG) .... JC
Jenny Craig [*Associated Press*] (SAG) .... JenCrg
Jenny Hunter's Kindergarten and Primary Training School, New York, NY [*Library symbol Library of Congress Obsolete*] (LCLS) .... NNJHK
Jenny Lind Island, NT [*ICAO location identifier*] (ICLI) .... CYUQ
Jenolan [*Australia Seismograph station code, US Geological Survey*] (SEIS) .... JNL
Jenpeg, MB [*FM radio station call letters*] .... CJEN
Jensen Beach, FL [*FM radio station call letters*] .... WHLG
Jensen Elementary School, Pasadena, TX [*Library symbol*] [*Library of Congress*] (LCLS) .... TxPJE
Jensen Interceptor Owners Club (EA) .... JIOC
Jensen-Salsbery Laboratories, Kansas City, KS [*Library symbol Library of Congress*] (LCLS) .... KKcJS
Jentaculum [*Breakfast*] [*Pharmacy*] .... JENTAC
Jentech Ventures Corp. [*Vancouver Stock Exchange symbol*] .... JCV
Jeopardize (ABBR) .... JEOPZ
Jeopardize (ABBR) .... JPRDZ
Jeopardized (ABBR) .... JEOPZD
Jeopardizing (ABBR) .... JEOPZG
Jeopardizing (ABBR) .... JPRDZG
Jeopardy (ABBR) .... JEOP
Jeopardy (BARN) .... Jep
Jeopardy (ABBR) .... JPRDY
Jepenssen Data Plan, Inc. [*ICAO designator*] (FAAC) .... XLD
Jequie [*Brazil*] [*Airport symbol*] (OAG) .... JEQ
Jerba/Zarzis [*Tunisia*] [*ICAO location identifier*] (ICLI) .... DTTJ
Jeremiah [*Old Testament book*] (BJA) .... Je
Jeremiah [*Old Testament book*] .... Jer
Jeremiah [*Old Testament book*] .... Jr
Jeremiah [*Old Testament book*] (BJA) .... Jer
Jeremias (BJA) .... Jer
Jeremie [*Haiti*] [*ICAO location identifier*] (ICLI) .... MTJE
Jeremy on Carriers [*A publication*] (DLA) .... Jer Car
Jeremy's Digest [*1817-49*] [*A publication*] (DLA) .... Jer Dig
Jeremy's Equity Jurisdiction [*A publication*] (DLA) .... Jer Eq Jur
Jeremy's Equity Jurisdiction [*A publication*] (DLA) .... Jeremy Eq
Jeremy's Equity Jurisdiction [*A publication*] (DLA) .... Jeremy Eq Jur
Jerez [*Spain ICAO location identifier*] (ICLI) .... LEJR
Jerez De La Frontera [*Spain*] [*Airport symbol*] (OAG) .... XRY
Jericho (BJA) .... Jer
Jericho [*Jordan*] [*ICAO location identifier*] (ICLI) .... OJJO
Jericho Public Library, Jericho, NY [*Library symbol Library of Congress*] (LCLS) .... NJer
Jericho Senior High School, Jericho, NY [*Library symbol Library of Congress*] (LCLS) .... NJerHS
Jerico Community Echo, Waucoma, IA [*Library symbol Library of Congress*] (LCLS) .... IaWauE

Jerked (ABBR) .... JRKD
Jerker (ABBR) .... JRKR
Jerkier (ABBR) .... JRKIR
Jerkiest (ABBR) .... JRKST
Jerkily (ABBR) .... JRKLY
Jerkin (ABBR) .... JRKN
Jerkiness (ABBR) .... JRKNS
Jerking (ABBR) .... JRKG
Jeroboam (WDAA) .... JEROB
[*The*] Jerome Biblical Commentary [*Englewood Cliffs, NJ*] [*A publication*] (BJA) .... JBC
Jerome, ID [*AM radio station call letters*] .... KART
Jerome, ID [*FM radio station call letters*] .... KMVX
Jerome Public Library, Jerome, ID [*Library symbol*] [*Library of Congress*] (LCLS) .... IdJ
Jerram Pharmaceuticals Ltd., Sands Pharmaceutical Division, Toronto, ON, Canada [*Library symbol Library of Congress*] (LCLS) .... CaOTJPS
Jerrold on Copyright [*A publication*] (DLA) .... Jerr Copyr
Jerry Campbell and Five Star Band Fan Club (EA) .... JCFSBFC
Jerry Jeff Walker Fan Club (EA) .... JJWFC
Jerry Reed Fan Club [*Defunct*] (EA) .... JRFC
Jerrybuild (ABBR) .... JRYBLD
Jerrybuilder (ABBR) .... JRYBLDR
Jerrybuilding (ABBR) .... JRYBLDG
Jerrybuilt (ABBR) .... JRYBLT
Jerry's Famous Deli [*NASDAQ symbol*] (TTSB) .... DELI
Jerry's Famous Deli, Inc. [*NASDAQ symbol*] (SAG) .... DELI
Jerrys Famous Deli, Inc. [*Associated Press*] (SAG) .... JryDeli
Jerry-Slough Virus [*Medicine*] (DMAA) .... JSV
Jersey [*Great Britain*] .... GBJ
Jersey [*Channel Islands*] [*Airport symbol*] (OAG) .... JER
Jersey [*Channel Islands*] [*Seismograph station code, US Geological Survey Closed*] (SEIS) .... JRS
Jersey (ABBR) .... JRSY
Jersey [*One of the Channel Islands*] (ROG) .... JSEY
Jersey Cattle Society [*British*] (DBA) .... JCS
Jersey Cent P&L 4%cmPfd [*NYSE symbol*] (TTSB) .... JYPPr
Jersey Cent P&L7.88% Pfd [*NYSE symbol*] (TTSB) .... JYPPrE
Jersey Central Power & Light [*Associated Press*] (SAG) .... JerC
Jersey Central Power & Light Co. [*NYSE symbol*] (SAG) .... JYP
Jersey Central Railroad .... JC
Jersey, Channel Islands [*British ICAO location identifier*] (ICLI) .... EGJJ
Jersey City Free Public Library, Jersey City, NJ [*Library symbol Library of Congress*] (LCLS) .... NjJ
Jersey City State College (GAGS) .... Jersey City St C
Jersey City State College, Jersey City, NJ [*OCLC symbol*] (OCLC) .... NJJ
Jersey City State College, Jersey City, NJ [*Library symbol Library of Congress*] (LCLS) .... NjJS
Jersey Committee of Resistance Workers and Deportees (EAIO) .... JCRWD
Jersey Community Hospital, Jerseyville, IL [*Library symbol Library of Congress*] (LCLS) .... IJeH
Jersey Community Unit, School District 100, Jerseyville, IL [*Library symbol Library of Congress*] (LCLS) .... IJeSD
Jersey Electric Co. [*British*] .... JEC
Jersey European [*ICAO designator*] (AD) .... JY
Jersey European Airways [*British ICAO designator*] (FAAC) .... JEA
Jersey European Airways [*ICAO designator*] (AD) .... JV
Jersey Farmers' Union [*British*] (DBA) .... JFU
Jersey Institute .... JI
Jersey Journal, Jersey City, NJ [*Library symbol Library of Congress*] (LCLS) .... NjJJJ
Jersey Microfilming, Clifton, NJ [*Library symbol Library of Congress*] (LCLS) .... JerM
Jersey. Ordres du Conseil [*A publication*] (DLA) .... OC
Jersey Shore, PA [*AM radio station call letters*] .... WJSA
Jersey Shore, PA [*FM radio station call letters*] .... WJSA-FM
Jersey Shore, PA [*FM radio station call letters*] (RBYB) .... WVRT
Jersey Wildlife Preservation Trust (EAIO) .... JWPT
Jerseyville & Eastern [*AAR code*] .... JE
Jerseyville Free Library, Jerseyville, IL [*Library symbol Library of Congress*] (LCLS) .... IJe
Jerseyville, IL [*AM radio station call letters*] .... WJBM
Jerseyville, IL [*FM radio station call letters*] .... WKBQ
Jerusalem [*Israel*] [*Seismograph station code, US Geological Survey*] (SEIS) .... JER
Jerusalem (BJA) .... Jerus
Jerusalem (ABBR) .... JLEM
Jerusalem [*Israel*] [*Airport symbol*] (OAG) .... JRS
Jerusalem [*Jordan*] [*ICAO location identifier*] (ICLI) .... OJJR
Jerusalem Academic Press (BJA) .... JAP
Jerusalem and the East Mission .... JEM
Jerusalem Avenue Junior High School, North Bellmore, NY [*Library symbol*] [*Library of Congress*] (LCLS) .... NNbeJJ
Jerusalem Bible .... JB
Jerusalem Institutions for the Blind (EA) .... KEREN-OR
Jerusalem Talmud (BJA) .... J
Jerusalem Talmud (BJA) .... Jer
Jerusalem Talmud (BJA) .... JT
Jerusalem Talmud. Pesahim (BJA) .... JerPes
Jerusalem Talmud. Yebamoth (BJA) .... JerYeb
[*The*] Jerusalem Targum of the Pentateuch (BJA) .... TargJer
Jerusalem und Seine Gelaende [*A publication*] (BJA) .... JG
Jerusalemer Warte (BJA) .... JerW
Jerushalmi (BJA) .... Jer
Jervis. Coroners [*9th ed.*] [*1957*] [*A publication*] (DLA) .... Jerv Cor

Jervis Library Association, Rome, NY [*Library symbol Library of Congress*] (LCLS) .... NRom
Jervis' New Rules [*A publication*] (DLA) .... Jerv NR
Jervis Public Library, Rome, NY [*OCLC symbol*] (OCLC) .... ZVA
Jes Air [*Bulgaria*] [*ICAO designator*] (FAAC) .... JES
Jesenwang [*Germany ICAO location identifier*] (ICLI) .... EDMJ
Jesness Behavior Checklist [*Psychology*] (DAVI) .... JBC
Jesness Inventory [*Psychology*] .... JI
Jesolo [*Italy*] [*Airport symbol*] (AD) .... JLO
Jesous Christos, Theou Uios Soter [*Jesus Christ, Son of God, Savior*] .... ICHTHYS
Jesse Couch Fan Club (EA) .... JCFC
Jesse Stuart Foundation (EA) .... JSF
Jessore [*Bangladesh*] [*Airport symbol*] (OAG) .... JSR
Jessore [*Bangladesh*] [*ICAO location identifier*] (ICLI) .... VGJR
Jessup Elementary School, Houston, TX [*Library symbol*] [*Library of Congress*] (LCLS) .... TxHJE
Jesuit (DSUE) .... JES
Jesuit Archives of the Province of Oregon, Spokane, WA [*Library symbol Library of Congress*] (LCLS) .... WaSpJ
Jesuit Association of Student Personnel Administrators (EA) .... JASPA
Jesuit Center for Social Studies [*Defunct*] (EA) .... JCSS
Jesuit Educational Association [*Later split into AJCU and JSEA*] (EA) .... JEA
Jesuit Fathers and Brothers (TOCD) .... SJ
Jesuit Fathers and Brothers, Society of Jesus (TOCD) .... sj
Jesuit Mission Office [*Australia*] .... JMO
Jesuit Office of Social Ministry [*Later, NOJSM*] (EA) .... JOSM
Jesuit Philosophical Association of the United States and Canada (EA) .... JPA
Jesuit Refugee Service/USA (EA) .... JRS/USA
Jesuit Scholastic Library, Spokane, WA [*Library symbol Library of Congress*] (LCLS) .... WaSpJS
Jesuit School of Theology in Chicago, Chicago, IL [*Library symbol Library of Congress*] (LCLS) .... ICJST
Jesuit Secondary Education Association (EA) .... JSEA
Jesuit Seismological Association (EA) .... JSA
Jesuit Seminary, Toronto, ON, Canada [*Library symbol Library of Congress*] (LCLS) .... CaOTJS
Jesuit Volunteer Corps: Northwest (EA) .... JVC
Jesuites/Bibliotheque, Saint-Jerome, PQ, Canada [*Library symbol Library of Congress*] (LCLS) .... CaQStJeJ
Jesuites/Bibliotheque, Saint-Jerome, Quebec [*Library symbol National Library of Canada*] (NLC) .... QSTJEJ
Jesuit-Krauss-McCormick Library, Chicago, IL [*Library symbol Library of Congress*] (LCLS) .... ICJKM
Jesuit-Krauss-McCormick Library, Chicago, IL [*OCLC symbol*] (OCLC) .... IDK
Jesuits in Communication in the US (EA) .... JESCOM
Jesup Citizen Herald, Jesup, IA [*Library symbol Library of Congress*] (LCLS) .... IaJesC
Jesup, GA [*Location identifier FAA*] (FAAL) .... JES
Jesup, GA [*FM radio station call letters*] .... WIFO
Jesup, GA [*AM radio station call letters*] .... WLOP
Jesup, GA [*FM radio station call letters*] .... WLPT
Jesus [*First and third letters of His name in Greek*] IC
Jesus (ROG) .... J
Jesus .... JES
Jesus Cares Refuge Incorporated [*Australia An association*] .... JCR
Jesus Christ .... JC
Jesus Christ Superstar [*Rock opera*] .... JCSS
Jesus Christus [*Jesus Christ*] [*Latin*] (ROG) .... JX
Jesus College [*Oxford or Cambridge*] [*England*] (DAS) .... JC
Jesus College [*Oxford or Cambridge*] [*England*] (ROG) .... JES COLL
Jesus College, Cambridge [*England*] (ROG) .... JCC
Jesus College, Oxford [*England*] (ROG) .... JCO
Jesus Hominum Salvator [*Jesus, Savior of Men*] (ROG) .... JHS
Jesus, Mary, and Joseph .... JMJ
Jesus Salvator Mundi [*Jesus the Savior of the World*] [*Latin*] (ROG) .... JSM
Jesus to the Communist World [*Later, CMCW*] (EA) .... JTTCW
Jet [*Aircraft*] .... J
Jet 14 Class Association (EA) J-14/CA
Jet Advance Warning System (PDAA) .... JAWS
Jet Age Conference .... JAC
Jet Age Malfunction (IAA) .... JAM
Jet Air Internacional Charters CA [*Venezuela*] [*ICAO designator*] (FAAC) .... INC
Jet Aircraft Coating .... JAC
Jet Aircraft Noise .... JAN
Jet Aircraft Noise Survey .... JANS
Jet Aircraft Noise Survey Research Program .... JANSRP
Jet Aircraft Starting Unit (AFM) .... JASU
Jet Alsace [*France ICAO designator*] (FAAC) .... JLS
Jet Approach and Landing Chart (AFM) .... JALC
Jet Approach Landing Charts (FAAC) .... JAL
Jet Aspen Air Lines, Inc. [*FAA designator*] (FAAC) .... JTX
Jet Assist Stop .... JASTOP
Jet Attitude Control System (KSC) .... JACS
Jet Augmented Wing Flap .... JAWF
Jet Aviation (SAA) .... JETAV
Jet Aviation, Business Jets AG [*Switzerland ICAO designator*] (FAAC) .... PJS
Jet Barrier .... J-B
Jet Black [*Derogatory nickname for a black person*] .... JB
Jet Blast Deflector .... JBD
Jet Bomb .... JB
Jet Business Airlines [*Belgium ICAO designator*] (FAAC) .... JAB
Jet Cargo-Liberia [*ICAO designator*] (FAAC) .... JCL
Jet Center Flight Training SA [*Spain ICAO designator*] (FAAC) .... JCF
Jet Circulation Control .... JCC
Jet Deflection Control (AAG) .... JDC
Jet Driver (KSC) .... JD
Jet East, Inc. [*ICAO designator*] (FAAC) .... JED
Jet Ejector System .... JES
Jet Engine .... JE
Jet Engine Base Maintenance .... JEBM
Jet Engine Base Maintenance - Return Rate (PDAA) .... JEBM-RR
Jet Engine Control Bearing .... JECB
Jet Engine Duct .... JED
Jet Engine Exhaust .... JEE
Jet Engine Field Maintenance .... JEFM
Jet Engine Fuel .... JEF
Jet Engine Intermediate Maintenance .... JEIM
Jet Engine Modulation (MCD) .... JEM
Jet Engine Processor .... JEP
Jet Engine Smoke Abatement Program .... JESAP
Jet Engine Thrust Augmentation Mix (SAA) .... JETAM
Jet Exhaust .... JE
Jet Express [*ICAO designator*] (AD) .... JI
Jet Express, Inc. [*ICAO designator*] (FAAC) .... JEX
Jet Express Ticketing System .... JETS
Jet Flap .... JF
Jet Flap Model .... JFM
Jet Flap Rotor .... JFR
Jet Flight Information (AFM) .... JFI
Jet Flying Belt (PDAA) .... JFB
Jet Form Corp. [*NASDAQ symbol*] (SAG) .... FORMF
Jet Form Corp. [*Associated Press*] (SAG) .... JetForm
Jet Freighters, Inc. [*ICAO designator*] (FAAC) .... CFT
Jet Fret [*France ICAO designator*] (FAAC) .... JFT
Jet Fuel .... J
Jet Fuel Starter .... JFS
Jet Fuel Thermal Oxidation Test [*or Tester*] [*Analytical chemistry*] [*Air Force*] .... JFTOT
Jet Fuel Thermal Stability .... JFTS
Jet Heritage Ltd. [*British ICAO designator*] (FAAC) .... JHL
Jet Impurity Survey Spectrometer [*Nuclear energy*] (NUCP) .... JISS
Jet Inlet System .... JIS
Jet Interaction (RDA) .... JI
Jet Interaction Control (MCD) .... JIC
Jet Interaction Fuel .... JIF
Jet Interaction Gas Generator .... JIGG
Jet Interaction / Secondary Injection .... JI/SI
Jet Interaction Steering .... JIS
Jet Interaction Test Apparatus (MCD) .... JITA
Jet Lift Aircraft .... JLA
Jet Lift Engine .... JLE
Jet Lift System .... JLS
Jet Mixing Flow .... JMF
Jet Navigation (AAG) .... J-N
Jet Navigation Chart .... JN
Jet Navigation Chart .... JNC
Jet Noise Survey .... JNS
Jet Operations Requirements .... JOR
Jet Penetration .... JP
Jet Penetration Approach .... JPAP
Jet Petroleum (AFM) .... JP
Jet Petroleum, Thermally Stable (DOMA) .... JPTS
Jet Pilot .... JP
Jet Pioneers Association of the United States of America (EA) .... JPA
Jet Pipe .... JP
Jet Pipe Temperature .... JPT
Jet Pipe Temperature Limiter (MCD) .... JPTL
Jet Plume Simulation .... JPS
Jet Power .... JP
Jet Propellant [*or Propulsion*] .... JP
Jet Propulsion Fuel .... JP
Jet Propulsion Laboratory [*Renamed H. Allen Smith Jet Propulsion Laboratory, 1973, after a retiring congressman. However, JPL is used officially*] [*California Institute of Technology Pasadena, CA*] [*NASA*] [*Research center*] .... JPL
Jet Propulsion Laboratory Field Station, Air Force Eastern Test Range .... JPL/ETR
Jet Propulsion Laboratory, Pasadena, CA [*Library symbol Library of Congress*] (LCLS) .... CPJP
Jet Propulsion Laboratory/Pilot Ocean Data System (MCD) .... JPL/PODS
Jet Propulsion Laboratory Self Testing and Repairing Computer [*California Institute of Technology*] (PDAA) .... JPL-STAR
Jet Publications [*DoD*] .... JP
Jet Pump [*Bioinstrumentation*] .... JP
Jet Reaction Control .... JRC
Jet Reaction Control System .... JRCS
Jet Refresher Training [*Navy*] (NVT) .... JRFTNG
Jet Rent SA [*Mexico ICAO designator*] (FAAC) .... JRN
Jet Repair Service .... JRS
Jet Research Center, Inc., Arlington, TX [*Library symbol Library of Congress*] (LCLS) .... TxArJ
Jet Research Laboratory (MCD) .... JRL
Jet Route [*Followed by identification*] .... J
Jet Runway Barrier [*Aviation*] (FAAC) .... J-Bar
Jet Select Logic (MCD) .... JSL
Jet Servisx SA de CV [*Mexico ICAO designator*] (FAAC) .... VIS
Jet Show Assembly .... JSA
Jet Stabilization .... JS
Jet Steering System .... JSS
Jet STOL [*Short Takeoff and Landing*] **Transport** [*Aircraft*] .... JST

Jet Strategic Airlift Capability [of Military Air Command] (AAG) ...... JSAC
Jet Stream ...... JS
Jet Stream ...... JTST
Jet Stream ...... JTSTR
Jet Strip System (PDAA) ...... JSS
Jet Study (AAG) ...... JS
Jet Tear-Down Facility (MCD) ...... JTF
Jet Test Vehicle ...... JTV
Jet Training Unit ...... JTU
Jet Transitional Training Unit [Navy] ...... JTTU
Jet Transport Landing Approach Simulator ...... JTLAS
Jet Utility Transport ...... JUT
Jet Vane Actuators ...... JVA
Jet Vane Control (MCD) ...... JVC
Jet Vapor Deposition [Coating technology] ...... JVD
Jet Ventilation [Medicine] ...... JV
Jet Way, Inc. [ICAO designator] (FAAC) ...... JWY
Jetag AB [Switzerland ICAO designator] (FAAC) ...... JAG
Jetair APS [Denmark ICAO designator] (FAAC) ...... FOX
Jet-Air Bedarfsflugunternehmen [Austria ICAO designator] (FAAC) ...... JTR
Jetall Holdings, Corp. [Canada ICAO designator] (FAAC) ...... JTL
Jet-Assisted Takeoff ...... JATO
Jetcom SA [Switzerland ICAO designator] (FAAC) ...... JCA
Jetcopter [Denmark ICAO designator] (FAAC) ...... JCP
Jetevator ...... JETR
Jetevator Assembly ...... JA
Jetevator Null Position Indicator ...... JNPI
Jetevator Sensor ...... JS
Jetflite OY [Finland ICAO designator] (FAAC) ...... JEF
Jet-Induced Circulation [Combustor] ...... JIC
Jet-Induced Lift ...... JIL
Jetliner (ABBR) ...... JETLNR
Jet-Piercing Machine ...... JPM
Jet-Propelled ...... JETP
Jet-Propelled Takeoff ...... JPTO
Jetronic Industries, Inc. [AMEX symbol] (SPSG) ...... JET
Jetronic Industries, Inc. [Associated Press] (SAG) ...... Jetronic
Jets Corporativos SA de CV [Mexico ICAO designator] (FAAC) ...... JTC
Jets Ejecutivos SA [Mexico ICAO designator] (FAAC) ...... JEJ
Jetsam (ABBR) ...... JET
Jetstream International Airlines [ICAO designator] (FAAC) ...... JIA
Jetstream Ltd. [Hungary ICAO designator] (FAAC) ...... JSH
Jetted (ABBR) ...... JETD
Jetting (ABBR) ...... JETG
Jettison ...... JET
Jettison ...... JETN
Jettison (KSC) ...... JETT
Jettison (MSA) ...... JTSN
Jettison and Washing Overboard ...... J & WO
Jettison Booster Package [NASA] ...... JBP
Jettison Control Module ...... JCM
Jettison Control Panel ...... JCP
Jettison Motor (KSC) ...... J/M
Jettison Pushbutton Switch ...... JPBS
Jettison Release Mechanism ...... JRM
Jettison Signal ...... JS
Jettisoning and Washing Overboard [Inventor] (ODBW) ...... jwo
Jetworld Airways Ltd. [Antigua and Barbuda] [ICAO designator] (FAAC) ...... JWA
Jeune Ballet de France ...... JBF
Jeunes Democrates Chretiens Europeens [European Young Christian Democrats - EYCD] (EA) ...... JDCE
Jeunesse Anarchiste Communiste [French student group] ...... JAC
Jeunesse Canada Monde (AC) ...... JCM
Jeunesse Chretienne Malgache [Malagasy Christian Youth] ...... JCM
Jeunesse de l'Unite Togolaise [Togolese Unity Youth] ...... JUT
Jeunesse Democratique Camerounaise [Cameroonian Democratic Youth] ...... JDC
Jeunesse du Kwilu-Kwango-Bateke [Kwilu-Kwango-Bateke Youth] ...... JKKB
Jeunesse du Mouvement National Congolaise - Lumumba [Youth of the Lumumba Wing of the Congolese National Movement] ...... JMNCL
Jeunesse du Rassemblement Democratique Africain [Youth of the African Democratic Rally] ...... JRDA
Jeunesse du Rassemblement Democratique Africain de Cote d'Ivoire [Youth of the African Democratic Rally of the Ivory Coast] ...... JRDACI
Jeunesse d'Union Dahomeene [Dahomean Youth Union] ...... JUD
Jeunesse d'Union Nationale Congolaise [Congolese National Youth Union] ...... JUNC
Jeunesse Etudiante Catholique Internationale [International Young Catholic Students] (EAIO) ...... JEC
Jeunesse Etudiante Catholique Internationale [International Young Catholic Students] ...... JECI
Jeunesse Independante Chretienne Internationale [International Independent Christian Youth - IICY] (EA) ...... JICI
Jeunesse Nationale Katangaise [Katangan National Youth] ...... JENAKAT
Jeunesse Ouvriere Catholique Canadienne [Young Canadian Catholic Workers] [Established 1930] ...... JOCC
Jeunesse Ouvriere Chretienne Internationale [International Young Christian Workers - IYCW] (EAIO) ...... JOCI
Jeunesse Ouvriere du Senegal [Senegalese Working Youth] ...... JOS
Jeunesse Ouvriere Marocaine [Moroccan Working Youth] ...... JOM
Jeunesse Populaire Senegalaise [Senegalese People's Youth] ...... JPS
Jeunesse pour Christ [Youth for Christ International - YFCI] (EA) ...... JPC
Jeunesse Progressiste Casamancaise [Casamance Progressive Youth] [Senegal] ...... JPC
Jeunesse Social Democrate [Social Democratic Youth] [Malagasy] ...... JSD

Jeunesse Socialiste Royale Khmere [Royal Cambodian Socialist Youth] [Political party] ...... JSRK
Jeunesse Travailleuse Oubanguienne [Ubangi Working Youth] ...... JTO
Jeunesse Universelle ...... JU
Jeunesses Europeennes Federalistes ...... JEF
Jeunesses Europeennes Liberales [Liberal European Youth] ...... JEL
Jever [Germany ICAO location identifier] (ICLI) ...... EDNJ
Jevons on Criminal Law [A publication] (DLA) ...... Jev Cr Law
Jevreiski Istoriski Muzej (BJA) ...... JIM
Jewel Bearing Assembly ...... JBA
Jewel Cave National Monument ...... JECA
Jewel Resources [Vancouver Stock Exchange symbol] ...... JRI
Jeweled-Orifice Misting Nozzle ...... JMN
Jeweled-Orifice Misting Nozzle ...... JOMN
Jeweled-Orifice Nozzle ...... JON
Jeweler (ABBR) ...... JLR
Jeweler ...... JWLR
Jewelers Board of Trade (EA) ...... JBT
Jewelers' Book Club (EA) ...... JBC
Jewelers Memorandum Bureau (EA) ...... JMB
Jewelers of America (EA) ...... JA
Jewelers Security Alliance of the US (EA) ...... JSA
Jewelers Shipping Association (EA) ...... JSA
Jewelers Vigilance Committee (EA) ...... JVC
Jewelery Distributors Association [British] (DBA) ...... JDA
Jeweller [British] (ADA) ...... JWLR
Jewellery [British] (ROG) ...... JEW
Jewelry (VRA) ...... jlry
Jewelry (WDAA) ...... JWLRY
Jewelry ...... JWLRY
Jewelry Crafts Association [Later, JMA] ...... JCA
Jewelry Industry Council (EA) ...... JIC
Jewelry Industry Distributors Association (EA) ...... JIDA
Jewelry Industry Tax Committee [Defunct] (EA) ...... JITC
Jewelry Manufacturers Association (EA) ...... JMA
Jewelry Manufacturers Guild (EA) ...... JMG
Jewelry Valuers' Council [Australia] ...... JVC
Jewels (ADA) ...... JLS
Jewels Horology (BARN) ...... J
Jewett Owners Club (EA) ...... JOC
Jewett-Cameron [Vancouver Stock Exchange symbol] ...... JCT
Jewett-Cameron Trading [NASDAQ symbol] (TTSB) ...... JCTCF
Jewett-Cameron Trading Co. Ltd. [NASDAQ symbol] (SAG) ...... JCTC
Jewett-Cameron Trading Co. Ltd. [Associated Press] (SAG) ...... JewettC
Jewish ...... J
Jewish ...... JEW
Jewish Academy of Arts and Sciences (EA) ...... JAAS
Jewish Agency for Israel [United Israel Appeal] [Absorbed by] (EA) ...... JAI
Jewish Agency for Palestine ...... JAFP
Jewish Agency for Palestine ...... JAP
Jewish Agricultural Society (EA) ...... JAS
Jewish Alcoholics, Chemically Dependent Persons, and Significant Others ...... JACS
Jewish Antiquities [Josephus] (BJA) ...... JosAnt
Jewish Apocryphal Literature [A publication] (BJA) ...... JAL
Jewish Aramaic (BJA) ...... JAr
Jewish Art, An Illustrated History [A publication] (BJA) ...... JA
Jewish Association for Retarded Citizens (EA) ...... JARC
Jewish Association for Services for the Aged (EA) ...... JASA
Jewish Autonomous Region [Eastern Siberia] ...... JAR
Jewish Board of Deputies [Australia] ...... JBD
Jewish Board of Guardians (BJA) ...... JBG
Jewish Book Council [of the National Jewish Welfare Board] [Later, JWBJBC] (EA) ...... JBC
Jewish Braille Institute of America (EA) ...... JBI
Jewish Braille Institute of America (EA) ...... JBIA
Jewish Burial Society [Australia] ...... JBS
Jewish Care [British] (EAIO) ...... JC
Jewish Cemetery Trust [Australia] ...... JCT
Jewish Ceremonial Art [A publication] (BJA) ...... JCA
Jewish Chaplain [Territorial Force] [Military British] (ROG) ...... J
Jewish Chaplains Council (EA) ...... JCC
Jewish Chautauqua Society (EA) ...... JCS
Jewish College, London [England] (ROG) ...... JEW COLL LOND
Jewish Colonization Association [British] ...... JCA
Jewish Committee for Israeli-Palestinian Peace (EA) ...... JCIPP
Jewish Committee for Relief Abroad ...... JCRA
Jewish Committee on the Middle East (EA) ...... JCOME
Jewish Communist Party [Political party] (BJA) ...... JCP
Jewish Community Center ...... JCC
Jewish Community Center, Samuel and Rebecca Astor Judaica Library, San Diego, CA [Library symbol Library of Congress] (LCLS) ...... CSdJ
Jewish Community Centers Association of North America (EA) ...... JCCANA
Jewish Community Information Center [Australia] ...... JCIC
[The] Jewish Community: Its History and Structure to the American Revolution [A publication] (BJA) ...... JC
Jewish Community News, Union, NJ [Library symbol Library of Congress] (LCLS) ...... NjUJ
Jewish Community Relations Council (BARN) ...... JCRC
Jewish Conciliation Board of America (EA) ...... JCBA
Jewish Convalescent Hospital, Chomedy, PQ, Canada [Library symbol Library of Congress] (LCLS) ...... CaQChJC
Jewish Cultural Clubs and Societies (EA) ...... JCCS
Jewish Defense League (EA) ...... JDL
Jewish Defense Organization (EA) ...... JDO

Jewish Defense Organization Youth Movement (EA) ... JDOYM
Jewish Division [*New York Public Library*] (BJA) ... JD
Jewish Documentation Centre [*See also BJVN*] (EAIO) ... JDC
Jewish Education Bureau [*British*] (CB) ... JEB
Jewish Education Service of North America (EA) ... JESNA
Jewish Educators Assembly (EA) ... JEA
Jewish Elite Person ... JEP
Jewish Encyclopaedia [*A publication*] (BJA) ... JE
Jewish Endowment for the Arts and Humanities ... JEAH
Jewish Family Name File [*Association for the Study of Jewish Languages*] [*Information service or system*] (CRD) ... JFNF
Jewish Family Purity (BJA) ... JFP
Jewish Family Service (EA) ... JFS
Jewish Federation of Camden County, Cherry Hill, NJ [*Library symbol Library of Congress*] (LCLS) ... NjChJ
Jewish Fighting Force Committee [*British*] ... JFFC
Jewish Folk Center [*Australia*] ... JFC
Jewish Folk Schools of New York (EA) ... JFSNY
Jewish Foundation for Education of Women (EA) ... JFEW
Jewish Free Loan Association (EA) ... JFLA
Jewish Friends Society (EA) ... JFS
Jewish Fund for Justice (EA) ... JFJ
Jewish Funeral Directors of America (EA) ... JFDA
Jewish Genealogical Society (EA) ... JGS
Jewish General Hospital, Institute of Community and Family Psychiatry, Montreal,PQ, Canada [*Library symbol Library of Congress*] (LCLS) ... CaQMJGI
Jewish General Hospital, Lady Davis Institute for Medical Research, Montreal, PQ, Canada [*Library symbol Library of Congress*] (LCLS) ... CaQMJGL
Jewish General Hospital, Montreal, PQ, Canada [*Library symbol Library of Congress*] (LCLS) ... CaQMJG
Jewish General Hospital, Montreal, Quebec [*Library symbol National Library of Canada*] (NLC) ... QMJG
Jewish Guild for the Blind (EA) ... JGB
Jewish Heritage [*A publication*] (BJA) ... JHe
Jewish Historical General Archives [*Jerusalem*] (BJA) ... JHGA
Jewish Historical Society of England ... JHSE
Jewish Historical Society of Greater Washington, Washington, DC [*Library symbol*] [*Library of Congress*] (LCLS) ... DJHi
Jewish Historical Society of Western Canada, Winnipeg, Manitoba [*Library symbol National Library of Canada*] (NLC) ... MWJHS
Jewish Historical Society, Vancouver, BC, Canada [*Library symbol*] [*Library of Congress*] (LCLS) ... CaBVaJH
Jewish Historical Society, Vancouver, British Columbia [*Library symbol National Library of Canada*] (BIB) ... BVAJH
Jewish Hospital, Louisville, KY [*OCLC symbol*] (OCLC) ... KLJ
Jewish Hospital, Medical Library, Cincinnati, OH [*Library symbol Library of Congress*] (LCLS) ... OCJH
Jewish Hospital, School of Nursing, Cincinnati, OH [*Library symbol Library of Congress*] (LCLS) ... OCJH-N
Jewish Immigrants Information Bureau (BJA) ... JIIB
Jewish Information and Referral Service Directory [*A publication*] (EAAP) ... JIRS
Jewish Information Bureau [*Defunct*] (EA) ... JIB
Jewish Information Society of America (EA) ... JIS
Jewish Institute for National Security Affairs (EA) ... JINSA
Jewish Institute of Religion ... JIR
Jewish Labor Bund (EA) ... JLB
Jewish Labor Committee (EA) ... JLC
Jewish Lads' Brigade [*British*] (DI) ... JLB
Jewish Lawyers Guild (EA) ... JLG
Jewish Ledger, Newark, NJ [*Library symbol Library of Congress*] (LCLS) ... NjNJL
Jewish Librarians Association [*Later, AJL*] (EA) ... JLA
Jewish Librarians Task Force (EA) ... JLTF
Jewish Liturgical Music Society of America (EA) ... JLMSA
Jewish Male [*Classified advertising*] ... JM
Jewish Media Service [*Defunct*] (EA) ... JMS
Jewish Minister and Cantors Association of America [*Later, JMCA*] (EA) ... JMCAA
Jewish Ministers Cantors Association of America and Canada (EA) ... JMCA
Jewish Ministers Cantors Association of America and Canada (EA) ... JMCAAC
Jewish Music Alliance (EA) ... JMA
Jewish Music Educators Association [*Defunct*] (EA) ... JMEA
Jewish Music Forum ... JMF
Jewish National and University Library ... JNUL
Jewish National and University Library, Hebrew University, Jerusalem, Israel [*Library symbol Library of Congress*] (LCLS) ... IsJJNL
Jewish National Fund (EA) ... JNF
Jewish National Fund of Australia ... JNFA
Jewish National Home for Asthmatic Children ... JNHAC
Jewish Nazi Victims Organization of America (EA) ... JNVOA
Jewish News Agency (BJA) ... JNA
Jewish News, Newark, NJ [*Library symbol Library of Congress*] (LCLS) ... NjNJN
Jewish News Service (BJA) ... JWNS
Jewish Occupational Council [*Later, NAJVS*] (EA) ... JOC
Jewish Palestine Exploration Society. Journal [*A publication*] (BJA) ... JPESJ
Jewish Palestinian Aramaic (BJA) ... JPA
Jewish Peace Fellowship (EA) ... JPF
Jewish Peace Lobby (EA) ... JPL
Jewish Penicillin Connoisseurs Association (EA) ... JPCA
Jewish People, Past and Present [*Jewish Encyclopedic Handbooks*] [*A publication*] (BJA) ... JPPP
Jewish Pharmaceutical Society of America (EA) ... JPSA
Jewish Philanthropic Fund of 1933 (EA) ... JPF
Jewish Policy Planning and Research Institute [*Synagogue Council of America*] ... JPPRI
Jewish Press [*Brooklyn, NY*] [*A publication*] (BJA) ... JP
Jewish Public Library, Montreal, PQ, Canada [*Library symbol Library of Congress*] (LCLS) ... CaQMJ
Jewish Public Library [*Bibliotheque Juive Publique, Montreal*] **Quebec** [*Library symbol National Library of Canada*] (NLC) ... QMJ
Jewish Public Library, Winnipeg, Manitoba [*Library symbol National Library of Canada*] (NLC) ... MWJP
Jewish Publication Society (EA) ... JPS
Jewish Publication Society of America (DGA) ... JPSA
Jewish Reconstructionist Foundation (EA) ... JRF
Jewish Record, Atlantic City, NJ [*Library symbol Library of Congress*] (LCLS) ... NjAcJ
Jewish Refugees Committee (EAIO) ... JRC
Jewish Resource Centre, Vancouver, BC, Canada [*Library symbol*] [*Library of Congress*] (LCLS) ... CaBVAJR
Jewish Resource Centre, Vancouver, British Columbia [*Library symbol National Library of Canada*] (BIB) ... BVAJR
Jewish Restitution Successor Organization (EA) ... JRSO
[*The*] **Jewish Right** (EA) ... JR
Jewish Royalty Association (EA) ... JRA
Jewish School [*British*] ... J
Jewish Social Democratic Party [*Political party*] (BJA) ... JSDP
Jewish Social Studies [*A publication*] (BRI) ... JSS
Jewish Socialist Verband of America [*Defunct*] (EA) ... JSVA
Jewish Socialist Youth Bund [*Later, MJSG*] (EA) ... JSYB
Jewish Society for Human Service [*British*] ... JSHS
Jewish Society for the Blind (EA) ... JSB
Jewish Society for the Deaf [*Later, New York Society for the Deaf*] (EA) ... JSD
Jewish Society of America ... JSA
Jewish Standard, Jersey City, NJ [*Library symbol Library of Congress*] (LCLS) ... NjJJ
Jewish Statistical Bureau (EA) ... JSB
Jewish Student Press Service (EA) ... JSPS
Jewish Symbols in the Greco-Roman Period [*A publication*] (BJA) ... JSGRP
Jewish Teachers Association - Morim (EA) ... JTA-M
Jewish Telegraphic Agency (EA) ... JTA
Jewish Television Network ... JTN
Jewish Theological Seminary of America ... JTSA
Jewish Theological Seminary of America, New York, NY [*Library symbol Library of Congress*] (LCLS) ... NNJ
Jewish Theological Seminary of America, New York, NY [*OCLC symbol*] (OCLC) ... VXJ
Jewish Thought and Civilization (BJA) ... JTC
Jewish Vacation Association [*Superseded by Association of Jewish Sponsored Camps*] (EA) ... JVA
Jewish Vegetarian Society - America [*Later, JVSNA*] (EA) ... JVS
Jewish Vegetarian Society-North America (EA) ... JVSNA
Jewish Vegetarians of North America (EA) ... JV
Jewish Visual Artists Association [*Defunct*] (EA) ... JVAA
Jewish Vocational Service Library, Chicago, IL [*Library symbol Library of Congress*] (LCLS) ... ICJV
Jewish Vocational Services ... JVS
[*The*] **Jewish War** [*A publication*] (BJA) ... JW
Jewish War Veterans of the USA (EA) ... JWV
Jewish War Veterans of the USA - National Ladies Auxiliary (EA) ... JWVA
Jewish War Veterans USA National Memorial (EA) ... JWVUSANM
[*The*] **Jewish Wars** [*of Josephus*] [*A publication*] (BJA) ... Wars
Jewish Welfare Society [*Australia*] ... JWS
Jewish Women's Resource Center (EA) ... JWRC
Jewish Yearbook of International Law [*A publication*] (DLA) ... Jew YB Int'l L
Jewish-American Princess [*Slang*] ... JAP
Jews' College, London, United Kingdom [*Library symbol Library of Congress*] (LCLS) ... UkLJ
Jews for Animal Rights (EA) ... JAR
Jews for Jesus (EA) ... JFJ
Jews for Jews [*Defunct*] (EA) ... JJ
Jews for Morality (EA) ... JFM
Jews for the Preservation of Firearms Ownership (EA) ... JPFO
[*The*] **Jews in NAZI Germany; A Handbook of Facts Regarding Their Present Situation** [*A publication*] (BJA) ... JNG
Jeypore [*India*] [*ICAO location identifier*] (ICLI) ... VEJP
Jezebel [*Sonobuoy*] **Exercise** [*Navy*] (NVT) ... JEZEX
J.F. Kennedy Elementary School, Babbit, MN [*Library symbol*] [*Library of Congress*] (LCLS) ... MnBabE
J.F. Kennedy High School, Babbitt, MN [*Library symbol*] [*Library of Congress*] (LCLS) ... MnBabH
JG Industries [*NASDAQ symbol*] (TTSB) ... JGIN
JG Industries, Inc. [*Associated Press*] (SAG) ... JG Ind
JG Industries, Inc. [*NASDAQ symbol*] (NQ) ... JGIN
JGC Corp. [*Formerly, Japan Gasoline Co. Ltd.*] ... JGC
Jhansi [*India*] [*ICAO location identifier*] (ICLI) ... VIJN
Jharkhand Coordination Committee [*Jharkhand Samanvaya Samiti*] [*India*] [*Political party*] ... JCC
Jharsuguda [*India*] [*ICAO location identifier*] (ICLI) ... VEJH
Jhunju [*South Korea ICAO location identifier*] (ICLI) ... RKJU
Jiadong [*China*] [*ICAO location identifier*] (ICLI) ... RCFS
Jian [*China*] [*ICAO location identifier*] (ICLI) ... ZSJA
Jiayi [*China*] [*ICAO location identifier*] (ICLI) ... RCKU
JIB, Inc. [*ICAO designator*] (FAAC) ... AXQ
Jibing (ABBR) ... JIBG
Jicamarca Radar Observatory [*Peru*] ... JRO
Jickling. Legal and Equitable Estates [*1829*] [*A publication*] (DLA) ... Jick Est
JICST [*Japan Information Center of Science and Technology*] **Electronic Information Processing Automatic Computer** (NITA) ... JEIPAC
Jidosha Kiki Co. Ltd. ... JKC

Jiffy (ABBR)	JFY
Jiffy Bag	JB
Jiffy Junction Connector	JJC
Jiffy Junction Single Wire Connector	JJSWC
Jiffy Junction Wire Connector	JJWC
Jig [Phonetic alphabet] [World War II] (DSUE)	J
Jig Grinder Head	JGH
Jig Grinding Machine	JGM
Jig Template (MSA)	JT
Jig Transit Central Y-Plane	JTCY-P
Jigger (ABBR)	JIGR
Jigger [Ship's rigging] (ROG)	JR
Jigging Information	JI
Jiggle (ABBR)	JIGL
Jiggled (ABBR)	JIGLD
Jiggling (ABBR)	JIGLG
Jiggly (ABBR)	JIGLY
Jigsaw (ABBR)	JGSW
Jijel [Algeria] [Airport symbol] (OAG)	GJL
Jijell/Taher [Algeria] [ICAO location identifier] (ICLI)	DAAV
JiJi Securities Data Service [JiJi Press Ltd.] [Japan Information service or system] (CRD)	JSD
Jijiga [Ethiopia] [ICAO location identifier] (ICLI)	HAJJ
Jilin Chemical Inc ADS [NYSE symbol] (TTSB)	JCC
Jilin Chemical Industrial Co. Ltd. [NYSE symbol] (SAG)	JCC
Jilin Chemical Industrial Co. Ltd. [Associated Press] (SAG)	JilinCh
Jillians Entertainment [NASDAQ symbol] (TTSB)	QBAL
Jillians Entertainment Corp. [Associated Press] (SAG)	JillEnt
Jillians Entertainment Corp. [NASDAQ symbol] (SAG)	QBAL
Jilong [China] [ICAO location identifier] (ICLI)	RCLU
Jilter (ABBR)	JLTR
Jim and Jesse Fan Club (EA)	JJFC
Jim Creek [Washington] [Seismograph station code, US Geological Survey] (SEIS)	JCW
Jim Hankins Air Service, Inc. [FAA designator] (FAAC)	HKN
Jim Hielms Private Coll'n [NASDAQ symbol] (TTSB)	JHPC
Jim Hjelms Private Collection [Associated Press] (SAG)	JHjelm
Jim Hjelms Private Collection [NASDAQ symbol] (SPSG)	JHPC
Jim Ratliff Air Service, Inc. [FAA designator] (FAAC)	RAS
Jim Smith Society (EA)	JSS
Jim Walter Research Corp., St. Petersburg, FL [Library symbol] [Library of Congress] (LCLS)	FSpW
JIMAP [Joint Institute for Marine and Atmospheric Research] Tsunami Research Effort [Marine science] (OSRA)	JTRE
JIMAR [Joint Institute for Marine and Atmospheric Research] Tsunami Research Effort (USDC)	JTRE
Jimi Hendrix Information Management Institute (EA)	JIMI
Jimma [Ethiopia] [ICAO location identifier] (ICLI)	HAJM
Jimma [Ethiopia] [Airport symbol] (OAG)	JIM
Jimmie Dale Fan Club (EA)	JDFC
Jimmy (ABBR)	JMY
Jimmy C. Newman Fan CLub (EA)	JCNFC
Jimmy Carter [James Earl Carter, Jr.] [US president, 1924-]	JC
Jimmy Carter Library, Atlanta, GA [Library symbol Library of Congress] (LCLS)	GAJC
Jimmy Kish "The Flying Cowboy" Fan Club (EA)	JKFCFC
Jimmy Murphy Fan Club (EA)	JMFC
Jimmy Swaggart Bible College Library, Baton Rouge, LA [Library symbol] [Library of Congress] (LCLS)	LBrJS
Jimmy Wakely Fan Club [Defunct] (EA)	JWFC
Jimmying (ABBR)	JN
Jim's Neighbors (EA)	JN
Jin Shin Do Foundation for Bodymind Acupressure (EA)	JSDF
Jinan [China] [Airport symbol] (OAG)	TNA
Jinan [China] [ICAO location identifier] (ICLI)	ZSTN
Jindabyne [Australia Seismograph station code, US Geological Survey Closed] (SEIS)	JIN
Jingdezhen [China] [Airport symbol] (OAG)	JDZ
Jingled (ABBR)	JINGLD
Jingling (ABBR)	JINGLG
Jinja [Uganda] [ICAO location identifier] (ICLI)	HUJI
Jinja [Uganda] [Airport symbol] (AD)	JIN
Jinjiang [China] [Airport symbol] (OAG)	JJN
Jinmen [China] [ICAO location identifier] (ICLI)	RCBS
Jinotega [Nicaragua] [Seismograph station code, US Geological Survey] (SEIS)	JIG
JINTACCS [Joint Interoperability of Tactical Command and Control System] Army Management Plan (MCD)	JAMP
JINTACCS [Joint Interoperability of Tactical Command and Control Systems] Automated Message Preparation System (MCD)	JAMPS
JIP/Areal Marketing Database [Toyo Keizai Shinposha Co. Ltd.] [Japan Information service or system] (CRD)	JIP/AMD
Jipijapa [Ecuador] [Airport symbol] (AD)	JIP
Jipijapa [Ecuador] [ICAO location identifier] (ICLI)	SEJI
Jiri [Nepal] [Airport symbol] (OAG)	JIR
Jiri [Nepal] [ICAO location identifier] (ICLI)	VNJI
Jiroft [Iran] [ICAO location identifier] (ICLI)	OIKJ
Jishu Kanri [Voluntary Management] [Japanese method for increasing productivity of industrial workers by involving them in planning]	JK
Jitter (ABBR)	JITR
Jitterbug (ABBR)	JITRBG
Jittered and Swept Active RADAR	JASAR
Jittery (ABBR)	JITRY
Jiuquan [China] [Airport symbol] (OAG)	CHW
Jiuquan [China] [ICAO location identifier] (ICLI)	ZLJQ

Jiwani [Pakistan] [Airport symbol] (OAG)	JIW
Jiwani [Pakistan] [ICAO location identifier] (ICLI)	OPJI
Jiyu-Minshuto [Liberal-Democratic Party] [Japan Political party]	JM
J.L. Richardson Associates, Ltd., Ottawa, ON, Canada [Library symbol] [Library of Congress] (LCLS)	CaOORIA
JLG Indus [NASDAQ symbol] (TTSB)	JLGI
JLG Industries, Inc. [Associated Press] (SAG)	JLG
JMAR Inds Wrrt [NASDAQ symbol] (TTSB)	JMARW
JMAR Industries [NASDAQ symbol] (SPSG)	JMAR
JMC Group [NASDAQ symbol] (TTSB)	JMCG
JMC Group, Inc. [Associated Press] (SAG)	JMC Gp
JMC Group, Inc. [NASDAQ symbol] (SAG)	JMCG
Joacaba [Brazil] [Airport symbol] (AD)	JCB
Joachim Bancorp [NASDAQ symbol] (TTSB)	JOAC
Joachim Bancorp, Inc. [NASDAQ symbol] (SAG)	JOAC
Joachim Bancorp, Inc. [Associated Press] (SAG)	Joachim
Joan Jett Fan Club (EA)	JJFC
Joan Lunden Fan Club [Defunct] (EA)	JLFC
Joanie Dale Fan Club (EA)	JDFC
Joannou & Paraskevaides [Construction company] [British]	J & P
Joao Pessoa [Brazil] [Airport symbol] (OAG)	JPA
Joao Pessoa/Presidente Castro Pinto [Brazil ICAO location identifier] (ICLI)	SBJP
Job (IEEE)	J
Job [Old Testament book]	Jb
Job (MCD)	JB
Job Accommodation Network [President's Committee on Employment of the Handicapped] [Information service or system] (IID)	JAN
Job Accounting Facility	JAF
Job Accounting Interface	JAI
Job Accounting Report System (MHDI)	JARS
Job Accounting System	JAS
Job Accounting Table	JAT
Job Activities Questionnaire	JAQ
Job Activity Survey	JAS
Job Aid	JA
Job Air Ltd. [Czechoslovakia] [FAA designator] (FAAC)	JBR
Job Analysis	JA
Job Analysis and Interest Measurement	JAIM
Job Analysis Memorandum	JAM
Job Analysis Memorandum Activity Chart	JAMAC
Job Analysis Schedule [Department of Labor]	JAS
Job Analysis System [Computer program]	JAS
Job Analysis Vocabulary (OICC)	JAV
Job and Function [Air Force] (AAG)	J & F
Job and Tape Planning System	JTPS
Job Appraisal Review (PDAA)	JAR
Job Area Acceptance Range (AAGC)	JAAR
Job Assembly Breakdown and Quality Control Section [Social Security Administration]	JABQC
Job Assignment Memorandum	JAM
Job Assistance Center (DOMA)	JAC
Job Attitude Scale [Employment test]	JAS
Job Bank (OICC)	JB
Job Bank Operations Review [Employment and Training Administration] [Department of Labor]	JBOR
Job Banks Opening Summary [Department of Labor]	JBOS
Job Book	JB
Job Catalog (HGAA)	JOBCAT
Job Center	JC
Job Change Notice [Form] (AAG)	JCN
Job Characteristics Inventory	JCI
Job Club	JC
Job Command Language (NITA)	JCL
Job Content Protection [UAW]	JCP
Job Control Block [Computer science] (BUR)	JCB
Job Control Card (MCD)	JCC
Job Control File Internal (IAA)	JCFI
Job Control File Source (IAA)	JCFS
Job Control Language [High-level programming language] [1979] [Computer science]	JCL
Job Control Language Automatic Generator [Computer science]	JCL-OMATIC
Job Control Language Generation [Computer science] (MHDB)	JCLGEN
Job Control Language Preprocessor [Computer science] (MHDB)	JCLPREP
Job Control Number	JCN
Job Control Program (CMD)	JCP
Job Control Statement [Computer science]	JCS
Job Control System (IAA)	JCS
Job Control Table (CMD)	JCT
Job Corps [Department of Labor]	JC
Job Corps Camp [Department of Labor]	JCC
Job Corps Opportunity Specialist [Department of Labor]	JCOS
Job Cost Sheet (DGA)	JCS
Job Creation Programme [Manpower Services Commission] (AIE)	JCP
Job Creation Scheme [Department of Employment] [British]	JCS
Job Cylinder Map [Computer science] (IBMDP)	JCM
Job Data Sheet (IEEE)	JDS
Job Delivery Orders (MCD)	JDO
Job Description [Department of Labor]	JD
Job Description Card	JDC
Job Description Index	JDI
Job Description Language [Computer science]	JDL
Job Description Library	JDL
Job Descriptor Language (NITA)	JDL
Job Development (OICC)	JD

Job Development Program ... JDP
Job Diagnosis Survey (PDAA) ... JDS
Job Drawing List (MCD) ... JDL
Job Effectiveness Prediction System [*Test for insurance company employees*] ... JEPS
Job Element Text (AFM) ... JET
Job English Training ... JET
Job Enlargement (MHDB) ... JE
Job Enrichment (MHDB) ... JE
Job Entry Central Services (MCD) ... JECS
Job Entry Control Language ... JECL
Job Entry Peripheral Services [*IBM Corp.*] (MCD) ... JEPS
Job Entry System [*or Subsystem*] [*IBM Corp.*] [*Computer science*] ... JES
Job Estimate (AAG) ... JE
Job Evaluation Policy Act of 1970 ... JEPA
Job Executive and Transport Satellite [*NCR Corp.*] ... JETS
Job File Control Block [*Computer science*] (BUR) ... JFCB
Job File Number ... JFN
Job File Table (PCM) ... JFT
Job Finder System ... JFS
Job Function Manual (AAG) ... JFM
Job Grading System for Trades and Labor Occupations ... JGTL
Job Guarantee Office of the United States (OICC) ... JGO-US
Job Guide Manual (PDAA) ... JGM
Job Hazard Analysis (PDAA) ... JHA
Job Hunter's Sourcebook [*A publication*] ... JHS
Job Ideas and Information Generator - Computer Assisted Learning (AIE) ... JIIG-CAL
Job Improvement Plan ... JIP
Job Improvement Request ... JIR
Job Information Block [*Computer science*] (BUR) ... JIB
Job Information Centre [*Canada*] ... JIC
Job Information Delivery System [*US Employment Service*] [*Department of Labor*] ... JIDS
Job Information Service [*Department of Labor*] ... JIS
Job Information Station [*Department of Labor*] (IAA) ... JIS
Job Information System (NITA) ... JIS
Job Information Test [*Military*] (AFM) ... JIT
Job Input System (NITA) ... JIS
Job Instruction ... JI
Job Instruction and Communication (PDAA) ... JIC
Job Instruction Manual ... JIM
Job Instruction Training ... JIT
Job Insurance [*Job Service*] (OICC) ... JI
Job Item Cost Code (MCD) ... JICC
Job Knowledge Test [*Military*] (AFM) ... JKT
Job Library [*Computer science*] ... JOBLIB
Job Management Operations System (PDAA) ... JMOS
Job Memory [*Computer science*] (MHDB) ... JMEM
Job Memory Switch Matrix ... JMSX
Job Method Learning (PDAA) ... JML
Job Methods Training ... JMT
Job Mix Optimization [*Computer science*] (MHDB) ... JOMO
Job Number ... JN
Job Operation Manual (AAG) ... JOM
Job Operations Report ... JOR
Job Opportunities in the Business Sector (WDAA) ... JOBS
Job Opportunity for Youth [*NASA employment program*] ... JOY
Job Opportunity Program (OICC) ... JOP
Job Order ... JO
Job Order Contracting ... JOC
Job Order Cost Accounting System (MCD) ... JOCAS
Job Order Costing (MHDI) ... JOC
Job Order Number (MCD) ... JON
Job Order/Program Control Number [*Army*] ... JO/PCN
Job Order Quantity [*Military*] (AFIT) ... JOQ
Job Order Request (AAG) ... JOR
Job Order Supplement (MCD) ... JOS
Job Organization Language [*1979*] [*Computer science*] (CSR) ... JOL
Job Orientation in Neighborhoods (AEBS) ... JOIN
Job Oriented Basic Skills [*Program*] [*Military*] ... JOBS
Job Pack Area [*Computer science*] (IBMDP) ... JPA
Job Parts List (AAG) ... JPL
Job Performance Aid ... JPA
Job Performance Evaluation (PDAA) ... JPE
Job Performance [*or Proficiency*] **Guide** (AFM) ... JPG
Job Performance Illustrations (MCD) ... JPI
Job Performance Manual (MCD) ... JPM
Job Performance Measure ... JPM
Job Placement [*Job Service*] (OICC) ... JP
Job Placement and Employment Training ... JPET
Job Planning Form ... JPF
Job Processing Unit ... JPU
Job Processing Word ... JPW
Job Processor ... JP
Job Progress Ticket ... JPT
Job Questionnaire ... JQ
Job Readiness Posture (OICC) ... JRP
Job Redesign Working Group ... JRWG
Job Rehearsal Scheme (AIE) ... JRS
Job Relations Training ... JRT
Job Release Analysis ... JRA
Job Release Scheme (PDAA) ... JRS
Job Rotation [*Computer science*] (MHDB) ... JR
Job Routed [*Military*] (AFIT) ... JR
Job Safety Analysis ... JSA
Job Safety and Health [*Bureau of National Affairs*] [*Information service or system*] (CRD) ... JOSH
Job Satisfaction Inventory [*Guidance*] ... JSI
Job Schedule Change Request ... JSCR
Job Schedule Items (MCD) ... JSI
Job Schedule Status (SAA) ... JSS
Job Search [*Job Training and Partnership Act*] (OICC) ... JBS
Job Search [*Job Training and Partnership Act*] (OICC) ... JS
Job Search Allowance ... JSA
Job Search and Relocation Assistance Projects (OICC) ... JSRA
Job Search Information ... JSI
Job Search Training Program ... JSTP
Job Seekers Guide to Private and Public Companies [*A publication*] ... JSG
Job Seeking Skills Training (OICC) ... JSST
Job Sensitivity Inventory [*Interpersonal skills and attitudes test*] ... JSI
Job Sequence Number ... JSN
Job Service (OICC) ... JS
Job Service Improvement Program [*Department of Labor*] ... JSIP
Job Service Matching Systems [*US Employment Service*] [*Department of Labor*] ... JSMS
Job Services File ... JSF
Job Shop Control System (MHDI) ... JSCS
Job Shop Simulation Program Generator (KSC) ... JSSPG
Job Shop Simulator ... JSS
Job Skills Education Program [*Military*] ... JSEP
Job Skills Training ... JST
Job Skills Training Course ... JSTC
Job Specification [*Department of Labor*] ... JS
Job Specification Language ... JSL
Job Step Control Block [*Computer science*] (BUR) ... JSCB
Job Step Index [*Computer science*] (IAA) ... JSI
Job Stream [*Computer science*] ... JS
Job Stream Manager [*Computer science*] (IAA) ... JSM
Job Support Program ... JSP
Job Swapping Memory [*Computer science*] (MHDB) ... JSWAP
Job Table [*Computer science*] (IAA) ... JT
Job Task Analysis ... JTA
Job Task Performance Test ... JTPT
Job Task Requirements Analysis (PDAA) ... JTRA
Job the Impatient (BJA) ... JIP
Job the Patient (BJA) ... JP
Job Training Assessment Program [*Vocational guidance test*] ... JOBTAP
Job Training Package ... JTP
Job Training Partnership Act [*Formerly, CETA*] [*1982*] ... JTPA
Job Training Partnership Administration ... JTPA
Job Training Program (OICC) ... JTP
Job Training Scheme [*Government initiative*] [*British*] ... JTS
Job Training Standard ... JTS
Job Transfer and Management (ACRL) ... JTM
Job Transfer and Manipulation [*Telecommunications*] (OSI) ... JTM
Job Transfer and Manipulation Protocol (NITA) ... JTMP
Job Unit Block [*Computer science*] (IAA) ... JUB
Job Work Folder (AABC) ... JWF
Job Work Order ... JWO
Jobbed (ABBR) ... JOBD
Jobber [*Merchant middleman*] ... J
Jobber ... JOB
Jobber (ABBR) ... JOBR
Jobbing (ABBR) ... JOBG
Jobbing Grinders' Provident Association [*A union*] [*British*] ... JGPA
Jobbing Printer [*A publication*] (DGA) ... JP
Jobholder (ABBR) ... JOBHLDR
Jobless Action (Australian Capital Territory) [*An association*] ... JA(ACT)
Job-Oriented Manual (AAG) ... JOM
Job-Oriented Organizational Structure (AAG) ... JOOS
Job-Oriented Training Standards (AFM) ... JOTS
Jobs Evaluation and Training ... JET
Jobs for America's Graduates [*An association*] (EA) ... JAG
Jobs for Employable Dependent Individuals Program [*Federal government*] ... JEDI
Jobs for the Future [*An association*] ... JFF
Jobs for Veterans National Committee [*Defunct*] (EA) ... JFV
Jobs Illustrated [*CD-ROM*] ... JILL
Jobs Impact Bulletin [*National Committee for Full Employment*] [*A publication*] ... JIB
Jobs in Energy (EA) ... JIE
Jobs Optional Program [*Combination job opportunities in the business sector and on the job training*] (OICC) ... JOP
Jobs or Income Now [*Students for a Democratic Society*] [*Defunct*] ... JOIN
Jobs with Peace National Network [*Later, NJWPC*] (EA) ... JWPNN
Job-Site Component ... JSC
Jobst Pump [*Medicine*] ... JP
Jockey (ABBR) ... JOCK
Jockey Club [*Later, TJC*] (EA) ... JC
[*The*] **Jockey Club** (EA) ... TJC
Jockey Club, Inc. [*NASDAQ symbol*] (SAG) ... JKCL
Jockey Club, Inc. [*Associated Press*] (SAG) ... JockeyC
Jockey's Association [*Defunct*] (EA) ... JA
Jockeys' Association [*British*] (DBA) ... JAGB
Jockeys' Guild (EA) ... JG
Jockstrap (ABBR) ... JOCK
Jocose [*or Jocular*] ... JOC
Jocular (ABBR) ... JOC

JODC [*Japan Oceanographic Data Center*] **On-Line Information and Data Exchange Service** [*Marine science*] (OSRA) .... JOIDES
Jodhpur [*India*] [*Airport symbol*] (OAG) .... JDH
Jodhpur [*India*] [*ICAO location identifier*] (ICLI) .... VIJU
Jodrell Bank Experimental Station [*British*] .... JBES
Joe Gallison Fan Club (EA) .... JGFC
Joe Stampley Fan Club [*Defunct*] (EA) .... JSFC
Joe Waters Fan Club (EA) .... JWFC
Joel [*Old Testament book*] .... JI
Joel [*Old Testament book*] (BJA) .... Jo
Joensuu [*Finland ICAO location identifier*] (ICLI) .... EFJO
Joensuu [*Finland*] [*Airport symbol*] (OAG) .... JOE
Joensuu [*Finland*] [*Seismograph station code, US Geological Survey Closed*] (SEIS) .... JOE
Jogged (ABBR) .... JOGD
Jogger (ABBR) .... JOGR
Jogging (ABBR) .... JOGG
Joggle [*Engineering*] .... JOG
Joggle (ABBR) .... JOGL
Joggle Blocks (MCD) .... JB
Joggle Die (MCD) .... JD
Joggled (ABBR) .... JOGLD
Joggling (ABBR) .... JOGLG
Jogyakarta [*Indonesia*] [*Airport symbol*] (OAG) .... JOG
Johan Mangku Negara [*Malaysian Honour*] .... JMN
Johannes Andreae [*Deceased, 1348*] [*Authority cited in pre-1607 legal work*] (DSA) .... Joan Andr
Johannes Baptista [*John the Baptist*] [*Authority cited in pre-1607 legal work*] (DSA) .... JB
Johannes Baptista Villalobos [*Authority cited in pre-1607 legal work*] (DSA) .... Joan Bapt Villalob
Johannes Bassianus [*Flourished, 12th century*] [*Authority cited in pre-1607 legal work*] (DSA) .... Jo B
Johannes Bassianus de Cremona [*Flourished, 12th century*] [*Authority cited in pre-1607 legal work*] (DSA) .... Jo Cre
Johannes Bassianus de Cremona [*Flourished, 12th century*] [*Authority cited in pre-1607 legal work*] (DSA) .... Jo de Cre
Johannes Bolognetus [*Deceased, 1575*] [*Authority cited in pre-1607 legal work*] (DSA) .... Joa Bologne
Johannes Bolognetus [*Deceased, 1575*] [*Authority cited in pre-1607 legal work*] (DSA) .... Joan Bologne
Johannes Borcholten [*Deceased, 1593*] [*Authority cited in pre-1607 legal work*] (DSA) .... Joan Borcholt
Johannes de Anania [*Deceased, 1457*] [*Authority cited in pre-1607 legal work*] (DSA) .... Jo de Ana
Johannes de Anania [*Deceased, 1457*] [*Authority cited in pre-1607 legal work*] (DSA) .... Jo de Anna
Johannes de Borbonio [*Flourished, 1317-30*] [*Authority cited in pre-1607 legal work*] (DSA) .... Jo de Bor
Johannes de Cesena [*Flourished, 13th century*] [*Authority cited in pre-1607 legal work*] (DSA) .... Joan de Ces
Johannes de Fintona [*Flourished, 13th century*] [*Authority cited in pre-1607 legal work*] (DSA) .... Jo de F
Johannes de Fintona [*Flourished, 13th century*] [*Authority cited in pre-1607 legal work*] (DSA) .... Jo de Fi
Johannes de Fintona [*Flourished, 13th century*] [*Authority cited in pre-1607 legal work*] (DSA) .... Jo F
Johannes de Imola [*Deceased, 1436*] [*Authority cited in pre-1607 legal work*] (DSA) .... Jo de Imol
Johannes de Imola [*Deceased, 1436*] [*Authority cited in pre-1607 legal work*] (DSA) .... Joa Imo
Johannes de Lignano [*Deceased, 1383*] [*Authority cited in pre-1607 legal work*] (DSA) .... Joan de Lign
Johannes de Monciaco [*Flourished, 1263-66*] [*Authority cited in pre-1607 legal work*] (DSA) .... Jo de Mo
Johannes Faventinus [*Deceased circa 1187*] [*Authority cited in pre-1607 legal work*] (DSA) .... Jo
Johannes Faventinus [*Deceased circa 1187*] [*Authority cited in pre-1607 legal work*] (DSA) .... Jo Fa
Johannes Faventinus [*Deceased circa 1187*] [*Authority cited in pre-1607 legal work*] (DSA) .... Jo Fav
Johannes Faventinus [*Deceased circa 1187*] [*Authority cited in pre-1607 legal work*] (DSA) .... Joan Fan
Johannes Franciscus Pavinus [*Flourished, 1448-82*] [*Authority cited in pre-1607 legal work*] (DSA) .... Joannes
Johannes Galensis [*Flourished, 13th century*] [*Authority cited in pre-1607 legal work*] (DSA) .... J
Johannes Galensis [*Flourished, 13th century*] [*Authority cited in pre-1607 legal work*] (DSA) .... Johs
Johannes Monachus [*Deceased, 1313*] [*Authority cited in pre-1607 legal work*] (DSA) .... Jo Mon
Johannes Monachus [*Deceased, 1313*] [*Authority cited in pre-1607 legal work*] (DSA) .... Joan Mon
Johannes Schwalm Historical Association (EA) .... JSHA
Johannes Teutonicus [*Deceased circa 1246*] [*Authority cited in pre-1607 legal work*] (DSA) .... Jo Te
Johannes Teutonicus [*Deceased circa 1246*] [*Authority cited in pre-1607 legal work*] (DSA) .... Joann
Johannes Teutonicus [*Deceased, 1246*] [*Authority cited in pre-1607 legal work*] (DSA) .... Joann Teut
Johannes Teutonicus [*Deceased circa 1246*] [*Authority cited in pre-1607 legal work*] (DSA) .... Joh Teut
Johannes Vaudus [*Flourished, 16th century*] [*Authority cited in pre-1607 legal work*] (DSA) .... Joan Vaud
Johannesburg [*South Africa*] [*ICAO location identifier*] (ICLI) .... FAJB

Johannesburg [*South Africa*] (ABBR) .... JHB
Johannesburg [*South Africa*] [*Airport symbol*] (OAG) .... JNB
Johannesburg [*South Africa*] [*Seismograph station code, US Geological Survey Closed*] (SEIS) .... JOH
Johannesburg, CA [*FM radio station call letters*] .... KRAJ
Johannesburg/Jan Smuts [*South Africa*] [*ICAO location identifier*] (ICLI) .... FAJS
Johannesburg Mounted Rifles [*British military*] (DMA) .... JMR
Johannesburg/Rand [*South Africa*] [*ICAO location identifier*] (ICLI) .... FAGM
Johannine (BJA) .... Joh
Johannis Lectura [*A publication*] (DSA) .... Jo Le
John [*New Testament book*] .... Jn
John [*New Testament book*] (BJA) .... Joh
John A. Andrew Clinical Society (EA) .... JAACS
John A. Graham Correctional Center, Hillsboro, IL [*Library symbol*] [*Library of Congress*] (LCLS) .... IHilbGC
John A. Johnson Elementary School, Two Harbors, MN [*Library symbol*] [*Library of Congress*] (LCLS) .... MnThE
John Abbott College Library [*EDUCATSS*] [*UTLAS symbol*] .... EUQ
John Abbott College, Ste.-Anne-De-Bellevue, PQ, Canada [*Library symbol Library of Congress*] (LCLS) .... CaQSTAJ
John Abbott College, Ste-Anne-De-Bellevue, Quebec [*Library symbol National Library of Canada*] (NLC) .... QSTAJ
John Adams [*US president, 1735-1826*] .... JA
John Alden Financial [*NYSE symbol*] (SPSG) .... JA
John and Mable Ringling Museum of Art, Sarasota, FL [*Library symbol Library of Congress*] (LCLS) .... FSR
John and Margaret Seidel [*Children of US importer after whom British sports car was named*] .... JOMAR
John and Mary Kirby Hospital, Monticello, IL [*Library symbol Library of Congress*] (LCLS) .... IMoH
John Anderson Fan Club [*Defunct*] (EA) .... JAFC
John Arpin Enterprises, Inc., Toronto, Ontario [*Library symbol National Library of Canada*] (NLC) .... OTJAE
John Augustus Foundation (EA) .... JAF
John B. Pierce Foundation Laboratory [*New Haven, CT*] .... JBP
John B. Wheeler Memorial Library, Musgrave Harbour, Newfoundland [*Library symbol National Library of Canada*] (NLC) .... NFMHJ
John B. Wheeler Memorial Library, Musgrave Harbour, NF, Canada [*Library symbol Library of Congress*] (LCLS) .... CaNfMHJ
John Bastyr College of Naturopathic Medicine, Seattle, WA [*Library symbol*] [*Library of Congress*] (LCLS) .... WaSJB
John Birch Society (EA) .... JBS
John Brown Anti-Klan Committee (EA) .... JBAKC
John Brown University [*Siloam Springs, AR*] .... JBU
John Brown University, Siloam Springs, AR [*OCLC symbol*] (OCLC) .... AKK
John Brown University, Siloam Springs, AR [*Library symbol Library of Congress*] (LCLS) .... ArSsJ
John Bull [*The typical Englishman*] .... JB
John Burroughs Association (EA) .... JBA
John Burroughs Memorial Association (EA) .... JBMA
John C. Hart Memorial Library, Shrub Oak, NY [*Library symbol Library of Congress*] (LCLS) .... NShr
John Carroll University [*University Heights, OH*] .... JCU
John Carroll University (GAGS) .... John Carroll U
John Carroll University, Cleveland, OH [*Library symbol Library of Congress*] (LCLS) .... OCIJC
John Carroll University, Grasselli Library, University Heights, OH [*OCLC symbol*] (OCLC) .... JCU
John Carter Brown Library, Providence, RI [*Library symbol Library of Congress*] (LCLS) .... RPJCB
John Chard Decoration [*British military*] (DMA) .... JCD
John Clark Elementary School, Rockville, MN [*Library symbol*] [*Library of Congress*] (LCLS) .... MnRvJ
John Conlee Fan Club (EA) .... JCFC
John Coutts Library Services [*ACCORD*] [*UTLAS symbol*] .... JOC
John Coutts Library Services Ltd., Niagara Falls, Ontario [*Library symbol National Library of Canada*] (NLC) .... ONFJC
John Crerar Library [*National Translation Center*] .... JCL
John Crerar Library, Chicago, IL [*OCLC symbol*] (OCLC) .... IAB
John Crerar Library, Chicago, IL [*Library symbol Library of Congress*] (LCLS) .... ICJ
John Crowe Productions, Inc. [*Houston, TX*] [*Telecommunications*] (TSSD) .... JCP
John D. Rockefeller III [*American philanthropist, 1906-1978*] JDR3
John Day, OR [*AM radio station call letters*] .... KJDY
John Deere Ltd., Hamilton, Ontario [*Library symbol National Library of Canada*] (NLC) .... OHJD
John Denver Early Warning Network (EA) .... JDEWN
John Denver Heart to Heart Fan Club (EA) .... JDHHFC
John Dewey [*Final letters of his first and last name used as a pseudonym*] [*American author, 1859-1952*] .... NY
John Dewey Society (EA) .... JDS
John Dolan Resource Library, Saskatchewan Association for the Mentally Retarded, Saskatoon, Saskatchewan [*Library symbol National Library of Canada*] (NLC) .... SSAMR
John E. Clegg Library, Central City, IA [*Library symbol Library of Congress*] (LCLS) .... IaCc
John E. Meyer Eye Foundation, Eye Foundation Hospital, Birmingham, AL [*Library symbol Library of Congress*] (LCLS) .... ABMF
John Ericsson Society (EA) .... JES
John F. Kennedy Center for Military Assistance (MCD) .... JFKCTRMA
John F. Kennedy First Day Cover Study Unit (EA) .... JFK FDC SU
John F. Kennedy High School, Bellmore, NY [*Library symbol*] [*Library of Congress*] (LCLS) .... NBellmKH
John F. Kennedy High School, Plainview, NY [*Library symbol Library of Congress*] (LCLS) .... NPIKH

John F. Kennedy Junior High School, Bethpage, NY [*Library symbol Library of Congress*] (LCLS) ... NBethKJ
John F. Kennedy Junior High School, Bethpage, NY [*Library symbol*] [*Library of Congress*] (LCLS) ... NBetKJ
John F. Kennedy Library ... JFKL
John F. Kennedy Library Foundation (EA) ... JFKLF
John F. Kennedy Library, Waltham, MA [*Library symbol Library of Congress*] (LCLS) ... MWalK
John F. Kennedy Memorial Hospital, Stratford, NJ [*Library symbol Library of Congress*] (LCLS) ... NjStrK
John F. Kennedy Middle School, Rockford, IL [*Library symbol*] [*Library of Congress*] (LCLS) ... IRoKM
John F. Kennedy Philatelic Society (EA) ... JFKPS
John F. Kennedy University, Orinda, CA [*Library symbol Library of Congress*] (LCLS) ... COriK
John F. Ross Collegiate Vocational Institute, Guelph, ON, Canada [*Library symbol*] [*Library of Congress*] (LCLS) ... CaOGJFR
John F. Ross Collegiate Vocational Institute, Guelph, Ontario [*Library symbol National Library of Canada*] (NLC) ... OGJFR
John Fitzgerald Kennedy [*US president, 1917-1963*] ... JFK
John Fitzgerald Kennedy Center for the Performing Arts ... JFKC
John Fitzgerald Kennedy National Historical Site ... JOKI
John Fitzgerald Kennedy Spaceflight Center [*Also known as KSC*] [*NASA*] ... JFKSC
John Flanagan [*Designer's mark, when appearing on US coins*] ... JF
John Fluke Manufacturing Co., Mountlake Terrace, WA [*Library symbol Library of Congress*] (LCLS) ... WaMtJF
John Forsyth Co., Inc. [*Toronto Stock Exchange symbol*] ... JFC
John Fox, Jr. Memorial Library, Paris, KY [*Library symbol Library of Congress*] (LCLS) ... KyParF
John Fricke Fan Club [*Defunct*] (EA) ... JFFC
John G. Shedd Aquarium, Chicago, IL [*Library symbol Library of Congress*] (LCLS) ... ICJSh
John G. Shedd Aquarium, Chicago, IL [*OCLC symbol*] (OCLC) ... IHW
John Gary International Fan Club (EA) ... JGIFC
John Gilbert Fan Club (EA) ... JGFC
John Gill Fan Club (EA) ... JGFC
John Graham Architect Engineer Ltd., Edmonton, Alberta [*Library symbol National Library of Canada*] (NLC) ... AEJGAE
John H. Burrows & Sons Ltd., Southend-On-Sea, United Kingdom [*Library symbol Library of Congress*] (LCLS) ... UkSsB
John H. Glenn High School, Huntington, NY [*Library symbol Library of Congress*] (LCLS) ... MHuGH
John H. Glenn High School, Huntington, NY [*Library symbol*] [*Library of Congress*] (LCLS) ... NHuGH
John H. Nelson Environmental Study Area [*University of Kansas*] [*Research center*] (RCD) ... NESA
John H. West Elementary School, Bethpage, NY [*Library symbol*] [*Library of Congress*] (LCLS) ... NBetWE
John Hancock Bk/Thrift Opp [*NYSE symbol*] (TTSB) ... BTO
John Hancock Income Securities Trust [*Associated Press*] (SAG) ... HanJS
John Hancock Income Securities Trust [*NYSE symbol*] (SPSG) ... JHS
John Hancock Inc. Sec [*NYSE symbol*] (TTSB) ... JHS
John Hancock Inv Tr [*NYSE symbol*] (TTSB) ... JHI
John Hancock Investors Trust [*Associated Press*] (SAG) ... HanJI
John Hancock Investors Trust [*NYSE symbol*] (SPSG) ... JHI
John Hancock Patr Gl Div Fd [*NYSE symbol*] (TTSB) ... PGD
John Hancock Patr Pfd Div Fd [*NYSE symbol*] (TTSB) ... PPF
John Hancock Patr Prem Dv Fd [*NYSE symbol*] (TTSB) ... PDF
John Hancock Patr Prem Dv II [*NYSE symbol*] (TTSB) ... PDT
John Hancock Patr Sel Div Tr [*NYSE symbol*] (TTSB) ... DIV
John Henry Cardinal Newman Honorary Society [*Defunct*] (EA) ... JHCNHS
John Henry Newman [*Initials used as pseudonym*] ... JHN
John Howard Association (EA) ... JHA
John Innes Institute [*British*] (ARC) ... JII
John Innes Manufacturers Association (DBA) ... JIMA
John J. Madden Mental Health Center, Training Staff Development Library, Hines, IL [*Library symbol Library of Congress*] (LCLS) ... IHineJ
John Jay College of Criminal Justice, New York, NY [*Library symbol Library of Congress*] (LCLS) ... NNJJ
John Jay College of Criminal Justice, New York, NY [*OCLC symbol*] (OCLC) ... VVJ
John Jay College of Criminal Justice of The City University of New York (GAGS) ... John Jay C (CUNY)
John Jermain Memorial Public Library, Sag Harbor, NY [*Library symbol Library of Congress*] (LCLS) ... NSh
John Judkyn Memorial (EA) ... JJM
John Krucek & Associates [*Telecommunications service*] (TSSD) ... JK & A
John L. Miller-Great Neck North High School, Great Neck, NY [*Library symbol*] [*Library of Congress*] (LCLS) ... NGrnMiS
John La Farge Institute (EA) ... JFI
John Lewis Childs Elementary School, Floral Park, NY [*Library symbol*] [*Library of Congress*] (LCLS) ... NFlpCE
John Lewis Partnership [*British*] (ECON) ... JLP
John Lovell & Son, City Directories Ltd., Montreal, PQ, Canada [*Library symbol Library of Congress*] (LCLS) ... CaQMJL
John Lovell & Son City Directories Ltd., Montreal, Quebec [*Library symbol National Library of Canada*] (NLC) ... QMJL
John M. Poindexter [*National Security Advisor during the Reagan Administration*] ... JMP
John Marshall Foundation (EA) ... JMF
John Marshall High School Library, Rochester, NY [*OCLC symbol*] (OCLC) ... RWS
John Marshall Law Journal [*A publication*] (DLA) ... John Marsh LJ
John Marshall Law Quarterly [*A publication*] (DLA) ... John Marsh LQ
John Marshall Law Quarterly [*A publication*] (DLA) ... John Marshall LQ
John Marshall Law School [*Chicago, IL*] (DLA) ... JMLS
John Marshall Law School (GAGS) ... John Marshall Law Sch
John Marshall Law School, Chicago, IL [*Library symbol Library of Congress*] (LCLS) ... ICJM
John Marshall Law School, Chicago, IL [*OCLC symbol*] (OCLC) ... IUJ
John McIntire Public Library, Zanesville, OH [*Library symbol Library of Congress*] (LCLS) ... OZav
John Menzies Library Services [*Information service or system*] (IID) ... JMLS
John Mercanti [*Designer's mark, when appearing on US coins*] ... JM
John Milton Hagen [*Antibody*] [*Immunology*] (DAVI) ... JMH
John Milton Society for the Blind [*Later, JMSB*] (EA) ... JMS
John Milton Society for the Blind (EA) ... JMSB
John Moores University [*British*] ... JMU
John Morgan Evans of Merthyr Tydil [*An association*] (EA) ... JMEMT
John Muir Institute for Environmental Studies [*Defunct*] (EA) ... JMI
John Muir National Historic Site ... JOMU
John Nurminen, OY [*Finland*] [*FAA designator*] (FAAC) ... JNA
John Nuveen 'A' [*NYSE symbol*] (TTSB) ... JNC
John of Tynemouth [*Deceased, 1221*] [*Authority cited in pre-1607 legal work*] (DSA) ... Jo T
John Oxley Journal [*A publication*] ... John Oxley J
John Pelham Historical Association (EA) ... JPHA
John Peter Smith Hospital, Fort Worth, TX [*Library symbol Library of Congress*] (LCLS) ... TxFJPS
John Philip Sousa Elementary School, Port Washington, NY [*Library symbol*] [*Library of Congress*] (LCLS) ... NPtwJSE
John Player Special [*Sponsor of British Lotus Formula I racing car*] ... JPS
John Quincy Adams [*US president, 1767-1848*] ... JQA
John R. Abney Collection, Edgefield County Library, Edgefield, SC [*Library symbol Library of Congress*] (LCLS) ... ScEA
John R. Kaufman, Jr., [*Sunbury*] **Public Library, Sunbury, PA** [*Library symbol Library of Congress*] (LCLS) ... PSu
John R. Sinnock [*Designer's mark, when appearing on US coins*] ... JRS
John R. Sinnock [*Designer's mark, when appearing on US coins*] ... JS
John Reich Collectors Society (EA) ... JRCS
John Ronald Renel Tolkien [*British author, 1892-1973*] ... JRRT
John Ross Ewing, Jr. [*Character in TV series "Dallas"*] ... JR
John Shaw's Justiciary Cases [*1848-52*] [*Scotland*] [*A publication*] (DLA) ... Shaw J
John Shaw's Justiciary Reports [*1848-52*] [*Scotland*] [*A publication*] (DLA) ... J Shaw
John Shaw's Justiciary Reports [*1848-52*] [*Scotland*] [*A publication*] (DLA) ... J Shaw Just
John Steinbeck House, Salinas, CA [*Library symbol Library of Congress*] (LCLS) ... CSalJS
John Steinbeck Society of America (EA) ... JSSA
John Street Elementary School, Franklin Square, NY [*Library symbol Library of Congress*] (LCLS) ... NFsJE
John Swaney Attendance Center, McNabb, IL [*Library symbol Library of Congress*] (LCLS) ... IMcSC
John T. and Catherine McArthur Foundation, Chicago, IL [*Library symbol*] [*Library of Congress*] (LCLS) ... ICJCM
John T. Mather Memorial Hospital, Port Jefferson, NY [*Library symbol Library of Congress*] (LCLS) ... NPjMH
John the Baptist ... JOBAPT
John the Divine ... JODIV
John the Evangelist ... JOEVANG
John Tomay Memorial Public Library, Georgetown, CO [*Library symbol Library of Congress*] (LCLS) ... CoGeo
John Tuck Elementary School, Redmond, OR [*Library symbol*] [*Library of Congress*] (LCLS) ... OrRedTE
John Tyler [*US president, 1790-1862*] ... JT
John Tyler Community College, Chester, VA [*Library symbol Library of Congress*] (LCLS) ... ViChT
John Von Neumann Computer Center Network (ACRL) ... JvNCnet
John Von Neumann National Supercomputer Center [*Princeton, NJ*] (GRD) ... JVNC
John Warner Hospital, Clinton, IL [*Library symbol Library of Congress*] (LCLS) ... ICIH
John Wesley College Library, Owosso, MI [*Inactive*] [*OCLC symbol*] (OCLC) ... EYJ
John Wesley College, Owosso, MI [*Library symbol Library of Congress*] (LCLS) ... MiOwJW
John Wiley [*& Sons*] [*Publisher*] ... JW
John Wiley & Sons [*Publisher*] (AAGC) ... Wiley
John Wiley & Sons, New York, NY [*Library symbol Library of Congress*] (LCLS) ... JwS
John Wood Community College, Quincy, IL [*Library symbol Library of Congress*] (LCLS) ... IQW
JOHNNIAC [*John's Integrator and Automatic Computer*] **Open Shop System** [*Time-sharing language*] [*Rand Corp. 1962*] [*Computer science*] ... JOSS
Johnnie [*Phonetic alphabet*] [*Royal Navy World War I*] (DSUE) ... J
Johnny [*Phonetic alphabet*] [*Pre-World War II*] (DSUE) ... J
Johnny Alfalfa Sprout [*Defunct*] (EA) ... JAS
Johnny and Jack Fan Club (EA) ... JJFC
Johnny Bernard Fan Club (EA) ... JBFC
Johnny Cash and June Carter Cash International Fan Club (EA) ... JCJCCIFC
Johnny Come Lately [*Slang*] ... JCL
Johnny Comfort International Fan Club [*Defunct*] (EA) ... JCIFC
Johnny Len Fan Club (EA) ... JLFC
Johnny Mathis International Fan Club (EA) ... JMIFC
Johnny Rodriguez Fan Club (EA) ... JRFC
John-Roger Foundation (EA) ... JRF
John's American Notaries [*A publication*] (DLA) ... John Am Not

Johns and Call Girls United Against Repression (EA) ... JACGUAR
Johns Hopkins University [*Maryland*] ... JHU
[*The*] **Johns Hopkins University** (GAGS) ... Johns Hopkins U
Johns Hopkins university, Alan Chesney Medical Archives, Baltimore, MD [*Library symbol*] [*Library of Congress*] (LCLS) ... MdBJ-C
Johns Hopkins University Applied Physics Laboratory [*Laurel, MD*] ... JHU/APL
Johns Hopkins University, Applied Physics Laboratory, Silver Spring, MD [*Library symbol Library of Congress*] (LCLS) ... MdBJ-A
Johns Hopkins University, Baltimore, MD [*OCLC symbol*] (OCLC) ... JHE
Johns Hopkins University, Baltimore, MD [*Library symbol Library of Congress*] (LCLS) ... MdBJ
Johns Hopkins University - Center for Research in Scientific Communication (PDAA) ... JHU-CRSC
Johns Hopkins University - Dyslexia and Dysgraphia Batteries ... JHU-DDB
Johns Hopkins University, George Peabody Library, Baltimore, MD [*Library symbol Library of Congress*] (LCLS) ... MdBJ-P
Johns Hopkins University, John Work Garrett Library, Baltimore, MD [*Library symbol Library of Congress*] (LCLS) ... MdBJ-G
Johns Hopkins University, School of Advanced International Studies, Washington, DC [*Library symbol Library of Congress*] (LCLS) ... MdBJ-AIS
Johns Hopkins University, School of Hygiene and Public Health, Maternal and Child Health-Population Dynamics Library, Baltimore, MD [*Library symbol Library of Congress*] (LCLS) ... MdBJ-H
Johns Hopkins University, Welch Medical Library, Baltimore, MD [*OCLC symbol*] (OCLC) ... JHW
Johns Hopkins University, William H. Welch Medical Library, Baltimore, MD [*Library symbol Library of Congress*] (LCLS) ... MdBJ-W
John's [*Von Neumann*] **Integrator and Automatic Computer** [*An early computer*] ... JOHNNIAC
Johns Manville Corp. (MCD) ... JM
Johns-Manville Corp., Corporate Information Center, Denver, CO [*OCLC symbol*] (OCLC) ... CJM
Johns-Manville Sales Corp., Corporate Information Center, Denver, CO [*Library symbol Library of Congress*] (LCLS) ... CoDJM
Johnson Air, Inc. [*ICAO designator*] (FAAC) ... JHN
Johnson and Hemming's English Chancery Reports [*70 English Reprint*] [*A publication*] (DLA) ... John & H
Johnson and Hemming's English Chancery Reports [*70 English Reprint*] [*A publication*] (DLA) ... Johns & H
Johnson and Hemming's English Chancery Reports [*70 English Reprint*] [*A publication*] (DLA) ... Johns & H (Eng)
Johnson and Hemming's English Chancery Reports [*70 English Reprint*] [*A publication*] (DLA) ... Johns & Hem
Johnson and Hemming's English Vice-Chancellors' Reports [*A publication*] (DLA) ... J & H
Johnson & Higgins, Willis, Faber Ltd., Montreal, Quebec [*Library symbol National Library of Canada*] (NLC) ... QMJHW
Johnson and Houghton's Institutes of Hindoo Law [*A publication*] (DLA) ... J & H Hind L
Johnson and Johnson [*Commercial firm*] (DAVI) ... J & J
Johnson & Johnson [*NYSE symbol*] (SPSG) ... JNJ
Johnson & Johnson [*Associated Press*] (SAG) ... JohnJn
Johnson & Johnson Dental Product Co., East Windsor, NJ [*Library symbol Library of Congress*] (LCLS) ... NjEwJJ
Johnson & Johnson Dental Products Co., Science Information Center, East Windsor,NJ [*OCLC symbol*] (OCLC) ... VJJ
Johnson & Johnson Ltd., Montreal, PQ, Canada [*Library symbol Library of Congress*] (LCLS) ... CaQMJJ
Johnson & Johnson Ltd., Montreal, Quebec [*Library symbol National Library of Canada*] (NLC) ... QMJJ
Johnson & Johnson, Research Center, New Brunswick, NJ [*Library symbol Library of Congress*] (LCLS) ... NjNbJJ
Johnson and Swanson, Law Library, Dallas, TX [*Library symbol Library of Congress*] (LCLS) ... TxDaJS
Johnson Associates Inc. (GAAI) ... JAI
Johnson Associates, Incorporated, Greenwich, CT [*Library symbol Library of Congress*] (LCLS) ... Jai
Johnson Bible College [*Tennessee*] ... JBC
Johnson Bible College, Knoxville, TN [*Library symbol Library of Congress*] (LCLS) ... TKimJ
Johnson C. Smith University, Charlotte, NC [*Library symbol Library of Congress*] (LCLS) ... NcCJ
Johnson C. Smith University, James B. Duke Memorial Library, Charlotte, NC [*OCLC symbol*] (OCLC) ... NCJ
Johnson Canyon [*California*] [*Seismograph station code, US Geological Survey*] (SEIS) ... JHC
Johnson City Medical Center Hospital, Learning Resources Center, Johnson City, TN [*Library symbol Library of Congress*] (LCLS) ... TJoMC
Johnson City, TN [*AM radio station call letters*] ... WETB
Johnson City, TN [*FM radio station call letters*] ... WETS
Johnson City, TN [*AM radio station call letters*] ... WJCW
Johnson City, TN [*Television station call letters*] ... WJHL
Johnson City, TN [*FM radio station call letters*] ... WQUT
Johnson City, TX [*Location identifier FAA*] (FAAL) ... JCY
Johnson City, TX [*FM radio station call letters*] ... KFAN
Johnson Controls [*NYSE symbol*] (TTSB) ... JCI
Johnson Controls, Corporate Information Center, Milwaukee, WI [*Library symbol Library of Congress*] (LCLS) ... WMJ
Johnson Controls, Inc. [*NYSE symbol*] (SPSG) ... JCI
Johnson Controls, Inc. [*Associated Press*] (SAG) ... JohnCn
Johnson County Community College, Overland Park, KS [*Library symbol Library of Congress*] (LCLS) ... KOvpJ
Johnson County Law Library, Olathe, KS [*Library symbol Library of Congress*] (LCLS) ... KOlJL
Johnson County Library, Buffalo, WY [*Library symbol Library of Congress*] (LCLS) ... WyBu
Johnson County Library, Kaycee Branch, Kaycee, WY [*Library symbol Library of Congress*] (LCLS) ... WyKc
Johnson County Library, Merriam, KS [*Library symbol Library of Congress*] (LCLS) ... KMrJ
Johnson County Mental Health Center, Mission, KS [*Library symbol Library of Congress*] (LCLS) ... KMiJ
Johnson County Museum, Franklin, IN [*Library symbol Library of Congress*] (LCLS) ... InFrlJM
Johnson County Public Library, Shawnee Mission, KS [*Library symbol Library of Congress*] (LCLS) ... KShm
Johnson County Recorder's Office, Franklin, IN [*Library symbol Library of Congress*] (LCLS) ... InFrlCR
Johnson Elementary School, Rockford, IL [*Library symbol*] [*Library of Congress*] (LCLS) ... IRoJoE
Johnson Flying Service [*Air carrier designation symbol*] ... JOHX
Johnson Free Public Library, Hackensack, NJ [*Library symbol Library of Congress*] (LCLS) ... NjHack
Johnson Informal Reading Inventory (EDAC) ... JIRI
Johnson, KS [*Location identifier FAA*] (FAAL) ... JHN
Johnson Matthey Bankers [*Commercial firm British*] ... JMB
Johnson Matthey Public Ltd. Co. [*Toronto Stock Exchange symbol*] ... JMP
Johnson Memorial Hospital and Nursing School, Dawson, MN [*Library symbol*] [*Library of Congress*] (LCLS) ... MnDawJH
Johnson Noise [*Thermal noise, that made by a resistor at a temperature above absolute zero*] ... JN
Johnson on Maritime Rights [*A publication*] (DLA) ... Johns Mar R
Johnson Reprint Corporation, New York, NY [*Library symbol Library of Congress*] (LCLS) ... JrC
Johnson Society (EA) ... JS
Johnson Society of London (EA) ... JSL
Johnson Space Center (USDC) ... JSC
Johnson State College, Johnson, VT [*OCLC symbol*] (OCLC) ... VTJ
Johnson State College, Johnson, VT [*Library symbol Library of Congress*] (LCLS) ... VtJoT
Johnson, VT [*FM radio station call letters*] ... WJSC
Johnson Worldwide Associates, Inc. [*Associated Press*] (SAG) ... JWA
Johnson Worldwide Associates, Inc. [*NASDAQ symbol*] (NQ) ... JWAI
Johnson Worldwide'A' [*NASDAQ symbol*] (TTSB) ... JWAIA
Johnson-Kenney Screening Test [*Psychology*] (DAVI) ... JKST
Johnson-O'Malley Act [*1934*] ... JOM
Johnson's Bills of Exchange [*2nd ed.*] [*1839*] [*A publication*] (DLA) ... Johns Bills
Johnson's Civil Law of Spain [*A publication*] (DLA) ... Johns Civ L Sp
Johnson's Ecclesiastical Law [*A publication*] (DLA) ... Johns Eccl L
Johnson's English Chancery Reports [*A publication*] (DLA) ... Johns Eng Ch
Johnson's English Chancery Reports [*A publication*] (DLA) ... Johns HRV
Johnson's English Dictionary [*A publication*] (DLA) ... John Dict
Johnson's English Vice-Chancellors' Reports [*A publication*] (DLA) ... John
Johnson's English Vice-Chancellors' Reports [*A publication*] (DLA) ... John Eng Ch
Johnson's English Vice-Chancellors' Reports [*A publication*] (DLA) ... Johns
Johnson's English Vice-Chancellors' Reports [*A publication*] (DLA) ... Johns Ch
Johnson's English Vice-Chancellors' Reports [*A publication*] (DLA) ... Johns VC
Johnson's English Vice-Chancellors' Reports [*A publication*] (DLA) ... Johns VC (Eng)
Johnson's English Vice-Chancellors' Reports [*A publication*] (DLA) ... Johnson
[*The*] **Johnsons Fan Club** (EA) ... TJFC
Johnson's Impeachment Trial [*A publication*] (DLA) ... Johns Tr
Johnson's Maryland Chancery Decisions [*A publication*] (DLA) ... Johns Ch
Johnson's Maryland Chancery Decisions [*A publication*] (DLA) ... Johns Dec
Johnson's Maryland Chancery Decisions [*A publication*] (DLA) ... Johnson
Johnson's Maryland Chancery Reports [*A publication*] (DLA) ... J Rep
Johnson's Maryland Chancery Reports [*A publication*] (DLA) ... John
Johnson's Maryland Chancery Reports [*A publication*] (DLA) ... Johns
Johnson's New York Cases [*or Reports*] [*A publication*] (DLA) ... JC
Johnson's New York Cases [*A publication*] (DLA) ... John Cas
Johnson's New York Cases [*A publication*] (DLA) ... Johns C
Johnson's New York Cases [*A publication*] (DLA) ... Johns Cas
Johnson's New York Cases [*A publication*] (DLA) ... Johns Cas (NY)
Johnson's New York Cases [*A publication*] (DLA) ... Johns Cases
Johnson's New York Chancery Reports [*A publication*] (DLA) ... J Ch
Johnson's New York Chancery Reports [*A publication*] (DLA) ... JCR
Johnson's New York Chancery Reports [*A publication*] (DLA) ... Jo Ch
Johnson's New York Chancery Reports [*A publication*] (DLA) ... Joh Ch Rep
Johnson's New York Chancery Reports [*A publication*] (DLA) ... John Ch Rep
Johnson's New York Chancery Reports [*A publication*] (DLA) ... John Chan
Johnson's New York Chancery Reports [*A publication*] (DLA) ... Johns Ch
Johnson's New York Chancery Reports [*A publication*] (DLA) ... Johns Ch Cas
Johnson's New York Chancery Reports [*A publication*] (DLA) ... Johns Ch (NY)
Johnson's New York Court of Errors Reports [*A publication*] (DLA) ... Johns Ct Err
Johnson's New York Reports [*A publication*] (DLA) ... J
Johnson's New York Reports [*A publication*] (DLA) ... J Rep
Johnson's New York Reports [*A publication*] (DLA) ... John
Johnson's New York Reports [*A publication*] (DLA) ... Johns (NY)
Johnson's New York Reports [*A publication*] (DLA) ... Johns R
Johnson's New York Reports [*A publication*] (DLA) ... Johnson
Johnson's New York Reports [*A publication*] (DLA) ... Johnson NYR
Johnson's New York Reports [*A publication*] (DLA) ... Johnson R
Johnson's New York Reports [*A publication*] (DLA) ... Johnson's Rep
Johnson's New York Reports [*A publication*] (DLA) ... JR
Johnson's New York Supreme Court Reports [*A publication*] (DLA) ... John
Johnson's New York Supreme Court Reports [*A publication*] (DLA) ... Johns
Johnson's New York Supreme Court Reports [*A publication*] (DLA) ... Johns Rep

Johnson's New Zealand Reports [*A publication*] (DLA) .... Johns NZ
Johnson's Patent Manual [*A publication*] (DLA) .... Johns Pat Man
Johnson's Quarto Dictionary [*A publication*] (DLA) .... Johnson's Quarto Dict
Johnson's Reports of Chase's United States Circuit Court Decisions [*A publication*] (DLA) .... J Rep
Johnson's Reports of Chase's United States Circuit Court Decisions [*A publication*] (DLA) .... Johns US
Johnson-Sea-Link I [*A submersible for deep sea studies*] .... JSLI
Johnsonville, SC [*FM radio station call letters*] (RBYB) .... WPDT
Johnston & Frye [*Vancouver Stock Exchange symbol*] .... JFS
Johnston Atoll [*MARC country of publication code Library of Congress*] (LCCP) .... ji
Johnston Atoll [*MARC geographic area code Library of Congress*] (LCCP) .... poji--
Johnston Atoll Chemical Agents Disposal System .... JACADS
Johnston City, IL [*AM radio station call letters*] .... WDDD
Johnston County Technical Institute, Smithfield, NC [*Library symbol Library of Congress*] (LCLS) .... NcSmJ
Johnston Industries [*NYSE symbol*] (TTSB) .... JII
Johnston Industries, Inc. [*NYSE symbol*] (SPSG) .... JII
Johnston Industries, Inc. [*Associated Press*] (SAG) .... Johnston
Johnston Island [*Airport symbol*] (OAG) .... JON
Johnston Island/Johnston Atoll [*Johnston Island*] [*ICAO location identifier*] (ICLI) .... PJON
Johnston, PA [*FM radio station call letters*] .... WMTZ
Johnston, SC [*AM radio station call letters*] .... WJES
Johnston, SC [*FM radio station call letters*] .... WKSX
Johnstone Point, AK [*Location identifier FAA*] (FAAL) .... JOH
Johnston's Institutes of the Laws of Spain [*A publication*] (DLA) .... Johnst Inst
Johnston's New Zealand Reports [*A publication*] (DLA) .... Johnst (NZ)
Johnstown [*Pennsylvania*] [*Airport symbol*] (OAG) .... JST
Johnstown America Indus [*NASDAQ symbol*] (TTSB) .... JAII
Johnstown America Industries, Inc. [*NASDAQ symbol*] (SAG) .... JAII
Johnstown America Industries, Inc. [*Associated Press*] (SAG) .... JohnstnA
Johnstown American Co. (MHDW) .... JAC
Johnstown & Stony Creek Rail Road Co. [*AAR code*] .... JSC
Johnstown, CO [*AM radio station call letters*] .... KHNC
Johnstown/Consolidated Realty Trust (MHDW) .... JCT
Johnstown Flood National Memorial .... JOFL
Johnstown, NY [*AM radio station call letters*] .... WIZR
Johnstown, NY [*FM radio station call letters*] .... WSRD
Johnstown, Oh [*FM radio station call letters*] (RBYB) .... WSMZ-FM
Johnstown, OH [*FM radio station call letters*] (RBYB) .... WTJY
Johnstown, PA [*Location identifier FAA*] (FAAL) .... JST
Johnstown, PA [*AM radio station call letters*] .... WCRO
Johnstown, PA [*FM radio station call letters*] .... WFRJ
Johnstown, PA [*FM radio station call letters*] .... WGLU
Johnstown, PA [*AM radio station call letters*] .... WJAC
Johnstown, PA [*Television station call letters*] .... WJAC-TV
Johnstown, PA [*FM radio station call letters*] .... WKYE
Johnstown, PA [*AM radio station call letters*] .... WNTJ
Johnstown, PA [*Television station call letters*] .... WTWB
Johnstown, PA [*Television station call letters*] .... WWCP
Johore Bahru [*Refers to Europeans named after Malaysian towns*] (DSUE) .... JB
Johore Bahru [*Malaysia*] [*Airport symbol*] (OAG) .... JHB
Johore Bahru [*Malaysia*] [*ICAO location identifier*] (ICLI) .... WMKJ
Johore Law Reports [*India*] [*A publication*] (DLA) .... JLR
Joigny [*France ICAO location identifier*] (ICLI) .... LFGK
Joilet in Illinois [*Diocesan abbreviation*] [*Illinois*] (TOCD) .... JOL
Join .... J
Join (MSA) .... JN
Join Airways (FAAC) .... JAWYS
Join in Progress [*Broadcasting*] (WDMC) .... JIP
Joinable (ABBR) .... JNB
Joinable Containers [*Shipping*] (DCTA) .... J
Joinder (ABBR) .... JNDR
Joined (AABC) .... JD
Joined (ABBR) .... JND
Joined by Enlistment [*Military*] .... JDENL
Joined by Induction [*Military*] .... JDIND
Joined by Reenlistment [*Military*] .... JDREENL
Joined From [*Military*] .... JDFR
Joiner [*Machinery*] .... J
Joiner (ABBR) .... JNR
Joiner (ABBR) .... JONR
Joiner Pilaster Fumetight [*Technical drawings*] .... JPFT
Joiner Pilaster Nontight [*Technical drawings*] .... JPNT
Joinery (ADA) .... JOIN
Joinery and Woodwork Employers' Federation [*British*] (BI) .... JWEF
Joinery Managers' Association [*British*] (BI) .... JMA
Joining [*Also, JNG*] [*Genetics*] .... J
Joining [*Also, J*] .... JNG
Joining Peptide [*Medicine*] (DMAA) .... JP
Joining Report (MCD) .... JOINREP
Joint .... J
Joint .... JNT
Joint .... JNT
Joint .... JT
Joint Academic Network [*Proposed supercomputer network*] .... JANET
Joint Academic Services Providers to Education and Research (AIE) .... JASPER
Joint Acceptance Plan (AAG) .... JAP
Joint Account .... JA
Joint Acoustic Surveillance System Model [*Military*] (CAAL) .... JASSM
Joint Acquisition Coordinating Board-Europe (AAGC) .... JACB-E
Joint Action Armed Forces .... JAAF
Joint Action Co. [*Marine Corps*] .... JAC
Joint Action in Community Service (EA) .... JACS
Joint Actions Control Office (AABC) .... JACO
Joint Activity Briefing [*Military*] (AFM) .... JAB
Joint Ad Hoc Working Group on Shipping [*ASEAN*] .... JAHWGS
Joint Administration Services .... JAS
Joint Administrative Committee [*Military*] .... JADC
Joint Administrative Instruction .... JAI
Joint Administrative Planning Section [*Joint Planning Staff*] [*World War II*] .... JAPS
Joint Advanced Fighter Engine .... JAFE
Joint Advanced Special Operations Radio System [*Military*] (RDA) .... JASORS
Joint Advanced Strike Technology [*DoD*] .... JAST
Joint Advanced Strike Technology [*Program*] [*Air Force*] [*Navy*] (DOMA) .... JAST
Joint Advanced Study Group .... JASG
Joint Advanced Study Group .... JASGP
Joint Advanced Tactical Command and Control System [*Military*] (SAA) .... JATCCS
Joint Advanced Tactical Command, Control, and Communications Program [*Military*] .... JATCCCP
Joint Advanced Tactical Command, Control, and Communications System [*Military*] (MCD) .... JATCCCS
Joint Advertising Directors of Recruiting [*Navy*] (NVT) .... JADOR
Joint Advisory Committee [*Military*] .... JAC
Joint Advisory Committee on Nutrition Education [*British*] .... JACNE
Joint Advisory Committee on Pets in Society [*British*] (DI) .... JACOPIS
Joint Advisory Survey Board [*British*] .... JASB
Joint Aerial Reconnaissance Interpretation Center (MCD) .... JARIC
Joint Aeronautical Materials Activity [*Military*] (AABC) .... JAMAC
Joint Agency for Municipal Securities Dealers .... JAMS
Joint Agency Training .... JAT
Joint Agent .... JA
Joint Agent (WDAA) .... JT AGT
Joint Agriculture Weather Facility [*Marine science*] (OSRA) .... JAWF
Joint Agriculture-Weather Facility (USDC) .... JAWF
Joint Air Attack Team [*Military*] (INF) .... JAAT
Joint Air Attack Team Tactics (MCD) .... JAATT
Joint Air Base Utilization Plan (MCD) .... JABUP
Joint Air Command Center [*Army*] (DOMA) .... JACC
Joint Air Communications of the Pacific .... JACSPAC
Joint Air Control and Coordination Center [*Air Force*] (AFM) .... JACCC
Joint Air Defense Board .... JADB
Joint Air Defense Division (SAA) .... JADD
Joint Air Defense Force (AAG) .... JADF
Joint Air Defense Interoperability Study .... JADIS
Joint Air Defense Operation Center .... JADOC
Joint Air Defense Operations [*Marine Corps*] (DOMA) .... JADO
Joint Air Defense Wing (SAA) .... JADW
Joint Air Force-NASA .... JAFNA
Joint Air Force-Navy Committee .... JAFNC
Joint Air Force-Navy Experiment (MUGU) .... JANE
Joint Air Intelligence Center (DOMA) .... JAIC
Joint Air Movements Board [*Military*] .... JAMB
Joint Air Operations Center [*Air Force*] .... JAOC
Joint Air Photo Center [*NATO*] (NATG) .... JAPC
Joint Air Reconnaissance Center [*NATO*] (NATG) .... JARC
Joint Air Reconnaissance Coordination Center [*Military*] (MCD) .... JARCC
Joint Air Reconnaissance Intelligence Board [*Australia*] .... JARIB
Joint Air Reconnaissance Intelligence Centre [*British*] .... JARIC
Joint Air Sea Interaction [*National Science Foundation/United Kingdom*] .... JASIN
Joint Air Support Tactics [*Military*] .... JAST
Joint Air Traffic Control Center [*Military*] .... JATCC
Joint Air Traffic Control RADAR Unit (IAA) .... JACTRU
Joint Air Training Plan .... JATP
Joint Air Transport Establishment [*Military British*] .... JATE
Joint Air Transportation Plan (AABC) .... JATP
Joint Air Transportation Service .... JATS
Joint Airborne Advance Party [*Military*] (AFM) .... JAAP
Joint Airborne/Air Transportability Training .... JA/ATT
Joint Airborne Communication and Command Post (IAA) .... JACCP
Joint Airborne Communications Center (MCD) .... JACC
Joint Airborne Communications Center and Command Post .... JACKPOT
Joint Airborne Communications Center/Command Post (AFM) .... JACC/CP
Joint Aircraft Committee [*World War II*] .... JAC
Joint Aircraft Hurricane Plan .... JAMHEP
Joint Air-Ground Instruction Team .... JAGIT
Joint Air-Ground Operations System [*Military*] .... JAGOS
Joint Airlift Allocations Board .... JAAB
Joint Airlift Allocations Committee .... JAAC
Joint Airlines Military Traffic Office .... JAMTO
Joint Airmiss Section [*Aviation*] (DA) .... JAS
Joint Airport Weather Studies [*National Center for Atmospheric Research*] .... JAWS
Joint Air-Sea Interaction Panel [*Federal Council for Science and Technology*] (NOAA) .... ASIP
Joint Air-Sea Interaction Program [*Marine science*] (OSRA) .... JASIN
Joint Air-Sea Interaction Program [*Global Atmospheric Research Program*] (USDC) .... JASIN
Joint Air-Surface Antisubmarine Action .... JASASA
Joint Air-to-Air Missile Requirement Study (MCD) .... JAAMRS
Joint Airworthiness Authority [*Aviation*] .... JAA
Joint Airworthiness Requirements (MCD) .... JAR
Joint Allied Command Western Approaches [*NATO*] (LAIN) .... JACWA
Joint Allied Communications Element (AFM) .... JACE
Joint Allied Military Petroleum Office [*NATO*] .... JAMPO

Joint Allocation Committee Civil Intelligence [*of US and Great Britain*] [*World War II*] ... JACCI
Joint Alternate Command Center [*Military*] (CINC) ... JACC
Joint Alternate Command Element ... JACE
Joint American Military Advisory Group ... JAMAG
Joint American Military Mission for Aid to Turkey (MUGU) ... JAMMAT
Joint American-Chinese Foul Up [*World War II slang*] [*Bowdlerized version*] ... JACFU
Joint Amphibious Board [*Military*] ... JAB
Joint Amphibious Task Force (NVT) ... JATF
Joint Analog Numeric Understanding System ... JANUS
Joint Analysed Make-up [*Computer-controlled attachment*] (PDAA) ... JAM
Joint and Combined Staff Officer School ... JCSOS
Joint and Several [*Legal shorthand*] (LWAP) ... JT & SEV
Joint Anglo-American Foul Up [*World War II slang*] [*Bowdlerized version*] ... JAAFU
Joint Animal By Products Parliamentary and Advisory Committee [*British*] (DBA) ... JABPPC
Joint Antiaircraft Operation Center [*NATO*] (NATG) ... JAAOC
Joint Antisatellite Study ... JASS
Joint Antisubmarine Action ... JASA
Joint Anti-Submarine School [*British military*] (DMA) ... JASS
Joint Antitactical Missile System (Provisional) [*Army*] (RDA) ... JATM
Joint Application Design [*Computer science*] ... JAD
Joint Application Design/Rapid Application Design [*Computer science*] ... JAD/RAD
Joint Apprenticeship and Training Committee [*Bureau of Apprenticeship and Training*] [*Department of Labor*] ... JATC
Joint Apprenticeship Committee ... JAC
Joint Apprenticeship Program [*Department of Labor*] ... JAP
Joint Arctic Weather Stations [*Canada-US*] ... JAWS
Joint Area of Operations (DOMA) ... JAO
Joint Area Petroleum Office ... JAPO
Joint Armed Forces Housing Referral Office (MCD) ... JAFHRO
Joint Armed Forces Publication ... JAFPUB
Joint Arms Control ... JAC
Joint Army and Navy ... JAN
Joint Army and Navy Committee on Welfare and Recreation ... JANCWR
Joint Army and Navy Munitions Board [*Terminated, 1947*] ... JANMB
Joint Army and Navy Technical Aeronautical Board ... JANTAB
Joint Army-Air Force ... JAAF
Joint Army-Air Force Adjustment Regulations ... JAAFAR
Joint Army-Air Force Air-Ground Study ... JAGS
Joint Army-Air Force Commercial Traffic Bulletin ... JAAFCTB
Joint Army-Air Force Master Plan for the Satisfaction of Army Meteorological Support Requirements (MCD) ... MAP/SAMSR
Joint Army-Air Force Procurement Circular ... JAAFPC
Joint Army-Navy Aircraft Instrument Action (MCD) ... JANAIA
Joint Army-Navy Aircraft Instrument Research ... JANAIR
Joint Army-Navy Assessment Committee [*World War II*] ... JANAC
Joint Army-Navy Ballistic Missile Committee ... JANBMC
Joint Army-Navy Board ... JB
Joint Army-Navy Communications ... JANCOM
Joint Army-Navy Experimental and Testing Board ... JANET
Joint Army-Navy Foul Up [*Military slang*] [*Bowdlerized version*] ... JANFU
Joint Army-Navy Grid System [*NATO*] ... JANGRID
Joint Army-Navy Information Center ... JANIC
Joint Army-Navy Intelligence Studies ... JANIS
Joint Army-Navy Machine Tools Committee (AAG) ... JANMAT
Joint Army-Navy Material ... JANMAT
Joint Army-Navy Ocean Terminal ... JANOT
Joint Army-Navy Petroleum Purchase Agency ... JANPPA
Joint Army-Navy Procedure ... JANP
Joint Army-Navy Publication ... JANP
Joint Army-Navy Specification (IAA) ... JANS
Joint Army-Navy Specification ... JANSPEC
Joint Army-Navy Standard [*NATO*] (NATG) ... JANSTD
Joint Army-Navy Tested Extra ... JANTX
Joint Army-Navy War Shipping Administration ... JANWSA
Joint Army-Navy-Air Force ... JANAF
Joint Army-Navy-Air Force Logistics Policy ... JANALP
Joint Army-Navy-Air Force Logistics Publication ... JANALP
Joint Army-Navy-Air Force, Pacific General Message [*Serially numbered*] (CINC) ... JANAFPAC
Joint Army-Navy-Air Force Procedure [*NATO*] (NATG) ... JANAP
Joint Army-Navy-Air Force Publication ... JANAP
Joint Army-Navy-Air Force Radiotelephone System (IAA) ... JANARS
Joint Army-Navy-Air Force Sea Transportation Message ... JANAST
Joint Aspiration [*Orthopedics*] (DAVI) ... jt asp
Joint Assault Signal Co. [*Small unit in Pacific amphibious warfare*] [*World War II*] ... JASCO
Joint Assessment and Initiatives Office [*Military*] ... JAIO
[*The*] **Joint Association of Classical Teachers** [*British*] ... JACT
Joint Association Survey [*American Petroleum Institute, Independent Petroleum Association of America, and Mid-Continent Oil and Gas Association*] ... JAS
Joint Atomic Energy Commission ... JAEC
Joint Atomic Energy Intelligence Center [*Military*] ... JAEIC
Joint Atomic Energy Intelligence Committee (KSC) ... JAEIC
Joint Atomic Exercise [*NATO*] (NATG) ... JAE
Joint Atomic Information Exchange Agency (SAA) ... JAIEA
Joint Atomic Information Exchange Group [*DoD*] ... JAIEG
Joint Atomic Weapons Planning Manual (AFM) ... JAWPM
Joint Atomic Weapons Publication System ... JAWPS
Joint Atomic Weapons Publications Board (AABC) ... JAWPB
Joint Attack Fighter [*Air Force*] [*Navy*] [*DoD*] (DOMA) ... JAF
Joint Attack of the Second Echelon (MCD) ... J-SAK
Joint Attack Weapon System [*Military*] (MCD) ... JAWS
Joint Author ... jt auth
Joint Automated Planning Support System [*of JOPS*] [*Military*] ... JAPSS
Joint Automatic Control Conference [*IEEE*] ... JACC
Joint Automatic Data Processing Unit ... JADPU
Joint Automatic Language Processing Group ... JALPG
Joint Aviation Requirement [*FAA*] (TAG) ... JAR
Joint Aviation Supply and Maintenance Material Management (DNAB) ... JASMMM
Joint Baltic American National Committee (EA) ... JBANC
Joint Bank-Fund Library, Washington, DC [*OCLC symbol*] (OCLC) ... DJB
Joint Bar ... JTB
Joint Blood Council [*Defunct*] (EA) ... JBC
Joint Blood Program Office (DOMA) ... JBPO
Joint Board of Directors, Army-Air Force Exchange Service (AABC) ... JBDAAFES
Joint Board on Future Storage of Atomic Weapons ... JBFSAW
Joint Bond ... JB
Joint Brazil-United States Defense Commission [*Terminated, 1977*] ... JBUSDC
Joint Brazil-United States Military Commission ... BMC
Joint Brazil-United States Military Commission ... JBUSMC
Joint Budget Committee (OICC) ... JBC
Joint Bus Military Traffic Office (AABC) ... JBMTO
Joint Cadet Executive [*British military*] (DMA) ... JCE
Joint Cadre Operation Control Group [*Military*] ... JCOCG
Joint Casualty Resolution Center (MCD) ... JCRC
Joint Casualty Resolution Center [*Established in 1973 to coordinate U.S. military activities regarding American MIA/POWs*] (VNW) ... JCRS
Joint CCOP/IOC Program of Research on the South Pacific [*Marine science*] (MSC) ... SOPAC
Joint Center for Energy Management [*Research center*] (RCD) ... JCEM
Joint Center for Graduate Study [*Research center*] (RCD) ... JCGS
Joint Center for Graduate Study, Richland, WA [*Library symbol*] [*Library of Congress*] (LCLS) ... WaRiJ
Joint Center for Lessons Learned (DOMA) ... JCLL
Joint Center for Political and Economic Studies (EA) ... JCPES
Joint Center for Political Studies [*Later, JCPES*] (EA) ... JCPS
Joint Center for the Study of Law and Human Genetics ... JCSLHG
Joint Center for Urban Studies of MIT [*Massachusetts Institute of Technology*] **and Harvard University** [*Research center*] (RCD) ... JCUS
Joint Central Air Defense Force (SAA) ... JCEADF
Joint Central Graves Registration Office [*Military*] (CINC) ... JCGRO
Joint Central Graves Registration Office (DOMA) ... JCGRO
Joint Chapters - Educational Council ... JCEC
Joint Checklist Working Group [*Military*] (AFIT) ... JCWG
Joint Chiefs of Staff [*Military*] ... JCOS
Joint Chiefs of Staff [*United States*] [*Military*] ... JCS
Joint Chiefs of Staff Alerting Network [*Military*] ... JCSAN
Joint Chiefs of Staff Alerting System (MCD) ... JCSAS
Joint Chiefs of Staff Automatic Conference Arranger [*Military*] (CET) ... JCS-ACA
Joint Chiefs of Staff Identification Badge [*Military decoration*] (GFGA) ... JCSIDBAD
Joint Chiefs of Staff Identification Badge [*Military decoration*] (AABC) ... JCSIdentBad
Joint Chiefs of Staff Interim Data Transmission Network [*Military*] (CET) ... JCSIDTN
Joint Chiefs of Staff Memorandum [*Military*] ... JCSM
Joint Chiefs of Staff National Military Command Center (DNAB) ... JCSNMCC
Joint Chiefs of Staff Organization [*Military*] (MCD) ... JCSO
Joint Chiefs of Staff Plans ... JCSP
Joint Chiefs of Staff Publications [*Military*] ... JCP
Joint Chiefs of Staff Publications [*Military*] ... JCSPUB
Joint Chiefs of Staff Representative, Europe [*NATO*] (NATG) ... JCSRE
Joint Chiefs of Staff (Special Assistant for Strategic Mobility) (DNAB) ... JCS(SASM)
Joint Chiefs of Staff Teletypwriter Conference Network [*Military*] (MCD) ... JCSTELECON
Joint Church Aid [*Biafra relief program in late 1960's*] [*Defunct*] ... JCA
Joint Church Aid - United States of America [*See also JCA*] [*Defunct*] (EA) ... JCA-USA
Joint Civil Affairs Committee ... JCAC
Joint Civil Defense Support Group ... JCDSG
Joint Civilian Employee Advisory Group [*Military*] (CINC) ... JCEAG
Joint Civilian Orientation Conference [*DoD*] ... JCOC
Joint Closed Loop Operations Test (SAA) ... JCLOT
Joint Collection Management Tools [*Army*] (RDA) ... JCMT
Joint Collection, Western Historical Manuscript Collection and State Historical,Columbia, MO [*Library symbol*] [*Library of Congress*] (LCLS) ... MoCoJ
Joint Combat Airspace Command and Control Course (DOMA) ... JCACC
Joint Combat Operations Center [*Navy*] (NVT) ... JCOC
Joint Combat Systems Integrating ... JCSI
Joint Combined System Test (KSC) ... JCST
Joint Command and Control Development Group [*DoD*] ... JCCDG
Joint Command and Control Requirements [*Military*] (GFGA) ... JCCR
Joint Command and Control Requirements Group [*Joint Chiefs of Staff*] [*DoD*] ... JCCRG
Joint Command and Control Standards Committee (AFM) ... JCCSC
Joint Command, Control, and Electronic Warfare School ... JCEWS
Joint Command Operations Center [*NATO*] (NATG) ... JCOC
Joint Command Post Exercise [*Military*] (AABC) ... JCPX
Joint Commission for Black Sea Fisheries ... JCBSF
Joint Commission of the Socialist Countries on Cooperation in the Field of Fisheries (PDAA) ... JCSCCF

Joint Commission on Accreditation of Healthcare Organizations [An association] .... JCAHO
Joint Commission on Accreditation of Hospitals [Later, JCAHO] (EA) .... JCAH
Joint Commission on Accreditation of Universities [Military] .... JCA
Joint Commission on Allied Health Personnel in Ophthalmology (EA) .... JCAHPO
Joint Commission on Applied Radioactivity .... JCAR
Joint Commission on Atomic Masses .... JCAM
Joint Commission on Competitive Safeguards and the Medical Aspects of Sports [Later, JCSMS] (EA) .... JCCSMAS
Joint Commission on Cooperation in the Field of Environmental Protection [US-USSR] [Marine science] (OSRA) .... JCCFEP
Joint Commission on Cooperation in the Field of Environmental Protection [US-USSR] (USDC) .... JCCFEP
Joint Commission on Dance and Theatre Accreditation (EA) .... JCDTA
Joint Commission on Hospital Accreditation .... JCHA
Joint Commission on Korea .... JCK
Joint Commission on Mental Health of Children .... JCMHC
Joint Commission on Mental Illness and Health [Defunct] (EA) .... JCMIH
Joint Commission on Political Prisoners and Refugees in French North Africa [World War II] .... JCPPRFNA
Joint Commission on Rural Reconstruction .... JCRR
Joint Commission on Sports Medicine and Science (EA) .... JCSMS
Joint Committe on Higher Surgical Training [Royal College of Surgeons] (PDAA) .... JCHST
Joint Committee for European Affairs [Defunct] (EA) .... JCEA
Joint Committee for the British Memorial Industry (DBA) .... JCBMI
Joint Committee of Cultural and Education Ministers [Australia] .... JCCEM
Joint Committee of Nordic Marine Technology [See also NSTM] (EAIO) .... JCNMT
Joint Committee of Nordic Master Tailors (EA) .... JCNMT
Joint Committee of the Nordic Natural Science Research Councils (EA) .... JCNNSRC
Joint Committee of the States to Study Alcoholic Beverage Laws (EA) .... JCSSAB
Joint Committee on Aboriginal Lands and Mining [Australia] .... JCALM
Joint Committee on Agricultural Research and Development [Agency for International Development] .... JCARD
Joint Committee on Atomic Energy [of the US Congress] [Terminated] .... JCAE
Joint Committee on Building Codes [Later, Model Code Standardization Council] (EA) .... JCBC
Joint Committee on College Teaching .... JCOT
Joint Committee on Contemporary China (EA) .... JCCC
Joint Committee on Continuing Legal Education [Later, ALI-ABA Committee on Con tinuing Professional Education] (EA) .... JCCLE
Joint Committee on Contraception (DMAA) .... JCC
Joint Committee on Cooperation in Studies of the World Ocean [US-USSR] [Marine science] (OSRA) .... JCCSWO
Joint Committee on Cooperation on Studies of the World Ocean [US-USSR] (USDC) .... JCCSWO
Joint Committee on Intersociety Coordination [Defunct] (EA) .... JCIC
Joint Committee on Library Education .... JCLE
Joint Committee on Mobility for the Disabled [British] .... JCMD
Joint Committee on New Weapons and Equipment .... JNW
Joint Committee on Powder Diffraction Standards (MCD) .... JCPDS
Joint [Congressional] Committee on Printing .... JCP
Joint Committee on Tactical Shelters (MCD) .... JOCOTAS
Joint Committee on Taxation [US Congress] .... JCT
Joint Committee on Television Transmission .... CMTT
Joint Committee [of Congress] on the Library of Congress .... JCLC
Joint Committee on the Union List of Serials .... JCULS
Joint Commonwealth/States Committee on the Adult Migration Education Program [Australia] .... JC/SCAMEP
Joint Communication Activity .... JCA
Joint Communications Agency [Military] .... JCA
Joint Communications and Electronics Working Group [NATO] (NATG) .... JCEWG
Joint Communications Board (MCD) .... JCB
Joint Communications Center (MCD) .... JCC
Joint Communications Center .... JCOMCEN
Joint Communications Contingency Station Activity (MCD) .... JCCSA
Joint Communications Electronic Warfare Simulation .... JCEW
Joint Communications Instruction .... JCI
Joint Communications Support Element [DoD] .... JCSE
Joint Communications Support Squadron .... JCSS
Joint Communications Systems Elements (MCD) .... JCSE
Joint Communications-Electronics Committee [Military] .... JCEC
Joint Communications-Electronics Committee, Pacific [Military] (CINC) .... JCECPAC
Joint Communications-Electronics Group [Military] .... JCEG
Joint Communications-Electronics Group [Military] .... JCEGP
Joint Communications-Electronics Nomenclature System [Military] .... JCENS
Joint Communications-Electronics Operating Instructions [Military] (CET) .... JCEOI
Joint Compound [Plumbing] .... JC
Joint Computer Bureau [Office of Population Census and Surveys] [British] .... JCB
Joint Computer Conference .... JCC
Joint Computer-Aided Acquisition and Logistic Support [DoD] .... JCALS
Joint Computer-Aided Acquisition Logistics System [Army] (RDA) .... JCALS
Joint COMSEC Coordination Center (MCD) .... JCCC
Joint Concept Review Committee (AAGC) .... JCRC
Joint Concepts and Evaluation Group [Military] (CINC) .... JCEG
Joint CONEX [Container Express] Control Agency .... JCCA
Joint Configuration Control Board [DoD] .... JCCB
Joint Configuration Control Committee [DoD] .... JCCC

Joint Conflict Model [Military] .... JCM
Joint Congressional Atomic Energy Commission (MUGU) .... JCAEC
Joint Conservation Group .... JCG
Joint Conservation Working Party [Australia Political party] .... JCWP
Joint Construction Agency .... JCA
Joint Consultative Board [NATO] (NATG) .... JCB
Joint Consultative Committee [of the National Joint Advisory Council] [British World War II] .... JCC
Joint Consultative Committee (NITA) .... JCC
Joint Contact Point Division [Desert Test Center] [Fort Douglas, UT] .... JCP
Joint Container Control Office (MCD) .... JCCO
Joint Continental Aerospace Defense Integration Staff [Military] (AABC) .... JCADIS
Joint Continental Defense Systems Integration Planning Staff [Air Force] .... JCDSIPS
Joint Contingency Task Group [Military] (VNW) .... JCTG
Joint Control Center (MCD) .... JCC
Joint Control Number .... JCN
Joint Conventional Ammunition Program [Army] .... JCAP
Joint Conventional Ammunition Program Coordinating Group [Army] .... JCAP-CG
Joint Coordinated Ammunition Production (MCD) .... JCAP
Joint Coordinating Committee on Fundamental Properties of Matter [US Department of Energy and USSR State Committee on Peaceful Uses of Atomic Energy] .... JCC-FPM
Joint Coordinating Group [Military] (AFIT) .... JCG
Joint Coordination Center (NVT) .... JCC
Joint Coordination Center Communications Network .... JCCOMNET
Joint Coordination Center, Far East [Military] (CINC) .... JCCFE
Joint Council for Repatriation .... JCR
Joint Council for Scientific and Technical Communication [British] .... JCSTC
Joint Council for the Welfare of Immigrants [British] (DI) .... JCWI
Joint Council of Allergy and Immunology (EA) .... JCAI
Joint Council of Fire Service Organizations [Defunct] (EA) .... JCFSO
Joint Council of Immunohistochemical Manufacturers .... JCIM
Joint Council of Language Associations [British] .... JCLA
Joint Council of Post Office Associations [South Africa] .... JCPOA
Joint Council on Economic Education (EA) .... JCEE
Joint Council on Educational Broadcasting [Later, JCET] (EA) .... JCEB
Joint Council on Educational Telecommunications [Defunct] (EA) .... JCET
Joint Council on Quantum Electronics (MCD) .... JCQE
Joint Council on Research in Pastoral Care and Counseling [Later, COMISS] (EA) .... JCRPCC
Joint Council to Improve Health Care of the Aged [Defunct] (EA) .... JCIHCA
Joint Countering Attack Helicopter Exercises (RDA) .... J-CATCH
Joint Crisis Communications Exercise Program (MCD) .... JCCEP
Joint Crisis Management Capability [DoD] .... JCMC
Joint Cruise Missile Program [or Project] Office (MCD) .... JCMPO
Joint Cultural Appeal (EA) .... JCA
Joint Custody Association (EA) .... JCA
Joint Customs Consultative Technical Committee [British] (DCTA) .... JCCTC
Joint Cutover Integrated Working Group [Military] (RDA) .... JCIWG
Joint Danube Fishery Commission [See also ZKRVD] [Zilina, Czechoslovakia] (EAIO) .... JDFC
Joint Data Systems Support Center [Military] .... JDSSC
Joint Declaration of Interest (DS) .... JDI
Joint Declaration of Principles .... JDP
Joint Defense Appeal [Defunct] (EA) .... JDA
Joint Defense Production Committee [Later, Joint War Production Committee] [World War II] .... JDPC
Joint Defense Space Communications Station .... JDSCS
Joint Defense Staff [NATO] (NATG) .... JDS
Joint Density of Electronic State [Semiconductor technology] (OA) .... JDES
Joint Department of Defense Configuration Management Committee (MCD) .... JDCMC
Joint Deployment Agency [DoD] .... JDA
Joint Deployment Community [Military] (INF) .... JDC
Joint Deployment System .... JDS
Joint Depot Maintenance Analysis Group [Military] .... JDMAG
Joint Deputy Chiefs of Staff [Military] .... JDCS
Joint Design Team [Military] .... JDT
Joint Determination (AFM) .... JD
Joint Development Agency [DoD] .... JDA
Joint Development Agreement [Business term] (PCM) .... JDA
Joint Development Community [DoD] .... JDC
Joint Development Objectives Plan (SAA) .... JDOP
Joint Development Program .... JDP
Joint Development Team (MCD) .... JDT
Joint Development Testing .... JDT
Joint Dictionary [Dictionary of US Military Terms for Joint Usage] [A publication] (AFM) .... JD
Joint Diploma in Management Accounting Services [British] .... JDipMA
Joint Direct Attack Munition (DOMA) .... JDAM
Joint Direct Attack Munitions [DoD] .... JDAM
Joint Direct Attack Program [Air Force] (DOMA) .... JDAP
Joint Directors of Laboratories [Military] .... JDL
Joint Directory of Higher Education [A publication] .... JDHE
Joint Disciplinary Scheme [British] .... JDS
Joint Dissemination Review Panels .... JDRP
Joint Doppler Operational Project [For tornado warning] [Meteorology] .... JDOP
Joint Duty Assignment (DOMA) .... JDA
Joint Duty Assignment List (DOMA) .... JDAL
Joint Duty Assignment Management Information System (DOMA) .... JDAMIS
Joint Eastern Air Defense Force (MUGU) .... JEADF
Joint Economic Committee of Congress .... JEC

Joint Economic Committee of Congress (MCD)	JECC
Joint Economic Team	JET
Joint Economy Board [Abolished, 1947] [Army-Navy]	JEB
Joint Editor	JT ED
Joint Educational Development (EA)	JED
Joint Efficiency Study (AIE)	JES
Joint Effort Against Lefthanded Complications	JELC
Joint Effort Evaluation Program [Military] (AFM)	JEEP
Joint Effort for Talent [Navy] (NG)	JET
Joint Electron Device Engineering Council (EA)	JEDEC
Joint Electron Tube Engineering Council [Later, JEDEC] (MCD)	JETEC
Joint Electronic Communications Nomenclature System [Military] (IAA)	JECNS
Joint Electronic Countermeasures Operation Section [NATO] (NATG)	JECMOS
Joint Electronic Data Interchange [International trade]	JEDI
Joint Electronic Payment Intitiative [Proposed] [Computer science]	JEPI
Joint Electronic Payments Initiative	JEPI
Joint Electronic Warfare Center (MCD)	JEWC
Joint Electronic Warfare Staff Officer Course (DOMA)	JEWSOC
Joint Electronics Board	JEB
Joint Electronics Information Agency	JEIA
Joint Electronics Type Designation System [Military] (AFM)	JETDS
Joint Electronics Type Designator [Military] (AABC)	JETD
Joint Electronics Type [Designation] System [Military] (NASA)	JETS
Joint Emergency Airlift Traffic Management Plan [DoD]	JEAT
Joint Emergency Defense Plan Europe [NATO] (NATG)	JEDPE
Joint Emergency Evacuation Plan [Military] (AABC)	JEEP
Joint Emergency Personnel Augmentation Plan [Military] (CINC)	JEPAP
Joint Emergency Relocation Site	JERS
Joint Endeavor Agreement	JEA
Joint Endeavor for Welfare, Education, and Liberation [Part of Grenadian political party, the New JEWEL Movement]	JEWEL
Joint Endeavor Manager	JEM
Joint Engagement Zone [Marine Corps] (DOMA)	JEZ
Joint Engine Project Office (MCD)	JEPO
Joint Engineering Agency	JEA
Joint Engineering and Data Management Information and Control System [Military]	JEDMICS
Joint Engineering Management Conference	JEMC
Joint Engineers [Army] (RDA)	JE
Joint Engineers Management Panel [Army] (RDA)	JEMP
Joint Enroute Terminal System [Canada] (MCD)	JETS
Joint Environmental Data Analysis Center [Army] [Marine science] (OSRA)	JEDA
Joint Environmental Effects Program [Military] (AFM)	JEEP
Joint Environmental Research Unit (MCD)	JERU
Joint Equipment Identification Team [Military] (CINC)	JEIT
Joint Establishment Experimental Pile [Nuclear reactor] [Norway]	JEEP
Joint Establishment for Nuclear Energy Research	JENER
Joint European Operations Communications Network	JEOCN
Joint European Semiconductor Silicon Initiative	JESSI
Joint European Submicron Silicon [Project]	JESSI
Joint European TOKAMAK [Toroidal Kamera Magnetic] [or Torus Nuclear reactor]	JET
Joint Evaluation Committee [NSF-UCAR]	JEC
Joint Executive Committee on Medicine and Biology	JECMB
Joint Exercise (NVT)	JEX
Joint Exercise Control Center (MCD)	JECC
Joint Exercise Control Group [Military] (AABC)	JXCG
Joint Exercise Manual (MCD)	JEM
Joint Exercise Planning Group [Military]	JEPG
Joint Exercise Planning Staff [NATO] (NATG)	JEPS
Joint Exercise Simulation System [DoD]	JESS
Joint Exercise Support System [Military]	JESS
Joint Experimental Helicopter Unit [British military] (DMA)	JEHU
Joint Expert Committee on Food Additives [FDA/WHO]	JECFA
Joint Exploratory Group [NATO] (NATG)	JEG
Joint Export Agent	JEA
Joint Export Association [Department of Commerce]	JEA
Joint Export Establishment Promotion [Trade exhibition] [Department of Commerce]	JEEP
Joint Export-Import Agency [Munich] [Allied German Occupation Forces]	JEIA
Joint Facilities Utilization Board [Military]	JFUB
Joint Feasibility Study Group [Air Force] (MCD)	JFSG
Joint Federal Travel Regulations (DOMA)	JFTR
Joint Fiction Reserve	JFR
Joint Field Training Exercise [Military]	JFTX
Joint Field Trial (NATG)	JFT
Joint Fighter Engine (DWSG)	JFE
Joint Filler [Technical drawings]	JF
Joint Financial Management Improvement Program	JFMIP
Joint Flight Acceptance Composite Test [Gemini] [NASA] (IAA)	JFAC
Joint Flight Acceptance Composite Test [Gemini] [NASA]	J-FACT
Joint Flight Test Control Group (AAG)	JFTCG
Joint Flow and Analysis System for Transportation [Model USA]	JFAST
Joint Fluid [Orthopedics] (DAVI)	JF
Joint Force [Military]	JF
Joint Force Air Component Commander (DOMA)	JFACC
Joint Force Commander [DoD]	JFC
Joint Force Development Process [or Program] [Army]	JFDP
Joint Force Headquarters [Military]	JFHQ
Joint Force Memorandum [Military]	JFM
Joint Force Signals Staff [Military]	JFSS
Joint Forces Land Component (DOMA)	JFLC
Joint Forces Land Component Commander (DOMA)	JFLCC
Joint Forecast System Project (USDC)	JFSP

Joint Forecast System Project [Marine science] (OSRA)	JFSP
Joint Foreign Exchange Agency [Berlin] [Post-World War II, Germany]	JFEA
Joint Foreign Intelligence Assistance Program (AFM)	JFIAP
Joint Formal Acceptance Inspection [NATO] (NATG)	JFAI
Joint Forward Air Controllers Training and Standards Unit [British]	JFACTSU
Joint Forward-Area Air Defense (MCD)	JFAAD
Joint Forward-Area Air Defense System	JFAADS
Joint Foundation Support (EA)	JFS
Joint Framework for Information Technology [British]	JFIT
Joint Free Public Library of Morristown and Morris Township, Morristown, NJ [Library symbol Library of Congress] (LCLS)	NjMo
Joint Frequency Allocation Panel	JFAP
Joint Frequency List	JFL
Joint Frequency Management Office (MCD)	JFMO
Joint Frequency Panel	JFP
Joint Fuze Task Group [Army]	JFTG
Joint General Staff [Military] (NATG)	JGS
Joint Global Ocean Flux Study [International experiment]	JGOFS
Joint Government Agencies Board (SSD)	JGAB
Joint Government Liaison Committee [Composed of Association of Brass and Bronze Ingot Manufacturers and Brass and Bronze Ingot Institute] (EA)	JGLC
Joint Group of Experts [Marine science] (MSC)	JGE
Joint Guidance and Control (KSC)	JG & C
Joint Headquarters [British military] (DMA)	JHQ
Joint Health Library, New York, NY [Library symbol Library of Congress Obsolete] (LCLS)	NNJH
Joint High Command (DNAB)	JHC
Joint Highway Research Project [Purdue University] [Research center] (RCD)	JHRP
Joint Household Goods Shipping Office [Military]	JHHGSO
Joint Household Goods Shipping Office, Washington Area [Military] (AABC)	JHGSOWA
Joint Hurricane Warning Center (CINC)	JHWC
Joint Hypocenter Determination [Earthquake study]	JHD
Joint Ice Center [Marine science] (MSC)	JIC
Joint Ice Center [US Navy] [Marine science] (OSRA)	JIC
Joint ICSU-UATI Coordinating Committee on Water Research (EAIO)	COWAR
Joint Identification (DNAB)	JI
Joint II March-May Study [Coastal Upwelling Ecosystems Analysis] (MSC)	MAM
Joint Imagery Interpretation Key Structure (MCD)	JIIKS
Joint Imagery Production Complex (DOMA)	JIPC
Joint Implementation Committee [Military] (SAA)	JIC
Joint Implementation Plan [Military]	JIP
Joint Industrial Conference on Hydraulic Standards	JICHS
Joint Industrial Council [Defunct] (EA)	JIC
Joint Industrial Measurement Programme (ACII)	JIMS
Joint Industry Board of the Electrical Industry (EA)	JIBEI
Joint Industry Committee for Cable Audience Research [Television] [British]	JICCAR
Joint Industry Committee for National Readership Surveys [British]	JICNARS
Joint Industry Committee for Poster Audience Surveys [British]	JICPAS
Joint Industry Committee for Radio Audience Research [British]	JICRAR
Joint Industry Committee for Television Advertising Research [Database producer]	JICTAR
Joint Industry Council (EAIO)	JIC
Joint Industry Group [An association] (EA)	JIG
Joint Industry Research Committee for Standardization of Miniature Precision Coaxial Connectors	JIRCSM
Joint Industry-Government Tall Structures Committee	JIGTSC
Joint In-Flight Data Transmission System [Army] (MCD)	JIFDATS
Joint In-Flight Transmission System [Army] (IEEE)	JIFTS
Joint Information and Retrieval System [DoD] (MCD)	JIRS
Joint Information Bureau [Military] (MCD)	JIB
Joint Information Liaison Office [Military]	JILO
Joint Information Office [Military]	JIO
Joint Information Search Unit Retrieval System (MCD)	JISR
Joint Input	JIP
Joint Input Processing (IEEE)	JIP
Joint Inspection Unit [United Nations]	JIU
Joint Installation Plan (AAG)	JIP
Joint Institute for Acoustics and Flight Sciences (MCD)	JIAFS
Joint Institute for Advancement of Flight Science [Research center] (RCD)	JIAFS
Joint Institute for Aeronautics and Acoustics [Stanford University] (PDAA)	JIAA
Joint Institute for Laboratory Astrophysics [University of Colorado, National Bureau of Standards] (EA)	JILA
Joint Institute for Laboratory Astrophysics-Information Center [University of Colorado] (PDAA)	JILA-IC
Joint Institute for Marine and Atmospheric Research [Honolulu, HI] [National Oceanic and Atmospheric Administration] (GRD)	JIMAR
Joint Institute for Study of the Atmosphere and Ocean [Seattle, WA] [University of Washington, NOAA] (GRD)	JISAO
Joint Institute of Food Safety and Applied Nutrition	JIFSAN
Joint Institute of Nuclear Research [Dubna, USSR]	JINR
Joint Insurance Committee [under the Trading with the Enemy Act] [World War II]	JIC
Joint Integrated Avionics Directorate (DOMA)	JIAD
Joint Integrated Avionics Working Group [DoD]	JIAWG
Joint Integrated Firepower [Task force] (MCD)	JIF
Joint Integrated Simulation (NASA)	JIS
Joint Integration Office [Department of Energy] [Albuquerque, NM] (GAAI)	JIO
Joint Intelligence Bureau [British] (MCD)	JIB
Joint Intelligence Center	JIC
Joint Intelligence Center, Africa	JICA

Joint Intelligence Center Pacific (DOMA)	JICPAC
Joint Intelligence Center, Pacific Ocean Areas	JICPOA
Joint Intelligence Collecting Agency	JICA
Joint Intelligence Collecting Agency, China, Burma, India [*World War II*]	JICACBI
Joint Intelligence Collecting Agency, Middle East [*World War II*]	JICAME
Joint Intelligence Collecting Agency, North Africa [*World War II*]	JICANA
Joint Intelligence Collecting Agency, Reception Committee [*Navy*]	JICARC
Joint Intelligence Committee	JIC
Joint Intelligence Coordination Staff [*Central Intelligence Agency*] (AABC)	JICS
Joint Intelligence Estimate for Planning (AFM)	JIEP
Joint Intelligence Group [*Military*]	JIG
Joint Intelligence Liaison Element (MCD)	JILE
Joint Intelligence Objectives Agency (MCD)	JIOA
Joint Intelligence Staff	JIS
Joint Intelligence Studies Publishing Board	JISPB
Joint Interest Audiovisual Requirements (MCD)	JIA
Joint Interest Test [*Navy*] (NG)	JIT
Joint Interface Implementation Program [*Army*] (MCD)	JIIP
Joint Interface Test Facility [*Army*] (RDA)	JITF
Joint Interface Test Force [*Military*] (RDA)	JITF
Joint Interim Working Party	JIWP
Joint International Coordination Group (MSC)	JICG
Joint Interoperability and Engineering Organization [*DoD*]	JIEO
Joint Interoperability of Tactical Command and Control Systems (MCD)	JINTACCS
Joint Interoperability of Tactical Command and Control Systems (DOMA)	JINTCCS
Joint Interrogation Center (MCD)	JIC
Joint Interrogation Facility (DOMA)	JIF
Joint Interservice Task Force (MCD)	JITF
Joint Interval Histogram [*Histology*] (DAVI)	JIH
Joint Investigation of the Southeastern Tropical Atlantic [*Angola, US*] (MSC)	JISETA
Joint IOC/WMO Group of Experts on IGOSS Technical Systems Design and Developmentand Service Requirements [*Marine science*] (MSC)	ITECH
Joint IOC/WMO Planning Group for IGOSS [*Marine science*] (MSC)	IPLAN
Joint Kinematics and Geometry (PDAA)	JOKING
Joint Labor Management Committee of the Retail Food Industry (EA)	JLMC
Joint Labor Relations Board	JLRB
Joint Land Use Advisory Committee	JLUAC
Joint Landing Force	JLF
Joint Landing Force Board	JLFB
Joint Least Squares [*Statistics*]	JLS
Joint Liaison Committee on Documents (DS)	JLCD
Joint Liaison Group (ECON)	JLG
Joint Lightweight 155mm Howitzer (RDA)	JLW-155
Joint Logistics and Personnel Policy Guidance [*Military*] (AFM)	JLPPG
Joint Logistics Commanders [*Military*]	JLC
Joint Logistics Commanders' Action Team [*Military*]	JLCAT
Joint Logistics Committee [*Military*]	JLC
Joint Logistics, Operations, Intelligence Center [*NATO*] (NATG)	JLOIC
Joint Logistics Over-the-Shore [*Military*] (RDA)	JLOTS
Joint Logistics Planning Board	JLPB
Joint Logistics Plans Committee [*Military*]	JLPC
Joint Logistics Plans Group [*Military*]	JLPG
Joint Logistics Review Board [*Military*]	JLRB
Joint Logistics Support Plan	JLSP
Joint Logistics System Command (DOMA)	JLSC
Joint Logistics Techniques and Procedures Board [*Military*]	JLTPB
Joint Long-Range Estimative Intelligence Document [*Military*]	JLREID
Joint Long-Range Proving Ground (KSC)	JLRPG
Joint Long-Range Strategic Appraisal [*Military*]	JLRSA
Joint Long-Range Strategic Estimates [*Military*]	JLRSE
Joint Long-Range Strategic Study [*Military*] (AFM)	JLRSS
Joint Man Machine (IAA)	JMM
Joint Management Team (MCD)	JMT
Joint Managing Director (DCTA)	JMD
Joint Manpower Program [*Military*] (CINC)	JMP
Joint Manual Direction Center [*Air Force*]	JMDC
Joint Maritime Commission	JMC
Joint Maritime Congress [*Washington, DC*] (EA)	JMC
Joint Maritime Information Element [*Coast Guard*]	JMIE
Joint Maritime Information Exchange	JMIE
Joint Materiel Priorities and Allocation Board [*Military*] (AABC)	JMPAB
Joint Matriculation Board [*British*]	J
Joint Matriculation Board [*British*] (DCTA)	JMB
Joint Maximum Effort	JME
Joint Medical Regulating Office (AABC)	JMRO
Joint Merchant Shipping Defence Committee [*General Council of British Shipping*] (DS)	JMSDC
Joint Merchant Vessels Board [*World War II*]	JMVB
Joint Meritorious Unit Award [*Military decoration*] (GFGA)	JMUA
Joint Message Center	JMC
Joint Meteorological Board (AAG)	JMB
Joint Meteorological Committee	JMC
Joint Meteorological Group [*DoD*]	JMG
Joint Meteorological Radio Propagation Committee [*British*] (MCD)	JMRP
Joint Meteorological Satellite Advisory Committee	JMSAC
Joint Meteorological Satellite Program Office	JMSPO
Joint Mexican-United States Defense Commission	JMUSDC
Joint Military Aircraft Hurricane Evacuation Plan (AFM)	JMAHEP
Joint Military Assistance Affairs Division (CINC)	JMAAD
Joint Military Commission [*US, North Vietnam, South Vietnam, Viet Cong*]	JMC
Joint Military Net Assessment [*A publication*] (RDA)	JMNA

Joint Military Packaging Training Center	JMPTC
Joint Military Potential Test (MCD)	JMPT
Joint Military Procurements Control [*World War II*]	JMPC
Joint Military Regulating Office	JMRO
Joint Military Task Group (MUGU)	JMTG
Joint Military Terminology Group (AFM)	JMTG
Joint Military Transportation Board	JMTB
Joint Military Transportation Committee	JMTC
Joint Mission Analysis	JMA
Joint Mission Element Need Statement (MCD)	JMENS
Joint Mission Essential Task List (DOMA)	JMETL
Joint Mobile Communications Center [*NATO*] (NATG)	JMCC
Joint Mobile Relay Center (MCD)	JMRC
Joint Modeling and Simulation Executive Panel [*DoD*]	JMSEP
Joint Monitor Display	JMD
Joint Movement Coordination Agency	JMCA
Joint Movements Branch [*NATO*] (NATG)	JMB
Joint Movements Coordinating Committee [*British*]	JMCC
Joint Movements Staff [*British*]	JMS
Joint Multichannel Trunking and Switching System (MCD)	JMTSS
Joint Munition Effectiveness Manual [*Navy*] (DOMA)	JMEMS
Joint Munitions Allocation Committee	JMAC
Joint Munitions Effectiveness Manual [*Military*] (AFM)	JMEM
Joint Munitions Effectiveness Manual Task Force (MCD)	JMEMTF
Joint Munitions Production Panel (MCD)	JMPP
Joint National Committee for Languages (EA)	JNCL
Joint National Council (AIE)	JNC
Joint National Media Research [*Database producer*]	JNMR
Joint Navigation Satellite Committee	JNSC
Joint Navy (IAA)	JNA
Joint Navy-Air Force	JNAF
Joint Negotiating Council [*British*] (DCTA)	JNC
Joint Network Scheme [*British*]	JNT
Joint Network Team [*British*] (NITA)	JNT
Joint North Sea Data Acquisition Project [*An informal group of Belgian, German, British, Dutch, and Swedish scientific institutes*] (PDAA)	JONSDAP
Joint North Sea Information Systems (PDAA)	JONSIS
Joint North Sea Wave Atmosphere Program [*Marine science*] (OSRA)	JONSWAP
Joint North Sea Wave Atmosphere Program [*Global Atmospheric Research Program*] (USDC)	JONSWAP
Joint North Sea Wave Project [*An informal group of Belgian, German, British, Dutch, and Swedish scientific institutes*] (PDAA)	JONSWAP
Joint Nuclear Accident Coordinating Center	JNACC
Joint Nuclear Planning Element (MCD)	JNPE
Joint Nuclear Plot (CINC)	JNP
Joint Nuclear Research Center [*EURATOM*]	JNRC
Joint Nuclear Research Institute [*Former USSR*]	JNRI
Joint Nuclear Weapons Publication Systems (MCD)	JNWPS
Joint Numerical Weather Prediction Unit (IAA)	JNWP
Joint Numerical Weather Prediction Unit	JNWPU
Joint Objective Area (NVT)	JOA
Joint Observation for Cometary Research (MCD)	JOCR
Joint Observing Program [*NASA*]	JOP
Joint Occupancy Date (MCD)	JOD
Joint Occupancy Plan Memorandum (AAG)	JOPM
Joint Ocean [*or Overseas*] Shipping Procedure	JOSPRO
Joint Ocean Surface Study	JOSS
Joint Ocean Wave Investigation Project [*US and Canadian venture*]	JOWIP
Joint Oceanographic Assembly [*Marine science*] (MSC)	JOA
Joint Oceanographic Institution (USDC)	JOI
Joint Oceanographic Institutions for Deep Earth Sampling	JOIDES
Joint Oceanographic Institutions, Inc. [*Research center*] (RCD)	JOI
Joint Oceanographic Research Group	JORG
Joint Oil Analysis Program [*Military*] (NVT)	JOAP
Joint Oil Analysis Program Coordinating Group (MCD)	JOAP-CG
Joint Oil Analysis Program Technical Support Center (MCD)	JOAP-TSC
Joint Oil Targets Committee [*World War II*]	JOTC
Joint Operating Agreement	JOA
Joint Operating Group [*SLA/ASIS*]	JOG
Joint Operating Plan	JOP
Joint Operation Planning and Execution System [*DoD*]	JOPES
Joint Operation Procedure (AAG)	JOP
Joint Operation Procedure Memorandum (AAG)	JOPM
Joint Operation Procedure Report (AAG)	JOPR
Joint Operational and Technical Reviews [*Military*] (AFIT)	JOTR
Joint Operational Compatibility Tests	J-OCT
Joint Operational Planning System [*Military*]	JOPS
Joint Operational Policies and Procedures (MCD)	JOPP
Joint Operational Report [*Military*] (AFM)	JOPREP
Joint Operational Tactical System [*Navy*] (DOMA)	JOTS
Joint Operational Test	JOT
Joint Operational Test and Evaluation (MCD)	JOT & E
Joint Operations Center	JOC
Joint Operations Control Center	JOCC
Joint Operations Evaluation Group (AABC)	JOEG
Joint Operations Evaluation Group, Vietnam [*Air Force*] (MCD)	JOEG-V
Joint Operations Graphics [*Military*]	JOG
Joint Operations Graphics - Air [*Military*] (PDAA)	JOG-A
Joint Operations Graphics - Ground (PDAA)	JOG-G
Joint Operations Group [*DoD*]	JOG
Joint Operations Interface Procedure (NASA)	JOIP
Joint Operations Interim Software (MCD)	JIS
Joint Operations Planning and Execution System [*Military*]	JOPES
Joint Operations Requirements [*Military*] (AFM)	JOR

Joint Operations Staff [*Military*] ... JOS
Joint Operations Support Activity Frankfurt [*National Security Agency*] ... JOSAF
Joint Optical Information Network [*Army*] ... JOIN
Joint Optical Range Instrumentation Type Designation System ... JORITDS
Joint Optoelectronics Project [*Japan*] [*Agreement for conducting cooperative global research*] ... JOP
Joint Opto-Electronics Research Scheme [*British*] ... JOERS
Joint Ordnance Commanders Group ... JOCG
Joint Ordnance Commanders Supply Group [*DoD*] ... JOCSG
Joint Organization ... JO
Joint Organization for Solar Observations ... JOSO
Joint Organizing Committee [*Global Atmospheric Research Program*] ... JOC
Joint Organizing Committee [*Marine science*] (OSRA) ... JOC
Joint Overseas Shipping Control Office ... JOSCO
Joint Overseas Switching System [*Military*] (AABC) ... JOSS
Joint Ownership [*Business term*] ... JO
Joint Pacific [*Military*] (CINC) ... JP
Joint Pacific Command Control Network (MCD) ... JPCC
Joint Pacific Voice [*Military*] (CINC) ... JPV
Joint Packaging Instruction ... JPI
Joint Panel on Oceanographic Tables and Standards [*Marine science*] [*United Nations*] (OSRA) ... JPOTS
Joint Parachute Test Facility [*DoD*] ... JPTF
Joint Passover Association of the City of New York (EA) ... JPA
Joint Peristimulus Time Histograms [*For study of physiology*] ... JPSTH
Joint Personal Property Shipping Office [*Military*] (DNAB) ... JPPSO
Joint Personal Property Shipping Office, Washington, DC [*Military*] (AABC) ... JPPSOWA
Joint Personnel Priority List ... JPPL
Joint Personnel Recovery Center [*Military*] ... JPRC
Joint Petroleum Coordination Center/Committee [*NATO*] (NATG) ... JPCC
Joint Petroleum Office ... JPO
Joint Photographic Experts Group [*International video standard*] (PCM) ... JPEG
Joint Photographic Experts Group [*Computer science*] ... jpeg
Joint Photographic Experts Group [*Antineoplastic drug*] ... JPEG
Joint Photographic Reconnaissance Organization [*World War II*] ... JPRO
Joint Photographic Type Designation System [*Military*] ... JPTDS
Joint Planning Activity [*DoD*] ... JPA
Joint Planning and Execution Community (DOMA) ... JPEC
Joint Planning and Scheduling Group ... JPSG
Joint Planning Board ... JPB
Joint Planning Center ... JPC
Joint Planning Committee ... JPC
Joint Planning Group [*NATO*] (NATG) ... JPG
Joint Planning Process [*Military*] (NVT) ... JPP
Joint Planning Staff [*US and Great Britain*] [*World War II*] ... JPS
Joint Policy Coordinating Group on Computer Resources Management (MCD) ... JPCG-CRM
Joint Policy Coordinating Group on Defense Integrated Materiel Management (AFIT) ... JPCG/DIMM
Joint Policy Coordinating Group on Depot Maintenance Interservicing ... JPCG-DMI
Joint Position Sense [*Medicine*] ... JPS
Joint Postwar Committee ... JPWC
Joint Potential Designator [*DoD*] ... JPD
Joint Power Conditioner ... JPC
Joint Power Conditions [*NASA*] (LAIN) ... JCP
Joint Power Generation Conference ... JPGC
Joint Precision Interdiction [*NATO*] (DOMA) ... JPI
Joint Primary Aircraft Training System [*Air Force*] [*Navy*] (DOMA) ... JPATS
Joint Primary Aircraft Training System ... JPATS
Joint Process Action Team ... JPAT
Joint Procurement Board [*Military*] (AABC) ... JPB
Joint Procurement Regulations [*of Army and Air Force*] ... JPR
Joint Production Board [*US and Great Britain*] ... JPB
Joint Production Committee [*British*] (DCTA) ... JPC
Joint Production Survey Committee ... JPSC
Joint Program Assessment Memorandum (MCD) ... JPAM
Joint Program for the Study of Abortion ... JPSA
Joint Program Integration Committee [*NASA*] (NASA) ... JPIC
Joint Program Management Office (MCD) ... JPMO
Joint Program Office [*Military*] (SDI) ... JPO
Joint Program Office for Biological Defense [*Army*] (RDA) ... JPO-BD
Joint Program Offrice-Transition Team [*DoD*] ... JPO-TT
Joint Program Plan (NASA) ... JPP
Joint Project Manager ... JPM
Joint Project Office [*or Officer*] ... JPO
Joint Projected Manpower Requirements [*Military*] (AABC) ... JPMR
Joint Psychological Warfare Committee (LAIN) ... JPWC
Joint Public Affairs Office (DOMA) ... JPAO
Joint Publications Research Service [*Department of Commerce*] ... JPRS
Joint Publications Research Service Translations - Government Use Only [*Department of Commerce*] ... JPRS-GUO
Joint Purchasing Board ... JPB
Joint RADAR Planning Group [*Military*] (CET) ... JRPG
Joint Radio Board ... JRB
Joint Rail Military Traffic Office (AABC) ... JRMTO
Joint Railroad Conference ... JRC
Joint Readiness Exercise (MCD) ... JRX
Joint Readiness Training Center [*Fort Chaffee, AR*] (INF) ... JRTC
Joint Readiness Training Center Instrumentation System [*DoD*] ... JRTC-IS
Joint Reconnaissance Board [*Military*] (AABC) ... JRB
Joint Reconnaissance Center [*Military*] (AFM) ... JRC
Joint Reconnaissance Control Center (MCD) ... JRCC
Joint Recovery Center (MCD) ... JRC
Joint Reentry System Working Group ... JRSWG
Joint Regional Continuing Committee [*Later, RCEAC*] [*Civil Defense*] ... JRCC
Joint Regional Reconnaissance Center [*NATO*] (NATG) ... JRRC
Joint Registered Publications Memorandum ... JRPM
Joint Reinforced Concrete Pavement ... JRCP
Joint Reporting Structure [*Military*] (AFM) ... JRS
Joint Representation Committee [*British*] (DCTA) ... JRC
Joint Requirements and Management Board [*Later, JROC*] [*Military*] ... JRMB
Joint Requirements Oversight Council [*Military*] ... JROC
Joint Requirements Planning (CDE) ... JRP
Joint Rescue Coordination Center [*Military*] (AFM) ... JRCC
Joint Research and Development Board [*1946-1947*] ... JRDB
Joint Research and Development Objectives Document [*Military*] (AABC) ... JRDOD
Joint Research and Test Activity (MCD) ... JRATA
Joint Research and Test Agency [*Terminated, 1966*] [*Military*] ... JRATA
Joint Research Center [*Commission of the European Communities*] ... JRC
Joint Research Center for Atom Technology [*Japan*] ... JRCAT
Joint Research Projects Office [*Army and NASA joint operation*] (RDA) ... JRPO
Joint Resistant Secure Communications [*DoD*] ... JRSC
Joint Resolution [*Usually, of the US Senate and House of Representatives*] ... JR
Joint Resource Assessment Data ... JRAD
Joint Resource Assessment Data Base Report [*Military*] (AABC) ... JADREP
Joint Resource Assessment Database ... JAD
Joint Resources Management Board [*Military*] ... JRMB
Joint Return (MHDB) ... JR
Joint Review ... JR
Joint Review Board (MCD) ... JRB
Joint Review Committee for Ophthalmic Medical Personnel (EA) ... JRCOMP
Joint Review Committee for Perfusion Education (DAVI) ... JRCPE
Joint Review Committee for Respiratory Therapy Education (EA) ... JRCRTE
Joint Review Committee for the Ophthalmic Medical Assistant (EA) ... JRCOMA
Joint Review Committee on Education for the Surgical Technologist (EA) ... JRCEST
Joint Review Committee on Education for the Surgical Technologist (DAVI) ... JRC-ST
Joint Review Committee on Education in Cardiovascular Technology (DAVI) ... JRC-CVT
Joint Review Committee on Education in Diagnostic Medical Sonography (EA) ... JRCDMS
Joint Review Committee on Education in Electroencephalographic [*Technology*] (DAVI) ... JRC-EEG
Joint Review Committee on Education in Radiologic Technology (EA) ... JRCERT
Joint Review Committee on Educational Programs for Physician Assistants (EA) ... JRCEPPA
Joint Review Committee on Educational Programs for Physician Assistants (EA) ... JRC-PA
Joint Review Committee on Educational Programs for the EMT [*Emergency MedicalTechnician*]-Paramedic (EA) ... JRCEMT-P
Joint Review Committee on Educational Programs for the EMT [*Emergency MedicalTechnician*]-Paramedic (EA) ... JRCEPEP
Joint Review Committee on Educational Programs in Nuclear Medicine Technology (DAVI) ... JRC-NMT
Joint School District Number One, Lake Geneva, WI [*Library symbol Library of Congress*] (LCLS) ... WLagSD
Joint Schools Committee for Academic Excellence Now (EA) ... JSCAEN
Joint Scientific Committee [*WMO/ICSU*] ... JSC
Joint Sealer Manufacturers Association ... JSMA
Joint Sealift Movements Board [*Military*] (AFM) ... JSMB
Joint Search and Rescue [*Military*] (DNAB) ... JSAR
Joint Search and Rescue Center [*Military*] (AABC) ... JSARC
Joint Search and Rescue Coordination Center (MCD) ... JSRCC
Joint Second Echelon Interdiction ... JSEI
Joint Security Area (MCD) ... JSA
Joint Security Assistance Memorandum [*Military*] ... JSAM
Joint Security Assistance Memorandum Supporting Analysis (MCD) ... JSAMSA
Joint Security Control ... JSC
Joint Security Force [*Army*] (INF) ... JSF
Joint Selection Committee ... JSC
Joint Service Achievement Medal [*Military decoration*] ... JSAM
Joint Service Advisory Group ... JSAG
Joint Service Agreement Report [*Defense Supply Agency*] ... JSAR
Joint Service Civil Engineering Research and Development Coordination Group [*Military*] (RDA) ... JSCERDCG
Joint Service Commendation Medal [*Military decoration*] (AFM) ... JSCM
Joint Service Committee [*Military*] ... JSC
Joint Service Common Airframe Multiple Purpose System [*Military*] (MCD) ... JSCAMPS
Joint Service Coordination Committee [*DoD*] ... JSCC
Joint Service Coordination Committee [*Military*] (DOMA) ... JSCC
Joint Service Cruise Missile Program Office (MCD) ... JSCMPO
Joint Service Fuze Plan [*Army*] ... JSFP
Joint Service Guidance and Control Committee ... JSGCC
Joint Service Induction Area ... JSIA
Joint Service Intelligence Manual ... JSIM
Joint Service Interior Intrusion Detection Devices [*Military*] (MCD) ... JSIID
Joint Service Interior Intrusion Detection System [*Military*] ... JSIIDS
Joint Service Intrusion Detection System [*Military*] (INF) ... J-SIDS
Joint Service Large Rocket Motor Disposal Office [*Army*] ... JSLRMDO
Joint Service Local Planning Committee ... JSLPC
Joint Service Meritorious Service Medal [*Military decoration*] ... JSMSM
Joint Service Office ... JSO
Joint Service Operational Requirement Statement (MCD) ... JSORS
Joint Service Program Management Review Committee [*Military*] ... JSPMRC

Joint Service Program Plan [Military] (RDA) .... JSPP
Joint Service Small Arms Management Committee (MCD) .... JSSAM
Joint Service Small Arms Panel (MCD) .... JSSAP
Joint Service Small Arms Program (RDA) .... JSSAP
Joint Service Small Arms Program Office [Dover, NJ] [Military] .... JSSAP
Joint Service Vertical-Lift Aircraft, Experimental [Military] (RDA) .... JVX
Joint Services [British military] (DMA) .... JS
Joint Services Actions Task Group (MCD) .... JSATG
Joint Services Automatic Testing Panel (AAGC) .... JSATP
Joint Services Commendation Medal (RDA) .... JSCOM
Joint Services Configuration Control Board [Military] (AFIT) .... JSCCB
Joint Services Development Program .... JSP
Joint Services Electronics Program [Military] .... JSEP
Joint Services Explosives Program (MCD) .... JSEXP
Joint Services Imagery Processing System [Military] .... JSIPS
Joint Services LASER-Guided Weapons Countermeasures (MCD) .... JSLGWCM
Joint Services Liaison Staff [British] .... JSLS
Joint Services Operational Notice .... JSON
Joint Services Operational Requirement [Military] .... JSOR
Joint Services Publication .... JSP
Joint Services Reading Panel [Military British] .... JSRP
Joint Services Review Committee .... JSRC
Joint Services Staff College [or Course] [Obsolete British] .... JSSC
Joint Services Staff Manual [Military British] .... JSSM
Joint Services Technical Publication Policy Committee [Ministry of Defence] (PDAA) .... JSTPPC
Joint Services Weapon Data Link (MCD) .... JSWDL
Joint Setup Cost .... JSC
Joint Ship Operations Center .... JSOC
Joint Ship Operations Committee .... JSOC
Joint Ship Repair Committee .... JSRC
Joint Shop Stewards Committee [British] .... JSSC
Joint Short-Range Technology (MCD) .... JSRT
Joint Simulation System [DoD] .... JSIMS
Joint Sobe Processing Center [Okinawa] [Military] .... JSPC
Joint Societies Employment Advisory Committee .... JSEAC
Joint Soil Moisture Experiment .... JSME
Joint Space Command Intelligence Center [Air Force] .... JSCIC
Joint Space Intelligence Center .... JSIC
Joint Space Narrowing [Medicine] .... JSN
Joint Spacelab Working Group [NASA] (NASA) .... JSLWG
Joint Spacing [Mining technology] .... JS
Joint Special Operations Area [Military] (INF) .... JSOA
Joint Special Operations Center (MCD) .... JSOC
Joint Special Operations Command [Military] .... JSOC
Joint Special Operations Force Institute [DoD] .... JSOFI
Joint Special Operations Support Element [DoD] .... JSOSE
Joint Special Operations Task Force [DoD] .... JSOTF
Joint Special Operations Task Force (DOMA) .... JSOTF
Joint Special Weapons Publications Board .... JSWPB
Joint Specialty Officer (DOMA) .... JSO
Joint Specialty Officer Nominee (DOMA) .... JSONOM
Joint Speech Research Unit [British] (NITA) .... JSRU
Joint Sponsored Research Agreement (GAVI) .... JSRA
Joint Staff [Military] (CINC) .... JS
Joint Staff Administrative Instruction [Military] .... JAI
Joint Staff Communications Office [Military] (AABC) .... JSCO
Joint Staff Consultative Committee [British] (DI) .... JSCC
Joint Staff Council [Japanese] [Military] (CINC) .... JSC
Joint Staff Memorandum (MCD) .... JSM
Joint Staff Mission [British World War II] .... JSM
Joint Staff Nuclear Planning Element (MCD) .... JSNPE
Joint Staff Pension Board [United Nations] .... JSPB
Joint Staff Pension Fund [United Nations] .... JSPF
Joint Staff Planners [Joint Chiefs of Staff] .... JSP
Joint Staff Support Information System [Military] (GFGA) .... JSSIS
Joint Staffing Review .... JSR
Joint Standing Committee (ADA) .... JSC
Joint Standing Committee on Library Cooperation [British] (NITA) .... JSCLC
Joint Standoff Weapons Program .... JSOW
Joint Statement of Agreed Principles [US-USSR] .... JSAP
Joint Statements of Requirements (DOMA) .... JSOR
Joint Stealth Strike Aircraft [DoD] (DOMA) .... JSSA
Joint Steering Committee for Revision of AACR [Anglo-American Cataloging Rules] .... JSCAACR
Joint Sticking Hemoglobin Universal Assay [Sickle cell anemia test] .... JOSHUA
Joint Stipulated Facts and Figures (AAGC) .... JSF
Joint Stock Co. (DLA) .... JNT STK CO
Joint Stock Land Banks [New Deal] .... JSLB
Joint Stock List [Military] (AFIT) .... JSL
Joint Strategic Bomber Study .... JSBS
Joint Strategic Capabilities [Military] .... JSC
Joint Strategic Capabilities Plan [Military] .... JSCP
Joint Strategic Committee [Military] .... JSC
Joint Strategic Connectivity Committee [Joint Chiefs of Staff] .... JSCS
Joint Strategic Connectivity Staff .... JSCS
Joint Strategic Objectives Plan [Military] .... JSOP
Joint Strategic Operations Command (MCD) .... JSOC
Joint Strategic Planning Document (MCD) .... JSPD
Joint Strategic Planning Document Supporting Analysis [Military] (AABC) .... JSPDSA
Joint Strategic Planning System [Military] .... JSPS
Joint Strategic Plans and Operations Group .... JSPOG
Joint Strategic Plans Committee [Military] .... JSPC
Joint Strategic Plans Group [Military] .... JSPG

Joint Strategic Review (DOMA) .... JSR
Joint Strategic Survey Committee [or Council] [DoD] .... JSSC
Joint Strategic Target Planning Agency (NATG) .... JSTPA
Joint Strategic Target Planning Staff [DoD] .... JSTPS
Joint Strategy and Action Committee [Defunct] (EA) .... JSAC
Joint Strike Fighter .... JSF
Joint Study Group on Military Resources Allocation Methodology (MCD) .... JSGOMRAM
Joint Subsidiary Plans Division [Military] (MUGU) .... JSPD
Joint Supply Council for Union of South Africa [World War II] .... JSCU
Joint Support [Military] (AFM) .... JS
Joint Support Command [Navy] .... JSC
Joint Support Item (DNAB) .... JSI
Joint Support List [Military] .... JSL
Joint Supportability Assessment [Army] .... JSA
Joint Suppression of Enemy Air Defenses [Military] (INF) .... J-SEAD
Joint [Maritime Administration - Navy] Surface-Effects Ship Program Office .... JSESPO
Joint Surveillance and Target Attack RADAR System .... JSTARS
Joint Surveillance System [FAA Air Force] .... JSS
Joint Surveillance Target Attack Radar System .... JSTARS
Joint Surveillance/Target Attack RADAR System Ground Station Module (RDA) .... JSTARS-GSM
Joint System Acceptance Test (MCD) .... JSAT
Joint System Operational Requirements [Document] (DOMA) .... JSORD
Joint System Test Plan [Initial Defense Communications Satellite Program] (DNAB) .... JSTP
Joint System Training Exercise [Military] .... JSTE
Joint Systematic Troop Review [Military] .... JSTR
Joint Systems Integration Planning Staff [Air Force] .... JSIPS
Joint Systems Test (KSC) .... JST
Joint Table of Allowance .... JTA
Joint Table of Distribution [Military] (AFM) .... JTD
Joint Tactical Aerial Reconnaissance/Surveillance [Military] (DNAB) .... JTARS
Joint Tactical Aerial Reconnaissance/Surveillance Mission Report [Military] (DNAB) .... JTARS MISREP
Joint Tactical Aids Detachment [Military] .... JTAD
Joint Tactical Air Control Center .... JTACC
Joint Tactical Air Support Board .... JTASB
Joint Tactical Area Communications System [Army] (RDA) .... JTACS
Joint Tactical Combat Training System [Military] .... JTCTS
Joint Tactical Command and Control and Communications System [Military] (RDA) .... JTC³S
Joint Tactical Command, Control, and Communications Agency [Military] .... JTC³A
Joint Tactical Command, Control, and Communications Agency (USGC) JTC3A
Joint Tactical Command, Control, and Communications System [Military] (MCD) .... JTCCCS
Joint Tactical Electric Vehicle [Military] .... JTEV
Joint Tactical Exploitation of National Systems [Army] (ADDR) .... J-TENS
Joint Tactical Fusion [Army] (RDA) .... JTF
Joint Tactical Fusion/All Source Analysis System (AAGC) .... JTF/ASAS
Joint Tactical Fusion Program [Military] (RDA) .... JTFP
Joint Tactical Fusion Program Management Office [Army] (RDA) .... JTFPMO
Joint Tactical Fusion System [Military] (LAIN) .... JTFS
Joint Tactical Ground Station [Army] (RDA) .... JTAGS
Joint Tactical Information Distribution System [DoD] .... JTIDS
Joint Tactical Information Distribution System .... JTIDS
Joint Tactical Microwave Landing System (MCD) .... JTMLS
Joint Tactical Missile System .... JTACMS
Joint Tactical Missile System - Army .... JTACMIS-A
Joint Tactical Missile System - Army .... JTACMS-A
Joint Tactical Multichannel Switch System (MCD) .... JTMSS
Joint Tactical Operations Center .... JTOC
Joint Tactical Radio [Army] .... JTR
Joint Tactical Support Activity .... JTSA
Joint Tactical Terminal/Common Integrated Broadcast System Module [Military] (RDA) .... JTT/CIBSM
Joint Tactical Unmanned Aerial Vehicle [DoD] .... JT-UAV
Joint Tactics, Techniques, and Procedures (DOMA) .... JTTP
Joint Tactics, Techniques, and Procedures Review Group .... JTTPRG
Joint Target Acquistion Ground Station [Military] .... JTAGS
Joint Target Intelligence Group [Military] (CINC) .... JTIG
Joint Targeting and Weapon Guidance (MCD) .... JTAWG
Joint Task Force [Military] .... JTF
Joint Task Force Alaska [Military] .... JTFAK
Joint Task Force Headquarters [Military] (MCD) .... JTFHQ
Joint Task Force Middle East (DOMA) .... JTFME
Joint Task Force Operating Area [Military] (NVT) .... JTFOA
Joint Task Force Report [Military] .... JTFREP
Joint Task Force Two [Sandia Base, NM] JTF2
Joint Task Force-Full Accounting [DoD] .... JTF-FA
Joint Task Group [Military] .... JTG
Joint Technical Advisory Committee [Electronics] .... JTAC
Joint Technical Architecture [Office of the Secretary of Defense] .... JTA
Joint Technical Architecture-Army .... JTA-Army
Joint Technical Committee (CDE) .... JTC
Joint Technical Configuration Control Group [Military] (AABC) .... JTCCG
Joint Technical Coordinating Group [Military] (MCD) .... JTCG
Joint Technical Coordinating Group [Military] .... JTCGP
Joint Technical Coordinating Group for Air Launched Non-Nuclear Ordnance [Military] (AFM) .... JTCG/ALNNO
Joint Technical Coordinating Group for Aircraft Survivability [Military] .... JTCG/AS

Joint Technical Coordinating Group for Data Link Acquisitions (MCD) ... JTCG-DLA
Joint Technical Coordinating Group for Depot Maintenance Interservicing [*Military*] (AFIT) ... JTCG-DMI
Joint Technical Coordinating Group for Electronic Equipment Reliability (MCD) ... JTCG-EER
Joint Technical Coordinating Group for Electronics Systems Reliability (MCD) ... JTCG-ESR
Joint Technical Coordinating Group for Munitions Development [*Military*] ... JTCG/MD
Joint Technical Coordinating Group for Munitions Effectiveness [*Military*] (AFM) ... JTCG/ME
Joint Technical Coordinating Group for Munitions Effectiveness [*Military*] ... JTCGP/ME
Joint Technical Coordinating Group for Tactical Air Control System [*Military*] ... JTCGP-TACS
Joint Technical Coordinating Group on Munitions Survivability [*Military*] (RDA) ... JTCG/MS
Joint Technical Coordinating Group on Simulators and Training Devi ces (MCD) ... JTCG-STD
Joint Technical Development Plan ... JTDP
Joint Technical Evaluation (MCD) ... JTE
Joint Technical Operations (AAG) ... JTO
Joint Technical Panel [*Aerospace*] ... JTP
Joint Technical Support Activity ... JTSA
Joint Technology Demonstrator Engine [*Air Force*] (MCD) ... JTDE
Joint Telecommunications Committee [*Military*] (AFM) ... JTC
Joint Telecommunications Resource Board [*Office of Science and Technology Policy*] [*Washington, DC*] (EGAO) ... JTRB
Joint Telecommunications Standards Coordinating Committee [*American National Standards Institute*] [*Telecommunications*] ... JTSCC
Joint Tenancy (MHDW) ... JT
Joint Tenancy Agreement [*Military*] ... JTA
Joint Tenant with Right of Survivorship [*Legal term*] (DLA) ... JTRS
Joint Tenants with Right of Survivorship [*Legal term*] ... JTWROS
Joint Termination Regulation ... JTR
Joint Terms of Reference (MCD) ... JTOR
Joint Test Action Group [*European automotive industry*] ... JTAG
Joint Test and Evaluation [*DoD*] ... JT & E
Joint Test and Evaluation Task Force [*Air Force*] ... JTETF
Joint Test Coordinating Committee (MCD) ... JTCC
Joint Test Directorate [*Military*] (CAAL) ... JTD
Joint Test Directorate Advanced Antiarmor Vehicle Evaluation [*Military*] (DNAB) ... JTDARMVAL
Joint Test Element ... JTE
Joint Test Exercises ... JTX
Joint Test Force [*Military*] ... JTF
Joint Test Group [*Nuclear energy*] (NRCH) ... JTG
Joint Test Organization [*Joint Tactical Communications Office*] [*Fort Huachuca, AZ*] ... JTO
Joint Theater Level Simulation [*Model*] [*DoD*] ... JTLS
Joint Theater Missile Defense [*DoD*] ... JTMD
Joint Theatre Reconnaissance Committee [*NATO*] (NATG) ... JTRC
Joint Track Data Storage ... JTDA
Joint Track Data Storage ... JTDS
Joint Trade Union Advisory Committee ... JTUAC
Joint Traffic Management Agency (MCD) ... JTMA
Joint Training Enhancement Committee [*Military*] ... JTEC
Joint Training Exercise [*Military*] ... JTX
Joint Training Group [*NASA*] (NASA) ... JTG
Joint Training Package ... JTP
Joint Training Scheme (AIE) ... JTS
Joint Training Standards [*Military*] (KSC) ... JTS
Joint Transform Correlator [*Instrumentation*] ... JTC
Joint Transportation Board [*Military*] ... JTB
Joint Transportation Intelligence Center [*MTMC*] (TAG) ... JTIC
Joint Transportation Movements Board [*Military*] (CINC) ... JTMB
Joint Travel Regulations ... JTR
Joint Travel Regulations ... JTRUS
Joint Travel Regulations, Department of Defense Civilian Personnel ... JTRCP
Joint Trials Subgroup [*NATO*] (NATG) ... JTSG
Joint Tropical Research Unit [*Australia*] ... JTRU
Joint Tsunami Research Effort ... JTRE
Joint Turbine Advanced Gas Generator [*DoD*] ... JTAGG
Joint Typhoon Warning Center ... JTWC
Joint UHF Modernization Project (MCD) ... JUMP
Joint Unconventional Warfare Assessment Team [*Military*] ... JUWAT
Joint Unconventional Warfare Command (MCD) ... JUWC
Joint Unconventional Warfare Task Force ... JUWTF
Joint Unconventional Warfare Task Force, Atlantic ... JUWTFA
Joint Underwriting Association [*Generic term*] (DHSM) ... JUA
Joint Unemployment, Vacancy, and Operating Statistics [*Department of Employment*] [*British*] ... JUVOS
Joint Uniform Military Pay Service [*or System*] ... JUMPS
Joint Uniform Military Pay System/Manpower Management System (DNAB) ... JUMPS/MMS
Joint Uniform Military Pay System - Reserve Components (MCD) ... JUMPS-RC
Joint Uniform Telephone Communications Precedence System (DNAB) ... JUTCPS
Joint Unit for Research on the Urban Environment [*British*] ... JURUE
Joint United Nations Programme on Acquired Immune Deficiency Syndrome (ECON) ... UNAIDS
Joint United States/Canada Civil Emergency Planning Committee ... JCEPC
Joint United States/Canada Industrial Mobilization Planning Committee [*NATO*] (NATG) ... JUSCIMPC
Joint United States Military Advisor Group-Korea (DOMA) ... JUSMAG-K
Joint United States Military Advisory and Planning Group ... JUSMAP
Joint United States Military Advisory Group ... JUSMAG
Joint United States Military Advisory Group to the Republic of the Philippines [*World War II*] ... JUSMAGPHIL
Joint United States Military Aid Group, Greece ... JUSMAGG
Joint United States Military Assistance Advisory Group ... JUSMAAG
Joint United States Military Assistance Group, Thailand ... JUSMAGTHAI
Joint United States Military Group ... JUSMG
Joint United States Military Group ... JUSMGP
Joint United States Military Mission for Aid to Turkey ... JUSMMAT
Joint United States Public Affairs Office [*Vietnam*] ... JUSPAO
Joint United States Strategic Committee ... JUSSC
Joint Universal Lessons Learned System (DOMA) ... JULLS
Joint University Libraries ... JUL
Joint University Libraries, George Peabody College for Teachers, Nashville, TN [*Library symbol Library of Congress*] (LCLS) ... TNJ-P
Joint University Libraries, Nashville, TN [*Library symbol Library of Congress*] (LCLS) ... TNJ
Joint University Libraries, Scarritt College for Christian Workers, Nashville, TN [*Library symbol Library of Congress*] (LCLS) ... TNJ-S
Joint University Libraries, Vanderbilt Medical Center, Nashville, TN [*Library symbol Library of Congress*] (LCLS) ... TNJ-M
Joint University Libraries, Vanderbilt School of Law, Nashville, TN [*Library symbol Library of Congress*] (LCLS) ... TNJ-L
Joint University Libraries, Vanderbilt School of Religion, Nashville, TN [*Library symbol Library of Congress*] (LCLS) ... TNJ-R
Joint Use [*Military*] (AFIT) ... JU
Joint User [*Telecommunications*] (TEL) ... JU
Joint Users Group [*Computer science*] ... JUG
Joint Users Requirements Group (NASA) ... JURG
Joint Utility Locating Information for Excavators [*Telecommunications*] (TEL) ... JULIE
Joint Utility Notification for Excavators (IEEE) ... JUNE
Joint Utilization Coordination Group [*DoD*] ... JUCG
Joint Venture [*Legal term*] (DLA) ... JNT VEN
Joint Venture [*Legal term Business term*] ... JV
Joint Venture Partners ... JVP
Joint Venture Scheme ... JVS
Joint Visual Information Services [*DoD*] (DOMA) ... JVIS
Joint Visually Integrated Display System (DOMA) ... JVIDS
Joint Vocational School ... JVS
Joint Vulnerability Board ... JVB
Joint Wages Board (DAS) ... JWB
Joint War Games Agency [*JCS*] [*DoD*] ... JWGA
Joint War Games Control Group [*Military*] (CINC) ... JWGCG
Joint War Plans Committee ... JWPC
Joint War Production Committee ... JWPC
Joint War Production Staff ... JWPS
Joint War Room [*Military*] ... JWR
Joint War Room Annex [*Military*] (CINC) ... JWRA
Joint Warfare ... JW
Joint Warfare Center [*DoD*] ... JWC
Joint Warfare Establishment [*British*] ... JWE
Joint Warfare Operations Center ... JNWOC
Joint Warfare Simulation Object Library [*DoD*] ... JWSOL
Joint Warfare Staff [*British*] ... JWS
Joint Warfighting Center [*DoD*] ... JWFC
Joint Warfighting Science and Technology Plan [*Defense Technical Information Center*] ... JWSTP
Joint Western Air Defense Force (MUGU) ... JWADF
Joint Whole Blood Center [*Military*] ... JWBC
Joint Whole Blood Control Agency (MCD) ... JWBCA
Joint Wideband Circuit Allocation and Requirement Group, Thailand [*Military*] (CINC) ... JOCARG
Joint WMO/IOC Group of Experts on Telecommunications (MSC) ... ITEL
Joint Working Group ... JOWOG
Joint Working Group [*Military*] ... JWG
Joint Working Group Meeting [*NASA*] (KSC) ... JWGM
Joint Working Group on River Inputs to Ocean Systems [*Marine science*] (MSC) ... RIOS
Joint Working Paper ... JWP
Joint Working Party (ADA) ... JWP
Joint-Army-Navy-NASA-Air Force Interagency Propulsion Committee (MCD) ... JANNAF
Jointed (ABBR) ... JNTD
Jointer (ABBR) ... JNTR
Jointly (ABBR) ... JNTLY
Jointly (ABBR) ... JNTY
Jointly ... JTLY
Jointly Endorsed Training [*Union-management*] ... JET
Jointly Sponsored Program for Foreign Libraries [*Defunct*] ... JSPFL
Jointly-Owned Contractor-Operated Facility (MCD) ... JOCO
Joint-Modeling and Simulation System ... J-Mass
Joint-Stock Bank [*Banking*] ... JSB
Joint-Stock Company ... JSC
Jointure (ABBR) ... JNTUR
Jointured (ABBR) ... JNTURD
Jointuring (ABBR) ... JNTURG
Joinville [*Brazil*] [*Airport symbol*] (OAG) ... JOI
Joinville [*Brazil ICAO location identifier*] (ICLI) ... SBJV
Joinville-Mussey [*France ICAO location identifier*] (ICLI) ... LFFJ
Joist [*Technical drawings*] ... J
Joists and Planks [*Technical drawings*] ... J & P
Jojoba Growers Association (EA) ... JGA

Joke to Come (WDMC) .... JTC
Jokester (ABBR) .... JOKSTR
Joking (ABBR) .... JOKG
Jokingly (ABBR) .... JOKGLY
Jokingly (ABBR) .... JOKGY
Jokkmokk [*Sweden ICAO location identifier*] (ICLI) .... ESNJ
Joliet Army Ammunition Plant (AABC) .... JAAP
Joliet, IL [*Location identifier FAA*] (FAAL) .... JOT
Joliet, IL [*FM radio station call letters*] .... WCSF
Joliet, IL [*Television station call letters*] .... WGBO
Joliet, IL [*FM radio station call letters*] .... WJCH
Joliet, IL [*AM radio station call letters*] .... WJOL
Joliet, IL [*FM radio station call letters*] .... WJTW
Joliet, IL [*FM radio station call letters*] .... WLLI
Joliet, IL [*AM radio station call letters*] .... WWHN
Joliet Junior College [*Illinois*] .... JJC
Joliet Public Library, Joliet, IL [*Library symbol Library of Congress*] (LCLS) .... IJol
Joliet Three-Minute Speech and Language Screen [*Test*] .... JMSLS
Joliette, PQ [*AM radio station call letters*] .... CJLM
Jollied (ABBR) .... JOLD
Jolly's Reaction [*Neurology*] (DAVI) .... JR
Jolo [*Philippines*] [*Airport symbol*] (OAG) .... JOL
Jolo, Sulu [*Philippines*] [*ICAO location identifier*] (ICLI) .... RPWJ
Jolon [*California*] [*Seismograph station code, US Geological Survey*] (SEIS) .... JOL
Jolt Beverage Co. Ltd. [*Vancouver Stock Exchange symbol*] .... JBV
Joltingly (ABBR) .... JOLTGLY
Joly Black Screen .... JBS
Joly Steam Calorimeter .... JSC
Jolys Regional Library, St. Pierre, Manitoba [*Library symbol National Library of Canada*] (NLC) .... MSTPJ
Jolys Regional Library, St. Pierre, MB, Canada [*Library symbol Library of Congress*] (LCLS) .... CaMStPJ
Jomalig, Quezon [*Philippines*] [*ICAO location identifier*] (ICLI) .... RPXJ
Jomsom [*Nepal*] [*Airport symbol*] (OAG) .... JMO
Jomsom [*Nepal*] [*ICAO location identifier*] (ICLI) .... VNJS
Jon Beryl Fan Club International (EA) .... JBFCI
Jonah [*Old Testament book*] .... Jon
Jonas [*Old Testament book*] [*Douay version*] .... JON
Jonas E. Salk Junior High School, Levittown, NY [*Library symbol*] [*Library of Congress*] (LCLS) .... NLevSJ
Jonathan [*Italy*] [*FAA designator*] (FAAC) .... JNT
Jonathan Bourne Public Library, Bourne, MA [*Library symbol*] [*Library of Congress*] (LCLS) .... MBou
Jonckheere Test [*Fisheries*] .... J
Jon-Erik Hexum Fan Club (EA) .... JEHFC
Jones and Cary's Irish Exchequer Reports [*1838-39*] [*A publication*] (DLA) .... J & C
Jones and Cary's Irish Exchequer Reports [*1838-39*] [*A publication*] (DLA) .... Jo & Car
Jones and Cary's Irish Exchequer Reports [*1838-39*] [*A publication*] (DLA) .... Jon & Car
Jones and Cary's Irish Exchequer Reports [*1838-39*] [*A publication*] (DLA) .... Jones & C
Jones and Haughton's Hindoo Law [*A publication*] (DLA) .... Jones & H Hind Law
Jones and La Touche's Irish Chancery Reports [*A publication*] (DLA) .... J & L
Jones and La Touche's Irish Chancery Reports [*A publication*] (DLA) .... J & La T
Jones and La Touche's Irish Chancery Reports [*A publication*] (DLA) .... Jo & La T
Jones and La Touche's Irish Chancery Reports [*A publication*] (DLA) .... Jon & L
Jones and La Touche's Irish Chancery Reports [*A publication*] (DLA) .... Jon & La T
Jones and La Touche's Irish Chancery Reports [*A publication*] (DLA) .... Jones & L
Jones and La Touche's Irish Chancery Reports [*A publication*] (DLA) .... Jones & L (Ir)
Jones and La Touche's Irish Chancery Reports [*A publication*] (DLA) .... Jones & La T
Jones and McMurtrie's Pennsylvania Supreme Court Reports [*A publication*] (DLA) .... Jones & McM
Jones and McMurtrie's Pennsylvania Supreme Court Reports [*A publication*] (DLA) .... Jones & McM (PA)
Jones and Spencer's Superior Court Reports [*33-61 New York*] [*A publication*] (DLA) .... J & S
Jones and Spencer's Superior Court Reports [*33-61 New York*] [*A publication*] (DLA) .... Jones & S
Jones and Spencer's Superior Court Reports [*33-61 New York*] [*A publication*] (DLA) .... Jones & Sp
Jones and Spencer's Superior Court Reports [*33-61 New York*] [*A publication*] (DLA) .... Jones & Spen
Jones and Spencer's Superior Court Reports [*33-61 New York*] [*A publication*] (DLA) .... JS
Jones and Varick's Laws of New York [*A publication*] (DLA) .... J & V
Jones and Varick's Laws of New York [*A publication*] (DLA) .... Jones & V Laws
Jones Apparel Group [*NYSE symbol*] (SPSG) .... JNY
Jones Apparel Group, Inc. [*Associated Press*] (SAG) .... JonesAp
Jones, Barclay, and Whittelsey's Reports [*31 Missouri*] [*A publication*] (DLA) .... Jones B & W (MO)
Jones, Barclay, and Whittelsey's Reports [*31 Missouri*] [*A publication*] (DLA) .... Jones Barclay & Whittelsey
Jones County Historical Society, Monticello, IA [*Library symbol*] [*Library of Congress*] (LCLS) .... IaMontHi
Jones County Historical Society, Monticello, IA [*Library symbol Library of Congress*] (LCLS) .... IaMontJHi
Jones County Junior College [*Ellisville, MS*] .... JCJC
Jones, Day, Reavis and Pogue, Law Library, Washington, DC [*Library symbol*] [*Library of Congress*] (LCLS) .... DJDR
Jones' Exchequer Proceedings Concerning Wales [*1939*] [*A publication*] (DLA) .... Jo Ex Pro W
Jones' History of the French Bar [*A publication*] (DLA) .... Jones Fr Bar
Jones' History of the French Bar [*A publication*] (DLA) .... Jones French Bar
Jones' Institutes of Hindoo Law [*A publication*] (DLA) .... Jones Inst
Jones Intercable [*NASDAQ symbol*] (TTSB) .... JOIN
Jones Intercable Cl'A' [*NASDAQ symbol*] (TTSB) .... JOINA
Jones Intercable, Inc. [*NASDAQ symbol*] (NQ) .... JOIN
Jones Intercable, Inc. [*Associated Press*] (SAG) .... JoneI
Jones Intercable, Inc. [*Associated Press*] (SAG) .... JonIcbl
Jones Intercable Inv Cl'A' [*AMEX symbol*] (TTSB) .... JTV
Jones Intercable Investors Ltd. [*Associated Press*] (SAG) .... JoneInt
Jones Intercable Investors Ltd. [*AMEX symbol*] (SPSG) .... JTV
Jones' Introduction to Legal Science [*A publication*] (DLA) .... Jones Intr
Jones' Irish Exchequer Reports [*A publication*] (DLA) .... Jo
Jones' Irish Exchequer Reports [*A publication*] (DLA) .... Jo Ex Ir
Jones' Irish Exchequer Reports [*A publication*] (DLA) .... Jon
Jones' Irish Exchequer Reports [*A publication*] (DLA) .... Jon Ex
Jones' Irish Exchequer Reports [*A publication*] (DLA) .... Jon Exch
Jones' Irish Exchequer Reports [*A publication*] (DLA) .... Jon Ir Exch
Jones' Irish Exchequer Reports [*A publication*] (DLA) .... Jones
Jones' Irish Exchequer Reports [*A publication*] (DLA) .... Jones Exch
Jones' Irish Exchequer Reports [*A publication*] (DLA) .... Jones Ir
Jones' Law of Bailments [*A publication*] (DLA) .... Jones B
Jones' Law of Bailments [*A publication*] (DLA) .... Jones Bailm
Jones' Law of Salvage [*A publication*] (DLA) .... Jones Salv
Jones' Law of Uses [*A publication*] (DLA) .... Jones Uses
Jones' Law Reports [*A publication*] (DLA) .... Jones L
Jones Library, Amherst, MA [*Library symbol Library of Congress*] (LCLS) .... MAJ
Jones Medical Indus [*NASDAQ symbol*] (TTSB) .... JMED
Jones Medical Industries, Inc. [*NASDAQ symbol*] (NQ) .... JMED
Jones Medical Industries, Inc. [*Associated Press*] (SAG) .... JonesM
Jones Memorial Hospital, Wellsville, NY [*Library symbol Library of Congress*] (LCLS) .... NWelH
Jones Memorial Library, Lynchburg, VA [*Library symbol Library of Congress*] (LCLS) ViL
Jones' North Carolina Equity Reports [*54-59*] [*1853-63*] [*A publication*] (DLA) .... Jones
Jones' North Carolina Equity Reports [*54-59*] [*1853-63*] [*A publication*] (DLA) .... Jones Eq
Jones' North Carolina Equity Reports [*54-59*] [*1853-63*] [*A publication*] (DLA) .... Jones Eq (NC)
Jones' North Carolina Law Reports [*A publication*] (DLA) .... Jones
Jones' North Carolina Law Reports [*A publication*] (DLA) .... Jones Law
Jones' North Carolina Law Reports [*A publication*] (DLA) .... Jones NC
Jones on Chattel Mortgages [*A publication*] (DLA) .... Jones Ch Mort
Jones on Land and Office Titles [*A publication*] (DLA) .... Jones L Of T
Jones on Libel [*1812*] [*A publication*] (DLA) .... Jones Lib
Jones on Mortgages [*A publication*] (DLA) .... Jones Mort
Jones on Pledges and Collateral Securities [*A publication*] (DLA) .... Jones Pledges
Jones on Railroad Securities [*A publication*] (DLA) .... Jones Securities
Jones on Railway Securities [*A publication*] (DLA) .... Jones Ry Sec
Jones Party [*Malta*] [*Political party*] (PPE) .... JP
Jones, Paul H., Romulus MI [*STAC*] .... JPH
Jones Plug [*Electricity*] (IAA) .... JP
Jones Plumbing Systems, Inc. [*Associated Press*] (SAG) .... JonesPl
Jones Plumbing Systems, Inc. [*AMEX symbol*] (SPSG) .... JPS
Jones' Reports [*22-30 Missouri*] [*A publication*] (DLA) .... Jones
Jones' Reports [*11, 12 Pennsylvania*] [*A publication*] (DLA) .... Jones
Jones' Reports [*43-48, 52-57, 61, 62 Alabama*] [*A publication*] (DLA) .... Jones
Jones' Reports [*11, 12 Pennsylvania*] [*A publication*] (DLA) .... Jones PA
Jones Spacelink Ltd. [*Associated Press*] (SAG) .... JonesSp
Jones' Treatise on Easements [*A publication*] (DLA) .... Jones Easem
Jones' Upper Canada Common Pleas Reports [*A publication*] (DLA) .... Jones
Jones' Upper Canada Common Pleas Reports [*A publication*] (DLA) .... Jones UC
Jonesboro [*Arkansas*] [*Airport symbol*] (OAG) .... JBR
Jonesboro, AR [*Location identifier FAA*] (FAAL) .... JBR
Jonesboro, AR [*Television station call letters*] .... KAIT
Jonesboro, AR [*FM radio station call letters*] (RBYB) .... KAOG
Jonesboro, AR [*FM radio station call letters*] .... KASU
Jonesboro, AR [*AM radio station call letters*] .... KBTM
Jonesboro, AR [*FM radio station call letters*] .... KDEZ
Jonesboro, AR [*FM radio station call letters*] .... KFIN
Jonesboro, AR [*FM radio station call letters*] .... KIYS
Jonesboro, AR [*AM radio station call letters*] .... KNEA
Jonesboro, AR [*Television station call letters*] .... KTEJ
Jonesboro, AR [*TV station call letters*] (RBYB) .... KVTJ-TV
Jonesboro, GA [*Location identifier FAA*] (FAAL) .... JOO
Jonesboro, LA [*Location identifier FAA*] (FAAL) .... JBL
Jonesboro, LA [*AM radio station call letters*] .... KTOC
Jonesboro, LA [*FM radio station call letters*] .... KTOC-FM
Jonesboro, Lake City & Eastern Railroad .... JLC & E
Jonesboro Public Library, Jonesboro, IN [*Library symbol Library of Congress*] (LCLS) .... InJo
Jonesborough, TN [*AM radio station call letters*] .... WKTP
Jonesville-Arlington Public Library, Jonesville, NC [*Library symbol Library of Congress*] (LCLS) .... NcJo
Jonkoping [*Sweden ICAO location identifier*] (ICLI) .... ESGJ
Jonkoping [*Sweden*] [*Airport symbol*] (OAG) .... JKG
Jonpol Explorations Ltd. [*Toronto Stock Exchange symbol*] .... JON
Jonquiere, PQ [*Television station call letters*] .... CFRS
Jonquiere, PQ [*FM radio station call letters*] .... CHOC
Jonquiere, PQ [*AM radio station call letters*] .... CKRS

Jonquil (ABBR) ... JNGL
Jonzac/Neulles [*France ICAO location identifier*] (ICLI) ... LFCJ
Jonzy's Universal Gopher Hierachy Excavation and Display [*Internet*] ... Jughead
Joodsch-Democratische Kiespartij [*Political party*] (BJA) ... JDK
JOPES [*Joint Operations, Planning, and Execution System*] **Training Org anization** (DOMA) ... JTO
Joplin [*Missouri*] [*Airport symbol*] (OAG) ... JLN
Joplin, MO [*Location identifier FAA*] (FAAL) ... JLN
Joplin, MO [*AM radio station call letters*] ... KFSB
Joplin, MO [*FM radio station call letters*] ... KJKT
Joplin, MO [*FM radio station call letters*] ... KOBC
Joplin, MO [*Television station call letters*] ... KODE
Joplin, MO [*Television station call letters*] ... KOZJ
Joplin, MO [*AM radio station call letters*] ... KQYX
Joplin, MO [*Television station call letters*] ... KSNF
Joplin, MO [*FM radio station call letters*] ... KSYN
Joplin, MO [*AM radio station call letters*] ... KWAS
Joplin, MO [*AM radio station call letters*] ... KXMS
Joplin, MO [*FM radio station call letters*] ... WMBH
Joplin Public Library, Joplin, MO [*Library symbol Library of Congress*] (LCLS) ... MoJo
Jordan [*MARC geographic area code Library of Congress*] (LCCP) ... a-jo--
Jordan [*MARC country of publication code Library of Congress*] (LCCP) ... jo
Jordan [*ANSI two-letter standard code*] (CNC) ... JO
Jordan [*ANSI three-letter standard code*] (CNC) ... JOR
Jordan (VRA) ... Jor
Jordan (ABBR) ... JORD
Jordan Amer Hldgs [*NASDAQ symbol*] (TTSB) ... JAHI
Jordan Amer Hldgs Wrrt [*NASDAQ symbol*] (TTSB) ... JAHIW
Jordan American Holdings, Inc. [*NASDAQ symbol*] (SAG) ... JAHI
Jordan American Holdings, Inc. [*Associated Press*] (SAG) ... Jordan
Jordan, Case, Taylor & McGrath [*Advertising agency*] ... JCT & M
Jordan Cosmological Theory ... JCT
Jordan Federation of Trade Unions ... JFTU
Jordan Information Bureau (EA) ... JIB
Jordan International Airline ... JIA
Jordan Is Palestine Committee (EA) ... JIPC
Jordan Left-Right Reversal Test [*Educational test*] ... JLRRT
Jordan, MT [*Location identifier FAA*] (FAAL) ... JDN
Jordan on Joint Stock Companies [*A publication*] (DLA) ... Jord Jt St Comp
Jordan Petroleum Ltd. [*Toronto Stock Exchange symbol*] ... JDN
Jordan Register (EA) ... JR
Jordan Valley High School, Jordan Valley, OR [*Library symbol Library of Congress*] (LCLS) ... OrJvHS
Jordan Watch [*Database*] [*Jordan & Sons Ltd.*] [*Information service or system*] (CRD) ... JW
Jordanian Air Force ... JAF
Jordanian Communist Party [*Political party*] (PD) ... JCP
Jordanian Dinar [*Monetary unit*] (BJA) ... JD
Jordanian News Agency ... JNA
Jordan's Parliamentary Journal [*A publication*] (DLA) ... Jord PJ
Jordan-Wentzel-Kramers-Brillouin [*Physics*] ... JWKB
Jorex Ltd. [*Toronto Stock Exchange symbol*] ... JX
Jorhat [*India*] [*Airport symbol*] (OAG) ... JRH
Jorhat [*India*] [*ICAO location identifier*] (ICLI) ... VEJT
Jorm Microlab, Inc., Cedar Rapids, IA [*Library symbol*] [*Library of Congress*] (LCLS) ... JmI
Joro Spider Toxin [*Biochemistry*] ... JSTX
Jos [*Nigeria*] [*ICAO location identifier*] (ICLI) ... DNJO
Jos [*Nigeria*] [*Airport symbol*] (OAG) ... JOS
Jos.A. Bank Clothiers [*NASDAQ symbol*] (TTSB) ... JOSB
Jose C. Paz/Dr. Mariano More [*Argentina ICAO location identifier*] (ICLI) ... SADJ
Jose de San Martin [*Argentina*] [*Airport symbol*] (OAG) ... JSM
Jose De San Martin [*Argentina ICAO location identifier*] (ICLI) ... SAWS
Jose Panganiban/PIM, Camarines Norte [*Philippines*] [*ICAO location identifier*] (ICLI) ... RPUP
Joseph (BJA) ... Jo
Joseph (BJA) ... Jos
Joseph A. Bank Clothers [*Associated Press*] (SAG) ... JosBank
Joseph A Bank Clothiers [*NASDAQ symbol*] (SAG) ... JOSB
Joseph A. Yablonski Memorial Clinic, Fredericktown, PA [*Library symbol Library of Congress*] (LCLS) ... PFredY
Joseph and Beven's Digest of Decisions [*Ceylon*] [*A publication*] (DLA) ... Jos & Bev
Joseph Brant Memorial Hospital, Burlington, Ontario [*Library symbol National Library of Canada*] (BIB) ... OBUJB
Joseph Conrad Society of America (EA) ... JCSA
Joseph E. Clouter Memorial Library, Catalina, Newfoundland [*Library symbol National Library of Canada*] (NLC) ... NFCAT
Joseph E. Clouter Memorial Library, Catalina, NF, Canada [*Library symbol Library of Congress*] (LCLS) ... CaNfCat
Joseph E. Seagram & Sons, Inc., New York, NY [*Library symbol Library of Congress*] (LCLS) ... NNSeag
Joseph E. Seagram & Sons Ltd., Technical Services, Lasalle, PQ, Canada [*Library symbol Library of Congress*] (LCLS) ... CaQMJES
Joseph Guzman & Associates, Inc. [*Palatine, IL*] [*Telecommunications Defunct*] (TSSD) ... JGA
Joseph M. Farley Nuclear Plant (NRCH) ... JFNP
Joseph Malins Crusade of Youth [*British*] (BI) ... JMCY
Joseph Mann Library, Two Rivers, WI [*Library symbol Library of Congress*] (LCLS) ... WTw
Joseph Pennell [*Specification-made paper*] ... JP
Joseph Preschool and Primary Self-Concept Screening Test [*Child development test*] [*Psychology*] ... JPPSST
Joseph R. McCarthy Foundation (EA) ... JRMF
Josephine Butler Society (EAIO) ... JBS
Josephine County Library System, Grants Pass, OR [*OCLC symbol*] (OCLC) ... OJL
Josephine Memorial Hospital, Grants Pass, OR [*Library symbol*] [*Library of Congress*] (LCLS) ... OrGH
Josephine-Louise Public Library, Walden, NY [*Library symbol Library of Congress*] (LCLS) ... NWald
Josephite Fathers (TOCD) ... cj
Josephite Fathers (TOCD) ... CJ
Joseph's Reports [*21 Nevada*] [*A publication*] (DLA) ... Jos
Josephson AttoWeber Switch [*Data processor circuitry*] ... JAWS
Josephson Interferometer [*Optics*] (IAA) ... JI
Josephson Junction [*Cryogenics*] (IAA) ... JJ
Josephson Transmission Line [*Physics*] ... JTL
Josephus (BJA) ... Jos
Josephus [*First century AD*] [*Classical studies*] (OCD) ... Joseph
Joshi Effect [*Physics*] ... JE
Joshua [*Old Testament book*] [*Freemasonry*] ... J
Joshua [*Old Testament book*] ... Jos
Joshua [*Old Testament book*] ... Josh
Joshua [*Old Testament book*] ... JS
Joshua Tree [*Nevada*] [*Seismograph station code, US Geological Survey Closed*] (SEIS) ... NYJ
Joshua Tree, CA [*FM radio station call letters*] ... KKJT
Joshua Tree National Monument ... JOTR
Josiah (BJA) ... Jos
Joslin Diabetes Center (EA) ... JDC
Joslin Diabetes Foundation, Inc. [*Later, JDC*] (EA) ... JDFI
Joslyn Art Museum, Omaha, NE [*Library symbol Library of Congress*] (LCLS) ... NbOJ
Joss Energy Ltd. [*Toronto Stock Exchange symbol*] ... JOS
JOSS-Based Expression Analyser for the Nineteen Hundred (NITA) ... JEAN
Jostens, Inc. [*NYSE symbol*] (SPSG) ... JOS
Jostens, Inc. [*Associated Press*] (SAG) ... Jostens
Josvafo [*Hungary*] [*Seismograph station code, US Geological Survey*] (SEIS) ... JOS
Jotted (ABBR) ... JOTD
Jotting (ABBR) ... JOTG
Jouf [*Saudi Arabia*] [*Airport symbol*] (OAG) ... AJF
Joule [*Symbol*] [*SI unit of energy*] (GPO) ... J
Joule [*Unit of work*] (ROG) ... WJ
Joule Ceramic Melter (PDAA) ... JCM
Joule Cycle [*Physics*] ... JC
Joule Effect [*Physics*] ... JE
Joule Heat Gradient (IEEE) ... JHG
Joule Impulse Generator [*Physics*] ... JIG
Joule Impulse Generator System [*Physics*] ... JIGS
Joule, Inc. [*AMEX symbol*] (SPSG) ... JOL
Joule per Coulomb [*Physics*] (DAVI) ... J/C
Joule per Kelvin [*Physics*] ... J/K
Joule per Kilogram [*Physics*] ... J/kg
Joule-Clausius Velocity [*Physics*] ... JCV
Joule-Rowland Method [*Physics*] ... JRM
Joules, Inc. [*Associated Press*] (SAG) ... Joule
Joule's Law [*Physics*] ... JL
Joule's Own Version of the International Algebraic [*or Algorithmic*] **Language** [*1958*] [*Computer science*] ... JOVIAL
Joules per Cubic Meter [*Physics*] ... J/M^3
Joules per Degree [*Physics*] (IAA) ... JDEG
Joules per Gram [*Physics*] (IAA) ... JG
Joules per Kilogram Kelvin ... J/(KG K)
Joules per Mole [*Physics*] ... J/MOL
Joules per Mole Kelvin [*Physics*] ... J/(MOL K)
Joules per Second (IDOE) ... J/s
Joules per Square Meter ... J/M^2
Joule-Thomson [*Physics*] ... J-T
Joule-Thomson Coefficient [*Physics*] ... JTC
Joule-Thomson Effect [*Physics*] ... JTE
Joule-Thomson Flow [*Physics*] ... JTF
Joule-Thomson High Pressure [*Physics*] ... JTHP
Joullie [*France*] [*Research code symbol*] ... LJ
Jour [*Day*] [*French*] ... j
Jour [*Day*] [*French*] ... JR
Jourdain Society [*British*] ... JS
Journal ... J
Journal (ROG) ... JL
Journal [*Online database field identifier*] ... JL
Journal ... JNL
Journal (ABBR) ... JOUR
Journal ... JOURN
Journal ... JR
Journal (ADA) ... jrl
Journal (DAVI) ... JRNL
Journal ... JRNL
Journal ... JRNL
Journal. Academy of Marketing Science [*A publication*] ... JAMS
Journal Access Service [*Center for Research Libraries*] ... JAS
Journal. American Academy of Matrimonial Lawyers [*A publication*] (DLA) ... JAAML
Journal. American Bankers Association [*A publication*] (DLA) ... J Am Bankers' Assn
Journal. American Trial Lawyers Association [*A publication*] (DLA) ... JATLA
Journal and Proceedings [*Australia A publication*] ... J & P
Journal and Proceedings. Australian Chemical Institute. [*A publication*] ... J & Proc Aust Chem Inst

Journal and Proceedings. Royal Society of Western Australia [*A publication*] ... J & Proc Roy Soc WA
Journal Announcement [*Dialog*] [*Searchable field*] [*Information service or system*] (NITA) ... JA
Journal Article Delivery Service [*Carnegie Mellon University*] ... JADS
Journal. Association of Law Teachers [*A publication*] (DLA) ... J Ass'n L Teachers
Journal. Association of Law Teachers [*A publication*] (DLA) ... J Assoc L Teachers
Journal. Association of Law Teachers [*A publication*] (DLA) ... JALT
Journal. Australian Indonesian Association [*A publication*] ... JAIA
Journal. Australian War Memorial [*A publication*] ... J Aus War M
Journal. Cancer Research Committee. University of Sydney [*A publication*] ... J Cancer Res Comm
Journal. Cincinnati Bar Association [*A publication*] (DLA) ... J Cin BA
Journal Citation (NITA) ... JC
Journal. Cleveland Bar Association [*A publication*] (DLA) ... Clev BJ
Journal Code [*Online database field identifier*] ... JC
Journal Coden [*Searchable fields*] (NITA) ... JC
Journal Control Table (IAA) ... JCT
Journal. Copyright Society of the USA [*A publication*] (DLA) ... J Copr Soc'y
Journal. Council for Scientific and Industrial Research (Australia) [*A publication*] ... JCSIR
Journal. Denning Law Society [*Tanzania*] [*A publication*] (DLA) ... J Denning L Soc'y
Journal. Denning Law Society [*Tanzania*] [*A publication*] (DLA) ... J Denning LS
Journal des Savants [*A publication*] (OCD) ... Journ Sav
Journal des Societes Civiles et Commerciales [*A publication*] (DLA) ... Jour Soc Civ
Journal des Tribunaux de Commerce [*A publication*] (DLA) ... Jour Trib Com
Journal. East African Swahili Committee [*A publication*] ... JEASC
Journal Editorial Committee (ACII) ... JEC
Journal Entries Transfer [*Computer science*] (MHDI) ... JET
Journal Folio (ROG) ... JF
Journal. Forensic Science Society [*A publication*] (DLA) ... J For Sci Soc
Journal. Historical Society of Nigeria [*A publication*] ... JHSN
Journal. Historical Society of South Australia [*A publication*] ... J Hist Soc SA
Journal Index ... JRNDEX
Journal. Indian Law Institute [*A publication*] (DLA) ... J Ind L Inst
Journal. Indian Law Teachers Association [*A publication*] (DLA) ... JILTA
Journal. Institute of Arbitrators [*A publication*] (DLA) ... J of Ins of Arbitrators
Journal. Institution of Electrical Engineers (1949-63) [*A publication*] ... J Inst Electr Eng (1949-63)
Journal. Institution of Electrical Engineers (1889-1940) [*A publication*] ... J Inst Electr Eng (1889-1940)
Journal. Institution of Engineers of Australia. [*A publication*] ... J Instn Eng Aust
Journal. International Commission of Jurists [*A publication*] (DLA) ... J Int'l Comm Jur
Journal. International Commission of Jurists [*A publication*] (DLA) ... JICJ
Journal. Kansas Bar Association [*A publication*] (DLA) ... J Kan B Ass'n
Journal. Law and Commerce Society [*Hong Kong*] [*A publication*] (DLA) ... JL & Com Soc
Journal. Law Society of Scotland [*A publication*] (DLA) ... JL Soc
Journal Name [*Online database field identifier*] ... JN
Journal. National Association of Referees in Bankruptcy [*A publication*] (DLA) ... JNA Referees Bank
Journal. National Conference of Referees in Bankruptcy [*A publication*] (DLA) ... JNC Referees Bank
Journal of Academic Librarianship [*A publication*] (BRI) ... JAL
Journal of Accountancy [*A publication*] (BRI) ... J Account
Journal of Accountancy [*A publication*] (DLA) ... J Acct
Journal of Adolescent & Adult Literacy [*A publication*] (BRI) ... JAAL
Journal of Advanced Education [*A publication*] ... J Adv Ed
Journal of Advanced Education [*A publication*] (ADA) ... JAE
Journal of Advertising Research [*Advertising Research Foundation*] [*A publication*] ... JAR
Journal of Aesthetic Education [*A publication*] (BRI) ... J Aes Ed
Journal of Aesthetics and Art Criticism [*A publication*] (BRI) ... JAAC
Journal of African History [*A publication*] ... JAH
Journal of African Law [*A publication*] (DLA) ... J African L
Journal of Agricultural Economics [*A publication*] ... JAE
Journal of Agricultural Industry, South Australia [*A publication*] ... J Agr Ind SA
Journal of Agricultural Taxation and Law [*A publication*] (DLA) ... J Agr Tax'n & L
Journal of Agriculture of Western Australia [*A publication*] ... J Agric W Aust
Journal of American Culture [*A publication*] (BRI) ... J Am Cult
Journal of American Folklore [*A publication*] (BRI) ... JAF
Journal of American History [*A publication*] (BRI) ... JAH
Journal of American Studies [*A publication*] (BRI) ... J Am St
Journal of Analytical Atomic Spectrometry [*Formerly, ARAAS*] [*A publication*] ... JAAS
Journal of Applied Chemistry [*A publication*] ... JAC
Journal of Aquatic Ecosystem Health [*A publication*] ... JAEH
Journal of Arts Management, Law & Society [*A publication*] (BRI) ... JAML
Journal of Asian Studies [*A publication*] (BRI) ... JAS
Journal of Atmospheric Sciences [*A publication*] (SSD) ... JAS
Journal of Australian Studies [*A publication*] ... J Aust Stud
Journal of Banking and Finance Law and Practice [*A publication*] ... JBFLP
Journal of Biblical Literature [*A publication*] (BRI) ... JBL
Journal of Biblical Literature [*A publication*] (OCD) ... Journ Bib Lit
Journal of Biological Inorganic Chemistry [*A publication*] ... JBIC
Journal of Black Studies [*A publication*] (BRI) ... J Bl St
Journal of Broadcasting and Electronic Media [*A publication*] (BRI) ... J Broadcst
Journal of Career Planning and Employment [*A publication*] (BRI) ... J Car P & E
Journal of Ceylon Law [*A publication*] (ILCA) ... J Ceylon Law
Journal of Ceylon Law [*Colombo, Ceylon*] [*A publication*] (DLA) ... J of Ceylon L
Journal of Chemical Education [*A publication*] (BRI) ... J Chem Ed
Journal of Chemical Education [*A publication*] (WDAA) ... JCE
Journal of Chromatographic Science [*A publication*] ... JCS
Journal of Chromatography [*A publication*] ... JC
Journal of Church and State [*A publication*] (BRI) ... J Ch St
Journal of Church and State [*A publication*] (DLA) ... J Church S
Journal of Clinical Psychiatry [*A publication*] (BRI) ... J ClinPsyc
Journal of Common Market Studies [*A publication*] (DLA) ... J Comm Mt Stud
Journal of Communication [*A publication*] (BRI) ... JC
Journal of Community Development [*A publication*] ... JCD
Journal of Comparative Corporate Law and Securities Regulation [*A publication*] (ILCA) ... Corp Law
Journal of Comparative Corporate Law and Securities Regulation [*A publication*] (ILCA) ... J Comp Corp L
Journal of Comparative Legislation and International Law [*A publication*] ... JCLIL
Journal of Computers in Math and Science Teaching (NITA) ... JCMST
Journal of Conational Law [*A publication*] (DLA) ... J Conat Law
Journal of Conational Law [*A publication*] (DLA) ... Jour Conat Law
Journal of Consumer Affairs [*A publication*] (BRI) ... J Con A
Journal of Contemporary Roman-Dutch Law [*A publication*] (DLA) ... J Contemp RDL
Journal of Contract Law [*Australia A publication*] ... JCL
Journal of Copyright, Entertainment, and Sports Law [*A publication*] (DLA) ... J Copyright Ent & Sports L
Journal of Copyright, Entertainment, and Sports Law [*A publication*] (DLA) ... J Copyright Entertainment Sports L
Journal of Corporate Taxation [*A publication*] (DLA) ... J Corp Tax'n
Journal of Criminal Law and Criminology [*A publication*] (DLA) ... J Crim L & Crim
Journal of Criminal Science [*A publication*] (DLA) ... J Crim Sci
Journal of Eastern African Research and Development [*A publication*] ... JEARD
Journal of Economic History [*A publication*] (BRI) ... JEH
Journal of Economic Literature [*A publication*] (BRI) ... JEL
Journal of Education [*A publication*] (ROG) ... J of E
Journal of Education [*A publication*] (BRI) ... JE
Journal of Electric Lighting [*A publication*] (ROG) ... J of EL
Journal of Electroanalytical Chemistry [*A publication*] ... JEAC
Journal of Energy and Development [*A publication*] (DLA) ... J Energy & Devel
Journal of English and Germanic Philology [*A publication*] (BRI) ... JEGP
Journal of Ethiopian Law [*A publication*] (DLA) ... J Eth L
Journal of Ethiopian Law [*Addis Ababa, Ethiopia*] [*A publication*] (DLA) ... J of Ethiop L
Journal of Fermentation Technology (1944-1976) [*Japan*] [*A publication*] ... J Ferment Technol (1944-1976)
Journal of Film & Video [*A publication*] (BRI) ... J Film & Vid
Journal of Geophysical Research ... JGR
Journal of Government Information [*A publication*] (BRI) ... J Gov Info
Journal of Higher Education [*A publication*] (BRI) ... J Hi E
Journal of Historical Geography [*A publication*] (BRI) ... J Hist G
Journal of Homosexuality [*A publication*] (BRI) ... J Homosex
Journal of Industrial Relations [*A publication*] ... J Ind R
Journal of Industrial Relations [*A publication*] ... J Indust Rel
Journal of Information Research Communications [*British*] (NITA) ... JIRC
Journal of Information Science [*A publication*] (NITA) ... JIS
Journal of Inorganic and Nuclear Chemistry [*A publication*] (WDAA) ... J INOR NUCL CHEM
Journal of Interdisciplinary History [*A publication*] (BRI) ... JIH
Journal of International and Comparative Law [*A publication*] (DLA) ... J Int'l & Comp L
Journal of International Business Studies [*A publication*] (BRI) ... JIB
Journal of International Law and Diplomacy [*A publication*] (DLA) ... J Int'l L & Dipl
Journal of International Law and Politics [*A publication*] (DLA) ... J Int'l L & Pol
Journal of Islamic and Comparative Law [*Nigeria*] [*A publication*] (DLA) ... J Islam & Comp L
Journal of Jurisprudence [*A publication*] (DLA) ... J Jur
Journal of Jurisprudence [*A publication*] (DLA) ... Jo Jur
Journal of Jurisprudence [*A publication*] (DLA) ... Jour Jur
Journal of Jurisprudence [*A publication*] (DLA) ... Journ Jur
Journal of Jurisprudence and Scottish Law Magazine [*A publication*] (DLA) ... Jour Jur Sc
Journal of Jurisprudence (Hall's) [*A publication*] (DLA) ... Hall Jour Jur
Journal of Jurisprudence (Hall's) [*A publication*] (DLA) ... Hall's J Jur
Journal of Juristic Papyrology [*A publication*] (DLA) ... J Jur Papyrol
Journal of Law [*A publication*] (DLA) ... Jour Law
Journal of Law and Education [*A publication*] (DLA) ... J Law & Ed
Journal of Law and Information Science [*A publication*] ... JL & Information Science
Journal of Law and Politics [*A publication*] (DLA) ... JL & Pol
Journal of Law and Religion [*A publication*] (DLA) ... JL & Religion
Journal of Law Reform [*A publication*] (DLA) ... J Law Reform
Journal of Marketing [*A publication*] (BRI) ... JM
Journal of Marriage and the Family [*A publication*] (BRI) ... JMF
Journal of Micrographics (NITA) ... JM
Journal of Military History [*A publication*] (BRI) ... J Mil H
Journal of Military History [*A publication*] ... J Mil H
Journal of Modern History [*A publication*] (BRI) ... JMH
Journal of Molecular Medicine [*A publication*] ... JMM
Journal of Multicultural Social Work [*A publication*] (BRI) ... JMSW
Journal of Negro Education [*A publication*] (BRI) ... JNE
Journal of Occupational Health and Safety - Australia and New Zealand [*A publication*] ... AJSH
Journal of Occupational Health and Safety - Australia and New Zealand [*A publication*] ... J Occup Health Safety
Journal of Occupational Health and Safety in Australia [*A publication*] ... J Occ Health Safety Aust
Journal of Organic Chemistry [*A publication*] ... JOC
Journal of Pacific History [*A publication*] ... J Pac H

Journal of Parapsychology [*A publication*] (BRI) ... JP
Journal of Parenteral Science and Technology [*A publication*] (EAAP) ... JPST
Journal of Peace Research [*A publication*] (BRI) ... JPR
Journal of Pedagogy [*New York*] [*A publication*] (ROG) ... J PED
Journal of Philology [*A publication*] (OCD) ... Journ Phil
Journal of Philosophy [*A publication*] (BRI) ... J Phil
Journal of Police Science and Administration [*A publication*] (DLA) ... J Pol Sci & Admin
Journal of Political Economy [*A publication*] (ROG) ... JP ECON
Journal of Political Economy [*A publication*] (BRI) ... JPE
Journal of Politics [*A publication*] (BRI) ... J Pol
Journal of Popular Culture [*A publication*] (BRI) ... JPC
Journal of Popular Film and Television [*A publication*] (BRI) ... J Pop F&TV
Journal of Product Innovation Management [*Product Development and Management Association*] [*A publication*] ... JPIM
Journal of Products Law (DLA) ... J Prod L
Journal of Professional Legal Education [*Australia A publication*] ... JPLE
Journal of Psychological Medicine and Medical Jurisprudence [*A publication*] (DLA) ... J Psychological Medicine
Journal of Psychological Medicine and Medical Jurisprudence [*A publication*] (DLA) ... Jour Ps Med
Journal of Purchasing and Materials Management [*A publication*] (AAGC) ... JPR
Journal of Quantum Electronics [*A publication*] (MCD) ... QE
Journal of Radio Law [*A publication*] (DLA) ... J Radio L
Journal of Radio Law [*A publication*] (DLA) ... Jo Radio Law
Journal of Rehabilitation Research and Development [*A publication*] (BRI) ... J Rehab RD
Journal of Religion [*A publication*] (BRI) ... JR
Journal of Reprints for Antitrust Law and Economics [*A publication*] (DLA) ... J Reprints Antitrust L & Econ
Journal of Ship Research [*A publication*] (DNAB) ... JSR
Journal of Social History [*A publication*] (BRI) ... J Soc H
Journal of South African Law [*A publication*] (ILCA) ... JSAL
Journal of Southern History [*A publication*] (BRI) ... JSH
Journal of Space Law (AAGC) ... J Space L
Journal of Spacecraft and Rockets [*A publication*] (AAGC) ... JSR
Journal of State Taxation [*A publication*] (DLA) ... J St Tax'n
Journal of Teacher Education [*A publication*] (BRI) ... J Teach Ed
Journal of Tertiary Educational Administration [*A publication*] ... J Tert Ed Admin
Journal of the American Academy of Religion [*A publication*] (BRI) ... JAAR
Journal of the American Medical Informatics Association [*A publication*] (DMAA) ... JAMIA
Journal of the Australian Natural Therapists Association [*A publication*] ... JANTA
Journal of the History of Ideas [*A publication*] (BRI) ... JHI
Journal of the House of Commons [*A publication*] (DLA) ... CJ
Journal of the House of Representatives [*United States*] [*A publication*] (DLA) ... JH
Journal of the Manchester Geographical Society [*A publication*] (ROG) ... J MAN GS
Journal of the Royal Agricultural Society [*A publication*] (ROG) ... JRAS
Journal of the Royal Colonial Institute (ROG) ... JRCI
Journal of the Royal United Service Institution [*A publication*] (ROG) ... JRUSI
Journal of Third World Studies [*A publication*] ... JTWS
Journal of Tropical Medicine and Hygiene [*A publication*] (WDAA) ... JTM & H
Journal of Urban History [*A publication*] (BRI) ... J Urban H
Journal of Vocational Education Research [*A publication*] (EAAP) ... JVER
Journal of Workforce Diversity [*A publication*] ... JWD
Journal of Youth Services in Libraries [*American Library Association*] ... JOYS
Journal Officiel des Communautes Europeennes [*Official Journal of the European Communities*] [*A publication*] (ILCA) ... JO
Journal Officiel des Communautes Europeennes [*Official Journal of the European Communities*] [*A publication*] (ILCA) ... Jo Comm Eur
Journal, Oxford, Nova Scotia [*Library symbol National Library of Canada*] (NLC) ... NSOJ
Journal, Oxford, NS, Canada [*Library symbol*] [*Library of Congress*] (LCLS) ... CaNSOJ
Journal pour l'Avancement des Soins Medicaux d'Urgence [*A publication*] ... JASMU
Journal. Roentgen Society [*A publication*] (ROG) ... JRS
Journal. Royal Historical Society of Queensland [*A publication*] ... JRHSQ
Journal. School Library Association of Queensland [*A publication*] ... J School Libr Ass Qd
Journal. Society of Commercial and Industrial Law [*A publication*] (ILCA) ... JS Com Ind L
Journal. Society of Comparative Legislation [*A publication*] (DLA) ... J Comp Leg
Journal. Society of Comparative Legislation [*A publication*] (DLA) ... J Soc'y Comp Leg
Journal. Society of Comparative Legislation [*A publication*] (DLA) ... Jour Comp Leg
Journal. State Bar of California [*A publication*] (DLA) ... J St Bar Calif
Journal. State Bar of California [*A publication*] (DLA) ... JBC
Journal. State Bar of California [*A publication*] (DLA) ... SBJ
Journal Status Central Operations Table (SAA) ... JSCO
Journal Supplement Abstract Service [*American Psychological Association*] ... JSAS
Journal. Sydney University Engineering Society. [*A publication*] ... J Syd Univ Eng Soc
Journal Voucher [*Accounting*] ... JV
Journalism ... J
Journalism (DD) ... Journ
Journalism (ABBR) ... JRNLM
Journalism (ABBR) ... JRNLSM
Journalism addition (WDMC) ... add
Journalism & Mass Communication Quarterly [*A publication*] (BRI) ... JMCQ
Journalism Association of Community Colleges (EA) ... JACC
Journalism Association of Junior Colleges [*Later, JACC*] ... JAJC
Journalism Education Association (EA) ... JEA
Journalism Quarterly [*A publication*] (BRI) ... JQ
Journalism School (WDMC) ... J school
Journalist ... JNLST
Journalist [*Navy rating*] ... JO
Journalist ... JRNIST
Journalist (ABBR) ... JRNLST
Journalist ... JRNLST
Journalist (ABBR) ... JRNLT
Journalist Biographies Master Index [*A publication*] ... JBMI
Journalist, First Class [*Navy rating*] ... JO1
Journalist, Second Class [*Navy rating*] ... JO2
Journalist, Third Class [*Navy rating*] ... JO3
Journalistic (ABBR) ... JRNLSTC
Journalistic (ABBR) ... JRNLTC
Journalistically (ABBR) ... JRNLTCY
Journalists Against Nuclear Extermination [*British*] (DI) ... JANE
Journalists, Authors and Poets on Stamps Study Unit (EA) ... JAPOS
Journalists' Club [*Australia*] ... JC
Journalistutbildningsutredningen [*Sweden*] ... JUBU
Journalization and Recovery System (PDAA) ... JARS
Journalize (ABBR) ... JRNLZ
Journalized (ABBR) ... JRNLZD
Journalizer (ABBR) ... JRNLZR
Journalizing (ABBR) ... JRNLZG
Journals (ADA) ... JNLS
Journals Access Service [*Center for Research Libraries*] ... JAS
Journals of the House of Commons [*A publication*] (DLA) ... Com Jour
Journals of the House of Lords [*England*] [*A publication*] (DLA) ... Lords Jour
Journey (WGA) ... JOUR
Journey (ABBR) ... JOURN
Journey (ABBR) ... JRNY
Journey ... JRNY
Journey to Work [*FHWA*] (TAG) ... J-T-W
Journeyed (ABBR) ... JRNYD
Journeying (ABBR) ... JRNYG
Journeyman ... JOUR
Journeyman (ABBR) ... JRNYMAN
Journeyman Bakers' and Confectioners Pension Society [*British*] (BI) ... JBCPS
Journeyman Training Program ... JTP
Journeymen Barbers, Hairdressers, Cosmetologists and Proprietors' International Union of America ... BHC
Journeymen Barbers, Hairdressers, Cosmetologists and Proprietors' International Union of America (EA) ... JBHCPIUA
Journeymen Curriers' Mutual Benefit Society [*A union*] [*British*] ... JCMBS
Journeymen Stone Cutters Association of North America [*Defunct*] ... JSA
Journeymen Stone Cutters Association of North America [*Defunct*] (EA) ... JSCA
Journeymen Under Specific Training in Construction Employment (PDAA) ... JUSTICE
Journey's End Motel Corp. [*Toronto Stock Exchange symbol*] ... JEM
Joutel Resources Ltd. [*Toronto Stock Exchange symbol*] ... JTL
JOVIAL Automated Verification System (MCD) ... JAVS
JOVIAL Compiler [*Computer science*] ... JC
JOVIAL Compiler Implementation Tool [*Computer science*] (MCD) ... JOCIT
JOVIAL Compiler Validation System [*Computer science*] ... JCVS
JOVIAL [*Joule's Own Version of the International Algorithmic Language*] **Control Program** [*Computer science*] ... JCP
JOVIAL [*Joule's Own Version of the International Algorithmic Language*] **Test Control Program** [*Computer science*] (SAA) ... JTCP
Jowett Car Club (EA) ... JCC
Jowitt's Dictionary of English Law [*2nd ed.*] [*1977*] [*A publication*] (DLA) ... Jow Dict
Joy [*Poland ICAO designator*] (FAAC) ... JOY
Joy. Admissibility of Confessions [*1842*] [*A publication*] (DLA) ... Joy Conf
Joy Industries Ltd. [*Vancouver Stock Exchange symbol*] ... JIL
Joy on Legal Education [*A publication*] (DLA) ... Joy Leg Ed
Joyce on Insurance [*A publication*] (DLA) ... Joyce Ins
Joyce on Limitations [*A publication*] (DLA) ... Joyce Lim
Joyce's Doctrines and Principles of Injunctions [*1877*] [*A publication*] (DLA) ... Joyce Prin Inj
Joyce's Law and Practice of Injunctions [*1872*] [*A publication*] (DLA) ... Joyce Prac Inj
Joygerms Unlimited (EA) ... JU
Joynes on Limitations [*A publication*] (DLA) ... Joyn Lim
Joy's Evidence of Accomplices [*1836*] [*A publication*] (DLA) ... Joy Acc
Joy's Evidence of Accomplices [*1836*] [*A publication*] (DLA) ... Joy Ev
Joy's Peremptory Challenge of Jurors [*1844*] [*A publication*] (DLA) ... Joy Chal
Jozini [*South Africa*] [*Seismograph station code, US Geological Survey*] (SEIS) ... JOZ
JP Foodservice [*NASDAQ symbol*] (TTSB) ... JPFS
JP Foodservice, Inc. [*Associated Press*] (SAG) ... JP Food
JP Foodservice, Inc. [*NASDAQ symbol*] (SAG) ... JPFS
J.P. Hunt, Inc. [*FAA designator*] (FAAC) ... RFX
J.P. McKenna Junior High School, Massapequa, NY [*Library symbol*] [*Library of Congress*] (LCLS) ... NmassMJ
JP Realty [*Associated Press*] (SAG) ... JP Rlty
JP Realty [*NYSE symbol*] (SPSG) ... JPR
JPE, Inc. [*Associated Press*] (SAG) ... JPE
JPE, Inc. [*NASDAQ symbol*] (SAG) ... JPEI
JPEG [*Joint Photographic Experts Group*] **File Interchange Format** [*Computer science*] (CDE) ... JFIF
JPL [*Jet Propulsion Laboratory*] **Astronautical Star Catalog** (KSC) ... JASC

JPL [Jet Propulsion Laboratory] Transient Radiation Analysis by Computer Program [NASA] .... JTRAC
JPM Co. [NASDAQ symbol] (TTSB) .... JPMC
JPM Co. (The) [Associated Press] (SAG) .... JPMCo
JPM Co. (The) [NASDAQ symbol] (SAG) .... JPMX
J-Q Resources, Inc. [Toronto Stock Exchange symbol] .... JQ
JR Energy Ltd. [Vancouver Stock Exchange symbol] .... JRE
JSB Financial [NASDAQ symbol] (TTSB) .... JSBF
JSB Financial, Inc. [Associated Press] (SAG) .... JSB Fn
JSB Financial, Inc. [NASDAQ symbol] (SPSG) .... JSBF
JSC [Johnson Space Center] Manual [NASA] (NASA) .... JSCM
JSC [Johnson Space Center] Payload Operations Center (MCD) .... JPOC
JSIMS [Joint Simulation (System)] Master Plan [DoD] .... JSMP
JSIMS [Joint Simulation (System)] Requirements Working Group [Military] .... JSRWG
JTF [Joint Task Force] Simulation [Model] [DoD] .... JTFS
JTPA [Job Training and Partnership Act] Annual Status Report (OICC) .... JASR
JTS Corp. [AMEX symbol] (SAG) .... JTS
JTS Corp. [Associated Press] (SAG) .... JTS Corp
JTwo Communications [Associated Press] (SAG) J2
JTwo Communications [Associated Press] (SAG) .... J2 Com
JTwo Communications [NASDAQ symbol] (SAG) .... JTWO
Juan Air (1979) Ltd. [Canada ICAO designator] (FAAC) .... WON
Juan de Fuca Ridge (USDC) .... JDFR
Juan de Fuca Ridge [Marine science] (OSRA) .... JdFR
Juana Diaz, PR [AM radio station call letters] .... WCGB
Juanda Flying School [Indonesia] [ICAO designator] (FAAC) .... JFS
Juanjui [Peru] [Airport symbol] (OAG) .... JJI
Juanjui [Peru] [ICAO location identifier] (ICLI) .... SPJI
Juan-les-Pins [France] [Airport symbol] (AD) .... JLP
Juba [Sudan] [ICAO location identifier] (ICLI) .... HSSJ
Juba [Sudan] [Airport symbol] (OAG) .... JUB
Jubail [Saudi Arabia] [ICAO location identifier] (ICLI) .... OEJB
Jubilate .... JUB
Jubilation - Paul Anka Admiration Society [Defunct] (EA) .... J-PAAS
Jubilee .... JBL
Jubilee Airways Ltd. [British ICAO designator] (FAAC) .... DKE
Jubilees [Pseudepigrapha] (BJA) .... Jub
Jucunde [Pleasantly] [Latin] .... JUCUND
Judaeo-Arabic [MARC language code Library of Congress] (LCCP) .... jrb
Judaeo-Persian .... J
Judaeo-Persian [MARC language code Library of Congress] (LCCP) .... jpr
Judah (WDAA) .... JUD
Judah and Swan's Jamaica Reports [1839] [A publication] (DLA) .... J & S
Judah and Swan's Jamaica Reports [1839] [A publication] (DLA) .... J & S Jam
Judah and Swan's Jamaica Reports [1839] [A publication] (DLA) .... Jud & Sw
Judah L. Magnes Memorial Museum, Rabbi Morris Goldstein Library, Berkeley, CA [Library symbol Library of Congress] (LCLS) .... CBM
Judaic (BJA) .... Jud
Judaica Captioned Film Center (EA) .... JCFC
Judaica Historical Philatelic Society (EA) .... JHPS
Judaisme Sepharadi (BJA) .... JS
Judas Priest Fan Club (EA) .... JPFC
Judd's Reports [4 Hawaii] [A publication] (DLA) .... Judd
Jude [New Testament book] (BJA) .... Jd
Judea (WDAA) .... JUD
Judean (BJA) .... Jud
Judean or Yahwistic [Used in biblical criticism to designate Yahwistic material] .... J
Judean Society (EA) .... JS
Judentum im Christlichen Religionsunterricht (BJA) .... JCRe
Judex [Judge] [Latin] .... J
Judge .... J
Judge .... JDG
Judge (WDAA) .... JUD
Judge .... JUDG
Judge Advocate [Legal term] (DLA) .... J Adv
Judge Advocate .... JA
Judge Advocate General [Military] (WDAA) .... J ADV GEN
Judge Advocate General [Air Force, Army, Navy] .... JAG
[The] Judge Advocate General [Army] .... TJAG
[The] Judge Advocate General Automated Army Legal System .... TAALS
Judge Advocate General Bulletin [Air Force A publication] (DLA) .... JAG Bull
Judge Advocate General Compilation of Court-Martial Orders [Navy A publication] (DLA) .... JAG Comp CMO (Navy)
Judge Advocate General Court-Martial Reports [Air Force A publication] (DLA) .... JAG CMR (AF)
Judge Advocate General, Department of National Defence [Jugeavocat General, Ministere de la Defense Nationale] Ottawa, Ontario [Library symbol National Library of Canada] (NLC) .... OONDJ
Judge Advocate General Digest of Opinions [A publication] (DLA) .... JAG Dig Op
Judge Advocate General Manual (Navy) [A publication] (DLA) .... JAG Man
Judge Advocate General of the Navy .... JAGN
Judge Advocate General's Area Representatives .... JAGAR
Judge Advocate General's Corps .... JAGC
[The] Judge Advocate General's Corps [Army] .... TJAGC
Judge Advocate General's Department [Air Force, Army] .... JAGD
Judge Advocate General's Department Reserve .... JAGDR
Judge Advocate General's Office .... JAGO
Judge Advocate General's Office Publications [Navy] .... NAVJAG
Judge Advocate General's School (DLA) .... JAGS
[The] Judge Advocate General's School, Army .... TJAGSA
Judge Advocate Library, Department of the Navy, Alexandria, VA [OCLC symbol] (OCLC) .... JAL
Judge Advocate of the Fleet .... JAF
Judge Advocates Association (EA) .... JAA

[The] Judge GTO International (EA) .... JGTOI
[The] Judge GTO International (EA) .... TJGTOI
Judge of Appeal .... JA
Judge of Probate [British] (ROG) .... JP
Judge of Probate [British] (ROG) .... JPROB
Judge of the Prize Court (DLA) .... JPC
Judge Prerogative Court, Canterbury [British] (ROG) .... J PR CT
Judged Perceived Noise Level (OA) .... JPNL
Judged Utility Decision Generator .... JUDGE
Judgement for the Defendant [Legal shorthand] (LWAP) .... JG/D
Judgement for the Plaintiff [Legal shorthand] (LWAP) .... JG/P
Judgement, Orientation, Memory, Abstraction, and Calculation [Medicine] (DAVI) .... JOMAC
Judgement Purchase Corp. .... JPC
Judges [Old Testament book] (BJA) .... Jg
Judges [Old Testament book] .... Jgs
Judges [Old Testament book] .... JJ
Judges [Old Testament book] (BJA) .... Ju
Judges [Old Testament book] (ROG) .... JUD
Judges [Old Testament book] .... Judg
Judges Library, Ontario Ministry of the Attorney General, Toronto, Ontario [Library symbol National Library of Canada] (NLC) .... OTJL
Judges, Marshals, and Constables Association .... JMCA
Judges of Appeal [Legal term] .... JJA
Judges' Rules [A publication] (DLA) .... JR
Judgment .... J
Judgment [Legal shorthand] (LWAP) .... JG
Judgment [Legal term] (ROG) .... JGT
Judgment (DCTA) .... JMT
Judgment .... JUD
Judgment .... JUDGT
Judgment Analysis [Psychology] .... JAN
Judgment Not Withstanding Verdict (HGAA) .... JNOV
Judgment, Orientation, Memory, Abstraction, and Calculation Intact [Medicine] (DAVI) .... JOMACI
Judgment Summons [British] (ROG) .... JS
Judgments, Gold Coast Colony [A publication] (DLA) .... Jud GCC
Judgments in the Supreme Court, Lagos [1884-92] [Nigeria] [A publication] (DLA) .... Lagos R
Judgments, Jamaica Supreme Court of Judicature [A publication] (DLA) .... Clark (Jam)
Judgments of Divisional and Full Courts, Gold Coast [A publication] (DLA) .... D & F
Judgments of the Federal Supreme Court [1956-61] [Nigeria] [A publication] (DLA) .... FSC (Nig)
Judgments of the Full Court, Privy Council, and Divisional Courts, Gold Coast [A publication] (DLA) .... Gold Coast
Judgments of the Supreme Court of Cyprus [A publication] (ILCA) .... JSC
Judgments of the Supreme Court of New South Wales for the District of Port Philip [1846-51] [A publication] (DLA) .... A'Beckett
Judgments of the Supreme Court of Nigeria [A publication] (DLA) .... SC (Nig)
Judgments of the West Indian Court of Appeal [A publication] (DLA) .... WICA
Judgments of the Windward Islands Court of Appeal [1866-1904] [A publication] (DLA) .... Greaves
Judgments of Upper Bench [England] [A publication] (DLA) .... Judg UB
Judicate, Inc. [NASDAQ symbol] (NQ) .... JUDG
Judicate, Inc. [Associated Press] (SAG) .... Judicate
Judicature (ROG) .... JUDE
Judicature .... JUDRE
Judicature Act (ROG) .... JA
Judicature Quarterly Review [1896] [A publication] (DLA) .... Jud QR
Judicial .... JUD
Judicial .... JUDIC
Judicial (ROG) .... JUDL
Judicial Appointments Project (EA) .... JAP
Judicial Assessor [Ghana] [A publication] (DLA) .... J As
Judicial Authority [British] .... JA
Judicial Chronicle [A publication] (DLA) .... Jud Chr
Judicial Commission of New South Wales [Australia] .... JCNSW
Judicial Committee of the Privy Council [A publication] (DLA) .... Jud Com PC
Judicial Committee of the Privy Council (DLA) .... PC
Judicial Conduct Reporter [A publication] (DLA) .... Jud Conduct Rep
Judicial Council (New York). Annual Reports [A publication] (DLA) .... Jud Coun (NY)
Judicial Council Reports [A publication] (DLA) .... JCR
Judicial Discipline and Disability Digest [American Judicature Society] [Information service or system] (CRD) .... JDDD
Judicial Education Teleseminar System [Defunct] (TSSD) .... JET
Judicial Officer [Department of Agriculture] (GFGA) .... JO
Judicial Officers Bulletin [A publication] .... JOB
Judicial Planning Council (OICC) .... JPC
Judicial Precedent Information Trace by Electronic Retrieval [Database] [Toyo Information Systems Co.] [Information service or system] (CRD) .... JUPITER
Judicial Recommendation against Deportation .... JRAD
Judicial Repository [New York] [A publication] (DLA) .... Jud Repos
Judicial Research Foundation [Defunct] .... JRF
Judicial Selection Project (EA) .... JSP
Judicial Separation [British] (ROG) .... JS
Judicial State Information System (OICC) .... JUSTIS
Judiciously Efficient Fixed Frame [Computer science] (MCD) .... JEFF
Judith [Old Testament book] [Roman Catholic canon] .... Jdt
Judith [Old Testament book] [Roman Catholic canon] (BJA) .... Jth
Judith [Old Testament book] [Roman Catholic canon] .... Jud
Judo Black Belt Federation [Later, USJE] .... JBBF

Judson College Library, Elgin, IL [*OCLC symbol*] (OCLC) ... IFH
Judson College, Marion, AL [*Library symbol Library of Congress*] (LCLS) ... AMaJ
Judson Dance Theater ... JDT
Judson Scott Is Number 1 Official Fan Club (EA) ... JSNOOFC
Judson Welliver Society (EA) ... JWS
Judy Farquharson Ltd. [*British*] ... JFL
Judy Fields Fan Club (EA) ... JFFC
Judy Garland Memorial Club (EA) ... JGMC
Juedische Volkspartei (BJA) ... JVP
Juedische Zeitschrift fuer Wissenschaft und Leben (A. Geiger) [*A publication*] (BJA) ... JZG
Juedische Zeremonialkunst [*A publication*] (BJA) ... JZ
Juedisches Gemeindeblatt fuer die Britische Zone [*A publication*] (BJA) ... JG
Juedisch-Palaestinisches Corpus Inscriptionum [*A publication*] (BJA) ... CI
Jugendwohlfahrtsgesetz [*Youth Welfare Law*] [*German*] (ILCA) ... JWG
Jugenheim [*Federal Republic of Germany*] [*Seismograph station code, US Geological Survey Closed*] (SEIS) ... JUG
Juggle Box ... JB
Juglans cinerea [*Butternut tree*] ... Jc
Juglans nigra [*Eastern black walnut*] ... Jn
Juglans regia [*Persian walnut*] ... Jr
Jugomaxillary [*Dentistry*] (DAVI) ... JM
Jugoslav (DSUE) ... JUG
Jugoslavia Study Group (EA) ... JSG
Jugoslovenska Demokratska Stranka [*Yugoslav Democratic Party*] [*Political party*] (PPE) ... JDS
Jugoslovenska Muslimanska Organizacija [*Yugoslav Moslem Organization*] [*Political party*] (PPE) ... JMO
Jugoslovenska Nacionalna Stranka [*Yugoslav National Party*] [*Political party*] (PPE) ... JNS
Jugoslovenska Radikalna Zajednica [*Yugoslav Radical Union*] [*Political party*] (PPE) ... JRZ
Jugoslovenska Radiotelevizija [*Association of Yugoslav Radio and Television Organizations*] (EY) ... JRT
Jugoslovenski Aerotransport [*Yugoslav Air Transport*] [*ICAO designator*] ... JAT
Jugoton [*Former Yugoslavia*] [*Record label*] ... Jug
Jugular [*Anatomy*] (DAVI) ... jug
Jugular Compression [*Test*] [*Neurology*] (DAVI) ... jug comp
Jugular Forainen [*Anatomy*] (DAVI) ... JF
Jugular Foramen Syndrome [*or Vernet's syndrome*] [*Medicine*] (DAVI) ... JFS
Jugular Vein [*Anatomy*] ... JV
Jugular Vein [*or Venous*] **Pulse** [*Medicine*] ... JVP
Jugular Venous [*Pressure and pulse*] [*Cardiology*] (DAVI) ... JV
Jugular Venous Catheter [*Medicine*] (DMAA) ... JVC
Jugular Venous Distention [*Medicine*] ... JVD
Jugular Venous Pressure [*Cardiology*] (DAVI) ... JVP
Jugular Venous Pulse Tracing [*Medicine*] ... JVPT
Jugulo [*To the Throat*] [*Pharmacy*] ... JUG
Jugulodigastric [*Node*] [*Gastroenterology*] (DAVI) ... JD
Juice ... J
Juice ... jc
Juice ... JC
Juice Newton Fan Club (EA) ... JNFC
[*The*] **Juilliard School** (GAGS) ... Juilliard
Juilliard School of Music, New York, NY [*Library symbol Library of Congress*] (LCLS) ... NNJu
Juist [*Germany ICAO location identifier*] (ICLI) ... EDWJ
Juist [*Germany Airport symbol Obsolete*] (OAG) ... JUI
Juiz De Fora [*Brazil*] [*Airport symbol*] (OAG) ... JDF
Juiz De Fora/Francisco De Assis [*Brazil ICAO location identifier*] (ICLI) ... SBJF
Jujamcyn Theaters [*Established by William McKnight, and named for his three grandchildren, Judy, James, and Cynthia*] ... JUJAMCYN
Jujuy [*Argentina*] [*Seismograph station code, US Geological Survey*] (SEIS) ... JUJ
Jujuy [*Argentina*] [*Airport symbol*] (OAG) ... JUJ
Jujuy [*Argentina ICAO location identifier*] (ICLI) ... SASJ
Jukebox (ABBR) ... JKBX
Jukeboxes [*Public-performance tariff class*] [*British*] ... JB
Julep (ABBR) ... JLEP
Julep (ROG) ... JU
Julepus [*Julep*] [*Pharmacy*] (ROG) ... JUL
Jules Verne Circle (EA) ... JVC
Julesburg Public Library, Julesburg, CO [*Library symbol Library of Congress*] (LCLS) ... CoJu
Julfa [*Iran*] [*ICAO location identifier*] (ICLI) ... OITJ
Julia Creek [*Australia Airport symbol*] (OAG) ... JCK
Julia MacRae [*Publisher*] [*British*] ... JM
Julia Morgan Association [*Defunct*] (EA) ... JMA
Julia Resources [*Vancouver Stock Exchange symbol*] ... JUR
Juliaca [*Peru*] [*Airport symbol*] (OAG) ... JUL
Juliaca [*Peru*] [*ICAO location identifier*] (ICLI) ... SPJL
Julian [*Calendar*] ... JUL
Julian, CA [*Location identifier FAA*] (FAAL) ... JLI
Julian, CA [*FM radio station call letters*] (RBYB) ... KLVW
Julian Date [*or Day*] ... JD
Julian Day Number ... JDN
Julian Day of Spring ... JDS
Julian Ephemeris Data (MCD) ... JED
Julian Messner [*Publisher's imprint*] ... JM
Julianehab [*Greenland*] [*ICAO location identifier*] (ICLI) ... BGJH
Julianehab [*Denmark*] [*Later, NAQ*] [*Geomagnetic observatory code*] ... JUL
Julianus Imperator [*332-363AD*] [*Classical studies*] (OCD) ... Julian
Julich [*Federal Republic of Germany*] [*Seismograph station code, US Geological Survey*] (SEIS) ... JUE
Julie [*Sonobuoy System*] **Automatic Search and Attack Plotter** [*Navy*] (MCD) ... JASAP
Julie [*Sonobuoy System*] **Automatic Sonic Data Analyzer** [*Navy*] ... JASDA
Julie [*Sonobuoy System*] **Exercise** [*Navy*] (NVT) ... JULIEX
Julie/Jezebel [*Sonobuoy Systems*] **Airborne Maintenance Operator Trainee** [*Navy*] (MCD) ... JAMOT
Julienhaab [*Greenland*] [*Airport symbol*] (AD) ... JJU
Julienne (ABBR) ... JLEN
Juliett [*Phonetic alphabet*] [*International*] (DSUE) ... J
Julio Iglesias Fan Club [*Defunct*] (EA) ... JIFC
Julius Caesar [*Shakespearean work*] ... JC
Julius Caesar [*Shakespearean work*] (BARN) ... Jul Caes
Julius Frontinus [*Roman soldier and author, 40-103*] (DLA) ... Jul Frontin
Julius Hartt Musical Foundation, Hartford, CT [*Library symbol Library of Congress*] (LCLS) ... CtHJH
Julius Paulus. Sententiae Receptae [*A publication*] (DLA) ... Paulus
July ... J
July ... JL
July (AFM) ... JUL
July (ODBW) ... Jul
July ... JY
July, October, January, and April [*Denotes quarterly payments of interest or dividends in these months*] [*Business term*] ... JOJA
Jumble (ABBR) ... JMBL
Jumbled (ABBR) ... JMBLD
Jumbling (ABBR) ... JMBLG
Jumbo Jet Transport ... JJT
Jumbo Oiler (DNAB) ... AO(J)
Jumbogroup Frequency Generator [*Bell System*] ... JFG
Jumbogroup Frequency Supply [*Bell System*] ... JFS
Jumbogroup Multiplex [*Bell System*] ... JMX
Jumla [*Nepal*] [*Airport symbol*] (OAG) ... JUM
Jumla [*Nepal*] [*ICAO location identifier*] (ICLI) ... VNJL
Jump [*Computer science*] ... JMP
Jump Address ... JA
Jump Address Register ... JAR
Jump If Above [*Computer science*] (PCM) ... JA
Jump If Above or Equal [*Computer science*] (PCM) ... JAE
Jump If Below [*Computer science*] (PCM) ... JB
Jump If Below or Equal [*Computer science*] (PCM) ... JBE
Jump If Equal [*Computer science*] (PCM) ... JE
Jump if Flag Set and Then Clear the Flag [*Computer science*] (NHD) ... JFCL
Jump If No Carry [*Computer science*] (PCM) ... JNC
Jump If Not Above [*Computer science*] (PCM) ... JNA
Jump If Not Above or Equal [*Computer science*] (PCM) ... JNAE
Jump If Not Below [*Computer science*] (PCM) ... JNB
Jump If Not Below or Equal [*Computer science*] (PCM) ... JNBE
Jump Indirectly [*Computer science*] ... JIN
Jump Not Equal [*Computer science*] (OA) ... JNE
Jump on Condition [*Computer science*] (BUR) ... JC
Jump on Condition [*Computer science*] ... JCN
Jump on Not Zero [*Computer science*] (PCM) ... JNZ
Jump on Zero [*Computer science*] (PCM) ... JZ
Jump Takeoff (WDAA) ... JTO
Jump to Subroutine [*Computer science*] (BUR) ... JSR
Jump to Subroutine Instruction [*Computer science*] ... JMS
Jump Unconditionally [*Computer science*] ... JUN
Jump Unit ... JU
Jump Walker [*Rehabilitation*] (DAVI) ... JW
Jumped (ABBR) ... JMPD
Jumper (MSA) ... JMPR
Jumper (IAA) ... JP
Jumpiness (ABBR) ... JMPNS
Jumping (ABBR) ... JMPG
Jumpmaster Personnel Inspection [*Army*] (ADDR) ... JMPI
Jumpoff (ABBR) ... JMPOF
JUMPS [*Joint Uniform Military Pay System*] **Action Memorandum** (NVT) ... JAM
JUMPS Army Coding System (MCD) ... JACS
JUMPS [*Joint Uniform Military Pay System*] **Automated Supplemental System-Active Component** [*Military*] ... JASS-AC
JUMPS [*Joint Uniform Military Pay System*] **Automated Support System** [*or Supplemental*] [*Military*] ... JASS
JUMPS [*Joint Uniform Military Pay System*] **Automated Support System - Reserve Corps** ... JASS-RC
JUMPS [*Joint Uniform Military Pay System*] **Field Procedures Handbook** (NVT) ... JFPH
JUMPS [*Joint Uniform Military Pay System*] **Leave Accounting System** (DNAB) ... JLAS
JUMPS [*Joint Uniform Military Payment System*] **Monthly Compute Output Listing** [*Military*] (AABC) ... JMCOL
Jump-to-Contact [*Physics*] ... JC
Juncos, PR [*AM radio station call letters*] ... WRRE
Junction ... J
Junction (ADA) ... JC
Junction (NITA) ... JCN
Junction [*Texas*] [*Seismograph station code, US Geological Survey*] (SEIS) ... JCT
Junction (AFM) ... JCT
Junction ... JCT
Junction [*Commonly used*] (OPSA) ... JCTION
Junction [*Commonly used*] (OPSA) ... JCTN
Junction ... JN
Junction (ADA) ... JNC
Junction (ABBR) ... JNCN
Junction (ABBR) ... JNT
Junction ... JUNC
Junction ... JUNCT
Junction [*Commonly used*] (OPSA) ... JUNCTION

Junction [Commonly used] (OPSA) .... JUNCTN
Junction [Commonly used] (OPSA) .... JUNCTON
Junction and Insulated Gate Field Effect Transistor (MCD) .... JIGFET
Junction Block [Automotive engineering] .... J/BLK
Junction Box [Technical drawings] .... JB
Junction Box Assembly .... JBA
Junction Center [Civil engineering] (IAA) .... JC
Junction City, KS [AM radio station call letters] .... KJCK
Junction City, KS [FM radio station call letters] .... KJCK-FM
Junction City, KY [AM radio station call letters] .... WDFB
Junction City Public Library, Junction City, OR [Library symbol Library of
   Congress] (LCLS) .... OrJc
Junction Current Recovery [in silicon devices] .... JCR
Junction Devices [JETDS nomenclature] [Military] (CET) .... J
Junction Diode Circuit .... JDC
Junction Emitting Avalanche Light .... JEAL
Junction Exchange [Telecommunications] (OA) .... JE
Junction Field-Effect Device .... JFED
Junction Field-Effect Transistor .... JFET
Junction Frequency [Telecommunications] (TEL) .... JF
Junction Gate (IAA) .... JUG
Junction Gate Field-Effect Transistor [Electronics] (IAA) .... JGFET
Junction Gate Field-Effect Transistor (TEL) .... JUGFET
Junction Gate Number .... JGN
Junction Grammar [Computer science] .... JG
Junction Grammar [Machine translation term] (NITA) .... JG
Junction Growth Technique .... JGT
Junction Isolation [Electronics] .... JI
Junction Latching Circulator .... JLC
Junction Light Output .... JLO
Junction Module [Deep Space Instrumentation Facility, NASA] .... JM
Junction Office [Telecommunications] (OA) .... JO
Junction Panel [or Point] [Electronics] .... JP
Junction Point (IAA) .... JCTPT
Junction Rack (KSC) .... JR
Junction Register (IAA) .... JRG
Junction Relay Set (IAA) .... JRS
Junction Tandem Exchange [Electronics] (IAA) .... JTE
Junction Temperature, Operating .... JTO
Junction Termination Extension (PDAA) .... JTE
Junction Transistor [Electronics] (IAA) .... JT
Junction, TX [Location identifier FAA] (FAAL) .... JCT
Junction, TX [FM radio station call letters] .... KAHO
Junction, TX [AM radio station call letters] .... KMBL
Junction Wide [Telecommunications] (OA) .... JW
Junction Wire Connector .... JWC
Junctional Epidermolysis Bullosa [Medicine] .... JEB
Junctional Escape [Cardiology] (DAVI) .... JE
Junctional Fold [Anatomy] (DAVI) .... JF
Junctional Premature Beat [Cardiology] .... JPB
Junctional Premature Contraction [Cardiology] .... JPC
Junctional Recovery Time [Medicine] (DMAA) .... JRT
Junctional Rhythm [Cardiology] .... JR
Junctional Slowing [Cardiology] (DAVI) .... JS
Junctions [Commonly used] (OPSA) .... JCTNS
Junctions [Postal Service standard] (OPSA) .... JCTS
Junctions .... JCTS
Junctions [Commonly used] (OPSA) .... JUNCTIONS
Junctor Frame [Telecommunications] (TEL) .... JF
Junctor Grouping Frame [Telecommunications] (TEL) .... JGF
Junctor Switch Frame [Telecommunications] (TEL) .... JSF
Juncture (ABBR) .... JNCUR
Juncture (ABBR) .... JNT
Jundah [Queensland] [Airport symbol] (AD) .... JUN
Jundt Growth Fund [NYSE symbol] (SPSG) .... JF
Jundt Growth Fund [Associated Press] (SAG) .... Jundt
June .... J
June .... JE
June (ROG) .... JN
June (ABBR) .... JNE
June .... JU
June (AFM) .... JUN
June (ODBW) .... Jun
June and December [Denotes semiannual payments of interest or dividends in
   these months] [Business term] .... J & D
June Carter Cash Fan Club (EA) .... JCCFC
June Grass [Test] [Medicine] (DAVI) .... JG
June Resources, Inc. [Vancouver Stock Exchange symbol] .... JNR
June, September, December, and March [Denotes quarterly payments of
   interest or dividends in these months] [Business term] .... JSDM
Juneau [Alaska] [Airport symbol] (OAG) .... JNU
Juneau [Diocesan abbreviation] [Alaska] (TOCD) .... JUN
Juneau [Alaska] [ICAO location identifier] (ICLI) .... PAJN
Juneau, AK [Location identifier FAA] (FAAL) .... JDL
Juneau, AK [Location identifier FAA] (FAAL) .... JNU
Juneau, AK [FM radio station call letters] (RBYB) .... KAKZ
Juneau, AK [FM radio station call letters] (RBYB) .... KAMT
Juneau, AK [AM radio station call letters] .... KINY
Juneau, AK [AM radio station call letters] .... KJNO
Juneau, AK [Television station call letters] .... KJUD
Juneau, AK [FM radio station call letters] .... KSUP
Juneau, AK [FM radio station call letters] .... KTKU
Juneau, AK [FM radio station call letters] .... KTOO
Juneau, AK [Television station call letters] .... KTOO-TV
Juneau Icefield Research Project [University of Idaho] [Research center] ...... JIRP

Juneau Memorial (Public) Library, Juneau, AK [Library symbol Library of
   Congress] (LCLS) .... AkJ
Juneau Public Library, Juneau, WI [Library symbol Library of Congress]
   (LCLS) .... WJu
Juneau, WI [Location identifier FAA] (FAAL) .... UNU
Juneau-Douglas High School, Douglas, AK [Library symbol] [Library of
   Congress] (LCLS) .... AkDJHS
June-July-August [Marine science] (OSRA) .... JJA
Jung Personality Questionnaire [Personality development test]
   [Psychology] .... JPQ
Junge Pioniero .... JP
Jungle .... J
Jungle (ABBR) .... JNGL
Jungle and Guerrilla Warfare Training Center [Army] .... JGWTC
Jungle Aviation & Radio Service, Inc. [Mission plane service] .... JAARS
Jungle Canopy Penetration .... JCP
Jungle Environmental Survival Training [Military] .... JEST
Jungle Exercise without Trees [British military] (DMA) .... JEWT
Jungle Message Encoder-Decoder (MCD) .... JMED
Jungle Operations Training Battalion [Military] .... JOTB
Jungle Operations Training Center [Army] (INF) .... JOTC
Jungle Penetrator [A helicopter rescue device] [Military] (VNW) .... JP
Jungle Warfare Course [Military] (MCD) .... JWC
Jungle Warfare School Trial and Development Wing [Johore Bahru,
   Malaysia] .... JWS/TD
Jungle Warfare Training Center [Army] .... JWTC
Jungsozialist [Young Socialist] [Germany] .... JUSO
Juniata College, Huntingdon, PA [Library symbol Library of Congress]
   (LCLS) .... PHuJ
Juniata College, Huntingdon, PA [OCLC symbol] (OCLC) .... PJU
Junin [Argentina ICAO location identifier] (ICLI) .... SAAJ
Junin Virus [Medicine] (DMAA) .... JV
Junior .... J
Junior (ROG) .... JN
Junior (EY) .... JNR
Junior .... JR
Junior (DD) .... Jr
Junior (WDMC) .... Jr
Junior .... JR
Junior .... JUN
Junior .... JUNR
Junior Achievement [Stamford, CT] (EA) .... JA
Junior Acting Field Captain [Military British] (ROG) .... JAFC
Junior Acting Field Officer [Military British] (ROG) .... JAFO
Junior Administrator Development Examination (AFM) .... JADE
Junior Admitting Resident [Medicine] (DAVI) .... JAR
Junior Ambassadors [Defunct] (EA) .... JA
Junior American Citizens [An association] (EA) .... JAC
Junior American Coin Klub (EA) .... JACK
Junior Aptitude Tests [Educational test] .... JAT
Junior Army and Navy Club [British] (DSUE) .... JANC
Junior Army-Navy Guild Organization [Organization of teenage daughters of
   military officers, who helped out in war work] [World War II] .... JANGO
Junior Assistant Cook [British military] (DMA) .... JACK
Junior Assistant Steward [British military] (DMA) .... JASTD
Junior Assistant Stores Accountant [British military] (DMA) .... JASA
Junior Assistant Writer [British military] (DMA) .... JAWTR
Junior Association of Commerce (BARN) .... JAC
Junior Astronomical Society (EAIO) .... JAS
Junior Beadle [Ancient Order of Foresters] .... JB
Junior Bird League [British] (BI) .... JBL
Junior Birdman [Slang] .... JB
Junior Bluejackets of America (EA) .... JBA
Junior Bookshelf [A publication] (BRI) .... JB
Junior Bowhunter Program (EA) .... JBP
Junior Catering Accountant [British military] (DMA) .... JCA
Junior Catholic Daughters of the Americas [Defunct] (EA) .... JCDA
Junior Chamber International (EAIO) .... JCI
Junior Chamber of Commerce (WDAA) .... JC
Junior Chamber of Commerce .... JC of C
Junior Chamber of Commerce .... JCC
Junior Classical League (EA) .... JCL
Junior Clergy Missionary Association [British] .... JCMA
Junior Clinicians [Medical students] (DAVI) .... JC
Junior College .... JC
Junior College (OICC) .... JUCO
Junior College District .... JCD
Junior College District, Kansas City, MO [OCLC symbol] (OCLC) .... MJC
Junior College Libraries Section [Association of College and Research
   Libraries] .... JCLS
Junior College of Albany, Albany, NY [Library symbol Library of Congress]
   (LCLS) .... NAIJ
Junior College of Flat River [Missouri] .... JCFR
Junior Collegiate Players [Later, Associate Collegiate Players] (EA) .... JCP
Junior Command Course [British military] (DMA) .... JCC
Junior Common Room [in British colleges and public schools] .... JCR
Junior Company Sergeant-Major [British military] (DMA) .... J/CSM
Junior Control Electrical Mechanic [British military] (DMA) .... JCEM
Junior Daughters of Peter Claver (EA) .... JDPC
Junior Deacon [Freemasonry] .... JD
Junior Dean .... JD
Junior Division [British military] (DMA) .... JD
Junior Duty Officer (MCD) .... JDO
Junior Electrical Mechanic (Air) [British military] (DMA) .... JEM(A)
Junior Electrical Mechanic (Air Weapon) [British military] (DMA) .... JEM(AW)

Junior Engineering Technical Society .... JETS
Junior Engineers' and Scientists' Summer Institute .... JESSI
Junior Enlisted Travel [Entitlement] (MCD) .... JET
Junior Executive Research Consultant [Fictitious position in Commerce Bank of Beverly Hills created for Jethro Bodine on the television show "The Beverly Hillbillies"] .... Jerc
Junior Eysenck Personality Inventory [Psychology] .... JEPI
Junior Fashion Fair International [British] (ITD) .... JFF
Junior Girls [School department] [British] (DI) .... JG
Junior Girls' Training Corps [British World War II] .... JGTC
Junior Grade .... JG
Junior Grand Deacon [Freemasonry] .... JGD
Junior Grand Warden [Freemasonry] .... JGW
Junior Guardsman [British military] (DMA) .... J/Gdsmn
Junior High School .... JHS
Junior High School (WDAA) .... JR HS
Junior Hospital Doctors Association [British] .... JHDA
Junior Hospital Medical Officer .... JHMO
Junior House Officer [Military] .... JHO
Junior Institute of Engineers .... JIE
Junior Institution of Engineers [British] .... JINSTE
Junior International Club (EA) .... JIC
Junior Judge [Legal term] (DLA) .... JJ
Junior Knights of Peter Claver (EA) .... JKPC
Junior Lance-Corporal [British military] (DMA) .... J/L/Cpl
Junior Lance-Sergeant [British military] (DMA) .... J/L/Sgt
Junior Leader [British military] (DMA) .... J/Ldr
Junior Leaders Regiment [British military] (DMA) .... JL
Junior Leaders Regiment [British military] (DMA) .... JLR
Junior Legacy Melbourne [Australia An association] .... JLM
Junior Life Saving [Red Cross] .... Jr LS
Junior Lodge, Independent Order of Odd Fellows (EA) .... JLIOOF
Junior Lord of the Treasury .... JLT
Junior Management Assistant .... JMA
Junior Marine [British military] (DMA) .... J/Mne
Junior Marine Engineering Mechanic [British military] (DMA) .... JMEM
Junior Medical Assistant [British military] (DMA) .... JMA
Junior Medical Student (DAVI) .... JMS
Junior Members Round Table [American Library Association] .... JMRT
Junior Military Aviator .... JMA
Junior Musician [British military] (DMA) .... J/Musn
Junior National Association for the Deaf [Defunct] (EA) .... JrNAD
Junior Naval Air Mechanic [British military] (DMA) .... JNAM
Junior Naval Airman [British military] (DMA) .... JNA
Junior Naval Command Course .... JNCC
Junior Naval Reserve Officer Training Corps .... JNROTC
Junior Non-Commissioned Officer [British military] (DMA) .... JNCO
Junior Observers of Meteorology [Trainees for government service to replace Weather Bureau men who had gone to war] [World War II] .... JOOMS
Junior Officer .... JO
Junior Officer Council [Army] .... JOC
Junior Officer of the Day [or Deck] [Navy] .... JOOD
Junior Officer of the Watch [Navy] .... JOOW
Junior Officer Professional Development Program [Army] (RDA) .... JOPD
Junior Officers and Professional Association .... JOPA
Junior Officers Common Training .... JOCT
Junior Offshore Group [Racing] [British] .... JOG
Junior Olympic Archery Development .... JOAD
Junior Olympic Pistol Championship [National Rifle Association] .... JOPC
Junior Olympic Rifle Championship [National Rifle Association] .... JORC
Junior Olympic Shooting Program [National Rifle Association] .... JOSP
Junior Optimist Clubs (EA) .... JOC
Junior Optimist Octagon International [Formerly, Optimist Octagon Clubs] (EA) .... OOC
Junior Order, Knights of Pythias (EA) .... JOKP
Junior Order United American Mechanics .... JOUAM
Junior Ordnance Electrical Mechanic [British military] (DMA) .... JOEM
Junior Panel Outdoor Advertising Association [Later, ESOAA] .... JPOAA
Junior Participating Tactical Data System [Also known as "Jeep"] (MCD) .... JPTDS
Junior Partner [i.e., a husband] [Slang] .... JP
Junior Philatelic Society [British] (BI) .... JPS
Junior Philatelic Society of America [Later, JPA] (EA) .... JPSA
Junior Philatelists of America (EA) .... JPA
Junior Principal [Freemasonry] (ROG) .... JP
Junior Probationer [British] (ROG) .... JP
Junior Professional Officer [United Nations] .... JPO
Junior Radio Electrical Mechanic [British military] (DMA) .... JREM
Junior Radio Operator [British military] (DMA) .... JRO
Junior Red Cross .... JRC
Junior Regimental Sergeant-Major [British military] (DMA) .... J/RSM
Junior Reserve Officers' Training Corps (AABC) .... JROTC
Junior Resident Note [Medical records] (DAVI) .... JRN
Junior Scholastic Aptitude Test [Education] (AEBS) .... JSAT
Junior Science and Humanities Symposia [Terminated, 1977] .... JSHS
Junior Seaman [British military] (DMA) .... JS
Junior Secondary School .... JSS
Junior Slovak Catholic Sokol (EA) .... JSCS
Junior South African Individual Scales [Intelligence test] .... JSAIS
Junior Staff Course [British] .... JSC
Junior Statesmen Foundation (EA) .... JSF
Junior Statesmen of America (EA) .... JSA
Junior Town Meeting League (EA) .... JTML
Junior Training Corps [British] .... JTC
Junior Under-Officer [British military] (DMA) .... JUO

Junior Varsity .... JV
Junior Vice Commander .... JVC
Junior Vice-President [Freemasonry] (ROG) .... JVP
Junior Victory Army [World War II] .... JVA
Junior Warden [Freemasonry] .... JW
Junior Wolf [A young philanderer] [Slang] .... JW
Junior Woodward [Ancient Order of Foresters] .... JW
Junior Year Abroad [Collegiate term] .... JYA
Juniorat des Freres du Sacre-Coeur, Bramptonville, Quebec [Library symbol National Library of Canada] (NLC) .... QBJ
Juniorat des Freres du Sacre-Coeur, Bromptonville, PQ, Canada [Library symbol Library of Congress] (LCLS) .... CaQBJ
Juniper (ABBR) .... JNPR
Juniper Features Ltd. [Associated Press] (SAG) .... JunF
Juniper Features Ltd. [NASDAQ symbol] (SAG) .... JUNI
Juniper Features Ltd. [Associated Press] (SAG) .... JuniprF
Juniper Features Wrr'A' [NASDAQ symbol] (TTSB) .... JUNIW
Juniper Features Wrrt'B' [NASDAQ symbol] (TTSB) .... JUNIZ
Juniperus [Juniper] [Pharmacy] (ROG) .... JUNIP
Junius (ROG) .... JUN
Junk [Ship's rigging] (ROG) .... JK
Junk Acronyms When Speaking [Program] .... JAWS
Junked (ABBR) .... JNKD
Junker [German aircraft type] [World War II] .... JU
Junkers-Motor [Junkers aircraft engine] [German military - World War II] .... JUMO
Junket (ABBR) .... JNKT
Junketed (ABBR) .... JNKTD
Junketer (ABBR) .... JNKTR
Junketing (ABBR) .... JNKTG
Junkie (ABBR) .... JNKI
Junking (ABBR) .... JNKG
Junkman (ABBR) .... JNKMA
Junkman-Shoeller Unit (MAE) .... JS
Juno Lighting [NASDAQ symbol] (TTSB) .... JUNO
Juno Lighting, Inc. [NASDAQ symbol] (NQ) .... JUNO
Juno Lighting, Inc. [Associated Press] (SAG) .... JunoLt
Junta Civico-Militar Cubana [An association] (EA) .... JCMC
Junta de Energia Nuclear [Spanish nuclear agency] .... JEN
Junta Democratica [Democratic Junta] [Spain Political party] (PPE) .... JD
Junta Internacional de Fiscalizacion de Estupefacientes [International Narcotics Control Board] .... JIFE
Junta Revolucionaria Cubana [Exile action group] .... JURE
Junta Socialista Unida [United Socialist Party] [Spain] .... JSU
Juntae (ROG) .... JUNT
Juntas de Accao Patriotica [Patriotic Action Boards] [Portuguese Political party] (PPE) .... JAP
Juntas de Ofensiva Nacional Sindicalista [Syndicalist Juntas of the National Offensive] [Spain Political party] (PPE) .... JONS
Jupiter .... J
Jupiter (KSC) .... JUP
Jupiter Atmospheric Probe .... JAP
Jupiter Entry Probe .... JEP
Jupiter, FL [Location identifier FAA] (FAAL) .... UTX
Jupiter, FL [FM radio station call letters] .... WJBW
Jupiter, FL [AM radio station call letters] .... WMLZ
Jupiter, FL [FM radio station call letters] (RBYB) .... WTPX-FM
Jupiter Flyby Mission [Aerospace] .... JFM
Jupiter Flyby Vehicle [Aerospace] .... JFV
Jupiter Inlet [NASA] (KSC) .... JI
Jupiter National, Inc. (SPSG) .... JPI
Jupiter National, Inc. [Associated Press] (SAG) .... JupNatl
Jupiter Orbiter [NASA] .... JO
Jupiter Orbiter Probe [Later, Project Galileo] [NASA] .... JOp
Jupiter Orbiter Satellite Lander [NASA] .... JO/SL
Jupiter Orbiting Vehicle for Exploration (MCD) .... JOVE
Jupiter, Saturn, and Pluto Mission (MCD) .... JSP
Jupiter, Saturn, Uranus, and Neptune (PDAA) .... JSUN
Jupiter-family Comets [Astronomy] .... JFC
Jupitor Resources Ltd. [Vancouver Stock Exchange symbol] .... JPT
Jurassic [Period, era, or system] [Geology] .... JUR
Jure Dignitatis [By Right of Rank] [Latin] (ROG) .... JUR DIG
Jure Uxoris [In Right of His Wife] [Latin] (ROG) .... JU
Juridical (ROG) .... JUR
Juridical Society Papers [1858-74] [Scotland] [A publication] (DLA) .... Jur Soc P
Juridical Society Papers [England] [A publication] (DLA) .... Jurid Soc'y Pap
Juridical Styles [Scotland] [A publication] (DLA) .... Jur St
Juridisk Tidsskrift [A publication] (ILCA) .... JT
Jurin Law [Electronics] .... JL
Juris [Of Law] [Latin] (ADA) .... J
Juris Baccalaureus [Bachelor of Laws] .... JB
Juris Canna Baccalaureus [Bachelor of Canon Law] .... J Can B
Juris Canna Doctor [Doctor of Canon Law] .... J Can D
Juris Canna Magister [Master of Canon Law] .... J Can M
Juris Canonici Baccalaureus [Bachelor of Canon Law] .... JCB
Juris Canonici Doctor [Doctor of Canon Law] [Latin] .... JCD
Juris Canonici Lector [Reader in Canon Law] .... JCL
Juris Canonici Licentiatus [Licentiate in Canon Law] .... JCL
Juris Civilis Baccalaureus [Bachelor of Civil Law] .... JCB
Juris Civilis Doctor [Doctor of Civil Law] [Latin] .... JCD
Juris Civilis Licentiatus [Licentiate of Civil Law] .... JCL
Juris Civilis Magister [Master of Civil Law] .... JCM
Juris Doctor [Doctor of Jurisprudence] [Latin] .... JD
Juris Doctor [Doctor of Law] [Latin] (ADA) .... JUR D
Juris Magister [Master of Laws] .... JM
Juris Utrisuque Doctor (DD) .... JUD

Juris Utriusque Doctor [Doctor of Both Laws; i.e., Canon and Civil Law] .... DUJ
Juris Utriusque Doctor [Doctor of Both Laws; i.e., Canon and Civil Law] .... JUD
Juris Utriusque Doctor [Doctor of Both Laws; i.e., Canon and Civil Law] .... JUDr
Juris Utriusque Doctor [Doctor of Both Laws; i.e., Canon and Civil Law] .... Jur Utr Dr
Juris Utriusque Doctor [Doctor of Both Laws; i.e., Canon and Civil Law] .... JVD
Juris Utriusque Licentiatus [Licentiate in Both Laws; i.e., Canon and Civil Law] .... JUL
Jurisconsult .... JC
Jurisconsult (ROG) .... JCT
Jurisconsulti [Counselors at Law] [Latin] (ROG) .... JCTI
Jurisconsultus [Counselor at Law] [Latin] (ROG) .... JCTUS
Jurisdiction [Legal shorthand] (LWAP) .... JD
Jurisdiction (ROG) .... JRISDON
Jurisdiction (AABC) .... JURIS
Jurisdiction .... JURISD
Jurisdiction (ROG) .... JURISDN
Jurisdiction (ROG) .... JURISDON
Jurisdictional [Legal shorthand] (LWAP) .... JDAL
Jurisdictional (ABBR) .... JRSDCNL
Jurisdictional Separation Process .... JSP
Jurisprudence (ABBR) .... JRSPDNC
Jurisprudence (ROG) .... JUR
Jurisprudence (ADA) .... JURIS
Jurisprudence .... JURISP
Jurisprudence (DLA) .... Jurispr
Jurisprudent (ABBR) .... JRSPDN
Jurisprudential (ABBR) .... JRSPDTL
Jurist (ABBR) .... JRST
[The] Jurist [Washington, DC] [A publication] (DLA) .... Jur
Jurist, or Law and Equity Reporter [New York] [A publication] (DLA) .... Jur NY
Jurist Reports [1873-78] [New Zealand] [A publication] (DLA) .... JR
Jurist Reports [18 vols.] [England] [A publication] (DLA) .... Jur
Jurist Reports, New Series, Cases in Mining Law [New Zealand] [A publication] (DLA) .... JRNSML
Jurist Reports, New Series, Cases in Mining Law [New Zealand] [A publication] (DLA) .... NZ Jur Mining Law
Jurist Reports, New Series, Court of Appeal [New Zealand] [A publication] (DLA) .... JRNSCA
Jurist Reports, New Series, Supreme Court [New Zealand] [A publication] (DLA) .... JRNSSC
Juristisches Informationssystem [Judicial Information System] [Federal Ministry of Justice Legal database] [Germany] (IID) .... JURIS
Jurong Town Corp. [Singapore] .... JTC
Juror .... JR
Juror (ABBR) .... JRR
Jurum Doctor [Doctor of Laws] [Latin] .... JD
Jury (ABBR) .... JRY
Jury [Ship's rigging] (ROG) .... JY
Jury Duty (WGA) .... JD
Jury Sittings (Faculty Cases) [Scotland] [A publication] (DLA) .... JS
Jury System Reform Society [British] .... JSRS
Jury Verdict Research, Inc. [Information service or system] (IID) .... JVR
Juryman (ABBR) .... JRYMA
Jus [Law] [Latin] .... J
Jus Liberorum Habens [Possessing the Right of Children] [Latin] .... ILH
Jus Navale Rhodiorum [A publication] (DLA) .... Jus Nav Rhod
Jusculum [Broth] [Pharmacy] (ROG) .... JUSC
Jusculum [Broth] [Pharmacy] .... Juscul
Jusculum Avenaceum [Gruel] [Pharmacy] (ROG) .... JUS AVEN
JUSE [Japanese Union of Scientists and Engineers] an Estimator of Phy sical Properties (NITA) .... JUSE-AESOPP
Jussi Bjorling Appreciation Society [British] (DBA) .... JBAS
Jussien (ROG) .... JUSS
Jussive .... JUSS
Just a Drop in the Basket Helps Keep New York Clean [Antilitter campaign] .... JADITBHKNYC
Just a Minute [Computer hacker terminology] (NHD) .... JAM
Just a Useful Device for You (PDAA) .... JUDY
Just Another Break-Even Situation [Slang] .... JABES
Just Another Confused Elephant .... JACE
Just Another Network [University of Waterloo] [Canada] .... JANET
Just Another Work Station [Jargon] (NITA) .... JAWS
Just Brand Names [Division of F. W. Woolworth Co.] .... J BRANNAM
Just Compensation [Business term] (MHDB) .... JC
Just Discriminable Change (IAA) .... JDC
Just For Feet [NASDAQ symbol] (SAG) .... FEET
Just For Feet, Inc. [Associated Press] (SAG) .... JstFeet
Just for Openers [An association] (EA) .... JFO
Just in Case (WDMC) .... JIC
Just in Time .... JIT
Just Jammin' Fresh and Def [Rap recording group] .... JJ FAD
Just Like Home [NASDAQ symbol] (TTSB) .... JLHC
Just Like Home, Inc. [NASDAQ symbol] (SAG) .... JLHC
Just Like Home, Inc. [Associated Press] (SAG) .... JustLHo
Just Looking [A browser] [Retail slang] .... JL
Just Not Noticeable Difference (MSA) .... JNND
Just Noticeable Difference [Psychology] .... JND
Just Noticeable Shift (PDAA) .... JNS
Just One Break (EA) .... JOB
Just, Participatory, and Sustainable Society [World Council of Churches] .... JPSS
Just Perceptible Color Difference [Telecommunications] (TEL) .... JPCD
Just Prior Condition [Computer science] .... JPC
Just Publishable Unit .... JPU
Just Scale .... JS

Just Toys [NASDAQ symbol] (TTSB) .... JUST
Just Toys, Inc. [NASDAQ symbol] (SAG) .... JUST
Just Toys, Inc. [Associated Press] (SAG) .... JustToys
Justerini and Brooks [Scotch] .... J & B
Justice [i.e., a judge; plural is JJ] .... J
Justice .... JSTC
Justice (ROG) .... JUS
Justice .... JUST
Justice Acquisition Regulation [A publication] (AAGC) .... JAR
Justice and Peace [An association Scotland] (EAIO) .... J & P
Justice Clerk .... JC
Justice Department .... JD
Justice Fellowship (EA) .... JF
Justice for Veteran Victims of the Veterans Administration (EA) .... JVVVA
Justice for Women (EA) .... JFW
Justice Institute of British Columbia, Instructional Service [UTLAS symbol] .... JIN
Justice Institute of British Columbia, Vancouver, BC, Canada [Library symbol Library of Congress] (LCLS) .... CaBVaJI
Justice Institute of British Columbia, Vancouver, British Columbia [Library symbol National Library of Canada] (NLC) .... BVAJI
Justice Itinerant [Legal term] (DLA) .... JUST ITIN
Justice Management Division [U.S. Department of Justice] (BARN) .... JMD
Justice Mining Corp. [Vancouver Stock Exchange symbol] .... JMC
Justice Now [An association] .... JN
Justice of Appeal [Legal term] (DLA) .... JA
Justice of the Common Pleas [Legal term] (DLA) .... JCP
Justice of the Common Pleas (ROG) .... JUST CP
Justice of the King's Bench (ROG) .... JKB
Justice of the King's Bench [British] (ROG) .... JUST KB
Justice of the King's Bench, Ireland (ROG) .... JKBIR
Justice of the Peace .... JP
Justice of the Peace and Local Government Review [A publication] (DLA) ...... JP
Justice of the Peace and Local Government Review [A publication] (DLA) .... JPJ
Justice of the Peace and Local Government Review [A publication] (DLA) .... Just P
Justice of the Peace and Local Government Review [A publication] (DLA) .... Just Peace
Justice of the Peace and Local Government Review Reports [A publication] (DLA) .... JPR
Justice of the Peace Clerk [British] (ROG) .... JPC
Justice of the Peace Fiscal [British] (ROG) .... JPF
Justice of the Peace Journal [A publication] .... JPJ
Justice of the Peace. Weekly Notes of Cases [England] [A publication] (DLA) .... JP
Justice of the Peace. Weekly Notes of Cases [England] [A publication] (DLA) .... JPJ
Justice of the Peace. Weekly Notes of Cases [England] [A publication] (DLA) .... JPJo
Justice of the Peace's Court [Legal term] (DLA) .... JP Ct
Justice of the Queen's Bench [Legal term] (DLA) .... JQB
Justice of the Supreme Court .... JSC
Justice of the Upper Bench [Legal term] (DLA) .... JUB
Justice Party [Turkey] [Political party] .... JP
Justice Procurement Regulation [A publication] (AAGC) .... JPR
Justice Retrieval and Inquiry System [Department of Justice] [Legal databank] [Information service or system] (IID) .... JURIS
Justice System Improvement Act [1979] .... JSIA
Justice System Interactive Model (PDAA) .... JUSSIM
Justice System Training Association [Defunct] (EA) .... JSTA
Justice Telecommunications Service [Department of Justice] (TSSD) .... JTS
Justices .... JJ
Justices' Clerks' Society [British] (DBA) .... JCS
Justices' Code [Oregon] [A publication] (DLA) .... Jus Code
Justices' Law Reporter [Pennsylvania] [A publication] (DLA) .... Just
Justices' Law Reporter [Pennsylvania] [A publication] (DLA) .... Just LR
Justices' Law Reporter [Pennsylvania] [A publication] (DLA) .... Justices' LR (PA)
Justices of Appeal [Legal term] (DLA) .... JJA
Justices of the Peace Association [Australia] .... JPA
Justices of the Supreme Court [Legal term] (DLA) .... JJSC
Justice's Sea Law [A publication] (DLA) .... Just SL
Justiciarius Anglie [Chief Justiciary of England] [Latin] (ROG) .... JUST ANGL
Justiciary [Legal term] (DLA) .... Just
Justiciary Cases [Scotland] [A publication] (DLA) .... J
Justiciary Cases [Scotland] [A publication] (DLA) .... JC
Justiciary Cases [Scotland] [A publication] (DLA) .... R(J)
Justiciary Reports [1893-1916] [Scotland] [A publication] (DLA) .... Adam
Justification (WDMC) .... J
Justification (AABC) .... JUST
Justification (ROG) .... JUSTIFON
Justification and Approval [Army] .... J & A
Justification and Approval (AAGC) .... J&A
Justification Code (LAIN) .... J-CODE
Justification for Authority to Negotiate [Military] .... JAN
Justification for Continued Operation [Nuclear energy] (NRCH) .... JCO
Justification for Non-Competitive Procurement (GFGA) .... JNCP
Justification for Other than Full and Open Competition (SSD) .... JOFOC
Justification for Other than Full and Open Competition (AAGC) .... JOTFOC
Justification of Major System New Start [Military] .... JMSNS
Justification Review Document (AAGC) .... JRD
Justification Service Digit [Telecommunications] (TEL) .... JSD
Justified .... J/S
Justifying Space [Typography] (DGA) .... JS
Justin (BJA) .... Just
Justin Indus [NASDAQ symbol] (TTSB) .... JSTN

Justin Industries, Inc. [*NASDAQ symbol*] (NQ) .... JSTN
Justin Industries, Inc. [*Associated Press*] (SAG) .... Justin
Justinian (ROG) .... JUST
Justinian [*483-565, Byzantine emperor*] [*Authority cited in pre-1607 legal
  work*] (DSA) .... Justin
Justinian [*Australia A publication*] .... Justn
Justinian Digesta [*Libri Pandectarum*] [*Legal*] (ROG) .... DIG
Justinian's Institutes [*A publication*] (DLA) .... Inst
Justinian's Institutes [*A publication*] (DLA) .... Just Inst
Just-In-Time [*Industry*] (ODBW) .... jit
Just-in-Time Inventory (TDOB) .... JIT
Justizminister [*Minister of Justice*] [*German*] (ILCA) .... JM
Justizministerium [*Ministry of Justice*] [*German*] (ILCA) .... JM
JustLife [*Defunct*] (EA) .... JL
Justus Liebig Universitatsbibliothek Giessen, Giessen/Lahn, Federal
  Republic of Germany [*Library symbol Library of Congress*] (LCLS) .... GyGiU
Juta's Daily Reporter [*South Africa*] [*A publication*] (DLA) ...... Juta
Juta's Daily Reporter, Cape Provincial Division [*South Africa*]
  [*A publication*] (DLA) .... JDR
Juta's Prize Cases [*South Africa*] [*A publication*] (DLA) .... Juta
Juta's South African Reports [*A publication*] (DLA) .... J
Juta's Supreme Court Cases [*1880-1910*] [*Cape Of Good Hope, South Africa*]
  [*A publication*] (DLA) .... SC Rep
Juta's Supreme Court Cases [*1880-1910*] [*Cape Of Good Hope, South Africa*]
  [*A publication*] (DLA) .... SCR
Juta's Supreme Court Reports [*1880-1910*] [*Cape Of Good Hope, South
  Africa*] [*A publication*] (DLA) .... Juta
Juta's Supreme Court Reports [*1880-1910*] [*Cape Of Good Hope, South
  Africa*] [*A publication*] (DLA) .... SC
Jute Carpet Backing Council (EA) .... JCBC
Jute Corp. of India .... JCI
Jute Importers' Association [*British*] (DBA) .... JIA
Jute Protection [*Telecommunications*] (TEL) .... JP
Jute-Asphalted [*Nonmetallic armor*] (AAG) .... J
Juticalpa [*Honduras*] [*ICAO location identifier*] (ICLI) .... MHJU
Juvancourt [*France ICAO location identifier*] (ICLI) .... FLQX
Juvenal [*Roman poet, 60-140AD*] [*Classical studies*] (ROG) ...... JUV
Juvenile .... J
Juvenile .... JUV
Juvenile .... JUVE
Juvenile .... JVNL
Juvenile (Amaurotic Idiocy) [*Medicine*] (DAVI) .... J
Juvenile Amaurotic Idiocy [*Medicine*] .... JAI
Juvenile and Domestic Relations Court [*Legal term*] (DLA) .... Juv & Dom Rel Ct
Juvenile Ankylosing Spondylitis [*Medicine*] (DMAA) .... JAS
Juvenile Arthritis Awareness Week [*Arthritis Foundation*] .... JAAW
Juvenile Atrophy [*Medicine*] (DAVI) .... JA
Juvenile Autoimmune Myasthenia Gravis [*Medicine*] (DAVI) ...... JAMG
Juvenile Calcaneal Fracture [*Medicine*] (DMAA) .... JCF
Juvenile Chronic Arthritis [*Medicine*] (DAVI) .... JCA
Juvenile Chronic Myelogenous [*or Myelocytic*] Leukemia [*Medicine*]
  (DMAA) .... JCML
Juvenile Court .... JC
Juvenile Court Journal [*A publication*] (DLA) .... Juv Ct J
Juvenile Delinquency [*or Delinquent*] .... JD
Juvenile Delinquency Act .... JDA
Juvenile Delinquency and Youth Development Office [*Federal
  government*] .... JDYD
Juvenile Delinquency Evaluation Project .... JDEP
Juvenile Dermatomyositis [*Medicine*] (DAVI) .... JDMS
Juvenile Diabetes [*Medicine*] (DAVI) .... JD
Juvenile Diabetes Foundation [*Later, JDFI*] (EA) .... JDF
Juvenile Diabetes Foundation International (EA) .... JDFI
Juvenile Diabetes Mellitus [*Medicine*] .... JDM

Juvenile General Paralysis [*Medicine*] (DAVI) .... JGP
Juvenile General Paresis [*Medicine*] (DMAA) .... JGP
Juvenile Hormone [*Entomology*] .... JH
Juvenile Hormone Analog [*Entomology*] .... JHA
Juvenile Hormone Binding Protein [*Entomology*] .... JHBP
Juvenile Hormone Esterase [*An enzyme*] .... JHE
Juvenile Hormone Mimic [*Entomology*] .... JHM
Juvenile Idiopathic Scoliosis [*Medicine*] (DMAA) .... JIS
Juvenile Justice [*Legal term*] (DLA) .... JUV JUST
Juvenile Justice and Delinquency Prevention .... JJDP
Juvenile Justice and Delinquency Prevention Act .... JJDPA
Juvenile Justice Planning Agency (OICC) .... JDPA
Juvenile Laryngeal Papilloma [*Medicine*] (DAVI) .... JLP
Juvenile Macular Degeneration [*Medicine*] (MEDA) .... JMD
Juvenile Missionary Association [*British*] (BI) .... JMA
Juvenile Myoclonic Epilepsy [*Medicine*] .... JME
Juvenile Offenders .... JO
Juvenile Offenders Learn the Truth [*Program*] .... JOLT
Juvenile Onset Diabetes [*Medicine*] .... JOD
Juvenile Onset Diabetes Mellitus [*Medicine*] .... JODM
Juvenile Open Angle Glaucoma [*Ophthalmology*] .... JOAG
Juvenile Opportunities Endeavor .... JOE
Juvenile Osteochondrititis Dissecans [*Medicine*] .... JODC
Juvenile Periodontist [*Dentistry*] (DAVI) .... JP
Juvenile Pilocytic Astrocytoma [*Medicine*] (DMAA) .... JPA
Juvenile Plantar Dermatosis [*Medicine*] (DAVI) .... JPD
Juvenile Probation Officer (OICC) .... JPO
Juvenile Products Manufacturers Association (EA) .... JPMA
Juvenile Rheumatoid Arthritis [*Also, JRA*] [*Medicine*] (DAVI) ...... JR
Juvenile Rheumatoid Arthritis [*Medicine*] .... JRA
Juvenile Templar [*Freemasonry*] .... JT
Juvenile Tropical Pancreatitis Syndrome [*Medicine*] (DMAA) ...... JTPS
Juvenile Xanthogranuloma [*Ophthalmology*] .... JXG
Juveniles in Need of Supervision [*Classification for delinquent children*] ...... JINS
Juvenis [*Young*] [*Latin*] .... JUV
Juventud Organizada del Pueblo en Armas [*Armed People's Organized
  Youth*] [*Guatemala*] (PD) .... JOPA
Juventud Peronista [*Peronist Youth*] [*Argentina*] .... JP
Juventud Trabajadora Peronista [*Working Peronist Youth*] [*Argentina*] ...... JTP
Juventud Universitaria Peronista [*University Peronist Youth*] [*Argentina*] ...... JUP
Juventud Uruguaya de Pie [*Upstanding Uruguayan Youth*] (PD) ...... JUP
Juventudes de Accion Popular [*Spanish*] (PPE) .... JAP
Juventudes Inconformes de Colombia [*Political party*] (EY) ...... JIC
Juvonen, K. W., Winnipeg, Manitoba CDA [*STAC*] .... JKW
Juxta [*Near*] [*Pharmacy*] .... JUXT
Juxta-Articular [*Orthopedics*] (DAVI) .... JA
Juxtaglomerular [*Histology*] .... JG
Juxtaglomerular Apparatus [*Histology*] .... JGA
Juxtaglomerular Cell Count [*Endocrinology*] .... JGCC
Juxtaglomerular Cell Tumor [*Histology*] (DAVI) .... JGCT
Juxtaglomerular Cells [*Histology*] .... JGC
Juxtaglomerular Granulation Index [*Endocrinology*] .... JGI
Juxtaglomerular Index [*Endocrinology*] .... JGI
Juxtamembrane Domain .... JM
Juxtaposition (WDAA) .... JUX
JV Avcom [*Russian Federation*] [*ICAO designator*] (FAAC) .... AOC
J.W. Smith Elementary School, Bemidji, MN [*Library symbol*] [*Library of
  Congress*] (LCLS) .... MnBemJE
Jwalamukhi [*India*] [*Seismograph station code, US Geological Survey
  Closed*] (SEIS) .... JWA
Jwaneng [*Botswana*] [*ICAO location identifier*] (ICLI) .... FBJW
JWB [*Jewish Welfare Board*] Jewish Book Council (EA) .... JWBJBC
Jydsk Teknologisk Institut [*Technological Institute of Jutland*] [*Denmark*] .... JTI
Jyvaskyla [*Finland ICAO location identifier*] (ICLI) .... EFJY
Jyvaskyla [*Finland*] [*Airport symbol*] (OAG) .... JYV

K
By Meaning

K (10³) Operations Per Second (NITA) .... KOPS
K & G Mens Center, Inc. [Associated Press] (SAG) .... KGMens
K & G Mens Center, Inc. [NASDAQ symbol] (SAG) .... MENS
K Capture [A type of radioactive decay] .... K
K, Li, and Na [For the chemical elements potassium, lithium, and sodium]
  [Beckman flame system Trademark] .... KLINA
K Mart Corp. [Associated Press] (SAG) .... K mart
K Mart Corp. [NYSE symbol] (SPSG) .... KM
K mart Financing Trust I [NYSE symbol] (SAG) .... KM
K mart Financing Trust I [Associated Press] (SAG) .... KmartF
K Swiss, Inc. [Associated Press] (SAG) .... K Swiss
K Swiss, Inc. [NASDAQ symbol] (SAG) .... KSWS
K Swiss Inc. 'A' [NASDAQ symbol] (TTSB) .... KSWS
K2 Del Aire SA de CV [Mexico ICAO designator] (FAAC) .... KDS
K2 Design, Inc. [Associated Press] (SAG) K2Desgn
K2 Design, Inc. [Associated Press] (SAG) K2Dsgn
K2 Design, Inc. [NASDAQ symbol] (SAG) .... KTWO
K-2 Resources, Inc. [Vancouver Stock Exchange symbol] .... KTR
Kaaba Resources [Vancouver Stock Exchange symbol] .... KBR
Ka-Ahari Resources [Vancouver Stock Exchange symbol] .... KLA
Kaanapali [Hawaii] [Airport symbol] (OAG) .... HKP
Kaanapali, Maui Island [Hawaii] [ICAO location identifier] (ICLI) .. PHKP
Kaapuna [Hawaii] [Seismograph station code, US Geological Survey]
  (SEIS) .... KUH
Kaatza Historical Museum, Lake Cowichan, British Columbia [Library
  symbol National Library of Canada] (NLC) .... BLCK
Kabaka Yekka [The King Alone] [Uganda Suspended] [Political party] ..... KY
Kabala [Sierra Leone] [ICAO location identifier] (ICLI) .... GFKB
Kabala [Sierra Leone] [Airport symbol] (OAG) .... KBA
Kabale [Uganda] [ICAO location identifier] (ICLI) .... HUKB
Kabalebo [Surinam] [ICAO location identifier] (ICLI) .... SMKA
Kabalega Falls [Uganda] [ICAO location identifier] (ICLI) .... HUKF
Kabalo [Zaire] [ICAO location identifier] (ICLI) .... FZRM
Kabalo [Zaire] [Airport symbol] (AD) .... KBO
Kabansk [Former USSR Seismograph station code, US Geological Survey]
  (SEIS) .... KAB
Kabarak [Kenya] [ICAO location identifier] (ICLI) .... HKKA
Kabataang Makabayan [Nationalist Youth] [Philippines] .... KM
Kabinda/Tunta [Zaire] [ICAO location identifier] (ICLI) .... FZWT
Kabo Air Travels [Nigeria] [ICAO designator] (FAAC) .... QNK
Kabombo [Zaire] [ICAO location identifier] (ICLI) .... FZRD
Kabompo [Zambia] [ICAO location identifier] (ICLI) .... FLPO
Kabre Dare [Ethiopia] [ICAO location identifier] (ICLI) .... HAKD
Kabri Dar [Ethiopia] [Airport symbol] (OAG) .... ABK
Kabuki Make-Up Syndrome [Medicine] (DMAA) .... KMS
Kabul [Afghanistan] [Seismograph station code, US Geological Survey]
  (SEIS) .... KAAO
Kabul [Afghanistan] [Airport symbol] (OAG) .... KBL
Kabul [Afghanistan] [Seismograph station code, US Geological Survey]
  (SEIS) .... KBL
Kabul [Afghanistan] [ICAO location identifier] (ICLI) .... OAKX
Kabul Ad [Afghanistan] [ICAO location identifier] (ICLI) .... OAKB
Kabushiki Goshi Kaisha [Partnership] [Japan] .... KGK
Kabushiki Kaishi [Joint stock company] [Japan] .... KK
Kabwe/Milliken [Zambia] [ICAO location identifier] (ICLI) ...... FLKW
Kabwum [Papua New Guinea] [Airport symbol] (OAG) .... KBM
Kach International (EA) .... KI
Kachin [MARC language code Library of Congress] (LCCP) ...... kac
Kachin Independence Army [Myanmar] [Political party] (EY) ...... KIA
Kachin Independence Organization [Myanmar] [Political party] (EY) .. KIO
Kachina Village, AZ [FM radio station call letters] .... KFLX
Kadena Air Base [Ryukyu Islands] [ICAO location identifier] (ICLI) ...... RODN
Kadena Air Base, Ryukyu Islands (NASA) .... KAD
Kadenz [Cadence] [Music] .... K
Kadhdhoo [Maldives] [ICAO location identifier] (ICLI) .... VRKD
Kadosh [Freemasonry] (ROG) .... KH
Kadrey Energy [Vancouver Stock Exchange symbol] .... KAD
Kadugli [Sudan] [ICAO location identifier] (ICLI) .... HSLI
Kaduna [Nigeria] [ICAO location identifier] (ICLI) .... DNKA
Kaduna [Nigeria] [Airport symbol] (OAG) .... KAD
Kaduna State Agricultural Development Project [Nigeria] (ECON) .. KADP
Kaedi [Mauritania] [ICAO location identifier] (ICLI) .... GQNK
Kaedi [Mauritania] [Airport symbol] (OAG) .... KED
Kaele [Cameroon] [ICAO location identifier] (ICLI) .... FKKH
Kaele [Cameroon] [Airport symbol] (AD) .... KLE
Kaempferol [Biochemistry] .... K

Kaena [Hawaii] [Seismograph station code, US Geological Survey] (SEIS) .... KAE
Kaena Point [Hawaii] [Seismograph station code, US Geological Survey
  Closed] (SEIS) .... KPH
Kaena Point Station [Hawaii] [Military] .... KPT
Kaffa People's Democratic Union [Ethiopia] [Political party] (EY) .... KPDU
Kaffaria [South Africa] (ROG) .... KAFFR
Kafka Society of America (EA) .... KSA
Kafrarian Mounted Rifles [British military] (DMA) .... KMR
Kafue International Air Services Ltd. [Zambia] [ICAO designator] (FAAC) ..... KAF
Kafue International Air Services Ltd. [Zambia] [FAA designator] (FAAC) .... KAF
Kagalaska [Alaska] [Seismograph station code, US Geological Survey]
  (SEIS) AD3
Kagerod [Sweden ICAO location identifier] (ICLI) .... ESMJ
Kagi [Papua New Guinea] [Airport symbol] (OAG) .... KGW
Kago Kaju [Sudan] [ICAO location identifier] (ICLI) .... HSKJ
Kagoshima [Japan] [Seismograph station code, US Geological Survey]
  (SEIS) .... KAG
Kagoshima [Japan] [Airport symbol] (OAG) .... KOJ
Kagoshima [Japan ICAO location identifier] (ICLI) .... RJFK
Kagoshima Space Center [Japan] .... KAG
Kagoshima Space Center [Japan] .... KSC
Kahal Kadosh. Holy Congregation (BJA) .... KK
Kahaluu, HI [FM radio station call letters] .... KLEO
Kahemba [Zaire] [ICAO location identifier] (ICLI) .... FZCF
Kahler Corp. [Associated Press] (SAG) .... Kahler
Kahler Corp. [NASDAQ symbol] (NQ) .... KHLR
Kahler Process Model [Computer science] .... KPM
KahlerRealty [NASDAQ symbol] (TTSB) .... KHLR
Kahlil Gibran Centennial Foundation (EA) .... KGCF
Kahn Intelligence Test (DMAA) .... KIT
Kahn Test of Symbol Arrangement [Psychology] .... KTSA
Kahnawake, PQ [FM radio station call letters] .... CKRK
Kahnooj [Iran] [ICAO location identifier] (ICLI) .... OIKW
Kahuku [Hawaii] [Seismograph station code, US Geological Survey] (SEIS) ..... KHU
Kahului [Hawaii] [Airport symbol] (OAG) .... OGG
Kahului, HI [AM radio station call letters] .... KNUI
Kahului, HI [FM radio station call letters] .... KNUI-FM
Kahului, HI [Location identifier FAA] (FAAL) .... OGG
Kahului, HI [Location identifier FAA] (FAAL) .... VYI
Kahului, Maui Island [Hawaii] [ICAO location identifier] (ICLI) ..... PHOG
Kai ta Loipa [And the Rest, And So Forth] .... ktl
Kai Tak [Hong Kong] [ICAO location identifier] (ICLI) .... VHKT
Kaiapit [New Guinea] [Airport symbol] (AD) .... KIA
Kaieteur [Guyana] [Airport symbol] (OAG) .... KAI
Kaieteur [Guyana] [ICAO location identifier] (ICLI) .... SYKA
Kaikohe [New Zealand] [Airport symbol Obsolete] (OAG) .... KKO
Kaikoura [New Zealand] [ICAO location identifier] (ICLI) .... NZKI
Kailashahar [India] [Airport symbol] (AD) .... IXH
Kailashahar [India] [ICAO location identifier] (ICLI) .... VEKR
Kailo [Zaire] [ICAO location identifier] (ICLI) .... FZOO
Kailua, HI [FM radio station call letters] .... KRTR
Kailua-Kona [Hawaii] [Seismograph station code, US Geological Survey]
  (SEIS) .... KKH
Kailua-Kona, HI [AM radio station call letters] .... KLEI
Kailua-Kona, HI [FM radio station call letters] .... KLUA
Kailua-Kona, HI [Location identifier FAA] (FAAL) .... KOA
Kaimana [Indonesia] [Airport symbol] (OAG) .... KNG
Kaimana (Utarom) [Indonesia] [ICAO location identifier] (ICLI) ... WASK
Kaimata [New Zealand] [Seismograph station code, US Geological Survey]
  (SEIS) .... KAI
Kainantu [New Guinea] [Airport symbol] (AD) .... KIU
Kainate-Binding Protein [Biochemistry] .... KBP
Ka-Inertial Launch and Leave System .... KILLS
Kainic Acid [Biochemistry] .... K
Kainic Acid [Biochemistry] .... K
Kainic Acid (DMAA) .... KA
Kainokawa [Japan] [Seismograph station code, US Geological Survey]
  (SEIS) .... KKW
Kaintiba [Papua New Guinea] [Airport symbol] (OAG) .... KZF
Kairouan [Tunisia] [ICAO location identifier] (ICLI) .... DTTK
Kai's Power Tools [Computer science] KPT3
Kai's Power Tools for Windows [HSC Software] (PCM) .... KPT
Kaisar-I-Hind [Indian medal] .... KIH
Kaiser [In radio call signs west of the Mississippi River] (ROG) .... KSR
Kaiser (ABBR) .... KSR
Kaiser Alum 8.255% 'PRIDES' [NYSE symbol] (TTSB) ...... KLUPrD

Kaiser Aluminum [*NYSE symbol*] (TTSB) ... KLU
Kaiser Aluminum & Chemical Corp. (MCD) ... KACC
Kaiser Aluminum & Chemical Corp. [*Associated Press*] (SAG) ... KaisA
Kaiser Aluminum & Chemical Corp. [*Associated Press*] (SAG) ... KaisAl
Kaiser Aluminum & Chemical Corp. [*NYSE symbol*] (SPSG) ... KLU
Kaiser Aluminum & Chemical Corp., Permanente, CA [*Library symbol Library of Congress*] (LCLS) ... CPermK
Kaiser Engineers (NRCH) ... KE
Kaiser Foundation Hospital, Doctor's Library, Los Angeles, CA [*Library symbol Library of Congress*] (LCLS) ... CLK-D
Kaiser Foundation Hospital, Los Angeles, CA [*Library symbol Library of Congress*] (LCLS) ... CLK
Kaiser Foundation Hospitals, Health Services Research Center, Portland, OR [*Library symbol Library of Congress*] (LCLS) ... OrPKF
Kaiser, MO [*Location identifier FAA*] (FAAL) ... SHY
Kaiser Permanente Medical Center, Health Science Library, Panorama City, CA [*Library symbol Library of Congress*] (LCLS) ... CPcK
Kaiser Resources, Inc. [*NASDAQ symbol*] (SAG) ... KRSC
Kaiser Steel Corp., Fontana, CA [*Library symbol Library of Congress*] (LCLS) ... CFonK
Kaiser Ventures [*NASDAQ symbol*] (TTSB) ... KRSC
Kaiser Ventures, Inc. [*Associated Press*] (SAG) ... KaisVent
Kaiser Ventures, Inc. [*NASDAQ symbol*] (SAG) ... KRSC
Kaiser Wilhelm [*King William*] [*Name of two Prussian kings and emperor of Germany*] (ROG) ... KW
Kaiser-Frazer Owners Club International (EA) ... KFOCI
Kaiser-Frazer Owners Clubs of America [*Later, KFOCI*] (EA) ... KFOC
Kaiserlautern [*Germany ICAO location identifier*] (ICLI) ... EDED
Kaiser-Permanente [*Diet*] ... K-P
Kaiser-Permanente Medical Center, Medical Library, Redwood City, CA [*Library symbol Library of Congress*] (LCLS) ... CRcK
Kaiser-Permanente Medical Center, San Francisco, CA [*Library symbol Library of Congress*] (LCLS) ... CSfK
Kaiserslautern [*Germany ICAO location identifier*] (ICLI) ... EDON
Kaiserslautern (Kapaun) [*Germany ICAO location identifier*] (ICLI) ... EDOS
Kaiserville [*Nevada*] [*Seismograph station code, US Geological Survey*] (SEIS) ... KVN
Kaitaia [*New Zealand*] [*Airport symbol*] (OAG) ... KAT
Kaitaia [*New Zealand*] [*ICAO location identifier*] (ICLI) ... NZKT
Kaitaia [*New Zealand*] [*ICAO location identifier*] (ICLI) ... NZKX
Kajaani [*Finland ICAO location identifier*] (ICLI) ... EFKI
Kajaani [*Finland*] [*Airport symbol*] (OAG) ... KAJ
Kajaani [*Finland*] [*Seismograph station code, US Geological Survey*] (SEIS) ... KJF
Kajaani [*Finland*] [*Seismograph station code, US Geological Survey Closed*] (SEIS) ... KJN
Kajagoogoo Fan Club [*Defunct*] (EA) ... KFC
Kajaki [*Afghanistan*] [*ICAO location identifier*] (ICLI) ... OAKJ
Kajiji [*Zaire*] [*ICAO location identifier*] (ICLI) ... FZCK
Kakamas [*South Africa*] [*ICAO location identifier*] (ICLI) ... FAKK
Kakamega [*Kenya*] [*ICAO location identifier*] (ICLI) ... HKKG
Kake [*Alaska*] [*Airport symbol*] (OAG) ... KAE
Kakemono (VRA) ... kakm
Kaken Chemical Co. [*Japan*] [*Research code symbol*] ... K
Kakhk [*Iran*] [*Seismograph station code, US Geological Survey*] (SEIS) ... KHI
Kakhonak [*Alaska*] [*Airport symbol*] (OAG) ... KNK
Kakioka [*Japan*] [*Seismograph station code, US Geological Survey*] (SEIS) ... KAK
Kakumbi [*Zambia*] [*ICAO location identifier*] (ICLI) ... FLKK
Kala [*Zaire*] [*ICAO location identifier*] (ICLI) ... FZFL
Kala Explorations [*Vancouver Stock Exchange symbol*] ... KLE
Kalaallit Nunaata Radioa [*Greenland*] (EY) ... KNR
Kalabahi/Mali [*Indonesia*] [*ICAO location identifier*] (ICLI) ... WRKM
Kalabo [*Zambia*] [*ICAO location identifier*] (ICLI) ... FLKL
Kalabo [*Zambia*] [*Airport symbol*] (OAG) ... KLB
Kalaleh [*Iran*] [*ICAO location identifier*] (ICLI) ... OINE
Kalallit Niuerfiat [*Greenland Trade*] (EY) ... KNI
Kalamata [*Greece*] [*Airport symbol*] (OAG) ... KLX
Kalamata [*Greece*] [*ICAO location identifier*] (ICLI) ... LGKL
Kalamazoo [*Michigan*] [*Airport symbol*] (OAG) ... AZO
Kalamazoo [*Diocesan abbreviation*] [*Michigan*] (TOCD) ... KAL
Kalamazoo Area Library Consortium [*Library network*] ... KETAL
Kalamazoo College, Kalamazoo, MI [*OCLC symbol*] (OCLC) ... EXK
Kalamazoo College, Kalamazoo, MI [*Library symbol Library of Congress*] (LCLS) ... MiKC
Kalamazoo Library System, Kalamazoo, MI [*OCLC symbol*] (OCLC) ... EXZ
Kalamazoo Library System, Kalamazoo, MI [*Library symbol Library of Congress*] (LCLS) ... MiKL
Kalamazoo, MI [*FM radio station call letters*] (RBYB) ... WAYK-FM
Kalamazoo, MI [*Television station call letters*] ... WGVK
Kalamazoo, MI [*FM radio station call letters*] ... WIDR
Kalamazoo, MI [*FM radio station call letters*] ... WKDS
Kalamazoo, MI [*AM radio station call letters*] ... WKMI
Kalamazoo, MI [*AM radio station call letters*] ... WKPR
Kalamazoo, MI [*AM radio station call letters*] ... WKZO
Kalamazoo, MI [*Television station call letters*] ... WLLA
Kalamazoo, MI [*FM radio station call letters*] ... WMUK
Kalamazoo, MI [*FM radio station call letters*] ... WQLR
Kalamazoo, MI [*AM radio station call letters*] ... WQSN
Kalamazoo, MI [*Television station call letters*] ... WWMT
Kalamazoo Public Library, Kalamazoo, MI [*Library symbol Library of Congress*] (LCLS) ... MiK
Kalamazoo Public School District, Kalamazoo, MI [*Library symbol Library of Congress*] (LCLS) ... MiKPSc
Kalamazoo Valley Community College, Kalamazoo, MI [*Library symbol Library of Congress*] (LCLS) ... MiKV
Kalamein [*Trademark*] ... KAL
Kalamein [*Trademark*] **Door** ... KALD
Kalamein [*Trademark*] **Door and Frame** ... KDF
Kalanchoe Virus 1 [*Plant pathology*] ... KV1
Kalasin/Ban Na Khu [*Thailand*] [*ICAO location identifier*] (ICLI) ... VTUA
Kalat [*Afghanistan*] [*ICAO location identifier*] (ICLI) ... OAKT
Kalat [*Pakistan*] [*ICAO location identifier*] (ICLI) ... OPKL
Kalaupapa [*Hawaii*] [*Airport symbol*] (OAG) ... LUP
Kalbarri [*Australia Airport symbol*] (OAG) ... KAX
Kaldar [*Afghanistan*] [*ICAO location identifier*] (ICLI) ... OAKR
Kaleidoscope (ABBR) ... KLDSOP
Kaleidoscope: Current World Data [*ABC-CLIO*] [*Information service or system*] (IID) ... KCWD
Kaleidoscopic (ABBR) ... KLDSOPC
Kalemi [*Zaire*] [*Airport symbol*] (OAG) ... FMI
Kalemie [*Zaire*] [*ICAO location identifier*] (ICLI) ... FZRF
Kalemyo [*Myanmar*] [*Airport symbol*] (OAG) ... KMV
Kalemyo [*Myanmar*] [*ICAO location identifier*] (ICLI) ... VBKM
Kalendae [*The Kalends*] [*First day of the ancient Roman month*] ... KAL
Kalendas [*Calends*] ... K
Kalengwa [*Zambia*] [*ICAO location identifier*] (ICLI) ... FLKG
Kalgoorlie [*Australia ICAO location identifier*] (ICLI) ... APKG
Kalgoorlie [*Australia Airport symbol*] (OAG) ... KGI
Kalgoorlie [*Australia Seismograph station code, US Geological Survey*] (SEIS) ... KLG
Kali Praeparatum [*Prepared Kali*] [*Carbonate of potash*] [*Pharmacy*] (ROG) ... KAL PPT
Kali Venture Corp. [*Vancouver Stock Exchange symbol*] ... KIV
Kaliber Resources Ltd. [*Vancouver Stock Exchange symbol*] ... KLI
Kalibo [*Philippines*] [*Airport symbol*] (OAG) ... KLO
Kalibo, Aklan [*Philippines*] [*ICAO location identifier*] (ICLI) ... RPVK
Kalijati [*Indonesia*] [*ICAO location identifier*] (ICLI) ... WIIK
Kalima [*Zaire*] [*ICAO location identifier*] (ICLI) ... FZOD
Kalima [*Zaire*] [*Airport symbol*] (AD) ... KLY
Kalima-Kamisuku [*Zaire*] [*ICAO location identifier*] (ICLI) ... FZOC
Kalini/Migalovo [*Former USSR ICAO location identifier*] (ICLI) ... UUEM
Kaliningrad [*Former USSR Geomagnetic observatory code*] ... KNG
Kaliophilite [*CIPW classification*] [*Geology*] ... kp
Kalispell [*Montana*] [*Airport symbol*] (OAG) ... FCA
Kalispell, MT [*Location identifier FAA*] (FAAL) ... FCA
Kalispell, MT [*FM radio station call letters*] ... KALS
Kalispell, MT [*FM radio station call letters*] ... KBBZ
Kalispell, MT [*Television station call letters*] ... KCFW
Kalispell, MT [*FM radio station call letters*] ... KDBR
Kalispell, MT [*AM radio station call letters*] ... KGEZ
Kalispell, MT [*AM radio station call letters*] ... KOFI
Kalispell, MT [*FM radio station call letters*] ... KOFI-FM
Kalispell, MT [*FM radio station call letters*] (RBYB) ... KSPL-FM
Kalispell, MT [*FM radio station call letters*] (RBYB) ... KUKL
Kalispell, MT [*Location identifier FAA*] (FAAL) ... SAK
Kalispell Regional Hospital, Kalispell, MT [*Library symbol Library of Congress*] (LCLS) ... MtKH
Kaliszer Leben (BJA) ... KL
Kaliszer Woch (BJA) ... KW
Kalitta Flying Service, Inc. [*FAA designator*] (FAAC) ... KFS
Kalium [*Potassium*] [*Chemical element*] ... K
Kalium [*Potassium*] [*Pharmacy*] ... KAL
Kalium [*Potassium*] **Phosphate Buffer** [*Biochemistry*] (DAVI) ... KPB
Kalix Air [*Nigeria*] [*FAA designator*] (FAAC) ... KLX
Kalixfors [*Sweden ICAO location identifier*] (ICLI) ... ESUK
Kalkar [*Germany ICAO location identifier*] (ICLI) ... EDNV
Kalkaska County Library, Kalkaska, MI [*Library symbol Library of Congress*] (LCLS) ... MiKa
Kalkaska, MI [*AM radio station call letters*] ... WKAL
Kalkaska, MI [*FM radio station call letters*] ... WKLT
Kallah (BJA) ... Kal
Kallah Rabbati (BJA) ... KalR
Kallah Rabbati (BJA) ... KR
Kalle Aktiengesellschaft, Litteraturabteilung, Wiesbaden-Biebrich, Germany [*Library symbol Library of Congress*] (LCLS) ... GyWK
Kallidin [*Biochemistry*] ... KD
Kallikrein (MEDA) ... Ka
Kallikrein Inactivator Unit [*Analytical biochemistry*] ... KIU
Kallikrein [*or Kininogenin*] **Inhibiting Unit** [*Hematology*] ... K
Kallikrein Unit (DMAA) ... KU
Kallikrein-Inhibiting Unit [*Analytical biochemistry*] (DAVI) ... KIU
Kallistatin (DMAA) ... KST
Kallitype (VRA) ... KATYP
Kallmann [*Syndrome*] [*Medicine*] (DMAA) ... KAL
Kalltalsperre [*Federal Republic of Germany*] [*Seismograph station code, US Geological Survey*] (SEIS) ... KLL
Kalman Automatic Sequential TMA [*Military*] (CAAL) ... KAST
Kalman Filter Theory ... KFT
Kalman Filtering System ... KFS
Kalmar [*Sweden ICAO location identifier*] (ICLI) ... ESMQ
Kalmar [*Sweden*] [*Airport symbol*] (OAG) ... KLR
Kalocsa [*Hungary*] [*Seismograph station code, US Geological Survey Closed*] (SEIS) ... KAL
Kalokol [*Kenya*] [*ICAO location identifier*] (ICLI) ... HKFG
Kalomo [*Zambia*] [*ICAO location identifier*] (ICLI) ... FLLO
Kalona News, Kalona, IA [*Library symbol Library of Congress*] (LCLS) ... IaKalN
Kalonda [*Zaire*] [*ICAO location identifier*] (ICLI) ... FZUV
Kalskag [*Alaska*] [*Airport symbol*] (OAG) ... KLG
Kaltag [*Alaska*] [*Airport symbol*] (OAG) ... KAL
Kalundborg [*Denmark ICAO location identifier*] (ICLI) ... EKKL
Kalundu [*Zambia*] [*ICAO location identifier*] (ICLI) ... FLKD

Kaluza-Klein [Theories] [Physics] .... KK
Kam Creed Mines Ltd. [Vancouver Stock Exchange symbol Toronto Stock Exchange symbol] .... KCM
Kamad Silver Co. Ltd. [Vancouver Stock Exchange symbol] .... KDS
Kamakura [Japan] [Seismograph station code, US Geological Survey Closed] (SEIS) .... KMK
Kamala Soela [Surinam] [ICAO location identifier] (ICLI) .... SMLA
Kamalpur [India] [Airport symbol] (AD) .... IXQ
Kamalpur [India] [ICAO location identifier] (ICLI) .... VEKM
Kaman Aircraft Corp. (MCD) .... KAC
Kaman Corp. [Associated Press] (SAG) .... Kaman
Kaman Corp. [NASDAQ symbol] (NQ) .... KAMN
Kaman Corp. Cl'A' [NASDAQ symbol] (TTSB) .... KAMNA
Kaman Cp $3.25 Ser 2 Cv Dep Pfd [NASDAQ symbol] (TTSB) ... KAMNZ
Kaman Sciences Corp., Nuclear Library, Colorado Springs, CO [Library symbol Library of Congress] (LCLS) .... CoCK
Kamanjab [Namibia] [ICAO location identifier] (ICLI) .... FAKJ
Kamar [Afghanistan] [ICAO location identifier] (ICLI) .... OAKM
Kamaran [People's Democratic Republic of Yemen] [ICAO location identifier] (ICLI) .... ODAN
Kamaran [Yemen] [ICAO location identifier] (ICLI) .... OYKM
Kamaran Island [South Arabia (Yemen)] [Airport symbol] (AD) ... KAM
Kamarang [Guyana] [Airport symbol] (OAG) .... KAR
Kamarang [Guyana] [ICAO location identifier] (ICLI) .... SYKM
Kamarata [Venezuela] [Airport symbol] (OAG) .... KTV
Kamarata, Bolivar [Venezuela ICAO location identifier] (ICLI) ... SVKM
Kamatanda [Zaire] [ICAO location identifier] (ICLI) .... FZQI
Kamba [MARC language code Library of Congress] (LCCP) ...... kam
Kambalda [Australia Airport symbol] (OAG) .... KDB
Kamdesh [Afghanistan] [ICAO location identifier] (ICLI) ...... OAKD
Kamehameha Early Education Program [Hawaii] (EDAC) ...... KEEP
Kamembe [Rwanda] [ICAO location identifier] (ICLI) .... HRZA
Kameradschaftpolizei (BJA) .... KAPO
Kamerun National Congress .... KNC
Kamerun National Democratic Party [Later, UNC] .... KNDP
Kames and Woodhouselee's Folio Dictionary, Scotch Court of Session [A publication] (DLA) .... F Dict
Kames and Woodhouselee's Folio Dictionary, Scotch Court of Session [A publication] (DLA) .... Fol Dic
Kames and Woodhouselee's Folio Dictionary, Scotch Court of Session [A publication] (DLA) .... Fol Dict
Kames and Woodhouselee's Folio Dictionary, Scotch Court of Session [A publication] (DLA) .... K & W
Kames and Woodhouselee's Folio Dictionary, Scotch Court of Session [A publication] (DLA) .... K & W Dic
Kames' Dictionary of Decisions, Scotch Court of Session [A publication] (DLA) .... Kam
Kames' Dictionary of Decisions, Scotch Court of Session [A publication] (DLA) .... Kames
Kames' Dictionary of Decisions, Scotch Court of Session [A publication] (DLA) .... Kames Dec
Kames' Dictionary of Decisions, Scotch Court of Session [A publication] (DLA) .... Kames Dict Dec
Kames' Elucidation of the Laws of Scotland [A publication] (DLA) .... Kam Eluc
Kames' Elucidation of the Laws of Scotland [A publication] (DLA) ..... Kames Elucid
Kames' Historical Law Tracts [Scotland] [A publication] (DLA) .... Kam L Tr
Kames' Principles of Equity [A publication] (DLA) .... Kam Eq
Kames' Principles of Equity [A publication] (DLA) .... Kames Eq
Kames' Remarkable Decisions [Scotland] [A publication] (DLA) ..... Kames Rem Dec
Kames' Remarkable Decisions, Scotch Court of Session [2 vols.] [1716-52] [A publication] (DLA) .... Kam
Kames' Remarkable Decisions, Scotch Court of Session [2 vols.] [1716-52] [A publication] (DLA) .... Kam Rem
Kames' Remarkable Decisions, Scotch Court of Session [2 vols.] [1716-52] [A publication] (DLA) .... Kames
Kames' Remarkable Decisions, Scotch Court of Session [2 vols.] [1716-52] [A publication] (DLA) .... Kames Rem
Kames' Select Decisions [Scotland] [A publication] (DLA) ...... Kam Sel
Kames' Select Decisions [Scotland] [A publication] (DLA) .. Kam Sel Dec
Kames' Select Decisions [Scotland] [A publication] (DLA) .. Kames Sel Dec
Kameshli [Syria] [Airport symbol] (OAG) .... KAC
Kameyama [Japan] [Seismograph station code, US Geological Survey] (SEIS) .... KAM
Kamigamo [Japan] [Seismograph station code, US Geological Survey Closed] (SEIS) .... KMM
Kamigoto [Japan ICAO location identifier] (ICLI) .... RJDK
Kamikineusu Station [Japan] [Seismograph station code, US Geological Survey] (SEIS) .... KMU
Kamileroi [Australia Airport symbol Obsolete] (OAG) .... KML
Kamimuroga [Japan] [Seismograph station code, US Geological Survey] (SEIS) .... KRJ
Kamina [Papua New Guinea] [Airport symbol] (OAG) .... KMF
Kamina [Zaire] [Airport symbol] (OAG) .... KMN
Kamina-Base [Zaire] [ICAO location identifier] (ICLI) .... FZSA
Kamina-Ville [Zaire] [ICAO location identifier] (ICLI) .... FZSB
Kamiraba [Papua New Guinea] [Airport symbol Obsolete] (OAG) ... KJU
Kamishli [Syria] [Airport symbol] (AD) .... KAC
Kamishly [Syria] [ICAO location identifier] (ICLI) .... OSKL
Kamituga [Zaire] [ICAO location identifier] (ICLI) .... FZPB
Kam-Kotia Mines Ltd. [Toronto Stock Exchange symbol] ...... KKL
Kamlode Resources, Inc. [Vancouver Stock Exchange symbol] ... KMD
Kamloops [Canada] [Airport symbol] (OAG) .... YKA
Kamloops, BC [Television station call letters] CBUFT-2
Kamloops, BC [AM radio station call letters] .... CFJC
Kamloops, BC [Television station call letters] .... CFJC-TV

Kamloops, BC [Television station call letters] .... CHKM
Kamloops, BC [AM radio station call letters] .... CHNL
Kamloops, BC [FM radio station call letters] .... CIFM
Kamloops, BC [FM radio station call letters] .... CKRV
Kamloops, BC [ICAO location identifier] (ICLI) .... CYKA
Kamloops CableNet [Vancouver Stock Exchange symbol] ...... KMC
Kamloops Museum, British Columbia [Library symbol National Library of Canada] (NLC) .... BKM
Kamloops Museum, Kamloops, BC, Canada [Library symbol Library of Congress] (LCLS) .... CaBKM
Kamloops Public Library, British Columbia [Library symbol National Library of Canada] (NLC) .... BK
Kamloops Public Library, Kamloops, BC, Canada [Library symbol Library of Congress] (LCLS) .... CaBK
Kammer der Technik .... KDT
Kammergericht [District Court, Berlin] [German] (DLA) .... KG
Kamov [Former USSR ICAO aircraft manufacturer identifier] (ICAO) ... KA
Kamp/Lintfort [Germany ICAO location identifier] (ICLI) ...... EDLC
Kampala [Uganda] [Airport symbol] (AD) .... KLA
Kampene [Zaire] [ICAO location identifier] (ICLI) .... FZOE
Kampfgeschwader [Bombardment wing] [German military - World War II] ... KG
Kampfwagen [Tank] [German military - World War II] .... KW
Kampfwagenkanone [Tank Gun] [German military - World War II] ... KWK
Kampground Owners Association [Phoenix, AZ] (EA) .... KOA
Kampgrounds of America .... KOA
Kampsville Reading Center, Kampsville, IL [Library symbol Library of Congress] (LCLS) .... IKampR
Kampuchean National United Front for National Salvation (PD) ... KNUFNS
Kampuchean [or Khmer] People's Revolutionary Party [Political party] (PD) .... KPRP
Kampuchean United Front for National Construction and Defence [Political party] (PPW) .... KUFNCD
Kams, TN [FM radio station call letters] .... WWST
Kamsar/Kawass [Guinea] [ICAO location identifier] (ICLI) ... GUKR
Kamuela [Hawaii] [Seismograph station code, US Geological Survey Closed] (SEIS) .... KML
Kamuela [Hawaii] [Airport symbol] (OAG) .... MUE
Kamuzu International [Malawi] [ICAO location identifier] (ICLI) ... FWKI
Kanaanaeische Inschriften [A publication] (BJA) .... KI
Kanaanaeische und Aramaeische Inschriften [A publication] (BJA) ... KAI
Kanab [Utah] [Seismograph station code, US Geological Survey] (SEIS) ... KNB
Kanab [Utah] [Airport symbol] (OAG) .... KNB
Kanab, UT [Location identifier FAA] (FAAL) .... KNB
Kanab, UT [FM radio station call letters] .... KONY-FM
Kanab, UT [Location identifier FAA] (FAAL) .... UNB
Kanabea [Papua New Guinea] [Airport symbol] (OAG) .... KEX
Kanabec County Historical Society, Mora, MN [Library symbol] [Library of Congress] (LCLS) .... MnMrHi
Kanada Esperanto-Asocio [Canadian Esperanto Association] ... KEA
Kanadska Slovenska Liga [Canadian Slovak League - CSL] ... KSL
Kanaf-Arkia Airlines Ltd. [Israel] [ICAO designator] (FAAC) ... KIZ
Kanaka Peak [California] [Seismograph station code, US Geological Survey] (SEIS) .... KPK
Kanamni [South Korea ICAO location identifier] (ICLI) .... RKSD
Kanamycin [Antibacterial compound] .... K
Kanamycin [Antibacterial compound] .... KM
Kanamycin Acetyltransferase [An enzyme] .... KAT
Kanamycin Resistant [Genetics] .... KANr
Kanamycin-Vancomycin [An antibiotic] (DAVI) .... KV
Kanamycin-Vancomycin Blood Agar [Microbiology] .... KVBA
Kanamycin-Vancomycin Labeled Blood Agar [Microbiology] ... KVLBA
Kananaskis Centre for Environmental Research [University of Calgary] [Research center] (RCD) .... KCER
Kananga [Zaire] [ICAO location identifier] (ICLI) .... FZUA
Kananga [Zaire] [Airport symbol] (OAG) .... KGA
Kanata High Technology Training Association [Canada] (EDAC) ... KHTTA
Kanata Public Library, Kanata, ON, Canada [Library symbol] [Library of Congress] (LCLS) .... CaOKAN
Kanata Public Library, Ontario [Library symbol National Library of Canada] (BIB) .... OKAN
[The] Kanawha Central Railway Co. [AAR code] .... KC
Kanawha County Public Library, Charleston, WV [Library symbol Library of Congress] (LCLS) .... WvC
Kanawha County Public Library, Charleston, WV [OCLC symbol] (OCLC) ... WVK
Kanawha Public Library, Kanawha, IA [Library symbol Library of Congress] (LCLS) .... IaKan
Kanawha Reporter, Kanawha, IA [Library symbol Library of Congress] (LCLS) .... IaKanR
Kanazawa [Japan] [Seismograph station code, US Geological Survey] (SEIS) .... KAN
Kanazawa/Komatsu [Japan ICAO location identifier] (ICLI) ... RJNK
Kancana Ventures Ltd. [Vancouver Stock Exchange symbol] ... KCV
Kanchanaburi [Thailand] [ICAO location identifier] (ICLI) ... VTBG
Kandahar [Afghanistan] [Airport symbol] (OAG) .... KDH
Kandahar [Afghanistan] [ICAO location identifier] (ICLI) ...... OAKN
Kandavu [Fiji] [Airport symbol] (OAG) .... KDV
Kandep [Papua New Guinea] [Airport symbol Obsolete] (OAG) ... KDP
K&G Men's Center [NQS] (TTSB) .... MENS
Kandi [Benin] [ICAO location identifier] (ICLI) .... DBBK
Kandiyohi Elementary School, Kandiyohi, MN [Library symbol] [Library of Congress] (LCLS) .... MnKaES
Kandla [India] [Airport symbol] (AD) .... IXY
Kandla [India] [ICAO location identifier] (ICLI) .... VAKE
Kandrian [Papua New Guinea] [Airport symbol] (OAG) .... KDR

[*The*] **Kandy-Kolored Tangerine-Flake Streamline Baby** [*Title of book by Tom Wolfe*] ... TKKTFSLB
Kane, PA [*FM radio station call letters*] ... WLMI
Kane, PA [*FM radio station call letters*] (RBYB) ... WPSB-FM
Kane, PA [*AM radio station call letters*] ... WQLE
Kaneb Energy Partners Ltd. (MHDW) ... KEP
Kaneb Pipe Line Partners Ltd. [*Associated Press*] (SAG) ... KanPip
Kaneb Pipe Line Partners LP [*Associated Press*] (SAG) ... KanPipSn
Kaneb Pipe Line Partners LP [*NYSE symbol*] (SAG) ... KPU
Kaneb Pipe Line PtnrsL.P. [*NYSE symbol*] (TTSB) ... KPP
Kaneb Pipe Ln Ptnrs LP Pref Ut [*NYSE symbol*] (TTSB) ... KPU
Kaneb Pipeline Partnership LP [*NYSE symbol*] (SPSG) ... KPP
Kaneb Services [*NYSE symbol*] (TTSB) ... KAB
Kaneb Services, Inc. [*NYSE symbol*] (SPSG) ... KAB
Kaneb Services, Inc. [*Associated Press*] (SAG) ... Kanb
Kaneb Services, Inc. [*Associated Press*] (SAG) ... Kaneb
Kaneb Svc Adj Rt A Pfd [*NYSE symbol*] (TTSB) ... KABPrA
Kanene [*Zaire*] [*ICAO location identifier*] (ICLI) ... FZSE
Kaneohe Bay, HI [*Location identifier FAA*] (FAAL) ... NKH
Kaneohe Bay Marine Corps Air Station, Oahu Island [*Hawaii*] [*ICAO location identifier*] (ICLI) ... PHNG
Kaneohe, HI [*TV station call letters*] (RBYB) ... KAPA
Kaneohe, HI [*FM radio station call letters*] ... KBLZ
Kaneohe, HI [*Location identifier FAA*] (FAAL) ... NGF
Kanfey-Ha'Emek Aviation [*Israel*] [*FAA designator*] (FAAC) ... KHE
Kang [*Botswana*] [*ICAO location identifier*] (ICLI) ... FBKG
Kangaroo (DSUE) ... KANGA
Kangaroo (ABBR) ... KNGR
Kangaroo Industries Association of Australia ... KIAA
Kangaroo Management Program [*Australia*] ... KMP
Kangaroo Management Zone ... KMZ
Kangaroo Marketing and Management Committee [*Australia*] ... KMMC
Kangaroo Protection Foundation (EA) ... KPF
Kangavar [*Iran*] [*ICAO location identifier*] (ICLI) ... OIHQ
Kangeld Resources Ltd. [*Vancouver Stock Exchange symbol*] ... KDR
Kangmar Thrust [*Geophysics*] ... KT
Kangnung [*South Korea ICAO location identifier*] (ICLI) ... RKNN
Kaniama [*Zaire*] [*ICAO location identifier*] (ICLI) ... FZTK
Kania-Sominka [*Zaire*] [*ICAO location identifier*] (ICLI) ... FZRG
Kanizkar Le'eyl [*As Mentioned Above*] [*Hebrew*] ... CANAL
Kanja [*Zambia*] [*ICAO location identifier*] (ICLI) ... FLKJ
Kankakee Bancorp [*AMEX symbol*] (TTSB) ... KNK
Kankakee Bancorp, Inc. [*AMEX symbol*] (SAG) ... KNK
Kankakee, Beaverville & Southern Railroad Co. [*AAR code*] ... KBSR
Kankakee Community College, Kankakee, IL [*Library symbol Library of Congress*] (LCLS) ... IKC
Kankakee, IL [*Location identifier FAA*] (FAAL) ... IKK
Kankakee, IL [*FM radio station call letters*] ... WBUS
Kankakee, IL [*AM radio station call letters*] ... WKAN
Kankakee, IL [*FM radio station call letters*] ... WLRT
Kankakee, IL [*FM radio station call letters*] ... WONU
Kankakee, IL [*FM radio station call letters*] (RBYB) ... WRZA-FM
Kankakee, IL [*FM radio station call letters*] ... WTKC
Kankakee, IL [*FM radio station call letters*] (RBYB) ... WVLI
Kankakkee Bancorp, Inc. [*Associated Press*] (SAG) ... KankakB
Kankan [*Guinea*] [*Airport symbol*] (AD) ... KNN
Kankan/Diankana [*Guinea*] [*ICAO location identifier*] (ICLI) ... GUXD
Kannada [*MARC language code Library of Congress*] (LCCP) ... kan
Kannapolis, NC [*TV station call letters*] (RBYB) ... WAXN-TV
Kannapolis, NC [*Television station call letters*] ... WKAY
Kannapolis, NC [*FM radio station call letters*] ... WRFX
Kannapolis, NC [*AM radio station call letters*] ... WRKB
Kano [*Nigeria*] [*ICAO location identifier*] (ICLI) ... DNKK
Kano [*Nigeria*] [*Airport symbol*] (OAG) ... KAN
Kano/Mallam Aminu International [*Nigeria*] [*ICAO location identifier*] (ICLI) ... DNKN
Kano, Nigeria [*Remote site*] [*NASA*] (NASA) ... KNO
Kano Transport International Ltd. KATI Air [*Nigeria*] [*ICAO designator*] (FAAC) ... KTI
Kanone [*Gun*] [*German military - World War II*] ... K
Kanonengranate [*Shell for a gun*] [*German military - World War II*] ... KGR
Kanoya [*Japan*] [*Geomagnetic observatory code*] ... KNY
Kanoya [*Japan ICAO location identifier*] (ICLI) ... RJFY
Kanozan [*Japan*] [*Geomagnetic observatory code*] ... KNZ
Kanpur [*India*] [*Airport symbol*] (OAG) ... KNU
Kanpur [*India*] [*ICAO location identifier*] (ICLI) ... VIKA
Kanpur/Chakeri [*India*] [*ICAO location identifier*] (ICLI) ... VICX
Kansai International Airport [*Japan*] ... KIA
Kansai International Airport Co. [*Japan*] ... KIAC
Kansai Research Reactor [*Japan*] ... KRR
Kansalaisvallen Liitto [*League of Civil Power*] [*Finland Political party*] (PPW) ... KL
Kansallinen Kokoomus [*National Coalition Party*] [*Finland*] [*Political party*] (EAIO) ... KOK
Kansallis-Osake-Pankki [*National Capital Stock Bank*] [*Finland*] ... KOP
Kansanvalistusseura [*Society for Culture and Education*] [*Finland*] (EAIO) ... KVS
Kansas ... KAN
Kansas (ODBW) ... Kan
Kansas (ODBW) ... Kans
Kansas (AFM) ... KANS
Kansas [*Obsolete*] (ROG) ... KAS
Kansas [*Postal code*] ... KS
Kansas [*MARC country of publication code Library of Congress*] (LCCP) ... ksu
Kansas [*MARC geographic area code Library of Congress*] (LCCP) ... n-us-ks
Kansas Academy of Family Physicians (SRA) ... KAFP
Kansas Administration Regulations [*A publication*] (DLA) ... Kan Admin Regs
Kansas Administrative Regulations [*A publication*] ... KAR
Kansas Advisory Council on Environmental Education (EDAC) ... KACEE
[*The*] **Kansas & Missouri Railway & Terminal Co.** [*Formerly, KMRT*] [*AAR code*] ... KM
[*The*] **Kansas & Missouri Railway & Terminal Co.** [*Later, KM*] [*AAR code*] ... KMRT
Kansas Appeals Reports [*A publication*] (DLA) ... Ka A
Kansas Appeals Reports [*A publication*] (DLA) ... Kan App
Kansas Appeals Reports [*A publication*] (DLA) ... Kans App
Kansas Appellate Reports [*A publication*] (DLA) ... Kan Ct App
Kansas Applied Remote Sensing Program [*University of Kansas*] [*Research center*] (RCD) ... KARS
Kansas Army Ammunition Plant (AABC) ... KAAP
Kansas Association of Chiefs of Police (SRA) ... KACP
Kansas Association of Marriage and Family Therapy (SRA) ... KAMFT
Kansas Association of Osteopathic Medicine (SRA) ... KAOM
Kansas Association of Private Career Schools (SRA) ... KAPCS
Kansas Association of Public Employees (SRA) ... KAPE
Kansas Association of School Boards (SRA) ... KASB
Kansas Association of School Librarians (SRA) ... KASL
Kansas Association of Soil Conservation Districts (SRA) ... KACD
Kansas Bankers Association (SRA) ... KBA
Kansas Bar Association (SRA) ... KBA
Kansas Chamber of Commerce and Industry (SRA) ... KCCI
Kansas Chiropractic Association (SRA) ... KCA
Kansas City [*Branch in the Federal Reserve regional banking system*] (BARN) ... J
Kansas City [*Missouri*] [*Slang*] ... KAYSEE
Kansas City [*Missouri*] [*Slang*] ... KC
Kansas City [*Missouri*] [*ICAO location identifier*] (ICLI) ... KMKM
Kansas City [*Missouri*] [*ICAO location identifier*] (ICLI) ... KNKA
Kansas City [*Missouri*] [*ICAO location identifier*] (ICLI) ... KRKC
Kansas City [*Missouri*] [*Airport symbol*] (OAG) ... MCI
Kansas City [*Missouri*] [*Airport symbol*] (OAG) ... MKC
Kansas City Area Hospital Association, Kansas City, MO [*Library symbol Library of Congress*] (LCLS) ... MoKHA
Kansas City Area Office [*Energy Research and Development Administration*] ... KCAO
Kansas City Arts Institute, Kansas City, MO [*Library symbol Library of Congress*] (LCLS) ... MoKAI
Kansas City Ballet ... KCB
Kansas City Bar Journal [*A publication*] (DLA) ... Kans BA
Kansas City Board of Trade ... KBOT
Kansas City College of Osteopathic Medicine, Kansas City, MO [*Library symbol Library of Congress*] (LCLS) ... MoKCO
Kansas City Connecting Railroad Co. [*AAR code*] ... KCC
Kansas City General Hospital, Kansas City, MO [*Library symbol Library of Congress*] (LCLS) ... MoKGH
Kansas City/International [*Missouri*] [*ICAO location identifier*] (ICLI) ... KMCI
Kansas City/Kansas City [*Missouri*] [*ICAO location identifier*] (ICLI) ... KMKC
Kansas City Kansas Public Schools, Kansas City, KS [*Library symbol*] [*Library of Congress*] (LCLS) ... KKcPS
Kansas City, Kaw Valley R. R., Inc. [*AAR code*] ... KVW
Kansas City, KS [*Location identifier FAA*] (FAAL) ... BGZ
Kansas City, KS [*Location identifier FAA*] (FAAL) ... KCK
Kansas City, KS [*FM radio station call letters*] ... KFKF
Kansas City, KS [*AM radio station call letters*] ... KNHN
Kansas City, KS [*FM radio station call letters*] ... KUDL
Kansas City Law Reporter [*A publication*] (DLA) ... Kan City L Rep
Kansas City Law Reporter [*A publication*] (DLA) ... Kan CL Rep
Kansas City Law Review [*A publication*] (DLA) ... Kan City L Rev
Kansas City Law Review [*A publication*] (DLA) ... KCR
Kansas City Life Ins [*NASDAQ symbol*] (TTSB) ... KCLI
Kansas City Life Insurance [*Associated Press*] (SAG) ... KnCtyL
Kansas City Life Insurance Co. [*NASDAQ symbol*] (NQ) ... KCLI
Kansas City, Memphis & Birmingham Railroad ... KCM & B
Kansas City Metropolitan Library Network Council [*Library network*] ... KCMLN
Kansas City, Mexico & Orient [*AAR code*] ... KCMO
Kansas City, MO [*Location identifier FAA*] (FAAL) ... DOT
Kansas City, MO [*FM radio station call letters*] ... KBEQ
Kansas City, MO [*AM radio station call letters*] ... KCMO
Kansas City, MO [*FM radio station call letters*] ... KCMO-FM
Kansas City, MO [*Television station call letters*] ... KCPT
Kansas City, MO [*Television station call letters*] ... KCTV
Kansas City, MO [*FM radio station call letters*] ... KCUR
Kansas City, MO [*TV station call letters*] (RBYB) ... KCWB-TV
Kansas City, MO [*AM radio station call letters*] ... KFEZ
Kansas City, MO [*FM radio station call letters*] ... KKFI
Kansas City, MO [*FM radio station call letters*] ... KLJC
Kansas City, MO [*FM radio station call letters*] ... KLTH
Kansas City, MO [*Television station call letters*] ... KMBC
Kansas City, MO [*AM radio station call letters*] ... KMBZ
Kansas City, MO [*FM radio station call letters*] ... KMXV
Kansas City, MO [*FM radio station call letters*] ... KPRS
Kansas City, MO [*AM radio station call letters*] ... KPRT
Kansas City, MO [*Television station call letters*] ... KSHB
Kansas City, MO [*Television station call letters*] ... KSMO
Kansas City, MO [*FM radio station call letters*] ... KXTR
Kansas City, MO [*Television station call letters*] ... KYFC
Kansas City, MO [*FM radio station call letters*] ... KYYS
Kansas City, MO [*Location identifier FAA*] (FAAL) ... MCI
Kansas City, MO [*Location identifier FAA*] (FAAL) ... MKM
Kansas City, MO [*Location identifier FAA*] (FAAL) ... PAJ
Kansas City, MO [*Location identifier FAA*] (FAAL) ... RIS
Kansas City, MO [*Location identifier FAA*] (FAAL) ... RNI
Kansas City, MO [*Location identifier FAA*] (FAAL) ... UQY

Kansas City, MO [*AM radio station call letters*] ... WDAF
Kansas City, MO [*Television station call letters*] ... WDAF-TV
Kansas City, MO [*AM radio station call letters*] ... WHB
Kansas City, MO [*Location identifier FAA*] (FAAL) ... ZKC
Kansas City Olathe [*Kansas*] [*ICAO location identifier*] (ICLI) ... KZKC
Kansas City P&L 3.80% Pfd [*NYSE symbol*] (TTSB) ... KLTPrA
Kansas City P&L 4.35% Pfd [*NYSE symbol*] (TTSB) ... KLTPrD
Kansas City P&L 4.50% Pfd [*NYSE symbol*] (TTSB) ... KLTPrE
Kansas City, Pittsburgh & Gulf Railroad ... KCP & G
Kansas City Plant ... KCP
Kansas City Plant [*Department of Energy*] [*Kansas City, MO*] (GAAI) ... KCP
Kansas City Plant (DOGT) ... KCP
Kansas City Power & Light Co. [*Associated Press*] (SAG) ... KCPL
Kansas City Power & Light Co. [*Associated Press*] (SAG) ... KCtyPL
Kansas City Power & Light Co. [*NYSE symbol*] (SPSG) ... KLT
Kansas City Public Library, Kansas City, KS [*Library symbol Library of Congress*] (LCLS) ... KKc
Kansas City Public Library, Kansas City, KS [*OCLC symbol*] (OCLC) ... KKC
Kansas City Public Library, Kansas City, MO [*OCLC symbol*] (OCLC) ... KCP
Kansas City Public Library, Kansas City, MO [*Library symbol Library of Congress*] (LCLS) ... MoK
Kansas City Public Service R. R. [*AAR code*] ... KCPS
Kansas City Pwr & Lt [*NYSE symbol*] (TTSB) ... KLT
Kansas City Records Center [*Military*] ... KCRC
Kansas City Regional Council for Higher Education [*Library network*] ... KCRCHE
Kansas City, St. Joseph & Council Bluffs Railroad ... KCStJ & CB
Kansas City Service Center [*IRS*] ... KCSC
Kansas City So. Ind. [*NYSE symbol*] (TTSB) ... KSU
Kansas City So. Ind 4% Pfd [*NYSE symbol*] (TTSB) ... KSUPr
Kansas City Southern Industries, Inc. [*Associated Press*] (SAG) ... KCSo
Kansas City Southern Industries, Inc. [*Associated Press*] (SAG) ... KCSou
Kansas City Southern Industries, Inc. [*NYSE symbol*] (SPSG) ... KSU
[*The*] **Kansas City Southern Railway Co.** [*AAR code*] ... KCS
Kansas City Standard [*Audio tape technology*] (EECA) ... KCS
Kansas City Terminal Railway Co. [*AAR code*] ... KCT
Kansas City Westport Belt [*AAR code*] ... KCWB
Kansas City-St. Joseph [*Diocesan abbreviation*] [*Missouri*] (TOCD) ... KC
Kansas Commission of Labor and Industry Workmen's Compensation Department Reports [*A publication*] (DLA) ... Kan CL & IWC
Kansas Committee for Prevention of Child Abuse (EDAC) ... KCPCA
Kansas Community Memorial Library, Kansas, IL [*Library symbol Library of Congress*] (LCLS) ... IKan
Kansas Community Unit School District, Kansas, IL [*Library symbol*] [*Library of Congress*] (LCLS) ... IKanSD
Kansas Contractors Association (SRA) ... KCA
Kansas Co-Operative Council (SRA) ... KCC
Kansas Cosmosphere and Space Center [*Hutchinson, KS*] ... KCSC
Kansas Digital Data System ... KANDIDATS
Kansas Education Dissemination/Diffusion System (EDAC) ... KEDDS
Kansas Flight Research Laboratory ... KFRL
Kansas Hospital Association (SRA) ... KHA
Kansas Individualized Curriculum Sequencing (EDAC) ... KICS
Kansas Information Circuit [*Library network*] ... KIC
Kansas Journal of Sociology ... KJS
Kansas Law Journal [*A publication*] (DLA) ... Kan LJ
Kansas Law Journal [*A publication*] (DLA) ... Kansas LJ
Kansas Lawyer [*A publication*] (DLA) ... Kan Law
Kansas Motor Carriers Association, Topeka KS [*STAC*] ... KSA
Kansas Neurological Institute, Topeka, KS [*Library symbol Library of Congress*] (LCLS) ... KTNI
Kansas Newman College [*Formerly, Sacred Heart College*] [*Wichita*] ... KNC
Kansas Newman College, Wichita, KS [*OCLC symbol*] (OCLC) ... KKN
Kansas Newman College, Wichita, KS [*Library symbol Library of Congress*] (LCLS) ... KWiK
Kansas, Oklahoma & Gulf Railway Co. ... KO & G
Kansas, Oklahoma & Gulf Railway Co. [*AAR code*] ... KOG
Kansas Pharmacists Association (SRA) ... KPhA
Kansas Reports [*A publication*] (DLA) ... Kans
Kansas Reports [*A publication*] (DLA) ... Kans R
Kansas Reports [*A publication*] (DLA) ... Kansas R
Kansas Reports [*A publication*] (DLA) ... Kas
Kansas Reports [*A publication*] (DLA) ... Kas R
Kansas Reports [*A publication*] (DLA) ... KS
Kansas River Basin ... KRB
Kansas Society of Association Executives (SRA) ... KSAE
Kansas State Corporation Commission Reports [*A publication*] (DLA) ... Kan SCC
Kansas State Historical Society, Topeka, KS [*Library symbol Library of Congress*] (LCLS) ... KHi
Kansas State Law Journal [*A publication*] (DLA) ... Kan St LJ
Kansas State Library, Law Department, Topeka, KS [*Library symbol Library of Congress*] (LCLS) ... K-L
Kansas State Library, Topeka, KS [*Library symbol Library of Congress*] (LCLS) ... K
Kansas State Teachers College ... KSTC
Kansas State Teachers College, Emporia, KS [*Library symbol Library of Congress Obsolete*] (LCLS) ... KEmT
Kansas State University ... KSU
Kansas State University, Farrell Library, Manhattan, KS [*OCLC symbol*] (OCLC) ... KKS
Kansas State University, Manhattan, KS [*Library symbol Library of Congress*] (LCLS) ... KMK
Kansas State University of Agriculture and Applied Science (GAGS) ... Kans St U
Kansas State University, Veterinary Medicine Library, Manhattan, KS [*Library symbol Library of Congress*] (LCLS) ... KMK-V
Kansas Statutes [*A publication*] (DLA) ... Kan Stat
Kansas Statutes, Annotated [*A publication*] (DLA) ... Kan Stat Ann
Kansas Statutes Annotated [*A publication*] (AAGC) ... Kan Stat Ann
Kansas Statutes, Annotated [*A publication*] ... KSA
Kansas Supreme Court Reports [*A publication*] (DLA) ... Kan
Kansas Telecommunications Association (SRA) ... KTA
Kansas Turfgrass Foundation (EA) ... KTF
Kansas University Lawyer [*A publication*] (DLA) ... Kan U Lawy
Kansas University Lawyer [*A publication*] (DLA) ... Kan Univ Lawy
Kansas Water Resources Research Institute [*Kansas State University*] [*Department of the Interior Research center*] (RCD) ... KWRRI
Kansas Wesleyan University [*Salina*] ... KWU
Kansas Wesleyan University, Salina, KS [*Library symbol Library of Congress*] (LCLS) ... KSalW
Kansas Wine and Spirits Wholesalers Association (SRA) ... KWSWA
Kansas-Oklahoma-Missouri League [*Old baseball league*] ... KOM
Kansimba [*Zaire*] [*ICAO location identifier*] (ICLI) ... FZRK
Kansu Province [*China, Mainland*] [*MARC geographic area code Library of Congress*] (LCCP) ... a-cc-ka
Kantchari [*Burkina Faso*] [*ICAO location identifier*] (ICLI) ... DHEL
Kantorberita Nasional Indonesia [*News service*] [*Indonesia*] (EY) ... KNI
Kantorei [*Record label*] [*Germany*] ... Kan
Kanuri [*MARC language code Library of Congress*] (LCCP) ... kau
Kanyau [*Zambia*] [*ICAO location identifier*] (ICLI) ... FLKU
Kanye [*Botswana*] [*ICAO location identifier*] (ICLI) ... FBKY
Kao/Kuabang [*Indonesia*] [*ICAO location identifier*] (ICLI) ... WAMK
Kaohsiung [*Takao*] [*Republic of China*] [*Seismograph station code, US Geological Survey*] (SEIS) ... KAU
Kaohsiung [*Taiwan*] [*Airport symbol*] (OAG) ... KHH
Kaohsiung [*Republic of China*] [*Seismograph station code, US Geological Survey Closed*] (SEIS) ... TWM
Kaohsiung [*Republic of China*] [*Seismograph station code, US Geological Survey*] (SEIS) ... TWM1
Kaohsiung Export Processing Zone [*Reexport manufacturing complex*] [*Taiwan*] ... KEPZ
Kaolack [*Senegal*] [*ICAO location identifier*] (ICLI) ... GOOK
Kaolack [*Senegal*] [*Airport symbol*] (AD) ... KLC
Kaolin (BARN) ... kao
Kaolin Cephalin Clotting Time (PDAA) ... KCCT
Kaolin Cephalin Time [*Clinical chemistry*] ... KCT
Kaolin Clay Producers Association (DGA) ... KCPA
Kaolin Clotting Time [*Clinical chemistry*] ... KCT
Kaolin Partial Thromboplastin Time [*Clinical chemistry*] (MAE) ... KPTT
Kaolinite [*A mineral*] ... Ka
Kaoma [*Zambia*] [*ICAO location identifier*] (ICLI) ... FLKO
Kaow Island [*Guyana*] [*ICAO location identifier*] (ICLI) ... SYKI
Kap Dan [*Greenland*] [*ICAO location identifier*] (ICLI) ... BGKD
Kap Resources [*Vancouver Stock Exchange symbol*] ... KAR
Kap Tobin [*Greenland*] [*ICAO location identifier*] (ICLI) ... BGKT
Kap Tobin [*Greenland*] [*Seismograph station code, US Geological Survey*] (SEIS) ... KTG
Kapanga [*Zaire*] [*ICAO location identifier*] (ICLI) ... FZSK
Kapapala Ranch [*Hawaii*] [*Seismograph station code, US Geological Survey*] (SEIS) ... KLH
Kapfenberg [*Austria ICAO location identifier*] (ICLI) ... LOGK
Kaphearst Resources [*Vancouver Stock Exchange symbol*] ... KAP
Kapiolani Community College, Honolulu, HI [*Library symbol Library of Congress*] (LCLS) ... HHK
Kapiri Mposhi [*Zambia*] [*ICAO location identifier*] (ICLI) ... FLKM
Kapit [*Malaysia*] [*Airport symbol*] (OAG) ... KPI
Kapit [*Indonesia*] [*ICAO location identifier*] (ICLI) ... WBGP
Kapitalist Birokrat [*Capitalist Bureaucrat*] [*Term for foreigner Indonesia*] ... KABIR
Kaplan, LA [*FM radio station call letters*] ... KMDL
Kaplan-Zuelzer [*Syndrome*] (DAVI) ... KZ
Kapoeta [*Sudan*] [*ICAO location identifier*] (ICLI) ... HSKP
Kapok (ABBR) ... KPK
Kaposi's Sarcoma [*Medicine*] ... KS
Kaposi's Sarcoma and Opportunistic Infection [*Infectious disease*] (DAVI) ... KS/OI
Kaposi's Sarcoma Associated Herpesvirus [*Medicine*] ... KSHV
Kaposi's Varicelliform Eruption [*Medicine Medicine*] (DMAA) ... KVE
Kappa [*Tenth letter of the Greek alaphabet*] (DAVI) ... K
Kappa Alpha Order ... KAO
Kappa Alpha Theta [*Sorority*] ... KAT
Kappa Application Language [*Artificial intelligence system*] [*IntelliCorp*] (PCM) ... KAL
Kappa Beta Pi [*Society*] ... KBP
Kappa Delta Pi [*Honor society*] (AEE) ... KDP
Kappa Delta Rho [*Fraternity*] ... KDR
Kappa Eta Kappa [*Fraternity*] ... KEK
Kappa Kappa Gamma [*Sorority*] ... KKG
Kappa Kappa Psi [*Society*] ... KKP
Kappa Mu Epsilon [*Society*] ... KME
Kappa Phi Kappa [*Fraternity*] ... KPK
Kappa Resources [*Vancouver Stock Exchange symbol*] ... KPC
Kappa Sigma Kappa [*Later, Theta Xi*] [*Fraternity*] ... KSK
Kapson Senior Quarters Corp. [*Associated Press*] (SAG) ... KapsnSn
Kapson Senior Quarters Corp. [*NASDAQ symbol*] (SAG) ... KPSQ
Kapuskasing [*Canada*] [*Airport symbol*] (OAG) ... YYU
Kapuskasing, ON [*Television station call letters*] ... CBLFT-4
Kapuskasing, ON [*AM radio station call letters*] ... CHYK
Kapuskasing, ON [*AM radio station call letters*] ... CKAP
Kapuskasing, ON [*ICAO location identifier*] (ICLI) ... CYYU
Kapuskasing Public Library, Kapuskasing, ON, Canada [*Library symbol Library of Congress*] (LCLS) ... CaOKap

Kapuskasing Public Library, Kapuskasing, ON, Canada [*Library symbol*] [*Library of Congress*] (LCLS) ... CaOKap
Kapuskasing Public Library, Ontario [*Library symbol National Library of Canada*] (NLC) ... OKAP
Kapuskasing Uplift [*Geology*] [*Canada*] ... KU
Kapustin Yar [*Test Facility*] [*US prefix for Soviet-Russian developmental missiles*] (DOMA) ... KY
Kar Kar [*Papua New Guinea*] [*Airport symbol*] (OAG) ... KRX
Karabiner [*Carbine*] [*German military - World War II*] ... KAR
Karachi [*Pakistan*] [*Seismograph station code, US Geological Survey*] (SEIS) ... KAR
Karachi [*Pakistan*] [*Airport symbol*] (OAG) ... KHI
Karachi [*Pakistan*] [*ICAO location identifier*] (ICLI) ... OPHQ
Karachi [*Pakistan*] [*ICAO location identifier*] (ICLI) ... OPKR
Karachi/International [*Pakistan*] [*ICAO location identifier*] (ICLI) ... OPKC
Karachi/Korangi Creek [*Pakistan*] [*ICAO location identifier*] (ICLI) ... OPKK
Karachi/Masroor [*Pakistan*] [*ICAO location identifier*] (ICLI) ... OPMR
Karachi/Shara-E-Faisal [*Pakistan*] [*ICAO location identifier*] (ICLI) ... OPSF
Karachi Stock Exchange [*Pakistan*] ... KSE
Karad [*India*] [*Seismograph station code, US Geological Survey*] (SEIS) ... KAD
Karadeniz Hava Yollari, AS [*Turkey*] [*FAA designator*] (FAAC) ... AZG
Karaganda [*Former USSR Geomagnetic observatory code*] ... KGD
Kar-Air [*ICAO designator*] (AD) ... KR
Kar-Air OY [*Finland ICAO designator*] (FAAC) ... KAR
Karaj [*Iran*] [*ICAO location identifier*] (ICLI) ... OIIJ
Karakalpak [*MARC language code Library of Congress*] (LCCP) ... kaa
Karakoram Highway [*Asia*] ... KKH
Karakul Fur Sheep Registry [*Later, AKFSR*] (EA) ... KFSR
Karamay [*China*] [*Airport symbol*] (OAG) ... KRY
Karanambo [*Guyana*] [*ICAO location identifier*] (ICLI) ... SYKR
Karaoke International Sing-Along Association (EA) ... KISA
Karapiro [*New Zealand*] [*Seismograph station code, US Geological Survey*] (SEIS) ... KRP
Karasabai [*Guyana*] [*Airport symbol*] (OAG) ... KRG
Karasabai [*Guyana*] [*ICAO location identifier*] (ICLI) ... SYKS
Karasburg [*Namibia*] [*ICAO location identifier*] (ICLI) ... FAKB
Karasu [*Former USSR Seismograph station code, US Geological Survey*] (SEIS) ... KRU
Karat [*A twenty-fourth part; unit of value for gold*] ... K
Karat (ABBR) ... KR
Karat [*Also, CT*] ... KT
Karate ... KRT
Karate (ABBR) ... KRTE
Karate Union of Great Britain ... KUGB
Karate Union of Great Britain National Championship ... KUGBNC
Karatin (ABBR) ... KRTN
Karato [*Papua New Guinea*] [*Airport symbol*] (OAG) ... KAF
Karavia [*Zaire*] [*Geomagnetic observatory code*] ... KVA
Karawa [*Zaire*] [*ICAO location identifier*] (ICLI) ... FZFS
Karen [*MARC language code Library of Congress*] (LCCP) ... kar
Karen Brooks Fan Club (EA) ... KBFC
Karen Carpenter Fan Club [*Defunct*] (EA) ... KCFC
Karen Horney Clinic (EA) ... KHC
Karen National Defense Organization [*Burma*] ... KNDO
Karen National Liberation Army [*Myanmar*] [*Political party*] ... KNLA
Karen National Liberation Front [*Myanmar*] [*Political party*] (PD) ... KNLF
Karen National Union [*Myanmar*] (PD) ... KNU
Karen National Unity Party [*Burma*] ... KNUP
Karen Silkwood Fund (EA) ... KSF
Karen Taylor-Good International Fan Club [*Defunct*] (EA) ... KTGIFC
Karenni National Progressive Party [*Myanmar*] [*Political party*] (EY) ... KNPP
Karenni Revolutionary Army [*Myanmar*] [*Political party*] (EY) ... KRA
Karez-I-Mir [*Afghanistan*] [*ICAO location identifier*] (ICLI) ... OAKZ
Karhunen-Loeve Transform [*Mathematics*] ... KLT
Kariba [*Zimbabwe*] [*Seismograph station code, US Geological Survey Closed*] (SEIS) ... KRB
Kariba Dam [*Zimbabwe*] [*Airport symbol*] (OAG) ... KAB
Kariba/Kariba [*Zimbabwe*] [*ICAO location identifier*] (ICLI) ... FVKB
Karibib [*Namibia*] [*ICAO location identifier*] (ICLI) ... FAKA
Karimui [*Papua New Guinea*] [*Airport symbol*] (OAG) ... KMR
Karin Lake Explorations [*Vancouver Stock Exchange symbol*] ... KRI
Karissimo Bene Merenti [*To the Most Dear and Well-Deserving*] [*Correspondence*] ... KBM
Karitane Mothercraft Society [*Australia*] ... KMS
Karkar Island [*Papua New Guinea*] [*Seismograph station code, US Geological Survey*] (SEIS) ... KKI
Kar-Kraft [*Automotive industry supplier*] ... KK
Karl Fischer [*Reagent*] [*Analytical chemistry*] ... KF
Karl Lagerfeld [*Fashion designer*] ... KL
Karl-Jaspers Foundation (EA) ... KJF
Karl-Jaspers Stiftung [*Karl-Jaspers Foundation - KJF*] (EA) ... KJS
Karl-Lorimar Home Video, Inc. ... K-L
Karlovy Vary [*Former Czechoslovakia*] [*Airport symbol*] (OAG) ... KLV
Karlovy Vary [*Former Czechoslovakia*] [*ICAO location identifier*] (ICLI) ... LKKV
Karlsborg [*Sweden ICAO location identifier*] (ICLI) ... ESIA
Karlshamn [*Sweden ICAO location identifier*] (ICLI) ... ESMC
Karlskoga [*Sweden ICAO location identifier*] (ICLI) ... ESKK
Karlskoga [*Sweden*] [*Airport symbol*] (OAG) ... KSK
Karlskrona [*Sweden*] [*Seismograph station code, US Geological Survey Closed*] (SEIS) ... KLS
Karlsruhe [*Germany ICAO location identifier*] (ICLI) ... EDIL
Karlsruhe [*Germany ICAO location identifier*] (ICLI) ... EDZK
Karlsruhe [*Federal Republic of Germany*] [*Seismograph station code, US Geological Survey*] (SEIS) ... KRL
Karlsruhe Architectural Language [*Computer science*] (CSR) ... KARL
Karlsruhe Charged Particle Group (NITA) ... KACHAPAG
Karlsruhe/Forchheim [*Germany ICAO location identifier*] (ICLI) ... EDTK
Karlsruhe Isochronous Cyclotron ... KIC
Karlsruhe - West [*Federal Republic of Germany*] [*Seismograph station code, US Geological Survey*] (SEIS) ... KRW
Karlstad [*Sweden ICAO location identifier*] (ICLI) ... ESSQ
Karlstad [*Sweden*] [*Airport symbol*] (OAG) ... KSD
Karlstad Elementary School, Karlstad, MN [*Library symbol*] [*Library of Congress*] (LCLS) ... MnKarE
Karluk [*Alaska*] [*Airport symbol*] (OAG) ... KYK
Karluk, AK [*Location identifier FAA*] (FAAL) ... KYK
Karluk Lake, AK [*Location identifier FAA*] (FAAL) ... KKL
Karma (ABBR) ... KRM
Karman Constant [*Physics*] ... KC
Karmann-Ghia [*Volkswagen model designation*] ... KG
Karmen Unit [*Medicine*] (MAE) ... KU
Karmic (ABBR) ... KRMC
Karnataka Watersheds Development ... KAWAD
Karntner Einheitsliste [*Carinthian Unity List*] [*Austria Political party*] (PPE) ... KEL
Karoi [*Zimbabwe*] [*ICAO location identifier*] (ICLI) ... FVKA
Karoi [*Zimbabwe*] [*Seismograph station code, US Geological Survey*] (SEIS) ... KRR
Karolinska Institutets Bibliotek och Informationscentral [*Karolinska Institute Library and Information Center*] [*Sweden Information service or system*] (IID) ... KIBIC
Karolinska Scales of Personality [*Medicine*] (DMAA) ... KSP
Karolus de Tocco [*Flourished, 13th century*] [*Authority cited in pre-1607 legal work*] (DSA) ... K
Karolus de Tocco [*Flourished, 13th century*] [*Authority cited in pre-1607 legal work*] (DSA) ... Ka
Karolus de Tocco [*Flourished, 13th century*] [*Authority cited in pre-1607 legal work*] (DSA) ... Kar
Karonga [*Malawi*] [*ICAO location identifier*] (ICLI) ... FWKA
Karonga [*Malawi*] [*Airport symbol*] (OAG) ... KGJ
Karpatair [*Hungary ICAO designator*] (FAAC) ... KPT
Karpathos [*Greece*] [*Airport symbol*] (OAG) ... AOK
Karpathos [*Greece*] [*ICAO location identifier*] (ICLI) ... LGKP
Karpeles Manuscript Library, Santa Barbara, CA [*Library symbol*] [*Library of Congress*] (LCLS) ... CStbK
Karr, Tuttle, Koch, Campbell, Mawer, Morrow, & Sax, Seattle, WA [*Library symbol*] [*Library of Congress*] (LCLS) ... WaSKTK
Karratha [*Australia ICAO location identifier*] (ICLI) ... APKA
Karratha [*Australia Seismograph station code, US Geological Survey Closed*] (SEIS) ... KAA
Karratha [*Australia Airport symbol*] (OAG) ... KTA
Karrington Health, Inc. [*NASDAQ symbol*] (SAG) ... KARR
Karrington Health, Inc. [*Associated Press*] (SAG) ... KarrHlth
Kars [*Turkey*] [*Airport symbol*] (AD) ... KAR
Kars [*Turkey ICAO location identifier*] (ICLI) ... LTCF
Karsamaki [*Finland ICAO location identifier*] (ICLI) ... EFKR
Karsanskaya [*Later, TFS*] [*Former USSR Geomagnetic observatory code*] ... KSI
Kart Industry Council ... KIC
Kart Marketing Association of America (EA) ... KMAA
Kartagener's Syndrome [*Medicine*] (DAVI) ... KS
Kartell Convent Blaetter (BJA) ... KCB
Kartell Convent Deutscher Studenten Juedischen Glaubens (BJA) ... KC
Kartell Zionistischer Verbindungen (BJA) ... KZV
Karuizawa [*Also, KRZ*] [*Japan*] [*Seismograph station code, US Geological Survey*] (SEIS) ... KAZ
Karuizawa [*Japan*] [*Also, KAZ*] [*Seismograph station code, US Geological Survey*] (SEIS) ... KRZ
Karumba [*Australia Airport symbol*] (OAG) ... KRB
Karuna Trust [*Multinational association based in England*] (EAIO) ... KT
Karup [*Denmark ICAO location identifier*] (ICLI) ... EKKA
Karup [*Denmark ICAO location identifier*] (ICLI) ... EKMC
Karup [*Denmark ICAO location identifier*] (ICLI) ... EKMK
Karup [*Denmark*] [*Airport symbol*] (OAG) ... KRP
Karyawan Pegawai Negeri [*Indonesia*] ... KARPEN
Karyopyknotic Index [*Cytology*] (MAE) ... KI
Karyopyknotic Index [*Cytology*] ... KPI
Karyotype [*Clinical chemistry*] ... K
Karyotype Instability [*Genetics*] ... KI
Karyovirus-II (ECON) ... K-II
Kasaan, AK [*Location identifier FAA*] (FAAL) ... KXA
Kasaba Bay [*Zambia*] [*ICAO location identifier*] (ICLI) ... FLKY
Kasaba Bay [*Zambia*] [*Airport symbol*] (OAG) ... ZKB
Kasaji [*Zaire*] [*ICAO location identifier*] (ICLI) ... FZSJ
Kasama [*Zambia*] [*ICAO location identifier*] (ICLI) ... FLKS
Kasama [*Zambia*] [*Airport symbol*] (OAG) ... KAA
Kasane [*Botswana*] [*ICAO location identifier*] (ICLI) ... FBKE
Kasatuan Aksi Mahasiswa Indonesia [*Political party*] (BARN) ... KAMI
Kasatuan Aksi Peladjar Indonesia [*Political party*] (BARN) ... KAPI
Kaschechewan [*Canada*] [*Airport symbol*] (OAG) ... ZKE
Kaschin-Beck Disease [*Medicine*] ... KBD
Kasempa [*Zambia*] [*ICAO location identifier*] (ICLI) ... FLPA
Kasenga [*Zaire*] [*ICAO location identifier*] (ICLI) ... FZQG
Kasese [*Zaire*] [*ICAO location identifier*] (ICLI) ... FZOS
Kasese [*Uganda*] [*ICAO location identifier*] (ICLI) ... HUKS
Kasese [*Uganda*] [*Airport symbol*] (OAG) ... KSE
Kasese/Kaniama [*Zaire*] [*ICAO location identifier*] (ICLI) ... FZTS
Kash n Karry Food Stores, Inc. [*NASDAQ symbol*] (SAG) ... KASH
Kash n Karry Food Stores, Inc. [*Associated Press*] (SAG) ... KashrK
Kash n'Karry Food Stores [*NASDAQ symbol*] (TTSB) ... KASH
Kashan [*Iran*] [*ICAO location identifier*] (ICLI) ... OIFK
Kashechewan Band Library, Kashechewan, ON, Canada [*Library symbol*] [*Library of Congress*] (LCLS) ... CaOKasB

Kashechewan Band Library, Ontario [*Library symbol National Library of Canada*] (BIB) ... OKB
Kashi [*China*] [*Airport symbol*] (OAG) ... KHG
Kashi [*China*] [*ICAO location identifier*] (ICLI) ... ZWSH
Kashia [*Zaire*] [*ICAO location identifier*] (ICLI) ... FZWI
Kashima [*Japan*] [*Seismograph station code, US Geological Survey*] (SEIS) ... KSJ
Kashin-Bek Disease [*Medicine*] (DMAA) ... KB
Kashiwara [*Japan*] [*Seismograph station code, US Geological Survey*] (SEIS) ... KAJ
Kashmar [*Iran*] [*ICAO location identifier*] (ICLI) ... OIMQ
Kashmir (VRA) ... Kash
Kashmir Law Journal [*India*] [*A publication*] (DLA) ... Kashmir LJ
Kashmiri [*MARC language code Library of Congress*] (LCCP) ... kas
Kashrut Observance (BJA) ... KO
Kasigluk [*Alaska*] [*Airport symbol*] (OAG) ... KUK
Kaskada Resources Ltd. [*Vancouver Stock Exchange symbol*] ... KAS
Kaskaska Library System, Smithton, IL [*Library symbol Library of Congress*] (LCLS) ... ISmK
Kaskaskia Library System [*Library network*] ... KLS
Kaskaskia Library System, Smithton, IL [*OCLC symbol*] (OCLC) ... IFG
Kasler Corp. [*Associated Press*] (SAG) ... Kasler Holding Co.
Kasler Holdings [*NYSE symbol*] (SPSG) ... KAS
Kaslo, BC [*FM radio station call letters*] ... CKZX-1
Kaslo Public Library, British Columbia [*Library symbol National Library of Canada*] (NLC) ... BKASL
Kaslo Public Library, Kaslo, BC, Canada [*Library symbol*] [*Library of Congress*] (LCLS) ... CaBKASL
Kasompe [*Zambia*] [*ICAO location identifier*] (ICLI) ... FLKE
Kasongo [*Zaire*] [*ICAO location identifier*] (ICLI) ... FZOK
Kasongo [*Zaire*] [*ICAO location identifier*] (ICLI) ... FZUF
Kasongo [*Zaire*] [*Airport symbol*] (AD) ... KGO
Kasos [*Greece*] [*ICAO location identifier*] (ICLI) ... LGKS
Kasos Island [*Greece*] [*Airport symbol*] (OAG) ... KSJ
Kasperske Hory [*Czechoslovakia*] [*Seismograph station code, US Geological Survey*] (SEIS) ... KHC
Kassala [*Sudan*] [*ICAO location identifier*] (ICLI) ... HSKA
Kassala [*Sudan*] [*Airport symbol*] (OAG) ... KSL
Kassan Resources [*Vancouver Stock Exchange symbol*] ... KSN
Kassel [*Germany Airport symbol*] (OAG) ... KSF
Kassel/Calden [*Germany ICAO location identifier*] (ICLI) ... EDVK
Kassel-Mittelfeld [*Germany ICAO location identifier*] (ICLI) ... EDVM
Kassian Benevolent Society in America (EA) ... KBSA
Kassinin [*Biochemistry*] ... Kass
Kastamonu [*Turkey*] [*Seismograph station code, US Geological Survey*] (SEIS) ... KAS
Kastamonu [*Turkey*] [*Airport symbol*] (AD) ... KXU
Kastamonu [*Turkey ICAO location identifier*] (ICLI) ... LTAL
Kasteli [*Greece*] [*ICAO location identifier*] (ICLI) ... LGTL
Kastelorizo [*Greece*] [*ICAO location identifier*] (ICLI) ... LGKJ
Kastoria [*Greece*] [*Airport symbol*] (OAG) ... KSO
Kastoria [*Greece*] [*ICAO location identifier*] (ICLI) ... LGKA
Kasumigaura [*Japan ICAO location identifier*] (ICLI) ... RJAK
Kasuminome [*Japan ICAO location identifier*] (ICLI) ... RJSU
Kasungu/Kasungu [*Malawi*] [*ICAO location identifier*] (ICLI) ... FWKG
Kasungu/Lifupa [*Malawi*] [*ICAO location identifier*] (ICLI) ... FWLP
Katabatic Wind ... KW
Katadyn Pocket Filter ... KPF
Katako, Kombe [*Zaire*] [*ICAO location identifier*] (ICLI) ... FZVG
Katal [*Unit of enzyme activity*] ... kat
Katalog Kandidatskikh i Doktorskikh Dissertatsii [*A bibliographic publication*] ... KKDD
Katanda Sur Rutshuru [*Zaire*] [*ICAO location identifier*] (ICLI) ... FZNK
Katchenovsky's Prize Law [*2nd ed.*] [*1867*] [*A publication*] (DLA) ... Katch Pr Law
Kate Greenaway Society (EA) ... KGS
Katechetische Blaetter [*Berlin-Grunewald*] [*A publication*] (BJA) ... KatechBR
Katende [*Zaire*] [*ICAO location identifier*] (ICLI) ... FZIK
Kateri Mission School, Grande Prairie, Alberta [*Library symbol National Library of Canada*] (BIB) ... AGPKS
Katete [*Zambia*] [*ICAO location identifier*] (ICLI) ... FLAT
Katherine [*Northern Territory, Australia*] [*Airport symbol*] (AD) ... KTR
Kathiawar Law Reports [*India*] [*A publication*] (DLA) ... KLR
Kathmandu [*Nepal*] [*ICAO location identifier*] (ICLI) ... VNSM
Kathmandu/International [*Nepal*] [*ICAO location identifier*] (ICLI) ... VNKT
Kathodal Closing [*Medicine*] ... KC
Kathodal Closing Contraction [*Medicine*] (DAVI) ... KSC
Kathodal Closing Tetanus [*Medicine*] ... KCT
Kathodal Closure Contraction [*Medicine*] ... KCC
Kathodal Closure Tetanus [*Medicine*] ... KCTE
Kathodal Duration [*Medicine*] ... KD
Kathodal Duration Contraction [*Medicine*] ... KDC
Kathodal Duration Tetanus [*Medicine*] ... KDT
Kathodal Duration Tetanus [*Medicine*] (ROG) ... KDTE
Kathodal Opening Contraction [*Medicine*] ... KOC
Kathode [*Cathode*] ... K
Kathode [*Cathode*] (AAG) ... KA
Kathode Dark Space ... KDS
Kathode Flicker Effect ... KFE
Kathode Heating Time ... KHT
Kathode Pulse Modulation ... KPM
Kathode Ray Furnace ... KRF
Kathode Ray Lamp ... KRL
Kathode Ray Oscilloscope ... KRO
Kathode Ray Tube (AAG) ... KRT
Kathode Ray Tube Oscillograph ... KRTO
Kathode Ray Tube Shield ... KRTS
Kathode Ray Tube Tester ... KRTT
Kathodenschilessungs-Tetanus [*or Kathodal closing tetanus*] [*Medicine*] (DAVI) ... KST
Kathodenschliessungs-Kontaktion [*or kathodal closing contraction*] [*Medicine*] (DAVI) ... KSK
Katholieke Arbeidersbeweging [*Netherlands*] ... KAB
Katholieke Film-Centrale [*Netherlands*] ... KFC
Katholieke Nationale Partij [*Catholic National Party*] [*Netherlands Political party*] (PPE) ... KNP
Katholieke Radio Omroep [*Catholic Broadcasting Association*] [*Netherlands*] ... KRO
Katholieke Volkspartij [*Catholic People's Party*] [*Netherlands Political party*] (PPE) ... KVP
Katholische Nachrichten-Agentur [*Catholic Press Agency*] [*Germany*] ... KNA
Katholische Welt-Bibelfoderation [*World Catholic Federation for the Biblical Apostolate - WCFBA*] (EAIO) ... KWBF
Katholisk Nederlands Persbureau [*Catholic Netherlands Press Agency*] [*Netherlands*] ... KNP
Kathy Lynn Sacra International Fan Club (EA) ... KLSIFC
Katihar [*India*] [*ICAO location identifier*] (ICLI) ... VEKH
Katipunang Manggagawang Pilipino [*Trade Union Congress of the Philippines*] (EY) ... KMP-TUCP
Katlanovo [*Yugoslavia*] [*Seismograph station code, US Geological Survey*] (SEIS) ... KAY
Katmai [*Alaska*] [*Seismograph station code, US Geological Survey*] (SEIS) ... KTM
Katmai National Monument ... KATM
Katmandu [*Nepal*] [*Airport symbol*] (OAG) ... KTM
Kato [*Guyana*] [*Airport symbol*] (OAG) ... KTO
Kato (Karto) [*Guyana*] [*ICAO location identifier*] (ICLI) ... SYKT
Katonah Village Library, Katonah, NY [*Library symbol Library of Congress*] (LCLS) ... NKa
Katoptric System [*Optics*] ... KS
Katorikku Shingaku [*Catholic Theology*] [*Tokyo*] [*A publication*] (BJA) ... KatShing
Katowice [*Poland*] [*Airport symbol*] (OAG) ... KTW
Katrineholm [*Sweden ICAO location identifier*] (ICLI) ... ESVK
Kattegat Air, AS [*Denmark ICAO designator*] (FAAC) ... KAT
Katten, Munchin & Zavis, Pearl, Greenburger & Galler, Chicago, IL [*Library symbol*] [*Library of Congress*] (LCLS) ... ICKMZ
Kattoo [*Ship's rigging*] (ROG) ... KO
Katubsanan sa Mamumio [*Philippine United Labor Congress*] ... KSM
Katubwe [*Zaire*] [*ICAO location identifier*] (ICLI) ... FZUT
Katumbi [*Malawi*] [*ICAO location identifier*] (ICLI) ... FWKB
Katuura [*Japan*] [*Seismograph station code, US Geological Survey Closed*] (SEIS) ... KTR
Katuura [*Japan*] [*Later, HTY*] [*Geomagnetic observatory code*] ... KTR
Katwe [*Zaire*] [*ICAO location identifier*] (ICLI) ... FZQH
Katy Indus [*NYSE symbol*] (TTSB) ... KT
Katy Industries, Inc. [*Formerly, Missour-Kansas-Texas R.R. Co., with Wall Street slang name of "Kathy"*] [*Associated Press*] (SAG) ... KatyInd
Katy Industries, Inc. [*Formerly, Missouri-Kansas-Texas R. R. Co., with Wall Street slang name of "Kathy"*] [*NYSE symbol*] (SPSG) ... KT
Katy, TX [*Television station call letters*] ... KNWS-TV
Katydid (ABBR) ... KTYD
Katz Adjustment Scales [*Psychology*] ... KAS
Katz Digital Technologies [*NASDAQ symbol*] (TTSB) ... KATC
Katz Digital Technologies, Inc. [*NASDAQ symbol*] (SAG) ... KATC
Katz Digital Technologies, Inc. [*Associated Press*] (SAG) ... KatzDig
Katz Media [*AMEX symbol*] (TTSB) ... KTZ
Katz Media Group, Inc. [*Associated Press*] (SAG) ... KatzM
Katz Media Group, Inc. [*AMEX symbol*] (SAG) ... KTZ
Katzman Automatic Imaging Telescope [*University of California*] ... KAIT
Kauai Public Library Association, Linhue, HI [*Library symbol Library of Congress*] (LCLS) ... HLK
Kauai Test Facility [*AEC*] ... KTF
Kaufbeuren [*Germany ICAO location identifier*] (ICLI) ... EDSK
Kaufel Group Ltd. [*Toronto Stock Exchange symbol*] ... KGL
Kaufhaus des Westens [*Department Store of the West*] [*Germany*] ... KaDeWe
Kaufman & Broad Home [*NYSE symbol*] (TTSB) ... KBH
Kaufman & Broad Home Corp. [*Associated Press*] (SAG) ... KaufBH
Kaufman & Broad Home Corp. [*NYSE symbol*] (SPSG) ... KBH
Kaufman & Broad Home Corp. [*Associated Press*] (SAG) ... KfBH
Kaufman & Broad, Inc. (MHDW) ... KB
Kaufman Assessment Battery for Children ... KABC
Kaufman Assessment Battery for Children [*Diagnostic assessment test*] (PAZ) ... K-ABC
Kaufman Developmental Scale [*Child development test*] ... KDS
Kaufman [*H. W.*] **Financial Group** [*Associated Press*] (SAG) ... KaufHW
Kaufman [*H. W.*] **Financial Group, Inc.** [*AMEX symbol*] (SPSG) ... HWK
Kaufman Infant and Preschool Scale [*Child development test*] [*Psychology*] ... KIPS
Kaufman Ion Thrustor ... KIT
Kaufman Test of Educational Achievement ... K-TEA
Kaufmann-Peterson Base [*Medicine*] (DMAA) ... KP
Kaufmann's Edition of Mackeldey's Civil Law [*A publication*] (DLA) ... Kauf Mack
Kaufmann's Edition of Mackeldey's Civil Law [*A publication*] (DLA) ... Kaufm Mackeld Civ Law
Kauhajoki [*Finland ICAO location identifier*] (ICLI) ... EFKJ
Kauhava [*Finland ICAO location identifier*] (ICLI) ... EFKA
Kauhava [*Finland*] [*Airport symbol*] (AD) ... KAU
Kaukauna Public Library, Kaukauna, WI [*Library symbol Library of Congress*] (LCLS) ... WKa
Kaukauna, WI [*FM radio station call letters*] ... WKFX
Kaukauna, WI [*FM radio station call letters*] (RBYB) ... WOGB-FM
Kaukauna, WI [*AM radio station call letters*] ... WSGC
Kaukura [*French Polynesia*] [*Airport symbol*] (OAG) ... KKR

Kaukura [French Polynesia] [ICAO location identifier] (ICLI) .... NTGK
Kaum-Tani Persatuan Indonesia [Indonesian Farmers' Party] [Surinam]
  [Political party] (PPW) .... KTPI
Kaunakakai, HI [Location identifier FAA] (FAAL) .... MKK
Kauppakorkeakoulu [Helsinki School of Economics], Helsinki, Finland [Library
  symbol Library of Congress] (LCLS) .... FiHK
Kauri-Butanol Value [Measure of relative solvent power] .... KB
Kautokeino [Norway ICAO location identifier] (ICLI) .... ENKA
Kavak [Turkey] [Seismograph station code, US Geological Survey] (SEIS) .... KVT
Kavala [Greece] [Airport symbol] (OAG) .... KVA
Kavala/Amigdhaleon [Greece] [ICAO location identifier] (ICLI) .... LGKM
Kavala/Khrisoupolis [Greece] [ICAO location identifier] (ICLI) .... LGKV
Kavanayen, Bolivar [Venezuela ICAO location identifier] (ICLI) .... SVKA
Kavieng [New Ireland] [Seismograph station code, US Geological Survey
  Closed] (SEIS) .... KAV
Kavieng [Papua New Guinea] [Airport symbol] (OAG) .... KVG
Kavieng [Papua New Guinea] [Seismograph station code, US Geological
  Survey] (SEIS) .... KVG
Kavieng [New Ireland] [Airport symbol] (AD) .... KVG
Kavik River, AK [Location identifier FAA] (FAAL) .... VIK
Kavouras, Inc. [ICAO designator] (FAAC) .... XKA
Kawah Idjen [Java] [Seismograph station code, US Geological Survey
  Closed] (SEIS) .... KIJ
Kawaihae, HI [FM radio station call letters] .... KWYI
Kawambwa [Zambia] [ICAO location identifier] (ICLI) .... FLKB
Kawasaki Automatic Power-Drive System [Kawasaki Motors Corp.] .... KAPS
Kawasaki Disease [Also, KS, MLNS] [Medicine] .... KD
Kawasaki Heavy Industries Ltd. [Japan ICAO aircraft manufacturer identifier]
  (ICAO) .... KH
Kawasaki Syndrome [Also, KD, MLNS] .... KS
Kawau Island [New Zealand] [Airport symbol] (AD) .... KWU
Kaweah Delta District Hospital, Visalia, CA [Library symbol Library of
  Congress] (LCLS) .... CViKD
Kawthaung [Myanmar] [Airport symbol] (OAG) .... KAW
Kawthaung [Myanmar] [ICAO location identifier] (ICLI) .... VBVP
Kay and Johnson's English Vice-Chancellors' Reports [69, 70 English
  Reprint] [A publication] (DLA) .... K & J
Kay and Johnson's English Vice-Chancellors' Reports [69, 70 English
  Reprint] [A publication] (DLA) .... Kay & J
Kay and Johnson's English Vice-Chancellors' Reports [69, 70 English
  Reprint] [A publication] (DLA) .... Kay & J (Eng)
Kay and Johnson's English Vice-Chancellors' Reports [69, 70 English
  Reprint] [A publication] (DLA) .... Kay & John
Kay and Johnson's English Vice-Chancellors' Reports [69, 70 English
  Reprint] [A publication] (DLA) .... Kay & Johns
Kay Kotts Assoc [NASDAQ symbol] (TTSB) .... KTAX
Kay. Shipmasters, and Seamen [2nd ed.] [1894] [A publication] (DLA) .... Kay Ship
Kaya [Burkina Faso] [ICAO location identifier] (ICLI) .... DHCA
Kayaba Industry Co. [Auto industry supplier] .... KYB
Kayak .... K
Kayak (ABBR) .... KYK
Kayak, Four Person (ADA) K4
Kayak Island [Alaska] [Seismograph station code, US Geological Survey]
  (SEIS) .... KYK
Kayak, Single Person (ADA) K1
Kayak, Two Person (ADA) K2
Kaydon Corp. [Associated Press] (SAG) .... Kaydon
Kaydon Corp. [NYSE symbol] (SAG) .... KDN
Kaye Group [NASDAQ symbol] (TTSB) .... KAYE
Kaye Group, Inc. [NASDAQ symbol] (SAG) .... KAYE
Kaye Group, Inc. [Associated Press] (SAG) .... KayeGrp
Kaye Kotts Assoc Wrrt [NASDAQ symbol] (TTSB) .... KTAXW
Kaye Kotts Associates, Inc. [Associated Press] (SAG) .... KayeK
Kaye Kotts Associates, Inc. [NASDAQ symbol] (SAG) .... KTAX
Kaye Kotts Associates, Inc. [Associated Press] (SAG) .... KyeKtts
Kayenta, AZ [Location identifier FAA] (FAAL) .... PBY
Kayes [Mali] [ICAO location identifier] (ICLI) .... GAKY
Kayes [Mali] [Airport symbol] (OAG) .... KYS
Kay's English Vice-Chancellors' Reports [69 English Reprint]
  [A publication] (DLA) .... Kay
Kay's English Vice-Chancellors' Reports [69 English Reprint]
  [A publication] (DLA) .... Kay (Eng)
Kayser .... K
Kayser [Surinam] [ICAO location identifier] (ICLI) .... SMKE
Kayser-Fleischer Ring [Medicine] (DMAA) .... KFR
Kayseri [Turkey] [Airport symbol] (OAG) .... ASR
Kayseri [Turkey] [Airport symbol] (AD) .... KYZ
Kayseri [Turkey ICAO location identifier] (ICLI) .... LTAM
Kayseri/Erkilet [Turkey ICAO location identifier] (ICLI) .... LTAU
Kazakh [MARC language code Library of Congress] (LCCP) .... kaz
Kazakh Soviet Socialist Republic [MARC geographic area code Library of
  Congress] (LCCP) .... e-ur-kz
Kazakh Soviet Socialist Republic .... KazSSR
Kazakh Soviet Socialist Republic [MARC country of publication code Library
  of Congress] (LCCP) .... e-ur-kz
Kazakhstan Airlines [ICAO designator] (FAAC) .... KAZAIR
Kazakhstan Airlines [ICAO designator] (FAAC) .... KZA
Kazan [Formerly, Kazanskaya] [Former USSR Geomagnetic observatory
  code] .... KNS
Kazan [Former USSR Airport symbol] (OAG) .... KZN
Kazan [Former USSR ICAO location identifier] (ICLI) .... UWKD
Kazan Aviation Institute .... KAI
Kazeroun [Iran] [ICAO location identifier] (ICLI) .... OISK
K-Band Circulator .... KBC
K-Band Feed .... KBF

K-Band Shuttle (SSD) .... KSH
K-Band Shuttle Forward (SSD) .... KSF
K-Band Shuttle Return (SSD) .... KSR
K-Band Simulation (SSD) .... K-SIM
K-Band, Single Access Forward (SSD) .... KSAF
K-Band, Single Access Return (SSD) .... KSAR
K-Band Waveguide Circulator .... KWC
KBK Capital [AMEX symbol] (TTSB) .... KBK
KBK Capital Corp. [AMEX symbol] (SAG) .... KBK
KBK Capital Corp. [Associated Press] (SAG) .... KBK Cap
KBK Capital Corp. [NASDAQ symbol] (SAG) .... KBKC
KCS Energy, Inc. [Formerly, KCS Group, Inc.] [NYSE symbol] (SPSG) .... KCS
KD Air Corp. [ICAO designator] (FAAC) .... KDC
KDD Engineering and Consulting Inc. (NITA) .... KEC
Kealakekua [Hawaii] [Seismograph station code, US Geological Survey
  Closed] (SEIS) .... KLK
Kealakekua, HI [FM radio station call letters] .... KAOY
Kealakekua, HI [AM radio station call letters] .... KKON
Kealakomo [Hawaii] [Seismograph station code, US Geological Survey
  Closed] (SEIS) .... KEA
Keamey, NE [FM radio station call letters] (RBYB) .... KLPR-FM
Keamy, AZ [FM radio station call letters] .... KZLZ
Kean College of New Jersey (GAGS) .... Kean C NJ
Kean College of New Jersey, Union, NJ [OCLC symbol] (OCLC) .... NJK
Kean College of New Jersey, Union, NJ [Library symbol Library of
  Congress] (LCLS) .... NjUN
Keanakolu [Hawaii] [Seismograph station code, US Geological Survey]
  (SEIS) .... KKU
Keane and Grant's English Registration Appeal Cases [1854-62]
  [A publication] (DLA) .... K & G
Keane and Grant's English Registration Appeal Cases [1854-62]
  [A publication] (DLA) .... K & Gr
Keane and Grant's English Registration Appeal Cases [1854-62]
  [A publication] (DLA) .... K & GRC
Keane and Grant's English Registration Appeal Cases [1854-62]
  [A publication] (DLA) .... Keane & Gr
Keane and Grant's English Registration Appeal Cases [1854-62]
  [A publication] (DLA) .... Keane & GRC
Keane, Inc. [AMEX symbol] (SPSG) .... KEA
Keane, Inc. [Associated Press] (SAG) .... Keane
Keansburg High School, Keansburg, NJ [Library symbol] [Library of
  Congress] (LCLS) .... NjKeHS
Kearfott Acceleration Integrating Gyroscope .... KAIG
Kearney [Nebraska] [Airport symbol] (OAG) .... EAR
Kearney and Area Public Library, Kearney, Ontario [Library symbol National
  Library of Canada] (NLC) .... OKEA
Kearney, NE [AM radio station call letters] .... KGFW
Kearney, NE [Television station call letters] .... KHGI
Kearney, NE [AM radio station call letters] .... KKPR
Kearney, NE [FM radio station call letters] .... KKPR-FM
Kearney, NE [FM radio station call letters] .... KQKY
Kearney, NE [FM radio station call letters] .... KRNY
Kearney, NE [FM radio station call letters] .... KSCV
Kearney Public Library, Kearney, NE [Library symbol Library of Congress]
  (LCLS) .... NbK
Kearney State College, Kearney, NE [OCLC symbol] (OCLC) .... KRS
Kearney State College, Kearney, NE [Library symbol Library of Congress]
  (LCLS) .... NbKS
Kearns, ON [Television station call letters] CFCL-2
Kearns, ON [Television station call letters] CITO-2
Kearns-Sayre Syndrome [Ophthalmology] .... KSS
Kearny Observer, Kearny, NJ [Library symbol Library of Congress] (LCLS).....NjKO
Kearny Public Library, Kearny, NJ [Library symbol Library of Congress]
  (LCLS) .... NjK
Keating, PA [Location identifier FAA] (FAAL) .... ETG
Keatinge's Family Settlements [1810] [A publication] (DLA) .... Keat Fam Sett
Keats-Shelley Association of America (EA) .... KSAA
Keats-Shelley Memorial Association [British] (DBA) .... K-SMA
Keavy, KY [FM radio station call letters] .... WVCT
Keban [Turkey] [Seismograph station code, US Geological Survey] (SEIS) ...... KEB
Kebar [Indonesia] [Airport symbol] (OAG) .... KEQ
Kebar [Indonesia] [ICAO location identifier] (ICLI) .... WASE
Keble College [Oxford University] (ROG) .... KEB COLL
Keble's English King's Bench Reports [83, 84 English Reprint]
  [A publication] (DLA) .... Keb
Keble's English King's Bench Reports [83, 84 English Reprint]
  [A publication] (DLA) .... Kebl
Keble's English King's Bench Reports [83, 84 English Reprint]
  [A publication] (DLA) .... Keble
Keble's English King's Bench Reports [83, 84 English Reprint]
  [A publication] (DLA) .... Keble (Eng)
Keble's Justice of the Peace [A publication] (DLA) .... Keb J
Keble's Statutes [A publication] (DLA) .... Keb Stat
Kechabta [Tunisia] [Seismograph station code, US Geological Survey]
  (SEIS) .... KCHT
Keck, Mahin, and Cate, Chicago, IL [Library symbol Library of Congress]
  (LCLS) .... ICKMC
Keck, Mahin & Cate, Chicago, IL [OCLC symbol] (OCLC) .... ILT
Kecskemet [Hungary] [Seismograph station code, US Geological Survey]
  (SEIS) .... KEC
Kedougou [Senegal] [ICAO location identifier] (ICLI) .... GOTK
Kedougou [Senegal] [Seismograph station code, US Geological Survey
  Closed] (SEIS) .... KDG
Kedougou [Senegal] [Seismograph station code, US Geological Survey]
  (SEIS) .... KDS

Kedougou [Senegal] [Seismograph station code, US Geological Survey Closed] (SEIS) .... KED
Kedougou [Senegal] [Airport symbol] (OAG) .... KGG
Keefer Resources, Inc. [Vancouver Stock Exchange symbol] .... KFR
Keekorok [Kenya] [ICAO location identifier] (ICLI) .... HKKE
Keel .... K
Keel (ROG) .... KL
Keel Bending (SSD) .... KB
Keel Blade Height [Botany] .... KBLH
Keel Blade Length [Botany] .... KBLL
Keel Blade Tip Reflex [Botany] .... KREX
Keel Depth Simulator .... KDS
Keel Shock Factor (NATG) .... KSF
Keel Torsion (SSD) .... KT
Keele Assessment of Auditory Style (DMAA) .... KAAS
Keeler, MI [Location identifier FAA] (FAAL) .... ELX
Keen Mountain [Virginia] [Seismograph station code, US Geological Survey Closed] (SEIS) .... KMV
Keen on the Job (ADA) .... KOJ
Keen on Waller [A coterie of women admirers of British stage actor, Lewis Waller (1860-1915)] (ROG) .... KOW
Keene [New Hampshire] [Airport symbol] (OAG) .... EEN
Keene, NH [Television station call letters] .... WEKW
Keene, NH [FM radio station call letters] .... WEVN
Keene, NH [AM radio station call letters] .... WKBK
Keene, NH [AM radio station call letters] .... WKNE
Keene, NH [FM radio station call letters] .... WKNE-FM
Keene, NH [FM radio station call letters] .... WKNH
Keene Public Library, Keene, NH [Library symbol Library of Congress] (LCLS) .... NhKe
Keene State College (GAGS) .... Keene St C
Keene State College, Keene, NH [OCLC symbol] (OCLC) .... KNM
Keene State College, Keene, NH [Library symbol Library of Congress] (LCLS) .... NhKeK
Keene, TX [FM radio station call letters] .... KJCR
Keeneland Association, Inc., Lexington, KY [Library symbol Library of Congress] (LCLS) .... KyLxK
Keener's Cases on Quasi Contracts [A publication] (DLA) .... Keener Quasi Contr
Keene's Cement Plaster [Technical drawings] .... KCP
Keene's Cement Plaster Ceiling [Technical drawings] .... KCPC
Keen's English Rolls Court Reports [48 English Reprint] [A publication] (DLA) .... Ke
Keen's English Rolls Court Reports [48 English Reprint] [A publication] (DLA) .... Keen
Keen's English Rolls Court Reports [48 English Reprint] [A publication] (DLA) .... Keen Ch
Keen's English Rolls Court Reports [48 English Reprint] [A publication] (DLA) .... Keen (Eng)
Keep America Beautiful (EA) .... KAB
Keep America Independent [Defunct] (EA) .... KAI
Keep Britain Tidy Group (DCTA) .... KBTG
Keep Buggering On [Perseverance] [Slang British] (DSUE) .... KBO
Keep Cost Order [Telecommunications] (TEL) .... KCO
Keep Fit Association [British] .... KFA
Keep Fit South Australia .... KFSA
Keep in Touch [Slang] (DNAB) .... KIT
Keep in View .... KIV
Keep It Dark [Say nothing about it] [Slang] .... KD
Keep It Short and Simple (MCD) .... KISS
Keep It Short and Sweet [Radio messages] .... KISS
Keep It Simple (ADA) .... KIS
Keep It Simple, Make It Fun .... KISMIF
Keep It Simple, Sir (SAA) .... KISS
Keep It Simple, Stupid [Bridge bidding term] .... KISS
Keep It Straight and Simple [Computer science] .... KISS
Keep Needle Open [Reference to intravenous fluid lines] (DAVI) .... KNO
Keep Off [i.e., avoid assuming the risk on an application, pending further investigation] [Insurance] .... KO
Keep Off Pounds Sensibly [Club] .... KOPS
Keep On [Continue] [Medicine] (DAVI) .... KO
Keep on Truckin' News [A publication] (EAAP) .... KOTN
Keep Open [Medicine] .... K/O
Keep Out of Reach of Children (DI) .... KOROC
Keep That Local Area Network Simple, Stupid [Telecommunications] .... KLANSS
Keep This Office Advised .... KEPOA
Keep Type Standing [Printing] .... KS
Keep Up [Typography] (DGA) .... KU
Keep Up the Good Work .... KUTGW
Keep Up to Date (KSC) .... KUTD
Keep Vein Open [Medicine] .... KVO
Keep Vein Open Cum [with] Dextrose 5% in Water [Pharmacology] (DAVI) .... KVO C D5W
Keep Your Mouth Shut .... KYMS
Keep-Alive Anode .... KAA
Keep-Alive Memory [Computer science] .... KAM
Keeper (ABBR) .... KPR
Keeper of the Privy Purse [British] .... KPP
Keephills Community Library, Alberta [Library symbol National Library of Canada] (NLC) .... AKEC
Keeping .... KPG
Keeping House of Ill Fame .... KHIF
Keeping the Army in the Public Eye [British military] (DMA) .... KAPE
Keeprite, Inc. [Toronto Stock Exchange symbol] .... KPT
Keepsake (ABBR) .... KPSK
Keeshond Club of America (EA) .... KCA

Keesings Contemporary Archives [A publication Also, an information service or system] .... KCA
Keesler Air Force Base [Mississippi] .... KAFB
Keesler Technical Training Center .... KTTC
Keesom Relationship .... KR
Keethanou School/Public Library, Stanley Mission, Saskatchewan [Library symbol National Library of Canada] (BIB) .... SSK
Keetmanshoop [South-West Africa] [Airport symbol] (OAG) .... KMP
Keetmanshoop/J. G. H. Van Der Wath [Namibia] [ICAO location identifier] (ICLI) .... FAKT
Keewatin Community College, The Pas, Manitoba [Library symbol National Library of Canada] (NLC) .... MTPK
Keewatin Community College, The Pas, MB, Canada [Library symbol Library of Congress] (LCLS) .... CaMTPK
Keewatin, Norman, and Rat Portage [Communities that merged to form town in Ontario, Canada] .... Kenora
Keewatin Public Library, Keewatin, MN [Library symbol] [Library of Congress] (LCLS) .... MnKee
Keewatin Public Library, Ontario [Library symbol National Library of Canada] (NLC) .... OKEE
Kefallinia [Greece] [ICAO location identifier] (ICLI) .... LGKF
Keflavik [Iceland] [ICAO location identifier] (ICLI) .... BIKF
Keflavik [Iceland] [Airport symbol] (AD) .... KEF
Keflin, Gentamicin, and Carbenicillin [Antibiotics] (DAVI) .... KGC
Keg .... K
Keg .... KG
Keg Restaurants Ltd. [Toronto Stock Exchange symbol Vancouver Stock Exchange symbol] .... KEG
Keg River Community Library, Alberta [Library symbol National Library of Canada] (NLC) .... AKC
Keg River Community Library, Keg River, AB, Canada [Library symbol Library of Congress] (LCLS) .... CaAKrC
Kegaska [Canada] [Airport symbol] (OAG) .... ZKG
Kegoayah Kozga Public Library, Nome, AK [Library symbol Library of Congress] (LCLS) .... AkN
Kehillath Anshe Mayriv (BJA) .... KAM
Kehr-Activated Sludge Process (PDAA) .... KASP
Keighley Central Library, Keighley, United Kingdom [Library symbol Library of Congress] (LCLS) .... UkK
Keil and Delitzsch Commentaries [A publication] (BJA) .... KDC
Keilinschriften und Geschichtsforschung [A publication] (BJA) .... KGF
Keilinschriftliche Bibliothek [Berlin] [A publication] (BJA) .... KB
Keilinschriftliche Bibliothek [A publication] (BJA) .... KiB
Keilinschriftliche Studien [A publication] (BJA) .... KST
Keillor House Museum, Dorchester, New Brunswick [Library symbol National Library of Canada] (NLC) .... NBDKH
Keilschrifttexte aus Assur Historischen Inhalts [A publication] (BJA) .... KAH
Keilschrifttexte aus Assur Historischen Inhalts [A publication] (BJA) .... KAHI
Keilschrifttexte aus Assur Juridischen Inhalts [A publication] (BJA) .... KAJ
Keilschrifttexte aus Assur Juridischen Inhalts [A publication] (BJA) .... KAJI
Keilschrifttexte aus Assur Religioesen Inhalts [A publication] (BJA) .... KAR
Keilschrifttexte aus Assur Religioesen Inhalts [A publication] (BJA) .... KARI
Keilschrifttexte aus Assur Verschiedenen Inhalts [A publication] (BJA) .... KAV
Keilschrifttexte aus Assur Verschiedenen Inhalts [A publication] (BJA) .... KAVI
Keilschrifttexte aus Boghazkoi [A publication] (BJA) .... KBo
Keilschrifttexte Medizinischen Inhalts [A publication] (BJA) .... KMI
Keilschrifturkunden aus Boghazkoi [A publication] (BJA) .... KUB
Keilway's English King's Bench Reports [72 English Reprint] [A publication] (DLA) .... Cro
Keilway's English King's Bench Reports [72 English Reprint] [A publication] (DLA) .... Croke
Keilway's English King's Bench Reports [72 English Reprint] [A publication] (DLA) .... Keil
Keilway's English King's Bench Reports [72 English Reprint] [A publication] (DLA) .... Keilw
Keilway's English King's Bench Reports [72 English Reprint] [A publication] (DLA) .... Keilw (Eng)
Keilway's English King's Bench Reports [72 English Reprint] [A publication] (DLA) .... Keilway
Keio University [EDUCATSS] [UTLAS symbol] .... KSL
Keio University, Tokyo, Japan [Library symbol Library of Congress] (LCLS) .... JTKU
Keith Keating Society for the Arts [Defunct] (EA) .... KKSA
Keith Martin Ballet Oregon .... KMBO
Keith Railway Equipment Co. [AAR code] .... KTX
Keith Sewell Fan Club (EA) .... KSFC
Keith, Wagener, Barker [Ophthalmology] .... KWB
Keithley Instruments [NYSE symbol] (TTSB) .... KEI
Keithley Instruments, Inc. [AMEX symbol] (SPSG) .... KEI
Keithley Instruments, Inc. [Associated Press] (SAG) .... Keithly
Keith-Wagener [Ophthalmology] .... KW
Keith-Welti-Ernst [Method] [Radiology] (DAVI) .... KWE
Keizer, OR [AM radio station call letters] .... KYKN
Kekaha, HI [Location identifier FAA] (FAAL) .... BKH
Kekaha, HI [FM radio station call letters] .... KAUI
Kekaha, Kauai, HI [Location identifier FAA] (FAAL) .... NBS
Kelafo [Ethiopia] [ICAO location identifier] (ICLI) .... HAKL
Kelan Resources [Vancouver Stock Exchange symbol] .... KLN
Kelardasht [Iran] [ICAO location identifier] (ICLI) .... OINQ
Kelco Co. [Research code symbol] .... B
Keld'Or Resources, Inc. [Vancouver Stock Exchange symbol] .... KEO
Kele/Kibangou [Congo] [ICAO location identifier] .... FCMK
Keleket X-Ray Corp. .... KXC
Keles [Later, TKT] [Former USSR Geomagnetic observatory code] .... KEL
Kelham's Norman French Law Dictionary [A publication] (DLA) .... Kelh

Kelham's Norman French Law Dictionary [*A publication*] (DLA) .... Kelh Dict
Kelham's Norman French Law Dictionary [*A publication*] (DLA) .... Kelham
Kelibia [*Tunisia*] [*ICAO location identifier*] (ICLI) .... DTTL
Kelim (BJA) .... Kel
Kelke's Judicature Acts [*A publication*] (DLA) .... Kelk Jud Acts
Kell [*Blood group*] .... K
Kell Factor (DMAA) .... K
Kell Negative [*Hematology*] (DAVI) .... KELN
Kelle [*Congo*] [*ICAO location identifier*] (ICLI) .... FCOK
Kelle [*Congo*] [*Airport symbol*] (OAG) .... KEE
Kellen's Reports [*146-55 Massachusetts*] [*A publication*] (DLA) .... Kellen
Keller, N. L., Washington DC [*STAC*] .... KNL
Keller, Rohrback, Law Library, Seattle, WA [*Library symbol*] [*Library of Congress*] (LCLS) .... WaSKR
Keller-Dorian, Berthon [*Method*] [*Photography*] .... KDB
Keller's Language [*1977*] [*Computer science*] (CSR) .... KL
Kelley Memorial Library, Salem, NH [*Library symbol Library of Congress*] (LCLS) .... NhS
Kelley Oil and Gas Corp. [*Associated Press*] (SAG) .... KellOG
Kelley Oil and Gas Corp. [*NASDAQ symbol*] (SAG) .... KOGC
Kelley-Kerr Energy [*Vancouver Stock Exchange symbol*] .... KYK
Kelli Warren Fan Club [*Defunct*] (EA) .... KWFC
Kellner Eye Piece .... KEP
Kellogg [*Idaho*] [*Seismograph station code, US Geological Survey*] (SEIS) .... KGI
Kellogg Biological Station [*Michigan State University*] .... KBS
Kellogg Community College, Battle Creek, MI [*OCLC symbol*] (OCLC) .... EEK
Kellogg Community College, Battle Creek, MI [*Library symbol Library of Congress*] (LCLS) .... MiBatK
Kellogg Co. [*NYSE symbol*] (SPSG) .... K
Kellogg Co. [*Associated Press*] (SAG) .... Kellogg
Kellogg National Fellowship Program .... KNFP
Kellogg Public Library, Kellogg, ID [*Library symbol*] [*Library of Congress*] (LCLS) .... IdKe
Kellogg Switchboard and Supply .... KSS
Kellogg Telecommunications Corp. [*Littleton, CO*] [*Telecommunications*] (TSSD) .... KTC
Kellstrom Inds Wrrt [*NASDAQ symbol*] (TTSB) .... KELLW
Kellstrom Industries [*NASDAQ symbol*] (TTSB) .... KELL
Kellstrom Industries, Inc. [*NASDAQ symbol*] (SAG) .... KELL
Kellstrom Industries, Inc. [*Associated Press*] (SAG) .... Kelstr
Kellstrom Industries, Inc. [*Associated Press*] (SAG) .... Kelstrm
Kellwood Co. [*Associated Press*] (SAG) .... Kellwood
Kellwood Co. [*NYSE symbol*] (SPSG) .... KWD
Kelly and Cobb's Reports [*4, 5 Georgia*] [*A publication*] (DLA) .... Kelly & C
Kelly and Cobb's Reports [*4, 5 Georgia*] [*A publication*] (DLA) .... Kelly & Cobb
Kelly Bushing [*Drilling*] (DICI) .... KB
Kelly, Douglas & Co. Ltd. [*Toronto Stock Exchange symbol*] .... KLD
Kelly on Contracts of Married Women [*A publication*] (DLA) .... Kel Cont
Kelly on Life Annuities [*A publication*] (DLA) .... Kel Life Ann
Kelly on Usury [*1835*] [*A publication*] (DLA) .... Kel Us
Kelly Russell Studios, Inc. [*Associated Press*] (SAG) .... KellyRus
Kelly Russell Studios, Inc. [*NASDAQ symbol*] (SAG) .... KRSI
Kelly Services, Inc. [*Associated Press*] (SAG) .... KellyS
Kelly Services, Inc. [*NASDAQ symbol*] (NQ) .... KELY
Kelly Services'A' [*NASDAQ symbol*] (TTSB) .... KELYA
Kelly Services'B' [*NASDAQ symbol*] (TTSB) .... KELYB
Kelly's Creek & Northwestern Railroad Co. [*AAR code*] .... KCNW
Kelly's Draftsman [*14th ed.*] [*1978*] [*A publication*] (DLA) .... Kel Draft
Kelly's Life Annuities [*1835*] [*A publication*] (DLA) .... Kel An
Kelly's Reports [*1-3 Georgia*] [*A publication*] (DLA) .... Kel GA
Kelly's Reports [*1-3 Georgia*] [*A publication*] (DLA) .... Kelly
Kelly's Scire Facias [*2nd ed.*] [*1849*] [*A publication*] (DLA) .... Kel Sc Fac
Kelly-Springfield Tire Co. .... KS
Kelman Phakoemulsification [*Ophthalmology*] (DAVI) .... KPE
Kelowna [*Canada*] [*Airport symbol*] (OAG) .... YLW
Kelowna, BC [*FM radio station call letters*] .... CBTK
Kelowna, BC [*Television station call letters*] .... CHBC
Kelowna, BC [*Television station call letters*] .... CHKL
Kelowna, BC [*FM radio station call letters*] .... CILK
Kelowna, BC [*FM radio station call letters*] (RBYB) .... CKBL
Kelowna, BC [*AM radio station call letters*] .... CKIQ
Kelowna, BC [*FM radio station call letters*] .... CKLZ
Kelowna, BC [*AM radio station call letters*] .... CKOV
Kelowna, BC [*ICAO location identifier*] (ICLI) .... CYLW
Kelowna Centennial Museum and Archives, British Columbia [*Library symbol National Library of Canada*] (NLC) .... BKOM
Kelowna Centennial Museum and Archives, Kelowna, BC, Canada [*Library symbol Library of Congress*] (LCLS) .... CaBKOM
Kelowna Flightcraft Air Charter Ltd. [*Canada ICAO designator*] (FAAC) .... KFA
Kelp [*Quality of the Bottom*] [*Nautical charts*] .... K
Kelsey Institute of Applied Arts and Sciences, Library Technician Program, Saskatoon,SK, Canada [*Library symbol*] [*Library of Congress*] (LCLS) .... CaSSKIL
Kelsey Institute of Applied Arts and Sciences, Saskatoon, Saskatchewan [*Library symbol National Library of Canada*] (NLC) .... SSSI
Kelsey Institute of Applied Arts and Sciences, Saskatoon, SK, Canada [*Library symbol Library of Congress*] (LCLS) .... CaSSSI
Kelsey-Hayes Canada Ltd. [*Toronto Stock Exchange symbol*] .... KEL
Kelseyville Free Library, Kelseyville, CA [*Library symbol Library of Congress*] (LCLS) .... CKel
Kelso Public Library, Kelso, WA [*Library symbol Library of Congress*] (LCLS) .... WaKel
Kelso Resources [*Vancouver Stock Exchange symbol*] .... KLS
Kelso, WA [*AM radio station call letters*] .... KLOG
Kelso, WA [*Location identifier FAA*] (FAAL) .... KLS
Kelso, WA [*FM radio station call letters*] .... KUKN
Kelso, WA [*Location identifier FAA*] (FAAL) .... LSO
Keltic, Inc. [*Toronto Stock Exchange symbol*] .... KTN
Keltic Society and the College of Druidism (EA) .... KS
Keluang [*Indonesia*] [*ICAO location identifier*] (ICLI) .... WIPV
Kelud [*Java*] [*Seismograph station code, US Geological Survey Closed*] (SEIS) .... KEL
Kelvin [*Symbol*] [*SI unit of thermodynamic temperature*] .... K
Kelvin Astatic Galvanometer [*Electronics*] .... KAG
Kelvin Circulation Theorem [*Physics*] .... KCT
Kelvin Double Bridge [*Physics*] .... KDB
Kelvin High School, Winnipeg, Manitoba [*Library symbol National Library of Canada*] (NLC) .... MWK
Kelvin High School, Winnipeg, MB, Canada [*Library symbol Library of Congress*] (LCLS) .... CaMWK
Kelvin Law [*Physics*] .... KL
Kelvin Square Meters per Watt .... K M^2/W
Kelvin Temperature Scale .... KTS
Kelvin-Helmholtz [*Waves*] [*Meteorology*] .... KH
Kelvin-Helmholtz Instability (PDAA) .... KHI
Kelvin-Varley Slide [*Electronics*] .... KVS
Ke-Macina [*Mali*] [*ICAO location identifier*] (ICLI) .... GAKM
Kemble [*British ICAO location identifier*] (ICLI) .... EGDK
Kemble's The Saxons in England [*A publication*] (DLA) .... Kemble Sax
Kemet Corp. [*Associated Press*] (SAG) .... Kemet
Kemet Corp. [*NASDAQ symbol*] (SAG) .... KMET
Kemgas Sydney, Inc. [*Vancouver Stock Exchange symbol*] .... KSI
Kemi [*Finland ICAO location identifier*] (ICLI) .... EFKE
Kemi [*Finland*] [*Airport symbol*] (OAG) .... KEM
Kemijarvi [*Finland ICAO location identifier*] (ICLI) .... EFKM
Kemmerer, WY [*Location identifier FAA*] (FAAL) .... EMM
Kemmerer, WY [*FM radio station call letters*] (RBYB) .... KAOX-FM
Kemmerer, WY [*AM radio station call letters*] .... KMER
Kemp Memorial Library, Ellerbe, NC [*Library symbol Library of Congress*] (LCLS) .... NcEl
Kemp Public Library, Wichita Falls, TX [*Library symbol Library of Congress*] (LCLS) .... TxWic
Kempa [*Zaire*] [*ICAO location identifier*] (ICLI) .... FZBG
Kemper Corp. [*NYSE symbol*] (SPSG) .... KEM
Kemper Corp. (MHDW) .... KEMC
Kemper Corp. [*Associated Press*] (SAG) .... Kemper
Kemper High Income [*NYSE symbol*] (SPSG) .... KHI
Kemper High Income Trust [*Associated Press*] (SAG) .... KmpHi
Kemper Interm Gvt Tr [*NYSE symbol*] (TTSB) .... KGT
Kemper Intermediate Government Trust [*NYSE symbol*] (SPSG) .... KGT
Kemper Intermediate Government Trust [*Associated Press*] (SAG) .... KmpIGv
Kemper Multi-Market Income [*NYSE symbol*] (SPSG) .... KMM
Kemper Multi-Market Income Trust [*Associated Press*] (SAG) .... KmpMI
Kemper Muni Income [*NYSE symbol*] (TTSB) .... KTF
Kemper Municipal Income Fund [*Associated Press*] (SAG) .... KmpMu
Kemper Municipal Income Fund [*NYSE symbol*] (CTT) .... KTF
Kemper Strategic Income [*AMEX symbol*] (TTSB) .... KST
Kemper Strategic Income Fund [*Associated Press*] (SAG) .... KmpSInc
Kemper Strategic Income Fund [*NYSE symbol*] (SAG) .... KST
Kemper Strategic Muni Tr [*NYSE symbol*] (TTSB) .... KSM
Kemper Strategic Municipal Income Trust [*Associated Press*] (SAG) .... KmpStr
Kemper Strategic Municipal Trust [*NYSE symbol*] (SPSG) .... KSM
Kempili [*Zaire*] [*ICAO location identifier*] (ICLI) .... FZBV
Kempsey [*Australia Airport symbol*] (OAG) .... KPS
Kempten/Durach [*Germany ICAO location identifier*] (ICLI) .... EDMK
Kemptville College of Agricultural Technology [*Canada*] (ARC) .... KCAT
Kemptville College of Agricultural Technology, Ontario [*Library symbol National Library of Canada*] (BIB) .... OKEMC
Kemptville Public Library, Ontario [*Library symbol National Library of Canada*] (NLC) .... OKEM
Kenai [*Alaska*] [*Airport symbol*] (OAG) .... ENA
Kenai [*Alaska*] [*ICAO location identifier*] (ICLI) .... PAEN
Kenai, AK [*Location identifier FAA*] (FAAL) .... DRF
Kenai, AK [*Location identifier FAA*] (FAAL) .... ENA
Kenai, AK [*Location identifier FAA*] (FAAL) .... IWW
Kenai, AK [*FM radio station call letters*] (RBYB) .... KDLL
Kenai, AK [*FM radio station call letters*] .... KWHQ
Kenai, AK [*AM radio station call letters*] .... KZXX
Kenai Central High School, Kenai, AK [*Library symbol Library of Congress*] (LCLS) .... AkKeH
Kenai Community Library, Inc., Kenai, AK [*Library symbol Library of Congress*] (LCLS) .... AkKe
Kenai Historical, Inc., Fort Kenai Museum, Kenai, AK [*Library symbol Library of Congress*] (LCLS) .... AkKeHi
Kenai Peninsula Borough [*Alaska*] .... KPB
Kenai Peninsula Community College, Soldotna, AK [*Library symbol*] [*Library of Congress*] (LCLS) .... AkSolK
Kenai Peninsula Libraries, Kenai, AK [*Library symbol Library of Congress*] (LCLS) .... AkKeK
Kenan Transport [*NASDAQ symbol*] (TTSB) .... KTCO
Kenan Transportation Co. [*Associated Press*] (SAG) .... Kenan
Kenan Transportation Co. [*NASDAQ symbol*] (NQ) .... KTCO
Kenan's Reports [*76-91 North Carolina*] [*A publication*] (DLA) .... Kenan
Kenansville, NC [*Location identifier FAA*] (FAAL) .... DPL
Kenar Resources [*Vancouver Stock Exchange symbol*] .... KNA
Kendall [*Record label*] .... Ken
Kendall Airlines [*Australia ICAO designator*] (FAAC) .... KDA
Kendall College, Evanston, IL [*Library symbol*] [*Library of Congress*] (LCLS) .... IEK
Kendall High School Library, Kendall, NY [*OCLC symbol*] (OCLC) .... RWT

Kendall Whaling Museum, Sharon, MA [*Library symbol Library of Congress*] (LCLS) ... MShaK
Kendall Young Library, Webster City, IA [*Library symbol Library of Congress*] (LCLS) ... IaWec
Kendall's Compound E [*Cortisone*] ... KE
Kendallville, IN [*AM radio station call letters*] ... WAWK
Kendallville, IN [*FM radio station call letters*] ... WBTU
Kendallville News-Sun, Kendallville, IN [*Library symbol Library of Congress*] (LCLS) ... InKendNS
Kendallville Public Library, Kendallville, IN [*Library symbol Library of Congress*] (LCLS) ... InKend
Kendari [*Indonesia*] [*Airport symbol*] (OAG) ... KDI
Kendari/Wolter Monginsidi [*Indonesia*] [*ICAO location identifier*] (ICLI) ... WAAU
Kendell Airlines [*ICAO designator*] (AD) ... KD
Kendrick & Co. [*Telecommunications service*] (TSSD) ... KENCO
Kene Thao [*Laos*] [*ICAO location identifier*] (ICLI) ... VLKT
Kenedy, TX [*FM radio station call letters*] ... KTNR
Kenedy-Karnes City, TX [*AM radio station call letters*] ... KAML
Kenema [*Sierra Leone*] [*ICAO location identifier*] (ICLI) ... GFKE
Kenema [*Sierra Leone*] [*Airport symbol*] (OAG) ... KEN
Kenergy Resource Corp. [*Vancouver Stock Exchange symbol*] ... KNY
Kenetech Corp. [*Associated Press*] (SAG) ... Kenetech
Kenetech Corp. [*Associated Press*] (SAG) ... Kentch
Kenetech Corp. [*NASDAQ symbol*] (SAG) ... KWND
KENETECH Cp 8.25% Cv Dep Pfd [*NASDAQ symbol*] (TTSB) ... KWNDZ
Kengate Resources [*Vancouver Stock Exchange symbol*] ... KGR
Kenge [*Zaire*] [*ICAO location identifier*] (ICLI) ... FZCS
Kengtung [*Myanmar*] [*Airport symbol*] (OAG) ... KET
Kengtung [*Myanmar*] [*ICAO location identifier*] (ICLI) ... VBKG
Kenhardt [*South Africa*] [*ICAO location identifier*] (ICLI) ... FAKH
Kenieba [*Mali*] [*ICAO location identifier*] (ICLI) ... GAKA
Kenieba [*Mali*] [*Airport symbol*] (OAG) ... KNZ
Keningau [*Malaysia*] [*Airport symbol*] (OAG) ... KGU
Keningau [*Malaysia*] [*ICAO location identifier*] (ICLI) ... WBKG
Kenitra/Tourisme [*Morocco*] [*ICAO location identifier*] (ICLI) ... GMMY
Kenly Public Library, Kenly, NC [*Library symbol*] [*Library of Congress*] (LCLS) ... NcKn
Kenmore Mercy Hospital, Medical Library, Buffalo, NY [*Library symbol*] [*Library of Congress*] (LCLS) ... NBuKMH
Kenn Borek Air Ltd. [*Canada ICAO designator*] (FAAC) ... KBA
Kennametal, Inc. [*Associated Press*] (SAG) ... Kennmtl
Kennametal, Inc. [*NYSE symbol*] (SPSG) ... KMT
Kennebunk, ME [*Location identifier FAA*] (FAAL) ... ENE
Kennebunk, ME [*FM radio station call letters*] ... WBQQ
Kennebunkport, ME [*FM radio station call letters*] ... WQEZ
Kennecott Co. Railroad [*AAR code*] ... KENN
Kennecott Copper Corp., Ledgemont Laboratory, Lexington, MA [*Library symbol Library of Congress*] (LCLS) ... MLexK
Kennedy Approved Parts List [*NASA*] (KSC) ... KAPL
Kennedy Athletic Recreation and Social [*NASA*] (KSC) ... KARS
Kennedy Booster Assembly Contractor (MCD) ... KBAC
Kennedy Elementary School, Great Neck, NY [*Library symbol Library of Congress*] (LCLS) ... NGrnKE
Kennedy Elementary School, Grimshaw, Alberta [*Library symbol National Library of Canada*] (BIB) ... AGWKS
Kennedy Elementary School, St. Joseph, MN [*Library symbol*] [*Library of Congress*] (LCLS) ... MnStjoKE
Kennedy Institute of Ethics, Washington, DC [*OCLC symbol*] (OCLC) ... KIE
Kennedy International Airport [*New York*] [*Airport symbol*] ... JFK
Kennedy Inventory Management System [*NASA*] (SSD) ... KIMS
Kennedy on Courts-Martial [*A publication*] (DLA) ... Kenn C Mar
Kennedy on Juries [*A publication*] (DLA) ... Kenn Jur
Kennedy Operating Instructions [*NASA*] (KSC) ... KOI
Kennedy Program Directive [*NASA*] (NASA) ... KPD
Kennedy Resources [*Vancouver Stock Exchange symbol*] ... KDY
Kennedy Space Center [*NASA*] ... K
Kennedy Space Center [*NASA*] ... KSC
Kennedy Space Center Area Permit [*NASA*] (MCD) ... KSCAP
Kennedy Space Center Avionics Test Set [*NASA*] (NASA) ... KATS
Kennedy Space Center Data Management System [*NASA*] (NASA) ... KDMS
Kennedy Space Center/Unmanned Launch Operations [*NASA*] ... KSC/ULO
Kennedy Space Center - Western Test Range Operations Division [*NASA*] ... KSC-WTROD
Kennedy Wilson, Inc. [*Associated Press*] (SAG) ... KdyWils
Kennedy Wilson, Inc. [*NASDAQ symbol*] (SAG) ... KWIC
Kennedya Yellow Mosaic Virus [*Plant pathology*] ... KYMV
Kennedy-Heaviside Layer [*Electronics*] ... KHL
Kennedy-King College of the City College of Chicago, Chicago, IL [*OCLC symbol*] (OCLC) ... IAN
Kennedy-King College of the City College of Chicago, Chicago, IL [*Library symbol Library of Congress*] (LCLS) ... ICKK
Kennedy's Chancery Practice [*2nd ed.*] [*1852-53*] [*A publication*] (DLA) ... Kenn Ch
Kennedy's Chancery Practice [*2nd ed.*] [*1852-53*] [*A publication*] (DLA) ... Kenn Pr
Kennedy-Thorndike Experiment ... KTE
Kennel (ABBR) ... KNL
Kennel ... KNL
Kennel Club ... KC
Kenneled (ABBR) ... KNLD
Kenneling (ABBR) ... KNLG
Kenner-Fecal Medium [*Organic chemistry*] (DAVI) ... KF
Kennesaw College, Marietta, GA [*OCLC symbol*] (OCLC) ... GKJ
Kennesaw College, Marietta, GA [*Library symbol Library of Congress*] (LCLS) ... GMarK
Kennesaw Mountain National Battlefield Park ... KEMO
Kenneth Cole Productions, Inc. [*Associated Press*] (SAG) ... KCole
Kenneth Cole Productions, Inc. [*Associated Press*] (SAG) ... KColePd
Kenneth Cole Productions, Inc. [*NYSE symbol*] (SAG) ... KCP
Kenneth Cole Productions'A' [*NYSE symbol*] (TTSB) ... KCP
Kenneth E. Johnson Environmental and Energy Center [*University of Alabama in Huntsville*] [*Research center*] (RCD) ... JEEC
Kenneth J. Lane [*Jewelry designer*] ... KJL
Kennett, MO [*AM radio station call letters*] ... KBOA
Kennett, MO [*AM radio station call letters*] (RBYB) ... KOTC
Kennett, MO [*FM radio station call letters*] ... KTMO
Kennett, MO [*FM radio station call letters*] (RBYB) ... KXOQ
Kennett, MO [*Location identifier FAA*] (FAAL) ... TKX
Kennett upon Impropriations [*A publication*] (DLA) ... Kenn Imp
Kennett upon Impropriations [*A publication*] (DLA) ... Kennett
Kennett's Glossary [*A publication*] (DLA) ... Kenn Gloss
Kennett's Glossary [*A publication*] (DLA) ... Kennett
Kennett's Glossary [*A publication*] (DLA) ... Kennett Gloss
Kennett's Parochial Antiquities [*A publication*] (DLA) ... Kenn Par Antiq
Kennett's Parochial Antiquities [*A publication*] (DLA) ... Kennett Par Ant
Kennett's Parochial Antiquities [*A publication*] (DLA) ... Paroch Ant
Kennewick General Hospital, Kennewick, WA [*Library symbol*] [*Library of Congress*] (LCLS) ... WaKeH
Kennewick, WA [*AM radio station call letters*] ... KONA
Kennewick, WA [*FM radio station call letters*] ... KONA-FM
Kennewick, WA [*AM radio station call letters*] ... KTCR
Kennewick, WA [*FM radio station call letters*] ... KTCV
Kennewick, WA [*Television station call letters*] ... KVEW
Kennnedy Disease [*Medicine*] (DMAA) ... KD
Kenny Antcliff Fan Club (EA) ... KAFC
Kenny Dale Fan Club (EA) ... KDFC
Kenny Information Systems [*Database producer*] (IID) ... KIS
Kenny Rehabilitation Institute, Minneapolis, MN [*Library symbol Library of Congress*] (LCLS) ... MnMK
Kenny Roberts and Bettyanne Fan Club [*Defunct*] (EA) ... KRBFC
Kenora [*Canada*] [*Airport symbol*] (OAG) ... YQK
Kenora, ON [*FM radio station call letters*] ... CBQX
Kenora, ON [*Television station call letters*] ... CBWAT
Kenora, ON [*Television station call letters*] ... CJBN
Kenora, ON [*AM radio station call letters*] ... CJRL
Kenora, ON [*ICAO location identifier*] (ICLI) ... CYQK
Kenora Public Library, Kenora, ON, Canada [*Library symbol Library of Congress*] (LCLS) ... CaOKe
Kenora Public Library, Ontario [*Library symbol National Library of Canada*] (NLC) ... OKE
Kenosha County Historical Association, Kenosha, WI [*Library symbol Library of Congress*] (LCLS) ... WKenHi
Kenosha Memorial Hospital, Kenosha, WI [*Library symbol Library of Congress*] (LCLS) ... WKenM
Kenosha Public Library, Kenosha, WI [*OCLC symbol*] (OCLC) ... WIK
Kenosha, WI [*Location identifier FAA*] (FAAL) ... ENW
Kenosha, WI [*Location identifier FAA*] (FAAL) ... PKW
Kenosha, WI [*FM radio station call letters*] ... WGTD
Kenosha, WI [*Television station call letters*] ... WHKE
Kenosha, WI [*FM radio station call letters*] ... WIIL
Kenosha, WI [*AM radio station call letters*] ... WLIP
Kenova, WV [*AM radio station call letters*] ... WTCR
Kenrick & Jefferson (DGA) ... K & J
Kenridge Mineral [*Vancouver Stock Exchange symbol*] ... KEN
Kensal Press [*Publisher*] [*British*] ... K
Kensett Public Library, Kensett, IA [*Library symbol Library of Congress*] (LCLS) ... IaKen
Kensey Nash [*NASDAQ symbol*] (TTSB) ... KNSY
Kensey Nash Corp. [*Associated Press*] (SAG) ... KenseyN
Kensey Nash Corp. [*NASDAQ symbol*] (SAG) ... KNSY
Kensington [*West London*] (ROG) ... KENS
Kensington and Chelsea Law Group [*British*] ... K & CL
Kensington Palace [*British*] ... KP
Kensington Palace Gardens [*British interrogation center*] ... KPM
Kensington Public School, Kensington, MN [*Library symbol*] [*Library of Congress*] (LCLS) ... MnKenS
Kensington-Johnson Elementary School, Great Neck, NY [*Library symbol Library of Congress*] (LCLS) ... NGrnKJE
Kent and County of London Yeomanry [*Military unit*] [*British*] ... KCLY
Kent and Radcliff's Law of New York, Revision of 1801 [*A publication*] (DLA) ... K & R
Kent and Radcliff's Law of New York, Revision of 1801 [*A publication*] (DLA) ... Kent & R St
Kent Automated Serials System [*Kent State University*] [*Automated library system*] (NITA) ... KASS
Kent Aviation Ltd. [*Canada ICAO designator*] (FAAC) ... KAH
Kent Barlow Information Associates [*British*] (NITA) ... KBIA
Kent County International Airport [*FAA*] (TAG) ... GRR
Kent County Library and Kent County Library System, Grand Rapids, MI [*OCLC symbol*] (OCLC) ... EXE
Kent County Public Library, Chatham, ON, Canada [*Library symbol Library of Congress*] (LCLS) ... CaOChaKC
Kent County Public Library, Chatham, Ontario [*Library symbol National Library of Canada*] (NLC) ... OCHAKC
Kent Electronics [*Associated Press*] (SAG) ... KentEl
Kent Electronics [*NYSE symbol*] (TTSB) ... KNT
Kent Electronics Corp. [*NYSE symbol*] (SPSG) ... KNT
Kent European Enterprises Ltd. [*British*] ... KEEL
Kent Executive Aviation Ltd. [*British ICAO designator*] (FAAC) ... KEA
Kent Financial Services [*NASDAQ symbol*] (SPSG) ... KENT
Kent Financial Services, Inc. [*Associated Press*] (SAG) ... KentFn
Kent Financial Svcs [*NASDAQ symbol*] (TTSB) ... KENT

Kent Infant Development Scale (EDAC) .... KID
Kent Infant Development Scale [*Neonatology*] (DAVI) .... KIDS
Kent Information Technology Conference (NITA) .... KIT
Kent International Airport [*British*] .... KIA
Kent Mathematics Project [*British*] (AIE) .... KMP
Kent Memorial Library, Suffield, CT [*Library symbol*] [*Library of Congress*] (LCLS) .... CtSuL
Kent, OH [*AM radio station call letters*] .... WJMP
Kent, OH [*FM radio station call letters*] .... WKSU
Kent, OH [*FM radio station call letters*] .... WNIR
Kent Scientific & Industrial Projects Ltd. [*University of Kent*] [*Research center British*] (IRUK) .... KSIP
Kent State University (GAGS) .... Kent St U
Kent State University [*Ohio*] .... KSU
Kent State University, Ashtabula Regional Campus, Ashtabula, OH [*Library symbol Library of Congress*] (LCLS) .... OAshtK
Kent State University, Columbiana Regional Campus, Salem, OH [*Library symbol Library of Congress*] (LCLS) .... OSalK
Kent State University, East Liverpool Regional Campus, East Liverpool, OH [*Library symbol Library of Congress*] (LCLS) .... OEalK
Kent State University, Kent, OH [*OCLC symbol*] (OCLC) .... KSU
Kent State University, Kent, OH [*Library symbol Library of Congress*] (LCLS) .... OKentU
Kent State University, School of Library Science, Kent, OH [*OCLC symbol*] (OCLC) .... KSS
Kent State University, Stark County Regional Campus, Canton, OH [*Library symbol Library of Congress*] (LCLS) .... OCanK
Kent State University, Stark County Regional Campus, Canton, OH [*OCLC symbol*] (OCLC) .... OCK
Kent State University, Trumbull Regional Campus, Warren, OH [*Library symbol Library of Congress OCLC symbol*] (LCLS) .... OWK
Kent State University, Tuscarawas County Regional Campus, New Philadelphia, OH [*Library symbol Library of Congress*] (LCLS) .... ONpK
Kent University On-Line System [*Computer science*] (PDAA) .... KOS
Kent Volunteer Fencibles [*British military*] (DMA) .... KVF
Kent Yeomanry [*Military unit*] [*British*] .... KY
Kentair (International) Ltd. [*British ICAO designator*] (FAAC) .... INK
Kent-Barlow Publications Ltd. [*Information service or system*] (IID) .... KBP
Kentek Information Sys [*NASDAQ symbol*] (TTSB) .... KNTK
Kentek Information Systems, Inc. [*Associated Press*] (SAG) .... Kentekl
Kentek Information Systems, Inc. [*NASDAQ symbol*] (SAG) .... KNTK
Kentfield [*California*] [*Seismograph station code, US Geological Survey*] (SEIS) .... KFC
Kentish .... K
Kentland Public Library, Kentland, IN [*Library symbol Library of Congress*] (LCLS) .... InKent
Kenton County Public Library, Covington, KY [*Library symbol Library of Congress*] (LCLS) .... KyCov
Kenton, DE [*Location identifier FAA*] (FAAL) .... ENO
Kenton Natural Resources Corp. [*Vancouver Stock Exchange symbol*] .... KNN
Kenton, OH [*FM radio station call letters*] .... WKTN
Kentron Programmatismou kai Oikonomikon Ereunon [*Centre of Planning and Economic Research*] [*Greece*] .... KEPE
Kent-Rosanoff Free Association Test [*Psychology*] .... K-R
Kent's Commentaries on American Law [*A publication*] (DLA) .... Kent
Kent's Commentaries on American Law [*A publication*] (DLA) .... Kent Com
Kent's Commentaries on American Law [*A publication*] (DLA) .... Kent Comm
Kent's Commentaries on American Law [*A publication*] (DLA) .... Kent's Commen
Kentucky .... KEN
Kentucky (ODBW) .... Ken
Kentucky (ODBW) .... Ky
Kentucky [*Postal code*] (AFM) .... KY
Kentucky [*MARC country of publication code Library of Congress*] (LCCP) .... kyu
Kentucky [*MARC geographic area code Library of Congress*] (LCCP) .... n-us-ky
Kentucky Academy of Family Physicians (SRA) .... KAFP
Kentucky Administration Regulations Service [*A publication*] (DLA) .... KY Admin Regs
Kentucky Administrative Register [*A publication*] (DLA) .... KY Admin Reg
Kentucky Administrative Regulations [*A publication*] (AAGC) .... KAR
Kentucky Administrative Regulations [*A publication*] (AAGC) .... Ky Admin Regs
Kentucky Allied Health Project (EDAC) .... KAHP
Kentucky & Indiana Terminal Railroad Co. [*AAR code*] .... KIT
Kentucky & Tennessee Railway [*AAR code*] .... KT
Kentucky Association for Marriage and Family Therapy (SRA) .... KAMFT
Kentucky Association of Electric Cooperatives (SRA) .... KAEC
Kentucky Association of Milk, Food, and Environmental Sanitarians (SRA) .... KAMFES
Kentucky Association of School Administrators (SRA) .... KASA
Kentucky Association of Secondary School Principals (SRA) .... KASSP
Kentucky Bar Association (SRA) .... KBA
Kentucky Broadcasters Association (SRA) .... KBA
Kentucky Callers Association (EA) .... KCA
Kentucky Cattlemen's Association (SRA) .... KCA
Kentucky Chamber of Commerce (SRA) .... KCC
Kentucky Coal Association (SRA) .... KCA
Kentucky Commentator [*A publication*] (DLA) .... KY Comment'r
Kentucky Cooperative Library and Information Project [*Library network*] .... KENCLIP
Kentucky Council on Higher Education, Frankfort, KY [*Library symbol*] [*Library of Congress*] (LCLS) .... KyFCE
Kentucky Court of Appeals Opinions [*A publication*] (DLA) .... KY Op
Kentucky Dam [*TVA*] .... KD
Kentucky Decisions (Sneed) [*2 Kentucky*] [*A publication*] (DLA) .... Ken Dec
Kentucky Department of Environmental Protection .... KDEP
Kentucky Department of Environmental Protection (DOGT) .... KDEP
Kentucky Department of Libraries and Archives, Kentucky Guide Project, Frankfort, KY [*Library symbol*] [*Library of Congress*] (LCLS) .... Ky-G
Kentucky Department of Libraries and Archives, Kentucky State Archives, Frankfort, KY [*Library symbol*] [*Library of Congress*] (LCLS) .... Ky-Ar
Kentucky Department of Libraries, Frankfort, KY [*Library symbol Library of Congress*] (LCLS) .... Ky
Kentucky Department of Libraries, Library Extension Division, Frankfort, KY [*OCLC symbol*] (OCLC) .... KSL
Kentucky Department of Libraries, Processing Center, Frankfort, KY [*OCLC symbol*] (OCLC) .... KSP
Kentucky Economic Information System [*University of Kentucky*] [*Lexington Database producer*] [*Information service or system*] .... KEIS
Kentucky Education Reform Act .... KERA
Kentucky Education Reform Act .... KERA
Kentucky Electric Steel [*NASDAQ symbol*] (TTSB) .... KESI
Kentucky Electric Steel Co. [*NASDAQ symbol*] (SAG) .... KESI
Kentucky Electric Steel Co. [*Associated Press*] (SAG) .... KntckyEl
Kentucky Enterprise Bancorp [*NASDAQ symbol*] (SAG) .... KEBI
Kentucky Enterprise Bancorp [*Associated Press*] (SAG) .... KentEnt
Kentucky Environmental Education Program (EDAC) .... KEEP
Kentucky Equine Respiratory Virus [*Veterinary science*] (DMAA) .... KERV
Kentucky First Bancorp [*AMEX symbol*] (TTSB) .... KYF
Kentucky First Bancorp, Inc. [*Associated Press*] (SAG) .... KY Fst
Kentucky First Bancorp, Inc. [*Associated Press*] (SAG) .... KY FstB
Kentucky First Bancorp, Inc. [*AMEX symbol*] (SAG) .... KYF
Kentucky Fried Chicken Corp. [*Later, KFC Corp.*] (ADA) .... KFC
Kentucky Guild of Artists and Craftsmen (SRA) .... KGAC
Kentucky Historical Society, Frankfort, KY [*Library symbol Library of Congress*] (LCLS) .... KyHi
Kentucky Hotel and Motel Association (SRA) .... KHMA
Kentucky Human Services Association (SRA) .... KHSA
Kentucky Industrial Development Council (SRA) .... KIDC
Kentucky Law Reporter [*A publication*] (DLA) .... K Law Rep
Kentucky Law Reporter [*A publication*] (DLA) .... Ken L Re
Kentucky Law Reporter [*A publication*] (DLA) .... Ken LR
Kentucky Law Reporter [*A publication*] (DLA) .... KLR
Kentucky Law Reporter [*A publication*] (DLA) .... KY L
Kentucky Law Reporter [*A publication*] (DLA) .... KY L Rep
Kentucky Law Reporter [*A publication*] (DLA) .... KY L Rptr
Kentucky Law Reporter [*A publication*] (DLA) .... KY Law Rep
Kentucky Law Reporter [*A publication*] (DLA) .... KY LR
Kentucky Law Reporter [*A publication*] (DLA) .... R
Kentucky Law Review [*A publication*] (DLA) .... KY L Rev
Kentucky Library for the Blind and Physically Handicapped, Frankfort, KY [*Library symbol Library of Congress*] (LCLS) .... Ky-BPH
Kentucky Medical Insurance Co. [*NASDAQ symbol*] (NQ) .... KYMD
Kentucky Medical Insurance Co. [*Associated Press*] (SAG) .... KyMed
Kentucky, Ohio, Michigan [*Medical library network*] .... KOM
Kentucky Opinions [*A publication*] (DLA) .... Ken Opin
Kentucky Opinions [*A publication*] (DLA) .... KY Opin
Kentucky Optometric Association (SRA) .... KOA
Kentucky Pharmacists Association (SRA) .... KPhA
Kentucky Power Co. [*NYSE symbol*] (SAG) .... KPC
Kentucky Power Co. [*Associated Press*] (SAG) KyPw25
Kentucky Pwr 8.72% Sr'A'Debs [*NYSE symbol*] (TTSB) .... KPC
Kentucky Reports [*A publication*] (AAGC) .... Ky
Kentucky Reports [*A publication*] (DLA) .... KY R
Kentucky Revised Statutes [*A publication*] .... KRS
Kentucky Revised Statutes [*A publication*] (DLA) .... KY Rev Stat
Kentucky Revised Statutes and Rules Service (Baldwin) [*A publication*] (DLA) .... KY Rev Stat & Rules Serv
Kentucky Society of Association Executives (SRA) .... KSAE
Kentucky State Bar Journal [*A publication*] (DLA) .... KBJ
Kentucky State Bar Journal [*A publication*] (DLA) .... KY SBJ
Kentucky State Bar Journal [*A publication*] (DLA) .... KY St BJ
Kentucky State University, Frankfort, KY [*Library symbol Library of Congress*] (LCLS) .... KyFSC
Kentucky State University, Frankfort, KY [*OCLC symbol*] (OCLC) .... KYS
Kentucky Supreme Court Reports [*1879-1951*] [*A publication*] (DLA) .... KY
Kentucky Telephone Association (SRA) .... KTA
Kentucky Thoroughbred Association (SRA) .... KTA
Kentucky Tourism Council (SRA) .... KTC
Kentucky Truck Plant [*Ford Motor Co.*] .... KTP
Kentucky Union List of Serials [*Library network*] .... KULS
Kentucky University (PDAA) .... KU
Kentucky Water Resources Research Institute [*University of Kentucky*] [*Lexington, KY*] [*Department of the Interior*] [*Research center*] (RCD) .... KWRRI
Kentucky Wesleyan College [*Owensboro*] .... KWC
Kentucky Wesleyan College, Owensboro, KY [*Library symbol Library of Congress*] (LCLS) .... KyOwK
Kentucky Workmen's Compensation Board Decisions [*A publication*] (DLA) .... KY WC Dec
Kentucky-Illinois-Tennessee League [*Old baseball league*] .... KITTY
Kentucky-Ohio-Michigan Regional Medical Library [*Library network*] .... KOMRMLN
Kentucky's Individualized Kindergartens (EDAC) .... KIK
Kentville, NS [*AM radio station call letters*] .... CKEN
Kentville, NS [*FM radio station call letters*] .... CKWM
Kentville Publishing, New Minas, Nova Scotia [*Library symbol National Library of Canada*] (NLC) .... NSNMK
Kentville Publishing, New Minas, NS, Canada [*Library symbol*] [*Library of Congress*] (LCLS) .... CaNSNmK
Kentwood, LA [*FM radio station call letters*] .... WYCT
Kentwood, MI [*AM radio station call letters*] .... WGVU
Kentwood, MI [*AM radio station call letters*] .... WKWM
Kenuz Airlines Ltd. [*Nigeria*] [*ICAO designator*] (FAAC) .... KNS

Kenwin Shops [*AMEX symbol*] (TTSB) .... KWN
Kenwin Shops, Inc. [*AMEX symbol*] (SPSG) .... KWN
Kenwood Elementary School, Bowling Green, OH [*Library symbol*] [*Library of Congress*] (LCLS) .... OBgKE
Kenworth Engine Governing System [*Automotive engineering*] .... KEGS
Kenworth Truck Co. .... KW
Kenya [*International vehicle registration*] (ODBW) .... EAK
Kenya [*MARC geographic area code Library of Congress*] (LCCP) .... f-ke--
Kenya [*MARC country of publication code Library of Congress*] (LCCP) .... ke
Kenya [*ANSI two-letter standard code*] (CNC) .... KE
Kenya [*ANSI three-letter standard code*] (CNC) .... KEN
Kenya (VRA) .... Ken
Kenya [*IYRU nationality code*] (IYR) .... KK
Kenya African Democratic Union [*Political party*] (PPW) .... KADU
Kenya African Movement .... KAM
Kenya African National Union [*Political party*] (PPW) .... KANU
Kenya African Union [*1944*] [*Political party*] (PPW) .... KAU
Kenya Air Force .... KAF
Kenya Airways [*ICAO designator*] (AD) .... KQ
Kenya Airways [*Airline flight code*] (ODBW) .... KQ
Kenya Airways Ltd. [*ICAO designator*] (FAAC) .... KQA
Kenya Federation of Labour .... KFL
Kenya Flamingo Airways Ltd. [*ICAO designator*] (FAAC) .... KFL
Kenya High Court Digest [*A publication*] (DLA) .... KHCD
Kenya Independent Squadron [*British military*] (DMA) .... KIS
Kenya Law Reports [*A publication*] (DLA) .... Kenya LR
Kenya Law Reports [*A publication*] (DLA) .... LRK
Kenya National Museum .... KNM
Kenya Navy .... KN
Kenya News Agency .... KNA
Kenya Petroleum and Oil Workers' Union .... KPOWU
Kenya Railways .... KR
Kenya Rangeland Ecological Monitoring Unit .... KREMU
Kenya Rift International Seismic Project .... KRISP
Kenya Shilling [*Monetary unit*] (IMH) .... KSH
Kenya Shilling [*Monetary unit*] (ODBW) .... KSh
Kenya Trypanosomiasis Research Institute .... KETRI
Kenya-Australia Society .... KAS
Kenyon College, Gambier, OH [*OCLC symbol*] (OCLC) .... KEN
Kenyon College, Gambier, OH [*Library symbol Library of Congress*] (LCLS) .... OGK
Kenyon Review [*A publication*] (BRI) .... Ken R
Kenyon's English King's Bench Reports [*A publication*] (DLA) .... K
Kenyon's English King's Bench Reports [*A publication*] (DLA) .... Ken
Kenyon's English King's Bench Reports [*A publication*] (DLA) .... Keny
Keogh Plan [*Business term*] .... KP
Keokuk Community College [*Iowa*] .... KCC
Keokuk County Courthouse, Sigourney, IA [*Library symbol*] [*Library of Congress*] (LCLS) .... IaSigCoC
Keokuk Gate City, Keokuk, IA [*Library symbol Library of Congress*] (LCLS) .... IaKG
Keokuk, IA [*Location identifier FAA*] (FAAL) .... EOK
Keokuk, IA [*AM radio station call letters*] .... KOKX
Keokuk, IA [*FM radio station call letters*] .... KOKX-FM
Keokuk, IA [*FM radio station call letters*] (RBYB) .... KRNQ-FM
Keokuk, IA [*FM radio station call letters*] .... KYAT
Keokuk Public Library, Keokuk, IA [*Library symbol Library of Congress*] (LCLS) .... IaK
Keokuk Savings Bank and Trust Co., Keokuk, IA [*Library symbol*] [*Library of Congress*] (LCLS) .... IaKS
Keonjhar [*India*] [*ICAO location identifier*] (ICLI) .... VEKJ
Keosauqua Public Library, Keosauqua, IA [*Library symbol Library of Congress*] (LCLS) .... IaKe
Keosippi Library Cooperative, Keokuk, IA [*Library symbol Library of Congress*] (LCLS) .... IaKK
Keota Eagle, Keota, IA [*Library symbol Library of Congress*] (LCLS) .... IaKeoE
Kep [*Viet Nam*] [*ICAO location identifier*] (ICLI) .... VVKP
Kepi [*Indonesia*] [*Airport symbol*] (OAG) .... KEI
Kepi [*Indonesia*] [*ICAO location identifier*] (ICLI) .... WAKP
Kerala Law Journal [*A publication*] (DLA) .... Kerala LJ
Kerang [*Victoria, Australia*] [*Airport symbol*] (AD) .... KRA
Keratin (DMAA) .... KRT
Keratin, Myosin, Epidermin, Fibrin [*Biochemistry*] .... KMEF
Keratinizing Desquamative Squamous Metaplasia [*Medicine*] .... KDSM
Keratinocyte Growth Factor [*Biochemistry*] .... KGF
Keratinocyte Growth Factor Receptor [*Biochemistry*] .... KGFR
Keratinocyte Growth Medium [*Cell culture*] .... KGM
Keratinocyte Precursor Cell .... KPC
Keratinocyte T-Cell Growth Factor [*Immunology*] .... KTGF
Keratinocyte-Conditioned Medium [*Biochemistry*] .... KCM
Keratitic Precipitate [*Ophthalmology*] .... KP
Keratitis [*Ophthalmology*] (DAVI) .... Kera
Keratitis, Ichthyosis, and Deafness Syndrome [*Medicine*] (DMAA) .... KID
Keratitis Punctata [*Ophthalmology*] .... KP
Keratoacanthoma [*Dermatology*] (DAVI) .... KA
Keratoconjunctivitis [*Ophthalmology*] .... KC
Keratoconjunctivitis Sicca [*Ophthalmology*] .... KCS
Keratoconus [*Ophthalmology*] (DAVI) .... KC
Keratoconus Posticus Circumscriptus [*Medicine*] (DMAA) .... KPC
Keratoma Climacterium [*Dermatology*] (DAVI) .... KC
Kerato-Refractive Society (EA) .... KRS
Keratosis Follicularis Spinulosa Decalvans [*Medicine*] (DMAA) .... KFSD
Keravat [*New Britain*] [*Seismograph station code, US Geological Survey Closed*] (SEIS) .... KET
Keravat [*New Britain*] [*Seismograph station code, US Geological Survey Closed*] (SEIS) .... KRT
KeraVision, Inc. [*NASDAQ symbol*] (SAG) .... KERA

KeraVision, Inc. [*Associated Press*] (SAG) .... KeraVis
KeraVision, Inc. [*Associated Press*] (SAG) .... KeraVs
Kerbing and Guttering [*British*] (ADA) .... K & G
Kerchief (ABBR) .... KRCHF
Kerekere [*Zaire*] [*ICAO location identifier*] (ICLI) .... FZJR
Kerema [*Papua New Guinea*] [*Airport symbol*] (OAG) .... KMA
Kerema [*Papua New Guinea*] [*Seismograph station code, US Geological Survey Closed*] (SEIS) .... KRG
Keremeos Museum, British Columbia [*Library symbol National Library of Canada*] (NLC) .... BKEM
Keremeos Museum, Keremeos, BC, Canada [*Library symbol*] [*Library of Congress*] (LCLS) .... CaBKEM
Keren Ami (BJA) .... KA
Keren Hajesod Ljisroel (BJA) .... KHL
Keren Hayesod (BJA) .... KH
Keren Kayemeth (BJA) .... KK
Keren Kayemeth Leisrael (BJA) .... KKL
Keren Mif'alim Konstruktiviyim [*Constructive Enterprises Fund*] (BJA) .... KMK
Keresztenydemokrata Neppart [*Christian Democratic People's Party*] [*Hungary Political party*] (EY) .... KDNP
Kerf Petroleums [*Vancouver Stock Exchange symbol*] .... KRF
Kerford and Box's Victorian Digest [*A publication*] (DLA) .... K & B Dig
Kericho [*Kenya*] [*ICAO location identifier*] (ICLI) .... HKKR
Kerikeri [*New Zealand*] [*Airport symbol*] (OAG) .... KKE
Kerithoth (BJA) .... Ker
Kerkhoven-Murdoch-Sunberg Elementary School, Kerkhoven, MN [*Library symbol*] [*Library of Congress*] (LCLS) .... MnKeES
Kerkhoven-Murdoch-Sunberg High School, Kerkhoven, MN [*Library symbol*] [*Library of Congress*] (LCLS) .... MnKeHS
Kerkhover-Murdock-Sunberg School, Murdock, MN [*Library symbol*] [*Library of Congress*] (LCLS) .... MnMuKS
Kerkira [*Greece*] [*ICAO location identifier*] (ICLI) .... LGKR
Kerkoven Public Library, Kerkoven, MN [*Library symbol*] [*Library of Congress*] (LCLS) .... MnKeP
Kerley Lines [*Radiology*] .... KL
Kerma (DMAA) .... K
Kermadec Islands [*MARC geographic area code Library of Congress*] (LCCP) .... poki--
Kerman [*Iran*] [*Airport symbol*] (OAG) .... KER
Kerman [*Iran*] [*ICAO location identifier*] (ICLI) .... OIKK
Kerman [*Iran*] [*ICAO location identifier*] (ICLI) .... OIKT
Kerman, CA [*FM radio station call letters*] .... KTAA
Kermanshah [*Iran*] [*Seismograph station code, US Geological Survey*] (SEIS) .... KER
Kermanshah [*Iran*] [*Airport symbol*] (AD) .... KSH
Kermit [*Texas*] [*Seismograph station code, US Geological Survey*] (SEIS) .... KIT
Kermit [*Texas*] [*Seismograph station code, US Geological Survey*] (SEIS) KM2
Kermit [*Texas*] [*Seismograph station code, US Geological Survey*] (SEIS) KM5
Kermit [*Texas*] [*Seismograph station code, US Geological Survey*] (SEIS) KM6
Kermit [*Texas*] [*Seismograph station code, US Geological Survey*] (SEIS) KM9
Kermit [*Texas*] [*Seismograph station code, US Geological Survey Closed*] (SEIS) .... KME
Kermit [*Texas*] [*Seismograph station code, US Geological Survey*] (SEIS) .... KT
Kermit [*Texas*] [*Seismograph station code, US Geological Survey*] (SEIS) .... KTE
Kermit [*Texas*] [*Seismograph station code, US Geological Survey Closed*] (SEIS) .... KTT
Kermit [*Texas*] [*Seismograph station code, US Geological Survey*] (SEIS) .... KTX
Kermit, TX [*AM radio station call letters*] .... KERB
Kermit, TX [*FM radio station call letters*] .... KERB-FM
Kern County Department of Health, Bakersfield, CA [*Library symbol Library of Congress*] (LCLS) .... CBaKDH
Kern County Library, Bakersfield, CA [*Library symbol Library of Congress*] (LCLS) .... CBaK
Kern County Library System [*Library network*] .... KCLS
Kern County Library System, Bakersfield, CA [*OCLC symbol*] (OCLC) .... KLC
Kern County Museum, Reference Library, Bakersfield, CA [*Library symbol Library of Congress*] (LCLS) .... CBaKM
Kern Medical Center, Bakersfield, CA [*Library symbol Library of Congress*] (LCLS) .... CBaH
Kern Wave [*Earthquakes*] .... K
Kernan's Reports [*11-14 New York*] [*A publication*] (DLA) .... Kern
Kernel (ABBR) .... KNRL
Kernel (ABBR) .... KRNL
Kernel APSE [*ADA Program Support Environment*] [*Computer science*] .... KAPSE
Kernel Migration Coefficient (PDAA) .... KMC
Kernel Multiple Processing System [*Computer science*] .... KMPS
Kernel Programming Interface [*Computer science*] .... KPI
Kernforschungsanlage [*Julich, Germany*] .... KFA
Kernforschungsanlage Julich, Julich, Germany [*Library symbol Library of Congress*] (LCLS) .... GyJuK
Kern's Reports [*100-116 Indiana*] [*A publication*] (DLA) .... Kern
Kernville, CA [*FM radio station call letters*] .... KCNQ
Kerosene (AAG) .... K
Kerosene (ABBR) .... KRSEN
Kerosene (MSA) .... KRSN
Kerosene, Alcohol, Acetic Acid, and Dioxane (DMAA) .... KAAD
Kerosine [*British*] .... KERO
Kerouane [*Guinea*] [*ICAO location identifier*] (ICLI) .... GUKE
Kerr Addison Mines Ltd. [*Toronto Stock Exchange symbol*] .... KER
Kerr Cell [*Optics*] .... KC
Kerr Center for Sustainable Agriculture [*Research center*] (RCD) .... KCSA
Kerr Constant [*Optics*] .... K
Kerr Effect [*Optics*] .... KE
Kerr Electro-Optical Effect [*Optics*] .... KEE
Kerr Group [*Associated Press*] (SAG) .... Kerr

Kerr Group [*Associated Press*] (SAG) .... KerrGp
Kerr Group [*NYSE symbol*] (SPSG) .... KGM
Kerr Group $1.70 Cv Pfd [*NYSE symbol*] (TTSB) ...... KMGPrD
Kerr Industrial Applications Center [*Southeastern Oklahoma State University*] [*Durant*] [*Information service or system*] (IID) ...... KIAC
Kerr Magneto-Optical Effect [*Optics*] .... KME
Kerr McGee Corp. [*Associated Press*] (SAG) ...... KerrMc
Kerr McGee Corp. [*NYSE symbol*] (SAG) .... KMG
Kerr on Ancient Lights [*A publication*] (DLA) ...... Kerr Anc L
Kerr on Injunctions [*A publication*] (DLA) ...... Kerr Inj
Kerr on Inter-State Extradition [*A publication*] (DLA) ...... Kerr Ext
Kerr on Receivers [*A publication*] (DLA) ...... Kerr Rec
Kerr Vector [*Optics*] .... KV
Kerr-Addison Mines [*TS, exchange symbol*] (TTSB) ...... KER
Kerr-Fourier [*Imaging*] .... KF
Kerrier [*England*] .... KERR
Kerrisdale Resources Ltd. [*Vancouver Stock Exchange symbol*] ...... KDL
Kerr-McGee [*NYSE symbol*] (TTSB) .... KMG
Kerr-McGee Corp. [*NYSE symbol Toronto Stock Exchange symbol*] (SPSG) ...... KMG
Kerr-McGee Corp., Oklahoma City, OK [*Library symbol Library of Congress*] (LCLS) .... OkOkK
Kerr's Actions at Law [*3rd ed.*] [*1861*] [*A publication*] (DLA) ...... Kerr Act
Kerr's Blackstone [*12th ed.*] [*1895*] [*A publication*] (DLA) ...... Kerr Black
Kerr's Discovery [*1870*] [*A publication*] (DLA) ...... Kerr Disc
Kerr's Fraud and Mistake [*7th ed.*] [*1952*] [*A publication*] (DLA) ...... Kerr F & M
Kerr's Fraud and Mistake [*7th ed.*] [*1952*] [*A publication*] (DLA) ...... Kerr Fr
Kerr's New Brunswick Reports [*A publication*] (DLA) ...... Kerr
Kerr's New Brunswick Reports [*A publication*] (DLA) ...... Kerr (NB)
Kerr's New Brunswick Reports [*A publication*] (DLA) ...... NBR Kerr
Kerr's Reports [*27-29 New York Civil Procedure*] [*A publication*] (DLA) ...... Kerr
Kerr's Reports [*18-22 Indiana*] [*A publication*] (DLA) ...... Kerr
Kerr's Student's Blackstone [*A publication*] (DLA) ...... Kerr Stu Black
Kerr's Water and Mineral Cases [*A publication*] (DLA) ...... Kerr W & M Cas
Kerrville, TX [*Location identifier FAA*] (FAAL) ...... ERV
Kerrville, TX [*AM radio station call letters*] ...... KERV
Kerrville, TX [*FM radio station call letters*] ...... KITE
Kerrville, TX [*Television station call letters*] ...... KRRT
Kerrville, TX [*FM radio station call letters*] ...... KRVL
Kerry [*County in Ireland*] (ROG) .... KER
Kerse's Manuscript Decisions, Scotch Court of Session [*A publication*] (DLA) .... Kerse
Kershaw County Library, Camden, SC [*Library symbol*] [*Library of Congress*] (LCLS) .... ScCam
Kershaw, SC [*AM radio station call letters*] ...... WKSC
Kersten Hurlk Group [*Commercial firm British*] ...... KH
Kerteh [*Malaysia*] [*ICAO location identifier*] (ICLI) ...... WMKE
Kerukunan Nasional [*Campaign for National Harmony*] [*Indonesia*] ..... KERUK-NASI
Kerwin Shops, Inc. [*Associated Press*] (SAG) ...... Kerwin
Kesatuan Aksi Guru Indonesia [*Action Front of Indonesian Teachers*] ...... KAGI
Kesatuan Aksi Sardjana Indonesia [*Action Front of Indonesian Scholars*] ...... KASI
Kesatuan Insaf Tanah Air [*National Consciousness Party*] [*Malaysia*] [*Political party*] ...... KITA
Keshequa Junior/Senior High School Library, Nunda, NY [*OCLC symbol*] (OCLC) ...... RWU
Keshm [*Afghanistan*] [*ICAO location identifier*] (ICLI) ...... OAEK
Keshod [*India*] [*Airport symbol*] (OAG) ...... IXK
Keshod [*India*] [*ICAO location identifier*] (ICLI) ...... VAKS
Keskustapuolue [*Center Party of Finland*] [*Political party*] (PPW) ...... KP
Kessel, WV [*Location identifier FAA*] (FAAL) ...... ESL
Kesselring Site [*Knolls Atomic Power Laboratory*] (GAAI) ...... KESS
Kessler Marketing Intelligence [*Information service or system*] (IID) ...... KMI
Kestrel (ABBR) .... KSTRL
Kestrel Energy [*NASDAQ symbol*] (TTSB) ...... KEST
Kestrel Energy, Inc. [*NASDAQ symbol*] (SAG) ...... KEST
Kestrel Energy, Inc. [*Associated Press*] (SAG) ...... Kestrel
Kestrel Interactive Development System [*Computer science*] ...... KIDS
Ketamine [*An anesthetic*] .... K
Ketamine [*An anesthetic*] .... KET
Ketamine [*An anesthetic*] .... KT
Ketapang [*Indonesia*] [*Airport symbol*] (OAG) ...... KTG
Ketapang/Rahadi Usman [*Indonesia*] [*ICAO location identifier*] (ICLI) ...... WIOK
Ketch (ROG) .... K
Ketch .... KCH
Ketch .... KTN
Ketchikan [*Alaska*] [*Airport symbol*] (OAG) ...... PAKT
Ketchikan [*Alaska*] [*ICAO location identifier*] (ICLI) ...... PAKT
Ketchikan, AK [*Location identifier FAA*] (FAAL) ...... CMJ
Ketchikan, AK [*Location identifier FAA*] (FAAL) ...... ECH
Ketchikan, AK [*FM radio station call letters*] (RBYB) ...... KFMJ-FM
Ketchikan, AK [*FM radio station call letters*] ...... KGTW
Ketchikan, AK [*Television station call letters*] (RBYB) ...... KNEB-TV
Ketchikan, AK [*FM radio station call letters*] ...... KRBD
Ketchikan, AK [*AM radio station call letters*] ...... KTKN
Ketchikan, AK [*Location identifier FAA*] (FAAL) ...... KTN
Ketchikan Community College, Ketchikan, AK [*Library symbol*] [*Library of Congress*] (LCLS) ...... AkKC
Ketchikan Gateway Borough School District, Ketchikan, AK [*Library symbol*] [*Library of Congress*] (LCLS) ...... AkKSD
Ketchikan Public Library, Ketchikan, AK [*Library symbol Library of Congress*] (LCLS) ...... AkK
Ketchum, McLeod & Grove, Inc., Pittsburgh, PA [*Library symbol Library of Congress*] (LCLS) ...... PPiK
Ketchum, OK [*FM radio station call letters*] ...... KGND
Ketchup (ABBR) .... KTCHP
Kete-Krachi [*Ghana*] [*ICAO location identifier*] (ICLI) ...... DGAE
Kethoxal Thiosemicarbazone [*An antiviral*] [*Pharmacology*] (DAVI) ...... KTS

Kethuboth (BJA) .... Ket
Kethuboth (BJA) .... Keth
Ketib (BJA) .... k
Keto Acid (DMAA) .... KA
Keto Isocaproic Acid (DMAA) .... KIC
Ketoacidosis [*Medicine*] .... KA
Ketoacyl-ACP Synthase [*An enzyme*] ...... KAS
Ketoaldonate Reductase [*An enzyme*] ...... KR
Ketobutyraldehyde Dimethyl Acetal [*Biochemistry*] ...... KBA
Ketoconazole (DMAA) .... KZ
Ketocyclazocine [*Biochemistry*] .... KC
Ketodeoxyoctonate [*Biochemistry*] ...... KDO
Keto-Diastix [*Miles Inc.*] [*Pharmacology*] (DAVI) ...... KD
Ketogenic Steroid [*Endocrinology*] ...... KGS
Ketogenic to Anti-Ketogenic [*Ratio*] [*In diets*] ...... K/A
Ketoglutarate (DMAA) .... KG
Ketoglutaric [*Biochemistry*] .... KG
Ketoisocaproate [*Biochemistry*] .... KIC
Ketoisovalerate [*Biochemistry*] ...... KIV
Ketol-Acid Reductoisomerase [*An enzyme*] ...... KARI
Keto-Laevo-Gulonic Acid [*Organic chemistry*] ...... KLG
Keto-L-glutonic (Acid) [*Biochemistry*] ...... KLG
Ketone [*Organic chemistry*] (ABBR) ...... KTON
Ketone Bodies [*Clinical chemistry*] ...... KB
Ketone Bodies [*Endocrinology*] (DAVI) ...... KET BD
Ketophenylbutazone [*or Kebuzone*] [*An antirheumatic*] (DAVI) ...... KPB
Ketoreductase [*An enzyme*] .... KR
Ketosteroid [*Endocrinology*] .... keto
Ketosteroid [*Endocrinology*] .... KS
Ketothiomethylbutyric Acid [*Organic chemistry*] ...... KTBA
Ketotifen [*Pharmacology*] .... K
Kettering Memorial Hospital, Kettering, OH [*Library symbol Library of Congress*] (LCLS) ...... OKetH
Kettering, OH [*FM radio station call letters*] ...... WKET
Kettering, OH [*FM radio station call letters*] ...... WLQT
Kettle (ABBR) .... KTL
Kettle River Museum, Midway, BC, Canada [*Library symbol*] [*Library of Congress*] (LCLS) ...... CaBMKRM
Kettle River Museum, Midway, British Columbia [*Library symbol National Library of Canada*] (NLC) ...... BMKRM
Kettle River Resources Ltd. [*Vancouver Stock Exchange symbol*] ...... KRR
Kettle Valley Railway Museum, Kelowna, BC, Canada [*Library symbol*] [*Library of Congress*] (LCLS) ...... CaBKRM
Kettle Valley Railway Museum, Kelowna, British Columbia [*Library symbol National Library of Canada*] (NLC) ...... BKRM
Kettledrum .... KD
Kettledrum (ABBR) .... KTLDR
Kettleson Memorial Library, Sitka, AK [*Library symbol Library of Congress*] (LCLS) ...... AkS
Keuka College, Keuka Park, NY [*Library symbol Library of Congress*] (LCLS) ...... NKpK
Keuka College, Lightner Library, Keuka Park, NY [*OCLC symbol*] (OCLC) ...... ZKC
Keuringsinstituut voor Waterleidingartikelen ...... KIWA
Kevin Collins Foundation for Missing Children (EA) ...... KCFMC
Kevlin Corp. [*Associated Press*] (SAG) ...... Kevlin
Kevlin Corp. [*NASDAQ symbol*] (NQ) ...... KVLM
Kevo [*Finland*] [*Seismograph station code, US Geological Survey*] (SEIS) ...... KEV
Kew [*England*] [*Seismograph station code, US Geological Survey Closed*] (SEIS) ...... KEW
Kewanee, IL [*Location identifier FAA*] (FAAL) ...... EZI
Kewanee, IL [*FM radio station call letters*] ...... WJRE
Kewanee, IL [*AM radio station call letters*] ...... WKEI
Kewanee, MS [*Location identifier FAA*] (FAAL) ...... EWA
Kewanee Public Library, Kewanee, IL [*OCLC symbol*] (OCLC) ...... IEV
Kewanee Public Library, Kewanee, IL [*Library symbol Library of Congress*] (LCLS) ...... IKe
Kewanna Observer, Kewanna, IN [*Library symbol Library of Congress*] (LCLS) ...... InKewO
Kewanna Public Library, Kewanna, IN [*Library symbol Library of Congress*] (LCLS) ...... InKew
Kewatin .... KEW
Kewaunee, Green Bay & Western R. R. [*AAR code*] ...... KGB
Kewaunee Nuclear Power Plant (NRCH) ...... KNPP
Kewaunee Scientific [*NASDAQ symbol*] (TTSB) ...... KEQU
Kewaunee Scientific Corp. [*Formerly, Kewaunee Science Equipment*] [*NASDAQ symbol*] (NQ) ...... KEQU
Kewaunee Scientific Corp. [*Associated Press*] (SAG) ...... KewnSc
Kewaunee, WI [*FM radio station call letters*] ...... WAUN
Keweenaw Research Center [*Houghton, MI*] [*Army Research center*] (GRD) ...... KRC
Keweenaw Rocket Launch Site [*University of Michigan*] ...... KRLS
Kex National Association (EA) .... K
Key .... KEY
Key [*Commonly used*] (OPSA) ...... KY
Key .... KY
Key (MCD) .... KY
Key Airlines [*ICAO designator*] (AD) ...... FS
Key Anacon Mines Ltd. [*Toronto Stock Exchange symbol*] ...... KEY
Key and Elphinstone's Conveyancing [*15th ed.*] [*1953-54*] [*A publication*] (DLA) ...... K & E Conv
Key and Elphinstone's Conveyancing [*15th ed.*] [*1953-54*] [*A publication*] (DLA) ...... Key & Elph Conv
Key and Lamp Units [*Telecommunications*] ...... KLU
Key Asset Protection Plan [*National Guard*] (INF) ...... KAPP

Key British Enterprises [*Dun & Bradstreet Ltd.*] [*Information service or system*] (IID) .... KBE
Key Buying Influence (WDMC) .... KBI
Key Call Receiver [*Telecommunications*] (TEL) .... KCR
Key Calling [*Telecommunications*] (IAA) .... KCG
Key Center for Mines [*University of Wollongong*] [*Australia*] .... KCM
Key Center for Statistical Services [*Deakin University*] [*Australia*] .... KCSS
Key Chain Collectors Club (EA) .... KCCC
Key Chain Tag and Mini License Plate Collectors Club [*Later, LPKCMLPCC*] (EA) .... KCTMLPCC
Key Clinical Finding [*Medicine*] (HCT) .... KCF
Key Club International (EA) .... KCI
Key Collectors International (EA) .... KCI
Key Colony Beach, FL [*FM radio station call letters*] .... WKKB
Key Configuration Element (DNAB) .... KCE
Key Configuration Studies (NASA) .... KCS
Key Control Characteristic .... KCC
Key Crude Prices [*Database*] [*Petroleum Intelligence Weekly*] [*Information service or system*] (CRD) .... KCP
Key Data Points (MCD) .... KDP
Key Data Station (NITA) .... KDS
Key Data Terminal .... KDT
Key Decision Point [*USCG*] (TAG) .... KDP
Key Defense Intelligence Issue (MCD) .... KDII
Key Definition (MHDB) .... KD
Key Definition Table [*Computer science*] (PCM) .... KDT
Key Depression per Hour [*Computer science*] (IAA) .... KDH
Key Development Plan [*Telecommunications*] (TEL) .... KDP
Key Display Operating System .... KDOS
Key Display System [*Computer science*] (MDG) .... KDS
Key Distribution Center (MCD) .... KDC
Key District Office [*IRS*] .... KDO
Key Element Search (MCD) .... KES
Key Energy Group [*AMEX symbol*] (SPSG) .... KEG
Key Energy Group [*Associated Press*] (SAG) .... KeyEng
Key Entry Processing .... KEP
Key Equipment [*Telecommunications*] (TEL) .... KE
Key Essential Item List [*Defense Supply Agency*] .... KEIL
Key Facilities List [*AEC*] .... KFL
Key Field .... KF
Key Field Sequential Access Method (NITA) .... KSAM
Key Financial Data (ADA) .... KFD
Key Gap [*Computer science*] (MHDI) .... KEG
Key Generator (MCD) .... KG
Key Generator Module .... KGM
Key Generator Receiver (MCD) .... KGR
Key Hole [*Reconnaissance satellite series*] (DOMA) .... KH
Key Indicators, Probes, and a Scoring Method [*Health care*] (HCT) .... KIPS
Key Indigenous Personnel (MCD) .... KIP
Key Industry [*Business term*] .... KI
Key Industry [*Business term*] (DS) .... KID
Key Integrative Social Systems .... KISS
Key Intelligence Position (AFM) .... KIP
Key Intelligence Question [*CIA*] .... KIQ
Key Intelligence Requirement (MCD) .... KIR
Key Intermediary Proteins (DAVI) .... KIP
Key Issue Tracking [*Database*] .... KIT
Key Largo, FL [*FM radio station call letters*] .... WZMQ
Key Learning Area [*Education*] .... KLA
Key Length [*Computer science*] (BUR) .... KL
Key Lever (IAA) .... KL
Key Lock Switch .... KLS
Key Locker .... KL
Key Makers' Trade Protection Society [*A union*] [*British*] .... KMTPS
Key Officers of Foreign Service Posts [*A publication*] .... KOFS
Key Operated Valve .... KOV
Key Operational Capability [*Military*] (RDA) .... KOC
Key Performance Indicator (TDOB) .... KPI
Key Personnel .... KP
Key Personnel Course (MCD) .... KPC
Key Personnel Upgrade Program [*National Guard*] .... KPUP
Key Phrase in Context .... KPIC
Key Point Error [*Computer science*] (IAA) .... KPE
Key Prep on Campus [*Slang*] .... KPOC
Key Product Characteristic .... KPC
Key Production [*NASDAQ symbol*] (TTSB) .... KPCI
Key Production Co. [*NYSE symbol*] (SAG) .... KP
Key Production Co., Inc. [*Associated Press*] (SAG) .... KeyPrd
Key Production Co., Inc. [*NASDAQ symbol*] (NQ) .... KPCI
Key Pulse Adapter [*Telecommunications*] (TEL) .... KPA
Key Pulse on Front Cord [*Telecommunications*] (TEL) .... KPF
Key Pulse Rate [*Cardiology*] (DAVI) .... KPR
Key Pulsing .... KP
Key Pulsing (MSA) .... KPLS
Key Records [*Record label*] .... KR
Key Register .... KR
Key Resource People [*US Chamber of Commerce*] .... KRP
Key Result Area .... KRA
Key Seated [*Freight*] .... KS
Key Sequenced Data Set (CMD) .... KSDS
Key Service Unit (IEEE) .... KSU
Key Stage [*Of National Curriculum*] [*British*] (AIE) .... KS
Key Station Terminal [*Computer science*] .... KST
Key Strokes per Hour .... KSH
Key Symbol Out of Context [*Computer science*] (DIT) .... KSOC

Key System Control Unit [*Telecommunications*] .... KSU
Key Technologies, Inc. [*NASDAQ symbol*] (SAG) .... KTEC
Key Technology [*NASDAQ symbol*] (TTSB) .... KTEC
Key Technology, Inc. [*Associated Press*] (SAG) .... KeyTech
Key Telephone Adapter [*Telecommunications*] (TEL) .... KTA
Key Telephone System [*Telecommunications*] (AAG) .... KTS
Key Telephone Unit .... KTU
Key to Disc System .... KDS
Key to Disk Operating System .... KDOS
Key to Disk Software .... KTDS
Key Transport Module .... KTM
Key Tronic Corp. [*NASDAQ symbol*] (TTSB) .... KTCC
Key Tronics Corp. [*Associated Press*] (SAG) .... Key Trn
Key Tronics Corp. [*NASDAQ symbol*] (NQ) .... KTCC
Key Verifier [*Computer science*] .... KV
Key Way .... KWY
Key West [*Florida*] [*Airport symbol*] (OAG) .... EYW
Key West [*Florida*] .... KW
Key West Art and Historical Society, Key West, FL [*Library symbol Library of Congress*] (LCLS) .... FKwHi
Key West, FL [*Location identifier FAA*] (FAAL) .... EYW
Key West, FL [*Location identifier FAA*] (FAAL) .... FIS
Key West, FL [*Location identifier FAA*] (FAAL) .... NQX
Key West, FL [*FM radio station call letters*] .... WAIL
Key West, FL [*FM radio station call letters*] .... WEOW
Key West, FL [*Television station call letters*] .... WEYS
Key West, FL [*FM radio station call letters*] .... WIIS
Key West, FL [*FM radio station call letters*] .... WJIR
Key West, FL [*AM radio station call letters*] .... WKIZ
Key West, FL [*FM radio station call letters*] .... WKRY
Key West, FL [*AM radio station call letters*] .... WKWF
Key West, FL [*FM radio station call letters*] .... WOZN
Key West, FL [*FM radio station call letters*] .... WSKP
Key West, FL [*FM radio station call letters*] .... WUNW
Key West, FL [*Television station call letters*] .... WWFD
Key West/Key West International [*Florida*] [*ICAO location identifier*] (ICLI) .... KEYW
Key West/Key West Naval Air Station [*Florida*] [*ICAO location identifier*] (ICLI) .... KNQX
Key Word [*Online database field identifier*] .... CLE
Key Word [*Online database field identifier*] .... KW
Key Word as a Dictionary Entry [*IBM*] [*Indexing system*] (NITA) .... KWADE
Key Word Online Catalogue Access .... KWOCA
Keyano College, Fort McMurray, Alberta [*Library symbol National Library of Canada*] (NLC) .... AFMK
Key-Auto-Key [*Computer science*] .... KAK
Keyboard [*Computer science*] .... KB
Keyboard .... KBD
Keyboard [*Computer science*] .... KEYBD
Keyboard (MSA) .... KYBD
Keyboard .... KYBRD
Keyboard and Display [*Computer science*] .... KAD
Keyboard and Display [*Computer science*] (MHDB) .... KD
Keyboard and Display Test (MCD) .... KDT
Keyboard and Printer Controller [*Computer science*] (NITA) .... KBPRC
Keyboard Assembly (DWSG) .... KBA
Keyboard Cathode Ray Tube (MCD) .... KCRT
Keyboard Change Button [*Computer science*] .... KCB
Keyboard Class Select / Statistics Output [*Computer science*] (MHDI) .... KCS/SO
Keyboard Common Contact [*Computer science*] .... KCC
Keyboard Configuration Studies (NASA) .... KCS
Keyboard Control Unit .... KCU
Keyboard Controlled Sequencer [*Computer science*] .... KCS
Keyboard Data Entry .... KDE
Keyboard Data Recorder [*Computer science*] .... KDR
Keyboard/Display (ACRL) .... K/D
Keyboard, Display, and Printer [*Computer science*] .... KDP
Keyboard Display Station [*Computer science*] (DA) .... KDS
Keyboard Display Terminal (MCD) .... KDT
Keyboard Display Unit (MCD) .... KDU
Keyboard Encoder [*Computer science*] .... KBE
Keyboard Encoder (NITA) .... KBENC
Keyboard Entry [*Computer science*] .... KBE
Keyboard Immortals [*Recording label*] .... KBI
Keyboard Input Device (MCD) .... KID
Keyboard Input Matrix [*Computer science*] .... KIM
Keyboard Input Printout [*Computer science*] (IEEE) .... KIPO
Keyboard Input Processor [*Computer science*] (NASA) .... KIP
Keyboard Input Simulation [*Computer science*] .... KIS
Keyboard Input Simulation-Noise-Problem Input [*Computer science*] (SAA) .... KSNOPI
Keyboard Input Stimulation Noise Problem Input (IAA) .... KISNOPI
Keyboard Interface Control Unit [*Computer science*] .... KICU
Keyboard Interface Module (MCD) .... KBIM
Keyboard Listener [*Computer science*] (MHDI) .... KBL
Keyboard Monitor [*Computer science*] .... KBM
Keyboard Monitor [*Digital Equipment Corp.*] .... KMON
Keyboard Perforator .... KP
Keyboard/Printer Control [*Computer science*] .... KPC
Keyboard Priority Controller [*Computer science*] (HGAA) .... KPC
Keyboard Process [*Computer science*] .... KBP
Keyboard Send and Receive [*Computer science*] .... KSR
Keyboard Send/Receive Terminal [*Computer science*] (MHDI) .... KSR/T
Keyboard Simulated Lateral Telling [*Computer science*] .... KSL
Keyboard Teachers Association (EA) .... KTA

Keyboard Typing Perforator (NITA) .... KTP
Keyboard Typing Reperforator [Computer science] .... KTR
Keyboard Unit [Computer science] (NASA) .... KBU
Keyboard Unit [Computer science] (NASA) .... KU
Keyboard/Video Switch [Computer science] .... KVS
Keyboard Visual Display Terminal (MCD) .... KVDT
Keyboard-Controlled Phototypesetter (NITA) .... KCP
Keyboards, Computers, and Software [A publication] .... KCS
Keychart Educational Equipment [for use with an electronic typewriter] .... KEE
Key-Click Filter .... KEY
KeyCorp [NYSE symbol] (SPSG) .... Keycorp
Keycorp [Associated Press] (SAG) .... Keycorp
Keycorp [Associated Press] (SAG) .... Keycp
KeyCorp 10% cm Dep Pfd [NYSE symbol] (TTSB) .... KEYPrA
Keycorp Industries [Vancouver Stock Exchange symbol] .... KYS
Keyed Address (IAA) .... KA
Keyed Alike [Locks] (ADA) .... KA
Keyed Display Console .... KDC
Keyed File Access Method [Computer science] (PDAA) .... KFAM
Keyed File Access System .... KFAS
Keyed File System [Computer science] .... KFS
Keyed Indexed Sequential Search .... KISS
Keyed Input Language .... KIL
Keyed Sequential Access Method [Computer science] (CMD) ...... KSAM
Keyed to Differ [Locks] (ADA) .... KD
Keyed Video Generator .... KVG
Keyed-Access, Erasable, Programmable Read-Only Memory [Computer science] .... KEPROM
Key-Edit Terminal Language [Computer science] (MHDI) .... KTL
Keyes' New York Court of Appeals Reports [A publication] (DLA) .... K
Keyes' New York Court of Appeals Reports [A publication] (DLA) .... Key
Keyes' New York Court of Appeals Reports [A publication] (DLA) .... Keyes
Keyes on Future Interest in Chattels [A publication] (DLA) .... Key Ch
Keyes on Future Interest in Lands [A publication] (DLA) .... Key Lands
Keyes on Remainders [A publication] (DLA) .... Key Rem
Keyette International (EA) .... KI
Keyfile Open Access Layer [Workflow automation software] (PCM) .... KOALA
Keyhole [United States reconnaissance satellite] (DOMA) .... KY
Keyhole (ABBR) .... KYHL
Keyhole Limpet Hemocyanin [Immunology] .... KLH
Keyhole Series [Optical reconnaissance satellites] .... KH
Keying Devices [JETDS nomenclature] [Military] (CET) .... KY
Keying Material [Computer science] (NVT) .... KEYMAT
Keying Relay .... KR
Keying Switching Station .... KSS
Keying Time [Computer order entry] .... KT
Keyletter-in-Context [Computer science] .... KLIC
Keylway's [or Keilway's] English King's Bench Reports [A publication] (DLA) .... Keyl
Keylway's [or Keilway's] English King's Bench Reports [A publication] (DLA) .... Keylway
KeyMath Diagnostic Arithmetic Test .... KMDAT
Keynote (ABBR) .... KYNT
Keynoting (ABBR) .... KYNTG
Key-On Engine-Off [Automotive engineering] .... KOEO
Key-On Engine-Running [Automotive engineering] .... KOER
Keyona College, Fort McMurray, AB, Canada [Library symbol Library of Congress] (LCLS) .... CaAFmK
Keyport Free Public Library, Keyport, NJ [Library symbol Library of Congress] (LCLS) .... NjKey
Keypunch [Computer science] .... KP
Keypunch Cabinet [Computer science] .... KPC
Keypunch Operator [Computer science] .... KPO
Keypunch Performance System [Computer science] (PDAA) .... KPS
Keypunch Replacement [Computer science] (MHDI) .... KPR
Keys [Commonly used] (OPSA) .... KEYS
Keys .... KYS
Keyseat (KSC) .... KST
Keyser, WV [FM radio station call letters] .... WCBC
Keyser, WV [AM radio station call letters] .... WKLP
Keyser, WV [FM radio station call letters] .... WQZK
Keyser-Mineral County Public and Potomac Valley Regional Library, Keyser, WV [Library symbol Library of Congress] (LCLS) .... WvK
Keyser's Stock Exchange [1850] [A publication] (DLA) .... Keys St Ex
Keyset [Navy] (NVT) .... KS
Keyset Central Multiplexer .... KCMX
Keyset Panel .... KSP
Keysort Multiple Selector .... KMS
Keystation Adapter Unit [Computer science] .... KAU
Keystation Control Language [Computer science] (MHDI) .... KCL
Keystation On-Line Business-Oriented Language [Computer science] .... KOBOL
Keyston Financial, Inc. [Associated Press] (SAG) .... KeyFn
Keystone .... KEYSTN
Keystone .... KS
Keystone (IAA) .... KS
Keystone (VRA) .... kyst
Keystone (ABBR) .... KYSTN
Keystone Air Services Ltd. [Canada ICAO designator] (FAAC) .... KEE
Keystone Association for Educational Data Systems (HGAA) .... KAEDS
Keystone Automotive Industries, Inc. [NASDAQ symbol] (SAG) .... KEYS
Keystone Automotive Industries, Inc. [Associated Press] (SAG) .... KeysAut
Keystone Bituminous Coal Association .... KBCA
Keystone Center [An association] (EA) .... KC
Keystone Consol Ind [NYSE symbol] (TTSB) .... KES
Keystone Consolidated Industries [Associated Press] (SAG) .... KeyCon
Keystone Consolidated Industries, Inc. [NYSE symbol] (SPSG) .... KES

Keystone Explorations [Vancouver Stock Exchange symbol] .... KYT
Keystone Financial [Associated Press] (SAG) .... KeystFn
Keystone Financial [NASDAQ symbol] (TTSB) .... KSTN
Keystone Financial, Inc. [NASDAQ symbol] (NQ) .... KSTN
Keystone Heritage Group [AMEX symbol] (TTSB) .... KHG
Keystone Heritage Group, Inc. [Associated Press] (SAG) .... KeysHer
Keystone Heritage Group, Inc. [AMEX symbol] (SAG) .... KHG
Keystone International [Associated Press] (SAG) .... KeyInt
Keystone International, Inc. [NYSE symbol] (SPSG) .... KII
Keystone Intl [NYSE symbol] (TTSB) .... KIL
Keystone Junior College [Pennsylvania] .... KJC
Keystone Junior College, La Plume, PA [Library symbol Library of Congress] (LCLS) .... PLapK
Keystone Public Library, Keystone, IA [Library symbol Library of Congress] (LCLS) .... IaKey
Keystone Visual Survey Test [Ophthalmology] .... KVST
Keystrokes Per Hour (NITA) .... KPH
Keyswitch Magic Relay Finder (IAA) .... KMRF
Key-to-Address Transformation [Computer science] (PDAA) .... KAT
Key-to-Disk Subsystem [Computer science] (MHDB) .... KDSS
Key-to-Disk-to-Tape (MCD) .... KDT
Keyword Adapted [Computer science] .... KWA
Keyword and Context [Indexing] (DIT) .... KWAC
Keyword and Universal Decimal Classification (PDAA) .... KWUC
Keyword Detection (NITA) .... KEYTECT
Keyword in Context [Indexing] .... KWIC
Keyword in Title [Indexing] .... KWIT
Keyword Index to Serial Titles [A publication] .... KIST
Keyword out of Context [Indexing] .... KWOC
Keyword out of Title [Indexing] .... KWOT
Keyword Transformation Unit [Computer science] (MHDI) .... KXU
Keyword Word in Permutation [Indexing] (PDAA) .... KWIP
Keyworded References to Archaeological Science [Department of Archaeology] [University of Leicester British] [Database] (NITA) .... KRAS
Keywords and Learning (AIE) .... KAL
Keywords Permuted (DIT) .... KEYPER
KFX, Inc. [AMEX symbol] (SAG) .... KFX
KFX Inc. [AMEX symbol] (TTSB) .... KFX
KFx, Inc. [Associated Press] (SAG) .... KFX Inc
KFx, Inc. [NASDAQ symbol] (SAG) .... KFXI
K.G. Parker Elementary School, Elk River, MN [Library symbol] [Library of Congress] (LCLS) .... MnErPE
KGB [Komitet Gossudarstvennoi Bezopasnosti] Agent .... K
Khabarovsk [Former USSR Geomagnetic observatory code] .... KHB
Khabarovsk [Former USSR Airport symbol] (OAG) .... KHV
Khabarovsk Commodity Exchange [Russian Federation] (EY) .... KHCE
Khabarovsk/Novy [Former USSR ICAO location identifier] (ICLI) .... UHHH
Khailkhal [Iran] [ICAO location identifier] (ICLI) .... OIGK
Khajuraho [India] [Airport symbol] (OAG) .... HJR
Khajuraho [India] [ICAO location identifier] (ICLI) .... VIKJ
Khaki Drill [British military] (DMA) .... KD
Khaksar Tehrik [Pakistan] [Political party] (FEA) .... KT
Khamampet [India] [ICAO location identifier] (ICLI) .... VOKM
Khamis Mushait [Saudi Arabia] [ICAO location identifier] (ICLI) .... OEKM
Khamtis [Myanmar] [Airport symbol] (OAG) .... KHM
Khan (ABBR) .... KN
Khancoban [Australia Seismograph station code, US Geological Survey] (SEIS) .... KHA
Khandwa [India] [ICAO location identifier] (ICLI) .... VAKD
Khaneh/Piranshahr [Iran] [ICAO location identifier] (ICLI) .... OITH
Khania/Souda [Greece] [ICAO location identifier] (ICLI) .... LGSA
Khan-Lewis Phonological Analysis [Speech evaluation test] .... KLPA
Khanty-Mansiysk [Former USSR ICAO location identifier] (ICLI) .... USHH
Khao San Pathet Lao [News agency] [Laos] (FEA) .... KPL
Khapalu [Pakistan] [Airport symbol] (AD) .... KPU
Khapcheranga [Former USSR Seismograph station code, US Geological Survey] (SEIS) .... KPC
Kharaghan [Iran] [ICAO location identifier] (ICLI) .... OIHG
Kharan [Pakistan] [ICAO location identifier] (ICLI) .... OPKN
Khark [Iran] [Airport symbol Obsolete] (OAG) .... KHK
Khark Island [Iran] [ICAO location identifier] (ICLI) .... OIBQ
Kharkov [Former USSR Airport symbol] (OAG) .... HRK
Kharkov Commodity and Raw Materials Exchange [Ukraine] (EY) .... KHCME
Khartoum [Sudan] [ICAO location identifier] (ICLI) .... HSSS
Khartoum [Sudan] [Airport symbol] (OAG) .... KRT
Khasab [Oman] [ICAO location identifier] (ICLI) .... OOKB
Khash [Iran] [ICAO location identifier] (ICLI) .... OIZK
Khashm El Girba [Sudan] [ICAO location identifier] (ICLI) .... HSKG
Khasi [MARC language code Library of Congress] (LCCP) .... kha
Khasm el Girba [Sudan] [Airport symbol] (AD) .... GBU
Khazar [Turkmenistan] [ICAO designator] (FAAC) .... KHR
Khe Sanh Combat Base [Vietnam] [Marine Corps] (VNW) .... KSCB
Kheis [Former USSR Seismograph station code, US Geological Survey] (SEIS) .... KHE
Kherson [USSR] [Airport symbol] (AD) .... KHE
Khezr Abad [Iran] [ICAO location identifier] (ICLI) .... OIYQ
Khios [Greece] [ICAO location identifier] (ICLI) .... LGHI
Khirbet (BJA) .... Kh
Khmer [Cambodia] Air Force (VNW) .... KAF
Khmer Insurgents [Cambodian rebel force] .... KI
Khmer People's National Liberation Front [Cambodia] [Political party] (PD) .... KPNLF
Khmer Rouge (BARN) .... KR
Khodzhikent [Former USSR Seismograph station code, US Geological Survey Closed] (SEIS) .... KDK

Khojaghar [*Afghanistan*] [*ICAO location identifier*] (ICLI) .... OAKG
Khomein [*Iran*] [*ICAO location identifier*] (ICLI) .... OIFW
Khomeini Shahr [*Iran*] [*ICAO location identifier*] (ICLI) .... OIFO
Khon Kaen [*Thailand*] [*Airport symbol*] (OAG) .... KKC
Khon Kaen [*Thailand*] [*ICAO location identifier*] (ICLI) .... VTUK
Khon Kaen/Nam Phung Dam [*Thailand*] [*ICAO location identifier*] (ICLI) .... VTUZ
Khong Island [*Laos*] [*ICAO location identifier*] (ICLI) .... VLKG
Khonj [*Iran*] [*ICAO location identifier*] (ICLI) .... OISX
Khor/Jandagh [*Iran*] [*ICAO location identifier*] (ICLI) .... OIYK
Khoram Dareh [*Iran*] [*ICAO location identifier*] (ICLI) .... OIIM
Khore Beyabanak [*Iran*] [*ICAO location identifier*] (ICLI) .... OIYN
Khorinsk [*Former USSR ICAO location identifier*] (ICLI) .... UIUH
Khorixas [*Namibia*] [*ICAO location identifier*] (ICLI) .... FAKX
Khorog [*Former USSR Seismograph station code, US Geological Survey*] (SEIS) .... KHO
Khorongon [*Former USSR Seismograph station code, US Geological Survey Closed*] (SEIS) .... KHR
Khorram Abad [*Iran*] [*ICAO location identifier*] (ICLI) .... OICK
Khors Aircompany [*Ukraine*] [*FAA designator*] (FAAC) .... KHO
Khortitsa-Air Ltd. [*Ukraine*] [*FAA designator*] (FAAC) .... PBZ
Khost [*Afghanistan*] [*Airport symbol Obsolete*] (OAG) .... KHT
Khost [*Afghanistan*] [*ICAO location identifier*] (ICLI) .... OAKS
Khost-O-Fering [*Afghanistan*] [*ICAO location identifier*] (ICLI) .... OAFG
Khotanese [*MARC language code Library of Congress*] (LCCP) .... kho
Khotanese Texts (BJA) .... KT
Khouribga [*Morocco*] [*ICAO location identifier*] (ICLI) .... GMMK
Khowai [*India*] [*Airport symbol*] (AD) .... IXN
Khowai [*India*] [*ICAO location identifier*] (ICLI) .... VEKW
Khoy [*Iran*] [*ICAO location identifier*] (ICLI) .... OITK
Khranit' Vechno [*To be Kept in Perpetuity*] [*KGB file status*] .... KhV
Khristianski Vostok (BJA) .... KhV
Khulna [*Bangladesh*] [*Airport symbol*] (AD) .... KHL
Khuzdar [*Pakistan*] [*Airport symbol*] (AD) .... KZR
Khuzdhar [*Pakistan*] [*ICAO location identifier*] (ICLI) .... OPKH
Khwahan [*Afghanistan*] [*ICAO location identifier*] (ICLI) .... OAHN
Khwai River Lodge [*Botswana*] [*ICAO location identifier*] (ICLI) .... FBKR
Kiana [*Alaska*] [*Airport symbol*] (OAG) .... IAN
Kiangsi Province [*China, Mainland*] [*MARC geographic area code Library of Congress*] (LCCP) .... a-cc-ki
Kiangsu Province [*China, Mainland*] [*MARC geographic area code Library of Congress*] (LCCP) .... a-cc-ku
Kiapupe [*Zaire*] [*ICAO location identifier*] (ICLI) .... FZOF
Kibangou [*Congo*] [*ICAO location identifier*] (ICLI) .... FCPG
Kibris Milli Turk Birligi [*Cypriot National Turkish Union*] (PPE) .... KMTB
Kibris Turk Hava Yollari Ltd. [*Turkey*] [*FAA designator*] (FAAC) .... KYV
Kick in the Afterdeck [*Bowdlerized version*] .... KITA
Kick It Off [*Slang*] (DOMA) .... KIO
Kick Plate .... KP
Kick Plate [*Building construction*] .... KPL
Kick Plate and Drip (AAG) .... KP & D
Kick Stage [*NASA*] (NASA) .... K/S
Kickback (MHDB) .... KB
Kickback Racket Act .... KRA
Kickdown [*Automotive engineering*] .... K/DN
Kicker [*Football*] .... K
Kickoff (MSA) .... KO
Kickoff Point [*Diamond drilling*] .... KOP
Kickpipe [*Building construction*] .... KP
Kid-Adult [*Television viewer aged 12-34*] .... Kidult
Kidal [*Mali*] [*ICAO location identifier*] (ICLI) .... GAKL
Kidd A [*Blood group*] (DAVI) .... Jk^a
Kidd B [*Blood group*] (DAVI) .... Jk^b
Kidd Creek Mines Ltd., Toronto, ON, Canada [*Library symbol*] [*Library of Congress*] (LCLS) .... CaOTKC
Kidd Creek Mines Ltd., Toronto, Ontario [*Library symbol National Library of Canada*] (NLC) .... OTKC
Kidd Resources Ltd. [*Vancouver Stock Exchange symbol*] .... KID
Kidderminster [*British depot code*] .... KDR
Kiddie .... KID
Kiddie Academy International, Inc. [*NASDAQ symbol*] (SAG) .... KAII
Kiddie Academy International, Inc. [*Associated Press*] (SAG) .... KidAInt
Kiddie Academy International, Inc. [*Associated Press*] (SAG) .... KiddAcInt
Kiddie Academy Intl [*NASDAQ symbol*] (TTSB) .... KAII
Kiddie Academy Intl Wrrt [*NASDAQ symbol*] (TTSB) .... KAIIW
Kiddie Products, Inc. [*NASDAQ symbol*] (NQ) .... KIDD
Kiddushin (BJA) .... Kid
Kideo Productions [*Associated Press*] (SAG) .... Kideo
Kideo Productions [*NASDAQ symbol*] (SAG) .... KIDO
Kidnap and Ransom [*Insurance terminology*] .... KNR
Kidnaping [*FBI standardized term*] .... KID
Kidnaping and Ransom [*Insurance policy*] .... K and R
Kidney [*Anatomy*] (MAE) .... K
Kidney [*Anatomy*] (DAVI) .... KID
Kidney and Lung Extract .... KLX
Kidney and Upper Bladder .... KUB
Kidney Bean Purple Acid Phosphatase [*An enzyme*] .... KBPAP
Kidney Disease Control Program [*Public Health Service*] .... KDCP
Kidney Disease Treatment Center (DMAA) .... KDC
Kidney Function [*Nephrology*] (DAVI) .... KF
Kidney Goldblatt Hypertension [*Medicine*] (DAVI) .... KGHT
Kidney Goldblatt Hypertension Scale .... KGH
Kidney, Liver, Spleen [*Medicine*] .... KLS
Kidney Lobe .... KL
Kidney Plasminogen Activator [*Anticlotting agent*] .... KPA
Kidney Pore .... KP
Kidney Protein [*Nephrology*] (DAVI) .... KP
Kidney Punch [*Medicine*] (DAVI) .... KP
Kidney Punch Test [*or Murphy's test*] (DAVI) .... KPT
Kidney Sac .... KS
Kidney Transplant [*Surgery*] (DAVI) .... KT
Kidney Transplant [*Medicine*] (DMAA) .... KT
Kidney Transplant Unit [*National Health Service*] [*British*] (DI) .... KTU
Kidney Ultrafiltration Rate [*Nephrology*] (DAVI) .... KUF
Kidney, Ureter, and Spleen [*Anatomy*] (MAH) .... KUS
Kidney, Ureter, Bladder [*X-ray*] .... KUB
Kidney Valve .... KV
Kidney-Fixing Antibody [*Immunology*] .... KFAB
Kidney-Specific Protein [*Medicine*] (DAVI) .... KSP
Kid-Powered Vehicle .... KPV
Kids Against Pollution .... KAP
Kids' Clubs Network (AIE) .... KCN
Kids for Saving Earth [*An association*] (EA) .... KSE
KIDS Fund (EA) .... KF
Kids of Preachers .... KP
Kidsgrove ALGOL [*Algorithmic Language*] **Digital Analogue Simulation** [*Computer science British*] .... KALDAS
Kiel Electron Telescope .... KET
Kiel Public Library, Kiel, WI [*Library symbol Library of Congress*] (LCLS) .... WKi
Kiel-Holtenau [*Germany ICAO location identifier*] (ICLI) .... EDCK
Kiena Gold Mines Ltd. [*Toronto Stock Exchange symbol*] .... KGM
Kienboeck's Unit [*of x-ray dosage*] (AAMN) X
Kienzle Input/Output Peripheral Interface .... KIOPI
Kienzle Input/Output Processor Interface (NITA) .... KIOPI
Kiernan Reentry Measurement Site .... KREMS
Kierowinctwo Walki Podziemnej (BJA) .... KWP
Kierowinctwo Walki Cywilnej (BJA) .... KWC
Kiersley Temperament Sorter [*Psychiatry*] (DAVI) .... KTS
Kieta [*Papua New Guinea*] [*Airport symbol*] (OAG) .... KIE
Kiev [*Former USSR Airport symbol*] (OAG) .... IEV
Kiev [*Former USSR Geomagnetic observatory code*] .... KIV
Kiev AAR Airlines [*Ukraine*] [*FAA designator*] (FAAC) .... AXA
Kiev Aviation Plant [*Ukraine*] [*FAA designator*] (FAAC) .... UAK
Kiev/Borispol [*Former USSR ICAO location identifier*] (ICLI) .... UKBB
Kiev Borispol Airport [*Former USSR Airport symbol*] (OAG) .... KBP
Kiev Universal Commodity Exchange [*Ukraine*] (EY) .... KUCE
Kiev/Zhulyany [*Former USSR ICAO location identifier*] (ICLI) .... UKKK
Kiffa [*Mauritania*] [*ICAO location identifier*] (ICLI) .... GQNF
Kiffa [*Mauritania*] [*Airport symbol*] (OAG) .... KFA
Kiftsgate [*England*] .... KIFTSG
Kigali [*Rwanda*] [*ICAO location identifier*] (ICLI) .... HRYR
Kigali [*Rwanda*] [*Airport symbol*] (OAG) .... KGL
Kigoma [*Tanzania*] [*ICAO location identifier*] (ICLI) .... HTKA
Kigoma [*Tanzania*] [*Airport symbol*] (OAG) .... TKQ
Kihei, HI [*AM radio station call letters*] .... KAOI
K-III Commun$2.875SrExPfd [*NYSE symbol*] (TTSB) .... KCCPr
K-III Communications [*NYSE symbol*] (TTSB) .... KCC
K-III Communications Corp. [*NYSE symbol*] (SPSG) .... KCC
K-III Communications Corp. [*Associated Press*] (SAG) .... K-III
Kiikala [*Finland ICAO location identifier*] (ICLI) .... EFIK
Kikai/Kikaigashima Island [*Japan ICAO location identifier*] (ICLI) .... RJKI
Kikaiga Shima [*Japan*] [*Airport symbol*] (OAG) .... KKX
Kikongo Sur Wamba [*Zaire*] [*ICAO location identifier*] (ICLI) .... FZCW
Kikori [*Papua New Guinea*] [*Airport symbol*] (OAG) .... KRI
Kikuyu [*MARC language code Library of Congress*] (LCCP) .... kik
Kikwit [*Zaire*] [*ICAO location identifier*] (ICLI) .... FZCA
Kikwit [*Zaire*] [*Airport symbol*] (OAG) .... KKW
Kilaguni [*Kenya*] [*ICAO location identifier*] (ICLI) .... HKKL
Kil'aim (BJA) .... Kil
Kilauea, HI [*FM radio station call letters*] (RBYB) .... KAQA-FM
Kilborn Engineering Ltd., Toronto, Ontario [*Library symbol National Library of Canada*] (NLC) .... OTKE
Kilbourn Public Library, Wisconsin Dells, WI [*Library symbol Library of Congress*] (LCLS) .... WWd
Kilburn's English Magistrates' Cases [*A publication*] (DLA) .... Kilb
Kilby Provincial Historic Park, Harrison Mills, British Columbia [*Library symbol National Library of Canada*] (NLC) .... BHMK
Kildare [*County in Ireland*] (ROG) .... KID
Kildare [*County in Ireland*] (ROG) .... KILD
Kilderkin [*Unit of measurement*] [*British*] (ROG) .... KIL
Kilderkin [*Unit of measurement*] [*British*] .... KILD
Kileen, TX [*TV station call letters*] (RBYB) .... KAKW
Kileen, TX [*AM radio station call letters*] .... KRMY
Kilembe Resources Ltd. [*Vancouver Stock Exchange symbol*] .... KIL
Kilenge Mission [*New Britain*] [*Seismograph station code, US Geological Survey*] (SEIS) .... KCM
Kilgore College, Kilgore, TX [*Library symbol Library of Congress*] (LCLS) .... TxKilC
Kilgore, TX [*AM radio station call letters*] .... KKTX
Kilgore, TX [*FM radio station call letters*] .... KKTX-FM
Kilgore, TX [*FM radio station call letters*] .... KTPB
Kilham Rat Virus [*Medicine*] .... KRV
Kili [*Marshall Islands*] [*Airport symbol*] (OAG) .... KIO
Kilimanjaro [*Tanzania*] [*ICAO location identifier*] (ICLI) .... HTKJ
Kilimanjaro [*Tanzania*] [*Airport symbol*] (OAG) .... JRO
Kilimatinde [*Tanzania*] [*ICAO location identifier*] (ICLI) .... HTKT
Kilkenny [*County in Ireland*] .... KILK
Kilkerran's Scotch Court of Session Decisions [*A publication*] (DLA) .... Kilk
Kilkerran's Scotch Court of Session Decisions [*A publication*] (DLA) .... Kilkerran
Kill Bad Name [*Marketing*] (WDMC) .... KBN
Kill Devil Hills, NC [*Location identifier FAA*] (FAAL) .... FFA
Kill Devil Hills, NC [*FM radio station call letters*] .... WCXL

Kill Probability (MCD)	KP
Kill Vehicle	KV
Killaloe/Bonnechere, ON [*ICAO location identifier*] (ICLI)	CYXI
Killaloe Public Library, Ontario [*Library symbol National Library of Canada*] (NLC)	OKIL
Killam Public Library, Alberta [*Library symbol National Library of Canada*] (NLC)	AKI
Killarney Oscillation [*Climatology*]	KO
Killdeer (ABBR)	KLDR
Killearn Properties [*AMEX symbol*] (TTSB)	KPL
Killearn Properties, Inc. [*Associated Press*] (SAG)	Kilern
Killearn Properties, Inc. [*AMEX symbol*] (SPSG)	KPI
Killed	K
Killed (AABC)	KD
Killed by Action [*In reference to the enemy*] [*Vietnam*] (VNW)	KBA
Killed by Air [*Military*]	KBA
Killed by Artillery [*In reference to the enemy*] [*Vietnam*] (VNW)	KBA
Killed by Helicopter [*In reference to the enemy*] [*Vietnam*]	KBH
Killed by Hostile Action [*Military*]	KHA
Killed in Action	ka
Killed in Action [*Military*]	KIA
Killed in Action - Body Not Recovered (MCD)	KIA - BNR
Killed Intracellular Bacteria [*Microbiology*] (DAVI)	KICB
Killed Measles-Virus Vaccine	KMV
Killed; Not Enemy Action [*Military*]	KNA
Killed Organism [*Medicine*] (DMAA)	KO
Killed Parenteral [*Vaccine*] [*Immunology*] (DAVI)	KP
Killed Parenteral Vaccine [*Immunology*] (DAVI)	KPV
Killed Poliomyelitis Vaccine [*Immunology*] (MAE)	PKV
Killed Target Detector [*Military*] (PDAA)	KTD
Killed Vaccine [*Immunology*] (MAE)	KV
Killed Virus [*Pharmacology*] (DAVI)	KV
Killed-Measles Vaccine [*Immunology*] (MAE)	MKV
Killeen [*Texas*] [*Airport symbol*] (OAG)	ILE
Killeen/Robert Gray Army Air Field [*Texas*] [*ICAO location identifier*] (ICLI)	KGRK
Killeen, TX [*Location identifier FAA*] (FAAL)	GRK
Killeen, TX [*Location identifier FAA*] (FAAL)	HLR
Killeen, TX [*Location identifier FAA*] (FAAL)	ILE
Killeen, TX [*FM radio station call letters*] (RBYB)	KAJZ-FM
Killeen, TX [*FM radio station call letters*]	KHHT
Killeen, TX [*FM radio station call letters*]	KIIZ
Killeen, TX [*FM radio station call letters*]	KNCT
Killer [*Cells*] [*Cytology*] (DAVI)	K
Killer as an Organized Sport [*Campus game*]	KAOS
Killer Weed [*Slang for phencyclidine; also called PCP and Sernyl*] (DAVI)	KW
Killer-Assistng Factor (DAVI)	KAF
Killer-Cell Inhibitory Receptor [*Immunology*]	KIR
Killick Gold Co. [*Vancouver Stock Exchange symbol*]	KLK
Killing (ABBR)	KLG
Killing Federal Officer	KFO
Killing Frost [*NWS*] (FAAC)	KFRST
Killing Zone [*Military British*]	KZ
Killington, VT [*FM radio station call letters*]	WEBK
Killjoy (ABBR)	KLJY
Kilman Phacoemulsification [*Medicine*] (MEDA)	KPE
Kilmarnock [*Postcode*] (ODBW)	KA
Kilmarnock Public Library, Central Library, Dick Institute, Kilmarnock, United Kingdom [*Library symbol Library of Congress*] (LCLS)	UkKi
Kilmarnock, VA [*FM radio station call letters*]	WKWI
Kiln, MS [*Location identifier FAA*] (FAAL)	AYI
Kiln-Dried [*Lumber*]	KD
Kiln-Dried After Treatment [*Lumber*]	KDAT
Kilo [*Phonetic alphabet*] [*International*] (DSUE)	K
Kilo [*A prefix meaning multiplied by 10³*] [*SI symbol*]	k
Kilo (WDMC)	k
Kilo (WDAA)	KI
Kilo Accounting Units (NASA)	KAU
Kilo British Thermal Unit (WDAA)	KBTU
Kilo BTU [*British Thermal Unit*]	KB
Kilo Characters per Second (IAA)	KCHS
Kilo Gray [*Absorbed dose*] [*Radiology*]	kGy
Kilo Symbols per Second (MCD)	KSPS
Kilo Yard	KYD
Kiloampere	kA
Kiloampere Hour (IAA)	KAH
Kilobar	kb
Kilobar	KBAR
Kilobase	kb
Kilobase Pairs [*Genetics*]	kbp
Kilobaud (IAA)	KB
KiloBIT [*Binary Digit*] [*Computer science*]	kb
KiloBITS [*Binary Digits*] per Second [*Transmission rate*] [*Computer science*] (TEL)	KBIT/S
KiloBITS [*Binary Digits*] per Second [*Transmission rate*] [*Computer science*]	kbps
Kilobits per Second [*Computer science*]	Kbps
KiloBITS [*Binary Digits*] per Second [*Transmission rate*] [*Computer science*]	kbs
Kilobyte [*10³ bytes*] [*Computer science*]	K
Kilobyte [*10³ bytes*] [*Computer science*]	KB
Kilobyte (NFD)	Kb
Kilobytes per Second [*Computer science*] (DOM)	KBps
Kilobytes Per Second (NITA)	KBPS
Kilobytes per Second [*Computer science*]	KBS
Kilocalorie	kc

Kilocalorie	kcal
Kilocharacter (BUR)	KC
Kilocharacter (MHDB)	kch
Kilocharacter (MHDB)	kchr
Kilocharacters per Second (IAA)	KCS
Kilocurie (IAA)	KC
Kilocurie (IDOE)	kc
Kilocurie (DEN)	kCi
Kilocurie (IAA)	KCU
Kilocycle	K
Kilocycle [*Radio*]	kc
Kilocycle (ABBR)	KLCCL
Kilocycles per Second	kcps
Kilocycles per Second	kcs
Kilocycles per Second [*Measurement*] (DAVI)	kd/sec
Kilodalton [*Molecular mass measure*]	kD
Kilodalton [*Physics*] [*Chemistry*] (DOG)	kDa
Kiloelectron Volt	keV
Kiloelectron Watt	keW
Kilogallons per Minute (MCD)	KGAL/MIN
Kilogauss	kG
Kilograin (BARN)	kgr
Kilogram [*Also, kg*] [*Symbol SI unit for mass*]	k
Kilogram [*Also, k*] [*Symbol SI unit for mass*]	kg
Kilogram (GAVI)	KG
Kilogram (AAGC)	Kg
Kilogram [*Also, k, kg*] [*SI unit for mass*] (DAVI)	kgm
Kilogram	KIL
Kilogram	KILO
Kilogram (ABBR)	KLGM
Kilogram (ROG)	KO
Kilogram Force per Meter	KGF/M
Kilogram Force per Square Centimeter	KGF/CM²
Kilogram Force per Square Meter	KGF/M²
Kilogram Weight (IAA)	KGWT
Kilogram-Calorie (IDOE)	kgc
Kilogram-Calorie	kgcal
Kilogram-Foot	kg-f
Kilogram-Force [*Unit of force*]	kgf
Kilogram-Meter	kg-m
Kilogram-Meter (IDOE)	kgm
Kilograms Oil Equivalent [*Petroleum industry*]	KOE
Kilograms per Cubic Meter	kg/cum
Kilograms per Cubic Meter	KG/M³
Kilograms per Cubic Meter (IDOE)	kg/m³
Kilograms per Hour (WDAA)	KG/HR
Kilograms per Joule	KG/J
Kilograms per Pascal Second Square Meter	KG/(PA S M²)
Kilograms per Second	kg/s
Kilograms per Second	kgps
Kilograms per Square Centimeter (DS)	kc
Kilograms per Square Meter	KG/M²
Kilograms Static Thrust (DOMA)	kgst
Kilohenry	KH
Kilohertz	kH
Kilohertz [*Electronics*]	kHz
Kilohertz [*FAA*] (TAG)	KHZ
Kilohertz [*Preferred form is kHz*] [*Electronics*] (MCD)	KZ
Kilohm	k
Kilohm (ABBR)	KO
Kilohm (MCD)	KOHM
Kilohm [*Formerly, K*] [*Unit of electrical resistance*] (DAVI)	kW
Kilo-Instructions per Second	KIPS
Kilojoule	kJ
Kilokayser	kK
Kilokelvin	KK
Kilolambert	kL
Kiloliter	KILOL
Kiloliter	kL
Kiloliters per Minute	KL/M
Kilomega	kM
Kilomega Hertz (MCD)	kMHZ
Kilomegacycle	kMc
Kilomegacycles per Second (AABC)	kMcs
Kilomegacycles per Sound [*Measurement*] (DAVI)	kMcps
Kilomegawatt (WGA)	kmw
Kilomegawatt-Hour (WGA)	kmwh
Kilometer (WDAA)	K
Kilometer	KIL
Kilometer	KILO
Kilometer	KILOM
Kilometer	KLM
Kilometer (ABBR)	KLMTR
Kilometer	km
Kilometer [*BTS*] (TAG)	KM
Kilometer Post	KP
Kilometers per Hour	KM/HR
Kilometers per Hour	kmh
Kilometers per Hour (AABC)	kmph
Kilometers per Hour	kph
Kilometers per Second	km/s
Kilometers per Second	kmps
Kilometers per Second (NASA)	KPS
Kilometer-Wave Orbiting Telescope [*NASA*]	KWOT
Kilometres in the Hour [*Rate of march*] [*Military British*]	KIH

Kilometric Wavelength [Radio astronomy] .... KOM
Kilomines [Zaire] [ICAO location identifier] (ICLI) .... FZKF
Kilonewton .... kN
Kilooersted .... kOe
Kilopackets per Second [Telecommunications] .... KPPS
Kiloparsec [Astronomy] .... kpc
Kilopascal .... kPa
Kilopond .... KP
Kilopondmeter .... Kpm
Kilopound (IAA) .... KIP
Kilopound (MCD) .... KLB
Kilopound-Force (WDAA) .... KLBF
Kilopounds per Square Inch (SAA) .... KSI
Kilopulse .... kp
Kilopulses per Second .... kpps
Kilorad (WDAA) .... KRAD
Kilorayleigh .... kR
Kiloroentgen .... kR
Kilostere .... KS
Kiloton [Nuclear equivalent of 1000 tons of high explosives] (AAG) .... KLT
Kiloton (ABBR) .... KLTN
Kiloton [Nuclear equivalent of 1000 tons of high explosives] .... kt
Kilourane (ABBR) .... KU
Kilovar .... kvar
Kilovar-Hour .... kvarh
Kilovolt .... kV
Kilovolt Alternating Current (IAA) .... KVAC
Kilovolt Ampere .... kVA
Kilovolt Constant Potential .... kVCP
Kilovolt Direct Current (IEEE) .... kVdc
Kilovolt Meter .... kVM
Kilovolt Peak .... kVP
Kilovolt-Ampere Hour .... kVAH
Kilovolt-Ampere Hour Meter (MSA) .... kVAhm
Kilovolt-Ampere Meter .... kVAM
Kilovolt-Ampere Reactive .... kVAr
Kilovolt-Ampere Reactive Hour (BARN) .... kilovar
[Reactive] Kilovolt-Ampere-Hour (IDOE) .... kVARh
Kilovolts, Direct Current (KSC) .... kDVC
Kilowatt (WDMC) .... K
Kilowatt (ABBR) .... KLWT
Kilowatt .... kW
Kilowatt (DFIT) .... KW
Kilowatt [DOE] (TAG) .... KW
Kilowatt Electric [DOE] (TAG) .... KWE
Kilowatt Foot (IAA) .... KWFT
Kilowatt Hour [DOE] (TAG) .... KWH
Kilowatt Isotope Power System (IEEE) .... KIPS
Kilowatt Meter .... kWm
Kilowatt, Thermal .... kWt
Kilowatt, Thermal .... kW(th)
Kilowatt-Hour .... kWh
Kilowatt-Hour (DFIT) .... KWH
Kilowatthour (ABBR) .... KWHR
Kilowatt-Hour .... kWhr
Kilowatt-Hour Electric .... kWhe
Kilowatt-Hour Meter .... KWHM
Kilowatts of Electric Energy .... kWe
Kilowatts per Square Meter .... KW/M²
Kilowatts Reactive .... kWr
Kiloword (BUR) .... KW
Kiloyards (MCD) .... KYDS
Kilter (ABBR) .... KLTR
Kilter Diagram .... KD
Kilusan ng Bangong Lipunan [New Society Movement] [Philippines] (PD) .... KBL
Kilusang Mabubukid ng Pilipnas [Philippine Peasant Federation] [Political party] .... KMP
Kilusang Mayo Uno [May First Movement] [Philippines] [Political party] .... KMU
Kilwa [Tanzania] [Airport symbol] (OAG) .... KIY
Kilwa Masoko [Tanzania] [ICAO location identifier] (ICLI) .... HTKI
Kim Jong Pil [South Korean politician] .... JP
Kimafu [Zaire] [ICAO location identifier] (ICLI) .... FZCX
Kimam [Indonesia] [Airport symbol] (OAG) .... KMM
Kimano II [Zaire] [ICAO location identifier] (ICLI) .... FZMP
Kimball Elementary School, Kimball, MN [Library symbol] [Library of Congress] (LCLS) .... MnKE
Kimball High School, Kimball, MN [Library symbol] [Library of Congress] (LCLS) .... MnKH
Kimball International, Inc. [NASDAQ symbol] (NQ) .... KBAL
Kimball International, Inc. [Associated Press] (SAG) .... Kimbal
Kimball Intl Cl'B' [NASDAQ symbol] (TTSB) .... KBALB
Kimball, NE [Location identifier FAA] (FAAL) .... IBM
Kimball, NE [AM radio station call letters] .... KIMB
Kimball Public Library, Kimball, MN [Library symbol] [Library of Congress] (LCLS) .... MnK
Kimball Public Library, Kimball, NE [Library symbol Library of Congress] (LCLS) .... NbKi
Kimbau [Zaire] [ICAO location identifier] (ICLI) .... FZDB
Kimbe [New Britain] [Seismograph station code, US Geological Survey Closed] (SEIS) .... KMB
Kimbel Unit (AAMN) .... KU
Kimbell Art Museum, Fort Worth, TX [Library symbol Library of Congress] (LCLS) .... TxFK
Kimberley [South Africa] [Seismograph station code, US Geological Survey] (SEIS) .... KIM

Kimberley [South Africa] [Airport symbol] (OAG) .... KIM
Kimberley and District Heritage Museum, Kimberley, BC, Canada [Library symbol] [Library of Congress] (LCLS) .... CaBKIHM
Kimberley and District Heritage Museum, Kimberley, British Columbia [Library symbol National Library of Canada] (NLC) .... BKIHM
Kimberley/B. J. Vorster [South Africa] [ICAO location identifier] (ICLI) .... FAKM
Kimberley Public Library, British Columbia [Library symbol National Library of Canada] (NLC) .... BKI
Kimberly Clark [Associated Press] (SAG) .... KimbClk
Kimberly McCullough Fan Club (EA) .... KMFC
Kimberly, OR [Location identifier FAA] (FAAL) .... IMB
Kimberly Public Library, Kimberly, ID [Library symbol] [Library of Congress] (LCLS) .... IdKi
Kimberly, WI [AM radio station call letters] .... WHBY
Kimberly-Clark [NYSE symbol] (TTSB) .... KMB
Kimberly-Clark Corp. [NYSE symbol] (SPSG) .... KMB
Kimberly-Clark Corp., Memphis, TN [Library symbol Library of Congress] (LCLS) .... TMK
Kimberly-Clark Corp., Research and Engineering Library, Neenah, WI [Library symbol Library of Congress] (LCLS) .... WNKC
Kimble Method for Controlled Devacuation .... KIMCODE
Kimchaek [North Korea ICAO location identifier] (ICLI) .... ZKKC
Kimco Realty [NYSE symbol] (SPSG) .... KIM
Kimco Realty Corp. [Associated Press] (SAG) .... Kimc
Kimco Realty Corp. [Associated Press] (SAG) .... Kimco
Kimco Rlty 7.75% Sr'A'Dep Pfd [NYSE symbol] (TTSB) .... KIMPrA
Kimco Rlty 8.50% Sr'B'Dep Pfd [NYSE symbol] (TTSB) .... KIMPrB
Kimco Rlty 8.375% Sr'C'Dep [NYSE symbol] (TTSB) .... KIMPrC
Kimhae/International [South Korea ICAO location identifier] (ICLI) .... RKPK
Kimmelstiel-Wilson [Medicine] .... KW
Kimmins Corp. [NYSE symbol] (TTSB) .... KVN
Kimmins Environmental Services [Associated Press] (SAG) .... KimEnv
Kimmins Environmental Services [NYSE symbol] (SPSG) .... KVN
K-Immunoglobulin Light Chains [Immunology] (DAVI) .... KM
Kimono (ABBR) .... KMNO
Kimpangu [Zaire] [ICAO location identifier] (ICLI) .... FZDU
Kimpoko [Zaire] [ICAO location identifier] (ICLI) .... FZAE
Kin Seeking Missing Military Personnel [Organization of parents with sons missing in action with purpose of supplementing US government search for missing personnel] [Post-World War II] .... KSMMP
Kina Kommunista Partja [Communist Party of China] [Political party] .... KKP
Kinai Technologies, Inc. [Formerly, Kinai Resources Corp.] [Vancouver Stock Exchange symbol] .... KTI
Kinark Corp. [AMEX symbol] (SPSG) .... KIN
Kinark Corp. [Associated Press] (SAG) .... Kinark
Kinase Insert .... KI
Kinase-Activating Factor [Organic chemistry] (DAVI) .... KAF
Kinase-Inducible Domain [Biochemistry] .... KID
Kincardine Branch, Bruce County Public Library, Ontario [Library symbol National Library of Canada] (NLC) .... OKI
Kincheng Banking Corp. [Hong Kong] .... KB
[A] Kind Of (MHDI) .... AKO
Kindale Public Library, Stephenville, Newfoundland [Library symbol National Library of Canada] (NLC) .... NFSK
Kindale Public Library, Stephenville, NF, Canada [Library symbol Library of Congress] (LCLS) .... CaNfSK
Kindamba [Congo] [ICAO location identifier] (ICLI) .... FCBK
Kindamba [Congo] [Airport symbol] (OAG) .... KNJ
Kinder (ABBR) .... KNDR
Kinder, Gentler [America] [In a George Bush speech during the 1989 Republican Convention] .... KG
Kinder-Care Learning Centers, Inc. [NASDAQ symbol] (SAG) .... KCLC
Kinder-Care Learning Centers, Inc. [Associated Press] (SAG) .... KndrL
Kinder-Care Learning Centers, Inc. [Associated Press] (SAG) .... KndrLr
Kinder-Care Learning Ctrs [NASDAQ symbol] (TTSB) .... KCLC
Kinder-Care Lrng Ctr Wrrt [NASDAQ symbol] (TTSB) .... KCLCW
Kindergarten .... K
Kindergarten .... KG
Kindergarten (WDAA) .... KIND
Kindergarten .... KINDERGTN
Kindergarten (ABBR) .... KNDGTN
Kindergarten (ABBR) .... KNDRG
Kindergarten Auditory Screening Test [Otorhinolaryngology] (DAVI) .... KAST
Kindergarten Evaluation for Learning Potential [McGraw Hill] .... KELP
Kindergarten Inventory of Developmental Skills [Child development test] .... KIDS
Kindergarten Language Screening Test .... KLST
Kindergarten Teachers Association (BARN) .... KTA
Kindergarten through 12th Grade (WDAA) K-12
Kindergartener (ABBR) .... KNDRGR
Kindersley, SK [AM radio station call letters] .... CFYM
Kindersley, SK [ICAO location identifier] (ICLI) .... CYKY
Kindest (ABBR) .... KNDST
Kindhearted (ABBR) .... KNDHTD
Kindheartedness (ABBR) .... KNDHTDNS
Kindia [Guinea] [ICAO location identifier] (ICLI) .... GUID
Kindle (ABBR) .... KNDL
Kindled (ABBR) .... KNDLD
Kindless (ABBR) .... KNDLES
Kindlier (ABBR) .... KNDLIR
Kindliest (ABBR) .... KNDLST
Kindliness (ABBR) .... KNDLNS
Kindling (ABBR) .... KNDLG
Kindly (ABBR) .... KNDLY
Kindly (ABBR) .... KNDY

Kindly Gunn Bunch [*Refers to the Metropolitan Transit Authority of New York City; Gunn is the MTA chairman*] .... KGB
Kindly Old Gentleman [*Slang*] .... KOG
Kindness (ABBR) .... KNDNS
Kindness in Nature's Defense [*Elementary school course*] .... KIND
Kindred (ABBR) .... KNDRD
Kindred, ND [*FM radio station call letters*] (RBYB) .... KPHT
Kindsbach [*Germany ICAO location identifier*] (ICLI) .... EDAC
Kindsbach [*Germany ICAO location identifier*] (ICLI) .... EDAK
Kindu [*Zaire*] [*ICAO location identifier*] (ICLI) .... FZOA
Kindu [*Zaire*] [*Airport symbol*] (OAG) .... KND
Kinematic Analysis Method .... KAM
Kinematic Bombing System .... KBS
Kinematic Synthesis (PDAA) .... KINSYM
Kinematic Viscosity .... KV
Kinematical Analysis Program .... KAP
Kinematics .... KNMTCS
Kinematograph Renter's Society .... KRS
Kinescope .... KIN
Kinescope .... KINE
Kinescope (ABBR) .... KNSCP
Kinescope Image Test and Evaluation System (MCD) .... KITES
Kinesin-Related Polypeptide [*Biochemistry*] .... KRP
Kinesthetic (AAG) .... K
Kinesthetic Anharmonic Oscillator [*Facetious term for a swing*] .... KAO
Kinesthetic Figural Aftereffects [*Also, KFAE*] [*Psychometrics*] .... KFA
Kinesthetic Figural Aftereffects [*Also, KFA*] [*Psychometrics*] .... KFAE
Kinetic (VRA) .... kin
Kinetic (ABBR) .... KNTC
Kinetic Analysis Using Over-Relaxation [*FORTRAN computer program*] [*Physical chemistry*] .... KORE
Kinetic Concepts [*NASDAQ symbol*] (TTSB) .... KNCI
Kinetic Concepts, Inc. [*Associated Press*] (SAG) .... Kinetic
Kinetic Concepts, Inc. [*NASDAQ symbol*] (NQ) .... KNCI
Kinetic Depth Effect [*Cognitive science*] .... KDE
Kinetic Energy [*Symbol*] [*IUPAC*] .... K
Kinetic Energy .... KE
Kinetic Energy [*Symbol*] [*IUPAC*] .... T
Kinetic Energy Anti-Satellite .... KEASAT
Kinetic Energy Missile (INF) .... KEM
Kinetic Energy Missile Vehicle [*Army*] .... KEM-V
Kinetic Energy Release .... KER
Kinetic Energy Release Distribution [*Of ions for spectral studies*] .... KERD
Kinetic Energy Released per Unit Mass (DEN) .... KERMA
Kinetic Energy Storage System .... KESS
Kinetic Energy Weapon Integrated Test Experiment (MCD) .... KITE
Kinetic Energy Weapons [*Military*] (RDA) .... KEW
Kinetic Energy-Training Projectile (MCD) .... KE-TP
Kinetic Experiment on Water Boiler [*Nuclear reactor*] .... KEWB
Kinetic Family Drawing [*Psychology*] .... KFD
Kinetic Family Drawing Test [*Psychology*] (DAVI) .... KFDT
Kinetic Fluid Induction .... KFI
Kinetic Hemolysis Curve [*Biochemistry*] (DAVI) .... KHC
Kinetic Intense Neutron Generator .... KING
Kinetic Isotope Effect [*Physical chemistry*] .... KIE
Kinetic Kill Vehicle (DOMA) .... KKV
Kinetic Measurement of Enzyme-Linked Immunosorbant Assay .... K-ELISA
Kinetic Momentum .... KM
Kinetic Monte Carlo [*Simulation*] .... KMC
Kinetic Percolation .... KP
Kinetic Potential .... KP
Kinetic Potential [*Symbol*] L
Kinetic Process Control .... KPC
Kinetic Reaction .... KR
Kinetic Resonance Raman Spectroscopy (DAVI) .... KRRS
Kinetic Ring Energy Storage System .... KRESS
Kinetic Theory .... KT
Kinetic Tree Theory (PDAA) .... KITT
Kinetically Designed Nozzle (NASA) .... KDN
Kinetic-Kill Vehicle [*Military*] (SDI) .... KKV
Kinetics and Catalysis .... KAC
Kinetics of Neutralization [*Chemistry*] .... KN
Kinetics of Nonhomogeneous Processes .... KNP
Kinetin [*Plant growth regulator*] .... KT
Kinetocardiogram [*Cardiology*] .... KCG
Kinetoplast DNA [*Deoxyribonucleic Acid*] [*Genetics*] (DOG) .... kDNA
Kinfolk (ABBR) .... KNFLK
King [*Chess, card games*] .... K
King [*Phonetic alphabet*] [*Royal Navy*] (DSUE) .... K
King [*Monetary unit*] [*Papua, New Guinea*] (BARN) .... K
King .... KG
King and Martyr [*Church calendars*] .... KM
King Aviation [*British ICAO designator*] (FAAC) .... KNG
King City, CA [*Location identifier FAA*] (FAAL) .... KIC
King City, CA [*FM radio station call letters*] .... KLFA
King City, CA [*AM radio station call letters*] .... KRKC
King City, CA [*FM radio station call letters*] .... KRKC-FM
King City Public Library, King City, CA [*Library symbol Library of Congress*] (LCLS) .... CK
King College, Bristol, TN [*Library symbol Library of Congress*] (LCLS) .... TBriK
King County Library System, Seattle, WA [*Library symbol Library of Congress*] (LCLS) .... WaSKC
King County Medical Society, Seattle, WA [*Library symbol Library of Congress*] (LCLS) .... WaSK
King Cove [*Alaska*] [*Airport symbol*] (OAG) .... KVC

King Cove, AK [*Location identifier FAA*] (FAAL) .... KVC
King Edward (ROG) .... KE
King Edward Point [*South Georgia Island*] [*Seismograph station code, US Geological Survey*] (SEIS) .... KEP
King Edward VII [*British*] .... KEVII
King Edward VIII [*British*] .... KEVIII
King Edward's Horse Regiment [*Military unit*] [*British*] .... KEH
King Edward's Own [*British military*] (DMA) .... KEO
King Edward's Own Cavalry [*British military*] (DMA) .... KEOC
King Edward's Own Lancers [*British military*] (DMA) .... KEOL
King Elementary School, Deer River, MN [*Library symbol*] [*Library of Congress*] (LCLS) .... MnDerE
King Elementary School, Rockford, IL [*Library symbol*] [*Library of Congress*] (LCLS) .... IRoKE
King Fahd International Airport [*Saudi Arabia*] .... KFIA
King Faisal Specialist Hospital and Research Center [*Saudi Arabia*] .... KFSH & RC
King George II [*British*] .... KGII
King George the Fifth's Own [*British military*] (DMA) .... KGVO
King George V [*British*] .... KGV
King George's Fund for Sailors [*British*] .... KGFS
King Island [*Australia ICAO location identifier*] (ICLI) .... AMKI
King Island [*Tasmania*] [*Airport symbol*] (OAG) .... KNS
King Jack Resources [*Vancouver Stock Exchange symbol*] .... KGJ
King James [*Version of the Bible*] (WDAA) .... KJ
King James Version [*or Authorized Version of the Bible, 1611*] .... KJV
King John [*Shakespearean work*] .... Jn
King Khalid Military City [*Saudi Arabia*] (DOMA) .... KKMC
King Khalid University Hospital [*Saudi Arabia*] .... KKUH
King Lear [*Shakespearean work*] .... Lr
King, NC [*AM radio station call letters*] .... WKTE
King of Arms .... KA
King of Our Hearts Elvis Presley Fan Club (EA) .... KOHEPFC
King Pin Angle [*Automotive engineering*] .... KA
King Pin Inclination [*Automotive engineering*] .... KPI
King Pin Offset [*Automotive engineering*] .... KPO
King Post .... KP
King Public Library, King, NC [*Library symbol Library of Congress*] (LCLS) .... NcKg
King, Queen, Jack Meld [*Canasta*] .... KQJM
King Ranch [*California*] [*Seismograph station code, US Geological Survey Closed*] (SEIS) .... KRC
King Research, Inc. [*Computer consultant*] [*Information service or system*] (IID) .... KRI
King Salmon [*Alaska*] [*Airport symbol*] (OAG) .... AKN
King Salmon [*Alaska*] [*ICAO location identifier*] (ICLI) .... PAKN
King Salmon-Naknek [*Alaska*] [*Airport symbol*] (AD) .... AKN
King Solomon [*Freemasonry*] (ROG) .... KS
King Solomon Resources [*Vancouver Stock Exchange symbol*] .... KFO
King Solomon's Temple [*Freemasonry*] .... KST
King Township Public Library, King City, ON, Canada [*Library symbol Library of Congress*] (LCLS) .... CaOKcKT
King Township Public Library, King City, Ontario [*Library symbol National Library of Canada*] (NLC) .... OKCKT
King World Prod'ns [*NYSE symbol*] (TTSB) .... KWP
King World Productions [*Associated Press*] (SAG) .... KingWd
King World Productions, Inc. [*NYSE symbol*] (SPSG) .... KWP
King-Armstrong Unit [*Clinical chemistry*] .... KA
King-Armstrong Unit [*Clinical chemistry*] .... KAU
Kingaroy [*Australia Airport symbol*] (OAG) .... KGY
Kingcome Navigation [*AAR code*] .... KNC
Kingdom (ROG) .... K
Kingdom (WGA) .... KDM
Kingdom .... KINGD
Kingdom .... KM
Kingdom (ABBR) .... KNGDM
Kingdom Resources Ltd. [*Vancouver Stock Exchange symbol*] .... KRL
King-Errington Resources Ltd. [*Vancouver Stock Exchange symbol*] .... KGE
Kingfish (ABBR) .... KNGFSH
Kingfisher (ABBR) .... KNGFSHR
Kingfisher, OK [*Location identifier FAA*] (FAAL) .... IFI
Kinglier (ABBR) .... KNGLR
Kingliest (ABBR) .... KNGLST
Kingliness (ABBR) .... KNGLNS
Kingly (ABBR) .... KNGLY
Kingly (ABBR) .... KNGY
Kingman [*Arizona*] [*Airport symbol*] (OAG) .... IGM
Kingman Aviation, Inc. [*ICAO designator*] (FAAC) .... GPA
Kingman, AZ [*AM radio station call letters*] .... KAAA
Kingman, AZ [*FM radio station call letters*] .... KGMN
Kingman, AZ [*Television station call letters*] .... KMOH
Kingman, AZ [*FM radio station call letters*] .... KRCY
Kingman, AZ [*FM radio station call letters*] .... KZZZ
Kingman City-Mohave County Library, Kingman, AZ [*Library symbol Library of Congress*] (LCLS) .... AzKiM
Kingman, KS [*FM radio station call letters*] (RBYB) .... KCVW-FM
Kingman, KS [*FM radio station call letters*] .... KTCM
Kingpin (ABBR) .... KNGPN
Kings [*Old Testament book*] (BJA) .... K
Kings [*Old Testament book*] .... Kgs
Kings [*Old Testament book*] .... Ki
Kings .... KK
King's African Rifles [*Military unit*] [*British*] .... KAR
King's and Queen's College of Physicians [*Ireland*] .... KQCP
King's Bad Bargain [*Undesirable serviceman*] [*Slang British*] (DSUE) .... KBB

Kings Bay Army Terminal .... KBART
Kings Beach, CA [*FM radio station call letters*] (RBYB) .... KBCH
Kings Beach, CA [*FM radio station call letters*] (RBYB) .... KHWG-FM
King's Bench [*of law courts*] [*British*] .... KB
King's Bench Court [*British*] .... KBC
King's Bench Division [*of law courts*] [*British*] (ROG) .... KBD
King's Bench Divisional Court [*England*] (DLA) .... KB Div'l Ct
King's Bench Divisional Court [*British*] .... KBDC
King's Bishop [*Chess*] .... KB
King's Bishop's Pawn [*Chess*] (IIA) .... KBP
King's Cheshire Yeomanry Cavalry [*British military*] (DMA) .... KCYC
King's College, Briarcliff Manor, NY [*Library symbol Library of Congress*] (LCLS) .... NBmK
King's College, Briarcliff Manor, NY [*OCLC symbol*] (OCLC) .... VZK
[*The*] **King's College, Edmonton, Alberta** [*Library symbol National Library of Canada*] (NLC) .... AEKC
King's College Hospital .... KCH
King's College, London .... KCL
King's College London [*British*] (IRUK) .... KQC
King's College, London, ON, Canada [*Library symbol Library of Congress*] (LCLS) .... CaOLK
King's College, London, Ontario [*Library symbol National Library of Canada*] (NLC) .... OLK
King's College School [*British*] .... KCS
King's College, Wilkes-Barre, PA [*OCLC symbol*] (OCLC) .... KOL
King's College, Wilkes-Barre, PA [*Library symbol Library of Congress*] (LCLS) .... PWbK
King's Colonials [*British military*] (DMA) .... KC
King's Commissioned Indian Officer [*British military*] (DMA) .... KCIO
King's Conflicting Cases [*Texas*] [*A publication*] (DLA) .... King's Con Cs
King's Conflicting Cases [*Texas*] [*A publication*] (DLA) .... King's Conf Ca
King's Counsel [*British*] .... KC
Kings County [*Sussex, New Brunswick*] (DAS) .... KC
Kings County Free Library, Hanford, CA [*Library symbol Library of Congress*] (LCLS) .... CHanK
Kings County Free Library, Hanford, CA [*OCLC symbol*] (OCLC) .... CKC
Kings County Historical Society, Sussex, NB, Canada [*Library symbol Library of Congress*] (LCLS) .... CaNBSuH
Kings County Historical Society, Sussex, New Brunswick [*Library symbol National Library of Canada*] (NLC) .... NBSUH
King's Cross [*British*] (ADA) .... KC
King's Daughters Public Library, Del Norte, CO [*Library symbol Library of Congress*] (LCLS) .... CoDn
King's Dragoon Guards [*Later, QDG*] [*Military unit*] [*British*] .... KDG
King's Empire Veterans [*British military*] (DMA) .... KEV
King's German Artillery [*British military*] (DMA) .... KGA
King's German Legion [*British military*] (DMA) .... KGL
King's Gurkha Officer [*British military*] (DMA) .... KGO
King's Harbour Master [*Obsolete British*] .... KHM
King's Hard Bargain [*British military slang for undesirable sailor or soldier*] .... KHB
King's Honorary Chaplain [*British*] .... KHC
King's Honorary Dental Surgeon [*British*] .... KHDS
King's Honorary Nursing Sister [*British*] .... KHNS
King's Hussars [*Military unit*] [*British*] .... KH
King's Knight [*Chess*] .... KKT
King's Knight's Pawn [*Chess*] (IIA) .... KKP
King's Knight's Pawn [*Chess*] (IIA) .... KKTP
King's Knight's Pawn [*Chess*] (BARN) .... KNP
Kings Landing Historical Settlement, Fredericton, NB, Canada [*Library symbol Library of Congress*] (LCLS) .... CaNBFKL
Kings Landing Historical Settlement, Fredericton, New Brunswick [*Library symbol National Library of Canada*] (NLC) .... NBFKL
King's Light Dragoons [*British military*] (DMA) .... KLD
King's Light Infantry [*Military unit*] [*British*] .... KLI
King's Magnetic Ore Separator (ROG) .... KMS
King's Medal [*or Medallist*] [*British*] .... KM
King's Messenger [*British*] (ROG) .... KM
Kings Mountain National Military Park .... KIMO
Kings Mountain, NC [*AM radio station call letters*] .... WKMT
King's Music Analysis Package [*King's College*] [*University of London*] [*British*] (NITA) .... KINGMAP
King's National Roll .... KNR
Kings Norton Mint [*British*] .... KN
King's Overseas Dominions Regiment [*British military*] (DMA) .... KODR
King's Own [*Military unit*] [*British*] .... KO
King's Own Borderers [*British military*] (DMA) .... KOB
King's Own Hussars [*British military*] (DMA) .... KOH
King's Own Light Infantry [*Military unit*] [*British*] .... KOLI
King's Own Royal [*Military unit*] [*British*] .... KOR
King's Own Royal Regiment [*Military unit*] [*British*] .... KORR
King's Own Scottish Borderers [*Military unit*] [*British*] .... KOSB
King's Own Yorkshire Light Infantry [*Military unit*] [*British*] .... KOYLI
King's Parade [*British*] (DSUE) .... KP
Kings Park State Hospital, Kings Park, NY [*Library symbol Library of Congress*] (LCLS) .... NKpaH
King's Pawn [*Chess*] (ADA) .... KP
King's Pleasure [*British*] .... KP
Kings Point Public Library, Kings Point, NF, Canada [*Library symbol Library of Congress*] (LCLS) .... CaNfKP
Kings Point Public Library, Newfoundland [*Library symbol National Library of Canada*] (NLC) .... NFKP
King's Police Medal .... KPM
King's Proctor [*British*] .... KP
King's Regiment [*Military unit*] [*British*] .... KR
Kings Regional Vocational School, Kentville, Nova Scotia [*Library symbol National Library of Canada*] (NLC) .... NSKKR
King's Regulations and Admiralty Instructions [*Navy British*] .... KR & AI
King's Regulations and Air Council Instructions [*British military*] (DMA) .... KR & ACI
King's Regulations and Orders for the Royal Canadian Air Force .... KR Air
King's Regulations and Orders for the Royal Canadian Army .... KR & O (Can)
King's Regulations and Orders for the Royal Canadian Navy .... KRCN
King's Regulations for the Army and the Army Reserves [*British*] .... KR
King's Remembrancer [*British*] .... KR
King's Reports [*5, 6 Louisiana*] [*A publication*] (DLA) .... King
Kings Road Entertainment, Inc. [*Associated Press*] (SAG) .... KngsRd
Kings Road Entertainment, Inc. [*NASDAQ symbol*] (NQ) .... KREN
Kings Road Entmt [*NASDAQ symbol*] (TTSB) .... KREN
King's Rook [*Chess*] .... KR
King's Rook's Pawn [*Chess*] .... KRP
King's Royal Irish [*Military unit*] [*British*] .... KRI
King's Royal Irish Hussars [*British military*] (DMA) .... KRIH
King's Royal Rifle Corps [*Military unit*] [*British*] .... KRRC
King's Royal Rifles [*Military unit*] [*British*] .... KRR
King's Scholar [*British*] .... KS
King's School, Canterbury (ROG) .... KSC
King's Serjeant [*British*] (ROG) .... KS
King's Shropshire Light Infantry [*Military unit*] [*British*] .... KSLI
King's Speech [*British*] .... KS
King's Tennessee Digest [*A publication*] (DLA) .... King Dig
Kings View Hospital, Reedley, CA [*Library symbol Library of Congress*] (LCLS) .... CReeK
Kingsbay [*Spitsbergen*] [*Seismograph station code, US Geological Survey*] (SEIS) .... KBS
Kingsborough Community College of the City University of New York, Brooklyn, NY [*Library symbol Library of Congress*] (LCLS) .... NBK
Kingsborough Community College of the City University of New York, Brooklyn, NY [*Library symbol*] [*Library of Congress*] (LCLS) .... NBKC
Kingsborough Community College of the City University of New York, Brooklyn, NY [*OCLC symbol*] (OCLC) .... YKC
Kingsbridge [*England*] .... KINGSBR
Kingsbrook Jewish Medical Center, Brooklyn, NY [*Library symbol Library of Congress*] (LCLS) .... NBJ
Kingsburg, CA [*FM radio station call letters*] (RBYB) .... KLVS-FM
Kingscote [*Australia Airport symbol*] (OAG) .... KGC
King's-Edgehill School, Windsor, Nova Scotia [*Library symbol National Library of Canada*] (NLC) .... NSWKE
King's-Edgehill School, Windsor, NS, Canada [*Library symbol*] [*Library of Congress*] (LCLS) .... CaNSWiKE
Kingsford, MI [*FM radio station call letters*] .... WEUL
Kingsize (ABBR) .... KNGSZ
Kingsland, GA [*FM radio station call letters*] .... WKBX
Kingsley, Kinsella, and Keeney [*Prominent citizens of Brooklyn; all three died within a year of each other, 1884-1885*] .... 3K's
Kingsley News-Tribune, Kingsley, IA [*Library symbol Library of Congress*] (LCLS) .... IaKiN
Kingsley Public Library, Kingsley, MI [*Library symbol Library of Congress*] (LCLS) .... MiKins
Kingsport Public Library, Kingsport, TN [*Library symbol Library of Congress*] (LCLS) .... TKi
Kingsport, TN [*FM radio station call letters*] (RBYB) .... WCQR-FM
Kingsport, TN [*FM radio station call letters*] .... WCSK
Kingsport, TN [*AM radio station call letters*] .... WKCV
Kingsport, TN [*AM radio station call letters*] .... WKIN
Kingsport, TN [*FM radio station call letters*] .... WKOS
Kingsport, TN [*AM radio station call letters*] .... WKPT
Kingsport, TN [*Television station call letters*] .... WKPT-TV
Kingsport, TN [*FM radio station call letters*] .... WTFM
Kingston [*Jamaica*] [*Airport symbol*] (OAG) .... KIN
Kingston [*Jamaica*] [*Seismograph station code, US Geological Survey*] (SEIS) .... KIN
Kingston [*Jamaica*] [*ICAO location identifier*] (ICLI) .... MKJK
Kingston [*Canada*] [*Airport symbol*] (OAG) .... YGK
Kingston Air Services [*Canada ICAO designator*] (FAAC) .... KAS
Kingston Community Public Library, Kingston, MI [*Library symbol Library of Congress*] (LCLS) .... MiKin
Kingston General Hospital, Ontario [*Library symbol National Library of Canada*] (NLC) .... OKGH
Kingston Hospital Libraries, Kingston, NY [*Library symbol Library of Congress*] (LCLS) .... NKiHL
Kingston Korner (EA) .... KK
Kingston Laboratories, Alcan International Ltd., Ontario [*Library symbol National Library of Canada*] (NLC) .... OKA
Kingston Military Products Division (SAA) .... KMPD
Kingston/Norman Manley International [*Jamaica*] [*ICAO location identifier*] (ICLI) .... MKJP
Kingston, NY [*Location identifier FAA*] (FAAL) .... IGN
Kingston, NY [*FM radio station call letters*] .... WAMK
Kingston, NY [*FM radio station call letters*] .... WBPM
Kingston, NY [*FM radio station call letters*] .... WFGB
Kingston, NY [*FM radio station call letters*] .... WFRH
Kingston, NY [*AM radio station call letters*] .... WGHQ
Kingston, NY [*AM radio station call letters*] .... WKNY
Kingston, NY [*Television station call letters*] (RBYB) .... WRNN-TV
Kingston, ON [*FM radio station call letters*] .... CBBK-FM
Kingston, ON [*AM radio station call letters*] .... CFFX
Kingston, ON [*FM radio station call letters*] .... CFLY
Kingston, ON [*FM radio station call letters*] .... CFMK
Kingston, ON [*FM radio station call letters*] .... CFRC

Kingston, ON [*AM radio station call letters*] ... CKLC
Kingston, ON [*Television station call letters*] ... CKWS
Kingston, ON [*ICAO location identifier*] (ICLI) ... CYGK
Kingston Public Library, Kingston, ON, Canada [*Library symbol Library of Congress*] (LCLS) ... CaOK
Kingston Public Library, Ontario [*Library symbol National Library of Canada*] (NLC) ... OK
Kingston Regional Cancer Center [*Canada*] (PDAA) ... KRCC
Kingston, RI [*FM radio station call letters*] ... WRIU
Kingston, TN [*AM radio station call letters*] ... WBBX
Kingston-Tinson [*Jamaica*] [*Airport symbol*] (OAG) ... KTP
Kingston-upon-Thames [*Postcode*] (ODBW) ... KT
Kingstown/Arnos Vale [*St. Vincent*] [*ICAO location identifier*] (ICLI) ... TVSV
Kingstree, SC [*Location identifier FAA*] (FAAL) ... CKI
Kingstree, SC [*FM radio station call letters*] (RBYB) ... WAOT
Kingstree, SC [*AM radio station call letters*] ... WDKD
Kingstree, SC [*FM radio station call letters*] (RBYB) ... WGSS-FM
Kingstree, SC [*FM radio station call letters*] ... WWKT
Kingsvale Resources [*Vancouver Stock Exchange symbol*] ... KVL
Kingsville Naval Air Station [*Texas*] [*ICAO location identifier*] (ICLI) ... KNQI
Kingsville, TX [*FM radio station call letters*] (RBYB) ... KFTX
Kingsville, TX [*AM radio station call letters*] (RBYB) ... KINE
Kingsville, TX [*FM radio station call letters*] (RBYB) ... KKBA
Kingsville, TX [*FM radio station call letters*] ... KTAI
Kingsville, TX [*Location identifier FAA*] (FAAL) ... NQI
Kingsville, TX [*Location identifier FAA*] (FAAL) ... TKB
Kingsway [*Record label*] ... Kings
Kingsway Branch, Burnaby Public Library, British Columbia [*Library symbol National Library of Canada*] (NLC) ... BBK
Kingwilliamstown [*South Africa*] [*ICAO location identifier*] (ICLI) ... FAWT
Kingwood Center Library, Mansfield, OH [*Library symbol Library of Congress*] (LCLS) ... OMansK
Kingwood, WV [*AM radio station call letters*] ... WFSP
Kingwood, WV [*FM radio station call letters*] ... WFSP-FM
Kingwood, WV [*FM radio station call letters*] ... WKMM
Kinhdom ... KNGDM
Kininogen [*Biochemistry*] ... KG
Kininogen (DMAA) ... KNG
Kinjo Gakuin University Library [*UTLAS symbol*] ... KUL
Kinkier (ABBR) ... KNKR
Kinkiest (ABBR) ... KNKST
Kinky Hair Disease [*Medicine*] (DMAA) ... KHD
Kinky Hair Syndrome [*Medicine*] (DMAA) ... KHS
Kinloss [*British ICAO location identifier*] (ICLI) ... EGQK
Kinnard Investments [*NASDAQ symbol*] (TTSB) ... KINN
Kinnard Investments, Inc. [*NASDAQ symbol*] (NQ) ... KINN
Kinnard Investments, Inc. [*Associated Press*] (SAG) ... Kinnard
Kinnear Public Library, McGill, NV [*Library symbol Library of Congress*] (LCLS) ... NvMcK
Kinney Public Library, City Hall, Kinney, MN [*Library symbol*] [*Library of Congress*] (LCLS) ... MnKin
Kinney's Law Dictionary and Glossary [*A publication*] (DLA) ... Kinney Law Dict & Glos
Kinnim (BJA) ... Kin
Kinomoto [*Japan*] [*Seismograph station code, US Geological Survey Closed*] (SEIS) ... KMT
Kinross Gold [*NYSE symbol*] (TTSB) ... KGC
Kinross Gold Corp. [*NYSE symbol*] (SAG) ... KGC
Kinross Gold Corp. [*Associated Press*] (SAG) ... Kinross
Kinross-Shire [*Former county in Scotland*] (WGA) ... KIN
Kinshasa [*Zaire*] [*Airport symbol*] (OAG) ... FIH
Kinshasa [*Zaire*] [*ICAO location identifier*] (ICLI) ... FZAZ
Kinshasa/N'Djili [*Zaire*] [*ICAO location identifier*] (ICLI) ... FZAA
Kinshasa/N'Dolo [*Zaire*] [*ICAO location identifier*] (ICLI) ... FZAB
Kinship (ABBR) ... KNSHP
Kinsman (ABBR) ... KNSMN
Kinston [*North Carolina*] [*Airport symbol*] (OAG) ... ISO
Kinston, NC [*Location identifier FAA*] (FAAL) ... ISO
Kinston, NC [*AM radio station call letters*] ... WELS
Kinston, NC [*FM radio station call letters*] (RBYB) ... WKNS
Kinston, NC [*AM radio station call letters*] (RBYB) ... WLNR
Kinston, NC [*AM radio station call letters*] ... WRNS
Kinston, NC [*FM radio station call letters*] ... WRNS-FM
Kinston, NC [*FM radio station call letters*] ... WZBR
Kinston-Lenoir County Public Library, Caswell Center Library, Kinston, NC [*Library symbol Library of Congress*] (LCLS) ... NcKC
Kinston-Lenoir County Public Library, Kinston, NC [*Library symbol Library of Congress*] (LCLS) ... NcK
Kinswoman (ABBR) ... KNSWMN
Kintbury [*England*] ... KINTB
Kinuso Municipal Library, Alberta [*Library symbol National Library of Canada*] (NLC) ... AKM
Kinuso Municipal Library, Kinuso, AB, Canada [*Library symbol*] [*Library of Congress*] (LCLS) ... CaAKM
Kinyarwanda [*MARC language code Library of Congress*] (LCCP) ... kin
Kiofi-Mosso [*Burundi*] [*ICAO location identifier*] (ICLI) ... HBBK
Kiosk (ABBR) ... KSK
Kiowa Business Committee [*An association*] ... KBC
Kiowa, CO [*Location identifier FAA*] (FAAL) ... IOC
Kiowa County Public Library, Eads, CO [*Library symbol Library of Congress*] (LCLS) ... CoE
Kiowa Industrial Development Commission ... KIDC
Kiowa-Comanche-Apache ... KCA
Kiowa-Commanche-Apache Intertribal Land Use Committee ... KCAILUC
Kip [*1000 lbs.*] ... K
Kip [*Monetary unit*] [*Laos*] ... K
Kip [*Thousands of Pounds*] **per Square Inch** ... KPSI
Kipapa [*Hawaii*] [*Seismograph station code, US Geological Survey*] (SEIS) ... KIP
Kipata' Katika [*Zaire*] [*ICAO location identifier*] (ICLI) ... FZDK
Kipling Society of North America - USA and Canada (EA) ... KS
Kiplinger's Personal Finance Magazine [*A publication*] (BRI) ... Kiplinger
Kipnuk [*Alaska*] [*Airport symbol*] (OAG) ... KPN
Kipnuk, AK [*Location identifier FAA*] (FAAL) ... IIK
Kipnuk, AK [*Location identifier FAA*] (FAAL) ... KPN
Kipp and Zonen Recorders ... K & Z
Kipp Relay ... KR
Kippe Brannon Fan Club [*Defunct*] (EA) ... KBFC
Kips [*Thousands of Pounds*] **per Square Foot** ... ksf
Kips [*Thousands of Pounds*] **per Square Inch** ... kpi
Kips [*Thousands of Pounds*] **per Square Inch** (MCD) ... KSI
Kipuka Nene [*Hawaii*] [*Seismograph station code, US Geological Survey*] (SEIS) ... KNH
Kipushia [*Zaire*] [*ICAO location identifier*] (ICLI) ... FZWF
Kira [*Papua New Guinea*] [*Airport symbol*] (OAG) ... KIQ
Kira Kira [*Solomon Islands*] [*Airport symbol*] (OAG) ... IRA
Kirbati Philatelic Society (EA) ... KPS
Kirby Corp. [*AMEX symbol*] (SPSG) ... KEX
Kirby Exploration Co., Inc. [*Associated Press*] (SAG) ... Kirby
Kirby's Connecticut Reports [*A publication*] (DLA) ... Kirby's Conn R
Kirby's Connecticut Reports [*A publication*] (DLA) ... Kirby's R
Kirby's Connecticut Reports [*A publication*] (DLA) ... Kirby's Rep
Kirby's Connecticut Reports and Supplement [*1785-89*] [*A publication*] (DLA) ... Kir
Kirby's Connecticut Reports and Supplement [*1785-89*] [*A publication*] (DLA) ... Kirb
Kirby's Connecticut Reports and Supplement [*1785-89*] [*A publication*] (DLA) ... Kirby
Kirbyville, TX [*Location identifier FAA*] (FAAL) ... BKB
Kirchenmusikalisches Jahrbuch [*A publication*] ... KJ
Kirchgons [*Germany ICAO location identifier*] (ICLI) ... EDIM
Kirchhoff Coda Migration [*For seismic wave imaging*] ... KCM
Kirchhoff Radiation Law [*Physics*] ... KRL
Kirchhoff's Current Law [*Electronics*] (IAA) ... KCL
Kirchhoff's Voltage Law (PDAA) ... KVL
Kirchner-French Memorial Library, Peterson, IA [*Library symbol Library of Congress*] (LCLS) ... IaPet
Kirchoff, H. H., St. Paul MN [*STAC*] ... KHH
Kirchoff Method [*Telecommunications*] (OA) ... KM
Kirensk [*Former USSR ICAO location identifier*] (ICLI) ... UIKK
Kirghiz [*MARC language code Library of Congress*] (LCCP) ... kir
Kirghiz Communist Party [*Political party*] ... KCP
Kirghiz Soviet Socialist Republic [*MARC geographic area code Library of Congress*] (LCCP) ... e-ur-kg
Kirghiz Soviet Socialist Republic [*MARC country of publication code Library of Congress*] (LCCP) ... kgr
Kirghiz Soviet Socialist Republic ... KirSSR
Kiri [*Zaire*] [*ICAO location identifier*] (ICLI) ... FZBT
Kiri [*Zaire*] [*Airport symbol*] (OAG) ... KRZ
Kiribati [*International civil aircraft marking*] (ODBW) ... T3
Kirin Brewery ADS [*NASDAQ symbol*] (TTSB) ... KNBWY
Kirin Brewery Co. Ltd. [*Associated Press*] (SAG) ... KirinBr
Kirin Brewery Co. Ltd. [*NASDAQ symbol*] (NQ) ... KNBW
Kirin Province [*China, Mainland*] [*MARC geographic area code Library of Congress*] (LCCP) ... a-cc-kr
Kiritimati Island [*Christmas Islands*] [*Kiribati*] [*ICAO location identifier*] (ICLI) ... PLCH
Kirjath Sepher [*Jerusalem*] (BJA) ... KirSeph
Kirjath Sepher [*Jerusalem*] (BJA) ... KS
Kirk (ROG) ... K
Kirkcaldy [*Seaport in Scotland*] ... KIRK
Kirkcudbrightshire [*County in Scotland*] ... KIRKCUDB
Kirkendall Public Library, Ankeny, IA [*Library symbol Library of Congress*] (LCLS) ... IaAnk
Kirkenes [*Norway*] [*Airport symbol*] (OAG) ... KKN
Kirkenes [*Norway*] [*Seismograph station code, US Geological Survey Closed*] (SEIS) ... KRK
Kirkenes/Hoybuktmoen [*Norway ICAO location identifier*] (ICLI) ... ENKR
Kirkjubaejar [*Iceland*] [*Airport symbol*] (AD) ... KBK
Kirkland & Ellis, Chicago, IL [*OCLC symbol*] (OCLC) ... IBM
Kirkland & Ellis, Chicago, IL [*Library symbol Library of Congress*] (LCLS) ... ICKE
Kirkland Lake [*Ontario*] [*Seismograph station code, US Geological Survey Closed*] (SEIS) ... KLC
Kirkland Lake [*Canada*] [*Airport symbol*] (OAG) ... YKX
Kirkland Lake Campus, Northern College, Ontario [*Library symbol National Library of Canada*] (NLC) ... OKLNC
Kirkland Lake, ON [*AM radio station call letters*] ... CJKL
Kirkland Municipal Library [*Bibliotheque Municipale de Kirkland*] **Quebec** [*Library symbol National Library of Canada*] (NLC) ... QK
Kirkland Municpal Library, Kirkland, PQ, Canada [*Library symbol*] [*Library of Congress*] (LCLS) ... CaQKi
Kirkland Town Library, Clinton, NY [*Library symbol*] [*Library of Congress*] (LCLS) ... NCPL
Kirkland, WA [*AM radio station call letters*] ... KARR
Kirklees Information Exchange [*Formerly, Huddersfield and District Information*] (NITA) ... KIE
Kirklin Public Library, Kirklin, IN [*Library symbol Library of Congress*] (LCLS) ... InKir
Kirksville [*Missouri*] [*Airport symbol*] (OAG) ... IRK
Kirksville College of Osteopathy and Surgery, Kirksville, MO [*Library symbol Library of Congress*] (LCLS) ... MoKiCO

Kirksville, MO [Location identifier FAA] (FAAL) .... IRK
Kirksville, MO [AM radio station call letters] .... KIRX
Kirksville, MO [FM radio station call letters] .... KLTE
Kirksville, MO [FM radio station call letters] .... KRXL
Kirksville, MO [FM radio station call letters] .... KTUF
Kirksville, MO [Television station call letters] .... KTVO
Kirkuk [Iraq] [Airport symbol] (AD) .... KIK
Kirkus Review [A publication] (BRI) .... KR
Kirkwall [British ICAO location identifier] (ICLI) .... EGPA
Kirkwall [Orkney Islands] [Airport symbol] (OAG) .... KOI
Kirkwall, Orkney [Postcode] (ODBW) .... KW
Kirkwood Community College, Cedar Rapids, IA [Library symbol Library of
  Congress] (LCLS) .... IaCrK
Kirlin Holding [NASDAQ symbol] (TTSB) .... KILN
Kirlin Holding Corp. [NASDAQ symbol] (SAG) .... KILN
Kirlin Holding Corp. [Associated Press] (SAG) .... Kirlin
Kirovabad [Former USSR Seismograph station code, US Geological Survey]
  (SEIS) .... KRV
Kirov-Kiev [Former USSR] .... K-K
Kirsch Technologies, Inc. [Software manufacturer] [St. Clair, MI] .... KTI
Kirschner [Wire] [Orthopedics] (DAVI) .... K
Kirsten Murine Sarcoma [Virus] [Oncology] (DAVI) .... KIMSA
Kirsten Murine Sarcoma Virus .... KI MUSV
Kirsten Murine Sarcoma Virus .... KiMSV
Kirsten Sarcoma Virus .... KiSV
Kirsten Sarcoma Virus in Normal Rat Kidney [Medicine] (DMAA) .... KNRK
Kirtland Air Force Base [New Mexico] .... KAFB
Kirtland Area Office [Department of Energy] .... KAO
Kirtland Area Office (DOGT) .... KAO
Kirtland Community College, Roscommon, MI [Library symbol Library of
  Congress] (LCLS) .... MiRoscK
Kirtland, NM [FM radio station call letters] .... KMYI
Kirtland on Practice in Surrogates' Courts [A publication] (DLA) .... Kirt Sur Pr
Kiruna [Sweden ICAO location identifier] (ICLI) .... ESNQ
Kiruna [Sweden] [Seismograph station code, US Geological Survey] (SEIS) ..... KIR
Kiruna [Sweden] [Geomagnetic observatory code] .... KIR
Kiruna [Sweden] [Airport symbol] (OAG) .... KRN
Kisan Mazdoor Praja Party [India] [Political party] .... KMPP
Kisangani [Zaire] [Airport symbol] (OAG) .... FKI
Kisangani [Zaire] [ICAO location identifier] (ICLI) .... FZIA
Kisangani/Bangoka [Zaire] [ICAO location identifier] (ICLI) .... FZIC
Kisaran/Aek Loba [Indonesia] [ICAO location identifier] (ICLI) .... WIML
Kisaran/Tanah Gambus [Indonesia] [ICAO location identifier] (ICLI) .... WIMK
Kisarazu [Japan ICAO location identifier] (ICLI) .... RJTK
Kisbee Air Ltd. [New Zealand] [ICAO designator] (FAAC) .... KSE
Kisbey on the Irish Land Law [A publication] (DLA) .... Kisb Ir Land L
Kisenge [Zaire] [ICAO location identifier] (ICLI) .... FZQP
Kisengwa [Zaire] [ICAO location identifier] (ICLI) .... FZWR
Kish Air [Iran] [ICAO designator] (FAAC) .... IRK
Kish Island [Iran] [Airport symbol] (OAG) .... KIH
Kish Island [Iran] [ICAO location identifier] (ICLI) .... OIBK
Kishinev [Former USSR Seismograph station code, US Geological Survey]
  (SEIS) .... KIS
Kishinev [Former USSR Airport symbol] (OAG) .... KIV
Kishinev [Former USSR ICAO location identifier] (ICLI) .... UKII
Kishwaukee Elementary School, Rockford, IL [Library symbol] [Library of
  Congress] (LCLS) .... IRoKiE
Kisii [Kenya] [ICAO location identifier] (ICLI) .... HKKS
Kisimayu [Somalia] [ICAO location identifier] (ICLI) .... HCMK
Kislovodsk [Former USSR ICAO location identifier] (ICLI) .... URMK
Kismayu [Somalia] [Airport symbol] (OAG) .... KMU
Kismet (ABBR) .... KSMT
Kiss [Correspondence] X
KISS [Knights in the Service of Satan] - Flaming Youth [Defunct] (EA) .... KFY
KISS [Knights in the Service of Satan] Konnection Fan Club (EA) .... KKFC
KISS [Knights in the Service of Satan] Rocks Fan Club (EA) .... KRFC
Kissable (ABBR) .... KSSB
Kissel Kar Klub (EA) .... KKK
Kisser (ABBR) .... KSSR
Kissidougou [Guinea] [ICAO location identifier] (ICLI) .... GUKU
Kissidougou [Guinea] [Airport symbol] (AD) .... KSI
Kissimmee, FL [Location identifier FAA] (FAAL) .... ISM
Kissimmee, FL [AM radio station call letters] .... WFIV
Kissimmee, FL [AM radio station call letters] .... WOTS
Kissimmee, FL [FM radio station call letters] (RBYB) .... WWKQ
Kisumu [Kenya] [ICAO location identifier] (ICLI) .... HKKI
Kisumu [Kenya] [Airport symbol] (OAG) .... KIS
Kit .... KT
Kit Carson Memorial Foundation, Inc., Taos, NM [Library symbol Library of
  Congress] (LCLS) .... NmTKC
Kit Collectors International (EA) .... KCI
Kit Configuration Notice (MCD) .... KCN
Kit Control Number [Navy] (NG) .... KCN
Kit Design Approach .... KDA
Kit Engineering Change Proposal (KSC) .... KECP
Kit, Individual Protection [British army] (INF) .... KIP
Kit Manufacturing Co. [AMEX symbol] (SPSG) .... KIT
Kit Manufacturing Co. [Associated Press] (SAG) .... Kit Mfg
Kit Mfg [AMEX symbol] (TTSB) .... KIT
Kit Munition Unit [Air Force] (MCD) .... KMU
Kit Quotation Request (MCD) .... KQR
Kit Shortage Notice .... KSN
Kit Upkeep Allowance [British] .... KUA
Kit Use Ratio [Statistics] .... KUR
Kita [Mali] [ICAO location identifier] (ICLI) .... GAKT

Kita Kyushu [Japan] [Airport symbol Obsolete] (OAG) .... KKJ
Kita-Daito [Japan] [Airport symbol] (OAG) .... KTD
Kitadaito [Ryukyu Islands] [ICAO location identifier] (ICLI) .... RORK
Kitakyushu [Japan ICAO location identifier] (ICLI) .... RJFR
Kitale [Kenya] [ICAO location identifier] (ICLI) .... HKKT
Kitale [Kenya] [Airport symbol] (AD) .... KTL
Kitchen .... K
Kitchen (AABC) .... KI
Kitchen (ADA) .... KIT
Kitchen (BARN) .... kitch
Kitchen .... KTCHN
Kitchen (ABBR) .... KTCN
Kitchen and Bath Industry Show West (ITD) .... KBIS
Kitchen and Bathroom .... KB
Kitchen and Dining Room [Real estate terminology] .... K & D
Kitchen Biddy [Female kitchen worker] [Restaurant slang] .... KB
Kitchen Cabinet Manufacturers Association (EA) .... KCMA
Kitchen, Company Level .... KCL
Kitchen/Dining Room [Classified advertising] (ADA) .... K/DR
Kitchen Exhaust (OA) .... KE
Kitchen Guild of America .... KGA
Kitchen Klutzs of America [Inactive] (EA) .... KKA
Kitchen Mechanic [Restaurant slang] .... KM
Kitchen Police [Kitchen helpers] [Military] .... KP
Kitchen Specialists Association [British] (DBA) .... KSA
Kitchen Table International [David D. Busch's vaporware software
  company] .... KTI
Kitchener, ON [FM radio station call letters] .... CFCA
Kitchener, ON [FM radio station call letters] .... CHYM
Kitchener, ON [Television station call letters] CICO-28
Kitchener, ON [Television station call letters] .... CKCO
Kitchener, ON [AM radio station call letters] .... CKGL
Kitchener, ON [AM radio station call letters] .... CKKW
Kitchener, ON [FM radio station call letters] .... CKWR
Kitchener Public Library, Kitchener, ON, Canada [Library symbol Library of
  Congress] (LCLS) .... CaOKit
Kitchener Public Library, Ontario [Library symbol National Library of
  Canada] (NLC) .... OKIT
Kitchener-Waterloo Academy of Medicine, Kitchener, Ontario [Library
  symbol National Library of Canada] (NLC) .... OWTA
Kitchener-Waterloo Academy of Medicine, Waterloo, ON, Canada [Library
  symbol Library of Congress] (LCLS) .... CaOWtA
Kitchener-Waterloo General Hospital, Waterloo, ON, Canada [Library symbol
  Library of Congress] (LCLS) .... CaOWtG
Kitchener-Waterloo Hospital, Kitchener, Ontario [Library symbol National
  Library of Canada] (NLC) .... OWTG
Kitchener-Waterloo Record, Kitchener, ON, Canada [Library symbol Library
  of Congress] (LCLS) .... CaOKitW
Kitchener-Waterloo Record, Kitchener, Ontario [Library symbol National
  Library of Canada] (NLC) .... OKITW
Kitchenette [Classified advertising] (ADA) .... K'ETTE
Kitchennette (ABBR) .... KTCNET
Kitchens, Bedrooms, and Bathrooms Equipment Exhibition [British]
  (ITD) .... KBB
Kitchens Design Drawing and Costing [Kitchens International DMS
  Electronics Ltd.] [Software package] (NCC) .... KIDDCOS
Kitchenware (ABBR) .... KTCNWR
Kitchigami Regional Library, Pine River, MN [Library symbol Library of
  Congress] (LCLS) .... MnPr
Kitchin on Courts [A publication] (DLA) .... Kitch Cts
Kitchin on Jurisdictions of Courts-Leet, Courts-Baron, Etc. [A publication]
  (DLA) .... Kit Ct
Kitchin on Jurisdictions of Courts-Leet, Courts-Baron, Etc. [A publication]
  (DLA) .... Kit Jur
Kitchin on Jurisdictions of Courts-Leet, Courts-Baron, Etc. [A publication]
  (DLA) .... Kitch
Kitchin on Jurisdictions of Courts-Leet, Courts-Baron, Etc. [A publication]
  (DLA) .... Kitch Courts
Kitchin's Retourna Brevium [4 eds.] [1581-92] [A publication] (DLA) .... Kit
Kitchin's Road Transport Law [19th ed.] [1978] [A publication]
  (DLA) .... Kit Rd Trans
Kite and Balloon Officer [Navy] .... KBO
Kite Balloon [Air Force] .... KB
Kite Balloon [Air Force] .... KYTOON
Kite Balloon Pilot .... KBP
Kite Trade Association International (EA) .... KTA
Kite Trade Association International [Later, KTA] (EA) .... KTAI
Kite-Supported Antenna .... KSA
Kithira [Greece] [Airport symbol] (OAG) .... KIT
Kithira [Greece] [ICAO location identifier] (ICLI) .... LGKC
Kitimat, BC [AM radio station call letters] .... CKTK
Kitimat Centennial Museum, British Columbia [Library symbol National
  Library of Canada] (NLC) .... BKCM
Kitimat Public Library, British Columbia [Library symbol National Library of
  Canada] (NLC) .... BKIT
Kitimat Public Library, Kitimat, BC, Canada [Library symbol] [Library of
  Congress] (LCLS) .... CaBKIT
Kiting (ABBR) .... KITG
Kiting Check [Investment] (MHDB) .... KC
Kiting Detection System (HGAA) .... KDS
Kiting Stock [Investment term] .... KS
Kitoi [Alaska] [Airport symbol] (OAG) .... KKB
Kitona-Base [Zaire] [ICAO location identifier] (ICLI) .... FZAI
Kitsaki School/Public Library, La Ronge, Saskatchewan [Library symbol
  National Library of Canada] (BIB) .... SLK

Kitsap Regional Library, Bremerton, WA [*Library symbol Library of Congress*] (LCLS) .... WaBr
Kitsch (ABBR) .... KTSC
Kitscoty Public Library, Alberta [*Library symbol National Library of Canada*] (NLC) .... AK
Kitscoty Public Library, Kitscoty, AB, Canada [*Library symbol*] [*Library of Congress*] (LCLS) .... CaAK
Kitt Peak National Observatory [*Tucson, AZ*] [*National Science Foundation*] .... KPNO
Kitt Peak National Observatory [*Tucson, AZ*] .... KPNOB
Kitt Peak National Observatory, Tucson, AZ [*Library symbol Library of Congress*] .... AzTK
Kitt Peak National Observatory, Tucson, AZ [*OCLC symbol*] (OCLC) .... KPO
Kittanning, PA [*AM radio station call letters*] .... WTYM
Kitten (ABBR) .... KITN
Kitten (ABBR) .... KTN
Kittenish (ABBR) .... KTNH
Kittery, ME [*FM radio station call letters*] .... WXBB
Kittila [*Finland ICAO location identifier*] (ICLI) .... EFKT
Kittila [*Finland*] [*Airport symbol*] (OAG) .... KTT
Kitting Instruction Sheet [*NASA*] (NASA) .... KIS
Kitting Notice [*NASA*] (NASA) .... KN
Kittrell College, Kittrell, NC [*Library symbol Library of Congress*] (LCLS) .... NcKiK
Kittrell Junior College, Kittrell, NC [*Inactive*] [*OCLC symbol*] (OCLC) .... KIT
Kitty (ABBR) .... KTY
Kitty Hawk Aircargo, Inc. [*ICAO designator*] (FAAC) .... PAI
Kitty Hawk Airways, Inc. [*ICAO designator*] (FAAC) .... KHA
Kitty Hawk, Inc. [*Associated Press*] (SAG) .... KittyHk
Kitty Hawk, Inc. [*NASDAQ symbol*] (SAG) .... KTTY
Kitty-Corner (ABBR) .... KTYCR
Kitty-Corner (ABBR) .... KU
Kitvei Ugarit (BJA) .... KIW
Kitwe [*Zambia*] [*Airport symbol*] (OAG) .... KIW
Kitz, Matheson, Green & MacIsaac Law Firm, Halifax, Nova Scotia [*Library symbol National Library of Canada*] (NLC) .... NSHKMGM
Kitz, Matheson, Green & MacIsaac Law Firm, Halifax, NS, Canada [*Library symbol Library of Congress*] (LCLS) .... CaNSHKMGM
Kitzingen [*Germany ICAO location identifier*] (ICLI) .... EDIN
Kiunga [*Papua New Guinea*] [*Airport symbol*] (OAG) .... UNG
Kiuruvesi [*Finland ICAO location identifier*] (ICLI) .... EFRV
Kivalina [*Alaska*] [*Airport symbol*] (OAG) .... KVL
Kivalina, AK [*Location identifier FAA*] (FAAL) .... KVL
Kives-Television [*In company name K-Tel International. Derived from name of company president and fact that it markets its products on television*] .... K-TEL
Kivijarvi [*Finland ICAO location identifier*] (ICLI) .... EFKV
Kiwai Island [*Papua New Guinea*] [*Airport symbol*] (OAG) .... KWX
Kiwanis International (EA) .... KI
Kiwanis International Accredited Representative .... KIAR
Kiwanis International - European Federation [*An association*] .... KI-EF
Kiwanis International Foundation [*An association*] .... KIF
Kiwi Growers of California (EA) .... KGC
KIWI International Air Lines, Inc. [*ICAO designator*] (FAAC) .... KIA
Kiwirok [*Indonesia*] [*ICAO location identifier*] (ICLI) .... WAJK
Kiyosumi [*Japan*] [*Seismograph station code, US Geological Survey Closed*] (SEIS) .... KIY
Kiyosumi - Telemeter [*Japan*] [*Seismograph station code, US Geological Survey*] (SEIS) .... KYS
Kizyl-Arvat [*Former USSR Seismograph station code, US Geological Survey*] (SEIS) .... KAT
Kjeller [*Norway ICAO location identifier*] (ICLI) .... ENKJ
KLA Instruments [*NASDAQ symbol*] (TTSB) .... KLAC
KLA Instruments Corp. [*Associated Press*] (SAG) .... KLA
KLA Instruments Corp. [*NASDAQ symbol*] (NQ) .... KLAC
Klaeger [*Plaintiff*] [*German*] (ILCA) .... KL
Klagenfurt [*Austria*] [*Airport symbol*] (OAG) .... KLU
Klagenfurt [*Austria ICAO location identifier*] (ICLI) .... LOWK
Klagenfurt [*Austria ICAO location identifier*] (ICLI) .... LOXK
Klamath County Library, Klamath Falls, OR [*OCLC symbol*] (OCLC) .... KCL
Klamath County Library, Klamath Falls, OR [*Library symbol Library of Congress*] (LCLS) .... OrK
Klamath Falls [*Oregon*] [*Seismograph station code, US Geological Survey*] (SEIS) .... KFO
Klamath Falls [*Oregon*] [*Airport symbol*] (OAG) .... LMT
Klamath Falls, OR [*AM radio station call letters*] .... KAGO
Klamath Falls, OR [*FM radio station call letters*] .... KAGO-FM
Klamath Falls, OR [*Television station call letters*] .... KDKF
Klamath Falls, OR [*AM radio station call letters*] .... KFLS
Klamath Falls, OR [*Television station call letters*] .... KFTS
Klamath Falls, OR [*FM radio station call letters*] .... KKRB
Klamath Falls, OR [*AM radio station call letters*] .... KLAD
Klamath Falls, OR [*FM radio station call letters*] .... KLAD-FM
Klamath Falls, OR [*Television station call letters*] .... KOTI
Klamath Falls, OR [*FM radio station call letters*] .... KSKF
Klamath Falls, OR [*FM radio station call letters*] .... KTEC
Klamath Falls, OR [*Location identifier FAA*] (FAAL) .... LFA
Klamath First Bancorp [*NASDAQ symbol*] (TTSB) .... KFBI
Klamath First Bancorp, Inc. [*NASDAQ symbol*] (SAG) .... KFBI
Klamath First Bancorp, Inc. [*Associated Press*] (SAG) .... Klamath
Klamath Northern Railway (MHDW) .... KNR
Klamath Northern Railway Co. [*Later, KNOR*] [*AAR code*] .... KN
Klamath Northern Railway Co. [*AAR code*] .... KNOR
Klang [*Musical Overtone*] [*German*] .... kl
Klassische Philologische Studien [*A publication*] (OCD) .... Klass Phil Stud
Klawock [*Alaska*] [*Airport symbol*] (OAG) .... KLW
KLD Associates, Inc., Huntington Station, NY [*Library symbol*] [*Library of Congress*] (LCLS) .... NHsK

KLD Associates, Inc., Huntington Station, NY [*Library symbol Library of Congress*] (LCLS) .... NHusk
Klebsiella [*Genus of microorganisms*] (DAVI) .... K
Klebsiella [*Genus of microorganisms*] (MAH) .... K
Klebsiella [*A genus of bacteria*] .... Klebs
Klebsiella, Enterobacter, Citrobacter [*Bacteriae*] [*Microbiology*] (DAVI) .... KEC
Klebsiella Pneumoniae [*Genus of microorganism*] (DAVI) .... KP
Klebs-Loeffler [*Bacteriology*] .... KL
Klebs-Loeffler Bacillus (AAMN) .... KL Bac
Kleena Kleene Gold Mines [*Vancouver Stock Exchange symbol*] .... KKE
Kleer-Vu Industries [*AMEX symbol*] (TTSB) .... KVU
Kleer-Vu Industries, Inc. [*Associated Press*] (SAG) .... KleerVu
Kleer-Vu Industries, Inc. [*AMEX symbol*] (SPSG) .... KVU
Kleihauer-Betke [*Stain*] [*Medicine*] (MEDA) .... K-B
Klein Brogel [*Belgium ICAO location identifier*] (ICLI) .... EBBL
Klein Offset Rotation [*Typography*] (DGA) .... KOR
Klein Paradox [*Physics*] .... KP
Kleine Beitraege zum Assyrischen Lexikon [*A publication*] .... KBAL
Kleine Flote [*Piccolo*] [*German*] .... KF
Kleine Schriften [*of various authors*] [*Classical studies*] (OCD) .... Kl Schr
Kleine Schriften zur Geschichte de Volkes Israel [*A. Alt*] [*A publication*] (BJA) .... KSch (Alt)
Kleine Schriften zur Geschichte des Volkes Israel [*A. Alt*] [*A publication*] (BJA) .... KSI
Kleine Texte fuer Theologische und Philosophische Vorlesungen [*A publication*] (BJA) .... KIT
Kleine-Levin [*Syndrome*] [*Medicine*] (DAVI) .... KL
Kleinert's, Inc. [*Associated Press*] (SAG) .... Kleinrt
Kleinert's, Inc. [*NASDAQ symbol*] (NQ) .... KLRT
Klein-Gordon Equation [*Physics*] .... KGE
Kleinkaliber [*Small Caliber*] [*German military*] .... KK
Kleinmann-Low [*Astronomy*] .... KL
Klein-Nishina Formula [*Physics*] .... KNF
Klein-Rydberg Method [*Physics*] .... KRM
Kleinsee [*South Africa*] [*ICAO location identifier*] (ICLI) .... FAKZ
Kleinwort Benson Aus [*NYSE symbol*] (TTSB) .... KBA
Kleinwort Benson Australian Income Fund, Inc. [*NYSE symbol*] (SPSG) .... KBA
Kleinwort Benson Australian Income Fund, Inc. [*Associated Press*] (SAG) .... KBAust
Kleinzee [*South Africa*] [*Airport symbol*] (OAG) .... KLZ
Klemm Flugzeugbau GmbH & Apparatebau Nabern [*Germany ICAO aircraft manufacturer identifier*] (ICAO) .... KL
Klenow Fragment [*Genetics*] .... KF
Kleptomania (ABBR) .... KLEPTO
Kleptomania (ABBR) .... KLPTMN
Kleptomaniac (ABBR) .... KLPTMNC
Klerksdorp [*South Africa*] [*ICAO location identifier*] (ICLI) .... FAKD
Klerusblatt [*Munich*] (BJA) .... KleBl
Kliatt Young Adult Paperback Book Guide [*A publication*] (BRI) .... Kliatt
Kligler Iron Agar [*Medium*] .... KIA
Klinefelter Syndrome and Associates (EA) .... KSA
Klinefelter-Reifenstein-Albright [*Syndrome*] [*Medicine*] (DAVI) .... KRA
Klinefelter's Syndrome [*Medicine*] .... KS
Klinge [*Germany*] [*Research code symbol*] .... K
Klinge [*Germany*] [*Research code symbol*] .... KD
Klingon Language Institute .... KLI
Klippan Control Reporting Point [*South Africa*] [*ICAO location identifier*] (ICLI) .... FAKN
Klippel-Feil [*Syndrome*] [*Neurology*] (DAVI) .... KF
Klippel-Feil Syndrome [*Medicine*] .... KFS
Klippel-Trenaunay [*Syndrome*] [*Medicine*] (DAVI) .... KT
Klippel-Trenaunay Support Group (EA) .... KTSG
Klippel-Trenaunay Syndrome [*Medicine*] (DMAA) .... KTS
Klippel-Trenaunay-Weber Syndrome [*Medicine*] (DMAA) .... KTW
Klippel-Trenaunay-Weber Syndrome [*Medicine*] (DMAA) .... KTWS
KLLM Transport Services, Inc. [*NASDAQ symbol*] (NQ) .... KLLM
KLLM Transport Sv [*NASDAQ symbol*] (TTSB) .... KLLM
KLM Cityhopper BV [*Netherlands ICAO designator*] (FAAC) .... KLC
KLM Helicopters NV [*Netherlands ICAO designator*] (FAAC) .... KLH
KLM Royal Dutch Air [*NYSE symbol*] (TTSB) .... KLM
KLM [*Koninklijke Luchtvaart Maatschappij*] **Royal Dutch Airlines** [*ICAO designator*] (OAG) .... KL
KLM Royal Dutch Airlines [*Netherlands ICAO designator*] (FAAC) .... KLM
KLM [*Koninklijke Luchtvaart Maatschappij*] **Royal Dutch Airlines** [*NYSE symbol*] (SPSG) .... KLM
Klondex Mines [*Vancouver Stock Exchange symbol*] .... KDX
Klondex Mines Ltd [*VS, exchange symbol*] (TTSB) .... KDX
Klondike National Historic Site, Parks Canada [*Lieu Historique National Klondike, Parcs Canada*] **Dawson City, Yukon** [*Library symbol National Library of Canada*] (NLC) .... YDPCK
Kloof Gold Mining ADR [*NASDAQ symbol*] (TTSB) .... KLOFY
Kloof Gold Mining Co. Ltd. [*NASDAQ symbol*] (NQ) .... KLOF
Kloof Gold Mining Co. Ltd. [*Associated Press*] (SAG) .... KloofG
Kloss, Low, and Hofmann [*Initialism is name of electronics company and brand name of its products*] .... KLH
Kluane National Park, Parks Canada [*Parc National Kluane, Parcs Canada*] **Haines Junction, Yukon** [*Library symbol National Library of Canada*] (NLC) .... YHJPCK
Kluang [*Malaysia*] [*Seismograph station code, US Geological Survey*] (SEIS) .... KGM
Kluang [*Malaysia*] [*ICAO location identifier*] (ICLI) .... WMAP
Klung Kidney-Heart-Lung [*Machine*] .... KKHL
Klutina [*Alaska*] [*Seismograph station code, US Geological Survey*] (SEIS) .... KLU
Kluver-Bucy Syndrome [*Psychiatry*] (DAVI) .... KBS
Klydonograph Type Gradient Recorder (IAA) .... KGR

Klynveld Peat Marwick Goerdeler [*Commercial firm British*] .... KPMG
Klystron .... K
Klystron Amplifier .... KLA
Klystron Frequency Multiplier .... KFM
Klystron Life Test .... KLT
Klystron Mount .... KM
Klystron Oscillator .... KLO
Klystron Oscillator .... KO
Klystron Phase Control .... KPC
Klystron Power Amplifier .... KPA
Klystron Power Supply .... KPS
Klystron Power Supply Modulator .... KPSM
Klyuchi [*Former USSR Seismograph station code, US Geological Survey*] (SEIS) .... KLY
Kmart [*NYSE symbol*] (TTSB) .... KM
KMS Fusion, Inc., Ann Arbor, MI [*Library symbol Library of Congress*] (LCLS) .... MiAaK
KN Energy [*NYSE symbol*] (TTSB) .... KNE
KN Energy, Inc. [*Associated Press*] (SAG) .... KN Engy
KN Energy, Inc. [*NYSE symbol*] (SPSG) .... KNE
Knackery and Pet Food Association [*Australia*] .... KPFA
Knape & Vogt Manufacturing Co. [*NASDAQ symbol*] (NQ) .... KNAP
Knape & Vogt Manufacturing Co. [*Associated Press*] (SAG) .... KnapeV
Knape & Vogt Mfg [*NASDAQ symbol*] (TTSB) .... KNAP
Knapp and Ombler's English Election Cases [*A publication*] (DLA) .... K & O
Knapp and Ombler's English Election Cases [*A publication*] (DLA) .... Kn & O
Knapp and Ombler's English Election Cases [*A publication*] (DLA) .... Kn & Omb
Knapp and Ombler's English Election Cases [*A publication*] (DLA) .... Knapp & O
Knapp Communications Corp. .... KCC
Knapp, Drewett & Sons Ltd., Kingston-Upon-Thames, United Kingdom [*Library symbol Library of Congress*] (LCLS) .... UkKuK
[*The*] **Knapp Press** [*Book publisher*] .... TKP
Knapp Time Metaphor Scale .... KTMS
Knapp's Privy Council Appeal Cases [*1829-36*] [*England*] [*A publication*] (DLA) .... Kn
Knapp's Privy Council Appeal Cases [*1829-36*] [*England*] [*A publication*] (DLA) .... Kn AC
Knapp's Privy Council Appeal Cases [*1829-36*] [*England*] [*A publication*] (DLA) .... Kn PC
Knapp's Privy Council Reports [*England*] [*A publication*] (DLA) .... Knapp
Knapp's Privy Council Reports [*England*] [*A publication*] (DLA) .... Rep
Knapsack (ABBR) .... KNPSK
Knapsack (AD) .... nap
Knapwell [*England*] .... KNAP
Knave (ABBR) .... KNV
Knavery (ABBR) .... KNVRY
Knavish (ABBR) .... KNVH
Knavishly (ABBR) .... KNVHLY
K-Nearest-Neighbor [*Algorithm*] .... KNN
Knee [*Anatomy*] (DAVI) .... K
Knee .... kn
Knee Bearing [*Prosthesis*] .... KB
Knee Board Training Device [*Military*] (MCD) .... KBTD
Knee Brace [*Technical drawings*] .... KB
Knee Disarticulation [*Medicine*] .... KD
Knee Jerk [*Medicine*] .... KJ
Knee Kick [*Neurology*] .... KK
Knee Orthosis [*Medicine*] .... KO
Knee Signature System [*Orthopedics*] .... KSS
Knee-Ankle Orthosis [*Medicine*] (DAVI) .... KAO
Knee-Ankle-Foot Orthosis [*Medicine*] .... KAFO
Kneecap (ABBR) .... KNECP
Kneedeep (ABBR) .... KNEDP
Knee-Foot-Ankel Orthosis [*Orthopedics*] (DAVI) .... KFAO
Kneeling (ABBR) .... KNELG
Knees to Chest [*Position*] [*Medicine*] (DAVI) .... KC
Kneller (ABBR) .... KNELR
Kneller Hall [*British military*] (DMA) .... KH
Knesset Israel (BJA) .... KI
[*The*] **Knickerbocker** [*L.L.*] **Company, Inc.** [*NASDAQ symbol*] (SAG) .... KNIC
[*The*] **Knickerbocker** [*L. L.*] **Co., Inc.** [*Associated Press*] (SAG) .... Knick
[*The*] **Knickerbocker** [*L. L.*] **Company, Inc.** [*Associated Press*] (SAG) .... KnickL
Knickerbocker L L Wrrt [*NASDAQ symbol*] (TTSB) .... KNWDV
Knickers (ABBR) .... KNKRS
Knickers Off Ready When I Come Home [*Correspondence*] (DSUE) .... NORWICH
Knie Resources, Inc. [*Vancouver Stock Exchange symbol*] .... KNE
Knife (ABBR) .... KNF
Knife and Fork [*Pharmacology*] (DAVI) .... knork
Knife and Fork Club International (EA) .... KFCI
Knife Blade .... KNBL
Knife Collectors Club (EA) .... KCC
Knife Edge .... KNED
Knife Switch .... KNSW
Knife Switch .... KS
Knifed (ABBR) .... KNFD
Knifelike (ABBR) .... KNFLK
Knifemakers Guild (EA) .... KG
Knifing (ABBR) .... KNFG
Knight [*Chess, card games*] .... K
Knight (ABBR) .... KN
Knight .... KNGHT
Knight (ABBR) .... KNGT
Knight (ABBR) .... KNHT
Knight [*British title*] .... KNT
Knight [*British title*] .... KT
Knight [*Chess*] .... KT
Knight [*Chess*] .... N
Knight Air Ltd. [*Canada ICAO designator*] (FAAC) .... KNA
Knight Bachelor .... Kt Bach
Knight Bachelor [*or Knight Companion*] **of the Order of the Bath** [*British*] .... KB
Knight Club (EA) .... KC
Knight Commander .... KC
Knight Commander of Court of Honor [*British*] .... KCCH
Knight Commander of [*the Order of*] **Pius IX** .... KCP
Knight Commander of [*the Order of*] **St. Gregory** [*British*] .... KCSG
Knight Commander of [*the Order of*] **St. John of Jerusalem** [*British*] .... KStJ
Knight Commander of St. Michael and St. George [*Facetiously translated, "Kindly Call Me God"*] [*British*] .... KCMG
Knight Commander of [*the Order of*] **St. Sylvester** .... KCSS
Knight Commander of the [*Order of the*] **Bath** [*British*] (GPO) .... KCB
Knight Commander of the [*Order of the*] **British Empire** .... KBE
Knight Commander of the [*Order of the*] **Crown** [*Belgium*] .... KCC
Knight Commander of the Guelphic Order of Hanover [*British*] .... KCH
Knight Commander of the Holy Sepulchre .... KCHS
Knight Commander of the [*Order of the*] **Indian Empire** [*British*] .... KCIE
Knight Commander of the Lion and the Sun .... KCLS
Knight Commander of the Order of St. Lazarus of Jerusalem (DD) .... KCLJ
Knight Commander of the Royal Victorian Order [*British*] .... KCVO
Knight Commander of the [*Order of the*] **Star of India** [*British*] .... KCSI
Knight Commander of the Temple [*Freemasonry*] (ROG) .... KCT
Knight Commander of the Tower and Sword [*Portugal*] (ROG) .... KCTS
Knight Elementary School, Randall, MN [*Library symbol*] [*Library of Congress*] (LCLS) .... MnRaKE
Knight Grand Commander .... KGC
Knight Grand Commander of the [*Order of the*] **Indian Empire** [*British*] .... GCIE
Knight Grand Commander of the [*Order of the*] **Star of India** [*British*] .... GCSI
Knight Grand Cross of St. Gregory the Great [*British*] .... GCSG
Knight Grand Cross of [*the Order of*] **St. John of Jerusalem** [*British*] .... GCStJ
Knight Grand Cross of St. Michael and St. George [*Facetiously translated "God Calls Me God"*] [*British*] .... GCMG
Knight Grand Cross of St. Sylvester [*British*] .... GCSS
Knight Grand Cross of the [*Order of the*] **Bath** [*British*] .... GCB
Knight Grand Cross of the [*Order of the*] **Bath** [*British*] .... KGCB
Knight Grand Cross of the [*Order of the*] **British Empire** .... GBE
Knight Grand Cross of the Guelphic Order of Hanover [*British*] .... GCH
Knight Grand Cross of the Legion of Honour [*British*] .... GCLH
Knight Grand Cross of the Order of St. Gregory the Great [*British*] (ADA) .... KGCSG
Knight Grand Cross of the Royal Victorian Order [*British*] .... GCVO
Knight Industries Two Thousand [*Acronym is name of computerized car in TV series "Knight Rider"*] .... KITT
Knight Kadosch [*Freemasonry*] .... K K-D-H
Knight Mareschal of Scotland (ROG) .... KT MAR SC
Knight of [*the Order of*] **Charles III of Spain** .... KCS
Knight of Ferdinand [*Spain*] .... KF
Knight of Grace, Order of St. John of Jerusalem .... KGStJ
Knight of Gustavus Vasa [*Sweden*] .... KGV
Knight of Hanover .... K of H
Knight of Honor .... KH
Knight of Justice, Order of St. John of Jerusalem .... KJStJ
Knight of Leopold [*Austria, Belgium*] (ROG) .... KL
Knight of [*the Order of*] **Leopold** [*Belgium*] .... KLB
Knight of [*the Order of*] **Leopold of Austria** .... KL
Knight of [*the Order of*] **Leopold of Austria** .... KLA
Knight of Malta .... KM
Knight of Maximilian Joseph [*Bavaria*] .... KMJ
Knight of Merit of Holstein .... KMH
Knight of Pius IX .... KP
Knight of Polonia Restituta [*British*] .... KPR
Knight of St. Andrew [*Russia*] [*Obsolete*] .... KA
Knight of St. Anne [*Russia*] [*Obsolete*] .... KSA
Knight of St. Benedict of Avis .... KBA
Knight of St. Columba .... KSC
Knight of St. Ferdinand [*Sicily*] (ROG) .... KSF
Knight of St. Ferdinand and Merit [*Italy*] .... KFM
Knight of St. Ferdinand and Merit [*Italy*] .... KSFM
Knight of St. George [*Russia*] [*Obsolete*] .... KSG
Knight of St. Gregory .... KSG
Knight of St. Hubert [*Bavaria*] .... KSH
Knight of St. Januarius [*Naples*] .... KSJ
Knight of St. Joachim .... KJ
Knight of St. John of Jerusalem [*Freemasonry*] (ROG) .... K ST J of J
Knight of [*the Order of*] **St. Lazarus of Jerusalem** [*British*] .... KLJ
Knight of [*the Order of*] **St. Lazarus of Jerusalem** [*British*] .... KSLJ
Knight of St. Maria Theresa [*Austria*] (ROG) .... KMT
Knight of Saint Michael and Saint George [*Ionian Islands*] .... KSM & SG
Knight of St. Patrick [*British*] .... KP
Knight of St. Stanislaus of Poland .... KSP
Knight of St. Sylvester .... KSS
Knight of Saint-Esprit [*France*] .... KSE
Knight of San Fernando [*Spain*] .... KSF
Knight of Tabor [*Freemasonry*] (ROG) .... KT
Knight of the Black Eagle [*Russia*] [*Obsolete*] .... KBE
Knight of the Blessed Sacrament .... KBS
Knight of the Crescent [*Turkey*] .... KC
Knight of the Eagle .... KE
Knight of the Eagle and Pelican [*Freemasonry*] .... KEP
Knight of the Elephant [*Denmark*] .... KE
Knight of [*the Order of*] **the Garter** [*British*] .... KG
Knight of the Golden Circle .... KGC

Knight of the Golden Fleece [Spain and Austria] .... KGF
Knight of the Grand Cross .... KGC
Knight of the Guelphic Order of Hanover [British] .... KGH
Knight of the Guelphic Order of Hanover [British] .... KH
Knight of the Holy Sepulchre .... KHS
Knight of the Holy Sepulchre of Jerusalem (DD) .... KHS
Knight of the Iron Crown [British] (ROG) .... KIC
Knight of the Legion of Honor [France] .... KLH
Knight of the Legion of Honour (DD) .... KLH
Knight of the Lion and Sun [Persia] (ROG) .... KLS
Knight of the Military and Hospitalier Order of St. Lazarus (DD) .... KLJ
Knight of the Netherlands Lion .... KNL
Knight of the [Order of the] Oak Crown .... KOC
Knight of the Order of Charles XIII of Sweden [Freemasonry] .... KCS
Knight of the Order of Malta (WDAA) .... KOM
Knight of the Order of Military Merit [Prussia] (ROG) .... KMM
Knight of the Order of St. John of Jerusalem (DD) .... KStJ
Knight of the (Order of the) Polar Star [Sweden] (ROG) .... KPS
Knight of the Red Cross [Freemasonry] .... KRC
Knight of the Red Eagle [Prussia] .... KRE
Knight of the [Order of the] Redeemer [Greece] .... KR
Knight of the Redeemer of Greece (ROG) .... KRG
Knight of [the Order of] the Royal Northern Star [Sweden] .... KNS
Knight of the Southern Star [Brazil] .... KSS
Knight of the Sovereign and Military Order of Malta (DD) .... KM
Knight of [the Order of] the Star of India [British] .... KSI
Knight of the Star of the East (ROG) .... KSE
Knight of the Sun and Lion [Persia] .... KSL
Knight of the Sword [of Sweden] .... KS
Knight of the Sword of Sweden .... KSS
Knight of the Thistle [British] .... KT
Knight of the Tower and Sword [Portugal] .... KTS
Knight of the White Eagle [Poland] .... KWE
Knight of William [Netherlands] .... KW
Knight of Windsor (ROG) .... KW
Knight Ridder, Inc. [Associated Press] (SAG) .... KnghtR
Knight Ridder Newspapers [Viewdata Corp.] [Videotex producer] (NITA) .... KRN
Knight Transportation [NASDAQ symbol] (SAG) .... KNGT
Knight Transportation [Associated Press] (SAG) .... KnightTr
Knighted .... KT
Knight-Errant (ABBR) .... KNGT-RNT
Knighthawk Air Express Ltd. [Canada ICAO designator] (FAAC) .... KNX
Knighthood .... K
Knighthood (ABBR) .... KNGTHD
Knightly (ABBR) .... KNGTLY
Knight-Ridder .... KR
Knight-Ridder Financial News [Database] (IT) .... KRFN
Knight-Ridder, Inc. [NYSE symbol] (SPSG) .... KRI
Knight-Ridder Information Inc. .... KRII
Knight's American Mechanical Dictionary [A publication] (DLA) .... Knight Mech Dict
Knights in the Service of Satan [Rock music group] .... KISS
Knight's Industrial Reports [A publication] (DLA) .... KIR
Knight's Industrial Reports [A publication] (DLA) .... Knight's Ind
Knight's Local Government Reports [A publication] (DLA) .... KLGR
Knight's Local Government Reports [A publication] (DLA) .... Kn LGR
Knight's Local Government Reports [A publication] (DLA) .... LGR
Knights of Aquarius Order (EAIO) .... KAO
Knights of Columbus (EA) .... K of C
Knights of Columbus .... KC
Knights of Equity (EA) .... KE
Knights of Jurisprudence .... KJ
Knights of King Arthur (EA) .... KKA
Knights of Labor .... K of L
Knights of Life Motorcycle Club (EA) .... KLMC
Knights of Lithuania (EA) .... K of L
Knights of Lithuania .... KL
Knights of Lithuania (EA) .... KOL
Knights of Peter Claver (EA) .... KPC
Knights of Pythias .... K of P
Knights of Pythias (EA) .... KP
Knights of St. John (EA) .... KSJ
Knights of St. John Supreme Commandery (EA) .... KSJSC
Knights of the Altar (EA) .... K/A
Knights of the Golden Eagle (EA) .... KGE
Knights of the Square Table (EA) .... NOST
Knights of Vartan (EA) .... KV
Knight's Pawn [Chess] (ROG) .... KT P
Knights Templar .... KT
Knightsbridge University [Denmark] (ECON) .... KU
Knightstown Banner, Knightstown, IN [Library symbol Library of Congress] (LCLS) .... InKniB
Knightstown, IN [FM radio station call letters] .... WKPW
Knightstown Public Library, Knightstown, IN [Library symbol Library of Congress] (LCLS) .... InKni
Knightway Air Charter Ltd. [British ICAO designator] (FAAC) .... KNT
Knigovedenie: Entsiklopedicheskil Slovar [A publication] .... KES
Knik Glacier [Alaska] [Seismograph station code, US Geological Survey] (SEIS) .... KNK
Knislinge [Sweden ICAO location identifier] (ICLI) .... ESFI
Knit .... K
Knit de Knit Texturing (IAA) .... KDK
Knit into Back [of Stitch] [Knitting] (BARN) .... Kb
Knit into Back of Stitch [Knitting] (BARN) .... Kb
Knitgoods Dyers and Processors Association .... KDPA

Knitted .... KNTTD
Knitted Dacron (MEDA) .... KD
Knitted Outerwear Foundation (EA) .... KOF
Knitted Textile Association (EA) .... KTA
Knitter (ABBR) .... KNITR
Knitting (ABBR) .... KNITG
Knitting .... KNT
Knitting Arts Expo (TSPED) .... KAE
Knitting Cylinder Lubrication (PDAA) .... KCL
[The] Knitting Guild of America (EA) .... TKGA
Knitting Industries Foundation [British] (DBA) .... KIF
Knitting Machine Manufacturers Association [Defunct] (EA) .... KMMA
Knitwear .... KNTWR
Knitwear Employers Association (EA) .... KEA
Knitwear Mill Representatives Association [Defunct] (EA) .... KMRA
Knitwise [Knitting] .... KW
Knob Door Fastener .... KDF
Knob Noster, MO [FM radio station call letters] .... KXKX
Knob Noster, MO [Location identifier FAA] (FAAL) .... SZL
Knob-Associated Histidine-Rich Protein [Cytology] .... KAHRP
Knobbier (ABBR) .... KNBR
Knobbiest (ABBR) .... KNBST
Knobby (ABBR) .... KNBY
Knobnoster/Whiteman Air Force Base [Missouri] [ICAO location identifier] (ICLI) .... KSZL
Knock [Cardiology] .... K
Knock Down Export [Automotive engineering] .... KDX
Knock Sensor [Automotive engineering] .... KS
Knockabout (ABBR) .... KNCKBT
Knockdown (ABBR) .... KNCKDN
Knockdown Resistance [Pesticide technology] .... KDR
Knocked Down [i.e., disassembled] .... KD
Knocked Down Flat .... KDF
Knocked Down, in Carloads .... KDCL
Knocked Down, in Less than Carloads .... KDLCL
Knocked Out [To write or produce something quickly] [Also called knock off] (WDMC) .... K/O
Knocked Out [Boxing] (DAVI) .... KO'd
Knocked-on-Atom .... KOA
Knocker (ABBR) .... KNCKR
Knock-knee (ABBR) .... KNCKKN
Knock-Off Wheels [Automotive accessory] .... KOW
Knockout (ABBR) .... KNCKOT
Knockout [Partly cut out or loosened area which can be easily removed, as in a junction box] [Technical drawings] .... KO
Knockout [Boxing] .... KO
Knockout Drops [A drug producing unconsciousness] [Slang] .... KO's
Knocks Eczema [Acronym, brand name for skin cream, said to be taken from this phrase] .... NOXZEMA
Knogo North America [AMEX symbol] (TTSB) .... KNA
Knogo North America, Inc. [AMEX symbol] (SAG) .... KNA
Knogo North America, Inc. [Associated Press] (SAG) .... KnogNA
Knoll (ABBR) .... KNL
Knoll .... KNL
Knoll [Commonly used] (OPSA) .... KNOL
Knoll [Commonly used] (OPSA) .... KNOLL
Knoll AG [Germany] [Research code symbol] .... D
Knolls (MCD) .... KNLS
Knolls .... KNLS
Knolls [Commonly used] (OPSA) .... KNOLLS
Knolls Atomic Power Laboratory [Schenectady, NY] [Department of Energy] .... KAPL
Knolls Atomic Power Plant .... KAPP
Knoop Hardness Number .... HK
Knoop Hardness Number .... KHN
Knot .... KN
Knot Area Ratio (PDAA) .... KAR
Knothole (ABBR) .... KNTHL
Knotless (ABBR) .... KNTLS
Knotlike (ABBR) .... KNTLK
Knots [Also, KT] [Nautical speed unit] .... K
Knots [Also, K] [Nautical speed unit] .... KT
Knots (ADA) .... KTS
Knots Calibrated Airspeed (MCD) .... KCAS
Knots Equivalent Airspeed (MCD) .... KEAS
Knots Indicated Airspeed (MCD) .... KIAS
Knots per Revolution .... KPR
Knots True Airspeed .... KTA
Knots True Airspeed [Navy] (NVT) .... KTAS
Knotted (ABBR) .... KNTD
Knotted List Structure (BUR) .... KLS
Knotting (ABBR) .... KNTG
Knotty (ABBR) .... KNTY
Knotty Pine .... KP
Know How Fund [European economic development fund] .... KHF
Know, Inc. (EA) .... KI
Know Problems of Hydrocephalus (EA) .... KPH
Know Your Body (DAVI) .... KYB
Know Your Customer [Business term] .... KYC
Know Your Customer [Investment term] (DFIT) .... KYC
Know Your Endorsers - Require Identification [Advice to businessmen and others who cash checks for the public] .... KYERI
Knowable (ABBR) .... KNWB
Knowbot [Computer program] (WDMC) .... bot
Knower (ABBR) .... KNWR

Know-How (ABBR) ... KNWHW
Knowing (ABBR) ... KNWG
Knowingly (ABBR) ... KNWGY
Knowingness (ABBR) ... KNWGNS
Knowledege Network of Washington (EDAC) ... KNOW-NET
Knowledge [*Record label*] ... Know
Knowledge (ABBR) ... KNWL
Knowledge (ABBR) ... KNWLDG
Knowledge, Absent Without Leave [*Army*] (ADDR) ... KAWOL
Knowledge Access System [*Interface*] ... KAS
Knowledge Acquisition System ... KAS
Knowledge and Distributed Intelligence ... KDI
Knowledge, Attitude, Skills, Habits [*Formula*] [*LIMRA*] ... KASH
Knowledge, Attitudes, and Behavior Survey [*Department of Health and Human Services*] (GFGA) ... KAB
Knowledge, Attitudes, and Practice [*Sociology*] ... KAP
Knowledge Availability Systems Center [*University of Pittsburgh*] ... KASC
Knowledge Base [*Computer science*] (IAA) ... KB
Knowledge Base Machine [*Computer science*] ... KBM
Knowledge Base Management System [*Computer science*] ... KBMS
Knowledge Based Management System ... KBMS
Knowledge Engineer [*Computer science*] ... KE
Knowledge Engineering Environment [*An artificial intelligence system*] ... KEE
Knowledge Engineering System [*Software Architecture and Engineering Inc.*] (NITA) ... KES
Knowledge Industry Publications, Inc. [*Telecommunications*] ... KIP
Knowledge Industry Publications, Inc. [*White Plains, NY*] [*Telecommunications Information service or system*] ... KIPI
Knowledge Industry Systems Concept [*Publishing and education*] [*Pronounced "kiss"*] ... KISC
Knowledge Information Processing [*Computer science*] ... KIP
Knowledge Information Processing Systems [*Computer science*] ... KIPS
Knowledge Information Skills and Curriculum [*Project*] (AIE) ... KISC
Knowledge Integrating Simulation System ... KISS
Knowledge Integrity [*Electronic information*] (IT) ... KI
Knowledge Interchange Format [*Computer science*] ... KIF
Knowledge Legacy of the Unavailable Expert [*Computer science*] (BTTJ) ... KLUE
Knowledge Management System [*Computer science*] ... KMS
Knowledge of Occupations Test [*Psychology*] (DAVI) ... KOT
Knowledge of Results [*Visual monitoring*] ... KOR
Knowledge of Results ... KR
Knowledge of Results Feedback ... KRF
Knowledge of Results Feedback Task (SAA) ... KRFT
Knowledge Processing System [*Expert system shell*] (NITA) ... KPS
Knowledge Query and Manipulation Language [*Computer science*] ... KQML
Knowledge Reigns Supreme Over Nearly Everyone [*Rap recording artist*] ... KRS-ONE
Knowledge Representation [*Computer science*] ... KR
Knowledge Representation Language ... KRL
Knowledge Representation Systems Trials Laboratory [*Pronounced "crystal"*] [*Artificial intelligence*] ... KRSTL
Knowledge Resource Center [*Computer-based information delivery system in libraries*] [*Generic term*] ... KRC
Knowledge Retrieval System [*KnowledgeSet Corp.*] ... KRS
Knowledge, Skills, and Abilities [*Psychology*] (DAVI) ... KSA
Knowledge Source (IAA) ... KS
Knowledgeability Brief (MCD) ... KB
Knowledgeable (ABBR) ... KNWLB
Knowledgeable (ABBR) ... KNWLDGB
Knowledge-Based Automated Design of Silencers [*Automotive engineering*] ... KADOS
Knowledge-Based Engineering [*Expert systems*] [*Computer-aided design*] ... KBE
Knowledge-Based Expert System ... KBES
Knowledge-Based Integrated Design System (DOMA) ... KIDS
Knowledge-Based Integrated Machine [*Computer science*] ... KIM
Knowledge-Based Logistics Planning Shell ... KBLPS
Knowledge-Based Machine Translation [*Computer science*] ... KBMT
Knowledge-Based Producibility Decision-Maker [*Productivity technology*] (RDA) ... KPD
Knowledge-Based Programming Assistant (PDAA) ... KBPA
Knowledge-Based Software Assistant [*Computer science*] ... KBSA
Knowledge-Based System [*Computer model*] [*Computer science*] ... KBS
Knowledge-Based System ... KNOBS
Knowledge-Based Systems Centre [*Polytechnic of the South Bank*] [*British*] (CB) ... KBSC
Knowles Electronics Manikin for Acoustic Research ... KEMAR
Knowles' Reports [*3 Rhode Island*] [*A publication*] (DLA) ... Knowles
Knowlton [*England*] ... KNOWLT
Known ... KN
Known (VRA) ... kn
Known Datum Point ... KDP
Known Drug Allergies [*Medicine*] (DMAA) ... KDA
Known Enemy Dead [*Military*] ... KED
Known Enemy Location [*Military*] ... KEL
Known Gambler [*Police slang*] ... KG
Known Geothermal Resource Area [*Department of the Interior*] ... KGRA
Known Recoverable Coal Resource Area (PDAA) ... KRCRA
Known Reference Point ... KRP
Known Segment Table [*Computer science*] (IAA) ... KST
Known-Distance [*Range*] [*Weaponry*] (INF) ... KD
Know-Nothing [*American political party, 1855-60*] ... KN
Know-Nothing (ABBR) ... KNWNTHG
Knox and Fitzhardinge's New South Wales Reports [*A publication*] (DLA) ... K & F NSW
Knox and Fitzhardinge's New South Wales Reports [*A publication*] (DLA) ... Knox & F
Knox College, Galesburg, IL [*OCLC symbol*] (OCLC) ... IBK
Knox College, Galesburg, IL [*Library symbol Library of Congress*] (LCLS) ... IGK
Knox College Library, University of Toronto [*UTLAS symbol*] ... KKC
Knox College, University of Toronto, Ontario [*Library symbol National Library of Canada*] (NLC) ... OTK
Knox College, University of Toronto, Toronto, ON, Canada [*Library symbol Library of Congress*] (LCLS) ... CaOTK
Knox County Daily News, Bicknell, IN [*Library symbol Library of Congress*] (LCLS) ... InBiKN
Knox County Public Library, Vincennes, IN [*OCLC symbol*] (OCLC) ... IMW
Knox, IN [*Location identifier FAA*] (FAAL) ... OXI
Knox, IN [*AM radio station call letters*] ... WKVI
Knox, IN [*FM radio station call letters*] ... WKVI-FM
Knox on Bengal Criminal Law [*A publication*] (DLA) ... Kn Cr Law
Knox on Civil Procedure in India [*A publication*] (DLA) ... Kn Civ Proc
Knox Ranch [*California*] [*Seismograph station code, US Geological Survey Closed*] (SEIS) ... KNO
Knox School, Thief River Falls, MN [*Library symbol*] [*Library of Congress*] (LCLS) ... MnTKS
Knox's Cube Test [*Short-term memory and attention span test*] ... KCT
Knox's New South Wales Reports [*A publication*] (DLA) ... Kn NSW
Knox's New South Wales Reports [*A publication*] (DLA) ... Knox
Knoxville [*Diocesan abbreviation*] [*Tennessee*] (TOCD) ... KNX
Knoxville [*Tennessee*] (ABBR) ... KNXV
Knoxville [*Tennessee*] [*Airport symbol*] (OAG) ... TYS
Knoxville Academy of Medicine, Knoxville, TN [*Library symbol Library of Congress*] (LCLS) ... TKAM
Knoxville Area Health Science Consortium [*Library network*] ... KAHSLC
Knoxville City School, Knoxville, TN [*Library symbol Library of Congress*] (LCLS) ... TKCS
Knoxville City School, Knoxville, TN [*OCLC symbol*] (OCLC) ... TKS
Knoxville Express, Knoxville, IA [*Library symbol Library of Congress*] (LCLS) ... IaKnE
Knoxville, IA [*AM radio station call letters*] ... KNIA
Knoxville, IA [*FM radio station call letters*] ... KRLS
Knoxville, IA [*Location identifier FAA*] (FAAL) ... OXV
Knoxville International Energy Exposition [*1982*] ... KIEE
Knoxville Journal, Knoxville, IA [*Library symbol Library of Congress*] (LCLS) ... IaKnJ
Knoxville/McGee Tyson [*Tennessee*] [*ICAO location identifier*] (ICLI) ... KTYS
Knoxville Public Library, Knoxville, IA [*Library symbol Library of Congress*] (LCLS) ... IaKn
Knoxville, TN [*Location identifier FAA*] (FAAL) ... BUI
Knoxville, TN [*Location identifier FAA*] (FAAL) ... DKX
Knoxville, TN [*Location identifier FAA*] (FAAL) ... SGK
Knoxville, TN [*Television station call letters*] ... WATE
Knoxville, TN [*Television station call letters*] ... WBIR
Knoxville, TN [*AM radio station call letters*] ... WEMG
Knoxville, TN [*AM radio station call letters*] ... WEZK
Knoxville, TN [*AM radio station call letters*] ... WHJM
Knoxville, TN [*FM radio station call letters*] ... WIMZ
Knoxville, TN [*AM radio station call letters*] ... WITA
Knoxville, TN [*AM radio station call letters*] ... WIVK
Knoxville, TN [*FM radio station call letters*] ... WIVK-FM
Knoxville, TN [*FM radio station call letters*] ... WJXB
Knoxville, TN [*FM radio station call letters*] ... WKCS
Knoxville, TN [*AM radio station call letters*] ... WKGN
Knoxville, TN [*AM radio station call letters*] ... WKNL
Knoxville, TN [*Television station call letters*] ... WKOP
Knoxville, TN [*Television station call letters*] ... WKXT
Knoxville, TN [*AM radio station call letters*] ... WKXV
Knoxville, TN [*AM radio station call letters*] (RBYB) ... WMEN
Knoxville, TN [*FM radio station call letters*] ... WQBB
Knoxville, TN [*AM radio station call letters*] ... WRJZ
Knoxville, TN [*Television station call letters*] ... WTNZ
Knoxville, TN [*FM radio station call letters*] ... WUOT
Knoxville, TN [*AM radio station call letters*] ... WUTK
Knoxville, TN [*FM radio station call letters*] ... WUTK-FM
Knoxville-Knox County Public Library, Knoxville, TN [*OCLC symbol*] (OCLC) ... TKL
Knuckle (ABBR) ... KNKL
Knuckle [*Automotive engineering*] ... KNU
Knuckle Buster University [*Facetious term*] ... KBU
Knuckle Cracking [*Orthopedics*] (DAVI) ... KC
Knuckle-Bender Splint [*Orthopedics*] (DAVI) ... KB
Knuckled (ABBR) ... KNKLD
Knuckling (ABBR) ... KNKLG
Knudsen Absolute Manometer [*Physics*] ... KAM
Knudsen Cosine Law [*Physics*] ... KCL
Knudsen Engineering Ltd., Perth, Ontario [*Library symbol National Library of Canada*] (BIB) ... OPKE
Knudsen Flow [*Physics*] ... KF
Knudsen Leaf Gauge [*Physics*] ... KLG
Knudsen Number ... K
Knudsen Number [*IUPAC*] ... Kn
Knurl [*Engineering*] ... KNRL
Knurling Tool ... KLTO
Koala Bear Park [*Adelaide*] [*Airport symbol*] (AD) ... KBP
Koala Corp. [*NASDAQ symbol*] (SAG) ... KARE
Koala Corp. [*Associated Press*] (SAG) ... Koala
Koala Preservation Society of New South Wales [*Australia*] ... KPSNSW
Koala Resources Ltd. [*Vancouver Stock Exchange symbol*] ... KOR
Kob Air Ltd. [*Uganda*] [*ICAO designator*] (FAAC) ... KOB

Koban [*Afghanistan*] [*ICAO location identifier*] (ICLI) ... OAKA
Kobe [*Japan*] [*Seismograph station code, US Geological Survey*] (SEIS) ... KOB
Kobe Gakuin University [*UTLAS symbol*] ... KGU
Kobe Marine Observatory (BARN) ... KMO
Kobe University. Law Review [*A publication*] (DLA) ... Kobe UL Rev
Kobe University Medical Mission to Indonesia ... KUMMI
Kobenhavn [*Denmark ICAO location identifier*] (ICLI) ... EKCA
Kobenhavn [*Denmark ICAO location identifier*] (ICLI) ... EKDK
Kobenhavn/Kastrup [*Denmark ICAO location identifier*] (ICLI) ... EKCH
Kobenhavn/Roskilde [*Denmark ICAO location identifier*] (ICLI) ... EKRK
Kobenhavns Universitetsbibliotekets [*University of Copenhagen*], Afdeling, Fiolstraede, Kobenhavn, Denmark [*Library symbol Library of Congress*] (LCLS) ... DnKU-S
Kobenhavns Universitetsbibliotekets [*University of Copenhagen*], Afdeling, Norre Alle, Kobenhavn, Denmark [*Library symbol Library of Congress*] (LCLS) ... DnKU
Koblenz [*Germany ICAO location identifier*] (ICLI) ... EDZN
Koblenz Procurement Center [*Federal Republic of Germany*] [*Military*] (NATG) ... KPC
Koblenz/Winningen [*Germany ICAO location identifier*] (ICLI) ... EDRK
Kobold Resources Ltd. [*Vancouver Stock Exchange symbol*] ... KBV
Kobuan [*Solomon Islands*] [*Seismograph station code, US Geological Survey Closed*] (SEIS) ... KOA
Kobuk [*Alaska*] [*Airport symbol*] (OAG) ... OBU
Kobuk, AK [*Location identifier FAA*] (FAAL) ... OBU
Koch, Neff, Oetlinger [*Germany*] (NITA) ... KNO
Kochel-Verzeichnis [*List of Mozart's works*] (IIA) ... KV
Kochi [*Japan*] [*Airport symbol*] (OAG) ... KCZ
Kochi [*Japan*] [*Seismograph station code, US Geological Survey*] (SEIS) ... KOC
Kochi [*Japan ICAO location identifier*] (ICLI) ... RJOK
Koch's Supreme Court Decisions [*Ceylon*] [*A publication*] (DLA) ... Koch
Kodachrome (VRA) ... KODCH
Kodaikanal [*India*] [*Geomagnetic observatory code*] ... KOD
Kodaikanal [*India*] [*Seismograph station code, US Geological Survey*] (SEIS) ... KOD
Kodak Automated Retrieval [*Kodak*] [*Microfilm office information system*] (NITA) ... KAR
Kodak Color Management System [*Eastman Kodak Co.*] (PCM) ... KCMS
Kodak Ektaprint Electronic Publishing System [*Hardware and software components*] [*Eastman Kodak Co.*] ... KEEPS
Kodak Image Enhancement ... KIE
Kodak Image Management System (HGAA) ... KIMS
Kodak Industrial Film ... KIF
Kodak Industrial X-Ray Film ... KIXF
Kodak Infrared Phosphor ... KIRP
Kodak Infrared Scope ... KIRS
Kodak Infrared Scope ... KIS
Kodak International Newspaper Snapshot Awards ... KINSA
Kodak Job Sheet ... KJS
Kodak Ltd., Recordak Division, London, United Kingdom [*Library symbol Library of Congress*] (LCLS) ... NRE-L
Kodak Metal Clad Plate (IAA) ... KMCP
Kodak Metal Etch Resist ... KMER
Kodak (Near East) Ltd., Beirut, Lebanon [*Library symbol Library of Congress*] (LCLS) ... NRE-B
Kodak Ortho Resist ... KOR
Kodak Photo Resist ... KPR
Kodak Photofabrication Center ... KPC
Kodak Process Resist [*Photography*] (DICI) ... KP
Kodak Reflex Camera ... KRC
Kodak Relief Plate ... KRP
Kodak Special Plate ... KSP
Kodak Standard [*Photography*] ... KS
Kodak Thin-Film Resist [*Cathode coating*] ... KTFR
Kodak Timing Negative Film ... KTNF
Kodak Unitized Engineering Data ... KUED
Kodak Vacuum Probe ... KVP
Kodak Versamat Processor ... KVP
Kodak Wratten Light Filter ... KWLF
Kodak X-Ray Film ... KXF
Kodalith (VRA) ... kdlth
Kodaly Music Education Institute of Australia ... KMEIA
Kodiak [*Alaska*] [*Airport symbol*] (OAG) ... ADQ
Kodiak [*Alaska*] [*Seismograph station code, US Geological Survey*] (SEIS) ... KDC
Kodiak [*Alaska*] [*Airport symbol*] (AD) ... NHB
Kodiak [*Alaska*] [*ICAO location identifier*] (ICLI) ... PADQ
Kodiak, AK [*Location identifier FAA*] (FAAL) ... FIB
Kodiak, AK [*FM radio station call letters*] ... KJJZ
Kodiak, AK [*FM radio station call letters*] ... KMXT
Kodiak, AK [*FM radio station call letters*] (RBYB) ... KRXX-FM
Kodiak, AK [*AM radio station call letters*] ... KVOK
Kodiak, AK [*Location identifier FAA*] (FAAL) ... NOJ
Kodiak, AK [*Location identifier FAA*] (FAAL) ... ODK
Kodiak, AK [*Location identifier FAA*] (FAAL) ... RWO
Kodiak Community College, Kodiak, AK [*Library symbol*] [*Library of Congress*] (LCLS) ... AkKoC
Kodiak High School Library, Kodiak, AK [*Library symbol Library of Congress*] (LCLS) ... AkKoH
Kodiak Historical Society, Kodiak, AK [*Library symbol Library of Congress*] (LCLS) ... AkKoHi
Kodiak/Municipal [*Alaska*] [*ICAO location identifier*] (ICLI) ... PAWD
Kodiak [*Alaska*] **Municipal Airport** [*Airport symbol Obsolete*] (OAG) ... KDK
Kodiak Public Library (A. Holmes Johnson Memorial Library), Kodiak, AK [*Library symbol Library of Congress*] (LCLS) ... AkKo
Kodiak Tracking Station [*NASA*] (MCD) ... KTS
Kodiak-Western Alaska Airlines, Inc. [*CAB official abbreviation*] ... KO
Kodoro [*Zaire*] [*ICAO location identifier*] (ICLI) ... FZER
Koechel [*Catalogue of Mozart's works*] (ODBW) ... K
Koeffler Golde-1 [*Cell line*] [*Cytology*] (DAVI) ... KG-1
Koehler and Baumgartner Lexikon in Veteris Testamenti Libros [*Leiden*] [*A publication*] (BJA) ... KoB
Koeln-Bonn [*Germany ICAO location identifier*] (ICLI) ... EDDK
Koeln-Bonn [*Germany ICAO location identifier*] (ICLI) ... EDNK
Koelner Bibliothekserschliessungssystem [*Automated library system*] (NITA) ... KOEBES
Koeln-Wahn [*Germany ICAO location identifier*] (ICLI) ... EDNB
Koeniglich [*Royal*] [*German*] ... KGL
Koff [*Type of ship*] (DS) ... KF
Koforidua [*Ghana*] [*ICAO location identifier*] (ICLI) ... DGKK
Kofu [*Japan*] [*Seismograph station code, US Geological Survey*] (SEIS) ... KOF
Koger Equity [*AMEX symbol*] (TTSB) ... KE
Koger Equity, Inc. [*AMEX symbol*] (CTT) ... KE
Koger Equity, Inc. [*Associated Press*] (SAG) ... KogEq
Koger Equity, Inc. [*Associated Press*] (SAG) ... KogrEq
Koger Equity Wrrt [*AMEX symbol*] (TTSB) ... KEWS
Kohala [*Hawaii*] [*Seismograph station code, US Geological Survey*] (SEIS) ... KOH
Kohat [*Pakistan*] [*ICAO location identifier*] (ICLI) ... OPKO
Kohat [*Pakistan*] [*ICAO location identifier*] (ICLI) ... OPKT
Kohelet (BJA) ... Koh
Kohelet Rabbah (BJA) ... KohR
Kohkiloyeh [*Iran*] [*ICAO location identifier*] (ICLI) ... OISW
Kohlberg Kravis Roberts & Co. ... KKR
Kohles, F. S., Montebello CA [*STAC*] ... KFS
Kohlman Evaluation of Living Skills [*Occupational therapy*] ... KELS
Kohls Corp. [*Associated Press*] (SAG) ... Kohls
Kohl's Corp. [*NYSE symbol*] (SPSG) ... KSS
Koinambe [*Papua New Guinea*] [*Airport symbol*] (OAG) ... KMB
Koingnaas [*South Africa*] [*Airport symbol*] (OAG) ... KIG
Koinonia Foundation (EA) ... KF
Kokanee Resources Ltd. [*Vancouver Stock Exchange symbol*] ... KKR
Kokkola [*Finland*] [*Airport symbol*] (OAG) ... KOK
Koko Head, HI [*Location identifier FAA*] (FAAL) ... CKH
Kokoda [*Papua New Guinea*] [*Airport symbol*] (OAG) ... KKD
Kokomo [*Indiana*] [*Airport symbol*] (OAG) ... OKK
Kokomo, IN [*Location identifier FAA*] (FAAL) ... OKK
Kokomo, IN [*AM radio station call letters*] ... WIOU
Kokomo, IN [*FM radio station call letters*] ... WIWC
Kokomo, IN [*Television station call letters*] ... WTTK
Kokomo, IN [*FM radio station call letters*] ... WWKI
Kokomo, IN [*FM radio station call letters*] ... WZWZ
Kokomo Public Library, Kokomo, IN [*OCLC symbol*] (OCLC) ... IKP
Kokomo Public Library, Kokomo, IN [*Library symbol Library of Congress*] (LCLS) ... InKo
Kokomo Tribune, Kokomo, IN [*Library symbol Library of Congress*] (LCLS) ... InKoT
Kokonao [*West Irian, Indonesia*] [*Airport symbol*] (AD) ... KOX
Kokonau [*Indonesia*] [*ICAO location identifier*] (ICLI) ... WABN
Kokoro [*Papua New Guinea*] [*Airport symbol*] (OAG) ... KOR
Kokoxili Suture [*Paleogeography*] ... KS
Koksijde [*Belgium ICAO location identifier*] (ICLI) ... EBFN
Kokuritsu Kokkai Toshokan [*National Diet Library*], Tokyo, Japan [*Library symbol Library of Congress*] (LCLS) ... JTNDL
Kokusai Denshin Denwa Co. Ltd. [*Telegraph & Telephone Corp.*] [*Tokyo, Japan*] [*Telecommunications*] ... KDD
Kokusai Koryu [*Japan Foundation*] (EAIO) ... KK
Kol [*Papua New Guinea*] [*Airport symbol*] (OAG) ... KQL
Kol Nidre (BJA) ... KN
Kol Yisroel [*Israeli Broadcasting Service*] ... KY
Kolaka/Pomalaa [*Indonesia*] [*ICAO location identifier*] (ICLI) ... WAAP
Kolberg [*Lesotho*] [*ICAO location identifier*] (ICLI) ... FXKB
Kolcsonos Segito Takarekpenztarak [*Mutual Savings Banks*] [*Hungarian*] ... KST
Kolda [*Senegal*] [*ICAO location identifier*] (ICLI) ... GOGK
Kolda [*Senegal*] [*Airport symbol*] (AD) ... KDA
Kole Sur Lukenie [*Zaire*] [*ICAO location identifier*] (ICLI) ... FZVC
Kolel Shomre Hachomos [*An association*] (EA) ... KSH
Kolel Shomre Hachomos/Reb Meir Baal Haness (EA) ... KSH/RMBH
Kolhapur [*India*] [*ICAO location identifier*] (ICLI) ... VAKP
Koliganek [*Alaska*] [*Airport symbol*] (OAG) ... KGK
Kol-Kol Airlines Ltd. [*Nigeria*] [*FAA designator*] (FAAC) ... KKL
Koll Real Estate Cv'A'Pfd [*NASDAQ symbol*] (TTSB) ... KREGP
Koll Real Estate Group [*Associated Press*] (SAG) ... KollRE
Koll Real Estate Group [*Associated Press*] (SAG) ... KollRl
Koll Real Estate Group [*NASDAQ symbol*] (SAG) ... KREG
Koll Real Estate Grp [*NASDAQ symbol*] (TTSB) ... KREG
Kollaborateur [*Nickname given Alain Robbe-Grillet*] [*World War II*] ... K
Kollmorgen Corp. [*NYSE symbol*] (SPSG) ... KOL
Kollmorgen Corp. [*Associated Press*] (SAG) ... Kolmor
Kollsman Integrated Flight Instrumentation System [*Aviation*] ... KIFIS
Kolmer, Kline, Kahn [*Test for syphilis*] [*Medicine*] (DAVI) ... KKK
Kolmer [*Test with*] **Reiter Protein** [*Serology*] ... KRP
Kolmogorov - Smirnov Test [*Statistics*] ... KS
Kolmogorov-Arnold-Moser [*Statistical mechanics*] ... KAM
Kolokani [*Mali*] [*ICAO location identifier*] (ICLI) ... GAKN
Kolokoso [*Zaire*] [*ICAO location identifier*] (ICLI) ... FZDL
Koloniale Rundschau (BJA) ... KR
Kolpashevo [*Former USSR ICAO location identifier*] (ICLI) ... UNCL
Kolson Quick Modality Test [*Education*] ... KQM
Kolwezi [*Zaire*] [*ICAO location identifier*] (ICLI) ... FZQM
Kolwezi [*Zaire*] [*Airport symbol*] (AD) ... KWZ
Kolyma-Avia [*Former USSR*] [*FAA designator*] (FAAC) ... KLI

Komaba [Japan] [Seismograph station code, US Geological Survey Closed] (SEIS) .... KOM

Komag, Inc. [NASDAQ symbol] (NQ) .... KMAG

Komag, Inc. [Associated Press] (SAG) .... Komag

Komakuk, YT [ICAO location identifier] (ICLI) .... CYAJ

Komati Power Station/Kragsentrale [South Africa] [ICAO location identifier] .... FAKG

Komatipoort [South Africa] [ICAO location identifier] (ICLI) .... FAKP

Komatsu [Japan] [Airport symbol] (OAG) .... KMQ

Komatsu America Corp. .... KAC

Komatsu America Industries Corp. .... KAIC

Komatsu America Manufacturing Corp. [Chattanooga, TN] .... KAMC

Komatsujima [Japan ICAO location identifier] (ICLI) .... RJOP

Komercni Bank [Czech Republic Bank] .... KB

Komercni Banka AS [Czech Republic] [Banking] .... KB

Komi Commodity Exchange [Russian Federation] (EY) .... KOCE

Komin-Yanga [Burkina Faso] [ICAO location identifier] (ICLI) .... DHEC

Komisarstvo za Evreiskiie Vuprosi [Bulgaria] (BJA) .... KEV

Komisja Koordynacyjna Zydowskich Instytucji Spolecznych (BJA) .... KKZIS

Komisja Koordynacyjna. Zydowskie Instytucje Opiekuncze (BJA) .... KK

Komitee fuer den Osten (BJA) .... KfdO

Komitet Domowy. Warsaw Ghetto (BJA) .... KD

Komitet Gosudarstvennoi Bezopasnosti [Committee of State Security] [Russian Secret Police Also satirically interpreted as Kontora Grubykh Banditov, or "Office of Crude Bandits"] .... KGB

Komitet Opiekunczy Miejski (BJA) .... KOM

Komma Dimokratikou Sosialismou [Party for Democratic Socialism] [Greek Political party] (PPE) .... KDS

Komma Georgiou Papandreou [Party of George Papandreou] [Greek Political party] (PPE) .... KGP

Komma Proodeftikon [Progressive Party] [Greek Political party] (PPE) .... KP

Komma Xiton Ethnikis Antistasseos ["X" National Resistance Party] [Political party] (PPE) X

Kommanditbolaget [Limited Partnership] [German] (ILCA) .... KB

Kommanditgesellschaft [Limited Partnership] [German] .... KG

Kommentar zum Alten Testament [A publication] (BJA) .... KAT

Kommentar zum Alten Testament [E. Sellin] [A publication] (BJA) .... KATSI

Kommentar zum Alten Testament [A publication] (BJA) .... KZAT

Kommentar zum Alten Testament [A publication] (BJA) .... SKAT

Kommentar zum Neuen Testament aus Talmud und Midrasch (H. L. Strack - F. Billerbeck) [A publication] (BJA) .... StB

Kommentare und Beitraege zum Alten und Neuen Testament [Duesseldorf] [A publication] (BJA) .... KomBeiANT

Kommerzielle Koordination [Former East German political party] .... KO-KO

Kommunal Statistisk DataBank [Danmarks Statistik] [Denmark Information service or system] (CRD) .... KSDB

Kommunista Ifjusagi Szovetseg [Communist Youth Organization] [Hungary] .... KISZ

Kommunistak Magyarorszagi Partja [Communist Party of Hungary] [Political party] (PPE) .... KMP

Kommunistesch Partei [Communist Party] [Luxembourg] [Political party] (PPE) .... KP

Kommunisticheskaia Partiia Ukrainy [Communist Party of the Ukraine] [Political party] .... KPU

Kommunisticheskaia Partiia Uzbekistana [Communist Party of Uzbekistan] [Political party] .... KPUZ

Kommunisticheskaya Partiya Sovetskogo Soyuza [Communist Party of the Soviet Union] [Political party] .... KPSS

Kommunistiko Komma Ellados [Communist Party of Greece] [Political party] (PPW) .... KKE

Kommunistiko Komma Ellados - Esoterikou [Communist Party of Greece - Interior] [Political party] (PPE) .... KKEes

Kommunistiko Komma Ellados - Esoterikou [Communist Party of Greece - Interior] [Political party] (PPW) .... KKES

Kommunistiko Komma Ellados - Exoterikou [Communist Party of Greece - Exterior] [Political party] (PPE) .... KKEex

Kommunistinen Tyovaenpuolue [Communist Workers' Party] [Finland] [Political party] (EY) .... KTP

Kommunistisch Partei vu Leetzebuerg [Communist Party of Luxembourg] [Political party] (PPW) .... KPL

Kommunistische Jugend Oesterreich [Communist Youth of Austria] .... KJO

Kommunistische Partei [Communist Party] [German Political party] (PPE) .... KP

Kommunistische Partei der Schweiz [Communist Party of Switzerland] [Political party] (PPW) .... KPS

Kommunistische Partei Deutschlands [Communist Party of Germany] [Political party] (PPW) .... KPD

Kommunistische Partei Deutschlands/Marxisten-Leninisten [Communist Party of Germany/Marxists-Leninists] [Political party] (PPW) .... KPD-ML

Kommunistische Partei Oesterreichs [Communist Party of Austria] [Political party] (PPW) .... KPO

Kommunistische Partij Suriname [Communist Party of Surinam] [Political party] (PPW) .... KPS

Kommunistische Partij van Belgie [Communist Party of Belgium] [See also PCB] [Political party] (PPE) .... KPB

Kommunistischer Bund Oesterrichs [Communist League of Austria] [Political party] (PPW) .... KBO

Kommunistischer Bund Westdeutschland [Communist League of West Germany] [Political party] (PPW) .... KBW

Kommunistischer Jugendverband Deutschlands [Communist Youth Club of Germany] [Political party] (PPW) .... KJVD

Kommunistiska Foerbundet Marxist-Leninisterna [Communist League of Marxist-Leninists] [Sweden Political party] (PPE) .... KFML

Komo-Manda [Papua New Guinea] [Airport symbol Obsolete] (OAG) .... KOM

Komondor Club of America (EA) .... KCA

Kompong Cham [Cambodia] [ICAO location identifier] (ICLI) .... VDKC

Kompong Chnang [Cambodia] [ICAO location identifier] (ICLI) .... VDKH

Komunisticka Partija Hrvatske [Communist Party of Croatia] [Political party] .... KPH

Komunisticka Partija Jugoslavije [Communist Party of Yugoslavia] [Political party] (PPE) .... KPJ

Komunisticka Strana Ceskoslovenska [Communist Party of Czechoslovakia] [Political party] (PPW) .... KSC

Komunisticka Strane Slovenska [Communist Party of Slovakia] [Former Czechoslovakia] [Political party] (PPW) .... KSS

Komunistycha Spilka Molodi Ukrainy .... KSMU

Komunistyczna Partia Polski [Communist Party of Poland (1925-1938)] [Political party] (PPE) .... KPP

Kona [Hawaii] [Airport symbol] (OAG) .... KOA

Kona Coffee Council [Defunct] (EA) .... KCC

Kona/Ke-Ahole, Hawaii Island [Hawaii] [ICAO location identifier] (ICLI) .... PHKO

Konark [India] [ICAO location identifier] (ICLI) .... VEKN

Konawaena [Hawaii] [Seismograph station code, US Geological Survey Closed] (SEIS) .... KNW

Konawaruk [Guyana] [Airport symbol Obsolete] (OAG) .... KKG

Konde [Zaire] [ICAO location identifier] (ICLI) .... FZAU

Kone [New Caledonia] [Airport symbol Obsolete] (OAG) .... KNQ

Kone [New Caledonia] [ICAO location identifier] (ICLI) .... NWWD

Kone Air Ltd. [Finland ICAO designator] (FAAC) .... KOA

Konedobu [Papua New Guinea] [Seismograph station code, US Geological Survey] (SEIS) .... KDB

Konferenz Europaeischer Kirchen [Conference of European Churches - CEC] (EA) .... KEK

Kong Kong [Malaysia] [ICAO location identifier] (ICLI) .... WMAO

Konge [Papua New Guinea] [Airport symbol] (OAG) .... KGB

Kongelige Bibliotek [Royal Library], Kobenhavn, Denmark [Library symbol Library of Congress] (LCLS) .... Dn

Kongiganak [Alaska] [Airport symbol] (OAG) .... KKH

Konglomerati Florida Foundation for Literature and the Book Arts (EA) .... KFFLBA

Kongo [MARC language code Library of Congress] (LCCP) .... kon

Kongo Boumba [Gabon] [Airport symbol] (AD) .... GKO

Kongolo [Zaire] [ICAO location identifier] (ICLI) .... FZRQ

Kongolo [Zaire] [Airport symbol] (OAG) .... KOO

Kongoussi [Burkina Faso] [ICAO location identifier] (ICLI) .... DHCG

Kongoussi [Upper Volta] [Airport symbol] (AD) .... ONU

Kongres Indian Muslim Malaysia [Malaysia Indian Moslem Congress] [Political party] (PPW) .... KIMMA

Kongres Liberalno-Demokratyczny [Liberal Democratic Congress] [Poland Political party] (EY) .... KLD

Kongsberg [Norway] [Seismograph station code, US Geological Survey] (SEIS) .... KON

Kongwa [Tanzania] [ICAO location identifier] (ICLI) .... HTKO

Konigsberg [Kaliningrad] [Former USSR Seismograph station code, US Geological Survey Closed] (SEIS) .... KNG

Koninklijk Besluit [Royal Decree] [Dutch] (ILCA) .... KB

Koninklijk Instituut van Inginieurs [Netherlands] (ACII) .... KIVI

Koninklijk Instituut voor de Tropen, Amsterdam, Netherlands [Library symbol Library of Congress] (LCLS) .... NeAT

Koninklijk Instituut voor Taal-, Land-, en Volkenkunde, Leiden, Netherlands [Library symbol Library of Congress] (LCLS) .... NeLV

Koninklijke Bibliotheek [Royal Library], The Hague, Netherlands [Library symbol Library of Congress] (LCLS) .... NeHKB

Koninklijke Java-China-Paketvaart Lijnen .... KJCPL

Koninklijke Luchtvaart Maatschappij [Royal Dutch Airlines] .... KLM

Koninklijke PTT Nederland [Post and telecommunications company] (ECON) .... KPN

Koninkrijk der Nederlanden [Kingdom of the Netherlands] [Dutch] (BARN) .... KdN

Konjak-I-Logar [Afghanistan] [ICAO location identifier] (ICLI) .... OAKL

Konkani [MARC language code Library of Congress] (LCCP) .... kok

Konkordanz zu den Qumrantexten [A publication] (BJA) .... KQT

Konrad Adenauer Stiftung [Germany Political party] .... KAS

Konservativ-Christlichsoziale Volkspartei [Conservative Christian-Social Party] [Switzerland Political party] (PPE) .... KCVP

Konservative Folkeparti [Conservative People's Party (Commonly called the Conservative Party)] [Denmark Political party] (PPE) .... KF

Konstam and Ward's Rating Appeals [1909-12] [A publication] (DLA) .... Konst & W Rat App

Konstam's Rating Appeals [1904-08] [A publication] (DLA) .... Konst Rat App

Konstanz [Germany ICAO location identifier] (ICLI) .... EDTZ

Konstitutionella Folkpartiet [Constitutional People's Party] [Finland Political party] (PPE) .... KFP

Kontra [Contra] [Music] .... K

Kontrabass [Double Bass] [Music] .... KB

Kontrafagott [Double Bassoon] [Organ stop Music] .... KF

Kontron Personal Instrumentation [Kontron Electronics] (NITA) .... KPI

Kontum [South Vietnam] [Airport symbol] (AD) .... KON

Konungariket Sverige [Kingdom of Sweden] (BARN) .... KS

Konya [Turkey] [Airport symbol] (AD) .... KYA

Konya [Turkey ICAO location identifier] (ICLI) .... LTAN

Konyvtartudomanyi es Modszertani Kozpont [Center for Library Science and Methodology] [Hungary] [Information service or system] (IID) .... KMK

Konzentrationslager [Concentration Camp] [German] (BJA) .... KL

Konzentrationslager [Concentration Camp] [Initials also used in medicine to indicate a psychiatric syndrome found in surviving victims of the World War II camps] [German] .... KZ

Koo Koo Roo [NASDAQ symbol] (TTSB) .... KKRO

Koo Koo Roo, Inc. [NASDAQ symbol] (SAG) .... KKRO

Koo Koo Roo, Inc. [Associated Press] (SAG) .... KooKR

Kookier (ABBR) .... KOOKR

Kookiest (ABBR) .... KOOKST

Koolatah [*Australia Airport symbol Obsolete*] (OAG) ... KOH
Kooperative Serbaguna Malaysia [*Bank*] ... KSM
Koor Indus Ltd ADS [*NYSE symbol*] (TTSB) ... KOR
Koor Industries Ltd. [*Associated Press*] (SAG) ... Koor
Koor Industries Ltd. [*NYSE symbol*] (SAG) ... KOR
Kooskia Public Library, Kooskia, ID [*Library symbol*] [*Library of Congress*] (LCLS) ... IdKo
Kootenai Medical Center, Medical Library, Couer d'Alene, ID [*Library symbol*] [*Library of Congress*] (LCLS) ... IdCH
Kootenay King Resources [*Vancouver Stock Exchange symbol*] ... KKG
Kopasker [*Iceland*] [*ICAO location identifier*] (ICLI) ... BIKP
Kopasker [*Iceland*] [*Airport symbol*] (OAG) ... OPA
Kopeck [*Monetary unit*] [*Former USSR*] ... K
Kopeck [*Monetary unit in Russia*] ... KOP
Kopeck (ABBR) ... KPCK
Kopiago [*Papua New Guinea*] [*Airport symbol*] (OAG) ... KPA
Kopin Corp. [*Associated Press*] (SAG) ... Kopin
Kopin Corp. [*NASDAQ symbol*] (SAG) ... KOPN
Koping [*Sweden ICAO location identifier*] (ICLI) ... ESVQ
Koplar Communications Center [*St. Louis, MO*] [*Telecommunications*] (TSSD) ... KCC
Koppel [*Federal Republic of Germany*] [*Seismograph station code, US Geological Survey*] (SEIS) ... KOE
Kopper Reppart [*Medium*] [*Biochemistry*] (DAVI) ... KR
Koppers Co., Inc., Research Department, Monroeville, PA [*Library symbol Library of Congress*] (LCLS) ... PMvK
Koppers Hydrate Process ... KHP
Koran (ROG) ... KOR
Korbach [*Germany ICAO location identifier*] (ICLI) ... EDGK
Korea [*MARC geographic area code Library of Congress*] (LCCP) ... a-kr--
Korea (VRA) ... Kor
Korea Advanced Institute of Science ... KIAS
Korea Advanced Institute of Science and Technology [*Seoul*] [*Information service or system*] (IID) ... KAIST
Korea Air Defense System (CINC) ... KADS
Korea Ammunition Management System (MCD) ... KAMS
Korea Australia Business Cooperation Council ... KABCC
Korea, Australia, New Zealand, and the United States ... KANZUS
Korea Development Bank ... KDB
Korea Development Finance Corp. ... KDFC
Korea Development Institute (ECON) ... KDI
Korea Economic Institute of America (EA) ... KEIA
Korea Electric Power ADS [*NYSE symbol*] (TTSB) ... KEP
Korea Electric Power Corp. [*NYSE symbol*] (SAG) ... KEP
Korea Electric Power Corp. [*Associated Press*] (SAG) ... KoreaElc
Korea Electric Power Corp. [*Associated Press*] (SAG) ... KorEIN
Korea Energy Development Organisation [*A consortium formed by the US, North Korea, and South Korea to finance and build reactors*] (ECON) ... KEDO
Korea Equity Fund [*NYSE symbol*] (SPSG) ... KEF
Korea Equity Fund [*Associated Press*] (SAG) ... KoreaEqt
Korea Exchange Bank (IMH) ... KEB
Korea Friendship Committee [*British*] (EAIO) ... KFC
Korea Fund [*NYSE symbol*] (TTSB) ... KE
Korea Fund, Inc. [*NYSE symbol*] (SPSG) ... KF
Korea Fund, Inc. [*Associated Press*] (SAG) ... Korea
Korea Housing Bank (IMH) ... KHB
Korea Institute for Industrial Economics and Trade (ECON) ... KIET
Korea Kuwait Banking Corp. ... KKBC
Korea Law Review [*A publication*] (DLA) ... Korea LR
Korea Limited Identification Zone ... KLIZ
Korea Microforms, Seoul, Korea [*Library symbol Library of Congress*] (LCLS) ... KoM
Korea Military Academy ... KMA
Korea Military Advisory Group [*United States*] ... KMAG
Korea Mobile Telecommunications [*Associated Press*] (SAG) ... KoreaM
Korea Mobile Telecommunications [*NYSE symbol*] (SAG) ... SKM
Korea National Party [*South Korea Political party*] (PPW) ... KNP
Korea, North [*MARC geographic area code Library of Congress*] (LCCP) ... a-kn--
Korea, North [*MARC country of publication code Library of Congress*] (LCCP) ... kn
Korea Ocean Research and Development Institute (USDC) ... KORDI
Korea Oceanographic Data Center [*Marine science*] (OSRA) ... KODC
Korea Oil Corp. ... KOCO
Korea Oil Storage Co. (CINC) ... KOSCO
Korea Procurement Agency ... KPA
Korea Scientific and Technical Information Centre (NITA) ... KORSTIC
Korea Scientific and Technological Information Center [*INSPEC operator*] ... KORSTIC
Korea Society (EA) ... KS
Korea, South [*MARC geographic area code Library of Congress*] (LCCP) ... a-ko--
Korea, South [*MARC country of publication code Library of Congress*] (LCCP) ... ko
Korea Stamp Society (EA) ... KSS
Korea Stock Exchange (ECON) ... KSE
Korea Tactical Target List (MCD) ... KTTL
Korea Tourist Association (EAIO) ... KTA
Korea Trade Advisory Group [*British Overseas Trade Board*] (DS) ... KTAG
Korea Trade Promotion Center (EA) ... KOTRA
Korea-American Commerce and Industry Association [*Later, KS*] ... KACIA
Korean [*MARC language code Library of Congress*] (LCCP) ... kor
Korean Affairs Institute (EA) ... KAI
Korean Air [*Airline flight code*] (ODBW) ... KE
Korean Air Intelligence System (MCD) ... KAIS
Korean Air Lines [*ICAO designator*] (AD) ... KE
Korean Air Lines Co. Ltd. [*ICAO designator*] (FAAC) ... KAL
Korean Air Lines, Inc. ... KAL
Korean Airways [*ICAO designator*] (AD) ... JS
Korean American Coalition (EA) ... KAC
Korean Army Training Center ... KATC
Korean Augmentation to the United States Army ... KATUSA
Korean Broadcasting System [*South Korea*] (FEA) ... KBS
Korean Central News Agency [*North Korea*] ... KCNA
Korean Centre of International PEN (EAIO) ... KPENC
Korean Chemical Society ... KCS
Korean Communications Zone [*Military*] ... KCOMZ
Korean Communist Party [*Political party North Korea*] (FEA) ... KCP
Korean Conflict Research Foundation [*Defunct*] ... KCRF
Korean Council of Organization [*South Korea*] ... KCLU
Korean Cultural and Freedom Foundation (EA) ... KCFF
Korean Democratic Party [*North Korea Political party*] (FEA) ... KDP
Korean Direct Hire ... KDH
Korean Federation of Education Associations ... KFEA
Korean Federation of Science and Technology ... KOFST
Korean Federation of Trade Unions [*North Korea*] ... KFTU
Korean Fighter Program ... KFP
Korean Foreign Exchange (IMH) ... KFX
Korean Hemorrhagic Fever [*Medicine*] ... KHF
Korean Institute for Human Rights (EA) ... KIHR
Korean Institute for Research in the Behavioral Sciences ... KIRBS
Korean Institute for Science and Technology ... KIST
Korean Institute of Electrical Engineers ... KIEE
Korean Institute of International Studies ... KIIS
Korean Intelligence Support System (DOMA) ... KISS
Korean International Telephone & Telegraph ... KITT
Korean Investment Fund [*NYSE symbol*] (SAG) ... KIF
Korean Investment Fund [*Associated Press*] (SAG) ... KoreaInv
Korean Journal of Comparative Law [*A publication*] (DLA) ... Korean J Comp L
Korean Journal of International Law [*A publication*] (DLA) ... Korean J Int'l L
Korean Journal of International Law [*A publication*] (DLA) ... Korean J of Internat L
Korean Labor Party [*Political party*] ... KLP
Korean Law [*A publication*] (DLA) ... Korean L
Korean Logistic Service Corps (CINC) ... KLSC
Korean Long Term Credit Bank ... KLTCB
Korean Marine Corps [*North Korea*] ... KMC
Korean Medical Association of America (EA) ... KMAS
Korean Military Assistance Group, Vietnam (VNW) ... KMAGV
Korean National Airlines ... KNA
Korean National Association (EA) ... KNA
Korean National Committee of the International Association on Water Pollution Research and Control (EAIO) ... KNCIAWPRC
Korean National Railroad (DCTA) ... KNR
Korean Overseas Development Co. [*Korean government agency*] ... KODCO
Korean Patriotic Women's Association in America [*Defunct*] (EA) ... KPWA
Korean Presidential Unit Citation [*Military award*] ... KPUC
Korean Scientists and Engineers Association in America (EA) ... KSEA
Korean Securities Dealers' Association (ECON) ... KSDA
Korean Service Corps ... KSC
Korean Service Medal [*Military decoration*] ... KSM
Korean Student Federation of the United States (EA) ... KSFUS
Korean Veterans International (EA) ... KVI
Korean War ... KW
Korean War Memorial (EA) ... KWM
Korean War Veterans Association (EA) ... KWVA
Korean War Veterans Memorial [*Defunct*] (EA) ... KWVM
Korean Welfare Society [*Australia*] ... KWS
Korean Wideband Network [*Communications*] [*Military*] (MCD) ... KWN
Korean Workers' Party [*North Korea Political party*] (PD) ... KWP
Korean-American Chamber of Commerce [*Later, AAACC*] ... KACC
Korean-American Cultural Foundation (EA) ... KACF
Korean-American Oil Co. ... KOAM
Korean-American Technical Cooperation Association ... KATCA
Korean-French Banking Corp. [*Acronym is based on foreign phrase*] (EY) ... SOGEKO
Korhogo [*Ivory Coast*] [*ICAO location identifier*] (ICLI) ... DIKO
Korhogo [*Ivory Coast*] [*Airport symbol*] (OAG) ... HGO
Korintji-Kaba-Dempo [*Sumatra*] [*Seismograph station code, US Geological Survey Closed*] (SEIS) ... KKD
Korla [*China*] [*Airport symbol*] (OAG) ... KRL
Koro [*Fiji*] [*Airport symbol*] (OAG) ... KXF
Koro [*Fiji*] [*ICAO location identifier*] (ICLI) ... NFNO
Koroba [*Papua New Guinea*] [*Airport symbol Obsolete*] (OAG) ... KDE
Koronadal [*Mindanao, Philippines*] [*Airport symbol*] (AD) ... KDL
Koror [*Palau Islands*] [*Seismograph station code, US Geological Survey Closed*] (SEIS) ... KOR
Koror [*Caroline Islands*] [*ICAO location identifier*] (ICLI) ... PTRO
Koror [*Palau Islands*] [*Airport symbol*] (OAG) ... ROR
Koroska Enotna Lista [*Carinthian Unity List*] [*Austria Political party*] (PPE) ... KEL
Korpus Bezpieczenstwa (BJA) ... KB
Korrespondenzblatt der Nachrichtenstelle fuer den Orient [*A publication*] (BJA) ... KNO
Korrespondenz-Blatt des Verbandes der Deutschen Juden [*A publication*] (BJA) ... KB
Korrespondenzblatt des Vereins zur Gruendung und Erhaltung der Akademie fuer dieWissenschaft des Judentums [*A publication*] (BJA) ... KAWJ
Korsakoff Syndrome [*Medicine Medicine*] (DMAA) ... KS
Korsakoff's Disease [*Medicine*] ... KD
Korsar [*Russian Federation*] [*ICAO designator*] (FAAC) ... KRS
Korteweg-deVries [*Equation*] [*Mathematics*] ... KdV
Kortrijk-Wevelgem [*Belgium ICAO location identifier*] (ICLI) ... EBKT
Koruna [*Monetary unit*] [*Former Czechoslovakia*] ... K
Koruna [*Czech Coin*] (BARN) ... Kc

Kos [Greece] [Airport symbol] (OAG) .... KGS
Kos [Greece] [ICAO location identifier] (ICLI) .... LGKO
Kosan Boka [Ivory Coast] [Seismograph station code, US Geological Survey]
 (SEIS) .... KIC
Kosciusko County Recorder's Office, Warsaw, IN [Library symbol Library of
 Congress] (LCLS) .... InWarsR
Kosciusko, MS [Location identifier FAA] (FAAL) .... OSX
Kosciusko, MS [FM radio station call letters] .... WBKJ
Kosciusko, MS [FM radio station call letters] .... WJTA
Kosciusko, MS [AM radio station call letters] .... WKOZ
Kosciuszko Foundation (EA) .... KF
Kosher .... K
Kosher (ABBR) .... KSHR
Kosher .... KSHR
Kosher Dining Club (BJA) .... KDC
Kosher Dining Hall (BJA) .... KDH
Kosher Kitchen (BJA) .... KK
Kosher Meal [Airline notation] .... KSML
Kosher Wine Institute (EA) .... KWI
Koshkonong Nuclear Plant (NRCH) .... KNP
Kosice [Former Czechoslovakia] [Airport symbol] (OAG) .... KSC
Kosice [Former Czechoslovakia] [ICAO location identifier] (ICLI) .... LKKZ
Kosmodemyansk [Former USSR Seismograph station code, US Geological
 Survey Closed] (SEIS) .... KOS
Kosmos [Publisher] [Holland] .... K
Kosovaair [Yugoslavia] [ICAO designator] (FAAC) .... KOS
Kosrae Island [Caroline Islands] [ICAO location identifier] (ICLI) .... PTTK
Koss Corp. [NASDAQ symbol] (SAG) .... KOSS
Kossuth County Advance, Algona, IA [Library symbol Library of Congress]
 (LCLS) .... IaAlgKA
Kossuth Foundation (EA) .... KF
Kosta [Sweden ICAO location identifier] (ICLI) .... ESFQ
Koster [South Africa] [Seismograph station code, US Geological Survey]
 (SEIS) .... KSR
Koster Vig [Denmark ICAO location identifier] (ICLI) .... EKMN
Kosterlitz-Thouless Theory [Physics] .... K-T
Kosterlitz-Thouless-Berezinskii Layers [Physics] .... KTB
Kosti [Sudan] [Airport symbol] (AD) .... KST
Kosti/Rabak [Sudan] [ICAO location identifier] (ICLI) .... HSKI
Koszalin [Poland] [Airport symbol] (OAG) .... OSZ
Kota [India] [Airport symbol] (OAG) .... KTU
Kota [India] [ICAO location identifier] (ICLI) .... VIKO
Kota Bahru/Sultan Ismail Petra [Malaysia] [ICAO location identifier]
 (ICLI) .... WMKC
Kota Bharu [Malaysia] [Airport symbol] (OAG) .... KBR
Kota Kinabalu [Malaysia] [Airport symbol] (OAG) .... BKI
Kota Kinabalu [Malaysia] [Seismograph station code, US Geological Survey]
 (SEIS) .... KKM
Kota Kinabalu [Malaysia] [ICAO location identifier] (ICLI) .... WBFC
Kota Kinabalu [Malaysia] [ICAO location identifier] (ICLI) .... WBKK
Kotabaru [West Irian, Indonesia] [Airport symbol] (AD) .... KBU
Kotabaru/Setagen [Indonesia] [ICAO location identifier] (ICLI) .... WRBK
Kotakoli [Zaire] [ICAO location identifier] (ICLI) .... FZFP
Kotal [Afghanistan] [ICAO location identifier] (ICLI) .... OATK
Kotamubagu/Mopait [Indonesia] [ICAO location identifier] (ICLI) .... WAMB
Kotas Joint Civil Aviation Enterprise [Former USSR] [FAA designator]
 (FAAC) .... KTS
Kotlas [Former USSR ICAO location identifier] (ICLI) .... ULAK
Kotlik [Alaska] [Airport symbol] (OAG) .... KOT
Kotoka International Airport [Ghana] .... KIA
Kotze and Barber's Transvaal (High Court) Reports [1885-88]
 [A publication] (DLA) .... K & B
Kotzebue [Alaska] [Seismograph station code, US Geological Survey]
 (SEIS) .... KTA
Kotzebue [Alaska] [Airport symbol] (OAG) .... OTZ
Kotzebue [Alaska] [ICAO location identifier] (ICLI) .... PAOT
Kotzebue, AK [Location identifier FAA] (FAAL) .... HHM
Kotzebue, AK [AM radio station call letters] .... KOTZ
Kotzebue Middle-High School, Kotzebue, AK [Library symbol] [Library of
 Congress] (LCLS) .... AkKzMHS
Kotze's Transvaal High Court Reports [South Africa] [A publication] (DLA) .... K
Kotze's Transvaal High Court Reports [South Africa] [A publication]
 (DLA) .... Kotze
Koudougou [Burkina Faso] [ICAO location identifier] (ICLI) .... DHCK
Koula Moutou [Gabon] [Airport symbol] (OAG) .... KOU
Koula-Moutou/Mabimbi [Gabon] [ICAO location identifier] (ICLI) .... FOGK
Koumac [New Caledonia] [Airport symbol] (OAG) .... KOC
Koumac [New Caledonia] [Seismograph station code, US Geological Survey]
 (SEIS) .... KOU
Koumac [New Caledonia] [ICAO location identifier] (ICLI) .... NWWK
Kountze/Silsbee, TX [Location identifier FAA] (FAAL) .... HRD
Koupela [Burkina Faso] [ICAO location identifier] (ICLI) .... DHEK
Kourday [Former USSR Seismograph station code, US Geological Survey
 Closed] (SEIS) .... KRD
Kouroussa [Guinea] [ICAO location identifier] (ICLI) .... GURS
Kousour [Djibouti] [Seismograph station code, US Geological Survey]
 (SEIS) .... KSU
Koussevitzky Music Foundation (EA) .... KMF
Koutaba [Cameroon] [Airport symbol] (OAG) .... KOB
Koutiala [Mali] [ICAO location identifier] (ICLI) .... GAKO
Kouts Times, Kouts, IN [Library symbol Library of Congress] (LCLS) .... InKouT
Kouyunjik [or Kuyounjik] [Collection of cuneiform tablets from Kuyounjik in the
 British Museum, London] (BJA) .... K
Kovar Air [Czechoslovakia] [ICAO designator] (FAAC) .... WOK
Kovats [Retention] Index .... KI

Kowanyama [Australia Airport symbol] (OAG) .... KWM
Kowkash Gold [Vancouver Stock Exchange symbol] .... KOW
[The] Kowloon Canton Railway [Hong Kong] (DCTA) .... KCR
Kowloon-Canton Railway Corp. [Commercial firm] [Hong Kong] .... KCRC
Koyama [Japan] [Seismograph station code, US Geological Survey Closed]
 (SEIS) .... KOY
Koyna Nagar [India] [Seismograph station code, US Geological Survey
 Closed] (SEIS) .... KNI
Koyukuk [Alaska] [Airport symbol] (OAG) .... KKA
Koyukuk [Alaska] [Airport symbol] (OAG) .... KYU
Koyukuk, AK [Location identifier FAA] (FAAL) .... KYU
Kozani [Greece] [Airport symbol] (OAG) .... KZI
Kozani [Greece] [Seismograph station code, US Geological Survey] (SEIS) ..... KZN
Kozani [Greece] [ICAO location identifier] (ICLI) .... LGKZ
Kozawa, Iwatsuru, and Kawaguchi [Factor involving injection of cancerous
 gastric juices into rabbits, named for its discoverers] [Medicine] .... KIK
Kozyrevsk [Former USSR Seismograph station code, US Geological Survey]
 (SEIS) .... KOZ
Kpelle [MARC language code Library of Congress] (LCCP) .... kpe
KPN [NYSE symbol] (SAG) .... KPN
Kradschuetzen-Bataillon [Motorcycle Battalion] [German military - World War
 II] .... KSB
Kraemer System .... KS
Kraepelin-Morel [Disease] [Psychiatry] (DAVI) .... KM
Kraft [Paper] (DGA) .... K
Kraft Black Liquor [Pulping technology] .... KBL
Kraft durch Freude [Strength through Joy Movement] [Pre-World War II]
 [German] .... KDF
Kraft, Inc., Law Library, Glenview, IL [Library symbol] [Library of Congress]
 (LCLS) .... IGlvK-L
Kraft Mill Effluent [Pulp and paper processing] .... KME
Kraft Paper Association [Later, API] (EA) .... KPA
Kraftco Corp., Research and Development Library, Glenview, IL [Library
 symbol Library of Congress] (LCLS) .... IGlvK
Kraftfahrwesen [Motor transport] [German military - World War II] .... K
Kraftrad [Motorcycle] [German military - World War II] .... K
Kraftverkehrsordnung fuer den Gueterfernverkehr mit Kraftfahrzeugen
 [Regulation for the Carriage of Goods by Motor Vehicles] [German Business
 term] (ILCA) .... KVO
Kraftwagen [Motor Vehicle] [German] .... KW
Kraftwerksunion [Germany] .... KWU
Krag-Jorgensen Rifle .... KRAG-JORG
Kraiaero [Russian Federation] [ICAO designator] (FAAC) .... KIO
Kraken (ABBR) .... KRKN
Krakow [Poland] [Seismograph station code, US Geological Survey] (SEIS) ..... KRA
Krakow [Poland] [Airport symbol] (OAG) .... KRK
Krakow/Balice [Poland ICAO location identifier] (ICLI) .... EPKK
Kralendijk/Flamingo, Bonaire Island [Netherlands Antilles] [ICAO location
 identifier] (ICLI) .... TNCB
Kramer Elementary School, Bethpage, NY [Library symbol Library of
 Congress] (LCLS) .... NBetKE
Kramers-Henneberger [Coordinate frame for electron movement] [Physics] ...... KH
Kramfors [Sweden ICAO location identifier] (ICLI) .... ESNK
Kramfors [Sweden] [Airport symbol] (OAG) .... KRF
Kraner Preschool Math Inventory [Educational test] .... KPMI
Krankenhaus Information System (DAVI) .... KIS
Krantor Corp. [NASDAQ symbol] (SAG) .... KRAN
Krantor Corp. [Associated Press] (SAG) .... Krantor
Krantor Corp. [Associated Press] (SAG) .... Krantr
Krantor Corp.Wrrt'A' [NASDAQ symbol] (TTSB) .... KRANW
Kranzco Realty Trust [Associated Press] (SAG) .... Kranzc
Kranzco Realty Trust [NYSE symbol] (SPSG) .... KRT
Krasnaya Polyana [Former USSR Seismograph station code, US Geological
 Survey Closed] (SEIS) .... KPR
Krasnodar [Former USSR Airport symbol] (OAG) .... KRR
Krasnodar [Former USSR ICAO location identifier] (ICLI) .... URKK
Krasnogorka [Former USSR Seismograph station code, US Geological Survey
 Closed] (SEIS) .... KRS
Krasnogorsk-3 [A 16mm film camera] (WDMC) K-3
Krasnoyarsk [Former USSR ICAO location identifier] (ICLI) .... UNKK
Kratie [Cambodia] [Airport symbol] (AD) .... KTI
Kratie [Cambodia] [ICAO location identifier] (ICLI) .... VDKT
Kratkie Soobshcheniia o Dokladakh i Polevykh Issledovaniiakh Instituta
 Istorii Materialnoi Kulturi [A publication] (BJA) .... KSIIMK
Krause's Furniture [NASDAQ symbol] (TTSB) .... SOFA
Krauses Furniture, Inc. [Associated Press] (SAG) .... Krause
Krauses Furniture, Inc. [Associated Press] (SAG) .... KrauseF
Krauses Furniture, Inc. [NASDAQ symbol] (SAG) .... SOFA
Kraus-Thomson Organization [Publisher] .... KO
Kraus-Thomson Organization [Publishing] .... KTO
Krazy Kat [Cartoon character by George Herriman] .... K
Krebs-Henseleit [Cycle] [or Ornithine cycle Analytical biochemistry] (DAVI) ...... KH
Krebs-Henseleit Bicarbonate [A buffer] [Analytical biochemistry] .... KHB
Krebs-Henseleit Buffer [Analytical biochemistry] (DMAA) .... KH
Krebs-Ringer Bicarbonate Buffer [Biochemistry] (DAVI) .... KRB
Krebs-Ringer Bicarbonate Buffer [Biochemistry] (DAVI) .... KRBB
Krebs-Ringer Bicarbonate Buffer [Containing] Glucose (DAVI) .... KRBG
Krebs-Ringer Bicarbonate Buffer with Glucose [Medicine] (DMAA) .... KRBG
Krebs-Ringer Bicarbonate Solution .... KRBS
Krebs-Ringer Bicarbonate Solution with Glucose .... KRBSG
Krebs-Ringer-Bicarbonate [Buffer solution] .... KRB
Krebs-Ringer-Bicarbonate Glucose-Albumin [Buffer solution] .... KRB-GA
Krebs-Ringer-Glucose [Buffer solution and growth medium] .... KRG
Krebs-Ringer-Phosphate [Buffer solution] .... KRP
Krebs-Ringer-Phosphate Buffer [Solution] .... KRPB

Krebs-Ringer-Phosphate Buffer Solution (MAE) .... KRPS
Kredietbank Luxembourgeoise [Luxembourg] .... KBL
Kreditanstalt fur Wiederaufbau [Finance] [Germany] ...... KfW
Kreeger, George W., Atlanta GA [STAC] .... KGW
Krefeld/Egelsberg [Germany ICAO location identifier] (ICLI) ...... EDLK
Kreisinger Development Laboratory (KSC) .... KDL
Kreisler Manufacturing Co. [Associated Press] (SAG) ...... Kreislr
Kreisler Manufacturing Co. [NASDAQ symbol] (NQ) ...... KRSL
Kreisler Mfg [NASDAQ symbol] (TTSB) .... KRSI
Kremers-Urban Co. (DAVI) .... K-U
Kremlin Kommandant .... KK
Kremmling, CO [FM radio station call letters] .... KRKM
Kremmling, CO [Location identifier FAA] (FAAL) .... RLG
Kremmling Public Library, Kremmling, CO [Library symbol Library of Congress] (LCLS) .... CoKr
Kremsmuenster [Austria] [Seismograph station code, US Geological Survey] (SEIS) .... KMR
Kresge Eye Institute .... KEI
Kresge Hearing Research Institute [University of Michigan] [Research center] .... KHRI
K-Resolved Inverse Photoelectron Spectroscopy .... KRIPES
Kress' Reports [2-12 Pennsylvania Superior Court] [166-194 Pennsylvania] [A publication] (DLA) .... Kress
Kreuzbein Lipomatous Syndrome [Medicine] (DMAA) .... KLS
Kreuzer [Monetary unit] [German] .... KR
Kreuzer [Monetary unit] [German] (ROG) .... KREUZ
KRG Management, Inc. [Toronto Stock Exchange symbol] ...... KRG
Kribi [Cameroon] [ICAO location identifier] (ICLI) .... FKKB
Kribi [Cameroon] [Airport symbol] (OAG) .... KBI
Krieger Data International Corp. [Vancouver Stock Exchange symbol] ...... KRD
Kriegs Dekoration [War Decoration] [German] .... KD
Kriegsausruestungsnachweisung [Table of Basic Allowances] [German military - World War II] .... KAN
Kriegsgefangener [Prisoner of War] [German] .... KGF
Kriegsgericht [War Tribunal] [German] .... KrG
Kriegsoffizier-Bewerber [Applicant for Wartime Commission] [German military - World War II] .... KOB
Kriegsstaerke-Nachweisung [Table of Organization] [German military - World War II] .... KSTN
Kriegstagebuch [War Diary] [German military - World War II] ...... KTB
Kriegsverdienstkreuz [War Service Cross] [German military decoration - World War II] .... KVK
Kriegsverwendungsfaehig [Fit for Active Service] [German military - World War II] .... KV
Kriel [South Africa] [ICAO location identifier] (ICLI) .... FAKL
Krilo [Former USSR] [FAA designator] (FAAC) .... KRI
Kriminalpolizei [Ordinary Criminal Police] [German] ...... KRIPO
Kris Kristofferson International Fan Club (EA) .... KKIFC
Krishnamurti Foundation of America (EA) .... KFA
Kristana Esperantista Ligo Internacia [International Christian Esperanto Association] (EAIO) .... KELI
Kristelig Folkpartiet [Christian People's Party] [Norway Political party] (PPE) .... KrF
Kristelig Forening for Unge Kvinder [Young Women's Christian Associations - YWCA] [Denmark] .... KFUK
Kristelig Forening for Unge Maend [Young Men's Christian Associations - YMCA] [Denmark] .... KFUM
Kristeligt Folkeparti [Christian People's Party] [Denmark Political party] (PPE) .... KrF
Kristen Demokratisk Samling [Christian Democratic Union] [Sweden Political party] (PPE) .... KDS
Kristiansand [Norway] [Airport symbol] (OAG) .... KRS
Kristiansand/Kjevik [Norway ICAO location identifier] (ICLI) ...... ENCN
Kristianstad [Sweden] [Airport symbol] (OAG) .... KID
Kristianstad/Everod [Sweden ICAO location identifier] (ICLI) ...... ESMK
Kristiansund [Norway] [Airport symbol] (OAG) .... KSU
Kristiansund/Kvernberget [Norway ICAO location identifier] (ICLI) ...... ENKB
Kroeber Anthropological Society (EA) .... KAS
Kroenig's Isthmus [Of resonance] [Medicine] .... KI
Kroger Co. [NYSE symbol] (TTSB) .... KR
[The] Kroger Co. [Associated Press] (SAG) .... Kroger
Kroh [Malaysia] [ICAO location identifier] (ICLI) .... WMBH
Kron Monjan [Afghanistan] [ICAO location identifier] (ICLI) ...... OAQM
Krona [Crown] [Monetary unit Faroe Islands] .... F KR
Krona [Monetary unit] [Iceland, Sweden] .... K
Krona [Crown] [Monetary unit Iceland, Sweden] (EY) .... KR
Krone [Crown] [Monetary unit Denmark, Norway] .... K
Krone (ABBR) .... KN
Krone [Crown] [Monetary unit Denmark, Norway] (EY) .... KR
Kronen (ABBR) .... KN
Kronig-Penny Model .... KPM
Kronos, Inc. [NASDAQ symbol] (SAG) .... KRON
Kronos, Inc. [Associated Press] (SAG) .... Kronos
Kroon [Monetary unit] [Estonia] .... K
Kroonstad [South Africa] [ICAO location identifier] (ICLI) ...... FAKS
Kru [MARC language code Library of Congress] (LCCP) ...... kro
Krueger-Ringier [Book manufacturer] .... K-R
KRUG International [NASDAQ symbol] (TTSB) .... KRUG
KRUG International Corp. [AMEX symbol] (SAG) .... KRG
KRUG International Corp. [NASDAQ symbol] (NQ) .... KRUG
KRUG Intl Wrrt [NASDAQ symbol] (TTSB) .... KRUGW
Krugersdorp [South Africa] [ICAO location identifier] (ICLI) ...... FAKR
Krupnokalibernyi Pulemyoy Vladimirova Heavy Machine Gun [Soviet-made weaponry used extensively by the People's Army of North Vietnam] (VNW) .... KPV HMG
Krupp Gun .... K

Krupp Quick-Firing Gun .... KQF
Krusa-Padborg [Denmark ICAO location identifier] (ICLI) ...... EKPB
Kruse Elementary School, Pasadena, TX [Library symbol] [Library of Congress] (LCLS) .... TxPKE
Kruskal-Wallis Test [Fisheries] .... KW
Kruunupyy [Finland ICAO location identifier] (ICLI) .... EFKK
Kryla [Ukraine] [FAA designator] (FAAC) .... KRL
Krypton [Chemical element] .... Kr
Krypton (ABBR) .... KRYPN
Krypton Absorption in Liquid Carbon Dioxide [Nuclear energy] (NRCH) ...... KALC
Krypton Exposure Technique (MCD) .... KET
Krypton Gas Bottling Station [Nuclear energy] (NRCH) ...... KGBS
Krypton Ion LASER .... KIL
Krypton LASER System .... KLS
Krystal Co. [NASDAQ symbol] (SAG) .... KRYS
Krystal Company [NASDAQ symbol] (TTSB) .... KRYSQ
Krystal Co. [Associated Press] (SAG) .... Krystal
KS Bancorp [NASDAQ symbol] (TTSB) .... KSAV
KS Bancorp, Inc. [Associated Press] (SAG) .... KS Bcp
KS Bancorp, Inc. [NASDAQ symbol] (SAG) .... KSAV
KS Nordic Air, Denmark [ICAO designator] (FAAC) .... NDI
Ksan Indian Village and Museum, Haselton, BC, Canada [Library symbol] [Library of Congress] (LCLS) .... CaBHKIM
Ksan Indian Village and Museum, Haselton, British Columbia [Library symbol National Library of Canada] (NLC) .... BHKIM
Ksar Es Souk [Seismograph station code, US Geological Survey Closed] (SEIS) .... KES
Ksara [Lebanon] [Geomagnetic observatory code] .... KSA
Ksara [Lebanon] [Seismograph station code, US Geological Survey] (SEIS) ..... KSA
KSB Bancorp [Associated Press] (SAG) .... KSB Bc
KSB Bancorp [NASDAQ symbol] (SAG) .... KSBK
KSC [Kennedy Space Center] Automated Payloads Notice [NASA] (NASA) .... K-APN
KSC [Kennedy Space Center] Automated Payloads Project Specification [NASA] (NASA) .... K-APPS
KSC [Kennedy Space Center] DOD Payloads Notice [Department of Defense] [NASA] (NASA) .... K-DPN
KSC [Kennedy Space Center] DOD Payloads Projects Specification [Department of Defense] [NASA] (NASA) .... K-DPPS
KSC [Kennedy Space Center] Handbook [NASA] (KSC) .... KHB
KSC [Kennedy Space Center] Management Instruction [NASA] (KSC) ...... KMI
KSC [Kennedy Space Center] MMSE Notice [Multiuse Mission Support Equipment] [NASA] (NASA) .... K-MMSEN
KSC [Kennedy Space Center] MMSE Project Specification [Multiuse Mission Support Equipment] [NASA] (NASA) .... K-MMSEPS
KSC [Kennedy Space Center] Notice [NASA] (NASA) .... KN
KSC [Kennedy Space Center] Operation Instruction [NASA] (NASA) ...... KOI
KSC [Kennedy Space Center] Organizational Manual [NASA] (NASA) ...... KOM
KSC [Kennedy Space Center] Program Requirements Document [NASA] (NASA) .... KPRD
KSC [Kennedy Space Center] Security Steering Committee [NASA] (SSD) .... KSSC
KSC [Kennedy Space Center] Shuttle Management [Document] [NASA] (NASA) .... K-SM
KSC [Kennedy Space Center] Shuttle Project Notice [NASA] (NASA) ...... K-SPN
KSC [Kennedy Space Center] Shuttle Project Specification [NASA] (NASA) .... K-SPS
KSC [Kennedy Space Center] Shuttle Project Station Set Specification [NASA] (NASA) .... K-SSS
KSC [Kennedy Space Center] Shuttle Test Station Notice [NASA] (GFGA) .... K-STSN
KSC [Kennedy Space Center] Shuttle Test Station Project Specification [NASA] (GFGA) .... K-STSPS
KSC [Kennedy Space Center] Space Transportation System Management [Document] [NASA] (NASA) .... K-STSM
KSC [Kennedy Space Center] Spacelab Notice [NASA] (NASA) ...... K-SLN
KSC [Kennedy Space Center] Spacelab Project Specification [NASA] (NASA) .... K-SLPS
Ksiaz [Poland] [Seismograph station code, US Geological Survey] (SEIS) .... KSP
Ktav Publishing House, Inc. [New York] (BJA) .... KPH
K-Tel International [NASDAQ symbol] (TTSB) .... KTEL
K-tel International, Inc. [Associated Press] (SAG) .... K-Tel
K-tel International, Inc. [NASDAQ symbol] (SAG) .... KTEL
K-Tel International, Inc. [Toronto Stock Exchange symbol] (SPSG) ...... KTL
KTI, Inc. [Associated Press] (SAG) .... KTI
KTI, Inc. [NASDAQ symbol] (SAG) .... KTIE
KTO Microform, Millwood, NY [Library symbol Library of Congress] (LCLS) ..... KtO
K-Tron International, Inc. [NASDAQ symbol] (NQ) .... KTII
K-Tron International, Inc. [Associated Press] (SAG) .... KTron
K-Tron Intl [NASDAQ symbol] (TTSB) .... KTII
KU Energy [NYSE symbol] (TTSB) .... KU
KU Energy Co. [NYSE symbol] (SPSG) .... KU
KU Energy Corp. [Associated Press] (SAG) .... KU Engy
Kuala Krai [Malaysia] [ICAO location identifier] (ICLI) .... WMAL
Kuala Lumpur [Malaysia] .... KL
Kuala Lumpur [Malaysia] [Seismograph station code, US Geological Survey] (SEIS) .... KLM
Kuala Lumpur [Malaysia] [Airport symbol] (OAG) .... KUL
Kuala Lumpur [Malaysia] [ICAO location identifier] (ICLI) ...... WMFC
Kuala Lumpur [Malaysia] [ICAO location identifier] (ICLI) ...... WMKS
Kuala Lumpur City Center [Malaysia] (ECON) .... KLCC
Kuala Lumpur/International [Malaysia] [ICAO location identifier] (ICLI) ...... WMKK
Kuala Lumpur Stock Exchange .... KLSE
Kuala Trengganu [Malaysia] [Airport symbol] (OAG) .... TGG

Kuala Trengganu/Sultan Mahmud [*Malaysia*] [*ICAO location identifier*] (ICLI) .... WMKN
Kuala Tungkal [*Indonesia*] [*ICAO location identifier*] (ICLI) .... WIPF
Kuantan [*Malaysia*] [*Airport symbol*] (OAG) .... KUA
Kuantan [*Malaysia*] [*ICAO location identifier*] (ICLI) .... WMKD
Ku-Band Antenna Feed Horn .... KAFH
Ku-Band Feed Horn .... KFH
Ku-Band Multiple Access (MCD) .... KMA
Ku-Band Signal Processor (MCD) .... KUSP
Ku-Band Single Access (MCD) .... KSA
Ku-Band Single Processor (MCD) .... KUSP
Kubbe [*Sweden ICAO location identifier*] (ICLI) .... ESNI
Kubelka-Munk [*Optics*] .... KM
Kubota Corp. [*Associated Press*] (SAG) .... Kubota
Kubota Corp. ADR [*NYSE symbol*] (SPSG) .... KUB
Kuching [*Malaysia*] [*Airport symbol*] (OAG) .... KCH
Kuching [*Malaysia*] [*ICAO location identifier*] (ICLI) .... WBGG
Kuching Employees and Labourers' Union [*Sarawak*] .... KELU
Kucino [*Former USSR Seismograph station code, US Geological Survey Closed*] (SEIS) .... KUC
Kud [*India*] [*ICAO location identifier*] (ICLI) .... VIKD
Kudat [*Malaysia*] [*Airport symbol*] (OAG) .... KUD
Kudat [*Malaysia*] [*ICAO location identifier*] (ICLI) .... WBKT
Kuder Interest Inventory [*Occupational information*] (OICC) .... KII
Kuder Occupational Interest Survey [*Aptitude and skills test*] .... KOIS
Kuder Performance Test [*Psychology*] (DAVI) .... KPT
Kuder Preference Record [*Psychology*] (DAVI) .... KPR
Kuder Preference Record - Personal [*Psychology*] .... KPR-P
Kuder Preference Record - Vocational [*Psychology*] (DAVI) .... KPR-V
Kuder Test [*Psychology*] (DAVI) .... KT
Kuder-Richardson Formula [*Education*] (AEE) .... K-R
Kuehne & Nagel Air Cargo Ltd. [*British*] .... KNAIR
Kuehnle, Kopp, & Kausch [*Auto industry supplier*] .... KKK
Kufra [*Libya*] [*ICAO location identifier*] (ICLI) .... HLKF
Kufrah [*Libya*] [*Airport symbol*] (OAG) .... AKF
Kugelberg-Welander Disease (DAVI) .... KW
Kugel-Stoloff [*Syndrome*] [*Medicine*] (DAVI) .... KS
Kuh Shi [*Republic of China*] [*Seismograph station code, US Geological Survey*] (SEIS) .... KSH
Kuhlman Corp. [*NYSE symbol*] (SPSG) .... KUH
Kuhlman Corp. [*Associated Press*] (SAG) .... Kuhlm
Kuhlmann-Anderson Intelligence Tests [*Education*] .... K-A
Kuhmo [*Finland ICAO location identifier*] (ICLI) .... EFKH
Kuhner, J. J., Cleveland OH [*STAC*] .... KJJ
Kuhns Zeitschrift fuer Vergleichende Sprachforschung [*A publication*] (BJA) .... KZ
Kuiper Airborne Observatory [*NASA*] .... KAO
Kuiper Belt Objects [*Planetary science*] .... KBO
Kuito/Bie [*Angola*] [*ICAO location identifier*] (ICLI) .... FNKU
Kuki National Assembly [*India*] [*Political party*] (PPW) .... KNA
Kulanka Afka Somalyed .... KAS
Kulicke & Soffa Ind [*NASDAQ symbol*] (TTSB) .... KLIC
Kulicke & Soffa Industries, Inc. [*NASDAQ symbol*] (NQ) .... KLIC
Kulicke & Soffa Industries, Inc. [*Associated Press*] (SAG) .... Kulcke
Kulik Lake, AK [*Location identifier FAA*] (FAAL) .... LKK
Kullback-Leibler [*Mathematics*] .... KL
Kulmbach [*Germany ICAO location identifier*] (ICLI) .... EDQK
Kulp's Luzerne Legal Register Reports [*Pennsylvania*] [*A publication*] (DLA) .... Kulp
Kulturbund .... KB
Kultusgemeinde (BJA) .... KG
Kulu [*India*] [*Airport symbol*] (AD) .... KUU
Kulu/Bhuntar [*India*] [*ICAO location identifier*] (ICLI) .... VIBR
Kulusuk [*Greenland*] [*ICAO location identifier*] (ICLI) .... BGKK
Kulusuk Island [*Greenland*] [*Airport symbol*] (AD) .... KUS
Kulutusosuuskuntien Keskusliitto [*Co-Operative Union*] [*Finland*] (EY) .... KK
Kulyab [*Former USSR Seismograph station code, US Geological Survey*] (SEIS) .... KUL
Kumagaya [*Japan*] [*Seismograph station code, US Geological Survey*] (SEIS) .... KMG
Kumamoto [*Japan*] [*Airport symbol*] (OAG) .... KMJ
Kumamoto [*Japan*] [*Seismograph station code, US Geological Survey*] (SEIS) .... KUM
Kumamoto [*Japan ICAO location identifier*] (ICLI) .... RJFT
Kumano [*Japan*] [*Seismograph station code, US Geological Survey*] (SEIS) .... KMN
Kumasi [*Ghana*] [*ICAO location identifier*] (ICLI) .... DGSI
Kumasi [*Ghana*] [*Airport symbol*] (OAG) .... KMS
Kume Jima [*Ryukyu Islands*] [*Seismograph station code, US Geological Survey*] (SEIS) .... KMJ
Kume Jima [*Ryukyu Islands*] [*ICAO location identifier*] (ICLI) .... ROKJ
Kume Jima [*Japan*] [*Airport symbol*] (OAG) .... UEO
Kumix Resources Corp. [*Vancouver Stock Exchange symbol*] .... KUX
Kumlinge [*Finland ICAO location identifier*] (ICLI) .... EFKG
Kummer, Kneser, and Kodaira [*Surfaces*] [*Mathematics*] K-3
Kumquat (ABBR) .... KMQUT
Kuna School/Comm Library, Kuna, ID [*Library symbol*] [*Library of Congress*] (LCLS) .... IdKu
Kundiawa [*Papua New Guinea*] [*Airport symbol*] (OAG) .... CMU
Kundu Introversion-Extraversion Inventory [*Personality development test*] [*Psychology*] .... KIEI
Kundu's Neurotic Personality Inventory [*Psychology*] .... KNPI
Kunduz [*Afghanistan*] [*ICAO location identifier*] (ICLI) .... OAUZ
Kunduz [*Afghanistan*] [*Airport symbol Obsolete*] (OAG) .... UND
Kungliga Automobil Klubben .... KAK
Kungliga Biblioteket, Bibliotheca Regia Holmiensis, Stockholm, Sweden [*Library symbol Library of Congress*] (LCLS) .... SwSKB
Kungliga Karolinska Mediko-Kirurgiska Institutes, Stockholm, Sweden [*Library symbol Library of Congress*] (LCLS) .... SwSKM
Kungliga Tekniska Hoegskolan [*Royal Institute of Technology*] [*Stockholm, Sweden*] (ARC) .... KTH
Kungliga Tekniska Hoegskolan [*Royal Institute of Technology*], Stockholm, Sweden [*Library symbol Library of Congress*] (LCLS) .... SwSK
Kungliga Tekniska Hogskolans Bibliotek [*Royal Institute of Technology Library*] [*Information service or system*] (IID) .... KTHB
Kungmiut [*Greenland*] [*ICAO location identifier*] (ICLI) .... BGKM
Kungtang [*Labor party*] [*Taiwan*] [*Political party*] (EY) .... KT
Kunia [*Hawaii*] [*ICAO location identifier*] (ICLI) .... PHKU
Kunia Coordinating Group (SAA) .... KUCOG
Kunia, Oahu, HI [*Location identifier FAA*] (FAAL) .... KUN
Kunia Operations Control Center Coordination Group (CINC) .... KOCCCG
Kunitz Pancreatic Trypsin Inhibitor [*Medicine*] (MAE) .... KPTI
Kunitz Protease Inhibitor [*Medicine*] .... KPI
Kunlun Mountain Region [*China, Mainland*] [*MARC geographic area code Library of Congress*] (LCCP) .... a-cck-
Kunming [*China*] [*Airport symbol*] (OAG) .... KMG
Kunming [*Republic of China*] [*Seismograph station code, US Geological Survey*] (SEIS) .... KUN
Kunming [*China*] [*ICAO location identifier*] (ICLI) .... ZPKM
Kunming/Wujiaba [*China*] [*ICAO location identifier*] (ICLI) .... ZPPP
Kunsan [*South Korea ICAO location identifier*] (ICLI) .... RKJK
Kunstgeschichte in Bildern [*A publication*] (OCD) .... KB
Kununurra [*Australia ICAO location identifier*] (ICLI) .... APKU
Kununurra [*Australia Seismograph station code, US Geological Survey*] (SEIS) .... KNA
Kununurra [*Australia Airport symbol*] (OAG) .... KNX
Kunzang Odsal Palyul Changchub Choling [*An association*] (EA) .... KOPCC
Kuomintang [*Nationalist Party of Taiwan*] [*Political party*] (PD) .... KMT
Kuopio [*Finland ICAO location identifier*] (ICLI) .... EFKU
Kuopio [*Finland*] [*Airport symbol*] (OAG) .... KUO
Kuopio Atherosclerosis Prevention Study .... KAPS
Kupang [*Indonesia*] [*Airport symbol*] (OAG) .... KOE
Kupang [*Timor*] [*Seismograph station code, US Geological Survey*] (SEIS) .... KUG
Kupang [*Timor*] [*Seismograph station code, US Geological Survey Closed*] (SEIS) .... KUP
Kupang/Eltari [*Indonesia*] [*ICAO location identifier*] (ICLI) .... WRKK
Kupang Sector [*Indonesia*] [*ICAO location identifier*] (ICLI) .... WRKZ
Kuparuk, AK [*Location identifier FAA*] (FAAL) .... PYC
Kuparuk, AK [*Location identifier FAA*] (FAAL) .... UBW
Kuparuk, AK [*Location identifier FAA*] (FAAL) .... UUK
Kupat Holim (BJA) .... KH
Kupat Holim Le-'Ovdim Le'umiyim [*A publication*] (BJA) .... KHL
Kupat Holim Year Book [*A publication*] (BJA) .... KHYB
Kupffer Cell [*Histology*] .... Kc
Kupffer Cell Conditioned Medium .... KCCM
Kupffer Cell Medium .... KCM
Kupiano [*Papua New Guinea*] [*Seismograph station code, US Geological Survey*] (SEIS) .... KPN
Kupiano [*Papua New Guinea*] [*Airport symbol*] (OAG) .... KUP
Kuqa [*China*] [*ICAO location identifier*] (ICLI) .... ZWKC
Kuranda [*Australia Seismograph station code, US Geological Survey Closed*] (SEIS) .... KDA
Kuratorium fuer die Tagungen der Nobelpreistrager [*Standing Committee for Nobel Prize Winners' Congresses - SCNPWC*] [*Germany*] (EA) .... KTN
Kuratorium fuer Technik in der Landwirtschaft .... KTL
Kurchatovium [*See also Rf*] [*Proposed name for chemical element 104*] .... Ku
Kurdish [*MARC language code Library of Congress*] (LCCP) .... kur
Kurdish Democratic Party [*Iran*] [*Political party*] .... KDP
Kurdish Democratic Party of Iran [*Political party*] (PPW) .... KDPI
Kurdish Democratic Party of Syria [*Political party*] .... KDPS
Kurdish Program (EA) .... KP
Kurdish Workers' Party [*Turkey Political party*] (PD) .... PKK
Kurdistan Revolutionary Party [*Iraq*] [*Political party*] (PPW) .... KRP
Kurdzhali [*Bulgaria*] [*Seismograph station code, US Geological Survey*] (SEIS) .... KDZ
Kure [*Japan*] [*Seismograph station code, US Geological Survey Closed*] (SEIS) .... KRE
Kuria [*Kiribati*] [*Airport symbol*] (OAG) .... KUC
Kurie Plot [*Physics*] .... KP
Kurilsk [*Former USSR Seismograph station code, US Geological Survey*] (SEIS) .... KUR
Kurmenty [*Former USSR Seismograph station code, US Geological Survey*] (SEIS) .... KRM
Kurram Militia [*British military*] (DMA) .... KM
Kursk State Air Enterprise [*Former USSR*] [*FAA designator*] (FAAC) .... KUS
Kurt Weill Foundation for Music (EA) .... KWFM
Kurth Memorial Library, Lufkin, TX [*Library symbol Library of Congress*] (LCLS) .... TxLufK
Kurtis-Kraft [*US racecar maker*] .... KK
Kurtis-Kraft Register [*Defunct*] (EA) .... KKR
Kurtosis [*The relative degree of flatness in the region about the mode of a frequency curve*] .... Ku
Kurukabaru [*Guyana*] [*ICAO location identifier*] (ICLI) .... SYKK
Kurukh [*MARC language code Library of Congress*] (LCCP) .... kru
Kurukshetra [*India*] [*Seismograph station code, US Geological Survey*] (SEIS) .... KKR
Kuruman [*South Africa*] [*ICAO location identifier*] (ICLI) .... FAKU
Kurupung [*Guyana*] [*Airport symbol*] (OAG) .... KPG
Kurus [*Monetary unit*] [*Turkey*] .... K
Kurze Sicht [*Short Sight*] [*German*] .... KS

Kurzer Handkommentar zum Alten Testament [*Tuebingen*] [*A publication*]
(BJA) ..... KHAT
Kurzer Handkommentar zum Alten Testament [*A publication*] (BJA) ..... KHK
Kurzes Bibelwoerterbuch [*A publication*] (BJA) ..... BW
Kurzgefasste Assyrische Grammatik [*A publication*] (BJA) ..... KgAG
Kurzgefasste Grammatik der Biblisch Aramaeischen Sprache [*A publication*] (BJA) ..... KgGBAS
Kurzgefasster Kommentar zu den Heiligen Schriften Alten und Neuen Testaments [*Munich*] [*A publication*] (BJA) ..... KK
Kurzgefasstes Exegetisches Handbuch zum Alten Testament [*Leipzig*] [*A publication*] (BJA) ..... KEH
Kurzgefasstes Exegetisches Handbuch zum Alten Testament [*Leipzig*] [*A publication*] (BJA) ..... KHB
Kurzweil Applied Intelligence [*Computer science*] ..... KAI
Kurzweil Applied Intelligence, Inc. [*NASDAQ symbol*] (SAG) ..... KURZ
Kurzweil Applied Intelligence, Inc. [*Associated Press*] (SAG) ..... Kurzweil
Kurzweil Data Entry Machine [*for optical character recognition*] ..... KDEM
Kurzweil Educational Systems, Inc. ..... KESI
Kurzweil Reading Machine ..... KRM
Kurzweil Voice Writer ..... KVW
Kurzweil VoiceSystem [*Voice-recognition computer device*] ..... KVS
Kusaie [*Caroline Islands*] [*ICAO location identifier*] (ICLI) ..... PTSA
Kush (BJA) ..... Ks
Kush Locke [*NASDAQ symbol*] (SAG) ..... KLOC
Kush Locke [*Associated Press*] (SAG) ..... KshLc
Kush Locke [*Associated Press*] (SAG) ..... KushLc
Kush Locke [*Associated Press*] (SAG) ..... KushLk
Kushan (VRA) ..... Kush
Kushi Macrobiotic Corp. [*NASDAQ symbol*] (SAG) ..... KMAC
Kushi Macrobiotic Corp. [*Associated Press*] (SAG) ..... Kushi
Kushi Macrobiotics [*NASDAQ symbol*] (TTSB) ..... KMAC
Kushi Macrobiotics Wrrt [*NASDAQ symbol*] (TTSB) ..... KMACW
Kushiro [*Japan*] [*Airport symbol*] (OAG) ..... KUH
Kushiro [*Japan*] [*Seismograph station code, US Geological Survey*] (SEIS) ..... KUS
Kushiro [*Japan ICAO location identifier*] (ICLI) ..... RJCK
Kushiro/Kenebetsu [*Japan ICAO location identifier*] (ICLI) ..... RJCS
Kushke Nosrat [*Iran*] [*ICAO location identifier*] (ICLI) ..... OIIC
Kushner-Locke [*NASDAQ symbol*] (TTSB) ..... KLOC
[The] Kushner-Locke Co. [*NASDAQ symbol*] (NQ) ..... KLOC
[The] Kushner-Locke Co. [*Associated Press*] (SAG) ..... KushLc
[The] Kushner-Locke Co. [*Associated Press*] (SAG) ..... KushLk
Kushner-Locke Wrrt [*NASDAQ symbol*] (TTSB) ..... KLOCW
Kushtia [*Bangladesh*] [*Airport symbol*] (AD) ..... KHS
Kuskokwin Consortium Library, Bethel, AK [*Library symbol Library of Congress*] (LCLS) ..... AkB
Kustbevakningen [*Sweden ICAO designator*] (FAAC) ..... KBV
Kustom Kemps of America (EA) ..... KKOA
Kustoms and Rodders Association of Canada ..... KARAC
Kutahya [*Turkey*] [*Airport symbol*] (AD) ..... KUT
Kutahya [*Turkey ICAO location identifier*] (ICLI) ..... LTBN
Kutaisi [*USSR*] [*Airport symbol*] (AD) ..... KTU
Kutchino [*Later, MOS*] [*Former USSR Geomagnetic observatory code*] ..... KTC
Kutenai [*MARC language code Library of Congress*] (LCCP) ..... kut
Kutkai [*Myanmar*] [*ICAO location identifier*] (ICLI) ..... VBKK
Kutsu-Ga-Hara [*Japan*] [*Seismograph station code, US Geological Survey*] (SEIS) ..... KUT
Kutta-Joukowski Force ..... KJF
Kuttim (BJA) ..... Kut
Kutusongo [*Zaire*] [*ICAO location identifier*] (ICLI) ..... FZVF
Kutztown [*Pennsylvania*] [*Seismograph station code, US Geological Survey*] (SEIS) ..... KTZ
Kutztown State College, Kutztown, PA [*OCLC symbol*] (OCLC) ..... KZS
Kutztown State College, Kutztown, PA [*Library symbol Library of Congress*] (LCLS) ..... PKuS
Kutztown University of Pennsylvania (GAGS) ..... Kutztown U
Kuujjuarapik, PQ [*ICAO location identifier*] (ICLI) ..... CYGW
Kuusamo [*Finland ICAO location identifier*] (ICLI) ..... EFKS
Kuusamo [*Finland*] [*Airport symbol*] (OAG) ..... KAO
Kuvasz Club of America (EA) ..... KCA
Kuwait [*MARC geographic area code Library of Congress*] (LCCP) ..... a-ku--
Kuwait [*MARC country of publication code Library of Congress*] (LCCP) ..... ku
Kuwait (ABBR) ..... KUW
Kuwait (VRA) ..... Kuw
Kuwait [*ANSI two-letter standard code*] (CNC) ..... KW
Kuwait [*Airport symbol*] (OAG) ..... KWI
Kuwait [*ANSI three-letter standard code*] (CNC) ..... KWT
Kuwait [*ICAO location identifier*] (ICLI) ..... OKAC
Kuwait [*IYRU nationality code*] (IYR) ..... Q
Kuwait Action Plan [*Advisory Committee on Pollution of the Sea*] ..... KAP
Kuwait Air Defense Force (MCD) ..... KADF
Kuwait Air Force [*Kuwait*] [*ICAO location identifier*] (ICLI) ..... OKAF
Kuwait Airways [*ICAO designator*] (AD) ..... KU
Kuwait Airways Corp. ..... KA
Kuwait Airways Corp. [*ICAO designator*] (FAAC) ..... KAC
Kuwait Directorate General of Civil Aviation [*Kuwait*] [*ICAO location identifier*] (ICLI) ..... OKAA
Kuwait Foreign Trading, Contracting & Investment Co. ..... KFTCIC
Kuwait French Bank ..... KFB
Kuwait Fund for Arab Economic Development ..... KFAED
Kuwait/International [*Kuwait*] [*ICAO location identifier*] (ICLI) ..... OKBK
Kuwait International Investment Co. ..... KIIC
Kuwait International NOTAM Office [*Kuwait*] [*ICAO location identifier*] (ICLI) ..... OKNO
Kuwait National Petroleum Co. ..... KNPC
Kuwait Oil Co. ..... KOC

Kuwait Television ..... KTV
Kuwaiti Air Force (DOMA) ..... KAF
Kuwaiti Dinar [*Monetary unit*] (BJA) ..... KD
Kuwaiti Dinar [*Monetary unit*] (DS) ..... KDI
Kuwaiti National Committee of the International Association on Water Pollution Research and Control (EAIO) ..... KNCIAWPRC
Kuwaiti [*Civil Affairs*] Task Force (DOMA) ..... KTF
Kuwaiti Theatre of Operation [*Operation Desert Storm*] ..... KTO
Kuybyshev/Kurumoch [*Former USSR ICAO location identifier*] (ICLI) ..... UWWW
Kuyper [*Indonesia*] [*Later, TNG*] [*Geomagnetic observatory code*] ..... KUY
Kuzbass Commodity and Raw Materials Exchange [*Russian Federation*] (EY) ..... KECME
Kuzell Institute for Arthritis Research [*Medical Research Institute at Pacific Medical Center*] [*Research center*] (RCD) ..... KIAR
Kuznetsk Commodity and Raw Materials Exchange [*Russian Federation*] (EY) ..... KCME
K-V Pharmaceutical Co. [*AMEX symbol*] (SPSG) ..... KV
K-V Pharmaceutical Co. [*Associated Press*] (SAG) ..... KV Ph
Kvakera Esperantista Societo [*Quaker Esperanto Society - QES*] (EAIO) ..... KES
Kveim-Seltzback (Test) [*Medicine*] ..... KS
KVH Industries [*NASDAQ symbol*] (TTSB) ..... KVHI
KVH Industries, Inc. [*NASDAQ symbol*] (SAG) ..... KVHI
KVH Industries, Inc. [*Associated Press*] (SAG) ..... KVHInd
Kvinnnens Frie Folkevalgte [*Women's Freely Elected Representatives*] [*Norway Political party*] (PPE) ..... KFF
Kvutzat Mesahake Kadur Regel Yehudit (BJA) ..... KMKRY
KW Resources Ltd. [*Vancouver Stock Exchange symbol*] ..... KWR
Kwacha [*Monetary unit*] [*Malawi, Zambia*] ..... K
Kwajalein [*Marshall Islands*] [*Airport symbol*] (OAG) ..... KWA
Kwajalein [*Marshall Islands*] [*ICAO location identifier*] (ICLI) ..... PKWA
Kwajalein Atoll (AABC) ..... KWAJ
Kwajalein Missile Range (AABC) ..... KMR
Kwajalein Standard Atmosphere ..... KSA
Kwajalein Test Site (MCD) ..... KTS
Kwakwani [*Guyana*] [*ICAO location identifier*] (ICLI) ..... SYKW
Kwamalasoemoetoe [*Surinam*] [*ICAO location identifier*] (ICLI) ..... SMSM
Kwanak [*South Korea ICAO location identifier*] (ICLI) ..... RKSH
Kwandaeri [*South Korea ICAO location identifier*] (ICLI) ..... RKNK
Kwangju [*South Korea ICAO location identifier*] (ICLI) ..... RKJJ
Kwangsi Chuang Autonomous Region [*China, Mainland*] [*MARC geographic area code Library of Congress*] (LCCP) ..... a-cc-kcz
Kwangtung Province [*China, Mainland*] [*MARC geographic area code Library of Congress*] (LCCP) ..... a-cc-kn
Kwansei Gakuin University. Law Review [*A publication*] (DLA) ..... Kwansei Gak L Rev
Kwantlen College Library [*UTLAS symbol*] ..... KWA
Kwantlen College, Surrey, BC, Canada [*Library symbol Library of Congress*] (LCLS) ..... CaBSKC
Kwantlen College, Surrey, British Columbia [*Library symbol National Library of Canada*] (NLC) ..... BSKC
Kwanza [*Monetary Unit*] [*Angola*] (BARN) ..... Kz
Kwanza (ODBW) ..... NKz
Kwartalnik dla Historji Zydow w Polsce [*A publication*] (BJA) ..... KZP
Kwashiorkormarasmus Syndrome [*Medicine*] (DMAA) ..... KMS
Kweichow Province [*China, Mainland*] [*MARC geographic area code Library of Congress*] (LCCP) ..... a-cc-kw
Kweiyang [*Republic of China*] [*Seismograph station code, US Geological Survey*] (SEIS) ..... KWA
Kweiyang [*China*] [*Airport symbol*] (AD) ..... KWE
Kwekwe [*Zimbabwe*] [*ICAO location identifier*] (ICLI) ..... FVKK
Kwethluk [*Alaska*] [*Airport symbol*] (OAG) ..... KWT
Kwethluk, AK [*Location identifier FAA*] (FAAL) ..... KWT
KWG Resources, Inc. [*Associated Press*] (SAG) ..... KWG Rs
KWG Resources, Inc. [*NASDAQ symbol*] (SAG) ..... KWGDF
KWIC Interactive Tagger [*University of Minnesota*] [*Text editing system*] (NITA) ..... KIT
Kwigillingok [*Alaska*] [*Airport symbol*] (OAG) ..... KWK
Kwigillingok, AK [*Location identifier FAA*] (FAAL) ..... GGV
Kwigillingok, AK [*Location identifier FAA*] (FAAL) ..... KWK
KWIK Products International Corp. [*Vancouver Stock Exchange symbol*] ..... KPI
Kwilu-Gongo [*Zaire*] [*ICAO location identifier*] (ICLI) ..... FZAW
K-Words Times Millions of Seconds [*Unit of measure*] (GFGA) ..... KMS
KXE6S Verein Chess Society (EA) ..... KVCS
Kyakhta [*Former USSR Seismograph station code, US Geological Survey Closed*] (SEIS) ..... KYA
Kyasanur Forest Disease ..... KFD
Kyat [*Monetary unit*] [*Myanmar*] ..... K
Kyaukpyu [*Myanmar*] [*Airport symbol*] (OAG) ..... KYP
Kyaukpyu [*Myanmar*] [*ICAO location identifier*] (ICLI) ..... VBKP
Kyauktaw [*Myanmar*] [*Airport symbol*] (OAG) ..... KYT
Kyauktu [*Myanmar*] [*ICAO location identifier*] (ICLI) ..... VBKU
Kyber Resources [*Vancouver Stock Exchange symbol*] ..... KYR
Kyburz Flat [*California*] [*Seismograph station code, US Geological Survey*] (SEIS) ..... KBF
Kyd on Awards [*A publication*] (DLA) ..... Kyd Aw
Kyd on Bills of Exchange [*A publication*] (DLA) ..... Kyd
Kyd on Bills of Exchange [*A publication*] (DLA) ..... Kyd Bills
Kyd on Corporations [*A publication*] (DLA) ..... Kyd Corp
Kyle Classification [*Library science*] ..... KC
Kyle Resources, Inc. [*Vancouver Stock Exchange symbol*] ..... KYL
Kymi [*Finland ICAO location identifier*] (ICLI) ..... EFKY
Kymograph (ABBR) ..... KYMO
Kynurenic Acid [*Biochemistry*] (OA) ..... KA
Kynurenic Acid (DMAA) ..... KYN
Kynurenine [*Biochemistry*] ..... KYN

Kyocera Corp. [*NYSE symbol*] (SPSG) .... KYO
Kyocera Corp. [*Associated Press*] (SAG) .... Kyocer
Kyocera Corp.ADR [*NYSE symbol*] (TTSB) .... KYO
Kyodo News International, Inc. [*Information service or system*] (IID) .... KNI
Kyosato Education Experiment Project [*Self-help program for Japanese farmers established by Americans in 1948*] .... KEEP
Kyoto [*Japan*] [*Seismograph station code, US Geological Survey*] (SEIS) .... KYO
Kyoto Encyclopedia of Genes and Genomes [*Computer network*] .... KEGG
Kyoto Law Review [*A publication*] (DLA) .... Kyoto L Rev
Kyoto Sangyo University [*UTLAS symbol*] .... KSU
Kyoto University, Kyoto, Japan [*Library symbol Library of Congress*] (LCLS) .... JKU
Kyoto University Reactor .... KUR
Kyphosis [*Orthopedics*] (DAVI) .... kyph
Kypriakes Aerogrammes [*Cyprus Airlines*] .... KA
Kypriakon Ethnikon Komma [*Cypriot National Party (1944-1960)*] [*Greek Cypriot*] [*Political party*] (PPE) .... KEK

Kyrghyzstan Airlines [*ICAO designator*] (FAAC) .... KGA
Kyrgyzstan Democratic Movement [*Political party*] .... KDM
Kyrie [*Liturgical*] .... KY
Kyritz [*Germany ICAO location identifier*] (ICLI) .... ETKZ
Kyrnair [*France ICAO designator*] (FAAC) .... KYN
Kyshe's Reports [*1808-90*] [*A publication*] (DLA) .... Kyshe
Kysor Indl [*NYSE symbol*] (TTSB) .... KZ
Kysor Industrial Corp. [*Associated Press*] (SAG) .... Kysor
Kysor Industrial Corp. [*NYSE symbol*] (SPSG) .... KZ
Kyungju [*South Korea ICAO location identifier*] (ICLI) .... RKTJ
Kyzen Corp. [*Associated Press*] (SAG) .... Kyzen
Kyzen Corp. [*NASDAQ symbol*] (SAG) .... KYZN
Kyzen Corp.'A' [*NASDAQ symbol*] (TTSB) .... KYZN
Kyzen Corp.Wrrt'A' [*NASDAQ symbol*] (TTSB) .... KYZNW
KZ Owners' Association [*Defunct*] (EA) .... KZOA
Kzyl-Orda [*Former USSR ICAO location identifier*] (ICLI) .... UAOO

L
By Meaning

L & B Financial, Inc. [*Associated Press*] (SAG) .... L & B Fin
L & B Financial, Inc. [*NASDAQ symbol*] (SAG) .... LBFI
L. C. Obourn High School Library, East Rochester, NY [*OCLC symbol*] (OCLC) .... RWV
L. Hungerford [*Record label*] [*Great Britain*] .... LH
L. M. Warren, Inc., Vancouver, BC, Canada [*Library symbol Library of Congress*] (LCLS) .... CaBVaLMW
L. M. Warren, Inc., Vancouver, British Columbia [*Library symbol National Library of Canada*] (NLC) .... BVALMW
L. P. Fisher Public Library, Woodstock, New Brunswick [*Library symbol National Library of Canada*] (NLC) .... NBW
L-5-Hydroxytryptophan [*Pharmacology*] (DAVI) L-5HTP
La Asunta [*Bolivia*] [*ICAO location identifier*] (ICLI) .... SLLA
La Barge, Inc. [*Associated Press*] (SAG) .... LaBarg
La Baule [*France*] [*Airport symbol*] (AD) .... LBY
La Baule/Escoublac [*France ICAO location identifier*] (ICLI) ..... LFRE
La Beata [*Ecuador*] [*ICAO location identifier*] (ICLI) .... SEBE
La Belle, FL [*Location identifier FAA*] (FAAL) .... LBV
La Belle, FL [*FM radio station call letters*] .... WKZY
La Bible. Bibliotheque de la Pleiade [*A publication*] (BJA) .... BPI
La Bible et les Peres [*A publication*] (BJA) .... BP
La Bibliotheque Deschatelets Peres Oblats [*Closed to the public*] **Ottawa, Ontario** [*Library symbol National Library of Canada*] (NLC) .... OOSJ
La Cecilia [*Ecuador*] [*ICAO location identifier*] (ICLI) .... SELC
La Ceiba [*Honduras*] [*Airport symbol*] (OAG) .... LCE
La Ceiba/Goloson Internacional [*Honduras*] [*ICAO location identifier*] (ICLI) .... MHLC
La Centrale des Bibliotheques [*Source file*] [*UTLAS symbol*] .... CEN
La China [*Bolivia*] [*ICAO location identifier*] (ICLI) .... SLLC
La Coloma [*Cuba ICAO location identifier*] (ICLI) .... MULM
La Coruna [*Spain*] [*Airport symbol*] (OAG) .... LCG
La Coruna [*Spain ICAO location identifier*] (ICLI) .... LECO
La Cosa Nostra [*Our Thing*] .... LCN
La Cote [*Switzerland ICAO location identifier*] (ICLI) .... LSGP
La Crescent, MN [*FM radio station call letters*] .... KQEG
La Crescent, MN [*FM radio station call letters*] .... KXLC
La Crete Community Library, Alberta [*Library symbol National Library of Canada*] (NLC) .... ALCC
La Crete Community Library, La Crete, AB, Canada [*Library symbol*] [*Library of Congress*] (LCLS) .... CaALcC
La Crosse [*A bunyavirus*] .... LAC
La Crosse [*Diocesan abbreviation*] [*Wisconsin*] (TOCD) LC
La Crosse Footwear, Inc. [*NASDAQ symbol*] (SAG) .... BOOT
La Crosse Lutheran Hospital, La Crosse, WI [*Library symbol Library of Congress*] (LCLS) .... WLacL
La Crosse Public Library, La Crosse, WI [*OCLC symbol*] (OCLC) ... GZX
La Crosse Public Library, La Crosse, WI [*Library symbol Library of Congress*] (LCLS) .... WLac
La Crosse, WI LX
La Crosse, WI [*FM radio station call letters*] .... WHLA
La Crosse, WI [*Television station call letters*] .... WHLA-TV
La Crosse, WI [*AM radio station call letters*] .... WIZM
La Crosse, WI [*FM radio station call letters*] .... WIZM-FM
La Crosse, WI [*Television station call letters*] .... WKBT
La Crosse, WI [*AM radio station call letters*] .... WKTY
La Crosse, WI [*Television station call letters*] .... WLAX
La Crosse, WI [*AM radio station call letters*] .... WLFN
La Crosse, WI [*FM radio station call letters*] .... WLSU
La Crosse, WI [*FM radio station call letters*] .... WLXR
La Crosse, WI [*FM radio station call letters*] .... WQCC
La Crosse, WI [*FM radio station call letters*] .... WSPL
La Crosse, WI [*Television station call letters*] .... WXOW
La Crosse [*Wisconsin*]/Winona [*Minnesota*] [*Airport symbol*] (OAG) .... LSE
La Cubana [*Cuba ICAO location identifier*] (ICLI) .... MUNA
La Cueva [*New Mexico*] [*Seismograph station code, US Geological Survey*] (SEIS) LCV
La Cueva [*Costa Rica*] [*ICAO location identifier*] (ICLI) .... MRLV
La Cumbre [*Argentina*] [*Airport symbol*] (AD) .... LCM
La Cumbre [*Argentina ICAO location identifier*] (ICLI) ...... SACC
La Cumbre Peak [*California*] [*Seismograph station code, US Geological Survey*] (SEIS) .... LPC
La Desirade [*Guadeloupe*] [*Airport symbol*] (OAG) .... DSD
La Divina Pastora, Bolivar [*Venezuela ICAO location identifier*] (ICLI) ... SVDP
La Ele [*Bolivia*] [*ICAO location identifier*] (ICLI) .... SLLE
La Esperanza [*Honduras*] [*ICAO location identifier*] (ICLI) ... MHLE
La Esperanza [*Bolivia*] [*ICAO location identifier*] (ICLI) ... SLEZ

La Estrella [*Ecuador*] [*ICAO location identifier*] (ICLI) .... SESO
La Fayette, GA [*AM radio station call letters*] .... WQCH
La Ferte-Alais [*France ICAO location identifier*] (ICLI) ..... LFFQ
La Ferte-Gaucher [*France ICAO location identifier*] (ICLI) ... LFFG
La Fleche/Thoree-Les-Pins [*France ICAO location identifier*] (ICLI) ... LFAL
La Flor [*Costa Rica*] [*ICAO location identifier*] (ICLI) ..... MRLF
La Foliniere [*France*] [*Seismograph station code, US Geological Survey*] (SEIS) .... FLN
La Follette, TN [*AM radio station call letters*] (RBYB) ..... WGLH
La Follette, TN [*AM radio station call letters*] .... WLAF
La Follette, TN [*FM radio station call letters*] .... WQLA-FM
La Fondation Canadienne de la Jeunesse (AC) .... FCJ
La Fontaine [*French author, 1621-1695*] (ROG) .... LA FONT
La Fosse Platinum Group, Inc. [*Toronto Stock Exchange symbol*] .... LF
La Frestal [*France*] [*Seismograph station code, US Geological Survey*] (SEIS) .... LFF
La Fria [*Venezuela*] [*Airport symbol*] (OAG) .... LFR
La Fria, Tachira [*Venezuela ICAO location identifier*] (ICLI) . SVLF
La Garroba [*Costa Rica*] [*ICAO location identifier*] (ICLI) . MRLG
LA Gear, Inc. [*NYSE symbol*] (CTT) .... LA
LA Gear, Inc. [*Associated Press*] (SAG) .... LA Gear
La Glace Community Library, Alberta [*Library symbol National Library of Canada*] (NLC) .... ALGC
La Glace Community Library, La Glace, AB, Canada [*Library symbol*] [*Library of Congress*] (LCLS) .... CaALgC
La Gloria [*Colombia*] [*Airport symbol*] (AD) .... LGL
La Grand'Combe [*France ICAO location identifier*] (ICLI) ..... LFTN
La Grande [*Canada*] [*Airport symbol*] (OAG) .... YGL
La Grande, OR [*FM radio station call letters*] .... KEOL
La Grande, OR [*AM radio station call letters*] .... KLBM
La Grande, OR [*Television station call letters*] .... KTVR
La Grande, OR [*FM radio station call letters*] .... KUBQ
La Grande, OR [*FM radio station call letters*] .... KWRL
La Grande, OR [*Location identifier FAA*] (FAAL) .... LGD
La Grande Public Library, La Grande, OR [*Library symbol Library of Congress*] (LCLS) .... OrLg
La Grande Riviere, PQ [*ICAO location identifier*] (ICLI) ..... CYGL
La Grange College, La Grange, GA [*Library symbol Library of Congress*] (LCLS) .... GLagC
La Grange College, La Grange, GA [*OCLC symbol*] (OCLC) ...... GLG
La Grange, GA [*Location identifier FAA*] (FAAL) .... LGC
La Grange, GA [*FM radio station call letters*] .... WJZF
La Grange, GA [*AM radio station call letters*] .... WLAG
La Grange, GA [*FM radio station call letters*] .... WOAK
La Grange, GA [*AM radio station call letters*] .... WTRP
La Grange, IL [*FM radio station call letters*] .... WLTL
La Grange, IL [*AM radio station call letters*] .... WTAQ
La Grange Park Library District, La Grange Park, IL [*Library symbol Library of Congress*] (LCLS) .... ILagp
La Grange Public Library, La Grange, IL [*Library symbol Library of Congress*] (LCLS) .... ILag
La Grange, TX [*FM radio station call letters*] .... KBUK
La Grange, TX [*AM radio station call letters*] .... KVLG
La Guaira [*Venzuela*] [*Airport symbol*] (AD) .... LAG
La Guera [*Morocco*] [*Airport symbol*] (AD) .... ZLG
LA Helicopter, Inc. [*ICAO designator*] (FAAC) .... LAH
La India [*Bolivia*] [*ICAO location identifier*] (ICLI) ...... SLLI
LA Industrial Group (NITA) .... LAIG
La Jolla [*California*] [*Seismograph station code, US Geological Survey Closed*] (SEIS) .... LJC
La Jolla Cancer Research Foundation [*Research center*] (RCD) . LJCRF
La Jolla Historical Society, La Jolla, CA [*Library symbol*] [*Library of Congress*] (LCLS) .... CLjHi
La Jolla Pharmaceutical [*Associated Press*] (SAG) .... LaJollPh
La Jolla Pharmaceutical [*Associated Press*] (SAG) .... LaJolP
La Jolla Pharmaceutical [*NASDAQ symbol*] (SAG) .... LJPC
La Jolla Pharmaceutical Wrrt [*NASDAQ symbol*] (TTSB) ..... LJPCW
La Julia [*Ecuador*] [*ICAO location identifier*] (ICLI) ...... SELJ
La Junta [*Colorado*] [*Airport symbol*] (AD) .... LHX
La Junta, CO [*FM radio station call letters*] .... KBLJ
La Junta, CO [*AM radio station call letters*] .... KBZZ
La Junta, CO [*Location identifier FAA*] (FAAL) .... LHX
La Leche League [*Local affiliates of LLLI*] (EA) LLL
La Leche League International (EA) LLL
La Libertad [*Guatemala*] [*ICAO location identifier*] (ICLI) . MGLL
La Ligia [*Costa Rica*] [*ICAO location identifier*] (ICLI) ... MRLI

La Loche Public Library, La Loche, SK, Canada [*Library symbol*] [*Library of Congress*] (LCLS) ... CaSLL

La Loche Public Library, Saskatchewan [*Library symbol National Library of Canada*] (NLC) ... SLL

La Lucha [*Costa Rica*] [*Seismograph station code, US Geological Survey*] (SEIS) ... LCR

La Lucha Farm [*Costa Rica*] [*Seismograph station code, US Geological Survey*] (SEIS) ... LLC

La Luz Mines Ltd. [*Toronto Stock Exchange symbol*] ... LAZ

La Luz, NM [*FM radio station call letters*] ... KPSA

La Madre [*Bolivia*] [*ICAO location identifier*] (ICLI) ... SLML

La Magnetotheque des Aveugles du Quebec, Montreal, PQ, Canada [*Library symbol*] [*Library of Congress*] (LCLS) ... CaQMMAQ

La Magnetotheque, Montreal, Quebec [*Library symbol National Library of Canada*] (NLC) ... QMMAQ

La Maison-Dieu [*Paris*] [*A publication*] (BJA) ... MD

La Malbaie [*Quebec*] [*Seismograph station code, US Geological Survey*] (SEIS) ... LMQ

La Malbaie, PQ [*FM radio station call letters*] ... CBV-6

La Man Corp. [*NASDAQ symbol*] (TTSB) ... LAMN

La Maruca [*Costa Rica*] [*ICAO location identifier*] (ICLI) ... MRLU

La Mina/Riohacha [*Colorado ICAO location identifier*] (ICLI) ... SKLM

La Mole [*France ICAO location identifier*] (ICLI) ... LFNM

La Montagne Noire [*France ICAO location identifier*] (ICLI) ... LFMG

La Motte Township Library, Palestine, IL [*Library symbol Library of Congress*] (LCLS) ... IPale

La Motte-Beuvron [*France ICAO location identifier*] (ICLI) ... LFFM

La Mourre [*France*] [*Seismograph station code, US Geological Survey*] (SEIS) ... LMR

La Nouvelle Clio [*Brussels*] [*A publication*] (BJA) ... NC

La Orchila - Dependencia Federal [*Venezuela ICAO location identifier*] (ICLI) ... SVLO

La Palma [*Canary Islands*] [*ICAO location identifier*] (ICLI) ... GCLA

La Palma [*El Salvador*] [*Seismograph station code, US Geological Survey*] (SEIS) ... LPS

La Palma [*Panama*] [*ICAO location identifier*] (ICLI) ... MPLP

La Palma [*Panama*] [*Airport symbol*] (OAG) ... PLP

La Paquita [*Costa Rica*] [*ICAO location identifier*] (ICLI) ... MRLA

La Paz [*Mexico*] [*Seismograph station code, US Geological Survey*] (SEIS) ... LAP

La Paz [*Mexico*] [*Airport symbol*] (OAG) ... LAP

La Paz [*Bolivia*] [*Seismograph station code, US Geological Survey*] (SEIS) ... LPB

La Paz [*Bolivia*] [*Airport symbol*] (OAG) ... LPB

La Paz [*San Calixto*] [*Bolivia*] [*Seismograph station code, US Geological Survey*] (SEIS) ... LPZ

La Paz [*Argentina ICAO location identifier*] (ICLI) ... SAMP

La Paz/General Manuel Marquez de Leon Internacional [*Mexico ICAO location identifier*] (ICLI) ... MMLP

La Paz/Kennedy Internacional [*Bolivia*] [*ICAO location identifier*] (ICLI) ... SLLP

La Pedrera [*Colombia*] [*Airport symbol*] (OAG) ... LPD

La Peregrina [*Puerto Rico*] [*Seismograph station code, US Geological Survey*] (SEIS) ... LPR

La Pine Senior High School, La Pine, OR [*Library symbol*] [*Library of Congress*] (LCLS) ... OrLpHS

La Place, LA [*FM radio station call letters*] ... WCKW

La Plata [*Argentina*] [*Seismograph station code, US Geological Survey*] (SEIS) ... LPA

La Plata [*Argentina*] [*Airport symbol*] (OAG) ... LPG

La Plata [*Argentina ICAO location identifier*] (ICLI) ... SADL

La Plata, MD [*AM radio station call letters*] (RBYB) ... WKIK

La Plata River and Basin [*MARC geographic area code Library of Congress*] (LCCP) ... sp----

La Pocatiere [*Quebec*] [*Seismograph station code, US Geological Survey*] (SEIS) ... POC

La Pocatiere, PQ [*FM radio station call letters*] ... CHOX

La Porte [*Indiana*] [*Airport symbol*] (OAG) ... LPO

La Porte City Progress-Review, La Porte City, IA [*Library symbol Library of Congress*] (LCLS) ... IaLpcPR

La Porte County Library, La Porte, IN [*OCLC symbol*] (OCLC) ... IMQ

La Porte, IN [*FM radio station call letters*] ... WCOE

La Porte, IN [*AM radio station call letters*] ... WLOI

La Porte Public Library, La Porte, IN [*Library symbol Library of Congress*] (LCLS) ... InLap

La Porte, TX [*Location identifier FAA*] (FAAL) ... JPA

La Pryor, TX [*Location identifier FAA*] (FAAL) ... CPZ

La Pryor, TX [*Location identifier FAA*] (FAAL) ... LKX

La Quiaca [*Argentina*] [*Seismograph station code, US Geological Survey Closed*] (SEIS) ... LQA

La Quiaca [*Argentina*] [*Geomagnetic observatory code*] ... LQA

La Quiaca [*Argentina ICAO location identifier*] (ICLI) ... SASQ

La Quinta, CA [*FM radio station call letters*] ... KUNA-FM

La Quinta Inns [*NYSE symbol*] (SAG) ... LQI

La Quinta Motor Inns Ltd. [*Associated Press*] (SAG) ... LaQuinta

La Rassegna Musicale [*A publication*] ... LRM

La Raza National Bar Association (EA) ... LRNBA

La Raza Unida Party (EA) ... LRUP

LA Reference, Special and Information Section [*British*] (NITA) ... LA RSIS

La Reole/Floudes [*France ICAO location identifier*] (ICLI) ... LFDR

La Republique des Citoyens du Monde [*Commonwealth of World Citizens*] ... RCM

La Retama Public Library, Corpus Cristi, TX [*Library symbol Library of Congress*] (LCLS) ... TxCc

La Reveil Juif. Sfax [*A publication*] (BJA) ... RJ

La Rioja [*Argentina*] [*Airport symbol*] (OAG) ... IRJ

La Rioja/Cap. V. Almandos Almonacid [*Argentina ICAO location identifier*] (ICLI) ... SANL

La Roca [*Costa Rica*] [*ICAO location identifier*] (ICLI) ... MRLR

La Rochelle [*France*] [*Airport symbol*] (OAG) ... LRH

La Rochelle/Laleu [*France ICAO location identifier*] (ICLI) ... LFBH

La Roche-Sur-Yon/Les Ajoncs [*France ICAO location identifier*] (ICLI) ... LFRI

La Romana [*Dominican Republic*] [*Airport symbol*] (OAG) ... LRM

La Romana [*Dominican Republic*] [*ICAO location identifier*] (ICLI) ... MDLR

La Ronge Public Library, Saskatchewan [*Library symbol National Library of Canada*] (NLC) ... SLA

La Ronge, SK [*FM radio station call letters*] ... CBKA

La Ronge, SK [*FM radio station call letters*] ... CBKA-FM

La Ronge, SK [*FM radio station call letters*] (RBYB) ... CJLR-FM

La Ronge, SK [*ICAO location identifier*] (ICLI) ... CYVC

La Sacra Bibbia (BJA) ... LSB

La Sacra Bibbia [*Turin*] [*A publication*] (BJA) ... SaBi

La Sacra Bibbia [*Turin*] [*A publication*] (BJA) ... SB

La Sainte Bible [*Pirot-Clamer*] [*Paris*] [*A publication*] (BJA) ... ClamB

La Sainte Bible [*A publication*] (BJA) ... SB

La Sainte Bible (1884) (Drioux) [*A publication*] (BJA) ... Dr

La Sainte Bible (1923) [*A. Crampon*] [*A publication*] (BJA) ... Cr

La Salette Seminary, Altamont, NY [*Library symbol Library of Congress*] (LCLS) ... NAltL

[*The*] **La Salle & Bureau County Railroad Co.** [*AAR code*] ... LSBC

La Salle College, Philadelphia, PA [*OCLC symbol*] (OCLC) ... LAS

La Salle College, Philadelphia, PA [*Library symbol Library of Congress*] (LCLS) ... PPLas

La Salle High School, Milwaukie, OR [*Library symbol Library of Congress*] (LCLS) ... OrMiLHS

La Salle, IL [*FM radio station call letters*] ... WAJK

La Salle, IL [*AM radio station call letters*] ... WLPO

La Salle, IL [*Television station call letters*] ... WWTO

La Salle Re Holdings Ltd. [*Associated Press*] (SAG) ... LaSalle

La Sarre, PQ [*AM radio station call letters*] ... CKLS

La Scie Public Library, La Scie, NF, Canada [*Library symbol Library of Congress*] (LCLS) ... CaNfLs

La Scie Public Library, Newfoundland [*Library symbol National Library of Canada*] (NLC) ... NFLS

La Selva [*Bolivia*] [*ICAO location identifier*] (ICLI) ... SLLV

La Serena [*Chile*] [*Airport symbol*] (AD) ... LSC

La Serena/La Florida [*Chile*] [*ICAO location identifier*] (ICLI) ... SCSE

La Sierra College, Arlington, CA [*Library symbol Library of Congress*] (LCLS) ... CArlS

La Societe Canadienne d'Aerophilatelie (AC) ... SCA

La Societe d'Histoire des Cantons de l'Est, Sherbrooke, Quebec [*Library symbol National Library of Canada*] (NLC) ... QSHERSH

La Societe Historique de Clair, Inc., Clair, NB, Canada [*Library symbol*] [*Library of Congress*] (LCLS) ... CaNBCISH

La Societe Historique de Clair, Inc., New Brunswick [*Library symbol National Library of Canada*] (NLC) ... NBCSH

La Societe Jersiaise (EAIO) ... LSJ

La Souterraine [*France*] [*Seismograph station code, US Geological Survey*] (SEIS) ... LSF

L.A. T Sportswear [*NASDAQ symbol*] (TTSB) ... LATS

LA T Sportswear, Inc. [*Associated Press*] (SAG) ... LA T Spt

LA T Sportswear, Inc. [*NASDAQ symbol*] (SAG) ... LATS

La Tabatiere [*Canada*] [*Airport symbol*] (OAG) ... ZLT

La Tapoa [*Niger*] [*ICAO location identifier*] (ICLI) ... DRRP

La Teko Resources Ltd. [*Vancouver Stock Exchange symbol*] ... LAO

La Teko Resources Ltd. [*NASDAQ symbol*] (SAG) ... LAOR

La Teko Resources Ltd. [*Associated Press*] (SAG) ... LaTeko

La Teko Resources Ltd [*NASDAQ symbol*] (TTSB) ... LAORF

La Themis [*Lower Canada*] [*A publication*] (DLA) ... L Th

La Themis [*A publication*] (DLA) ... La Th

La Themis [*A publication*] (DLA) ... Them

La Themis (Lower Canada) [*A publication*] (DLA) ... La Them LC

La Tour-Du-Pin-Cessieu [*France ICAO location identifier*] (ICLI) ... LFKP

La Trobe University Staff Association [*Australia*] ... LTUSA

La Tuque, PQ [*Television station call letters*] ... CBVT-2

La Tuque, PQ [*AM radio station call letters*] ... CFLM

La Tuyere a Reverse Aval [*Concorde*] ... TRA

La Union [*Honduras*] [*Airport symbol Obsolete*] (OAG) ... LUI

La Vente par Correspondance [*Mail Order*] [*Business term French*] ... VPC

La Verendrye Management Corp. [*Toronto Stock Exchange symbol*] ... LVY

La Verne, CA [*Location identifier FAA*] (FAAL) ... POC

La Verne College, La Verne, CA [*Library symbol Library of Congress*] (LCLS) ... CLavC

La Verne University, La Verne, CA [*OCLC symbol*] (OCLC) ... CLV

La Victoria (Ex Casado) [*Paraguay*] [*ICAO location identifier*] (ICLI) ... SGLV

La Yolanda [*Costa Rica*] [*ICAO location identifier*] (ICLI) ... MRLY

Laake Oy [*Finland*] [*Research code symbol*] ... B

Laarbruch [*Germany ICAO location identifier*] (ICLI) ... EDUL

Laayoune [*Morocco*] [*Airport symbol*] (OAG) ... EUN

Lab. Anphar [*France*] [*Research code symbol*] ... ANP

Lab. Aron [*France*] [*Research code symbol*] ... LA

Lab. Dausse [*France*] [*Research code symbol*] ... LD

LAB Flying Service [*ICAO designator*] (AD) ... JF

Lab. Funai [*Japan*] [*Research code symbol*] ... F

Lab. J. Uriach & Cia. SA [*Spain*] [*Research code symbol*] ... UR

Lab. Jacques Logeais [*France*] [*Research code symbol*] ... JL

Lab. Lafon [*France*] [*Research code symbol*] ... LL

Lab. Miquel [*Spain*] [*Research code symbol*] ... AD

Lab. Miquel [*Spain*] [*Research code symbol*] ... MI

Lab. Roland-Marie [*France*] [*Research code symbol*] ... RM

Lab. Sopharga [*France*] [*Research code symbol*] ... C

Lab. UPSA [*France*] [*Research code symbol*] ... UP

Lab. Wander [*France*] [*Research code symbol*] ... LW

Laban Art of Movement Guild [Later, LG] (EA) .... LAMG
Laban/Bartenieff Institute of Movement Studies (EA) .... LBIMS
Laban Guild [Formerly, LAMG]⁺ (EA) .... LG
Laban Institute of Movement Studies [Later, LBIMS] (EA) .... LIMS
Laban ng Demokratikong Pilipino [Democratic Filipino's Struggle] [Political party] .... LDP
LaBarge, Inc. [AMEX symbol] (SPSG) .... LB
Labasa [Fiji] [Airport symbol] (OAG) .... LBS
Labatt [John] Ltd. [Toronto Stock Exchange symbol Vancouver Stock Exchange symbol] .... LBT
Labatt's California District Court Reports [1857-58] [A publication] (DLA) ...... Lab
Labatt's Central Research Library, London, ON, Canada [Library symbol Library of Congress] (LCLS) .... CaOLLCR
Labatt's Central Research Library, London, Ontario [Library symbol National Library of Canada] (NLC) .... OLLCR
Labaz [Belgium, France] [Research code symbol] L
Labe [Guinea] [Airport symbol] (AD) .... LEK
Labe/Tata [Guinea] [ICAO location identifier] (ICLI) .... GULB
Label (MDG) L
Label [or Labelling] (IAA) .... LAB
Label (MSA) .... LBL
Label .... LBL
Label as Such [Pharmacology] (CDAI) .... LAS
Label Clause LC
Label Definition (IAA) .... LD
Label Information Area (CMD) .... LIA
Label Manufacturers National Association [Defunct] .... LMNA
Label Printing Industries of America (EA) .... LPIA
Labeled Lymphoblast [Oncology] (DMAA) .... LBL
Labeled Release [Mars life detection experiment] .... LR
Labeling Index [Measurement of cell labeling] LI
Labelled Plan Display (PDAA) .... LPD
Labelled RADAR Display (PDAA) .... LRD
Labetalol [Pharmacology] L
Labete [Solomon Islands] [Seismograph station code, US Geological Survey] (SEIS) .... LBT
Labial [Dentistry] .... La
Labial Nerve [Anatomy] .... LbN
Labile Aggregation-Stimulating Substance [Hematology] .... LASS
Labile Particulate Organic Carbon [Environmental science] .... LPOC
Labindustries [Commercial firm] .... L/I
Labiocervical [Dentistry] .... LaC
Labiogingival [Dentistry] .... LaG
Labioglossolaryngeal [Dentistry] (DAVI) .... LGL
Labioglossopharyngeal [Dentistry] (DAVI) .... LGP
Labioincisal [Dentistry] .... LAI
Labiolingual [Dentistry] .... LaL
Labiolingual [Dentistry] .... LALI
Labiomental [Lip and chin] [Dentistry] (DAVI) .... LM
Labionasal [lip and nose] [Otorhinolaryngology] (DAVI) .... LN
Labis [Malaysia] [ICAO location identifier] (ICLI) .... WMAQ
Lablab [Papua New Guinea] [Airport symbol] (OAG) .... LAB
Labmin Resources Ltd. [Toronto Stock Exchange symbol] .... LAB
Labologists Society [Farnborough, Hampshire, England] (EAIO) .... LS
LabOne, Inc. [Associated Press] (SAG) .... LabOne
LabOne, Inc. [NASDAQ symbol] (SAG) .... LABS
Labor L
Labor .... LAB
Labor .... Lbr
Labor Advisory Board [New Deal] .... LAB
Labor Agreement Information Retrieval System [Office of Management and Budget] .... LAIRS
Labor Agreement Settlement Data [Cast Metals Association] [A publication] .... LASD
Labor and Automation Bulletin [A publication] (DLA) .... Lab & Auto Bull
Labor and Delivery [Area of a hospital] .... L & D
Labor and Delivery [Obstetrics] (DAVI) .... LD
Labor and Material Bond .... L & M
Labor and Production Effectiveness Reporting System [DoD] .... LAPERS
Labor Arbitration and Dispute Settlements [A publication] (DLA) .... Lab Arb & Disp Settl
Labor Arbitration Awards [Commerce Clearing House] [A publication] .... ARB
Labor Arbitration Awards [Commerce Clearing House] [A publication] (DLA) .... Lab Arb Awards
Labor Arbitration Awards (Commerce Clearing House) [A publication] (DLA) .... CCH Lab Arb Awards
Labor Arbitration Information System [LRP Publications] [Information service or system] (CRD) .... LAIS
Labor Arbitration Reports [A publication] (DLA) .... LA
Labor Arbitration Reports [Bureau of National Affairs] [A publication] (DLA) .... Lab Arb
Labor Arbitration Reports [Bureau of National Affairs] [A publication] (DLA) .... LAR
Labor Area .... LA
Labor Area Summary [Employment and Training Administration] [Department of Labor] .... LAS
Labor Case Comments [Cast Metals Association] [A publication] LCC
Labor Cases [A publication] (DLA) LC
Labor Cases (Commerce Clearing House) [A publication] (DLA) .... CCH Lab Cas
Labor Class Code (DNAB) LCC
Labor Code [A publication] (DLA) .... Labor C
Labor Code (DNAB) LC
Labor Committee for Safe Energy and Full Employment [Defunct] (EA) .... LCSEFE
Labor Congress of Liberia LCL

Labor Cooperative Educational and Publishing Society [Defunct] (EA) ..... LCEPS
Labor Cost Index LCI
Labor Council for Latin American Advancement (EA) .... LCLAA
Labor Council of New South Wales [Australia] .... LCNSW
Labor Daily [A publication] .... LD
Labor Data Collection (MCD) .... LDC
Labor Day Committee [Australia] .... LDC
Labor, Delivery, Recovery, Post-Partum [Medicine] (MEDA) .... LDRP
Labor, Delivery, Recovery Room [Medicine] .... LDR
Labor Department .... LD
Labor Department, Research Library, Baton Rouge, LA [Library symbol Library of Congress] (LCLS) .... LBrL
Labor Developments Abroad [A publication] .... LDA
Labor Dispute (DLA) .... LD
Labor Education Advancement Program .... LEAP
Labor Education and Research Project (EA) .... LERP
Labor Exchange .... LE
Labor Heritage Foundation (EA) .... LHF
Labor Historians [Defunct] (EA) .... LH
Labor Hour [In contract work] .... LH
Labor Information Database [International Labor Office] [Information service or system] (IID) .... LID
Labor Institute of Public Affairs (EA) .... LIPA
Labor Intensive (MHDW) LI
Labor Investing for Tomorrow [Department of Labor] .... LIFT
Labor Law Reporter [Commerce Clearing House] [A publication] (DLA) .... Lab L Rep
Labor Law Reporter (Commerce Clearing House) [A publication] (DLA) .... CCH Lab L Rep
Labor Law Reporter (Commerce Clearing House) [A publication] (DLA) .... CCH LLR
Labor Letter [Cast Metals Association] [A publication] LL
Labor Management Maritime Committee, Inc. (EA) .... LMMCI
Labor Market Advisory Councils [Department of Labor and Department of Health, Education, and Welfare] [Terminated, 1982] (EGAO) .... LMAC
Labor Market and Occupational Information (OICC) .... LMOI
Labor Market Area .... LMA
Labor Market Bulletin (OICC) .... LMB
Labor Market Characteristics (OICC) .... LMC
Labor Market Exposure [Work Incentive Program] .... LME
Labor Market Information [Department of Labor] .... LMI
Labor Market Information - Analytical Table Series [Department of Labor - Employment and Training Administration] (OICC) .... LMI-ATS
Labor Market Information System [Department of Labor] .... LMIS
Labor Market Training Needs .... LMTN
Labor Mobility Demonstration .... LMD
Labor Mobility Project [Department of Labor] .... LMP
Labor of Genetic Disease Research [National Institutes of Health] .... LGDR
Labor Old Guard [Australia An association] .... LOG
Labor Organization Reporting System [Department of Labor] (GFGA) .... LORS
Labor Policy Advisory Committee for Multilateral Trade Negotiations [Terminated, 1980] (EGAO) .... LPAC
Labor Policy Association (EA) .... LPA
Labor Protection Plan .... LPP
Labor Relations and Research Center [University of Massachusetts] .... LRRC
Labor Relations Guide (Prentice-Hall, Inc.) [A publication] (DLA) .... Lab Rel Guide (P-H)
Labor Relations Reference Manual [A publication] (DLA) .... LRM
Labor Relations Reference Manual [Bureau of National Affairs] [A publication] (DLA) .... LRRM
Labor Relations Specialist (AAGC) .... LRS
Labor Relations Week [Bureau of National Affairs] [Information service or system] (CRD) .... LRW
Labor Reports (OICC) .... LR
Labor Research Association (EA) .... LRA
Labor Review [A publication] .... LR
Labor Room [Obstetrics] .... LR
Labor Sector Advisory Committee [Terminated, 1980] (EGAO) .... LSAC
Labor Service [Military] .... LS
Labor Service Unit [Military] .... LSU
Labor Services Agency (AABC) .... LSA
Labor Socialist Committee [Australia] .... LSC
Labor Statistics [Database] [Department of Labor] .... LABSTAT
Labor Studies Center [AFL-CIO] .... LSC
Labor Surplus Area .... LSA
Labor Turnover Statistics (OICC) .... LTS
Labor Union (OICC) .... LU
Labor Utilization (MCD) .... LABUT
Labor Zionist Alliance (EA) .... LZA
Labor Zionist Organization of America - Poale Zion [Later, LZA] (EA) .... LZOA
Laboratoire d'Analyse Statistique des Langues Anciennes [Laboratory for the Statistical Analysis of Ancient Languages] [University of Liege, Belgium] .... LASLA
Laboratoire de Police Scientifique, Montreal, Quebec [Library symbol National Library of Canada] (NLC) .... QMJLP
Laboratoire de Recherche en Administration et Politique Scolaires [Canada] .... LABRAPS
Laboratoire de Recherche en Sciences de l'Administration [Laval University] [Canada Research center] (RCD) .... LRSA
Laboratoire de Recherche en Sciences Immobilieres [University of Quebec at Montreal] [Research center] (RCD) .... LARSI
Laboratoire de Recherche sur l'Emploi, la Repartition, et la Securite du Revenu [University of Quebec at Montreal] [Research center] (RCD) .... LABREV
Laboratoire de Recherches en Optique et Laser [Laval University] [Canada Research center] (RCD) .... LROL

Laboratoire de Sante Publique du Quebec, Ste. Anne de Bellevue, PQ, Canada [Library symbol] [Library of Congress] (LCLS) .... CaQSABS

Laboratoire de Sante Publique du Quebec, Ste-Anne-De-Bellevue, Quebec [Library symbol National Library of Canada] (NLC) .... QSABS

Laboratoire des Sciences de l'Activite Physique [Laval University] [Canada Research center] (RCD) .... LABSAP

Laboratoire d'Etudes Politiques et Administratives [Universite Laval, Quebec] [Canada] .... LEPA

Laboratoire d'Oceanographie Dynamique et de Climatologie [France] [Marine science] (OSRA) .... LODYC

Laboratoires Abbott Ltee, Montreal, PQ, Canada [Library symbol] [Library of Congress] (LCLS) .... CaQMLA

Laboratoires Abbott Ltee, Montreal, Quebec [Library symbol National Library of Canada] (NLC) .... QMLA

Laboratoires Bruneau & Cie [France] [Research code symbol] .... LBC

Laboratoires Nordic, Inc., Kirkland, Quebec [Library symbol National Library of Canada] (BIB) .... QKLN

Laboratories and Test (NASA) .... L & T

Laboratories' Applied Physiology Branch [Army] .... LAPB

Laboratories for Astrophysics and Space Research [University of Chicago] [Research center] .... LASR

Laboratories for Molecular Neuroendocrinology and Diabetes [Tulane University] [Research center] (RCD) .... LMNED

Laboratories Low Level Linked List (NITA) LLLLL

Laboratories Low-Level Linked List Language [Bell Systems] (DIT) L6

Laboratories Low-Level Linked List Language [Bell Systems] (MCD) LLLLLL

Laboratories Management Information System .... LABMIS

Laboratories of Applied Sciences [University of Chicago] (MCD) .... LAS

Laboratorio Chile ADS [NYSE symbol] (TTSB) .... LBC

Laboratorio Chile SA [Associated Press] (SAG) .... LabChile

Laboratorio Chile SA [NYSE symbol] (SAG) .... LBC

Laboratorio de Fisica e Engenharia Nucleores [Portugal] .... LFEN

Laboratory L

Laboratory (AFM) .... LAB

Laboratory (WDMC) .... lab

Laboratory .... LAB

Laboratory (MAE) .... LB

Laboratory Accreditation Program [Department of Commerce] .... LAP

Laboratory Admission Baseline Studies .... LABS

Laboratory, Alberta Agriculture, Edmonton, Alberta [Library symbol Obsolete National Library of Canada] (NLC) .... AEAGL

Laboratory and Checkout (NASA) .... L & C

Laboratory Animal Breeders Association (EA) .... LABA

Laboratory Animal Dander Allergy (DAVI) .... LADA

Laboratory Animal Data Bank [Battelle Memorial Institute] [Columbus, OH No longer available online] [Information service or system] (IID) .... LADB

Laboratory Animal Management and Business Systems [Computer science] .... LAMBS

Laboratory Animal Management Association (EA) .... LAMA

Laboratory Animal Science Association [British] .... LASA

Laboratory Attendant [Ranking title] [British Royal Navy] L

Laboratory Automated Calibration System (MCD) .... LACS

Laboratory Automated Data Management .... LADM

Laboratory Automation System .... LAS

Laboratory Branch Complement Fixation [Clinical chemistry] .... LBCF

Laboratory Bulletin .... LB

Laboratory Centre for Disease Control [Canada] .... LCDC

Laboratory Centre for Disease Control, Health Protection Branch, Department of National Health and Welfare [Laboratoire de Lutte Contre la Maladie, DirectionGenerale de la Protection de la Sante, Ministere de la Sante Nationale et du Bi en-Etre Social] Ottawa, Ontario [Library symbol National Library of Canada] (NLC) .... OONHL

Laboratory Command [Adelphi, MD] [Army] (RDA) .... LABCOM

Laboratory Computer Online Inquiry .... LACONIQ

Laboratory Configured Fire Units (MCD) .... LCFU

Laboratory Contract Manager (MCD) .... LCM

Laboratory Corp. Amer Hldgs Wrrt [NYSE symbol] (TTSB) .... LH

Laboratory Corp. of America Holdings [Associated Press] (SAG) .... LabCp

Laboratory Corp. of America Holdings [NYSE symbol] (SAG) .... LH

Laboratory Craftsman (ADA) LC

Laboratory Data (MAE) .... LD

Laboratory Data Control [Commercial firm] .... LDC

Laboratory Data Integrity Program [Environmental Protection Agency] (GFGA) .... LDIP

Laboratory Data Management System [IBM Corp.] .... LDMS

Laboratory Data Processor (IAA) .... LDP

Laboratory Designated Area (AFIT) .... LDA

Laboratory Distribution Panel .... LDP

Laboratory Education Advancement Program [Department of Labor] .... LEAP

Laboratory Electronics Technician (IAA) .... LET

Laboratory Environment Model .... LEM

Laboratory Equipment Corp. [Auto industry supplier] .... LABECO

Laboratory Equipment Exhibition (TSPED) .... LABEX

Laboratory Evaluation (MUGU) .... LE

Laboratory Evaluation and Accreditation Program .... LEAP

Laboratory Evaluation Program [Environmental Protection Agency] (GFGA) .... LEP

Laboratory Evening Academic Program (SAA) .... LEAP

Laboratory Experimental Research Facility [Army] (RDA) .... LERF

Laboratory Facilities Request (MCD) .... LFR

Laboratory for Agricultural Remote Sensing .... LARS

Laboratory for Applications of Remote Sensing [Purdue University] [Research center] (RCD) .... LARS

Laboratory for Applications of Remote Sensing System for Aircraft Analysis [NASA] (GFGA) .... LARSSYAA

Laboratory for Applied Biophysics [MIT] (MCD) .... LAB

Laboratory for Atmospheric and Space Physics [University of Colorado] [Research center] .... LASP

Laboratory for Atomic and Solid State Physics [Cornell University] [Research center] (RCD) .... LASSP

Laboratory for Computational Statistics [Stanford University] (PDAA) .... LCS

Laboratory for Computer and Communications Research [Simon Fraser University] [Canada Research center] (RCD) .... LCCR

Laboratory for Computer Science [Massachusetts Institute of Technology] [Research center] (RCD) .... LCS

Laboratory for Computer Science Research [Rutgers University] [Research center] (RCD) .... LCSR

Laboratory for Computer-Aided Design and Analysis in the Molecular Sciences [Washington State University] [Research center] (RCD) .... CADAMS

Laboratory for Electromagnetic and Electronic Systems [Massachusetts Institute of Technology] [Research center] (RCD) .... LEES

Laboratory for Electronics (DNAB) .... LFE

Laboratory for Energy-Related Health Research [University of California-Davis] [Department of Energy] (GRD) .... LEHR

Laboratory for Environmental Data Research [National Oceanic and Atmospheric Administration] .... LEDR

Laboratory for Environmental Studies [Ohio State University] [Research center] (RCD) .... LES

Laboratory for Experimental Medicine and Surgery in Primates [New York University] [Research center] .... LEMSIP

Laboratory for High Energy Astrophysics [Greenbelt, MD] [NASA] (GRD) .... LHEA

Laboratory for Information and Decision Systems [Massachusetts Institute of Technology] [Research center] (RCD) .... LIDS

Laboratory for Information Science in Agriculture [Research center Defunct] (RCD) .... LISA

Laboratory for Insulation Research [MIT] (MCD) .... LIR

Laboratory for International Fuzzy Engineering Research [Japan] .... LIFE

Laboratory for LASER Energetics [University of Rochester] [Research center] .... LLE

Laboratory for Mathematics and Statistics [University of California at San Diego] [Research center] (RCD) .... LMS

Laboratory for Meteorology and Earth Sciences [NASA] .... LMES

Laboratory for Nuclear Science [MIT] (MCD) .... LNS

Laboratory for Pest Control Application Technology [Ohio State University] [Research center] (RCD) .... LPCAT

Laboratory for Research on the Structure of Matter [University of Pennsylvania] .... LRSM

Laboratory for Space Research [Netherlands] .... LSR

Laboratory for Surface Science and Technology [University of Maine at Orono] [Research center] (RCD) .... LASST

Laboratory for Surface Studies [University of Wisconsin, Milwaukee] [Research center] (RCD) .... LSS

Laboratory for the Structure of Matter [Navy] (PDAA) .... LSM

Laboratory Graduate Participation [Oak Ridge National Laboratory] .... LGP

Laboratory Hazards Bulletin [Royal Society of Chemistry] [Information service or system] (IID) .... LHB

Laboratory Information Bulletin (GNE) .... LIB

Laboratory Information Management System .... LIMS

Laboratory Information Systems (DNAB) .... LABIS

Laboratory Information Systems .... LIS

Laboratory Institute of Merchandising [New York, NY] .... LIM

Laboratory Instrument Computer [Medical analyzer] .... LINC

Laboratory Instrument Data Acquisition .... LIDAS

Laboratory Interface Language [Programming language] LIL

Laboratory Interface Peripheral Subsystem [Computer science] .... LIPS

Laboratory Journal of Australasia [A publication] .... Lab J Aust

Laboratory Management Division .... LMD

Laboratory Manager .... LM

Laboratory Materiel Control Activity (AFIT) .... LMCA

Laboratory Microscope .... LM

Laboratory Module (MCD) .... LM

Laboratory Module Computer Program .... LMCP

Laboratory Module Simulation Equipment .... LMSE

Laboratory of Advertising Performance [McGraw-Hill] .... LAP

Laboratory of Architecture and Planning [Massachusetts Institute of Technology] [Research center] (RCD) .... LAP

Laboratory of Atmospheric Sciences [National Science Foundation] .... LAS

Laboratory of Biochemical Risk Analysis (GNE) .... LBRA

Laboratory of Biomedical and Environmental Sciences [Research center] (RCD) .... LBES

Laboratory of Blood and Blood Products [Public Health Service] .... LBBP

Laboratory of Brain Evolution and Behavior [National Institute of Mental Health] .... LBEB

Laboratory of Cellular Immunology [University of Arizona] [Research center] (RCD) LCI

Laboratory of Chemical and Solid-State Physics [MIT] (MCD) .... LCSSP

Laboratory of Electro-Modeling [Former USSR] .... LEM

Laboratory of Electronics [Rockefeller University] [Research center] (RCD) .... LE

Laboratory of Genetics (GNE) .... LG

Laboratory of Hygiene, Ottawa, ON, Canada [Library symbol Library of Congress Obsolete] (LCLS) .... CaOOH

Laboratory of Infectious Diseases [Later, Laboratory of Viral Diseases] [NIAID] .... LID

Laboratory of Molecular and Integrative Neuroscience (GNE) .... LMIN

Laboratory of Molecular Biophysics (GNE) .... LMB

Laboratory of Molecular Carcinogensis (GNE) .... LMC

Laboratory of Molecular Genetics (GNE) .... LMG

Laboratory of Molecular Structure [Massachusetts Institute of Technology] .... LMS

Laboratory of Nuclear Medicine and Radiation Biology .... LNMRB

Laboratory of Physiological Hygiene [*University of Minnesota*] [*Research center*] (RCD) ... LPH
Laboratory of Pulmonary Pathobiology (GNE) ... LPP
Laboratory of Renewable Resources Engineering [*Purdue University*] ... LORRE
Laboratory of Reproductive and Developmental Toxicology (GNE) ... LRDT
Laboratory of Research in Human and Social Ecology [*University of Quebec at Montreal*] [*Canada Research center*] (RCD) ... LAREHS
Laboratory of the Government Chemist [*Research center British*] (IRC) ... LGC
Laboratory of Virology and Rickettsial Diseases ... LVR
Laboratory Office Building ... LOB
Laboratory Office Network Experiment [*DoD*] ... LONEX
Laboratory Office Network System [*DoD*] ... LONS
Laboratory, Ontario Ministry of the Environment, Rexdale, Ontario [*Library symbol National Library of Canada*] (NLC) ... OTMENL
Laboratory Operating Instructions (MCD) ... LOI
Laboratory Operating System [*NASA*] ... LOS
Laboratory Operations Support Center [*NASA*] (SSD) ... LOSC
Laboratory Outfitting (SSD) ... LO
Laboratory Peripheral System ... LPS
Laboratory Precision Connector (IAA) ... LPC
Laboratory Procedure [*Medicine*] (BABM) ... LAB PROC
Laboratory Procedure ... LP
Laboratory Procurement Supply Office ... LPSO
Laboratory Program for Computer-Assisted Learning (IAA) ... LOCAL
Laboratory Program Summary (MCD) ... LPS
Laboratory Pulse Compression ... LPC
Laboratory Pulse Compression Loop ... LPCL
Laboratory Reactor ... LR
Laboratory Reagent ... LR
Laboratory Recoil Simulator (MCD) ... LRS
Laboratory Reference (MAE) ... LR
Laboratory Release System (MCD) ... LRS
Laboratory Report ... LR
Laboratory Research Cooperative Program [*Scientific Services Program*] [*Army*] (RDA) ... LRCP
Laboratory Review Office [*Army*] (RDA) ... LRO
Laboratory Rocket ... LABROC
Laboratory Services, Ontario Ministry of Health, Toronto, Ontario [*Library symbol National Library of Canada*] (NLC) ... OTDHL
Laboratory Services Section, Food Production and Marketing Branch, Agriculture Canada [*Section des Services d'Analyse, Direction de la Production et de la Commercialisation des Aliments, Agriculture Canada*] **Ottawa, Ontario** [*Library symbol National Library of Canada*] (NLC) ... OOAGFP
Laboratory Simulation Facility (MCD) ... LSF
Laboratory Space Allocation Plan (MCD) ... LSAP
Laboratory Specialists Amer [*NASDAQ symbol*] (TTSB) ... LABZ
Laboratory Specialists of America, Inc. [*Associated Press*] (SAG) ... LabSpc
Laboratory Specialists of America, Inc. [*Associated Press*] (SAG) ... LabSpec
Laboratory Specialists of America, Inc. [*NASDAQ symbol*] (SAG) ... LABZ
Laboratory Specialists Wrrt [*NASDAQ symbol*] (TTSB) ... LABZW
Laboratory Support Equipment (SSD) ... LSE
Laboratory Support Service ... LSS
Laboratory System ... LS
Laboratory Technologies Corp. (PCM) ... LAB TECH
Laboratory Test (IAA) ... LT
Laboratory Test Handbook ... LTH
Laboratory Test Set ... LTS
Laboratory Unit Operation ... LUO
Laboratory Vehicle (MCD) ... LV
Laboratory Vehicle Checkout Procedure ... LVCP
Laboratory Vehicle Development ... LVD
Laboratory Vehicle Procedure Simulator ... LVPS
Laboratory Vehicle Support Facility ... LVSF
Laboratory Vehicle System Segment ... LVSS
Laboratory Virtual Instrument Engineering Workbench ... LabVIEW
Laboratory Workbench ... LWB
Laboratory-Certifying Scientist [*Analytical chemistry*] ... LCS
Laboratoy Corp. Amer Hldgs Wrrt [*NYSE symbol*] (TTSB) ... LH.WS
Labor-Delivery-Recovery Suite (HCT) ... LDRS
Labor-Delivery-Recovery-Postpartum Suite (HCT) ... LDRPS
Laborer ... LABR
Laborer ... LBR
Laborers' International Union of North America (EA) ... LIUNA
Laborers Political League (EA) ... LPL
Labor-Force Participation ... LFP
Labor-Industry Coalition for International Trade [*Washington, DC*] (EA) ... LICIT
Labor-Management Advisory Committee [*Terminated, 1974*] [*Cost of Living Council*] (EGAO) ... LMAC
Labor-Management Relations ... LMR
Labor-Management Relations Act [*1947*] ... LMRA
Labor-Management Relations Service of the US Conference of Mayors (EA) ... LMRS
Labor-Management Relations Staff [*Department of Agriculture*] (GFGA) ... LMRS
Labor-Management Reporting and Disclosure Act [*1959*] ... LMRDA
Labor-Management Reporting and Disclosure Act - Investigative Matter [*FBI standardized term*] ... LMRDA-IM
Labor-Management Services Administration [*Department of Labor*] ... LMSA
Labor-Management Welfare-Pension [*Reports*] [*Department of Labor*] ... LMWP
Labor's League for Political Education [*AFL*] [*Later merged into Committee on Political Education of AFL-CIO*] ... LLPE
Labor's Old Guard Socialists [*Australia An association*] ... LOGS
Laboulaye [*Argentina ICAO location identifier*] (ICLI) ... SAOL
Labour and Co-Operative Party [*British*] ... LAB-CO-OP
Labour and Industry [*A publication*] ... Lab Ind
Labour Appeal Cases [*India*] [*A publication*] (DLA) ... Lab AC
Labour Appeal Cases [*India*] [*A publication*] (ILCA) ... LAC
Labour Arbitration Cases [*Canada Law Book, Inc.*] [*Information service or system A publication A publication*] (CRD) ... LAC
Labour Campaign Electoral Reform [*British*] [*An association*] (DBA) ... LCER
Labour Canada [*See also TRAVC*] ... LC
Labour Canada [*Travail Canada*] **Ottawa, Ontario** [*Library symbol National Library of Canada*] (NLC) ... OOL
Labour College of Canada, Ottawa, ON, Canada [*Library symbol Library of Congress*] (LCLS) ... CaOOLC
Labour College of Canada, Ottawa, Ontario [*Library symbol National Library of Canada*] (NLC) ... OOLC
Labour Coordinating Committee [*British*] ... LCC
Labour Corps [*British military*] (DMA) ... LC
Labour Cost Research Associates Ltd. [*British*] (ECON) ... LCRA
Labour Exchange Managers' Federation [*A union*] [*British*] ... LEMF
Labour Force Survey [*Canada*] ... LFS
Labour History [*A publication*] ... Lab His
Labour Information Database [*International Labour Office*] [*Information service or system*] (IID) ... LABORINFO
Labour Market Planning and Information Resource Centre, Saskatchewan Department of Advanced Education and Manpower, Regina, Saskatchewan [*Library symbol National Library of Canada*] (NLC) ... SRAEL
Labour Mobility [*British*] ... LM
Labour Party [*British Political party*] ... LAB
Labour Party of Dominica [*Political party*] (EY) ... LPD
Labour Party of South Africa [*Political party*] (PPW) ... LP
Labour Party Young Socialists [*British Political party*] ... LPYS
Labour Progressive Party [*Canadian communist party*] ... LPP
Labour Protection League [*A union*] [*British*] ... LPL
Labour Relations Board [*Canada*] ... LRB
Labour Representation Committee [*Northern Ireland*] (PPW) ... LRC
Labour Research Department [*Trade union*] [*British*] ... LRD
Labour Research Library, Manitoba Department of Labour and Manpower, Winnipeg, Manitoba [*Library symbol National Library of Canada*] (NLC) ... MWLR
Labour Staff Association [*National Coal Board*] [*British*] ... LSA
Labour Supply Board [*British*] ... LSB
Labour Supply Inspector [*British*] ... LSI
Labrador [*Canada*] ... LAB
Labrador [*Postal code*] [*Canada*] ... LB
Labrador Airways [*ICAO designator*] (AD) ... WJ
Labrador Airways Ltd. [*Canada ICAO designator*] (FAAC) ... LAL
Labrador City, NF [*AM radio station call letters*] ... CBDQ
Labrador City, NF [*Television station call letters*] ... CBNLT
Labrador City, NF [*FM radio station call letters*] ... CJRM
Labrador City Public Library, Newfoundland [*Library symbol National Library of Canada*] (NLC) ... NFL
Labrador City Regional Library, Labrador City, NF, Canada [*Library symbol Library of Congress*] (LCLS) ... CaNfL
Labrador Institute of Northern Studies [*Memorial University of Newfoundland*] [*Canada Research center*] (RCD) ... LINS
Labrador Inuit Association, Nain, Newfoundland [*Library symbol National Library of Canada*] (NLC) ... NFNLI
Labrador Inuit Association, Nain, NF, Canada [*Library symbol*] [*Library of Congress*] (LCLS) ... CaNfNaLI
Labrador Retriever [*Dog breed*] ... LAB
Labrador Retriever Club (EA) ... LRC
Labrador Sea Water [*Oceanography*] ... LSW
Labrador Unit Association, Nain, Newfoundland [*Library symbol National Library of Canada*] (NLC) ... NFNLI
Labrea [*Brazil*] [*Airport symbol*] (AD) ... LBR
Labrea [*Brazil ICAO location identifier*] (ICLI) ... SBLB
Labs. Dr. J. Auclair [*France*] [*Research code symbol*] ... D
Labuan [*Island in Malaysia*] (ROG) ... LAB
Labuan [*Malaysia*] [*Airport symbol*] (OAG) ... LBU
Labuan [*Malaysia*] [*ICAO location identifier*] (ICLI) ... WBKL
Labuha [*Indonesia*] [*Airport symbol*] (OAG) ... LAH
Labuhan Bilik/Ajamu [*Indonesia*] [*ICAO location identifier*] (ICLI) ... WIMA
Labuhu/Usman Sadik [*Indonesia*] [*ICAO location identifier*] (ICLI) ... WAPH
Labyrinth [*Engineering*] ... LBYR
Labyrinth Air Induction Silencer [*Automotive engineering*] ... LAIS
Labyrinth Air Induction System [*Automotive engineering*] ... LAIS
Labyrinth Pack [*Engineering*] ... LBYRPK
Labyrinthine Defect [*Physiology*] (MAE) ... LD
Labyrinthine Righting Reflex [*Physiology*] ... LRR
Lac Du Bonnet, MB [*Television station call letters*] ... CBWT-2
Lac La Biche [*Canada Airport symbol*] ... YLB
Lac La Biche, AB [*Television station call letters*] ... CFRN-5
Lac La Biche, AB [*FM radio station call letters*] ... CFWE
Lac La Biche Public Library, Alberta [*Library symbol National Library of Canada*] (NLC) ... ALLB
Lac La Biche Public Library, Lac La Biche, AB, Canada [*Library symbol*] [*Library of Congress*] (LCLS) ... CaALlb
Lac La Ronge [*Canada*] [*Airport symbol*] (OAG) ... YVC
Lac Megantic, PQ [*AM radio station call letters*] ... CKFL
Lacana Mining Corp. [*Toronto Stock Exchange symbol*] ... LCA
Lac-Coated Urea Fertilizer ... LCU
Lace and Embroidery Association of America [*Later, Lace Importers Association*] (EA) ... LEAA
Lace Research Association [*British*] ... LRA
Lacerated Wound ... LW
Laceration [*Medicine*] ... LAC
Lacerations and Contusions [*Medicine*] (DAVI) ... lac & cont
Lacerta [*Constellation*] ... Lac
Lacerta [*Constellation*] ... Lacr

Lac-Etchemin, PQ [*FM radio station call letters*] ... CFIN

Lacey, WA [*AM radio station call letters*] (RBYB) ... KBRD

Lacey, WA [*AM radio station call letters*] ... KTOL

Lacey's Digest of Railroad Decisions [*A publication*] (DLA) ... Lac RR Dig

Lacey's Digest of Railroad Decisions [*A publication*] (DLA) ... Lacey Dig

Lachar-Wrobel Critical Items [*Psychology*] (DAVI) ... LWCT

Lachen/Speyerdorf [*Germany ICAO location identifier*] (ICLI) ... EDRL

Laches [*of Plato*] [*Classical studies*] (OCD) ... La

Laches [*of Plato*] [*Classical studies*] (OCD) ... Lach

Lachute, PQ [*FM radio station call letters*] ... CJLA

Lack Characteristics of Desirable Investment [*Moody's bond rating*] [*Investment term*] ... B

Lack of Fusion ... LOF

Lack of Moral Fibre [*British military*] (DMA) ... LMF

Lackawanna & Wyoming Valley Railway Co. [*Absorbed into Consolidated Rail Corp.*] [*AAR code*] ... LWV

Lackawanna Bar Association Law Library, Scranton, PA [*Library symbol Library of Congress*] (LCLS) ... PScLL

Lackawanna Bar Reporter [*Pennsylvania*] [*A publication*] (DLA) ... Lack Bar R

Lackawanna Bar Reporter [*Pennsylvania*] [*A publication*] (DLA) ... Lackawanna B

Lackawanna County Reports [*Pennsylvania*] [*A publication*] (DLA) ... Lack Co (PA)

Lackawanna Legal News [*Pennsylvania*] [*A publication*] (DLA) ... Lack Leg N

Lackawanna Legal News [*Pennsylvania*] [*A publication*] (DLA) ... Lack Leg News (PA)

Lackawanna Legal News [*Pennsylvania*] [*A publication*] (DLA) ... Lack LN

Lackawanna Legal News [*Pennsylvania*] [*A publication*] (DLA) ... Lacka Leg News

Lackawanna Legal Record [*Pennsylvania*] [*A publication*] (DLA) ... Lack Leg R

Lackawanna Legal Record [*Pennsylvania*] [*A publication*] (DLA) ... Lack Leg Rec

Lackawanna Legal Record [*Pennsylvania*] [*A publication*] (DLA) ... Lack LR

Lackawaxen & Stourbridge Railroad Corp. [*AAR code*] ... LASB

Lackland Aircraft Reactors Operations Office (SAA) ... LAROO

Laclede Gas [*NYSE symbol*] (TTSB) ... LG

Laclede Gas Co. [*Associated Press*] (SAG) ... LaclGas

Laclede Gas Co. [*NYSE symbol*] (SPSG) ... LG

Laclede Steel [*NASDAQ symbol*] (TTSB) ... LCLD

Laclede Steel Co. [*Associated Press*] (SAG) ... LacledeSt

Laclede Steel Co. [*NASDAQ symbol*] (SAG) ... LCLD

Lacombe, LA [*FM radio station call letters*] ... KPXF

Lacombe, LA [*FM radio station call letters*] (RBYB) ... WYLA-FM

Lacombe Public Library, Alberta [*Library symbol National Library of Canada*] (NLC) ... ALAC

Laconia [*New Hampshire*] [*Airport symbol*] (OAG) ... LCI

Laconia, NH [*Location identifier FAA*] (FAAL) ... BLO

Laconia, NH [*Location identifier FAA*] (FAAL) ... LCI

Laconia, NH [*AM radio station call letters*] ... WEMJ

Laconia, NH [*AM radio station call letters*] ... WEZS

Laconia, NH [*FM radio station call letters*] ... WLNH

Lacquer (WDAA) ... LAC

Lacquer (VRA) ... lac

Lacquer ... LACQ

Lacquer ... LAQ

Lacquer (KSC) ... LIC

Lacquer Insulating Compound ... LIC

L'Acquisition Numerique et Televisualisation d'Images Organisees en Pages d'Ecriture [*French videotex system*] ... ANTIOPE

Lacrimal [*Ophthalmology*] (DAVI) ... lacr

Lacrimatory Factor [*Food technology*] ... LF

LaCrosse [*A virus*] ... LAC

Lacrosse [*British*] (ROG) ... LAX

LaCrosse Boiling Water Reactor [*Also, LCBWR*] ... LACBWR

LaCrosse Boiling Water Reactor [*Also, LACBWR*] ... LCBWR

LaCrosse Footwear [*NASDAQ symbol*] (TTSB) ... BOOT

LaCrosse Footwear, Inc. [*NASDAQ symbol*] (SAG) ... BOOT

LaCrosse Footwear, Inc. [*Associated Press*] (SAG) ... LaCrose

Lacrosse Foundation (EA) ... LF

Lacrosse Regional News, La Crosse, IN [*Library symbol Library of Congress*] (LCLS) ... InLacN

Lacrosse Victoria [*Australia An association*] ... LV

LaCrosse, WI [*FM radio station call letters*] (RBYB) ... WTRV-FM

Lact-Aid International [*Commercial firm*] (EA) ... LAI

Lactalbumin [*Biochemistry*] ... LA

Lactalbumin Hydrolysate [*Biochemistry*] (MAE) ... LAH

Lactate [*or Lactating*] (AAMN) ... lact

Lactate Dehydrogenase [*Also, LD, LDH*] [*An enzyme*] ... LAD

Lactate Dehydrogenase [*Also, LAD, LDH*] [*An enzyme*] ... LD

Lactate Dehydrogenase [*Also, LAD, LD*] [*An enzyme*] ... LDH

Lactate Extraction [*Medicine*] (DMAA) ... LE

Lactate/Pyruvate [*Ratio*] ... L/P

Lactate Threshold [*Biochemistry*] ... LaT

Lactated Ringer [*Medicine*] ... LR

Lactated Ringer's Solution [*Intravenous solution*] ... LRS

Lactate-Pyruvate Ratio (MAE) ... LPR

Lactating [*Medicine*] (MAE) ... lact

Lactating Rat Serum Factor [*Immunology*] ... LRSF

Lactation (WDAA) ... LAC

Lactation Consultant [*Medicine*] (MEDA) ... LC

Lactic Acid [*Biochemistry*] ... LA

Lactic Acid [*Biochemistry*] (DAVI) ... LACT

Lactic Acid Bacteria [*Food microbiology*] ... LAB

Lactic Acid Dehydrogenase [*See also LDH*] [*An enzyme*] ... LAD

Lactic Acid Dehydrogenase [*An enzyme*] (DAVI) ... LADH

Lactic Acid Mineral (DMAA) ... LM

Lactic Dehydrogenase (DMAA) ... LDG

Lactic Dehydrogenase Isoenzymes (DAVI) ... LDHI

Lactic Dehydrogenase Isoenzymes (DAVI) ... LDISO

Lactic Dehydrogenase Virus ... LDV

Lactic Dehydrogenase-C (DMAA) ... LDHC

Lactic Dehydrogenase-K (DMAA) ... LDHK

Lactis Recentis [*New Milk*] [*Pharmacy*] (ROG) ... LAC REC

Lactoalbumin-Yeastolate [*Cell growth medium*] ... LY

Lactobacillus ... L

Lactobacillus bulgaricus Factor [*Biochemistry*] ... LBF

Lactobacillus Lactis Dorner Factor [*Vitamin B_{12}*] [*Also, APA, APAF, EF*] ... LLD

Lactobacillus Maintenance Medium [*Microbiology*] ... LMM

Lactobacillus Selector [*Microbiology*] (DAVI) ... LBS

Lactobacillus Viridescens [*Biochemistry*] (DAVI) ... LV

Lactoferrin [*Biochemistry*] ... LF

Lactoferrin [*Biochemistry*] (MAE) ... LFN

Lactogenic Hormone [*Also, LTH, PR, PRL*] [*Endocrinology*] ... LGH

Lactogenic Hormone [*Also, LGH, PR, PRL*] [*Endocrinology*] ... LTH

Lactone Terminated Polybutadiene [*Organic chemistry*] (MCD) ... LTPB

Lactose [*Cardiology*] (DAVI) ... LAC

Lactose Broth [*Microbiology*] ... LB

Lactose Coliform Count [*Medicine*] (BABM) ... LCC

Lactose Malabsorption [*Gastroenterology*] ... LM

Lactose Saccharose Urea [*Cell growth medium*] ... LSU

Lactose/Sucrose [*Ratio*] ... L/S

Lactose Tolerance [*Gastroenterology*] (DAVI) ... LAC T

Lactose, Yeast, and Peptone Agar [*Medicine*] (DMAA) ... LYP

Lactose-Free Diet ... LFD

Lacus Mortis [*Lunar area*] ... LM

Lacus Somniorum [*Lunar area*] ... LS

Lacy J. Dalton Fan Club (EA) ... LJDFC

Ladd Consolidated Community School District 94, Ladd, IL [*Library symbol Library of Congress*] (LCLS) ... ILadSD

Ladd Furniture [*NASDAQ symbol*] (SAG) ... LADF

Ladd Furniture, Inc. [*Associated Press*] (SAG) ... LaddFr

Ladd Mountain [*Washington*] [*Seismograph station code, US Geological Survey*] (SEIS) ... LMW

Ladd Public Library, Ladd, IL [*Library symbol Library of Congress*] (LCLS) ... ILad

Ladder (MSA) ... LAD

Ladder Rung (AAG) ... LR

Ladder Static Logic ... LSL

Ladd-Franklin Theory [*Color vision*] ... LFT

Ladd's Reports [*59-64 New Hampshire*] [*A publication*] (DLA) ... Ladd

Ladeco Cargo, SA [*Chile*] [*FAA designator*] (FAAC) ... LDC

Ladestreifen [*Ammunition Clip*] [*German military - World War II*] ... L

Ladies' After Thoughts on Equal Rights [*Acronym is used as name of association*] [*Defunct*] (EA) ... LATER

Ladies Against Women (EA) ... LAW

Ladies Amateur Fencing Union [*British*] (DBA) ... LAFU

Ladies Apparel Contractors Association (EA) ... LACA

Ladies Auxiliary, Military Order of the Purple Heart, United States of America (EA) ... LAMOPH

Ladies' Auxiliary of the American Beekeeping Federation (EA) ... LAABF

Ladies Auxiliary to the National Dental Association [*Later, ANDA*] (EA) ... LANDA

Ladies Auxiliary to the Veterans of Foreign Wars of the United States (EA) ... LAVFWUS

Ladies Golf Union ... LGU

Ladies' Hermitage Association (EA) ... LHA

Ladies Hermitage Association, Hermitage, TN [*Library symbol Library of Congress*] (LCLS) ... THer

Ladies' Home Mission Union [*British*] (BI) ... LHMU

Ladies' Kayak, Four Person (ADA) ... LK4

Ladies' Kayak, Single Person (ADA) ... LK1

Ladies' Kayak, Two Person (ADA) ... LK2

Ladies Kennel Association [*British*] (BI) ... LKA

Ladies Kennel Association of America (EA) ... LKA of A

Ladies Kennel Association of America (EA) ... LKAA

Ladies Left Handed ... LLH

Ladies Love Cool James [*Rap recording artist, James Todd Smith*] ... LL COOL J

Ladies of Bethany (TOCD) ... LB

Ladies of Retreads (EA) ... LOR

Ladies of the Grand Army of the Republic (EA) ... LGAR

Ladies Oriental Shrine of North America (EA) ... LOS of NA

Ladies Pennsylvania Slovak Catholic Union (EA) ... LPSCU

Ladies Professional Bowlers Tour (EA) ... LPBT

Ladies Professional Golf Association (EA) ... LPGA

Ladies Shoemakers' Society [*A union*] [*British*] ... LSS

Ladies' Touring Kayak, Single Person (ADA) ... LTK1

Lading (WDAA) ... LDG

Ladinian [*Geology*] ... L

Ladino [*MARC language code Library of Congress*] (LCCP) ... lad

Ladle Refining Furnace [*Nuclear energy*] (NUCP) ... LRF

Ladner, Downs, Barristers & Solicitors, Vancouver, British Columbia [*Library symbol National Library of Canada*] (NLC) ... BVALD

Ladoeanie [*Surinam*] [*ICAO location identifier*] (ICLI) ... SMDO

Ladoga-Clark Township Public Library, Ladoga, IN [*Library symbol Library of Congress*] (LCLS) ... InLad

Ladouanie [*Suriname*] [*Airport symbol*] (OAG) ... LDO

Ladron Mountain [*New Mexico*] [*Seismograph station code, US Geological Survey*] (SEIS) ... LAD

Ladson, SC [*FM radio station call letters*] ... WKCL

Lady [*or Ladyship*] ... L

Lady Bird Johnson [*Mrs. Lyndon Baines Johnson*] ... LBJ

Lady Boss ... LB

Lady Davis Institute for Medical Research, Jewish General Hospital, Montreal, Quebec [*Library symbol National Library of Canada*] (NLC) ... QMJGL

Lady Day [*March 25, the Feast of the Annunciation*] [*British*] ... LD

Lady Franklin Point, NT [*ICAO location identifier*] (ICLI) ... CYUJ

Lady [*of the Order of the*] **Garter** (BARN) ... LG
Lady Jockeys Association [*British*] (DBA) ... LJA
Lady Licentiate of Arts [*Scotland*] ... LLA
Lady Literate in Arts [*British*] ... LLA
Lady Luck Gaming Corp. [*Associated Press*] (SAG) ... LadyLuck
Lady Luck Gaming Corp. [*NASDAQ symbol*] (SAG) ... LUCK
Lady Luck Gaming'A' [*NASDAQ symbol*] (TTSB) ... LUCK
Lady Margaret Boat Club [*of St. John's College, Cambridge*] [*British*] ... LMBC
Lady Margaret Hall [*Oxford University*] ... LMH
[*A*] **Lady of England** [*Pseudonym used by Charlotte Maria Tucker, 19th-century author of children's books*] ... ALOE
"Lady of the House" [*Advertising*] (DOAD) ... LOH
Lady of the House [*Telephone marketing*] (WDMC) ... loh
Lady Robyn Resources, Inc. [*Vancouver Stock Exchange symbol*] ... LRY
Ladybrand [*South Africa*] [*ICAO location identifier*] (ICLI) ... FALB
Ladycliff College, Highland Falls, NY [*Library symbol Library of Congress*] (LCLS) ... NHigfL
Lady's Realm [*A publication*] (ROG) ... LR
Ladyship (BARN) ... Ladp
Ladyship [*or Lordship*] ... LDP
Ladyship [*or Lordship*] ... LP
Ladysmith [*South Africa*] [*ICAO location identifier*] (ICLI) ... FALY
Ladysmith [*South Africa*] [*Airport symbol*] (OAG) ... LAY
Ladysmith, WI [*Location identifier FAA*] (FAAL) ... RCX
Ladysmith, WI [*FM radio station call letters*] ... WJBL
Ladysmith, WI [*AM radio station call letters*] ... WLDY
Ladysmith, WI [*FM radio station call letters*] ... WWIB
Lae [*Papua New Guinea*] [*ICAO location identifier*] (ICLI) ... AYLA
Lae [*Papua New Guinea*] [*Airport symbol*] (OAG) ... LAE
Lae [*Papua New Guinea*] [*Seismograph station code, US Geological Survey Closed*] (SEIS) ... LAE
Lae [*Papua New Guinea*] [*Seismograph station code, US Geological Survey*] (SEIS) ... LAT
Lae [*Marshall Islands*] [*Airport symbol*] (OAG) ... LML
Lae-City [*Papua New Guinea*] [*Airport symbol*] (OAG) ... LAC
Laennec's Cirrhosis [*Medicine*] (MAE) ... LC
Laeso [*Denmark ICAO location identifier*] (ICLI) ... EKLS
Laetolil Hominid ... LH
Laevo-Mandelonitrile-beta-glucuronic Acid [*Possible anticancer compound*] ... LAETRILE
Laevus [*Left*] [*Pharmacy*] ... LAEV
Lafarge Canada, Inc. [*Toronto Stock Exchange symbol*] ... LCI
Lafarge Corp. [*NYSE symbol*] (SPSG) ... LAF
Lafarge Corp. [*Associated Press*] (SAG) ... Lafarge
Lafayette [*Rhode Island*] [*Seismograph station code, US Geological Survey Closed*] (SEIS) ... LAF
Lafayette [*Indiana*] [*Airport symbol*] (OAG) ... LAF
Lafayette [*Diocesan abbreviation*] [*Louisiana*] (TOCD) ... LAF
Lafayette [*Diocesan abbreviation*] [*Indiana*] (TOCD) ... LFT
Lafayette [*Louisiana*] [*Airport symbol*] (OAG) ... LFT
Lafayette American Bank & Trust [*NASDAQ symbol*] (SAG) ... LABK
Lafayette American Bank & Trust [*Associated Press*] (SAG) ... LafayABk
Lafayette American Bk & Tr [*NASDAQ symbol*] (TTSB) ... LABK
Lafayette College, Easton, PA [*OCLC symbol*] (OCLC) ... LAF
Lafayette College, Easton, PA [*Library symbol Library of Congress*] (LCLS) ... PEL
Lafayette Elementary School, Willmar, MN [*Library symbol*] [*Library of Congress*] (LCLS) ... MNWiLES
Lafayette, FL [*FM radio station call letters*] (RBYB) ... WWFO
Lafayette Flying Corps [*World War I*] ... LFC
Lafayette General Hospital, Buffalo, NY [*Library symbol Library of Congress*] (LCLS) ... NBuLH
Lafayette, IN [*Location identifier FAA*] (FAAL) ... BVT
Lafayette, IN [*Location identifier FAA*] (FAAL) ... LAF
Lafayette, IN [*AM radio station call letters*] ... WASK
Lafayette, IN [*FM radio station call letters*] ... WAZY
Lafayette, IN [*AM radio station call letters*] ... WCFY
Lafayette, IN [*FM radio station call letters*] ... WJEF
Lafayette, IN [*FM radio station call letters*] ... WKHY
Lafayette, IN [*FM radio station call letters*] ... WKOA
Lafayette, IN [*Television station call letters*] ... WLFI
Lafayette Industries [*NASDAQ symbol*] (TTSB) ... LAFIE
Lafayette Industries, Inc. [*Associated Press*] (SAG) ... Lafay
Lafayette Industries, Inc. [*Associated Press*] (SAG) ... Lafaye
Lafayette Industries, Inc. [*NASDAQ symbol*] (SAG) ... LAFI
Lafayette Industries Wrrt [*NASDAQ symbol*] (TTSB) ... LAFWE
Lafayette Journal and Courier, Lafayette, IN [*Library symbol Library of Congress*] (LCLS) ... InLJC
Lafayette, LA [*AM radio station call letters*] ... KACY
Lafayette, LA [*Television station call letters*] ... KADN
Lafayette, LA [*Television station call letters*] ... KATC
Lafayette, LA [*AM radio station call letters*] (RBYB) ... KDYS-AM
Lafayette, LA [*AM radio station call letters*] ... KJCB
Lafayette, LA [*Television station call letters*] ... KLFY
Lafayette, LA [*Television station call letters*] ... KLPB
Lafayette, LA [*AM radio station call letters*] ... KPEL
Lafayette, LA [*FM radio station call letters*] ... KRRQ
Lafayette, LA [*FM radio station call letters*] ... KRVS
Lafayette, LA [*FM radio station call letters*] ... KSJY
Lafayette, LA [*FM radio station call letters*] ... KSMB
Lafayette, LA [*FM radio station call letters*] ... KTDY
Lafayette, LA [*AM radio station call letters*] ... KVOL
Lafayette, LA [*Location identifier FAA*] (FAAL) ... LFT
Lafayette, LA [*Location identifier FAA*] (FAAL) ... LKM
Lafayette Public Library, Lafayette, CO [*Library symbol Library of Congress*] (LCLS) ... CoLaf
Lafayette Public Library, Lafayette, LA [*Library symbol Library of Congress*] (LCLS) ... LLafL
Lafayette Radio Electronics Corp. ... LRE
Lafayette/Regional [*Louisiana*] [*ICAO location identifier*] (ICLI) ... KLFT
Lafayette School Corp., Lafayette, IN [*OCLC symbol*] (OCLC) ... ILA
Lafayette Schools System, Lafayette, IN [*Library symbol Library of Congress*] (LCLS) ... InLS
Lafayette, TN [*Location identifier FAA*] (FAAL) ... LFB
Lafayette, TN [*AM radio station call letters*] ... WEEN
Lafayette, TN [*FM radio station call letters*] ... WLCT
Lafayette Township, IN [*FM radio station call letters*] ... WCYT
Lafferty Transportation [*AAR code*] ... LTC
Lafleur, Brown & De Granpre, Montreal, Quebec [*Library symbol National Library of Canada*] (BIB) ... QMLBD
Lafond Public Library, Alberta [*Library symbol National Library of Canada*] (NLC) ... ALAF
Lafond Public Library, Lafond, AB, Canada [*Library symbol*] [*Library of Congress*] (LCLS) ... CaALaf
Lafourche Parish Library, Thibodaux, LA [*Library symbol Library of Congress*] (LCLS) ... LTL
LaFrancis Hardiman Early Childhood Center, Wyandanch, NY [*Library symbol*] [*Library of Congress*] (LCLS) ... NWyaHEC
Lag Amplifier ... LA
Lag Angle (IAA) ... LA
Lag Bolt [*Technical drawings*] ... LB
Lag Line Filter ... LLF
Lagena [*Flask*] [*Latin*] ... Lag
Lager (ABBR) ... LGR
Laggard (ABBR) ... LGRD
Lagged Reserve Accounting [*Banking*] ... LRA
Lagged Reserve Requirement [*Finance*] ... LRR
Lagging [*Engineering*] ... LAG
Laghman [*Afghanistan*] [*ICAO location identifier*] (ICLI) ... OALN
Laghouat [*Algeria*] [*ICAO location identifier*] (ICLI) ... DAUL
Laghouat [*Algeria*] [*Airport symbol*] (AD) ... LOO
Lagniappe (ABBR) ... LGNAP
Lago Agrio [*Ecuador*] [*Airport symbol*] (OAG) ... LGQ
Lago Agrio [*Ecuador*] [*ICAO location identifier*] (ICLI) ... SELA
Lago Argentino [*Argentina*] [*Airport symbol*] (OAG) ... ING
Lago Argentino [*Argentina ICAO location identifier*] (ICLI) ... SAWA
Lago De Cote [*Costa Rica*] [*Seismograph station code, US Geological Survey*] (SEIS) ... AR2
Lago Musters [*Argentina ICAO location identifier*] (ICLI) ... SAVM
Lago Verde [*Peru*] [*ICAO location identifier*] (ICLI) ... SPLV
Lagoa Santa [*Brazil ICAO location identifier*] (ICLI) ... SBLS
Lagonda Club, US Section (EA) ... LC
Lagoon [*Maps and charts*] ... LAG
Lagoon [*Board on Geographic Names*] ... LAGN
Lagoon [*Maps and charts*] (ROG) ... LG
Lagoon (ADA) ... LGN
Lagoon (ABBR) ... LGON
Lagoons [*Maps and charts*] (ROG) ... LGS
Lagos [*Nigeria*] [*Airport symbol*] (OAG) ... LOS
Lagos [*Portugal ICAO location identifier*] (ICLI) ... LPLG
Lagos App [*Nigeria*] [*ICAO location identifier*] (ICLI) ... DNLL
Lagos High Court Reports [*A publication*] (DLA) ... Lagos HCR
Lagos/Murtala Muhammed [*Nigeria*] [*ICAO location identifier*] (ICLI) ... DNMM
Lagos Notes and Records [*A publication*] ... LNR
LaGrange College (GAGS) ... LaGrange C
LaGrange County Historical Society, LaGrange, IN [*Library symbol Library of Congress*] (LCLS) ... InLagHi
LaGrange County Library, LaGrange, IN [*Library symbol Library of Congress*] (LCLS) ... InLag
Lagrange Differential Equation ... LDE
Lagrange, IN [*FM radio station call letters*] ... WTHD
LaGrange News and Standard, LaGrange, IN [*Library symbol*] [*Library of Congress*] (LCLS) ... InLagNS
Lagrange-Helmholtz Equation ... LHE
Lagrangian Function ... L
Lagrangian Stochastic Dispersion Model [*Marine science*] (OSRA) ... LSDM
Lagrangian Stochastic Dispersion Model (USDC) ... LSDM
LaGuardia Airport [*New York*] (CDAI) ... LGA
LaGuardia Automated Library System [*LaGuardia Community College*] [*Information service or system*] (IID) ... LALS
LaGuardia Community College Library [*UTLAS symbol*] ... LAG
LaGuardia Community College of the City University of New York, Long Island Cit y, NY [*Library symbol Library of Congress*] (LCLS) ... NLicL
Lague [*Congo*] [*ICAO location identifier*] (ICLI) ... FCBL
Lagulanda (BJA) ... La
Laguna Beach-Santa Ana [*California*] [*Airport symbol*] (AD) ... SNA
Laguna Choclococha [*Peru*] [*ICAO location identifier*] (ICLI) ... SPNH
Laguna Larga [*Argentina ICAO location identifier*] (ICLI) ... SACL
Laguna Loa [*Bolivia*] [*ICAO location identifier*] (ICLI) ... SLLL
Laguna Peak [*California*] [*Seismograph station code, US Geological Survey*] (SEIS) ... BLG
Laguna Peak Tracking and Injection Station ... LPTIS
Lagunas [*Peru*] [*ICAO location identifier*] (ICLI) ... SPGS
Lagunillas [*Venezuela*] [*Seismograph station code, US Geological Survey*] (SEIS) ... LGN
Lagunillas [*Venezuela*] [*Airport symbol*] (AD) ... LGY
Lahad Datu [*Malaysia*] [*Airport symbol*] (OAG) ... LDU
Lahad Datu [*Malaysia*] [*ICAO location identifier*] (ICLI) ... WBKD
Lahaina, HI [*FM radio station call letters*] ... KLHI
Lahaina, HI [*FM radio station call letters*] ... KPOA
Lahaina-Kaanapali & Pacific Railroad [*Hawaii*] ... LK & PRR

Lahey Clinic Foundation, Boston, MA [*Library symbol Library of Congress*] (LCLS) ... MBLC
Lahijan [*Iran*] [*ICAO location identifier*] (ICLI) ... OIGN
Lahnda [*MARC language code Library of Congress*] (LCCP) ... lah
Lahoma, OK [*FM radio station call letters*] ... KMKZ
Lahore [*Pakistan*] [*Seismograph station code, US Geological Survey Closed*] (SEIS) ... LAH
Lahore [*Pakistan*] [*Airport symbol*] (OAG) ... LHE
Lahore [*Pakistan*] [*ICAO location identifier*] (ICLI) ... OPLA
Lahore [*Pakistan*] [*ICAO location identifier*] (ICLI) ... OPLR
Lahore Cases [*India*] [*A publication*] (DLA) ... Lah Cas
Lahore Law Journal [*India*] [*A publication*] (DLA) ... Lah LJ
Lahore Law Journal [*India*] [*A publication*] (DLA) ... LLJ
Lahore Law Times [*India*] [*A publication*] (DLA) ... Lah LT
Lahore Law Times [*India*] [*A publication*] (DLA) ... Lahore L Times
Lahore Law Times [*India*] [*A publication*] (DLA) ... LLT
Lahore Light Horse [*British military*] (DMA) ... LLH
Lahore/Walton [*Pakistan*] [*ICAO location identifier*] (ICLI) ... OPLH
Lahr [*Germany ICAO location identifier*] (ICLI) ... EDAN
Lahr/Bader Area [*Germany*] ... LBA
Lahu National Army [*Myanmar*] [*Political party*] (EY) ... LNA
Lai [*Chad*] [*ICAO location identifier*] (ICLI) ... FTTH
Lai [*Chad*] [*Airport symbol*] (AD) ... LTC
Laici per il Terzo Mondo [*Italy*] ... LTM
Laid Off, Lack of Work [*Unemployment insurance and the Bureau of Labor Statistics*] (OICC) ... LOLW
Laidlaw, Inc. [*Associated Press*] (SAG) ... LaidlwA
Laidlaw, Inc. [*Associated Press*] (SAG) ... LaidlwB
Laidlaw Inc. [*NYSE symbol*] (SAG) ... LDW
Laidlaw One 5.75% Ex Nts 2000 [*NYSE symbol*] (TTSB) ... UXL
Laidlaw One, Inc. [*Associated Press*] (SAG) ... Ldlw COO
Laidlaw One, Inc. [*Associated Press*] (SAG) ... LdlwOOO
Laidlaw One, Inc. [*NYSE symbol*] (SAG) ... UXL
Laidlaw Transportation Ltd. [*Toronto Stock Exchange symbol*] ... LDM
L'Aigle/Saint-Michel [*France ICAO location identifier*] (ICLI) ... LFOL
Laiko Enotiko Komma [*Populist Union Party*] [*Greece*] [*Political party*] (PPE) ... LEK
Laiko Komma [*Populist Party*] [*Greece*] [*Political party*] (PPE) ... LK
Laingsburg Public Library, Laingsburg, MI [*Library symbol Library of Congress*] (LCLS) ... MiLai
Laira [*Plymouth*] [*British depot code*] ... LA
Laird Group, Inc. [*Toronto Stock Exchange symbol*] ... LGR
Laja [*Bolivia*] [*ICAO location identifier*] (ICLI) ... SLLJ
Lajas, PR [*AM radio station call letters*] ... WAVB
Lajas, PR [*FM radio station call letters*] ... WCFI
Lajes [*Brazil*] [*Airport symbol*] (OAG) ... LAJ
Lajes [*Brazil*] [*Airport symbol*] (AD) ... LJZ
Lajes [*Brazil ICAO location identifier*] (ICLI) ... SBLJ
Lajes, Terceira Island [*Portugal ICAO location identifier*] (ICLI) ... LPLA
Lakas ng Bayan [*Peoples' Power Movement - Fight*] [*Philippines*] [*Political party*] (PPW) ... LABAN
Lake [*Maps and charts*] ... L
Lake [*Commonly used*] (OPSA) ... LAKE
Lake ... LK
Lake [*Board on Geographic Names*] (MCD) ... LK
Lake Acidification Mitigation Project [*Environmental Protection Agency*] (GFGA) ... LAMP
Lake Agassiz Regional Library, Moorhead, MN [*Library symbol Library of Congress*] (LCLS) ... MnMohL
Lake Air Helicopters Ltd. [*British ICAO designator*] (FAAC) ... LKR
Lake Aircraft [*ICAO aircraft manufacturer identifier*] (ICAO) ... LA
Lake and Rail ... L & R
Lake Ariel Bancorp [*NASDAQ symbol*] (SAG) ... LABN
Lake Ariel Bancorp [*Associated Press*] (SAG) ... LakeAriel
Lake Arrowhead, CA [*FM radio station call letters*] (RBYB) ... KCXX
Lake Benton Public Library, Lake Benton, MN [*Library symbol*] [*Library of Congress*] (LCLS) ... MnLb
Lake Benton Public Schools, Lake Benton, MN [*Library symbol*] [*Library of Congress*] (LCLS) ... MnLbPS
Lake Carriers' Association (EA) ... LCA
Lake Central Airlines ... LC
Lake Central Airlines ... LCA
Lake Chabot [*California*] [*Seismograph station code, US Geological Survey*] (SEIS) ... LKC
Lake Champlain & Moriah Rail Road Co. [*AAR code*] ... LCM
Lake Champlain Research Consortium [*Marine science*] (OSRA) ... LCRC
Lake Champlain Research Consortium (USDC) ... LCRC
Lake Charles [*Louisiana*] [*Airport symbol*] (OAG) ... LCH
Lake Charles [*Diocesan abbreviation*] [*Louisiana*] (TOCD) ... LKC
Lake Charles, LA [*AM radio station call letters*] ... KAOK
Lake Charles, LA [*FM radio station call letters*] ... KBIU
Lake Charles, LA [*FM radio station call letters*] ... KHLA
Lake Charles, LA [*AM radio station call letters*] ... KLCL
Lake Charles, LA [*Television station call letters*] ... KLTL
Lake Charles, LA [*FM radio station call letters*] ... KOJO
Lake Charles, LA [*Television station call letters*] ... KPLC
Lake Charles, LA [*Television station call letters*] ... KVHP
Lake Charles, LA [*AM radio station call letters*] ... KXZZ
Lake Charles, LA [*FM radio station call letters*] ... KYKZ
Lake Charles, LA [*FM radio station call letters*] ... KZWA
Lake Charles, LA [*Location identifier FAA*] (FAAL) ... LCH
Lake Charles/Lake Charles [*Louisiana*] [*ICAO location identifier*] (ICLI) ... KLCH
Lake Charles Memorial Hospital [*Lake Charles, LA*] ... LCMH
Lake Charles Public Library, Lake Charles, LA [*Library symbol Library of Congress*] (LCLS) ... LLc
Lake City, AR [*FM radio station call letters*] (RBYB) ... KDXY-FM
Lake City Army Ammunition Plant (AABC) ... LCAAP
Lake City Elementary School, Lake City, MI [*Library symbol*] [*Library of Congress*] (LCLS) ... MiLacES
Lake City, FL [*AM radio station call letters*] ... WDSR
Lake City, FL [*AM radio station call letters*] ... WGRO
Lake City, FL [*FM radio station call letters*] ... WNFB
Lake City, FL [*FM radio station call letters*] ... WOLR
Lake City Graphic, Lake City, IA [*Library symbol Library of Congress*] (LCLS) ... IaLcG
Lake City High School, Lake City, MI [*Library symbol*] [*Library of Congress*] (LCLS) ... MiLacHS
Lake City, MI [*FM radio station call letters*] (RBYB) ... WNHB
Lake City, MN [*FM radio station call letters*] ... KMFX
Lake City Public Library, Lake City, CO [*Library symbol Library of Congress*] (LCLS) ... CoLc
Lake City Public Library, Lake City, CO [*Library symbol*] [*Library of Congress*] (LCLS) ... CoLcP
Lake City, SC [*AM radio station call letters*] ... WRIP
Lake City, SC [*FM radio station call letters*] ... WWFN
Lake County Library, Lakeview, OR [*Library symbol*] [*Library of Congress*] (LCLS) ... OrLak
Lake County Public Library, Leadville, CO [*Library symbol Library of Congress*] (LCLS) ... CoLe
Lake County Public Library, Merrillville, IN [*OCLC symbol*] (OCLC) ... ILC
Lake County Public Library, Merrillville, IN [*Library symbol Library of Congress*] (LCLS) ... InMerL
Lake County Star, Crown Point, IN [*Library symbol Library of Congress*] (LCLS) ... InCrpLS
Lake Dallas, TX [*Television station call letters*] ... KLDT
[*The*] **Lake Erie & Eastern Railroad Co.** [*AAR code*] ... LEE
Lake Erie & Fort Wayne Railroad Co. [*AAR code*] ... LEFW
[*The*] **Lake Erie & Northern Railway Co.** [*AAR code*] ... LEN
Lake Erie Cleanup Committee [*Defunct*] (EA) ... LECC
Lake Erie College [*Painesville, OH*] ... LEC
Lake Erie College, Painesville, OH [*OCLC symbol*] (OCLC) ... LEC
Lake Erie College, Painesville, OH [*Library symbol Library of Congress*] (LCLS) ... OPaL
Lake Erie Environmental Studies ... LEES
Lake Erie, Franklin & Clarion Railroad Co. [*AAR code*] ... LEF
Lake Erie Information Forecasting System [*Marine science*] (OSRA) ... LEIFS
Lake Erie Information Forecasting System (USDC) ... LEIFS
Lake Erie Regional Library, London, ON, Canada [*Library symbol Library of Congress*] (LCLS) ... CaOLLE
Lake Erie Regional Library System, London, Ontario [*Library symbol National Library of Canada*] (NLC) ... OLLE
Lake Erie Steam Association [*Defunct*] ... LESA
Lake Evaporation and Thermodynamics Model [*Marine science*] (OSRA) ... LETM
Lake Evaporation and Thermodynamics Model (USDC) ... LETM
Lake Evella [*Australia Airport symbol*] (OAG) ... LEL
Lake Exploration Module [*University of Wisconsin*] ... LEM
Lake Forest College [*Illinois*] ... LFC
Lake Forest College, Lake Forest, IL [*OCLC symbol*] (OCLC) ... IAK
Lake Forest College, Lake Forest, IL [*Library symbol Library of Congress*] (LCLS) ... ILfC
Lake Forest, IL [*FM radio station call letters*] ... WMXM
Lake Forest Library, Lake Forest, IL [*Library symbol Library of Congress*] (LCLS) ... ILf
Lake Forest Library, Lake Forest, IL [*OCLC symbol*] (OCLC) ... JAI
Lake Fork Canyon [*New Mexico*] [*Seismograph station code, US Geological Survey*] (SEIS) ... LFC
[*The*] **Lake Front Dock & Railroad Terminal Co.** [*Formerly, LDT*] [*AAR code*] ... LDRT
[*The*] **Lake Front Dock & Railroad Terminal Co.** [*Later, LDRT*] [*AAR code*] ... LDT
Lake Geneva Public Library, Lake Geneva, WI [*Library symbol Library of Congress*] (LCLS) ... WLag
Lake Geneva, WI [*AM radio station call letters*] (RBYB) ... WAUX
Lake Geneva, WI [*FM radio station call letters*] ... WLKG
Lake George [*Uganda*] [*ICAO location identifier*] (ICLI) ... HULA
Lake George, NY [*FM radio station call letters*] ... WCKM
Lake Harbour, NT [*ICAO location identifier*] (ICLI) ... CYLC
Lake Havasu Air Service [*ICAO designator*] (FAAC) ... HCA
Lake Havasu City [*Arizona*] [*Airport symbol*] (OAG) ... LHU
Lake Havasu City, AZ [*FM radio station call letters*] ... KBBC
Lake Havasu City, AZ [*AM radio station call letters*] ... KFWJ
Lake Havasu City, AZ [*FM radio station call letters*] ... KJCC
Lake Havasu City, AZ [*FM radio station call letters*] ... KNLB
Lake Havasu City, AZ [*FM radio station call letters*] ... KZUL
Lake Havasu City Public Library, Lake Havasu City, AZ [*Library symbol Library of Congress*] (LCLS) ... AzLhc
Lake Helena [*Montana*] [*Seismograph station code, US Geological Survey Closed*] (SEIS) ... LHM
Lake Hiawatha Public Library, Lake Hiawatha, NJ [*Library symbol Library of Congress*] (LCLS) ... NjLh
Lake Hopatcong Historical Society, Lake Hopatcong, NJ [*Library symbol Library of Congress*] (LCLS) ... NjLaHi
Lake Hughes, CA [*Location identifier FAA*] (FAAL) ... LHS
Lake Isabella, CA [*AM radio station call letters*] ... KVLI
Lake Isabella, CA [*FM radio station call letters*] ... KVLI-FM
Lake Itasca Forestry and Biological Station, Lake Itasca, MN [*Library symbol Library of Congress*] (LCLS) ... MnLaiL
Lake Jackson [*Texas*] [*Airport symbol*] (OAG) ... LJN
Lake Jackson, TX [*Location identifier FAA*] (FAAL) ... BRR
Lake Jackson, TX [*FM radio station call letters*] (RBYB) ... KTBZ
Lake Jackson, TX [*FM radio station call letters*] (RBYB) ... KYBJ

Lake Jackson, TX [*Location identifier FAA*] (FAAL) .... LBX
Lake Land College, Mattoon, IL [*Library symbol Library of Congress*] (LCLS) .... ImatLC
Lake Lillian Public Library, Lake Lillian, MN [*Library symbol*] [*Library of Congress*] (LCLS) .... MnLl
Lake Linden-Hubbell Public School Library, Lake Linden, MI [*Library symbol Library of Congress*] (LCLS) .... MiLaI
Lake Luzerne, NY [*FM radio station call letters*] .... WBAR
Lake Manyara [*Tanzania*] [*ICAO location identifier*] (ICLI) .... HTLM
Lake Mead National Recreation Area .... LAME
Lake Michigan College, Benton Harbor, MI [*Library symbol Library of Congress*] (LCLS) .... MiBhL
Lake Michigan Federation (EA) .... LMF
Lake Mills Graphic, Lake Mills, IA [*Library symbol Library of Congress*] (LCLS) .... IaLmG
Lake Minchumina [*Alaska*] [*Airport symbol*] (OAG) .... LMA
Lake Mountain [*Utah*] [*Seismograph station code, US Geological Survey*] (SEIS) .... LMU
Lake Murray [*Papua New Guinea*] [*Airport symbol*] (OAG) .... LMY
Lake Of The Ozarks [*Missouri*] [*Airport symbol*] (OAG) .... AIZ
Lake of the Woods High School, Baudette, MN [*Library symbol*] [*Library of Congress*] (LCLS) .... MnBauLH
Lake Ontario Cement Ltd. [*Toronto Stock Exchange symbol*] .... LOP
Lake Ontario Ordnance Works .... LOOW
Lake Ontario Regional Library System, Kingston, ON, Canada [*Library symbol Library of Congress*] (LCLS) .... CaOKL
Lake Ontario Regional Library System, Kingston, Ontario [*Library symbol Obsolete National Library of Canada*] (NLC) .... OKL
Lake Oswego High School, Lake Oswego, OR [*Library symbol Library of Congress*] (LCLS) .... OrLoHS
Lake Oswego Junior High School, Lake Oswego, OR [*Library symbol Library of Congress*] (LCLS) .... OrLoJS
Lake Oswego, OR [*FM radio station call letters*] .... KKJZ
Lake Oswego, OR [*AM radio station call letters*] (RBYB) .... KKSL
Lake Oswego Public Library, Lake Oswego, OR [*Library symbol Library of Congress*] (LCLS) .... OrLo
Lake Ozark, MO [*FM radio station call letters*] .... KQUL
Lake Park Elementary School, Lake Park, MN [*Library symbol*] [*Library of Congress*] (LCLS) .... MnLkpE
Lake Park High School, Lake Park, MN [*Library symbol*] [*Library of Congress*] (LCLS) .... MnLkpH
Lake Park News, Lake Park, IA [*Library symbol Library of Congress*] (LCLS) .... IaLpN
Lake Placid, FL [*AM radio station call letters*] .... WWTK
Lake Placid, NY [*Location identifier FAA*] (FAAL) .... LKP
Lake Placid, NY [*AM radio station call letters*] .... WIRD
Lake Placid, NY [*FM radio station call letters*] .... WLPW
Lake Placid Public Library, Lake Placid, NY [*Library symbol Library of Congress*] (LCLS) .... NLp
Lake Placid School of Art, Fine Arts Library, Lake Placid, NY [*Library symbol Library of Congress*] (LCLS) .... NLpSA
Lake Placid-Saranac Lake [*New York*] [*Airport symbol*] (AD) .... SLK
Lake Ponask Gold Corp. [*Toronto Stock Exchange symbol*] .... LPG
Lake Providence, LA [*Location identifier FAA*] (FAAL) .... BLE
Lake Providence, LA [*AM radio station call letters*] .... KLPL
Lake Providence, LA [*FM radio station call letters*] .... KLPL-FM
Lake Providence, Texarkana & Western R. R. [*AAR code*] .... LPTW
Lake Region Hospital, Fergus Falls, MN [*Library symbol Library of Congress*] (LCLS) .... MnFfH
Lake Region Junior College, Devils Lake, ND [*Library symbol Library of Congress*] (LCLS) .... NdDeL
Lake Reporting Service .... LRS
Lake Ronkonkoma, NY [*FM radio station call letters*] .... WSHR
Lake Shore & Michigan Southern Railway .... LS & MS
Lake Shore Hospital, Irving, NY [*Library symbol Library of Congress*] (LCLS) .... NIrvH
Lake Shore Mines Ltd. [*Toronto Stock Exchange symbol*] .... LKK
Lake State Airways [*ICAO designator*] (AD) .... NT
Lake Success, NY [*FM radio station call letters*] .... WYNY
Lake Superior (BARN) .... L Sup
Lake Superior & Ishpeming Railroad Co. [*AAR code*] .... LSI
Lake Superior State College [*Sault Ste. Marie, MI*] .... LSSC
Lake Superior State College, Sault Ste. Marie, MI [*OCLC symbol*] (OCLC) .... EZL
Lake Superior State College, Sault Ste. Marie, MI [*Library symbol Library of Congress*] (LCLS) .... MiSsL
Lake Superior State University [*Michigan*] .... LSSU
Lake Superior Terminal & Transfer Railway Co. [*AAR code*] .... LSTT
Lake Survey Center [*National Oceanic and Atmospheric Administration*] .... LSC
Lake Tahoe [*California*] [*Airport symbol*] (OAG) .... TVL
[*The*] **Lake Terminal Railroad Co.** [*AAR code*] .... LT
Lake Ventures Ltd. [*Vancouver Stock Exchange symbol*] .... LKV
Lake Vessel Reporting System .... LAVERS
Lake View Memorial Hospital, Doctor's Library, Danville, IL [*Library symbol Library of Congress*] (LCLS) .... IDanviL
Lake View Public Library, Lake View, IA [*Library symbol Library of Congress*] (LCLS) .... IaLv
Lake View Resort, Lake View, IA [*Library symbol Library of Congress*] (LCLS) .... IaLvR
Lake Villa District Library, Lake Villa, IL [*Library symbol Library of Congress*] (LCLS) ILv
Lake Villa District Library, Lake Villa, IL [*OCLC symbol*] (OCLC) .... JAS
Lake Village, AR [*FM radio station call letters*] (RBYB) .... KDTL-FM
Lake Village, AR [*FM radio station call letters*] .... KEGT
Lake Village, AR [*FM radio station call letters*] .... KUUZ
Lake Village Library, Lake Village, IN [*Library symbol Library of Congress*] (LCLS) .... InLv
Lake Wales, FL [*AM radio station call letters*] .... WIPC
Lake Warning [*or Weather*] **Bulletin** [*National Weather Service*] [*A publication*] .... LAWEB
Lake Wisdom [*Papua New Guinea*] [*Seismograph station code, US Geological Survey*] (SEIS) .... LKW
Lake Worth, FL [*Television station call letters*] .... WHBI
Lake Worth, FL [*AM radio station call letters*] .... WLVS
Lake Worth Public Library, Lake Worth, FL [*Library symbol Library of Congress*] (LCLS) .... FLw
Lakeba [*Fiji*] [*Airport symbol*] (OAG) .... LKB
Laked Kanamycin-Vancomycin [*Agar*] [*Microbiology*] .... LKV
Lakedell and Area Community Library, Westerose, Alberta [*Library symbol National Library of Canada*] (NLC) .... ALAAC
Lakefield Public Library, Ontario [*Library symbol National Library of Canada*] (NLC) .... OLA
Lakehead Pipe Line Partners Ltd. [*Associated Press*] (SAG) .... LakehdP
Lakehead Pipe Line Partners Ltd. [*NYSE symbol*] (SPSG) .... LHP
Lakehead Pipe Line Ptrs L.P. [*NYSE symbol*] (TTSB) .... LHP
Lakehead Psychiatric Hospital, Staff Library, Thunder Bay, ON, Canada [*Library symbol Library of Congress*] (LCLS) .... CaOTBLP
Lakehead University [*Thunder Bay*] [*Ontario*] [*Seismograph station code, US Geological Survey*] (SEIS) .... LHC
Lakehead University, Audio Library Services of Northwestern Ontario, Thunder Bay, ON, Canada [*Library symbol*] [*Library of Congress*] (LCLS) .... CaOTBLA
Lakehead University, Department of Geography, Thunder Bay, ON, Canada [*Library symbol Library of Congress*] (LCLS) .... CaOPALG
Lakehead University, Faculty of Education, Thunder Bay, ON, Canada [*Library symbol Library of Congress*] (LCLS) .... CaOPALE
Lakehead University Library [*UTLAS symbol*] .... LHD
Lakehead University School of Library Technology [*Canada*] .... LUSOLT
Lakehead University, School of Library Technology, Thunder Bay, ON, Canada [*Library symbol*] [*Library of Congress*] (LCLS) .... CaOTBLL
Lakehead University, Thunder Bay, ON, Canada [*Library symbol Library of Congress*] (LCLS) .... CAOPAL
Lakehead University, Thunder Bay, Ontario [*Library symbol National Library of Canada*] (NLC) .... OPAL
Lakehurst/Lakehurst Naval Air Station [*New Jersey*] [*ICAO location identifier*] (ICLI) .... KNEL
Lakehurst, NJ [*Location identifier FAA*] (FAAL) .... NEL
Lakehurst, NJ [*Location identifier FAA*] (FAAL) .... NFW
Lakeland [*Florida*] [*Airport symbol*] (AD) .... LAL
Lakeland [*ICAO designator*] (AD) .... YQ
Lakeland Aviation [*ICAO designator*] (FAAC) .... LKL
Lakeland College, Sheboygan, WI [*OCLC symbol*] (OCLC) .... WIL
Lakeland College, Sheboygan, WI [*Library symbol Library of Congress*] (LCLS) .... WSheL
Lakeland College, Vermilion, AB, Canada [*Library symbol Library of Congress*] (LCLS) .... CaAVC
Lakeland College, Vermilion, Alberta [*Library symbol National Library of Canada*] (NLC) .... AVC
Lakeland Counseling Center, Elkhorn, WI [*Library symbol Library of Congress*] (LCLS) .... WEILC
Lakeland First Fianancial Group, Inc. [*Associated Press*] (SAG) .... LakldFt
Lakeland, FL [*Location identifier FAA*] (FAAL) .... LAL
Lakeland, FL [*FM radio station call letters*] .... WCIE
Lakeland, FL [*AM radio station call letters*] .... WLKF
Lakeland, FL [*AM radio station call letters*] .... WONN
Lakeland, FL [*FM radio station call letters*] (RBYB) .... WSJT-FM
Lakeland, FL [*Television station call letters*] .... WTMV
Lakeland, FL [*AM radio station call letters*] .... WWAB
Lakeland, FL [*FM radio station call letters*] .... WYFO
Lakeland, GA [*FM radio station call letters*] .... WHFE
Lakeland Hospital, Elkhorn, WI [*Library symbol Library of Congress*] (LCLS) .... WEIL
Lakeland Indus [*NASDAQ symbol*] (TTSB) .... LAKE
Lakeland Industries, Inc. [*NASDAQ symbol*] (SAG) .... LAKE
Lakeland Industries, Inc. [*Associated Press*] (SAG) .... Lakelnd
Lakeland Library Cooperative [*Library network*] LLC
Lakeland Library Region, North Battleford, Saskatchewan [*Library symbol National Library of Canada*] (NLC) .... SNB
Lakeland Library Region, North Battleford, SK, Canada [*Library symbol Library of Congress*] (LCLS) .... CaSNB
Lakeland Public Library, Lakeland, FL [*Library symbol*] [*Library of Congress*] (LCLS) .... FLl
Lakeland Regional Library, Killarney, Manitoba [*Library symbol National Library of Canada*] (NLC) .... MKL
Lakeland Regional Library, Killarney, MB, Canada [*Library symbol Library of Congress*] (LCLS) .... CaMKL
Lakeland Village School, Medical Lake, WA [*Library symbol Library of Congress*] (LCLS) .... WaMeL
Lakemba [*Fiji*] [*ICAO location identifier*] (ICLI) .... NFNK
Lakenheath [*British ICAO location identifier*] (ICLI) .... EGUL
Lakeport, CA [*FM radio station call letters*] .... KNTI
Lakeport, CA [*AM radio station call letters*] .... KXBX
Lakeport, CA [*FM radio station call letters*] .... KXBX-FM
Lakeport Carnegie Public Library, Lakeport, CA [*Library symbol Library of Congress*] (LCLS) .... CLp
Laker Airways [*ICAO designator*] (AD) .... GK
Laker Airways (Bahamas) Ltd. [*ICAO designator*] (FAAC) .... LBH
Laker Resources [*Vancouver Stock Exchange symbol*] .... LAK
Lakeridge High School, Lake Oswego, OR [*Library symbol Library of Congress*] (LCLS) .... OrLoLHS

Lakes [*Commonly used*] (OPSA) ..... LAKES
Lakes [*Commonly used*] (OPSA) ..... LKS
Lakes ..... LKS
Lakes District Museum, Burns Lake, BC, Canada [*Library symbol*] [*Library of Congress*] (LCLS) ..... CaBBLM
Lakes District Museum, Burns Lake, British Columbia [*Library symbol National Library of Canada*] (NLC) ..... BBLM
Lakes Region Sled Dog Club (EA) ..... LRSDC
Lakeshore General Hospital, Community Health Department, Montreal, PQ, Canada [*Library symbol*] [*Library of Congress*] (LCLS) ..... CaQMLGC
Lakeshore General Hospital, Pointe-Claire, PQ, Canada [*Library symbol Library of Congress*] (LCLS) ..... CaQMLG
Lakeshore General Hospital [*Hopital General du Lakeshore*] **Pointe-Claire, Quebec** [*Library symbol National Library of Canada*] (NLC) ..... QMLG
Lakeshore Mental Health Institute, Staff Library, Knoxville, TN [*Library symbol Library of Congress*] (LCLS) ..... TKLMI
Lakeshore Technical Institute, Educational Resource Center, Cleveland, WI [*Library symbol Library of Congress*] (LCLS) ..... WClI
Lakeside & Marblehead R. R. [*AAR code*] ..... LSM
Lakeside Aviation Ltd. [*British ICAO designator*] (FAAC) ..... LKS
Lakeside Elementary School, Merrick, NY [*Library symbol*] [*Library of Congress*] (LCLS) ..... NMerkLE
Lakeside Hospital, Cleveland, OH [*Library symbol Library of Congress*] (LCLS) ..... OClLH
Lakeside Hospital, Copiague, NY [*Library symbol Library of Congress*] (LCLS) ..... NCopH
Lakeside Hospital, Kansas City, MO [*Library symbol Library of Congress*] (LCLS) ..... MoKLH
Lakeside Hospital, Memphis, TN [*Library symbol Library of Congress*] (LCLS) ..... TML
Lakeside Intermediate Media Center, Chisago City, MN [*Library symbol*] [*Library of Congress*] (LCLS) ..... MnCgL
Lakeside Laboratories, Inc. [*Research code symbol*] ..... EX
Lakeside Laboratories, Inc. [*Research code symbol*] ..... JB
Lakeside Laboratories, Milwaukee, WI [*Library symbol Library of Congress*] (LCLS) ..... WML
Lakeside Public Library, Lakeside, AZ [*Library symbol Library of Congress*] (LCLS) ..... AzLa
Lake-Sumter Community College, Leesburg, FL [*Library symbol Library of Congress*] (LCLS) ..... FLeL
Lakeview Financial [*NASDAQ symbol*] (TTSB) ..... LVSB
Lakeview Financial Corp. [*Associated Press*] (SAG) ..... LakevwF
Lakeview Financial Corp. [*NASDAQ symbol*] (SAG) ..... LVSB
Lakeview, MI [*FM radio station call letters*] ..... WPLB
Lakeview, OR [*Location identifier FAA*] (FAAL) ..... GOS
Lakeview, OR [*AM radio station call letters*] ..... KQIK
Lakeview, OR [*FM radio station call letters*] ..... KQIK-FM
Lakeview, OR [*Location identifier FAA*] (FAAL) ..... LKV
Lakeview Public Library, Rockville Centre, NY [*Library symbol Library of Congress*] (LCLS) ..... NRockL
Lakeview School, Worthington, MN [*Library symbol*] [*Library of Congress*] (LCLS) ..... MnWoLS
Lakeville Elementary School, Great Neck, NY [*Library symbol Library of Congress*] (LCLS) ..... NGrnLE
Lakeville, MN [*FM radio station call letters*] ..... KREV
Lakeville, MN [*Location identifier FAA*] (FAAL) ..... LVN
Lakewide Management Plan [*Great Lakes*] [*Environmental Protection Agency*] ..... LAMP
Lakewood Board of Education, Lakewood, OH [*Inactive*] [*OCLC symbol*] (OCLC) ..... LBE
Lakewood Board of Education, Lakewood, OH [*Library symbol Library of Congress*] (LCLS) ..... OLakB
Lakewood, CO [*FM radio station call letters*] ..... KWMX
Lakewood, CO [*AM radio station call letters*] ..... KYGO
Lakewood Community College, White Bear Lake, MN [*Library symbol Library of Congress*] (LCLS) ..... MnWbIL
Lakewood Elementary School, Duluth, MN [*Library symbol*] [*Library of Congress*] (LCLS) ..... MnDuLWE
Lakewood Forest Products Ltd. [*Vancouver Stock Exchange symbol*] ..... LST
Lakewood General Hospital and Convalescent Center, Tacoma, WA [*Library symbol Library of Congress*] (LCLS) ..... WaTLG
Lakewood Golf Course [*California*] [*Seismograph station code, US Geological Survey*] (SEIS) ..... LGC
Lakewood Mining [*Vancouver Stock Exchange symbol*] ..... LKW
Lakewood, NJ [*AM radio station call letters*] ..... WOBM
Lakewood Public Library, Lakewood, NJ [*Library symbol Library of Congress*] (LCLS) ..... NjLak
Lakewood Public Library, Lakewood, OH [*OCLC symbol*] (OCLC) ..... LAP
Lakewood Public Library, Lakewood, OH [*Library symbol Library of Congress*] (LCLS) ..... OLak
Lakewood Regional Library, Lakewood, CO [*Library symbol Library of Congress*] (LCLS) ..... CoLak
Lakewood, WA [*AM radio station call letters*] ..... KLAY
Lakewood, WA [*FM radio station call letters*] (RBYB) ..... KNTB-FM
Lakewood, WA [*AM radio station call letters*] ..... KNTE
Lakey Clinic Medical Center [*Burlington, MA*] LC
Laki-Lorand Factor [*Factor XIII*] [*Also, FSF Hematology*] ..... LLF
Lakin, KS [*Television station call letters*] ..... KSWK
Lakselv [*Norway*] [*Airport symbol*] (OAG) ..... LKL
Lal [*Afghanistan*] [*ICAO location identifier*] (ICLI) ..... OALL
L-Alanine [*Biochemistry*] (DAVI) ..... L-Ala
Lali [*Iran*] [*ICAO location identifier*] (ICLI) ..... OIAL
Lalibela [*Ethiopia*] [*ICAO location identifier*] (ICLI) ..... HALL
Lalibella [*Ethiopia*] [*Airport symbol*] (OAG) LLI
Lalitpur [*India*] [*ICAO location identifier*] (ICLI) ..... VILP
Lalmonirhat [*Bangladesh*] [*Airport symbol*] (AD) ..... LLJ
Lalmonirhat [*Bangladesh*] [*ICAO location identifier*] (ICLI) ..... VGLM
Lalor's Cyclopaedia of Political Science, Political Economy, Etc. [*A publication*] (DLA) ..... Lalor Pol Econ
Lalor's Law of Real Property [*A publication*] (DLA) ..... Lal RP
Lalor's Supplement to Hill and Denio's New York Reports [*A publication*] (DLA) ..... H & D
Lalor's Supplement to Hill and Denio's New York Reports [*A publication*] (DLA) ..... Hill & D
Lalor's Supplement to Hill and Denio's New York Reports [*A publication*] (DLA) ..... Hill & Den
Lalor's Supplement to Hill and Denio's New York Reports [*A publication*] (DLA) ..... Hill & Den Supp
Lalor's Supplement to Hill and Denio's New York Reports [*A publication*] (DLA) ..... L Sup H & D
Lalor's Supplement to Hill and Denio's New York Reports [*A publication*] (DLA) ..... Lalor
Lalor's Supplement to Hill and Denio's New York Reports [*A publication*] (DLA) ..... Lalor Supp
Lalor's Supplement to Hill and Denio's New York Reports [*A publication*] (DLA) ..... Lalor's Supp
Lalor's Supplement to Hill and Denio's New York Reports [*A publication*] (DLA) ..... Lalor's Supp (Hill and Denio)
Lalouila [*Congo*] [*ICAO location identifier*] (ICLI) ..... FCBA
L'Alpe D'Huez [*France ICAO location identifier*] (ICLI) ..... LFHU
Lam Research [*NASDAQ symbol*] (TTSB) ..... LRCX
Lam Research Corp. [*Associated Press*] (SAG) ..... LamRsch
Lam Research Corp. [*NASDAQ symbol*] (SAG) ..... LRCX
LAMA [*Library Administration and Management Association*] **Buildings and Equipment Section** ..... LAMA BES
Lama Foundation (EA) ..... LA
Lama Foundation (EA) ..... LF
LAMA [*Library Administration and Management Association*] **Fund Raising and Financial Development Section** ..... LAMA FRFDS
LAMA [*Library Administration and Management Association*] **Library Organization and Management Section** ..... LAMA LOMS
LAMA [*Library Administration and Management Association*] **Personnel Administration Section** ..... LAMA PAS
LAMA [*Library Administration and Management Association*] **Public Relations Section** ..... LAMA PRS
LAMA [*Library Administration and Management Association*] **Statistics Section** ..... LAMA SS
LAMA [*Library Administration and Management Association*] **Systems and Services Section** ..... LAMA SASS
LAMA [*Library Administration and Management Association*] **Systems and Services Section** ..... LAMA SSS
Lamacarena [*Colombia*] [*Airport symbol Obsolete*] (OAG) ..... LMC
LaMan Corp. [*Associated Press*] (SAG) ..... LaMan
Lamap [*New Hebrides*] [*Seismograph station code, US Geological Survey*] (SEIS) ..... LMP
Lamap [*Vanuatu*] [*Airport symbol*] (OAG) ..... LPM
Lamap [*Vanuatu*] [*ICAO location identifier*] (ICLI) ..... NVSL
Lamar [*Colorado*] [*Airport symbol*] (OAG) ..... LAA
Lamar Carnegie Public Library, Lamar, CO [*Library symbol Library of Congress*] (LCLS) ..... CoLam
Lamar, CO [*AM radio station call letters*] ..... KLMR
Lamar, CO [*FM radio station call letters*] ..... KSEC
Lamar, CO [*FM radio station call letters*] ..... KVAY
Lamar, CO [*Location identifier FAA*] (FAAL) ..... LAA
Lamar Community College, Lamar, CO [*Library symbol Library of Congress*] (LCLS) ..... CoLamC
Lamar, MO [*FM radio station call letters*] ..... KHST
Lamar, MO [*Location identifier FAA*] (FAAL) ..... LLU
Lamar University (GAGS) ..... Lamar U
Lamar University, Beaumont, TX [*Library symbol Library of Congress*] (LCLS) ..... TxBeaL
Lamar University, Beaumont, TX [*OCLC symbol*] (OCLC) ..... TXR
Lamar University-Orange, Orange, TX [*Library symbol*] [*Library of Congress*] (LCLS) ..... TxOrL
Lamarck [*Biology*] (BARN) ..... Lam
Lamar's Reports [*25-40 Florida*] [*A publication*] (DLA) ..... Lamar
Lamas [*Peru*] [*ICAO location identifier*] (ICLI) ..... SPSL
Lamb Committee (EA) LC
Lamb Dysentery Bacillus [*Medicine*] (DMAA) ..... LDB
Lamb Weather Type [*Meteorology*] ..... LWT
Lamba [*MARC language code Library of Congress*] (LCCP) ..... lam
Lambair Ltd. [*Canada ICAO designator*] (FAAC) ..... LWL
Lambard's Archaionomia [*A publication*] (DLA) ..... Lamb
Lambard's Archaionomia [*A publication*] (DLA) ..... Lamb Arch
Lambard's Archaionomia [*A publication*] (DLA) ..... Lamb Archaion
Lambard's Archeion [*1635*] [*A publication*] (DLA) ..... Lamb
Lambard's Archeion [*1635*] [*A publication*] (ILCA) ..... Lamb Arch
Lambard's Duties of Constables, Etc. [*A publication*] (DLA) ..... Lamb Const
Lambard's Eirenarcha [*A publication*] (DLA) ..... Eir
Lambard's Eirenarcha [*A publication*] (DLA) ..... Lamb
Lambard's Eirenarcha [*A publication*] (DLA) ..... Lamb Eir
Lambard's Eirenarcha [*A publication*] (DLA) ..... Lamb Eiren
Lambard's Explication [*A publication*] (DLA) ..... Lamb
Lambard's Explication [*A publication*] (DLA) ..... Lamb Explic
Lambarene [*Gabon*] [*ICAO location identifier*] (ICLI) ..... FOGR
Lambarene [*Gabon*] [*Airport symbol*] (OAG) ..... LBQ
Lambasa [*Fiji*] [*ICAO location identifier*] (ICLI) ..... NFNL
Lambda (WDAA) L
Lambda Alpha ..... LA
Lambda Amateur Radio Club (EA) ..... LARC

Lambda Book Report [A publication] (BRI) .... Lam Bk Rpt
Lambda Gamma Delta [Society] .... LGD
Lambda Kappa Sigma (EA) .... LKS
Lambda Legal Defense and Education Fund (EA) .... LLDEF
Lambda Limiting Process .... LLP
Lambda Mercantile Corp. [Toronto Stock Exchange symbol] .... LME
Lambeg Industrial Research Association [British] (IRUK) .... LIRA
Lambert [Unit of luminance] [Preferred unit is lx, Lux] L
Lambert (IDOE) L
Lambert [Unit of luminance] [Preferred unit is lx, Lux] (ADA) .... La
Lambert [Unit of luminance] [Preferred unit is lx, Lux] .... Lam
Lambert Cosine Law [Physics] LCL
Lambert-Eaton Myasthenic Syndrome [Medicine] .... LES
Lamberton Public Library, Lamberton, MN [Library symbol] [Library of
   Congress] (LCLS) .... MnLam
Lamberton School, Lamberton, MN [Library symbol] [Library of Congress]
   (LCLS) .... MnLamS
Lambert's Law of Dower [A publication] (DLA) .... Lamb Dow
Lambertus de Ramponibus [Deceased, 1304] [Authority cited in pre-1607
   legal work] (DSA) .... La de Rampo
Lambertus de Ramponibus [Deceased, 1304] [Authority cited in pre-1607
   legal work] (DSA) .... Lab
Lambertus de Ramponibus [Deceased, 1304] [Authority cited in pre-1607
   legal work] (DSA) .... Lam
Lambertus de Ramponibus [Deceased, 1304] [Authority cited in pre-1607
   legal work] (DSA) .... Lamb de Ramp
Lambertus de Salinis [Flourished, 14th century] [Authority cited in pre-1607
   legal work] (DSA) .... Lamber de Sal
Lambertville Beacon, Lambertville, NJ [Library symbol Library of Congress]
   (LCLS) .... NjLamB
Lambeth [Degrees granted by Archbishop of Canterbury] [British] (ROG) .... LAMB
Lambeth Information Network [Information service or system] [British]
   (NITA) .... LINK
Lambeth Public Libraries, Tate Central Library, London, United Kingdom
   [Library symbol Library of Congress] (LCLS) .... UkLLT
Lamborghini Club America (EA) .... LCA
Lambourne [England] .... LAMB
Lamb-Retherford Shift [Physics] .... LRS
Lamb's Reports [103-105 Wisconsin] [A publication] (DLA) .... Lamb
Lambton College of Applied Arts and Technology, Sarnia, ON, Canada
   [Library symbol Library of Congress] (LCLS) .... CaOSLC
Lambton College of Applied Arts and Technology, Sarnia, Ontario [Library
   symbol National Library of Canada] (NLC) .... OSLC
Lambton County Public Library, Wyoming, ON, Canada [Library symbol
   Library of Congress] (LCLS) .... CaOWyL
Lambton County Public Library, Wyoming, Ontario [Library symbol National
   Library of Canada] (NLC) .... OWYL
Lambuth College, Jackson, TN [Library symbol Library of Congress]
   (LCLS) .... TJaLam
Lamda Airlines [Greece] [ICAO designator] (FAAC) .... LMD
Lamellar Body [Physiology] .... LB
Lamellar Keratoplasty [Ophthalmology] .... LKP
Lamellar Phase [Physical chemistry] .... La
Lamellar Strip [Botany] .... LS
Lamen Bay [Vanuata] [Airport symbol] (OAG) .... LNB
Lamen-Bay [Vanuatu] [ICAO location identifier] (ICLI) .... NVSM
Lameness [Used by immigration officials] [Obsolete] L
Lamentation over the Destruction of Sumer and Ur (BJA) .... LSU
Lamentations [Old Testament book] (BJA) .... La
Lamentations [Old Testament book] .... Lam
Lamentations [Old Testament book] .... LM
Lamentations over the Destruction of Ur (BJA) .... LU
Lamentations Rabbah (BJA) .... LamR
Lamerd [Iran] [ICAO location identifier] (ICLI) .... OISR
Lamesa, TX [FM radio station call letters] .... KIOL
Lamesa, TX [FM radio station call letters] .... KMMX
Lamesa, TX [AM radio station call letters] .... KPET
Lamesa, TX [Location identifier FAA] (FAAL) .... LSA
Lametia-Terme [Italy] [Airport symbol] (OAG) .... SUF
Lamezia/Terme [Italy ICAO location identifier] (ICLI) .... LICA
Lamidada [Nepal] [ICAO location identifier] (ICLI) .... VNLD
Lamidanda [Nepal] [Airport symbol] (OAG) .... LDN
Lamina [Medicine] (DAVI) .... LAM
Lamina Densa [Dermatology] .... LD
Lamina Lucida [Dermatology] LL
Lamina Monopolar Cell [Cytology] .... LMC
Lamina Precursor Cell [Neurology] .... LPC
Lamina Propria Lymphocyte [Hematology] .... LPL
Laminar Air Flow Room (DMAA) .... LAFR
Laminar Air Navigation and Anticollision [Air Force] .... LANAC
Laminar Airflow (KSC) .... LAF
Laminar Airflow Room [Medicine] (DAVI) .... LaFr
Laminar Airflow Unit [Medicine] (DAVI) .... LAFU
Laminar Angular Rate Sensor [Navy] .... LARS
Laminar Boundary Layer .... LBL
Laminar Boundary-Layer Separation .... LBLS
Laminar Boundary-Layer Separation .... LBS
Laminar Defect Examination (IEEE) .... LDE
Laminar Flow Control [Aerodynamics] .... LFC
Laminar Flow Element [Engineering] .... LFE
Laminar Flow Torch [For plasma generation] .... LFT
Laminar Flow Zone .... LFZ
Laminar-Flow Reactor [Engineering] .... LFR
Laminate (MSA) .... LAM
Laminate .... LMNT

Laminate Council of America [Defunct] (EA) .... LCA
Laminated (VRA) .... lam
Laminated (WDMC) .... lam
Laminated .... LAMTD
Laminated Diatom Ooze [Oceanography] .... LDO
Laminated Ferrite Memory System (MCD) .... LFMS
Laminated Fiberglass Insulation Producers Association [Defunct] (EA) .... LFIPA
Laminated Foil Manufacturers' Association [Defunct] .... LFMA
Laminated Metal Part .... LMP
Laminated Object Manufacturing [Desktop manufacturing] .... LOM
Laminated Overlay Transistor [Electronics] (IAA) .... LOT
Laminated Plastics Fabricators Association [British] (BI) .... LPFA
Laminated Polyethylene Film .... LP
Laminated Safety Glass [Automotive engineering] .... LSG
Laminated SONAR Transistor .... LST
Laminated Synthetic High Voltage .... LSHV
Laminated TEFLON .... LT
Laminated-Veneer Lumber LVL
Laminating .... LMNTNG
Laminating Materials Association [Oradell, NJ] (EA) .... LMA
Laminating Technologies, Inc. [Associated Press] (SAG) .... Lamin
Laminating Technologies, Inc. [Associated Press] (SAG) .... Laminat
Laminating Technologies, Inc. [NASDAQ symbol] (SAG) .... LAMT
Laminators Safety Glass Association (EA) .... LSGA
Laminectomy [Medicine] .... LAM
Laminectomy and Fusion [Medicine] (DAVI) .... lam & fus
Lamington [Papua New Guinea] [Seismograph station code, US Geological
   Survey] (SEIS) .... LMG
Laminin A (DMAA) .... LAMA
Laminin B Receptor (DMAA) .... LAMBR
Laminin C (DMAA) .... LAMC
L-Amino Acid Oxidase [An enzyme] .... LAAO
Laminogram (MAE) .... lam
Laminotomy [Medicine] (DAVI) .... lami
Lamium Mild Mosaic Virus [Plant pathology] .... LMMV
Lamocks [Republic of China] [Seismograph station code, US Geological
   Survey] (SEIS) .... LMC
LaMoille Community Unit, School District 303, LaMoille, IL [Library symbol
   Library of Congress] (LCLS) .... ILamSD
Lamoille Valley Railroad Co. [AAR code] .... LVRC
LaMoille-Clarion District Library, LaMoille, IL [Library symbol Library of
   Congress] (LCLS) .... ILam
Lamoni Chronicle, Lamoni, IA [Library symbol Library of Congress] (LCLS) .... IaLC
Lamoni, IA [Location identifier FAA] (FAAL) .... LMN
Lamoni Public Library, Lamoni, IA [Library symbol Library of Congress]
   (LCLS) .... IaL
Lamoni Public Library, Lamoni, IA [Library symbol] [Library of Congress]
   (LCLS) .... IaLL
Lamont Doherty Geological Observatory [Marine science] (OSRA) .... LDGO
Lamont Geological Observatory [Later, L-DGO] [Columbia University] .... LGO
Lamont Leader, Lamont, IA [Library symbol Library of Congress]
   (LCLS) .... IaLamtL
Lamont Public Library, Alberta [Library symbol National Library of Canada]
   (NLC) .... ALAM
Lamont Public Library, Lamont, AB, Canada [Library symbol] [Library of
   Congress] (LCLS) .... CaALam
Lamont-Doherty Geological Observatory [Formerly, LGO] [Columbia
   University] .... L-DGO
Lamp L
Lamp [Automotive engineering] .... LP
Lamp and Shade Institute of America [Defunct] (EA) .... LSIA
Lamp Dimmer Unit (MCD) .... LDU
Lamp Driver .... LD
Lamp Heat Flux .... LHF
Lamp Lumen Depreciation .... LLD
Lamp of Hope Project [An association] (EA) .... LHP
Lamp Oil .... LO
Lampang [Thailand] [Seismograph station code, US Geological Survey]
   (SEIS) .... LPT
Lampang [Thailand] [Airport symbol] (OAG) .... LPT
Lampang [Thailand] [ICAO location identifier] (ICLI) .... VTCL
Lampasas, TX [AM radio station call letters] .... KCYL
Lampasas, TX [FM radio station call letters] .... KUTZ
Lampasas, TX [Location identifier FAA] (FAAL) .... LZZ
Lampblack .... LMPBLK
Lampedusa [Italy ICAO location identifier] (ICLI) .... LICD
Lampedusa [Italy] [Airport symbol] (OAG) .... LMP
Lampholder .... LPHLDR
Lamphole (ABBR) .... LH
Lamport & Holt Line [Steamship] (MHDB) .... L & H
Lamp-Pumped LASER (MCD) .... LPL
LAMPS [Light Airborne Multipurpose System] Element Coordinator [Navy]
   (CAAL) .... LEC
LAMPS Shipboard Element (MCD) .... LASE
Lamsn & Sessions [NYSE symbol] (TTSB) .... LMS
[The] Lamson & Sessions Co. [Associated Press] (SAG) .... LamSes
[The] Lamson & Sessions Co. [NYSE symbol] (SPSG) .... LMS
Lamto [Ivory Coast] [Seismograph station code, US Geological Survey]
   (SEIS) LIC
Lamu [Kenya] [ICAO location identifier] (ICLI) .... HKLU
Lamu [Kenya] [Airport symbol] (OAG) .... LAU
LAN [Linked Access Network] Automatic Inventory [Brightwork Development,
   Inc.] [Computer science] (PCM) .... LAI
Lan Chile [Airline flight code] (ODBW) .... LA

LAN [*Local Area Network*] **Dealers Association** (CDE) .... LANDA
LAN [*Local Area Network*] **Emulation** [*Computer science*] .... LE
LAN [*Local Area Network*] **Emulation Client** [*Telecommunications*] (ACRL) .... LEC
LAN [*Local Area Network*] **Emulation Configuration Server** [*Telecommunications*] (ACRL) .... LECS
LAN [*Local Area Network*] **Emulation Server** [*Telecommunications*] (ACRL) .... LES
LAN [*Local Area Network*] **Interface Card** (PCM) .... LANIC
LAN [*Linked Access Network*] **Network Manager** .... LNM
LAN [*Linked Access Network*]/WAN Exchange [*Wide Area Network*] [*Telecommunications*] .... LWX
Lana Gold Corp. [*Vancouver Stock Exchange symbol*] .... LAL
Lanai City [*Hawaii*] [*Airport symbol*] (OAG) .... LNY
Lanai City, HI [*FM radio station call letters*] .... KONI
Lanai City, Lanai Island [*Hawaii*] [*ICAO location identifier*] (ICLI) .... PHNY
Lanark Union Public Library, Lanark, Ontario [*Library symbol National Library of Canada*] (BIB) .... OLAU
Lanarkshire [*County in Scotland*] .... LAN
Lanarkshire Rifle Volunteers [*British military*] (DMA) .... LRV
Lancashire [*County in England*] .... LANCS
Lancashire & Yorkshire Railway [*British*] .... LYR
Lancashire Enterprise Ltd. [*British*] (ECON) .... LEL
Lancashire Flats [*British*] (DCTA) L
[*The*] **Lancashire Fusiliers** [*Military unit*] [*British*] .... LF
Lancashire Hussars Yeomanry [*British military*] (DMA) .... LHY
Lancashire Rifle Volunteers [*British military*] (DMA) .... LRV
Lancashire Volunteer Artillery [*British military*] (DMA) .... LVA
Lancaster [*Postcode*] (ODBW) .... LA
Lancaster [*England*] (ROG) .... LANC
Lancaster [*Pennsylvania*] [*Airport symbol*] (OAG) .... LNS
Lancaster & Chester Railway Co. [*AAR code*] LC
Lancaster Bible College, Lancaster, PA [*OCLC symbol*] (OCLC) .... LBB
Lancaster Branch, Stormont, Dundas, and Glengarry County Library, Ontario [*Library symbol National Library of Canada*] (BIB) .... OLSDG
Lancaster, CA [*Location identifier FAA*] (FAAL) .... GWF
Lancaster, CA [*AM radio station call letters*] .... KAVL
Lancaster, CA [*FM radio station call letters*] .... KGMX
Lancaster, CA [*AM radio station call letters*] .... KHJJ
Lancaster, CA [*FM radio station call letters*] (RBYB) .... KTLW
Lancaster, CA [*Location identifier FAA*] (FAAL) .... WJF
Lancaster Colony [*NASDAQ symbol*] (SAG) .... LANC
Lancaster Colony [*Associated Press*] (SAG) .... Lancastr
Lancaster County Historical Society, Lancaster, PA [*Library symbol Library of Congress*] (LCLS) .... PLHi
Lancaster County Library, Lancaster, PA [*OCLC symbol*] (OCLC) .... LKC
Lancaster County Library, Lancaster, PA [*Library symbol Library of Congress*] (LCLS) .... PL
Lancaster County Library, Lancaster, SC [*Library symbol*] [*Library of Congress*] (LCLS) .... ScLan
Lancaster Finishing School [*British military*] (DMA) .... LFS
Lancaster, KY [*AM radio station call letters*] .... WKYY
Lancaster, KY [*FM radio station call letters*] .... WRNZ
Lancaster Law Review [*A publication*] (DLA) .... Lanc L Rev
Lancaster Law Review [*A publication*] (DLA) .... Lanc Law Rev
Lancaster Law Review [*A publication*] (DLA) .... LLR
Lancaster Mennonite Conference Historical Society, Lancaster, PA [*Library symbol Library of Congress*] (LCLS) .... PLMHi
Lancaster Mennonite Historical Society (EA) .... LMHS
Lancaster, NY [*AM radio station call letters*] .... WXRL
Lancaster, OH [*Location identifier FAA*] (FAAL) .... LHQ
Lancaster, OH [*FM radio station call letters*] .... WFCO
Lancaster, OH [*FM radio station call letters*] .... WHOK
Lancaster, OH [*AM radio station call letters*] .... WLOH
Lancaster, OH [*FM radio station call letters*] .... WSWZ
Lancaster, PA [*Location identifier FAA*] (FAAL) .... LRP
Lancaster, PA [*FM radio station call letters*] .... WDAC
Lancaster, PA [*FM radio station call letters*] .... WFNM
Lancaster, PA [*Television station call letters*] .... WGAL
Lancaster, PA [*FM radio station call letters*] .... WJTL
Lancaster, PA [*AM radio station call letters*] .... WLAN
Lancaster, PA [*FM radio station call letters*] .... WLAN-FM
Lancaster, PA [*FM radio station call letters*] .... WLCH
Lancaster, PA [*AM radio station call letters*] .... WLPA
Lancaster, PA [*Television station call letters*] .... WLYH
Lancaster, PA [*FM radio station call letters*] .... WROZ
Lancaster Public School, Lancaster, MN [*Library symbol*] [*Library of Congress*] (LCLS) .... MnLanS
Lancaster Resources [*Vancouver Stock Exchange symbol*] .... LCS
Lancaster Review [*Pennsylvania*] [*A publication*] (DLA) .... Lanc Rev
Lancaster, SC [*Location identifier FAA*] (FAAL) .... LKR
Lancaster, SC [*AM radio station call letters*] .... WAGL
Lancaster, SC [*FM radio station call letters*] .... WRHM
Lancaster Theological Seminary of the United Church of Christ, Lancaster, PA [*Library symbol Library of Congress*] (LCLS) .... PLT
Lancaster Town Library, Lancaster, MA [*Library symbol Library of Congress*] (LCLS) .... MLanc
Lancaster, TX [*Location identifier FAA*] (FAAL) .... LNC
Lancaster, WI [*AM radio station call letters*] .... WGLR
Lancaster, WI [*FM radio station call letters*] .... WGLR-FM
Lancaster, WI [*FM radio station call letters*] .... WJTY
Lancastrian [*Of the royal house of Lancaster*] [*British*] (ROG) .... LA
Lancastrian Volunteers [*British military*] (DMA) LV
Lance (WGA) .... LCE
Lance .... LNC
Lance Corporal [*Marine Corps*] E3
Lance Corporal LC
Lance Corporal .... LCPL
Lance Havidar [*Military British*] .... L/Hadr
Lance, Inc. [*Associated Press*] (SAG) .... Lance
Lance, Inc. [*NASDAQ symbol*] (SAG) .... LNCE
Lance Information Retrieval System .... LIRS
Lance Sergeant [*British military*] (DMA) .... L/Sgt
Lance-Bombardier [*British military*] (DMA) .... L/Bdr
Lance-Bubbling-Equilibrium [*Steelmaking*] .... LBE
Lance-Corporal [*Military British*] (ROG) .... L-CORP
Lance-Corporal of Horse [*British military*] (DMA) .... L/COH
Lancellottus [*Authority cited in pre-1607 legal work*] (DSA) .... Lanc
Lancellottus Galiaula [*Flourished, 16th century*] [*Authority cited in pre-1607 legal work*] (DSA) .... Lancell Galiaul
Lance-Naik [*British military*] (DMA) .... L/Nk
Lancer [*Military British*] (ROG) .... LANC
Lancer [*Military British*] (DMA) .... Lr
Lancer Corp. [*AMEX symbol*] (SPSG) .... LAN
Lancer Corp. [*Associated Press*] (SAG) .... Lancer
Lancer Orthodontics [*NASDAQ symbol*] (TTSB) .... LANZ
Lancer Orthodontics, Inc. [*NASDAQ symbol*] (SAG) .... LANZ
Lancer Orthodontics, Inc. [*Associated Press*] (SAG) .... LncrOrt
Lancer Resources [*Vancouver Stock Exchange symbol*] .... LNC
Lancers L
Lanchow [*Republic of China*] [*Seismograph station code, US Geological Survey Closed*] (SEIS) .... LAN
Lanchow [*Republic of China*] [*Seismograph station code, US Geological Survey*] (SEIS) .... LZH
Lancia Motor Club [*Ledbury, Herefordshire, England*] (EAIO) .... LMC
Lancit Media Productions [*NASDAQ symbol*] (TTSB) .... LNCT
Lancit Media Productions Ltd. [*Associated Press*] (SAG) .... Lancit
Lancit Media Productions Ltd. [*NASDAQ symbol*] (SAG) .... LNCT
LanClient Control Manager [*Computer science*] .... LCCM
Land L
Land [*Postal Service standard*] (OPSA) .... LAND
Land .... LD
Land Acoustical Monitoring System [*NASA*] .... LAMS
Land Acquisition and Management Schemes [*British*] .... LAMS
Land Agent [*Ministry of Agriculture, Fisheries, and Food*] [*British*] .... LA
Land Agents' Society [*British*] (DI) .... LAS
Land Air Warfare Committee [*Military*] .... LAWC
Land and Approach System for Space Vehicles [*NASA*] (KSC) .... LASSV
Land and Facilities Development Administration [*HUD*] .... LFDA
Land and Sea Interaction Laboratory [*Environmental Science Services Administration*] .... LASIL
Land and Sea Interaction Laboratory [*Environmental Science Services Administration*] (NOAA) .... LSIL
Land and Valuation Review Tribunal [*Northern Territory, Australia*] .... LVRT
Land and Water Conservation Fund [*Department of the Interior*] .... LWCF
Land and Water Conservation Fund (GNE) .... LWCF
Land and Water Systems [*Michigan*] .... LAWS
Land Attack Mode [*Navy*] (CAAL) .... LAM
Land Authority for Wales .... LAW
Land Bank Commission .... LBC
Land Based .... LB
Land Capability Classes [*Agriculture*] LCC
Land Combat Missile .... LCM
Land Combat Support Set (NATG) .... LCSS
Land Combat Support System (DWSG) .... LCSS
Land Combat Support Systems .... LCSS
Land Combat System .... LCS
Land Combat System Study (AFIT) .... LCSS
Land Commander, North Norway [*NATO*] (NATG) .... LCNN
Land Commission [*British*] LC
Land Compensation Act [*Town planning*] [*British*] .... LCA
Land Compensation Reports [*A publication*] (ILCA) .... LCR
Land Component Commander (MCD) LCC
Land Condition-Trend Analysis [*Army*] (RDA) .... LCTA
Land Court [*Legal*] [*British*] LC
Land Court Cases [*New South Wales*] [*A publication*] (DLA) LCC
Land Decisions, United States [*A publication*] (DLA) .... Land Dec
Land Development Accounting System (MHDB) .... LANDAC
Land Development Aircraft (PDAA) .... LDA
Land Development Contractors' Association [*Australia*] .... LDCA
Land Development Law Reporter [*A publication*] (DLA) .... LDLR
Land Disposal Facility .... LDF
Land Disposal Restrictions [*Environmental Protection Agency*] .... LDR
Land Disposal Restrictions Task Force [*Environmental Protection Agency*] (GFGA) .... LDRTF
Land Educational Associates Foundation [*Defunct*] (EA) .... LEAF
Land Equivalent Ratio [*Agriculture*] .... LER
Land Evaluation and Site Assessment System [*Department of Agriculture*] .... LESA
Land Exercise [*Marine Corps*] .... LEX
Land Force Adriatic [*British Royal Marines*] [*World War II*] .... LFA
Land Force, Airmobility [*NATO*] (NATG) .... LFA
Land Force Tactical Doctrine Working Party [*NASA*] (MCD) .... LFTDWP
Land Forces [*Military British*] .... LF
Land Forces Classification System (AABC) .... LFCS
Land Forces Logistics Working Party (MCD) .... LFLWP
Land Grant (DLA) .... L/G
Land Grant (MHDB) .... Ld Gt
Land Hydrological and Meteorological Station [*ITU designation*] (DEN) .... FLH
Land Improvement Contractors of America (EA) .... LICA
Land Information and Analysis [*Program*] [*Department of the Interior*] .... LIA
Land Institute [*An association*] (EA) LI

Land Integrated Equipment for Tactical Systems (MCD) ... LIETS
Land Interface Sub-Working Group [*NATO*] (NATG) ... LISWG
Land Laws Service [*Australia A publication*] ... LLS
Land Level Facility [*Navy*] ... LLF
Land Line Frequency Modulation (AAG) ... LLFM
Land Line of Communications [*Military*] ... LLOC
Land Lines Assembly [*Ground Communications Facility, NASA*] ... LLSA
Land Lines Communications Facilities (FAAC) ... LICOF
Land Locomotion Division [*Army Tank-Automotive Command*] [*Warren, MI*] ... LL
Land Locomotion Laboratory [*Army*] ... LL
Land Locomotion Laboratory [*Army*] ... LLL
Land Mammal Ages [*Paleontology*] ... LMA
Land Management Society of Western Australia ... LMSWA
Land Margin Ecosystem Research [*Marine science*] (OSRA) ... LMER
Land Margin Ecosystem Research (USDC) ... LMER
Land Mass Simulator ... LMS
Land Mine [*Military*] ... LM
Land Mobile ... LM
Land Mobile Communications Council (EA) ... LMCC
Land Mobile Radio (NITA) ... LMR
Land Mobile Satellite Service [*Rockwell International Corp.*] ... LMSS
Land Mobile Service (DA) ... LMS
Land Mobile Station [*ITU designation*] (NATG) ... ML
Land Navigation System ... LNS
Land O' Lakes, WI [*Location identifier FAA*] (FAAL) ... LNL
Land Observation Satellite (PDAA) ... LOS
[*The*] **Land of the Bible: A Historical Geography** [*A publication*] (BJA) ... LOB
Land Office Decisions, United States [*A publication*] (DLA) ... L Dec
Land Office Decisions, United States [*A publication*] (DLA) ... LD
Land O'Lakes [*Wisconsin*] [*Airport symbol*] (AD) ... LNL
Land Ordnance Engineering Branch [*Canada Military*] (PDAA) ... LORE
Land Ordnance Maintenance Management Information System (PDAA) ... LOMMIS
Land Ownership Survey ... LOS
Land Plane ... LP
Land Protection Council [*Victoria, Australia*] ... LPC
Land Registry [*British*] ... LAR
Land Registry (DLA) ... LR
Land Remote Sensing Commercialization Act [*1984*] ... LRSCA
Land Remote Sensing Satellite System (GFGA) ... LANDSAT
Land Reports, by Roche, Dillon, and Kehoe [*1881-82*] [*Ireland*] [*A publication*] (DLA) ... Land Com Rep
Land Reports, by Roche, Dillon, and Kehoe [*1881-82*] [*Ireland*] [*A publication*] (DLA) ... Land Comp Rep
Land Resource Research Centre [*Canada*] (IRC) ... LRRC
Land Resources Development Centre [*British*] (ARC) ... LRDC
Land Resources Group ... LRG
Land Resources Management (MCD) ... LRM
Land Resources Research Institute [*Agriculture Canada*] [*Formerly, Soil Research Institute*] [*Research center*] (RCD) ... LRRI
Land Revenue Records and Enrollments Office [*British*] ... LRRO
Land Rover Owners Association (EA) ... LROA
Land Rover Owners Association, USA (EA) ... LROA USA
Land Satellite [*Marine science*] (OSRA) ... LANDSAT
Land Satellite (USDC) ... LANDSAT
Land Sea Rescue (NASA) ... LSR
Land Service ... LS
Land Service Assistant [*Ministry of Agriculture, Fisheries, and Food*] [*British*] ... LSA
Land Settlement Association [*British*] ... LSA
Land Site Marshalling Team [*Military*] ... LSMT
Land Special Security Force [*Army*] (AABC) ... LSSF
Land Speed Record [*Auto racing*] ... LSR
Land Station [*ITU designation*] (CET) ... FL
Land Surface Parmeterization [*Environmental science*] ... LSP
Land Surveying Program [*Association of Independent Colleges and Schools specialization code*] ... LS
Land Surveyor ... LS
Land Surveyors' Licensing Board [*Western Australia*] ... LSLB
Land Tax Rulings [*Australia A publication*] ... LT Rulings
Land Technical Library, Department of National Defence [*Bibliotheque Technique (Terre), Ministere de la Defense Nationale*] **Ottawa, Ontario** [*Library symbol National Library of Canada*] (NLC) ... OONDLT
Land Tenure Center [*University of Wisconsin*] [*Research center*] ... LTC
Land Title Trust (DLA) ... LTT
Land Titles Division [*South Australia*] ... LTD
Land Training Installations (NATG) ... LTI
Land Transport Corps [*British military*] (DMA) ... LTC
Land Transport Vehicle (NVT) ... LTV
Land Transportation [*FCC*] (NTCM) ... L
Land Treatment Demonstration [*or Unit*] (GNE) ... LTD(U)
Land Treatment Unit [*Waste disposal*] ... LTU
Land Trust Alliance (EA) ... LTA
Land Trust Commission (BARN) ... LTC
Land Trust Exchange [*Later, LTA*] (EA) ... LTE
Land Use Adjustment Program ... LUAP
Land Use and Cover Change [*Environmental studies*] (ECON) ... LUCC
Land Use and Environment Law Review [*A publication*] (DLA) ... Land Use & Env't L Rev
Land Use and Planning [*British*] ... LUP
Land Use and Requirements Study (MCD) ... LURS
Land Use and Transport Planning [*British*] ... LUTP
Land Use Concurrence [*Acquisition of real estate for the use of US forces on a rent-free basis*] [*Vietnam*] ... LUC
Land Use Data ... LUDA
Land Use Designation [*US Forest Service*] ... LUD
Land Use Game Simulation ... LUGS
Land Use Management Information System [*NASA*] ... LUMIS
Land Use Planning Reports [*A publication*] (DLA) ... Land U Pl Rep
Land Use Trade Off Model (DICI) ... LUTOM
Land Utilization Survey (WDAA) ... LUS
Land Valuation Boards of Review [*Australia*] ... LVBR
Land Value (ADA) ... LV
Land Valuers' Licensing Board [*Western Australia*] ... LVLB
Land Warfare [*formerly, Limited War*] **Laboratory** [*Army*] ... LWL
Land-Air Integrated Reduction System (MUGU) ... LAIRS
Landair Services [*NASDAQ symbol*] (SAG) ... LAND
Landair Services [*Associated Press*] (SAG) ... Landair
Land-Air Synergic Homogeneous Ultra-Processor (SAA) ... LASHUP
Land-Air White Sands (MUGU) ... LAIWS
Land-Attack Standard Missile ... LASM
Landauer, Inc. [*Associated Press*] (SAG) ... Landaur
Landauer, Inc. [*AMEX symbol*] (SPSG) ... LDR
L&B Financial [*NASDAQ symbol*] (TTSB) ... LBFL
Land-Based Evaluation Facility [*Military*] (CAAL) ... LBEF
Land-Based Marine Pollution ... LBMP
Land-Based Multimission Naval Aircraft (MCD) ... LMNA
Land-Based Plant (NRCH) ... LBP
Land-Based Sources [*of Marine Pollution*] [*Marine science*] (OSRA) ... LBS
Land-Based Sources of Marine Pollution (USDC) ... LBS
Land-Based Tanker [*Aircraft*] (DOMA) ... LBT
Land-Based Test Facility (DNAB) ... LBTF
Land-Based Test Site ... LBTS
Land-Bearing Equipment [*Military*] (INF) ... LBE
Land-Covered Earth (OA) ... LCE
Lande Splitting Factor ... LSF
Landec Corp. [*NASDAQ symbol*] (TTSB) ... LNDC
Landed Duty Free ... LDF
Landed Duty Paid [*Military*] ... LDP
Landed Estate Companies Association [*British*] (BI) ... LECA
Landed Estates Court [*England*] (DLA) ... Land Est C
Landed Estates Courts Commission [*England*] (DLA) ... LEC
Landed Gentry ... LG
Landed Terms ... LT
Landelijke Knokplogen [*Netherlands Regional Action Groups*] [*World War II*] ... LKP
Landelijke Organistatie [*Netherlands underground organization*] [*World War II*] ... LO
Lander College, Greenwood, SC [*Library symbol Library of Congress*] (LCLS) ... ScGrwL
Lander College, Larry A. Jackson Library, Greenwood, SC [*OCLC symbol*] (OCLC) ... SLG
Lander Dynamic Test Model [*NASA*] ... LDTM
Lander Electrical Interface Simulator [*NASA*] ... LEIS
Lander Local Time [*NASA*] ... LLT
Lander Radio Subsystem [*NASA*] ... LRS
Lander Static Test Model [*NASA*] ... LSTM
Lander Trajectory Reconstruction [*Program*] [*NASA*] ... LTR
Lander, WY [*Television station call letters*] ... KCWC
Lander, WY [*FM radio station call letters*] ... KDLY
Lander, WY [*Television station call letters*] ... KGWL
Lander, WY [*AM radio station call letters*] ... KOVE
Lander, WY [*Location identifier FAA*] (FAAL) ... LND
Landers [*California*] [*Seismograph station code, US Geological Survey*] (SEIS) ... LAC
Landesarbeitsgericht [*Provincial Labor Court of Appeal*] [*German*] (ILCA) ... LArbG
Landes-Entschaedigungsamt (BJA) ... LEA
LANDesk Client Manager Technology [*Intel*] [*Computer science*] ... LDCM
Landeskartellbehoerde [*Provincial Cartel Authority*] [*German*] (DLA) ... LKartB
Landesring der Unabhaengigen [*Independent Party*] [*Switzerland Political party*] (PPE) ... LdU
Landesschuetzeneinheit [*Regional defense force*] [*German military - World War II*] ... LS
Landesverband der Israelitischen Religionsgemeinde (BJA) ... LIRG
Landfall Technique School [*Navy*] ... LTS
Landfill ... LNDFLL
Landfill Gas ... LFG
Landgericht [*Regional Court*] [*German*] (ILCA) ... LG
Land-Grant College of Agriculture ... LGCA
Land-Grant University ... LGU
Landing ... L
Landing [*Commonly used*] (OPSA) ... LANDING
Landing [*Maps and charts*] (AFM) ... LDG
Landing [*Maps and charts*] (KSC) ... LNDG
Landing ... LNDG
Landing [*Commonly used*] (OPSA) ... LNDNG
Landing Account [*Shipping*] ... L/A
Landing Aid [*Navigation*] (IAA) ... LAN
Landing Aids Control Building [*NASA*] (NASA) ... LACB
Landing and Approach System, Spiral-Oriented ... LASSO
Landing and Ascent [*NASA*] ... L & A
Landing and Deceleration [*NASA*] (NASA) ... L & D
Landing and Delivery [*Shipping*] (DS) ... Ldg & Dly
Landing and Ferry Operations Panel [*NASA*] (NASA) ... LFOP
Landing and Recovery (KSC) ... L & R
Landing and Recovery Division [*NASA*] ... LRD
Landing and Takeoff ... LTO
Landing Approach Simulator ... LAS
Landing Assist Device [*Aviation*] (NG) ... LAD
Landing Barge ... LB

Landing Barge, Emergency Repair	LBE
Landing Barge Flak [*British military*] (DMA)	LBF
Landing Barge, Kitchen	LBK
Landing Barge Oiler [*British military*] (DMA)	LBO
Landing Barge Water [*British military*] (DMA)	LBW
Landing Beach [*Navy*]	LB
Landing Boat, Support [*Navy symbol*]	LBS
Landing Boat, Vehicle [*Navy symbol Obsolete*]	LBV
Landing Book [*Tea trade*] (ROG)	L/B
Landing Control Center	LCC
Landing Control Logic Unit [*Aviation*] (OA)	LCLU
Landing Craft	LANCRA
Landing Craft	LC
Landing Craft, Air Cushion [*Navy symbol*]	LCAC
Landing Craft and Amphibious Vehicle Assignment Table	LCAVAT
Landing Craft and Bases [*Military*]	LANCRAB
Landing Craft and Bases [*Military*] (AFIT)	LANDCRA
Landing Craft and Bases [*Military*] (AABC)	LANDCRAB
Landing Craft and Bases, Europe [*Navy*]	LANCRABEU
Landing Craft and Bases, Northwest African Waters [*World War II Navy*]	LANCRABNAW
Landing Craft, Armored [*Used in Vietnam by the French to transport their engineer units*] (VNW)	LCA
Landing Craft, Assault [*Navy ship symbol*]	LCA
Landing Craft, Assault, Experimental [*Navy ship symbol*]	LCAX
Landing Craft, Assault (Flamethrower) [*British military*] (DMA)	LCA(FT)
Landing Craft, Assault (Hedgerow)	LCA(H)
Landing Craft, Assault (Obstacle Clearance) [*British military*] (DMA)	LCA(OC)
Landing Craft, Control	LCC
Landing Craft Control Officer [*Military*]	LCCO
Landing Craft Control Primary [*Military*]	LCCP
Landing Craft, Emergency Repair	LCE
Landing Craft, Engine Overhaul Parties	LCEOP
Landing Craft, Flak	LCF
Landing Craft, Flotilla, Pacific Fleet	LCFLOTSPAC
Landing Craft, Group	LCGP
Landing Craft Gun (MCD)	LCG
Landing Craft, Gun (Large)	LCG(L)
Landing Craft, Gun (Medium)	LCG(M)
Landing Craft, Gun (Small) [*British military*] (DMA)	LCG(S)
Landing Craft, Gunboat	LCG
Landing Craft Headquarters [*British military*] (DMA)	LCH
Landing Craft (Heavy) (ADA)	LCH
Landing Craft Hospital [*British military*] (DMA)	LCH
Landing Craft, Hydrofoil, Experimental [*Navy symbol*]	LVHX
Landing Craft, Infantry [*Obsolete*]	LCI
Landing Craft, Infantry (Ammunition)	LCI(A)
Landing Craft, Infantry (Demolition) [*British military*] (DMA)	LCI(D)
Landing Craft, Infantry, Division	LCIDIV
Landing Craft, Infantry, Flotilla [*Obsolete*]	LCIFLOT
Landing Craft, Infantry (Flotilla Flagship) [*Navy symbol*]	LC(FF)
Landing Craft, Infantry, Group	LCIGRP
Landing Craft, Infantry, Gunboat [*Obsolete*]	LCI(G)
Landing Craft, Infantry (Gunboat) [*Navy symbol Obsolete*]	LSI(G)
Landing Craft, Infantry, Large [*Obsolete*]	LCIL
Landing Craft, Infantry, Large, Flotilla [*Obsolete*]	LCILFLOT
Landing Craft, Infantry (Medium) [*British military*] (DMA)	LCI(M)
Landing Craft, Infantry (Mortar) [*Navy symbol Obsolete*]	LSI(M)
Landing Craft, Infantry (Mortar Ship) [*Obsolete*]	LCI(M)
Landing Craft, Infantry (Rocket) [*Navy symbol Obsolete*]	LSI(R)
Landing Craft, Infantry (Rocket Ship) [*Obsolete*]	LCI(R)
Landing Craft, Infantry (Small) [*British military*] (DMA)	LCI(S)
Landing Craft, Kitchen	LCK
Landing Craft, Logistic [*British military*] (DMA)	LCL
Landing Craft, Material Supply Officer	LCMSO
Landing Craft, Mechanised (Gun) [*British military*] (DMA)	LCM(G)
Landing Craft, Mechanised (Rocket) [*British military*] (DMA)	LCM(R)
Landing Craft, Mechanized [*Navy symbol*]	LCM
Landing Craft, Mechanized, MKII [*Navy symbol*]	LCM(2)
Landing Craft, Mechanized, MKIII [*Navy symbol*]	LCM(3)
Landing Craft, Mechanized, MKVI [*Navy symbol*]	LCM6
Landing Craft, Mechanized, MKVIII [*Navy symbol*]	LCM8
Landing Craft, Medium [*Navy*]	LCM
Landing Craft, Navigation [*Obsolete*]	LCN
Landing Craft, Obstruction Clearance Unit	LCOCU
Landing Craft Officer [*British*] (ADA)	LCO
Landing Craft, Personnel	LCP
Landing Craft, Personnel, Large [*Navy symbol*]	LCPL
Landing Craft, Personnel Leader	LCPLR
Landing Craft, Personnel (Medium)	LCP(M)
Landing Craft, Personnel (Nested) [*Obsolete*]	LCP(N)
Landing Craft, Personnel (Plastic)	LCP(P)
Landing Craft, Personnel, Ramped [*Navy symbol*]	LCPR
Landing Craft, Personnel (Small) [*British military*] (DMA)	LCP(S)
Landing Craft, Personnel (Survey)	LCP(SY)
Landing Craft, Personnel (Utility) [*British military*] (DMA)	LCP(U)
Landing Craft, Raiding [*British*]	LCR
Landing Craft, Recovery Unit	LCRU
Landing Craft, Repair Ship [*Navy symbol*]	ARL
Landing Craft, Rocket [*British military*] (DMA)	LCR
Landing Craft, Rubber	LCR
Landing Craft, Rubber (Large) [*Obsolete*]	LCR(L)
Landing Craft, Rubber (Rocket)	LCR(R)
Landing Craft, Rubber (Small) [*Obsolete*]	LCR(S)
Landing Craft, Support	LCS

Landing Craft, Support (Large) [*Obsolete*]	LCS(L)
Landing Craft, Support (Medium)	LCS(M)
Landing Craft, Support (Rocket)	LCS(R)
Landing Craft, Support (Small), MKI [*Navy symbol Obsolete*]	LCS(S)
Landing Craft, Swimmer Reconnaissance [*Navy symbol*]	LCSR
Landing Craft, Swimmer Recovery (Light) [*Navy symbol*] (NVT)	LCSR(L)
Landing Craft, Tank [*Navy symbol*]	LCT
Landing Craft, Tank (Armored)	LCT(A)
Landing Craft, Tank (Hospital) [*British military*] (DMA)	LCT(H)
Landing Craft, Tank (Rocket)	LCT(R)
Landing Craft, Tank (Slow)	LCT(S)
Landing Craft, Utility [*Navy symbol*]	LCU
Landing Craft, Vehicle [*Navy symbol*]	LCB
Landing Craft, Vehicle [*Navy symbol*]	LCV
Landing Craft, Vehicle, Personnel [*Navy symbol NATO*]	LCVP
Landing/Deceleration Subsystem [*NASA*] (NASA)	LDS
Landing, Deservicing, and Safing [*NASA*] (KSC)	LDS
Landing Direction Finding Station [*Aviation*] (IAA)	LDFSTN
Landing Direction Indicator [*ICAO*] (FAAC)	LDI
Landing Direction Light [*Aviation*] (IAA)	LDL
Landing Directional Aid [*FAA*] (TAG)	LDA
Landing Distance [*Aviation*] (IAA)	LD
Landing Distance Available [*FAA*] (TAG)	LDA
Landing Distance Available [*FAA*] (FAAC)	LDA
Landing Dynamics Computer Program [*NASA*]	LDCP
Landing Elementary School, Glen Cove, NY [*Library symbol*] [*Library of Congress*] (LCLS)	NGlcLE
Landing Exercise [*Navy*] (CAAL)	LANDEX
Landing Exercise [*Navy*] (NVT)	LDEX
Landing Force [*Military*]	LANDFOR
Landing Force [*Navy*] (NVT)	LF
Landing Force Air Support Control Unit [*Navy*]	LANDFORASCU
Landing Force Amphibious Support Vehicle (SAA)	LFASV
Landing Force Assault Amphibious Vehicle (MCD)	LFAAV
Landing Force Aviation	LFA
Landing Force Bulletin [*Marine Corps*]	LFB
Landing Force Integrated Communications System [*Marine Corps*]	LFICS
Landing Force Intelligence Center [*Navy*] (DNAB)	LFIC
Landing Force Logistics Afloat (MCD)	LFLA
Landing Force Manual [*Marine Corps, Navy*]	LFM
Landing Force Naval Gunfire Team	LFNGFT
Landing Force Operation Center [*Navy*] (CAAL)	LFOC
Landing Force Operational Reserve Material [*Navy*] (NVT)	LFORM
Landing Force Organizational Systems Study	LFUSS
Landing Force Support Party [*Navy*] (ANA)	LFSP
Landing Force Support Ship [*Navy*]	LFSS
Landing Force Support Vehicle (MCD)	LFSV
Landing Force Support Weapon	LFSW
Landing Force Training Command [*Navy*] (NVT)	LFTC
Landing Force Training Command, Atlantic [*Navy*]	LANFORTRACOMLANT
Landing Force Training Command, Pacific [*Navy*] (DNAB)	LFTCPAC
Landing Force Training Unit [*Marine Corps*] (DNAB)	LANFORTRAU
Landing Force Training Unit [*Marine Corps*]	LFTU
Landing Gear [*Aircraft*]	LG
Landing Gear, Avionics Systems Package (MCD)	LASPAC
Landing Gear Warning	LGW
Landing Ground [*Navy*]	LG
Landing Ground, Emergency [*British military*] (DMA)	LGE
Landing Group [*Navy*] (NVT)	LG
Landing Guidance System [*Aerospace*]	LGS
Landing Helicopter Assault	LHA
Landing Line Teletype	LDTTY
Landing Observer Signal System (MSA)	LOSS
Landing Observer Signal System	LOSSYS
Landing Operations Area [*NASA*] (NASA)	LOA
Landing Operations Center (MCD)	LOC
Landing Operations Working Group [*NASA*] (NASA)	LOWG
Landing Performance Score (MCD)	LPS
Landing Personnel Helicopter [*British*] (NATG)	LPH
Landing Platform, Dock	LPD
Landing Platform Vehicle [*Navy British*]	LPV
Landing Point [*British military*] (DMA)	LP
Landing Point Designator [*Apollo*] [*NASA*]	LPD
Landing Pontoon Vehicle [*Military*]	LPV
Landing RADAR	LR
Landing Report (WDAA)	LR
Landing Rights Airport [*US Customs*]	LRA
Landing Safety Officer (MCD)	LSO
Landing, Separation Simulator (MCD)	LSS
Landing Ship	LS
Landing Ship, Assault [*Navy British*]	LSA
Landing Ship, Bombardment	LSB
Landing Ship Carrier [*British military*] (DMA)	LSC
Landing Ship Deck	LSD
Landing Ship, Dock [*Navy symbol*]	LSD
Landing Ship, Emergency Repair	LSE
Landing Ship, Experimental	LSX
Landing Ship, Fighter Direction [*British military*] (DMA)	LSF
Landing Ship, Flotilla Flagship [*Navy symbol Obsolete*]	LSFF
Landing Ship, Gantry	LSG
Landing Ship, Gun [*British military*] (DMA)	LSG
Landing Ship, Headquarters	LSH
Landing Ship, Headquarters [*British military*] (DMA)	LSHQ
Landing Ship, Headquarters (Large)	LSH(L)
Landing Ship, Headquarters (Small)	LSH(S)

Landing Ship, Heavy ..... LSH
Landing Ship, Helicopter/Landing Ship, Fighter Direction (DNAB) ..... LSH/LSF
Landing Ship, Infantry [*Navy symbol*] ..... LSI
Landing Ship, Infantry (Hand-Hoisted Boats) [*British*] ..... LSI(H)
Landing Ship, Infantry (Large) [*Obsolete*] ..... LSI(L)
Landing Ship, Infantry (Medium) [*British*] ..... LSI(M)
Landing Ship, Infantry (Small) ..... LSI(S)
Landing Ship, Logistic [*British*] ..... LSL
Landing Ship, Material Supply Officer ..... LSMSO
Landing Ship, Medium [*Navy symbol*] ..... LSM
Landing Ship, Medium (Rocket) [*Later, LFR*] [*Navy symbol*] ..... LSM(R)
Landing Ship Personnel [*British military*] (DMA) ..... LSP
Landing Ship, Rocket (NATG) ..... LSR
Landing Ship Squadron (CINC) ..... LANSHIPRON
Landing Ship Sternchute [*British military*] (DMA) ..... LSS
Landing Ship, Support (NATG) ..... LSS
Landing Ship Support, Large [*Military*] (VNW) ..... LSSL
Landing Ship, Tank [*Navy symbol*] ..... LST
Landing Ship, Tank (Casualty Evacuation) [*Navy symbol Obsolete*] ..... LST(H)
Landing Ship, Tank (Hospital) [*British military*] (DMA) ..... LST(H)
Landing Ship Transport (MCD) ..... LST
Landing Ship (Utility) [*Navy symbol*] ..... LSTS
Landing Ship, Utility [*Navy symbol Obsolete*] ..... LSU
Landing Ship, Vehicle [*Navy symbol*] ..... LSV
Landing Ship, Vehicle and Personnel [*Navy symbol*] ..... LSVP
Landing Side [*Air Force*] ..... LS
Landing Signal Enlisted [*Military*] ..... LSE
Landing Signal Officer ..... LSO
Landing Signal Officer Trainer [*Navy*] ..... LSOT
Landing Site (KSC) ..... LS
Landing, Storage, Delivery [*Business term*] ..... LSD
Landing Supply Activity ..... LSA
Landing Support Battalion (DNAB) ..... LDGSPTBN
Landing Support Group/Logistics Support Unit (DNAB) ..... LSG/LSU
Landing Support Officer [*Navy*] ..... LSO
Landing Support Platoon [*Navy*] (DNAB) ..... LNDSPTPLT
Landing Team ..... LT
Landing Traffic [*Aviation*] (FAAC) ..... LTFC
Landing Vehicle LV
Landing Vehicle, Airfoil ..... LVA
Landing Vehicle, Assault [*Navy symbol*] ..... LVA
Landing Vehicle, Hydrofoil ..... LVH
Landing Vehicle, Tracked (Armored) [*Turret Type*] ..... LVT (A)
Landing Vehicle, Tracked (Armored) (Mark I) [*"Water Buffalo," Turret Type*] ..... LVT (A) (1)
Landing Vehicle, Tracked (Armored) (Mark II) [*"Water Buffalo," Canopy Type*] ..... LV (A) (2)
Landing Vehicle, Tracked (Armored) (Mark IV) ..... LVT (A) (4)
Landing Vehicle, Tracked (Armored) (Mark V) ..... LVT (A) (5)
Landing Vehicle, Tracked, Command (NVT) ..... LVTC
Landing Vehicle, Tracked, Command, Experimental (MCD) ..... LVTCX
Landing Vehicle, Tracked, Engineer [*Model 1*] ..... LVTE
Landing Vehicle, Tracked, Howitzer [*Model 6*] ..... LVTH
Landing Vehicle, Tracked, Personnel (AABC) ..... LVTP
Landing Vehicle, Tracked Personnel, Command [*Marine Corps*] (VNW) ..... LVTP-CMD
Landing Vehicle, Tracked, Personnel, Experimental (MCD) ..... LVTPX
Landing Vehicle, Tracked, Recovery, Experimental (MCD) ..... LVTRX
Landing Vehicle, Tracked, Retriever (NVT) ..... LVTR
Landing Vehicle, Tracked (Rocket) [*British military*] (DMA) ..... LVT(R)
Landing Vehicle, Tracked (Unarmored) [*Navy symbol*] ..... LVT
Landing Vehicle, Tracked (Unarmored) ..... LVTU
Landing Vehicle, Tracked (Unarmored) (Mark I) [*"Alligator"*] [*Navy symbol*] ..... LVT (1)
Landing Vehicle, Tracked (Unarmored) (Mark II) [*"Water Buffalo"*] [*Navy symbol*] ..... LVT (2)
Landing Vehicle, Tracked (Unarmored) (Mark III) [*Navy symbol*] ..... LVT (3)
Landing Vehicle, Tracked (Unarmored) (Mark IV) ..... LVT (4)
Landing Vehicle, Wheeled ..... LVW
Landing Zone ..... LZ
Landing Zone Control Center [*Air Force*] (IAA) ..... LZCC
Landing Zone Control Officer [*Air Force*] (AFM) ..... LZCO
Landing Zone Locator ..... LZL
Landing-Gear-Extended Speed [*Aviation*] ..... VLE
Landing-Site Determination [*NASA*] (KSC) ..... LSD
Landing-Site Indicator [*Aviation*] ..... LASI
Landing-Site Supervisor ..... LSS
Landivisiau [*France ICAO location identifier*] (ICLI) ..... LFRJ
Landline [*Aviation*] LL
Land-Line [*Telecommunications*] (TEL) LL
Landline Telephony [*Aviation*] (DA) ..... LTF
Land-Line Teletypewriter [*Military*] (IAA) ..... LLT
Landline Teletypewriter [*Military*] ..... LLTT
Landline Teletypewriter [*Military*] ..... LLTTY
Landline Teletypewriter [*Military*] ..... LTT
Landlocked and Geographically Disadvantaged States [*Developing countries*] ..... LLGDS
Landlord (ROG) ..... LANDLD
Landlord [*Legal shorthand*] (LWAP) LL
Landlord and Tenant [*A publication*] (DLA) ..... L & T
Landmark (KSC) ..... LDMK
Landmark (KSC) ..... LM
Landmark (NASA) ..... LMK
Landmark ..... LNDMRK
Landmark Bancorp [*Associated Press*] (SAG) ..... LdmkBc
Landmark Bancorp [*NASDAQ symbol*] (SAG) ..... LMBC
Landmark Bancshares [*Associated Press*] (SAG) ..... LandBnc
Landmark Bancshares [*NASDAQ symbol*] (SAG) ..... LARK
Landmark Bancshares [*NASDAQ symbol*] (TTSB) ..... LARK
Landmark Corp. [*Toronto Stock Exchange symbol*] ..... LMK
Landmark Graphics [*NASDAQ symbol*] (SAG) ..... LMRK
Landmark Graphics Corp. [*Associated Press*] (SAG) ..... LdmkGph
Landmark Line of Sight (KSC) ..... LLOS
Landmark Resources Ltd. [*Vancouver Stock Exchange symbol*] ..... LDR
Landmarks of American Popular Culture [*A publication*] ..... LAPC
Landmarks Preservation Commission [*New York City*] ..... LPC
Land-Ocean Interaction in the Costal Zone [*International Geosphere Biosphere Programme*] ..... LOICZ
Land-Ocean-Climate Satellite [*Marine science*] (OSRA) ..... LOCS
Landplane L
Landpower Education Fund ..... LEF
Land-Rover Register 1947-1951 [*Petersfield, Hampshire, England*] (EAIO) ..... LRR
Landry-Guillain-Barre (Syndrome) [*Medicine*] ..... LGB
Landry-Guillain-Barre Syndrome [*Medicine*] (DMAA) ..... LGBS
Landry's Seafood Restaurants [*NASDAQ symbol*] (TTSB) ..... LDRY
Landrys Seafood Restaurants, Inc. [*Associated Press*] (SAG) ..... Landrys
Landrys Seafood Restaurants, Inc. [*NASDAQ symbol*] (SAG) ..... LDRY
Lands and Forests Commission [*Australia*] ..... LFC
Lands' End [*NYSE symbol*] (SPSG) ..... LE
Land's End for Order [*Shipping*] ..... LEFO
Land's End, Inc. [*Associated Press*] (SAG) ..... LandsE
Land's End/St. Just [*British ICAO location identifier*] (ICLI) ..... EGHC
Lands Tribunal [*Legal*] [*British*] ..... LT
Lands Tribunal Rating Appeals [*Legal*] [*British*] ..... LTRA
Lands Tribunal Rules [*Town planning*] [*British*] ..... LTR
LANDSAT Earthnet Data Availability [*ESA-Earthnet Programme Office*] [*Database*] ..... LEDA
LANDSAT [*Land Remote Sensing Satellite System*] **Sensor** [*NASA*] (SSD) ..... LAS
Landsberg [*Germany ICAO location identifier*] (ICLI) ..... EDSA
Landscape ..... LANDSC
Landscape (VRA) ..... ldscp
Landscape ..... LNDSCP
Landscape Architectural Accreditation Board (GAGS) ..... LAAB
Landscape Architecture Foundation (EA) ..... LAF
Landscape Contractors' Association of New South Wales [*Australia*] ..... LCANSW
Landscape Contractors Association of Victoria [*Australia*] ..... LCAV
Landscape Institute [*British*] LI
Landscape Nursery Council (EA) ..... LANCO
Landscape Nursery Council (EA) ..... LNC
Landscape Research Group [*Lutterworth, Leicestershire, England*] (EAIO) ..... LRG
Landscaping ..... LANDSCPG
Landsdowne Public Library, Ontario [*Library symbol National Library of Canada*] (BIB) ..... OLAN
Landshut [*Germany ICAO location identifier*] (ICLI) ..... EDML
Landsing Pacific Fund [*Associated Press*] (SAG) ..... LndsPc
Landsing Pacific Fund [*AMEX symbol*] (CTT) ..... LPF
Landskrona [*Sweden ICAO location identifier*] (ICLI) ..... ESHE
Landskrona/Viarp [*Sweden ICAO location identifier*] (ICLI) ..... ESML
Landslide [*Washington*] [*Seismograph station code, US Geological Survey Closed*] (SEIS) ..... LSW
Landsorganisasjonen i Norge [*Norwegian Federation of Trade Unions*] ..... LO
Landsorganisationen i Sverige [*Swedish Federation of Trade Unions*] ..... LO
Landstar System [*NASDAQ symbol*] (TTSB) ..... LSTR
Landstar System, Inc. [*NASDAQ symbol*] (SAG) ..... LSTR
Landstar Systems, Inc. [*Associated Press*] (SAG) ..... Landstr
Landsteiner-Wiener [*Serum*] ..... LW
Landstuhl [*Germany ICAO location identifier*] (ICLI) ..... EDIP
Landstuhl Army Regional Medical Center [*Germany*] ..... LARMC
Landsverk-Wollan [*Radiation survey meter*] ..... L-W
Landulfus Acconzaioco [*Flourished, 13th century*] [*Authority cited in pre-1607 legal work*] (DSA) L
Landulfus Acconzaioco [*Flourished, 13th century*] [*Authority cited in pre-1607 legal work*] (DSA) ..... La
Landulfus Acconzaioco [*Flourished, 13th century*] [*Authority cited in pre-1607 legal work*] (DSA) ..... Lan
Landulfus Acconzaioco [*Flourished, 13th century*] [*Authority cited in pre-1607 legal work*] (DSA) ..... Lan Acon
Landwirtschaftsversorgungsamt [*German Land Economic Supply Office*] [*Post-World War II*] ..... LWV
Lane L
Lane ..... LA
Lane [*Commonly used*] (OPSA) ..... LANE
Lane [*Commonly used*] (OPSA) ..... LANES
Lane ..... LN
Lane (MCD) ..... LN
Lane Brody Fan Club (EA) ..... LBFC
Lane Bryant, Inc. ..... LB
Lane College, Jackson, TN [*Library symbol Library of Congress*] (LCLS) ..... TJaL
Lane Community College, Eugene, OR [*OCLC symbol*] (OCLC) ..... OLE
Lane Community College, Eugene, OR [*Library symbol Library of Congress*] (LCLS) ..... OrEL
Lane Control Signal ..... LCS
Lane County Archives, Eugene, OR [*Library symbol Library of Congress*] (LCLS) ..... OrECoAr
Lane County Law Library, Eugene, OR [*Library symbol Library of Congress*] (LCLS) ..... OrECoL
Lane County Museum [*Formerly, Lane County Pioneer Museum*], **Eugene, OR** [*Library symbol Library of Congress*] (LCLS) ..... OrEPM
Lane Grader [*Slang for an army instructor*] (VNW) ..... LG
Lane Photograph Method ..... LPM

Lane, Powell, Moss & Miller Library, Seattle, WA [Library symbol] [Library of Congress] (LCLS) .... WaSLP
Lane Public Library, Hamilton, OH [Library symbol Library of Congress] (LCLS) .... OHa
Lane Public Library, Hamilton, OH [OCLC symbol] (OCLC) .... OLN
Lane Sensing System [Automotive engineering] .... LSS
Laneas Aeraes Trans Costa Rica SA [ICAO designator] (FAAC) .... TCR
Lane's English Exchequer Reports [1605-12] [A publication] (DLA) .... La
Lane's English Exchequer Reports [1605-12] [A publication] (DLA) .... Lane
Lanett, AL [AM radio station call letters] (RBYB) .... WDWZ-AM
Lanett, AL [AM radio station call letters] .... WRLD
Laney College, Oakland, CA [Library symbol Library of Congress] (LCLS) .... COLC
Lanfrancus [Deceased, 1089] [Authority cited in pre-1607 legal work] (DSA) .... La
Lanfrancus [Deceased, 1089] [Authority cited in pre-1607 legal work] (DSA) .... Laf
Lanfrancus [Deceased, 1089] [Authority cited in pre-1607 legal work] (DSA) .... Lan
Lanfrancus Cremensis [Deceased, 1229] [Authority cited in pre-1607 legal work] (DSA) .... La
Lanfrancus Cremensis [Deceased, 1229] [Authority cited in pre-1607 legal work] (DSA) .... Laf
Lanfrancus Cremensis [Deceased, 1229] [Authority cited in pre-1607 legal work] (DSA) .... Lan
Lanfrancus Cremensis [Deceased, 1229] [Authority cited in pre-1607 legal work] (DSA) .... Lan Cre
Lang, Michener, Lash & Johnston, Ottawa, Ontario [Library symbol National Library of Canada] (BIB) .... OOLML
Langage de Programmation et de Gestion [French computer language] .... LPG
Langara, BC [ICAO location identifier] (ICLI) .... CYLA
Langat Encephalitis [Medicine] .... LGT
Langatabbetje [Surinam] [ICAO location identifier] (ICLI) .... SMLT
Langdell's Cases in Equity Pleading [A publication] (DLA) .... Lang Eq Pl
Langdell's Cases on Contracts [A publication] (DLA) .... Lang Cont
Langdell's Cases on Contracts [A publication] (DLA) .... Lang Cont
Langdell's Cases on Contracts [A publication] (DLA) .... Langd Cont
Langdell's Cases on Contracts [A publication] (DLA) .... LC Cont
Langdell's Cases on the Law of Sales [A publication] (DLA) .... Lang Ca Sales
Langdell's Cases on the Law of Sales [A publication] (DLA) .... Lang Sales
Langdell's Cases on the Law of Sales [A publication] (DLA) .... LC Sales
Langdell's Summary of Equity Pleading [A publication] (DLA) .... Lang Eq Pl
Langdell's Summary of the Law of Contracts [A publication] (DLA) .... Lang Cont
Langdell's Summary of the Law of Contracts [A publication] (DLA) .... Lang Sum Cont
Langdell's Summary of the Law of Contracts [A publication] (DLA) .... Langd Cont
Langdon, ND [AM radio station call letters] .... KNDK
Langdon, ND [FM radio station call letters] .... KNDK-FM
Lange Sicht [Long Sight] [German] .... LS
Langebaanweg [South Africa] [ICAO location identifier] (ICLI) .... FALW
Langenlebarn [Austria ICAO location identifier] (ICLI) .... LOXT
Langenthal [Switzerland ICAO location identifier] (ICLI) .... LSPL
Langeoog [Germany ICAO location identifier] (ICLI) .... EDWL
Langer Biomechanics Group [NASDAQ symbol] (SAG) .... GAIT
[The] Langer Biomechanics Group, Inc. [Associated Press] (SAG) .... Langer
Langer Biomechanics Grp [NASDAQ symbol] (TTSB) .... GAIT
Langerhans' Cell Granule [Anatomy] .... LCG
Langerhans' Cell Granulomatosis [Oncology] .... LCG
Langerhans' Cells [Medicine] LC
Langerood [Iran] [ICAO location identifier] (ICLI) .... OIGL
Langford Lodge [British ICAO location identifier] (ICLI) .... EGAL
Langgur [Indonesia] [Airport symbol] (OAG) .... LUV
Langgur/Dumatubun [Indonesia] [ICAO location identifier] (ICLI) .... WAPL
Langila [Cape Gloucester] [New Britain] [Seismograph station code, US Geological Survey] (SEIS) .... LAG
Langimar [Papua New Guinea] [Airport symbol] (OAG) .... LNM
Langkawi [Malaysia] [Airport symbol] (OAG) .... LGK
Langkawi [Malaysia] [ICAO location identifier] (ICLI) .... WMAM
Langkho [Myanmar] [ICAO location identifier] (ICLI) .... VBLO
Langley [Unit of sun's heat] (IAA) .... LAN
Langley [England] .... LANG
Langley [Unit of sun's heat] .... LY
Langley Aeronautical Laboratory [NASA] .... LAL
Langley Air Force Base (MCD) .... LAFB
Langley Centennial Museum and National Exhibition Centre, Fort Langley, British Columbia [Library symbol National Library of Canada] (NLC) .... BFLCM
Langley Complex Coordination [Device] [NASA] LCC
Langley Memorial Aeronautical Laboratory [NASA] (AAG) .... LMAL
Langley Research Center [NASA] .... LARC
Langley Research Center [NASA] .... LRC
Langley Transonic Dynamics Tunnel [NASA] (KSC) .... LTDT
Langley Unitary Plan Wind Tunnel [NASA] (KSC) .... LUPWT
Langley Working Paper [NASA] .... LWP
Langley-Porter Neuropsychiatric Institute, San Francisco, CA [Library symbol Library of Congress] (LCLS) .... CSfLP
Langley's Trustees' Act [A publication] (DLA) .... Lang Tr
Langlois Public Library, Langlois, OR [Library symbol Library of Congress] (LCLS) .... OrLan
Langmuir [Unit of measure] L
Langmuir Circulation [Geophysics] LC
Langmuir Dark Space [Electronics] .... LDS
Langmuir Diffusion Pump [Engineering] .... LDP
Langmuir-Blodgitt Technique [Optics] (EECA) .... LB
Langmuir-Hinshelwood Mechanism [Chemistry] .... LH
Langmuir-Hinshelwood-Hougen-Watson Rate Equation [Chemical kinetics] .... LHHW
Langogne/L'Esperon [France ICAO location identifier] (ICLI) .... LFHL
Langor (ABBR) .... LGOR
Langorous (ABBR) .... LGORU

Langorously (ABBR) .... LGORUY
Langsam Library Online Information Services [University of Cincinnati] (OLDSS) .... LOIS
Langston, OK [FM radio station call letters] .... KALU
Langston University, Langston, OK [Library symbol Library of Congress] (LCLS) .... OkLaU
Langtang [Nepal] [ICAO location identifier] (ICLI) .... VNLT
Langtry Flying Group Ltd. [British] [FAA designator] (FAAC) .... PAP
Language L
Language [Online database field identifier] .... LA
Language (AFM) .... LANG
Language .... LANG
Language [Online database field identifier] .... LG
Language Access to Distributed Data with Error Recovery .... LADDER
Language Acquisition Device .... LAD
Language Age [Score] .... LA
Language Analog [Project] .... LANA
Language and Assembly Language [Computer science] (DNAB) .... LASS
Language and Culture Atlas of Ashkenazic Jewry [A publication] (BJA) .... LCAAJ
Language and Language Behavior Abstracts [Sociological Abstracts] [Database] (NITA) .... LLBA
Language and Mode Converter [Computer science] (TEL) .... LAMC
Language and Society Centre [Monash University] [Australia] .... LSC
Language and Systems Together [Programming language] [Baytec Bay City, MI] .... LAST
Language Aptitude Test [Military] (AFM) .... LAT
Language Arts [A publication] (BRI) .... LA
Language Assessment Remediation and Screening Procedure [for the language impaired] .... LARSP
Language Assessment Scales [Test] .... LAS
Language Central Facility [Computer science] (IEEE) .... LCF
Language Code [Online database field identifier] LC
Language Conversion Program [Computer science] (BUR) .... LCP
Language Data Processing (MSA) .... LDP
Language Dependent Translator .... LDT
Language Description Language [Computer science] .... LDL
Language Experience .... LEXP
Language Experience Approach [Education] .... LEA
Language for ALGOL [Algorithmic Language] **Compiler Extension** [Computer science] (CSR) .... LACE
Language for Automated Logic and System Design [Computer science] (CSR) .... LALSD
Language for Computer Design (CSR) .... LCD
Language for Conversational Computing (MDG) LCC
Language for Export Research Center [University of Western Sydney] [Australia] .... LERC
Language for Expressing Associative Procedures [Computer science] .... LEAP
Language for Manufacturing Business and Distribution Activity (IAA) .... LAMBDA
Language for Programming-in-the-Small [Computer science] (MHDI) .... LPS
Language for Simulation of Computer Architecture (CSR) .... LASCAR
Language for Symbolic Simulation .... LSS
Language for Systems Development .... LSD
Language for the On-Line Investigation and Transformation of Abstractions [Computer science] .... LOLITA
Language for Users' Needs and Aims (NITA) .... LUNA
Language for Utility Checkout and Instrumentation Development .... LUCID
Language for Your Remote Instruction by Computer [Computer science] (MDG) .... LYRIC
Language Foundation of Australia .... LFA
Language Identity Code [Army] (INF) LIC
Language Imitation Test .... LIT
Language Implementation System (IAA) .... LIS
Language Improvement to Facilitate Education of Hearing-Impaired Children [A project of NEA] .... LIFE
Language in Society [A publication] (BRI) .... Lang Soc
Language Information Network and Clearinghouse System [Center for Applied Linguistics] [Washington, DC] .... LINCS
Language Information Network Coordination [Education] (AIE) .... LINC
Language Instruction for Recent Immigrants through Computer Technology (EDAC) .... LIRIC
Language Interface Facility with Ellipsis and Recursion [Computer science] (MHDI) .... LIFER
Language Interface Module (NITA) .... LIM
Language Interpretation Module .... LIM
Language Inventory for Teachers [Child development test] .... LIT
Language Laboratory [Research center] (RCD) .... UCBLL
Language, Literacy and Numeracy .... LLN
Language, Literacy and Numeracy Skills Taskforce [Australia] .... LL & N
Language Media Format (CET) .... LMF
Language Modalities Test for Aphasia [Psychology] .... LMTA
Language of Functions and Graphs (AIE) .... LEG
Language of Temporal Ordering of Specifications [Computer science] .... LOTOS
Language Organization Voicing Esperanto .... LOVE
[A] Language Oriented to Flight Engineering and Testing [NASA] (KSC) .... ALOFT
Language Processing and Debugging [Computer science] (BUR) .... LPD
Language Processor Unit .... LPU
Language Proficiency Test [Military] (AFM) .... LPT
Language Research in Progress (DIT) .... LRIP
Language Sampling and Analysis [Educational test] .... LSA
Language Specification (IEEE) .... LS
Language Structure Group [CODASYL] .... LSG
Language Support System (IAA) .... LSS
Language System FORTRAN [Computer science] .... LSF

Language Teaching Information Centre [British] (CB) .... LTIC
Language Teaching System .... LTS
Language Testing and Curriculum Center [Griffith University] [Australia] ...... LTCC
Language Testing Center [University of Melbourne] [Australia] ...... LTC
Language Training Detachment [Defense Language Institute] (DNAB) .... LTD
Language Translation [Computer science] .... LT
Language Translation System .... LTS
Language Understander Translator and Editor (NITA) .... LUTE
Language, Unseamanlike [Slang Military] (DNAB) .... LUL
Language Used to Communicate Information System Design .... LUCID
Language Used to Conceal Actual Meaning .... LUTCAM
Language-Based Learning Impairment [Neurology] LLI
Language-Independent Macro Processor (PDAA) .... LIMP
Language-Oriented System Analysis Table (IAA) .... LOSAT
Languages and Linguistics [Educational Resources Information Center (ERIC) Clearinghouse] [Center for Applied Linguistics] (PAZ) .... FL
Languages Other than English .... LOTE
Languages Services Centre [South Australia] .... LSC
Language-Structured Auditory Retention Span Test .... LARS
Langue d'Oc [MARC language code Library of Congress] (LCCP) .... lan
Langwelle [Long Wave] [German] (MCD) .... LW
Lanham Housing Act (DLA) .... LHA
Lanier Academic Motivational Program [Military] .... LAMP
Lanier Lake Regional and Gwinnett County Library, Lawrenceville, GA [Library symbol Library of Congress] (LCLS) .... GL
Lanier Library Association, Inc., Tryon, NC [Library symbol Library of Congress] (LCLS) .... NcTy
Lanka Estate Workers' Union [Ceylon] .... LEWU
Lanka Jatika Estate Workers' Union [Ceylon National Estate Workers' Union] .... LJEWU
Lanka Prajatantrawadi Party [Ceylon] .... LPP
Lanka Sama Samaja Party [Sri Lanka Equal Society Party] [Political party] (PPW) .... LSSP
Lankalink Aircargo (Pvp) Ltd. [Sri Lanka] [FAA designator] (FAAC) LLC
Lanmer Consultants Ltd., Niagara Falls, ON, Canada [Library symbol Library of Congress] (LCLS) .... CaONfLC
Lanmer Consultants Ltd., Niagara Falls, Ontario [Library symbol National Library of Canada] (NLC) .... ONFLC
L'Annee Epigraphique [A publication] (OCD) .... AE
Lannet Data Communications Ltd. [NASDAQ symbol] (SAG) .... LANT
Lannet Data Communictions Ltd. [Associated Press] (SAG) .... Lannet
Lannion [France] [Airport symbol] (OAG) .... LAI
Lannion/Servel [France ICAO location identifier] (ICLI) .... LFRO
Lanoptics Ltd. [Associated Press] (SAG) .... Lanoptic
Lanoptics Ltd. [NASDAQ symbol] (SAG) .... LNOP
LanOptics Ltd [NASDAQ symbol] (TTSB) .... LNOPF
Lanpar Technologies, Inc. [Toronto Stock Exchange symbol] .... LPR
Lansa, SRL [Honduras] [ICAO designator] (ICDA) .... UL
Lansco Resources [Vancouver Stock Exchange symbol] .... LNS
Lansdale, PA [AM radio station call letters] .... WNPV
Lansdowne House, ON [ICAO location identifier] (ICLI) .... CYLH
Lansdowne Minerals [Vancouver Stock Exchange symbol] .... LNM
L'Anse Au Loup Public Library, L'Anse Au Loup, NF, Canada [Library symbol Library of Congress] (LCLS) .... CaNfLa
L'Anse Au Loup Public Library, Newfoundland [Library symbol National Library of Canada] (NLC) .... NFLA
L'Anse, MI [FM radio station call letters] (RBYB) .... WCUP
L'Anse Township School and Public Library, L'Anse, MI [Library symbol Library of Congress] (LCLS) .... MiLan
Lanseria [South Africa] [ICAO location identifier] (ICLI) .... FALA
Lansford, PA [AM radio station call letters] .... WLSH
Lansing [Michigan] [Airport symbol] (OAG) .... LAN
Lansing/Capital Region [Michigan] [ICAO location identifier] (ICLI) ...... KLAN
Lansing Community College, Lansing, MI [OCLC symbol] (OCLC) .... EEL
Lansing Community College, Lansing, MI [Library symbol Library of Congress] (LCLS) .... MiLC
Lansing General Hospital [Michigan] .... LGH
Lansing General Hospital Library, Lansing, MI [Library symbol] [Library of Congress] (LCLS) .... MiLGH
Lansing, IL [FM radio station call letters] .... WEJM
Lansing Library Service, Oakland, CA [Library symbol Library of Congress] (LCLS) .... COL
Lansing, MI [Location identifier FAA] (FAAL) .... CPQ
Lansing, MI [Location identifier FAA] (FAAL) .... LAN
Lansing, MI [FM radio station call letters] (RBYB) .... WHZZ
Lansing, MI [AM radio station call letters] .... WILS
Lansing, MI [FM radio station call letters] .... WITL
Lansing, MI [FM radio station call letters] .... WITL-FM
Lansing, MI [AM radio station call letters] .... WJIM
Lansing, MI [FM radio station call letters] .... WJIM-FM
Lansing, MI [Television station call letters] .... WLAJ
Lansing, MI [Television station call letters] .... WLNS
Lansing, MI [Television station call letters] .... WLNZ
Lansing, MI [Television station call letters] .... WSYM
Lansing Public Library, Lansing, IL [Library symbol Library of Congress] (LCLS) .... ILa
Lansing Public Library, Lansing, MI [OCLC symbol] (OCLC) .... EEP
Lansing Public Library, Lansing, MI [Library symbol Library of Congress] (LCLS) .... MiL
Lansing's New York Supreme Court Reports [A publication] (DLA) L
Lansing's New York Supreme Court Reports [A publication] (DLA) ...... Lans
Lansing's Select Cases in Chancery [1824, 1826] [New York] [A publication] (DLA) L
Lansing's Select Cases in Chancery [1824, 1826] [New York] [A publication] (DLA) .... Lans Ch

Lansing's Select Cases in Chancery [1824, 1826] [New York] [A publication] (DLA) .... Lans Sel Cas
Lanslevillard [France] [Seismograph station code, US Geological Survey] (SEIS) .... LNS
LANTCOM ELINT Center (MCD) .... LEC
LANTCOM Integrated Command and Control Management Information System (MCD) .... LANTICOMIS
Lanterman-Petris-Short Act [Psychology] (DAVI) .... LPS
Lantern (MSA) .... LTRN
Lantern Slide [Photography] .... LS
Lantern Slide (VRA) .... LTRN
Lanthanide [Chemical element] (WGA) .... Ln
Lanthanide Ion Probe Spectroscopy .... LIPS
Lanthanide Shift Reagent [Spectroscopy] .... LSR
Lanthanide-Induced Shift [Spectroscopy] .... LIS
Lanthanide-Ion Induced Chemical Shift [Spectroscopy] .... LIS
Lanthanum [Chemical element; symbol is La] L
Lanthanum [Chemical element] .... La
Lanthanum/Calcium/Manganese/Oxygen [Inorganic chemistry] .... LCMO
Lanthanum Magnesium Double Nitrate .... LMN
Lanthanum Strontium Copper Oxide [Inorganic chemistry] .... LSCO
Lanthanum-Barium-Copper-Oxide [Inorganic chemistry] .... LBCO
Lanveoc/Poulmic [France ICAO location identifier] (ICLI) .... LFRL
LanVision Systems [NASDAQ symbol] (TTSB) .... LANV
Lanyard .... LNYD
Lanyard Release Switch .... LRS
Lanyu [Republic of China] [Seismograph station code, US Geological Survey] (SEIS) .... LAY
Lanyu [China] [ICAO location identifier] (ICLI) .... RCLY
Lanywa [Myanmar] [ICAO location identifier] (ICLI) .... VBLY
Lanzhou [China] [Airport symbol] (OAG) .... LHW
Lanzhou [China] [ICAO location identifier] (ICLI) .... ZLHW
Lanzhou City [China] [ICAO location identifier] (ICLI) .... ZLAN
Lanzhou/Zhongchuan [China] [ICAO location identifier] (ICLI) .... ZLLL
Lao [MARC language code Library of Congress] (LCCP) .... lao
Lao Aviation [Laos] [ICAO designator] (ICDA) .... QV
Lao Aviaton [Laos] [ICAO designator] (FAAC) .... LAO
Lao Civil Servants' Union .... LCSU
Lao Pen Kang [Laotian Neutralist Party] (CINC) .... LPK
Lao People's Democratic Republic .... LPDR
Lao Peoples Liberation Army (CINC) .... LPLA
Lao People's Revolutionary Party [Phak Pasason Pativat Lao] [Political party] (PPW) .... LPRP
Laoag [Philippines] [Airport symbol] (OAG) .... LAO
Laoag/International, Ilocos Norte [Philippines] [ICAO location identifier] (ICLI) .... RPML
Laokay [Viet Nam] [ICAO location identifier] (ICLI) .... VVLK
Laon/Chambry [France ICAO location identifier] (ICLI) .... LFAF
Laona & Northern Railway Co. [AAR code] .... LNO
Laos [MARC geographic area code Library of Congress] (LCCP) .... a-ls--
Laos [or Lao People's Democratic Republic] [ANSI two-letter standard code] (CNC) .... LA
Laos [or Lao People's Democratic Republic] [ANSI three-letter standard code] (CNC) .... LAO
Laos [MARC country of publication code Library of Congress] (LCCP) .... ls
Laos [International civil aircraft marking] (ODBW) .... RDPL
Laos Ammunition Procedures (CINC) .... LAMP
Laos and Thailand Military Assistance .... LATH
Laotian Cultural and Research Center (EA) .... LCRC
Lap Joint Strength .... LJS
Lapalisse-Perigny [France ICAO location identifier] (ICLI) .... LFHX
Laparoscopic Bilateral Partial Salpingectomies [Gynecology] (DAVI) ...... LS BPS
Laparoscopic Tubal Banding [Ligation] (DAVI) .... LTB
Laparoscopic Tubal Ligation [Gynecology] (DAVI) .... LSTL
Laparoscopic Tubal Ligation [Gynecology] (DAVI) .... LTL
Laparoscopic Ultrasonography [Medicine] .... LUS
Laparoscopically-Assisted Vaginal Hysterectomy [Medicine] .... LAVH
Laparoscopy [Medicine] .... lap
Laparotomy [Medicine] .... LAP
Laparotomy [Sponges] (DAVI) .... LAP
Lapeer, MI [AM radio station call letters] .... WLSP
Lapeer, MI [AM radio station call letters] .... WMPC
Lapeer, MI [FM radio station call letters] .... WWGZ
Lapel Review, Lapel, IN [Library symbol Library of Congress] (LCLS) .... InLaR
Laperriere's Speaker's Decisions [Canada] [A publication] (DLA) .... Lap Dec
Lapidary .... LAPDRY
Lapideum [Stony] [Latin] (MAE) .... lapid
Lapidus Airfloat System (DAVI) .... LAS
Lapis Lazuli (VRA) ll
Laplace Transform [Mathematics] .... LT
Laplace Transformation Estimator .... LTE
Laplace-Carson Transform [Mathematics] .... LCT
Laplace-Stieltjes Transform .... LST
Lapland .... LAP
LapLink Remote Access [Traveling Software, Inc.] [Computer science] (PCM) .... LLRA
LaPorte County Historical Society, LaPorte, IN [Library symbol Library of Congress] (LCLS) .... InLapHi
LaPorte Herald-Argus, LaPorte, IN [Library symbol Library of Congress] (LCLS) .... InLapHA
Laporte, PA [FM radio station call letters] (RBYB) .... WRPA-FM
Laporte Public School, Laporte, MN [Library symbol] [Library of Congress] (LCLS) .... MnLapS
Lapp [MARC language code Library of Congress] (LCCP) .... lap
Lapped Orthogonal Transform [Telecommunications] .... LOT

Lapped Seam (DNAB) ... LS
Lapped Transform [*Telecommunications*] ... LT
Lappeenranta [*Finland ICAO location identifier*] (ICLI) ... EFLP
Lappeenranta [*Finland*] [*Airport symbol*] (OAG) ... LPP
Lapping [*Electricity*] ... LPG
Lappish [*Language, etc.*] (ROG) ... LAPP
LAPS Observing System Simulation (USDC) ... LOSS
LAPS [*Local Analysis and Prediction System*] **Observing System Stimulation** [*Marine science*] (OSRA) ... LOSS
Lapse Ratio [*Insurance*] ... LR
Laptop [*Computer*] (BARN) ... LT
Laptop Automated Aid Positioning System [*Coast Guard*] [*Computer science*] (DOMA) ... LAAPS
Lap-Top Expansion [*Computer science*] ... LTX
Lapu-Lapu/Mactan International [*Philippines*] [*ICAO location identifier*] (ICLI) ... RPMT
Lapus de Castiglionchio [*Flourished, 1353-81*] [*Authority cited in pre-1607 legal work*] (DSA) ... La
Lapus de Castiglionchio [*Flourished, 1353-81*] [*Authority cited in pre-1607 legal work*] (DSA) ... La de Castigl
Lapus de Castiglionchio [*Flourished, 1353-81*] [*Authority cited in pre-1607 legal work*] (DSA) ... Lap
Lapus Tatti [*Flourished, 14th century*] [*Authority cited in pre-1607 legal work*] (DSA) ... La
Lar [*Iran*] [*ICAO location identifier*] (ICLI) ... OISL
LAR Transregional, Linhas Aereas Regionais SA [*Portugal ICAO designator*] (FAAC) ... PDF
Laramide Resources Ltd. [*Vancouver Stock Exchange symbol*] ... LAM
Laramie [*Wyoming*] [*Seismograph station code, US Geological Survey*] (SEIS) ... LAR
Laramie [*Wyoming*] [*Airport symbol*] (OAG) ... LAR
Laramie County Community College, Cheyenne, WY [*Library symbol Library of Congress*] (LCLS) ... WyCC
Laramie County Library System, Cheyenne, WY [*Library symbol Library of Congress*] (LCLS) ... WyC
Laramie County Library System, Cheyenne, WY [*OCLC symbol*] (OCLC) ... WYL
Laramie County Medical Society, Cheyenne, WY [*Library symbol Library of Congress*] (LCLS) ... WyCMS
Laramie Energy Research Center [*Department of Energy*] ... LERC
Laramie Energy Technology Center [*Department of Energy*] (GRD) ... LETC
Laramie, North Park & Western Railroad (IIA) ... LNP & W
Laramie Project Office [*Laramie, WY*] [*Department of Energy*] (GRD) ... LPO
Laramie, WY [*FM radio station call letters*] ... KCGY
Laramie, WY [*FM radio station call letters*] ... KIMX
Laramie, WY [*FM radio station call letters*] ... KKNG
Laramie, WY [*AM radio station call letters*] ... KLDI
Laramie, WY [*AM radio station call letters*] ... KOWB
Laramie, WY [*FM radio station call letters*] ... KRQU
Laramie, WY [*FM radio station call letters*] ... KUWR
Laramie, WY [*Location identifier FAA*] (FAAL) ... LAR
Larantuka [*Indonesia*] [*Airport symbol*] (OAG) ... LKA
Larantuka/Gewayentana [*Indonesia*] [*ICAO location identifier*] (ICLI) ... WRKL
LARC Instruction Assembly ... LISA
LARC Instruction Simulator ... LIS
Larceny [*FBI standardized term*] ... L
Larceny [*Legal shorthand*] (LWAP) ... LAR
Larceny [*FBI standardized term*] ... LARC
Larceny and Receiving ... L & R
Larch Mountain Correctional Center, Resident Library, Yacolt, WA [*Library symbol Library of Congress*] (LCLS) ... WaYacL-R
Larch Mountain Correctional Center, Staff Library, Yacolt, WA [*Library symbol Library of Congress*] (LCLS) ... WaYacL
Larch Resources Ltd. [*Vancouver Stock Exchange symbol*] ... LCH
Larchmont Public Library, Larchmont, NY [*Library symbol Library of Congress*] (LCLS) ... NLar
Larder Lake Public Library, Ontario [*Library symbol National Library of Canada*] (BIB) ... OLL
Larder Resources, Inc. [*Toronto Stock Exchange symbol*] ... LRS
Laredo [*Texas*] [*Airport symbol*] (AD) ... LOI
Laredo [*Texas*] [*Airport symbol*] (OAG) ... LRD
Laredo Air, Inc. [*ICAO designator*] (FAAC) ... LRD
Laredo/International [*Texas*] [*ICAO location identifier*] (ICLI) ... KLRD
Laredo Junior College [*Texas*] ... LJC
Laredo Junior College, Laredo, TX [*OCLC symbol*] (OCLC) ... TLJ
Laredo Junior College, Laredo, TX [*Library symbol Library of Congress*] (LCLS) ... TxLarC
Laredo Petroleums [*Vancouver Stock Exchange symbol*] ... LPD
Laredo Public Library, Laredo, TX [*Library symbol Library of Congress*] (LCLS) ... TxLar
Laredo State University, Laredo, TX [*OCLC symbol*] (OCLC) ... TLS
Laredo State University, Laredo, TX [*Library symbol Library of Congress*] (LCLS) ... TxLarU
Laredo, TX [*FM radio station call letters*] ... KBNL
Laredo, TX [*AM radio station call letters*] ... KDOS
Laredo, TX [*Television station call letters*] ... KGNS
Laredo, TX [*FM radio station call letters*] ... KHOY
Laredo, TX [*FM radio station call letters*] ... KJBZ
Laredo, TX [*AM radio station call letters*] ... KLAR
Laredo, TX [*Television station call letters*] ... KLDO
Laredo, TX [*FM radio station call letters*] ... KOYE
Laredo, TX [*FM radio station call letters*] ... KRRG
Laredo, TX [*AM radio station call letters*] ... KVOZ
Laredo, TX [*Television station call letters*] ... KVTV
Laredo, TX [*FM radio station call letters*] ... KZTQ
Laredo, TX [*Location identifier FAA*] (FAAL) ... LOI
Lares [*Puerto Rico*] [*Seismograph station code, US Geological Survey*] (SEIS) ... LRS
Lares, PR [*AM radio station call letters*] ... WGDL
Largamente [*Easily*] [*Music*] ... LARG
Large [*Size designation for clothing, etc.*] ... L
Large (WDMC) ... l
Large ... LG
Large (MSA) ... LGE
Large Acrocentric Chromosome [*Medicine*] ... LAC
Large Advanced Mirror Program [*Military*] (SDI) ... LAMP
Large Aircraft Carrier [*Navy symbol Obsolete*] ... CVB
Large Aircraft Start System (DWSG) ... LASS
Large Amount [*Medicine*] ... LA
Large Amplitude Late Arrival [*Seismology*] ... LALA
Large Amplitude Multimode Aerospace Research Simulator ... LAMARS
Large Amplitude Simulator ... LAS
Large Amplitude SLOSH [*Sea, Lake, Overland Surge from Hurricanes*] [*NASA*] ... LAMPS
Large and Medium Lymphocytes [*Medicine*] ... LML
Large and Small Capital Letters (WDMC) ... C & sc
Large and Small Capital Letters (WDMC) ... csc
Large Angle and Spectrometric Coronagraph Experiment [*For observation of the sun*] ... LASCO
Large Angle Tagger (MCD) ... LAT
Large Angle Torque (MCD) ... LAT
Large Antenna Multifrequency Microwave Radiometer (MCD) ... LAMMR
Large Aperture [*Photography*] (ROG) ... LA
Large Aperture Infrared Telescope System ... LAIRTS
Large Aperture Microwave Radiometer (SSD) ... LAMR
Large Aperture Scanning Telescope (TEL) ... LAST
Large Aperture Seismic Array [*Nuclear detection device*] ... LASA
Large Aperture Seismic Experiment [*Geophysical survey*] ... LASE
Large Aperture Solenoid Spectrometer [*Stanford Linear Accelerator Center*] ... LASS
Large Area Coverage [*Marine science*] (OSRA) ... LAC
Large Area Crop Inventory Experiment [*NASA*] ... LACIE
Large Area Crop Inventory Program [*NASA*] (NASA) ... LACIP
Large Area Detector [*Instrumentation*] ... LAD
Large Area Display ... LAD
Large Area Electronic Display ... LAED
Large Area Electronic Display Panel ... LAEDP
Large Area Electronic Panel ... LAEP
Large Area/Mobile Projected Smoke System [*Military*] (RDA) ... LA/MPSS
Large Area Modular Array of Reflectors [*Astronomy*] ... LAMAR
Large Area Multi Object Fiber Spectroscopic Telescope [*Proposed, China*] ... LAMOST
Large Area Nozzle Delivery of Fuel Air Explosive (RDA) ... LANDFAE
Large Area Panel ... LAP
Large Area Record Reader (IAA) ... LARR
Large Area Screening Systems (MCD) ... LASS
Large Area Sky Survey ... LASS
Large Area Solar Array ... LASA
Large Area Solar Cell Array ... LASCA
Large Area Transmission Density (MCD) ... LATD
Large Artificial Nerve [*or Neuron*] **Network** ... LANNET
Large Assembly Order (MCD) ... LAO
Large Astronomical Satellite [*ESRO*] ... LAS
Large Atypical Mole Syndrome [*Medicine*] ... LAMS
Large Atypical Nevus Syndrome [*Medicine*] ... LANS
Large Automatic Navigational Buoy [*Shipping*] (DS) ... LANBY
Large Automatic Research Computer [*or Calculator*] ... LARC
Large Base Unit [*Telecommunications*] ... LBU
Large Basin Runoff Model [*Marine science*] (OSRA) ... LBRM
Large Basin Runoff Model (USDC) ... LBRM
Large Bile Duct [*Medicine*] (DMAA) ... LBD
Large Binocular Telescope ... LBT
Large Blast Load Generator (PDAA) ... LBLG
Large Blast Simulator ... LBS
Large Bore Cannon (MCD) ... LBC
Large Bowel [*Anatomy*] ... LB
Large Bowel Obstruction [*Medicine*] ... LBO
Large Bright Quasar Survey [*Astronomy*] ... LBQS
Large Bulb Ship ... LBS
Large Caliber Soft Recoil [*Weaponry*] (MCD) ... LCSR
Large Caliber Weapon Systems Laboratory [*ARRADCOM*] (RDA) ... LCWSL
Large Calorie (DMAA) ... Cal
Large Capacity Cassette [*Electronic printing*] (DGA) ... LCC
Large Capacity Core Storage [*Computer science*] (MDG) ... LCCS
Large Capacity [*or Core*] **Storage** [*Computer science*] ... LCS
Large Case [*Indicator*] [*IRS*] ... LC
Large Catapult Lighter [*Navy symbol Obsolete*] ... AVC
Large Cavitation Channel [*Pressurized water tunnel to test submarines and ship models*] [*Navy*] ... LCC
Large Cell [*Lymphoma classification*] ... LC
Large Cell Lung Carcinoma [*Oncology*] (DAVI) ... LCLC
Large Climate-Moderating Envelope [*Energy-conserving form of architecture*] ... LCME
Large Close-Up (ADA) ... LCU
Large Cloud Particle-Size Spectrometer ... LCPS
Large Coil Program [*Physics*] ... LCP
Large Coil Test Facility (MCD) ... LCTF
Large Combatant (DNAB) ... LGCOMB
Large Component Handling System [*Nuclear energy*] (NRCH) ... LCHS
Large Component Test Loop [*Nuclear energy*] ... LCTL
Large Components Test Installation [*Nuclear energy*] (NRCH) ... LCTI

Large Compound Vesicle [Biochemistry]	LCV
Large Compressor Colorimeter (MCD)	LCC
Large Computer Project (IAA)	LCP
Large Computerized [Private] Branch Exchange (MHDI)	LCBX
Large Co-Ops Network [British]	LCN
Large Core Storage [Computer science] (OA)	LCS
Large Cosmic X-Ray Telescope (PDAA)	LCXT
Large Covered Lighter [Non-self-propelled] [Navy symbol]	YFNB
Large Cruiser [Navy symbol Obsolete]	CB
Large Dense-Core Vesicle [Neurobiology]	LDCV
Large Dense-Cored Vesicle [Medicine] (DMAA)	LDV
Large Deployable Antenna Shuttle Experiment [NASA] (PDAA)	LDASE
Large Deployable Reflector [Astronomy]	LDR
Large Developmental Plant [Project] [Department of Energy]	LDP
Large Diameter Component Cask [Nuclear energy] (NRCH)	LDCC
Large Diameter Core (SAA)	LDC
Large Diameter Gravity Corer [Nuclear energy] (NUCP)	LGC
Large Disk Storage [Computer science] (IEEE)	LDS
Large Dollar [Indicator] [IRS]	LD
Large Earth Survey Telescope	LEST
Large Earth-Based [formerly, European] Solar Telescope	LEST
Large Eddy Breakup Device [Aerodynamics]	LEBU
Large Eddy Simulation [For modelling fluid flow]	LES
Large Einsteinium Activation Program	LEAP
Large Electronic Display	LED
Large Electronic Display Panel	LEDP
Large Electronic Panel	LEP
Large Electron-Positron [Accelerator] [in Europe]	LEP
Large End (OA)	LE
Large Engineering Loop [NASA] (NRCH)	LEL
Large Experimental Aquifer Program [Oregon Graduate Institute of Science and Technology] [Research center] (RCD)	LEAP
Large Extension Node [Telecommunications] (LAIN)	LEN
Large, External Transformation Sensitive [Glycoprotein] [Also known as CSP Cytochemistry]	LETS
Large Families of America [Defunct] (EA)	LFA
Large Field of View [Radiology] (DAVI)	LFOV
Large Field of View [Radiology] (DAVI)	LFV
Large Flat Plate	LFP
Large Flight Envelope (MCD)	LFE
Large Follow-On	LFO
Large for Gestational Age [Pediatrics]	LGA
Large Format Camera [Space exploration]	LFC
Large Formation Flyer (SSD)	LFF
Large German Telescope [Acronym is based on German phrase]	DGT
Large Glucagon Immunoreactivity [Immunochemistry]	LGI
Large Grain	LG
Large Granular Leukocyte [Hematology]	LGL
Large Granular Lymphocyte [Hematology]	LGL
Large Granular Vesicle (OA)	LGV
Large Gray Ship [Slang Navy]	LGS
Large Green Soft [Stool] [Gastroenterology] (DAVI)	LGS
Large Group Display (MCD)	LGD
Large Group Health Plan [Department of Health and Human Services] (GFGA)	LGHP
Large Group View Display (MCD)	LGVD
Large Guided Missile Motorboat [Navy symbol] (DNAB)	PTFG
Large Hadron Collider [Nuclear physics] (ECON)	LHC
Large Harbor Tug [Self-propelled] [Navy symbol]	YTB
Large Heavy Seeds [Botany]	LH
Large Hydrofoil Hybrid Ship	Lahhs
Large Immersion Lens	LIL
Large Infrared Telescope	LIRTS
Large Integrated Circuit [Electronics]	LIC
Large Integrated Monolithic Array Computer (MCD)	LIMAC
Large Interactive Surface [Automated drafting table that serves as a computer input and output device]	LIS
Large Internet Packet [Computer science] (PCM)	LIP
Large Inventory Top-Tier Site [Industrial hazard designation] [British]	LITTS
Large Ion Lithophile Element [Geochemistry]	LILE
Large Jet Engine Department [NASA] (KSC)	LJED
Large Launch Vehicle Planning Group [NASA]	LLVPG
Large Leak Test Rig [Nuclear energy] (NRCH)	LLTR
Large Letter	LL
Large Light Seeds [Botany]	LL
Large Local Exchange [Telecommunications] (TEL)	LLE
Large Local Reaction [Medicine] (DMAA)	LLR
Large Loop Excision of the Transformation Zone [Medicine]	LLETZ
Large Lymphocyte [Medicine]	LL
Large Magellanic Cloud [Astronomy]	LMC
Large Marine Ecosystem	LME
Large, Medium Speed RO/RO [Roll On/Roll Off] [Navy]	LMSR
Large Memory [Computer science]	LM
Large Metoscale Area (PDAA)	LMSA
Large Millimeter Telescope [US-Mexico project] [Proposed, 1994]	LMT
Large Model Access (MCD)	LMA
Large Monopolar Cell [Anatomy]	LMC
Large Mouth Bass [Pisciculture]	LM
Large Multifunctional Protease [Medicine] (DMAA)	LMP
Large Myelinated Fiber [Neuroanatomy]	LMF
Large Navigation Buoy [Marine science] (MSC)	LNB
Large Neuronal Polypeptide [Medicine] (DMAA)	LNP
Large Number Hypothesis [Medicine] (DMAA)	LNH
Large Object Salvage System [Navy]	LOSS
Large Off-Line Retrieval Text Base Access System	LORBAS

Large Opaque Vesicle [Medicine] (DMAA)	LOV
Large Open-Area Floor	LOAF
Large Optical Cavity [LASER design]	LOC
Large Optical Reflector	LOR
Large Optical Tracker - Aerospace	LOTAS
Large Optics Demonstration Experiment [DoD]	LODE
Large Optics Diamond Turning Machine (SDI)	LODTM
Large Orbital Research Laboratory [NASA]	LORL
Large Orbital X-Ray Telescope [NASA]	LOXT
Large Orbiting Earth Resources Observatory (IEEE)	LOERO
Large Orbiting Telescope (MCD)	LOT
Large Order Assembly Planning System (MCD)	LOAPS
Large Organic Debris [Pisciculture]	LOD
Large Overland Transporter System (MCD)	LOTS
Large Paper Proofs	LPP
Large Particle	LP
Large Payload Test Vehicle [Air Force]	LPTV
Large Phased-Array RADAR	LAPAR
Large Phased-Array RADAR	LPAR
Large Pointing System (MCD)	LPS
Large Post	LP
Large Power Plant Effluent Study (NRCH)	LAPPES
Large Print Video Terminal	LPVT
Large Radio Observatory (KSC)	LRO
Large Radioisotope Heat Source [NASA] (IAA)	LRHS
Large Radioisotope Heat Source Capsule [NASA] (KSC)	LRHSC
Large Repair Parts Transporter (MCD)	LRPT
Large Repairs to Hull	LRP
Large Retractable Solar Cell Array	LRSCA
Large Ring	LR
Large Ring Sparger [Engineering]	LRS
Large Rotating Plug [Nuclear energy] (NRCH)	LRP
Large Scale (ABBR)	LGSC
Large Scale Integration Development	LSID
Large Science Aperture [Spectrometer]	LSA
Large Screen Color Television System (NASA)	LASCOT
Large Screen Display	LSD
Large Screen Display System	LSDS
Large Screen RADAR Indicator	LSRI
Large Seed-Blanket Reactor	LSBR
Large Shallow-Draught [Bulk carrier] (PDAA)	LSD
Large Ship Reactor	LSR
Large Single Copy Region [Of a chromosome] [Genetics]	LSC
Large Sky Area Multi-Objects Fiber Spectroscopic Telescope [China]	LAMOST
Large Sodium Disposal Facility [Nuclear energy] (NRCH)	LSDF
Large Solar Concentrator (SSD)	LSC
Large Solar Observatory [NASA]	LSO
Large Solid Motor [Aerospace]	LSM
Large Space Antenna (SSD)	LSA
Large Space Structure (IEEE)	LSS
Large Space System (IEEE)	LSS
Large Space Telescope [Later, Space Telescope] [NASA]	LST
Large Spherical Array	LSA
Large Steam Turbine-Generator	LST-G
Large Steel Desk [Position given to ex-astronauts]	LSD
Large Stellar Telescope (KSC)	LST
Large Structure Technology Experiment (SSD)	LSTE
Large Submetacentric Chromosome [Medicine]	LSC
Large Subsonic Tunnel [NASA]	LST
Large Surface Effect Ship (PDAA)	LSES
Large Table Electroplotter [Computer science]	LTE
Large Tactical Command Ship [Navy symbol Obsolete]	CBC
Large Terminal Repeats [Genetics] (DAVI)	LTE
Large Test Vessel [Nuclear energy] (NRCH)	LTV
Large Thrust per Element	LTE
Large Transformed Cell [Medicine] (DMAA)	LTC
Large Transmitter Coated with Paraffin	LT-P
Large Transmitter Coated with Silicon Rubber	LT-SR
Large Transport Airplane	LTA
Large Tug [Army]	LT
Large Ultimate Size [Telecommunications] (TEL)	LUS
Large Undisturbed-Bottom Sampler (PDAA)	LUBS
Large Unilamellar Vesicle [Pharmacy Biochemistry]	LUV
Large Unstained Cells [Cytology]	LUC
Large Vacuum Chamber [Army]	LVC
Large Vertical Aperture Antenna [Aviation]	LVA
Large Vessel Hematocrit (MAE)	LVH
Large Virus-Like Particle	LVLP
Large Volume Filtration System [Environmental chemistry]	LVFS
Large Volume Parenterals [Medicine]	LVP
Large White Kidney [Medicine] (DMAA)	LWK
Large Woody Debris [Pisciculture]	LWD
Large X-Ray Survey Experiment (PDAA)	LAXRAY
Large-Amplitude, Slow Wave Activity [Encephalography]	LSWA
Large-Angle Spectrometric Coronagraph [Marine science] (OSRA)	LASCO
Large-Angle Spectrometric Coronagraph [USDC]	LASCO
Large-Angle Spectroscopic Coronagraph [Instrumentation]	LASCO
Large-Animal Anesthesia Machine [Instrumentation]	LAAM
Large-Area Processing [For fabricating multichip modules]	LAP
Large-Area-Counter [Astronomy] [Instrumentation]	LAC
Large-Component Cleaning Vessel [Nuclear energy] (NRCH)	LCCV
Large-Core Memory [Computer science]	LCM
Large-Ion Lithophile	LIL
Largely (ABBR)	LGY
Largeness (ABBR)	LGNS

Large-Paper Edition [of a book]	LP
Large-Probe Atmospheric Structure [NASA]	LAS
Large-Probe Gas Chromatograph [NASA]	LGC
Large-Probe Nephelometer [NASA]	LN
Large-Probe Neutral Mass Spectrometer [NASA]	LNMS
Large-Probe Solar Net Flux Radiometer [NASA]	LSFR
Larger (WGA)	LGR
Larger Word [Computer science]	LWD
Large-Sample Scanning Tunneling Mode [Microscopy]	LSTM
Large-Scale Compound Integration	LSCI
Large-Scale Computer	LSC
Large-Scale Disturbance Field	SL
Large-Scale Dynamical System (PDAA)	LSDS
Large-Scale Equipment (MCD)	LSE
Large-Scale General Purpose	LSGP
Large-Scale Geostrophic [Marine science] (OSRA)	LSG
Large-Scale Hybrid Integration	LSHI
Large-Scale Integrated Circuit [Electronics] (KSC)	LSIC
Large-Scale Integration [of circuits] [Electronics]	LSI
Large-Scale Integration Computer	LSIC
Large-Scale Integration Technology (IAA)	LSIT
Large-Scale Linear Integration (IAA)	LSLI
Large-Scale Melt Facility [Nuclear reactor test unit]	LMF
Large-Scale Operations Management Test (RDA)	LSOMT
Large-Scale Standard (IAA)	LSS
Large-Scale Structure [Cosmology]	LSS
Large-Solid Propellant Booster Program [Aerospace] (IAA)	LSPBP
Largest (ABBR)	LGT
Largest Feasible Steerable Telescope	LF
Largest Frame (ACRL)	LPT
Largest Processing Time First [Computer science] (MHDB)	LSI
Largest Single Item (AFM)	LV
Largest Vessel [British] (ADA)	LARGO
Larghetto [Slow] [Music] (ROG)	LGHET
Larghetto (ABBR)	LARG
Largo [Very Slow] [Music] (ROG)	LGO
Largo (ABBR)	WNZE
Largo, FL [AM radio station call letters]	WNZE
Largo, FL [AM radio station call letters] (RBYB)	WZTM-AM
Lariat Oil & Gas Ltd. [Toronto Stock Exchange symbol]	LAR
Larimer Memorial Library, Palatka, FL [Library symbol Library of Congress] (LCLS)	FPa
Larissa [Greece] [ICAO location identifier] (ICLI)	LGLR
Larissa [Greece] [Airport symbol] (OAG)	LRA
Larizza Industries, Inc. [Associated Press] (SAG)	Larizz
Larizza Industries, Inc. [AMEX symbol] (SPSG)	LII
Larkana [Pakistan] [Airport symbol] (AD)	LKW
Larkspur Public Library, Larkspur, CA [Library symbol Library of Congress] (LCLS)	CLar
Lar-Linile Aeriene Romance [Romania] [ICAO designator] (FAAC)	RLA
Larnaca [Cyprus] [Airport symbol] (OAG)	LCA
Larnaca [Cyprus] [ICAO location identifier] (ICLI)	LCLK
Larned, KS [AM radio station call letters]	KANS
Larned, KS [FM radio station call letters] (RBYB)	KGTR
Larned, KS [Location identifier FAA] (FAAL)	LQR
Larned State Hospital, Larned, KS [Library symbol Library of Congress] (LCLS)	KLaSH
LaRoche College, Pittsburgh, PA [OCLC symbol] (OCLC)	PLR
LaRoche College, Pittsburgh, PA [Library symbol Library of Congress] (LCLS)	PPiL
Laron-Type Dwarfism [Medicine]	LTD
Larose, LA [FM radio station call letters]	KLRZ
La-Rouche-Sur-Yon [France] [Airport symbol]	ELM
Larrimore, William M., San Francisco CA [STAC]	LWM
Larry Gatlin and the Gatlin Brothers Fan Club (EA)	LGGBFC
Larry Gatlin and the Gatlin Brothers International Fan Club (EA)	LGGBIFC
Larscom Inc. [NASDAQ symbol] (SAG)	LARS
Larscom Inc. [Associated Press] (SAG)	Larscom
Larsen and Toubro Ltd. [India] [Commercial firm]	LT
Larsen Bay [Alaska] [Airport symbol] (OAG)	KLN
Larson Davis [NASDAQ symbol] (TTSB)	LDII
Larson-Davis [Associated Press] (SAG)	LarDav
Larson-Davis [NASDAQ symbol] (SAG)	LDII
Larva [Biology]	L
Larval Chamber [Botany]	LC
Larval Heart	LH
Larval Hemolymph Protein [Entomology]	LHP
Larval Operculum	LO
Laryak [Former USSR ICAO location identifier] (ICLI)	USRL
Laryngeal [Otorhinolaryngology] (DAVI)	laryn
Laryngeal Mask [Medicine] (DMAA)	LM
Laryngeal Muscle (BABM)	LM
Laryngeal Pharyngeal [Medicine]	LP
Laryngeal Sound Discrimination [Medicine] (DMAA)	LSD
Laryngectomee Association of New South Wales [Australia]	LANSW
Laryngectomy [Medicine] (MAE)	LG
Laryngitis [Otorhinolaryngology] (DAVI)	laryn
Laryngofissure (MAE)	LF
Laryngologist	LARYNGLGST
Laryngologist (DAVI)	Laryngol
Laryngology	LAR
Laryngology	Laryng
Laryngology	LARYNGLGY
Laryngology	LARYNGOL
Laryngoscopy [Otorhinolaryngology] (DAVI)	laryn

Laryngo-Tracheal Bronchitis	LTB
Larynx [Anatomy] (DAVI)	lar
Laryssa Lauret Fan Club (EA)	LLFC
Las Acacias [Argentina] [Geomagnetic observatory code]	ACS
Las Animas Public Library, Las Animas, CO [Library symbol Library of Congress] (LCLS)	CoLas
Las Anod [Somalia] [ICAO location identifier] (ICLI)	HCMP
Las Clavellinas [Cuba ICAO location identifier] (ICLI)	MUCV
Las Cruces [New Mexico] [Airport symbol] (OAG)	LRU
Las Cruces [Diocesan abbreviation] [New Mexico] (TOCD)	LSC
Las Cruces, NM [AM radio station call letters]	KGRT
Las Cruces, NM [FM radio station call letters]	KGRT-FM
Las Cruces, NM [AM radio station call letters]	KOBE
Las Cruces, NM [FM radio station call letters]	KROL
Las Cruces, NM [FM radio station call letters]	KRUX
Las Cruces, NM [FM radio station call letters]	KRWG
Las Cruces, NM [Television station call letters]	KRWG-TV
Las Cruces, NM [AM radio station call letters] (RBYB)	KXDA
Las Cruces, NM [Television station call letters]	KZIA
Las Cruces, NM [Location identifier FAA] (FAAL)	LCR
Las Cruces, NM [Location identifier FAA] (FAAL)	LRU
Las Heras [Argentina ICAO location identifier] (ICLI)	SAVH
Las Hermanas [Later, LH-USA] (EA)	LH
Las Hermanas de Juan Diego (TOCD)	HJD
Las Hermanas-United States of America (EA)	LH-USA
Las Lomas [Costa Rica] [ICAO location identifier] (ICLI)	MRLL
Las Lomitas [Argentina ICAO location identifier] (ICLI)	SATK
Las Mesas [Puerto Rico] [Seismograph station code, US Geological Survey] (SEIS)	LSP
Las Oblatas de Jesus Sacerdote [Oblates of Jesus the Priest] [Roman Catholic women's religious order]	OJS
Las Palmas [Canary Islands] [Airport symbol] (OAG)	LPA
Las Palmas [Peru] [ICAO location identifier] (ICLI)	SPLP
Las Piedras [Venezuela] [Airport symbol] (OAG)	LSP
Las Trancas [Costa Rica] [ICAO location identifier] (ICLI)	MRLT
Las Tunas [Cuba ICAO location identifier] (ICLI)	MUVT
Las Tunas [Cuba] [Airport symbol] (OAG)	VTU
Las Vegas [New Mexico] [ICAO location identifier] (ICLI)	KLVS
Las Vegas [Nevada] [Airport symbol] (OAG)	LAS
Las Vegas [Diocesan abbreviation] [Nevada] (TOCD)	LAV
Las Vegas [Nevada] [Seismograph station code, US Geological Survey] (SEIS)	LVN
Las Vegas [Nevada] [Seismograph station code, US Geological Survey] (SEIS)	LVW
Las Vegas Airlines [ICAO designator] (AD)	TQ
Las Vegas Carnegie Library, Las Vegas, NM [Library symbol Library of Congress] (LCLS)	NmLv
Las Vegas Disc Golf & Tennis [NASDAQ symbol] (TTSB)	LVDG
Las Vegas Discount Golf & Tennis [NASDAQ symbol] (SAG)	LVDG
Las Vegas Discount Golf & Tennis, Inc. [Associated Press] (SAG)	LasVDsc
Las Vegas Entertainment Network [Associated Press] (SAG)	LasVE
Las Vegas Entertainment Network [Associated Press] (SAG)	LasVEE
Las Vegas Entertainment Network [Associated Press] (SAG)	LasVEnt
Las Vegas Entertainment Network [NASDAQ symbol] (SAG)	LVEN
Las Vegas Entmt Ntwk [NASDAQ symbol] (TTSB)	LVEN
Las Vegas Entmt Ntwk Wrrt'A' [NASDAQ symbol] (TTSB)	LVENW
Las Vegas Entmt Ntwk Wrrt'B' [NASDAQ symbol] (TTSB)	LVENZ
Las Vegas Major League Sports [Associated Press] (SAG)	LasVMaj
Las Vegas/McCarran International [Nevada] [ICAO location identifier] (ICLI)	KLAS
Las Vegas Mjr League Sports [NASDAQ symbol] (TTSB)	LVTD
Las Vegas/Nellis Air Force Base [Nevada] [ICAO location identifier] (ICLI)	KLSV
Las Vegas, NM [FM radio station call letters]	KBAC
Las Vegas, NM [FM radio station call letters]	KEDP
Las Vegas, NM [AM radio station call letters]	KFUN
Las Vegas, NM [FM radio station call letters]	KLVF
Las Vegas, NM [AM radio station call letters]	KNMX
Las Vegas, NM [Location identifier FAA] (FAAL)	LVS
Las Vegas [Nevada] North Terminal [Airport symbol] (OAG)	VGT
Las Vegas, NV [Location identifier FAA] (FAAL)	AUI
Las Vegas, NV [Location identifier FAA] (FAAL)	DIQ
Las Vegas, NV [FM radio station call letters]	KCEP
Las Vegas, NV [AM radio station call letters]	KDWN
Las Vegas, NV [FM radio station call letters]	KEDG
Las Vegas, NV [FM radio station call letters]	KENO
Las Vegas, NV [FM radio station call letters]	KEYV
Las Vegas, NV [Television station call letters]	KFBT
Las Vegas, NV [FM radio station call letters]	KFMS-FM
Las Vegas, NV [FM radio station call letters]	KILA
Las Vegas, NV [Television station call letters] (RBYB)	KINC
Las Vegas, NV [Television station call letters]	KKLZ
Las Vegas, NV [AM radio station call letters]	KKVV
Las Vegas, NV [Television station call letters]	KLAS
Las Vegas, NV [AM radio station call letters]	KLAV
Las Vegas, NV [FM radio station call letters]	KLUC-FM
Las Vegas, NV [Television station call letters]	KLVX
Las Vegas, NV [FM radio station call letters]	KNPR
Las Vegas, NV [FM radio station call letters]	KOMP
Las Vegas, NV [AM radio station call letters]	KORK
Las Vegas, NV [FM radio station call letters]	KRBO
Las Vegas, NV [Television station call letters]	KRLR
Las Vegas, NV [AM radio station call letters] (RBYB)	KRLV
Las Vegas, NV [FM radio station call letters] (RBYB)	KSNE-FM
Las Vegas, NV [Television station call letters]	KTNV
Las Vegas, NV [FM radio station call letters]	KUNV

Las Vegas, NV [*Television station call letters*] (RBYB) .... KUPN
Las Vegas, NV [*Television station call letters*] .... KVBC
Las Vegas, NV [*FM radio station call letters*] (RBYB) .... KVBC-FM
Las Vegas, NV [*FM radio station call letters*] .... KXPT
Las Vegas, NV [*Location identifier FAA*] (FAAL) .... LAS
Las Vegas, NV [*Location identifier FAA*] (FAAL) .... LSV
Las Vegas, NV [*Location identifier FAA*] (FAAL) .... VGT
Las Vegas Public Library, Las Vegas, NV [*Library symbol Library of Congress*] (LCLS) .... NvL
Las Vegas, TX [*FM radio station call letters*] (RBYB) .... KBGO-FM
Lasa Array [*Montana*] [*Seismograph station code, US Geological Survey*] (SEIS) .... LAO
Lasa B Ring [*Montana*] [*Seismograph station code, US Geological Survey*] (SEIS) .... LB
Lasa C Ring [*Montana*] [*Seismograph station code, US Geological Survey*] (SEIS) LC
Lasa D Ring [*Montana*] [*Seismograph station code, US Geological Survey*] (SEIS) .... LD
LaSall Re Holdings [*NASDAQ symbol*] (TTSB) .... LSREF
LaSalle County Board for Developmentally Disabled, Ottawa, IL [*Library symbol Library of Congress*] (LCLS) .... IOtBD
LaSalle County Cooperative Extension, Ottawa, IL [*Library symbol Library of Congress*] (LCLS) .... IOtCE
LaSalle County Educational Service Region, Ottawa, IL [*Library symbol Library of Congress*] (LCLS) .... IOtES
LaSalle County Regional Planning Commission, Ottawa, IL [*Library symbol Library of Congress*] (LCLS) .... IOtRP
LaSalle, IL [*FM radio station call letters*] (RBYB) .... WNIW-FM
LaSalle Parish Library, Jena, LA [*Library symbol Library of Congress*] (LCLS) .... LJeL
LaSalle Public Library, LaSalle, IL [*Library symbol Library of Congress*] (LCLS) .... ILas
LaSalle Re Holdings Ltd. [*NASDAQ symbol*] (SAG) .... LSREF
LaSalle-Peru Township High School, LaSalle, IL [*Library symbol Library of Congress*] (LCLS) .... ILasSD
Lasallian Sisters (Vietnam) (TOCD) .... LS
LaSallian Volunteer Movement (EA) .... LVM
Lascelles' Horse Warranty [*2nd ed.*] [*1880*] [*A publication*] (DLA) .... Lasc H War
Lascelles on Juvenile Offenders [*A publication*] (DLA) .... Lasc Juv Off
Lasell Junior College [*Newton, MA*] .... LJC
Laser L
Laser (VRA) .... lsr
Laser .... LSR
LASER Absolute Gravimeter .... LAG
LASER Absorption Spectrometer .... LAS
LASER Absorption Wave (PDAA) .... LAW
LASER Acoustic Delay .... LAD
LASER Acquisition and Direction .... LAD
LASER Acquisition and Tracking (OA) .... LAT
LASER Acquisition Device (MCD) .... LAD
LASER Active Boresight System (PDAA) .... LABS
LASER Actuator Director System [*DoD*] .... LADS
LASER Advanced Development Center (IAA) .... LADC
LASER Aerospace Communications Experiment .... LACE
LASER [*Light Amplification by Stimulated Emission of Radiation*] Aiming Module .... LAM
LASER Aiming Simulation (PDAA) .... LASIM
LASER Air Defense .... LAD
LASER Air Defense System .... LADS
LASER Airborne Depth Sounder .... LADS
LASER Airborne Photographic Scanning System [*Navy*] .... LAPSS
LASER Air-to-Air Gunnery Simulator [*Military*] (CAAL) .... LATAG
LASER Alarm Locator System .... LALS
LASER Altimeter [*NASA*] .... LA
LASER Amplifier Chain .... LAC
Laser and Electro-Optics Manufacturers' Association (EA) .... LEMA
LASER and Electro-Optics Manufacturers' Association .... LEOMA
LASER and FLIR [*Forward-Looking Infrared*] Test Set [*Air Force*] .... LAFTS
LASER and MASER Patents .... LAMP
LASER and Mixing Program .... LAMP
LASER Angioplasty [*Cardiology*] (DMAA) .... LA
LASER Angular Rate Sensor [*or Scanner*] .... LARS
LASER Antiflash System .... LAS
LASER Anti-Satellite Weapon (LAIN) .... LASA
LASER Antitank Semiactive Homing .... LASH
LASER Applications in Close Air Support [*Air Force*] .... LACAS
LASER Applications Research Center (RCD) .... LARC
LASER Applications System Study [*Military*] .... LASS
Laser Assisted In-Situ Keratomileusis [*Ophthalmology*] .... LASIK
Laser Association of America [*Later, LEMA*] (EA) .... LAA
LASER Atmospheric Transmission Test .... LATT
LASER Atmospheric Visibility and Contamination (PDAA) .... LAVAC
LASER Atmospheric Wind Sounder [*NASA*] .... LAWS
LASER Attack System .... LAS
LASER Attenuator Assembly .... LAA
LASER [*Gyro*] Axis (IEEE) .... LA
LASER Bank Management System [*Computer science*] .... LMS
LASER Beam Analyzer (IAA) .... LBA
LASER Beam Cutting [*Welding*] .... LBC
LASER Beam Cutting - Air .... LBC-A
LASER Beam Cutting - Evaporative .... LBC-EV
LASER Beam Cutting - Inert Gas .... LBC-IG
LASER Beam Cutting - Oxygen .... LBC-O
LASER Beam Image Reproducer .... LBIR
LASER Beam Machine (IAA) .... LBM

LASER Beam Position Indicator .... LBPI
LASER Beam Position Indicator System .... LBPIS
Laser Beam Printer (NITA) .... LBP
LASER Beam Recorder [*or Recording*] .... LBR
LASER Beam Rider (RDA) .... LBR
LASER Beam Rider Guidance (MCD) .... LBRG
LASER Beam Surgery .... LBS
LASER Beam Welding .... LBW
LASER Bibliography (MCD) .... LABIB
LASER Bombing System .... LBS
Laser Capture Microdissection [*Biochemistry*] .... LCM
LASER Chemical Vapor Deposition [*Coating technology*] .... LCVD
LASER Cloud Mapper .... LCM
LASER Code Control Panel (MCD) .... LCCP
LASER Coherence Techniques Section .... LCTS
LASER Communication (SSD) .... LACO
LASER Communication Satellite Experiment [*NASA*] .... LCSE
LASER Communications (MCD) .... LASERCOM
LASER Communications System .... LCS
LASER Compatible Vidicon LCV
LASER Cooling Unit (MCD) .... LCU
Laser Corp. [*Associated Press*] (SAG) .... LasrCp
Laser Corp. [*NASDAQ symbol*] (SAG) .... LSER
LASER Countermeasure .... LCM
LASER Countermeasure System [*Military*] (INF) .... LCMS
LASER Crosswind System (RDA) .... LCS
LASER Deep Space .... LDS
LASER Designation Battlefield Obscuration Simulator (RDA) .... LDBOS
LASER Designator Range (MCD) .... LDR
LASER Designator Rangefinding Module (RDA) .... LDRM
LASER Designator Search System .... LDSS
LASER Designator System [*Rangefinder*] (MCD) .... LDS
LASER Designator Weapon System Simulation (RDA) .... LDWSS
LASER Desorption [*of ions for analysis*] .... LD
LASER Desorption Ionization [*Spectroscopy*] .... LDI
LASER Desorption Mass Spectrometry .... LDMS
LASER Desorption Time-of-Flight [*Spectrometry*] .... LDTOF
LASER Detection and Analysis System (MCD) .... LDAS
LASER Detection and Ranging .... LADAR
Laser Detection System .... LDS
LASER Detector Diode .... LDD
LASER Diode .... LD
LASER Diode Driver .... LDD
LASER Discectomy [*Spinal surgery*] .... LD
LASER Discharge Capacitor (IAA) .... LDC
LASER Discharge Tube .... LDT
LASER Discrimination RADAR System .... LDRS
LASER Distance Measuring Equipment (DNAB) .... LDME
LASER Distance Measuring Instrument .... LDMI
LASER Distance Measuring System .... LDMS
LASER Doppler Anemometry .... LDA
LASER Doppler RADAR (MCD) .... LADAR
LASER Doppler RADAR (IAA) .... LOPPLAR
LASER Doppler Velocimeter .... LDV
LASER Drilling Machine .... LDM
LASER Drilling System .... LDS
LASER/Electro/Optic Measurement Alignment System .... LEOMA
LASER Electron Paramagnetic Resonance .... LEPR
LASER Electronic Computer .... LEC
LASER Electronics (MCD) .... LE
LASER Electro-Optical Alignment Pole for Surveying [*NASA*] .... LEAPS
LASER Energy Evaluator (PDAA) .... LEE
LASER Energy Monitor .... LEM
LASER Engineering and Application of Prototype System (MCD) .... LEAPS
LASER Enhanced NMR [*Nuclear Magnetic Resonance*] Spectroscopy .... LENS
LASER Excitation Spectroscopy .... LES
LASER Excited Fluorescence .... LEF
LASER Exhaust Measurement .... LEM
LASER Experimental Package .... LEK
LASER Experimental Research Kit .... LERK
LASER Feedback Microscope .... LFM
LASER/Fiber-Optic (MCD) .... LFO
LASER Fire Control System .... LFCS
LASER Flash Lamp .... LFL
LASER Flash Tube .... LFT
LASER Fluorescence Spectroscopy .... LFS
LASER Force Microscope .... LFM
LASER Fusion Breeder Reactor .... LFBR
LASER Fusion Feasibility Project [*Nuclear fusion*] .... LFFP
LASER Geodynamic Satellite [*NASA*] (PDAA) .... LAGEO
LASER Geodynamic Satellite [*NASA*] .... LAGEOS
LASER Ground Mapper .... LGM
LASER Ground Mapping System .... LGMS
LASER Guidance System (MCD) .... LGS
LASER Gyro (MCD) .... LG
LASER Gyro Interface Unit (NASA) .... LGIU
LASER HELLFIRE Missile Evaluation (MCD) .... LHME
LASER Hole Drilling System .... LHDS
LASER Homing and Warning System [*Military*] (PDAA) .... LAHAWS
LASER Illumination Detection System .... LIDS
LASER Illuminator System .... LIS
LASER Illuminator Targeting Equipment .... LITE
LASER Image Converter LIC
LASER Image Display (MCD) .... LID
LASER Image Generator (MCD) .... LIG

LASER Indirect Fire Semiactive ... LISA
Laser Indus Ltd, Ord [*AMEX symbol*] (TTSB) ... LAS
Laser Industries Ltd. [*AMEX symbol*] (SPSG) ... LAS
Laser Industries Ltd. [*Associated Press*] (SAG) ... Laser
LASER Inertial Aided Synthetic Aperture RADAR (MCD) ... LIASAR
LASER Inertial Measurement Unit (MCD) ... LIMU
LASER Inertial Navigation Attack System (IAA) ... LINAS
LASER Inertial Navigation System (MCD) ... LINS
LASER In-Flight Obstacle Detection Device ... LIODD
LASER Infrared Countermeasures Demonstration System [*Air Force*] ... LIDS
LASER Infrared RADAR (IEEE) ... LIDAR
LASER Initiated Transfer Energy Subsystem [*Detonator, developed by US Navy*] ... LITES
LASER Initiating Explosive Device ... LIED
LASER Injection Diode ... LID
LASER In-Space Technology Experiment ... LITE
Laser Institute of America (EA) ... LIA
LASER Intelligence (MCD) ... LASINT
LASER Intensity Direction and Ranging (IEEE) ... LIDAR
Laser Intensity Modulation System [*Computer science*] ... LIMOS
LASER Intercept and Technical Exploitation System (MCD) ... LITES
LASER Intercept Capability [*Military*] (CAAL) ... LIC
LASER Interface Control Electronics (MCD) ... LICE
LASER Interference Filter ... LIF
LASER Interferometer System ... LIS
LASER Interferometric Holography ... LIH
LASER Interferometry Gravitational Wave Observatory [*Proposed*] ... LIGO
LASER Intrusion Detector ... LID
LASER Intrusion Device (MCD) ... LID
LASER Ionization Based on Resonant Saturation [*Physics*] ... LIBORS
LASER Isotope Dating ... LID
LASER Isotope Separation ... LIS
LASER Isotope Separation Program ... LISP
LASER Kit Combination Lock ... LKCL
LASER Light Detector ... LLD
LASER Light Pump ... LLP
LASER Light Scattering [*Physical chemistry*] ... LLS
LASER Light Scattering Spectroscopy ... LLSS
LASER Light Source ... LLS
LASER Light Source Station ... LLSS
LASER Lightning Rod System (PDAA) ... LLRS
LASER Line Scanner ... LLS
LASER Line Scanner Aerial Camera ... LLSAC
LASER Machine (IAA) ... LM
LASER Magnetic Resonance (MCD) ... LMR
LASER Magnetic Stage ... LMS
LASER Magnetic Storage International ... LMS
LASER Mapping System ... LMS
LASER Marksmanship Trainer (MCD) ... LMT
LASER Mass Spectrometer ... LMS
LASER Master Oscillator ... LMO
LASER Maverick (MCD) ... LMAV
Laser Microbeam Program [*Research center*] (RCD) ... LAMP
LASER Microprobe Mass Analyzer [*Spectrometry*] ... LAMMA
LASER Microprobe Mass Spectrometry [*or Spectroscopy*] ... LAMMS
LASER Microprobe Mass Spectrometry [*or Spectroscopy*] ... LMMS
LASER Microspectral Analysis ... LMA
LASER Microwave Division [*Army*] ... LMD
LASER Microwelder ... LMW
LASER Milling Gauge ... LMG
LASER Mirror Coating ... LMC
LASER Nephelometry [*Analytical biochemistry*] ... LN
LASER Night Sensor ... LNS
LASER Obstacle Terrain Avoidance Warning System ... LOTAWS
LASER Optical Guidance Integration Concept [*Missile guidance*] ... LOGIC
LASER Optical Modulator ... LOM
LASER Optical Ranging and Designation System ... LORADS
LASER Opto-Acoustic ... LOA
LASER Optoacoustic Detection ... LOAD
Laser Pacific Media Corp. [*Associated Press*] (SAG) ... LasPMd
Laser Pacific Media Corp. [*NASDAQ symbol*] (SAG) ... LPAC
LASER Particle Monitor (PDAA) ... LPM
LASER Particulate Spectrometer [*NASA*] ... LPS
LASER Phase Macroscope ... LPM
Laser Photocoagulation [*Ophthalmology*] (DAVI) ... LPC
LASER Photoionization Spectroscopy ... LAPIS
LASER Planning and Coordination Group [*Energy Research and Development Administration*] ... LPCG
LASER Plasmadynamic Converter ... LPDC
LASER Polarization Detector ... LPD
LASER Power Supply ... LPS
LASER Precision Microfabrication (IAA) ... LPM
LASER Printer Adapter ... LPA
Laser Printing System (NITA) ... LPS
LASER Profile System ... LAPS
LASER Propulsion Test (SSD) ... LPT
LASER Pyrolysis Technique [*Inorganic synthesis*] ... LPT
LASER RADAR Cross Section ... LRCS
LASER RADAR Fuze ... LRF
LASER RADAR Intelligence Acquisition Technology ... LARIAT
LASER Radiation Receiver ... LRR
LASER Raman Scattering ... LRS
LASER Raman Spectroscopy ... LRS
LASER Range-Finder ... LRF
LASER Range-Finder and Marked Target Receiver (MCD) ... LRF/MTR
LASER Range-Finder and Marked Target Seeker (MCD) ... LRMTS
LASER Range-Finder Controller (MCD) ... LRFC
LASER Range-Finder/Designator (MCD) ... LRF/D
LASER Range-Finder Theodolite ... LRT
LASER Ranger and Designator (MCD) ... LRD
LASER Ranger Finder/Solid State Computer (MCD) ... LRF/SSC
LASER Ranging and Designation System [*Military*] (CAAL) ... LRDS
LASER Ranging and Tracking System (RDA) ... LRTS
LASER Ranging Bombing System ... LRBS
LASER Ranging Retroreflection [*Also, LRRR*] [*Initialism pronounced "LR-cubed" Apollo 11 experiment*] [*NASA*] ... LR3
LASER Ranging Retroreflection [*Also, LR3*] [*Pronounced "LR-cubed" Apollo 11 experiment*] [*NASA*] ... LRRR
LASER Ranging System ... LRS
LASER Raster Scanner ... LRS
LASER [*Gyro*] **Reference Axis** (IEEE) ... LRA
LASER Reflectance Spectrometer (SSD) ... LRS
LASER Relay Communication Equipment ... LRCE
LASER Research Kit ... LRK
LASER Retinal Photocoagulator ... LRP
LASER Scan Inspection System (PDAA) ... LSIS
LASER Scanning Confocal Microscopy ... LSCM
LASER Scanning Microscope ... LSM
LASER Search and Secure Observer (CET) ... LASSO
LASER Semiactive Missile ... LASAM
LASER Semiactive Missile (DNAB) ... LASM
LASER Shutterable Image Sensor ... LSIS
Laser Sight, Inc. [*NASDAQ symbol*] (SAG) ... LASE
Laser Sight, Inc. [*Associated Press*] (SAG) ... LsrSght
LASER Signal Device ... LSD
LASER Slicing Machine ... LSM
LASER Source Signature Simulator ... LSSS
LASER Spectral Control ... LSC
LASER Spectral Control Technique ... LSCT
LASER Spillover and Reflectivity (MCD) ... LASOR
LASER Spot Tracker (MCD) ... LST
LASER Spot Tracker/Strike Camera (MCD) ... LST/CAM
LASER Spot Tracker / Strike Camera ... LST/SCAM
LASER Spot Welder ... LSW
Laser Storm [*NASDAQ symbol*] (TTSB) ... LAZR
Laser Storm, Inc. [*Associated Press*] (SAG) ... LaserSt
Laser Storm, Inc. [*NASDAQ symbol*] (SAG) ... LAZR
Laser Storm Unit [*NASDAQ symbol*] (TTSB) ... LAZRU
Laser Storm Wrrt [*NASDAQ symbol*] (TTSB) ... LAZRW
LASER Submarine Range-Finder ... LSRF
LASER Surface Interaction ... LSI
LASER Synchronization from Stationary Orbit (IEEE) ... LASSO
LASER System ... LS
LASER Tank Fire Control System ... LTFCS
LASER Tank Range-Finder ... LTR
LASER Tank Range-Finder ... LTRF
LASER Target Designator ... LTD
LASER Target Designator/Ranger (DWSG) ... LTD/R
LASER Target Designator Receiver ... LTDR
LASER Target Designator Scoring System (MCD) ... LTDSS
LASER Target Designator System (MCD) ... LTDS
LASER Target Interface Device (RDA) ... LTID
LASER Target Interface System ... LTIS
LASER Target Marker (RDA) ... LTM
LASER Target Marker Ranger [*Aviation*] (OA) ... LTMR
LASER Target Recognition [*Military*] (CAAL) ... LTR
LASER Target Recognition System ... LTRS
LASER Target Simulator (MCD) ... LTS
LASER Target Tracker ... LTT
Laser Technics [*Associated Press*] (SAG) ... Lasertech
Laser Technics [*NASDAQ symbol*] (SAG) ... LASX
Laser Technics, Inc. [*Associated Press*] (SAG) ... Lasrtch
Laser Technology [*AMEX symbol*] (TTSB) ... LSR
Laser Technology, Inc. [*AMEX symbol*] (SPSG) ... LSR
Laser Technology, Inc. [*Associated Press*] (SAG) ... LsrTc
Laser Technology, Inc. [*Associated Press*] (SAG) ... LsrTech
LASER Technology Program Office [*Navy*] ... LTPO
Laser Technology Wrrt [*AMEX symbol*] (TTSB) ... LSR.WS
LASER Terminal Homing Engagement Simulator (PDAA) ... LATHES
LASER Terrain Follower ... LTF
LASER Terrain Following System ... LTFS
LASER Test Set (MCD) ... LTS
LASER Time Sharing (PDAA) ... LTS
LASER Transceiver Device ... LXD
LASER Transfer Module [*Telecommunications*] (LAIN) ... LTM
LASER Trimming (PDAA) ... LT
LASER Variable Neutral Density ... LVND
LASER Vector Scoring System (DWSG) ... LVSS
LASER Velocimeter ... LV
LASER Vibration Sensor Inspection Test System [*Army*] (RDA) ... LVS/ITS
Laser Video Network [*NASDAQ symbol*] (SAG) ... LVNI
Laser Video Network [*NASDAQ symbol*] (TTSB) ... LVNI
Laser Video Network, Inc. [*Associated Press*] (SAG) ... LsrV
Laser Video Network, Inc. [*Associated Press*] (SAG) ... LsrVd
Laser Video Network, Inc. [*Associated Press*] (SAG) ... LsrVide
Laser Video Network Wrrt'A' [*NASDAQ symbol*] (TTSB) ... LVNIW
Laser Video Network Wrrt'B' [*NASDAQ symbol*] (TTSB) ... LVNIZ
LASER Viewdata Information Service (NITA) ... L-VIS
Laser Vision Centers [*NASDAQ symbol*] (TTSB) ... LVCI
Laser Vision Centers, Inc. [*Associated Press*] (SAG) ... LsrVis

Laser Vision Centers, Inc. [Associated Press] (SAG) .... LsrVs
Laser Vision Centers, Inc. [NASDAQ symbol] (SAG) LVCI
LASER Vision Read-Only Memory .... LV-ROM
LASER Warning Receiver (MCD) .... LWR
LASER Weapon System (MCD) .... LWS
LASER Weapon System Demonstrator [Military] .... LWSD
LASER Welder/Driller (PDAA) .... LWD
LASER Welder Unit .... LWU
LASER Window Test Apparatus [Air Force] .... LWTA
LASER without Inversion .... LWI
LASER-Acoustic Time Reversal Expansion and Compression (MCD) ..... LATREC
LASER-Activated Geodetic Satellite [AFCRL] .... LAGS
LASER-Activated Recession Compensator (MCD) .... LARC
LASER-Activated Reflecting Geodetic Optical Satellite .... LARGOS
LASER-Activated Semiconductor Switch (IAA) .... LASS
LASER-Activated Silicon Switch (MCD) .... LASS
LASER-Aided Rocket (MCD) .... LAR
LASER-Aided Rocket System [Military] (CAAL) .... LARS
LASER-Articulated Robotic System .... LARS
Laser-Assisted Chemical Vapor Deposition [Coating technology] .... LCVD
LASER-Assisted Uvulopalatoplasty [Medicine] (DMAA) .... LAUP
LASER-Augmented Airborne TOW Sight [Army] (MCD) .... LAAT
LASER-Augmented Airborne Track .... LAAT
LASER-Augmented Air-Rescue System (PDAA) .... LAARS
LASER-Augmented Target Acquisition and Recognition System (MCD) .... LATAR
LASER-Augmented Target Acquisition System .... LATAS
LASERcom Space Measurement Unit (IEEE) .... LSMU
LASER-Energized Explosive Device .... LEED
LASER-Engineered Net Shaping .... LENS
LASER-Enhanced Ionization [Spectrometry] .... LEI
LASER-Excited Atomic Fluorescent Spectrometry .... LEAFS
LASER-Excited Shpol'skii Spectrometry .... LESS
Lasergate Sys Wrrt [NASDAQ symbol] .... LSGTW
Lasergate Systems [NASDAQ symbol] (TTSB) .... LSGT
Lasergate Systems, Inc. [Associated Press] (SAG) .... Lasergte
Lasergate Systems, Inc. [Associated Press] (SAG) .... Lasrgt
Lasergate Systems, Inc. [NASDAQ symbol] (SAG) .... LSGT
LASERgraphics Film Recorder (PCM) .... LFR
LASER-Guided Bomb .... LGB
LASER-Guided Dispenser Munition (PDAA) .... LGDM
LASER-Guided Missile System (MCD) .... LAGUMS
LASER-Guided Munition .... LGM
LASER-Guided Projectile (MCD) .... LGP
Laser-Guided Weapon (DOMA) .... LGW
LASER-Guided Weapons Counter-Measure (PDAA) .... LGWCM
LASER-Guided Weapons Systems (IEEE) .... LGWS
LASER-Hardened Materials Evaluation Laboratory .... LHMEL
LASER-Heated Pedestal Growth [Crystal growing technology] .... LHPG
LASER-Improved Naval Combat Equipment (PDAA) .... LINCE
LASER-Induced Breakdown Spectroscopy .... LIBS
LASER-Induced Chemical Vapor Deposition [Photovoltaic energy systems] .... LICVD
LASER-Induced Chemistry (RDA) LIC
Laser-Induced Chlorophyll Fluorescence [Analytical biochemistry] .... LICF
LASER-Induced Cut and Patch .... LICAP
LASER-Induced Damage Testing .... LIDT
LASER-Induced Fluorescence [Physical chemistry] .... LIF
LASER-Induced Fluorescence and Environmental Sensing [NASA] .... LIFES
LASER-Induced Fluorescence Emission .... LIFE
LASER-Induced Fluorescence Spectroscopy .... LIFS
LASER-Induced Infrared Photochemistry .... LIIP
LASER-Induced Ion-Mass Analyzer [Instrumentation] .... LIMA
LASERInduced Microgrough Structures [Surface Technology] .... LIMS
LASER-Induced Modulation of Infrared in Silicon .... LIMIRIS
LASER-Induced Optoacoustic Spectroscopy .... LIOAS
LASER-Induced Photoacoustic Spectroscopy .... LIPAS
LASER-Induced Photodissociation and Fluorescence [Coal technology] ..... LIPF
LASER-Induced Plasma [Spectroscopy] .... LIP
LASER-Induced Pressure Pulse [Medicine] (DMAA) .... LIPP
LASER-Induced Separation (MCD) .... LIS
Laser-Induced Thermal Desorption .... LITD
LASER-Integrated Navigation/Attack System (MCD) .... LINAS
LaserMaster Technologies [NASDAQ symbol] (TTSB) .... LMTS
LaserMaster Technologies, Inc. [Associated Press] (SAG) .... LasrmTc
LaserMaster Technologies, Inc. [NASDAQ symbol] (SAG) .... LMTS
Laser-pac Media [NASDAQ symbol] (TTSB) .... LPAC
LASER-Produced Plasma .... LPP
Laser-Protective Visor (DOMA) .... LPV
LASER-Pumped-LASER .... LPL
LASER-RADAR (MCD) .... LR
LASERS in Graphics (DGA) .... LIG
Lasers in Publishing Users Group (EA) .... LPUG
LASER-Scan Confocal Microscope .... LSCM
Laserscope [NASDAQ symbol] (SAG) .... LSCP
Laserscope, Inc. [Associated Press] (SAG) .... Lasrscp
LASER-Selective Demagnetization [Analytical technique] .... LSD
Lasersight Inc. [NASDAQ symbol] (TTSB) .... LASE
LASER-Supported Absorption (PDAA) .... LSA
LASER-Supported Absorption-Wave (PDAA) .... LSAW
LASER-Supported Combustion (MCD) .... LSC
LASER-Supported Detonation Waves (MCD) .... LSD
Lasertechnics Inc. [NASDAQ symbol] (TTSB) .... LASX
LASER-to-Electric Energy Conversion (SSD) .... LEEC
LASER-Triggered Spark Gap .... LTSG

LASER-Triggered Switch (MCD) .... LTS
LaserVision [Videodisc system] LV
Lasham [British ICAO location identifier] (ICLI) .... EGHL
Lasham [England] [Airport symbol] .... QLA
Lashenden/Headcorn [British ICAO location identifier] (ICLI) .... EGKH
Lashing [Engineering] .... LSHG
Lashio [Myanmar] [Airport symbol] (OAG) .... LSH
Lashio [Myanmar] [ICAO location identifier] (ICLI) .... VBLS
Lasir Gold, Inc. [Vancouver Stock Exchange symbol] .... LAI
Lasmo Canada, Inc. [Toronto Stock Exchange symbol] .... LMO
Lasmo Ltd. [Associated Press] (SAG) .... Lasmo
LASMO pic ADS [NYSE symbol] (TTSB) .... LSO
Lasmo PLC [NYSE symbol] (SAG) .... LSO
LASMO plc Sr'A'Pref ADS [NYSE symbol] (TTSB) .... LSOPrA
L-Asparaginase [Also, L, L-ase, L-asnase, L-Asp] [An enzyme, an antineoplastic] .... A
L-Asparaginase [Also, A, L-ase, L-asnase, L-Asp] [An enzyme, an antineoplastic] L
L-Asparaginase [Also, A, L, L-Asp, L-asnase] [An enzyme, an antineoplastic] .... L-Ase
L-Asparaginase [Also, A, L, L-ase, L-Asp] [An enzyme, an antineoplastic] .... L-Asnase
L-Asparaginase [Also, A, L, L-ase, L-asnase] [An enzyme, an antineoplastic] .... L-Asp
L-Asparaginase and Methotrexate [Antineoplastic drug regimen] (DAVI) .... LAM
L-Asparaginase, Ifosfamide, and Methotrexate [Antineoplastic drug regimen] (DAVI) .... AIM
L-Asparaginase, Prednisone, Oncovin [Vincristine], Cytarabine, Adriamycin [Antineoplastic drug regimen] .... LAPOCA
Lasqueti Island Historical Society, Hawkshaw Ranch, Hawkshaw, BC, Canada [Library symbol] [Library of Congress] (LCLS) .... CaBLIHS
Lassa-Fever Virus .... LFV
Lassen County Free Library, Susanville, CA [Library symbol Library of Congress] (LCLS) .... CSuLas
Lassen Volcanic National Park .... LAVO
Lassiter [Tennessee] [Seismograph station code, US Geological Survey Closed] (SEIS) DY2
Lassiter Corners [Tennessee] [Seismograph station code, US Geological Survey Closed] (SEIS) DY5
L'Association Canadienne des Centres d'Action Benevole (AC) .... l'ACCAB
L'Association Canadienne des Ludotheques et des Centres de Ressources pour la Famille [Canadian Association of Toy Libraries and Parent Resource Centers] [See also TLRC] (EAIO) .... LCRF
L'Association Canadienne des Producteurs d'Acier (AC) .... ACPA
L'Association Canadienne du Camionnage (AC) .... ACC
L'Association Canadienne pour les Jeunes Enfants (AC) .... L'ACJE
L'Association de la Neurofibromatose du Quebec (AC) .... ANFQ
L'Association de Spina-Bifida et d'Hydrocephalie du Quebec (AC) .... ASBHQ
L'Association Dentaire Canadienne (AC) .... L'ADC
L'Association des Hoteliers de la Province de Quebec [Province of Quebec Hotel Keepers' Association] (AC) .... AHPQ
L'Association pour la Recherche contre le Cancer [Association for Research Against Can cer] [France] .... ARC
L'Association Quebecoise des Organismes Regionaux de Concertation et de Developpement (AC) .... L'AQORCD
Last [Wool weight] .... LA
Last (ROG) LL
Last (BUR) .... LST
Last (ROG) .... LT
Last Appearance Datum [Geology] .... LAD
Last Brochure .... LB
Last Byte In (ECII) .... LBI
Last Calls Meter [Telecommunications] (NITA) .... LCM
Last Card LC
Last Card Program Start (IAA) .... LCP
Last Card Total (IAA) .... LCT
Last Cast Syndrome [Fictitious fishing malady] .... LCS
Last Chance Filter (MCD) .... LCF
Last Chance Forever (EA) .... LCF
Last Clear Chance [Legal shorthand] (LWAP) LCC
Last Come, First Served Preemptive Resume (PDAA) .... LCFSPR
Last Complete Program (WDAA) .... LCP
Last Data Sample (IAA) .... LDS
Last Day of Attendance .... LDA
Last Day of the Month (AFM) .... LDM
Last Field Address (IAA) .... LFA
Last Frame Address Register .... LFAR
Last Frame Indicator .... LFI
Last Frame of Action [Cinematography] (WDMC) .... LFOA
Last Glacial Maximum [Climatology] .... LGM
Last Half [of month] [Business term] (DS) .... LH
Last Harvest [An association] (EA) .... LH
Last Hope [Facetious name for Chrysler's 1993 sedans] .... LH
Last In, First Out [Queuing technique] [Accounting] .... LIFO
Last In, Still Here [Accounting] (ADA) .... LISH
Last In, Still There [Accounting] .... LIST
Last Instruction Cycle (IAA) LIC
Last Instruction Readout Cycle (IAA) .... LIROC
Last Interglacial Period [Climatology] .... LIG
Last Known Address (LAIN) .... LKA
Last Known Port (MCD) .... LKNPT
Last Known Position (MCD) .... LKNPOS
Last Known Position [Aviation] (NVT) .... LKP
Last Maneuver Calculation [Orbit identification] .... LAMC
Last Manufacturers Association [Defunct] (EA) .... LMA

Last Meal Furnished	LMF
Last Menstrual Period [Medicine]	LMP
Last Month's Forecast (MCD)	LMF
Last Name Unknown	LNU
Last Normal Menstrual Period [Medicine]	LNMP
Last Offer Binding Arbitration [Labor negotiations]	LOBA
[The] Last One [A microcomputer program manufactured by DJ-AI]	TLO
Last Operation Completed [Computer science]	LOP
Last Page Generator (NASA)	LPG
Last Paid [Military]	LP
Last Papanicolaou Smear [Gynecology] (DAVI)	LPS
Last Pass Heat Sink Welding [Nuclear energy] (NUCP)	LPHSW
Last Performance	LP
Last Period Satisfied [IRS]	LPS
Last Pinedale Glacial Maximum [Climatology]	LPGM
Last Post (WDAA)	LP
Last Premidcourse Orbit	LAPM
Last Quarter [Moon phase]	LQ
Last Radio Contact [Aviation]	LARCT
Last Record (IAA)	LR
Last Regular Menstrual Period [Gynecology] (DMAA)	LRMP
Last Renewal	LR
Last Resort Target [Military]	LRT
Last Resort Target [Military]	LRTGT
Last Return Amount [IRS]	LRA
Last Return Filed [IRS]	LRF
Last Revision Date Routine	LRDR
Last Safe Date [Marine insurance] (DS)	LSD
Last Satellite Position [Navy Navigation Satellite System] (DNAB)	LAST
Last Significant Character (ECII)	LSC
Last Speed Rating [of a horse]	LSR
Last Standing Order	LSO
Last Telecast (NTCM)	LT
Last Telecast (WDMC)	LT
Last Telecast (WDMC)	LTC
Last Trunk Busy [Telecommunications] (TEL)	LTB
Last Vehicle [Railroads] (ROG)	LV
Last Word (IAA)	LW
Last Word Address	LWA
Last Year but Not This [Fundraising]	LYBNT
Last Year's Model [Merchandising slang]	LY
Last Year's Model [Marketing] (WDAA)	LYM
Last-Come, First-Served	LCFS
Lastenausgleichsgesetz (BJA)	LAG
Lastensegler; Lastensegelflugzeug [Cargo transport glider] [German military - World War II]	LS
Last-In, Last-Out [Accounting]	LILO
Lasting	LSTNG
Lastourville [Gabon] [ICAO location identifier] (ICLI)	FOOR
Lastourville [Gabon] [Airport symbol] (OAG)	LTL
Lastp-Linhas Aereas de Sao Tome e Principe [ICAO designator] (FAAC)	OTN
L'Astrologie Chaldeenne [A publication] (BJA)	ACh
Lat [Monetary unit] [Latvia]	L
Latacunga [Ecuador] [ICAO location identifier] (ICLI)	SELT
Latakia [Syria] [Airport symbol] (OAG)	LTK
Latakia/Latakia [Syria] [ICAO location identifier] (ICLI)	OSLK
Latakia Type Tobacco [Shipping]	LTT
Latch (NASA)	LAT
Latch (MSA)	LCH
Latch and Lock (DAC)	L & L
Latch and Plaster (DAC)	L & P
Latch Checking Switch (MSA)	LCSW
Latch, Lock, and Bolt (DAC)	LL & B
Latch Side	LS
Latch Up Screen	LUS
Latcharter [Latvia] [FAA designator] (FAAC)	LTC
Latchford Senior Citizens Group, Latchford, ON, Canada [Library symbol] [Library of Congress] (LCLS)	CaOLfSCG
Latchford Senior Citizens Group, Ontario [Library symbol National Library of Canada] (BIB)	OLSCG
Latching [Electronics]	L
Latching Relay (IAA)	LRY
Latching Relay Matrix	LRM
Latching Semiconductor Diode	LSD
Latch's English King's Bench Reports [1625-28] [A publication] (DLA)	Lat
Latch's English King's Bench Reports [1625-28] [A publication] (DLA)	Latch
Late	L
Late (WDMC)	l
Late (VRA)	la
Late Abortion [Medicine] (DMAA)	LA
Late Ambulatory Monitoring [Medicine]	LAM
Late Antigen [Biochemistry]	LA
Late Assessment of Thrombolytic Efficacy [Cardiology study]	LATE
Late Asthmatic Response [Medicine] (DAVI)	LAR
Late Babylonian (BJA)	LB
Late Babylonian Astronomical and Related Texts (BJA)	LBAT
Late Bronze [Age] (BJA)	LB
Late Change Message [Aviation] (DA)	LCM
Late Choice Call (NITA)	LCC
Late Choice Call Meter [Telecommunications] (NITA)	LCCM
Late Clamped [Umbilical cord]	LC
Late Commitment [Reason for missed interception] [Military]	LC
Late Cortical Cerebellar Atrophy [Neurology]	LCCA
Late Cutaneous Anaphylactic Reaction [Immunology]	LCAR
Late Cutaneous Reaction [Immunology]	LCR

Late Direct Injection Stratified Charge	L-DISC
Late Distal Cortical Tubule [Medicine] (DMAA)	LDCT
Late Effects Study Group [for Hodgkins disease]	LESG
Late Finish Time	LFT
Late Flight Plan	LFP
Late Generalized Tuberculosis [Medicine]	LGT
Late Glacial Stage [Paleontology]	LGS
Late Great Chevrolet Association (EA)	LGCA
Late Greek [or Low Greek] [Language] (BARN)	LGk
Late Heavy Bombardment [Planetary history]	LHB
Late Hebrew (WDAA)	L HEB
Late Helladic (BJA)	LH
Late Hyperpolarizing Potential [Neurophysiology]	LHP
Late Infantile Amaurotic Familial Idiocy [Medicine] (MAE)	LIAFI
Late Iron [Age] (BJA)	LI
Late Latent Infection [Medicine]	LLI
Late Latin [Language, etc.]	LL
Late Luteal Phase Dysphoric Disorder [Gynecology]	LLPDD
Late Minoan 1A [Archaeology]	LM1A
Late Minoan 1B [Archaeology]	LM1B
Late Model [Class of racing cars]	LM
Late Onset Cerebellar Ataxia [Medicine]	LOCA
Late Operating Contact [Symbol] (DEN)	Y
Late Phase Reaction [or Response] [Medicine]	LPR
Late Phoenician (BJA)	LPh
Late Pleistocene Origins [Ecology]	LPO
Late Position Report [Report of a flight which is off flight plan]	LPR
Late Positive Component (MAE)	LPC
Late Postpartum Hemorrhage [Medicine] (DMAA)	LPPH
Late Procurement Request [Air Force] (AFM)	LPR
Late Punic (BJA)	LPu
Late Reaction [Medicine] (DMAA)	LAR
Late Receptor Potential [Photoreceptor] [Physiology]	LRP
Late Renal Failure [Medicine]	LRF
Late Scramble [Reason for missed interception] [Military]	LS
Late Shock [Medicine]	LS
Late Start Time	LST
Late Stone Age	LSA
Late Systolic Click [Cardiology] (DAVI)	LSC
Late Systolic Murmur (MAE)	LSM
Late Warning	LW
Late-Differentiation Antigen [Immunology]	LDA
Lateen [Ship's rigging] (ROG)	LN
Latency Relaxation	LR
Latent	LAT
Latent Cancer Fatalities (PDAA)	LCF
Latent Heat	L
Latent Heat (IAA)	LH
Latent Image Memory	LIM
Latent Information Parameter	LIP
Latent Iron-Binding Capacity [Clinical chemistry]	LIBC
Latent Lethality [Radiation casualty criterion] [Army]	LL
Latent Membrane Potential [Medicine] (DMAA)	LMP
Latent Membrane Protein [Genetics]	LMP
Latent Period [Physiology]	LP
Latent Photographic Image	LPI
Latent Variable [Data analysis]	LV
[The] Later Roman Empire [A publication] (OCD)	Later Rom Emp
Lateral (IAA)	L
Lateral (KSC)	LAT
Lateral (VRA)	lat
Lateral (MSA)	LATL
Lateral (DNAB)	LATR
Lateral	LATRL
Lateral [RADAR]	X
Lateral Acceleration Response Time	LART
Lateral Acceleration Sensing System (PDAA)	LASS
Lateral Accelerometer Assembly (MCD)	LAA
Lateral Access Network (NITA)	LAN
Lateral Awareness and Directionality Test [Sensorimotor skills test]	LAD
Lateral Channel Stop (IAA)	LCS
Lateral Choroid Plexus (PDAA)	LCP
Lateral Collateral Ligament [Anatomy]	LCL
Lateral Component	LC
Lateral Control System (MUGU)	LCS
Lateral Direction (MCD)	LD
Lateral Dispersion (MCD)	LATDISP
Lateral Dorsal [Anatomy]	LD
Lateral Dorsal Tract [Neuroanatomy]	LDT
Lateral Double-Diffused Metal-Oxide Semiconductor (MCD)	LDMOS
Lateral Drift	LD
Lateral Efferent Bundle [Neuroanatomy]	LEB
Lateral Electrical Spine Stimulation [Orthopedics] (DAVI)	LESS
Lateral Electronic Guidance System [Automotive engineering]	LEGS
Lateral Element	LE
Lateral Epicondyle [Anatomy]	LE
Lateral Epithelial Space [Anatomy] (DAVI)	LES
Lateral Eye Movement	LEM
Lateral Femoral Condyle [Anatomy]	LFC
Lateral Force Microscopy [Morphology]	LFM
Lateral Forebrain Bundle	LFB
Lateral Gastrocnemius	LG
Lateral Geniculate Body	LGB
Lateral Geniculate Nucleus	LGN
Lateral Geniculate Nucleus Dorsal [Neuroanatomy]	LGND

Lateral Giant Interneuron [*Neurobiology*] ... LGI
Lateral Habenular (Nucleus) [*Neuroanatomy*] ... LHb
Lateral Head Displacement [*Sperm*] [*Medicine*] (DMAA) ... LHD
Lateral Homing Depth Charge ... LHDC
Lateral Hypothalamic [*or Hypothalamus*] ... LH
Lateral Hypothalamic Area ... LHA
Lateral Intercellular Space (PDAA) ... LIS
Lateral Intraparietal Area [*Anatomy*] ... LIP
Lateral Joint Line [*Orthopedics*] (DAVI) ... LJL
Lateral Lemniscus [*Neuroanatomy*] ... LL
Lateral Line [*Invertebrate zoology*] ... LL
Lateral Lip ... LL
Lateral Malleolus [*Anatomy*] ... LM
Lateral Meniscectomy [*Orthopedics*] (DAVI) ... lat men
Lateral Meniscus [*Anatomy*] ... LM
Lateral Mesencephalic Nucleus [*Brain anatomy*] ... LMN
Lateral Motoneuron [*Neurobiology*] ... LMN
Lateral Motor Column [*of the spinal cord*] [*Neurobiology*] ... LMC
Lateral Nasal Gland [*Anatomy*] ... LNG
Lateral Navigation [*Provides computer description of aircraft's planned lateral flight path*] (GAVI) ... LNAV
Lateral Neuropil [*Neurology*] ... LN
Lateral Nuclear Stratum [*Medicine*] (DMAA) ... LNS
Lateral Oblique [*X-ray view*] (DAVI) ... LO
Lateral Offset Active Light (GAVI) ... OFST
Lateral Olfactory Tract ... LOT
Lateral Pharyngeal Wall [*Medicine*] (DMAA) ... LPW
Lateral Photoelectric Detector (PDAA) ... LPD
Lateral Premotor System (DMAA) ... LPS
Lateral Preoptic [*Brain anatomy*] ... LPO
Lateral Pterygoid Muscle (DMAA) ... LPM
Lateral Pterygoid Plate [*Medicine*] (DMAA) ... LPP
Lateral Pyloric [*Neuron*] ... LP
Lateral Reach-Through Device (PDAA) ... LRThD
Lateral Rectus [*Muscle*] [*Anatomy*] ... LR
Lateral Reversal [*Typography*] (DGA) ... LR
Lateral Root [*Botany*] ... LR
Lateral Separation Focus Sensor (PDAA) ... LSFS
Lateral Septum ... LS
Lateral Series Servo (MCD) ... LSS
Lateral Shear Interferometer (PDAA) ... LSI
Lateral Simulated Ground Plane [*Aerodynamics*] ... LSGP
Lateral Sinus Thrombophlebitis [*Medicine*] (MEDA) ... LST
Lateral Spherical Aberration ... LSA
Lateral Spinothalamic Tract [*Neurology*] (DAVI) ... LST
Lateral Subsylvian Cortex [*Neuroanatomy*] ... LS
Lateral Superior Geniculate Artery [*Anatomy*] ... LSG
Lateral Superior Olive [*Brain anatomy*] ... LSO
Lateral Superlattice [*Physics*] ... LSL
Lateral Suspensor [*Ligament*] [*Anatomy*] (DAVI) ... LS
Lateral Test Simulator (IAA) ... LTS
Lateral Tire Run-Out [*Automotive engineering*] ... LTRO
Lateral Tooth ... LT
Lateral Touch Neuron [*of a leech*] ... Tl
Lateral Transitional Phase Shift [*Optics*] ... LTPS
Lateral Triceps Brachii [*Medicine*] ... LT
Lateral Vascularized Patellar Tendon Graft [*Orthopedics*] ... LVPTG
Lateral Ventricle [*Neuroanatomy*] ... LV
Lateral Vestibular Nucleus [*Neuroanatomy*] ... LV
Lateral Vestibular Nucleus [*Medicine*] (DMAA) ... LVN
Lateral Vestibulospinal Tract [*Medicine*] (DMAA) ... LVST
Lateral Wall [*Image on transesophageal echocardiography*] [*Cardiology*] (DAVI) ... LW
Lateral Wheel Run-Out [*Automotive engineering*] ... LWRO
Lateralis Dorsalis [*Neuroanatomy*] ... LD
Laterality Preference Schedule [*Psychology*] ... LPS
Laterality Quotient [*Neuropsychology*] ... LQ
Laterally Compounded Fresnel Lens Optical Landing System ... LCFLOLS
Laterally to the Pedunculus Cerebellaris Superior [*Medicine*] ... LPCS
Lateri Admoveatum [*Let It Be Applied to the Side*] [*Pharmacy*] ... LAT ADMOV
Lateri Dolente [*To the Painful Side*] [*Pharmacy*] ... LAT DOL
Latest Arrival Date (AABC) ... LAD
Latest Closing Time ... LCT
Latest Cost Estimate (NATG) ... LCE
Latest Epicardial Activation [*Cardiology*] ... LEA
Latest Estimate [*Business term*] ... LE
Latest Finish Date ... LFD
Latest Finish Time ... LFT
Latest Information Selected and Abstracted for Researchers and Decision-Makers [*Database*] ... LISARD
Latest Information Selected and Abstracted for Researchers and Decision-Makers [*Database*] ... LISD
Latest Recommended Posting Times [*Business term*] (DCTA) ... LPT
Latest Reporting Period [*Business term*] ... LRP
Latest Revised Estimate (MCD) ... LRE
Latest Scram Set Point (NRCH) ... LSSP
Latest Start Date ... LSD
Latest Time [*Business term*] ... LT
Latest Time Information of Value [*Military*] (AFM) ... LTIOV
Latest Time over Target (AFM) ... LTOT
Latex (DMAA) ... L
Latex (VRA) ... ltx
Latex Agglutination [*Test*] [*Clinical chemistry*] ... LA
Latex Agglutination Inhibition Test [*for pregnancy*] [*Medicine*] ... LAIT
Latex Agglutination Test [*Clinical chemistry*] ... LAT
Latex Agglutination-Inhibition (PDAA) ... LAI
Latex and Resorcinol Formaldehyde ... LRF
Latex Direct Agglutination Reaction [*Medicine*] (DMAA) ... LDAR
Latex Fixation [*Test*] [*Medicine*] ... LF
Latex Fixation Test [*Medicine*] ... LFT
Latex Flocculation Test [*Clinical chemistry*] ... LFT
Latex Foam Rubber Council [*Defunct*] (EA) ... LFRC
Latex Particle Agglutination [*Immunochemistry*] (DAVI) ... LPA
Latex Res Inc. [*NASDAQ symbol*] (TTSB) ... LATX
Latex Resources [*Associated Press*] (SAG) ... Latex
Latex Resources [*Associated Press*] (SAG) ... LatexRs
Latex Resources, Inc. [*NASDAQ symbol*] (SAG) ... LATX
Latex Resources Wrrt [*NASDAQ symbol*] (TTSB) ... LTXW
Latex-Modified Concrete (PDAA) ... LMC
Lath Renders' Trade Association [*A union*] [*British*] ... LRTA
Latham & Watkins, Chicago, IL [*Library symbol*] [*Library of Congress*] (LCLS) ... ICLW
Latham on the Law of Window Lights [*A publication*] (DLA) ... Lath Wind L
Lathe [*Division in the county of Kent*] [*British*] ... LA
Lathe Control System ... LCS
Lathe Fixture (MCD) ... LF
Lathing ... LTHG
Lathrop, CA [*Location identifier FAA*] (FAAL) ... LRO
Lathrop Elementary School, Rockford, IL [*Library symbol*] [*Library of Congress*] (LCLS) ... IRoLE
Lathrop High School, Fairbanks, AK [*Library symbol*] [*Library of Congress*] (LCLS) ... AkFLHS
Lathrop Park Youth Camp, Walsenburg, CO [*Library symbol Library of Congress*] (LCLS) ... CoWaL
Lathrop's Reports [*115-145 Massachusetts*] [*A publication*] (DLA) ... Lath
Lathrop's Reports [*115-145 Massachusetts*] [*A publication*] (DLA) ... Lathrop
Lathwell Resources Ltd. [*Vancouver Stock Exchange symbol*] ... LAT
Latin ... L
Latin ... LAT
Latin [*MARC language code Library of Congress*] (LCCP) ... lat
Latin Amer Casinos [*NASDAQ symbol*] (TTSB) ... LACI
Latin Amer Casinos Wrrt [*NASDAQ symbol*] (TTSB) ... LACIW
Latin America [*MARC geographic area code Library of Congress*] (LCCP) ... cl----
Latin America ... LA
Latin America Antiquity [*A publication*] ... L A Ant
Latin America Bureau [*British*] (EAIO) ... LAB
Latin America Center [*Acronym is based on foreign phrase Belgium*] ... SAGO
Latin America Common Market [*Proposed*] ... LACM
Latin America Dollar Income Fund [*Associated Press*] (SAG) ... LatADIr
Latin America Dollar Inc.Fd [*NYSE symbol*] (TTSB) ... LBF
Latin America Dollar, Inc. Fund [*NYSE symbol*] (SPSG) ... LBF
Latin America Equity Fd [*NYSE symbol*] (TTSB) ... LAQ
Latin America Equity Fund [*NYSE symbol*] (SPSG) ... LAQ
Latin America Equity Fund [*Associated Press*] (SAG) ... LatAEqt
Latin America Growth Fund, Inc. [*Associated Press*] (SAG) ... LatinAGr
Latin America Inv Fd [*NYSE symbol*] (TTSB) ... LAM
Latin America Microform Project, Center for Research Libraries, Chicago, IL [*Library symbol*] [*Library of Congress*] (LCLS) ... ICRL-LA
Latin America Mission (EA) ... LAM
Latin America Parents Association (EA) ... LAPA
Latin America Resource Center and Clearinghouse [*Defunct*] (EA) ... LARCCH
Latin America Science Cooperation Office (MSC) ... LASCO
Latin America Trade Union Federation (NATG) ... LATUF
Latin American Agribusiness Development Corp. ... LAAD
Latin American Air Intelligence Brief (MCD) ... LAAIB
Latin American and Caribbean Center [*Florida International University*] [*Research center*] (RCD) ... LACC
Latin American and Caribbean Council for Self-Management (EAIO) ... LACCSM
Latin American and Caribbean Health Sciences Literature (IID) ... LILACS
Latin American and Caribbean International Moving [*Panama*] (EAIO) ... LACIM
Latin American and Caribbean Movers Association (EAIO) ... LACMA
Latin American and Caribbean Solidarity Association (EA) ... LACASA
Latin American and Caribbean Studies Center [*University of Illinois*] [*Research center*] (RCD) ... CLACS
Latin American and Caribbean Women's Health Network (EAIO) ... LCWHN
Latin American Anthropology Group (EA) ... LAAG
Latin American Antiquity [*A publication*] (BRI) ... LA Ant
Latin American Association for Afro-Asian Studies [*Mexico*] (EAIO) ... LAAAAS
Latin American Association for Social Psychology [*Formerly, Latin American Social Psychology Committee*] (EA) ... LAASP
Latin American Association for the Development and Integration of Women [*See also ALADIM*] [*Chile*] (EAIO) ... LAADIW
Latin American Association for the Study of the Liver [*Mexico*] (EAIO) ... LAASL
Latin American Association of Archives [*See also ALA*] (EAIO) ... LAAA
Latin American Association of Behavior Analysis and Modification [*Uruguay*] (EAIO) ... LAABAM
Latin American Association of Environmental Mutagens, Carcinogens, and Teratogens Societies [*Mexico*] (EAIO) ... LAAEMCTS
Latin American Association of Freight and Transport Agents [*Paraguay*] (EAIO) ... LAFTA
Latin American Association of Medical Schools and Faculties [*See also ALAFEM*] [*Ecuador*] (EAIO) ... LAAMSF
Latin American Association of National Academies of Medicine (EA) ... ALANAM
Latin American Association of Pharmaceutical Industries [*See also ALIFAR*] (EAIO) ... LAAPI
Latin American Banking Federation [*Bogota, Colombia*] (EA) ... LABF
Latin American Bibliographic Foundation, Redlands, CA [*Library symbol*] [*Library of Congress*] (LCLS) ... CRedlL
Latin American Blind Union [*See also ULAC*] [*Uruguay*] (EAIO) ... LABU
Latin American Book Programs [*Defunct*] ... LABP

Latin American Casinos, Inc. [*Associated Press*] (SAG) .... LACas
Latin American Casinos, Inc. [*NASDAQ symbol*] (SAG) .... LACI
Latin American Casinos, Inc. [*Associated Press*] (SAG) .... LatACas
Latin American Civil Aviation Commission [*See also CLAC*] (EAIO) .... LACAC
Latin American Confederation of Clinical Biochemistry [*Colombia*] (EAIO) .... LACCB
Latin American Confederation of Tourist Organizations [*Argentina*] (EAIO) .... LAFTO
Latin American Confederation of YMCAs [*See also CLACJ*] (EAIO) .... LACYMCA
Latin American Constitutional Law Association [*Argentina*] (EAIO) .... LACLA
Latin American Cooperative Acquisitions Program [*or Project*] .... LACAP
Latin American Data Bank [*University of Florida*] (IID) .... LADB
Latin American Data Base [*An association*] (EA) .... LADB
Latin American Discovery Fd [*NYSE symbol*] (TTSB) .... LDF
Latin American Discovery Fund [*Associated Press*] (SAG) .... LatADis
Latin American Discovery Fund [*NYSE symbol*] (SPSG) .... LDF
Latin American Federation of Thermalism and Climatism [*See also FLT*] [*Argentina*] (EAIO) .... LAFTC
Latin American Female [*Classified advertising*] (DMAA) .... LAF
Latin American Football League [*British*] .... LAFL
Latin American Growth Fd [*NYSE symbol*] (TTSB) .... LLF
Latin American Hospital Federation [*Mexico*] (EAIO) .... LAHF
Latin American Human Rights Association (EA) .... ALDHU
Latin American Indian Literatures Association (EA) .... LAILA
Latin American Industrialists Association [*Uruguay*] (EAIO) .... LAIA
Latin American Institute [*University of New Mexico*] [*Research center*] (RCD) .... LAI
Latin American Institute for Information and Computer Sciences [*Chile*] (PDAA) .... LAIICS
Latin American Institute for Transnational Studies (EA) .... LAITS
Latin American Institute of Educational Communication [*Mexico*] (EAIO) .... LAIEC
Latin American Institute of Social Doctrine and Social Studies [*Chile*] (EAIO) .... LAISDSS
Latin American Integration Association [*Trade association of Argentina, Bolivia, Brazil, Chile, Colombia, Ecuador, Mexico, Paraguay, Peru, Uruguay, and Venezuela*] (BARN) .... ALADI
Latin American Integration Association [*Formerly, LAFTA*] [*See also ALADI Uruguay*] (EAIO) .... LAIA
Latin American Investment Fund [*NYSE symbol*] (SPSG) .... LAM
Latin American Investment Fund [*Associated Press*] (SAG) .... LatAInv
Latin American Journal of Politics, Economics, and Law [*A publication*] (DLA) .... LAJPEL
Latin American Male (DAVI) .... LAM
Latin American Manufacturers Association [*Washington, DC*] (EA) .... LAMA
Latin American Military Communications System .... LAMCS
Latin American Mission [*Air Force*] .... LAM
Latin American Newsletters [*British Information service or system*] (IID) .... LAN
Latin American Office of Aerospace Research [*Air Force*] .... LAOAR
Latin American Paper Money Society (EA) .... LAPMS
Latin American Parliament [*See also PLA*] [*Colombia*] (EAIO) .... LAP
Latin American Philatelic Society (EA) .... LAPS
Latin American, Portuguese, and Spanish [*Division*] [*Library of Congress*] .... LAPS
Latin American Railways Association (EA) .... LARA
Latin American Regional Office [*United Nations Food and Agricultural Organization*] (BARN) .... LARO
Latin American Rural Sociological Association (EAIO) .... LARSA
Latin American Scholarship Program of American Universities (EA) .... LASPAU
Latin American Secretariat for Academic Services [*Defunct*] .... LASAS
Latin American Serial Documents .... LASD
Latin American Social Sciences Council [*Argentina Database producer*] (EA) .... LASSC
Latin American Society of Hepatology [*See also SLH*] (EAIO) .... LASH
Latin American Studies Association (EA) .... LASA
Latin American Tax Law Institute [*Uruguay*] (EAIO) .... LATLI
Latin American Trade Advisory Group [*British Overseas Trade Board*] (DS) .... LATAG
Latin American Working Group [*Canada*] (CROSS) .... LAWG
Latin American-American Communications Systems (PDAA) .... LAMCS
Latin American-Caribbean Labor Institute (EA) .... LALI
Latin and Mediterranean Group for Sport Medicine (EA) .... LMGSM
Latin Languages Speaking Allergists [*See also GAILL*] (EAIO) .... LLSA
Latin Liturgy Association (EA) .... LLA
Latin Mass Society (EAIO) .... LMS
Latin Mediterranean Medical Union [*See also UMML*] [*Mantua, Italy*] (EAIO) .... LMMU
Latin Monetary Union [*Established in 1865*] .... LMU
Latin Old Style (ADA) .... LOS
Latina [*Italy ICAO location identifier*] (ICLI) .... LIRL
Latin-American Forestry Commission .... LAFC
Latin-American Free Trade Association [*Later, LAIA*] .... LAFTA
Latinamerika-Institutet, Stockholm, Sweden [*Library symbol Library of Congress*] (LCLS) .... SwSL
Latitude L
Latitude .... LAT
Latitude (ADA) .... LATD
Latitude and Longitude Indicator LLI
Latitude Data Computer .... LDC
Latitude/Longitude (IEEE) .... L/L
Latitude of Target .... LAT
Latitudinal Species-Diversity Gradient [*Biodiversity*] .... LSDG
Latpass [*Latvia*] [*FAA designator*] (FAAC) .... LTP
Latrine (DSUE) .... LAT
Latrine Urinal Shower Toilet [*A unit of mobility equipment*] [*Military*] .... LUST
Latrobe [*Pennsylvania*] [*Airport symbol*] (OAG) .... LBE
LaTrobe Library Journal [*A publication*] .... LLJ
Latrobe, PA [*Location identifier FAA*] (FAAL) .... BHU
Latrobe, PA [*Location identifier FAA*] (FAAL) .... LBE
Latrobe, PA [*AM radio station call letters*] .... WCNS
Latrobe, PA [*AM radio station call letters*] .... WQTW
LaTrobe University, Bundoora, V, Australia [*Library symbol Library of Congress*] (LCLS) .... AuBL
Latrobe's Justice [*A publication*] (DLA) .... Lat Jus
Latronico [*Italy ICAO location identifier*] (ICLI) .... LIBU
Latrunculin-A [*A toxin*] .... LAT-A
Latrunculin-B [*A toxin*] .... LAT-B
Latter .... LTTR
Latter-Day Saints [*Mormons*] .... LDS
Latter-Day Saints Genealogical Library, Mesa, AZ [*Library symbol Library of Congress*] (LCLS) .... AzML
Latter-Day Saints Museum, Salt Lake City, UT [*Library symbol Library of Congress*] (LCLS) .... USIL
Lattey's Privy Council Practice [*1869*] [*A publication*] (DLA) .... Latt Pr C Pr
Lattice (MSA) .... LTC
Lattice Assessment Program [*Civil Defense*] .... LAP
Lattice Girder Floor Association [*British*] (DBA) .... LGFA
Lattice Screen Editor [*Program editor*] .... LSE
Lattice Semiconductor [*NASDAQ symbol*] (TTSB) .... LSCC
Lattice Semiconductor Corp. [*Associated Press*] (SAG) .... Lattice
Lattice Semiconductor Corp. [*NASDAQ symbol*] (SAG) .... LSCC
Lattice Test Reactor .... LTR
Lattice-Preferred Orientation [*Geophysics*] .... LPO
Latus [*Wide*] [*Pharmacy*] .... LAT
Latvia .... LAT
Latvia (VRA) .... Latv
Latvian .... Latv
Latvian [*MARC language code Library of Congress*] (LCCP) .... lav
Latvian Airlines [*ICAO designator*] (FAAC) .... LTL
Latvian Association of Foresters in the United States [*Defunct*] (EA) .... LAFUS
Latvian Association of South Australia .... LA(SA)
Latvian Choir Association of the US (EA) .... LCAUS
Latvian Green Party [*Political party*] (EY) .... LZP
Latvian National Foundation [*Stockholm, Sweden*] (EAIO) .... LNF
Latvian Popular Front [*Political party Defunct*] (EAIO) .... LPF
Latvian Soviet Socialist Republic [*MARC geographic area code Library of Congress*] (LCCP) .... e-ur-lv
Latvian Soviet Socialist Republic .... LatSSR
Latvian Soviet Socialist Republic [*MARC country of publication code Library of Congress*] (LCCP) .... lvr
Latvian Telegraph Agency (EY) .... LETA
Latvijas Socialdemokratiska Stradnieku Partija [*Lativian Social Democratic Workers' Party*] [*Political party*] (EAIO) .... LSDSP
Latvijas Tautas Fronte [*Popular Front of Latvia*] [*Political party*] (EY) .... LTF
Latymer Upper School Cadet Corps [*British military*] (DMA) .... LUSCC
Laubach Literacy Action (EA) .... LLA
Laubach Literacy Fund [*Later, LLI*] (EA) .... LLF
Laubach Literacy International (EA) LLI
Laucala Island [*Fiji*] [*Airport symbol*] (OAG) .... LUC
Laucks Foundation (EA) .... LF
Lauda Air [*Austria ICAO designator*] (FAAC) .... LDA
Lauda Air [*Italy ICAO designator*] (FAAC) .... LDI
Laudatur [*Latin*] L
Lauder [*New Zealand*] [*Geomagnetic observatory code*] .... LAU
Lauder (Estee) Co. [*NYSE symbol*] (TTSB) .... EL
Lauderdale County Hospital, Ripley, TN [*Library symbol Library of Congress*] (LCLS) .... TRipLH
Lauerer Markin Gibbs, Inc. [*Maumee, OH*] [*Telecommunications*] (TSSD) .... LMG
Laufend Rechnung [*Current Account*] [*German Business term*] .... IR
Laufenden Monats [*Of the Current Month*] [*German*] .... LM
Laugh (ABBR) .... LGH
Laugh Lovers (EA) LL
Laugh Out Loud [*Internet language*] [*Computer science*] .... LOL
Laugh Out Very Loud [*Internet language*] [*Computer science*] .... LOVL
Laughable (ABBR) .... LGHB
Laughably (ABBR) .... LGHBY
Laughed (ABBR) .... LGHD
Laugher (ABBR) .... LGHR
Laughing (ABBR) .... LGHG
Laughing Out Loud .... LOL
Laughingly (ABBR) .... LGHGY
Laughlin, NV [*FM radio station call letters*] .... KADD
Laughlin, NV [*AM radio station call letters*] (RBYB) .... KLSQ
Laughlin, NV [*FM radio station call letters*] (RBYB) .... KLUK
Laughter (ABBR) .... LGHTR
Laughter Therapy (EA) .... LT
Laumontite [*A zeolite*] .... LAU
Launceston [*Australia ICAO location identifier*] (ICLI) .... AMLT
Launceston [*Municipal borough in England*] .... LAUNC
Launceston [*Tasmania*] [*Airport symbol*] (OAG) .... LST
Launceston Technical College [*Australia*] .... LTC
Launch [*or Launcher*] L
Launch (MSA) .... LANH
Launch .... LCH
Launch (AAG) .... LNCH
Launch Abort [*NASA*] (KSC) .... LA
Launch Abort Guide Simulation [*NASA*] (NASA) .... LAGS
Launch Abort Interface Unit [*NASA*] (MCD) .... LAIU
Launch Acceptability Region (MCD) .... LAR
Launch Aft .... LA

Launch Alert Receiver (DNAB) .... LAR
Launch Analyst [*Aerospace*] (AAG) .... LA
Launch Analyst Panel [*Aerospace*] (AAG) .... LAP
Launch Analyst's Console [*Aerospace*] (AAG) .... LAC
Launch and Flight Division [*Ballistic Research Laboratory*] (RDA) .... LFD
Launch and Flight Operations System .... LFOS
Launch and Ground Support Equipment .... L/GSE
Launch and Impact (AFM) .... L & I
Launch and Landing [*NASA*] (NASA) LL
Launch and Landing Computational Facilities [*NASA*] (NASA) .... LLCF
Launch and Landing Interface Unit (MCD) .... LLIU
Launch and Landing Project [*NASA*] (NASA) .... LLP
Launch and Landing Project Office [*NASA*] (NASA) .... LLPO
Launch and Landing Site (MCD) .... LLS
Launch and Recovery Platform (DNAB) .... LARP
Launch and Recovery System [*NASA*] .... LARS
Launch and Servicing (AAG) .... L & S
Launch Angle Condition Evaluator .... LACE
Launch Area [*NASA*] (KSC) .... LA
Launch Area Antenna (MCD) .... LAA
Launch Area Supervisor (AFM) .... LAS
Launch Area Support Ship .... LASS
Launch Automatic Checkout Equipment .... LACE
Launch Auxiliary System .... LAS
Launch Axis, Horizontal (MCD) .... LAH
Launch Axis, Vertical (MCD) .... LAV
Launch Azimuth [*NASA*] (KSC) .... LA
Launch Base Support [*Air Force*] .... LBS
Launch Blast Simulator (MUGU) .... LBS
Launch Boost (MCD) .... LB
Launch Bunker (MUGU) .... LB
Launch Bus (NASA) .... LB
Launch Captain's Control Panel [*Navy*] (CAAL) .... LCCP
Launch Center LC
Launch Checkout and Countdown System [*Aerospace*] (IAA) .... LCCS
Launch Command and Control LCC
Launch Commit Criteria (MCD) LCC
Launch Commit Criteria Document [*NASA*] (NASA) .... LCCD
Launch Complex LC
Launch Complex LCX
Launch Complex Assessment Report [*NASA*] (KSC) .... LCAR
Launch Complex Engineer [*NASA*] (KSC) .... LCE
Launch Complex Equipment .... LCE
Launch Complex Facility Console [*NASA*] (IAA) .... LCFC
Launch Complex Instrumentation (IAA) LCI
Launch Complex Operational Support Equipment .... LCOSE
Launch Complex Safety Officer (IAA) .... LCSO
Launch Complex Set .... LCS
Launch Complex Telemetry Trailer .... LCTT
Launch Complex Work Flow (IAA) .... LCWF
Launch Conference [*Aerospace*] (AAG) LC
Launch Control [*Aerospace*] (AAG) .... L/C
Launch Control Amplifier [*NASA*] (NASA) .... LCA
Launch Control Analyst [*NASA*] (AAG) .... LCA
Launch Control and Checkout System [*Aerospace*] (IAA) .... LCCS
Launch Control and Monitoring System [*NASA*] (AAG) .... LCMS
Launch Control and Sequencer System .... LCSS
Launch Control and Status Monitor .... LCSM
Launch [*or Launcher*] **Control Area** [*Missiles*] .... LCA
Launch Control Building [*NASA*] .... LCB
Launch Control Center [*NASA*] LCC
Launch Control Center Measuring Station [*NASA*] (KSC) .... LCCMS
Launch Control Complex Facility Console [*NASA*] (IAA) .... LCCFC
Launch Control Console LCC
Launch Control Design [*NASA*] (AAG) .... LCD
Launch Control Equipment (AAG) .... LCE
Launch Control Equipment Building (AFM) .... LCEB
Launch Control Facility .... LCF
Launch Control Facility Simulator [*NASA*] (IAA) .... LCFS
Launch Control Monitor (MCD) .... LCM
Launch Control Officer's Console (AAG) .... LCOC
Launch Control Officer's Panel (AAG) .... LCOP
Launch Control Operation (MCD) .... LCO
Launch Control Panel .... LCP
Launch Control Post (MCD) .... LCP
Launch Control Room (MCD) .... LCR
Launch Control Room (AAG) .... LCRM
Launch Control Safety Officer (MCD) .... LCSO
Launch Control Sequence (AAG) .... LCS
Launch Control Simulator .... LCS
Launch Control Station .... LCS
Launch Control Support Building [*Missiles*] .... LCSB
Launch Control System [*or Subsystem*] .... LCS
Launch Control System Simulator [*NASA*] (IAA) .... LCSS
Launch Control Trailer .... LCT
Launch Control Training Building [*NASA*] (IAA) .... LCTB
Launch Control Transfer Switching Unit [*Aerospace*] (AAG) .... LCTSU
Launch Control Unit (MCD) .... LCU
Launch Coolant System Control Unit (AAG) .... LCSCU
Launch Coordinator [*NASA*] LC
Launch Corridor [*Aerospace*] (AAG) LC
Launch Cost [*Aerospace*] LC
Launch Count [*NASA*] (KSC) LC
Launch Countdown [*NASA*] (NASA) LC
Launch Countdown [*NASA*] (NASA) .... LCD
Launch Countdown [*NASA*] (NASA) .... LCT
Launch Countdown Exercise [*NASA*] (AFM) .... LCE
Launch Crew Member (AAG) .... LCM
Launch Crew Quarters (AFM) .... LCQ
Launch Critical (MCD) LC
Launch Critical Spare Parts List [*NASA*] (KSC) .... LCSPL
Launch Critical Support Items [*NASA*] (KSC) .... LCSI
Launch Data Bus [*Computer science*] (MCD) .... LDB
Launch Data Interface Unit (MCD) .... LDIU
Launch Data System [*NASA*] (KSC) .... LDS
Launch Detection Satellite [*Former USSR*] .... LDS
Launch Director [*NASA*] (KSC) .... LD
Launch Division Officer [*Missiles*] (MUGU) .... LDO
Launch Effects Simulator .... LES
Launch Effects Trainer [*Weaponry*] (MCD) .... LET
Launch Eject .... LE
Launch Eject Gas Generator .... LEGG
Launch Eject Test .... LET
Launch Electronics .... LE
Launch Electronics Equipment .... LEE
Launch Electronics System Test .... LEST
Launch Enable Alarm (MCD) .... LEA
Launch Enable Logic Unit .... LELU
Launch Enable System Turret (IAA) .... LEST
Launch Enable Unit .... LEU
Launch Enabling System .... LES
Launch Enclosure Maintenance [*Aerospace*] (IAA) .... LEM
Launch Encounter [*NASA*] (KSC) .... L/E
Launch/Entry Helmet (MCD) .... LEH
Launch/Entry Suit [*NASA*] .... LES
Launch Environment, Mission, Type, Design Number, and Series [*Missiles*] (AFM) .... LMTDNS
Launch Environmental Simulator (MCD) .... LES
Launch Equipment Evaluation Set (MCD) .... LEES
Launch Equipment Shop (MCD) .... LES
Launch Equipment Test .... LET
Launch Equipment Test Facility [*NASA*] (NASA) .... LETF
Launch Equipment Test Set (MCD) .... LETS
Launch Escape [*NASA*] (KSC) .... LE
Launch Escape Assembly [*NASA*] (KSC) .... LEA
Launch Escape Control [*NASA*] (KSC) .... LEC
Launch Escape Control Area [*NASA*] (KSC) .... LECA
Launch Escape Monitor (MCD) .... LEM
Launch Escape Motor [*NASA*] .... LEM
Launch Escape Propulsion System [*NASA*] .... LEPS
Launch Escape Stabilization and Control System [*NASA*] (IAA) .... LESCS
Launch Escape System [*or Subsystem*] [*NASA*] .... LES
Launch Escape System Control [*NASA*] (KSC) .... LESC
Launch Escape System Simulator [*NASA*] (IAA) .... LESS
Launch Escape Tower [*NASA*] (MCD) .... LET
Launch Escape Tower Canard System [*NASA*] (IAA) .... LETCS
Launch Escape Vehicle [*NASA*] .... LEV
Launch Facility .... LF
Launch Facility Equipment Building [*Missiles*] .... LFEB
Launch Facility Security System [*NASA*] (KSC) .... LFSS
Launch Facility Simulator .... LFS
Launch Facility Trainer .... LFT
Launch First Motion .... LFM
Launch Forward .... LF
Launch Guidance Computer .... LGC
Launch in Process [*NASA*] (IAA) .... LIP
Launch Information Exchange Facility [*NASA*] .... LIEF
Launch Instant Selector .... LIS
Launch Instructions (SAA) LI
Launch Landing Test Data System (MCD) .... LLTDS
Launch Left (MCD) LL
Launch Maintenance Conference Network [*Aerospace*] (AAG) .... LMCN
Launch Missile Control Network (IAA) .... LMCN
Launch Mission Rules [*NASA*] (KSC) .... LMR
Launch Mission Rules Document [*NASA*] (KSC) .... LMRD
Launch Module .... LM
Launch Module / Defense Unit Platform .... LM/DUP
Launch Monitor Console [*or Control*] [*NASA*] (IAA) .... LMC
Launch Monitor Equipment [*NASA*] (KSC) .... LME
Launch Monitor Room [*NASA*] (MCD) .... LMR
Launch Motor Test .... LMT
Launch Mount (AFM) .... LM
Launch Network Test .... LNT
Launch Network Verification Test (IAA) .... LNVT
Launch Numerical Aperture [*Telecommunications*] (TEL) .... LNA
Launch on Assessment [*Military*] .... LOA
Launch on Attack [*Military*] .... LOA
Launch on Search [*Navy*] (CAAL) .... LOS
Launch on Warning [*Missiles*] .... LOW
Launch Operations [*or Operator*] [*NASA*] .... LO
Launch Operations Agency [*NASA*] (KSC) .... LOA
Launch Operations and Test Vehicle [*NASA*] (KSC) .... LOTV
Launch Operations Area (MCD) .... LOA
Launch Operations Branch [*NASA*] .... LOB
Launch Operations Building [*NASA*] .... LOB
Launch Operations Center [*NASA*] .... LOC
Launch Operations Complex .... LOC
Launch Operations Control .... LOC
Launch Operations Control Center .... LOCC
Launch Operations Directive [*or Director*] [*NASA*] .... LOD

Launch Operations Division [*NASA*] (KSC)	LOD
Launch Operations Manager [*NASA*]	LOM
Launch Operations [*or Operator's*] Panel [*NASA*]	LOP
Launch Operations Planning Group	LOPG
Launch Operations Simulation Model	LOSM
Launch Operations System [*NASA*] (KSC)	LOS
Launch Operations Television System	LOTS
Launch Operator's Console [*Aerospace*] (AAG)	LOC
Launch Optical Trajectory System [*NASA*] (IAA)	LOTS
Launch Optional Selector (IAA)	LOS
Launch Pad (KSC)	LP
Launch Pad Interface Assembly	LPIA
Launch Pad Lightning Warning System [*NASA*] (KSC)	LPLWS
Launch Panel	LP
Launch Phase Analyst	LPA
Launch Phase Simulator [*NASA*]	LPS
Launch Pitch Rate Control	LPRC
Launch Platform	LP
Launch Platform Detected [*Navy*] (CAAL)	LPD
Launch Pod Container [*General Support Rocket System*] (MCD)	LPC
Launch Point Determination	LPD
Launch Preparation Equipment (AABC)	LPE
Launch Preparation Equipment Compartment (AABC)	LPEC
Launch Preparation Equipment Monitor (MCD)	LPEM
Launch Preparation Equipment Set (AABC)	LPES
Launch Preparation Equipment Vault (MCD)	LPEV
Launch Preparations Group [*NASA*]	LPG
Launch Procedure Document [*NASA*] (KSC)	LPD
Launch Processing System [*NASA*] (KSC)	LPS
Launch Processing System / Central Data Subsystem [*Military*]	LPS/CDS
Launch Program Requirement Document [*NASA*] (IAA)	LPRD
Launch Rate Factor	LRF
Launch Readiness Demonstration [*NASA*] (KSC)	LRD
Launch Readiness Report [*or Review*] [*NASA*] (KSC)	LRR
Launch Readiness Verification [*NASA*] (NASA)	LRV
Launch Recoil Simulator	LRS
Launch, Recovery, and Transport [*Vehicle*]	LRT
Launch/Recovery Visual Landing Aid Change (MCD)	LRC
Launch/Reentry (MCD)	L/R
Launch Reliability (MCD)	LR
Launch Right (MCD)	LR
Launch Safe-and-Arm Device	LSAD
Launch/Safety Officer [*NASA*]	LSO
Launch Sequence (MCD)	LS
Launch Sequence and Control Equipment	LSCE
Launch Sequence and Interlock Document [*NASA*] (NASA)	LSID
Launch Sequence Applications Program (MCD)	LSAP
Launch Sequence Control	LSC
Launch Sequence Plan [*NASA*] (IAA)	LSP
Launch Sequence Simulator	LSS
Launch Sequencer [*Navy*] (CAAL)	LSEQ
Launch Sequencer Equipment [*NASA*]	LSE
Launch Service	LS
Launch Service Building	LSB
Launch Services Agreement (MCD)	LSA
Launch Set	LS
Launch Signal Responder (AAG)	LSR
Launch Signature Simulator (MCD)	LSS
Launch Simulator (MUGU)	LS
Launch Site [*NASA*] (MCD)	LS
Launch Site Accommodations Handbook [*NASA*] (NASA)	LSAH
Launch Site Maintenance [*NASA*] (IAA)	LSM
Launch Site Recovery [*NASA*] (KSC)	LSR
Launch Site Recovery Commander [*NASA*] (KSC)	LSRC
Launch Site Support Manager [*NASA*] (NASA)	LSSM
Launch Site Support Plan (MCD)	LSSP
Launch Site Support Team (MCD)	LSST
Launch Site Transportation Equipment [*NASA*] (NASA)	LSTE
Launch Station (MCD)	LS
Launch Station Equipment	LSE
Launch Station Test Set (MCD)	LSTS
Launch Station Test Set Radio Frequency Adapter (MCD)	LSTSRFA
Launch Status Summarizer	LSS
Launch/Storage Container	L/SC
Launch Success Indicator	LSI
Launch Support Division [*NASA*] (KSC)	LSD
Launch Support Equipment [*NASA*] (AAG)	LSE
Launch Support Equipment - Engineering Division [*NASA*] (KSC)	LSEED
Launch Support Facility [*NASA*] (KSC)	LSF
Launch Support Operations Contractor (SSD)	LSOC
Launch Support Requirement [*NASA*] (KSC)	LSR
Launch Support Section [*NASA*]	LSS
Launch Support System [*NASA*] (KSC)	LSS
Launch Support Team [*NASA*] (KSC)	LST
Launch Systems Data	LSD
Launch Telemetry Station	LTS
Launch Telemetry System	LTS
Launch Test [*NASA*] (IAA)	LT
Launch Test Area	LTA
Launch Test Directive [*NASA*] (KSC)	LTD
Launch Test Set	LTS
Launch Test Vehicles	LTV
Launch Test Working Group	LTWG
Launch to Eject	LTE
Launch Tracking [*or Trajectory*] Data System	LTDS

Launch Tracking Station	LTS
Launch Tracking System	LTS
Launch Umbilical Tower [*NASA*]	LUT
Launch under Attack [*Nuclear warfare option*]	LUA
Launch Utility Mode	LUM
Launch Vehicle (MCD)	LV
Launch Vehicle Alarm System [*NASA*] (IAA)	LVAS
Launch Vehicle and Propulsion [*NASA*] (IAA)	LVAP
Launch Vehicle and Propulsion Program [*NASA*]	LVPP
Launch Vehicle Assessment Report [*or Review*] [*NASA*] (KSC)	LVAR
Launch Vehicle Availability [*NASA*]	LVA
Launch Vehicle Data Adapter [*NASA*]	LVDA
Launch Vehicle Data Center [*NASA*] (KSC)	LVDC
Launch Vehicle Deployment Assembly [*NASA*] (MCD)	LVDA
Launch Vehicle Digital Computer [*NASA*]	LVDC
Launch Vehicle Engine (IAA)	LVE
Launch Vehicle Flight Control	LVFC
Launch Vehicle Flight Control System	LVFCS
Launch Vehicle Ground Support Equipment [*NASA*] (KSC)	LVGSE
Launch Vehicle Guidance Computer [*NASA*]	LVGC
Launch Vehicle Instrumentation Systems [*NASA*] (KSC)	LVIS
Launch Vehicle Material (MCD)	LVM
Launch Vehicle Mission Peculiar	LVMP
Launch Vehicle Monitor	LVM
Launch Vehicle Operations	LVO
Launch Vehicle Operations Division [*NASA*] (IAA)	LVOD
Launch Vehicle Planning Group [*Aerospace*] (AAG)	LVPG
Launch Vehicle Pressure Display [*NASA*] (KSC)	LVPD
Launch Vehicle Recovery System [*NASA*] (IAA)	LVRS
Launch Vehicle Safety System Test Set [*NASA*] (IAA)	LVSSTS
Launch Vehicle Simulator [*NASA*] (IAA)	LVS
Launch Vehicle Study Group [*NASA*] (KSC)	LVSG
Launch Vehicle Systems Engineer [*NASA*] (SAA)	LVSE
Launch Vehicle Test Conductor [*NASA*] (KSC)	LTC
Launch Vehicle Test Conductor [*NASA*] (KSC)	LVTC
Launch Verification [*NASA*] (IAA)	LV
Launch Warning Receiver [*Electronic countermeasure device*] [*Military*] (VNW)	LWR
Launch Window [*Aerospace*] (AAG)	LW
Launch Window Display [*Aerospace*] (MCD)	LWD
Launch Window Width [*Aerospace*]	LWW
Launch Zone Display	LZD
Launch Zone Display Flag	LZDF
Launch Zone Flag	LZF
Launch Zone Override	LZO
Launcher (AAG)	LCHR
Launcher	LNCHR
Launcher Adapter Electronics (MCD)	LAE
Launcher Adapter Missile Test Set	LAMTS
Launcher Adapter Rail (MCD)	LAR
Launcher Air Filtration Facility	LAFF
Launcher Aircraft Unit	LAU
Launcher and Missile Simulator	LAMSIM
Launcher Armament Unit [*Navy*] (DOMA)	LAU
Launcher Assignment Console	LAC
Launcher Avionics Packages (MCD)	LAPS
Launcher Booster Unit	LBU
Launcher Captain Control System [*Military*] (NVT)	LCCS
Launcher Control and Monitoring Panel	LCMP
Launcher Control Indicator [*Missiles*] (AABC)	LCI
Launcher Control Test Panel	LCTP
Launcher Electronic Module [*Military*] (RDA)	LEM
Launcher Electronic Unit (MCD)	LEU
Launcher Equipment Room [*Missiles*]	LER
Launcher Group [*Army*]	LG
Launcher Handling Procedure	LHP
Launcher Interchange Circuit (IAA)	LIC
Launcher Load Dolly	LLD
Launcher Loader Module	LLM
Launcher Maintenance Trainer Course	LMTC
Launcher Operation Control Panel	LOCP
Launcher Operation Station	LOS
Launcher Order and Capture Computer (MCD)	LOCC
Launcher Plant Assembly (IAA)	LPA
Launcher Preparation Control Panel	LPCP
Launcher Preparation Control Panel	LPP
Launcher Relay Assembly [*Navy*] (CAAL)	LRA
Launcher Selector Unit	LSU
Launcher Status Multiplexer (MSA)	LSM
Launcher Status Panel (MCD)	LSP
Launcher Support Building	LSB
Launcher Support Structure [*Navy*] (CAAL)	LSS
Launcher Switching Unit [*Navy*] (CAAL)	LSU
Launcher System Angles Matched [*Navy*] (CAAL)	LSAM
Launcher Tube Azimuth Datum Line	LTADL
Launcher Tube Longitudinal Axis	LTLA
Launcher Tube Vertical Centerline	LTVC
Launcher Umbilical Tower Transporter [*NASA*] (KSC)	LUTT
Launcher, Zero Length [*British military*] (DMA)	LZL
Launching Charging Header	LCH
Launching Control [*Military*]	LC
Launching Control Office [*or Officer*] [*Military*]	LCO
Launching Division [*Missiles*] (MUGU)	LD
Launching Equipment	LE
Launching Equipment Checkout Set	LECS

Launching Platoon [*Army*] ... LP
Launching Point Vertical (NATG) ... LPV
Launching Position Indicator ... LPI
Launching Reference Point ... LRP
Launching System ... LS
Launching System Module ... LSM
Launching System Module Console [*Navy*] (CAAL) ... LSMC
Launderer ... LDRER
Laundrette Association of Australia ... LAA
Laundromat ... LNDRMT
Laundry (MSA) ... LAU
Laundry (AFM) ... LDRY
Laundry ... LDY
Laundry ... LNDRY
Laundry and Cleaners Allied Trades Association [*Later, TCATA*] (EA) ... LACATA
Laundry and Cleaners Allied Trades Association [*Later, TCATA*] ... LCATA
Laundry and Decontamination Drycleaning System [*Military*] (DWSG) ... LADDS
Laundry and Decontamination Drycleaning System [*Military*] (DWSG) ... LDDCS
Laundry and Dry Cleaning International Union ... LDC
Laundry and Dry Cleaning Operations [*Military*] ... LDCO
Laundry Chute (MSA) ... LC
Laundry, Cleaning, and Dye House Workers' International Union [*Later, Textile Processors, Service Trades, Health Care, Professional, and Technical Employees International Union*] (EA) ... LCDHWIU
Laundry, Dry Cleaning, and Dye House Workers' International Union [*Later, Textile Processors, Service Trades, Health Care, Professional, and Technical Employees International Union*] ... LWIU
Laundry Tray ... LT
Laundry Waste Treatment System [*Nuclear energy*] (NRCH) ... LWTS
Laupheim [*Germany ICAO location identifier*] (ICLI) ... EDPM
Laura [*Australia Airport symbol Obsolete*] (OAG) ... LUU
Laura Branigan Fan Club (EA) ... LBFC
Laura Hendler Fan Club (EA) ... LHFC
Laura Ingalls Wilder Memorial Society (EA) ... LIWMS
Laura Ingalls Wilder - Rose Wilder Lane Home and Museum, Mansfield, MO [*Library symbol Library of Congress*] (LCLS) ... MoManW
Laura Lee McBride Fan Club (EA) ... LLMFC
Laura Station [*Australia Airport symbol Obsolete*] (OAG) ... LUT
Lauralee Bell Fan Club (EA) ... LBFC
Laurasia Resources Ltd. [*Toronto Stock Exchange symbol*] ... LUR
Laureate [*Numismatics*] ... LUR
Laureate in Arts ... LA
Laureate in English Literature ... LEL
Laureate of Arts ... AL
Laureate of Arts ... LC
Laureate of Letters ... LC
Laureate of Philosophy ... LP
Laureate of Science ... L Sc
Laurel [*Costa Rica*] [*ICAO location identifier*] (ICLI) ... MRLE
Laurel and Hardy [*The film comedy team of Stan Laurel and Oliver Hardy*] ... L & H
Laurel Bancorp, Inc. [*NASDAQ symbol*] (SAG) ... LAUR
Laurel Bancorp, Inc. [*Associated Press*] (SAG) ... LaurelBc
Laurel Cap Group [*NASDAQ symbol*] (TTSB) ... LARL
Laurel Capital Group [*NASDAQ symbol*] (SAG) ... LARL
Laurel Capital Group [*Associated Press*] (SAG) ... LaurlCa
Laurel, DE [*FM radio station call letters*] ... WDNO
Laurel Explorations Ltd. [*Vancouver Stock Exchange symbol*] ... LAX
Laurel/Hattiesburg [*Mississippi*] [*Airport symbol*] (OAG) ... PIB
Laurel Library Association, Laurel, MS [*Library symbol Library of Congress*] (LCLS) ... MsL
Laurel, MD [*AM radio station call letters*] ... WILC
Laurel, MS [*Location identifier FAA*] (FAAL) ... LUL
Laurel, MS [*Location identifier FAA*] (FAAL) ... THJ
Laurel, MS [*AM radio station call letters*] ... WAML
Laurel, MS [*Television station call letters*] ... WDAM
Laurel, MS [*AM radio station call letters*] ... WLAU
Laurel, MS [*FM radio station call letters*] (RBYB) ... WMXI-FM
Laurel, MS [*FM radio station call letters*] ... WNSL
Laurel, MS [*AM radio station call letters*] ... WQIS
Laurel, MT [*AM radio station call letters*] ... KBSR
Laurel, MT [*FM radio station call letters*] ... KRSQ
Lauren Rogers Library and Museum of Art, Laurel, MS [*Library symbol Library of Congress*] (LCLS) ... MsLE
Laurence-Moon Syndrome [*Medicine*] ... LMS
Laurence-Moon-Bardet-Biedl Syndrome [*Medicine*] (DMAA) ... LMBB
Laurence-Moon-Bardet-Biedl Syndrome [*Medicine*] ... LMBBS
Laurence-Moon-Bardet-Biedl Syndrome Network [*An association*] (EA) ... LMBBSN
Laurence-Moon-Biedl [*Medicine*] ... LMB
Laurence-Moon-Biedl Syndrome [*Medicine*] ... LMBS
Laurence's Primogeniture [*1878*] [*A publication*] (DLA) ... Laur Prim
Laurence's Reports of the High Court of Griqualand [*1882-1910*] [*South Africa*] [*A publication*] (DLA) ... Laurence
Laurens County Library, Laurens, SC [*Library symbol Library of Congress*] (LCLS) ... ScLau
Lauren's High Court Cases [*South Africa*] [*A publication*] (DLA) ... Laur HC Ca
Laurens Public Library, Laurens, IA [*Library symbol Library of Congress*] (LCLS) ... IaLau
Laurens, SC [*Location identifier FAA*] (FAAL) ... LUX
Laurens, SC [*AM radio station call letters*] ... WLBG
Laurens Sun, Laurens, IA [*Library symbol Library of Congress*] (LCLS) ... IaLauS
Laurentian Bank of Canada [*Toronto Stock Exchange symbol*] ... LB
Laurentian Forest Research Center [*Canadian Forestry Service*] [*Research center*] (RCD) ... LFRC
Laurentian Forestry Centre, Canadian Forestry Service [*Centre de Foresterie des Laurentides, Service Canadien des Forets*] **Ste.-Foy, Quebec** [*Library symbol National Library of Canada*] (NLC) ... QQMF
Laurentian Group Corp. [*Toronto Stock Exchange symbol*] ... LGC
Laurentian Library [*Classical studies*] (OCD) ... Laur
Laurentian Life Insurance Co., Inc. [*Toronto Stock Exchange symbol*] ... LL
Laurentian University Library [*UTLAS symbol*] ... LAU
Laurentian University, Sudbury, ON, Canada [*Library symbol Library of Congress*] (LCLS) ... CaOSuL
Laurentian University [*Universite Laurentienne*] **Sudbury, Ontario** [*Library symbol National Library of Canada*] (NLC) ... OSUL
Laurentide Ice Sheet [*Climatology*] ... LIS
Laurentius de Pallatis [*Flourished, 16th century*] [*Authority cited in pre-1607 legal work*] (DSA) ... Laur de Palat
Laurentius de Pinu [*Deceased, 1397*] [*Authority cited in pre-1607 legal work*] (DSA) ... Lau de Pin
Laurentius de Rodulphis [*Flourished, 15th century*] [*Authority cited in pre-1607 legal work*] (DSA) ... Lauren de Rodul
Laurentius Hispanus [*Deceased, 1248*] [*Authority cited in pre-1607 legal work*] (DSA) ... L
Laurentius Hispanus [*Deceased, 1248*] [*Authority cited in pre-1607 legal work*] (DSA) ... La
Laurentius Hispanus [*Deceased, 1248*] [*Authority cited in pre-1607 legal work*] (DSA) ... Lau
Laurentius Hispanus [*Deceased, 1248*] [*Authority cited in pre-1607 legal work*] (DSA) ... Laur
Laurentius Hispanus [*Deceased, 1248*] [*Authority cited in pre-1607 legal work*] (DSA) ... Lauren
Lauric [*or Lauroyl or Lauryl*] **Isopropanolamide** [*Also, LPA*] [*Organic chemistry*] ... LIPA
Lauric [*or Lauroyl or Lauryl*] **Isopropanolamide** [*Also, LIPA*] [*Organic chemistry*] ... LPA
Laurie Hill Library, Heron, MT [*Library symbol*] [*Library of Congress*] (LCLS) ... MtHe
Laurinburg & Southern Railroad Co. (IIA) ... L & S
Laurinburg & Southern Railroad Co. [*AAR code*] ... LRS
Laurinburg, NC [*FM radio station call letters*] ... WAZZ
Laurinburg, NC [*AM radio station call letters*] ... WEWO
Laurinburg, NC [*AM radio station call letters*] ... WLNC
Lauritz Melchior Heldentenor Foundation (EA) ... LMHF
Lauro/Viceroy/Global Joint Service [*Shipping*] (DS) ... LVG
Lauroyl Peroxide [*Organic chemistry*] ... LPO
Lauryl Diethanolamide [*Also, LDE*] [*Organic chemistry*] ... LDA
Lauryl Diethanolamide [*Also, LDA*] [*Organic chemistry*] ... LDE
Lauryl Sulfate Tryptose [*Growth medium*] ... LST
Lauryldimethylamine Oxide [*Detergent*] ... LDAO
Laurylpyridinium Chloride [*Also, DPC*] [*Organic chemistry*] ... LPC
Lauryltrimethylammonium Chloride [*Organic chemistry*] ... LTMAC
Laus Deo [*Praise to God*] [*Latin*] ... LD
Laus Deo et Gloria [*Praise and Glory Be to God*] [*Latin*] ... LDEG
Laus Deo Semper [*Praise to God Always*] [*Latin*] ... LDS
Laus Sit Jesu et Mariae [*Praise Be to Jesus and Mary*] [*Latin*] ... LSJM
Laus Verbo Incarnato [*Praise to the Incarnate Word*] [*Latin*] ... LVI
Lausanne/Blecherette [*Switzerland ICAO location identifier*] (ICLI) ... LSGL
Laussat's Equity Practice in Pennsylvania [*A publication*] (DLA) ... Lauss Eq
Lauterbrunnen [*Switzerland ICAO location identifier*] (ICLI) ... LSXL
Lauthala Islands [*Fiji*] [*ICAO location identifier*] (ICLI) ... NFNH
Laut-und Formenlehre des Aegyptisch-Aramaeisch [*A publication*] (BJA) ... LFIAA
Lava [*Maps and charts*] ... LA
Lava (WGA) ... LV
Lava Beds National Monument ... LABE
Lava Capital Corp. [*Toronto Stock Exchange symbol*] ... LVA
Lavacrum Palladis [*of Callimachus*] [*Classical studies*] (OCD) ... Lav Pall
Laval/Entrammes [*France ICAO location identifier*] (ICLI) ... LFOV
Laval, PQ [*FM radio station call letters*] ... CFGL
Laval Theologique et Philosophique [*Quebec*] [*A publication*] (BJA) ... LavalTPh
Lavaliere [*Lapel microphone*] (NTCM) ... LAV
Lavalin Environment, Inc., Montreal, Quebec [*Library symbol National Library of Canada*] (BIB) ... QMLAVE
Lavalin Environnement, Montreal, Quebec [*Library symbol National Library of Canada*] (NLC) ... QMAMA
Lavalin, Inc., Montreal, Quebec [*Library symbol National Library of Canada*] (BIB) ... QMLAV
Lavalin Industries, Inc. [*Toronto Stock Exchange symbol*] ... LVI
Lavalin Services, Inc., Calgary, AB, Canada [*Library symbol*] [*Library of Congress*] (LCLS) ... CaACLa
Lavalin Services, Inc., Calgary, Alberta [*Library symbol National Library of Canada*] (NLC) ... ACLA
Lavan Island [*Iran*] [*ICAO location identifier*] (ICLI) ... OIBV
Lavatory (DSUE) ... LA
Lavatory (KSC) ... LAV
Lavatory [*Slang*] (DSUE) ... LAVO
Lavatory Basin ... LB
Lavender [*Botany*] ... L
Lavender [*Philately*] ... lav
Lavendula [*Lavender*] [*Pharmacology*] (ROG) ... LAVEND
Laventhol & Horwath, Toronto, Ontario, [*Library symbol National Library of Canada*] (BIB) ... OTLH
Laverack Barracks [*Australia ICAO location identifier*] (ICLI) ... ABLK
Laverda Owner's Club (EA) ... LOC
Laverda SpA [*Italy ICAO aircraft manufacturer identifier*] (ICAO) ... LV
Laverne and Shirley [*Television program*] ... L & S
Laverton [*Australia ICAO location identifier*] (ICLI) ... AMLV
Laverton [*Australia Airport symbol*] (OAG) ... LVO

LaVeta Public Library, LaVeta, CO [*Library symbol Library of Congress*] (LCLS) ... CoLav
Lavochkin [*USSR aircraft type*] [*World War II*] ... LA
Lavrentiya [*Former USSR ICAO location identifier*] (ICLI) ... UHML
Lavumisa [*Swaziland*] [*ICAO location identifier*] (ICLI) ... FDGL
Law ... L
Law Advertiser [*1823-31*] [*A publication*] (DLA) ... L Advertiser
Law Advertiser [*1823-31*] [*A publication*] (DLA) ... Law Advert
Law Agent ... LA
Law Almanac [*New York*] [*A publication*] (DLA) ... Law Alm
Law Amendment Journal [*1855-58*] [*A publication*] (DLA) ... Law Am Jour
Law Amendment Journal [*1855-58*] [*A publication*] (DLA) ... Law Amdt J
Law and Communication [*A publication*] (DLA) ... L & Comm
Law and Computer Technology [*A publication*] (DLA) ... L & Computer Tech
Law and Contemporary Problems [*A publication*] (LWAP) ... L & CONTEM PROB
Law and Equity Reporter [*United States*] [*A publication*] (DLA) ... L & Eq Rep
Law and Equity Reporter [*New York*] [*A publication*] (DLA) ... Law & Eq Rep
Law and History Review [*A publication*] (DLA) ... Law & Hist Rev
Law and Legal Information Directory [*A publication*] ... LLD
Law and Legislation in the German Democratic Republic [*A publication*] (DLA) ... L & Leg GDR
Law and Legislation in the German Democratic Republic [*A publication*] (DLA) ... L & Legis in GDR
Law and Legislation in the German Democratic Republic [*A publication*] (DLA) ... Law & Legisl in the German Dem Rep
Law and Legislative Reference Library, Augusta, ME [*Library symbol Library of Congress*] (LCLS) ... Me-LR
Law and Liberty [*A publication*] (DLA) ... L & Lib
Law and Liberty [*A publication*] (DLA) ... Law & Lib
Law and Liberty Project [*Defunct*] (EA) ... LLP
Law and Order [*A publication*] (DLA) ... L & Order
Law and Policy in International Business [*ABA*] [*A publication*] (AAGC) ... LPIB
Law and Political Science Section [*Association of College and Research Libraries*] ... LPSS
Law and Psychology Review [*A publication*] (DLA) ... L & Psych Rev
Law and Psychology Review [*A publication*] (DLA) ... L & Psychology Rev
Law and Psychology Review [*A publication*] (DLA) ... Law & Psychology Rev
Law and Social Change [*A publication*] (DLA) ... Law & Soc
Law and Society Association (EA) ... LSA
Law Association for Asia and the Pacific [*Australia*] ... LAAP
Law Association of Victoria [*Australia*] ... LAV
Law Book Adviser [*A publication*] (DLA) ... L Book Adviser
Law Book Review Digest and Current Legal Bibliography [*A publication*] (DLA) ... Law Bk Rev Dig
Law Bulletin [*Zambia*] [*A publication*] (DLA) ... Law Bull
Law Bulletin and Brief [*A publication*] (DLA) ... Law Bul & Br
Law Bulletin. State University of Iowa [*A publication*] (DLA) ... Law Bul IA
Law Cases, William I to Richard I [*England*] [*A publication*] (DLA) ... Law Cas Wm I
Law Centres Federation [*British*] (DBA) ... LCF
Law Certificate ... LLC
Law Chronicle [*England*] [*A publication*] (DLA) ... L Chr
Law Chronicle [*England*] [*A publication*] (DLA) ... L Chron
Law Chronicle [*England*] [*A publication*] (DLA) ... Law Chr
Law Chronicle [*South Africa*] [*A publication*] (ILCA) ... Law Chr
Law Chronicle and Auction Record [*A publication*] (DLA) ... Law Chr & Auct Rec
Law Chronicle and Journal of Jurisprudence [*A publication*] (DLA) ... Law Chr & Jour Jur
Law Chronicle and Law Students' Magazine [*A publication*] (DLA) ... L Chron & L Stud Mag
Law Chronicle and Law Students' Magazine (New Series) [*A publication*] (DLA) ... L Chron & L Stud Mag (NS)
Law Clerk (DLA) ... Law Cl
Law Clerk Record [*1910-11*] [*A publication*] (DLA) ... Law Cl Rec
Law Commentary [*A publication*] (DLA) ... L Comment
Law Commentary [*A publication*] (DLA) ... L Comment'y
Law Commission (DLA) ... Law Com
Law Commission (DLA) ... LC
Law Commission Report [*A publication*] (DLA) ... Law Com
Law Commission Working Paper [*A publication*] (DLA) ... LCWP
Law Companies Group, Inc., Kennesaw, GA [*Library symbol*] [*Library of Congress*] (LCLS) ... GKLC
Law Council of Australia. Business Law Section. Bulletin [*A publication*] ... LCABLS Bull
Law Council of the Australian Capital Territory ... LCACT
Law Court (DLA) ... L Ct
Law Courts ... LC
Law Department Bulletin, Union Pacific Railroad Co. [*A publication*] (DLA) ... Law Dept Bull
Law Dictionary [*A publication*] (DLA) ... L Dict
Law Dictionary [*A publication*] (DLA) ... LD
Law Division (DLA) ... L Div
Law Encounter Severity Scale [*Personality development test*] [*Psychology*] ... LESS
Law Enforcement ... LE
Law Enforcement Access Field [*Telecommunications*] ... LEAF
Law Enforcement Agencies (DOMA) ... LEA
Law Enforcement Assistance Act ... LEAA
Law Enforcement Assistance Administration [*Closed, functions transferred to Office of Justice Assistance, Research, and Statistics*] [*Department of Justice*] ... LEAA
Law Enforcement Assistance Administration. Legal Opinions [*A publication*] (DLA) ... LEAA Legal Op
Law Enforcement Assistance Program (EA) ... LEA
Law Enforcement Automated Data System (IEEE) ... LEADS
Law Enforcement Data System ... LEDS
Law Enforcement Detachment [*Coast Guard*] ... LEDET
Law Enforcement Division [*National Park Service*] ... LED
Law Enforcement Education Program [*Department of Justice*] ... LEEP
Law Enforcement Explorer Post [*Boy Scouts*] ... LEEP
Law Enforcement Group (WDAA) ... LEG
Law Enforcement Information Management Section [*An association*] (EA) ... LEIM
Law Enforcement Information Network ... LEIN
Law Enforcement Intelligence Units [*An association*] (EA) ... LEIU
Law Enforcement Manpower Resources Allocation [*IBM program product*] ... LEMRAS
Law Enforcement Manual [*IRS*] ... LEM
Law Enforcement Memorial Foundation (EA) ... LEMF
Law Enforcement Memorial Research Project (EA) ... LEMRP
Law Enforcement Officer (MCD) ... LEO
Law Enforcement Planning Commission ... LEPC
[*A*] **Law Enforcement Roundtable** [*Information service or system*] (IID) ... ALERT
Law Enforcement Security Access Position ... LESAP
Law Enforcement Squadron ... LES
Law Enforcement Standards Laboratory [*National Institute of Standards and Technology*] ... LESL
Law Enforcement Standards Program [*National Institute of Law Enforcement and Criminal Justice*] ... LESP
Law Enforcement Study Unit [*of the American Topical Association*] (EA) ... LESU
Law Enforcement Teletype [*or Teletypewriter*] **Service** [*Phoenix, AZ*] ... LETS
Law Enforcement Television Network ... LETN
Law Examination Journal [*A publication*] (DLA) ... Law Ex J
Law Examination Reporter [*A publication*] (DLA) ... Law Ex Rep
Law for the Australian Businessman [*A publication*] ... ABL
Law Foundation of Tasmania [*Australia*] ... LFT
Law French (DLA) ... L Fr
Law French (DLA) ... LF
Law French Dictionary [*A publication*] (DLA) ... Law Fr Dict
Law Gazette [*A publication*] (DLA) ... L Gaz
Law Gazette [*A publication*] (DLA) ... Law Gaz
Law Glossary (DLA) ... LG
Law Guardian [*A publication*] (DLA) ... L Guard
Law in American Society [*A publication*] (DLA) ... L Am Soc
Law in American Society [*A publication*] (DLA) ... L Am Soc'y
Law in Context [*A publication*] ... Law in Cont
Law in Context [*Australia A publication*] ... LIC
Law in Eastern Europe [*A publication*] (DLA) ... L East Eur
Law in Eastern Europe [*A publication*] (DLA) ... L in Eastern Eur
Law in Eastern Europe [*A publication*] (DLA) ... LIEE
Law in Society [*A publication*] (DLA) ... L in Soc'y
Law in Transition Journal [*A publication*] (DLA) ... L in Trans J
Law in Transition Quarterly [*A publication*] (DLA) ... L in Trans Q
Law in Transition Quarterly [*A publication*] (DLA) ... L Trans Q
Law Institute News [*Australia A publication*] ... LIN
Law Intelligencer [*United States*] [*A publication*] (DLA) ... L Intell
Law Intelligencer [*United States*] [*A publication*] (DLA) ... Law Int
Law Journal, County Courts Reporter [*A publication*] (DLA) ... LJCC
Law Journal, Exchequer in Equity [*England*] [*A publication*] (DLA) ... LJ Ex Eq
Law Journal, Irish [*1933-34*] [*A publication*] (DLA) ... LJ Ir
Law Journal, Irish Free State [*1931-32*] [*A publication*] (DLA) ... LJIFS
Law Journal, King's Bench, Old Series [*England*] [*A publication*] (DLA) ... LJKB OS
Law Journal (Law Tracts) [*England*] [*A publication*] (DLA) ... LJLT
Law Journal (Lower Canada) [*A publication*] (DLA) ... LJLC
Law Journal. Marut Bunnag International Law Office [*A publication*] (DLA) ... LJ of the Marut Bunnag Internat L Off
Law Journal, Matrimonial [*England*] [*A publication*] (DLA) ... LJ Mat
Law Journal, Matrimonial [*England*] [*A publication*] (DLA) ... LJ Mat (Eng)
Law Journal, New Series [*England*] [*A publication*] (DLA) ... LJ NS
Law Journal, New Series, Admiralty [*A publication*] (DLA) ... LJ Adm
Law Journal, New Series, Chancery [*A publication*] (DLA) ... Law J Ch
Law Journal, New Series, Common Law, Magistrates Cases (Discontinued) [*A publication*] (DLA) ... LJ Mag
Law Journal, New Series, Divorce and Matrimonial [*England*] [*A publication*] (DLA) ... LJ Mat Cas
Law Journal, New Series, English Queen's Bench [*A publication*] (DLA) ... Law JQB
Law Journal, New Series, English Queen's Bench [*A publication*] (DLA) ... Law Jr QB
Law Journal, New Series, Exchequer [*A publication*] (DLA) ... Law J Exch
Law Journal Newspaper [*England*] [*A publication*] (DLA) ... L Jo
Law Journal Newspaper [*1866-1965*] [*A publication*] ... LJ
Law Journal Newspaper [*1866-1965*] [*A publication*] (DLA) ... LJ News
Law Journal Newspaper [*England*] [*A publication*] (DLA) ... LJ News (Eng)
Law Journal Newspaper [*1866-1965*] [*A publication*] (DLA) ... LJ Newsp
Law Journal Newspaper, County Court Appeals [*England*] [*A publication*] (DLA) ... LJCCA
Law Journal Newspaper, County Court Appeals [*England*] [*A publication*] (DLA) ... LJNCCA
Law Journal Newspaper, County Court Reports [*England*] [*A publication*] (DLA) ... LJNCCR
Law Journal, Notes of Cases [*England*] [*A publication*] (DLA) ... L Jo NC
Law Journal, Notes of Cases [*A publication*] (DLA) ... LJNC
Law Journal, Notes of Cases [*England*] [*A publication*] (DLA) ... LJNC (Eng)
Law Journal of Upper Canada [*A publication*] (DLA) ... LJUC
Law Journal, Old Series [*1822-31*] [*London*] [*A publication*] (DLA) ... LJ OS
Law Journal, Old Series, Chancery [*1822-23*] [*A publication*] (DLA) ... LJ OS Ch
Law Journal, Old Series, Common Pleas [*1822-31*] [*A publication*] (DLA) ... LJ OS CP
Law Journal, Old Series, Exchequer [*1830-31*] [*A publication*] (DLA) ... LJ OS Ex

Law Journal, Old Series, King's Bench [*1822-31*] [*A publication*] (DLA) ... LJ OS KB
Law Journal, Old Series, Magistrates' Cases [*1826-31*] [*A publication*] (ILCA) ... LJOSMC
Law Journal, Probate and Matrimonial [*England*] [*A publication*] (DLA) ... LJ Prob & Mat
Law Journal, Probate and Matrimonial [*England*] [*A publication*] (DLA) ... LJ Prob (Eng)
Law Journal, Probate and Matrimonial [*England*] [*A publication*] (DLA) ... LJP & M
Law Journal, Probate and Matrimonial, New Series [*England*] [*A publication*] (DLA) ... LJ Prob NS (Eng)
Law Journal, Probate Division [*A publication*] (DLA) ... Law JPD
Law Journal Reports [*A publication*] (DLA) ... Law J
Law Journal Reports [*A publication*] (DLA) ... Law Jour
Law Journal Reports [*A publication*] (DLA) ... LJ Rep
Law Journal Reports [*A publication*] ... LJR
Law Journal Reports [*England*] [*A publication*] (DLA) ... LJR (Eng)
Law Journal Reports, Admiralty, New Series [*1865-75*] [*A publication*] (DLA) ... LJ Adm NS
Law Journal Reports, Bankruptcy [*A publication*] (DLA) ... LJ Bank
Law Journal Reports, Bankruptcy [*A publication*] (DLA) ... LJ Bankr
Law Journal Reports, Bankruptcy [*A publication*] (DLA) ... LJ Bk
Law Journal Reports, Chancery, New Series [*1831-1946*] [*A publication*] (DLA) ... LJ Eq
Law Journal Reports, Chancery, Old Series [*1822-31*] [*England*] [*A publication*] (DLA) ... LJ Ch (OS)
Law Journal Reports, Common Pleas Decisions [*England*] [*A publication*] (DLA) ... LJCP
Law Journal Reports, Common Pleas Decisions [*England*] [*A publication*] (DLA) ... LJCP (Eng)
Law Journal Reports, Common Pleas Decisions [*England*] [*A publication*] (DLA) ... LJCPD
Law Journal Reports, Common Pleas Decisions, New Series [*1831-75*] [*A publication*] (DLA) ... LJCP NS
Law Journal Reports, Common Pleas, New Series [*England*] [*A publication*] (DLA) ... LJCP NS (Eng)
Law Journal Reports, Common Pleas, Old Series [*England*] [*A publication*] (DLA) ... LJCP (OS)
Law Journal Reports, Exchequer, Old Series [*A publication*] (DLA) ... LJ Exch (OS)
Law Journal Reports, King's Bench [*A publication*] (DLA) ... LJKB
Law Journal Reports, King's Bench [*England*] [*A publication*] (DLA) ... LJKB (Eng)
Law Journal Reports, King's Bench, New Series [*A publication*] (DLA) ... LJKB NS
Law Journal Reports, King's Bench, New Series [*England*] [*A publication*] (DLA) ... LJKB NS (Eng)
Law Journal Reports, Magistrates' Cases [*1822-31*] [*A publication*] (DLA) ... LJ Mag Cas
Law Journal Reports, Magistrates' Cases [*England*] [*A publication*] (DLA) ... LJ Mag Cas (Eng)
Law Journal Reports, Magistrates' Cases, New Series [*1831-96*] [*A publication*] (DLA) ... LJ Mag Cas NS
Law Journal Reports, Magistrates' Cases, New Series [*England*] [*A publication*] (DLA) ... LJ Mag Cas NS (Eng)
Law Journal Reports, Matrimonial, Probate, and Admiralty [*England*] [*A publication*] (DLA) ... LJMPA
Law Journal Reports, New Series [*A publication*] (DLA) ... LJ Rep NS
Law Journal Reports, New Series, Admiralty [*England*] [*A publication*] (DLA) ... LJ Adm NS (Eng)
Law Journal Reports, New Series, Appeals [*A publication*] (DLA) ... LJ App
Law Journal Reports, New Series, Bankruptcy [*A publication*] (DLA) ... LJ Bank NS
Law Journal Reports, New Series, Bankruptcy [*England*] [*A publication*] (DLA) ... LJ Bankr NS (Eng)
Law Journal Reports, New Series, Bankruptcy [*A publication*] (DLA) ... LJ Bcy
Law Journal Reports, New Series, Chancery [*A publication*] (DLA) ... LJ Ch
Law Journal Reports, New Series, Chancery [*England*] [*A publication*] (DLA) ... LJ Ch (Eng)
Law Journal Reports, New Series, Chancery [*England*] [*A publication*] (DLA) ... LJ Ch NS (Eng)
Law Journal Reports, New Series, Common Pleas [*England*] [*A publication*] (DLA) ... LJC
Law Journal Reports, New Series, Crown Cases Reserved [*England*] [*A publication*] (DLA) ... LJCCR
Law Journal Reports, New Series, Crown Cases Reserved [*England*] [*A publication*] (DLA) ... LJCCR (NS)
Law Journal Reports, New Series, Divorce and Matrimonial [*England*] [*A publication*] (DLA) ... LJD & M
Law Journal Reports, New Series, Ecclesiastical Cases [*A publication*] (DLA) ... LJ Ecc
Law Journal Reports, New Series, Ecclesiastical Cases [*A publication*] (DLA) ... LJ Eccl
Law Journal Reports, New Series, Exchequer [*1831-75*] [*A publication*] (DLA) ... LJ Exch NS
Law Journal Reports, New Series, Exchequer Division [*England*] [*A publication*] (DLA) ... LJ Ex
Law Journal Reports, New Series, Exchequer Division [*England*] [*A publication*] (DLA) ... LJ Ex D
Law Journal Reports, New Series, Exchequer Division [*England*] [*A publication*] (DLA) ... LJ Exch
Law Journal Reports, New Series, Exchequer Division [*England*] [*A publication*] (DLA) ... LJ Exch (Eng)
Law Journal Reports, New Series, Exchequer Division [*England*] [*A publication*] (DLA) ... LJ Exch NS (Eng)
Law Journal Reports, New Series, House of Lords [*England*] [*A publication*] (DLA) ... LJHL
Law Journal Reports, New Series, Magistrates' Cases [*England*] [*A publication*] (DLA) ... LJM Cas
Law Journal Reports, New Series, Magistrates' Cases [*England*] [*A publication*] (DLA) ... LJMC
Law Journal Reports, New Series, Privy Council [*England*] [*A publication*] (DLA) ... LJ PC NS
Law Journal Reports, New Series, Privy Council [*England*] [*A publication*] (DLA) ... LJP
Law Journal Reports, New Series, Probate and Matrimonial [*1858-59, 1866-75*] [*A publication*] (DLA) ... LJ Prob
Law Journal Reports, New Series, Probate and Matrimonial [*1858-59, 1866-75*] [*A publication*] (DLA) ... LJ Prob NS
Law Journal Reports, New Series, Probate, Divorce, and Admiralty [*1875-1946*] [*A publication*] (DLA) ... Law JPD & A
Law Journal Reports, New Series, Probate, Divorce, and Admiralty [*1875-1946*] [*A publication*] (DLA) ... LJPD & A
Law Journal Reports, New Series, Probate, Divorce, and Admiralty [*England*] [*A publication*] (DLA) ... LJPD & Adm
Law Journal Reports, New Series, Probate, Matrimonial, and Admiralty [*England*] [*A publication*] (DLA) ... LJPM & A
Law Journal Reports, New Series, Queen's Bench [*England*] [*A publication*] (DLA) ... LJQB
Law Journal Reports, New Series, Queen's Bench [*England*] [*A publication*] (DLA) ... LJQB (Eng)
Law Journal Reports, New Series, Queen's Bench [*1831-1946*] [*A publication*] (DLA) ... LJQB NS
Law Journal Reports, New Series, Queen's Bench Division [*England*] [*A publication*] (DLA) ... LJQBD
Law Journal Reports, New Series, Queen's Bench Division [*England*] [*A publication*] (DLA) ... LJQBD NS
Law Journal Reports, Old Series, Magistrates' Cases [*England*] [*A publication*] (DLA) ... LJMCOS
Law Journal Reports, Privy Council [*England*] [*A publication*] (DLA) ... LJ PC (Eng)
Law Journal Reports, Privy Council [*England*] [*A publication*] (DLA) ... LJPC
Law Journal Reports, Probate, Divorce, and Admiralty [*England*] [*A publication*] (DLA) ... LJP
Law Journal Reports, Queen's Bench, New Series [*England*] [*A publication*] (DLA) ... LJQB NS (Eng)
Law Journal (Smith) [*England*] [*A publication*] (DLA) ... Sm LJ
Law Journal. Student Bar Association. Ohio State University [*A publication*] (DLA) ... OSLJ
Law Judge (DLA) ... LJ
Law Latin ... LL
Law Latin ... LLAT
Law Latin Dictionary [*A publication*] (DLA) ... Law Lat Dic
Law Library Association of St. Louis, St. Louis, MO [*Library symbol Library of Congress*] (LCLS) ... MoSL
Law Library, Bell Canada, Montreal, Quebec [*Library symbol National Library of Canada*] (NLC) ... QMBL
Law Library, British Columbia, Ministry of the Attorney General, Victoria, British Columbia [*Library symbol National Library of Canada*] (NLC) ... BVIAGL
Law Library, C-I-L, Inc., North York, Ontario [*Library symbol National Library of Canada*] (NLC) ... OTCILL
Law Library, Cox, Downie & Co., Halifax, Nova Scotia [*Library symbol National Library of Canada*] (NLC) ... NSHCD
Law Library Foundation, Victoria, BC, Canada [*Library symbol Library of Congress*] (LCLS) ... CaBViL
Law Library Foundation, Victoria, British Columbia [*Library symbol National Library of Canada Obsolete*] (NLC) ... BVIL
Law Library, Manufacturers Life Insurance Co., Toronto, Ontario [*Library symbol National Library of Canada*] (BIB) ... OTML
Law Library, McGill University, Montreal, Quebec [*Library symbol National Library of Canada*] (NLC) ... QMML
Law Library, McInnes, Cooper & Robertson, Halifax, Nova Scotia [*Library symbol National Library of Canada*] (NLC) ... NSHMCR
Law Library, New Series [*Philadelphia, PA*] [*A publication*] (DLA) ... Law Lib NS
Law Library, New Series [*Philadelphia Reprint of English Treatises*] [*A publication*] (DLA) ... LL NS
Law Library, Newfoundland Department of Justice, St. John's, Newfoundland [*Library symbol National Library of Canada*] (NLC) ... NFSJL
Law Library News [*A publication*] (DLA) ... Law Lib N
Law Library of Congress United Association of Employees ... LLCUNAE
Law Library of Louisiana, New Orleans, LA [*Library symbol Library of Congress*] (LCLS) ... L-L
Law Library of Louisiana, New Orleans, LA [*OCLC symbol*] (OCLC) ... LNL
Law Library, Patterson, Smith, Mathews & Grant, Truro, Nova Scotia [*Library symbol National Library of Canada*] (NLC) ... NSTPS
Law Library, Queen's University, Kingston, Ontario [*Library symbol National Library of Canada*] (NLC) ... OKQL
Law Library, University of Alberta, Edmonton, Alberta [*Library symbol National Library of Canada*] (NLC) ... AEUL
Law Library, University of British Columbia, Vancouver, British Columbia [*Library symbol National Library of Canada*] (NLC) ... BVAUL
Law Library, University of Calgary, Alberta [*Library symbol National Library of Canada*] (BIB) ... ACUL
Law Library, University of New Brunswick, Fredericton, New Brunswick [*Library symbol National Library of Canada*] (NLC) ... NBFUL
Law Library, University of Saskatchewan, Saskatoon, Saskatchewan [*Library symbol National Library of Canada*] (NLC) ... SSUL
Law Library, University of Victoria, British Columbia [*Library symbol National Library of Canada*] (NLC) ... BVIVL
Law Library, University of Western Ontario, London, Ontario [*Library symbol National Library of Canada*] (NLC) ... OLUL
Law Library, University of Windsor, Ontario [*Library symbol National Library of Canada*] (NLC) ... OWAL

Law Library, York University, Toronto, Ontario [*Library symbol National Library of Canada*] (NLC) ... OTYL
Law List (ILCA) ... LL
Law Magazine [*A publication*] (DLA) ... Law Mag
Law Magazine and Law Review [*A publication*] (DLA) ... L Mag & LR
Law Magazine and Law Review [*A publication*] (DLA) ... Law Mag & Law Rev
Law Magazine and Law Review [*A publication*] (DLA) ... LM & LR
Law Magazine and Review [*A publication*] (DLA) ... L Mag & Rev
Law Magazine and Review [*A publication*] (ROG) ... LAW M
Law Magazine and Review [*A publication*] (DLA) ... Law Mag & R
Law Magazine and Review [*A publication*] (DLA) ... Law Mag & Rev
Law News [*A publication*] (DLA) ... Law N
Law Notes, American Bar Association Section of General Practice [*A publication*] (DLA) ... LN
Law Notes, England [*A publication*] (DLA) ... L Notes
Law Notes for the General Practitioner [*A publication*] (DLA) ... L Notes Gen Pract
Law Notes, London [*A publication*] (DLA) ... LN
Law Observer [*1872*] [*India*] [*A publication*] (DLA) ... LO
Law of Corresponding States [*Physics*] ... LCS
Law of Initial Value [*Joseph Wilder*] ... LIV
Law of the Alemanni [*A publication*] (DLA) ... L Alem
Law of the Iterated Logarithm (PDAA) ... LIL
Law of the Ripuarians [*A publication*] (DLA) ... L Ripuar
Law of the Sea [*United Nations*] (ASF) ... LOS
Law of the Sea Conference [*United Nations*] (MSC) ... LOSC
Law of the Sea Conference [*United Nations*] ... LSC
Law of the Sea Convention [*Australia*] ... LOSC
Law of the Sea Information System (GNE) ... LOSIS
Law of the Sea Institute (EA) ... LSI
Law of the Sea Treaty (MCD) ... LOST
Law Office Economics and Management [*A publication*] (DLA) ... L Off Econ & Mgt
Law Office Managemnt and Accounting System (HGAA) ... LOMAS
Law Officer ... LO
Law Officers' Department [*British*] ... LOD
Law on Church Building Societies [*A publication*] (DLA) ... Law Ch Bdg Soc
Law on Church Wardens [*A publication*] (DLA) ... Law Ch Ward
Law Opinions [*A publication*] (DLA) ... LO
Law Opinions [*A publication*] (DLA) ... O
Law Pamphlet (ROG) ... LP
Law Quarterly Review [*A publication*] (BRI) ... Law Q Rev
Law Record [*1911-12*] [*India*] [*A publication*] (DLA) ... LR
Law Recorder [*Dublin, Ireland*] [*A publication*] (DLA) ... L Rec
Law Recorder [*Dublin, Ireland*] [*A publication*] (DLA) ... L Record
Law Recorder [*1827-31*] [*Ireland*] [*A publication*] (DLA) ... Law Rec
Law Recorder [*1827-38*] [*Ireland*] [*A publication*] (DLA) ... LR
Law Recorder, First Series [*Ireland*] [*A publication*] (DLA) ... Ir L Rec 1st Ser
Law Recorder, First Series [*Ireland*] [*A publication*] (DLA) ... L Rec OS
Law Recorder, First Series [*Ireland*] [*A publication*] (DLA) ... Law Rec (OS)
Law Recorder, New Series [*Ireland*] [*A publication*] (DLA) ... Ir L Rec NS
Law Recorder, New Series [*Ireland*] [*A publication*] (DLA) ... L Rec NS
Law Recorder, New Series [*Ireland*] [*A publication*] (DLA) ... Law Rec (NS)
Law Recorder (Sierra Leone) [*A publication*] (ILCA) ... Sierra Leone L Rec
Law Reform Commission [*Canada*] ... LRC
Law Reform Commission of New South Wales [*Australia*] ... LRCNSW
Law Reform Commission of Tasmania [*Australia*] ... LRTC
Law Reform Commission, Ottawa, ON, Canada [*Library symbol Library of Congress*] (LCLS) ... CaOOLR
Law Reform Commission [*Commission de Reforme du Droit*] **Ottawa, Ontario** [*Library symbol National Library of Canada*] (NLC) ... OOLR
Law Reform Committee (DLA) ... Law Ref Com
Law Reform Committee (DLA) ... Law Ref Cttee
Law Reform Committee (DLA) ... LRC
Law Register [*1880-1909*] [*A publication*] (DLA) ... LR
Law Register, Chicago [*A publication*] (DLA) ... Law Reg
Law Reporter [*England*] [*A publication*] (DLA) ... Law Rep
Law Reporter [*1821-22*] [*A publication*] (DLA) ... LR
Law Reporter [*Boston*] [*A publication*] (DLA) ... Month Law Rep
Law Reporter, Montreal [*A publication*] (DLA) ... L Rep Mont
Law Reporter, Montreal [*Canada*] [*A publication*] (DLA) ... R & M
Law Reporter (Ramsey and Morin) [*Canada*] [*A publication*] (DLA) ... Law Rep
Law Reporter (Ramsey and Morin) [*Canada*] [*A publication*] (DLA) ... Law Repr
Law Reporter (Toronto) [*A publication*] (DLA) ... Law Rep (Tor)
Law Reports [*England*] [*A publication*] (DLA) ... Law Rep
Law Reports, Admiralty and Ecclesiastical Cases [*1865-75*] [*A publication*] (DLA) ... Law Rep A & E
Law Reports, Admiralty and Ecclesiastical Cases [*1865-75*] [*A publication*] (DLA) ... LR Adm & Ecc
Law Reports, Admiralty and Ecclesiastical Cases [*1865-75*] [*A publication*] (DLA) ... LR Adm & Eccl
Law Reports, Admiralty and Ecclesiastical Cases [*England*] [*A publication*] (DLA) ... LR Adm & Eccl (Eng)
Law Reports, Appeal Cases [*England*] [*A publication*] (DLA) ... AC
Law Reports, Appeal Cases [*England*] [*A publication*] (DLA) ... App Cas
Law Reports, Appeal Cases [*England*] [*A publication*] (DLA) ... Law Rep App Cas
Law Reports, British Burma [*A publication*] (DLA) ... LR Burm
Law Reports, British Burma [*A publication*] (DLA) ... LR Burma
Law Reports, British Guiana [*1890-1955*] [*A publication*] (DLA) ... LRBG
Law Reports, Chancery Appeal Cases [*1865-75*] [*England*] [*A publication*] (DLA) ... Ch App
Law Reports, Chancery Appeal Cases [*England*] [*A publication*] (DLA) ... Law Rep Ch
Law Reports, Chancery Appeal Cases [*England*] [*A publication*] (DLA) ... Law Rep Ch App
Law Reports, Chancery Appeal Cases [*England*] [*A publication*] (DLA) ... LR Ch
Law Reports, Chancery Appeal Cases [*England*] [*A publication*] (DLA) ... LR Ch (Eng)
Law Reports, Chancery Division [*A publication*] (DLA) ... Law Rep Ch D
Law Reports, Chancery Division, English Supreme Court of Judicature [*A publication*] (DLA) ... LR Ch D (Eng)
Law Reports, Chancery Division, English Supreme Court of Judicature [*A publication*] (DLA) ... LR Ch Div (Eng)
Law Reports, Common Pleas [*England*] [*A publication*] (DLA) ... CP
Law Reports, Common Pleas [*England*] [*A publication*] (DLA) ... Law Rep CP
Law Reports, Common Pleas [*1865-75*] [*England*] [*A publication*] (DLA) ... LRCP
Law Reports, Common Pleas [*England*] [*A publication*] (DLA) ... LRCP (Eng)
Law Reports, Common Pleas Division [*England*] [*A publication*] (DLA) ... CPD
Law Reports, Common Pleas Division [*England*] [*A publication*] (DLA) ... Law Rep CPD
Law Reports, Common Pleas Division [*England*] [*A publication*] (DLA) ... LRCP Div
Law Reports, Court of Appeals of Eastern Africa [*A publication*] (DLA) ... EACA
Law Reports, Court of Appeals of New Zealand [*A publication*] (DLA) ... LRCA
Law Reports, Crown Cases [*A publication*] (DLA) ... Law Rep CC
Law Reports, Crown Cases Reserved [*England*] [*A publication*] (DLA) ... LR Cr Cas Res
Law Reports, Crown Cases Reserved [*England*] [*A publication*] (DLA) ... LRCCR
Law Reports Digest [*A publication*] (DLA) ... Law Rep Dig
Law Reports Digest [*A publication*] (DLA) ... LR Dig
Law Reports, East Africa [*A publication*] (DLA) ... LREA
Law Reports, English and Irish Appeal Cases [*A publication*] (DLA) ... Eng & Ir App
Law Reports, English and Irish Appeal Cases [*A publication*] (DLA) ... Eng Ir App
Law Reports, English and Irish Appeals [*1866-75*] [*A publication*] (DLA) ... LR Eng & Ir App
Law Reports, English and Irish Appeals and Peerage Claims, House of Lords [*England*] [*A publication*] (DLA) ... LRHL
Law Reports, English and Irish Appeals and Peerage Claims, House of Lords [*England*] [*A publication*] (DLA) ... LRHL (Eng)
Law Reports, Equity Cases [*A publication*] (DLA) ... Law Rep Eq
Law Reports, Exchequer [*A publication*] (DLA) ... Law Rep Ex
Law Reports, Exchequer Division [*England*] [*A publication*] (DLA) ... Ex D
Law Reports, Exchequer Division [*England*] [*A publication*] (ILCA) ... Ex Div
Law Reports, Exchequer Division [*England*] [*A publication*] (DLA) ... Law Rep Ex D
Law Reports, Exchequer Division [*England*] [*A publication*] (DLA) ... LR Ex D
Law Reports, Exchequer Division [*England*] [*A publication*] (DLA) ... LR Exch Div
Law Reports, House of Lords, English and Irish Appeal Cases [*A publication*] (DLA) ... Law Rep HL
Law Reports, House of Lords, English and Irish Appeals [*1866-75*] [*A publication*] (DLA) ... E & I App
Law Reports, House of Lords, English and Irish Appeals [*1866-75*] [*A publication*] (DLA) ... HL
Law Reports, House of Lords, English and Irish Appeals [*1866-75*] [*A publication*] (DLA) ... LRE & I App
Law Reports, House of Lords, Scotch and Divorce Appeal Cases [*1866-75*] [*A publication*] (DLA) ... LRHL Sc App Cas
Law Reports, Indian Appeals [*A publication*] (DLA) ... Ind App
Law Reports, Indian Appeals [*A publication*] (DLA) ... Law Rep Ind App
Law Reports, Ireland [*1878-1893*] [*A publication*] ... LRIr
Law Reports, Irish [*A publication*] (DLA) ... Law Rep Ir
Law Reports, Irish [*A publication*] (DLA) ... LR Ir
Law Reports, Miscellaneous Division [*A publication*] (DLA) ... Law Rep Misc D
Law Reports, Miscellaneous Division [*A publication*] (DLA) ... LR Misc D
Law Reports, New Series [*New York*] [*A publication*] (DLA) ... Law Rep NS
Law Reports, New South Wales Supreme Court [*A publication*] (DLA) ... LRNSW
Law Reports, New Zealand [*A publication*] (DLA) ... LRNZ
Law Reports, New Zealand Supreme Court [*A publication*] (DLA) ... LRSC
Law Reports of Supreme Court of Sarawak, North Borneo, and Brunei [*A publication*] (DLA) ... SCR
Law Reports of the District Court of Tel Aviv [*A publication*] (BJA) ... TALR
Law Reports, Privy Council, Appeal Cases [*England*] [*A publication*] (DLA) ... Law Rep PC
Law Reports, Privy Council, Appeal Cases [*England*] [*A publication*] (DLA) ... PC App
Law Reports, Privy Council, Indian Appeals [*India*] [*A publication*] (DLA) ... IA
Law Reports, Privy Council, Indian Appeals [*India*] [*A publication*] (DLA) ... Indian App
Law Reports, Probate [*A publication*] (DLA) ... Law Rep P
Law Reports, Probate and Divorce [*England*] [*A publication*] (DLA) ... P & D
Law Reports, Probate and Divorce [*England*] [*A publication*] (DLA) ... Pr & Div
Law Reports, Probate and Divorce Cases [*A publication*] (DLA) ... Law Rep P & D
Law Reports, Probate and Matrimonial [*1866-75*] [*A publication*] (DLA) ... LRP & M
Law Reports, Probate and Matrimonial Cases [*England*] [*A publication*] (DLA) ... P & M
Law Reports, Probate Division [*A publication*] (DLA) ... LRPD
Law Reports, Probate Division [*England*] [*A publication*] (DLA) ... P Div
Law Reports, Probate Division [*England*] [*A publication*] (DLA) ... Prob
Law Reports, Probate Division [*1891*] [*England*] [*A publication*] (DLA) ... Prob (1891)
Law Reports, Probate, Divorce, and Admiralty [*Since 1890*] [*England*] [*A publication*] (DLA) ... P
Law Reports, Probate, Divorce, and Admiralty Division [*1875-90*] [*England*] [*A publication*] (DLA) ... PD
Law Reports, Queen's Bench [*A publication*] (DLA) ... Law Rep QB
Law Reports, Queen's Bench Division [*A publication*] (DLA) ... Law Rep QBD
Law Reports, Restrictive Practices Cases [*1958-72*] [*A publication*] (DLA) ... LRRP
Law Reports, Scotch and Divorce Appeal Cases, House of Lords [*A publication*] (DLA) ... Law Rep HL Sc

Law Reports, Scotch and Divorce Appeals [1866-75] [A publication] (DLA) .... LRS & D App
Law Reports, Scotch and Divorce Appeals [A publication] (DLA) .... Sc & Div
Law Reports, Scotch Appeals [A publication] (DLA) .... LR Sc App
Law Reports, Scotch Appeals [A publication] (DLA) .... LR Sc Div App
Law Reports, Sierra Leone Series [A publication] (DLA) .... LRSL
Law Reports, Sierra Leone Series [A publication] (ILCA) .... Sierra Leone LR
Law Repository [A publication] (DLA) .... L Repos
Law Reprints, New York, NY [Library symbol] [Library of Congress] (LCLS) .... NNLR
Law Review and Quarterly Journal [London] [A publication] (DLA) .... L Rev & Quart J
Law Review and Quarterly Journal [London] [A publication] (DLA) .... Law Rev & Qu J
Law Review Digest [A publication] (DLA) .... L Rev Dig
Law Review Journal [A publication] (DLA) .... Law Rev J
Law Review Quarterly [Albany, NY] [A publication] (DLA) .... Law Rev Qu
Law Review. University of Detroit [A publication] (DLA) .... L Rev U Detroit
Law Review. University of Detroit [A publication] (DLA) .... Law Rev U Det
Law School Admission Council (EDAC) .... LSAC
Law School Admission Council/Law School Admission Services (EA) .... LSAC/LSAS
Law School Admission Services (EDAC) .... LSAS
Law School Admission Test .... LSAT
Law School Aptitude Test (GAGS) .... LSAT
Law School Computer Group [Defunct] (EA) .... LSCG
Law School, Dalhousie University, Halifax, Nova Scotia [Library symbol National Library of Canada] (NLC) .... NSHDL
Law School Data Assembly Service (GAGS) .... LSDAS
Law School Library, University of Georgia, Athens, GA [OCLC symbol] (OCLC) .... GUB
Law School Record [Chicago] [A publication] (DLA) .... Law School Rec
Law School Review. Toronto University [A publication] (DLA) .... Law School Rev
Law Schools On-Line (AAGC) .... LSO
Law Services Association [British] (DBA) .... LSA
Law Society (WDAA) .... LS
Law Society. Gazette [A publication] .... Law Soc G
Law Society of Alberta, Calgary, AB, Canada [Library symbol Library of Congress] (LCLS) .... CaACL
Law Society of Alberta, Calgary, Alberta [Library symbol National Library of Canada] (NLC) .... ACL
Law Society of British Columbia, Vancouver, BC, Canada [Library symbol Library of Congress] (LCLS) .... CaBVaL
Law Society of Manitoba, Winnipeg, Manitoba [Library symbol National Library of Canada] (NLC) .... MWL
Law Society of Manitoba, Winnipeg, MB, Canada [Library symbol Library of Congress] (LCLS) .... CaMWL
Law Society of Massachusetts. Journal [A publication] (DLA) .... Law Soc Jo
Law Society of New South Wales [Australia] .... LSNSW
Law Society of Newfoundland, St. John's, Newfoundland [Library symbol National Library of Canada] (NLC) .... NFSLS
Law Society of Newfoundland, St. John's, NF, Canada [Library symbol Library of Congress] (LCLS) .... CaNfSLS
Law Society of Prince Edward Island, Charlottetown, PE, Canada [Library symbol Library of Congress] (LCLS) .... CaPCLS
Law Society of Prince Edward Island, Charlottetown, Prince Edward Island [Library symbol National Library of Canada] (NLC) .... PCLS
Law Society of Saskatchewan Libraries, Regina [Library symbol National Library of Canada] (BIB) .... SRLS
Law Society of Scotland .... LSS
Law Society of Scotland. Journal [A publication] (DLA) .... J Law Soc'y Scotland
Law Society of Scotland. Journal [A publication] (DLA) .... Law Soc'y Scotl
Law Society of South Australia .... LSSA
Law Society of Tasmania [Australia] .... LST
Law Society of Tasmania. Newsletter [A publication] .... Law Soc Tas NL
Law Society of the Australian Capital Territory. Newsletter [A publication] .... Law Soc ACT NL
Law Society of the Northern Territory [Australia] .... LSNT
Law Society of Upper Canada [UTLAS symbol] .... LSU
Law Society of Upper Canada, Toronto, ON, Canada [Library symbol Library of Congress] (LCLS) .... CaOTLS
Law Society of Upper Canada, Toronto, Ontario [Library symbol National Library of Canada] (NLC) .... OTLS
Law Society of Western Australia .... LSWA
Law Student [A publication] (ILCA) .... Law Stud
Law Student (DLA) .... LS
Law Student Division [American Bar Association] (BARN) .... LSD
Law Student Division - American Bar Association (EA) .... ABA/LSD
Law Students Association for Buyers' Education in Labeling [Student legal action organization] .... LABEL
Law Students Civil Rights Research Council (EA) .... LSCRRC
Law Students Exposing Advertising Deceptions [Student legal action organization] .... LEAD
Law Students' Helper [A publication] (DLA) .... L Stud H
Law Students' Helper [A publication] (DLA) .... L Stud Helper
Law Students' Helper [A publication] (ILCA) .... Law Stu H
Law Students' Helper [A publication] (DLA) .... Lw Stu H
Law Students' Journal [A publication] (DLA) .... L Stud J
Law Students' Magazine [A publication] (DLA) .... L Stu Mag
Law Students' Magazine [A publication] (DLA) .... Law Stu Mag
Law Students' Magazine [A publication] (DLA) .... Law Stud Mag
Law Students' Magazine. New Series [A publication] (ILCA) .... L Stu Mag NS
Law Students' Magazine. New Series [A publication] (DLA) .... Law Stud Mag NS
Law Students' Magazine. Old Series [A publication] (ILCA) .... L Stu Mag OS
Law Teacher [A publication] (DLA) .... Law Tchr

Law Times Bankruptcy Reports [United States] [A publication] (DLA) .... ALTBR
Law Times Bankruptcy Reports [United States] [A publication] (DLA) .... LTB
Law Times Journal [A publication] (DLA) .... LT
Law Times Journal [A publication] (DLA) .... LTJ
Law Times Journal (England) [A publication] (DLA) .... L T (Eng)
Law Times Journal (England) [A publication] (DLA) .... LT Jo (Eng)
Law Times. New Series [Pennsylvania] [A publication] (DLA) .... Law T NS
Law Times. New Series [Pennsylvania] [A publication] (DLA) .... Law Times (NS)
Law Times. New Series [Pennsylvania] [A publication] (DLA) .... LT NS
Law Times. New Series [England] [A publication] (DLA) .... LT NS (Eng)
Law Times Newspaper [A publication] (DLA) .... LT
Law Times, Old Series [Luzerne, PA] [A publication] (DLA) .... Law Times (OS)
Law Times, Old Series [British] .... LTOS
Law Times Reports [A publication] (DLA) .... Law T
Law Times Reports [British] .... LT
Law Times Reports, New Series [England] [A publication] (DLA) .... Law T NS
Law Times Reports, New Series [England] [A publication] (DLA) .... Law T Rep NS
Law Times Reports, New Series [England] [A publication] (DLA) .... LT NS
Law Times Reports, New Series [England] [A publication] (DLA) .... LT Rep
Law Times Reports, New Series [England] [A publication] (DLA) .... LT Rep NS
Law Times Reports, New Series [England] [A publication] (DLA) .... LTR
Law Times Reports, New Series [England] [A publication] (DLA) .... LTR NS
Law Times Reports, Old Series [England] [A publication] (DLA) .... Law T Rep OS
Law Times Reports, Old Series [England] [A publication] (DLA) .... LT OS
Law Tracts [A publication] (DLA) .... Law Tr
Law Weekly [A publication] (DLA) .... Law W
Law Weekly [A publication] (DLA) .... LW
Law-abiding Citizen (BARN) .... LAC
Lawas [Malaysia] [Airport symbol] (OAG) .... LWY
Lawas [Malaysia] [ICAO location identifier] (ICLI) .... WBGW
LAWASIA [Law Association for Asia and the Pacific] Human Rights Bulletin [A publication] .... LAWASIA HRB
LAWASIA. Journal of the Law Association for Asia and the Western Pacific [A publication] (DLA) .... LAWASIA
LAWASIA [Law Association for Asia and the Pacific] Law Journal [A publication] (DLA) .... LAWASIA LJ
Lawes on Charterparties [1813] [A publication] (DLA) .... Law Ch P
Lawes on Charterparties [1813] [A publication] (DLA) .... Lawes Ch
Lawes on Pleading [A publication] (DLA) .... Lawes Pl
Lawes' Pleading in Assumpsit [1810] [A publication] (DLA) .... Law Pl
Lawes' Pleading in Civil Actions [1806] [A publication] (DLA) .... Law Pl
Lawesson Reagent [Organic chemistry] .... LR
Lawful Permanent Resident [Department of Justice] .... LPR
Lawless Container Corp., North Tonawanda, NY [Library symbol Library of Congress] (LCLS) .... NNotL
Lawn and Garden Manufacturers Association [Defunct] (EA) .... LAGMA
Lawn Faucet (MSA) .... LF
Lawn Hill [Australia Airport symbol Obsolete] (OAG) .... LWH
Lawn Institute (EA) LI
Lawn Mower Institute [Later, OPEI] .... LMI
Lawn Tennis .... LT
Lawn Tennis Association (EAIO) .... LTA
Lawn Tennis Ball Convention [British] (BI) .... LTBC
Lawn Tennis Club [British] .... LTC
Lawn Tennis Registered Coaches Association [British] (BI) .... LTRCA
Lawn Tennis Writers' Association of America [Later, USTWA] (EA) .... LTWA
Lawndale Railway & Industrial Co. [Terminated AAR code] .... LRI
Lawndale Transportation Co. [AAR code] .... LDTC
Lawn-O-Gram [A publication] (EAAP) .... LOG
Law-Related Education (AEE) .... LRE
Lawrence [Kansas] [Seismograph station code, US Geological Survey] (SEIS) .... LAW
Lawrence [Kansas] [Airport symbol] (OAG) .... LWC
Lawrence [Massachusetts] [Airport symbol] (AD) .... LWM
Lawrence Aviation, Inc. [ICAO designator] (FAAC) .... LAR
Lawrence Berkeley Laboratory [Berkeley, CA] [Department of Energy] (GRD) .... LBL
Lawrence Country Day School, Hewlett, NY [Library symbol] [Library of Congress] (LCLS) .... NHewLD
Lawrence County Historical Society, Bedford, IN [Library symbol Library of Congress] (LCLS) .... InBLHi
Lawrence County Public Library, Monticello, MS [Library symbol Library of Congress] (LCLS) .... MsMo
Lawrence County Recorder's Office, Bedford, IN [Library symbol Library of Congress] (LCLS) .... InBCR
Lawrence Experiment Station [Agar] [Medicine] (BABM) .... LES
Lawrence Free Public Library, Lawrence, KS [Library symbol Library of Congress] (LCLS) .... KLaw
Lawrence Free Public Library, Lawrence, MA [Library symbol Library of Congress] (LCLS) .... MLaw
Lawrence High Court Reports [Griqualand] [A publication] (DLA) .... Lawr
Lawrence High School, Cedarhurst, NY [Library symbol] [Library of Congress] (LCLS) .... NCedHS
Lawrence Ins. Group [AMEX symbol] (TTSB) .... LWR
Lawrence Institute of Technology [Later, Lawrence Technological University] .... LIT
Lawrence Institute of Technology, Southfield, MI [OCLC symbol] (OCLC) .... EYL
Lawrence Institute of Technology, Southfield, MI [Library symbol Library of Congress] (LCLS) .... MiSfL
Lawrence Insurance Group [AMEX symbol] (SPSG) .... LWR
Lawrence Insurance Group, Inc. [Associated Press] (SAG) .... LawrG
Lawrence Junior High School, Lawrence, NY [Library symbol Library of Congress] (LCLS) .... NLawJH
Lawrence Junior High School, Uniondale, NY [Library symbol Library of Congress] (LCLS) .... NUnLJ

Lawrence, KS [*FM radio station call letters*] .... KANU
Lawrence, KS [*FM radio station call letters*] .... KJHK
Lawrence, KS [*AM radio station call letters*] .... KLWN
Lawrence, KS [*FM radio station call letters*] .... KLZR
Lawrence, KS [*Television station call letters*] .... KMCI
Lawrence Law Journal [*A publication*] (DLA) .... Law LJ
Lawrence Livermore Laboratory [*Also, LLNL*] [*University of California*] LLL
Lawrence Livermore National Laboratory [*Also, LLL*] [*Livermore, CA*] [*Department of Energy*] (GRD) .... LLNL
Lawrence Lowery Apperception Test .... LLAT
Lawrence, MA [*Location identifier FAA*] (FAAL) .... HGX
Lawrence, MA [*Location identifier FAA*] (FAAL) .... LWM
Lawrence, MA [*AM radio station call letters*] .... WCCM
Lawrence, MA [*FM radio station call letters*] .... WEGQ
Lawrence, MA [*Television station call letters*] .... WMFP
Lawrence Memorial Library, Windsor, NC [*Library symbol Library of Congress*] (LCLS) .... NcWind
Lawrence Microfilming Service, Fuquay-Varina, NC [*Library symbol Library of Congress*] (LCLS) .... LawM
Lawrence Mining [*Vancouver Stock Exchange symbol*] .... LWE
Lawrence Radiation Laboratory [*Livermore*] [*Later, Lawrence Livermore Laboratory University of California*] .... LRL
Lawrence Radiation Laboratory FORTRAN [*Programming language*] [*1961*] (CSR) .... LRLTRAN
Lawrence Radiation Laboratory, Livermore [*Later, Lawrence Livermore Laboratory*] [*University of California*] .... LRL-L
Lawrence Radiation Laboratory Translator (IEEE) .... LRLTRAN
Lawrence Road Junior High School, Hempstead, NY [*Library symbol*] [*Library of Congress*] (LCLS) .... NHemLJ
Lawrence Savings Bank [*Associated Press*] (SAG) .... LawrSB
Lawrence Savings Bank [*NASDAQ symbol*] (SAG) .... LSBX
Lawrence Senior High School, Lawrence, NY [*Library symbol*] [*Library of Congress*] (LCLS) .... NLawSH
Lawrence Technological University .... LTU
Lawrence Township Library, Lawrenceville, IL [*Library symbol Library of Congress*] (LCLS) .... ILaw
Lawrence Traffic Bureau Inc., Kansas City MO [*STAC*] .... LTB
Lawrence University, Appleton, WI [*Library symbol Library of Congress*] (LCLS) .... WAL
Lawrence University, Appleton, WI [*OCLC symbol*] (OCLC) .... WIB
Lawrence Welk .... LW
Lawrenceburg, KY [*FM radio station call letters*] .... WKYL
Lawrenceburg Public Library, Lawrenceburg, IN [*Library symbol Library of Congress*] (LCLS) .... InLaw
Lawrenceburg, TN [*Location identifier FAA*] (FAAL) .... LRT
Lawrenceburg, TN [*AM radio station call letters*] .... WDXE
Lawrenceburg, TN [*FM radio station call letters*] .... WDXE-FM
Lawrenceburg, TN [*FM radio station call letters*] .... WLLX
Lawrenceburg, TN [*AM radio station call letters*] .... WWLX
Lawrence's Edition of Wheaton on International Law [*A publication*] (DLA) .... Law Wheat
Lawrence's Edition of Wheaton on International Law [*A publication*] (DLA) .... Lawr Wh
Lawrence's First Comptroller's Decisions [*United States*] [*A publication*] (DLA) .... Lawrence Comp Dec
Lawrence's First Comptroller's Decisions [*United States*] [*A publication*] (DLA) .... Lawrence Compt Dec
Lawrence's Reports [*20 Ohio*] [*A publication*] (DLA) .... Lawrence
Lawrence's Visitation and Search [*A publication*] (DLA) .... Law V & S
Lawrenceville [*Illinois*] [*Airport symbol Obsolete*] (OAG) .... LWV
Lawrenceville, IL [*AM radio station call letters*] .... WAKO
Lawrenceville, IL [*FM radio station call letters*] .... WAKO-FM
Lawrenceville, NJ [*FM radio station call letters*] .... WRRC
Lawrenceville, VA [*Location identifier FAA*] (FAAL) LVL
Lawrenceville, VA [*FM radio station call letters*] .... WHFD
Lawrenceville, VA [*AM radio station call letters*] .... WLES
Lawrencium [*Original symbol, Lw, changed in 1963*] [*Chemical element*] .... Lr
Lawrencium [*Symbol changed, 1963, to Lr*] [*Chemical element*] .... Lw
Laws (ROG) LL
Law's Digest of United States Patent Cases [*A publication*] (DLA) .... Law Pat Dig
Law's Ecclesiastical Law [*2nd ed.*] [*1844*] [*A publication*] (DLA) .... Law Ecc Law
Laws for Construction of Programs (MHDB) .... LCP
Law's Jurisdiction of the Federal Courts [*A publication*] (DLA) .... Law Jur
Laws of Athelstan [*A publication*] (DLA) .... LL Athelst
Laws of Burgundians [*A publication*] (DLA) .... LL Burgund
Laws of Delaware [*A publication*] (DLA) .... Del Laws
Laws of Edward the Confessor [*A publication*] (DLA) .... LL Edw Conf
Laws of Eshnunna (BJA) .... LE
Laws of Henry I [*A publication*] (DLA) .... LL Hen I
Laws of Illinois [*A publication*] (DLA) .... Ill Laws
Laws of Ina [*A publication*] (DLA) .... LL Inse
Laws of King Canute [*or Knut*] [*A publication*] (DLA) .... LL Canuti R
Laws of King Henry the First [*A publication*] (DLA) .... Leg HI
(Laws of) Lipit-Ishtar (BJA) LI
Laws of Malcolm, King of Scotland [*A publication*] (DLA) .... LL Malcom R Scott
Laws of Maryland [*A publication*] (DLA) .... MD Laws
Laws of Minnesota [*A publication*] (DLA) .... Minn Laws
Laws of Missouri [*A publication*] (DLA) .... MO Laws
Laws of Montana [*A publication*] (DLA) .... Mont Laws
Laws of New York [*A publication*] (DLA) .... LNY
Laws of North Dakota [*A publication*] (DLA) .... ND Sess Laws
Laws of Oleron [*Maritime law*] [*A publication*] (DLA) .... Leg Oler
Laws of Puerto Rico Annotated [*A publication*] .... LPRA
Laws of Puerto Rico, Annotated [*A publication*] (DLA) .... PR Laws Ann
Laws of the Canal Zone [*A publication*] (DLA) .... LCZ
Laws of the General Assembly of the Commonwealth of Pennsylvania [*A publication*] (DLA) .... PA Laws
Laws of the Lombards [*A publication*] (DLA) .... LL Longobard
Laws of the State of Israel (BJA) .... LSI
Laws of the United States [*A publication*] (DLA) .... LUS
Laws of the Visigoths [*A publication*] (DLA) .... LL Wisegotho
Laws of Ur Nammu (BJA) .... LU
Laws of Virginia [*A publication*] (DLA) LV
Laws of War (MCD) .... LOW
Laws of William the Bastard [*A publication*] (DLA) .... LL Wm Noth
Laws of William the Conqueror [*A publication*] (DLA) .... LL Wm Conq
Laws of Wisby [*Maritime law*] [*A publication*] (DLA) .... Leg Wisb
Laws of Wisby [*Maritime law*] [*A publication*] (DLA) .... Wisb
Laws of Women [*A publication*] (DLA) .... Laws Wom
Law's Practice in United States Courts [*A publication*] (DLA) .... Law Pr
Law's Practice in United States Courts [*A publication*] (DLA) .... Law US Cts
Laws Relating to the Navy Annotated [*Military law*] .... LRNA
Law's United States Patent Cases [*A publication*] (DLA) .... Law Pat
Lawson & Jones Ltd. [*Toronto Stock Exchange symbol*] .... LJ
Lawson Army Airfield [*Fort Benning, GA*] (MCD) .... LAAF
Lawson, I. C., St. Paul MN [*STAC*] LIC
Lawson Mardon Group Ltd. [*Toronto Stock Exchange symbol*] .... LMP
Lawson Memorial Library, Willmar, MN [*Library symbol*] [*Library of Congress*] (LCLS) .... MnWil
Lawson on Contracts [*A publication*] (DLA) .... Law Con
Lawson on Contracts [*A publication*] (DLA) .... Laws Cont
Lawson on Expert and Opinion Evidence [*A publication*] (DLA) .... Lawson Exp Ev
Lawson on Presumptive Evidence [*A publication*] (DLA) .... Lawson Pres Ev
Lawson on Rights, Remedies, and Practice [*A publication*] (DLA) .... Lawson Rights Rem & Pr
Lawson on the Law of Usages and Customs [*A publication*] (DLA) .... Lawson Usages & Cust
Lawson Products [*NASDAQ symbol*] (SAG) .... LAWS
Lawson Products, Inc. [*Associated Press*] (SAG) .... Lawsn
Lawson's Classroom Test of Formal Reasoning (EDAC) .... CTFR
Lawson's Notes of Decisions, Registration [*A publication*] (DLA) L
Lawson's Registration Cases [*England*] [*A publication*] (DLA) .... Law Reg Cas
Lawson's Registration Cases, Irish [*1885-1914*] [*A publication*] (DLA) .... Laws Reg Cas
Lawter International, Inc. [*NYSE symbol*] (SPSG) .... LAW
Lawter International, Inc. [*Associated Press*] (SAG) .... Lawter
Lawter Intl [*NYSE symbol*] (TTSB) .... LAW
Lawton [*Oklahoma*] [*Airport symbol*] (OAG) .... LAW
Lawton, OK [*FM radio station call letters*] .... KBZQ
Lawton, OK [*FM radio station call letters*] .... KCCU
Lawton, OK [*FM radio station call letters*] (RBYB) .... KIRQ
Lawton, OK [*FM radio station call letters*] (RBYB) .... KJMZ-FM
Lawton, OK [*AM radio station call letters*] .... KKRX
Lawton, OK [*FM radio station call letters*] .... KKRX-FM
Lawton, OK [*FM radio station call letters*] .... KLAW
Lawton, OK [*FM radio station call letters*] (RBYB) .... KMGZ
Lawton, OK [*AM radio station call letters*] .... KSWO
Lawton, OK [*Television station call letters*] .... KSWO-TV
Lawton, OK [*FM radio station call letters*] .... KVRS
Lawton, OK [*FM radio station call letters*] .... KVRW
Lawton, OK [*FM radio station call letters*] .... KZCD
Lawton, OK [*Location identifier FAA*] (FAAL) .... LAW
Lawton Public Library, Lawton, MI [*Library symbol Library of Congress*] (LCLS) .... MiLaw
Lawton Public Library, Lawton, OK [*OCLC symbol*] (OCLC) .... LPL
Lawton Public Library, Lawton, OK [*Library symbol Library of Congress*] (LCLS) .... OkL
Lawyer (ADA) .... LAW
Lawyer (DLA) .... Lawy
Lawyer .... LWYR
Lawyer and Banker [*A publication*] (DLA) .... L & Bank
Lawyer and Banker [*New Orleans*] [*A publication*] (DLA) .... Law & Bank
Lawyer and Banker and Central Law Journal [*A publication*] (DLA) .... Law & Banker
Lawyer and Banker and Central Law Journal [*A publication*] (DLA) .... Lawyer & Banker
Lawyer and Magistrate Magazine [*1898-99*] [*Dublin*] [*A publication*] (DLA) .... Law & Mag
Lawyer and Magistrate Magazine [*1898-99*] [*Dublin*] [*A publication*] (DLA) .... Law & Mag Mag
Lawyer Referral Service .... LRS
Lawyer-Pilots Bar Association (EA) .... LPBA
Lawyers Alliance for Nuclear Arms Control [*Later, LAWS*] (EA) .... LANAC
Lawyers Alliance for World Security (EA) .... LAWS
Lawyers' and Bankers' Quarterly [*A publication*] (DLA) .... Law & Bank
Lawyer's and Magistrate's Magazine [*A publication*] (DLA) .... Law & Magis Mag
Lawyers' Campaign to Free Nelson Mandela [*Defunct*] (EA) .... LCFNM
Lawyers Christian Fellowship (EA) .... LCF
Lawyers' Committee for Civil Rights under Law (EA) .... LCCRUL
Lawyers Committee for Human Rights (EA) .... LCHR
Lawyers Committee for International Human Rights (EA) .... LCIHR
Lawyers Committee for the Enforcement of Animal Protection Law (EA) .... LCEAPL
Lawyers' Committee News [*A publication*] (DLA) .... Law Committee News
Lawyers Committee on Central America [*Defunct*] (EA) .... LCCA
Lawyers' Committee on Nuclear Policy (EA) .... LCNP
Lawyers Co-Operative Publishing Co. (DLA) .... Lawyers Co-Op
Lawyers Co-Operative Publishing Co. [*Rochester, NY*] .... LCP
Lawyers' Edition, United States Supreme Court Reports [*A publication*] (DLA) .... L Ed

Lawyers' Edition, United States Supreme Court Reports [A publication] (DLA) .... L Ed (US)

Lawyer's Edition, United States Supreme Court Reports [A publication] (DLA) .... Law Ed

Lawyers' Edition, United States Supreme Court Reports [A publication] (DLA) .... LE

Lawyers' Edition, United States Supreme Court Reports [A publication] (DLA) .... USL Ed

Lawyers' Edition, United States Supreme Court Reports, Second Series [A publication] (DLA) .... L Ed 2d

Lawyer's Edition, United States Supreme Court Reports, Second Series [A publication] (DLA) .... LE 2d

Lawyers' Edition, United States Supreme Court Reports, Second Series [A publication] (DLA) .... USL Ed 2d

Lawyers Engaged in Alternative Dispute Resolution [Australia An association] .... LEADR

Lawyers for an Independent Judiciary [Defunct] (EA) .... LIJ

Lawyers for Civil Justice (EA) .... LCJ

Lawyers for Nuclear Disarmament [Defunct] (EAIO) .... LND

Lawyers Guild Monthly [A publication] (DLA) .... Law Guild M

Lawyers' Law Books [1977] [A publication] (ILCA) .... LLB

Lawyers, Layers, and Limos [Television broadcasting industry] LLL

Lawyers Linked by MODEM [Computer bulletin board system] [FIDO] .... LLM

Lawyers' Magazine [A publication] (DLA) .... Lawy Mag

Lawyers Protecting People from Malicious and Unjustified Lawsuits (EA) .... LPPMUL

Lawyers' Reports, Annotated [A publication] (DLA) .... LA

Lawyers' Reports, Annotated [A publication] (DLA) .... La An

Lawyers' Reports, Annotated [A publication] (DLA) .... Lawy Rep Ann

Lawyers' Reports, Annotated [A publication] (DLA) .... Lawyers' Rep Ann

Lawyers' Reports, Annotated [A publication] (DLA) .... Lawyers' Rep Annotated

Lawyers' Reports, Annotated [A publication] (DLA) .... LR Ann

Lawyers' Reports, Annotated [A publication] (DLA) .... LRA

Lawyers' Reports, Annotated, New Series [A publication] (DLA) .... LRA NS

Lawyers' Review [A publication] (DLA) .... Lawy Rev

Lawyers' Review [A publication] (DLA) .... Lawyers' Rev

Lawyers Tile [NYSE symbol] (TTSB) .... LTI

Lawyers Title Corp. [NYSE symbol] (SAG) .... LTI

Lawyers Title Corp. [Associated Press] (SAG) .... LwyrTitl

Lawyers' Title Guaranty Funds Newsletter [A publication] (DLA) .... LTGF Newl

Laxa [Sweden ICAO location identifier] (ICLI) .... ESSH

Laxative [Medicine] (DAVI) .... las

Laxative [Pharmacy] .... lax

Laxative Abuse Syndrome [Medicine] (DAVI) .... LAS

Laxative of Choice [Medicine] .... LOC

Lay Helpers' Association [British] .... LHA

Lay Mission-Helpers Association (EA) .... LMHA

Lay Observer (ILCA) .... LO

Lay Preacher .... LP

Lay Reader (ROG) .... LR

"Lay" Source (BJA) L

Lay Volunteers International Association .... LVIA

Layaway of Industrial Facilities (AABC) .... LIF

Layer [Officer's rating] [British Royal Navy] L

Layer (MSA) .... LYR

Layer Cloud [Meteorology] (DA) .... LYR

Layer Depth .... LD

Layer Detection (SAA) .... LAYDET

Layer Management Entity [Telecommunications] .... LME

Layer Primitive Equation (MHDI) .... LPE

Layer Rating [British military] (DMA) .... LR

Layered Defense System (MCD) .... LDS

Layered Device Driver Architecture [Microsoft Corp.] [Computer science] (PCM) .... LADDR

Layered Half Space .... LHS

Layered Metal Phosphates [Physical chemistry] .... LMP

Layered Synthetic Microstructure [For optical instruments] .... LSM

Laying-Up Position [British military] (DMA) .... LUP

Layman Tithing Foundation (EA) .... LTF

Layman-Oriented Language (IAA) .... LOLA

Layman's Bible Commentary [London] [A publication] (BJA) .... LBC

Laymen's Commission of the American Council of Christian Churches (EA) .... LCACCC

Laymen's Home Missionary Movement (EA) .... LHMM

Laymen's League (EA) LL

Laymen's National Bible Association (EA) .... LNBA

Laymen's National Bible Committee [Formerly, LNC] [Later, LNBA] (EA) .... LNBC

Laymen's National Committee [Later, LNBC] .... LNC

Laymen's Overseas Service [Acronym is now used as official name of the organization] .... LAOS

Layne Christensen Co. [NASDAQ symbol] (SAG) .... LAYN

Layne Christensen Co. [NASDAQ symbol] (TTSB) .... LAYN

Layne Christensen Co. [Associated Press] (SAG) .... Layne

Layne, Inc. [NASDAQ symbol] (SAG) .... LAYN

Layne, Inc. [Associated Press] (SAG) .... Layne

Layne Texas Co., Houston, TX [Library symbol Library of Congress] (LCLS) .... TxHLT

Layos, Hollywood [Record label] .... Layos

Layout [Graphic arts] .... LO

Layout (VRA) .... lyot

Layout (MSA) .... LYT

Layout and Manuscript [Advertising] (WDMC) .... L & M

Layout and Manuscript [Publishing] (WDMC) .... L&M

Layout Generator [Ergonomics] .... LAYGEN

Layout of Passenger Accommodation (MCD) .... LOPA

Layout Template (MCD) .... LT

Layout Work Order (MCD) .... LWO

Lay's English Chancery Reports [A publication] (DLA) .... Lay

Layton School of Art [Wisconsin] .... LSA

La-Z Boy Chair [NYSE symbol] (TTSB) .... LZB

La-Z Boy Chair Co. [Associated Press] (SAG) .... LaZ Boy

La-Z Boy Chair Co. [NYSE symbol] (SPSG) .... LZB

Lazare Kaplan International, Inc. [Associated Press] (SAG) .... LazKap

Lazare Kaplan International, Inc. [AMEX symbol] (SPSG) .... LKI

Lazare Kaplan Intl [AMEX symbol] (TTSB) .... LKI

Lazarev [Later, NVL] [Former USSR Geomagnetic observatory code] .... LZV

Lazaro Cardenas [Mexico ICAO location identifier] (ICLI) .... MMLC

Lazurus Distributors [Vancouver Stock Exchange symbol] .... LZR

Lazy Bay, AK [Location identifier FAA] (FAAL) .... ALZ

Lazy Leukocyte Syndrome [Medicine] .... LLS

L-Band Digital Phase Shifter .... LDPS

L-Band Electronic Frequency Converter .... LEFC

L-Band Frequency Converter .... LFC

L-Band Phase Shifter .... LPS

L-Band Radiometer (MCD) .... LBR

L-Band Tetrode .... LBT

L-Band Transmitter .... LBT

LCA-Vision [NASDAQ symbol] (TTSB) .... LCAV

LCI International [Associated Press] (SAG) .... LC Intl

LCI International [NYSE symbol] (SAG) LCI

LCI International [Associated Press] (SAG) .... LCI Int

LCI Intl 5% Cv Exch Pfd [NYSE symbol] (TTSB) .... LCIPr

LCS Industries [NASDAQ symbol] (SAG) .... LCSI

LCS Industries, Inc. [Associated Press] (SAG) .... LCS

LDEF [Long-Duration Exposure Facility] Assembly and Transportation System [NASA] (NASA) .... LATS

LDI Corp. [Associated Press] (SAG) .... LDI Cp

LDI Corp. [NASDAQ symbol] (SAG) .... LDIC

LDI [Low Density Lipoprotein] Receptor-Related Protein [Biochemistry] .... LRP

L-DOPA Test [Endocrinology] .... LDT

Le Blanc [France ICAO location identifier] (ICLI) .... LFEL

Le Bonheur Children's Medical Center, Health Sciences Library, Memphis, TN [Library symbol Library of Congress] (LCLS) .... TMLBC

Le Boreal Express, Montreal, Quebec [Library symbol National Library of Canada] (NLC) .... QTB

Le Bourget Airport [France] .... LBG

Le Castellet [France ICAO location identifier] (ICLI) .... LFMQ

Le Cercle Concours d'Elegance (EA) LCC

Le Grand, CA [FM radio station call letters] .... KEFR

Le Gros Scouts [British military] (DMA) .... LS

Le Groupe Opus Communications, Inc. [Vancouver Stock Exchange symbol] .... LOC

Le Groupe SOBECO, Montreal, PQ, Canada [Library symbol Library of Congress] (LCLS) .... CaQMSOB

Le Groupe SOBECO, Montreal, Quebec [Library symbol National Library of Canada] (NLC) .... QMSOB

Le Havre [France] [Airport symbol] (OAG) .... LEH

Le Havre/Octeville [France ICAO location identifier] (ICLI) .... LFOH

Le Havre/Saint-Romain [France ICAO location identifier] (ICLI) .... LFOY

Le Iscrizioni Fenicie e Puniche delle Colonie in Occidente (BJA) .... ICO

Le Luc/Le Cannet [France ICAO location identifier] (ICLI) .... LFMC

Le Maitre Phonetique [A publication] (BJA) .... MF

Le Mans [France] [Seismograph station code, US Geological Survey Closed] (SEIS) .... LMF

Le Mans/Arnage [France ICAO location identifier] (ICLI) .... LFRM

Le Marchant's Gardner Peerage Case [A publication] (DLA) .... Le Mar

Le Mars, IA [FM radio station call letters] .... KKMA

Le Mars, IA [AM radio station call letters] .... KLEM

Le Mars Public Library, Le Mars, IA [Library symbol Library of Congress] (LCLS) .... IaLem

Le Mazet-De-Romanin [France ICAO location identifier] (ICLI) .... LFNZ

Le Musee de St-Isidore, Inc., New Brunswick [Library symbol National Library of Canada] (NLC) .... NBSTIM

Le Musee de St-Isidore, Inc., St. Isidore, NB, Canada [Library symbol Library of Congress] (LCLS) .... CaNBStiM

Le Musee Historique de Tracadie, New Brunswick [Library symbol National Library of Canada] (NLC) .... NBTM

Le Musee Historique de Tracadie, Tracadie, NB, Canada [Library symbol Library of Congress] (LCLS) .... CaNBTM

Le Mussee du Royal 22e Regiment et la Regie du Royal 22e Regiment, Quebec, Quebec [Library symbol National Library of Canada] (NLC) .... QQMR

Le Parti de la Guadeloupe [Political party] (EY) .... LPG

Le Pertre [France] [Seismograph station code, US Geological Survey] (SEIS) .... LPF

Le Plessis-Belleville [France ICAO location identifier] (ICLI) .... LFPP

Le Point Air [France ICAO designator] (ICDA) .... FW

Le Point Air [France ICAO designator] (FAAC) .... POA

Le Pouchou [France] [Seismograph station code, US Geological Survey] (SEIS) .... LPO

Le Puy/Loudes [France ICAO location identifier] (ICLI) .... LFHP

Le Regiment de Trois-Rivieres [British military] (DMA) .... RTR

Le Roy, IL [FM radio station call letters] .... WBWN

Le Sueur-Waseca Regional Library, Waseca, MN [Library symbol Library of Congress] (LCLS) .... MnWas

LE [Lupus Erythematosus] Support Club (EA) .... LESC

Le Syllabaire Accadien [A publication] (BJA) .... SA

Le Touquet [France] [Airport symbol] (OAG) .... LTQ

Le Touquet/Paris-Plage [France ICAO location identifier] (ICLI) .... LFAT

Le Village Historique Acadien, Caraquet, NB, Canada [Library symbol Library of Congress] (LCLS) .... CaNBCVHA

Le Village Historique Acadien, Caraquet, New Brunswick [*Library symbol National Library of Canada*] (NLC) .... NBCVHA
Leach Public Library, Wahpeton, ND [*Library symbol Library of Congress*] (LCLS) .... NdWah
Leachate (Detection) Collection and Removal System (GNE) .... L(D)CRS
Leaching Rate [*Nuclear energy*] (NUCP) .... LR
Leach-Precipitate Float (BARN) .... LPF
Leach's Cases in Crown Law [*A publication*] (DLA) .... Leach CL
Leach's Club Cases [*London*] [*A publication*] (DLA) .... Leach Cl Cas
Leach's Crown Cases, King's Bench [*England*] [*A publication*] (DLA) .... Leach CC
Leach's English Crown Cases [*1730-1815*] [*A publication*] (DLA) LCC
Leach's English Crown Cases [*1730-1815*] [*A publication*] (DLA) .... Leach
Leach's English Crown Cases [*1730-1815*] [*A publication*] (DLA) .... Leach Cr Cas
Lead [*or Leads*] [*Publishing*] .... LD
Lead (WDMC) .... ld
Lead [*South Dakota*] [*Seismograph station code, US Geological Survey Closed*] (SEIS) .... LEA
Lead [*BTS*] (TAG) .... PB
Lead .... Pb
Lead Acid Battery .... LAB
Lead Adapter [*Electric equipment*] .... LA
Lead Agency Official (MHDB) .... LAO
Lead Air Jet Service [*France ICAO designator*] (FAAC) .... LEA
Lead Air Materiel Area [*Air Force*] .... LAMA
Lead Allowance Parts List .... LAPL
Lead Allowance Parts List System (DNAB) .... LAPLS
Lead Amplifier .... LA
Lead Angle (MSA) .... LA
Lead Angle Error .... LAE
Lead Belly Society (EA) .... LBS
Lead Computing Gun Sight .... LCGS
Lead Computing Gyro (MCD) .... LCG
Lead Computing Gyroscope Unit (MCD) .... LCGU
Lead Computing Optical Sight .... LCOS
Lead Computing Optical Sighting System (MCD) .... LCOSS
Lead Contractors Association [*British*] (EAIO) .... LCA
Lead Covered [*or Coated*] LC
Lead Covered Cable [*Telecommunications*] (TEL) LCC
Lead Design Supervisor [*Engineering*] .... LDS
Lead Development Association [*British*] (EAIO) .... LDA
Lead Engineer (AAG) .... LE
Lead Experiment [*Marine science*] (OSRA) .... LEADEX
Lead Experiment (USDC) .... LEADEX
Lead Hydrogen Purge System [*Nuclear energy*] (IEEE) .... LHPS
Lead Industries Association [*New York, NY*] (EA) .... LIA
Lead Industries Development Council [*British*] (DAS) .... LIDC
Lead Inventory Control Point (NG) .... LICP
Lead Joint Runner .... LJR
Lead Pencil Manufacturers Association [*Later, Pencil Makers Association*] (EA) .... LPMA
Lead Piping Engineer .... LPE
Lead Reactor Manufacturer (NRCH) .... LRM
Lead Red Blood Count [*For lead poisoning*] [*Medicine*] (DAVI) .... Pb-RBC
Lead Resistance Compensator .... LRC
Lead Screw Position Pick-Off .... LSPPO
Lead, SD [*Television station call letters*] .... KHSD
Lead, SD [*Television station call letters*] .... KIVV
Lead Sheath (AAG) L
Lead Sheet [*Military*] .... LS
Lead Spring Assembly .... LSA
Lead Sulfide Detection .... LSD
Lead Sulfide Thin Film .... LSTF
Lead Systems Integration .... LSI
Lead Technical Information Bureau [*British*] (BI) .... LTIB
Lead Telluride Crystal [*Photoconductor*] .... LTC
Lead, Test, Probe (DWSG) .... LTP
Lead Tetraacetate [*Organic chemistry*] .... LTA
Lead Tetraacetate-Schiff (Reaction) [*Clinical chemistry*] .... LTAS
Lead Time (NG) .... LT
Lead Time Matrix (MCD) .... LTM
Lead to Come [*Publishing*] (WDMC) .... LTC
Lead To Come [*Copyediting*] (WDMC) .... LTK
Lead Zirconate Titanate [*Ferroelectric material*] .... LZT
Lead [*Plumbum*] **Zirconate-Titanate** [*Piezoelectric transducer*] .... PZT
Leadam and Baldwin's Select Cases before the King's Council [*England*] [*A publication*] (DLA) .... L & B
Leadam's Select Cases before King's Council in the Star Chamber [*Selden Society Publications, Vols. 16, 25*] [*A publication*] (DLA) .... Leadam
Lead-Coated Copper (OA) LCC
Lead-Coated Metal [*Technical drawings*] .... LCM
Leaded .... LED
Leader (ADA) L
Leader (AFM) .... LDR
Leader .... LDR
Leader Authenticity Scale [*Psychology*] (EDAC) .... LAS
Leader Behavior Description Questionnaire [*Psychology*] .... LBDQ
Leader, Berwick, Nova Scotia [*Library symbol National Library of Canada*] (NLC) .... NSBLE
Leader, Berwick, NS, Canada [*Library symbol*] [*Library of Congress*] (LCLS) .... CaNSBeLE
Leader, Company Procurement [*Military*] (AFIT) .... LCP
Leader Development Study [*Army*] .... LDS
Leader Dogs for the Blind (EA) .... LDB
Leader Effectiveness and Adaptability Description [*Test*] .... LEAD
Leader Effectiveness Training [*A course of study*] .... LET

Leader Financial [*NASDAQ symbol*] (TTSB) .... LFCT
Leader Financial Corp. [*Associated Press*] (SAG) .... LeadrFn
Leader Financial Corp. [*NASDAQ symbol*] (SAG) .... LFCT
Leader Internode Ratio [*Botany*] .... LIR
Leader Law Reports [*Ceylon*] [*A publication*] (DLA) .... Lead
Leader Law Reports [*South Africa*] [*A publication*] (DLA) .... Lead LR
Leader Law Reports [*South Africa*] [*A publication*] (DLA) .... LLR
LEADER Mechanical Analysis and Retrieval of Text (NITA) .... LEADERMART
Leader Preparation Course .... LPC
Leader Preparation Program .... LPP
Leader Publications, Lyndhurst, NJ [*Library symbol Library of Congress*] (LCLS) .... NjLyL
Leader Resources, Inc. [*Vancouver Stock Exchange symbol*] .... LEA
Leader Sequence (DMAA) L
Leader Training Program [*Army*] .... LTP
Leaderless Group Discussion .... LGD
Leader-Post Ltd., Regina, Saskatchewan [*Library symbol National Library of Canada*] (NLC) .... SRLP
Leader-Post, Regina, SK, Canada [*Library symbol Library of Congress*] (LCLS) .... CaSRLP
Leaders Equity Corp. [*Vancouver Stock Exchange symbol*] .... LDQ
Leaders of Religion [*A publication*] .... LR
Leaders of Science [*A publication*] .... LS
Leaders Reaction Course [*Military training*] (INF) .... LRC
Leadership .... LDRSHP
Leadership (AFM) .... LDRSP
Leadership .... LEDSHP
Leadership .... LSHIP
Leadership Ability Evaluation [*Psychology*] .... LAE
Leadership and Education for Advancement of Phoenix [*Arizona*] .... LEAP
Leadership and Excellence in Alzheimer's Disease Award Program [*Department of Health and Human Services*] (GFGA) .... LEAD
Leadership and Management Development Center [*Maxwell Air Force Base, AL*] .... LMDC
Leadership and Management Education and Training [*Navy*] .... LMET
Leadership and Management Training [*Navy*] (NVT) .... LMT
Leadership and World Society [*Defunct*] .... LAWS
Leadership Appraisal Survey [*Interpersonal skills and attitudes test*] .... LAS
Leadership Assessment and Development Program [*Army*] (INF) .... LADP
Leadership Career Counseling Officer (DNAB) .... LCCO
Leadership Conference of Women Religious of the USA (EA) .... LCWR
Leadership Conference on Civil Rights (EA) .... LCCR
Leadership Council of Aging Organizations (EA) .... LCAO
Leadership Councils of America (EA) .... LCA
Leadership Development Projects [*National Science Foundation*] .... LDP
Leadership, Education, and Development [*US Army Corps of Engineers*] .... LEAD
Leadership Education and Development USA (EA) .... LEAD USA
Leadership for Environment and Development Institute [*Non-profit organization*] (ECON) .... LEAD
Leadership in Educational Administration Development .... LEAD
Leadership Institute (EA) LI
Leadership Opinion Questionnaire [*Test*] .... LOQ
Leadership Potential Rating [*Army*] (AABC) .... LPR
Leadership Project [*Defunct*] (EA) .... LP
Leadership Q-Sort Test [*Psychology*] .... LQST
Lead-Free .... LF
Lead-Free Glass .... LFG
Lead-In Flight Training [*Air Force*] (DOMA) .... LIFT
Lead-In Lighting [*or Lights*] [*Aviation*] .... LDIN
Lead-In Light-System [*Aviation*] LIL
Lead-In Training [*Air Force*] (DOMA) .... LIT
Leading (MSA) .... LD
Leading (WDMC) .... ld
Leading .... LDG
Leading Air Mechanic [*British military*] (DMA) .... LAM
Leading Aircraft Woman [*RAF*] [*British*] .... LACW
Leading Aircraft Woman [*RAF*] [*British*] .... LAW
Leading Aircraftsman [*RAF*] [*British*] .... LA
Leading Aircraftsman [*RAF*] [*British*] .... LAC
Leading Aircrewman [*British military*] (DMA) .... LACMN
Leading Article (ROG) .... LA
Leading Cases (DLA) LC
Leading Cases, Annotated [*A publication*] (DLA) .... LCA
Leading Cases in Equity, by White and Tudor [*A publication*] (DLA) .... Lead Cas Eq
Leading Cases in Equity, by White and Tudor [*A publication*] (DLA) .... Lead Cas in Eq
Leading Cases in Equity, by White and Tudor [*England*] [*A publication*] (DLA) .... Lead Cas in Eq (Eng)
Leading Cases on Buddhist Law [*A publication*] (DLA) .... Chan Toon
Leading Catering Accountant [*British military*] (DMA) .... LCA
Leading Catholic Layman LCL
Leading Chief Petty Officer (DNAB) .... LCPO
Leading Control Electrical Mechanic [*British military*] (DMA) .... LCEM
Leading Cook [*British military*] .... L Ck
Leading Deep Recess [*Rotary automotive engine*] .... LDR
Leading Economic Indicator .... LEI
Leading Edge [*Aerospace*] .... LE
Leading Edge Airborne PANAR .... LEAP
Leading Edge Delay [*Aviation*] (IAA) .... LD
Leading Edge Environment .... LEE
Leading Edge Extension [*Aviation*] .... LEX
Leading Edge Flap [*Aviation*] .... LEF
Leading Edge Flap Control System [*Aviation*] .... LEFCS
Leading Edge Mean Aerodynamic Chord .... LEMAC

Leading Edge Radius (MSA)	LER
Leading Edge Root Extension [Aviation]	LERX
Leading Edge Slats (MCD)	LES
Leading Edge Structure Subsystem [Aviation] (NASA)	LESS
Leading Edge Tracker	LET
Leading Edge Tracker System	LETS
Leading Edge - Trailing Edge [Aerodynamics]	LE-TE
Leading Electrical Mechanic (Air) [British military] (DMA)	LEM(A)
Leading Electrical Mechanic (Air Weapon) [British military] (DMA)	LEM(AW)
Leading Electrical Mechanician	LEM
Leading Field Activity (MCD)	LFA
Leading Light [Navigation signal]	LDGLT
Leading Mechanician	LM
Leading Medical Assistant [British military] (DMA)	LMA
Leading National Advertiser	LNA
Leading Note [Music] (ROG)	LN
Leading Ones Detector [Computer science]	LOD
Leading Ordnance Electrical Mechanic (Air) [British military] (DMA)	LOEM(A)
Leading Patrolman [Navy British] (DI)	LPM
Leading Physical Trainer [British military] (DMA)	LPT
Leading Radio Electrical Mechanic (Air) [British military] (DMA)	LREM(A)
Leading Radio Operator [British military] (DMA)	LRO
Leading Radio Operator (General) [British military] (DMA)	LRO(G)
Leading Radio Operator (Warfare) [British military] (DMA)	LRO(W)
Leading Regulator [British]	LREG
Leading Seaman [Navy British] (DMA)	L/Smn
Leading Seaman [Navy British]	LS
Leading Seaman Clearance Diver	LSCD
Leading Sick Bay Attendant [Navy British]	LSBA
Leading Signal Unit [Telecommunications] (TEL)	LSU
Leading Steward [British military] (DMA)	LSTD
Leading Stoker	LS
Leading Stores Accountant [British military] (DMA)	LSA
Leading Supply Assistant (WDAA)	LSA
Leading Telegraphist	L/T
Leading Telegraphist	Ldg Tel
Leading Torpedoman [Navy British]	LT
Leading Torpedoman [Navy British]	LTM
Leading Torpedoman [Navy British] (DMA)	LTO
Leading Underwriters' Agreement for Marine Cargo Business (DS)	LUAMC
Leading Underwriters' Agreement for Marine Hull Business (DS)	LUAMH
Leading WREN [Women's Royal Naval Service] Air Mechanic [British military] (DMA)	LWRENAM
Leading WREN [Women's Royal Naval Service] Cinema Operator [British military] (DMA)	LWRENCINE
Leading WREN [Women's Royal Naval Service] Dental Hygienist [British military] (DMA)	LWRENDHYG
Leading WREN [Women's Royal Naval Service] Dental Surgery Assistant [British military] (DMA)	LWRENDSA
Leading WREN [Women's Royal Naval Service] Education Assistant [British military] (DMA)	LWRENEDUC
Leading WREN [Women's Royal Naval Service] Meteorologist [British military] (DMA)	LWRENMET
Leading WREN [Women's Royal Naval Service] Motor Transport Driver [British military] (DMA)	LWRENMT
Leading WREN [Women's Royal Naval Service] Photographer [British military] (DMA)	LWRENPHOT
Leading WREN [Women's Royal Naval Service] Quarters Assistant [British military] (DMA)	LWRENQA
Leading WREN [Women's Royal Naval Service] Radio Electrical Mechanic [British military] (DMA)	LWRENREM
Leading WREN [Women's Royal Naval Service] Radio Operator (Morse) [British military] (DMA)	LWRENRO(M)
Leading WREN [Women's Royal Naval Service] Steward [British military] (DMA)	LWRENSTD
Leading WREN [Women's Royal Naval Service] Stores Assistant (Clothes) [British military] (DMA)	LWRENS(C)
Leading WREN [Women's Royal Naval Service] Stores Assistant (Stores) [British military] (DMA)	LWRENS(S)
Leading WREN [Women's Royal Naval Service] Stores Assistant (Victualling) [British military] (DMA)	LWRENS(V)
Leading WREN [Women's Royal Naval Service] Telephonist [British military] (DMA)	LWRENTEL
Leading WREN [Women's Royal Naval Service] Training Support Assistant [British military] (DMA)	LWRENTSA
Leading WREN [Women's Royal Naval Service] Weapon Analyst [British military] (DMA)	LWRENWA
Leading WREN [Women's Royal Naval Service] Writer (General) [British military] (DMA)	LWRENWTR(G)
Leading WREN [Women's Royal Naval Service] Writer (Pay) [British military] (DMA)	LWRENWTR(P)
Leading WREN [Women's Royal Naval Service] Writer (Shorthand) [British military] (DMA)	LWRENWTR(S)
Leading Writer [British military] (DMA)	LWTR
Lead-in-Light System [FAA] (TAG)	LDIN
Lead-in-Steel Analyser (PDAA)	LISA
Leadless Ceramic Chip Carrier [Electronics]	LCCC
Leadless Chip Carrier [Motorola, Inc.]	LCC
Leadless Inverted Device	LID
Leadless Land Grid Array [Electronics] (EECA)	LLGA
Leadless Sealed Device (PDAA)	LSD
Leadore Community Library, Leadore, ID [Library symbol] [Library of Congress] (LCLS)	IdLe
Lead-Sheathed Steel-Taped	Isst
Lead-Tin Overlay [Automotive engineering]	LTO
Leadville [Nevada] [Seismograph station code, US Geological Survey Closed] (SEIS)	LDV
Leadville, CO [Location identifier FAA] (FAAL)	LXV
Leadville, CO [Location identifier FAA] (FAAL)	SWN
Leadville Corp. [NASDAQ symbol] (SAG)	LEAD
Leadville Corp. [Associated Press] (SAG)	Leadvle
Lead-Zinc Producers Committee (EA)	LZPC
Leaf [Bibliography] [Botany]	L
Leaf [Bibliography] (ROG)	LF
Leaf (VRA)	lf
Leaf Abscission [Botany]	LA
Leaf Area Duration [Botany]	LAD
Leaf Area Index [Forestry]	LAI
Leaf Area Ratio [Botany]	LAR
Leaf Length [Botany]	LFLEN
Leaf Length [Botany]	LFLGTH
Leaf Persistence [Botany]	LFPER
Leaf Plastochron Index [Botany]	LPI
Leaf Protein [Food industry]	LP
Leaf Protein Concentrate [Food industry]	LPC
Leaf Pubescence [Botany]	LFPUB
Leaf Rapids Public Library, Leaf Rapids, MB, Canada [Library symbol Library of Congress] (LCLS)	CaMLR
Leaf Rapids Public Library, Manitoba [Library symbol National Library of Canada] (NLC)	MLR
Leaf Rust [Plant Pathology]	LR
Leaf Spring [Automotive engineering]	LS
Leaf Tobacco Exporters Association (EA)	LTEA
Leafage (ABBR)	LFAG
Leafhopper A Virus [Medicine] (DMAA)	LAV
Leafier (ABBR)	LFR
Leafiest (ABBR)	LFT
Leafiness (ABBR)	LFNS
Leafless (ABBR)	LFLS
Leaflet	L
Leaflet (WGA)	LF
Leaflet (ADA)	LFT
Leaflet Artillery Round [PSYOP] (RDA)	LAR
Leaflet Dispensing Pod	LDP
Leaflet Rolling Machine [PSYOP] (RDA)	LRM
Leaf-Mold (ROG)	LMD
Lea-Francis Owners Club [British] (EAIO)	LFOC
Leafstalk (ABBR)	LFSTK
Leafy (ABBR)	LFY
Leafy Greens Council (EA)	LGC
League	L
League [Unit of measurement]	LEA
League	LEA
League (WDAA)	LGE
League (ABBR)	LGU
League (ROG)	LL
League Against Cruel Sports (EA)	LACS
League Against Nuclear Dangers [Defunct] (EA)	LAND
League Championship Series [Baseball]	LCS
League City, TX [Location identifier FAA] (FAAL)	SPX
League for Democracy and Peace [Myanmar] [Political party] (EY)	LDP
League for Ecological Democracy (EA)	LED
League for Emotionally Disturbed Children	LEDC
League for Equitable General Aviation Legislation (EA)	LEGAL
League for Industrial Democracy (EA)	LID
League for Innovation in the Community College (EA)	LICC
League for International Food Education [Defunct] (EA)	LIFE
League for Less Noise	LLN
League for Liberty (EA)	LFL
League for Mutual Aid [Defunct] (EA)	LMA
League for National Advancement [Papua New Guinea] [Political party] (EY)	LNA
League for National Labor in Israel (EA)	LNLI
League for Programming Freedom (EA)	LPF
League for Religious Freedom in Israel [Later, American Friends of Religious Freedom in Israel] (EA)	LRFI
League for Religious Labor in Eretz Israel (EA)	LRLEI
League for Socialist Action [Canada] (EA)	LSA
League for Socialist Reconstruction [Later, IUP] (EA)	LSR
League for the Advancement of States' Equal Rights	LASER
League for the Defense of Human Rights in Romania [Paris, France] (EAIO)	LDHRR
League for the Exchange of Commonwealth Teachers (EA)	LECT
League for the Revolutionary Party (EA)	LRP
League for Yiddish [Later, LYI] (EA)	LY
League for Yiddish, Inc. (EA)	LYI
League International for Creditors (DCTA)	LIC
League of Advertising Agencies [New York, NY] (EA)	LAA
League of American Theatres and Producers (EA)	LATP
League of American Wheelman/Bicycle USA (EA)	LAW/BUSA
League of American Wheelmen	LAW
League of Americans of Ukrainian Descent (EA)	LAUD
League of Arab States [Tunis, Tunisia]	LAS
League of Arab States Documentation and Information Center [Information service or system] (IID)	ALDOC
League of Canadian Poets [Canada] (EAIO)	LCP
League of Communists [Former Yugoslavia]	LC
League of Communists - Movement for Yugoslavia [Political party]	LC-MY
League of Communists of Croatia - Party of Democratic Reform [Political party]	LCC-PDR

League of Communists of Macedonia - Party for Democratic Reform [*Political party*] ..... LCM-PDR
League of Communists of Slovenia - Party of Democratic Reform [*Political party*] ..... LCS-PDR
League of Communists of Yugoslavia [*Savez Komunista Jugoslavije*] [*Political party*] (PPW) ..... LCY
League of Composers (EA) LC
League of Conservation Voters (EA) LCV
League of Disabled Voters (EA) ..... LDV
League of Distilled Spirits Rectifiers [*Defunct*] ..... LDSR
League of Empire Loyalists [*British*] ..... LEL
League of Federal Recreation Associations (EA) ..... LFRA
League of Filipino Students ..... LFS
League of Finnish-American Societies (EAIO) ..... LFAS
League of Friendship [*Defunct*] (EA) ..... LF
League of Historic American Theatres (EA) ..... LHAT
League of Home Help [*Australia An association*] ..... LHH
League of Housewives [*Also known as HOW*] ..... LOH
League of IBM [*International Business Machines Corp.*] **Employee Credit Unions** (EA) ..... LICU
League of IBM [*International Business Machines Corp.*] **Employee Credit Unions** [*Later, LICU*] (EA) ..... LIECU
League of International Red Cross Societies ..... LICROSS
League of Lefthanders [*Defunct*] (EA) ..... LOL
League of Mercy [*Salvation Army*] ..... LOM
League of Nations [*1919-1946*] ..... L of N
League of Nations [*1919-1946*] ..... LN
League of Nations. Official Journal [*A publication*] (DLA) ..... League of Nations Off J
League of Nations. Official Journal [*A publication*] (DLA) ..... League of Nations OJ
League of Nations. Official Journal. Special Supplement [*A publication*] (DLA) ..... League of Nations OJ Spec Supp
League of Nations Treaty Series [*A publication*] (DLA) ..... LNTS
League of Nations Union ..... LNU
League of New York Theatres [*Later, LNYTP*] (EA) ..... LNYT
League of New York Theatres and Producers (EA) ..... LNYTP
League of Night Adoration in the Home [*Later, NAH*] (EA) ..... LNAH
League of Off-Broadway Theatres and Producers [*Later, OBL*] (EA) ..... LOBTP
League of Off-Broadway Theatres and Producers (EA) ..... OBL
League of Pace Amendment Advocates (EA) ..... LPAA
League of Prayer for Unity [*Defunct*] (EA) ..... LPU
League of Professional Craftsmen [*British*] (DBA) ..... LPC
League of Professional Theatre Training Programs [*Defunct*] (EA) ..... LPTTP
League of Red Cross and Red Crescent Societies [*Switzerland*] (EA) ..... LRCS
League of Red Cross Societies ..... LORCS
League of Red Cross Societies ..... LRCS
League of Red Cross Societies Development Program ..... RCSDP
League of Religious Settlements (EA) ..... LRS
League of Resident Theaters (EA) ..... LORT
League of Rural Voters Education Project (EA) ..... LRVEP
League of Safe Drivers [*British*] (BI) ..... LSD
League of St. Dymphna (EA) ..... LOSD
League of Shut-In Sodalists (EA) ..... LSIS
League of Socialist Youth of Croatia [*Political party*] ..... LSYC
League of Tarcisians (EA) ..... LT
League of Tarcisians of the Sacred Heart [*Later, LT*] (EA) ..... LTSH
League of Tasmanian Wheelmen [*Australia*] ..... LTW
League of the Cross [*Roman Catholic religious order*] (ROG) LC
League of the Kingdom of God [*Church of England*] ..... LKG
League of the Norden Associations (EA) ..... LNA
League of Ukrainian Catholics of America (EA) ..... LUC
League of United Latin American Citizens (EA) ..... LULAC
League of Women Composers [*Later, ILWC*] (EA) ..... LWC
League of Women Voters Education Fund (EA) ..... LWVEF
League of Women Voters of the United States ..... LWV
League of Women Voters of the United States (EA) ..... LWVUS
League of Women Voters of Victoria [*Australia*] ..... LWVV
League of Young Liberals [*British*] (ROG) ..... LYL
League to Abolish Billionaires [*Fictitious organization mentioned in Donald Duck comic by Carl Barks*] ..... LTAB
League to Save Lake Tahoe (EA) ..... LSLT
League to Uphold Congregational Principles [*Defunct*] (EA) ..... LUCP
Leagued (ABBR) ..... LGUD
Leaguing (ABBR) ..... LGUG
Leak (KSC) ..... LK
Leak Control System [*Nuclear energy*] (NRCH) ..... LCS
Leak Detection [*Nuclear energy*] (IAA) ..... LD
Leak Detection and Repair [*Chemical engineering*] ..... LDAR
Leak Detection System [*Nuclear energy*] (NRCH) ..... LDS
Leak Detection Technology Association (EA) ..... LDTA
Leakage (MSA) ..... LKG
Leakage and Breakage (WDAA) ..... LKG & BKG
Leakage and Breakage (IAA) ..... LKGABKG
Leakage Collection System [*Nuclear energy*] (NRCH) ..... LCS
Leakage of Information [*British World War II*] LI
Leakage Resistance Limit ..... LRL
Leake and Bullen's Precedents of Pleading [*A publication*] (DLA) ..... L & B Prec
Leake County Library, Carthage, MS [*Library symbol Library of Congress*] (LCLS) ..... MsCar
Leake on Contracts [*1861-1931*] [*A publication*] (DLA) ..... Leake
Leake on Contracts [*1861-1931*] [*A publication*] (DLA) ..... Leake Cont
Leake's Digest of the Law of Property in Land [*A publication*] (DLA) ..... Leake
Leake's Digest of the Law of Property in Land [*A publication*] (DLA) ..... Leake Land
Leakesville, MS [*Location identifier FAA*] (FAAL) ..... GCV
Leaking Underground Storage Tank [*Environmental chemistry*] ..... LUST
Leakoff [*Mechanical engineering*] ..... LOFF
Leak-Off Test ..... LOT
Leak-X Environmental [*NASDAQ symbol*] (TTSB) ..... LEAK
Leak-X Environmental Corp. [*NASDAQ symbol*] (SAG) ..... LEAK
Leak-X Environmental Corp. [*Associated Press*] (SAG) ..... LeakX
Leak-X Environmental Wrrt [*NASDAQ symbol*] (TTSB) ..... LEAKW
Leaky Pipe Antenna ..... LPA
Leaky Valve [*Nuclear energy*] (NRCH) LV
Leaming and Spicer's Laws, Grants, Concessions, and Original Constitutions [*New Jersey*] [*A publication*] (DLA) ..... Leam & Spic
Leamington [*British depot code*] ..... LMTN
Leamington, ON [*FM radio station call letters*] ..... CHYR
Leamington Public Library, Ontario [*Library symbol National Library of Canada*] (NLC) ..... OLE
Lean Best Torque [*Automotive engineering*] ..... LBT
Lean Body Mass [*Exercise*] ..... LBM
Lean Body Weight [*Medicine*] (DMAA) ..... LBW
Lean Line (EA) LL
Lean Misfire Limb (PDAA) ..... LML
Lean Misfire Limit [*Automotive engine testing*] ..... LML
Leander High School, Leander, TX [*Library symbol*] [*Library of Congress*] (LCLS) ..... TxLeaHS
Leap and Stamp [*Dance terminology*] ..... LAMP
Leap Group, Inc. (The) [*NASDAQ symbol*] (SAG) ..... LEAP
Leap Group, Inc. (The) [*Associated Press*] (SAG) ..... LeapGrp
Leapfrog Configuration [*Circuit theory*] (IEEE) ..... LF
Leap-Frog Test ..... LFT
Leapingwell on the Roman Civil Law [*A publication*] (DLA) ..... Leap Rom Civ L
Leap-Second ..... L-S
Lear [*ICAO aircraft manufacturer identifier*] (ICAO) ..... LR
Lear Corp. [*NYSE symbol*] (TTSB) ..... LEA
Lear Integrated Flight Equipment (MCD) ..... LIFE
Lear Oil & Gas Corp. [*Vancouver Stock Exchange symbol*] ..... LEO
Lear Seating Co. [*NYSE symbol*] (SAG) ..... LEA
Lear Seating Co. [*Associated Press*] (SAG) ..... LearSeat
Lear Siegler Inc. (NITA) ..... LSI
Learmonth [*Australia ICAO location identifier*] (ICLI) ..... APLM
Learmonth [*Australia Airport symbol*] (OAG) ..... LEA
Learmonth & Burchett Management Systems [*British*] (NITA) ..... LBMS
Learmouth & Burchett Management Systems, Inc. [*NASDAQ symbol*] (SAG) ..... LBMSY
Learmouth & Burchett Management Systems, Inc. [*Associated Press*] (SAG) ..... LearBur
Learmouth & Burchett Mgt ADS [*NASDAQ symbol*] (TTSB) ..... LBMSY
Learn [*Database*] ..... LEAR
Learn, Execute, and Diagnose ..... LEAD
Learned Doctor of Laws ..... LDL
Learned Information [*Database originator and marketer*] (NITA) LI
Learned Society Board (ACII) ..... LSB
Learner L
Learner-Approved Motorcycle ..... LAM
Learner-Centered Instruction (PDAA) LCI
Learning [*Denotes learning drivers before they receive their automobile driving licenses*] [*British*] L
Learning ..... LRNG
Learning Ability Test [*Military*] (AFM) ..... LAT
Learning about Basic Science [*Education program*] ..... LABS
Learning Accomplishment Profile [*Psychology*] ..... LAP
Learning Achievement through Saturated Educational Resources ..... LASER
Learning Activity (ADA) ..... LA
Learning Activity Package (EDAC) ..... LAP
Learning Activity Packet (AEE) ..... LAP
Learning and Recognition System [*GTE*] ..... LARS
Learning and the Law [*A publication*] (DLA) ..... Learn & L
Learning and the Law [*A publication*] (DLA) ..... Learn & Law
Learning Assistance Center [*Stanford University*] ..... LAC
[*The*] **Learning Channel** [*Cable-television system*] ..... TLC
Learning Classifier System [*Computer science*] ..... LCS
Learning Climate Questionnaire [*Medicine*] (DMAA) ..... LCQ
Learning Co. [*NASDAQ symbol*] (SAG) ..... LRNG
Learning Co. [*Associated Press*] (SAG) ..... LrngCo
Learning Curve (MSA) LC
Learning Curve Factor ..... LCF
Learning Disabilities Association of America (EA) ..... LDA
Learning Disabilities Association of Canada (EAIO) ..... LDAC
Learning Disabilities Association of Quebec (AC) ..... LDAQ
Learning Disabilities/Differences ..... LD
Learning Disabilities Research Institute [*University of Virginia*] (EDAC) ..... LDRI
Learning Disabilities Teacher Consultant ..... LDTC
Learning Disability [*or Learning-Disabled*] ..... LD
Learning Disability Center ..... LDC
Learning Disability Rating Procedure [*Educational test*] ..... LDRP
Learning Disabled Student SIG [*Special Interest Group*] (EA) ..... LDSSIG
Learning Disordered Children ..... LDC
Learning Efficiency Test [*Educational test*] ..... LET
[*The*] **Learning Exchange** [*Defunct*] (EA) ..... TLE
Learning Expectancy Level [*Education*] ..... LEL
Learning Experience Approach [*Education*] (EDAC) ..... LEA
Learning Experience for Technical Students [*NASA*] ..... LETS
Learning Experience Guides for Nursing Students [*Series of films, games, slides, etc.*] ..... LEGS
Learning Handicapped ..... LH
Learning in a Free Environment [*Education program*] ..... LIFE
Learning in Dialog (PDAA) ..... LIDIA
Learning Independence Through Computers, Inc. ..... LING

Learning Institute of North Carolina .... LINC
Learning Materials Information Store (PDAA) .... LERMISTOR
Learning Methods Test [*Mills*] [*Education*] .... LMT
Learning Objective .... LO
Learning of Middle Size Task [*Psychology*] .... LMST
Learning Opportunity [*Education*] .... LOP
Learning Preference Inventory .... LPI
Learning Quotient .... LQ
Learning Research and Development Center [*University of Pittsburgh*] [*Research center*] .... LRDC
Learning Resource Center .... LRC
Learning Resource Centre, Agnes Macleod Memorial Library, University of Alberta Hospitals, Edmonton, Alberta [*Library symbol National Library of Canada*] (BIB) .... AEUAH
Learning Resource Centre, BNR Ltd., Toronto, Ontario [*Library symbol National Library of Canada*] (NLC) .... OTBNR
Learning Resource Centre, Conestoga College of Applied Arts and Technology, Kitchener, Ontario [*Library symbol National Library of Canada*] (NLC) .... OKITC
Learning Resource Centre, Woodland Campus, Saskatchewan Institute of Applied Science and Technology, Prince Albert, Saskatchewan [*Library symbol National Library of Canada*] (BIB) .... SPAW
Learning Resources Centre, David Thompson Library, Nelson, British Columbia [*Library symbol National Library of Canada*] (BIB) .... BNND
Learning Resources Centre, Georgian College of Applied Arts and Technology, Orillia, Ontario [*Library symbol National Library of Canada*] (NLC) .... OORIGC
Learning Resources Centre, Red River Community College, Winnipeg, Manitoba [*Library symbol National Library of Canada*] (NLC) .... MWRR
Learning Resources Development Group [*British*] (DBA) .... LRDG
Learning Resources Institute (EA) .... LRI
Learning Resources Network (EA) .... LERN
Learning Skills Center Reading and Study Skills Program [*Cornell University*] [*Research center*] (RCD) .... LSC
Learning Step .... LS
Learning Style Identification Scale [*Educational test*] .... LSIS
Learning Style Inventory [*Occupational therapy*] .... LSI
Learning Styles Inventory-Primary Version [*Occupational therapy*] (EDAC) .... LSI-P
Learning Systems and Access Branch [*Education*] (AIE) .... LSAB
Learning Systems Institute [*Florida State University*] [*Research center*] (RCD) .... LSI
Learning Systems Model (EDAC) .... LSM
Learning Technology Dissemination Initiative (AIE) .... LTDI
Learning through Industry and Voluntary Educators [*Community education program*] .... LIVE
Learning Through Listening [*Recording for the blind*] .... LTL
Learning to Look .... LTL
[*The*] Learning Tree [*UTLAS symbol*] .... LTR
Learning Tree International, Inc. [*Associated Press*] (SAG) .... LrnTree
Learning Tree Intl. [*NASDAQ symbol*] (TTSB) .... LTRE
[*The*] Learning Tree, Mississauga, ON, Canada [*Library symbol*] [*Library of Congress*] (LCLS) .... CaOMLT
[*The*] Learning Tree, Mississauga, Ontario [*Library symbol National Library of Canada*] (NLC) .... OMLT
Learnng .... LEARN
LeaRonal, Inc. [*Associated Press*] (SAG) .... LearnI
LeaRonal, Inc. [*NYSE symbol*] (SPSG) .... LRI
Lea's Tennessee Reports [*A publication*] (DLA) .... BJ Lea
Lea's Tennessee Reports [*A publication*] (DLA) .... Lea
Lease .... LE
Lease .... LS
Lease [*Legal shorthand*] (LWAP) .... LS
Lease (ROG) .... LSE
Lease Automatic Custody Transfer .... LACT
Lease Base Machine Inventory (MHDB) .... LBMI
Lease Electronic Accounting System (IEEE) .... LEAS
Lease Expenditure Request (MCD) .... LER
Lease or Loan LL
Lease Production Revenue System - 5 File [*Petroleum Information Corp.*] [*Information service or system*] (CRD) LPR-5
Lease Production Revenue System - 10 File [*Petroleum Information Corp.*] [*Information service or system*] (CRD) LPR-10
Lease Rental Agreement (MHDB) .... LRA
Lease to Ownership Plan .... LTOP
Lease with Option to Purchase (AAGC) .... LWOP
Lease-A-Plane International [*ICAO designator*] (FAAC) .... LPL
Leased (WGA) .... LSD
Leased Attached Pallet (SSD) .... LAP
Leased Bachelor Housing [*Military*] (DNAB) .... LBH
Leased Circuit Digital Data Service [*British Telecom*] (EECA) .... LCDDS
Leased Interfacility Nas Communications System [*FAA*] (TAG) .... LINCS
Leased Line [*Private telephone or Teletype line*] [*Telecommunications*] LL
Leased Line Adapter [*Telecommunications*] .... LLA
Leased Line Adaptor (NITA) .... LLA
Leased Long Lines Program (NATG) .... LLP
Leased Management Agreement [*Radio*] [*Television*] (WDMC) .... LMA
Leased Satellite (NITA) .... LEASAT
Leased Satellite [*Military*] (CAAL) .... LESAT
Leased Satellite Communications (NVT) .... LEASAT
Leased Spacecraft Bus (SSD) .... LSB
Leased Teletypewriter Service .... TWL
Lease-Financial Accounting Control System (MHDB) .... LEAS-FACS
Leasehold (ROG) L
Leasehold [*Legal term*] (DLA) .... L/H

Leasehold (ROG) .... LHOLD
Leasehold .... LSHLD
Leasehold Area (ADA) .... LA
Leasehold Ground Rent (ROG) .... LGR
Leasing .... LEASE
Leasing Edge [*NASDAQ symbol*] (TTSB) .... LECE
Leasing Edge cm Cv'A'Pfd [*NASDAQ symbol*] (TTSB) .... LECEP
Leasing Edge Corp. [*Associated Press*] (SAG) .... LeasEd
Leasing Edge Corp. [*NASDAQ symbol*] (SAG) .... LECE
Leasing Edge Corp. [*Associated Press*] (SAG) .... LsEd
Leasing Edge Wrrt'A' [*NASDAQ symbol*] (TTSB) .... LECEZ
Leasing Edge Wrrt'B' [*NASDAQ symbol*] (TTSB) .... LECEL
Leasing Solutions [*NASDAQ symbol*] (TTSB) .... LSSI
Leasing Solutions, Inc. [*Associated Press*] (SAG) .... LsgSolu
Leasing Solutions, Inc. [*NASDAQ symbol*] (SAG) .... LSSI
Least Coincidence Voltage Detection (MDG) .... LCVD
Least Common BIT [*Binary Digit*] (MCD) .... LCB
Least [*or Lowest*] Common Denominator [*or Divisor*] [*Mathematics*] .... LCD
Least [*or Lowest*] Common Factor [*Mathematics*] .... LCF
Least Common Multiple [*Mathematics*] .... LCM
Least Concave Majorant [*Statistics*] .... LCM
Least Cost Estimating and Scheduling (IAA) .... LCES
Least Cost Feed Formulation System (ADA) .... LCF
Least Count LC
Least Depth [*Nautical charts*] .... LD
Least Energy Principle .... LEP
Least Fatal Dose .... LFD
Least Frequency Unit (NITA) .... LFU
Least Frequent (AEBS) .... LF
Least Frequently Used [*Computer science*] .... LFU
Least Incompatible [*Laboratory science*] (DAVI) LIC
Least Input for the Most Output [*Business term*] .... LIMO
Least Material Condition (MSA) .... LMC
Least Mean Square (IEEE) .... LMS
Least Negative Down Level (IAA) .... LNDL
Least Newtonian Path (IAA) .... LNP
Least Objectionable Program [*Television*] .... LOP
Least Perceptible Difference [*Psychology*] .... LPD
Least Positive Uplevel (IAA) .... LPUL
Least Publishable Unit [*of research data*] .... LPU
Least Recently Used [*Replacement algorithm*] [*Computer science*] .... LRU
Least Recently Used Master [*Computer science*] .... LRM
Least Repairable Unit (IAA) .... LRU
Least Replaceable Unit (IAA) .... LRU
Least Restrictive Alternative [*For the education of the handicapped*] .... LRA
Least Restrictive Environment [*For the education of the handicapped*] .... LRE
Least Significant (IEEE) .... LS
Least Significant (IAA) .... LSIG
Least Significant BIT [*or Byte*] [*Data compaction*] .... LSB
Least Significant Byte [*Data compaction*] [*Computer science*] .... LSBY
Least Significant Character (IEEE) .... LSC
Least Significant Decade (IAA) .... LSD
Least Significant Difference [*Statistics*] .... LSD
Least Significant Digit [*Data compaction*] (MUGU) .... LSD
Least Significant Portion (MCD) .... LSP
Least Significant Position (CMD) .... LSP
Least Significant Word (MCD) .... LSW
Least Square Center (IAA) .... LSC
Least Square Complex Exponential [*Mathematics*] .... LSCE
Least Square Fit .... LSF
Least Square Mean [*Mathematical statistics*] .... LSM
Least Square Polynomial Fit (IAA) .... LSPF
Least Squares [*Mathematical statistics*] .... LS
Least Squares Circle [*Manufacturing term*] .... LSC
Least Squares Estimator [*Statistics*] .... LSE
Least [*or Lowest*] Upper Bound .... LUB
Least Used, First Out [*Computer science*] .... LUFO
Least Voltage Coincidence Detector .... LVCD
Least Widely Used and Least Taught Languages (AIE) .... LWULT
Least-Common Bigram [*Computer science*] (BYTE) .... LCB
Least-Cost Estimating and Scheduling System .... LESS
Least-Cost Routing [*Telecommunications*] .... LCR
Least-Developed Developing Country [*Trade status*] .... LDDC
Least-Preferred Co-Worker [*Management term*] .... LPC
Least-Squares Collocation [*Mathematics*] .... LSC
Leather L
Leather .... LEA
Leather (VRA) .... lea
Leather (ROG) .... LEATH
Leather [*Automotive advertising*] .... LTH
Leather (KSC) .... LTHR
Leather .... LTHR
Leather and Associated Trades Show [*British*] (ITD) .... LATS
Leather Apparel Association (EA) .... LAA
Leather Dressers' Old Society [*A union*] [*British*] .... LDOS
Leather Dressers' Union [*British*] .... LDU
Leather Factory [*AMEX symbol*] (TTSB) .... TLF
Leather Factory, Inc. [*Associated Press*] (SAG) .... LeathFac
Leather Factory, Inc. [*AMEX symbol*] (SPSG) .... TLF
Leather Finishers' Society [*A union*] [*British*] .... LFS
Leather Industries of America (EA) .... LIA
Leather Industry Suppliers Associates [*British*] (DBA) .... LISA
Leather, Leather Goods, Fur [*Department of Employment*] [*British*] .... LLGF
Leather or Rubber Covered [*Freight*] .... L or RC

Leather Personnel Carriers [*i.e., boots*] [*Slang Army*]	LPC
Leather Producers' Association for England, Scotland, and Wales (BI)	LPA
Leather Workers International Union of America (EA)	LWIU
Leather Workers International Union of America	LWU
Leathercraft Guild (EA)	LG
Leathercrafters' Association of Queensland [*Australia*]	LAQ
Leatherhead [*City in England*]	LEATH
Leatherhead Food Research Association [*British*] (ARC)	LFRA
Leathery Pocket [*of pineapple*]	LP
Leave	L
Leave	LEA
Leave (AFM)	LV
Leave (WGA)	LVE
Leave Address (DNAB)	L/A
Leave Advance [*Military*]	L/A
Leave and Earnings Statement [*Military*] (AABC)	LES
Leave and Liberty (WDAA)	L & L
Leave and Upkeep Period [*Military*] (NVT)	LVUPK
Leave Authorization Balance [*Air Force*] (AFM)	LAB
Leave Edge (DGA)	LE
Leave Message [*Word processing*]	LM
Leave of Absence	LOA
Leave on Pass	LOP
Leave One Out at a Time [*Data analysis*]	LOO
Leave Rations [*Military*]	LEAVERATS
Leave Rations [*Military*]	LR
Leave Rations [*Military*] (DNAB)	LVRATS
Leave Rations, Sick Leave [*Military*] (DNAB)	LVRATS SL
Leave Rations, Special Leave [*Military*] (DNAB)	LVRATS SPEC
Leave to Appeal Refused [*Legal term*] (ADA)	LR
Leave Trapping Mode (SAA)	LTM
Leave Travel Allowance	LTA
Leave with Pay (KSC)	LWP
Leave without Pay	LWOP
Leave Word [*Telecommunications*] (TEL)	LW
Leaved	lvd
Leavenworth, KS [*Location identifier FAA*] (FAAL)	FLV
Leavenworth, KS [*AM radio station call letters*]	KKLO
Leavenworth, KS [*FM radio station call letters*]	KQRC-FM
Leavenworth Public Library, Leavenworth, KS [*Library symbol Library of Congress*] (LCLS)	KLe
Leavers Lace Manufacturers of America [*Defunct*] (EA)	LLMA
Leaves	LEVS
Leaves	LL
Leaves [*Bibliography*]	LVS
Leaves (MSA)	LVS
Leavesden [*British ICAO location identifier*] (ICLI)	EGTI
Leaving	LVG
Leaving Air Defense Identification Zone	LADIZ
Leaving Scene of an Accident [*Traffic offense charge*]	LSA
Lebakeng [*Lesotho*] [*ICAO location identifier*] (ICLI)	FXLK
Lebanese Air Transport [*ICAO designator*] (FAAC)	LAQ
Lebanese Armed Revolutionary Faction	LARF
Lebanese Forces	LF
Lebanese Information and Research Center (EA)	LIRC
Lebanese International Airways	LIA
Lebanese Kidnap [*Victims*] [*American hostages held in Beirut*]	LEBNAP
Lebanese Moslem Association [*Australia*]	LMA
Lebanese National Movement [*Political party*] (PPW)	LNM
Lebanese National Patriotic Forces [*Political party*]	LNPF
Lebanese Revolutionary Party [*Political party*] (PD)	LRP
Lebanese-American Society of Greater New York [*Defunct*] (EA)	LAS
Lebanon [*MARC geographic area code Library of Congress*] (LCCP)	a-le--
Lebanon [*ANSI two-letter standard code*] (CNC)	LB
Lebanon [*ANSI three-letter standard code*] (CNC)	LBN
Lebanon [*MARC country of publication code Library of Congress*] (LCCP)	le
Lebanon [*New Hampshire*] [*Airport symbol*] (OAG)	LEB
Lebanon (VRA)	Leb
Lebanon Airport Development Corp. [*ICAO designator*] (FAAC)	LAD
Lebanon Community Hospital, Lebanon, OR [*Library symbol*] [*Library of Congress*] (LCLS)	OrLeH
Lebanon Correctional Institution Library, Lebanon, OH [*Library symbol Library of Congress*] (LCLS)	OLeC
Lebanon County Historical Society, Lebanon, PA [*Library symbol Library of Congress*] (LCLS)	PLebHi
Lebanon County Legal Journal [*Pennsylvania*] [*A publication*] (DLA)	Lebanon
Lebanon County Legal Journal [*Pennsylvania*] [*A publication*] (DLA)	Lebanon Co LJ (PA)
Lebanon High School, Lebanon, IL [*Library symbol Library of Congress*] (LCLS)	ILebHS
Lebanon Historical Society, Lebanon, NH [*Library symbol Library of Congress*] (LCLS)	NhLeHi
Lebanon, IN [*FM radio station call letters*]	WIRE
Lebanon, KY [*AM radio station call letters*]	WLBN
Lebanon, KY [*FM radio station call letters*]	WLSK
Lebanon, MO [*FM radio station call letters*]	KCLQ
Lebanon, MO [*FM radio station call letters*]	KIRK
Lebanon, MO [*AM radio station call letters*]	KJEL
Lebanon, MO [*AM radio station call letters*]	KLWT
Lebanon, MO [*Location identifier FAA*] (FAAL)	LBO
Lebanon, NH [*Location identifier FAA*] (FAAL)	DVR
Lebanon, NH [*Location identifier FAA*] (FAAL)	IVV
Lebanon, NH [*Location identifier FAA*] (FAAL)	LAH
Lebanon, NH [*Location identifier FAA*] (FAAL)	LEB
Lebanon, NH [*FM radio station call letters*] (RBYB)	WNBX-FM
Lebanon, NH [*FM radio station call letters*]	WUVR

Lebanon, OH [*FM radio station call letters*]	WMMA
Lebanon, OR [*AM radio station call letters*] (RBYB)	KGAL
Lebanon, OR [*AM radio station call letters*]	KSHO
Lebanon, OR [*AM radio station call letters*]	KXPC
Lebanon, PA [*AM radio station call letters*]	WADV
Lebanon, PA [*AM radio station call letters*]	WLBR
Lebanon, PA [*AM radio station call letters*]	WQIC
Lebanon Public Library, Lebanon, IL [*Library symbol Library of Congress*] (LCLS)	ILeb
Lebanon Public Library, Lebanon, IN [*Library symbol Library of Congress*] (LCLS)	InLeb
Lebanon Public Library, Lebanon, NH [*Library symbol Library of Congress*] (LCLS)	NhLe
Lebanon Public Library, Lebanon, OH [*Library symbol Library of Congress*] (LCLS)	OLe
Lebanon Reporter, Lebanon, IN [*Library symbol Library of Congress*] (LCLS)	InLebR
Lebanon, TN [*FM radio station call letters*]	WANT
Lebanon, TN [*AM radio station call letters*]	WCOR
Lebanon, TN [*FM radio station call letters*]	WFMQ
Lebanon, TN [*Television station call letters*]	WJFB
Lebanon, TN [*FM radio station call letters*]	WQDQ
Lebanon, TN [*FM radio station call letters*]	WYHY
Lebanon, VA [*FM radio station call letters*]	WLRV
Lebanon, VA [*FM radio station call letters*]	WXLZ
Lebanon Valley College [*Pennsylvania*]	LVC
Lebanon Valley College, Annville, PA [*OCLC symbol*] (OCLC)	LVC
Lebanon Valley College, Annville, PA [*Library symbol Library of Congress*] (LCLS)	PAnL
Lebap [*Turkmenistan*] [*ICAO designator*] (FAAC)	LEB
Lebendige Seelsorge (BJA)	LebSeels
Lebensalter [*Chronological Age*] [*Psychology*]	LA
Leber's Congenital Amaurosis [*Medicine*] (DAVI)	LCA
Leber's Hereditary Optic Neuropathy [*Ophthalmology*]	LHON
Leboulou [*Congo*] [*ICAO location identifier*] (ICLI)	FCML
Lebowa People's Party [*South Africa*] [*Political party*] (PPW)	LPP
Lec Refrigeration Ltd. [*British ICAO designator*] (FAAC)	WLMS
Lecanto, FL [*FM radio station call letters*]	LIBN
Lecce [*Italy ICAO location identifier*] (ICLI)	LOF
Lecherous Old Fool [*Slang*]	EDSL
Lechfeld [*Germany ICAO location identifier*] (ICLI)	LECH
Lechters, Inc. [*NASDAQ symbol*] (SAG)	Lechters
Lechters, Inc. [*Associated Press*] (SAG)	LBS
Lecithin Bile State [*Medicine*]	L/S
Lecithin/Sphingomyelin [*Ratio*] [*Clinical chemistry*]	LSR
Lecithin/Sphingomyelin Ratio [*Medicine*] (DMAA)	LCAT
Lecithin-Cholesterol Acyltransferase [*An enzyme*]	LRAT
Lecithin-Retinol Acyltransferase [*An enzyme*]	EDNL
Leck [*Germany ICAO location identifier*] (ICLI)	QMUEC
L'Ecole de Criminologie, Universite de Montreal, Quebec [*Library symbol National Library of Canada*] (NLC)	EGXV
Leconfield [*British ICAO location identifier*] (ICLI)	FOGL
Leconi [*Gabon*] [*ICAO location identifier*] (ICLI)	EPA
L'Economie des Pays Arabes [*A publication*] (BJA)	LCA
LeConte Airlines [*ICAO designator*] (FAAC)	LCRY
LeCroy Corp. [*NASDAQ symbol*] (SAG)	LeCroy
LeCroy Corp. [*Associated Press*] (SAG)	LECT
LecTec Corp. [*NASDAQ symbol*] (SAG)	Lectec
LecTec Corp. [*Associated Press*] (SAG)	LECT
Lectern (ROG)	LECAM
Lectin Adhesion Molecule [*Biochemistry*]	LECAM
Lectin-Cellular Adhesion Molecule [*Biochemistry*]	LDCC
Lectin-Dependent Cell-Mediated Cytotoxicity [*Biochemistry*]	LD
Lectio Divina [*Paris*] [*A publication*] (BJA)	lectn
Lectionary (VRA)	LE
Lector (ROG)	LB
Lectori Benevolo [*To the Kind (or Gentle) Reader*] [*Latin*]	LBS
Lectori Benevolo Salutem [*To the Kind (or Gentle) Reader, Greeting*] [*Latin*]	LS
Lectori Salutem [*Latin*]	LECTO
Lectotype	Lect y V
Lectura y Vida [*A publication*]	LEC
Lecture	LECT
Lecture [*or Lecturer*]	LECT
Lecture	LB
Lecture Bottle [*Shipment of gas products*] [*Union Carbide Corp.*]	LECTR
Lecturer	LECTR
Lecturer	LIC
Lecturer in Charge (ADA)	LORA
Lecturer-Oriented Response Analysis (PDAA)	LDV
Lectus Developments Ltd. [*Vancouver Stock Exchange symbol*]	CaOTLP
Ledbury Park Junior High School, Toronto, ON, Canada [*Library symbol Library of Congress*] (LCLS)	OTLP
Ledbury Park Junior High School, Toronto, Ontario [*Library symbol National Library of Canada*] (NLC)	LCF
Lederberg-Coxeter-Frucht [*Notation*] [*Graph theory, mathematics*]	LF
Lederer Foundation (EA)	CL
Lederle Laboratories [*Research code symbol*]	L
Lederle Laboratories [*Research code symbol*]	LL
Lederle Laboratories [*Research code symbol*]	YLL
Lederle Laboratories, Pearl River, NY [*OCLC symbol*] (OCLC)	Le
Ledge	LDR
Ledger (ADA)	LED
Ledger	LR
Ledger (ROG)	

Ledger Account (ROG) .... LA
Ledger Asset .... LA
Ledger Card Computer (MHDB) LCC
Ledger Folio (ROG) .... LED FO
Ledger Folio .... LF
Leduc Public Library, Alberta [Library symbol National Library of Canada]
(NLC) .... ALE
Ledyard, CT [FM radio station call letters] .... WBMW
Lee College, Baytown, TX [Library symbol Library of Congress] (LCLS) .... TxByL
Lee College, Cleveland, TN [Library symbol Library of Congress] (LCLS) ...... TCleL
Lee College, Cleveland, TN [OCLC symbol] (OCLC) .... TLC
Lee County Central Electric [AAR code] .... LCCE
Lee County Historical Society, Museum Library, Loachapoka, AL [Library symbol Library of Congress] (LCLS) .... ALoaLHi
Lee County Library, Sanford, NC [Library symbol Library of Congress]
(LCLS) .... NcSaL
Lee County Library, Sanford, NC [Library symbol] [Library of Congress]
(LCLS) .... NcSaLCL
Lee County Library System, Fort Myers, FL [Library symbol] [Library of Congress] (LCLS) .... FFmL
Lee County Public Library, Bishopville, SC [Library symbol] [Library of Congress] (LCLS) .... ScBi
Lee County Public Library, Fort Meyers, FL [Library symbol Library of Congress] (LCLS) .... FFm
Lee, David M., Los Angeles CA [STAC] .... LDM
Lee Elementary School, Hicksville, NY [Library symbol Library of Congress]
(LCLS) .... NHickLE
Lee Enterprises [NYSE symbol] (TTSB) .... LEE
Lee Enterprises, Inc. [NYSE symbol] (SPSG) .... LEE
Lee Enterprises, Inc. [Associated Press] (SAG) .... LeeEnt
Lee on Captures [A publication] (DLA) .... Lee Cap
Lee Pharmaceuticals [Associated Press] (SAG) .... LeePhr
Lee Pharmaceuticals [AMEX symbol] (SPSG) .... LPH
Lee Road Elementary School, Levittown, NY [Library symbol] [Library of Congress] (LCLS) .... NLevLE
Lee Stocking Island, Exuma Island [Bahamas] [ICAO location identifier]
(ICLI) .... MYES
Lee Town News, Des Moines, IA [Library symbol Library of Congress]
(LCLS) .... IaDmLN
Lee White Tritium [Clotting Time] [Hematology] (DAVI) .... LEE W
Leeds [British ICAO location identifier] (ICLI) .... EGRY
Leeds [Utah] [Seismograph station code, US Geological Survey] (SEIS) .... LEE
Leeds and Bradford [British ICAO location identifier] (ICLI) .... EGNM
Leeds and Liverpool Canal [Shipping] [British] (ROG) .... L & LC
Leeds/Bradford [England] [Airport symbol] (OAG) .... LBA
Leeds Central Helicopters [British] [FAA designator] (FAAC) .... LEH
Leeds City Library, Leeds, United Kingdom [Library symbol Library of Congress] (LCLS) .... UkLe
Leeds Federal Svgs Bk [NASDAQ symbol] (TTSB) .... LFED
Leeds FSB [Associated Press] (SAG) .... LeedsFdl
Leeds FSB [NASDAQ symbol] (SAG) .... LFED
Leeds University Institute of Education [British] (AIE) .... LUIE
Leeds Volunteers [British military] (DMA) LV
Lee-Enfield [British military] (DMA) .... LE
Lee-Itawamba Regional Library, Tupelo, MS [Library symbol Library of Congress] (LCLS) .... MsT
Leek Yellow Stripe Virus [Plant pathology] .... LYSV
Leelanau Township Library, Northport, MI [Library symbol Library of Congress] (LCLS) .... MiNop
Leembruggen and Asirvatham's Appeal Court Reports [Ceylon]
[A publication] (DLA) .... L & A
Lee-Metford [British military] (DMA) .... LM
Leeming [British ICAO location identifier] (ICLI) .... EGXE
Lee-On-Solent [British ICAO location identifier] (ICLI) .... EGUS
Leepertown Consolidated Community School District 175, Bureau, IL
[Library symbol Library of Congress] (LCLS) .... IBureLSD
Leepertown Township Library, Bureau, IL [Library symbol Library of Congress] (LCLS) .... IBure
Leer-Nuttermoor [Germany ICAO location identifier] (ICLI) .... EDWF
Lee's Abstracts of Title [1843] [A publication] (DLA) .... Lee Abs
Lee's Dictionary of Practice [A publication] (DLA) .... Lee Dict
Lee's English Ecclesiastical Reports [A publication] (DLA) .... Lee
Lee's English Ecclesiastical Reports [A publication] (DLA) .... Lee Eccl
Lee's English King's Bench Cases Tempore Hardwicke [1733-38] [England]
[A publication] (DLA) .... Lee T Hard
Lee's English King's Bench Cases Tempore Hardwicke [1733-38] [England]
[A publication] (DLA) .... Lee T Hardw
Lee's English King's Bench Reports Tempore Hardwicke [1733-38]
[A publication] (DLA) .... Lee & H
Lee's English King's Bench Reports Tempore Hardwicke [1733-38]
[A publication] (DLA) .... Rep T Hard
Lee's English King's Bench Reports Tempore Hardwicke [1733-38]
[A publication] (DLA) .... Rep T Hardw
Lee's English King's Bench Reports Tempore Hardwicke, Annaly Edition
[1733-38] [A publication] (DLA) .... Annaly
Lees Junior College [Jackson, KY] .... LJC
Lee's Law and Practice of Bankruptcy [3rd ed.] [1887] [A publication]
(DLA) .... Lee Bank
Lee's Laws of Shipping [A publication] (DLA) .... Lee Ship
Lee's Multidifferential Agar [Brewery bacteria culture medium] .... LMDA
Lee's Reports [9-12 California] [A publication] (DLA) .... Lee
Lee's Summit Hospital, Lee's Summit, MO [Library symbol Library of Congress] (LCLS) .... MoLeeH
Lees Summit Public School District, Lees Summit, MO [Library symbol]
[Library of Congress] (LCLS) .... MoLeeS

Leesburg, FL [Location identifier FAA] (FAAL) .... LEE
Leesburg, FL [Television station call letters] .... WACX
Leesburg, FL [AM radio station call letters] .... WLBE
Leesburg, FL [TV radio station call letters] (RBYB) .... WLCB-TV
Leesburg, FL [AM radio station call letters] .... WQBQ
Leesburg, FL [FM radio station call letters] .... WXXL
Leesburg, GA [FM radio station call letters] (RBYB) .... WJAD
Leesburg Public Library, Leesburg, FL [Library symbol] [Library of Congress] (LCLS) .... FLe
Leesburg, VA [Location identifier FAA] (FAAL) .... GFG
Leesburg, VA [AM radio station call letters] .... WAGE
Leese's Reports [26 Nebraska] [A publication] (DLA) .... Leese
Lees-Hromas-Webb [Theory] .... LHW
Lees-McRae College, Banner Elk, NC [Library symbol Library of Congress]
(LCLS) .... NcBaneL
Leesona Corp. (KSC) LC
Leesona Moos Laboratory .... LML
Leesville, LA [FM radio station call letters] .... KJAE
Leesville, LA [AM radio station call letters] .... KLLA
Leesville, LA [FM radio station call letters] .... KVVP
Leesville State School, Leesville, LA [Library symbol Library of Congress]
(LCLS) .... LLeS
Lee-Tse-Goldberg-Lowe [Theory] .... LTGL
Leeuwarden [Netherlands ICAO location identifier] (ICLI) .... EHLW
Leeward L
Leeward Community College, Pearl City, HI [Library symbol Library of Congress] (LCLS) .... HPcL
Leeward Islands (BARN) .... Le Is
Leeward Islands (BARN) LI
Leeward Islands [MARC geographic area code Library of Congress]
(LCCP) .... nwli--
Leeward Islands Air Transport (1974) Ltd. [Antigua and Barbuda] [ICAO designator] (FAAC) .... LIA
Leeward Islands Air Transport Services Ltd. [Humorous interpretation: Luggage in Another Town] [Airline] .... LIAT
Lee-Whedon Memorial Library, Medina, NY [Library symbol Library of Congress] (LCLS) .... NMed
Lee-White Clotting Time [Hematology] .... LWCT
Lee-White Method [Hematology] (MAE) .... LW
Lefevre's Parliamentary Decisions, by Bourke [England] [A publication]
(DLA) .... Lef Dec
Lefroy and Cassel's Practice Cases [1881-83] [Ontario] [A publication]
(ILCA) .... L & C
Lefroy and Cassel's Practice Cases [1881-83] [Ontario] [A publication]
(DLA) .... Lef & Cas
Lefroy's Irish Criminal Law [A publication] (DLA) .... Lef Cr L
Lefroy's Railroad and Canal Cases [England] [A publication] (DLA) .... Lefroy
Lefschetz Center for Dynamical Systems [Brown University] [Research center] (RCD) .... LCDS
Left [Politics] L
Left [Direction] L
Left (WDMC) l
Left (ECII) .... LF
Left (ABBR) .... LFT
Left (VRA) .... lft
Left .... LT
Left Acromio-Dorso-Anterior [A fetal position] [Obstetrics] .... LADA
Left Acromio-Dorso-Posterior [A fetal position] [Obstetrics] .... LADP
Left Add, Right Subtract [Army field artillery technique] (INF) .... LARS
Left Aft Propulsion System [or Subsystem] (NASA) .... LAPS
Left and Below [Medicine] .... L & B
Left and Right .... L & R
Left Angle .... LA
Left Angulation [Orthopedics] (DAVI) .... LA
Left Anterior Descending [Artery] .... LAD
Left Anterior Descending Artery [Anatomy] (DAVI) .... LADA
Left Anterior Descending Coronary Artery [Anatomy] .... LADC
Left Anterior Descending Coronary Artery [Medicine] (MEDA) .... LADCA
Left Anterior Descending Diagonal [Branch of coronary artery] [Anatomy]
(DAVI) .... LADD
Left Anterior Digestive [Gland] .... LAD
Left Anterior Fascicle [Anatomy] .... LAF
Left Anterior Fascicular Block [Cardiology] .... LAFB
Left Anterior Hemiblock [Cardiology] .... LAH
Left Anterior Hemiblock [Medicine] (MEDA) .... LAHB
Left Anterior Measurement (DAVI) .... LAM
Left Anterior Oblique [Cardiology] .... LAO
Left Anterior Occipital [Position] [Obstetrics] (DAVI) .... LAO
Left Anterior Small Thoracotomy [Medicine] (DMAA) .... LAST
Left Anterior Thigh [Medicine] .... LAT
Left Anterior-Superior [Anatomy] (DAVI) .... LAS
Left Anterior-Superior Fascicular Block [Cardiology] (DAVI) .... LASFB
Left Anterosuperior Hemiblock [Cardiology] (DAVI) .... LASH
Left Arithmetic Element .... LAE
Left Arm [Medicine] .... LA
Left Arm Reclining [or Recumbent] [Medicine] .... LAR
Left Arm Sitting [Blood pressure and pulse measurement] [Cardiology]
(DAVI) .... LAS
Left Arterial Pressure [Cardiology] (DAVI) .... LAP
Left Artial Myxoma [Cardiology] (DAVI) .... LAM
Left Artrial Involvement [Medicine] (MEDA) .... LAI
Left Ascension .... LA
Left Atrial Abnormality [Medicine] (MEDA) .... LAA
Left Atrial [or Avricular] Appendage [Cardiology] (DAVI) .... LA
Left Atrial Ball-Valve Thrombus [Cardiology] (DAVI) .... LABVT

Left Atrial Contraction [*Cardiology*] (DAVI)	LAC
Left Atrial Emptying Index [*Medicine*] (DMAA)	LAEI
Left Atrial Enlargement [*Cardiology*]	LAE
Left Atrial Hypertrophy [*Cardiology*]	LAH
Left Atrial Neovascularization [*Cardiology*] (DAVI)	LANV
Left Atrial Overloading [*Cardiology*] (DAVI)	LAO
Left Atrial Posterior Wall [*Cardiology*] (DAVI)	LAPW
Left Atrial Pressure [*Cardiology*]	LAP
Left Atrial Transesophageal Pacing Test [*Medicine*] (DMAA)	LATPT
Left Atrial Transmural Pressure [*Medicine*] (DMAA)	LATP
Left Atrial Volume in End Diastole [*Medicine*] (DMAA)	LAEDV
Left Atrial Wall [*Medicine*] (DMAA)	LAW
Left Atrium [*Anatomy*]	LA
Left Attack Wing [*Women's lacrosse position*]	LA
Left Auricle [*Anatomy*]	LA
Left Axilla (KSC)	LAL
Left Axillary Line [*Medicine*] (DMAA)	LAL
Left Axis Deviation [*Medicine*]	LAD
Left Axis Deviation Minimal [*Cardiology*] (DAVI)	LAD-MIN
Left Back [*Football*] (WDAA)	LB
Left Bank	LBK
Left Basal Artery [*Medicine*] (DMAA)	LBA
Left Base [*Aviation*] (FAAC)	LB
Left Book Club [*Founded in the 1930's by publisher Victor Gollancz*] [*Defunct British*]	LBC
Left Border [*Genetics*]	LB
Left Border Cardiac Dullness [*Cardiology*]	LBCD
Left Border of Dullness [*Cardiology*]	LBD
Left Bounded Context [*Computer science*] (MHDB)	LBC
Left Brachial Vein [*Cardiology*] (DAVI)	LBV
Left Breast [*Medicine*] (DMAA)	LB
Left Breast Biopsy (DAVI)	LBB
Left Breast Biopsy Examination [*Medicine*] (AAMN)	LBBX
Left Buccal Ganglion [*Medicine*]	LBG
Left Buffer Memory (GFGA)	LBM
Left Bundle [*Cardiology*] (DMAA)	LB
Left Bundle Branch [*Cardiology*] (AAMN)	LBB
Left Bundle Branch Block [*Cardiology*]	LBBB
Left Bundle Branch System Block [*Cardiology*]	LBBSB
Left Bundle-Branch [*Cardiology*] (DAVI)	LB
Left Buttock [*Medicine*]	LB
Left Buttock Line (MCD)	LBL
Left Carotid Artery [*Cardiology*] (DAVI)	LCA
Left Caudate Nucleus [*Medicine*] (DMAA)	LCN
Left Center [*A stage direction*]	LC
Left Center Entrance [*Theater*] (WDMC)	LCE
Left Cerebral Ganglion [*Medicine*]	LCG
Left Chest [*Medicine*] (KSC)	LC
Left Circular Polarization	LCP
Left Circularly Polarized Light	LCPL
Left Circumflex (Artery) [*Anatomy*]	LC
Left Circumflex Artery [*Anatomy*]	LCF
Left Circumflex Coronary Artery [*Medicine*] (DMAA)	LCC
Left Circumflex Coronary Artery [*Anatomy*]	LCCA
Left Circumflex Coronary Artery [*Cardiology*] (DAVI)	LCX
Left Common Carotid Artery [*Cardiology*] (DAVI)	LCCA
Left Common Femoral [*Artery*] [*Anatomy*] (DAVI)	LCF
Left Cornerback [*Football*]	LCB
Left Coronary Artery [*Cardiology*]	LCA
Left Costal Margin [*Medicine*]	LCM
Left Defense	LD
Left Defense Wing [*Women's lacrosse position*]	LDW
Left Deltoid [*Medicine*]	LD
Left Digestive Gland	LDG
Left Direct Inguinal Hernia [*Medicine*] (DMAA)	LDIH
Left Door [*Theater*]	LD
Left Dorso-Anterior [*A fetal position*] [*Obstetrics*]	LDA
Left Dorso-Posterior [*A fetal position*] [*Obstetrics*]	LDP
Left Dorsotransverse [*Medicine*] (DMAA)	LDT
Left Ear (DMAA)	LE
Left Ear, Cold Stimulus [*Medicine*] (MEDA)	LC
Left Ear, Warm Stimulus [*Medicine*] (MEDA)	LW
Left End	LE
Left Exotropia [*Ophthalmology*]	LXT
Left Extremity	LE
Left Extremity Venous Tracing [*Cardiology*] (DAVI)	LEVT
Left Eye [*Opthalmology*] (DAVI)	L
Left Eye	LE
Left Femoral Artery [*Anatomy*]	LFA
Left Femoral Hernia [*Medicine*]	LFH
Left Field [*or Fielder*] [*Baseball*]	LF
Left Foot	LF
Left Forward [*Football*]	LF
Left Front	LF
Left Front Fluid Temperature [*Brake system*] [*Automotive engineering*]	LFFT
Left Front Lining Temperature [*Brake system*] [*Automotive engineering*]	LFLT
Left Frontal Craniotomy [*Medicine*] (DMAA)	LFA
Left Frontoanterior [*A fetal position*] [*Obstetrics*]	LFA
Left Frontolateral [*Medicine*] (DMAA)	LFL
Left Frontoposterior [*A fetal position*] [*Obstetrics*]	LFP
Left Frontotransverse [*A fetal position*] [*Obstetrics*]	LFT
Left Fullback [*Soccer*]	LB
Left Fullback [*Soccer*]	LF
Left Fullback [*Soccer*]	LFB
Left Gluteus [*Medicine*]	LG
Left Green Network [*An association*] (EA)	LGN
Left Guard [*Football*]	LG
Left Half (WDAA)	LH
Left Half Indicators, Off Test (SAA)	LFT
Left Half Plane (IAA)	LHP
Left Half Word	LHW
Left Halfback [*Soccer*]	LH
Left Halfback [*Soccer*]	LHB
Left Hand [*Music*] (ROG)	L
Left Hand	LH
Left Hand Grip (DMAA)	LHG
Left Hand, Right Hand (IAA)	LHRH
Left Hand World [*British*] [*An association*] (DBA)	LHW
Left Heart Assistance [*Cardiology*]	LHA
Left Heart Failure [*Medicine*]	LHF
Left Heart Strain [*Medicine*]	LHS
Left Hemiparesis [*Medicine*] (MEDA)	LHP
Left Hemisphere Lesion [*Neurology*] (DAVI)	LHL
Left Hepatic Artery [*Medicine*] (DMAA)	LHA
Left Hepatic Lobe [*Anatomy*]	LHL
Left Hyperphoria [*Ophthalmology*]	LH
Left Hypertropia [*Ophthalmology*]	LHT
Left Hypochondrium [*Medicine*]	LHC
Left Iliac Crest [*Anatomy*] (DAVI)	LIC
Left Iliac Fossa [*Medicine*]	LIF
Left Iliac Region [*Medicine*] (MAE)	LIR
Left in Bottle (MAE)	LIB
Left in Place [*Telecommunications*] (TEL)	LI
Left Inboard (MCD)	LIB
Left Inboard Elevon [*Aviation*] (MCD)	LIE
Left Inferior Oblique [*Anatomy*] (DAVI)	LIO
Left Inferior Rectus [*Muscle*] [*Ophthalmology and surgery*] (DAVI)	LIR
Left Inguinal Hernia [*Medicine*]	LIH
Left Innominate Vein [*Medicine*] (MAE)	LIV
Left Intercostal Margin [*Anatomy*]	LICM
Left Intercostal Space [*Cardiology*] (MAE)	LICS
Left Intercostal Space [*Cardiology*]	LIS
Left Internal Carotid [*Artery*] [*Anatomy*] (DAVI)	LIC
Left Internal Carotid Artery [*Anatomy*] (DAVI)	LICA
Left Internal Jugular Vein [*Medicine*] (DMAA)	LIJ
Left Internal Mammary Artery [*Anatomy*] (AAMN)	LIMA
Left Kidney [*Medicine*]	LK
Left Kidney [*Anatomy*] (DAVI)	LKID
Left Knee Right [*Guitar playing*]	LKR
Left Knee Vertical [*Guitar playing*]	LKV
Left Lateral [*Anatomy*] (DAVI)	LL
Left Lateral [*Radiology*] (DAVI)	LLAT
Left Lateral [*Anatomy*] (DAVI)	LLT
Left Lateral [*Medicine*] (MAE)	lt lat
Left Lateral Border [*Medicine*] (DMAA)	LLB
Left Lateral Decubitus [*Medicine*] (AAMN)	LLD
Left Lateral Femoral [*Site of injection*] [*Medicine*]	LLF
Left Lateral Flexion [*Medicine*] (DMAA)	LLF
Left Lateral Rectus [*Eye muscle*] (BABM)	LLR
Left Lateral Rotation [*Medicine*]	LLR
Left Lateral Thigh [*Medicine*]	LLT
Left Lateral Ventricular Preexcitation [*Medicine*] (DMAA)	LLVP
Left Leg (MAE)	LL
Left Line Contactor (MCD)	LLC
Left Linebacker (WGA)	LLB
Left Long Leg Brace [*Medicine*]	LLLB
Left Lower [*Medicine*]	LL
Left Lower Border of Cardiac Dullness [*Cardiology*]	LLBCD
Left Lower Extremity [*Medicine*]	LLE
Left Lower Eyelid [*Medicine*]	LLL
Left Lower Limb [*Anatomy*] (DAVI)	LLL
Left Lower Lobe [*of lung*] [*Medicine*]	LLL
Left Lower Quadrant [*of abdomen*] [*Medicine*]	LLQ
Left Lower Scapular Border [*Medicine*] (DMAA)	LLSB
Left Lower Sternal Border [*Anatomy*] (DAVI)	LLSB
Left Lower Zone [*Medicine*] (DMAA)	LLZ
Left Lumbar Region [*Medicine*] (MAE)	LLR
Left Lung [*Medicine*]	LL
Left Main Coronary Artery [*Anatomy*]	LMCA
Left Main Coronary Artery Disease	LMCAD
Left Main Gear (MCD)	LMG
Left Main-Stem Bronchus [*Medicine*] (MEDA)	LMB
Left Male (MSA)	LM
Left Medial Deltoid [*Injection Site*]	LMD
Left Medial Rectus [*Eye muscle*] (BABM)	LMR
Left Mediolateral [*Episiotomy*] [*Obstetrics*]	LML
Left Mediolateral Episiotomy [*Obstetrics*] (MAE)	LME
Left Mentoanterior [*A fetal position*] [*Obstetrics*]	LMA
Left Mentolateral [*Episiotomy*] [*Obstetrics*]	LML
Left Mentoposterior [*A fetal position*] [*Obstetrics*]	LMP
Left Mentotransverse [*A fetal position*] [*Obstetrics*]	LMT
Left Mid (NASA)	LM
Left Middle Cerebral Artery [*Medicine*] (MAE)	LMCA
Left Middle Ear Exploration [*Otorhinolaryngology*] (DAVI)	LMEE
Left Middle Finger (DMAA)	LMF
Left Middle Lobe [*of lung*] (DAVI)	LML
Left minus Right [*Stereo signals*] (NTCM)	L - R
Left Minus Right Double Sideband (IAA)	LRDSB
Left Most BIT [*Binary Digit*] [*Computer science*] (MHDB)	LMB
Left Nationalists [*Spain Political party*] (PPW)	NE

Left Oblique Inguinal Hernia [Medicine] (DMAA)	LOIH
Left Occipitoanterior [A fetal position] [Obstetrics]	LOA
Left Occipitolateral [A fetal position] [Obstetrics]	LOL
Left Occipitoposterior [A fetal position] [Obstetrics]	LOP
Left Occipitotransverse [A fetal position] [Obstetrics]	LOT
Left of Baseline	LOB
Left on Base [Baseball]	LB
Left on Base [Baseball]	LOB
Left Otitis Media [Medicine] (CPH)	LOM
Left Otitis Media Suppurative Acute [Medicine]	LOMSA
Left Otitis Media Suppurative, Chronic [Medicine] (MEDA)	LOMSACh
Left Otitis Media Suppurative Chronic [Medicine]	LOMSCH
Left Out of Battle [British]	LOB
Left Outboard (MCD)	LO
Left Outboard (MCD)	LOB
Left Outboard Elevon [Aviation] (MCD)	LOE
Left Outer Thigh [Injection site]	LOT
Left Outside Position [Dancing]	LOP
Left Pectoral Fin [Fish anatomy]	LP
Left Pleural Ganglion [Medicine]	LPLG
Left plus Right [Stereo signals] (NTCM)	L + R
Left Posterio Occipital [A fetal position] (DAVI)	LPO
Left Posterior [Medicine] (MEDA)	L POST
Left Posterior Fascicle [Anatomy]	LPF
Left Posterior Fascicular Block [Cardiology]	LPFB
Left Posterior Hemiblock [Cardiology]	LPH
Left Posterior Oblique [Cardiology] (MAE)	LPO
Left Posterior Ventricular Preexcitation [Medicine] (DMAA)	LPVP
Left Posterior-Inferior [Medicine] (DMAA)	LPI
Left Pulmonary Artery [Anatomy]	LPA
Left Pulmonary Vein [Anatomy]	LPV
Left Radical Mastectomy [Medicine] (MAE)	LRM
Left Radical Neck Dissection [Surgical procedure] (DAVI)	LRND
Left Rear	LR
Left Rear Fluid Temperature [Brake system] [Automotive engineering]	LRFT
Left Rear Lining Temperature [Brake system] [Automotive engineering]	LRLT
left Renal Artery [Anatomy] (DAVI)	LRA
Left Renal Vein [Anatomy] (DAVI)	LRV
Left Rudder (MCD)	LR
Left Sacroanterior [A fetal position, the breech position] [Obstetrics]	LSA
Left Sacroanterior Position [of the fetus] [Obstetrics]	SLA
Left Sacrolateral [A fetal position] [Obstetrics]	LSL
Left Sacroposterior [A fetal position, the breech position] [Obstetrics]	LSP
Left Sacroposterior Position [of the fetus] [Obstetrics]	SLP
Left Sacrotransverse [A fetal position] [Obstetrics]	LST
Left Sacrum [Medicine] (KSC)	LS
Left Safety [Football] (DICI)	LS
Left Salivary [Gland]	LSAL
Left Salpingo-Oophorectomy [Gynecology] (CPH)	LSO
Left Scapuloanterior [A fetal position] [Obstetrics]	LScA
Left Scapuloanterior Position [of the fetus] [Obstetrics]	Sc LA
Left Scapuloposterior [A fetal position] [Obstetrics]	LScP
Left Scapuloposterior Position [of the fetus] [Obstetrics]	Sc LP
Left Second Entrance [Theater]	LSE
Left Shift	LS
Left Short Leg Brace [Medicine]	LSLB
Left Side	LS
Left Sign (IAA)	LS
Left Span (MAE)	LSp
Left Stage Center [A stage direction]	LSC
Left Stellate Ganglion Stimulation [Physiology]	LSGS
Left Sternal Border	LSB
Left Sternal Edge [Cardiology]	LSE
Left Store (SAA)	LST
Left Subclavian Artery [Anatomy] (AAMN)	LSA
Left Subclavian Artery [Anatomy] (DAVI)	LSCA
Left Subclavian Vein [Anatomy] (DAVI)	LSCV
Left Subclavian Vein [Anatomy]	LSV
Left Superior Rectus [Muscle] [Medicine] (DMAA)	LSR
Left Tackle [Football]	LT
Left Test Register (IAA)	LTR
Left Thigh	LT
Left to Count (DAVI)	LTC
Left to Right [Ratio] (DAVI)	L/R
Left to Right	L-R
Left to Right (MAE)	LR
Left to Right (DMAA)	L-R
Left Traffic Pattern [Aviation] (FAAC)	LP
Left [or Levo] Transposition of the Great Arteries [Also called corrected transposition] [Cardiology] (DAVI)	LTGA
Left Trendelenburg [Position] [Surgery] (DAVI)	LTren
Left Triceps [Anatomy] (DAVI)	LT
Left Umbilical Junction Box [Aerospace] (AAG)	LUJB
Left Unity Group [European political movement] (ECON)	LU
Left Upper [Medicine]	LU
Left Upper Arm [Medicine]	LUA
Left Upper Entrance [Theater]	LUE
Left Upper Extremity [Medicine]	LUE
Left Upper Extremity [Anatomy] (DMAA)	LUE
Left Upper Eyelid [Medicine]	LUL
Left Upper Limb [Medicine]	LUL
Left Upper Lobe [of lung] [Medicine]	LUL
Left Upper Lobe Bronchus [Anatomy]	LUB
Left Upper Outer Quadrant [of abdomen] [Medicine]	LUOQ
Left Upper Quadrant [of abdomen] [Medicine]	LUQ

Left Upper Sternal Border [Anatomy] (DAVI)	LUSB
Left Ureteral Orifice [Medicine]	LUO
Left Vastus Lateralis [Anatomy] (DAVI)	LVL
Left Ventral Fin [Fish anatomy]	LV
Left Ventral Gluteal [Injection site]	LVG
Left Ventricle [Cardiology]	LV
Left Ventricle Assist Device [Cardiology]	LVAD
Left Ventricle Assist System [Cardiology]	LVAS
Left Ventricle Internal Diameter [Cardiology]	LVID
Left Ventricle Outflow [Medicine] (DMAA)	LVO
Left Ventricle to Aorta Pressure Gradient [Cardiology] (DAVI)	AoP
Left Ventricular Aneurysm [Cardiology]	LVA
Left Ventricular Assist Device [An artificial organ]	LVD
Left Ventricular Assistance [Cardiology]	LVA
Left Ventricular Bypass [Cardiology]	LVB
Left Ventricular Cardiac Work Index [Physiology]	LCWI
Left Ventricular Developed Pressure [Medicine] (DMAA)	LVDP
Left Ventricular Diastolic Pressure [Cardiology]	LVDP
Left Ventricular Diastolic Volume [Cardiology] (MAE)	LVDV
Left Ventricular Dimension [Cardiology] (DMAA)	LVDI
Left Ventricular Dimension in Enddiastole [Cardiology] (DMAA)	LVDd
Left Ventricular Dysfunction [Cardiology] (DAVI)	LVD
Left Ventricular Ejection [Medicine] (DMAA)	LVE
Left Ventricular Ejection Fraction [Time] [Cardiology]	LVEF
Left Ventricular Ejection Time [Cardiology]	LVET
Left Ventricular Ejection Time Index [Cardiology]	LVETI
Left Ventricular End-Diastolic [Cardiology]	LVED
Left Ventricular End-Diastolic Circumference [Cardiology] (MAE)	LVEDC
Left Ventricular End-Diastolic Dimension [Cardiology]	LVEDD
Left Ventricular End-Diastolic Pressure [Cardiology] (MAE)	LVd
Left Ventricular End-Diastolic Pressure [Cardiology]	LVEDP
Left Ventricular End-Diastolic Pressure [Cardiology] (MAE)	LVEP
Left Ventricular End-Diastolic Volume [Cardiology]	LVEDV
Left Ventricular Endocardial Half [Cardiology] (DAVI)	LVEndo
Left Ventricular Enlargement [Cardiology]	LVE
Left Ventricular Epicardial Half [Cardiology] (DAVI)	LVEpi
Left Ventricular Failure [Cardiology]	LVF
Left Ventricular Filling Pressure [Cardiology]	LVFP
Left Ventricular Hypertrophy [Cardiology]	LVH
Left Ventricular Initial Diastolic Pressure [Cardiology] (AAMN)	LVIDP
Left Ventricular Insufficiency [Cardiology] (MAE)	LVI
Left Ventricular Internal Dimension [Cardiology] (DAVI)	LVID
Left Ventricular Ischemia [Medicine] (DMAA)	LVI
Left Ventricular Mass [Cardiology]	LVM
Left Ventricular Muscle Mass [Cardiology] (DAVI)	LVMM
Left Ventricular Outflow Tract [Cardiology] (CPH)	LVOT
left Ventricular Overactivity [Cardiology] (DAVI)	LVO
Left Ventricular Overactivity [Cardiology] (DAVI)	LVOA
Left Ventricular Peak Filling Rate [Cardiology] (DMAA)	LVPFR
Left Ventricular Posterior Wall [Cardiology] (DMAA)	LVPW
Left Ventricular Posterior Wall Thickness [Cardiology] (DAVI)	LVPWT
Left Ventricular Pressure [Cardiology]	LVP
Left Ventricular Pump [Cardiology]	LVP
Left Ventricular Septal Wall [Cardiology] (DAVI)	LVSW
Left Ventricular Strain [Cardiology] (DAVI)	LVS
Left Ventricular Strain [Cardiology]	LVS
Left Ventricular Stroke Volume [Cardiology]	LVSV
Left Ventricular Stroke Work [Cardiology]	LVSW
Left Ventricular Stroke Work Index [Cardiology]	LVSWI
Left Ventricular Subendocardia Lischemia [Cardiology] (DMAA)	LVSEMI
Left Ventricular Systolic Pressure [Cardiology]	LVSP
Left Ventricular Systolic Pressure Mean [Cardiology] (MAE)	LVs
Left Ventricular Tension [Cardiology] (MAE)	LVT
Left Ventricular Volume [Cardiology]	LVV
Left Ventricular Wall [Anatomy]	LVW
Left Ventricular Wall Thickness [Cardiology] (DMAA)	LVWT
Left Ventricular Work [Cardiology]	LVW
Left Ventricular Work Index [Cardiology]	LVWI
Left Ventriculography [Medicine]	LVG
Left Ventrogluteal [Anatomy] (DAVI)	LVG
Left Ventrolateral Gluteal [Site of injection] [Medicine]	LVLG
Left Visceral Ganglion [Medicine]	LVG
Left Visual Acuity [Medicine]	LVA
Left Visual Field [Psychometrics]	LVF
Left Wing	LW
Left Wing Down [Aviation]	LWD
Left Zero (IAA)	LZ
Left Zero Print (IAA)	LZP
Left-End-of-Tape	LEOT
Left-Hand Chain (MHDI)	LHC
Left-Hand Circular [Polarization] (IEEE)	LHC
Left-Hand Circularly Polarized [LASER waves]	LHCP
Left-Hand Circularly Polarized Mode (IAA)	LHM
Left-Hand Control (IAA)	LHCTL
Left-Hand Drive [AEC]	LHD
Left-Hand Drive [AEC]	LHDR
Left-Hand Equipment Bay [NASA] (KSC)	LHEB
Left-Hand Forward Equipment Bay [NASA] (KSC)	LHFEB
Left-Hand Head	LHH
Left-Hand Page (DGA)	LHP
Left-Hand Page (WDMC)	lhp
Left-Hand Panel	
Left-Hand Rule	LHR
Left-Hand Side	LHS
Left-Hand Side Console [NASA] (KSC)	LHSC

Left-Hand Side Storage Container [NASA] (KSC) .... LHSSC
Left-Hand Thread .... LHTH
Lefthanded (ABBR) .... LFTHDD
Left-Handed Pitcher [Baseball] .... LHP
Lefthandedly (ABBR) .... LFTHDY
Left-Handers Against the World [Defunct] (EA) .... LAW
Lefthanders International (EA) .... LHI
Left-In Telephone [Telecommunications] (TEL) .... LEF
Leftist (ABBR) .... LFTT
Leftover (ABBR) .... LFTOV
Left-Right Indicator .... LRI
Left-Sided Colon Cancer [Oncology] .... LSC
Leftwing (ABBR) .... LFTWG
Leftwinger (ABBR) .... LFTWR
Leg (IAA) .... LG
Leg before Wicket [Cricket] .... LBW
Leg Bye [Cricket] .... LB
Leg Exercise [Sports medicine] .... LE
Leg Godt [Play Well] [Acronym is brand of child's building toy] [Denmark] ...... LEGO
Leg Length Discrepancy [Orthopedics] (DAVI) .... LLD
Leg Multiple [Telegraph] [Telecommunications] (TEL) .... LM
Leg Negative Pressure (PDAA) .... LNP
LEG [Liquefied Energy Gas] Volume Measuring System .... LVMS
Lega dei Giovani Somali [Somali Youth League] .... LGS
Lega Lombarda [Italy] [Political party] (ECED) LL
Legacies (ROG) .... LEGS
Legacy (ROG) .... LEGY
Legacy (ABBR) .... LGCY
Legacy: A Journal of American Women Writers [A publication] (BRI) .... Legacy
Legacy Coordinating Council [Australia] LCC
Legacy Encapsulation Methodology .... LEM
Legacy Encapsulation Technology .... LET
Legacy International Youth Program [Later, LIYTP] (EA) .... LIYP
Legacy International Youth Training Program (EA) .... LIYTP
Legacy Resource Management Program (DOMA) .... LRMP
Legacy Software [NASDAQ symbol] (TTSB) .... LGCY
Legacy Software, Inc. [Associated Press] (SAG) .... LgacySft
Legacy Software, Inc. [NASDAQ symbol] (SAG) .... LGCY
Legal (AFM) .... LEG
Legal (ABBR) .... LGL
Legal .... LGL
Legal Abbreviations [Database] .... LABB
Legal Action Group [British] (DBA) .... LAG
Legal Advertiser [Chicago] [A publication] (DLA) .... Legal Adv
Legal Adviser .... LA
Legal Adviser [Chicago] [A publication] (DLA) .... Leg Adv
Legal Adviser [Denver] [A publication] (DLA) .... Legal Adv
Legal Advisory Committee [of NYSE] .... LAC
Legal Advocates for Women (EA) .... LAW
Legal Aid Commission of New South Wales [Australia] .... LACNSW
Legal Aid Commission of Queensland [Australia] .... LACQLD
Legal Aid Commission of Tasmania [Australia] .... LACT
Legal Aid Commission of the Northern Territory [Australia] .... LACNT
Legal Aid Commission of Western Australia .... LACWA
Legal Aid Office .... LAO
Legal Aid Review Committee .... LARC
Legal Aid Society (WDAA) .... LAS
Legal Aid Task Force .... LATF
Legal Aid Warranty [Fund providing legal services in case of arrest] .... LAW
Legal and Educational Aid to the Poor [Center] .... LEAP
Legal and Insurance Reporter [Pennsylvania] [A publication] (DLA) ..... Leg & Ins R
Legal and Insurance Reporter [Philadelphia, PA] [A publication]
    (DLA) .... Leg & Ins Rep
Legal and Insurance Reporter [Philadelphia, PA] [A publication]
    (DLA) .... Leg & Ins Rept
Legal and Magnanimous Side [Sarcastic reference to the government of
    Vietnam and its allies] (VNW) .... L & M
Legal Aspects of Medical Practice [A publication] (DLA) .... Legal Asp Med Prac
Legal Asset [Business term] .... LA
Legal Assistance for the Elderly .... LATE
Legal Assistance Officer .... LAO
Legal Assistant Management Association (EA) .... LAMA
Legal Associate Member of the Royal Town Planning Institute [British]
    (DBQ) .... LAMRTPI
Legal Attache [FBI agent posted at an American embassy] .... LEGAT
Legal Automated Army-Wide .... LAAW
Legal Bibliography [A publication] (DLA) .... Leg Bibl
Legal Bond [Investment term] .... LB
Legal Branch, Department of External Affairs [Direction des Operations
    Juridiques, Ministere des Affaires Exterieures] Ottawa, Ontario [Library
    symbol National Library of Canada] (NLC) .... OOELB
Legal Chronicle Reports [Pottsville, PA] [A publication] (DLA) .... Leg Chron Rep
Legal Chronicle Reports, Edited by Foster [Pennsylvania] [A publication]
    (DLA) .... Foster
Legal Chronicle Reports, Edited by Foster [Pennsylvania] [A publication]
    (DLA) .... Leg Chron
Legal Committee (MCD) LC
Legal Counsel for the Elderly (EA) .... LCE
Legal Currency (ADA) LC
Legal Department, Steinberg, Inc., Montreal, Quebec [Library symbol
    National Library of Canada] (NLC) .... QMST
Legal Deposit (ADA) .... LD
Legal Discriminator (MCD) .... LD
Legal Division [Coast Guard] L

Legal Education Institute, United States Civil Service Commission
    (DLA) .... LEICSC
Legal Electronic Network and Database (IID) .... LEGEND
Legal Enforcement Policy Division [Environmental Protection Agency]
    (GFGA) .... LEPD
Legal Environmental Assistance Foundation (EA) .... LEAF
Legal Examiner [London or New York] [1831-35; 1862-68; 1869-72]
    [A publication] (DLA) .... Leg Exam
Legal Examiner and Law Chronicle [London] [A publication]
    (DLA) .... Leg Exam & LC
Legal Examiner and Medical Jurist [London] [A publication]
    (DLA) .... Leg Exam & Med J
Legal Examiner, New Series [England] [A publication] (DLA) ..... Leg Exam NS
Legal Examiner Weekly Reporter [A publication] (DLA) ..... Leg Exam WR
Legal Exchange [Des Moines, IA] [A publication] (DLA) .... Leg Exch
Legal Fees and Costs Board [Australia] .... LFCB
Legal Gazette [A publication] (DLA) .... Leg Gaz
Legal Gazette (Pennsylvania) [A publication] (DLA) .... Legal Gaz (PA)
Legal Gazette (Pennsylvania) [A publication] (DLA) .... PA Leg Gaz
Legal Gazette (Pennsylvania) [A publication] (DLA) .... PA LG
Legal Gazette Reports (Campbell) [Pennsylvania] [A publication]
    (DLA) .... PA Leg Gaz
Legal Gazette Reports (Campbell) [Pennsylvania] [A publication] (DLA) ..... PA LG
Legal Guide [A publication] (DLA) .... Leg G
Legal Holiday (MHDW) .... LH
Legal Industry Advisory Council (EA) .... LIAC
Legal Information and Reference Services [General Accounting Office]
    (IID) .... LIRS
Legal Information Bulletin [A publication] (DLA) .... Leg Inf Bul
Legal Information On-Line [Ministry of Labour] [Hamilton, ON] [Information
    service or system] (IID) .... LIOL
Legal Information Through Electronics [Air Force] .... LITE
Legal Inquirer [London] [A publication] (DLA) .... Leg Inq
Legal Intelligencer [A publication] (DLA) .... Leg Int
Legal Intelligencer [A publication] (DLA) .... Leg Intel
Legal Intelligencer [A publication] (DLA) .... Leg Intell
Legal Intelligencer [A publication] (DLA) .... Leg Intl
Legal Intelligencer [A publication] (DLA) .... Legal Int
Legal Intelligencer [A publication] (DLA) .... Legal Intel
Legal Intelligencer [A publication] (DLA) .... Legal Intell
Legal Intelligencer [A publication] (DLA) LI
Legal Inverse Path [Physics] .... LIP
Legal Issues of European Integration [A publication] (ILCA) ..... Leg Issues
Legal Journals Index [Information service or system] (IID) .... LJI
Legal Maxims with Observations by George Frederick Wharton
    [A publication] (DLA) .... Whart
Legal Medicine .... LM
Legal Member of the Royal Town Planning Institute [British] (DBQ) ..... LMRTPI
Legal Member of the Town Planning Institute [British] (DLA) .... LMTPI
Legal Miscellany [Ceylon] [A publication] (DLA) .... Leg Misc
Legal Miscellany and Review [India] [A publication] (DLA) ..... Leg Misc & Rev
Legal News [Canada] [A publication] (DLA) .... Leg News
Legal News [Canada] [A publication] (DLA) .... LN
Legal Notes on Local Government [New York] [A publication] (DLA) ..... Leg Notes
Legal Notice (OICC) .... LN
Legal Notification [Ghana] [A publication] (DLA) .... LN
Legal Observer [London] [A publication] (DLA) .... Leg Obs
Legal Observer [London] [A publication] (DLA) .... Legal Obser
Legal Observer [British] .... LO
Legal Observer and Solicitor's Journal [London] [A publication] (DLA) ..... Leg Obs
Legal Office Information System .... LOIS
Legal Officer .... LO
Legal Opinion [Pennsylvania] [A publication] (DLA) .... Leg Op
Legal Opinion [Pennsylvania] [A publication] (DLA) .... Leg Ops (PA)
Legal Opinion [1870-73] [A publication] (DLA) .... LO
Legal Practices Update [A publication] .... LPU
Legal Practitioner and Solicitor's Journal [1846-47, 1849-51]
    [A publication] (DLA) .... Leg Pract & Sol J
Legal Practitioners' Admission Board [Australia] .... LPAB
Legal Practitioners Complaints Committee [South Australia] .... LPCC
Legal Practitioners Disciplinary Tribunal [South Australia] .... LPDT
Legal Process [British] .... LP
Legal Procurator (WDAA) .... LP
Legal Public Library, Alberta [Library symbol National Library of Canada]
    (NLC) .... ALEG
Legal Public Library, Legal, AB, Canada [Library symbol] [Library of
    Congress] (LCLS) .... CaALEG
Legal Rate of Interest [Business term] (MHDB) .... LROI
Legal Record [Detroit, MI] [A publication] (DLA) .... Leg Rec
Legal Record Reports [Pennsylvania] [A publication] (DLA) .... Leg R
Legal Record Reports [Pennsylvania] [A publication] (DLA) .... Leg Rec Rep
Legal Reference Centre, Manufacturers' Life Insurance Co., Waterloo,
    Ontario [Library symbol National Library of Canada] (BIB) .... OWTM
Legal Reformer [1819-20] [A publication] (DLA) .... Leg Ref
Legal Remembrancer [Calcutta] [A publication] (DLA) .... Leg Rem
Legal Reporter [1840-43] [Ireland] [A publication] (DLA) .... Leg Rep
Legal Reporter [Australia A publication] .... Legal Rep
Legal Reporter, Irish Courts [A publication] (DLA) .... Leg Rep (Ir)
Legal Reporter, New Series [Tennessee] [A publication] (DLA) .... Legal Rep
Legal Reporter Parallel to Shannon Cases [Tennessee] [A publication]
    (DLA) .... Leg R (Tenn)
Legal Reporter Special Leave Supplement [A publication] .... Leg Rep SL
Legal Research Center [NASDAQ symbol] (TTSB) .... LRCI
Legal Research Center, Inc. [Associated Press] (SAG) .... LegalR
Legal Research Center, Inc. [NASDAQ symbol] (SAG) .... LRCI

Legal Research Service [*Registered service mark*] (IID) ..... LEXIS
Legal Reserve (MHDW) ..... LR
Legal Resource Centre, Legal Services Society, Vancouver, British Columbia [*Library symbol National Library of Canada*] (NLC) ..... BVALS
Legal Resource Index [*Information Access Corp.*] [*Bibliographic database*] [*Information service or system*] (IID) ..... LRI
Legal Response; Child Advocacy and Protection [*A publication*] (DLA) ..... Legal Resp Child Adv Protection
Legal Review [*1812-13*] [*London*] [*A publication*] (DLA) ..... Leg Rev
Legal Scholastic Aptitude Test (HGAA) ..... LSAT
Legal Scroll ..... LS
Legal Services Corp. [*Government agency*] ..... LSC
Legal Services, Environment Canada [*Services Juridiques, Environnement Canada*] **Ottawa, Ontario** [*Library symbol National Library of Canada*] (NLC) ..... OOELS
Legal Services for Children (EA) ..... LSC
Legal Services for Prisoners with Children (EA) ..... LSPC
Legal Services for the Elderly (EA) ..... LSE
Legal Services for the Elderly Poor [*Later, LSE*] (EA) ..... LSEP
Legal Services Group ..... LSG
Legal Support Inspection [*Clean Water Act*] [*Environmental Protection Agency*] (EPA) ..... LSI
Legal Support Services Branch [*General Accounting Office*] [*Information service or system*] (IID) ..... LSSB
Legal Technology Group [*Information service or system*] (IID) ..... LTG
Legal Tender [*Currency*] ..... LT
Legal Tender Cases [*A publication*] (DLA) ..... Leg T Cas
Legal Title [*Business term*] ..... LT
Legal Training [*Navy British*] ..... lt
Legal Volt LV
Legal Weight (WDAA) ..... LEG WT
Legal World [*India*] [*A publication*] (DLA) ..... Leg W
Legal Year Book [*London*] [*A publication*] (DLA) ..... Leg YB
Legalise Cannabis Campaign [*British*] (DBA) LCC
Legalism (ABBR) ..... LGLM
Legalist (ABBR) ..... LGLST
Legalistic (ABBR) ..... LGLSTC
Legalistic (ABBR) ..... LGLTC
Legalistically (ABBR) ..... LGLSTCY
Legality (ABBR) ..... LGLT
Legalization (ABBR) ..... LGLZN
Legalize (ABBR) ..... LGLZ
Legalize Marijuana [*Acronym is used for name of an organization*] ..... LEMAR
Legalized (ABBR) ..... LGLZD
Legalizing (ABBR) ..... LGLZG
Legally (ABBR) ..... LGLY
Legally Committed (BABM) ..... LEG COM
Legally Correct Interpretation [*of the ABM treaty*] LCI
Legally Oriented Language [*Programming language project*] [*British*] (NITA) ..... LEGOL
Legally Separated (MAE) ..... LS
Leganda [*Congo*] [*ICAO location identifier*] (ICLI) ..... FCPE
Legaspi [*Philippines*] [*Seismograph station code, US Geological Survey*] (SEIS) ..... LGP
Legaspi [*Philippines*] [*Airport symbol*] (OAG) ..... LGP
Legate ..... LEG
Legate (ABBR) ..... LGT
Legatee (ABBR) ..... LGTE
Legatio ad Gaium [*of Philo Judaeus*] [*Classical studies*] (OCD) ..... Leg
Legation (ABBR) ..... LGTN
Legato [*Smoothly and Connectedly*] [*Music*] ..... LEG
Legato (ABBR) ..... LGTO
Legato Systems [*NASDAQ symbol*] (TTSB) ..... LGTO
Legato Systems, Inc. [*Associated Press*] (SAG) ..... Legato
Legato Systems, Inc. [*NASDAQ symbol*] (SAG) ..... LGTO
Legazpi, Albay [*Philippines*] [*ICAO location identifier*] (ICLI) ..... RPMP
Leg-Calve-Perthes Disease [*Medicine*] ..... L-C-P
Lege Artis [*According to the Art*] [*Pharmacy*] ..... LA
Lege Quaeso [*Please Read*] [*Latin*] ..... LQ
Legend [*Numismatics*] ..... LEG
Legend ..... legd
Legend (VRA) ..... lgd
Legend (ABBR) ..... LGND
Legend Properties, Inc. [*Associated Press*] (SAG) ..... Legend
Legend Properties, Inc. [*NASDAQ symbol*] (SAG) ..... LPRO
Legendary (ABBR) ..... LGNDY
Legerdemain (ABBR) ..... LGDMN
Leges [*Laws*] [*Latin*] (ROG) L
Leges [*Laws*] [*Latin*] (ILCA) ..... Leg
Leges [*Laws*] [*Latin*] LL
Leges Alfredi [*Laws of King Alfred*] [*Latin A publication*] (DLA) ..... Leg Alfred
Leges Alfredi [*Laws of King Alfred*] [*Latin A publication*] (DLA) ..... LL Alfredi
Leges Canuti [*Laws of King Canute or Knut*] [*Latin A publication*] (DLA) ..... Leg Canut
Leges Edmundi [*Laws of King Edmund*] [*Latin A publication*] (DLA) ..... Leg Edm
Leges Ethelredi [*Laws of King Ethelred*] [*Latin A publication*] (DLA) ..... Leg Ethel
Leges Portuum [*A publication*] (DLA) ..... Leg Port
Legg Mason, Inc. [*Associated Press*] (SAG) ..... LeggMas
Legg Mason, Inc. [*NYSE symbol*] (SPSG) ..... LM
Legge [*Law, Act, Statute*] [*Italian*] (ILCA) L
Legge on Outlawry [*A publication*] (DLA) ..... Leg Out
Legge on Outlawry [*A publication*] (DLA) ..... Legg Out
Leggett & Platt [*NYSE symbol*] (TTSB) ..... LEG
Leggett & Platt, Inc. [*NYSE symbol*] (SPSG) ..... LEG
Leggett & Platt, Inc. [*Associated Press*] (SAG) ..... LegPlat
Leggett on Bills of Lading [*A publication*] (DLA) ..... Legg Bills L
Leggett's Reports [*India*] [*A publication*] (DLA) ..... Legg
Leggiero [*Light and Rapid*] [*Music*] ..... LEGG
Leggiero [*Light and Rapid*] [*Music*] ..... Leggo
Legging (ABBR) ..... LGG
Leggoons Inc. [*NASDAQ symbol*] (TTSB) ..... LGNS
Leggo's Chancery Forms [*Ontario*] [*A publication*] (DLA) ..... Leg Ch Forms
Leggo's Chancery Practice [*Ontario*] [*A publication*] (DLA) ..... Leg Ch Pr
Leggy (ABBR) ..... LGY
Leghorn (ABBR) ..... LGHN
Legibility (ABBR) ..... LGBT
Legible (ABBR) ..... LGB
Legibly (ABBR) ..... LGBY
Leg-Inducing Membrane [*Entomology*] ..... LIM
Legion (ABBR) ..... LGN
Legion ..... LGN
Legion d'Honneur [*French decoration*] ..... L d'H
Legion d'Honneur [*French decoration*] ..... LH
Legion of Christ the King [*Defunct*] (EA) ..... LCK
Legion of Frontiersmen [*British military*] (DMA) ..... LF
Legion of Greeks from Egypt and the Middle East [*Australia An association*] ..... LGEME
Legion of Guardsmen (EA) ..... LOG
Legion of Merit [*Military decoration*] ..... LM
Legion of Merit [*Military award*] ..... LOM
Legion of Valor of the United States of America (EA) ..... LVUSA
Legion of Young Polish Women (EA) ..... LYPW
Legion Resources Ltd. [*Vancouver Stock Exchange symbol*] ..... LGN
Legionaire (ABBR) ..... LGNAR
Legionaries of Christ [*Roman Catholic men's religious order*] LC
Legionaries of Christ (TOCD) lc
Legionarios del Trabajo in America (EA) ..... LTA
Legionary (ABBR) ..... LGNY
Legionella [*A bacteria*] (DAVI) L
Legionella-Like Organisms [*Medicine*] ..... LLO
Legionnaire's Disease ..... LD
Legionnaires Disease Bacillus [*Medicine*] (DMAA) ..... LDB
Legionnaire's Disease Bacterium ..... LDB
Legis Comparativae Magister [*Master of Comparative Law*] [*Latin*] (WGA) ..... LCM
Legislate (ABBR) ..... LGLA
Legislated (ABBR) ..... LGLAD
Legislating (ABBR) ..... LGLAG
Legislation [*or Legislature*] ..... LEG
Legislation ..... LEGISLN
Legislation [*Legal shorthand*] (LWAP) ..... LEGISN
Legislation (ABBR) ..... LGLAN
Legislative [*or Legislature*] ..... LEGIS
Legislative (ADA) ..... LEGISL
Legislative [*Legal shorthand*] (LWAP) ..... LEGISV
Legislative ..... Legve
Legislative (ABBR) ..... LGLAY
Legislative Action on Smoking and Health (EA) ..... LASH
Legislative Affairs ..... LA
Legislative Alliance of Creative Arts Therapies [*Defunct*] (EA) ..... LACAT
Legislative and Liaison [*Military*] ..... L & L
Legislative Assembly ..... LA
Legislative Assembly of New South Wales [*Australia*] ..... LANSW
Legislative Assembly of Queensland [*Australia*] ..... LAQ
Legislative Assembly of the Australian Capital Territory ..... LAACT
Legislative Assembly of the Northern Territory [*Australia*] ..... LANT
Legislative Assembly of Victoria [*Australia*] ..... LAV
Legislative Assembly of Western Australia ..... LAWA
Legislative Assistant [*US Congress*] ..... LA
Legislative Authorization Program Information System [*General Accounting Office*] [*Defunct*] (IID) ..... LAPIS
Legislative Council [*British*] LC
Legislative Council [*Hong Kong*] (ECON) ..... Legco
Legislative Council for Photogrammetry [*Later, MAPPS*] (EA) ..... LCP
Legislative Council of Colorado, Denver, CO [*Library symbol Library of Congress*] (LCLS) ..... CoDLC
Legislative Council of New South Wales [*Australia*] ..... LCNSW
Legislative Council of South Australia ..... LCSA
Legislative Council of Tasmania [*Australia*] ..... LCT
Legislative Council of Victoria [*Australia*] LCV
Legislative Council of Western Australia ..... LCWA
Legislative Data Base [*Department of Energy*] [*Information service or system*] (IID) ..... LDB
Legislative Department [*Generic term*] (ROG) ..... LD
Legislative Extended Assistance Group [*University of Iowa*] [*Research center*] (RCD) ..... LEAG
Legislative Indexing Vocabulary LIV
Legislative Information and Status System [*for House of Representatives*] ..... LEGIS
Legislative Information Network Corp. [*Information service or system*] (IID) ..... LINC
Legislative Information Service [*New Jersey State Legislature*] [*Trenton*] [*Information service or system*] (IID) ..... LIS
Legislative Information System [*National Conference of State Legislatures*] [*Information service or system*] (IID) ..... LIS
Legislative Instrument [*Ghana*] [*1960-*] [*A publication*] (ILCA) LI
Legislative Liaison LL
Legislative Liaison Office (AAGC) ..... LLO
Legislative Library Board, Legislative Reference Library, Austin, TX [*Library symbol Library of Congress*] (LCLS) ..... TxAuL

Legislative Library [*Bibliotheque Legislative*] **Fredericton, New Brunswick** [*Library symbol National Library of Canada*] (NLC) .... NBFL

Legislative Library, Halifax, Nova Scotia [*Library symbol National Library of Canada*] (NLC) .... NSHL

Legislative Library, Halifax, NS, Canada [*Library symbol Library of Congress*] (LCLS) .... CaNSHL

Legislative Library of British Columbia [*UTLAS symbol*] .... LEG

Legislative Library of Manitoba, Winnipeg, Manitoba [*Library symbol National Library of Canada*] (NLC) .... MWP

Legislative Library of Ontario, Toronto, Ontario [*Library symbol National Library of Canada*] (NLC) .... OTL

Legislative Library of Saskatchewan, Office of the Archives Division, Regina, SK, Canada [*Library symbol Library of Congress*] (LCLS) .... CaSRA

Legislative Library of Saskatchewan, Regina, Saskatchewan [*Library symbol National Library of Canada*] (NLC) .... SRL

Legislative Library of Saskatchewan, Regina, SK, Canada [*Library symbol Library of Congress*] (LCLS) .... CaSRL

Legislative Library, St. John's, Newfoundland [*Library symbol National Library of Canada*] (NLC) .... NFSL

Legislative Library, St. John's, NF, Canada [*Library symbol Library of Congress*] (LCLS) .... CaNfSL

Legislative Library, Victoria, BC, Canada [*Library symbol Library of Congress*] (LCLS) .... CaBViP

Legislative Library, Victoria, British Columbia [*Library symbol National Library of Canada*] (NLC) .... BVIP

Legislative/Political Action Team .... L/PAT

Legislative Proposal (GFGA) .... LP

Legislative Reference Library - Minnesota Document Collection, St. Paul, MN [*OCLC symbol*] (OCLC) .... MLD

Legislative Reference Service [*Later, Congressional Research Service*] [*Library of Congress*] .... LRS

Legislative Research Commission, Library, Frankfort, KY [*Library symbol*] [*Library of Congress*] (LCLS) .... KyFLR

Legislative Service Center [*Washington State Legislature*] [*Information service or system*] (IID) .... LSC

Legislative Strategy Group [*Reagan administration*] .... LSG

Legislative Studies Quarterly [*A publication*] (DLA) .... Legis Stud Q

Legislator [*Legal shorthand*] (LWAP) .... LEGISOR

Legislator (ABBR) .... LGLAR

Legislators, Lawyers, and Lead [*Forces mustered by opponents of proposed nuclear-waste burial sites*] .... 3L's

Legislature [*Legal shorthand*] (LWAP) .... LEGISURE

Legislature (ABBR) .... LGLAR

Legit [*He, or She, Reads*] [*Latin*] .... LEG

Legitimacy Declaration Act [*British*] (ROG) .... LDA

Legitimate L

Legitimate .... LEGIT

Legitimate (DSUE) .... LGITMA

Legitimate (ABBR) .... LA

Legitimate Access [*British police term*] LC

Legitimate Child .... LGITMAD

Legitimated (ABBR) .... LGITMY

Legitimately (ABBR) .... LGITMAG

Legitimating (ABBR) .... LGITIT

Legitimist (ABBR) .... LGITIZ

Legitimize (ABBR) .... LGITIZD

Legitimized (ABBR) .... LGITIZG

Legitimizing (ABBR) .... LGITMC

Legitmacy (ABBR) ....

L'Eglise Historique St-Henri-de-Barachois, Robichaud, NB, Canada [*Library symbol*] [*Library of Congress*] (LCLS) .... CaNBReH

L'Eglise Historique St-Henri-De-Barachois, Robichaud, New Brunswick [*Library symbol National Library of Canada*] (NLC) .... NBREH

Legrest Pin Handle .... LPH

Leguleian [*1850-65*] [*A publication*] (DLA) .... Legul

Legum [*Of Laws*] [*Latin*] (ADA) LL

Legum [*Latin*] .... LA

Legum Allegoriae [*Philo*] (BJA) .... LB

Legum Baccalaureus [*Bachelor of Laws*] .... LLB

Legum Baccalaureus [*Bachelor of Laws*] [*Latin*] .... LLD

Legum Doctor [*Doctor of Laws*] [*Latin*] .... LLM

Legum Magister [*Master of Laws*] [*Latin*] .... LGU

Legume (ABBR) .... LYV

Legume Yellows Virus [*Plant pathology*] .... LGUNU

Leguminous (ABBR) .... LEG

Legunt [*They Read*] [*Latin*] (ADA) IXL

Leh [*India*] [*Airport symbol*] (OAG) .... WCKT

Lehigh Acres, FL [*FM radio station call letters*] .... WWCL

Lehigh Acres, FL [*AM radio station call letters*] .... LEANS

Lehigh Analog Simulator (IAA) ....

[*The*] Lehigh & Hudson River Railway Co. [*Absorbed into Consolidated Rail Corp.*] .... L & HR

[*The*] Lehigh & Hudson River Railway Co. [*Absorbed into Consolidated Rail Corp.*] [*AAR code*] .... LHR

Lehigh & New England Railway Co. [*Absorbed into Consolidated Rail Corp.*] .... L & NE

Lehigh & New England Railway Co. [*Absorbed into Consolidated Rail Corp.*] [*AAR code*] .... LNE

Lehigh Automatic Device for Efficient Retrieval [*Center for Information Sciences, Lehigh University*] [*Bethlehem, PA*] [*Computer science*] .... LEADER

Lehigh County Historical Society, Allentown, PA [*Library symbol Library of Congress*] (LCLS) .... PAtL

Lehigh County Law Journal [*Pennsylvania*] [*A publication*] (DLA) .... Leh

Lehigh County Law Journal [*Pennsylvania*] [*A publication*] (DLA) .... Leh Co LJ (PA)

Lehigh County Law Journal [*A publication*] (DLA) .... Leh LJ

Lehigh County Law Journal [*Pennsylvania*] [*A publication*] (DLA) .... Lehigh Co LJ

Lehigh County Law Journal [*Pennsylvania*] [*A publication*] (DLA) .... Lehigh LJ

Lehigh Group [*NYSE symbol*] (TTSB) .... LEI

Lehigh Group, Inc. [*Formerly, LUI Group*] [*Associated Press*] (SAG) .... LehighGp

Lehigh Group, Inc. [*Formerly, LUI Group*] [*NYSE symbol*] (SAG) LVI

Lehigh University (GAGS) .... Lehigh U

Lehigh University, Bethlehem, PA [*OCLC symbol*] (OCLC) .... LYU

Lehigh University, Bethlehem, PA [*Library symbol Library of Congress*] (LCLS) .... PBL

Lehigh University Computing Center [*Pennsylvania*] [*Research center*] (RCD) .... LUCC

Lehigh Valley Association of Independent College Libraries [*Library network*] .... LVAIC

Lehigh Valley Law Reporter [*Pennsylvania*] [*A publication*] (DLA) .... Leh VLR (PA)

Lehigh Valley Law Reporter [*Pennsylvania*] [*A publication*] (DLA) .... Lehigh

Lehigh Valley Law Reporter [*Pennsylvania*] [*A publication*] (DLA) .... Lehigh Val L Rep

Lehigh Valley Law Reporter [*Pennsylvania*] [*A publication*] (DLA) .... Lehigh Val Law Rep

Lehigh Valley Law Reporter [*Pennsylvania*] [*A publication*] (DLA) .... Lehigh Val LR

Lehigh Valley Law Reporter [*Pennsylvania*] [*A publication*] (DLA) .... LV Rep

Lehigh Valley Railroad Co. [*Absorbed into Consolidated Rail Corp.*] [*AAR code*] LV

Lehigh Valley Railroad Co. [*Absorbed into Consolidated Rail Corp.*] .... LVRR

Lehighton, PA [*Location identifier FAA*] (FAAL) .... LQX

Lehighton, PA [*AM radio station call letters*] .... WYNS

Lehman Br Amgen'YEELD ''97 [*AMEX symbol*] (TTSB) .... AYN

Lehman Br G1 Tele'SUNS'2000 [*AMEX symbol*] (TTSB) .... SXT

Lehman Br Hldg 8.30%'QUICS' [*NYSE symbol*] (TTSB) .... LEQ

Lehman Br Holdngs [*NYSE symbol*] (TTSB) .... LEH

Lehman Br Micron'YEELD''97 [*AMEX symbol*] (TTSB) .... MUY

Lehman Br Reg'l Bk'SUNS' 1996 [*AMEX symbol*] (TTSB) .... BKG

Lehman Brothers [*NYSE symbol*] (SAG) .... LEH

Lehman Brothers [*Associated Press*] (SAG) LehBr35

Lehman Brothers [*Associated Press*] (SAG) .... LehmBr

Lehman Brothers [*Associated Press*] (SAG) .... LehSTc

Lehman Brothers [*NYSE symbol*] (SAG) .... LEQ

Lehman Brothers Holdings, Inc. [*Associated Press*] (SAG) .... LehAMGN

Lehman Brothers Holdings, Inc. [*Associated Press*] (SAG) .... LehORCL

Lehman Brothers, Inc. [*AMEX symbol*] (SAG) .... AYN

Lehman Brothers, Inc. [*AMEX symbol*] (SAG) .... BKG

Lehman Brothers, Inc. [*AMEX symbol*] (SAG) .... EXA

Lehman Brothers, Inc. [*Associated Press*] (SAG) .... LB Eur

Lehman Brothers, Inc. [*Associated Press*] (SAG) .... LehGTel

Lehman Brothers, Inc. [*Associated Press*] (SAG) .... LeHK

Lehman Brothers, Inc. [*Associated Press*] (SAG) .... LehMU

Lehman Brothers, Inc. [*Associated Press*] (SAG) .... LehRgBk

Lehman Brothers, Inc. [*Associated Press*] (SAG) .... LeJY

Lehman Brothers, Inc. [*AMEX symbol*] (SAG) .... LHW

Lehman Brothers, Inc. [*AMEX symbol*] (SAG) .... LYN

Lehman Brothers, Inc. [*AMEX symbol*] (SAG) .... MUY

Lehman Brothers, Inc. [*AMEX symbol*] (SAG) .... SXT

Lehman Brothers, Inc. [*AMEX symbol*] (SAG) .... YBW

Lehman Brothers Latin American Growth Fund [*NYSE symbol*] (SAG) .... LLF

Lehman Caves National Monument .... LECA

Lehman Caves National Monument, Baker, NV [*Library symbol Library of Congress*] (LCLS) .... NvBL

Lehman College, Bronx, NY [*OCLC symbol*] (OCLC) .... VYL

Lehman Corp., New York, NY [*Library symbol Library of Congress*] (LCLS) .... NNLehman

Lehman Investment Opportunity Note .... LION

Lehn & Fink Products Co., Montvale, NJ [*Library symbol Library of Congress*] (LCLS) .... NjMovL

Lehndorff Canadian Prop. [*Limited Partnership Units*] [*Toronto Stock Exchange symbol*] .... LCP

Lehu [*Papua New Guinea*] [*Airport symbol*] (OAG) .... LHP

Leibovitz-Emory Medium [*Microbiology*] .... LEM

Leibovitz-Emory Medium for Viral Cultures [*Microbiology*] .... LEV

Leicester [*British ICAO location identifier*] (ICLI) .... EGBG

Leicester Intravenous Magnesium Intervention Trial [*Cardiology study*] .... LIMIT

Leicester, MA [*AM radio station call letters*] .... WVNE

Leicester Records [*Municipal Courts, 1103-1603*] [*England*] [*A publication*] (DLA) .... Bateson

Leicester's Straits Law Reports [*Malaya*] [*A publication*] (DLA) .... SLR Leic

Leicester's Straits Law Reports [*Malaya*] [*A publication*] (DLA) .... SLR Leicester

Leicestershire [*County in England*] (ROG) .... LEIC

Leicestershire [*County in England*] .... LEICS

Leicestershire and Derbyshire Yeomanry [*Military unit*] [*British*] .... LDY

Leicestershire Imperial Yeomanry [*British military*] (DMA) .... LIY

Leicestershire Regiment [*Military unit*] [*British*] .... LR

Leicestershire Technical Information Service [*British*] (NITA) .... LETIS

Leicestershire Yeomanry Cavalry (Prince Albert's Own) [*British military*] (DMA) .... LYC

Leicestershire Yeomanry (Prince Albert's Own) [*British military*] (DMA) .... LY

Leichte Infanteriegeschuetz [*Light Infantry Howitzer*] [*German military - World War II*] .... LIG

Leichte Infanteriekolonne [*Light Infantry Supply Column*] [*German military - World War II*] .... LIK

Leichtgeschuetz [*Light gun for airborne operations*] [*German military - World War II*] .... LG

Leichtverwundet; Leichtverwundeter [*Slightly wounded; minor casualty*] [*German military - World War II*] .... LEV

Leiden-Berkeley Deep Survey [*Astronomy*] .... LBDS

Leif Ericson Society International (EA) .... LESI

Leigh and Cave's English Crown Cases Reserved [*1861-65*] [*A publication*] (DLA) .... L & C

Leigh and Cave's English Crown Cases Reserved [*1861-65*] [*A publication*] (DLA) ... L & CCC
Leigh and Cave's English Crown Cases Reserved [*1861-65*] [*A publication*] (DLA) ... Le & Ca
Leigh and Cave's English Crown Cases Reserved [*1861-65*] [*A publication*] (DLA) ... Leigh & C
Leigh and Cave's English Crown Cases Reserved [*1861-65*] [*A publication*] (DLA) ... Leigh & CCC
Leigh and Dalzell. Conversion of Property [*1825*] [*A publication*] (DLA) ... L & D Conv
Leigh and Dalzell. Conversion of Property [*1825*] [*A publication*] (DLA) ... Leigh & D Conv
Leigh and Le Marchant. Elections [*4th ed.*] [*1885*] [*A publication*] (DLA) ... L & LeM
Leigh and Le Marchant. Elections [*4th ed.*] [*1885*] [*A publication*] (DLA) ... Leigh & LM Elec
Leigh Creek [*Australia ICAO location identifier*] (ICLI) ... AALC
Leigh Creek [*Australia ICAO location identifier*] (ICLI) ... APLC
Leigh Creek [*Australia Airport symbol*] (OAG) ... LGH
Leigh Instruments Ltd. [*Toronto Stock Exchange symbol*] ... LHI
Leigh Instruments Ltd., Carleton Place, ON, Canada [*Library symbol Library of Congress*] (LCLS) ... CaOCpL
Leigh Instruments Ltd., Carleton Place, Ontario [*Library symbol National Library of Canada*] (NLC) ... OCPL
Leigh Light [*British military*] (DMA) ... L/L
Leigh McCloskey Fan Club (EA) ... LMFC
Leigh's Abridgment of the Law of Nisi Prius [*1838*] [*A publication*] (DLA) ... Leigh Abr
Leigh's Abridgment of the Law of Nisi Prius [*1838*] [*A publication*] (DLA) ... Leigh NP
Leigh's Game Act [*A publication*] (DLA) ... Leigh GA
Leigh's Virginia Supreme Court Reports [*1829-42*] [*A publication*] (DLA) ... Leigh
Leigh's Virginia Supreme Court Reports [*1829-42*] [*A publication*] (DLA) ... Leigh (VA)
Leighton Barracks [*Germany ICAO location identifier*] (ICLI) ... EDOY
Leijona [*Record label*] [*Finland*] ... Lei
Leinster [*Australia Airport symbol*] (OAG) ... LER
Leinster Regiment [*Military unit*] [*British*] (ROG) ... LEINS R
Leiomyblastoma [*Pathology*] (DAVI) ... LMB
Leiomyoblastoma [*Medicine*] ... LB
Leiomyoma [*Gynecology*] (DAVI) ... leio
Leiomyosarcoma [*Oncology*] ... LMS
Leiomyosarcoma [*Medicine*] ... LS
Leipheim [*Germany ICAO location identifier*] (ICLI) ... EDSD
Leipzig [*Germany ICAO location identifier*] (ICLI) ... ETLS
Leipzig [*German Democratic Republic*] [*Seismograph station code, US Geological Survey Closed*] (SEIS) ... LEI
Leipzig [*City in East Germany*] (ROG) ... LEIP
Leipzig [*Germany Airport symbol*] (OAG) ... LEJ
Leipzig [*City and district in East Germany*] (ROG) ... LPZ
Leipzig/Mockau [*Germany ICAO location identifier*] (ICLI) ... ETLM
Leipziger Aegyptologische Studien [*A publication*] (BJA) ... LAS
Leipziger Semitische Studien [*A publication*] (BJA) ... LSS
Leipziger Studien zur Klassischen Philosophie [*A publication*] (OCD) ... Leipz Stud
Leiria [*Portugal ICAO location identifier*] (ICLI) ... LPJF
Leirvogur [*Iceland*] [*Geomagnetic observatory code*] ... LRV
Leishman-Donovan (Bodies) [*Microbiology*] ... L-D
Leishmania [*Microbiology*] (MAE) ... L
Leishmania braziliensis braziliensis [*Microbiology*] ... Lbb
Leisure ... LSRE
Leisure ... LSUR
Leisure Activities Blank [*Vocational guidance test*] ... LAB
Leisure & Hotel Appointments [*Recruitment for the hotel, leisure, and travel industries*] [*British*] ... LHA
Leisure and Outdoor Furniture Association [*British*] (DBA) ... LOFA
Leisure Concepts [*NASDAQ symbol*] (SAG) ... LCIC
Leisure Counseling [*Medicine*] (MEDA) ... LC
Leisure Diagnostic Battery [*Psychology*] (EDAC) ... LDB
Leisure International Airways Ltd. [*British ICAO designator*] (FAAC) ... ULE
Leisure, Recreation, and Tourism Abstracts [*Database*] [*Commonwealth Agricultural Bureaux International*] [*Information service or system*] (CRD) ... LRTA
Leisure Studies Association [*British*] ... LSA
Leisure Time Activity ... LTA
Leisure-Interest Class (MEDA) ... LIC
LeisureLine [*Footscray Institute of Technology Library*] [*Database*] [*Information service or system*] (IID) ... LEIS
Leisureways Marketing [*Associated Press*] (SAG) ... LeisMkt
Leisureways Marketing [*NASDAQ symbol*] (SAG) ... LMLA
Leisureways Marketing Ltd [*NASDAQ symbol*] (TTSB) ... LMLAF
Leitchfield, KY [*FM radio station call letters*] ... WKHG
Leitchfield, KY [*AM radio station call letters*] ... WMTL
Leitender Ingenieur [*Chief Engineer*] [*German military - World War II*] ... LI
Leiter Adult Intelligence Scale [*Intelligence test*] [*Psychology*] ... LAIS
Leiter International Performance Scale [*Psychology*] ... LIPS
Leiter International Performance Test [*Psychology*] (DAVI) ... LIPT
Leith. Blackstone on Real Property [*2nd ed.*] [*1880*] [*A publication*] (DLA) ... Leith Black
Leith's Real Property Statutes [*Ontario*] [*A publication*] (DLA) ... Leith R Pr
Leitrim [*County in Ireland*] (ROG) ... LEIT
Leitrim [*County in Ireland*] (ROG) ... LEITR
Lek [*Monetary unit*] [*Albania*] (BARN) ... L
Lek [*Monetary unit*] [*Albania*] ... LK
Lekana [*Congo*] [*Airport symbol*] (OAG) ... LKC
Lekhwair [*Oman*] [*ICAO location identifier*] (ICLI) ... OOLK
Leknes [*Norway ICAO location identifier*] (ICLI) ... ENLK
Leknes [*Norway*] [*Airport symbol*] (OAG) ... LKN
Leksaker, Bibliotek [*Program providing meaningful toys for mentally disturbed children; operates on the same principle as a lending library.*] [*Name formed from Swedish words for "playthings" and "library"*] ... LEKOTEK
Leksikon fun der Nayer Yidisher Literatur [*New York*] [*A publication*] (BJA) ... LNYL
Lekythos (VRA) ... lekyt
Leland Community Unit, School District 1, Leland, IL [*Library symbol Library of Congress*] (LCLS) ... ILelSD
Leland, MI [*FM radio station call letters*] ... WIAR
Leland, MS [*FM radio station call letters*] ... WBAD
Leland, MS [*AM radio station call letters*] ... WESY
Leland, MS [*FM radio station call letters*] ... WIQQ
Leland, NC [*AM radio station call letters*] ... WAAV
Leland, NC [*FM radio station call letters*] (RBYB) ... WAAV-FM
Leland, NC [*FM radio station call letters*] (RBYB) ... WAAV-FM
Leland Township Public Library, Leland, MI [*Library symbol Library of Congress*] (LCLS) ... MiLe
Lely and Foulkes' Elections [*3rd ed.*] [*1887*] [*A publication*] (DLA) ... Lely & F Elec
Lely and Foulkes' Judicature Acts [*4th ed.*] [*1883*] [*A publication*] (DLA) ... Lely & F Jud Acts
Lely and Foulkes' Licensing Acts [*3rd ed.*] [*1887*] [*A publication*] (DLA) ... Lely & F Lic Acts
Lely's Regulation of Railway Acts [*1873*] [*A publication*] (DLA) ... Lely Railw
Lelystad [*Netherlands ICAO location identifier*] (ICLI) ... EHLE
LEM [*Lunar Excursion Module*] **Dummy Guidance Equipment** [*NASA*] (KSC) ... LDGE
LEM [*Lunar Excursion Module*] **Guidance Equipment** [*NASA*] (KSC) ... LGE
LEM [*Lunar Excursion Module*] **Mission Simulator** [*NASA*] ... LMS
LEM [*Lunar Excursion Module*] **Optical Tracking System** [*NASA*] (KSC) ... LOTS
LEM [*Lunar Excursion Module*] **Partial Guidance Equipment** [*NASA*] (KSC) ... LPGE
LEM Test Article (MCD) ... LTA
LEM [*Lunar Excursion Module*] **Test Procedure** [*NASA*] (KSC) ... LTP
LeMans America (EA) ... LA
Lemars, IA [*Location identifier FAA*] (FAAL) ... LRJ
Lembaga Ilmu Pengetahuan Indonesia, Pusat Dokumentasi Ilmiah Nasional, Jakarta, Indonesia [*Library symbol Library of Congress*] (LCLS) ... IeDL
Lembaga Ilmu Pengetahuan Indonesia, Pusat Dokumentasi Ilmiah Nasional, Jakarta, Indonesia [*Library symbol*] [*Library of Congress*] (LCLS) ... IeDLIP
Lembang [*Java*] [*Seismograph station code, US Geological Survey*] (SEIS) ... LEM
Lemko Association of US and Canada (EA) ... LA
Lemming Resources, Inc. [*Vancouver Stock Exchange symbol*] ... LMM
Lemmon High School Library, Lemmon, SD [*Library symbol Library of Congress*] (LCLS) ... SdLemH
Lemmon Public Library, Lemmon, SD [*Library symbol Library of Congress*] (LCLS) ... SdLem
Lemmon, SD [*AM radio station call letters*] ... KBJM
Lemmon, SD [*Location identifier FAA*] (FAAL) ... LEM
Lemnos [*Greece*] [*Airport symbol*] (OAG) ... LXS
Lemon [*Philately*] ... lem
Lemon Administrative Committee (EA) ... LAC
Lemonthyme [*Tasmania*] [*Seismograph station code, US Geological Survey Closed*] (SEIS) ... LMT
Lemoore, CA [*AM radio station call letters*] ... KJOP
Lemoore, CA [*Location identifier FAA*] (FAAL) ... NLC
LeMoyne College, Syracuse, NY [*Library symbol Library of Congress*] (LCLS) ... NSyL
LeMoyne College, Syracuse, NY [*OCLC symbol*] (OCLC) ... VFL
LeMoyne-Owen College, Memphis, TN [*OCLC symbol*] (OCLC) ... LOC
LeMoyne-Owen College, Memphis, TN [*Library symbol Library of Congress*] (LCLS) ... TMLO
Lempel Zev [*Computer science*] ... LZ
Lempel-Zev-Welch [*Compression*] [*Computer science*] (PCM) ... LZW
Lempira [*Monetary unit*] [*Honduras*] ... L
Lempira [*Monetary unit*] [*Honduras*] ... LP
Lemvig [*Denmark ICAO location identifier*] (ICLI) ... EKLV
Lemwerder [*Germany ICAO location identifier*] (ICLI) ... EDWD
Lenad Subgroup [*Leucite, nephelite, halite, thenardite*] [*CIPW classification Geology*] ... L
Lenakel [*Vanuatu*] [*ICAO location identifier*] (ICLI) ... NVVK
Lenawee County Library, Adrian, MI [*Library symbol Library of Congress*] (LCLS) ... MiAdL
Lenawee County Railroad Co., Inc. [*AAR code*] ... LCRC
Lencourt Ltd. [*Toronto Stock Exchange symbol*] ... LCT
Lender of Last Resort ... LLR
Lending Library ... LL
Lending Library Unit ... LLU
Lending Rate [*Banking*] (MHDW) ... LR
Lend-Lease [*Bill*] [*World War II*] ... LL
Lend-Lease Administration [*Defunct*] ... LLA
Lend-Lease Liaison Office [*World War II*] ... LLLO
Lenex [*Poland ICAO designator*] (FAAC) ... LNX
Lengeh [*Iran*] [*Airport symbol*] (AD) ... LNH
Length [*Symbol*] [*IUPAC*] ... l
Length [*or Lengthwise*] ... L
Length (IAA) ... LE
Length ... LEN
Length ... LENGTH
Length (MSA) ... LG
Length ... LGH

Length (AFM) ... LGTH
Length (VRA) ... lgth
Length (IAA) ... LNG
Length [*of a boat*] **at Waterline** ... LWL
Length/Beam Ratio (DNAB) ... L/B
Length Between Perpendiculars [*Technical drawings*] ... LBP
Length, Breadth, Height ... LBH
Length Indicator [*Computer science*] (TNIG) ... LI
Length, Mass, Time [*Physics*] ... LMT
Length of Adjacency Process (MHDB) ... LOAP
Length of Chord (MSA) ... LC
Length of Column [*Military*] (GFGA) ... LGTHCOLM
Length of Curve (MSA) ... LCRV
Length of Day ... LOD
Length of Effectiveness for Magnetic-Field Antennae ... LEM
Length of Flowering Period [*Botany*] ... LFL
Length of Hospitalization ... LOH
Length of Lead [*Actual*] [*Technical drawings*] ... LOL
Length of Leaf at Widest Portion [*Botany*] ... LFWID
Length of Mean Turn ... LMT
Length of Patient Stay [*Medicine*] (AABC) ... LOPS
Length of Perpendiculars ... LPP
Length of Service ... LOS
Length of Stay ... LOS
Length of Stroke ... LS
Length Over-All [*Technical drawings*] ... LOA
Length to Width Ratio [*Of a leaf*] [*Botany*] ... LENWID
Length-Diameter Ratio ... LD
Length-Diameter Ratio ... LDR
Lengthen (ABBR) ... LGTHN
Lengthened (ROG) ... LENGTHD
Lengthened (ABBR) ... LGTHND
Lengthening (ABBR) ... LGTHNG
Lengthier (ABBR) ... LGTHR
Lengthiest (ABBR) ... LGTHT
Lengthily (ABBR) ... LGTHIY
Lengthiness (ABBR) ... LGTHNS
Lengthwise (ABBR) ... LGTHWS
Lengthy (ABBR) ... LGTHY
Lengyel-Kerman-Vargar [*Rating*] [*Psychology*] (DAVI) ... LKV
Leninakan [*Former USSR Seismograph station code, US Geological Survey*] (SEIS) ... LEN
Leningrad [*Former USSR Airport symbol*] (OAG) ... LED
Leningrad [*Former USSR Seismograph station code, US Geological Survey Closed*] (SEIS) ... LNN
Leningrad [*Former USSR Geomagnetic observatory code*] ... LNN
Leningrad Institute of Metals [*Former USSR*] (MCD) ... LIM
Leningrad International Management Institute [*Joint Venture between Bocconi University, Italy and Leningrad University*] (ECON) ... LIMI
Leningrad Prison Psychiatric Hospital [*Later, LSPH*] ... LPPH
Leningrad/Pulkovo [*Former USSR ICAO location identifier*] (ICLI) ... ULLL
Leningrad Special Psychiatric Hospital [*Formerly, LPPH*] ... LSPH
Leningradskii Universitet, Nauchnaia Biblioteka Imeni Gor'kogo [*Leningrad State University, Gor'kii Scientific Library*], Leningrad, Soviet Union [*Library symbol Library of Congress*] (LCLS) ... RuLU-N
Leniter [*Gently*] [*Pharmacy*] ... LENIT
Lenkoran [*Former USSR Seismograph station code, US Geological Survey*] (SEIS) ... LNK
Lenkurt Electric Co., Burnaby, BC, Canada [*Library symbol Library of Congress*] (LCLS) ... CaBBL
Lenkurt Electric Co., Burnaby, British Columbia [*Library symbol National Library of Canada*] (NLC) ... BBL
Lenkurt Electric Co., San Carlos, CA [*Library symbol Library of Congress*] (LCLS) ... CScL
Lennar Corp. [*NYSE symbol*] (SPSG) ... LEN
Lennar Corp. [*Associated Press*] (SAG) ... Lennar
Lennard-Jones [*Physical chemistry*] ... LJ
Lennon Sisters Fan Club (EA) ... LSFC
Lennox Airways [*Kenya*] [*ICAO designator*] (FAAC) ... LAK
Lennox Airways, Gambia Ltd. [*ICAO designator*] (FAAC) ... GLN
Lennox and Addington Counties Public Libraries, Napanee, ON, Canada [*Library symbol Library of Congress*] (LCLS) ... CaONaLAC
Lennox and Addington Counties Public Library, Napanee, Ontario [*Library symbol National Library of Canada*] (NLC) ... ONLAC
Lennox & Addington County Library, Camden East Branch, Camden East, ON, Canada [*Library symbol*] [*Library of Congress*] (LCLS) ... CaOCELAC
Lennox & Addington County Library, Enterprise Branch, Enterprise, ON, Canada [*Library symbol*] [*Library of Congress*] (LCLS) ... CaOENLA
Lennox & Addington County Library, Odessa Branch, Odessa, ON, Canada [*Library symbol*] [*Library of Congress*] (LCLS) ... CaOODLAC
Lennox & Addington County Library, Stella Branch, Stella, ON, Canada [*Library symbol*] [*Library of Congress*] (LCLS) ... CaOSLA
Lennox & Addington County Public Library, Amherstview Branch, Amherstview, ON, Canada [*Library symbol*] [*Library of Congress*] (LCLS) ... CaOALAC
Lennox & Addington County Public Library, Bath Branch, Bath, ON, Canada [*Library symbol*] [*Library of Congress*] (LCLS) ... CaOBLAC
Lennox and Addington Historical Society, Napanee, Ontario [*Library symbol National Library of Canada*] (BIB) ... ONLAH
Lennox and Addington Museum, Napanee, ON, Canada [*Library symbol Library of Congress*] (LCLS) ... CaONaLAM
Lennox and Addington Museum, Napanee, Ontario [*Library symbol National Library of Canada*] (NLC) ... ONLAM
Lennox High School Library, Lennox, SD [*Library symbol Library of Congress*] (LCLS) ... SdLeH
Lennoxville-Ascot Historical Society Museum, Lennoxville, Quebec [*Library symbol National Library of Canada*] (NLC) ... QLAH
Lenoir City, TN [*AM radio station call letters*] ... WBLC
Lenoir City, TN [*AM radio station call letters*] ... WLIL
Lenoir City, TN [*FM radio station call letters*] ... WLIL-FM
Lenoir Community College, Kinston, NC [*Library symbol Library of Congress*] (LCLS) ... NcKL
Lenoir, NC [*AM radio station call letters*] ... WJRI
Lenoir, NC [*AM radio station call letters*] ... WKGX
Lenoir, NC [*FM radio station call letters*] ... WKVS
Lenoir Rhyne College [*Hickory, NC*] ... LRC
Lenoir Rhyne College, Hickory, NC [*Library symbol Library of Congress*] (LCLS) ... NcHyL
Lenora Explorations Ltd. [*Toronto Stock Exchange symbol*] ... LEN
Lenox College, Hopkinton, IA [*Library symbol Library of Congress*] (LCLS) ... IaHoL
Lenox Elementary School, Baldwin, NY [*Library symbol Library of Congress*] (LCLS) ... NBaldLE
Lenox Hill Hospital, Medical Library, New York, NY [*Library symbol Library of Congress*] (LCLS) ... NNLH
Lenox Township Library, New Haven, MI [*Library symbol Library of Congress*] (LCLS) ... MiNhL
Lens ... L
Lens/Benifontaine [*France ICAO location identifier*] (ICLI) ... LFQL
Lens Board [*Mechanical engineering*] ... LNBD
Lens Culinaris Lectin ... LCL
Lens Electronic Automatic Design (IAA) ... LEAD
Lens Extraction, Oculus Dexter [*Right eye*] [*Ophthalmology*] (DAVI) ... LEOD
Lens Quality [*Optics*] ... LQ
Lens Sign Convention ... LSC
Lens Speed [*Mechanical engineering*] ... LNSP
Lens-End-Lamp ... LEL
Lensibavia [*Former USSR*] [*FAA designator*] (FAAC) ... LSB
Lens-Modulated Oscillator ... LMO
Lens-Pinhole Spatial Filter (PDAA) ... LPSF
Lent Reading (ROG) ... LR
Lentando [*With Increasing Slowness*] [*Music*] (ROG) ... LENTO
Lente Insulin [*Pharmacology*] (DAVI) ... L
Lenticular Opacity [*Ophthalmology*] (DAVI) ... LO
Lentigines, EKG Abnormalities, Ocular Hypertelorism, Pulmonary Stenosis, Abnormalities of Genitalia, Retardation of Growth, and Deafness Syndrome [*Medicine*] (DMAA) ... LEOPARD
Lentigo Maligna [*Oncology*] ... LM
Lentigo Maligna Melanoma [*Oncology*] ... LMM
Lentini Aviation, Inc. [*ICAO designator*] (FAAC) ... LEN
Lento [*Very Slow*] [*Music*] (ROG) ... LNTO
Lentz Peace Research Laboratory (EA) ... LPRL
Lenwood, CA [*FM radio station call letters*] ... KGXY
Lenwood, CA [*FM radio station call letters*] ... KIXW
Leo [*Burkina Faso*] [*ICAO location identifier*] (ICLI) ... DHCL
Leo (WDAA) ... L
Leo Baeck Institute (EA) ... LBI
Leo Baeck Institute, New York, NY [*Library symbol Library of Congress*] (LCLS) ... NNLBI
Leo F. Giblyn Elementary School, Freeport, NY [*Library symbol*] [*Library of Congress*] (LCLS) ... NFreeGE
Leo Minor [*Constellation*] ... LMi
Leo Minor [*Constellation*] ... LMin
Leo Pharm. Products [*Denmark*] [*Research code symbol*] ... VD
Leo Taxi Aereo SA de CV [*Mexico ICAO designator*] (FAAC) ... LTX
Leominster Historical Society, Inc., Leominster, MA [*Library symbol*] [*Library of Congress*] (LCLS) ... MLeoHi
Leominster, MA [*AM radio station call letters*] (RBYB) ... WCMX
Leominster Public Library, Leominster, MA [*Library symbol Library of Congress*] (LCLS) ... MLeo
Leon [*Spain ICAO location identifier*] (ICLI) ... LELN
Leon [*Mexico*] [*Airport symbol*] (OAG) ... LEN
Leon [*Mexico*] [*Seismograph station code, US Geological Survey*] (SEIS) ... LNM
Leon [*Mexico ICAO location identifier*] (ICLI) ... MMLO
Leon Cerro Gordo [*Mexico*] [*Seismograph station code, US Geological Survey*] (SEIS) ... LCG
Leon/Fanor Urroz [*Nicaragua*] [*ICAO location identifier*] (ICLI) ... MNLN
Leon Jordan Fan Club (EA) ... LJFC
Leon Journal-Reporter, Leon, IA [*Library symbol Library of Congress*] (LCLS) ... IaLeoJR
Leon Public Library, Leon, IA [*Library symbol Library of Congress*] (LCLS) ... IaLeo
Leon Velarde/Shiringayoc O Hda. Mejia [*Peru*] [*ICAO location identifier*] (ICLI) ... SPOV
Leona, TX [*Location identifier FAA*] (FAAL) ... LOA
Leonard [*Unit for cathode rays*] ... Le
Leonard Nimoy Fan Club (EA) ... LNFC
Leonard Nimoy Fan Club, Spotlight (EAIO) ... LNFCS
Leonard Wood Memorial [*American Leprosy Foundation*] (EA) ... LWM
Leonard Wood Memorial [*Later, LWM*] [*Also known as American Leprosy Foundation*] (EA) ... WOODMEM
Leonard Wood Memorial for the Eradication of Leprosy [*Later, LWM*] (EA) ... LWMEL
Leonard's King's Bench, Common Pleas, and Exchequer Reports [*England*] [*A publication*] (DLA) ... Leon
Leonard's King's Bench Reports [*1540-1615*] [*England*] [*A publication*] (DLA) ... Leo
Leonard's Louisiana Digest of United States Cases [*A publication*] (DLA) ... Leon LA Dig
Leonard's Precedents in County Courts [*1869*] [*A publication*] (DLA) ... Leon Prec
Leonardus [*Authority cited in pre-1607 legal work*] (DSA) ... Leo

Leoncito [*Argentina*] [*Seismograph station code, US Geological Survey*] (SEIS) .... LEO
Leone [*Monetary unit*] [*Sierra Leone*] .... LE
Leone, AS [*AM radio station call letters*] .... WVUV
Leonhartsberger Flugunternchmen GmbH [*Austria ICAO designator*] (FAAC) .... LFU
Leonia Public Library, Leonia, NJ [*Library symbol Library of Congress*] (LCLS) .... NjLe
Leon-Jefferson Library System [*Library network*] .... LCPL
Leon-Jefferson-Wakulla County Public Library, Tallahassee, FL [*Library symbol Library of Congress*] (LCLS) .... FTaL
Leonora [*Australia Airport symbol*] (OAG) .... LNO
Leon's Furniture Ltd. [*Toronto Stock Exchange symbol*] .... LNF
Leopair SA [*Switzerland ICAO designator*] (FAAC) .... LEO
Leopold Stokowski Society (EA) .... LSS
Leopold Stokowski Society of America (EA) .... LSSA
Leopold-Franzens Universitat Insbruck, Insbruck, Austria [*Library symbol Library of Congress*] (LCLS) .... AsIU
Leota Christian School, Leota, MN [*Library symbol*] [*Library of Congress*] (LCLS) .... MnLeoCS
Leoti, KS [*FM radio station call letters*] (RBYB) .... KSKZ
Lep Group Ltd. [*NASDAQ symbol*] (SAG) .... LEPG
Leparoscopically Assisted Vaginal Hysterectomy [*Medicine*] .... LAVH
Lepetit [*Italy*] [*Research code symbol*] L
Lepetit [*Italy*] [*Research code symbol*] .... P
Lepide Dictum [*Wittily Said*] [*Latin*] (ADA) .... LD
Lepidocrocite [*A mineral*] L
Lepidoptera [*Entomology*] .... Lep
Lepidoptera Research Foundation (EA) .... LRF
Lepidopterists' Society (EA) .... LEPSOC
Lepidopterists' Society .... LS
Lepista Nuda [*A fungus*] .... LN
Lepromatous-Type Leprosy [*Animal pathology*] LL
Leprosy Mission [*Australia An association*] .... LM
Leprosy Relief Association [*British*] (DI) .... LEPRA
Leptocytes [*Biochemistry*] (DAVI) .... LEPT
Leptomeningeal Metastasis .... LM
Leptosphaeria korrea [*A fungus*] .... Lk
Leptosphaerulina Trifolii [*A fungus*] .... Lt
Leptosphaerulinia briosiana [*A fungus*] .... Lb
Leptospira [*A bacteria*] (DAVI) L
Leptospira [*Genus of bacteria*] .... Lept
Leptospirosis Agglutinins [*Biochemistry*] (DAVI) .... LEPTOS
Leptotrichia [*A bacteria*] (DAVI) L
Lepus [*Constellation*] .... Lep
Lepus [*Constellation*] .... Leps
L'Equilibre Biologique [*France*] [*Research code symbol*] .... EB
L'Equilibre Biologique [*France*] [*Research code symbol*] .... OHB
Lereh [*Indonesia*] [*ICAO location identifier*] (ICLI) .... WAJL
Leribe [*Lesotho*] [*ICAO location identifier*] (ICLI) .... FXLR
Lerner and Loewe [*Composers*] .... L&L
Lernout & Hauspie [*A speech products manufacturer*] (PCM) .... L&H
Lernout & Hauspie Speech Pds [*NASDAQ symbol*] (TTSB) .... LHSPF
Lernout & Hauspie Speech Products [*NASDAQ symbol*] (SAG) .... LHSP
Lernout & Hauspie Speech Products [*Associated Press*] (SAG) .... LrnHaus
Leros [*Greece*] [*ICAO location identifier*] (ICLI) .... LGLE
LeRoy Historical Society, LeRoy, NY [*Library symbol Library of Congress*] (LCLS) .... NLerHi
LeRoy Public Library, LeRoy, MI [*Library symbol Library of Congress*] (LCLS) .... MiLer
Leroy Van Dyke International Fan Club (EA) .... LVDIFC
Lerwick [*United Kingdom*] [*Geomagnetic observatory code*] .... LER
Lerwick [*Scotland*] [*Airport symbol*] (OAG) .... LSI
Lerwick [*Scotland*] **Tingwall Airport** [*Airport symbol*] (OAG) .... LWK
Les Apocryphes de l'Ancien Testament [*A publication*] (BJA) .... AAT
Les Arrets de la Cour Federale [*Legal database, Department of Justice*] [*Canada*] (NITA) .... ACF
Les Arrets de la Cour Supreme [*Legal database*] [*Canada*] (NITA) .... ACS
Les Brown's Encyclopedia of Television [*A publication*] .... LBETV
Les Buteaux [*France*] [*Seismograph station code, US Geological Survey*] (SEIS) .... LBF
Les Cercles des Jeunes Naturalistes (AC) .... CJN
Les Codes Larcier [*A publication*] (ILCA) CL
Les Conseillers Samson Belair, Inc., Sherbrooke, PQ, Canada [*Library symbol*] [*Library of Congress*] (LCLS) .... CaQSherSB
Les Conseillers Samson Belair, Inc., Sherbrooke, Quebec [*Library symbol National Library of Canada*] (NLC) .... QSHERSB
Les Dames d'Escoffier (EA) .... LDE
Les Eplatures [*Switzerland ICAO location identifier*] (ICLI) .... LSGC
Les Fusiliers Mont Royal [*British military*] (DMA) .... FMR
Les Hieroglyphes Hittites [*A publication*] (BJA) .... HH
Les Industries Harnois, St. Thomas de Joliette, PQ, Canada [*Library symbol*] [*Library of Congress*] (LCLS) .... CaQSttH
Les Industries Harnois, St-Thomas-De-Joliette, Quebec [*Library symbol National Library of Canada*] (NLC) .... QSTTH
Les Miserables [*Musical based on Victor Hugo's novel*] .... Les Miz
Les Mureaux [*France ICAO location identifier*] (ICLI) .... LFXU
Les Papyrus Fouad I [*A publication*] (OCD) .... PFouad
Les Quatre Saisons [*Record label*] [*France*] .... LQS
Les Quatre Saisons [*Record label*] [*France*] .... QS
Les Rejaudoux [*France*] [*Seismograph station code, US Geological Survey*] (SEIS) .... RJF
Les Sables D'Olonne/Talmont [*France ICAO location identifier*] (ICLI) .... LFOO
Les Sagesses du Proche-Orient Ancien. Colloque de Strasbourg [*1962*]. Travaux du Centre d'Etudes Superieurs Specialise d'Histoire des Religions de Strassbourg [*Paris*] [*A publication*] (BJA) .... SPOA
Les Saintes [*Guadeloupe*] [*Airport symbol*] (OAG) .... LSS
Les Saintes/Terre-De-Haut [*French Antilles*] [*ICAO location identifier*] (ICLI) .... TFFS
Les Traductions Tessier SCC (Division de Multiscript International), Ottawa, Ontario [*Library symbol National Library of Canada*] (BIB) .... OOTRAT
Lesbian (DSUE) .... LES
lesbian [*Psychology*] (DAVI) .... lessy
Lesbian and Gay Associated Engineers and Scientists [*Later, NOGLSTP*] (EA) .... LGAES
Lesbian and Gay Bands of America (EA) .... LGBA
Lesbian and Gay Caucus of Public Health Workers (EA) .... LGCPHW
Lesbian and Gay Medical Association [*Defunct*] (EAIO) .... LGMA
Lesbian and Gay People in Medicine [*Later, LGBPM*] (EA) .... LGPIM
Lesbian, Bisexual, and Gay United Employees at AT & T .... LEAGUE
Lesbian Feminist Liberation (EA) .... LFL
Lesbian, Gay, and Bisexual People in Medicine (EA) .... LGBPM
Lesbian/Gay Rights Monitoring Group (EA) .... LGRMG
Lesbian Herstory Educational Foundation (EA) .... LHEF
Lesbian Mothers National Defense Fund (EA) .... LMNDF
Lesbian Resource Center (EA) .... LRC
Lesbian Rights Project [*Later, NCLR*] (EA) .... LRP
Lesbian Until Graduation .... LUG
Leschetizky Association (EA) .... LA
Lesch-Nyhan [*Medicine*] .... L-N
Lesch-Nyhan Syndrome [*Medicine*] .... LNS
Lesco, Inc. [*Associated Press*] (SAG) .... Lesco
Lesco, Inc. [*NASDAQ symbol*] (SAG) .... LSCO
Lese [*Papua New Guinea*] [*Airport symbol*] (OAG) .... LNG
Leshonenu [*Jerusalem*] (BJA) .... Lesh
Lesion Expansion Rate [*Pathology*] .... LR
Lesion Number [*Pathology*] .... LN
Lesley College, Cambridge, MA [*Library symbol Library of Congress*] (LCLS) .... MCL
Lesley College, Cambridge, MA [*Library symbol*] [*Library of Congress*] (LCLS) .... MCLC
Lesley Gore Fan Club (EA) .... LGFC
Leslie Charleson Fan Club (EA) .... LCFC
Leslie R. Foss Public Library, Center Line, MI [*Library symbol Library of Congress*] (LCLS) .... MiCen
Leslie-Lohman Gay Art Foundation (EA) .... LLGAF
Leslies Poolmart [*NASDAQ symbol*] (SAG) .... LESL
Leslie's Poolmart [*NASDAQ symbol*] (TTSB) .... LESL
Leslie's Poolmart, Inc. [*Associated Press*] (SAG) .... LesPol
Lesnwith [*England*] .... LESNW
Lesobeng [*Lesotho*] [*ICAO location identifier*] (ICLI) .... FXLS
Lesobeng [*Lesotho*] [*Airport symbol*] (OAG) .... LES
Lesotho [*Aircraft nationality and registration mark*] (FAAC) 7P
Lesotho [*MARC geographic area code Library of Congress*] (LCCP) .... f-lo--
Lesotho [*MARC country of publication code Library of Congress*] (LCCP) .... lo
Lesotho [*ANSI two-letter standard code*] (CNC) .... LS
Lesotho [*ANSI three-letter standard code*] (CNC) .... LSO
Lesotho Airways [*ICAO designator*] (AD) .... QL
Lesotho Airways Corp. [*ICAO designator*] (FAAC) .... LAI
Lesotho Highlands Development Authority (ECON) .... LHDA
Lesotho Highlands Water Project (ECON) .... LHWP
Lesotho Liberation Army (PD) .... LLA
Lesotho National Broadcasting Service [*South Africa*] .... LNBS
Lesotho National Development Corp. .... LNDC
Lesotho Telecommunications Corp. [*Ministry of Transport and Communications*] [*Lesotho*] (TSSD) .... LTC
Lesotho Union of Journalists (EAIO) .... LUJ
Lesozavodsk [*Former USSR Seismograph station code, US Geological Survey Closed*] (SEIS) .... LES
Lesparre/St. Laurent Du Medoc [*France ICAO location identifier*] (ICLI) .... LFDU
L'Esprit Createur [*A publication*] (BRI) .... L'Esprit
Less .... LS
Less Active Tetragonal (PDAA) .... LAT
Less Developed Country .... LDC
Less Industrialized Country (MHDW) LIC
Less Infant Fatality Everywhere [*In association name, Project LIFE*] .... LIFE
Less Prosperous Country .... LPC
Less Sleep and More Speed [*Hobo slang*] .... LS and MS
Less Than (IBMDP) .... LT
Less Than .... LTU
Less Than Fair Value [*Business term*] .... LTFV
Less Than Full Container Load .... LFCL
Less than Honorable Discharge [*Military*] (VNW) .... LTH
Less than Lethal (INF) .... LTL
Less than or Equal .... LE
Less than Release Unit [*Army*] (AABC) .... LRU
Less than Truckload [*Under 24,000 pounds*] .... LTL
Less than Truckload [*Under 24,000 pounds*] (WGA) .... LTT
Less than Truckload Cargo (MCD) .... LTC
Less than Truckload Lot [*Under 24,000 pounds*] (MHDW) .... LCT
Lessay [*France ICAO location identifier*] (ICLI) .... LFOM
Lesser (DAVI) L
Lesser Antilles (VRA) .... L Anti
Lesser Antilles [*MARC geographic area code Library of Congress*] (LCCP) .... nwla--
Lesser Included Offense .... LIO
Lesser of Costs or Charges [*Medicine*] (GFGA) LCC
Lesser of Two Evils [*Politics*] .... LOTE
Lessing Society (EA) .... LS

Lessio Intellectuale Europeo [*Research Institute*] [*Consiglio Nationale delle Richerche*] [*Italy*] (NITA) ..... LIE

Lesson Administrative Instructions [*Military*] ..... LAI

Lesson Analysis Design Approach ..... LADA

Lesson Assembly Program (IEEE) ..... LAP

Lesson Content Analysis ..... LCA

Lesson Design Approach (MCD) ..... LDA

Lesson Plan ..... LP

Lesson Specification Document (MCD) ..... LSD

Lesson Translator (NVT) ..... L-TRAN

Lessons Learned LL

Lessor ..... LSSR

Less-than-Carload [*Under 60,000 pounds*] LCL

Less-than-Carload Lot (DFIT) LCL

Less-than-Container Load [*Shipping*] LCL

Lester and Butler's Supplement to Lester's Georgia Reports [*A publication*] (DLA) ..... Lest & But

Lester and Butler's Supplement to Lester's Georgia Reports [*A publication*] (DLA) ..... Lester & B

Lester and Butler's Supplement to Lester's Georgia Reports [*A publication*] (DLA) ..... Lester Supp

Lester & Orpen Dennys [*Canadian publisher*] ..... L & OD

Lester B. Forman Central Library, Fairport, NY [*OCLC symbol*] (OCLC) ..... RWW

Lester B. Pearson College of the Pacific, Victoria, BC, Canada [*Library symbol Library of Congress*] (LCLS) ..... CaBViLBP

Lester B. Pearson College of the Pacific, Victoria, British Columbia [*Library symbol National Library of Canada*] (NLC) ..... BVILBP

Lester Park Elementary School, Duluth, MN [*Library symbol*] [*Library of Congress*] (LCLS) ..... MnDuLPE

Lester Prairie Public School, Lester Prairie, MN [*Library symbol*] [*Library of Congress*] (LCLS) ..... MnLepPS

Lester's Decisions in Public Land Cases [*A publication*] (DLA) ..... Lest PL

Lester's Reports [*31-33 Georgia*] [*A publication*] (DLA) ..... Lester

Let Me See Correspondence [*Business term*] ..... LMSC

Let Nicaragua Live [*An association Defunct*] (EA) ..... LNL

Let Others Share Equally [*Slogan opposing President Gerald R. Ford's anti-inflation WIN campaign*] ..... LOSE

Letaba Airways [*ICAO designator*] (AD) ..... LK

Letaba Airways [*South Africa ICAO designator*] (FAAC) ..... LKZ

Letchworth Indep Bancshares [*NASDAQ symbol*] (TTSB) ..... LEBC

Letchworth Indep Bcshs Wrrt [*NASDAQ symbol*] (TTSB) ..... LEBCW

Letchworth Independent Bancshares Corp. [*NASDAQ symbol*] (SAG) ..... LEBC

Letchworth Independent Bancshares Corp. [*Associated Press*] (SAG) ..... Letch

Letchworth Independent Bancshares Corp. [*Associated Press*] (SAG) ..... LetchInd

Letchworth Junior/Senior High School Library, Gainesville, NY [*OCLC symbol*] (OCLC) ..... RWX

Letdown [*Nuclear energy*] (NRCH) ..... LD

Letdown [*Nuclear energy*] (NRCH) ..... LTD

Letdown Storage Tank [*Nuclear energy*] (NRCH) ..... LDST

Letdown Terrain Clearance (DNAB) ..... LTC

Letelier-Moffitt Memorial Fund for Human Rights [*Later, LMMFHR/IPS*] (EA) ..... LMMFHR

Letelier-Moffitt Memorial Fund for Human Rights/Institute for Policy Studies (EA) ..... LMMFHR/IPS

Lethal L

Lethal [*Pharmacology*] (DAVI) ..... leth

Lethal (ABBR) ..... LHAL

Lethal Agent Disposal Process Optimization Program (MCD) ..... LADPOP

Lethal Aid for Bomber Penetration (MCD) ..... LABP

Lethal Area [*Of indirect-fire weapon systems*] [*Military*] ..... LA

Lethal Area Data Reduction and Plotting (SAA) ..... LADRAP

Lethal Area Estimate ..... LAE

Lethal Concentration LC

Lethal Concentration Low (ERG) ..... LC^{Lo}

Lethal Concentration, Median [*Lethal for 50% of test group*] ..... LC_{50}

Lethal Defense System (MCD) ..... LDS

Lethal Dose ..... LD

Lethal Dose Low (ERG) ..... LD^{Lo}

Lethal Dose, Median [*Also, MLD*] [*Lethal for 50% of test group*] ..... LD_{50}

Lethal Graft-Versus-Host Disease [*Medicine*] (DMAA) ..... LGVHD

Lethal Ground Range (MCD) ..... LGR

Lethal Material ..... LM

Lethal Weapon [*A motion picture*] ..... LW

Lethal Yellowing [*Plant pathology*] ..... LY

Lethality and Target Hardening [*Military*] (SDI) ..... L & TH

Lethality Assessment Program ..... LAP

Lethality End Game Simulation (MCD) ..... LEGS

Lethbridge [*Canada*] [*Airport symbol*] (OAG) ..... YQL

Lethbridge, AB [*Television station call letters*] CFCN-TV-5

Lethbridge, AB [*FM radio station call letters*] ..... CFRV

Lethbridge, AB [*Television station call letters*] CISA-7

Lethbridge, AB [*AM radio station call letters*] ..... CJOC

Lethbridge, AB [*AM radio station call letters*] ..... CKRX

Lethbridge, AB [*FM radio station call letters*] CKUA-2

Lethbridge, AB [*ICAO location identifier*] (ICLI) ..... CYQL

Lethbridge College, Alberta [*Library symbol National Library of Canada*] (NLC) ..... ALC

Lethbridge College, Lethbridge, AB, Canada [*Library symbol Library of Congress*] (LCLS) ..... CaALC

Lethbridge Public Library [*UTLAS symbol*] ..... LPL

Lethbridge Public Library, Alberta [*Library symbol National Library of Canada*] (NLC) ..... AL

Lethbridge Public Library, Lethbridge, AB, Canada [*Library symbol Library of Congress*] (LCLS) ..... CaAL

Lethbridge Rehabilitation Centre, Montreal, PQ, Canada [*Library symbol Library of Congress*] (LCLS) ..... CaQMLR

Lethem [*Guyana*] [*Airport symbol*] (OAG) ..... LTM

Lethem [*Guyana*] [*ICAO location identifier*] (ICLI) ..... SYLT

Leticia [*Colombia*] [*Airport symbol*] (OAG) ..... LET

Leticia/Alfredo Vasquez Cobo [*Colorado ICAO location identifier*] (ICLI) ..... SKLT

Letitia Elizabeth Landon [*English poet and novelist, 1802-1839*] ..... LEL

LeTourneau College, Longview, TX [*OCLC symbol*] (OCLC) ..... TLT

LeTourneau College, Longview, TX [*Library symbol Library of Congress*] (LCLS) ..... TxLoL

Let's Discuss ..... LD

Let's Face It [*Later, AFLFI*] [*An association*] (EA) ..... LFI

Let's Have Better Mottoes Association [*A mythical association*] (EA) ..... LHBMA

Let's Improve Future Environment ..... LIFE

Let's Improve Today's Education [*Newsletter*] ..... LITE

Let's Make a Deal [*TV program*] ..... LMAD

Let's Omit Superfluous Expenses [*Slogan opposing President Gerald R. Ford's anti-inflation WIN campaign*] ..... LOSE

Let's Stick It to Them [*Acronym used as book title*] ..... LSITT

Let's Tax Plutocrats [*Humorous interpretation of LTP - Limit on Tax Preferences*] ..... LTP

Letseng [*Lesotho*] [*ICAO location identifier*] (ICLI) ..... FXLT

Letter L

Letter ..... LET

Letter [*Online database field identifier*] ..... LR

Letter ..... LT

Letter (AFM) ..... LTR

Letter ..... LTR

Letter Appointment in Mail ..... POINTMAIL

Letter Box ..... LB

Letter Box Number [*Viet Cong equivalent to the US APO*] ..... LBN

Letter Box Study Group [*British*] (DBA) ..... LBSG

Letter Carrier Depot (DD) ..... LCD

Letter Carrier Presort [*Canadian postal term*] (NFD) ..... LCP

Letter Carrier Route Evaluation System [*Postal Service*] ..... LCRES

Letter Carriers' Union of Canada ..... LCUC

Letter Contract LC

Letter Description (PDAA) ..... LD

Letter Enjoyers Association (EA) ..... LEA

Letter Exchange (EA) ..... LEX

Letter Follows (NOAA) ..... LETFO

Letter Input Processing [*Printing*] (DGA) ..... LIP

Letter Mail Code Sort System [*Postal Service*] ..... LMCSS

Letter of Acceptance ..... LOA

Letter of Activation [*Military*] ..... LA

Letter of Agreement ..... LOA

Letter of Agreement and Acceptance ..... LOAA

Letter of Aristeas (Pseudepigrapha) (BJA) ..... Arist

Letter of Authority ..... L/A

Letter of Authorization ..... LOA

Letter of Comment ..... LOC

Letter of Compliance [*Program*] [*Coast Guard*] ..... LOC

Letter of Consent ..... LOC

Letter of Credit (DFIT) ..... L/C

Letter of Credit LC

Letter of Credit ..... LCr

Letter of Credit Control System [*Department of Housing and Urban Development*] (GFGA) ..... LOCCS

Letter of Deposit [*Banking*] ..... L/D

Letter of Determination of Dependency ..... LDD

Letter of Evaluation ..... LOE

Letter of Execution (MCD) ..... LOE

Letter of Finding (GFGA) ..... LOF

Letter of General Representation (PDAA) ..... LGR

Letter of Indemnity (DS) ..... L/I

Letter of Instruction ..... LOI

Letter of Intent (DFIT) ..... L/I

Letter of Intent LI

Letter of Intent (MCD) ..... LOI

Letter of Interest (NG) ..... LOI

Letter of Introduction (ADA) LI

Letter of Introduction ..... LOI

Letter of Moral Intent [*Business term*] ..... LOMI

Letter of No Objection [*FDA*] ..... LONO

Letter of Notification ..... LON

Letter of Offer ..... L/O

Letter of Offer and Acceptance (MCD) ..... LOA

Letter of Promulgation [*Navy*] (NVT) ..... LOP

Letter of Proposal [*Military*] (AFM) ..... LOP

Letter of Repair/Analysis (AAGC) ..... LOR/A

Letter of Request (AFIT) ..... LOR

Letter of Transmittal (MCD) ..... LOT

Letter of Transmittal (MCD) ..... LT

Letter of Understanding [*Nuclear energy*] (NRCH) ..... LOU

Letter Orders ..... LO

Letter Quality (PCM) ..... LQ

Letter Quality Printer [*Computer science*] ..... LQP

Letter Report ..... LR

Letter Requirement ..... LR

Letter Requirement - Quick Reaction [*Army*] ..... LR-QR

Letter Service ..... LS

Letter Signed [*Manuscript descriptions*] ..... LS

Letter Signed [*Handwritten signature*] (WDMC) ..... ls

Letter Sorting Machine [*US Postal Service*] ..... LSM

Letter Stock ..... LS

Letter Telegram ... LT
Letter to the Editor ... LTE
Letter Writing with Automatic Send-Receive (IAA) ... LASR
Lettera di Credito [*Letter of Credit*] [*Italian Business term*] ... L/C
Lettera di Transporto Aereo [*Air Waybill*] [*Italian Business term*] ... LTA
Letterer-Siwe Disease [*Medicine*] (DMAA) ... LESD
Lettering (ADA) ... LTG
Lettering Faded ... LF
Lettering Piece (ROG) ... LP
Letterkenny Army Depot [*Pennsylvania*] (AABC) ... LEAD
Letterman Army Institute of Research [*San Francisco, CA*] ... LAIR
Letterman Army Medical Center (AABC) ... LAMC
Letter-Numerical [*system*] (DAVI) ... L/N
Letterpress (ADA) ... L/P
Letterpress ... LTP
Letterpress ... LTRPRS
Letterpress ... LTRPRS
Letterpress to Offset Conversion (DGA) ... LOC
Letters ... LETT
Letters ... LRES
Letters Abroad (EA) ... LA
Letters and Cards [*US Postal Service*] ... LC
Letters and Inscriptions of Hammurabi [*A publication*] (BJA) ... LIH
Letters in Digit Strings [*Psychology*] ... LID
Letters in Words [*Psychology*] ... LIW
Letters of Credit ... LOC
Letters of the First Babylonian Dynasty [*A publication*] (BJA) ... LFBD
Letters of Undertaking [*RSPA*] (TAG) ... LOU
Letters Patent (ROG) ... L/PAT
Letters Patent (ROG) ... LP
Letters Per Minute (WDMC) ... lpm
Letters Shift [*Teleprinters*] ... LTRS
Letter-Type Technical Directive [*Navy*] (NG) ... LTTD
Letter-Writing Support System (PDAA) ... LWSS
Lettish [*Latvian*] (ROG) ... LET
Lettish [*Latvian*] (ROG) ... LETT
Lettre d'Avis [*Letter of Advice*] [*French*] ... L/A
Lettre de Credit [*Letter of Credit*] [*French*] ... L/CR
Lettre de Credit [*Letter of Credit*] [*Business term*] [*French*] ... LC
Lettre de Transport Aerien [*Air Waybill*] [*French Business term*] ... LTA
Lettuce Infectious Yellows Virus ... LIYV
Lettuce Mosaic Virus ... LMV
Lettuce Necrotic Yellows Virus ... LNYV
Lettuce Speckles Mottle Virus [*Plant pathology*] ... LSMV
Letzeburger Chreschtliche Gewerkschaftsbond [*Confederation of Christian Trade Unions of Luxembourg*] ... LCGB
Letzeburger Sozialistesch Arbechter Partei [*Socialist Workers' Party of Luxembourg*] [*Political party*] (PPE) ... LSAP
Leu [*Monetary unit*] [*Romania*] ... L
Leucadia National [*NYSE symbol*] (TTSB) ... LUK
Leucadia National Corp. [*Associated Press*] (SAG) ... LeucNtl
Leucadia National Corp. [*NYSE symbol*] (SPSG) ... LUK
Leuchars [*British ICAO location identifier*] (ICLI) ... EGQL
Leucine [*One-letter symbol; see Leu*] [*An amino acid*] ... L
Leucine [*Also, L*] [*An amino acid*] ... Leu
Leucine [*An amino acid*] (DOG) ... leu
Leucine Acetylsalicylate [*Biochemistry*] (DAVI) ... LAS
Leucine Aminopeptidase [*Also, LP, LPAP*] [*An enzyme*] ... LA
Leucine Aminopeptidase [*Also, LA, LP*] [*An enzyme*] ... LAP
Leucine Aminopeptidase [*Also, LA, LAP*] [*An enzyme*] ... LP
Leucine Enkephalin [*Biochemistry*] ... LE
Leucine, Isoleucine, and Valine Binding Protein [*Biochemistry*] (DMAA) ... LIV-BP
Leucine Nitroanilide [*Biochemistry*] ... LNA
Leucine Tolerance Test [*Clinical chemistry*] (AAMN) ... LTT
Leucine Zipper [*Protein structure*] ... LZ
Leucine-Binding Protein [*Biochemistry*] ... LBP
Leucine-Rich Amelogenin Polypeptide [*Biochemistry of dental enamel*] ... LRAP
Leucine-Rich Glycoprotein ... LRG
Leucine-Rich Repeat [*Biochemistry*] ... LRR
Leucine-Rich Repeats [*Genetics*] ... LRR
Leucite [*CIPW classification*] [*Geology*] ... lc
Leucocyte Elastase [*An enzyme*] ... LE
Leucocyte Pyrogen [*Immunology*] ... LP
Leuconostoc [*An algae*] [*Biochemistry*] (DAVI) ... L
Leucosulfakinin [*Biochemistry*] ... LSK
Leucotomy [*European term for lobotomy*] (DSUE) ... LEUC
Leucotriene A [*Clinical pharmacology*] ... LTA
Leucotriene B [*Clinical pharmacology*] ... LTB
Leucotriene E [*Clinical pharmacology*] ... LTE
Leucotriene F [*Clinical pharmacology*] ... LTF
Leucovorin (DMAA) ... LEU
Leucyl-Transfer Ribonucleic Acid [*Biochemistry*] (DAVI) ... LARS
Leukemia [*Oncology*] ... LE
Leukemia [*Medicine*] ... Leuk
Leukemia Antigen [*Immunochemistry*] (DAVI) ... LA
Leukemia Cell-Derived Inhibitory Activity [*Hematology*] (DAVI) ... LIA
Leukemia Inhibitory Factor [*Oncology*] ... LIF
Leukemia Inhibitory Factor Receptor [*Biochemistry*] ... LIFR
Leukemia Society of America ... LS
Leukemia Society of America (EA) ... LSA
Leukemia Virus [*Hematology*] (MAE) ... LV
Leukemia-Associated Antigen [*Immunochemistry*] (DAVI) ... LAA
Leukemia-Associated Inhibiting Activity [*Medicine*] ... LIA
Leukemia-Like Reaction [*Hematology*] ... LLR
Leukemic Reticuloendotheliosis [*Medicine*] (AAMN) ... LRE
Leukeran [*Chlorambucil*], Methotrexate, Fluorouracil [*Antineoplastic drug regimen*] ... LMF
Leukoagglutinating [*Immunochemistry*] ... LA
Leukocyte [*Biochemistry*] (DAVI) ... LEUK
Leukocyte [*Hematology*] ... leuko
Leukocyte Adherence Inhibition [*Immunochemistry*] ... LAI
Leukocyte Adherence Inhibition Factor (DAVI) ... LAIF
Leukocyte Adhesion Deficiency [*Medicine*] ... LAD
Leukocyte Adhesion Receptor [*Immunology*] ... LAR
Leukocyte Alkaline Phosphatase [*An enzyme*] ... LAP
Leukocyte Alkaline Phosphatase [*Biochemistry*] (DAVI) ... LEUKAP
Leukocyte Alkaline Phosphatase Activity [*Biochemistry*] ... LAPA
Leukocyte Antigen-Related [*Medicine*] (DMAA) ... LAR
Leukocyte Ascorbic Acid [*Clinical chemistry*] (AAMN) ... LAA
Leukocyte Automatic Recognition Computer [*Blood counting*] ... LARC
Leukocyte Common Antigen [*Immunochemistry*] ... LCA
Leukocyte Differential Count [*Medicine*] (MEDA) ... LDC
Leukocyte Endothelial Cell-Cell Adhesion Molecule [*Cytology*] ... LECCAM
Leukocyte Equivalent Unit (DMAA) ... LEU
Leukocyte Esterase Enzyme Immunoassay ... LE-EIA
Leukocyte Feeder Layer [*Medicine*] (DMAA) ... LFL
Leukocyte Function-Associated Antigen [*Immunology*] ... LFA
Leukocyte Histamine Release [*Test*] ... LHR
Leukocyte Inhibition Factor [*Hematology*] ... LIF
Leukocyte Interferon [*Genetics*] ... LeIF
Leukocyte Migration Inhibition [*Hematology*] ... LMI
Leukocyte Migration Inhibition Factor [*Hematology*] (DMAA) ... LMIF
Leukocyte Mitogenic Factor [*Medicine*] ... LMF
Leukocyte Particle Counter [*Instrumentation*] ... LPC
Leukocyte Tyrosine Kinase [*An enzyme*] ... LTK
Leukocyte-Activated Killer [*Cells*] [*Oncology*] (DAVI) ... LAK
Leukocyte-Activating Factor [*Immunochemistry*] ... LAF
Leukocyte-Antigen Sensitivity Testing [*Medicine*] (MEDA) ... LAST
Leukocyte-Associates Herpes Virus [*Medicine*] (DAVI) ... LAHV
Leukocyte-Conditioned Medium [*Microbiology*] ... LCM
Leukocyte-Expressed Seven-Transmembrane-Domain Receptor [*Biochemistry*] ... LESTR
Leukocyte-Poor [*Hematology*] ... LP
Leukocyte-Specific Antinuclear Antibody [*Hematology*] (DMAA) ... LSANA
Leukocytic Endogenous Mediator [*Immunochemistry*] ... LEM
Leukocytoelastic Angitis [*Cardiology*] (DAVI) ... LCCA
Leukocytosi-Inducing Factor [*Hematology*] (DAVI) ... LIF
Leukocytosis-Promoting Factor [*Hematology*] ... LPF
Leukoencephalomalacia [*Veterinary medicine*] ... LEM
Leukoerythroblastic Reaction [*Biochemistry*] (DAVI) ... L-ERX
Leukoerythrogenetic (MAE) ... LE
Leukogglutination (DMAA) ... LA
Leukokinesis-Enhancing Factor [*Medicine*] (DMAA) ... LEF
Leukotactic Factor Activity [*Medicine*] (DMAA) ... LFA
Leukotriene [*Clinical pharmacology*] ... LT
Leukotriene C [*Clinical pharmacology*] ... LTC
Leukotriene D [*Clinical pharmacology*] ... LTD
Leukotriene Receptor Antagonist [*Biochemistry*] ... LTRA
Leuo Leucine Methylester [*Biochemistry*] ... LLME
Leuprlide [*Antineoplastic drug*] (CDI) ... LEUP
Leuprolide Acetate (DMAA) ... LA
Leurocristine [*Oncovin, Vincristine*] [*Also, O, V, VC, VCR*] [*Antineoplastic drug*] ... LCR
Leurs Altesses Imperiales [*Their Imperial Highnesses*] [*French*] ... LLAAII
Leurs Altesses Royales [*Their Royal Highnesses*] [*French*] ... LLAARR
Leurs Eminences [*Their Eminences*] [*French*] ... LLEE
Leurs Excellences [*Their Excellencies*] [*French*] ... LLEE
Leurs Majestes [*Their Majesties*] [*French*] ... LLMM
Leutkirch/Unterzeil [*Germany ICAO location identifier*] (ICLI) ... EDYL
Lev [*Monetary unit*] [*Bulgaria*] ... L
Lev [*Monetary unit*] [*Bulgaria*] ... LV
Lev Scientific Industries Ltd. [*Vancouver Stock Exchange symbol*] ... LEV
Levack Branch, Onaping Falls Public Library, Ontario [*Library symbol National Library of Canada*] (NLC) ... OLOF
Levaldigi [*Italy ICAO location identifier*] (ICLI) ... LIMZ
Levamisole [*Antineoplastic drug*] (CDI) ... LEV
Levant ... LEV
Levator [*Muscle*] [*Medicine*] (MEDA) ... lev
Levator Ani [*Anatomy*] ... LA
Levator Palpebrae Superioris [*Muscle*] [*Anatomy*] (AAMN) ... LPS
Level (KSC) ... L
Level ... LEV
Level (AAG) ... LVL
Level (VRA) ... lvl
Level 1 Trauma Center [*Medicine*] (DMAA) ... L1TC
Level above Threshold ... LAT
Level Absolute (SSD) ... LA
Level Alarm [*Engineering*] ... LA
Level Amplifier (IAA) ... LA
Level and Density Recorder Switch [*Nuclear energy*] (NRCH) ... L/DRS
Level Bombing Wind Offset Computer [*Military*] (IAA) ... LBWOC
Level Control ... LC
Level Control Function [*Computer science*] ... LCF
Level Control Valve (MCD) ... LCV
Level Crossing ... LC
Level Crossing Rate (IAA) ... LCR
Level Crossing Resonance [*Physical chemistry*] ... LCR
Level Decision Circuit ... LDC
Level Delay Time ... LDT
Level Detector ... LD

Level Detector (MSA) .... LDET
Level Detector (KSC) .... LDT
Level Discriminator .... LD
Level Discriminator (MSA) .... LDISCR
Level Distribution Recorder .... LDR
Level Equivalent (SSD) .... LEQ
Level Gauge .... LG
Level Indicating Alarm [Engineering] .... LIA
Level Indicator LI
Level Indicator Controller (NRCH) LIC
Level Indicator Recorder [Electronics] (ECII) .... LIR
Level Indicator Recorder Controller [Electronics] (ECII) .... LIRC
Level Indicator Recording Switch (NRCH) .... LIRS
Level Island, AK [Location identifier FAA] (FAAL) .... LVD
Level Island, AK [Location identifier FAA] (FAAL) .... SQM
Level Measuring Set [for test signals] [Telecommunications] (TEL) ..... LMS
Level Meter .... LM
Level of Aspiration Board [Psychology] .... LAB
Level of Authority [Military] (AFIT) .... LOA
Level of Care [Medicine] (GFGA) .... LOC
Level of Concern [Environmental Protection Agency] (ERG) .... LOC
Level of Consciousness [Medicine] .... LOC
Level of Detail (MCD) .... LOD
Level of Effort (KSC) .... LOE
Level of Free Convection [Meteorology] .... LFC
Level of Greatest Item Control [DoD] .... LOGIC
Level of Incompetence (DMAA) .... LOI
Level of Injury [Neurology] (DAVI) .... LOI
Level of Maintenance (MCD) .... LOM
Level of No Motion [Oceanography] .... LNM
Level of Rehabilitation Scale-I [Medicine] (DAVI) .... LORS-I
Level of Repair .... LOR
Level of Repair Analysis (MCD) .... LORA
Level of Repair Analysis Program .... LORAP
Level of Repair for Aeronautical Material (PDAA) .... LORAM
Level of Service [BTS] (TAG) .... LOS
Level of Study [Online database field identifier] LV
Level Off .... LO
Level Off [Aviation] (FAAC) .... LVLOF
Level One Communications [NASDAQ symbol] (TTSB) ..... LEVL
Level One Communications, Inc. [Associated Press] (SAG) .... LevelOne
Level One Communications, Inc. [NASDAQ symbol] (SAG) ..... LEVL
Level Recorder .... LR
Level Recording Controller .... LRC
Level Recording Switch (NRCH) .... LRS
Level Reference Base .... LRB
Level Regulator (NRCH) .... LR
Level Removable Instrument Assembly [Nuclear energy] (IEEE) ..... LRIA
Level Sensitive Scan Design (MCD) .... LSSD
Level Sensor Demonstration .... LSD
Level Sensor Gradiometer .... LSG
Level Set Point (NRCH) .... LSP
Level Setter .... LS
Level Shift Amplifier .... LSA
Level Shifter (NITA) .... LVLSH
Level Switch .... LS
Level Table (MHDB) .... LEVTAB
Level Transmitter (NRCH) .... LT
Level Trigger .... LT
Leveling Control Amplifier .... LCA
Leveling Control System .... LCS
Leveling/Sharpening Aggressions Test [Psychology] (EDAC) ..... LSAT
Leveling Torquer Amplifier .... LTA
Levelized Energy Adjustment Clause (NRCH) .... LEAC
Levelized Energy Cost .... LEC
Levelland Energy [Vancouver Stock Exchange symbol] LVL
Levelland, TX [AM radio station call letters] .... KLVT
Levelland, TX [FM radio station call letters] .... KLVT-FM
Levelland, TX [Location identifier FAA] (FAAL) .... LLN
Levelock [Alaska] [Airport symbol] (OAG) .... KLL
Levelometer .... LEVMETR
Levels-of-Processing [Psychology] .... LOP
Levend Joods Geloof (Liberaal Joodse Gemeente) (BJA) ..... LJG
Levengood Oil & Gas, Inc. [Vancouver Stock Exchange symbol] ..... LVG
Levenson's Internal, Powerful Others, and Chance Scales (EDAC) ..... LIPC
Lever L
Lever .... LEV
Lever (MSA) .... LVR
Lever .... LVR
Lever Lock (MCD) LL
Leverage Contract [Business term] LC
Leverage Transaction Merchant (MHDI) .... LTM
Leveraged Buy-Out .... LBO
Leveraged Employee Stock Ownership Plan [Procter & Gamble Co.] ..... LESOP
Leveraged Management Buy-Out .... LMBO
Leverkusen [Germany ICAO location identifier] (ICLI) ..... EDKL
Levesque, Beaubien & Co. [Toronto Stock Exchange symbol] ..... LBC
Leviathan Gas Pipeline [Associated Press] (SAG) .... LevGas
Leviathan Gas PL Partners Ltd. [NYSE symbol] (SPSG) ..... LEV
Leviathan Gas PLPtnrs LP [NYSE symbol] (TTSB) .... LEV
Levin Tube [Medicine] .... LT
Levinge's Irish Justice of the Peace [A publication] (DLA) ..... Lev JP
Levinthal-Coles-Lillie Bodies [Microbiology] LCL
Levinz's Entries [England] [A publication] (DLA) .... Lev Ent

Levinz's King's Bench and Common Pleas Reports [1660-97] [England]
  [A publication] (DLA) .... Lev
Levis [Light] [Pharmacy] .... LEV
Levi's International Commercial Law [2nd ed.] [1863] [A publication]
  (DLA) .... Levi Com L
Levi's Mercantile Law [1854] [A publication] (DLA) ..... Levi Merc L
Levis, PQ [FM radio station call letters] .... CFLS
Levitated Spherator (PDAA) .... LSP
Leviter [Lightly] [Pharmacy] .... LEVIT
Leviticus [Old Testament book] .... Lev
Leviticus [Old Testament book] (ROG) .... LEVIT
Leviticus [Old Testament book] Lv
Leviticus Rabbah (BJA) .... LevR
Leviticus Rabbah (BJA) .... LR
Levittown Memorial Education Center, Levittown, NY [Library symbol]
  [Library of Congress] (LCLS) .... NLevEC
Levittown, PR [FM radio station call letters] .... WKVN
Levittown Public Library, Levittown, NY [Library symbol Library of
  Congress] (LCLS) .... NLev
Levittown-Fairless Hills, PA [AM radio station call letters] ..... WBCB
Levitz Furniture [NYSE symbol] (TTSB) .... LFI
Levitz Furniture, Inc. [Associated Press] (SAG) .... Levitz
Levitz Furniture, Inc. [NYSE symbol] (SPSG) .... LFI
Levo [or Laevo] [Configuration in chemical structure] L
Levo-alpha-Acetylmethadol [Drug alternative to methadone] ..... LAAM
Levobunolol [Also, LBUN] [Biochemistry] .... LB
Levobunolol [Also, LB] [Biochemistry] .... LBUN
Levo-Carnitine Chloride [Biochemistry] LCC
Levo-Dihydroxyphenylalanine [Pharmacology] .... L-DOPA
Levodopa [Obstetrics] (DAVI) .... LD
Levon Resources Ltd. [Toronto Stock Exchange symbol Vancouver Stock
  Exchange symbol] .... LVN
Levorotary [or Levorotatory] [Chemistry] l
Levorotatory [Optics] [Chemistry] (DOG) L
Levorotatory [Optics] [Chemistry] (DOG) .... lev
Levothyroxine [Pharmacy] .... LT
Levtech Medical Technologies Ltd. [Vancouver Stock Exchange symbol] ..... LMT
Levulinic Acid [Organic chemistry] .... LA
Levulose (10 Percent) in Water L-10-W
Levy [Alaska] [Seismograph station code, US Geological Survey] (SEIS) ..... LVY
Levy Industries Ltd. [Toronto Stock Exchange symbol] ..... LE
Levyne [A zeolite] .... LEV
Lew David Feldman [New York bookseller; phonetic spelling of his initials
  forms name of company] .... EL DIEFF
Lew DeWitt Fan Club [Defunct] (EA) .... LDFC
Lewd and Lascivious .... L & L
Lewes, DE [FM radio station call letters] .... WXJN
Lewin on Trusts [A publication] (DLA) .... Lew Tr
Lewin on Trusts [A publication] (DLA) .... Lewin
Lewin's Appportionment [1869] [A publication] (DLA) ..... Lew App
Lewin's English Crown Cases [A publication] (DLA) ..... Lew CC
Lewin's English Crown Cases [A publication] (DLA) ..... Lewin CC (Eng)
Lewin's English Crown Cases Reserved [1822-38] [A publication] (DLA) ..... Lew
Lewin's English Crown Cases Reserved [1822-38] [A publication]
  (DLA) .... Lewin CC
Lewin's English Crown Cases Reserved [A publication] (DLA) ..... Lewin Cr Cas
Lewis [Blood group] .... Le
Lewis [Rat strain] .... LEW
Lewis and Clark College (GAGS) .... Lewis & Clark C
Lewis and Clark College, Portland, OR [OCLC symbol] (OCLC) ..... OLP
Lewis and Clark College, Portland, OR [Library symbol Library of Congress]
  (LCLS) .... OrPL
Lewis and Clark Community College, Godfrey, IL [Library symbol Library of
  Congress] (LCLS) .... IGoL
Lewis and Clark Library System [Library network] .... LCLS
Lewis and Clark Library System, Alhambra, Alhambra, IL [Library symbol
  Library of Congress] (LCLS) .... IEdL-A
Lewis and Clark Library System, Chesterfield, Chesterfield, IL [Library
  symbol Library of Congress] (LCLS) .... IEdL-C
Lewis and Clark Library System, Edwardsville, IL [Library symbol Library of
  Congress] (LCLS) .... IEdL
Lewis and Clark Library System, Edwardsville, IL [OCLC symbol] (OCLC) ..... IEU
Lewis and Clark Library System, Hamel, Hamel, IL [Library symbol Library of
  Congress] (LCLS) .... IEdL-H
Lewis and Clark Library System, Hillsboro Prison, Edwardsville, IL [Library
  symbol Library of Congress] (LCLS) .... IEdL-HP
Lewis and Clark Library System, Livingston, Livingston, IL [Library symbol
  Library of Congress] (LCLS) .... IEdL-L
Lewis and Clark Library System, Marine, Marine, IL [Library symbol Library
  of Congress] (LCLS) .... IEdL-M
Lewis and Clark Library System, Mulberry Grove, Mulberry Grove, IL
  [Library symbol Library of Congress] (LCLS) .... IEdL-Mg
Lewis and Clark Library System, Palmyra, Palmyra, IL [Library symbol
  Library of Congress] (LCLS) .... IEdL-P
Lewis and Clark Library System, St. Jacob, St. Jacob, IL [Library symbol
  Library of Congress] (LCLS) .... IEdL-StJ
Lewis and Clark Library System, Shipman, Shipman, IL [Library symbol
  Library of Congress] (LCLS) .... IEdL-Sh
Lewis and Clark Regional Library [Library network] ..... LCRL
Lewis and Clark Society of America (EA) .... LCSA
Lewis and Clark Trail Heritage Foundation (EA) .... LCTHF
Lewis & Roca, Phoenix, AZ [Library symbol] [Library of Congress]
  (LCLS) .... AzPhL
Lewis' Appeals Reports [29-35 Missouri] [A publication] (DLA) ..... Lewis
Lewis Carroll Society of North America (EA) .... LCNA

Lewis County District Library, Kamiah Branch, Kamiah, ID [*Library symbol*] [*Library of Congress*] (LCLS) ... IdNp-K
Lewis County Free District Library, Nez Perce, ID [*Library symbol*] [*Library of Congress*] (LCLS) ... IdNP
Lewis County General Hospital, Medical Library, Lowville, NY [*Library symbol Library of Congress*] (LCLS) ... NLowLH
Lewis' Criminal Law [*A publication*] (DLA) ... Lew CL
Lewis D. and John J. Gilbert, Corporate Democracy (EA) ... CD
Lewis' Digest of United States Criminal Law [*A publication*] (DLA) ... Lew Dig Cr L
Lewis' Digest of United States Criminal Law [*A publication*] (DLA) ... Lew US Cr L
Lewis' East India Penal Code [*A publication*] (DLA) ... Lew Ind Pen
Lewis' Election Manual [*A publication*] (DLA) ... Lew Elec
Lewis Expandable Adjustable Prosthesis [*Orthopedics*] ... LEAP
Lewis Flight Propulsion Laboratory [*NASA*] ... LFPL
Lewis Flight Propulsion Research Laboratory [*NASA*] (MUGU) ... LFPRL
Lewis Ginter Botanical Gardens, Inc., Richmond, VA [*Library symbol*] [*Library of Congress*] (LCLS) ... ViRBG
Lewis Gun ... LG
Lewis, IN [*Location identifier FAA*] (FAAL) ... LEU
Lewis' Kentucky Law Reporter [*A publication*] (DLA) ... Lewis
Lewis' Law of Perpetuities [*A publication*] (DLA) ... Lew Perp
Lewis' Law of Perpetuities [*A publication*] (DLA) ... Lewis Perp
Lewis' Leading Cases on Public Land Law [*A publication*] (DLA) ... Lew L Cas
Lewis Lung Carcinoma [*Oncology*] ... 3LL
Lewis, M. H., Winchester VA [*STAC*] ... LMH
Lewis Number [*IUPAC*] ... Le
Lewis on Bonds and Securities [*A publication*] (DLA) ... Lew B & S
Lewis on Eminent Domain [*A publication*] (DLA) ... Lewis Em Dom
Lewis on Equity Drafting [*A publication*] (DLA) ... Lew Eq Dr
Lewis on Land Titles in Philadelphia [*A publication*] (DLA) ... Lew LT
Lewis on Stocks, Bonds, Etc. [*A publication*] (DLA) ... Lew St
Lewis' Principles of Conveyancing [*A publication*] (DLA) ... Lew Conv
Lewis Public Library, Lewis, IA [*Library symbol Library of Congress*] (LCLS) ... IaLew
Lewis' Reports [*Nevada*] [*A publication*] (DLA) ... Lew
Lewis' Reports [*Missouri*] [*A publication*] (DLA) ... Lew
Lewis' Reports [*Nevada*] [*A publication*] (DLA) ... Lewis
Lewis Research Center [*NASA*] (KSC) ... LERC
Lewis Research Center [*NASA*] ... LRC
Lewis Space Flight Center (MCD) ... LSPC
Lewis University, College of Law, Glen Ellyn, IL [*Library symbol Library of Congress*] (LCLS) ... ILocL-L
Lewis University, Lockport, IL [*OCLC symbol*] (OCLC) ... ICX
Lewis University, Lockport, IL [*Library symbol Library of Congress*] (LCLS) ... ILocL
Lewis x Brown Norway [*Rat strain*] ... LBN
Lewis Zero Gravity Facility ... LZGF
Lewisburg, PA [*FM radio station call letters*] (RBYB) ... WCXR
Lewisburg, PA [*FM radio station call letters*] ... WGRC
Lewisburg, PA [*AM radio station call letters*] ... WTGC
Lewisburg, PA [*FM radio station call letters*] ... WVBU
Lewisburg, TN [*Location identifier FAA*] (FAAL) ... LUG
Lewisburg, TN [*AM radio station call letters*] ... WAXO
Lewisburg, TN [*AM radio station call letters*] ... WJJM
Lewisburg, TN [*FM radio station call letters*] ... WJJM-FM
Lewisburg, WV [*Location identifier FAA*] (FAAL) ... LWB
Lewisburg, WV [*FM radio station call letters*] ... WKCJ
Lewisburg, WV [*Television station call letters*] ... WVGV
Lewisburg, WV [*TV station call letters*] (RBYB) ... WVSX-TV
Lewis-Clark State College, Lewiston, ID [*Library symbol Library of Congress*] (LCLS) ... IdLN
Lewisite [*War gas*] [*Army symbol*] ... L
Lewisite-Mustard Gas Mix [*for land mines*] [*Army symbol*] ... LH
Lewisporte Public Library, Lewisporte, NF, Canada [*Library symbol Library of Congress*] (LCLS) ... CaNfLe
Lewisporte Public Library, Newfoundland [*Library symbol National Library of Canada*] (NLC) ... NFLE
Lewiston [*Maine*] [*Airport symbol*] (OAG) ... LEW
Lewiston [*Idaho*] [*Airport symbol*] (OAG) ... LWS
Lewiston City Library, Lewiston, ID [*Library symbol*] [*Library of Congress*] (LCLS) ... IdL
Lewiston Elementary Schools, Camelot Elementary School, Lewiston, ID [*Library symbol*] [*Library of Congress*] (LCLS) ... IdLES-CM
Lewiston Elementary Schools, Centennial Elementary School, Lewiston, ID [*Library symbol*] [*Library of Congress*] (LCLS) ... IdLES-CN
Lewiston Elementary Schools, Lewiston, ID [*Library symbol*] [*Library of Congress*] (LCLS) ... IdLES
Lewiston Elementary Schools, McGhee Elementary School, Lewiston, ID [*Library symbol*] [*Library of Congress*] (LCLS) ... IdLES-MG
Lewiston Elementary Schools, McSorley Elementary School, Lewiston, ID [*Library symbol*] [*Library of Congress*] (LCLS) ... IdLES-MS
Lewiston Elementary Schools, Orchards Elementary School, Lewiston, ID [*Library symbol*] [*Library of Congress*] (LCLS) ... IdLES-OR
Lewiston Elementary Schools, Webster Elementary School, Lewiston, ID [*Library symbol*] [*Library of Congress*] (LCLS) ... IdLES-WB
Lewiston Elementary Schools, Whitman Elementary School, Lewiston, ID [*Library symbol*] [*Library of Congress*] (LCLS) ... IdLES-WH
Lewiston High School, Lewiston, ID [*Library symbol*] [*Library of Congress*] (LCLS) ... IdLHS
Lewiston, ID [*FM radio station call letters*] ... KATW
Lewiston, ID [*Television station call letters*] ... KLEW
Lewiston, ID [*FM radio station call letters*] ... KLHS
Lewiston, ID [*FM radio station call letters*] ... KMOK
Lewiston, ID [*AM radio station call letters*] ... KOZE
Lewiston, ID [*FM radio station call letters*] ... KOZE-FM
Lewiston, ID [*AM radio station call letters*] ... KRLC
Lewiston, ME [*FM radio station call letters*] ... WCYI
Lewiston, ME [*FM radio station call letters*] ... WRBC
Lewiston, ME [*FM radio station call letters*] ... WTHT
Lewiston ME [*AM radio station call letters*] ... WTME
Lewiston, ME [*Television station call letters*] ... WWLA
Lewiston, ME [*AM radio station call letters*] ... WZOU
Lewiston Public Library, Lewiston, ME [*Library symbol Library of Congress*] (LCLS) ... MeL
Lewiston Public Library, Lewiston, MI [*Library symbol Library of Congress*] (LCLS) ... MiLew
Lewiston Public Library, Lewiston, NY [*Library symbol Library of Congress*] (LCLS) ... NLew
Lewiston Public Library, Lewiston, UT [*Library symbol Library of Congress*] (LCLS) ... ULew
Lewistown [*Montana*] [*Airport symbol*] (OAG) ... LWT
Lewistown City Library, Lewistown, MT [*Library symbol Library of Congress*] (LCLS) ... MtLe
Lewistown, MT [*FM radio station call letters*] ... KLCM
Lewistown, MT [*AM radio station call letters*] ... KXLO
Lewistown, PA [*FM radio station call letters*] (RBYB) ... WANU-FM
Lewistown, PA [*FM radio station call letters*] ... WCHX
Lewistown, PA [*AM radio station call letters*] ... WIEZ
Lewistown, PA [*AM radio station call letters*] ... WKVA
Lewistown, PA [*FM radio station call letters*] ... WMRF
Lewisville Aquatic Ecosystem Research Facility [*Texas*] ... LAERF
Lewisville Aquatic Ecosystem Research Facility [*Army*] ... LAERF
Lewisville, NC [*AM radio station call letters*] ... WSGH
Lewisville Public Library, Lewisville, ID [*Library symbol*] [*Library of Congress*] (LCLS) ... LdLew
Lex Custumaria [*Latin A publication*] (DLA) ... Lex Cust
Lex Maneriorum [*Latin A publication*] (DLA) ... Lex Man
Lex Mercatoria Americana [*Latin A publication*] (DLA) ... Lex Mer Am
Lex Operator Gene ... LOp
Lex Parliamentaria [*Latin A publication*] (DLA) ... Lex Parl
Lex Vehicle Leasing [*British*] ... LVL
Lexden [*England*] ... LEXD
Lexical (BJA) ... Lex
Lexical (ABBR) ... LEXI
Lexical Functional Grammar [*Artificial intelligence*] ... LFG
Lexical Rule [*Linguistics*] ... L
Lexical-Graphical Composer Printer [*Photocomposition*] ... LGCP
Lexicographer (ABBR) ... LEX
Lexicographer (ABBR) ... LEXICO
Lexicographer (ABBR) ... LEXPHR
Lexicography ... LEXICOG
Lexicography (ABBR) ... LEXPHY
Lexicography Information Service [*Germany Computer science*] ... LEXIS
Lexicological (ABBR) ... LEXOGL
Lexicologist (ABBR) ... LEXOGT
Lexicology (ABBR) ... LEXOG
Lexicon ... LEX
Lexicon (ABBR) ... LEXN
Lexicon Hebraicum et Aramaicum Veteris Testamenti [*Rome*] [*A publication*] (BJA) ... LVT
Lexicon in Veteris Testamenti Libros [*A publication*] (BJA) ... LVTL
Lexicon in Veteris Testamenti Libros. Supplementum [*L. Koehler and W. Baumgartner*] [*A publication*] (BJA) ... KBL
Lexicon Messanense [*Classical studies*] (OCD) ... Lex Mess
Lexicon of Inconspicuously Ambiguous Recommendations [*Term coined by Robert J. Thornton of Lehigh University*] ... LIAR
Lexicon Syriacum [*A publication*] (BJA) ... LexSyr
Lexington [*Kentucky*] [*Seismograph station code, US Geological Survey*] (SEIS) ... LEK
Lexington [*Virginia*] [*Seismograph station code, US Geological Survey Closed*] (SEIS) ... LEX
Lexington [*Diocesan abbreviation*] [*Kentucky*] (TOCD) ... LEX
Lexington, AL [*AM radio station call letters*] ... WKNI
Lexington Army Depot [*Kentucky*] (AFIT) ... LXAD
Lexington B & L Financial Corp. [*Associated Press*] (SAG) ... LexBLF
Lexington B & L Financial Corp. [*NASDAQ symbol*] (SAG) ... LXMO
Lexington Bluegrass Depot Activity [*Kentucky*] [*Army*] ... LBDA
Lexington Corporate Prop [*NYSE symbol*] (TTSB) ... LXP
Lexington Corporate Properties [*Associated Press*] (SAG) ... LexCrpP
Lexington Corporate Properties [*NYSE symbol*] (SAG) ... LXP
Lexington County Circulating Library, Batesburg, SC [*Library symbol Library of Congress*] (LCLS) ... ScBa
Lexington Design Group (SAA) ... LDG
Lexington Development Branch (SAA) ... LDB
Lexington Developmental Scales [*Child development test*] ... LDS
Lexington/Frankfort [*Kentucky*] [*Airport symbol*] (OAG) ... LEX
Lexington Global Asset Managers, Inc. [*Associated Press*] (SAG) ... LexGlbl
Lexington Global Asset Managers, Inc. [*NASDAQ symbol*] (SAG) ... LGAM
Lexington Global Assets Mgrs [*NASDAQ symbol*] (TTSB) ... LGAM
Lexington Group in Transportation History (EA) ... LGTH
Lexington Historical Society, Lexington, MA [*Library symbol Library of Congress*] (LCLS) ... MLexHi
Lexington, KY [*Location identifier FAA*] (FAAL) ... GNJ
Lexington, KY [*Location identifier FAA*] (FAAL) ... LSD
Lexington, KY [*Location identifier FAA*] (FAAL) ... SEN
Lexington, KY [*Television station call letters*] ... WKLE
Lexington, KY [*FM radio station call letters*] ... WKQQ
Lexington, KY [*Television station call letters*] ... WKYT
Lexington, KY [*AM radio station call letters*] ... WLAP
Lexington, KY [*Television station call letters*] ... WLEX

Lexington, KY [*AM radio station call letters*] ..... WLXG
Lexington, KY [*FM radio station call letters*] ..... WMXL
Lexington, KY [*FM radio station call letters*] ..... WRFL
Lexington, KY [*Television station call letters*] ..... WTVQ
Lexington, KY [*FM radio station call letters*] ..... WUKY
Lexington, KY [*AM radio station call letters*] ..... WVLK
Lexington, KY [*FM radio station call letters*] ..... WVLK-FM
Lexington, MI [*FM radio station call letters*] ..... WBTI
Lexington, MO [*FM radio station call letters*] ..... KISF
Lexington, MO [*AM radio station call letters*] ..... KLEX
Lexington, MS [*FM radio station call letters*] ..... WAGR
Lexington, MS [*AM radio station call letters*] ..... WXTN
Lexington, NC [*Location identifier FAA*] (FAAL) ..... EXX
Lexington, NC [*TV station call letters*] (RBYB) ..... WBFX-TV
Lexington, NC [*Television station call letters*] ..... WEJC
Lexington, NC [*AM radio station call letters*] ..... WLXN
Lexington, NC [*FM radio station call letters*] ..... WWGL
Lexington, NE [*FM radio station call letters*] ..... KLNE
Lexington, NE [*Television station call letters*] ..... KLNE-TV
Lexington, NE [*AM radio station call letters*] ..... KRVN
Lexington, NE [*FM radio station call letters*] ..... KRVN-FM
Lexington, NE [*Location identifier FAA*] (FAAL) ..... LXN
Lexington, OK [*Location identifier FAA*] (FAAL) ..... HMY
Lexington Park Library, Lexington Park, MD [*Library symbol Library of Congress*] (LCLS) ..... MdLxp
Lexington Park, MD [*FM radio station call letters*] ..... WMDM
Lexington Park, MD [*AM radio station call letters*] ..... WPTX
Lexington Public Library, Lexington, KY [*Library symbol Library of Congress*] (LCLS) ..... KyLx
Lexington Resources Ltd. [*Vancouver Stock Exchange symbol*] ..... LXN
Lexington, SC [*AM radio station call letters*] ..... WLGO
Lexington, SC [*FM radio station call letters*] ..... WLXC
Lexington Technical Institute, Lexington, KY [*OCLC symbol*] (OCLC) ..... KUT
Lexington Technical Institute, Lexington, KY [*Library symbol Library of Congress*] (LCLS) ..... KyLxTI
Lexington Theological Seminary, Lexington, KY [*Library symbol Library of Congress*] (LCLS) ..... KyLxCB
Lexington, TN [*AM radio station call letters*] ..... WDXL
Lexington, TN [*Television station call letters*] ..... WLJT
Lexington, TN [*FM radio station call letters*] ..... WZLT
Lexington, VA [*FM radio station call letters*] ..... WLUR
Lexington, VA [*FM radio station call letters*] ..... WMRL
Lexington, VA [*AM radio station call letters*] ..... WREL
Lexington-Blue Grass Army Depot [*Kentucky*] (AABC) ..... LBAD
Lexington-Fayette, KY [*FM radio station call letters*] ..... WJGG
Lexington-Fayette, KY [*FM radio station call letters*] (RBYB) ..... WLKT-FM
Lexmark International Group [*Associated Press*] (SAG) ..... Lexmrk
Lexmark International Group [*NYSE symbol*] (SAG) ..... LXK
Lexmark Intl Group'A' [*NYSE symbol*] (TTSB) ..... LXK
L'Express, Inc. [*ICAO designator*] (FAAC) ..... LEX
Leyden [*Netherlands*] (ROG) ..... LEYD
Leydig-Cell Tumor in Wistar Rat [*Medicine*] (DMAA) ..... LTW
Leydig's Cells [*Endocrinology*] LC
Leyland Cars [*Leyland Daf Ltd.*] LC
Ley's English Court of Wards Reports [*A publication*] (DLA) ..... Ley
Ley's English Court of Wards Reports [*A publication*] (DLA) ..... Ley Wards
Ley's English King's Bench Reports [*1608-29*] [*A publication*] (DLA) ..... Leigh
Ley's English King's Bench Reports [*1608-29*] [*A publication*] (DLA) ..... Ley
Lezignan-Corbieres [*France ICAO location identifier*] (ICLI) ..... LFMZ
L.F. Smith Elementary School, South Houston, TX [*Library symbol*] [*Library of Congress*] (LCLS) ..... TxShoSE
LFP Holdings, Inc. [*Toronto Stock Exchange symbol*] ..... LFP
LFS Bancorp [*Associated Press*] (SAG) ..... LFS Bcp
LFS Bancorp [*NASDAQ symbol*] (SAG) ..... LFSB
LFU Leonhartsberger Flugunternehmen Gesellschaft MbH [*Austria*] [*FAA designator*] (FAAC) ..... LFU
LG & E Energy [*NYSE symbol*] (SPSG) ..... LGE
LGA: Local Government Administration [*A publication*] ..... LGA
L-Glutamic [*acid*] **and L-Alanine** [*Copolymer*] ..... GA
L-Glutamic [*acid*] **and L-Lysine** [*Copolymer*] ..... GL
L-Gulanolactone Oxidase [*An enzyme*] ..... GLO
Lhasa [*Tibet*] [*Seismograph station code, US Geological Survey Closed*] (SEIS) ..... LHA
Lhasa [*Tibet*] [*Seismograph station code, US Geological Survey*] (SEIS) ..... LSA
Lhasa [*China*] [*Airport symbol*] (OAG) ..... LXA
Lhasa [*China*] [*ICAO location identifier*] (ICLI) ..... ZULS
L-Histidinol [*Biochemistry*] ..... L-HTL
Lhok Sukon [*Indonesia*] [*ICAO location identifier*] (ICLI) ..... WITL
Liability ..... LBLTY
Liability [*Insurance*] LI
Liability ..... LIAB
Liability (ABBR) ..... LIABT
Liability (ABBR) ..... LIBT
Liability Damage Waiver [*Insurance*] ..... LDW
Liability Management (TDOB) ..... LM
Liability Policy [*Information service or system*] (DOAD) ..... LP
Liable (ABBR) ..... LIBL
Liaison [*Airplane designation*] L
Liaison ..... LIA
Liaison (AFM) ..... LN
Liaison Branch [*BUPERS*] ..... LB
Liaison Call Sheet ..... LCS
Liaison Change Notice ..... LCN
Liaison Committee for Mediterranean Citrus Fruit Culture [*See also CLAM*] [*Madrid, Spain*] (EAIO) ..... LCMCFC
Liaison Committee of Cooperating Oil and Gas Associations (EA) ..... LCCOGA
Liaison Committee of Development Non-Governmental Organizations to the European Communities [*Belgium*] (EAIO) ..... LC NGO-EC
Liaison Committee of European Bicycle Manufacturers [*Belgium*] (EAIO) ..... LCEBM
Liaison Committee of European Motorcycle Manufacturers [*Belgium*] (EAIO) ..... LCEMM
Liaison Committee of the Architects of United Europe [*EC*] (ECED) ..... LCAUE
Liaison Committee of the European Economic Community Steel Tube Industry [*Defunct*] (EAIO) ..... LCEECSTI
Liaison Committee of the Rice Starch Manufacturers of the EEC [*Belgium*] (EAIO) ..... LCRSMEEC
Liaison Committee of Women's International Organisations [*British*] (DI) ..... LCWIO
Liaison Committee on Graduate Medical Education ..... LCGME
Liaison Committee on Medical Education (EA) ..... LCME
Liaison Engineering Order ..... LEO
Liaison Group for International Educational Exchange (EA) ..... LGIEE
Liaison, Interface, Coupling, Technology Transfer ..... LINCOTT
Liaison Internationale des Industries de l'Alimentation [*International Liaison for the Food Industries*] ..... LIDIA
Liaison Office [*or Officer*] ..... LO
Liaison Office Support ..... LOS
Liaison Officer [*Military*] ..... LINO
Liaison Officer [*Military*] ..... LNO
Liaison Officer Coordinator [*Air Force*] (AFM) ..... LOC
Liaison Report (AAG) ..... LR
Liaison Request (AAG) ..... LR
Liaison Residency Endorsement Committee [*RRCEM*] [*Superseded by*] (EA) ..... LREC
Liaison-Cargo [*Air Force*] LC
Liang-Chow [*Republic of China*] [*Seismograph station code, US Geological Survey Closed*] (SEIS) LCC
Liaoning Province [*China, Mainland*] [*MARC geographic area code Library of Congress*] (LCCP) ..... a-cc-lp
Libbey, Inc. [*NYSE symbol*] (SPSG) ..... LBY
Libbey, Inc. [*Associated Press*] (SAG) ..... Libbey
Libbey-Owens-Ford Glass Co. [*Auto industry supplier*] ..... LOF
Libbey-Owens-Ford Glass Co., Corporate Library, Toledo, OH [*Library symbol Library of Congress*] (LCLS) ..... OTLO
Libbey-Owens-Ford Glass Co., Technical Library, Toledo, OH [*Library symbol Library of Congress*] (LCLS) ..... OTL
Libby Army Airfield ..... LAAF
Libby Dam [*Montana*] [*Seismograph station code, US Geological Survey*] (SEIS) ..... LDM
Libby High School, Libby, MT [*Library symbol*] [*Library of Congress*] (LCLS) ..... MtLibH
Libby Junior High School, Libby, MT [*Library symbol*] [*Library of Congress*] (LCLS) ..... MtLibJ
Libby, MT [*AM radio station call letters*] ..... KLCB
Libby, MT [*FM radio station call letters*] ..... KTNY
Libby, MT [*Location identifier FAA*] (FAAL) ..... LYI
Libel and Slander [*Legal term*] (DLA) ..... LIB & SL
Libel Defense Resource Center (EA) ..... LDRC
Libenge [*Zaire*] [*ICAO location identifier*] (ICLI) ..... FZFA
Libenge [*Zaire*] [*Airport symbol Obsolete*] (OAG) ..... LIE
Liber [*Book*] [*Latin*] L
Liber [*Book*] [*Latin*] ..... LIB
Liber Antiquitatum Biblicarum. Pseudo-Philo (BJA) ..... LAB
Liber Assisarum [*Book of Assizes, or pleas of the crown*] [*Pt. 5 of Year Books*] [*A publication*] (DLA) ..... Ass
Liber Assisarum [*Book of Assizes, or pleas of the crown*] [*Pt. 5 of Year Books*] [*A publication*] (DLA) ..... Lib Ass
Liber Feudorum [*Book of Feuds*] [*At the end of the Corpus Juris Civilis*] [*A publication*] (DLA) ..... Lib Feud
Liber Niger [*Black Book*] [*A publication*] (DLA) ..... LN
Liber Sextus Decretalium [*A publication*] (DSA) ..... Sext
Libera Confederazione Generale Italiana dei Lavoratori [*Free Italian General Confederation of Workers*] ..... LCGIL
Libera Federazione Italiana Lavoratori Industrie Estrattive [*Free Italian Federation of Workers in Mining Industries*] ..... LFILIE
Liberaalinen Kansanpuolue [*Liberal People's Party*] [*Finland Political party*] (PPE) ..... LKP
Liberace Club of Las Vegas (EA) LCLV
Liberal [*Politics*] L
Liberal [*Kansas*] [*Airport symbol*] (OAG) ..... LBL
Liberal ..... LIB
Liberal ..... LIBL
Liberal [*Especially in negative political context*] ..... L-word
Liberal Academic Complex ..... LAC
Liberal Action Group for Electoral Reform [*British*] (DI) ..... LAGER
Liberal Alliance [*Political party*] [*British*] ..... All
Liberal Arts ..... LA
Liberal Conservative LC
Liberal Country League [*Australia*] (BARN) LCL
Liberal Country Party [*Australia*] (BARN) ..... LCP
Liberal, Democratic, and Reformist Group [*European political movement*] (ECON) ..... LDR
Liberal, Democratic and Reformist Group [*See also GLDR*] (EAIO) ..... LDRG
Liberal Democratic Party [*Slovenia*] [*Political party*] (EY) ..... LDP
Liberal Demokratische Partei [*Liberal Democratic Party*] [*Germany Political party*] (PPE) ..... LDP
Liberal Education for Adoptive Families (EA) ..... LEAF
Liberal European Youth ..... LEY
Liberal Industrial Relations Association [*British*] ..... LIRA

Liberal International [*World Liberal Union*] [*British*] (EAIO) LI
Liberal International (British Group) [*World Liberal Union*] (EAIO) .... LibInt(BG)
Liberal, KS [*FM radio station call letters*] .... KLDG
Liberal, KS [*AM radio station call letters*] .... KSCB
Liberal, KS [*FM radio station call letters*] .... KSCB-FM
Liberal, KS [*FM radio station call letters*] .... KSLS
Liberal, KS [*AM radio station call letters*] .... KYUU
Liberal, KS [*FM radio station call letters*] .... KZQD
Liberal, KS [*Location identifier FAA*] (FAAL) .... LBL
Liberal/National Party [*Political party Australia*] .... LNP
Liberal Party [*Canada*] (PPW) .... LP
Liberal Party of Nova Scotia, Halifax [*Library symbol National Library of Canada*] (BIB) .... NSHLP
Liberal Party of Nova Scotia, Halifax, NS, Canada [*Library symbol*] [*Library of Congress*] (LCLS) .... CaNSHLP
Liberal Party of Wales [*Political party*] .... LPW
Liberal Party Organization [*British*] .... LPO
Liberal Religious Educators Association (EA) .... LREDA
Liberal Religious Peace Fellowship (EA) .... LRPF
Liberal Religious Youth .... LRY
Liberal Socialist Party [*Egypt*] [*Political party*] (PPW) .... LSP
Liberala Folkpartiet [*Liberal People's Party*] [*Finland Political party*] (PPE) .... LFP
Liberal-Democratic Party of Japan [*Jiyu-Minshuto*] [*Political party*] (PPW) .... LDP
Liberal-Demokratische Partei Deutschlands [*Liberal Democratic Party of Germany*] [*Political party*] (PPW) .... LDPD
Liberal-Demokratische Union der Schweiz [*Liberal Democratic Union of Switzerland*] [*Political party*] (PPE) .... LIDUS
Liberale Partei der Schweiz [*Liberal Party of Switzerland*] [*Political party*] (PPE) .... LPS
Liberale Partei Oesterreichs [*Liberal Party of Austria*] [*Political party*] (PPE) .... LPO
Liberale Staatspartij [*Liberal State Party*] [*Netherlands Political party*] (PPE) .... LSP
Liberalium Artium Magister [*Master of the Liberal Arts*] .... LAM
Liberalize (ABBR) .... LIBRLZ
Liberalizing (ABBR) .... LIBLZG
Liberal-Labour Alliance [*British*] (DSUE) .... LIB LAB
Liberal-National Country Party [*Australia Political party*] (PPW) .... L-NCP
Liberalsoziale Union [*Liberal Social Union*] [*Germany Political party*] (PPW) .... LSU
Liberalt Centrum [*Liberal Center*] [*Denmark Political party*] (PPE) LC
Liberal-Unionist [*British*] (ROG) .... LU
Liberated (ABBR) .... LIBERD
Liberated Areas Committee [*World War II*] .... LAC
Liberating (ABBR) .... LIBERG
Liberation .... LIB
Liberation (ABBR) .... LIBERN
Liberation, Absorption, Distribution, Metabolism, Excretion [*Medicine*] (DAVI) .... LADME
Liberation Action Party [*Trinidad and Tobago*] [*Political party*] (PPW) .... LAP
Liberation Broadcasting Station (CINC) .... LBS
Liberation Kanake Socialiste [*Socialist Kanak Liberation*] [*New Caledonia*] (PD) .... LKS
Liberation Movement of the German Reich [*An association*] (EAIO) .... LMGR
Liberation News Agency [*Vietnam*] .... LNA
Liberation News Service (EA) .... LNS
Liberation Support Movement Information Center (EA) .... LSM
Liberation Tigers of Tamil Eelam [*Sri Lanka*] .... LTTE
Liberator (ABBR) .... LIBERR
Liberator Atlanta [*An association*] (EA) .... LA
Liberator Bomber Aircraft [*British*] (DSUE) .... LIB
Liberator Lake, AK [*Location identifier FAA*] (FAAL) .... LLK
Liberator Party [*Guyana*] [*Political party*] (PPW) .... LP
Liberia [*MARC geographic area code Library of Congress*] (LCCP) .... f-lb--
Liberia [*MARC country of publication code Library of Congress*] (LCCP) .... lb
Liberia [*ANSI three-letter standard code*] (CNC) .... LBR
Liberia (ABBR) LI
Liberia .... Lib
Liberia (VRA) .... Liber
Liberia [*Costa Rica*] [*Airport symbol*] (OAG) .... LIR
Liberia [*ANSI two-letter standard code*] (CNC) .... LR
Liberia International Foundation for Elevation .... LIFE
Liberia Military Mission [*US*] .... LIBMISH
Liberia National Shipping Line (EY) .... LNSL
Liberia Refining Co. .... LRC
Liberia Research and Information Project (EA) .... LRIP
Liberia Telecommunications Corp. (IMH) .... LTC
Liberia/Tomas Guardia Internacional [*Costa Rica*] [*ICAO location identifier*] (ICLI) .... MRLB
Liberia Unification Party [*Political party*] .... LUP
Liberian American-Swedish Minerals Co. .... LAMCO
Liberian International American Corporation [*New York*] .... LIAC
Liberian Iron Ore Ltd. [*Toronto Stock Exchange symbol*] .... LIO
Liberian Law Reports [*A publication*] (ILCA) .... LLR
Liberian Liberal Party [*Political party*] (EY) .... LLP
Liberian News Agency (EY) .... LINA
Liberian People's Party [*Political party*] (EY) .... LPP
Liberian Philatelic Society [*Defunct*] (EA) .... LPS
Liberian Shipowners Council (EA) .... LSC
Liberian World Airlines, Inc. [*ICAO designator*] (FAAC) .... LWA
Libertarian Alliance [*British*] (EAIO) .... LA
Libertarian Conservative .... LIBCON
Libertarian Council of Churches [*Defunct*] (EA) LCC
Libertarian Defense Caucus [*Defunct*] (EA) .... LDC
Libertarian Education Institute (EA) .... LEI
Libertarian Foundation for Human Assistance (EAIO) .... LiFHAS
Libertarian Futurist Society (EA) .... LFS
Libertarian Humanist Association (EA) .... LHA
Libertarian Information Service [*An association*] (EA) .... LIS
Libertarian International (EA) LI
Libertarian Party [*Australia Political party*] .... LNP
Libertarian Party (EA) .... LP
Libertarian Party Abolitionist Caucus (EA) .... LPAC
Libertarian Republican Alliance (EA) .... LRA
Libertarian Republican Organizing Committee [*Defunct*] (EA) .... LROC
Libertarian SIG [*Special Interest Group*] (EA) .... LibSIG
Libertarians for Animal Rights (EA) .... LFAR
Libertarians for Gay and Lesbian Concerns (EA) .... LGLC
Libertarians for Life (EA) .... LFL
Liberte Chretienne [*A publication*] (BJA) .... LChr
Liberte Investors [*Formerly, Lomas & Nettleton Mortgage Investors*] [*NYSE symbol*] (SPSG) .... LBI
Liberte Investors, Inc. [*Associated Press*] (SAG) .... Liberte
Liberte, Liberation, et Liberation Nationale [*French resistance movement*] [*World War II*] LLL
Liberty .... LBRT
Liberty .... LBRTY
Liberty [*Geographical division*] [*British*] .... LIB
Liberty (ABBR) .... LIBT
Liberty All Star Growth [*NYSE symbol*] (SAG) .... ASG
Liberty All Star Growth [*Associated Press*] (SAG) .... LbtyASG
Liberty ALL-STAR Eqty [*NYSE symbol*] (TTSB) .... USA
Liberty All-Star Equity [*Associated Press*] (SAG) .... LbtyASE
Liberty All-Star Equity [*NYSE symbol*] (SPSG) .... USA
Liberty ALL-STAR Growth Fd [*NYSE symbol*] (TTSB) .... ASG
Liberty Amendment Committee of the USA (EA) .... LAC
Liberty Amendment Committee of the USA (EA) .... LACUSA
Liberty Bancorp, Inc. [*NASDAQ symbol*] (SAG) .... LBCI
Liberty Bancorp, Inc. [*Associated Press*] (SAG) .... LbtyBc
Liberty Bancorp, Inc., Oklahoma [*NASDAQ symbol*] (SAG) .... LBNA
Liberty Bancorp(OK) [*NASDAQ symbol*] (TTSB) .... LBNA
Liberty Baptist College [*Virginia*] .... LBC
Liberty Baptist College, Lynchburg, VA [*Library symbol*] [*Library of Congress*] (LCLS) .... ViLLB
Liberty Bell Communications, Inc. [*Detroit, MI*] [*Telecommunications*] (TSSD) .... LBC
Liberty Bell Matchcover Club (EA) .... LBMC
Liberty Broadcasting Network [*Cable-television system*] .... LBN
Liberty City Library, Liberty, TX [*Library symbol Library of Congress*] (LCLS) .... TxLib
Liberty Corp. [*NYSE symbol*] (SPSG) LC
Liberty Corp. [*Associated Press*] (SAG) .... LibtyCp
Liberty County Library, Chester, MT [*Library symbol*] [*Library of Congress*] (LCLS) .... MtChe
Liberty Federation (EA) .... LF
Liberty Financial Companies, Inc. [*NYSE symbol*] (SAG) L
Liberty Financial Companies, Inc. [*Associated Press*] (SAG) .... LibFin
Liberty Financial Cos. [*NYSE symbol*] (TTSB) L
Liberty Godparent Ministry (EA) .... LGM
Liberty Herald, Liberty, IN [*Library symbol Library of Congress*] (LCLS) .... InLibH
Liberty Hill [*South Carolina*] [*Seismograph station code, US Geological Survey*] (SEIS) .... LHS
Liberty Homes Cl'A' [*NASDAQ symbol*] (TTSB) .... LIBHA
Liberty Homes Cl'B' [*NASDAQ symbol*] (TTSB) .... LIBHB
Liberty Homes, Inc. [*Associated Press*] (SAG) .... LbtyH
Liberty Homes, Inc. [*NASDAQ symbol*] (SAG) .... LIBH
Liberty, KY [*AM radio station call letters*] .... WKDO
Liberty, KY [*FM radio station call letters*] .... WKDO-FM
Liberty Lobby (EA) LL
Liberty, MO [*FM radio station call letters*] (RBYB) .... KCIY
Liberty, MO [*AM radio station call letters*] (RBYB) .... KCXL
Liberty, MO [*FM radio station call letters*] .... KWJC
Liberty Mutual Insurance Co. .... LMIC
Liberty National Bank [*NASDAQ symbol*] (SAG) .... LIBC
Liberty National Bank [*Huntington Beach, CA*] [*Associated Press*] (SAG) .... LibNBk
Liberty, NC [*Location identifier FAA*] (FAAL) .... LIB
Liberty, NY [*AM radio station call letters*] .... WVOS
Liberty, NY [*FM radio station call letters*] .... WVOS-FM
Liberty Property Trust [*Associated Press*] (SAG) .... LibtProp
Liberty Property Trust [*NYSE symbol*] (SAG) .... LRY
Liberty Public Library, Liberty, NY [*Library symbol Library of Congress*] (LCLS) .... NLib
Liberty Public Schools District, Liberty, MO [*Library symbol*] [*Library of Congress*] (LCLS) .... MoLiPS
Liberty Seated Collectors Club (EA) .... LSCC
Liberty Technologies [*NASDAQ symbol*] (TTSB) .... LIBT
Liberty Technologies, Inc. [*Associated Press*] (SAG) .... LibrtyTc
Liberty Technologies, Inc. [*NASDAQ symbol*] (SAG) .... LIBT
Liberty Term Trust [*Associated Press*] (SAG) .... LbtTrm
Liberty Term Trust-1999 [*NYSE symbol*] (SPSG) .... LTT
Liberty to the Captives [*Later, ACAT*] (EA) .... LTC
Liberty Tree Network [*An association*] (EA) .... LTN
Liberty, TX [*AM radio station call letters*] .... KPXE
Liberty, TX [*FM radio station call letters*] .... KSHN
Liberty-Bell Mines, Inc. [*Vancouver Stock Exchange symbol*] .... LBM
Libourne/Artiques De Lussac [*France ICAO location identifier*] (ICLI) .... LFDI
Libra [*Pound*] L
Libra [*Pound*] [*Latin*] (AAG) .... lb
Libra [*Pound*] .... LIB
Libra [*Constellation*] .... Lib
Libra [*Constellation*] .... Libr
Libra Energy, Inc. [*Vancouver Stock Exchange symbol*] .... LBE
Libra Industries, Inc. [*Vancouver Stock Exchange symbol*] .... LBI

Librairie Pointe-Aux-Trembles, Quebec [*Library symbol National Library of Canada*] (NLC) .... QMLPT
Librairies Flammarion [*ACCORD*] [*UTLAS symbol*] .... FLA
Librairies Flammarion, Montreal, Quebec [*Library symbol National Library of Canada*] (NLC) .... QMLF
Librarian (WDAA) .... LBR
Librarian (DLA) .... Lib
Librarian (WGA) .... LIBN
Librarian (EY) .... LIBR
Librarian .... LIBRN
Librarian .... LIBRN
[*The*] Librarian and the Machine [*A publication*] .... L & M
Librarian/Online [*Database*] (MHDI) .... LIB/OL
Librarians Antidefamation League .... LADLE
Librarians Automation Group [*Australia*] (NITA) .... LAG
Librarians' Christian Fellowship [*British*] (DBA) .... LCF
Librarians Committee of the Associated Colleges of Central Kansas [*Library network*] .... ACCK
Librarians for Nuclear Arms Control [*Defunct*] (EA) .... LNAC
Librarians Inquiry Terminal (IT) .... LIT
Librarians of Institutes and Schools of Education [*British*] (DBA) .... LISE
Librarians United to Fight Costly, Silly, Unnecessary Serial Title Changes [*Defunct*] (EA) .... LUTFCSUSTC
Librarianship and Archives Old Students' Association (DGA) .... LAOSA
Libraries & Culture [*A publication*] (BRI) .... Lib & Cult
Libraries and Our Civilizations [*A publication*] .... LOC
Libraries Board of South Australia .... LBSA
Libraries Consultative Committee [*Australia*] LCC
Libraries Copyright Committee [*Australia*] LCC
Libraries Division, Agriculture Canada [*Division des Bibliotheques, Agriculture Canada*] Ottawa, Ontario [*Library symbol National Library of Canada*] (NLC) .... OOAG
Libraries for Prisons [*An association*] (EA) .... LFP
Libraries for the Blind and Physically Handicapped [*Automated system*] .... LBPH
Libraries in North Staffordshire and South Cheshire in Cooperation [*British*] (NITA) .... LINOSCO
Libraries of Affiliated Teaching Hospitals - School of Medicine [*Library network*] .... LATH
Libraries of Idaho Teletype Network - Academics [*Library network*] .... LITTY
Libraries of the Social Sciences [*Australia An association*] .... LOTSS
Libraries Serving Special Populations Section [*Association of Specialized and Cooperative Library Agencies*] .... LSSPS
Libraries Unlimited [*Library network*] .... LU
Library L
Library (MSA) .... LBRY
Library .... LBRY
Library (AFM) .... LIB
Library [*A publication*] (BRI) .... Lib
Library (VRA) .... libr
Library .... LIBR
Library (ABBR) .... LIBRY
Library Access and Sixth-Form Studies [*British*] (AIE) .... LASS
Library Access Program .... LAP
Library Acquisition Program [*Computer program*] .... LIBACC
Library Acquisition Services System Online [*Suggested name for the Library of Cogress computer system*] .... LASSO
Library Acquisitions Information System .... LAIS
Library Acquisitions: Practice and Theory [*A publication*] .... LAPT
Library Addition and Maintenance Program .... LAMP
Library Administration and Management .... LA & M
Library Administration and Management Association (EA) .... LAMA
Library Administration Division [*American Library Association*] [*Later, LAMA*] (EA) .... LAD
Library Administration Division, Library Organization and Management Section [*American Library Association*] (AEBS) .... LAD-LOMS
Library Advisory Council [*Department of Education and Science*] [*British*] (NITA) .... LAC
Library Advisory Council, Dawson Creek, BC, Canada [*Library symbol Library of Congress*] (LCLS) .... CaBDCL
Library Advisory Council, Dawson Creek, British Columbia [*Library symbol National Library of Canada*] (NLC) .... BDCL
Library Advisory Council for England (NITA) .... LACE
Library Advocacy Now [*American Library Association*] .... LAN
Library Affairs Committee of the Associated Mid-Florida Colleges [*Library network*] .... LAC of AMFC
Library Allard, St. Georges, Manitoba [*Library symbol National Library of Canada*] (BIB) .... MSTGA
Library, Amphibious Warfare (DNAB) .... LAW
Library and Audio-Visual Services, George Brown College of Applied Arts and Technology, Toronto, Ontario [*Library symbol National Library of Canada*] (BIB) .... OTGB
Library & Information Consultants Ltd. [*Information service or system*] (IID) .... LINC
Library and Information for the Northwest [*Program of the Fred Meyer Charitable Trust*] .... LIRN
Library and Information Network [*Planned Parenthood Federation of America, Inc.*] [*Information service or system*] (IID) .... LINK
Library and Information Plans [*British*] .... LIPS
Library and Information Research Group [*Bristol Polytechnic Library*] [*British Information service or system*] (IID) .... LIRG
Library and Information Research News [*A publication*] (NITA) .... LIRN
Library and Information Resources (NITA) .... LIR
Library and Information Scholarship Today [*A publication*] .... LISST
Library and Information Science .... LIS

Library and Information Science Students Attitudes, Demographics, and Aspirations Survey [*American Libraries Association*] .... LISSADA
Library and Information Science Trends .... LIST
Library and Information Service .... LIS
Library and Information Service Automated Retrieval of Data (NITA) .... LISARD
Library and Information Service to Industry and Commerce (NITA) .... LISIC
Library and Information Services [*Institution of Mining and Metallurgy*] [*British Information service or system*] (IID) .... LIS
Library and Information Services Council [*British*] .... LISC
Library and Information Services Division [*National Oceanic and Atmospheric Administration*] (NITA) .... LISD
Library and Information Services, Tees-Side (IEEE) .... LIST
Library and Information Services Today [*A publication*] .... LIST
Library and Information Software Package (PDAA) .... LISP
Library and Information Statistics Unit (AIE) .... LISU
Library and Information Technology Association (EA) .... LITA
Library and Information Technology Associaton of the ALA (NITA) .... LITA
Library and Information Unit .... LIU
Library and Records Center, Crows Nest Resources Ltd., Calgary, Alberta [*Library symbol National Library of Canada*] (NLC) .... ACCNR
Library & Records Centre, Alsands Energy Ltd., Calgary, Alberta [*Library symbol National Library of Canada*] (NLC) .... ACAEL
Library and Resource Collection, Yoho National Park, Field, British Columbia [*Library symbol National Library of Canada*] (NLC) .... BFY
Library Assistants Certificate [*City and Guilds Institute*] [*British*] (NITA) .... LAC
Library Association [*British*] (NITA) .... LA
Library Association [*British*] .... LA
Library Association Government Libraries Group (PDAA) .... LAGLG
Library Association Information Technology Group [*British*] (NITA) .... LAIT
Library Association Information Technology Group (AIE) .... LAITG
Library Association, London, United Kingdom [*Library symbol Library of Congress*] (LCLS) .... UkLLA
Library Association National Council for Educational Technology (NITA) .... LANCET
Library Association of Ireland (EAIO) .... LAI
Library Association of La Jolla, La Jolla, CA [*Library symbol Library of Congress Obsolete*] (LCLS) .... CLjL
Library Association of Portland [*Public Library for Portland and Multnomah County*], Portland, OR [*Library symbol Library of Congress*] (LCLS) .... OrP
Library Association of the United Kingdom .... LAUK
Library Association Publishing Ltd. [*British*] .... LAPL
Library Association Record [*A publication*] (BRI) .... LAR
Library Association Reference and Special Information Section (PDAA) .... LARSIS
Library Association Year Book [*A publication*] (DGA) .... LAYB
Library Association's Annual Conference [*British*] .... LAAC
Library at Jamesburg, Jamesburg, NJ [*Library symbol Library of Congress*] (LCLS) .... NjJa
Library Automated Service System (IAA) .... LASS
Library Automated Systems Information Exchange [*Australia*] (NITA) .... LASIE
Library Automation .... LA
Library Automation and Networks .... LAN
Library Automation Research and Consulting Association (NITA) .... LARC
Library Automation Research and Consulting Services (IAA) .... LARC
Library Automation Services [*Oxford University*] .... LAS
Library Automation Systems and Services Options Study [*Advisory committee*] (NITA) .... LASSOS
Library Awareness Program [*FBI*] .... LAP
Library Bibliographies and Indexes [*A publication*] .... LBI
Library Binding Institute (EA) .... LBI
Library Board of Western Australia, State Bibliographical Centre, Perth, WA, Australia [*Library symbol Library of Congress*] (LCLS) .... AuPL
Library Bookseller (NITA) .... LB
Library Bulletin .... LB
Library Cat Society (EA) .... LCS
Library Catalogue (WDAA) .... LIB CAT
Library Club of America [*Defunct*] (EA) .... LCA
Library Collection Management System (NITA) .... LCMS
Library Co. of Burlington, Burlington, NJ [*Library symbol Library of Congress*] (LCLS) .... NjBu
Library Co. of Philadelphia, Philadelphia, PA [*Library symbol Library of Congress*] (LCLS) .... PPL
Library Computer System [*University of Illinois*] [*Library network*] .... LCS
Library Construction Kit [*Microsoft Corp.*] [*Computer science*] (PCM) .... LCK
Library Control Language (OA) LCL
Library Control System [*Ohio State Library*] [*Columbus*] [*Information service or system*] (IID) .... LCS
Library Cooperative of Macomb [*Library network*] .... LNM
Library Council of Metropolitan Milwaukee [*Wisconsin*] [*Library network*] .... LCOMM
Library Development Center [*Columbia University*] .... LDC
Library Development Commission, Victoria, BC, Canada [*Library symbol Library of Congress*] (LCLS) .... CaBViLDC
Library Development Consultants, Inc. [*Information service or system*] (IID) .... LDC
Library Development Team .... LDT
Library Edition (ADA) .... LE
Library Editor (MHDI) .... LIBE
Library Editor (MHDI) .... LIBEDIT
Library Education Division [*American Library Association*] [*Defunct*] .... LED
Library Education Experimental Project [*Syracuse University*] .... LEEP
Library Education Group of the Library Association (NITA) .... LEG
Library Education Services, Data Logic Canada, Ottawa, Ontario [*Library symbol National Library of Canada*] (NLC) .... OODLC
Library Entrance Online .... LEO

Library Equipment Institute [American Library Association] .... LEI
Library Experimental Automated Demonstration System [Computer science] .... LEADS
Library for Intercultural Studies, Inc., New York, NY [Library symbol Library of Congress] (LCLS) .... NNIS
Library Foundation for Voluntary Organizations [Defunct] (EA) .... LFVO
Library Fundraising Resource Center [American Library Association] .... LFRC
Library General Information Survey [of the National Center for Educational Statistics] .... LIBGIS
Library Hi Tech [Pierian Press, Inc.] [Information service or system A publication] (IID) .... LHT
Library Hi Tech News [A publication] .... LHTN
Library History Round Table [American Library Association] ...... LHRT
Library History Seminar .... LHS
Library Holdings Ratio per Inhabitant .... LHO ratio
Library Index Search and Transcribe .... LIST
Library Information Access System [Pennsylvania State University Libraries] [University Park] [Information service or system] (IID) .... LIAS
Library Information and Enquiry System .... LIES
Library Information and On-Line Network Service [New York Public Library] [Information service or system] (IID) .... LIONS
Library Information Center [Lunar and Planetary Institute] [Information service or system] (IID) LIC
Library Information Management System [University of Maryland] .... LIMS
Library Information Network Exchange Services [Australia A publication] .... LINES
Library Information OnLine [International Atomic Energy Agency] [United Nations] (DUND) .... LION
Library Information Plan (AIE) .... LIP
Library Information Retrieval Service [Oregon State University] [Information service or system] .... LIRS
Library Information Retrieval System [California Institute of Technology] [Pasadena, CA] .... LIRS
Library Information Search and Retrieval Data System [US Navy] (NITA) .... LISARD
Library Information Search and Retrieval Data System (IEEE) .... LIZARDS
Library Information Service [or System] [The Royal Library Database] [Information service or system] (IID) .... LIBRIS
Library Information System [Georgetown University] [Information service or system] .... LIS
Library Information System Time-Sharing .... LISTS
Library Instruction Materials Bank [Loughborough University of Technology] [Information service or system] (IID) .... LIMB
Library Instruction Round Table [American Library Association] .... LIRT
Library Interface Systems, Inc. [Information service or system] (IID) .... LISI
Library Internet Browsing Software .... LIBS
Library Issue Document (NVT) .... LID
Library Journal [A publication] (BRI) .... LJ
Library Labels [Antiquarian book trade] .... L/L
Library Maintenance Routine (IAA) .... LMR
Library Maintenance System (PDAA) .... LMS
Library Management (MHDB) .... LIBMAN
Library Management and Retrieval System [Navy Information service or system] (IID) .... LMARS
Library Management Network, Inc. [Information service or system] (IID) .... LMN
Library Management Research Unit (NITA) .... LMRU
Library Management System .... LMS
Library Master File [FORTRAN program] .... LIBMAS
Library Material Preservation Manual .... LMPM
Library Material Processed .... LMP
Library Materials Management System .... LMMS
Library/Media Technical Assistant .... LMTA
Library Merge Program [Computer program] .... LIBMRG
Library Microfilm & Materials Co. .... LMM
Library Micromation News (NITA) .... LMN
Library Network Analysis Theory .... LIBNAT
Library Network of SIBIL Users (EAIO) .... LNSU
Library of Ancient Semitic Inscriptions (BJA) .... LASI
Library of Art [A publication] .... LA
Library of Congress .... L of C
Library of Congress LC
Library of Congress (WDAA) .... LIB CONG
Library of Congress .... LIBCON
Library of Congress .... LOC
Library of Congress - American Doctoral Dissertations [A bibliographic publication] .... LC-ADD
Library of Congress and National Union Catalog Author Lists, 1942-1962 [A publication] .... LC/NUC
Library of Congress Authority File [Source file] [UTLAS symbol] .... LCA
Library of Congress Automation Techniques Exchange .... LOCATE
Library of Congress Card Number (NITA) LC
Library of Congress Catalog Card Number (NITA) .... LCCCN
Library of Congress Catalog-Card Number .... LCCN
Library of Congress Catalogue Card (WDAA) LCCC
Library of Congress Classification LC
Library of Congress Classification LCC
Library of Congress Classification - Additions and Changes [A publication] .... LCAC
Library of Congress Classification Schedules [A publication] .... LCCS
Library of Congress COBRA [Source file] [UTLAS symbol] .... CBRA
Library of Congress Computer Catalog (NITA) LCCC
Library of Congress Current MARC [Machine-Readable Catalog] File (NITA) .... LCCMARC
Library of Congress/English [Database on English language monographs] (NITA) .... LIBCON/E

Library of Congress Films [Source file] [UTLAS symbol] .... LCF
Library of Congress, Government Printing Office [Source file] [UTLAS symbol] .... GPO
Library of Congress. Information Bulletin [A publication] .... LCIB
Library of Congress Information System [Library of Congress Information service or system] (IID) .... LOCIS
Library of Congress, Interlibrary Loan Department [UTLAS symbol] LCL
Library of Congress Machine Readable Catalog [Washington, DC] [Bibliographic database] [Library of Congress] .... LC MARC
Library of Congress Maps [Source file] [UTLAS symbol] .... LCM
Library of Congress MARC [Machine-Readable Catalog] Files (NITA) ...... LCMARC
Library of Congress Minimal Level Cataloguing [Source file] [UTLAS symbol] .... LCML
Library of Congress Music [Source file] [UTLAS symbol] .... LCU
Library of Congress, National Library Service for the Blind and Physically Handicapped, Music Library, Washington, DC [Library symbol Library of Congress] (LCLS) .... DLC-BM
Library of Congress, National Library Service for the Blind and Physically Handicapped, Washington, DC [Library symbol Library of Congress] (LCLS) .... DLC-B
Library of Congress Number (MCD) .... LCN
Library of Congress. Quarterly Journal [A publication] (DLA) .... Lib Cong Q
Library of Congress Subject Headings [Formerly, SHDC] [A publication] ..... LCSH
Library of Congress, Washington, DC [Library symbol Library of Congress OCLC symbol] (OCLC) .... DLC
Library of Devotion [A publication] .... LD
Library of Dianetics and Scientology, Silver Spring, MD [Library symbol Library of Congress] (LCLS) .... MdSsD
Library of Early Novelists [A publication] .... LEN
Library of English Classics [A publication] .... LEC
Library of Exact Philosophy .... LEP
Library of Industrial and Commercial Education and Training .... LICET
Library of International Relations, Chicago, IL [Library symbol Library of Congress] (LCLS) .... ICIntR
Library of Jewish Information (BJA) .... LJI
Library of Law and Equity [A publication] (DLA) .... Lib L & Eq
Library of Literary History [A publication] .... LLH
Library of Living Thought [A publication] .... LLT
Library of New South Wales, Mitchell Library, Sydney, NSW, Astralia [Library symbol Library of Congress] (LCLS) .... AuSN-M
Library of New South Wales, Sydney, NSW, Australia [Library symbol Library of Congress] (LCLS) .... AuSN
Library of Parliament [Canada] .... LP
Library of Parliament, Ottawa, ON, Canada [Library symbol Library of Congress] (LCLS) .... CaOOP
Library of Parliament [Bibliotheque du Parlement] Ottawa, Ontario [Library symbol National Library of Canada] (NLC) .... OOP
Library of Philosophy [A publication] .... LP
Library of Poultney Bigelow, Malden-On-Hudson, NY [Library symbol] [Library of Congress] (LCLS) .... NMh
Library of Romance [A publication] .... LRA
Library of Standard Biographies [A publication] .... LSB
[The] Library of the Palestine Pilgrims' Text Society (BJA) .... LPPTS
Library of Useful Stories [A publication] .... LUS
Library of Vehicles, Los Angeles, CA [Library symbol Library of Congress] (LCLS) CLV
Library On-Line Acquisitions [Washington State University] [Data processing system] .... LOLA
Library On-Line Information and Text Access [Oregon State University] [Corvallis, OR Data processing system] .... LOLITA
Library Online Information Services [Morehead State University] (OLDSS) ..... LOIS
Library Order Information System [Computer system] [Library of Congress Obsolete] .... LOIS
Library Organization and Management Section [Library Administration Division of ALA] .... LOMS
Library Orientation/Bibliographic Instruction [Florida Library Association caucus] .... LOBI
Library Orientation/Instruction Exchange [Library network] .... LOEX
Library Processes System [Educomp] [Information service or system] (IID) .... LPS
Library Program, Cataloging Department, Recreation Service, Fort Polk, LA [Library symbol Library of Congress] (LCLS) .... LFtp
Library Public Relations Council (EA) .... LPRC
Library Quarterly [A publication] (BRI) .... LQ
Library Reports & Research Service, Inc. [Information service or system] (IID) .... LRRS
Library Reproduction Service, Microfilm Co. of California, Los Angeles, CA [Library symbol Library of Congress] (LCLS) .... LRS
Library Research Center [University of Illinois] (IID) .... LRC
Library Research Round Table [American Library Association] .... LRRT
Library Resources & Information Centre, Brockville Psychiatric Hospital, Ontario [Library symbol National Library of Canada] (NLC) .... OBRPH
Library Resources & Technical Services [Association for Library Collections and Technical Services] [American Library Association] .... LRTS
Library Resources Coordinating Committee of the University of London (NITA) .... LRCC
Library Resources Exhibition [British] .... LRE
Library Resources, Inc. [Subsidiary of Encyclopaedia Britannica] .... LRI
Library Resources, Incorporated, Chicago, IL [Library symbol Library of Congress] (LCLS) .... LrI
Library Review [A publication] (BRI) .... LR
Library Routine Management System .... LRMS
Library Rubber Stamps [Antiquarian book trade] .... L/R/S
Library Science .... LS
Library Science Abstracts [A publication] .... LSA

Library Science Library, McGill University, Montreal, Quebec [*Library symbol National Library of Canada*] (NLC) ...... QMMLS
Library Science Student Organization ...... LSSO
Library Search ...... LS
Library Service Centre, Winnipeg School Division No. 1, Winnipeg, MB, Canada [*Library symbol Library of Congress*] (LCLS) ...... CaMWLC
Library Service to Developmentally Disabled Persons Membership Activity Group [*Association of Specialized and Cooperative Library Agencies*] [*American Library Association*] ...... LSSDDPMAG
Library Service to People with Visual or Physical Disabilities Forum [*Association of Specialized and Cooperative Library Agencies*] [*American Library Association*] ...... LSPVPD
Library Service to Prisoners Forum [*Association of Specialized and Cooperative Library Agencies*] ...... LSPF
Library Service to the Blind and Physically Handicapped Forum [*Association of Specialized and Cooperative Library Agencies*] ...... LSBPHF
Library Service to the Blind Round Table ...... LSBRT
Library Service to the Deaf Forum [*Association of Specialized and Cooperative Library Agencies*] ...... LSDF
Library Service to the Developmentally Disabled Persons Forum [*Association of Specialized and Cooperative Library Agencies*] [*American Library Association*] ...... LSSDPF
Library Service to the Disadvantaged Committee ...... LSD
Library Service to the Impaired Elderly Forum [*Association of Specialized and Cooperative Library Agencies*] ...... LSIEF
Library Services ...... LS
Library Services Act [*1956*] ...... LSA
Library Services and Construction Act [*1963*] ...... LSCA
Library Services Authority Act (NITA) ...... LSAA
Library Services Branch, Alberta Department of Health, Edmonton, Alberta [*Library symbol National Library of Canada*] (BIB) ...... AEHE
Library Services Branch, Government of the Yukon, Whitehorse, Yukon [*Library symbol National Library of Canada*] (NLC) ...... YWLS
Library Services Branch, Ministry of Provincial Secretary and Governement Services, Victoria, British Columbia [*Library symbol National Library of Canada*] (NLC) ...... BVILSB
Library Services Branch, Ministry of Provincial Secretary and Government Services, Cranbrook, British Columbia [*Library symbol National Library of Canada*] (NLC) ...... BCRLSB
Library Services Branch, Ministry of Provincial Secretary and Government Services, Dawson Creek, British Columbia [*Library symbol National Library of Canada*] (NLC) ...... BDCLSB
Library Services Branch, Ministry of Provincial Secretary and Government Services, Prince George, British Columbia [*Library symbol National Library of Canada*] (NLC) ...... BPGLSB
Library Services, Brandon General Hospital, Manitoba [*Library symbol National Library of Canada*] (NLC) ...... MBGH
Library Services Center, Midwestern Regional Library System [*UTLAS symbol*] ...... LSC
Library Services Center of Missouri [*Library network*] ...... LSC
Library Services, Colonel Belcher Hospital, Calgary, Alberta [*Library symbol National Library of Canada*] (BIB) ...... ACCB
Library Services Division, Health Protection Branch, Health and Welfare Canada [*Service de Bibliotheque, Direction Generale de la Protection de la Sante, Sante et Bien-Etre Social Canada*] Ottawa, Ontario [*Library symbol National Library of Canada*] (NLC) ...... OONHHP
Library Services, Health Sciences Centre, Winnipeg, Manitoba [*Library symbol National Library of Canada*] (NLC) ...... MWHS
Library Services Network [*Library network*] ...... LISN
Library Services, Policy, Communications, and Information Branch, Health and Welfare Canada [*Services de Bibliotheque, Direction Generale de la Politique, des Communications, et de l'Information, Sante et Bien-Etre Social Canada*] Ottawa, Ontario [*Library symbol National Library of Canada*] (NLC) ...... OONHPP
Library Services, Rocky View General Hospital, Calgary, Alberta [*Library symbol National Library of Canada*] (BIB) ...... ACRVH
Library Services to the Handicapped, Alberta Culture [*UTLAS symbol*] ...... LSH
Library Set [*Computer program*] ...... LIBSET
Library Software Archives [*Computer science*] (TNIG) ...... LIBSOFT
Library Software Package (ADA) ...... LSP
Library Storage Unit ...... LSU
Library Studies Program, Concordia University [*EDUCATSS*] [*UTLAS symbol*] ...... EUC
Library Studies Program, Concordia University, Montreal, Quebec [*Library symbol National Library of Canada*] (NLC) ...... QMGLS
Library Studies Program, Memorial University of Newfoundland, St. John's, Newfoundland [*Library symbol National Library of Canada*] (BIB) ...... NFSMLS
Library System [*Computer program*] ...... LIBSYS
Library Systems Analysis ...... LISA
Library Systems and Services, Inc. [*Information service or system*] (IID) ...... LSSI
Library Systems Centre, National Library of Canada [*Centre des Systemes de Bibliotheque, Bibliotheque Nationale du Canada*] Ottawa, Ontario [*Library symbol National Library of Canada*] (NLC) ...... OONLD
Library Talk [*A publication*] (BRI) ...... LT
Library Technical Assistant ...... LTA
Library Technical Centre [*Polytechnic of Central London*] (NITA) ...... LTC
Library Technical Services [*Library network*] ...... LTS
Library Technician Program, Algonquin College [*EDUCATSS*] [*UTLAS symbol*] ...... EUO
Library Technician Program, Algonquin College of Applied Arts & Technology, Ottawa, Ontario [*Library symbol National Library of Canada*] (NLC) ...... OOACL
Library Technician Program, Fraser Valley College [*EDUCATSS*] [*UTLAS symbol*] ...... EUF

Library Technician Program, Fraser Valley College, Abbotsford, British Columbia, [*Library symbol National Library of Canada*] (NLC) ...... BABFVL
Library Technician Program, Kelsey Institute [*EDUCATSS*] [*UTLAS symbol*] ...... EUK
Library Technician Program, Kelsey Institute of Applied Arts & Sciences, Saskatoon, Saskatchewan [*Library symbol National Library of Canada*] (NLC) ...... SSKIL
Library Technician Program, Mohawk College [*EDUCATSS*] [*UTLAS symbol*] ...... EUH
Library Technician Program, Mohawk College of Applied Arts & Technology, Hamilton, Ontario [*Library symbol National Library of Canada*] (NLC) ...... OHMCL
Library Technician Program, Niagara College [*EDUCATSS*] [*UTLAS symbol*] ...... EUN
Library Technician Program, Niagara College of Applied Arts & Technology, Welland, Ontario [*Library symbol National Library of Canada*] (NLC) ...... OWENL
Library Technician Program, Red River Community College [*EDUCATSS*] [*UTLAS symbol*] ...... EUR
Library Technician Program, Red River Community College, Winnipeg, Manitoba, LS [*National Library of Canada*] (NLC) ...... MWRRL
Library Technician Program, Vancouver Community College [*EDUCATSS*] [*UTLAS symbol*] ...... EUV
Library Technician Program, Vancouver Community College, British Columbia [*Library symbol National Library of Canada*] (NLC) ...... BVAVCLT
Library Techniques, Seneca College [*EDUCATSS*] [*UTLAS symbol*] ...... EUS
Library Techniques, Seneca College of Applied Arts and Technology, Willowdale, Ontario [*Library symbol National Library of Canada*] (NLC) ...... OTSCLT
Library Techniques, Sheridan College [*EDUCATSS*] [*UTLAS symbol*] ...... EUD
Library Techniques, Sheridan College, Oakville, Ontario [*Library symbol National Library of Canada*] (NLC) ...... OOAKSCL
Library Technology Program [*Formerly, Library Technology Project*] [*ALA*] [*Defunct*] ...... LTP
Library Technology Reports [*American Library Association*] ...... LTR
Library User Information System [*Detroit, MI*] [*Library network*] ...... LUIS
Library Users of America (EA) ...... LUA
Library Utility [*Computer science*] ...... LU
Library Video Network [*Video producer*] ...... LVN
Library Wholesale Services [*Information service or system*] (IID) ...... LWS
Library-Anthropology Resource Group ...... LARG
Library-College Associates [*Defunct*] (EA) ...... LCA
Librascope Operations Control System ...... LOCS
Librating Equidistant Observer ...... LEO
Libration [*Space exploration*] L
Librettist [*MARC relator code*] [*Library of Congress*] (LCCP) ...... lbt
Libretto [*Music*] ...... LIB
Libreville [*Gabon*] [*ICAO location identifier*] (ICLI) ...... FOOO
Libreville [*Gabon*] [*ICAO location identifier*] (ICLI) ...... FOOV
Libreville [*Gabon*] [*Airport symbol*] (OAG) ...... LBV
Libreville/Leon M'Ba [*Gabon*] [*ICAO location identifier*] (ICLI) ...... FOOL
Libri Coloniarum [*Classical studies*] (OCD) ...... Lib Colon
Libri Feudorum [*A publication*] (DSA) ...... F
Libri Veteris Testamenti (BJA) ...... LibVT
LIBRIS Intercept [*Sweden*] (NITA) ...... LIBCEPT
Librium [*Pharmacology*] (DAVI) ...... LIBR
Libya [*Aircraft nationality and registration mark*] 5A
Libya [*MARC geographic area code Library of Congress*] (LCCP) ...... f-ly--
Libya [*License plate code assigned to foreign diplomats in the US*] ...... FM
Libya [*ANSI three-letter standard code*] (CNC) ...... LBY
Libya [*ANSI two-letter standard code*] (CNC) ...... LY
Libya [*MARC country of publication code Library of Congress*] (LCCP) ...... ly
Libya National Oil Co. ...... LNOC
Libyan Arab Airlines [*ICAO designator*] (AD) ...... LN
Libyan Arab Company for Air Cargo [*ICAO designator*] (FAAC) ...... LCR
Libyan Arab Foreign Bank ...... LAFB
Libyan Desert Glass [*Archeology*] ...... LDG
Libyan Dinar [*Monetary unit*] (BJA) ...... LD
Libyan Federation of Labor and Professional Unions ...... LFLPU
Libyan General Workers' Federation ...... LGWF
Libyan-American Reconstruction Commission ...... LARC
Licence in Administration [*Canada*] (DD) ...... LScAdmin
Licence in Economics [*Canada*] (DD) ...... LScEco
Licence in Science (Economics) [*British*] (DI) ...... LSc(Econ)
Licence in Social Science [*British*] ...... LScSoc
Licence in Social Science [*British*] ...... ScSocL
Licence in the Science of Optometry [*Canada*] (DD) ...... LScO
Licenciado en Derecho [*Licentiate in Law*] [*Spanish*] ...... Lic en Der
Licenciado en Filosofia [*Licentiate in Philosophy*] [*Spanish*] ...... Lic en Fil
Licenciate in Midwifery of the Royal College of Physicians [*British*] ...... LMRCP
Licenciatus [*Academic Qualification*] [*Latin*] L
Licencie en Droit [*Licentiate in Law*] [*French*] ...... L en D
Licencie en Sciences Comptables [*Licentiate of Accounting*] (DD) ...... LScCompt
Licencie es Lettres [*Licentiate in Letters*] [*French*] (EY) ...... L es L
Licencie es Lettres [*Licentiate in Letters*] [*French*] (BARN) ...... Lest
Licencie es Sciences [*Licentiate of Sciences*] [*French*] ...... L es SC
Licencie es Sciences [*Licentiate in Science*] [*French*] (BARN) ...... LesS
Licensable (ABBR) ...... LICB
License L
License (KSC) LIC
License (ROG) ...... LICE
License Economic Sciences [*Canada*] (DD) ...... LEconSc
License in Civil Law LL
License Inquiry [*Police*] LI

License Plate, Key Chain, and Mini License Plate Collectors Club (EA) .... LPKCMLPCC
License Plate Reader .... LPR
License Review Group [*Nuclear energy*] (NRCH) .... LRG
License to Export Uranium (NRCH) .... LEU
Licensed .... LCNSD
Licensed (ROG) .... LICD
Licensed Acupuncturist [*Medicine*] .... LAc
Licensed Aircraft Engineers' Notice (DNAB) .... LAE NOTE
Licensed Aircraft Maintenance Engineer (ADA) .... LAME
Licensed Animal Slaughterers and Salvage Association [*British*] (BI) .... LASSA
Licensed Beverage Distributors (SRA) .... LBD
Licensed Beverage Industries [*Later, DISCUS*] (EA) .... LBI
Licensed Beverage Information Council (EA) .... LBIC
Licensed Clinical Psychologist .... LCP
Licensed Clinical Social Worker (MEDA) .... LCSW
Licensed Clinical Social Worker [*Medicine*] .... LCSW
Licensed Clubs Association of Australia .... LCAA
Licensed Clubs Association of New South Wales [*Australia*] .... LCANSW
Licensed Clubs Association of South Australia .... LCASA
Licensed Clubs Association of Tasmania [*Australia*] .... LCAT
Licensed Clubs Association of the Australian Capital Territory .... LCAACT
Licensed Company Auditor [*British*] .... LCA
Licensed Deposit-Taking Institution [*British*] .... LDT
Licensed Driver's Waiver (BARN) .... LDW
Licensed Financial Institution .... LFI
Licensed Fishing Boat .... LFB
Licensed Hotel Motel .... LHM
Licensed Massage Therapist [*Medicine*] .... LMT
Licensed Merchandisers' Association [*Later, ILMA*] (EA) .... LMA
Licensed Motor Dealer .... LMD
Licensed Motor Repairer .... LMR
Licensed Nurse .... LN
Licensed Officer [*US Merchant Marine*] .... LO
Licensed Pearl Producers' Association [*Australia*] .... LPPA
Licensed Physical Therapist .... LPT
Licensed Practical Nurse .... LPN
Licensed Practical Nurses Association of Florida (SRA) .... LPNAF
Licensed Preacher .... LPR
Licensed Professional Counselor .... LPC
Licensed Shorthand Writer .... LSW
Licensed Surveyor [*British*] (ADA) .... LS
Licensed Taxi Drivers' Association [*British*] (DBA) .... LTDA
Licensed to Practice [*Medicine*] L
Licensed Veterinary Technician .... LVT
Licensed Victualer LV
Licensed Victuallers' Defence League of England and Wales (BI) .... LVDL
Licensed Victuallers' National Defence League [*British*] (DI) .... LVNDL
Licensed Visiting Nurse .... LVN
Licensed Vocational Nurse .... LVN
Licensed Vocational Nurses Association of Texas (SRA) .... LVNAT
Licensee [*MARC relator code*] [*Library of Congress*] (LCCP) .... lse
Licensee Contractor Vendor Inspection Report Program [*Nuclear energy*] (NRCH) .... LCVIP
Licensee Event Report [*Nuclear energy*] (NRCH) .... LER
Licensing (ABBR) .... LICG
Licensing Act (DLA) .... LA
Licensing Appeals Tribunal [*Australia*] .... LAT
Licensing Assistant (NRCH) .... LA
Licensing Authorities Office .... LAO
Licensing Authority (DCTA) .... LA
Licensing Commission of Tasmania [*Australia*] .... LCT
Licensing Country [*Dialog*] [*Searchable field*] [*Information service or system*] (NITA) LC
Licensing Executives Society (EA) .... LES
Licensing Industry Association [*Later, ILMA*] (EA) .... LIA
Licensing Information Service (IID) .... LIS
Licensing Online Retrieval Data (NRCH) .... LORD
Licensing On-Line Retrieval Data System (NRCH) .... LORDS
Licensing Project Manager [*Nuclear energy*] (NRCH) .... LPM
Licensing Registration [*British*] .... LR
Licensing Support System [*Department of Energy*] (EGAO) .... LSS
Licensing Technical Review [*Nuclear energy*] (NRCH) .... L-TR
Licensor [*MARC relator code*] [*Library of Congress*] (LCCP) .... lso
Licensure Information System [*Public Health Service*] [*Georgetown University Medical Center*] (IID) .... LIS
Licentiate L
Licentiate LIC
Licentiate Architect Member of the Incorporated Association of Architects and Surveyors [*British*] (DAS) .... LMIAA
Licentiate in Accountancy (DD) .... LIA
Licentiate in Acupuncture [*British*] .... LicAc
Licentiate in Agricultural Science .... LSA
Licentiate in Agronomy [*British*] .... Lic Agro
Licentiate in Arts .... LA
Licentiate in Civil Engineering (WDAA) .... LCE
Licentiate in Commercial Science (DD) .... LScC
Licentiate in Commercial Science .... LScCom
Licentiate in Commercial Science (DD) .... LScComm
Licentiate in Composition, Royal Academy of Music [*British*] (ROG) .... L COMP RAM
Licentiate in Dental Science [*British*] .... LDSc
Licentiate in Dental Surgery .... LDS
Licentiate in Dental Surgery (Ireland) .... LDSI
Licentiate in Dental Surgery of the Royal College of Physicians and Surgeons of Glasgow [*British*] .... LDSRCPS Glas
Licentiate in Dental Surgery of the Royal College of Surgeons [*British*] .... LDSRCS
Licentiate in Dental Surgery of the Royal College of Surgeons in Ireland .... LDSRCS Irel
Licentiate in Dental Surgery of the Royal College of Surgeons of Edinburgh [*British*] .... LDSRCS Edin
Licentiate in Dental Surgery of the Royal College of Surgeons of Edinburgh (DI) .... LDSRCSEd
Licentiate in Dental Surgery of the Royal College of Surgeons of England .... LDSRCS Eng
Licentiate in Dentistry [*British*] (ROG) .... LD
Licentiate in Divinity .... L Div
Licentiate in Divinity (DAS) .... LD
Licentiate in Economic Sciences (WDAA) .... LIC ECON
Licentiate in Economics and Finance .... LEF
Licentiate in Health, Dublin (ROG) .... LHD
Licentiate in Laws LLL
Licentiate in Letters .... Litt L
Licentiate in Medicine .... Lic Med
Licentiate in Medicine .... LM
Licentiate in Medicine .... ML
Licentiate in Medicine and Surgery (DAVI) .... LMed & Ch
Licentiate in Medicine and Surgery [*British*] .... LMS
Licentiate in Medicine and Surgery of the Society of Apothecaries [*British*] .... LMSSA
Licentiate in Midwifery .... LM
Licentiate in Midwifery .... ML
Licentiate in Music (WDAA) .... LM
Licentiate in Music of the London College of Music [*British*] (DBQ) .... LMusLCM
Licentiate in Music, Trinity College of Music, London [*British*] (DBQ) .... LMusTCL
Licentiate in Obstectric Science (DAVI) .... LAO
Licentiate in Obstetrical Science .... LOS
Licentiate in Philosophy .... Fil Lic
Licentiate in Philosophy [*British*] .... Lic Phil
Licentiate in Philosophy .... Ph L
Licentiate in Religion (DD) .... LScRel
Licentiate in Religious Education .... LRE
Licentiate in Sacred Scriptures .... LSSc
Licentiate in Sacred Theology [*British*] .... LST
Licentiate in Sacred Theology (GAGS) .... STL
Licentiate in Sanitary Science [*British*] (ROG) .... LSSC
Licentiate in Science .... LS
Licentiate in Science (DD) .... LSc
Licentiate in Social, Economic, & Political Sciences (DD) .... LSSE
Licentiate in Surgery .... LS
Licentiate in Teaching [*British*] .... LT
Licentiate in Technology [*British*] .... Lic Tech
Licentiate in the Technology of Surface Coatings [*British*] (DBQ) .... LTSC
Licentiate in Theology .... L Th
Licentiate in Theology [*British*] .... Lic Theol
Licentiate in Theology .... LT
Licentiate in Theology .... Th L
Licentiate in Tropical Medicine [*British*] .... LTM
Licentiate, Institute of Sales and Marketing Executives (ADA) .... LISM
Licentiate Member of the Association of Business and Administrative Computing [*British*] (DBQ) .... LABAC
Licentiate Member of the Royal Society of Health [*British*] .... LMRSH
Licentiate Ministers and Certified Mediums Society (EA) .... LMCMS
Licentiate of Canon Law [*British*] LCL
Licentiate of Civil Law LCL
Licentiate of Cost and Management Institute [*British*] .... LCMI
Licentiate of Dental Medicine .... LDM
Licentiate of Guildhall School of Music [*British*] .... LGSM
Licentiate of Instruction [*or Licentiate Instructor*] LI
Licentiate of Letters (WDAA) .... L LETT
Licentiate of Medical Council of Canada .... LMCC
Licentiate of Music .... LMus
Licentiate of Pharmacy .... Ph L
Licentiate of Philosophy .... LPh
Licentiate of Philosophy [*British*] .... Phil Lic
Licentiate of Physicians and Surgeons of America .... LCP & SA
Licentiate of Sacred Scripture .... SSL
Licentiate of the Ambulance Service Institute [*British*] (DBQ) .... LASI
Licentiate of the Apothecaries' Company [*British*] .... LAC
Licentiate of the Apothecaries' Hall [*Dublin*] .... LAH
Licentiate of the Art of Obstetrics [*British*] .... LAO
Licentiate of the Associated Board of Royal Schools of Music [*British*] .... LAB
Licentiate of the Association of Cost and Executive Accountants [*British*] (DBQ) .... LCEA
Licentiate of the British Institute of Professional Photography (DBQ) .... LBIPP
Licentiate of the British Institute of Surgical Technologists (DBQ) .... LBIST
Licentiate of the British Society of Commerce (DBQ) .... LBSC
Licentiate of the Chartered Institute of Building [*British*] (DI) .... LCIOB
Licentiate of the College of Physicians and Surgeons [*British*] .... LCPS
Licentiate of the College of Preceptors [*British*] .... LCP
Licentiate of the College of Speech Therapists [*British*] .... LCST
Licentiate of the Construction Surveyors' Institute [*British*] (DBQ) .... LCSI
Licentiate of the Corporation of Executives and Administrators [*British*] (DBQ) .... LFBA
Licentiate of the Faculty of Architects and Surveyors [*British*] (DBQ) .... LFS
Licentiate of the Faculty of Commerce and Industry [*British*] (DBQ) .... LFCI
Licentiate of the Faculty of Physicians and Surgeons [*British*] .... LFPS
Licentiate of the Faculty of Physicians and Surgeons, Glasgow (ROG) .... LFPSG

Licentiate of the Faculty of Secretaries [*British*] (DBQ) .... LFCS
Licentiate of the Guild of Cleaners and Launderers [*British*] (DBQ) .... LGCL
Licentiate of the Hotel, Catering, and Institutional Management Association [*British*] (DBQ) .... LHCIMA
Licentiate of the Imperial Society of Teachers of Dancing [*British*] .... LISTD
Licentiate of the Incorporated Guild of Church Musicians [*British*] (ROG) .... LIGCM
Licentiate of the Incorporated Society of Musicians (ROG) .... LISM
Licentiate of the Institute of Administrative Accountants [*British*] (DBQ) .... LAAI
Licentiate of the Institute of British Bakers (DBQ) .... LInstBB
Licentiate of the Institute of Burial and Cremation Administration [*British*] (DBQ) .... LInstBCA
Licentiate of the Institute of Business Administration .... LIBA
Licentiate of the Institute of Chiropodists [*British*] .... LCh
Licentiate of the Institute of Clerks of Works of Great Britain, Inc. (DBQ) .... LICW
Licentiate of the Institute of Health Service Administrators [*British*] (DBQ) .... LHA
Licentiate of the Institute of Heraldic and Genealogical Studies [*British*] (DBQ) .... LHG
Licentiate of the Institute of Housing Managers [*British*] (DI) .... LIHM
Licentiate of the Institute of Leisure and Amenity Management [*British*] (DBQ) .... LILAM
Licentiate of the Institute of Mathematics and Its Applications [*British*] (DBQ) .... LIMA
Licentiate of the Institute of Metal Finishing [*British*] (DBQ) .... LIMF
Licentiate of the Institute of Park and Recreation Administration [*British*] (DI) .... LInstPRA
Licentiate of the Institute of Physics [*British*] .... L Inst P
Licentiate of the Institute of Population Registration [*British*] (DBQ) .... LIR
Licentiate of the Institution of Body Engineers [*British*] (DBQ) .... LBEI
Licentiate of the International Faculty of Arts [*British*] .... LIFA
Licentiate of the King's and Queen's College of Physicians of Ireland .... LKQCPI
Licentiate of the London College of Music [*British*] (DBQ) .... LLCM
Licentiate of the London College of Music (Teacher's Diploma) [*British*] .... LLCM(TD)
Licentiate of the London College of Osteopathy .... LLCO
Licentiate of the Medical College of Canada (DD) .... LMCC
Licentiate of the National College of Rubber Technology [*British*] (DI) .... LNCRT
Licentiate of the National Council of Psychotherapists [*British*] .... LCNP
Licentiate of the Physicians Guild [*British*] .... LPG
Licentiate of the Plastics and Rubber Institute [*British*] (DBQ) .... LPRI
Licentiate of the Royal Academy of Dancing [*British*] .... LRAD
Licentiate of the Royal Academy of Music [*British*] (EY) .... LRAM
Licentiate of the Royal College of Music [*British*] .... LRCM
Licentiate of the Royal College of Physicians [*British*] .... LRCP
Licentiate of the Royal College of Physicians and Surgeons of Glasgow (DI) .... LRCPSGlasg
Licentiate of the Royal College of Physicians and Surgeons of Ireland (AAMN) .... LRCP & SI
Licentiate of the Royal College of Physicians and the College of Surgeons of Edinburgh, and of the Faculty of Physicians and Surgeons of Glasgow (ROG) .... LRCP & S
Licentiate of the Royal College of Physicians (Edinburgh) .... LRCPE
Licentiate of the Royal College of Physicians of Ireland .... LRCP Irel
Licentiate of the Royal College of Physicians of Ireland .... LRCPI
Licentiate of the Royal College of Surgeons [*British*] .... LRCS
Licentiate of the Royal College of Surgeons (Edinburgh) (DI) .... LRCS (Edin)
Licentiate of the Royal College of Surgeons (Edinburgh) .... LRCSE
Licentiate of the Royal College of Surgeons in Ireland .... LRCS Irel
Licentiate of the Royal College of Surgeons in Ireland .... LRCSI
Licentiate of the Royal College of Veterinary Surgeons [*British*] .... LRCVS
Licentiate of the Royal Conservatory of Toronto [*Canada*] .... LRCT
Licentiate of the Royal Faculty of Physicians and Surgeons [*British*] .... LRFPS
Licentiate of the Royal Faculty of Physicians and Surgeons, Glasgow .... LRFPS(G)
Licentiate of the Royal Institute of British Architects .... LRIBA
Licentiate of the Royal Institute of Chemistry [*British*] .... LRIC
Licentiate of the Royal Photographic Society [*British*] (DBQ) .... LRPS
Licentiate of the Royal School of Music, London [*British*] .... LRSM
Licentiate of the Royal Society of Chemistry [*British*] (DBQ) .... LRSC
Licentiate of the Society of Apothecaries [*British*] .... LSA
Licentiate of the Society of Industrial Artists [*British*] .... LSIA
Licentiate of the Speech and Drama Association (ADA) .... LSDA
Licentiate of the Textile Institute [*British*] (DBQ) .... LTI
Licentiate of the Toronto Conservatory of Music [*Canada*] .... LTCM
Licentiate of the Victoria College of Music [*London*] (ROG) .... LVCM
Licentiate of the Welsh College of Music and Drama [*British*] (DBQ) .... LWCMD
Licentiate of Trinity College of Music, London [*British*] .... LTCL
Licentiate Surveyor Member of the Incorporated Association of Architects and Surveyors [*British*] (DAS) .... LMIAS
Licentiateship of the London School of Polymer Technology [*British*] (DBQ) .... LLSPT
Licentiatus Chirurgiae [*Licentiate in Surgery*] .... L Ch
Lichen Amyloidosis [*Dermatology*] (DAVI) .... LA
Lichen Chronicus Simplex [*Dermatology*] (DAVI) .... LCS
Lichen Planus-Like Lesion [*Medicine*] (DMAA) .... LPL
Lichen Ruber Planus (DMAA) .... LRP
Lichen Sclerosis et Atrophicus [*Dermatology*] .... LSA
Lichenoid Keratosis [*Medicine*] (DMAA) .... LK
Lichfield [*City in England*] (ROG) .... LICH
Lichinga [*Mozambique*] [*ICAO location identifier*] (ICLI) .... FQLC
Lichinga [*Mozambique*] [*Airport symbol*] (OAG) VXC
Licht Sammler [*Light Collector*] [*Fluorescent plastic used in commercial displays*] [*German*] .... LISA
Lichtenburg [*South Africa*] [*ICAO location identifier*] (ICLI) .... FALI
Lichtenfels [*Germany ICAO location identifier*] (ICLI) .... EDQL
Lid, Sclera, and Conjunctiva [*Opthalmology*] (DAVI) .... LSC
Lid Tank .... LT
Lid Tank Shielding Facility [*Nuclear energy*] (NRCH) .... LTSF
Lidak Pharmaceuticals [*NASDAQ symbol*] (SAG) .... LDAK
Lidak Pharmaceuticals [*Associated Press*] (SAG) .... Lidak
LIDAK Pharmaceuticals'A' [*NASDAQ symbol*] (TTSB) .... LDAKA
LIDAR [*Light Detection and Ranging*] **Atmosphere Sensing Experiment** .... LASE
LIDAR [*Light Detection and Ranging*] **Atmospheric Sounder and Altimeter** .... LASA
Lidco Industries, Inc. [*Toronto Stock Exchange symbol*] .... LID
Liddell and Scott [*Greek-English Lexicon, 9th ed., revised by H. Stuart Jones*] [*A publication*] (OCD) .... LSJ
Lidkoping [*Sweden ICAO location identifier*] (ICLI) .... ESGL
Lido Elementary School, Long Beach, NY [*Library symbol Library of Congress*] (LCLS) .... NLobLE
Lidocaine [*Topical anesthetic*] L
Lidocaine [*Topical anesthetic*] (WDAA) .... LIDOC
Lidocaine Blood Concentration (DMAA) .... LBC
Lidocaine, Epinephrine, and Tetracaine Solution [*Medicine*] (DMAA) .... LET
Lidocaine Tissue Concentration [*Medicine*] (DMAA) .... LTC
Lidoflazine [*A vasodilator*] L
Lieber on Civil Liberty and Self Government [*A publication*] (DLA) .... Lieber Civ Lib
Liebermann-Burchard [*Reaction*] [*Medicine*] (MEDA) .... L-B
Lieber's Hermeneutics [*A publication*] (DLA) .... Lieb Herm
Liechtenstein [*MARC geographic area code Library of Congress*] (LCCP) .... e-lh--
Liechtenstein [*IYRU nationality code*] (IYR) .... FL
Liechtenstein [*MARC country of publication code Library of Congress*] (LCCP) .... lh
Liechtenstein [*ANSI two-letter standard code*] (CNC) LI
Liechtenstein [*ANSI three-letter standard code*] (CNC) .... LIE
Liechtenstein (ABBR) .... LIECH
Liechtenstein .... Liecht
Liechtenstein Global Trust .... LGT
Liederkranz [*Type of cheese*] (BJA) .... LK
Liederkranz Foundation (EA) .... LF
Lief (ABBR) .... LIF
Liefdezusters van de H. Carolus Borromeus [*Sisters of Charity of St. Charles Borromeo - SCSCB*] (EAIO) .... LCB
Liege [*Belgium*] [*Airport symbol*] (OAG) .... LGG
Liege (ABBR) .... LIG
Liege/Bierset [*Belgium ICAO location identifier*] (ICLI) .... EBLG
Liege/Bierset [*Belgium ICAO location identifier*] (ICLI) .... EBLH
Lien .... LN
Lient Trief Mixed [*Cement*] .... LTM
Lient Trief Pure [*Cement*] .... LTP
Lies [*Read*] [*German*] L
Lietuviu Darbininku Susivienijimas [*Association of Lithuanian Workers*] (EA) .... LDS
Lietuviu Krikscioniu Demokratu Partija [*Lithuanian Christian Democratic Party*] [*Political party*] (PPE) .... LKDP
Lietuviy Demokraty Partija [*Lithuanian Democratic Party*] [*Political party*] (PPE) .... LDP
Lietuvos Komunisty Partija [*Communist Party of Lithuania*] [*Political party*] (PPE) .... LKP
Lietuvos Revoliuciniu Socialistu Liaudininkai Partija [*Revolutionary Socialist Populists Party of Lithuania*] [*Political party*] (PPE) .... LRSLP
Lietuvos Socialdemokratu Partija [*Social Democratic Party of Lithuania*] [*Political party*] (EAIO) .... LDSP
Lietuvos Socialdemokratu Partija [*Lithuanian Social Democratic Party*] [*Political party*] (PPE) .... LSDP
Lietuvos Socialdemokratu Partijos Uzsienio Delegatura [*Lithuanian Social Democratic Party*] (EAIO) .... LSPUD
Lietuvos Socialistu Liaudininkai Demokratu Partija [*Socialist Populists Democratic Party of Lithuania*] [*Political party*] (PPE) .... LSLDP
Lietuvos Socialistu Liaudininkai Partija [*Socialist Populists Party of Lithuania*] [*Political party*] (PPE) .... LSLP
Lietuvos TSR Valstybine Respublikine Biblioteka [*National Library of Lithuania*], Vilnius, Lithuania [*Library symbol Library of Congress*] (LCLS) .... Lit
Lieutenancy (ABBR) .... LIEUTC
Lieutenancy (ABBR) .... LIEUTE
Lieutenant [*Navy British*] L
Lieutenant (EY) .... LIEUT
Lieutenant (EY) .... LT
Lieutenant .... LT
Lieutenant [*Navy*] O3
Lieutenant Colonel .... LCOL
Lieutenant Colonel (AABC) .... LTC
Lieutenant Colonel .... LTCOL
Lieutenant Colonel [*Air Force, Army, Marine Corps*] O5
Lieutenant Commander LC
Lieutenant Commander (AAG) .... LCDR
Lieutenant Commander [*Navy British*] .... LCr
Lieutenant Commander (DNAB) .... LT COMDR
Lieutenant Commander (GFGA) .... LTC
Lieutenant Commander .... LTCDR
Lieutenant Commander (DNAB) .... LTCOM
Lieutenant Commander [*Navy*] O4
Lieutenant (Engineer) .... LT(E)
Lieutenant Field Marshal .... LFM
Lieutenant General [*British*] (ROG) .... LG
Lieutenant General [*Navy British*] .... LGen
Lieutenant General (AABC) .... LTG
Lieutenant General .... LTGEN

Lieutenant General [*Air Force, Army, Marine Corps*] O9
Lieutenant Governor (WGA) .... LT Gov
Lieutenant Grand Commander [*Freemasonry*] .... LTGC
Lieutenant Junior Grade [*Navy*] .... Lieut Jg
Lieutenant Junior Grade [*Navy*] .... LTJG
Lieutenant Junior Grade [*Navy*] O2
Lieutenant of the Victorian Order [*Canada*] (DD) .... LVO
Lieutenant of Treasury [*British*] .... LT T
Lieutenant, Royal Marines [*Navy British*] (ROG) .... RML
Lieutenant (Special) .... LT(Sp)
Lieutenant-at-Arms [*British*] .... LA
Lieutenant-at-Arms [*British*] (DMA) .... LAA
Lieutenant-Colonel [*British military*] (DMA) .... Lieut-Col
Lieutenant-Commander [*British military*] (DMA) .... Lt-Comm
Lieutenant-General [*British military*] (DMA) .... Lieut-Gen
Life [*Insurance*] L
Life (ABBR) .... LF
Life Action Ministries (EA) .... LAM
Life Adjustment Inventory [*Psychology*] .... LAI
Life after Divorce Is Eventually Sane (EA) .... LADIES
Life Agency Cashiers Association of the United States and Canada (EA) .... LACA
Life Agency Management Program [*GAMC*] .... LAMP
Life Amendment Political Action Committee [*Defunct*] (EA) .... LAPAC
[*The*] **Life and Times of Eddie Roberts** [*TV program*] .... LATER
Life and Unit Trust Intermediaries Regulatory Organisation [*British*] .... LUTIRO
Life Assurance and Unit Trust Regulatory Organisation [*British*] .... LAUTRO
Life Assurance of Scotland [*Commercial firm*] .... LAS
Life Assurance Premium Relief [*Business term*] .... LAPR
Life Assurance Relief [*British*] .... LAR
Life Bancorp [*NASDAQ symbol*] (TTSB) .... LIFB
Life Bancorp, Inc. [*NASDAQ symbol*] (SAG) .... LIFB
Life Bancorp, Inc. [*Associated Press*] (SAG) .... Life Bcp
LIFE Bible College, Los Angeles, CA [*Library symbol Library of Congress*] (LCLS) CLLI
Life Blower Bearing .... LBB
"Life Can Be Beautiful" [*Old radio program; nicknamed "Elsie Beebee"*] .... LCBB
Life Care [*Medicine*] (BABM) LC
Life Care Services .... LCS
Life Change Unit [*Psychometrics*] .... LCU
Life College, Marietta, GA [*Library symbol*] [*Library of Congress*] (LCLS) .... GMarLC
Life Communicators Association [*Des Moines, IA*] (EA) .... LCA
Life Component Tester .... LCT
Life Cycle Analysis [*or Assessment*] [*Environmental science*] .... LCA
Life Cycle Cost Analysis (MCD) .... LCCA
Life Cycle Cost / Design to Cost .... LCC/DTC
Life Cycle Cost in Design [*Computer program released by US Army Construction Engineering Research Laboratory*] (RDA) .... LCCID
Life Cycle Cost of Ownership (MCD) .... LCCO
Life Cycle Cost Tracking System [*Social Security Administration*] .... LCCTS
Life Cycle Hypothesis [*Economics*] .... LCH
Life Cycle Inventory [*Environmental engineering*] LCI
Life Cycle Management Planning [*Army*] .... LCMP
Life Cycle Manager (MCD) .... LCM
Life Cycle Material Manager (MCD) .... LCMM
Life Cycle Software Support .... LCSS
Life Detection Instrument .... LDI
Life Environmental Testing (IAA) .... LET
Life Events [*or Expectancy*] **Inventory** .... LEI
Life Events Questionnaire [*Psychology*] (EDAC) .... LEQ
Life Expectancy [*Military*] .... LF-EX
Life Experiences Survey [*Psychology*] .... LES
Life Extension Foundation (EA) .... LEF
Life Fellow Imperial Institute [*British*] (ROG) .... LFIINST
Life Float .... LF
Life Guards [*Military unit*] [*British*] .... LG
Life (Health and Accident) Cases [*Commerce Clearing House*] [*A publication*] (DLA) .... Life C
Life (Health and Accident) Cases [*Commerce Clearing House*] [*A publication*] (DLA) .... Life Cas
Life (Health and Accident) Cases, Second Series [*Commerce Clearing House*] [*A publication*] (DLA) .... Life Cas 2d
Life Health Monitoring Program (BABM) .... LHMP
Life History Questionnaire [*Psychology*] (DAVI) .... LHQ
Life History Recorder Set [*or System*] (MCD) .... LHRS
Life in One Position [*Telecommunications*] (TEL) .... LIOP
Life Insurance Act [*Australia*] .... LIA
Life Insurance Adjustment Bureau [*Defunct*] (EA) .... LIAB
Life Insurance Advertisers Association [*Later, LCA*] (EA) .... LAA
Life Insurance Agency Management Association [*Later, LIMRA*] .... LIAMA
Life Insurance Association [*British*] (DBA) .... LIA
Life Insurance Association of America [*Later, ACLI*] (EA) .... LIAA
Life Insurance Committee for a Nuclear Disarmament (EA) .... LICND
Life Insurance Committee for a Nuclear Weapons Freeze [*Later, LICND*] (EA) .... LICNWF
Life Insurance Co. Income Tax Act of 1959 .... LICITA
Life Insurance Co. Tax Act of 1955 .... LICTA
Life Insurance Index [*A publication*] LII
Life Insurance Marketing and Research Association [*Hartford, CT*] (EA) .... LIMRA
Life Insurance Medical Research Fund [*Defunct*] .... LIMRF
Life Insurance Policy .... LIP
Life Insurance Sales Research Bureau [*Later, LIMRA*] .... LISRB
Life Insurance Society of America (EA) .... LISA
Life Insurance Society of New York (SRA) .... LISNY
Life Insurance Trust (DLA) .... LIT
Life Insurers Conference [*Richmond, VA*] (EA) LIC
Life Interpersonal History Enquiry [*Test*] [*Psychology*] .... LIPHE
Life Issues in Formal Education (EA) .... LIFE
Life Jacket .... LJ
Life Line International (EA) LLI
Life Management Institute [*Life Office Management Association*] .... LMI
Life Med Sciences [*NASDAQ symbol*] (TTSB) .... CHAI
Life Med Sciences Wrrt 'A' [*NASDAQ symbol*] (TTSB) .... CHAIW
Life Med Sciences Wrrt'B' [*NASDAQ symbol*] (TTSB) .... CHAIZ
Life Medical Sciences [*NASDAQ symbol*] (SAG) .... CHAI
Life Medical Sciences [*Associated Press*] (SAG) .... LfeMd
Life Medical Sciences [*Associated Press*] (SAG) .... LfeMed
Life Medical Sciences [*Associated Press*] (SAG) .... LfMd
Life Member of Engineering Institute of Canada .... LMEIC
Life of Josephus (BJA) .... JosLife
Life of Josephus (BJA) .... JVita
Life of Program .... LOP
[*The*] **Life of the Spirit** [*London*] [*A publication*] (BJA) .... LifeSpir
Life of Type (AFIT) .... LOT
Life Office Management Association [*Atlanta, GA*] (EA) .... LOMA
Life Offices' Association [*British*] (DCTA) .... LOA
Life Orientation (Survey) .... LIFO
Life Partners [*Associated Press*] (SAG) .... LifePart
Life Partners Group [*NYSE symbol*] (TTSB) .... LPG
Life Partners Group, Inc. [*NYSE symbol*] (SPSG) .... LPG
Life Policy [*Insurance*] .... L/P
Life Policy [*Insurance*] (DCTA) .... L/POL
Life Preserver .... LPRSVR
Life Preserver Unit .... LPU
Life Probability Function .... LPF
Life Re [*NYSE symbol*] (TTSB) .... LRE
Life Re Corp. [*Associated Press*] (SAG) .... LifeRe
Life Real Estate [*NYSE symbol*] (SPSG) .... LRE
Life/Revisit [*NASA*] (KSC) .... L/R
Life Role Expectations Inventory (EDAC) .... LREI
Life Safety Box .... LSB
Life Safety Code .... LSC
Life Satisfaction Index [*Medicine*] (DMAA) .... LSI
Life Saving Appliance [*or Apparatus*] (DS) .... LSA
Life Saving Service (WDAA) .... LSS
Life Science (NASA) .... LS
Life Science Experiment (MUGU) .... LSE
Life Science Module [*NASA*] (NASA) .... LSM
Life Science Payloads Development Facility (MCD) .... LSPDF
Life Science Research Ltd. [*British*] (IRUK) .... LSR
Life Science Research Module (MCD) .... LSRM
Life Sciences Flight Experiment [*NASA*] (NASA) .... LSFE
Life Sciences Laboratory (AAG) .... LSL
Life Sciences Organizations and Agencies Directory [*A publication*] .... LSOAD
Life Sciences Research Office [*NASA*] (KSC) .... LSRO
Life Sciences Shuttle Research Centrifuge [*NASA*] (NASA) .... LSSRC
Life Sciences Space Laboratory [*NASA*] (NASA) .... LSSL
Life Sciences Strategic Planning Study Committee [*NASA*] .... LSSPSC
Life Sciences Support Facility [*NASA*] (NASA) .... LSSF
Life Services Network of Illinois (SRA) .... LSN
Life Services System [*For the disabled*] .... LSS
Life Size (VRA) .... lf sz
Life Space Interviewing [*Teaching technique*] .... LSI
Life Span .... LSp
Life, Sport, and Drama [*A publication British*] .... LSD
Life Style Analysis [*Psychology*] .... LSA
Life Support (AAG) .... LS
Life Support and Environmental Control System (IEEE) .... LSECS
Life Support and Environmental System (IAA) .... LSES
Life Support Equipment (KSC) .... LSE
Life Support Evaluator (SAA) .... LSE
Life Support for Trauma And Transport [*Northrop Grumman*] (PS) .... LSTAT
Life Support Package [*Diving apparatus*] .... LSP
Life Support System [*or Subsystem*] .... LSS
Life Support Systems Project Office [*NASA*] (MCD) .... LSSPO
Life Support Umbilical [*NASA*] .... LSU
Life Support Unit [*NASA*] (KSC) .... LSU
Life System (MCD) .... LS
Life Systems Officer [*NASA*] (KSC) .... LSO
Life Technologies [*NASDAQ symbol*] (TTSB) .... LTEK
Life Technologies, Inc. [*Associated Press*] (SAG) .... LfeTch
Life Technology (MCD) .... VITEK
Life Test Data Logger (CAAL) .... LTDL
Life Test Model .... LTM
Life Test Vehicle .... LTV
Life Underwriter Training Council [*Washington, DC*] (EA) .... LUTC
Life Underwriter Training Course .... LUTC
Life Underwriters Association of Canada .... LUAC
Life Underwriters Political Action Committee .... LUPAC
Life USA Holding, Inc. [*Associated Press*] (SAG) .... LfeUSA
Life USA Holding, Inc. [*NASDAQ symbol*] (SAG) .... LUSA
Life USA Holdings [*NASDAQ symbol*] (TTSB) .... LUSA
Lifeblood (ABBR) .... LFBD
Lifeboat (AAG) .... LB
Lifeboat (ABBR) .... LFBT
Lifeboat Deck .... LD
Lifeboat Station [*Coast Guard*] .... LB
Lifeboat Station [*Coast Guard*] .... LIFESTA
Lifecell Corp. [*NASDAQ symbol*] (SAG) .... LIFC

Lifecell Corp. [Associated Press] (SAG) .... Lifecell
Lifecore Biomedical [NASDAQ symbol] (TTSB) .... LCBM
LifeCore Biomedical, Inc. [NASDAQ symbol] (SAG) .... LCBM
LifeCore Biomedical, Inc. [Associated Press] (SAG) .... Lifecore
Life-Cycle Cost Estimate (AABC) .... LCCE
Life-Cycle Costing [or Costs] [DoD] LCC
Life-Cycle Logistic Support Cost (PDAA) .... LCLSC
Life-Cycle Management Model (AABC) .... LCMM
Life-Cycle Management System .... LCMS
Life-Cycle Productivity System .... LPS
Life-Cycle Software Engineering [Army] (RDA) .... LCSE
Life-Cycle Software Engineering Center [Army] .... LCSEC
Life-Cycle Software Engineering Center [Army] .... LSEC
Life-Cycle Software Support Center [Army] .... LCSSC
Life-Cycle Software Support Environment [Army] .... LCSSE
Life-Cycle Survivability (MSA) .... LCS
Life-Cycle Systems Management Model .... LCSMM
Lifegain Institute (EA) LI
Life-Giving Unselfish Middle-Class Parent Survivors [Facetious term coined by columnist Erma Bombeck to describe the Yuppies' progenitors] [Lifestyle classification] .... Lumps
Lifeguard (ABBR) .... LFGRD
Lifelessly (ABBR) .... LFLSY
Lifelike (ABBR) .... LFLK
Lifeline (ABBR) .... LFLN
Lifeline Foundation (EA) .... LF
Lifeline Systems [NASDAQ symbol] (SAG) .... LIFE
Lifeline Systems [NASDAQ symbol] (TTSB) .... LIFE
Lifeline Systems, Inc. [Associated Press] (SAG) .... LfelneS
LifeQuest Medical [NASDAQ symbol] (TTSB) .... LQMD
LifeQuest Medical, Inc. [Associated Press] (SAG) .... LfeQst
LifeQuest Medical, Inc. [NASDAQ symbol] (SAG) .... LQMD
Lifer (ABBR) .... LFR
LifeRate Systems [NQS] (TTSB) .... LRSI
LifeRate Systems, Inc. [Associated Press] (SAG) .... LifeRte
LifeRate Systems, Inc. [NASDAQ symbol] (SAG) .... LRSI
Lifesaver (ABBR) .... LFSV
Lifesaving (MSA) .... LSVG
Lifesaving Service [Coast Guard] .... LS
Lifesaving Station [Nautical charts] .... LSS
Lifesize (ABBR) .... LFSZ
Lifespan Resources [An association] (EA) .... LR
Life-Span Study [Environmental science] (FFDE) .... LSS
Lifestyle [Wire service code] (NTCM) L
Lifestyle (ABBR) .... LFST
Lifestyle Beverage Corp. [Vancouver Stock Exchange symbol] .... LSB
[The] Lifestyles Organization (EA) .... LO
[The] Lifestyles Organization (EA) .... TLO
Life-Sustaining Treatment [Medicine] (DMAA) .... LST
Lifetime (ABBR) .... LFTM
Lifetime [Cable television channel] .... LIFE
Lifetime Book of Money Management [A publication] .... LBMM
Lifetime Element Advancing Program .... LEAP
Lifetime Evaluation and Analysis of Heterogeneous System (PDAA) .... LEAHS
Lifetime Hoan [NASDAQ symbol] (TTSB) .... LCUT
Lifetime Hoan Corp. [NASDAQ symbol] (SAG) .... LCUT
Lifetime Hoan Corp. [Associated Press] (SAG) .... LifeHoan
Lifetime Medical Television .... LMT
Lifetime Reproductive Success [Demographics] .... LRS
Lifetime Sports Education Project [of Lifetime Sports Foundation] .... LSEP
Lifetrends Behavioral Systems, Inc. [Vancouver Stock Exchange symbol] .... LTS
Lifeway Foods [NASDAQ symbol] (SAG) .... LWAY
Lifeway Foods, Inc. [Associated Press] (SAG) .... Lifeway
Lifework (ABBR) .... LFWK
Lifou/Ouanaham, Iles Loyaute [New Caledonia] [ICAO location identifier] (ICLI) .... NWWL
Li-Fraumeni Syndrome [Oncology] .... LFS
Lifschultz Inds [NASDAQ symbol] (TTSB) .... LIFF
Lifschultz Industries, Inc. [NASDAQ symbol] (SAG) .... LIFF
Lifschultz Industries, Inc. [Associated Press] (SAG) .... Lifschlt
Lifshitz-Slyozov-Wagner Theory of Mineral Recrystallization L
Lift .... L & LC
Lift and Lift Cruise (MCD) .... L & LC
Lift Improvement Device (MCD) .... LID
Lift Owners' Association of Victoria [Australia] .... LOAV
Lift Unit Frame [Shipping] (DS) .... LUF
Lift Vector (NASA) LV
Lift-Drag [Ratio] .... L:D
Lift-Drag [Ratio] (MCD) .... LTD
Lifting (MSA) .... LFT
Lifting (ABBR) .... LIFTG
Lifting Ascent Vehicle .... LAV
Lifting Body Development .... LBD
Lifting Body Program Office [NASA] .... LBPO
Lifting Body Research Vehicle .... LBRV
Lifting Condensation Level [Meteorology] LCL
Lifting Entry Vehicle .... LEV
Lifting Equipment Engineers Association [British] (EAIO) .... LEEA
Lifting Equipment Manufacturers Association [British] (BI) .... LEMA
Lifting Eye .... LE
Lifting Fair Air Intake [Hovercraft] .... LFAI
Lifting Fan [Hovercraft] .... LF
Lifting Fan Intake [Hovercraft] .... LFI
Lifting Index [Ergonometrics] LI
Lifting of Aerodynamic Decelerators (PDAA) .... LOADS

Lifting Reentry Vehicle (MCD) .... LRV
Lifting-Body Airship (PDAA) .... LBA
Liftoff (ABBR) .... LFTF
Lift-Off (AAG) .... LO
Lift-Off Acquisition System .... LOAS
Lift-Off Elevation and Azimuth Programmer .... LEAP
Lift-Off Simulator [NASA] (NASA) .... LOS
Lift-Off Speed [Aviation code] (AIA) v1of
Lift-off Speed (GAVI) .... VLOF
Lift-Off Time [Aerospace] (MCD) .... LOT
Lift-Off Time and Update .... LTU
Lift-Off Transmission Subsystem (IAA) .... LTS
Lift-On/Lift-Off .... LO/LO
Lift-Right Bounded-Context [Computer science] (MHDI) .... LRBC
Lifts and Cranes Appeals Tribunal [Australia] .... LCAT
Lifts Not Operating [Skiing] .... NO
Lifts Operating [Skiing] .... OPR
Lift-Up Door [Technical drawings] .... LUD
Lifu [Loyalty Islands] [Airport symbol] (OAG) .... LIF
Lifuka [Tonga Islands] [Airport symbol] (OAG) .... HPA
Liga Apararii Nationale Crestine [League of National Christian Defense] [Romania] [Political party] (PPE) .... LANC
Liga Armada Gallega [Armed Galician League] [Spain] (PD) .... LAG
Liga Comunista Internacionalista [International Communist League] [Portugal Political party] (PPE) LCI
Liga de Uniao e Acao Revolucionaria [Portugal] .... LUAR
Liga Ibero-Americana de Astronomia [Ibero-American Astronomy League] (EAIO) .... LIADA
Liga International (EA) LI
Liga Medicorum Homoeopathica Internationalis [International Homoeopathic Medical League] (EA) .... LMHI
Ligament [or Ligamentum] L
Ligament (ABBR) .... LGMN
Ligament [or Ligamentum] .... LIG
Ligament [Anatomy] (DAVI) .... LIG
Ligament Augmentation Device [Sports medicine] .... LAD
Ligaments [or Ligamenti] .... LIGG
Ligand [Chemistry] .... LB
Ligand Binding Domain [Genetics] .... LB
Ligand Hyperfine Structure .... LHFS
Ligand Pharmaceuticals 'B' [NASDAQ symbol] (TTSB) .... LGND
Ligand Pharmaceuticals, Inc. [NASDAQ symbol] (SAG) .... LGND
Ligand Pharmaceuticals, Inc. [Associated Press] (SAG) .... Ligand
Ligand-Binding Assay [Analytical biochemistry] .... LBA
Ligand-Binding Domain [Biochemistry] .... LBD
Ligand-Driven Light-Induced Spin Changes [Physics] .... LD-LISC
Ligand-Field Theory [Physical chemistry] .... LFT
Ligand-Responsive Transcription Factor [Genetics] .... LTF
Ligand-to-Metal Charge Transfer [Physical chemistry] .... LMCT
Ligas Populares de 28 de Febrero [February 28 Popular Leagues] [El Salvador] (PD) LP-28
Ligase Chain Reaction [Genetics] .... LCR
Ligated [or Ligation] [Medicine] .... LIG
Ligating and Dividing Stapler [Used surgical procedures] (DAVI) .... LDS
Ligation-Mediated Polymerase Chain Reaction [Genetics] .... LMPCR
Ligature (ABBR) .... LGTR
Ligature (DGA) .... LIG
Ligature [Surgery] (DAVI) .... ligg
Ligatured (ABBR) .... LGTRD
Ligaturing (ABBR) .... LGTRG
Liggett & Myers, Inc. [Later, Liggett Group, Inc.], Durham, NC [Library symbol Library of Congress] (LCLS) .... NcDurL
Light [Chain] [Biochemistry, immunochemistry] L
Light .... LGT
Light .... LGT
Light (ABBR) .... LHT
Light [Commonly used] (OPSA) .... LIGHT
Light (WDMC) .... lt
Light (AAG) .... LT
Light (VRA) .... lt
Light Aid Detachment [Military British] .... LAD
Light Air Defense Artillery [Army] .... LADA
Light Airborne ASW [Antisubmarine Warfare] Vehicle .... LAAV
Light Airborne Multiple Package System .... LAMPS
Light Airborne Multipurpose System [Navy] (MCD) .... LAMP
Light Airborne Multipurpose System [Navy] .... LAMPS
Light Airborne Multipurpose System Standard Operating Procedures Manual [Navy] (DNAB) .... LAMPSOP
Light Aircraft Binary Information Link .... LABIL
Light Aircraft Manufacturers' Association (EA) .... LAMA
Light Air-to-Surface Semiautomatic Optical [French missile] .... LASSO
Light Ale (ADA) .... LA
Light Alloy .... LA
Light All-Weather Missile (MCD) .... LAWM
Light Alternating (IAA) .... LTALT
Light Amphibious Cargo Vehicle (MCD) .... LACV
Light Amphibious Resupply Craft .... LARC
Light Amplification by Stimulated Emission of Radiation [Acronym was coined in 1957 by scientist Gordon Gould] .... LASER
Light Amplification by Stimulated Emission of Radiation (WDMC) .... laser
Light Amplification by Stimulated Emission of Radiation Computer Output Microfilm (EECA) .... LASERCOM
Light and Accommodation [Optometry] .... L & A
Light and Accommodation [Ophthalmology] (DAVI) .... L & A
Light and Variable [Referring to wind] LV

Light Antiaircraft [Guns] ..... LAA
Light Antiaircraft Control Center (NATG) ..... LAACC
Light Antiaircraft Missile ..... LAAM
Light Antiaircraft Missile Battalion (MUGU) ..... LAAMBN
Light Antiarmor Weapon [Military] (RDA) ..... LAW
Light Antitank Weapon ..... LAW
Light Antitank Weapon System (LAIN) ..... LAWS
Light Area Defense (MCD) ..... LAD
Light Area Defense System (MCD) ..... LADS
Light Area Weapon ..... LAW
Light Armed Reconnaissance Aircraft [Air Force] ..... LARA
Light Armor [Telecommunications] (TEL) ..... LA
Light Armor Antitank System (MCD) ..... LAAS
Light Armored Assault Battalion [Marine Corps] ..... LAAB
Light Armored Combat Vehicle ..... LACV
Light Armored Infantry [Marine Corps] (DOMA) ..... LAI
Light Armored Squad Carrier ..... LASC
Light Armored Turret System (MCD) ..... LATS
Light Armored Vehicle [Army] (RDA) ..... LAV
Light Armored Vehicle / Air Defense [Army] (DWSG) ..... LAV/AD
Light Armored Vehicle/Air Defense System [Army] ..... LAV/ADS
Light Armored Vehicle, Air Force (LAIN) ..... LAV-AF
Light Armored Vehicle - Antitank [Canada] ..... LAV-AT
Light Armored Vehicle Battalion [Marine Corps] (DOMA) ..... LAVB
Light Armored Vehicle-Assault Gun [Marine Corps] (DOMA) ..... LAV-AG
Light Armoured Fighting Vehicle [British military] (DMA) ..... LAFV
Light Armoured Motor Brigade [British military] (DMA) ..... LAMB
Light Army Aircraft ..... LAA
Light Artillery ..... LA
Light Artillery Rocket (MCD) ..... LAR
Light Artillery Rocket System (NATG) ..... LARS
Light Artillery Tractor [British military] (DMA) ..... LAT
Light Assault Antitank Weapon ..... LAAW
Light Assault Bridge [Military program] (INF) ..... LAB
Light Assault Floating Bridge [British military] (DMA) ..... LAFB
Light Assault Weapon ..... LAW
Light Atomic Gas Oil [Petroleum product] ..... LAGO
Light Attack Aircraft [Symbol] (MCD) ..... VAL
Light Attack Battalion (INF) ..... LAB
Light Attack Navigation and Bombing System (MCD) ..... LANABS
Light Attack Turbofan Single Aircraft [Aviation] ..... LATS
Light Attack Weapon ..... LAW
Light Attack Weapons School, Pacific (DNAB) ..... LATKWEPSCOLPAC
Light Attack Wing [Navy] (NVT) ..... LATWING
Light Attendant Station [Coast Guard] ..... LAR
Light Aviation Special Support Operations ..... LASSO
Light Battalion [British military] (DMA) ..... LB
Light Bay [Horse racing] ..... LTB
Light Beam Deflection ..... LBD
Light Beam Oscillograph ..... LBO
Light Beam Pickup ..... LBP
Light Behind Camera [Photographic technique] ..... LIBEC
Light Blend [Horticulture] ..... LtBI
Light Bombardment [Air Force] ..... LB
Light Bomber [Air Force] ..... LB
Light Bomber Strike [Air Force] (NATG) ..... LBS
Light Bracket (AAG) ..... LB
Light Capital Technology (PDAA) ..... LCT
Light Car [British] LC
Light Cargo Ship [Navy symbol] ..... AKL
Light Case [Military] (NATG) LC
Light Center Length LCL
Light Chain [Immunoglobulin] LC
Light Chain Deposition Disease [Medicine] (DMAA) ..... LCDD
Light Chopping Reticle ..... LCR
Light Combat Aircraft [Military] ..... LCA
Light Commercial Vehicle LCV
Light Commercial Vehicle Association (EA) ..... LCVA
Light Compact Performance [Filtration systems] [Automotive engineering] ..... LCP
Light Company [British military] (DMA) LC
Light Control [Technical drawings] LC
Light Corner Wear [Deltiology] ..... LT/COR/WR
Light Crease [Deltiology] ..... LT/CR
Light Cruiser [Navy symbol] CL
Light Cruiser Squadron [British military] (DMA) ..... LCS
Light Current (IAA) LC
Light Cycle Oil [Petrochemical technology] ..... LCO
Light Dependent Resistor ..... LDR
Light Destroyer (ADA) ..... DDL
Light Detection and Ranging ..... LIDAR
Light Diesel Oil (IAA) ..... LDO
Light Difference [Difference between amounts of light perceptible to the two eyes] [Ophthalmology] ..... LD
Light Digital FACSIMILE [Machine] ..... LDF
Light Direction Center [Military] ..... LDC
Light Displacement Ton [MARAD] (TAG) ..... LDT
Light Distillate Feedstock (PDAA) ..... LDF
Light Distillate Spirit (PDAA) ..... LDS
Light Distribution Box (AAG) ..... LDB
Light Division Direct Support [Artillery system] (MCD) ..... LDDS
Light Dragoons [Military unit] [British] ..... LD
Light Driver (IAA) ..... LD
Light Duty [Automotive engineering] ..... L/D
Light Duty Diesel Vehicle [VDOT] (TAG) ..... LDDV
Light Edge Tool and Allied Trades Association [British] (BI) ..... LETATA

Light Edge Wear [Deltiology] ..... LT/ED/WR
Light Effector Mediator System [Plant physiology] ..... LEM
Light Efficiency Radiator [General Motors Corp.] [Automotive engineering] ..... LER
Light Emission via Inelastic Tunnelling (IAA) ..... LEIT
Light Ends Fractionating Unit [Petroleum technology] ..... LEFU
Light Energy Converter [Telecommunications] (TEL) ..... LEC
Light Equipment ..... LE
Light Equipment Maintenance (MCD) ..... LEM
Light Equipment Maintenance Co. (MCD) ..... LEMCO
Light Equipment Transporter (MCD) ..... LET
Light/Escort Carrier [Ship symbol] (NATG) ..... CVL/CVE
Light European Combat Aircraft (PDAA) ..... LECA
Light Evaluation Plan (MCD) ..... LEP
Light Exo-Atmospheric Projectile [Formerly, Lightweight] (DOMA) ..... LEAP
Light Experimental Supercruiser (MCD) ..... LES
Light Exposure Speed [Photography] (OA) ..... LES
Light Fastness Ink (DGA) ..... LF
Light Field Artillery Tactical Data System (GFGA) ..... LFATDS
Light Field Battery [British military] (DMA) ..... LFB
Light Fighter Course [Army] ..... LFC
Light Filter Factor ..... LFF
Light Fire Team [Military] (CINC) ..... LFT
Light Foot Quantizer ..... LFQ
Light Freight Agent (ADA) ..... LFA
Light Frigate ..... FFL
Light from the Ancient Past, the Archeological Background of Judaism and Christianity [Jack Finegan] [A publication] (BJA) ..... FLAP
Light Fuel Oil (BARN) ..... LFO
Light Future Armored Combat System [Tank] ..... LFACS
Light Gas Gun ..... LGG
Light Gas Oil [Fuel technology] ..... LGO
Light Green ..... LG
Light Ground Station Module ..... LGSM
Light Ground-Attack Fighter ..... LGAF
Light Gun ..... LG
Light Harvesting Complex ..... LHC
Light Heavy-Duty Diesel Engine [Motor vehicle specifications] ..... LHDDE
Light Helicopter [Military] (RDA) ..... LH
Light Helicopter, Attack [Computer test vehicle] ..... LHA
Light Helicopter, Experimental [Army] (RDA) ..... LHX
Light Helicopter Fireteam [Navy] (NVT) ..... LHFT
Light Helicopter Turbine Engine Co. [US Army contractor] ..... LHTEC
Light Helicopters [Army] (RDA) ..... LHX
Light Horse [Cavalry] ..... LH
Light Horse Volunteers [British military] (DMA) ..... LHV
Light Hydrocarbon [Organic chemistry] ..... LHC
Light Industrial Gas Heat Transfer ..... LIGHT
Light Infantry LI
Light Infantry [British military] (DMA) ..... Lt Inf
Light Infantry Division [Army] (INF) ..... LID
Light Infantry Volunteers [Military unit] [British] LIV
Light Intensity High ..... LIH
Light Intensity Low LIL
Light Intensity Medium ..... LIM
Light Intensity Modulation Direct OverWrite [Computer science] ..... LIMDOW
Light Interface Technology [Signal transmission] ..... LIT
Light Intratheater Transport [Air Force] ..... LIT
Light Ion Beam (PDAA) ..... LIB
Light Ion Trough ..... LIT
Light Line [Military] LL
Light Living Library (EA) LLL
Light Load (AAG) LL
Light Lock LL
Light Lorry [British] LL
Light Loss Factor [Floodlighting] ..... LLF
Light Lyne Optical Correlation (MCD) ..... LILOC
Light Machine Gun ..... LM
Light Machine Gun ..... LMG
Light Maintenance ..... LM
Light Marching Pack [Military] ..... LMP
Light Medium Tactical Vehicle [Army] (RDA) ..... LMTV
Light Meromyosin [Biochemistry] ..... LMM
Light Metal ..... LM
Light Metal Founders Association [British] (DBA) ..... LMFA
Light Metal Hydride ..... LMH
Light Metal Products ..... LMP
Light Microscope ..... LM
Light Microscopy Trace Analysis ..... LMTA
Light Military Electronics Equipment ..... LMEE
Light Military Hovercraft (PDAA) ..... LMH
Light Minelayer [Later, MMD] [Navy symbol] ..... DM
Light Minimum [Medicine] ..... LM
Light Mitochondrial Extract (OA) ..... LME
Light Mobile Protected Gun (INF) ..... LMPG
Light Modulation Recording ..... LMR
Light Motorized Infantry Battalion (INF) ..... LMIB
Light Music [Canadian Broadcasting Corp. record series prefix] ..... LM
Light Night Striking Force [British military] (DMA) ..... LNSF
Light Non-Aqueous Phase Liquids ..... LNAPL
Light Observation Aircraft ..... LOA
Light Observation Helicopter ..... LOH
Light Observation Helicopter Avionics Package (MCD) ..... LOHAP
Light Observation Helicopter Target Acquisition Designation System (MCD) ..... LOHTADS
Light Observation Light-Armored Aircraft ..... LOLA

Light Observation Utility Helicopter (NATG)	LOUH
Light of Divine Truth Foundation (EA)	LDTF
Light of the Night Sky [Galaxy]	LONS
Light of Yoga Society (EA)	LYS
Light on Dark	LD
Light Opera of Manhattan	LOOM
Light Operated Typewriter	LOT
Light Output Ratio (WDAA)	LOR
Light Output Ratio Working (PDAA)	LORW
Light Patrol Car [British]	LPC
Light Patrol Frigate (ADA)	LPF
Light Pen	LP
Light Pen Tracking (MCD)	LPT
Light Pen Value (IAA)	LPV
Light Perception [Ophthalmology]	LP
Light Perception [Ophthalmology]	LPerc
Light Perception Only [Ophthalmology]	LPO
Light Photographic Squadron	LIGHTPHOTORON
Light Photographic Squadron	LTPHOTORON
Light Projection [Ophthalmology]	LProj
Light Pulse [Embryology]	LP
Light Pulser Array	LPA
Light Pulser Matrix	LPM
Light Radiation Sensor	LRS
Light Rail Rapid Transit [TRB] (TAG)	LRRT
Light Rail Transit	LRT
Light Rail Transit Association [Milton, Keynes, England] (EAIO)	LRTA
Light Rail Vehicle	LRV
Light Railway Loads [British]	LRL
Light Railway Research Society of Australia	LRRSA
Light Railway Transport League [British] (DCTA)	LRTL
Light Rapid Comfortable [Train system]	LRC
Light Rare Earth Elements [Chemistry]	LREE
Light Reaction (MAE)	LR
Light Reconnaissance Vehicle [Military]	LRV
Light Recreational Vehicle [Mitsubishi minivan]	LRV
Light Reflective Capacitor [Electronics] (DA)	LRC
Light Reflex [Medicine] (AAMN)	LR
Light Repair Car [British]	LRC
Light Repair Section [British military] (DMA)	LRS
Light Repair Truck [British]	LRT
Light Replaceable Assemblies	LRA
Light Responsive Element [Chemistry]	LRE
Light Salvage Ship [Navy symbol] (VNW)	LLC
Light Savers USA [NASDAQ symbol] (TTSB)	LTSV
Light Savers USA, Inc. [Associated Press] (SAG)	LightSav
Light Savers USA, Inc. [NASDAQ symbol] (SAG)	LTSV
Light Scatter Index	LSI
Light Scattering Photometer	LSP
Light SEAL [Sea, Air, and Land] Support Boat [Navy] (DNAB)	LSSB
Light SEAL [Sea, Air, and Land] Support Craft [Navy symbol]	L
Light Sense	LS
Light Sequence Flasher System (DWSG)	LSFS
Light Shield/Star Tracker (NASA)	LS/ST
Light Ship	LS
Light Ship (IAA)	LSH
Light Source	LS
Light Spot Scanner	LSS
Light Station [Coast Guard] (IAA)	LSTN
Light Station [Coast Guard]	LTSTA
Light Stopping Reticle	LSR
Light, Straight Run [Petroleum technology]	LSR
Light Strike Aircraft [Military] (PDAA)	LSA
Light Support Weapon (MCD)	LSW
Light Sussex [Poultry]	LS
Light Switch	LTSW
Light Switch	LTR
Light Tactical Raft	LTT
Light Tactical Transport (MCD)	LTT
Light Tactical Transport Aircraft System [Helicopter] [Military] (RDA)	LTTAS
Light Tactile Stimulation [Neurology] (DAVI)	LTS
Light Tank	LT
Light Tapping Storage (IAA)	LITASTOR
Light Temporarily Extinguished [Navigation]	TE
Light Terminal (PDAA)	LT
Light Terminal Complexes	LTC
Light Test (IAA)	LT
Light Training Helicopter (WDAA)	LTH
Light Transmission Index	LTI
Light Transmittance Difference Meter	LTDM
Light Transport Plane [Single-engine] [Navy symbol]	VG
Light Trap	LT
Light Truck [British]	LT
Light Truck On-Off Road	LTOOR
Light Units, Times Square [Electronics]	LUTS
Light Utility Glider	LUG
Light Utility Vehicle [Pickup truck]	LUV
Light Utilization More Efficient (MCD)	LUME
Light Vacuum Gas Oil [Petroleum technology]	LVGO
Light Value [Photography] (DICI)	LV
Light Value System [Photography] (BARN)	LVS
Light Valve Display	LVD
Light Valve Projector	LVP
Light Variegated Maize	LV
Light Vehicle [British military] (DMA)	LV

Light Vehicle Mine [Military]	LVM
Light Virgin Naphtha (PDAA)	LVN
Light Wall	LW
Light Warning	LW
Light Warning (Station)	LW(STA)
Light Waste Storage Tank (IEEE)	LWST
Light Weight [Technical drawings]	LW
Light Weight / Air Warning	LW/AW
Light Weight Sheet Molding Compound	LW-SWC
Light Year	LTYR
Light Year	LY
Light-Activated Programmable Unijunction Transistor	LAPUT
Light-Activated Silicon Switch	LASS
Light-Activated Silicon-Controlled Rectifier	LASCR
Light-Activated Silicon-Controlled Switch (MCD)	LASCS
Light-Activated Switch	LAS
Light-Addressable Potentiometric Sensor [Semiconductor]	LAPS
Light-Armed Helicopter [Military] (PDAA)	LAH
Light-Beam Transmissometer (PDAA)	LBT
Light-Dark [Ratio] [Ophthalmology] (DAVI)	L/D
Light-Dark [Cycles]	LD
Light-Dark Discrimination [Ophthalmology]	LDD
Light-Dependent Diode [Instrumentation]	LDD
Light-Duty Diesel Truck [Automotive emissions]	LDDT
Light-Duty Gasoline Vehicle	LDGV
Light-Duty Lathe Engine	LDLE
Light-Duty Truck	LDT
Light-Duty Vehicle	LDV
Lighted	LGTD
Lighted (ABBR)	LHTD
Lighted Buoy [USCG] (TAG)	LB
Lighted Independent of Computer	LIOC
Lighted Pushbutton (ECII)	LPB
[The] Lighted Way [An association] (EA)	TLW
Light-Emitting Array	LEA
Light-Emitting Chemical Compound [Marking agent for equipment used in night operations] [Military] (VNW)	LEC
Light-Emitting Diode [Display component]	LED
Light-Emitting Diode Display	LEDD
Light-Emitting Diode Recorder (MCD)	LEDR
Light-Emitting Electrochemical Cell [Chemistry]	LEC
Light-Emitting Film (IEEE)	LEF
Light-Emitting Numerics	LEN
Light-Emitting Polymer	LEP
Light-Emitting Resistor [Computer hacker terminology] (NHD)	LER
Light-Emitting Switch [Electronics] (OA)	LES
Light-Emitting Switch Control [Electronics] (OA)	LESC
Lighten (ABBR)	LGTN
Lighten (ABBR)	LHTEN
Lightened (ABBR)	LHTEND
Lightener (ABBR)	LGTR
Lightening (ABBR)	LHTENG
Lightening	LTG
Lightening Hole [Engineering]	LTGH
Lighter	LGHTR
Lighter (ABBR)	LHTR
Lighter	LTR
Lighter Aboard Ship [Barge-carrying ship]	LASH
Lighter, Air Cushion Vehicle, 30 Tons [Military] (MCD)	LACV-30
Lighter, Air-Cushion Vehicle [Usually used in combination with numerals] [Military] (RDA)	LACV
Lighter, Ambulance [Navy symbol Obsolete]	YH
Lighter, Ammunition [Navy symbol]	YE
Lighter, Amphibian Heavy Lift	LAMP-H
Lighter, Amphibious, Resupply, Cargo [Vessel]	LARC
Lighter, Amphibious, Resupply, Cargo-Five Ton [Vessel] (DNAB)	LARC-V
Lighter Association (EA)	LA
Lighter Collectors' International Society [Defunct] (EA)	LCIS
Lighter Electronics Guidance System (MCD)	LEGS
Lighter, Over-the-Shore [Missions] [For air-cushion vehicles] (RDA)	LOTS
Lighter (Special Purpose) [Non-self-propelled] [Navy symbol]	YFNX
Lighter than Air Society [An association] (PDAA)	LTAS
Lighterage	LTGE
Lighterage Assembly Area	LAA
Lighterage Limits	LL
Lighterage Pontoon [Navy symbol] (DNAB)	YWN
Lightermen, Stevedores, and Dockers	LSD
Lighter-than-Air [Aircraft]	LA
Lighter-than-Air [Aircraft]	LTA
Lighter-than-Air [Aircraft] [Navy symbol] (MUGU)	ZZ
Lighter-than-Air Submarine Simulator	LASS
Lightest (ABBR)	LHTST
Light-Expanded Clay Aggregate (DAC)	LECA
Lightface [Type]	LF
Lightface Type (WDMC)	lf
Lightfingered (ABBR)	LGTFGR
Light-Float [Navigation]	LTF
Lightfooted (ABBR)	LGTFTD
Lightfootedly (ABBR)	LGTFTY
Light-Gun Amplifier	LGA
Light-Gun Pulse Generator	LGG
Light-Harvesting Chlorophyll Protein Complex [Botany]	LHPC
Lighthawk [An association] (EA)	LH
Lightheaded (ABBR)	LGTHD
Lightheadedly (ABBR)	LGTHDY

Lighthearted (ABBR) ... LGTHRTD
Lightheartedly (ABBR) ... LGTHRTY
Lightheartedness (ABBR) ... LGTHRTNS
Lighthouse (ABBR) ... LGTHS
Lighthouse [*Maps and charts*] ... LH
Lighthouse ... LTHO
Lighthouse Automation and Modernization Project [*US Coast Guard*] (PDAA) ... LAMP
Lighthouse, Fixed [*Maps and charts*] (ROG) ... LHF
Lighthouse, Floating [*Maps and charts*] (ROG) ... LHFI
Lighthouse, Intermittent [*Maps and charts*] (ROG) ... LHI
Lighthouse Keepers Association (EA) ... LKA
Lighthouse Publishing Ltd., Bridgewater, Nova Scotia [*Library symbol National Library of Canada*] (NLC) ... NSBL
Lighthouse Publishing Ltd., Bridgewater, NS, Canada [*Library symbol*] [*Library of Congress*] (LCLS) ... CaNSBL
Lighthouse Resources, Inc. [*Vancouver Stock Exchange symbol*] ... LSR
Lighthouse, Revolving [*Maps and charts*] (ROG) ... LHR
Lighthouse Service [*Coast Guard*] ... LS
Lighthouse Study Unit (EA) ... LSU
Lighthouse Tender [*Navy symbol Obsolete*] ... AGL
Lighthouse Tender ... LHT
Lighthouse Tender [*Coast Guard symbol*] (DNAB) ... WYTM
Lighthouse Transmitter Receiver (IAA) ... LHTR
Light-Induced Absorbance Change ... LIAC
Light-Induced Excited Spin State Trapping [*Physics*] ... LIESST
Lighting [*As part of a code*] ... L
Lighting (ABBR) ... LGTG
Lighting (ABBR) ... LHTG
Lighting (ABBR) ... LIGHT
Lighting ... LIGHT
Lighting ... LTG
Lighting and Power ... L & P
Lighting Control Assembly [*NASA*] (KSC) ... LCA
Lighting Design Lumen (PDAA) ... LDL
Lighting Designer (NTCM) ... LD
Lighting Director (NTCM) ... LD
Lighting Director Engineer (NTCM) ... LDE
Lighting Equipment Manufacturers' Association (DAC) ... LEMA
Lighting Industry Federation [*British*] (DBA) ... LIF
Lighting Panel (IAA) ... LP
Lighting Research Institute (EA) ... LRI
Lighting Supervisor [*Television*] ... LS
Lighting System ... LS
Lighting Test Set (KSC) ... LTS
Lighting-Electrical Materials Distributors Association (EA) ... LEMDA
Lighting-Power Density ... LPD
Light-Intensity Detector (MSA) ... LTID
Lightly (ABBR) ... LGTY
Lightly (ABBR) ... LHTY
Lightly Armored Structure Vulnerability Estimation Methodology (MCD) ... LASVEM
Lightly Canceled ... LC
Lightly Doped Drain (MCD) ... LDD
Lightly Hinged [*Philately*] ... LH
Lightly Included [*Colored gemstone grade*] ... LI
Lightly Treated Coated [*Papermaking*] ... LTC
Lightly Wounded in Action ... LWA
Lightminded (ABBR) ... LGTMDD
Lightmindedly (ABBR) ... LGTMDY
Lightning [*Meteorology*] ... L
Lightning (ABBR) ... LGTNG
Lightning (ABBR) ... LHTNG
Lightning (ABBR) ... LIGHT
Lightning [*Meteorology*] ... LTG
Lightning (ADA) ... LTN
Lightning [*Meteorology*] ... LTNG
Lightning and Radio-Emission Detector [*Instrumentation*] ... LRD
Lightning and Transients Research Institute [*St. Paul, MN*] (MCD) ... LTRI
Lightning Arrester ... LA
Lightning Arrester (IAA) ... LTNGARR
Lightning Cloud-to-Air [*NWS*] (FAAC) ... LTGCA
Lightning Cloud-to-Cloud [*NWS*] (FAAC) ... LTGCC
Lightning Cloud-to-Cloud, Cloud-to-Ground [*NWS*] (FAAC) ... LTGCCCG
Lightning Cloud-to-Ground [*NWS*] (FAAC) ... LTGCG
Lightning Cloud-to-Water [*NWS*] (FAAC) ... LTGCW
Lightning Correlation ... LICOR
Lightning Creek Mines Ltd. [*Vancouver Stock Exchange symbol*] ... LCM
Lightning Detection and Ranging System [*Meteorology*] ... LDAR
Lightning Detection Network [*Electric Power Research Institute*] ... LDN
Lightning Hole [*Electronics*] ... LGTH
Lightning in Clouds [*NWS*] (FAAC) ... LTGIC
Lightning Loss Exclusion [*Insurance*] ... LLE
Lightning Mapper Sensor [*NASA*] ... LMS
Lightning Minerals [*Vancouver Stock Exchange symbol*] ... LTG
Lightning Position and Tracing System (MCD) ... LPATS
Lightning Protection Institute (EA) ... LPI
Lightning Protection System [*Boating*] ... LPS
Lightning Sensor [*Aviation*] ... LS
Lightning Training Flight [*British military*] (DMA) ... LTF
Lightning Warning Set [*Air Force*] ... LWS
Lightning Warning System [*NASA*] (NASA) ... LWS
Lightning-Induced Electron Precipitation [*Atmospheric physics*] ... LEP
Light-Off Catalyst [*Exhaust emissions*] [*Automotive engineering*] ... LOC
Light-Off Detector [*Military*] (CAAL) ... LOD
Light-Off Examination [*Navy*] (NVT) ... LOE
Light-Off Temperature [*For steady-state combustion*] ... LOT
Light-Off Time [*Exhaust emissions*] [*Automotive engineering*] ... LOT
Light-Optic Microscope (MSA) ... LOM
LightPath Technol Wrrt 'A' [*NASDAQ symbol*] (TTSB) ... LPTHW
LightPath Technol Wrrt 'B' [*NASDAQ symbol*] (TTSB) ... LPTHZ
LightPath Technologes'A' [*NASDAQ symbol*] (TTSB) ... LPTHA
LightPath Technologies, Inc. [*Associated Press*] (SAG) ... LightP
LightPath Technologies, Inc. [*NASDAQ symbol*] (SAG) ... LPTH
LightPath Technologies Unit [*NASDAQ symbol*] (TTSB) ... LPTHU
Lightproof [*Technical drawings*] ... LP
Lightproof [*Technical drawings*] (IAA) ... LTPR
Lightproof Louver [*Technical drawings*] ... LPL
Lightproof Shade [*Technical drawings*] ... LPS
Lightproof Vent [*Technical drawings*] ... LPV
Lights [*Postal Service standard*] (OPSA) ... LGTS
Lights ... LGTS
Lights [*Commonly used*] (OPSA) ... LIGHTS
Lights Advisory Committee [*General Council of British Shipping*] (DS) ... LAC
Lights Monitor Module [*Automotive engineering*] ... LMM
Light's Retention Scale [*Test*] ... LRS
Light-Saturated Hydrocarbon [*Organic chemistry*] ... LSHC
Light-Scattering Response [*Biology*] ... LSR
Light-Sensing Device (IAA) ... LSD
Light-Sensitive Relay ... LSR
Light-Sensitive Resistor ... LSR
Light-Sensitive Tube ... LST
Lightship [*Navy symbol Obsolete*] ... AL
Lightship [*Coast Guard symbol*] (DNAB) ... WLV
Lightship Screen File [*Computer science*] ... LSF
Light-to-Dark Ratio ... LDR
Light-Travel-Time [*Astronomy*] ... LTT
Light-Vehicle Animation Simulation [*Accident reconstruction*] [*Automotive engineering*] ... LVAS
Light-Vehicle Dynamics Simulation [*Accident reconstruction*] [*Automotive engineering*] ... LVDS
Light-Vessel [*Navigation*] ... LTV
Light-Vessel [*Navigation*] ... LV
Light-Warning RADAR Set (NATG) ... LWS
Light-Water Breeder [*Reactor*] ... LWB
Light-Water Breeder Reactor ... LWBR
Light-Water Critical Assembly [*Nuclear reactor*] [*Japan*] ... LWCA
Light-Water Moderated, Gas-Cooled Reactor (IAA) ... LWGCR
Light-Water Reactor ... LWR
Light-Water-Cooled, Graphic-Moderated (IAA) ... LWGR
Light-Water-Cooled, Graphite-Moderated Reactor (NRCH) ... LGR
Light-Water-Cooled, Heavy-Water-Moderated Reactor (NRCH) ... LWCHW
Lightweight (ABBR) ... LGTWT
Lightweight ... LTWT
Lightweight Acoustic Processing and Display System [*British military*] (DMA) ... LAPADS
Lightweight Advanced Inertial Reference Sphere ... LAIRS
Lightweight Advanced Super-Responsive Engine [*Automotive engineering*] ... LASRE
Lightweight Aggregate Producers Association (EA) ... LAPA
Lightweight Air Defense System (MCD) ... LADS
Lightweight Airborne Navigation System (MCD) ... LANS
Lightweight Airborne Thermal Imaging System (MCD) ... LATIS
Lightweight Aircraft-to-Surface Vessel [*Military*] ... LWASV
Light-Weight Air-to-Air Missile (MCD) ... LWAAM
Lightweight Amphibious Container Handler (MCD) ... LACH
Lightweight Analog Motor (MCD) ... LAM
Lightweight Antenna Kit ... LAK
Lightweight Antenna Terminal Seeker ... LATS
Lightweight Armor ... LWA
Lightweight Attack and/or Reconnaissance (NATG) ... LWAR
Lightweight Battlefield Surveillance Device ... LBSD
Lightweight Broadband Antenna Kit ... LBAK
Lightweight Camouflage Screen System (MCD) ... LCSS
Lightweight Camouflage Screen System (MCD) ... LWCSS
Lightweight Ceramic Dome ... LCD
Lightweight Coated [*Paper*] ... LWC
Lightweight Coated Gravure [*Paper*] (DGA) ... LWCG
Lightweight Coated Offset [*Paper*] (DGA) ... LWCO
Lightweight Collapsible Pillolo Tank ... LCPT
Lightweight Communication Kit (MCD) ... LICK
Lightweight Company Mortar System ... LWCMS
Lightweight Concrete [*Technical drawings*] ... LWC
Lightweight Container Handler (MCD) ... LWCH
Lightweight Crewman Communication Umbilical (MCD) ... LCCU
Lightweight Cycle Association of Great Britian (DBA) ... LCAofGB
Lightweight Cycle Manufacturers Association [*British*] (DBA) ... LCMA
Lightweight Decontamination System (INF) ... LDS
Lightweight Deployable Communications System [*Army*] ... LDC
Lightweight Director Group [*Military*] (CAAL) ... LWDG
Lightweight Directory Access Protocol [*Computer science*] ... LDAP
Lightweight Directory Access Protocol [*Computer science*] ... LDAP
Lightweight Directory Access Protocol [*Computer science*] ... LDAP
Lightweight Directory Access Protocol [*Computer utility tool*] (PCM) ... LDAP
Lightweight Doppler Navigation System (MCD) ... LDNS
Lightweight Electronic Locating and Tracking System ... LELTS
Lightweight Exoatmospheric Advanced Projectile [*Military*] (SDI) ... LEAP
Lightweight Fighter [*Air Force*] ... LWF
Lightweight Fighter Joint Test Force [*Air Force*] ... LWFJTF
Lightweight Fire Control System [*Military*] (CAAL) ... LWFCS

Lightweight Gun (NG) ... LWG
Lightweight Gun Mount [*Military*] (CAAL) ... LWGM
Lightweight Headset [*Apollo*] [*NASA*] ... LWHS
Lightweight High-Velocity Rifle ... LWHVR
Lightweight Hydraulic System [*Navy aviation*] ... LHS
Lightweight Individual Combat Clothing and Equipment (AABC) ... LINCLOE
Lightweight Individual Special Purpose [*Weaponry*] ... LISP
Lightweight Individual Weapon (PDAA) ... LIW
Lightweight Inertial Navigation System [*Air Force*] ... LINS
Lightweight Inertial Northseeking Equipmet (SAA) ... LINE
Lightweight Insulating Concrete [*Technical drawings*] ... LWIC
Lightweight Integrated Shelter System (DWSG) ... LISS
Lightweight Intermediate Caliber Gun System (MCD) ... LICGS
Lightweight LASER Designator ... LWLD
Lightweight LASER [*Light Amplification by Stimulated Emission of Radiation*] **Designator Range Finder** [*DoD*] ... LLDR
Lightweight LASER Target Designator ... LLTD
Lightweight Launcher (MCD) ... LWL
Lightweight Leader Computer [*Army*] (INF) ... LLC
Light-Weight Low-Cost (PDAA) ... LWLC
Lightweight Man-Transportable Radio Direction-Finding System [*Army*] ... LMRDFS
Lightweight Marking System [*British Army*] ... LIMAS
Lightweight Multifunction Tactical Beacon System (MCD) ... LMTBS
Lightweight Multipurpose Missile System (MCD) ... LMMS
Lightweight Optronic Director (MCD) ... LIOD
Lightweight Presentation Protocol [*Telecommunications*] (ACRL) ... LPP
Lightweight RADAR (NATG) ... LW
Lightweight RADAR Missile (MCD) ... LWRM
Lightweight RADAR Set ... LRS
Lightweight RADAR Unit (NATG) ... LWRU
Lightweight Ramjet Missile (MCD) ... LRM
Lightweight Reconnaissance Aircraft (NATG) ... LWRECCE
Lightweight Remote Procedure Call [*Computer science*] ... LRPC
Lightweight Search RADAR (IAA) ... LWSR
Lightweight Ship SATCOM Set [*Navy*] (CAAL) ... LSSS
Lightweight Sight ... LWS
Lightweight Sports [*Concept car*] [*Automotive engineering*] ... LWS
Lightweight Strike and Reconnaissance Aircraft (NATG) ... LWSR
Lightweight Strike and Reconnaissance Aircraft (Reconnaissance Role) (NATG) ... LWSR(R)
Lightweight Strike and Reconnaissance Aircraft (Strike Role) (NATG) ... LWSR(S)
Lightweight Strike Fighter [*NATO Air Forces*] ... LSF
Lightweight Strike Fighter [*NATO Air Forces*] ... LWSF
Lightweight System ... LWS
Lightweight Tactical Fire Direction System [*Artillery*] [*Army*] (INF) ... LTACFIRE
Lightweight Target Designator ... LTD
Lightweight Torpedo [*Now Mk 50*] (DOMA) ... LWT
Lightweight Transponder ... LWT
Lightweight Type [*Anchor gear*] ... LWT
Light-Weight Van ... LWV
Lightweight Video Reconnaissance System [*Military*] (INF) ... LVRS
Lightweight Weapon ... LWW
Lightweight Weapons Sight ... LWWS
Lightweight Weather RADAR Set ... LWRS
Lightwood-Albright [*Syndrome*] [*Nephrology*] (DAVI) ... LA
Lightyear (ABBR) ... LGTYR
Lignes Aerienne Seychelles [*ICAO designator*] (FAAC) ... LAS
Lignes Aeriennes Canadiennes Pacifiques ... LACP
Lignes Nationales Aeriennes - Linacongo [*Congo*] [*ICAO designator*] (FAAC) ... GCB
Lignin-Carbohydrate Complex [*Organic chemistry*] ... LCC
Lignin-Hemicellulose-Cellulose [*A complex found in plants*] ... LHC
Lignite (WDAA) ... L
Lignosulfonate [*Pulp and paper processing*] ... LS
Lignum [*Wood*] [*Latin*] ... Lign
Lignum Vitae [*Botany*] ... LGNMVTE
Ligo Internacia de Blindaj Esperantistoj [*International League of Blind Esperantists - ILBE*] (EAIO) ... LIBE
Ligo Samseksamaj Geesperantistoj [*Richmond, Surrey, England*] (EAIO) ... LSG
Ligonier Advance-Leader, Ligonier, IN [*Library symbol Library of Congress*] (LCLS) ... InLigAL
Ligonier, IN [*FM radio station call letters*] ... WLNB
Ligon's Digest [*Alabama*] [*A publication*] (DLA) ... Lig Dig
Ligue Canadienne des Composeurs [*Canadian League of Composers - CLC*] ... LCC
Ligue Communiste des Travailleurs [*Communist Workers' League*] [*Senegal*] [*Political party*] (PPW) ... LCT
Ligue Communiste (Marxiste-Leniniste) du Canada [*Canadian Communist League (Marxist-Leninist)*] ... LC(ML)C
Ligue Communiste Revolutionnaire [*Revolutionary Communist League*] [*France Political party*] (PPW) ... LCR
Ligue de Foyer [*Salvation Army Home League - SAHL*] (EAIO) ... LF
Ligue Democratique - Mouvement pour le Parti des Travailleurs [*Democratic League - Movement for the Workers' Party*] [*Senegal*] [*Political party*] (PPW) ... LD-MPT
Ligue des Bibliotheques Europeennes de Recherche [*League of European Research Libraries*] (EAIO) ... LIBER
Ligue des Droits de l'Homme [*France*] ... LDH
Ligue des Originaires de Cote d'Ivoire [*League of Ivory Coast Natives*] ... LOCI
Ligue Europeenne de Natation [*European Swimming Federation*] [*Sweden*] (EAIO) ... LEN
Ligue Europeenne pour une Nouvelle Societe [*European League for a New Society - ELNS*] [*Paris, France*] (EAIO) ... LIENS
Ligue Generale des Travailleurs Angolais [*General League of Angolan Workers in Exile*] ... LGTA
Ligue Guineenne des Droits de l'Homme [*Guinea*] [*Political party*] (EY) ... LGDHC
Ligue Internationale Contre la Concurrence Deloyale [*International League Against Unfair Competition*] (EAIO) ... LICCD
Ligue Internationale Contre le Racisme et l'Antisemitisme [*International League Against Racism and Antisemitism*] ... LICA
Ligue Internationale Contre le Racisme et l'Antisemitisme [*France*] ... LICRA
Ligue Internationale de Femmes pour la Paix et la Liberte [*Women's International League for Peace and Freedom - WILPF*] (EAIO) ... LIFPL
Ligue Internationale de Femmes pour la Paix et la Liberte, Section Francaise (EAIO) ... LIFPL/SF
Ligue Internationale de Hockey sur Glace [*International Ice Hockey Federation*] ... LIHG
Ligue Internationale de la Librairie Ancienne [*International League of Antiquarian Booksellers - ILAB*] (EAIO) ... LILA
Ligue Internationale de la Representation Commerciale [*International League of Commercial Travelers and Agents - ILCTA*] (EAIO) ... LI
Ligue Internationale de la Representation Commerciale [*International League of Commercial Travelers and Agents - ILCTA*] (EAIO) ... LIRC
Ligue Internationale des Droits de l'Animal [*International League for Animal Rights*] (EAIO) ... LIDA
Ligue Internationale du Droit de la Concurrence [*International League for Competition Law*] [*Paris, France*] (EA) ... LIDC
Ligue Marxiste Revolutionnaire [*Revolutionary Marxist League*] [*Switzerland Political party*] (PPW) ... LMR
Ligue Monarchiste du Canada [*Monarchist League of Canada*] (EAIO) ... LMC
Ligue Patriotique pour le Developpement [*Burkina Faso*] [*Political party*] (EY) ... LIPAD
Ligue Populaire Africaine pour l'Independance [*African People's League for Independence*] [*Djibouti*] ... LPAI
Ligue Suisse des Droits de l'Homme [*Switzerland*] ... LSDH
Ligue Universelle [*Esperantiste*] ... LU
Ligula Length Index ... LLI
Lihir Gold ADS [*NASDAQ symbol*] (TTSB) ... LIHRY
Lihir Gold Ltd. [*Associated Press*] (SAG) ... LihirGld
Lihir Gold Ltd. [*NASDAQ symbol*] (SAG) ... LIHRY
Lihue [*Hawaii*] [*Airport symbol*] (OAG) ... LIH
Lihue, HI [*FM radio station call letters*] ... KFMN
Lihue, HI [*AM radio station call letters*] ... KQNG
Lihue, HI [*FM radio station call letters*] ... KQNG-FM
Lihue, Kauai Island [*Hawaii*] [*ICAO location identifier*] (ICLI) ... PHLI
Like Kind and Quality (Metal) [*Auto repair*] ... LKQ
Like Type (FAAC) ... LKTYP
Likelihood Ratio [*Statistics*] ... LR
Likelihood Ratio Test [*Statistics*] ... LRT
Likely (FAAC) ... LKLY
Likely Operational Range [*Navy*] (ANA) ... LOR
Like-Sexed ... LS
Likiep [*Marshall Islands*] [*Airport symbol*] (OAG) ... LIK
Likoma [*Malawi*] [*ICAO location identifier*] (ICLI) ... FWLK
Likud-Herut USA (EA) ... LHUSA
Lilabari [*India*] [*Airport symbol*] (OAG) ... IXI
Lilabari/North Lakhimpur [*India*] [*ICAO location identifier*] (ICLI) ... VELR
Lilac ... L
Lilac (ROG) ... LI
Lilac (ROG) ... LIL
Lilac Chlorotic Leafspot Virus [*Plant pathology*] ... LCLV
Lilac Mottle Virus [*Plant pathology*] ... LIMV
Lilac Ring Mottle Virus [*Plant pathology*] ... LRMV
Lilangeni [*Monetary unit*] [*Swaziland*] (BARN) ... L
Lilayi [*Zambia*] [*ICAO location identifier*] (ICLI) ... FLLY
Lille [*France*] [*Airport symbol*] (OAG) ... LIL
Lille [*France*] [*Seismograph station code, US Geological Survey Closed*] (SEIS) ... LIL
Lille/Lesquin [*France ICAO location identifier*] (ICLI) ... LFQQ
Lille/Marcq-En-Baroeul [*France ICAO location identifier*] (ICLI) ... LFQO
Lillehammer [*Norway*] [*Seismograph station code, US Geological Survey*] (SEIS) ... LHN
Lillian Vernon [*AMEX symbol*] (TTSB) ... LVC
Lillian Vernon Corp. [*Associated Press*] (SAG) ... LilVern
Lillian Vernon Corp. [*AMEX symbol*] (SPSG) ... LVC
Lillick, Mchose & Charles, San Francisco, CA [*Library symbol*] [*Library of Congress*] (LCLS) ... CSfLMC
Lillie M. Evans Memorial Library, Princeville, IL [*Library symbol Library of Congress*] (LCLS) ... IPriv
Lillie M. Evans Memorial Library, Princeville, IL [*OCLC symbol*] (OCLC) ... ISQ
Lillington, NC [*AM radio station call letters*] ... WLLN
Lilliput Edison Screw ... LES
Lilliputian (ABBR) ... LIL
Lilliputian Bottle Club (EA) ... LBC
Lillooet [*British Columbia*] [*Seismograph station code, US Geological Survey Closed*] (SEIS) ... LLL
Lillooet Museum, British Columbia [*Library symbol National Library of Canada*] (NLC) ... BLIM
Lillooet Museum, Lillooet, BC, Canada [*Library symbol*] [*Library of Congress*] (LCLS) ... CaBLIM
Lilly [*Eli*] [*Associated Press*] (SAG) ... LillyEli
Lilly [*Eli*] **and Co.** [*Associated Press*] (SAG) ... Lilly
Lilly [*Eli*] **& Co.** [*Associated Press*] (SAG) ... LillyE
Lilly [*Eli*] **& Co.** [*NYSE symbol*] (SPSG) ... LLY
Lilly Contingent Payment Units [*AMEX symbol*] (SPSG) ... HYU
Lilly CtgntPymt Units [*AMEX symbol*] (TTSB) ... HYU
Lilly (Eli) [*NYSE symbol*] (TTSB) ... LLY
Lilly Industries, Inc. [*NYSE symbol*] (SAG) ... LI

Lilly Industries, Inc. [*Associated Press*] (SAG) .... LillyInd
Lilly Industries 'A' [*NYSE symbol*] (TTSB) LI
Lilly Pike Sullivan Municipal Library, Enfield, NC [*Library symbol Library of Congress*] (LCLS) .... NcEn
Lilly's Abridgment [*England*] [*A publication*] (DLA) .... L Abr
Lilly's Abridgment [*England*] [*A publication*] (DLA) .... Lil Abr
Lilly's Abridgment [*England*] [*A publication*] (DLA) .... Lilly Abr
Lilly's Assize Reports [*1688-93*] [*A publication*] (DLA) .... Lib Plac
Lilly's Conveyancer [*A publication*] (DLA) .... Lil Conv
Lilly's English Assize Reports [*1688-93*] [*A publication*] (DLA) Lil
Lilly's Entries [*England*] [*A publication*] (DLA) .... Lill Ent
Lilly's Practical Register [*A publication*] (ILCA) .... Lil Reg
Lilly's Practical Register [*A publication*] (DLA) .... LPR
Lilly's Reports and Pleadings of Cases in Assize [*170 English Reprint*] [*1688-93*] [*A publication*] (DLA) .... Lilly
Lilly's Reports and Pleadings of Cases in Assize [*170 English Reprint*] [*1688-93*] [*A publication*] (DLA) .... Lilly Assize
Lilly's Reports and Pleadings of Cases in Assize [*170 English Reprint*] [*1688-93*] [*A publication*] (DLA) .... Lilly Assize (Eng)
Lilongwe [*Malawi*] [*ICAO location identifier*] (ICLI) .... FWHQ
Lilongwe [*Malawi*] [*ICAO location identifier*] (ICLI) .... FWLL
Lilongwe [*Malawi*] [*Airport symbol*] (OAG) .... LLW
Lily Symptomless Virus [*Plant pathology*] .... LSV
Lily Virus X [*Plant pathology*] LVX
Lima [*Phonetic alphabet*] [*International*] (DSUE) L
Lima [*Ohio*] [*Airport symbol*] (OAG) .... LIA
Lima [*Peru*] [*Airport symbol*] (OAG) .... LIM
Lima [*Peru*] [*Seismograph station code, US Geological Survey*] (SEIS) .... LIM
Lima [*Magdalena*] [*Peru*] [*Seismograph station code, US Geological Survey*] (SEIS) LM2
Lima [*Peru*] [*ICAO location identifier*] (ICLI) .... SPLI
Lima Army Modification Center (RDA) .... LAMC
Lima Army Tank Plant [*Ohio*] .... LATP
Lima Bean Advisory Board [*Superseded by California Dry Bean Advisory Board*] (EA) .... LBAB
Lima Bean Agar [*Microbiology*] .... LBA
Lima Bean (trypsin) Inhibitor [*Biochemistry*] .... LBI
Lima Blas [*Malaysia*] [*ICAO location identifier*] (ICLI) .... WMAT
Lima, OH [*Location identifier FAA*] (FAAL) .... AOH
Lima, OH [*Location identifier FAA*] (FAAL) .... LYL
Lima, OH [*AM radio station call letters*] .... WCIT
Lima, OH [*FM radio station call letters*] .... WGLE
Lima, OH [*AM radio station call letters*] .... WIMA
Lima, OH [*FM radio station call letters*] .... WIMT
Lima, OH [*Television station call letters*] .... WLIO
Lima, OH [*FM radio station call letters*] (RBYB) .... WLJM-FM
Lima, OH [*FM radio station call letters*] .... WLSR
Lima, OH [*FM radio station call letters*] .... WTGN
Lima, OH [*Television station call letters*] .... WTLW
Lima, OH [*FM radio station call letters*] .... WYRX
Lima Public Library, Lima, NY [*Library symbol Library of Congress*] (LCLS) .... NL
Lima Public Library, Lima, OH [*OCLC symbol*] (OCLC) .... LIM
Lima Public Library, Lima, OH [*Library symbol Library of Congress*] (LCLS) .... OLima
Lima-Callao/Internacional Jorge Chavez [*Peru*] [*ICAO location identifier*] (ICLI) .... SPIM
Limas Bulgarian Airlines [*ICAO designator*] (FAAC) .... LBA
Limay [*Nicaragua*] [*Seismograph station code, US Geological Survey*] (SEIS) .... LIY
Limb Blood Flow (AAMN) .... LBF
Limb Girdle Muscular Dystrophy [*Medicine*] .... LGMD
Limb Infrared Monitor of the Stratosphere .... LIMS
Limb Load Monitor .... LLM
Limb Radiance Inversion Radiometer .... LRIR
Limb Sounder (SSD) .... LIMS
Limb Volume Measuring System .... LVMS
Limbang [*Malaysia*] [*Airport symbol*] (OAG) .... LMN
Limbang [*Malaysia*] [*ICAO location identifier*] (ICLI) .... WBGJ
Limber (MSA) .... LIM
Limberlost State Memorial, Geneva, IN [*Library symbol Library of Congress*] (LCLS) .... InGeL
Limbic System [*Brain anatomy*] .... LS
Limbless Soldiers' Association of New South Wales [*Australia*] .... LSANSW
Limbless Soldiers' Association of Queensland [*Australia*] .... LSAQ
Limbless Soldiers' Association of South Australia .... LSASA
Limbless Soldiers' Association of Victoria [*Australia*] .... LSAV
Limb-Motion Sensor [*System*] .... LIMS
Limb-Scanning Infrared Radiometer .... LSIR
Lime L
Lime Acres [*South Africa*] [*ICAO location identifier*] (ICLI) .... FALC
Lime and Cement Mortar (DAC) .... L & CM
Lime, Cement, and Flyash (PDAA) .... LCF
Lime Fly Ash [*Aggregate*] (DICI) .... LFA
Lime Juice, Scotch, Drambuie [*A cocktail*] (IIA) .... LSD
Lime Mortar (DAC) .... LM
Lime Springs Herald, Lime Springs, IA [*Library symbol Library of Congress*] (LCLS) .... IaLsH
Lime-Ammonium-Nitrate [*Fertilizer*] .... LAN
Lime-Magnesium Carbonate .... LMC
Limen or Threshold [*Psychology*] L
Limerent Object [*One who is the object of obsessional romantic love*] .... LO
Limerick [*County in Ireland*] (ROG) .... LIM
Limerick Generation Station [*Nuclear energy*] (NRCH) .... LGS
Limes [*Boundary*] [*Pharmacology*] (DAVI) L
Limes [*Limit*] [*Latin*] .... lim
Limes Reacting Dose of Diphtheria Toxin [*Medicine*] (DMAA) .... Lr

Limestone [*Petrology*] L
Limestone [*Petrology*] .... limest
Limestone [*Technical drawings*] .... LMS
Limestone (VRA) L
Limestone [*Petrology*] (AAG) .... lmst
Limestone (AAG) .... LS
Limestone College, Gaffney, SC [*Library symbol Library of Congress*] (LCLS) .... ScGaL
Limestone Community High School, Bartonville, IL [*Library symbol Library of Congress*] (LCLS) .... IBartL
Limestone High School, Bartonville, IL [*OCLC symbol*] (OCLC) .... IQY
Limestone Injection/Multistage Burner .... LIMB
Limestone/Loring Air Force Base [*Maine*] [*ICAO location identifier*] (ICLI) .... KLIZ
Limestone, ME [*Location identifier FAA*] (FAAL) .... LIZ
Limestone-Injection, Multi-Stage Burner (GNE) .... LIMB
Lime-Sulphur-Synthetic-Solution [*Hydrometallurgy*] .... LSSS
Limewood (VRA) .... lmwd
Liminal [*or Least*] Sensation [*Psychology*] .... LS
Limit L
Limit .... LIM
Limit (IAA) .... LM
Limit (AFM) .... LMT
Limit .... LMT
Limit (DEN) .... LT
Limit Address Register [*Computer science*] .... LAR
Limit Control Register [*Navy Navigation Satellite System*] (DNAB) .... LCR
Limit of Advance [*Army*] (DOMA) .... LOA
Limit of Basic Aircraft (MCD) .... LBA
Limit of Detection .... LOD
Limit of Error on Inventory Difference .... LEID
Limit of Flocculation .... LF
Limit of Impurities .... LOI
Limit of Liability (MCD) .... LOL
Limit of Proportionality [*Mechanics*] (IAA) .... LP
Limit of Quantitation [*Analytical chemistry*] .... LOQ
Limit of Stack Register .... LOSR
Limit of Visibility .... LOV
Limit on Tax Preferences .... LTP
Limit Order Switching (PDAA) .... LOS
Limit Register .... LR
Limit Signaling Comparator .... LSC
Limit Switch (NRCH) .... LIMSW
Limit Switch [*Electronics*] .... LS
Limit Switch [*Electronics*] .... LSW
Limit Switch Closed [*Electronics*] (IAA) .... LSCL
Limit Switch Forward [*Electronics*] (IAA) .... LSF
Limit Switch Open [*Electronics*] (IAA) .... LSOP
Limit Switch Reverse [*Electronics*] (IAA) .... LSR
Limit Switch Up [*Electronics*] (IAA) .... LSU
Limit to Topographic Development [*Of hillsides*] [*Geology*] .... LTD
Limit Value LV
Limitation [*Dialog*] [*Searchable field*] [*Information service or system*] (NITA) .... LM
Limitation of Action [*Legal term*] (DLA) .... LIM ACT
Limitation of Cost (AAGC) .... LOC
Limitation of Cost Clause (AAGC) .... LOCC
Limitation of Funds (AAGC) .... LOF
Limitation of Government Obligation (MCD) .... LOGO
Limitation of Motion [*Neurology*] (DAVI) .... LOM
Limitation of Movement .... LOM
Limitation of Supplies Order [*World War II*] .... LIMOSO
Limited (DLA) L
Limited .... LD
Limited (ROG) .... LIMD
Limited (AAMN) .... lmtd
Limited [*British corporation*] (EY) .... LTD
Limited (DD) .... Ltd
Limited .... LTD
Limited (NFD) .... Ltd
Limited (DAVI) .... ltd
Limited Access Authorization [*Military*] (GFGA) .... LAA
Limited Air Weather Reporting Certificate (IAA) .... LAWRC
Limited Amateur Operator's Certificate of Proficiency [*Radio*] .... LAOCP
Limited Amplifier Filter .... LAF
Limited Area .... LA
Limited Area Coverage [*Data*] .... LAC
Limited Area HIBU [*Hydrological Institute and Belgrade University*] (USDC) .... LAHM
Limited Area Mesoscale Prediction System (MCD) .... LAMPS
Limited Area Model [*Marine science*] (OSRA) .... LAM
Limited Area Networks (NITA) .... LmAN
Limited Assignment Status [*Military*] .... LAS
Limited Assortment Store (WDMC) .... LAS
Limited Attack Defense System .... LADS
Limited Aviation Weather Reporting Station [*FAA*] (TAG) .... LAWRS
Limited Aviation Weather Reporting Station (FAAC) .... LAWRS
Limited Axial Power Distribution (IEEE) .... LAPD
Limited Base [*Air Force*] (AFM) .... LB
Limited Benefits [*Unemployment insurance*] (OICC) .... LB
Limited Broadcasting License [*Australia*] .... LBL
Limited Calendar Life, Controlled Item .... LCL/CI
Limited Capability Buoy .... LCB
Limited Capability Configuration [*Army*] (DOMA) LCC
Limited Channel Logout LCL
Limited Configuration Atomic Orbital (MCD) .... LCAO
Limited Conventional War [*Description of Vietnam War*] [*DoD*] (VNW) .... LCW
Limited Coordinating (NG) LC

Limited Data Block (KSC) ... LDB
Limited Depository Account ... LDA
Limited Depot Maintenance Work Requirements ... LDMWR
Limited Disease [*Medicine*] ... LD
Limited Distance Data Service [*Telecommunications*] ... LDDS
Limited Distance Data Set [*Modem*] (NITA) ... LDDS
Limited Distance Line Adapter ... LDLA
Limited Distribution [*Military*] (AFIT) ... LIMDIS
Limited Duty (MCD) ... LIMDU
Limited Duty Officer [*Navy*] ... LDO
Limited Early Site [*Nuclear energy*] (NRCH) ... LES
Limited Early Site Review [*Nuclear energy*] (NRCH) ... LESR
Limited Edition (ADA) ... LE
Limited Edition [*Publishing*] ... LTD ED
Limited Editions Club ... LEC
Limited Employee Retirement Account (IEEE) ... LERA
Limited English Proficiency ... LEP
Limited English Speaking (OICC) ... LES
Limited Entry Decision Table ... LEDT
Limited Environmental Test (MCD) ... LET
Limited Fanout-Free (MHDB) ... LFF
Limited Fine Mesh ... LFM
Limited First-Strike Capability ... LFSC
Limited Flying Quality ... LFQ
Limited Frequency Band ... LFB
Limited Functional English Literacy ... LIFEL
Limited Hold ... LH
Limited Implementation Program [*FAA*] (TAG) ... LIP
[*The*] **Limited, Inc.** [*Associated Press*] (SAG) ... Limitd
[*The*] **Limited, Inc.** [*NYSE symbol*] (SPSG) ... LTD
Limited Information Estimation ... LIE
Limited Information Maximum Likelihood [*Econometrics*] ... LIML
Limited Initial Operating Production (MCD) ... LIOP
Limited Instrument Departure (MCD) ... LID
Limited Intelligent Agent [*Virtual reality technology*] (PS) ... LIA
Limited Joint Mobility [*Medicine*] (DMAA) ... LJM
Limited Liability [*Finance*] ... LL
Limited Liability Company ... LLC
Limited Life Component (MCD) ... LLC
Limited Life Item (MCD) ... LLI
Limited Locus Allowed [*Legal*] (ROG) ... LLA
Limited Mass Search [*Chromatography*] ... LMS
Limited National Agency Check (AFM) ... LNAC
Limited Night Recovery System (PDAA) ... LNRS
Limited Nuclear Option [*Military*] (MCD) ... LNO
Limited Official Use Only [*Military*] ... LOUO
Limited Operating Base (AFM) ... LOB
Limited Operating Life ... LOL
Limited Operational Capability (CET) ... LOC
Limited Operational Capability for Europe [*DoD*] ... LOCE
Limited Operational Readiness Inspection (MCD) ... LORI
Limited Operational Strategy ... LOS
Limited Operational Test ... LOT
Limited Operational-Life Items [*NASA*] (NASA) ... LOLI
Limited- or Non-English Speaking Handicapped Student ... LONESHS
Limited Order [*Business term*] ... LO
Limited Paperback Editions ... LPE
Limited Partner in Brokers Firm [*London Stock Exchange*] ... LB
Limited Partner in Dual Capacity Firm [*London Stock Exchange*] ... LD
Limited Partner in Jobbers Firm [*London Stock Exchange*] ... LJ
Limited Partnership ... LP
Limited Partnership Investment Review [*Information service or system*] (IID) ... LPIR
Limited Period Appointment [*Short-term employment*] [*British*] ... LPA
Limited Planning (MCD) ... LP
Limited Preliminary Flight Rating Test ... LPFRT
Limited Procurement ... LP
Limited Procurement Test ... LPT
Limited Procurement, Urgent (MCD) ... LPU
Limited Production (AABC) ... LP
Limited Production Option [*Automotive engineering*] ... LPO
Limited Production - Test (AABC) ... LP-T
Limited Production - Urgent (AABC) ... LP-U
Limited Proprietorship [*Business term*] ... LP
Limited Purpose Agency (OICC) ... LPA
Limited Quantity [*Refers to a test performed on a scanty specimen*] [*Biochemistry*] (DAVI) ... LTDQ
Limited Raman LASER ... LRL
Limited Range Intercept [*Telecommunications Navy*] (ANA) ... LRI
Limited Rate Production ... LRP
Limited Reaction Processing [*Semiconductor technology*] ... LRP
Limited Recoverable (IEEE) ... LR
Limited Register Machine ... LRM
Limited Remaining Radiation Service [*Unit*] [*Military*] ... LRRS
Limited Remote [*or Radio*] **Communication Outlet** ... LRCO
Limited Resources Specialty (AFM) ... LRS
Limited Rights to Delivered Data ... LRDD
Limited Saturation Device (PDAA) ... LSD
Limited Scientific and Technical Aerospace Reports [*NASA*] (MCD) ... LSTAR
Limited Serial Project Slip ... LSPS
Limited Service Storage Facility ... LSSF
Limited Signed Edition (ADA) ... LSE
Limited Space Charge Accumulation Mode [*Telecommunications*] (NITA) ... LSA mode
Limited Space-Charge Accumulation [*Electronics*] ... LSA
Limited Space-Charge Drift [*Electronics*] (IAA) ... LSD
Limited Speech Recognition (PDAA) ... LISPER
Limited Standard (IAA) ... LTDSTD
Limited Storage Site (AABC) ... LSS
Limited Style Run ... LSR
Limited Subgroup (NATG) ... LSG
Ltd. Systems [*Vancouver Stock Exchange symbol*] ... PLI
Limited Technical Evaluation (MCD) ... LTE
Limited Term Employee (OICC) ... LT
Limited Test Ban [*Nuclear testing*] ... LTB
Limited Test Ban Treaty [*Signed in 1963; prohibits testing of nuclear devices in certain environments*] ... LTBT
Limited Test Equipment ... LTE
Limited to Interrogations (MCD) ... LTI
Limited to Searches (MCD) ... LSR
Limited Treadmill Test [*Medicine*] (DMAA) ... LTT
Limited Underwater Breathing Apparatus (NG) ... LUBA
Limited User Test [*Military*] (RDA) ... LUT
Limited Visibility Study (MCD) ... LV
Limited War ... LW
Limited War Capabilities Study ... LWCS
Limited War Capability (AAG) ... LWR
Limited War - Counterinsurgency ... LW-COIN
Limited War Laboratory [*Military*] (IIA) ... LWL
Limited War Office [*Air Force*] (MCD) ... LWO
Limited War Plan ... LWP
Limited Warfare Intelligence Reduction Complex ... LWIRC
Limited Warning Operation ... LWO
Limited Work Authorizations [*Nuclear energy*] ... LWA
Limited-Amplitude, Controlled-Decay (PDAA) ... LACD
Limited-Area Fine-Mesh Model [*Marine science*] (OSRA) ... LFM
Limited-Area Fine-Mesh Model (USDC) ... LFM
Limited-Distance MODEM [*Computer science*] ... LDM
Limited-Overs Cricket Information Group [*British*] (DBA) ... LOCIG
Limited-Slip Differential [*Automotive engineering*] ... LSD
Limitee [*Limited*] [*French*] ... Ltee
Limiter [*Electronics*] (ECII) ... LIM
Limiter ... LIMR
Limiter [*Electronics*] ... LMTR
Limiting (MSA) ... LMTG
Limiting Actual Exposure Time (KSC) ... LAET
Limiting Admissible Concentration ... LAC
Limiting Conditions for Operation [*Nuclear energy*] (NRCH) ... LCO
Limiting Date ... LIMDAT
Limiting Dilution Analyses [*Analytical biochemistry*] ... LDA
Limiting Dilution Cloning [*Biochemistry*] ... LDC
Limiting Dome Height [*Automotive metal stamping*] ... LDH
Limiting Drawing Ratio (MCD) ... LDR
Limiting Equivalent Exposure Time (MUGU) ... LEET
Limiting Factor (MCD) ... LIMFAC
Limiting Fragmentation [*Physics*] (OA) ... LF
Limiting Interval Availability ... LIA
Limiting Interval Reliability ... LIR
Limiting Isorrheic Concentration [*Medicine*] ... LIC
Limiting Level ... LL
Limiting Lines of Approach [*Navy*] (NVT) ... LLA
Limiting Lines of Quiet Approach [*Navy*] (NVT) ... LLQA
Limiting Lines of Snorkel Approach [*Navy*] (NVT) ... LLSNA
Limiting Lines of Submerged Approach [*Navy*] (NVT) ... LLSUA
Limiting Lines of Surfaced Approach [*Navy*] (NVT) ... LLSA
Limiting Nose Dive [*Aerospace*] ... LND
Limiting Oxygen Concentration [*For ignition*] ... LOC
Limiting Oxygen Index ... LOI
Limiting Pressure Velocity (PDAA) ... LPV
Limiting Quality (IAA) ... LQ
Limiting Safety System Setting [*Nuclear energy*] (NRCH) ... LSSS
Limiting System Utilization Factor (MHDB) ... LUF
Limiting Viscosity Number ... LVN
Limitless ... LMTLSS
Limits and Fits [*System*] [*Precision of tolerance*] [*Automotive engineering*] ... LAF
Limits of Error ... LE
Limits of Error on Material Unaccounted For ... LEMUF
Limits to Acceptable Change [*Park tourism management*] ... LAC
Limits-to-Throughput Model [*Environmental science*] ... LTM
Limitswitch Down [*Electronics*] (IAA) ... LSD
Limnological Research Center [*University of Minnesota*] [*Research center*] (RCD) ... LRC
Limnology ... LIMNOL
Limnos [*Greece*] [*ICAO location identifier*] (ICLI) ... IGLM
Limoges [*France*] [*Airport symbol*] (OAG) ... LIG
Limoges/Bellegarde [*France ICAO location identifier*] (ICLI) ... LFBL
Limoges/Romanet [*France ICAO location identifier*] (ICLI) ... LFXF
Limon [*Costa Rica*] [*Airport symbol*] (OAG) ... LIO
Limon [*Ecuador*] [*ICAO location identifier*] (ICLI) ... SELN
Limon [*Honduras*] [*Airport symbol*] (AD) ... UBG
Limon, CO [*AM radio station call letters*] (RBYB) ... KLIM
Limon, CO [*Location identifier FAA*] (FAAL) ... LIC
Limon/Limon Internacional [*Costa Rica*] [*ICAO location identifier*] (ICLI) ... MRLM
Limon Memorial Public Library, Limon, CO [*Library symbol Library of Congress*] (LCLS) ... CoLim
Limoncocha [*Ecuador*] [*ICAO location identifier*] (ICLI) ... SELI
Limonene [*Organic chemistry*] ... LIM
Limonis [*Of Lemon*] [*Pharmacy*] (ROG) ... LIMON
Limousine (DSUE) ... LIMO
Limousine ... LIMO

Limousine Industry Manufacturers Organization (EA) .... LIMO
Limp [*Binding*] [*Publishing*] .... LP
Limp Cloth [*Bookbinding*] (DGA) LC
Limpet Assembly Modular [*Navy*] (CAAL) .... LAM
Limulus Amebocyte Lysate .... LAL
Limulus Amebocyte Lysate Method .... LALM
Limulus Lysate Assay (DMAA) .... LLA
Lin Television Corp. [*Associated Press*] (SAG) .... LinTelev
Lin Television Corp. [*NASDAQ symbol*] (SAG) .... LNTV
LINAC Stretcher Ring [*Design for an electron accelerator*] .... LSR
Lina-Congo [*ICAO designator*] (AD) .... GC
Linair-Hungarian Regional Airlines [*FAA designator*] (FAAC) .... LIN
Linamar Machine Ltd. [*Toronto Stock Exchange symbol*] .... LNR
Linaria Public Library, Alberta [*Library symbol National Library of Canada*] (NLC) .... ALI
Lincare Holdings [*NASDAQ symbol*] (TTSB) .... LNCR
Lincare Holdings, Inc. [*Associated Press*] (SAG) .... Lincare
Lincare Holdings, Inc. [*NASDAQ symbol*] (SAG) .... LNCR
Lincln Natl $3.00 Cv Pfd [*NYSE symbol*] (TTSB) .... LNCPr
Lincln Natl Cv Sec [*NYSE symbol*] (TTSB) .... LNV
Lincoln [*Nebraska*] [*Seismograph station code, US Geological Survey Closed*] (SEIS) .... LIN
Lincoln [*Diocesan abbreviation*] [*Nebraska*] (TOCD) .... LIN
Lincoln [*Nebraska*] [*Airport symbol*] (OAG) .... LNK
Lincoln Air Force Base (AAG) .... LAFB
Lincoln Airlines, Inc. [*ICAO designator*] (FAAC) .... LUX
Lincoln Boyhood National Memorial .... LIBO
Lincoln Boyhood National Memorial, Lincoln City, IN [*Library symbol Library of Congress*] (LCLS) .... InLcLM
Lincoln Calibration Sphere .... LCS
Lincoln Capital Corp. [*Toronto Stock Exchange symbol*] LCC
Lincoln Cent Collectors Society (EA) .... SLCC
Lincoln Center for the Performing Arts (EA) .... LCPA
Lincoln Christian College, Lincoln, IL [*Library symbol Library of Congress*] (LCLS) .... ILinL
Lincoln Christian College, Lincoln, IL [*OCLC symbol*] (OCLC) .... JAN
Lincoln City Libraries, Lincoln, NE [*Library symbol Library of Congress*] (LCLS) .... NbL
Lincoln City Libraries, Lincoln, NE [*Library symbol*] [*Library of Congress*] (LCLS) .... NbLL
Lincoln City, OR [*AM radio station call letters*] .... KBCH
Lincoln City, OR [*FM radio station call letters*] .... KSND
Lincoln Continental Owners Club (EA) .... LCOC
Lincoln Cosmopolitan Owners Registry [*Defunct*] (EA) .... LCOR
Lincoln County Free Library, Libby, MT [*Library symbol*] [*Library of Congress*] (LCLS) .... MtLib
Lincoln County Library, Afton Branch, Afton, WY [*Library symbol Library of Congress*] (LCLS) .... WyA
Lincoln County Library, Kemmerer, WY [*Library symbol Library of Congress*] (LCLS) .... WyKe
Lincoln County Memorial Library, Lincolnton, NC [*Library symbol Library of Congress*] (LCLS) .... NcLiL
Lincoln County Senior High School, Eureka, MT [*Library symbol*] [*Library of Congress*] (LCLS) .... MtELH
Lincoln Educational Foundation [*Defunct*] (EA) .... LEF
Lincoln Electric [*NASDAQ symbol*] (TTSB) .... LECO
Lincoln Electric 'A' [*NASDAQ symbol*] (TTSB) .... LECOA
[*The*] **Lincoln Electric Co.** [*NASDAQ symbol*] (SAG) .... LECO
[*The*] **Lincoln Electric Co.** [*Associated Press*] (SAG) .... LincEl
Lincoln Electric Co. (The) [*Associated Press*] (SAG) .... LincElA
Lincoln Elementary School, Alexandria, MN [*Library symbol*] [*Library of Congress*] (LCLS) .... MnAleLE
Lincoln Elementary School, Bemidji, MN [*Library symbol*] [*Library of Congress*] (LCLS) .... MnBemLE
Lincoln Elementary School, Brainerd, MN [*Library symbol*] [*Library of Congress*] (LCLS) .... MnBrLE
Lincoln Elementary School, Crookston, MN [*Library symbol*] [*Library of Congress*] (LCLS) .... MnCrLE
Lincoln Elementary School, Detroit Lakes, MN [*Library symbol*] [*Library of Congress*] (LCLS) .... MnDlLe
Lincoln Elementary School, Duluth, MN [*Library symbol*] [*Library of Congress*] (LCLS) .... MnDuLE
Lincoln Elementary School, Glencoe, MN [*Library symbol*] [*Library of Congress*] (LCLS) .... MnGLES
Lincoln Elementary School, Little Falls, MN [*Library symbol*] [*Library of Congress*] (LCLS) .... MnLfLE
Lincoln Elementary School, St. Cloud, MN [*Library symbol*] [*Library of Congress*] (LCLS) .... MnStclL
Lincoln Elementary School, Willmar, MN [*Library symbol*] [*Library of Congress*] (LCLS) .... MnWilLiS
Lincoln Elementary School, Wright, MN [*Library symbol*] [*Library of Congress*] (LCLS) .... MnWriLE
Lincoln Elementary-High School, Ivanhoe, MN [*Library symbol*] [*Library of Congress*] (LCLS) .... MnIvEHS
Lincoln Experimental Satellite [*Lincoln Laboratory, MIT*] .... LES
Lincoln Experimental Satellite Operations Center (MCD) .... LESOC
Lincoln Experimental Terminal [*NASA*] .... LET
Lincoln First Bank of Rochester Library Service, Rochester, NY [*OCLC symbol*] (OCLC) .... RXQ
Lincoln First Bank of Rochester, Rochester, NY [*Library symbol Library of Congress*] (LCLS) .... NRLF
Lincoln Health Sciences Library Group [*Library network*] .... LHSLG
Lincoln Herald, Lincoln Park, NJ [*Library symbol Library of Congress*] (LCLS) .... NjLpH
Lincoln Heritage Trail Foundation (EA) .... LHTF
Lincoln High School, Thief River Falls, MN [*Library symbol*] [*Library of Congress*] (LCLS) .... MnTLH
Lincoln Highway Association [*Motoring history organization*] .... LHA
Lincoln Hospital, Bronx, NY [*OCLC symbol*] (OCLC) .... ZLH
Lincoln, IL [*Location identifier FAA*] (FAAL) .... AAA
Lincoln, IL [*FM radio station call letters*] .... WLNX
Lincoln, IL [*AM radio station call letters*] .... WPRC
Lincoln, IL [*AM radio station call letters*] (RBYB) .... WVAX-AM
Lincoln, IL [*FM radio station call letters*] .... WWTE
Lincoln, IL [*FM radio station call letters*] (RBYB) .... WYXY-FM
Lincoln Information Storage and Associative Retrieval System [*Lincoln Laboratory*] [*Massachusetts Institute of Technology*] (NITA) .... LISTAR
Lincoln Information Storage and Retrieval [*MIT*] .... LISTAR
Lincoln Institute for Research and Education (EA) .... LIRE
Lincoln Junior High School, LaSalle, IL [*Library symbol Library of Congress*] (LCLS) .... ILasL
Lincoln Laboratory [*MIT*] (MCD) LL
Lincoln Laboratory Boolean Algebra Minimizer (IAA) .... LLBAM
Lincoln Land Community College, Springfield, IL [*Library symbol Library of Congress*] (LCLS) .... ISLC
Lincoln Library of Essential Information LL
Lincoln Library, Springfield, IL [*OCLC symbol*] (OCLC) .... ILM
Lincoln Library, Springfield, IL [*Library symbol Library of Congress*] (LCLS) .... ISL
Lincoln, ME [*Location identifier FAA*] (FAAL) .... LRG
Lincoln, ME [*FM radio station call letters*] .... WHMX
Lincoln, ME [*AM radio station call letters*] .... WTOX
Lincoln Memorial University [*Tennessee*] .... LMU
Lincoln Memorial University, Harrogate, TN [*Library symbol Library of Congress*] (LCLS) .... THaroL
Lincoln Mercury [*Division of Ford Motor Co.*] .... LM
Lincoln Middle School, Rockford, IL [*Library symbol*] [*Library of Congress*] (LCLS) .... IRoLM
Lincoln Model Elementary School, Staples, MN [*Library symbol*] [*Library of Congress*] (LCLS) .... MnStLE
Lincoln/Municipal [*Nebraska*] [*ICAO location identifier*] (ICLI) .... KLNK
Lincoln National Convertible Securities Fund, Inc. [*Associated Press*] (SAG) .... LncNtC
Lincoln National Convertible Securities Fund, Inc. [*NYSE symbol*] (SPSG) .... LNV
Lincoln National Corp. [*Associated Press*] (SAG) .... LincN
Lincoln National Corp. [*Associated Press*] (SAG) .... LincNatl
Lincoln National Corp. [*NYSE symbol*] (SPSG) .... LNC
Lincoln National Corp. Capital I [*Associated Press*] (SAG) .... LincN
Lincoln National Corp. Capital I [*NYSE symbol*] (SAG) .... LNC
Lincoln National Corp. Capital II [*Associated Press*] (SAG) .... LincN
Lincoln National Corp. Capital II [*NYSE symbol*] (SAG) .... LNC
Lincoln National Income Fund, Inc. [*Associated Press*] (SAG) .... LincNIF
Lincoln National Income Fund, Inc. [*Formerly, Lincoln National Direct Placement Fund, Inc.*] [*NYSE symbol*] (SPSG) .... LND
Lincoln National Life Foundation, Fort Wayne, IN [*Library symbol Library of Congress*] (LCLS) .... InFwL
Lincoln Natl Corp. [*NYSE symbol*] (TTSB) .... LNC
Lincoln Natl Income Fd [*NYSE symbol*] (TTSB) .... LND
Lincoln, NE [*FM radio station call letters*] .... KEZG
Lincoln, NE [*FM radio station call letters*] .... KFBN
Lincoln, NE [*FM radio station call letters*] .... KFGE
Lincoln, NE [*AM radio station call letters*] .... KFOR
Lincoln, NE [*FM radio station call letters*] .... KFRX
Lincoln, NE [*FM radio station call letters*] (RBYB) .... KGDE
Lincoln, NE [*AM radio station call letters*] .... KHAT
Lincoln, NE [*FM radio station call letters*] .... KIBZ
Lincoln, NE [*FM radio station call letters*] (RBYB) .... KKUL-FM
Lincoln, NE [*FM radio station call letters*] (RBYB) .... KLCV-FM
Lincoln, NE [*FM radio station call letters*] .... KLDZ
Lincoln, NE [*AM radio station call letters*] .... KLIN
Lincoln, NE [*TV station call letters*] (RBYB) .... KLKN-TV
Lincoln, NE [*AM radio station call letters*] .... KMEM
Lincoln, NE [*FM radio station call letters*] (RBYB) .... KNET-FM
Lincoln, NE [*Television station call letters*] .... KOLN
Lincoln, NE [*FM radio station call letters*] .... KRNU
Lincoln, NE [*FM radio station call letters*] .... KUCV
Lincoln, NE [*Television station call letters*] .... KUON
Lincoln, NE [*FM radio station call letters*] .... KZUM
Lincoln, NE [*Location identifier FAA*] (FAAL) .... OCZ
Lincoln, Nebraska Air National Guard [*FAA designator*] (FAAC) .... GDQ
Lincoln Orchard Mesa Elementary School, Grand Junction, CO [*Library symbol Library of Congress*] (LCLS) .... CoGjLOE
Lincoln Orens School, Island Park, NY [*Library symbol*] [*Library of Congress*] (LCLS) .... NIpL
Lincoln Owners Club (EA) .... LOC
Lincoln Parish Library, Ruston, LA [*Library symbol Library of Congress*] (LCLS) .... LRuLP
Lincoln Park Elementary School, Grand Junction, CO [*Library symbol Library of Congress*] (LCLS) .... CoGjLPE
Lincoln Park Public Library, Lincoln Park, NJ [*Library symbol Library of Congress*] (LCLS) .... NjLp
Lincoln Public Library, Fleming Branch, Beamsville, ON, Canada [*Library symbol*] [*Library of Congress*] (LCLS) .... CaOBeLF
Lincoln Public Library, Lincoln, CA [*Library symbol Library of Congress*] (LCLS) CLi
Lincoln Public Library, Lincoln, CA [*Library symbol*] [*Library of Congress*] (LCLS) .... CLiP
Lincoln Red [*Livestock terminology*] .... LR
Lincoln Red Cattle Society [*British*] (DBA) .... LRCS
Lincoln Red Cattle Society of Australia .... LRCSA

Lincoln Research Laboratory .... LRL
Lincoln Resign Formulation .... LRF
Lincoln Resources, Inc. [*Vancouver Stock Exchange symbol*] .... LNN
Lincoln Savings Bank [*Associated Press*] (SAG) .... LincSB
Lincoln School [*California*] [*Seismograph station code, US Geological Survey*] (SEIS) .... LOC
Lincoln School, Floodwood, MN [*Library symbol*] [*Library of Congress*] (LCLS) .... MnFILS
Lincoln Sesquicentennial Committee [*Terminated, 1960*] [*Government agency*] .... LSC
Lincoln Snacks [*NASDAQ symbol*] (TTSB) .... SNAX
Lincoln Snacks Co. [*Associated Press*] (SAG) .... LincSnk
Lincoln Snacks Co. [*NASDAQ symbol*] (SAG) .... SNAX
Lincoln Society of Philately [*Defunct*] (EA) .... LSP
Lincoln Telecmmun [*NASDAQ symbol*] (TTSB) .... LTEC
Lincoln Telecommunications Co. [*Associated Press*] (SAG) .... LincTel
Lincoln Township Public Library, Stevensville, MI [*Library symbol Library of Congress*] (LCLS) .... MiSte
Lincoln Trail Libraries, Champaign, IL [*Library symbol Library of Congress*] (LCLS) .... IChamL
Lincoln Trail Libraries System [*Library network*] .... LTLS
Lincoln Trail Libraries System, Champaign, IL [*OCLC symbol*] (OCLC) .... IHI
Lincoln Tube Process Specification (SAA) .... LTPS
Lincoln University (GAGS) .... Lincoln U
Lincoln University, Jefferson City, MO [*Library symbol Library of Congress*] (LCLS) .... MoJcL
Lincoln University, Lincoln University, PA [*OCLC symbol*] (OCLC) .... LZU
Lincoln University, Lincoln University, PA [*Library symbol Library of Congress*] (LCLS) .... PLuL
Lincoln University, PA [*FM radio station call letters*] .... WLIU
Lincoln Zephyr Owner's Club (EA) .... LZOC
Lincoln-Lawrence-Franklin Regional Library, Brookhaven, MS [*Library symbol Library of Congress*] (LCLS) .... MsBr
Lincoln's Inn [*London*] [*One of the Inns of Court*] LI
Lincoln's Inn Library [*A publication*] (DLA) LIL
Lincolnshire [*County in England*] .... LINC
Lincolnshire [*County in England*] .... LINCS
Lincolnshire Vintage Vehicle Club [*British*] (DCTA) LVVC
Lincolnton, NC [*AM radio station call letters*] .... WLON
Lincolnwood Community Reading Center, Raymond, IL [*Library symbol Library of Congress*] (LCLS) .... IRayL
Lincolnwood Public Library District, Lincolnwood, IL [*OCLC symbol*] (OCLC) .... ILE
Lincolnwood Public Library, Lincolnwood, IL [*Library symbol Library of Congress*] (LCLS) .... ILinw
Lincomycin Cosynthetic Factor [*Biochemistry*] .... LCF
Lincroft, NJ [*FM radio station call letters*] .... WBJB
Linctus [*Tincture*] [*Pharmacy*] (ROG) .... LINCT
Linda Gray's Official Fan Club (EA) .... LGOFC
Linda Hall Library, Kansas City, MO [*Library symbol Library of Congress*] (LCLS) .... MoKL
Lindal Cedar Homes [*NASDAQ symbol*] (SAG) .... LNDL
Lindal Cedar Homes, Inc. [*Associated Press*] (SAG) .... LindlH
Lindamood Auditory Conceptualization Test .... LAC
Lindamood Auditory Conceptualization Test [*Psychology*] (DAVI) .... LAC
Lindas Diversified Holdings [*NASDAQ symbol*] (SAG) .... LINC
Lindas Diversified Holdings [*Associated Press*] (SAG) .... LindasDiv
Linda's Flame Roasted Chicken [*NASDAQ symbol*] (TTSB) .... LINCA
Lindas Flame Roasted Chicken, Inc. [*Associated Press*] (SAG) .... Linda
Lindas Flame Roasted Chicken, Inc. [*Associated Press*] (SAG) .... LindasCh
Linda's Flame Rstd Ckn Wrrt'A' [*NASDAQ symbol*] (TTSB) .... LINCW
Linda's Flame Rstd Ckn Wrrt'B' [*NASDAQ symbol*] (TTSB) .... LINCZ
Lindasw Diversified Holdings [*Associated Press*] (SAG) .... Linda
Lindberg Corp. [*NASDAQ symbol*] (SAG) .... LIND
Lindberg Corp. [*Associated Press*] (SAG) .... Lindbrg
Lindblad Resonance [*Planetary science*] .... LR
Lindell Boulevard School, Long Beach, NY [*Library symbol Library of Congress*] (LCLS) .... NLobLS
Lindeman Island [*Australia Airport symbol*] .... LDC
Linden [*Record label*] .... Lin
Linden [*Guyana*] [*ICAO location identifier*] (ICLI) .... SYLD
Linden, AL [*FM radio station call letters*] .... WINL
Linden, AL [*FM radio station call letters*] .... WNPT
Linden, CA [*Location identifier FAA*] (FAAL) .... LIN
Linden Free Public Library, Linden, NJ [*Library symbol Library of Congress*] (LCLS) .... NjLin
Linden Municipal Library, Alberta [*Library symbol National Library of Canada*] (NLC) .... ALM
Linden Municipal Library, Linden, AB, Canada [*Library symbol Library of Congress*] (LCLS) .... CaALiM
Linden, NJ [*Location identifier FAA*] (FAAL) .... LDJ
Linden, NJ [*Television station call letters*] .... WNJU
Linden Public Library, Linden, IN [*Library symbol Library of Congress*] (LCLS) .... InLind
Linden, VA [*Location identifier FAA*] (FAAL) .... LDN
Lindenhurst High School, Lindenhurst, NY [*Library symbol*] [*Library of Congress*] (LCLS) .... NLinHS
Lindenhurst Junior High School, Lindenhurst, NY [*Library symbol*] [*Library of Congress*] (LCLS) .... NLinJS
Lindenhurst Memorial Library, Lindenhurst, NY [*Library symbol Library of Congress*] (LCLS) .... NLin
Lindenwood (VRA) .... lindwd
Lindenwood College, St. Charles, MO [*OCLC symbol*] (OCLC) .... MOQ
Lindenwood College, St. Charles, MO [*Library symbol Library of Congress*] (LCLS) .... MoStcL
Lindewoode's Provinciales [*A publication*] (DLA) .... Lind Pr
Lindheimer Astronomical Research Center [*Northwestern University*] .... LARC
Lindi [*Tanzania*] [*ICAO location identifier*] (ICLI) .... HTLI
Lindi [*Tanzania*] [*Airport symbol*] (OAG) .... LDI
Lindley on Partnership [*A publication*] (DLA) .... Lind Part
Lindley on Partnership [*A publication*] (DLA) .... Lindl Copartn
Lindley on Partnership [*A publication*] (DLA) .... Lindl Partn
Lindley on Partnership [*A publication*] (DLA) .... Lindley P
Lindley on Partnership [*A publication*] (DLA) .... Lindley Part
Lindley's Law of Companies [*A publication*] (DLA) .... Lindley
Lindley's Law of Companies [*A publication*] (DLA) .... Lindley Comp
Lindley's Study of Jurisprudence [*A publication*] (DLA) .... Lind Jur
Lindner Elementary School, Malverne, NY [*Library symbol Library of Congress*] (LCLS) .... NMalvLE
Lindquist Investment Co., Inc. [*ICAO designator*] (FAAC) .... SWS
Lindsay Aviation, Inc. [*ICAO designator*] (FAAC) .... LSY
Lindsay, CA [*FM radio station call letters*] .... KZPO
Lindsay Manufacturing [*NASDAQ symbol*] (SAG) .... LINZ
Lindsay Manufacturing Co. [*Associated Press*] (SAG) .... Lindsy
Lindsay Mfg [*NASDAQ symbol*] (TTSB) .... LINZ
Lindsay, OK [*FM radio station call letters*] .... KBLP
Lindsay, ON [*AM radio station call letters*] .... CKLY
Lindsay on Probates [*A publication*] (DLA) .... Lind Prob
Lindsay Public Library, Lindsay, ON, Canada [*Library symbol Library of Congress*] (LCLS) .... CaOLi
Lindsay Public Library, Ontario [*Library symbol National Library of Canada*] (NLC) .... OLI
Lindsay Wagner's Official Fan Club (EA) .... LWOFC
Lindsborg, KS [*FM radio station call letters*] .... KQNS
Lindsey Wilson College [*Columbia, KY*] .... LWC
Lindsey Wilson College, Columbia, KY [*Library symbol Library of Congress*] (LCLS) .... KyColW
Lindside, WV [*FM radio station call letters*] .... WHFI
Lindstrom Public Library, Lindstrom, MN [*Library symbol*] [*Library of Congress*] (LCLS) .... MnLi
Lindtorp [*Denmark ICAO location identifier*] (ICLI) .... EKHO
Line L
Line (WDMC) l
Line (WDAA) .... LIN
Line (AAG) .... LN
Line (VRA) .... ln
Line Access Point [*Telecommunications*] (TEL) .... LAP
Line Access Unit (NITA) .... LAU
Line Adapter [*Computer science*] (CMD) .... LA
Line Adapter Unit [*Computer science*] .... LAU
Line Adaptor (NITA) .... LA
Line Addressable Random Access Memory [*Computer science*] (MDG) .... LARAM
Line Amplifier and Super Sync Mixer .... LASS
Line Amplifier and Super Sync Mixer (MSA) .... LASSM
Line and Half Line [*Illustration*] (DGA) .... LHL
Line and Halftone [*Illustration*] (DGA) .... LHT
Line and Halftone Combined [*Illustration*] (DGA) .... L & HTC
Line and Terminal [*Telecommunications*] (TEL) .... L & T
Line Apparatus Shop [*Telecommunications*] (OA) .... LAS
Line Assembly (AAG) L
Line Automatic Reperforator (CET) .... LARP
Line Balance Converter .... LBC
Line Balancing Network [*Telecommunications*] (TEL) .... LBN
Line Binder Post (IAA) .... LBP
Line Buffer [*Computer science*] .... LB
Line Buffer System [*Computer science*] .... LBS
Line Building Out .... LBO
Line Busy .... LB
Line Circuit [*Telecommunications*] LC
Line Clearance Airdrome [*Air Force*] .... LCA
Line Coding Storage .... LCS
Line Collector LC
Line Concentrator LC
Line Concentrator Module .... LCM
Line Connection LC
Line Connector (NITA) LC
Line Construction Tools [*JETDS nomenclature*] [*Military*] (CET) LC
Line Contractor (MCD) LC
Line Control LC
Line Control Adapter .... LCA
Line Control Block [*Computer science*] .... LCB
Line Control Module [*Telecommunications*] (TEL) .... LCM
Line Control Unit [*Data communications*] .... LCU
Line Control Word .... LCW
Line Coupling Unit (NASA) .... LCU
Line Crosser [*Deserter*] [*Military*] LC
Line Current Disconnect (HGAA) .... LCD
Line Directional Coupler .... LDC
Line Dolly (MCD) .... LD
Line Drawing (MSA) .... LD
Line Drawing Analyzer [*Cybernetics*] .... LINDA
Line Driver .... LD
Line Driver/Terminal Equipment (MCD) .... LD/TE
Line Driver Unit [*Computer communication*] (MCD) .... LDU
Line Driver-Receiver [*Computer communication*] (TEL) .... LDR
Line Driving Amplifier .... LDA
Line Echo Wave Pattern .... LEWP
Line Editor [*Computer science*] (MHDI) .... LINED
Line Embossing Device [*Computer science*] .... LED
Line Equalizing Amplifier (AFM) .... LEA

Line Equipment [*Telecommunications*] (TEL) .... LE
Line Equipment Assignment and Display System [*GTE Corp.*] .... LEADS
Line Equipped [*Telecommunications*] (TEL) .... LEQ
Line Error Recording Block (MCD) .... LERB
Line Exchange [*Telecommunications*] .... LEX
Line Expansion Function .... LEF
Line Fault Detector [*Telecommunications*] (TEL) .... LFD
Line Feed [*Control character*] [*Computer science*] .... LF
Line Feed [*Computer science*] (DOM) .... LF
Line Finder [*Teletype*] .... LF
Line for Line [*Typesetting*] (WDMC) .... L/L
Line Frequency Rejection (IAA) .... LFR
Line Gate Number [*Computer science*] .... LGN
Line Generator [*Computer science*] .... LG
Line Graph (OA) .... LG
Line Group Controller (ACRL) .... LGC
Line Impedance Stabilization Network .... LISA
Line Impedance Stabilization Network .... LISN
Line Information Database [*Telecommunications*] (ACRL) .... LIDB
Line Information Storage and Retrieval [*Information service or system*] (NITA) .... LISR
Line Information Store [*Telecommunications*] (TEL) .... LIS
Line Insulation Monitor (PDAA) .... LIM
Line Insulation Test [*Telecommunications*] .... LIT
Line Integral Refractometer .... LIR
Line Interface Base [*Telecommunications*] .... LIB
Line Interface Handler .... LIH
Line Interface Module .... LIM
Line Interface Unit [*Data communications*] .... LIU
Line Intermediate Distributing Frame .... LIDF
Line Islands Experiment [*National Science Foundation*] .... LIE
Line Islands Experiment [*Marine science*] (OSRA) .... LIE
Line Isolation Device [*Telecommunications*] (NITA) .... LID
Line Isolation Switch [*Reactor level switch*] (IEEE) .... LIS
Line Isolation Unit [*Electronics*] .... LIU
Line Item (AABC) LI
Line Item Description (MCD) .... LID
Line Item Number (AABC) .... LIN
Line Item Value LIV
Line Judge [*Football*] .... LJ
Line Leg [*Telegraph*] [*Telecommunications*] (TEL) LL
Line Length Ciceros [*Typography*] (DGA) LC
Line Length Remainder [*Graphic arts*] (DGA) .... LLR
Line Link (IAA) LL
Line Link Frame [*Telecommunications*] (TEL) .... LLF
Line Link Network [*Bell System*] .... LLN
Line Link Pulsing [*Telecommunications*] .... LLP
Line Map Editing Console .... LMEC
Line Mark (IAA) .... LM
Line Monitor/Recorder (MCD) .... LMR
Line Monitor Unit .... LMU
Line Occupancy .... LO
Line of Arrested Growth [*Biology*] .... LAG
Line of Assurance .... LOA
Line of Balance .... LOB
Line of Bearing [*Navy*] (NVT) .... LOB
Line of Bearing Sensor .... LSNSR
Line of Bomb Release (NATG) .... LBR
Line of Business [*Used in corporate reports to Federal Trade Commission*] .... LOB
Line of Code .... LOC
Line of Communication [*Military*] LC
Line of Communication [*Military*] .... LOC
Line of Communication Combat Zone [*Military*] .... LOCCOZO
Line of Contact [*Military*] LC
Line of Contact (MCD) .... LOC
Line of Correction .... LOC
Line of Credit [*Business term*] .... L/C
Line of Dance .... LOD
Line of Departure [*Military*] .... LD
Line of Departure [*Military*] (AFM) .... LOD
Line of Departure Is Friendly Forward Disposition [*Army*] (AABC) .... LD Is FFD
Line of Departure Is Present Positions [*Military*] (AABC) .... LD Is PPOS
Line of Departure/Line of Contact [*Army*] (ADDR) .... LD/LC
Line of Direction .... LOD
Line of Duty [*Military*] .... LD
Line of Duty [*Military*] .... LOD
Line of Effort (MCD) .... LOE
Line of Equipment [*Telecommunications*] (TEL) .... LEQ
Line of Fire .... LOF
Line of Force .... LOF
Line of Induction .... LOI
Line of Launch [*Navy*] (CAAL) .... LOL
Line of Least Resistance .... LLR
Line of Nodes .... LON
Line of Position [*Electronics*] .... LOP
Line of Power (WDAA) .... LOP
Line (of Print) [*Publishing*] (NTCM) L
Line of Scrimmage [*Football*] .... LOS
Line of Sight .... LOS
Line of Sight-Forward Light [*DoD*] .... LOS-FL
Line of Supply .... LOS
Line Office [*Marine science*] (OSRA) .... LO
Line Office (USDC) .... LO
Line Oriented Evaluation (GAVI) .... LOE
Line Oriented Flight Training (MCD) .... LOFT

Line Out of Service [*Telecommunications*] (TEL) .... LOS
Line Output Transformer (IAA) .... LOPT
Line Output Unit [*Printing*] (DGA) .... LOU
Line Overhead (ACRL) .... LOH
Line Pair [*Philately*] .... lp
Line Pressure .... LP
Line Printer [*Computer science*] .... LP
Line Printer [*Computer science*] (NASA) .... LPR
Line Printer [*Computer science*] .... LPT
Line Printer [*Computer science*] (DOM) .... LPT
Line Printer [*Computer science*] (MSA) .... LPTR
Line Printer Daemon (PCM) .... LPD
Line Printer Remote (PCM) .... LPR
Line Procedure Specifications (CMD) .... LPS
Line Processing Unit .... LPU
Line Program Selector (IAA) .... LPS
Line Protection Switching System [*Bell System*] .... LPSS
Line Receiver .... LR
Line Receiver/Line Driver (MCD) .... LR/LD
Line Receiving Amplifier (MSA) .... LRA
Line Rectifier Circuit .... LRC
Line Relay .... LR
Line Removable Unit .... LRU
Line Replaceable Unit (AFM) .... LRU
Line Replaceable Unit Power Supply (MCD) .... LRUPS
Line Replacement Module .... LRM
Line Scan (DEN) .... LS
Line Scan Image Generator (OA) .... LSIG
Line Scan Tube .... LST
Line Scanner System .... LSS
Line Segment Block [*Computer science*] .... LSB
Line Select Module (NITA) .... LSM
Line Selection Module [*Telecommunications*] (TEL) .... LSM
Line Selection Unit [*Telecommunications*] (IAA) .... LSU
Line Sensing Amplifier (IAA) .... LSA
Line Sharing Adaptor (NITA) .... LSA
Line Signal Detector .... LSD
Line Source Range (IAA) .... LSR
Line Spectrum Pair (IAA) .... LSP
Line Speed .... LS
Line Spread Function (MCD) .... LSF
Line Squall [*Meteorology*] (WDAA) .... KQ
Line Squall [*ICAO*] (FAAC) .... LSQ
Line Stabilization Network .... LSN
Line Stabilized Oscillator .... LSO
Line Station Assembly Order (MCD) .... LSAO
Line Status Verifier [*Telecommunications*] (TEL) .... LSV
Line Stretcher .... LS
Line Switch [*Telecommunications*] (TEL) .... LS
Line Switch [*Telecommunications*] (IAA) .... LSW
Line Switch Frame [*Telecommunications*] (TEL) .... LSF
Line Synchronizing Pulse .... LSP
Line Telecommunications .... L/T
Line Telegraphy .... LT
Line Term Buffer [*Computer science*] (AABC) .... LTB
Line Terminal Control (IAA) .... LTC
Line Terminating Equipment (ACRL) .... LTE
Line Terminating Unit (CET) .... LTU
Line Termination Equipment [*Telecommunications*] (TEL) .... LTE
Line Termination Unit (NITA) .... LTU
Line Terminator .... LT
Line Time Clock .... LTC
Line Traffic Coordinator (CET) .... LTC
Line Transfer Device .... LTD
Line Transient Suppression .... LTS
Line Transition Monitoring (NITA) .... LTM
Line/Trunk (MCD) .... LUNK
Line Trunk Group [*Telecommunications*] .... LTG
Line Trunk Group [*Telecommunications*] (ACRL) .... LTG
Line Trunk Scanner Register [*Computer science*] (IAA) .... LTSR
Line Type Modulation [*Radio*] .... LTM
Line Type Processor [*Radio*] (IAA) .... LTP
Line Unit (IAA) .... LU
Line Unit [*Computer science*] (BUR) .... LUT
Line Utilization Cable Assignment System (MCD) .... LUCAS
Line Voltage Monitor .... LVM
Line Voltage Regulator .... LVR
Line Width, Black-to-White-Ratio, Area, Fixation Point .... LBAF
Linea Aerea Aerosanta [*Chile*] [*ICAO designator*] (FAAC) .... SON
Linea Aerea del Cobre Ltda. [*Chile*] [*ICAO designator*] (FAAC) .... LCO
Linea Aerea del Cobre SA [*Chile*] (EY) .... LADECO
Linea Aerea Nacional [*National Airline*] [*Chile*] .... LAN
Linea Aerea Nacional de Chile [*Chilean airline*] [*ICAO designator*] (OAG) .... LA
Linea Aerea Nacional de Chile [*ICAO designator*] (FAAC) .... LAN
Linea Aerea Nacional (Lansa) [*Dominican Republic*] [*ICAO designator*] (FAAC) .... LSA
Linea Aerea Peruana [*Peruvian State Airlines*] .... AEROPERU
Linea Aerea Privadas Argentina [*ICAO designator*] (FAAC) .... LPR
Linea Aerea TACA de Venezuela .... TACAV
Linea Aerea Tama [*Chile*] [*ICAO designator*] (FAAC) .... LTA
Linea Aerea Taxpa Ltda. [*Chile*] [*ICAO designator*] (FAAC) .... TXP
Linea Aeropostal Venezolana [*Venezuela*] [*ICAO designator*] (FAAC) .... LAV
Linea Federal Argentina SEM [*ICAO designator*] (FAAC) .... FED
Lineal (MSA) .... LIN
Lineal Feet .... LF

Linear (KSC) ... LIN
Linear Absorption Coefficient ... LAC
Linear [*Electron*] **Accelerator** ... LINAC
Linear Accelerator Regenerator Reactor (BARN) ... LARR
Linear Accelerator Tube ... LAT
Linear Accelerator-Driven Reactor (BARN) ... LADR
Linear Accelerometer Unit (PDAA) ... LAU
Linear Acoustic Vernier Analyzer (CAAL) ... LAVA
Linear Aeronautical Chart (BARN) ... LAC
Linear Alcohol Ethoxylate [*Surfactant*] ... LAE
Linear Alkylbenzene [*Organic chemistry*] ... LAB
Linear Alkylbenzene Sulfonate [*Surfactant*] ... LAS
Linear Amplifier for Various Applications (IEEE) ... LAVA
Linear Amplitude-Continuous (PDAA) ... LAC
Linear Analysis and Design of Structure (IAA) ... LADS
Linear Arithmetic [*Computer science*] ... LA
Linear Arithmetic Processor (IAA) ... LAP
Linear Array Hybrid Assembly (PDAA) ... LAHA
Linear Assembly ... LA
Linear Augmented Plane-Wave [*Physics*] ... LAPW
Linear Ball Bushing ... LBB
Linear Beam Tube ... LBT
Linear CMOS [*Complementary Metal Oxide Semiconductor*] [*Texas Instruments*] (NITA) ... LinCMOS
Linear Collision Sequence (MCD) ... LCS
Linear Combination ... LC
Linear Combination of Atomic Orbitals [*Physical chemistry*] ... LCAO
Linear Combination of Atomic Orbitals to Form Molecular Orbitals by a Self-Consistent Field [*Quantum mechanics*] ... LCAO-MO-SCF
Linear Combination of [*Semi-localized*] **Band Orbitals** [*Atomic physics*] ... LCBO
Linear Combination of Gaussian Orbitals [*Atomic physics*] ... LCGO
Linear Combination of Muffin Tin Orbitals [*Atomic physics*] ... LMTO
Linear Combination of Rydberg Orbitals [*Atomic physics*] ... LCRO
Linear Combination of Virtual Atomic Orbitals [*Physical chemistry*] ... LCVAO
Linear Combination Technique [*Nuclear science*] (OA) ... LCT
Linear Complementary Metal-Oxide Semiconductor [*Electronics*] (EECA) ... LINCMOS
Linear Composition (PDAA) ... LINCO
Linear Count Rate Meter (NRCH) ... LCRM
Linear Crystal Oxygen Free Copper [*Cable component*] (NITA) ... LC OFC
Linear Cutting Cord [*Aircraft escape technology*] (PDAA) ... LCC
Linear Decision ... LD
Linear Decision Rule ... LDR
Linear Delta Modulation ... LDM
Linear Detonating Cord (MSA) ... LDC
Linear Dichroism [*Spectra*] ... LD
Linear Differential Equation ... LDE
Linear Differential Transformer ... LDT
Linear Differential Vector ... LDV
Linear Differential Vector Equation ... LDVE
Linear Diophantine Object ... LDO
Linear Discriminant Analysis ... LDA
Linear Discriminant Classification Tree [*Mathematics*] ... LDCT
Linear Discriminant Function [*Mathematics*] ... LDF
Linear Displacement Analysis (DAVI) ... LDA
Linear Displacement Gauge ... LDG
Linear Displacement Indicator ... LDI
Linear Displacement Transduced (MCD) ... LDT
Linear Driving Force ... LDF
Linear Dynamic Analyzer (IAA) ... LDA
Linear Dynamic Range ... LDR
Linear Dynamic System ... LDS
Linear Econometric Modeling System (BUR) ... LEMS
Linear Electric Field Effect (PDAA) ... LEFE
Linear Electric Motor [*Magnetic rapid-transit car*] (PS) ... LEM
Linear Electrical Network ... LEN
Linear Embedding Algorithm (PDAA) ... LEA
Linear Energy Transfer [*Radiology*] ... LET
Linear Error Correcting Code (IAA) ... LECC
Linear Expansion [*Physics*] ... LE
Linear Feedback Shift Register ... LFSR
Linear Feet per Minute ... LFM
Linear Field Line ... LFL
Linear File [*Computer file*] (NITA) ... LF
Linear Filter ... LF
Linear Flash Tube ... LFT
Linear Flow Reactor [*Chemical engineering*] ... LFR
Linear Foot ... LF
Linear Foot (ADA) ... LFT
Linear Foot ... LINFT
Linear Free Energy Relationship ... LFER
Linear Frequency Modulation (CAAL) ... LFM
Linear Frequency Modulation on Pulse (MCD) ... LFMOP
Linear Friction Welding [*Environmental science*] ... LFW
Linear Function Interpolator ... LFI
Linear Gate ... LG
Linear Gate and Integrator (MHDB) ... LGI
Linear Heat Generation Rate [*Nuclear energy*] (NRCH) ... LHGR
Linear Hybrid ... LH
Linear Imaging Device (MCD) ... LID
Linear/Imaging Self-Scanner Sensor (MCD) ... LISS
Linear Induction Accelerator (MCD) ... LIA
Linear Induction Motor [*Magnetic rapid-transit car*] ... LIM
Linear Induction Motor Propulsion System ... LIMPS
Linear Induction Motor Research Vehicle [*Magnetic rapid-transit car*] ... LIMRV
Linear Induction Motor Test Vehicle [*Magnetic rapid-transit car*] ... LIMTV
Linear Information Processing Language [*High-order programming language*] [*Computer science*] (IEEE) ... LIPL
Linear Integrated Circuit ... LIC
Linear Interpolation [*Computer science*] (NHD) ... LERP
Linear Interpolator (IAA) ... LI
Linear, Invariant (PDAA) ... LIV
Linear Kalman Filter ... LKF
Linear Learning Machine [*Data analysis*] ... LLM
Linear Least Squares [*Mathematics*] ... LLS
Linear Log Potentiometer ... LLP
Linear Low-Density Polyethylene [*Plastics technology*] ... LLDPE
Linear, Lumped, Finite, Passive, Bilateral ... LLFPB
Linear Master Oscillator ... LMO
Linear Matched Filter (IEEE) ... LMF
Linear Measuring System ... LMS
Linear Meter ... LM
Linear Meters per Hour (IAA) ... LINMH
Linear, Minimum Variance Estimation (PDAA) ... LMVE
Linear Modulation ... LM
Linear Motion Bearing ... LMB
Linear Multiple Regression (IAA) ... LMR
Linear Multistep Formula (PDAA) ... LMF
Linear Multi-Step Method (PDAA) ... LMM
Linear Nearest Neighbor (MHDB) ... LNN
Linear Nested Region Analysis (PDAA) ... LNRA
Linear No-Threshold [*Risk model*] ... LNT
Linear Omnidirectional Airspeed System (PDAA) ... LORAS
Linear One-Step Transition [*Mathematical model for social grouping*] ... LOST
Linear Optical Trajectory [*Vision*] ... LOT
Linear Output Hall Effect Transducer ... LOHET
Linear Parameter Estimation [*Physical chemistry*] ... LPE
Linear Partial Information (PDAA) ... LPI
Linear Phase ... LP
Linear Phase Code Modulation ... LPCM
Linear Phase with Equal Ripple Error (IAA) ... LPERE
Linear Phasing Device [*Telecommunications*] (OA) ... LPD
Linear Photodiode Array [*Instrumentation*] ... LPDA
Linear Photopolymerization [*Organic chemistry*] ... LPP
Linear Poisson-Boltzmann Equation [*Physical chemistry*] ... LPBE
Linear Polarization ... LP
Linear Polarization Resistance (MCD) ... LPR
Linear Polarized Wave ... LPW
Linear Polyethylene [*Organic chemistry*] ... LPE
Linear Power Amplifier ... LPA
Linear Power Controller ... LPC
Linear Prediction [*Computer science*] ... LP
Linear Prediction Code ... LPC
Linear Prediction with Singular Value Decomposition [*Computer science*] ... LPSVD
Linear Predictive Coding [*Digital coding technique*] [*Telecommunications*] ... LPC
Linear Profile Scan [*Medicine*] (DMAA) ... LPS
Linear Programmed Thermal Degradation [*Instrumentation*] ... LPTD
Linear Programmed Thermal Degradation - Mass Spectroscopy [*Instrumentation*] ... LPTD-MS
Linear Programming [*Computer science*] ... LP
Linear Programming File Generator [*Computer science*] (IAA) ... LPFGEN
Linear Programming Language (NITA) ... LP
Linear Programming Language [*Intertechnique*] [*French Computer science*] ... LPL
Linear Programming Mathematical Optimization Subroutine System (IAA) ... LPMOSS
Linear Programming Matrix Generation (IAA) ... LPMATGEN
Linear Programming Solution (IAA) ... LPSOL
Linear Programming System [*Computer science*] ... LPS
Linear Programming under Uncertainty [*Computer science*] ... LPUU
Linear Pulse Sector (OA) ... LPS
Linear Pulse-Code Modulation [*Computer science*] ... LPCM
Linear Pulse-Height Analyzer Spectrum Analysis (PDAA) ... LPASA
Linear Quadratic [*Mathematics*] ... LQ
Linear Quadratic Gaussian (MCD) ... LQG
Linear Quadratic Problem [*Mathematics*] ... LQP
Linear Quantizer (IAA) ... LQT
Linear, Quasi Invariant (PDAA) ... LQIV
Linear Radial Transmission Filter [*Photography*] ... LRTF
Linear Referencing System [*FHWA*] (TAG) ... LRS
Linear Regression [*Mathematics*] ... LR
Linear Responsibility Charting (PDAA) ... LRC
Linear Rocket Engine System (PDAA) ... LRES
Linear Rotary Differential Capacitance Transducer [*Instrumentation*] ... LRDCT
Linear Rule of Cumulative Damage (PDAA) ... LRCD
Linear Seal Ring ... LSR
Linear Sedimentation Rate [*Geology*] ... LSR
Linear Select Memory ... LSM
Linear Selenium Photocell ... LSP
Linear Selenium Photocell ... LSPC
Linear Sequential Circuit ... LSC
Linear Sequential Machine ... LSM
Linear Sequential Network (MUGU) ... LSN
Linear Servo Actuator ... LSA
Linear Shift-Varying (PDAA) ... LSV
Linear Slope Controlled (PDAA) ... LSC
Linear Solvation Energy Relationship [*Physical chemistry*] ... LSER
Linear Sound Ranging Base (PDAA) ... LSRB
Linear Stochastic Optimal Control and Estimation [*Computer program*] ... LSOCE
Linear Strip Ion Thruster ... LSIT

Linear Structural Relationships (NITA)	LISREL
Linear Sweep Voltammograms [Electrochemistry]	LSV
Linear Synchronous Motor (IAA)	LSM
Linear Synchronous Motor [TRB] (TAG)	LSM
Linear Systems Analysis	LISA
Linear Systems Analysis Program [Statistics]	LSAP
Linear Tangent Guidance (MCD)	LTG
Linear Technology Corp. [Associated Press] (SAG)	LinearT
Linear Technology Corp. [NASDAQ symbol] (TTSB)	LLTC
Linear Technology, Inc. [Toronto Stock Exchange symbol]	LTI
Linear Threshold Element [Computer science]	LTE
Linear Time Base Oscillator	LTBO
Linear Time Invariant (IAA)	LTI
Linear Time Plot (MUGU)	LTP
Linear Time-Varying Network	LTN
Linear Transformation Converter (IAA)	LTC
Linear Transformer Read Only Memory [Computer science] (IAA)	LTROM
Linear Transmission Channel	LTC
Linear Transport Drive	LTD
Linear Tumor Diameter [Oncology]	LTD
Linear Unbiased Estimator [Statistics]	LUE
Linear Utility Prediction Function [Mathematics]	LUPF
Linear Variable Differential Transformer	LVDT
Linear Variable Differential Transformer - Primary	LVDT-PRIM
Linear Variable Differential Transformer - Secondary	LVDT-SEC
Linear Variable Displacement Transducer	LVDT
Linear Variable Inductance Transducer	LVIT
Linear Vector Equation	LVE
Linear Vector Function	LVF
Linear Velocity	LV
Linear Velocity Displacement Transformer (IEEE)	LVDT
Linear Velocity Transducer	LVT
Linear Voltage Differential Transformer (NASA)	LVDT
Linear Xenon Flash Tube	LXFT
Linear Xenon Tube	LXT
Linear Yard (AFM)	LY
Linear-Analogue Self Assessment (DMAA)	LASA
Linear-Analogue Self-Assessment-Pristman (DMAA)	LASA-P
Linear-Analogue Self-Assessment-Selby (DMAA)	LASA-S
Linear-Bounded Automaton	LBA
Linear-Elastic Analysis Program [SIA Computer Services] [Software package] (NCC)	LEAP
Linear-Elastic Fracture Mechanics	LEFM
Linear-Elastic Matrix Analysis Routine	LAMAR
Linear-Energy Spectrophotofluorometry	LEF
Linear-Energy Transfer Spectrometer [Radiology] (KSC)	LETS
Linear-Energy Transfer System [Radiology]	LETS
Linearity Test Set	LTS
Linearized Augmented Plane Wave [Physical chemistry]	LAPW
Linearized High-Resolution Wind-Field Flow [Model] [Marine science] (OSRA)	LFLOW
Linearized High-Resolution Wind-Field Flow [Model] (USDC)	LFLOW
Linear-Load Field Effect Transistor [Electronics] (PDAA)	LLFET
Linear-Logarithmic (IEEE)	LINLOG
Linearly Frequency-Modulated Pulse	LIFMOP
Linearly Organized Chemical Code for Use in Computer Systems (DIT)	LINCO
Linearly Polarized Mode [Telecommunications] (TEL)	LPM
Linear-Motor Resonant-Piston Compressor [Navy]	LMRPC
Linear-Shaped Charge	LSC
Lineas Aereas Allegro SA de CV [Mexico ICAO designator] (FAAC)	GRO
Lineas Aereas Canarias SA [Spain ICAO designator] (FAAC)	LCN
Lineas Aereas Colombianas Ltd. [Colombia] [ICAO designator] (FAAC)	LAE
Lineas Aereas Costarricenses SA [Costa Rica] [ICAO designator] (FAAC)	LACAS
Lineas Aereas Costarricenses SA [Costa Rica] [ICAO designator] (FAAC)	LRC
Lineas Aereas Costarricenses Sociedad Anonima [Airline] [Costa Rica]	LACSA
Lineas Aereas Costarricenses, Sociedad Anonima (LACSA) [Costa Rica] [ICAO designator] (ICDA)	LR
Lineas Aereas de Ixtlan SA de CV [Mexico ICAO designator] (FAAC)	IXT
Lineas Aereas de Nicaragua, SA [Nicaraguan airline]	LANICA
Lineas Aereas del Caribe [Colombia] [ICAO designator] (FAAC)	LIC
Lineas Aereas del Estada [Argentine Air Force airline]	LADE
Lineas Aereas del Estado [Argentina ICAO designator] (FAAC)	LDE
Lineas Aereas del Humaya, SA de CV [Mexico] [FAA designator] (FAAC)	UMA
Lineas Aereas du Espanalos [Iberia] [Spain ICAO designator]	IB
Lineas Aereas Eldorado Ltd. [Colombia] [ICAO designator] (FAAC)	EDR
Lineas Aereas Iberoamericanas [Chile] [FAA designator] (FAAC)	IBA
Lineas Aereas Latur SA de CV [Mexico ICAO designator] (FAAC)	LUR
Lineas Aereas Mexicana, Sociedad Anonima	LAMSA
Lineas Aereas Nacionales Consolidadas Sociedad Anonima	LANSA
Lineas Aereas Paraguayas [Paraguay] [ICAO designator] (FAAC)	LAP
Lineas Aereas Paraguayas Sociedad Anonima [Airline] [Paraguay]	LAPSA
Lineas Aereas Petroleras [Colombia] [ICAO designator] (FAAC)	APT
Lineas Aereas Postales Espanoles [Airline] [Spain]	LAPE
Lineas Aereas Privadas Argentinas [ICAO designator] (AD)	MJ
Lineas Aereas Suramericanas Ltd. [Colombia] [ICAO designator] (FAAC)	LAU
Lineas Navieras Bolivianas [Shipping line] [Bolivia] (EY)	LINABOL
Linebacker [Football]	LB
Line-Carrying	LC
Linecaster Control (DGA)	LCC
Lined	LND
Lined Hollow Charge	LHC
Line-Drop Compensator (MSA)	LDC
Linee Aeree Transcontinentali Italiane	LATI
Line-Haul Tractor (DOMA)	LHT
Lineman (AABC)	LMN
Linen [Deltiology]	L
Linen (ADA)	LIN
Linen (VRA)	lin
Linen	lin
Linen and Lace Paper Institute [Later, SSI] (EA)	LLPI
Linen Industry Research Association [British] (BI)	LIRA
Linen Press (ADA)	LP
Linen Supply Association of America [Later, TRSA] (EA)	LSAA
Linen Trade Association (EA)	LTA
Linen-Faced Paper (DGA)	L/F
Line-of-Flight (MCD)	LOF
Line-of-Sight - Air Defense [DoD]	LOS-AD
Line-of-Sight - Antitank [DoD]	LOS-AT
Line-of-Sight Expendables (DNAB)	LOSE
Line-of-Sight - Forward [DoD]	LOS-F
Line-of-Sight - Forward Heavy [DoD]	LOS-FH
Line-of-Sight Rate (MCD)	LOSR
Line-of-Sight - Rear [DoD]	LOS-R
Line-of-Sight - Repeater Placement Program (IAA)	LOSARP
Line-of-Sight Task Force Communications [Military] (CAAL)	LOSTFC
Line-of-Sight Task Force Communications System [Military]	LOSTFCS
Line-of-Sight Test Fixture	LOSTF
Line-Oriented Protocol	LOP
Line-Oriented Simulation (GAVI)	LOS
Liner [Nautical]	L
Liner	LNR
Lines	LL
Lines (WDMC)	ll
Lines Dose [Medicine]	L
Lines Layout (MCD)	LL
Lines of Communication Designators (MCD)	LOCD
Lines of Communications Ports (AABC)	LOCPORT
Lines per Hour [Printing]	LPH
Lines per Inch [Printing]	LPI
Lines per Millimeter (AAG)	LMM
Lines per Millimeter (WDAA)	LPM
Lines per Minute [Computer science]	L/M
Lines per Minute (IDOE)	l/m
Lines per Minute (IDOE)	lpm
Lines per Minute [Computer science]	LPM
Lines per Page	LPP
Lines per Second (WDAA)	L/S
Lines per Second [Computer science]	LPS
Lines per Vertical Inch (WDMC)	li
Line-Scanning Mode [Microscopy]	LSM
Line-Sequential (IAA)	LS
Line-Sequential Color Composite (IEEE)	LSCC
Line-Sharing Adapter	LSA
Line-Sharing Device	LSD
Line-Sharing Unit	LSU
Linesville, PA [FM radio station call letters]	WVCC
Line-Throwing Projectile (NG)	LTP
Line-to-Disk [Computer science] (MHDI)	LINDI
Line-to-Ground (IAA)	LG
Line-to-Line (MCD)	L-L
Line-to-Line	LTL
Line-to-Line to Ground (IAA)	LLG
Line-Up	LU
Lineville, AL [AM radio station call letters]	WZZX
Linfen [Republic of China] [Seismograph station code, US Geological Survey] (SEIS)	LNF
Linfield College (GAGS)	Linfield C
Linfield College, McMinnville, OR [OCLC symbol] (OCLC)	OLC
Linfield College, McMinnville, OR [Library symbol Library of Congress] (LCLS)	OrMcL
Lingayen, Pangasinan [Philippines] [ICAO location identifier] (ICLI)	RPUG
Lingerie	LNGR
[The] Lingerie and Corsetry Exhibition [British] (ITD)	LACE
Lingerie Manufacturers Association [Later, IAMA] (EA)	LMA
Ling-Temco-Vought [LTV] [ICAO aircraft manufacturer identifier] (ICAO)	TE
Ling-Temco-Vought Co.	LTV
Lingua Cosmica [Artificial language consisting of radio signals of varying lengths and frequencies]	LINCOS
Lingua Tertii Imperii [A study of the abuse of language under Nazism by Viktor Klemperer]	LTI
Lingual [Dentistry]	L
Lingual Antimicrobial Peptide [Biochemistry]	LAP
Lingual Antimicrobial Peptide [Medicine]	LAP
Lingual Developmental Groove (DMAA)	LDG
Lingual Skills Required [Civil service]	LSR
Linguere [Senegal] [ICAO location identifier] (ICLI)	GOOG
Linguistic Analysis of Spanish Colonial Documents	LASCODOCS
Linguistic Analysis of Speech Samples (DAVI)	LASS
Linguistic Analysis System (ECII)	LINGUA
Linguistic Association of Canada and the United States (EA)	LACUS
Linguistic Atlas of the Middle and South Atlantic States	LAMSAS
Linguistic Atlas of the United States and Canada [1930]	LAUSC
Linguistic Atlas of the Upper Midwest	LAUM
Linguistic Data Consortium [Defense Advanced Research Projects Agency]	LDC
Linguistic Minorities Project [Education] (AIE)	LMP
Linguistic Problems	LP
Linguistic Society of America (EA)	LSA

Linguistic Survey of the Ottawa Valley [*Carleton University*] [*Canada Research center*] (RCD) .... LSOV
Linguistic-Kinesic [*Psychiatry*] .... L-K
Linguistics .... LING
Linguistics Association of Great Britain .... LAGB
Linguistics Documentation Center [*University of Ottawa*] [*Database*] [*Canada*] (NITA) .... LDC
Linguistics of Visual English [*Sign language system for the hearing impaired*] .... LOVE
Linguistics Research Center [*University of Texas at Austin*] [*Research center*] (RCD) .... LRC
Linguistics Research Laboratory [*Gallaudet College*] [*Research center*] (RCD) .... LRL
Linguistics Research System .... LA
Linguoaxial [*Dentistry*] .... LAC
Linguoaxiocervical [*Dentistry*] .... LAG
Linguoaxiogingival [*Dentistry*] LC
Linguocervical [*Dentistry*] .... LD
Linguodistal [*Dentistry*] .... LG
Linguogingival [*Dentistry*] LI
Linguoincisal [*Dentistry*] .... LM
Linguomesial [*Dentistry*] .... LO
Linguoocclusal [*Dentistry*] .... LP
Linguopulpal [*Dentistry*] .... LP
Linhas Aereas da Guine-Bissau [*Airline*] [*Guinea-Bissau*] .... LAGB
Linhas Aereas da Guine-Bissau [*ICAO designator*] (AD) .... YZ
Linhas Aereas de Mocambique [*Mozambique*] [*ICAO designator*] (FAAC) .... LAM
Linhas Aereas Regionais SA [*Portugal ICAO designator*] (FAAC) .... LAR
Liniment .... LIN
Liniment .... LINIM
Lining .... LG
Lining .... LNG
Lining (MSA) .... LUT
Lining Up Table (DGA) .... Linium
Linium Technology Corp. [*Associated Press*] (SAG) .... Linium
Linjeflyg [*ICAO designator*] (AD) .... LF
Link L
Link LI
Link .... LK
Link (KSC) .... LNK
Link .... LAP
Link Access Procedure [*Telecommunications*] (TEL) .... LAP
Link Access Procedure [*or Protocol*] Balanced [*Telecommunications*] .... LAPB
Link Access Procedure for MODEMs [*Communications protocol*] [*Computer science*] (PCM) .... LAPM
Link Access Procedure Half-Duplex [*Telecommunications*] (ACRL) .... LAPX
Link Access Procedure to Frame Mode Bearer Services [*Telecommunications*] (ACRL) .... LAPF
Link Access Procedure-D [*Telecommunications*] (DOM) .... LAPD
Link Access Protocol [*Telecommunications*] .... LAP
Link Access Protocol, B Channel [*Telecommunications*] .... LAPB
Link Access Protocol, D Channel [*Telecommunications*] .... LAPD
Link Active Scheduler (ACII) .... LAS
Link Address (IAA) .... LA
Link Airways of Australia [*Australia ICAO designator*] (FAAC) .... LAW
Link Allotter .... LA
Link Analysis .... LSL
Link and Selector Language .... LB
Link Babler [*Telecommunications*] (ECII) .... LCNT
Link Celestial Navigation Trainer LC
Link Circuit LC
Link Control [*Telecommunications*] (OSI) .... LCP
Link Control Procedure [*Telecommunications*] .... LCP
Link Control Protocol [*Telecommunications*] (ACRL) LCC
Link Control Standard Controller [*Telecommunications*] (ECII) .... LCS
Link Control Station [*Telecommunications*] (ECII) .... LCU
Link Control Unit [*Telecommunications*] (TEL) .... LEIP
Link Eleven Improvement Program (DOMA) .... LH
Link Header (ACRL) .... LH
Link House Books [*Publisher*] [*British*] .... LIS
Link Information Sciences (BUR) .... LIFT
Link Intellectual Functions Tester .... LIU
Link Interface Unit [*Telecommunications*] (ECII) LLI
Link Layer Interface [*Computer science*] (PCM) .... LPDU
Link Layer Protocol Data Unit [*Telecommunications*] (OSI) .... LSAP
Link Layer Service Access Point .... LSDU
Link Layer Service Data Unit LL
Link Level [*Telecommunications*] .... LLCS
Link Level Communications Subsystem [*NCR Corp.*] .... LILO
Link Loader (IAA) .... LMI
Link Management Interface [*Computer science*] .... LM
Link Manager .... LME
Link Monitor Equipment (MCD) .... LN
Link Number (MHDB) .... LOW
Link Orderwire Project .... LPA
Link Pack Area [*Computer science*] (MCD) .... LPVS
Link Packetized Voice Subsystem [*Telecommunications*] (ACRL) .... LPP
Link Peripheral Processor (ACRL) .... LP
Link Printer (ACRL) .... LPC
Link Priority Change [*NASA*] (KSC) .... LQA
Link Quality Analysis (PDAA) .... LR
Link Resources, Inc. [*Vancouver Stock Exchange symbol*] .... LRU
Link Retraction Unit (KSC) .... LS
Link State (ACRL) .... LSP
Link State Packet [*Telecommunications*] .... LSL
Link Support Layer .... LT
Link Terminal [*Telecommunications*] (TEL) .... LT

Link Terminal Simulator .... LTS
Link Testing (NITA) .... LT
Link Trainer Instructor .... LT
Link Utilization Efficiency .... LUE
Linkage (MSA) .... LKGE
Linkage, Ability, Interest [*Fundraising term*] (NFD) .... L-A-I
Linkage Control Language [*Computer science*] (BUR) LCL
Linkage Control Table [*Telecommunications*] (IAA) .... LCT
Linkage Disequilibrium [*Genetics*] .... LD
Linkage Editor (IAA) .... LE
Linkage Editor [*Computer science*] .... LIED
Linkage Editor [*Computer science*] (IAA) .... LNKEDT
Linkage Equilibrium [*Genetics*] .... LE
Linkage Group [*Genetics*] (OA) .... LG
Linkage System Diagnostic (IAA) .... LSD
Linked Access Network .... LAN
Linked Access Network Resource Extension and Service .... LANRES
Linked Access Network Transport Management System [*Telecommunications*] .... LANTMS
Linked Administrative Statistical Sample [*Social Security Administration*] (GFGA) .... LASS
Linked Cluster Network [*Chemistry*] .... LCN
Linked Compressor and Expander (NATG) .... LINCOMPEX
Linked Cross Sectional (PDAA) .... LCS
Linked Indexed Sequential Access .... LISA
Linked Object Code (TEL) .... LOC
Linked Operational Capability (DOMA) .... LOC
Linked Systems Project [*of the Library of Congress*] .... LSP
Linked Systems Protocol [*Computer science*] (TNIG) .... LSP
Linked Term [*Online database field identifier*] .... LT
Linked Vertical Well [*Coal gastification*] (DICI) .... LVW
Link-Edit Language [*Computer science*] .... LEL
Linker Directive [*Telecommunications*] (TEL) .... LD
Linker Polypeptide [*Biochemistry*] .... LP
Linker Scanning [*Mutants*] [*Genetics*] .... LS
Linking (IAA) .... LKG
Linking Industry and School Education (AIE) .... LIASE
Linking Loader (IAA) LL
Linking Relocating Loader .... LRL
Linking Segment Subprogram .... LSS
Linkless Ammunition Loading System (MCD) .... LALS
Linkoeping [*Sweden*] [*Airport symbol*] (OAG) .... LPI
Linkoping/Malmen [*Sweden ICAO location identifier*] (ICLI) .... ESCF
Linkoping/SAAB [*Sweden ICAO location identifier*] (ICLI) .... ESSL
Linkport [*Electronics*] (ECII) .... LP
Linkport Controller [*Electronics*] (ECII) .... LPC
Linkport Extension [*Electronics*] (ECII) .... LPE
Links and Chargers (NATG) LC
Linksozialisten [*Left Socialists*] [*Austria Political party*] (PPE) .... LS
Linn County Heritage Society, Cedar Rapids, IA [*Library symbol Library of Congress*] (LCLS) .... IaCrL
Linn News-Letter, Central City, IA [*Library symbol Library of Congress*] (LCLS) .... IaCcL
Linn on the Laws of the Province of Pennsylvania [*A publication*] (DLA) .... Linn Laws Prov PA
Linnaean L
Linnaean Society .... LA
Linnaean Society of London .... LSL
Linnaean Society of New York (EA) .... LSNY
Linnaeus .... LINN
Linn-Benton Community College, Albany, OR [*OCLC symbol*] (OCLC) .... OLX
Linn-Benton Community College, Albany, OR [*Library symbol Library of Congress*] (LCLS) .... OrAlC
Linnean Society [*Australia*] .... LS
Linn's Index of Pennsylvania Reports [*A publication*] (DLA) .... Linn Ind
Linocut (VRA) .... lino
Linoleic Acid (AAMN) .... LA
Linoleic Acid Depression [*Clinical chemistry*] (AAMN) .... LAD
Linoletic Acid-Like Activity (PDAA) .... LALA
Linoleum .... LINO
Linoleum (MSA) .... LINOL
Linoleum .... LNLM
Linoleum Base [*Technical drawings*] .... LB
Linoleum Floor [*Technical drawings*] .... LF
Linomatic Operating Unit [*Printing*] (DGA) .... LOU
Linomatic Tape System [*Typography*] (DGA) .... LTS
Linotronic [*Computer science*] .... Lino
Linotype .... LINO
Lins [*Brazil ICAO location identifier*] (ICLI) .... SBLN
Linseed Association Terms [*Shipping*] .... LAT
Linseed Oil (VRA) .... lnsd
Linseed Oil (PDAA) .... LSO
L'Institut National Canadien pour les Aveugles (AC) .... L'INCA
Lintel .... LNTL
Lintel [*Technical drawings*] .... LTL
L'Internationale Liberale IL
Lintex Minerals [*Vancouver Stock Exchange symbol*] .... LXM
Linton Daily Citizen, Linton, IN [*Library symbol Library of Congress*] (LCLS) .... InLintC
Linton, IN [*AM radio station call letters*] .... WBTO
Linton, IN [*FM radio station call letters*] .... WQTY
Linton Kwesi Johnson [*British musician*] .... LKJ
Linton Public Library, Linton, IN [*Library symbol Library of Congress*] (LCLS) .... InLint
Linton-On-Ouse [*British ICAO location identifier*] (ICLI) .... EGXU

Linton-on-Ouse FTU [*British ICAO designator*] (FAAC) ... LOP
Lintronics International Ltd. [*Vancouver Stock Exchange symbol*] ... LTX
Linus Pauling Institute of Science and Medicine [*Research center*] (RCD) ... LPI
Linville, NC [*Television station call letters*] ... WUNE
Linz [*Austria*] [*Airport symbol*] (OAG) ... LNZ
Linz [*Austria ICAO location identifier*] (ICLI) ... LOWL
Linz and Donawetz [*Furnace*] [*Metallurgy Named after two plant sites in Austria*] ... LD
Lio Matu [*Malaysia*] [*ICAO location identifier*] (ICLI) ... WBGO
Lion Brewery [*NASDAQ symbol*] (TTSB) ... MALT
Lion Brewery, Inc. (The) [*Associated Press*] (SAG) ... LionBrw
Lion Brewery, Inc. (The) [*NASDAQ symbol*] (SAG) ... MALT
Lionair SA [*Luxembourg*] [*ICAO designator*] (FAAC) ... LIR
Lionel Collectors Club of America (EA) ... LCCA
Lionel Railroader Club (EA) ... LRC
Lions Blind Sports Foundation (EA) ... LBSF
Lions Clubs International (EA) ... LCI
Lion's Head Branch, Bruce County Public Library, Ontario [*Library symbol National Library of Canada*] (NLC) ... OLIH
Lions International [*Later, LCI*] (EA) ... LI
Lions International Stamp Club (EA) ... LISC
Lions Philatelic Unit (EA) ... LPU
Lions-Air, AG [*Switzerland*] [*FAA designator*] (FAAC) ... LEU
Liottite [*A zeolite*] ... LIO
Lip ... L
Lip Nerve ... LN
Lipa/Fernando Air Base, Batangas [*Philippines*] [*ICAO location identifier*] (ICLI) ... RPUL
Lipari [*Lipari Islands*] [*Seismograph station code, US Geological Survey*] (SEIS) ... LLI
Lipase (MAE) ... LPS
Lipase B (DMAA) ... LIPB
Lipase D (DMAA) ... LIPD
Lipemic [*Cardiology*] (DAVI) ... lip
Lipenius' Bibliotheca Juridica [*A publication*] (DLA) ... Lip Bib Jur
Lipid Body [*Biochemistry*] (MAE) ... LB
Lipid Cytosome [*Biochemistry*] (MAE) ... LC
Lipid Hydrocarbon [*Biochemistry*] ... LH
Lipid Hydrocarbon Inclusions [*Biochemistry*] (DAVI) ... LHI
Lipid Mobilizing Hormone [*Endocrinology*] ... LM
Lipid Mobilizing Hormone [*Endocrinology*] ... LMH
Lipid Profile [*Cardiology*] (DAVI) ... LIP P
Lipid Research Center [*Washington University*] [*Research center*] (RCD) ... LRC
Lipid Research Clinics ... LRC
Lipid Research Clinics Coronary Primary Prevention Trial [*Cardiology*] ... LRCCPPT
Lipid Soluble Secondary Antioxidants [*Biochemistry*] ... LSSA
Lipid Transfer Protein [*Biochemistry*] ... LTP
Lipid-Bound Sialic Acid [*Analytical biochemistry*] ... LBSA
Lipid-Bound Sialic Acid [*Biochemistry*] (DAVI) ... LSA
Lipizzan Association of America (EA) ... LAA
Lipkovo [*Yugoslavia*] [*Seismograph station code, US Geological Survey*] (SEIS) ... LIP
Lipman Management Resources Ltd. (NITA) ... LMR
Lipnur [*Indonesia*] [*ICAO aircraft manufacturer identifier*] (ICAO) ... NU
Lipoamide Dehydrogenase [*An enzyme*] ... LAD
Lipoarabinomannan [*Biochemistry*] ... LAM
Lipoate [*Also called Lipoic acid*] [*Biochemistry*] (DAVI) ... Lip
Lipoate Transacetylase [*An enzyme*] ... LTA
Lipo-Chitooligosaccharide [*Botany*] ... LCO
Lipocortin (DMAA) ... LPC
Lipoid [*Biochemistry*] ... L
Lipophosphoglycan [*Biochemistry*] ... LPG
Lipopolysaccharide [*Biochemistry*] ... LPS
Lipopolysaccharide-Binding Protein [*Biochemistry*] ... LBP
Lipoprotein [*Biochemistry*] ... Lp
Lipoprotein A [*Biochemistry*] ... LpA
Lipoprotein B [*Biochemistry*] ... LpB
Lipoprotein C [*Biochemistry*] ... LpC
Lipoprotein D [*Biochemistry*] ... LpD
Lipoprotein Deficient Human Serum ... LPDS
Lipoprotein E [*Biochemistry*] ... LpE
Lipoprotein Electrophoresis [*Biochemistry*] ... LEP
Lipoprotein Electrophoresis [*Biochemistry*] ... LPE
Lipoprotein Lipase [*An enzyme*] ... LPL
Lipoprotein Lipase [*An enzyme*] (DAVI) ... LPP
Lipoprotein Lipase Activity [*Medicine*] (DMAA) ... LPLA
Lipoprotein Lipase Inactivation System [*Biochemistry*] (DAVI) ... LPLIS
Lipoprotein-Associated Coagulation Inhibitor [*Hematology*] ... LACI
Lipoprotein-Deficient Fraction [*Medicine*] (DMAA) ... LPDF
Lipoprotein-X [*Biochemistry*] (MAE) ... Lp-X
Liporotein Receptor-Related Protein [*Biochemistry*] ... LRP
Liposoluble Neutral Fraction (OA) ... LNF
Liposome $1.9375 Cv Dep'A'Pfd [*NASDAQ symbol*] (TTSB) ... LIPOZ
Liposome Co. [*NASDAQ symbol*] (SAG) ... LIPO
[*The*] **Liposome Co., Inc.** [*Associated Press*] (SAG) ... Liposm
[*The*] **Liposome Co., Inc.** [*Associated Press*] (SAG) ... Lipsm
Liposome Encapsulated Hemoglobin [*Biochemistry*] ... LEH
Liposome Immunoassay [*Clinical chemistry*] ... LIA
Liposome Immunosensor [*Electrochemistry*] ... LIS
Liposome-Antibody-Complement [*Immunochemistry*] ... LAC
Liposome-Encapsulated Amikacin [*Bactericide*] ... LEAK
Liposome-Encapulated Gentamicin [*Bactericide*] ... LEGEN
Lipoteichoic Acid [*Biochemistry*] ... LTA
Lipothiamide-Pyrophosphate ... LTPP
Lipotropic Factor [*Choline*] [*Biochemistry*] ... LTF
Lipotropin (DMAA) ... LPT
Lipotropin Hormone [*Endocrinology*] ... LPH
Lipoxin A [*Biochemistry*] ... LXA
Lipoxin B [*Biochemistry*] ... LXB
Lippitt's Massachusetts Criminal Law [*A publication*] (DLA) ... Lipp Cr L
Liquefied ... LQFD
Liquefied Energy Gas ... LEG
Liquefied Gaseous Fuels Spill Test Facility (USDC) ... LGFSTP
Liquefied Natural Gas ... LNG
Liquefied Natural Petroleum ... LNP
Liquefied Petroleum [*Gas*] ... LP
Liquefied Petroleum Gas ... LPG
Liquefied Petroleum Gas Industry Technical Association [*British*] ... LPGITA
Liquefied Refinery Gas ... LRG
Liquest International Marketing [*Vancouver Stock Exchange symbol*] ... LIQ
Liqueur [*Solution*] [*Pharmacy*] ... liq
Liqui-Box Corp. [*NASDAQ symbol*] (SAG) ... LIQB
Liqui-Box Corp. [*Associated Press*] (SAG) ... LiquiBox
Liquid [*Chemistry*] ... (l)
Liquid (AAG) ... LIQ
Liquid (ECII) ... LIQD
Liquid ... lq
Liquid ... LQD
Liquid ... LQD
Liquid Affinity Chromatography ... LAC
Liquid Agent Detector (AABC) ... LAD
Liquid Air (NASA) ... LAIR
Liquid Air Accumulator Rocket ... LAAR
Liquid Air Collection Engine ... LACE
Liquid Air Cycle Engine [*Aerospace plane engine concept*] ... LACE
Liquid Air Rocket ... LAR
Liquid and Solid Industrial Control Association (EA) ... LSICA
Liquid Asset [*Business term*] ... LA
Liquid Asset and Government Securities (ADA) ... LGS
Liquid Boost Module (MCD) ... LBM
Liquid Capacity ... LC
Liquid Chromatographic Reactor ... LCR
Liquid Chromatographs with Electrochemical Detection ... LCEC
Liquid Chromatography ... LC
Liquid Chromatography/Infrared ... LC/IR
Liquid Chromatography/Mass Spectrometry ... LC/MS
Liquid Chromatography plus Pulsed Amperometric Detection [*Analytical chemistry*] ... LC-PAD
Liquid, Complex Fertilizer (PDAA) ... LCF
Liquid Composite Molding [*Materials science*] ... LCM
Liquid Conditioned Microclimate System [*Army*] (RDA) ... LCMCS
Liquid Controlled Solid (KSC) ... LCS
Liquid Cooling and Ventilation Garment [*NASA*] (NASA) ... LCVG
Liquid Cooling System ... LCS
Liquid Core Nuclear Rocket ... LCNR
Liquid Crystal ... LC
Liquid Crystal (IDOE) ... LIX
Liquid Crystal Analog ... LCA
Liquid Crystal Cell (IEEE) ... LCC
Liquid Crystal Digital [*Battery-powered wristwatch*] ... LCD
Liquid Crystal Diode ... LCD
Liquid Crystal Display ... LCD
Liquid Crystal Induced Circular Dichroism [*Spectroscopy*] ... LCICD
Liquid Crystal Institute [*Kent State University*] (PDAA) ... LCI
Liquid Crystal Quartz (WGA) ... LCQ
Liquid Crystal Shutter [*Epson*] [*Printer technology*] ... LCS
Liquid Crystal Thermography ... LCT
Liquid Crystal Visual Display [*Electronics*] (EECA) ... LVD
Liquid Crystalline Polymer Research Center [*University of Connecticut*] [*Research center*] (RCD) ... LCPRC
Liquid Curing Medium ... LCM
Liquid Cyclone Process [*for making high-protein edible cottonseed flour*] ... LCP
Liquid Cyclone Processed Cottonseed Flour ... LCPC
Liquid Delay Line ... LDL
Liquid, Diesel-Cycle, Supercharged ... LDS
Liquid Drop ... LD
Liquid Droplet Radiator (MCD) ... LDR
Liquid Effluents Data System [*Environmental Protection Agency*] (GFGA) ... LEDS
Liquid Element Display ... LED
Liquid Emulsion Membrane [*Separation technology*] ... LEM
Liquid Encapsulated Czochralski [*Crystal growing technique*] (IEEE) ... LEC
Liquid Encapsulated Kyropoulos [*Crystal growing technique*] ... LEK
Liquid Encapsulation Zone-Refining (PDAA) ... LEZOR
Liquid Encapsulation-Vertical Gradient Freeze (PDAA) ... LE-VGF
Liquid Engine Air-Augmented Package (MCD) ... LEAP
Liquid Expanded Film ... LEF
Liquid Filtration System ... LFS
Liquid Flow System ... LFS
Liquid Fluidized Bed Reactor ... LFBR
Liquid Fluidized Bed Reactor Critical Experiment ... LFBR-CX
Liquid Fuel ... LIFU
Liquid Fuel Rocket (IAA) ... LIQFRKT
Liquid Fuel Systems Maintenance Technician/Specialist [*Aerospace*] (AAG) ... LFSMT/S
Liquid Gas ... LG
Liquid Gas Tank ... LGT
Liquid Granule Applicator [*Device used to disperse pesticides*] ... LIGA
Liquid Helium (IAA) ... LH
Liquid Helium ... LHE

Liquid Helium Temperature (PDAA)	LHeT
Liquid High Activity Waste [Nuclear energy] (NUCP)	LHAW
Liquid High Level Waste [Nuclear energy] (NUCP)	LHLW
Liquid Hourly Space Velocity [Fluid dynamics]	LHSV
Liquid Hydrogen	LH
Liquid Hydrogen [NASA]	LH$_2$
Liquid Hydrogen Container	LHC
Liquid Hydrogen System Complex [NASA] (KSC)	LHSC
Liquid Hydrogen Vessel	LHV
Liquid Immersion Development [Reprography]	LID
Liquid in Glass	LQGLS
Liquid Injection Electric Thruster [NASA] (NASA)	LINJET
Liquid Injection Molding	LIM
Liquid Injection Molding	LIM
Liquid Injection Technique (IEEE)	LIT
Liquid Injection Thrust Vector Control	LITVC
Liquid Injector Spray Pattern (MCD)	LISP
Liquid Interface Diffusion	LID
Liquid Ionization [Spectrometric instrumentation]	LI
Liquid Junction Potential	LJP
Liquid Large-Bore Cannon (MCD)	LLBC
Liquid Level (ECII)	LL
Liquid Level Control	LLC
Liquid Level Control Switch	LLCS
Liquid Level Controller (ECII)	LLI
Liquid Level Indicator	LLI
Liquid Level Monitor Port Plug [Nuclear energy] (NRCH)	LLMPP
Liquid Level Sensor	LLS
Liquid Level Switch (IAA)	LLS
Liquid Limit (IEEE)	LL
Liquid/Liquid Extraction [Laboratory procedure]	L/L
Liquid Liquid Phase Transfer Catalysis [Physical chemistry]	LL-PTC
Liquid Low Activity Waste [Nuclear energy] (NUCP)	LLAW
Liquid Low Level Waste [Nuclear energy] (NUCP)	LLLW
Liquid Measuring System	LMS
Liquid Media Concentrate [Cell culture]	LMC
Liquid Medium Active Waste (NUCP)	LMAW
Liquid Medium Level Waste [Nuclear energy] (NUCP)	LMLW
Liquid Membrane	LM
Liquid Membrane Extraction [Separation science and technology]	LME
Liquid Mercury Engine	LME
Liquid Mercury Isolator	LMI
Liquid Metal	LM
Liquid Metal Breeder [Reactor]	LIMB
Liquid Metal Cooled Demonstration (IAA)	LMCD
Liquid Metal Cooled Reactor	LMCR
Liquid Metal Cycle	LMC
Liquid Metal Detector	LMD
Liquid Metal Embrittlement (MCD)	LME
Liquid Metal Engineering Center [Energy Research and Development Administration]	LMEC
Liquid Metal Fast Breeder Reactor	LMFBR
Liquid Metal Fuel	LMF
Liquid Metal Fueled Reactor	LMFR
Liquid Metal Fueled Reactor Experiment	LMFRE
Liquid Metal Heat Exchanger (NRCH)	LMHX
Liquid Metal Ion Gun [Surface analysis]	LMIG
Liquid Metal Ion Source	LMIS
Liquid Metal Ionization [Spectrometry]	LMI
Liquid Metal Magnetohydrodynamics	LMMHD
Liquid Metal Plasma Valve (IAA)	LMP
Liquid Metal Reactor	LMR
Liquid Metal Slip Ring	LMSE
Liquid Metal System	LMS
Liquid Metal Thorium Breeder Reactor	LMTBR
Liquid Metals Information Center [AEC]	LMIC
Liquid Metals Safety Committee [AEC] (MCD)	LMSC
Liquid Methane Gas	LMG
Liquid Molding Resin [Organic chemistry]	LMR
Liquid Money Market [Banking]	LMM
Liquid Monopropellant	LMP
Liquid Natural Gas [BTS] [DOE] (TAG)	LNG
Liquid Natural Rubber	LNR
Liquid Nitrogen (AFM)	LIN
Liquid Nitrogen	LN
Liquid Nitrogen [NASA] (NASA)	LN$_2$
Liquid Nitrogen Evaporator	LNE
Liquid Nitrogen Processing	LNP
Liquid Nitrogen Refrigeration	LNR
Liquid Nitrogen Temperature (IAA)	LNT
Liquid Nitrogen Transfer System	LNTS
Liquid Organic Compound	LOC
Liquid Oxygen	LO
Liquid Oxygen [Also, LOX] [NASA] (KSC)	LO$_2$
Liquid Oxygen [Also, LO$_2$]	LOX
Liquid Oxygen and Liquid Hydrogen	LOX/LH
Liquid Oxygen Expert System (NITA)	LOX
Liquid Oxygen Maintenance Panel (AAG)	LMP
Liquid Oxygen Petrol, Guided Aircraft Projectile	LOP-GAP
Liquid Oxygen Start Tank (AAG)	LST
Liquid Oxygen	LOZ
Liquid Ozone	LO
Liquid Pathway Generic Study [Nuclear energy] (NRCH)	LPGS
Liquid Penetrant Testing [or Examination] [Nuclear energy] (NRCH)	LPT
Liquid Phase [Chemistry]	LP
Liquid Phase Chemical Vapor Deposition [Photovoltaic energy systems]	LPCVD

Liquid Phase Epitaxy [Magnetic film]	LPE
Liquid Phase Flow Reactor (KSC)	LPFR
Liquid Phase Methanation [Fuel chemistry]	LPM
Liquid Phase Methanation/Shift Reaction [Fuel chemistry]	LPM/S
Liquid Phase Oxidation [Chemical processing]	LPO
Liquid Phase Processing [Chemistry]	LPP
Liquid Pressure Filter	LPF
Liquid Processing Unit	LPU
Liquid Propane Gas	LPG
Liquid Propane-Gas Shutoff [NFPA pre-fire planning symbol] (NFPA)	LPG
Liquid Propellant	LP
Liquid Propellant Analysis	LPA
Liquid Propellant Applied Research Motor	LPARM
Liquid Propellant Gas Generator	LPGG
Liquid Propellant Gun (NASA)	LPG
Liquid Propellant Information Agency [Johns Hopkins Univeristy]	LPIA
Liquid Propellant Intercontinental Ballistic Missile [Military] (IAA)	LPICBM
Liquid Propellant Rocket [Air Force]	LPR
Liquid Propellant Rocket Engine [Air Force]	LPRE
Liquid RADWASTE System (NRCH)	LRS
Liquid Reaction Molding	LRM
Liquid Redox Sulfur Recovery [Processes for removing hydrogen sulfide from gases]	LRSR
Liquid Rheostat	LRh
Liquid Rocket	LR
Liquid Rocket Engine	LRE
Liquid Rocket Fuel (MCD)	LRF
Liquid Rocket Motor (KSC)	LRM
Liquid Rocket Propulsion Laboratory [Army] (IEEE)	LRPL
Liquid Sample Kit	LSK
Liquid Scintillation [Chemical analysis]	LS
Liquid Scintillation Analyzer [Chemistry]	LSA
Liquid Scintillation Cocktail [Analytical chemistry]	LSC
Liquid Scintillation Counter [or Counting]	LSC
Liquid Scintillation Spectrometer	LSS
Liquid Scintillator Neutrino Detector [Physics]	LSND
Liquid Secondary Injection Thrust Vector Control (PDAA)	LSITV
Liquid Secondary Ion Mass Spectrometry	LSIMS
Liquid Sensor (AAG)	LS
Liquid Slip Ring	LSR
Liquid Smoke Condensate	LSC
Liquid Solid Chromatography	LSC
Liquid Steady State (PDAA)	LIQSS
Liquid Storage Tank (AAG)	LST
Liquid Strand Burning Rate (MCD)	LSBR
Liquid Test Rig [Apollo] [NASA]	LTR
Liquid Thermal Flowmeter	LTF
Liquid Toned [Copier] [Reprography]	LT
Liquid Toner Transfer [Typography] (DGA)	LTT
Liquid Transient (PDAA)	LIQT
Liquid Upper Stage (NASA)	LUS
Liquid Vapor Equilibrium	LVE
Liquid Vapor Interface	LVI
Liquid, Vee, Diesel-Cycle, Supercharged	LVDS
Liquid Volume Charge Density [Automotive fuel systems]	LVCD
Liquid Waste and Sludge Transporter Council (EA)	LWSTC
Liquid Waste Management System [Nuclear energy] (NRCH)	LWMS
Liquid Waste Monitor [Nuclear energy] (IEEE)	LWM
Liquid Waste Processing [Nuclear energy] (NRCH)	LWP
Liquid Waste Processing System [Nuclear energy] (NRCH)	LWPS
Liquid Waste Release [Nuclear energy] (IEEE)	LWR
Liquid Waste Test Tank [Nuclear energy] (IEEE)	LWTT
Liquid Waste Treatment (MCD)	LWT
Liquid Water Content	LWC
Liquid Whole Egg	LWE
Liquidate (ROG)	LIQDTE
Liquidating Dividend [Investment term] (DFIT)	C
Liquidation (MCD)	LIQ
Liquidation	LIQUON
Liquidator (ROG)	LIQOR
Liquidator	LQDR
Liquid-Cooled Garment [Spacesuit]	LCG
Liquid-Cooled Naturally Aspirated Diesel Engine	LCNADE
Liquid-Cooled Spark Ignition Engine	LCSIE
Liquid-Cooled Turbocharged Diesel Engine	LCTCDE
Liquid-Cooled Undergarment (MCD)	LCUG
Liquid-Crystal Displays [Computer science]	LCDS
Liquid-Crystal Light Valve (IEEE)	LCLV
Liquid-Crystal Polymer [Organic chemistry]	LCP
Liquid-Cushion Electroplating Cell [Steel production]	LCC
Liquide Cephalo-Rachidien [Cerebrospinal Fluid] [French]	LCR
Liquid-Fueled Ramjet [Navy] (MCD)	LFRJ
Liquid-Fueled Ramjet [Navy] (MCD)	LIFRAM
Liquid-Fueled Ramjet Engine Demonstration [Navy] (MCD)	LFRED
Liquid-Fuelled Thermo-Electric Generator (PDAA)	LFTEG
Liquid-Holding Recovery [of bacterial cells]	LHR
Liquid-Ion Exchange Chromatography (PDAA)	LXC
Liquidity [Business term]	L
Liquidity Preference [Economics]	LP
Liquidity-Money Supply [Economics]	LM
Liquid-Like Intermediate Transistory	LLIT
Liquid-Liquid Chromatography	LLC
Liquid-Liquid Equilibria [Physical chemistry]	LLE
Liquid-Liquid Extraction	LLE
Liquido Cefaloraquideo [Cerebrospinal Fluid] [Spanish]	LCR

Liquidometer ... LQMETR
Liquid-Phase Sintering (MCD) ... LPS
Liquid-Protein Diet ... LPD
Liquids from Coal ... LFC
Liquids Solids Contact ... LSC
Liquid-Solid Extraction [*Chemistry*] ... LSE
Liquid-State Submerged Fermentation [*Biochemistry*] ... LSF
Liquidus [*Liquid*] [*Pharmacy*] (ROG) ... LIQUID
Liquid-Vapor Bubble [*Chemical engineering*] ... LVB
Liquid-Water Path [*Meteorology*] ... LWP
Liquid-Yield Option Note [*Merrill Lynch & Co.*] [*Finance*] ... LYON
Liquified Gaseous Fuels Spill Test Facility [*Department of Energy*] ... LGFSTF
Liquified Petroleum Gas Industry Technical Committee ... LPGITC
Liquified Petroleum Gas Industry Technical Committee (MCD) ... LPGTC
Liquified Petroleum Gas Report [*American Petroleum Institute*] [*Database*] ... LPGS
Liquitex (VRA) ... lqtx
Liquor (DAVI) ... L
Liquor ... LIQ
Liquor ... LQR
Liquor ... LQR
Liquor Carbonis Detergens [*Coal tar solution*] [*Medicine*] ... LCD
Liquor Control Board [*Canada*] ... LCB
Liquor Control Commission ... LCC
Liquor Control Law Service (Commerce Clearing House) [*A publication*] (DLA) ... Liquor Cont L Serv (CCH)
Liquor Law ... LL
Liquor Licensing Board [*Australian Capital Territory*] ... LLB
Liquor Merchants' Association [*Australia*] ... LMA
Liquor Merchants' Association of Australia ... LMAA
Liquor Merchants Association of Queensland [*Australia*] ... LMAQ
Liquor Stores Association of New South Wales [*Australia*] ... LSANSW
Liquor Stores' Association of Victoria [*Aerospace*] ... LSAV
Liquor Stores' Association of Western Australia ... LSAWA
Lira [*Uganda*] [*ICAO location identifier*] (ICLI) ... HULI
Lira [*Monetary unit*] [*Italy*] ... L
Lira [*Monetary unit*] [*Italy*] ... lir
[*Maltese*] **Lira** [*Monetary Unit*] [*Malta*] (BARN) ... Lm
Lira Nuova [*Monetary unit*] [*Italy*] (ROG) ... LN
Lira Toscana [*Tuscany Pound*] [*Monetary unit*] [*Italian*] (ROG) ... LT
Lira Turca [*Turkish Pound*] [*Monetary unit*] [*Italian*] (ROG) ... LT
Lirangu [*Sudan*] [*ICAO location identifier*] (ICLI) ... HSLR
Lire Italiane [*Italian Lire*] [*Monetary unit*] ... Lit
Lisa Madonia Memorial Fund [*An association*] (EA) ... LMMF
Lisala [*Zaire*] [*ICAO location identifier*] (ICLI) ... FZGA
Lisala [*Zaire*] [*Airport symbol*] (OAG) ... LIQ
Lisboa [*Portugal ICAO location identifier*] (ICLI) ... LPAM
Lisboa [*Portugal ICAO location identifier*] (ICLI) ... LPMG
Lisboa [*Portugal ICAO location identifier*] (ICLI) ... LPPC
Lisboa [*Portugal ICAO location identifier*] (ICLI) ... LPPT
Lisbon [*Portugal*] [*Seismograph station code, US Geological Survey*] (SEIS) ... LIS
Lisbon [*Portugal*] [*Airport symbol*] (OAG) ... LIS
Lisbon, ND [*AM radio station call letters*] ... KQLX
Lisbon, ND [*FM radio station call letters*] ... KQLX-FM
Lisbon, NH [*FM radio station call letters*] ... WLTN
Lishan [*China*] [*ICAO location identifier*] (ICLI) ... RCLS
Liskeard [*Municipal borough in England*] ... LISK
Lisle Fellowship (EA) ... LF
Lisle Library District, Lisle, IL [*Library symbol Library of Congress*] (LCLS) ... IL
Lismore [*Australia Airport symbol*] (OAG) ... LSY
LISP Extended Algebraic Facility ... LEAF
Lissamine Rhodamine B [*Fluorescent dye*] ... LRB
List (MSA) ... L
List and Index Society [*British*] (NITA) ... LIS
List Assembly Programming [*Computer science*] ... LAP
List Down ... LD
List Execution Condition (IAA) ... LEC
List Handling Facility ... LHF
List Management System ... LMS
List of Applicable Material (MCD) ... LOAM
List of Applicable Publications [*Air Force*] ... LOAP
List of Applicable Technical Orders [*Military*] (AFIT) ... LATO
List of Assessed Contractors [*Military*] (RDA) ... LAC
List of Assessed Spares (MCD) ... LOAS
List of Cancelled Items ... LOCI
List of Chosen Descriptors (PDAA) ... LCD
List of Command Signals (MCD) ... LCS
List of Common Abbreviations in Training and Education (AIE) ... LOCATE
List of Deleted Items (NG) ... LODI
List of Drawings [*USN*] (MCD) ... LD
List of Drawings ... LOD
List of Effective Cards (NVT) ... LOEC
List of Effective Pages (NVT) ... LEP
List of Effective Pages (NVT) ... LOEP
List of Instruments and Controls (DNAB) ... LIC
List of Interchangeable Parts and Assemblies ... LIPA
List of Items (AABC) ... LOI
List of Items Requiring Special Handling ... LIRSH
List of Journals Indexed (DMAA) ... LJI
List of Material [*DoD*] ... LM
List of Materials (AAG) ... L/M
List of Materials (CET) ... LOM
List of Measurement Points (NASA) ... LMP
List of Modifications (AFM) ... LOM
List of Physical Dimensions (NASA) ... LPDM
List of Publications [*National Institute of Standards and Technology*] ... LP
List of Required Documents (NVT) ... LORD
List of Sections Affected (AAGC) ... LSA
List of Selected File Numbers (AABC) ... LSFN
List of Specifications (NATG) ... LS
List of Specifications and Standards (MSA) ... LSST
List of Standard/Modified Hand Tools (MCD) ... LSMHT
List of Successful Bidders [*DoD*] ... LSB
List on Tape (IAA) ... LOT
List per Inch (IAA) ... LPI
List Price (BARN) ... LP
List Processing [*Programming language*] [*Facetious translation: "Lots of Insane, Stupid Parentheses"*] [*Computer science*] ... LISP
List Processing Language [*Computer science*] (IEEE) ... LPL
List Processor [*Standard programming language*] [*1958*] [*Computer science*] ... LISP
List Processor [*Standard programming language*] [*1958*] [*Computer science*] (BUR) ... LP
List Program Generator (IAA) ... LPG
List Test Resister (PDAA) ... LTR
List Total [*Banking*] ... LS
List Up ... LU
List Updated Sort and Total (PDAA) ... LUST
Lista [*Norway ICAO location identifier*] (ICLI) ... ENLI
Liste de Noms Geographiques [*A publication*] (BJA) ... LNG
Listed [*Stock exchange term*] ... L
Listed Address [*Telecommunications*] (TEL) ... LA
Listed Company Advisory Committee [*of NYSE*] ... LCAC
Listed Directory Number [*Bell System*] ... LDN
Listed Property Trust ... LPT
Listed Securities ... LS
Listen (IAA) ... LTN
Listen before Talk (IAA) ... LBT
Listen Before Transmission Multiple Access (PDAA) ... LBTMA
Listen for Pleasure [*Audio books*] ... LFP
Listen to the Band (EA) ... LTTB
Listen While Talk (IAA) ... LWT
Listen While Transmission Multiple Access [*Telecommunications*] (PDAA) ... LWTMA
Listener Active State (IAA) ... LACS
Listener Addressed State (IAA) ... LADS
Listener Function (IAA) ... LF
Listener Idle State (IAA) ... LIDS
Listening Comprehension Group Test ... LCGT
Listening Post [*In symbol only*] ... L
Listening Post ... LP
Listening Room, York University, Toronto, Ontario [*Library symbol National Library of Canada*] (NLC) ... OTYLR
Lister Hill National Center for Biomedical Communications [*National Library of Medicine*] [*Information service or system*] (IID) ... LHNCBC
Lister Hill System [*Search system*] ... ELHILL
Listeria [*A bacteria*] (DAVI) ... L
Listeria Monocytogenes [*Microorganism*] ... LM
Listing Agent [*Classified advertising*] (ADA) ... LA
Listing Exchange ... LEX
Listing of a Program in a File [*Computer science*] ... LST
Listing of Oil and Gas Opportunities [*Online Resource Exchange, Inc.*] [*Database*] ... PSI-LOGO
Listing Requirement [*Investment term*] ... LR
Listing Site Inspection [*Environmental science*] (FFDE) ... LSI
Listing-Time Limit (MSA) ... LTL
Listowel Public Library, Listowel, ON, Canada [*Library symbol*] [*Library of Congress*] (LCLS) ... CaOLIS
Listowel Public Library, Ontario [*Library symbol National Library of Canada*] (NLC) ... OLIS
Lists of Parts (NATG) ... LP
ListServ Simple Mail Transport Protocol [*L-Soft International, Inc.*] [*Computer science*] ... LSMTP
Lisuride Hydrogen Maleate [*Pharmacology*] ... LHM
Lit ... L
Litag K.G. [*Austria*] [*FAA designator*] (FAAC) ... LNZ
Litany (ROG) ... LIT
Litas [*Monetary unit*] [*Lithuania*] ... L
Litchfield & Madison [*AAR code*] ... LM
Litchfield Carnegie Public Library, Litchfield, IL [*Library symbol Library of Congress*] (LCLS) ... ILit
Litchfield Community Unit, School District 12, Litchfield, IL [*Library symbol Library of Congress*] (LCLS) ... ILitSD
Litchfield, CT [*FM radio station call letters*] ... WZBG
Litchfield District Library, Litchfield, MI [*Library symbol Library of Congress*] (LCLS) ... MiLit
Litchfield Financial [*NASDAQ symbol*] (TTSB) ... LTCH
Litchfield Financial Corp. [*Associated Press*] (SAG) ... LitchFin
Litchfield Financial Corp. [*NASDAQ symbol*] (SAG) ... LTCH
Litchfield Historical Society, Litchfield, CT [*Library symbol Library of Congress*] (LCLS) ... CtLHi
Litchfield, IL [*Location identifier FAA*] (FAAL) ... LTD
Litchfield, IL [*AM radio station call letters*] ... WSMI
Litchfield, IL [*FM radio station call letters*] ... WSMI-FM
Litchfield Institute (EA) ... LI
Litchfield, MI [*Location identifier FAA*] (FAAL) ... LFD
Litchfield, MN [*AM radio station call letters*] ... KLFD
Litchfield Park Public Library, Litchfield Park, AZ [*Library symbol Library of Congress*] (LCLS) ... AzLp

Litchfield Public Library, Litchfield, MN [*Library symbol*] [*Library of Congress*] (LCLS) ... MnLit
Litchfield Senior High School, Litchfield, MN [*Library symbol*] [*Library of Congress*] (LCLS) ... MnLitSH
Litcom Library, Melville, NY [*Library symbol Library of Congress*] (LCLS) .... NMelL
Liter [*Also, l*] [*Metric measure of volume*] ... L
Liter ... l
Liter (IDOE) ... l
Liter [*Metric measure of volume*] (MCD) ... LI
Liter [*Metric measure of volume*] ... LIT
Liter [*Metric measure of volume*] ... LT
Liter (ECII) ... l
Liter per Meter Day ... L/(M D)
Litera Dominicalis [*Sunday Letter*] ... LD
Litera Scripta Manet [*The Written Word Remains*] [*Latin*] (ADA) ... LSM
Literacy ... LIT
Literacy and Evangelism International (EA) ... LEI
Literacy and Learning Program ... LLP
Literacy International ... LITINT
Literacy Volunteers of America (EA) ... LVA
Literal ... LIT
Literarische Keilschrifttexte aus Assur [*A publication*] (BJA) ... LKA
Literarische Keilschrifttexte aus Uruk [*A publication*] (BJA) ... LKU
Literary ... LIT
Literary and Historical Society of Quebec [*Societe Litteraire et Historique de Quebec*] Quebec [*Library symbol National Library of Canada*] (NLC) ... QQLH
Literary and Historical Society of Quebec, Quebec, PQ, Canada [*Library symbol of Congress*] (LCLS) ... CaQQLH
Literary, Artistic, Political, or Scientific [*Value*] [*In obscenity law, a criterion established by the 1973 case of Miller Versus California*] ... LAPS
[*A*] Literary Atlas and Gazetteer of the British Isles [*A publication*] ... LAG
Literary Criticism (WGA) ... Lit Crit
Literary Criticism [*A publication*] ... LCI
Literary Criticism Index [*A publication*] ... LG
[*The*] Literary Guild ... LITIR
Literary Information and Retrieval [*Computer science*] ... LITIR
Literary Information Bases for Research and Instruction [*American Philological Association*] [*An association*] (NITA) ... LIBRI
Literary Landmarks Association (EA) ... LLA
Literary Lives [*A publication*] ... LL
Literary Magazine Review [*A publication*] (BRI) ... LMR
Literary Market Place [*A publication*] ... LMP
Literary Society Foundation (EA) ... LSF
Literary Translators Association of Canada (EAIO) ... LTAC
Literate ... L
Literate in Arts ... LA
Literaturbericht (BJA) ... Lber
Literaturdienst Medizin und Umwelt [*Literature Service in Medicine and Environment*] [*Austrian National Institute for Public Health*] [*Information service or system*] (IID) ... LID
Literaturdokumentation zur Arbeitsmarkt- und Berufsforschung [*Deutsche Bundesanstalt fuer Arbeit*] [*Germany Information service or system*] (CRD) ... LitDokAB
Literature ... LIT
Literature ... lit
Literature (WDMC) ... lit
Literature and Religion of Israel [*A publication*] ... LRI
Literature Attached to Charts [*Nursing program*] ... LATCH
Literature Criticism from 1400 to 1800 [*A publication*] ... LC
Literature in North Queensland [*A publication*] ... LINQ
Literature in Nursing Kardex ... LINK
Literature Information and Retrieval [*Database on Victorian studies literature*] [*University of Alberta*] [*Canada*] (NITA) ... LITIR
Literature Intelligence (MCD) ... LITINT
Literature Management System ... LMS
Literature on Modern Art ... LOMA
Literature Primers [*A publication*] ... LPA
Literature Retrieval System [*Computer science*] ... LIRES
Literature Retrieval System - Multiple Searching, Complete Text [*Computer science*] ... LIRES-MC
Literature Search ... LS
Literatures of the World [*A publication*] ... LW
Literaturinformationssystem [*Literature Information System*] [*North Rhine-Westphalia Institute for Air Pollution Control*] [*Information service or system*] (IID) ... LISDOK
Literaturnachweise [*Literature Compilations Database*] [*Fraunhofer Society*] (IID) ... LINA
Liters per Day (KSC) ... LPD
Liters per Hour (KSC) ... LPH
Liters per Minute ... L/M
Liters per Minute ... L/MIN
Liters per Minute (MCD) ... LPM
Liters per Second [*SI symbol*] ... l/s
Liters per Second [*Respiration*] [*Medicine*] (DAVI) ... l/sec
Liters per Second (KSC) ... LPS
Liters per Second per Person (ECON) ... lsp
Liters per Square Meter Day ... L/(M² D)
Litha-Alumina-Silicate [*Inorganic chemistry*] ... LAS
Lithiated Vanadium Oxide [*Battery technology*] ... LVO
Lithium [*Chemical element*] (ROG) ... L
Lithium [*Chemical element*] ... Li
Lithium [*Pharmacy*] (DAVI) ... LITH
Lithium Aluminum Deuteride [*Inorganic chemistry*] ... LAD
Lithium Aluminum Hydride [*Inorganic chemistry*] ... LAH
Lithium Aluminum Pentahydride (MCD) ... LAPH
Lithium Aluminum Tri-tert-Butoxyhydride [*Organic chemistry*] ... LATB
Lithium Boron Oxide [*Inorganic chemistry*] ... LBO
Lithium Bromide (DNAB) ... LB

Lithium Bromide (DNAB) ... LITH BRO
Lithium Carbonate [*Pharmacology*] (DAVI) ... $LiCO_3$
Lithium/Chromium-Oxide [*Type of battery*] ... LiCrOx
Lithium Cooled Reactor Experiment ... LCRE
Lithium Corp. of America, Ellestad Research Library, Bessemer City, NC [*Library symbol Library of Congress*] (LCLS) ... NcBesL
Lithium Diisopropylamide [*Organic chemistry*] ... LDA
Lithium Diodosalicylate [*Organic chemistry*] ... LIS
Lithium Excretion Test [*Clinical chemistry*] ... LET
Lithium Hydroxide (NASA) ... LiOH
Lithium Ion Drift Semiconductor ... LIDS
Lithium Ion Storage Battery (PCM) ... LISB
Lithium Isopropylcyclohexylamide [*Organic chemistry*] ... LICA
Lithium Metal Sulfide ... LiMS
Lithium Niobate (PDAA) ... LNB
Lithium Nitrate Ammoniate [*Inorganic chemistry*] ... LNA
Lithium Nuclear Microprobe ... LNM
Lithium Organic Battery ... LiO
Lithium Perchlorate Ammoniate [*Inorganic chemistry*] ... LPA
Lithium Polymer Battery ... LPB
Lithium Thallium Tartrate [*Inorganic chemistry*] ... LTT
Lithocholate [*Biochemistry*] ... LC
Lithocholic Acid [*Biochemistry*] ... LCA
Lithogenic Grain Size [*An indicator of wind intensity*] ... LGS
Lithograph [*or Lithography*] (WDAA) ... LI
Lithograph [*or Lithography*] (ROG) ... LITH
Lithograph (WDMC) ... lith
Lithograph (WDMC) ... litho
Lithograph ... LITHO
Lithograph ... LITHO
Lithograph (AABC) ... litho
Lithograph (VRA) ... litho
Lithograph (WDMC) ... lithog
Lithographed (ROG) ... LITHD
Lithographer [*Navy rating*] ... LI
Lithographer ... LITHOR
Lithographer [*MARC relator code*] [*Library of Congress*] (LCCP) ... ltg
Lithographer, First Class [*Navy rating*] ... LI1
Lithographer, Second Class [*Navy rating*] ... LI2
Lithographer, Third Class [*Navy rating*] ... LI3
Lithographers and Photoengravers International Union [*Later, Graphic Arts International Union*] ... LPIU
Lithographers and Printers National Association [*Later, PIA*] (EA) ... LPNA
Lithographers National Association ... LNA
Lithographic (WDMC) ... lith
Lithographic (WDMC) ... litho
Lithographic ... LITHOC
Lithographic (WDMC) ... lithog
Lithographic Engravers and Plate Makers Association (EA) ... LEPMA
Lithographic Galvanoforming Abformung [*Materials science*] ... LIGA
Lithographic Institute of Australia ... LIA
Lithographic Preparatory Services Association [*Later, GPA*] (EA) ... LPSA
Lithographic Technical Foundation [*Later, GATF*] (MSA) ... LTF
Lithographing ... LITHOG
Lithographing (WDMC) ... lith
Lithography (WDMC) ... litho
Lithography (WDMC) ... lithog
Lithography ... LITHOG
Lithography ... LITHOY
Lithology (BARN) ... lithol
Lithophane Collectors Club (EA) ... LiCC
Lithosphere-Asthenosphere Boundary [*Geology*] ... LAB
Lithospheric Seismic Profile in Britain (PDAA) ... LISPB
Lithotomy [*Medicine*] ... LITHOT
Lithotripsy [*Medicine*] (DAVI) ... litho
Lithuania (ROG) ... LITH
Lithuania (VRA) ... Lith
Lithuanian [*MARC language code Library of Congress*] (LCCP) ... lit
Lithuanian [*Language, etc.*] ... LITH
Lithuanian ... LITHUAN
Lithuanian Airlines [*ICAO designator*] (FAAC) ... LIL
Lithuanian Alliance of America (EA) ... LAA
Lithuanian American Community (EA) ... LAC
Lithuanian American National Alliance (EA) ... LANA
Lithuanian American Roman Catholic Federation (EA) ... LARCF
Lithuanian Apostolate for Lithuanian Catholics [*Diocesan abbreviation*] (TOCD) ... LIT
Lithuanian Boy Scouts (EA) ... LBS
Lithuanian Catholic Academy of Sciences (EA) ... LCAS
Lithuanian Catholic Alliance (EA) ... LCA
Lithuanian Catholic Federation Ateitis (EA) ... LCFA
Lithuanian Catholic Press Society (EA) ... LCPS
Lithuanian Catholic Religious Aid (EA) ... LCRA
Lithuanian Catholic Students' Association "Ateitis" (EA) ... SAS
Lithuanian Catholic Women (EA) ... LCW
Lithuanian Catholic Youth Association Ateitis (EA) ... MAS
Lithuanian Chamber of Commerce of America (EA) ... LCCA
Lithuanian Cultural Society [*Defunct*] (EA) ... LCS
Lithuanian Information Center [*Defunct*] (EA) ... LIC
Lithuanian National Foundation (EA) ... LNF
Lithuanian National League of America (EA) ... LNLA
Lithuanian Numismatic Association (EA) ... LNA
Lithuanian Philatelic Society of New York (EA) ... LPSNY
Lithuanian Regeneration Association (EA) ... LRA
Lithuanian Roman Catholic Alliance of America [*Later, LCA*] (EA) ... LRCA
Lithuanian Roman Catholic Federation of America (EA) ... LRCFA

Lithuanian Roman Catholic Priests' League of America (EA) .... LRCPLA
Lithuanian Scouts Association (EA) .... LSA
Lithuanian Soviet Socialist Republic [*MARC geographic area code Library of Congress*] (LCCP) .... e-ur-li
Lithuanian Soviet Socialist Republic [*MARC country of publication code Library of Congress*] (LCCP) .... lir
Lithuanian Soviet Socialist Republic .... LithSSR
Lithuanian State Privatisation Agency .... LSPA
Lithuanian Student Scout Association [*Later, Lithuanian Scouts Association College Division*] (EA) .... LSSA
Lithuanian Students Association (EA) .... LSA
Lithuanian Veterans Association Ramove (EA) .... LVAR
Lithuanian World Community (EA) .... LWC
Lithuanian World Youth Association Communications Center [*Defunct*] (EA) .... LWYACC
Lithuanian-American Catholic Services [*Defunct*] (EA) .... LACS
Lithuanian-American Community of the USA [*Later, LAC*] (EA) .... LACUSA
Lithuanian-American Information Center [*Defunct*] .... LAIC
Litigation [*A publication*] (DLA) .... Litig
Litigation (ROG) .... LITIGON
Litre (ROG) LL
Littelfuse, Inc. [*NASDAQ symbol*] (SAG) .... LFUS
Littelfuse, Inc. [*Associated Press*] (SAG) .... Litelfuse
Littelfuse, Inc. [*Associated Press*] (SAG) .... Litfse
Littelfuse Inc. Wrrt'A' [*NASDAQ symbol*] (TTSB) .... LFUSW
Littell [*Kentucky*] [*A publication*] (DLA) .... Litt (KY)
Littell and Swigert's Digest of Statute Law [*Kentucky*] [*A publication*] (DLA) .... Litt & S St Law
Littell's Kentucky Reports [*A publication*] (DLA) .... Lit
Littell's Kentucky Reports [*A publication*] (DLA) .... Littell
Littell's Kentucky Supreme Court Reports [*1822-24*] [*A publication*] (DLA) ..... Litt
Littell's Select Kentucky Cases [*A publication*] (DLA) .... Lit Sel Ca
Littell's Select Kentucky Cases [*A publication*] (DLA) .... Litt Sel Cas
Littell's Statute Law [*Kentucky*] [*A publication*] (DLA) .... Litt Comp Laws
Litter (WDAA) .... LIT
Litter Bearer (AABC) .... LB
Litter Hook .... LH
Litter Patient .... LP
Litterae [*Letters*] [*Latin*] (ADA) .... LIT
Litterae Humaniores [*Classic literature*] [*Latin*] (ROG) .... LIT HUM
Litterarum Baccalaureus [*Bachelor of Letters or Literature*] [*Latin*] .... LB
Litterarum Baccalaureus [*Bachelor of Letters or Literature*] [*Latin*] .... Lit B
Litterarum Baccalaureus [*Bachelor of Letters or Literature*] [*Latin*] .... Litt B
Litterarum Doctor [*Doctor of Letters or Literature*] [*Latin*] (ROG) .... LD
Litterarum Doctor [*Doctor of Letters or Literature*] [*Latin*] .... Lit D
Litterarum Doctor [*Doctor of Letters or Literature*] [*Latin*] .... Litt D
Litterarum Humaniorum Doctor [*Doctor of Humane Letters*] [*Latin*] .... LHD
Litterateur [*French*] (ROG) .... LITT
Little L
Little (ABBR) LIL
Little .... Lit
Little .... LTL
Little .... LTL
Little America [*Antarctica*] [*Seismograph station code, US Geological Survey Closed*] (SEIS) .... LAA
Little Athletics Association [*Australia*] .... LAA
Little Bear Resources [*Vancouver Stock Exchange symbol*] .... LBR
Little Big Horn Associates (EA) .... LBHA
Little Big Horn College, Crow Agency, MT [*Library symbol*] [*Library of Congress*] (LCLS) .... MtCaC
[*The*] **Little Black Book** [*Cygnet Technologies, Inc.*] [*Database software*] .... LBB
Little Black Devils [*Nickname given to the 90th Battalion of the Winnipeg Rifles during the Northwest Rebellion in 1885*] .... LBD
Little Black Dress [*Women's fashions*] .... LBD
Little Books on Art [*A publication*] .... LBA
Little Books on Religion [*A publication*] .... LBR
Little Brothers of Saint Francis (TOCD) .... ibsf
Little Brothers of Saint Francis (TOCD) .... LBSF
Little Brothers of the Good Shepherd (TOCD) .... BGS
Little Brothers of the Good Shepherd (TOCD) .... bgs
Little Brown Job [*Unidentified bird, to a bird watcher*] .... LBJ
Little Buffalo School, Cadotte Lake, Alberta [*Library symbol National Library of Canada*] (BIB) .... ACLLS
Little Butte [*Montana*] [*Seismograph station code, US Geological Survey Closed*] (SEIS) .... LBM
Little Carter Cay [*NASA*] (KSC) LCC
Little Cayman [*West Indies*] [*Airport symbol*] (OAG) .... LYB
Little Cayman/Boddenfield [*Cayman Islands*] [*ICAO location identifier*] (ICLI) .... MWCL
Little Change (FAAC) .... LTLCG
Little Change in Temperature [*NWS*] (FAAC) .... LCTMP
Little City Foundation (EA) .... LCF
Little Company of Mary, Nursing Sisters [*Roman Catholic religious order*] .... LCM
Little Computer Person [*Activision computer game*] .... LCP
Little Current Public Library, Ontario [*Library symbol National Library of Canada*] (NLC) .... OLICU
Little Daughters of St. Joseph [*Roman Catholic religious order*] .... LDSJ
Little Diomede Island, AK [*Location identifier FAA*] (FAAL) .... LDD
Little Eagle, SD [*FM radio station call letters*] (RBYB) .... KLND
Little Falls Bancorp [*NASDAQ symbol*] (TTSB) .... LFBI
Little Falls Community High School, Little Falls, MN [*Library symbol*] [*Library of Congress*] (LCLS) .... MnLfH
Little Falls Community Middle School, Little Falls, MN [*Library symbol*] [*Library of Congress*] (LCLS) .... MnLfM
Little Falls Free Public Library, Little Falls, NJ [*Library symbol Library of Congress*] (LCLS) .... NjLf
Little Falls, MN [*FM radio station call letters*] .... KFML
Little Falls, MN [*AM radio station call letters*] .... KLTF
Little Falls, MN [*Location identifier FAA*] (FAAL) LXL
Little Falls, MN [*FM radio station call letters*] .... WYRQ
Little Falls, MN [*Location identifier FAA*] (FAAL) .... XCR
Little Falls, NY [*AM radio station call letters*] .... WLFH
Little Falls, NY [*FM radio station call letters*] .... WOWB
Little Falls Public Library, Little Falls, NY [*Library symbol Library of Congress*] (LCLS) .... NLf
Little Flower Mission League (EA) .... LFML
Little Franciscan Sisters of Mary [*Roman Catholic religious order*] .... PFM
Little Grand Rapids [*Canada*] [*Airport symbol*] (OAG) .... ZGR
Little Green Men [*British term for space signals*] .... LGM
Little Green Mountain [*Idaho*] [*Seismograph station code, US Geological Survey Closed*] (SEIS) .... LGM
Little Guides [*A publication*] .... LG
Little Ice Age [*Geoscience*] .... LIA
Little Italy Restoration Association .... LIRA
Little Joe [*Early developmental spacecraft*] [*NASA*] .... LJ
Little Joe Launch Vehicle [*NASA*] .... LJLV
Little John [*Rocket*] [*Military*] (AABC) .... LJ
Little John Launcher [*Military*] .... LJL
Little John Rocket [*Military*] .... LJR
Little Lake Resources Ltd. [*Vancouver Stock Exchange symbol*] .... LLK
Little League [*Baseball*] LL
Little League Baseball (EA) .... LLB
Little League Foundation (EA) .... LLF
Little Library [*A publication*] .... LLA
Little Maria Mountains [*California*] [*Seismograph station code, US Geological Survey*] (SEIS) .... LTM
Little Mission for the Deaf-Mute [*See also PMS*] [*Rome, Italy*] (EAIO) .... LMDM
Little Missionary Sisters of Charity (TOCD) .... LMSC
Little Missionary Sisters of Charity [*Roman Catholic religious order*] .... PMC
Little Mountain [*Utah*] [*Seismograph station code, US Geological Survey*] (SEIS) .... LTU
Little Nash Rambler Club (EA) .... LNRC
Little Old Ladies in Tennis Shoes [*Facetious reference to minor league baseball*] .... LOLITS
Little Old Lady [*Slang*] .... LOL
Little Old Man [*Slang*] (DAVI) .... LOM
Little Oxford Dictionary [*A publication*] .... LOD
Little People of America (EA) .... LPA
Little Rabbit Valley [*California*] [*Seismograph station code, US Geological Survey*] (SEIS) .... LRV
Little Raleigh [*North Carolina*] [*Seismograph station code, US Geological Survey*] (SEIS) .... RNC
Little Red Air Service [*Canada ICAO designator*] (FAAC) .... LRA
Little Rock [*Arkansas*] [*Airport symbol*] (OAG) .... LIT
Little Rock [*Diocesan abbreviation*] [*Arkansas*] (TOCD) .... LR
Little Rock [*Arkansas*] [*Seismograph station code, US Geological Survey Closed*] (SEIS) .... LRA
Little Rock/Adams Field [*Arkansas*] [*ICAO location identifier*] (ICLI) .... KLIT
Little Rock, AR [*AM radio station call letters*] .... KAAY
Little Rock, AR [*FM radio station call letters*] .... KABF
Little Rock, AR [*Television station call letters*] .... KARK
Little Rock, AR [*AM radio station call letters*] .... KARN
Little Rock, AR [*Television station call letters*] .... KATV
Little Rock, AR [*Television station call letters*] .... KETS
Little Rock, AR [*AM radio station call letters*] (RBYB) .... KEZQ
Little Rock, AR [*AM radio station call letters*] .... KITA
Little Rock, AR [*AM radio station call letters*] .... KJBN
Little Rock, AR [*FM radio station call letters*] .... KKPT
Little Rock, AR [*FM radio station call letters*] .... KLRE
Little Rock, AR [*Television station call letters*] .... KLRT
Little Rock, AR [*FM radio station call letters*] .... KSSN
Little Rock, AR [*AM radio station call letters*] (RBYB) .... KSYG
Little Rock, AR [*FM radio station call letters*] (RBYB) .... KSYG-FM
Little Rock, AR [*Television station call letters*] .... KTHV
Little Rock, AR [*FM radio station call letters*] .... KUAR
Little Rock, AR [*AM radio station call letters*] .... KURB
Little Rock, AR [*FM radio station call letters*] .... KURB-FM
Little Rock, AR [*Television station call letters*] .... KVUT
Little Rock, AR [*FM radio station call letters*] .... KYFX
Little Rock, AR [*Location identifier FAA*] (FAAL) .... TYV
Little Rock Cotton Exchange [*Defunct*] .... LRCE
Little Rock Port Railroad [*AAR code*] .... LRPA
Little Rock Public Library, Little Rock, AR [*Library symbol Library of Congress*] (LCLS) .... ArL
Little Rock University [*Merged with University of Arkansas*] .... LRU
Little S Positive [*Laboratory science*] (DAVI) .... SLIT
Little Servant Sisters of the Immaculate Conception (TOCD) .... LSIC
Little Sisters of Carmel .... LSC
Little Sisters of Jesus [*See also PSJ*] [*Italy*] (EAIO) .... LSJ
Little Sisters of Jesus and Mary (TOCD) .... LSJM
Little Sisters of the Assumption [*See also PSA*] [*France*] (EAIO) .... LSA
Little Sisters of the Gospel (France) (TOCD) .... LSG
Little Sisters of the Poor [*Roman Catholic religious order*] .... LSP
Little Sitkin Island [*Alaska*] [*Seismograph station code, US Geological Survey Closed*] (SEIS) .... LSI
Little Skull Mountain [*Nevada*] [*Seismograph station code, US Geological Survey*] (SEIS) .... LSM
Little Stock (MHDW) .... LS
Little Switzerland [*NASDAQ symbol*] (TTSB) .... LSVI

Little Switzerland, Inc. [*NASDAQ symbol*] (SAG) .... LSVI
Little Switzerland, Inc. [*Associated Press*] (SAG) .... LtSwtz
Little Theatre Guild [*British*] (DBA) .... LTG
Little Way Circle [*An association*] (EA) .... LWC
Little Whale Cay, Berry Island [*Bahamas*] [*ICAO location identifier*] (ICLI) ... MYBX
Little Wood River District Library, Carey, ID [*Library symbol*] [*Library of Congress*] (LCLS) .... IdCar
Little Workers of the Sacred Heart (TOCD) .... POSC
Littlefield, Adams [*AMEX symbol*] (TTSB) .... LFA
Littlefield, Adams & Co. [*AMEX symbol*] (SPSG) .... LFA
Littlefield, [*Adams*] & Co. [*Associated Press*] (SAG) .... LitfldAd
Littlefield, TX [*AM radio station call letters*] .... KZZN
Littlefield, TX [*Location identifier FAA*] (FAAL) .... LIU
Littlefork Elementary School, Littlefork, MN [*Library symbol*] [*Library of Congress*] (LCLS) .... MnLfoE
Littlefork High School, Littlefork, MN [*Library symbol*] [*Library of Congress*] (LCLS) .... MnLfoH
Little-Known Fan [*of science fiction or fantastic literature*] [*See also BNF*] .... LNF
Littleton and Blatchley's Insurance Digest [*A publication*] (DLA) ...... L & B Ins Dig
Littleton and Blatchley's Insurance Digest [*A publication*] (DLA) .... Lit & Bl Dig
Littleton, CO [*AM radio station call letters*] .... KDKO
Littleton, NH [*Television station call letters*] .... WLED
Littleton, NH [*AM radio station call letters*] .... WLTN
Littleton, NH [*FM radio station call letters*] .... WMTK
Littleton Public Library, Littleton, NC [*Library symbol Library of Congress*] (LCLS) .... NcLit
Littleton's English Common Pleas and Exchequer Reports [*A publication*] (DLA) .... Litt Rep
Littleton's English Common Pleas and Exchequer Reports [*A publication*] (DLA) .... Littleton
Littleton's English Common Pleas Reports [*A publication*] (DLA) ...... Lit
Littleton's English Common Pleas Reports [*A publication*] (DLA) ...... Litt
Littleton's Tenures [*A publication*] (DLA) .... Lit
Littleton's Tenures [*A publication*] (DLA) .... Litt Ten
Littleton's Tenures [*A publication*] (DSA) .... Ten
Litton Airborne Search RADAR Mark Two [*Canada*] (PDAA) ... LASR-2
Litton Business-Oriented Language (IAA) .... LIBOL
Litton Computer Services [*Information service or system*] (IID) ... LCS
Litton Educational Publishing, Inc. .... LEPI
Litton Graphics Standard (MCD) .... LGS
Litton Indus [*NYSE symbol*] (TTSB) .... LIT
Litton Indus,$2 B Pfd [*NYSE symbol*] (TTSB) .... LITPrB
Litton Industries, Inc. [*NYSE symbol*] (SPSG) .... LIT
Litton Industries, Inc. [*Associated Press*] (SAG) .... Litton
Litton Industries, Inc., Beverly Hills, CA [*Library symbol Library of Congress*] (LCLS) .... CBevL
Litton Industries, Inc., Guidance and Central Systems Division, Engineering Library, Woodland Hills, CA [*Library symbol Library of Congress*] (LCLS) .... CWohL
Litton Industries Privacy System .... LIPS
Litton Systems Canada Ltd., Rexdale, ON, Canada [*Library symbol*] [*Library of Congress*] (LCLS) .... CaOTLSC
Litton Systems Canada Ltd., Rexdale, Ontario [*Library symbol National Library of Canada*] (NLC) .... OTLSC
Litton Systems Ltd. (MCD) .... LSL
Littoral Environment Observation [*Program*] [*Oceanography*] ... LEO
Lituanus Foundation (EA) .... LF
Liturgical Arts Society (EA) .... LAS
Liturgical Conference (EA) LC
Liturgical Fragments from Qumran. Cave One (BJA) 1QPrayers
Liturgie und Moenchtum [*A publication*] (BJA) .... LitMo
Liturgie und Moenchtum [*A publication*] (BJA) .... LM
Liturgies (ROG) .... LITURG
Liturgy .... LIT
Liturgy (VRA) .... litg
Liturgy (VRA) .... LITZ
Litzendraht [*Wire*] [*German*] .... LITZ
Liuski International [*NASDAQ symbol*] (TTSB) .... LSK
Liuski International, Inc. [*Associated Press*] (SAG) ...... Liuski
Liuski International, Inc. [*NASDAQ symbol*] (SAG) ...... LSKI
Live [*Wiring code*] [*British*] L
Live Action (NTCM) .... LA
Live Action Camera (WDMC) .... LAC
Live Aid Foundation (EA) .... LAF
Live Animals Board [*IATA*] (DS) .... LAB
Live Assembly Area (MCD) .... LAA
Live Birth .... LB
Live Entertainment [*NASDAQ symbol*] (TTSB) .... LIVE
LIVE Entertainment, Inc. [*Associated Press*] (SAG) ...... LiveEn
LIVE Entertainment, Inc. [*Associated Press*] (SAG) ...... LiveEnt
Live Entmt cm Cv'B' Pfd [*NASDAQ symbol*] (TTSB) ...... LIVEP
Live Environment Testing .... LET
Live Environment Testing with SAGE (MCD) .... LETS
Live Environment Training [*Military*] (ADDR) .... LET
Live Exercise [*Military exercise in which live forces participate*] (NATG) .... LIVEX
Live Fire .... LF
Live Fire Component (MCD) .... LFC
Live Fire Evaluation Manikin [*Perceptronics, Inc.*] [*Military*] ... LIFEMAN
Live Fire Evasive Target System [*Army*] (INF) .... LFETS
Live Fire Exercise [*Army*] (INF) .... LFX
Live Fire Test .... LFT
Live Fire Test and Evaluation [*Required testing for major weapon system and munition programs*] [*Military*] (RDA) .... LFT & E
Live Fire Test and Evaluation (DOMA) .... LFT & E
Live Firing Program Analysis Group [*Military*] (CAAL) ... LFPAG
Live Flying (NATG) .... LF

Live Food Singles Club - World Wide [*Defunct*] (EA) ...... LFSCWW
Live Letter-Drop [*Espionage*] .... LLD
Live Load LL
Live Load Punch .... LLP
Live Missile Assembly Facility .... LMAF
Live Oak, FL [*Television station call letters*] .... WFXU
Live Oak, FL [*AM radio station call letters*] .... WQHL
Live Oak, FL [*FM radio station call letters*] .... WQHL-FM
Live Oak, Perry & Gulf Railroad (IIA) .... LOP & G
Live Oak, Perry & South Georgia Railway Co. [*AAR code*] ... LPSG
Live Oak Society (EA) .... LOS
Live Poliomyelitis Vaccine [*Immunology*] (MAE) .... PLV
Live Test Demonstration .... LTD
Live Traffic Model [*Telecommunications*] (TEL) .... LTM
Live Vaccine [*Medicine*] LV
Live Virus [*Medicine*] (MAE) LV
Live Zero (IAA) .... LZ
Live-Alone Person [*Lifestyle classification*] .... Lappie
Lived [*or Living*] LIV
Live-Fire Exercises [*Army*] (INF) .... LFX
Live-Free, Inc. [*An association*] (EA) .... L-FI
Live-In Lover [*Slang*] (DSUE) LIL
Lively Branch, Walden Public Library, Ontario [*Library symbol National Library of Canada*] (NLC) .... OWLI
Livengood, AK [*Location identifier FAA*] (FAAL) LIV
Livens Projector [*Military*] .... LP
Livent, Inc. [*Associated Press*] (SAG) .... Livent
Livent Inc. [*NASDAQ symbol*] (TTSB) .... LVNTE
Livent, Inc. [*NASDAQ symbol*] (SAG) .... LVNTF
Liver (MAE) L
Liver Alcohol Dehydrogenase [*An enzyme*] .... LADH
Liver and Iron (DMAA) .... L&I
Liver and Spleen [*Medicine*] .... LS
Liver Battery Test [*Gastroenterology*] (DAVI) LIV
Liver Blood Flow [*Physiology*] .... LBF
Liver Cell Adhesion Molecule [*Cytology*] .... LCAM
Liver Cell Dysplasia [*Medicine*] .... LCD
Liver Cell Tumor [*Medicine*] (DMAA) .... LCT
Liver Cirrhosis [*Medicine*] LC
Liver Copper Concentration [*Physiology*] .... LCuC
Liver Disease [*Gastroenterology*] (DAVI) .... ID
Liver Extract [*Protein/lipid substance*] [*Immunology*] ...... LEx
Liver Extract [*Protein/lipid substance*] [*Immunology*] LX
Liver Fraction Elevated [*Gastroenterology*] (DAVI) ...... LVER
Liver Function Series [*Clinical chemistry*] .... LFS
Liver Function Test [*Medicine*] .... LFT
Liver Infusion Agar [*Germination medium*] .... LIA
Liver, Iron, Red Bone Marrow .... LIRBM
Liver, Kidney, Spleen [*Medicine*] .... LKS
Liver, Kidney, Spleen, Bladder [*Medicine*] (DMAA) ...... LKSB
Liver, Kidneys, and Spleen (DAVI) .... LKS
Liver, Kidneys, and Spleen Not Palpable [*On physical examination*] (DAVI) .... LKS NP
Liver Lactate Dehydrogenase [*An enzyme*] (DAVI) ...... LLDH
Liver Membrane Antigen [*Immunochemistry*] .... LM-Ag
Liver Membrane Autoantibody [*Immunochemistry*] ...... LMA
Liver Microsomal Band 2 .... LM2
Liver Plasma Membrane .... LPM
Liver Protein [*Medicine*] .... LP
Liver Pyruvate Kinase [*Medicine*] (DMAA) .... LPK
Liver Regenerating Serum Factor [*Medicine*] (DMAA) ... LRSF
Liver Residue Factor [*Molybdenum*] [*Medicine*] .... LRF
Liver, Spleen, Kidney [*Medicine*] .... LSK
Liver/Spleen Ratio [*Medicine*] (DMAA) .... LSR
Liver to Plasma Concentration Ratio (MAE) .... LP
Liver Yang Exuberance Syndrome [*Medicine*] (DMAA) ... LYES
Liver-Kidney Microsomal [*Antibody*] [*Medicine*] (DMAA) ... LKM
Livermore Action Group [*Defunct*] (EA) .... LAG
Livermore Atomic Research Computer .... LARC
Livermore, CA [*FM radio station call letters*] .... KKIQ
Livermore, CA [*Location identifier FAA*] (FAAL) ...... LVK
Livermore Library, Livermore, CA [*Library symbol Library of Congress*] (LCLS) CLiv
Livermore on Principal and Agent [*A publication*] (DLA) ...... Liv Ag
Livermore on Principal and Agent [*A publication*] (DLA) ...... Liverm Ag
Livermore on Principal and Agent [*A publication*] (DLA) ...... Livermore Ag
Livermore Pool Type Reactor .... LPTR
Livermore Research Laboratory [*University of California*] (KSC) ... LRL
Livermore Water Boiler [*Nuclear reactor*] [*Dismantled*] ... LIWB
Livermore's Dissertation on the Contrariety of Laws [*A publication*] (DLA) .... Liv Dis
Liverpool [*British ICAO location identifier*] (ICLI) ...... EGGP
Liverpool [*British ICAO location identifier*] (ICLI) ...... EGGQ
Liverpool [*Postcode*] (ODBW) L
Liverpool (ROG) LIV
Liverpool [*England*] [*Airport symbol*] (OAG) .... LPL
Liverpool (ROG) .... L'POOL
Liverpool [*England*] .... LVPL
Liverpool [*England*] [*Seismograph station code, US Geological Survey Closed*] (SEIS) .... LVR
Liverpool Academy [*British*] .... LA
Liverpool Academy of Arts [*England*] .... LAA
Liverpool and District Scientific Industrial and Research Library Advisory Council [*Library cooperative scheme*] [*British*] (NITA) ... LADSIRLAC

Liverpool Daily Post & Echo Ltd., Liverpool, United Kingdom [*Library symbol Library of Congress*] (LCLS) .... UkLiP

Liverpool Daily Post and Echo, Ltd., Liverpool, United Kingdom [*Library symbol*] [*Library of Congress*] (LCLS) .... UkLiPE

Liverpool Marine Biological Committee [*British*] (BARN) .... LMBC

Liverpool, NS [*FM radio station call letters*] CKBW-1

Liverpool Post and Mercury [*A publication*] (ROG) .... LP & M

Liverpool Public Libraries, Liverpool, United Kingdom [*Library symbol Library of Congress*] (LCLS) .... UkLi

Liverpool Quay Terms (DS) .... LQT

Liverpool Underwriters Association (DS) .... LUA

Liver-Specific [*Membrane*] Lipoprotein (DAVI) .... LSP

Liver-Specific Protein .... LSP

Liver-Spleen Scan [*Medicine*] (MEDA) .... LSS

Liver-Spleen-Kidney Megaly [*Medicine*] .... LSKM

Livery LV

Lives With (ADA) .... LW

Livestock (DCTA) .... LS

Livestock .... LVSTCK

Livestock .... LVSTK

Livestock Agent .... LSA

Livestock and Grain Producers' Association of New South Wales [*Australia*] .... LGPANSW

Livestock and Meat Authority [*Queensland, Australia*] .... LMA

Livestock and Meat Authority of Queensland [*Australia*] .... LMAQ

Livestock and Range Research Station [*Department of Agriculture*] (GRD) .... LARRS

Livestock Auction Markets Association (EA) .... LAMA

Livestock Auctioneers' Market Committee [*British*] (DBA) .... LAMC

Livestock Conservation Institute (EA) LCI

Livestock Equipment Council [*Defunct*] (EA) .... LEC

Livestock Feed Program .... LFP

Livestock Husbandry Adviser [*Ministry of Agriculture, Fisheries, and Food*] [*British*] .... LHA

Livestock Industry Institute (EA) LII

Livestock Industry Promotion Council [*Australia*] .... LIPC

Livestock Marketing Association (EA) .... LMA

Livestock Merchandising Institute [*Later, LII*] (EA) .... LMI

Livestock Publications Council (EA) .... LPC

Livestock Unit .... LSU

Living (DAVI) L

Living (DAVI) LIV

Living .... LVNG

Living Allowance .... LA

Living and Active (DAVI) .... L & A

Living and Well .... L & W

Living Aquatic Resources Sector [*Aquaculture*] .... LARS

Living Arts Foundation (EA) .... LAF

Living Bank (EA) .... LB

Living Benefits Rider [*Insurance*] (WYGK) .... LBR

Living Centers of America [*NYSE symbol*] (SAG) .... LCA

Living Centers of America, Inc. [*Associated Press*] (SAG) .... LivngCtr

Living Children LC

Living Church Foundation (EA) .... LCF

Living Colour Fan Club (EA) .... LCFC

Living Country Blues [*A publication*] .... LCB

Living Donor [*Medicine*] .... LD

Living/Dying Project (EA) .... L/DP

Living Female Child [*Medicine*] (DMAA) .... LFC

Living in Family Environments .... LIFE

Living Male Child [*Medicine*] (DMAA) .... LMC

Living Marine Resource [*Marine science*] (OSRA) .... LMR

Living Marine Resource (USDC) .... LMR

Living Masters of Music [*A publication*] .... LMM

Living Modified Organism .... LMO

Living Personnel Management Authorization Document [*DoD*] .... LPMAD

Living Plant Growers Association (EA) .... LPGA

Living Quarters Allowance [*Air Force*] (AFM) .... LQA

Living Related Donor [*Medicine*] .... LRD

Living Related Donor Transplant [*Medicine*] (DMAA) .... LRDT

Living Related Renal Transplantation [*Medicine*] .... LRTx

Living Renal Donor [*Nephrology*] (DAVI) .... LRD

Living Room (ROG) L

Living Room (BARN) .... liv rm

Living Room .... LR

Living Skin Equivalent [*Synthetic organ*] .... LSE

Living Standards Management Study [*International Monetary Fund*] .... LSMS

Living Stream Prayer Circle (EA) .... LSPC

Living Structures Tank (WDAA) .... LST

Living Table of Organization and Equipment [*Army*] (INF) .... LTOE

Living Together Arrangement .... LTA

Living Together Partner [*Lifestyle classification*] .... LTP

Living Together Relationship .... LTR

Living Tree Center (EA) .... LTC

Living under Canvas [*British military*] (DMA) .... LUC

Living Unrelated Renal Transplantation [*Medicine*] .... LURTx

Living Utility Module [*NASA*] (KSC) .... LUM

Living with Cancer [*An association*] (EA) .... LWC

Livingston, CA [*FM radio station call letters*] .... KNTO

Livingston Community Consolidated School District, Livingston, IL [*Library symbol Library of Congress*] (LCLS) .... ILivSD

Livingston County Archives, Geneseo, NY [*Library symbol Library of Congress*] (LCLS) .... NGenoA

Livingston Elementary Schools, Livingston, MT [*Library symbol*] [*Library of Congress*] (LCLS) .... MtLvSD

Livingston Middle School, Livingston, MT [*Library symbol*] [*Library of Congress*] (LCLS) .... MtLvMS

Livingston, MT [*FM radio station call letters*] (RBYB) .... KPKX

Livingston, MT [*AM radio station call letters*] .... KPRK

Livingston, MT [*Location identifier FAA*] (FAAL) .... LVM

Livingston Parish Library, Livingston, LA [*Library symbol Library of Congress*] (LCLS) LLiLi

Livingston Public Library, Livingston, MT [*Library symbol*] [*Library of Congress*] (LCLS) .... MtLv

Livingston, TN [*Location identifier FAA*] (FAAL) .... LVT

Livingston, TN [*FM radio station call letters*] .... WCSD

Livingston, TN [*AM radio station call letters*] .... WLIV

Livingston, TX [*AM radio station call letters*] .... KETX

Livingston, TX [*FM radio station call letters*] .... KETX-FM

Livingston University (GAGS) .... Livingston U

Livingston University, Livingston, AL [*Library symbol Library of Congress*] (LCLS) .... ALT

Livingstone [*Zambia*] [*ICAO location identifier*] (ICLI) .... FLLI

Livingstone [*Zambia*] [*Airport symbol*] (OAG) LVI

Livingstone College, Salisbury, NC [*Library symbol Library of Congress*] (LCLS) .... NcSalL

Livingstone Energy [*Vancouver Stock Exchange symbol*] LIV

Livingston's Cases in Error [*New York*] [*A publication*] (DLA) .... Liv Cas

Livingston's Judicial Opinions [*New York*] [*A publication*] (DLA) .... Liv Jud Cas

Livingston's Judicial Opinions [*New York*] [*A publication*] (DLA) .... Liv Jud Op

Livingston's Judicial Opinions [*New York*] [*A publication*] (DLA) .... Liv Judic Op

Livingston's Law Magazine [*New York*] [*A publication*] (DLA) .... Liv L Mag

Livingston's Law Magazine [*New York*] [*A publication*] (DLA) .... Liv Law Mag

Livingston's Law Register [*New York*] [*A publication*] (DLA) .... Liv L Reg

Livingston's Louisiana Criminal Code [*A publication*] (DLA) .... Liv La Cr Code

Livingston's Mayor's Court Reports [*New York*] [*A publication*] (DLA) Liv

Livingston's System of United States Penal Codes [*A publication*] (DLA) .... Liv US Pen Co

Livingston-Steuben-Wyoming BOCES [*Boards of Cooperative Educational Services*], Educational Communications Center, Geneseo, NY [*OCLC symbol*] (OCLC) .... WLS

Livingston-Steuben-Wyoming Educational Communication Center (BOCES), Geneseo, NY [*Library symbol Library of Congress*] (LCLS) .... NGenoLS

Livonia Avon & Lakeville Railroad (MHDB) .... LA & LR

Livonia, Avon & Lakeville Railroad Corp. [*AAR code*] .... LAL

Livonia Career/Technical Center .... LC/TC

Livonia High School Library, Livonia, NY [*OCLC symbol*] (OCLC) .... RWY

Livonia, MI [*AM radio station call letters*] .... WCAR

Livonia Public Schools, Livonia, MI [*OCLC symbol*] (OCLC) .... EYI

Livonia Public Schools, Livonia, MI [*Library symbol Library of Congress*] (LCLS) .... MiLivPS

Livorno [*Italy*] [*Seismograph station code, US Geological Survey Closed*] (SEIS) LIV

Livraison [*Delivery*] [*French*] LIV

Livramento [*Brazil*] [*Airport symbol*] (OAG) .... LVB

Livre [*Monetary unit*] [*Obsolete French*] L

Livre [*Book or Pound*] [*French*] LIV

Livre [*Monetary unit*] [*Obsolete French*] (ROG) LV

Livres Bibliotheque Saclay Database [*Commissariat a l'Energie Atomique*] [*France Information service or system*] (CRD) .... LIBISAC

Livros Tecnicos e Cientificos Editora Ltda. [*Brazil*] .... LTC

Livy [*Roman historian, c. 10BC*] (ROG) LIV

Liz Claiborne [*NYSE symbol*] (TTSB) .... LIZ

Liz Claiborne, Inc. [*NYSE symbol*] (SAG) .... LIZ

Liza Minnelli Fan Club (EA) .... LMFC

Lizard (MSA) .... LIZ

Lizard Butte District Library, Marsing, ID [*Library symbol*] [*Library of Congress*] (LCLS) .... IdMar

Lizard Island [*Australia Airport symbol*] (OAG) .... LZR

Lizar's Scotch Exchequer Cases [*A publication*] (DLA) .... Liz Sc Exch

Lizar's Scotch Exchequer Cases [*A publication*] (DLA) .... Lizars

Ljubljana [*Slovenia*] [*Seismograph station code, US Geological Survey*] (SEIS) .... LJU

Ljubljana [*Slovenia*] [*Airport symbol*] (OAG) .... LJU

Ljubljana [*Former Yugoslavia*] [*ICAO location identifier*] (ICLI) .... LYLJ

Ljungby/Feringe [*Sweden ICAO location identifier*] (ICLI) .... ESMG

Ljungbyhed [*Sweden ICAO location identifier*] (ICLI) .... ESDA

Ljusdal [*Sweden ICAO location identifier*] (ICLI) .... ESUL

LK Resources Ltd. [*Toronto Stock Exchange symbol*] .... LKR

LL & E Royalty Trust [*Associated Press*] (SAG) .... LLE Ry

LL & E Royalty Trust UBI [*NYSE symbol*] (SPSG) .... LRT

Lladro Collectors Society (EA) .... LCS

Llama Association of North America (EA) .... LANA

Llanada [*California*] [*Seismograph station code, US Geological Survey*] (SEIS) .... LLA

Llanbedr [*British ICAO location identifier*] (ICLI) .... EGOD

Llandaff (ROG) .... LLAN

LL&E Royalty Tr UBI [*NYSE symbol*] (TTSB) .... LRT

Llandore [*Welsh depot code*] .... LDR

Llanelly [*Welsh depot code*] .... LLY

Llanelly & Mynydd Mawr Railway [*Wales*] .... LMM

Llano Estacado Center for Advanced Professional Studies and Research [*Eastern New Mexico University*] [*Research center*] (RCD) .... LECAPSR

Llano, TX [*FM radio station call letters*] (RBYB) .... KBAE

Llano, TX [*Television station call letters*] .... KXAM-TV

Llano, TX [*Location identifier FAA*] (FAAL) .... LLO

Llantrisant [*Welsh depot code*] .... LTS

Lloyd Aereo Boliviano [*ICAO designator*] (AD) .... LB

Lloyd Aereo Boliviano SA [*Lloyd Bolivian Air Line*] .... LAB

Lloyd Aereo Boliviano SA [Bolivia] [ICAO designator] (FAAC) ... LLB
Lloyd and Goold's Irish Chancery Reports Tempore Plunkett [A publication] (DLA) ... Cas T Plunk
Lloyd and Goold's Irish Chancery Reports Tempore Plunkett [A publication] (DLA) ... L & G Temp Plunk
Lloyd and Goold's Irish Chancery Reports Tempore Plunkett [A publication] (DLA) ... L & GT Plunk
Lloyd and Goold's Irish Chancery Reports Tempore Plunkett [A publication] (DLA) ... L & GTP
Lloyd and Goold's Irish Chancery Reports Tempore Plunkett [A publication] (DLA) ... Ll & GT Pl
Lloyd and Goold's Irish Chancery Reports Tempore Plunkett [A publication] (DLA) ... Ll & GTP
Lloyd and Goold's Irish Chancery Reports Tempore Plunkett [A publication] (DLA) ... Lloyd & Goold (T Plunkett) (Ir)
Lloyd and Goold's Irish Chancery Reports Tempore Sugden [1835] [A publication] (DLA) ... L & G Temp Sugd
Lloyd and Goold's Irish Chancery Reports Tempore Sugden [1835] [A publication] (DLA) ... L & GT Sug
Lloyd and Goold's Irish Chancery Reports Tempore Sugden [1835] [A publication] (DLA) ... L & GTS
Lloyd and Goold's Irish Chancery Reports Tempore Sugden [1835] [A publication] (DLA) ... Ll & GTS
Lloyd and Goold's Irish Chancery Reports Tempore Sugden [A publication] (DLA) ... Lloyd & Goold (T Sugden) (Ir)
Lloyd and Welsby's English Commercial and Mercantile Cases [1829-30] [A publication] (DLA) ... L & W
Lloyd and Welsby's English Commercial and Mercantile Cases [1829-30] [A publication] (DLA) ... L & Welsb
Lloyd and Welsby's English Commercial Cases [A publication] (DLA) ... Ll & Wels
Lloyd and Welsby's English Mercantile Cases [A publication] (DLA) ... Ll & W
Lloyd and Welsby's English Mercantile Cases [A publication] (DLA) ... Lloyd & W
Lloyd Library and Museum, Cincinnati, OH [Library symbol Library of Congress] (LCLS) ... OCLloyd
Lloyd Library and Museum, Cincinnati, OH [OCLC symbol] (OCLC) ... OLM
Lloyd on Prohibition [1849] [A publication] (DLA) ... Ll Pr
Lloyd on Succession Laws [1877] [A publication] (DLA) ... Ll Suc
Lloyd on Trade-Marks [A publication] (DLA) ... Ll Tr M
Lloyd Shaw Foundation (EA) ... LSF
Lloyd Wood Fan Club [Defunct] (EA) ... LWFC
lloyd Your Trans-Australian Airline [ICAO designator] (AD) ... UD
Lloydminster [Canada] [Airport symbol] (OAG) ... YLL
Lloydminster, AB [Television station call letters] ... CITL
Lloydminster, AB [AM radio station call letters] ... CKSA
Lloydminster, AB [Television station call letters] ... CKSA-TV
Lloydminster, AB [ICAO location identifier] (ICLI) ... CYLL
Lloydminster Public Library, Lloydminster, SK, Canada [Library symbol Library of Congress] (LCLS) ... CaSL
Lloydminster Public Library, Saskatchewan [Library symbol National Library of Canada] (NLC) ... SL
Lloyd's Agent ... L/A
Lloyd's American Trust Fund (AIA) ... LATF
Lloyds & BOLSA [Bank of London & South America] International Bank Ltd. [British] ... LBI
Lloyd's Aviation Claims Centre (AIA) ... LACC
Lloyd's Aviation Department (AIA) ... LAD
Lloyd's Aviation Underwriters Association [British] (DBA) ... LAUA
Lloyds Bank International (ADA) ... LBI
Lloyd's Canadian Trust Fund (AIA) ... LCTF
Lloyd's Compensation for Lands, Etc. [6th ed.] [1895] [A publication] (DLA) ... Ll Comp
Lloyd's County Courts Practice [A publication] (DLA) ... Ll CC Pr
Lloyd's Insurance Brokers Committee (AIA) ... LIBC
Lloyd's International Private Banking [Finance] ... LIPB
Lloyd's List Law Reports [England] [A publication] (DLA) ... Ll L Rep
Lloyd's List Law Reports [England] [A publication] (DLA) ... Ll List LR
Lloyd's List Law Reports [England] [A publication] (DLA) ... Ll LLR
Lloyd's List Law Reports [England] [A publication] (DLA) ... Ll LR
Lloyd's List Law Reports [England] [A publication] (DLA) ... Ll Rep
Lloyd's List Law Reports [England] [A publication] (DLA) ... Lloyd LR
Lloyd's List Law Reports [England] [A publication] (DLA) ... Lloyd's List LR
Lloyd's List Law Reports [England] [A publication] (DLA) ... Lloyd's Rep
Lloyd's List Prize Cases Reports [England] [A publication] (DLA) ... Ll L Pr Cas
Lloyd's List Prize Cases Reports [England] [A publication] (DLA) ... Ll Pr Cas
Lloyd's List Prize Cases Reports [England] [A publication] (DLA) ... Lloyd Pr Cas
Lloyd's List Prize Cases Reports [England] [A publication] (DLA) ... Lloyd's Pr Cas
Lloyd's List Prize Cases Reports [London] [A publication] (DLA) ... Lloyd's Prize Cas
Lloyd's List Prize Cases Reports, New Series [1939-53] [A publication] (DLA) ... Ll Pr Cas NS
Lloyd's List Prize Cases Reports, Second Series [1939-53] [A publication] (DLA) ... Ll R Pr Cas
Lloyd's List Prize Cases Reports, Second Series [1939-53] [A publication] (DLA) ... Lloyd Pr Cas NS
Lloyd's Machinery Certificate [Shipping] ... LMC
Lloyds Maritime and Commercial Law Quarterly [A publication] (DLA) ... LMCLQ
Lloyd's Maritime Information Services Ltd. [Information service or system] (IID) ... LMIS
Lloyd's Maritime Law Newsletter [A publication] (DLA) ... Ll Mar LN
Lloyd's Maritime Law Newsletter [A publication] (DLA) ... Lloyd's Mar LN
Lloyd's Motor Underwriters Association [British] (DBA) ... LMUA
Lloyd's of London Press [British] ... LLP
Lloyd's Policy Signing Office [Lloyd's of London] ... LPSO
Lloyd's Refrigerating Machinery Certificate ... LRMC
Lloyd's Register of Shipping ... LR
Lloyd's Register of Shipping ... LRS
Lloyd's Registry Building Certificate ... LRBC
Lloyd's Statutes of Practical Utility [A publication] (DLA) ... Ll St
Lloyd's Supreme Court of Judicature Acts [1875] [A publication] (DLA) ... Ll Jud Act
Lloyd's Underwriters' Association [British] (DBA) ... LUA
Lloyd's Underwriters Claims Office (AIA) ... LUCO
Lloyd's Underwriters Non-Marine Claims Office (AIA) ... LUNCO
Lloyd's Universal Register of Shipping [British] (ROG) ... UR
Llurimaguas [Ecuador] [ICAO location identifier] (ICLI) ... SELL
Llymphocryptovirus ... LCV
LM [Lunar Module] Change Directive [NASA] (KSC) ... LCD
LM [Lunar Module] Guidance Computer [NASA] ... LGC
LM [Lunar Module] Interface Control Specification [NASA] (KSC) ... LIS
LM [Lunar Module] Mission Programmer [NASA] (KSC) ... LMP
LM [Lunar Module] Optical Rendezvous System [NASA] ... LORS
LM [Lunar Module] Plan [NASA] (KSC) ... LPL
LM [Lunar Module] Replaceable Package [NASA] ... LRP
LM [Lunar Module] Specification [NASA] (KSC) ... LSP
LM [Lunar Module] Test Article [NASA] ... LTA
LMX Resources Ltd. [Vancouver Stock Exchange symbol] ... LMX
LNG [Liquefied Natural Gas] Seabed Supported System ... L3S
LNH Real Estate Investment Trust (SPSG) ... LHC
LNH REIT, Inc. [NYSE symbol] (SAG) ... LHC
LNH REIT [Real Estate Investment Trust], Inc. [Associated Press] (SAG) ... LNH
Lo Ta'aseh (BJA) ... LT
Load (MDG) ... L
Load [or Loader] (AAG) ... LD
Load Acceptance Module ... LAM
Load Accumulator ... LAC
Load Accumulator with Magnitude (HGAA) ... LACM
Load Accumulator with Magnitude ... LAM
Load Address (IAA) ... LA
Load Address (IAA) ... LAD
Load Address Immediate (BUR) ... LAI
Load Adjuster (CET) ... LA
Load Adjuster Reference Datum (IAA) ... LARD
Load Alleviation and Mode Stabilization ... LAMS
Load Allocation [Environmental science] (FFDE) ... LA
Load and Go (NITA) ... LAG
Load and Go Assembler (BUR) ... LAG
Load and Go FORTRAN [Computer science] ... GOTRAN
Load, Assemble, Pack [Army] (AABC) ... LAP
Load Balance System [Telecommunications] (TEL) ... LBS
Load Bank [Computer science] (KSC) ... LB
Load Bank and Jump [Computer science] ... LBJ
Load Bearing System ... LBS
Load Bit Field [Computer science] (IAA) ... LBF
Load Buffer Memory [Computer science] ... LBM
Load Bus Contactor [Aviation] ... LBC
Load Carrier ... LC
Load Cell ... LC
Load Cell Platform ... LCP
Load Center (MSA) ... LC
Load Channel (IAA) ... LCH
Load Circuit Efficiency ... LCE
Load Classification Group (DA) ... LCG
Load Classification Number (AFM) ... LCN
Load Complement Register (IAA) ... LCR
Load Computer [or Controller] (MCD) ... LC
Load Contactor ... LC
Load Control Valve [Engineering] ... LCV
Load Controller Assembly (NASA) ... LCA
Load Controlling Crewman [Helicopter] [Navy] ... LCC
Load Current Contacting Aiding ... LCCA
Load D-Bank and Jump [Computer science] ... LDJ
Load Determining Bolt ... LDB
Load Distribution Matrix (IAA) ... LDM
Load Division Fault ... LDF
Load Draught (IAA) ... LD
Load Drawer Computer (MCD) ... LDC
Load Effective Address [Computer science] ... LEA
Load Equalization Net [Aircraft arresting barrier] [Trademark] ... LEN
Load External Memory Address Register ... LXMAR
Load Factor (IAA) ... LDF
Load Factor ... LF
Load Factor Error Sensor (MCD) ... LOFES
Load Frequency Control (IEEE) ... LFC
Load Graphics Table [Computer science] ... GRAFTABL
Load, Haul, Dump [Mining] ... LHD
Load I-Bank and Jump [Computer science] ... LIS
Load Impedance Stabilization Network [Electrical engineering] ... LISN
Load Index [Tires] [Automotive engineering] ... LI
Load Index from Address ... LXA
Load Index from Decrement ... LXD
Load Indicator ... LDI
LOAD [Low-Altitude Defense] Interceptor Subsystem Development Plan ... LISDP
Load Interface Circuit (MCD) ... LIC
Load Limit (WDAA) ... LD LMT
Load Line [Shipping] (DS) ... LL
Load Line Method ... LLM
Load List (MSA) ... LL
Load List File (AFIT) ... LLF
Load Matching Network ... LMN

Load Matching Switch ..... LMS
Load Measurement System (NASA) ..... LMS
Load Memory Lockout Register ..... LMLR
Load Module (MCD) ..... LM
Load Module Generator (IAA) ..... LMGEN
Load Module Librarian (MHDB) ..... LLIB
Load Multiple [*Computer command*] (PCM) ..... LM
Load Number ..... LN
Load on Top [*Oil tankers*] ..... LOT
Load On-Call [*Computer science*] ..... LOCAL
Load Optimization and Passenger Acceptance Control [*Airport computer*] ..... LOPAC
Load over the Side ..... LOTS
Load Overcurrent ..... LOC
Load per Unit of Length ..... w
Load Point (BUR) ..... LP
Load Point Photocell ..... LPPC
Load Program Status Word (IAA) ..... LPSW
Load Ratio ..... LR
Load Ratio Control (MSA) ..... LRC
Load Ratio Transformer (IAA) ..... LRT
Load Real Address (HGAA) ..... LRA
Load Reference Axis ..... LRA
Load Rejection (NRCH) ..... LR
Load Relief Control System ..... LRCS
Load Request Block (IAA) ..... LRB
Load Resistance (IDOE) ..... R_L
Load Sharing Network ..... LSN
Load Sheet Fuel [*Aviation*] (DA) ..... LSF
Load Shifting Resistor (MSA) ..... LSR
LOAD [*Low Altitude Defense*] **Simulation Center** ..... LSC
Load Standardization Crew (MCD) ..... LSC
Load Storage Register ..... LSR
Load Storage Unit [*Computer science*] ..... LSU
Load System (MCD) ..... L/S
LOAD [*Low Altitude Defense*] **System Requirements Simulation** ..... LSRS
Load Tap Changing ..... LTC
Load Task Register [*Computer science*] (PCM) ..... LTR
Load Test (MCD) ..... L/T
LOAD [*Low Altitude Defense*] **Test Planning Working Group** ..... LTPWG
Load Threshold Value (DA) ..... LTV
Load Ton Mile (IAA) ..... LTM
Load Transfer Switch ..... LTS
Load Unit ..... LU
Load, Unload, Cool, Fracture (PDAA) ..... LUCF
Load, Update, Subset ..... LUS
Load Upper Immediate [*Computer science*] ..... LUI
Load Vertical LV
Load Water Plane ..... LWP
Load Waterline ..... LWL
Load Wear Index ..... LWI
Loadable Control Storage [*Computer science*] (NITA) ..... LCS
Load-Bearing Axis ..... LBA
Load-Bearing Equipment (INF) ..... LBE
Load-Bearing Surface (MCD) ..... LBS
Load-Bearing Vest [*Military*] (INF) ..... LBV
Load-Carrying Ability (IAA) ..... LCA
Load-Carrying Equipment (MCD) ..... LCE
Load-Compensated Diode Transistor Logic [*Computer science*] ..... LCDTL
Load-Compensating (MSA) LC
Loaded ..... LDD
Loaded Applicator Impedance ..... LAI
Loaded Deployability [*Posture*] [*Military*] (DOMA) ..... LD
Loaded Equipment Section ..... LES
Loaded Motional Impedance ..... LMI
Loaded on Trailers or Wagons [*Freight*] ..... LOTW
Loaded Program Request Block [*Computer science*] (BUR) ..... LPRB
Loaded Radial Tire Run-Out [*Automotive engineering*] ..... LRTRO
Loaded Radial Wheel Run-Out [*Automotive engineering*] ..... LRWRO
Loaded Vehicle Weight [*Automotive engineering*] ..... LVW
Loaded, Waiting Orders or Assignment [*Navy*] ..... LODOR
Loader (MSA) ..... LDR
Loader ..... LODR
Loader/Editor/Verifier [*Telecommunications*] (TEL) ..... LEV
Loader Storage Unit Support Program [*Computer science*] (MHDI) ..... LSUP
Loader Trainer (MCD) ..... LT
Loader-Transporter [*British military*] (DMA) ..... LT
Load-High [*Computer science*] (PCM) ..... LH
Load-Indicating Relay (IAA) ..... LIR
Load-Indicating Relay (MSA) ..... LIRLY
Load-Indicating Resistor (IAA) ..... LIR
Loading ..... LDG
Loading ..... LDNG
Loading and Handling Corrective Action Program ..... LOHAC
Loading and Unloading ..... L & U
Loading Assembling and Packing ..... LAP
Loading Coil [*Telecommunications*] (TEL) LC
Loading Coil Case [*Telecommunications*] (TEL) LCC
Loading Control Program (IAA) ..... LCP
Loading Dock (MCD) ..... LD
Loading Dock Equipment Manufacturers Association (EA) ..... LODEM
Loading Dose ..... LD
Loading Exercise [*Military*] (NVT) ..... LOADEX
Loading Ramp ..... LR
Loading Splice [*Telecommunications*] (TEL) ..... LS
Loading Training Captive Carry Missile (MCD) ..... LTCCM
Loading Valve (MCD) LV
Loading Zone ..... LZ
Load-Limiting Resistor ..... LLR
Load-Limiting Resistor (MSA) ..... LLRES
Loadmaster Systems, Inc. [*Vancouver Stock Exchange symbol*] ..... LMS
Load-Resistor Relay (MSA) ..... LR
Loads [*Military*] ..... LDS
Loads Control Group [*Prepares supplies to be airlifted*] [*Military*] ..... LCG
Loads/Environmental Spectra Survey (MCD) ..... L/ESS
Load-Sensing Proportioning and Bypass Valve ..... LSPBV
Loaf ..... LF
Loaf ..... LF
Loaf [*Commonly used*] (OPSA) ..... LOAF
Loam [*Agronomy*] L
Loam [*Type of soil*] (ROG) ..... LO
Loan ..... LN
Loan Accounting Information System [*Agency for International Development*] ..... LAIS
Loan Amount [*Dialog*] [*Searchable field*] [*Information service or system*] (NITA) ..... LA
Loan Application Processing System ..... LAPS
Loan Capital [*Business term*] LC
Loan Crowd [*Investment term*] LC
Loan Forgiveness (DICI) ..... LF
Loan Guaranty Revolving Fund ..... LGRF
Loan Policy Board [*of SBA*] [*Abolished, 1965*] ..... LPB
Loan Production Office [*Banking*] ..... LPO
Loan Production System [*Department of Veterans Affairs*] ..... LPS
Loan Rate [*Banking*] ..... LR
Loan Repayment Program [*Department of Health and Human Services*] (GFGA) ..... LRP
Loan Word (BJA) ..... lw
Loanda [*Brazil*] [*Airport symbol*] (AD) ..... LOP
Loaned Executives Assignment Program [*American Association of Advertising Agencies lobbying group*] ..... LEAP
Loans and Discounts [*Banking*] ..... L & D
Loan-to-Value Ratio [*Finance*] ..... LTV
Lobatse [*Botswana*] [*ICAO location identifier*] (ICLI) ..... FBLO
Lobatsi [*Botswana*] [*Airport symbol*] (AD) ..... LOQ
Lobby ..... LBBY
Lobby Europeen des Femmes [*European Women's Lobby*] [*Belgium*] (EAIO) ..... LEF
Lobbyist Systems Corp. [*Information service or system*] (IID) ..... LSC
Lobbyists and Lawyers for Campaign Finance Reform (EA) ..... LLCFR
Lobe [*Of a leaf*] [*Botany*] L
Lobe Attachment Module [*Computer science*] ..... LAM
Lobe Attachment Unit [*Computer science*] (ACRL) ..... LAM
Lobe Switching (IAA) ..... LS
Lobe-Dominated Quasar [*Astronomy*] ..... LDQ
Lobelville, TN [*FM radio station call letters*] ..... WFGZ
Lobe-On Receive Only [*Electronic counter-countermeasures*] ..... LORO
Lobingier's Extra-Territorial Cases [*United States Court for China*] [*A publication*] (DLA) ..... Exter Ca
Lobingier's Extra-Territorial Cases [*United States Court for China*] [*A publication*] (DLA) ..... Extra Ca
Lobingier's Extra-Territorial Cases [*United States Court for China*] [*A publication*] (DLA) ..... Lobin
Lobito [*Angola*] [*ICAO location identifier*] (ICLI) ..... FNLB
Lobito [*Angola*] [*Airport symbol*] (AD) ..... LOB
Lobitos [*Peru*] [*ICAO location identifier*] (ICLI) ..... SPLT
Loblaw Companies Ltd. [*Toronto Stock Exchange symbol Vancouver Stock Exchange symbol*] L
Loblaw Cos. [*TS, exchange symbol*] (TTSB) L
Lobo Wildlife Lodge [*Tanzania*] [*ICAO location identifier*] (ICLI) ..... HTLO
Lobrego, Fortin [*Paraguay*] [*ICAO location identifier*] (ICLI) ..... SGLO
Lobster ..... LBSTR
Lobular Carcinoma in Situ [*Medicine*] (AAMN) ..... LCIS
Lobular Giant Movement Detector (PDAA) ..... LGMD
Lobular Glomerulonephritis [*Medicine*] (MAE) ..... LGN
Lobular in Situ [*Medicine*] ..... LIS
Lobuloalveolar [*Medicine*] (DAVI) ..... LA
Lobuloalveolar-Ductal [*Medicine*] (DAVI) ..... LADu
Lobus Parolfactorius (PDAA) ..... LPO
LOCA [*Loss-of-Coolant Accident*] **Core Melt** [*Nuclear energy*] (NRCH) ..... LCM
Loca Sancta [*A publication*] (BJA) ..... LS
Local [*Broadcasting program*] (NTCM) L
Local (WDMC) l
Local LCL
Local (AFM) LCL
Local [*Navy*] ..... Lo
Local ..... LOC
Local Aboriginal Education Consultative Group [*Australia*] ..... LAECG
Local Aboriginal Employment Promotion Committee [*Australia*] ..... LAEPC
Local Access and Transport Area ..... LATA
Local Access Network Directory [*Frye Computer Systems*] [*Telecommunications*] (PCM) ..... LAND
Local Access Port [*Telecommunications*] (ACRL) ..... LAP
Local Access Transport Area [*Telecommunications*] ..... LATA
Local Acquisition RADAR (CET) ..... LAR
Local Adaptation Syndrome [*Medicine*] ..... LAS
Local Address ..... LA
Local Address Space ..... LAS
Local Adjunct Language (PDAA) ..... LAL

Local Administration of Vocational Education and Practical Arts (OICC) .... LAVEPA

Local Administrative Tool Kit [AT & T] [Software development and integration tools] (NITA) .... LATK

Local Advisory Board Procedural Regulation (Office of Rent Stabilization) [Economic Stabilization Agency] [A publication] (DLA) .... LABPR

Local Advisory Council [British labor] .... LAC

Local Advisory Council [British labor] .... LAC

Local Agency Check (AFM) .... LA

Local Agent .... LASU

Local Air Supply Unit [British military] (DMA) .... LASU

Local Air Warning .... LAW

Local Air Wing (DNAB) .... LAW

Local Airport Advisory [Aviation] (FAAC) .... LAA

Local Alarm (NRCH) .... LA

Local Alcoholism Reception Center .... LARC

Local Alignment System [Optics] .... LAS

Local Analysis and Prediction [Marine science] (OSRA) .... LAP

Local Analysis and Prediction [Branch] (USDC) .... LAP

Local Analysis and Prediction System (USDC) .... LAPS

Local Analysis and Prediction System [Marine science] (OSRA) .... LAPS

Local and Remote Printing [Computer science] .... LARP

Local and Remote Printing Station [Computer science] .... LARPS

Local and Short Haul Carriers National Conference (EA) .... LSHCNC

Local Anesthetic [Medicine] .... LA

Local Angle of Attack (MCD) .... AOAL

Local Antiair Warfare (NVT) .... LAAW

Local Antiair Warfare Commander (NVT) .... LAAWC

Local Apparent Noon [Navigation] .... LAN

Local Apparent Time (MSA) .... LAT

Local Apparent Time .... LAPT

Local Application Numerical Control [Sony Corp.] (DOM) .... LANC

Local Approvals Review Program .... LARP

Local Area Broadcast (NVT) .... LAB

Local Area Communications Network (DMAA) .... LACN

Local Area Coverage [Meteorology] .... LAC

Local Area Data Service [Telecommunications] (ACRL) .... LADS

Local Area Data Set .... LADS

Local Area Data Transport [AT & T] .... LADT

Local Area Digital Transmission (WGA) .... LADT

Local Area Multiuser Board [American Micronics] [Computer science] .... LAMB

Local Area Network [Telecommunications] .... LAN

Local Area Network Controller for Ethernet [Mostek] (NITA) .... LANCE

Local Area Network Emulation [Telecommunications] (ACRL) .... LANE

Local Area Network Exchange .... LANX

Local Area Network / Program Design Language (LAIN) .... LAN/PDL

Local Area Network Reference Model .... LAN/RM

Local Area Network System [Telecommunications] .... LANS

Local Area Networks [Information Gatekeepers, Inc.] [No longer available online] [Information service or system] (CRD) .... LAN

Local Area Screening .... LAS

Local Area Sensor System [Military] (LAIN) .... LASS

Local Area Signaling Service [Bell Laboratories] .... LASS

Local Area Signaling Services [Telecommunications] (ACRL) .... LASS

Local Area Telecommunications, Inc. [Digital microwave carrier] [New York, NY] (TSSD) .... LOCATE

Local Area Transport [Telecommunications] .... LAT

Local Area Unemployment Statistics (OICC) .... LAUS

Local Area Vaxcluster (USDC) .... LAVc

Local Area Wireless Network [O'Neill Communications, Inc.] [Computer science] (PCM) .... LAWN

Local Asymptotic Relative Efficiency [Statistics] .... LARE

Local Attached Support Processor .... LASP

Local Authorities' Conditions of Service Advisory Board [British] (DCTA) .... LACSAB

Local Authorities' Coordinating Body on Training Standards [British] .... LACOTS

Local Authorities Historic Buildings Act [Town planning] [British] .... LAHB

Local Authorities (Land) Act [Town planning] [British] .... LA(L)A

Local Authorities' Management Services and Computer Committee [British] .... LAMSAC

Local Authorities' Mutual Investment Trust [British] .... LAMIT

Local Authorities Ordnance Survey Committee [British] .... LAOSC

Local Authorities Research and Intelligence Association [British] .... LARIA

Local Authorities School Meals Equipment Consortium .... LASMEC

Local Authority .... LA

Local Authority Associations Group of Work Related Non-Advanced Further Education (AIE) .... LAAGOWRNAFE

Local Authority Catering Advisory Service (AIE) .... LACAS

Local Authority Financial Information System (PDAA) .... LAFIS

Local Authority Financial Institution System (AIE) .... LAFIS

Local Authority Fire Brigade [British] .... LAFB

Local Authority Health Services [British] .... LAHS

Local Authority Land Use Classification (PDAA) .... LALUC

Local Authority Management Information System (PDAA) .... LAMIS

Local Authority Social Services [British] .... LASS

Local Authority Valuers Association [British] (DBA) .... LAVA

Local Authority Valuers Association [British] (DBA) .... LAPIS

Local Automated Personnel Information System (DNAB) .... LAPIS

Local Automatic Circuit Exchange [Telecommunications] .... LACE

Local Automatic Message Accounting [Telecommunications] (TEL) .... LAMA

Local Baggage Committee [IATA] (DS) .... LBC

Local Base Rescue [Air Force] (AFM) .... LBR

Local Batch (IAA) .... LB

Local Battery [Radio] .... LB

Local Battery .... LBA

Local Battery Apparatus .... LBA

Local Battery Magneto Call Telephone Exchange (IAA) .... LBMCTX

Local Battery Signaling [Telecommunications] (IAA) .... LBS

Local Battery Supply [Telecommunications] (IAA) .... LBS

Local Battery Switchboard [Telecommunications] (IAA) .... LBS

Local Battery System [Telecommunications] (IAA) .... LBS

Local Battery Telephone [Telecommunications] (IAA) .... LBT

Local Battery Telephone Exchange [Telecommunications] (IAA) .... LBTX

Local Battery Telephone Set [Telecommunications] (IAA) .... LBTS

Local Battery Telephone Switchboard [Telecommunications] (IAA) .... LBTS

Local Battery with Buzzer Calling Telephone Exchange [Telecommunications] (IAA) .... LBWBUZCALTX

Local Battery with Magneto and Buzzer Calling Telephone Exchange [Telecommunications] (IAA) .... LBWMABCTX

Local Board .... LB

Local Board Memoranda .... LBM

Local Board of Health [British] .... LBH

Local Boards of the Selective Service System .... LBSS

Local Bus Adapter [Computer science] .... LBA

Local Bus Adaptor (NITA) .... LBA

Local Bus Controller .... LBC

Local Bus Video .... LBV

Local Calibration Procedure .... LCP

Local Call [Followed by telephone number] LC

Local Cartage National Conference [Later, LSHCNC] .... LCNC

Local Cataloguing Service (NITA) .... LOCAS

Local Cerebral Blood Flow [Medicine] .... LCBF

Local Cerebral Glucose Utilization [Biochemistry] .... LCGU

Local Cerebral Metabolic Rate for Glucose [Brain research] .... LCMRGlc

Local Change Control Board (MCD) .... LCCB

Local Channel (CET) LC

Local Circuit Switched Network .... LCSN

Local City Hospital (DAVI) .... LCH

Local Civil Defense Operating Systems Evaluation Model (PDAA) .... LCDOSEM

Local Civil Noon (ADA) .... LCN

Local Civil Time .... LCT

Local Climatological Data [A publication] .... LCD

Local Collaborative Projects [Between business and education] [British] .... LCP

Local Combat Air Patrol .... LCAP

Local Command Headquarters [NATO] (NATG) .... LCHQ

Local Commandant, Military Police [British military] (DMA) .... LCMP

Local Committee Operations Manual [A publication] (EAAP) .... LCOM

Local Communication Network (ACRL) .... LCN

Local Communications Adapter [IBM Corp.] .... LCA

Local Communications Area (KSC) LCC

Local Communications Complex LCC

Local Communications Console LCC

Local Communications Network (GAVI) .... LCN

Local Communications Service Order .... LCSO

Local Communications Services [British] .... LCS

Local Communications Services/Information Services (NITA) .... LCS/IS

Local Community (ADA) .... LOCOM

Local Computer Network .... LCN

Local Concentrator Switching Unit [Telecommunications] (TEL) .... LCSU

Local Configuration Control Board (AABC) .... LCCB

Local Control Console (CAAL) LCC

Local Control Facility [FAA] (TAG) .... LCF

Local Control Hydraulic Panel .... LCHP

Local Control Number (MCD) .... LCN

Local Control Panel (CAAL) .... LCP

Local Control Point [Telecommunications] (TEL) .... LCP

Local Control Unit (IAA) .... LCU

Local Control Valve [Nuclear energy] (NRCH) LCV

Local Cooperation Agreement [Army Corps of Engineers] .... LCA

Local Coordinating Committee LCC

Local Coordinator (FAAC) .... LOCOR

Local Core Alignment [Telecommunications] (NITA) .... LCA

Local Correlation-Tracking [Instrumental technique] .... LCT

Local Course Improvement [National Science Foundation] (EDAC) .... LOCI

Local Courts and Municipal Gazette [Toronto, ON] [A publication] (DLA) .... Loc Ct Gaz

Local Courts and Municipal Gazette [Toronto, ON] [A publication] (DLA) .... Local Ct & Mun Gaz

Local Cycle Fatigue (IEEE) .... LCF

Local Damage Assessment Model (PDAA) .... LDAM

Local Damping Control [Automotive engineering] .... LDC

Local Data Administrator .... LDA

Local Data Base System (MHDI) .... LDBS

Local Data Buffer (IAA) .... LDB

Local Data Concentrator [Telecommunications] .... LDD

Local Data Distribution .... LDD

Local Data Manager .... LDM

Local Data Package (KSC) .... LDP

Local Data Processor (AABC) .... LDT

Local Daylight Saving Time .... LDT

Local Defence Volunteers [Later called Home Guards] [British World War II] .... LDV

Local Defense Center .... LDC

Local Defense District Craft .... LODC

Local Defense Forces .... LDF

Local Delivery .... LD

Local Density Functional Theory [Chemistry] .... LDF

Local Density of Electron States [Physical chemistry] .... LDOS

Local Density of States [Solid state physics] .... LDOS

Local Dental Officer .... LDO

Local Dentist (DAVI) .... LDDS

Local Departmental Committee [British labor] .... LDC

Local Descriptor Table [Computer science] .... LDT

Local Design Agency (MCD) .... LDA
Local Development Company .... LDC
Local Development District .... LDD
Local DGPS [*Differential*] [*Global Positioning System*] (GAVI) .... LDGPS
Local Digital Distribution Subsystem .... LDDS
Local Digital Message Exchange (AABC) .... LDMX
Local Digital Switch [*Telecommunications*] (TEL) .... LDS
Local Director (DCTA) .... LD
Local Directory (ACRL) .... LD
Local Disease .... LOCD
Local Display Adapter (MHDB) .... LDA
Local Display Controller .... LDC
Local Distributed Data Interface [*Telecommunications*] .... LDDI
Local Distribution Company .... LDC
Local Distribution Service [*Cable TV network*] (NITA) .... LDS
Local Distribution Service Unit (IAA) .... LDSU
Local Distribution System [*or Service*] [*Cable television*] (MDG) .... LDS
Local Doctor of Dental Surgery (MAE) .... LDDS
Local Dynamics Experiment [*Marine science*] (MSC) .... LDE
Local Economic Consequences Study [*Military*] .... LECS
Local Economic Development Corp. .... LEDC
Local Education Agencies (PAZ) .... LEAs
Local Education Agency [*School district*] [*HEW*] (OICC) .... LEA
Local Education Authorities (ECON) .... LEAS
Local Education Authorities and Schools Item Banking [*Project*] (AIE) .... LEASIB
Local Education Authorities Project for School Management Training (AIE) .... LEAP
Local Education Authority [*British*] .... LEA
Local Education Authority Training Grants Scheme (AIE) .... LEATGS
Local Effective Mole Fraction [*Chemistry*] .... LEMF
Local Elected Official (OICC) .... LEO
Local Elected Officials Project of the Center for Innovative Diplomacy [*Defunct*] (EA) .... LEOPCID
Local Emergency Management Officer .... LEMO
Local Emergency Operations Controller .... LEOC
Local Emergency Planning Committee [*Hazardous waste*] .... LEPC
Local Emergency Planning Committee [*For hazard analysis*] .... LEPC
Local Employment Act [*Town planning*] [*British*] .... LEA
Local Employment Committee [*Department of Employment*] [*British*] .... LEC
Local Employment Development Initiative [*Australia*] .... LEDI
Local Employment Network (AIE) .... LEN
Local Engineering Change [*DoD*] .... LEC
Local Engineering Control Office [*Telecommunications*] (TEL) .... LECO
Local Engineering Instruction (DNAB) .... LEI
Local Engineering Specifications [*DoD*] .... LES
Local Engineering Standard (IAA) .... LES
Local Enterprise Companies [*Scotland*] (ECON) .... LECS
Local Enterprise Program .... LEP
Local Enterprise Trust [*British*] .... LET
Local Entry Network (NITA) .... LEN
Local Ethernet Bridge [*RAD Network Devices, Inc.*] .... LEB
Local Exchange [*Telecommunications*] (TEL) .... LE
Local Exchange Area Planning Simulation [*Bell Laboratories*] .... LEAPS
Local Exchange Carrier [*Telecommunications*] (PCM) .... LEC
Local Exchange/Packet Handler (ACRL) .... LE/PH
Local Exchange Test Bed [*Telecommunications*] (TEL) .... LETB
Local Excitatory State .... LES
Local Exhaust Ventilation [*Hazardous material control*] .... LEV
Local Export Control [*British*] (DS) .... LEC
Local Feed Junctor [*Telecommunications*] (NITA) .... LFJ
Local Field Potential [*Neurobiology*] .... LEP
Local Field Potential [*Electrophysiology*] .... LFP
Local File Manager .... LFM
Local Files Check .... LFC
Local Film .... LF
Local Flow Management/Profile Descent .... LFM/PD
Local Flying Area [*Aviation*] (DA) .... LFA
Local Force [*Viet Cong combat force*] .... LF
Local Form Session Identifier (ACRL) .... LFSID
Local Format Storage .... LFS
Local Forms Control [*Computer science*] (CMD) .... LFC
Local Freight Agent .... LFA
Local Frequency Distribution .... LFD
Local Geomagnetic Time .... LGT
Local Glucose Utilization [*Physiology*] .... LGU
Local Government (ADA) .... LG
Local Government Administration .... LGA
Local Government Advisory Board [*Tasmania, Australia*] .... LGAB
Local Government and Magisterial Reports [*England*] [*A publication*] (DLA) .... Local Gov
Local Government and Magisterial Reports [*England*] [*A publication*] (DLA) .... Local Gov't
Local Government Area (ADA) .... LGA
Local Government Association of New South Wales [*Australia*] .... LGANSW
Local Government Association of South Australia .... LGASA
Local Government Association of the Northern Territory [*Australia*] .... LGANT
Local Government Audit [*British*] .... LGA
Local Government Auditors' Association of New South Wales [*Australia*] .... LGAANSW
Local Government Auditors' Board [*Queensland, Australia*] .... LGAB
Local Government Board .... LGB
Local Government Board Office [*British*] .... LGBO
Local Government Boundaries Commission [*New South Wales, Australia*] .... LGBC
Local Government Boundary Commission for England .... LGBCE
Local Government Center [*Database producer*] (EA) .... LGC
Local Government Chronicle [*1855*] [*A publication*] (DLA) .... LGC
Local Government Chronicle [*London, England*] [*A publication*] (DLA) .... Loc Gov Chron
Local Government Chronicle and Magisterial Reporter [*London*] [*A publication*] (DLA) .... Loc Govt Chr & Mag Rep
Local Government Clerks' Association [*Australia*] .... LGCA
Local Government Clerks' Association of New South Wales [*Australia*] .... LGCANSW
Local Government Clerks' Board [*Queensland, Australia*] .... LGCB
Local Government Clerks' Certificate .... LGCC
Local Government Commission [*Victoria, Australia*] .... LGC
Local Government Council .... LGC
Local Government Electrical Engineering Qualifications Committee [*Australia*] .... LGEEQC
Local Government Electricity Association of New South Wales [*Australia*] .... LGEANSW
Local Government Energy Management Program .... LGEMP
Local Government Engineer .... LGE
Local Government Engineering Qualifications Committee [*Australia*] .... LGEQC
Local Government Engineers' Association of New South Wales [*Australia*] .... LGEANSW
Local Government Financial System (MHDB) .... LGFS
Local Government Grants Commission .... LGGC
Local Government Information Center .... LOGIC
Local Government Information Network [*Information service or system*] .... LOGIN
Local Government Information Unit [*British*] .... LGIU
Local Government Journal [*A publication*] (ROG) .... LGJ
Local Government Journal of Western Australia [*A publication*] .... Local Govt Jl WA
Local Government Library [*A publication*] .... LGL
Local Government Management [*A publication*] .... LGM
Local Government Management Board (AIE) .... LGMB
Local Government Office .... LGO
Local Government Operational Research Unit [*British*] (DI) .... LGORU
Local Government Qualifications Board [*Victoria, Australia*] .... LGQB
Local Government Reorganization [*British*] .... LGR
Local Government Reports [*England*] [*A publication*] (DLA) .... LGR
Local Government Reports [*England*] [*A publication*] (DLA) .... LGR (Eng)
Local Government Reports [*New Zealand*] [*A publication*] (DLA) .... NZLGR
Local Government Reports of Australia [*A publication*] (DLA) .... Local Gov R Aust
Local Government Services Bureau [*South Australia*] .... LGSB
Local Government Superannuation Board [*Queensland, Australia*] .... LGSB
Local Government Town Planners' Board [*Queensland, Australia*] .... LGTPB
Local Government Training Board [*British*] .... LGTB
Local Government Valuers' Committee [*New South Wales, Australia*] .... LGVC
Local Graphics Library [*Cambridge Computer Graphics Ltd.*] [*Software package*] (NCC) .... LGL
Local Head Office [*British*] (DCTA) .... LHO
Local Health Authority [*British*] .... LHA
Local Health Councils [*Scotland*] (DAVI) .... LHC
Local Healthcare Executive Group (HCT) .... LHEG
Local Hemolysis in Gel (PDAA) .... LHG
Local Horizontal .... LH
Local Hour Angle [*Navigation*] .... LHA
Local Hour Angle of Mean Sun .... LHAMS
Local Hour Angle of True Sun .... LHATS
Local Housing Authority .... LHA
Local Import Control [*British*] (DS) LIC
Local Inclusive Tour (DCTA) .... LIT
Local Income Tax (PDAA) .... LIT
Local Indigenous Civilian [*Military*] LIC
Local Industry Advisory Committee [*Civil defense*] .... LIAC
Local Information Network for Universal Service [*Telecommunications service*] (TSSD) .... LINUS
Local Initiatives Program [*Canada*] .... LIP
Local Initiatives Support Corp. (EA) .... LISC
Local Input/Output Nozzle [*Computer science*] .... LION
Local Interagency Coordinating Council LICC
Local Interconnect Option [*Wang Laboratories, Inc.*] (BYTE) .... LIO
Local Interneuron [*Neuroanatomy*] LI
Local Interstellar Cloud [*Astronomy*] LIC
Local Irradiation (MAE) LX
Local Issue Data [*Telecommunications*] (TEL) .... LID
Local Job Entry .... LJE
Local Job Processing (IAA) .... LJP
Local Joint Consultative Committee [*British*] (DCTA) .... LJCC
Local Junction Switching Unit [*Telecommunications*] (TEL) .... LJSU
Local Labour Market Information/Intelligence [*British*] (AIE) .... LLMI
Local Language Program .... LLP
Local Leak Rate Test [*Nuclear energy*] (NRCH) .... LLRT
Local Leak Rate Test [*Nuclear energy*] (IEEE) .... LRT
Local Lesion [*Pathology*] LL
Local Level Control [*Electronics*] LLC
Local Library System [*OCLC*] .... LLS
Local Line [*Telecommunications*] LL
Local Line Feed [*Telecommunications*] (DNAB) .... LOC LF
Local Line Network [*Telecommunications*] (NITA) .... LLN
Local Linearization LL
Local Lockout (IAA) .... LLO
Local Loop Access Ring [*Telecommunications*] (ACRL) .... LLAR
Local Loopback (MHDB) LL
Local Maintenance and Management of Facilities [*Military*] (AABC) .... LMMF
Local Management Committee .... LMC
Local Management Interface [*Telecommunications*] (ACRL) .... LMI

Local Management of Schools [British]	LMS
Local Manual Attempt Recording (TEL)	LOMAR
Local Manufacture (AAG)	LM
Local Marshalling Areas (MCD)	LMA
Local Mate Competition [Entomology]	LMC
Local Maximum Likelihood Estimates [Statistics]	LMLE
Local Mean Time (AFM)	LMT
Local Measured Service [Telecommunications] (TEL)	LMS
Local Medical Committee [British]	LMC
Local Medical Doctor	LMD
Local Memory	LM
Local Memory Bus Interface [Computer science]	LMBI
Local Memory Image	LMI
Local Message Box (NATG)	LMB
Local Message Metering Service [Telecommunications] (TEL)	LMMS
Local Message Switched Network	LMSN
Local Militia [British military] (DMA)	LM
Local Missile Selector (IAA)	LMS
Local Multipoint Distribution Service [Telecommunications]	LMDS
Local Multipoint Distribution System [Telecommunications] (ACRL)	LMDS
Local Multipoint Distribution Systems [Broadcasting term]	LMDS
Local Name Base [Computer science]	LNB
Local Nasal Immunotherapy	LNIT
Local National	LN
Local National Forces [SEATO] (CINC)	LNF
Local Nationals, Direct Hire [Military] (AABC)	LNDH
Local Nature Reserve (PDAA)	LNR
Local Naval Commander	LNC
Local Navy Authority	LNA
Local Navy Supervising Activity	LNSA
Local Neglect of Differential Overlap [Physical chemistry]	LNDO
Local Network Emulator	LNE
Local Networks, Edmonton, AB, Canada [Library symbol] [Library of Congress] (LCLS)	CaAELN
Local Networks, Edmonton, Alberta [Library symbol National Library of Canada] (NLC)	AELN
Local Non-Switched Network	LNSN
Local Notice to Mariners	LNM
Local Number Dialed [Telecommunications] (TEL)	LND
Local Number Dialling [Telecommunications] (NITA)	LND
Local Numbering Area [Telecommunications] (TEL)	LNA
Local Office	LO
Local Office Microcomputer Project (NITA)	LOMP
Local Office Online Payment System [Unemployment insurance]	LOOPS
Local Office Project [Department of Health and Social Security] [British]	LOP
Local Officials' Administration Network [An association]	LOAN
Local Off-Net Access Line [Telecommunications] (TEL)	LONAL
Local Online Network System	LONS
Local On-Scene Commander [Military] (DNAB)	LOSC
Local Operating Procedures (AFM)	LOP
Local Operating Station (DNAB)	LOS
Local Operating System (IAA)	LOS
Local Operational Plot	LOP
Local Order	LO
Local Original Channel [Cable television broadcasting]	LOC
Local Origination [Television programming]	LO
Local Oscillator [Electronics]	LO
Local Oscillator Filter [Electronics]	LOF
Local Oscillator Frequency [Electronics]	LOF
Local Osteolytic Hypercalcemia [Endocrinology]	LOH
Local Overseas Allowance [British military] (DMA)	LOA
Local Oxidation of Polysilicon over Silicon [Transistor technology]	LOPOS
Local Oxidation of Silicon [Transistor technology]	LOCOS
Local Oxidation of Silicon on Sapphire [Transistor technology] (IAA)	LOSOS
Local Packet Switched Network	LPSN
Local Pastors [British]	LP
Local Patching Panel	LPP
Local Pay Authority (AIE)	LPA
Local Payment of Airline (MCD)	LOPA
Local Payment Receipt (AABC)	LPR
Local Planning Assistance (OICC)	LPA
Local Planning Authority [British] (DCTA)	LPA
Local Point Warning [Military]	LPW
Local Population Studies Society [British]	LPSS
Local Post (EA)	LOPO
Local Post Collectors Society (EA)	LPCS
Local Power Density (NRCH)	LPD
Local Power Range Monitor (NRCH)	LPRM
Local Primary Reference Source	LPRS
Local Process Control Host (IAA)	LPCH
Local Process Specification (NG)	LPS
Local Processing Agency [Department of Housing and Urban Development] (GFGA)	LPA
Local Processor Link	LPL
Local Processor Memory (IAA)	LPM
Local Procurement [Military]	LP
Local Procurement Direct [Military]	LPD
Local Public Agency	LPA
Local Public Document Room (GFGA)	LPDR
Local Public Employment Office	LPEO
Local Public Transportation	LPT
Local Public Works Act (OICC)	LPWA
Local Purchase (AFM)	LP
Local Purchase Order	LOCPURO
Local Purchase Order	LPO

Local Qualitative Radio [Ratings] (NTCM)	LQR
Local Radio Luminosity Function [Cosmology]	LRLF
Local Radiotherapy	LRT
Local Reference Beam [Holography]	LRB
Local Regional Access Node (MCD)	LRAN
Local/Remote [Telecommunications] (TEL)	L/R
Local/Remote Control Unit	L/RCU
Local Resource Enhancement [Biology]	LRE
Local Scientific Survey Module [NASA]	LSSM
Local Service Access Point [Telecommunications] (OSI)	LSAP
Local Service for Mobiles [Computer science]	LSM
Local Service Planning System [Telecommunications] (TEL)	LSPS
Local Servicing Control Center [Telecommunications] (TEL)	LSCC
Local Servicing Control Unit [Telecommunications] (TEL)	LSCU
Local Session Identification [Computer science] (IBMDP)	LSID
Local Shared Resources [Computer science] (IBMDP)	LSR
Local Side Effects [Pharmacology] (DAVI)	LSE
Local Sidereal Time (MSA)	LSDT
Local Sidereal Time	LST
Local Solar Time	LST
Local Spin Density [Physics]	LSD
Local Spinal Glucose Utilization [Medicine]	LSGU
Local Standard of Rest [Galactic science]	LSR
Local Standard Time	LST
Local Stock Number	LSN
Local Storage Address Register (IAA)	LSAR
Local Storage Function Register	LSFR
Local Storage Register (NITA)	LSR
Local Storage Unit [Computer science]	LSU
Local Store	LS
Local Store Data Register	LSDR
Local Store Pointer	LSP
Local Summer Time [Astronomy] (IAA)	LST
Local Sunrise	LSR
Local Sunset	LS
Local Sunset Time (WDMC)	LS
Local Supercluster [Cosmology]	LSC
Local Supervising Authority	LSA
Local Switching Centre [Telecommunications] (NITA)	LSC
Local Switching Replacement Planning [Telecommunications] (TEL)	LSRP
Local Switching System General Requirement [Telecommunications]	LSSGR
Local Switching Unit [Telecommunications] (TEL)	LSU
Local Synchronization Subsystem [Telecommunications] (TEL)	LSS
Local Synchronization Utility [Telecommunications] (TEL)	LSU
Local System Queue Area [Computer science] (BUR)	LSQA
Local Tactical Grid [Military] (NVT)	LTG
Local Tax Office [British]	LTO
Local Telephone Circuit [Telecommunications] (TEL)	LTC
Local Telephone Exchange (NITA)	LTE
Local Terminal Controller	LTC
Local Test Desk [Telecommunications] (KSC)	LTD
Local Thermal Equilibrium [Physical chemistry]	LTE
Local Thermodynamic Equilibrium [or Equivalent] [Astronautics, astrophysics]	LTE
Local Time	LT
Local Tourism Plan	LTP
Local Track Quality (NVT)	LTQ
Local Training Area (MCD)	LTA
Local Training Flight	LTF
Local Training Plan [Job Training and Partnership Act] (OICC)	LTP
Local Urgent Mail [British]	LUM
Local User Terminal	LUT
Local Utah Freight Bureau, Omaha NE [STAC]	LUF
Local Vehicle Licensing Office [British]	LVLO
Local Vertical (KSC)	L/V
Local Vertical and Orbit Plane	LVOP
Local Vertical/Local Horizontal (NASA)	LVLH
Local Vertical/Relative Velocity Vector	LV/RVV
Local Veterans Employment Representative [Department of Labor]	LVER
Local Veterinary Inspector [British]	LVI
Local Virtual Address	LVA
Local Wage Rate	LWR
Local Welfare Authority [British]	LWA
Local Welfare Authority Full Time [British]	LWF
Local Winter Time [Astronomy] (IAA)	LWT
Local Works Managing Budget [British Armed Forces]	LWMB
Local Zone Time	LZT
Local-Area Telephone Authority [Telecommunications]	LATA
Local-Battery Talking, Common-Battery Signaling [Telecommunications] (TEL)	LBT CBS
Local-Density (Functional) Approximation [Physical chemistry]	LDA
Local-Density Functional Equation (MCD)	LDF
Localization Code (IAA)	LC
Localized Collagen Dystrophy [Medicine] (DAVI)	LCD
Localized Corrosion (PDAA)	LC
Localized Gain Region (PDAA)	LGR
Localized Hypertrophic Neuropathy [Medicine]	LHN
Localized Induction Approximation [Mathematics]	LIA
Localized Juvenile Periodontitis [Dentistry]	LJP
Localized Leukocyte Mobilization	LLM
Localized Magnetic Resonance (DAVI)	LMR
Localized Plaque Formation [Dentistry] (MAE)	LPF
Localized Vibrational Mode (PDAA)	LVM
Localizer (CET)	LCL
Localizer (IAA)	LCLZR

Localizer .... LCZR
Localizer [ICAO designator] (CET) .... LLZ
Localizer (MSA) .... LOC
Localizer Directional Aid [Aviation] .... LDA
Localizer Line of Sight .... LOC
Localizer Station [ITU designation] (CET) .... RLL
Locally Assigned Convoy Route Carrier Code .... LACRC
Locally Assigned Reporting Code [Munitions reports] (AFM) ... LARC
Locally Defined Neighborhood .... LDN
Locally Engaged .... LE
Locally Engaged Staff .... LES
Locally Enlisted Personnel [British military] (DMA) .... LEP
Locally Excited [Physical chemistry] .... LE
Locally Funded (AFM) .... LF
Locally Generated Income (MCD) .... LGI
Locally Integrated Software Architecture [Apple microcomputer] [Computer science] .... LISA
Locally Manufactured Equipment .... LME
Locally Most Powerful Rank Test [Statistics] .... LMPRT
Locally One-Dimensional (OA) .... LOD
Locally Unwanted Land Use [i.e. garbage incinerators, prisons, roads, etc.] .... LULU
Locally-Normalized Discrete Correlation Function [Mathematics] ... LNDCF
Locally-Originated Program [Broadcasting] (NTCM) .... LOP
Locally-Oxidized Complementary Metal-Oxide Semiconductor (PDAA) .... LOCMOS
Locally-Weighted Scatterplot Smoother [Medicine] .... LOWESS
Local-Pair [Superconductivity] .... LP
LocalTalk Link Access Protocol [Computer science] (ACRL) ... LLAP
Locarno [Switzerland ICAO location identifier] (ICLI) .... LSZL
LOCAS Users Group (NITA) .... LUG
Locate (MSA) .... LCT
Locate (MSA) .... LOC
Locate Drum Address (CET) .... LDA
Locate in Europe Information Retrieval System [University of Strathclyde] [Glasgow, Scotland] [Information service or system] (IID) ... EUROLOC
Locate in Scotland [Investment group] (ECON) .... LIS
Located (AFM) .... LCTD
Locating Head [Engineering] (OA) .... LH
Locating Point [Optical tooling] .... LP
Location .... LCTN
Location .... LCTN
Location (AFM) .... LOC
Location (VRA) .... loc
Location (DAVI) .... LOCAT
Location .... LOCN
Location [Symbol on map] X
Location Aid Device (MCD) .... LAD
Location and Movement Analysis System (MCD) .... LAMAS
Location Audit Program [Navy] (NG) .... LAP
Location, Command, and Telemetry (IAA) .... LCT
Location Counter [Computer science] LC
Location Counter [Computer science] .... LCNTR
Location Counter [Computer science] .... LOC
Location Dependent .... LOD
Location Evaluation Recognition and Statistical Comparison (PDAA) ... LERSC
Location File (MCD) .... LOCF
Location/Identification Transmitter [NASA] .... LIT
Location Identifier (IAA) LI
Location Identifier [FAA] (TAG) .... LOCID
Location Identifiers [A publication FAA] .... LOID
Location of Launching Site [Army] .... LOLAS
Location of Miss and Hit [Marksmanship training] [Army] (INF) ... LOMAH
Location of Offices Bureau [British] .... LOB
Location Stack Register .... LSR
Location Transactivating Region [Medicine] (DMAA) .... LTR
Location-Based Entertainment .... LBE
Locative (Case) [Linguistics] I
Locative (Case) [Linguistics] .... LOC
Locator [Compass] L
Locator [Compass] (DA) .... Latr
Locator .... LCTR
Locator at Back Course Marker (PDAA) .... LBCM
Locator at Middle Marker [Aviation] .... LMM
Locator at Outer Marker [Aviation] .... LOM
Locator Back Marker [Aviation] (DA) .... LBM
Locator Beacon L
Locator File [Information retrieval] .... LO
Locator Inner Marker [Aviation] (DA) .... LIM
Locator Lists [Army] LL
Locator Map in Source (IAA) .... LOMIS
Locavia 49 [France ICAO designator] (FAAC) .... LOC
Loccenius. De Jure Maritimo [A publication] (DLA) .... Locc
Loch L
Loch Ness Investigation Bureau [Inactive] (EA) .... LNIB
Loch Ness Phenomena Investigation Bureau [Later, LNIB] ... LNPIB
Locher Evers International Ltd. .... LEI
Lochgilphead [Scotland] [Airport symbol] (OAG) .... LPH
Lochiel Exploration Ltd. [Toronto Stock Exchange symbol] ... LHX
Loch's Horse [British military] (DMA) .... LH
Lock .... LCK
Lock [Postal Service standard] (OPSA) .... LCK
Lock [Automotive engineering] .... LK
Lock [Commonly used] (OPSA) .... LOCK
Lock Actuator (MCD) .... LA

Lock Forward .... LF
Lock Haven [Pennsylvania] [Airport symbol] (AD) .... LHV
Lock Haven, PA [Location identifier FAA] (FAAL) .... LHV
Lock Haven, PA [AM radio station call letters] .... WBPZ
Lock Haven, PA [FM radio station call letters] .... WSNU
Lock Haven State College, Lock Haven, PA [OCLC symbol] (OCLC) ... LQS
Lock Haven State College, Lock Haven, PA [Library symbol Library of Congress] (LCLS) .... PLhS
Lock Museum of America (EA) .... LMA
Lock on Track .... LOT
Lock Performance Monitoring System [DOD] [COE] (TAG) ... LPMS
Lock Pillar (AAG) .... LPLR
Lock Pointer Table .... LPT
Lock Rail .... LR
Lock Range (IAA) .... LR
Lock Up (ADA) .... LU
Lock Washer [Automotive engineering] .... LK/WA
Lock Washer [Automotive engineering] .... LKWASH
Locke Egg Serum [Medicine] (MAE) .... LES
Locke Rich Minerals [Vancouver Stock Exchange symbol] ... LKM
Locked (KSC) .... LKD
Locked Closed LC
Locked Door Seclusion [Medicine] (DMAA) .... LDS
Locked Octal (IAA) .... LOKTAL
Locked Open [Technical drawings] .... LO
Locked Oscillator .... LO
Locked Oscillator-Quadrature Grid [Computer science] ... LO-QG
Locked Rotor .... LKROT
Locked Shut (NRCH) .... LS
Locked-In Device (MSA) .... LID
Locked-On RADAR Bearing Indicator .... LORBI
Locked-Rotor Amperes (MSA) .... LRA
Lockeport Little School Museum, Lockeport, NS, Canada [Library symbol] [Library of Congress] (LCLS) .... CaNSLoLS
Lockeport Little School Museum, Nova Scotia [Library symbol National Library of Canada] (NLC) .... NSLLS
Locker (DNAB) .... LCKR
Locker .... LCKR
Locker (KSC) .... LKR
Locker Door Hydraulic Cylinder .... LDHC
Locke's Game Laws [5th ed.] [1866] [A publication] (DLA) ... Lock GL
Locket (ROG) .... LKT
Lockhart Elementary School, Massapequa, NY [Library symbol Library of Congress] (LCLS) .... NMassLE
Lockhart Rivers [Australia Airport symbol] (OAG) .... IRG
Lockhart, TX [AM radio station call letters] .... KFIT
Lockhead Petroleum Services Ltd., New Westminster, BC, Canada [Library symbol Library of Congress] (LCLS) ... CaBNWLP
Lockheed Air Terminal, Inc. [Subsidiary of Lockheed Aircraft Corp.] ... LAT
Lockheed Air Terminal, Inc. [Guam] [ICAO designator] (FAAC) ... XLG
Lockheed Aircraft Corp. [ICAO aircraft manufacturer identifier] (ICAO) ... L
Lockheed Aircraft Corp. [ICAO designator] (FAAC) .... LAC
Lockheed Airline System Simulation (PDAA) .... LASS
Lockheed Antisubmarine Warfare Systems Organization ... LAWSO
Lockheed Command and Tracking (IAA) .... LOCT
Lockheed DataPlan, Inc. [Information service or system] (IID) ... LDI
Lockheed Duats [ICAO designator] (FAAC) .... XDD
Lockheed Electronics Assembly Program .... LEAP
Lockheed Electronics Corp. [Subsidiary of Lockheed Aircraft Corp.] ... LEC
Lockheed Emergency Reset Timer (IAA) .... LERT
Lockheed Engineers for National Deployment (SAA) ...... LEND
Lockheed Information Systems (NITA) .... LIS
Lockheed Maintenance Recording System .... LMRS
Lockheed Martin [NYSE symbol] (TTSB) .... LMT
Lockheed Martin Corp. [NYSE symbol] (SAG) .... LMT
Lockheed Martin Corp. [Associated Press] (SAG) .... LockhM
Lockheed Martin Energy Systems, Inc. (GAAI) .... LMES
Lockheed Martin Idaho Technologies (GAAI) .... LMIT
Lockheed Martin Launch Vehicle .... LMLV
Lockheed Missile and Space Division (IAA) .... LMSD
Lockheed Missile Beacon (IAA) .... LOMB
Lockheed Missile System (MCD) .... LMS
Lockheed Missiles & Space Corp. [Subsidiary of Lockheed Aircraft Corp.] ... LMSC
Lockheed Missiles & Space Corp., Palo Alto, CA [Library symbol Library of Congress] (LCLS) .... CPaL
Lockheed Multiprocessor Simulation System (IEEE) .... LOMUSS
Lockheed Optical Communications and Tracking System ... LOCATS
Lockheed Petroleum Services Ltd., New Westminster, British Columbia [Library symbol National Library of Canada] (NLC) ... BNWLP
Lockheed Propulsion Co. [Division of Lockheed Aircraft Corp.] (KSC) ... LPC
Lockheed Radio Command (MUGU) .... LORC
Lockheed Space Operations Co. .... LSOC
Lockheed Standards .... LS
Lockheed Tracking and Control System .... LOCTRACS
Lockheed Training Reactor .... LTR
Lockheed Underwater Missile Facility (AAG) .... LUMF
Lockheed-California Co. [Division of Lockheed Aircraft Corp.] (MCD) ... CALAC
Lockheed-California Co. [Division of Lockheed Aircraft Corp.] ... LCC
Lockheed-California Co., Burbank, CA [Library symbol Library of Congress] (LCLS) .... CBbL
Lockheed-Georgia Co., Scientific and Technical Information Department, Marietta, GA [Library symbol Library of Congress] (LCLS) ... GMarLG
Lock-In .... LKN
Lock-In Amplifier (MAE) .... LIA
Locking [Lamp base type] (NTCM) L

Locking (KSC) ... LKG
Locknut (MSA) ... LKNT
Lock-On ... LO
Lock-On after Launch [*Weaponry*] (CAAL) ... LOAL
Lock-On Before Launch [*Missile*] (DOMA) ... LOBL
Lock-On Completed (MCD) ... LOC
Lock-On Initiated (MCD) ... LOI
Lock-Out ... LO
Lockout Relay (MCD) ... LOR
Lockport, IL [*FM radio station call letters*] ... WLRA
Lockport Memorial Hospital, Doctor's Library, Lockport, NY [*Library symbol Library of Congress*] (LCLS) ... NLockH
Lockport, NY [*AM radio station call letters*] ... WLVL
Lockport Public Library, Lockport, NY [*Library symbol Library of Congress*] (LCLS) ... NLock
Lockport Township Public Library, Lockport, IL [*Library symbol Library of Congress*] (LCLS) ... ILoc
Locks ... LCKS
Locks ... LCKS
Locks [*Commonly used*] (OPSA) ... LOCKS
Lockscrew ... LKSCR
Locksmith ... LOKSMTH
Locksmith ... LSMITH
Locksmith Security Association (EA) ... LSA
Lockup ... LKUP
Lock-Up Garage ... LUG
Lock-Up Solenoid [*Automotive engineering*] ... LUS
Lockwood Petroleum, Inc. [*Vancouver Stock Exchange symbol*] ... LOK
Lockwood Torday & Carlisle Ltd. [*British*] ... LTC
Lockwood's Reversed Cases [*New York*] [*A publication*] (DLA) ... Lock Rev Ca
Lockwood's Reversed Cases [*New York*] [*A publication*] (DLA) ... Lock Rev Cas
Loco [*Place*] [*Latin*] ... LO
Loco [*As Written*] [*Music*] ... LO
Loco [*Place*] [*Latin*] (WGA) ... LOC
Loco Citato [*In the Place Cited*] [*Latin*] ... LC
Loco Citato [*In the Place Cited*] [*Latin*] ... LO CIT
Loco Citato [*In the Place Cited*] [*Latin*] ... LOC CIT
Loco Dolenti [*To the Painful Spot*] [*Pharmacy*] ... LOC DOL
Loco Laudato [*In the Place Quoted*] [*Latin*] ... LL
Loco Laudato [*In the Place Quoted*] [*Latin*] ... LOC LAUD
Loco Primo Citato [*In the Place First Cited*] [*Latin*] (ILCA) ... Loc Primo Cit
Loco Prius Citato [*In the Place First Cited*] [*Latin*] (ADA) ... LOC PRIUS CIT
Loco Sub Citato [*In the Place Cited Below*] [*Latin*] (ROG) ... LSC
Loco Supra Citato [*In the Place Cited Above*] [*Latin*] ... LSC
Locomotion (WDAA) ... LOCO
Locomotive (AABC) ... LOCO
Locomotive ... LOCOM
Locomotive and Allied Manufacturers' Association [*British*] (BI) ... LAMA
Locomotive and Carriage Institution of Great Britain and Eire (BI) ... LCIGB
Locomotive Club of Great Britain (BI) ... LCGB
Locomotive Engineers Mutual Life and Accident Insurance Association (EA) ... LEML & AIA
Locomotive Maintenance Officers' Association (EA) ... LMOA
Locomotor Neuron [*Neurology*] ... LMN
Locomotor Respiratory Coupling [*Physiology*] ... LRC
Loctite Corp. [*NYSE symbol*] (SPSG) ... LOC
Loctite Corp. [*Associated Press*] (SAG) ... Loctite
L'Octogone, Bibliotheque Municipale de LaSalle, Quebec [*UTLAS symbol*] ... LSQ
L'Octogone, Centre de la Culture, La Salle, PQ, Canada [*Library symbol*] [*Library of Congress*] (LCLS) ... CaQLsO
L'Octogone, Centre de la Culture, La Salle, Quebec [*Library symbol National Library of Canada*] (NLC) ... QLSO
Locum Tenens [*In the Place Of*] [*Latin*] ... LT
Locus [*Place*] [*Latin*] ... L
Locus Activation Region [*Genetics*] ... LAR
Locus Allowed (ROG) ... LA
Locus Ceruleus [*Brain anatomy*] ... LC
Locus Control Region [*Genetics*] ... LCR
Locus Monumenti [*Place of the Monument*] [*Latin*] ... LM
Locus of Control [*Psychology*] ... LC
Locus of Control Interview [*Psychology*] ... LCI
Locus of Radius ... L/R
Locus Sepulchri [*Place of the Sepulchre*] [*Latin*] ... LS
Locus Sigilli [*Place of the Seal*] [*Legal term Latin*] ... LS
Locus Standi Reports [*England*] [*A publication*] (DLA) ... Locus Standi
Locus Standi Reports [*A publication*] (DLA) ... LSR
Locust (MSA) ... LCT
Locust Bean Gum (OA) ... LBG
Locust Elementary School, Garden City, NY [*Library symbol*] [*Library of Congress*] (LCLS) ... NGcLE
Locust Grove, OK [*FM radio station call letters*] ... KEMX
Locust Valley High School, Locust Valley, NY [*Library symbol Library of Congress*] (LCLS) ... NLvHS
Locust Valley Intermediate School, Locust Valley, NY [*Library symbol Library of Congress*] (LCLS) ... NLvI
Locust Valley Public Library, Locust Valley, NY [*Library symbol Library of Congress*] (LCLS) ... NLv
Loda Public Library, Loda, IL [*Library symbol Library of Congress*] (LCLS) ... ILod
Lodar [*South Arabia*] [*Airport symbol*] (AD) ... LDR
Lode Resources Corp. [*Vancouver Stock Exchange symbol*] ... LRC
Lodestar Energy, Inc. [*Vancouver Stock Exchange symbol*] ... LOT
Lodge ... L
Lodge [*or Lodging*] (MCD) ... LDG
Lodge ... LDG
Lodge [*Commonly used*] (OPSA) ... LDGE
Lodge [*Commonly used*] (OPSA) ... LODG
Lodge [*Commonly used*] (OPSA) ... LODGE
Lodge of Instruction [*Freemasonry*] ... LOI
Lodge of Perfection [*Freemasonry*] (DAS) ... L of P
LodgeNet Entertainment [*NASDAQ symbol*] (TTSB) ... LNET
Lodgenet Entertainment Corp. [*NASDAQ symbol*] (SAG) ... LNET
Lodgenet Entertainment Corp. [*Associated Press*] (SAG) ... LodgEnt
Lodge-Pole Pine [*Utility pole*] [*Telecommunications*] (TEL) ... LP
Lodges [*Freemasonry*] (ROG) ... LL
Lodging Allowance [*British military*] (DMA) ... LA
Lodging Allowance [*British military*] (DMA) ... LgA
Lodging and Pay Allowance [*British military*] (DMA) ... L & PA
Lodi, CA [*AM radio station call letters*] ... KCVR
Lodi, CA [*FM radio station call letters*] ... KWIN
Lodi District Vintners Association (EA) ... LDVA
Lodi Memorial Library, Lodi, NJ [*Library symbol Library of Congress*] (LCLS) ... NjL
Lodi Metals, Inc. [*Vancouver Stock Exchange symbol*] ... LOD
Lodi Public Library, Lodi, CA [*Library symbol Library of Congress*] (LCLS) ... CLod
Lodja [*Zaire*] [*ICAO location identifier*] (ICLI) ... FZVA
Lodja [*Zaire*] [*Airport symbol*] (OAG) ... LJA
Lodwar [*Kenya*] [*ICAO location identifier*] (ICLI) ... HKLO
Lodz [*Poland*] [*Airport symbol*] (AD) ... LDZ
Lodzer Idishe Dramatishe Aktyorn (BJA) ... LIDA
Lodzer Young Men's Benevolent Society (EA) ... LYMBS
Loeb Classical Library. Harvard University Press [*A publication*] (BJA) ... LCL
Loehmann's Inc. [*NASDAQ symbol*] (TTSB) ... LOEH
Loei [*Thailand*] [*Airport symbol Obsolete*] (OAG) ... LOE
Loei [*Thailand*] [*ICAO location identifier*] (ICLI) ... VTUL
Loer, C. M., Reno NV [*STAC*] ... LCM
Loeser, Luftfarhtgesellschaft GmbH [*Germany ICAO designator*] (FAAC) ... LOE
Loess Hills Historical Society of Monona County, Whiting, IA [*Library symbol*] [*Library of Congress*] (LCLS) ... IaWhHi
Loevinger Sentence Completion Test (EDAC) ... LSCT
Loewen Group [*NASDAQ symbol*] (TTSB) ... LWNGF
Loewen Group Cap Ser'A' 'MIPS' [*NYSE symbol*] (TTSB) ... LWNPr
Loewen Group Capital Ltd. [*NYSE symbol*] (SAG) ... LWN
Loewen Group Capital LP [*Associated Press*] (SAG) ... LoewenG
Loewen Group, Inc. [*Associated Press*] (SAG) ... Loewen
Loewen Group, Inc. [*Toronto Stock Exchange symbol*] ... LWN
Loewen, Ondaatje, McCutcheon, Inc. [*Toronto Stock Exchange symbol Vancouver Stock Exchange symbol*] ... LOM
Loewenthal Papers [*Shanghai/Washington, DC*] [*A publication*] (BJA) ... LP
Loew's Corp. [*Formerly, Loew's Theatres, Inc.*] [*Associated Press*] (SAG) ... Loews
Loew's Corp. [*Formerly, Loew's Theatres, Inc.*] [*NYSE symbol*] (SPSG) ... LTR
Lofexidine (DMAA) ... LOF
Lofft on the Law of Libels [*A publication*] (DLA) ... Lofft Lib
Lofft's Elements of Universal Law [*A publication*] (DLA) ... Lofft Un L
Lofft's English King's Bench Reports [*1772-74*] [*A publication*] (DLA) ... Lofft
Lofft's English King's Bench Reports [*1772-74*] [*A publication*] (DLA) ... Lofft's Rep
Lofft's English King's Bench Reports [*1772-74*] [*A publication*] (DLA) ... Loft
Lofft's Maxims, Appended to Lofft's Reports [*A publication*] (DLA) ... Lofft Append
Loft Bomb Release Computer (MCD) ... LBRC
Loft Dried Paper (DGA) ... LD
LOFT [*Loss-of-Fluid Test*] **Lead Rod** (GAAI) ... LLR
Loft Line (MSA) ... LL
Loftier (ABBR) ... LFTIR
Loftiest (ABBR) ... LFTIT
Loftiness (ABBR) ... LFTINS
Lofty (ABBR) ... LFTY
Log Analyzer Processor [*Computer science*] ... LA
Log Book ... LB
Log Cabin [*Alabama*] [*Seismograph station code, US Geological Survey*] (SEIS) ... LCA
Log Cabin Federation (EA) ... LCF
Log Conversion Voltmeter ... LCVM
Log Count Rate [*Nuclear energy*] (NRCH) ... LCR
Log Dose Response [*Biochemical analysis*] ... LDR
Log File Editor (NITA) ... LOGFED
Log File Editor Processor [*Computer science*] ... LOGFED
Log Homes Council (EA) ... LHC
Log House Builder's Association of North America (EA) ... LHBANA
Log Mean Temperature ... LMT
Log Neutralization Index [*Microbiology*] ... LNI
Log Periodic [*Antenna*] (NATG) ... LP
Log Periodic Antenna ... LPA
Log Periodic Array Antenna ... LPAA
Log Periodic Broadband Antenna ... LPBBA
Log Periodic Dipole ... LPD
Log Periodic Dipole Antenna [*Military*] (CAAL) ... LPDA
Log Periodic Dipole Array ... LPDA
Log Periodic Scattering Array ... LPSA
Log Periodic V [*Antenna*] ... LPV
Log Recording [*Computer science*] ... LOGREC
Log Run [*Lumber*] ... LR
Log Voltmeter Converter ... LVC
Logal Educational Software & Systems Ltd. [*Associated Press*] (SAG) ... LogalEd
Logal Educational Software & Systems Ltd. [*NASDAQ symbol*] (SAG) ... LOGL
Logal Educational Softwr&Sys [*NASDAQ symbol*] (TTSB) ... LOGLF
Logan [*Utah*] [*Airport symbol*] (OAG) ... LGU
Logan [*Utah*] [*Seismograph station code, US Geological Survey Closed*] (SEIS) ... LOG
Logan Brothers Book Co. ... LB

Logan College of Chiropractic, Chesterfield, MO [Library symbol] [Library of Congress] (LCLS) .... MoCheL
Logan Herald-Observer, Logan, IA [Library symbol Library of Congress] (LCLS) .... IaLoH
Logan Junior High School, Princeton, IL [Library symbol Library of Congress] (LCLS) .... IPriLH
Logan Mines Ltd. [Vancouver Stock Exchange symbol] .... LOG
Logan, OH [AM radio station call letters] .... WLGN
Logan, OH [FM radio station call letters] .... WLGN-FM
Logan Public Library, Logan, UT [OCLC symbol] (OCLC) .... UUD
Logan, UT [Location identifier FAA] (FAAL) .... CCH
Logan, UT [FM radio station call letters] .... KBLQ
Logan, UT [AM radio station call letters] .... KLGN
Logan, UT [FM radio station call letters] .... KUSU
Logan, UT [FM radio station call letters] .... KVFM
Logan, UT [FM radio station call letters] .... KVNU
Logan, UT [Location identifier FAA] (FAAL) .... LGU
Logan, WV [AM radio station call letters] .... WLOG
Logan, WV [AM radio station call letters] .... WVOW
Logan, WV [FM radio station call letters] .... WVOW-FM
Loganair [ICAO designator] (AD) LC
Loganair Ltd. [British ICAO designator] (FAAC) .... LOG
Loganberry (ABBR) .... LGBR
Loganberry (ABBR) .... LGNBRY
Logan-Hocking County District Library, Logan, OH [Library symbol Library of Congress] (LCLS) .... OLogC
Loganiar Ltd. [British] .... LG
Logan-Keck-Stickney [Method] .... LKS
Logan's Compendium of Ancient Law [A publication] (DLA) .... Log Comp
Logan's Roadhouse [NASDAQ symbol] (TTSB) .... RDHS
Logan's Roadhouse, Inc. [Associated Press] (SAG) .... Logans
Logansort Financial [NASDAQ symbol] (TTSB) .... LOGN
Logansport Financial Corp. [NASDAQ symbol] (SAG) .... LOGN
Logansport Financial Corp. [Associated Press] (SAG) .... Lognspt
Logansport, IN [Location identifier FAA] (FAAL) .... GGP
Logansport, IN [FM radio station call letters] .... WLHM
Logansport, IN [AM radio station call letters] .... WSAL
Logansport-Cass County Public Library, Logansport, IN [Library symbol Library of Congress] (LCLS) .... InLog
Logar [Afghanistan] [ICAO location identifier] (ICLI) .... OALG
Logarithm [Mathematics] L
Logarithm [Mathematics] .... LOG
Logarithm (IDOE) .... log
Logarithm (Natural) [Mathematics] .... ln
Logarithm of the Odds .... LOD
Logarithm of the Odds [Favoring linkage] [Genetics] (DOG) .... lod
Logarithm Tangent Bearing (IAA) .... LOGTANBG
Logarithm to the Base e [Mathematics] (DAVI) .... log$_e$
Logarithmic Amplifier .... LA
Logarithmic Amplifier (IEEE) .... LOAMP
Logarithmic Amplifier (IAA) .... LOGAMP
Logarithmic Computing Instrument .... LOCI
Logarithmic Computing Instrument (HGAA) .... LOGI
Logarithmic Correlators Ratiometer (PDAA) .... LCR
Logarithmic Decrement (IAA) .... LOGDEC
Logarithmic Fast Time Constant .... LOGFTC
Logarithmic Feedback Element [Computer science] .... LFE
Logarithmic Histogram Scanning [Mass spectrometry] .... LGH
Logarithmic Intermediate Frequency Amplifier (IAA) .... LOGIFAMP
Logarithmic Mean Temperature Difference .... LMTD
Logarithmic Mean Temperature Difference (IAA) .... LOGMTD
Logarithmic Outline [or Online] Processing System for Analog Data (IEEE) .... LOPAD
Logarithmic Periodic Antenna (MCD) .... LPA
Logarithmic Radiation Monitor (NRCH) .... LRM
Logarithmic Ratio Module .... LRM
Logarithmic Series Distribution [Statistics] .... LSD
Logarithmic Video Amplifier (IAA) .... LVA
Logger (ABBR) .... LGGR
Loggerhead (ABBR) .... LGGRHD
Loggia (VRA) .... log
Logging .... LOG
Logic .... LGC
Logic (MSA) .... LGC
Logic .... LOG
Logic Analysis for Maintenance Planning (MHDB) .... LAMP
Logic Analysis System [Rohde and Schwartz] [Germany] (NITA) .... LAS
Logic and Adder (IAA) .... LAD
Logic and Control Simulation (NITA) .... LOCS
Logic and Control Simulator [Computer science] (BUR) .... LOCS
Logic and Information Network Compiler II [Computer science] (HGAA) .... LINEII
Logic and Test Function Drawer [Computer science] (MCD) .... LTFD
Logic Automated Stimulus and Response (MCD) .... LASAR
Logic Block Diagram (IAA) .... LBD
Logic Bucket Number (NITA) .... LBN
Logic Bus Monitor [Computer science] (CET) .... LBM
Logic Cell (IAA) LC
Logic Cell Array (IAA) .... LCA
Logic Clock Pulse Generator [Computer science] .... LCPG
Logic Control Block .... LCB
Logic Control Output Module (MCD) .... LCOM
Logic Corp. LC
Logic Design Data [Telecommunications] (TEL) .... LDD
Logic Design Translator [Computer science] .... LDT
Logic Devices [NASDAQ symbol] (TTSB) .... LOGC

Logic Devices, Inc. [NASDAQ symbol] (SAG) .... LOGC
Logic Devices, Inc. [Associated Press] (SAG) .... LogicD
Logic Driver [Computer science] .... LD
Logic Element .... LE
Logic Enhanced Memory .... LEM
Logic Fault Simulator [Computer science] .... LFS
Logic Flow Chart [Computer science] .... LFC
Logic Function .... LF
Logic Gate Expander [Computer science] .... LGE
Logic Generating Language [Computer science] .... LOGEL
Logic In, Documents Out (PDAA) .... LIDO
Logic Inference per Second (IAA) .... LIPS
Logic Level Driver [Computer science] (MCD) .... LLD
Logic Link Control [Network interfacing] (NITA) LLC
Logic Master Tape (IAA) .... LMT
Logic Model [Fault isolation device] [Army] (MCD) .... LOGMOD
Logic Module [Computer science] (MCD) .... LM
Logic of Computers Operating System (MCD) .... LOCOSS
Logic Probe .... LP
Logic Processor (IAA) .... LOP
Logic Refresh Control Unit .... LRCU
Logic State Analyzer (IAA) .... LSA
Logic Tables (IEEE) .... LOGTAB
Logic Theorist [or Theory] [Computer science] .... LT
Logic Theory Machine (SAA) .... LTM
Logic Time Analyzer (IAA) .... LTA
Logic Tree .... LT
Logic Tree Trouble-Shooting Aid (PDAA) .... LTTA
Logic Works [NASDAQ symbol] (TTSB) .... LGWX
Logic Works, Inc. [NASDAQ symbol] (SAG) .... LGWX
Logic Works, Inc. [Associated Press] (SAG) .... Logic
Logical (ABBR) .... LGCL
Logical .... LGCL
Logical Acknowledgement Message [Aviation] (DA) .... LAM
Logical Address .... LA
Logical Address Strobe .... LAS
Logical Algorithmic Language [Computer science] (CSR) .... LOGAL
Logical Algorithmic Language [Computer science] .... LOGALGOL
Logical Analysis Device .... LAD
Logical Analyzer of Hypothesis (IEEE) .... LAH
Logical Applications Group [Social Security Administration] .... LAG
Logical Aptitude Device (BUR) .... LAD
Logical Block .... LB
Logical Block Address [Computer science] .... LBA
Logical Channel (PDAA) LC
Logical Channel Fill .... LCF
Logical Channel Group Number [Telecommunications] (OSI) .... LCGN
Logical Channel Number [Computer science] (TNIG) .... LCN
Logical Channel Queue [Computer science] .... LCH
Logical Channel Queue [Computer science] (BUR) .... LCQ
Logical Channel Termination .... LCT
Logical Channel Termination (NITA) .... LCT
Logical Channels Switching Program (MHDB) .... LCSP
Logical Commands .... LOGANDS
Logical Communications, Inc. [East Norwalk, CT] [Telecommunications] (TSSD) .... LOGICOM
Logical Comparative LOFAR LCL
Logical Compare Accumulator with Storage (SAA) .... LAS
Logical Data Definition Language (IAA) .... LDDL
Logical Data Language [Computer science] (IAA) .... LDL
Logical Database .... LDB
Logical Database Designer [Computer science] .... LDD
Logical Design .... LD
Logical Design Translator (NITA) .... LDT
Logical Device Address [Computer science] (IBMDP) .... LDA
Logical Device Order [Computer science] (IBMDP) .... LDO
Logical Device Table (IAA) .... LDT
Logical Display List (MCD) .... LDL
Logical End of Media .... LEM
Logical Equipment Table .... LET
Logical Error Detection .... LED
Logical File [Computer science] (BUR) .... LF
Logical File Name .... LFN
Logical File Number [Computer science] (MCD) .... LFN
Logical File Structure [Computer science] (OA) .... LFS
Logical File System (IAA) .... LFS
Logical Group Number [Computer science] (IBMDP) .... LGN
Logical Hardware Interface Description [Computer science] .... LHID
Logical Identification (MCD) .... LID
Logical Inference Tester [NASA] .... LOGIT
Logical Inferences per Second [Processing power units] [Computer science] .... LIPS
Logical Input/Output Control System [Computer science] .... LIOCS
Logical Inquiry and Update System .... LINUS
Logical Language .... LOGLAN
Logical Language Group [An association] (EA) .... LLG
Logical Line Group [Computer science] (IBMDP) .... LLG
Logical Link Control [Telecommunications] LLC
Logical Link Identifier (ACRL) LLI
Logical Mapping Table .... LMT
Logical Memory Level .... LML
Logical Module (NITA) .... LM
Logical Network Machine (MHDB) .... LNM
Logical Operation (AAG) .... LO
Logical Organizing and Gathering of Information Knowledge (MHDI) .... LOGIK

Logical Page Identifier .... LIPID
Logical Page Identifier (BUR) .... LPID
Logical Page Number (BUR) .... LPN
Logical Processor and Computer .... LOGIPAC
Logical Program .... LOGRAM
Logical Record .... LR
Logical Record Access [Computer science] (MHDB) .... LRA
Logical Record Address (NITA) .... LRA
Logical Record Length .... LRL
Logical Record Location .... LRL
Logical Record Processor (IAA) .... LRP
Logical Records of Fixed Length (MCD) .... LRECL
Logical Shift Left [Computer science] .... LSL
Logical Shift Right [Computer science] .... LSR
Logical Signal Processor (IAA) .... LSP
Logical Structure: The Timing and the Sequencing of Synchronous/
  Asynchronous Machines [Computer science] (CSR) .... LOTIS
Logical Sum [Computer science] .... LS
Logical Systems Design Methodology (NITA) .... LSDM
Logical Timing Sequencing (NITA) .... LOTIS
Logical Track Header .... LTH
Logical Transient Area .... LTA
Logical Twin Forward Pointer (MHDI) .... LTF
Logical Unit [Computer science] .... LU
Logical Unit and Checker (NITA) .... LUCK
Logical Unit Block [Computer science] .... LUB
Logical Unit Number .... LUN
Logical Unit of Information (IAA) .... LUI
Logical Unit Services Manager (MHDB) .... LUSVC
Logical Unit to Logical Unit .... LULU
Logical Units of Work [Computer science] (BYTE) .... LUW
Logical Weakness [Used in correcting manuscripts, etc.] .... LW
Logicality (ABBR) .... LGCLT
Logically (ABBR) .... LGCLY
Logically Integrated FORTRAN Translator [UNIVAC] .... LIFT
Logically Organized Data Entry, Storage, and Recording .... LODESTAR
Logically Passive Function .... LPF
Logically Passive Self-Dual .... LPSD
Logicheskii Yazyk dlia Predstavleniya Algoritmov Sinteza Releinykh
  Ustroistv [A Programming Language for Logic and Coding Algorithm] [Book
  title] .... LYpAS
Logician (ABBR) .... LGCN
Logic-in-Memory Array .... LIMA
Logicon Corp. [Associated Press] (SAG) .... Logicon
Logicon, Inc. [NYSE symbol] (SPSG) .... LGN
Logicon Input/Output Network .... LI/ON
Logicon Products [Vancouver Stock Exchange symbol] .... LPS
Logiealmond [Scotland] [Seismograph station code, US Geological Survey]
  (SEIS) .... ELO
Logilab, Inc., Charlebois, PQ, Canada [Library symbol] [Library of Congress]
  (LCLS) .... CaQCbL
Logilab, Inc., Charlebois, Quebec [Library symbol National Library of
  Canada] (NLC) .... QCL
Log-Inject-Log [Petroleum technology] LIL
Logistec Corp. [Toronto Stock Exchange symbol] .... LGT
Logistic (ABBR) .... LGSTC
Logistic (ABBR) .... LGTIC
Logistic .... LOGISTC
Logistic and Command Assessment of Projects [Army] .... LOGCAP
Logistic Applications of Automated Marking and Reading Symbols
  [DoD] .... LOGMARS
Logistic Approval Data .... LAD
Logistic Area Material Readiness List [Military] (AFIT) .... LAMRL
Logistic Assistance Office Command Interest Flasher [Military]
  (AABC) .... LAOCIF
Logistic Availability Factor (CAAL) .... LAF
Logistic Capability Estimate (MCD) .... LCE
Logistic Capability Plan [Navy] .... LCP
Logistic Capability Plan - Fiscal Year [Navy] (NG) .... LCP-FY
Logistic Center [Army] .... LOG CTR
Logistic Change Report [Military] (AFM) .... LCR
Logistic Communications (CET) .... LOGCOM
Logistic Control Activity (AABC) .... LCA
Logistic Control Code [Military] (AABC) LCC
Logistic Control Shipping Instruction (AAG) .... LCSI
Logistic Delay Time (CAAL) .... LDT
Logistic Effectiveness (CAAL) .... LE
Logistic Element Action Proposal (MCD) .... LEAP
Logistic Element Alternatives Process (MCD) .... LEAP
Logistic Element Manager .... LEM
Logistic Engine Generator Set (DWSG) .... LEGS
Logistic Escape Trunk (CAAL) .... LET
Logistic Evaluation .... LE
Logistic Evaluation Agency [Army] .... LEA
Logistic Evaluation Group .... LEG
Logistic Event and Assessment Program .... LEAP
Logistic Factors File (DOMA) .... LFF
Logistic Guidance Memorandum .... LGM
Logistic Improvement Program [Military] .... LOGIMP
Logistic Index (CAAL) LI
Logistic Inventory Management System [North American Rockwell] .... LIMS
Logistic Joint Work Group [DoD] .... LJWG
Logistic Management Advisory Committee .... LOMAC
Logistic Management of the Turnaround (MCD) .... LMT
Logistic Movement Center [Military] (CAAL) .... LMC

Logistic Movement Coordination Center [Navy] (ANA) .... LMCC
Logistic Operation Center [Military] .... LOC
Logistic Operation - Streamline [Military] (AABC) .... LOS
Logistic Oriented Schools [Army] .... LOS
Logistic Policy Statement [Navy] .... LPS
Logistic Readiness Report [Navy] (CINC) .... REDLOG
Logistic Readiness Review [Navy] .... LRR
Logistic Regression [Medicine] .... LR
Logistic Review Group [Military] (CAAL) .... LRG
Logistic Shelter Air Transportable .... LSAT
Logistic Status Review .... LSR
Logistic Support Agreement [Military] (CAAL) .... LSA
Logistic Support Aircraft (MCD) .... LSA
Logistic Support Analysis .... LSA
Logistic Support Analysis Control Number (MCD) .... LSACN
Logistic Support Analysis/Logistic Support Analysis Record [Army]
  (RDA) .... LSA/LSAR
Logistic Support Analysis Plan [or Program] [Army] .... LSAP
Logistic Support Analysis Process [Navy] .... LSAP
Logistic Support Analysis Record (RDA) .... LSAR
Logistic Support and Mobilization Plan [Military] (NVT) .... LSMP
Logistic Support Area (NVT) .... LSA
Logistic Support Base (NVT) .... LSB
Logistic Support Cadre (MCD) .... LSC
Logistic Support Control Point [Military] (AFM) .... LSCP
Logistic Support Coordination Meeting [Military] (MCD) .... LSCM
Logistic Support Data Responsibility Matrix (MCD) .... LSDRM
Logistic Support Force [Military] .... LSF
Logistic Support Impact .... LSI
Logistic Support Maintenance Equipment (MCD) .... LSME
Logistic Support Manager .... LSM
Logistic Support Plan for Preoperational Support (MCD) .... LSPPS
Logistic Support Plan Summary .... LSPS
Logistic Support Readiness Date .... LSRD
Logistic Support Requirement Analysis (MCD) .... LSRA
Logistic Support Resource Funds [Army] .... LSRF
Logistic Support Squadron (AAG) .... LSS
Logistic Support System (AABC) .... LSS
Logistic Support System Characteristics (AAG) .... LSSC
Logistic Supportability Index .... LSI
Logistic System Analysis [Navy] .... LSA
Logistic System Feasibility Analysis (AABC) .... LSFA
Logistic System Quality Control Program [Military] (AFIT) .... LSQCP
Logistic System Support Activity [Army] .... LSSA
Logistic System Support Agency .... LSSA
Logistic System Support Center [Army] .... LSSC
Logistic Technical Data [Navy] .... LTD
Logistic Unit Productivity System [Army] .... LURS
Logistic Work Group [NATO] (NATG) .... LWG
Logistical (ABBR) .... LGSTCL
Logistical (ABBR) .... LGTICL
Logistical Base Command [Korea] .... LBC
Logistical Command .... LOGCMD
Logistical Command .... LOGCOMD
Logistical Exercise [Army] (AABC) .... LOGEX
Logistical Expediting Group .... LEG
Logistical Force Structure Assessment (MCD) .... LFSA
Logistical Operational Control Key [Army] (AABC) .... LOCK
Logistical Operations Control Center [Army] .... LOCC
Logistical Ratio [Army] .... LOGR
Logistical Reassignment [Military] (AFIT) .... LR
Logistical Requirement .... LR
Logistical Status Report [Military] (INF) .... LOGSTAT
Logistical Support [Army] .... LS
Logistical Support Center [Army] .... LSC
Logistical Support Operations Center [Army] .... LSOC
Logistical Unit (NATG) .... LU
Logistical Vehicle System .... LVS
Logistic-Automated Support System (SSD) .... LASS
Logistician (ABBR) .... LGSTCN
Logistician .... LOG
Logistician .... LOGSTCN
Logistics (KSC) .... LOG
Logistics Action Worksheet .... LAW
Logistics Activation Task Force [Air Force] (MCD) .... LATAF
Logistics Air Network [Air Force] .... LOGAIRNET
Logistics Airlift [Military] .... LOGAIR
Logistics Analysis Model [Army] (RDA) .... LOGAM
Logistics Analysis Simulation System .... LASS
Logistics Anchor Desk [Army] (RDA) .... LAD
Logistics and Acquisition Management Program [Army] (RDA) .... LOGAMP
Logistics and Material Planning Team (NATG) .... LMPT
Logistics and Support (NASA) .... L & S
Logistics Area Coordinator (MCD) .... LAC
Logistics Area Officer (MCD) .... LAO
Logistics Assessment and Assistance Team (MCD) .... LAAT
[A] Logistics Assessment of the Readiness to Mobilize [Military] .... ALARM
Logistics Asset Support Estimate .... LASE
Logistics Assets Requirements Model (PDAA) .... LARM
Logistics Assistance and Instruction Team [Military] (AABC) .... LAIT
Logistics Assistance Office [or Officer] [Army Materiel Command] .... LAO
Logistics Assistance Program .... LAP
Logistics Assistance Representative [Army] (DOMA) .... LAR
Logistics Assistance Team .... LAT
Logistics Attack Model [BDM Corp.] (MCD) .... LOGATAK

Logistics Automated Information System [*Marine Corps*] (DOMA) .... LOGAIS
Logistics Automated Supply System .... LASS
Logistics Automation Master PLan [*Military*] .... LAMP
Logistics Ballistic Missile Network [*Air Force*] .... LOGBALNET
Logistics Capability .... LOGCAP
Logistics Center [*Army*] .... LOGC
Logistics Center (MCD) .... LOGCEN
Logistics Center Advisory Board (MCD) .... LOGCAB
Logistics Center Involvement in Army Model Improvement Program .... LOGC-AMIP
Logistics Civil Augmentation Program [*Army*] .... LOGCAP
Logistics Civilian Career Enhancement Program [*Military*] .... LCCEP
Logistics Combat Support Vehicle Family (MCD) .... LCSVF
Logistics Command (IAA) LC
Logistics Command (MCD) .... LOGCOM
Logistics Command Central Information System [*British*] ...... LOGCCIS
Logistics Command Management System .... LCMS
Logistics Communications Division [*Military*] .... LCD
Logistics Composite Model .... LCOM
Logistics Control Area (IAA) .... LCA
Logistics Control Center [*Military*] (INF) LCC
Logistics Control Center System .... LCCS
Logistics Control Group [*Air Materiel Command*] (AAG) ... LCG
Logistics Control Number (MCD) .... LCN
Logistics Control Office [*Military*] (AABC) .... LCO
Logistics Control Office, Atlantic [*Military*] .... LCOA
Logistics Control Office, Pacific [*Military*] (AABC) .... LCOP
Logistics Coordination (NVT) .... LOGCOR
Logistics Coordination Center [*NATO*] LCC
Logistics Cost Analysis Data (MCD) .... LCAD
Logistics Cost Analysis Model (MCD) .... LOCAM
Logistics Cost Model (PDAA) .... LOGCOST
Logistics Data Bank (NASA) .... LDB
Logistics Data Center [*Army*] (AABC) .... LDC
Logistics Data Element Standardization and Management Office [*DoD*] (AABC) .... LOGDESMO
Logistics Data Element Standardization and Management Process (IEEE) .... LODESMP
Logistics Data Element Standardization and Management Program [*DoD*] (AABC) .... LOGDESMAP
Logistics Data Package .... LDP
Logistics Data Sheet .... LDS
Logistics Database .... LOGDB
Logistics Demonstration (MCD) .... LD
Logistics Development Program (DOMA) .... LDP
Logistics Division [*Supreme Headquarters, Allied Powers Europe*] (NATG) .... LOGDIV
Logistics Doctrine and Systems Agency [*Army*] (MCD) ..... LDSA
Logistics Doctrine and Systems Office [*Army*] ...... LDSO
Logistics Doctrine Systems and Readiness Agency [*Army*] (AABC) .... LDSRA
Logistics Document (MCD) .... LD
Logistics Echelons above Division in Europe (MCD) ...... LEADER
Logistics Efficiencies to Increase Army Power (MCD) ..... LEAP
Logistics Electronic Information Delivery System .... LEIDS
Logistics Engineering Analysis (NASA) .... LEA
Logistics Engineering Directorate [*ARRCOM*] (RDA) ...... LED
Logistics Entry Vehicle .... LEV
Logistics Evaluation Activity [*Army*] .... LEA
Logistics Evaluation and Review .... LEAR
Logistics Evaluation and Review Integrated Flight Equipment [*Aviation*] (IAA) .... LIFE
Logistics Evaluation and Review Synchronization (IAA) ...... LEARSYN
Logistics Evaluation Exercise .... LEE
Logistics Executive Development Course [*Army*] ..... LEDC
Logistics Feasibility System .... LFS
Logistics/Ferry Station .... LFS
Logistics Force [*Military*] .... LOGFOR
Logistics Group [*Military*] .... LG
Logistics Helicopter (NVT) .... LOGHELO
Logistics Identification Document (NASA) .... LID
Logistics Indoctrination Course [*Military*] (DNAB) LIC
Logistics Information Management Support System [*Military*] ..... LIMSS
Logistics Instructions [*Military*] LI
Logistics Intelligence Data Base (AABC) .... LIDB
Logistics Intelligence File (AABC) .... LIF
Logistics Intelligence File Europe .... LIFE
Logistics Inventory Disposition Order (AAG) .... LIDO
Logistics Item Data Systems [*DoD*] .... LIDS
Logistics Item Identification Guide [*Military*] (AFM) ..... LIIG
Logistics, Maintenance, and Repair (IAA) .... LOMAR
Logistics Management Association of Australia ..... LMAA
Logistics Management Center [*Army*] (MCD) ...... LMC
Logistics Management Committee (AAGC) .... LOMC
Logistics Management Course for Auditors [*Army*] ..... LMCA
Logistics Management Data [*Military*] (MCD) ..... LMD
Logistics Management Engineering, Inc. [*Annapolis, MD*] [*Telecommunications*] (TSSD) .... LME
Logistics Management Engineering Team [*Military*] ...... LOGMET
Logistics Management Information System [*Marine Corps*] (GFGA) ...... LMIS
Logistics Management Information System [*USACC*] ...... LOGMIS
Logistics Management Institute [*Bethesda, MD*] [*Research center*] (AFM) ...... LMI
Logistics Management Office [*Army*] .... LMO
Logistics Management Specialist (MCD) .... LMS
Logistics Management Systems Center [*Military*] ..... LMSC
Logistics Management Team [*Navy*] .... LMT

Logistics Manager (MCD) .... LM
Logistics Master Planning System .... LOGMAPS
Logistics Master Schedules (MCD) .... LMS
Logistics Material Control Activity [*Military*] ...... LMCA
Logistics Module [*Simulation games*] [*Army*] (SSD) ..... LGM
Logistics Module [*Simulation games*] [*Army*] (SSD) ..... LM
Logistics Module [*Simulation games*] [*Army*] (INF) ..... LOGMOD
Logistics Network (MCD) .... LOGNET
Logistics Offensive .... LO
Logistics Officer Program [*Army*] .... LOP
Logistics Operating Base .... LOB
Logistics Operating Information System (AABC) ..... LOGOIS
Logistics Organization Planning Unit .... LOPU
Logistics over the Shore [*Military*] .... LOTS
Logistics Package [*Army*] (INF) .... LOGPAC
Logistics Performance Indicator (PDAA) .... LPI
Logistics Performance Measurement and Evaluation System (AABC) ...... LPMES
Logistics Pipeline Analysis [*Military*] (MCD) .... LPA
Logistics Planning and Reporting Code [*Military*] ..... LPRCO
Logistics Planning and Requirements Simplification System [*Army*] (RDA) .... LOGPARS
Logistics Planning Study (MCD) .... LPS
Logistics Plans .... LOGP
Logistics Policy and Procedures for Contingency Operations [*DARCOM*] (CINC) .... LP & P
Logistics Program Management System [*Air Force*] (AFIT) ..... LPMS
Logistics Readiness Center [*Air Force*] .... LRC
Logistics Readiness Condition System [*DARCOM*] (MCD) ...... LOGCON
Logistics Readiness Elements (MCD) .... LRE
Logistics Readiness Officer [*Military*] (AABC) ...... LRO
Logistics Readiness Rating Report [*DoD*] .... LR^3
Logistics Reassignment Task Group [*DoD*] (MCD) ..... LRTG
Logistics Release Point [*Army*] (INF) .... LRP
Logistics Replenishment (NVT) .... LOGREP
Logistics Representative [*Navy*] (NVT) .... LOGREP
Logistics Requirements (NVT) .... LOGREQ
Logistics Requirements Allocation Sheet (SSD) ..... LRAS
Logistics Requirements Determination (MCD) ...... LRD
Logistics Requirements System [*Navy*] .... LRS
Logistics Research Project, George Washington University ...... LRP/GWU
Logistics Review and Analysis Office [*US Army Defense Ammunition Center and School*] .... LRAO
Logistics Section [*of an Army or Marine Corps division general staff, or Marine brigade or aircraft wing general staff; also, the officer in charge of this section*] G-4
Logistics Section [*of a joint military staff; also, the officer in charge of this section*] J-4
Logistics Section [*in Army brigades or smaller units, and in Marine Corps units smaller than a brigade; also, the officer in charge of this section*] S-4
Logistics Service [*Military*] (NVT) .... LOGSVC
Logistics Spares List (KSC) .... LSL
Logistics Special Assistance Team (MCD) .... LOGSAT
Logistics Squadron [*Military*] .... LS
Logistics Storage and Retrieval System (MCD) ..... LOGSAR
Logistics Structure and Composition System (AABC) ...... LOGSACS
Logistics Studies Office [*Army*] (RDA) .... LSO
Logistics Studies Steering Group (AABC) .... LSSG
Logistics Summary (NVT) .... LOGSUM
Logistics Supply Area .... LSA
Logistics Support .... LOGSUP
Logistics Support Alternative [*or Analysis*] Model (MCD) ...... LOGSAM
Logistics Support Alternative [*or Analysis*] Model (MCD) ...... LSAM
Logistics Support Analysis .... LSA
Logistics Support Cost Analysis (NASA) .... LSCA
Logistics Support Element .... LSE
Logistics Support Equipment [*Military*] (MCD) ..... LSE
Logistics Support Field Office [*Federal disaster planning*] ..... LSFO
Logistics Support Group (AAG) .... LSG
Logistics Support Management Information [*NASA*] (NASA) ..... LSMI
Logistics Support Plan .... LSP
Logistics Support Requirements (NG) .... LSR
Logistics Support Squadron [*Military*] .... LSGSS
Logistics Support Unit [*Military*] (NVT) .... LSU
Logistics Support Vessel [*Military*] .... LSV
Logistics Supportability (AABC) .... LOGS
Logistics Supportability Evaluation Team [*Military*] (AFIT) ..... LSET
Logistics Sustainability Analysis Feasibility Estimator (DOMA) ..... LOGSAFE
Logistics Sustaining Base [*Military*] (RDA) .... LSB
Logistics System Master Plan [*Army*] .... LOGMAP
Logistics System Plan [*Navy DoD*] .... LOG PLAN
Logistics Systems Division [*Air Force*] .... LSD
Logistics Systems Laboratory .... LSL
Logistics Systems Policy Committee [*Navy*] ...... LSPC
Logistics Systems Review Committee [*DARCOM*] (MCD) ...... LSRC
Logistics Test Squadron [*Military*] .... LTS
Logistics to Relay Converter (MCD) .... LRC
Logistics Transport by Land [*Military*] .... LOGLAND
Logistics Transport by Sea [*Military*] .... LOGSEA
Logistics Unit Productivity Study [*or System*] [*Army*] ..... LUPS
Logistics Vehicle System .... LVS
Logistics Wing [*Military*] .... LW
Logistics-over-the-Beach Base [*Military*] (VNW) ..... LOB
Loglan Institute (EA) LI
Log-Likelihood Ratio (PDAA) .... LLR
Log-Likelihood Ratio Representation (MHDB) ...... LLRR

Lognes/Emerainville [France ICAO location identifier] (ICLI) ... LFPL
Logo Forum on Compuserve [Defunct] (EA) ... LFC
Logo Resources Ltd. [Vancouver Stock Exchange symbol] ... LGO
Logogram (BJA) ... log
Logographic (BJA) ... log
Logotype [Advertising] (DSUE) ... LOGO
Log-Out Analysis (NITA) ... LOA
Log-Periodic Loop Antenna (PDAA) ... LPLA
Logrono [Spain ICAO location identifier] (ICLI) ... LELO
Logrono [Spain] [Seismograph station code, US Geological Survey] (SEIS) ... LGR
Log-Skidder [Tires] (DICI) ... LS
Log-Slope Difference [Statistics] ... LSD
Logsplitter Manufacturers Association [Defunct] (EA) ... LMA
Lohame Herut Yisrael (BJA) ... LHY
Lohathla [South Africa] [ICAO location identifier] (ICLI) ... FALH
Loh's Sinfully Good Ice Cream & Cookies, Inc. [Vancouver Stock Exchange symbol] ... LSG
Loide Aereo Nacional, SA [Brazilian airline] ... LAP
Loikaw [Myanmar] [Airport symbol] (OAG) ... LIW
Loikaw [Myanmar] [ICAO location identifier] (ICLI) ... VBLK
Loire Base Section [World War II] ... LBS
Lois des Batiments [A publication] (DLA) ... Lois Batim
Lois Recentes du Canada [A publication] (DLA) ... Lois Rec
Loita Armada Revolucionaria [Armed Revolutionary Struggle] [Spain] (PD) ... LAR
Loitering [FBI standardized term] ... LOIT
Loitering with Intent [British] (DSUE) ... LI
Loitokitok [Kenya] [ICAO location identifier] (ICLI) ... HKLT
Loja [Ecuador] [Airport symbol] (OAG) ... LOH
Loja (La Toma) [Ecuador] [ICAO location identifier] (ICLI) ... SELO
Lo-Jack Corp. [Associated Press] (SAG) ... LoJack
LoJack Corp. [NASDAQ symbol] (SAG) ... LOJN
Loki Gold Corp. [Vancouver Stock Exchange symbol] ... LKI
Loki Ranging Transponder ... LRT
Lokichoggio [Kenya] [ICAO location identifier] (ICLI) ... HKLK
Lokitaung [Kenya] [ICAO location identifier] (ICLI) ... HKLG
Lokolela [Zaire] [ICAO location identifier] (ICLI) ... FZEG
Lokutu [Zaire] [ICAO location identifier] (ICLI) ... FZIZ
Lo-Linua [Vanuatu] [ICAO location identifier] (ICLI) ... NVSD
Lolium Enation Virus [Plant pathology] ... LEV
Lolium Mottle Virus [Plant pathology] ... LOMV
Lollipop Daycare [Vancouver Stock Exchange symbol] ... LLP
Lollipop Power [An association] (EA) ... LP
Lollipop Power Books (EA) ... LPB
Lolo (Bantu) [MARC language code Library of Congress] (LCCP) ... lol
Loma Del Porvenir [Bolivia] [ICAO location identifier] (ICLI) ... SLDP
Loma Elementary, Loma, CO [Library symbol Library of Congress] (LCLS) ... CoLmE
Loma Larga [Ecuador] [ICAO location identifier] (ICLI) ... SELM
Loma Linda University (GAGS) ... Loma Linda U
Loma Linda University, Loma Linda, CA [Library symbol Library of Congress] (LCLS) ... CLolC
Loma Linda University, Loma Linda, CA [OCLC symbol] (OCLC) ... LLU
Loma Linda University, Riverside Campus, Riverside, CA [Library symbol Library of Congress] (LCLS) ... CRivL
Lomak Petroleum [NASDAQ symbol] (TTSB) ... LOMK
Lomak Petroleum, Inc. [Associated Press] (SAG) ... Lomak
Lomak Petroleum, Inc. [NASDAQ symbol] (SAG) ... LOMK
Lomas Data Products [Marlboro, MA] [Computer manufacturer] ... LDP
Lomas Financial Corp. [NYSE symbol] (SPSG) ... LFC
Lomas Helicopters Ltd. [British ICAO designator] (FAAC) ... LMS
Lomas's City Hall Reporter [New York] [A publication] (DLA) ... Lom CH Rep
Lomax on Executors [A publication] (DLA) ... Lom Ex
Lomax on Executors [A publication] (DLA) ... Lomax Ex'rs
Lomax's Digest of Real Property [A publication] (DLA) ... Lom Dig
Lombard-Dowell [Broth medium] [Microbiology] ... LD
Lombard-Dowell Egg Yolk Agar [Microbiology] ... LD-EYA
Lombard-Dowell Neomycin Egg Yolk Agar [Microbiology] ... LD-NEYA
Lombo [Zaire] [ICAO location identifier] (ICLI) ... FZFN
Lome [Togo] [Airport symbol] (OAG) ... LFW
Lome [Togo] [Seismograph station code, US Geological Survey] (SEIS) ... LOM
Lome/Tokoin [Togo] [ICAO location identifier] (ICLI) ... DXXX
Lomela [Zaire] [ICAO location identifier] (ICLI) ... FZVE
Lometa, TX [FM radio station call letters] (RBYB) ... KACQ
Lomie [Cameroon] [ICAO location identifier] (ICLI) ... FKAL
Lomir Shoyn Davenen (BJA) ... LSD
Lomira, WI [FM radio station call letters] ... WFDL
Lommel and Steinkopf [German name for mustard gas, taken from two of the chemists who helped develop it as a chemical warfare agent] ... LOST
Lommen Health Science Library, University of South Dakota, Vermillion, SD [OCLC symbol] (OCLC) ... USF
Lommis [Switzerland ICAO location identifier] (ICLI) ... LSZT
Lomond Public Library, Alberta [Library symbol National Library of Canada] (NLC) ... ALOMO
Lomond Publications, Inc. [Telecommunications service] (TSSD) ... LPI
Lompoc [California] [Seismograph station code, US Geological Survey] (SEIS) ... BLP
Lompoc, CA [FM radio station call letters] (RBYB) ... KAKV-FM
Lompoc, CA [FM radio station call letters] (RBYB) ... KAOH-FM
Lompoc, CA [FM radio station call letters] ... KBOX
Lompoc, CA [AM radio station call letters] ... KCLL
Lompoc, CA [AM radio station call letters] ... KLOM
Lompoc, CA [AM radio station call letters] ... KRQK
Lompoc, CA [AM radio station call letters] ... KTME
Lompoc, CA [Location identifier FAA] (FAAL) ... LPC
Lompoc, CA [Location identifier FAA] (FAAL) ... SVJ

Lompoc, CA [Location identifier FAA] (FAAL) ... VBG
Lompoc Public Library, Lompoc, CA [Library symbol Library of Congress] (LCLS) ... CLom
Lompoc/Vandenberg Air Force Base [California] [ICAO location identifier] (ICLI) ... KVBG
Lon Morris College [Texas] ... LMC
Lon Morris College, Jacksonville, TX [Library symbol Library of Congress] (LCLS) ... TxJaL
Londolovit [Papua New Guinea] [Airport symbol Obsolete] (OAG) ... LNV
London [British ICAO location identifier] (ICLI) ... EGGA
London [British ICAO location identifier] (ICLI) ... EGGB
London [British ICAO location identifier] (ICLI) ... EGGC
London [British ICAO location identifier] (ICLI) ... EGGO
London [British ICAO location identifier] (ICLI) ... EGLW
London [British ICAO location identifier] (ICLI) ... EGRB
London [British ICAO location identifier] (ICLI) ... EGWI
London [Phonetic alphabet] [Royal Navy World War I Pre-World War II] (DSUE) ... L
London [England] ... L
London [Ontario] [Seismograph station code, US Geological Survey] (SEIS) ... LDN
London [England] ... LDN
London [Ontario] [Seismograph station code, US Geological Survey] (SEIS) ... LND
London [England] [Airport symbol] (OAG) ... LON
London [Record label] [Export issues of English Decca - mainly USA, Canada, etc.] ... Lon
London ... LOND
London [Kentucky] [Airport symbol] (OAG) ... LOZ
London [Canada] [Airport symbol] (OAG) ... YXU
London Academy of Music ... LAM
[The] London Academy of Music and Dramatic Art ... LAMDA
London Aero Motor Services ... LAMS
London Air Defence Area [British military] (DMA) ... LADA
London Air Traffic Control Center [British ICAO location identifier] (ICLI) ... EGTT
London Airport ... LAP
London Airport Cargo Electronic-Data-Processing Scheme ... LACES
London Airtours Ltd. [British ICAO designator] (FAAC) ... LAJ
London Air-Traffic Control Center ... LATCC
London Allowance [British military] (DMA) ... LnA
London Amenity and Transport Association ... LATA
London Amusement Guide ... LAG
London & Blackwall Railway [British] (ROG) ... L & BR
London and Continental Advertising Holdings [British] ... LCAH
London and Edinburgh Trust [British] ... LET
London and India Docks [Shipping] [British] (ROG) ... L & ID
London and International School of Acting [British] ... LISA
London & North Eastern Railway [British] ... LNER
London & North Eastern Railway Group [British] ... LNERG
London & North Western Railway [British] ... LNWR
London & Overseas Freight ADS [NASDAQ symbol] (TTSB) ... LOFSY
London and Overseas Freighter ... LOF
London & Overseas Freightliners [NASDAQ symbol] (SAG) ... LOFS
London & Overseas Freightliners [Associated Press] (SAG) ... LondOvr
London & Port Stanley Railway Co. [AAR code] ... LPS
London & Scottish Marine Oil [British] ... LASMO
London and Scottish Rifle Volunteers [Military British] (ROG) ... LSRV
London and South Eastern Library Region [Information service or system] (IID) ... LASER
London & South-Western Railway (ROG) ... L & SWR
London & South-Western Railway (ROG) ... LSWR
London Appreciation Society ... LAS
London Association for the Teaching of English [British] (AIE) ... LATE
London Bacon Buyers' Association Ltd. [British] ... LBBA
London Ballet Circle ... LBC
London Bankruptcy Court ... LBC
London Board of Education, London, ON, Canada [Library symbol Library of Congress] (LCLS) ... CaOLB
London Board of Education, Ontario [Library symbol National Library of Canada] (NLC) ... OLB
London Book Fair [England] ... LBF
London Borough [England] ... LB
London Boroughs Association [British] (DCTA) ... LBA
London Bridge ... LB
London, Brighton & South Coast Railway [British] ... LBSCR
London Broadcasting Co. ... LBC
London Bullion Market Association ... LBMA
London Business Aviation [British ICAO designator] (FAAC) ... LBS
London Business School [England] ... LBS
London Centre for Biotechnology [British] (IRUK) ... LCB
London Centre for Marine Technology [British] (IRUK) ... LCMT
London Chamber of Commerce [British] (DAS) ... LCC
London Chamber of Commerce and Industry [British] (DCTA) ... LCCI
London Chamber of Commerce Examinations Board [British] (AIE) ... LCCEB
London, Chatham & Dover Railway [British] ... LCDR
London Church Choir Association ... LCCA
London City [British ICAO location identifier] (ICLI) ... EGLL
London City Airport [British] ... LCA
London City Airways [ICAO designator] (AD) ... II
London City Mission ... LCM
London Classification of Business Studies [Library classification scheme] [British] (NITA) ... LCBS
London Clause [Business term] ... LC
London Club (EA) ... LC
London College of Divinity ... LCD
London College of Music (ROG) ... LCM
London College of Printing ... LCP

London Communications Committee [*World War II*] LCC
London Contemporary Dance Theatre ..... LCDT
London Contemporary Dance Theatre [*Defunct*] ..... LCDT
London Controlling Section [*British military*] (DMA) ..... LCS
London Corn Trade Association ..... LCTA
London Council of Social Service ..... LCSS
London County Council [*or Councillor*] [*Later, GLC*] LCC
London Court of International Arbitration ..... LCIA
London Daily Price [*British*] ..... LDP
London Diocesan Board of Education ..... LDBE
London Diocesan Fund ..... LDF
London Diocesan Home Mission [*or Missionary*] ..... LDHM
London Dipole Theory ..... LDT
London Discount Market Association [*British*] (MHDW) ..... LDMA
London Docklands Development Corp. [*British*] (ECON) ..... LDDC
London Docks ..... LD
London Dumping Convention [*Sets standards for disposal of wastes in oceans*] ..... LDC
London East Training and Enterprise Council [*British*] (AIE) ..... LETEC
London Education Classification [*Library classification system*] (NITA) ..... LEC
London Electric Railway ..... LER
London Electricity Board ..... LEB
London Encyclopedia [*A publication*] (DLA) ..... Lond
London Enterprise Agency ..... LEntA
London European Airways PLC [*British ICAO designator*] (FAAC) ..... LON
London Executive Aviation Ltd. [*British*] [*FAA designator*] (FAAC) ..... LNX
London Festival Ballet ..... LFB
London Festival Ballet's Ensemble Group LFB2
London Film Festival ..... LFF
London Financial [*NASDAQ symbol*] (TTSB) ..... LONF
London Fire Brigade ..... LFB
London Flight Centre (Stansted) Ltd. [*British ICAO designator*] (FAAC) ..... LOV
London Flights (Biggin Hill) Ltd. [*British ICAO designator*] (FAAC) ..... LNF
London/Gatwick [*British ICAO location identifier*] (ICLI) ..... EGKK
London General Omnibus Co. [*British*] (DCTA) ..... LGOC
London Grand Rank [*Freemasonry*] ..... LGR
London Gregorian Choral Association ..... LGCA
London, Havre, Antwerp, Rouen [*Shipping route*] (ROG) ..... LHAR
London/Heathrow [*British ICAO location identifier*] (ICLI) ..... EGLN
London Historical Museums, London, ON, Canada [*Library symbol*] [*Library of Congress*] (LCLS) ..... CaOLHM
London Historical Museums, Ontario [*Library symbol National Library of Canada*] (BIB) ..... OLHM
London Hospital Medical College [*British*] (DI) ..... LHMC
London, Hull, Antwerp, or Rotterdam [*Shipping route*] ..... LHAR
London Industrial Group [*British*] ..... LIG
London Insurance and Reinsurance Market Association (ECON) ..... LIRMA
London Interbank Bid Rate [*Finance British*] ..... LIBID
London Interbank Median Average Rate ..... LIMEAN
London Interbank Offered [*Rate*] [*Reference point for syndicated bank loans*] ..... LIBO
London Interbank Offered Rate [*Reference point for syndicated bank loans*] ..... LIBOR
London International [*Record label*] [*Great Britain, USA, etc.*] LI
London International College [*British*] LIC
London International Festival of Theatre [*British*] ..... LIFT
London International Financial Futures Exchange Ltd. [*London, England*] ..... LIFFE
London International Freight Terminal (DS) ..... LIFT
London International Furniture Show [*British*] (ITD) ..... LIFS
London International Group Ltd. [*NASDAQ symbol*] (SAG) ..... LOND
London International Group PLC [*Associated Press*] (SAG) ..... LondInt
London Intl Group plc ADS [*NASDAQ symbol*] (TTSB) ..... LONDY
London Investment Trust [*British*] ..... LIT
London Jurist [*1854*] [*A publication*] (DLA) ..... Jur
London Jurist, New Series [*A publication*] (DLA) ..... Lond Jur NS
London Jurist Reports [*England*] [*A publication*] (DLA) ..... Lond Jur
London Juvenile Court (DAS) ..... LJC
London, KY [*AM radio station call letters*] ..... WFTG
London, KY [*AM radio station call letters*] (RBYB) ..... WGWM-AM
London, KY [*AM radio station call letters*] ..... WMAK
London, KY [*FM radio station call letters*] ..... WWEL
London, KY [*FM radio station call letters*] (RBYB) ..... WYGE
London Labour Party [*British Political party*] ..... LLP
London Landed Terms [*Shipping*] ..... LLT
London Law Magazine [*A publication*] (DLA) ..... Lond LM
London Meat Futures Exchange [*British*] ..... LMFE
London Metal Exchange ..... LME
London Microfilming Services Ltd., London, ON, Canada [*Library symbol Library of Congress*] (LCLS) ..... LmS
London, Midland & Scottish Railway [*British*] (DCTA) ..... LM & Sc R
London, Midland & Scottish Railway [*British*] ..... LMS
London, Midland & Scottish Railway [*British*] ..... LMSR
London Missionary Society ..... LMS
London Montessori Centre [*British*] (AIE) ..... LMC
London Munitions Assignments Board [*World War II*] ..... LMAB
London Normal School ..... LNS
London Office ..... LO
London, OH [*Location identifier FAA*] (FAAL) ..... UYF
London, OH [*FM radio station call letters*] ..... WCKX
London, ON [*FM radio station call letters*] ..... CBBL-FM
London, ON [*FM radio station call letters*] ..... CBCL-FM
London, ON [*AM radio station call letters*] ..... CFPL
London, ON [*FM radio station call letters*] ..... CFPL-FM
London, ON [*Television station call letters*] ..... CFPL-TV
London, ON [*FM radio station call letters*] ..... CHRW
London, ON [*Television station call letters*] CICO-18
London, ON [*FM radio station call letters*] ..... CIQM
London, ON [*FM radio station call letters*] CIXX
London, ON [*FM radio station call letters*] CJBC-4
London, ON [*AM radio station call letters*] ..... CJBK
London, ON [*FM radio station call letters*] ..... CJBX
London, ON [*Radio station call letters*] [*1930's*] ..... CJGC
London, ON [*AM radio station call letters*] ..... CKSL
London, ON [*ICAO location identifier*] (ICLI) ..... CYXU
London Online Local Authorities (NITA) ..... LOLA
London Operatic and Dramatic Society (ROG) ..... LO & DS
London Orphan Asylum (ROG) ..... LOA
London Overseas Mail Office ..... LOMO
London Over-the-Counter Market [*Information service or system*] (IID) ..... LOTC
London Pacific Group Ltd. [*Associated Press*] (SAG) ..... LondonP
London Pacific Group Ltd. [*NASDAQ symbol*] (SAG) ..... LPGL
London Pacific Grp ADS [*NASDAQ symbol*] (TTSB) ..... LPGLY
London Parcels Delivery Co. ..... LPDC
London Particular [*Marsala*] ..... LP
London Passenger Transport Board ..... LPTB
London Philharmonic Orchestra ..... LPO
London Potato Futures Association [*London Stock Exchange*] ..... LPFA
London Press Exchange ..... LPE
London Press Service ..... LPS
London Printing and Kindred Trades Federation (DGA) ..... LP & KTF
London Procurement Field Office ..... LPFO
London Property Register [*London Research Centre*] [*British Information service or system*] (IID) ..... LPR
London Psychiatric Hospital, Ontario [*Library symbol National Library of Canada*] (NLC) ..... OLPH
London Public Library and Art Museum, London, ON, Canada [*Library symbol Library of Congress*] (LCLS) ..... CaOL
London Public Library, Ontario [*Library symbol National Library of Canada*] (NLC) ..... OL
London Radio Workshop [*Independent Local Radio*] [*British*] ..... LRW
London Rank [*Freemasonry*] ..... LR
London Reading Test [*Educational test*] ..... LRT
London Record Society [*British*] (ILCA) ..... LRS
London Regional Art Gallery, London, ON, Canada [*Library symbol*] [*Library of Congress*] (LCLS) ..... CaOLRAG
London Regional Art Gallery, Ontario [*Library symbol National Library of Canada*] (NLC) ..... OLRAG
London Regional Examining Board [*British*] (AIE) ..... LREB
London Regional Federation [*League of Nations Union*] ..... LRF
London Regional Passengers Committee [*British*] (ECON) ..... LRPC
London Regional Transport ..... LRT
London Research Center, Agriculture Canada [*Centre de Recherches de London, Agriculture Canada*] **London, Ontario** [*Library symbol National Library of Canada*] (NLC) ..... OLAG
London Review of Books [*A publication*] (BRI) ..... Lon R Bks
London Rifle Brigade [*Military unit*] [*British*] ..... LRB
London Rowing Club ..... LRC
London Salvage Corps ..... LSC
London School Board ..... LSB
London School of Economics ..... LSE
London School of Hygiene ..... LSH
London School of Hygiene and Tropical Medicine (DAVI) ..... LSHTM
London School of Medicine for Women (ROG) ..... LSMW
London School of Polymer Technology [*British*] (AIE) ..... LSPT
London Scottish [*Army regiment*] ..... LS
London Scottish Cadet Corps [*British military*] (DMA) ..... LSCC
London Silver Corp. [*Vancouver Stock Exchange symbol*] ..... LDN
[*The*] **London Sinfonietta** ..... LS
London Small Arms Co. [*Military*] ..... LSAC
London Society of Music Engravers [*British*] (DGA) ..... LSME
London Specialist Software Systems (NITA) LS3
London Stage Information Bank [*Lawrence University*] [*Information service or system*] (IID) ..... LSIB
London/Stansted [*British ICAO location identifier*] (ICLI) ..... EGSS
London Stock Exchange ..... LSE
London Symphony Orchestra ..... LSO
London Tanker Broker Panel ..... LTBP
London Teaching Hospitals [*National Health Service*] [*British*] (DI) ..... LTH
London, Tilbury & Southend Railway [*British*] ..... LT & S
London, Tilbury & Southend Railway [*British*] (ROG) ..... LT & SR
London Tourist Board [*British*] (DCTA) ..... LTB
London Transport ..... LT
London Transport Board [*British*] ..... LTB
London Transport Executive ..... LTE
London Underground Ltd. [*British*] (ECON) ..... LUL
London Underground Railway ..... LUR
London Union List of Periodicals ..... LULOP
London United Investments [*British*] ..... LUI
London University Computer Services (IAA) ..... LUCS
London University Officers Training Corps [*British military*] (DMA) ..... LUOTC
London Urban Resource Centre, London, ON, Canada [*Library symbol Library of Congress*] (LCLS) ..... CaOLURC
London Urban Resource Centre, Ontario [*Library symbol National Library of Canada*] (NLC) ..... OLURC
London Vintage Taxi Association - American Section (EA) ..... LVTA
London Voluntary Service Council [*British*] ..... LVSC
London Volunteer Regiment [*British military*] (DMA) ..... LVR
London Weekend Television [*England*] ..... LWT
Londonderry [*County in Ireland*] (ROG) ..... DERRY

Londonderry [*County in Ireland*] (ROG) ... LDERRY
Londonderry [*Northern Ireland*] [*Airport symbol*] (OAG) ... LDY
Londonderry/Eglinton [*British ICAO location identifier*] (ICLI) ... EGAE
London-Ducretet-Thomson [*Record label*] [*Great Britain, USA, etc.*] ... LT
London-Eyring-Polanyi-Sato Method [*Reaction dynamics*] ... LEPS
London-Gatwick [*England*] [*Airport symbol*] (OAG) ... LGW
London-Heathrow [*England*] [*Airport symbol*] (OAG) ... LHR
London-Oiseau-Lyre [*Record label*] [*Great Britain, USA, etc.*] ... LOL
London's Central Criminal Court [*England*] (AD) ... Old Bailey
London's Traded Options Market [*British*] (ECON) ... LTOM
Londrina [*Brazil*] [*Airport symbol*] (OAG) ... LDB
Londrina [*Brazil ICAO location identifier*] (ICLI) ... SBLO
Lone Grove, OK [*FM radio station call letters*] ... KYNZ
Lone Indian Fellowship [*Later, Lone Indian Fellowship and Lone Scout Alumni*] (EA) ... LIF
Lone Indian Fellowship and Lone Scout Alumni (EA) ... LIFLSA
Lone Jack Resources Ltd. [*Vancouver Stock Exchange symbol*] ... LJR
Lone Mountain College, San Francisco, CA [*Library symbol Library of Congress*] (LCLS) ... CSfLM
Lone Oak Road [*California*] [*Seismograph station code, US Geological Survey*] (SEIS) ... LRC
Lone Parents' Family Support Service - Birthright [*Australia*] ... LPFSSB
Lone Pine Public Library, Didsbury, Alberta [*Library symbol National Library of Canada*] (NLC) ... ADILP
Lone Replaceable Unit (MCD) ... LRU
Lone Rock, WI [*Location identifier FAA*] (FAAL) ... LNR
Lone Signal Unit [*Telecommunications*] (TEL) ... LSU
Lone Signalling Unit (NITA) ... LSU
Lone Star [*Missouri*] [*Seismograph station code, US Geological Survey*] (SEIS) ... LST
Lone Star Army Ammunition Plant (AABC) ... LSAAP
Lone Star Gas Co., Dallas, TX [*Library symbol Library of Congress*] (LCLS) ... TxDaL
Lone Star Indus [*NYSE symbol*] (TTSB) ... LCE
Lone Star Indus Wrrt [*NYSE symbol*] (TTSB) ... LCE.WS
Lone Star Industries [*Associated Press*] (SAG) ... LnStr
Lone Star Industries [*Associated Press*] (SAG) ... LnStrInd
Lone Star Industries, Inc. [*Formerly, Lone Star Cement Corp.*] [*NYSE symbol*] (SPSG) ... LCE
Lone Star Steakhouse & Saloon, Inc. [*Associated Press*] (SAG) ... LneSStk
Lone Star Steakhouse & Saloon, Inc. [*NASDAQ symbol*] (SAG) ... STAR
Lone Star Steakhouse/Saloon [*NASDAQ symbol*] (TTSB) ... STAR
Lone Star Technologies [*Associated Press*] (SAG) ... LoneStar
Lone Star Technologies [*NASDAQ symbol*] (SAG) ... LSST
Lone Star Technologies, Inc. [*Associated Press*] (SAG) ... LoneStr
Lone Star, TX [*Location identifier FAA*] (FAAL) ... LST
Lone Tree Reporter, Lone Tree, IA [*Library symbol Library of Congress*] (LCLS) ... IaLtR
Lone Tree Road [*California*] [*Seismograph station code, US Geological Survey*] (SEIS) ... LTR
Lonekin [*Myanmar*] [*ICAO location identifier*] (ICLI) ... VBLN
Lonely, AK [*Location identifier FAA*] (FAAL) ... HES
Lonely, AK [*Location identifier FAA*] (FAAL) ... HUG
Lonely, AK [*Location identifier FAA*] (FAAL) ... LNI
Loners of America [*An association*] (EA) ... LA
Loners on Wheels (EA) ... LOW
Lonesome Pine Regional Library, Wise, VA [*Library symbol*] [*Library of Congress*] (LCLS) ... ViWis
Long ... L
Long (KSC) ... LG
Long ... LNG
Long Acting Thyroid Stimulator-Protector [*Endocrinology*] ... LATS-P
Long Address Form (NITA) ... LAF
Long Aerial Mine [*Military*] ... LAM
Long Akah [*Indonesia*] [*ICAO location identifier*] (ICLI) ... WBGL
Long Akha [*Malaysia*] [*Airport symbol*] (AD) ... KLH
Long and Russell's Election Cases [*Massachusetts*] [*A publication*] (DLA) ... Long & R
Long Arm Cast [*Medicine*] (MEDA) ... LAC
Long Arm Posterior Molded Splint [*Medicine*] (MEDA) ... LAPMS
Long Atip [*Malaysia*] [*ICAO location identifier*] (ICLI) ... WBGA
Long Baseline Position and Rates [*Guidance and tracking system*] [*Air Force*] ... LOPAR
Long Baseline RADAR ... LOBAR
Long Bawan [*Indonesia*] [*Airport symbol*] (OAG) ... LBW
Long Bawan/Juvai Semaring [*Indonesia*] [*ICAO location identifier*] (ICLI) ... WRLB
Long Beach [*California*] [*ICAO location identifier*] (ICLI) ... KLGB
Long Beach [*California*] [*Airport symbol*] (OAG) ... LGB
Long Beach Bar Bulletin [*A publication*] (DLA) ... Long Beach B Bull
Long Beach, CA [*FM radio station call letters*] (RBYB) ... KBUE
Long Beach, CA [*AM radio station call letters*] ... KFRN
Long Beach, CA [*AM radio station call letters*] ... KGER
Long Beach, CA [*FM radio station call letters*] ... KLAX
Long Beach, CA [*FM radio station call letters*] ... KLON
Long Beach, CA [*Location identifier FAA*] (FAAL) ... LGB
Long Beach, CA [*Location identifier FAA*] (FAAL) ... NMO
Long Beach City College [*California*] ... LBCC
Long Beach City College, Business and Technology Division, Long Beach, CA [*Library symbol Library of Congress*] (LCLS) ... CLobC-B
Long Beach City College, Long Beach, CA [*Library symbol Library of Congress*] (LCLS) ... CLobC
Long Beach Junior High School, Long Beach, NY [*Library symbol Library of Congress*] (LCLS) ... NLobJH
Long Beach Memorial Hospital, Long Beach, CA [*Library symbol Library of Congress*] (LCLS) ... CLobM
Long Beach Memorial Hospital, Long Beach, NY [*Library symbol Library of Congress*] (LCLS) ... NLobH
Long Beach Middle School, Long Beach, NY [*Library symbol*] [*Library of Congress*] (LCLS) ... NLobM
Long Beach, MS [*FM radio station call letters*] ... WJZD
Long Beach Naval Shipyard (DNAB) ... LBNS
Long Beach Naval Shipyard (MUGU) ... LBNSY
Long Beach Public Library, Long Beach, CA [*OCLC symbol*] (OCLC) ... CLB
Long Beach Public Library, Long Beach, CA [*Library symbol Library of Congress*] (LCLS) ... CLob
Long Beach Public Library, Long Beach, MS [*Library symbol Library of Congress*] (LCLS) ... MsLb
Long Beach Public Library, Long Beach, NY [*Library symbol Library of Congress*] (LCLS) ... NLob
Long Beach Senior High School, Long Beach, NY [*Library symbol Library of Congress*] (LCLS) ... NLobSH
Long Beach Test Facility [*Missiles*] ... LBTF
Long Beach, WA [*FM radio station call letters*] ... KKEE
Long Bill [*Business term*] ... LB
Long Bill of Exchange [*Business term*] (MHDW) ... LBE
Long Binh [*Vietnam*] ... LB
Long Binh Jail [*Vietnam*] ... LBJ
Long Binh Subarea [*Vietnam*] ... LBSA
Long Bone or Pelvic Fracture [*Medicine*] (DMAA) ... LBPF
Long Branch, NJ [*FM radio station call letters*] ... WZVU
Long Branch Public Library, Long Branch, NJ [*Library symbol Library of Congress*] (LCLS) ... NjLob
Long Calcined Ton [*Bauxite, etc.*] ... LCT
Long Core [*Drilling program*] ... LOCO
Long Day [*Botany*] ... LD
Long Day Care ... LDC
Long Delay ... LD
Long Distance ... LD
Long Distance Infrared Flash Camera (PDAA) ... LODIF
Long Distance Love [*An association*] (EA) ... LDL
Long Distance Navigation (FAAC) ... LODISNAV
Long Distance Running Directors Association (EA) ... LDRDA
Long Distance Savers ... LDS
Long Distance Swimmer ... LDS
Long Distance Telephone [*Telecommunications*] (IAA) ... LDTEL
Long Distance Transmission (BUR) ... LDT
Long Distance/USA, Inc. [*Honolulu, HI*] [*Telecommunications*] (TSSD) ... LD/USA
Long Distance Walkers Association [*British*] (DBA) ... LDWA
Long Double Upright Brace [*Medicine*] ... LDUB
Long Dry Ton ... LDT
Long Duration ... LD
Long Dwell Time RADAR (NATG) ... LDTR
Long Endurance Breathing Apparatus (PDAA) ... LEBA
Long [*Term*] **Equity Anticipation Securities** [*Finance*] ... LEARS
Long Eye Relief (MCD) ... LER
Long Feeder Route Analysis Program [*Bell System*] ... LFRAP
Long Fiber Injection ... LFI
Long Fiber Thermoplastic Resin ... LFTPR
Long Filename (PCM) ... LFN
Long Flashing Light [*Navigation signal*] ... LFl
Long Geng [*Malaysia*] [*ICAO location identifier*] (ICLI) ... WBGE
Long Haul Fuel Conservation System ... LHFCS
Long Instruction Word [*Teraplex*] [*Computer science*] ... LIW
Long Interspered Nuclcotide Elements [*Genetics*] ... LINEs
Long Interspersed Element Sequence [*Genetics*] ... LINE
Long Interspersed Nuclear Element [*Genetics*] ... LINE
Long Island ... LI
Long Island Airlines [*ICAO designator*] (AD) ... YL
Long Island, AK [*AM radio station call letters*] ... KABN
Long Island Association of Commerce and Industry, Jericho, NY [*Library symbol Library of Congress*] (LCLS) ... NJerC
Long Island Bancorp [*NASDAQ symbol*] (TTSB) ... LISB
Long Island Bancorp, Inc. [*Associated Press*] (SAG) ... LI Bcp
Long Island Bancorp, Inc. [*NASDAQ symbol*] (SAG) ... LISB
Long Island Biological Association ... LIBA
Long Island College Hospital, Brooklyn, NY [*Library symbol Library of Congress*] (LCLS) ... NBLiCH
Long Island Doctors' Hospital, Roslyn Heights, NY [*Library symbol Library of Congress*] (LCLS) ... NRhDH
Long Island Early Fliers Club (EA) ... LIEFC
Long Island Expressway (BARN) ... LIE
Long Island Historical Society, Brooklyn, NY [*Library symbol Library of Congress*] (LCLS) ... NBLiHi
Long Island Jewish Hospital, New Hyde Park, NY [*Library symbol Library of Congress*] (LCLS) ... NNhpJ
Long Island Library Resources Council [*Bellport, NY*] [*Library network*] ... LILRC
Long Island Library Resources Council, Inc., Bellport, NY [*Library symbol Library of Congress*] (LCLS) ... NBelL
Long Island Light'g [*NYSE symbol*] (TTSB) ... LIL
Long Island Lighting Co. [*Formerly, LLT*] [*NYSE symbol*] (SPSG) ... LIL
Long Island Lighting Co. [*Associated Press*] (SAG) ... LILCo
Long Island Lighting Co., Hicksville, NY [*Library symbol*] [*Library of Congress*] (LCLS) ... NHlckL
Long Island Lighting Co., Hicksville, NY [*Library symbol Library of Congress*] (LCLS) ... NHvL
Long Island Ltg 5% B Pfd [*NYSE symbol*] (TTSB) ... LILPrB
Long Island Ltg 4.35% Cv E Pfd [*NYSE symbol*] (TTSB) ... LILPrE
Long Island Ltg, 5.75% Cv I Pfd [*NYSE symbol*] (TTSB) ... LILPrI
Long Island Ltg 7.05% Pfd [*NYSE symbol*] (TTSB) ... LILPrQ
Long Island Ltg 7.66% Pfd [*NYSE symbol*] (TTSB) ... LILPrC

Long Island Ltg 7.95% Pfd [NYSE symbol] (TTSB) .... LILPrA
Long Island [New York] MacArthur [Airport symbol] (OAG) .... ISP
[The] Long Island Rail Road Co. [AAR code] LI
[The] Long Island Rail Road Co. .... LIRR
Long Island Republic [New York] [Airport symbol] (OAG) .... FRG
Long Island Sports Network [Cable-television system] .... LISN
Long Island University [Brooklyn, NY] .... LIU
Long Island University (Brooklyn Campus) (GAGS) .... LIU
Long Island University, Brooklyn, NY [Library symbol Library of Congress]
  (LCLS) .... NBLiU
Long Island University, C. W. Post Center, Greenvale, NY [Library symbol
  Library of Congress] (LCLS) .... NGvP
Long Island University, C. W. Post Center, Greenvale, NY [OCLC symbol]
  (OCLC) VXX
Long Island University Press (DGA) .... LIUP
Long Island University, Southampton College, Southampton, NY [Library
  symbol Library of Congress] (LCLS) .... NSoaS
Long Jump .... LJ
Long Lama [Malaysia] [Airport symbol] (AD) .... LLM
Long Latency Response [Neurology] .... LLR
Long Lead (NASA) LL
Long Lead Item (MUGU) LLI
Long Lead Item List LLIL
Long Lead List (MCD) LLL
Long Lead Part .... LLP
Long Lead Repair Part .... LLRP
Long Lead Time .... LLT
Long Lead Time Items (AAG) .... LLTI
Long Lead Time Items List (NASA) LLIL
Long Lead Time Items List [Military] (CAAL) .... LLTIL
Long Lead Time Material (DNAB) .... LLTM
Long Leadtime/Items List .... LL/L
Long Leaf Yellow Pine [Lumber] .... LLYP
Long Left Shift (SAA) .... LLS
Long Leg Brace [Orthopedics] .... LLB
Long Leg Cast [Orthopedics] LLC
Long Leg Posterior Molded Splint [Medicine] (MEDA) .... LLPMS
Long Leg Splint [Orthopedics] (DAVI) .... LLS
Long Lellang [Malaysia] [Airport symbol] (OAG) .... LGL
Long Length Record (IAA) .... LLR
Long Life Recording and Data Storage (MCD) .... LLRDS
Long Life Space System (IAA) .... LLSS
Long Life Valve LLV
Long Life Vehicle [Automotive engineering] LLV
Long Line [Telecommunications] (MCD) LL
Long Line Azimuth [Survey] .... LOLA
Long Line Effect .... LLE
Long Line Equipment [Telecommunications] (TEL) .... LLE
Long Line Loiter [Aircraft] LLL
Long Line Voice Interface Rack (SSD) .... LLVIR
Long Lines Coordination (NATG) LLC
Long Magazine Lee-Enfield [British military] (DMA) .... LMLE
Long Market Value [Investment term] .... LMV
Long Mawang [Indonesia] [ICAO location identifier] (ICLI) ... WRLN
Long Measure (ROG) .... LM
Long Meter [Music] .... LM
Long Meter Double [Music] .... LMD
Long Module (MCD) .... LM
Long Normal Superchron [Geology] .... LNS
Long on Irrigation [A publication] (DLA) .... Long Irr
Long on Sales of Personal Property [A publication] (DLA) .. Long S
Long Open Reading [Frame] [Genetics] .... LOR
Long Part Number .... LPN
Long Particular [or Peculiar] Metre [Music] .... LPM
Long Path Gas [Spectroscopy] .... LPG
Long Path Infrared .... LOPAIR
Long Period .... LP
Long Periodic Perturbation .... LPP
Long Persistence .... LP
Long Picot .... LP
Long Play [VHS recorder mode] (NTCM) .... LP
Long Play Talkdown .... LPTD
Long Playing [Phonograph record] .... LP
Long Position [Investment term] .... LP
Long Prairie Elementary School, Long Prairie, MN [Library symbol] [Library
  of Congress] (LCLS) .... MnLpE
Long Prairie High School, Long Prairie, MN [Library symbol] [Library of
  Congress] (LCLS) .... MnLpH
Long Prairie, MN [AM radio station call letters] .... KEYL
Long Prairie Public Library, Long Prairie, MN [Library symbol] [Library of
  Congress] (LCLS) .... MnLp
Long Primer .... LP
Long Provost .... LP
Long Pulse - Continuous Wave (NG) .... LP-CW
Long Pulse LASER .... LPL
Long Quinto [Pt. 10 of Year Books] [A publication] (DSA) .. L5
Long Quinto [Pt. 10 of Year Books] [A publication] (DLA) .. Long Q
Long Range .... LR
Long Range .... LRG
Long Range Air-to-Air Missile [Air Force] .... LRAAM
Long Range Communications (NTCM) .... LRC
Long Range Desert Group [British Army] [World War II] .. LRDG
Long Range Navigation [FAA] (TAG) .... LRNAV
Long Reduced Rate [Taxation] (WDAA) .... LRR
Long Reference Number .... LRN

Long Reference Number Code .... LRNC
Long Regulatory Region [Genetics] .... LRR
Long Reversed Superchron [Geology] .... LRS
Long Rifle .... LR
Long Right Shift .... LRS
Long Ring Timer .... LRT
Long, Rolling Sea [Meteorology] L
Long Run [Economics] .... LR
Long Sault Branch, Stormont, Dundas, and Glengarry County Public
  Library, Ontario [Library symbol National Library of Canada] (BIB) ...... OLSSDG
Long Semado [Malaysia] [Airport symbol] (OAG) .... LSM
Long Semado [Malaysia] [ICAO location identifier] (ICLI) .. WBGD
Long Seridan [Malaysia] [Airport symbol] (OAG) .... ODN
Long Service (ADA) .... LS
Long Service and Good Conduct (ADA) .... LSGC
Long Service and Good Conduct Medal [Military decoration British] ...... LS & GCM
Long Service Leave (ADA) .... LSL
Long Shoot Terminal Bud [Botany] .... LSTB
Long Shot [A photograph or motion picture sequence taken from a distance] ..... LS
Long Side .... LSD
Long Sight (WDAA) .... LS
Long Sleeves [Dressmaking] .... LS
Long, Slow Distance [Training method for runners] ..... LSD
Long Sukang [Malaysia] [Airport symbol] (OAG) .... LSU
Long Tank Delta .... LTD
Long Tank Thrust-Augmented (PDAA) .... LTTA
Long Tank Thrust-Augmented Delta (PDAA) .... LTTAD
Long Tank Thrust-Augmented Thor .... LTTAT
Long Taper (WDAA) .... LG TPR
Long Taper .... LTPR
Long Term .... LT
Long Term Costing [Military] (RDA) .... LTC
Long Term Credit Bank [Japan] (ECON) .... LTCB
Long Term Ecological Research [National Science Foundation] ..... LTER
Long Term Projections [Townsend-Greenspan & Co., Inc.] [Database] .. LTP
Long Terminal Repeat [or Redundancy] [Genetics] ...... LTR
Long Throw [Speaker system] .... LT
Long Time Constant (IEEE) .... LTC
Long Time Low Temperature [Food processing] .... LTLT
Long Time, No See [Computer science] (DOM) .... LTNS
Long to Short [Computer utility tool] (PCM) .... LTOS
Long Ton [2240 pounds] (WDAA) .... LG TN
Long Ton [2240 pounds] .... LT
Long Ton [2240 pounds] .... LTON
Long Ton Unit .... LTU
Long Tons Discharged or Loaded .... LOTON
Long Tour [Military] (GFGA) .... LT
Long Trailing Wire Antenna (MCD) .... LTWA
Long Treble [Crocheting] (ROG) .... LT
Long Treble [Knitting] .... LTR
Long Tube Vertical .... LTV
Long Valley [New Jersey] [Seismograph station code, US Geological Survey]
  (SEIS) .... LVNJ
Long Vertical Left LVL
Long Vertical Right .... LVR
Long Wave (FAAC) .... LGWV
Long Wave [Radio] .... LW
Long Wavelength Infrared (MCD) .... LWI
Long Wavelength Infrared .... LWIR
Long Wavelength Infrared Illuminator .... LWII
Long Wavelength Redundant [Camera for spectra] ...... LWR
Long Wheelbase .... LWB
Long Wire Antenna .... LWA
Longacre [James B.] [Designer's mark, when appearing on US coins] L
Long-Acting [Pharmacy] .... LA
Long-Acting Neuroleptic [Pharmacology] (DAVI) .... LAN
Long-Acting Theophylline [Pharmacology] .... LAT
Long-Acting Thyroid Stimulator [Endocrinology] ...... LATS
Longana [Vanuata] [Airport symbol] (OAG) .... LOD
Longana [Vanuatu] [ICAO location identifier] (ICLI) .... NVSG
Long-Arm [Cast] [Orthopedics] (DAVI) .... LA
Long-Arm Navicular Cast [Orthopedics] (DAVI) .... LANC
Long-Arm Splint [Orthopedics] (DAVI) .... LAS
Long-Baseline Interferometer [or Interferometry] (PDAA) .. LBI
Long-Baseline Tiltmeter [For earthquake study] .... LBT
Longboat Resources, Inc. [Vancouver Stock Exchange symbol] ...... LRI
Longbow Apache [Helicoptor] [Army] (RDA) .... LBA
Longbow Apache-Tactical Engagement Simulation System .... LBA-TESS
Longbow Fire Control RADAR (DWSG) .... LBFCR
Longbow Hellfire Seeker (DWSG) .... LBHS
Long-Burning Target Indicator [British military] (DMA) .. LBTI
Long-Chain [Triglyceride] [Biochemistry] (MAE) LC
Long-Chain Branching [Organic chemistry] .... LCB
Long-Chain Fatty Acids [Organic chemistry] .... LCFA
Long-Chain Monoglyceride [Biochemistry] (MAE) ...... LCMG
Long-Chain Polysaturated Fatty Acid [Biochemistry] (MAE) .. LCP
Long-Chain Triglyceride [Biochemistry] .... LCT
Long-Day Plant [Botany] .... LDP
Long-Delay Monostable [Circuitry] .... LDM
Long-Delayed Echo .... LDE
Long-Distance Call .... LDC
Long-Distance Communications .... LDC
Long-Distance Control System (IEEE) .... LDCS
Long-Distance Dialing Center (IAA) .... LDDC
Long-Distance Diesel Oil (PDAA) .... LDDO

Long-Distance Discount Service [*Telecommunications*] .... LDDS
Long-Distance Dispersal [*Botany*] .... LDD
Long-Distance Medium Frequency Omni Range (IAA) .... LOMOR
Long-Distance Navigation Aid .... LDNA
Long-Distance Navigation System, Global [*Air Force*] .... NAVAGLOBE
Long-Distance Oil [*Service mark*] [*Amoco Oil Co.*] .... LDO
Long-Distance Range Finder (SSD) .... LDRF
Long-Distance Xerography [*Xerox Corp.*] [*Communications facsimile system*] .... LDX
Long-Duration Auxiliary Power System (NG) .... LDAPS
Long-Duration Exposure .... LDE
Long-Duration Exposure Facility [*NASA*] .... LDEF
Longear Sunfish [*Ichthyology*] .... Ls
Long-Endurance Aircraft .... LEA
Long-Endurance Experimental Research Submarine (SAA) .... LEERS
Long-Endurance Patrolling Torpedo .... LEPT
Longer (WGA) .... LGR
Longer Combination Vehicle [*Trucks hauling multiple trailers*] LCV
Longeron [*Aerospace engineering*] .... LONGN
Longer-Range Intermediate-Range Nuclear Forces .... LRINF
Longest Activity from Longest Project .... LALP
Longest Operation First .... LOF
Longest Path .... LP
Longest Perpendicular [*IOR*] [*Yacht racing*] .... LP
Longest Queue .... LNQ
Longest Remaining Processing Time (PDAA) .... LRPT
Long-Evans Rat .... LE
Longevity (AFM) .... LONGV
Longevity Quotient [*Demography*] .... LQ
Longfellow House, Longfellow National Historic Site, Cambridge, MA [*Library symbol Library of Congress*] (LCLS) .... MCLong
Longfellow Poetry Society (EA) .... LPS
Long-Fiber Thermoplastic .... LFT
Longfield and Townsend's Irish Exchequer Reports [*1841-42*] [*A publication*] (DLA) .... L & T
Longfield and Townsend's Irish Exchequer Reports [*1841-42*] [*A publication*] (DLA) .... Long & T
Longfield and Townsend's Irish Exchequer Reports [*1841-42*] [*A publication*] (DLA) .... Longf & T
Longfield on Distress and Replevin [*A publication*] (DLA) .... Longf Dist
Longford [*County in Ireland*] (ROG) .... LFD
Longford [*County in Ireland*] (WGA) .... Long
Longford [*County in Ireland*] (ROG) .... LONGF
Longford [*County in Ireland*] .... LONGFD
Longhaul Customer Modem [*Telecommunications*] (NITA) .... LCM
Longhaul Customer Modem Adapter [*Telecommunications*] (NITA) .... LCMA
Long-Haul Network (RDA) .... LHN
Long-Haul Optical Transmission Set [*Telecommunications*] (EECA) .... LHOTS
Longhorn Army Ammunition Plant (MCD) .... LAAP
Longhorn Army Ammunition Plant (AABC) .... LHAAP
Longhorn Steaks [*NASDAQ symbol*] (TTSB) .... LOHO
Longhorn Steaks, Inc. [*Associated Press*] (SAG) .... LngStk
Longhorn Steaks, Inc. [*NASDAQ symbol*] (SAG) .... LOHO
Long-Interspersed Repeated Segments [*of DNA*] [*Genetics*] (DAVI) .... LINES
Longitude .... G
Longitude L
Longitude (ABBR) .... LGTUD
Longitude .... LO
Longitude (KSC) .... LON
Longitude (AFM) .... LONG
Longitude and Latitude Indicator LLI
Longitude Independent Reset .... LIR
Longitude of Launch .... LOL
Longitude of the Ascending Node .... LAN
Longitudinal (ABBR) .... LGTUDL
Longitudinal (VRA) .... longit
Longitudinal Acoustic [*Spectroscopy*] .... LA
Longitudinal Acoustic [*or Acoustical*] **Mode** [*Spectroscopy*] .... LAM
Longitudinal Aerodynamic Characteristics .... LAC
Longitudinal Air Spring .... LAS
Longitudinal Chromatic Aberration .... LCA
Longitudinal Ciliated Groove of Filament .... LCGF
Longitudinal Diameter .... LD
Longitudinal Direct Substitution Imputation Procedure [*Bureau of the Census*] (GFGA) .... LDS
Longitudinal Division [*Cytology*] .... LD
Longitudinal Electric Pressure Wave .... LEPW
Longitudinal Employer-Employee Data File [*Social Security Administration*] .... LEED
Longitudinal Establishment Data [*Bureau of the Census*] (GFGA) .... LED
Longitudinal Expansion Joint [*Technical drawings*] .... LEJ
Longitudinal Fame Developing and Conducting System (PDAA) .... LODACS
Longitudinal Field Modulator .... LFM
Longitudinal Interval (ADA) LI
Longitudinal Interval Follow-Up Evaluation (MEDA) .... LIFE
Longitudinal Muscle [*Anatomy*] .... LM
Longitudinal Muscles of Pinnule .... LMP
Longitudinal Optic .... LO
Longitudinal Parity [*Telecommunications*] (TEL) .... LP
Longitudinal Parity Check [*Telecommunications*] (IAA) .... LPC
Longitudinal Position of Center of Buoyancy .... LCB
Longitudinal Position of Center of Flotation .... LCF
Longitudinal Position of Center of Gravity .... LCG
Longitudinal Pressure Wave .... LPW
Longitudinal Primary Care [*Medicine*] (DMAA) .... LPC
Longitudinal Redundancy Check [*Computer science*] .... LRC
Longitudinal Redundancy Check Character [*Telecommunications*] (TEL) .... LRCC
Longitudinal Redundancy Check Register [*Telecommunications*] (IAA) .... LRCR
Longitudinal Relaxation Time Constant [*Radiology*] (DAVI) T1
Longitudinal Retirement History Survey [*Social Security Administration*] (GFGA) .... LRHS
Longitudinal Ridge of Basal Fold .... LRBF
Longitudinal Ridge of Dorsal Lip .... LRDL
Longitudinal Ridge of Lateral Lip .... LRLL
Longitudinal Section .... LS
Longitudinal Section Magnetic [*Electronics*] (OA) .... LSM
Longitudinal Spherical Aberration .... LSA
Longitudinal Stability Augmentation System [*Aviation*] (DA) .... LSAS
Longitudinal Staggering (IAA) .... LS
Longitudinal Static Stability .... LSS
Longitudinal Static Stability Augmentation System (MCD) .... LSSAS
Longitudinal Studies Branch [*Department of Education*] (GFGA) .... LSB
Longitudinal Study of American Youth [*Northern Illinois University*] [*Education*] .... LSAY
Longitudinal Study of the Aging [*Department of Health and Human Services*] (GFGA) .... LSOA
Longitudinal Time Code (NTCM) .... LTC
Longitudinal Time Constant .... LTC
Longitudinal Triangular Ripples [*Oceanography*] .... LTR
Longitudinal Velocity Sorting Tube .... LVST
Longitudinal Video Recording .... LVR
Longitudinally (ABBR) .... LGTUDY
Longitudinally Applied Paper Insulation [*Telecommunications*] (TEL) .... LPI
Longitudinally Excited Atmosphere [*LASER technology*] (EECA) .... LEA
Longitudinally in Homogeneous Traveling Waves (MCD) .... LITW
Longitudinal-Section Electric (IEEE) .... LSE
Longlac Public Library, Ontario [*Library symbol National Library of Canada*] (NLC) .... OLO
Long-Lasting Depolarization [*Neurophysiology*] .... LLD
Long-Leg Brace (DMAA) .... LLB
Long-Leg Walking Cast [*Orthopedics*] (DAVI) .... LLWC
Long-Linking Carbon LLC
Longman's Dictionary of Contemporary English [*A publication*] .... LDOCE
Longman's Elementary Science Manuals [*A publication*] .... LESM
Longmeadow Historical Society, Longmeadow, MA [*Library symbol Library of Congress*] (LCLS) .... MLonHi
Longmire [*Washington*] [*Seismograph station code, US Geological Survey*] (SEIS) .... LON
Longmont, CO [*FM radio station call letters*] .... KCDC
Longmont, CO [*TV station call letters*] (RBYB) .... KDEN-TV
Longmont, CO [*AM radio station call letters*] .... KLMO
Longmont, CO [*FM radio station call letters*] .... KQKS
Longmont, CO [*Television station call letters*] .... KZJG
Longmont Public Library, Longmont, CO [*Library symbol Library of Congress*] (LCLS) .... CoLo
Longmoor Military Railway [*British military*] (DMA) .... LMR
Longold Resources, Inc. [*Vancouver Stock Exchange symbol*] .... LG
Longovilo [*Chile*] [*Seismograph station code, US Geological Survey*] (SEIS) .... LNV
Long-Pass [*Absorption cell*] .... LP
Long-Period Pulses [*Volcanology*] .... LPP
Long-Period Tremor [*Volcanology*] .... LPT
Long-Playing Record (IAA) .... LPR
Long-Playing Rocket [*Aerospace*] .... LPR
Long-Range Accuracy [*RADAR*] .... LORAC
Long-Range Acoustic Propagation .... LRAP
Long-Range Acoustic Propagation Project .... LRAPP
Long-Range Active Detection .... LORAD
Long-Range Active Detection and Communications System .... LORADAC
Long-Range Active Duty Program [*Army*] .... LRADP
Long-Range Adaption (MCD) .... LORA
Long-Range Addition (NVT) .... LORA
Long-Range Aerospace Observation Platform .... LRAOP
Long-Range Aid to Navigation [*Military*] (DOMA) .... LORAN
Long-Range Air Antisubmarine Warfare Capable Aircraft (MCD) .... LRAACA
Long-Range Air Army [*Former USSR*] (MCD) .... LRAA
Long-Range Air Defense (AABC) .... LORAD
Long-Range Air Defense Missile (MCD) .... LRADM
Long-Range Air Force .... LRAF
Long-Range Airborne ASW [*Antisubmarine Warfare*] **System** (MCD) .... LORAAS
Long-Range Airborne ASW [*Antisubmarine Warfare*] **System** (MCD) .... LRAAS
Long-Range Aircraft Rocket (NG) .... LAR
Long-Range Air-to-Surface Missile (MCD) .... LRASM
Long-Range Air-to-Surface Vessel (IAA) .... LRASV
Long-Range and Detection RADAR (NATG) .... LORD
Long-Range and Tactical Navigation System .... LORTAN
Long-Range Antisubmarine Capability Aircraft .... LAASCA
Long-Range Antitank [*Army*] (INF) .... LRAT
Long-Range Antitank Guided Weapon [*British military*] (DMA) .... LRATGW
Long-Range Approach and Landing System (PDAA) .... LRALS
Long-Range Area Homing .... LORAH
Long-Range Area RADAR for Intrusion Detection and Tracking .... LARIAT
Long-Range Assessments and Research [*Program*] [*Department of State*] [*Washington, DC*] .... LAR
Long-Range Assistance Strategy (CINC) .... LAS
Long-Range Attitude and Event [*Instrumentation system*] .... LORAE
Long-Range Automatic Measuring Station [*Meteorology*] .... LORAMS
Long-Range Autonomous Submersible .... LRAS
Long-Range Aviation [*Army*] (AABC) .... LRA
Long-Range Ballistic Missile .... LRBM
Long-Range Ballistic Rocket .... LRBR

Long-Range Bombardment Round .... LRBR
Long-Range Capability Objective [Air Force] .... LRCO
Long-Range Chemical LASER (MCD) .... LRCL
Long-Range Climb (MCD) .... LRC
Long-Range Combat Aircraft .... LRCA
Long-Range Construction Program [Military] .... LRCP
Long-Range Conventional Cruise Missile (MCD) .... LRCCM
Long-Range Conventional Standoff Weapon [Military] .... LRCSOW
Long-Range Conventional Standoff Weapon (MCD) .... LRCSW
Long-Range Conventional Standoff Weapon .... LRSOW
Long-Range Cruise [Aircraft speed] .... LRC
Long-Range Cruise Missile [Navy] .... LRCM
Long-Range Data [RADAR] .... LRD
Long-Range Development Program (IAA) .... LRDP
Long-Range Development Unit .... LRDU
Long-Range Dual-Mission Missile (MCD) .... LRDMM
Long-Range Early Warning (NATG) .... LREW
Long-Range Early Warning System (NATG) .... LREWS
Long-Range Earth Current Communications .... LOREC
Long-Range Earth Sensor .... LRES
Long-Range Echo Level Indicator .... LORELEI
Long-Range Effects Research Program [Marine science] (OSRA) .... L-RERP
Long-Range Effects Research Program (USDC) .... L-RERP
Long-Range Electronic Warfare Plan [Military] (CAAL) .... LREWP
Long-Range, Electro-Optical Reconnaissance System .... LOREORS
Long-Range Energy Development and Supply (PDAA) .... LORENDAS
Long-Range Facility [Telecommunications] (TEL) .... LRF
Long-Range Flight .... LRF
Long-Range Forecasting System (TEL) .... LRFS
Long-Range Generation Planning Problem [Energy] .... LRGPP
Long-Range Guidance (MCD) .... LRG
Long-Range Guided Bomb (MCD) .... LRGB
Long-Range - Home on Jam .... LORA-HOJ
Long-Range Impact Point (MUGU) .... LRIP
Long-Range Indicator .... LRI
Long-Range Input (CET) .... LRI
Long-Range Input Monitor [RADAR] .... LRIM
Long-Range Inspector .... LRI
Long-Range Interceptor .... LRI
Long-Range International (DOMA) .... LRI
Long-Range Logistics Guidance [Air Force] .... LRLG
Long-Range Maritime Patrol [Aircraft] (NATG) .... LRMP
Long-Range Metal Object Detection System (MCD) .... LORMODS
Long-Range Missile Launcher .... LRM
Long-Range Missile Launcher [Military] (IAA) .... LRML
Long-Range Multipurpose Naval Aircraft (HGAA) .... LMNA
Long-Range Navigation .... LORAN
Long-Range Navigation (IDOE) .... loran
Long-Range Navigation .... LRN
Long-Range Navigation Doppler Inertial (DNAB) .... LORAN D
Long-Range Navigation Double Master .... LORAN DM
Long-Range Navigation Double Slave .... LORAN DS
Long-Range Navigation Master .... LORAN M
Long-Range Navigation Slave .... LORAN S
Long-Range Navigation System [Aviation] .... LRNS
Long-Range Night Observation Device [Army] (AABC) .... LRNOD
Long-Range Objectives [Navy] .... LRO
Long-Range Objectives Group [Navy] (MCD) .... LROG
Long-Range Oblique Photography .... LOROP
Long-Range Open Ocean Patrol [Navy] (NVT) .... LOOP
Long-Range Order .... LRO
Long-Range Overwater Diffusion [Experiment] [Marine science] (OSRA) .... LROD
Long-Range Overwater Diffusion [Experiment] (USDC) .... LROD
Long-Range Passive Homing System .... LORAPH
Long-Range Passive Location System (PDAA) .... LRPLS
Long-Range Path (IEEE) .... LRP
Long-Range Patrol [Pronounced "lurp"] [Formerly, LRRP] [Army] (AABC) .... LRP
Long-Range Patrol Aircraft (MCD) .... LRPA
Long-Range Penetration .... LRP
Long-Range Penetration Group [Military World War II] .... LRPG
Long-Range Planning for School Improvement [Pennsylvania] (EDAC) .... LRPSI
Long-Range Planning Ground Rules (AAG) .... LRPGR
Long-Range Planning Purpose Document .... LRPPD
Long-Range Planning Service [Stanford Research Institute] [Assists businesses in investment activities] (IID) .... LRPS
Long-Range Planning Task Group [Oversaw military strategy in Vietnam] (VNW) .... LORAPL
Long-Range Plans (NVT) .... LRP
Long-Range Position-Determining System [Army] (RDA) .... LRPDS
Long-Range Positioning System .... LRPS
Long-Range Procurement Estimate (PDAA) .... LRPE
Long-Range Propulsion Plan (MCD) .... LRPP
Long-Range Proving Ground [Air Force] .... LRPG
Long-Range Proving Ground Automatic Computer (IEEE) .... LORPGAC
Long-Range Proving Ground Division [Air Force] .... LRPGD
Long-Range RADAR .... LRR
Long-Range RADAR Input .... LRI
Long-Range RADAR Site (OA) .... LRRS
Long-Range Radio Navigation (ACRL) .... LORAN
Long-Range Radiotelephone (DNAB) .... LR/RT
Long-Range Radiotelephone .... LRT
Long-Range Reconnaissance (MCD) .... LRR
Long-Range Reconnaissance Detachment .... LRRD
Long-Range Reconnaissance Patrol [Pronounced "lurp"] [Later, LRP] [Army] (AABC) .... LRRP

Long-Range Reference Retroreflectance Instrument [Bicycle test] [National Institute of Standards and Technology] .... LRRI
Long-Range Requirements [Navy] .... LRR
Long-Range Research, Development, and Acquisition Plan (RDA) .... LRRDAP
Long-Range Resource and Management Forecast .... LRR & MF
Long-Range Rocket (MUGU) .... LRR
Long-Range Schedule (SAA) .... LRS
Long-Range Science and Technology Plan [Army] .... LRS & TP
Long-Range Scientific Technical Planning Program (NG) .... LRSTPP
Long-Range Search .... LRS
Long-Range Seismograph Measurements (MCD) .... LRSM
Long-Range Service Life Analysis (MCD) .... LRSLA
Long-Range Sniper Rifle (PDAA) .... LRSR
Long-Range SOF [Special Operation Force] Insertion (DOMA) .... LRSI
Long-Range SONAR .... LORS
Long-Range Special Unit [Military] .... LORSU
Long-Range Stand-Off Missile .... LRSOM
Long-Range Station Keeping (NG) .... LRSK
Long-Range Steerable Antenna (MCD) .... LORSA
Long-Range Strategic Planning (PDAA) .... LRSP
Long-Range Strategic Studies [Military] (AFIT) .... LRSS
Long-Range Study .... LRS
Long-Range Submarine Communications (AAG) .... LORSAC
Long-Range Surface-to-Air Guided Weapon (IAA) .... LRSAGW
Long-Range Surface-to-Air Missile (NATG) .... LRSAM
Long-Range Surveillance [Military] (INF) .... LRS
Long-Range Surveillance Co. [Military] (INF) .... LRSC
Long-Range Surveillance Detachment [Military] (INF) .... LRSD
Long-Range Surveillance Leader [Military] (INF) .... LRSL
Long-Range Surveillance Outpost (MCD) .... LRSO
Long-Range Surveillance Unit [Military] (INF) .... LRSU
Long-Range Surveillance Unit Base Radio Station [Military] (INF) .... LRSUBRS
Long-Range Survey System [Military] .... LRSS
Long-Range Systems Forecast .... LRSF
Long-Range Tactical Strike Missile (MCD) .... LTSM
Long-Range Technical Forecast (IEEE) .... LRTF
Long-Range Technical Plan (PDAA) .... LRTP
Long-Range Theater Nuclear Force [Military] .... LRTNF
Long-Range Theater Nuclear Weapons [Military] .... LRTNW
Long-Range Training and Rotation Plan .... LORTRAP
Long-Range Training Mission [Military] .... LRTM
Long-Range Transport [Navy British] .... LRT
Long-Range Transport of Atmospheric Pollutants .... LRTAP
Long-Range Typhon [Navy] (NG) .... LRT
Long-Range Video (MCD) .... LRV
Longreach [Australia ICAO location identifier] (ICLI) .... ABLR
Longreach [Australia Airport symbol] (OAG) .... LRE
Long-Reach Detonator [Explosive] .... LRD
Longreach Resources Ltd. [Vancouver Stock Exchange symbol] .... LRR
Long-Route Engineering Study [Bell System] .... LORES
Long-Run Average Cost Curve [Economics] .... LAC
Long-Run Average Costs [Marketing] .... LRAC
Long-Run Average Total Costs [Economics] .... LRATC
Long-Run Deal Effect [Marketing] .... LRDE
Long-Run Incremental Cost [Business term] (ADA) .... LRIC
Long-Run Marginal Cost Curve [Economics] .... LMC
Long-Run Marginal Costs .... LRMC
Long-Run Price Effect [Marketing] .... LRPE
Long-Running Thermal Precipitation (DICI) .... LRTP
Longs Drug Stores [NYSE symbol] (TTSB) .... LDG
Longs Drug Stores [Associated Press] (SAG) .... LongDrg
Longs Drug Stores Corp. [NYSE symbol] (SPSG) .... LDG
Longs Drug Stores Corp. [Associated Press] (SAG) .... LongDr
Longshore and Harbor Workers' Compensation Act (AAGC) .... LHWCA
Longshore Case Management System [Department of Labor] (GFGA) .... LCMS
Longshoremen's and Harbor Workers' Compensation Act (DLA) .... LHCA
Longshoremen's and Warehousemen's Union International .... LWUI
Longstaff Bluff, NT [ICAO location identifier] (ICLI) .... CYUV
Long-Tailed Pair [Electronics] (OA) .... LTP
Longtan [China] [ICAO location identifier] (ICLI) .... RCDI
Longterm Ambulatory Physiological Surveillance Equipment (PDAA) .... LAPSE
Long-Term and Expanded Program of Oceanic Exploration and Research .... LEPOR
Long-Term and Expanded Program of Oceanic Research and Exploration (BARN) .... LEPORE
Long-Term Arrangements [Department of State] .... LTA
Long-Term Average (CAAL) .... LTA
Long-Term Bone Marrow Culture [Cell culture] .... LTBMC
Long-Term Capital Gain .... LTCG
Long-Term Capital Loss .... LTCL
Long-Term Care [Medicine] .... LTC
Long-Term Care Campaign (EA) .... LTCC
Long-Term Care Facility [Medicine] .... LTCF
Long-Term Care Facility [Medicine] (DAVI) .... LTCF
Long-Term Care Minimum Data Set [Department of Health and Human Services] (GFGA) .... LTCMDS
Long-Term Care Statistics Branch [Department of Health and Human Services] (GFGA) .... LTCSB
Long-Term Communications Improvement Plan (NATG) .... LOTCIP
Long-Term Contract (ADA) .... LTC
Long-Term Credit Bank of Japan, Ltd. (ECON) .... LTCB
Long-Term Defense Program [NATO] (MCD) .... LTDP
Long-Term Depression [Neurophysiology] .... LTD
Long-Term Disability .... LTD
Long-Term Ecological Research .... LTER

Long-Term Economic Deterioration [*Department of Commerce*] ..... LTED
Long-Term Effect ..... LTE
Long-Term Effects of Dredging Operations [*Coastal Engineering Research Center*] ..... LEDO
Long-Term Enhancement [*Neurophysiology*] ..... LTE
Long-Term Equilibration [*Analytical chemistry*] ..... LTE
Long-Term Equipment Plan [*Military*] (RDA) ..... LTEP
Long-Term Equity Anticipation Securities [*Investment term*] (DFIT) ..... LEAPS
Long-Term Equity Anticipations [*Business term*] ..... LEAP
Long-Term/Frequency Modulation ..... LT/FM
Long-Term Goals (DAVI) ..... LTG
Long-Term Heart Rate (PDAA) ..... LHR
Long-Term Heat Aging ..... LTHA
Long-Term Holiday (MHDB) ..... LTH
Long-Term Incentive Plan ..... LTIP
Long-Term Integration (CAAL) ..... LTI
Long-Term Lapse Survey [*LIMRA*] ..... LTLS
Long-Term Memory ..... LTM
Long-Term Multilineage Reconstituting [*Cytology*] ..... LTMR
Long-Term Multilineage Reconstituting Stem Cell [*Cytology*] ..... LTMRSC
Long-Term Nephelometer [*Instrumentation*] ..... LTN
Long-Term Nonprogessor [*Of the human immune deficiency virus*] ..... LTNP
Long-Term Ocean Bottom Settlement Test for Engineering Research [*Navy project*] ..... LOBSTER
Long-Term Parenteral Nutrition (PDAA) ..... LTPN
Long-Term Pavement Performance [*FHWA*] (TAG) ..... LTPP
Long-Term Potentiation [*Neurophysiology*] ..... LTP
Long-Term Prime Rate [*Finance*] ..... LTPR
Long-Term Procedural Language ..... LTPL
Long-Term Public Expenditure [*British*] ..... LTPE
Long-Term Quality-Control [*Analytical chemistry*] ..... LTQC
Long-Term Requirement Plan (NATG) ..... LTRP
Long-Term Reserve [*British military*] (DMA) ..... LTR
Long-Term Revitalization (OA) ..... LTR
Long-Term Scientific Study [*NATO Defense Research Group*] (MCD) ..... LTSS
Long-Term Stability ..... LTS
Long-Term Stability Test [*Chemistry*] ..... LST
Long-Term Standard [*Lamp for spectrometry*] ..... LTS
Long-Term Stay [*in hospital*] [*British*] ..... LT
Long-Term Storage [*Memory*] [*Computer science*] ..... LTS
Long-Term Survival [*Medicine*] (DMAA) ..... LTS
Long-Term Tape Recorder ..... LTTR
Long-Term Training (MCD) ..... LTT
Long-Term Trend [*Finance*] (MHDI) ..... LTT
Long-Term Unemployed ..... LTU
Long-Term Upper Ocean Study ..... LOTUS
Long-Term Vibration ..... LTV
Long-Term Waviness [*Metal surface finish*] ..... LTW
Long-Term Worldwide Air Defense Study [*Army*] (AABC) ..... LOTADS
Long-Term Zonal Earth Energy Budget Experiment [*Spacecraft*] [*NASA*] ..... LZEEBE
Longtree [*England*] ..... LONGT
Long-Tube Recirculation [*Evaporator*] ..... LTR
Longueuil, PQ [*FM radio station call letters*] (RBYB) ..... CHAA-FM
Longueuil, PQ [*FM radio station call letters*] ..... CIEL
Longus [*Long*] [*Pharmacy*] ..... LONG
Longuyon/Villette [*France ICAO location identifier*] (ICLI) ..... LFGS
Longview [*Texas*] [*Airport symbol*] (OAG) ..... GGG
Longview Community College, Lee's Summit, MO [*Library symbol Library of Congress*] (LCLS) ..... MoLeeL
Longview Fibre [*NYSE symbol*] (TTSB) ..... LFB
Longview Fibre Co. [*NYSE symbol*] (CTT) ..... LFB
Longview Fibre Co. [*Associated Press*] (SAG) ..... LongvF
Longview/Gregg County [*Texas*] [*ICAO location identifier*] (ICLI) ..... KGGG
Longview Municipal Library, Alberta [*Library symbol National Library of Canada*] (NLC) ..... ALOM
Longview Municipal Library, Longview, AB, Canada [*Library symbol Library of Congress*] (LCLS) ..... CaALoM
Longview, Portland & Northern Railway Co. [*AAR code*] ..... LPN
Longview Public Library, Longview, WA [*Library symbol Library of Congress*] (LCLS) ..... WaLo
Longview, TX [*AM radio station call letters*] ..... KARW
Longview, TX [*AM radio station call letters*] ..... KFRO
Longview, TX [*Television station call letters*] ..... KFXK
Longview, TX [*FM radio station call letters*] ..... KYKX
Longview, WA [*AM radio station call letters*] ..... KBAM
Longview, WA [*AM radio station call letters*] ..... KEDO
Longview, WA [*FM radio station call letters*] ..... KJVH
Longview, WA [*FM radio station call letters*] ..... KLYK
Longview, WA [*FM radio station call letters*] ..... KZOE
Longwave Club of America (EA) ..... LWCA
Long-Wave Pass Filter (PDAA) ..... LWPF
Long-Wave Radiation ..... LWR
Long-Wavelength Oscillation [*Astrophysics*] ..... LWO
Longwood College (GAGS) ..... Longwood C
Longwood College, Farmville, VA [*Library symbol Library of Congress*] (LCLS) ..... ViFarL
Longwood Gardens [*Kennett Square, PA*] ..... LG
Longwood Gardens Library, Kennett Square, PA [*OCLC symbol*] (OCLC) ..... LWG
Longwood Gardens Library, Kennett Square, PA [*Library symbol Library of Congress*] (LCLS) ..... PKsL
Long-Working Distance [*Microscopy*] ..... LWD
Longworth House Office Building ..... LHOB
Longyear [*Norway*] [*Airport symbol*] (OAG) ..... LYR
Lonicera Latent Virus [*Plant pathology*] LLV
Lonoke, AR [*FM radio station call letters*] ..... KMZX
Lonorore [*Vanuata*] [*Airport symbol*] (OAG) ..... LNE
Lonorore [*New Hebrides*] [*Seismograph station code, US Geological Survey*] (SEIS) ..... LNR
Lonorore [*Vanuatu*] [*ICAO location identifier*] (ICLI) ..... NVSO
Lons Le Saunier/Courlaoux [*France ICAO location identifier*] (ICLI) ..... LFGL
Lonsdale's Statute Criminal Law [*A publication*] (DLA) ..... Lons Cr L
Lonvest Corp. [*Toronto Stock Exchange symbol Vancouver Stock Exchange symbol*] ..... LNV
Lonza Aktiengesellschaft, Zentralbibliothek, Basel, Switzerland [*Library symbol Library of Congress*] (LCLS) ..... SzBaL
Loogootee, IN [*FM radio station call letters*] (RBYB) ..... WBHW-FM
Loogootee Tribune, Loogootee, IN [*Library symbol Library of Congress*] (LCLS) ..... InLooT
Look Ahead (IAA) ..... LA
Look Ahead Carry Generator [*Computer science*] (NITA) ..... LAHCG
Look Ahead on Fault [*Computer science*] (MHDB) ..... LOF
Look Ahead Variable Acceleration [*Computer science*] (MHDB) ..... LAVA
Look Angles of Celestial Bodies (KSC) ..... LACB
Look at Me (IAA) ..... LAM
Lookahead Carry Generator [*Computer science*] (IAA) ..... LCG
Lookahead Left to Right [*Computer science*] ..... LALR
Lookdown/Shootdown (MCD) ..... LDSD
Looking (MSA) ..... LKG
Looking for Party [*Telecommunications*] (TEL) ..... LK
Looking for Work ..... LFW
Looking Up [*An association*] (EA) ..... LU
Lookout (MSA) ..... LKT
Look-Out [*Navy British*] ..... LO
Look-Out Aiming Sight [*Military*] (PDAA) ..... LAS
Lookout Assist Device [*Navigation*] (OA) ..... LAD
Lookout Mountain Air Force Station ..... LMAFS
Lookout Mountain Laboratories [*California*] (SAA) ..... LML
Lookout Mountain Observatory [*California*] [*Seismograph station code, US Geological Survey Closed*] (SEIS) ..... LMO
Lookout Mountain Observatory [*California*] [*Seismograph station code, US Geological Survey*] (SEIS) ..... LMS
Lookout Mountain School for Boys, Golden, CO [*Library symbol Library of Congress*] (LCLS) ..... CoGLM
Lookout Mountain, TN [*AM radio station call letters*] ..... WFLI
Lookout Post (IAA) ..... LOP
Lookthrough (LAIN) ..... LT
Lookup Dictionary Adaptor Program (IEEE) ..... LADAPT
Lookup Dictionary Print Program (IEEE) ..... LPRINT
Lookup Table [*Computer science*] (BYTE) ..... LUT
Loomis-Wood Diagram [*Physics*] ..... LWD
Loop [*Fingerprint description*] L
Loop [*Postal Service standard*] (OPSA) ..... LOOP
Loop [*Commonly used*] (OPSA) ..... LOOPS
Loop [*Knitting*] ..... LP
Loop Activity Tracking Information System [*Telecommunications*] (TEL) ..... LATIS
Loop Actuating Signal (SAA) ..... LAS
Loop Adder and Multiplier (NITA) ..... LAM
Loop Addition and Modification [*Computer science*] ..... LAM
Loop Antenna (DEN) ..... LA
Loop Cable Record Inventory System (MCD) ..... LCRIS
Loop Carrier Analysis Program [*Bell System*] ..... LCAP
Loop Check (MUGU) ..... L/C
Loop College, Chicago, IL [*OCLC symbol*] (OCLC) ..... IBJ
Loop College, Chicago, IL [*Library symbol Library of Congress*] (LCLS) ..... ICLoop
Loop Control System [*Nuclear energy*] (NRCH) ..... LCS
Loop Current Step Response Method (IEEE) ..... LCSRM
Loop Diagram ..... LD
Loop Electrosurgical Excision Procedure [*Medicine*] ..... LEEP
Loop Error Signal ..... LES
Loop Extender [*Telecommunications*] (TEL) ..... LE
Loop Extension Amplifier ..... LEA
Loop Feedback Signal ..... LFS
Loop Fluidized Bed [*Chemical engineering*] ..... LFB
Loop Gain ..... LG
Loop Gap Resonator [*Spectrometry*] ..... LGR
Loop Ground Multiplexer (MCD) ..... LGM
Loop Handling Machine [*Nuclear energy*] (NRCH) ..... LHM
Loop Handling System [*Nuclear energy*] (NRCH) ..... LHS
Loop Input Signal ..... LIS
Loop Insertion Cell [*Nuclear energy*] (NRCH) LIC
Loop Interface Address ..... LIA
Loop Key Generator (MCD) ..... LKG
Loop Maintenance Operations System [*Formerly, MLR*] [*Bell System*] ..... LMOS
Loop Multiplexer ..... LM
Loop of Henle [*Medicine*] (DMAA) ..... LOH
Loop of Intestine LI
Loop Output Signal (CET) ..... LOS
Loop Preparation Cask [*Nuclear energy*] (NRCH) ..... LPC
Loop Preparation Equipment [*Nuclear energy*] (NRCH) ..... LPE
Loop Regenerative Repeater ..... LRR
Loop Sampling Module ..... LSM
Loop Shorting Relay (MCD) ..... LSR
Loop Station Connector (MHDB) ..... LSC
Loop Switching System [*Telecommunications*] ..... LSS
Loop Test [*Aerospace*] (AAG) ..... L/T
Loop Test Conference [*Aerospace*] (AAG) ..... LTC
Loop-Control [*Relay*] (IEEE) ..... LPC
Loop-Disconnect [*Telecommunications*] (TEL) ..... LD
Looper [*Computer science*] (MDG) L

Looper Position Regulator ... LPR
Loops [*Military decoration*] (AABC) ... Lps
Loose ... LSE
Loose Actors Revolving Company [*for producing plays; members include actors George C. Scott and Rod Steiger*] ... LARC
Loose Bladder Construction [*Ball*] (DICI) ... LBC
Loose Body [*Medicine*] ... LB
Loose Bowel Movement [*Medicine*] (CPH) ... LBM
Loose Container Load [*Shipping*] (IMH) ... LCL
Loose Coupler ... LC
Loose Cubic Meter (DAC) ... LCM
Loose Cubic Yard (DAC) ... LCY
Loose Fuel-Rod Shipping Basket (GAAI) ... LFRSB
Loose Granular Snow [*Skiing condition*] ... LSGR
Loose Leaf ... LL
Loose Leaf and Blank Book Manufacturers Association [*Later, ABPM*] (EA) ... LLBBMA
Loose Leaf Ledger ... LLL
Loose or in Packages [*Freight*] ... LOPKGS
Loose or on Skids [*Freight*] ... LSE SKDS
Loose Shot ... LS
Loose Snow on Runway [*NWS*] (FAAC) ... LSR
Loose Snow on Runway-Patchy [*Aviation*] (DNAB) ... LSR-P
Loosely Coupled Network [*Telecommunications*] (OSI) ... LCN
Loose-Parts Monitoring System [*Nuclear energy*] (NRCH) ... LPMS
Loose-Parts-Monitor Assembly [*Nuclear energy*] (NRCH) ... LPMA
Lop Buri [*Thailand*] [*ICAO location identifier*] (ICLI) ... VTBL
Lop Buri/Sa Pran Nak [*Thailand*] [*ICAO location identifier*] (ICLI) ... VTBH
Lop Rabbit Club of America (EA) ... LRCA
Loparskaya [*Formerly, Murmansk*] [*Former USSR Geomagnetic observatory code*] ... MMK
Lopez Island [*Washington*] [*Airport symbol*] (OAG) ... LPS
Lopez Island Library District, Lopez, WA [*Library symbol*] [*Library of Congress*] (LCLS) ... WaLop
LOPO [*Local Post*] **Collectors Society** (EA) ... LCS
Loquitur [*He, or She, Speaks*] [*Latin*] ... LOQ
[*The*] **Lorain & West Virginia Railway Co.** [*AAR code*] ... LAWV
Lorain County Community College, Elyria, OH [*Library symbol Library of Congress*] (LCLS) ... OElyL
Lorain, OH [*Location identifier FAA*] (FAAL) ... LQG
Lorain, OH [*FM radio station call letters*] ... WNZN
Lorain, OH [*AM radio station call letters*] ... WRKG
Lorain, OH [*Television station call letters*] ... WUAB
Lorain, OH [*FM radio station call letters*] ... WZLE
Lorain Public Library, Lorain, OH [*OCLC symbol*] (OCLC) ... LXP
Lorain Public Library, Lorain, OH [*Library symbol Library of Congress*] (LCLS) ... OLor
Loraine Mine [*South Africa*] [*ICAO location identifier*] (ICLI) ... FALM
Loral Corp. [*NYSE symbol*] (SPSG) ... LOR
Loral Corp. [*Associated Press*] (SAG) ... Loral
Loral Electro-Optical Systems Corp. ... LEOS
Loral Space Communications [*NYS*] (TTSB) ... LOR
Loralai [*Pakistan*] [*ICAO location identifier*] (ICLI) ... OPLL
LORAN [*Long-Range Navigation*] (IAA) ... L
LORAN [*Long-Range Aid to Navigation*] ... LRN
LORAN Airborne Navigation System (IEEE) ... LANS
LORAN [*Long-Range Navigation*] **Automatic Vehicle Monitoring** (PDAA) ... LAVM
LORAN Inertial Command Air-Launched Missile ... LICALM
LORAN Inertial System ... LINS
LORAN Integrated Engineering Program ... LIEP
LORAN Integrated Engineering Program, Shed Light ... LIEPS
LORAN Monitor Station ... LORMONSTA
LORAN Navigation Chart [*Air Force*] ... LNC
LORAN/OMEGA Course and Tracking Equipment (MCD) ... LOCATE
LORAN Operational Training School ... LOTS
LORAN Station [*ITU designation*] (CET) ... RLN
LORAN Transmitting Station ... LORSTA
LORAN-Aided Weapons Delivery System ... LAWDS
Loras College (GAGS) ... Loras C
Loras College, Dubuque, IA [*Library symbol Library of Congress*] (LCLS) ... IaDuL
Loras College, Dubuque, IA [*OCLC symbol*] (OCLC) ... IOL
Lorazepam [*A tranquilizer*] ... L
Lorazepam [*A tranquilizer*] ... LOR
Lorazepam [*Also, L, LOR*] [*Antiepileptic drug*] ... LZP
Lorcan Resources Ltd. [*Vancouver Stock Exchange symbol*] ... LOA
Lorcha [*Ship's rigging*] (ROG) ... LOR
Lord [*or Lordship*] ... L
Lord ... LD
Lord (WGA) ... Lo
Lord Advocate [*British*] (DAS) ... L Adv
Lord Advocate of Scotland (DLA) ... LA
Lord Advocate of Scotland ... LAS
Lord Birkenhead's Judgments, House of Lords [*England*] [*A publication*] (DLA) ... Ld Birk
Lord Brougham's Speeches [*A publication*] (DLA) ... Ld Br Sp
Lord Chamberlain [*British*] ... LC
Lord Chancellor (DLA) ... C
Lord Chancellor [*British*] (ROG) ... L CH
Lord Chancellor [*British*] ... LC
Lord Chancellor's Department [*British*] ... LCD
Lord Chancellor's Legal Aid Advisory Committee [*British*] (DLA) ... LAAC
Lord Chancellor's Office [*British*] (DLA) ... LCO
Lord Chief Baron [*British*] ... LCB
Lord Chief Justice [*British A publication*] (DLA) ... CJ
Lord Chief Justice [*British*] ... LCJ
Lord Corp. Research and Development Library, Cary, NC [*Library symbol*] [*Library of Congress*] (LCLS) ... NcCyL
Lord Elgin High School, Burlington, ON, Canada [*Library symbol Library of Congress*] (LCLS) ... CaOBUL
Lord Elgin High School, Burlington, Ontario [*Library symbol National Library of Canada*] (NLC) ... OBUL
Lord Fairfax Community College, Learning Resources Center, Middletown, VA [*Library symbol Library of Congress*] (LCLS) ... ViMidL
Lord Great Chamberlain [*British A publication*] (DLA) ... LGC
Lord High Admiral [*British*] ... LHA
Lord High Chancellor [*British*] ... LHC
Lord High Treasurer [*British*] ... LHT
Lord Howe Island [*Australia ICAO location identifier*] (ICLI) ... ASLH
Lord Howe Island [*Australia Airport symbol*] (OAG) ... LDH
Lord Jesus Christ (ROG) ... LJC
Lord Justice ... LJ
Lord Justice Clerk of Scotland (DAS) ... LJCS
Lord Justice General [*British*] ... LJG
Lord Justice of Appeal ... LJA
Lord Keeper [*of the Great Seal*] [*British*] (ROG) ... LK
Lord Kenyon's English King's Bench Reports [*1753-59*] [*A publication*] (DLA) ... Ld Ken
Lord Kenyon's English King's Bench Reports [*1753-59*] [*A publication*] (DLA) ... Ld Kenyon
Lord Kenyon's English King's Bench Reports [*1753-59*] [*A publication*] (DLA) ... Ld Kenyon (Eng)
Lord Kenyon's English King's Bench Reports, Notes, Edited by Hanmer [*A publication*] (ILCA) ... Hanm
Lord Kenyon's English King's Bench Reports, Notes, Edited by Hanmer [*A publication*] (DLA) ... Hanmer
Lord Lieutenant ... LL
Lord Lieutenant of Ireland ... LLI
Lord Mansfield's Decisions [*1799-1814*] [*England*] [*A publication*] (DLA) ... Evans
Lord Mayor ... LDM
Lord Mayor ... LM
Lord of Creation ... LOC
[*The*] **Lord of the Rings** [*A trilogy*] ... LOTR
Lord President of the Court of Session, Scotland (DLA) ... LP
Lord President's Committee [*British*] ... LPC
Lord Privy Seal [*British*] ... LPS
Lord Provost [*British*] ... LP
Lord Raymond's English King's Bench Reports [*3 vols.*] [*A publication*] (DLA) ... Raym Ld
Lord Raymond's King's Bench and Common Pleas Reports [*1694-1732*] [*A publication*] (DLA) ... Ld Ray
Lord Raymond's King's Bench and Common Pleas Reports [*1694-1732*] [*A publication*] (DLA) ... Ld Raym
Lord River Gold [*Vancouver Stock Exchange symbol*] ... LRD
Lord Ruthven Assembly [*An association*] (EA) ... LRA
Lord Selkirk Regional School, Selkirk, Manitoba [*Library symbol National Library of Canada*] (NLC) ... MSEL
Lord Selkirk Regional School, Selkirk, MB, Canada [*Library symbol Library of Congress*] (LCLS) ... CaMSeL
Lord Treasurer's Remembrancer [*British*] ... LTR
Lordosis [*Medicine*] ... LORD
Lordosis Quotients [*Medicine*] ... LQ
Lords ... LL
Lord's Acre Plan (EA) ... LAP
Lord's Day Alliance of the United States (EA) ... LDA
Lord's Day Observance Society [*British*] ... LDOS
Lords Justices ... LJJ
Lords Justices ... LLJJ
Lords of the Privy Council Lower Provinces Code [*India*] [*A publication*] (DLA) ... LPC
Lordsburg, NM [*FM radio station call letters*] ... KXKK
Lordsburg, NM [*Location identifier FAA*] (FAAL) ... LSB
Lordsburg-Hidalgo Public Library, Lordsburg, NM [*Library symbol Library of Congress*] (LCLS) ... NmLor
Lordship [*British*] ... LDP
Loredi Resources Ltd. [*Vancouver Stock Exchange symbol*] ... LDI
Lorentz Doppler Profile [*Physics*] ... LDP
Lorentz Double Refraction [*Physics*] ... LDR
Lorentz Reciprocal Theorem ... LRT
Lorentz Unit [*Electronics*] ... L
Lorentz-Polarization [*Optics*] ... LP
Lorenz Domination [*Statistics*] ... LDOM
Lorenzo, TX [*FM radio station call letters*] ... KKCL
Lorenz's Appeal Reports [*Ceylon*] [*A publication*] (DLA) ... Lorenz App R
Lorenz's Ceylon Reports [*A publication*] (DLA) ... Lorenz
Lorenz's Ceylon Reports [*A publication*] (ILCA) ... Lorenz Rep
Loreto [*Mexico*] [*Airport symbol*] (OAG) ... LTO
Loreto [*Mexico ICAO location identifier*] (ICLI) ... MMLT
Loretta Lynn Fan Club (EA) ... LLFC
Loretto Geriatric Center, Educational Resource Center, Syracuse, NY [*Library symbol Library of Congress*] (LCLS) ... NSyLG
Loretto Heights College [*Denver, CO*] ... LHC
Loretto Heights College, Denver, CO [*OCLC symbol*] (OCLC) ... COL
Loretto Heights College, Denver, CO [*Library symbol Library of Congress*] (LCLS) ... CoLH
Loretto in Kansas City, Kansas City, MO [*Library symbol Library of Congress*] (LCLS) ... MoKLo
Loretto Junior College [*Kentucky*] ... LJC
Loretto, PA [*AM radio station call letters*] (RBYB) ... WEBG-AM
Loretto, PA [*AM radio station call letters*] ... WJRV
Lorgues [*France*] [*Seismograph station code, US Geological Survey*] (SEIS) ... LRG

Lori Corp. [*Associated Press*] (SAG) .... LoriCp
Lori Corp. [*AMEX symbol*] (SPSG) .... LRC
Lori Robin Smith International Fan Club (EA) .... LRSIFC
Lorica [*Colombia*] [*Airport symbol*] (AD) .... LRI
Loricrin (DMAA) .... LOR
Lorient [*France*] [*Airport symbol*] (OAG) .... LRT
Lorient/Lann-Bihoue [*France ICAO location identifier*] (ICLI) .... LFRH
Lorillard Research Center, Greensboro, NC [*Library symbol Library of Congress*] (LCLS) .... NcGL
Lorimer. Institutes of Law [*A publication*] (ILCA) .... Lor Inst
Lorimer's Handbook of Scotch Law [*A publication*] (DLA) .... Lor Sc L
Loring and Russell's Election Cases in Massachusetts [*A publication*] (DLA) .... L & R
Loring and Russell's Election Cases in Massachusetts [*A publication*] (DLA) .... L & R Election Cases
Loring and Russell's Election Cases in Massachusetts [*A publication*] (DLA) .... Lor & Russ
Loring and Russell's Election Cases in Massachusetts [*A publication*] (DLA) .... Loring & Russel El Cases
Loring and Russell's Election Cases in Massachusetts [*A publication*] (DLA) .... Loring & Russell
Loring and Russell's Election Cases in Massachusetts [*A publication*] (DLA) .... Mass EC L & R
Loring and Russell's Election Cases in Massachusetts [*A publication*] (DLA) .... Mass Election Cases
Loris, SC [*Location identifier FAA*] (FAAL) .... BEZ
Loris, SC [*AM radio station call letters*] .... WLSC
Loris, SC [*FM radio station call letters*] .... WVCO
Lorman, MS [*FM radio station call letters*] .... WPRL
Lormes [*Somee*] [*France*] [*Seismograph station code, US Geological Survey*] (SEIS) .... LOR
Lornex Mining Corp. [*Vancouver Stock Exchange symbol*] .... LMN
Loronix Info Systems [*NASDAQ symbol*] (TTSB) .... LORX
Loronix Information Systems, Inc. [*Associated Press*] (SAG) .... Loronix
Loronix Information Systems, Inc. [*NASDAQ symbol*] (SAG) .... LORX
Lorraine [*Australia Airport symbol Obsolete*] (OAG) .... LOA
Lorraine Publishing, Inc., Bordentown, NJ [*Library symbol Library of Congress*] (LCLS) .... NjBorL
Lorry Command Vehicle [*British military*] (DMA) LCV
Lorry with Gas Containers [*British*] .... LGC
Lorry-Mounted Crane Association [*British*] (BI) .... LMCA
Los Alamitos, CA [*Location identifier FAA*] (FAAL) .... SLI
Los Alamitos/Los Alamitos Naval Air Station [*California*] [*ICAO location identifier*] (ICLI) .... KNTB
Los Alamos [*New Mexico*] [*Airport symbol*] (OAG) .... LAM
Los Alamos [*New Mexico*] [*Seismograph station code, US Geological Survey*] (SEIS) .... LOA
Los Alamos [*Ecuador*] [*ICAO location identifier*] (ICLI) .... SEAL
Los Alamos Area Office [*Energy Research and Development Administration*] .... LAAO
Los Alamos Digital Image Enhancement Software (PDAA) .... LADIES
Los Alamos Fourier Transform Spectrometer [*Department of Energy*] (GRD) .... LAFTS
Los Alamos Fuel Model [*Department of Energy*] (GFGA) .... LAFM
Los Alamos Medium Energy Facility .... LAMEF
Los Alamos Meson Physics Facility [*Later, Clinton P. Anderson Meson Physics Facility at Los Alamos*] [*Department of Energy*] .... LAMPF
Los Alamos Molten Plutonium Program .... LAMPP
Los Alamos Molten Plutonium Reactor Experiment .... LAMPRE
Los Alamos National Laboratory [*Los Alamos, NM*] [*Department of Energy*] .... LANL
Los Alamos National Scientific Laboratories [*New Mexico*] .... LANSL
Los Alamos Neutron Scattering Center .... LANSCE
Los Alamos, NM [*FM radio station call letters*] .... KBOM
Los Alamos, NM [*FM radio station call letters*] .... KEFE
Los Alamos, NM [*AM radio station call letters*] .... KRSN
Los Alamos, NM [*FM radio station call letters*] .... KTMN
Los Alamos, NM [*Location identifier FAA*] (FAAL) .... LAM
Los Alamos Power Reactor .... LAPR
Los Alamos Power Reactor Experiment .... LAPRE
Los Alamos Scientific Laboratory [*USAEC*] (MCD) .... LA
Los Alamos Scientific Laboratory [*USAEC*] (MCD) .... LAMS
Los Alamos Scientific Laboratory [*USAEC*] .... LASL
Los Alamos Scientific Laboratory, Los Alamos, NM [*Library symbol Library of Congress*] (LCLS) .... NmLaS
Los Alamos Scientific Laboratory, Medical Library, Los Alamos, NM [*Library symbol Library of Congress*] (LCLS) .... NmLaS-M
Los Alamos Water Boiler (NRCH) .... LAMB
Los Alamos Water Boiler [*Nuclear reactor*] (NRCH) .... LAWB
Los Altos, CA [*FM radio station call letters*] (RBYB) .... KFFG
Los Altos, CA [*FM radio station call letters*] .... KFJC
Los Angeles [*California*] [*ICAO location identifier*] (ICLI) .... KRLA
Los Angeles [*California*] [*Slang*] .... LA
Los Angeles [*California*] [*Airport symbol*] (OAG) .... LAX
Los Angeles (GAVI) .... LAX
Los Angeles Air Defense Sector [*ADC*] .... LAADS
Los Angeles Air Force Station .... LAAFS
Los Angeles Air Procurement District .... LAAPD
Los Angeles Air Procurement District .... LAPD
Los Angeles Air Service, Inc. .... LAAS
Los Angeles Aircraft Division [*Rockwell International*] .... LAAD
Los Angeles Airways, Inc. .... LAA
Los Angeles Baptist College and Theological Seminary, Newhall, CA [*Library symbol Library of Congress*] (LCLS) .... CNeBC
Los Angeles Bar Association. Bulletin [*A publication*] (DLA) .... Los Angeles BAB
Los Angeles Branch [*AEC*] .... LAB
Los Angeles, CA [*Location identifier FAA*] (FAAL) .... CFN
Los Angeles, CA [*Location identifier FAA*] (FAAL) .... GPE
Los Angeles, CA [*Location identifier FAA*] (FAAL) .... HQB
Los Angeles, CA [*Location identifier FAA*] (FAAL) .... IAS
Los Angeles, CA [*AM radio station call letters*] .... KABC
Los Angeles, CA [*Television station call letters*] .... KABC-TV
Los Angeles, CA [*FM radio station call letters*] .... KBIG
Los Angeles, CA [*Television station call letters*] .... KCAL-TV
Los Angeles, CA [*FM radio station call letters*] .... KCBS
Los Angeles, CA [*Television station call letters*] .... KCBS-TV
Los Angeles, CA [*Television station call letters*] .... KCET
Los Angeles, CA [*Television station call letters*] .... KCOP
Los Angeles, CA [*Television station call letters*] .... KEEF
Los Angeles, CA [*AM radio station call letters*] .... KFI
Los Angeles, CA [*FM radio station call letters*] .... KFSG
Los Angeles, CA [*AM radio station call letters*] .... KFWB
Los Angeles, CA [*AM radio station call letters*] .... KGFJ
Los Angeles, CA [*FM radio station call letters*] (RBYB) .... KIBB-FM
Los Angeles, CA [*AM radio station call letters*] .... KIIS
Los Angeles, CA [*FM radio station call letters*] .... KIIS-FM
Los Angeles, CA [*FM radio station call letters*] .... KKBT
Los Angeles, CA [*FM radio station call letters*] .... KKGO-FM
Los Angeles, CA [*AM radio station call letters*] .... KKHJ
Los Angeles, CA [*FM radio station call letters*] .... KKLA
Los Angeles, CA [*AM radio station call letters*] .... KLAC
Los Angeles, CA [*Television station call letters*] .... KLCS
Los Angeles, CA [*FM radio station call letters*] .... KLOS
Los Angeles, CA [*FM radio station call letters*] .... KLSX
Los Angeles, CA [*FM radio station call letters*] .... KLVE
Los Angeles, CA [*Television station call letters*] .... KMEX
Los Angeles, CA [*AM radio station call letters*] .... KMPC
Los Angeles, CA [*Television station call letters*] .... KNBC
Los Angeles, CA [*AM radio station call letters*] .... KNX
Los Angeles, CA [*FM radio station call letters*] .... KOST
Los Angeles, CA [*FM radio station call letters*] .... KPFK
Los Angeles, CA [*FM radio station call letters*] .... KPWR
Los Angeles, CA [*FM radio station call letters*] .... KRTH
Los Angeles, CA [*Television station call letters*] .... KTLA
Los Angeles, CA [*AM radio station call letters*] .... KTNQ
Los Angeles, CA [*Television station call letters*] .... KTTV
Los Angeles, CA [*FM radio station call letters*] .... KTWV
Los Angeles, CA [*FM radio station call letters*] .... KUSC
Los Angeles, CA [*Television station call letters*] .... KWHY
Los Angeles, CA [*AM radio station call letters*] .... KWKW
Los Angeles, CA [*AM radio station call letters*] .... KXED
Los Angeles, CA [*FM radio station call letters*] .... KXEZ
Los Angeles, CA [*FM radio station call letters*] .... KXLU
Los Angeles, CA [*AM radio station call letters*] (RBYB) .... KXMG-AM
Los Angeles, CA [*AM radio station call letters*] (RBYB) .... KYPA-AM
Los Angeles, CA [*FM radio station call letters*] .... KYSR
Los Angeles, CA [*FM radio station call letters*] .... KZLA
Los Angeles, CA [*Location identifier FAA*] (FAAL) .... MKZ
Los Angeles, CA [*Location identifier FAA*] (FAAL) .... OSS
Los Angeles, CA [*Location identifier FAA*] (FAAL) .... UWU
Los Angeles, CA [*Location identifier FAA*] (FAAL) .... WHP
Los Angeles, CA [*Location identifier FAA*] (FAAL) .... ZLA
Los Angeles Catalyst Study [*Environmental Protection Agency*] .... LACS
Los Angeles Chamber of Commerce, Research Library, Los Angeles, CA [*Library symbol Library of Congress*] (LCLS) CLCC
Los Angeles City College [*California*] .... LACC
Los Angeles City College, Los Angeles, CA [*Library symbol Library of Congress*] (LCLS) CLCiC
Los Angeles City Historical Society, Malibu, CA [*Library symbol*] [*Library of Congress*] (LCLS) .... CMalHi
Los Angeles College of Chiropractic, Glendale, CA [*Library symbol Library of Congress*] (LCLS) .... CGlCC
Los Angeles College of Optometry [*California*] .... LACO
Los Angeles College of Optometry, Los Angeles, CA [*Library symbol Library of Congress*] (LCLS) .... CLCO
Los Angeles Copyright Society (EA) .... LACS
Los Angeles County Air Pollution Control District Library, Los Angeles, CA [*Library symbol Library of Congress*] (LCLS) .... CLCAPF
Los Angeles County Civil Service Commission, Los Angeles, CA [*Library symbol Library of Congress*] (LCLS) .... CLCCS
Los Angeles County General Hospital, Los Angeles, CA [*Library symbol Library of Congress*] (LCLS) .... CLCGH
Los Angeles County Health Department, Los Angeles, CA [*Library symbol Library of Congress*] (LCLS) .... CLCP
Los Angeles County Law Library, Los Angeles, CA [*Library symbol Library of Congress*] (LCLS) CLL
Los Angeles County Medical Association, Los Angeles, CA [*Library symbol Library of Congress*] (LCLS) .... CLM
Los Angeles County Museum of Art .... LACMA
Los Angeles County Museum of Art, Los Angeles, CA [*OCLC symbol*] (OCLC) .... CAM
Los Angeles County Museum of Art, Los Angeles, CA [*Library symbol Library of Congress*] (LCLS) .... CLCMAr
Los Angeles County Museum of Natural History, Los Angeles, CA [*Library symbol Library of Congress*] (LCLS) .... CLCM
Los Angeles County Public Library, Los Angeles, CA [*Library symbol Library of Congress*] (LCLS) .... CLCo
Los Angeles County Public Library, Los Angeles, CA [*Library symbol*] [*Library of Congress*] (LCLS) .... CLCoP

Los Angeles County/University of Southern California Medical Center (DAVI) .... LAC/USC

Los Angeles Educational Alliance for Restructuring Now [Education-reform project] (ECON) .... LEARN

Los Angeles Free Press [A publication] .... FREEP

Los Angeles Grain Exchange (EA) .... LAGE

Los Angeles Harbor Junior College, Wilmington, CA [Library symbol Library of Congress] (LCLS) .... CLHJ

Los Angeles/International [California] [ICAO location identifier] (ICLI) .... KLAX

Los Angeles International Fern Society (EA) .... LAIFS

Los Angeles Junction Railway Co. [AAR code] .... LAJ

Los Angeles Kings Fan Club (EA) .... LAKFC

Los Angeles Law Review [A publication] (DLA) .... Los Angeles L Rev

Los Angeles Multiple Corridor Identification System (SAA) .... LAMCIS

Los Angeles Neurological Medical Group, Inc., Los Angeles, CA [Library symbol Library of Congress] (LCLS) .... CLIN

Los Angeles Olympic Organizing Committee (EA) .... LAOOC

Los Angeles Ordnance District [Military] (AAG) .... LAOD

Los Angeles Pacific College [California] .... LAPC

Los Angeles Pacific College, Los Angeles, CA [Library symbol Library of Congress] (LCLS) .... CLPC

Los Angeles Palmdale [California] [ICAO location identifier] (ICLI) .... KZLA

Los Angeles Procurement Agency [Army] .... LAPA

Los Angeles Procurement Field Office .... LAPFO

Los Angeles Public Library .... LAPL

Los Angeles Public Library, Los Angeles, CA [Library symbol Library of Congress] (LCLS) CL

Los Angeles Public Library, Municipal Reference Library, Los Angeles, CA [Library symbol Library of Congress] (LCLS) .... CL-MR

Los Angeles Public Library, Police Department Library, Los Angeles, CA [Library symbol Library of Congress] (LCLS) .... CL-MP

Los Angeles Public Library, Water and Power Department Library, Los Angeles, CA [Library symbol Library of Congress] (LCLS) .... CL-MW

Los Angeles Theater Center [California] .... LATC

Los Angeles Times [A publication] .... LAT

Los Angeles Times Book Review [A publication] (BRI) .... LATBR

Los Angeles Times, Los Angeles, CA [Library symbol Library of Congress] (LCLS) .... CLT

Los Angeles Times News Service .... LATNS

Los Angeles Union Passenger Terminal [AAR code] .... LAPT

Los Angeles Valley College, Van Nuys, CA [Library symbol Library of Congress] (LCLS) .... CVnL

Los Banos, CA [FM radio station call letters] .... KHTN

Los Banos, CA [AM radio station call letters] .... KLBS

Los Banos, CA [FM radio station call letters] .... KQLB

Los Banos, CA [Location identifier FAA] (FAAL) .... LSN

Los Brasiles/Carlos Ulloa [Nicaragua] [ICAO location identifier] (ICLI) .... MNBR

Los Cabos [Mexico] [Airport symbol] (OAG) .... SJD

Los Californianos (EA) LC

Los Cedros/Uraba [Colorado ICAO location identifier] (ICLI) .... SKLC

Los Chiles [Costa Rica] [Airport symbol] (OAG) .... LSL

Los Chiles [Costa Rica] [ICAO location identifier] (ICLI) .... MRLC

Los Gatos, CA [FM radio station call letters] .... KRTY

Los Gatos Memorial Library, Los Gatos, CA [Library symbol Library of Congress] (LCLS) .... CLg

Los Hermanos de Juan Diego (TOCD) .... HJD

Los Lunas [FM radio station call letters] .... KIOT

Los Lunas, NM [FM radio station call letters] (RBYB) .... KDNR

Los Madonnas College, Pittsburg, CA [Library symbol] [Library of Congress] (LCLS) .... CPiC

Los Mochis [Mexico] [Airport symbol] (OAG) .... LMM

Los Mochis [Mexico ICAO location identifier] (ICLI) .... MMLM

Los Ninos International Adoption Center .... LNIAC

Los Osos-Baywood Park, CA [FM radio station call letters] .... KSTT

Los Pinos Mountain [New Mexico] [Seismograph station code, US Geological Survey] (SEIS) .... LPM

Los Queltehues [Chile] [Seismograph station code, US Geological Survey] (SEIS) .... LQT

Los Ranchos de Albuquerque, NM [AM radio station call letters] .... KALY

Los Ranchos de Albuquerque, NM [AM radio station call letters] (RBYB) .... KHFN

Los Ranchos de Albuquerque, NM [AM radio station call letters] (RBYB) .... KNML-AM

Los Roques, Dependencia Federal [Venezuela ICAO location identifier] (ICLI) .... SVRS

Los Tajibos [Bolivia] [ICAO location identifier] (ICLI) .... SLLT

Los Trancos Woods [California] [Seismograph station code, US Geological Survey] (SEIS) .... LTW

Los Ybanez, TX [FM radio station call letters] .... KYMI

Losing Inventory Manager [Army] (AABC) .... LIM

Losing Pitcher [Baseball] .... LP

Los-Ionic-Strength Saline Solution [Medicine] (MEDA) .... LISS

Loss and Damage .... L & D

Loss and Damage (IAA) .... LD

Loss and Damage Review [A publication] (DLA) .... Loss & Dam Rev

Loss Entry Form [Insurance] .... LEF

Loss Exchange Ratio (MCD) .... LER

Loss Executives Association [Parsippany, NJ] (EA) .... LEA

Loss Factor [Electronics] (IAA) .... LSF

Loss Frequency Method [Insurance] .... LFM

Loss in Weight .... LIW

Loss Information Service [Insurance] .... LIS

Loss Margin (IAA) .... LM

Loss of Clock Detector .... LCD

Loss of Consciousness [Medicine] .... LOC

Loss of Contact (IAA) LC

Loss of Coolant (GAAI) .... LOC

Loss of Electric Power .... LOEP

Loss of Feedwater [Nuclear energy] (NRCH) .... LOF

Loss of Feedwater [Nuclear energy] (NRCH) .... LOFW

Loss of Flow [Nuclear energy] (NRCH) .... LOF

Loss of Flow Accident [Nuclear energy] (NRCH) .... LOFA

Loss of Flow [or Fluid] Test Facility [Nuclear energy] .... LOFT

Loss of Fluid (BARN) .... LOF

Loss of Forced Circulation [Nuclear energy] (NRCH) .... LOFC

Loss of Heat Sink [Nuclear energy] (NRCH) .... LOHS

Loss of Heterozygosity [Genetics] .... LOH

Loss of Imprinting [Genetics] .... LOI

Loss of Interim Status [Environmental Protection Agency] .... LOIS

Loss of Load Probability [Nuclear energy] (IEEE) .... LOLP

Loss of Main Feedwater [Nuclear energy] (NRCH) .... LOMF

Loss of Mesodermal Competence [Developmental biology] .... LMC

Loss of Motion [Medicine] .... LOM

Loss of Normal Power (IEEE) .... LNP

Loss of Offsite Power [Nuclear energy] (NRCH) .... LOOP

Loss of Offsite Power [Nuclear energy] (NRCH) .... LOP

Loss of Offsite Power [Nuclear energy] (NRCH) .... LOSP

Loss of Pay [Court-martial sentence] [Marine Corps] .... LP

Loss of Pipe Integrity [Nuclear energy] (NRCH) .... LOPI

Loss of Righting Reflex [Medicine] (DMAA) .... LOR

Loss of Righting Reflex [Medicine] .... LRR

Loss of Sight .... LOS

Loss of Signal .... LOS

Loss of Synchronization .... LOS

Loss of System Pressure [Nuclear energy] (NRCH) .... LOSP

Loss of Vehicle (KSC) .... LOV

Loss of Visibility (NASA) .... LOV

Loss of Vision (DAVI) .... LOV

Loss on Ignition [Analytical chemistry] .... LOI

Loss Ratio Reserve Method [Insurance] .... LRRM

Loss Report [Aircrew/aircraft] .... LOSREP

Loss' Security Regulations [A publication] (DLA) .... Loss Sec Reg

Lossiemouth [British ICAO location identifier] (ICLI) .... EGQS

Lossiemouth FTU [British ICAO designator] (FAAC) .... LOS

Lossless Digital Integrator (IAA) .... LDI

Lossless Reciprocal Embedding (IAA) .... LRE

Loss-of-Coolant Accident [Nuclear energy] .... LOCA

Loss-of-Coolant Experiment [Nuclear energy] .... LOCE

Loss-of-Coolant Flow [Nuclear energy] (NRCH) .... LOCF

Loss-of-Coolant Protection [Nuclear energy] (NRCH) .... LOCP

Loss-of-Fluid Test (GAAI) .... LOFT

Lost [Sports statistics] L

Lost [RADAR] L

Lost by Inventory (DNAB) .... LBI

Lost Calls Cleared [Telecommunications] (NITA) LCC

Lost Calls Held [Telecommunications] (NITA) .... LCH

Lost Cause Press, Louisville, KY [Library symbol Library of Congress] (LCLS) .... LCP

Lost Chord Clubs (EA) LCC

Lost Circulation Material [Oil well drilling] .... LCM

Lost Creek, WV [FM radio station call letters] .... WOTR

Lost Heartbeat [An attractive girl] [Slang] .... LHB

Lost in Space Fannish Alliance (EA) .... LISFA

Lost Item Replacement (MCD) .... LIR

Lost Lake Resources Ltd. [Vancouver Stock Exchange symbol] .... LSO

Lost Music Network [Defunct] (EA) .... LMN

Lost Nation Press, Lost Nation, IA [Library symbol Library of Congress] (LCLS) .... IaLnP

Lost on Foul [Boxing] .... LF

Lost Parts Replacement Authorization (MCD) .... LPRA

Lost Planes [An association] (EA) .... LP

Lost River, AK [Location identifier FAA] (FAAL) .... LSR

Lost River District Library, Arco, ID [Library symbol] [Library of Congress] (LCLS) .... IdAr

Lost Seska [Defunct] (EA) .... LS

Lost Time Injury [Industrial plant safety] .... LTI

Lost Wax (VRA) .... lstwx

Lostant Community Library, Lostant, IL [Library symbol Library of Congress] (LCLS) .... ILos

Lostant Consolidated Community School District 25, Lostant, IL [Library symbol Library of Congress] (LCLS) .... ILosSD

Lostant Consolidated High School District 400, Lostant, IL [Library symbol Library of Congress] (LCLS) .... ILosHSD

Lostwithiel [Municipal borough in England] .... LOSTW

Losuia [Papua New Guinea] [Airport symbol] (OAG) .... LSA

Lot .... LT

Lot Acceptance Test (NASA) .... LAT

Lot Fraction Reliability Deviation [Quality control] .... LFRD

Lot Indices LI

Lot Number .... LN

Lot Rejection Report .... LRR

Lot Sensitive Plan (PDAA) .... LSP

LOT [Limited Operational Test] Support Services [Military] (DWSG) .... LSS

Lot Time (SAA) .... LT

Lot Time Order .... LTO

Lot Tolerance Fraction Reliability Deviation [Quality control] .... LTFRD

Lot Tolerance Percent Defective [Quality control] (MSA) .... LTPD

Lotarius [Flourished, 1191-1212] [Authority cited in pre-1607 legal work] (DSA) .... Lo

Lotarius Rosario de Cremona [Deceased, 1227] [Authority cited in pre-1607 legal work] (DSA) .... Lot

Lot-Car Load ... LCL
Lotharian Regiment [*Military British*] (ROG) ... LOTH R
Lothario (ABBR) ... LHAR
Lothian and Berwick Cavalry [*British military*] (DMA) ... LBC
Lothians and Border Horse [*British military*] (DMA) ... L & B
Loti [*Monetary unit*] [*Lesotho*] (BARN) ... L
Lotio [*Lotion*] [*Pharmacy*] ... LOT
Loto-Quebec, Centre de Documentation, Montreal, PQ, Canada [*Library symbol*] [*Library of Congress*] (LCLS) ... CaQMLQ
Lotru [*Romania*] [*Seismograph station code, US Geological Survey*] (SEIS) ... LOT
Lot-Size Inventory Management Interpolation Technique (BUR) ... LIMIT
Lotta Continua [*Continuous Struggle*] [*Italy Political party*] (PPE) ... LC
Lotteries Commission of South Australia ... LCSA
Lotteries Commission of Western Australia ... LCWA
Lottery Collectors Society (EA) ... LCS
Lottery Enterprises [*NASDAQ symbol*] (TTSB) ... LOTO
Lottery Enterprises, Inc. [*Associated Press*] (SAG) ... LotteryE
Lottery Promotion Co. [*British*] (ECON) ... LPC
Lotto World [*NASDAQ symbol*] (TTSB) ... LTTO
Lotto World, Inc. [*Associated Press*] (SAG) ... LottoW
Lotto World, Inc. [*NASDAQ symbol*] (SAG) ... LTTO
Lot-Truck Load ... LTL
Lotus 1-2-3 Users' Association ... L123UA
Lotus Cortina of America Register [*Defunct*] (EA) ... LCAR
Lotus Cosmetics International Ltd. [*Vancouver Stock Exchange symbol*] ... LTC
Lotus Extended Applications Facility ... LEAF
Lotus/Intel/Microsoft [*Computer science*] ... LIM
Lotus International Character Set [*Printer technology*] (PCM) ... LICS
Lotus Lantern International Buddhist Center [*South Korea*] (EAIO) ... LLIBC
Lotus West (EA) ... LW
Lotus-Intel-Microsoft Expanded Memory Specification [*Computer science*] (BTTJ) ... LIM-EMS
Lou Christie International Fan Club (EA) ... LCIFC
Loubomo [*Congo*] [*Airport symbol*] (OAG) ... DIS
Loubomo [*Congo*] [*ICAO location identifier*] (ICLI) ... FCPL
Loud and Clear ... LC
Loud Speaking Telephone (NITA) ... LST
Loudima [*Congo*] [*ICAO location identifier*] (ICLI) ... FCPD
Loudness Contour Selector ... LCS
Loudness Discomfort Level (MAE) ... LDL
Loudness Equivalent [*Medicine*] (DMAA) ... Leq
Loudness Level ... LL
Loudness Unit ... LU
Loudon, TN [*AM radio station call letters*] ... WLOD
Loudon, TN [*FM radio station call letters*] ... WNOX
Loudon, TN [*FM radio station call letters*] ... WXST
Loudonville, NY [*FM radio station call letters*] ... WVCR
Loudonville, OH [*FM radio station call letters*] ... WBZW
Loudonville Public Library, Loudonville, OH [*Library symbol Library of Congress*] (LCLS) ... OLou
Loudspeaker ... LS
Loudspeaker (TEL) ... LSPK
Loudspeaker Acoustical Labyrinth ... LAL
Loudspeaker Acoustical Phase-Inverter ... LAP
Loudspeaker Amplifier (DWSG) ... LSA
Loudun [*France ICAO location identifier*] (ICLI) ... LFDL
Loufoula [*Congo*] [*ICAO location identifier*] (ICLI) ... FCMF
Lough [*Maps and charts*] ... L
Loughborough University Computerized Information and Drawings Project [*British*] ... LUCID
Loughborough University of Technology [*British*] (IRUK) ... LUT
Loughborough's Digest of Statute Law [*Kentucky*] [*A publication*] (DLA) ... St Law
Lougheed, AB [*Television station call letters*] ... CFRN-7
Lougheed Public Library, Alberta [*Library symbol National Library of Canada*] (NLC) ... ALO
Louis A. Warren Lincoln Library and Museum, Fort Wayne, IN [*Library symbol*] [*Library of Congress*] (LCLS) ... InFwLW
Louis A. Weiss Memorial Hospital, Chicago, IL [*Library symbol Library of Congress*] (LCLS) ... ICWeH
Louis Armstrong Memorial Project ... LAMP
Louis Braille Foundation for Blind Musicians [*Defunct*] (EA) ... LBF
Louis Comfort Tiffany [*Signature on the art glass designed by Tiffany*] ... LCT
Louis Dreyfus Natural Gas [*NYSE symbol*] (TTSB) ... LD
Louis Dreyfus Natural Gas [*Associated Press*] (SAG) ... LDryNG
Louis Dreyfus Natural Gas Holdings Corp. [*NYSE symbol*] (SPSG) ... LD
Louis Finkelstein Institute for Religious and Social Studies (EA) ... LFIRSS
Louis, Holland, Callaway [*Advertising agency*] ... LHC
Louis Latzer Memorial Library, Highland, IL [*Library symbol Library of Congress*] (LCLS) ... IHig
Louis Leakey - Korongo [*Anthropological skull*] ... LLK
Louis Trichardt [*South Africa*] [*ICAO location identifier*] (ICLI) ... FALO
Louis Trichardt [*South Africa*] [*ICAO location identifier*] (ICLI) ... FALT
Louis Trichardt [*South Africa*] [*Airport symbol*] (OAG) ... LCD
Louis Trichardt [*South Africa*] [*Seismograph station code, US Geological Survey*] (SEIS) ... LTT
Louis Vuitton [*Initials used as a pattern on Vuitton luggage, handbags, etc.*] ... LV
Louis Vuitton Moet-Hennessy [*Commercial firm*] [*Belgium*] ... LVMH
Louis XIV, James II, Mary, Prince of Wales [*Jacobite toast*] ... LIMP
Louisa County Courthouse, Wapello, IA [*Library symbol*] [*Library of Congress*] (LCLS) ... IaWapCoC
Louisa, KY [*FM radio station call letters*] ... WSAC
Louisa, KY [*AM radio station call letters*] ... WVKY
Louisa May Alcott Memorial Association (EA) ... LMAMA
Louisa, VA [*FM radio station call letters*] ... WLSA
Louis-Allen Power Supply ... LAPS
Louisbourg Archives, Louisbourg, NS, Canada [*Library symbol Library of Congress*] (LCLS) ... CaNSLA
Louisbourg Archives, Nova Scotia [*Library symbol National Library of Canada*] (NLC) ... NSLA
Louisburg College, Louisburg, NC [*Library symbol Library of Congress*] (LCLS) ... NcLoC
Louisburg, NC [*Location identifier FAA*] (FAAL) ... LFN
Louisburg, NC [*FM radio station call letters*] ... WHLQ
Louisburg, NC [*AM radio station call letters*] ... WYRN
Louise Mandrell Fan Club (EA) ... LMFC
Louiseville G&E 5% Pfd [*NASDAQ symbol*] (TTSB) ... LGASP
Louisiana [*Postal code*] (AFM) ... LA
Louisiana [*MARC country of publication code Library of Congress*] (LCCP) ... lau
Louisiana ... LOU
Louisiana [*MARC geographic area code Library of Congress*] (LCCP) ... n-us-la
Louisiana [*Peru*] [*ICAO location identifier*] (ICLI) ... SPLA
Louisiana Administrative Code [*A publication*] (DLA) ... LA Admin Code
Louisiana Administrative Register [*A publication*] (DLA) ... LA Admin Reg
Louisiana & Arkansas Railway Co. ... L & A
Louisiana & Arkansas Railway Co. [*AAR code*] ... LA
[*The*] **Louisiana & North West Railroad Co.** [*AAR code*] ... LNW
[*The*] **Louisiana & Pine Bluff Railway Co.** [*AAR code*] ... LPB
Louisiana Annual Reports [*A publication*] (DLA) ... Annual R
Louisiana Annual Reports [*A publication*] (DLA) ... L Ann
Louisiana Annual Reports [*A publication*] (DLA) ... LA A
Louisiana Annual Reports [*A publication*] (DLA) ... LA An R
Louisiana Annual Reports [*A publication*] (DLA) ... LA An Rep
Louisiana Annual Reports [*A publication*] (DLA) ... LA Ann
Louisiana Annual Reports [*A publication*] (DLA) ... LA Ann Reps
Louisiana Annual Reports [*A publication*] (DLA) ... Louisiana Ann
Louisiana Annual Reports [*A publication*] (DLA) ... Louisiana Ann Rep
Louisiana Annuals [*A publication*] (DLA) ... A
Louisiana Army Ammunition Plant (AABC) ... LAAP
Louisiana Arts and Science Center, Baton Rouge, LA [*Library symbol*] [*Library of Congress*] (LCLS) ... LBrLAS
Louisiana Association for Health, Physical Education, Recreation, and Dance (SRA) ... LAHPERD
Louisiana Association of Business Educators (EDAC) ... LABE
Louisiana Association of Criminal Defense Lawyers (SRA) ... LACDL
Louisiana Bankers Association (SRA) ... LBA
Louisiana Bar. Official Publication of the Louisiana State Bar Association [*A publication*] (DLA) ... LA Bar
Louisiana Cattlemen's Association (SRA) ... LCA
Louisiana Chemical Association (SRA) ... LCA
Louisiana College, Pineville, LA [*Library symbol Library of Congress*] (LCLS) ... LPiL
Louisiana Commerce Department, Research Library, Baton Rouge, LA [*Library symbol Library of Congress*] (LCLS) ... LBrC
Louisiana Constitution [*A publication*] (DLA) ... LA Const Art
Louisiana Council on Economic Education (EDAC) ... LCEE
Louisiana Court of Appeals (Parish of Orleans) (DLA) ... LA A (Orleans)
Louisiana Court of Appeals (Parish of Orleans) (DLA) ... LA App (Orleans)
Louisiana Courts of Appeal Reports [*A publication*] (DLA) ... L Ap
Louisiana Courts of Appeal Reports [*A publication*] (DLA) ... LA A
Louisiana Courts of Appeal Reports [*A publication*] (DLA) ... LA App
Louisiana Department of Health and Human Resources, Office of Youth Services, Baton Rouge, LA [*Library symbol Library of Congress*] (LCLS) ... LBrHR-Y
Louisiana Department of Health and Human Resources, Policy Planning and Evaluation Office, Baton Rouge, LA [*Library symbol Library of Congress*] (LCLS) ... LBrHR
Louisiana Department of State, State Archives and Records, Baton Rouge, LA [*Library symbol Library of Congress*] (LCLS) ... L-Ar
Louisiana Eastern Railroad [*AAR code*] ... LE
Louisiana Education Department, Baton Rouge, LA [*Library symbol Library of Congress*] (LCLS) ... LBrEd
Louisiana Farm Bureau Federation (SRA) ... LFBF
Louisiana Government Information Network [*Louisiana State Library*] [*Baton Rouge*] [*Information service or system*] (IID) ... LaGIN
Louisiana Historical Association, Memorial Hall, New Orleans, LA [*Library symbol Library of Congress*] (LCLS) ... LNHA
Louisiana Historical Society, New Orleans, LA [*Library symbol Library of Congress*] (LCLS) ... LHi
Louisiana Independent Administrators Association (SRA) ... LIAA
Louisiana Independent Automobile Dealers Association (SRA) ... LIADA
Louisiana Independent Physicians Association, Inc. ... LIPA
Louisiana Information Processing Authority, Baton Rouge, LA [*Library symbol Library of Congress*] (LCLS) ... LBrIPA
Louisiana Insurers' Conference (SRA) ... LIC
Louisiana Justice Department, Huey P. Long Library, Baton Rouge, LA [*Library symbol Library of Congress*] (LCLS) ... LBrJ
Louisiana Land & Exploration Co. [*Associated Press*] (SAG) ... LaLand
Louisiana Land & Exploration Co. [*NYSE symbol Toronto Stock Exchange symbol*] ... LLX
Louisiana Land/Exp [*NYSE symbol*] (TTSB) ... LLX
Louisiana Law Journal [*New Orleans*] [*A publication*] (DLA) ... LA LJ
Louisiana Law Journal [*A publication*] (DLA) ... Lou L Jour
Louisiana Law Journal [*New Orleans*] [*A publication*] (DLA) ... Lou LJ
Louisiana Legal News [*A publication*] (DLA) ... Lou Leg N
Louisiana Legislative Council, Reference Division, Baton Rouge, LA [*Library symbol Library of Congress*] (LCLS) ... LBrLC
Louisiana Masonic Grand Lodge, New Orleans, LA [*Library symbol Library of Congress*] (LCLS) ... LNFM
Louisiana Meat Industry Association (SRA) ... LMIA
Louisiana Midland Railway Co. (IIA) ... LM

Louisiana Midland Railway Co. [Later, LMT] [AAR code] .... LMD
Louisiana Midland Transport [AAR code] .... LMT
Louisiana Mining Corp. [Vancouver Stock Exchange symbol] .... LMG
Louisiana, MO [FM radio station call letters] .... KJFM
Louisiana Motor Freight Bureau [STAC] .... LAM
Louisiana Motor Transport Association (SRA) .... LMTA
Louisiana National Bank [Baton Rouge] (TSSD) .... LNB
Louisiana Numerical Register [Louisiana State Library] [Baton Rouge, LA]
    [Library network] .... LNR
Louisiana Offshore Oil Port [Group of major oil companies] .... LOOP
Louisiana Pacific [NYSE symbol] (TTSB) .... LPX
Louisiana Pecan Growers' Association (EA) .... LPGA
Louisiana Pest Control Association (SRA) .... LPCA
Louisiana Pharmacists Association (SRA) .... LPA
Louisiana Polytechnical Institute .... LPI
Louisiana Power & Light Co. [Associated Press] (SAG) .... LaPL
Louisiana Power & Light Co. [NYSE symbol] (SPSG) .... LPL
Louisiana Presbyterian Theological Seminary .... LPTS
Louisiana Press Association (SRA) .... LPA
Louisiana Primary Care Association (SRA) .... LPCA
Louisiana Psychological Association (SRA) .... LPA
Louisiana Realtors Association (SRA) .... LRA
Louisiana Register [A publication] (AAGC) .... LR
Louisiana Reports [A publication] (DLA) L
Louisiana Reports [A publication] (DLA) .... LA
Louisiana Reports [A publication] (DLA) .... LA R
Louisiana Reports [A publication] (DLA) .... LA Rep
Louisiana Reports [A publication] (DLA) .... Law Rep
Louisiana Reports [A publication] (DLA) .... Lou R
Louisiana Reports [A publication] (DLA) .... Lou Reps
Louisiana Reports [A publication] (DLA) .... Louis Rep
Louisiana Reports [A publication] (DLA) .... Louisiana Rep
Louisiana Reports [A publication] (DLA) .... LR
Louisiana Restaurant Association (SRA) .... LRA
Louisiana Retailers Association (SRA) .... LRA
Louisiana Revenue Department, Research Department, Baton Rouge, LA
    [Library symbol Library of Congress] (LCLS) .... LBrR
Louisiana Session Law Service [A publication] (DLA) .... LA Sess Law Serv
Louisiana Soft Drink Association (SRA) .... LSDA
Louisiana Southern Railway Co. [AAR code] .... LSO
Louisiana State at Baton Rouge, Eighteenth Century Short Title Catalogue,
    Baton Rouge, LA [Library symbol Library of Congress] (LCLS) .... LU-ECT
Louisiana State Department of Agriculture, Research Library, Baton
    Rouge, LA [Library symbol Library of Congress] (LCLS) .... LBrAg
Louisiana State Library, Baton Rouge, LA [Library symbol Library of
    Congress] (LCLS) L
Louisiana State Library, Baton Rouge, LA [OCLC symbol] (OCLC) .... LSL
Louisiana State Library, Department for the Blind and Physically
    Handicapped, Baton Rouge, LA [Library symbol Library of Congress]
    (LCLS) .... L-BPH
Louisiana State Library, Processing Center, Baton Rouge, LA [OCLC
    symbol] (OCLC) .... LSM
Louisiana State Medical Society (SRA) .... LSMS
Louisiana State Museum, New Orleans, LA [Library symbol Library of
    Congress] (LCLS) .... L-M
Louisiana State Penitentiary, Angola, LA [Library symbol Library of
    Congress] (LCLS) .... LAnP
Louisiana State University .... LSU
Louisiana State University and Agricultural and Mechanical College
    (GAGS) .... LSU
Louisiana State University, Baton Rouge, LA [Library symbol Library of
    Congress] (LCLS) .... LU
Louisiana State University, Baton Rouge, LA [OCLC symbol] (OCLC) .... LUU
Louisiana State University, Chemistry Library, Baton Rouge, LA [Library
    symbol Library of Congress] (LCLS) .... LU-C
Louisiana State University, Department of Archives and Manuscripts,
    Baton Rouge,LA [Library symbol Library of Congress] (LCLS) .... LU-Ar
Louisiana State University, Graduate School of Library Science, Baton
    Rouge, LA [OCLC symbol] .... LLS
Louisiana State University in Alexandria, Alexandria, LA [Library symbol
    Library of Congress] (LCLS) .... LU-A
Louisiana State University in Eunice, Eunice, LA [Library symbol Library of
    Congress] (LCLS) .... LU-E
Louisiana State University in New Orleans [Later, University of New
    Orleans] .... LSUNO
Louisiana State University in Shreveport, Library, Shreveport, LA [OCLC
    symbol] (OCLC) .... LUS
Louisiana State University in Shreveport, Medical Center Library,
    Shreveport, LA [Library symbol Library of Congress] (LCLS) .... LU-SM
Louisiana State University in Shreveport, Shreveport, LA [Library symbol
    Library of Congress] (LCLS) .... LU-S
Louisiana State University, Law Library, Baton Rouge, LA [Library symbol
    Library of Congress] (LCLS) .... LU-L
Louisiana State University, Medical Center, New Orleans, LA [Library
    symbol Library of Congress] (LCLS) .... LU-M
Louisiana State University Medicine Center (GAGS) .... LSU Med Cent
Louisiana State University. Quarterly [A publication] (DLA) .... LA SUQ
Louisiana State University, School of Veterinary Medicine, Medical Library,
    Baton Rouge, LA [Library symbol Library of Congress] (LCLS) .... LU-V
Louisiana State University Shreveport (GAGS) .... LSU Shreveport
Louisiana Statutes, Annotated [A publication] (DLA) .... LSA
Louisiana Sugar Exchange (EA) .... LSE
Louisiana Supreme Court Condensed Reports [A publication]
    (DLA) .... Cond Lou'a Reps

Louisiana Supreme Court Condensed Reports [A publication]
    (DLA) .... Condensed Rep
Louisiana Supreme Court Reports [A publication] (DLA) .... LA
Louisiana Sweet Potato Commission .... LSPC
Louisiana Tech University (GAGS) .... La Tech U
Louisiana Technical University, Ruston, LA [Library symbol Library of
    Congress] (LCLS) .... LRuL
Louisiana Term Reports (Martin) [A publication] (DLA) .... LA TR
Louisiana Term Reports, New Series (Martin) [1823-30] [A publication]
    (DLA) .... LA TR (NS)
Louisiana Thoroughbred Breeders Association (SRA) .... LTBA
Louisiana Training Institute, Bridge City Library, Bridge City, LA [Library
    symbol Library of Congress] (LCLS) .... LBrcTI
Louisiana Training Institute, Monroe, LA [Library symbol Library of
    Congress] (LCLS) .... LMTI
Louisiana Transportation Research Center [Louisiana State University]
    [Research center] (RCD) .... LTRC
Louisiana Travel Promotion Association (SRA) .... LTPA
Louisiana Trial Lawyers Association (SRA) .... LTLA
Louisiana Union Catalog [Library network] .... LUC
Louisiana Universities Marine Consortium .... LUMCON
Louisiana Universities Marine Consortium, Chauvin, LA [Library symbol
    Library of Congress] (LCLS) .... LChaMC
Louisiana Veterinary Medical Association (SRA) .... LVMA
Louisiana Water Resources Research Institute [Louisiana State University]
    [Department of the Interior] [Research center] (RCD) .... LWRRI
Louisiana-Alabama-Mississippi Automated Clearing House
    Association .... LAMACHA
Louisiana-Pacific Corp. [Associated Press] (SAG) .... LaPac
Louisiana-Pacific Corp. [NYSE symbol] (SPSG) .... LPX
Louisiana-Texas Experiment [Gulf Marine Minerals Management] [Marine
    science] (OSRA) .... LATEX
Louisiana-Texas Experiment [Gulf Marine Minerals Management]
    (USDC) .... LATEX
Louisville [Diocesan abbreviation] [Kentucky] (TOCD) L
Louisville [Kentucky] [Airport symbol] (OAG) .... SDF
Louisville, AL [Television station call letters] .... WGIQ
Louisville & Nashville Railroad Co. .... L & N
Louisville & Nashville Railroad Co. .... L & NRR
Louisville & Wadley Railway Co. [AAR code] .... LW
Louisville Behavior Check List [Psychology] .... LBCL
Louisville/Bowman [Kentucky] [ICAO location identifier] (ICLI) .... KLOU
Louisville Fear Survey for Children [Psychology] .... LFSC
Louisville Free Public Library, Louisville, KY [OCLC symbol] (OCLC) .... KLP
Louisville Free Public Library, Louisville, KY [Library symbol Library of
    Congress] (LCLS) .... KyLo
Louisville, GA [AM radio station call letters] .... WPEH
Louisville, GA [FM radio station call letters] .... WPEH-FM
Louisville Gas & Electric Co. [NASDAQ symbol] (SAG) .... LGAS
Louisville Gas & Electric Co. [Associated Press] (SAG) .... LouG
Louisville Gas & Electric Co. [Associated Press] (SAG) .... LouG 5
Louisville, KY [Location identifier FAA] (FAAL) .... ADO
Louisville, KY [Location identifier FAA] (FAAL) .... BQM
Louisville, KY [Location identifier FAA] (FAAL) .... LJC
Louisville, KY [Location identifier FAA] (FAAL) .... LKS
Louisville, KY [Location identifier FAA] (FAAL) .... LOU
Louisville, KY [Location identifier FAA] (FAAL) .... PYJ
Louisville, KY [FM radio station call letters] .... WAMZ
Louisville, KY [Television station call letters] .... WAVE
Louisville, KY [AM radio station call letters] .... WAVG
Louisville, KY [Television station call letters] .... WBNA
Louisville, KY [FM radio station call letters] .... WDJX
Louisville, KY [Television station call letters] .... WDRB
Louisville, KY [AM radio station call letters] .... WFIA
Louisville, KY [FM radio station call letters] .... WFPK
Louisville, KY [FM radio station call letters] .... WFPL
Louisville, KY [AM radio station call letters] .... WHAS
Louisville, KY [Television station call letters] .... WHAS-TV
Louisville, KY [AM radio station call letters] (RBYB) .... WHKW
Louisville, KY [Television station call letters] .... WKMJ
Louisville, KY [Television station call letters] .... WKPC
Louisville, KY [Television station call letters] .... WLKY
Louisville, KY [AM radio station call letters] .... WLLV
Louisville, KY [AM radio station call letters] .... WLOU
Louisville, KY [FM radio station call letters] .... WLRS
Louisville, KY [FM radio station call letters] .... WQLL
Louisville, KY [FM radio station call letters] (RBYB) .... WSJW-FM
Louisville, KY [FM radio station call letters] .... WTFX
Louisville, KY [AM radio station call letters] .... WTMT
Louisville, KY [FM radio station call letters] .... WUOL
Louisville, KY [FM radio station call letters] .... WVEZ
Louisville, KY [AM radio station call letters] .... WWKY
Louisville Medical Library, Louisville, KY [Library symbol Library of
    Congress] (LCLS) .... KyLoM
Louisville, MS [Location identifier FAA] (FAAL) .... LMS
Louisville, MS [AM radio station call letters] .... WLSM
Louisville, MS [FM radio station call letters] .... WLSM-FM
Louisville Municipal College [Kentucky] .... LMC
Louisville, New Albany & Corydon Railroad Co. [AAR code] .... LNAC
Louisville Orchestra [Record label] .... LO
Louisville Presbyterian Seminary, Louisville, KY [Library symbol Library of
    Congress] (LCLS) .... KyLoL
Louisville Public Library, Louisville, CO [Library symbol Library of
    Congress] (LCLS) .... CoLou
Loukanyi [Congo] [ICAO location identifier] (ICLI) .... FCPY

Loukolela [*Congo*] [*ICAO location identifier*] (ICLI) ... FCOL
Loumana [*Burkina Faso*] [*ICAO location identifier*] (ICLI) ... DHOL
Loumic Resources Ltd. [*Vancouver Stock Exchange symbol*] ... LOO
Lounge ... LNG
Lounge [*Classified advertising*] (ADA) ... Lnge
Lounge/Dining Room [*Classified advertising*] (ADA) ... L/DR
Loup City Township Library, Loup City, NE [*Library symbol Library of Congress*] (LCLS) ... NbLo
Lourdes Public Library, Lourdes, NF, Canada [*Library symbol Library of Congress*] (LCLS) ... CaNfLo
Lourdes Public Library, Newfoundland [*Library symbol National Library of Canada*] (NLC) ... NFLO
Lourdes/Tarbes [*France*] [*Airport symbol*] (OAG) ... LDE
Lourenco Marques [*Mozambique*] [*Seismograph station code, US Geological Survey*] (SEIS) ... LMM
Louse-Borne Relapsing Fever [*Medicine*] (AAMN) ... LBRF
Lousiana Maneuvers [*Military*] ... LAM
Lousy Paying Guest [*Hotel slang*] ... LPG
Loutete [*Congo*] [*ICAO location identifier*] (ICLI) ... FCBT
Louth [*County in Ireland*] (ROG) ... LO
Louth [*County in Ireland*] (WGA) ... Lou
Loutit Library, Grand Haven, MI [*Library symbol Library of Congress*] (LCLS) ... MiGh
Louver (MSA) ... LVR
Louver Opening ... LVO
Louvered Door (AAG) ... LVD
Lovat Scouts [*British military*] (DMA) ... LS
Love [*Phonetic alphabet*] [*World War II*] (DSUE) ... L
Love and Kisses [*Correspondence*] ... L & K
Love and Liquor (IIA) ... L & L
Love Attitudes Inventory [*Premarital relations test*] [*Psychology*] ... LAI
Love Canal Homeowners Association (EA) ... LCHA
Love Games Won [*Tennis*] ... LGW
Love in Action International (EA) ... LIAI
"Love Is All" for Enge (EA) ... LAE
Love Is Feeding Everyone (EA) ... LIFE
Love Notes [*An association*] (EA) ... LN
Love Object ... LO
Love Project (EA) ... LP
Love, Togetherness, and Devotion [*Rock music group*] ... LT & D
Love Token Society (EA) ... LTS
Love Wave [*Earthquakes*] ... Lq
Lovejoy Unit, District 188, Lovejoy, IL [*Library symbol Library of Congress*] (LCLS) ... ILovjD
Lovelace Aerosol Particle Separator [*Lovelace Foundation for Medical Education and Research*] (PDAA) ... LAPS
Lovelace Foundation for Medical Education and Research [*Reorganized to form Lovelace Medical Foundation and Lovelace Biomedical and Environmental Research Institute*] ... LF
Lovelace Foundation for Medical Education and Research [*Reorganized to form Lovelace Medical Foundation and Lovelace Biomedical and Environmental Research Institute*] (MCD) ... LFMER
Lovelace Foundation for Medical Education and Research, Albuquerque, NM [*Library symbol Library of Congress*] (LCLS) ... NmAL
Loveland, CO [*AM radio station call letters*] ... KLOV
Loveland, CO [*FM radio station call letters*] ... KTRR
Loveland Public Library, Loveland, CO [*Library symbol Library of Congress*] (LCLS) ... CoLov
Lovell-Powell [*Wyoming*] [*Airport symbol*] (AD) ... POY
Lovelock [*Nevada*] [*Airport symbol Obsolete*] (OAG) ... LOL
Lovelock [*Nevada*] [*Seismograph station code, US Geological Survey Closed*] (SEIS) ... LVK
Love-N-Addiction [*An association*] (EA) ... LNA
Loverboy Fan Club (EA) ... LFC
[*A*] **Lover's Complaint** [*Shakespearean work*] ... LC
Lovers of the Holy Cross Sisters (TOCD) ... LHC
Lovers of the Stinking Rose (EA) ... LSR
Love's Labour's Lost [*Shakespearean work*] ... LLL
Loves Park, IL [*FM radio station call letters*] ... WGSL
Loves Park, IL [*AM radio station call letters*] ... WLUV
Loves Park, IL [*FM radio station call letters*] ... WLUV-FM
Lovesy on Arbitration [*1867*] [*A publication*] (DLA) ... Lov Arb
Lovesy's Bankruptcy Act [*1869, 1870*] [*A publication*] (DLA) ... Love Bank
Lovington, NM [*AM radio station call letters*] ... KLEA
Lovington, NM [*FM radio station call letters*] ... KLEA-FM
Lovington, NM [*Location identifier FAA*] (FAAL) ... LGX
Lovington Public Library, Lovington, NM [*Library symbol Library of Congress*] (LCLS) ... NmLov
Lovo [*Sweden*] [*Geomagnetic observatory code*] ... LOV
Lovozero [*Former USSR Geomagnetic observatory code*] ... LOZ
Low [*or Lower*] ... L
Low (IDOE) ... l
Low (IDOE) ... lo
Low (KSC) ... LO
Low [*Automotive advertising*] ... LW
Low Accuracy ... LOAC
Low Achievers Project [*Education*] (AIE) ... LAP
Low Active Waste [*Nuclear energy*] ... LAW
Low Affinity-High Capacity [*Medicine*] (DMAA) ... LAHC
Low Air Loss ... LAL
Low Air Speed (MCD) ... LAS
Low Alcohol [*Trademark of Anheuser-Busch, Inc.*] ... LA
Low Alcohol Drinking [*Rat strain*] ... LAD
Low Altitude ... LA
Low Altitude Air Defense Battalion [*Navy*] (ANA) ... LAADBN
Low Amplitude Contraction [*Neurology*] (DAVI) ... LAC
Low- and High-Pressure Oxygen ... LHOX
Low and Medium Bleeding Frequency [*Medicine*] ... LMBF
Low and Medium Frequency ... LMF
Low Angle [*RADAR*] (DEN) ... LA
Low Angle Electron Diffraction (PDAA) ... LAED
Low Anxiety (MAE) ... LA
Low Atmospheric Pressure (DAVI) ... LAP
Low Attaining Pupils in Secondary Schools (AIE) ... LAPS
Low Back [*Disorder*] [*Medicine*] ... LB
Low Back Bending (DMAA) ... LBB
Low Back Injury [*Medicine*] (DMAA) ... LBI
Low Back Pain Questionnaire [*Medicine*] (DMAA) ... LBPQ
Low Back Strain (DAVI) ... LBS
Low Back Syndrome [*Medicine*] (DMAA) ... LBS
Low Back Tenderness [*Medicine*] (DMAA) ... LBT
Low Background Epifluorescence Microscopy ... LBEFM
Low Band (AAG) ... LB
Low Bandpass Transformer ... LBT
Low Bay (KSC) ... LB
Low Bay Dolly Tug (NASA) ... LBDT
Low Birth Rate ... LBR
Low Birth Weight [*Obstetrics*] ... LBW
Low BIT [*Binary Digit*] **Rate** [*Computer science*] (MCD) ... LBR
Low BIT [*Binary Digit*] **Rate Voice** [*Telecommunications*] ... LBRV
Low BIT [*Binary Digit*] **Test** [*Computer science*] (IEEE) ... LBT
Low Blood Pressure [*Medicine*] ... LBP
Low Body Weight ... LBW
Low BTU Gas (MCD) ... LBG
Low Cab Forward [*Automotive engineering*] ... LCF
Low Cab Forward [*Truck configuration*] ... LCF
Low Calcium [*Diet*] (DAVI) ... lo calc
Low Calorie (AAMN) ... LC
Low Calorie (MAE) ... lo cal
Low Calorific Value [*of a fuel*] ... LCV
Low Capacitance [*Cable*] [*Bell System*] ... LOCAP
Low Carbon [*Content, as low-carbon steel*] ... LC
Low Cardiac Output [*Cardiology*] ... LCO
Low Cardiac Output Syndrome [*Medicine*] (DMAA) ... LCOS
Low Center of Gravity [*Tractor engineering*] ... LCG
Low Cervical Caesarean Section ... LCCS
Low Cervical Transverse [*Position*] [*Obstetrics*] (DAVI) ... LCT
Low Cervical Vertical [*Incision*] [*Obstetrics*] (DAVI) ... LCV
Low Coefficient of Friction [*Aerodynamics*] ... LCF
Low [*Altitude*] **Combat Air Patrol** (NVT) ... LOCAP
Low Complexity Color Display [*Video technology*] (EECA) ... LCCD
Low Compression [*Automotive engineering*] ... L/C
Low Compression Ratio [*Automotive engineering*] (IAA) ... LCR
Low Conditioners [*Psychology*] ... LC
Low Constant [*or Continuous*] **Suction** [*Surgical procedure*] (DAVI) ... LCS
Low Coolant ... LCOLNT
Low Core Threshold (NITA) ... LOW
Low Cost Color [*Computer science*] (CDE) ... LC
Low Cost Drifter [*Marine science*] (OSRA) ... LCD
Low Cost Junction [*Optical fibre equipment*] (NITA) ... LCJ
Low Cost Module (IAA) ... LCM
Low Cost Range ... LCR
Low Cost Terminal [*Telecommunications*] (LAIN) ... LCT
Low Cost Uncooled Sensor Prototype [*Army*] ... LOCUSP
Low Count Range [*Nuclear energy*] (NUCP) ... LCR
Low Cross Range ... LCR
Low Cross-Range Orbiter (KSC) ... LCRO
Low Current Diode Transistor Logic [*Electronics*] (IAA) ... LCDTL
Low Data Rate [*RADAR*] ... LDR
Low Data Rate [*RADAR*] (IAA) ... LDRT
Low Data Rate Auxiliary [*RADAR*] ... LDRA
Low Data Rate Input [*RADAR*] ... LDRI
Low Data Rate Integrated Acoustic Communications System [*Military*] (CAAL) ... LDRIACS
Low Data Rate UHF [*Ultra-High Frequency*] **Satellite** [*RADAR*] (MCD) ... LODUS
Low Data Register [*Computer science*] ... LDR
Low Density ... LD
Low Density (IAA) ... LOD
Low Density Lipoprotein [*Biochemistry*] ... LDLP
Low Density-Reinforced Reaction Injection Molding ... LD-RRIM
Low Dimensional Structures and Devices [*British*] ... LDSD
Low Dispersion [*Optics*] ... LD
Low Door (WDAA) ... LD
Low Dose [*Medicine*] ... LD
Low Dose Rate [*Medicine*] ... LDR
Low Drag ... LD
Low Drop Out ... LDO
Low Dust ... LD
Low Dutch [*Language, etc.*] ... LD
Low Dynamic ... LD
Low Earth Orbit ... LEO
Low Earth Orbit Satellite (MCD) ... LEOS
Low Earth Orbit Satellites (ACRL) ... LEOS
Low Efficiency ... LE
Low Egg Passage [*Rabies vaccine*] ... LEP
Low Emissions Paint Consortium ... LEPC
Low Emissions Partnership ... LEP
Low Emitter Concentration (PDAA) ... LEC
Low Energy (CAAL) ... LE

Low Energy LASER [Light Amplification by Stimulated Emission of Radiation] [Military] .... LEL
Low Entry [Truck cab] .... LE
Low Entry Networking (MCD) .... LEN
Low Erucic Acid Rapeseed [Plant variety] .... LEAR
Low Erucic Acid Rapeseed Oil (PDAA) .... LERSO
Low Explosive [Military] .... LE
Low Fat [Diet] .... LF
Low Fat and Cholesterol Diet (DMAA) .... LFC
Low Fighter Engagement Zone (PDAA) .... LOFEZ
Low Flange (DICI) .... LF
Low Flow Alarm (IEEE) .... LFA
Low Flyer, Defense Mode .... LFDM
Low Foliage Forager [Ecology] .... LF
Low Foliage Nester [Ecology] .... LN
Low Food Density [Ecology] .... LF
Low Force .... LF
Low Forceps [Delivery] [Obstetrics] .... LF
Low Frequency .... LF
Low Frequency (WDMC) .... lf
Low Frequency Active (DOMA) .... LFA
Low Frequency Intersection (FAAC) .... LFNT
Low Frequency Jet Ventilation [Medicine] .... LFJV
Low Frequency, Medium Frequency .... LF/MF
Low Frequency Radio Range (TAG) .... LFR
Low Frequency, Very Low Frequency (IAA) .... LFVLF
Low Friction Arthroplasty [Orthopedics] (DAVI) .... LFA
Low Front End Cost [Engineering] .... LOFRECO
Low Functioning Autism .... LFA
Low Gelling Temperature [Analytical biochemistry] .... LGT
Low German [Language, etc.] .... LG
Low German [Language, etc.] (ROG) .... LGER
Low Glucose [Medicine] .... LG
Low Gravity Orbit .... LGO
Low Greek [Language, etc.] .... LGR
Low Ground Pressure .... LGP
Low Group Receiving Unit .... LGR
Low Group Transmitting Unit .... LGT
Low Head [Nuclear energy] (NRCH) .... LH
Low Heat Rejection Engine [Mechanical engineering] .... LHRE
Low heat Release [Adiabatic engines] [Automotive engineering] .... LHR
Low Heat [or Heating] Value (MCD) .... LHV
Low Impact Resistant Supports [FAA] (TAG) .... LIRS
Low Impulsiveness (MAE) LI
Low Impulsiveness, High Anxiety (MAE) .... LIHA
Low Impulsiveness, Low Anxiety (MAE) .... LILA
Low in Volatiles [Commercial grading] LV
Low Income Country LIC
Low Income Cut-Off [Canada] .... LICO
Low Income Energy Assistance [Later, LIHEAP] [Block grant] .... LIEA
Low Income Family Emancipation Society .... LIFE
Low Income Family Emergency Center .... LIFE
Low Income Home Energy Assistance Program [Formerly, LIEA] [Block grant] .... LIHEAP
Low Income Housing Development Corp. [North Carolina] (EA) .... LIHDC
Low Income Housing Information Service (EA) .... LIHIS
Low Income Housing Preservation and Resident Homeownership Act of 1990 .... LIHPRHA
Low Income, Parents Supporting [Lifestyle classification] .... Lips
Low Index [NWS] (FAAC) LX
Low Inductance Stripline (IAA) .... LIS
Low Inertia Clutch LIC
Low Input Reduced Tillage [Cropping systems] (GNE) .... LIRT
Low Intensity LI
Low Intensity - Direct Current .... LIDC
Low Intensity Runway Edge Lights [FAA] (TAG) .... LIRL
Low Intensity Two-Color Approach Slope Indicator [Aviation] (DA) .... LITAS
Low Interest Rate Currency (MHDW) .... LIRC
Low Interfacial Tension [Physical chemistry] .... LIFT
Low Intermittent Suction [Medicine] (MEDA) .... LIS
Low Internal Phase [Emulsion chemistry] .... LIP
Low Investment Vehicle LIV
Low Isotonic Strength Titrator .... LIST
Low Jet Route (ADA) .... LJR
Low Latin [Language, etc.] LL
Low Level LL
Low Level Language [Computer programming] (NTCM) LLL
Low Level Liquid Waste [Nuclear energy] (NUCP) .... LLLW
Low Level Waste Policy Act [1980] (NUCP) .... LLPA
Low Level Wind Shear [Aviation] (FAAC) .... LLWS
Low Level Wind Shear Alert System [Aviation] (FAAC) .... LLWAS
Low Level Windshear Alert System .... LLWAS
Low Light and Thermal Imaging System (PDAA) .... LLATIS
Low Light Level LLL
Low Liquid Cutoff LLC
Low Liquid Level [Engineering] LLL
Low Load [Finance] LL
Low Loaders (DCTA) .... LO
Low Low Alarm (ECII) .... LLA
Low Low Pond Level (IEEE) .... LLPL
Low Lunar Orbit .... LLO
Low Magnetic Saturation Garnet .... LMSG
Low Mass Vehicle .... LMV
Low Meaningfulness [Psychology] .... LM
Low/Medium (MCD) .... L/M

Low Melting Point .... LMP
Low Middling Clause [Business term] .... LMC
Low Modulus Direction [Mechanical testing] .... LMD
Low Moisture Activity [Brake system] [Automotive engineering] .... LMA
Low Molecular [Chemistry] .... LM
Low Molecular Weight .... LMW
Low Molecular-Weight Kininogen [Biochemistry] .... LMWK
Low Needle Position [on dial] .... LNP
Low Nitric Oxide [Combustion technology] .... LNCFS
Low Nitrogen Oxide Burner [Combustion technology] .... LNB
Low Noise (IAA) .... LN
Low Noise .... LONO
Low Nonessential Air Pressure (IEEE) .... LNAP
Low Oblique [Aerospace] .... LO
Low Observable (DOMA) .... LO
Low Oil Agglomeration [Coal processing] .... LOA
Low Order [Computer science] (OA) .... LO
Low Ordinary (IAA) .... LO
Low Osmolar Contrast Agent [Medicine] .... LOCA
Low Out of Range Alarm (ECII) .... LORA
Low Outlet Forceps [Delivery] [Obstetrics] (DAVI) .... LOF
Low Output Syndrome (MAE) .... LOS
Low Oxidation State Metallic Ion [Nuclear energy] (NUCP) .... LOMI
Low Pass [Electronics] .... LP
Low Pay Unit [British] .... LPU
Low Performance .... LP
Low Period Dipole .... LPD
Low Placed Conus Medullaris [Medicine] (DMAA) .... LPCM
Low Point .... LP
Low Point [Technical drawings] .... LPT
Low Polar Latitude [Geophysics] .... LPL
Low Population Zone (NRCH) .... LPZ
Low Power [Microscopy] .... LP
Low Power Distress Transmitter [Aviation] (DA) .... LPDT
Low Power Output (MSA) .... LPO
Low Power Relay Transmitter .... LPRT
Low Pressure .... LP
Low Pressure Permanent Mould (PDAA) .... LPPM
Low Pressure Turbocharger .... LPT
Low Pressurization Pressure Test Transmitter (IEEE) .... LPPT
Low Primary (IAA) .... LP
Low Probability of Exploitation (PDAA) .... LPE
Low Probability of Intercept (NVT) .... LPI
Low Probability of Intercept Antijam Secure Airborne Radio System (MCD) .... LASARS
Low Probability of Interest .... LPI
Low Protein [Nutrition] .... LP
Low Protein Diet .... LPD
Low Pulse Recurrence Frequency (MCD) .... LPRF
Low Rate Encoding [Telecommunications] (LAIN) .... LRE
Low Rate Forward [Ecology] .... lf
Low Rate Production (RDA) .... LRP
Low Rate Reverse [Ecology] .... lr
Low Reduction (NITA) .... LR
Low Refraction Layer .... LRF
Low Register (IAA) .... LR
Low Resistance (IAA) .... LR
Low Resolution [Computer science] .... LO-RES
Low Resolution Imaging Spectrograph [Instrumentation] .... LRIS
Low Resolution Imaging Spectrograph [Instrumentation] .... LRIS
Low Rigging Penalty [IOR] [Yacht racing] .... LRP
Low Right Atrium [Anatomy] .... LRA
Low Rigid Frame (PDAA) .... LRES
Low Risk .... LR
Low Running Rate (KSC) .... LBR
Low Salt [Dietetics] .... LS
Low Saturated Fat [Diet] (DAVI) .... LSF
Low Season [Airline fare code] L
Low Secondary (IAA) .... LS
Low Section Height [Automotive engineering] .... LSH
Low Serum-Bound Iron (MAE) .... LBI
Low Sight Lobe .... LSL
Low Silhouette Blade [Aircraft] .... LSB
Low Similarity [Psychology] .... LS
Low Sodium [Dietetics] (DAVI) .... LoNa
Low Specific Activity [Radioisotope] .... LSA
Low Speed Line Adaptor (NITA) .... LSLA
Low Steam .... LSTM
Low Steamline Flow Test (IEEE) .... LSFT
Low Stocking Rate [Agriculture] (OA) .... LSR
Low Styrene Emission Gelcoat .... LSEG
Low Sulphur Heavy Stock (PDAA) .... LSHS
Low Supersonic Transport (PDAA) .... LSSTA
Low Support Program (OICC) .... LSP
Low Temperature .... LT
Low Temperature .... LTEMP
Low Temperature Aftercooled [Automotive engineering] .... LTA
Low Temperature Coal Distillers Association [British] (DBA) .... LTCDA
Low Temperature Oxidation [Physical chemistry] .... LTO
Low Temperature Research Facility [NASA] .... LTRF
Low Temperature Research Station [British] .... LTRS
Low Temperature Teatment [Materials science] .... LTT
Low Tension .... LT
Low Thermal Expansion [Synthetic ceramic] .... LO-X
Low Thermal Mass (PDAA) .... LTM

Low Threshold Spike [*Neurochemistry*] ... LTS
Low Tire-Pressure Warning System [*Automotive engineering*] ... LTPWS
Low Torque ... LT
Low Torque ... LTQ
Low Transverse [*incision*] [*Obstetrics*] (DAVI) ... LT
Low Transverse Cesarean Section [*Medicine*] (MEDA) ... LTCS
Low Turret Half ... LTH
Low Velocity [*British military*] (DMA) ... LV
Low Velocity Air Drop [*Military vehicle specifications*] ... LVAD
Low Velocity Friction Apparatus (PDAA) ... LVFA
Low Very High Frequency (IAA) ... LVHF
Low Vision Aid [*Ophthalmology*] ... LVA
Low Voltage ... LV
Low Volume ... LV
Low Volume Eye Test (DMAA) ... LVET
Low Vulnerability Ammunition [*Military*] (RDA) ... LOVA
Low Water [*Tides and currents*] ... LW
Low Water Full and Change [*Tides and currents*] ... LWF & C
Low Water of Spring Tide ... LWS
Low Waterline ... LWL
Low Watermark ... LWM
Low Waterplane (PDAA) ... LWP
Low Wave (WDAA) ... LW
Low Wing [*Aviation*] (AIA) ... LW
Low-Accuracy Data/Designation [*System*] (MUGU) ... LAD
Low-Accuracy RADAR Data Transmission System ... LARDS
Low-Acid Waste [*Nuclear energy*] (NRCH) ... LAW
Low-Affinity Choline Transport ... LACT
Low-Alloy Steel ... LAS
Low-Altitude Air Defense Identification and Engagement Study ... LADIES
Low-Altitude Air Defense [*or Delivery*] **System** ... LAADS
Low-Altitude Air Dropped Stores (MCD) ... LAADS
Low-Altitude Airfield Attack System (MCD) ... LAAAS
Low-Altitude Alert [*Air traffic control*] ... LALA
Low-Altitude Alerting System ... LAAS
Low-Altitude Attack ... LAA
Low-Altitude Bombing [*Military*] ... LAB
Low-Altitude Bombing Position Indicator Equipment [*Military*] ... LABPIE
Low-Altitude Bombing System [*Air Force*] ... LABS
Low-Altitude Clear-Air Turbulence (MCD) ... LOCAT
Low-Altitude Close Air Support [*Military*] ... LACAS
Low-Altitude Contour Matching (MCD) ... LACOM
Low-Altitude Control Area ... LACA
Low-Altitude Coverage RADAR ... LACR
Low-Altitude Cruise (MCD) ... LAC
Low-Altitude Defense (MCD) ... LOAD
Low-Altitude Defense System (MCD) ... LADS
Low-Altitude Defense System ... LOADS
Low-Altitude Detection System [*Air Force*] ... LADS
Low-Altitude Dispenser ... LAD
Low-Altitude Dispensing System [*Missiles*] ... LADS
Low-Altitude Drive on Ground (IAA) ... LADOG
Low-Altitude Drogue Delivery (AFM) ... LADD
Low-Altitude Drop Test [*NASA*] ... LADT
Low-Altitude Forward Air Defense System (PDAA) ... LOFADS
Low-Altitude Forward Area Air Defense (AABC) ... LOFAAD
Low-Altitude Forward Area Anti-Aircraft Defense System [*Army*] ... LOFAADS
Low-Altitude, High-Speed ... LAHS
Low-Altitude/High-Velocity Experiment ... LAHIVE
Low-Altitude Hold [*Military*] (CAAL) ... LAH
Low-Altitude Indicator ... LAI
Low-Altitude Inertial Navigation System [*Air Force*] ... LAINS
Low-Altitude LASER Air Defense System ... LOLAD
Low-Altitude Low-Light Level ... LALLL
Low-Altitude Manned Penetrator ... LAMP
Low-Altitude Missile (MCD) ... LAM
Low-Altitude Multiburst Code (MCD) ... LAMB
Low-Altitude Navigation and Targeting Infrared [*System*] **for Night** [*Aviation*] ... LANTIRN
Low-Altitude Night Attack (DOMA) ... LANA
Low-Altitude Observation ... LALO
Low-Altitude Parachute Extraction System [*Military*] ... LAPES
Low-Altitude Penetrating Attack Missile [*Proposed*] ... LAPAM
Low-Altitude Penetration ... LAP
Low-Altitude Performance ... LAP
Low-Altitude Proximity Sensor (MCD) ... LAPS
Low-Altitude Pursuit Dive on Ground (MCD) ... LAPDOG
Low-Altitude Qualification Test [*Balloon*] ... LAQT
Low-Altitude RADAR Altimeter [*Air Force*] ... LARA
Low-Altitude RADAR Fuzing (CET) ... LARF
Low-Altitude RADAR Interface System (MCD) ... LARIS
Low-Altitude RADAR System (NATG) ... LARS
Low-Altitude Release ... LAR
Low-Altitude Research Vehicle (IAA) ... LARV
Low-Altitude Research Vehicular Advancements ... LARVA
Low-Altitude Retro Rocket System (DWSG) ... LARRS
Low-Altitude Ride Control [*Shock-absorbing system*] [*Aviation*] (MCD) ... LARC
Low-Altitude Safety and Targeting Equipment (DWSG) ... LASTE
Low-Altitude Satellite ... LAS
Low-Altitude Satellite Studies of Ionospheric Irregularities ... LASSII
Low-Altitude Search Option [*Search mode of the BOMARC guidance system*] ... LASO
Low-Altitude Short-Range Missile ... LASRAM
Low-Altitude Short-Range Missile ... LASRM
Low-Altitude Space Platform (MCD) ... LASP
Low-Altitude Supersonic Research Missile ... LASRM
Low-Altitude Supersonic Target (RDA) ... LAST
Low-Altitude Supersonic Vehicle [*Formerly, SLAM*] [*Air Force*] ... LASV
Low-Altitude Surface Vehicle (WDAA) ... LASV
Low-Altitude Surface-to-Air Missiles (NATG) ... LOSAM
Low-Altitude Surveillance Platform (MCD) ... LASP
Low-Altitude Surveillance RADAR ... LASR
Low-Altitude Tactical Navigation ... LATN
Low-Altitude Tactics (DOMA) ... LAT
Low-Altitude Unmanned Reconnaissance Aircraft (DOMA) ... LAURA
Low-Altitude Vulnerability Model [*Aerospace*] (MCD) ... LAVM
Low-Altitude Warning (MCD) ... LAW
Low-Altitude Warning System (NVT) ... LAWS
Low-Angle Dolly ... LAD
Low-Angle LASER Light Scattering ... LALLS
Low-Angle Low-Drag ... LALD
Low-Angle Polycrystalline Silicon Sheet [*Photovoltaic energy systems*] ... LAPSS
Low-Angle Reentry [*Aerospace*] (MCD) ... LAR
Low-Angle Re-Entry Maneuvering Re-Entry Vehicle (PDAA) ... LARM
Low-Angle Silicon Sheet [*Photovoltaic energy systems*] ... LASS
Low-Angle Track (CAAL) ... LAT
Low-Angle X-Ray Scattering (MCD) ... LAXS
Low-Approach Navigation Director System [*Aircraft landing aid*] [*Air Force*] ... LANDIS
Low-Aspect Ratio ... LAR
Low-Attack Mode (MCD) ... LAM
Low-Back Pain [*Medicine*] ... LBP
Lowband Color [*Broadcasting*] (NTCM) ... LBC
Lowband Monochrome [*Broadcasting*] (NTCM) ... LBM
Low-Barrier Hydrogen Bond [*Enzymology*] ... LBHB
Low-Birth-Weight Infant [*Obstetrics*] (MAE) ... LBWI
Low-Birth-Weight Infant [*Obstetrics*] ... LOWBI
Low-Byte Enable ... LBEN
Low-Calcium Pyroxene [*Mineralogy*] ... LCP
Low-Capacity Link [*Telecommunications*] (OA) ... LCL
Low-Capacity Microwave Link ... LCML
Low-Carbon Ferrochrome [*Metallurgy*] ... LCF
Low-Cement Castable [*Ceramics*] ... LCC
Low-Contrast Resolution Test [*Optics*] ... LCRT
Low-Cost Air Target (MCD) ... LOCAT
Low-Cost Alternate LASER Seeker (MCD) ... LOCALS
Low-Cost Anti-Armor Submunitions [*Military*] ... LOCAAS
Low-Cost Arrays for Detection of Infrared (PDAA) ... LADIR
Low-Cost Attack RADAR ... LCAR
Low-Cost Automation (WDAA) ... LCA
Low-Cost Automation Centre [*British*] ... LCAC
Low-Cost Classifier (MCD) ... LCC
Low-Cost Cockpit Procedures Trainer (MCD) ... LCCPT
Low-Cost Composite Weapon (MCD) ... LCCW
Low-Cost Computer Attachment (IAA) ... LCCA
Low-Cost Computer Attachment (IAA) ... LOCA
Low-Cost Controllable Booster (MCD) ... LCCB
Low-Cost Development System [*National Semiconductor Corp.*] ... LCDS
Low-Cost Electronic Warfare Suite (NVT) ... LCEWS
Low-Cost Encryption Device [*Military*] (GFGA) ... LCED
Low-Cost Expendable [*Refers to payload type*] [*NASA*] ... LCE
Low-Cost Expendable Harassment Vehicle [*Air Force*] (MCD) ... LCEHV
Low-Cost Generator ... LCG
Low-Cost Graphics Terminal/Interactive Graphics System (PDAA) ... LCGT/IGS
Low-Cost Indirect-Fire Training Round [*Army*] (INF) ... LITR
Low-Cost Inertial ... LCI
Low-Cost Inertial Guidance Subsystem (MCD) ... LCIGS
Low-Cost Interceptor (MCD) ... LOCI
Low-Cost LASER Seeker (MCD) ... LCS
Low-Cost Launch Vehicle [*NASA*] (KSC) ... LCLV
Low-Cost Lightweight Missile (MCD) ... LCLM
Low-Cost Modular Spacecraft [*NASA*] ... LCMS
Low-Cost Motor Demonstration (MCD) ... LCMD
Low-Cost Night Vision Aid (MCD) ... LCNVA
Low-Cost Night Vision Goggles (MCD) ... LCNVG
Low-Cost Part Task Trainer (MCD) ... LCPTT
Low-Cost Powered Dispenser ... LOCPOD
Low-Cost Production (WDAA) ... LCP
Low-Cost Propulsion Integration Study (MCD) ... LCPIS
Low-Cost Readout Station [*NASA*] ... LCRS
Low-Cost Reusable [*Refers to payload type*] [*NASA*] ... LCR
Low-Cost Risk Reduction (PDAA) ... LCRR
Low-Cost Silicon Solar Array Project ... LCSSAP
Low-Cost Solar Array (IEEE) ... LSA
Low-Cost Solid Logic Technology (IAA) ... LCSLT
Low-Cost Sonobuoy (DOMA) ... LCS
Low-Cost Systems Office [*NASA*] (PDAA) ... LCSO
Low-Cost Tactical RADAR (DNAB) ... LOCO TAC
Low-Cost Technology (PDAA) ... LCT
Low-Cost Visual-Approach Slope Indicator (DNAB) ... LCVASI
Low-Cost Weapon Delivery System (MCD) ... LCWDS
Low-Cost-to-Produce Classifier (MCD) ... LCPC
Low-Coverage Acquisiton RADAR (PDAA) ... LCAR
Low-Cycle Fatigue [*Rocket engine*] ... LCF
Low-Cycle Fatigue Counter (PDAA) ... LCFC
Low-Cycle High-Temperature Fatigue [*Rocket engine*] ... LCHTF
Low-Density Amorph [*Materials science*] ... LDA
Low-Density Data (KSC) ... LDD
Low-Density Data System ... LDDS
Low-Density Gas ... LDG

Low-Density Indication (MCD) ... LDI
Low-Density Lipoprotein [*Biochemistry*] ... LDL
Low-Density Lipoprotein Apheresis [*Medicine*] (DMAA) ... LDLA
Low-Density Lipoprotein Receptor [*Biochemistry*] ... LDLR
Low-Density Lipoprotein-Cholesterol [*Biochemistry*] ... LDL-C
Low-Density Microsome [*Cytology*] ... LDM
Low-Density Oil [*Petroleum industry*] ... LDO
Low-Density Overlay [*Plywood*] ... LDO
Low-Density Phenolic Nylon [*Polymer*] ... LDPN
Low-Density Polyethylene [*Polymer*] ... LDPE
Low-Density, Recorder ... LDR
Low-Density Reinforced Reaction Injection Molding [*Plastics*] ... LDRRIM
Low-Density Structural Reaction Injection Molding [*Plastics*] ... LD-SRIM
Low-Dispersion Automatic Cannon System ... LODACS
Low-Dollar Value ... LDV
Low-Dose Unfractionated Heparin [*Medicine*] (DMAA) ... LDUH
Low-Dose Urea in Invert Sugar (AAMN) ... LUIS
Low-Drag Bomb ... LDB
Low-Drag Boundary Layer Control [*Military*] ... LDBLC
Low-Drag General Purpose (MCD) ... LDGP
Lowe Limit of Detection [*Also, LLD*] [*Analytical chemistry*] ... LLOD
Lowe Technical School, Windsor, ON, Canada [*Library symbol Library of Congress*] (LCLS) ... CaOWL
Lowe Technical School, Windsor, Ontario [*Library symbol National Library of Canada*] (NLC) ... OWL
Low-Echo-Centroid [*Geology*] ... LEC
Low-Elevation (CAAL) ... Low-E
Lowell, AR [*FM radio station call letters*] ... KKZQ
Lowell City Library, Lowell, MA [*Library symbol Library of Congress*] (LCLS) ... MLow
Lowell Elementary School, Brainerd, MN [*Library symbol*] [*Library of Congress*] (LCLS) ... MnBrLoE
Lowell Elementary School, Duluth, MN [*Library symbol*] [*Library of Congress*] (LCLS) ... MnDuLOE
Lowell, IN [*FM radio station call letters*] ... WZVN
Lowell, MA [*AM radio station call letters*] ... WCAP
Lowell, MA [*FM radio station call letters*] ... WJUL
Lowell, MA [*AM radio station call letters*] ... WLLH
Lowell, MA [*FM radio station call letters*] (RBYB) ... WOAZ-FM
Lowell, MA [*FM radio station call letters*] ... WSSH
Lowell Public Library, Lowell, IN [*Library symbol Library of Congress*] (LCLS) ... InLow
Lowell State College, Lowell, MA [*Library symbol Library of Congress Obsolete*] (LCLS) ... MLowTC
Lowell Technological Institute [*Massachusetts*] ... LTI
Lowell Technological Institute, Lowell, MA [*Library symbol Library of Congress Obsolete*] (LCLS) ... MLowT
Lowell Technological Institute Research Foundation (MCD) ... LTIRF
Lowell Tribune, Lowell, IN [*Library symbol Library of Congress*] (LCLS) ... InLowT
Lowell's Decisions [*A publication*] (DLA) ... Low Dec (F)
Lowell's District Court Reports [*United States, Massachusetts District*] [*A publication*] (DLA) ... Low
Lowell's District Court Reports [*United States, Massachusetts District*] [*A publication*] (DLA) ... Low Dis
Lowell's District Court Reports [*United States, Massachusetts District*] [*A publication*] (DLA) ... Lowell
Low-Emission Vehicle Certification Board [*Terminated, 1980*] [*Environmental Protection Agency*] ... LEVCB
Low-Emissions Bus ... LEB
Low-Emissions Truck ... LET
Low-Emissions Vehicle ... LEV
Low-Emissivity [*Glass*] ... LOW-E
Low-End Torque [*Automotive engineering*] ... LET
Low-Energy All-Purpose (Collimator) [*Radiology*] ... LEAP
Low-Energy Antiproton Ring [*Particle physics*] ... LEAR
Low-Energy Charged Particle [*Atomic physics*] ... LECP
Low-Energy Deasphalting [*Petroleum refining*] ... LEDA
Low-Energy Detector ... LED
Low-Energy Detonating Cord (SAA) ... LEDC
Low-Energy Diffraction ... LED
Low-Energy Electron Beam Irradiation [*Physics*] ... LEEBI
Low-Energy Electron Diffraction [*Spectroscopy*] ... LEED
Low-Energy Electron Microscopy ... LEEM
Low-Energy Electron Reflection (IEEE) ... LEER
Low-Energy Gamma Monitor ... LEGM
Low-Energy Ion Detector ... LEID
Low-Energy Ion Scattering [*For study of surfaces*] ... LEIS
Low-Energy Ion Scattering Spectroscopy ... LEISS
Low-Energy LASER System ... LELS
Low-Energy Magnetic Electron Spectrum (IAA) ... LEMES
Low-Energy Magnetospheric Particle Analyzer [*Atomic physics*] ... LEMPA
Low-Energy Molecular Scattering (MCD) ... LEMS
Low-Energy Particle Telescope ... LEPT
Low-Energy Photon Detector [*Environmental Protection Agency*] ... LEPD
Low-Energy Proton-Electron Differential Energy Analyzer [*NASA*] ... LEPEDEA
Low-Energy Recoil Ion Spectroscopy ... LERIS
Low-Energy Speech Transmission ... LEST
Low-Energy Sputter ... LES
Low-Energy Telescope [*Geophysics*] ... LET
Low-Energy Telescope System [*Geophysics*] ... LETS
Low-Energy-Electron-Induced X-Ray Spectrometry ... LEEIXS
Lowenfeld Kaleidoblocs [*Psychological testing*] ... LK
Lowenfeld Mosaic Test [*Psychology*] ... LMT
Low-Enriched Uranium [*Nuclear energy*] ... LEU
Lowenstein-Jensen [*Growth medium*] ... L-J
Lowenstein-Jensen Growth Medium (MAE) ... LJM
Lower (VRA) ... low
Lower ... LOWR
Lower (ADA) ... LR
Lower (AAG) ... LWR
Lower Abdominal Surgery (DAVI) ... LAS
Lower Acceptable Mean Maximum Pressure (SAA) ... LAMMP
Lower Acceptance Level ... LAL
Lower Achieving Pupils Project [*British*] ... LAPP
Lower Airspace (WDAA) ... LAS
Lower Airspace RADAR Advisory Service [*British*] (DA) ... LARS
Lower and Upper [*Anatomy*] ... L & U
Lower Arithmetic Unit (IAA) ... LAU
Lower Arkansas Valley Regional Library, Las Animas, CO [*Library symbol Library of Congress*] (LCLS) ... CoLasA
Lower Arm ... LA
Lower Atmosphere Composition and Temperature Experiment [*National Science Foundation*] ... LACATE
Lower Atmosphere Research Satellite (SSD) ... LARS
Lower Back Disability [*Medicine*] ... LBD
Lower Ball Joint [*Automotive engineering*] ... LBJ
Lower Bearing ... LB
Lower Body Negative Pressure [*Boots*] [*Space flight equipment*] [*NASA*] ... LBNP
Lower Body Negative Pressure Device [*Space flight equipment*] [*NASA*] ... LBNPD
Lower Bound [*Computer science*] ... LB
Lower Bound [*Computer science*] ... LWB
Lower Bow [*Music*] (ROG) ... L
Lower Brace (MCD) ... LB
Lower Branchial Filament ... LBRF
Lower Burma Printed Judgments [*A publication*] (DLA) ... PJLB
Lower Burma Rulings [*India*] [*A publication*] (DLA) ... LBR
Lower California ... LC
Lower Canada ... LC
Lower Canada Arms Collectors Association, Montreal, PQ, Canada [*Library symbol Library of Congress*] (LCLS) ... CaQMLCA
Lower Canada Arms Collectors Association, Montreal, Quebec [*Library symbol National Library of Canada*] (NLC) ... QMLCA
Lower Canada Civil Code [*A publication*] (DLA) ... LCCC
Lower Canada Civil Procedure [*A publication*] (DLA) ... LCCP
Lower Canada College, Montreal, PQ, Canada [*Library symbol Library of Congress*] (LCLS) ... CaQMLCC
Lower Canada College Montreal, Quebec [*Library symbol National Library of Canada*] (NLC) ... QMLCC
Lower Canada Jurist [*A publication*] (DLA) ... LC Jur
Lower Canada Jurist [*A publication*] (DLA) ... Low Can Jur
Lower Canada Jurist [*A publication*] (DLA) ... Low Can Jurist
Lower Canada Jurist [*A publication*] (DLA) ... Lower Can Jur
Lower Canada Jurist, Montreal [*1848-91*] [*A publication*] (DLA) ... LCJ
Lower Canada Jurist, Quebec [*1848-91*] [*A publication*] (DLA) ... J
Lower Canada Law Journal [*A publication*] (DLA) ... LCL Jo
Lower Canada Law Journal [*A publication*] (DLA) ... LCLJ
Lower Canada Law Journal [*A publication*] (DLA) ... LJ
Lower Canada Law Journal [*A publication*] (DLA) ... Low Can LJ
Lower Canada Reports [*A publication*] (DLA) ... LCR
Lower Canada Reports [*A publication*] (DLA) ... Low Can
Lower Canada Reports [*A publication*] (DLA) ... Low Can R
Lower Canada Reports [*A publication*] (DLA) ... Low Can Rep
Lower Canada Reports (Decisions des Tribunaux du Bas-Canada) [*1850-67*] [*A publication*] (DLA) ... DTBC
Lower Canada Seignorial Questions Reports [*A publication*] (DLA) ... LC Rep S Qu
Lower Canada Seignorial Questions Reports [*A publication*] (DLA) ... Low C Seign
Lower Canada Seignorial Questions Reports [*A publication*] (DLA) ... Low Can Rep SQ
Lower Canada Seignorial Questions Reports [*A publication*] (DLA) ... Lower Can SQ
Lower Canada Seignorial Questions Reports [*A publication*] (DLA) ... Seign Rep
Lower Character (IAA) ... LC
Lower Circulating Reflux [*Chemical engineering*] ... LCR
Lower Class - Double [*or Dual*] **Income, No Kids** [*Lifestyle classification*] ... L-Dink
Lower Colorado River Authority ... LCRA
Lower Columbia College, Longview, WA [*Library symbol Library of Congress*] (LCLS) ... WaLoL
Lower Confidence Limit [*Statistics*] ... LCL
Lower Conformance Altitude (SAA) ... LCAL
Lower Control (IAA) ... LC
Lower Control Limit [*QCR*] ... LCL
Lower Control Unit (WDAA) ... LCU
Lower Cost Processor (MCD) ... LCP
Lower Courts and Municipal Gazette [*Canada*] [*A publication*] (DLA) ... LC & M Gaz
Lower Courts Gazette [*Ontario*] [*A publication*] (DLA) ... LCG
Lower Critical End Points [*Supercritical extraction*] ... LCEP
Lower Critical Ordering Transition [*Polymer physics*] ... LCOT
Lower Critical-Solution-Temperature ... LCST
Lower Cylinder ... LC
Lower Dead Center ... LDC
Lower Deck ... LD
Lower Deck ... LDK
Lower Detectable Limit [*Chemical analysis*] ... LDL
Lower Deviation Level (AABC) ... LDL
Lower Earnings Limit (MHDB) ... LEL
Lower Eastside Action Project [*New York City*] ... LEAP
Lower Echelon Automatic Switchboard ... LEAS

Lower Electrical Limit (NRCH) ... LEL
Lower Elevated Serum Cholesterol [*Acronym is trade name of Dow Chemical*] ... LORELCO
Lower Emissions Dispatch [*Environmental Protection Agency*] ... LED
Lower End Plug (IEEE) ... LEP
Lower Epidermal Cell [*Botany*] ... LEC
Lower Epidermis [*Botany*] ... LE
Lower Equipment Bay [*Apollo*] [*NASA*] ... LEB
Lower Esophageal High Pressure Zone [*Gastroenterology*] (DAVI) ... LEHPZ
Lower Esophageal Sphincter [*Medicine*] ... LES
Lower Esophageal Sphincter Pressure [*Medicine*] ... LESP
Lower Excess Air [*Combustion technology*] ... LEA
Lower Explosive Limit [*of fuel vapor*] ... LEL
Lower Extremity [*Medicine*] ... L/EXT
Lower Extremity [*Medicine*] ... LE
Lower Extremity [*Anatomy*] (DMAA) ... LX
Lower Extremity Amputation [*Medicine*] (DMAA) ... LEA
Lower Extremity Venous Tracing [*Cardiology*] (DAVI) ... LEVT
Lower Fascial Height [*Medicine*] ... LFH
Lower Figure of Merit ... LFM
Lower Flammable Limit ... LFL
Lower Fort Garry National Historic Park, Parks Canada [*Parc Historique National Lower Fort Garry, Parcs Canada*] **Selkirk, Manitoba** [*Library symbol National Library of Canada*] (NLC) ... MSPCL
Lower Genital Tract Infection [*Medicine*] (DMAA) ... LGTI
Lower Group Stop (NRCH) ... LGS
Lower Half ... LH
Lower Hemispherical (MCD) ... LH
Lower High-Water [*Tides and currents*] ... LHW
Lower High-Water Interval [*Tides and currents*] ... LHWI
Lower Hold [*Shipping*] ... LH
Lower Hold [*Shipping*] (DS) ... Lw
Lower Hour Angle [*Navigation*] ... LHA
Lower Hybrid Resonance ... LHR
Lower Hybrid Resonance Heating (MCD) ... LHH
Lower Inlet Module [*Nuclear energy*] (NRCH) ... LIM
Lower Inner Quadrant [*Anatomy*] ... LIQ
Lower Inventory for Tomorrow [*A program of the Canadian government to bring heavy stocks of wheat into line with demand by paying farmers not to produce*] ... LIFT
Lower Kuskokwim School District, Media Center, Bethel, AK [*Library symbol*] [*Library of Congress*] (LCLS) ... AkBSD
Lower Laterals [*Botany*] ... LL
Lower Left ... LL
Lower Left Abdomen [*Injection Site*] ... LLA
Lower Leg ... LL
Lower Leg Artery [*Anatomy*] ... LOLA
Lower Leg Brace [*Medicine*] ... LLB
Lower Leg Vein [*Anatomy*] ... LOLV
Lower Leg Venule [*Anatomy*] ... LOLVE
Lower Level Computer Software Component ... LLCSC
Lower Level End Item Subdivision [*Army*] (AABC) ... LLEIS
Lower Lid [*Ophthalmology*] ... LL
Lower Limb [*Lower edge of sun, moon, etc.*] [*Navigation*] ... LL
Lower Limen [*Psychology*] ... LL
Lower Limit ... LL
Lower Limit of a Class Interval [*Psychology*] ... l
Lower Limit of Detection [*Spectrometry*] ... LLD
Lower Lip [*Anatomy*] (DAVI) ... LL
Lower Lip Length [*Medicine*] ... LLL
Lower Living Standard Income Level [*CETA*] [*Department of Labor*] ... LLSIL
Lower Lobe [*Medicine*] ... LL
Lower Low Water [*Tides and currents*] ... LLW
Lower Low-Water Interval [*Tides and currents*] ... LLWI
Lower Magazine [*Typography*] ... LM
Lower Mainland Regional Planning Board, New Westminster, BC, Canada [*Library symbol Library of Congress*] (LCLS) ... CaBNWL
Lower Mainland Regional Planning Board, New Westminster, British Columbia [*Library symbol National Library of Canada*] (NLC) ... BNWL
Lower Medium [*Moody's bond rating*] ... Baa
Lower Medium [*Standard & Poor's bond rating*] [*Investment term*] ... BB
Lower Mid Fuselage (NASA) ... LMF
Lower Middle Income Country ... LMIC
Lower Midwest ... LMW
Lower Mississippi Valley Division [*Army Engineers*] ... LMVD
Lower Motor [*Neurology*] ... LM
Lower Motor Neuron [*Anatomy*] ... LMN
Lower Motor Neuron Lesion [*Medicine*] ... LMNL
Lower North Atlantic Deep Water [*Oceanography*] ... LNADW
Lower O-Esophageal Sphincter Pressure [*Medicine*] (DMAA) ... LOS(P)
Lower of Cost or Market (TDOB) ... LCL
Lower of Cost or Market ... LCM
Lower Operator Rate [*Telecommunications British*] ... LOR
Lower Outer Quadrant [*Anatomy*] ... LOQ
Lower Outer Tube ... LOT
Lower Panel (IAA) ... LP
Lower Peninsula [*Michigan*] ... LP
Lower Provinces Code [*India*] [*A publication*] (DLA) ... Low Pr Code
Lower Pump Cubicle (IEEE) ... LPC
Lower Radicular Obstetrical Paralysis [*Medicine*] (DMAA) ... LROP
Lower Rail [*Typography*] ... LR
Lower Reject Limit Median (SAA) ... LRLM
Lower Reject Limit Median ... LRM
Lower Respiratory Infection [*Medicine*] ... LRI
Lower Respiratory Tract [*Medicine*] ... LRT
Lower Respiratory Tract Illness (DAVI) ... LRTI
Lower Respiratory Tract Infection [*Medicine*] (ADA) ... LRTI
Lower Rib Cage [*Anatomy*] ... LRC
Lower Right ... LR
Lower Right Abdomen [*Injection site*] ... LRA
Lower Right Quadrant (MAE) ... LRQ
Lower Rule ... LR
Lower Segment Caesarean Section [*Medicine*] ... LSCS
Lower Sequential Permissive (NRCH) ... LSP
Lower Side Frequency [*Electronics*] (ECII) ... LSF
Lower Sideband [*Data transmission*] ... LSB
Lower Solution Point ... LSP
Lower Specified Limit ... LSL
Lower Sprocket (ECII) ... LS
Lower Sternal Edge [*Cardiology*] ... LSE
Lower Structure ... LS
Lower Surface Center Line ... LSCL
Lower Thermal Comfort Threshold [*Environmental heating*] ... LTCT
Lower Third [*Referring to long bones*] [*Orthopedics*] (DAVI) ... L/3
Lower Torso ... LT
Lower Torso Assembly [*Aerospace*] (MCD) ... LTA
Lower Transition Altitude (SAA) ... LTAL
Lower Trip Point ... LTP
Lower Unit Costs and Related Earnings (MHDB) ... LUCRE
Lower Yield Point [*Medicine*] (DMAA) ... LYP
Lowercase [*i.e., small letters*] [*Typography*] ... LC
Lowercase (WDMC) ... lc
Lowercase Alphabet ... LCA
Lowercase-Alphabet Length [*Typesetting*] (WDMC) ... lca
Lower-Deck Attitude [*British military*] (DMA) ... LDA
Lower-Extremity Amputation Protocol [*Orthopedics*] ... LEAP
Lower-Half Assembly ... LHA
Lower-Sideband Suppressed Carrier (IDOE) ... LSSC
Lower-Speed Service-Deriving [*Telecommunications*] (TSSD) ... LSSD
Lowe's Companies, Inc. [*NYSE symbol*] (SPSG) ... LOW
Lowe's Companies, Inc. [*Associated Press*] (SAG) ... Lowes
Lowe's Cos. [*NYSE symbol*] (TTSB) ... LOW
Lowe's Syndrome Association (EA) ... LSA
Lowest [*Moody's bond rating*] [*Investment term*] ... C
Lowest (MSA) ... LWST
Lowest Achievable Emission Rate [*Environmental Protection Agency*] ... LAER
Lowest Astronomical Tide (PDAA) ... LAT
Lowest Astronomical Tide of the Foreseeable Future (PDAA) ... LATOFF
Lowest Astronomical Tide of the Month (PDAA) ... LATOM
Lowest Astronomical Tide of the Year (PDAA) ... LATOY
Lowest Common Multiple [*Mathematics*] ... LCM
Lowest Cost of Ownership ... LCO
Lowest Designated Assembly ... LDA
Lowest Effect Level [*Toxicology*] ... LEL
Lowest Effective Power ... LEP
Lowest Effective Toxic Dose [*Medicine*] (DMAA) ... LETD
Lowest Emitting Dose [*Medicine*] (DMAA) ... LED
Lowest Empty Molecular Orbital [*Medicine*] (DMAA) ... LEMO
Lowest Fare Routing [*Travel industry*] ... LFR
Lowest Level Remove-Replace (SAA) ... LLRR
Lowest Maintenance Level (MCD) ... LML
Lowest Maximum Range ... LMR
Lowest Observed Adverse Effect Level (EG) ... LOAEL
Lowest Observed Effect Concentration [*Environmental Technology*] ... LOEC
Lowest Observed Effect Level [*Toxicology*] ... LOEL
Lowest Offer [*Business term*] ... LO
Lowest Operating Frequency (IEEE) ... LOF
Lowest Planned Level of Maintenance (SAA) ... LPLM
Lowest Possible Airfare ... LPF
Lowest Quadrant ... LQ
Lowest Quadrille ... LQ
Lowest Quantity Determinable [*Analytical chemistry*] ... LQD
Lowest Repairable Unit (MCD) ... LRU
Lowest Replacement Unit (MCD) ... LRU
Lowest Required Radiated Power ... LRRP
Lowest Safe Altitude [*Aviation*] (DA) ... LSALT
Lowest Significant Dose [*Toxicology*] ... LSD
Lowest Temperature [*NWS*] (FAAC) ... LOTMP
Lowest Temperature Equaled for All Time [*NWS*] (FAAC) ... LOEAT
Lowest Temperature Equaled for the Month [*NWS*] (FAAC) ... LOEFM
Lowest Temperature Equaled So Early [*NWS*] (FAAC) ... LOESE
Lowest Temperature Equaled So Late [*NWS*] (FAAC) ... LOESL
Lowest Temperature Exceeded for All Time [*NWS*] (FAAC) ... LOXAT
Lowest Temperature Exceeded for the Month [*NWS*] (FAAC) ... LOXFM
Lowest Temperature Exceeded So Early [*NWS*] (FAAC) ... LOXSE
lowest Temperature Exceeded So Late [*NWS*] (FAAC) ... LOXSL
Lowest Total Overall Cost (MHDI) ... LTOC
Lowest Unoccupied Molecular Orbital [*Atomic physics*] ... LUMO
Lowest Usable [*or Useful*] **Frequency** [*Radio*] ... LUF
Lowest Usable [*or Useful*] **High-Frequency** [*Radio*] ... LUHF
Lowest-Observed-Effect Level [*Environmental science*] (FFDE) ... LOEL
Low-Excess-Air [*Combustion technology*] ... LEA
Low-Fat Diet ... LFD
Low-Field Magnetometer [*Instrumentation*] ... LFM
Low-Fluence [*Physics*] ... LF
Low-Flux Reactor ... LFR
Low-Flying Aerial Target [*Military*] (CAAL) ... LOFAT
Low-Forceps Delivery [*Obstetrics*] ... LFD
Low-Frequency Accelerometer Flutter (MCD) ... LFAF
Low-Frequency Accelerometer Modes (MCD) ... LFAM

Low-Frequency Accelerometer POGO [Polar Orbiting Geophysical Observatory] [NASA] (NASA) .... LFAP
Low-Frequency Acoustic Vernier Analyzer (NVT) .... LAVA
Low-Frequency Acquisition and Ranging .... LOFAR
Low-Frequency Active Sonar (DOMA) .... LFAS
Low-Frequency Analysis and Recording [Sonobuoys] [Navy] .... LOFAR
Low-Frequency Analysis and Recording (MCD) .... LOWFAR
Low-Frequency Beacon .... LFB
Low-Frequency Choke (DEN) .... LFC
Low-Frequency Correction (CET) .... LFC
Low-Frequency Cross-Modulation [Electronics] (OA) .... LFCM
Low-Frequency Current .... LFC
Low-Frequency Decoy .... LFD
Low-Frequency Direction Finder (MCD) .... LFDF
Low-Frequency Disturbance .... LFD
Low-Frequency Field-Effect Transistor [Electronics] (OA) .... LFFET
Low-Frequency Filter (IAA) .... LFF
Low-Frequency Generator .... LFG
Low-Frequency Gravity Gradiometer .... LFGG
Low-Frequency Hearing Loss (DMAA) .... LFHL
Low-Frequency Inductor .... LFI
Low-Frequency Instruments and Measurement (MCD) .... LFIM
Low-Frequency Intersection .... LFINT
Low-Frequency Jammer .... LFJ
Low-Frequency Magnetic [Field] .... LFM
Low-Frequency Microwave Radiometer .... LFMR
Low-Frequency Modulation .... LFM
Low-Frequency Navigation System (NG) .... LFNS
Low-Frequency Omnidirectional Radio Range .... LOR
Low-Frequency Oscillation (MCD) .... LOFO
Low-Frequency Oscillator .... LFO
Low-Frequency Outer Marker (MSA) .... LFOM
Low-Frequency Outer Marker .... LOM
Low-Frequency Phase Shifter [Telecommunications] .... LFPS
Low-Frequency Plasma Wave .... LFPW
Low-Frequency Positive Pressure Ventilation [Medicine] (DMAA) .... LFPPV
Low-Frequency Prediction [Marine science] (OSRA) .... LEP
Low-Frequency Prediction (USDC) .... LFP
Low-Frequency Pulsed Electromagnetic Field .... LFPEF
Low-Frequency Radio Range (MCD) .... LFRR
Low-Frequency Range (MCD) .... LFR
Low-Frequency Resistance (IDOE) .... R_{LF}
Low-Frequency Stimulation [Neurophysiology] .... LFS
Low-Frequency Stimulation [Neurophysiology] .... LFS
Low-Frequency Telescope [NASA] .... LOFT
Low-Frequency Tetanus [Medicine] (DMAA) .... LFT
Low-Frequency Timing Assembly (IAA) .... LFTA
Low-Frequency Transduction .... LFT
Low-Frequency Transionospheric Satellite .... LOFTI
Low-Frequency Transmit System (DWSG) .... LTS
Low-Frequency Vibration .... LFV
Low-G Accelerometer Calibration System [NASA] .... LOGACS
Low-G Accelerometer System [NASA] .... LGAS
Low-Gain Antenna .... LGA
Low-Grade Dysplasia [Medicine] .... LGD
Low-Grade Squamous Intraepithelial Lesion [Medicine] .... LSIL
Low-Head Safety Injection [Nuclear energy] (NRCH) .... LHSI
Low-Heat-Rejection Engine [Mechanical engineering] (RDA) .... LHR
Low-Impact Aerobics .... LIA
Low-Impact Switch (MCD) .... LIS
Low-Impedance Transmission .... LIT
Low-Input Landscaping LIL
Low-Input Sustainable Agriculture .... LISA
Low-Input Voltage (KSC) LIV
Low-Input Voltage Conversion and Regulation .... LIVCR
Low-Input Voltage Converter LIVC
Low-Input Voltage Regulation .... LIVR
Low-Intensity Conflict [Military] LIC
Low-Intensity Large Area [Headlight] .... LILAC
Low-Intensity Reciprocity Failure [Of photographic emulsions] .... LIRF
Low-Intensity Runway Lighting .... LIRL
Low-Intensity Sonication [Chemistry] .... LIS
Low-Intensity Test Reactor [ORNL] .... LITR
Low-Intensity X-Ray Imaging Scope .... LIXISCOPE
Low-Iodine Diet [Medicine] .... LID
Low-Ionic-Strength Saline [Medicine] (DMAA) .... LISS
Low-Ionization Filament Component [Galactic science] .... LIF
Low-Ionization Nuclear Emission-Line Region [Spectroscopy] .... LINER
Low-Iron, Manganese-Enriched [Meteorite] .... LIME
Low-Iron-Content Monoethanolamine .... LIMEA
Low-Key Maintenance .... LKM
Lowland-Southern Hybrid [Hemoglobin phenotype of Rana pipiens] .... LSH
Low-Level Acceleration Measurement Apparatus .... LLAMA
Low-Level Air Defence [Navy British] .... LLAD
Low-Level Analog (MCD) .... LLA
Low-Level Bombsight (NATG) .... LLBS
Low-Level Compaction Station [Nuclear energy] (NRCH) .... LLCS
Low-Level Detector (IEEE) .... LLD
Low-Level Differential Logic (IAA) .... LLDL
Low-Level Dose [Nuclear energy] (NRCH) .... LLD
Low-Level Extraction [Military aviation] .... LOLEX
Low-Level Flux Monitor [Nuclear energy] (NRCH) .... LLFM
Low-Level Graded Exercise Test [Cardiology] (DAVI) .... LL-GXT
Low-Level Graphical Language (PDAA) .... LLGL
Low-Level Heating [Nuclear energy] (OA) .... LLH

Low-Level Input Voltage LLIV
Low-Level Interface LLI
Low-Level Jet [Marine science] (OSRA) .... LLJ
Low-Level Jet (USDC) .... LLJ
Low-Level Language [Computer programming] .... LOWL
Low-Level LASER Television .... LLLTV
Low-Level Liquid Waste Tank [Nuclear energy] (NRCH) .... LLLWT
Low-Level Logic LLL
Low-Level Multiplexer .... LLM
Low-Level Night Operations [Aviation] .... LLNO
Low-Level Oil Alarm (IAA) .... LOLA
Low-Level Output Voltage .... LLOV
Low-Level Penetration Bomb .... LPB
Low-Level Pumping Station (ADA) .... LLPS
Low-Level Radiation .... LLR
Low-Level Radio Frequency .... LLRF
Low-Level Radio Modulator .... LLRM
Low-Level Radioactive Waste .... LLW
Low-Level Radioactive Waste Policy Act of 1980 (GAAI) .... LLRWPA
Low-Level Radioactive Waste Policy Amendments Act of 1985 (GAAI) .... LLRWPAA
Low-Level Radiological Waste [U.S. Army Corps of Engineers] .... LLRW
Low-Level Reactor Test (IEEE) .... LLRT
Low-Level Resistance [to disease] .... LLR
Low-Level Sensor (KSC) .... LLS
Low-Level Service [Computer science] .... LLS
Low-Level Signaling Unit [Telecommunications] (TEL) .... LLSU
Low-Level Solid [Nuclear energy] (NRCH) .... LLS
Low-Level Solid Waste Storage Vault [Nuclear energy] (NRCH) .... LLSWV
Low-Level Sounding System [for measuring weather conditions] .... LLSS
Low-Level Storage Vault [Nuclear energy] (NRCH) .... LLSV
Low-Level Surface-to-Air Guided Weapon (IAA) .... LLSAGW
Low-Level Terminal .... LLT
Low-Level Transit Time .... LLTR
Low-Level Tritiated Water Processing Subsystem (MCD) .... LLTWP
Low-Level Turbulence .... LLT
Low-Level Waste [Nuclear energy] (NRCH) .... LLW
Low-Level Waste .... LLW
Low-Level Waste Disposal Development and Demonstration .... LLWDDD
Low-Level Waste Management Program (GAAI) .... LLWMP
Low-Level Waste Storage Vault [Nuclear energy] (NRCH) .... LLWSV
Low-Level Weapons Delivery System (MCD) .... LLDS
Low-Level Windshear Alert System [Marine science] (OSRA) .... LLWAS
Low-Level Windshear Alert System (USDC) .... LLWAS
Low-Level-LASER Guided Bomb .... LLLGB
Low-Level-Run-In (MCD) .... LLRI
Low-Light Television .... LLT
Low-Light-Level Television [Night vision device] [Military] (RDA) .... LLLTV
Low-Light-Level Television [Night vision device] [Military] .... LLLTV
Low-Light-Level Television [Military] (DOMA) .... LLLTV
Low-Light-Level Television [Night vision device] [Military] .... LLTV
Low-Limit Temperature Control Systems .... LLTCS
Low-Low Frequency Acoustics (DOMA) .... LLFA
Low-Maintenance Battery (MCD) .... LMB
Low-Mass X-Ray Binary [Star system] .... LMXB
Low-Melting (OA) .... LM
Low-Mintage Coin Club (EA) .... LMCC
Low-Molecular Weight [Chemistry] .... LMW
Low-Molecular-Weight Dextran [Medicine] .... LMD
Low-Molecular-Weight Dextran (MAE) .... LMDX
Low-Molecular-Weight Dextran [Medicine] (AAMN) .... LMWD
Low-Molecular-Weight Heparin [Biochemistry] .... LMWH
Low-Molecular-Weight Hydrocarbon (MCD) .... LMWHC
Low-Molecular-Weight Inhibitor [of protease activity] .... LMI
Low-Molecular-Weight Polypeptide [Biochemistry] .... LMP
Low-Molecular-Weight Proteinuria [Medicine] .... LMWP
Lowndes and Maxwell's English Bail Court Cases [1852-54] [A publication] (DLA) .... Bail CC
Lowndes and Maxwell's English Bail Court Cases [1852-54] [A publication] (DLA) .... Bail Cr Rep
Lowndes and Maxwell's English Bail Court Cases [1852-54] [A publication] (DLA) .... Bail Ct Cas
Lowndes and Maxwell's English Bail Court Cases [1852-54] [A publication] (DLA) .... Bail Ct Rep
Lowndes and Maxwell's English Bail Court Reports [1852-54] [A publication] (DLA) .... Lown & M
Lowndes and Maxwell's English Bail Court Reports [1852-54] [A publication] (DLA) .... Lownd & M
Lowndes and Maxwell's English Bail Court Reports [1852-54] [A publication] (DLA) .... Lowndes & M
Lowndes and Maxwell's English Bail Court Reports [1852-54] [A publication] (DLA) .... Lowndes & M (Eng)
Lowndes and Maxwell's English Practice Cases [1852-54] [A publication] (DLA) .... L & M
Lowndes County Library System, Columbus, MS [Library symbol Library of Congress] (LCLS) .... MsCol
Lowndes' General Average [10th ed.] [1975] [A publication] (DLA) .... Lownd Av
Lowndes, Maxwell, and Pollock's English Bail Court Practice Reports [1850-51] [A publication] (DLA) .... LM & P
Lowndes, Maxwell, and Pollock's English Bail Court Practice Reports [1850-51] [A publication] (DLA) .... Pr Rep BC
Lowndes, Maxwell, and Pollock's English Bail Court Reports [1850-51] [A publication] (DLA) .... Lown M & P
Lowndes, Maxwell, and Pollock's English Bail Court Reports [1850-51] [A publication] (DLA) .... Lownd M & P

Lowndes, Maxwell, and Pollock's English Bail Court Reports [*1850-51*] [*A publication*] (DLA) ... Lowndes M & P
Lowndes on Collisions at Sea [*A publication*] (DLA) ... Lownd Col
Lowndes on Copyright [*A publication*] (DLA) ... Lownd Cop
Lowndes on Insurance [*A publication*] (DLA) ... Lownd Ins
Lowndes on Legacies [*A publication*] (DLA) ... Lown Leg
Lowndes on Legacies [*A publication*] (DLA) ... Lownd Leg
Lown-Ganong-Levine [*Syndrome*] [*Medicine*] ... LGL
Low-Noise Amplifier [*Satellite communications*] ... LNA
Low-Noise Antenna ... LNA
Low-Noise Block [*Satellite communications*] ... LNB
Low-Noise Block Feed [*Satellite communications*] ... LNBF
Low-Noise Cable ... LNC
Low-Noise Converter [*Satellite communications*] ... LNC
Low-Noise Emission Product (GFGA) ... LNEP
Low-Noise Feed [*Satellite communications*] ... LNF
Low-Noise Level Margin ... LNLM
Low-Noise Receiver ... LNR
Low-Noise Traveling Wave Amplifier ... LNTWA
Low-Noise Traveling Wave Tube Amplifier (IAA) ... LNTWTA
Low-Observability Reentry Vehicle ... LORV
Low-Observable Technology (MCD) ... LOT
Low-Operating Current Light-Emitting Diode ... LOCLED
Low-Order Memory (CET) ... LOM
Low-Order Position [*Military*] (AFIT) ... LOP
Low-Pass Filter [*Electronics*] ... LPF
Lowpass Filter (MSA) ... LPFL
Low-Pass Network [*Electronics*] ... LPN
Low-Performance Drone ... LPD
Low-Power Acquisition RADAR ... LOPAR
Low-Power Amplifier (CET) ... LPA
Low-Power Atmospheric Compensation Experiment [*Strategic Defense Initiative*] ... LACE
Low-Power Boiler [*US reactor*] ... LOPO
Low-Power Channel (IAA) ... LPC
Low-Power Counter ... LPC
Low-Power Difference (IEEE) ... LPD
Low-Power Diode Transistor Logic [*Electronics*] (IAA) ... LPDTL
Low-Power Field [*Microscopy*] ... LPF
Low-Power Illuminator (NATG) ... LPI
Low-Power Illuminator Signal Source (MCD) ... LPISS
Low-Power Injection [*Nuclear energy*] (NRCH) ... LPI
Low-Power Interrupt (MCD) ... LPI
Low-Power Logic ... LPL
Low-Power Physics (IEEE) ... LPP
Low-Power Radio Frequency (MCD) ... LPRF
Low-Power Range Monitor [*Nuclear energy*] (NRCH) ... LPRM
Low-Power Reactor Assembly [*University of Illinois*] (NRCH) ... LOPRA
Low-Power Research Reactor ... LPRR
Low-Power Schottky [*Electronics*] ... LPS
Low-Power Schottky [*Electronics*] ... LS
Low-Power Schottky Transistor-Transistor Logic [*Electronics*] (IAA) ... LPSTTL
Low-Power Schottky Transistor-Transistor Logic [*Electronics*] ... LSTTL
Low-Power Self-Screening Noise Jammer [*Military*] (CAAL) ... LPSSNJ
Low-Power Spread Spectrum RADAR (PDAA) ... LPSSR
Low-Power Television ... LPTV
Low-Power Test ... LPT
Low-Power Test Facility [*Nuclear energy*] ... LPTF
Low-Power Transistor-Transistor Logic ... LPTTL
Low-Power Transistor-Transistor Logic (IEEE) ... LTTL
Low-Power Unit (CAAL) ... LPU
Low-Powered Fan Marker (MUGU) ... LFM
Low-Powered Fan Marker (MSA) ... LPFM
Low-Powered, Very-High-Frequency Omnirange ... LVOR
Low-Pressure Alarm (IEEE) ... LPA
Low-Pressure Chamber Technician [*Navy*] ... LPC
Low-Pressure Chemical Vapor Deposition [*Semiconductor technology*] ... LPCVD
Low-Pressure Combustion Chamber ... LPCC
Low-Pressure Composite ... LPC
Low-Pressure Compressor ... LPC
Low-Pressure Coolant Injection [*Nuclear energy*] (NRCH) ... LPCI
Low-Pressure Coolant Injection System [*Nuclear energy*] (NRCH) ... LPCIS
Low-Pressure Coolant Recirculation System [*Nuclear energy*] (IEEE) ... LPCRS
Low-Pressure Core Spray System [*Nuclear energy*] (NRCH) ... LPCS
Low-Pressure Cut-Off [*Air conditioning system*] [*Automotive engineering*] ... LPCO
Low-Pressure Cylinder [*Especially, a locomotive cylinder*] ... LP
Low-Pressure Difference (IEEE) ... LPD
Low-Pressure Fuel Pump (KSC) ... LPFP
Low-Pressure Fuel Turbopump ... LPFT
Low-Pressure Fuel Turbopump (NASA) ... LPFTP
Low-Pressure Gas (NRCH) ... LPG
Low-Pressure Heating Boiler ... LPHB
Low-Pressure Index ... LPI
Low-Pressure Injection [*Nuclear energy*] (NRCH) ... LPI
Low-Pressure Injection System [*Nuclear energy*] (NRCH) ... LPIS
Low-Pressure Liquefied Natural Gases (NRCH) ... LPLNG
Low-Pressure Low-Temperature Molding Compound ... LPL?TMC
Low-Pressure Molding Compound (MCD) ... LMC
Low-Pressure Molding Compound [*Environmental science*] ... LPMC
Low-Pressure Molding Compound ... LPMC
Low-Pressure Noble Gas Processing (NRCH) ... LPNGP
Low-Pressure Oil-Filled [*Cable*] (DICI) ... LPOF
Low-Pressure Oxidizer Turbopump (NASA) ... LPOP
Low-Pressure Oxidizer Turbopump (MCD) ... LPOT
Low-Pressure Oxidizer Turbopump (NASA) ... LPOTP
Low-Pressure Oxygen ... LPO
Low-Pressure Oxygen (AFM) ... LPOX
Low-Pressure Plasma Sprayed [*Thermal barrier coating*] ... LPPS
Low-Pressure Recirculation System (NRCH) ... LPRS
Low-Pressure Safety Injection [*Nuclear energy*] (NRCH) ... LPSI
Low-Pressure Safety Injection Pump [*Nuclear energy*] (NRCH) ... LPSIP
Low-Pressure Sand [*Casting*] [*Automotive engineering*] ... LPS
Low-Pressure Scram [*Nuclear energy*] (IEEE) ... LPS
Low-Pressure Separator [*Chemical engineering*] ... LPS
Low-Pressure Service Water [*Nuclear energy*] (NRCH) ... LPSW
Low-Pressure Side Temperature Sensor [*Air conditioning system*] [*Automotive engineering*] ... LSTS
Low-Pressure Sodium ... LPS
Low-Pressure Solenoid Valve ... LPSV
Low-Pressure Suction Air Conveyor (PDAA) ... LSAC
Low-Pressure Test ... LPT
Low-Pressure Transducer ... LPT
Low-Pressure Turbine [*Nuclear energy*] (NRCH) ... LPT
Low-Pressure Turbine [*on a ship*] (DS) ... LPTB
Low-Pressure-Pipe System [*Waste water treatment*] ... LPP
Low-Priority Key [*Computer science*] ... LK
Low-Probability Behavior ... LPB
Low-Probability Intercept RADAR ... LPIR
Low-Profile ... LO-PRO
Low-Profile Bioprosthesis [*Medicine*] (DMAA) ... LPBP
Low-Profile Flange ... LPF
Low-Quality Recruiting Report (DNAB) ... LQRR
Lowrance Electronics [*NASDAQ symbol*] (SAG) ... LEIX
Lowrance Electronics, Inc. [*Associated Press*] (SAG) ... Lowranc
Low-Range Airspeed System (MCD) ... LORAS
Low-Range Force Gauge ... LRFG
Low-Rate Engineering Decommutator Executive [*Computer program*] [*NASA Viking Mission*] ... DECOM
Low-Rate Initial Production (RDA) ... LRIP
Low-Rate Station ... LRS
Low-Renin Essential Hypertension [*Medicine*] ... LREH
Low-Resistance Ohmmeter ... LRO
Low-Resolution Facsimile [*Telecommunications*] (TEL) ... LRFAX
Low-Resolution Infrared Radiometer ... LRIR
Low-Resolution Infrared Radiometer (MSA) ... LRIRR
Low-Resolution Non-Scanning Radiometer (MCD) ... LRNR
Low-Resolution Omnidirectional Radiometer (MCD) ... LROR
Lowry Air Force Base (SAA) ... LAFB
Lowry, SD [*FM radio station call letters*] (RBYB) ... KMLO-FM
Lowry, SD [*Television station call letters*] ... KQSD
Lowry, SD [*FM radio station call letters*] ... KSQD
Lowry Technical Training Center [*Air Force*] (AFM) ... LTTC
Low-Salinity Plume [*Oceanography*] ... LSP
Low-Ship Impact Ranging [*Navy*] (CAAL) ... LSIR
Low-Signature Vehicle [*Hazardous materials control*] ... LSV
Low-Sodium Diet (DMAA) ... LS
Low-Sodium Diet (DMAA) ... LSD
Low-Sodium Meal [*Airline notation*] (ADA) ... NSML
Low-Solvent Technology (GNE) ... LST
Low-Speed ... LS
Low-Speed Access to a Computer (PDAA) ... LSAC
Low-Speed Adapter (IAA) ... LSA
Low-Speed Black and White [*Photography*] ... LBW
Low-Speed Breaker Relay (IEEE) ... LSB
Low-Speed Buffer (CET) ... LSB
Low-Speed Card Punch [*Computer science*] (AABC) ... LSCP
Low-Speed Compound Terminal (CET) ... LSCT
Low-Speed Concentrator ... LSC
Low-Speed Data ... LSD
Low-Speed Data Channel ... LDC
Low-Speed Data Service [*RCA Global Communications, Inc.*] [*Piscataway, NJ*] [*Telecommunications*] (TSSD) ... LSDS
Low-Speed Digital System ... LSDS
Low-Speed Encoder (IAA) ... LSE
Low-Speed Fuel Air Explosive ... LSFAE
Low-Speed Logic (IAA) ... LSL
Low-Speed MODEM (IAA) ... LSM
Low-Speed Multiline Controller (MHDB) ... LSMLC
Low-Speed Multiplexer Arrangement ... LSMA
Low-Speed Output Adapter (MHDB) ... LOA
Low-Speed Packet Switched Data [*Computer science*] (ACRL) ... LSPSD
Low-Speed Paper Tape Punch [*Telecommunications*] (AABC) ... LSPTP
Low-Speed Paper Tape Reader [*Telecommunications*] (TEL) ... LSPTR
Low-Speed Printer ... LSP
Low-Speed Pulse Restorer (MCD) ... LSPR
Low-Speed Reader ... LSR
Low-Speed Wind Tunnel (MCD) ... LSWT
Low-Spin Folding Fin Aircraft Rocket (IEEE) ... LSFFAR
Low-Stress Grinding (DICI) ... LSG
Low-Styrene Emission ... LSE
Low-Styrene-Emission Laminating Resin ... LSELR
Low-Sulfate Medium [*Microbiology*] ... LSM
Low-Sulfur Diesel Fuel [*Petroleum marketing*] ... LSD
Low-Sulfur Fuel Oil ... LSFO
Low-Surface-Brightness [*Galaxies - astronomy*] ... LSB
Low-Tar Content [*of cigarettes*] ... LTC
Low-Temperature Arc Vapor Deposition [*Coating technology*] ... LTAVD
Low-Temperature Ashing [*Analytical chemistry*] ... LTA
Low-Temperature Carbonization ... LTC
Low-Temperature Catalyst ... LTC

Low-Temperature Coefficient .... LTC
Low-Temperature Cooling .... LTC
Low-Temperature Drying .... LTD
Low-Temperature Flow Test [Lubricant technology] .... LTFT
Low-Temperature Fuel Cell [Energy source] .... LTFC
Low-Temperature Herschel (OA) .... LTH
Low-Temperature Holding .... LTH
Low-Temperature Isomerization [Organic chemistry] .... LTI
Low-Temperature Isotope .... LTI
Low-Temperature Magnetic Force Microscope .... LTMFM
Low-Temperature Multieffect Distillation [Chemical engineering] .... LTMED
Low-Temperature Neutron Irradiation Facility [Oak Ridge, TN] [Oak Ridge National Laboratory] [Department of Energy] (GRD) .... LTNIF
Low-Temperature Noble Gas Process [Nuclear energy] (NRCH) .... LTNGP
Low-Temperature Optical Facility .... LTOF
Low-Temperature Orthorhombic [Crystallography] .... LTO
Low-Temperature Passivation (PDAA) .... LTP
Low-Temperature Phase (PDAA) .... LTP
Low-Temperature Phosphorimetry [Analytical chemistry] .... LTP
Low-Temperature Physics .... LTP
Low-Temperature Polymer (IAA) .... LTP
Low-Temperature Reactor [Chemical engineering] .... LTR
Low-Temperature Reusable Surface Insulation (NASA) .... LRSI
Low-Temperature Scanning Electron Microscopy .... LTSEM
Low-Temperature Semiconductor [Electronics] .... LTSC
Low-Temperature Separation .... LTS
Low-Temperature Smoking (PDAA) .... LTS
Low-Temperature Superconducting Device Electronics (DOMA) .... LTSDE
Low-Temperature Test .... LTT
Low-Temperature Tetragonal [Crystallography] .... LTT
Low-Temperature Thermomechanical Treatment .... LTTMT
Low-Temperature X-Ray Diffraction [Instrumentation] .... LTXRD
Low-Tension (Battery) (DEN) .... LT(B)
Low-Tension Current (IAA) .... LTC
Low-Tension Winding (IAA) .... LTW
Low-Threshold Test Ban Treaty [Proposed] .... LTTBT
Low-Thrust Engine .... LTE
Low-to-High (MDG) .... L/H
Low-to-Medium-Altitude Air Defense (AABC) .... LOMAD
Low-Trajectory Missiles (NRCH) .... LTM
Low-Turbulence Pressure Tunnel [NASA] .... LTPT
Low-Value Materiel (MCD) .... LVM
Low-Value Product .... LVP
Low-Variation Medical Condition .... LVMC
Low-Velocity Anomaly [Seismology] .... LVA
Low-Velocity Detonation [or Drop] .... LVD
Low-Velocity Layer [Geophysics] (OA) LVL
Low-Velocity Scanning .... LVS
Low-VHF [Very-High-Frequency] Transmitter-Receiver .... LVTR
[The] Lowville & Beaver River Railroad Co. [AAR code] .... LBR
Lowville, NY [FM radio station call letters] .... WLLG
Low-Viscosity Index (IAA) LVI
Low-Viscosity Zone .... LVZ
Low-Visibility Landing Simulation [Program] [Air Force] .... LOVISIM
Low-Visibility, Moving Target Acquisition and Strike [Military] .... LVMTAS
Low-Voltage Activated [Neurochemistry] .... LVA
Low-Voltage Avalanche [Electronics] (IAA) .... LVA
Low-Voltage Bias .... LVB
Low-Voltage Capacitor LVC
Low-Voltage Circuit Tester (MCD) .... LVCT
Low-Voltage Cutoff [Battery] LVC
Low-Voltage Direct Current .... LVDC
Low-Voltage Drop (CET) .... LVD
Low-Voltage Electrical Stimulation [Meat treatment] .... LVES
Low-Voltage Fast [Electronics] .... LVF
Low-Voltage Foci (MAE) .... LVF
Low-Voltage Neon .... LVN
Low-Voltage Plate .... LVP
Low-Voltage Power Supply .... LVPS
Low-Voltage Protection [Electronics] .... LVP
Low-Voltage Rack .... LVR
Low-Voltage Ramjet .... LVRJ
Low-Voltage Relay .... LVR
Low-Voltage Release [Electronics] .... LVR
Low-Voltage Release [Electronics] .... LVRLSE
Low-Voltage Release (Continuous Effect) [Electronics] (DNAB) .... LVR(CE)
Low-Voltage Release Effect [Electronics] (MSA) .... LVRE
Low-Voltage Tubular .... LVT
Low-Volume High-Velocity (IEEE) .... LVHV
Low-Volume Ramjet (MCD) .... LVR
Low-Volume Ramjet .... LVRJ
Low-Volume Ramjet Inlet System .... LVRIS
Low-Water Data [Marine science] (OSRA) .... LWD
Low-Water Data (USDC) .... LWD
Low-Water Datum .... LWD
Low-Water Interval .... LWI
Low-Water Ordinary Spring [Tides] .... LWOS
Low-Water Ordinary Spring Tides .... LWOST
Low-Water Quadrature .... LWQ
Low-Water Sensitivity [Brake fluid designation] .... LWS
Low-Water-Tolerant Brake Fluid [Automotive engineering] .... LWTF
Low-Wind Energy Conversion System (PDAA) .... LWECS
Low-Yield Fallout Trajectory (DNAB) .... LYFT
Low-Yield Test Ban Treaty .... LYTBT
LOX [Liquid Oxygen] Clean LC

Loxoseles reclusus - Phospholipase D [An enzyme] .... Lox-PLD
Loyal Christian Benefit Association [Erie, PA] (EA) .... LCBA
Loyal Edinburgh Volunteers [British military] (DMA) .... LEV
Loyal Escorts of the Green Garters (EA) .... LEGGS
Loyal, Free, Industrious Society of Wheelwrights and Blacksmiths [A union] [British] .... LFISWB
Loyal Independent Sheffield Volunteers [British military] (DMA) .... LISV
Loyal Knights of the Round Table (EA) .... LKRT
Loyal Legion of the Medal of Honor (EA) .... LLMH
Loyal London Volunteers [British military] (DMA) LLV
Loyal Lusitanian League [British military] (DMA) LLL
Loyal Orange Institution of United States of America (EA) .... LOIUSA
Loyal Orange Institution of Victoria [Australia] (EA) .... LOIV
Loyal Orange Ladies Institution (EA) .... LOLI
Loyal Orange Lodge .... LOL
Loyal Order of Ancient Shepherds [British] (BI) .... LOAS
Loyal Order of Catfish Lovers (EA) .... LOCL
Loyal Order of Moose (EA) .... LOM
Loyal Order of Moose (EA) .... LOOM
Loyal Order of the Boar (EA) .... LOB
Loyal Regiment [Military British] .... LR
Loyal Suffolk Hussars [British military] (DMA) .... LSH
Loyal Wheelwrights' and Blacksmiths' Society [A union] [British] .... LWBS
Loyalist Association of Workers [Trade union] [Northern Ireland] .... LAW
Loyalist College of Applied Arts and Technology, Belleville, ON, Canada [Library symbol Library of Congress] (LCLS) .... CaOBelL
Loyalist College of Applied Arts and Technology, Belleville, Ontario [Library symbol National Library of Canada] (NLC) .... OBEL
Loyalty L
Loyalty (AABC) .... LOY
Loyalty Review Board [Abolished, 1953] [Civil Service Commission] .... LRB
Loyengalani [Kenya] [ICAO location identifier] (ICLI) .... HKLY
Loyola Campus, Concordia University, Montreal, Quebec [Library symbol National Library of Canada] (NLC) .... QML
Loyola Capital [NASDAQ symbol] (SAG) .... LOYC
Loyola Capital Corp. [Associated Press] (SAG) .... Loyola
Loyola College (Maryland) (GAGS) .... Loyola C (Md)
Loyola Consumer Protection Journal [Los Angeles] [A publication] (DLA) .... Loy Con Prot J
Loyola Digest [A publication] (DLA) .... Loy Dig
Loyola Digest [A publication] (DLA) .... Loyola Dig
Loyola Law Journal [New Orleans] [1920-32] [A publication] (DLA) .... Loy LJ
Loyola Law Journal [A publication] (DLA) .... Loyola LJ
Loyola Lawyer [A publication] (DLA) .... Loy Law
Loyola Marymount University [Los Angeles, CA] .... LMU
Loyola Marymount University (Los Angeles) (GAGS) .... Loyola Marymount U
Loyola Marymount University, Los Angeles, CA [Library symbol Library of Congress] (LCLS) .... CLLoy
Loyola Marymount University, Orange Campus, Orange, CA [Library symbol Library of Congress] (LCLS) .... COrL
Loyola - Notre Dame Library, Inc., Baltimore, MD [OCLC symbol] (OCLC) .... LOY
Loyola - Notre Dame Library, Inc., Baltimore, MD [Library symbol Library of Congress] (LCLS) .... MdBLN
Loyola University, Career Information Center, New Orleans, LA [OCLC symbol] (OCLC) LLC
Loyola University, Chicago, IL [OCLC symbol] (OCLC) .... IAL
Loyola University, Chicago, IL [Library symbol Library of Congress] (LCLS) ICL
Loyola University, Dental School, Chicago, IL [Library symbol Library of Congress] (LCLS) .... ICL-D
Loyola University, Julia Deal Lewis Library, Chicago, IL [Library symbol Library of Congress] (LCLS) .... ICL-B
Loyola University, Law Library, Chicago, IL [Library symbol] [Library of Congress] (LCLS) .... ICL-L
Loyola University, Law Library, New Orleans, LA [OCLC symbol] (OCLC) .... LLT
Loyola University, Law Library, New Orleans, LA [Library symbol Library of Congress] (LCLS) .... LNL-L
Loyola University. Law Review [Chicago] [A publication] (DLA) .... Loyola Univ L Rev
Loyola University. Law Review (Chicago) [A publication] (DLA) .... Loyola ULJ (Chicago)
Loyola University (Louisiana) (GAGS) .... Loyola U (La)
Loyola University, New Orleans, LA [OCLC symbol] (OCLC) .... LLM
Loyola University, New Orleans, LA [Library symbol Library of Congress] (LCLS) .... LNL
Loyola University of Chicago (GAGS) .... Loyola U Chicago
Loyola University of Los Angeles [Later, Loyola Marymount University] .... LULA
Loyola University, Pharmacy Library, New Orleans, LA [Library symbol Library of Congress] (LCLS) .... LNL-Phar
Loyola University School of Law (DLA) .... LUSL
Loyola University, School of Medicine, Maywood, IL [Library symbol Library of Congress] (LCLS) .... ICL-M
Lozenge [Pharmacy] (DAVI) .... LOZ
L-Phenylalanin, Procarbazine, Adriamycin, Methotrexate [Antineoplastic drug regimen] (DAVI) .... L-PAM
L-Phenylalanine Mustard [Melphalan] [Also, A, M, MPH, MPL] [Antineoplastic drug] .... L-PAM
L-Phenylalanine Mustard, 5-Fluorouracil, Methotrexate [Antineoplastic drug regimen] (DAVI) .... PMF
L-Phenylalanine Mustard and 5-Fluorouracil [Antineoplastic drug regimen] (DAVI) .... PF
LRU [Line Replaceable Unit] Identification and Maintenance Requirements Catalog (NASA) .... LIMRC
LSB Bancshares, Inc. North Carolina [NASDAQ symbol] (SAG) .... LXBK
LSB Bancshares, Inc. of North Carolina [Associated Press] (SAG) .... LSB NC
LSB Bancshares(NC) [NASDAQ symbol] (TTSB) .... LXBK

LSB Financial [*NASDAQ symbol*] (TTSB) ... LSBI
LSB Financial Corp. [*Associated Press*] (SAG) ... LSB Fn
LSB Financial Corp. [*Associated Press*] (SAG) ... LSB Fncl
LSB Financial Corp. [*NASDAQ symbol*] (SAG) ... LSBI
LSB Ind $3.25 Cv Exch Pfd [*NYSE symbol*] (TTSB) ... LSBPrC
LSB Industries [*NYSE symbol*] (TTSB) ... LSB
LSB Industries, Inc. [*NYSE symbol*] (SAG) ... LSB
LSB Industries, Inc. [*Associated Press*] (SAG) ... LSB Ind
L-Serine-O-Phosphate [*Biochemistry*] ... LSOP
LSI Industries [*NASDAQ symbol*] (TTSB) ... LYTS
LSI Industries, Inc. [*Associated Press*] (SAG) ... LSI Ind
LSI Industries, Inc. [*Associated Press*] (SAG) ... LSI Inds
LSI Industries, Inc. [*NASDAQ symbol*] (SAG) ... LYTS
LSI Logic [*NYSE symbol*] (TTSB) ... LSI
LSI Logic Corp. [*NYSE symbol*] (SPSG) ... LSI
LSI Logic Corp. [*Associated Press*] (SAG) ... LSI Log
LSI Logic Corp. of Canada, Inc. [*Toronto Stock Exchange symbol*] ... LSC
LTC Properties [*NYSE symbol*] (TTSB) ... LTC
LTC Properties, Inc. [*NYSE symbol*] (SPSG) ... LTC
LTC Properties, Inc. [*Associated Press*] (SAG) ... LTC Prp
LTE International Airways SA [*Spain*] [*FAA designator*] (FAAC) ... LTE
LTU [*Lufttransport Unternehmen Sud*] **GmbH** [*Germany ICAO designator*] (FAAC) ... LTS
LTV Aerospace & Defense Co., Buffalo, NY [*Library symbol*] [*Library of Congress*] (LCLS) ... NBuLTV
LTV Corp. [*Formerly, Ling-Temco-Vought, Inc.*] [*NYSE symbol*] (SPSG) ... LTV
LTV Jet Fleet Corp. [*ICAO designator*] (FAAC) ... JFC
LTX Corp. [*Associated Press*] (SAG) ... LTX
LTX Corp. [*NASDAQ symbol*] (SAG) ... LTXX
L-Type Multiplex [*Telecommunications*] (TEL) ... LMX
Luampa [*Zambia*] [*ICAO location identifier*] (ICLI) ... FLLU
Luanda [*Angola*] [*ICAO location identifier*] (ICLI) ... FNAN
Luanda [*Angola*] [*Airport symbol*] (OAG) ... LAD
Luanda [*Angola*] [*Seismograph station code, US Geological Survey Closed*] (SEIS) ... LUA
Luanda/4 De Fevereiro [*Angola*] [*ICAO location identifier*] (ICLI) ... FNLU
Luanda Belas [*Angola*] [*Geomagnetic observatory code*] ... LUA
Luang Prabang [*Laos*] [*Airport symbol*] (AD) ... LPQ
Luang Prabang [*Laos*] [*ICAO location identifier*] (ICLI) ... VLLB
Luanshya [*Zambia*] [*ICAO location identifier*] (ICLI) ... FLLA
Luau [*Angola*] [*ICAO location identifier*] (ICLI) ... FNUA
Luba [*MARC language code Library of Congress*] (LCCP) ... lub
Lubang, Occidental Mindoro [*Philippines*] [*ICAO location identifier*] (ICLI) ... RPXG
Lubango [*Angola*] [*ICAO location identifier*] (ICLI) ... FNUB
Lubango [*Angola*] [*Airport symbol*] (OAG) ... SDD
Lubao [*Zaire*] [*ICAO location identifier*] (ICLI) ... FZWS
Lubavitch Women's Organization (EA) ... LWO
Lubavitch Youth Organization (EA) ... LYO
Lubbock [*Texas*] [*Airport symbol*] (OAG) ... LBB
Lubbock [*Texas*] [*Seismograph station code, US Geological Survey*] (SEIS) ... LUB
Lubbock Christian College, Lubbock, TX [*Library symbol Library of Congress*] (LCLS) ... TxLC
Lubbock City-County Libraries, Lubbock, TX [*Library symbol Library of Congress*] (LCLS) ... TxL
Lubbock/Reese Air Force Base [*Texas*] [*ICAO location identifier*] (ICLI) ... KREE
Lubbock/Regional [*Texas*] [*ICAO location identifier*] (ICLI) ... KLBB
Lubbock, TX [*Television station call letters*] ... KAMC
Lubbock, TX [*FM radio station call letters*] ... KAMY
Lubbock, TX [*AM radio station call letters*] (RBYB) ... KBZO
Lubbock, TX [*Television station call letters*] ... KCBD
Lubbock, TX [*FM radio station call letters*] ... KEJS
Lubbock, TX [*FM radio station call letters*] ... KFMX
Lubbock, TX [*AM radio station call letters*] ... KFYO
Lubbock, TX [*Television station call letters*] ... KJTV
Lubbock, TX [*AM radio station call letters*] ... KKAM
Lubbock, TX [*Television station call letters*] ... KLBK
Lubbock, TX [*AM radio station call letters*] ... KLFB
Lubbock, TX [*AM radio station call letters*] ... KLLL
Lubbock, TX [*FM radio station call letters*] ... KLLL-FM
Lubbock, TX [*FM radio station call letters*] ... KOHM
Lubbock, TX [*FM radio station call letters*] ... KONE
Lubbock, TX [*Television station call letters*] (RBYB) ... KPTB
Lubbock, TX [*AM radio station call letters*] (RBYB) ... KRFE
Lubbock, TX [*FM radio station call letters*] ... KRLB
Lubbock, TX [*FM radio station call letters*] ... KTXT
Lubbock, TX [*Television station call letters*] ... KTXT-TV
Lubbock, TX [*AM radio station call letters*] ... KXTQ
Lubbock, TX [*FM radio station call letters*] ... KXTQ-FM
Lubbock, TX [*FM radio station call letters*] ... KYFT
Lubbock, TX [*FM radio station call letters*] ... KZII
Lubbock, TX [*Location identifier FAA*] (FAAL) ... LBB
Lubbock, TX [*Location identifier FAA*] (FAAL) ... LDT
Lubbock, TX [*Location identifier FAA*] (FAAL) ... REE
Lubbock, TX [*Location identifier FAA*] (FAAL) ... RVO
Lube and Oil Filter ... LOF
Lube, Oil, and Filter [*Automobile servicing*] ... LOF
Lube Oil Fill, Transfer, and Purification System (DNAB) ... LOFTPS
Lube Oil Storage Tank (NRCH) ... LOST
Lube on Equity Pleading [*A publication*] (DLA) ... Lube Eq
Lube on Equity Pleading [*A publication*] (DLA) ... Lube PL
Lubero [*Zaire*] [*ICAO location identifier*] (ICLI) ... FZNF
Lubondaie [*Zaire*] [*ICAO location identifier*] (ICLI) ... FZUE
Lubrecht Forest [*Montana*] [*Seismograph station code, US Geological Survey Closed*] (SEIS) ... LFM
Lubricant (WDAA) ... LUB
Lubricant ... LUBR
Lubricant (MSA) ... LUBT
Lubricant, Arctic, Weapon [*Military*] (INF) ... LAW
Lubricant, Small Arms [*Weaponry*] [*Military*] (VNW) ... LSA
Lubricant Test Monitoring System [*Automotive engineering*] ... LTMS
Lubricate [*or Lubrication*] (AAG) ... LUB
Lubricate (ADA) ... LUBE
Lubricate (ADA) ... LUBR
Lubricating Oil ... LO
Lubricating Oil ... LUBO
Lubricating Oil Pump (MSA) ... LOP
Lubrication ... LUBEE
Lubrication Chart ... LC
Lubrication Instructions [*Marine Corps*] ... LI
Lubrication Order ... LO
Lubricity Index (IAA) ... LI
[*The*] **Lubrizol Corp.** [*Associated Press*] (SAG) ... Lubrizol
[*The*] **Lubrizol Corp.** [*NYSE symbol*] (SPSG) ... LZ
Lubudi [*Zaire*] [*ICAO location identifier*] (ICLI) ... FZQU
Lubudi [*Zaire*] [*Seismograph station code, US Geological Survey*] (SEIS) ... LBC
Lubumbashi [*Zaire*] [*Airport symbol*] (OAG) ... FBM
Lubumbashi/Karavia [*Zaire*] [*ICAO location identifier*] (ICLI) ... FZQO
Lubumbashi/Luano [*Zaire*] [*ICAO location identifier*] (ICLI) ... FZQA
Luby's Cafeterias [*NYSE symbol*] (TTSB) ... LUB
Luby's Cafeterias, Inc. [*NYSE symbol*] (SPSG) ... LUB
Luby's Cafeterias, Inc. [*Associated Press*] (SAG) ... Lubys
Lucan [*39-65AD*] [*Classical studies*] (OCD) ... Luc
Lucas Air Transport [*ICAO designator*] (AD) ... ZI
Lucas: an Evangelical History Review [*A publication*] (APTA) ... Luc
Lucas County Historical Society, Lucas, IA [*Library symbol Library of Congress*] (LCLS) ... IaLuHi
Lucas Industries Noise Centre [*Research center British*] (IRUK) ... LINC
Lucas' Reports [*Modern Reports, Part X*] [*A publication*] (DLA) ... Luc
Lucas' Reports [*Modern Reports, Part X*] [*A publication*] (DLA) ... Lucas
Lucas, William J., Albuquerque NM [*STAC*] ... LWJ
Lucas-Sargent Proposition [*Economics*] ... LSP
Lucas-Sumitomo Brakes [*Auto industry supplier*] ... LSB
Lucasvarity PLC [*Associated Press*] (SAG) ... LucasV
Lucasvarity PLC [*NYSE symbol*] (SAG) ... LVA
Luce Primo [*At Daybreak*] [*Pharmacy*] ... LUC PRIM
Lucedale, MS [*AM radio station call letters*] ... WRBE
Lucedale, MS [*FM radio station call letters*] ... WRBE-FM
Lucena, Quezon [*Philippines*] [*ICAO location identifier*] (ICLI) ... RPUE
Lucent Technologies [*NYSE symbol*] (TTSB) ... LU
Lucent Technologies, Inc. [*NYSE symbol*] (SAG) ... LU
Lucent Technologies, Inc. [*Associated Press*] (SAG) ... Lucent
Lucerne Australian Latent Virus [*Plant pathology*] ... LALV
Lucerne Enation Virus [*Plant pathology*] ... LUEV
Lucerne Transient Streak Virus [*Plant pathology*] ... LTSV
Lucerne Valley, CA [*FM radio station call letters*] ... KIXA
Lucero Resources Corp. [*Vancouver Stock Exchange symbol*] ... LCR
Lucey C. Laney High School, Augusta, GA [*Library symbol Library of Congress*] (LCLS) ... GAuL
Luchow/Rehbeck [*Germany ICAO location identifier*] (ICLI) ... EDHC
Luchtvaart Historische Vereniging [*Society of Aeronautical Historians*] [*Netherlands Defunct*] (EAIO) ... LHV
Luciano Pavarotti Appreciation Society [*British*] (DBA) ... LPAS
Lucifer (WDAA) ... LUC
Lucifer Yellow [*A dye*] [*Organic chemistry*] ... LY
Luciferase [*An enzyme*] ... LUC
Lucilius [*Second century BC*] [*Classical studies*] (OCD) ... Lucil
Lucille Farms [*NASDAQ symbol*] (TTSB) ... LUCY
Lucille Farms, Inc. [*Associated Press*] (SAG) ... Lucile
Lucille Farms, Inc. [*Associated Press*] (SAG) ... LucileFr
Lucille Farms, Inc. [*NASDAQ symbol*] (SAG) ... LUCY
Lucin, UT [*Location identifier FAA*] (FAAL) ... LCU
Lucis Trust (EA) ... LT
Lucke Tumor Herpesvirus ... LTHV
Lucknow [*India*] [*Airport symbol*] (OAG) ... LKO
Lucknow [*City in India*] (ROG) ... LUCKN
Lucknow [*India*] [*ICAO location identifier*] (ICLI) ... VILK
Lucknow Branch, Bruce County Public Library, Ontario [*Library symbol National Library of Canada*] (NLC) ... OLUC
Lucky ... LCKY
Lucky 7 Exploration [*Vancouver Stock Exchange symbol*] ... LKS
Lucky Break Gold [*Vancouver Stock Exchange symbol*] ... LBG
Lucky Mee Family Association (EA) ... LMFA
Lucky Strike Means Fine Tobacco [*Advertising slogan*] ... LS/MFT
Lucky Strike Resources [*Vancouver Stock Exchange symbol*] ... LKY
Luclle Farm Wrrt [*NASDAQ symbol*] (TTSB) ... LUCYW
Luc-Luong Dac-Viet [*Vietnamese special forces*] ... LLDV
Lucor, Inc. [*Associated Press*] (SAG) ... Lucor
Lucor, Inc. [*NASDAQ symbol*] (SAG) ... LUCR
Lucor Inc.'A' [*NASDAQ symbol*] (TTSB) ... LUCR
[*The Rape of*] **Lucrece** [*Shakespearean Work*] (BARN) ... Lucr
Lucretius [*Roman poet, 96-55BC*] [*Classical studies*] (ROG) ... LUCR
Lucullus [*of Plutarch*] [*Classical studies*] (OCD) ... Luc
Lucullus or Academica Posteriora [*of Cicero*] [*Classical studies*] (OCD) ... Luc
Ludao [*China*] [*ICAO location identifier*] (ICLI) ... RCGI
Ludden's Reports [*43, 44 Maine*] [*A publication*] (DLA) ... Ludd
Ludden's Reports [*43, 44 Maine*] [*A publication*] (DLA) ... Ludden
Luderitz [*Namibia*] [*ICAO location identifier*] (ICLI) ... FALZ
Luderitz [*South-West Africa*] [*Airport symbol*] (OAG) ... LUD
Luder's Election Cases [*England*] [*A publication*] (DLA) ... Lud EC
Luder's Election Cases [*England*] [*A publication*] (DLA) ... Lud El Cas

Luder's Election Cases [*England*] [*A publication*] (DLA) ... Luder Elec Cas
Luder's Election Cases [*England*] [*A publication*] (DLA) ... Luders Elec Cas (Eng)
Ludhaiha [*India*] [*ICAO location identifier*] (ICLI) ... VILD
Ludington & Northern Railway [*AAR code*] ... LUN
Ludington, MI [*Location identifier FAA*] (FAAL) ... LDM
Ludington, MI [*AM radio station call letters*] ... WKLA
Ludington, MI [*FM radio station call letters*] ... WKLA-FM
Ludington Public Library, Bryn Mawr, PA [*Library symbol Library of Congress*] (LCLS) ... PBmL
Ludington Public Library, Ludington, MI [*Library symbol Library of Congress*] (LCLS) ... MiLud
Ludlow and Jenkyns on the Law of Trade-Marks [*A publication*] (DLA) ... L & J Tr Mar
Ludlow and Jenkyns on Trade-Marks [*A publication*] (DLA) ... Lud & J Tr M
Ludlow Aviation, Inc. [*FAA designator*] (FAAC) ... PTQ
Ludlow Bone Bed Member [*England*] [*Geology*] ... LBBM
Ludlow, CA [*FM radio station call letters*] ... KDUQ
Ludlow, CA [*FM radio station call letters*] (RBYB) ... KHWZ-FM
Ludlum School, Hempstead, NY [*Library symbol*] [*Library of Congress*] (LCLS) ... NHemLE
Ludovicus Bologninus [*Deceased, 1508*] [*Authority cited in pre-1607 legal work*] (DSA) ... Lud Bolog
Ludovicus Bologninus [*Deceased, 1508*] [*Authority cited in pre-1607 legal work*] (DSA) ... Ludo Bolog
Ludovicus Gozzadini [*Deceased, 1536*] [*Authority cited in pre-1607 legal work*] (DSA) ... Lud Gozad
Ludovicus Pontanus de Roma [*Deceased, 1439*] [*Authority cited in pre-1607 legal work*] (DSA) ... Lud de Ro
Ludovicus Pontanus de Roma [*Deceased, 1439*] [*Authority cited in pre-1607 legal work*] (DSA) ... Ludo
Ludovicus Pontanus de Roma [*Deceased, 1439*] [*Authority cited in pre-1607 legal work*] (DSA) ... Ludo Ro
Ludvika [*Sweden ICAO location identifier*] (ICLI) ... ESSG
Ludwig Maxmilians Universitatsbibliothek Munchen, Munich, Federal Republic of Germany [*Library symbol Library of Congress*] (LCLS) ... GyMLM
Ludwig's Angina [*Medicine*] (DAVI) ... LA
Ludwigsburg [*Germany ICAO location identifier*] (ICLI) ... EDIR
Ludwigshafen-Unfallklinik [*Germany ICAO location identifier*] (ICLI) ... EDGL
Luebeck/Blankensee [*Germany ICAO location identifier*] (ICLI) ... EDHL
Luebo [*Zaire*] [*ICAO location identifier*] (ICLI) ... FZUN
Luena [*Angola*] [*ICAO location identifier*] (ICLI) ... FNUE
Luena [*Zaire*] [*ICAO location identifier*] (ICLI) ... FZTL
Luena [*Angola*] [*Airport symbol*] (OAG) ... LUO
Lues [*or Syphilis*] [*Medicine*] (DAVI) ... L
Lues [*Syphilis*] [*Latin*] (WDAA) ... LU
Lues Hereditaria [*Medicine*] ... LH
Lues I [*Primary syphilis*] [*Infectious diseases*] (DAVI) ... LI
Lues II [*or Secondary syphilis*] [*Infectious diseases*] (DAVI) ... LII
Lues III [*Teritiary syphilis*] [*Infectious diseases*] (DAVI) ... LIII
Lufkin/Angelina County [*Texas*] [*ICAO location identifier*] (ICLI) ... KLFK
Lufkin Industries [*NASDAQ symbol*] (TTSB) ... LUFK
Lufkin Industries, Inc. [*NASDAQ symbol*] (SAG) ... LUFK
Lufkin Industries, Inc. [*Associated Press*] (SAG) ... Lufkin
Lufkin/Nacogdoches [*Texas*] [*Airport symbol*] (OAG) ... LFK
Lufkin, TX [*FM radio station call letters*] ... KLDN
Lufkin, TX [*AM radio station call letters*] ... KRBA
Lufkin, TX [*FM radio station call letters*] ... KSWP
Lufkin, TX [*Television station call letters*] ... KTRE-TV
Lufkin, TX [*FM radio station call letters*] ... KUEZ
Lufkin, TX [*FM radio station call letters*] ... KYKS
Lufkin, TX [*Location identifier FAA*] (FAAL) ... LFK
Luftfahrzeug Service - Aircraft Service [*Austria ICAO designator*] (FAAC) ... LFS
Lufthansa (ABBR) ... LH
Lufthansa Cargo, AG [*Germany*] [*FAA designator*] (FAAC) ... GEC
Lufthansa Cityline [*Germany ICAO designator*] (FAAC) ... CLH
Lufthansa German Airlines [*ICAO designator*] (AD) ... LH
Luftmine [*Aerial mine*] [*German military - World War II*] ... LM
Luftnachrichten-Regiment [*Air forces signal regiment*] [*German military - World War II*] ... LNR
Luftschiff Zeppelin 1 ... LZ1
Luftschutzraum [*Air-Raid Shelter*] [*German military - World War II*] ... LSR
Lufttarhtgesellschaft Walter GmbH [*Germany ICAO designator*] (FAAC) ... LGW
Lufttransport Unternehmen GmbH [*Germany ICAO designator*] (FAAC) ... LTU
Lufttransport-Sud [*Airline*] [*Germany*] ... LTS
Luftuberlegenheits Flugzeug (Air Superiority) [*German*] (MCD) ... AS-FLUGZEUG
Luftwaffe (ABBR) ... LFTWF
Lug Terminal ... LT
Lugalbanda and Enmerkar (BJA) ... LE
Lugalbanda Epos (BJA) ... LE
Luganda [*MARC language code Library of Congress*] (LCCP) ... lug
Lugano [*Switzerland ICAO location identifier*] (ICLI) ... LSZA
Lugano [*Switzerland*] [*Airport symbol*] (OAG) ... LUG
Lugano Resources Ltd. [*Vancouver Stock Exchange symbol*] ... LUG
Luganville [*New Hebrides*] [*Seismograph station code, US Geological Survey*] (SEIS) ... LUG
Lugdunum [*Lyons*] [*Imprint*] (ROG) ... LUGD
Lugdunum Batavorum [*Leyden*] [*Imprint*] (ROG) ... LUG BAT
Luggage (ABBR) ... LGAG
Luggage ... LUG
Luggage ... LUGG
Luggage and Leather Goods Manufacturers of America (EA) ... LLGMA
Luggage and Leather Goods Salesmen's Association of America (EA) ... LLG
Luggage Compartment [*Automotive engineering*] ... L/COMPT
Lugger [*Ship's rigging*] (ROG) ... LR
Lugger [*Boat*] ... LUG
Lugh Ferrandi [*Somalia*] [*ICAO location identifier*] (ICLI) ... HCMJ
Lugo [*Spain ICAO location identifier*] (ICLI) ... LELU
Lugsail (ABBR) ... LGSL
Lugubrious (ABBR) ... LGBRU
Lugubriously (ABBR) ... LGBRUY
Luheki [*Zaire*] [*ICAO location identifier*] (ICLI) ... FZAX
Luis Palau Evangelistic Association (EA) ... LPEA
Luisa [*Zaire*] [*ICAO location identifier*] (ICLI) ... FZUG
Luiseno [*MARC language code Library of Congress*] (LCCP) ... lui
Luishi [*Zaire*] [*ICAO location identifier*] (ICLI) ... FZQW
Luitingh [*Holland*] ... L
Luiz Munoz Marin International Airport [*FAA*] (TAG) ... SJU
Lukala [*Zaire*] [*ICAO location identifier*] (ICLI) ... FZAP
Luke [*New Testament book*] ... Lk
Lukens, Inc. [*NYSE symbol*] (SPSG) ... LUC
Lukens, Inc. [*Associated Press*] (SAG) ... Lukens
Lukens Med [*NASDAQ symbol*] (TTSB) ... LUKN
Lukens Medical Corp. [*Associated Press*] (SAG) ... LukMed
Lukens Medical Corp. [*NASDAQ symbol*] (SAG) ... LUKN
Lukens Steel Co., Coatesville, PA [*Library symbol Library of Congress Obsolete*] (LCLS) ... PCtvL
Lukla [*Nepal*] [*Airport symbol*] (OAG) ... LUA
Lukla [*Nepal*] [*ICAO location identifier*] (ICLI) ... VNLK
Lukombe-Batwa [*Zaire*] [*ICAO location identifier*] (ICLI) ... FZVK
Lukulu [*Zambia*] [*ICAO location identifier*] (ICLI) ... FLLK
Lukulu [*Zambia*] [*Airport symbol*] (AD) ... LXU
Lukuni [*Zaire*] [*ICAO location identifier*] (ICLI) ... FZDC
Lukuzi [*Zambia*] [*ICAO location identifier*] (ICLI) ... FLKZ
LULAC [*League of United Latin American Citizens*] **National Educational Service Centers** (EA) ... LNESC
Lulea [*Sweden*] [*Airport symbol*] (OAG) ... LLA
Lulea/Kallax [*Sweden ICAO location identifier*] (ICLI) ... ESPA
Luling, TX [*FM radio station call letters*] (RBYB) ... KAMX
Lulingu-Tshioka [*Zaire*] [*ICAO location identifier*] (ICLI) ... FZOG
Lulov, Esrog, Arrovos, Hadassim (BJA) ... LEAH
Luluabourg [*Zaire*] [*Airport symbol*] (AD) ... LLB
Luma Chroma Chroma [*Photo CD channels*] (PCM) ... YCC
Lumbago (WDAA) ... LUM
Lumbar [*Medicine*] ... L
Lumbar [*Anatomy*] (DAVI) ... Lu
Lumbar [*Medicine*] (WDAA) ... LUM
Lumbar [*Medicine*] (MAE) ... lumb
Lumbar Back Pain [*Medicine*] (DMAA) ... LBP
Lumbar Back Strain [*Medicine*] (DMAA) ... LBS
Lumbar Laminectomy [*Medicine*] (DAVI) ... Llam
Lumbar Length [*Anatomy*] (DAVI) ... LL
Lumbar Motion Monitor [*Ergonometrics*] ... LMM
Lumbar Puncture [*Medicine*] ... LMP
Lumbar Puncture [*Medicine*] ... LP
Lumbar Spine [*Medicine*] (DMAA) ... LS
Lumbar Spine [*Medicine*] (DHSM) ... LSP
Lumbar Spine Index [*Medicine*] (DMAA) ... LSI
Lumbar Traction [*Orthopedics*] (DAVI) ... LT
Lumbar Vertebra [*Medicine*] ... LV
Lumbar-Peritoneal [*Shunt*] (DAVI) ... LP
Lumber (KSC) ... LBR
Lumber ... LMBR
Lumber (WDAA) ... LUM
Lumber Dealers Research Council [*Defunct*] (EA) ... LDRC
Lumber Recovery Factor ... LRF
Lumber Transfer and Distribution ... LTD
Lumber [*Timber*], Winter, North Atlantic [*Vessel load line mark*] ... LWNA
Lumbermen's Association of Texas (SRA) ... LAT
Lumberton, MS [*FM radio station call letters*] ... WLUN
Lumberton, NC [*Location identifier FAA*] (FAAL) ... LBT
Lumberton, NC [*Location identifier FAA*] (FAAL) ... RSY
Lumberton, NC [*AM radio station call letters*] ... WAGR
Lumberton, NC [*FM radio station call letters*] ... WJSK
Lumberton, NC [*FM radio station call letters*] ... WKML
Lumberton, NC [*AM radio station call letters*] ... WTSB
Lumberton, NC [*Television station call letters*] (RBYB) ... WUNU
Lumbo [*Mozambique*] [*ICAO location identifier*] (ICLI) ... FQLU
Lumbosacral [*Medicine*] ... LS
Lumbosacral Orthosis [*Medicine*] ... LSO
Lumbosacral Spine [*Medicine*] (MEDA) ... LSS
Lumbosacroiliac Orthosis [*Medicine*] ... LSIO
Lumen [*Unit of luminous flux*] ... L
Lumen (IDOE) ... l
Lumen [*Anatomy*] (DAVI) ... L
Lumen (IDOE) ... lm
Lumen [*Symbol*] [*SI unit of luminous flux*] ... LM
Lumen [*Anatomy*] ... Lu
Lumen [*Record label*] [*France*] ... Lum
Lumen and Glare Calculations [*Facet Ltd.*] [*Software package*] (NCC) ... LUGL
Lumen Gentium [*Dogmatic Constitution on the Church*] [*Vatican II document*] ... LG
Lumen Hour (ADA) ... LHR
Lumen Hour (IAA) ... LMH
Lumen Hour (IAA) ... LMHR
Lumen Hour ... LUH
Lumen per Square Foot (WDAA) ... LM/FT^2
Lumen per Square Foot (IAA) ... LMSQFT
Lumen per Square Meter (WDAA) ... LM/M^2
Lumen Second (IAA) ... LMSEC
Lumen-Hour (IDOE) ... lm-hr
Lumens per Second (MCD) ... LM/S

Lumens per Square Centimeter .... LM/CM²
Lumens per Square Foot (WDAA) .... L/FT²
Lumens per Square Foot (IDOE) .... lm/ft²
Lumens per Square Meter (IDOE) .... lm/m²
Lumens per Watt (IDOE) .... l/W
Lumens per Watt .... lm/W
Lumens per Watt (CET) .... lp/W
Lumens per Watt (ADA) .... LW
Lumex, Inc. [AMEX symbol] (SPSG) .... LUM
Lumex, Inc. [Associated Press] (SAG) .... Lumex
Lumi [Papua New Guinea] [Airport symbol] (OAG) .... LMI
Lumid Pau [Guyana] [ICAO location identifier] (ICLI) .... SYLP
Luminaire Dirt Depreciation [Floodlighting] L
Luminance (DMAA) .... Y
Luminance .... Y/C
Luminance, Color .... Y/C
Luminescence and Fluorescence Immunoassay [Clinical chemistry] .... LFIA
Luminescence Detector (SSD) .... LD
Luminescence Digital Imaging Microscopy .... LDIM
Luminescence Diode (IAA) .... LD
Luminescence Enzyme Immunoassay [Clinical chemistry] .... LEIA
Luminescence Immunoassay [Clinical chemistry] .... LIA
Luminescences Emission Monitor .... LEM
Luminescent Pigment Tattooing .... LPT
Luminescent Solar Concentrator .... LSC
Luminescent Stamp Club [Defunct] (EA) .... LSC
Luminometer Number [Hydrocarbon fuel rating] .... LN
Luminosity (WDMC) .... US
Luminosity Class [Astronomy] (IAA) LC
Luminosity to Mass [Ratio] [Astronomy] .... L/M
Luminous (MSA) .... LUM
Luminous Blue Variables [Astronomy] .... LBV
Luminous Efficiency [Physics] (BARN) .... K
Luminous Flux [Physics] .... F
Luminous Intensity [Symbol] [IUPAC] I
Luminous Wall Firing (DICI) .... LWF
Lumisys, Inc. [NASDAQ symbol] (SAG) .... LUMI
Lumisys, Inc. [Associated Press] (SAG) .... Lumisys
Lumley on Bastardy [A publication] (DLA) .... Lum Bast
Lumley on Bye-Laws [A publication] (DLA) .... Lum BL
Lumley on the Law of Annuities [A publication] (DLA) .... Lum Ann
Lumley on the Law of Settlements [A publication] (DLA) .... Lum Sett
Lumley's Parliamentary Practice [A publication] (DLA) .... Lum Parl Pr
Lumley's Poor Law Cases [1834-42] [A publication] (DLA) .... Lum PL Cas
Lumley's Poor Law Cases [1834-42] [A publication] (DLA) .... Lum PLC
Lumley's Poor Law Cases [1834-42] [A publication] (DLA) .... Lumley PLC
Lumley's Public Health Acts [12th ed.] [1950-55 and supplements] [A publication] (DLA) .... Lum Pub H
Lummer-Brodhun Cube [Physics] .... LBC
Lummer-Gehreke Plate [Physics] .... LGP
Lummus Co. Canada Ltd., Willowdale, ON, Canada [Library symbol Library of Congress] (LCLS) .... CaOTLCC
Lummus Co. Canada Ltd., Willowdale, Ontario [Library symbol National Library of Canada] (NLC) .... OTLCC
Lummus Crest, Inc. [Telecommunications service] (TSSD) LCI
Lumonics, Inc. [Toronto Stock Exchange symbol] .... LUM
Lumonics, Inc., Kanata, ON, Canada [Library symbol] [Library of Congress] (LCLS) .... CaOKanLU
Lumonics, Inc., Kanata, Ontario [Library symbol National Library of Canada] (NLC) .... OKLU
Lump Sum .... LS
Lumped Burnable Poison Rod [Assembly] [Nuclear energy] (NRCH) .... LBPR
Lumped Constant Dispersion .... LCD
Lumped Element Circulator .... LEC
Lumped Element Hybrid Microwave Integrated Circuit [Electronics] (LAIN) .... LEHMIC
Lumped, Linear, Parametric Network .... LLPN
Lumped Selection Filter [Telecommunications] (OA) .... LSF
Lumped Shell Analysis Method .... LSAM
Lumped-Parameter Calorimeter [Heat measure] .... LPC
Lumpkin, GA [FM radio station call letters] .... WKCN
Lumpkin's Reports [59-77 Georgia] [A publication] (DLA) .... Lumpkin
Lump-Sum Contract .... LSC
Lump-Sum Death Payment .... LSDP
Lump-Sum Distribution [Banking] .... LSD
Lump-Sum Leave Payment [Military] (DNAB) .... LSL
Lump-Sum Leave Payment [Air Force] (AFM) .... LSLP
Lump-Sum Leave Payment, Basic Pay [Military] (DNAB) .... LSLBP
Lump-Sum Leave Payment, Personal Money Allowance [Military] (DNAB) .... LSL PMA
Lump-Sum Leave Payment, Quarters [Military] (DNAB) .... LSL QTRS
Lump-Sum Leave Payment, Subsistence [Military] (DNAB) .... LSL SUBS
Lump-Sum Payment to Air Force Reserve Officers .... LSPAFRO
Lump-Sum Wage Payments (MCD) .... LSWP
Lumsden Public Library, Lumsden, NF, Canada [Library symbol Library of Congress] (LCLS) .... CaNfLu
Lumsden Public Library, Newfoundland [Library symbol National Library of Canada] (NLC) .... NFLU
Lunacharskoye [Former USSR Seismograph station code, US Geological Survey Closed] (SEIS) .... LNC
Lunacy [FBI standardized term] .... LNCY
Lunar (KSC) .... LUN
Lunar Aeronautical Chart [Air Force] .... LAC
Lunar Analysis and Mapping Program [NASA] (IAA) .... LAMP
Lunar and Interplanetary Vehicle [Aerospace] (AFM) LIV

Lunar and Planetary [Aerospace] (IAA) .... LP
Lunar and Planetary Bibliography [Lunar and Planetary Institute] [Information service or system] (IID) .... LPB
Lunar and Planetary Ephemerides Assembly [Space Flight Operations Facility, NASA] .... LPE
Lunar and Planetary Horizon Scanner [Aerospace] .... LPHS
Lunar and Planetary Institute [University Space Research Association] [Research center] (RCD) .... LPI
Lunar and Planetary Institute Bibliographic Search Service [University Space Research Association] [Information service or system] (IID) .... LPIBSS
Lunar and Planetary Laboratory [University of Arizona] [Research center] (MCD) .... LPL
Lunar and Planetary Program .... L & PP
Lunar and Planetary Working Group [Aerospace] (IAA) .... LPWG
Lunar Applications of a Spent Stage [Aerospace] (MCD) .... LASS
Lunar Applications of a Spent Stage in Orbit [Aerospace] (MCD) .... LASSO
Lunar Atlas Chart [Aerospace] (SAA) .... LAC
Lunar Atmosphere Detector [Aerospace] .... LAD
Lunar Atmospheric Composition Experiment [Apollo] [NASA] .... LACE
Lunar Attitude System [Aerospace] .... LAS
Lunar Breaking Module [NASA] (IAA) .... LBM
Lunar Communication [System] [Aerospace] .... LUCOM
Lunar Communications Relay Unit [Apollo] [NASA] .... LCRU
Lunar Corp. [Associated Press] (SAG) .... Lunar
Lunar Corp. [NASDAQ symbol] (SAG) .... LUNR
Lunar Cycle Test One [Aerospace] LCT-1
Lunar Day (KSC) .... LD
Lunar Deep Seismic Sounding [Aerospace] (MCD) .... LDSS
Lunar Distance Measuring System [Aerospace] .... LDMS
Lunar Docking [NASA] (IAA) .... LD
Lunar Docking Events Controller [NASA] (MCD) .... LDEC
Lunar Drill [NASA] (KSC) .... LD
Lunar Drill System [NASA] .... LDS
Lunar Dust and Earth Return [NASA] (IAA) .... LUSTER
Lunar Dust Detector [NASA] .... LDD
Lunar Ejecta and Meteorites [Experiment] [NASA] .... LEAM
Lunar Ephemeris .... LE
Lunar Equatorial Zone [Army Map Service] .... LEZ
Lunar Equipment Conveyor [Aerospace] .... LEC
Lunar Escape Ambulance Pack [Aerospace] .... LEAP
Lunar Escape System [Aerospace] .... LES
Lunar Escape System Simulator [NASA] .... LESS
Lunar Escape Vehicle (IAA) .... LEV
Lunar Excursion Module [Later, LM] [NASA] .... LEM
Lunar Excursion Module Descent Engine [NASA] (MCD) .... LEMDE
Lunar Excursion Module Test Vehicle [NASA] (IAA) .... LTV
Lunar Excursion Module Track [NASA] (IAA) .... LEMT
Lunar Excursion Vehicle [Aerospace] .... LEV
Lunar Experiment Telemetry System [Aerospace] .... LETS
Lunar Exploration Module [NASA] (IAA) .... LEM
Lunar Exploration Office [NASA] .... LEO
Lunar Exploration Science Working Group [NASA] .... LEXSWG
Lunar Exploration System for Apollo [NASA] .... LESA
Lunar Extravehicular Visor Assembly [NASA] (KSC) .... LEVVA
Lunar Facsimile Capsule [NASA] (KSC) .... LFC
Lunar Far Horizon (KSC) .... LFH
Lunar Farside Chart [Air Force] .... LFC
Lunar Flying Unit [NASA] .... LFU
Lunar Flying Vehicle [NASA] .... LFV
Lunar Gas Chromatograph .... LGC
Lunar Geological Camera [NASA] (KSC) .... LGC
Lunar Geological Equipment [NASA] .... LGE
Lunar Geological Exploration Camera (PDAA) .... LGEC
Lunar Geology Investigation [NASA] .... LGI
Lunar Geophysical Surface .... LGS
Lunar Geoscience Observer (MCD) .... LGO
Lunar Gravity Simulator [Aerospace] .... LGS
Lunar Gravity Simulator [Aerospace] (MCD) .... LUNARG
Lunar Hand Tool [NASA] .... LHT
Lunar Horizon Sensor [Aerospace] .... LHS
Lunar Impact Probe [Aerospace] .... LIP
Lunar Impact Vehicle [NASA] (KSC) .... LIVE
Lunar Instrument Carrier [NASA] (KSC) LIC
Lunar International Laboratory LIL
Lunar International Observer Network [NASA] .... LION
Lunar Interplanetary Monitoring Probe (IAA) .... LIMP
Lunar Ionosphere Detector (PDAA) .... LID
Lunar Landing [NASA] (KSC) LL
Lunar Landing Mission [NASA] .... LLM
Lunar Landing Module [NASA] (MCD) .... LLM
Lunar Landing Program [NASA] .... LLP
Lunar Landing Research Facility [Aerospace] .... LLRF
Lunar Landing Research Vehicle [Aerospace] .... LLRV
Lunar Landing Simulator [Aerospace] (AAG) .... LLS
Lunar Landing Training Vehicle [Aerospace] .... LLTV
Lunar Landing Vehicle [NASA] LLV
Lunar LASER Range-Finder [Aerospace] .... LLRF
Lunar LASER Ranging [Aerospace] .... LLR
Lunar Logistics Supply Vehicle [NASA] (IAA) .... LLSV
Lunar Logistics System [NASA] .... LLS
Lunar Logistics System [NASA] .... LULS
Lunar Logistics System Vehicle [NASA] .... LLSV
Lunar Logistics Vehicle [NASA] LLV
Lunar Mapping and Survey System [NASA] (MCD) .... LMSS
Lunar Mapping System [Aerospace] .... LUMAS

Lunar Mass Spectrometer [*NASA*] ... LMS
Lunar Measuring System [*Aerospace*] ... LMS
Lunar Meteoroid Analyzer [*NASA*] ... LMA
Lunar Meteoroid Detector [*NASA*] ... LMD
Lunar Meteoroid Detector-Analyzer [*NASA*] ... LMDA
Lunar Mission ... LM
Lunar Module [*Formerly, LEM*] [*NASA*] ... LM
Lunar Module Adapter [*NASA*] (MCD) ... LMA
Lunar Module Apollo Telescope Mount [*NASA*] (MCD) ... LM/ATM
Lunar Module Ascent Engine [*NASA*] ... LMAE
Lunar Module Descent Engine [*NASA*] ... LMDE
Lunar Module Engine [*NASA*] ... LME
Lunar Module Guidance Computer [*NASA*] (KSC) ... LMGC
Lunar Module/Lunar Roving Vehicle [*NASA*] ... LM/LRV
Lunar Module Pilot [*Apollo*] [*NASA*] ... LMP
Lunar Module Procedures Simulator [*NASA*] ... LMPS
Lunar Module Rendezvous RADAR [*NASA*] ... LMRR
Lunar Module Rendezvous Simulator [*NASA*] (IAA) ... LMRS
Lunar Module Replaceable Assembly [*NASA*] (IAA) ... LRAS
Lunar Module Replaceable Package [*NASA*] (KSC) ... LMRP
Lunar Module Simulator [*NASA*] (SSD) ... LMS
Lunar Near Horizon [*NASA*] (KSC) ... LNH
Lunar Neutron Probe [*NASA*] (KSC) ... LNP
Lunar Optical-UVIR [*Ultraviolet Infrared*] **Synthesis Array** [*NASA*] ... LOUISA
Lunar Orbit and Landing Approach [*Simulator*] [*NASA*] ... LOLA
Lunar Orbit Insertion [*NASA*] ... LOI
Lunar Orbit Plane [*NASA*] (IAA) ... LOP
Lunar Orbit Plane Change [*NASA*] ... LOPC
Lunar Orbit [*or Orbital*] **Rendezvous** [*NASA*] ... LOR
Lunar Orbit Space Station [*NASA*] ... LOSS
Lunar Orbital Map [*Air Force*] ... LOM
Lunar Orbital Mission [*NASA*] (KSC) ... LOM
Lunar Orbital Photocraft [*NASA*] (IAA) ... LOPC
Lunar Orbital Survey System [*NASA*] (KSC) ... LOSS
Lunar Orbiter [*Aerospace*] (MCD) ... LO
Lunar Orbiter Data Conversion System [*Aerospace*] ... LODCS
Lunar Orbiter Data Printer [*Aerospace*] ... LODP
Lunar Orbiter Photographic Project [*Aerospace*] ... LOPP
Lunar Orbiting Photographic System [*Aerospace*] ... LOPS
Lunar Orbiting Reconnaissance System [*Aerospace*] ... LORS
Lunar Orbiting Satellite [*or Spacecraft*] [*Aerospace*] (MCD) ... LOS
Lunar Orbiting Vehicle for Emergency Rescue (PDAA) ... LOVER
Lunar Parking Orbit [*Apollo*] [*NASA*] ... LPO
Lunar Payload Module [*Aerospace*] (MCD) ... LPM
Lunar Penetrometer System [*Aerospace*] ... LPS
Lunar Pilotage System [*Aerospace*] ... LPS
Lunar Polar Orbiter [*NASA*] ... LPO
Lunar Portable Magnetometer [*Apollo*] [*NASA*] ... LPM
Lunar Precepts Positioner [*Aerospace*] ... LPP
Lunar Program Office [*NASA*] (IAA) ... LPO
Lunar Projects Laboratory ... LPL
Lunar Pyrotechnic Control Assembly [*Aerospace*] ... LPCA
Lunar Ranging Experiment [*Aerospace*] ... LURE
Lunar Receiving Laboratory [*NASA*] ... LRL
Lunar Reconnaissance [*or Rendezvous*] **Mission** [*Aerospace*] ... LRM
Lunar Reconnaissance Module [*Aerospace*] ... LRM
Lunar Research Laboratory [*NASA*] (DAVI) ... LRL
Lunar Resources Ltd. [*Vancouver Stock Exchange symbol*] ... LNA
Lunar Retrograde Engine [*NASA*] (KSC) ... LRE
Lunar Rover [*or Roving*] **Vehicle** [*NASA*] ... LRV
Lunar Sample Analysis Planning Team [*NASA*] ... LSAPT
Lunar Sample Preliminary Examination Team [*NASA*] ... LSPET
Lunar Satellite Tracking Data [*NASA*] (KSC) ... LSTD
Lunar Science Institute [*Houston*] ... LSI
Lunar Science Institute, Houston, TX [*Library symbol Library of Congress*] (LCLS) ... TxHLS
Lunar Science Natural Language Information System (PDAA) ... LSNLIS
Lunar Scientific Facility [*NASA*] (KSC) ... LSF
Lunar Seismic Profiling Experiment [*NASA*] ... LSPE
Lunar Shuttle Vehicle [*Aerospace*] (AAG) ... LSV
Lunar Soil Stimulant [*NASA*] (KSC) ... LSS
Lunar Space Tug (PDAA) ... LSSTA
Lunar Spectral Photometrics [*Aerospace*] ... LSP
Lunar Support Equipment [*Aerospace*] (IAA) ... LSE
Lunar Surface (KSC) ... LS
Lunar Surface (PDAA) ... LUSURF
Lunar Surface Base [*NASA*] (KSC) ... LSB
Lunar Surface Data Acquisition Camera [*Aerospace*] ... LDAC
Lunar Surface Drill [*Aerospace*] ... LSD
Lunar Surface Experiment [*NASA*] ... LSE
Lunar Surface Experiment Package [*NASA*] ... LSEP
Lunar Surface Exploration Vehicle [*Aerospace*] ... LSEV
Lunar Surface Explorer Simulation Program [*Aerospace*] (MCD) ... LUSEX
Lunar Surface Gravimeter [*Apollo*] [*NASA*] ... LSG
Lunar Surface Inspection [*Aerospace*] ... LUSI
Lunar Surface Instrument [*Aerospace*] ... LSI
Lunar Surface Magnetometer [*NASA*] ... LSM
Lunar Surface Operations Planning [*NASA*] (KSC) ... LSOP
Lunar Surface Probe [*Aerospace*] ... LSP
Lunar Surface Project Office [*NASA*] (KSC) ... LSPO
Lunar Surface Rendezvous [*NASA*] (KSC) ... LSR
Lunar Surface Return Container [*NASA*] (KSC) ... LSRC
Lunar Surface Roving Vehicle [*Aerospace*] ... LSRV
Lunar Surface Sampling Device [*Aerospace*] ... LSSD
Lunar Surface Scientific Module [*NASA*] ... LSSM
Lunar Surface Telescope [*NASA*] ... LST
Lunar Surface Thermal Simulator [*NASA*] (KSC) ... LSTS
Lunar Surface Transponder [*Aerospace*] ... LST
Lunar Surface Ultraviolet [*Camera*] [*NASA*] ... LSUV
Lunar Surface Vehicle [*Aerospace*] ... LSV
Lunar Surface Vehicle Communications [*Aerospace*] ... LSVC
Lunar Survey Probe [*NASA*] (IAA) ... LSP
Lunar Survey Probe Delivery System [*NASA*] (SAA) ... LSPDS
Lunar Survey Sensor [*NASA*] (KSC) ... LSS
Lunar Survey Viewfinder [*Aerospace*] ... LSV
Lunar Surveying System [*Aerospace*] ... LSS
Lunar Surveying System Program [*Aerospace*] ... LSSP
Lunar Tele-Operations Model 1 [*Mooncolony modeling*] ... LTM1
Lunar Terrain [*or Topographic*] **Camera** [*NASA*] ... LTC
Lunar Terrain Measuring System [*Aerospace*] ... LTMS
Lunar Terrestrial Age ... LTERR
Lunar Test Table [*Aerospace*] ... LTT
Lunar Tidal Perturbation ... LTP
Lunar Touchdown System [*NASA*] (IAA) ... LTS
Lunar Trajectory Injection Vehicle [*NASA*] (KSC) ... LTIV
Lunar Traverse Gravimeter [*Experiment*] [*NASA*] ... LTG
Lunar Ultraviolet Observatory [*NASA*] ... LUVO
Lunar-Anchored Interplanetary Monitoring Platform [*Aerospace*] (MCD) ... LAIMP
Lunar-Anchored Interplanetary Monitoring Platform [*Aerospace*] ... LIMP
Lunar-Environment Construction and Operations Simulator [*NASA*] (IAA) ... LECOS
Lunar-Environment Sample Container [*Apollo*] [*NASA*] ... LESC
Lunch (CDAI) ... L
Lunch ... Lch
Lunch Break ... LB
Luncheon Voucher [*British*] ... LV
Lund [*Sweden ICAO location identifier*] (ICLI) ... ESMN
Lund [*Sweden*] [*Seismograph station code, US Geological Survey Closed*] (SEIS) ... LUN
Lund International [*NASDAQ symbol*] (TTSB) ... LUND
Lund International Holdings, Inc. [*NASDAQ symbol*] (SAG) ... LUND
Lund International Holdings, Inc. [*Associated Press*] (SAG) ... LundInt
Lund on Patents [*A publication*] (DLA) ... Lund Pat
Lundazi [*Zambia*] [*ICAO location identifier*] (ICLI) ... FLLD
Lundin Explorations [*Vancouver Stock Exchange symbol*] ... LUD
Lunds Universitet [*University of Lund*], Lund, Sweden [*Library symbol Library of Congress*] (LCLS) ... SwLU
Lundy Collectors Club (EA) ... LCC
Luneberg Lens Commutator [*Physics*] ... LLC
Luneberg Lens Rapid Commutator [*Physics*] ... LLRC
Luneberg Rapid Commutator [*Physics*] ... LRC
Luneburg [*Germany ICAO location identifier*] (ICLI) ... EDHG
Lunenburg Heritage Society, Lunenburg, NS, Canada [*Library symbol*] [*Library of Congress*] (LCLS) ... CaNSLuHS
Lunenburg Heritage Society, Nova Scotia [*Library symbol National Library of Canada*] (NLC) ... NSLHS
Lunette ... LUN
Lunette (VRA) ... lun
Luneville/Croismare [*France ICAO location identifier*] (ICLI) ... LFQC
Lung [*Anatomy*] (DAVI) ... L
Lung Basement Membrane [*Medicine*] (DMAA) ... LBM
Lung Configuration Recorder ... LCR
Lung Damaging Particle ... LDP
Lung Hageman Factor Activator [*Medicine*] (DMAA) ... LHFA
Lung Rate Counter ... LRC
Lung Serum Simulant (PDAA) ... LSS
Lung Sounds [*Medicine*] ... LS
Lung Volume (MAE) ... LV
Lung Water ... LW
Lung-Body Weight Ratio [*Medicine*] (MAE) ... LBWR
Lung-Imaging Fluorescent Endoscope [*Medicine*] (ECON) ... LIFE
Luning [*Nevada*] [*Seismograph station code, US Geological Survey Closed*] (SEIS) ... LNG
L'Union Territoriale des Syndicats Professionelles Caledoniens [*Territorial Federation of New Caledonian Unions of Private Employees*] ... LTSPC
Lunn Industries [*NASDAQ symbol*] (SAG) ... LUNN
Lunn Industries, Inc. [*Associated Press*] (SAG) ... LunnI
Lunping [*Taiwan*] [*Geomagnetic observatory code*] ... LNP
Luogo [*As Written*] [*Music*] ... LUO
Luong Nam Tha [*Laos*] [*ICAO location identifier*] (ICLI) ... VLLN
Luong Namtha [*Laos*] [*Airport symbol*] (AD) ... LXG
Luozi [*Zaire*] [*ICAO location identifier*] (ICLI) ... FZAL
Lupenga Air Charters [*Zambia*] [*ICAO designator*] (FAAC) ... LUP
Lupin, NT [*ICAO location identifier*] (ICLI) ... CYWO
Lupron, Vinblastine, Adriamycin, Mutamycin [*Antineoplastic drug*] (CDI) ... L-VAM
Lupulus [*Hops*] [*Pharmacy*] (ROG) ... LUPUL
Lupus [*Constellation*] ... Lup
Lupus [*Constellation*] ... Lupi
Lupus Anticoagulant [*Immunochemistry*] ... LAC
Lupus Association of New South Wales [*Australia*] ... LANSW
Lupus Erythematosus [*Hematology*] ... LE
Lupus Erythematosus Anonymous (EA) ... LEANON
Lupus Erythematosus Disseminatus [*Medicine*] ... LED
Lupus Erythematosus Factor [*Medicine*] (DMAA) ... LEF
Lupus Erythematosus Preparation [*Hematology*] (CPH) ... LE Prep
Lupus Erythematosus Preparation [*Hematology*] (DAVI) ... LEP
Lupus Erythematosus, Systemic [*Medicine*] (MAE) ... LES
Lupus Foundation of America (EA) ... LFA
Lupus Network (EA) ... LN
Lupus-Type Inclusions [*Medicine*] (DMAA) ... LTI

Luray, VA [*Location identifier FAA*] (FAAL) ... LUA
Luray, VA [*FM radio station call letters*] ... WLCC
Luray, VA [*AM radio station call letters*] ... WRAA
Luray, VA [*FM radio station call letters*] ... WYFT
Lure/Malbouhans [*France ICAO location identifier*] (ICLI) ... LFYL
Luria [*L.*] **& Sons, Inc.** [*NYSE symbol*] (SAG) ... LUR
Luria [*L.*] **& Sons, Inc.** [*Associated Press*] (SAG) ... Luria
Luria Broth [*For cultivation of cells*] ... LB
Luria (L)& Son [*NYSE symbol*] (TTSB) ... LUR
Luria-Nebraska Neuropsychological Battery ... LNNB
Lusaka [*Zambia*] [*ICAO location identifier*] (ICLI) ... FLFI
Lusaka [*Zambia*] [*ICAO location identifier*] (ICLI) ... FLHQ
Lusaka [*Zambia*] [*ICAO location identifier*] (ICLI) ... FLLC
Lusaka [*Zambia*] [*Airport symbol*] (OAG) ... LUN
Lusaka [*Zambia*] [*Seismograph station code, US Geological Survey*] (SEIS) ... LUS
Lusaka/International [*Zambia*] [*ICAO location identifier*] (ICLI) ... FLLS
Lusambo [*Zaire*] [*ICAO location identifier*] (ICLI) ... FZVI
Lusanga [*Zaire*] [*ICAO location identifier*] (ICLI) ... FZCE
Luscar Ltd., Edmonton, AB, Canada [*Library symbol*] [*Library of Congress*] (LCLS) ... CaAEL
Luscar Ltd., Edmonton, Alberta [*Library symbol National Library of Canada*] (NLC) ... AEL
Luscher Color Test [*Psychology*] (DAVI) ... LCT
Luscombe Association (EA) ... LA
Lushington on Prize Law [*A publication*] (DLA) ... Lush Pr L
Lushington's English Admiralty Reports [*1859-62*] [*A publication*] (DLA) ... Lush
Lushington's English Admiralty Reports [*1859-62*] [*A publication*] (DLA) ... Lush Adm
Lushoto [*Tanzania*] [*Airport symbol*] (AD) ... LUY
Lush's Common Law Practice [*A publication*] (DLA) ... Lush Pr
Lusiana [*Czechoslovakia*] [*ICAO designator*] (FAAC) ... LUB
Lusinga [*Zaire*] [*ICAO location identifier*] (ICLI) ... FZRL
Lusingando [*Coaxingly*] [*Music*] ... LUSING
Lusitanair-Transportes Aereos Comercials SA [*Portugal ICAO designator*] (FAAC) ... LUS
Lusk, WY [*Location identifier FAA*] (FAAL) ... LSK
Luso-American Education Foundation (EA) ... LAEF
Luso-American Fraternal Federation (EA) ... LAFF
Luso-Americano, Newark, NJ [*Library symbol Library of Congress*] (LCLS) ... NjNL
Lussazione Congenita dell'Anca [*Congenital Hip Dislocation*] [*Italian Medicine*] ... LCA
Luster Paper [*Photography*] (DGA) ... LP
Lustre (VRA) ... lus
Lustrous (WDAA) ... LUST
Lute Society [*Harrow, England*] (EAIO) ... LS
Lute Society of America (EA) ... LSA
Luteal Angiogenic Factor [*Biochemistry*] ... LAF
Luteal Phase Defect [*Gynecology*] (DAVI) ... LPD
Luteinization Inhibitor [*Endocrinology*] ... LI
Luteinization Stimulator [*Endocrinology*] ... LS
Luteinized Unruptured Follicle [*Medicine*] (DMAA) ... LUF
Luteinized Unruptured Follicle Syndrome [*Medicine*] (DMAA) ... LUFS
Luteinizing Hormone Antiserum [*Endocrinology*] ... LHAS
Luteinizing Hormone Receptor Binding Inhibitor [*Endocrinology*] ... LHRBI
Luteinizing-Hormone [*Also, ICSH, LSH*] [*Endocrinology*] ... LH
Luteinizing-Hormone Releasing Factor [*Also, GnRF, GnRH, LH-RH, LH-RH/FSH-RH, LRF, LRH*] [*Endocrinology*] ... LH-RF
Luteinizing-Hormone Releasing Factor [*Also, GnRF, GnRH, LH-RF, LH-RH, LH-RH/FSH-RH, LRH*] [*Endocrinology*] ... LRF
Luteinizing-Hormone Releasing Hormone [*Also, GnRF, GnRH, LH-RF, LH-RH/FSH-RH, LRF, LRH*] [*Endocrinology*] ... LH-RH
Luteinizing-Hormone Releasing Hormone [*Also, GnRF, GnRH, LH-RF, LH-RH, LH-RH/FSH-RH, LRF*] [*Endocrinology*] ... LRH
Luteinizing-Hormone Releasing Hormone/Follicle-Stimulating Hormone Releasing Hormone [*Also, GnRF, GnRH, LH-RF, LH-RH, LRF, LRH*] [*Endocrinology*] ... LH-RH/FSH-RH
Lutein-Stimulating Hormone [*Also, ICSH, LH*] [*Endocrinology*] ... LSH
Luteolin [*Botany*] ... L
Luteotrophic Hormone [*Also, PR, PRL*] [*Endocrinology*] ... LTH
Lutesvile, MO [*FM radio station call letters*] (RBYB) ... KMHM-FM
Lutesville, MO [*FM radio station call letters*] ... KQUA
Lutetia Parisiorum [*Paris*] [*Imprint*] (ROG) ... LUT PAR
Lutetia Parisiorum [*Paris*] [*Imprint*] (ROG) ... LUTET
Lutetium [*Chemical element*] ... Lu
Lutetium, Silicon, and Oxygen [*Inorganic chemistry*] ... LSO
Luteum [*Yellow*] [*Latin*] ... LUT
Luther College, Decorah, IA [*Library symbol Library of Congress*] (LCLS) ... IaDL
Luther College, Decorah, IA [*OCLC symbol*] (OCLC) ... IOH
Luther College, Regina, Saskatchewan [*Library symbol National Library of Canada*] (NLC) ... SRLC
Luther College, Regina, SK, Canada [*Library symbol Library of Congress*] (LCLS) ... CaSRLC
Luther College, Teaneck, NJ [*Library symbol Library of Congress*] (LCLS) ... NjTeaL
Luther Family Association ... LFA
Luther Hospital, Eau Claire, WI [*Library symbol Library of Congress*] (LCLS) ... WEL
Luther Hospital, Eau Claire, WI [*Library symbol*] [*Library of Congress*] (LCLS) ... WELH
Luther Hospital Sentence Completions [*Nursing school test*] ... LHSC
Luther League [*Defunct*] (EA) ... LL
Luther League of America [*Later, LL*] ... LLA
Luther Med Products [*NASDAQ symbol*] (TTSB) ... LUTH
Luther Medical Products [*NASDAQ symbol*] (SAG) ... LUTH
Luther Medical Products, Inc. [*Associated Press*] (SAG) ... LuthMed
Luther Public Library, Luther, MI [*Library symbol*] [*Library of Congress*] (LCLS) ... MiLut
Luther Theological Seminary, St. Paul, MN [*Library symbol Library of Congress Obsolete*] (LCLS) ... MnSL
Lutheran [*Blood group*] ... Lu
Lutheran ... LUTH
Lutheran ... LUTH
Lutheran Academy for Scholarship [*Defunct*] (EA) ... LAS
Lutheran Benevolent Association (EA) ... LBA
Lutheran Bible Translators (EA) ... LBT
Lutheran Braille Evangelism Association (EA) ... LBEA
Lutheran Braille Workers (EA) ... LBW
Lutheran Brethren Schools, Fergus Falls, MN [*Library symbol Library of Congress*] (LCLS) ... MnFfL
Lutheran Brotherhood Foundation Reformation Library, St. Paul, MN [*Library symbol*] [*Library of Congress*] (LCLS) ... MnSLBF
Lutheran Campus Ministry Association [*Defunct*] (EA) ... LCMA
Lutheran Church and Indian People [*An association Defunct*] (EA) ... LUCHIP
Lutheran Church in America [*Later, ELCA*] ... LCA
Lutheran Church in America Foundation ... LCAF
Lutheran Church Library Association (EA) ... LCLA
Lutheran Church Men of America ... LCMA
Lutheran Church - Missouri Synod ... LCMS
Lutheran Church Women [*Defunct*] (EA) ... LCW
Lutheran Churches of the Reformation ... LCR
Lutheran Coalition on Latin America (EA) ... LUCOLA
Lutheran Collegiate Association [*Defunct*] (EA) ... LCA
Lutheran Council [*British*] (DBA) ... LC
Lutheran Council in Canada, Winnipeg, Manitoba [*Library symbol National Library of Canada*] (NLC) ... MWLCC
Lutheran Council in Canada, Winnipeg, MB, Canada [*Library symbol Library of Congress*] (LCLS) ... CaMWLCC
Lutheran Council in the USA [*Defunct*] (EA) ... LC/USA
Lutheran Council in the USA, New York, NY [*Library symbol Library of Congress*] (LCLS) ... NNLC
Lutheran Deaconess Association (EA) ... LDA
Lutheran Deaconess Conference (EA) ... LDC
Lutheran Deaconess Hospital, Minneapolis, MN [*Library symbol Library of Congress*] (LCLS) ... MnMLD
Lutheran Education Association (EA) ... LEA
Lutheran Educational Conference of North America (EA) ... LECNA
Lutheran Foundation for Religious Drama (EA) ... LFD
Lutheran Fraternities of America (EA) ... LFA
Lutheran Free Church (WDAA) ... LFC
Lutheran General Health Care System (EA) ... LGHCS
Lutheran General Hospital, Park Ridge, IL [*OCLC symbol*] (OCLC) ... IBO
Lutheran General Hospital, Park Ridge, IL [*Library symbol Library of Congress*] (LCLS) ... IParkL
Lutheran Historical Conference (EA) ... LHC
Lutheran Historical Society, Gettysburg, PA [*Library symbol Library of Congress*] (LCLS) ... PGL-Hi
Lutheran Hospital Association of America (EA) ... LHA
Lutheran Hospital of Maryland, Baltimore, MD [*Library symbol Library of Congress*] (LCLS) ... MdBLH
Lutheran Hospital of Milwaukee, Milwaukee, WI [*Library symbol Library of Congress*] (LCLS) ... WMLH
Lutheran Hospitals and Homes Society of America (EA) ... LHHS
Lutheran Human Relations Association of America (EA) ... LHRAA
Lutheran Immigration and Refugee Service (EA) ... LIRS
Lutheran Immigration Service [*Later, LIRS*] (EA) ... LIS
Lutheran Institute of Human Ecology (EA) ... LIHE
Lutheran Laymen's League [*Later, ILLL*] (EA) ... LLL
Lutheran Medical Mission Association [*Defunct*] (EA) ... LMMA
Lutheran Mission Societies (EA) ... LMS
Lutheran News Service [*Lutheran Church in America*] [*Information service or system*] (IID) ... LNS
Lutheran Outdoors Ministry Association [*Later, NLOMA*] (EA) ... LOMA
Lutheran Peace Fellowship (EA) ... LPF
Lutheran Resources Commission (EA) ... LRC
Lutheran Resources Commission - Washington [*Later, LRC*] (EA) ... LRC-W
Lutheran School of Messiah Elementary Library, Grand Junction, CO [*Library symbol*] [*Library of Congress*] (LCLS) ... CoGjL
Lutheran School of Theology, Chicago, IL [*Library symbol Library of Congress*] (LCLS) ... ICLT
Lutheran Seminary, University of Saskatchewan, Saskatoon, Saskatchewan [*Library symbol National Library of Canada*] (NLC) ... SSULS
Lutheran Seminary, University of Saskatchewan, Saskatoon, SK, Canada [*Library symbol Library of Congress*] (LCLS) ... CaSSULS
Lutheran Social Service System [*An association*] ... LSS
Lutheran Society for Worship, Music, and the Arts [*Later, Liturgical Conference*] ... LSWMA
Lutheran Student Movement - USA (EA) ... LSM-USA
Lutheran Theological Journal [*A publication*] (APTA) ... LTJ
Lutheran Theological Seminary, Gettysburg, PA [*Library symbol Library of Congress*] (LCLS) ... PGL
Lutheran Theological Seminary, Philadelphia, PA [*OCLC symbol*] (OCLC) ... PLT
Lutheran Theological Seminary, Philadelphia, PA [*Library symbol Library of Congress*] (LCLS) ... PPLT
Lutheran Theological Southern Seminary, Columbia, SC [*Library symbol Library of Congress*] (LCLS) ... ScCoT
Lutheran Volunteer Corps (EA) ... LVC
Lutheran Welfare Services [*Australia*] ... LWS
Lutheran Women's Missionary League [*Later, ILWML*] (EA) ... LWML
Lutheran World Federation [*See also FLM*] [*Geneva, Switzerland*] (EAIO) ... LWF

Lutheran World Federation United States of America National Committee (EA) .... LWFUSANC
Lutheran World Relief (EA) .... LWR
Lutheran Youth Fellowship (EA) .... LYF
Lutherans Concerned/North America (EA) .... LC/NA
Lutherans for Life (EA) .... LFL
Luther-Northwestern Seminary, St. Paul, MN [*Library symbol Library of Congress*] (LCLS) .... MnSLN
Luthiers Mercantile International [*Healdsburg, CA*] [*Commercial firm*] .... LMI
Lutlag [*Limited Company*] [*Norwegian*] LL
Luton [*British ICAO location identifier*] (ICLI) .... EGGW
Luton [*England*] [*Airport symbol*] (OAG) .... LTN
Luton Analogue Computing Engine [*British*] (DEN) .... LACE
Luton College of Higher Education (AIE) .... LCHE
Luton Information Service (NITA) .... LUTIS
Lutshatsha [*Zaire*] [*ICAO location identifier*] (ICLI) .... FZUU
Lutte Ouvriere [*Workers' Struggle*] [*France Political party*] (PPW) .... LO
Lutwyche's English Common Pleas Reports [*A publication*] (DLA) .... Lutw E
Lutwyche's English Election Cases [*A publication*] (DLA) .... Lut Elec Cas
Lutwyche's English Registration Appeal Cases [*1843-45*] [*A publication*] (DLA) .... Lut RC
Lutwyche's English Registration Cases [*A publication*] (DLA) .... Lutw Reg Cas
Lutwyche's Entries [*1704; 1718*] [*A publication*] (DLA) .... Lut Ent
Lutz Mountain Heritage Foundation, Inc., Moncton, NB, Canada [*Library symbol*] [*Library of Congress*] (LCLS) .... CaNBMoLM
Lutz Mountain Heritage Foundation, Inc., Moncton, New Brunswick [*Library symbol National Library of Canada*] (NLC) .... NBMOLM
Luverne, MN [*FM radio station call letters*] .... KLQL
Luverne, MN [*AM radio station call letters*] .... KQAD
Luvers of David Jones United (EA) .... LDJU
Luvua [*Zaire*] [*ICAO location identifier*] (ICLI) .... FZRO
Luwuk [*Indonesia*] [*Airport symbol*] (OAG) .... LUW
Luwuk/Bubung [*Indonesia*] [*ICAO location identifier*] (ICLI) .... WAMW
Lux [*Symbol*] [*SI unit of luminance*] lx
Lux [*Light*] [*Latin*] LX
Lux e Tenebris [*Light Out of Darkness*] [*Freemasonry*] [*Latin*] .... LET
Lux Second .... LX S
Luxair-Societe Luxembourgeoise de Navigation Aerienne SA [*Germany ICAO designator*] (FAAC) .... LGL
Luxembourg [*MARC geographic area code Library of Congress*] (LCCP) .... e-lu--
Luxembourg L
Luxembourg [*ANSI two-letter standard code*] (CNC) .... LU
Luxembourg [*MARC country of publication code Library of Congress*] (LCCP) .... lu
Luxembourg [*Seismograph station code, US Geological Survey*] (SEIS) .... LUX
Luxembourg [*Airport symbol*] (OAG) .... LUX
Luxembourg [*ANSI three-letter standard code*] (CNC) .... LUX
Luxembourg (VRA) .... Lux
Luxembourg .... Luxem
Luxembourg Brotherhood of America (EA) .... LBA
Luxembourg Income Study [*Economics*] .... LIS
Luxembourg/Luxembourg [*ICAO location identifier*] (ICLI) .... ELLX
Luxembourg Philatelic Study Club [*Defunct*] (EA) .... LPSC
Luxembourg Stock Exchange .... LSE
Luxeuil/Saint-Sauveur [*France ICAO location identifier*] (ICLI) .... LFSX
Luxol Fast Blue [*Biological stain*] .... LFB
Luxor [*Egypt*] [*ICAO location identifier*] (ICLI) .... HELX
Luxor [*Egypt*] [*Airport symbol*] (OAG) .... LXR
Luxottica Group [*Associated Press*] (SAG) .... Luxottca
Luxottica Group ADS [*NYSE symbol*] (SPSG) .... LUX
Luxtec Corp. [*Associated Press*] (SAG) .... Luxtec
Luxtec Corp. [*AMEX symbol*] (SAG) .... LXU
Luxury [*In automobile model name "Cordia L"*] L
Luxury [*or Luxurious*] [*Classified advertising*] (ADA) .... LUX
Luxury, Leisure, Longevity [*Economics*] .... 3L's
Luxury Sport [*In automobile model name "Cordia LS"*] .... LS
Luxury Sport Coupe .... LSC
Luxury Sport Euro [*Automobile model designation*] [*General Motors Corp. - Cadillac*] .... LSE
Luxury Sport Utility Vehicle .... LSUV
Luxury Tax (MHDB) .... LT
Luya [*Peru*] [*ICAO location identifier*] (ICLI) .... SPYA
Luzern-Beromunster [*Switzerland ICAO location identifier*] (ICLI) .... LSPZ
Luzerne County Community College [*Nanticoke, PA*] (TSSD) LCCC
Luzerne Law Journal [*Pennsylvania*] [*A publication*] (DLA) .... Luz LJ
Luzerne Law Journal [*Pennsylvania*] [*A publication*] (DLA) .... Luzerne LJ (PA)
Luzerne Law Times [*Pennsylvania*] [*A publication*] (DLA) .... Luz Law T
Luzerne Law Times. New Series [*Pennsylvania*] [*A publication*] (DLA) .... Luz LT (NS)
Luzerne Law Times. Old Series [*Pennsylvania*] [*A publication*] (DLA) .... Luz LT (OS)
Luzerne Legal Observer [*Pennsylvania*] [*A publication*] (DLA) .... Luz Leg Obs
Luzerne Legal Observer [*Pennsylvania*] [*A publication*] (DLA) .... Luz LO
Luzerne Legal Observer [*Pennsylvania*] [*A publication*] (DLA) .... Luzerne Leg Obs (PA)
Luzerne Legal Register Reports [*Pennsylvania*] [*A publication*] (DLA) .... Luz Leg Reg Rep
Luzerne Legal Register Reports [*Pennsylvania*] [*A publication*] (DLA) .... Luzerne Leg Reg R (PA)
Luzerne Legal Register Reports (Continuation of Kulp) [*Pennsylvania*] [*A publication*] (DLA) .... Luz L Reg Rep
Luzon Engineer District [*Army World War II*] .... LUZED
LVMH Moet Hennessey Louis Vuitton [*Associated Press*] (SAG) .... LVMH
LVMH Moet-Hennessey Louis Vuitton [*NASDAQ symbol*] (SAG) .... LVMH
LVMH Most Henn Lou Vttn ADS [*NASDAQ symbol*] (TTSB) .... LVMHY
Lvov [*Ukraine*] [*Seismograph station code, US Geological Survey*] (SEIS) LVV
Lvov [*Former USSR ICAO location identifier*] (ICLI) .... UKLL
LVOV Airlines [*Ukraine*] [*FAA designator*] (FAAC) .... UKW
Lwiro [*Zaire*] [*Seismograph station code, US Geological Survey*] (SEIS) .... LWI
Lwow [*Former USSR Airport symbol*] (OAG) .... LWO
LXE, Inc. [*Associated Press*] (SAG) .... LXE
LXE, Inc. [*NASDAQ symbol*] (SAG) .... LXEI
LXR Biotechnology [*AMEX symbol*] (TTSB) .... LXR
LXR Biotechnology, Inc. [*AMEX symbol*] (SAG) .... LXR
LXR Biotechnology, Inc. [*Associated Press*] (SAG) .... LXRBiot
Lyallpur [*Pakistan*] [*Airport symbol*] (AD) .... LYP
Lyapunov Characteristic Exponent [*Mathematics*] .... LCE
Lycee d'Enseignement General et Technologique [*High School for General and Technical Studies*] [*French*] (BARN) .... LEGT
Lycee d'Enseignement Professionel [*Professional Secondary School for AdvancedStudies*] [*French*] (BARN) .... LEP
Lychnis Ringspot Virus [*Plant pathology*] .... LRSV
Lycksele [*Sweden ICAO location identifier*] (ICLI) .... ESNL
Lycksele [*Sweden*] [*Geomagnetic observatory code*] .... LYS
Lycoming College, Williamsport, PA [*OCLC symbol*] (OCLC) .... LYC
Lycoming College, Williamsport, PA [*Library symbol Library of Congress*] (LCLS) .... PWmL
Lycoming Reporter [*Pennsylvania*] [*A publication*] (DLA) .... Lycoming
Lycoming Reporter [*Pennsylvania*] [*A publication*] (DLA) .... Lycoming R (PA)
Lycophron [*Third century BC*] [*Classical studies*] (OCD) .... Lycoph
Lycos Inc. [*NASDAQ symbol*] (TTSB) .... LCOS
Lycurgus [*of Plutarch*] [*Fourth century BC*] [*Classical studies*] (OCD) .... Lyc
Lycurgus [*of Plutarch*] [*Fourth century BC*] [*Classical studies*] (OCD) .... Lycurg
Lydall, Inc. [*NYSE symbol*] (SPSG) .... LDL
Lydall, Inc. [*Associated Press*] (SAG) .... Lydall
Lydd [*British ICAO location identifier*] (ICLI) .... EGMD
Lydd [*England*] [*Airport symbol*] .... LYX
Lydenburg [*South Africa*] [*ICAO location identifier*] (ICLI) .... FALL
Lydenburg Platinum Ltd. [*Associated Press*] (SAG) .... Lydnbg
Lydenburg Platinum Ltd ADR [*NASDAQ symbol*] (TTSB) .... LYDPY
Lydney [*British depot code*] .... LYD
Lykens Valley Railroad Co. [*AAR code*] .... LKVY
Lyman [*Spectrography*] .... Ly
Lyman [*Washington*] [*Seismograph station code, US Geological Survey*] (SEIS) .... LYW
Lyman Continuum [*Spectroscopy*] (OA) LC
Lyman Laboratory of Physics [*Harvard*] (MCD) .... LLP
Lyman Limit System [*Spectroscopy*] .... LLS
Lyman-Birge-Hopfield [*System*] [*Physics*] (MUGU) .... LBH
Lyme Borreliosis Foundation (EA) .... LBF
Lyme Disease [*Medicine*] .... LD
Lyme Disease Foundation .... LDF
Lympangiosium [*Medicine*] .... LAG
Lymph [*A fluid*] [*Biochemistry*] (DAVI) L
Lymph [*or Lymphatic*] (WDAA) .... LYM
Lymph Glands [*Medicine*] .... LG
Lymph Node [*Medicine*] .... LN
Lymph Node Biopsy [*Surgical procedure*] (DAVI) .... LNB
Lymph Node Cell [*Medicine*] .... LNC
Lymph Node Dissection [*Medicine*] .... LND
Lymph Node Enlargement [*Medicine*] (DMAA) .... LNE
Lymph Node Lymphocyte [*Medicine*] (DMAA) .... LNL
Lymph Node Metastases [*Oncology*] .... LNM
Lymph Node Permeability Factor [*Immunology*] .... LNPF
Lymph Node Region [*Medicine*] (DAVI) .... LNR
Lymph Node T Cells [*Immunology*] .... LNTC
Lymphadenopathy [*Medicine*] .... LA
Lymphadenopathy Syndrome [*Medicine*] .... LAS
Lymphadenopathy-Associated Virus .... LAV
Lymphadenopathy-Associated Virus (PDAA) .... LAVI
Lymphadenosis Benigna Cutis [*Medicine*] (DMAA) .... LBC
Lymphangiogram [*or Lymphangiography*] .... LAG
Lymphangioleiomyomatosis [*Medicine*] .... LAM
Lymphoblastic Lymphoma [*Oncology*] .... LBL
Lymphoblastic Lymphoma [*Oncology*] (DAVI) LL
Lymphoblastic Transformation Test [*Biochemistry*] (DAVI) .... LTT
Lymphoblastoid B-Cell Line [*Genetics*] .... LBCL
Lymphoblastoid Cell Line LCL
Lymphocyte [*Biochemistry*] (DAVI) L
Lymphocyte .... LYM
Lymphocyte .... LYMPH
Lymphocyte Activating Factor [*Immunology*] .... LAF
Lymphocyte Antibody-Lymphocytolytic Interaction [*Medicine*] (DMAA) .... LALI
Lymphocyte Chemoattractant Factor [*Biochemistry*] .... LCF
Lymphocyte Conditioned Medium [*Hematology*] .... LCM
Lymphocyte Cytosol Polypeptide [*Medicine*] (DMAA) .... LCP
Lymphocyte Defined [*Immunology*] .... LD
Lymphocyte Depletion [*Hematology*] .... LD
Lymphocyte Derived Chemotactic Factor [*Biochemistry*] .... LDCF
Lymphocyte Determined Membrane Antigen [*Immunology*] .... LYDMA
Lymphocyte Function-Associated Antigen [*Immunochemistry*] .... LFA
Lymphocyte Migration Index .... LMI
Lymphocyte Mitogenic Factor [*Endocrinology, hematology*] .... LMF
Lymphocyte Proliferative Response [*Immunology*] .... LPR
Lymphocyte Separation Medium [*Medicine*] .... LSM
Lymphocyte Specific Gravity Distribution [*Medicine*] .... LSGD
Lymphocyte to Polymorph Ratio [*Hematology*] .... L/P
Lymphocyte Transformation [*Hematology*] .... LT
Lymphocyte Transformation Test [*Medicine*] .... LTT
Lymphocyte Transforming Factor [*Immunology*] .... LTF
Lymphocyte-Activating Determinant (DAVI) .... LAD

Lymphocyte-Associated Virus .... LAV
Lymphocyte-Dependent Antibody [*Immunology*] .... LDA
Lymphocyte-Depletion Hodgkin's Disease [*Medicine*] .... LDHD
Lymphocyte-Induced Angiogenesis [*Immunology*] .... LIA
Lymphocyte-Mediated Cytotoxicity [*Also, LMC*] [*Immunology*] LC
Lymphocyte-Mediated Cytotoxicity [*Also, LC*] [*Immunology*] .... LMC
Lymphocytes [*Medicine*] (BABM) .... Lymphos
Lymphocyte-Stimulating Factor [*Biochemistry*] .... LSF
Lymphocytic Choriomeningitis [*Medicine*] .... LCM
Lymphocytic Choriomeningitis Virus .... LCMV
Lymphocytic Leukemia (MAE) LCL
Lymphocytic Leukemia, Chronic (MAE) LLC
Lymphocytic Leukemia Virus LLV
Lymphocytic Lymphosarcoma [*Oncology*] LCL
Lymphocytic Meningpolyradiculitis [*Medicine*] (DMAA) .... LMR
Lymphocytical Determined [*Hematology*] (DAVI) .... LD
Lymphocytosis-Promoting Factor [*Hematology*] (DAVI) .... LPF
Lymphocytosis-Stimulating Hormone [*Endocrinology*] .... LSH
Lymphocytotoxic Antibodies [*Immunochemistry*] .... LCTA
Lymphocytotoxicity [*Medicine*] (DMAA) .... LCT
Lymphocytotoxicity Test [*Hematology*] .... LCT
Lymphogranuloma [*Pathology*] (DAVI) L
Lymphogranuloma Venereum [*Medicine*] .... LGV
Lymphoid Blast Crisis of Chronic Myeloid Leukemia [*Oncology*] .... LBC/CML
Lymphoid Cellular Infiltration [*Oncology*] LI
Lymphoid Enhancer Factor [*Biochemistry*] .... LEF
Lymphoid Interstitial Pneumonitis [*Medicine*] .... LIP
Lymphoid Plasma [*Hematology*] (MAE) .... LP
Lymphoid Predominance [*Medicine*] (AAMN) .... LP
Lymphoid Tissue [*Biology*] .... LT
Lymphoid Tissue Mononuclear Cell [*Physiology*] .... LTMC
Lymphoid-Enhanced Binding Factor [*Medicine*] (DMAA) .... LEF
Lymphokine [*Immunochemistry*] .... LK
Lymphokine-Activated Killer [*Cells*] [*Immunotherapy*] .... LAK
Lymphoma Cell Line [*Oncology*] LCL
Lymphoma/Leukemia [*Oncology*] .... L/L
Lymphomatoid Granulomatosis [*Medicine*] .... LYG
Lymphomyeloid Complex [*Medicine*] .... LMC
Lymphopathia Venereum (MAE) .... LPV
Lymphoproliferative Disease [*Oncology*] .... LPD
Lymphosarcoma [*Medicine*] .... LS
Lymphosarcoma [*Medicine*] .... LSa
Lymphosarcoma [*Medicine*] (AAMN) .... Lyp
Lymphosarcoma Cell [*Oncology*] (DAVI) .... LSAR
Lymphosarcoma Cell Leukemia [*Medicine*] (DMAA) .... LSCI
Lymphosarcoma - Reticulum Cell Sarcoma [*Oncology*] (MAE) .... LSA/RCS
Lymphotoxin [*Immunochemistry*] .... LT
Lymphotropic Papovavirus .... LPV
Lymph-Plasma [*Ratio*] [*Laboratory science*] (DAVI) .... L/P
Lymph-Plasma Ratio [*Hematology*] (MAE) .... LP
Lympne [*England*] [*Airport symbol*] (AD) .... LYM
Lyn Branch, Elizabethtown Township Public Library, Ontario [*Library symbol National Library of Canada*] (BIB) .... OLELB
Lynbrook High School, Lynbrook NY [*Library symbol*] [*Library of Congress*] (LCLS) .... NLynHS
Lynbrook South Middle School, Lynbrook, NY [*Library symbol*] [*Library of Congress*] (LCLS) .... NLynSM
Lynch Corp. [*AMEX symbol*] (SPSG) .... LGL
Lynch Corp. [*Associated Press*] (SAG) .... LynchC
Lynch Flying Service, Inc. [*ICAO designator*] (FAAC) .... LCH
Lynch, Young & Associates [*Newport Beach, CA*] [*Telecommunications*] (TSSD) .... LYA
Lynchburg [*Virginia*] [*Airport symbol*] (OAG) .... LYH
Lynchburg College (GAGS) .... Lynchburg C
Lynchburg College, Lynchburg, VA [*Library symbol Library of Congress*] (LCLS) ViLC
Lynchburg Pool Reactor .... LPR
Lynchburg Source Reactor .... LSR
Lynchburg Technology Center (GAAI) .... LTC
Lynchburg, VA [*AM radio station call letters*] .... WBRG
Lynchburg, VA [*FM radio station call letters*] .... WGOL
Lynchburg, VA [*FM radio station call letters*] .... WJJX
Lynchburg, VA [*Television station call letters*] .... WJPR
Lynchburg, VA [*AM radio station call letters*] .... WKPA
Lynchburg, VA [*AM radio station call letters*] .... WLLL
Lynchburg, VA [*FM radio station call letters*] .... WLNI
Lynchburg, VA [*AM radio station call letters*] .... WLVA
Lynchburg, VA [*FM radio station call letters*] .... WLYK
Lynchburg, VA [*FM radio station call letters*] .... WRVL
Lynchburg, VA [*Television station call letters*] .... WSET
Lynchburg, VA [*AM radio station call letters*] .... WVLR
Lynchburg, VA [*FM radio station call letters*] .... WWMC
Lynchburg, VA [*AM radio station call letters*] .... WWOD
Lynd Public Library, Lynd, MN [*Library symbol*] [*Library of Congress*] (LCLS) .... MnLyPS
Lynden, WA [*FM radio station call letters*] .... KLYN
Lynden, WA [*FM radio station call letters*] (RBYB) .... KWPZ-FM
Lyndhurst Branch, Rideau Lakes Union Library, Ontario [*Library symbol National Library of Canada*] (BIB) .... OLRL
Lyndhurst Public Library, Lyndhurst, NJ [*Library symbol Library of Congress*] (LCLS) .... NjLy
Lyndon B. Johnson Library .... LBJL
Lyndon B. Johnson School of Public Affairs, Lyndon Baines Johnson Library, Austin, TX [*Library symbol Library of Congress*] (LCLS) .... TxAuLBJ
Lyndon B. Johnson Space Center (MSC) .... LBJSC
Lyndon Baines Johnson [*US president, 1908-1973*] .... LBJ
Lyndon State College, Lyndonville, VT [*Library symbol Library of Congress*] (LCLS) .... VtLyL
Lyndon, VT [*FM radio station call letters*] .... WGMT
Lyndonville Historical Society, Lyndonville, NY [*Library symbol Library of Congress*] (LCLS) .... NLyndHi
Lyndonville, VT [*Location identifier FAA*] (FAAL) LLX
Lyndonville, VT [*FM radio station call letters*] .... WWLR
Lyndwood's Provinciales [*A publication*] (DLA) .... Lynd
Lyndwood's Provinciales [*A publication*] (DLA) .... Lynd Prov
Lyndwood's Provinciales [*A publication*] (DLA) .... Lyndw Prov
Lyne on Leases for Lives [*A publication*] (DLA) .... Lyne Lea
Lyne on Renewals [*A publication*] (DLA) .... Lyne on Renew
Lyneham [*British ICAO location identifier*] (ICLI) .... EGDL
Lyneham, FTU [*British*] [*FAA designator*] (FAAC) .... LYE
Lyne's Irish Chancery Cases (Wallis) [*1766-91*] [*A publication*] (DLA) .... Lyne
Lynn Anderson Fan Club (EA) .... LAFC
Lynn G. Haskin School, Sandwich, IL [*Library symbol Library of Congress*] (LCLS) .... ISanH
Lynn Lake [*Canada*] [*Airport symbol Obsolete*] (OAG) .... YYL
Lynn Lake, MB [*ICAO location identifier*] (ICLI) .... CYYL
Lynn, MA [*FM radio station call letters*] .... WFNX
Lynn, MA [*AM radio station call letters*] .... WLYN
Lynn Public Library, Lynn, MA [*Library symbol Library of Congress*] (LCLS) .... MLy
Lynn Public Library, Lynn, MA [*Library symbol*] [*Library of Congress*] (LCLS) .... MLyL
Lynn-01, AK [*Location identifier FAA*] (FAAL) .... JDL
Lynngold Resources, Inc. [*Toronto Stock Exchange symbol*] .... LY
Lynnville, IL [*FM radio station call letters*] .... WEAI
Lynnwood Arts Centre, Simcoe, ON, Canada [*Library symbol Library of Congress*] (LCLS) .... CaOSiL
Lynton Aviation [*British ICAO designator*] (FAAC) .... LYN
Lynwood Arts Centre, Simcoe, Ontario [*Library symbol National Library of Canada*] (NLC) .... OSIL
Lynx [*Constellation*] .... Lyn
Lynx-Canada Explorations Ltd. [*Toronto Stock Exchange symbol*] .... LYX
Lyon [*France*] [*Airport symbol*] (OAG) .... LYS
Lyon Air [*France ICAO designator*] (FAAC) .... LYA
Lyon and Redman on Bills of Sale [*A publication*] (DLA) .... Lyon & R BS
Lyon/Bron [*France ICAO location identifier*] (ICLI) .... LFLY
Lyon/Corbas [*France ICAO location identifier*] (ICLI) .... LFHJ
Lyon County Courthouse, Rock Rapids, IA [*Library symbol Library of Congress*] (LCLS) .... IaRrLCoC
Lyon County News, George, IA [*Library symbol Library of Congress*] (LCLS) .... IaGeoN
Lyon county Register, George, IA [*Library symbol*] [*Library of Congress*] (LCLS) .... IaGeoR
Lyon County Reporter, Rock Rapids, IA [*Library symbol Library of Congress*] (LCLS) .... IaRrLR
Lyon/Mont-Verdun [*France ICAO location identifier*] (ICLI) .... LFXV
Lyon on the Laws of India [*A publication*] (DLA) .... Lyon Ind L
Lyon/Satolas [*France ICAO location identifier*] (ICLI) .... LFLL
Lyon-Brindas [*France ICAO location identifier*] (ICLI) .... LFKL
Lyondell Petrochem [*NYSE symbol*] (TTSB) .... LYO
Lyondell Petrochemical [*NYSE symbol*] (SPSG) .... LYO
Lyondell Petrochemical Co. [*Associated Press*] (SAG) .... Lyondl
Lyon's Electronic Office .... LEO
Lyons Electronic Office [*J. Lyons & Co*] [*British*] (NITA) .... LEO
Lyons, GA [*AM radio station call letters*] .... WBBT
Lyons, GA [*FM radio station call letters*] .... WLYU
Lyon's Institutes of Justinian [*A publication*] (DLA) .... Lyon Just
Lyons, KS [*FM radio station call letters*] .... KSKU
Lyons, KS [*Location identifier FAA*] (FAAL) .... LYO
Lyons Public Library, Lyons, IL [*Library symbol Library of Congress*] (LCLS) .... ILy
Lyons Public Library, Lyons, MI [*Library symbol Library of Congress*] (LCLS) .... MiLy
Lyons Township Junior College [*Illinois*] .... LTJC
Lyophilized [*Medicine*] (DMAA) .... LYO
Lyophilized Allantoic Fluid [*Endocrinology*] .... LAF
Lyophilized Anterior Pituitary [*Endocrinology*] .... LAP
Lyotropic Liquid Crystals [*Physical chemistry*] LLC
Lyra [*Constellation*] .... Lyr
Lyric [*or Lyrical*] .... LYR
Lyrichord [*Record label*] .... Lyr
Lyricist [*MARC relator code*] [*Library of Congress*] (LCCP) .... lyr
Lyrics and Lyricists [*Long running New York show*] .... L&L
Lysander [*of Plutarch*] [*Classical studies*] (OCD) .... Lys
Lysander Gold [*Vancouver Stock Exchange symbol*] .... LYS
Lysergic Acid Cryptoethelane (IIA) .... LACE
Lysergic Acid Diethylamide [*or Lysergsaeure Diethylamid*] [*Hallucinogenic drug*] .... LSD
Lysergic Acid Morpholide .... LSM
Lysias [*Fifth century BC*] [*Classical studies*] (OCD) .... Lys
Lysinated Rhodamine Dextran [*Cytology*] .... LRD
Lysine [*One-letter symbol; see Lys*] .... K
Lysine [*Also, K*] [*An amino acid*] .... Lys
Lysine (DMAA) .... LYS
Lysine [*An amino acid*] (DOG) .... lys
Lysine Acetylsalicylate [*Biochemistry*] .... LAS
Lysine Iron Agar [*Microbiology*] .... LIA
Lysine Methyl Ester [*Biochemistry*] .... LME
Lysine Vasopressin [*Antidiuretic hormone*] .... LVP
Lysine Vasotonin [*Adrenergic agent*] .... LVT

Lysine-Binding Site [*Hematology*] .... LBS
Lysinoalanine [*An amino acid*] .... LAL
Lysinuric Protein Intolerance [*Medicine*] (DMAA) .... LPI
Lysistrata [*of Aristophanes*] [*Classical studies*] (OCD) .... Lys
Lysodren (DMAA) .... LYS
Lysolecithin [*Biochemistry*] LL
Lysolecithin (DMAA) .... LLT
Lysophosphatidic Acid [*Biochemistry*] .... LPA
Lysophosphatidic Acid Acyltransferase [*An enzyme*] .... LPAAT
Lysophosphatidylcholine [*Also, Lyso-PC*] [*Biochemistry*] ...... LPC
Lysophosphatidylcholine [*Also, LPC*] [*Biochemistry*] .... Lyso-PC
Lysophosphatidylethanolamine [*Biochemistry*] .... LPE
Lysophospholipase [*An enzyme*] .... LPL
Lysopine Dehydrogenase [*An enzyme*] .... LpDH
Lysopine Dehydrogenase (BABM) .... LpOH
Lysosome [*Biochemistry*] (DAVI) L
Lysosome [*Cytology*] .... LYS

Lysosome-Associated Membrane Protein [*Biochemistry*] .... LAMP
Lysozyme [*Also, LZM*] [*An enzyme*] .... LYS
Lysozyme [*Medicine*] (DMAA) .... LYZ
Lysozyme [*An enzyme*] .... LZM
Lysyl [*Enzymology*] .... LYS
Lysyl Oxidase [*An enzyme*] .... LO
Lytes Electrolytes [*Medicine*] (DMAA) .... LYS
Lythway Press [*British*] .... LP
Lytic Capacity [*Clinical chemistry*] LC
Lytle, TX [*FM radio station call letters*] .... KXPZ
Lytta [*A Blistering Fly*] [*Pharmacy*] (ROG) .... LYTT
Lytton, BC [*ICAO location identifier*] (ICLI) .... CYLY
Lytton Minerals Ltd. [*Toronto Stock Exchange symbol Vancouver Stock Exchange symbol*] .... LTL
Lytton Star, Sac City, IA [*Library symbol Library of Congress*] (LCLS) .... IaSacLS
Lyudmila Zhivkova International Foundation (EAIO) .... LZIF
Lyxose [*As substituent on nucleoside*] [*Biochemistry*] I
Lyxose [*Also, I*] [*A sugar*] .... Lyx

M
By Meaning

M/A/R/C INC. [*NASDAQ symbol*] (TTSB) .... MARC
M. Alice Chapin Memorial Library, Marion, MI [*Library symbol Library of Congress*] (LCLS) .... MiMar
M & M Aviation, Inc. [*ICAO designator*] (FAAC) .... GSP
M & M Porcupine Gold Mines [*Vancouver Stock Exchange symbol*] .... MMP
M & S [*Modeling and Simulation*] Executive Agent [*Army*] .... MSEA
M. D. Anderson Hospital and Tumor Institute [*Houston, TX*] .... MDAH
M. H. de Young Memorial Museum, San Francisco, CA [*Library symbol Library of Congress*] (LCLS) .... CSfDeY
M H Meyerson & Co. Wrtt [*NASDAQ symbol*] (TTSB) .... MHMYW
M. I. Hummel Club (EA) .... MIHC
M/I Schottenstein Homes [*NYSE symbol*] (TTSB) .... NHO
M/I Schottenstein Homes, Inc. [*NYSE symbol*] (SPSG) .... MHO
M. L. Cass Petroleum [*Vancouver Stock Exchange symbol*] .... MLO
M. M. Dillon Ltd., Willowdale, Ontario [*Library symbol National Library of Canada*] (NLC) .... OWMMD
M McWhorter Technologies [*NYSE symbol*] (TTSB) .... MWT
M/S Jet Airways Ltd. [*India*] [*FAA designator*] (FAAC) .... JAI
M12 [*Hawaii*] [*Seismograph station code, US Geological Survey Closed*] (SEIS) M12
MA [*Military Assistance*] Articles and Services List [*DoD*] .... MASL
Maamba [*Zambia*] [*ICAO location identifier*] (ICLI) .... FLMB
Maanpuolustuksen ja Turvallisuuden Ammattijaerjestoet [*Defence and Security Employees Union*] [*Finalnd*] (EY) .... MJAJ
Ma'arbae (BJA) .... Ma
Maars [*Alaska*] [*Seismograph station code, US Geological Survey*] (SEIS) .... MRS
Maart [*March*] [*Dutch*] (AD) .... Mrt
Ma'aser Sheni (BJA) .... Ma'asSh
Ma'aser Sheni (BJA) .... MS
Ma'aser Sheni (BJA) .... MSh
Ma'aserot (BJA) .... Ma
Ma'asroth (BJA) .... Ma'as
Maastricht [*Germany ICAO location identifier*] (ICLI) .... EDDY
Maastricht [*Netherlands*] [*Airport symbol*] (OAG) .... MST
Maastricht Automatic Data Processing and Display System [*Air traffic control*] .... MADAP
Maastricht Economic Research Institute on Innovation and Technology .... MERIT
Maastricht Referendum Campaign [*British*] (ECON) .... MARC
Maastricht School of Management [*Netherlands*] .... MSM
Maastricht/Zuid-Limburg [*Netherlands ICAO location identifier*] (ICLI) .... EHBK
Maastrichtial [*Paleontology*] .... MAA
Maatschappij [*Joint Stock Company*] [*Netherlands*] .... MIJ
Maatschappij [*Company*] [*Dutch*] (AD) .... Mpy
Mabaruma [*Guyana*] [*ICAO location identifier*] (ICLI) .... SYMB
Mabaruma [*Guyana*] [*Airport symbol*] (OAG) .... USI
Mabel Tainter Memorial Free Library, Menomonie, WI [*Library symbol Library of Congress*] (LCLS) .... WMen
MAC [*McDonnell Aircraft Corporation*] Acquisition and Attack Trainer (MCD) .... MAAT
MAC Automated Deployment Reporting System [*Military*] (GFGA) .... MACADS
MAC Aviation SL [*Spain ICAO designator*] (FAAC) .... MAO
MAC Aviation, S.L. [*Spain*] [*FAA designator*] (FAAC) .... MAQ
Mac Dan Aviation Corp. [*ICAO designator*] (FAAC) .... MCN
Mac Knight Airlines [*ICAO designator*] (AD) .... MT
Mac Library System [*Computer Advanced Software Products - CASPR*] [*Cupertino, CA*] [*Information service or system*] (IID) .... MLS
MAC [*Massive Algebraic Computation*] Symbolic Manipulator [*Programming language*] [*1969*] (CSR) .... MACSYMA
MAC Technical Services Co. (GAAI) .... MACTEC
Mac [*Apple's Mackintosh computer*] Terminal Emulation Program .... MacTEP
MAC [*Military Airlift Command*] Transportation Authorization (AFM) .... MTA
Macadam (ADA) .... MAC
Macae [*Brazil*] [*Airport symbol*] (OAG) .... MEA
Macae [*Brazil ICAO location identifier*] (ICLI) .... SBME
Macalester College, St. Paul, MN [*Library symbol Library of Congress*] (LCLS) .... MnSM
Macalester College, Weyerhaeuser Library, St. Paul, MN [*OCLC symbol*] (OCLC) .... MAC
Macalpin on Money Lenders [*A publication*] (DLA) .... Macalp Mon L
Mac-Am Resources Corp. [*Vancouver Stock Exchange symbol*] .... MCM
MacAndrew [*Alcoholism scale*] .... MAC
Macao [*MARC geographic area code Library of Congress*] (LCCP) .... a-mh--
Macao [*MARC country of publication code Library of Congress*] (LCCP) .... mh
Macao Federation of Trade Unions .... MFTU
Macapa [*Brazil*] [*Airport symbol*] (OAG) .... MCP

Macapa/Internacional [*Brazil ICAO location identifier*] (ICLI) .... SBMQ
Macara [*Ecuador*] [*Airport symbol*] (OAG) .... MRR
Macara [*Ecuador*] [*ICAO location identifier*] (ICLI) .... SEMA
Macaroni .... MCRN
MacArthue/West Elementary School, Duluth MN [*Library symbol*] [*Library of Congress*] (LCLS) .... MnDuMWE
MacArthur and Mackey's District of Columbia Reports [*A publication*] (DLA) .... McArth & M
MacArthur and Mackey's District of Columbia Supreme Court Reports [*A publication*] (DLA) .... MacAr & M
MacArthur and Mackey's District of Columbia Supreme Court Reports [*A publication*] (DLA) .... MacAr & Mackey
MacArthur and Mackey's District of Columbia Supreme Court Reports [*A publication*] (DLA) .... MacArth & M
MacArthur and Mackey's District of Columbia Supreme Court Reports [*A publication*] (DLA) .... MacArth & M (Dist Col)
MacArthur and Mackey's District of Columbia Supreme Court Reports [*A publication*] (DLA) .... MacArthur & M
Macarthur Gruen Party [*Political party Australia*] .... MGP
MacArthur, Nimitz, and Spaatz [*Nickname for World War II command structure of Douglas MacArthur, Chester W. Nimitz, and Carl A. Spaatz*] .... MACNIMAATZ
MacArthur on Courts-Martial [*A publication*] (DLA) .... MacArth Ct Mar
MacArthur's Patent Cases [*District of Columbia*] [*A publication*] (DLA) .... Mac A Pat Cas
MacArthur's Patent Cases [*A publication*] (DLA) .... MacAr
MacArthur's Patent Cases [*District of Columbia*] [*A publication*] (DLA) .... MacAr Pat Cas
MacArthur's Patent Cases [*A publication*] (DLA) .... MacArth
MacArthur's Patent Cases [*United States*] [*A publication*] (DLA) .... MacArth Pat Cas
MacArthur's Patent Cases [*A publication*] (DLA) .... MacArthur
MacArthur's Patent Cases [*United States*] [*A publication*] (DLA) .... MacArthur Pat Cas
MacArthur's Reports [*8-10 District of Columbia*] [*A publication*] (DLA) .... MacAr
MacArthur's Reports [*8-10 District of Columbia*] [*A publication*] (DLA) .... MacArth
MacArthur's Reports [*8-10 District of Columbia*] [*A publication*] (DLA) .... MacArthur
Macas [*Ecuador*] [*ICAO location identifier*] (ICLI) .... SEMC
Macaskie on Executors, Etc. [*A publication*] (DLA) .... Macask Ex
Macassey's New Zealand Reports [*A publication*] (DLA) .... Mac
Macassey's New Zealand Reports [*A publication*] (DLA) .... Mac NZ
Macassey's New Zealand Reports [*A publication*] (DLA) .... Macas
Macau [*ANSI three-letter standard code*] (CNC) .... MAC
Macau [*ANSI two-letter standard code*] (CNC) .... MO
Macau [*Macau*] [*ICAO location identifier*] (ICLI) .... VMMC
Macaulay Land Use Research Institute, Aberdeen [*British*] (IRUK) .... MLURI
Macaulay's History of England [*A publication*] (DLA) .... Macaulay Hist Eng
Macbeth [*Shakespearean work*] .... Mac
Macbeth [*Shakespearean work*] (BARN) .... Macb
Macbride Museum Society (EA) .... MMS
MACC Private Equities [*NASDAQ symbol*] (TTSB) .... MACC
MACC Private Equities, Inc. [*NASDAQ symbol*] (SAG) .... MACC
Maccabees [*Old Testament book*] [*Roman Catholic canon*] (ROG) .... MAC
Maccabees [*Old Testament book*] [*Roman Catholic canon*] .... Macc
Maccabees [*Old Testament book*] [*Roman Catholic canon*] .... Mc
[*The*] Maccabees [*Southfield, MI*] (EA) .... TM
Maccabi World Union [*Ramat Gan, Israel*] (EAIO) .... MWU
Maccala's Breach of Promise Cases [*A publication*] (DLA) .... Macc Cas
Maccala's Reports [*Modern Reports, Part X*] [*1710-25*] [*A publication*] (DLA) .... Maccl
MacCarthy's Irish Land Cases [*A publication*] (DLA) .... MacCarthy
MacCartney Clan Society (EA) .... MCS
Macclenny, FL [*FM radio station call letters*] .... WJXR
Macclesfield's Trial (Impeachment) [*1725*] [*London*] [*A publication*] (DLA) .... Maccl Tr
MacConkey [*Agar*] [*Microbiology*] .... MAC
MACDAC system (NITA) .... MACDACsys
MacDermid, Inc. [*NASDAQ symbol*] (NQ) .... MACD
MacDermid, Inc. [*Associated Press*] .... MacDrmd
MacDevitt's Irish Land Cases [*1882-84*] [*A publication*] (DLA) .... MacDev
MacDevitt's Irish Land Commissioner's Reports [*A publication*] (DLA) .... MacD
MacDonald Agricultural Services Ltd. [*British*] (SAG) .... MAS
Macdonald College Library, Ste-Anne-De-Bellevue, Quebec [*Library symbol National Library of Canada*] (NLC) .... QMAC
Macdonald, Dettwiler & Associates Ltd., Richmond, British Columbia [*Library symbol National Library of Canada*] (NLC) .... BRMD
Macdonald Museum, Middleton, Nova Scotia [*Library symbol National Library of Canada*] (NLC) .... NSMM

Macdonald Museum, Middleton, NS, Canada [Library symbol] [Library of Congress] (LCLS) ... CaNSMiM
MacDonald Ophthalmic Foundation, Toronto, ON, Canada [Library symbol Library of Congress] (LCLS) ... CaOTMOF
MacDonald Ophthalmic Foundation, Toronto, Ontario [Library symbol National Library of Canada] (NLC) ... OTMOF
MacDonald Science Library, Dalhousie University, Halifax, Nova Scotia [Library symbol National Library of Canada] (NLC) ... NSHDS
MacDonald-Cartier Highway [Canada] ... M-C
Macdonell's State Trials [1820-58] [A publication] (DLA) ... St Tr NS
Macdougall's Jamaica Reports [A publication] (DLA) ... Mac R
Macdougall's Jamaica Reports [A publication] (DLA) ... Macd Jam
Macdowall's Institute of Laws of Scotland [3 vols.] [1751-53] [A publication] (DLA) ... Bankt
Mace Security International [NASDAQ symbol] (SAG) ... MACE
Mace Security International [Associated Press] (SAG) ... MaceSec
Mace Security Intl [NASDAQ symbol] (TTSB) ... MACE
Mace Utilities Sector Editor [Computer science] ... MUSE
Macedonia ... Maced
Macedonia AS [Yugoslavia] [ICAO designator] (FAAC) ... MDO
Macedonian [MARC language code Library of Congress] (LCCP) ... mac
Macedonian ... MACED
Macedonian Educational and Cultural Association [Australia] ... MECA
Macedonian Literary Association [Australia] ... MLA
Macedonian Patriotic Organization of US and Canada (EA) ... MPO
Macedonian Seleucid Era (BJA) ... SelMac
Maceio [Brazil] [Airport symbol] (OAG) ... MCZ
Maceio/Palmares [Brazil ICAO location identifier] (ICLI) ... SBMO
Macenta [Guinea] [ICAO location identifier] (ICLI) ... GUMA
Macenta [Guinea] [Airport symbol] (AD) ... MCA
Macera & Jarzyna, Ottawa, ON, Canada [Library symbol] [Library of Congress] (LCLS) ... CaOOMJ
Macera & Jarzyna, Ottawa, Ontario [Library symbol National Library of Canada] (BIB) ... OOMJ
Macerare [Macerate] [Pharmacy] ... M
Macerare [Macerate] [Pharmacy] ... MAC
Macerare [Macerate] [Pharmacy] ... MACER
Macerich Co. [NYSE symbol] (SAG) ... MAC
Macerich Co. [Associated Press] (SAG) ... Macerich
Macfarland's Digest of Mining Cases [A publication] (DLA) ... Macf Min
MacFarlane's Practice of the Court of Sessions [A publication] (DLA) ... MacF Pr
MacFarlane's Scotch Jury Court Reports [1838-39] [A publication] (DLA) ... MacF
MacFarlane's Scotch Jury Court Reports [1838-39] [A publication] (DLA) ... MacFar
MacFarlane's Scotch Jury Court Reports [1838-39] [A publication] (DLA) ... M'F R
MacFarlane's Scotch Jury Trials [A publication] (DLA) ... MacF
MacFarlane's Scotch Jury Trials [A publication] (DLA) ... MacFarl
MacFarlane's Scotch Jury Trials [A publication] (DLA) ... MacFarlane
Macfie on Copyright [A publication] (DLA) ... Macf Cop
Macfie Resources [Vancouver Stock Exchange symbol] ... MFR
MacFrugal's Bargains [Formerly, Pic'n'Save Corp.] [NYSE symbol] (SPSG) ... MFI
MacFrugals Bargains Close Outs [Associated Press] (SAG) ... MacFrug
MacFrugals Bargains Closeouts [NYSE symbol] (TTSB) ... MFI
MacGillivray and Parkington's Insurance Law [6th ed.] [1975] [A publication] (DLA) ... MacGillivray & Parkington
MacGillivray's Copyright Cases [1901-49] [A publication] (DLA) ... Mac CC
MacGillivray's Copyright Cases [1901-49] [A publication] (DLA) ... MacG CC
MacGillivray's Copyright Cases [1901-49] [A publication] (DLA) ... MCC
MacGregor Sports & Fitness [NASDAQ symbol] (TTSB) ... MACG
MacGregor Sports & Fitness, Inc. [Associated Press] (SAG) ... MacG
MacGregor Sports & Fitness, Inc. [NASDAQ symbol] (SAG) ... MACG
MacGregor Sports & Fitness, Inc. [Associated Press] (SAG) ... MacG S
MacGregor Sports & Fitness, Inc. [Associated Press] (SAG) ... MacG Sp
MacGregor Sports&Fitness Wrrt [NASDAQ symbol] (TTSB) ... MACGW
Mach Aids to Surface-to-Air Missile Development (IAA) ... MASD
Mach/Airspeed Indicator (GAVI) ... M/ASI
Mach Indicated ... MI
Mach Max Operating (GAVI) ... MMO
Mach Meter Reading (MCD) ... MMR
Mach Number ... M
Mach Number [IUPAC] ... Ma
Mach Number Indicated (MCD) ... MNI
Machabees [Old Testament book] [Douay version] ... MACH
Machala [Ecuador] [Airport symbol] (OAG) ... MCH
Machala [Ecuador] [ICAO location identifier] (ICLI) ... SEMH
Machaneng [Botswana] [ICAO location identifier] (ICLI) ... FBMG
Mache Unit [Measure of radium emanation from solutions] (AAMN) ... Mu
Macheezmo Mouse Restaurants [NASDAQ symbol] (TTSB) ... MMRI
Macheezmo Mouse Restaurants, Inc. [Associated Press] (SAG) ... Macheez
Macheezmo Mouse Restaurants, Inc. [NASDAQ symbol] (SAG) ... MMRI
Machias, ME [AM radio station call letters] (RBYB) ... WALZ
Machias, ME [AM radio station call letters] (RBYB) ... WALZ-AM
Machias, ME ... WALZ-FM
Machinability Data Center [Computerized search services] [Metcut Research Associates, Inc.] ... MACHDC
Machinability Data Center [Computerized search service] [Metcut Research Associates, Inc.] (IID) ... MDC
Machine ... M
Machine (ROG) ... M/C
Machine (ROG) ... M/E
Machine [or Machinery] ... MACH
Machine ... MACH
Machine ... MACH
Machine ... MCHN
Machine Accessory [Tool] (AAG) ... MCAC

Machine Accountant [Navy] ... MA
Machine Accountant, First Class [Navy] ... MA1
Machine Accountant, Seaman [Navy] ... MASN
Machine Accountant, Second Class [Navy] ... MA2
Machine Accountant, Third Class [Navy] ... MA3
Machine Accounting School ... MAS
Machine Aids to Nike-X [Army] (AABC) ... MANIX
Machine Analysis Display ... MAD
Machine Analysis Table (IAA) ... MAT
Machine Analyzer Package (PDAA) ... MAP
Machine and Hull History File Card (DNAB) ... MHHFC
Machine ANSI Data ... MAD
Machine Applications to Technical Information Center Operations ... MATICO
Machine Augmented Manual Scheduling System (MCD) ... MAMSS
Machine Automated Parts System (MCD) ... MAPS
Machine Automated Realty Service ... MARS
Machine Automated Speech Transcription (PDAA) ... MAST
Machine Automatically Generating Production Inventory Evaluation [Computer science] (IEEE) ... MAGPIE
Machine Available Time [Computer science] ... MAT
Machine Bolt [Technical drawings] ... MB
Machine Cancel Society (EA) ... MCS
Machine Cancellation [Philately] ... MC
Machine Centralized Control System (DWSG) ... MCCS
Machine Chain Manufacturers Association (EA) ... MCMA
Machine Channel Handler (ECII) ... MCH
Machine Check [Computer science] (IAA) ... MC
Machine Check Analysis and Recording (BUR) ... MCAR
Machine Check Extended Logout ... MCEL
Machine Check Handle (NITA) ... MCH
Machine Check Interrupt (NITA) ... MCI
Machine Check Interruption [Computer science] (BUR) ... MCI
Machine Check Interruption Code [Computer science] ... MCIC
Machine Check Recording and Recovery [Computer science] ... MCRR
Machine Coated Board (DGA) ... MCB
Machine Code (IAA) ... MC
Machine Communication with Digital Automatic Computer ... MACDAC
Machine Console ... MC
Machine Control Medium (MCD) ... MCM
Machine Control Unit ... MCU
Machine Cycle (IAA) ... MC
Machine Dependent Data (OA) ... MDD
Machine Direction Paper (DGA) ... MACH D
Machine Dried Paper (DGA) ... MD
Machine Examination Teaching, Evaluation, and Re-education (PDAA) ... METER
Machine Finish [Paper] ... MF
Machine for Automatic Graphics Interface to a Computer ... MAGIC
Machine Gaming Division [Queensland, Australia] ... MGD
Machine Group (MUGU) ... MACHGR
Machine Gun (MUGU) ... MG
Machine Gun Guards [British military] (DMA) ... MGG
Machine Gun LASER (MCD) ... MGL
Machine Gun Officer [British military] (DMA) ... MGO
Machine Gun Regiment [British military] (DMA) ... MGR
Machine Gun School [British military] (DMA) ... MGS
Machine Gunner [British military] (DMA) ... MG
Machine Independent ... MI
Machine Independent Data Management System [Defense Intelligence Agency] (MCD) ... MIDMS
Machine Independent Microprogramming Language ... MIMOLA
Machine Independent Package (DGA) ... MIP
Machine Independent Systems Effectiveness Data System (MCD) ... MISED
Machine Instruction Processor [Computer science] (BUR) ... MIP
Machine Intelligence (RDA) ... MI
Machine Interface Terminal [Tangram Computer Aided Engineering] [Software package] (NCC) ... MIT
Machine Interface Unit (HGAA) ... MIU
Machine Knife and Bayonet Workers' Union [British] ... MKBWU
Machine Knife Association (EA) ... MKA
Machine Knife Manufacturers Association (EA) ... MKMA
Machine Language [Computer science] ... ML
Machine Language Debugger [National Computer Sharing Service] ... MLD
Machine Language Instruction ... MLI
Machine Language Printed Circuit Boards [Computer science] (IEEE) ... MLPCB
Machine Language Program [Computer science] ... MLP
Machine Level Control [Computer science] ... MLC
Machine Literature Searching [Computer science] (DIT) ... MLS
Machine Made Paper (DGA) ... MM
Machine Operation (AFM) ... MO
Machine Parts Fabrication ... MPF
Machine Parts Inspection Plans (MCD) ... MPIP
Machine Pistol [Military] (IIA) ... MP
Machine Power Transmission Association (AD) ... MPTA
Machine Pressed ... MP
Machine Printers and Engravers Association of the United States (EA) ... MPEA
Machine Printers and Engravers Association of the United States (DGA) ... MPEAUS
Machine Printers' Beneficial Association [Later, MPEA] ... MPBA
Machine Processing Section [National Security Agency] ... MPRO
Machine Punch Card ... MPC
Machine Readable Archives Division [Public Archives of Canada] [Information service or system] (IID) ... MRA
Machine Readable Library Information [British Library] [Information service or system] (IID) ... MERLIN
Machine Receipt ... M/R

Machine Record (AD) .... mr
Machine Records .... MR
Machine Records Activity .... MRA
Machine Records Installation [*Military*] .... MRI
Machine Records Unit [*Computer science*] .... MRU
Machine Referenced and Coordinated Outline .... MARCO
Machine Representation Language .... MRL
Machine Retrieval System .... MARS
Machine Rifle .... MR
Machine Rifle (AD) .... mr
Machine Ruling (DGA) .... MACH R
Machine Screw .... MS
Machine Screw (AD) .... ms
Machine Screw .... MSCR
Machine Screw Jack .... MSJ
Machine Selection (IEEE) .... MS
Machine Shock Test .... MST
Machine Shop (MHDB) .... Mshp
Machine Specification Language .... MSL
Machine Status Register [*Computer science*] (OA) .... MSR
Machine Status Word [*Computer science*] .... MSW
Machine Steel .... MS
Machine Steel (AD) .... ms
Machine Steel .... MST
Machine Strap Makers' Society [*A union*] [*British*] .... MSMS
Machine Stress Rated .... MSR
Machine Survey and Installation Report .... MSIR
Machine Tool .... MT
Machine Tool Builders' Association .... MTBA
Machine Tool Control .... MTC
Machine Tool Control Unit (IAA) .... MCU
Machine Tool Forum .... MTF
Machine Tool Industry Research Association [*Research center British*] .... MTIRA
Machine Tool Retrofit Program .... MTRP
Machine Tool Technologies Association [*British*] (EAIO) .... MTTA
Machine Tool Technology Program [*Association of Independent Colleges and Schools specialization code*] .... MT
Machine Tool Trades Association (ACII) .... MTTA
Machine Tool Trades' Association (NADA) .... MTTA
Machine Tool Trigger Order Program (MHDB) .... MTTOP
Machine Tool Wire .... MTW
Machine Tools Industry (MCD) .... MTI
Machine Translation [*Computer science*] .... MT
Machine Trim Compensator (AAG) .... MTC
Machine Unit .... MU
Machine User Symbiotic Environment (PDAA) .... MUSE
Machine User Symbolic Environment (IAA) .... MUSE
Machine Utilization Index [*Computer science*] .... MUI
Machine Utilization Report Generator .... MURG
Machine Utilization Report Generator (DNAB) .... MUST
Machine Utilization Report System [*Computer science*] (IAA) .... MURS
Machine Utilization Reporting System (PDAA) .... MURS
Machine Utilization Statistical Information Collection (IAA) .... MUSIC
Machine Vision Association [*Later, MVA/SME*] (EA) .... MVA
Machine Vision Association [*Society of Manufacturing Engineers*] (EA) .... MVA/SME
Machine Word (IAA) .... MW
Machine Yield [*Agriculture*] (OA) .... MY
Machine-Aided Cognition [*Computer project*] [*Massachusetts Institute of Technology*] .... MAC
Machine-Aided Composition and Editing .... MACE
Machine-Aided Drafting System (IEEE) .... MADS
Machine-Aided Graphics for Illustration and Composition [*Bell Telephone*] .... MAGIC
Machine-Aided Index (NITA) .... MAI
Machine-Aided Indexing (KSC) .... MAI
Machine-Aided Information and Dissemination Systems .... MAIDS
Machine-Aided Manufacturing Information [*Computer science*] .... MAMI
Machine-Aided Planning, Scheduling, and Control .... MAPSAC
Machine-Aided Program for Preparation of Instruction Data .... MAPID
Machine-Aided Realization System .... MARS
Machine-Aided Technical Processing System [*Yale University Library*] [*New Haven, CT*] [*Computer science*] .... MATPS
Machine-Aided Translation (NITA) .... MAT
Machine-Aided Translation Editing (PDAA) .... MATE
Machine-Assisted Detection and Classification (NVT) .... MADC
Machine-Assisted Educational System for Teaching by Remote Operation (IEEE) .... MAESTRO
Machine-Assisted Realization of the Virtual Electronic Library [*Information service or system Library of Congress*] .... MARVEL
Machine-Assisted Reference Section [*American Library Association*] [*Information service or system*] (IID) .... MARS
Machine-Assisted Reference Service [*St. Paul Public Library*] (OLDSS) .... MARS
Machine-Assisted Translation .... MAT
Machine-Assisted Vendor Information Network .... MAVIN
Machine-Check Handler [*Computer science*] (MCD) .... MCH
Machined .... MCHND
Machined Hemispherical Shell .... MHS
Machined Metal Part .... MMP
Machined Part Requisition (MCD) .... MPR
Machined Surface .... MASU
Machine-Finish Paper (WDMC) .... mf
Machine-Glazed [*Poster paper*] .... MG
Machine-Gun Artillery Division [*Former USSR*] .... MGAD
Machine-Gun Car [*or Carrier*] [*British*] .... MGC
Machine-Gun Combination [*British*] .... MGC
Machine-Gun Co. [*or Corps*] .... MGC
Machine-Independent Telemetry-Oriented Language [*Computer science*] (IEEE) .... MITOL
Machine-Made and Machine-Assisted Index [*Computer science*] (IAA) .... MAMMAX
Machine-Made Snow [*Skiing*] .... MM
Machine-Oriented Higher Order Language [*Computer science*] (MHDI) .... MOHOL
Machine-Oriented High-Level Language [*Computer science*] (HGAA) .... MOHILL
Machine-Oriented Language [*Programming language*] .... MOL
Machine-Oriented Language (AD) .... mol
Machine-Prepared Wiring Data [*Telecommunications*] (TEL) .... MPWD
Machine-Pressed Bales .... MPB
Machiner .... MACHR
Machine-Readable Cards .... MARC
Machine-Readable Catalog (NITA) .... MARC
Machine-Readable Cataloging [*Library of Congress*] .... MARC
Machine-Readable Cataloguing - Serials (ADA) .... MARC-S
Machine-Readable Code (IAA) .... MARC
Machine-Readable Code .... MRC
Machine-Readable Collections Reading Room [*Library of Congress*] (IT) .... MRCRR
Machine-Readable Data Files .... MRDF
Machine-Readable Data Files [*Computer science*] (AD) .... mrdf
Machine-Readable Form of Bibliographic Information [*American Library Association*] .... MARBI
Machine-Readable Government Information Task Force [*Government Documents Round Table*] [*American Library Association*] .... MRGITF
Machine-Readable Passport (DA) .... MRP
Machine-Readable Passport (AD) .... mrp
Machine-Readable Record (MCD) .... MRR
Machine-Readable Shelf List [*Carleton University*] [*Canada*] (NITA) .... MARSL
Machine-Readable Tapes [*Computer science*] .... MRT
Machinery (ROG) .... MACHY
Machinery .... MACHY
Machinery (MSA) .... MCHRY
Machinery (ROG) .... MCHY
Machinery (IAA) .... MCY
Machinery .... MM
Machinery Alteration .... MACHALT
Machinery and Allied Products Institute (MHDI) .... MAPI
Machinery and Fixed Equipment [*British*] .... MFE
Machinery and Occupational Safety Act [*Environmental science*] .... MOS
Machinery and Optics .... M & O
Machinery Certificate [*Shipping*] .... MC
Machinery Dealers National Association (EA) .... MDNA
Machinery Dealers' National Information System .... MDNIS
Machinery Defective, Government-Furnished (DNAB) .... MDG
Machinery Diagnostic Consultant [*Software program*] .... MDC
Machinery Failure Prevention Technology (RDA) .... MFPT
Machinery Forward (DS) .... Mchy fwd
Machinery Haulers Association Agent, Saint Paul MN [*STAC*] .... MHA
Machinery Installation Certificate .... MIC
Machinery Maintenance Engineering Center (AFIT) .... MMEC
Machinery Numeral [*Marine insurance*] (DS) .... MN
Machinery of Government [*British*] .... MG
Machinery of Government .... MOG
Machinery of Government, Parliamentary Procedure [*British*] .... MG(P)
Machinery Overhaul Co. .... MOCO
Machinery, Plant Control System [*Navy*] .... MPCS
Machinery, Plant Control System Operator Trainer [*Navy*] .... MPCSOT
Machinery Repairman [*Navy rating*] .... MR
Machinery Repairman, Chief [*Navy rating*] .... MRC
Machinery Repairman, First Class [*Navy rating*] MR1
Machinery Repairman, Master Chief [*Navy rating*] .... MRCM
Machinery Repairman, Seaman [*Navy rating*] .... MRSN
Machinery Repairman, Seaman Apprentice [*Navy rating*] .... MRSA
Machinery Repairman, Second Class [*Navy rating*] MR2
Machinery Repairman, Senior Chief [*Navy rating*] .... MRCS
Machinery Repairman, Third Class [*Navy rating*] MR3
Machinery Safety Tag .... MST
Machinery Survey [*Shipping*] .... MS
Machinery Users' Association [*British*] (BI) .... MUA
Machinery-Metals Export Club [*Later, International Industrial Marketing Club*] (EA) .... MMEC
Machines for Coordinated Multiprocessing .... MCM
Machine-Tractor Stations .... MTS
Machining .... MACHG
Machining Arbor [*Tool*] (AAG) .... MCAR
Machining Data Bank [*PERA*] [*Software package*] (NCC) .... MACBANK
Machining Optimisation [*PERA*] [*Software package*] (NCC) .... MACOPT
Machining System (IAA) .... MS
Machining Technology Association of the Society of Manufacturing Engineers (EA) .... MTA/SME
Machining-Intensive Durable Goods [*Manufacturing*] .... MDG
Machinist (WDAA) .... MACH
Machinist .... MACHST
Machinist (MSA) .... MCHST
Machinists and Aerospace Workers (DICI) .... MAW
Machinist's Mate [*Navy rating*] .... MM
Machinist's Mate, Chief [*Navy rating*] .... MMC
Machinist's Mate, Construction Battalion, Equipment Operator [*Navy rating*] .... MMCBE
Machinist's Mate, Engineman [*Navy rating*] .... MME
Machinist's Mate, First Class [*Navy rating*] MM1

Machinist's Mate, Industrial Gas Generating Mechanic [*Navy rating*] ..... MMG
Machinist's Mate, Master Chief [*Navy rating*] ..... MMCM
Machinist's Mate, Refrigeration [*Navy rating*] ..... MMR
Machinist's Mate, Second Class [*Navy rating*] MM2
Machinist's Mate, Senior Chief [*Navy rating*] ..... MMCS
Machinist's Mate, Ship Repair [*Navy rating*] ..... MMSR
Machinist's Mate, Ship Repair, Engine Operator [*Navy rating*] ..... MMSRE
Machinist's Mate, Ship Repair, Inside Machinist [*Navy rating*] ..... MMSRS
Machinist's Mate, Ship Repair, Instrument Maker [*Navy rating*] ..... MMSRI
Machinist's Mate, Ship Repair, Outside Machinist [*Navy rating*] ..... MMSRO
Machinist's Mate, Shop Mechanic [*Navy rating*] ..... MMS
Machinist's Mate, Third Class [*Navy rating*] MM3
Machinists Non-Partisan Political League (EA) ..... MNPL
Machinists Non-Partisan Political League (EA) ..... MN-PPL
Machinists Vise Association [*Later, HTI*] (EA) ..... MVA
Machismo [*Spanish*] (DSUE) ..... MACHO
Machover Draw-A-Person Test [*Psychology*] ..... MDAP
Machrihanish [*British ICAO location identifier*] (ICLI) ..... EGQJ
Macht Sich Wichtig (BJA) ..... MSW
Machynlleth [*Welsh depot code*] ..... MCH
Macintosh [*Computer science*] (WDMC) ..... Mac
Macintosh Application System [*Computer science*] (CDE) ..... MAS
Macintosh Development System [*Computer science*] ..... MDS
Macintosh File System [*Computer science*] ..... MFS
MacIntosh Gallery, University of Western Ontario, London, Ontario [*Library symbol National Library of Canada*] (NLC) ..... OLUMG
Macintosh Operating System [*Computer science*] (CDE) ..... Mac OS
Macintosh Programmer's Workshop [*Computer science*] (BTTJ) ..... MPW
Macintosh Special Interest Group of Mensa (EA) ..... MSIGM
Macintosh User Group [*Computer science*] (WDMC) ..... MUG
Macintosh User Group [*Computer science*] (CDE) ..... MUG
Mack Vickery Fan Club (EA) ..... MVFC
Mackay [*Australia ICAO location identifier*] (ICLI) ..... ABMK
Mackay [*Australia Airport symbol*] (OAG) ..... MKY
Mackay. Court of Session Practice [*A publication*] (ILCA) ..... Mack Ct Sess
Mackay District Library, Mackay, ID [*Library symbol*] [*Library of Congress*] (LCLS) ..... IdMac
Mackay's Law of Property [*1882*] [*A publication*] (DLA) ..... Mack Law of Prop
Mackeldey on Modern Civil Law [*A publication*] (DLA) ..... Mack CL
Mackeldey on Modern Civil Law [*A publication*] (DLA) ..... Mackeld
Mackeldey on Modern Civil Law [*A publication*] (DLA) ..... Mackeld Civil Law
Mackeldey on Roman Law [*A publication*] (DLA) ..... Mackeld
Mackeldey on Roman Law [*A publication*] (DLA) ..... Mackeld Rom Law
Mackeldey's Handbook of the Roman Law [*A publication*] (DLA) ..... Rom Law
Mackenzie ..... MACK
Mackenzie Art Gallery [*University of Regina*] [*Canada Research center*] (RCD) ..... MAGI
Mackenzie, BC [*AM radio station call letters*] ..... CKMK
Mackenzie Financial [*NASDAQ symbol*] (TTSB) ..... MKFCF
Mackenzie Financial Corp. [*Associated Press*] (SAG) ..... MackFn
Mackenzie Financial Corp. [*Toronto Stock Exchange symbol*] ..... MKF
Mackenzie Financial Corp. [*NASDAQ symbol*] (SAG) ..... MKFC
Mackenzie on Bills of Lading [*A publication*] (DLA) ..... Mack BL
Mackenzie Public Library, British Columbia [*Library symbol National Library of Canada*] (NLC) ..... BMK
Mackenzie-Papineau Battalion [*Canada*] ..... Mac-Paps
Mackenzie's Institutes of the Law of Scotland [*9 eds.*] [*1684-1758*] [*A publication*] (DLA) ..... Mack Inst
Mackenzie's Observations on Acts of Parliament [*1675, etc.*] [*Scotland*] [*A publication*] (DLA) ..... Mack Obs
Mackenzie's Studies in Roman Law [*A publication*] (DLA) ..... Mack Rom Law
Mackenzie's Treatise on Criminal Law [*4th ed.*] [*1678-1758 Scotland*] [*A publication*] (DLA) ..... Mack Cr L
Mackenzie's Treatise on Criminal Law [*4 eds.*] [*1678-1758 Scotland*] [*A publication*] (DLA) ..... Mack Crim
Mackerel [*Pimp*] [*Slang*] (DSUE) ..... MAC
Mackeson and Forbes' Judicature Acts [*A publication*] (DLA) ..... Mack & F Jud A
Mackey International Airlines [*ICAO designator*] (AD) ..... MI
Mackey International, Inc. [*USA*] [*ICAO designator*] (OAG) ..... MI
Mackey's District of Columbia Reports [*12-20 District of Columbia*] [*A publication*] (DLA) ..... Mackey
Mackie Designs [*NASDAQ symbol*] (TTSB) ..... MKIE
Mackie Designs, Inc. [*Associated Press*] (SAG) ..... Mackie
Mackie Designs, Inc. [*NASDAQ symbol*] (SAG) ..... MKIE
Mackinac Island Public Library, Mackinac Island, MI [*Library symbol Library of Congress*] (LCLS) ..... MiMaci
Mackinac Transportation Co. [*AAR code*] ..... MCTR
Mackinaw City, MI [*FM radio station call letters*] (RBYB) ..... WLJZ
Mackinaw City Public Library, Mackinaw City, MI [*Library symbol Library of Congress*] (LCLS) ..... MiMack
Mackinaw Township Library, Mackinaw, IL [*OCLC symbol*] (OCLC) ..... IER
Mackinnon Road [*Kenya*] [*ICAO location identifier*] (ICLI) ..... HKMR
Mackintosh (DSUE) ..... MAC
Mackintosh's Law of Nature and Nations [*5th ed.*] [*1835*] [*A publication*] (DLA) ..... Mack Nat
Macknight Airlines [*Australia ICAO designator*] (FAAC) ..... MTD
Maclachlan on Merchant Shipping [*A publication*] (DLA) ..... Macl Sh
Maclachlan on Merchant Shipping [*A publication*] (DLA) ..... Macl Shipp
Maclaren Engineering, Winnipeg, Manitoba [*Library symbol National Library of Canada*] (NLC) ..... MWME
MacLaren Engineering, Winnipeg, MB, Canada [*Library symbol Library of Congress*] (LCLS) ..... CaMWME
MacLaren Marex, Dartmouth, NS, Canada [*Library symbol Library of Congress*] (LCLS) ..... CaNSDMM
Maclaren on Wills and Successions [*A publication*] (DLA) ..... Macl
MacLaren Plansearch Ltd., Dartmouth, Nova Scotia [*Library symbol National Library of Canada*] (NLC) ..... NSDMM
MacLaren Plansearch Ltd., Dartmouth, NS, Canada [*Library symbol Library of Congress*] (LCLS) ..... CaNSDMP
Maclaurin's Remarkable Cases [*1670-1773*] [*Scotland*] [*A publication*] (DLA) ..... Macl Rem Cas
Maclaurin's Scotch Criminal Decisions [*A publication*] (DLA) ..... Macl
Maclean and Robinson's Scotch Appeal Cases [*1839*] [*A publication*] (DLA) ..... M & R
Maclean and Robinson's Scotch Appeal Cases [*1839*] [*A publication*] (DLA) ..... M & Rob
Maclean and Robinson's Scotch Appeal Cases [*1839*] [*A publication*] (DLA) ..... Mac & Rob
Maclean and Robinson's Scotch Appeal Cases [*1839*] [*A publication*] (DLA) ..... Mac R
Maclean and Robinson's Scotch Appeal Cases [*9 English Reprint*] [*A publication*] (DLA) ..... Macl & R
Maclean and Robinson's Scotch Appeal Cases [*9 English Reprint*] [*A publication*] (DLA) ..... Macl & Rob
Maclean and Robinson's Scotch Appeal Cases [*9 English Reprint*] [*A publication*] (DLA) ..... Maclean & R
Maclean and Robinson's Scotch Appeal Cases [*9 English Reprint*] [*A publication*] (DLA) ..... Maclean & R (Sc)
Maclean Hunter Ltd. [*Toronto Stock Exchange symbol*] ..... MHP
MacLean-Hunter Ltd., Toronto, ON, Canada [*Library symbol Library of Congress*] (LCLS) ..... CaOTMH
Maclean's [*A publication*] (BRI) ..... Mac
Macleod Dixon Library, Calgary, AB, Canada [*Library symbol Library of Congress*] (LCLS) ..... CaACMD
Macleod Dixon Library, Calgary, Alberta [*Library symbol National Library of Canada*] (NLC) ..... ACMD
Macleod's Theory and Practice of Banking [*A publication*] (DLA) ..... Macl Bank
Maclura Mosaic Virus [*Plant pathology*] ..... MAMV
MacMillan Bloedel Ltd. [*Associated Press*] (SAG) ..... MB
MacMillan Bloedel Ltd. [*NASDAQ symbol*] (NQ) ..... MMBL
MacMillan Bloedel Ltd., Nanaimo, BC, Canada [*Library symbol Library of Congress*] (LCLS) ..... CaBNaMBL
MacMillan Bloedel Ltd., Nanaimo, British Columbia [*Library symbol National Library of Canada*] (NLC) ..... BNMBL
MacMillan Bloedel Ltd., Vancouver, British Columbia [*Library symbol National Library of Canada*] (NLC) ..... BVAMBL
MacMillan Bloedel Research Ltd., Vancouver, BC, Canada [*Library symbol Library of Congress*] (LCLS) ..... CaBVaMB
MacMillan Bloedel Research Ltd., Vancouver, BC, Canada [*Library symbol Library of Congress*] (LCLS) ..... CaBVaMBL
MacMillan Bloedel Research Ltd., Vancouver, British Columbia [*Library symbol National Library of Canada*] (NLC) ..... BVAMB
MacMillan Gold [*Vancouver Stock Exchange symbol*] ..... MMG
MacMillan-Bloedel [*NASDAQ symbol*] (TTSB) ..... MMBLF
Macmillan's Commercial Series [*A publication*] ..... MCS
Macmillan's Manuals for Students [*A publication*] ..... MMS
Macmillan's Manuals for Teachers [*A publication*] ..... MMT
MacMurray College, Jacksonville, IL [*OCLC symbol*] (OCLC) ICI
MacMurray College, Jacksonville, IL [*Library symbol Library of Congress*] (LCLS) ..... IJMac
Macnaghten and Gordon's English Chancery Reports [*A publication*] (DLA) ..... M & G
Macnaghten and Gordon's English Chancery Reports [*A publication*] (DLA) ..... M & Gord
Macnaghten and Gordon's English Chancery Reports [*A publication*] (DLA) ..... Mac & G
Macnaghten and Gordon's English Chancery Reports [*A publication*] (DLA) ..... Macn & G
Macnaghten and Gordon's English Chancery Reports [*A publication*] (DLA) ..... Macn & G (Eng)
Macnaghten on Courts-Martial [*A publication*] (DLA) ..... Macn CM
Macnaghten's Criminal Evidence [*A publication*] (DLA) ..... Macn Cr Ev
Macnaghten's Elements of Hindu Law [*A publication*] (DLA) ..... Macn El Hind L
Macnaghten's English Chancery Reports [*A publication*] (DLA) ..... Mac
Macnaghten's Hindu Law [*India*] [*A publication*] (DLA) ..... FMacn
Macnaghten's Hindu Law Cases [*India*] [*A publication*] (DLA) ..... Macn
Macnaghten's Nizamut Adalat Cases [*1805-50*] [*Bengal, India*] [*A publication*] (DLA) ..... Macn
Macnaghten's Nizamut Adalat Reports [*Bengal, India*] [*A publication*] (DLA) ..... Macn NA Beng
Macnaghten's Select Cases in Chancery Tempore King [*A publication*] (DLA) ..... Macn
Macnaghten's Select Cases in Chancery Tempore King [*A publication*] (DLA) ..... McNagh
Macnaghten's Select Cases, Sadr Diwani Adalat [*1791-1858*] [*Bengal, India*] [*A publication*] (DLA) ..... Macn
Macnaghten's Select Cases, Sadr Diwani Adalat [*1791-1858*] [*Bengal, India*] [*A publication*] (DLA) ..... Macn SDA
Macnally's Rules of Evidence [*A publication*] (DLA) ..... McNal Ev
Macnally's Rules of Evidence on Pleas of the Crown [*A publication*] (DLA) ..... Macn Ev
Macnamara's Nullities and Irregularities in Law [*1842*] [*A publication*] (DLA) ..... Macn Nul
MacNeal Memorial Hospital, Berwyn, IL [*Library symbol Library of Congress*] (LCLS) ..... IBerMH
MacNeal-Schwendler [*AMEX symbol*] (TTSB) ..... MNS
[*The*] **MacNeal-Schwendler Corp.** [*Associated Press*] (SAG) ..... MacNSc
[*The*] **MacNeal-Schwendler Corp.** [*AMEX symbol*] (SPSG) ..... MNS
[*The*] **MacNeal-Schwendler Corp.** ..... MSC
MacNeil [*Herman A.*] [*Designer's mark, when appearing on US coins*] ..... M

MacNeill Industrial, Inc. [*Vancouver Stock Exchange symbol*] ... MCE
MACOM [*Major Command*] **Outstanding Excess Report** ... MOER
MACOM [*Major Command*] **Telephone Modernizations Program** ... MTMP
Macomb County Community College [*Michigan*] ... MCCC
Macomb County Community College, Warren, MI [*Library symbol Library of Congress*] (LCLS) ... MiWarM
Macomb County Library, Mt. Clemens, MI [*OCLC symbol*] (OCLC) ... EYB
Macomb County Library, Mount Clemens, MI [*Library symbol Library of Congress*] (LCLS) ... MiMtcM
Macomb, IL [*Location identifier FAA*] (FAAL) ... MQB
Macomb, IL [*FM radio station call letters*] ... WIUM
Macomb, IL [*FM radio station call letters*] ... WIUS
Macomb, IL [*FM radio station call letters*] ... WJEQ
Macomb, IL [*FM radio station call letters*] ... WKAI
Macomb, IL [*AM radio station call letters*] ... WLRB
Macomb, IL [*Television station call letters*] ... WMEC
Macomb on Courts-Martial [*A publication*] (DLA) ... Mac CM
Macomb on Courts-Martial [*A publication*] (DLA) ... Macomb CM
Macomer [*Italy ICAO location identifier*] (ICLI) ... LIEM
Macon [*Georgia*] [*Airport symbol*] (OAG) ... MCN
Macon/Charnay [*France ICAO location identifier*] (ICLI) ... LFLM
Macon County Public Library, Franklin, NC [*Library symbol Library of Congress*] (LCLS) ... NcFr
Macon, Dublin & Savannah Railroad (IIA) ... MD & S
Macon, GA [*Location identifier FAA*] (FAAL) ... MAC
Macon, GA [*FM radio station call letters*] ... WAYS
Macon, GA [*AM radio station call letters*] ... WBML
Macon, GA [*AM radio station call letters*] ... WDDO
Macon, GA [*AM radio station call letters*] ... WDEN
Macon, GA [*FM radio station call letters*] ... WDEN-FM
Macon, GA [*Television station call letters*] ... WGNM
Macon, GA [*Television station call letters*] ... WGXA
Macon, GA [*AM radio station call letters*] ... WMAZ
Macon, GA [*Television station call letters*] ... WMAZ-TV
Macon, GA [*Television station call letters*] ... WMGT
Macon, GA [*FM radio station call letters*] ... WMKS
Macon, GA [*AM radio station call letters*] (RBYB) ... WMWR-AM
Macon, GA [*AM radio station call letters*] ... WNEX
Macon, GA [*FM radio station call letters*] ... WPEZ
Macon Junior College, Macon, GA [*Library symbol Library of Congress*] (LCLS) ... GMJ
Macon Junior College, Macon, GA [*OCLC symbol*] (OCLC) ... GOM
Macon, MO [*AM radio station call letters*] ... KLTI
Macon, MO [*Location identifier FAA*] (FAAL) ... MCM
Macon/Robins Air Force Base [*Georgia*] [*ICAO location identifier*] (ICLI) ... KWRB
Macon Terminal Co. [*AAR code*] ... MTCO
Macon/Warner Robins, GA [*Location identifier FAA*] (FAAL) ... WRB
Macosa-Associated Lymphoid Tissue [*Medicine*] ... MALT
Macoupin Community District 1, Carlinville, IL [*Library symbol Library of Congress*] (LCLS) ... ICarlMCD
Macoupin Community District 3, Girard, IL [*Library symbol Library of Congress*] (LCLS) ... IGirMCD
Macoupin Community District 4, Virden, IL [*Library symbol Library of Congress*] (LCLS) ... IVirdMCD
Macoupin Community, District 5, Mount Olive, IL [*Library symbol Library of Congress*] (LCLS) ... IMtoMCD
Macoupin Community District 6, Staunton, IL [*Library symbol Library of Congress*] (LCLS) ... IStauMCD
Macoupin Community District 7, Gillespie, IL [*Library symbol Library of Congress*] (LCLS) ... IGillMCD
Macoupin Community District 8, Bunker Hill, IL [*Library symbol Library of Congress*] (LCLS) ... IBunMCD
Macoupin Community Unit, District 9, Piasa, IL [*Library symbol Library of Congress*] (LCLS) ... IPiaMCD
Macpherson, Lee, and Bell [*Scotland*] [*A publication*] (DLA) ... Macph L & B
Macpherson, Lee, and Bell's Scotch Session Cases [*A publication*] (DLA) ... Macph
Macpherson on Infancy [*A publication*] (DLA) ... Macph Inf
Macpherson's Practice of the Judicial Committee of the Privy Council [*A publication*] (DLA) ... Macph Jud Com
Macpherson's Practice of the Judicial Committee of the Privy Council [*2nd ed.*] [*1873*] [*A publication*] (DLA) ... Macph Pr C
Macpherson's Privy Council Practice [*A publication*] (DLA) ... Macph Priv Counc
Macpherson's Scotch Court of Session Cases [*1862-73*] [*A publication*] (DLA) ... Macph
Macpherson's Scotch Session Cases [*1862-73*] [*A publication*] (DLA) ... M
Macquarie Island [*Australia ICAO location identifier*] (ICLI) ... AMMQ
Macquarie Island [*Australia Seismograph station code, US Geological Survey*] (SEIS) ... MCQ
Macquarie Island [*Australia Seismograph station code, US Geological Survey Closed*] (SEIS) ... MQI
Macquarie Law Students Journal [*A publication*] ... MLSJ
Macquarie University Caving Group [*Australia*] ... MUCG
Macquarie University Law School Foundation [*Australia*] ... MULSF
Macquarie University, North Ryde, NSW, Australia [*Library symbol Library of Congress*] (LCLS) ... AuNrM
Macqueen's Debates on Life-Peerage Questions [*A publication*] (DLA) ... Macq D
Macqueen's Marriage, Divorce, and Legitimacy [*2nd ed.*] [*1860*] [*A publication*] (DLA) ... Macq Mar
Macqueen's Marriage, Divorce, and Legitmacy [*2nd ed.*] [*1860*] [*A publication*] (DLA) ... Macq Div
Macqueen's Rights and Liabilities of Husband and Wife [*4th ed.*] [*1905*] [*A publication*] (DLA) ... Macq H & W
Macqueen's Scotch Appeal Cases, House of Lords [*A publication*] (DLA) ... Macq
Macqueen's Scotch Appeal Cases, House of Lords [*A publication*] (DLA) ... Macq HL Cas
Macqueen's Scotch Appeal Cases, House of Lords [*A publication*] (DLA) ... Macq Sc App Cas
Macqueen's Scotch Appeal Cases, House of Lords [*A publication*] (DLA) ... Mcq
Macquest Resources Ltd. [*Toronto Stock Exchange symbol*] ... MQT
Macrae and Hertslet's English Insolvency Cases [*1847-52*] [*A publication*] (DLA) ... Mac & I
Macrae and Hertslet's English Insolvency Cases [*1847-52*] [*A publication*] (DLA) ... Macr & H
MACRIT [*Manpower Authorization Criteria*] **Planning Factors Study** [*Army*] ... MPFS
Macro Arithmetic Processor [*Computer science*] (MDG) ... MAP
Macro Assembler [*Computer language*] (PCM) ... MASM
Macro Control Processor [*Computer science*] (IAA) ... MACP
Macro Data (IAA) ... MD
Macro Description Language [*Computer science*] (BUR) ... MDL
Macro Directory [*Computer science*] (IAA) ... MD
Macro Editor/Debugger [*Personics Corp.*] [*Computer science*] (PCM) ... MED
Macro Observation Module [*Microscopy*] ... MOM
Macro Operation Symbolic Assembler and Information Compiler [*Computer science*] (IEEE) ... MOSAIC
Macro Output System [*NASA*] (KSC) ... MOIST
[*A*] **Macro Programming Language** [*Computer science*] ... AMPL
Macro Programming Language [*Computer application*] (PCM) ... MPL
Macro Read-Only Memory [*Computer science*] ... MROM
Macro Selection Compiler [*Computer science*] (BUR) ... MSC
Macro Society (EA) ... MS
[*Enhanced*] **Macro Version of Common Assembler Language** [*Interdata*] (NITA) ... MACROCAL
Macroaddress Bus ... MAB
Macroaddress Register ... MAR
Macroaggregated Albumin [*Medicine*] ... MAA
Macroaggregated Ferrous Hydroxide [*Medicine*] (MAE) ... MAFH
Macroaggregated Radioiodinated Albumin [*Radiology*] [*Pharmacy*] (DAVI) ... MARIA
Macroassembler (MHDI) ... MACRO
Macroassembler ... MAS
Macroassembly Language [*Computer science*] (BUR) ... MAL
Macroassembly Program [*Computer science*] ... MAP
Macro-Associative Processor Programming Language [*Computer science*] (PDAA) ... MAPPLE
Macro-Based Display Oriented Language [*Raytheon Co.*] ... MACROL
MacRobertson Miller Airline Services [*Australia*] ... MMA
MacRobertson-Miller Airline Service [*ICAO designator*] (AD) ... MV
Macrobii [*of Lucian*] [*Classical studies*] (OCD) ... Macr
Macrobius [*Late fourth and early fifth century AD*] [*Classical studies*] (OCD) ... Macrob
Macroblock Design ... MBD
MacroChem Corp. [*Associated Press*] (SAG) ... Macr
MacroChem Corp. [*Associated Press*] (SAG) ... Macrch
MacroChem Corp. [*Associated Press*] (SAG) ... MacroCh
MacroChem Corp. [*NASDAQ symbol*] (NQ) ... MCHM
Macrochem Corp. Wrrt'A' [*NASDAQ symbol*] (TTSB) ... MCHML
Macrochem Corp. Wrrt'AA' [*NASDAQ symbol*] (TTSB) ... MCHMM
Macrochem Corp. Wrrt'X' [*NASDAQ symbol*] (TTSB) ... MCHMN
Macrocytic/Normochromic [*Anemia*] [*Hematology*] (DAVI) ... M/E
Macrocytosis [*Hematology*] (DAVI) ... MACR
Macrocytosis [*Hematology*] (DAVI) ... MACRO
Macrodefect Free [*Materials science*] ... MDF
Macrogenerator [*SEMIS*] ... MAG
Macroglobulin-Trypsin [*Complex*] (DAVI) ... M-T
Macroglobulin-Trypsin Complex [*Medicine*] (BABM) ... M-T
Macroinstruction (ECII) ... MACRO
Macroinstruction Compiler Assembler [*Computer science*] ... MICA
Macrolibrary (MHDI) ... maclib
Macromedia, Inc. [*NASDAQ symbol*] (SAG) ... MACR
Macromedia, Inc. [*Associated Press*] (SAG) ... Macrmd
Macromicromodular Hyperplasia [*Medicine*] ... MMH
Macromind Utility Disk ... MUD
Macromodular System [*Computer science*] (IEEE) ... MS
Macromodule and Digital Differential Analyzer Machine [*Computer science*] ... MADDAM
Macromolecular ... MACMOL
Macronix Intl ADR [*NASDAQ symbol*] (TTSB) ... MXICY
Macronutrient Additives [*Fat substituted for food*] ... MA
Macro-Oriented Business Language [*Computer science*] ... MOBL
Macro-Oriented Business Language [*Computer science*] (AD) ... mobl
Macro-Ovalocyte [*Biochemistry*] (DAVI) ... MACC
Macrophage Activating Factor [*Biochemistry*] ... MAF
Macrophage Agglutination Factor [*Biochemistry*] (MAE) ... MAggF
Macrophage and Granulocyte Inducer [*Biochemistry*] ... MGI
Macrophage Chemotactic Factor [*Immunochemistry*] (MAE) ... MCF
Macrophage Derived Growth Factor [*Biochemistry*] ... MDGF
Macrophage Electrophoretic Migration [*Clinical chemistry*] (AAMN) ... MEM
Macrophage Electrophoretic Mobility Test (MAE) ... MEM
Macrophage Growth Factor (PDAA) ... MGF
Macrophage Inflammatory Protein [*Biochemistry*] ... MIP
Macrophage Inhibitory Factor [*Immunology*] ... MIF
Macrophage Migration Inhibition [*Cytology*] ... MMI
Macrophage Rich ... MR
Macrophage Scavenger Receptor [*Immunology*] ... MSR
Macrophage Spreading Factor [*Hematology*] ... MSF
Macrophage Stimulating Protein [*Biochemistry*] ... MSP
Macrophage-Capping Protein [*Biochemistry*] ... MCP

Macrophage-Colony Stimulating Factor [Biochemistry] .... M-CSF
Macrophage-Induced Protein [Biochemistry] .... MIP
Macroprocessor (MHDB) .... macp
Macroprocessor (MHDI) .... MACRO
Macroprocessor .... MP
Macrory's Patent Cases [England] [A publication] (DLA) .... Mac Pat Cas
Macrory's Patent Cases [England] [A publication] (DLA) .... Mac PC
Macrory's Patent Cases [England] [A publication] (DLA) .... Macr
Macrory's Patent Cases [England] [A publication] (DLA) .... Macr P Cas
Macrory's Patent Cases [England] [A publication] (DLA) .... Macr Pat Cas
Macroscopic Quantum Coherence [Physics] .... MQC
Macroscopic Quantum Tunneling [Quantum mechanics] .... MQT
Macrosiphum avenae Virus .... MAV
Macrotext Editor (MHDB) .... MATEX
Macrotrends International [Vancouver Stock Exchange symbol] .... MIT
Macrotrends Ventures, Inc. [Vancouver Stock Exchange symbol] .... MVI
Macrovalocytes [Microbiology] (DAVI) .... M-OVAL
MacSweeney on Mines, Quarries, and Minerals [5 eds.] [1884-1922] [A publication] (DLA) .... MacS
Macular Degeneration [Ophthalmology] .... MD
Macular Degeneration Task Force [Medicine] .... MDTF
Macular Edema [Ophthalmology] (DAVI) .... ME
MACV [Military Assistance Command, Vietnam] **Office of Information** (VNW) .... MACOI
Mad Art Lover .... MAL
MAD [Magnetic Anomaly Detector] **Hunting Circle** (NVT) .... MHC
MAD Operational Effectiveness (DNAB) .... MOE
Mad World Campaign [An association Defunct] (EA) .... MWC
Madagascar .... Mad
Madagascar (ROG) .... MADAG
Madagascar [Malagasy Republic] (VRA) .... Madag
Madagascar [ANSI three-letter standard code] (CNC) .... MDG
Madagascar [ANSI two-letter standard code] (CNC) .... MG
Madagasikara Otronin'ny Malagasy [Formerly, MONIMA] [Madagascar Led by Malagasy] .... MOMA
Madam .... MAD
Madam (DSUE) .... MAM
Madam (WGA) .... Mdm
Madame (ROG) .... MDE
Madame .... MDME
Madang [Papua New Guinea] [ICAO location identifier] (ICLI) .... AYMD
Madang [Papua New Guinea] [Seismograph station code, US Geological Survey] (SEIS) .... MAD
Madang [Papua New Guinea] [Airport symbol] (OAG) .... MAG
Madang [Papua New Guinea] [Seismograph station code, US Geological Survey] (SEIS) .... MDG
Madang Air Services [Australia] .... MAS
Madawaska, ME [FM radio station call letters] .... WCXX
Madawaska, ME [AM radio station call letters] .... WSJR
Madawaska Valley District High School, Barry's Bay, ON, Canada [Library symbol] [Library of Congress] (LCLS) .... CaOBBMV
Madawaska Valley District High School, Barry's Bay, Ontario [Library symbol National Library of Canada] (NLC) .... OBBMV
Madbury, NH [AM radio station call letters] .... WWNH
Madchen-Bibel-Kreise [Bible Reading Circles] [German] .... MBK
Madden on Registration of Deeds [A publication] (DLA) .... Mad Reg
Madden Steven Ltd. [Associated Press] (SAG) .... Madden
Madden Steven Ltd. [Associated Press] (SAG) .... Madn
Madden Steven Ltd. [NASDAQ symbol] (SAG) .... SHOO
Madden (Steven) Ltd [NASDAQ symbol] (TTSB) .... SHOO
Madden (Steven) Wrrt'B' [NASDAQ symbol] (TTSB) .... SHOOZ
Maddock and Geldart's English Chancery Reports [1815-22] [A publication] (DLA) .... M & G
Maddock and Geldart's English Chancery Reports [1815-22] [A publication] (DLA) .... M & Gel
Maddock and Geldart's English Chancery Reports [A publication] (DLA) .... Mad & Gel
Maddock and Geldart's English Chancery Reports [A publication] (DLA) .... Madd & G
Maddock and Geldart's English Chancery Reports [A publication] (DLA) .... Madd & Gel
Maddock's English Chancery Practice [3rd ed.] [1837] [A publication] (DLA) .... Mad Ch Pr
Maddock's English Chancery Practice [A publication] (DLA) .... Madd Ch Pr
Maddock's English Chancery Reports [56 English Reprint] [1815-22] [A publication] (DLA) .... Mad
Maddock's English Chancery Reports [A publication] (DLA) .... Madd
Maddock's English Chancery Reports [56 English Reprint] [1815-22] [A publication] (DLA) .... Madd Ch
Maddock's English Chancery Reports [56 English Reprint] [A publication] (DLA) .... Madd Ch (Eng)
Maddock's Reports [9-18 Montana] [A publication] (DLA) .... Mad
Maddona Resources Corp. [Vancouver Stock Exchange symbol] .... MNO
Maddox and Bach's Reports [19 Montana] [A publication] (DLA) .... Mad & B
Maddox and Bach's Reports [19 Montana] [A publication] (DLA) .... Madd & B
Maddox's Reports [9-18 Montana] [A publication] (DLA) .... Madd
Made in Canada [Business term] .... MIC
Made Merchantable .... MM
Made on Assembly .... MOA
Made Over Democrat [Facetious translation referring to Mods - Moderate Republicans] .... Mod
Made to Order (ODBW) .... MTO
Madeco SA [NYSE symbol] (SPSG) .... MAD
Madeco SA [Associated Press] (SAG) .... Madeco
Madeco S.A. ADS [NYSE symbol] (TTSB) .... MAD
Madeira Abyssal Plain [Geology] .... MAP
Madeira Islands [MARC geographic area code Library of Congress] (LCCP) .... lnma--
Madeira Islands .... Mad Isls
Madeleine Mines Ltd. [Toronto Stock Exchange symbol] .... MN
Madelian Thomas Completion Stories [Psychology] (DAVI) .... MTCS
Mademoiselle .... MDLLE
Mademoiselle [Miss] [French] (EY) .... MLLE
Madera, CA [AM radio station call letters] .... KHOT
Madera, CA [FM radio station call letters] .... KMMM
Madera, CA [FM radio station call letters] .... KZFO
Madera, CA [Location identifier FAA] (FAAL) .... MAE
Madera County Free Public Library, Madera, CA [Library symbol Library of Congress] (LCLS) .... CMa
Maderas y Sinteticos [NYSE symbol] (SPSG) .... MYS
Maderas y Sinteticos ADS [NYSE symbol] (TTSB) .... MYS
Maderas y Sinteticos Sociedad Anonima [Associated Press] (SAG) .... MaderSin
Made-Up Textiles Association [British] (DBA) .... MUTA
Madge Networks N.V. [NASDAQ symbol] (TTSB) .... MADGF
Madge NV [NASDAQ symbol] (SAG) .... MADG
Madge NV [Associated Press] (SAG) .... Madge
Madge NV [Associated Press] (SAG) .... MadgeNt
Madhya Bharat Law Reports [India] [A publication] (DLA) .... MBLR
Madidi [Bolivia] [ICAO location identifier] (ICLI) .... SLMD
Madigan Army Medical Center (AABC) .... MAMC
Madill [S.] **Ltd.** [Vancouver Stock Exchange symbol] .... MDL
Madill, OK [AM radio station call letters] .... KMAD
Madill, OK [FM radio station call letters] .... KMAD-FM
Madinah [Saudi Arabia] [ICAO location identifier] (ICLI) .... OEMA
Madin-Darby Bovine Kidney [Cell line] .... MDBK
Madin-Darby Canine Kidney [Cell line] .... MDCK
Madingou [Congo] [ICAO location identifier] (ICLI) .... FCBG
Madinhae (BJA) .... Md
Madirovalo [Malagasy] [Airport symbol] (AD) .... WMV
Madisn Gas & Elec [NASDAQ symbol] (TTSB) .... MDSN
Madison [Diocesan abbreviation] [Wisconsin] (TOCD) .... MAD
Madison [Wisconsin] [Seismograph station code, US Geological Survey Closed] (SEIS) .... MDS
Madison [Wisconsin] [Airport symbol] (OAG) .... MSN
Madison Academic Computing Center [University of Wisconsin - Madison] [Information service or system Research center] .... MACC
Madison Academy, Madison College, TN [Library symbol Library of Congress] (LCLS) .... TMadM
Madison, AL [AM radio station call letters] (RBYB) .... WUMP
Madison Area Library Council [Library network] .... MALC
Madison Area Technical College, Madison, WI [Library symbol Library of Congress] (LCLS) .... WMaTC
Madison Avenue General Ideas Committee [New York City] .... MAGIC
Madison Avenue Sports Car Driving and Chowder Society (EA) .... MASCDCS
Madison Bancshares Group [NASDAQ symbol] (SAG) .... MADB
Madison Bancshares Group [NASDAQ symbol] (TTSB) .... MADB
Madison Bancshares Group [Associated Press] (SAG) .... MadsBn
Madison Center for Educational Affairs (EA) .... MCEA
Madison Chromosome [Genetics] (DAVI) RM-1
Madison Community, Unit 12, Madison, IL [Library symbol Library of Congress] (LCLS) .... IMadCU
Madison County Library, Canton, MS [Library symbol Library of Congress] (LCLS) .... MsCaM
Madison County Library District, Rexburg, ID [Library symbol] [Library of Congress] (LCLS) .... IdR
Madison County Public Library, Marshall, NC [Library symbol Library of Congress] (LCLS) .... NcMarM
Madison, CT [Location identifier FAA] (FAAL) .... MAD
Madison Daily Courier, Madison, IN [Library symbol Library of Congress] (LCLS) .... InMadC
Madison Eagle, Madison, NJ [Library symbol Library of Congress] (LCLS) .... NjME
Madison Elementary School, St. Cloud, MN [Library symbol] [Library of Congress] (LCLS) .... MnStclM
Madison, FL [AM radio station call letters] .... WMAF
Madison, GA [AM radio station call letters] .... WYTH
Madison Gas & Electric Co. [Associated Press] (SAG) .... MadGE
Madison Gas & Electric Co. [NASDAQ symbol] (NQ) .... MDSN
Madison General Hospital, Madison, WI [Library symbol Library of Congress] (LCLS) .... WMaG
Madison General Hospital, School of Nursing, Madison, WI [Library symbol Library of Congress] (LCLS) .... WMaG-N
Madison Group Assoc [NASDAQ symbol] (TTSB) .... MADI
Madison Historical Society, Madison, NJ [Library symbol Library of Congress] (LCLS) .... NjMHi
Madison Holdings Ltd. [Vancouver Stock Exchange symbol] .... MDH
Madison, IN [Location identifier FAA] (FAAL) .... IMS
Madison, IN [Location identifier FAA] (FAAL) .... MDN
Madison, IN [AM radio station call letters] .... WORX
Madison, IN [FM radio station call letters] .... WORX-FM
Madison, IN [AM radio station call letters] (RBYB) .... WXGO-AM
Madison Junction [Wyoming] [Seismograph station code, US Geological Survey Closed] (SEIS) .... MJW
Madison, ME [FM radio station call letters] .... WHAA
Madison, ME [FM radio station call letters] (RBYB) .... WIGY
Madison Memorial Hospital, Medical Library, Rexburg, ID [Library symbol] [Library of Congress] (LCLS) .... IDRH
Madison Memorial Hospital, Rexburg, ID [Library symbol] [Library of Congress] (LCLS) .... IdRMH
Madison, MN [Location identifier FAA] (FAAL) .... DXX
Madison, MN [FM radio station call letters] .... KLQP

Madison, MS [*Location identifier FAA*] (FAAL) .... MBO
Madison, NJ [*FM radio station call letters*] .... WMNJ
Madison Parish Library, Tallulah, LA [*Library symbol Library of Congress*] (LCLS) .... LTaM
[*The*] **Madison Project** (EA) .... TMP
Madison Public Library, Madison, IL [*Library symbol Library of Congress*] (LCLS) .... IMad
Madison Public Library, Madison, NC [*Library symbol Library of Congress*] (LCLS) .... NcMad
Madison Public Library, Madison, WI [*OCLC symbol*] (OCLC) .... WIM
Madison Public Library, Madison, WI [*Library symbol Library of Congress*] (LCLS) .... WMa
Madison Railway Co., Inc. [*AAR code*] .... MDRY
Madison, SD [*FM radio station call letters*] (RBYB) .... KAMM
Madison, SD [*AM radio station call letters*] .... KJAM
Madison, SD [*FM radio station call letters*] .... KJAM-FM
Madison, SD [*Location identifier FAA*] (FAAL) .... MDS
Madison Square Garden [*New York, NY*] (NADA) .... MSG
Madison Square Garden Network [*Cable-television system*] .... MSG
Madison, TN [*AM radio station call letters*] (RBYB) .... WCKD
Madison Township Historical Society, Matawan, NJ [*Library symbol Library of Congress*] (LCLS) .... NjMatHi
Madison/Truax Field [*Wisconsin*] [*ICAO location identifier*] (ICLI) .... KMSN
Madison, WI [*Location identifier FAA*] (FAAL) .... DSZ
Madison, WI [*Location identifier FAA*] (FAAL) .... TAX
Madison, WI [*FM radio station call letters*] .... WERN
Madison, WI [*AM radio station call letters*] .... WHA
Madison, WI [*Television station call letters*] .... WHA-TV
Madison, WI [*AM radio station call letters*] .... WHIT
Madison, WI [*AM radio station call letters*] .... WIBA
Madison, WI [*FM radio station call letters*] .... WIBA-FM
Madison, WI [*Television station call letters*] .... WISC
Madison, WI [*Television station call letters*] .... WKOW
Madison, WI [*FM radio station call letters*] .... WMGN
Madison, WI [*Television station call letters*] .... WMSN
Madison, WI [*Television station call letters*] .... WMTV
Madison, WI [*FM radio station call letters*] .... WNWC
Madison, WI [*FM radio station call letters*] .... WORT
Madison, WI [*AM radio station call letters*] .... WTDY
Madison, WI [*AM radio station call letters*] .... WTSO
Madison, WI [*FM radio station call letters*] .... WZEE
Madison, WV [*AM radio station call letters*] .... WZAC
Madison-Jefferson County Public Library, Madison, IN [*Library symbol Library of Congress*] (LCLS) .... InMad
Madisonville Community College, Media Center, Madisonville, KY [*Library symbol Library of Congress*] (LCLS) .... KyMadC
Madisonville, KY [*AM radio station call letters*] .... WFMW
Madisonville, KY [*Television station call letters*] .... WKMA
Madisonville, KY [*FM radio station call letters*] .... WKTG
Madisonville, KY [*Television station call letters*] .... WLCN
Madisonville, KY [*FM radio station call letters*] .... WSOF
Madisonville, KY [*AM radio station call letters*] .... WTTL
Madisonville, KY [*FM radio station call letters*] (RBYB) .... WZEZ-FM
Madisonville, TN [*Location identifier FAA*] (FAAL) .... MNV
Madisonville, TN [*AM radio station call letters*] .... WRKQ
Madisonville, TN [*FM radio station call letters*] .... WYGO
Madisonville, TX [*FM radio station call letters*] .... KAGG
Madisonville, TX [*AM radio station call letters*] .... KMVL
Madisonville, TX [*FM radio station call letters*] (RBYB) .... KMVL-FM
Madiun/Iswahyudi [*Indonesia*] [*ICAO location identifier*] (ICLI) .... WIAR
Madjelis Permusiawaratan Rakat [*People's Deliberative Assembly*] [*Indonesia*] (AD) .... MPR
Madly Enthusiastic about Grapes .... MEG
Madness Network News (EA) .... MNN
Mado Robin Society [*Defunct*] (EA) .... MRS
Madoc Public Library, Ontario [*Library symbol National Library of Canada*] (BIB) .... OMAD
Madonna [*Our Lady*] [*Italian*] (AD) .... Mona
Madonna College, Livonia, MI [*OCLC symbol*] (OCLC) .... EYZ
Madonna College, Livonia, MI [*Library symbol Library of Congress*] (LCLS) .... MiLivM
Madonna Heights High School, Huntington, NY [*Library symbol*] [*Library of Congress*] (LCLS) .... NHuMHS
Madonna House Apostolate [*Combermere, ON*] (EAIO) .... MHA
Madonna House Library, Combermere, Ontario [*Library symbol National Library of Canada*] (NLC) .... OCMH
Madonna International Fan Club [*Defunct*] (EA) .... MIFC
Madonna Plan (EA) .... MP
Madox's Barona Anglia [*A publication*] (DLA) .... Mad Bar
Madox's Firma Burgi [*A publication*] (DLA) .... Mad Fir Burg
Madox's Formulare Anglicanum [*A publication*] (DLA) .... Mad Form
Madox's Formulare Anglicanum [*A publication*] (DLA) .... Mad Form Angl
Madox's Formulare Anglicanum [*A publication*] (DLA) .... Madox
Madox's History of the Exchequer [*A publication*] (DLA) .... Mad Exch
Madox's History of the Exchequer [*A publication*] (DLA) .... Mad Hist Exch
Madox's History of the Exchequer [*A publication*] (DLA) .... Madox
Madras [*India*] [*Airport symbol*] (OAG) .... MAA
Madras [*India*] (ROG) .... MADR
Madras [*India*] [*Seismograph station code, US Geological Survey*] (SEIS) .... MDR
Madras [*India*] [*ICAO location identifier*] (ICLI) .... VOMF
Madras [*India*] [*ICAO location identifier*] (ICLI) .... VOMM
Madras Army Native Hospital Corps [*British military*] (DMA) .... MANHC
Madras Artillery [*British military*] (DMA) .... MA
Madras Civil Service [*British*] .... MCS
Madras Code [*India*] [*A publication*] (DLA) .... Mad Co
Madras Criminal Cases [*A publication*] (DLA) .... M Cr C
Madras European Regiment [*British military*] (DMA) .... MER
Madras High Court Reports [*India*] [*A publication*] (DLA) .... Mad
Madras High Court Reports [*India*] [*A publication*] (DLA) .... Mad HC
Madras High Court Reports [*India*] [*A publication*] (DLA) .... MHC
Madras High Court Reports [*India*] [*A publication*] (DLA) .... MHCR
Madras High School, Madras, OR [*Library symbol*] [*Library of Congress*] (LCLS) .... OrMadHS
Madras Infantry [*British*] .... MI
Madras Junior High School, Madras, OR [*Library symbol*] [*Library of Congress*] (LCLS) .... OrMadJH
Madras Jurist [*India*] [*A publication*] (DLA) .... Mad Jur
Madras Jurist [*India*] [*A publication*] (DLA) .... MJ
Madras Lancers [*British military*] (DMA) .... ML
Madras Law Journal and Reports [*India*] [*A publication*] (DLA) .... Madras LJ
Madras Law Reporter [*India*] [*A publication*] (DLA) .... Mad L Rep
Madras Law Reporter [*India*] [*A publication*] (DLA) .... Mad Law Rep
Madras Law Times [*India*] [*A publication*] (DLA) .... Mad LT
Madras Law Times [*India*] [*A publication*] (DLA) .... MLT
Madras Law Weekly [*India*] [*A publication*] (DLA) .... Mad LW
Madras Law Weekly [*India*] [*A publication*] (DLA) .... MLW
Madras Light Cavalry [*British military*] (DMA) .... MLC
Madras Native Infantry [*British*] .... MNI
Madras Sadr Diwani Adalat Reports [*India*] [*A publication*] (DLA) .... Mad SDAR
Madras Sadr Diwani Adalat Reports [*India*] [*A publication*] (DLA) .... SDA Mad
Madras Select Decrees [*A publication*] (DLA) .... Mad Sel Dec
Madras Staff Corps [*British*] .... MSC
Madras Subordinate Medical Department [*British military*] (DMA) .... MSMD
Madras Weekly Notes [*A publication*] (DLA) .... Mad WN
Madras Weekly Notes [*India*] [*A publication*] (DLA) .... MWN
Madras Weekly Notes, Criminal Cases [*India*] [*A publication*] (DLA) .... Mad WNCC
Madras Weekly Notes, Criminal Cases [*India*] [*A publication*] (DLA) .... MWNCC
Madrepores [*Quality of the bottom*] [*Nautical charts*] .... Mds
Madres de los Desamparados [*Mothers of the Helpless*] [*Roman Catholic religious order*] .... MD
Madrid [*Spain ICAO location identifier*] (ICLI) .... LEAC
Madrid [*Spain ICAO location identifier*] (ICLI) .... LECA
Madrid [*Spain ICAO location identifier*] (ICLI) .... LECM
Madrid [*Spain ICAO location identifier*] (ICLI) .... LEEE
Madrid [*Spain ICAO location identifier*] (ICLI) .... LEMM
Madrid [*Spain ICAO location identifier*] (ICLI) .... LESP
Madrid [*Spain*] [*Airport symbol*] (OAG) .... MAD
Madrid [*Spain*] .... MAD
Madrid [*Spain*] [*Seismograph station code, US Geological Survey Closed*] (SEIS) .... MDD
Madrid/Barajas [*Spain ICAO location identifier*] (ICLI) .... LEMD
Madrid/Cuatro Vientos [*Spain ICAO location identifier*] (ICLI) .... LEVS
Madrid Deep Space Communications Complex .... MDSCC
Madrid/Getafe [*Spain ICAO location identifier*] (ICLI) .... LEGT
Madrid Interbank Offered Rate (MHDW) .... MIBOR
Madrid Predict [*Orbit identification*] .... MDPR
Madrid, Spain [*Spaceflight Tracking and Data Network*] [*NASA*] .... MAX
Madrid Stock-Exchange Index [*Spain*] (ECON) .... MSCI
Madrid/Torrejon [*Spain ICAO location identifier*] (ICLI) .... LETO
Madritum [*Madrid*] [*Imprint*] [*Latin*] (ROG) .... MADR
Madrona Resources, Inc. [*Vancouver Stock Exchange symbol*] .... MDS
Madurai [*India*] [*Airport symbol*] (OAG) .... IXM
Madurai [*India*] [*ICAO location identifier*] (ICLI) .... VOMD
Mae Hong Son [*Thailand*] [*Airport symbol*] (OAG) .... HGN
Mae Hong Son [*Thailand*] [*ICAO location identifier*] (ICLI) .... VTCH
Mae Hong Son/Khun Yuam [*Thailand*] [*ICAO location identifier*] (ICLI) .... VTCK
Mae Hong Son/Mae Sariang [*Thailand*] [*ICAO location identifier*] (ICLI) .... VTCS
Mae Hong Son/Pai [*Thailand*] [*ICAO location identifier*] (ICLI) .... VTCI
Mae Smythe Elementary School, Pasadena, TX [*Library symbol*] [*Library of Congress*] (LCLS) .... TxPSE
Maebashi [*Japan*] [*Seismograph station code, US Geological Survey*] (SEIS) .... MAE
Maelzel's Metronome [*Music*] .... MM
Maersk Air IS [*Denmark ICAO designator*] (FAAC) .... DMA
Maersk Commuter IS [*Netherlands ICAO designator*] (FAAC) .... MAE
Maestoso [*Majestic*] [*Music*] .... Maes
Maestoso [*Majestic*] [*Music*] .... MAESTO
Maestretti [*Italy*] [*Research code symbol*] .... LM
Maestro [*Record label*] [*Belgium, etc.*] .... Mae
Maestro (AD) .... Mro
Maestro GG1MasterGG2 [*Italian*] (AD) .... Mo
Maeventec Employers Rated Almanac [*Maeventec*] [*Information service or system*] (CRD) .... MERA
Maeventec Travel Information [*Maeventec*] [*Information service or system*] (CRD) .... MTI
Maewo-Naone [*Vanuatu*] [*ICAO location identifier*] (ICLI) .... NVSN
MAF Bancorp [*NASDAQ symbol*] (SPSG) .... MAFB
MAF Bancorp, Inc. [*Associated Press*] (SAG) .... MAF Bcp
Mafco Consolidated Group [*Associated Press*] (SAG) .... Mafco
Mafco Consolidated Group [*NYSE symbol*] (SAG) .... MFO
Mafeking [*South Africa*] [*Airport symbol*] (OAG) .... MFK
Mafeking, MB [*Television station call letters*] .... CBWYT
Mafeteng [*Lesotho*] [*ICAO location identifier*] (ICLI) .... FXMF
Mafia [*Tanzania*] [*ICAO location identifier*] (ICLI) .... HTMA
Mafia Islands [*Tanzania*] [*Airport symbol*] (OAG) .... MFA
Mafic Granulite [*Geology*] .... mg
Mafikeng [*South Africa*] [*ICAO location identifier*] (ICLI) .... FAMK
Mafinga [*Tanzania*] [*ICAO location identifier*] (ICLI) .... HTSH
Mafraq [*Jordan*] [*ICAO location identifier*] (ICLI) .... OJMF

Magadan [*Former USSR Seismograph station code, US Geological Survey*] (SEIS) ... MAG
Magadan [*Later, FUR*] [*Former USSR Geomagnetic observatory code*] ... MGD
Magadan 1 [*Former USSR Seismograph station code, US Geological Survey*] (SEIS) ... MGD
Magadan Airlines [*Russian Federation*] [*ICAO designator*] (FAAC) ... MVL
Magadi [*Kenya*] [*ICAO location identifier*] (ICLI) ... HKMG
Magadi [*India*] [*ICAO location identifier*] (ICLI) ... VOMG
Magahi [*MARC language code Library of Congress*] (LCCP) ... mag
Magainin Pharmaceuticals [*NASDAQ symbol*] (SPSG) ... MAGN
Magainin Pharmaceuticals [*Associated Press*] (SAG) ... MagPhr
Magal Security Systems [*Commercial firm Associated Press*] (SAG) ... Magal
Magal Security Systems [*NASDAQ symbol*] (SAG) ... MAGS
Magal Security Systems Ltd [*NASDAQ symbol*] (TTSB) ... MAGSF
Magalia [*California*] [*Seismograph station code, US Geological Survey*] (SEIS) ... MGL
Magalia, CA [*FM radio station call letters*] ... KLVC
Magangue [*Colombia*] [*Airport symbol*] (AD) ... MGN
Magangue/Baracoa [*Colorado ICAO location identifier*] (ICLI) ... SKMG
Magazine (VRA) ... mag
Magazine (AFM) ... MAG
Magazine ... MAG
Magazine [*Slang*] (WDMC) ... mag
Magazine ... MAG
Magazine ... Magz
Magazine (ABBR) ... MGN
Magazine Advertising Bureau [*of MPA*] ... MAB
Magazine Advertising Sales Club (EA) ... MASC
Magazine and Paperback Marketing Institute (EA) ... MPMI
Magazine and Periodical Publishers Exhibition (NITA) ... MAPPEX
Magazine Antiques [*A publication*] (BRI) ... Mag Antiq
Magazine Capacity [*Military*] ... MAGCAP
Magazine Cartoonists Guild [*Later, CG*] (EA) ... MCG
Magazine Flooding and Sprinkling ... MF & S
Magazine Index [*Information Access Corp.*] [*Information service or system*] (IID) ... MI
Magazine Industry Market Place [*A publication*] ... MIMP
Magazine Lee-Enfield [*British military*] (DMA) ... MLE
Magazine Lee-Metford [*British military*] (DMA) ... MLM
Magazine of Fantasy and Science Fiction [*A publication*] (BRI) ... MFSF
Magazine of History [*A publication*] (BRI) ... M of Hist
Magazine Page Exposure [*Publishing*] (WDMC) ... MPX
Magazine Page Interactive Editor (DGA) ... MAGPIE
Magazine Printers Section (EA) ... MPS
Magazine Promotion Group [*Defunct*] (EA) ... MPG
Magazine Publisher's Association (NTCM) ... MPA
Magazine Publishers of America [*New York, NY Database producer*] (IID) ... MPA
Magazine Research, Inc. (AD) ... MRI
Magazine Shippers Association ... MSA
Magazine-Catalog [*Advertising*] ... Magalog
Magazines for Friendship [*An association*] (EA) ... MF
Magazines for Industry [*An association*] ... MFI
Magcobar Corp., Houston, TX [*Library symbol Library of Congress*] (LCLS) ... TxHMa
Magdalen College [*Oxford University*] (ROG) ... MAGD
Magdalen College School Cadets [*British military*] (DMA) ... MCSC
Magdalen Island [*Quebec*] [*Airport symbol*] (AD) ... YGR
Magdalena [*Bolivia*] [*ICAO location identifier*] (ICLI) ... SLMG
Magdalena Milpas Altas [*Guatemala*] [*Seismograph station code, US Geological Survey*] (SEIS) ... MMG
Magdalene College, Cambridge University [*England*] (ROG) ... MAGD
Magdalene College, Cambridge University [*England*] (ROG) ... MCC
Magdalenian (VRA) ... Magdl
Magdeburg [*Germany ICAO location identifier*] (ICLI) ... ETMG
Magec Aviation Ltd. [*British ICAO designator*] (FAAC) ... MGC
Magee, MS [*FM radio station call letters*] ... WKXI
Magellan Health Svcs [*AMEX symbol*] (TTSB) ... MGL
Magellan Petroleum [*Exchange Symbol*] (TTSB) ... MPC
Magellan Petroleum Corp. [*Associated Press*] (SAG) ... MagelPt
Magellan Petroleum Corp. [*NASDAQ symbol*] (NQ) ... MPET
Magellan Resources Corp. [*Vancouver Stock Exchange symbol*] ... MGS
Magellan Restauraunt System [*Associated Press*] (SAG) ... MagelRst
Magelssen Elementary School, Fosston, MN [*Library symbol*] [*Library of Congress*] (LCLS) ... MnFtME
Magen David Adom [*Israel's Red Cross Service*] ... MDA
Magen on Insurance [*A publication*] (DLA) ... Mag Ins
Magenta (WDMC) ... M
Magenta (WDMC) ... m
Magenta (ROG) ... MAG
Magenta (ROG) ... MG
Magenta Development Corp. [*Vancouver Stock Exchange symbol*] ... MGT
Magestic Agency for Joint Intelligence ... MAJI
Maggie Mines [*Vancouver Stock Exchange symbol*] ... MAG
Maggioni & C. [*Italy*] [*Research code symbol*] ... MG
Maggiore [*Major*] [*Music*] ... MAGG
Maggot (ABBR) ... MGOT
Maghemite [*A mineral*] ... Mg
Maghemite, Inc. [*Vancouver Stock Exchange symbol*] ... MHT
Maghreb (BJA) ... Magh
Maghreb-Arabe Presse [*Maghreb Arab Press Agency*] [*Morocco*] ... MAP
Magic (ABBR) ... MGC
Magic ... MGC
Magic Angle Sample Spinning [*Spectroscopy*] ... MASS
Magic Angle Spinning [*Spectroscopy*] ... MAS
Magic Angle Spinning Nuclear Magnetic Resonance [*Spectroscopy*] ... MASNMR
Magic Answer Extractor [*Database*] ... MAX
Magic Circle [*An association*] (EA) ... MC
Magic Collectors' Association (EA) ... MCA
Magic Dealers Association [*Later, IMDA*] ... MDA
Magic Eye (DEN) ... ME
Magic Eye Tube ... MET
Magic Foods, Inc. [*Vancouver Stock Exchange symbol*] ... MFD
Magic Kingdom [*Walt Disney World*] ... MK
Magic Kingdom Club [*Walt Disney Productions*] ... MKC
Magic Lantern Film Society [*An association*] ... MLFS
Magic Lantern Society of the United States and Canada (EA) ... ML
Magic Restaurants [*NASDAQ symbol*] (TTSB) ... MGIKQ
Magic Restaurants Wrrt [*NASDAQ symbol*] (TTSB) ... MGIWQ
Magic Software Enterprises [*Associated Press*] (SAG) ... MagSft
Magic Software Enterprises [*NASDAQ symbol*] (TTSB) ... MGICF
Magic Software Enterprises, Inc. [*NASDAQ symbol*] (SAG) ... MGIC
Magic Tee (IAA) ... MT
Magic Valley Regional Library System [*Library network*] ... MVLS
Magic Valley Regional Medical Center, Medical Library, Twin Falls, ID [*Library symbol*] [*Library of Congress*] (LCLS) ... IdTfH
Magical (ABBR) ... MGCL
Magical Blend [*A publication*] ... Mag Bl
Magical Blend [*A publication*] (BRI) ... Mag Bl
Magical Youths International (EA) ... MYI
Magically (ABBR) ... MGCLY
Magician (ABBR) ... MGCN
Magic-Tone Records [*Record label*] ... MTR
Magister [*Master*] [*Latin*] ... M
Magister [*Master*] [*Latin*] ... mgr
Magister [*Master*] [*Latin*] (ROG) ... MR
Magister Architecturae [*Master of Architecture*] [*Latin*] ... Mag Arch
Magister Artium [*Master of Arts*] [*Latin*] ... MA
Magister Chirurgiae [*Master of Surgery*] [*Latin*] ... M Ch
Magister Chirurgiae [*Master of Surgery*] ... M Chir
Magister Chirurgiae [*Master of Surgery*] ... MC
Magister Chirurgiae Dentalis [*Master of Dental Surgery*] ... M Ch D
Magister in Arte Ingeniaria [*Master of Engineering*] ... MAI
Magister Melendus [*Flourished, 1188-1209*] [*Authority cited in pre-1607 legal work*] (DSA) ... MM
Magister Pharmaciae [*Master of Pharmacy*] [*Latin*] ... Mag Pharm
Magister Philosophiae [*Master of Philosophy*] [*Latin*] ... Mag Phil
Magister Philosophiae Facultatis Theologicae [*Latin*] ... Mag Phil Fac Theol
Magister Rerum Naturalium [*Latin*] ... Mag Rer Nat
Magister Rerum Socialium Oeconomicarumque [*Latin*] ... Mag Rer Soc Oec
Magister Scientia Dentalis [*Master of Dental Science*] [*British*] ... MScD
Magister Theologiae [*Master of Theology*] [*Latin*] ... Mag Theol
Magisterial (ABBR) ... MGSTL
Magisterial Cases [*England*] [*A publication*] (DLA) ... Mag Cas
Magistrae Piae Venerini [*Religious Venerini Sisters*] [*Roman Catholic religious order*] ... MPV
Magistrate ... M
[*The*] **Magistrate** [*London*] [*A publication*] (DLA) ... Mag
[*The*] **Magistrate** [*Australia A publication*] (ILCA) ... Mag
Magistrate ... MAGIS
Magistrate ... MAGSTR
Magistrate (ABBR) ... MGSTRA
Magistrate and Constable [*A publication*] (DLA) ... Mag & Con
Magistrate and Constable [*A publication*] (DLA) ... Mag & Const
Magistrate and Constable [*Pennsylvania*] [*A publication*] (DLA) ... Magis & Const (PA)
Magistrate and Municipal and Parochial Lawyer [*London*] [*A publication*] (DLA) ... Mag
Magistrate and Municipal and Parochial Lawyer [*A publication*] (DLA) ... Mag & M & PL
Magistrate and Municipal and Parochial Lawyer [*A publication*] (DLA) ... Mag Mun Par Law
Magistrates (ROG) ... MAGS
Magistrates' Appeal Cases [*A publication*] (DLA) ... MAC
Magistrates' Cases [*Reprinted from Law Journal Reports*] [*1892-1910*] [*A publication*] (DLA) ... Mag Cas
Magistrates Cases [*Legal term British*] ... MC
Magistrates' Court (DLA) ... Mag Ct
Magistrates' Court (DLA) ... Magis Ct
Magistrates' Court Decisions [*New Zealand*] [*A publication*] (DLA) ... MCD
Magistrates' Court Reports [*New Zealand*] [*A publication*] (DLA) ... MCR
Magistrates' Court Reports (New Zealand) [*A publication*] (ILCA) ... MCR (NZ)
[*The*] **Magistrates of the Roman Republic** [*A publication*] (OCD) ... MRR
Magma (ABBR) ... MGMA
Magma Arizona Railroad Co. [*Later, MAA*] [*AAR code*] ... MA
Magma Arizona Railroad Co. [*AAR code*] ... MAA
Magma Copper Co. [*Associated Press*] (SAG) ... MagC
Magma Copper Co. [*Associated Press*] (SAG) ... Magmc
Magma Copper Co. [*NYSE symbol*] (SPSG) ... MCU
Magna Bancorp [*Associated Press*] (SAG) ... MagnaBb
Magna Bancorp [*NASDAQ symbol*] (SAG) ... MGNL
Magna Bibliotheca Anglo-Judaica (BJA) ... MBAJ
Magna Britannia [*Great Britain*] [*Latin*] (ROG) ... MAG BRIT
Magna Brittannia, Gallia, et Hibernia [*Great Britain, France, and Ireland*] [*Latin*] (ROG) ... MBG & H
Magna Carta Dames, National Society (EA) ... MCD
Magna Charta [*or Carta*] [*Great Charter*] [*Latin*] [*A publication*] (DLA) ... Mag Char
Magna Group, Inc. [*Associated Press*] (SAG) ... MagGp
Magna Group, Inc. [*NASDAQ symbol*] (NQ) ... MAGI
Magna International, Inc. [*Associated Press*] (SAG) ... Magnal
Magna International, Inc. [*Toronto Stock Exchange symbol*] ... MG

Magna International, Inc. [*NYSE symbol*] (SPSG) .... MGA
Magna International, Inc., Markham, Ontario [*Library symbol National Library of Canada*] (BIB) .... OMMI
Magna Moralia [*of Aristotle*] [*Classical studies*] (OCD) .... Mag Mor
Magna Ventures Ltd. [*Vancouver Stock Exchange symbol*] .... MVN
Magnaflux .... M
Magna-Lab 'A' [*NASDAQ symbol*] (TTSB) .... MAGLA
Magna-Lab, Inc. [*NASDAQ symbol*] (SAG) .... MAGL
Magna-Lab, Inc. [*Associated Press*] (SAG) .... Magna
Magna-Lab, Inc. [*Associated Press*] (SAG) .... MagnaL
Magna-Lab, Inc. [*Associated Press*] (SAG) .... Mgna
Magna-Lab Unit [*NASDAQ symbol*] (TTSB) .... MAGLU
Magna-Lab Wrrt 'A' [*NASDAQ symbol*] (TTSB) .... MAGLW
Magna-Lab Wrrt 'B' [*NASDAQ symbol*] (TTSB) .... MAGLZ
Magna-Lab Wrrt 'E' [*NASDAQ symbol*] (TTSB) .... MAGLL
Magnanimity (ABBR) .... MGNMT
Magnanimous (ABBR) .... MGNMU
Magnanimous Green Leprechaun .... MGL
Magnate (ABBR) .... MGNT
Magnatek, Inc. [*Associated Press*] (SAG) .... Magntk
Magnavox Co., Fort Wayne, IN [*Library symbol Library of Congress*] (LCLS) .... InFwM
Magnavox Doppler and Ranging RADAR (NG) .... MAGDARR
Magnavox Electronic Data Image Apparatus .... MEDIA
Magnesia-Alumina-Silicate [*Inorganic chemistry*] .... MAS
Magnesia-Buffered Zinc Oxide (PDAA) .... MBZ
Magnesiowustite [*Mineralogy*] .... MW
Magnesite and Chrome Brickmakers Association [*British*] (DBA) .... MCBA
Magnesium [*Chemical symbol is Mg*] .... MAG
Magnesium (VRA) .... magns
Magnesium [*Chemical element*] .... Mg
Magnesium [*Chemical symbol is Mg*] .... MGNSM
Magnesium Aspartate Hydrochloride [*Antihypertensive*] .... MAH
Magnesium Association [*Later, IMA*] (EA) .... MA
Magnesium Chlorate [*Inorganic chemistry*] .... MC
Magnesium Citrate [*Pharmacy*] .... mag cit
Magnesium Deficiency [*Medicine*] (DMAA) .... MD
Magnesium Elektron Ltd. [*British*] (IRUK) .... MEL
Magnesium Excretion [*Medicine*] (DAVI) .... $U_{Mg}V$
Magnesium Flat Cell .... MFC
Magnesium Industry Council [*British*] (BI) .... MIC
Magnesium Methyl Carbonate [*Organic chemistry*] .... MMC
Magnesium Oxide [*Magnesium-based alloy*] .... MAGNOX
Magnesium Oxide [*Acronym is trademark of Basic Chemicals*] .... MAGOX
Magnesium Pemoline [*Pharmacology*] .... MPL
Magnesium Pyridoxal Phosphate Glutamate [*Biochemistry*] .... MPPG
Magnesium Sulfate [*Pharmacology*] (DAVI) .... mag sulf
Magnesium Sulfate, Glycerine, and Water (Enema) [*Medicine*] .... MGW
Magnesium-Aluminum Hydroxide [*Commercial antacid*] .... MAALOX
Magnesium-Thorium [*Inorganic chemistry*] .... MAG-THOR
Magnet (ABBR) .... MGNT
Magnetawan Area Union Public Library, Magnetawan, Ontario [*Library symbol National Library of Canada*] (NLC) .... OMAU
Magnetech Corp. [*Associated Press*] (SAG) .... MagCp
MagneTek, Inc. [*NYSE symbol*] (SPSG) .... MAG
Magnetic .... M
Magnetic (AFM) .... MAG
Magnetic (WDMC) .... mag
Magnetic (ROG) .... MAGN
Magnetic (ABBR) .... MGNETC
Magnetic .... MGNTC
Magnetic .... MT
Magnetic Abrasion Resistant Coating (IAA) .... MARC
Magnetic Acoustic Detection of Mines (DOMA) .... MADOM
Magnetic Airborne Detector [*Navy*] .... MAD
Magnetic Airborne Recording System .... MARS
Magnetic Aircraft Weapons Link .... MAWL
Magnetic Amplification of Microwave Integrated Emissions (IEEE) .... MAMIE
Magnetic Amplifier .... MA
Magnetic Amplifier .... MAGAMP
Magnetic Amplifier (IDOE) .... magamp
Magnetic Amplifier Bridge .... MAB
Magnetic Amplifier Output .... MAO
Magnetic Amplifier Output Stage .... MAOS
Magnetic Amplifier Relay .... MAR
Magnetic and Germanium Integer Calculator (DEN) .... MAGIC
Magnetic Anisotropy Field .... MAF
Magnetic Annular Arc (IEEE) .... MAARC
Magnetic Annular Shock Tube .... MAST
Magnetic Anomaly Detection [*or Detector*] .... MAD
Magnetic Anomaly Detection and Identification Ranging (MCD) .... MADAIR
Magnetic Anomaly Detection Exercise (NVT) .... MADEX
Magnetic Anomaly Detector Contact Man (NVT) .... MADMAN
Magnetic Anomaly Detector Vectoring [*Military*] (CAAL) .... MADVEC
Magnetic Antibody Immunoassay .... MAIA
Magnetic Anti-Intrusion Detector (PDAA) .... MAID
Magnetic Anti-Intrusion Detector/Magnetic Intrusion Line Sensor (MCD) .... MAID/MILES
Magnetic Armature (MSA) .... MG
Magnetic Armature Loudspeaker .... MAL
Magnetic Attitude Control .... MAC
Magnetic Attitude Prediction .... MGAP
Magnetic Attitude Spin Coil .... MASC
Magnetic Automatic Calculator (DEN) .... MAC
Magnetic Automatic Navigation [*System*] (RDA) .... MAN

Magnetic Azimuth Detector (MCD) .... MAD
Magnetic Bearing [*Navigation*] (DNAB) .... MAGBRG
Magnetic Bearing [*Navigation*] .... MB
Magnetic Bias Coil (IIA) .... MBC
Magnetic Bias Control (DNAB) .... MBC
Magnetic Brake [*Industrial control*] (IEEE) .... MB
Magnetic Bubble Memory [*Computer science*] .... MBM
Magnetic Bubble Unit (NITA) .... MBU
Magnetic Capability and Safety System (NVT) .... MACAS
Magnetic Card [*Electronics*] (ECII) .... MAGCARD
Magnetic Card [*Word processing*] .... MC
Magnetic Card and Tape Unit (IAA) .... MCT
Magnetic Card Memory [*Computer science*] (IAA) .... MCM
Magnetic Card Reader [*Computer science*] .... MCR
Magnetic Card Selecting (DNAB) .... MCS
Magnetic Card Selectric Typewriter (NITA) .... MC/ST
Magnetic Card "Selectric" Typewriter [*IBM Corp.*] .... MCST
Magnetic Card Unit [*Computer science*] (IAA) .... MCU
Magnetic Cast Iron (IAA) .... MAGCI
Magnetic Cast Steel (IAA) .... MAGCS
Magnetic Character Reader [*Computer science*] (IEEE) .... MCR
Magnetic Character Recognition [*Computer science*] (BUR) .... MCR
Magnetic Character Typewriter (PDAA) .... MCT
Magnetic Circular Dichroism .... MCD
Magnetic Circular X-Ray Dichroism [*Light polarization*] .... MCXD
Magnetic Circularly Polarized Luminescence [*Spectroscopy*] .... MCPL
Magnetic Clutch .... MC
Magnetic Compass Record Book .... MCRB
Magnetic Compass Table (DNAB) .... MCT
Magnetic Compensator Group .... MCG
Magnetic Confinement Fusion [*Physics*] .... MCF
Magnetic Confinement Reactor .... MCR
Magnetic Core .... MC
Magnetic Core Memory [*Computer science*] .... MCM
Magnetic Core Tape .... MCT
Magnetic Core Tester .... MCT
Magnetic Core Transistor Relay (IAA) .... MTR
Magnetic Coupling System (MCD) .... MCS
Magnetic Course [*Navigation*] .... MC
Magnetic Crack Definer [*Aviation*] .... MCD
Magnetic Cushion Vehicle (IEEE) .... MCV
Magnetic Czochralski Process [*Crystallization*] .... MCZ
Magnetic Decision Element [*Computer science*] (BUR) .... MDE
Magnetic Deflection [*Cathode-ray tube*] (DEN) .... MD
Magnetic Deflection Amplifier .... MDA
Magnetic Deflection Yoke .... MDY
Magnetic Delay Line .... MDL
Magnetic Detection Indicator (IAA) .... MDI
Magnetic Detection of Submarines [*British military*] (DMA) .... MDS
Magnetic Device Evaluator [*Computer science*] .... MADE
Magnetic Digital Versatile Disc .... M-DVD
Magnetic Digital-Pulse Generator .... MDPG
Magnetic Dipole Radiation .... MDR
Magnetic Dipole Spark Transmitter (NASA) .... MAPOLE
Magnetic Direction Finding [*Meteorology*] .... MDF
Magnetic Direction Indicator .... MDI
Magnetic Disc Memory .... MDM
Magnetic Disc Recorder (NTCM) .... MDR
Magnetic Disk [*Computer science*] (BUR) .... MD
Magnetic Disk Control Unit .... MDCU
Magnetic Disk Drive .... MDD
Magnetic Disk Storage [*Computer science*] (IAA) .... MDS
Magnetic Disk Storage Device [*Computer science*] .... MDSD
Magnetic Document Reader (IAA) .... MDR
Magnetic Double Layer .... MDL
Magnetic Drum .... MD
Magnetic Drum Data Processing Machine (IAA) .... MDDPM
Magnetic Drum Digital Differential Analyzer .... MADDIDA
Magnetic Drum Head .... MDH
Magnetic Drum Memorex [*Computer science*] (IAA) .... MDM
Magnetic Drum Module [*Computer science*] .... DM
Magnetic Drum RADAR Equipment .... MADRE
Magnetic Drum Receiving Equipment .... MADRE
Magnetic Drum Recorder .... MDR
Magnetic Drum Storage [*Computer science*] (IAA) .... MDS
Magnetic Drum Storage System .... MDSS
Magnetic Drum System .... MDS
Magnetic Electron Multiplier (PDAA) .... MEM
Magnetic Emulsion Spectrometer .... MESS
Magnetic Energy Product .... MEP
Magnetic Engineering Associates, Inc. .... MEA
Magnetic Environment Measuring Equipment (CAAL) .... MEME
Magnetic Estimation (OA) .... ME
Magnetic Field .... MF
Magnetic Field Calibration System .... MFCS
Magnetic Field Code .... MAFCO
Magnetic Field Dependent Resistor (IAA) .... MDR
Magnetic Field Energy .... MFE
Magnetic Field Explorer [*NASA*] .... MFE
Magnetic Field Indicator .... MFI
Magnetic Field Integral Equation (PDAA) .... MFIE
Magnetic Field Intensity .... MFI
Magnetic Field Line .... MFL
Magnetic Field Monitor [*NASA*] .... MFM
Magnetic Field Perturbation .... MFP

Magnetic Field Satellite [*NASA*] (MCD) .... MAGSAT
Magnetic Field Strength .... MFS
Magnetic Field Vector .... MFV
Magnetic Field-Induced Superconductivity .... MFIS
Magnetic Film Counter .... MFC
Magnetic Film Handler (CMD) .... MFH
Magnetic Film Strip Recorder .... MFSR
Magnetic Flight Test Recording System .... MFTRS
Magnetic Flip-Flop [*Computer science*] .... MFF
Magnetic Flow Transmitter .... MFT
Magnetic Fluid [*Physics*] .... MF
Magnetic Flux [*Symbol*] (ROG) .... N
Magnetic Flux [*or Flow*] Density .... b
Magnetic Focus [*of cathode-ray tube*] (DEN) .... MF
Magnetic Force Microscope .... MFM
Magnetic Force Upset [*Metals*] .... MFU
Magnetic Force Upset Welding [*Metals*] .... MFUW
Magnetic Forming Machine .... MFM
Magnetic Frequency Detector .... MFD
Magnetic Fusion Advisory Committee [*Department of Energy*] [*Washington, DC*] .... MFAC
Magnetic Fusion Energy .... MFE
Magnetic Fusion Energy Research Network [*Department of Energy*] .... MFENET
Magnetic Fusion Engineering Act .... MFEA
Magnetic Head [*or Heading*] .... MH
Magnetic Heading Reference System .... MHRS
Magnetic Heading System (AAG) .... MHS
Magnetic Heart Vector [*Cardiology*] .... MHV
Magnetic Immunochemistry [*Laboratory analysis*] .... MAGIC
Magnetic Indicator Loop (NVT) .... MIL
Magnetic Induction (DAS) .... B
Magnetic Induction Field [*Radiology*] (DAVI) .... Bp
Magnetic Induction Nuclear Gyroscope .... MING
Magnetic Induction Plasma Engine .... MIPE
Magnetic Injection Gun (IEEE) .... MIG
Magnetic Ink Character [*Computer science*] (HGAA) .... MIC
Magnetic Ink Character Recognition [*Banking*] [*Computer science*] .... MICR
Magnetic Ink Character Recognition / Magnetic Ink Mark Recognition (BTTJ) .... MICR/MIMR
Magnetic Ink Mark Recognition .... MIMR
Magnetic Ink Read .... MIR
Magnetic Insulation Test Experiment .... MITE
Magnetic Integrator Neuron Duplicator .... MIND
Magnetic Interaction Mechanism .... MIM
Magnetic Intrusion Detector (NVT) .... MAGID
Magnetic Intrusion Line Sensor (PDAA) .... MILES
Magnetic Ionization Experiment .... MIX
Magnetic Isotope Effect [*Physics*] .... MIE
Magnetic Latch (MUGU) .... MAGLATCH
Magnetic Latching [*Electronics*] (OA) .... ML
Magnetic Latching Relay (MCD) .... MLR
Magnetic Ledger Card (CMD) .... MLC
Magnetic Ledger Card Unit [*Computer science*] (MHDB) .... MLCU
Magnetic Lens Assembly .... MLA
Magnetic Level Indicator .... MLI
Magnetic Levitation Transportation .... MLT
Magnetic Levitation Vehicle (BARN) .... MLV
Magnetic Linear Birefringence (MCD) .... MLB
Magnetic Local Time .... MLT
Magnetic Logic Computer .... MAGLOC
Magnetic Materials Producers Association (EA) .... MMPA
Magnetic Materials Products Association (AAGC) .... MMPA
Magnetic Memory Record (NITA) .... MMR
Magnetic Metal-Oxide-Semiconductor Field-Effect Transistor (PDAA) .... MAGFET
Magnetic Minesweeping (MSA) .... MMS
Magnetic Mirror Device .... MMD
Magnetic Modulator .... MAGMOD
Magnetic Modulator (SAA) .... MAGNETTOR
Magnetic Moment [*Symbol*] (DEN) .... M
Magnetic North .... MN
Magnetic Optic Converter .... MOC
Magnetic Optical Display .... MOD
Magnetic Particle .... MP
Magnetic Particle Brake .... MPB
Magnetic Particle Clutch .... MPC
Magnetic Particle Inspection .... MPI
Magnetic Particle Inspection (AD) .... mpi
Magnetic Particle Testing [*Nuclear energy*] (NRCH) .... MPT
Magnetic Particle Testing [*Nuclear energy*] (IEEE) .... MT
Magnetic Peripherals Inc. (NITA) .... MPI
Magnetic Phase Modulator .... MPM
Magnetic Pickup [*Electronics*] .... MPU
Magnetic Polarization [*Symbol*] (DEN) .... M
Magnetic Polarization Vector .... MPV
Magnetic Pole Strength .... MPS
Magnetic Poparization [*Physics*] (BARN) .... J
Magnetic Porous Glass [*Materials science*] .... MPG
Magnetic Powder Core Association (EA) .... MPCA
Magnetic Press, Inc. [*Information service or system*] (IID) .... MPI
Magnetic Pressure (NVT) .... MP
Magnetic Quantum Number [*Atomic physics*] [*Symbol*] .... m
Magnetic Quantum Number [*Atomic physics*] .... MQN
Magnetic Radiation Generator .... MRG
Magnetic Radiation Generator (AD) .... mrg
Magnetic Raman Optical Activity [*Spectrometry*] .... MROA
Magnetic Random-Access Memory [*Computer science*] (PS) .... MRAM
Magnetic Reaction Analyzer (PDAA) .... MRA
Magnetic Recorder [*or Recording*] (IAA) .... MGREC
Magnetic Recorder (DEN) .... MR
Magnetic Recording Boresight [*or Borescope*] .... MRB
Magnetic Recording Head .... MRH
Magnetic Recording Industry Association [*Later, Electronic Industries Association*] (EA) .... MRIA
Magnetic Rectifier Control .... MRC
Magnetic Rectifier Control (AD) .... mrc
Magnetic Reed Rotary Switch .... MRRS
Magnetic Reed Switch .... MRS
Magnetic Research Corp. (MCD) .... MRC
Magnetic Resonance .... MR
Magnetic Resonance Gyro (MCD) .... MRG
Magnetic Resonance Imaging [*Medicine*] .... MRI
Magnetic Resonance Imaging [*Medical*] .... MRI
Magnetic Resonance Spectrum .... MRS
Magnetic Resonating (AD) .... MR
Magnetic Rubber Inspection (AD) .... mri
Magnetic Scalar Potential .... MSP
Magnetic Sensing Intrusion Device [*Remote sensor*] [*Also, M-SID*] [*Military*] (VNW) .... MAGNA-SID
Magnetic Sensing Intrusion Device [*Remote sensor*] [*Also, MAGNA-SID*] [*Military*] (VNW) .... M-SID
Magnetic Shield Simulator (PDAA) .... MAGSIM
Magnetic Shift Register .... MSR
Magnetic Shock Pulse Generator (IAA) .... MSPG
Magnetic Silencing Facility [*Kingsburg, GA*] (DWSG) .... MSF
Magnetic Silencing Range [*Navy*] (DOMA) .... MSR
Magnetic Silencing Ranger (DWSG) .... MSR
Magnetic Solar Daily Variation .... S
Magnetic South .... MS
Magnetic Spark Spectrometer (PDAA) .... MSS
Magnetic Speed Variable Assist [*General Motors*] [*Power steering*] .... MSVA
Magnetic Stereotaxis System [*Surgery*] .... MSS
Magnetic Stirrer [*Biotechnology*] .... MS
Magnetic Storage [*Computer science*] .... MS
Magnetic Storage Drum [*Computer science*] .... MSD
Magnetic Storage Drum System [*Computer science*] .... MSDS
Magnetic Storage Ring [*Computer science*] .... MSR
Magnetic Storm Satellite [*Air Force/NASA*] .... MSS
Magnetic Strain Energy .... MSE
Magnetic Strip (IAA) .... MS
Magnetic Stripe Reader (IAA) .... MSR
Magnetic Superresolution .... MSR
Magnetic Surface Current .... MSC
Magnetic Surfaces Laboratory .... MSL
Magnetic Susceptibility [*Physics*] (DAVI) .... X_m
Magnetic Susceptibility Bridge .... MSB
Magnetic Synchron (IAA) .... MS
Magnetic Tape .... MT
Magnetic Tape Accessory [*General Electric Co.*] .... MTA
Magnetic Tape and Telemetry (MCD) .... MTTM
Magnetic Tape Cassette [*Computer science*] .... MTC
Magnetic Tape Channel [*Computer science*] .... MTC
Magnetic Tape Channel (NITA) .... MTCH
Magnetic Tape Command [*Computer science*] (IAA) .... MTC
Magnetic Tape Control [*Computer science*] .... MTC
Magnetic Tape Control Interface (MCD) .... MTCI
Magnetic Tape Control Unit [*Computer science*] .... MTCU
Magnetic Tape Controller (NITA) .... MAGTC
Magnetic Tape Controller (NITA) .... MTC
Magnetic Tape Disk (MCD) .... MTD
Magnetic Tape Disk [*Computer science*] (NASA) .... MTDSK
Magnetic Tape Disk .... MTDSK
Magnetic Tape Encoder [*Computer science*] (IAA) .... MTE
Magnetic Tape Field Scan [*Computer science*] .... MFC
Magnetic Tape Field Search [*Computer science*] .... MFS
Magnetic Tape Handler [*Computer science*] .... MTH
Magnetic Tape Loader .... MTL
Magnetic Tape Message .... MTM
Magnetic Tape Module (IAA) .... MTMOD
Magnetic Tape Operating System (NITA) .... MTOS
Magnetic Tape Operations System [*Computer science*] (NRCH) .... MTOS
Magnetic Tape Operator (MCD) .... MTO
Magnetic Tape Processor (NITA) .... MTP
Magnetic Tape Programming System [*Computer science*] (IEEE) .... MTPS
Magnetic Tape Reader (NITA) .... MTR
Magnetic Tape Recorder .... MTR
Magnetic Tape Recorder End .... MTRE
Magnetic Tape Recorder Set .... MTRS
Magnetic Tape Recorder Start .... MTRS
Magnetic Tape Reformatting System [*Hewlett-Packard Co.*] .... MTRS
Magnetic Tape Search Unit [*Computer science*] .... MTSU
Magnetic Tape Selectric Composer [*IBM Corp.*] .... MTSC
Magnetic Tape Selectric Typewriter (NITA) .... MT/ST
Magnetic Tape Selectric Typewriter [*IBM Corp.*] .... MTST
Magnetic Tape Station [*Computer science*] (CET) .... MTS
Magnetic Tape Storage [*Computer science*] (IAA) .... MTS
Magnetic Tape Storage System .... MTSS
Magnetic Tape System [*Computer science*] .... MTS
Magnetic Tape Terminal [*Computer science*] .... MTT
Magnetic Tape Terminal Equipment [*Computer science*] (CET) .... MTTE
Magnetic Tape to Microfilm .... MT/MF

Magnetic Tape Transmissions (CET)	MTM's
Magnetic Tape Transport [Computer science] (IEEE)	MTT
Magnetic Tape Transport Interface [Computer science] (MCD)	MTTI
Magnetic Tape Transport Replacement (DWSG)	MTTR
Magnetic Tape Unit [Computer science]	MTU
Magnetic Technologies [NASDAQ symbol] (TTSB)	MTCC
Magnetic Tracker (MUGU)	MAGTRAC
Magnetic Trap Stability Experiment (IEEE)	MTSE
Magnetic, True, and Grid Heading Select (MCD)	MTGHS
Magnetic Tube	MT
Magnetic Type System [Computer science] (IAA)	MTS
Magnetic Unloading System	MUS
Magnetic Variation (MCD)	M/V
Magnetic Vector Potential [Symbol] (DEN)	A
Magnetic Vector Potential	MVP
Magnetic Video Camera [Sony Corp.]	MAVICA
Magnetic Video Card (NITA)	MAVICA
Magnetic Voltage Stabilizer	MVS
Magnetic Wire Shift Register	MWSR
Magnetic-Acoustic-Pressure (NVT)	MAP
Magnetically (ABBR)	MGNETCY
Magnetically Enhanced Reactive Ion Etching [By plasmas]	MERIE
Magnetically Impelled Arc Butt [Welding] (MCD)	MIAB
Magnetically Induced Velocity Charge [Southwest Research Institute]	MIVC
Magnetically Insulated Diode [Physics]	MID
Magnetically Insulated Macroparticle Accelerator System	MIMAS
Magnetically Settable Counter	MSC
Magnetically Supported Vehicle	MSV
Magnetically Suspended Momentum Wheel	MSMW
Magnetically-Coupled Transformer (IAA)	MCT
Magnetically-Levitated [High-speed ground transportation]	MAG-LEV
Magnetically-levitated Linear Motor Vehicle	MLX01
Magnetically-Linked Solenoid (MCD)	MLS
Magnetically-Modulated Microwave Reflection [Spectrometer]	MMR
Magnetic-Bubble Domain Device [Computer science] (IEEE)	MBD
Magnetic-Field Modulation [Computer science] (PCM)	MFM
Magnetic-Operated Limit Switch	MOLS
Magnetic-Resonance Imager (AD)	mri
Magnetic-Resonance Spectroscopy [Biochemistry] (ECON)	MRS
Magnetics International Ltd. [Toronto Stock Exchange symbol]	MGI
Magnetics Technology [Associated Press] (SAG)	MagTch
Magnetics Technology [NASDAQ symbol] (SAG)	MTCC
Magnetism (ABBR)	MGNETSM
Magnetite [CIPW classification] [Geology]	mt
Magnetite-Hematite [Geology]	MH
Magnetization (ABBR)	MGNETZ
Magnetization Transfer Contrast [Imaging technique]	MTC
Magnetize [or Magnetized] (ABBR)	MGNETZ
Magnetized	MGNTZD
Magnetized Concentration [Lunar]	MAGCON
Magnetized Ionized Gas	MIG
Magnetized Orange Pipe [Minesweeping device] [Navy]	MOP
Magnetizing Force [Symbol] (DEN)	H
Magneto (KSC)	MAG
Magneto [Generator]	MGN
Magneto	MGNTO
Magneto Cumulative Generator (MCD)	MCG
Magneto [or Magnetic] Field Generators [JETDS Nomenclature] [Military] (CET)	MF
Magnetocardiogram	MCG
Magnetocardiogram	MKG
Magnetocardiograph (IDOE)	MCG
Magnetocrystalline Anisotropy [Physics]	MCA
Magneto-Dynamic Positioning	MBP
Magnetoelastic	ME
Magneto-Elastic Resonance (PDAA)	MER
Magnetoelastic Static Hysteresis (MCD)	MSH
Magneto-Electronic (PDAA)	ME
Magnetoencephalogram [Medicine]	MEG
Magnetoencephalography [Medicine] (ECON)	MEG
Magnetofluid Mechanic	MFM
Magnetofluiddynamic	MFD
Magnetogasdynamic	MGD
Magnetogasdynamics Laboratory [MIT] (MCD)	ML
Magnetohydrodynamic [Simulation] [Marine science] (OSRA)	MHD
Magnetohydrodynamic Conversion [Nuclear energy] (NRCH)	MHDC
Magnetohydrodynamic Generator (PDAA)	MHDG
Magnetohydrodynamic LASER (PDAA)	MHDL
Magnetohydrodynamics [Electric power]	MHD
Magnetoionic Wave Component	MWC
Magnetokinetic Wave	MKW
Magnetometer [or Magnetometry]	MAG
Magnetometer (ABBR)	MGNETMTR
Magnetometer	MGTMTR
Magnetometer Satellite (NASA)	MAGSAT
Magnetomotive Force (KSC)	MF
Magnetomotive Force	mmf
Magnetomotive Hammer System	MHS
Magneto-Optic [Computer science]	MO
Magneto-Optic Kerr Effect	MOKE
Magneto-Optic Rotary Dispersion (PDAA)	MORD
Magneto-Optical (PCM)	MO
Magneto-Optical [Physics]	MO
Magneto-Optical Disc [Digital audio technology]	MOD
Magneto-Optical Disc (AD)	mod

Magneto-Optical Display Memory	MDM
Magneto-Optical Display Memory	MODM
Magneto-Optical Rotation	MOR
Magneto-Optical System (AD)	MOS
Magneto-Optical Trap [Physics]	MOT
Magnetooptically Detected Spin Conversion [Physics]	MODSC
Magnetopause [In a magnetic field]	MP
Magnetoplasmadynamic	MPD
Magnetoplasmadynamic Thruster [Electric thruster type]	MPDT
Magnetoplasmadynamics (AD)	mpd
Magnetopneumogram [Medicine]	MPG
Magnetoresistive	MR
Magnetoresistive Extended [Computer science]	MRX
Magnetorheological Finishing [Optics manufacturing] (RDA)	MRF
Magnetosphere-Thermosphere Explorer [NASA]	MTE
Magnetospheric Multiprobe (SSD)	MMP
Magnetospheric Particle Detector (MCD)	MPD
Magnetospheric Radio Burst	MRB
Magnetostatic [Telecommunications] (IAA)	MS
Magnetostatic Backward Volume Wave [Telecommunications] (TEL)	MSBVW
Magnetostatic Forward Volume Wave [Telecommunications] (TEL)	MSFVW
Magnetostatic Surface Wave [Telecommunications] (TEL)	MSSW
Magnetostatic Waves [Telecommunications] (TEL)	MSW
Magnetostriction	MS
Magnetostrictive Delay Line	MSDL
Magnetostrictive Transducer	MST
Magnetotactic, Many-Celled Prokaryote [Biology]	MMP
Magnetotactic Multicellular Aggregate [Microbiology]	MMA
Magnetotelluric [Geological surveying]	MT
Magnetron (MDG)	M
Magnetron (CET)	MAG
Magnetron [Electricity]	MAGN
Magnetron Beam Switching	MBS
Magnetron Branch [Electronics] (OA)	MB
Magnetron Cutoff	MCO
Magnetron Ion Etching [Semiconductor technology]	MIE
Magnifiable (ABBR)	MGNFIB
Magnification (NTCM)	M
Magnification	MAG
Magnification	
Magnification (ABBR)	magnif
Magnificence (ABBR)	MGNFIN
Magnificent (ABBR)	MGNFNC
Magnificently (ABBR)	MGNFNT
Magnified (ABBR)	MGNFTY
Magnifier (ABBR)	MGNFID
Magnify (MSA)	MGNFIR
Magnify (ABBR)	MGF
Magnifying	MGNFI
Magnifying (ABBR)	MGFG
Magnifying Power (IIA)	MGNFIG
Magnitude	MP
Magnitude	M
Magnitude (AFM)	MAG
Magnitude	MAG
Magnitude	MAGTD
Magnitude (ABBR)	MGNTUD
Magnitude Estimation	ME
Magnitude Estimation Scaling (MCD)	MAGES
Magnitude of Rotation	MR
Magnitude Square of the Complex Coherence (PDAA)	MSC
Magnocellular Neuroendocrine Cell [Medicine] (DMAA)	MgC
Magnocellular Neurosecretory Cells	MNC
Magnocellular Nucleus [of anterior neostriatum] [Neurology] (DAVI)	MAN
Magnolia, AR [Location identifier FAA] (FAAL)	AGO
Magnolia, AR [AM radio station call letters]	KVMA
Magnolia, AR [FM radio station call letters]	KVMA-FM
Magnolia School, Long Beach, NY [Library symbol Library of Congress] (LCLS)	NLobMS
[The] Magnolia Society (EA)	TMS
Magnum (WDAA)	MAG
Magnum Airlines [ICAO designator] (AD)	LE
Magnum Airlines [ICAO designator] (AD)	MQ
Magnum Pete $1.10 Cv'C'Pfd [AMEX symbol] (TTSB)	MPMPrEC
Magnum Petroleum [Associated Press] (SAG)	MagnPet
Magnum Petroleum [Associated Press] (SAG)	MagP
Magnum Petroleum [Associated Press] (SAG)	MagPet
Magnum Petroleum [Associated Press] (SAG)	MagPt
Magnum Petroleum [AMEX symbol] (SAG)	MPM
Magnum Resources [Vancouver Stock Exchange symbol]	MNH
Magnum Rifle Powder (DICI)	MRP
Magnus [Large] [Pharmacy]	MAG
Magnus [Great] [Latin] (ADA)	MAGN
Magnus and Estrin on Companies [5th ed.] [1978] [A publication] (DLA)	Mag & E Comp
Magnus Rotulus [Great Roll of the Exchequer] [Latin A publication] (DLA)	Mag Rot
Magnus Rotulus Pipae [Great Roll of the Pipe] [Latin A publication] (DLA)	Magna Rot Pip
Magnuson Fishery Conservation and Management Act [1976] [Also, FCMA]	MFCMA
Magog, PQ [FM radio station call letters]	CIMO
Magog [China] [ICAO location identifier] (ICLI)	RCQC
Magovern-Cromie [Prosthesis] (AAMN)	M-C
Magrath Public Library, Alberta [Library symbol National Library of Canada] (NLC)	AM

Magrath's South Carolina Digest [*A publication*] (DLA) .... Mag Dig
Magruder's Reports [*1, 2 Maryland*] [*A publication*] (DLA) .... Mag
Magruder's Reports [*1, 2 Maryland*] [*A publication*] (DLA) .... Mag (MD)
Magruder's Reports [*1, 2 Maryland*] [*A publication*] (DLA) .... Magruder
MAGTF [*Marine Air Ground Task Force*] **All-Source Fusion Center**
    (DOMA) .... MAFC
MAGTF [*Marine Air-Ground Task Force*] **Automated Services Center**
    (GFGA) .... MASC
MAGTF [*Marine Air-Ground Task Force*] **Decision-Support System**
    (DOMA) .... MDSS
MAGTF [*Marine Air-Ground Task Force*] **Tactical Warfare Simulation**
    [*DoD*] .... MTWS
Maguayo [*Puerto Rico*] [*Seismograph station code, US Geological Survey*]
    (SEIS) .... MGP
Magwe [*Myanmar*] [*Airport symbol*] (OAG) .... MWQ
Magwe [*Myanmar*] [*ICAO location identifier*] (ICLI) .... VBMW
Magyar [*Language, etc.*] (ROG) .... MAG
Magyar Allamvasutak [*Hungarian State Railways*] .... MAV
Magyar Communion of Friends (EA) .... MCF
Magyar Demokrata Forum [*Hungarian Democratic Forum*] [*Political party*]
    (EY) .... MDF
Magyar Dolgozok Partja [*Hungarian Workers' Party*] [*Political party*] (PPE) .... MDP
Magyar Elet Mozgalma [*Movement of Hungarian Life*] [*Political party*]
    (PPE) .... MEM
Magyar Elet Partja [*Party of Hungarian Life*] [*Political party*] (PPE) .... MEP
Magyar Izraelitak Orszagos Kepviselete (BJA) .... MIOK
Magyar Kommunista Part [*Hungarian Communist Party*] [*Political party*]
    (PPE) .... MKP
Magyar Megujulas Partja [*Party of Hungarian Renewal*] [*Political party*]
    (PPE) .... MMP
Magyar Muza [*Record label*] [*Hungary*] .... Magy
Magyar Nemzeti Fueggetlensegi Front [*Hungarian National Independence
    Front*] [*Political party*] .... MNFF
Magyar Nemzeti Fueggetlensegi Part [*Hungarian National Independence
    Party*] [*Political party*] (PPE) .... MNFP
Magyar Orszagos Leveltar, Budapest, Hungary [*Library symbol Library of
    Congress*] (LCLS) .... Hu-Ar
Magyar Orvostudomanyi Tarsasagok Szovetsege [*Federation of Hungarian
    Medical Societies*] (EAIO) .... MOTESZ
Magyar Statisztikai Kozlemenyek [*Hungary*] .... MSK
Magyar Szocial Demokrata Part [*Hungarian Social Democratic Party*] [*Political
    party*] (PPE) .... MSZDP
Magyar Szocialista Munkaspart [*Hungarian Socialist Workers' Party*] [*Political
    party*] (PPE) .... MSZMP
Magyar Szocialista Part [*Hungarian Socialist Party*] [*Political party*] (EY) .... MSzP
Magyar Tavviati Iroda [*Hungarian News Agency*] (BARN) .... MTI
Magyar Tudomanyos Akademia Konyvtara [*Hungarian Academy of Sciences
    Library*] (IID) .... MTAK
Magyar Zsido Lexikon [*A publication*] (BJA) .... MZsL
Magyar Zsidok Vilagszovetsege [*World Federation of Hungarian Jews*]
    (EAIO) .... MZV
Magyarorszagi Szocialdemokrata Part [*Hungarian Social-Democratic Party*]
    [*Political party*] (EY) .... SzDP
Mahabad [*Iran*] [*ICAO location identifier*] (ICLI) .... OITB
Mahableshwar [*India*] [*Seismograph station code, US Geological Survey
    Closed*] (SEIS) .... MAH
Mahad [*India*] [*ICAO location identifier*] (ICLI) .... VOMH
Mahaffy and Dodson's Road Traffic [*3rd ed.*] [*1961*] [*A publication*]
    (DLA) .... Mah & DRT
Mahagi [*Zaire*] [*ICAO location identifier*] (ICLI) .... FZKC
Mahajana Eksath Peramuna [*People's United Front*] [*Sri Lanka*] [*Political
    party*] (PPW) .... MEP
Mahajanga/Amborovy [*Madagascar*] [*ICAO location identifier*] (ICLI) .... FMNM
Mahallat [*Iran*] [*ICAO location identifier*] (ICLI) .... OIIH
Mahanoro [*Madagascar*] [*ICAO location identifier*] (ICLI) .... FMMH
Mahanoro [*Madagascar*] [*Airport symbol*] (OAG) .... VVB
Maharashtra Ekikaran Samithi [*India*] [*Political party*] (PPW) .... MES
Maharashtra Law Journal [*India*] [*A publication*] (DLA) .... Mah LJ
Maharashtra Law Journal [*India*] [*A publication*] (DLA) .... Maharashtra LJ
Maharashtra Prajatantra Congress [*India*] [*Political party*] (PPW) .... MPC
Maharashtra Progressive Congress [*India*] [*Political party*] (PPW) .... MPC
Maharashtra Socialist Congress [*India*] [*Political party*] (PPW) .... MSC
Maharashtrawadi Gomantak [*India*] [*Political party*] (PPW) .... MG
Maharishi International University [*Fairfield, IA*] .... MIU
Maharishi International University, Fairfield, IA [*Library symbol Library of
    Congress*] (LCLS) .... IaFairM
Maharishi International University, Fairfield, IA [*OCLC symbol*] (OCLC) .... MIU
Mahaska County Historical Society, Oskaloosa, IA [*Library symbol Library of
    Congress*] (LCLS) .... IaOskMHi
Mahaska Investment [*NASDAQ symbol*] (TTSB) .... OSKY
Mahaska Investment Co. [*Associated Press*] (SAG) .... Mahaska
Mahaska Investment Co. [*NASDAQ symbol*] (SAG) .... OSKY
Mahdia [*Guyana*] [*Airport symbol*] (OAG) .... MHA
Mahdia [*Guyana*] [*ICAO location identifier*] (ICLI) .... SYMD
Mahe Island [*Seychelles Islands*] [*Airport symbol*] (OAG) .... SEZ
Mahe/Seychelles International (ICLI) .... FSSS
Mahendranagar [*Nepal*] [*ICAO location identifier*] (ICLI) .... VNMN
Mahendranagar [*Nepal*] [*Airport symbol*] (OAG) .... XMG
Maher, Inc. [*Toronto Stock Exchange symbol*] .... MHS
Mahfid [*South Arabia*] [*Airport symbol*] (AD) .... MJZ
Mahfooz Aviation [*Gambia*] [*FAA designator*] (FAAC) .... MZS
Mahmood Abad [*Iran*] [*ICAO location identifier*] (ICLI) .... OINM
Mahnomen Elementary School, Mahnomen, MN [*Library symbol*] [*Library of
    Congress*] (LCLS) .... MnMaE

Mahnomen High School, Mahnomen, MN [*Library symbol*] [*Library of
    Congress*] (LCLS) .... MnMah
Mahogany (VRA) .... mah
Mahogany (MSA) .... MAH
Mahogany (DSUE) .... MAHOG
Mahogany (WGA) .... MHG
Mahogany Association (EA) .... MA
Mahogany Minerals [*Vancouver Stock Exchange symbol*] .... MOY
Mahomet, IL [*FM radio station call letters*] (RBYB) .... WGKC-FM
Mahomet, IL [*FM radio station call letters*] .... WHZT
Mahomet Township Public Library, Mahomet, IL [*Library symbol Library of
    Congress*] (LCLS) .... IMah
Mahommedanism (ROG) .... MAH
Mahon [*Spain*] [*Airport symbol*] (OAG) .... MAH
Mahon/Menorca [*Spain ICAO location identifier*] (ICLI) .... LEMH
Mahoning Valley Historical Society, Arms Museum, Youngstown, OH
    [*Library symbol Library of Congress*] (LCLS) .... OYMHi
Mahopac Library Association, Mahopac, NY [*Library symbol Library of
    Congress*] (LCLS) .... NMah
Mahri, Suqutri, and Shahri (BJA) .... MSA
Mahwah, NJ [*FM radio station call letters*] .... WRPR
Mahzor Vitry [*A publication*] (BJA) .... MV
Mahzor Yanai (BJA) .... MY
MAI Systems [*AMEX symbol*] (TTSB) .... NOW
MAI Systems Corp. [*Associated Press*] (SAG) .... MAI Sy
MAI Systems Corp. [*Associated Press*] (SAG) .... MAI Sys
MAI Systems Corp. [*AMEX symbol*] (SAG) .... NOW
Maiana [*Kiribati*] [*Airport symbol*] (OAG) .... MNK
Maiana [*Kiribati*] [*ICAO location identifier*] (ICLI) .... NGMA
MAIC Holdings [*NASDAQ symbol*] (TTSB) .... MAIC
MAIC Holdings, Inc. [*NASDAQ symbol*] (SAG) .... MAIC
MAIC Holdings, Inc. [*Associated Press*] (SAG) .... MAIC Hld
Maicao [*Colombia*] [*Airport symbol*] (OAG) .... MCJ
MAICO Micrographics, Inc., Wormleysburg, PA [*Library symbol*] [*Library of
    Congress*] (LCLS) .... McInc
M.A.I.D. ADS [*NASDAQ symbol*] (TTSB) .... M
Maiden .... MDN
Maiden Race [*Horse racing*] .... MA
Maids of Athena (EA) .... MAID
Maidstone [*Municipal borough in England*] .... M & D
Maidstone & District Motor Services Ltd. [*British*] (DCTA) .... MPC
Maidstone Paper Converters [*Commercial firm British*] .... DNMA
Maiduguri [*Nigeria*] [*ICAO location identifier*] (ICLI) .... MIU
Maiduguri [*Nigeria*] [*Airport symbol*] (OAG) .... VEG
Maikwak [*Guyana*] [*Airport symbol*] (OAG) .... M
Mail .... ML
Mail Advertising Service Association International [*Bethesda, MD*] .... MASA
Mail Advertising Service Association International (EA) .... MASAI
Mail Advertising Service Association International. Quarterly Business
    Outlook [*A publication*] .... QBO
Mail Application Programming Interface [*Computer science*] (PCM) .... MAPI
Mail Applications Program Interface [*Microsoft Corp.*] .... MAPI
Mail Boxes Etc. [*NASDAQ symbol*] (NQ) .... MAIL
Mail Boxes Etc. [*Associated Press*] (SAG) .... MailBx
Mail Boxes Etc. USA [*San Diego, CA*] [*Telecommunications*] (TSSD) .... MBE
Mail Chute (DAC) .... MC
Mail Chute (AAG) .... MCH
Mail Classification Center (DNAB) .... MCC
Mail Control Authority (AFM) .... MCA
Mail Distribution Schedule [*Air Force*] (AFM) .... MDS
Mail Distribution Scheme [*Army*] .... MDS
Mail Distribution Scheme / Military Post Office Location List
    (DNAB) .... MDS-MPOLL
Mail Exchange [*Computer science*] .... MX
Mail File Requirement [*Code*] [*Computer science*] .... MFR
Mail for Tots (EA) .... MFT
Mail Handler [*Computer science*] .... MH
Mail Handling System [*Computer science*] .... MHS
Mail Order [*Business term*] .... MO
Mail Order (AD) .... mo
Mail Order Association of America (EA) .... MOAA
Mail Order Buyer (WDMC) .... MOB
Mail Order Department [*Business term*] .... MOD
Mail Order Publisher Authority (PDAA) .... MOPA
Mail Order Traders Association (MHDB) .... MOTA
Mail Payment [*Banking*] .... M/P
Mail Payment (AD) .... mp
Mail Preference Service [*Direct Mail Advertising Association*] .... MPS
Mail Readership Measurement .... MRM
Mail Readership Measurement (AD) .... mrm
Mail Steamer .... MS
Mail Stop .... M/S
Mail Systems Management Association [*New York, NY*] (EA) .... MSMA
Mail Transfer .... MT
Mail Tray (AAG) .... MT
Mail Unit (KSC) .... MU
Mail Users' Association [*British*] .... MUA
Mail Will Be Addressed to Show .... MWBAS
Mailbox (AAG) .... MB
Mailbox Club [*Later, MCI*] (EA) .... MBC
Mailer .... MLR
Mailer's Postmark Permit .... MPP
Mailer's Postmark Permit Club (EA) .... MPPC
Mailers Technical Advisory Committee (EA) .... MTAC

Mailgram	MGM
Mailing	MLG
Mailing Address Only [Military] (AABC)	MAO
Mailing Label and Directory Lookup Package (PDAA)	MLDLP
Mailing List Brokers Professional Association [Defunct] (EA)	MLBPA
Mailing List User and Supplier Association [Defunct] (EA)	ML/USA
Mailing-List Manager [Type of database]	MLM
Mailly-Le-Camp [France ICAO location identifier] (ICLI)	LFXL
Mail-Order Action Line [Direct marketing association] (WDMC)	MOAL
Mailorder Association of Nurserymen [Defunct] (EA)	MAN
Mail-Order Delivery	MOD
Mail-Order Protection Scheme [British]	MOPS
Mailstop Code	MSC
Mail-Well, Inc. [Associated Press] (SAG)	MailWell
Mail-Well, Inc. [NASDAQ symbol] (SAG)	MLWL
Maimama [Afghanistan] [ICAO location identifier] (ICLI)	OAMN
Maimana [Afghanistan] [Airport symbol Obsolete] (OAG)	MMZ
Maimonides Hospital and Home for the Aged, Montreal, PQ, Canada [Library symbol Library of Congress] (LCLS)	CaQMMHH
Maimonides Hospital Geriatric Center [Centre Hospitalier Geriatrique Maimonides], Montreal, Quebec [Library symbol National Library of Canada] (NLC)	QMMHH
Main	M
Main [Menu] [Computer science] [Telecommunications]	m
Main	MN
Main (AAG)	MN
Main Air Display Plot	MADP
Main Alarm (IAA)	MA
Main Amplifier (OA)	MA
Main and Reheat Steam System [Nuclear energy] (NRCH)	MRSS
Main Arithmetic Processor (IAA)	MAP
Main Armament Group	MAG
Main Array Signal Band	MASB
Main Assembly Drawing	MAD
Main Ballast	MB
Main Ballast Tank	MBT
Main "Bang" Suppressor	MBS
Main Bang Synchronization Pulse (IAA)	MBSP
Main Base [Air Force] (AFM)	MB
Main Base Visit (NASA)	MBV
Main Battery [Guns]	MB
Main Battle Air Vehicle [Military] (PDAA)	MBAV
Main Battle Area (AABC)	MBA
Main Battle Line [Military] (IAA)	MBL
Main Battle Tank	MBT
Main Battle Tank Distribution/Redistribution Plan (MCD)	MBTD/RP
Main Beach Signal Station (IAA)	MBSS
Main Beam Avoidance Maneuver	MBAM
Main Beam Clutter	MBC
Main Boundary Fault [Geophysics]	MBF
Main Boundary Thrust [Geology]	MBT
Main Buffer Storage (IAA)	MBS
Main Bus (MCD)	MB
Main Bus A,B, or C (NASA)	MNA,B,C
Main Bus-Switching Assembly (SSD)	MBSA
Main Cabin	MC
Main Call Process [Telecommunications] (TEL)	MCP
Main Carrier Acquisition Unit (MCD)	MCAU
Main Central Thrust [Geophysics]	MCT
Main Chamber [NASA] (KSC)	M/C
Main Chamber Oxidizer Valve [NASA] (KSC)	MCOV
Main Channel	MC
Main Chute (KSC)	MC
Main Civilian Occupation	MCO
Main Cock	MC
Main Color [Crocheting]	MC
Main Combustion Chamber (NASA)	MCC
Main Communications Center	MCC
Main Compution System	MCS
Main Condensate Pump [Navy] (CAAL)	MCP
Main Condenser [Nuclear energy] (NRCH)	MC
Main Condenser Evacuation System [Nuclear energy] (NRCH)	MCES
Main Console Assembly [NASA] (KSC)	MCA
Main Control Board (NRCH)	MCB
Main Control Circuit (IAA)	MCC
Main Control Console [Diving apparatus]	MCC
Main Control Room (IEEE)	MCR
Main Control Room Habitability [Nuclear energy] (NRCH)	MCRH
Main Control Room Habitability System [Nuclear energy] (NRCH)	MCRHS
Main Control Station [Nuclear energy] (IAA)	MCS
Main Control Tank (MSA)	MCT
Main Control Unit (IAA)	MCU
Main Coolant (MSA)	MC
Main Coolant Pump (NVT)	MCP
Main Coronary Artery [Cardiology] (DAVI)	MCA
Main Data Path	MDP
Main DC [Direct Current] Power Distributor Assembly (MCD)	MPD
Main Deck [Naval engineering]	MD
Main Defense Line (IAA)	MDL
Main Device Scheduler (IAA)	MDS
Main Display Console	MAC
Main Display Console	MDC
Main Display Panel (SAA)	MDP
Main Distributing Frame [Bell System]	MDF
Main Distribution Assembly (NASA)	MDA

Main Distribution Assembly	MDA
Main Distribution Control Assembly (MCD)	MDCA
Main Distribution Equipment (IAA)	MDE
Main Distribution Frame (NITA)	MDF
Main Dressing Station	MDS
Main Droite [With the Right Hand] [Music]	MD
Main Drum (CET)	MD
Main Duct	MD
Main Economic Indicators (NITA)	MEI
Main Electronic Unit (INF)	MEU
Main Electronics Assembly (MCD)	MEA
Main Electronics Box (NASA)	MEB
Main Electronics Box	MEB
Main Engine (KSC)	ME
Main Engine Burnout (NASA)	MEBO
Main Engine Computational Facilities [NASA] (NASA)	MECF
Main Engine Console (AAG)	MEC
Main Engine Controller [NASA] (NASA)	MEC
Main Engine Controller Assembly [NASA] (NASA)	MECA
Main Engine Cutoff [Aerospace] (AAG)	MEC
Main Engine Cutoff [Aerospace]	MECO
Main Engine Ignition [Aerospace]	MEI
Main Engine Ignition [Aerospace] (KSC)	MEIG
Main Engine Ignition [Aerospace]	MEIGN
Main Engine Interface Unit (MCD)	MEIU
Main Engine Propellant (MCD)	MEP
Main Engine Room [Navy] (CAAL)	MER
Main Engine Start [NASA] (KSC)	MES
Main Engine Thrust Vector Control (MCD)	METVC
Main Entry [Library Science] [Online database field identifier]	ME
Main Entry Point (NASA)	MEP
Main Entry Point	MEP
Main Equipment Supplier (NATG)	MES
Main Evaluation Center (NVT)	MEC
[The] Main Event [A publication]	TME
Main Feed [Technical drawings]	MF
Main Feed (MCD)	MFD
Main Feed Booster Pump (NVT)	MFBP
Main Feed Power [Nuclear energy] (NRCH)	MFP
Main Feed Pump (NVT)	MFP
Main Feed Pump Turbine Condenser [Nuclear energy] (NRCH)	MFPTC
Main Feedwater [Nuclear energy] (NRCH)	MFW
Main Feedwater Line [Nuclear energy] (NRCH)	MFL
Main Feedwater Line Break [Nuclear energy] (NRCH)	MFWLB
Main Feedwater Pump [Nuclear energy] (NRCH)	MFP
Main Feedwater Pump Turbine [Nuclear energy] (NRCH)	MFPT
Main Feedwater Valve [Nuclear energy] (NRCH)	MFV
Main Feedwater Valve [Nuclear energy] (NRCH)	MFWV
Main Fire Support Element (AABC)	MFSE
Main Fixed Earth Station [NASA] (PDAA)	MFES
Main Force [Military]	MF
Main Force Patrol [In movie "Mad Max"]	MFP
Main Frame	MNFRM
Main Fuel Control (MCD)	MFC
Main Fuel Valve (KSC)	MFV
Main Gauche [With the Left Hand] [Music]	MG
Main Gear Box (MCD)	MGB
Main Generator (IAA)	MG
Main Hatch	MH
Main Heat Transport System [Nuclear energy] (NRCH)	MHTS
Main Himalayan Thrust [Geology]	MHT
Main Immunogenic Region [Immunology]	MIR
Main Injector Neutrino Oscillation Search [Particle Physics]	MINOS
Main Instrument Console and Readout Stations (NATG)	MICRS
Main Instrument Panel (MCD)	MIP
Main Instrumentation Van [NASA]	MIV
Main Jet [Automotive engineering]	MJ
Main Landing Gear	MLG
Main Line [Business term]	ML
Main Line of Defense	MLD
Main Line of Resistance	MLR
Main Lobe	ML
Main Lobe Clutter	MLC
Main LOX [Liquid Oxygen] Valve [NASA] (KSC)	MLV
Main Lube Oil [System] (NRCH)	MLO
Main Magnetization Winding [Telecommunications] (OA)	MMW
Main Mantle Thrust [Geology]	MMT
Main Mediterranean Naval Intelligence Center [Navy]	MMNIC
Main Memory	MM
Main Memory Address Register	MMAR
Main Memory Interface (NITA)	MMI
Main Memory Register	MMR
Main Memory Unit	MMU
Main Meteorological Office	MMO
Main Metering [Automotive engineering]	M/MTRG
Main Metering Jet [Automotive engineering]	MMJ
Main Metering Jet-Primary [Automotive engineering]	MMJP
Main Metering Jet-Secondary [Automotive engineering]	MMJS
Main Missile Battery	MMBAT
Main Module (NASA)	MM
Main Network [Telecommunications] (TEL)	MN
Main Network Switching Center [Telecommunications] (TEL)	MNSC
Main Olfactory Bulb [Anatomy]	MOB
Main Operating Base	MOB
Main Operating Base LASER	MOBL

Main Oxidizer Valve (KSC) ... MOV
Main Pancreatic Duct [*Anatomy*] ... MPD
Main Parachute (MCD) ... M/P
Main Parachute Support Structure (NASA) ... MPSS
Main Parachute Support Structure ... MPSS
Main Phase (IEEE) ... MP
Main Political Administration [*of the Army and Navy*] [*Russian*] (DOMA) ... MPA
Main Port (AD) ... mnpo
Main Power Distribution Box (SSD) ... MPDB
Main Power Switch ... MPS
Main Power Unit ... MPU
Main Propellant Valve Actuator (MCD) ... MPVA
Main Propulsion (DNAB) ... MP
Main Propulsion Assistant ... MPA
Main Propulsion Motor ... MPM
Main Propulsion System [*or Subsystem*] [*NASA*] (KSC) ... MPS
Main Propulsion Test [*NASA*] (NASA) ... MPT
Main Propulsion Test Article [*NASA*] ... MPTA
Main Propulsion Test Article (AD) ... mpta
Main Propulsion Test Facility [*NASA*] (NASA) ... MPTF
Main Propulsion Test Facility [*NASA*] ... MPTF
Main Propulsion Test Program (MCD) ... MPTP
Main Propulsion Unit ... MPU
Main Pulmonary Artery [*Anatomy*] ... MPA
Main Rail Launcher (DWSG) ... MRL
Main Renal Artery Stenosis [*Medicine*] (DMAA) ... MRAS
Main Repair Group [*British military*] (DMA) ... MRG
Main Resource Unit ... MRU
Main St. & Main [*NASDAQ symbol*] (TTSB) ... MAIN
Main St. & Main, Inc. [*NASDAQ symbol*] (SAG) ... MAIN
Main St. & Main, Inc. [*Associated Press*] (SAG) ... MainSt
Main/Satellite/Tributary Network [*Telecommunications*] (ACRL) ... M/N/T
Main Sea Level (AAG) ... MSL
Main Sequence [*Astronomy*] ... MS
Main Signal Office [*British*] ... MSO
Main Stage (IAA) ... MS
Main Steam (NRCH) ... MS
Main Steam and Feed Water System (IEEE) ... MSFS
Main Steam Isolation Signal [*Nuclear energy*] (NRCH) ... MSIS
Main Steam Isolation Valve [*Nuclear energy*] (NRCH) ... MSIV
Main Steam Isolation Valve Leakage Control System [*Nuclear energy*] (NRCH) ... MSIVLCS
Main Steam Line [*Nuclear energy*] (NRCH) ... MSL
Main Steam Line Accident [*Nuclear energy*] (NRCH) ... MSLA
Main Steam Line Break [*Nuclear energy*] (NRCH) ... MSLB
Main Steam Line Isolation Valve Sealings System [*Nuclear energy*] (NRCH) ... MSLIVSS
Main Steam Radiation Monitor (IEEE) ... MSRM
Main Steam Radiation System (IEEE) ... MSRS
Main Steam Relief Valve [*Nuclear energy*] (NRCH) ... MSRV
Main Steam Supply System [*Nuclear energy*] (NRCH) ... MSSS
Main Steam System [*Nuclear energy*] (NRCH) ... MSS
Main Steamline Break [*Nuclear energy*] (NRCH) ... MSB
Main Storage ... MS
Main Storage Control [*Computer science*] (BUR) ... MSC
Main Storage Control Element [*Computer science*] (IEEE) ... MSCE
Main Storage Data Register [*Computer science*] (IAA) ... MSDR
Main Storage Database ... MSDB
Main Storage Stock Control [*Computer science*] (IAA) ... MSSC
Main Storage Unit [*Computer science*] ... MSU
Main Store Allocator ... MSA
Main Stream Flow Control Valve [*Nuclear energy*] (NUCP) ... MSFCV
Main Street BankGroup, Inc. [*Associated Press*] (SAG) ... MainStB
Main Street Elementary School, Port Washington, NY [*Library symbol Library of Congress*] (LCLS) ... NPtwMSE
Main Supply Road [*or Route*] ... MSR
Main Supply Route/Alternative Supply Route (MCD) ... MSR/ASR
Main Support Base [*Air Force*] (AFM) ... MSB
Main Support Battalion [*Army*] (INF) ... MSB
Main Support Battalion [*Army*] (DOMA) ... MSB
Main Support Structure (NRCH) ... MSS
Main Switch ... MS
Main Switch (AD) ... ms
Main Switchboard ... MSB
Main Switching Centre [*Telecommunications*] (NITA) ... MSC
Main Switching Unit [*Telecommunications*] (NITA) ... MSU
Main Tank Gun [*Army*] ... MTG
Main Tank Gunfire/Weapon Effects Signature Simulator (MCD) ... MTG/WESS
Main Tank Injection ... MTI
Main Technical Directorate (RDA) ... MTD
Main Telecommunication Network [*United Nations*] (EY) ... MTN
Main Telescope ... MT
Main Terminal Board ... MTB
Main Time Base [*Electronics*] ... MTB
Main Timing Register ... MTR
Main Traffic Group [*Telecommunications*] (TEL) ... MTG
Main Transfer Line (MCD) ... MTL
Main Trawl Winch ... MTW
Main Trunk Circuit [*World Meteorological Organization*] [*Telecommunications*] (TEL) ... MTC
Main Trunk System [*Telecommunications*] (TEL) ... MTS
Main Turbine Control Valve (IEEE) ... MTCV
Main Turbine / Gearing Unit (PDAA) ... MTGU
Main Turbogenerator ... MTG
Main Valve Actuator (NASA) ... MVA
Main Valve Actuator ... MVA
Main Verb [*Linguistics*] ... MV
Main Yankee Atomic Power Plant (NRCH) ... MYAPP
Maina Air Ltd. [*Nigeria*] [*FAA designator*] (FAAC) ... MNI
Main-Belt Asteroid [*Astronomy*] ... MBA
Mainbullau [*Germany ICAO location identifier*] (ICLI) ... EDFU
Main-d'Oeuvre Indigene [*Indigenous Manpower*] [*Congo - Leopoldville*] ... MOI
Maine [*Postal code*] ... ME
Maine [*MARC country of publication code Library of Congress*] (LCCP) ... meu
Maine [*MARC geographic area code Library of Congress*] (LCCP) ... n-us-me
Maine Agriculture Experiment Station [*University of Maine at Orono*] [*Research center*] (RCD) ... MAES
Maine/Anjou Cattle Breeders' Association of Australia ... MACBAA
Maine Aquaculture Innovation Center [*University of Maine*] [*Research center*] (RCD) ... MAIC
Maine Association of Engineers (SRA) ... MAE
Maine Association of Life Underwriters (SRA) ... MALU
Maine Aviation Corp. [*ICAO designator*] (FAAC) ... MAT
Maine Central Railroad Co. [*AAR code*] ... MEC
Maine Central Road Railroad (MHDB) ... MCRR
Maine Charitable Mechanic Association, Portland, ME [*Library symbol Library of Congress*] (LCLS) ... MePM
Maine Criminal Justice Academy, Waterville, ME [*OCLC symbol*] (OCLC) ... MEJ
Maine Debris Information Office [*National Oceanic and Atmospheric Administration*] ... MDIO
Maine Department of Environmental Protection ... MDEP
Maine Department of Environmental Protection (DOGT) ... MDEP
Maine Department of Inland Fisheries and Wildlife, Fishery Research Management Division [*Research center*] (RCD) ... MDIF & W
Maine Department of Transportation, Augusta, ME [*OCLC symbol*] (OCLC) ... MED
Maine Government Register [*A publication*] (AAGC) ... Me Gov't Reg
Maine Historical Society, Portland, ME [*Library symbol Library of Congress*] (LCLS) ... MeHi
Maine Indian Claims Settlement Act [*1980*] ... MICSA
Maine Legislative Service [*A publication*] (DLA) ... ME Legis Serv
Maine Lobster Fishermen's Association (EA) ... MLFA
Maine Lobstermen's Association (EA) ... MLA
Maine Maritime Academy, Castine, ME [*Library symbol Library of Congress*] (LCLS) ... MeCasM
Maine Maritime Academy, Castine, ME [*OCLC symbol*] (OCLC) ... MMM
Maine Maritime Museum, Bath, ME [*Library symbol*] [*Library of Congress*] (LCLS) ... MeBathM
Maine Medical Center, Portland, ME [*Library symbol Library of Congress*] (LCLS) ... MePMC
Maine Motor Rate Bureau, Portland ME [*STAC*] ... MEB
Maine Office of Energy Resources Library, Augusta, ME [*OCLC symbol*] (OCLC) ... MEE
Maine Personnel and Guidance Association (AD) ... MPGA
Maine Potato Board (EA) ... MPB
Maine Potato Council [*Later, MPB*] (EA) ... MPC
Maine Public Service [*AMEX symbol*] (TTSB) ... MAP
Maine Public Service Co. [*AMEX symbol*] (SPSG) ... MAP
Maine Public Service Co. [*Associated Press*] (SAG) ... MePS
Maine Public Utilities Commission Reports [*A publication*] (DLA) ... Maine PUR
Maine Reports [*A publication*] (DLA) ... Maine
Maine Reports [*A publication*] (DLA) ... Maine R
Maine Reports [*A publication*] (DLA) ... Maine Rep
Maine Reports (AAGC) ... Me
Maine Revised Statutes [*A publication*] (DLA) ... ME Rev Stat
Maine Revised Statutes, Annotated [*A publication*] (DLA) ... ME Rev Stat Ann
Maine Revised Statutes Annotated [*West*] [*A publication*] (AAGC) ... Me Rev Stat Ann
Maine Revised Statutes, Annotated [*A publication*] (DLA) ... MRSA
Maine Sardine Council (EA) ... MSC
Maine Sardine Packers Association (EA) ... MSPA
Maine State Department of Environmental Protection and Department of Conservation, Augusta, ME [*OCLC symbol*] (OCLC) ... MER
Maine State Department of Human Services, Augusta, ME [*Library symbol Library of Congress*] (LCLS) ... MeAMH
Maine State Department of Human Services, Augusta, ME [*OCLC symbol*] (OCLC) ... MEH
Maine State Department of Marine Resources, West Boothbay Harbor, ME [*OCLC symbol*] (OCLC) ... MMR
Maine State Library, Augusta, ME [*Library symbol Library of Congress*] (LCLS) ... Me
Maine State Library, Augusta, ME [*OCLC symbol*] (OCLC) ... MEA
Maine State Library, Bookmobiles, Augusta, ME [*OCLC symbol*] (OCLC) ... MEK
Maine State Library Service for the Blind and Physically Handicapped, Augusta, ME [*Library symbol Library of Congress*] (LCLS) ... Me-BPH
Maine State Museum, Augusta, ME [*Library symbol Library of Congress*] (LCLS) ... MeAMM
Maine State Museum, Augusta, ME [*OCLC symbol*] (OCLC) ... MEM
Maine State Planning Office, Augusta, ME [*Library symbol Library of Congress*] (LCLS) ... MaMP
Maine State Planning Office, Augusta, ME [*Library symbol*] [*Library of Congress*] (LCLS) ... MeAMP
Maine State Planning Office, Augusta, ME [*OCLC symbol*] (OCLC) ... MES
Maine Supreme Judicial Court Reports [*A publication*] (DLA) ... ME
Maine Wholesale Lobster Dealers Association [*Defunct*] (EA) ... MWLDA
Maine's Ancient Law [*A publication*] (DLA) ... Mai Anc L
Maine's Ancient Law [*A publication*] (DLA) ... Maine Anc Law
Maine's History of Institutions [*A publication*] (DLA) ... Mai Inst
Maine's Reports [*A publication*] (DLA) ... Mai
Maine-Soroa [*Niger*] [*ICAO location identifier*] (ICLI) ... DRZM

Mainframe (NITA) ... M/F
Mainframe Interface to Libraries Online [*Illinois Library Computer Systems Office online union catalog*] ... MILO
Mainframe Termination [*Telecommunications*] (TEL) ... MFT
Main-Group Ureilite [*Meteorite component*] ... MGU
Mainland (MUGU) ... ML
Mainland (FAAC) ... MNLD
Mainland China [*MARC country of publication code Library of Congress*] (LCCP) ... cc
Mainland Journal, Pleasantville, NJ [*Library symbol Library of Congress*] (LCLS) ... NjPleM
Mainline Automated Clearance System [*Interstate trucking*] [*Highway safety*] ... MACS
Mainline Information Display and Automation System [*Salford Electrical Instruments*] (NITA) ... MIDAS
Mainly (FAAC) ... MNLY
Mainly about Books [*A publication*] ... MAB
Mainly about Nature [*A publication*] ... MAN
Mainly about People [*A publication*] ... MAP
Mainly English-Speaking ... MES
Mains Army Depot [*Germany*] ... MZAD
Mains Cable Group [*British*] (DBA) ... MCG
Mains Propres [*Personal Delivery*] [*French*] ... MP
Mainsail ... MNSL
Mainsail Hoist Lenght [*IOR*] ... P
Mainsborne Telecontrol System (NITA) ... MTS
Main-Sequence Turnoff [*Stellar physics*] ... MSTO
Mainstage [*NASA*] (KSC) ... M/S
Main-Stem Node [*Botany*] ... MSN
Mainstream Corporation Tax ... MCT
Mainstream Data, Inc. [*Associated Press*] (SAG) ... MainDta
Mainstream Data, Inc. [*NASDAQ symbol*] (SAG) ... MSDI
Mainstream of American Thought (AD) ... moAt
Mainstream of Republican Thought (AD) ... moRt
Mainstreamed Special Educator Model (EDAC) ... MSEM
MainStreet BankGroup [*NASDAQ symbol*] (TTSB) ... MSBC
MainStreet BankGroup, Inc. [*NASDAQ symbol*] (SAG) ... MSBC
Maintain ... MNTN
Maintain (AD) ... mntn
Maintain at Least (Altitude) [*Aviation*] (FAAC) ... MAL
Maintain Flight Level [*Aviation*] ... MFL
Maintain Production Schedules ... MAPROS
Maintain System History Program [*IBM Corp.*] ... MSHP
Maintain Visual Separation [*Aviation*] ... MVSP
Maintain Well to Right of Course [*Aviation*] (FAAC) ... MWRC
Maintainability [*or Maintenance*] (MCD) ... M
Maintainability Action Request (MCD) ... MAR
Maintainability and Reliability (AD) ... m & r
Maintainability and Reliability Cost-Effectiveness Program (IEEE) ... MARCEP
Maintainability and Repairs (AD) ... m & r
Maintainability Data Baseline (MCD) ... MDBL
Maintainability Demonstration (MCD) ... MD
Maintainability Demonstration Plan (MCD) ... MDP
Maintainability Demonstration Report (MCD) ... MDR
Maintainability Design Approach ... MDA
Maintainability Design Baseline (MCD) ... MDBL
Maintainability Design Data Sheets (MCD) ... MDDS
Maintainability Engineering Design Handbook ... MEDH
Maintainability Evaluation (NASA) ... MYVAL
Maintainability Evaluation ... MYVAL
Maintainability Evaluation and Tracking System (MCD) ... METS
Maintainability Evaluation Process (MCD) ... MEP
Maintainability Index Prediction Procedure ... MIPP
Maintainability of Software Analysis Tool (MCD) ... MAT
Maintainability Plan ... MP
Maintainability Problem Report (NASA) ... MPR
Maintainability Program Plan ... MPP
Maintainability Program Requirements (AD) ... MPR
Maintainability Report ... MR
Maintainability Requirements Group (AD) ... MRG
Maintainability Review Team [*Navy*] (NG) ... MRT
Maintainability Task Analyses (NASA) ... MYTA
Maintainability Task Analyses ... MYTA
Maintainable Electronics Component Assembly ... MECA
Maintained ... maintd
Maintained [*Automotive advertising*] ... MNT
Maintained (AD) ... mntnd
Maintained Load (WDAA) ... ML
Maintainer Instructional Package (MCD) ... MIP
Maintaining (AD) ... mntng
Maintaining, Preparing, and Processing Executive Reports [*Computer science*] (CDE) ... MAPPER
Maintaining, Preparing and Producing Executive Reports (NITA) ... MAPPER
Maintenace Index Page (DNAB) ... MID
Maintenance ... MA
Maintenance ... MA
Maintenance ... MAIN
Maintenance (NASA) ... MAIN
Maintenance (AFM) ... MAINT
Maintenance (ROG) ... MAINTCE
Maintenance [*Automotive advertising*] ... MAINTN
Maintenance [*Freight*] ... MAINTNCE
Maintenance (AD) ... mntnc
Maintenance ... MNTNC
Maintenance [*Telecommunications*] (TEL) ... MTCE

Maintenance Ability (KSC) ... MA
Maintenance Access Terminal [*Aviation*] ... MAT
Maintenance Action Data Form [*Military*] (CAAL) ... MADF
Maintenance Action Form ... MAF
Maintenance Action Form / Technical Directives Compliance [*Military*] (DNAB) ... MAF/TDC
Maintenance Action Request ... MAR
Maintenance Actions ... MA
Maintenance Actions per Flight Hour (MCD) ... MA/FH
Maintenance Actions per Interval (MCD) ... MA/INT
Maintenance Activities and Resources Simulation [*Computer science*] ... MARS
Maintenance Activity Management System [*Military*] ... MAMS
Maintenance Administration Panel (ACRL) ... MAP
Maintenance Advisory Committee [*NSIA*] ... MAC
Maintenance Aided Computer-HAWK-[*Homing All The Way Killer*]-Intelligence/Institutional/Instructor [*Military*] ... MACH III
Maintenance Air Abort [*Air Force*] (AFIT) ... MAAB
Maintenance Air Abort Rate [*Air Force*] (AFIT) ... MAABR
Maintenance Alert Directive [*Aviation*] ... MAD
Maintenance Alert Network [*RCA*] ... MAN
Maintenance Allocation Chart [*Military*] ... MAC
Maintenance Allocation Chart and System Maintenance (MCD) ... MAC/SM
Maintenance Analysis (KSC) ... M/A
Maintenance Analysis and Planning (NASA) ... MA & P
Maintenance Analysis and Procedures System [*Computer science*] ... MAPS
Maintenance Analysis and Recording Systems ... MARS
Maintenance Analysis and Structural Integration Information System ... MASSIIS
Maintenance Analysis Center [*FAA*] ... MAC
Maintenance Analysis Checkout Equipment ... MACE
Maintenance Analysis Data [*or Diagram*] (MCD) ... MAD
Maintenance Analysis, Detection, and Reporting System [*Computer science*] (AFM) ... MADARS
Maintenance Analysis Procedure [*Computer science*] ... MAP
Maintenance Analysis Program [*NASA*] (KSC) ... MAP
Maintenance Analysis Repair Set ... MARS
Maintenance Analysis Report (MCD) ... MAR
Maintenance Analysis Review Technique ... MART
Maintenance Analysis Task Sheet ... MATS
Maintenance Analysis Test Set ... MATS
Maintenance Analysis Unit ... MAU
Maintenance Analyzer Working Group (MCD) ... MWG
Maintenance and Administration Panel [*Bell System*] ... MAAP
Maintenance and Assembly (MCD) ... M & A
Maintenance and Calibration ... M/C
Maintenance and Checkout (NASA) ... M & C
Maintenance and Checkout Facility [*NASA*] (KSC) ... MCF
Maintenance and Checkout Station [*NASA*] (NASA) ... MCS
Maintenance and Construction [*Computer science*] (IAA) ... MAC
Maintenance and Construction Management Information System [*Computer science*] ... MACMIS
Maintenance and Cure [*Legal shorthand*] (LWAP) ... M & C
Maintenance and Diagnosis System [*Military*] (CAAL) ... MADS
Maintenance and Diagnostic Logic Display [*Burroughs*] (NITA) ... MDL
Maintenance and Electricity Equipment Vault (MCD) ... MEEV
Maintenance and Engineering Inspection ... MEI
Maintenance and Equipment (NATG) ... M & E
Maintenance and Handling Equipment ... MHE
Maintenance and Logistics Space [*System*] ... MALOS
Maintenance and Material Management [*Navy*] ... 3M
Maintenance and Material Management [*Navy*] ... MMM
Maintenance and Material Management Information System ... MMMIS
Maintenance and Material Management Project Center [*Navy*] ... MMMPC
Maintenance and Material Management System (KSC) ... MMMS
Maintenance and Operating [*Factor*] (NG) ... MO
Maintenance and Operation (MCD) ... M & O
Maintenance and Operation [*Army*] (AFIT) ... MAO
Maintenance and Operational Data Presentation Study (AAG) ... MODAPS
Maintenance and Operations Branch [*BUPERS*] ... M & OB
Maintenance and Overhaul ... M & O
Maintenance and Overhaul (AD) ... m & o
Maintenance and Refurbishment (NASA) ... M & R
Maintenance and Refurbishment (MCD) ... MAR
Maintenance and Refurbishment ... M+R
Maintenance and Refurbishment Facility [*NASA*] (KSC) ... MRF
Maintenance and Reliability Kit [*Military*] (NVT) ... MARK
Maintenance and Reliability Simulation Model (PDAA) ... MRSM
Maintenance and Repair ... M & R
Maintenance and Repair ... MAR
Maintenance and Repair ... M+R
Maintenance and Repair Craft [*Military*] ... MRC
Maintenance and Repair Cycle ... MRC
Maintenance and Repair Detachment ... M & RDET
Maintenance And Repair Inspection Program [*Military*] (DNAB) ... MARIP
Maintenance and Repair of Real Property [*Military*] ... MRRP
Maintenance and Repair Support Items ... MRSI
Maintenance and Service ... MS
Maintenance and Service (AD) ... ms
Maintenance and Service Subsystem (IAA) ... MSSS
Maintenance and Services (AFIT) ... MAS
Maintenance and Status Unit [*Telecommunications*] (TEL) ... MSU
Maintenance and Supply ... M & S
Maintenance and Supply (AD) ... M & S
Maintenance and Supply ... MANDS
Maintenance and Supply (AFIT) ... MAS

Maintenance and Supply Facility Management (AFIT) .... MASFM
Maintenance and Supply Squadron [Air Force] .... M & SSq
Maintenance and Support (DNAB) .... MAINTSUPP
Maintenance and Support Network .... MSN
Maintenance and Test (AAG) .... M & T
Maintenance and Test Assemblies [JETDS nomenclature] .... M
Maintenance and Training [in complex equipment] .... MAINTRAIN
Maintenance Antijam Console [Air Force] .... MAJAC
Maintenance Appraisal Team (MCD) .... MAT
Maintenance Area [Military British] .... MA
Maintenance Assembly and Check-Out Model (PDAA) .... MACOM
Maintenance, Assembly, and Disassembly .... MAD
Maintenance Assist Module .... MAM
Maintenance Assist Modules (MCD) .... MAMS
Maintenance Assistance and Instruction Team [Army] (AABC) .... MAIT
Maintenance Assistance and Repair System [Military] .... MARS
Maintenance Assistance Vehicle (MCD) .... MAV
Maintenance Assumes Monitor [Aviation] (FAAC) .... MAM
Maintenance Augmenting Unit (NG) .... MAU
Maintenance Automated Data Management .... MADM
Maintenance Automatic Integration Director [Computer science] .... MAID
Maintenance Availability .... MA
Maintenance Battalion (DNAB) .... MAINTBN
Maintenance between Hardware Mission Failures [Quality control] .... MTBHMF
Maintenance, Bureau of Yards and Docks [Budget category] [Obsolete; see FEC] [Navy] .... MBY & D
Maintenance Busy [Telecommunications] (TEL) .... MB
Maintenance Capability Audit [Military] (CAAL) .... MCA
Maintenance Center (MCD) .... MC
Maintenance Channel Transmit Receiver Register (MHDI) .... MCHTR
Maintenance Check (FAAC) .... MCK
Maintenance Checkoff .... MCO
Maintenance Checkoff List .... MCL
Maintenance Cleaning Equipment (MCD) .... MCE
Maintenance Command [Obsolete Air Force British] .... MC
Maintenance Communications Net (MCD) .... MCN
Maintenance Computing and Recording System .... MCRS
Maintenance Condemnation Factor (MCD) .... MCF
Maintenance Console (MCD) .... MACON
Maintenance Console .... MC
Maintenance Console Control Panel .... MCCP
Maintenance Contractor Logistic Support [Army] .... MCLS
Maintenance Control and Display System [NASA] (NASA) .... MCDS
Maintenance Control and Statistics Process [Telecommunications] (TEL) .... MCSP
Maintenance Control Center [Telecommunications] (AFM) .... MCC
Maintenance Control Circuit (IAA) .... MCC
Maintenance Control Department [Military] (DNAB) .... MCD
Maintenance Control Information System (IEEE) .... MCIS
Maintenance Control Manual [Canadian Airlines International] .... MCM
Maintenance Control Module [Telecommunications] (TEL) .... MCM
Maintenance Control Number .... MCN
Maintenance Control Panel [Navy] (CAAL) .... MCP
Maintenance Control Point (NG) .... MCP
Maintenance Control Report .... MCR
Maintenance Control Section [DCE] .... MCS
Maintenance Control System [NASA] (IAA) .... MCS
Maintenance Control Unit [Computer science] .... MCU
Maintenance Cost System (MCD) .... MCS
[The] Maintenance Council of the American Trucking Associations (EA) .... TMC
Maintenance Cycle (MCD) .... MC
Maintenance Data Analysis (MCD) .... MDA
Maintenance Data Bank .... MDB
Maintenance Data Center (MCD) .... MDC
Maintenance Data Collection [Military] (AFM) .... MDC
Maintenance Data Collection Report (MCD) .... MDCR
Maintenance Data Collection System [or Subsystem] [Navy] .... MDCS
Maintenance Data Management Schedule .... MDMS
Maintenance Data Program (MCD) .... MDP
Maintenance Data Report [Army] (AABC) .... MDR
Maintenance Data System (MCD) .... MDS
Maintenance Data Unit (MCD) .... MDU
Maintenance Decision Support System .... MDSS
Maintenance Demand Rate (NASA) .... MDR
Maintenance Demand Time (MCD) .... MDT
Maintenance Demonstration [DoD] .... M-DEMO
Maintenance Dependency Chart (IEEE) .... MDC
Maintenance Depot Assistance [Air Force] (AFM) .... MDA
Maintenance Depot Fabrication .... MDF
Maintenance Depot Material Control .... MDM
Maintenance Depot Production .... MDP
Maintenance Design Approach .... MDA
Maintenance Design Disclosure .... MDD
Maintenance Design Requirement .... MDR
Maintenance/Development [Effort ratio] .... M/D
Maintenance Development Officer (MCD) .... MDO
Maintenance Diagnostic Assistance Module [Military] (CAAL) .... MADAM
Maintenance Diagnostic Logic [Computer science] (BUR) .... MDL
Maintenance Diagnostic Processor (NITA) .... MDP
Maintenance Diagnostic Program [Computer science] (IAA) .... MDP
Maintenance Diagnostic System (MCD) .... MDS
Maintenance Diagnostic Unit .... MDU
Maintenance Display Panel (MCD) .... MDP
Maintenance Documentation [Bell System] (IAA) .... MD
Maintenance Documentation System [Bell System] .... MDS

Maintenance Dose [Medicine] .... MD
Maintenance Douglas Process Manual .... MDPM
Maintenance Downtime (MCD) .... MDT
Maintenance Due Date (NVT) .... MDD
Maintenance Effectiveness Inspection (MCD) .... MEI
Maintenance Efficiency Factor .... MEF
Maintenance Electrolyte Solution [Physiology] .... MES
Maintenance Engineer .... MAE
Maintenance Engineering Analyses Control Number [DoD] .... MEACN
Maintenance Engineering Analysis .... MEA
Maintenance Engineering Analysis Board .... MEAB
Maintenance Engineering Analysis Data .... MEAD
Maintenance Engineering Analysis Data System .... MEADS
Maintenance Engineering Analysis Program .... MEAP
Maintenance Engineering Analysis Record [or Report] .... MEAR
Maintenance Engineering Analysis Request [NASA] (NASA) .... MEAR
Maintenance Engineering Analysis Work Sheet (DNAB) .... MEAWS
Maintenance Engineering Change Request (MCD) .... MECR
Maintenance Engineering Data Storage and Retrieval System (NG) .... MEDSARS
Maintenance Engineering Evaluation (MCD) .... MEE
Maintenance Engineering Exchange .... MENEX
Maintenance Engineering Investigation [DoD] .... MEI
Maintenance Engineering Order [NASA] (KSC) .... MEO
Maintenance Engineering Report .... MER
Maintenance Engineering Review Team [Navy] (NG) .... MERT
Maintenance Engineering Support Analysis [Military] (CAAL) .... MESA
Maintenance Engineering Support Team (MCD) .... MEST
Maintenance Engineering Technique .... MET
Maintenance Engineering Working Group [NASA] (NASA) .... MEWG
Maintenance Equipment .... ME
Maintenance Equipment Floor Valve (NRCH) .... MEFV
Maintenance Evaluation (MCD) .... ME
Maintenance Evaluation Inspection (MCD) .... MEI
Maintenance Evaluation Team .... MET
Maintenance Expenditure Limit (MCD) .... MEL
Maintenance Factor .... MF
Maintenance Float [Military] .... MF
Maintenance Float Distribution Point [Computer science] (NATG) .... MFDP
Maintenance Floor Valve (NRCH) .... MFV
Maintenance Fuel .... MF
Maintenance Ground Abort [Air Force] (AFIT) .... MGAB
Maintenance Ground Abort Rate [Air Force] (AFIT) .... MGABR
Maintenance Ground Equipment [Formerly, GSF] .... MGE
Maintenance Ground Equipment Section .... MGES
Maintenance Ground Equipment Utilization Sheets .... MGEUS
Maintenance Ground Point .... MGP
Maintenance Ground Support Equipment .... MGSE
Maintenance Ground Support Equipment-Environmental Controls and Mechanisms (SAA) .... MGSE-ECM
Maintenance Handbook .... MH
Maintenance Handbook .... MHB
Maintenance Hazard Analysis (MCD) .... MHA
Maintenance Hemodialysis [Nephrology] (CPH) .... MH
Maintenance Hemodialysis [Medicine] (DMAA) .... MHD
Maintenance Identification Code [Military] (CAAL) .... MIC
Maintenance Implementation Plan [FAA] (TAG) .... MIP
Maintenance Improvement Program .... MIP
Maintenance Incident Log Report [Navy] (CAAL) .... MILR
Maintenance Index Code (DNAB) .... MIC
Maintenance Index Page .... MIP
Maintenance Indicator System [TACOM] [Army] (RDA) .... MIS
Maintenance Information Authorizing System (MCD) .... MIAS
Maintenance Information Automated Retrieval System [DoD] .... MIARS
Maintenance Information Center [Navy] (NG) .... MIC
Maintenance Information Chart [DoD] .... MIC
Maintenance Information Concerning [the repair and operation of] Missile Systems .... MICOMS
Maintenance Information Retrieval Aid .... MIRAID
Maintenance Information System [Military] (NVT) .... MAIS
Maintenance Information System for Quality (MCD) .... MIS-Q
Maintenance Infusion Rate [Medicine] .... MIR
Maintenance Inspection Report .... MIR
Maintenance Instruction (AAG) .... MI
Maintenance Instructions Manual [DoD] .... MIM
Maintenance Integrated Data Access System (MCD) .... MIDAS
Maintenance Interface Machine (NITA) .... MIM
Maintenance Interservice [or Intersupport] Management Office [DARCOM] (AFIT) .... MISMO
Maintenance Interservice Office [Air Force] (AFIT) .... MISO
Maintenance Interservice Support Group Center (MCD) .... MISG-C
Maintenance Inventory Center [Air Force] (AFIT) .... MIC
Maintenance Inventory Control System [Bell System] .... MICS
Maintenance Jettison System [NASA] .... MJS
Maintenance Job Request .... MJR
Maintenance Laboratory (MUGU) .... ML
Maintenance Level Function .... MLF
Maintenance Loading Sheet (MCD) .... MLS
Maintenance/Logistics Observer Report .... MLOR
Maintenance Loop (MCD) .... M/L
Maintenance Loop Recorder (MCD) .... M/LR
Maintenance Management and Control System (MCD) .... MMACS
Maintenance Management Center .... MMC
Maintenance Management Course [Army] .... MMC
Maintenance Management Data System [Military] (CAAL) .... MMDS
Maintenance Management Division [Army] (INF) .... MMD

Maintenance Management Engineering Team [Military]	MMET
Maintenance Management Field Office [Military] (MCD)	MMFO
Maintenance Management Functional Coordinating Group [Army]	MMFCG
Maintenance Management Improvement Program (MCD)	MMIP
Maintenance Management Information and Control (MCD)	MMIC
Maintenance Management Information and Control System	MMICS
Maintenance Management Information System [Military] (AFM)	MMIS
Maintenance Management Level [Military]	MML
Maintenance Management Manual	MMM
Maintenance Management Plan	MMP
Maintenance Management Review (MCD)	MMR
Maintenance Management Review Board (MCD)	MMRB
Maintenance Management Software	MMS
Maintenance Management System	MMS
Maintenance Management Systems Improvement Project [Air Force] (DOMA)	MMSIP
Maintenance Man-Hours (NG)	MMH
Maintenance Man-Hours	MMHR
Maintenance Man-Hours per Flight Hours	MMH/FH
Maintenance Man-Hours per Flight Hours (MCD)	MMHR/FH
Maintenance Man-Hours per Operating Hours (MCD)	MMH/OH
Maintenance Man-Hours per Sortie [Aerospace] (MCD)	MMH/S
Maintenance Man-Minute	MMM
Maintenance Manual	MM
Maintenance Material Control Officer (DNAB)	MMCO
Maintenance Message Process [Telecommunications] (TEL)	MMP
Maintenance Mode Operational Equipment Checkout Box (MCD)	MMOECB
Maintenance Monitor	MM
Maintenance Monitor Panel (MCD)	MMP
Maintenance/Nonconformance Record (MCD)	MNR
Maintenance of Air/FMF [Fleet Marine Force] Expeditionary Equipment (NG)	MAFE
Maintenance of Close Contact	MCC
Maintenance of Deception	MOD
Maintenance of Deception/Operation	MOD/OP
Maintenance of Effort [Medicare Act]	MOE
Maintenance of Hercules Capability (SAA)	MOHEC
Maintenance of Membership [Labor unions]	M of M
Maintenance of Property	MOP
Maintenance of Real Property Facilities (AABC)	MRPF
Maintenance of True Bearing	MTB
Maintenance of Way [Railroading]	M of W
Maintenance Officer (MCD)	MO
Maintenance Operating Instruction [Air Force Logistics Command]	MOI
Maintenance Operating Procedure (MCD)	MOP
Maintenance Operational Check	MOC
Maintenance Operations Center [Military]	MOC
Maintenance Operations Control [Canadian Airlines International]	MOC
Maintenance Operations Control File (MCD)	MOCF
Maintenance Operations Management (MCD)	MOM
Maintenance Operations Protocol (ACRL)	MOP
Maintenance Operations Section [Marine Corps] (DOMA)	MOS
Maintenance/Organization (MCD)	M/O
Maintenance Outline Procedure [Nuclear energy] (NRCH)	MOP
Maintenance Overload Factor Reporting System	MOFARS
Maintenance Panel (AAG)	MP
Maintenance Part (AD)	mp
Maintenance Part Task Trainer [Army]	MPTT
Maintenance Parts Breakdown (KSC)	MPB
Maintenance Parts Catalog	MPC
Maintenance Parts Handbook	MPH
Maintenance Parts Kit (MSA)	MPK
Maintenance Parts Lists	MPL
Maintenance Performance System [DoD]	MPS
Maintenance Period	MP
Maintenance Personnel Roster	MPR
Maintenance Plan	MP
Maintenance Planning [Database] (NASA)	MPLN
Maintenance Planning [Data base]	MPLN
Maintenance Planning Analysis (MCD)	MPA
Maintenance Planning and Control (MCD)	MP & C
Maintenance Planning and Control	MP&C
Maintenance Planning Data Manual (MUGU)	MPDM
Maintenance Planning Manual (NG)	MPM
Maintenance Plant at Ober Ramstadt [Army] (MCD)	MPOR
Maintenance Point	MP
Maintenance Policy Council [DoD Washington, DC]	MPC
Maintenance Policy Document [Deep Space Instrumentation Facility, NASA]	MPD
Maintenance Posture Improvement Program (MCD)	MPIP
Maintenance Prints	MP
Maintenance Priority Code	MPC
Maintenance Problem Summary	MPS
Maintenance Procedure (MCD)	MP
Maintenance Procedure Chart	MPC
Maintenance Program	MP
Maintenance Program Analysis Report	MPAR
Maintenance Program Management [Military] (AABC)	MPM
Maintenance Program Operations Management [Military] (AABC)	MPOM
Maintenance Quality Specialist (MCD)	MQS
Maintenance Rally Point [Military] (INF)	MRP
Maintenance Ratio (MCD)	MR
Maintenance Ratio Intermediate Forward	MRIF
Maintenance Readiness Training (DNAB)	MRT
Maintenance Real Property (NVT)	MRP

Maintenance Repair and Minor Construction [Program] [Air Force]	MAREMIC
Maintenance, Repair, and Operating (AD)	mro
Maintenance, Repair, and Operating Supplies (AAGC)	MRO
Maintenance, Repair, and Operation	MRO
Maintenance, Repair, and Operation of Facility (KSC)	MROF
Maintenance, Repair, and Overhaul	MRO
Maintenance, Repair, and Service	MRS
Maintenance Repair Facility	MRF
Maintenance Repair Frequency	MRF
Maintenance Repair Level (MCD)	MRL
Maintenance Repair Spares Instruction (MCD)	MRSI
Maintenance, Repairs, and Replacements [Military]	MRR
Maintenance Replaceable Unit (MCD)	MRU
Maintenance Replacement Factor (NG)	MRF
Maintenance Replacement Factor (AD)	mrf
Maintenance, Replacement, Removal (AFIT)	MRR
Maintenance Report Order (SAA)	MRO
Maintenance, Reporting, and Management [Military] (MCD)	MRM
Maintenance Reporting System [Army]	MRS
Maintenance Required Not Developed (MSA)	MRND
Maintenance Requirement Card	MRC
Maintenance Requirement Development Activity [Military] (CAAL)	MRDA
Maintenance Requirement Interim Support Asset Notice (MCD)	MRISAN
Maintenance Requirement Substantiated (MSA)	MRS
Maintenance Requirements General (MCD)	MRG
Maintenance Requirements List (MCD)	MRL
Maintenance Requirements Review Board [Military] (AFIT)	MRRB
Maintenance Requirements Review Team (MUGU)	MRRT
Maintenance Requirements Task Analysis (AD)	MRTA
Maintenance Responsibility File (MCD)	MRF
Maintenance Review	MR
Maintenance Review Board (MCD)	MRB
Maintenance Safety and Protection Equipment (AFIT)	MSPE
Maintenance Safety Data Sheets (MCD)	MSDS
Maintenance Schedule (DA)	MS
Maintenance Schedule Code (PDAA)	MASCO
Maintenance Service Plan	MSP
Maintenance Service Unit (IAA)	MSU
Maintenance Shop and Warehouse (NRCH)	MS & W
Maintenance Signal Data Cassette (MCD)	MSDC
Maintenance Signal Data Converter (MCD)	MSDC
Maintenance Signal Data Recorder (MCD)	MSDR
Maintenance Signal Data Recording Set [or System] (MCD)	MSDRS
Maintenance Signal Unit [Telecommunications] (TEL)	MSU
Maintenance Significant Items (NASA)	MSI
Maintenance Source File (MCD)	MSF
Maintenance Squadron	MS
Maintenance Standard	MS
Maintenance Standard Book	MSB
Maintenance Standard Order	MSO
Maintenance Standard Tests [Military]	MST
Maintenance Standardization and Evaluation Team (MCD)	MSET
Maintenance Standardization Evaluation Program [Air Force] (AFM)	MSEP
Maintenance Standards Study (MCD)	MSS
Maintenance Status System (MCD)	MSS
Maintenance Steering Group (MCD)	MSG
Maintenance Strategy Diagraming Technique (IEEE)	MSDT
Maintenance Superintendent [Military] (AFIT)	MS
Maintenance Supply Item	MSI
Maintenance Supply Liaison [Air Force] (AFM)	MSL
Maintenance Supply Office (DNAB)	MAINTSUPOFC
Maintenance Supply Services Agency (NATG)	MSSA
Maintenance Supply Services System (NATG)	MSSS
Maintenance Support Activity	MSA
Maintenance Support Base [Military]	MSB
Maintenance Support Center (MCD)	MSC
Maintenance Support Concept Model (MCD)	MASC
Maintenance Support Equipment [Deep Space Instrumentation Facility, NASA]	MSE
Maintenance Support Equipment Center	MSEC
Maintenance Support Index	MSI
Maintenance Support Logistics Group [Military] (CAAL)	MSLG
Maintenance Support Management File (MCD)	MSMF
Maintenance Support Office [Navy]	MAINTSUPPORTOFF
Maintenance Support Office [Navy]	MSO
Maintenance Support Office Instructions [Navy]	MSOINST
Maintenance Support Plan [or Program] [Army]	MSP
Maintenance Support Positive	MS +
Maintenance Support Schedule [Air Force] (AFM)	MSS
Maintenance Support Team (MCD)	MST
Maintenance Support Test Package [Military]	MSTP
Maintenance Support Vessel	MSV
Maintenance Surveillance Procedure (IEEE)	MSP
Maintenance System (ACII)	MS
Maintenance Task Analysis	MTA
Maintenance Task Analysis	MTA
Maintenance Task Cycle	MTC
Maintenance Task Demand File (MCD)	MTD
Maintenance Task Information System (NG)	MTIS
Maintenance Task Monitor (MCD)	MTM
Maintenance Tasks Distribution	MTD
Maintenance Technical Directive (SAA)	MTD
Maintenance Technician (NOAA)	MATEC
Maintenance Technician (MUGU)	MT
Maintenance Technology Development	MTD

Maintenance Technology Office [*Air Force Logistics Command*] .... MTO
Maintenance Test and Support Equipment .... MT & SE
Maintenance Test Equipment (MCD) .... MTE
Maintenance Test Equipment Catalog (MCD) .... MTEC
Maintenance Test Equipment Certification Procedure (SAA) .... MTECP
Maintenance Test Equipment Certification Requirement (SAA) .... MTECR
Maintenance Test Equipment, Electrical (NASA) .... MTEE
Maintenance Test Equipment, Electronic (NASA) .... MTEEC
Maintenance Test Equipment, Fluid (NASA) .... MTEF
Maintenance Test Equipment Module (MCD) .... MTEM
Maintenance Test Equipment, Optical (NASA) .... MTEO
Maintenance Test Flight (MCD) .... MTF
Maintenance Test Module .... MTP
Maintenance Test Package (MCD) .... MTSP
Maintenance Test Support Package [*Army*] .... MT
Maintenance Time .... MTB
Maintenance Time Budget .... MTC
Maintenance Time Constraint (IEEE) .... M/F
Maintenance to Flight [*Ratio*] .... M/O
Maintenance to Operation [*Ratio*] .... MT
Maintenance Trailer .... MT
Maintenance Trainer (MCD) .... MTD
Maintenance Training Department .... MTEA
Maintenance Training Effectiveness Analysis [*Army*] .... MTE
Maintenance Training Equipment (MCD) .... MTF
Maintenance Training Flight [*Military*] .... MTS
Maintenance Training Set (MCD) .... MTT
Maintenance Training Team (MCD) .... MTU
Maintenance Training Unit .... MTS
Maintenance Transmittal Sheet .... MU
Maintenance Unit [*Military*] .... MUS
Maintenance Utilization Sheet .... MVP
Maintenance Verification Plan .... MV
Maintenance Version (IAA) .... MWO
Maintenance Work Order .... MWR
Maintenance Work Request [*or Requirement*] .... MFL
Maintenance-Free Lifetime (PDAA) .... MOSS
Maintenance-Operations Support Set (AFM) .... moss
Maintenance-Operations Support Set (AD) .... m/o
Maintenance-to-Operation (AD) .... FMMO
Maintirano [*Madagascar*] [*ICAO location identifier*] (ICLI) .... FMMO
Maintirano [*Madagascar*] [*Airport symbol*] (OAG) .... MXT
Mainwater Feed Isolation Valve [*Nuclear energy*] (NRCH) .... MFIV
Mainz Army Maintenance Plant (MCD) .... MAMP
Maio [*Cape Verde Islands*] [*Airport symbol*] (OAG) .... MMO
Maio, Maio Island [*Cape Verde*] [*ICAO location identifier*] (ICLI) .... GVMA
Maiquetia [*Venezuela*] [*Airport symbol*] (AD) .... MIQ
Maiquetia [*Venezuelan airport*] (AD) .... MQI
Maiquetia [*Venezuela ICAO location identifier*] (ICLI) .... SVZM
Maiquetia [*Venezuela ICAO location identifier*] (ICLI) .... SVZZ
Maisach [*Federal Republic of Germany*] [*Geomagnetic observatory code*] .... MSC
Maislin Industries Ltd. [*Toronto Stock Exchange symbol*] .... MLI
Maison [*House*] [*French*] (AD) .... mon
Maison de la Fondation Europeenne (EAIO) .... MFE
Maison Generalice des Soeurs du Bon Pasteur, Ste-Foy, Quebec [*Library symbol National Library of Canada*] (NLC) .... QSFBP
Maison Master Keyed [*Locks*] (ADA) .... MMK
Maithili [*MARC language code Library of Congress*] (LCCP) .... mai
Maitland [*Australia Airport symbol*] (OAG) .... MTL
Maitland's Manuscript Session Cases [*Scotland*] [*A publication*] (DLA) .... Maitland
Maitland's Pleas of the Crown, [*1221*] [*England*] [*A publication*] (DLA) ...... Maitland
Maitland's Pleas of the Crown, County of Gloucester [*A publication*] (DLA) .... Mait Gl
Maitland's Select Pleas of the Crown [*A publication*] (DLA) .... Mait
Maitland's Select Pleas of the Crown [*A publication*] (DLA) .... Maitland
Maitre [*Barrister, Advocate*] [*French*] (ROG) .... ME
Maitre en Administration Publique [*Master of Public Administration*] .... MAP
Maitre en Ingenierie [*Master of Engineering*] [*French*] .... MIng
Maitre en Theologie Pastorale [*Master in Pastoral Theology*] [*French*] ...... MThPast
Maitre es Arts [*Master of Arts*] [*French*] .... MesA
Maitre es Sciences Appliquees [*Master of Applied Science*] [*French*] .... MScA
Maitrise en Fiscalite (DD) .... MFisc
Maitrise en Ingenierie [*Master of Engineering*] (DD) .... MIng
Maius [*May*] [*Latin*] .... MAI
Maiz Dulce [*Race of maize*] .... M-D
Maize Bushy Stunt Mycoplasm [*Plant pathology*] .... MBSM
Maize Chlorotic Dwarf Virus [*Plant pathology*] .... MCDV
Maize Chlorotic Mottle Virus [*Plant pathology*] .... MCMOV
Maize Chlorotic Mottle Virus [*Plant pathology*] .... MCMV
Maize Dwarf Mosaic Virus [*Plant pathology*] .... MDM
Maize Dwarf Mosaic Virus [*Plant pathology*] .... MDMV
Maize Dwarf Ringspot Virus [*Plant pathology*] .... MDRSV
Maize Mosaic Virus [*Plant pathology*] .... MMV
Maize Oil (PDAA) .... MO
Maize Rayado Fino Virus [*Plant pathology*] .... MRFV
Maize Rough Dwarf Virus [*Plant pathology*] .... MRDV
Maize Sterile Stunt Virus [*Plant pathology*] .... MSSV
Maize Streak Virus [*Plant pathology*] .... MSV
Maize Stripe [*Plant pathology*] .... MStp
Maize Stripe Virus [*Plant pathology*] .... MStpV
Maize Stripe Virus [*Plant pathology*] .... MSTV
Maize White Line Mosaic Virus [*Plant pathology*] .... MWLMV
Maizuru [*Japan*] [*Seismograph station code, US Geological Survey Closed*] (SEIS) .... MAI
Majana [*Cuba ICAO location identifier*] (ICLI) .... MUJA

Majestic .... MJSTC
Majestic Airlines, Inc. [*ICAO designator*] (FAAC) .... MAJ
Majestic Circle, Military Order of Lady Bugs of USA (EA) .... MOLB
Majestic Contractors Ltd. [*Toronto Stock Exchange symbol*] .... MJC
Majestic Eagles (EA) .... ME
Majestic Electronic Stores, Inc. [*Toronto Stock Exchange symbol*] .... MAJ
Majestic Resources [*Vancouver Stock Exchange symbol*] .... MTC
Majestic Wine Warehouses [*Commercial firm*] [*British*] .... MWW
Majesties .... MM
Majesty .... M
Majesty Resources [*Vancouver Stock Exchange symbol*] .... MJY
Maji [*Ethiopia*] [*ICAO location identifier*] (ICLI) .... HAMJ
Maji [*Ethiopia*] [*Airport symbol*] (AD) .... MJI
Maji Controlled [*A security classification*] .... MAJIC
Majma [*Saudi Arabia*] [*Airport symbol*] (AD) .... MJH
Majma'a al-Fiqh al-Islami [*Islamic Jurisprudence Academy - IJA*] (EAIO) .... IFA
Majolica [*Ceramics*] (ROG) .... MAJ
Majolica (VRA) .... maj
Major [*Cycle*] .... M
Major (DSUE) .... MA
Major [*Military*] (AABC) .... MAJ
Major [*Record label*] .... Mjr
Major .... MJR
Major [*Air Force, Army, Marine Corps*] O4
Major 20th-Century Writers [*A publication*] .... MTCW
Major Academic Field .... MAF
Major Accident Reporting System [*Engineering*] .... MARS
Major Accident Response Exercise (MCD) .... MARE
Major Account Response Evaluation (MCD) .... MARE
Major Acquisition Decision Point [*Military*] (MCD) .... MADP
Major Action Significantly Affecting the Quality of the Human Environment (DNAB) .... MASAQUE
Major Activity Center .... MAC
Major Air Command [*Later, MAJCOM*] .... MAC
Major Air Command Controlled [*Units*] .... MAJCON
Major Air Disaster (PDAA) .... MAD
Major Aircraft Accident (MCD) .... MAA
Major Aircraft Review [*Navy*] .... MAR
Major Ambulatory Categories [*Patient classification system*] (DAVI) .... MAC
Major Analytical Instrumentation Center [*University of Florida*] [*Research center*] (RCD) .... MAIC
Major Analytical Instruments Facility [*Case Western Reserve University*] [*Research center*] (RCD) .... MAIF
Major Appliance Consumer Action Panel (EA) .... MACAP
Major Army Command (AABC) .... MACOM
Major Army Command Management Information System .... MACMIS
Major Army Field Command (AABC) .... MAFC
Major Army Subcommand (AABC) .... SUBMACOM
Major Assembly Checkout [*NASA*] (NASA) .... MACO
Major Assembly Direct Labor Reporting (MCD) .... MADLR
Major Assembly Labor and Performance (MCD) .... MALP
Major Assembly Performance System (MCD) .... MAPS
Major Assembly Release [*Military*] (AABC) .... MAR
Major Attack Option [*Military*] (MCD) .... MAO
Major Authors and Illustrators for Children and Young Adults [*A publication*] .... MAICYA
Major Automated Information System Review Council [*Army*] .... MAISARC
Major Automated Information Systems Review Council [*Army*] .... MAISRC
Major Automated System Review Council [*Military*] .... MASRC
Major Basic Protein .... MBP
Major Business Development Initiative .... MBDI
Major Caliber Lightweight Gun [*Navy*] (MCD) .... MCLG
Major Caliber Lightweight Gun [*Navy*] (NG) .... MCLWG
Major Capital Improvement [*Justification for rent increase*] .... MCI
Major Category Code (MCD) .... MCC
Major City Code [*IRS*] .... MCC
Major City Earth Stations [*Telecommunications*] (TSSD) .... MCES
Major Claimant/Priority Rating Indicator (MCD) .... MC/PRI
Major Command [*Formerly, Major Air Command*] [*Military*] .... MAJCOM
Major Command of Primary Responsibility [*Air Force*] (AFM) .... MCOPR
Major Command Orientation Program [*Air Force*] (AFM) .... MCOP
Major Command Worldwide Ammunition Reporting System [*Army*] .... MWARS
Major Commands Material Readiness List (AFIT) .... COMRL
Major Communications Relay Ship [*Navy symbol*] .... AGMR
Major Component .... MC
Major Component Schedule (AAG) .... MCS
Major Coronary Arteries [*Cardiology*] .... MCA
Major Cost Proposal System (MCD) .... MCPS
Major Crime Unit [*Elite police squad on television series "Crime Story"*] .... MCU
Major Cycle .... MC
Major Defense Acquisition Program (AAGC) .... MDAP
Major Defense Equipment (MCD) .... MDE
Major Defense Equipment List .... MDEL
Major Depressive Disorder [*Psychiatry*] .... MDD
Major Design Review (KSC) .... MDR
Major Diagnostic Categories [*Medicine*] .... MDC
Major Electronics Procurement .... MEP
Major Emitting Facility [*Environmental Protection Agency*] .... MEF
Major End Item .... MEI
Major Energy Users' Group [*British*] .... MEUG
Major Engine Overhaul .... MEO
Major Engineering Test Item (AAG) .... METI
Major Equipment File (MCD) .... MEF
Major Events Committee [*Victoria, Australia*] .... MEC
Major Extinction Position [*Polarizer-Analyzer*] .... MEP

Major Facilitator [Biochemistry] .... MF
Major Fleet Escort .... MFE
Major Fleet Escort Study [Navy] (CAAL) .... MFES
Major Force Issues [Army] (AABC) .... MFI
Major Force Oriented Issue [Military] (AFM) .... MFOI
Major Force Program [Air Force] (AFIT) .... MFP
Major Fraction Thereof .... MFCT
Major Fraction Thereof .... MFT
Major Fuel Burning Installation (GFGA) .... MFBI
Major Function (MCD) .... MF
Major Function Overlay (MCD) .... MFO
Major Functional Group [NASA] (KSC) .... MFG
Major Gain Control .... MGC
Major General .... M GEN
Major General (AFM) .... MAJ GEN
Major General .... MG
Major General [Air Force, Army, Marine Corps] O8
Major General Commandant [Marine Corps] .... MGC
Major General, General Staff .... MGGS
Major Ground Test (NASA) .... MGT
Major Hazard Incident Data Service [Atomic Energy Authority] [British
    Information service or system] (IID) .... MHIDAS
Major Histocompatibility Complex [Immunology] .... MHC
Major Histocompatibility Region [Immunology] .... MHR
Major Histocompatibility System [Immunology] .... MHS
Major Homology Region [Biochemistry] .... MHR
Major Immunogene Complex [Genetics] (DOG) .... MIC
Major Improvements in Electronic Effectiveness through Advanced
    Technology (MCD) .... MIEETAT
Major Incident Room Index and Action Management [Police computer]
    [British] .... MIRIAM
Major Incidents Computer Application (PDAA) .... MICA
Major Indoor Soccer League [Defunct] (EA) .... MISL
Major Indoor Soccer League Players Association (EA) .... MISLPA
Major International Narcotics Traffickers [Register] [Drug Enforcement
    Administration] .... MINT
Major Intrinsic Protein [Biochemistry] .... MIP
Major Investigation for Low-Frequency Ocean Bottom Loss Experiments
    [Marine science] (MSC) .... Mainlobe
Major Issue (MCD) .... MI
Major Item [Military] .... MI
Major Item Automated System [Army Materiel Command] (AABC) ... MIAS
Major Item Data File (AABC) .... MIDF
Major Item Distribution Plan (AABC) .... MIDP
Major Item Management System (AABC) .... MIMS
Major Item Material Excess [Air Force] (AFIT) .... MIMEX
Major Item Removal Frequency [Army Aviation Systems Command] ... MIRF
Major Item Repair Parts List (NATG) .... MIRPL
Major Item Special Study [Army Aviation Systems Command] ... MISS
Major Item Status Report .... MISR
Major Item Supply Management Agency .... MISMA
Major Items Automated Management (AAGC) .... MIAM
Major Items Data Agency [Military] .... MIDA
Major Items of Equipment .... MIE
Major Karyotypic Abnormalities [Medicine] .... MAKA
Major Land Resource Area [USDA topographic characterization] ... MLRA
Major Landing Craft .... MLC
Major Late Promoter [Genetics] .... MLP
Major Late Promotor [Biochemistry] .... MLP
Major Late Transcription Factor [Genetics] .... MLTF
Major League [Baseball] .... ML
Major League Baseball .... MLB
Major League Baseball Players Association .... BPA
Major League Baseball Players Association (EA) .... MLBPA
Major League Scouting Bureau [Baseball] .... MLSB
Major League Umpires Association .... MLU
Major League Umpires Association (EA) .... MLUA
Major Legislation of Congress [Data processing system] [Congressional
    Research Service] .... MLC
Major Line Component [of NOAA] (NOAA) .... MLC
Major Lobe (MSA) .... ML
Major Logistical Control Headquarters (MCD) .... MLCH
Major Machine Accessory (MCD) .... MMA
Major Machine Equipment (MCD) .... MME
Major Mail Users of Australia .... MMUA
Major Maintenance Availability (MHDB) .... MMA
Major Market Index .... MMI
Major Medical [Insurance] .... MM
Major Missile Component List .... MMCL
Major Mission and Support Category .... MM & SC
Major Mission and Support Category .... MMASC
Major Mode (KSC) .... MM
Major Movable Equipment (MEDA) .... MME
Major NATO Command [or Commander] (NATG) .... MNC
Major Objective (KSC) .... MO
Major Operating System [Army] (AABC) .... MOS
Major Operations Data System (NVT) .... MODS
Major Organizational Entity (MCD) .... MOE
Major Outer Membrane Protein [Biochemistry] .... MOMP
Major Overhaul Program [Navy] .... MOP
Major Oversea Depot and Installation Method [Army] .... MODI
Major Oversea Depot Method [Army] .... MODM
Major Peace Treaties of Modern History, 1648-1967 [A publication]
    (DLA) .... MPTMH
Major Program (CAAL) .... MP

Major Program Memorandum [Military] .... MPM
Major Program Objective (MCD) .... MPO
Major Program Proposal (AAG) .... MPP
Major Project Funding .... MPF
Major Project Manager .... MPM
Major Projects Association [British] (DBA) .... MPA
Major Range and Test Facility Base [Military] (CAAL) ... MRTFB
Major Readiness Command (MCD) .... MRC
Major Realty [NASDAQ symbol] (TTSB) .... MAJR
Major Realty Corp. [NASDAQ symbol] (SAG) .... MAJR
Major Realty Corp. [Associated Press] (SAG) .... MajRty
Major Regional Contingency (DOMA) .... MRC
Major Research Equipment .... MRE
Major Retail Center .... MRC
Major Role Therapy [Schizophrenia] .... MRT
Major Seismic Disturbance .... MSD
Major Ship Satellite Terminal .... MASST
Major Shipboard SATCOM Terminal (MCD) .... MASST
Major Soccer League (BARN) .... MSL
Major Source Enforcement Effort [Environmental Protection Agency]
    (GFGA) .... MSEE
Major Source of Employment .... MSE
Major State Register (MHDB) .... MAJSR
Major Stationary Source [Environmental Protection Agency] ... MSS
Major Subcontract (MCD) .... MSC
Major Subcontract Change Coordination (MCD) .... MSCC
Major Subcontract Change Request/Approval (MCD) .... MSCR/A
Major Subcontractor .... MSK
Major Subject [Military] .... MS
Major Subject (AD) .... ms
Major Subject Descriptor [Online database field identifier] ... MJ
Major Subordinate Command [Military] .... MSC
Major Subordinate Command Liaison Officer .... MSC LNO
Major Support Element (DOMA) .... MSE
Major Symphony Managers Association (EA) .... MSMA
Major System Mode (CAAL) .... MSM
Major Systems Acquisitions [OMB Circular] (AAGC) A-109
Major Test Article (NASA) .... MTA
Major Training Area [Army] .... MTA
Major Trauma Outcome Study [American College of Surgeons Committee on
    Trauma] .... MTOS
Major Trouble Report (MCD) .... MTR
Major Unit Assembly Area (MCD) .... MUAA
Major United States Army Reserve Command (AABC) .... MUSARC
Major Urban Resource Library [Department of Education] (GFGA) ... MURL
Major Weapon System [Manager] (MCD) .... MWS
Major Wingfield Club (EA) .... MWC
Major World Air Route Area .... MWARA
Major World Authors [A publication] .... MWA
Major-General in Charge of Administration [British] ...... MGA
Major-General, Royal Artillery [Army British] .... MGRA
Major-General, Royal Marines [British military] (DMA) ... MGRM
Majority (KSC) .... MAJ
Majority (ROG) .... MAJY
Majority Agency for Joint Intelligence .... MAJI
Majority Congress Committee [Defunct] (EA) .... MCC
Majority Rule Association (EA) .... MARA
Majority Stockholder .... MS
Majority-Vote Technique [Parapsychology] .... MV
Majors Electronic Data Interchange Communications System [Computer
    science] .... MEDICS
Majorteck Industries [Vancouver Stock Exchange symbol] ... MJT
Majunga [Madagascar] [Airport symbol] (OAG) .... MJN
Majuro [Marshall Islands] [Airport symbol] (OAG) .... MAJ
Majuro [Marshall Islands] [ICAO location identifier] (ICLI) ... PKMJ
Makabana [Congo] [ICAO location identifier] (ICLI) ...... FCPA
Makabana [Congo] [Airport symbol] (AD) .... KMK
Makai Undersea Test Range (DNAB) .... MUTR
Makalamabedi [Botswana] [ICAO location identifier] (ICLI) ... FBMM
Makale [Ethiopia] [ICAO location identifier] (ICLI) .... HAMK
Makale [Ethiopia] [Airport symbol] (OAG) .... MQX
Makale/Pongtiku [Indonesia] [ICAO location identifier] (ICLI) ... WAAT
Makaopuhi [Hawaii] [Seismograph station code, US Geological Survey]
    (SEIS) .... MKA
Makapuu Oceanic Center [Hawaii] (AD) .... MOC
Makassar [Celebes] [Seismograph station code, US Geological Survey]
    (SEIS) .... MKS
Makassar [Sulawesi, Indonesia] [Airport symbol] (AD) ... MSR
Makawao, HI [FM radio station call letters] .... KDLX
Make .... M
Make and Mend .... M & M
Make Busy (IAA) .... MBY
Make Descent From [Aviation] (FAAC) .... MDFR
Make Directory [Computer science] .... MD
Make Directory [Computer science] .... MKDIR
Make From (SAA) .... M/F
Make Good .... MG
Make Good a Magnetic Track of (Degrees) [Aviation] (FAAC) ... MGMT
Make Good All Works Distributed [Legal term] (BARN) ... MGAWD
Make Necessary Transfer [Military] (DNAB) .... MAKETRANS
Make Offer .... MO
Make on Arrival (NASA) .... MOA
Make on Installation (SAA) .... MOI
Make or Buy [Economics] .... MOB
Make or Buy (AD) .... mob

Make or Subcontract Authorization (AAG) .... MSCA
Make per Drawing (SAA) .... MPD
Make Ready / Put Away (DNAB) .... MR/PA
Make Suitable Substitution .... MAKSUTSUB
Make Suitable Substitution .... MSS
Make Today Count (EA) .... MTC
Make-a-Picture Story [*Psychological testing*] .... MAPS
Make-a-Wish Foundation [*Later, MWFA*] (EA) .... MWF
Make-a-Wish Foundation of America (EA) .... MWFA
Make-before-Break .... MBB
Make-Break .... M-B
Make-Break Keying (IAA) .... MBK
Makedonski Aviotrnasport-Macedonian Airline [*FAA designator*] (FAAC) .... MAK
Makemo [*French Polynesia*] [*Airport symbol*] (OAG) .... MKP
Makemo [*French Polynesia*] [*ICAO location identifier*] (ICLI) .... NTGA
Make-or-Buy Authorization (AAG) .... MBA
Make-or-Buy Data Record (KSC) .... MBDR
Maker .... MKR
Maker (VRA) .... mkr
Maker Interchange Format [*Computer science*] (CDE) .... MIF
Makerere-University Zoology Museum [*Uganda*] .... MUZM
Makers of British Art [*A publication*] .... MBA
Makers of Canada [*A publication*] .... MC
Makers of National History [*A publication*] .... MNH
Makeup .... MKUP
Makeup (NRCH) .... MU
Makeup and Purification [*Nuclear energy*] (NRCH) .... MU & P
Makeup Demineralizer Waste Neutralizer Tank (IEEE) .... MUDWNT
Makeup Feed [*Boiler*] .... MUF
Makeup Feed [*Boiler*] .... MUFD
Make-Up Gas [*Chemical engineering*] .... MUG
Make-Up Pay (MHDB) .... MUP
Makeup Tank [*Nuclear energy*] (NRCH) .... MUT
Makeup Water Treatment (IEEE) .... MWT
Makeyevka [*Former USSR Seismograph station code, US Geological Survey Closed*] (SEIS) .... MKY
Makhachkala [*Former USSR Seismograph station code, US Geological Survey*] (SEIS) .... MAK
Makhshirin (BJA) .... Makhsh
Makhshirin (BJA) .... Maks
Makhshirin (BJA) .... Maksh
Makimono (VRA) .... makm
Makin [*Kiribati*] [*Airport symbol*] (OAG) .... MTK
Makin [*Kiribati*] [*ICAO location identifier*] (ICLI) .... NGMN
Makindu [*Kenya*] [*ICAO location identifier*] (ICLI) .... HKMU
Making .... MAK
Making .... MKG
Making Capacity (IAA) .... MC
Making Objects [*Research test*] [*Psychology*] .... MO
Making of the Nations [*A publication*] .... MN
Makita Corp. [*Associated Press*] (SAG) .... Makita
Makita Corp. [*NASDAQ symbol*] (SAG) .... MKTA
Makita Corp. [*NASDAQ symbol*] (TTSB) .... MKTAY
Makkabi Hazair (BJA) .... MH
Makkoth (BJA) .... MAK
Mako Marine International, Inc. [*NASDAQ symbol*] (SAG) .... MAKO
Mako Marine International, Inc. [*Associated Press*] (SAG) .... MakoM
Mako Marine Intl. [*NASDAQ symbol*] (TTSB) .... MAKO
Mako Marine Intl. 'Unit' [*NASDAQ symbol*] (TTSB) .... MAKOU
Makokola Club [*Malawi*] [*ICAO location identifier*] (ICLI) .... FWCM
Makokou [*Gabon*] [*Airport symbol*] (OAG) .... MKU
Makokou/Epassengue [*Gabon*] [*ICAO location identifier*] (ICLI) .... FOOK
Makou [*Iran*] [*ICAO location identifier*] (ICLI) .... OITU
Makoua [*Congo*] [*ICAO location identifier*] (ICLI) .... FCOM
Makoua [*Congo*] [*Airport symbol*] (OAG) .... MKJ
Makung [*Taiwan*] [*Airport symbol*] (OAG) .... MZG
Makung Airlines [*Taiwan*] [*ICAO designator*] (FAAC) .... MKO
Makurdi [*Nigeria*] [*ICAO location identifier*] (ICLI) .... DNMK
Makurdi [*Nigeria*] [*Airport symbol*] (OAG) .... MDI
Makus Resources, Inc. [*Vancouver Stock Exchange symbol*] .... MQU
Mala Services Ltd. [*British*] [*FAA designator*] (FAAC) LCL
Malabang [*Philippines*] [*Airport symbol*] (OAG) .... MLP
Malabang, Lanao Del Sur [*Philippines*] [*ICAO location identifier*] (ICLI) .... RPWM
Malabar [*Java*] [*Seismograph station code, US Geological Survey Closed*] (SEIS) .... MLB
Malabar Law Quarterly [*A publication*] (DLA) .... MLQ
Malabar Volunteer Rifles [*British military*] (DMA) .... MVR
Malabo [*Equatorial Guinea*] [*Airport symbol*] (OAG) .... SSG
Malabo, Isla De Macias, Nguema Biyoga [*Equatorial Guinea*] [*ICAO location identifier*] (ICLI) .... FGSL
Malacatan [*Guatemala*] [*ICAO location identifier*] (ICLI) .... MGML
Malacca [*Malaysia*] [*Airport symbol*] (OAG) .... MKZ
Malacca [*Malaysia*] [*ICAO location identifier*] (ICLI) .... WMKM
Malachi [*Old Testament book*] .... Mal
Malachi [*Old Testament book*] (BJA) .... MI
Malachi [*Old Testament book*] .... ML
Malachias [*Old testament book*] [*Douay version*] .... MAL
Malachite Green [*A dye*] .... MG
Malachite Green Leucocyanite (OA) .... MGL
Malacology .... MALAC
Malacoota [*New South Wales, Australia*] [*Airport symbol*] (AD) .... XMC
Malad City, ID [*Location identifier FAA*] (FAAL) .... MLD
Malad Range [*Idaho*] [*Seismograph station code, US Geological Survey*] (SEIS) .... MLI
Maladapted Behavior Record [*Personality development test*] [*Psychology*] .... MBR

Maladjusted Child [*Social Work*] [*British*] (DSUE) .... MALAD
Maladjustment Score [*Psychology*] .... MS
Malaga [*Spain*] [*Airport symbol*] (OAG) .... AGP
Malaga [*Spain ICAO location identifier*] (ICLI) .... LEMG
Malaga [*Spain*] [*Seismograph station code, US Geological Survey*] (SEIS) .... MAL
Malagasi Republic [*Madagascar*] [*MARC geographic area code Library of Congress*] (LCCP) .... f-mg--
Malagasy [*MARC language code Library of Congress*] (LCCP) .... mla
Malagasy Republic (VRA) .... Madag
Malagasy Republic .... Malag Rep
Malagasy Republic [*Madagascar*] [*MARC country of publication code Library of Congress*] (LCCP) .... mg
Malaimbandy [*Madagascar*] [*ICAO location identifier*] (ICLI) .... FMMC
Malaimbandy [*Madagascar*] [*Airport symbol*] (OAG) .... WML
Malakal [*Sudan*] [*ICAO location identifier*] (ICLI) .... HSSM
Malakal [*Sudan*] [*Airport symbol*] (OAG) .... MAK
Malakoff, TX [*FM radio station call letters*] .... KCKL
Malalane [*South Africa*] [*ICAO location identifier*] (ICLI) .... FAMN
Malalaua [*Papua New Guinea*] [*Airport symbol*] (OAG) .... MLQ
Malamala [*South Africa*] [*ICAO location identifier*] (ICLI) .... FAMD
Malan Realty Investors [*NYSE symbol*] (SAG) .... MAL
Malan Realty Investors [*Associated Press*] (SAG) .... MalanR
Malang [*Indonesia*] [*Airport symbol*] (OAG) .... MLG
Malang/Abdul Rachman Saleh [*Indonesia*] [*ICAO location identifier*] (ICLI) ..... WIAS
Malanga [*Zaire*] [*ICAO location identifier*] (ICLI) .... FZDA
Malange [*Angola*] [*Airport symbol*] (OAG) .... MEG
Malanje [*Angola*] [*ICAO location identifier*] (ICLI) .... FNMA
Malargue [*Argentina ICAO location identifier*] (ICLI) .... SAMM
Malaria [*Infectious diseases*] (DAVI) .... MALAR
Malaria Control Detachment [*Army World War II*] .... MCD
Malaria Control in War Areas [*Later, Centers for Disease Control*] .... MCWA
Malaria Control Unit [*Army World War II*] .... MCU
Malaria Eradication Special Account .... MESA
Malaria Immune Globulin .... MIG
Malaria Philatelists International (EA) .... MPI
Malaria Research Centre [*India*] .... MRC
Malaria Survey Unit [*Army World War II*] .... MSU
Malaria Therapy [*British*] .... MT
Malarial Parasites [*Infectious diseases Laboratory and respiratory*] (DAVI) ...... MALA
Malariology Technician [*Navy*] .... MAL
Malartic Hygrade Gold Mines Ltd. (MHDW) .... MHG
Malartic Hygrade Gold Mines Ltd. [*Vancouver Stock Exchange symbol*] .... MYC
Malartic, PQ [*Television station call letters*] .... CBVD
Malaspina [*Alaska*] [*Seismograph station code, US Geological Survey*] (SEIS) .... MLA
Malaspina [*Alaska*] [*Seismograph station code, US Geological Survey*] (SEIS) .... MLP
Malaspina College Learning Resources Centre [*UTLAS symbol*] .... MAL
Malaspina College, Nanaimo, BC, Canada [*Library symbol Library of Congress*] (LCLS) .... CaBNM
Malaspina College, Nanaimo, British Columbia [*Library symbol National Library of Canada*] (NLC) .... BNM
Malate .... MAL
Malate Dehydrogenase [*Also, MDH*] [*An enzyme*] .... MD
Malate Dehydrogenase [*Also, MD*] [*An enzyme*] .... MDH
Malatya [*Turkey*] [*Airport symbol*] (OAG) .... MLX
Malatya/Erhac [*Turkey ICAO location identifier*] (ICLI) .... LTAO
Malatya/Erhac [*Turkey ICAO location identifier*] (ICLI) .... LTAT
Malavi [*Iran*] [*ICAO location identifier*] (ICLI) .... OICY
Malawi [*Aircraft nationality and registration mark*] (FAAC) 7QY
Malawi [*MARC geographic area code Library of Congress*] (LCCP) .... f-mw--
Malawi [*MARC country of publication code Library of Congress*] (LCCP) .... mw
Malawi [*ANSI two-letter standard code*] (CNC) .... MW
Malawi [*ANSI three-letter standard code*] (CNC) .... MWI
Malawi Congress Party [*Nyasaland*] [*Political party*] (PPW) .... MCP
Malawi Kwacha [*Monetary unit*] .... MK
Malawi Nyika National Park (AD) .... MNNP
Malawi Rural Finance Co. Ltd. .... MRFC
Malawi Socialist Labour Party [*Political party*] (EY) .... MSLP
Malawi Women's League .... MWL
Malay (WDAA) .... MAL
Malay [*MARC language code Library of Congress*] (LCCP) .... may
Malay National Party [*Political party*] (AD) .... MNP
Malay National Party (NADA) .... MNP
Malay Nationalist Revolutionary Party of Malaya [*Partai Kebangsaan Melayu Revolusioner Malaya*] [*Political party*] (PPW) .... MNRPM
Malaya [*MARC geographic area code Library of Congress*] (LCCP) .... am----
Malaya Law Review [*A publication*] (DLA) .... Mal L Rev
Malayalam [*MARC language code Library of Congress*] (LCCP) .... mal
Malayan (AABC) .... MAL
Malayan Airways Ltd. .... MAL
Malayan Cases [*1908-58*] [*A publication*] (DLA) .... MC
Malayan Communist Party [*Political party*] .... MCP
Malayan Law Reports [*1950-54*] [*A publication*] (DLA) .... MLR
Malayan National Liberation Front [*Singapore*] [*Political party*] (PD) .... MNLF
Malayan People's Anti-Japanese Army [*World War II*] .... MPAJA
Malayan People's Anti-Japanese Union [*World War II*] .... MPAJU
Malayan People's Liberation Army .... MPLA
Malayan People's Liberation League .... MPLL
Malayan Planning Unit [*World War II*] .... MPU
Malayan Races Liberation Army .... MRLA
Malayan Rubber Fund Board (AD) .... MRFB
Malayan Union Law Reports [*1946-47*] [*A publication*] (ILCA) .... MULR
Malaya-Philippines-Indonesia .... MAPHILINDO
Malaybalay, Bukidon [*Philippines*] [*ICAO location identifier*] (ICLI) .... RPWY

Malayer [Iran] [ICAO location identifier] (ICLI) .... OIHM
Malayo-Polynesian [MARC language code Library of Congress] (LCCP) .... map
Malaysia [Aircraft nationality and registration mark] (FAAC) 9M
Malaysia [MARC geographic area code Library of Congress] (LCCP) .... a-my--
Malaysia (WDAA) .... MAL
Malaysia (VRA) .... Malay
Malaysia [IYRU nationality code] [ANSI two-letter standard code] (CNC) .... MY
Malaysia [MARC country of publication code Library of Congress] (LCCP) .... my
Malaysia [ANSI three-letter standard code] (CNC) .... MYS
Malaysia Airlines [Airline flight code] (ODBW) .... MH
Malaysia East Asia Satellite .... MEASAT
Malaysia Fund [NYSE symbol] (TTSB) .... MF
Malaysia Fund, Inc. [Associated Press] (SAG) .... Malaysa
Malaysia Fund, Inc. [NYSE symbol] (SPSG) .... MF
Malaysia High Commission, Ottawa, Ontario [Library symbol National Library of Canada] (NLC) .... OOMHC
Malaysia International Chamber of Commerce and Industry (EAIO) .... MICCI
Malaysia, Singapore, and Brunei Association [British] (DBA) .... MSBA
Malaysia Singapore Australia Society .... MSAS
Malaysia Tourist Information Center (EA) .... MTIC
Malaysian Air Lines .... MAL
Malaysian Airline System [ICAO designator] (FAAC) .... MAS
Malaysian Airline System [ICAO designator] (AD) .... MH
Malaysian Aquatic Sciences and Fisheries Information System [Marine science] (OSRA) .... MAFIS
Malaysian Book Publishers' Association (EAIO) .... MABOPA
Malaysian Chinese Association [Political party] (PPW) .... MCA
Malaysian Cocoa Butter .... MCB
Malaysian Indian Congress [Political party] (PPW) .... MIC
Malaysian International Shipping Corp. (DS) .... MISC
Malaysian MARC (NITA) .... MALMARC
Malaysian Multimedia Super Corridor .... MSC
Malaysian National Liberation League (NADA) .... MNLL
Malaysian Newspaper Publishers' Association (EAIO) .... MNPA
Malaysian Peasants Front [Political party] (AD) .... MPF
Malaysian Refrigerator Co. (AD) .... MRCo
Malaysian Rubber Bureau (EA) .... MRB
Malaysian Rubber Exchange and Licensing Board (AD) .... MRELB
Malaysian Rubber Producers' Research Association [Research center British] (IRC) .... MRPRA
Malaysian Rubber Research and Development Board (AD) .... MRRDB
Malaysian Students' Organization [Australia] .... MSO
Malaysian Tin Bureau [Defunct] (EA) .... MTB
Malaysian University of Science and Technology .... MUST
Malaysian Youth Movement .... ABIM
Malaysian-American Chamber of Commerce [Later, AAACC] .... MACC
Malaysian-American Electronics Industry .... MAEI
Malaysia-Singapore Airlines .... MSA
Malcolm Baldrige National Quality Award [Department of Commerce] ...... MBNQA
Malcolm X College of the City College of Chicago, Chicago, IL [Library symbol Library of Congress] (LCLS) .... ICMX
Malcolm X Liberation University .... MXLU
Malcolm's Legal and Judicial Ethics [A publication] (DLA) .... Malcolm Ethics
Malda [India] [ICAO location identifier] (ICLI) .... VEMH
Malden [Missouri] [Seismograph station code, US Geological Survey Closed] (SEIS) .... MLD
Malden Hospital [Malden, MA] .... MH
Malden, MO [FM radio station call letters] .... KMAL
Malden, MO [AM radio station call letters] .... KTCB
Malden, MO [Location identifier FAA] (FAAL) .... MAW
Malden Public Library, Malden, MA [Library symbol Library of Congress] (LCLS) .... MMal
Maldive Islands .... Mald Isls
Maldives [Aircraft nationality and registration mark] (FAAC) 8Q
Maldives [MARC geographic area code Library of Congress] (LCCP) .... i-xc--
Maldives [ANSI three-letter standard code] (CNC) .... MDV
Maldives [ANSI two-letter standard code] (CNC) .... MV
Maldives [MARC country of publication code Library of Congress] (LCCP) xc
Maldives Association of the Tourism Industry (EY) .... MATI
Maldives International Airlines [ICAO designator] (AD) .... RQ
Maldives News Bureau (EY) .... MNB
Maldonado/Base Aeronaval C/C Carlos A. Curbelo [Uruguay] [ICAO location identifier] (ICLI) .... SULS
Male [Electronics] .... M
Male (DD) .... m
Male .... M
Male (DAVI) .... Ma
Male [Maldives] [Airport symbol] (OAG) .... MLE
Male, Altered Animal (DMAA) .... M/A
Male, Altered Animal (DMAA) .... MALT
Male and Female [Components, as of connecting devices] .... M & F
Male and Female Homosexual Association of Great Britain .... MANDFHAB
Male Bonding Alert [Screenwriter's lexicon] .... MBA
Male Bowhunter Aided [International Bowhunting Organization] [Class equipment] .... MBA
Male, Castrated Animal (DMAA) .... M/C
Male Chauvinist Pig [Feminist term] .... MCP
Male Chromosome .... Y
Male Electronic Genital Stimulator [Developed by Biosonics, Inc.] .... MEGS
Male Equivalents [Entomology] .... ME
Male, Female, Handicapped, Veteran (BARN) .... m/f/h/v
Male/Female - Married/Widow [or Widower]/Single .... MF/MWS
Male Impotence Test [Psychology] .... MIT
Male/International [Maldives] [ICAO location identifier] (ICLI) .... VRMM
Male Liberation Foundation (EA) .... MLF

Male or Female .... MorF
Male or Female (NHD) .... MORF
Male Oriental (AD) .... m/O
Male Pattern Baldness (AD) .... mpb
Male Pipe Thread (AD) .... mpt
Male Pipe Thread (MSA) .... MPT
Male Pronucleus Growth Factor [Biochemistry] .... MPGF
Male Seniors [International Bowhunting Organization] [Class equipment] .... MSR
Male Servant .... MS
Male Sexual Biomass [Botany] .... MSB
Male Specific Antigen (PDAA) .... MSA
Male Sterile-Facilitated Recurrent Selection Population [Plant breeding] .... MSFRSP
Male Threaded .... MTHRD
Male to Female [Ratio] .... MF
Male Treated with DOC [Deoxycorticosterone] .... MD
Male Urban Professional [Lifestyle classification] .... Muppy
Maleated Bovine Serum Albumin [Medicine] (DMAA) .... Mal-BSA
Malebo [Zaire] [ICAO location identifier] (ICLI) .... FZBN
Male-Female Longevity Difference .... MFLD
Malefiloane [Lesotho] [ICAO location identifier] (ICLI) .... FXML
Maleic Anhydride [Also, MAH] [Organic chemistry] .... MA
Maleic Anhydride [Also, MA] [Organic chemistry] .... MAH
Maleic Hydrazide [Plant growth regulator] .... MH
Maleimidobenzoyl N-Hydroxysuccinimide [Organic chemistry] .... MBS
Malekolon [Papua New Guinea] [Airport symbol] (OAG) .... MKN
Male-Pattern Baldness .... MPB
Malerei und Zeichnung [A publication] (OCD) .... Malerei u Zeichn
Males, Density Of [Ecology] .... MDEN
Malev-Hungarian Airlines [ICAO designator] (FAAC) .... MAH
Maleyl [Biochemistry] .... Mal
Maleylated Bovine Serum Albumin [Biochemistry] .... MBSA
Malfunction (KSC) .... MAL
Malfunction .... MAL
Malfunction (KSC) .... MALF
Malfunction Alert [Computer science] (BUR) .... MFA
Malfunction Analysis Branch [NASA] .... MAB
Malfunction Analysis, Detection, and Recording [Computer science] .... MADAR
Malfunction Analysis, Detection, and Recording Subsystem [Computer science] .... MADARS
Malfunction and Data Recorder [Computer science] (IAA) .... MADAR
Malfunction Array RADAR .... MAR
Malfunction Detection (NASA) .... MD
Malfunction Detection (NASA) .... MFD
Malfunction Detection Analysis and Recording [NASA] (KSC) .... MDAR
Malfunction Detection Analysis, Recording, and Training System .... MADARTS
Malfunction Detection and Recording [Checkout system for aircraft] [Air Force] .... MADREC
Malfunction Detection Package .... MDP
Malfunction Detection System [Gemini] [NASA] .... MDS
Malfunction Detector Analyzer (PDAA) .... MDA
Malfunction Display and Control System (MCD) .... MDCS
Malfunction Indicator Light [Automotive engineering] .... MIL
Malfunction Insertion and Display Unit [Aviation] .... MIDU
Malfunction Insertion Unit [Aviation] .... MIU
Malfunction Investigation Laboratory .... MIL
Malfunction Investigation Report [NASA] (KSC) .... MIR
Malfunction Investigation Support Laboratory [NASA] (KSC) .... MISL
Malfunction Investigations File (MCD) .... MIF
Malfunction Rate .... MFR
Malfunction Rate Detection System (DNAB) .... MRDS
Malfunction Receiver .... MFR
Malfunction Reporting Program [Navy] .... MRP
Malfunction Reporting System [Boeing] .... MRS
Malfunction Verification Test (MCD) .... MVT
Malfunctioned Equipment Corrective Action .... MECA
Malfunctioning Display (DA) .... MFD
Malfunction-Linked People .... MLP
Malheur County Library, Ontario, OR [Library symbol Library of Congress] (LCLS) .... OrOn
Malheur Memorial Hospital, J. J. Sarazin Memorial Library, Nyssa, OR [Library symbol Library of Congress] (LCLS) .... OrNyMH
Malheur National Wildlife Refuge [Oregon] (AD) .... MNWR
Mali [MARC geographic area code Library of Congress] (LCCP) .... f-ml--
Mali [ANSI two-letter standard code] (CNC) .... ML
Mali [MARC country of publication code Library of Congress] (LCCP) .... ml
Mali [ANSI three-letter standard code] (CNC) .... MLI
Mali [International civil aircraft marking] (ODBW) .... TZ
Mali Franc [Monetary unit] .... MF
Maliair Ltd. [British ICAO designator] (FAAC) .... MAK
Maliana [East Timor] [ICAO location identifier] (ICLI) .... WPMN
Malic Dehydrogenase [An enzyme] (MAE) .... MD
"Malic" Enzyme .... ME
Malicious [FBI standardized term] .... MAL
Malicious Call Identification [Telecommunications] (TEL) .... MCI
Malicious Call Identification [Telecommunications] (DOM) .... MCID
Malicious Destruction of Property .... MDOP
Malicious Destruction of Property .... MDP
Malicious False Alarm [Firefighting] .... MFA
Malicious Mischief [Legal term] (DLA) .... MAL MISCH
Malicious Prosecution [Legal term] (DLA) .... MAL PROS
Malignancy-Associated Changes [Cancer] .... MAC
Malignancy-Associated Humoral Hypercalcemia [Medicine] (DMAA) .... MAHH
Malignancy-Associated Hypercalcemia [Oncology] .... MAH
Malignant [Medicine] .... M

Malignant [*Medicine*] .... malig
Malignant Angioendotheliomatosis [*Oncology*] .... MA
Malignant Angioendotheliomatosis [*Oncology*] .... MAE
Malignant Arrhythmia [*Medicine*] (DMAA) .... MA
Malignant Fibrous Histiocytoma [*Oncology*] .... MFH
Malignant Histiocytosis [*Medicine*] .... MH
Malignant Hyperpyrexia [*Medicine*] .... MH
Malignant Hyperthermia [*Medicine*] .... MH
Malignant Hyperthermia Association of the United States (EA) .... MHAUS
Malignant Hyperthermia Resistance [*Medicine*] (DMAA) .... MHR
Malignant Hyperthermia Susceptible [*Medicine*] .... MHS
Malignant Hypothermia Susceptible [*Patients*] [*Emergency medicine*] (DAVI) .... MHS
Malignant Lymphoma [*Oncology*] .... ML
Malignant Lymphoma/Centroblastic-Centrocytic [*Oncology*] .... ML/CB-CC
Malignant Lymphoma/Centrocytic [*Oncology*] .... ML/CC
Malignant Lymphoma/Lymphoblastic [*Oncology*] .... ML/LB
Malignant Lymphoma/Lymphoplasmacytoid [*Oncology*] .... ML/LPC
Malignant Melanoma [*Oncology*] .... MM
Malignant Mixed Muellerian Tumor [*Oncology*] .... MMMT
Malignant Papillary Mesothelioma [*Medicine*] .... MPM
Malignant Peripheral Nerve Sheath Tumor .... MPNST
Malignant Persistent Positional Nystagmus [*Medicine*] (DMAA) .... MPPN
Malignant Small Cell Tumor [*Oncology*] .... MSCT
Malignant Teratoma [*Oncology*] .... MT
Malignant Teratoma, Anaplastic [*Medicine*] (DMAA) .... MTA
Malignant Teratoma Intermediate [*Oncology*] (MAE) .... MTI
malignant Teratoma Undifferentiated [*Oncology*] (DAVI) .... MTU
Malignant Trophoblastic Teratoma [*Oncology*] (MAE) .... MTT
Malignant Ventricular Arrhythmias [*Cardiology*] (DAVI) .... MVA
Malili [*Indonesia*] [*ICAO location identifier*] (ICLI) .... WAAI
Malimpung [*Indonesia*] [*ICAO location identifier*] (ICLI) .... WAAG
Malinau [*Indonesia*] [*ICAO location identifier*] (ICLI) .... WRLM
Malindi [*Kenya*] [*ICAO location identifier*] (ICLI) .... HKML
Malindi [*Kenya*] [*Airport symbol*] (OAG) .... MYD
Mali-Tinbouctou Air Service [*ICAO designator*] (FAAC) .... HBM
Maljamar, NM [*FM radio station call letters*] .... KMTH
Maljamar, NM [*FM radio station call letters*] .... KWMW
Malka Resources Ltd. [*Vancouver Stock Exchange symbol*] .... MLU
Mall [*Postal Service standard*] (OPSA) .... MALL
Mall Airways [*ICAO designator*] (AD) .... FH
Mall Airways, Inc. [*ICAO designator*] (FAAC) .... MLS
Mallaig Public Library, Alberta [*Library symbol National Library of Canada*] (NLC) .... AMAL
Mallaig Public Library, Mallaig, AB, Canada [*Library symbol*] [*Library of Congress*] (LCLS) .... CaAMal
Mallard Public Library, Mallard, IA [*Library symbol Library of Congress*] (LCLS) .... IaMall
Malleable (MSA) .... MAL
Malleable (KSC) .... MALL
Malleable .... MALL
Malleable Cast Iron .... MCI
Malleable Chain Manufacturers Institute [*Later, American Chain Association*] .... MCMI
Malleable Founders' Society [*Later, Iron Castings Society - ICS*] .... MFS
Malleable Iron .... MI
Malleable Iron Pipe .... MIP
Malleable Research and Development Foundation (AD) .... MR&DF
Mallinckrodt Chemical Works [*Later, Mallinckrodt, Inc.*] .... MCW
Mallinckrodt Chemical Works [*Later, Mallinckrodt, Inc.*], St. Louis, MO [*Library symbol Library of Congress*] (LCLS) .... MoSMal
Mallinckrodt Group [*Formerly, IMCERA Group*] [*Associated Press*] (SAG) .... Malinc
Mallinckrodt Group [*Formerly, IMCERA Group*] [*Associated Press*] (SAG) .... Malinckr
Mallinckrodt Group [*Formerly, IMCERA Group*] [*NYSE symbol*] (SAG) .... MKG
Mallinckrodt, Inc. [*Research code symbol*] .... MP
Mallincrodt Group 4% Pfd [*NYSE symbol*] (TTSB) .... MKGPr
Mallon Resources [*NASDAQ symbol*] (TTSB) .... MLRC
Mallon Resources Corp. [*Associated Press*] (SAG) .... Mallon
Mallon Resources Corp. [*NASDAQ symbol*] (CTT) .... MLRC
Mallory Body [*Medicine*] .... MB
Mallory Body Cytokeratin [*Medicine*] .... MBCK
Mallory's Irish Chancery Reports [*A publication*] (DLA) .... Mallory
Mallory's Modern Entries [*A publication*] (DLA) .... Mall Ent
Mallory-Weiss Syndrome [*Medicine*] (MEDA) .... M-W
Malmesbury [*South Africa*] [*ICAO location identifier*] (ICLI) .... FAMY
Malmo [*Sweden ICAO location identifier*] (ICLI) .... ESMM
Malmo [*Sweden*] [*Airport symbol*] (OAG) .... MMA
Malmo Aviation AB [*Sweden ICAO designator*] (FAAC) .... SCW
Malmo/Harbour [*Sweden ICAO location identifier*] (ICLI) .... ESHM
Malmo/Sturup [*Sweden ICAO location identifier*] (ICLI) .... ESMS
Malmstrom Air Force Base [*Montana*] (KSC) .... MAFB
Maloelap [*Marshall Islands*] [*Airport symbol*] (OAG) .... MAV
Malolactic Fermentation .... MLF
Malolo Lailai [*Fiji*] [*ICAO location identifier*] (ICLI) .... NFFO
Malololailai [*Fiji*] [*Airport symbol*] (OAG) .... PTF
Malonaldehyde [*Organic chemistry*] .... MA
Malonate [*Organic chemistry*] .... mal
Malondialdehyde [*Biochemistry*] .... MDA
Malone [*New York*] [*Airport symbol*] (AD) .... MAL
Malone College, Canton, OH [*OCLC symbol*] (OCLC) .... MAL
Malone College, Canton, OH [*Library symbol Library of Congress*] (LCLS) .... OCanM
Malone, NY [*Location identifier FAA*] (FAAL) .... MAL
Malone, NY [*AM radio station call letters*] .... WICY
Malone, NY [*FM radio station call letters*] .... WSLO
Malone, NY [*FM radio station call letters*] .... WVNV
Malone Society (EA) .... MS
Maloti [*Plural of Loti*] [*Monetary Unit*] [*Lesotho*] (BARN) .... M
Malpractice Association (EA) .... MA
Malraux Society (EAIO) .... RMR
Malt Extract [*Microbiology*] .... ME
Malt Extract Agar [*Culture media*] .... MEA
Malt House .... MH
Malt Research Institute [*Later, NMRI*] .... MRI
Malta [*Aircraft nationality and registration mark*] (FAAC) 9H
Malta [*MARC geographic area code Library of Congress*] (LCCP) .... e-mm--
Malta [*Malta*] [*ICAO location identifier*] (ICLI) .... LMMM
Malta (WDAA) .... MAL
Malta [*Airport symbol*] (OAG) .... MLA
Malta [*ANSI three-letter standard code*] (CNC) .... MLT
Malta [*MARC country of publication code Library of Congress*] (LCCP) .... mm
Malta [*IYRU nationality code*] [*ANSI two-letter standard code*] (CNC) .... MT
Malta Air Charter Co. Ltd. [*ICAO designator*] (FAAC) .... MAC
Malta Bend, MO [*FM radio station call letters*] .... KRLI
Malta Fencible Artillery [*British*] .... MFA
Malta International Business Authority (EY) .... MIBA
Malta Labor Party [*Political party*] (PPW) .... MLP
Malta/Luqa [*Malta*] [*ICAO location identifier*] (ICLI) .... LMML
Malta, MT [*FM radio station call letters*] .... KMMR
Malta, MT [*Location identifier FAA*] (FAAL) .... MLK
Malta Workers Party [*Political party*] (PPE) .... MWP
Maltahohe [*Namibia*] [*ICAO location identifier*] (ICLI) .... FAMH
maltase-to-Lactase [*Ratio*] [*Biochemistry*] (DAVI) .... M:L
Maltbie's Appellate Procedure [*A publication*] (DLA) .... Conn App Proc
Maltby on Courts-Martial [*A publication*] (DLA) .... Malt CM
Maltese (DSUE) .... MALT
Maltese [*MARC language code Library of Congress*] (LCCP) .... mlt
Maltese Australian Women's Association .... MAWA
Maltese Falcon Society [*Defunct*] (EA) .... MFS
Maltese Light Infantry [*British military*] (DMA) .... MLI
Maltese-American Benevolent Society (EA) .... MABS
Malting and Brewing Industry Barley Technical Committee [*Australia*] .... MBIBTC
Malting Barley Improvement Association (EA) .... MBIA
Maltose-Binding Protein [*Biochemistry*] .... MBP
Maltsters Association [*British*] (DBA) .... MAGB
Maltwood Art Museum, University of Victoria, British Columbia [*Library symbol National Library of Canada*] (NLC) .... BVIMH
Malum [*Ill*] [*Latin*] (MAE) .... mal
Malung [*Sweden ICAO location identifier*] (ICLI) .... ESVM
Malung School, Roseau, MN [*Library symbol*] [*Library of Congress*] (LCLS) .... MnRosMS
Malva [*Mallow*] [*Pharmacy*] (ROG) .... MALV
Malva Yellows Virus [*Plant pathology*] .... MYV
Malvalic Acid (PDAA) .... MA
Malvaux [*France*] [*Seismograph station code, US Geological Survey*] (SEIS) .... MLV
Malvern [*British ICAO location identifier*] (ICLI) .... EGRE
Malvern, AR [*AM radio station call letters*] .... KBOK
Malvern, AR [*FM radio station call letters*] .... KBOK-FM
Malvern, AR [*FM radio station call letters*] .... KISI
Malvern, AR [*Location identifier FAA*] (FAAL) .... MVQ
Malvern Leader, Malvern, IA [*Library symbol Library of Congress*] (LCLS) .... IaMalvL
Malvern Program Analysis System (NITA) .... MALPAS
Malvern Public Library, Malvern, IA [*Library symbol Library of Congress*] (LCLS) .... IaMalv
Malverne Public Library, Malverne, NY [*Library symbol Library of Congress*] (LCLS) .... NMalv
Malverne Senior High School, Malverne, NY [*Library symbol*] [*Library of Congress*] (LCLS) .... NMalvSH
Malwa Bhil Corps [*British military*] (DMA) .... MBC
Malye Karmakuly [*Former USSR Geomagnetic observatory code*] .... MAY
Malynes' Ancient Law Merchant [*A publication*] (DLA) .... Mal Law M
Malynes' Lex Mercatoria [*3 eds.*] [*1622-36*] [*A publication*] (DLA) .... Mal Lex Merc
Malynes' Lex Mercatoria [*3 eds.*] [*1622-36*] [*A publication*] (DLA) .... Malynes
MAM Aviation Ltd. [*British ICAO designator*] (ICDA) .... MF
MAM Aviation Ltd. [*British ICAO designator*] (FAAC) .... WSY
Mamai [*Papua New Guinea*] [*Airport symbol*] (OAG) .... MAP
Mamaia [*Romania*] [*Airport symbol*] (AD) .... XMM
Mamaroneck Free Library, Mamaroneck, NY [*Library symbol Library of Congress*] (LCLS) .... NMam
Mamaroneck Free Library, Mamaroneck, NY [*Library symbol*] [*Library of Congress*] (LCLS) .... NMamL
Mamas and the Papas Fan Club (EA) .... MPFC
Mamassani [*Iran*] [*ICAO location identifier*] (ICLI) .... OISM
Mambajao [*Philippines*] [*Seismograph station code, US Geological Survey Closed*] (SEIS) .... MAM
Mambone [*Mozambique*] [*Airport symbol*] (AD) .... MBM
Mamburao [*Philippines*] [*Airport symbol*] (OAG) .... MBO
Mamburao, Occidental Mindoro [*Philippines*] [*ICAO location identifier*] (ICLI) .... RPUM
Mamfe [*Cameroon*] [*ICAO location identifier*] (ICLI) .... FKKF
Mamfe [*Cameroon*] [*Airport symbol*] (OAG) .... MMF
Mamie Doud Eisenhower Public Library, Broomfield, CO [*Library symbol Library of Congress*] (LCLS) .... CoBro
Mamie Van Doren Fan Club (EA) .... MVDFC
Mamitupo [*Panama*] [*Airport symbol*] (OAG) .... MPI
Mamma (DSUE) .... MA
Mammal Society (EAIO) .... MS
Mammalian Selectivity Ratio (FFDE) .... MSR

Mammary Ascites Tumor [Oncology] ... MAT
Mammary Carcinoma [Oncology] ... MAC
Mammary Gland [Anatomy] ... MG
Mammary Tumor [Medicine] ... MT
Mammary Tumor Agent (DOG) ... MTA
Mammary Tumor Virus ... MTV
Mammillothalamic Tract [Neuroanatomy] ... MTT
Mammilothalamic Tract [Anatomy] ... MT
Mammography ... MAMGRAPHY
Mammography [Gynecology] (DAVI) ... mammo
Mammoth Cave National Park ... MACA
Mammoth Decimal Arithmetic Program [NASA] (KSC) ... MADCAP
Mammoth Hot Springs [Wyoming] [Seismograph station code, US Geological Survey] (SEIS) ... MHS
Mammoth Lakes [California] [Airport symbol] (OAG) ... MMH
Mammoth Lakes, CA [FM radio station call letters] ... KMMT
Mammoth Lakes, CA [Location identifier FAA] (FAAL) ... MMH
Mammoth Public Library, Mammoth, AZ [Library symbol Library of Congress] (LCLS) ... AzMa
Mammoth Spring, AR [FM radio station call letters] ... KAMS
Mammotropic Hormone [Endocrinology] ... MH
Mampikony [Madagascar] [ICAO location identifier] (ICLI) ... FMNP
Mampikony [Malagasy] [Airport symbol] (AD) ... WMP
Mamuju [Indonesia] [Airport symbol] (OAG) ... MJU
Mamuju/Tampa Padang [Indonesia] [ICAO location identifier] (ICLI) ... WAAJ
Man [Ivory Coast] [ICAO location identifier] (ICLI) ... DIMN
Man ... M
Man [Ivory Coast] [Airport symbol] (OAG) ... MJC
Man - A Course of Study [Title of social-studies course] [National Science Foundation] ... MACOS
Man and Computer (DIT) ... MAC
Man and LASER (MCD) ... MAL
Man and the Biosphere Program [UNESCO] [Paris, France] ... MAB
Man Communication and Display for an Automatic Computer (PDAA) ... MACDAC
Man Computer Graphics [Computer science] (MCD) ... MCG
Man Day ... M/D
Man Days Lost (NUCP) ... MDL
Man Hours per Operating Hour [Maintenance] (RDA) ... MH/OH
Man In, Machine Out [Computer science] ... MIMO
Man in Space ... MIS
Man in Space Simulator ... MISS
Man in Space Soonest ... MISS
Man in Space Sophisticated (MUGU) ... MISSOPH
Man in the Street [The average man] [Usually "Mr. Mits" See also T C MITS] ... MITS
Man/Machine ... M/M
Man/Machine Assembly Analysis (MCD) ... MMAA
Man Machine System for the Optimum Design and Construction of Buildings (PDAA) ... MODCON
Man Marketing Council [New York City] ... MMC
Man, Material, Machinery, Methods [Statistical process control] ... MMMM
Man on the Street (WDMC) ... MOS
Man [or Manual] Orbital Operations Safety Equipment [Space life raft] [NASA] ... MOOSE
Man Out of Space Easiest ... MOOSE
Man Overboard and Breakdown Light (AD) ... mob lt
Man Position Locator ... MPL
Man Station [Military] ... MS
Man System Integration (IAA) ... MSI
Man/Vehicular User Equipment ... MVUE
Man Watchers (EA) ... MW
Man Week ... MW
Man Worn LASER Detector [Assembly] (MCD) ... MWLD
Man, WV [Location identifier FAA] (FAAL) ... GTC
Man Year ... MY
Mana [Fiji] [Airport symbol] (OAG) ... MNF
Mana Pools Game Reserve [Rhodesia] (AD) ... MPGR
Manado [Celebes] [Seismograph station code, US Geological Survey] (SEIS) ... MNI
Manado/Sam Ratulangi [Indonesia] [ICAO location identifier] (ICLI) ... WAMM
Manage ... MANAG
Manage (ABBR) ... MGE
Manage Old Vehicles Easily [Performance Data Services, Inc.] [Software] ... MOVE
Manageability (ABBR) ... MGBT
Manageability (ABBR) ... MGEBT
Manageable (ABBR) ... MGB
Manageable (ABBR) ... MGEB
Manageably (ABBR) ... MGBY
Manageably (ABBR) ... MGEBY
Managed ... MGD
Managed (ABBR) ... MGED
Managed Approach Reservoir [FAA] (TAG) ... MAR
Managed Care [Insurance] (WYGK) ... MC
Managed Care Solutions [NQS] (TTSB) ... MCSX
Managed Care Solutions, Inc. [NASDAQ symbol] (SAG) ... MCSX
Managed Care Solutions, Inc. [Associated Press] (SAG) ... MgdCare
Managed Change Technique [Management] ... MCT
Managed Competition ... MC
Managed Cost Improvement (NRCH) ... MCI
Managed Data Network ... MDN
Managed Data Network Services (NITA) ... MDNS
Managed Futures Trade Association (EA) ... MFTA
Managed High Income Portfolio [NYSE symbol] (SPSG) ... MHY
Managed High Inc. Portfolio [NYSE symbol] (TTSB) ... MHY
Managed High Yield Fd [NYSE symbol] (TTSB) ... PHT
Managed High Yield Fund [Associated Press] (SAG) ... MgHiYld
Managed High-Income Income Portfolio [Associated Press] (SAG) ... MgdHi
Managed Internet Service [Computer science] ... MIS
Managed Muni Portfolio [NYSE symbol] (TTSB) ... MMU
Managed Muni Portfolio II [NYSE symbol] (TTSB) ... MTU
Managed Municipal Portfolio II [NYSE symbol] (SPSG) ... MTU
Managed Municipal Portfolio [NYSE symbol] (SPSG) ... MMU
Managed Municipals Portfolio [Associated Press] (SAG) ... MgdMun
Managed Municipals Portfolio II [Associated Press] (SAG) ... MgdMun2
Managed Object [Telecommunications] (OSI) ... MO
Managed Object Conformance Statement [Telecommunications] (OSI) ... MOCS
Managed On-the-Job Training (DNAB) ... MOJT
Managed Service Organization [Health Insurance] ... MSO
Managed Thermactor Air [Automotive engineering] ... MTA
Management (WDAA) ... MAN
Management ... MANG
Management (ROG) ... MANGT
Management (ABBR) ... MGENT
Management ... MGMNT
Management (KSC) ... MGMT
Management (DD) ... mgmt
Management ... MGMT
Management ... MGMT
Management (AFM) ... MGT
Management (ADA) ... MNGMT
Management ... Mngt
Management (DAVI) ... mx
Management Access to Records ... MATR
Management Accounting and Payroll System (NITA) ... MAPS
Management Accounting and Performance System ... MAPS
Management Accounting Maintenance Advertising, Inc. ... MAMA
Management Accounting System ... MAS
Management Action Reporting System (MCD) ... MARS
Management Administration [Department of Labor Statistics] (OICC) ... MA
Management Administration Control System ... MACS
Management Adviser ... MA
Management Advisory Committee [Environmental Protection Agency] (GFGA) ... MAC
Management Advisory Group [Environmental Protection Agency] (GFGA) ... MAG
Management Advisory Services ... MAS
Management Advisory System using Computerized Optimization Techniques (PDAA) ... MASCOT
Management Advisory Team (NRCH) ... MAT
Management Analysis and Planning System ... MAPS
Management Analysis Course (Class O) [Navy] (DNAB) ... MAC(O)
Management Analysis Division [NASA] (MCD) ... MAD
Management Analysis Memorandum [DoD] (MCD) ... MAM
Management Analysis of Key Resource Operations [Military] ... MAKRO
Management Analysis Officer [Air Force] ... MGTANALYSO
Management Analysis [or Assessment] Program ... MAP
Management Analysis Report [DoD] (MCD) ... MAR
Management Analysis Reporting Information on the Naval Environment System (NG) ... MARINE
Management Analysis Reporting System [Computer science] ... MARS
Management and Administration ... M & A
Management and Administration Manual (NRCH) ... MAM
Management and Administrative Reporting Subsystem [Department of Health and Human Services] (GFGA) ... MARS
Management and Administrative Statistics (OICC) ... MAS
Management and Budget Office (MCD) ... MBO
Management and Command Ashore (NVT) ... MCA
Management & Computer Services, Inc. [Information service or system] (IID) ... MACS
Management and Contracts Information Service ... MACIS
Management and Cost Visibility System (SSD) ... MCVS
Management and Equipment Evaluation Program ... MEEP
Management and Graduate Item Bank [Reasoning skills test] ... MGIB
Management & Industrial Consultants ... MIC
Management and Information System Staff [United Nations Development Program] ... MISS
Management and Investment Companies Program ... MICP
Management and Logistics [NATO] (NATG) ... M and L
Management and Maintenance Inspection (NVT) ... MMI
Management and Marketing Abstracts [PIRA] [Bibliographic database] [British] ... MMA
Management and Operating Contractor (ODBW) ... MOC
Management & Operation of Public Services Section [Reference and User Services Association] [American Library Association] ... MOPSS
Management and Operation of User Services Section ... MOUSS
Management and Organisation in Secondary Schools (AIE) ... MOSS
Management and Organization ... M & O
Management and Organization (AD) ... m & o
Management and Organization Division [Environmental Protection Agency] (GFGA) ... MOD
Management and Personnel Office (AIE) ... MPO
Management and Personnel Office (ODBW) ... MPO
Management and Planning Committee [Library of Congress] ... MAP
Management and Programming (IAA) ... MAP
Management and Scientific Information System [Air Force] ... MASIS
Management and Technical Services Company (AAGC) ... MATSCO
Management Application Protocol (ACRL) ... MAP
Management Application Protocol Data Unit [Telecommunications] (OSI) ... MAPDU
Management Applications in a Computer Environment (IEEE) ... MACE

Management Appraisal Survey [*Test*] ... MAS
Management Assessment Report (MCD) ... MAR
Management Assessment Review (MCD) ... MAR
Management Assistance Corporation of America (AAGC) ... MACA
Management Assistance for Profits ... MAP
Management Assistance Group [*Washington, DC*] (EA) ... MAG
Management Association of Private Photogrammetric Surveyors (EA) ... MAPPS
Management Assurance of Safety, Adequacy, and Reliability (MHDB) ... MASAR
Management Audit Information System ... MAIS
Management Automated Information Display System (KSC) ... MAIDS
Management Baseline (NASA) ... MB
Management Board (ACII) ... MB
Management Buy-Out ... MBO
Management Buy-Out ... MBO
Management Buy-Out ... MNBO
Management by Exception ... MBE
Management by Exception [*Management technique*] (IAA) ... MBX
Management by Goals and Objectives (MCD) ... MGO
Management by Initiative [*Management technique*] ... MBI
Management by Objectives [*Management technique*] [*Facetious translations: "Management by Oblivion," and "Management by Others"*] ... MBO
Management by Objectives and Results [*Management technique*] (MCD) ... MBOR
Management by Results [*Management technique*] ... MBR
Management by System [*Management technique*] (IAA) ... MBS
Management by Talking Around [*Business term*] ... MTA
Management by Walking About [*or Wandering Around*] [*Facetious translation of MBO - Management by Objectives*] ... MBWA
Management by Walking Around ... MWA
Management Change Notice (MCD) ... MCN
Management Coaching Relations Test ... MCR
Management Committee (IAA) ... MC
Management Communication Consultants, Inc. [*Cincinnati, OH*] (TSSD) ... MCC
Management Communications and Data System (SSD) ... MCDS
Management Communications and Data System Hardware (SSD) ... MCDSH
Management Consultants Association [*British*] (DCTA) ... MCA
Management Consultants International, Inc. [*Information service or system*] (IID) ... MCI
Management Consultation Services Unit [*LIMRA*] ... MCSU
Management Contents [*Information Access Co.*] [*Information service or system*] (IID) ... MC
Management Control Activity ... MCA
Management Control Authority (NVT) ... MCA
Management Control Center [*Computer science*] (BUR) ... MCC
Management Control Data System [*Computer science*] (IAA) ... MCDS
Management Control - Material Management (IEEE) ... MCMM
Management Control Number [*Army*] (AABC) ... MCN
Management Control Plan ... MCP
Management Control Review (AAGC) ... MCR
Management Control System (MCD) ... MCS
Management Control Systems List [*DoD*] ... MCSL
Management Control Systems Research Project (SAA) ... MCSRP
Management Control Unit (PDAA) ... MCU
Management Council of the American Trucking Association [*Defunct*] (EA) ... MCATA
Management Data (MCD) ... MD
Management Data Charting and Review (IAA) ... MADCAR
Management Data List (AABC) ... MDL
Management Data Online Status/Inquiry System (MCD) ... MDOSIS
Management Data Query System [*Computer science*] ... MDQS
Management Data Reporting System (MCD) ... MDRS
Management Data Service Center ... MDSC
Management Data System (NASA) ... MDS
Management Database (ACRL) ... MDB
Management Decision Package [*DoD*] ... MDEP
Management Decisions Development Corporation [*Canada*] (NITA) ... MDDC
Management Development Adviser (AIE) ... MDA
Management Development Course (MCD) ... MDC
Management Development Institute (MCD) ... MDI
Management Development Programme [*British*] (DCTA) ... MDP
Management Directive ... MD
Management Division [*Environmental Protection Agency*] (GFGA) ... MD
Management Education Institute [*Arthur D. Little, Inc.*] ... MEI
Management Education Training and Development (AIE) ... METD
Management Effectiveness Inspection ... MEI
Management Engineer [*Air Force*] ... MGTENGR
Management Engineering (KSC) ... ME
Management Engineering Flight [*Air Force*] ... MEF
Management Engineering Program [*Air Force*] (AFM) ... MEP
Management Engineering Squadron [*Air Force*] ... MES
Management Engineering Squadron [*Air Force*] ... MESq
Management Engineering Steering Committee for Embedded Computer Resources (MCD) ... MEC-ECR
Management Engineering Team [*Air Force*] (AFM) ... MET
Management Evaluation [*Food Stamp Program*] [*Department of Agriculture*] (GFGA) ... ME
Management Evaluation Group [*Department of State*] ... MEG
Management Evaluation Program (AAG) ... MEP
Management Expense Ratio ... MER
Management Experten-Nachweis [*Management Experts Data Base*] [*Society for Business Information*] [*Information service or system*] (IID) ... MANEX
Management Farm Information Service (PDAA) ... MAFIS
Management Forum [*A publication*] ... Man For
Management Forum [*A publication*] ... Mgmt Forum
Management Framework Plan ... MFP
Management Games Institute [*Raytheon Co.*] ... MGI
Management Group Codes (MCD) ... MGC
Management Implementation Plan (MCD) ... MIP
Management Improvement and Cost Reduction Project Reporting System ... MICR
Management Improvement and Evaluation ... MIE
Management Improvement and Operating Plan [*Department of Housing and Urban Development*] (GFGA) ... MIO
Management Improvement Board (AAG) ... MIB
Management Improvement Plan ... MIP
Management Improvement Program [*Military*] ... MIP
Management Incentive Program ... MIP
Management Indicator Code (MCD) ... MIC
Management Information (CAAL) ... MI
Management Information and Analysis Group (MCD) ... MIAG
Management Information and Control System [*Navy*] ... MICS
Management Information and Data Systems (NVT) ... MIDS
Management Information and Data Systems Division [*Environmental Protection Agency*] (GFGA) ... MIDSD
Management Information and Development Aids System (SSD) ... MIDAS
Management Information and Display System [*NASA*] ... MIRADS
Management Information and Instructional Systems Activity (DNAB) ... MIISA
Management Information and Instructional Systems Activity Detachment (DNAB) ... MIISADET
Management Information and Instructional Systems Activity Unit (DNAB) ... MIISAU
Management Information and Text System ... MITS
Management Information Base ... MIB
Management Information Bases [*Compaq*] [*Computer science*] ... MIBs
Management Information Block [*Computer science*] ... MIB
Management Information Capability for Enforcement [*Environmental Protection Agency*] (GFGA) ... MICE
Management Information Center ... MIC
Management Information Centre, Privy Council Office [*Regie Interne de l'Information, Bureau du Conseil Prive*] **Ottawa, Ontario** [*Library symbol National Library of Canada*] (NLC) ... OOPC
Management Information Control Liaison Officers (MCD) ... MICLO
Management Information Coordinating Group [*Navy*] ... MICG
Management Information Corp. [*Cherry Hill, NJ*] [*Information service or system*] (IID) ... MIC
Management Information Display System (MCD) ... MIDS
Management Information Element [*Telecommunications*] (OSI) ... MIE
Management Information File [*Computer science*] (PCM) ... MIF
Management Information for COPICS [*Communications Oriented Production Information and Control System*] **Users** [*IBM Corp.*] ... MI-COPICS
Management Information for Decision and Control ... MIDAC
Management Information Format [*Computer science*] ... MIF
Management Information Format File [*Computer science*] ... MIFF
Management Information Guide [*Reference series*] ... MIG
Management Information Office [*or Officer*] [*Air Force*] (AFM) ... MIO
Management Information Planning and Accountancy Service (MHDI) ... MIPAS
Management Information Progress Sheets (MCD) ... MIPS
Management Information Protocol [*Telecommunications*] (OSI) ... MIP
Management Information Report ... MIR
Management Information Report Access without Computer Languages [*Computer science*] (IEEE) ... MIRACL
Management Information Reporting and Review of Operational Resources System ... MIRROR
Management Information Research Assistance Center (AABC) ... MIRAC
Management Information Science ... MIS
Management Information Service ... MIS
Management Information Specialist ... MIS
Management Information Strategy ... MIS
Management Information System [*Generic term*] ... MIS
Management Information System Development Office (DNAB) ... MISDO
Management Information System Executive Group (DNAB) ... MISEG
Management Information System for Expenditure Reporting (PDAA) ... MISER
Management Information System Improvement Plan ... MISIP
Management Information System Laboratory ... MISL
Management Information System Plan ... MISP
Management Information System Symbolic Interpretive Language [*Computer science*] (MCD) ... MISSIL
Management Information Systems [*Corporation for Public Broadcasting*] [*Information service or system*] (IID) ... MIS
Management Information Systems Control Officer (MCD) ... MICO
Management Information Systems Directorate [*Army Missile Command*] [*Redstone Arsenal, AL*] ... MISD
Management Information Systems Economic Analysis ... MISEA
Management Information Systems for Vocational Education (OICC) ... MISVE
Management Information Systems Inventory and Analysis System [*Navy*] ... MISIAS
Management Information Systems Office (AABC) ... MISO
Management Information Systems Research Center [*University of Minnesota*] [*Research center*] (RCD) ... MISRC
Management Information Systems Task Force (SAA) ... MISTAF
Management Information Tree [*Telecommunications*] (OSI) ... MIT
Management Institute for National Development ... MIND
Management Integrated Control System ... MICS
Management Integrated Data Accumulating System ... MIDAS
Management Integrated System (TEL) ... MIS
Management Integration Consortium ... MIC
Management Integration Office [*NASA*] (NASA) ... MIO
Management Interest Inventory [*Test*] ... MII
Management Intern ... MI
Management Intern Program ... MIP
Management Inventory on Managing Change [*Test*] ... MIMC

Management Inventory on Modern Management [*Test*] ..... MIMM
Management Inventory on Time Management [*Test*] ..... MITM
Management Job Description (PDAA) ..... MJD
Management Job Review [*LIMRA*] ..... MJR
Management Level ..... ML
Management Level Chart [*Military*] (AFIT) ..... MLC
Management Level Code [*Military*] (AFIT) ..... MLC
Management List ..... ML
Management List - Consolidated ..... ML-C
Management List - Navy (NVT) ..... MLN
Management Manual (KSC) ..... MM
Management Milestone Records [*Navy*] (NG) ..... MMR
Management Need Statement (AAGC) ..... MNS
Management Network (MCD) ..... MN
Management Numerical Control Information System (MCD) ..... MNCIS
Management of Acquisition Logistics Course (AAGC) ..... MALC
Management of Advanced Automation Technology Center [*Worcester Polytechnic Institute*] [*Research center*] (RCD) ..... MAAT
Management of Atmospheric Data for Evaluation and Research [*Marine science*] (OSRA) ..... MADER
Management of Atmospheric Data for Evaluation and Research (USDC) ..... MADER
Management of Change ..... MOC
Management of Defense Acquisition Contracts Course [*DoD*] (RDA) ..... MDACC
Management of Enlisted Bonus Recipients ..... MAEBR
Management of Expenditure and Resident-Linked Information Network [*Computer science*] ..... MERLIN
Management of Items Subject to Repair [*Air Force*] (AFM) ..... MISTR
Management of Migration [*of wastewaters*] ..... MOM
Management of Motives Index [*Test*] ..... MMI
Management of Objectives with Dollars through Employees [*Department of Agriculture*] ..... MODE
Management of Officer Grade Authorization (MCD) ..... MOGA
Management of Radiographic Environments [*Radiology*] (DAVI) ..... MORE
Management of Repair Parts Expenditure [*Army*] (PDAA) ..... MARPEX
Management of Technology ..... MOT
Management of Traffic Operations [*Federal Highway Administration*] ..... MAGTOP
Management of Value Engineering ..... MOVE
Management Office ..... MO
Management Office, Office, Chief of Staff ..... MOO C of S
Management On-Line Data System [*University of Syracuse*] ..... MOLDS
Management Operating Ratios (NG) ..... MOR
Management Operating System ..... MOS
Management Operation System Technique ..... MOST
Management Operations Audit [*Navy*] (NG) ..... MOA
Management Operations Officer [*Social Security Administration*] ..... MOO
Management Operations Staff [*Environmental Protection Agency*] (GFGA) ..... MOS
Management Order (NOAA) ..... MO
Management Order Ship Status Reporting System (MCD) ..... MOSSRS
Management Orientation School [*LIMRA*] ..... MOS
Management Orientation Study Course [*LIMRA*] ..... MOSC
Management Oversight and Risk Tree (NASA) ..... MORT
Management Oversight and Risk Tree ..... MORT
Management Package (NASA) ..... MP
Management Partnerships International, Inc. (IID) ..... MPI
Management Plan ..... MP
Management Planning and Control System ..... MP & CS
Management Planning and Control System [*IBM Corp.*] ..... MPACS
Management Planning and Evaluation Staff [*Environmental Protection Agency*] (GFGA) ..... MPES
Management Policy and Directives ..... MPD
Management Policy Statement ..... MPS
Management Practices in TOE Units [*Military*] (GFGA) ..... MAP-TOE
Management Problem-Knowledge Coupler ..... MPKC
[*The*] **Management Processor** (MCD) ..... TMP
Management Professionals Association [*Madras, India*] (EA) ..... MPA
Management Program for Executives (ECON) ..... MPE
Management Program Review [*NASA*] (NASA) ..... MPR
Management Program Review ..... MPR
Management Program Review Report [*NASA*] (MCD) ..... MPRR
Management Quarterly Magazine [*A publication*] (EAAP) ..... MQ
Management Recruiters International (HGAA) ..... MRI
Management Relations Survey [*Test*] ..... MRS
Management Report Generator [*Randolph Data Services, Inc.*] [*Software package*] [*Computer science*] (IEEE) ..... MARGEN
Management Reporting System ..... MRS
Management Reports and Statistics ..... MARS
Management Requirements (MCD) ..... MR
Management Research Center [*University of Wisconsin - Milwaukee*] [*Research center*] (RCD) ..... MRC
Management Research Corp. [*Shelbyville, IN*] [*Information service or system*] (IID) ..... MRC
Management Research Groups [*British*] ..... MRG
Management Reserve (MCD) ..... MR
Management Resources Accounting System ..... MRAS
Management Responsibility Matrix ..... MRM
Management Review and Analysis Program (AD) ..... MRAP
Management Review and Improvement Program [*Department of Labor*] ..... MRIP
Management Review Meeting (AFIT) ..... MRM
Management Review Officer ..... MRO
Management Review System (NASA) ..... MRS
Management Scheduling and Control System [*Telecommunications*] (TEL) ..... MSCS
Management Science [*Computer science*] (BUR) ..... MS
Management Science America, Inc., Atlanta, GA [*Library symbol Library of Congress*] (LCLS) ..... GAMSA
Management Science Associates, Inc. [*Information service or system*] (IID) ..... MSA
Management Science Department, General Foods, Inc., Don Mills, Ontario [*Library symbol National Library of Canada*] (NLC) ..... OTGFM
Management Science of America (HGAA) ..... MSA
Management Science Office ..... MSO
Management Science Systems (IEEE) ..... MSS
Management Sciences Library, Bell Canada, Montreal, Quebec [*Library symbol Obsolete National Library of Canada*] (NLC) ..... QMBMS
Management Sciences Research Project [*University of California*] (MCD) ..... MSRP
Management Selection Ltd. ..... MSL
Management Service Center [*Marine science*] (OSRA) ..... MSC
Management Service Center (USDC) ..... MSC
Management Service Organization ..... MSO
Management Services (KSC) ..... MS
Management Services Contractor [*INTELSAT*] ..... MSC
Management Services Department [*British*] (DCTA) ..... MSD
Management Services Department Library, Municipality of Metropolitan Toronto, Ontario [*Library symbol National Library of Canada*] (BIB) ..... OTMSM
Management Services Division (NITA) ..... MSD
Management Signal Unit [*Telecommunications*] (TEL) ..... MSU
Management Skills - Knowledge Profile [*Business term*] ..... MSKP
Management Staff [*Environmental Protection Agency*] (GFGA) ..... MS
Management Statistics Subsystem (TEL) ..... MSS
Management Summary Sheets (MCD) ..... MSS
Management Supplier Selection (AAG) ..... MSS
Management Support Staff [*Social Security Administration*] ..... MSS
Management Support System [*Marine science*] (OSRA) ..... MSS
Management Support System (USDC) ..... MSS
Management Support Unit ..... MSU
Management Survey Team (AAG) ..... MST
Management System (OICC) ..... MS
Management System Analysis ..... MSA
Management System Evaluation Review (NG) ..... MSER
Management System for Support Contracts [*Social Security Administration*] ..... MSSC
Management System Programmers Ltd. (NITA) ..... MSP
Management Systems Concept (PDAA) ..... MASC
Management Systems Development Office ..... MSDO
Management Systems Division [*Environmental Protection Agency*] (EPA) ..... MSD
Management Systems Laboratories [*Virginia Polytechnic Institute and State University*] [*Research center*] (RCD) ..... MSL
Management Systems Office [*NASA*] ..... MSO
Management Systems Representative (MCD) ..... MSR
Management Systems Study (MCD) ..... MSS
Management Systems Summary List ..... MSSL
Management Systems Training Council [*British*] ..... MSTC
Management Systems Unit ..... MSU
Management Team ..... MT
Management Technical Applications Plan (MCD) ..... MTAP
Management Technologies [*NASDAQ symbol*] (TTSB) ..... MTCI
Management Technologies, Inc. [*Associated Press*] (SAG) ..... MgtTch
Management Technologies, Inc. [*NASDAQ symbol*] (NQ) ..... MTCI
Management Television [*Air Force*] (AFM) ..... MTV
Management Tracking System [*Environmental Protection Agency*] (EPA) ..... MTS
Management Training Program [*of Center for Research in Business and Economics, University of Houston*] ..... MANTRAP
Management Transactions Audit [*Test*] ..... MTA
Management Trial Exercise [*Career orientation simulation*] ..... MATRIX
Management/Union Consultative Group [*Australia*] ..... MUCG
Management Unit [*Aviation*] ..... MU
Management Update and Retrieval System (NRCH) ..... MUR
Management Verification Consortium (AIE) ..... MVC
Management Work Station (BUR) ..... MWS
Management Working Group [*Army*] (RDA) ..... MWG
Management World [*Administrative Management Society*] [*A publication*] ..... MW
Management-Initiated Early Retirement (ADA) ..... MIER
Management-Labor Policy Committee ..... MLPC
Management-Oriented Budget Information System ..... MOBIS
Management-Oriented Computing (MHDB) ..... MOC
Manager [*or Managing*] (EY) ..... MAN
Manager ..... MANGR
Manager (ROG) ..... MANR
Manager (ABBR) ..... MGER
Manager (AFM) ..... MGR
Manager (DD) ..... mgr
Manager ..... MGR
Manager (ODBW) ..... Mgr
Manager ..... MGR
Manager ..... MNGR
Manager, Antisubmarine Warfare Systems Project [*Navy*] ..... MASWSP
Manager, Antisubmarine Warfare Systems Project Office [*Navy*] ..... MASWSPO
Manager Integrated Dictionary Week [*Manager Software Products*] (EA) ..... MIDWEEK
Manager of Aviation ..... MA
Manager on Duty ..... MOD
Manager Owner User Systems Engineer (OA) ..... MOUSE
Manager Software Products Ltd. (NITA) ..... MSP
Manager Support Programs (MCD) ..... MSP
Manager, Traffic Department ..... MTD
Manager, Transportation Department ..... MTD
Manageress (ROG) ..... MANGRSS
Manageress (ROG) ..... MGRESS

Managerial (ABBR) ... MGERL
Managerial (ABBR) ... MGRL
Managerial ... MGRL
Managerial, Administrative, Technical, and Supervisory Association [*British*] (DCTA) ... MATSA
Managerial and Professional Job Functions Inventory [*Test*] ... MP-JFI
Managerial Grid ... MG
Managerial Philosophies Scale [*Test*] ... MPS
Manager's Assistant (DCTA) ... MA
Manager's Discretionary Limit (DCTA) ... MDL
Manager's Guide ... MG
Managers, Proprietors, and Officials ... MPO
Managership of Soldier Training, Education, and Readiness with Knowledge and Excellence Year-Round [*Army*] (INF) ... MASTER KEY
Manager-to-Manager (ACRL) ... M2M
Managing (DD) ... man
Managing (ABBR) ... MGEG
Managing (ABBR) ... MGG
Managing (ABBR) ... MNG
Managing (MSA) ... MNGNG
Managing ... MNGNG
Managing and Marketing Sales Association [*British*] (DBA) ... MAMSA
Managing Civilians to Budget [*Army*] ... MCB
Managing Company Expansion [*Manpower Services Commission*] [*British*] ... MACE
Managing Director ... MD
Managing Director of Royal Ordnance Factories [*British*] (RDA) ... MDROF
Managing Director Posts [*British*] (DCTA) ... MDP
Managing Editor (DGA) ... MAN ED
Managing Editor ... ME
Managing General Agent [*Insurance*] ... MGA
Managing Printer [*A publication*] (DGA) ... MP
Managing the Modern Laboratory [*A publication*] ... MML
Managing Your Money [*MECA Software, Inc.*] (PCM) ... MYM
Managment Domain [*Telecommunications*] (OSI) ... MD
Managment List - Consolidated (IID) ... M-CL
Managua [*Nicaragua*] [*Airport symbol*] (OAG) ... MGA
Managua [*Cuba ICAO location identifier*] (ICLI) ... MUMG
Managua/Augusto Cesar Sandino [*Nicaragua*] [*ICAO location identifier*] (ICLI) ... MNMG
Manahawkin, NJ [*FM radio station call letters*] ... WJRZ
Manahawkin, NJ [*FM radio station call letters*] (RBYB) ... WNJM-FM
Manahawkin, NJ [*FM radio station call letters*] ... WYRS
Manakara [*Madagascar*] [*ICAO location identifier*] (ICLI) ... FMSK
Manakara [*Madagascar*] [*Airport symbol*] (OAG) ... WVK
Manalta Coal Ltd., Information Centre, Calgary, AB, Canada [*Library symbol*] [*Library of Congress*] (LCLS) ... CaACMC
Mananara [*Madagascar*] [*Airport symbol*] (OAG) ... WMR
Mananara-Nord [*Madagascar*] [*ICAO location identifier*] (ICLI) ... FMNC
Manang [*Nepal*] [*ICAO location identifier*] (ICLI) ... VNMA
Mananjary [*Madagascar*] [*ICAO location identifier*] (ICLI) ... FMSM
Mananjary [*Madagascar*] [*Airport symbol*] (OAG) ... MNJ
Manantiales [*Argentina*] [*Seismograph station code, US Geological Survey*] (SEIS) ... MAA
Manari [*Papua New Guinea*] [*Airport symbol*] (OAG) ... MRM
Manari [*Guyana*] [*ICAO location identifier*] (ICLI) ... SYMN
Manasquan Public Library, Manasquan, NJ [*Library symbol Library of Congress*] (LCLS) ... NjMan
Manassa Elementary School, Manassa, CO [*Library symbol*] [*Library of Congress*] (LCLS) ... CoManaES
Manassas [*Virginia*] [*Airport symbol*] (OAG) ... MNZ
Manassas National Battlefield Park ... MANA
Manassas, VA [*Location identifier FAA*] (FAAL) ... HEF
Manassas, VA [*FM radio station call letters*] ... WJFK
Manassas, VA [*AM radio station call letters*] ... WKDV
Manassas, VA [*Television station call letters*] ... WVVI
Manatee County Library System, Bradenton, FL [*Library symbol Library of Congress*] (LCLS) ... FBr
Manatee Junior College, Bradenton, FL [*Library symbol Library of Congress*] (LCLS) ... FBrM
Manati [*Cuba ICAO location identifier*] (ICLI) ... MUTI
Manati, PR [*AM radio station call letters*] ... WMNT
Manati, PR [*Radio expansion station*] (RBYB) ... WMTI Exp Stn
Manati, PR [*FM radio station call letters*] ... WNRT
Manatron, Inc. [*NASDAQ symbol*] (NQ) ... MANA
Manatron, Inc. [*Associated Press*] (SAG) ... Mantrn
Manaung [*Myanmar*] [*ICAO location identifier*] (ICLI) ... VBMN
Manaus [*Brazil*] [*Airport symbol*] (OAG) ... MAO
Manaus (AD) ... Mns
Manaus [*Brazil ICAO location identifier*] (ICLI) ... SBMU
Manaus/Eduardo Gomes [*Brazil ICAO location identifier*] (ICLI) ... SBEG
Manaus/Ponta Pelada [*Brazil ICAO location identifier*] (ICLI) ... SBMN
Manawa Public Library, Manawa, WI [*Library symbol Library of Congress*] (LCLS) ... WMan
Manby on Fines [*A publication*] (DLA) ... Manb Fines
Manby's Abridgement of Coke's Reports [*A publication*] (DLA) ... Manb Coke
Mancando [*Dying Away*] [*Music*] ... Man
Mancando [*Decreasing in Loudness*] [*Music*] ... MANC
Mancando [*Decreasing in Loudness*] [*Music*] ... MANCO
Mancando [*Decreasing in Loudness*] [*Music*] (ROG) ... MANDO
Man-Carried Automatic Navigator (MCD) ... MANCAN
Man-Carrying Motion Generator [*Space-flight simulation*] ... MCMG
Man-Carrying Test Vehicle (MCD) ... MCTV
Mancelona Township Library, Mancelona, MI [*Library symbol Library of Congress*] (LCLS) ... MiManc
Manchester [*British ICAO location identifier*] (ICLI) ... EGRC
Manchester (ROG) ... M/C
Manchester [*England*] [*Airport symbol*] (OAG) ... MAN
Manchester [*England*] ... MANCH
Manchester [*County in England*] (ROG) ... M'CHR
Manchester [*County in England*] (ROG) ... M'CHTR
Manchester [*New Hampshire*] [*Airport symbol*] (OAG) ... MHT
Manchester [*City in England*] (ROG) ... M'TER
Manchester Academy of Fine Arts [*British*] ... MAFA
Manchester & Milford Railway [*Wales*] ... M & M
Manchester Automatic Digital Machine [*Manchester University*] [*British*] (DEN) ... MADAM
Manchester Automatic Digital Machine [*Manchester University*] [*British*] ... MADM
Manchester/Barton [*British ICAO location identifier*] (ICLI) ... EGCB
Manchester Business School [*England*] ... MBS
Manchester City Library, Manchester, NH [*Library symbol Library of Congress*] (LCLS) ... NhM
Manchester College, North Manchester, IN [*OCLC symbol*] (OCLC) ... IMN
Manchester College, North Manchester, IN [*Library symbol Library of Congress*] (LCLS) ... InNomanC
Manchester College, North Manchester, IN [*Library symbol*] [*Library of Congress*] (LCLS) ... InNomMC
Manchester Community College, Manchester, CT [*Library symbol Library of Congress*] (LCLS) ... CtManC
Manchester Court Leet Records [*A publication*] (DLA) ... Harland
Manchester, CT [*AM radio station call letters*] ... WLAT
Manchester, GA [*AM radio station call letters*] ... WFDR
Manchester, GA [*FM radio station call letters*] ... WVFJ
Manchester General Ability Test [*Education*] (AEBS) ... MGAT
Manchester Historical Society, Manchester, MA [*Library symbol Library of Congress*] (LCLS) ... MManHi
Manchester, IA [*FM radio station call letters*] ... KMCH
Manchester International [*British ICAO location identifier*] (ICLI) ... EGCC
Manchester International Airport [*British*] (DS) ... MIA
Manchester International Freight Terminal [*British*] (DS) ... MIFT
Manchester, KY [*AM radio station call letters*] ... WKLB
Manchester, KY [*FM radio station call letters*] ... WTBK
Manchester, KY [*FM radio station call letters*] ... WWLT
Manchester, KY [*AM radio station call letters*] ... WWXL
Manchester Law Students' Chronicle [*A publication*] (DLA) ... Man LS Chron
Manchester Law Students' Journal [*A publication*] (DLA) ... Man LSJ
Manchester Metropolitan University [*British*] (AIE) ... MMU
Manchester, NH [*Location identifier FAA*] (FAAL) ... DRY
Manchester, NH [*Location identifier FAA*] (FAAL) ... MHT
Manchester, NH [*AM radio station call letters*] ... WFEA
Manchester, NH [*AM radio station call letters*] ... WGIR
Manchester, NH [*FM radio station call letters*] ... WGIR-FM
Manchester, NH [*AM radio station call letters*] ... WKBR
Manchester, NH [*FM radio station call letters*] ... WLMW
Manchester, NH [*Television station call letters*] ... WMUR
Manchester, NH [*FM radio station call letters*] ... WRND
Manchester, NH [*FM radio station call letters*] ... WZID
Manchester, OH [*FM radio station call letters*] ... WAGX
Manchester Open College Federation [*British*] (AIE) ... MOCF
Manchester Press, Manchester, IA [*Library symbol Library of Congress*] (LCLS) ... IaMancP
Manchester Public Libraries, Central Library, Manchester, United Kingdom [*Library symbol Library of Congress*] (LCLS) ... UkMa
Manchester Publishing Co., Lakehurst, NJ [*Library symbol Library of Congress*] (LCLS) ... NjLakhM
Manchester Resources Corp. [*Vancouver Stock Exchange symbol*] ... MHO
Manchester Scales of Social Adaptation [*Psychology*] ... MSSA
Manchester, Sheffield & Lincolnshire Railway [*Later, Great Central*] [*British*] (ROG) ... MS & LR
Manchester Ship Canal ... MSC
Manchester Terminal Unit (NITA) ... MTU
Manchester, TN [*FM radio station call letters*] ... WFTZ
Manchester, TN [*AM radio station call letters*] ... WMSR
Manchester, TN [*FM radio station call letters*] ... WWTN
Manchester Township Library, Manchester, MI [*Library symbol Library of Congress*] (LCLS) ... MiMan
Manchester University Press [*Manchester, England*] ... MUP
Manchester University Software System (NITA) ... MUSS
Manchester, VT [*FM radio station call letters*] ... WEQX
Manchuria ... Manch
Man-Computer Interactive Data Access System ... McIDAS
Mancos Elementary School, Mancos, CO [*Library symbol*] [*Library of Congress*] (LCLS) ... CoMaEL
Mancos Public Library, Mancos, CO [*Library symbol Library of Congress*] (LCLS) ... CoMa
Mancunium [*Signature of the Bishops of Manchester*] (ROG) ... MANCUN
Mandabe [*Madagascar*] [*ICAO location identifier*] (ICLI) ... FMSC
Mandabe [*Madagascar*] [*Airport symbol*] (OAG) ... WMD
Mandaic (BJA) ... Mand
Mandaic Dictionary [*Oxford*] [*A publication*] (BJA) ... MdD
Mandala Airlines PT [*Indonesia*] [*ICAO designator*] (FAAC) ... MDL
Mandala Holistic Health [*Defunct*] (EA) ... MHH
Mandalay [*Myanmar*] [*Airport symbol*] (OAG) ... MDL
Mandalay [*Burma*] [*Airport symbol*] (AD) ... MDL
Mandalay [*Burma*] [*Seismograph station code, US Geological Survey Closed*] (SEIS) ... MND
Mandalay [*Myanmar*] [*ICAO location identifier*] (ICLI) ... VBRM
Mandalay Elementary School, Wantagh, NY [*Library symbol Library of Congress*] (LCLS) ... NWanME
Mandamus [*We Command*] [*Latin*] (ADA) ... MAND
Mandan, ND [*FM radio station call letters*] ... KNDR

Mandan Public Library, Mandan, ND [*Library symbol Library of Congress*] (LCLS) ..... NdMan
Mandarian Airlines [*ICAO designator*] (FAAC) ..... MDA
Mandarin Capital Corp. [*Vancouver Stock Exchange symbol*] ..... MCC
Mandasor [*India*] [*ICAO location identifier*] (ICLI) ..... VIMS
Mandated Territory ..... MT
Mandato de Accion y Unidad Nacional [*Mandate of Action and National Unity*] [*Bolivia*] [*Political party*] (PPW) ..... MAN
Mandatory (KSC) ..... M
Mandatory ..... M
Mandatory (AABC) ..... MAND
Mandatory Advertising Association [*Automotive retailing*] ..... MAA
Mandatory Annual Audit Requirement (AAGC) ..... MAAR
Mandatory Broadcast Zone [*Telecommunications*] (DA) ..... MBZ
Mandatory Continuing Education ..... MCE
Mandatory Continuing Legal Education [*Australia A publication*] ..... MCLE
Mandatory Date of Transportation [*Military*] ..... MDT
Mandatory Frequency (DA) ..... MF
Mandatory Incident and Defect Reporting (NATG) ..... MIDR
Mandatory Independent Taxation [*British*] (DI) ..... MIT
Mandatory Inspection Point (KSC) ..... MIP
Mandatory Inspection Report (MCD) ..... MIR
Mandatory Modification and Inspection Summary [*Aviation*] (DA) ..... MAMIS
Mandatory Occurrence Reporting ..... MOR
Mandatory Oil Import Program ..... MOIP
Mandatory Parts List [*DoD*] ..... MPL
Mandatory Product Control ..... MPC
Mandatory Product Control Items (MCD) ..... MPCI
Mandatory RADAR Service Area ..... MRSA
Mandatory Recovery Items Code (MCD) ..... MRIC
Mandatory Recovery Items List (MCD) ..... MRIL
Mandatory Removal Roster [*Army*] ..... MRR
Mandatory Resource Group (MCD) ..... MRG
Mandatory Retirement Age Law of 1978 (WYGK) ..... MRAL
Mandatory Retirement Date [*Army*] (AABC) ..... MRD
Mandatory Second Surgical Opinion [*Health insurance*] (GHCT) ..... MSO
Mandatory Securities Valuation Reserve [*National Association of Insurance Commissioners*] ..... MSVR
Mandatum sine Clausula [*Authority without Restriction*] [*Latin*] ..... MSC
Mandel Social Adjustment Scale [*Psychology*] ..... MSAS
Mandela Bush Negro Liberation Movement [*Suriname*] [*Political party*] (EY) ..... BBM
Mandelate Racemase [*An enzyme*] ..... MR
Mandelic Acid [*Organic chemistry*] (AAMN) ..... MA
Mandella Resources Ltd. [*Vancouver Stock Exchange symbol*] ..... MLL
Mandera [*Kenya*] [*ICAO location identifier*] (ICLI) ..... HKMA
Mandera [*Kenya*] [*Airport symbol*] (OAG) ..... NDE
Mandeville [*Jamaica*] [*Airport symbol Obsolete*] (OAG) ..... MVJ
Mandibar [*Dentistry*] (DAVI) ..... mand
Mandible ..... MAND
Mandibular Line [*Jaw anatomy*] ..... ML
Mandibular Nerve [*Anatomy*] ..... MdN
Mandibular Orthopedic Repositioning Appliance [*Dentistry*] ..... MORA
Mandibular Vestibulolingual Sulcoplasty [*Surgery*] ..... MVLS
Mandingo [*MARC language code Library of Congress*] (LCCP) ..... man
Mandolin [*Music*] ..... MAND
Mandorla (VRA) ..... mandl
Mandrel [*Mechanical engineering*] ..... MDRL
Mandritsara [*Madagascar*] [*ICAO location identifier*] (ICLI) ..... FMNX
Mandritsara [*Madagascar*] [*Airport symbol*] (OAG) ..... WMA
Mandusa Resources Ltd. [*Vancouver Stock Exchange symbol*] ..... MSA
Mane [*Morning*] [*Pharmacy*] ..... M
Mane [*Morning*] [*Pharmacy*] ..... MAN
Mane et Nocte [*Morning and Night*] [*Pharmacy*] ..... M et N
Mane et Nocte [*Morning and night*] [*Latin*] [*Pharmacy*] (DAVI) ..... m et n
Mane Primo [*Early in the Morning*] [*Pharmacy*] ..... MAN PR
Mane Primo [*Early in the Morning*] [*Pharmacy*] (ROG) ..... MPR
Manege [*Horsemanship*] [*French*] ..... MAN
Manetti Roberts [*Italy*] [*Research code symbol*] ..... SC
Manetti Roberts [*Italy*] [*Research code symbol*] ..... SCO
Maneuver (KSC) ..... MNVR
Maneuver ..... MNVR
Maneuver (AABC) ..... MVR
Maneuver Analysis and Command ..... MAC
Maneuver Analysis and Command Group ..... MACG
Maneuver and Fire Support Team (MCD) ..... MANFIST
Maneuver Area Command [*Army*] ..... MAC
Maneuver Arms Tactical Protective System [*Army*] (RDA) ..... MANTAPS
Maneuver Control Functional Segment [*Army*] (RDA) ..... MCFS
Maneuver Control System [*Computer science*] ..... MCS
Maneuver Control System / Common Hardware System [*Computer science*] ..... MCS/CHS
Maneuver Criteria Evaluation Program [*Army*] ..... MCEP
Maneuver Director Headquarters [*Military*] ..... MDH
Maneuver Force Air Defense ..... MFAD
Maneuver Limited Altitude (GAVI) ..... MLA
Maneuver Load Alleviation [*Aviation*] ..... MLA
Maneuver Load Control [*Aviation*] ..... MLC
Maneuver Motor Array (MCD) ..... MMA
Maneuver, Objective, Offensive, Surprise, Economy of Force, Mass, Unity of Command, Simplicity, Security [*Basic principles of war*] [*See also MOSS MOUSE*] ..... MOOSEMUSS
Maneuver, Objective, Security, Surprise, Mass, Offensive, Unity of Command, Simplicity, Economy of Force [*Basic principles of war*] [*See also MOOSEMUSS*] (MCD) ..... MOSS MOUSE
Maneuver Operations Program System [*NASA*] ..... MOPS
Maneuver Planning Table [*NASA*] ..... MPT
Maneuver Propulsion Assembly (MCD) ..... MPA
Maneuver Right Area [*Army*] ..... MRA
Maneuver Training Command [*Army*] (AABC) ..... MTC
Maneuverability Augmentation System for Tactical Air Combat Simulation (PDAA) ..... MASTACS
Maneuverable AntiRADAR Vehicle (MCD) ..... MARV
Maneuverable Ballistic Reentry Vehicle ..... MBRV
Maneuverable Recoverable Space Vehicle ..... MRSV
Maneuverable Reentry Technology Investigation ..... MARTI
Maneuverable Reentry Vehicle (AABC) ..... MARV
Maneuverable Satellite Landing System (MUGU) ..... MSLS
Maneuvering (KSC) ..... MANUV
Maneuvering and Navigation System [*Military*] (IAA) ..... MANAV
Maneuvering and Seakeeping ..... MASK
Maneuvering Attack System (MCD) ..... MAS
Maneuvering Decoy (MCD) ..... MANDEC
Maneuvering Element [*Military*] (AABC) ..... MEL
Maneuvering Reentry Control and Ablation Studies ..... MARCAN
Maneuvering Reentry Control and Ablation Studies (MCD) ..... MARCAS
Maneuvering Reentry Vehicle ..... MRV
Maneuvering Reentry Vehicle for Low-Level Penetration (MCD) ..... MRVLP
Maneuvering Room Equipment Panel (DNAB) ..... MREP
Maneuvering Satellite Propulsion System (MCD) ..... MSPS
Maneuvering Ship [*In speed triangle of relative movement problems*] ..... M
Maneuvering Target Test Vechicle ..... MTTV
Maneuvering Technology Vehicle ..... MTV
Maneuvering Unit (KSC) ..... MU
Maneuvering Work Platform [*NASA*] ..... MWP
Maneuvers and Exercises (NATG) ..... M & E
Manga [*Burkina Faso*] [*ICAO location identifier*] (ICLI) ..... DHCM
Manga [*Papua New Guinea*] [*Airport symbol*] (OAG) ..... MGP
Mangahao [*New Zealand*] [*Seismograph station code, US Geological Survey*] (SEIS) ..... MNG
Mangaia [*Cook Islands*] [*Airport symbol*] (OAG) ..... MGS
Mangaia [*Cook Islands*] [*ICAO location identifier*] (ICLI) ..... NCMG
Mangalore [*India*] [*Airport symbol*] (OAG) ..... IXE
Mangalore [*India*] [*ICAO location identifier*] (ICLI) ..... VOML
Manganese [*Chemical element*] ..... Mn
Manganese Alkaline Battery ..... MAB
Manganese Centre (EA) ..... MC
Manganese Nodule Program [*For sampling on ocean floor*] ..... MANOP
Manganese Oxide Mesoporous Structure [*Inorganic Chemistry*] ..... MOMS
Manganese Oxide Thin Film ..... MOTF
Manganese Superoxide Dismutase ..... MnSOD
Manganese Tetraphenylporphine Sulfonate [*Organic chemistry*] ..... MnTPPS
Manganese Zinc Ferrite ..... MZF
Manganese-Enhanced Austenitic Nitrogen Steel ..... MEAN
Manged Care Organization ..... MCO
Mangla [*New Mirpur*] [*Pakistan*] [*Seismograph station code, US Geological Survey*] (SEIS) ..... MNL
Mangla [*Pakistan*] [*Airport symbol*] (AD) ..... MWP
Mangla [*Pakistan*] [*ICAO location identifier*] (ICLI) ..... OPMA
Manglaralto [*Ecuador*] [*ICAO location identifier*] (ICLI) ..... SEML
Mango Resources [*Vancouver Stock Exchange symbol*] ..... MRH
Mangochi [*Malawi*] [*ICAO location identifier*] (ICLI) ..... FWMG
Mangole [*Indonesia*] [*ICAO location identifier*] (ICLI) ..... WAPE
Mangrove [*Maps and charts*] ..... Mg
Mangrove Cay [*Bahamas*] [*Airport symbol*] (OAG) ..... MAY
Manhasset Junior High School, Manhasset, NY [*Library symbol*] [*Library of Congress*] (LCLS) ..... NManhJH
Manhasset Junior-Senior High School, Manhasset, NY [*Library symbol Library of Congress*] (LCLS) ..... NManhJSH
Manhasset Medical Center Hospital, Manhasset, NY [*Library symbol Library of Congress*] (LCLS) ..... NManhM
Manhasset Public Library, Manhasset, NY [*Library symbol Library of Congress*] (LCLS) ..... NManh
Manhasset Senior High School, Manhasset, NY [*Library symbol*] [*Library of Congress*] (LCLS) ..... NManhSH
Manhattan ..... MAN
Manhattan [*Kansas*] [*Seismograph station code, US Geological Survey*] (SEIS) ..... MHK
Manhattan [*Kansas*] [*Airport symbol*] (OAG) ..... MHK
Manhattan [*Kansas*] [*Seismograph station code, US Geological Survey Closed*] (SEIS) ..... MHT
Manhattan Bagel [*NASDAQ symbol*] (TTSB) ..... BGLS
Manhattan Bagel Company, Inc. [*NASDAQ symbol*] (SAG) ..... BGLS
Manhattan Bagel Co., Inc. [*Associated Press*] (SAG) ..... ManBagel
Manhattan Bible College [*Kansas*] ..... MBC
Manhattan Bowery Corp. (EA) ..... MBC
Manhattan Bowery Project (EA) ..... MBP
Manhattan Cable TV, Inc. [*New York, NY*] [*Telecommunications*] (TSSD) ..... MCTV
Manhattan Chess Club (EA) ..... MCC
Manhattan Christian College, Manhattan, KS [*Library symbol*] [*Library of Congress*] (LCLS) ..... KMC
Manhattan College (GAGS) ..... Manhattan C
Manhattan College, Library, Bronx, NY [*OCLC symbol*] (OCLC) ..... ZMC
Manhattan College, New York, NY [*Library symbol Library of Congress*] (LCLS) ..... NNMan
Manhattan District Declassified Code [*AEC*] ..... MDDC
Manhattan Drug Co. ..... MDC
Manhattan Engineer District [*Developed atomic bomb; dissolved, 1946*] ..... MED
Manhattan Institute for Policy Research (EA) ..... MIPR
Manhattan, KS [*AM radio station call letters*] ..... KKSU

Manhattan, KS [*AM radio station call letters*] .... KMAN
Manhattan, KS [*FM radio station call letters*] .... KMKF
Manhattan, KS [*FM radio station call letters*] .... KSDB
Manhattan, KS [*FM radio station call letters*] (RBYB) ... KXBZ-FM
Manhattan, KS [*Location identifier FAA*] (FAAL) .... MHK
Manhattan, KS [*Location identifier FAA*] .... MQD
Manhattan Life Insurance [*NASDAQ symbol*] (TTSB) ..... MLIC
Manhattan Life Insurance Co. [*Associated Press*] (SAG) .. ManhLfe
Manhattan Life Insurance Co. [*NASDAQ symbol*] (SAG) .. MLIC
Manhattan Mineral [*Vancouver Stock Exchange symbol*] .. MHN
Manhattan Miniature Camera Club (EA) .... MMCC
Manhattan National Corp. [*NYSE symbol*] (SPSG) .... MLC
Manhattan Public Library, Manhattan, KS [*Library symbol Library of Congress*] (LCLS) .... KM
Manhattan Publishing Group (EA) .... MPG
Manhattan Ryegrass Growers Association (EA) .... MRGA
Manhattan School of Music (GAGS) .... Manhattan Sch Music
Manhattan School of Music .... MSM
Manhattan School of Music, New York, NY [*Library symbol Library of Congress*] (LCLS) .... NNMSM
Manhattan State Hospital, New York, NY [*Library symbol Library of Congress*] (LCLS) .... NNMS
Manhattan Theater Club .... MTC
Manhattanville College (GAGS) .... Manhattanville C
Manhattanville College, Purchase, NY [*Library symbol Library of Congress*] (LCLS) .... NPurMC
Manhattanville College, Purchase, NY [*OCLC symbol*] (OCLC) ... VYE
Manhay [*Belgium*] [*Geomagnetic observatory code*] ...... MAB
Manhole (AAG) .... MH
Manhole .... MC
Manhole Cover .... MH
Man-Hour (MCD) .... MHR
Man-Hour .... MHA
Man-Hour Accounting (NVT) .... MARS
Manhour Accounting and Reporting System .... MARS
Man-Hour Accounting and Reporting System [*Military*] (MCD) .. MHAC
Man-Hour Accounting Card .... MHAS
Man-Hour Accounting System (DNAB) .... ME
Man-Hours Earned .... MH/FH
Man-Hours per Flying Hour [*Air Force*] (DNAB) .... MHPH
Man-Hours per Flying Hour [*Air Force*] (AFIT) .... MHS
Man-Hours per Sortie [*Air Force*] (AFIT) .... MAD
Manhunter Assignment Device [*Computer science*] .... MDI
Manic Depression Interval [*Course*] .... MDDA
Manic Depressive and Depressive Association [*Later, NDMDA*] (EA) ... MDDA
Manic Depressive Illness .... MDI
Manic Depressive Psychosis .... MDP
Manic-Depressive .... MD
Manic-Depressive Association (EA) .... M
Manichaean Middle Persian .... MRE
Manicore [*Brazil*] [*Airport symbol*] (AD) .... SBMY
Manicore [*Brazil ICAO location identifier*] (ICLI) .... SBMY
Manicouagan [*Quebec*] [*Seismograph station code, US Geological Survey*] (SEIS) .... MNQ
Manicouagan [*Quebec*] [*Airport symbol*] (AD) .... YMV
Manifest (AABC) .... MAN
Manifest .... MANFST
Manifest .... MANIF
Manifest .... MFST
Manifest Achievement (AAMN) .... MA
Manifest Anxiety .... MA
Manifest Anxiety Scale [*Psychology*] .... MAS
Manifest Hypermetropia [*Medicine*] .... Hm
Manifest Information Management System (GAAI) .... MIMS
Manifest Needs Questionnaire (EDAC) .... MNQ
Manifestable (ABBR) .... MFSTB
Manifestation [*Medicine*] .... manifest
Manifestation (ABBR) .... MFSTN
Manifested (ABBR) .... MFSTD
Manifesting (ABBR) .... MFSTG
Manifesto (VRA) .... manif
Manifesto (ABBR) .... MFSTO
Manifold (KSC) .... MANF
Manifold .... MANF
Manifold .... MANI
Manifold [*Automotive engineering*] .... MFD
Manifold [*Paper*] (DGA) .... MFLD
Manifold (KSC) .... MNFD
Manifold (ECII) .... MNFLD
Manifold (KSC) .... MAP
Manifold Absolute Pressure .... MAP
Manifold Air Pressure .... MAPS
Manifold Air Pressure Sensor [*Automotive engineering*] .. MAPS
Manifold Air Temperature [*Automotive engineering*] .... MAT
Manifold Charge Temperature [*Automotive engineering*] . MCT
Manifold Control Valve [*Automotive engineering*] ...... MCV
Manifold Ignition Primary Charge .... MIPC
Manifold Interest Schedule .... MIS
Manifold Pressure .... MP
Manifold Pressure .... mp
Manifold Pressure (AD) .... MST
Manifold Surface Temperature [*Automotive engineering*] . MST
Manifold Surface Temperature Sensor [*Automotive engineering*] .. MSTS
Manifold Vacuum [*Automotive engineering*] .... MV
Manifold Vacuum Sensor [*Automotive engineering*] ...... MVS
Manifold Vacuum Zone Switch [*Automotive engineering*] . MVZS
Manifold-Regulator Accumulator Charging [*Formerly, NCP*] (AAG) .. MRAC
Manifold-Regulator Accumulator Charging (AD) .... mrac

Manihi [*French Polynesia*] [*ICAO location identifier*] (ICLI) ... NTGI
Manihi [*French Polynesia*] [*Airport symbol*] (OAG) ... XMH
Maniilaq Association (EA) .... MA
Manila [*Rope*] .... M
Manila [*Philippines*] [*Seismograph station code, US Geological Survey*] (SEIS) .... MAN
Manila [*Philippines*] [*Airport symbol*] (OAG) .... MNL
Manila, AR [*Location identifier FAA*] (FAAL) .... MXA
Manila Electric Railroad & Light Company [*Still known by acronym, although official name now Manila Electric Company*] ... MERALCO
Manila Hemp Association [*British*] (DBA) .... MHA
Manila/International [*Philippines*] [*ICAO location identifier*] (ICLI) ... RPMM
Manila International Airport .... MIA
Manilla (ADA) .... MAN
Manilla Times, Manilla, IA [*Library symbol Library of Congress*] (LCLS) .... IaManT
Maningrida [*Australia Airport symbol Obsolete*] (OAG) . MNG
Man-in-the-Loop [*Army*] .... MITL
Man-in-the-Loop Simulator [*Military*] .... MITLS
Man-in-the-Loop Trajectory Optimization Program [*NASA*] . MILTOP
Man-in-the-Sea Program [*Navy*] .... MITS
Manipulate [*Medicine*] (MAE) .... man
Manipulated Information Rate Processor .... MIRP
Manipulation [*Medicine*] .... manip
Manipulation Language (NITA) .... ML
Manipulative Communications Cover [*Military*] (ADDR) .. MCC
Manipulative Communications Deception [*Military*] (NVT) . MCD
Manipulative Electronics Deception (MCD) .... MED
Manipulative Learning Operation [*in laboratory work*] . MLO
Manipulator Controller Interface Unit (NASA) .... MCIU
Manipulator Controller Power Conditioner (MCD) .... MCPC
Manipulator Deployment Facility (MCD) .... MDF
Manipulator Deployment Mechanism (MCD) .... MDM
Manipulator Development Facility [*NASA*] (NASA) .... MDF
Manipulator Foot Restraint (NASA) .... MFR
Manipulator Foot Restraint .... MFR
Manipulator Handset Controller (MCD) .... MHC
Manipulator Handset Controller (MCD) .... MHSC
Manipulator Interactive Kinematics Evaluator (SSD) ..... MIKE
Manipulator Jettison System [*or Subsystem*] (MCD) ..... MJS
Manipulator Jettison System .... MJS
Manipulator Language [*Computer science*] .... ML
Manipulator Positioning Latches (MCD) .... MPL
Manipulator Positioning Mechanism (NASA) .... MPM
Manipulator Repair Shop (NRCH) .... MRS
Manipulator Retention Latch [*or Lock*] (NASA) .... MRL
Manipulator/Teleoperator Control Technology (SSD) ...... MTCT
Manipulus [*A Handful*] [*Pharmacy*] .... M
Manipulus [*A Handful*] [*Pharmacy*] .... MAN
Manipulus [*A Handful*] [*Pharmacy*] .... Manip
Manipur People's Party [*India*] [*Political party*] (PPW) . MPP
Manistee [*Michigan*] [*Airport symbol*] (OAG) .... MBL
Manistee & Northeastern Railroad (IIA) .... M & NE
Manistee & Repton R. R. [*AAR code*] .... MAR
Manistee County Library, Manistee, MI [*Library symbol Library of Congress*] (LCLS) .... MiMani
Manistee, MI [*Television station call letters*] .... WCMW
Manistee, MI [*AM radio station call letters*] .... WMTE
Manistee, MI [*FM radio station call letters*] (RBYB) .. WVXM
Manistee, MI [*FM radio station call letters*] .... WXYQ
Manistee Railroad .... MRR
Manistique & Lake Superior R. R. [*AAR code*] .... MLS
Manistique, MI [*Location identifier FAA*] (FAAL) ...... ISQ
Manistique, MI [*AM radio station call letters*] .... WTIQ
Maniti Sugar [*Stock exchange symbol*] (AD) .... MNU
Manitoba [*Canada*] (DD) .... Man
Manitoba [*Canadian province*] .... MAN
Manitoba [*Canadian province*] .... MANIT
Manitoba [*Canadian province*] [*Postal code*] .... MB
Manitoba [*MARC country of publication code Library of Congress*] (LCCP) .. mbc
Manitoba [*MARC geographic area code Library of Congress*] (LCCP) .. n-cn-mb
Manitoba and Saskatchewan Tax Reporter (Commerce Clearing House) [*A publication*] (DLA) ..... Man & Sask Tax Rep (CCH)
Manitoba Association for Educational Data Systems [*Canada*] (EDAC) .... MAN-AEDS
Manitoba Association of Architects [*1914*] [*Canada*] (NGC) .. MAA
Manitoba Association of Registered Nurses, Winnipeg, Manitoba [*Library symbol National Library of Canada*] (NLC) .. MWARN
Manitoba Association of Registered Nurses, Winnipeg, MB, Canada [*Library symbol Library of Congress*] (LCLS) .. CaMWARN
Manitoba Bar News [*A publication*] (ILCA) .... Man B News
Manitoba Cancer Treatment and Research Foundation, Winnipeg, Manitoba [*Library symbol National Library of Canada*] (NLC) .. MWCT
Manitoba Cancer Treatment and Research Foundation, Winnipeg, MB, Canada [*Library symbol Library of Congress*] (LCLS) .. CaMWCT
Manitoba Consumer's Bureau, Winnipeg, Manitoba [*Library symbol National Library of Canada*] (NLC) .. MWCCI
Manitoba Department of Agriculture, Winnipeg, Manitoba [*Library symbol National Library of Canada*] (NLC) .. MWA
Manitoba Department of Consumer and Corporate Affairs, Winnipeg, Manitoba [*Library symbol Obsolete National Library of Canada*] (NLC) .. MWCCA
Manitoba Department of Consumer and Corporate Affairs, Winnipeg, MB, Canada [*Library symbol Library of Congress*] (LCLS) .. CaMWCCA

Manitoba Department of Consumer, Corporate, and Internal Services, Consumers' Bureau, Winnipeg, MB, Canada [Library symbol Library of Congress] (LCLS) .... CaMWCCI

Manitoba Department of Economic Development, Winnipeg, Manitoba [Library symbol National Library of Canada] (NLC) .... MWIC

Manitoba Department of Education, Special Materials Services, Winnipeg, MB, Canada [Library symbol] [Library of Congress] (LCLS) .... CaMWESM

Manitoba Department of Education, Winnipeg, Manitoba [Library symbol National Library of Canada] (NLC) .... MWE

Manitoba Department of Education, Winnipeg, MB, Canada [Library symbol Library of Congress] (LCLS) .... CaMWE

Manitoba Department of Environment and Workplace Safety and Health, Winnipeg, MB, Canada [Library symbol] [Library of Congress] (LCLS) .... CaMWEWSH

Manitoba Department of Environment, Workplace Safety, and Health [UTLAS symbol] .... MEW

Manitoba Department of Environment, Workplace Safety and Health, Winnipeg, Manitoba [Library symbol National Library of Canada] (NLC) .... MWEWSH

Manitoba Department of Finance, Winnipeg, Manitoba [Library symbol National Library of Canada] (NLC) .... MWFI

Manitoba Department of Finance, Winnipeg, MB, Canada [Library symbol Library of Congress] (LCLS) .... CaMWFI

Manitoba Department of Fitness, Recreation and Sport, Winnipeg, Manitoba [Library symbol National Library of Canada] (NLC) ...... MWFRS

Manitoba Department of Fitness, Recreation and Sport, Winnipeg, MB, Canada [Library symbol] [Library of Congress] (LCLS) .... CaMWFRS

Manitoba Department of Health and Community Service, Winnipeg, MB, Canada [Library symbol Library of Congress] (LCLS) .... CaMWHP

Manitoba Department of Industry and Commerce, Winnipeg, MB, Canada [Library symbol Library of Congress] (LCLS) .... CaMWIC

Manitoba Department of Labour, Labour Research Library, Winnipeg, MB, Canada [Library symbol Library of Congress] (LCLS) .... CaMWLR

Manitoba Department of Mines, Natural Resources and Environment, Natural Resources and Environment Division, Winnipeg, MB, Canada [Closed] [Library symbol] [Library of Congress] (LCLS) .... CaMWNR

Manitoba Department of Mines, Resource and Environmental Management, Mineral Resources Division, Winnipeg, MB, Canada [Library symbol] [Library of Congress] (LCLS) .... CaMWMR

Manitoba Department of Municipal Affairs, Administration Branch, Winnipeg, MB, Canada [Library symbol Library of Congress] (LCLS) .... CaMWAMA

Manitoba Department of Municipal Affairs, Winnipeg, Manitoba [Library symbol National Library of Canada] (NLC) .... MWMA

Manitoba Department of Natural Resources, Park Management Library, Winnipeg, MB,Canada [Library symbol Library of Congress] (LCLS) .... CaMWPNR

Manitoba Department of Renewable Resources, Winnipeg, Manitoba [Library symbol National Library of Canada] (NLC) .... MWDRR

Manitoba Department of Renewable Resources, Winnipeg, MB, Canada [Library symbol Library of Congress] (LCLS) .... CaMWDRR

Manitoba. Department of Tourism, Recreation, and Cultural Affairs, Winnipeg, MB,Canada [Library symbol Library of Congress] (LCLS) .... CaMWTRC

Manitoba Energy and Mines, Winnipeg, Manitoba [Library symbol National Library of Canada] (NLC) .... MWEMM

Manitoba Environmental Management Division, Winnipeg, Manitoba [Library symbol National Library of Canada] (NLC) .... MWEM

Manitoba Environmental Management Division, Winnipeg, MB, Canada [Library symbol Library of Congress] (LCLS) .... CaMWEM

Manitoba Gazette [A publication] (DLA) .... Man Gaz

Manitoba Health Organizations, Winnipeg, Manitoba [Library symbol National Library of Canada] (NLC) .... MWHO

Manitoba Health Services Commission, Winnipeg, Manitoba [Library symbol National Library of Canada] (NLC) .... MWHSC

Manitoba Health Services Commission, Winnipeg, MB, Canada [Library symbol Library of Congress] (LCLS) .... CaMWHSC

Manitoba Hydro, Winnipeg, Manitoba [Library symbol National Library of Canada] (NLC) .... MWH

Manitoba Hydro, Winnipeg, MB, Canada [Library symbol Library of Congress] (LCLS) .... CaMWH

Manitoba Journal of Counselling [A publication] .... MJC

Manitoba Law Reports [Canada] [A publication] (DLA) .... Man

Manitoba Law Reports [Canada A publication] (DLA) .... Man LR

Manitoba Law Reports [Canada A publication] (DLA) .... Manitoba

Manitoba Law Reports [Canada] [A publication] (DLA) .... Manitoba L (Can)

Manitoba Law Reports [Canada] [A publication] (DLA) .... MLR

Manitoba Law Reports [Canada] [A publication] (DLA) .... MR

Manitoba Museum of Man & Nature, Winnipeg, Manitoba [Library symbol National Library of Canada] (NLC) .... MWMM

Manitoba Museum of Man and Nature, Winnipeg, MB, Canada [Library symbol Library of Congress] (LCLS) .... CaMWMM

[The] Manitoba Network [Canada] [Computer science] (TNIG) .... MBnet

Manitoba Pool Elevators Library, Winnipeg, Manitoba [Library symbol National Library of Canada] (NLC) .... MWMPE

Manitoba Probation Services, Winnipeg, Manitoba [Library symbol National Library of Canada] (NLC) .... MWPS

Manitoba Probation Services, Winnipeg, MB, Canada [Library symbol Library of Congress] (LCLS) .... CaMWPS

Manitoba Properties, Inc. [Toronto Stock Exchange symbol Vancouver Stock Exchange symbol] .... MPI

Manitoba Queen's Bench Tempore Wood, by Armour [A publication] (DLA) .... Armour

Manitoba Regional Library, Secretary of State Canada [Bibliotheque Regionale du Manitoba, Secretariat d'Etat], Winnipeg, Manitoba [Library symbol National Library of Canada] (NLC) .... MWSS

Manitoba Reports [Maritime Law Book Co. Ltd.] [Information service or system A publication A publication] (DLA) .... Man R

Manitoba Reports, by Carey [1875] [A publication] (ILCA) .... Carey

Manitoba Reports, by Carey [1875] [A publication] (DLA) .... Carey MR

Manitoba Reports Tempore Wood [Canada] [A publication] (DLA) .... Man RT Wood

Manitoba Reports Tempore Wood [Canada] [A publication] (DLA) .... Man T Wood

Manitoba Reports Tempore Wood [Canada A publication] (DLA) .... Rep T Wood

Manitoba Reports Tempore Wood [Canada] [A publication] (DLA) .... RTW

Manitoba Reports Tempore Wood [Canada A publication] (DLA) .... Temp Wood

Manitoba Research Council [Research center] (RCD) .... MRC

Manitoba Research Council, Winnipeg, Manitoba [Library symbol National Library of Canada] (NLC) .... MWMRC

Manitoba Research Council, Winnipeg, MB, Canada [Library symbol Library of Congress] (LCLS) .... CaMWMRC

Manitoba Revised Statutes [Canada] [A publication] (DLA) .... Man Rev Stat

Manitoba School, Portage La Prairie, Manitoba [Library symbol National Library of Canada] (NLC) .... MPLPM

Manitoba School, Portage La Prairie, MB, Canada [Library symbol Library of Congress] (LCLS) .... CaMPlpM

Manitoba Society of Artists [1925] [Canada] (NGC) .... MSA

Manitoba Statutes [Canada] [A publication] (DLA) .... Man Stat

Manitoba Teachers Society, Winnipeg, MB, Canada [Library symbol Library of Congress] (LCLS) .... CaMWMTS

Manitoba Teachers Socity, Winnipeg, Manitoba [Library symbol National Library of Canada] (NLC) .... MWMTS

Manitoba Technical Institute [Canada] .... MTI

Manitoba Telephone System [Telecommunications service] (TSSD) .... MTS

Manitoba Telephone System, Winnipeg, Manitoba [Library symbol National Library of Canada] (NLC) .... MWTS

Manitoba Telephone System, Winnipeg, MB, Canada [Library symbol Library of Congress] (LCLS) .... CaMWTS

Manitoba Theater Center, Winnipeg, Manitoba [Library symbol National Library of Canada] (NLC) .... MWMTC

Manitoba Theater Center, Winnipeg, MB, Canada [Library symbol Library of Congress] (LCLS) .... CaMWMTC

Manitoba Veterinarian Services, Branch Library, Winnipeg, MB, Canada [Library symbol Library of Congress] (LCLS) .... CaMWVS

Manitoba Workplace Safety and Health Division, Winnipeg, Manitoba [Library symbol National Library of Canada] (NLC) .... MWWSH

Manitou & Pike's Peak Railway .... M & PP

Manitou Library (Ojibway of Manitou Rapids Indian Band), Manitou Rapids, Ontario [Library symbol National Library of Canada] (BIB) .... OMRM

Manitou Reef Resources [Vancouver Stock Exchange symbol] .... MNF

Manitou Springs, CO [FM radio station call letters] (RBYB) .... KBIQ-FM

Manitou Springs, CO [FM radio station call letters] .... KCME

Manitou Springs, CO [FM radio station call letters] .... KIKX

Manitou Springs, CO [AM radio station call letters] .... KXRE

Manitou Springs Public Library, Manitou Springs, CO [Library symbol Library of Congress] (LCLS) .... CoMs

Manitoulin Air Services Ltd. [Canada ICAO designator] (FAAC) .... MTO

Manitoulin Secondary School Library, West Bay, Ontario [Library symbol National Library of Canada] (BIB) .... OWBMS

Manitouwadge, ON [Television station call letters] CBLAT-1

Manitouwadge Public Library, Manitouwadge, ON, Canada [Library symbol] [Library of Congress] (LCLS) .... CaOMan

Manitouwadge Public Library, Ontario [Library symbol National Library of Canada] (NLC) .... OMAN

Manitowoc [Wisconsin] [Airport symbol] (OAG) .... MTW

Manitowoc Calumet Counties Library System [Library network] .... M/CCFLS

Manitowoc Co. [NYSE symbol] (SPSG) .... MTW

[The] Manitowoc Co., Inc. [Associated Press] (SAG) .... Manitw

Manitowoc Public Library, Manitowoc, WI [OCLC symbol] (OCLC) .... WIA

Manitowoc Public Library, Manitowoc, WI [Library symbol Library of Congress] (LCLS) .... WMani

Manitowoc, WI [FM radio station call letters] .... WLTU

Manitowoc, WI [AM radio station call letters] .... WOMT

Manitowoc, WI [FM radio station call letters] .... WQTC

Maniwacki, PQ [AM radio station call letters] .... CKMG

Maniwaki [Quebec] [Seismograph station code, US Geological Survey] (SEIS) .... MIQ

Maniwaki, PQ [AM radio station call letters] CBOF-1

Maniwaki, PQ [FM radio station call letters] .... CHGA

Maniwaki, PQ [ICAO location identifier] (ICLI) .... CYMW

Manizales [Colombia] [Airport symbol] (OAG) .... MZL

Manizales/La Nubia [Colorado ICAO location identifier] (ICLI) .... SKMZ

Manja [Madagascar] [ICAO location identifier] (ICLI) .... FMSJ

Manja [Madagascar] [Airport symbol] (OAG) .... MJA

Manjil [Iran] [ICAO location identifier] (ICLI) .... OIGM

Man-Job Match [Military] .... MJM

Mankato [Minnesota] [Airport symbol] (OAG) .... MKT

Mankato Area Vocational-Technical Institute, North Mankato, MN [Library symbol Library of Congress] (LCLS) .... MnNmT

Mankato Industrial Corp. [Automotive industry supplier] .... MICO

Mankato, KS [Location identifier FAA] (FAAL) .... TKO

Mankato, MN [FM radio station call letters] .... KEEZ

Mankato, MN [Television station call letters] .... KEYC

Mankato, MN [FM radio station call letters] .... KMSU

Mankato, MN [AM radio station call letters] .... KTOE

Mankato, MN [AM radio station call letters] .... KYSM

Mankato, MN [FM radio station call letters] .... KYSM-FM

Mankato, MN [Location identifier FAA] (FAAL) .... MKT

Mankato State College [Later, Mankato State University] [Minnesota] .... MSC

Mankato State College [*Later, Mankato State University*], Mankato, MN [*Library symbol Library of Congress*] (LCLS) .... MnManS
Mankato State University (GAGS) .... Mankato St U
Mankato State University, Mankato, MN [*OCLC symbol*] (OCLC) .... MNM
Mankind Research Foundation (EA) .... MRF
Mankoya [*Zambia*] [*Airport symbol*] (AD) .... MNK
Manley Hot Springs [*Alaska*] [*Airport symbol*] (OAG) .... MLY
Manley Hot Springs, AK [*Location identifier FAA*] (FAAL) .... MLY
Manlius, NY [*FM radio station call letters*] .... WAQX
Manly Signal, Manly, IA [*Library symbol Library of Congress*] (LCLS) .... IaManyS
Man-Machine Communication [*Computer science*] .... MMC
Man-Machine Integration Branch [*Ames Research Center*] [*NASA*] .... MMIB
Man-Machine Integration Design and Analysis System (GAVI) .... MIDAS
Man-Machine Interaction (NITA) .... MMI
Man-Machine Interactive Processing System (PDAA) .... MMIPS
Man-Machine Interface .... MMI
Man-Machine Interrogation Technique .... MMIT
Man-Machine Language [*Computer science*] (TEL) .... MML
Man-Machine Partnership Translation [*Telecommunications*] (IEEE) .... MMPT
Man-Machine System (MCD) .... MMS
Man-Machine System Analysis [*Engineering*] .... MMSA
Manmade [*Diamonds*] .... MM
Man-Made Fiber Producers Association [*Later, MMFPAI*] (EA) .... MMFPA
Man-Made Fiber Producers Association, Inc. (EA) .... MMFPAI
Man-Made Fibres Producers Committee [*British*] (DBA) .... MFPC
Man-Made Fibres Producing Industry Training Board [*British*] (BI) .... MMFITB
Man-Made Mineral Fiber .... MMMF
Man-Made Soling Association Ltd. [*British*] (BI) .... MANSA
Man-Month (AFM) .... MM
Mann Oil Resources, Inc. [*Vancouver Stock Exchange symbol*] .... MAN
Manna [*Pharmacy*] (ROG) .... MANN
Mannan-Binding Lectin [*Immunology*] .... MBL
Manned Activity Scheduling System [*NASA*] .... MASS
Manned Aerial Surveillance .... MAS
Manned Aerial Vehicle for Surveillance (MCD) .... MAVS
Manned Aerodynamic Reusable Spaceship .... MARS
Manned Air Combat Simulation (MCD) .... MACS
Manned and Operational (MUGU) .... M/O
Manned Antisubmarine Helicopter .... MASH
Manned Apollo Operations [*NASA*] (KSC) .... MAO
Manned Astronautical Research Station [*Space laboratory*] .... MARS
Manned Attack Torpedo Carrying Helicopter (PDAA) .... MATCH
Manned Circumlunar Mission .... MCM
Manned Command/Reconnaissance Vehicle .... MCRV
Manned Control Car [*Nuclear energy*] .... MCC
Manned Core (SSD) .... MC
Manned Data Insertion Unit (KSC) .... MDIU
Manned Deep Space Vehicle .... MDSV
Manned Earth Orbit .... MEO
Manned Earth Orbit Laboratory (IAA) .... MEOL
Manned Earth Orbit Mission .... MEOM
Manned Earth Reconnaissance [*Naval Air Electronic Systems Command project*] .... MER
Manned Earth-Satellite Terminal Evolving from Earth-to-Orbit Ferry Rockets (SAA) .... METEOR
Manned Entry Vehicle .... MEV
Manned Environmental Systems Assessment [*NASA*] .... MESA
Manned, Evasive Target Tank [*Army*] .... METT
Manned Exploration Site (MCD) .... MES
Manned Extravehicular Manipulating Unit (MCD) .... MEMU
Manned Extravehicular Operation .... MEO
Manned Flight Awareness [*NASA*] (NASA) .... MFA
Manned Flight Awareness Program [*NASA*] (KSC) .... MFAP
Manned Flight Engineering Division [*NASA*] .... MFED
Manned Flight Operations Directive [*NASA*] (KSC) .... MFOD
Manned Flying System (MCD) .... MFS
Manned Geosynchronous Spacecraft Servicer (SSD) .... MGSS
Manned Hypersonic Test Vehicle (MCD) .... MHTV
Manned Hypersonic Vehicle .... MHV
Manned Information and Communications Facility (SAA) .... MANICOM
Manned Interactive Control Stations (MCD) .... MICS
Manned Interceptor Integration Team (SAA) .... MIIT
Manned Interceptor SAGE Evaluation Routine (MCD) .... MISER
Manned Interceptor Simulation Program .... MISP
Manned Lifting Entry Vehicle (MCD) .... MLEV
Manned Lunar Exploration [*NASA*] (AAG) .... MLE
Manned Lunar Exploration Program [*NASA*] (KSC) .... MLEP
Manned Lunar Landing [*NASA*] .... MLL
Manned Lunar Landing and Return [*NASA*] .... MALLAR
Manned Lunar Landing Program [*NASA*] .... MLLP
Manned Lunar Orbiter [*NASA*] .... MLO
Manned Lunar Roving Vehicle [*NASA*] (PDAA) .... MLRV
Manned Lunar Surface [*NASA*] .... MLS
Manned Lunar Test [*NASA*] (KSC) .... MLT
Manned Lunar Vehicle Program [*NASA*] (AAG) .... MLVP
Manned Maneuverable Space System .... MMSS
Manned Maneuvering Module [*Aerospace*] (IIA) .... MMM
Manned Maneuvering Unit [*Aerospace*] .... MMU
Manned Mars and Venus Exploration Studies .... MAVES
Manned Mars Flyby Vehicle [*Aerospace*] .... MMFV
Manned Mars Mission [*NASA*] .... MMM
Manned Military Recovery System (SAA) .... MMRS
Manned Military System Capability Vehicle .... MMSCV
Manned One-Day Mission [*NASA*] .... MODM
Manned Open Sea Experiment Station (NOAA) .... MOSES
Manned Orbit Transfer Vehicle (MCD) .... MOTV
Manned Orbital Development Station [*See also MODS, MOSS, MTSS*] [*Air Force/NASA*] .... MOD
Manned Orbital Development Station [*See also MOD, MOSS, MTSS*] [*Air Force/NASA*] .... MODS
Manned Orbital Flight [*NASA*] (NASA) .... MOF
Manned Orbital Oceanographic Survey System Experiment .... MOOSSE
Manned Orbital Platform .... MOP
Manned Orbital Research and Development System .... MORDS
Manned Orbital Research Facility [*NASA*] (MCD) .... MORF
Manned Orbital [*or Orbiting*] **Research Laboratory** [*NASA*] .... MORL
Manned Orbital Solar Telescope .... MOST
Manned Orbital Space Station [*or System*] [*See also MOD, MODS, MTSS Air Force/NASA*] .... MOSS
Manned Orbital Station (AAG) .... MOS
Manned Orbital Systems Concept (AD) .... mosc
Manned Orbital Systems Concepts [*NASA*] .... MOSC
Manned Orbital Telescope [*NASA*] .... MOT
Manned Orbital Weapon Station [*or System*] .... MOWS
Manned Orbiter (MCD) .... MO
Manned Orbiting Laboratory [*NASA*] .... MOL
Manned Orbiting Laboratory / Altitude Control and Transmission System (DNAB) .... MOL/ACTS
Manned Orbiting Laboratory Test-Oriented Language [*NASA*] (MCD) .... MOLTOL
Manned Orbiting Mission [*NASA*] .... MOM
Manned Orbiting Vehicle [*NASA*] .... MOV
Manned Reconnaissance Satellite [*Air Force*] .... MRS
Manned Repeater Station [*Telecommunications*] (OA) .... MRS
Manned Research on Celestial Bodies Committee [*International Academy of Astronautics*] .... MARECEBO
Manned Reusable Payload .... MRP
Manned Reusable Payload (AD) .... mrp
Manned Reusable Product (AD) .... mrp
Manned Revolving Space Systems Simulator (AD) .... mrsss
Manned Rotating Platform .... MRP
Manned Rovolving Simulated Space Station (SAA) .... MRSS
Manned Satellite .... MANSAT
Manned Satellite Inspection System .... MSIS
Manned Satellite Inspector .... MSI
Manned Scientific Orbital Laboratory [*NASA*] (IAA) .... MSOL
Manned Shuttle Comprehensive Optimization and Targeting [*NASA*] .... MASCOT
Manned Solar Observatory (MCD) .... MSO
Manned Space Flight [*NASA*] (KSC) .... MSF
Manned Space Flight and Launch Vehicles [*Panel*] .... MSFLV
Manned Space Flight Control Center [*Air Force*] .... MSCC
Manned Space Flight Data Processing System [*NASA*] .... MSFDPS
Manned Space Flight Experiments Board [*NASA*] (KSC) .... MSFEB
Manned Space Flight Headquarters [*NASA*] .... MSFH
Manned Space Flight Laboratory [*NASA*] (IAA) .... MSFL
Manned Space Flight Network [*NASA*] .... MSFN
Manned Space Flight Network Operations Center [*NASA*] (KSC) .... MSFNOC
Manned Space Flight Operations [*NASA*] (KSC) .... MSFO
Manned Space Flight Program [*NASA*] (KSC) .... MSFP
Manned Space Flight Subcommittee [*NASA*] (AAG) .... MSFS
Manned Space Flight Support Group (MCD) .... MSFSG
Manned Space Flight Support Project Office [*NASA*] (IAA) .... MASSPO
Manned Space Flight Support Requirements Documentation [*NASA*] .... MSFSRD
Manned Space Flight System [*NASA*] (IAA) .... MSFS
Manned Space Laboratory [*NASA*] (IAA) .... MSL
Manned Space Network [*NASA*] (MCD) .... MSN
Manned Space Station [*NASA*] .... MSS
Manned Space Station Communications System [*NASA*] .... MSSCS
Manned Space Station Simulator [*NASA*] (MUGU) .... MSSS
Manned Space Vehicle [*NASA*] (AAG) .... MSV
Manned Spacecraft Center [*Later, Johnson Space Center*] [*NASA*] .... MSC
Manned Spacecraft Engineer (MCD) .... MSE
Manned Spacecraft Operations [*NASA*] (KSC) .... MSCO
Manned Spacecraft Operations [*NASA*] (KSC) .... MSO
Manned Spacecraft Operations Building [*NASA*] (KSC) .... MSOB
Manned Spacecraft Operations Building .... MSOB
Manned Spacecraft Test Center [*NASA*] (KSC) .... MSTC
Manned Static Space Simulator .... MSSS
Manned Station (IAA) .... MS
Manned Supersonic Test Vehicle (MCD) .... MSTV
Manned Support Module [*NASA*] (NASA) .... MSM
Manned Teller System .... MTS
Manned Test Operations Board [*NASA*] .... MTOB
Manned Test Space System [*See also MOD, MODS, MOSS*] [*Air Force/NASA*] .... MTSS
Manned [*or Manual*] **Thrust Vector Control** (MCD) .... MTVC
Manned Undersea [*or Underwater*] **Activity** [*Marine science*] .... MUA
Manned Undersea Science and Technology [*Marine science*] (MSC) .... MUS & T
Manned Undersea Science and Technology [*Marine science*] (OSRA) .... MUST
Manned Undersea Science and Technology (USDC) .... MUST
Manned Undersea Station .... MUST
Manned Underwater Laboratories [*Marine science*] (MSC) .... MUL
Manned Underwater Station .... MUS
Manned Underwater Station .... MUWS
Manned Upperstage Reusable Payload .... MURP
Manned Vehicle .... MV
Manned Venus Flyby Vehicle .... MVFV
Manned Vertical Flight (MCD) .... MVF
Manned-Unmanned Environmental Research Station (MSC) .... MUMMERS
Manned-Unmanned Lunar Explorer .... MULE
Mannequin and Models' Guild of Australia .... MMGA

Manner Common among Business Men ...... MCABM
Manner of Performance [Officer rating] ...... MOP
Manner of Performance Rating (AD) ...... mopr
Manner of Performing Rating ...... MOPR
Mannerism (VRA) ...... Mnrsm
Mannes College of Music [New York, NY] ...... MCM
Mannes College of Music, New York, NY [Library symbol Library of Congress] (LCLS) ...... NNMC
Mannesman Tally (NITA) ...... MT
Mannheim [Germany Airport symbol] (OAG) ...... MHG
Mannheimer Versorgungs und Verkehrsgesellschaft [Germany] ...... MVV
Mannheim-Neuostheim [Germany ICAO location identifier] (ICLI) ...... EDFM
Manning, AB [Television station call letters] CBXAT-3
Manning and Granger's English Common Pleas Reports [A publication] (DLA) ...... M & G
Manning and Granger's English Common Pleas Reports [A publication] (DLA) ...... Man & G
Manning and Granger's English Common Pleas Reports [A publication] (DLA) ...... Mann & G (Eng)
Manning & Napier Information Services ...... MNIS
Manning and Ryland's English King's Bench Reports [1827-30] [A publication] (DLA) ...... M & R
Manning and Ryland's English King's Bench Reports [1827-30] [A publication] (DLA) ...... Man & R
Manning and Ryland's English King's Bench Reports [1827-30] [A publication] (DLA) ...... Man & Ry
Manning and Ryland's English King's Bench Reports [1827-30] [A publication] (ILCA) ...... Man & Ry KB
Manning and Ryland's English King's Bench Reports [1827-30] [A publication] (DLA) ...... Mann & R
Manning and Ryland's English King's Bench Reports [1827-30] [A publication] (DLA) ...... Mann & R (Eng)
Manning and Ryland's English Magistrates' Cases [1827-30] [A publication] (DLA) ...... M & RMC
Manning and Ryland's English Magistrates' Cases [1827-30] [A publication] (DLA) ...... Man & R
Manning and Ryland's English Magistrates' Cases [1827-30] [A publication] (DLA) ...... Man & Ry
Manning and Ryland's English Magistrates' Cases [1827-30] [A publication] (DLA) ...... Man & Ry Mag
Manning and Ryland's English Magistrates' Cases [1827-30] [A publication] (DLA) ...... Man & Ry Mag Cas
Manning and Ryland's English Magistrates' Cases [1827-30] [A publication] (DLA) ...... Man & Ry MC
Manning and Ryland's English Magistrates' Cases [1827-30] [A publication] (DLA) ...... Mann & R
Manning and Scott's English Common Bench Reports [IX] [A publication] (DLA) ...... M & S
Manning and Scott's English Common Bench Reports, Old Series [IX] [A publication] (DLA) ...... Man & S
Manning and Scott's English Common Bench Reports, Old Series [IX] [A publication] (DLA) ...... Man & Sc
Manning [Greg] Auctions, Inc. [NASDAQ symbol] (SAG) ...... GMAI
Manning [Greg] Auctions, Inc. [Associated Press] (SAG) ...... GMann
Manning [Greg] Auctions, Inc. [Associated Press] (SAG) ...... GManning
Manning Control Authority (MCD) ...... MCA
Manning, Granger, and Scott's English Common Bench Reports [135-39 English Reprint] [1845-56] [A publication] (DLA) ...... Mann G & S
Manning, Granger, and Scott's English Common Bench Reports, Old Series [I-VIII] [A publication] (DLA) ...... Man G & S
Manning, Granger, and Scott's English Common Bench Reports, Old Series [I-VIII] [A publication] (DLA) ...... Man Gr & S
Manning, Granger, and Scott's English Common Bench Reports, Old Series [I-VIII] [A publication] (DLA) ...... Mann G & S (Eng)
Manning, Granger, and Scott's English Common Pleas Reports [1845-56] [A publication] (DLA) ...... MG & S
Manning Monitor, Manning, IA [Library symbol Library of Congress] (LCLS) ...... IaMannM
Manning Municipal Library, Alberta [Library symbol National Library of Canada] (NLC) ...... AMAM
Manning Municipal Library, Manning, AB, Canada [Library symbol] [Library of Congress] (LCLS) ...... CaAMaM
Manning on Bills and Notes [A publication] (DLA) ...... Mann Bills
Manning, SC [Location identifier FAA] (FAAL) ...... MNI
Manning, SC [FM radio station call letters] ...... WHLZ
Manning, SC [AM radio station call letters] ...... WYMB
Manning Table and Equipment List ...... MTEL
Manning Unit Group [Air Force] (AFM) ...... MUG
Manning's Commentaries on the Law of Nations [A publication] (DLA) ...... Man Int Law
Manning's Commentaries on the Law of Nations [A publication] (DLA) ...... Mann Com
Manning's Commentaries on the Law of Nations [A publication] (DLA) ...... Mann Nat
Manning's Digest of the Nisi Prius Reports [England] [A publication] (DLA) ...... Mann
Manning's English Court of Revision Reports [A publication] (DLA) ...... Mann
Manning's English Election Cases (Court of Revision) [A publication] (DLA) ...... Man El Cas
Manning's English Exchequer Practice [A publication] (DLA) ...... Man Exch Pr
Manning's English Exchequer Practice [A publication] (DLA) ...... Mann Ex Pr
Manning's Reports [1 Michigan] [A publication] (DLA) ...... Man
Manning's Reports [1 Michigan] [A publication] (DLA) ...... Mann
Manning's Reports [1 Michigan] [A publication] (DLA) ...... Manning

Manning's Reports, English Revision Court [1832-35] [A publication] (DLA) ...... Man
Manning's Revision Cases [1832-35] [A publication] (DLA) ...... Mann EC
Manning's Unreported Cases [Louisiana] [A publication] (DLA) ...... Man Unr Cases
Manning's Unreported Cases [Louisiana] [A publication] (DLA) ...... Man Unrep Cas
Manning's Unreported Cases [Louisiana] [A publication] (DLA) ...... Man Unrep Cas (LA)
Manning's Unreported Cases [Louisiana] [A publication] (DLA) ...... Mann Unrep Cas
Manning's Unreported Cases [Louisiana] [A publication] (DLA) ...... Manning
Manning's Unreported Cases [Louisiana] [A publication] (DLA) ...... Manning LA
Manning's Unreported Cases [Louisiana] [A publication] (DLA) ...... Manning's UC
Manning's Unreported Cases [Louisiana] [A publication] (DLA) ...... Manning's Unrep Cases
Mannington, WV [FM radio station call letters] ...... WTUS
Mannion Air Charter, Inc. [ICAO designator] (FAAC) ...... MAN
Mannion Air Charter, Inc. [Air carrier designation symbol] ...... MANX
Mannito-Egg Yolk Polymyxin (OA) ...... MYP
Mannitol [Organic chemistry] ...... M
Mannitol Hexanitrate [Organic chemistry] ...... MHN
Mannitol Salt Agar (MAE) ...... MSA
Mannlicher Collectors Association (EA) ...... MCA
Mannlicher Rifle ...... MANN
Mannlicher-Schoenauer (AD) ...... M/S
Mannose [A sugar] ...... Man
Mannose Phosphate Receptor [Biochemistry] ...... MPR
Mannose Resistant [Biochemistry] ...... MR
Mannose Sensitive [Biochemistry] ...... MS
Mannose-6-Phosphate [Chemistry] (DAVI) MAN-6-P
Mannose-Binding Protein C [Biochemistry] ...... MBP-C
Mannosephosphate Isomerase [An enzyme] ...... MPI
Mannose-Resistant Hemagglutination ...... MRHA
Mannsville, KY [FM radio station call letters] (RBYB) ...... WVLC
Mannville Oil & Gas Ltd. [Toronto Stock Exchange symbol] ...... MOG
Mannville Public Library, Alberta [Library symbol National Library of Canada] (NLC) ...... AMAN
Mannville Public Library, Mannville, AB, Canada [Library symbol] [Library of Congress] (LCLS) ...... CaAMan
Mano [Hand] [Spanish] ...... M
Mano Destra [With the Right Hand] [Music] ...... MD
Mano River Union [See also UFM] (EAIO) ...... MRU
Mano Sinistra [With the Left Hand] [Music] ...... MS
Manobo [MARC language code Library of Congress] (LCCP) ...... mno
Manoel Ribas [Brazil ICAO location identifier] (ICLI) ...... SBMR
Manokotak [Alaska] [Airport symbol] (OAG) ...... KMO
Manokwari [Indonesia] [Airport symbol] (OAG) ...... MKW
Manokwari/Rendani [Indonesia] [ICAO location identifier] (ICLI) ...... WASR
Manometer ...... MANO
Manono [Zaire] [ICAO location identifier] (ICLI) ...... FZRA
Manono [Zaire] [Airport symbol] (OAG) ...... MNO
Man-on-the-Move [Military slang] (DNAB) ...... MOM
Man-on-the-Move Communications ...... MOMCOMS
Man-on-the-Street Interview [Journalism] ...... MOS
Man-Operated Propulsion System ...... MOPS
Manor [Commonly used] (OPSA) ...... MANOR
Manor ...... MNR
Manor (MCD) ...... MNR
Manor Care [NYSE symbol] (TTSB) ...... MNR
Manor Care, Inc. [Associated Press] (SAG) ...... ManorCr
Manor Care, Inc. [NYSE symbol] (SPSG) ...... MNR
Manorhaven Elementary School, Port Washington, NY [Library symbol Library of Congress] (LCLS) ...... NptwME
Manorial Society of Great Britain (EAIO) ...... MSGB
Manor-Oaks-William R. Bowie School, New Hyde Park, NY [Library symbol] [Library of Congress] (LCLS) ...... NNhpME
Manors [Commonly used] (OPSA) ...... MANORS
Manors [Postal Service standard] (OPSA) ...... MNRS
Manors ...... MNRS
Manotick Public Library, Ontario [Library symbol National Library of Canada] (NLC) ...... OMANO
Man-Overboard ...... MOB
Manpack ...... mpk
Manpack Battery Pack ...... MBP
Manpack Loop Antenna ...... MLA
Manpack Personnel Detector-Chemical [Officially the Olfractronic Personnel Detector] [Military] (VNW) ...... MPD-C
Manpack Tactical Intelligence System ...... MANTIS
Manpack Unit (MCD) ...... MPU
Man-Portable Air Defense (AABC) ...... MANPAD
Man-Portable Air Defense System (MCD) ...... MANPADS
Manportable Cannon Thermal Night Sight (MCD) ...... MCTNS
Man-Portable Illuminator ...... MPI
Manportable MILSTAR [Military Strategic and Tactical Relay] Terminal [Army] ...... MMT
Manportable Office System [Army] (RDA) ...... MPOS
Man-Portable Radio Direction-Finding System ...... MRDFS
Manpower (KSC) ...... MANPWR
Manpower [A publication] ...... MAP
Manpower (AFM) ...... MNPWR
Manpower ...... MNPWR
Manpower ...... MP
Manpower (AABC) ...... MPR
Manpower Absorption Plan [Department of Labor] ...... MAP
Manpower Administration [Later, Employment and Training Administration] [Department of Labor] ...... MA
Manpower Advisory Committee (OICC) ...... MAC

Manpower Allocation and Accounting Subsystem [*Air Force*] (AFM) .... MAAS
Manpower Allocation Requirement Criteria [*Military*] (RDA) ..... MARC
Manpower Allocation/Requirements Plan [*Navy*] ..... MARP
Manpower Analysis and Planning Society (EA) ..... MAPS
Manpower Analysis Paper ..... MAP
Manpower and Career Development Agency ..... MCDA
Manpower and Community College Counselor Training Program
   (OICC) ..... MCCTP
Manpower and Equipment Force Packaging [*Military*] ..... MEFPAK
Manpower and Immigration [*Canada*] ..... M & I
Manpower and Logistics Analysis ..... M & LA
Manpower and Logistics Analysis (MCD) ..... MALA
Manpower and Organization [*Military*] ..... M & O
Manpower and Organization Division [*Air Force*] ..... MOD
Manpower and Personnel (MCD) ..... MP
Manpower and Personnel Administration [*Military British*] ..... MPA
Manpower and Personnel Council [*DoD*] ..... MPC
Manpower and Personnel Integration [*Military*] (RDA) ..... MANPRINT
Manpower and Personnel Management Information System [*Navy*] ..... MAPMIS
Manpower and Personnel Management Information System Manual
   [*Navy*] (DNAB) ..... MAPMISMAN
Manpower and Personnel Plan [*Army*] (AABC) ..... MAPP
Manpower and Personnel Research Laboratory [*Army Research Institute for*
   the Behavioral and Social Sciences] (RDA) ..... MPRL
Manpower and Production Projections [*LIMRA*] ..... MAPP
Manpower and Production Survey [*LIMRA*] ..... MAPS
Manpower and Reserve Affairs ..... M & RA
Manpower and Talent Clearinghouse ..... MATCH
Manpower and Training (DOMA) ..... MPT
Manpower and Training Research Information System [*DoD Information*
   service or system] (IID) ..... MATRIS
Manpower Area Planning System [*Under CAMPS*] ..... MAPS
Manpower Assistance Project [*Department of Labor*] ..... MAP
Manpower Authorization Criteria [*Army*] ..... MACRIT
Manpower Authorization File ..... MAF
Manpower Authorization Request for Change [*Air Force*] ..... MARC
Manpower Authorization Voucher ..... MAV
Manpower Business Training Institute ..... MBTI
Manpower Commission (NADA) ..... MC
Manpower Consultative Service [*Canada*] (PDAA) ..... MCS
Manpower Control Report ..... MCR
Manpower Data Automated System (DNAB) ..... MDAS
Manpower Data Relay Station (IAA) ..... MDRS
Manpower Determination Model [*Military*] ..... MDM
Manpower Development and Training Act [*1962*] [*Later, CETA Department of*
   Labor] ..... MDTA
Manpower Development Program [*Department of Labor*] ..... MDP
Manpower Development Program [*Department of Labor*] ..... MPDP
Manpower Education Institute (EA) ..... MEI
Manpower Employment Assistance Training [*Act*] [*Pennsylvania*] ..... MEAT
Manpower Estimate (AAG) ..... ME
Manpower Estimate Report (AAGC) ..... MER
Manpower Estimating Relationships (MCD) ..... MER
Manpower Evaluation Report [*Military*] ..... MER
Manpower for a Clean Environment [*Water Pollution Control*
   Federation] ..... MANFORCE
Manpower Force Packaging [*Military*] ..... MANFOR
Manpower Forces and Readiness [*Military*] ..... MF & R
Manpower, Inc. [*NYSE symbol*] (SPSG) ..... MAN
Manpower, Inc. [*Associated Press*] (SAG) ..... Manpwl
Manpower Information Division [*Navy*] ..... MID
Manpower Information Retrieval System (IEEE) ..... MIRS
Manpower Information System (MCD) ..... MIS
Manpower Intelligence and Planning Division (AIE) ..... MIPD
Manpower Management Information ..... MMI
Manpower Management Planning Board ..... MMPB
Manpower Management Staff [*NATO*] (NATG) ..... MMS
Manpower Management System [*Marine Corps*] ..... MMS
Manpower, Materials, Money ..... 3M's
Manpower Needs [*Military*] ..... MPNE
Manpower Operations Data System [*Employment and Training Administration*]
   [*Department of Labor*] ..... MODS
Manpower, Personnel, and Training ..... MPT
Manpower, Personnel, and Training Analysis ..... MPTA
Manpower Personnel and Training Information System [*Navy*] ..... MAPTIS
Manpower, Personnel, and Training Support [*Military*] (CAAL) ..... MPTS
Manpower Personnel Assignment Document (AFM) ..... MPAD
Manpower Personnel, Navy (DOMA) ..... MPN
Manpower, Personnel, Training, and Safety [*Army*] ..... MPTS
Manpower Planning Council ..... MPC
Manpower Planning Model ..... MPM
Manpower Planning Quota (PDAA) ..... MPQ
Manpower Policy and Requirements Branch [*Department of Defence*]
   [*Australia*] ..... MPR
Manpower Priorities Committee ..... MPC
Manpower Requirements ..... MR
Manpower Requirements Analysis Report [*Military*] ..... MRAR
Manpower Requirements and Resources Control System [*Navy*]
   (NVT) ..... MARRCS
Manpower Requirements Change [*Military*] (GFGA) ..... MRC
Manpower Requirements Criteria [*Army*] ..... MARC
Manpower Research and Data Analysis Center [*DoD*] (NVT) ..... MARDAC
Manpower Research and Data Analysis Center [*DoD*] (DNAB) ..... MRDAC
Manpower, Reserve Affairs and Logistics (MCD) ..... MRA & L
Manpower Resource Identification Code [*Military*] ..... M-RIC

Manpower Resources Accounting System [*Air Force*] ..... MRAS
Manpower Resources Research and Development Center [*Army*]
   (RDA) ..... MANRRDC
Manpower Services Branch [*Military*] (MCD) ..... MSB
Manpower Services Commission [*British*] ..... MSC
Manpower Source Listing (MCD) ..... MSL
Manpower System (NRCH) ..... MPS
Manpower Systems Work Group ..... MANSWG
Manpower Systems Work Group ..... MSWG
Manpower Tradeoff Methodology [*Military*] ..... MTM
Manpower, Training, and Personnel (MCD) ..... MANTRAPERS
Manpower Training Association (AEBS) ..... MTA
Manpower Training Institute ..... MTI
Manpower Training Services ..... MTS
Manpower Utilisation and Payment Structure [*Imperial Chemical Industries*]
   [*British*] ..... MUPS
Manpower Utilization and Control System ..... MUACS
Manpower Utilization Report (MCD) ..... MUR
Manpower Utilization System and Techniques [*Department of State*] ..... MUST
Manpower Validation Program ..... MVP
Manpower Voucher [*Army*] (AABC) ..... MV
Man-Powered Aircraft ..... MPA
Man-Powered Vehicle ..... MPV
Manpower-Needs Forecasting (MCD) ..... MPNF
Manpower-Planning Quota (AD) ..... mpq
MANPRINT [*Manpower and Personnel Integration*] Coordination Team
   [*Army*] ..... MCT
MANPRINT [*Manpower and Personnel Integration*] Joint Working Group
   [*Army*] ..... MJWG
MANPRINT [*Manpower and Personnel Integration*] Staff Officer Course
   [*Military*] (RDA) ..... MSOC
Manridge Explorations Ltd. [*Toronto Stock Exchange symbol*] ..... MRG
Man's Environments - Display Implication and Applications (PDAA) ..... MEDIA
Man's Impact on Coastal and Estuarine Ecosystems [*Marine science*]
   [*United Nations*] (OSRA) ..... MICE
Mansa [*Zambia*] [*ICAO location identifier*] (ICLI) ..... FLMA
Mansa [*Zambia*] [*Airport symbol*] (AD) ..... FZB
Mansa [*Zambia*] [*Airport symbol*] (OAG) ..... MNS
Mansel on Costs [*A publication*] (DLA) ..... Mans on C
Mansel on Demurrer [*1828*] [*A publication*] (DLA) ..... Man Dem
Mansel on Demurrer [*1828*] [*A publication*] (DLA) ..... Mans Dem
Mansel on Limitations [*1839*] [*A publication*] (DLA) ..... Man Lim
Mansel on Limitations [*1839*] [*A publication*] (DLA) ..... Mans Lim
Mansfield [*Ohio*] [*Airport symbol*] (OAG) ..... MFD
Mansfield Historical Society, Mansfield Center, CT [*Library symbol Library of*
   Congress] (LCLS) ..... CtMaHi
Mansfield, LA [*FM radio station call letters*] ..... KJVC
Mansfield, LA [*FM radio station call letters*] ..... KORI
Mansfield, LA [*Location identifier FAA*] (FAAL) ..... MSD
Mansfield, MA [*Location identifier FAA*] (FAAL) ..... IHM
Mansfield, MO [*FM radio station call letters*] ..... KTRI
Mansfield, OH [*Location identifier FAA*] (FAAL) ..... MFD
Mansfield, OH [*AM radio station call letters*] ..... WMAN
Mansfield, OH [*Television station call letters*] ..... WMFD
Mansfield, OH [*FM radio station call letters*] ..... WOSV
Mansfield, OH [*FM radio station call letters*] ..... WVMC
Mansfield, OH [*FM radio station call letters*] ..... WVNO
Mansfield, OH [*FM radio station call letters*] ..... WYHT
Mansfield, PA [*FM radio station call letters*] ..... WNTE
Mansfield Park [*Novel by Jane Austen*] ..... MP
Mansfield Public Library, Mansfield, OH [*Library symbol Library of*
   Congress] (LCLS) ..... OMans
Mansfield State College, Mansfield, PA [*OCLC symbol*] (OCLC) ..... MAN
Mansfield State College, Mansfield, PA [*Library symbol Library of Congress*]
   (LCLS) ..... PManM
Mansfield University of Pennsylvania (GAGS) ..... Mansfield U
Mansfield-Richland County Public Library, Mansfield, OH [*OCLC symbol*]
   (OCLC) ..... OMN
Mansfield's Digest of Statutes [*Arkansas*] [*A publication*] (DLA) ..... Mansf Dig
Mansfield's Reports [*49-52 Arkansas*] [*A publication*] (DLA) ..... Mans
Manshead [*England*] ..... MANSH
Mansion House Association on Transport, Inc. [*British*] (BI) ..... MHA
Mansiones ..... MANS
Mansions ..... M/S
Manslaughter ..... MANS
Mansoa [*Guinea-Bissau*] [*ICAO location identifier*] (ICLI) ..... GGMS
Manson Creek Resources Ltd. [*Vancouver Stock Exchange symbol*] ..... MCK
Manson Evaluation [*Psychology*] ..... ME
Manson Impact Structure [*Iowa*] [*Geology*] ..... MIS
Manson Journal, Manson, IA [*Library symbol Library of Congress*]
   (LCLS) ..... IaMansJ
Manson's English Bankruptcy and Winding-Up Cases [*A publication*]
   (DLA) ..... Mans
Manson's English Bankruptcy and Winding-Up Cases [*A publication*]
   (DLA) ..... Manson
Manson's English Bankruptcy and Winding-Up Cases [*A publication*]
   (DLA) ..... Manson Bankr Cas
Manson's English Bankruptcy Cases [*A publication*] (DLA) ..... Man
Manson's English Bankruptcy Cases [*A publication*] (DLA) ..... Manson (Eng)
Manston [*British ICAO location identifier*] (ICLI) ..... EGMH
Manston [*British ICAO location identifier*] (ICLI) ..... EGUM
Manston [*England*] [*Airport symbol*] (AD) ..... MSE
Man-Systems Integration Standard (SSD) ..... MSIS
Manta [*Ecuador*] [*Airport symbol*] (OAG) ..... MEC
Manta [*Ecuador*] [*ICAO location identifier*] (ICLI) ..... SEMT

Mantagu and MacArthur's English Bankruptcy Reports [*1826-30*] [*A publication*] (DLA) .... Mont & M Bankr (Eng)
Manteca, CA [*FM radio station call letters*] .... KVFX
Manteigas [*Portugal*] [*Seismograph station code, US Geological Survey*] (SEIS) .... MTE
Mantellate Sisters, Servants of Mary of Blue Island (TOCD) .... OSM
Man-Tended Approach (SSD) .... MTA
Man-Tended Capability (SSD) .... MTC
Man-Tended Committee (SSD) .... MTC
Man-Tended Free Flyer (MCD) .... MTFF
Man-Tended Operation (SSD) .... MTO
Man-Tended Reference Configuration (SSD) .... MTRC
Man-Tended Review Board (SSD) .... MTRB
Manteo, NC [*Location identifier FAA*] (FAAL) .... MQI
Manteo, NC [*Location identifier FAA*] (FAAL) .... RBX
Manteo, NC [*FM radio station call letters*] .... WVOD
Mantes-Cherence [*France ICAO location identifier*] (ICLI) .... LFFC
Manti City Library, Manti, UT [*Library symbol Library of Congress*] (LCLS) .... UMan
Manti, UT [*AM radio station call letters*] .... KMTI
Manti, UT [*FM radio station call letters*] .... KMXU
Mantissa [*Decimal portion of a logarithm*] .... M
Mantle Arm Index .... MAI
Mantle Bouguer Anomaly [*Geology*] .... MBA
Mantle Cavity .... MC
Mantle Collar .... MC
Mantle Floor .... MF
Mantle Length .... ML
Mantle Lip .... ML
Mantle Nerve .... MN
Mantle Tentacle .... MT
Mantle Vessel .... MV
Mantle Width Index .... MWI
Mantle Zone .... MZ
Manton [*Australia Seismograph station code, US Geological Survey*] (SEIS) .... MTN
Manton Public Library, Manton, MI [*Library symbol Library of Congress*] (LCLS) .... MiMant
Mantoux Diameter (MAE) .... MD
Mantrust Asahi Airways PT [*Indonesia*] [*ICAO designator*] (FAAC) .... MTS
Mantsonyane [*Lesotho*] [*ICAO location identifier*] (ICLI) .... FXMN
Manu [*Peru*] [*ICAO location identifier*] (ICLI) .... SPNU
Manu Dextra [*With the Right Hand*] [*Latin*] .... MD
Manu Propria [*In documents, after king's signature*] [*Italian*] .... MP
Manuae [*Cook Islands*] [*ICAO location identifier*] (ICLI) .... NCMN
Manual .... M
Manual .... MA
Manual (KSC) .... MAN
Manual [*A handbook*] (WDMC) .... man
Manual (IAA) .... MANL
Manual .... MN
Manual (MSA) .... MNL
Manual A1 Simplex [*Aviation*] .... MAS
Manual Abell-Kendall [*Clinical chemistry*] .... MAK
Manual Adaptive TMA [*Target Motion Analysis*] **Estimator** [*Navy*] (ANA) .... MATE
Manual Adjusting [*Automotive engineering*] .... M/ADJ
Manual Aircraft Data Input System (MCD) .... MADIS
Manual Aircraft Display Information System [*Military*] (CAAL) .... MADIS
Manual Amendment .... MANAM
Manual Angle Tracking Capability .... MANTRAC
Manual Arts Therapist .... MAT
Manual Assisted Gaming of Integrated Combat (PDAA) .... MAGIC
Manual Authority File .... MAF
Manual/Automatic Separation and Flotation Equipment (DNAB) .... MAN/SAFE
Manual Battery Control (AAG) .... MBC
Manual Board [*Telecommunications*] (NITA) .... MBD
Manual Bomb Hoist .... MBH
Manual Brake [*Automotive engineering*] .... M/BRK
Manual Burst Disable (AABC) .... MBD
Manual Business Systems Association [*British*] (DBA) .... MBSA
Manual Change Order (MSA) .... MCO
Manual Change Request (MSA) .... MCR
Manual Clock [*Computer science*] (MDG) .... MK
Manual Code (NITA) .... MC
Manual Combat Center [*Air Force*] .... MCC
Manual Command-to-Line-of-Sight [*Missile guidance system*] (INF) .... MCLOS
Manual Communication Module [*Telecommunication device for the deaf*] .... MCM
Manual Communications Unit .... CTC
Manual Computer Makeready (DGA) .... MCM
Manual Control .... MC
Manual Control Center [*Air Force*] .... MCC
Manual Control Device .... MCD
Manual Control Number .... MCN
Manual Control Panel .... MCP
Manual Control Unit .... MCU
Manual Damper (OA) .... MD
Manual d'Archeologie Biblique [*A publication*] (BJA) .... MAB
Manual Data .... MD
Manual Data Input [*SAGE*] .... MDI
Manual Data Input Function [*Computer science*] .... MDIF
Manual Data Input Section [*Computer science*] .... MDIS
Manual Data Input System [*Computer science*] .... MDIS
Manual Data Input Unit [*Computer science*] .... MDIU
Manual Data Relay Center (MCD) .... MDRC
Manual Data Room .... MDR
Manual Data Supervisor [*Computer science*] (IAA) .... MDS
Manual Data Technician [*Computer science*] (IAA) .... MDT
Manual Dilation of the Anus (AAMN) .... MDA
Manual Direct (NASA) .... MD
Manual Direction Center [*Air Force*] (AFM) .... MDC
Manual Direction Finder [*Radio*] .... MDF
Manual Disconnect (MCD) .... MD
Manual Electron Device .... MED
Manual Emergency Controls [*Aerospace*] (KSC) .... MEC
Manual Entry Device .... MED
Manual Entry Panel [*Military*] (CAAL) .... MEP
Manual Entry System [*or Subsystem*] (IEEE) .... MES
Manual Equipment Checkout (NG) .... MECO
Manual Fault Isolation Test .... MFIT
Manual Five Speed [*DOE*] (TAG) M5
Manual Flight Control System [*NASA*] .... MFCS
Manual for Administration of the Hands-On Component (MCD) .... MAHOC
Manual for Courts-Martial .... MCM
Manual Frequency Control .... MFC
Manual Fuel Cutoff (AAG) .... MFCO
Manual Gain Control .... MGC
Manual Governing Valve Control [*Nuclear energy*] (NRCH) .... MGVC
Manual Group (NRCH) .... MG
Manual High-Voltage Power Supply .... MHVPS
Manual Hold [*Telecommunications*] .... MH
Manual Index Page [*SNMMMS*] .... MIP
Manual Individual [*Nuclear energy*] (NRCH) .... MI
Manual Input [*Computer science*] .... MANIP
Manual Input [*Computer science*] .... MI
Manual Input Buffer [*Computer science*] .... MIB
Manual Input Processing [*or Program*] [*Computer science*] .... MIP
Manual Input Room (SAA) .... MIR
Manual Inputs-Tracks (SAA) .... MIT
Manual Intervention and Display .... MAID
Manual Intervention and Observation Simulator (AAG) .... MINOS
Manual Intervention Facility .... MIF
Manual Launch - RADAR Search .... MLRS
Manual Loader (AAG) .... ML
Manual Local (IAA) .... ML
Manual Low-Voltage Power Supply .... MLVPS
Manual Master Direction Center .... MMDC
Manual Maximal Displacement [*Sports medicine*] .... MM
Manual Metal Arc [*Welding*] .... MMA
Manual Mode Space Simulator .... MMSS
Manual Molder Shielded Arc .... MMSA
Manual Morse (MCD) .... MM
Manual Muscle Test .... MMT
Manual of Air Force Law [*British*] .... MAFL
Manual of Clinical Immunology [*A publication*] .... MCI
Manual of Clinical Microbiology [*A publication*] .... MCM
Manual of Courts-Martial, United States .... MCMUS
Manual of Engineering Instructions .... MEI
Manual of Field Engineering [*British military*] (DMA) .... MFE
Manual of Investigative and Operational Guidelines [*FBI*] .... MIOG
Manual of Meat Inspection Procedures [*of the USDA*] .... MMIP
Manual of Military Law [*British*] .... MML
Manual of Operations .... MANOP
Manual of Patent Examining Procedures .... MPEP
Manual of Practice (GNE) .... MOP
Manual of Qualification for Advancement .... MQA
Manual of the Medical Department [*Navy*] .... MANMED
Manual of the Medical Department [*Navy*] .... MANMEDDEPT
Manual of the Medical Department [*Navy*] .... MMD
Manual of Tumor Nomenclature [*Medicine*] (DHSM) .... MOTNAC
Manual on the Control of Government Property in the Possession of Contractors .... MCGPPC
Manual on Uniform Traffic Control Devices [*Highway engineering*] [*A publication*] .... MUTCD
Manual on Uniform Traffic Control Traffic Control Devices [*Federal Housing Adminstration*] .... MUTCD
Manual Operation (AD) .... mo
Manual Operations Control .... MOC
Manual Operations Panel .... MOP
Manual or Automatic (NRCH) .... M/A
Manual or Automatic Ultrasonic Laboratory Test .... MAULT
Manual Orientation (MCD) .... MO
Manual Output .... MO
Manual Overdrive [*Automotive engineering*] .... MOD
Manual Override Panel (AAG) .... MOP
Manual Override Switch .... MOS
Manual Overseas Visa System .... MOVS
Manual Oxygen Control Valve (NASA) .... MOCV
Manual Oxygen Control Valve .... MOCV
Manual Phase Shifter .... MPS
Manual Plot Entry (MCD) .... MPE
Manual Pointing Controller (MCD) .... MPC
Manual Proportional [*Attitude control system of Mercury spacecraft*] .... MP
Manual Propositional Control System (AAG) .... MPCS
Manual Pulser .... MP
Manual RADAR Reconnaissance Exploitation (MCD) .... MARRE
Manual RADAR Reconnaissance Exploitation System [*Air Force*] .... MARRES
Manual Removal [*Medicine*] .... MR
Manual Reporting Post (NATG) .... MRP
Manual Ringdown [*Telecommunications*] (TEL) .... MRD
Manual Safety Switch .... MSS
Manual Select Keyboard [*Computer science*] (KSC) .... MSK
Manual Sequential (NRCH) .... MS

Manual SHORAD [*Short Range Air Defense*] **Control System** (RDA) ... MSCS
Manual SHORAD [*Short Range Air Defense*] **Control System** [*Army*] ... MSD
Manual Slave Direction Center [*RADAR site*] ... MSDC
Manual Sliding Roof [*Automotive accessory*] ... MSR
Manual Supplement ... MS
Manual Sustainer Cutoff [*NASA*] (KSC) ... MSCO
Manual Switching Position (IAA) ... MSP
Manual System (DCTA) ... MS
Manual System Training Program (SAA) ... MSTP
Manual Target Acquisition (MCD) ... MTA
Manual Templating Model (MCD) ... MATEM
Manual Terrain Avoidance RADAR ... MTAR
Manual Test ... MT
Manual Testing System [*Sports medicine*] ... MTS
Manual Track While Scan ... MTWS
Manual Traffic Control (MCD) ... MTC
Manual Transaxle ... MTX
Manual Transmission [*Automotive engineering*] ... M/T
Manual Transmission [*Automotive engineering*] ... M/TRANS
Manual Trim in Motion [*Aviation*] ... MTIM
Manual Troubleshooting Procedures [*Army*] ... MTP
Manual Unit Test Set ... MUTS
Manual Update Service (NITA) ... MUS
Manual Valve (MCD) ... MV
Manual Versus Automatic Transmission Study (MCD) ... MATS
Manual Visas for Overseas System [*Australia*] ... MANVOS
Manual Volume Control ... MVC
Manual Wire Wrap ... MWW
Manual Wire Wrap Fixture ... MWWF
Manual Word ... MW
Manual-Automatic Multipoint Apparatus (MCD) ... MAMA
Manually Aided Tracking Enhancement (MCD) ... MATE
Manually Entered Identification Library (CAAL) ... MEIDL
Manually Operated ... MO
Manually Operated Plotting Board ... MOPB
Manually Operated Plotting Board (AD) ... mopb
Manually Operated Visual Landing Aid System (NG) ... MOVLAS
Manually Variable Phase Shifter ... MVPS
Manually-Assisted Universal Deviator ... MAUD
Manually-Operated Changeover [*Computer science*] ... MOX
Manually-Operated Lift Truck (DWSG) ... MOLT
Manual-Off-Automatic (KSC) ... MOA
Manuals of Elementary Science [*A publication*] ... MES
Manuals of Engineering Practice [*ASCE*] ... MEP
Manuel Antonio Noriega [*Military commander and de facto ruler of Panama*] ... MAN
Manufactory (ABBR) ... MFRY
Manufactory (ABBR) ... MFY
Manufacture ... MAN
Manufacture (DAVI) ... manu
Manufacture (WGA) ... MF
Manufacture [*or Manufacturer*] (AFM) ... MFR
Manufacture (DD) ... mfr
Manufacture ... MFR
Manufacture (ADA) ... MFRE
Manufacture Procedure Manual (KSC) ... MPM
Manufactured ... MANFRD
Manufactured (ROG) ... MANUFD
Manufactured ... MFD
Manufactured (ABBR) ... MFRD
Manufactured Buildings Association [*Defunct*] (EA) ... MBA
Manufactured Gas Plant [*Environmental biotechnology*] ... MGP
Manufactured Home Communities [*NYSE symbol*] (SPSG) ... MHC
Manufactured Home Communities, Inc. [*Associated Press*] (SAG) ... ManufHm
Manufactured Home Estates ... MHE
Manufactured Housing Institute (EA) ... MHI
Manufactured Housing Task Force [*Defunct*] (EA) ... MHTF
Manufacturer (WDAA) ... MAN
Manufacturer (WGA) ... MANF
Manufacturer ... MANFR
Manufacturer [*or Manufacturing*] (ROG) ... MANUF
Manufacturer ... MFGR
Manufacturer (ABBR) ... MFRR
Manufacturer Standard Paint Color [*Motor vehicle specification*] ... MSPC
Manufacturers' Agents Association of Great Britain and Ireland (BI) ... MAA
Manufacturers Agents National Association (EA) ... MANA
Manufacturers Aircraft Association [*Supersedes AMA*] [*Defunct*] (EA) ... MAA
Manufacturers Alliance for Productivity and Innovation (EA) ... MAPI
Manufacturers and Contractors ... M & C
Manufacturers Assistance in Verifying, Identification in Cataloging ... MAVERICK
Manufacturers' Assistance Program [*Michigan State Department of Commerce*] [*Lansing, MI*] [*Information service or system*] (IID) ... MAP
Manufacturers Association of Robes, Leisurewear, Shirts, and Rainwear [*Defunct*] (EA) ... MARLSR
Manufacturers' Consumer Advertising ... MCA
Manufacturers Council on Color and Appearance [*Defunct*] (EA) ... MCCA
Manufacturers Delegated Testing (NITA) ... MDT
Manufacturer's Designated Fuel [*Automotive engineering*] ... MDF
Manufacturers Educational Drug Information Association ... MEDIA
Manufacturer's Excise Tax ... MET
Manufacturers Hanover Trust Co. [*of Manufacturers Hanover Corp.*] [*Nickname: "Manny Hanny"*] ... MHT
Manufacturers Item Correlation Key ... MICK
Manufacturers' Junction Railway Co. [*AAR code*] ... MJ
Manufacturers Life Capital Corp., Inc. [*Toronto Stock Exchange symbol*] ... MLC
Manufacturers' Monthly [*A publication*] ... Mfurers Mon
Manufacturer's Name (NITA) ... MN
Manufacturers Number ... MFRN
Manufacturers of Aerial Devices and Digger-Derricks Council (EA) ... MADDDC
Manufacturers of Domestic Unvented Supply Systems Equipment [*British*] (DBA) ... MODUSSE
Manufacturers of Emission Controls Association (EA) ... MECA
Manufacturers of Illumination Products (EA) ... MIP
Manufacturers of Telescoping and Articulating Cranes Council (EA) ... MOTACC
Manufacturers Operations Division [*Environmental Protection Agency*] (GFGA) ... MOD
Manufacturer's Output ... MO
Manufacturers Output Policy [*Insurance*] ... MOP
Manufacturers Part Number (MCD) ... MPN
Manufacturer's Productivity Network [*Hewlett-Packard Co.*] ... MPN
Manufacturers Radio Frequency Advisory Committee (EA) ... MRFAC
Manufacturers Railway Co. [*AAR code*] ... MRS
Manufacturer's Recommended Price (ODBW) ... MRP
Manufacturer's Representative ... MR
Manufacturers Representatives Educational Research Foundation [*Rolling Meadows, IL*] (EA) ... MRERF
Manufacturers Representatives of America (EA) ... MRA
Manufacturers Standard Gauge ... MSG
Manufacturers Standardization Society (AAGC) ... MSS
Manufacturers Standardization Society of the Valve and Fittings Industry (EA) ... MSS
Manufacturers Standardization Society of the Valve and Fittings Industry (EA) ... MSSVFI
Manufacturer's Statement of Origin ... MSO
Manufacturer's Statement of Origin [*Automobile sales*] ... MSO
Manufacturer's Suggested Retail Price ... MSRP
Manufacturers Surgical Trade Association [*Later, HIMA*] (EA) ... MSTA
Manufacturer's Weight Empty (DA) ... MWE
Manufacturer's Working Cell Bank [*Cell line*] ... MWCB
Manufactures ... MFS
Manufactures Empty Weight (MCD) ... MEW
Manufacturing (ROG) ... MANFG
Manufacturing ... MANFRG
Manufacturing (ADA) ... MANUFG
Manufacturing (AFM) ... MFG
Manufacturing (DD) ... mfg
Manufacturing ... MFG
Manufacturing ... MFRG
Manufacturing ... MG
Manufacturing, Accounting and Product Information Central System (NITA) ... MAPICS
Manufacturing, Accounting, and Production Information Control System [*IBM Corp.*] ... MAPICS
Manufacturing Action Request (MCD) ... MAR
Manufacturing Activity Projection ... MAP
Manufacturing Advisory Service (DCTA) ... MAS
Manufacturing Aids Program Requirements (AAG) ... MAPR
Manufacturing Analysis of Engineering Change (MCD) ... MAEC
Manufacturing and Automated Design Engineering ... MADE
Manufacturing and Consulting Services (PCM) ... MCS
Manufacturing and Cost Control System (IAA) ... MACCS
Manufacturing and Distribution Control System ... MDCS
Manufacturing and Engineering Assembly Parts List [*File*] ... MEAPL
Manufacturing and Engineering Support (IAA) ... MAES
Manufacturing and Inspection Record (KSC) ... M & IR
Manufacturing and Inspection Record (KSC) ... MAIR
Manufacturing and Inspection Record ... MAIR
Manufacturing and Management [*A publication*] ... Manufacturing Mgmt
Manufacturing and Resource Planning System [*Cincom Systems Ltd.*] [*Software package*] (NCC) ... MRPS
Manufacturing and Technology Laboratory ... MTL
Manufacturing and Testing Process (KSC) ... M & TP
Manufacturing Assembly ... MA
Manufacturing Assembly and Test (MCD) ... MA & T
Manufacturing Assembly Drawing ... MAD
Manufacturing Assembly Parts List ... MAPL
Manufacturing Assembly Report (IAA) ... MAR
Manufacturing Assembly Specification ... MAS
Manufacturing Automation Protocol [*Data communications standards*] ... MAP
Manufacturing Automation Protocol/One [*Local area network*] [*Industrial Networking, Inc.*] ... MAP/One
Manufacturing Automation Protocol / Technical Office Protocol (BTTJ) ... MAP/TOP
Manufacturing, Build, and Flow Plan (NASA) ... MBFP
Manufacturing Change (IAA) ... MC
Manufacturing Change Analysis (MCD) ... MCA
Manufacturing Change Notice ... MCN
Manufacturing Change Point ... MCP
Manufacturing Change Request ... MCR
Manufacturing Chemists Association [*Later, CMA*] (EA) ... MCA
Manufacturing Confectioners' Commercial Travellers Association [*British*] (BI) ... MCCTA
Manufacturing Construction Document (SAA) ... MCD
Manufacturing Control Language [*Computer science*] (MCD) ... MCL
Manufacturing Control Number ... MCN
Manufacturing Control System ... MCS
Manufacturing Controls and Requirements ... MC & R
Manufacturing Cost Collection System ... MACCS
Manufacturing Cost Control Program [*DoD*] ... MCCP
Manufacturing Council of Victoria [*Australia*] ... MCV

Manufacturing Cycle Effectiveness	MCE
Manufacturing Data Retrieval System (NASA)	MADRE
Manufacturing Data Retrieval System	MADRE
Manufacturing Data Retrieval System	MDRS
Manufacturing Data Retrieval System (NASA)	MDRS
Manufacturing Data Systems Inc. (NITA)	MDSI
Manufacturing Day Number (MCD)	MDN
Manufacturing Defect Analyzer [Automotive engineering]	MDA
Manufacturing Department Change Analysis Commitment (SAA)	MDCAC
Manufacturing Design Change Analysis	MDCA
Manufacturing Development and Process Request (AAG)	MDPR
Manufacturing Electron Beam Exposure System (IAA)	MEBES
Manufacturing Energy Consumption Survey [Department of Energy] (GFGA)	MECS
Manufacturing Engineering (MCD)	ME
Manufacturing Engineering Analysis	MEA
Manufacturing Engineering and Cost Control Applications (NITA)	MECCA
Manufacturing Engineering Applications Center [Worchester Polytechnic Institute] [Research center] (RCD)	MEAC
Manufacturing Engineering Council (EA)	MEC
Manufacturing Engineering Document (SAA)	MED
Manufacturing Engineering Education Foundation	MEEF
Manufacturing Engineering Management Operations System (MCD)	MEMOS
Manufacturing Engineering Plan	MEP
Manufacturing Engineering Work Order (MCD)	MEWO
Manufacturing Evaluation Board (MCD)	MEB
Manufacturing Extension Partnership [National Institute for Science and Technology]	MEP
Manufacturing Fit Test	MFT
Manufacturing Flow and Building Plan (NASA)	MFBP
Manufacturing Impact Item (MCD)	MII
Manufacturing in Space	MS
Manufacturing Index (MCD)	MI
Manufacturing Industries [Department of Employment] [British]	MI
Manufacturing Industries Advisory Council (NADA)	MIAC
Manufacturing Industry Products Division (MCD)	MIPD
Manufacturing Information and Control System	MIACS
Manufacturing Information and Control System (OA)	MICS
Manufacturing Information Memorandum	MIM
Manufacturing Information System [Computer science] (BUR)	MIS
Manufacturing Information System Support Integrated Online [Computer science] (MHDI)	MISSION
Manufacturing Inspector (FAAC)	MI
Manufacturing Instruction (MSA)	MI
Manufacturing Jewelers and Silversmiths of America (EA)	MJSA
Manufacturing Jewelers Golf Association (EA)	MJGA
Manufacturing Jewelers Sales Association	MJSA
[A] Manufacturing Language [Computer science]	AML
Manufacturing Lead Time	MLT
Manufacturing License (NRCH)	ML
Manufacturing License Agreement	MLA
Manufacturing Load Boards (MCD)	MLB
Manufacturing Management (PDAA)	MANMAM
Manufacturing Management (MHDI)	MANMAN
Manufacturing Management	MM
Manufacturing Management Accounting System (PDAA)	MMAS
Manufacturing Management Accounting Systems (MHDI)	MMAS
Manufacturing Manual (AAG)	MM
Manufacturing Material Planning System (MHDB)	MMPS
Manufacturing Message Format Service (NITA)	MMFS
Manufacturing Message Format System	MMPS
Manufacturing Message Interface [Data communications standards]	MMI
Manufacturing Message [or Messaging] Specification [or Standard] [Computer science]	MMS
Manufacturing Messaging Format Standards [Automotive engineering]	MMFS
Manufacturing Methods and Technology [Program] [Army Materiel Command] (RDA)	MM & T
Manufacturing Methods Committee	MMC
Manufacturing Methods Procedure (MCD)	MMP
Manufacturing Methods Technology (AAGC)	MMT
Manufacturing Monitoring System [Computer science] (IBMDP)	MMS
Manufacturing Operating System [IBM Corp.]	MOS
Manufacturing Operation and Tooling	MOT
Manufacturing Operation Record (NASA)	MOR
Manufacturing Operation Record	MOR
Manufacturing Operations Development and Integration Laboratory	MODIL
Manufacturing Operations Short Event Scheduling	MOSES
Manufacturing Operations Survey (MCD)	MOS
Manufacturing or Testing Process (KSC)	MOTP
Manufacturing Order (NASA)	MO
Manufacturing Other Charges (AD)	moc
Manufacturing Outline	MO
Manufacturing Outreach Center	MOC
Manufacturing Parts List (AAG)	MPL
Manufacturing Parts Record (KSC)	MPR
Manufacturing Plan Change	MPC
Manufacturing Plan Control Board (AD)	MPCB
Manufacturing, Planning, and Control [Arthur Anderson & Co.] [Software package] (NCC)	MAC-PAC
Manufacturing, Planning, and Control	MPC
Manufacturing Planning and Control System (PDAA)	MANUPACS
Manufacturing Planning Change Coordination (MCD)	MPCC
Manufacturing Planning Review (MCD)	MPR
Manufacturing Process	MP
Manufacturing Process Control Document (KSC)	MPCD

Manufacturing Process Instructions	MPI
Manufacturing Process Specification (AAG)	MPS
Manufacturing Production Order (NRCH)	MPO
Manufacturing Quality Assurance	MQA
Manufacturing Quality Control (MCD)	MQC
Manufacturing Reference Line	MRL
Manufacturing Requirements Planning [Purchasing computer program] (PCM)	MRP
Manufacturing Requisition	MR
Manufacturing Research and Design Group [McMaster University] [Canada Research center] (RCD)	MRDG
Manufacturing Research Corp. of Ontario [Research center Canada] (RCD)	MRCO
Manufacturing Research Laboratory	MRL
Manufacturing Resource Control [Kongsberg Vaapenfabrikk] [Software package] (NCC)	MRC
Manufacturing Resource Control System [Deritend Computer Bureau Ltd.] [Software package] (NCC)	MARC
Manufacturing Resource Planning [Computer science]	MRP
Manufacturing Rework Order	MRO
Manufacturing Run-In	MRI
Manufacturing Science Finance [A union] [British]	MSF
Manufacturing Sequence Outline (MCD)	MSO
Manufacturing Service Request (MCD)	MSR
Manufacturing Shop Manual (SAA)	MSM
Manufacturing Specification (AAG)	MS
Manufacturing Specification Request (AAG)	MSR
Manufacturing Standard	MS
Manufacturing Standards and Specifications for Textbooks	MSST
Manufacturing Standards Manual	MSM
Manufacturing Status (AAG)	MS
Manufacturing Support	MS
[The] Manufacturing System [Burroughs Machines Ltd.] [Software package] (NCC)	TMS
Manufacturing Systems and Technology Center [Baltimore, MD] [Westinghouse Electric Corp.]	MSTC
Manufacturing Systems Engineering	MSE
Manufacturing Technical Order (SAA)	MTO
Manufacturing Technical Procedure [NASA] (NASA)	MTP
Manufacturing Technology	MANTECH
Manufacturing Technology (RDA)	MT
Manufacturing Technology Advisory Group [DoD] (RDA)	MTAG
Manufacturing Technology Center	MTC
Manufacturing Technology Centre of New Brunswick [Research center] (RCD)	MTC
Manufacturing Technology Development (RDA)	MTD
Manufacturing Technology Directorate [Army] (RDA)	MTD
Manufacturing Technology Division [Air Force]	MTD
Manufacturing Technology Facility [US Army Communications-Electronics Command] [Fort Monmouth, NJ] (RDA)	MTF
Manufacturing Technology Information Analysis Center [DoD Information service or system] (IID)	MTIAC
Manufacturing Technology Program [Aviation Systems Command] (RDA)	MTP
Manufacturing Technology Projects [Manufacturing Technology Information Analysis Center] [Information service or system] (CRD)	MTP
Manufacturing Technology Section [Navy]	MTS
Manufacturing Test Data System (IEEE)	MTDS
Manufacturing Test Procedure	MTP
Manufacturing under Licence [British] (DS)	MUL
Manufacturing USA [A publication]	MUSA
Manufacturing Value Added	MVA
Manufacturing Verification (NASA)	MV
Manufacturing Week (MCD)	MW
Manufacturing Work Authority	MWA
Manufacturing Work Order	MWO
Manufacturing Zone (MHDB)	M-ZONE
Manufaturing Execution System [Engineering]	MES
Manugistics Group [NASDAQ symbol] (TTSB)	MANU
Manugistics Group, Inc. [NASDAQ symbol] (SAG)	MANU
Manugistics Group, Inc. [Associated Press] (SAG)	Manugist
Manumission Cases in New Jersey, by Bloomfield [A publication] (DLA)	Man Cas
Manumu [Papua New Guinea] [Airport symbol] (OAG)	UUU
Manure (ROG)	MA
Manus [Papua New Guinea] [Airport symbol] (OAG)	MAS
Manus Island [Bismarck Archipelago] [Airport symbol] (AD)	MAS
Manuscript (VRA)	ms
Manuscript (WDAA)	MS
Manuscript (WDMC)	ms
Manuscript Decisions [Comptroller General] [United States] [A publication] (DLA)	MsD
Manuscript Division, Public Archives [Division des Manuscrits, Archives Publiques] Ottawa, Ontario [Library symbol National Library of Canada] (NLC)	OOAMS
Manuscript, Inner Temple [A publication] (DLA)	Ms IT
Manuscript, Lincoln's Inn [A publication] (DLA)	Ms LI
Manuscript, Middle Temple [A publication] (DLA)	MS MT
Manuscript of Deuteronomy 32 from Qumran. Cave 4 (BJA)	4QDeut32
Manuscript on Paper	MOP
Manuscript on Vellum	MOV
Manuscript Reports [A publication] (DLA)	MS
Manuscript, Signed	MSS
Manuscript Society (EA)	MS
Manuscripta [Manuscripts] [Latin]	MSS
Manuscripts, Signed	MSSS

Manuscriptum [*Manuscript*] [*Latin*] ... MS
Man-Vehicle Laboratory [*Massachusetts Institute of Technology*] [*Research center*] (RCD) ... MVL
Manville Corp. [*Associated Press*] (SAG) ... Manvl
Manville Corp. [*Associated Press*] (SAG) ... Manvlle
Manville Corp. [*NYSE symbol*] (CTT) ... MVL
Man-Week (NASA) ... MW
Manwood's Forest Laws [*1592, 1598, 1615*] [*A publication*] (DLA) ... Manw
Manwood's Forest Laws [*1592, 1598, 1615*] [*A publication*] (DLA) ... Manw For Law
Manwood's Forest Laws [*1592, 1598, 1615*] [*A publication*] (DLA) ... Manwood
Man-Worn LASER Device [*Army*] ... MWLD
Man-Worn Receiver (MCD) ... MWR
Manx [*MARC language code Library of Congress*] (LCCP) ... max
Manx Airlines [*Airline flight code*] (ODBW) ... JE
Manx Airlines (Europe) Ltd. [*British ICAO designator*] (FAAC) ... MXE
Manx Airlines Ltd. ... MA
Manx Airlines Ltd. ... MN
Manx Airlines Ltd. [*British ICAO designator*] (FAAC) ... MNX
Manx Gaelic (AD) ... Mnx
Manx National Farmers Union [*British*] (DBA) ... MNFU
Many, LA [*AM radio station call letters*] ... KWLA
Many, LA [*FM radio station call letters*] ... KWLV
Many, LA [*Location identifier FAA*] (FAAL) ... MMY
Many Worlds Interpretation [*Term coined by authors John Barrow and Frank Tipler in their book, "The Anthropic Cosmological Principle"*] ... MWI
Many-Body Alloy [*Metallurgy*] ... MBA
Many-Body Perturbation Theory [*Physics*] ... MBPT
Many-Body Theory [*Physics*] (BARN) ... MBT
Man-Year (AFM) ... MY
Man-Year-Space [*Army*] (AABC) ... MYS
Many-Element LASER ... MEL
Manzanillo [*Mexico ICAO location identifier*] (ICLI) ... MMZO
Manzanillo [*Mexico*] [*Seismograph station code, US Geological Survey*] (SEIS) ... MNZ
Manzanillo (AD) ... Mnzlo
Manzanillo [*Cuba ICAO location identifier*] (ICLI) ... MUMI
Manzanillo [*Cuba ICAO location identifier*] (ICLI) ... MUMZ
Manzanillo [*Cuba*] [*Airport symbol*] (OAG) ... MZO
Manzanillo [*Mexico*] [*Airport symbol*] (OAG) ... ZLO
Manzanita Lake [*California*] [*Seismograph station code, US Geological Survey*] (SEIS) ... MLC
Manzanola Public Library, Manzanola, CO [*Library symbol Library of Congress*] (LCLS) ... CoManz
Manzini [*Swaziland*] [*Airport symbol*] (OAG) ... MTS
Manzini/Matsapa [*Swaziland*] [*ICAO location identifier*] (ICLI) ... FDMS
Mao [*Chad*] [*Airport symbol*] (AD) ... AMO
Mao [*Chad*] [*ICAO location identifier*] (ICLI) ... FTTU
Maof Airlines [*Israel*] [*ICAO designator*] (ICDA) ... MG
Maoist Reorganization Movement of the Party of the Proletariat [*Political party*] (AD) ... MRPP
Maoist Revolutionary Communist Party [*Political party*] (AD) ... MRCP
Maoist Revolutionary Communist Party (NADA) ... MRCP
Maori [*MARC language code Library of Congress*] (LCCP) ... mao
Maota [*Western Samoa*] [*ICAO location identifier*] (ICLI) ... NSMA
Map ... M
Map Analysis ... MA
Map Analysis System [*Computer science*] ... MANS
Map and Air Photo Library, McGill University, Montreal, Quebec [*Library symbol National Library of Canada*] (NLC) ... QMMG
Map and Atlas Collection, University of Manitoba, Winnipeg, Manitoba [*Library symbol National Library of Canada*] (NLC) ... MWUM
Map and Chart Information System (MHDB) ... MCIS
Map and Data Viewer [*NASA*] (KSC) ... M & DV
Map and Data Viewer [*NASA*] (KSC) ... MDV
Map and Geography Round Table [*American Library Association*] ... MAGERT
Map and Visual Display ... MVD
Map Collection, Douglas Library, Queen's University, Kingston, Ontario [*Library symbol National Library of Canada*] (NLC) ... OKQMA
Map Collectors' Circle [*Defunct*] (EA) ... MCC
Map Distance (ADA) ... MD
Map Division, University of British Columbia, Vancouver, British Columbia [*Library symbol National Library of Canada*] (NLC) ... BVAUM
Map Editing Console ... MEC
Map Exercise [*Military*] (INF) ... MAPEX
Map Exercise Computer Assistance (MCD) ... MECA
Map Generator (MHDI) ... MAPGEN
Map Information Assembly and Display System ... MIADS
Map Information Office [*US Geological Survey*] ... MIO
MAP [*Medical Assistance Programs*] **International** (EA) ... MAP
MAP International, Brunswick, GA [*Library symbol*] [*Library of Congress*] (LCLS) ... GBruM
MAP International, Wheaton, IL [*OCLC symbol*] (OCLC) ... IPT
MAP International, Wheaton, IL [*Library symbol Library of Congress*] (LCLS) ... IWM
Map Library, Dalhousie University, Halifax, Nova Scotia [*Library symbol National Library of Canada*] (NLC) ... NSHDMA
Map Library, Energy, Mines and Resources Canada [*Cartotheque, Energie, Mines et Ressources Canada*] **Ottawa, Ontario** [*Library symbol National Library of Canada*] (NLC) ... OOSMM
Map Library, McMaster University, Hamilton, Ontario [*Library symbol National Library of Canada*] (NLC) ... OHMM
Map Library, Simon Fraser University, Burnaby, British Columbia [*Library symbol National Library of Canada*] (NLC) ... BVASM
Map Library, Trent University, Peterborough, Ontario [*Library symbol National Library of Canada*] (NLC) ... OPETM
Map Library, University of Calgary, Alberta [*Library symbol National Library of Canada*] (NLC) ... ACUMA
Map Library, University of Ottawa [*Cartotheque, Universite d'Ottawa*] **Ontario** [*Library symbol National Library of Canada*] (NLC) ... OOUMA
Map Library, University of Toronto, Ontario [*Library symbol National Library of Canada*] (NLC) ... OTUMA
Map Maneuver Exercise (MCD) ... MMEX
Map Margin Top Line (SAA) ... MMTLN
MAP [*Manufacturing Automation Protocol*]/One Applications Services [*Software*] [*Automotive engineering*] ... MAS
MAP [*Manufacturing Automation Protocol*]/One System Software [*Industrial Networking, Inc.*] ... MSS
Map Online Users Group (EA) ... MOUG
Map Pictorial Display ... MPD
Map Reading (AD) ... M/R
Map Reading (AD) ... m/r
Map Reading ... MR
Map Reference ... MR
Map Reference (AD) ... mr
Map Room, Government Documents Department, University of New Brunswick, Fredericton, New Brunswick [*Library symbol National Library of Canada*] (NLC) ... NBFUM
Map Unit (DOG) ... mu
MAPCO, Inc. [*Associated Press*] (SAG) ... MAPCO
MAPCO, Inc. [*NYSE symbol*] (SPSG) ... MDA
Mapinfo Corp. [*Associated Press*] (SAG) ... MapInfo
Mapinfo Corp. [*NASDAQ symbol*] (SAG) ... MAPS
Mapiri [*Bolivia*] [*ICAO location identifier*] (ICLI) ... SLMP
Maple (DAC) ... mpl
Maple ... MPL
Maple Air Services Ltd. [*Canada ICAO designator*] (FAAC) ... MAD
Maple Flooring Manufacturers Association (EA) ... MFMA
Maple Lake Elementary School, Maple Lake, MN [*Library symbol*] [*Library of Congress*] (LCLS) ... MNMIE
Maple Lake High, Maple Lake, MN [*Library symbol*] [*Library of Congress*] (LCLS) ... MnMIH
Maple Lane School, Staff Library, Centralia, WA [*Library symbol Library of Congress*] (LCLS) ... WaCeM
Maple Leaf Club (EA) ... MLC
Maple Leaf Foods [*Toronto Stock Exchange symbol*] (SPSG) ... MLF
Maple Leaf Gardens Ltd. [*Toronto Stock Exchange symbol*] ... ML
Maple Rapids Public Library, Maple Rapids, MI [*Library symbol*] [*Library of Congress*] (LCLS) ... MiMaRP
Maple Ridge Museum, British Columbia [*Library symbol National Library of Canada*] (NLC) ... BMRM
Maple Ridge Museum, Maple Ridge, BC, Canada [*Library symbol*] [*Library of Congress*] (LCLS) ... CaBMRM
Maple Shade Progress Press, Maple Shade, NJ [*Library symbol Library of Congress*] (LCLS) ... NjMsP
Maple Shade Public Library, Maple Shade, NJ [*Library symbol Library of Congress*] (LCLS) ... NjMs
Maple Sugar [*or Syrup*] **Urine** [*Medicine*] (DMAA) ... MSU
Maple Sugar [*or Syrup*] **Urine Disease** [*Medicine*] ... MSUD
Maple Syrup Council (EA) ... MSC
Maple Technology Ltd. [*Vancouver Stock Exchange symbol*] ... MPL
Maple Valley Explorations Ltd. [*Vancouver Stock Exchange symbol*] ... MVE
Maple Woods Community College, Kansas City, MO [*Library symbol Library of Congress*] (LCLS) ... MoKMW
Maples, MO [*Location identifier FAA*] (FAAL) ... MAP
Mapleton, IA [*Location identifier FAA*] (FAAL) ... MEY
Mapleton Press, Mapleton, IA [*Library symbol Library of Congress*] (LCLS) ... IaMapP
Mapleton Public Library, Mapleton, IA [*Library symbol Library of Congress*] (LCLS) ... IaMap
Maplewood Elementary School, Huntington Station, NY [*Library symbol*] [*Library of Congress*] (LCLS) ... NHsME
Maplewood Memorial Library, Maplewood, NJ [*Library symbol Library of Congress*] (LCLS) ... NjMap
Maplewood, MN [*AM radio station call letters*] ... WCTS
Maplex Management & Holdings Ltd. [*Toronto Stock Exchange symbol*] ... MMH
Maplin Telecommunications (NITA) ... MAPTEL
Map-Matching Location - Estimation System [*Aviation*] ... MMLES
Mapped Programming Executive [*Systems Engineering Laboratories U.S.*] (NITA) ... MPX
Mapped Real-Time Disk Operating System [*Computer science*] (MDG) ... MRDOS
Mapper Application Interface [*Computer science*] ... MAI
Mapper Sweep Generator ... MSG
Mapping (MSA) ... MAP
Mapping and Charting Establishment, Department of National Defence [*Service de la Cartographie, Ministere de la Defense Nationale*] **Ottawa, Ontario** [*Library symbol National Library of Canada*] (NLC) ... OONDMC
Mapping and Charting Research Laboratory [*Ohio State University*] (MCD) ... MCRL
Mapping and Charting Squadron [*Air Force*] ... M & CSq
Mapping and Geodesy [*Army*] (AABC) ... M & G
Mapping and Reconnaissance Ku-Band Airborne RADAR ... MARKAR
Mapping and Survey System (KSC) ... M & SS
Mapping Camera ... MC
Mapping Camera System ... MCS
Mapping, Charting, and Geodesy [*Air Force*] (AFM) ... MC & G
Mapping, Charting, and Geodesy [*Activity*] (MCD) ... MCAG
Mapping, Charting, and Geodesy/Military Geography Information [*DoD*] ... MC & G/MGI
Mapping, Charting, and Geodesy/Military Geography Information [*DoD*] (MCD) ... MCAG/MGI

Mapping Cylinder Neighborhood .... MCN
Mapping Field (ACRL) .... MPF
Mapping of Disease .... MOD
Mapping Supervisor Gap Filler (SAA) .... MSG
Maps and Charts [Interservice] [NATO] .... MC
Mapua [Papua New Guinea] [Airport symbol Obsolete] (OAG) .... MPU
Maputo [Mozambique] [ICAO location identifier] (ICLI) .... FQMA
Maputo [Mozambique] [Airport symbol] .... LUM
Maputo [Mozambique] [Airport symbol] (OAG) .... MPM
Maputo [Mozambique] [Geomagnetic observatory code] .... MPO
Maquela [Angola] [ICAO location identifier] (ICLI) .... FNMQ
Maquette (VRA) .... maq
Maquinchao [Argentina ICAO location identifier] (ICLI) .... SAVQ
Maquoketa Community Press, Maquoketa, IA [Library symbol Library of Congress] (LCLS) .... IaMaqP
Maquoketa Free Public Library, Maquoketa, IA [Library symbol Library of Congress] (LCLS) .... IaMaq
Maquoketa, IA [FM radio station call letters] .... KMAQ-FM
Maquoketa, IA [Location identifier FAA] (FAAL) .... OQW
Mar Del Plata [Argentina] [Airport symbol] (OAG) .... MDQ
Mar Del Plata [Argentina ICAO location identifier] (ICLI) .... SAZM
Mara Lodges [Kenya] [Airport symbol] (OAG) .... MRE
Mara Township Public Library, Orillia, Ontario [Library symbol National Library of Canada] (BIB) .... OORIMT
Maraba [Brazil] [Airport symbol] (OAG) .... MAB
Maraba [Brazil ICAO location identifier] (ICLI) .... SBMA
Maraba/Carajas [Brazil ICAO location identifier] (ICLI) .... SBCJ
Maracaibo [Venezuela] [Airport symbol] (OAG) .... MAR
Maracaibo/La Chinita Internacional, Zulia [Venezuela ICAO location identifier] (ICLI) .... SVMC
Maracay [Venezuela] [Airport symbol] (OAG) .... MYC
Maracay/Centro Nacional de Comunicaciones/Meteorologicos, Aragua [Venezuela ICAO location identifier] (ICLI) .... SVMR
Maracay/El Libertador, Base Aerea Aragua [Venezuela ICAO location identifier] (ICLI) .... SVBL
Maracay/Mariscal Sucre, Base Aerea Aragua [Venezuela ICAO location identifier] (ICLI) .... SVBS
Maradi [Niger] [ICAO location identifier] (ICLI) .... DRRM
Maradi [Niger] [Airport symbol] (OAG) .... MFQ
Maragheh [Iran] [ICAO location identifier] (ICLI) .... OITM
Marakei [Kiribati] [Airport symbol] (OAG) .... MZK
Marakei [Kiribati] [ICAO location identifier] (ICLI) .... NGMK
Marala [Congo] [ICAO location identifier] (ICLI) .... FCMR
Maralal [Kenya] [ICAO location identifier] (ICLI) .... HKMI
Marampa [Sierra Leone] [ICAO location identifier] (ICLI) .... GFMP
Marana, AZ [FM radio station call letters] .... KOHT
Marana, AZ [Location identifier FAA] (FAAL) .... MZJ
Maranatha Gospel Bottle Crusade [Later, CEM] (EA) .... MGBC
Marand [Iran] [ICAO location identifier] (ICLI) .... OITD
Maraschino Cherry and Glace Fruit Processors (EA) .... MCGFP
Marathi [MARC language code Library of Congress] (LCCP) .... mar
Marathon [Greece] [ICAO location identifier] (ICLI) .... LGMR
Marathon .... MRTHN
Marathon [Florida] [Airport symbol] (OAG) .... MTH
Marathon Boat Racers Association .... MBRA
Marathon County Public Library, Wausau, WI [OCLC symbol] (OCLC) .... WIW
Marathon, FL [FM radio station call letters] .... WAVK
Marathon, FL [AM radio station call letters] .... WFFG
Marathon, FL [FM radio station call letters] .... WGMX
Marathon, FL [FM radio station call letters] (RBYB) .... WKTS
Marathon Health Care Center, Wausau, WI [Library symbol Library of Congress] (LCLS) .... WWsMC
Marathon Minerals [Vancouver Stock Exchange symbol] .... MMN
Marathon Oil Co., Technical Information Section, Littleton, CO [Library symbol Library of Congress] (LCLS) .... CoLiM
Marathon, ON [Television station call letters] CBLAT-4
Marathon, ON [FM radio station call letters] .... CFNO
Marathon Public Library, Marathon, IA [Library symbol Library of Congress] (LCLS) .... IaMara
Marathon Public Library, Ontario [Library symbol National Library of Canada] (NLC) .... OMAR
Marathon, TX [Location identifier FAA] (FAAL) .... IMP
Marathon, WI [FM radio station call letters] (RBYB) .... WKQH
Marau [Solomon Islands] [Airport symbol] (OAG) .... RUS
Marble (VRA) .... marb
Marble (AAG) .... MR
Marble [Technical drawings] .... MRB
Marble .... MRBL
Marble and Granite Association [British] (BI) .... MGA
Marble Bar [Australia Airport symbol] (OAG) .... MBB
Marble Bar [Australia Seismograph station code, US Geological Survey] (SEIS) .... MBL
Marble Bar - Town [Australia Seismograph station code, US Geological Survey Closed] (SEIS) .... MBT
Marble Base (AAG) .... MRB
Marble Base (AD) .... mrb
Marble Collectors Society of America (EA) .... MCSA
Marble Collectors Unlimited (EA) .... MCU
Marble Falls, TX [Location identifier FAA] (FAAL) .... MFS
Marble Financial Corp. [Associated Press] (SAG) .... MarbFn
Marble Financial Corp. [NASDAQ symbol] (NQ) .... MRBL
Marble Floor (AAG) .... MRF
Marble Floor (AD) .... mrf
Marble Hall [South Africa] [ICAO location identifier] (ICLI) .... FAMI
Marble Hill Nuclear Generating Station (NRCH) .... MHNGS

Marble Hill Nuclear Power Station (NRCH) .... MHNPS
Marble Institute of America (EA) .... MIA
Marble Polishers' Trade Union Society [British] .... MPTUS
Marble Public Library, Marble, MN [Library symbol] [Library of Congress] (LCLS) .... MnMarb
Marble Rock Public Library, Marble Rock, IA [Library symbol Library of Congress] (LCLS) .... IaMbr
Marble Threshold (AAG) .... MRT
Marble Workers' Trade Union [British] .... MWTU
Marbled [Edges or sides of cover] [Bookbinding] (ROG) .... MARB
Marbled Edges [Bookbinding] .... ME
Marbled Paper (DGA) .... MP
Marbled Paper Sides [Bookbinding] .... MPS
Marbled Paper Sides (AD) .... mps
Marblehead Historical Society, Marblehead, MA [Library symbol Library of Congress] (LCLS) .... MMhHi
Marble-in-the-Hole [Game used in psychometrics] .... MITH
Marburger Theologische Studien (BJA) .... MbThSt
Marburg-Schoenstadt [Germany ICAO location identifier] (ICLI) .... EDFN
MARC [Machine-Readable Cataloging] Automated Serials System (PDAA) .... MASS
MARC Development Office (NITA) .... MDO
MARC Five (NITA) .... MARCIVE
MARC, Inc. [NASDAQ symbol] (SAG) .... MARC
MARC [Machine-Readable Cataloging] International Format .... MIF
MARC Israel (NITA) .... MARC IS
MARC Library of Congress (NITA) .... MARC(LC)
MARC [Machine-Readable Cataloging] Quebecois [Source file] [UTLAS symbol] .... MQ
MARC [Machine-Readable Cataloging] Record Management System .... MRMS
MARC [Machine-Readable Cataloging] Records Distribution Service [National Library of Canada] (IID) .... MRDS
MARC Serials (NITA) .... MARC(S)
MARC (United Kingdom) (NITA) .... MARC(UK)
MARC Users Group (NITA) .... MUG
MARC Video Disc Library System (NITA) .... MARVLS
Marca Registrada [Registered Trademark] [Spanish] .... MR
Marcala [Honduras] [ICAO location identifier] (ICLI) .... MHMA
Marcam Corp. [Associated Press] (SAG) .... Marcam
Marcam Corp. [NASDAQ symbol] .... MCAM
Marcana Petroleum Ltd. [Vancouver Stock Exchange symbol] .... MCP
Marcaptan Terminated Polybutadiene (PDAA) .... MTB
Marcato [Emphasized] [Music] .... MARC
MARC-Based Automated Serials System (NITA) .... MASS
Marcella Sembrich Memorial Studio, Bolton Landing, NY [Library symbol] [Library of Congress] (LCLS) .... NBolS
Marcellus [of Plutarch] [Classical studies] (OCD) .... Marc
Marcellus Free Library, Marcellus, NY [Library symbol Library of Congress] (LCLS) .... NMar
Marcellus Township Library, Marcellus, MI [Library symbol Library of Congress] (LCLS) .... MiMarc
March .... M
March .... MA
March (AFM) .... MAR
March .... MCH
March .... MR
March and September [Denotes semiannual payments of interest or dividends in these months] [Business term] .... M & S
March for Life (EA) .... ML
March Helicopters Ltd. [British ICAO designator] (FAAC) .... MAR
March, June, September, and December [Denotes quarterly payments of interest or dividends in these months] [Business term] .... MJSD
March of Dimes Birth Defects Foundation (EA) .... MDBDF
[The] March of Time [Radio and motion picture series] .... MOT
March on Drugs [An association] .... MOD
March Order [Military] .... MO
March Resources [Vancouver Stock Exchange symbol] .... MHL
Marchand [Merchant, Trader] [French] .... MD
March-Bender Factor [Physiology] .... MB
Marche a Terme des Instruments Financiere [French stock exchange] .... MATIF
Marche a Terme des Instruments Financiers [French Financial Futures Market] .... MATIF
Marche de l'Europe [March of Europe] (EAIO) .... ME
Marche des Options Negociables sur Actions [Options exchange] [France] (EY) .... MONA
Marche des Options Negotiables de Paris [French Traded Options Market] (ODBW) .... MONEP
Marche International des Programmes de Television [Cannes Film Festival] [France] .... MIPTV
Marche International des Programmes de Television International [International Marketplace for Buyers and Sellers of Television Programs] (NTCM) .... MIP
Marches (ROG) .... MRS
Marching Bands of America (EA) .... MBA
Marching Pack (DNAB) .... MP
Marchioness .... MARCH
March's Action for Slander and Arbitrament [A publication] (DLA) .... Ma
March's Brooke's New Cases [1651] [England] [A publication] (DLA) .... Mar Br
March's English King's Bench and Common Pleas Reports [A publication] (DLA) .... March
March's English King's Bench Reports [1639-42] [A publication] (DLA) .... March
March's New Cases [1639-42] [A publication] (DLA) .... Mar NR
March's New Cases, English King's Bench [1639-42] [A publication] (DLA) .... Mar NC

March's New Cases, English King's Bench [*1639-42*] [*A publication*] (DLA) ... March NC
March's New Cases, English King's Bench [*1639-42*] [*A publication*] (DLA) ... March NR
March's New Cases, English King's Bench and Common Pleas Reports [*A publication*] (DLA) ... March N
March's Translation of Brooke's New Cases, English King's Bench [*82 English Reprint*] [*A publication*] (DLA) ... March
Marchwood Engineering Laboratories [*Research center British*] (IRUK) ... MEL
Marcive, Inc., San Antonio, TX [*Library symbol*] [*Library of Congress*] (LCLS) ... MvI
Marcive Users Group [*Library network*] ... MUG
Marco, FL [*FM radio station call letters*] ... WAVV
Marco, FL [*FM radio station call letters*] ... WGUF
Marco Island [*Florida*] [*Airport symbol*] (OAG) ... MRK
Marco Island Airways [*ICAO designator*] (AD) ... LS
Marco Island, FL [*Location identifier FAA*] (FAAL) ... MKY
Marco Island, FL [*AM radio station call letters*] ... WODX
Marco Polo Club (EA) ... MPC
Marco Resources [*Vancouver Stock Exchange symbol*] ... MAL
Marconi Advanced Sample Facility (NITA) ... MASF
Marconi Automatic Relay System (IEEE) ... MARS
Marconi Command and Control Systems Ltd. (NITA) ... MCCSL
Marconi Electronic Devices Ltd. [*British*] (IRUK) ... MEDL
Marconi Fast Tuning (MCD) ... MFT
Marconi Industries [*General Electric Co.*] [*British*] ... MI
Marconi Integrated Design and Test Automation [*Marconi Industries*] [*Telecommunications British*] ... MIDATA
Marconi Self-Tuning (IAA) ... MST
Marconi Underwater Systems Ltd. [*British*] ... MUSL
Marconi Wireless Telegraph [*Telecommunications*] (IAA) ... MWT
Marconi-Franklin Antenna ... MFA
Marcos Juarez [*Argentina ICAO location identifier*] (ICLI) ... SAOM
Marcos Owners Club [*Formerly, Marcos Club*] (EA) ... MOC
Marcum Natural Gas Service, Inc. [*NASDAQ symbol*] (SAG) ... MGAS
Marcum Natural Gas Services, Inc. [*Associated Press*] (SAG) ... MarcNG
Marcum Natural Gas Svcs [*NASDAQ symbol*] (TTSB) ... MGAS
Marcus [*of Scriptores Historiae Augustae*] [*Classical studies*] (OCD) ... Marc
Marcus Antoninus [*of Scriptores Historiae Augustae*] [*Classical studies*] (OCD) ... M Ant
Marcus Antonius Blancus [*Deceased, 1548*] [*Authority cited in pre-1607 legal work*] (DSA) ... Marcus An
Marcus Antonius Blancus [*Deceased, 1548*] [*Authority cited in pre-1607 legal work*] (DSA) ... Marcus Anto
[*The*] **Marcus Corp.** [*Associated Press*] (SAG) ... Marcus
[*The*] **Marcus Corp.** [*NYSE symbol*] (SPSG) ... MCS
Marcus Gunn (Pupil) [*Ophthalmology*] ... MG
Marcus Island [*Japan*] [*Seismograph station code, US Geological Survey*] (SEIS) ... MCS
Marcus Mantua Benavidius [*Deceased, 1582*] [*Authority cited in pre-1607 legal work*] (DSA) ... Mar Mant
Marcus Mantua Benavidius [*Deceased, 1582*] [*Authority cited in pre-1607 legal work*] (DSA) ... Marc Mant
Marcus Public Library, Marcus, IA [*Library symbol Library of Congress*] (LCLS) ... IaMarc
Marcus Tullius Cicero [*Roman orator and author, 106-43 BC*] ... MTC
Marcy Psychiatric Center, Marcy, NY [*Library symbol Library of Congress*] (LCLS) ... NMarcP
Marcy's Conveyancing Statutes [*5th ed.*] [*1893*] [*A publication*] (DLA) ... Mar Conv St
Marcy's Epitome of Conveyancing [*1881*] [*A publication*] (DLA) ... Mar Conv
Mardan Test Set ... MTS
Marden-Walker Syndrome [*Medicine*] (DMAA) ... MWS
Mare [*Thoroughbred racing*] ... M
Mare [*Loyalty Islands*] [*Airport symbol*] (OAG) ... MEE
Mare Crisium [*Sea of Crises*] [*Lunar area*] ... MC
Mare Feccunditatis [*Sea of Fertility*] [*Lunar area*] ... MF
Mare Frigoris [*Sea of Cold*] [*Lunar area*] ... MFr
Mare Humorum [*Sea of Moisture*] [*Lunar area*] ... MH
Mare Humorum-Helmet [*Lunar area*] ... MH-H
Mare Imbrium [*Sea of Showers*] [*Lunar area*] ... MI
Mare Island, California [*Site of naval base*] ... MI
Mare Island Division [*San Francisco Bay Naval Shipyard, Vallejo, CA*] ... MID
Mare Island Naval Shipyard [*Also, MINSY*] [*Later, MID*] ... MINS
Mare Island Naval Shipyard [*Also, MINS*] [*Later, MID*] ... MINSY
Mare/La Roche, Iles Loyaute [*New Caledonia*] [*ICAO location identifier*] (ICLI) ... NWWR
Mare Nectaris [*Sea of Nectar*] [*Lunar area*] ... MN
Mare Nubium [*Sea of Clouds*] [*Lunar area*] ... MNu
Mare Serenitatis [*Sea of Serenity*] [*Lunar area*] ... MS
Mare Serenitatis [*Sea of Serenity*] [*Lunar area*] ... MS-2
Mare Tranquillitatis [*Sea of Tranquility*] [*Lunar area*] ... MT
Mare Vaporum [*Sea of Vapor*] [*Lunar area*] ... MV
Mareb [*Yemen*] [*Airport symbol Obsolete*] (OAG) ... MYN
Marek's Disease [*Avian pathology*] ... MD
Marek's Disease Herpesvirus [*Medicine*] (DMAA) ... MDHV
Marek's Disease Virus [*Avian pathology*] ... MDV
Marek's Herpesvirus Disease [*Avian pathology*] (MAE) ... MHVD
Marema Tlou Freedom Party [*Lesotho*] ... MTFP
Marengo Pioneer-Republican, Marengo, IA [*Library symbol Library of Congress*] (LCLS) ... IaMarePR
Marengo Public Library, Marengo, IA [*Library symbol Library of Congress*] (LCLS) ... IaMare
Marfa, TX [*Location identifier FAA*] (FAAL) ... MRF
Marfan Syndrome [*Medicine*] ... MFS
Margahayu/Sulaiman [*Indonesia*] [*ICAO location identifier*] (ICLI) ... WIAK
Margaret (AD) ... Mog
Margaret C. Hanson Normal School, New Orleans, LA [*Library symbol Library of Congress Obsolete*] (LCLS) ... LNM
Margaret Chase Smith Library Center, Skowhegan, ME [*Library symbol*] [*Library of Congress*] (LCLS) ... MeSkS
Margaret Morris Movement [*British*] (BI) ... MMM
Margaret Reaney Memorial Library, St. Johnsville, NY [*Library symbol*] [*Library of Congress*] (LCLS) ... NStj
Margaret Sanger Research Bureau [*Defunct*] (EA) ... MSRB
Margaret Welch Memorial Library, Longville, MN [*Library symbol*] [*Library of Congress*] (LCLS) ... MnLon
Margaret Woodbury Strong Museum, Rochester, NY [*Library symbol Library of Congress*] (LCLS) ... NRMW
Margaret Woodbury Strong Museum, Rochester, NY [*OCLC symbol*] (OCLC) ... VZM
Margarine ... MARG
Margarine (ADA) ... MARGE
Margarine and Shortening Manufacturers Association (EAIO) ... MSMA
Margarita/Internacional del Caribe Gral Santiago Marino, Neuva Esparta [*Venezuela ICAO location identifier*] (ICLI) ... SVMG
Margate [*South Africa*] [*ICAO location identifier*] (ICLI) ... FAMG
Margate [*South Africa*] [*Airport symbol*] (OAG) ... MGH
Margate Air Services [*South Africa ICAO designator*] (FAAC) ... MGT
Margate City, NJ [*FM radio station call letters*] ... WTTH
Margate Industries [*NASDAQ symbol*] (TTSB) ... CGUL
Margate Public Library, Margate, United Kingdom [*Library symbol Library of Congress*] (LCLS) ... UkMg
Margate Ventures [*NASDAQ symbol*] (NQ) ... CGUL
Margate Ventures [*Associated Press*] (SAG) ... Margate
Marge Enterprises [*Vancouver Stock Exchange symbol*] ... MGE
Margin (DAVI) ... MAR
Margin [*or Marginal*] ... MARG
Margin (WDMC) ... marg
Margin (DAVI) ... MG
Margin (ROG) ... MGIN
Margin [*Accounting*] ... MGN
Margin (AD) ... mrg
Margin Account [*Investment term*] ... MA
Margin Buccal [*Medicine*] (MAE) ... MB
Margin Call [*Banking, investments*] ... MC
Margin of Exposure [*Toxicology*] ... MOE
Margin of Profit [*Accounting*] ... MOP
Margin of Safety [*Business term*] ... MOS
Margin of Safety [*Engineering*] ... MS
Margin of Safety (AD) ... ms
Marginal (ROG) ... MARGL
Marginal (AAG) ... MG
Marginal (MSA) ... MGL
Marginal Absolute Certainty Equivalent [*Statistics*] ... MACE
Marginal Check [*Computer*] ... MC
Marginal Checking (NITA) ... MC
Marginal Checking and Distribution ... MCD
Marginal Cost [*Business term*] ... MC
Marginal Cost Efficiency [*Marketing*] ... MCE
Marginal Credit [*Business term*] ... M/C
Marginal Credit (DFIT) ... MC
Marginal Efficiency of Capital [*Economics*] ... MEC
Marginal Efficiency of Investment ... MEI
Marginal Granulocyte Pool [*Hematology*] ... MGP
Marginal Ice Zone [*Oceanography*] ... MIZ
Marginal Ice Zone Experiment [*Oceanography*] ... MIZEX
Marginal Income [*Economics*] ... MI
Marginal Lending Rate [*Finance*] ... MLR
Marginal Net Value ... MNV
Marginal Physical Product [*Economics*] ... MP
Marginal Physical Product [*Agriculture*] ... MPP
Marginal Physical Product (AD) ... mpp
Marginal Producers Cost [*Engineering economics*] ... MPC
Marginal Product ... MP
Marginal Propensity to Consume [*Economics*] ... MPC
Marginal Propensity to Consume (AD) ... mpc
Marginal Propensity to Import [*Economics*] ... m
Marginal Propensity to Import [*Economics*] ... MPM
Marginal Propensity to Invest [*Economics*] ... MPI
Marginal Propensity to Invest (AD) ... mpi
Marginal Propensity to Save [*Economics*] ... MPS
Marginal Propensity to Tax [*Economics*] ... MPT
Marginal Propensity to Tax [*Economics*] ... t
Marginal Rate of Substitution [*Economics*] ... MRS
Marginal Rate of Substitution (AD) ... mrs
Marginal Rate of Technical Substitution (AD) ... mrts
Marginal Rate of Technical Substitution [*Ecology*] ... MRTS
Marginal Relative Certainty Effect [*Statistics*] ... MRCE
Marginal Return [*Army*] (AABC) ... MR
Marginal Revenue [*Economics*] ... MR
Marginal Revenue (AD) ... mr
Marginal Revenue/Average Physical Product [*Economics*] ... MRAP
Marginal Revenue/Marginal Physical Product [*Economics*] ... MRMP
Marginal Revenue Product [*Economics*] ... MRP
Marginal Revenue Product (AD) ... mrp
Marginal Sea Ice Zone Pacific [*Marine science*] (MSC) ... MIZPAC
Marginal Terrain Assault Bridge [*Military*] (RDA) ... MTAB
Marginal Terrain Vehicle ... MTV
Marginal Utility [*Economics*] ... MU

Marginal Value Analysis (MCD) ... MVA
Marginal Value of Product [*Agriculture*] ... MVP
Marginal Value Theorem [*Mathematical model developed by Dr. Eric Charnov*] ... MVT
Marginal Wage [*Economics*] ... MW
Marginal Wings [*Botany*] ... MW
Marginal Zone [*Neurology*] ... MZ
Marginalia (ABBR) ... MGNIA
Marginalia (AD) ... mrg
Marginality (ABBR) ... MGNLT
Marginally (ABBR) ... MGNLY
Marginally Indigent Defendant ... MID
Marginally Learning Disabled ... MLD
Margination (ABBR) ... MGNAN
Margo Nursery Farms [*Associated Press*] (SAG) ... Margo
Margo Nursery Farms [*NASDAQ symbol*] (TTSB) ... MRGO
Margo Nursery Farms, Inc. [*NASDAQ symbol*] (NQ) ... MRGO
Mar-Gold Resources [*Vancouver Stock Exchange symbol*] ... MAR
Marham [*British ICAO location identifier*] (ICLI) ... EGYM
Mari Sandoz Library Network [*Library network*] ... MSLN
Maria [*Mary*] ... M
Maria College, Albany, NY [*Library symbol Library of Congress*] (LCLS) ... NAIM
Maria Elisa Gonzales Farelas [*Mexico*] [*FAA designator*] (FAAC) ... FRL
Maria Mitchell Association (EA) ... MMA
Maria Regina College, Library, Syracuse, NY [*OCLC symbol*] (OCLC) ... ZUT
Maria Regina College, Syracuse, NY [*Library symbol Library of Congress*] (LCLS) ... NSyMR
Mariah Resources Ltd. [*Vancouver Stock Exchange symbol*] ... MRS
Marian College, Indianapolis, IN [*OCLC symbol*] (OCLC) ... IMI
Marian College, Indianapolis, IN [*Library symbol Library of Congress*] (LCLS) ... InIM
Marian College of Fond Du Lac, Fond Du Lac, WI [*Library symbol Library of Congress*] (LCLS) ... WFonM
Marian Minerals [*Vancouver Stock Exchange symbol*] ... MAR
Marian Movement of Priests (EA) ... MMP
Marian Sisters of the Diocese of Lincoln (TOCD) ... MS
Marian Society of Dominican Catechists (TOCD) ... OP
Mariana Islands (VRA) ... CM
Mariana Islands [*MARC geographic area code Library of Congress*] (LCCP) ... poxd--
Marianapolis College, Montreal, Quebec [*Library symbol National Library of Canada*] (NLC) ... QMMAR
Marianas Political Status Commission ... MPSC
Marianas-Bonins Command ... MARBO
Marianas-Bonins Group ... MABO
Marianist Sisters (TOCD) ... MR
Marianitas (TOCD) ... RM
Marianna [*Florida*] [*Airport symbol*] (AD) ... MAI
Marianna & Blountstown [*Railroad*] (MHDB) ... M & B
Marianna & Blountstown Railroad Co. (IIA) ... M & B
Marianna & Blountstown Railroad Co. [*AAR code*] ... MBT
Marianna, AR [*FM radio station call letters*] ... KAKJ
Marianna, AR [*AM radio station call letters*] ... KZOT
Marianna Black Library, Bryson City, NC [*Library symbol Library of Congress*] (LCLS) ... NcBc
Marianna, FL [*Location identifier FAA*] (FAAL) ... MAI
Marianna, FL [*Location identifier FAA*] (FAAL) ... SMY
Marianna, FL [*FM radio station call letters*] ... WBNF
Marianna, FL [*FM radio station call letters*] ... WJAQ
Marianna, FL [*FM radio station call letters*] ... WJNF
Marianna, FL [*AM radio station call letters*] ... WTOT
Marianna, FL [*AM radio station call letters*] ... WTYS
Marianus Socinus [*Authority cited in pre-1607 legal work*] (DSA) ... Maria Soci
Marianus Socinus, the Elder [*Deceased, 1467*] [*Authority cited in pre-1607 legal work*] (DSA) ... Socin Sen
Mariazell [*Austria*] [*Seismograph station code, US Geological Survey*] (SEIS) ... MZA
Marib [*Yemen*] [*ICAO location identifier*] (ICLI) ... OYMB
Maribo [*Denmark ICAO location identifier*] (ICLI) ... EKMB
Maribor [*Former Yugoslavia*] [*ICAO location identifier*] (ICLI) ... LYMB
Maribor [*Former Yugoslavia*] [*Airport symbol*] (OAG) ... MBX
Maricao, PR [*FM radio station call letters*] ... WAEL
Maricopa County Community College, Phoenix, AZ [*Library symbol Library of Congress*] (LCLS) ... AzPhMC
Maricopa County Free Library, Phoenix, AZ [*Library symbol Library of Congress*] (LCLS) ... AzPhM
Maricopa County Law Library, Phoenix, AZ [*Library symbol Library of Congress*] (LCLS) ... AzPhML
Maricopa County Medical Society, Phoenix, AZ [*Library symbol Library of Congress*] (LCLS) ... AzPhMM
Maridi [*Sudan*] [*ICAO location identifier*] (ICLI) ... HSMD
Marie Fleche Memorial Library, Berlin, NJ [*Library symbol Library of Congress*] (LCLS) ... NjBerl
Marie Galante [*French Antilles*] [*Airport symbol*] (OAG) ... GBJ
Marie S. Penney Memorial Library, Ramea, Newfoundland [*Library symbol National Library of Canada*] (NLC) ... NFRP
Marie S. Penney Memorial Library, Ramea, NF, Canada [*Library symbol Library of Congress*] (LCLS) ... CaNfRP
Marie-Galante Island [*Guadeloupe*] [*Airport symbol*] (AD) ... GJB
Mariehamn [*Finland ICAO location identifier*] (ICLI) ... EFMA
Mariehamn [*Finland*] [*Airport symbol*] (OAG) ... MHQ
Mariental [*Namibia*] [*ICAO location identifier*] (ICLI) ... FAML
Mariepskop [*South Africa*] [*ICAO location identifier*] (ICLI) ... FAMR
Marietta College, Marietta, OH [*OCLC symbol*] (OCLC) ... MRC
Marietta College, Marietta, OH [*Library symbol Library of Congress*] (LCLS) ... OMC
Marietta Corp. [*Associated Press*] (SAG) ... Mariet
Marietta Corp. [*NASDAQ symbol*] (NQ) ... MRTA
Marietta/Dobbins Air Force Base [*Georgia*] [*ICAO location identifier*] (ICLI) ... KMGE
Marietta, GA [*Location identifier FAA*] (FAAL) ... DJR
Marietta, GA [*Location identifier FAA*] (FAAL) ... DOB
Marietta, GA [*Location identifier FAA*] (FAAL) ... MGE
Marietta, GA [*Location identifier FAA*] (FAAL) ... NCQ
Marietta, GA [*Location identifier FAA*] (FAAL) ... NFP
Marietta, GA [*Location identifier FAA*] (FAAL) ... RYY
Marietta, GA [*AM radio station call letters*] ... WFOM
Marietta, GA [*AM radio station call letters*] ... WFTD
Marietta, GA [*FM radio station call letters*] ... WGHR
Marietta, GA [*FM radio station call letters*] ... WKHX
Marietta, OH [*FM radio station call letters*] ... WCMO
Marietta, OH [*AM radio station call letters*] ... WMOA
Marietta, OH [*FM radio station call letters*] ... WMRT
Marietta, OH [*FM radio station call letters*] (RBYB) ... WURN
Marietta, OH [*FM radio station call letters*] (RBYB) ... WYLI
Marietta, PA [*FM radio station call letters*] ... WRFH
Marietta Resources [*Vancouver Stock Exchange symbol*] ... MRT
MariFarms, Inc. [*Later, Marine Harvest International*] [*AMEX symbol*] (SPSG) ... MRF
Marigny-Le-Grand [*France ICAO location identifier*] (ICLI) ... LFYM
Marigold Library System, Strathmore, AB, Canada [*Library symbol Library of Congress*] (LCLS) ... CaASMLS
Marigold Library System, Strathmore, Alberta [*Library symbol National Library of Canada*] (NLC) ... ASMLS
Marigold Society of America (EA) ... MSA
Marijuana ... MJ
Marijuana Cigarette [*Slang*] (DSUE) ... MARI
Marijuana Detection Dog (DNAB) ... MDD
Marijuana Review [*A publication*] (DLA) ... Marijuana Rev
Marijuana Smoke ... MS
Marilia [*Brazil*] [*Airport symbol*] (OAG) ... MII
Marilia [*Brazil ICAO location identifier*] (ICLI) ... SBML
Marilyn Monroe [*American motion picture star, 1926-1962*] ... MM
Marilyn Monroe Fan Club - Marilyn Forever (EA) ... MMFC-MF
Marilyn Monroe International Fan Club (EA) ... MMIFC
Marilyn Resources [*Vancouver Stock Exchange symbol*] ... MRY
Marimba [*Music*] ... MAR
Marimba and Fife Inspectors Association [*Women's tongue-in-cheek organization*] [*Defunct*] ... MAFIA
Marin County Free Library, San Rafael, CA [*Library symbol Library of Congress*] (LCLS) ... CSrCL
Marin Self-Publishers Association (EA) ... MSPA
Marina ... MRNA
Marina Association of America [*Defunct*] (EA) ... MAA
Marina, CA [*FM radio station call letters*] ... KRQC
Marina Development Group [*Commercial firm*] [*British*] ... MDG
Marina Di Campo [*Italy ICAO location identifier*] (ICLI) ... LIRJ
Marina Di Ginosa [*Italy ICAO location identifier*] (ICLI) ... LIBH
Marina di Massa [*Italy*] [*Airport symbol*] (AD) ... QMM
Marina Ltd Partnership [*NASDAQ symbol*] (TTSB) ... MRNCZ
MARINALG International, World Association of Seaweed Processors (EA) ... WASP
Marinduque [*Philippines*] [*Airport symbol*] (OAG) ... MRQ
Marinduque/Gasan, Marinduque [*Philippines*] [*ICAO location identifier*] (ICLI) ... RPUW
Marine [*Insurance*] ... M
Marine [*FCC*] (NTCM) ... M
Marine (MSA) ... MAR
Marine [*British military*] (DMA) ... Mne
Marine ... MRNE
Marine Accessories and Services Association [*Later, NAMPS*] (EA) ... MASA
Marine Accidents Requiring Rescue (OA) ... MARR
Marine Account Reconciliation Service ... MARS
Marine Acoustical Services ... MAS
Marine Advisory Program [*Marine science*] (MSC) ... MAP
Marine Advisory Service [*See also NMAS*] [*National Oceanic and Atmospheric Administration Information service or system*] (IID) ... MAS
Marine Advisory Unit ... MARADVU
Marine Advisory Unit [*Marine Corps*] ... MAU
Marine Aerial Refueler/Transport Squadron [*Navy symbol*] (NVT) ... VMGR
Marine Aerosol and Gas Exchange [*Marine science*] (OSRA) ... MAGE
Marine Aerosol and Gas Exchange (USDC) ... MAGE
Marine Affairs Council [*Marine science*] (MSC) ... MAC
Marine Aide-de-Camp to the King [*British Admiralty*] ... MADCK
Marine Air Base ... MAB
Marine Air Base Defense Wing ... MABDW
Marine Air Base Squadron ... MABRON
Marine Air Base Squadron ... MABS
Marine Air Command and Control System (NVT) ... MACCS
Marine Air Control Group ... MACG
Marine Air Control Squadron ... MACS
Marine Air Control Squadron ... MACSQ
Marine Air Depot, Miramar [*California*] ... MAIRMAR
Marine Air Depot Squadron ... MADEPSQ
Marine Air [*or Aviation*] **Detachment** ... MAD
Marine Air Detection (AFIT) ... MAD
Marine Air Facility ... MAF
Marine Air Ground Intelligence System ... MAGIS
Marine Air Group (VNW) ... MAG

Marine Air Regulating Squadron ... MAREGSQ
Marine Air Reserve Training Command ... MARTC
Marine Air Reserve Training Command ... MARTCOM
Marine Air Reserve Training Detachment ... MARTD
Marine Air Support Control Unit ... MASCU
Marine Air Support Group ... MASG
Marine Air Support RADAR Teams (IEEE) ... MASRT
Marine Air Support RADAR Unit [*DoD*] ... MASRU
Marine Air Support Squadron ... MASS
Marine Air Support Squadron Detachment (DNAB) ... MASSDET
Marine Air Tactical [*later, Traffic*] **Control Unit** [*Marine Corps*] ... MATCU
Marine Air Temperature [*Meteorology*] ... MAT
Marine Air Traffic Control and Landing System [*Navy*] ... MATCALS
Marine Air Traffic Control Squadron (DNAB) ... MATCS
Marine Air Traffic Control Squadron Detachment (DNAB) ... MATCSDET
Marine Air Traffic Unit ... MATU
Marine Air Warning Squadron ... MAWS
Marine Air Weapons Training Unit (MCD) ... MAWTU
Marine Air West Coast ... MAWC
Marine Air Wing ... MAW
Marine Air Wing Pacific ... MAWP
Marine Aircraft Base Defense Group ... MABDG
Marine Aircraft Experimental Establishment ... MAEE
Marine Aircraft Experimental Laboratory [*British*] ... MAEL
Marine Aircraft [*or Aviation*] **Group** ... MAG
Marine Aircraft Maintenance Squadron ... MAMRON
Marine Aircraft Repair Squadron ... MARS
Marine Aircraft Wing ... MARAIRWING
Marine Air-Droppable Area Marker (MCD) ... MADAM
Marine Air-Ground Task Force (AFM) ... MAGTAF
Marine Air-Ground Task Force (NVT) ... MAGTF
Marine All Weather Fighter Training Squadron ... MARALLWEAFITRARON
Marine All-Weather Attack Training Squadron [*Navy symbol*] (DNAB) ... VMAT(AW)
Marine Amphibious Brigade ... MAB
Marine Amphibious Brigade Field Exercise (NVT) ... MABFEX
Marine Amphibious Brigade Landing Exercise (NVT) ... MABLEX
Marine Amphibious Corps ... MAC
Marine Amphibious Force (AABC) ... MAF
Marine Amphibious Force Air Support Airfield (MCD) ... MAFASA
Marine Amphibious Force Field Exercise [*Military*] (NVT) ... MAFFEX
Marine Amphibious Force Landing Exercise [*Military*] (NVT) ... MAFLEX
Marine Amphibious Ready Group (MCD) ... MARG
Marine Amphibious Unit (NVT) ... MAU
Marine Amphibious Unit Landing Exercise (NVT) ... MAULEX
Marine and Allied Industries Training Association (AIE) ... MAITA
Marine & Aviation Management International [*British ICAO designator*] (FAAC) ... MMM
Marine and Estuarine Protected Area ... MEPA
Marine and Freshwater Biomedical Science (GNE) ... MFBS
Marine & Industrial ... M & I
Marine and Ports Council of Australia (AD) ... MPCA
Marine Antiair Warfare Exercise (NVT) ... MARAAWEX
Marine Aspects of Earth System History [*Research programs*] ... MESH
Marine Assessment Research Division [*Now Ocean Environmental Research Division*] (USDC) ... MARD
Marine Assessment Research Division [*Marine science*] (OSRA) ... MARD
Marine Associated Services Technology Systems Exposition [*Canada*] (ITD) ... MASTS
Marine Attack Helicopter Squadron (VNW) ... HMA
Marine Attack Squadron [*Navy symbol*] (NVT) ... VMA
Marine Attack Squadron (All-Weather) [*Navy symbol*] (NVT) ... VMA(AW)
Marine Attack Training Squadron [*Navy symbol*] (DNAB) ... VMAT
Marine Automated Flowcharting Analysis System ... MAFAS
Marine Automatic Meteorological Observing Station [*Automatic system*] ... MAMOS
Marine Automatic Telephone Weather Answering Service [*Marine science*] (MSC) ... MATWAS
Marine Aviation Training Support Group (DNAB) ... MATSG
Marine Aviation Training Support Squadron (DNAB) ... MATSS
Marine Aviation Weapons and Tactics Squadron ... MAWTS
Marine Bank [*Board on Geographic Names*] ... BNKM
Marine Barracks ... MARBKS
Marine Barracks ... MB
Marine Barracks, Naval Air Station ... MBNAS
Marine Barracks, Naval Ammunition Depot ... MBNAD
Marine Barracks, Naval Mine Depot ... MBNMD
Marine Barracks, Naval Operating Base ... MBNOB
Marine Barracks, Naval Station ... MBNS
Marine Barracks, Navy Yard ... MBNYD
Marine Barracks, Submarine Base ... MBSB
Marine Base ... MB
Marine Base Air Warning System ... MBAWS
Marine Base Defense Group ... MBDG
Marine Biological Association [*British*] ... MBA
Marine Biological Association of the United Kingdom (ARC) ... MBAUK
Marine Biological Laboratory ... MBL
Marine Biological Laboratory, Woods Hole, MA [*Library symbol Library of Congress*] (LCLS) ... MWhB
Marine Biology Research Centre [*University of Moncton*] [*Canada*] (IRC) ... MBRC
Marine Biomedical Center [*Duke University*] [*Research center*] (RCD) ... MBC
Marine Biomedical Institute [*University of Texas*] [*Research center*] (RCD) ... MBI
Marine Board (EA) ... MB
Marine Board of Queensland [*Australia*] ... MBQ
Marine Board of Victoria [*Australia*] ... MBV
Marine Boundary Layer [*Oceanography*] ... MBL
Marine Brigade ... MARBRIG
Marine Broadcast Station [*ITU designation*] (CET) ... FCB
Marine Builders Training Trust (AIE) ... MBTT
Marine Carrier Qualifications (NVT) ... MCARQUALS
Marine Casualty Statistics (OA) ... MCS
Marine Centralized Automatic Control System (PDAA) ... MCACS
Marine City, MI [*AM radio station call letters*] ... WIFN
Marine Class ... MA
Marine Climatological Summaries Scheme [*World Meteorological Organization*] [*United Nations*] (DUND) ... MCSS
Marine Communications Detachment (DNAB) ... MARCOMMDET
Marine Communications Satellites (NITA) ... MARECS
Marine Composite Reconnaissance [*Photo*] **Squadron** [*Navy symbol*] ... VMCJ
Marine Computer System (PDAA) ... MARCS
Marine Conservation Society [*British*] ... MCS
Marine Construction Battalion ... MCB
Marine Cooks and Stewards Union ... MCS
Marine Corps [*When used as prefix with plane designation*] ... M
Marine Corps ... MARCOR
Marine Corps ... MARCORPS
Marine Corps ... MC
Marine Corps Absentee Collection Unit (DNAB) ... MARCORABSCOLLUNIT
Marine Corps Absentee Collection Unit Detachment (DNAB) ... MARCORASBCOLLUNITDET
Marine Corps Accrued Military Pay System (NG) ... MARCAMP
Marine Corps Achievement Medal [*Military decoration*] ... MCAM
Marine Corps Administrative Detachment (DNAB) ... MARCORADMINDET
Marine Corps Air Base ... MCAB
Marine Corps Air Depot ... MCAD
Marine Corps Air Facility ... MCAF
Marine Corps Air Facility (DOMA) ... MCAF
Marine Corps Air Field ... MCAF
Marine Corps Air Ground Combat Training Center (MCD) ... MCAGCTC
Marine Corps Air Station ... MCAS
Marine Corps Air Station (Helicopter) (FAAC) ... MCAS(H)
Marine Corps Air-Ground Combat Center [*Twenty-nine Palms, Calif.*] (DOMA) ... MCAGCC
Marine Corps Air-Ground Intelligence Center (MCD) ... MAGIC
Marine Corps Association (EA) ... MCA
Marine Corps Automated Readiness Evaluation System ... MARES
Marine Corps Automated Readiness Evaluation System/Status of Forces ... MARES/FORSTAT
Marine Corps Automated Test System (DWSG) ... MCATS
Marine Corps Auxiliary Air Facility ... MCAAF
Marine Corps Auxiliary Air Station ... MCAAS
Marine Corps Auxiliary Landing Field ... MCALF
Marine Corps Aviation Association (EA) ... MCAA
Marine Corps Aviation Cadet ... MARCAD
Marine Corps Base ... MCB
Marine Corps Basic School ... MARBASSCOL
Marine Corps Brevet Medal ... MCBM
Marine Corps Capabilities Plan (DOMA) ... MCCP
Marine Corps Capabilities Plan (MCD) ... MCP
Marine Corps Central Design and Programming Activity (DNAB) ... MCCDPA
Marine Corps Clothing Depot ... MCCD
Marine Corps Combat Correspondents Association (EA) ... MCCCA
Marine Corps Combat Development Command [*Quantico, VA*] (GRD) ... MCCDC
Marine Corps Combat Readiness Evaluation System ... MCCRES
Marine Corps Combat Readiness Training Group ... MCCRTG
Marine Corps Commandant ... MCC
Marine Corps Communications Electronics School (DNAB) ... MCCES
Marine Corps Component Navy Advisory Group (CINC) ... MARCOMNAVADGRU
Marine Corps Development and Education Command ... MCDEC
Marine Corps Disbursing Office ... MARCORDISBOF
Marine Corps District (DNAB) ... MCD
Marine Corps Education Center ... MCEC
Marine Corps Emergency Actions Center ... MCEAC
Marine Corps Enlisted Commissioning Education Program (DNAB) ... MECEP
Marine Corps Environmentally Controlled Medical System (MCD) ... MCEMS
Marine Corps Equipment Board ... MCEB
Marine Corps Exchange ... MCX
Marine Corps Exchange Manual (SAA) ... MCXM
Marine Corps Exchange Service Branch (DNAB) ... MCXSERV
Marine Corps Expeditionary Shelter System (MCD) ... MCESS
Marine Corps Finance Center (DNAB) ... MARFINCEN
Marine Corps Freight Office ... MCFO
Marine Corps Gazette [*A publication*] (BRI) ... Mar Crp G
Marine Corps Gazette [*A publication*] (DOMA) ... MCG
Marine Corps Good Conduct Medal ... MCGCM
Marine Corps Ground-Controlled Interceptor Squadron (IAA) ... MCGCIS
Marine Corps Gun Howitzer (MCD) ... MCGH
Marine Corps Historical Center (DNAB) ... MARCORHISTCEN
Marine Corps Historical Foundation (EA) ... MCHF
Marine Corps Institute ... MCI
Marine Corps Integrated Maintenance Management System ... MIMMS
Marine Corps Integrated Manpower Management Information System ... MIMMIS
Marine Corps Intelligence Center (DOMA) ... MCIC
Marine Corps Key Experiences Evaluation System (MCD) ... MCKEES
Marine Corps Landing Force Development Center ... MCLFDC
Marine Corps League (EA) ... MCL
Marine Corps League Auxiliary (EA) ... MCLA
Marine Corps Level of Repair Analysis ... MCLORA
Marine Corps Logistic Support Base, Atlantic (MCD) ... MCLSBLANT

Marine Corps Logistic Support Base, Pacific (MCD) ... MCLSBPAC
Marine Corps Logistics Base (DOMA) ... MCLB
Marine Corps Long-Range Plans ... MLRP
Marine Corps Manual ... MARCORMAN
Marine Corps Manual ... MCM
Marine Corps Memorial Commission ... MCMC
Marine Corps Midrange Objectives Plan (MCD) ... MMRP
Marine Corps Mountain Warfare Training Center [*Bridgeport, CA*] ... MCMWTC
Marine Corps Movement Coordination Center (DNAB) ... MCMCC
Marine Corps Mustang Association (EA) ... MCMA
Marine Corps - Navy Publicity Bureau (SAA) ... MCNPB
Marine Corps Officer ... MCO
Marine Corps Operational Test and Evaluation Activity (CAAL) ... MCOTEA
Marine Corps Operations Analysis Group ... MCOAG
Marine Corps Order ... MCO
Marine Corps Ordnance Publication ... MCOP
Marine Corps Outlying Landing Field ... MCOLF
Marine Corps Personnel Manual ... MARCORPERSMAN
Marine Corps Personnel Manual (SAA) ... MCPM
Marine Corps Procurement District ... MCPD
Marine Corps Program Decision Meeting (DOMA) ... MCPDM
Marine Corps Program Progress Report ... MCPPR
Marine Corps Publications [*Later, NAVMC*] ... NMC
Marine Corps Recruit Depot ... MCRD
Marine Corps Recruit Depot ... MCRDEP
Marine Corps Recruit Option Center ... MCROC
Marine Corps Recruiting Command ... MCRC
Marine Corps Recruiting Station ... MCRS
Marine Corps Recruiting Substation ... MCRSS
Marine Corps Remote Area Approach and Landing System (MCD) ... MRAALS
Marine Corps Representative (DNAB) ... MARCOREP
Marine Corps Representative (SAA) ... MCR
Marine Corps Requirements Document (MCD) ... MCRD
Marine Corps Research, Development, and Acquisition Command [*Quantico, VA*] (GRD) ... MCRDAC
Marine Corps Reserve ... MCR
Marine Corps Reserve Bulletin Board System (DOMA) ... MCRBBS
Marine Corps Reserve Landing Exercise (NVT) ... MARLEX
Marine Corps Reserve Officers Association (EA) ... MCROA
Marine Corps Reserve/Recruitment District ... MCRRD
Marine Corps Reserve Ribbon ... MCRR
Marine Corps Reserve Support Center ... MCRSC
Marine Corps Reserve Training (NVT) ... MARESTNG
Marine Corps Reserve Training Center ... MARCORESTRACEN
Marine Corps Reserve Training Center ... MRTC
Marine Corps School [*Quantico, VA*] ... MCS
Marine Corps Security Force (DNAB) ... MCSF
Marine Corps Shipping Order (NG) ... MARSO
Marine Corps Shoulder-Launched Multipurpose Assault Weapon (MCD) ... MCSMAW
Marine Corps Special Orders (SAA) ... MCSO
Marine Corps Station ... MCS
Marine Corps Stock [*or Supply*] **Lists** ... MCSL
Marine Corps Supply Activity [*Obsolete*] ... MCS
Marine Corps Supply Activity [*Obsolete*] (NVT) ... MCSA
Marine Corps Supply Center ... MCSC
Marine Corps Supply Depot ... MARCORSUPDEP
Marine Corps Supply Depot (MUGU) ... MCSD
Marine Corps System Command (DOMA) ... MCSYSCOM
Marine Corps Systems Command (DOMA) ... MARCORSYSCOM
Marine Corps Systems Command ... MARCORSYSCOM
Marine Corps Tactical Command and Control System (MCD) ... MTCACS
Marine Corps Tactical Data System (AFIT) ... MTADS
Marine Corps Tactical Systems and Support Activity [*Camp Pendleton, CA*] (GRD) ... MCTSSA
Marine Corps Tank Full-Crew Interactive Simulator Trainer ... MCTFIST
Marine Corps Test Support Element (MCD) ... MCTSE
Marine Corps Unified Materiel Management System ... MUMMS
Marine Corps Uniform Board [*Washington, DC*] (EGAO) ... MCUB
Marine Corps Women's Reserve ... MCWR
Marine Corrosion Research Laboratory [*Navy*] (PDAA) ... MCRL
Marine Court Reporter (McAdam's) [*New York*] [*A publication*] (DLA) ... Marine Ct R
Marine Craft [*British military*] (DMA) ... MC
Marine Craft Radio Installation ... MCRI
Marine Cranking Amperes [*Battery*] [*Automotive engineering*] ... MCA
Marine Data Logger System ... MDLS
Marine Detachment ... MARDET
Marine Detachment ... MD
Marine Diesel Oil ... MDO
Marine Differential Analyzer ... MARDAN
Marine Distress Signal (IAA) ... MDS
Marine Division ... MARDIV
Marine Drilling [*NASDAQ symbol*] (TTSB) ... MDCO
Marine Drilling Co. [*Associated Press*] (SAG) ... MarDrl
Marine Drilling Co. [*NASDAQ symbol*] (NQ) ... MDCO
Marine Dynamics Branch, Canada Institute for Scientific and Technical Information, National Research Council [*Direction de la Dynamique Marine Institut Canadien de l'Information Scientifique et Technique, Conseil National de Recherches*], St. John's, Newfoundland [*Library symbol National Library of Canada*] (NLC) ... NFSNM
Marine Early Warning ... MEW
Marine Ecological Database System [*Marine science*] (OSRA) ... MEDS
Marine Ecological Database System (USDC) ... MEDS
Marine Ecosystem Research Laboratory [*University of Rhode Island*] [*Research center*] ... MERL
Marine Ecosystem Study in Tropical Areas [*Marine science*] (MSC) ... MESTA
Marine Ecosystems Analysis [*Pollution-monitoring project*] ... MESA
Marine Electric Power Plant (PDAA) ... MEPP
Marine Electronic Technical Unit (MUGU) ... METU
Marine Emergency Operations Center [*Western Australia*] ... MEOC
Marine Engine ... ME
Marine Engine Condition Monitor (PDAA) ... MECOM
Marine Engine Manufacturers Association [*Formerly, OMMA*] (EA) ... MEMA
Marine Engineer (PGP) ... Mar Eng
Marine Engineer ... ME
Marine Engineer Officer [*British*] ... MEO
Marine Engineer Officer of the Watch [*British*] ... MEOOW
Marine Engineer Officer's Writer [*British military*] (DMA) ... MEOW
Marine Engineering Artificer [*Navy rating British*] ... MEA
Marine Engineering Laboratory [*Navy*] ... MEL
Marine Engineering Laboratory - Annapolis [*Navy*] (DNAB) ... MEL-A
Marine Engineering Mechanic [*Navy rating British*] ... MEM
Marine Engineers' Association [*A union*] [*British*] ... MEA
Marine Engineers' Beneficial Association ... MEBA
Marine Environment Protection Committee [*IMCO*] (MSC) ... MEPC
Marine Environment Studies Laboratory [*Marine science*] (OSRA) ... MESL
Marine Environmental Activities [*Marine science*] (MSC) ... MEA
Marine Environmental Data Information Referral System [*UNESCO*] [*Paris, France*] ... MEDI
Marine Environmental Data Service [*Canada*] (NOAA) ... MEDS
Marine Environmental Management Office [*Marine science*] (MSC) ... MEMO
Marine Environmental Observation and Forecasting (NOAA) ... MEOF
Marine Environmental Prediction Task Group [*US government*] [*Terminated, 1969*] ... MAREP
Marine Environmental Quality [*Marine science*] (MSC) ... MEQ
Marine Environmental Quality Committee [*Marine science*] (OSRA) ... MEQC
Marine Environmental Response [*USCG*] (TAG) ... MER
Marine Environmental Sciences Consortium [*Library network*] ... MESC
Marine Environmental Sciences Consortium, Dauphin Island, AL [*Library symbol*] [*Library of Congress*] (LCLS) ... ADaiM
Marine Environmental Testing and Electro-Optical Radiation (MCD) ... METEOR
Marine Expeditionary Brigade ... MEB
Marine Expeditionary Brigade Field Exercise (NVT) ... MEBFEX
Marine Expeditionary Brigade Landing Exercise ... MEBLEX
Marine Expeditionary Corps (NVT) ... MEC
Marine Expeditionary Force ... MEF
Marine Expeditionary Force Field Exercise (NVT) ... MEFFEX
Marine Expeditionary Force Landing Exercise (NVT) ... MEFLEX
Marine Expeditionary Unit ... MEU
Marine Expeditionary Unit Landing Exercise (NVT) ... MEULEX
Marine Expeditionary Unit Service Support Group (DOMA) ... MSSG
Marine Express (AABC) ... MARINEX
Marine Fighter Attack Squadron [*Navy symbol*] (NVT) ... VMFA
Marine Fighter Attack Training Squadron [*Navy symbol*] ... VMFAT
Marine Fighter Bomber Squadron [*Navy symbol*] ... VMBF
Marine Fighter Squadron [*Navy symbol*] ... VMF
Marine Fighter Squadron (All-Weather) [*Navy symbol*] (NVT) ... VMF(AW)
Marine Fire Detection Control Center ... MFDCC
Marine Firing Exercise (NVT) ... MARFIREX
Marine Fisheries Advisory Committee [*Department of Commerce Washington, DC*] (EGAO) ... MAFAC
Marine Fishery Reserve ... MFR
Marine Fleet Air ... MARFAIR
Marine Fleet Air, West Coast ... MARFAIRWEST
Marine Fleet Air, West Coast ... MFAIRWEST
Marine Fleet Air, West Coast ... MFWC
Marine Forces [*Element of a Joint Task Force*] ... MARFOR
Marine Forecast [*Pronounced "mayfor"*] ... MAFOR
Marine Forecast Unit [*National Weather Service*] ... MFU
Marine Fuel Oil ... MFO
Marine Garrison Force ... MARGARFOR
Marine Gene Probe Laboratory [*Dalhousie University*] [*Canada*] ... MGPL
Marine General Workers' Federation ... MWF
Marine Geological Institute [*Indonesia*] [*Marine science*] (OSRA) ... MGI
Marine Geophysical Survey [*NOO*] ... MGS
Marine Glider Squadron [*Navy symbol*] ... VML
Marine Gunner ... MG
Marine Gunner ... MGUN
Marine Helicopter Experimental Squadron ... HMX
Marine Helicopter Experimental Squadron One [*Organized in 1947 for the development and study of helicopter tactics*] ... HMX-1
Marine Helicopter Landing Exercise (NVT) ... MARHELILEX
Marine Helicopter Squadron ... HM
Marine Helicopter Squadron Attack (NVT) ... HMA
Marine Helicopter Squadron Heavy ... HMH
Marine Helicopter Squadron Light ... HML
Marine Helicopter Squadron Medium ... HMM
Marine Helicopter Training Group (NVT) ... MHTG
Marine Historical Association [*Later, MSM*] (EA) ... MHA
Marine Hospital Service [*Public Health Service*] ... MHS
Marine Hydrophysical Institute ... MHI
Marine Index Bureau ... MIB
Marine Inertial Navigation Data Assimilation Computer (IEEE) ... MINDAC
Marine Information and Advisory Service [*Institute of Oceanographic Sciences*] [*Databank*] [*British*] (IID) ... MIAS
Marine Information Centre [*Information service or system*] (IID) ... MIC
Marine Information Management [*Marine science*] (MSC) ... MIM
Marine Information System (NITA) ... MIS

Marine Inspection Office [*Coast Guard*] ... MIO
Marine Inspection Operations [*USCG*] (TAG) ... MIO
Marine Institute of Technology and Graduate Studies [*Baltimore*] ... MITGS
Marine Instrument Training Squadron ... MARINTRARON
Marine Instrumentation Laboratory [*Marine science*] (OSRA) ... MIL
Marine Instrumentation Laboratory (USDC) ... MIL
Marine Insurance ... MI
Marine Insurance Policy ... MIP
Marine Integrated Fire and Air Support System ... MIFASS
Marine Integrated Logistics System ... MILS
Marine Integrated Personnel and Logistics Subsystem ... MIPLOGS
Marine Integrated Personnel System (MCD) ... MIPS
Marine Investigation (LAIN) ... MI
Marine Isotope Stage [*Climatology*] ... MIS
Marine Jet ... MJ
Marine Liaison Office (DNAB) ... MARLNO
Marine Liaison Officer (DOMA) ... MARLO
Marine Librarians Association (EA) ... MLA
Marine Life and Geochemical Studies [*Marine science*] (MSC) ... MARLAGS
Marine Life Research Group [*Scripps Institution of Oceanography*] ... MLRG
Marine Life Research Program ... MLRP
Marine Life Resources [*Program*] ... MLR
Marine Light Infantry [*Navy British*] (ROG) ... MLI
Marine Ltd. [*Associated Press*] (SAG) ... MarnLP
Marine Ltd. Partnership [*Associated Press*] (SAG) ... MarnLP
Marine Ltd. Partnership [*NASDAQ symbol*] (SAG) ... MRNC
Marine Logistical Command (VNW) ... MARLOG
Marine Mammal Act [*1972*] (MSC) ... MMA
Marine Mammal Commission [*Marine science*] (MSC) ... MMC
Marine Mammal Events Program (EA) ... MMEP
Marine Mammal Health and Stranding Response Act ... MMHSRA
Marine Mammals Protection Act [*1972*] ... MMPA
Marine Manufacturers Safety Equipment Association (EA) ... SEA
Marine Maritime Academy ... MMA
Marine Mechanical Engineer ... Mar Mech E
Marine Medium and Heavy Patrol Bomber Squadron [*Land-based and seaplane*] [*Navy symbol*] ... VMB
Marine Meteorological Service ... MARMETS
Marine Meteorological Services [*Marine science*] (MSC) ... MAMS
Marine Meteorological Services System [*WMO*] (MSC) ... MMSS
Marine Midland Banks, Inc. [*Associated Press*] (SAG) ... MarM
Marine Midland Banks, Inc. [*NYSE symbol*] (SPSG) ... MMB
Marine Midland Services Corp., Technical Information Center, Buffalo, NY [*Library symbol Library of Congress*] (LCLS) ... NBuMM
Marine Minerals Technology [*National Oceanic and Atmospheric Administration*] ... MMT
Marine Minerals Technology Center [*National Oceanic and Atmospheric Administration*] ... MMTC
Marine Motor Association (ROG) ... MMA
Marine Multipurpose Missile (DNAB) ... MMM
Marine Museum of the Great Lakes at Kingston, Kingston, ON, Canada [*Library symbol Library of Congress*] (LCLS) ... CaOKMM
Marine Museum of the Great Lakes at Kingston, Ontario [*Library symbol National Library of Canada*] (NLC) ... OKMM
Marine National Bank (California) [*Associated Press*] (SAG) ... MarNB
Marine National Bank (California) [*Associated Press*] (SAG) ... MarNBk
Marine National Bank (California) [*NASDAQ symbol*] (SAG) ... MNBK
Marine Nat'l Bank [*NASDAQ symbol*] (TTSB) ... MNBK
Marine Natl Bk Irvine CA Wrrt [*NASDAQ symbol*] (TTSB) ... MNBKW
Marine Navigating Light ... MNL
Marine Navigating Light System ... MNLS
Marine Navigation (NITA) ... MARNA
Marine Night Fighter Squadron [*Navy symbol*] ... VMF(N)
Marine Observation Satellite [*Japan*] ... MOS
Marine Observation Squadron [*Navy symbol*] ... VMO
Marine Observation Squadron (Artillery Spotting) [*Navy symbol*] ... VMO(AS)
Marine Occupational Standard (DNAB) ... MOS
Marine Office of America (AD) ... MOA
Marine Officer Instructor (DOMA) ... MOI
Marine Officer's Attendant [*British military*] (DMA) ... MOA
Marine Oil Pickup Service [*Marine science*] (MSC) ... MOPS
Marine Oil Transportation [*AAR code*] ... MOT
Marine Operation Center [*NASA*] (NASA) ... MOC
Marine Operation Center ... MOC
Marine Operational Training Group ... MOTG
Marine Operations and Instrumentation Laboratory [*Marine science*] (OSRA) ... MOIL
Marine Operations and Instrumentation Laboratory (USDC) ... MOIL
Marine Operations Division [*Environmental Protection Agency*] (GFGA) ... MOD
Marine Oxidation/Fermentation ... MOF
Marine Petrol Tr [*NASDAQ symbol*] (TTSB) ... MRPS
Marine Petroleum and Minerals Advisory Committee [*Terminated, 1976*] [*National Oceanic and Atmospheric Administration*] (NOAA) ... MP & MAC
Marine Petroleum Trust [*NASDAQ symbol*] (NQ) ... MARP
Marine Petroleum Trust [*Associated Press*] (SAG) ... MarPet
Marine Photographic Squadron [*Navy symbol*] ... VMD
Marine Physical Environmental Prediction ... MARPEP
Marine Physical Laboratory [*Research center*] (RCD) ... MPL
Marine Physician Assistant (AD) ... MPA
Marine Physics Laboratory [*Scripps*] ... MPL
Marine Plastic Pollution Research and Control Act ... MPPRCA
Marine Police ... MP
Marine Policy Center (GNE) ... MPC
Marine Pollution ... MP
Marine Pollution Control Unit [*Department of Transportation*] ... MPCU
Marine Pollution Incident [*Marine science*] (OSRA) ... MPI
Marine Pollution Information Centre [*Marine Biological Association of the United Kingdom*] (IID) ... MARPIC
Marine Pollution Management Group [*British*] ... MPMG
Marine Pollution Monitoring Management Group (ASF) ... MPMMG
Marine Pollution [*or Petroleum*] **Monitoring Pilot Project** [*Marine science*] (MSC) ... MAPMOPP
Marine Pollution Retrieval System [*BTS*] (TAG) ... MPRS
Marine Polymetalic Sulfide ... MPS
Marine Power Plant (PDAA) ... MPP
Marine Prepositioned Ships Program ... MPS
Marine Preservation Association ... MPA
Marine Products Development Irradiator ... MPDI
Marine Profile Data Base (GNE) ... MARPRO
Marine Protection, Research, and Sanctuaries Act [*1972*] ... MPRSA
Marine Protein Concentrate [*See also FPC*] (MSC) ... MPC
Marine Protein Concentrate (AD) ... mpc
Marine Provost [*British military*] (DMA) ... MP
Marine RADAR Interrogator-Transponder (PDAA) ... MRIT
Marine Radio Beacon Station [*ITU designation*] (CET) ... RLM
Marine Recreational Fishing [*Marine science*] (MSC) ... MRF
Marine Recreational Fishing Statistics Survey [*Marine science*] (OSRA) ... MRESS
Marine Recreational Fishing Statistics Survey (USDC) ... MRFSS
Marine Reporting Station [*National Weather Service*] ... MARS
Marine Research Committee ... MRC
Marine Research Corp. [*Marine science*] (OSRA) ... MRC
Marine Research Corporation (USDC) ... MRC
Marine Research Group of Victoria [*Australia*] ... MRGV
Marine Research Institute ... MRI
Marine Reserve Aviation Supply Training Unit (DNAB) ... MRASTU
Marine Resources and Engineering Development Act [*1966*] (MSC) ... MREDA
Marine Resources Council ... MRC
Marine Resources Development Foundation ... MRDF
Marine Resources Information Center [*Massachusetts Institute of Technology*] (NOAA) ... MARIC
Marine Resources Monitoring, Assessment, and Prediction [*National Oceanic and Atmospheric Administration*] ... MARMAP
Marine Resources Research Division [*Marine science*] (OSRA) ... MRRD
Marine Resources Research Division [*Now Ocean Environment Research Division*] (USDC) ... MRRD
Marine Resources Research Institute [*South Carolina Wildlife and Marine Resources Department*] [*Research center*] (RCD) ... MRRI
Marine Retailers Association of America (EA) ... MRAA
Marine Safety Agency (NADA) ... MSA
Marine Safety Council [*Coast Guard*] ... MSC
Marine Safety Information System [*Coast Guard*] (MSC) ... MSIS
Marine Safety Management System [*BTS*] (TAG) ... MSMS
Marine Safety Manual [*Coast Guard*] [*A publication*] (DLA) ... MSM
Marine Safety Office (MCD) ... MSO
Marine Safety Services [*British*] (DCTA) ... MSS
Marine Safety Training and Assistance Team [*RSPA*] (TAG) ... MSTAT
Marine Sanitation Device ... MSD
Marine Science Activities [*Program*] [*Coast Guard*] ... MSA
Marine Science Center [*Oregon State University*] [*Research center*] (RCD) ... MSC
Marine Science Council [*Marine science*] (MSC) ... MSC
Marine Science Division [*Instrument Society of America*] (MSC) ... MASID
Marine Science Institute [*University of California, Santa Barbara*] [*Research center*] (RCD) ... MSI
Marine Science Institute [*Philippines*] ... MSI
Marine Sciences Affairs Staff [*A publication*] ... MSAS
Marine Sciences Directorate [*Canada*] (MSC) ... MSD
Marine Sciences Research Center [*State University of New York at Stony Brook*] [*Research center*] (RCD) ... MSRC
Marine Sciences Research Laboratory [*Canada*] (MSC) ... MSRL
Marine Scientific Equipment Service [*British*] ... MSES
Marine Scout Bombing Squadron [*Navy symbol*] ... VMSB
Marine Search and Attack System (PDAA) ... MARSAS
Marine Security Guard ... MSG
Marine Security Program [*FHWA*] (TAG) ... MSP
Marine Service Squadron ... SMS
Marine Services Engineer Officer [*Navy British*] ... MSEO
Marine Services Research Division [*Marine science*] (OSRA) ... MSRD
Marine Services Research Division [*Now Coastal and Arctic Research Division*] (USDC) ... MSRD
Marine Signal Detachment (SAA) ... MSD
Marine Society of the City of New York (EA) ... MSCNY
Marine Spill Response Corp. [*An association*] ... MSRC
Marine Stable Element ... MAST
Marine Staff Officers (EA) ... MSO
Marine Stewards' Association [*Australia*] ... MSA
Marine Support Battalion (DNAB) ... MARSPTBN
Marine Surface Contre Avions (SAA) ... MASURCA
Marine Systems Acquisition Review Council (MCD) ... MSARC
Marine Systems Laboratory [*Smithsonian Institution*] ... MSL
Marine Systems Operational Compiler ... MSOC
Marine Tactical Air Control and Landing System ... MTACLS
Marine Tactical Command and Control System (MCD) ... MTACCS
Marine Tactical Data (IAA) ... MTDA
Marine Tactical Data System ... MTDS
Marine Tactical Electronic Warfare Squadron [*Navy symbol*] (DNAB) ... VMAQ
Marine Tactical Reconnaissance Squadron [*Navy symbol*] (DNAB) ... VMFP
Marine Tactical Reconnaissance Squadron Detachment [*Navy symbol*] (DNAB) ... VMFPDET
Marine Technology Directorate [*British*] ... MTD
Marine Technology Society (EA) ... MTS

Marine Terminal Fuel Separator (MCD) .... MTFS
Marine Terminal Fuel Tankage System (MCD) .... MTFTS
Marine Terminal Tankage System (MCD) .... MTTS
Marine Test Boat .... MTB
Marine Toebreak Data System (NG) .... MTDS
Marine Torpedo Bomber Squadron [*Navy symbol*] .... VMTB
Marine Towing and Transportation Employers Association [*Defunct*] (EA) .... MTTEA
Marine Trades Association [*British*] (DBA) .... MTA
Marine Training and Replacement Command (SAA) .... MT&RC
Marine Training and Replacement Commands .... MARTRA & REPLCOMS
Marine Transport Squadron [*Navy symbol*] .... VMR
Marine Unit Training (NVT) .... MARUNITNG
Marine Unit Vietnam (VNW) .... MUV
Marine Utility Squadron [*Navy symbol*] .... VMJ
Marine Vapor Control System .... MVCS
Marine Vapor Recovery System (GNE) .... MVRS
Marine Weather Service (NOAA) .... MWS
Marine Wildlife Preservation Fund .... MWPF
Marine Wing Communication Squadron .... MWCS
Marine Wing Facilities Squadron .... MWFS
Marine Wing Headquarters Group .... MWHG
Marine Wing Headquarters Squadron (NVT) .... MWHS
Marine Wing Headquarters Squadron Detachment (DNAB) .... MWHSDET
Marine Wing Staff Ground (MCD) .... MWSGR
Marine Wing Support Group (NVT) .... MWSG
Marine Wing Support Group Detachment (DNAB) .... MWSGDET
Marine Wing Support Squadron [*Navy*] (ANA) .... MWSS
Marine Wing Weapon Unit .... MWWU
Marine-Aided Inertial Navigation System (PDAA) .... MAINS
Marineartillerieabteilung [*Naval Coast Artillery Battalion*] [*German military - World War II*] .... MAA
Marine-Estuarine-Environmental Sciences (PDAA) .... MEES
Marine-Finish Slate (MSA) .... MFS
Marine-Kuestenartillerie [*Naval Coast Artillery*] [*German military - World War II*] .... MKA
Mariner Explorations [*Vancouver Stock Exchange symbol*] .... MEX
Mariner Health Group [*NASDAQ symbol*] (TTSB) .... MRNR
Mariner Health Group, Inc. [*Associated Press*] (SAG) .... MarinerH
Mariner Health Group, Inc. [*NASDAQ symbol*] (SAG) .... MRNR
Mariner Jupiter Orbit [*NASA*] .... MJO
Mariner Jupiter-Saturn [*NASA*] .... MJS
Mariner Jupiter-Uranus [*Mission*] [*NASA*] .... MJU
Mariner Mars Project [*NASA*] .... MM
Mariner Venus Project [*NASA*] .... MV
Mariner Venus-Mercury Project [*NASA*] .... MVM
Mariner-Like Elements [*Genetics*] .... MLE
Mariners [*Seattle Baseball Team*] (AD) .... Ms
Mariners' Church, Detroit, MI [*Library symbol Library of Congress*] (LCLS) .... MiDMch
Mariners' Museum, Newport News, VA [*Library symbol Library of Congress*] (LCLS) .... ViNeM
Marinette, Tomahawk & Western Railroad Co. [*AAR code*] .... MTW
Marinette, WI [*FM radio station call letters*] .... WLST
Marinette, WI [*AM radio station call letters*] .... WMAM
Maringa [*Brazil*] [*Airport symbol*] (OAG) .... MGF
Maringa [*Brazil ICAO location identifier*] (ICLI) .... SBMG
Marino Di Ravenna [*Italy ICAO location identifier*] (ICLI) .... LIVM
Marinus de Caramanico [*Flourished, 1269-85*] [*Authority cited in pre-1607 legal work*] (DSA) .... M
Marinus de Caramanico [*Flourished, 1269-85*] [*Authority cited in pre-1607 legal work*] (DSA) .... Mari
Marinus Freccia [*Flourished, 16th century*] [*Authority cited in pre-1607 legal work*] (DSA) .... Marin Frecc
Mariological Society of America (EA) .... MSA
Marion [*South Africa*] [*Geomagnetic observatory code*] .... MRN
Marion [*Illinois*] [*Airport symbol*] (OAG) .... MWA
Marion [*Indiana*] [*Airport symbol*] (AD) .... MZZ
Marion, AL [*AM radio station call letters*] .... WAJO
Marion, AR [*FM radio station call letters*] .... KFTH
Marion Capital Holdings [*NASDAQ symbol*] (NQ) .... MARN
Marion Capital Holdings, Inc. [*Associated Press*] (SAG) .... MarCap
Marion Carnegie Library, Marion, IA [*Library symbol Library of Congress*] (LCLS) .... IaMari
Marion Carnegie Library, Marion, IL [*Library symbol*] [*Library of Congress*] (LCLS) .... Imari
Marion Carnegie Public Library, Marion, OH [*Library symbol Library of Congress*] (LCLS) .... OMarion
Marion Chronicle Tribune, Marion, IN [*Library symbol Library of Congress*] (LCLS) .... InMarCT
Marion College, Marion, IN [*OCLC symbol*] (OCLC) .... IMC
Marion College, Marion, IN [*Library symbol Library of Congress*] (LCLS) .... InMarC
Marion County Historical Society, Fairmont, WV [*Library symbol Library of Congress*] (LCLS) .... WvFMHi
Marion County Historical Society, Salem, OR [*Library symbol*] [*Library of Congress*] (LCLS) .... OrSaMHi
Marion County Library, Marion, SC [*Library symbol*] [*Library of Congress*] (LCLS) .... ScMar
Marion County Library, Yellville, AR [*Library symbol Library of Congress*] (LCLS) .... ArY
Marion County News, Pleasantville, IA [*Library symbol Library of Congress*] (LCLS) .... IaPleN
Marion County Public Library, Fairmont, WV [*Library symbol Library of Congress*] (LCLS) .... WvF
Marion Downs [*Queensland*] [*Airport symbol*] (AD) .... MXD
Marion, IL [*FM radio station call letters*] .... WDDD
Marion, IL [*AM radio station call letters*] .... WGGH
Marion, IL [*Television station call letters*] .... WTCT
Marion, IN [*Location identifier FAA*] (FAAL) .... MZZ
Marion, IN [*AM radio station call letters*] .... WBAT
Marion, IN [*FM radio station call letters*] (RBYB) .... WBSW-FM
Marion, IN [*AM radio station call letters*] .... WGOM
Marion, IN [*FM radio station call letters*] .... WMRI
Marion, IN [*Television station call letters*] (RBYB) .... WNDY-TV
Marion Island [*South Africa*] [*ICAO location identifier*] (ICLI) .... FAME
Marion Junior College, Marion, VA [*Library symbol Library of Congress*] (LCLS) .... ViMarC
Marion, KY [*AM radio station call letters*] .... WMJL
Marion, KY [*FM radio station call letters*] .... WMJL-FM
Marion Laboratories, Inc. .... Mar
Marion Laboratories, Inc., Kansas City, MO [*Library symbol Library of Congress*] (LCLS) .... MoKML
Marion, MA [*FM radio station call letters*] .... WWTA
Marion, MS [*FM radio station call letters*] .... WZMP
Marion, MS [*FM radio station call letters*] (RBYB) .... WZRW-FM
Marion, NC [*AM radio station call letters*] .... WBRM
Marion, OH [*Location identifier FAA*] (FAAL) .... BUD
Marion, OH [*Location identifier FAA*] (FAAL) .... MNN
Marion, OH [*FM radio station call letters*] .... WDIF
Marion, OH [*AM radio station call letters*] .... WMRN
Marion, OH [*FM radio station call letters*] .... WMRN-FM
Marion Power Shovel [*Stock exchange symbol*] (AD) .... MNV
Marion Public Library, Marion, IN [*Library symbol Library of Congress*] (LCLS) .... InMar
Marion Public Library, Marion, IN [*OCLC symbol*] (OCLC) .... XMP
Marion Public Library, Marion, OH [*OCLC symbol*] (OCLC) .... OMP
Marion, SC [*Location identifier FAA*] (FAAL) .... MAO
Marion, SC [*FM radio station call letters*] .... WCMG
Marion, SC [*FM radio station call letters*] .... WKSY
Marion Sentinel, Marion, IA [*Library symbol Library of Congress*] (LCLS) .... IaManS
Marion Street Elementary School, Lynbrook, NY [*Library symbol*] [*Library of Congress*] (LCLS) .... NLynME
Marion, TX [*AM radio station call letters*] .... KBIB
Marion, VA [*Location identifier FAA*] (FAAL) .... MYX
Marion, VA [*AM radio station call letters*] .... WMEV
Marion, VA [*FM radio station call letters*] .... WMEV-FM
Marion, VA [*Television station call letters*] .... WMSY
Marion, VA [*AM radio station call letters*] .... WOLD
Marion, VA [*FM radio station call letters*] .... WOLD-FM
Marion, VA [*FM radio station call letters*] .... WVTR
Marionette and Puppet .... MUPPET
Mariposa, CA [*FM radio station call letters*] .... KROW
Mariposa, CA [*FM radio station call letters*] .... KUBB
Mariposa County Free Library, Mariposa, CA [*Library symbol Library of Congress*] (LCLS) .... CMar
Mariposa Folk Foundation (EAIO) .... MFF
Mariposa Museum and History Center, Resource Library, Mariposa, CA [*Library symbol*] [*Library of Congress*] (LCLS) .... CMarM
Mariposa Resources, Inc. [*Vancouver Stock Exchange symbol*] .... MPR
Mariquita [*Colombia*] [*Airport symbol*] (OAG) .... MQU
Mariquita/Mariquita [*Colorado ICAO location identifier*] (ICLI) .... SKMQ
Marisa Christina [*NASDAQ symbol*] (TTSB) .... MRSA
Marisa Christina, Inc. [*Associated Press*] (SAG) .... MarisaC
Marisa Christina, Inc. [*NASDAQ symbol*] (SAG) .... MRSA
Mariscal Estigarribia [*Paraguay*] [*ICAO location identifier*] (ICLI) .... SGME
[*The*] **Marist Brothers** (TOCD) .... FMS
Marist Brothers (TOCD) .... fms
Marist College and Seminary, Framingham Center, MA [*Library symbol Library of Congress*] (LCLS) .... MFmcM
Marist College, Poughkeepsie, NY [*Library symbol Library of Congress*] (LCLS) .... NPM
Marist College, Washington, DC [*Library symbol Library of Congress*] (LCLS) .... DMarC
Marist Fathers (TOCD) .... sm
Marist Missionary Sisters (TOCD) .... SMSM
Marist Seminary, Washington, DC [*Library symbol Library of Congress*] (LCLS) .... DMarS
Marist Sisters Congregation of Mary (TOCD) .... SM
Marital Attitude Evaluation [*Psychology*] .... MATE
Marital History .... MH
Marital Roles Inventory [*Psychology*] .... MRI
Marital Satisfaction Inventory [*Psychology*] .... MSI
Marital Satisfaction Scale [*Psychology*] (DAVI) .... MSS
Marital Status [*Army*] (AABC) .... MARSTA
Marital Status .... MS
Marital Status Code [*IRS*] .... MSC
Maritime .... MAR
Maritime .... MARIT
Maritime (AD) .... mrtm
Maritime .... MRTM
Maritime Action Group [*Non-carrier naval task group*] (DOMA) .... MAG
Maritime Administration [*Also, MARAD, MARITADMIN*] [*Department of Transportation*] .... MA
Maritime Administration [*Also, MA, MARITADMIN*] [*Department of Transportation*] .... MARAD
Maritime Administration [*Also, MA, MARAD*] [*Department of Transportation*] (MUGU) .... MARITADMIN
Maritime Administration Office of Research and Development [*Washington, DC*] .... MA-RD
Maritime Administration Report [*Department of Commerce*] .... MAR

Maritime Administration Transport Planning Mobilization [*Federal emergency order*] .... MA-TPM
Maritime Advisory Committee [*Terminated, 1968*] .... MAC
Maritime Air Command [*Canada NATO*] (NATG) .... MAC
Maritime Air Control Authority [*NATO*] (NATG) .... MACA
Maritime Air, Eastern Atlantic (DNAB) .... MAIREASTLANT
Maritime Air Forces Mediterranean [*NATO*] (DNAB) .... MAIRMED
Maritime Air Forces Mediterranean [*NATO*] (NATG) .... MARAIRMED
Maritime Air Group [*Canada*] .... MAG
Maritime Air Radio Organization [*NATO*] (NATG) .... MARO
Maritime Air Superiority (NVT) .... MAS
Maritime Air Superiority Exercise (NVT) .... MASEX
Maritime Air Telecommunications Organization [*NATO*] (NATG) .... MATELO
Maritime Aircraft Weather Code (NATG) .... MAWEC
Maritime Airfield (NATG) .... MARITA
Maritime Antarctic [*Air Mass*] [*Meteorology*] (BARN) .... ma
Maritime Anti-Standing SONAR System (DNAB) .... MASS
Maritime Application Bridge System (OA) .... MABS
Maritime Arctic [*Cold Air*] [*Meteorology*] (BARN) .... mAk
Maritime Arctic Warm [*Air Mass*] [*Meteorology*] (BARN) .... mAw
Maritime Association of the Port of New York [*Later, MAPONY/NJ*] (EA) .... MAPNY
Maritime Association of the Port of New York (EA) .... MAPONY
Maritime Association of the Port of New York/New Jersey (EA) .... MAPONY/NJ
Maritime, Aviation, and Transport Insurance (DLA) .... MAT
Maritime Bank of Israel (BJA) .... MBI
Maritime Cargo Transportation Conference [*of MTRB*] .... MCTC
Maritime Cases, by Crockford and Cox [*1860-71*] [*A publication*] (DLA).... Mar Cas
Maritime Central Airways .... MAR
Maritime Central Analysis Team [*NATO*] (NATG) .... MCAT
Maritime Central Planning Team [*NATO*] (NATG) .... MCPT
Maritime Coal, Railway & Power Co. Ltd. [*AAR code*] .... MCRP
Maritime Command [*Canada, since 1964*] .... MARCOM
Maritime Command Museum, Canadian Forces Base, Halifax, Nova Scotia [*Library symbol National Library of Canada*] (BIB) .... NSHCFM
Maritime Command Operational Research Branch [*Canada*] .... MC/ORB
Maritime Command Operational Research Division [*Canada*] .... MC/ORD
Maritime Command Operational Team Training [*Canadian Navy*] .... MARCOT
Maritime Command Pacific [*Canada, since 1964*] .... MARPAC
Maritime Commission (DNAB) .... MARCOMM
Maritime Commission .... MARITCOM
Maritime Commission [*of Department of Commerce*] [*Merged with Federal Maritime Commission*] .... MC
Maritime Commission Decisions .... MCD
Maritime Commission, Emergency Ship .... MCE
Maritime Commission, Victory Ship .... MCV
Maritime Communication Subsystem [*INTELSAT/INMARSAT*] .... MCS
Maritime Communications Satellite .... MARECS
Maritime Conference Archives, Halifax, NS, Canada [*Library symbol*] [*Library of Congress*] (LCLS) .... CaNSMCA
Maritime Conservatory of Music, Halifax, Nova Scotia [*Library symbol National Library of Canada*] (NLC) .... NSHMC
Maritime Contingency Force [*NATO*] (NATG) .... MARCONFOR
Maritime Contingency Forces, Atlantic [*NATO*] (NATG) .... MARCONFORLANT
Maritime Contingency Plans (NATG) .... MARCONP
Maritime Control Area .... MCA
Maritime Coordination Center .... MCC
Maritime Data Network [*Lloyd's Maritime Data Network Ltd.*] [*Stamford, CT Database*] .... MARDATA
Maritime Data System (IAA) .... MARIDAS
Maritime Defense Zone [*Navy*] [*Coast Guard*] (DOMA) .... MARDEZ
Maritime Defense Zone [*Program for drug interdiction*] .... MDZ
Maritime Education and Training Act of 1980 .... META
Maritime Electric Co. Ltd. [*Toronto Stock Exchange symbol*] .... MEC
Maritime Employers Association (NADA) .... MEA
Maritime Engineering [*Canadian Navy*] .... MARE
Maritime Environment Protection Committee (NADA) .... MEPC
Maritime Federation of the World (NADA) .... MFW
Maritime Forces Pacific Operational Research Team [*Canada*] .... MARPAC/ORT
Maritime Fruit Carriers [*Steamship*] (MHDW) .... MFC
Maritime Gas-Cooled Reactor .... MGCR
Maritime Gas-Cooled Reactor Critical Experiment .... MGCR-CX
Maritime Group Headquarters, Halifax, Nova Scotia, Canada .... CANAIRFAX
Maritime Headquarters (NVT) .... MHQ
Maritime History Archive, Memorial University, St. John's, Newfoundland [*Library symbol National Library of Canada*] (BIB) .... NFSMMH
Maritime Index Bureau (NADA) .... MIB
Maritime Industrial Development Area [*Navy*] .... MIDAS
Maritime Information Association [*British*] (EAIO) .... MIA
Maritime Institute for Research and Industrial Development [*Washington, DC*] (EA) .... MIRAID
Maritime Interception Force (DOMA) .... MIF
Maritime Interception Operations [*Coast Guard*] (DOMA) .... MIO
Maritime Labor Board [*Terminated, 1942*] .... MLB
Maritime Law Association of the US (EA) .... MLA
Maritime Law Book Key Number Data Base [*Maritime Law Book Co. Ltd.*] [*Canada Information service or system*] (CRD) .... MLB
Maritime Law Cases, by Crockford [*1860-71*] [*A publication*] (DLA) .... Mar LC
Maritime Law Cases, First Series, by Crockford [*1860-71*] [*A publication*] (DLA) .... Mar LR
Maritime Law Cases (New Series), by Aspinall [*1870-1940*] [*A publication*] (DLA) .... Mar L Cas (NS)
Maritime Law Cases, New Series, by Aspinall [*1870-1940*] [*England*] [*A publication*] (DLA) .... Mar LC NS

Maritime Law Cases, New Series, by Aspinall [*1870-1940*] [*A publication*] (DLA) .... Mar LR
Maritime Law Reports [*A publication*] (DLA) .... Mar R
Maritime Life Assurance Co. [*Toronto Stock Exchange symbol*] .... MMF
Maritime Maintenance Barge .... MARBARGE
Maritime Mobile .... MM
Maritime Mobile Coastal Telegraphy .... MMCT
Maritime Mobile Phone .... MMP
Maritime Mobile Phone Coastal .... MMPC
Maritime Mobile Phone Distress and Calling .... MMPDC
Maritime Mobile Telegraph .... MMT
Maritime Mobile Telegraph Distress and Calling .... MMTDC
Maritime Mobile Telegraphy Calling .... MMTC
Maritime Museum of British Columbia, Victoria, BC, Canada [*Library symbol Library of Congress*] (LCLS) .... CaBViMM
Maritime Museum of British Columbia, Victoria, British Columbia [*Library symbol National Library of Canada*] (NLC) .... BVIMM
Maritime Museum of the Atlantic, Halifax, Nova Scotia [*Library symbol National Library of Canada*] (NLC) .... NSHMM
Maritime Museum of the Atlantic Library, Halifax, NS, Canada [*Library symbol Library of Congress*] (LCLS) .... CaNSHMM
Maritime Museum, Vancouver, BC, Canada [*Library symbol Library of Congress*] (LCLS) .... CaBVaMM
Maritime Museum, Vancouver, British Columbia [*Library symbol National Library of Canada*] (NLC) .... BVAMM
Maritime Notes and Queries [*1873-1900*] [*A publication*] (DLA) .... Mar N & Q
Maritime Officer Production Study [*Canadian Navy*] .... MOPS
Maritime Operational Intelligence Summary .... MOIS
Maritime Operational Intelligence Summary (MCD) .... MOS
Maritime Operations .... MAROPS
Maritime Orbital Test Satellite .... MAROTS
Maritime Other Ranks Production Study [*Canadian Navy*] .... MORPS
Maritime Patrol (NATG) .... MP
Maritime Patrol Aircraft (NATG) .... MPA
Maritime Patrol Aircraft (AD) .... mpa
Maritime Patrol Airship Study .... MPAS
Maritime Patrol Force (MCD) .... MPF
Maritime Patrol Group .... MPG
Maritime Patrol/Reconnaissance Attack Aircraft (NATG) .... MP/VAP
Maritime Polar Air Mass .... MP
Maritime Polar Air Mass (MSA) .... MPAM
Maritime Polar Air Mass (AD) .... mpam
Maritime Polar [*Air Mass*] Warm [*Meteorology*] (BARN) .... mPw
Maritime Policy [*British*] (ROG) .... MP
Maritime Pollution Convention [*1978*] (DS) .... MARPOL
Maritime Postmark Society [*Later, USCS*] (EA) .... MPS
Maritime Prepositioned Equipment and Supplies [*Navy*] (ANA) .... MPE/S
Maritime Prepositioning Force (DOMA) .... MPF
Maritime Prepositioning Ship (MCD) .... MPS
Maritime Prepositioning Ship .... TAKX
Maritime Prepositioning Ship Squadron (DOMA) .... MPSRON
Maritime Prepositioning Squadron (DOMA) .... MPS
Maritime Provinces [*MARC geographic area code Library of Congress*] (LCCP) .... n-cnm-
Maritime Provinces Higher Education Commission (AD) .... MPHEC
Maritime Provinces Reports [*Canada*] [*A publication*] (DLA) .... Mar Prov
Maritime Provinces Reports [*Canada*] [*A publication*] (DLA) .... MPR
Maritime Radio Direction Finding .... MRDF
Maritime Radio Executive [*British*] .... MRE
Maritime Radionavigation .... MRN
Maritime Radionavigation Mobile Station [*ITU designation*] (CET) .... RM
Maritime Rear Link (MCD) .... MRL
Maritime Reconnaissance (NATG) .... MR
Maritime Reconnaissance Unit [*British military*] (DMA) .... MRU
Maritime Regiment .... MR
Maritime Remote Sensing (MCD) .... MARSEN
Maritime Rescue Coordination Center [*Australia*] .... MRCC
Maritime Rescue Sub-Center [*Canada*] .... MRSC
Maritime Research Department [*An association Inactive*] (EA) .... MRD
Maritime Research Information Service [*National Academy of Sciences*] .... MRIS
Maritime Resource Management Service [*Service d'Amenagement des Ressources des Maritimes*] Amherst, Nova Scotia [*Library symbol National Library of Canada*] (NLC) .... NSAMRMS
Maritime Resource Management Service, Amherst, NS, Canada [*Library symbol Library of Congress*] (LCLS) .... CaNSAMRMS
Maritime Royal Artillery [*British military*] (DMA) .... MRA
Maritime Safety Agency (NADA) .... MSA
Maritime Safety Committee [*Advisory Committee on Pollution of the Sea*] .... MSC
Maritime Satellite [*COMSAT*] .... MARSAT
Maritime Satellite System [*COMSAT*] .... MARISAT
Maritime Satellite System [*COMSAT*] .... MARSATS
Maritime School of Social Work, Halifax, Nova Scotia [*Library symbol National Library of Canada*] (NLC) .... NSHSW
Maritime School of Social Work, Halifax, NS, Canada [*Library symbol Library of Congress*] (LCLS) .... CaNSHSW
Maritime Sector Operations Center [*NATO*] (NATG) .... MSOC
Maritime Self-Defense Force [*Japan*] .... MSDF
Maritime Service Committee [*New York, NY*] (EA) .... MSC
Maritime Services Board of New South Wales [*Australia*] .... MSBNSW
Maritime Shore Patrol .... MSP
Maritime Staff Defense Force (CINC) .... MSDF
Maritime Strike Plan .... MARISP
Maritime Studies Group [*Military*] (VNW) .... MSG
Maritime Subsidy Board [*Maritime Administration*] [*Department of Commerce*] .... MSB

Maritime Support Service .... MSS
Maritime Surface and Subsurface [*Canadian Navy*] .... MARS
Maritime Tactical Data Exchange (NATG) .... MTDE
Maritime Tactical Schools (MCD) .... MTS
Maritime Technical Information Facility [*Maritime Administration*] [*Database producer*] (IID) .... MTIF
Maritime Technical Library, Department of National Defence [*Bibliotheque Technique (Mer), Ministere de la Defense Nationale*] **Ottawa, Ontario** [*Library symbol National Library of Canada*] (NLC) .... OONDMT
Maritime Telegraph & Telephone Co. Ltd. [*Toronto Stock Exchange symbol*] .... MTT
Maritime Telegraph & Telephone, Information Resource Centre, Halifax, NS, Canada [*Library symbol Library of Congress*] (LCLS) .... CaNSHMTT
Maritime Trades Department, AFL-CIO [*American Federation of Labor and Congress of Industrial Organizations*] (EA) .... MTD
Maritime Training Association (EA) .... MTA
Maritime Transport Committee [*OECD*] (DS) .... MTC
Maritime Transport Committee of the Organization for Economic Cooperation and Development [*France*] (EAIO) .... MTCOECD
Maritime Transportation Research Board [*National Research Council*] .... MTRB
Maritime Tropical Air Mass .... MT
Maritime Tropical Air Mass (MSA) .... MTAM
Maritime Union of Australia .... MUA
Maritime Warfare School [*Canadian Navy*] .... MWFS
Maritimes Forest Research Centre [*Research center*] (RCD) .... MFRC
Maritimes Forest Research Centre, Environment Canada [*Centre de Recherches Forestieres des Maritimes, Environnement Canada*] **Fredericton, New Brunswick** [*Library symbol National Library of Canada*] (NLC) .... NBFE
Maritimes Law Reporter (Commerce Clearing House) [*A publication*] (DLA) .... Maritimes L Rep (CCH)
Maritime-Self-Defense .... MSD
Maritrans, Inc. [*Associated Press*] (SAG) .... Maritrn
Maritrans, Inc. [*NYSE symbol*] (SPSG) .... TUG
Maritus [*Bridegroom*] [*Latin*] .... M
Maritzburg (ROG) .... MARITZ
Marius [*of Plutarch*] [*Classical studies*] (OCD) .... Mar
Marius. Concerning Bills of Exchange [*4 eds.*] [*1651-84*] [*A publication*] (DLA) .... Marius
Marius on Bills of Exchange [*A publication*] (DLA) .... Mar Bills
Marius Salomonius [*Deceased, 1557*] [*Authority cited in pre-1607 legal work*] (DSA) .... Mar Sal
Marivan [*Iran*] [*ICAO location identifier*] (ICLI) .... OITY
Marjorie Mayrock Center for CIS [*Commonwealth of Independent States*] **and East European Research** [*Israel*] (EAIO) .... MMCSEER
Marjorie Webster Junior College [*Washington, DC*] .... MWJC
Mark [*Monetary unit*] [*German*] (GPO) .... M
Mark [*Coin*] (ROG) .... MA
Mark (KSC) .... MK
Mark [*Ammunition*] (NATG) .... MK
Mark [*New Testament book*] .... Mk
Mark (WDMC) .... mk
Mark .... MRK
Mark (VRA) .... mrk
Mark Aero [*Air carrier designation symbol*] .... MARX
Mark Centers Trust [*Associated Press*] (SAG) .... MarkCtr
Mark Centers Trust [*NYSE symbol*] (SPSG) .... MCT
Mark Cross [*Initials often used as pattern on Mark Cross leather goods*] .... MC
Mark der Deutschen Notenbank [*Mark of the German Bank of Issue*] [*Later, M*] (EG) .... MDN
Mark Document Reader [*Trademark*] [*Bell & Howell*] .... MDR
Mark Forward [*Papers*] [*British*] .... MF
Mark IV Industries [*NYSE symbol*] (TTSB) IV
Mark IV Industries, Inc. [*NYSE symbol*] (SPSG) IV
Mark IV Industries, Inc. [*Associated Press*] (SAG) .... MarkIV
Mark Lindsay International Fan Club [*Defunct*] (EA) .... MLIFC
Mark Mason (ROG) .... MM
Mark Master [*Freemasonry*] .... MM
Mark Master Mason [*Freemasonry*] .... MMM
Mark Morris Dance Group .... MMDG
Mark of the Beast [*Disparaging term for 19th century Protestant clerical waistcoats that had Catholic influences*] .... MB
Mark of the Craft [*Freemasonry*] .... MC
Mark Off .... MO
Mark on Top (NVT) .... MOT
Mark Resources, Inc. [*Toronto Stock Exchange symbol*] .... MKC
Mark Russell (AD) .... MR
Mark Sense (NITA) .... MS
Mark Sense Form (MCD) .... MSF
Mark Sense Reading .... MSR
Mark Sense Source Data Automation Test and Analysis (MCD) .... MASSDATA
Mark Sensing (MSA) .... MS
Mark Sheet Reader [*Computer science*] (BUR) .... MSR
Mark Skinner Public Library, Manchester, VT [*Library symbol Library of Congress*] (LCLS) .... VtMan
Mark Slade Fan Club (EA) .... MSFC
Mark Solutions [*NASDAQ symbol*] (TTSB) .... MCSI
Mark Solutions, Inc. [*Associated Press*] (SAG) .... MarkSol
Mark Solutions, Inc. [*NASDAQ symbol*] (SAG) .... MCSI
Mark Template [*Tool*] .... MKTP
Mark Trunk (IAA) .... MT
Mark Twain Association (EA) .... MTA
Mark Twain Bancshares, Inc. [*Associated Press*] (SAG) .... MkTwain
Mark Twain Bancshares, Inc. [*NYSE symbol*] (SAG) .... MTB
Mark Twain Bancshares, Inc. [*NASDAQ symbol*] (NQ) .... MTWN
Mark Twain Bancshrs [*NASDAQ symbol*] (TTSB) .... MTWN
Mark Twain Boyhood Home Associates (EA) .... MTBHA
Mark Twain Home Board (EA) .... MTHB
Mark Twain Library Association, Redding, CT [*Library symbol*] [*Library of Congress*] (LCLS) .... CtRe
Mark Twain Memorial (EA) .... MTM
Mark Twain Memorial, Hartford, CT [*Library symbol Library of Congress*] (LCLS) .... CtHMTH
Mark Twain Museum, Hannibal, MO [*Library symbol Library of Congress*] (LCLS) .... MoHM
Mark Twain Research Foundation (EA) .... MTRF
Mark Twain School, Thief River Falls, MN [*Library symbol*] [*Library of Congress*] (LCLS) .... MnTMT
Mark Twain Shrine, Mark Twain State Park, Florida, MO [*Library symbol Library of Congress*] (LCLS) .... MoFIM
Mark Twain Society [*Defunct*] (EA) .... MTS
Mark V Petroleums & Mines [*Vancouver Stock Exchange symbol*] .... MRV
Mark VII [*NASDAQ symbol*] (TTSB) .... MVII
Mark VII, Inc. [*Associated Press*] (SAG) .... MarkVII
Mark VII, Inc. [*NASDAQ symbol*] (SAG) .... MVII
Mark West Springs [*California*] [*Seismograph station code, US Geological Survey*] (SEIS) .... MAC
Mark XII Output and Monitoring System (SAA) .... MOM
MarkAir (GAVI) .... BF
Markair, Inc. [*ICAO designator*] (FAAC) .... MRK
Markala [*Mali*] [*ICAO location identifier*] (ICLI) .... GAMA
Markby's Elements of Law [*6th ed.*] [*1905*] [*A publication*] (DLA) .... Mark El
Markdale Public Library, Ontario [*Library symbol National Library of Canada*] (NLC) .... OMARK
Marked (MSA) .... MKD
Marked [*Computer science*] (MDG) .... MRKD
Marked (AD) .... mrkd
Marked Capacity [*Freight cars*] .... MC
Marked Cocontraction [*Medicine*] .... MCC
Marked Dullness [*on Auscultation*] [*Medicine*] (DAVI) .... M_2
Marked For .... M/F
Marked Stack Control Word .... MSCW
Marked Temperature Inversion [*Aviation*] (DA) .... MTI
Marked Tree, AR [*FM radio station call letters*] .... KERC
Marked Tree, AR [*FM radio station call letters*] (RBYB) .... KJBR-FM
Markel Corp. [*NASDAQ symbol*] (NQ) .... MAKL
Markel Corp. [*Associated Press*] (SAG) .... Markel
Markel Financial Holdings Ltd. [*Toronto Stock Exchange symbol*] .... MFH
Marker [*Beacon*] (AFM) .... M
Marker [*Beacon*] .... MKR
Marker (WGA) .... MRKR
Marker (AD) .... mrkr
Marker and Cell [*Computing technique*] [*NASA*] .... MAC
Marker Beacon Receiver .... MBR
Marker International [*Associated Press*] (SAG) .... MarkerI
Marker International [*NASDAQ symbol*] (SAG) .... MRKR
Marker Intl. [*NASDAQ symbol*] (TTSB) .... MRKR
Marker Light Indicator .... MLI
Marker Pulse Conversion [*Telecommunications*] (TEL) .... MPC
Marker Signal Attenuation .... MSA
Marker Switch (IAA) .... MS
Marker-Adder Generator .... MAG
Market .... MAR
Market .... Mark
Market (VRA) .... mark
Market .... MKT
Market .... MKT
Market (WDMC) .... mkt
Market Administration (HCT) .... MA
Market Advisory Service [*British Overseas Trade Board*] (DS) .... MAS
Market Analysis and Information Database [*MAID Systems Ltd.*] [*British Information service or system*] (IID) .... MAID
Market Analysis and Reference System [*Vancouver stock exchange computer system*] [*Canada*] .... MARS
Market Analysis Guide - Intercity Communications [*AT & T*] .... MAGIC
Market Analysis Report Generator [*Computer science*] .... MARG
Market and Opinion Research International [*Polling organization*] .... MORI
Market and Opinion Research International [*Polling organization*] (ODBW) .... Mori
Market Average [*Investment term*] .... MA
Market Basket Survey [*Business term*] .... MBS
Market Buy Market [*Information service or system*] (IID) .... MBM
Market Capacity (ADA) .... MC
Market Center Limit Order File [*Investment term*] (DICI) .... MCLOF
Market Compilation and Research Bureau, Inc. [*North Hollywood, CA*] [*Information service or system*] (IID) .... MCRB
Market Data Retrieval [*Westport, CT*] [*Information service or system*] (IID) .... MDR
Market Data System [*NYSE*] .... MDS
Market Day [*British*] .... MD
Market Decision System (HGAA) .... MDS
Market Decisions, Inc. [*Information service or system*] (IID) .... MDI
Market Development Index [*Business term*] (DOAD) .... MDI
Market Economy Country .... MEC
Market Entry Guarantee Scheme [*Board of Trade*] [*British*] (DI) .... MEGS
Market Exchange Rates [*Monetary conversion rate*] (ECON) .... MER
Market Facts [*NASDAQ symbol*] (TTSB) .... MFAC
Market Facts, Inc. [*NASDAQ symbol*] (NQ) .... MFAC
Market Facts, Inc. [*Associated Press*] (SAG) .... MktFct
Market Gardeners' Association of Western Australia .... MGAWA
Market Identifiers [*Dun's Marketing Services*] [*Database*] .... MI
Market if Touched [*Stock exchange term*] .... MIT

Market Impact Clearance .... MIC
Market Impact Study .... MIS
Market Intelligence Report .... MINTEL
Market Intelligence Research Co. [*Palo Alto, CA*] (TSSD) .... MIRC
Market Investigation [*Army*] .... MI
Market Milk Producers' Council [*Australia*] .... MMPC
Market Odd-Lot Execution (PDAA) .... MOLE
Market Odd-Lot Execution System [*Computer science*] (MHDI) .... MOLE
Market Opening Sector Specific (AD) .... MOSS
Market Opinion Research, Inc. [*Information service or system*] (IID) .... MOR
Market Oversight Surveillance System .... MOSS
Market Performance Committee [*of NYSE*] .... MPC
Market Price [*Business term*] .... MP
Market Research and Analysis .... MR & A
Market Research Corp. of America .... MCA
Market Research Corp. of America (AD) .... MRCA
Market Research Corp. of America (NADA) .... MRCA
Market Research Council .... MRC
Market Research Information System [*Bell System*] .... MRIS
Market Research Society [*British*] .... MRS
Market Science Associates, Inc. [*Information service or system*] (IID) .... MSA
Market Share Reporter [*A publication*] .... MSR
Market Stabilization Price [*Department of Agriculture*] .... MSP
Market Structures and Trends on Italy [*Databank Ltd.*] [*British*] (ECON) .... MAST
Market Technicians Association (NADA) .... MTA
Market Town [*Geographical division*] [*British*] .... MT
Market Trend Index [*Associated Equipment Distributors program*] .... MATRIX
Market Value .... MV
Market Value [*Insurance*] .... MVal
Market Value Added .... MVA
Market Value Appraiser (DD) .... MVA
Marketable Equity Securities [*Investment term*] (DICI) .... MES
Market-Auction Preferred Stock .... MAPS
Market-by-Market Allocation [*Business term*] (DOAD) .... MBM
Marketer .... MRKTR
Marketfax Infoservices Ltd. [*Vancouver Stock Exchange symbol*] .... MFI
Marketing .... MKTG
Marketing (DD) .... mktg
Marketing .... MKTG
Marketing (WDMC) .... mktg
Marketing .... MKTNG
Marketing Action Planner [*National Association of Printers and Lithographers*] [*A publication*] .... MAP
Marketing, Advertising, and Promotions Solutions Exhibition [*British*] (ITD) .... MAPS
Marketing Agents for Food Service Industry (EA) .... MAFSI
Marketing Aids Group .... MAG
Marketing and Advertising General Information Centre [*Datasolve Ltd.*] [*British Information service or system*] .... MAGIC
Marketing and Advertising Reference Service (NITA) .... MARS
Marketing and Distributive Education Association [*Later, MEA*] (EA) .... MDEA
Marketing and Product Line Evaluation (PDAA) .... MAPLE
Marketing and Promotion Association [*British*] .... MPA
Marketing And Research Counselors Inc. [*Irving, TX*] (WDMC) .... M/A/R/C
Marketing & Sales Division (ACII) .... M&S
Marketing and Training Institute (EA) .... MTI
Marketing and Transportation Situation [*Series*] [*A publication*] .... MTS
Marketing Assistance (MCD) .... MA
Marketing Assistance Program [*Department of Agriculture*] .... MAP
Marketing Assistance Test .... MAT
Marketing Center [*Veterans Administration*] .... MC
Marketing Communications Executives International [*Dallas, TX*] (EA) .... MCEI
Marketing Communications Research Center [*Later, CMC*] .... MCRC
Marketing Concepts, Inc. [*New York, NY*] [*Telecommunications*] (TSSD) .... MCI
Marketing Data Management System [*British*] .... MDMS
[*A*] **Marketing Decision Simulation** [*Game*] .... MARKSIM
Marketing Economics Institute Ltd. [*New York, NY*] .... MEI
Marketing Education Association (EA) .... MEA
Marketing, Engineering, and Business Services [*Telecommunications*] (TEL) .... MEBS
Marketing Freedom Index [*OPEC*] [*Business term*] .... MFI
Marketing Information Data Systems, Inc. [*Information service or system*] (IID) .... MIDS
Marketing Information Network [*Information service or system*] (IID) .... MIN
Marketing Information System .... MIS
Marketing Information System .... MkIS
Marketing Intelligence Corp. [*Information service or system*] (IID) .... MIC
Marketing International Corp. [*Washington, DC*] (TSSD) .... MIC
Marketing of Investments Board [*Finance British*] .... MIB
Marketing of Investments Board Organising Committee [*British*] .... MIBOC
Marketing of Public Library Services Section [*Public Library Association*] .... MPLSS
Marketing Organization (AD) .... MO
Marketing Programs and Services Group, Inc. [*Gaithersburg, MD*] [*Information service or system Telecommunications*] (TSSD) .... MPSG
Marketing Quota .... MQ
Marketing Requirement Document .... MRD
Marketing Research Association [*Chicago, IL*] (EA) .... MRA
Marketing Research Division [*of AMS, Department of Agriculture*] .... MR
Marketing Research Library .... MRL
Marketing Research Trade Association [*Later, MRA*] (EA) .... MRTA
Marketing Science Institute [*Cambridge, MA*] (EA) .... MSI
Marketing Service Representative .... MSR
Marketing Services Conference [*LIMRA*] .... MSC
Marketing Services Group .... MSGI
Marketing Services Officer [*Insurance*] .... MSO
Marketing Strategy [*Simulation package developed by Professors Jean-Claude Larreche and Hubert Gatignon*] .... MARKSTRAT
Marketing Support Representative .... MSR
Marketing Technical Services .... MTS
MarketLink, Inc. [*NASDAQ symbol*] (SAG) .... MKTL
MarketLink, Inc. [*Associated Press*] (SAG) .... MktLink
Market-Oriented, Sector-Selective [*or Specific*] [*Trade negotiations between United States and Japan*] .... MOSS
Marketplace .... MRKTPLC
Markets (AD) .... Mrkts
Market-Value Accounting [*Banking*] (ECON) .... MVA
Market-Value Transmission [*Pricing concept*] .... MVT
Markham District Historical Museum, Markham, ON, Canada [*Library symbol*] [*Library of Congress*] (LCLS) .... CaOMaHM
Markham District Historical Museum, Ontario [*Library symbol National Library of Canada*] (BIB) .... OMAHM
Markham High School, Markham, ON, Canada [*Library symbol Library of Congress*] (LCLS) .... CaOMaH
Markham High School, Ontario [*Library symbol National Library of Canada*] (NLC) .... OMAH
Markham Prayer Card Apostolate (EA) .... MPCA
Markham Public Library, Markham, IL [*Library symbol Library of Congress*] (LCLS) .... IMar
Markham Public Library, Markham, ON, Canada [*Library symbol Library of Congress*] (LCLS) .... CaOMa
Markham Public Library, Ontario [*Library symbol National Library of Canada*] (NLC) .... OMA
Marking .... MKG
Marking (AD) .... mrkg
Marking and Stenciling (AD) .... m/s
Marking Device Association (EA) .... MDA
Marking Diagram Master (MCD) .... MDM
Marking of Overseas Shipments .... MOS
Markings .... MKGS
Markings Center Brief (MCD) .... MCB
Markka [*Monetary unit*] [*Finland*] .... F MK
Markka [*Monetary unit*] [*Finland*] .... M
Markka [*Monetary unit*] [*Finland*] (GPO) .... MK
Markka [*Monetary unit*] [*Finland*] .... Mkk
Markle Foundation, New York, NY [*Library symbol Library of Congress*] (LCLS) .... NNMF
Markov Game Planar Intercept-Evasion Package [*Computer science*] .... MAGPIE
Markov Random Field [*Mathematics*] .... MRF
Markov Renewal Program .... MRP
Marks and Sayre's Reports [*108 Alabama*] [*A publication*] (DLA) .... Marks & Sayre
Marks' and Sayre's Reports [*108 Alabama*] [*A publication*] (DLA) .... Marks & Sayre's
Marks & Spencer [*English department store chain*] .... M & S
Marks & Spencer Canada, Inc. [*Toronto Stock Exchange symbol*] .... MKS
Marks Banco (ROG) .... MB
Marks Bros Jewelers [*NASDAQ symbol*] (TTSB) .... MBJI
Marks Bros. Jewelers, Inc. [*Associated Press*] (SAG) .... MarksBr
Marks Bros. Jewelers, Inc. [*NASDAQ symbol*] (SAG) .... MBJI
Marks, MS [*Location identifier FAA*] (FAAL) .... MMS
Marks, MS [*AM radio station call letters*] .... WQMA
Mark's Work Wearhouse Ltd. [*Toronto Stock Exchange symbol*] .... MWW
Marksman [*British military*] (DMA) .... M
Marksman [*Marine Corps*] .... MKM
Marksman [*Marine Corps*] .... MKS
Marksman Qualification Badge [*Military decoration*] (AABC) .... MkmQualBad
Marksmanship and Gunnery LASER Device (RDA) .... MAGLAD
Marksmanship Qualification Order [*Marine Corps*] .... MQO
Marksmanship Training (NVT) .... MKSTNG
Marksmanship Training Unit (AABC) .... MKTU
Marksville, LA [*AM radio station call letters*] .... KAPB
Marksville, LA [*FM radio station call letters*] .... KAPB-FM
Marksville, LA [*Location identifier FAA*] (FAAL) .... MKV
Mark-to-Market [*Securities*] .... MTM
Markup .... MU
Mark-Up Language [*Computer science*] .... ML
Markway Resources Ltd. [*Vancouver Stock Exchange symbol*] .... MAK
MarkWest Hydrocarbon, Inc. [*Associated Press*] (SAG) .... MarkWst
MarkWest Hydrocarbon, Inc. [*NASDAQ symbol*] (SAG) .... MWHX
Marky Cattle Association (EA) .... MCA
Marl [*Quality of the bottom*] [*Nautical charts*] .... MI
Marl/Loemuhle [*Germany ICAO location identifier*] (ICLI) .... EDLM
Marla [*Australia Airport symbol*] (OAG) .... MRP
Marlat Resources Ltd. [*Vancouver Stock Exchange symbol*] .... MLA
Marlboro [*Vermont*] [*Seismograph station code, US Geological Survey*] (SEIS) .... MARL
Marlboro College, Marlboro, VT [*Library symbol Library of Congress*] (LCLS) .... VtMarC
Marlboro County Public Library, Bennettsville, SC [*Library symbol*] [*Library of Congress*] (LCLS) .... ScBen
Marlborough (ROG) .... MARLB
Marlborough, MA [*Television station call letters*] .... WHSH
Marlborough, MA [*AM radio station call letters*] .... WSRO
Marlborough Productions Ltd. [*Vancouver Stock Exchange symbol*] .... MPD
Marlborough Public Library, Marlborough, MA [*Library symbol Library of Congress*] (LCLS) .... MMar
Marlborough Technical Management [*British*] .... MTM
Marlette, MI [*FM radio station call letters*] .... WBGV
Marlette Township Library, Marlette, MI [*Library symbol Library of Congress*] (LCLS) .... MiMarl

Marley Mines Ltd. [Vancouver Stock Exchange symbol] .... MYM
Marley, Scrooge, and Cratchit [Accounting agency] .... MS & C
Marley Vehicle Leasing [Commercial firm British] .... MVL
Marlin Developments [Vancouver Stock Exchange symbol] .... MND
Marlin Owners' Club (EA) .... MOC
Marlin, TX [FM radio station call letters] .... KEYR
Marlin-Rockwell Corp. (AD) .... MRC
Marlow, OK [FM radio station call letters] .... KFXI
Marlowe Society of America (EA) .... MSA
Marlowe-Crowne Social Desirability Scale [Medicine] (DMAA) .... MCSDS
Marlton Technologies [AMEX symbol] (TTSB) .... MTY
Marlton Technologies, Inc. [Associated Press] (SAG) .... Marlton
Marlton Technologies, Inc. [AMEX symbol] (SPSG) .... MTY
Marman Expansion Joint .... MEJ
Marmande/Virazeil [France ICAO location identifier] (ICLI) .... LFDM
Marmon Club (EA) .... MC
Marmor Parium [Classical studies] (OCD) .... Marm Par
Marmora, Deloro, and Lake Union Public Library, Marmora, Ontario [Library symbol National Library of Canada] (BIB) .... OMDL
Marmorilik [Greenland] [ICAO location identifier] (ICLI) .... BGMM
Marmul/Nasir [Oman] [ICAO location identifier] (ICLI) .... OONR
Maroa, IL [FM radio station call letters] (RBYB) .... WDKR-FM
Maroantsetra [Madagascar] [ICAO location identifier] (ICLI) .... FMNR
Maroantsetra [Madagascar] [Airport symbol] (OAG) .... WMN
Maron [Java] [Seismograph station code, US Geological Survey Closed] (SEIS) .... MAJ
Marondera [Zimbabwe] [ICAO location identifier] (ICLI) .... FVMA
Maroochydore [Australia ICAO location identifier] (ICLI) .... ABMC
Maroochydore [Australia Airport symbol] (OAG) .... MCY
Maroon [Philately] .... mar
Maroua [Cameroon] [Airport symbol] (OAG) .... MVR
Maroua/Salak [Cameroon] [ICAO location identifier] (ICLI) .... FKKL
Maroua/Ville [Cameroon] [ICAO location identifier] (ICLI) .... FKKA
Marquandia Society (EA) .... MS
Marquardt Corp. [Stock exchange symbol] (AD) .... MRQ
Marquardt Navair Fuel [A boron slurry propellant for spacecraft] .... MARNAF
Marque de Commerce [Trademark] .... MC
Marque Deposee [Trademark] .... MD
Marquee Group, Inc. (The) [Associated Press] (SAG) .... MarqG
Marquee Group, Inc. (The) [Associated Press] (SAG) .... MarqGrp
Marquee Group, Inc. (The) [NASDAQ symbol] (SAG) .... MRQE
Marquest Medical Products [NASDAQ symbol] (TTSB) .... MMPI
Marquest Medical Products, Inc. [Associated Press] (SAG) .... Marqst
Marquest Medical Products, Inc. [NASDAQ symbol] (NQ) .... MMPI
Marquetry (VRA) .... marq
Marquetry Society of America (EA) .... MSA
Marquette [Diocesan abbreviation] [Michigan] (TOCD) .... MAR
Marquette [Michigan] [Airport symbol] (OAG) .... MQT
Marquette & Huron Mountain Railroad Co., Inc. [AAR code] .... MHCO
Marquette Business Review [A publication] (DLA) .... Marquette Bus Rev
Marquette County Historical Society, John M. Longyear Memorial Library, Marquette, MI [Library symbol Library of Congress] (LCLS) .... MiMarqHi
Marquette Electronics, Inc. [NASDAQ symbol] (SPSG) .... MARQ
Marquette Electronics, Inc. [Associated Press] (SAG) .... MarqEl
Marquette Electronics 'A' [NASDAQ symbol] (TTSB) .... MARQA
Marquette High School, Ottawa, IL [Library symbol Library of Congress] (LCLS) .... IOtM
Marquette League for Catholic Indian Missions [Defunct] (EA) .... MLCIM
Marquette/Marquette County [Michigan] [ICAO location identifier] (ICLI) .... KMQT
Marquette Medical Systems, Inc. [NASDAQ symbol] (SAG) .... MARQ
Marquette Medical Systems, Inc. [Associated Press] (SAG) .... MarqMed
Marquette, MI [Location identifier FAA] (FAAL) .... DSN
Marquette, MI [AM radio station call letters] .... WDMJ
Marquette, MI [FM radio station call letters] .... WFXD
Marquette, MI [FM radio station call letters] .... WHWL
Marquette, MI [Television station call letters] .... WLUC
Marquette, MI [FM radio station call letters] .... WNMU
Marquette, MI [Television station call letters] .... WNMU-TV
Marquette, MI [FM radio station call letters] .... WUPK
Marquette, MI [FM radio station call letters] .... WUPX
Marquette University (GAGS) .... Marquette U
Marquette University, College of Nursing, Milwaukee, WI [Library symbol Library of Congress] (LCLS) .... WMM-N
Marquette University, Milwaukee, WI [OCLC symbol] (OCLC) .... GZQ
Marquette University, Milwaukee, WI [Library symbol Library of Congress] (LCLS) .... WMM
Marquette University, School of Law, Milwaukee, WI [Library symbol Library of Congress] (LCLS) .... WMM-L
Marquette-Alger Intermediate School District, Learning Materials Center, Marquette, MI [Library symbol Library of Congress] (LCLS) .... MiMarqAS
Marquis [or Marquess] .... M
Marquis [or Marquess] .... MARQ
Marquis Academic Media [Publisher] .... MAM
Marquis Giuseppe Scicluna International University Foundation (EA) .... MGSIUF
Marquis, SK [Television station call letters] .... CKMJ
Marquis Who's Who [Marquis Who's Who, Inc.] [Information service or system A publication] .... MWW
Marquise [Marchioness] [French] (ROG) .... MSC
Marquoketa, IA [AM radio station call letters] .... KMAQ
Marr, Cahalan & Dunn [Law firm] .... MCD
Marrack's European Assurance Cases [England] [A publication] (DLA) .... Marr
Marrakech [Morocco] [Airport symbol] (OAG) .... RAK
Marrakech/Menara [Morocco] [ICAO location identifier] (ICLI) .... GMMX
Marree [Australia Airport symbol Obsolete] (OAG) .... RRE
Marriage (DLA) .... Marr

Marriage (ROG) .... MARRE
Marriage Adjustment Form [Psychology] .... MAF
Marriage Adjustment Inventory [Psychology] .... MAI
Marriage Adjustment Sentence Completion Survey [Psychology] .... MASCS
Marriage Analysis [Psychology] .... MA
Marriage and Family Counseling Certificate (PGP) .... MFCC
Marriage and Family Therapist [Psychology] .... MFT
Marriage Certificate .... MC
Marriage Dissolved .... M Dis
Marriage Encounter .... ME
Marriage Evaluation [Marital relations test] .... ME
Marriage, Family, and Child Counseling (PGP) .... MFCC
Marriage, Family, and Child Counselor [Psychology] (DAVI) .... MFCC
Marriage Guidance Council [British] .... MGC
Marriage Guidance South Australia .... MGSA
Marriage Guidance Western Australia .... MGWA
Marriage Law Defence Union [British] .... MLDU
Marriage Law Reform Association [British] .... MLRA
Marriage License (WDAA) .... MAR LIC
[A] Marriage Prediction Schedule [Premarital relations test] .... AMPS
Marriage Prediction Schedule [Psychology] .... MPS
Marriage Role Expectation Inventory [Psychology] .... MREI
Marriage Settlement [Legal term] (DLA) .... MARR SETTL
Marriage-Personality Inventory [Psychology] .... MPI
Married .... M
Married .... MAR
Married (ROG) .... MARRD
Married .... MD
Married Americans for Tax Equality .... MATE
Married Couple (ADA) .... MC
Married Enlisted Men's Quarters .... MEMQ
Married Enlisted Quarters .... MEQ
Married Man's Allowance [Taxes] [British] .... MMA
Married Officer Quarters .... MOQ
Married Women's Association [British] (DBA) .... MWA
Married Women's Property Act [1882] [British] (AIA) .... MWPA
Marriott International [NYSE symbol] (SPSG) .... MAR
Marriott International [Associated Press] (SAG) .... Marriott
Marriott's English Admiralty Reports [A publication] (DLA) .... Marr Adm
Marriott's Formulare Instrumentorum [Admiralty Court] [1802] [A publication] (DLA) .... Marr Form
Marromeu [Mozambique] [Airport symbol] (AD) .... MEU
Marrow Granulocyte Reserves [Hematology] .... MGR
Marrow Neutrophil Reserve [Medicine] .... MNR
Marrow Production Rate [Hematology] .... MPR
Marrow Release Rate [Hematology] .... MRR
Marrow Stromal Cell [Biochemistry] .... MSC
Marrupa [Mozambique] [ICAO location identifier] (ICLI) .... FQMR
Mars .... M
Mars Aeronomy Mission (MCD) .... MAM
Mars Aeronomy Orbiter (MCD) .... MAO
Mars Approach Sensor .... MAS
Mars Ascent Vehicle [NASA] .... MAV
Mars Atmosphere Density Sensor .... MADS
Mars Atmosphere Probe .... MAP
Mars Atmospheric Water Detection [NASA] .... MAWD
Mars Consortium .... MARCON
Mars Departure Window [Aerospace] .... MDW
Mars Entry Probe .... MEP
Mars Environmental Survey [NASA] .... MESUR
Mars: Evolution of Its Climate and Atmosphere [Planetary science project] .... MECA
Mars Excursion Mission [NASA] (IAA) .... MEM
Mars Excursion Module .... MEM
Mars Flyby Vehicle [Aerospace] .... MFV
Mars General Circulation Model [For planetary weather study] .... MGGM
Mars Geoscience/Climatology Orbiter .... MGCO
Mars Global Surveyor [NASA] .... MGS
Mars Hill College [North Carolina] .... MHC
Mars Hill College, Mars Hill, NC [OCLC symbol] (OCLC) .... NCM
Mars Hill College, Mars Hill, NC [Library symbol Library of Congress] (LCLS) .... NcMhC
Mars Hill, NC [FM radio station call letters] .... WVMH
Mars In-situ-utilization Sample Return [Computer science] .... MISR
Mars Investigation Group [Defunct] (EA) .... MIG
Mars Mission Module .... MMM
Mars Observer Mission (MCD) .... MO
Mars Orbit Ejection (MCD) .... MOE
Mars Orbit [or Orbital] Insertion [Aerospace] .... MOI
Mars Orbital Rendezvous .... MOR
Mars Orbiter [NASA] (KSC) .... MO
Mars Oxident Experiment [NASA] .... MOX
Mars Probe Lander [Aerospace] .... MPL
Mars Roving Vehicle [NASA] (PDAA) .... MRV
Mars Soil [or Surface] Sample Return .... MSSR
Mars Spinning Support Module [NASA] (KSC) .... MSSM
MARS [Modular Airborne Recorder System] Supplemental Data (GFGA) .... MSD
Mars Surface Module (MCD) .... MSM
Mars Surface Operation .... MSO
MARS [Military Affiliate Radio System] Technical Service (CET) .... MTS
[The] Mars Upper Atmosphere Dynamics, Energetics and Evolution Spacecraft [NASA] (ECON) .... MUADEE
Mars Volatiles and Climate Survey [NASA] .... MVACS
Marsa Brega [Libya] [ICAO location identifier] (ICLI) .... HLMB
Marsa Brega [Libya] [Airport symbol] (AD) .... LMQ

Marsabit [*Kenya*] [*ICAO location identifier*] (ICLI) ... HKMB
Marsabit National Park [*Kenya*] (AD) ... MNP
Marschkolonne [*March Column*] [*German military - World War II*] ... MK
Marsden's Collisions at Sea [*11th ed.*] [*1961*] [*A publication*] (DLA) ... Mars Coll
Marsden's English Admiralty [*A publication*] (DLA) ... Mars Adm
Marsden's Select Pleas in the Court of Admiralty [*Selden Society Publications, Vols. 6, 11*] [*A publication*] (DLA) ... Mars
Marseille [*France*] [*Airport symbol*] (OAG) ... MRS
Marseille/Marignane [*France ICAO location identifier*] (ICLI) ... LFML
Marseilles [*France*] [*Seismograph station code, US Geological Survey Closed*] (SEIS) ... MAR
Marseilles High School, Marseilles, IL [*Library symbol Library of Congress*] (LCLS) ... IMarseHS
Marseilles, IL [*Location identifier FAA*] (FAAL) ... MMO
Marseilles, IL [*FM radio station call letters*] ... WKOT
Marseilles Public Library, Marseilles, IL [*Library symbol Library of Congress*] (LCLS) ... IMarse
Marsh [*Maps and charts*] ... Ma
Marsh (ADA) ... MRSH
Marsh & McLennan [*NYSE symbol*] (TTSB) ... MMC
Marsh & McLennan Companies, Inc. [*NYSE symbol*] (SPSG) ... MMC
Marsh & McLennan Companies, Inc. [*Associated Press*] (SAG) ... MrshMc
Marsh Harbour [*Bahamas*] [*Airport symbol*] (OAG) ... MHH
Marsh Harbour, Abaco Island [*Bahamas*] [*ICAO location identifier*] (ICLI) ... MYAM
Marsh Supermarkets, Inc. [*NASDAQ symbol*] (NQ) ... MARS
Marsh Supermarkets, Inc. [*Associated Press*] (SAG) ... MrshS
Marsh Supermarkets, Inc. [*Associated Press*] (SAG) ... MrshSu
Marsh Supermkts'A' [*NASDAQ symbol*] (TTSB) ... MARSA
Marsh Supermkts'B' [*NASDAQ symbol*] (TTSB) ... MARSB
Marshal ... M
Marshal (ROG) ... MAR
Marshal (ROG) ... MARSHL
Marshal (BARN) ... Mshl
Marshal of the Royal Air Force [*British*] ... MRAF
Marshal Sprayable Ablative [*NASA*] ... MSA
Marshaling Area [*Military*] ... MA
Marshaling Area Control Group [*Military*] (AABC) ... MACG
Marshaling Area Control Officer [*Military*] (AABC) ... MACO
Marshaling Yards [*Military*] ... M/Y
Marshall [*Alaska*] [*Airport symbol*] (OAG) ... MLL
Marshall [*Minnesota*] [*Airport symbol*] (OAG) ... MML
Marshall ... MRSHLL
Marshall, AK [*Location identifier FAA*] (FAAL) ... MLL
Marshall & Ilsley [*NASDAQ symbol*] (TTSB) ... MRIS
Marshall & Ilsley Bank ... M & I
Marshall & Isley Corp. [*Associated Press*] (SAG) ... Marshl
Marshall & Isley Corp. [*Associated Press*] (SAG) ... MarshIls
Marshall & Isley Corp. [*NASDAQ symbol*] (NQ) ... MRIS
Marshall and Sevestre's Appeals [*1862-64*] [*Bengal, India*] [*A publication*] (DLA) ... Mar
Marshall and Sevestre's Appeals [*1862-64*] [*Bengal, India*] [*A publication*] (DLA) ... Marsh
Marshall and Swift Cost Index (DICI) ... M & S
Marshall and Wood's Abridgment [*A publication*] (DLA) ... M & W Abr
Marshall, AR [*FM radio station call letters*] ... KBCN
Marshall, AR [*AM radio station call letters*] ... KCGS
Marshall Booster Assembly Contractor (MCD) ... MBAC
Marshall County Historical Society Library, Plymouth, IN [*Library symbol Library of Congress*] (LCLS) ... InPlyHi
Marshall County Library, Holly Springs, MS [*Library symbol Library of Congress*] (LCLS) ... MsHos
Marshall Drummond McCall, Inc. [*Toronto Stock Exchange symbol*] ... MDM
Marshall Energy Ltd. [*Vancouver Stock Exchange symbol*] ... MSE
Marshall, IL [*FM radio station call letters*] ... WMMC
Marshall Indus [*NYSE symbol*] (TTSB) ... MI
Marshall Industries [*NYSE symbol*] (SPSG) ... MI
Marshall Industries [*Associated Press*] (SAG) ... Mrshllnd
Marshall [*Space Flight Center*] **Information Retrieval and Display System** [*NASA*] (PDAA) ... MIRADS
Marshall Islands [*ANSI two-letter standard code*] (CNC) ... MH
Marshall Islands [*ANSI three-letter standard code*] (CNC) ... MHL
Marshall Islands ... MI
Marshall Islands [*MARC geographic area code Library of Congress*] (LCCP) ... poxe--
Marshall Islands (VRA) ... TT
Marshall Manual (SSD) ... MM
Marshall, MI [*FM radio station call letters*] ... WELL
Marshall, MI [*FM radio station call letters*] (RBYB) ... WRCC-FM
Marshall, MN [*FM radio station call letters*] ... KBJJ
Marshall, MN [*FM radio station call letters*] ... KKCK
Marshall, MN [*AM radio station call letters*] ... KMHL
Marshall, MN [*Location identifier FAA*] (FAAL) ... MML
Marshall, MO [*AM radio station call letters*] ... KMMO
Marshall, MO [*FM radio station call letters*] ... KMMO-FM
Marshall, MO [*FM radio station call letters*] ... KMVC
Marshall, MO [*Location identifier FAA*] (FAAL) ... MHL
Marshall, NC [*AM radio station call letters*] ... WHBK
Marshall of Cambridge (Engineering) Ltd. [*British ICAO designator*] (FAAC) ... MCE
Marshall on Marine Insurance [*A publication*] (DLA) ... Marsh Ins
Marshall on Railways as Carriers [*A publication*] (DLA) ... Marsh Car
Marshall on Railways as Carriers [*A publication*] (DLA) ... Marsh Ry
Marshall on the Federal Constitution [*A publication*] (DLA) ... Marsh Dec
Marshall on the Law of Costs [*A publication*] (DLA) ... Marsh Costs
Marshall Plan of the Mind [*BBC radio program*] (ECON) ... MPM
Marshall Public Library, Marshall, IL [*Library symbol Library of Congress*] (LCLS) ... IMars
Marshall Public Library, Marshall, MI [*Library symbol Library of Congress*] (LCLS) ... MiMars
Marshall School, Duluth, MN [*Library symbol*] [*Library of Congress*] (LCLS) ... MnDuMS
Marshall School, Hempstead, NY [*Library symbol*] [*Library of Congress*] (LCLS) ... NHemME
Marshall Space Flight Center [*Also known as GCMSC*] [*NASA*] ... MSFC
Marshall Steel Ltd. [*Toronto Stock Exchange symbol*] ... MS
Marshall System for Aerospace Simulation [*Programming language*] [*1966-68*] (CSR) ... MARSYAS
Marshall, TX [*Location identifier FAA*] (FAAL) ... ASL
Marshall, TX [*FM radio station call letters*] ... KBWC
Marshall, TX [*AM radio station call letters*] ... KMHT
Marshall, TX [*FM radio station call letters*] ... KZEY-FM
Marshall University (GAGS) ... Marshall U
Marshall University, Huntington, WV [*OCLC symbol*] (OCLC) ... WVH
Marshall University, Huntington, WV [*Library symbol Library of Congress*] (LCLS) ... WvHuM
Marshall - University of Michigan Probe [*Rocket flight*] ... MUMP
Marshall-Lyon County Library, Marshall, MN [*Library symbol Library of Congress*] (LCLS) ... MnMar
Marshall-Lyon County Library, Marshall, MN [*Library symbol*] [*Library of Congress*] (LCLS) ... MnMarC
Marshall-Macklin-Monaghan Library, Don Mills, Ontario [*Library symbol National Library of Canada*] (NLC) ... OTMMM
Marshall-Marchetti Procedure [*Medicine*] (MAE) ... MM
Marshall-Marchetti-Krantz [*Procedure*] [*Medicine*] (MEDA) ... MMK
Marshall-Marchetti-Krantz [*Cystourethropexy*] [*Medicine*] (DAVI) ... MMK
Marshall's Air [*ICAO designator*] (AD) ... HS
Marshall's Ceylon Reports [*A publication*] (DLA) ... Marsh Ceylon
Marshall's Circuit Court Decisions [*United States*] [*A publication*] (DLA) ... Marsh
Marshall's Circuit Court Decisions, by Brockenbrough [*United States*] [*A publication*] (DLA) ... Marsh Dec
Marshall's Circuit Court Reports [*United States*] [*A publication*] (DLA) ... Mar
Marshall's Constitutional Opinions [*A publication*] (DLA) ... Marsh Op
Marshall's Duties and Obligations of Railway Companies [*A publication*] (DLA) ... Marsh Ry
Marshall's English Common Pleas Reports [*1814-16*] [*A publication*] (DLA) ... Marsh
Marshall's English Common Pleas Reports [*A publication*] (DLA) ... Marsh CP
Marshall's English Common Pleas Reports [*A publication*] (DLA) ... Marsh (Eng)
Marshall's High Court Reports [*Bengal*] [*A publication*] (DLA) ... Marsh
Marshall's Posse (EA) ... MP
Marshall's Reports [*Kentucky*] [*A publication*] (DLA) ... JJ Marsh (KY)
Marshall's Reports [*Ceylon*] [*A publication*] (DLA) ... Mar
Marshall's Reports [*Bengal*] [*A publication*] (DLA) ... Mar
Marshall's Reports [*Kentucky*] [*A publication*] (DLA) ... Mar
Marshall's Reports [*Ceylon*] [*A publication*] (DLA) ... Marsh
Marshall's Reports [*4 Utah*] [*A publication*] (DLA) ... Marsh
Marshall's Reports [*Kentucky*] [*A publication*] (DLA) ... Marsh
Marshall's Reports [*Bengal*] [*A publication*] (DLA) ... Marsh Beng
Marshall's Reports [*Calcutta*] [*A publication*] (DLA) ... Marsh Calc
Marshall's Reports [*Kentucky*] [*A publication*] (DLA) ... Marsh (KY)
Marshall's Reports [*Bengal*] [*A publication*] (DLA) ... Marshall
Marshalls-Gilberts Area ... MARGILSAREA
Marshalltown Financial [*NASDAQ symbol*] (TTSB) ... MFCX
Marshalltown Financial Corp. [*Associated Press*] (SAG) ... MarshFn
Marshalltown Financial Corp. [*NASDAQ symbol*] (SAG) ... MFCX
Marshalltown, IA [*Location identifier FAA*] (FAAL) ... EMD
Marshalltown, IA [*AM radio station call letters*] ... KDAO
Marshalltown, IA [*AM radio station call letters*] ... KFJB
Marshalltown, IA [*FM radio station call letters*] ... KXIA
Marshalltown, IA [*Location identifier FAA*] (FAAL) ... MIW
Marshalltown Junior College [*Iowa*] ... MJC
Marshalltown Public Library, Marshalltown, IA [*Library symbol Library of Congress*] (LCLS) ... IaMa
Marshalltown Times-Republican, Marshalltown, IA [*Library symbol Library of Congress*] (LCLS) ... IaMaTR
Marsh-Bender [*Factor*] [*Muscle tissue*] ... MB
Marshfield [*Wisconsin*] [*Airport symbol*] (OAG) ... MFI
Marshfield Clinic, Marshfield, WI [*Library symbol Library of Congress*] (LCLS) ... WMarC
Marshfield, MA [*FM radio station call letters*] ... WATD
Marshfield, MO [*FM radio station call letters*] (RBYB) ... KKLH-FM
Marshfield, MO [*AM radio station call letters*] ... KMRF
Marshfield, MO [*FM radio station call letters*] ... KTOZ
Marshfield, WI [*Location identifier FAA*] (FAAL) ... DUS
Marshfield, WI [*Location identifier FAA*] (FAAL) ... GIZ
Marshfield, WI [*Location identifier FAA*] (FAAL) ... MFI
Marshfield, WI [*AM radio station call letters*] ... WDLB
Marshfield, WI [*FM radio station call letters*] ... WLJY
Marst on Sicca [*England*] ... MARSTSIC
Marstons Mills Public Library, Marstons Mills, MA [*Library symbol Library of Congress*] (LCLS) ... MMam
Martec Ltd., Halifax, Nova Scotia [*Library symbol National Library of Canada*] (NLC) ... NSHML
Martek Biosciences, Inc. [*Associated Press*] (SAG) ... Martek
Martek Biosciences, Inc. [*NASDAQ symbol*] (SAG) ... MATK
Martel Oil & Gas [*Vancouver Stock Exchange symbol*] ... MRL
Marten Falls Band Library, Ogoki Post, Ontario [*Library symbol National Library of Canada*] (BIB) ... OOPMF
Marten Transport [*NASDAQ symbol*] (TTSB) ... MRTN

Marten Transport Ltd. [*Associated Press*] (SAG) ... Marten
Marten Transport Ltd. [*NASDAQ symbol*] (NQ) ... MRTN
Martens' Law of Nations [*A publication*] (DLA) ... Mart Law Nat
Martens Polarization Photometer [*Physics*] ... MPP
Martha and the Muffins [*Musical group*] ... M & M
Martha Graham School of Contemporary Dance [*New York, NY*] ... MGSCD
Martha Movement (EA) ... MM
Martha Washington Cases [*A publication*] (DLA) ... Marth W Ca
Martha's Vineyard [*Massachusetts*] [*Airport symbol*] (OAG) ... MVY
Martha's Vineyard, MA [*Location identifier FAA*] (FAAL) ... BXH
Martial [*Roman poet of the first century AD*] (ROG) ... MAR
Martial [*Roman poet, 40-104AD*] [*Classical studies*] (OCD) ... Mart
Martial Arts Commission [*British*] (DI) ... MAC
Martial Arts Control Board [*Victoria, Australia*] ... MACB
Martian Exploratory Rocket Glide Vehicle ... MERGV
Martian Surface and Atmosphere through Time [*NASA*] ... MSATT
Martian Surface Vehicle ... MSV
Martin and Yerger's Tennessee Reports [*8 Tennessee*] [*1825-28*] [*A publication*] (DLA) ... M & Y
Martin and Yerger's Tennessee Reports [*8 Tennessee*] [*1825-28*] [*A publication*] (DLA) ... M and Yerger's Rep
Martin and Yerger's Tennessee Reports [*8 Tennessee*] [*1825-28*] [*A publication*] (DLA) ... M & YR
Martin and Yerger's Tennessee Reports [*8 Tennessee*] [*1825-28*] [*A publication*] (DLA) ... Mar & Yer
Martin and Yerger's Tennessee Reports [*8 Tennessee*] [*1825-28*] [*A publication*] (DLA) ... Mart & Y
Martin and Yerger's Tennessee Reports [*8 Tennessee*] [*1825-28*] [*A publication*] (DLA) ... Mart & Y (Tenn)
Martin and Yerger's Tennessee Reports [*8 Tennessee*] [*1825-28*] [*A publication*] (DLA) ... Mart & Yer
Martin and Yerger's Tennessee Reports [*8 Tennessee*] [*1825-28*] [*A publication*] (DLA) ... Mart & Yerg
Martin Automatic Data-Reduction Equipment ... MADRE
Martin Automatic Rapid Test and Control ... MARTAC
Martin Automatic Reporting System ... MARS
Martin Aviation Services [*ICAO designator*] (FAAC) ... XMA
Martin Color-Fi, Inc. [*Associated Press*] (SAG) ... MartCol
Martin Color-Fi, Inc. [*NASDAQ symbol*] (SAG) ... MRCF
Martin Color-FI [*NASDAQ symbol*] (TTSB) ... MRCF
Martin Co. (MCD) ... MC
Martin Co. Division [*Martin-Marietta Corp.*] [*ICAO aircraft manufacturer identifier*] (ICAO) ... M
Martin County Democrat, Shoals, IN [*Library symbol Library of Congress*] (LCLS) ... InShoD
Martin County Historical Society, Shoals, IN [*Library symbol Library of Congress*] (LCLS) ... InShoHi
Martin County Library, Fairmont, MN [*Library symbol Library of Congress*] (LCLS) ... MnFa
Martin County Public Library, Stuart, FL [*Library symbol Library of Congress*] (LCLS) ... FStuM
Martin Goffman Associates (IID) ... MGA
Martin Industries [*NASDAQ symbol*] (TTSB) ... MTIN
Martin Industries, Inc. [*Associated Press*] (SAG) ... MartnIn
Martin Industries, Inc. [*NASDAQ symbol*] (SAG) ... MTIN
Martin Infrared Tracker ... MIRTAK
Martin Infrared Tracker (SAA) ... MIRTRAK
Martin, KY [*AM radio station call letters*] ... WMDJ
Martin Landau Aficionados [*An association*] ... MLA
Martin Lawrence Ltd. [*Associated Press*] (SAG) ... MartnL
Martin Lawrence Limited Editions [*NYSE symbol*] (SAG) ... MLE
Martin Lawrence Ltd Editions [*NYSE symbol*] (TTSB) ... MLE
Martin Luther King Elementary School, Wyandanch, NY [*Library symbol*] [*Library of Congress*] (LCLS) ... NWyaKE
Martin Luther King III ... MLKIII
Martin Luther King, Jr. ... MLK
Martin Luther King, Jr., Center for Nonviolent Social Change (EA) ... MLKCNSC
Martin Luther King, Jr., Center for Social Change [*Later, MLKCNSC*] (EA) ... MLKCSC
Martin Luther King, Jr., Memorial Center, Atlanta, GA [*Library symbol Library of Congress*] (LCLS) ... GAMK
Martin Luther King Junior Papers Project, Stanford University Libraries, Stanford, CA [*Library symbol*] [*Library of Congress*] (LCLS) ... CStMLK
Martin Luther King Memorial Hospital, Kansas City, MO [*Library symbol Library of Congress*] (LCLS) ... MoKKM
Martin Luther's German Version of the Bible [*A publication*] (BJA) ... Lth
Martin Marietta Corp. ... M-M
Martin Marietta Corp. (KSC) ... MMC
Martin Marietta Corp., Research Library, Denver, CO [*Library symbol Library of Congress*] (LCLS) ... CoDMM
Martin Marietta Corp., RIAS Library, Baltimore, MD [*Library symbol Library of Congress*] (LCLS) ... MdBGM-N
Martin Marietta Corp., Science and Technology Library, Baltimore, MD [*Library symbol Library of Congress*] (LCLS) ... MdBGM-E
Martin Marietta Data Systems ... MMDS
Martin Marietta, Diehl, Thorn-EMI, Thomson [*Army*] ... MDT2
Martin Marietta International ... MMI
Martin Marietta Materials [*Associated Press*] (SAG) ... MartMM
Martin Marietta Materials [*NYSE symbol*] (SAG) ... MLM
Martin Marietta Missile Electronics Division [*Military*] ... MMME
Martin Marietta Missile System [*Military*] ... MMMS
Martin Memorial Library, Williamston, NC [*Library symbol Library of Congress*] (LCLS) ... NcWill
Martin Memorial [*York City and County*] **Library, York, PA** [*Library symbol Library of Congress*] (LCLS) ... PY
Martin Memorial [*York City and County*] **Library, York, PA** [*OCLC symbol*] (OCLC) ... PYM
Martin Monsen Regional Library, Naknek, AK [*Library symbol Library of Congress*] (LCLS) ... AkNak
Martin Nuclear Division [*AEC*] (MCD) ... MND
Martin on Executors [*A publication*] (DLA) ... Mart Ex
Martin, SD [*FM radio station call letters*] ... KZSD
Martin, SD [*Television station call letters*] ... KZSD-TV
Martin Steinberg Center for Jewish Artists - American Jewish Congress [*Defunct*] (EA) ... MSCJA-AJC
Martin Steinberg Center of the American Jewish Congress (EA) ... MSCAJC
Martin Technical Institute, Williamston, NC [*Library symbol Library of Congress*] (LCLS) ... NcWillM
Martin Thin-Film Electronic Circuit ... MARTEC
Martin, TN [*AM radio station call letters*] ... WCMT
Martin, TN [*FM radio station call letters*] ... WCMT-FM
Martin, TN [*FM radio station call letters*] ... WUTM
Martin Van Buren [*US president, 1782-1862*] ... MVB
Martin Van Buren Fan Club (EA) ... MVBFC
Martina Franca [*Italy ICAO location identifier*] (ICLI) ... LIBX
Martinair Holland NV [*Netherlands ICAO designator*] (FAAC) ... MPH
Martinaire [*ICAO designator*] (FAAC) ... MRA
Martin-Baker Ltd. [*British ICAO designator*] (FAAC) ... MBE
Martinek-Zaichkowsky Self-Concept Scale for Children [*Child development test*] ... MZSCS
Martinez (AD) ... Mrtnz
Martinez, GA [*FM radio station call letters*] ... WGOR
Martinez, GA [*FM radio station call letters*] ... WKBG
Martingana [*Ship's rigging*] (ROG) ... MA
Martini & Rossi ... M&R
Martini-Enfield [*Rifle*] ... M-E
Martini-Henry [*Rifle*] ... M-H
Martinique [*West Indies*] (WDAA) ... MART
Martinique [*MARC country of publication code Library of Congress*] (LCCP) ... mq
Martinique [*ANSI two-letter standard code*] (CNC) ... MQ
Martinique [*West Indies*] (WDAA) ... MQE
Martinique (AD) ... Mqe
Martinique (AD) ... Mrt
Martinique [*ANSI three-letter standard code*] (CNC) ... MTQ
Martinique [*MARC geographic area code Library of Congress*] (LCCP) ... nwmq--
Martinique Communist Party [*Political party*] ... MCP
Martin-Lewis [*Medium*] [*Microbiology*] ... M-L
Martin's Chancery Decisions [*Arkansas*] [*A publication*] (DLA) ... Martin's Chy
Martin's Circuit Court Reports [*1 North Carolina*] [*A publication*] (DLA) ... Mart USCC
Martin's Condensed Louisiana Reports [*A publication*] (DLA) ... Mart Cond LA
Martin's Decisions in Equity [*Arkansas*] [*A publication*] (DLA) ... Mart Ark
Martin's Index to Virginia Reports [*A publication*] (DLA) ... Martin Index
Martin's Louisiana Reports [*A publication*] (DLA) ... Mar
Martin's Louisiana Reports [*A publication*] (DLA) ... Mar LA
Martin's Louisiana Reports [*A publication*] (DLA) ... Mart Rep
Martin's Louisiana Reports [*A publication*] (DLA) ... Martin
Martin's Louisiana Reports [*A publication*] (DLA) ... Martin's LA Rep
Martin's Louisiana Reports [*A publication*] (DLA) ... Martin's Louisiana R
Martin's Louisiana Reports, New Series [*A publication*] (DLA) ... Lou Rep NS
Martin's Louisiana Reports, New Series [*A publication*] (DLA) ... Mar NS
Martin's Louisiana Reports, New Series [*A publication*] (DLA) ... Mart NS
Martin's Louisiana Reports, New Series [*A publication*] (DLA) ... Mart NS (LA)
Martin's Louisiana Reports, New Series [*A publication*] (DLA) ... Mart Rep NS
Martin's Louisiana Reports, New Series [*A publication*] (DLA) ... Martin (Lou) NS
Martin's Louisiana Reports, New Series [*A publication*] (DLA) ... Martin's LA Rep NS
Martin's Louisiana Reports, New Series [*A publication*] (DLA) ... Martin's NS
Martin's Louisiana Reports, New Series [*A publication*] (DLA) ... Martin's R NS
Martin's Louisiana Reports, New Series [*A publication*] (DLA) ... MNS
Martin's Louisiana Reports, New Series [*A publication*] (DLA) ... New Series
Martin's Louisiana Reports, Old and New Series [*A publication*] (DLA) ... Mart LA
Martin's Louisiana Reports, Old Series [*A publication*] (DLA) ... Mart OS (LA)
Martin's Louisiana Term Reports [*1809-30*] [*A publication*] (DLA) ... Mart
Martin's Mining Cases [*Canada*] [*A publication*] (DLA) ... Mart MC
Martin's Mining Cases [*British Columbia*] [*A publication*] (DLA) ... MCC
Martin's North Carolina Reports [*1 North Carolina*] [*A publication*] (DLA) ... Mar
Martin's North Carolina Reports [*1 North Carolina*] [*A publication*] (DLA) ... Mar NC
Martin's North Carolina Reports [*1 North Carolina*] [*A publication*] (DLA) ... Mart
Martin's North Carolina Reports [*1 North Carolina*] [*A publication*] (DLA) ... Mart NC
Martin's North Carolina Reports [*1 North Carolina*] [*A publication*] (DLA) ... Martin
Martin's Practice of Conveyancing [*A publication*] (DLA) ... Mart Conv
Martin's Recital Book [*A publication*] (DLA) ... Mar Rec B
Martin's Reports [*21-30 Georgia*] [*A publication*] (DLA) ... Mart GA
Martin's Reports [*54-70 Indiana*] [*A publication*] (DLA) ... Mart Ind
Martin's Reports [*21-30, 54-70 Georgia*] [*A publication*] (DLA) ... Martin
Martin's Reports of Mining Cases [*Canada*] [*A publication*] (DLA) ... MM Cas
Martin's Reports of Mining Cases [*Canada*] [*A publication*] (DLA) ... MMC
Martin's Scarlet Blue [*Histologic stain*] ... MSB
Martinsburg, PA [*AM radio station call letters*] ... WJSM
Martinsburg, PA [*FM radio station call letters*] ... WJSM-FM
Martinsburg, WV [*Location identifier FAA*] (FAAL) ... EXW
Martinsburg, WV [*Location identifier FAA*] (FAAL) ... MRB
Martinsburg, WV [*Location identifier FAA*] (FAAL) ... VYJ
Martinsburg, WV [*AM radio station call letters*] ... WEPM
Martinsburg, WV [*FM radio station call letters*] ... WKMZ
Martinsburg, WV [*AM radio station call letters*] ... WRNR
Martinsburg, WV [*TV station call letters*] (RBYB) ... WSHE-TV

Martinsburg, WV [*FM radio station call letters*] ... WVEP
Martinsburg, WV [*Television station call letters*] ... WYVN
Martinsburg-Berkeley County Public Library, Martinsburg, WV [*Library symbol Library of Congress*] (LCLS) ... WvMa
Martinsried Institute for Protein Sequences [*Database producer*] ... MIPS
Martinsville Community Unit Schools District, Martinsville, IL [*Library symbol*] [*Library of Congress*] (LCLS) ... IMartSD
Martinsville, IN [*FM radio station call letters*] ... WCBK
Martinsville, IN [*AM radio station call letters*] ... WMCB
Martinsville Township Library, Martinsville, IL [*Library symbol Library of Congress*] (LCLS) ... IMart
Martinsville, VA [*Location identifier FAA*] (FAAL) ... BRJ
Martinsville, VA [*Location identifier FAA*] (FAAL) ... MTV
Martinsville, VA [*AM radio station call letters*] ... WHEE
Martinsville, VA [*AM radio station call letters*] ... WMVA
Martinsville, VA [*FM radio station call letters*] ... WPIM
Martinsville, VA [*FM radio station call letters*] ... WROV
Martinus Caratti de Laude [*Flourished, 1438-45*] [*Authority cited in pre-1607 legal work*] (DSA) ... Mar de Lau
Martinus Caratti de Laude [*Flourished, 1438-45*] [*Authority cited in pre-1607 legal work*] (DSA) ... Mart Laud
Martinus de Caramanico [*Flourished, 1269-85*] [*Authority cited in pre-1607 legal work*] (DSA) ... Ma
Martinus de Fano [*Deceased circa 1275*] [*Authority cited in pre-1607 legal work*] (DSA) ... M Fa
Martinus de Fano [*Deceased circa 1275*] [*Authority cited in pre-1607 legal work*] (DSA) ... Mar Fa
Martinus de Fano [*Deceased circa 1275*] [*Authority cited in pre-1607 legal work*] (DSA) ... Mar Fan
Martinus de Fano [*Deceased circa 1275*] [*Authority cited in pre-1607 legal work*] (DSA) ... MF
Martinus Gosia [*Authority cited in pre-1607 legal work*] (DSA) ... M
Martinus Gosia [*Authority cited in pre-1607 legal work*] (DSA) ... Ma
Martinus Gosia [*Authority cited in pre-1607 legal work*] (DSA) ... Mart
Martinus Gosia [*Authority cited in pre-1607 legal work*] (DSA) ... MG
Martinus Sillimanus [*Flourished, 13th century*] [*Authority cited in pre-1607 legal work*] (DSA) ... Mar Sill
Martinus Zamorensis [*Flourished, 13th century*] [*Authority cited in pre-1607 legal work*] (DSA) ... M
Martis Peak [*California*] [*Seismograph station code, US Geological Survey*] (SEIS) ... MPK
Martius [*March*] [*Latin*] ... MART
Martyr ... M
Martyr ... MART
Martyrdom (VRA) ... mtydm
Martyrdom of Isaiah [*Pseudepigrapha*] (BJA) ... MartIs
Martyrdom of Isaiah [*Pseudepigrapha*] (BJA) ... MartIsa
Martyres [*Martyrs*] ... MM
Marudi [*Malaysia*] [*Airport symbol*] (OAG) ... MUR
Marudi [*Indonesia*] [*ICAO location identifier*] (ICLI) ... WBGM
Maruman Integrated Circuits (NITA) ... MIC
Maruranawa [*Guyana*] [*ICAO location identifier*] (ICLI) ... SYMW
Maruzen Co. Ltd. [*UTLAS symbol*] ... MZN
Maruzen International Co., Inc. [*Information service or system*] (IID) ... MIC
Maruzen Online Network [*Maruzen Co. Ltd.*] [*Japan Telecommunications*] ... MARUNET
Maruzen Scientific Information Service Center [*Maruzen Co. Ltd.*] [*Japan Telecommunications*] ... MASIS
Marvel Entertainment Corp. [*Associated Press*] (SAG) ... Marvel
Marvel Entertainment Group [*NYSE symbol*] (SPSG) ... MRV
Marvel Entertainment Grp [*NYS*] (TTSB) ... MRV
Marvelous (DSUE) ... MARV
Marvel's Reports [*Delaware*] [*A publication*] (DLA) ... Mar
Marvel's Reports [*15-16 Delaware*] [*A publication*] (DLA) ... Marv
Marvel's Reports [*15-16 Delaware*] [*A publication*] (DLA) ... Marv (Del)
Marvel's Reports [*15-16 Delaware*] [*A publication*] (DLA) ... Marvel
Marvin Duchow Music Library, McGill University, Montreal, Quebec [*Library symbol National Library of Canada*] (NLC) ... QMMMDM
Marvin Ltd. [*British ICAO designator*] (FAAC) ... MVN
Marvin on General Average [*A publication*] (DLA) ... Mar Av
Marvin on General Average [*A publication*] (DLA) ... Marv Av
Marvin on Wreck and Salvage [*A publication*] (DLA) ... Mar Wr & S
Marvin on Wreck and Salvage [*A publication*] (DLA) ... Marv Wr & S
Marvin's Legal Bibliography [*A publication*] (DLA) ... Mar Leg Bib
Marvin's Legal Bibliography [*A publication*] (DLA) ... Marv Leg Bib
Marwari [*MARC language code Library of Congress*] (LCCP) ... mwr
Marwayne Public Library, Alberta [*Library symbol National Library of Canada*] (NLC) ... AMAR
Marwayne Public Library, Marwayne, AB, Canada [*Library symbol*] [*Library of Congress*] (LCLS) ... CaAMar
Marx, Engels, Lenin, Stalin, October Revolution [*Given name popular in Russia after the Bolshevik Revolution*] ... MELSOR
Marxism-Leninism-Mao Tse-Tung Thought [*Ideologies guiding the New People's Army, a guerrilla movement in the Philippines*] ... MLMTT
Marxist [*Politics*] ... M
Marxist All-Ethiopian Socialist Movement [*Political party*] (PD) ... MAESON
Marxist on Drugs [*Mods - Facetious translation referring to Moderate Republicians*] ... Mod
Marxist Progressive Labor Party [*Political party*] (AD) ... MPLP
Marxisten-Leninisten Oesterreichs [*Marxists-Leninists of Austria*] [*Political party*] (PPE) ... MLO
Marxist-Leninist Armed Propaganda Unit [*Turkey*] ... MLAPU
Marxist-Leninist Communist Party [*Bolivia*] [*Political party*] (PPW) ... PC-ML
Marxist-Leninist Party of the USA (EA) ... MLP USA
Mary [*Former USSR Seismograph station code, US Geological Survey Closed*] (SEIS) ... MRY
Mary Allen Junior College, Crockett, TX [*Library symbol Library of Congress*] (LCLS) ... TxCrMA
Mary Baker Eddy [*Founder of Christian Science*] ... MBE
Mary Baldwin College [*Virginia*] ... MBC
Mary Baldwin College, Staunton, VA [*Library symbol Library of Congress*] (LCLS) ... ViStM
Mary Baldwin College, Staunton, VA [*OCLC symbol*] (OCLC) ... VMB
Mary Bridge Children's Health Center, Tacoma, WA [*Library symbol Library of Congress*] (LCLS) ... WaTCH
Mary C. Rauchholz Memorial Library, Hemlock, MI [*Library symbol Library of Congress*] (LCLS) ... MiHem
Mary Cheney Library, Manchester, CT [*Library symbol Library of Congress*] (LCLS) ... CtMan
Mary Cheney Library, Manchester, CT [*OCLC symbol*] (OCLC) ... MCP
Mary College, Bismarck, ND [*Library symbol Library of Congress*] (LCLS) ... NdBM
Mary College, Library, Bismarck, ND [*OCLC symbol*] (OCLC) ... NDM
Mary Ellen, Dorothy, Chuck, Ann [*Famous Canadian resort, named for the owners' children*] ... MEDOCHAN
Mary Ellen Resources Ltd. [*Vancouver Stock Exchange symbol*] ... MYE
Mary Esther/Eglin Air Field Auxiliary [*Florida*] [*ICAO location identifier*] (ICLI) ... KHRT
Mary Esther, FL [*Location identifier FAA*] (FAAL) ... HRT
Mary Esther, FL [*Location identifier FAA*] (FAAL) ... REZ
Mary Esther, FL [*FM radio station call letters*] ... WYZB
Mary Glawgow Publications [*Publisher*] [*British*] ... MGP
Mary Hardin-Baylor College, Belton, TX [*OCLC symbol*] (OCLC) ... MHB
Mary Hardin-Baylor College, Belton, TX [*Library symbol Library of Congress*] (LCLS) ... TxBelM
Mary Hartman, Mary Hartman [*Initialism is shortened form of television program title*] [*Also, MH2*] ... M^{2H2}
Mary Hartman, Mary Hartman [*Initialism is shortened form of television program title*] [*Also, M^{2H2}*] ... MH2
Mary Hawkins Memorial Library, Saltspring Island Public Library, Ganges, BritishColumbia [*Library symbol National Library of Canada*] (NLC) ... BGSI
Mary Holmes College, West Point, MS [*OCLC symbol*] (OCLC) ... MHC
Mary Holmes College, West Point, MS [*Library symbol Library of Congress*] (LCLS) ... MsWpMH
Mary Immaculate Hospital, School of Nursing, Jamaica, NY [*Library symbol Library of Congress*] (LCLS) ... NJMI
Mary Immaculate Seminary [*Pennsylvania*] ... MIS
Mary Immaculate Seminary, Northampton, PA [*Library symbol Library of Congress*] (LCLS) ... PNohM
Mary J. Drexel Home, Gladwyne, PA [*Library symbol Library of Congress Obsolete*] (LCLS) ... PGladM
Mary J. L. Black Library, Thunder Bay, ON, Canada [*Library symbol Library of Congress*] (LCLS) ... CaOTBMB
Mary J. L. Black Library, Thunder Bay, Ontario [*Library symbol National Library of Canada*] (NLC) ... OTBMB
Mary Jo Cattlett Fan Club (EA) ... MCFC
Mary L. Cook Public Library, Waynesville, OH [*Library symbol Library of Congress*] (LCLS) ... OWay
Mary Lyon School, Minnesota Correctional Facility, Sauk Centre, MN [*Library symbol*] [*Library of Congress*] (LCLS) ... MnScML
Mary MacDonald Elementary School, Silver Bay, MN [*Library symbol*] [*Library of Congress*] (LCLS) ... MnSibME
Mary Manse College, Toledo, OH [*Library symbol Library of Congress*] (LCLS) ... OTMM
Mary Morstan's Companions [*An association*] ... MMC
Mary P. Shelton Library, Georgetown, OH [*Library symbol Library of Congress*] (LCLS) ... OGeo
Mary (Queen of England) (DLA) ... Mar
Mary Queen of Scots Society (EAIO) ... MQSS
Mary S. Biesecker Public Library, Somerset, PA [*Library symbol Library of Congress*] (LCLS) ... PSom
Mary Stuart Society of America (EA) ... MSS
Mary Tyler Moore [*Actress after whom film studio MTM Enterprises is named*] ... MTM
Mary Washington College [*University of Virginia*] ... MWC
Mary Washington College, Fredericksburg, VA [*OCLC symbol*] (OCLC) ... VMW
Mary Washington College of the University of Virginia, Fredericksburg, VA [*Library symbol Library of Congress*] (LCLS) ... ViFreM
Mary Wilson Fan Club (EA) ... MWFC
Maryborough [*Australia Airport symbol*] (OAG) ... MBH
Marycrest College, Davenport, IA [*Library symbol Library of Congress*] (LCLS) ... IaDaMC
Marycrest College, Davenport, IA [*OCLC symbol*] (OCLC) ... IOR
Marygrove College (GAGS) ... Marygrove C
Marygrove College, Detroit, MI [*Library symbol Library of Congress*] (LCLS) ... MiDM
Maryheart Crusaders (EA) ... MC
Maryknoll Associate Lay Missioners (EA) ... MALM
Maryknoll Center for Justice Concerns (EA) ... MCJC
Maryknoll Fathers, Catholic Foreign Mission Society of America (TOCD) ... mm
Maryknoll Fathers Seminary, Maryknoll, NY [*Library symbol Library of Congress*] (LCLS) ... NMyM
Maryknoll Missioners [*Catholic Foreign Mission Society*] [*Roman Catholic religious order*] ... MM
Maryknoll Seminary, Glen Ellyn, IL [*Library symbol Library of Congress*] (LCLS) ... IGleM
Maryknoll Sisters of St. Dominic (TOCD) ... MM
Maryland [*Postal code*] ... MD
Maryland [*MARC country of publication code Library of Congress*] (LCCP) ... mdu
Maryland [*MARC geographic area code Library of Congress*] (LCCP) ... n-us-md

Maryland Academic Library Center for Automated Processing (NITA) .... MALCAP
Maryland & Delaware Railroad Co. [*AAR code*] .... MDDE
Maryland & Pennsylvania Railroad Co. (IIA) .... M & P
Maryland & Pennsylvania Railroad Co. [*AAR code*] .... MPA
Maryland Appellate Reports [*A publication*] (DLA) .... MD A
Maryland Appellate Reports [*A publication*] (DLA) .... MD App
Maryland Association of Certified Public Accountants (SRA) .... MACPA
Maryland Association of Health Maintenance Organizations (SRA) .... MAHMO
Maryland Automated Geographic Information System [*Maryland State Department of State Planning*] [*Information service or system*] (IID) .... MAGI
Maryland Automotive Reclamation Corp. [*Automotive materials recycling project*] .... MARC
Maryland Chancery Decisions [*A publication*] (DLA) .... Maryland Ch Dec
Maryland Chancery Decisions [*A publication*] (DLA) .... MD Ch D
Maryland Chancery Decisions [*A publication*] (DLA) .... MD Ch Dec
Maryland Chancery Decisions [*A publication*] (DLA) .... MD Chan
Maryland Chancery Decisions [*A publication*] (DLA) .... MD Chan Dec
Maryland Chancery Reports, by Johnson [*4 vols.*] [*A publication*] (DLA) .... MD Ch
Maryland College for Women, Lutherville, MD [*Library symbol Library of Congress*] (LCLS) .... MdLuW
Maryland Committee for Children (EDAC) .... MCC
Maryland Constitution [*A publication*] (DLA) .... MD Const
Maryland Department of Legislative Reference, Baltimore, MD [*Library symbol Library of Congress*] (LCLS) .... Md-LR
Maryland Department of Mental Hygiene, Baltimore, MD [*Library symbol Library of Congress*] (LCLS) .... Md-MH
Maryland Fed Bancorp [*NASDAQ symbol*] (TTSB) .... MFSL
Maryland Federal Bancorp, Inc. [*Associated Press*] (SAG) .... MdFdBc
Maryland Federal Bancorp, Inc. [*NASDAQ symbol*] (NQ) .... MFSL
Maryland Functional Mathematics Test (EDAC) .... MFMT
Maryland Functional Reading Test (EDAC) .... MFRT
Maryland Functional Writing Program (EDAC) .... MFWP
Maryland Historical Society, Baltimore, MD [*Library symbol Library of Congress*] (LCLS) .... MdHi
Maryland House of Corrections, Jessup, MD [*Library symbol Library of Congress*] (LCLS) .... MdJC
Maryland Independent Truckers and Drivers Association [*Later, ITDA*] (EA) .... MITDA
Maryland Institute College of Art (GAGS) .... Md Inst C Art
Maryland Institute, School of Fine and Applied Arts, Baltimore, MD [*Library symbol Library of Congress*] (LCLS) .... MdBMI
Maryland Interlibrary Loan (NITA) .... MILO
Maryland Interlibrary Organization [*Information service or system*] (IID) .... MILO
Maryland Journal of International Law and Trade [*A publication*] (DLA) .... Md J Int'l L & Trade
Maryland Law Encyclopedia [*A publication*] (DLA) .... MLE
Maryland Law Journal and Real Estate Record [*A publication*] (DLA) .... Mar LJ
Maryland Law Record [*A publication*] (DLA) .... Mar L Rec
Maryland Law Record [*Baltimore*] [*A publication*] (DLA) .... MD L Rec
Maryland Law Record [*A publication*] (DLA) .... MLR
Maryland Law Reporter [*Baltimore*] [*A publication*] (DLA) .... MD L Rep
Maryland Library Center for Automated Processing [*Library network*] .... MALCAP
Maryland Online User Group (NITA) .... MOUG
Maryland Parent Attitude Survey [*Psychology*] .... MPAS
Maryland Personnel and Guidance Association (AD) .... MPGA
Maryland Port Authority (AD) .... mpa
Maryland Preschool Self-Concept Scale (EDAC) .... MPSS
Maryland Probation, Patrol and Corrections Association (AD) .... MPPCA
Maryland Psychiatric Research Center [*University of Maryland*] [*Research center*] (RCD) .... MPRC
Maryland Public Television [*Owings Mills*] [*Information service or system Telecommunications*] (TSSD) .... MPT
Maryland Reports [*A publication*] (DLA) .... Mary
Maryland Reports [*A publication*] (DLA) .... Maryland
Maryland Reports [*A publication*] (DLA) .... MD
Maryland Reports [*A publication*] (DLA) .... MD R
Maryland Reports [*A publication*] (DLA) .... MD Rep
Maryland School for the Deaf, Frederick, MD [*Library symbol*] [*Library of Congress*] (LCLS) .... MdFreSD
Maryland State Bar Association, Report [*A publication*] (DLA) .... Mr SBA
Maryland State Board of Contract Appeals (AAGC) .... MSBCA
Maryland State College [*Merged with University of Maryland*] .... MSC
Maryland State Department of Natural Resources, Annapolis, MD [*Library symbol Library of Congress*] (LCLS) .... Md-NR
Maryland State Law Library, Annapolis, MD [*Library symbol Library of Congress*] (LCLS) .... Md-LL
Maryland State Library, Annapolis, MD [*Library symbol Library of Congress*] (LCLS) .... Md
Maryland State Planning Commission, Baltimore, MD [*Library symbol Library of Congress*] (LCLS) .... Md-SP
Maryland State Police [*FAA designator*] (FAAC) .... TRP
Maryland State Teachers College .... MSTC
Maryland Workmen's Compensation Cases [*A publication*] (DLA) .... MD WCC
Maryland-National Capital Park and Planning Commission .... MNCPPC
Marylebone Cricket Club [*Governing body for cricket*] .... MCC
Marylhurst College, Marylhurst, OR [*Library symbol Library of Congress*] (LCLS) .... OrMaC
Marymount College, Arlington, VA [*Library symbol Library of Congress*] (LCLS) .... ViArM
Marymount College, Palos Verdes Estates, CA [*Library symbol Library of Congress Obsolete*] (LCLS) .... CPvMC
Marymount College, Salina, KS [*Library symbol Library of Congress*] (LCLS) .... KSalM
Marymount College, Tarrytown, NY [*Library symbol Library of Congress*] (LCLS) .... NTaM
Marymount Manhattan College [*New York, NY*] .... MMC
Marymount Manhattan College, New York, NY [*Library symbol Library of Congress*] (LCLS) .... NNMa
Maryport (AD) .... Mpt
Marystown, NF [*Television station call letters*] CBNT-3
Marystown, NF [*AM radio station call letters*] .... CHCM
Marystown, NF [*FM radio station call letters*] .... CIOZ
Marystown Public Library, Marystown, NF, Canada [*Library symbol Library of Congress*] (LCLS) .... CaNfMa
Marystown Public Library, Newfoundland [*Library symbol National Library of Canada*] (NLC) .... NFMA
Marysvale [*Utah*] [*Seismograph station code, US Geological Survey*] (SEIS) .... MSU
Marysville [*California*] [*Airport symbol*] (AD) .... MYV
Marysville/Beale Air Force Base [*California*] [*ICAO location identifier*] (ICLI) .... KBAB
Marysville, CA [*Location identifier FAA*] (FAAL) .... BAB
Marysville, CA [*AM radio station call letters*] .... KMYC
Marysville, CA [*FM radio station call letters*] .... KSXX
Marysville, CA [*Location identifier FAA*] (FAAL) .... MYV
Marysville City Library, Marysville, CA [*Library symbol Library of Congress*] (LCLS) .... CMary
Marysville, KS [*AM radio station call letters*] .... KNDY
Marysville, KS [*FM radio station call letters*] .... KNDY-FM
Marysville, KS [*Location identifier FAA*] (FAAL) .... MYZ
Marysville, OH [*Location identifier FAA*] (FAAL) .... MRT
Marysville, OH [*FM radio station call letters*] .... WAKS
Marysville, OH [*AM radio station call letters*] .... WUCO
Marysville Public Library, Marysville, MI [*Library symbol Library of Congress*] (LCLS) .... MiMary
Maryville College, Maryville, TN [*Library symbol Library of Congress*] (LCLS) .... TMaryC
Maryville College of the Sacred Heart [*Missouri*] .... MCSH
Maryville College, St. Louis, MO [*Library symbol Library of Congress*] (LCLS) .... MoSMa
Maryville College, St. Louis, MO [*OCLC symbol*] (OCLC) .... MVC
Maryville, MO [*Location identifier FAA*] (FAAL) .... EVU
Maryville, MO [*AM radio station call letters*] .... KNIM
Maryville, MO [*FM radio station call letters*] .... KNIM-FM
Maryville, MO [*FM radio station call letters*] .... KXCV
Maryville Reading Center, Maryville, IL [*Library symbol Library of Congress*] (LCLS) .... IMaryR
Maryville, TN [*AM radio station call letters*] .... WGAP
Maryville, TN [*FM radio station call letters*] .... WGAP-FM
Maryville, TN [*AM radio station call letters*] (RBYB) .... WKCE
Maryville University of St. Louis (GAGS) .... Maryville U
Marywood College (GAGS) .... Marywood C
Marywood College, Scranton, PA [*Library symbol Library of Congress*] (LCLS) .... PScM
Marzo [*March*] [*Spanish*] (AD) .... mrz
Mas o Menos [*More or Less*] [*Spanish*] (AD) .... m/ o m/
Masa County School District 51, Union Catalog, Grand Junction, CO [*Library symbol*] [*Library of Congress*] (LCLS) .... CoGjSD-U
Masachapa [*Nicaragua*] [*Seismograph station code, US Geological Survey*] (SEIS) .... MCH
Masada of the Zionist Organization of America (EA) .... MZOA
Masada Security Holdings, Inc. [*Associated Press*] (SAG) .... MasdSec
Masada Security Holdings, Inc. [*NASDAQ symbol*] (SAG) .... MSDA
Masada, the Holocaust Survivors Organization (EA) .... MHSO
Masai [*MARC language code Library of Congress*] (LCCP) .... mas
Masamba [*Indonesia*] [*Airport symbol*] (OAG) .... MXB
Masamba/Andi Jemma [*Indonesia*] [*ICAO location identifier*] (ICLI) .... WAAM
Masamuna [*Zaire*] [*ICAO location identifier*] (ICLI) .... FZDM
Masasi [*Tanzania*] [*ICAO location identifier*] (ICLI) .... HTMI
Masasi [*Tanzania*] [*Airport symbol*] (OAG) .... XMI
Masbate [*Philippines*] [*Airport symbol*] (OAG) .... MBT
Masbate [*Philippines*] [*ICAO location identifier*] (ICLI) .... RPVM
Mascara [*Algeria*] [*Airport symbol*] (OAG) .... MUW
Maschinenfabrik Augsburg-Nuernburg [*Manufacturer of diesel engines*] .... MAN
Maschinengewehr-Eisenbeton-Unterstand [*Machine-Gun-Iron-Reinforced Concrete Emplacement*] [*German "pill box," battlefield redoubts World War I*] .... MABU
Maschinengewehr-Eisenbeton-Unterstand [*Machine-Gun-Iron-Concrete-Emplacement*] [*German "pill box," battlefield redoubts World War I*] .... MEBU
Maschinengewehr-Zieleinrichtung [*Machine-Gun Sighting Mechanism*] [*German military - World War II*] .... MGZ
Maschinengewehr-Zielfernrohr [*Machine-Gun Telescopic Sight*] [*German military - World War II*] .... MGZF
Maschinenpistole [*Submachine Gun*] [*German*] (AD) .... MP
Masco Corp. [*NYSE symbol*] (SPSG) .... MAS
Masco Corp. [*Associated Press*] (SAG) .... Masco
Masco Tech Inc. Cv Pfd [*NYSE symbol*] (TTSB) .... MSXPr
Mascot Gold Mines Ltd. [*Toronto Stock Exchange symbol Vancouver Stock Exchange symbol*] .... MSG
Mascota [*Mexico*] [*Airport symbol*] (AD) .... MSX
Mascotech [*Commercial firm Associated Press*] (SAG) .... Mascot
Mascotech [*Commercial firm Associated Press*] (SAG) .... Mascotch
MascoTech, Inc. [*NYSE symbol*] (SPSG) .... MSX
Mascoutah High School, Mascoutah, IL [*Library symbol Library of Congress*] (LCLS) .... IMasHS
Mascoutah Public Library, Mascoutah, IL [*Library symbol Library of Congress*] (LCLS) .... IMas
Masculine .... M
Masculine .... MAS
Masculine .... MASC

Masculine Chromosome Pair .... XY
Masculinity-Femininity (AEBS) .... MF
Masectomy Association of Great Britain .... MAGB
Maserati Information Exchange (EA) .... MIE
Maserati Owners Club of North America (EAIO) .... MOCNA
Maseru [*Lesotho*] [*Airport symbol*] (OAG) .... MSU
Maseru/Leabua Jonathan [*Lesotho*] [*ICAO location identifier*] (ICLI) .... FXMU
Maseru Moshoeshoe International [*Lesotho*] [*ICAO location identifier*] (ICLI) .... FXMM
Mashai Store [*Lesotho*] [*ICAO location identifier*] (ICLI) .... FXMS
Mashhad [*Iran*] [*Seismograph station code, US Geological Survey*] (SEIS) .... MAIO
Mashhad [*Iran*] [*Airport symbol*] (OAG) .... MHD
Mashhad [*Iran*] [*Seismograph station code, US Geological Survey*] (SEIS) .... MHI
Mashhad [*Iran*] [*Seismograph station code, US Geological Survey Closed*] (SEIS) .... MSH
Mashhad [*Iran*] [*ICAO location identifier*] (ICLI) .... OIMM
Mashhad [*Iran*] [*ICAO location identifier*] (ICLI) .... OIMV
Mashhad University [*Iran*] [*Seismograph station code, US Geological Survey*] (SEIS) .... MUI
Mashonaland (ROG) .... MASHONLD
Mashonaland Mounted Police [*British military*] (DMA) .... MMP
Mashpee, MA [*FM radio station call letters*] (RBYB) .... WWKJ-FM
Masi-Manimba [*Zaire*] [*ICAO location identifier*] (ICLI) .... FZCV
Masindi [*Uganda*] [*ICAO location identifier*] (ICLI) .... HUMI
Masirah [*Oman*] [*ICAO location identifier*] (ICLI) .... OOMA
Masisea [*Peru*] [*ICAO location identifier*] (ICLI) .... SPSS
Masjed Soleiman [*Iran*] [*ICAO location identifier*] (ICLI) .... OIAI
Masjed Soleyman [*Iran*] [*Airport symbol*] (AD) .... MJX
Mask [*Computer science*] .... MK
Mask [*Computer science*] (IAA) .... MSK
Mask Index Register .... MXR
Mask Programmable Logic Array (NITA) .... MPLA
Mask Programmed Read-Only Memory [*Computer science*] .... MPROM
Mask Register .... MR
Mask Shop Information System [*Bell Laboratories*] .... MSIS
Mask Superposition Error [*Computer science*] (IAA) .... MSE
Maskali [*Djibouti*] [*Seismograph station code, US Geological Survey*] (SEIS) .... MKL
Masked Read-Only Memory [*Computer science*] .... MROM
Masked Terrain Map [*Military*] .... MTM
Masked Terrain Trainer [*Military*] .... MTT
Masking Beacon (IAA) .... MEACON
Masking Level Difference [*Hearing*] .... MLD
Masking Parameter Printout [*Computer science*] .... MAPP
Masking Pattern Universal Sub-Band Integrated Coding and Multiplexing [*Broadcasting*] .... MUSICAM
Masking Template [*Tool*] (AAG) .... MATP
Masking Template (MCD) .... MT
Maskolen [*Indonesia*] [*ICAO location identifier*] (ICLI) .... WRKF
Maslach Burnout Inventory .... MBI
Masland Corp. [*Associated Press*] (SAG) .... Masland
Masland Corp. [*NASDAQ symbol*] (SAG) .... MSLD
Masling Commuter Services [*ICAO designator*] (AD) .... EK
Masochism (CDAI) .... M
Mason (ROG) .... M
Mason [*or Masonry*] (ROG) .... MAS
Mason .... MSN
Mason & Hanger-Silas Mason Co., Inc. (RDA) .... MHSM
Mason & Hanger-Silas Mason Co., Inc., Pantex Plant Library, Amarillo, TX [*Library symbol Library of Congress*] (LCLS) .... TxAmM
Mason Butte [*Idaho*] [*Seismograph station code, US Geological Survey Closed*] (SEIS) .... MAS
Mason City [*Iowa*] [*Airport symbol*] (OAG) .... MCW
Mason City & Clear Lake R. R. [*AAR code*] .... MCCL
Mason City Globe-Gazette, Mason City, IA [*Library symbol Library of Congress*] (LCLS) .... IaMcG
Mason City Globe-Gazette, Mason City, IA [*Library symbol*] [*Library of Congress*] (LCLS) .... IaMcGG
Mason City, IA [*FM radio station call letters*] .... KCMR
Mason City, IA [*AM radio station call letters*] .... KGLO
Mason City, IA [*FM radio station call letters*] .... KIAI
Mason City, IA [*Television station call letters*] .... KIMT
Mason City, IA [*FM radio station call letters*] .... KLSS-FM
Mason City, IA [*AM radio station call letters*] .... KRIB
Mason City, IA [*AM radio station call letters*] .... KRNI
Mason City, IA [*FM radio station call letters*] .... KUNY
Mason City, IA [*Television station call letters*] .... KYIN
Mason City, IA [*Location identifier FAA*] (FAAL) .... MCW
Mason City Junior College [*Iowa*] .... MCJC
Mason City Public Library, Mason City, IA [*Library symbol Library of Congress*] (LCLS) .... IaMc
Mason Contractors Association of America (EA) .... MCAA
Mason County Library, Scottville, MI [*Library symbol Library of Congress*] (LCLS) .... MiSc
Mason Dixon International Fan Club (EA) .... MDFC
Mason Memorial Public Library, Buda, IL [*Library symbol Library of Congress*] (LCLS) .... IBud
Mason Memorial Public Library, Buda, IL [*OCLC symbol*] (OCLC) .... IVB
Mason, MI [*AM radio station call letters*] .... WUNN
Mason Public Library, Mason, OH [*Library symbol Library of Congress*] (LCLS) .... OMsn
Mason-Dixon Bancshares [*NASDAQ symbol*] (TTSB) .... MSDX
Mason-Dixon Bancshares, Inc. [*Associated Press*] (SAG) .... MasonDix
Mason-Dixon Bancshares, Inc. [*NASDAQ symbol*] (SAG) .... MSDX
Masonic .... MSNC
Masonic Grand Lodge, Denver, CO [*Library symbol Library of Congress*] (LCLS) .... CoDFM
Masonic Grand Lodge, Fargo, ND [*Library symbol*] [*Library of Congress*] (LCLS) .... NdFMG
Masonic Grand Lodge Library, Fargo, ND [*Library symbol Library of Congress*] (LCLS) .... NdFM
Masonic Grand Lodge of Texas, Waco, TX [*Library symbol Library of Congress*] (LCLS) .... TxWFM
Masonic Hall (ROG) .... MH
Masonic Homes Executives' Association of North America (EA) .... MHEANA
Masonic Library, Meridian, MS [*Library symbol Library of Congress*] (LCLS) .... MsMFM
Masonic Library of Southern California, Los Angeles, CA [*Library symbol Library of Congress*] (LCLS) .... CLMas
Masonic Medical Research Laboratory, Library, Utica, NY [*OCLC symbol*] (OCLC) .... ZUU
Masonic Medical Research Laboratory, Utica, NY [*Library symbol Library of Congress*] (LCLS) .... NUtMM
Masonic Relief Association of the United States and Canada (AD) .... MRAUSCAN
Masonic Relief Association of USA and Canada (EA) .... MRA
Masonic Service Association of the United States (EA) .... MSA
Masonic Study Unit [*American Topical Association*] (EA) .... MSU
Masonic Temple Library, Providence, RI [*Library symbol Library of Congress*] (LCLS) .... RPMa
Masonic Youth Welfare Fund [*Australia*] .... MYWF
Masonite (VRA) .... masn
Masonite Hydropress Die (MSA) .... MHPD
Mason-Pfizer Monkey Virus .... MPMV
Mason-Pfizer Virus [*Medicine*] (AD) .... M-P v
Masonry (VRA) .... mas
Masonry .... MASON
Masonry .... MSNRY
Masonry (MSA) .... MSRY
Masonry Industry Committee (EA) .... MIC
Masonry Opening [*Technical drawings*] .... MO
Masonry Opening (AD) .... mo
[*The*] **Masonry Society** (EA) .... TMS
Mason's New England Civil Practice [*A publication*] (DLA) .... Mas NE Pr
[*The*] **Masons (of detroit)** [*Rock music group*] .... TM(od)
Mason's United States Circuit Court Reports [*A publication*] (DLA) .... Mas
Mason's United States Circuit Court Reports [*A publication*] (DLA) .... Mason
Mason's United States Circuit Court Reports [*A publication*] (DLA) .... Mason CCR
Mason's United States Circuit Court Reports [*A publication*] (DLA) .... Mason Circt Ct R
Mason's United States Circuit Court Reports [*A publication*] (DLA) .... Mason R
Mason's United States Circuit Court Reports [*A publication*] (DLA) .... Mason US
Mason's United States Circuit Court Reports [*A publication*] (DLA) .... Mason US Circ Ct Rep
Mason's United States Circuit Court Reports [*A publication*] (DLA) .... Mason USR
Mason's United States Circuit Court Reports [*A publication*] (DLA) .... Mason's R
Mason's United States Circuit Court Reports [*A publication*] (DLA) .... Mason's Rep
Mason's United States Code, Annotated [*A publication*] (DLA) .... Mason's Code
Masontown, PA [*FM radio station call letters*] .... WRIJ
Masorah (BJA) .... Mas
Masoreten des Ostens (BJA) .... MdO
Masoreten des Westens (BJA) .... MdW
Masoretic Text [*of the Bible*] [*Hebrew tradition*] .... MT
Masque [*Record label*] .... Msq
Mass [*Symbol*] [*IUPAC*] .... m
Mass Absorption Coefficient .... MAC
Mass Accumulation Rate [*Geology*] .... MAR
Mass Addition Boundary Layer Program [*NASA*] .... MABL
Mass Air Flow [*Automotive engineering*] .... MAF
Mass Air Flow .... MAF
Mass Air Sequential Electronic Fuel Injection [*Automotive engineering*] .... MASEFI
Mass Analyzer .... MA
Mass Analyzer Detector .... MAD
Mass and Charge Spectroscopy .... MACS
Mass and Meals [*Refers to nuns who appear only at these activities*] .... M & M's
Mass Balance .... MB
Mass Balance Area (NUCP) .... MBA
Mass Casualties [*Military*] (AABC) .... MASSCAL
Mass Casualty Supplement [*Military*] .... MCS
Mass Change Log (MCD) .... MCL
Mass Communication (NTCM) .... MC
Mass Concentration [*Medicine*] (MAE) .... masc
Mass Concentration [*of gravitational pull*] .... MASCON
Mass Concentration (BARN) .... maskon
Mass Concentration [*Medicine*] (DMAA) .... massc
Mass Conference of Chief Librarians of Public Higher Educational Institutions [*Library network*] .... MCCLPHEI
Mass Control Module .... MCM
Mass Core Memory Unit (MCD) .... MCMU
Mass Culturing Technique [*Microbiology*] .... MCT
Mass Data Storage Facility .... MDSF
Mass Democratic Movement [*Political coalition*] [*South Africa*] .... MDM
Mass Destruction Weapons .... MDW
Mass Digital Storage .... MDS
Mass Digital Storage System .... MDSS
Mass Driver Reaction Engine [*Aerospace*] .... MDRE
Mass Energy Equivalent .... MEE
Mass Energy Relationship .... MER
Mass Expulsion System (MCD) .... MES
Mass Finishing Job Shops Association (EA) .... MFJSA

Mass Flow Controller [*Engineering*] ... MFC
Mass Flow of Air [*Aviation*] (DA) ... M_a
Mass Flow of Fuel [*Aviation*] (DA) ... M_f
Mass Fraction Burn [*Automotive engine combustion analysis*] ... MFB
Mass Health & Education Tax-Exempt [*AMEX symbol*] (SPSG) ... MHE
Mass Hlth & Edu Tax-Exempt Tr [*AMEX symbol*] (TTSB) ... MHE
Mass in Earth Orbit [*NASA*] ... MEO
Mass Inertia Excitation ... MIE
Mass Loaded Transducer ... MLT
Mass Marketing Insurance Institute (EA) ... MMII
Mass Media Ministries [*An association*] ... MMM
Mass Median Diameter ... MMD
Mass Median Equivalent Diameter [*of airborne particles*] ... MMED
Mass Memory (NASA) ... MM
Mass Memory Control Subsystem (TEL) ... MMCS
Mass Memory Data Base ... MMDB
Mass Memory Database (NASA) ... MMDB
Mass Memory Storage Device (DWSG) ... MMSD
Mass Memory Store [*Computer science*] (IEEE) ... MMS
Mass Memory Subsystem [*Aviation*] ... MMS
Mass Memory Test (NASA) ... MMT
Mass Memory Unit ... MMU
Mass Merchandising Distributors' Association (EA) ... MMDA
Mass Miniature Radiography ... MMR
Mass Model [*Computer program*] ... MASMOD
Mass Mutual Participating Investors [*NYSE symbol*] (CTT) ... MPV
Mass Number [*Symbol*] ... A
Mass Observation ... MO
Mass Observation (AD) ... mo
Mass of Vehicle ... MOV
Mass Optical Storage Technologies [*Computer science*] ... MOST
Mass Properties (MCD) ... MP
Mass Properties Engineering Section ... MPES
Mass Properties Management Plan (NASA) ... MPMP
Mass Psychogenic Illness ... MPI
Mass Radiography Unit ... MRU
Mass Radiography Unit (AD) ... mru
Mass Random Access Data Storage [*Computer science*] ... MRADS
Mass Random Access Disk [*Computer science*] ... MRAD
Mass Rapid Transit (AD) ... MRT
Mass Rapid Transit System (AD) ... MRTS
Mass Rapid Transport [*British*] ... MRT
Mass Resolving Power [*Physics*] ... MRP
Mass Retailing Institute [*Formerly, Mass Merchandising Research Institute*] [*Later, NMRI*] ... MRI
Mass Scatterable Mine (RDA) ... MSM
Mass Selector Detector [*Gas chromatography*] ... MSD
Mass Sensor Demonstration ... MSD
Mass Service Mainline Cable Systems ... MSMLCS
Mass Spectral Information System ... MSIS
Mass Spectral Search System [*National Bureau of Standards, Environmental Protection Agency, and National Institutes of Health*] [*Database*] ... MSSS
Mass Spectral Search System-Wiley [*Cornell University*] [*Database*] ... MSSSW
Mass Spectrography ... MS
Mass Spectrometer Leak Detector (NRCH) ... MSLD
Mass Spectrometer Leak Detector ... MSLD
Mass Spectrometer Outgasing (KSC) ... MSO
Mass Spectrometer Tube ... MST
Mass Spectrometric (AD) ... ms
Mass Spectrometric Immunoassay ... MSIA
Mass Spectrometric Isotope Dilution ... MSID
Mass Spectrometry ... MS
Mass Spectrometry Bulletin [*Mass Spectrometry Data Centre*] [*Bibliographic database*] [*British*] ... MSB
Mass Spectrometry Data Centre [*Royal Society of Chemistry*] (IID) ... MSDC
Mass Spectrometry/Mass Spectrometry ... MS/MS
Mass Stimulated Vehicles (MCD) ... MSV
Mass Storage [*Computer science*] ... MS
Mass Storage Adapter ... MSA
Mass Storage Control [*Computer science*] (BUR) ... MSC
Mass Storage Control Protocol (NITA) ... MSCP
Mass Storage Control System [*Computer science*] (IAA) ... MSCS
Mass Storage Control Table Create [*Computer science*] (MHDI) ... MSCTC
Mass Storage Controller (NITA) ... MSC
Mass Storage Device [*Computer science*] ... MSD
Mass Storage Editor [*Computer science*] (MCD) ... MSE
Mass Storage Facility [*Computer science*] (IBMDP) ... MSF
Mass Storage Input-Output [*Computer science*] (IEEE) ... MSIO
Mass Storage Operating System [*Control Data Corp.*] [*Computer science*] (NVT) ... MSOS
Mass Storage Processor [*Honeywell, Inc.*] ... MSP
Mass Storage Resident [*Computer science*] (IEEE) ... MSR
Mass Storage Service [*Computer science*] ... MSS
Mass Storage System [*Computer science*] ... MSS
Mass Storage System Communications (NITA) ... MSSC
Mass Storage System Communicator [*Computer science*] (IBMDP) ... MSSC
Mass Storage System Control [*Computer science*] (BUR) ... MSSC
Mass Storage Task [*Computer science*] (NOAA) ... MST
Mass Storage Task Group [*CODASYL*] ... MSTG
Mass Storage Unit [*Computer science*] (NASA) ... MSU
Mass Storage Volume ... MSV
Mass Storage Volume Control [*Computer science*] (BUR) ... MSVC
Mass Storage Volume Inventory [*Computer science*] (IAA) ... MSVI
Mass Tape Duplicator/Verifier [*Computer science*] (MCD) ... MTD
Mass Target Sensor ... MTS
Mass, Tenderness, Rebound [*On abdominal examination*] [*Gastroenterology*] (DAVI) ... MTR
Mass Termination System [*Computer science*] (IEEE) ... MTS
Mass Thermal Analysis (MCD) ... MTA
Mass to Charge Ratio ... m-z
Mass to Luminosity [*Ratio*] [*Astronomy*] ... M/L
Mass Transfer Coefficient [*Symbol*] [*IUPAC*] ... k
Mass Transfer Coefficient ... MTC
Mass Transfer Factor [*Physics*] (DAVI) ... jM
Mass Transfer Limiting Current (PDAA) ... MTLC
Mass Transfer Zone [*Chemical engineering*] ... MTZ
Mass Transit Railway (DS) ... MTR
Mass Unbalance Input [*Computer science*] ... MUI
Mass Unbalance Spin ... MUS
Mass Units ... MU
Mass Unity Sounding in Concert [*Duke Ellington definition of music*] ... MUSIC
Mass X-Ray ... MXR
Massa [*A Mass*] [*Pharmacy*] ... MASS
Massa Pilularum [*A Pill Mass*] [*Pharmacy*] ... MAS PIL
Massa Pilularum [*A Pill Mass*] [*Pharmacy*] ... Mass Pil
Massa Pilularum [*A Pill Mass*] [*Pharmacy*] (ROG) ... MP
Massachusettensis Medicinae Societatis Socius [*Fellow of the Massachusetts Medical Society*] ... MMSS
Massachusetts [*Postal code*] ... MA
Massachusetts (AFM) ... MASS
Massachusetts [*MARC country of publication code Library of Congress*] (LCCP) ... mau
Massachusetts [*MARC geographic area code Library of Congress*] (LCCP) ... n-us-ma
Massachusetts Acoustical Drywall-Interior Contractors Association (SRA) ... MADICA
Massachusetts Advance Legislative Service [*Lawyers Co-Operative Publishing Co.*] [*A publication*] (DLA) ... Mass Adv Legis Serv
Massachusetts Advance Sheets [*A publication*] (DLA) ... Mass Adv Sh
Massachusetts Advance Sheets [*A publication*] (DLA) ... Mass Adv Sheets
Massachusetts Aggregates and Asphalt Pavement Association (SRA) ... MAAPA
Massachusetts Appeals Court Advance Sheets [*A publication*] (DLA) ... Mass App Ct Adv Sh
Massachusetts Appeals Court Reports [*A publication*] (DLA) ... MA A
Massachusetts Appeals Court Reports [*A publication*] (DLA) ... Mass App Ct
Massachusetts Appeals Court Reports [*A publication*] (DLA) ... Mass App Rep
Massachusetts Appellate Decisions [*A publication*] (DLA) ... Mass AD
Massachusetts Appellate Decisions [*A publication*] (DLA) ... Mass App Dec
Massachusetts Appellate Division Reports [*A publication*] (DLA) ... App Div Rep
Massachusetts Appellate Division Reports [*A publication*] (DLA) ... Mass ADR
Massachusetts Appellate Division Reports [*A publication*] (DLA) ... Mass App Div
Massachusetts Association of 766 Approved Private Schools (SRA) ... MAAPS
Massachusetts Association of Community Rehabilitation Organizations (SRA) ... MACRO
Massachusetts Association of Land Surveyors and Civil Engineers (SRA) ... MALSCE
Massachusetts Association of Life Underwriters (SRA) ... MALU
Massachusetts Attorney General Reports [*A publication*] (DLA) ... OAG Massachusetts
Massachusetts Bay (GAAI) ... MASS
Massachusetts Bay Community College [*Wellesley*] ... MBCC
Massachusetts Bay Community College, Watertown, MA [*Library symbol Library of Congress*] (LCLS) ... MWatM
Massachusetts Bay Transportation Authority [*Formerly, MTA*] ... MBTA
Massachusetts Board of Conciliation and Arbitration Reports [*A publication*] (DLA) ... Mass BC & A
Massachusetts Bureau of Library Extension, Boston, MA [*Library symbol Library of Congress*] (LCLS) ... MBBL
Massachusetts Central [*AAR code*] ... MCER
Massachusetts College of Art (GAGS) ... Mass C Art
Massachusetts College of Art, Boston, MA [*OCLC symbol*] (OCLC) ... MAR
Massachusetts College of Art, Boston, MA [*Library symbol Library of Congress*] (LCLS) ... MBMSA
Massachusetts College of Optometry ... MCO
Massachusetts College of Pharmacy (GAGS) ... Mass C Pharmacy
Massachusetts College of Pharmacy [*Boston*] ... MCP
Massachusetts College of Pharmacy, Boston, MA [*Library symbol Library of Congress*] (LCLS) ... MBP
Massachusetts Controverted Election Cases [*A publication*] (DLA) ... Mass Cont Election Cushing S & J
Massachusetts Council for the Humanities [*Defunct*] (EA) ... MCH
Massachusetts. Department of Industrial Accidents. Bulletin [*A publication*] (DLA) ... Mass DIA
Massachusetts Division of Unemployment Compensation Digest of Board of Review Decisions [*A publication*] (DLA) ... Mass UC Dig
Massachusetts Division of Unemployment Compensation Opinions [*A publication*] (DLA) ... Mass UC Ops
Massachusetts Election Cases [*A publication*] (DLA) ... Mass Elec Ca
Massachusetts Election Cases [*A publication*] (DLA) ... Mass Elec Cas
Massachusetts Financial Services ... MFS
Massachusetts General Hospital (DAVI) ... MGH
Massachusetts General Hospital, Treadwell Library, Boston, MA [*Library symbol Library of Congress*] (LCLS) ... MBMGH-T
Massachusetts General Hospital, Treadwell Library, Boston, MA [*OCLC symbol*] (OCLC) ... MGH
Massachusetts General Hospital Utility Multiprogramming System [*Programming language*] ... MUMPS
Massachusetts General Laws [*A publication*] (DLA) ... Mass Gen Laws
Massachusetts General Laws Annotated [*A publication*] ... MGLA

Massachusetts General Laws, Annotated (West) [*A publication*] (DLA) ..... Mass Gen Laws Ann (West)
Massachusetts Grand Lodge, F & AM, Boston, MA [*Library symbol Library of Congress*] (LCLS) ..... MBFM
Massachusetts Health & Education Tax Exempt Trust [*Associated Press*] (SAG) ..... MassHe
Massachusetts Historical Society, Boston, MA [*OCLC symbol*] (OCLC) ..... MAH
Massachusetts Historical Society, Boston, MA [*Library symbol Library of Congress*] (LCLS) ..... MHi
Massachusetts Horticultural Society, Boston, MA [*Library symbol Library of Congress*] (LCLS) ..... MBH
Massachusetts Independent Auto Dealers Association (SRA) ..... MAIADA
Massachusetts Industrial Accident Board Reports of Cases [*A publication*] (DLA) ..... Mass IAB
Massachusetts Institute of Technology [*Facetious translation: "Made in Taiwan" because of large number of Asian-American students*] ..... MIT
Massachusetts Institute of Technology (GAGS) ..... MIT
Massachusetts Institute of Technology [*ICAO designator*] (FAAC) ..... MTH
Massachusetts Institute of Technology, Cambridge, MA [*Library symbol Library of Congress*] (LCLS) ..... MCM
Massachusetts Institute of Technology, Cambridge, MA [*OCLC symbol*] (OCLC) ..... MYG
Massachusetts Institute of Technology, Francis Russell Hart Nautical Museum, Cambridge, MA [*Library symbol Library of Congress*] (LCLS) ..... MCM-H
Massachusetts Institute of Technology Information Laboratory Automatic Coding ..... MITILAC
Massachusetts Institute of Technology Instrumentation Laboratory (SAA) ..... MITIL
Massachusetts Institute of Technology/Lincoln Laboratory (AAG) ..... MIT/LL
Massachusetts Institute of Technology, Lincoln Laboratory, Lexington, MA [*OCLC symbol*] (OCLC) ..... LIN
Massachusetts Institute of Technology, Lincoln Laboratory, Lexington, MA [*Library symbol Library of Congress*] (LCLS) ..... MCM-L
Massachusetts Institute of Technology/Naval Supersonic Laboratory (AAG) ..... MIT/NSL
Massachusetts Institute of Technology Reactor ..... MITR
Massachusetts Institute of Technology Research Establishment (NATG) ..... MITRE
Massachusetts Institute of Technology Sea Grant Program (NOAA) ..... MITSG
Massachusetts Institute of Technology/Servomechanisms Laboratory (AAG) ..... MIT/SmL
Massachusetts Institute of Technology/Sloan Laboratory (AAG) ..... MIT/SL
Massachusetts Institute of Technology/Spectroscopy Laboratory (AAG) ..... MIT/SpL
Massachusetts Institute of Technology, University Film Study Center, Cambridge, MA [*Library symbol Library of Congress*] (LCLS) ..... MCM-F
Massachusetts Investors Trust ..... MIT
Massachusetts Labor Relations Commission Decisions [*A publication*] (DLA) ..... Mass LRC Dec
Massachusetts Maritime Academy [*Buzzards Bay*] ..... MMA
Massachusetts Maritime Academy, Buzzards Bay, MA [*Library symbol Library of Congress*] (LCLS) ..... MBbM
Massachusetts Maritime Academy, Captain C. H. Hurley Library, Buzzards Bay, MA [*OCLC symbol*] (OCLC) ..... MMA
Massachusetts Microelectronics Center [*Research center*] (RCD) M2C
Massachusetts Microelectronics Center [*Research center*] (RCD) ..... MMC
Massachusetts Military Academy ..... MMA
Massachusetts Natural Heritage Program [*Massachusetts State Division of Fisheries and Wildlife*] [*Information service or system*] (IID) ..... MA-NHP
Massachusetts Organization for the Repeal of Abortion Laws ..... MORAL
Massachusetts Organized Crime Control Council (AD) ..... MOCCC
Massachusetts Regional Library for the Blind and Physically Handicapped, PerkinsSchool for the Blind, Watertown, MA [*Library symbol*] [*Library of Congress*] (LCLS) ..... MWatP-BP
Massachusetts Register [*A publication*] (AAGC) ..... Ma Reg
Massachusetts Register [*A publication*] (DLA) ..... Mass Admin Reg
Massachusetts Reports [*A publication*] (DLA) ..... MA
Massachusetts Reports [*A publication*] (DLA) ..... Mas
Massachusetts Reports [*A publication*] (DLA) ..... Mas R
Massachusetts Reports [*A publication*] (DLA) ..... Mas Rep
Massachusetts Reports [*A publication*] (DLA) ..... Mass R
Massachusetts Reports [*A publication*] (DLA) ..... Mass Rep
Massachusetts Reports Supplement [*A publication*] (AAGC) ..... Mass Supp
Massachusetts School of Art ..... MSA
Massachusetts Secretary of State, Archives Division, Boston, MA [*Library symbol Library of Congress*] (LCLS) ..... M-Ar
Massachusetts State Board of Conciliation and Arbitration Reports [*A publication*] (DLA) ..... Mass St BC & A
Massachusetts State Library, Boston, MA [*Library symbol Library of Congress*] (LCLS) ..... M
Massachusetts State Library, Boston, MA [*OCLC symbol*] (OCLC) ..... MAS
Massachusetts State Teachers College ..... MSTC
Massachusetts Supreme Judicial Court Reports [*A publication*] (DLA) ..... Mass
Massachusetts Unemployment Compensation Commission Opinions [*A publication*] (DLA) ..... Mass UCC Op
Massachusetts Volunteer Militia (HGAA) ..... MVM
Massachusetts Workmen's Compensation Cases [*A publication*] (DLA) ..... Mass WCC
Massage ..... M
Massage ..... MASS
Massage ..... MSG
Massage (DAVI) ..... MSS
Massage ..... MIKE
Mass-Analyzed Ion Kinetic Energy ..... MIKE
Mass-Analyzed Ion Kinetic Energy Spectrometry ..... MIKES
Massapequa General Hospital, Seaford, NY [*Library symbol Library of Congress*] (LCLS) ..... NSeaMH
Massapequa Public Library, Massapequa, NY [*Library symbol Library of Congress*] (LCLS) ..... NMass
Massasoit Community College, West Bridgewater, MA [*Library symbol Library of Congress*] (LCLS) ..... MWbriM
Massawa [*Ethiopia*] [*ICAO location identifier*] (ICLI) ..... HAMS
Massawa [*Ethiopia*] [*Airport symbol*] (OAG) ..... MSW
MASSBANK Corp. [*NASDAQ symbol*] (NQ) ..... MASB
Massbank Corp. [*Associated Press*] (SAG) ..... Massbnk
Masse. Le Droit Commercial [*A publication*] (DLA) ..... Mass Dr Com
Masseketh (BJA) ..... Mas
Massena [*New York*] [*Seismograph station code, US Geological Survey*] (SEIS) ..... MSNY
Massena [*New York*] [*Airport symbol*] (OAG) ..... MSS
Massena Memorial Hospital, Massena, NY [*Library symbol*] [*Library of Congress*] (LCLS) ..... NMasMH
Massena, NY [*AM radio station call letters*] ..... WMSA
Massena, NY [*AM radio station call letters*] ..... WYBG
Massena Public Library, Massena, NY [*Library symbol*] [*Library of Congress*] (LCLS) ..... NMasL
Massena/Richards Field [*New York*] [*ICAO location identifier*] (ICLI) ..... KMSS
[*The*] **Massena Terminal Railroad Co.** [*AAR code*] ..... MSTR
Massenet Society/American Branch (EA) ..... MS/AB
Massenet Society and Lovers of French Music [*Later, MSAB*] (EA) ..... MSLFM
Massenya [*Chad*] [*Airport symbol*] (AD) ..... MYC
Masses or Tumors [*Medicine*] (CPH) ..... M/T
Masset [*Canada*] [*Airport symbol*] (OAG) ..... ZMT
Masseur [*Ranking title*] [*British Royal Navy*] ..... M
Massey and Township Public Library, Ontario [*Library symbol Library network*] (NLC) ..... OMAST
Massey College in the University of Toronto, Toronto, ON, Canada [*Library symbol Library of Congress*] (LCLS) ..... CaOTMC
Massey College, Toronto, Ontario [*Library symbol National Library of Canada*] (NLC) ..... OTMC
Massey University School of Aviation [*New Zealand*] [*ICAO designator*] (FAAC) ..... MSY
Massieu Function [*Symbol*] [*IUPAC*] ..... J
Massillon, OH [*AM radio station call letters*] ..... WTIG
Massillon Public Library, Massillon, OH [*Library symbol Library of Congress*] (LCLS) ..... OMas
Massio [*Ethiopia*] [*Airport symbol*] (AD) ..... MZX
Massive [*Agriculture*] ..... M
Massive Algebraic Computation [*Programming language*] [*1958*] [*Computer science*] (CSR) ..... MAC
Massive Analog Recording Technical Instrument for Nebulous Indications ..... MARTINI
Massive Attack Option (MCD) ..... MAO
Massive Black Hole [*Galactic science*] ..... MBH
Massive Compact Halo Object [*Astrophysics*] ..... MACHO
Massive Compact Halo Object [*Cosmology*] ..... MACHO
Massive Compact Halo Objects [*Astronomy*] ..... MACHO
Massive Dark Object [*Galactic science*] ..... MDO
Massive Economic Neighborhood Development [*New York City*] ..... MEND
Massive Hepatic Necrosis [*Medicine*] (MAE) ..... MHN
Massive Liver Metastasis [*Oncology*] ..... MLM
Massive Nuclear Retaliation (AAG) ..... MNR
Massive Nuclear Retaliation (AD) ..... mnr
Massive Offshore Surf Zone ..... MOSZ
Massive Open Systems Environment Standard [*Computer science*] ..... MOSES
Massive Periretinal Proliferation [*Ophthalmology*] (DAVI) ..... MPP
Massive Resources Ltd. [*Vancouver Stock Exchange symbol*] ..... MAV
Massive Selective Retaliatory Power (NATG) ..... MSRP
Massive Surf Zone ..... MSZ
Massive Vitreous Retraction (MAE) ..... MVR
Massive Vitreous Retractor [*Blade*] [*Ophthalmology*] (DAVI) ..... MVR
Massively Parallel Processor [*Image processing*] ..... MPP
Masslo [*Ethiopia*] [*ICAO location identifier*] (ICLI) ..... HAML
Mass-Median Aerodynamic Diameter [*of particles*] ..... MMAD
MassMutual Corporate Investors [*NYSE symbol*] (SPSG) ..... MCI
MassMutual Corporate Investors, Inc. [*Associated Press*] (SAG) ..... MasCp
MassMutual Corp. Inv [*NYSE symbol*] (TTSB) ..... MCI
MassMutual Participation Investors [*Associated Press*] (SAG) ..... MasPrt
MassMutual Participation Investors [*NYSE symbol*] (SAG) ..... MPV
MassMutual Part'n Inv [*NYSE symbol*] (TTSB) ..... MPV
Massora Finalis (BJA) ..... MF
Massorah Magna [*or Massora Magna*] (BJA) ..... MM
Massorah Parva [*or Massora Parva*] (BJA) ..... MP
Masspequa High School, Massapequa, NY [*Library symbol*] [*Library of Congress*] (LCLS) ..... NMassHS
Mass-Separating Agent [*Chemical engineering*] ..... MSA
Mass-Transfer Rate [*Chemical engineering*] ..... MTR
Mass-Transport-Limited [*Chemical engineering*] ..... MTL
Mast (IAA) ..... MT
Mast Aerial (IAA) ..... MA
Mast Cell ..... MC
Mast Cell Degranulating [*or Destroying*] **Peptide** [*Biochemistry*] ..... MCD
Mast Cell Degranulation Test [*Medicine*] (DAVI) ..... MCDT
Mast Check System ..... MCS
Mast Connection System (SAA) ..... MCS
Mast Controller (DNAB) ..... MC
Mast Hull Loop ..... MHL
Mast Mount Visionics (MCD) ..... MMV
Mast Mount Visionics System (MCD) ..... MMVS
Mast Mounted Sight ..... MMS

Mast Mounted Sight System (MCD)	MMSS
Mast Mounted Signal (MCD)	MMS
Mast Section (IAA)	MS
Mastaba (VRA)	mstb
Mast-Cell Growth Factor [Cytology]	MGF
Mastec, Inc. [Associated Press] (SAG)	Mastec
Mastec, Inc. [NASDAQ symbol] (SAG)	MASX
Mastech Corp. [NASDAQ symbol] (SAG)	MAST
Mastech Corp. [Associated Press] (SAG)	Mastech
Mastectomy [Medicine] (AAMN)	MAST
Master	M
Master (MSA)	MA
Master	MA
Master (DSUE)	MAS
Master (ROG)	MAST
Master [British military] (DMA)	MR
Master (AD)	Mr
Master (MCD)	MST
Master	MSTR
Master (VRA)	mstr
Master	MSTR
Master	MSTR
Master Accession Document [Computer science] (BUR)	MAD
Master Account Title [Office of Management and Budget]	MAT
Master Acoustical Console [Army]	MAC
Master Acquisition Bus [Computer science] (MCD)	MAB
Master Activation Phasing Schedule (IAA)	MAPS
Master Activation Schedule (AAG)	MAS
Master Activity Data Management (DNAB)	MADMAN
Master Activity Programming	MAP
Master Address File [US Census Bureau]	MAF
Master Agility Excellent	MX
Master Air Data [Computer]	MAD
Master Air Pilot	MAP
Master Air Waybill [Shipping] (DS)	MAWB
Master Aircraft Crewman Badge [Military decoration] (AABC)	MastAcftCrmnBad
Master Aircraft Crewman Badge [Military decoration] (GFGA)	MSTACCMB
Master Alarm	MA
Master Allowance Parts List [Military] (CAAL)	MAPL
Master Analysis Scheme [Monitoring technique]	MAS
Master and Slave Oscillator Array (PDAA)	MASOA
Master Angular Reference (IAA)	MAR
Master Antenna Television	MATV
Master Appraisal File [Real estate]	MAF
Master Area Interest Decks (MCD)	MAID
Master Area Reference File [Bureau of the Census] (GFGA)	MARF
Master Army Aviator	MAA
Master Army Aviator (AABC)	MASTARAV
Master Army Aviator Badge [Military decoration]	Mast AR Av Bad
Master Army Aviator Badge [Military decoration] (GFGA)	MSTARAVB
Master Assistant [British military] (DMA)	MA
Master Attack Plan [Military] (DOMA)	MAP
Master Attitude Reference System	MARS
Master Audit File (SSD)	MAF
Master Augmentation Unit [Navy] (DOMA)	MAU
Master Authorization List	MAL
Master Availability Reference File [Army Electronics Command]	MARF
Master Bakers' Association [Australia]	MBA
Master Bedroom [Real estate]	MBR
Master Beneficiary Record [Social Security Administration]	MBR
Master Bibliographic File (ADA)	MBF
Master Bibliographic System (ADA)	MBS
Master Bidders' List (NG)	MBL
Master Boat Builders' Association of Queensland [Australia]	MBBAQ
Master Boot Record [Computer science] (PCM)	MBR
Master Brewers Association of the Americas (EA)	MBAA
Master Builders Federation [British] (BI)	MBF
Master Bus Controller [Computer science]	MBC
Master Butchers' Association of New South Wales [Australia]	MBANSW
Master Buy Plan (AAGC)	MBP
Master Calendar Control System [New York City courts' speedup system]	MCCS
Master Car Builder	MCB
Master Car Builders' Association [Later, CDOA]	MCBA
Master Car Builders' Rules	MCBR
Master Carvers Association [British] (DBA)	MCA
Master Caution and Warning [NASA] (KSC)	MC & W
Master Caution and Warning	MC&W
Master Cell Bank [Cell line]	MCB
Master Central Timing System [NASA]	MCTS
Master Change (IAA)	MC
Master Change Committee	MCC
Master Change Compliance Record	MCCR
Master Change Log	MCL
Master Change Notice (KSC)	MCN
Master Change Proposal (KSC)	MCP
Master Change Record	MCR
Master Change Record (AAGC)	MCR
Master Chief Aircraft Maintenanceman [Navy rating]	AFCM
Master Chief Aircrew Survival Equipmentman [Formerly, Master Chief Parachute R igger] [Navy rating]	PRCM
Master Chief Aviation Boatswain's Mate [Navy rating]	ABCM
Master Chief Avionics Technician [Navy rating]	AVCM
Master Chief Builder [Navy rating]	BUCM
Master Chief Constructionman [Navy rating]	CUCM

Master Chief Damage Controlman [Navy rating]	DCCM
Master Chief Data Processing Technician [Formerly, MACM] [Navy rating]	DPCM
Master Chief Equipmentman [Navy rating]	EQCM
Master Chief Gunner's Mate, Technician [Navy rating]	GMTCM
Master Chief Hull Maintenance Technician [Formerly, SFCM] [Navy rating]	HTCM
Master Chief Illustrator Draftsman [Navy rating]	DMCM
Master Chief Instrumentman [Navy rating]	IMCM
Master Chief Interior Communications Electrician [Navy rating]	ICCM
Master Chief Journalist [Navy rating]	JOCM
Master Chief Lithographer [Navy rating]	LICM
Master Chief Machine Accountant [Later, DPCM] [Navy rating]	MACM
Master Chief Mess Management Specialist [Formerly, SDCM] [Navy rating]	MSCM
Master Chief Navy Counselor [Navy rating] (DNAB)	NCCM
Master Chief Opticalman [Navy rating]	OMCM
Master Chief Patternmaker [Navy rating]	PMCM
Master Chief Personnelman [Navy rating]	PNCM
Master Chief Petty Officer [Navy]	E9
Master Chief Petty Officer [Navy]	MCPO
Master Chief Petty Officer of Command [Navy]	MCPOC
Master Chief Petty Officer of the Coast Guard	E9
Master Chief Petty Officer of the Fleet [or Force] (DNAB)	MCPOF
Master Chief Petty Officer of the Navy	MCPON
Master Chief Photographer's Mate [Navy rating]	PHCM
Master Chief Photographic Intelligenceman [Navy rating]	PTCM
Master Chief Postal Clerk [Navy rating]	PCCM
Master Chief Precision Instrumentman [Navy rating]	PICM
Master Chief Quartermaster [Navy rating]	QMCM
Master Chief RADARman [Navy rating]	RDCM
Master Chief Radioman [Navy rating]	RMCM
Master Chief Shipfitter [Later, HTCM] [Navy rating]	SFCM
Master Chief Ship's Serviceman [Navy rating]	SHCM
Master Chief Signalman [Navy rating]	SMCM
Master Chief SONAR Technician [Navy rating]	STCM
Master Chief SONARman [Navy rating]	SOCM
Master Chief Steam Propulsionman [Navy rating]	SPCM
Master Chief Steelworker [Navy rating]	SWCM
Master Chief Steward [Later, MSCM] [Navy rating]	SDCM
Master Chief Storekeeper [Navy rating]	SKCM
Master Chief Torpedoman's Mate [Navy rating]	TMCM
Master Chief TRADEVMAN [Training Devices Man] [Navy rating]	TDCM
Master Circuit System	MCS
Master Civilian Facilities Listing [DoD]	MCFL
Master Class Code File (MCD)	MCCF
Master Cleaners' Association of South Australia [Australia]	MCASA
Master Clear Line (IAA)	MCL
Master Clerical Data [Management system]	MCD
Master Clinical Science (DAVI)	MCISci
Master Clock (IAA)	MC
Master Clock	MCLK
Master Clock Assembly	MCA
Master Clock Receiver	MCR
Master Clock Unit	MCU
Master Code Database (MCD)	MCDB
Master Code File	MCF
Master Combat Data System Plan [Military] (CAAL)	MCDSP
Master Commandant	MC
Master Commander [Navy British] (ROG)	MC
Master Communications (PDAA)	MASCOM
Master Community Antenna	MCA
Master Component List (MCD)	MCL
Master Component Repair List	MCRL
Master Component Rework Capability (MCD)	MCRC
Master Composite Specification (MCD)	MCS
Master Computer Program [NASA] (KSC)	MCP
Master Configuration Index (MCD)	MCI
Master Configuration List	MCL
Master Construction Specification [Canada]	GMS
Master Container Freight [MARAD] (TAG)	MCFS
Master Control (MCD)	MAC
Master Control	MC
Master Control and Data Buffer Storage Unit	MCDBSU
Master Control and Interface Unit [NASA] (NASA)	MCIU
Master Control and User Interface Software Subsystem [Space Flight Operations Facility, NASA]	MCUIS
Master Control Assembly [NASA] (NASA)	MCA
Master Control Assembly	MCA
Master Control Card [IRS]	MCC
Master Control Center (NATG)	MCC
Master Control Console	MCC
Master Control Executive (IAA)	MACE
Master Control File	MCF
Master Control Gauge (IAA)	MCG
Master Control List	MCL
Master Control Module	MCM
Master Control Number	MCN
Master Control Program [Burroughs Corp.]	MCP
Master Control Program [Computer science] (ECII)	MPC
Master Control Program / Advanced System (HGAA)	MCP/AS
Master Control Record System (AABC)	MCR
Master Control Register	MCR
Master Control Relay [Manufacturing term]	MCR
Master Control Room (MCD)	MCR

Master Control Routine	MCR
Master Control Set (IAA)	MCS
Master Control Station (NRCH)	MCS
Master Control System [or Subsystem]	MCS
Master Control Unit	MCU
Master Controller Processor Unit (MCD)	MCPU
Master Cook [Navy]	MCK
Master Craftsmen's Association [British] (DBA)	MCA
Master Cross-Reference File	MCRF
Master Cross-Reference List	MCRL
Master Cross-Reference List	MRCL
Master Cross-Reference List	RL
Master Cylinder [Automotive engineering]	M/CYL
Master Data Center, Inc. [Information service or system] (IID)	MDC
Master Data Control Console	MDCC
Master Data Control System [Computer science] (IAA)	MDCS
Master Data File (AFIT)	MDF
Master Data Index	MADI
Master Data Library [NASA]	MDL
Master Data Record (NG)	MDR
Master Database (MCD)	MDB
Master Decommissioning Plan [Nuclear energy] (NRCH)	MDP
Master Delivery Schedule (AAG)	MDS
Master Design Award	MDA
Master Design Plan (MCD)	MDP
Master Development Schedule (KSC)	MDS
Master Diagram (MCD)	MD
Master Digital Command System	MDCS
Master Digital Data Tape (PDAA)	MDDT
Master Dimension (NASA)	MD
Master Dimension Information	MDI
Master Dimension Specification (MSA)	MDS
Master Direction Center [Air Force]	MDC
Master Direction Indicator	MDI
Master Directory [NASA Information service or system] (IID)	MD
Master Directory File [Computer science]	MDF
Master Discrepancy Report (AAG)	MDR
Master Display Panel (KSC)	MDP
Master Distribution Box [Missile system] [Army]	MDB
Master Distribution Frame [Electronics] (ECII)	MDF
Master Diver [Navy]	DM
Master Diver Badge [Military decoration]	Mast Div Bad
Master Diver Badge [Military decoration] (GFGA)	MSTDIVB
Master Diversion Airfield (AIA)	MDA
Master Document File [Computer science]	MDF
Master Drawing List	MDL
Master Drawings Association (EA)	MDA
Master Driver Unit	MDU
Master Drum Sender	MDS
Master Dyers Association (EA)	MDA
Master Electric (IAA)	MAE
Master Electrical Common Connector Assembly (MCD)	MECCA
Master Electronics Board	MEB
Master Employee Record [DoD]	MER
Master Engine Control Unit	MECU
Master Engineering Drawing Data File System	MEDDF
Master Enumeration District List [Bureau of Census]	MEDList
Master Equatorial	ME
Master Equipment Allowance [or Authorization] List [Military]	MEAL
Master Equipment List [Military] (NG)	MEL
Master Equipment List Identification [Military] (IAA)	MELI
Master Equipment List Index [Military] (KSC)	MELI
Master Equipment Management Index [Air Force] (AFM)	MEMI
Master Equipment Management List [Air Force] (AFM)	MEML
Master Equipment Number [Military] (NG)	MEN
Master Erection Schedule (DNAB)	MES
Master Evaluation Center (MCD)	MEC
Master Evaluation Plan [Army]	MEP
Master Event Controller [NASA] (NASA)	MEC
Master Event Sequence Controller (KSC)	MESC
Master Events Timer (MCD)	MET
Master Explosive Ordnance Disposal Badge [Military decoration] (GFGA)	MSTEODBAD
Master Fabrication Schedule (DNAB)	MFS
Master Facility Inventory [Department of Health and Human Services] (GFGA)	MFI
Master Facility Register [Nuclear energy]	MFR
Master Facility Tool	MAF
Master Facility Tool (MCD)	MFOM
Master, Faculty of Occupational Medicine (DAVI)	MFOM
Master Farriers' Association of New South Wales [Australia]	MFANSW
Master Fencers Association (NADA)	MFA
Master Fencers Association	M/F
Master File	MFA
Master File Activities [Computer science]	MFA
Master File Change Activity [Computer science] (MCD)	MFCA
Master File Copy [Computer science] (KSC)	MFC
Master File Directory [Computer science]	MFD
Master File Maintenance [Computer science]	MFM
Master File Program [Computer science]	MFP
Master File Replacement System [Computer science]	MFRS
Master File Tax [Code] [IRS]	MFT
Master Fish Merchants' Association of New South Wales [Australia]	MFMANSW
Master Fitness Trainer [Army] (INF)	MFT
Master Fixture	MSFX
Master Flight Surgeon Badge [Military decoration] (GFGA)	MSTFLSB

Master Flight Test Assignment Document (NASA)	MFTAD
Master Flight Test Assignments Document [NASA]	MFTAD
Master Floor Sanders Association (NADA)	MFSA
Master Flow Controller [Nuclear energy] (NRCH)	MFC
Master Force List [DoD]	MFL
Master Frame	MF
Master Frame Recognize (MCD)	MFR
Master Freight File	MFF
Master Frequency Oscillator (NG)	MFO
Master Frequency Record [FCC list] (NTCM)	MFR
Master Fund Control List [Air Force] (AFM)	MFCL
Master Furriers Guild of America (EA)	MFGA
Master Gauge	MSGA
Master Gemology Association (EA)	MGA
Master Gemology Society [Defunct] (EA)	MGS
Master General of the Ordnance [Army British]	MGO
Master Generator [Telecommunications] (OA)	MG
Master Glaziers Karate International [Associated Press] (SAG)	MstG
Master Glaziers Karate International [Associated Press] (SAG)	MstGlaz
Master Glaziers Karate Intl. [NASDAQ symbol] (SAG)	KICK
Master Glaziers Karate Intl [NASDAQ symbol] (TTSB)	KICK
Master Glaziers Karate Wrrt'A' [NASDAQ symbol] (TTSB)	KICKW
Master Glaziers Karate Wrrt'B' [NASDAQ symbol] (TTSB)	KICKZ
Master Government-Furnished Equipment List (NVT)	MGFEL
Master Ground-Controller Interception RADAR (NATG)	MGCI
Master Group Information System [AT & T]	MAGI
Master Group Multiplexer	MGM
Master Gunnery Sergeant [Marine Corps]	E9
Master Gunnery Sergeant [Marine Corps] (DNAB)	MGSGT
Master Gunnery Sergeant [Marine Corps]	MGYSGT
Master Hairdressers' Association of Western Australia	MHAWA
Master Herbalist	MH
Master History File	MHF
Master Horizontal Bomber	MHB
Master Hosts [An association Defunct] (EA)	MH
Master Hotel Supplier [Educational Institute of the American Hotel and M otel Association] [Designation awarded by]	MHS
Master House Movers' Association [Australia]	MHMA
Master Imagery Exchange Format (MCD)	MIEF
Master Implementation Schedule [NATO Air Defense Ground Environment] (NATG)	MIS
Master Improvement Program (AFIT)	MIP
Master in Accounting Science (DD)	MAccSc
Master in Administration of Justice (PGP)	M Adm J
Master in Chemical Analysis	MChemA
Master in Commercial Science (DD)	MCommSc
Master in Commercial Science (DD)	MScComm
Master in Commercial Sciences	MScCom
Master in Communication (DD)	MCommun
Master in Engineering and Public Administration	M Eng & PA
Master in Engineering and Public Administration	MEPA
Master in Human Resource Department (PGP)	MHRD
Master in International Economics and Management (ECON)	MIEM
Master in Land Economy	MLandEc
Master in Media Management	MMM
Master in Pastoral Studies	MPast
Master in Pharmacy	Ph M
Master in Political and Institutional Administration	MPIA
Master in Professional Geophysics	M Pr Gph
Master in Psychiatric Nursing (GAGS)	MPN
Master in Psychiatric Occupational Therapy (GAGS)	MPOT
Master in Public Policy [National University of Singapore]	MPP
Master in Regional Planning (DD)	MRP
Master in Teaching (PGP)	MIT
Master in Teaching English as a Second Language (PGP)	MTESL
Master in the Teaching of Mathematics (PGP)	MTM
Master Indentured Parts List	MIPL
Master Index	MI
Master Index Assembly Outline [Paper]	MIAO
Master Index File	MIF
Master Index List (MCD)	MIL
Master Index of Allowable Parts Lists [Navy]	MIAPL
Master Index of Repairables (MCD)	MIR
Master Index Pulse Generator	MIPG
Master Index Remote Access Capability (MHDI)	MIRAC
Master Information Paper [Military] (CAAL)	MIP
Master Input/Output Processor (NITA)	MIOP
Master Instruction Book	MIB
Master Instruction Tape [Computer science]	MIT
Master Instrumentation List	MIL
Master Instrumentation Timing Equipment (CET)	MITE
Master Insurance Program	MIP
Master Integrated Schedule (AAG)	MIS
Master Interconnect Board (MCD)	MIB
Master Interface Network (MCD)	MINW
Master Intern Training Plan [Military]	MITP
Master International Frequency List	MIFL
Master International Frequency Register	MIFR
Master Interrupt Control [Computer science] (OA)	MIC
Master Inventory File (AFIT)	MIF
Master Inventory Record	MIR
Master Item (MSA)	MI
Master Item File (MCD)	MIF
Master Item Identification Control System	MIICS
Master Item Identification List	MIIL

Master Item Identification List (AABC) .... MIL
Master Item Intelligence File .... MIIF
Master Jet Base [Navy] (NVT) .... MJB
Master Kennel Association [Commercial firm] (EA) .... MKA
Master Key [Locks] (ADA) .... MK
Master Labor Contract (AABC) .... MLC
Master Laboratory Station .... MLS
Master Layout .... MSLO
Master Layout Duplicate (MSA) .... MLD
Master Layout Original (MSA) .... MLO
Master Library Tape [Computer science] .... MLT
Master Limited Partnership .... MLP
Master Lines Layout (MSA) .... MLL
Master List of Medical Indexing Terms .... MALIMET
Master List of Outstanding Items [Military] (DNAB) .... MLOI
Master Listing Index .... MLI
Master Lock, Skeleton Key .... MLSK
Master Locksmiths Association [British] (BI) .... MLA
Master Logistics Plan (AABC) .... MLP
Master Logistics Review Board (AAG) .... MLRB
Master Logistics Review Committee (AAG) .... MLRC
Master Makeup and Display .... MMD
Master Mason [Freemasonry] .... MM
Master Material Erection Schedule [Shipbuilding] (NG) .... MMES
Master Material Ordering and Delivery Schedule (DNAB) .... MMODS
Master Material Review Board (NADA) .... MMRB
Master Materiel Support Record .... MMSR
Master Measurement and Control List (MCD) .... MMCL
Master Measurement Database (NASA) .... MMDB
Master Measurements List (NASA) .... MML
Master Mechanic .... MM
Master Member of the Institute of Executives and Managers [British] (DBQ) .... MIEM
Master Menu Board [Military] .... MMB
Master Message Display Console (MCD) .... MMDC
Master Microfiche Record .... MMR
Master Military Pay File (AABC) .... MMPF
Master Minimum Equipment List (DA) .... MMEL
Master Missile System Training Program (SAA) .... MMSTP
Master Mobilization Plan [DoD] .... MMP
Master Model (MCD) .... MAM
Master Monitor .... MM
Master Monitor Criteria Data File .... MMCD
Master Monitor Display .... MMD
Master Mortician .... Mor M
Master Multiattribute Utility (IEEE) .... MMAU
Master Music Printers and Engravers Association (DGA) .... MMP
Master Navigator [Air Force] .... MN
Master Negative Assembly [Monophoto] (DGA) .... MNA
Master of Accountancy [or Accounting] .... M Acc
Master of Accountancy (PGP) .... M Acct
Master of Accountancy (PGP) .... M Accy
Master of Accountancy (PGP) .... M Acy
Master of Accountancy and Financial Information Systems (PGP) .... MAFIS
Master of Accounting .... M Ac
Master of Accounting .... M Acco
Master of Accounting (PGP) .... M Acct
Master of Accounting (GAGS) .... MAcc
Master of Accounting Information Systems (PGP) .... MAIS
Master of Accounting Science .... MAS
Master of Accounts .... M Accs
Master of Actuarial Science .... MAS
Master of Acupuncture (PGP) .... M Ac
Master of Acupuncture and Traditional Chinese Medicine (PGP) .... MATCM
Master of Administration (PGP) .... M Ad
Master of Administration .... M Adm
Master of Administration (PGP) .... M Admin
Master of Administration .... MAdmin
Master of Administration in Vocational Education (PGP) .... M Ad VE
Master of Administration in Vocational Education (PGP) .... MAV Ed
Master of Administration Management (PGP) .... M Adm Mgt
Master of Administrative Arts (GAGS) .... MAA
Master of Administrative Engineering .... M Adm E
Master of Administrative Science (PGP) .... MAS
Master of Administrative Studies .... M Admin
Master of Administrative Studies (ADA) .... MAS
Master of Adult and Occupational Education (PGP) .... MAOE
Master of Adult Education (PGP) .... M Ad Ed
Master of Advanced Studies in Architecture (PGP) .... MASA
Master of Aeronautical and Astronomical Engineering (GAGS) .... MAAE
Master of Aeronautical Engineering .... M Ae E
Master of Aeronautical Engineering .... M Ae Eng
Master of Aeronautical Engineering .... M Aero E
Master of Aeronautical Engineering .... M Aero Eng
Master of Aeronautical Engineering (WDAA) .... MAE
Master of Aeronautical Science .... M Ae S
Master of Aeronautical Science .... M Ae Sc
Master of Aeronautical Science (GAGS) .... MAS
Master of Aeronautics .... M Ae
Master of Aeronautics and Astronautics (GAGS) .... MAA
Master of Aerospace Engineering (PGP) .... M Aero E
Master of Aerospace Engineering (PGP) .... MAE
Master of Aerospace Operations Management (GAGS) .... MAOM
Master of Agribusiness Management (PGP) .... MABM
Master of Agricultural Business and Economics (WGA) .... MABE

Master of Agricultural Business and Finance .... MABF
Master of Agricultural Development Economics .... MADE
Master of Agricultural Development Economics (ADA) .... MAgDevEc
Master of Agricultural Development Economics .... MAgrDevEc
Master of Agricultural Economics .... M Ag Ec
Master of Agricultural Economics (PGP) .... MAE
Master of Agricultural Economics .... MAgrEc
Master of Agricultural Education .... M Ag Ed
Master of Agricultural Education (PGP) .... MAE
Master of Agricultural Engineering .... M Agr E
Master of Agricultural Engineering .... M Agr Eng
Master of Agricultural Engineering (GAGS) .... MAE
Master of Agricultural Extension (GAGS) .... MAE
Master of Agricultural Extension (GAGS) .... MAgExt
Master of Agricultural Management and Resource Development (GAGS) .... MAMRD
Master of Agricultural Science .... M Agr S
Master of Agricultural Science .... M Agr Sc
Master of Agricultural Science .... MAgrSci
Master of Agricultural Science (ADA) .... MAgSc
Master of Agricultural Science .... MAgSci
Master of Agricultural Science (DD) .... MASc
Master of Agricultural Studies (ADA) .... MAgrSt
Master of Agricultural Studies .... MAgSt
Master of Agriculture .... M Ag
Master of Agriculture .... M Agr
Master of Agriculture .... M Agric
Master of Agriculture and Management (PGP) .... MAM
Master of Air Conditioning Education (NADA) .... MACE
Master of Air Conditioning Engineering .... MAC Eng
Master of Air Conditioning Engineering .... MACE
Master of Anesthesiology Education (PGP) .... M Anesth Ed
Master of Animal Medicine (GAGS) .... MAM
Master of Animal Science, University of Liverpool [British] (DBQ) .... MAnimSc
Master of Applied Art (GAGS) .... MAA
Master of Applied Arts .... MAA
Master of Applied Chemistry .... MA Chem
Master of Applied Communication Theory and Methodology (PGP) .... MACTM
Master of Applied Development and Health (PGP) .... MADH
Master of Applied Epidemiology .... MAppEpidem
Master of Applied Geography (PGP) .... MAG
Master of Applied Human and Community Development (PGP) .... MAHCD
Master of Applied Linguistics .... MAppLing
Master of Applied Linguistics and Exegesis (PGP) .... MLE
Master of Applied Literature (GAGS) .... MApplLit
Master of Applied Mathematical Science (PGP) .... MAM Sc
Master of Applied Mathematical Sciences (PGP) .... MAMS
Master of Applied Mathematics (PGP) .... M Ap Ma
Master of Applied Mathematics (GAGS) .... MApplM
Master of Applied Mechanics .... MA Mech
Master of Applied Mechanics (PGP) .... MAM
Master of Applied Molecular Biology (PGP) .... MAMB
Master of Applied Psychology (PGP) .... MAP
Master of Applied Psychology .... MAppPsych
Master of Applied Psychology (ADA) .... MPsychApp
Master of Applied Science .... MA Sc
Master of Applied Science .... MAppSc
Master of Applied Science .... MAppSci
Master of Applied Science (GAGS) .... MApSc
Master of Applied Science .... MAS
Master of Applied Science (DD) .... MScA
Master of Applied Science - Built Environment .... MAppSc-BltEnvir
Master of Applied Science in Social Ecology .... MAppSc(SocEcol)
Master of Applied Science - Medical Physics .... MAppSc-MedPhys
Master of Applied Spirituality (PGP) .... MAS
Master of Applied Statistics (PGP) .... M Ap Stat
Master of Applied Statistics (PGP) .... M Appl Stat
Master of Applied Statistics (GAGS) .... MAS
Master of Applied Statistics .... MAStat
Master of Aquaculture (PGP) .... M Aq
Master of Aquacultures (GAGS) .... MAq
Master of Architectural Design .... M Arch Des
Master of Architectural Engineering .... M Arch E
Master of Architectural Engineering .... M Arch Eng
Master of Architectural Engineering (GAGS) .... MArch
Master of Architectural History (PGP) .... M Arch H
Master of Architectural History (GAGS) .... MArchH
Master of Architectural Studies (PGP) .... M Arch Studies
Master of Architectural Studies (PGP) .... MS Arch St
Master of Architecture .... M Ar
Master of Architecture .... M Arch
Master of Architecture .... M of Arch
Master of Architecture in City Planning .... M Arch in CP
Master of Architecture in Urban Design (PGP) .... M Arch UD
Master of Architecture in Urban Design (GAGS) .... MArchUD
Master of Archival Studies (GAGS) .... MAS
Master of Archival Studies .... MAS
Master of Archive Administration, University of Liverpool [British] (DBQ) .... MArAd
Master of Archives Administration (ADA) .... MArchivAdmin
Master of Art Education .... MAE
Master of Art of Oratory .... MAO
Master of Art, Royal College of Art .... M Art (RCA)
Master of Arts (NADA) .... AM
Master of Arts .... MA

Master of Arts Administration (GAGS) ... MAd
Master of Arts and Letters ... MARL
Master of Arts and Sciences ... M Ar Sc
Master of Arts and Sciences (NADA) ... MArSci
Master of Arts (Asian Studies) ... MA(AsianStudies)
Master of Arts (Drama) ... MA(Drama)
Master of Arts in Accountancy (PGP) ... MACY
Master of Arts in Acupuncture and Oriental Medicine (PGP) ... M Ac OM
Master of Arts in Adult Education (GAGS) ... MAdEd
Master of Arts in Alcoholism and Drug Abuse Ministry (PGP) ... MA ADAM
Master of Arts in American Studies (GAGS) ... MAAmSt
Master of Arts in Applied Behavioral Sciences (GAGS) ... MAABS
Master of Arts in Applied Economics (GAGS) ... MAAE
Master of Arts in Applied Organizational Management (PGP) ... MAAOM
Master of Arts in Applied Theology (PGP) ... MAAT
Master of Arts in Architecture ... MA Arch
Master of Arts in Art Therapy (GAGS) ... MAAT
Master of Arts in Arts Administration (PGP) ... MAAA
Master of Arts in Behavior Science (GAGS) ... MABS
Master of Arts in Biblical Studies (PGP) ... MABS
Master of Arts in Business (PGP) ... MAB
Master of Arts in Business Education ... MABE
Master of Arts in Children's Literature and Reading ... MA(ChildLit/Reading)
Master of Arts in Christian Education (PGP) ... MACE
Master of Arts in Christian Ministries (PGP) ... MACM
Master of Arts in Church History (PGP) ... MACH
Master of Arts in Church Music (PGP) ... MACM
Master of Arts in Church Social Services (PGP) ... MACSS
Master of Arts in Civil Engineering ... MACE
Master of Arts in Classroom Psychology (PGP) ... MACL
Master of Arts in College Teaching ... MACT
Master of Arts in Communication (PGP) ... MA Comm
Master of Arts in Communication (GAGS) ... MAC
Master of Arts in Communication Arts ... MACA
Master of Arts in Communications ... MA in Comm
Master of Arts in Community College Teaching (GAGS) ... MACCT
Master of Arts in Community Psychology (PGP) ... MACP
Master of Arts in Computer Applications (GAGS) ... MACA
Master of Arts in Computer Education (PGP) ... MACE
Master of Arts in Counseling (PGP) ... MAC
Master of Arts in Counseling (PGP) ... MACO
Master of Arts in Counseling Psychology (PGP) ... MACP
Master of Arts in Counseling Psychology: Art Therapy (PGP) ... MACAT
Master of Arts in Criminological Studies ... MACrimStudies
Master of Arts in Dispute Resolution (PGP) ... MADR
Master of Arts in Economic and Social Studies [*University of Manchester*] [*British*] ... MA (Econ)
Master of Arts in Economic Studies [*Universities of Newcastle and Sheffield*] [*British*] ... MA (Econ)
Master of Arts in Economics (PGP) ... MA Ec
Master of Arts in Economics ... MAEC
Master of Arts in Education ... MA Ed
Master of Arts in Education (PGP) ... MA EdU
Master of Arts in Education ... MAE
Master of Arts in English (PGP) ... MAE
Master of Arts in English Teaching (PGP) ... MAET
Master of Arts in Environmental Sciences (PGP) ... MAES
Master of Arts in Family Counseling (GAGS) ... MAFC
Master of Arts in Finance (PGP) ... MAF
Master of Arts in Foreign Language and Literature (PGP) ... MAFLL
Master of Arts in Gerontological Psychology (PGP) ... MAGP
Master of Arts in Hebrew Education (BJA) ... MAHE
Master of Arts in Hebrew Letters (PGP) ... MAHL
Master of Arts in History Teaching (PGP) ... MAHT
Master of Arts in Home Economics and Family Ecology (GAGS) ... MAHE&FE
Master of Arts in Home Economics and Family Ecology (PGP) ... MAHEFE
Master of Arts in Human Ecology (GAGS) ... MAHE
Master of Arts in Human Resource Management (GAGS) ... MAHRM
Master of Arts in Human Service Management (GAGS) ... MAHSM
Master of Arts in Humanities (GAGS) ... MAH
Master of Arts in Industrial Arts (PGP) ... MAIA
Master of Arts in Industrial Relations ... MAIR
Master of Arts in Intercultural Studies (PGP) ... MAICS
Master of Arts in Interdisciplinary Studies (GAGS) ... MAIS
Master of Arts in Interior Design (GAGS) ... MAID
Master of Arts in Interior Design (PGP) ... MAIND
Master of Arts in International Affairs (GAGS) ... MAIA
Master of Arts in International Communications (PGP) ... MAIIC
Master of Arts in International Diplomacy (GAGS) ... MAID
Master of Arts in International Relations (GAGS) ... MAIR
Master of Arts in International Studies (GAGS) ... MAIS
Master of Arts in Jewish Communal Service (BJA) ... MAJCS
Master of Arts in Jewish Communal Studies and Social Work (BJA) ... MAJCSSW
Master of Arts in Jewish Education (PGP) ... MAJ Ed
Master of Arts in Jewish Education (BJA) ... MAJE
Master of Arts in Jewish Studies (PGP) ... MAJS
Master of Arts in Journalism (GAGS) ... MAJ
Master of Arts in Journalism and Communication (PGP) ... MAJC
Master of Arts in Judaic Studies (BJA) ... MAJS
Master of Arts in Labor and Employment Relations (PGP) ... MALER
Master of Arts in Language Teaching (GAGS) ... MALT
Master of Arts in Latin American Studies (PGP) ... MALAS
Master of Arts in Law and Diplomacy ... MALD
Master of Arts in Law and Diplomacy (GAGS) ... MALD
Master of Arts in Liberal Arts (PGP) ... MALA
Master of Arts in Liberal Learning (PGP) ... MALL
Master of Arts in Liberal Studies ... MALS
Master of Arts in Library and Information Science (PGP) ... MALIS
Master of Arts in Library Science (NADA) ... AMLS
Master of Arts in Library Science ... AMLS
Master of Arts in Library Science ... MALS
Master of Arts in Library Service (NADA) ... MALS
Master of Arts in Liturgical Arts (PGP) ... MALA
Master of Arts in Management (PGP) ... MA Mgt
Master of Arts in Management ... MAM
Master of Arts in Marriage and Family Counseling (GAGS) ... MAMFC
Master of Arts in Marriage and Family Therapy (PGP) ... MAMFT
Master of Arts in Marriage, Family, and Child Counseling (PGP) ... MAMFCC
Master of Arts in Mass Communication (PGP) ... MAMC
Master of Arts in Ministry (PGP) ... MA Min
Master of Arts in Ministry Management (PGP) ... MAMM
Master of Arts in Missions (PGP) ... MA Missions
Master of Arts in Missions/Evangelism (PGP) ... MAME
Master of Arts in Music ... MA (Mus)
Master of Arts in New Testament (PGP) ... MANT
Master of Arts in Occupational Therapy ... MAOT
Master of Arts in Old Testament (PGP) ... MAOT
Master of Arts in Pacific Rim Studies (GAGS) ... MAPRS
Master of Arts in Pastoral Care and Counseling (PGP) ... MAPCC
Master of Arts in Pastoral Counseling (PGP) ... MAPC
Master of Arts in Pastoral Ministry (PGP) ... MAP Min
Master of Arts in Pastoral Ministry (PGP) ... MAPM
Master of Arts in Pastoral Music (PGP) ... MAPM
Master of Arts in Pastoral Studies (PGP) ... MAPS
Master of Arts in Physical Education (GAGS) ... MAPE
Master of Arts in Planning (PGP) ... MAP
Master of Arts in Political Economy (PGP) ... MAPE
Master of Arts in Professional Writing (PGP) ... MAPW
Master of Arts in Psychology (PGP) ... MA Ps
Master of Arts in Psychology (PGP) ... MA Psych
Master of Arts in Psychology (GAGS) ... MAPsych
Master of Arts in Public Administration (GAGS) ... MAPA
Master of Arts in Public Administration in Spanish (PGP) ... MAPAS
Master of Arts in Public Affairs (GAGS) ... MAPA
Master of Arts in Public Policy (GAGS) ... MAPP
Master of Arts in Public Service ... MAPS
Master of Arts in Religion ... MAR
Master of Arts in Religion (GAGS) ... MAR
Master of Arts in Religion and Theology (PGP) ... MART
Master of Arts in Religious Communication (PGP) ... MARC
Master of Arts in Religious Education (PGP) ... MARE
Master of Arts in Religious Leadership (PGP) ... MARL
Master of Arts in Religious Studies (PGP) ... AMRS
Master of Arts in Religious Studies (PGP) ... MARS
Master of Arts in Research ... AM(R)
Master of Arts in Research (GAGS) ... MAR
Master of Arts in Sacred Music (BJA) ... MASM
Master of Arts in School Media Librarianship (PGP) ... MAML
Master of Arts in Social Science (ADA) ... MA(SS)
Master of Arts in Social Studies (NADA) ... MASocStud
Master of Arts in Social Work ... MASW
Master of Arts in Special Studies (PGP) ... MASS
Master of Arts in Spiritual Direction (PGP) ... MASD
Master of Arts in Substance Abuse Counseling (PGP) ... MASAC
Master of Arts in Teacher Education ... MA (T Ed)
Master of Arts in Teaching ... AM in T
Master of Arts in Teaching ... AMT
Master of Arts in Teaching ... MAT
Master of Arts in Teaching ... MA(T)
Master of Arts in Teaching English as a Second Language (PGP) ... MATESL
Master of Arts in Teaching English to Speakers of Other Languages (PGP) ... MATESOL
Master of Arts in Teaching English to Speakers of Other Languages ... MA(TESOL)
Master of Arts in Teaching Foreign Language (PGP) ... MATFL
Master of Arts in Teaching of Languages (PGP) ... MATL
Master of Arts in Teaching of Mathematics (PGP) ... MATM
Master of Arts in Teaching of Science (PGP) ... MATS
Master of Arts in Textiles (PGP) ... MATEX
Master of Arts in the Teaching of English ... MATE
Master of Arts in Theological Studies (PGP) ... MATS
Master of Arts in Theology (PGP) ... MA Th
Master of Arts in Theology ... MA Theol
Master of Arts in Theology (PGP) ... MAT
Master of Arts in Theology ... MA(Th)
Master of Arts in Theology ... STM
Master of Arts in Therapy (PGP) ... MATH
Master of Arts in Urban Affairs (GAGS) ... MAUA
Master of Arts in Urban and Regional Planning (GAGS) ... MAURP
Master of Arts in Urban Design (GAGS) ... MAUD
Master of Arts in Urban Planning ... MA in Urb Pl
Master of Arts in Worship (PGP) ... MAW
Master of Arts in Writing (GAGS) ... MAW
Master of Arts (Landscape Design), University of Manchester [*British*] (DBQ) ... MA(LD)
Master of Arts (Library Science) ... MA(LibSc)
Master of Arts Management (PGP) ... MAM
Master of Arts - Ministry (PGP) ... MAM
Master of Arts (Research) (PGP) ... MA(R)

Master of Arts, Royal College of Art (Photography) [*British*] (DBQ) .... MA(RCA)
Master of Arts (Social Sciences), University of Glasgow [*British*] (DBQ) .... MA(SocSci)
Master of Arts (Social Studies) .... MA (Social Studies)
Master of Arts with Honours (ADA) .... MA(Hons)
Master of Associated Medical Sciences (PGP) .... MAMS
Master of Association Management (PGP) .... MAM
Master of Association Science .... M As S
Master of Association Science .... M As Sc
Master of Audiology .... MAud
Master of Automobile Engineering .... M Au E
Master of Automobile Engineering .... M Au Eng
Master of Automotive Engineering (PGP) .... MAE
Master of Avian Medicine (PGP) .... MAM
Master of Aviation Management (GAGS) .... MAM
Master of Back Stabbin', Cork Screwin', and Dirty Dealin' [*Self-conferred degree held by Mordecai Jones in 1967 movie "The Flim-Flam Man"*] .... MBSCSDD
Master of Bacteriology .... Ms B
Master of Basic Science .... MBS
Master of Beauty Culture .... MBC
Master of Behavioral Health Care Management (PGP) .... MBHCM
Master of Behavioral Science (GAGS) .... MBS
Master of Behavioural Science .... MBSc
Master of Behavioural Sciences (ADA) .... MBehaviouralSc
Master of Bilingual Education (PGP) .... MBE
Master of Bioengineering (PGP) .... M Bio E
Master of Bioethics .... MBioEth
Master of Biological and Agricultural Engineering (PGP) .... MBAE
Master of Biological Chemistry .... M Bi Ch
Master of Biological Chemistry (NADA) .... MBiChem
Master of Biological Engineering .... M Bi E
Master of Biological Engineering (NADA) .... MBiEng
Master of Biological Illustration (GAGS) .... MBI
Master of Biological Physics .... M Bi Phy
Master of Biological Sciences .... M Bi S
Master of Biomathematics (PGP) .... M Biomath
Master of Biomedical Engineering (ADA) .... MBiomedE
Master of Bioradiology .... M Biorad
Master of Biosystems and Agricultural Engineering (PGP) .... MBAE
Master of Biotechnology .... MBiotech
Master of Brand Management (GAGS) .... MBM
Master of Building (ADA) .... MBldg
Master of Building (ADA) .... MBuild
Master of Building Construction (PGP) .... MBC
Master of Building Management (ADA) .... MBM
Master of Building Science .... MBdgSc
Master of Building Science (ADA) .... MBldgSc
Master of Building Science .... MBldSc
Master of Building Science (GAGS) .... MBS
Master of Business (ADA) .... MBus
Master of Business - Accountancy .... MBus-Accy
Master of Business Administration .... MB Adm
Master of Business Administration .... MBA
Master of Business Administration (GAGS) .... MBA
Master of Business Administration (ADA) .... MBusAd
Master of Business Administration - Experienced Professionals (PGP) .... MBA-EP
Master of Business Administration in Actuarial Science .... MBAAS
Master of Business Administration in Aviation (PGP) .... MBAA
Master of Business Administration in International Business (GAGS) .... MBAIB
Master of Business Administration in International Trade (PGP) .... MBAIT
Master of Business Administration - Physician's Executive (PGP) .... MBA-PE
Master of Business and Public Administration .... MBPA
Master of Business and Public Management .... MBPM
Master of Business and Technology .... MBT
Master of Business - Communication .... MBus-Comn
Master of Business Economics .... MBE
Master of Business Economics (GAGS) .... MBE
Master of Business Education .... M Bus Ed
Master of Business Education .... MB Ed
Master of Business Education .... MBE
Master of Business Education (GAGS) .... MBE
Master of Business in Telecommunication Management (PGP) .... MBATM
Master of Business Information Science (PGP) .... MBSI
Master of Business Information Systems .... MBIS
Master of Business (Information Technology) .... MB (IT)
Master of Business Management .... MBM
Master of Business - Management .... MBus-Mgt
Master of Business Management and Software Engineering (PGP) .... MBMSE
Master of Business Science .... MB Sc
Master of Business Taxation (GAGS) .... MBT
Master of Canon Law .... M Can L
Master of Canon Law (PGP) .... MCL
Master of Cement Engineering .... M Ce Eng
Master of Ceramic Engineering .... M Cer E
Master of Ceremonies .... EMCEE
Master of Ceremonies .... MC
Master of Ceremonies (WDMC) .... MC
Master of Chemical Engineering .... M Ch E
Master of Chemical Engineering .... M Chem E
Master of Chemical Engineering (GAGS) .... MCE
Master of Chemistry .... MC
Master of Chemistry (ADA) .... MChem
Master of Chiropody .... M Cp
Master of Christian Education .... M Chr Ed
Master of Christian Education .... MCE
Master of Christian Ministry (PGP) .... MCM
Master of Christian Science .... CSM
Master of Christian Training .... MCT
Master of Chromatics [*British*] .... MChrom
Master of Church Management (PGP) .... MCM
Master of Church Music .... MCM
Master of City and Regional Planning (GAGS) .... MCRP
Master of City Planning (GAGS) .... MCP
Master of City Planning .... MCP
Master of Civic Design .... MCD
Master of Civil Engineering (PGP) .... M Civil E
Master of Civil Engineering .... MC Eng
Master of Civil Engineering .... MCE
Master of Civil Engineering (GAGS) .... MCE
Master of Civil Engineering (Melbourne University) .... MCE(Melb)
Master of Civil Law .... MCL
Master of Classics .... MC
Master of Clinical Biochemistry .... MCB
Master of Clinical Biochemistry .... MClBiochem
Master of Clinical Dentistry (PGP) .... M Cl D
Master of Clinical Gerontology (PGP) .... MCG
Master of Clinical Microbiology (PGP) .... MCM
Master of Clinical Nutrition .... MCN
Master of Clinical Psychology .... MClinPsych
Master of Clinical Psychology (ADA) .... MClinPsychol
Master of Clinical Science (PGP) .... M Cl Sc
Master of Clinical Science (ADA) .... MClinSc
Master of Clinical Science (ADA) .... MClSc
Master of Clinical Science (PGP) .... MCS
Master of Cognitive Science .... MCogSc
Master of Commerce .... M Com
Master of Commerce .... M of C
Master of Commerce (GAGS) .... MC
Master of Commerce (ADA) .... MComm
Master of Commerce and Administration (ROG) .... M Comm
Master of Commercial Administration .... M Com Adm
Master of Commercial Arts .... MCA
Master of Commercial Aviation (PGP) .... MCA
Master of Commercial Education .... MC Ed
Master of Commercial Law .... LLM Com
Master of Commercial Science .... M Com Sc
Master of Commercial Science .... MC Sc
Master of Commercial Science .... MCS
Master of Commercial Service .... MC Se
Master of Communication (GAGS) .... MC
Master of Communication Arts (PGP) .... MCA
Master of Communication Disorders (GAGS) .... MCD
Master of Communication Studies (PGP) .... MCS
Master of Community Dental Health, University of Birmingham [*British*] (DBQ) .... MCDH
Master of Community Economic Development (PGP) .... MCED
Master of Community Health .... M Comm H
Master of Community Health (GAGS) .... MCH
Master of Community Planning (GAGS) .... MCP
Master of Community Psychology (PGP) .... MCP
Master of Comparative Jurisprudence .... MCJ
Master of Comparative Law (DLA) .... LLCM
Master of Comparative Law (GAGS) .... LLCM
Master of Comparative Law .... M Comp L
Master of Comparative Law .... MCL
Master of Comparative Law (NADA) .... MCompLaw
Master of Comparative Religion .... MCR
Master of Computer and Information Science (PGP) .... MCIS
Master of Computer Engineering (PGP) .... M Comp E
Master of Computer Information Systems (GAGS) .... MCIS
Master of Computer Science (PGP) .... MC Sc
Master of Computer Science .... MComSc
Master of Computer Science (WGA) .... MCS
Master of Computer Science (GAGS) .... MCS
Master of Computer Science and Engineering (GAGS) .... MCSE
Master of Computing .... M Comp
Master of Congress [*British*] (DAS) .... MC
Master of Construction Management (PGP) .... MCM
Master of Construction Science/Management (PGP) .... MCSM
Master of Continuing Education (PGP) .... MC Ed
Master of Cosmology .... M Co
Master of Counseling (PGP) .... M Coun
Master of Counseling (GAGS) .... MC
Master of Counseling Psychology (GAGS) .... MCP
Master of Counselling (Education) (ADA) .... MCouns(Ed)
Master of Creative Arts .... MCA
Master of Creative Arts in Therapy (PGP) .... MCAT
Master of Criminal Justice (GAGS) .... MCJ
Master of Criminal Justice Administration (GAGS) .... MCJA
Master of Criminology .... M Cr
Master of Criminology (GAGS) .... MCrim
Master of Curriculum Studies .... MCurrSt
Master of Curriculum Studies .... MCurrStud
Master of Decision Sciences (PGP) .... M Dec S
Master of Decision Sciences (GAGS) .... MDS
Master of Defence Studies .... MDefStudies
Master of Dental Medicine .... DDM
Master of Dental Science [*British*] .... M Dent Sc

Master of Dental Science [British]	MD Sc
Master of Dental Science (GAGS)	MDS
Master of Dental Science (DAVI)	MScD
Master of Dental Science	MScD
Master of Dental Surgery	MDS
Master of Design	M Des
Master of Design, Royal College of Art	M Des (RCA)
Master of Design Studies (PGP)	M Des S
Master of Design Studies (GAGS)	MDesS
Master of Design Studies	MDesSt
Master of Development Adminstration (PGP)	MDA
Master of Development Management	MDM
Master of Developmental Economics (PGP)	MDE
Master of Didactics	M Did
Master of Didactics	MDI
Master of Diesel Engineering	M Di E
Master of Diesel Engineering	M Di Eng
Master of Dietetics (GAGS)	MSD
Master of Diplomacy	M Dip
Master of Dispute Resolution (PGP)	MDR
Master of Distance Education (PGP)	MDE
Master of Divine Literature	MDL
Master of Divinity	DM
Master of Divinity	M Div
Master of Domestic Economy (NADA)	MDE
Master of Dramatic Art	MDA
Master of Early Childhood Education	MECEd
Master of Economic Science (ADA)	MEconS
Master of Economic Studies (ADA)	MEconSt
Master of Economics	M Ec
Master of Economics (PGP)	M Econ
Master of Economics	MEcon
Master of Economics in Regional Planning (ADA)	MEc(Reg Plan)
Master of Economics of Development	MEcDev
Master of Ecosystem Management (PGP)	MEM
Master of Education	Ed M
Master of Education	M Ed
Master of Education	ME
Master of Education (Educational Psychology), University of Birmingham [British] (DBQ)	MEd(Ed/Psych)
Master of Education in Business Teacher Education	Ed M in BT Ed
Master of Education in Creative Arts	MEdCA
Master of Education in Guidance and Counselling	MEd(Guid&Coun)
Master of Education in Library Science (WDAA)	M ED L SC
Master of Education in Library Science	M Ed LS
Master of Education in Physical Education	Ed M in Phy Ed
Master of Education in Rural Education	MEd(RuralEd)
Master of Education in Special Education (ADA)	MEd(SpEd)
Master of Education in Teaching (PGP)	M Ed T
Master of Education in Teaching (GAGS)	MET
Master of Education (Mathematics)	MEd(Maths)
Master of Education of the Deaf (GAGS)	MED
Master of Education - Professional Development (PGP)	MEPD
Master of Education (Special Education)	MEd(SpecEd)
Master of Educational Administration (ADA)	MEdAd
Master of Educational Administration (ADA)	MEdAdm
Master of Educational Administration	MEdAdmin
Master of Educational Ministry (PGP)	MEM
Master of Educational Psychology (ADA)	MEdPsych
Master of Educational Studies (ADA)	MEdSt
Master of Educational Studies	MEdStud
Master of Electrical and Computer Engineering (PGP)	MECE
Master of Electrical Engineering (PGP)	M Elec E
Master of Electrical Engineering	ME Eng
Master of Electrical Engineering	MEE
Master of Electrochemical Engineering	ME Ch E
Master of Electrochemical Engineering	MECE
Master of Elementary Didactics	MED
Master of Elements	M El
Master of Elements	ME
Master of Elocution	M Elo
Master of Emergency Medical Service (PGP)	MEMS
Master of Energy Resources (GAGS)	MER
Master of Engineering	M Eng
Master of Engineering (PGP)	M Engr
Master of Engineering (WDAA)	MA E
Master of Engineering	ME
Master of Engineering Administration	MEA
Master of Engineering and Public Administration (NADA)	MEngPA
Master of Engineering and Technology Management (PGP)	METM
Master of Engineering Architecture (GAGS)	MEA
Master of Engineering (Chemical) (ADA)	MEC
Master of Engineering Chemistry	ME(Chem)
Master of Engineering (Electrical) (ADA)	ME(Elec)
Master of Engineering in Manufacturing Systems (GAGS)	MEMS
Master of Engineering Management (PGP)	M Eng Mgt
Master of Engineering Management	MEM
Master of Engineering Management (GAGS)	MEM
Master of Engineering (Mechanical) (ADA)	ME(Mech)
Master of Engineering Physics	ME Phy
Master of Engineering Physics	MEP
Master of Engineering (Research)	ME(Res)
Master of Engineering Science	M Eng Sc
Master of Engineering Science	ME Sc
Master of Engineering Science	MEngS

Master of Engineering Sciences	MES
Master of Engineering Studies (ADA)	MEngSt
Master of Engineering Studies	MES
Master of English	M En
Master of English	M Eng
Master of English Divinity	MED
Master of English Language (PGP)	MEL
Master of English Literature	MEL
Master of Entomology	M Ent
Master of Environment (PGP)	M Env
Master of Environmental Design (PGP)	M Env Des
Master of Environmental Design (GAGS)	MED
Master of Environmental Design (DD)	MEDes
Master of Environmental Design Studies (PGP)	MEDS
Master of Environmental Engineering (PGP)	M Env E
Master of Environmental Engineering (PGP)	M Envir E
Master of Environmental Engineering (PGP)	MENVEGR
Master of Environmental Engineering and Management (PGP)	MEEM
Master of Environmental Management (PGP)	MEM
Master of Environmental Planning	MEnvPlan
Master of Environmental Planning (GAGS)	MEP
Master of Environmental Pollution Control (GAGS)	MEPC
Master of Environmental Science (PGP)	M En S
Master of Environmental Science (PGP)	M Env Sc
Master of Environmental Science	MEnvS
Master of Environmental Science (GAGS)	MEnvS
Master of Environmental Science (ADA)	MEnvSc
Master of Environmental Science (DD)	MES
Master of Environmental Science (PGP)	MESM
Master of Environmental Studies (DD)	MEnv
Master of Environmental Studies	MEnvS
Master of Environmental Studies (ADA)	MEnvSt
Master of Environmental Studies (ADA)	MEnvStud
Master of Environmental Studies	MEnvStudies
Master of Environmental Studies (PGP)	MES
Master of Exercise and Sport Sciences (PGP)	MESS
Master of Experimental Statistics (GAGS)	MExSt
Master of Expression	M Ex
Master of Extension Education (PGP)	M Ext Ed
Master of Extension Education (GAGS)	MExtEd
Master of Family and Consumer Sciences (PGP)	MFCS
Master of Family Life	MFL
Master of Family Studies (GAGS)	MFS
Master of Family Therapy (GAGS)	MFT
Master of Finance (PGP)	M Fin
Master of Finance	MF
Master of Finance	MFin
Master of Finance and Banking (PGP)	MFB
Master of Financial Economics (PGP)	MFE
Master of Financial Management (ADA)	MFM
Master of Financial Management (PGP)	MSFM
Master of Financial Studies	MFinStud
Master of Fine Arts	MFA
Master of Fine Arts in Music (WDAA)	MFAMUS
Master of Fine Arts in Writing (PGP)	MFAW
Master of Fine Arts International [British]	MAI
Master of Fisheries and Aquatic Science (PGP)	MFAS
Master of Fisheries Science	MFSc
Master of Food Science	MFS
Master of Foreign Service	MFS
Master of Foreign Study	MFS
Master of Foreign Trade	MFT
Master of Forensic Science (GAGS)	MFS
Master of Forest Conservation (PGP)	MFC
Master of Forest Engineering	MF Eng
Master of Forest Engineering	MFE
Master of Forest Resources (GAGS)	MFR
Master of Forest Resources and Conservation (PGP)	MFRC
Master of Forest Science (ADA)	MForSc
Master of Forest Science (GAGS)	MFS
Master of Forest Studies (PGP)	MFS
Master of Forestry	MF
Master of Forestry	MFor
Master of Fox Hounds	MFH
Master of French (PGP)	M Fr
Master of French Studies (PGP)	MFS
Master of Gas Technology (GAGS)	MGT
Master of General Engineering (PGP)	M Gen E
Master of General Studies (ADA)	MGenStud
Master of General Studies (GAGS)	MGS
Master of Geological Engineering	M Ge E
Master of Geological Engineering	M Ge Eng
Master of Geological Engineering (PGP)	M Geo E
Master of Geological Engineering	M Geol E
Master of Geological Engineering (GAGS)	MGE
Master of Geological Engineering (NADA)	MGE
Master of Geological Engineering (NADA)	MGeolEng
Master of Gerontological Studies (GAGS)	MGS
Master of Government Administration (GAGS)	MGA
Master of Graphic Design (PGP)	MGD
Master of Group Process and Group Psychotherapy (PGP)	MGPGP
Master of Gynaecology and Obstetrics (ADA)	MGO
Master of Hamburgerology [McDonald's Corp. Hamburger University]	MH
Master of Health (GAGS)	MH
Master of Health Administration	MHA

Master of Health Administration (ADA) .... MHealthAdmin
Master of Health Care Administration (GAGS) .... MHCA
Master of Health Education (GAGS) .... MHE
Master of Health Education (GAGS) .... MHEd
Master of Health Management Systems (PGP) .... MHMS
Master of Health Personnel Education (ADA) .... MHPEd
Master of Health, Physical Education, and Recreation .... MH PE & R
Master of Health Planning (ADA) .... MHP
Master of Health Professions (PGP) .... MHP
Master of Health Professions Education (PGP) .... MHPE
Master of Health Science Education (PGP) .... MHSE
Master of Health Sciences (PGP) .... MH Sc
Master of Health Sciences (PGP) .... MHS
Master of Health Services (GAGS) .... MHS
Master of Health Services Administration (GAGS) .... MHSA
Master of Health Services Administration (DD) .... MHSA
Master of Hebrew Letters (BJA) .... MHL
Master of Hebrew Literature (BJA) .... MAHL
Master of Hebrew Literature .... MHL
Master of Heritage Preservation (GAGS) .... MHP
Master of Higher Education (GAGS) .... MHE
Master of Higher Education .... MHEd
Master of Highway Engineering .... M Hi E
Master of Highway Engineering .... M Hi Eng
Master of Highway Engineering (NADA) .... MHE
Master of Hispanic Studies (PGP) .... MHS
Master of Historical Administration and Museum Studies (GAGS) .... MHAMS
Master of Historical Preservation (GAGS) .... MHP
Master of Home Economics (PGP) .... MH Ec
Master of Home Economics .... MHE
Master of Home Economics (GAGS) .... MHE
Master of Home Economics Education .... MHE Ed
Master of Home Economics Education (NADA) .... MHEE
Master of Home Economics Education (NADA) .... MHEEd
Master of Home Economics Engineering (NADA) .... MHE
Master of Horticultural Science .... MHortSc
Master of Horticulture .... M Hor
Master of Horticulture .... MH
Master of Hospital Administration .... MHA
Master of Hotel Management (PGP) .... MHM
Master of Hotel, Restaurant, and Institutional Management (PGP) .... MHRIM
Master of Hounds [British] .... MH
Master of Household Economy .... M Ho Ec
Master of Household Science .... M Ho Sc
Master of Human Development (PGP) .... MHD
Master of Human Ecology (PGP) .... MHE
Master of Human Kinetics (GAGS) .... MHK
Master of Human Movement Studies (ADA) .... MHMS
Master of Human Resources (GAGS) .... MHR
Master of Human Resources and Industrial Relations (PGP) .... MHRIR
Master of Human Resources and Organization Development (PGP) .... MHROD
Master of Human Resources Management (PGP) .... MHRM
Master of Human Services (PGP) .... M Hum Svcs
Master of Human Services (GAGS) .... MAHS
Master of Human Services (GAGS) .... MHS
Master of Human Services Administration (PGP) .... MHSA
Master of Human-Computer Interaction (PGP) .... MHCI
Master of Humane Letters [or Master of the More Humane Letters] .... LHM
Master of Humane Letters .... MHL
Master of Humane Studies (PGP) .... MHS
Master of Humanics .... MH
Master of Humanities .... HM
Master of Humanities .... M Hu
Master of Humanities .... M Hum
Master of Humanities (GAGS) .... MH
Master of Humanities in Philosophy (PGP) .... MHP
Master of Hygiene .... M Hy
Master of Hygiene .... M Hyg
Master of Hygiene .... MH
Master of Individualized Studies (GAGS) .... MIS
Master of Industrial Administration (GAGS) .... MIndAdm
Master of Industrial and Labor Relations .... MILR
Master of Industrial Arts .... MIA
Master of Industrial Design .... MID
Master of Industrial Education (PGP) .... M In Ed
Master of Industrial Education .... MIndEd
Master of Industrial Engineering .... MI Eng
Master of Industrial Engineering .... MIE
Master of Industrial Engineering (GAGS) .... MIE
Master of Industrial Engineering Management (PGP) .... MIE Mgmt
Master of Industrial Health .... MIH
Master of Industrial Management .... MIM
Master of Industrial Relations .... MIR
Master of Industrial Technology (PGP) .... MIT
Master of Information and Library Science (GAGS) .... MILS
Master of Information Science (PGP) .... MIS
Master of Information Services (GAGS) .... MIS
Master of Information Studies (PGP) .... MI St
Master of Information Systems .... MInfSys
Master of Information Systems (PGP) .... MIS
Master of Information Technology and Communication .... MInfoTech
Master of Initial Teaching (PGP) .... MIT
Master of Instruction (PGP) .... MI
Master of Instruction .... MI
Master of Insurance (GAGS) .... MI

Master of Insurance .... MIN
Master of Integrated Manufacturing Systems (PGP) .... MIMS
Master of Intellectual Property (PGP) .... MIP
Master of Intercultural Administration (PGP) .... MIA
Master of Interdisciplinary Studies (GAGS) .... MIS
Master of Interior Architectural Engineering .... M I Arch Eng
Master of Interior Architecture .... M I Arch
Master of Interior Architecture (PGP) .... MI Arch
Master of Interior Design (GAGS) .... MID
Master of Internal Affairs (NADA) .... MIA
Master of International Administration (PGP) .... MIA
Master of International Affairs .... MIA
Master of International Affairs (GAGS) .... MIA
Master of International and Intercultural Management (PGP) .... MIIM
Master of International Business (GAGS) .... MIB
Master of International Business Administration (GAGS) .... MIBA
Master of International Business Studies .... MIBS
Master of International Health Management (PGP) .... MIHM
Master of International Journalism (PGP) .... MIJ
Master of International Law .... MIntLaw
Master of International Management .... MIM
Master of International Management (DD) .... MIM
Master of International Management of Technology (PGP) .... MIMOT
Master of International Medicine (NADA) .... MIntMed
Master of International Public Administration (GAGS) .... MIPA
Master of International Public Policy (GAGS) .... MIPP
Master of International Service .... MIS
Master of International Studies (PGP) .... MIS
Master of Irrigation Engineering .... MIE
Master of Japanese Studies (ADA) .... MJS
Master of Jewish Education (PGP) .... MJ Ed
Master of Jewish Pedagogy .... MJP
Master of Journalism .... MJ
Master of Journalism in New Media Management (GAGS) .... MJNMM
Master of Judaic Studies (PGP) .... MJS
Master of Judicial Science .... JSM
Master of Juridical Science (DLA) .... MJS
Master of Jurisprudence .... Jur M
Master of Jurisprudence .... MJ
Master of Jurisprudence .... MJur
Master of Justice Administration (PGP) .... MJA
Master of Justice Policy and Management (PGP) .... MJPM
Master of Kinesiology (PGP) .... M Kin
Master of Labor and Human Resources (PGP) .... MLHR
Master of Labor and Industrial Relations (GAGS) .... MLIR
Master of Labor Relations and Human Resources (PGP) .... MLRHR
Master of Laboratory Animal Science (PGP) .... MLAS
Master of Land Economy .... MLE
Master of Landscape Architecture (PGP) .... M Land Arch
Master of Landscape Architecture .... ML Arch
Master of Landscape Architecture .... MLA
Master of Landscape Architecture [Canada] (DD) .... MLandArch
Master of Landscape Architecture in Urban Development (GAGS) .... MLAUD
Master of Landscape Design .... ML Des
Master of Landscape Design .... MLD
Master of Landscape Engineering .... ML Eng
Master of Landscape Management .... MLM
Master of Languages [British] (DBQ) .... MLing
Master of Latin Letters .... M La L
Master of Latin Literature .... MLL
Master of Law (GAGS) .... LLM
Master of Law and Social Policy (GAGS) .... MLSP
Master of Law and Taxation (GAGS) .... ML&T
Master of Law and Taxation .... MLT
Master of Law Librarianship .... ML Libr
Master of Law Librarianship (ILCA) .... MLL
Master of Laws (PGP) .... LL M
Master of Laws .... LLM
Master of Laws .... ML
Master of Laws in Comparative Law .... LLM (CL)
Master of Laws in International Law .... LLM (Int L)
Master of Legal Studies .... MLegS
Master of Legal Studies (GAGS) .... MLS
Master of Letters .... Litt M
Master of Letters .... M Lit
Master of Letters .... M Litt
Master of Letters .... ML
Master of Liberal Arts (PGP) .... ALM
Master of Liberal Arts .... LAM
Master of Liberal Arts (GAGS) .... MLA
Master of Liberal Studies (GAGS) .... MLS
Master of Librarianship (PGP) .... M Libr
Master of Librarianship (GAGS) .... ML
Master of Librarianship .... MLib
Master of Librarianship .... MLS
Master of Library and Information Science .... MLIS
Master of Library Media (PGP) .... MLM
Master of Library Science (BARN) .... M Lib Sc
Master of Library Science .... MLS
Master of Library Science (NADA) .... MLibSci
Master of Library Science (GAGS) .... MLS
Master of Library Science .... MLS
Master of Library Science and International Technology (PGP) .... MLSIT
Master of Library Services (PGP) .... MLS
Master of Library Studies .... MLS

Master of Life Science	LSM
Master of Life Science (GAGS)	MLS
Master of Literary Interpretation	MLI
Master of Literary Studies (ADA)	MLitSt
Master of Literature	Lit M
Master of Literature	M Lit
Master of Literature	ML
Master of Literature	MLitt
Master of Liturgical Music (PGP)	M Lit M
Master of Liturgical Music (GAGS)	MLitM
Master of Management (PGP)	M Mgmt
Master of Management (PGP)	M Mgt
Master of Management	MM
Master of Management (GAGS)	MM
Master of Management	MMgt
Master of Management and Administration, Cranfield Institute of Technology [British] (DBQ)	MMA
Master of Management Engineering (NADA)	MMgtEng
Master of Management in Hospitality (PGP)	MMH
Master of Management in Manufacturing (PGP)	MMM
Master of Management Information Systems (GAGS)	MMIS
Master of Management Science (GAGS)	MMS
Master of Management Science (GAGS)	MMSc
Master of Management Studies	MMS
Master of Manpower Administration (GAGS)	MMA
Master of Manufacturing (PGP)	MOM
Master of Manufacturing Engineering (PGP)	MME
Master of Manufacturing Systems Engineering (PGP)	MMSE
Master of Marine Affairs (GAGS)	MMA
Master of Marine Engineering	M Ma E
Master of Marine Engineering	M Ma Eng
Master of Marine Policy (GAGS)	MMP
Master of Marine Science (GAGS)	MMS
Master of Marine Science (GAGS)	MMSc
Master of Marketing Research (GAGS)	MMR
Master of Marketing Science (PGP)	MMS
Master of Marriage and Family Therapy (GAGS)	MMFT
Master of Marriage, Family and Child Counseling (GAGS)	MMFCC
Master of Mass Communication (GAGS)	MMC
Master of Material Engineering (GAGS)	MME
Master of Material Science and Engineering (PGP)	M Mat SE
Master of Materials Engineering (PGP)	M Mtl E
Master of Materials Science (GAGS)	MMS
Master of Mathematics (PGP)	M Math
Master of Mathematics (GAGS)	MM
Master of Mathematics	MMath
Master of Mathematics for Educators (PGP)	MME
Master of Mechanic Arts	AMM
Master of Mechanical and Aerospace Engineering (PGP)	MMAE
Master of Mechanical Engineering	M Mech E
Master of Mechanical Engineering	MM Eng
Master of Mechanical Engineering	MME
Master of Mechanical Engineering (GAGS)	MME
Master of Mechanical Engineering (NADA)	MMechEng
Master of Mechanical Science	MM Sc
Master of Mechanical Science	MMS
Master of Media Arts (PGP)	MMA
Master of Medical Art (GAGS)	MMA
Master of Medical Biochemistry (GAGS)	MMB
Master of Medical Education	MMedEd
Master of Medical Humanities (PGP)	MMH
Master of Medical Management (PGP)	MMM
Master of Medical Science	M Med Sc
Master of Medical Science	M Sc Med
Master of Medical Science	MM Sc
Master of Medical Science	MMS
Master of Medical Science (GAGS)	MMSc
Master of Medical Science	MSM
Master of Medical Science (NADA)	MSMed
Master of Medical Technology	MMT
Master of Medicine	M Med
Master of Medicine	MM
Master of Medicine (Anaesthesia)	MMedAnaes
Master of Medicine (Cardiology)	MMedCardiol
Master of Medicine (Community Medicine)	MMed(CM)
Master of Medicine (Diagnostic Radiology)	MMedRadD
Master of Medicine (Paediatrics)	MMedPaed
Master of Medicine (Pathology)	MMedPath
Master of Medicine (Venereology)	MMedVen
Master of Metal Engineering (PGP)	M Mtl E
Master of Metallurgical and Materials Engineering (PGP)	MMME
Master of Metallurgical Engineering	M Met E
Master of Metallurgy	M Met
Master of Metallurgy and Engineering, University of Sheffield [British] (DBQ)	MMetEng
Master of Metaphysics	M Me
Master of Metaphysics	Me M
Master of Microbiology	M Mic
Master of Midwifery	MMidwif
Master of Midwifery, Society of Apothecaries	MMSA
Master of Military Art and Science (MCD)	MMAS
Master of Military Science	M Sci Mil
Master of Mineral Engineering (GAGS)	MME
Master of Mining and Metallurgy (DD)	MIMM
Master of Mining Engineering	M Mi E
Master of Mining Engineering	MME
Master of Mining Engineering (NADA)	MMiEng
Master of Mining Management	MMinMgt
Master of Ministries (PGP)	M Min
Master of Ministry (PGP)	MM
Master of Ministry Management (PGP)	MMM
Master of Missiology (PGP)	M Miss
Master of Modern Languages	MML
Master of Modern Studies (PGP)	MM
Master of Modern Studies (PGP)	MMS
Master of Movement Therapy (GAGS)	MMT
Master of Municipal Administration	MM Adm
Master of Municipal Administration	MMA
Master of Museum Practice (GAGS)	MMP
Master of Museum Studies (PGP)	MM St
Master of Music (PGP)	M Mu
Master of Music	M Mus
Master of Music	MM
Master of Music (GAGS)	MM
Master of Music (GAGS)	MMu
Master of Music (GAGS)	MMus
Master of Music Composition, University of Manchester [British] (DBQ)	MusMComp
Master of Music Education (PGP)	M Mu Ed
Master of Music Education	M Mus Ed
Master of Music Education	MM Ed
Master of Music Education	MME
Master of Music Education	Mus Ed M
Master of Music in Church Music (PGP)	MMCM
Master of Music in Music Education	M Mus (Mus Ed)
Master of Music in Music Literature	M Mus (Mus Lit)
Master of Music in Public School Music	M Mus (PSM)
Master of Music in Wind Instruments	M Mus (W Inst)
Master of Music Performance (PGP)	MMP
Master of Music Performance, University of Manchester [British] (DBQ)	MusMPerf
Master of Music, Royal College of Music	M Mus (RCM)
Master of Music Teaching (GAGS)	MMT
Master of Musical Art (GAGS)	MMA
Master of Musical Arts	MMA
Master of Natural Resource Management (PGP)	MNRM
Master of Natural Resources (ADA)	MNatRes
Master of Natural Science (PGP)	M Nat Sci
Master of Natural Science (GAGS)	MNatSci
Master of Natural Sciences (GAGS)	MNS
Master of Naval Architecture	MN Arch
Master of Naval Engineering	MN Eng
Master of Naval Engineering	MNE
Master of Navigation	M Na
Master of Nonprofit Administration (GAGS)	MNA
Master of Nonprofit Management (PGP)	MNM
Master of Nonprofit Organization (PGP)	MNO
Master of Nuclear Engineering	MNE
Master of Nuclear Science (GAGS)	MNS
Master of Nuclear Science (GAGS)	MNucSc
Master of Nurse Anesthesia (PGP)	MNA
Master of Nursing (BARN)	M Nurs
Master of Nursing	MN
Master of Nursing (NADA)	MNurs
Master of Nursing	MNursing
Master of Nursing Administration	MNA
Master of Nursing Education	MN Ed
Master of Nursing Science	MN Sc
Master of Nursing Science	MNS
Master of Nutritional Science	MNS
Master of Nutritional Science	MNutrSc
Master of Nutritional Sciences (GAGS)	MNS
Master of Obstetric Art (DAVI)	AOM
Master of Obstetrics	MO
Master of Obstetrics and Gynaecology	MO & G
Master of Obstetrics and Gynecology (AD)	MOG
Master of Occupational Health (PGP)	MOH
Master of Occupational Health and Safety	MOHS
Master of Occupational Information and Guidance	MOIG
Master of Occupational Therapy (ADA)	MOccThy
Master of Occupational Therapy (GAGS)	MOT
Master of Ocean Engineering (GAGS)	MOE
Master of Oceanographic Engineering (PGP)	M Oc E
Master of Oceanographic Engineering (GAGS)	MOcE
Master of Operations Research (PGP)	MOR
Master of Ophthalmological Surgery (NADA)	MSOphthal
Master of Optometry	M Opt
Master of Optometry (GAGS)	MOpt
Master of Optometry (ADA)	MOptom
Master of Oral English	MOE
Master of Oratory	M Or
Master of Oratory	MO
Master of Organizational Behavior (GAGS)	MOB
Master of Organizational Development (GAGS)	MOD
Master of Organizational Leadership (PGP)	MOL
Master of Oriental Languages	MOL
Master of Oriental Learning	MOL
Master of Orthopaedic Surgery	M Ch Orth
Master of Osteopathy	MO
Master of Oto-Rhino-Laryngological Surgery	M Ch Otol

Master of Otter Hounds ... MOH
Master of Pacific International Affairs (GAGS) ... MPIA
Master of Paediatrics ... MPaed
Master of Painting ... M Pa
Master of Painting ... MP
Master of Park, Recreation, and Tourism Management (GAGS) ... MPRTM
Master of Pastoral Counseling (PGP) ... MPC
Master of Pastoral Studies (PGP) ... MPS
Master of Pastoral Theology (PGP) ... M Th Past
Master of Pastoral Theology (PGP) ... MPT
Master of Patent Law ... MPL
Master of Pedagogy ... M Pd
Master of Pedagogy ... Pd M
Master of Pedagogy ... Ped M
Master of Performing Arts (PGP) ... M Perf A
Master of Personnel and Employee Relations (GAGS) ... MPER
Master of Personnel Counseling (GAGS) ... MPC
Master of Personnel Management (GAGS) ... MPM
Master of Personnel Service (GAGS) ... MPS
Master of Personnel Services ... MPS
Master of Pest Management (PGP) ... MPM
Master of Pest Management (DD) ... MPM
Master of Petroleum Engineering ... M Pe E
Master of Petroleum Engineering ... M Pe Eng
Master of Petroleum Engineering (GAGS) ... MPetE
Master of Pharmaceutical Chemistry ... M Ph C
Master of Pharmaceutical Chemistry ... M Phar C
Master of Pharmacy ... M Phar
Master of Pharmacy ... M Pharm
Master of Pharmacy (GAGS) ... MP
Master of Pharmacy ... Pharm M
Master of Philosophical Foundations (PGP) ... M Phil F
Master of Philosophy ... M Ph
Master of Philosophy ... M Phil
Master of Philosophy ... Ph M
Master of Philosophy (PGP) ... Phil M
Master of Philosophy (GAGS) ... PhilM
Master of Photography ... M Pho
Master of Physic Sciences ... M Ps Sc
Master of Physical Activity Studies (PGP) ... MPAS
Master of Physical Biology ... MPB
Master of Physical Education ... MPE
Master of Physical Education ... MPEd
Master of Physical Education and Health ... MPH
Master of Physical Planning (NADA) ... MPP
Master of Physical Science ... M Ph S
Master of Physical Science ... M Ph Sc
Master of Physical Therapy (GAGS) ... MPT
Master of Physician Assistant (PGP) ... MPA
Master of Physician Assistant Studies (PGP) ... MPAS
Master of Physics ... M Phy
Master of Physics (DD) ... MPhysics
Master of Physiotherapy [*British*] (ADA) ... MPhty
Master of Planning (PGP) ... M Pl
Master of Planning (GAGS) ... MP
Master of Planning ... MPl
Master of Planning ... MPlan
Master of Planning Studies ... MPlanStud
Master of Planning Studies ... MPlanStudies
Master of Plant Protection and Pest Management (GAGS) ... MPPPM
Master of Polar and Ocean Science ... MPOSC
Master of Policy ... MPol
Master of Policy and Administration ... MPolAdmin
Master of Policy and Law ... MPolLaw
Master of Policy Sciences (PGP) ... MPS
Master of Polite Literature ... MPL
Master of Political Economy [*British*] (ADA) ... MPolEcon
Master of Political Science (PGP) ... M Pol
Master of Political Science ... M Pol Sc
Master of Political Science (GAGS) ... MPS
Master of Preventive Medicine ... M Pr M
Master of Preventive Medicine and Public Health (GAGS) ... MPM&PH
Master of Preventive Veterinary Medicine (GAGS) ... MPVM
Master of Probability and Statistics (PGP) ... M Prob S
Master of Process Engineering, University of Sheffield [*British*] (DBQ) ... MProcEng
Master of Product Design (GAGS) ... MPD
Master of Professional Accountancy (PGP) ... M Pr A
Master of Professional Accountancy ... M Prof Acc
Master of Professional Accountancy (PGP) ... MP Acc
Master of Professional Accountancy [*or Accounting*] ... MPA
Master of Professional Accounting (PGP) ... MP Acc
Master of Professional Accounting (PGP) ... MP Acct
Master of Professional Accounting (GAGS) ... MPA
Master of Professional Accounting (NADA) ... MPA
Master of Professional Accounting (GAGS) ... MProfAcc
Master of Professional Arts ... MPA
Master of Professional Counseling (PGP) ... MPC
Master of Professional Management (PGP) ... MPM
Master of Professional Meteorology (PGP) ... M Pr Met
Master of Professional Meteorology (GAGS) ... MPrMet
Master of Professional Pastoral (PGP) ... M Prof Past
Master of Professional Studies (PGP) ... MPS
Master of Professional Studies in Human Relations ... MPS
Master of Professional Studies in Real Estate (PGP) ... MPSRE
Master of Professional Studies-Hospital and Health Services Administration ... MPS-HHSA
Master of Project Management (PGP) ... MPM
Master of Psychiatric Social Work (NADA) ... MPSW
Master of Psychological Management ... MPM
Master of Psychological Medicine ... M Psy Med
Master of Psychological Medicine (ADA) ... MPM
Master of Psychological Medicine, University of Liverpool [*British*] (DBQ) ... MPsychMed
Master of Psychological Science (GAGS) ... MPsSc
Master of Psychology ... M Ps
Master of Psychology (PGP) ... M Psych
Master of Psychology ... MPsych
Master of Psychology ... MPsychol
Master of Psychology (PGP) ... Psy M
Master of Psychology (Clinical) ... MPsych(Clin)
Master of Psychology (Education) ... MPsych(Ed)
Master of Psychology Orientation (NADA) ... MPsO
Master of Psycho-Therapy ... M Ps Th
Master of Psychotherapy ... MPsychTh
Master of Public Accounting (GAGS) ... MPAcc
Master of Public Administration ... M Pub Adm
Master of Public Administration ... MP Adm
Master of Public Administration ... MPA
Master of Public Administration (GAGS) ... MPA
Master of Public Administration ... MPubAdmin
Master of Public Affairs (PGP) ... MP Aff
Master of Public Affairs ... MPA
Master of Public Affairs and Urban and Regional Planning (PGP) ... MPA-URP
Master of Public and International Affairs (GAGS) ... MPIA
Master of Public and Private Management ... MPPM
Master of Public Communication (PGP) ... MPC
Master of Public Health ... MPH
Master of Public Health and Tropical Medicine (GAGS) ... MPH&TM
Master of Public Health and Tropical Medicine ... MPHTM
Master of Public Health Education ... MPH Ed
Master of Public Health Education (PGP) ... MPHE
Master of Public Health Engineering (NADA) ... MEPH
Master of Public Health Engineering ... MPH Eng
Master of Public Health Engineering ... MPHE
Master of Public Health Nursing ... MPHN
Master of Public Law ... MPL
Master of Public Law ... MPubLaw
Master of Public Management ... MPM
Master of Public Management (GAGS) ... MPM
Master of Public Management and Administration ... MPMA
Master of Public Policy ... MPP
Master of Public Policy ... MPubPol
Master of Public Policy Administration (GAGS) ... MPPA
Master of Public Policy and Urban Planning (PGP) ... MPPUP
Master of Public School Art ... MPSA
Master of Public School Music ... MPSM
Master of Public Service (GAGS) ... MPS
Master of Public Works (PGP) ... MPW
Master of Publishing (PGP) ... M Pub
Master of Quality Management (PGP) ... MQM
Master of Quantitative Systems ... MQS
Master of Radio and Television Engineering ... MRT Eng
Master of Radio and Television Engineering ... MRTE
Master of Radio Engineering ... M Ra E
Master of Radio Engineering ... M Ra Eng
Master of Radiology ... M Rad
Master of Radiology (Radiodiagnosis) ... M Rad (D)
Master of Radiology (Radiotherapy) ... M Rad (T)
Master of Real Estate and Construction Management (GAGS) ... MRECM
Master of Real Estate Development (GAGS) ... MRED
Master of Recreation Administration (GAGS) ... MRA
Master of Recreation and Parks Administration (GAGS) ... MRPA
Master of Recreation Education (GAGS) ... MREd
Master of Recreation Resources (F6) Administration (PGP) ... MRRA
Master of Refrigeration Engineering ... M Re E
Master of Refrigeration Engineering ... M Re Eng
Master of Refrigeration Engineering (NADA) ... MRefEng
Master of Regional and City Planning (PGP) ... MRCP
Master of Regional and Community Planning (GAGS) ... MRCP
Master of Regional and Town Planning ... MRTP
Master of Regional Planning ... MRP
Master of Regional Science (ADA) ... MRegSc
Master of Rehabilitation Administration (GAGS) ... MRA
Master of Rehabilitation Counseling ... MRC
Master of Religion ... M Re
Master of Religion (PGP) ... M Rel
Master of Religious Education (PGP) ... M Rel Ed
Master of Religious Education ... MR Ed
Master of Religious Education ... MRE
Master of Religious Education (GAGS) ... MRelEd
Master of Religious Guidance ... MRG
Master of Resource Administration (GAGS) ... MRA
Master of Resource and Environmental Studies ... MResEnvS
Master of Resource and Environmental Studies ... MResEnvSt
Master of Resource Management (GAGS) ... MRM
Master of Resource Science ... MResSc
Master of Retailing ... M Ret
Master of Roentgenology ... Roent M
Master of Rural and Town Planning (GAGS) ... MRTP

Master of Rural Engineering .... M Ru E
Master of Rural Engineering .... M Ru Eng
Master of Rural Science [*British*] (ADA) .... MRSc
Master of Rural Science [*British*] (ADA) .... MRurSc
Master of Russian History .... MRH
Master of Sacred Letters .... MS Litt
Master of Sacred Literature .... MSL
Master of Sacred Ministry (PGP) .... MSM
Master of Sacred Music .... MSM
Master of Sacred Music (BJA) .... SMM
Master of Sacred Sciences .... M Sa Sc
Master of Sacred Theology .... MST
Master of Sacred Theology (GAGS) .... MST
Master of Sacred Theology (NADA) .... STM
Master of Safety Science .... MSafetySc
Master of Safety Science .... MSafSc
Master of Sanitary Education .... MS Ed
Master of Sanitary Engineering .... MS Eng
Master of Sanitary Engineering .... MSE
Master of Sanitary Science .... M San Sc
Master of Sanitary Science .... MS Sc
Master of Sanitary Science .... MSS
Master of Sanitary Science and Public Health (GAGS) .... MSanSc&PH
Master of Sanitation .... M San
Master of School Administration (PGP) .... MSA
Master of School Music .... M Sch Mus
Master of School Psychology (PGP) .... MSP
Master of Science .... M Sc
Master of Science [*Facetious translation "More of the Same"*] .... MS
Master of Science (GAGS) .... MS
Master of Science [*Academic degree*] (AIE) .... MSc
Master of Science .... Sc M
Master of Science .... SM
Master of Science (Acoustics) (ADA) .... MSc(Acoustics)
Master of Science Administration (PGP) .... MSA
Master of Science (Aeromedicine) .... MSc(AeroMed)
Master of Science (Agricultural Economics) (ADA) .... MSc(AgricE)
Master of Science (Agricultural Economics) (ADA) .... MSc(AgricEc)
Master of Science (Agriculture) .... MSc(Ag)
Master of Science and Arts .... MSA
Master of Science and English Literature .... MSEL
Master of Science (Applied) (PGP) .... M Sc A
Master of Science (Applied) (ADA) .... MSc(Appl)
Master of Science (Architectural) (Conservation) .... MSc(Arch)(Cons)
Master of Science (Architecture) .... MSc(Arch)
Master of Science (Biochemistry) .... MSc(Biochem)
Master of Science (Biotechnology) (ADA) .... MSc(Biotech)
Master of Science (Building Services) (ADA) .... MSc(BuildServ)
Master of Science (Community Medicine) .... MSc(CommMed)
Master of Science Education (GAGS) .... MSEd
Master of Science (Engineering) .... M Sc (Eng)
Master of Science (Engineering) .... MSc(Engg)
Master of Science (Epidemiology) .... MSc(Epid)
Master of Science (Home Science) .... MSc(HomeScience)
Master of Science in Accountancy .... MS/Accy
Master of Science in Accountancy .... MSA
Master of Science in Accounting (PGP) .... MS Acct
Master of Science in Accounting (GAGS) .... MSA
Master of Science in Accounting .... MSAc
Master of Science in Accounting (PGP) .... MSACC
Master of Science in Acquisition and Contract Management (PGP) .... MSACM
Master of Science in Administration (PGP) .... MS Admin
Master of Science in Administration (GAGS) .... MSA
Master of Science in Advanced Technology (PGP) .... MSAT
Master of Science in Aeronautical and Astronautical Engineering (GAGS) .... MSAAE
Master of Science in Aeronautical Engineering .... MS in Aero E
Master of Science in Aeronautical Engineering .... MSAE
Master of Science in Aerospace Engineering (GAGS) .... MSAE
Master of Science in Aerospace Engineering (PGP) .... MSAER
Master of Science in Agricultural Economics .... MS in Ag Ec
Master of Science in Agricultural Education .... MS in Ag E
Master of Science in Agricultural Education .... MS in Agr Ed
Master of Science in Agricultural Engineering .... M Sc in Agr Eng
Master of Science in Agricultural Engineering .... MS (Ag E)
Master of Science in Agricultural Engineering .... MS in AN
Master of Science in Agricultural Engineering (PGP) .... MSAE
Master of Science in Agricultural Engineering (NADA) .... MSAgrEng
Master of Science in Agricultural Extension .... M Sc in Agr Ex
Master of Science in Agriculture .... MS (Ag)
Master of Science in Agriculture .... MS Agr
Master of Science in Agriculture .... MS in Ag
Master of Science in Agriculture .... MS in Agr
Master of Science in Agriculture .... MSA
Master of Science in Agriculture (GAGS) .... MSAg
Master of Science in Agriculture .... MScAgri
Master of Science in Agriculture .... MSc(Agric)
Master of Science in Anesthesia (PGP) .... MSA
Master of Science in Anthropology (PGP) .... MSA
Master of Science in Applied Mechanics .... MSAM
Master of Science in Applied Physics (PGP) .... MSAP
Master of Science in Applied Psychology (PGP) .... MSAP
Master of Science in Applied Science (GAGS) .... MSApSc
Master of Science in Architectural Engineering (PGP) .... MSAE
Master of Science in Architectural Studies (GAGS) .... MSAS
Master of Science in Architectural Studies (PGP) .... SM Arch S
Master of Science in Architecture .... M Sc (Architecture)
Master of Science in Architecture .... MS Arch
Master of Science in Art Education (PGP) .... MSAE
Master of Science in Artificial Intelligence (GAGS) .... MSAI
Master of Science in Astronautics and Aeronautics (PGP) .... MSAA
Master of Science in Audiology and Speech .... MS in Aud & Sp
Master of Science in Basic Medical Science (PGP) .... MSBMS
Master of Science in Bioengineering (PGP) .... MSBENG
Master of Science in Biological and Agricultural Engineering (PGP) .... MSBAE
Master of Science in Biological Sciences .... MS in Bl Sc
Master of Science in Biomedical Communications (PGP) .... M Sc BMC
Master of Science in Biomedical Engineering (GAGS) .... MSBE
Master of Science in Biomedical Engineering (PGP) .... MSBME
Master of Science in Biosystems and Agricultural Engineering (PGP) .... MSBAE
Master of Science in Building Construction .... MSBC
Master of Science in Building Technology (PGP) .... SMBT
Master of Science in Business .... MS Bus
Master of Science in Business .... MSB
Master of Science in Business Administration .... MS in BA
Master of Science in Business Administration .... MSBA
Master of Science in Business Education (PGP) .... MSBE
Master of Science in Business Management (PGP) .... MSBM
Master of Science in Ceramic Engineering .... MS (Cer E)
Master of Science in Ceramic Engineering .... MS in Cer E
Master of Science in Ceramic Technology .... MS in Cer Tech
Master of Science in Ceramics .... MS in Cer
Master of Science in Ceramics (ADA) .... MSc(Cer)
Master of Science in Chemical Engineering (PGP) .... MS Ch E
Master of Science in Chemical Engineering .... MS in Ch E
Master of Science in Chemical Engineering .... MS in Ch Eng
Master of Science in Chemical Engineering .... MSChE
Master of Science in Chemical Engineering (GAGS) .... MSChE
Master of Science in Chemical Engineering .... MSE
Master of Science in Chemical Technology [*British*] (ADA) .... MScChemTech
Master of Science in Chemistry .... MS in Ch
Master of Science in Christian Counseling (PGP) .... MSCC
Master of Science in Chromo-Electronic Science .... M Sc CE
Master of Science in City and Regional Planning .... MS in CRP
Master of Science in City and Regional Planning (PGP) .... MSCRP
Master of Science in Civil and Environmental Engineering (PGP) .... MSCEE
Master of Science in Civil Engineering .... MS in CE
Master of Science in Civil Engineering [*British*] (ADA) .... MScCE
Master of Science in Civil Engineering .... MSCE
Master of Science in Civil Engineering .... SMCE
Master of Science in Civil Engineering Management (PGP) .... MSCEM
Master of Science in Clinical Engineering (PGP) .... MSCE
Master of Science in Clinical Epidemiology (PGP) .... MSCE
Master of Science in Clinical Laboratory Science (PGP) .... MSCLS
Master of Science in Clinical Laboratory Studies (PGP) .... MSCLS
Master of Science in Clinical Nutrition (PGP) .... MSCNU
Master of Science in Commerce .... MS in C
Master of Science in Commerce (PGP) .... MSC
Master of Science in Commerce (DD) .... MSC
Master of Science in Commerce (DD) .... MScC
Master of Science in Commercial and Business Administration .... MS in C & BA
Master of Science in Communication (PGP) .... MSC
Master of Science in Communication Disorders (PGP) .... MSCD
Master of Science in Communication Disorders (PGP) .... MSCDIS
Master of Science in Communication Sciences and Disorders (PGP) .... MSCSD
Master of Science in Community and Regional Planning (PGP) .... MSCRP
Master of Science in Community Planning .... MSCP
Master of Science in Computational Finance (PGP) .... MSCF
Master of Science in Computer and Systems Engineering (PGP) .... MSCSE
Master of Science in Computer Engineering (PGP) .... MS Cp E
Master of Science in Computer Engineering (GAGS) .... MSCE
Master of Science in Computer Information Science (PGP) .... MSCIS
Master of Science in Computer Information Systems .... MSCIS
Master of Science in Computer Science (PGP) .... M Sc CS
Master of Science in Computer Science .... MSCS
Master of Science in Computer Science and Engineering (PGP) .... MSCSE
Master of Science in Computer-Based Information Systems .... MSIS
Master of Science in Conservation .... MS Cons
Master of Science in Conservation .... MS in Con
Master of Science in Continuing Education (GAGS) .... MSCEd
Master of Science in Counseling (PGP) .... MS Coun
Master of Science in Counseling (GAGS) .... MSC
Master of Science in Counseling Psychology (PGP) .... MSCP
Master of Science in Criminal Justice (WGA) .... MSCJ
Master of Science in Criminal Justice Administration (PGP) .... MSCJA
Master of Science in Dendrology .... SM Dendrol
Master of Science in Dentistry .... MS Dent
Master of Science in Dentistry (GAGS) .... MScD
Master of Science in Dentistry .... MSc(Dent)
Master of Science in Dentistry .... MSD
Master of Science in Dermatology .... MS in Derm
Master of Science in Dermatology (NADA) .... MSDerm
Master of Science in Design .... MS Des
Master of Science in Design (PGP) .... MSD
Master of Science in Design and Development (PGP) .... MSDD
Master of Science in Dietetics .... MS in Dt
Master of Science in Dietetics (PGP) .... MSD
Master of Science in Economics .... M Sc (Econ)
Master of Science in Economics (PGP) .... MS Eco
Master of Science in Economics (PGP) .... MS Econ

Master of Science in Economics (DD) .... MScEcon
Master of Science in Education .... M Sc Ed
Master of Science in Education .... MS Ed
Master of Science in Education (PGP) .... MS EdU
Master of Science in Education .... MS in E
Master of Science in Education .... MS in Ed
Master of Science in Education .... MSE
Master of Science in Education (GAGS) .... MSE
Master of Science in Electrical and Computer Engineering (PGP) .... MSECE
Master of Science in Electrical Engineering .... M Sc EE
Master of Science in Electrical Engineering .... M Sc (Elec Eng)
Master of Science in Electrical Engineering .... MS Elect E
Master of Science in Electrical Engineering .... MS in EE
Master of Science in Electrical Engineering .... MSEE
Master of Science in Electrical Engineering (GAGS) .... MSEE
Master of Science in Electrical Engineering .... SMEE
Master of Science in Electronics [*British*] (ADA) .... MSc(Elec)
Master of Science in Energy Resources (GAGS) .... MSER
Master of Science in Engineering (PGP) .... M Sc E
Master of Science in Engineering (PGP) .... M Sc Engr
Master of Science in Engineering .... MS Eng
Master of Science in Engineering (PGP) .... MS Engr
Master of Science in Engineering .... MS in E
Master of Science in Engineering (DD) .... MScE
Master of Science in Engineering .... MSE
Master of Science in Engineering and Mining (GAGS) .... MSEM
Master of Science in Engineering - Electrical .... MSE (Elec)
Master of Science in Engineering Management .... MS in E Mgt
Master of Science in Engineering Management (PGP) .... MSE Mgt
Master of Science in Engineering Management (PGP) .... MSEM
Master of Science in Engineering Management (GAGS) .... MSEMgt
Master of Science in Engineering Mechanics .... MS in EM
Master of Science in Engineering Mechanics .... MS in Mech
Master of Science in Engineering Mechanics .... MSEM
Master of Science in Engineering Mechanics (GAGS) .... MSEMech
Master of Science in Engineering of Mines .... MS in EM
Master of Science in Engineering of Mines (PGP) .... MSEM
Master of Science in Engineering Physics .... MS in EP
Master of Science in Engineering Science (PGP) .... MS Engr Sci
Master of Science in Engineering Science [*or Sciences*] .... MS in ES
Master of Science in Engineering Science (PGP) .... MSES
Master of Science in Engineering Science and Mechanics (PGP) .... MSESM
Master of Science in Entomology .... MS Ent
Master of Science in Environmental Engineering (PGP) .... MS En E
Master of Science in Environmental Engineering (PGP) .... MS Env E
Master of Science in Environmental Engineering (GAGS) .... MSEE
Master of Science in Environmental Engineering (GAGS) .... MSEnvrE
Master of Science in Environmental Health (PGP) .... MSEH
Master of Science in Environmental Law (PGP) .... MSEL
Master of Science in Environmental Management (PGP) .... MSEM
Master of Science in Environmental Management (PGP) .... MSEVM
Master of Science in Environmental Studies (PGP) .... MSES
Master of Science in Environmental Technology Management (PGP) .... MSETM
Master of Science in Exercise and Sport Studies (GAGS) .... MSESS
Master of Science in Exercise Physiology (PGP) .... MSP Ex
Master of Science in Experimental Surgery (PGP) .... MS Exp Surg
Master of Science in Family Studies (PGP) .... MSFAM
Master of Science in Family Studies (PGP) .... MSFS
Master of Science in Finance .... MSF
Master of Science in Financial Services (PGP) .... MSFS
Master of Science in Foreign Service (GAGS) .... MSFS
Master of Science in Forensic Science (GAGS) .... MSFS
Master of Science in Forest Engineering (PGP) .... M Sc FE
Master of Science in Forest Management .... MSFM
Master of Science in Forestry (PGP) .... M Sc F
Master of Science in Forestry .... M Sc (For)
Master of Science in Forestry .... MS For
Master of Science in Forestry .... MS in For
Master of Science in Forestry (PGP) .... MSFOR
Master of Science in Game Management .... MSG Mgt
Master of Science in General Engineering .... MS in GE
Master of Science in General Science and Mathematics .... MS in GSM
Master of Science in Genetic Counseling (PGP) .... MSGC
Master of Science in Geological Engineering (PGP) .... MS Geo E
Master of Science in Geological Engineering (NADA) .... MSGE
Master of Science in Geology .... SM Geol
Master of Science in Geophysical Engineering .... MS in Gp Engr
Master of Science in Gerontology (GAGS) .... MSG
Master of Science in Government Management .... MSGM
Master of Science in Health Administration (PGP) .... MSHA
Master of Science in Health and Physical Education .... MSH & Ph Ed
Master of Science in Health and Safety (GAGS) .... MSHS
Master of Science in Health Education (PGP) .... MSH Ed
Master of Science in Health Professions (PGP) .... MSHP
Master of Science in Health Science (PGP) .... MSHS
Master of Science in Health Science Education (PGP) .... MSHSE
Master of Science in Health Systems (GAGS) .... MSHS
Master of Science in Home Economics .... MS in H Ec
Master of Science in Home Economics .... MS in HE
Master of Science in Home Economics .... MSH Ec
Master of Science in Home Economics .... MSHE
Master of Science in Horticulture .... MS Hort
Master of Science in Horticulture [*British*] (ADA) .... MSc(Hort)
Master of Science in Horticulture (NADA) .... MSH
Master of Science in Hospice (PGP) .... MSH
Master of Science in Hospital Administration .... MSHA
Master of Science in Human and Consumer Science (PGP) .... MSHCS
Master of Science in Human Environmental Sciences (PGP) .... MSHES
Master of Science in Human Relations .... MS in HR
Master of Science in Human Resources (PGP) .... MSHR
Master of Science in Human Resources Management (PGP) .... MSHRM
Master of Science in Human Service Administration (PGP) .... MSHSA
Master of Science in Hydraulic Engineering .... MSHE
Master of Science in Hygiene .... MS Hyg
Master of Science in Hygiene (NADA) .... MSH
Master of Science in Hygiene (DAVI) .... MSHy
Master of Science in Hygiene .... Sc M in Hyg
Master of Science in Hygiene .... SM in Hyg
Master of Science in Industrial Administration .... MSIA
Master of Science in Industrial Design .... MS in ID
Master of Science in Industrial Education .... MS in Ind Ed
Master of Science in Industrial Engineering .... MS in IE
Master of Science in Industrial Engineering .... MS Ind E
Master of Science in Industrial Engineering .... MSIE
Master of Science in Industrial Engineering (GAGS) .... MSIE
Master of Science in Industrial Engineering (NADA) .... MSIndEng
Master of Science in Industrial Engineering and Operations Research (GAGS) .... MSIEOR
Master of Science in Industrial Management .... MS in IM
Master of Science in Industrial Management .... MSIM
Master of Science in Industrial Relations (GAGS) .... MSIR
Master of Science in Industrial Technology (PGP) .... MSIT
Master of Science in Information Management (GAGS) .... MSIM
Master of Science in Information Management and Communication (PGP) .... MSIMC
Master of Science in Information Processing and Communications (PGP) .... MSIPC
Master of Science in Information Science (GAGS) .... MSIS
Master of Science in Information Systems (PGP) .... MSIS
Master of Science in Instruction (PGP) .... MSI
Master of Science in Insurance .... MSI
Master of Science in Interdisciplinary Studies (PGP) .... MSIS
Master of Science in International Adminstration (PGP) .... MSIA
Master of Science in International Affairs (GAGS) .... MSIA
Master of Science in International Banking (PGP) .... MSIBK
Master of Science in International Business (PGP) .... MSIB
Master of Science in International Economics (PGP) .... MSIE
Master of Science in International Logistics (PGP) .... MSIL
Master of Science in Japanese Business Studies (PGP) .... MSJBS
Master of Science in Jewish Studies (PGP) .... MSJS
Master of Science in Journalism .... MSJ
Master of Science in Judicial Administration (GAGS) .... MSJA
Master of Science in Justice and Public Safety (PGP) .... MSJPS
Master of Science in Justice and Public Service (GAGS) .... MSJPS
Master of Science in Kinesiology (GAGS) .... MSK
Master of Science in Labor and Industrial Relations .... MSLIR
Master of Science in Language .... MSL
Master of Science in Law and Society (DLA) .... MSLS
Master of Science in Legal Administration (PGP) .... MSLA
Master of Science in Librarianship (PGP) .... MSL
Master of Science in Library Science .... MS in LS
Master of Science in Library Science .... MSLS
Master of Science in Library Science .... MSLSc
Master of Science in Limnology (PGP) .... MSL
Master of Science in Linguistics .... MSL
Master of Science in Logistics Systems (PGP) .... MSLS
Master of Science in Management (PGP) .... MS Mgt
Master of Science in Management .... MSM
Master of Science in Management (GAGS) .... MSMgt
Master of Science in Management and Computer Science (PGP) .... MSMCS
Master of Science in Management Engineering .... MS Mgt E
Master of Science in Management Information Systems (PGP) .... MSMIS
Master of Science in Management of Technology (PGP) .... MS Mot
Master of Science in Management of Technology (PGP) .... MSMOT
Master of Science in Management Science (PGP) .... MSMS
Master of Science in Management Systems Analysis (PGP) .... MSMSA
Master of Science in Manufacturing Engineering (PGP) .... MS Mfg E
Master of Science in Manufacturing Engineering (PGP) .... MSMFE
Master of Science in Manufacturing Management (PGP) .... MSMM
Master of Science in Manufacturing Systems Engineering (PGP) .... MS Mf SE
Master of Science in Manufacturing Systems Engineering (PGP) .... MSMSE
Master of Science in Marketing Communication (GAGS) .... MSMC
Master of Science in Mass Communication (GAGS) .... MSMC
Master of Science in Material Science and Engineering (PGP) .... MS Mat SE
Master of Science in Material Science Engineering (PGP) .... MSMSE
Master of Science in Materials Engineering (PGP) .... MS Mat
Master of Science in Materials Engineering (PGP) .... MS Mat E
Master of Science in Materials Engineering (PGP) .... MS Mt E
Master of Science in Materials Engineering (PGP) .... MSMAE
Master of Science in Materials Science Engineering (GAGS) .... MSMatSE
Master of Science in Mathematics and Science Education (GAGS) .... MSMSEd
Master of Science in Mathematics Education (PGP) .... MSME
Master of Science in Mechanical Engineering .... M Sc in ME
Master of Science in Mechanical Engineering .... M Sc (Mech Eng)
Master of Science in Mechanical Engineering .... MS in ME
Master of Science in Mechanical Engineering .... MS Mech E
Master of Science in Mechanical Engineering .... MSME
Master of Science in Media Arts and Sciences (PGP) .... MSMAS
Master of Science in Medical Illustration (GAGS) .... MSMI
Master of Science in Medical Sciences (PGP) .... MSMS

Master of Science in Medical Technology (GAGS)	MSMT
Master of Science in Medicine	MS in Med
Master of Science in Medicine [British] (ADA)	MScMed
Master of Science in Metallurgical Engineering	MS in Met E
Master of Science in Metallurgical Engineering	MS Met E
Master of Science in Metallurgy	M Sc Met
Master of Science in Metallurgy	MS in Met
Master of Science in Metallurgy	MS Metr
Master of Science in Meteorology (PGP)	MS Min
Master of Science in Mining (PGP)	MSc(Min)
Master of Science in Mining [British] (ADA)	MS Min E
Master of Science in Mining Engineering (PGP)	MS in Mus
Master of Science in Music	MSM
Master of Science in Music	MSMus
Master of Science in Music (NADA)	MS in Mus Ed
Master of Science in Music Education	MSMusEd
Master of Science in Music Education (NADA)	MSc(NatResMgt)
Master of Science in Natural Resources Management	MSNS
Master of Science in Natural Science (PGP)	MS Nsurg
Master of Science in Neurosurgery (PGP)	MS in Nucl E
Master of Science in Nuclear Engineering	MSNE
Master of Science in Nuclear Engineering (GAGS)	MSNuclEng
Master of Science in Nuclear Engineering (NADA)	MS in NT
Master of Science in Nuclear Technology	MSNA
Master of Science in Nurse Anesthesia (GAGS)	M Sc N
Master of Science in Nursing (PGP)	MS in N
Master of Science in Nursing	MScN
Master of Science in Nursing	MSN
Master of Science in Nursing	MSN
Master of Science in Nursing (GAGS)	MSNA
Master of Science in Nursing Administration (GAGS)	MS in N Ed
Master of Science in Nursing Education	MS in NE
Master of Science in Nursing Education	MS in Nr Ed
Master of Science in Nursing Education	MSNEd
Master of Science in Nursing Education (NADA)	MSN(R)
Master of Science in Nursing (Research) (PGP)	MSc(Nutr)
Master of Science in Nutrition [British] (ADA)	MSOT
Master of Science in Occupational Technology (PGP)	MSOT
Master of Science in Occupational Therapy (GAGS)	MSOE
Master of Science in Ocean Engineering (PGP)	MSOR
Master of Science in Operations Research (GAGS)	MScOptom
Master of Science in Optometry (ADA)	MSOM
Master of Science in Organization and Management (PGP)	MSOB
Master of Science in Organizational Behavior	MSOD
Master of Science in Organizational Development (GAGS)	MS Orn Hort
Master of Science in Ornamental Horticulture	MSO
Master of Science in Orthodontics (GAGS)	M Sc (Ost)
Master of Science in Osteopathy	MS Otol
Master of Science in Otolaryngology (PGP)	MSPIR
Master of Science in Personnel and Industrial Relations	MSPNGE
Master of Science in Petroleum and Natural Gas Engineering (PGP)	MS in PE
Master of Science in Petroleum Engineering	MS in Pet E
Master of Science in Petroleum Engineering	MS Pet E
Master of Science in Petroleum Engineering (PGP)	MSPE
Master of Science in Petroleum Engineering (PGP)	MSPetE
Master of Science in Petroleum Engineering (GAGS)	MSPetEng
Master of Science in Petroleum Engineering (NADA)	MS in PRE
Master of Science in Petroleum Refining Engineering	MS in Phar
Master of Science in Pharmacy	MS Phr
Master of Science in Pharmacy (PGP)	MScPhm
Master of Science in Pharmacy (ADA)	MSP
Master of Science in Pharmacy	MSPharm
Master of Science in Pharmacy (NADA)	MSPHR
Master of Science in Pharmacy (PGP)	MS in P Ed
Master of Science in Physical Education	MS in PE
Master of Science in Physical Education	MSPE
Master of Science in Physical Education	
Master of Science in Physical Medicine and Rehabilitation (PGP)	MSPM Rehab
Master of Science in Physical Therapy (PGP)	M Sc PT
Master of Science in Physical Therapy (GAGS)	MSPT
Master of Science in Physics	MS in Phy
Master of Science in Physiological Optics (PGP)	MS Phys Op
Master of Science in Physiology of Exercise (GAGS)	MSPEx
Master of Science in Planning (PGP)	M Sc P
Master of Science in Planning (PGP)	M Sc Pl
Master of Science in Planning (PGP)	MSP
Master of Science in Planning Studies (PGP)	MSPS
Master of Science in Polymers (GAGS)	MSPoly
Master of Science in Poultry Husbandry	MSPH
Master of Science in Poultry Science	MS in Py Sc
Master of Science in Professional Accountancy (PGP)	MSPA
Master of Science in Psychological Services (GAGS)	MSPS
Master of Science in Psychology (PGP)	MSPG
Master of Science in Public Administration	MS in PA
Master of Science in Public Administration (GAGS)	MSPA
Master of Science in Public Health	MS in PH
Master of Science in Public Health	MSPH
Master of Science in Public Health Education	MSPH Ed
Master of Science in Public Health Engineering	MSPHE
Master of Science in Public School Music	MS in PSM
Master of Science in Radiation Science (GAGS)	MSRadSc
Master of Science in Radiological Medical Physics (PGP)	MSRMP
Master of Science in Radiology	MS in Rad
Master of Science in Real Estate and Urban Affairs	MSRE
Master of Science in Recreation	MS in Rec

Master of Science in Recreation (NADA)	MSRec
Master of Science in Recreation Administration (PGP)	MSRA
Master of Science in Recreational Studies (PGP)	MSRS
Master of Science in Religious Education (PGP)	MSRE
Master of Science in Research	MS (R)
Master of Science in Resource Conservation (PGP)	MSRC
Master of Science in Retailing	MS in Ret
Master of Science in Retailing (NADA)	MSRet
Master of Science in Safety (GAGS)	MSS
Master of Science in Sanitary Engineering	MSSanE
Master of Science in Sanitary Engineering	MSSE
Master of Science in Sanitary Engineering (NADA)	MSSEng
Master of Science in Sanitary Engineering	SMSanE
Master of Science in Sanitary Science	MS in SS
Master of Science in Science Management (PGP)	MSSM
Master of Science in Science Teaching	MSST
Master of Science in Science Teaching (GAGS)	MSST
Master of Science in Secondary Education of Students (who are Deaf or Hard of Hearing)	MSSE
Master of Science in Social Administration (GAGS)	MSSA
Master of Science in Social Science	MSSS
Master of Science in Social Service	MS in SS
Master of Science in Social Work	MS in SW
Master of Science in Social Work	MSSW
Master of Science in Special Education (PGP)	MS Sp Ed
Master of Science in Speech	MS in Sp
Master of Science in Speech and Hearing	MSS & H
Master of Science in Speech and Hearing (PGP)	MSSH
Master of Science in Speech and Language (PGP)	MSSL
Master of Science in Statistics (PGP)	MS Stat
Master of Science in Statistics (GAGS)	MSStat
Master of Science in Statistics (PGP)	MSTA
Master of Science in Strategic Intelligence (PGP)	MSSI
Master of Science in Structural Engineering (NADA)	MSStEng
Master of Science in Surgery (PGP)	MS Surg
Master of Science in Systems Management (PGP)	MSSM
Master of Science in Systems Science (PGP)	MS Sy Sc
Master of Science in Taxation	MST
Master of Science in Taxation (GAGS)	MST
Master of Science in Teacher Education	MS (T Ed)
Master of Science in Teaching (PGP)	M Sc T
Master of Science in Teaching (GAGS)	MScT
Master of Science in Teaching	MST
Master of Science in Teaching a Second Language (GAGS)	MSTSL
Master of Science in Teaching Mathematics (PGP)	MSTM
Master of Science in Technical Education (PGP)	MST Ed
Master of Science in Technical Education (PGP)	MSTE
Master of Science in Technical Education (GAGS)	MSTEd
Master of Science in Technology	M Sc Tech
Master of Science in Technology Management (GAGS)	MSTM
Master of Science in Telecommunications (PGP)	MSTC
Master of Science in Textile Chemistry (PGP)	MS Text Chem
Master of Science in Textiles (PGP)	MS Text
Master of Science in Textiles (GAGS)	MSText
Master of Science in the Economic Aspects of Chemistry	MSEC
Master of Science in the Social Sciences	M Sc (Social Sciences)
Master of Science in Tourism (GAGS)	MST
Master of Science in Trade and Industrial Education	MS in T & I
Master of Science in Transportation (NADA)	MSTrans
Master of Science in Transportation Engineering	MS in Trans E
Master of Science in Transportation Engineering (GAGS)	MSTE
Master of Science in Transportation Engineering (NADA)	MSTransE
Master of Science in Tropical Medicine (GAGS)	MSTM
Master of Science in Urban Design (GAGS)	MSUD
Master of Science in Urban Environmental Systems Management (PGP)	MSUESM
Master of Science in Visual Studies (PGP)	SM Vis S
Master of Science in Water Resources and Environmental Engineering (PGP)	MSWREE
Master of Science (Industrial Design) (ADA)	MSC(IndDes)
Master of Science/Industry Work Study	MS/IWS
Master of Science, London	M Sc (Lond)
Master of Science/Management Information Systems	MS/MIS
Master of Science (Medical)	MSc(Med)
Master of Science (Neurochemistry)	MSc(NeuChem)
Master of Science (Nutrition)	MSc(Nut)
Master of Science (Occupational Medicine)	MSc(OccMed)
Master of Science (Ophthalmology)	MSc(Ophth)
Master of Science (Rehabilitation Medicine)	MSc(Rehab)
Master of Science (Research) in Physical Therapy (PGP)	MS(R)PT
Master of Science (Social Science)	M Sc (Soc Sci)
Master of Science Teaching (GAGS)	MScT
Master of Science Teaching (GAGS)	MST
Master of Science Technology (PGP)	MST
Master of Scientific Agriculture	MSA
Master of Scientific Didactics	MS Di
Master of Scientific Didactics	MSD
Master of Scientific Studies (ADA)	MScSt
Master of Secondary School Science (GAGS)	MSecSchSci
Master of Secondary Teaching (GAGS)	MST
Master of Secretarial Arts	M Se A
Master of Secretarial Science	M Se Sc
Master of Secretarial Studies	M Se St
Master of Selected Studies (PGP)	MSS
Master of Service Management (PGP)	MSM

Master of Social Administration (GAGS)	MScA
Master of Social Administration	MSocAdmin
Master of Social and Industrial Relations	MSIR
Master of Social Planning and Development (ADA)	MSPD
Master of Social Policy	MSocPol
Master of Social Psychology (PGP)	MSP
Master of Social Science	M So Sc
Master of Social Science (PGP)	M Soc Sc
Master of Social Science	MS Sc
Master of Social Science	MSS
Master of Social Sciences	MSocSc
Master of Social Sciences	MSocSci
Master of Social Service	M So Se
Master of Social Service	MSS
Master of Social Service (GAGS)	MSS
Master of Social Studies	MSocSt
Master of Social Studies (ADA)	MSocStud
Master of Social Studies	MSS
Master of Social Welfare	MSW
Master of Social Welfare and Administration Planning	MSWAP
Master of Social Work	M So W
Master of Social Work	MSocWk
Master of Social Work	MSW
Master of Sociology	M So
Master of Sociology (PGP)	M Soc
Master of Sociology	MS
Master of Sociology (ADA)	MSoc
Master of Software Engineering (PGP)	M Sw En
Master of Software Engineering (GAGS)	MSE
Master of Special Education (PGP)	M Sp Ed
Master of Special Education (PGP)	MES
Master of Special Education	MSpecEd
Master of Special Education	MSpEd
Master of Speech	M Sp
Master of Speech Communication (GAGS)	MSC
Master of Speech Pathology (PGP)	MSP
Master of Speech Pathology and Audiology (PGP)	MSPA
Master of Speech Pathology and Audiology (GAGS)	MSSPA
Master of Speech Therapy (ADA)	MSpThy
Master of Speech Therapy (GAGS)	MST
Master of Speech-Language Pathology (PGP)	MSLP
Master of Sport Administration (GAGS)	MSA
Master of Sport Science (GAGS)	MSS
Master of Staghounds	MSH
Master of Statistics	M St
Master of Statistics (PGP)	M Stat
Master of Statistics	MStat
Master of Structural Engineering	M St E
Master of Structural Engineering	M St Eng
Master of Studies in Law	MSL
Master of Studies, University of Oxford [British] (DBQ)	MSt
Master of Surgery (DD)	ChM
Master of Surgery (DD)	CM
Master of Surgery	M Sur
Master of Surgery	MS
Master of Surgery (BABM)	MSurg
Master of Surgery (DAVI)	MSurg
Master of Surgery (NADA)	MSurgery
Master of Surgery (Orthopedic)	MS(Orth)
Master of Surgical Science, University of Dundee [British] (DBQ)	MSSc
Master of Surveying	MSurv
Master of Surveying and Mapping	MSurvMap
Master of Surveying Science	MSurvSc
Master of Systematic Theology	M Sy Th
Master of Systems Engineering	MSE
Master of Systems Technology (PGP)	MST
Master of Tax Accounting (GAGS)	MTA
Master of Taxation (PGP)	M Tax
Master of Taxation (GAGS)	MT
Master of Taxation	MTX
Master of Teacher Education (PGP)	MTE
Master of Teaching	MST
Master of Teaching	MT
Master of Teaching (GAGS)	MT
Master of Teaching Arts (GAGS)	MTA
Master of Teaching of Science (GAGS)	MTS
Master of Teaching Speech Communication (GAGS)	MTSC
Master of Technical and Professional Writing (GAGS)	MTPW
Master of Technical and Scientific Communication (GAGS)	MTSC
Master of Technical Science	M Sc Tech
Master of Technology	M Tech
Master of Technology (GAGS)	MT
Master of Technology for International Development (PGP)	MTID
Master of Telecommunications Engineering (NADA)	MTelEng
Master of Television	M TV
Master of Textile Chemistry	MT Ch
Master of Textile Chemistry	MTC
Master of Textile Design	MT Des
Master of Textile Dyeing	MTD
Master of Textile Engineering	MT Eng
Master of Textile Engineering	MTE
Master of Textile Technology	MTT
Master of Textiles (PGP)	MT
Master of Textiles (NADA)	MText
Master of the Acupuncture Association [British] (DBQ)	MAcA
Master of the Art of Obstetrics	MAO
Master of the British Arts Association (DBQ)	MBA
Master of the Built Environment (ADA)	MBEnv
Master of the Fox Hunt (DD)	MFH
[The] Master of the Free School, Margate [Pseudonym used by Zachariah Cozens]	TMOTFSM
Master of the Horse [British] (ROG)	MH
Master of the Hunt	MH
Master of the Queen's Music [British] (AD)	MQM
Master of the Rolls	MR
Master of the Science of Forestry [or Master of Science in Forestry]	MScF
Master of the Science of Forestry	MSF
Master of the Science of Law	M Sc L
Master of the Science of Medicine	M Sc M
Master of the Science of Oratory	M Or Sc
Master of the Science of Oratory	M Sc O
Master of the Science of Oratory	MSO
Master of the Science of Theology	STM
Master of the University	MUniv
Master of Theater Arts (GAGS)	MTA
Master of Theatre Arts	MThA
Master of Theological Studies (WGA)	MTS
Master of Theological Studies Counseling (PGP)	MTSC
Master of Theology	M Th
Master of Theology	M Theol
Master of Theology	TheolM
Master of Theology (GAGS)	ThM
Master of Theology and Ministry (PGP)	MTM
Master of Total Quality Management (PGP)	MTQM
Master of Town and Country Planning (ADA)	MTCP
Master of Town and Country Planning	MTP
Master of Town and Regional Planning [British] (ADA)	MTRP
Master of Town Planning	MTP
Master of Toxicology (PGP)	M Tox
Master of Toxicology (GAGS)	MTox
Master of Traditional Chinese Medicine (PGP)	MTCM
Master of Traditional Oriental Medicine (PGP)	MTOM
Master of Transpersonal Psychology (PGP)	MTP
Master of Transport Design	MTD
Master of Transport Economics	MTransEc
Master of Transport Management	MTM
Master of Tropical Health	MTH
Master of Tropical Medicine	MTM
Master of Tropical Medicine and Hygiene (GAGS)	MTMH
Master of Urban Affairs (GAGS)	MUA
Master of Urban and Regional Planning	MUrbRegPlg
Master of Urban and Regional Planning	MURP
Master of Urban and Regional Planning (PGP)	MURPL
Master of Urban and Rural Planning (GAGS)	MURP
Master of Urban Architecture (GAGS)	MUA
Master of Urban Design (GAGS)	MUD
Master of Urban Design	MUrbDes(Arch)
Master of Urban Planning	MUP
Master of Urban Planning and Policy (GAGS)	MUPP
Master of Urban Planning, Design, and Development (PGP)	MUPDD
Master of Urban Studies (ADA)	MUS
Master of Urban Systems Engineering (PGP)	MU Sys E
Master of Valuation Sciences (GAGS)	MVS
Master of Veterinary Clinical Studies	MVetClinStud
Master of Veterinary Medicine	MDV
Master of Veterinary Medicine (NADA)	MVetMed
Master of Veterinary Medicine	MVM
Master of Veterinary Science (PGP)	M Vet Sc
Master of Veterinary Science	MV Sc
Master of Veterinary Science [British] (ADA)	MVetSc
Master of Veterinary Science (NADA)	MVetSci
Master of Veterinary Studies	MVetSt
Master of Veterinary Studies	MVS
Master of Veterinary Studies (ADA)	MVSt
Master of Veterinary Surgery	MVS
Master of Visual Arts (GAGS)	MVA
Master of Vocational and Technical Education (PGP)	MVT Ed
Master of Vocational Counseling (GAGS)	MSVC
Master of Vocational Education	MV Ed
Master of Vocational Education (NADA)	MVE
Master of Vocational Technical Education (GAGS)	MVTE
Master of Water Resources Administration (PGP)	MWRA
Master of Welfare Policy	MWP
Master of Wine [Bestowed by the Worshipful Company of Vintners, one of the ancient guilds in the City of London]	MW
Master of Women's Studies (PGP)	MWS
Master of Wood and Paper Science (GAGS)	MWPS
Master of Wood Technology	MWT
Master of Zoological Science	MZ Sc
Master of Zoology Science (GAGS)	MZS
Master Operability Test (CAAL)	MOT
Master Operating Panel (CAAL)	MOP
Master Operating System [Sperry UNIVAC]	MOS
Master Operation Control (AD)	moc
Master Operational Computer [or Controller]	MOC
Master Operational Recording Tape [SAGE]	MORT
Master Operational Recording Tape Address Table (IAA)	MAT
Master Operations Center	MOC
Master Operations Console	MOC
Master Operations Control	MOC

Master Operations Control Center (SAA)	MOCC
Master Operations Control System (KSC)	MOCS
Master Ordnance Configuration File [Navy]	MOC
Master Ordnance Systems Pattern File [Navy]	MOSP
Master Oscilator Power Amplifier (AD)	mopa
Master Oscilator (AD)	mo
Master Oscillator [Radio]	MO
Master Oscillator Power Amplifier [Radio]	MOPA
Master Oscillator Power Amplifier RADAR (AD)	MOPAR
Master Oscillator-Power Amplifier RADAR (AD)	mopar
Master Painters, Decorators, and Signwriters Association (AD)	MPDSA
Master Painters, Decorators and Signwriters' Association of New South Wales [Australia]	MPDSANSW
Master Parachutist Badge [Military decoration] (AABC)	MastPrchtBad
Master Parachutist Badge [Military decoration]	MRPARABAD
Master Parachutist Badge [Military decoration] (GFGA)	MSTPRCHT
Master Part Dimensioned (MCD)	MAPD
Master Part Number (MCD)	MPN
Master Parts Card	MPC
Master Parts File (MCD)	MPF
Master Parts List	MPL
Master Parts Reference List	MPRL
Master Pastry Cooks Association (AD)	MPCA
Master Pastrycooks' Association [Australia]	MPA
Master Patch Panel [Air Force] (MCD)	MPP
Master Patient Index (MEDA)	MPI
Master Patternmakers' Association of New South Wales [Australia]	MPANSW
Master Performance System	MPS
Master Personnel Administration	MPA
Master Personnel Record	MPERR
Master Petroleum Material Requirements Plan (MCD)	MPMRP
Master Phasing Chart (MCD)	MPC
Master Photo Dealers' and Finishers' Association [Later, PMA] (EA)	MPDFA
Master Photographers Association (AD)	MPA
Master Photographers Association of Great Britain (BI)	MPA
Master Plan for Academic Computing (AD)	MPAC
Master Plan for Computing Services (AD)	MPCS
Master Plan for Data Processing and Information Systems (AD)	MPDPIS
Master Plan Works Breakdown Structure (AD)	MPWBS
Master Planner, Inc. [ICAO designator] (FAAC)	MPL
Master Planning Schedule (MCD)	MPS
Master Plate [Tool] (AAG)	MSPE
Master Plumbers and Mechanical Contractors Association of New South Wales [Australia]	MPMCANSW
Master Plumbers and Mechanical Contractors' Association of Victoria [Australia]	MPMCAV
Master Plumbers and Mechanical Contractors' Association of Western Australia	MPMCAWA
Master Pointer [Computer science] (BYTE)	MP
Master Poulterers' Association of New South Wales [Australia]	MPANSW
Master Poultry Processors' Association of Victoria [Australia]	MPPAV
Master Power Regulator	MPR
Master Printer (DGA)	MP
Master Printers and Engravers Association of the United States (AD)	MPEAUS
Master Printers Annual [A publication] (DGA)	MP
Master Printers of America (EA)	MPA
Master Problem Status Manual	MPSM
Master Production Planning Schedule [Air Force] (AFIT)	MPPS
Master Production Schedule	MPS
Master Program Chart (MCD)	MPC
Master Program of Instruction [Army] (AABC)	MPOI
Master Program Phasing Chart (MCD)	MPPC
Master Program Plan (NG)	MPP
Master Program Planning Schedule	MPPS
Master Program Schedule (NASA)	MPS
Master Project Assignment (MCD)	MPA
Master Project Summary [Civil Defense]	MPS
Master Quality Characteristic List (MCD)	MQCL
Master Quality Review Report File [IRS]	QRRF
Master RADAR Tracking Station	MARTS
Master RADAR Tracking Station	MRTS
Master RADAR Training System	MARTS
Master Radio Frequency List (NATG)	MRFL
Master Real-Time Circulation Controller (PDAA)	MARCCO
Master Record Repository (MCD)	MRR
Master Reference Buoy [Navy] (NVT)	MRB
Master Reference Gyro (PDAA)	MRG
Master Relay [Electrical] (DICI)	MR
Master Remote Query Interface System [Computer science]	MARQUIS
Master Remote Slave Station (MCD)	MRSS
Master Repair List (AFIT)	MRL
Master Repair Schedule [Air Force] (AFM)	MRS
Master Repairable Item List	MRIL
Master Report List	MRL
Master Requirements Code	MRC
Master Requirements Directory [Military] (AFM)	MRD
Master Reset (MCD)	MR
Master Resources & Developments Ltd. [Vancouver Stock Exchange symbol]	MSD
Master Restationing Plan [DoD]	MRP
Master Retail Milk Vendors Association (AD)	MRMVA
Master Retailers Association (AD)	MRA
Master Routing (SAA)	MR
Master Routing Control (SAA)	MRC

Master Safeguards and Security Agreements (DOMA)	MSSA
Master Save List [Military] (AFIT)	MSL
Master Scenario Events List (MCD)	MSEL
Master Scene [Major script sequence] (NTCM)	MS
Master Schedule and Milestone Chart (MCD)	MSMC
Master Scheduler (CMD)	MS
Master Scheduling Letter	MSL
Master Scheduling Manager	MSM
Master/Senior/Chief Petty Officer of the Command (DNAB)	M/S/CPO
Master Sensitized Material Print (MSA)	MSMP
Master Sensor Data Record [For spacecraft]	MSDR
Master Separation Events Controller (MCD)	MSEC
Master Sequence Controller (NASA)	MSC
Master Sequencer	M/SEQ
Master Sequencer (AAG)	MS
Master Sergeant [Air Force]	E7
Master Sergeant [Army, Marine Corps]	E8
Master Sergeant	MS
Master Sergeant [Army] (AABC)	MSG
Master Sergeant	MSGT
Master Serial Number (AAG)	MSN
Master Ship Acquisition Milestone Plan	MSAMP
Master Ships Configuration Index (MCD)	MSCI
Master Ships Configuration List (MCD)	MSCL
Master Shot [Film production] (NTCM)	MS
Master Shuttle Verification Plan (MCD)	MSP
Master Shuttle Verification Plan (MCD)	MSVP
Master Sign Makers' Association (NADA)	MSMA
Master Sign Makers' Association [British] (BI)	MSMAN
Master Simulation Data System (Model) [Army]	MSDS
Master Simulator Control Console (MCD)	MSCC
Master Simulator Program (NVT)	MSP
Master Slave D Flip Flop (NITA)	MSDFF
Master Slave Flipflop [Nuclear energy] (IAA)	MSFF
Master Slave Manipulator [Nuclear energy]	MSM
Master Source File [Computer science] (BUR)	MSF
Master Source Program Library Tape [Computer science] (BUR)	MSPLT
Master Space Allocation Plan (MCD)	MSAP
Master Spares Positioning Resolver [Data processing]	MSPR
Master Standard Data	MSD
Master Station Subsystem	MSS
Master Status Chart	MSC
Master Steward [Marine Corps]	MSTD
Master Stock Item Record	MSIR
Master Stock Record (DNAB)	MSR
Master Stone Masons' Association of Victoria [Australia]	MSMAV
Master Support List (MCD)	MSL
Master Surgeon Dentist	MSD
Master Surveillance Station [Air Force]	MSS
Master Switch (IAA)	MASW
Master Switch	MS
Master Switch (AD)	ms
Master Switch	MSW
Master Switching Station (MCD)	MSS
Master Synchronization [Telecommunications] (TEL)	MSYNC
Master Synchronizer (CET)	MS
Master Synchronizer (MSA)	MSYNC
Master System Schedule (MCD)	MSS
Master System Tape (IAA)	MASTAP
Master Table of Contents (IAA)	MTC
Master Tailored Interest File [Navy] (NG)	MTIF
Master Tape (AAG)	MSTA
Master Tape Control	MTC
Master Tape Data	MTD
Master Tape Loading	MTL
Master Tape Loading Program	MTLP
Master Tape Validation	MTVAL
Master Teacher (ADA)	MT
Master Technical Sergeant [Marine Corps]	MTSGT
Master Technical Sergeant (Commissary) [Marine Corps]	MTSGT(C)
Master Template	MSTP
Master Terminal Operator (IAA)	MTO
Master Terminal Unit [Instrumentation]	MTU
Master Test Plan (KSC)	MTP
Master Test Station	MTS
Master Textile Printers Association (EA)	MTPA
Master Thrust Control [or Controller] [NASA] (NASA)	MTC
Master Time Display	MTD
Master Time Unit	MTU
Master Timer	MT
Master Timer Assembly	MTA
Master Timing and Control Circuit	MTCC
Master Timing Oscillator (MCD)	MTO
Master Timing Schedule	MTS
Master Timing System	MTS
Master Tool (NASA)	MT
Master Tool Record (SAA)	MTR
Master Tracking Data [NASA]	MTD
Master Tracking Data File [NASA]	MTDF
Master Training Concept [Problem solving]	MTC
Master Training File [Computer science]	MTRF
Master Training Plan [Navy] (ANA)	MTP
Master Transportation Plan (AAG)	MTP
Master Trigger Unit (IAA)	MTU
Master Typography Program (DNAB)	MTP

Master Unit (NASA) ... MU
Master Urgency List [*Navy*] ... MUL
Master User Directory (MHDI) ... MUD
Master Vellum Center [*Jet Propulsion Laboratory, NASA*] ... MVC
Master Verification Plan (MCD) ... MVP
Master Verification Process Requirement (SSD) ... MVPR
Master Verification Requirement (SSD) ... MVR
Master Vision Screener (PDAA) ... MAVIS
Master Volume Control (NASA) ... MVC
Master Warning Light (IAA) ... MLW
Master Warrant Officer [*Canadian Forces, since 1964*] ... MWO
Master Warrant Officer Training [*DoD*] ... MWOT
Master Water Data Index [*US Geological Survey*] [*Information service or system*] (CRD) ... MWDI
Master Weavers Institute (EA) ... MWI
Master Work Book (NASA) ... MWB
Master Work Order (AAG) ... MWO
Master-at-Arms [*Navy*] ... MA
Master-at-Arms [*Navy*] ... MAA
MasterCard [*Credit card*] ... MC
MasterCard Automated Point-of-Sale Program ... MAPP
Mastercard International [*New York, NY*] (EA) ... MC
Master-General [*Military British*] ... MG
Mastergroup Multiplex [*AT & T*] ... MMX
Mastergroup Surveillance System [*AT & T*] ... MSS
Master-Group Translator [*Telecommunications*] (TEL) ... MGT
Master-Locating RADAR (AABC) ... MLR
Masterman's Parliamentary Elections [*1880*] [*A publication*] (DLA) ... Mast El
Masterpiece Theatre [*Public television*] ... MPI
Masters ... MM
Masters Aerospace Operations Management [*Air Force*] ... MAEROSPOPNSMGT
Masters and Johnson Institute [*St. Louis, MO*] [*Formerly, Reproductive Biology Research Foundation*] [*Research center*] ... MJI
Master's Decisions (Patents) [*A publication*] (DLA) ... MD
Masters Deerhounds Association [*British*] (DBA) ... MDHA
Masters Degree in Energy and Environmental Management and Economics (ECON) ... MEDEA
Masters Degree in International Economics and Management (ECON) ... MIEM
Masters in Hotel, Restaurant, Tourism, and Administration (PGP) ... MHRTA
Master's Intelligent Terminal System [*Software package*] [*Nippon Kokan*] ... MITS
Master's Men of the National Association of Free Will Baptists (EA) ... MMNAFWB
Masters of Disaster [*Computer hacker gang*] ... MOD
Masters of Earth Resources Management (PGP) ... MERM
Masters of Foxhounds Association [*British*] (BI) ... MFHA
Masters of Foxhounds Association of America [*Later, American Master of Foxhounds Association*] (EA) ... MFAA
Masters of Foxhounds Club of America and England [*Defunct*] (EA) ... MFCAE
Masters of Medicine [*A publication*] ... MMA
Masters Retailers Association (NADA) ... MRA
Master's Supreme Court Reports [*25-28 Canada*] [*A publication*] (DLA) ... Mast
Masters Track and Field Committee (EA) ... MTFC
Master-Scale Television ... MSTV
Masterseal [*Record label*] ... MSL
Master-Servant [*Legal shorthand*] (LWAP) ... M-S
Mastership in Food Control [*British*] (DBQ) ... MFC
Master-Slave [*Computer science*] (MHDI) ... MS
Masterspec 2 [*Production Systems for Architects & Engineers, Inc.*] [*Information service or system*] (IID) ... M2
Masterton [*New Zealand*] [*Airport symbol*] (OAG) ... MRO
Masthead (MSA) ... MHD
Mastic ... MSTC
Mastic Asphalt Advisory Council [*British*] (BI) ... MAAC
Mastic Asphalt Council and Employers Federation [*British*] (DBA) ... MACEF
Mastic Asphalt Employers' Federation [*British*] (BI) ... MAEF
Mastic Floor [*Technical drawings*] ... MF
Mastic Joint [*Technical drawings*] ... MJ
Mastic Point [*Andros Islands, Bahamas*] [*Airport symbol*] (AD) ... MSK
Mastiche [*Mastic*] [*Pharmacy*] (ROG) ... MASTICH
Mastics-Moriches-Shirley Community Library, Mastic Beach, NY [*Library symbol Library of Congress*] (LCLS) ... NMb
Mastiff Club of America (EA) ... MCA
Mastiff Club of America (EA) ... MCOA
Mastitis-Metritis-Agalactia Syndrome [*Medicine*] (DMAA) ... MMA
Mastoid [*Medicine*] ... MAST
Mastoid Air Cell System [*Anatomy*] ... MACS
Mastuj [*Pakistan*] [*Airport symbol*] (AD) ... MJP
Mastung [*Pakistan*] [*Airport symbol*] (AD) ... MAU
Masurium ... MA
Masvingo [*Zimbabwe*] [*Airport symbol*] (OAG) ... FTV
Masvingo/Masvingo [*Zimbabwe*] [*ICAO location identifier*] (ICLI) ... FVMV
Mat ... MT
Mat Molding Reaction Injection Molding [*Plastics technology*] ... MMRIM
Matabeleland Mounted Police [*British military*] (DMA) ... MMP
Matabeng Store [*Lesotho*] [*ICAO location identifier*] (ICLI) ... FXMT
Matabeng Village [*Lesotho*] [*ICAO location identifier*] (ICLI) ... FXMV
Matachewan Consolidated Mines Ltd. [*Toronto Stock Exchange symbol*] ... MAT
Matadi [*Zaire*] [*ICAO location identifier*] (ICLI) ... FZAM
Matadi [*Zaire*] [*Airport symbol Obsolete*] (OAG) ... MAT
Matador Automatic RADAR Command ... MARC
Matagami [*Canada*] [*Airport symbol*] (OAG) ... YNM
Matagami, PQ [*ICAO location identifier*] (ICLI) ... CYNM
Matagorda Island, TX [*Location identifier FAA*] (FAAL) ... MGI
Matahambre [*Cuba ICAO location identifier*] (ICLI) ... MUMH
Matair Ltd. [*British ICAO designator*] (FAAC) ... MAO
Mataiva [*French Polynesia*] [*Airport symbol*] (OAG) ... MVT
Mataiva [*French Polynesia*] [*ICAO location identifier*] (ICLI) ... NTGV
Matam [*Senegal*] [*Airport symbol*] (OAG) ... MAX
Matam [*Senegal*] [*Seismograph station code, US Geological Survey Closed*] (SEIS) ... MMS
Matam/Ouro Sogui [*Senegal*] [*ICAO location identifier*] (ICLI) ... GOSM
Matamoros [*Mexico*] [*Airport symbol*] (OAG) ... MAM
Matamoros Internacional [*Mexico ICAO location identifier*] (ICLI) ... MMMA
Matane [*Canada*] [*Airport symbol*] (OAG) ... YME
Matane, PQ [*AM radio station call letters*] ... CBGA
Matane, PQ [*Television station call letters*] ... CBGAT
Matane, PQ [*FM radio station call letters*] ... CHOE
Matane, PQ [*AM radio station call letters*] ... CHRM
Matanza/Aeroclub Universita Rio [*Argentina ICAO location identifier*] (ICLI) ... SADZ
Matanzas [*Cuba ICAO location identifier*] (ICLI) ... MUMT
Matara Cases [*Ceylon*] [*A publication*] (DLA) ... MC
Mataram [*Indonesia*] [*Airport symbol*] (OAG) ... AMI
Mataram/Selaparang [*Indonesia*] [*ICAO location identifier*] (ICLI) ... WRRA
Matari [*Zaire*] [*ICAO location identifier*] (ICLI) ... FZDT
Matatiele [*South Africa*] [*ICAO location identifier*] (ICLI) ... FAMA
Matav-Cable Systems Media Ltd. [*NASDAQ symbol*] (SAG) ... MATV
Matav-Cable Systems Media Ltd. [*Associated Press*] (SAG) ... MatvCab
Matawan Joint Free Public Library, Matawan, NJ [*Library symbol Library of Congress*] (LCLS) ... NjMat
Match Dissolve [*Cinematography*] (WDMC) ... MD
Match Flip Flop [*Computer science*] (MHDI) ... MFF
Match Indicator Code (MCD) ... MIC
Match Institute [*Defunct*] (EA) ... MI
Match Problems [*Research test*] [*Psychology*] ... MP
Matchbox Collectors Club [*Defunct*] (EA) ... MCC
Matched and Beaded ... M & B
Matched and Lost [*Business term*] ... M & L
Matched and Lost [*Investment term*] (DFIT) ... M&L
Matched Angle (OA) ... MA
Matched Crystal Filters ... MCF
Matched Filter Performance ... MFP
Matched Logistic Regression [*Statistics*] ... MLR
Matched Memory Cycle [*Computer science*] ... MMC
Matched Power Gain ... MPG
Matched Sale-Purchase Agreement [*Business term*] ... MSP
Matched Set [*Philately*] ... MS
Matched Set (AD) ... ms
Matched Spatial Filter [*Optics*] ... MSF
Matched Transmission Line ... MTL
Matchedash Public Library, Coldwater, Ontario [*Library symbol National Library of Canada*] (BIB) ... OCM
Matched-Pairs Signed-Rank Test [*Statistics*] ... MPSRT
Matching Abacus Test [*Parapsychology*] ... MAT
Matching Aid to Restore States Habitat (GNE) ... MARSH
Matching Alcoholism Treatments to Client Heterogeneity ... MATCH
Matching Available Student Time to Educational Resources [*Computer science*] ... MASTER
Matching Familiar Figures [*Psychology*] ... MFF
Matching Familiar Figures Test [*Education*] ... MFFT
Matching Funds (OICC) ... MF
Matching Logic and Adder ... MLA
Mate [*of a ship*] ... M
Mate and Ferry [*NASA*] (NASA) ... MF
Mate and Ferry ... MF
Mate/Demate Device [*NASA*] (NASA) ... MDD
Mate/Demate Facility [*NASA*] (NASA) ... MDF
Mate/Demate Stiff Leg Derrick (MCD) ... MDSD
Mate/Demate Stiff Leg Derrick ... MDSLD
Mate/Demate Stiffleg Derrick ... MDSD
Mate With (MCD) ... M/W
MATEC Corp. [*Associated Press*] (SAG) ... Matec
MATEC Corp. [*AMEX symbol*] (SPSG) ... MXC
Mated Cast Iron Pair ... MCIP
Mated Elements [*or Events*] **Simulator** [*NASA*] (MCD) ... MES
Mated Elements Simulator ... MES
Mated Events Simulator ... MES
Mated Ground Vibration Test (NASA) ... MGVT
Mated Vertical Ground Vibration Test [*NASA*] (NASA) ... MVGVT
Mategua [*Bolivia*] [*ICAO location identifier*] (ICLI) ... SLMW
Matehematical Association of Western Australia ... MAWA
Matei [*Fiji*] [*ICAO location identifier*] (ICLI) ... NFNM
Mater [*Mother*] [*Latin*] ... M
Mater [*Mother*] [*Latin*] (ADA) ... MA
Mater Dei College, Ogdensburg, NY [*Library symbol Library of Congress*] (LCLS) ... NOgM
Mater Dei High School, Breese, IL [*Library symbol Library of Congress*] (LCLS) ... IBreMHS
Mater Lectionis (BJA) ... ML
Materia Medica (ROG) ... MM
Material (AFM) ... MAT
Material (VRA) ... mat
Material ... MATER
Material (KSC) ... MATL
Material ... Matrl
Material ... MIL
Material ... MTL
Material (KSC) ... MTL
Material ... MTRL
Material (FAAC) ... MTRL

Material Ablation with Chemically Active Boundary Layers in Reentry [*NASA*] .... MACABRE
Material Access Area [*Nuclear energy*] (NRCH) .... MAA
Material Access Authorization Program [*Nuclear energy*] (NRCH) .... MAAP
Material Accountability Recoverability Code .... MARC
Material Acquisition (NG) .... MATACQ
Material Acquisition Decision Process [*Military*] (MCD) .... MADP
Material Acquisition Guidance Letter (MCD) .... MAGL
Material Acquisition Management Application [*Suggested name for the Library of Congress computer system*] .... MAMA
Material Acquisition Manager [*Army*] (AAGC) .... MAM
Material Acquisition Process [*or Program*] (MCD) .... MAP
Material Action Reporting System (MCD) .... MARS
Material Activity Schedule .... MAS
Material Adjustment Order (MCD) .... MAO
Material Analysis Data .... MAD
Material and Equipment [*Nuclear energy*] (NRCH) .... M & E
Material and Equipment [*Nuclear energy*] (IAA) .... MAE
Material and Personnel Handling Equipment (NASA) .... MPHE
Material and Process .... M & P
Material and Toxicology System .... MATS
Material Annex Item [*Military*] .... MAI
Material Annex Line Item [*Military*] .... MALI
Material Annex Line Item Progress Report [*Military*] (NG) .... MALIPR
Material Annex/Weapons Dictionary [*Military*] .... MA/WD
Material Application Evaluation Board [*NASA*] (MCD) .... MAEB
Material Application Service [*NASA*] (IAA) .... MAS
Material Applications Board .... MAB
Material Assistance Designated [*Report*] (MCD) .... MAD
Material Authorization (KSC) .... MA
Material Authorization .... MA
Material Automated Information System .... MAIN
Material Automated Inventory Network (MCD) .... MAIN
Material Availability Commitment (AAG) .... MAC
Material Availability Date (CET) .... MAD
Material Availability Report [*NASA*] (KSC) .... MAR
Material Availability Request .... MAR
Material Availability Schedule .... MAS
Material Balance .... MB
Material Balance Area [*Nuclear energy*] .... MBA
Material Balance Report [*Nuclear energy*] .... MBR
Material Category .... MATCAT
Material Category Code (MCD) .... MCC
Material Change Notice (MCD) .... MCN
Material Characterization Center [*For nuclear wastes*] .... MCC
Material Classification Board (DNAB) .... MCB
Material Code (MCD) .... MC
Material Complaint Notice .... MCN
Material Concept Investigation (MCD) .... MCI
Material Condition Reporting System .... MCRS
Material Condition Status Report [*Military*] .... MCSR
Material Control (AAG) .... MC
Material Control Adjustment .... MCA
Material Control and Accountability (NRCH) .... MCA
Material Control and Accountability .... MC&A
Material Control and Accounting [*Nuclear energy*] (NRCH) .... MC & A
Material Control Area (AAG) .... MCA
Material Control Code .... MCC
Material Control Coordinator (MCD) .... MCC
Material Control Officer (MCD) .... MATCONOFF
Material Control Order Additional Material .... MCOAM
Material Coordinating Agency .... MCA
Material Co-Ordination Division (Naval) [*British*] .... MatCo-Ord(N)
Material Cross-Reference List (MCD) .... MCRL
Material Data Administrator (DNAB) .... MDA
Material Data Collection System [*NASA*] (KSC) .... MDCS
Material Date of Arrival (DNAB) .... MDOA
Material Deficiency Reports [*Program*] .... MDR
Material Delivery Expeditor Unit (DNAB) .... MDEU
Material Departmental Instruction .... MDI
Material Deviation List [*Military*] .... MDL
Material Directory Data Sheet (MCD) .... MDDS
Material Disposal Authority .... MDA
Material Distribution Board (DNAB) .... MDB
Material Electrocardiogram (MCD) .... MECG
Material Engineering Laboratory .... MEL
Material Evaluation Rocket Motor .... MERM
Material Expediting [*Program*] (DNAB) .... MATEX
Material Experiment Analysis .... MEA
Material Factor .... MF
Material False Statement [*Nuclear energy*] (NUCP) .... MFS
Material Fielding Agreement [*Army*] .... MFA
Material Fielding Operations (MCD) .... MFO
Material Handling and Management Society (EAIO) .... MHMS
Material Handling Area .... MHA
Material Handling Association of Quebec (AC) .... MHAQ
Material Handling Crane [*Autocrane*] (MCD) .... MHC
Material Handling Equipment Distributors Association (EA) .... MHEDA
Material Handling Institute (EA) .... MHI
Material Handling Unit (AFIT) .... MHU
Material Identification Accounting Code .... MIAC
Material Identification and Control (DNAB) .... MIC
Material Improvement Plan [*or Program*] [*Aviation*] .... MIP
Material Improvement Team (MCD) .... MIT
Material in Transit (MCD) .... MIT

Material Information Control and Information System (MCD) .... MICIS
Material Information Flow Device [*Military*] (AFM) .... MIFD
Material Information Flow System [*Military*] (AFM) .... MIFS
Material Information Management System (MCD) .... MIMS
Material Inspection [*Navy*] (NVT) .... MATINSP
Material Inspection [*Navy*] .... MI
Material Inspection and Receiving Report [*Military*] (KSC) .... MI & RR
Material Inspection and Receiving Report [*Military*] .... MIRR
Material Inspection Report [*Navy*] .... MIR
Material Inspection Service [*Navy*] (AAGC) .... INSMAT
Material Inspection Service [*Navy*] .... MIS
Material Introduction Team .... MIT
Material Inventory Control .... MIC
Material Inventory Control and Inventory System (NASA) .... MICIS
Material Inventory Control System [*NASA*] (SSD) .... MICS
Material Investigators Reactor [*NASA*] .... MIR
Material List (MSA) .... ML
Material, Maintenance, and Distribution (MCD) .... MMD
Material Maintenance Management (MCD) .... MMM
Material Management Accountability System (NASA) .... MMAS
Material Management Aggregation Code (MCD) .... MMAC
Material Management and Accounting System (AAGC) .... MMAS
Material Management Center Theater Supply [*Army*] .... MMCTS
Material Management Field Office .... MMFO
Material Manual and Memorandum (AAG) .... MM & M
Material Manufacturing Authorization (AAG) .... MMA
Material Mark .... MMK
Material Military Establishment [*Formerly, OSRD*] (MCD) .... MME
Material Movement Priority Designator (DNAB) .... MMPD
Material Need (Abbreviated) (MCD) .... MN(A)
Material Need Document [*DoD*] .... MND
Material Need Engineering Development (MCD) .... MN ED
Material Number .... MN
Material on Job Date [*Telecommunications*] (TEL) .... MOJ
Material Ordering and Delivery Schedule (DNAB) .... MODS
Material Ordering Guide [*Shipbuilding*] .... MOG
Material Ordering Schedule .... MOS
Material Other than Grape [*Wine making*] .... MOG
Material Overhead (AD) .... moh
Material Pass (AAG) .... MP
Material Performance Branch [*Air Force*] .... MPB
Material Planning Schedule and Control [*Division of Inspection Offices, Navy*] .... MPSC
Material Planning Study .... MPS
Material Planning System [*Manufacturing management*] .... MPS
Material Process and Inspection Specification (AAG) .... MP & IS
Material Process Instruction (AD) .... MPI
Material Processing Laboratory (SSD) .... MPL
Material Processing Procedure (NASA) .... MPP
Material Processing Specification (NASA) .... MPS
Material Processing System .... MPS
Material Processing System .... MPS
Material Professional [*Army*] .... MP
Material Properties Bibliographic Data System [*Purdue University*] [*Database*] .... MPBDS
Material Properties Numerical Data System [*Purdue University*] [*Database*] .... MPNDS
Material Property Damage (DNAB) .... MPD
Material Purchase Contracts Control .... MPCC
Material Purchase Requisition .... MPR
Material Readiness Index System [*Military*] .... MRIS
Material Readiness Report (MCD) .... MRR
Material Receipt Discrepancy Notice (AD) .... MRDN
Material Receipt Discrepancy Record .... MRDR
Material Receipt Voucher (AD) .... mrv
Material Receiving Instruction [*Bechtel*] [*Nuclear energy*] (NRCH) .... MRI
Material Receiving Report .... MATL RR
Material Receiving [*Inspection*] Report [*Nuclear energy*] (NRCH) .... MRR
Material Recorder Notice (AD) .... MRN
Material Recovery Unit .... MRU
Material Redistribution [*Program*] (DNAB) .... MATRED
Material Redistribution and Disposal .... MR & D
Material Redistribution and Disposal Administration .... MR & DA
Material Redistribution Center .... MRC
Material Rejection Report .... MRR
Material Reliability Program [*Military*] (AFIT) .... MRP
Material Reliability Report (MCD) .... MRR
Material Removal Rate (MCD) .... MRR
Material Request [*or Requisition*] (MCD) .... MR
Material Request [*or Requirement*] Summary .... MRS
Material Requested .... MATRE
Material Requested Being Supplied [*Military*] .... MATSO
Material Requested Is Not Available .... MATNO
Material Required Date .... MRD
Material Requirements Deck (AAG) .... MRD
Material Requirements Drawing (MCD) .... MRD
Material Requirements Estimation System [*Navy*] .... MRES
Material Requirements for Stock Balance .... MRSB
Material Requirements Lists .... MRL
Material Requirements Planning [*Pronounced "merp"*] .... MRP
Material Requirements Planning List [*Navy*] .... MRPL
Material Requisition .... MATL REQ
Material Research and Production Methods (MCD) .... MRPM
Material Reserve Planning .... MRP
Material Resource Planning (ACII) .... MRP

Material Response Study	MARS
Material Returned to Store [NASA] (KSC)	MRS
Material Review [Aviation] (AAG)	MR
Material Review Activity	MRA
Material Review Board [Aviation] (MCD)	MRB
Material Review Central Control [Aviation] (MCD)	MRCC
Material Review Disposition [Aviation]	MRD
Material Review Disposition Record (NASA)	MRDR
Material Review Group [Aviation]	MRG
Material Review Item [Aviation]	MRI
Material Review Record [or Reports] [Aviation] (MCD)	MRR
Material Review Request	MRR
Material Review - Ships Record (MCD)	MR-SR
Material Review Tag [Aviation] (MCD)	MRT
Material Routing Slip	MRS
Material Safety Data	MSD
Material Safety Data Sheet (GNE)	MSDS
Material Safety Data Sheets [Occupational Health Services, Inc.] [Information service or system]	MSDS
Material Safety Task Group [Air Force] (AFM)	MSTG
Material Safety Task Group [Air Force]	MSTGP
Material Sales Order	MSO
Material Salvage Unit	MSU
Material Sciences [NYSE symbol] (TTSB)	MSC
Material Sciences Corp. [Associated Press] (SAG)	MatSci
Material Sciences Corp. [NYSE symbol] (SPSG)	MSC
Material Service Area (NASA)	MSA
Material Service Area	MSA
Material Source Code	MSC
Material Specification (AAGC)	E SPEC
Material Specifications	MS
Material Standard (AD)	MS
Material Status Report [AEC]	MSR
Material Stores Area (KSC)	MSA
Material Supply Notice (AAG)	MSN
Material Support	MS
Material Support Branch [NASA] (KSC)	MSB
Material Support Data (MCD)	MSD
Material Support Date (DOMA)	MSD
Material Support Plan [or Program]	MSP
Material Surveillance Assembly [Nuclear energy] (NRCH)	MSA
Material Test (IAA)	MT
Material Test Procedure Pamphlet	MTPP
Material Test Specification (MSA)	MTS
Material Test Work Order (SAA)	MTWO
Material Testing Center	MTC
Material Testing Technology (MCD)	MTT
Material Thickness Indicator	MTI
Material Transfer (NRCH)	MT
Material Transfer, Information Transfer, Control Transfer, Energy Transfer	MICE
Material Transfer Recorder [LASER] [Army]	MTR
Material Turned into Stores	MTIS
Material Unaccounted For [Nuclear energy]	MUF
Material Utilization Reference File [Military]	MURF
Materialien zum Sumerischen Lexikon. B. Landsberger. Patrologiae Cursus Completus. Series Latina [A publication] (BJA)	MSL
Material-in-Process Engineering Request	MPER
Materials Acquisition Sub-System [Computer science]	MASS
Materials Advisory Board [Later, NMAB] [NAS-NRC]	MAB
Materials Analysis Co.	MAC
Materials Analysis, Tracking, and Control [Johnson Space Center data system] [NASA] (NASA)	MATCO
Materials and Activities for Teachers and Children	MATCH
Materials and Coatings (SSD)	MAC
Materials and Components Development and Testing Association [Paisley College of Technology] [British] (IRUK)	MACDATA
Materials and Ecological Testing Laboratory [Research center] (RCD)	METL
Materials and Facilities (MCD)	M & F
Materials and Maintenance (NASA)	M & M
Materials and Mechanics Research Center [Army] (MCD)	MMRC
Materials and Methods Standards Association (EA)	MMSA
Materials and Molecular Research Division [Lawrence Berkeley Laboratory] [Research center] (RCD)	MMRD
Materials and Others	M & O
Materials and Plant Protection [Nuclear energy] (NRCH)	M & PP
Materials and Process Engineering (MCD)	M & PE
Materials and Process Requirement [Navy]	MPR
Materials and Processes (AD)	m & p
Materials and Processes Acceptance Requirement	MAPAR
Materials and Resources Information Service (NITA)	MARIS
Materials and Science Toxicology Laboratory [University of Tennessee] [Research center] (RCD)	MSTLAB
Materials and Services [NASA] (KSC)	M & S
Materials and Structures (SDI)	M & S
Materials and Structures Division [NASA]	MSD
Materials and Structures Laboratory [Texas A & M University] [Research center] (RCD)	MSL
Materials Application Advisory Board [NASA] (NASA)	MAAB
Materials Applications Board (MCD)	MAB
Materials Business File [American Society for Metals, The Institute for Metals] [Information service or system] (IID)	MBF
Materials Centre Library, University of Calgary, Alberta [Library symbol National Library of Canada] (NLC)	ACUMC
Materials Committee (MCD)	MC

Materials Compatibility in Sodium [Nuclear energy] (NRCH)	MCIS
Materials Control and Verification Program [NASA] (NASA)	MCVP
Materials Control Information System (MHDB)	MCIS
Materials Control Plan (NASA)	MCP
Materials Cost Index	MCI
Materials Database Steel and Iron [German Iron and Steel Engineers Association] [Ceased operation] [Information service or system] (IID)	STEELFACTS
Materials Department [David W. Taylor Naval Ship Research and Development Center] [Annapolis, MD]	MAT
Materials Dissemination Center [Institute for Development of Educational Activities]	MDC
Materials Engineer	Mat E
Materials, Engineering, and Advanced Test Reactor (SAA)	MEATR
Materials Engineering Code	MEC
Materials Engineering Research Laboratory [NASA] (NASA)	MERL
Materials Engineering Research Laboratory Ltd. [British] (IRC)	MERL
Materials Equipment Requirements List (NASA)	MERL
Materials Equipment Requirements List	MERL
Materials Evaluation (PDAA)	ME
Materials Evaluation and Development Laboratory [General Services Administration]	MEDL
Materials Evaluation Laboratory (MCD)	MEL
Materials Experiment Assembly	MEA
Materials Finishes and Processes (MCD)	MF & P
Materials Flow Management [Manufacturing]	MFM
Materials for the Assyrian Dictionary (BJA)	MAD
Materials Handling (NATG)	MH
Materials Handling and Construction Equipment (DNAB)	MH-CE
Materials Handling Equipment [Military] (AFM)	MHE
Materials Handling Support System [Military] (AFM)	MHSS
Materials Irradiation Chamber	MIC
Materials Joining Tool	MJT
Materials Laboratory Library, Nova Scotia Department of Transportation, Windsor Junction, Nova Scotia [Library symbol National Library of Canada] (NLC)	NSWJT
Materials Management [Nuclear energy]	MM
Materials Management Institute	MMI
Materials Marketing Associates [Hartford, CT] (EA)	MMA
Materials Measurement (IEEE)	MM
Materials Methods Research and Engineering (MCD)	MMRE
Materials Open-Test Assembly [Nuclear energy] (NRCH)	MOTA
Materials Physics Division [Air Force]	MPD
Materials Preparation Center [Ames, IA] [Ames Laboratory] [Department of Energy] (GRD)	MPC
Materials Preparation Program (SAA)	MPP
Materials Processing Center [Massachusetts Institute of Technology] [Research center] (RCD)	MPC
Materials Processing Facility [NASA] (KSC)	MPF
Materials Processing in Space	MPS
Materials Processing in Space [NASA]	MPS
Materials Processing Technology Laboratory (SSD)	MPTL
Materials Program Code (AD)	mpc
Materials Properties Branch [Army] (RDA)	MPB
Materials Properties Council (EA)	MPC
Materials Proximity Detector	MPD
Materials Quality Assurance Directorate [Ministry of Defence] [British]	MQAD
Materials Recovery Facility [for recycling of glass, plastics, etc.]	MRF
Materials Requirement Analysis (PDAA)	MRA
Materials Requirement Planning System (HGAA)	MRPS
Materials Research and Protection Methods (SAA)	MRAPM
Materials Research and Standards (AD)	MR & S
Materials Research Center [Northwestern University] (RCD)	MRC
Materials Research Center [Lehigh University] (RCD)	MRC
Materials Research Corp.	MRC
Materials Research Laboratories [National Science Foundation] [Research center]	MRL
Materials Research Society (EA)	MRS
Materials Review Area (AAG)	MRA
Materials Review Crib (AAG)	MRC
Materials Science	MS
Materials Science and Engineering	MS & E
Materials Science and Engineering Commission [British]	MSEC
Materials Science and Manufacturing in Space [Program] [NASA]	MS/MS
Materials Science Center [Cornell University]	MSC
Materials Science Double Rack	MSDR
Materials Service Center [NASA] (NASA)	MSC
Materials Summary Acceptance Document (MCD)	MSAD
Materials Synthesis and Processing [National Science Foundation]	MS & P
Materials Technology Institute of the Chemical Process Industries (EA)	MTI
Materials Technology Laboratory [Watertown, MA] [Army] (RDA)	MTL
Materials Test (IEEE)	MT
Materials Test Loop [Nuclear energy] (NRCH)	MTL
Materials Testing Activity (MCD)	MTA
Materials Testing and Technology Program	MTTP
Materials Testing Branch [Kennedy Space Center]	MTB
Materials Testing Branch [NASA]	MTB
Materials Testing Reactor	MTR
Materials Testing Report	MTR
Materials Transportation Bureau [Department of Transportation]	MTB
Materials Usage Agreement (NASA)	MUA
Materials-by-Design [Chemical engineering]	MBD
Materials-Evaluation Subcaliber Rocket Motor (SAA)	MESROM
Materials-Process-Product Model (PDAA)	MPPM
Materiel [Military] (AFM)	MAT

Materiel [*Military*] ... MATL
Materiel ... MATL
Materiel Acquisition and Delivery [*Military*] ... MAD
Materiel Acquisition and Integrated Logistics Support ... MAILS
Materiel Acquisition and Readiness Executive Development [*Program*] [*Army*] (RDA) ... MARED
Materiel Acquisition Decision Review [*Army*] ... MADR
Materiel Acquisition Management Plan ... MAMP
Materiel Acquisition Management Program [*Army*] (RDA) ... MAM
Materiel Acquisition Management System ... MAMS
Materiel Acquisition Plan [*Army*] ... MAP
Materiel Acquisition Resource Committee [*Military*] ... MARC
Materiel Acquisition Resource System [*Military*] ... MARS
Materiel Acquisition Review Board [*Army*] ... MARB
Materiel Allowance List [*Military*] ... MAL
Materiel and Supply Section [*of an air staff; also, officer in charge of this section*] [*Air Force*] ... A-4
Materiel Asset Redistribution Center Europe [*Military*] ... MARCE
Materiel Category Structure Code [*Military*] ... MCSC
Materiel Change [*Military*] ... MC
Materiel Change Management ... MCM
Materiel Command [*Army*] (AABC) ... MATCOM
Materiel Command [*Air Force*] ... MC
Materiel Command, Europe ... MATCOMEUR
Materiel Command Procedure [*Military*] ... MCP
Materiel Concept [*Army*] ... MC
Materiel Deployment/Acceptance Plan (MCD) ... MDAP
Materiel Deployment Schedule ... MDS
Materiel Deterioration Prevention and Control [*Program*] [*Army*] (RDA) ... MADPAC
Materiel Developer ... MATDEV
Materiel Developer [*Army*] ... MD
Materiel Developer's Test Program [*Military*] ... MDTP
Materiel Development and Logistic Command [*Army - replaced Ordnance, Engineer, Signal, Chemical and Quartermaster Overall Commands*] ... MDLC
Materiel Development and Readiness Command [*Formerly, AMC*] [*See also DARCOM*] [*Army*] ... MDRC
Materiel Essential to Reconstitution Operations [*Air Force*] (AFM) ... METRO
Materiel Field Test (MCD) ... MFT
Materiel Fielding Plan ... MFP
Materiel Fielding Plan/Materiel Transfer Plan [*Army*] (RDA) ... MFP/MTP
Materiel Fielding Team [*Army*] (RDA) ... MFT
Materiel Handling Equipment [*Army*] (INF) ... MHE
Materiel Identification and New Item Control Technique [*AFLC*] ... MINT
Materiel Improvement Project [*Military*] ... MIP
Materiel Inventory Data Acquisition System ... MIDAS
Materiel Management Center [*Military*] (AABC) ... MMC
Materiel Management Code [*Military*] (AFM) ... MMC
Materiel Management Decision [*Military*] ... MMD
Materiel Management Division [*Army*] ... MMD
Materiel Management Optimization Program [*DoD*] ... MATMOP
Materiel Management Review [*DoD*] ... MMR
Materiel Management Review Board (AFIT) ... MMRB
Materiel Management Training Center [*Military*] ... MMTC
Materiel Need Statement [*Army*] ... MNS
Materiel Needs [*Army*] ... MN
Materiel Obligation Validation (AFIT) ... MOV
Materiel Performance Package [*Military*] (AFM) ... MPP
Materiel Planning Study [*Army*] ... MPS
Materiel Procurement Priorities Review Board [*Army*] (AABC) ... MPPRB
Materiel Procurement Priorities Review Committee [*Army*] (RDA) ... MPPRC
Materiel Program Code [*Air Force*] (AFM) ... MPC
Materiel Readiness [*Army*] ... MR
Materiel Readiness Authorization List [*Military*] ... MRAL
Materiel Readiness Command [*Military*] ... MRC
Materiel Readiness Expediter [*Army*] ... MRE
Materiel Readiness Officer (MCD) ... MRO
Materiel Readiness Report [*Army*] (AABC) ... MRR
Materiel Readiness Reporting System [*Army*] ... MRRS
Materiel Readiness Support Activity [*Army*] (RDA) ... MRSA
Materiel Readiness Support Agency [*Navy*] ... MRSA
Materiel Redistribution Division [*Army*] (AFIT) ... MRD
Materiel Release Confirmation [*Army*] (AABC) ... MRC
Materiel Release Denial [*Army*] (AABC) ... MATRD
Materiel Release Denial [*Military*] (AABC) ... MRD
Materiel Release Order [*Air Force*] ... MRO
Materiel Release Review Board [*Military*] ... MRRB
Materiel Repair Requirement List [*Military*] (AFIT) ... MRRL
Materiel Repair System [*Air Force*] (AFM) ... MRS
Materiel Request History and Status ... MRHS
Materiel Request History and Storage File ... MRHSF
Materiel Requirements Document [*Army*] ... MRD
Materiel Requirements List [*Military*] ... MRL
Materiel Requirements Review Board [*Military*] (AFIT) ... MRRB
Materiel Requirements Review Committee [*Military*] ... MRRC
Materiel Returns Program [*Military*] (AFIT) ... MRP
Materiel Screening Code [*DoD*] (AFIT) ... MSC
Materiel Squadron ... MATS
Materiel Status [*Military*] ... MATSTAT
Materiel Status Committee [*Military*] (AABC) ... MSC
Materiel Status Evaluation [*Army*] (AABC) ... MSE
Materiel Status Office (MCD) ... MSO
Materiel Studies Review Committee [*Army*] ... MSRC
Materiel Support Center (MCD) ... MSC
Materiel Support Command (MCD) ... MSC
Materiel Support Planning Guidance [*Military*] (AABC) ... MSPG
Materiel System Requirements Specification [*Military*] ... MSRS
Materiel Test Procedure [*Army*] ... MTP
Materiel Testing Command [*Merged with Weapons and Mobility Command*] [*Army*] ... MTC
Materiel Testing Directorate [*Army*] (RDA) ... MTD
Materiel Transfer Agreement [*DoD*] ... MTA
Materiel Transfer Plan [*Army*] ... MTP
Materiel Utilization Control Office (AFIT) ... MUCO
Maternal (WDAA) ... MATERN
Maternal and Child Health Block Grant [*Department of Health and Human Services*] (GFGA) ... MCHBG
Maternal and Child Health Service (EA) ... MCHS
Maternal and Child Health Services [*Generic term*] (DHSM) ... MCH
Maternal and Infant Care [*Medicine*] ... MIC
Maternal Deprivation (MAE) ... MD
Maternal Deprivation Syndrome [*Medicine*] (DMAA) ... MDS
Maternal Diabetes Mellitus [*Medicine*] ... MDM
Maternal Electrocardiogram [*Cardiology*] [*Obstetrics*] (DAVI) ... MECG
Maternal Grandfather (AAMN) ... MGF
Maternal Grandmother (AAMN) ... MGM
Maternal Mortality Rate [*Gynecology*] ... MMR
Maternal Resistance Factor (BARN) ... MRF
Maternal Serum Alpha Fetoprotein [*Clinical chemistry*] ... MSAFP
Maternity ... MAT
Maternity (WDAA) ... MATERN
Maternity ... MTRNTY
Maternity and Child Welfare [*Medicine British*] ... M and CW
Maternity and Maternity Services [*British*] ... MMS
Maternity and Surgical (AD) ... M&S
Maternity Center Association (EA) ... MCA
Mates Receipt (AD) ... M/R
Mate's Receipt ... MR
Matewan BancShares [*NASDAQ symbol*] (TTSB) ... MATE
Matewan BancShares [*Associated Press*] (SAG) ... Mtewan
Matewan BancShares, Inc. [*NASDAQ symbol*] (SAG) ... MATE
Matewan BancShares, Inc. [*Associated Press*] (SAG) ... Matewan
Matewan Bancshrs 7.5% Cv'A'Pfd [*NASDAQ symbol*] (TTSB) ... MATEP
Matewan, WV [*AM radio station call letters*] ... WHJC
Matewan, WV [*FM radio station call letters*] ... WVKM
Math Acceleration Unit (NITA) ... MAU
Math Analysis Library (MCD) ... MALIB
Math Error [*IRS*] ... ME
Math Model (KSC) ... MM
Math Model Test (MCD) ... MMT
Math Network Curriculum Project (EDAC) ... MNCP
Mathematical ... MATHL
Mathematical Advisory Unit [*Ministry of Transport*] [*British*] ... MAU
Mathematical Analysis of a Perception and Preference ... MAPP
Mathematical Analysis of Downtime (DNAB) ... MAD
Mathematical Analysis of Requirements for Career Information Appraisal ... MARCIA
Mathematical Analysis without Programming [*Computer science*] ... MAP
Mathematical Analyzer, Numerical Integrator and Computer ... MANIAC
Mathematical and Functional Subroutine Library (MHDB) ... MFSL
Mathematical and Physical Sciences and Engineering (IEEE) ... MPE
Mathematical Applications Group, Inc. (MCD) ... MAGI
Mathematical Association [*British*] (BI) ... MA
Mathematical Association of America (EA) ... MAA
Mathematical Association of South Australia ... MASA
Mathematical Automata Theory ... MAT
Mathematical Center (IAA) ... MC
Mathematical Code System ... MCS
Mathematical Cuneiform Texts [*A publication*] (BJA) ... MCT
Mathematical Didactics [*Fachinformationszentrum Energie, Physik, Mathematik GmbH*] [*Database*] ... MATHDI
Mathematical Expectation [*Statistics*] (DAVI) ... E
Mathematical Foundation of Computer Science (PDAA) ... MFCS
Mathematical Laboratory [*Programming language*] (CSR) ... MATHLAB
Mathematical Modeling and Reliability Transducer (MCD) ... MART
Mathematical Off-Print Service [*American Mathematical Society*] ... MOS
Mathematical Operations Computer ... MOC
Mathematical, Optical, and Philosophical Instrument Makers' Society [*A union*] [*British*] ... MOPIMS
Mathematical Package (IAA) ... MATHPAC
Mathematical, Physical, and Engineering Science (AD) ... MPES
Mathematical Problem-Solving Project [*National Science Foundation*] ... MPSP
Mathematical Programming [*Computer science*] ... MP
Mathematical Programming Language [*Computer science*] (PDAA) ... MPL
Mathematical Programming Language [*Computer science*] (AD) ... mpl
Mathematical Programming Society [*Voorburg, Netherlands*] (EAIO) ... MPS
Mathematical Programming System [*Computer science*] ... MPS
Mathematical Programming System Control Language [*1974*] [*Computer science*] (CSR) ... MPSCL
Mathematical Programming System Extended [*IBM Corp.*] [*Computer science*] ... MPSX
Mathematical Sciences Institute [*Cornell University*] [*Research center*] (RCD) ... MSI
Mathematical Sciences Research Institute [*University of California, Berkeley*] (PDAA) ... MSRI
Mathematical Sciences Research Institute [*University of Minnesota*] (PDAA) ... MSRI
Mathematical Study Unit [*American Topical Association*] (EA) ... MSU
Mathematical Tables and Other Aids to Computation ... MTAC
Mathematician (AFM) ... MATHN

Mathematics [Secondary school course] [British] .... M
Mathematics (EY) .... MATH
Mathematics (DD) .... Math
Mathematics .... MATHS
Mathematics Abstracts [Fachinformationszentrum Karlsruhe GmbH]
  [Information service or system] .... MATH
Mathematics and Computer Division [Supreme Headquarters Allied Powers
  Europe] (NATG) .... MCD
Mathematics Anxiety Rating Scale [Psychology] .... MARS
Mathematics Applied to novel Situations Test (EDAC) .... MANS
Mathematics Attitude Scale (EDAC) .... MAS
Mathematics Computation Laboratory [General Services Administration] ...... MCL
Mathematics Diagnostic/Prescriptive Inventory (EDAC) .... MDPI
Mathematics Education for Gifted Secondary School Students Project
  (EDAC) .... MEGSSS
Mathematics Functional Literacy Test (EDAC) .... MFLT
Mathematics in Recognizable Form Automatically Compiled [Computer
  science] .... MIRFAC
Mathematics in Society Project (AIE) .... MISP
Mathematics Model .... MM
Mathematics of Computation (IEEE) .... MCOM
Mathematics Olympiads for Elementary Schools (EDAC) .... MOES
Mathematics, Physics, Chemistry (AD) .... mpc
Mathematics Research Center (MCD) .... MRC
Mathematics Resources Project [National Science Foundation] .... MRP
Mathematics/Science/Computer .... MSC
Mathematics Teacher [A publication] (BRI) .... Math T
Matheson, Coleman & Bell [Commercial firm] .... MCB
Matheson Memorial Library, Elkhorn, WI [Library symbol Library of
  Congress] (LCLS) .... WEI
Matheson Public Library, Matheson, ON, Canada [Library symbol Library of
  Congress] (LCLS) .... CaOMat
Matheson Public Library, Ontario [Library symbol National Library of
  Canada] (NLC) .... OMAT
Matheus de Mathesillanis [Flourished, 1381-1402] [Authority cited in pre-1607
  legal work] (DSA) .... Ma
Matheus de Mathesillanis [Flourished, 1381-1402] [Authority cited in pre-1607
  legal work] (DSA) .... Ma de Ma
Matheus de Mathesillanis [Flourished, 1381-1402] [Authority cited in pre-1607
  legal work] (DSA) .... Ma de Math
Matheus de Mathesillanis [Flourished, 1381-1402] [Authority cited in pre-1607
  legal work] (DSA) .... Math
Mathews Memorial Library, Mathews, VA [Library symbol Library of
  Congress] (LCLS) .... ViMat
Mathews on Landlord and Tenant [A publication] (DLA) .... Mat L & T
Mathews on Presumptive Evidence [A publication] (DLA) .... Math Pres Ev
Mathews on the Law of Partnership [A publication] (DLA) .... Mat Part
Mathews on the Law of Portions [A publication] (DLA) .... Mat Por
Mathias-Soave-Redlich-Kwong [Equation of state] .... MSRK
Mathieu's Quebec Reports [A publication] (DLA) .... Math
Mathieu's Quebec Revised Reports [A publication] (DLA) .... RJR
Mathieu's Quebec Revised Reports [A publication] (DLA) .... RJRQ
Mathis Society [Defunct] (EA) .... MS
Mathsoft, Inc. [NASDAQ symbol] (SAG) .... MATH
Mathsoft, Inc. [Associated Press] (SAG) .... Mathsft
Matiaro [Cook Islands] [ICAO location identifier] (ICLI) .... NCMR
Matilda J. Gibson Memorial Library, Creston, IA [Library symbol Library of
  Congress] (LCLS) .... IaCres
Matinee .... M
Matinee .... MAT
Mating Sequence and Control (NASA) .... MS
Matins [Early morning prayers] .... M
Matins (ROG) .... MAT
Matka [Yugoslavia] [Seismograph station code, US Geological Survey]
  (SEIS) .... MYG
Matlack Systems [NYSE symbol] (TTSB) .... MLK
Matlack Systems, Inc. [Associated Press] (SAG) .... Matlack
Matlack Systems, Inc. [NYSE symbol] (CTT) .... MLK
Mato Grosso [Brazil] [Airport symbol] (AD) .... MGO
Matriculate (ROG) .... MATR
Matriculation .... MATRIC
Matrimonial (ROG) .... MATRL
Matrimonial and Family Law [New York, NY A publication] .... MFL
Matrimonial and Family Life [A publication] .... MFL
Matrimonial Causes Rules [A publication] (DLA) .... MCR
Matrimonial Matters [Slang] (DSUE) .... MATS
Matrimonio Duxit [Led into Matrimony] [Latin] (ROG) .... MD
Matrimonium [Matrimony] [Latin] .... MM
Matritech, Inc. [Associated Press] (SAG) .... Matritch
Matritech, Inc. [Associated Press] (SAG) .... Matrtc
Matritech, Inc. [NASDAQ symbol] (SAG) .... NMPS
Matrix .... M
Matrix .... M
Matrix .... MAT
Matrix (MSA) .... MAT
Matrix (IAA) .... MTX
Matrix (BUR) .... MX
Matrix Algebra General Interpretive Coding (IEEE) .... MAGIC
Matrix Algebra Interpretive Program (IEEE) .... MAIP
Matrix Analogies Test [Intelligence test] .... MAT
Matrix Analogies Test - Expanded Form [Intelligence test] .... MAT-EF
Matrix Analogies Test - Short Form [Intelligence test] .... MAT-SF
Matrix Analysis of Insider Threat [Nuclear energy] (NRCH) .... MAIT
Matrix Analysis Subsystem (MCD) .... MASS
Matrix Antigen [Biochemistry] .... MA

Matrix Arithmetic Expression .... MAE
Matrix Attachment Region [Genetics] .... MAR
Matrix Automation through EMATS [Military] (MCD) .... MATE
Matrix Capital Corp. [Associated Press] (SAG) .... MatrCap
Matrix Capital Corp. [NASDAQ symbol] (SAG) .... MTXC
Matrix Case Arrangement (DGA) .... MCA
Matrix Connector Punched Card Programmer [Computer science]
  (IEEE) .... MACON
Matrix Difference Equation .... MDE
Matrix Electrostatic Writing Technique .... MEWT
Matrix Generating and Reporting System [Computer science] (PDAA) ...... MAGEN
Matrix Generator and Report Writer [Computer science] .... MGRW
Matrix Generator Language [Computer science] (BUR) .... MGL
Matrix Glass [Geology] .... MG
Matrix Information and Directory Services, Inc. .... MIDS
Matrix Inversion Program [Computer science] (BUR) .... MIP
Matrix Ion Species Ratio [Spectroscopy] .... MISR
Matrix Isolation and Electron Spin Resonance [Analytical chemistry] .... MIESR
Matrix Iteration Method of Unfolding Spectra [Computer science] .... MIMUSA
Matrix Laboratory [Computer science] .... MATLAB
Matrix Language [Computer science] (IEEE) .... MATLAN
Matrix Light Valve .... MLV
Matrix Log-In Memory .... MLIM
Matrix Math Extensions (PCM) .... MMX
Matrix Memory (MHDI) .... MXM
Matrix Metalloproteinase [An enzyme] .... MMP
Matrix - National Module .... MX-NM
Matrix of Environmental Residuals for Energy Systems [Computerized
  information system] .... MERES
Matrix Operations Programming .... MOP
Matrix Operations Programming Combination of Estimates .... MOPCOM
Matrix Output Amplifier .... MOA
Matrix Pharmaceutical [NASDAQ symbol] (TTSB) .... MATX
Matrix Pharmaceutical, Inc. [Associated Press] (SAG) .... MatrxPh
Matrix Pharmaceutical, Inc. [NASDAQ symbol] (SAG) .... MATX
Matrix Processing Peptidase [An enzyme] .... MPP
Matrix Program Board .... MPB
Matrix Reducibility Algorithm (PDAA) .... MRA
Matrix Scheme for Algorithms (PDAA) .... MSA
Matrix Service [NASDAQ symbol] (TTSB) .... MTRX
Matrix Service Co. [Associated Press] (SAG) .... MatrxSv
Matrix Service Co. [Associated Press] (SAG) .... MatrxSv
Matrix Service Corp. [NASDAQ symbol] (NQ) .... MTRX
Matrix Solid-Phase Dispersion [Analytical chemistry] .... MSPD
Matrix Spike .... MS
Matrix Spike Duplicate .... MSD
Matrix Test Facility (MCD) .... MTF
Matrix-Addressed Liquid Crystal Display .... MALCD
Matrix-Assisted LASER Desorption Ionization [Spectroscopy] .... MALDI
Matrix-Assisted LASER Desorption Mass Spectrometry .... MALDMS
Matrix-Assisted Laser Ionizaion [Spectrometry] .... MALI
Matron [British military] (DMA) .... M
Matron .... MATR
Matron-in-Chief [Navy British] .... M-in-C
Matrons of Hospitals Association (ROG) .... M of HA
Matrox Graphics Architecture [Matrox Eletronics Systems Ltd.] (PCM) .... MGA
Matsaile [Lesotho] [ICAO location identifier] (ICLI) .... FXMA
Matson Public Library, Princeton, IL [Library symbol Library of Congress]
  (LCLS) .... IPri
Matson's Reports [22-24 Connecticut] [A publication] (DLA) .... Mats
Matson's Reports [22-24 Connecticut] [A publication] (DLA) .... Matson
Matsqui-Sumas-Abbotsford Museum, Abbotsford, British Columbia [Library
  symbol National Library of Canada] (NLC) .... BAM
Matsue [Japan] [Seismograph station code, US Geological Survey] (SEIS) ...... MTS
Matsumoto [Japan] [Airport symbol] (OAG) .... MMJ
Matsumoto [Japan] [Seismograph station code, US Geological Survey]
  (SEIS) .... MTM
Matsumoto [Japan ICAO location identifier] (ICLI) .... RJAF
Matsushima [Japan ICAO location identifier] (ICLI) .... RJST
Matsushiro [Japan] [Seismograph station code, US Geological Survey]
  (SEIS) .... MAJO
Matsushiro [Japan] [Seismograph station code, US Geological Survey]
  (SEIS) .... MAT
Matsushita El Ind ADR [NYSE symbol] (TTSB) .... MC
Matsushita Electric Corp. of America (IAA) .... MECA
Matsushita Electric Industrial Co. Ltd. [Associated Press] (SAG) .... Matsu
Matsushita Electric Industrial Co. Ltd. [NYSE symbol] (SPSG) .... MC
Matsuyama [Japan] [Seismograph station code, US Geological Survey]
  (SEIS) .... MTY
Matsuyama [Japan] [Airport symbol] (OAG) .... MYJ
Matsuyama [Japan ICAO location identifier] (ICLI) .... RJOM
Matt Art [Paper] (DGA) .... MA
Matt Dillon Fan Club (EA) .... MDFC
Mattachine Society of New York [Defunct] (EA) .... MSNY
Mattagami Band Public Library, Gogama, Ontario [Library symbol National
  Library of Canada] (NLC) .... OGMB
Mattamuskeet National Wildlife Refuge [North Carolina] (AD) .... MNWR
Mattatuck Museum of the Mattatuck Historical Society, Waterbury, CT
  [Library symbol] [Library of Congress] (LCLS) .... CtWMHi
Mattawa Public Library, Ontario [Library symbol National Library of Canada]
  (NLC) .... OMATT
Matte One Side [Aluminum] M1S
Matte Two Sides [Aluminum] M2S
Mattel, Inc. [NYSE symbol] (SPSG) .... MAT
Mattel, Inc. [Associated Press] (SAG) .... Mattel

Matter (ROG) ... MRE
[*A*] **Matter of Crime** [*Novel by Matthew Bruccoli*] ... AMOC
[*A*] **Matter of Fact** [*Pierian Press, Inc.*] [*Information service or system*] (IID) ... AMOF
Matter of Public Importance (ADA) ... MPI
Matter-Anti-Matter (PDAA) ... MAM
Mattes [*Quality of the bottom*] [*Nautical charts*] ... Ma
Matteson Public Library, Matteson, IL [*Library symbol Library of Congress*] (LCLS) ... IMatt
Matt-Finish Structural Facing Units [*Technical drawings*] ... MFSFU
Matthaeus de Afflictis [*Deceased, 1528*] [*Authority cited in pre-1607 legal work*] (DSA) ... Mathe de Afflcti
Matthaeus de Afflictis [*Deceased, 1528*] [*Authority cited in pre-1607 legal work*] (DSA) ... Matthe de Affli
Matthaeus Gribaldus [*Deceased, 1564*] [*Authority cited in pre-1607 legal work*] (DSA) ... Matth Gribal
Matthaeus Nerutius [*Flourished, 16th century*] [*Authority cited in pre-1607 legal work*] (DSA) ... Math N
Mattheus de Mathesillanis [*Flourished, 1381-1402*] [*Authority cited in pre-1607 legal work*] (DSA) ... Mat
Matthew [*New Testament book*] ... MAT
Matthew [*New Testament book*] ... Matt
Matthew [*New Testament book*] ... Mt
Matthew and Bangs' Illinois Circuit Court Reports [*A publication*] (DLA) ... Ill CC
Matthew Arnold [*English poet, 1822-1888*] [*Initial used as pseudonym*] ... A
Matthew Paris. Historia Minor [*A publication*] (DLA) ... Mat Par
Matthew Paris. Historia Minor [*A publication*] (DLA) ... Mat Paris
Matthew Pelosi [*Designer's mark when appearing on US coins*] ... MP
Matthew Town, Great Inagua Island [*Bahamas*] [*ICAO location identifier*] (ICLI) ... MYIG
Matthews' Digest of Criminal Law [*A publication*] (DLA) ... Matth Cr L
Matthews' Executors and Administrators [*2nd ed.*] [*1839*] [*A publication*] (DLA) ... Matth Exe
Matthews' Guide to Commissioner in Chancery [*A publication*] (DLA) ... Matth Com
Matthews International Corp. [*Associated Press*] (SAG) ... MatthwInt
Matthews International Corp. [*NASDAQ symbol*] (SAG) ... MATW
Matthews Intl. 'A' [*NASDAQ symbol*] (TTSB) ... MATW
Matthews on Partnership [*A publication*] (DLA) ... Matth Part
Matthews on Presumptive Evidence [*A publication*] (DLA) ... Matth Pr Ev
Matthews Public Library, Matthews, IN [*Library symbol Library of Congress*] (LCLS) ... InMat
Matthews' Reports [*6-9 West Virginia*] [*A publication*] (DLA) ... Matthews
Matthews' Reports [*75 Virginia*] [*A publication*] (DLA) ... Matthews
Matthews Ridge [*Guyana*] [*Airport symbol*] (OAG) ... MWJ
Matthews Ridge [*Guyana*] [*ICAO location identifier*] (ICLI) ... SYMR
Matthews Studio Equipment Group [*NASDAQ symbol*] (NQ) ... MATT
Matthews Studio Equipment Group [*Associated Press*] (SAG) ... MatthwSt
Matthias M. Hoffman Public Library, Dyersville, IA [*Library symbol Library of Congress*] (LCLS) ... IaDy
Mattice-Val Cote Public Library, Mattice, Ontario [*Library symbol National Library of Canada*] (BIB) ... OMVC
Mattis Dementia Rating Scale [*Medicine*] (DMAA) ... MDRS
Mattituck Free Library, Mattituck, NY [*Library symbol Library of Congress*] (LCLS) ... NMat
Mattoon [*Illinois*] [*Airport symbol*] (OAG) ... MTO
Mattoon, IL [*AM radio station call letters*] ... WLBH
Mattoon, IL [*FM radio station call letters*] ... WLBH-FM
Mattoon, IL [*FM radio station call letters*] ... WLKL
Mattoon, IL [*FM radio station call letters*] ... WMCI
Mattoon Public Library, Mattoon, IL [*Library symbol*] [*Library of Congress*] (LCLS) ... IMat
Mattress ... MATRS
Mattress (MSA) ... MTRS
Mattress and Palliasse Makers' Society [*A union*] [*British*] ... MPMS
Mattson Technology [*NASDAQ symbol*] (TTSB) ... MTSN
Mattson Technology, Inc. [*Associated Press*] (SAG) ... Mattson
Mattson Technology, Inc. [*NASDAQ symbol*] (SAG) ... MTSN
Matua [*Former USSR Seismograph station code, US Geological Survey*] (SEIS) ... MAU
Matupit Island [*New Britain*] [*Seismograph station code, US Geological Survey*] (SEIS) ... MPT
Maturation Index (MAE) ... MI
Maturational Age [*Also, Development Age*] [*Medical term*] (PAZ) ... MA
Maturation-Inducing Substance [*Endocrinology*] ... MIS
Maturation-Promoting Factor [*Cytology*] ... MPF
Mature ... M
Mature Adult [*Film and video classification*] ... MA
Mature Age Allowance ... MAA
Mature Age Student (ADA) ... MAS
Mature Audiences [*Movie rating*] [*Replaced by GP*] ... M
Mature Australia [*An association*] ... MA
Mature Equivalent (OA) ... ME
Mature Market Institute [*An association Defunct*] (EA) ... MMI
Mature Motion Pictures (AD) ... Ms
Mature Outlook (EA) ... MO
Mature Students' Association [*British*] (BI) ... MSA
Mature Upwardly Mobile Mommy [*Lifestyle classification*] ... Mummy
Matured ... MAT
Matured Bonds [*Investment term*] (DFIT) ... M
Mature-Onset Diabetes Mellitus (MAE) ... MODM
Maturin [*Venezuela*] [*Airport symbol*] (OAG) ... MUN
Maturin/Internacional, Monagas [*Venezuela ICAO location identifier*] (ICLI) ... SVMT
Maturity ... MAT
Maturity [*Business term*] ... MTY
Maturity Date [*Banking*] ... MD
Maturity News Service ... MNS
Maturity Onset Diabetes [*Medicine*] ... MOD
Maturity Onset Diabetes of the Young [*Medicine*] (DMAA) ... MODY
Maturity Phase ... MP
Matutinal (ADA) ... MAT
Matutinus [*In the Morning*] [*Pharmacy*] ... MATUT
Matzner Suburban Newspapers, Wayne, NJ [*Library symbol Library of Congress*] (LCLS) ... NjWMN
Maubeuge/Elesmes [*France ICAO location identifier*] (ICLI) ... LFQJ
Maubois, Mocquot, and Vassal [*Cheesemaking*] ... MMV
Maude and Pollock's Law of Merchant Shipping [*A publication*] (DLA) ... M & P Sh
Maude and Pollock's Law of Merchant Shipping [*A publication*] (DLA) ... Mau & Pol Sh
Maude and Pollock's Law of Merchant Shipping [*A publication*] (DLA) ... Maude & P
Maude and Pollock's Law of Merchant Shipping [*A publication*] (DLA) ... Maude & P Mer Shipp
Maude and Pollock's Law of Merchant Shipping [*A publication*] (DLA) ... Maude & P Shipp
Maude Shunk Public Library, Menomonee Falls, WI [*OCLC symbol*] (OCLC) ... WMF
Maudsley on Mental Responsibility [*A publication*] (DLA) ... Maud Ment Res
Maudsley Personality Inventory [*Psychology*] ... MPI
Maues [*Brazil*] [*Airport symbol*] (AD) ... MBZ
Maugham's Attorneys, Solicitors, and Agents [*1825*] [*A publication*] (DLA) ... Maug Att
Maugham's Literary Property [*1828*] [*A publication*] (DLA) ... Maugh Lit Pr
Maugham's Outlines of Criminal Law [*2nd ed.*] [*1842*] [*A publication*] (DLA) ... Maug Cr L
Maugham's Outlines of Law [*1837*] [*A publication*] (DLA) ... Maug Law
Maugham's Outlines of Real Property Law [*1842*] [*A publication*] (DLA) ... Maugh RP
Maugham's Outlines of the Jurisdiction [*1838*] [*A publication*] (DLA) ... Maug Jur
Maugham's Statutes Relating to Attorneys, Etc. [*1839*] [*A publication*] (DLA) ... Maug Att
Maui Airlines, Inc. [*ICAO designator*] (FAAC) ... OWL
Maui Community College [*Hawaii*] ... MCC
Maui County Free Library, Wailuku, HI [*Library symbol Library of Congress*] (LCLS) ... HWM
Maui Optical Tracking and Identification Facility [*Hawaii*] [*Air Force*] ... MOTIF
Maui Volcanic Complex [*Geology*] ... MVC
Mauke [*Cook Islands*] [*Airport symbol*] (OAG) ... MUK
Mauke [*Cook Islands*] [*ICAO location identifier*] (ICLI) ... NCMK
Maule Aircraft Corp. [*ICAO aircraft manufacturer identifier*] (ICAO) ... ML
Maule and Selwyn's English King's Bench Reports [*A publication*] (DLA) ... M & S
Maule and Selwyn's English King's Bench Reports [*A publication*] (DLA) ... Mau & Sel
Maule and Selwyn's English King's Bench Reports [*A publication*] (DLA) ... Maul & Sel
Maule and Selwyn's English King's Bench Reports [*A publication*] (DLA) ... Maule & S
Mauler Feasibility Validation Program ... MFVP
Mauler Seeker Head ... MSH
Maumee, OH [*FM radio station call letters*] ... WYSZ
Maumelle, AR [*FM radio station call letters*] ... KOLL
Maumere [*Indonesia*] [*Airport symbol*] (OAG) ... MOF
Maumere/Wai Oti [*Indonesia*] [*ICAO location identifier*] (ICLI) ... WRKC
Maun [*Botswana*] [*ICAO location identifier*] (ICLI) ... FBMN
Maun [*Botswana*] [*Airport symbol*] (OAG) ... MUB
Mauna Kea [*Hawaii*] [*Seismograph station code, US Geological Survey*] (SEIS) ... MKH
Mauna Kea Observatory [*Hawaii*] (BARN) ... MKO
Mauna Loa [*Hawaii*] [*Seismograph station code, US Geological Survey*] (SEIS) ... MLH
Mauna Loa 2 [*Hawaii*] [*Seismograph station code, US Geological Survey*] (SEIS) ... MLX
Mauna Loa Macadamia Partners Ltd. [*Associated Press*] (SAG) ... MauLoa
Mauna Loa Macadamia Partners LP [*NYSE symbol*] (SPSG) ... NUT
Mauna Loa Macadamia'A' [*NYSE symbol*] (TTSB) ... NUT
Mauna Loa Observatory [*Hawaii*] [*National Weather Service*] ... MLO
Mauna Olu College [*Maui*] (AD) ... MOC
Maunawili, HI [*AM radio station call letters*] ... KULA
Maupiti [*French Polynesia*] [*Airport symbol*] (OAG) ... MAU
Maupiti [*French Polynesia*] [*ICAO location identifier*] (ICLI) ... NTTP
Maurer, B. B., Chicago IL [*STAC*] ... MBB
Maurer Kunst Geselle [*Fellowcraft*] [*Freemasonry*] [*German*] ... MKG
Maurice, LA [*FM radio station call letters*] ... KFXZ
Maurice Lamontagne Institute, Fisheries and Oceans Canada [*Institut Maurice Lamontagne, Peches et Oceans Canada*], Mont-Joli, Quebec [*Library symbol National Library of Canada*] (NLC) ... QQPSM
Maurice Rose [*Germany ICAO location identifier*] (ICLI) ... EDEN
Maurice-Farman [*British military*] (DMA) ... MF
Mauricio [*Mauritius*] [*Spanish*] (AD) ... Mrc
Mauricius [*Authority cited in pre-1607 legal work*] (DSA) ... Mau
Mauritania [*MARC geographic area code Library of Congress*] (LCCP) ... f-mu--
Mauritania ... Maur
Mauritania ... Maurit
Mauritania (VRA) ... Maurti
Mauritania [*ANSI two-letter standard code*] (CNC) ... MR
Mauritania [*ANSI three-letter standard code*] (CNC) ... MRT
Mauritania [*MARC country of publication code Library of Congress*] (LCCP) ... mu

Mauritania [*International vehicle registration*] (ODBW) .... RIM
Mauritanian Party for Renewal [*Political party*] (EY) .... MPR
Mauritian Socialist Movement [*Political party*] .... MSM
Mauritius [*Aircraft nationality and registration mark*] (FAAC) 3B
Mauritius [*MARC geographic area code Library of Congress*] (LCCP) .... i-mf--
Mauritius (ROG) .... MAU
Mauritius .... Maur
Mauritius [*MARC country of publication code Library of Congress*] (LCCP) .... mf
Mauritius (AD) .... Mrts
Mauritius [*Airport symbol*] (OAG) .... MRU
Mauritius .... MS
Mauritius [*ANSI two-letter standard code*] (CNC) .... MU
Mauritius [*ANSI three-letter standard code*] (CNC) .... MUS
Mauritius Decisions [*A publication*] (DLA) .... Maur Dec
Mauritius Decisions [*A publication*] (DLA) .... MR
Mauritius Flight Information Center [*ICAO location identifier*] (ICLI) .... FIMM
Mauritius Freeport Authority .... MFA
Mauritius Island [*Mascarene Islands*] [*Seismograph station code, US Geological Survey Closed*] (SEIS) .... MRI
Mauritius Labor Party [*Political party*] (PPW) .... MLP
Mauritius Law Reporter [*A publication*] (DLA) .... MLR
Mauritius Reports [*A publication*] (DLA) .... MR
Mauritius Reports, by Bruzard [*1842-45*] [*A publication*] (DLA) .... Bruzard
Mauritius/Sir Seewoosagur Ramgoolam International [*ICAO location identifier*] (ICLI) .... FIMP
Mauritius Rupee [*Monetary unit*] (AD) .... M rps
Maury Center for Ocean Science [*Washington, DC*] .... MC
Mauser Rifle .... MAUS
Mausoleum (VRA) .... mauso
Mauston Public Library, Mauston, WI [*Library symbol Library of Congress*] (LCLS) .... WMau
Mauston, WI [*AM radio station call letters*] .... WRJC
Mauston, WI [*FM radio station call letters*] .... WRJC-FM
Mauthner [*Cell*] [*Neurology*] .... M
Mauve [*Philately*] (ROG) .... MV
Mauve [*Philately*] (ROG) .... MVE
Maverick Interim Report .... MIR
Maverick Naturalite Beef Corp. [*Vancouver Stock Exchange symbol*] .... MNB
Maverick Tube [*NASDAQ symbol*] (TTSB) .... MAVK
Maverick Tube Corp. [*NASDAQ symbol*] (SAG) .... MAVK
Maverick Tube Corp. [*Associated Press*] (SAG) .... MavTube
Mavesa SA ADS [*NYSE symbol*] (SAG) .... MAV
Mavesa SA ADS [*Associated Press*] (SAG) .... Mavesa
Mavinza [*Congo*] [*ICAO location identifier*] (ICLI) .... FCMA
Mavis, Paul A., South Bend IN [*STAC*] .... MPL
Mavtech Holdings, Inc. [*Toronto Stock Exchange symbol*] .... MGI
Mawashi [*Ryukyu Islands*] [*Seismograph station code, US Geological Survey Closed*] (SEIS) .... MWS
Mawson [*Antarctica*] [*Seismograph station code, US Geological Survey*] (SEIS) .... MAW
Max & Erma's Restaurants [*NASDAQ symbol*] (TTSB) .... MAXE
Max & Erma's Restaurants, Inc. [*NASDAQ symbol*] (NQ) .... MAXE
Max & Erma's Restaurants, Inc. [*Associated Press*] (SAG) .... MaxEr
Max Minerals, Inc. [*Vancouver Stock Exchange symbol*] .... MXS
Max Planck Institute (AD) .... MPI
Max Sea Food SA de CV [*El Salvador*] [*ICAO designator*] (FAAC) .... MSF
Max Steiner Memorial Society (EA) .... MSMS
Max-Aviation [*Canada ICAO designator*] (FAAC) .... MAV
Max-Aviation [*Canada*] [*FAA designator*] (FAAC) .... MAX
Maxco, Inc. [*NASDAQ symbol*] (NQ) .... MAXC
Maxco, Inc. [*Associated Press*] (SAG) .... Maxco
Maxey Flats, Kentucky [*Commercial waste site*] (GAAI) .... MFKY
Maxey Flats Radioactive Protective Association (EA) .... MFRPA
Maxfield-Buchholz Scale of Social Maturity [*Psychology*] .... MBSSM
Maxicare Health Plans [*NASDAQ symbol*] (TTSB) .... MAXI
Maxicare Health Plans, Inc. [*Associated Press*] (SAG) .... MaxcrHlt
Maxicare Health Plans, Inc. [*NASDAQ symbol*] (NQ) .... MAXI
Maxilla [*Jawbone*] .... MAX
Maxillary Mandibular Odentectomy Alveolectomy [*Dentistry*] (DAVI) .... MMOA
Maxillary Nerve [*Neuroanatomy*] .... MxN
Maxillary Process .... MP
Maxillofacial Prosthesis Laboratory [*WRAMC*] (RDA) .... MPL
Maxillofacial Surgery [*Medical specialty*] (DHSM) .... MFS
Maxim (ROG) .... MAX
Maxim Development Ltd. [*Vancouver Stock Exchange symbol*] .... MDV
Maxim Group [*Associated Press*] (SAG) .... MaximGp
Maxim Group [*NASDAQ symbol*] (SAG) .... MAXM
Maxim Integrated Prod [*NASDAQ symbol*] (TTSB) .... MXIM
Maxim Integrated Products, Inc. [*Associated Press*] (SAG) .... Maxim
Maxim Integrated Products, Inc. [*NASDAQ symbol*] (NQ) .... MXIM
Maxim Nordenfelt Gun .... MN
Maxim Pharmaceuticals, Inc. [*Associated Press*] (SAG) .... MaximPh
Maxim Pharmaceuticals, Inc. [*Associated Press*] (SAG) .... MaxmP
Maxim Pharmaceuticals, Inc. [*AMEX symbol*] (SAG) .... MMP
Maxima (WDAA) .... MAX
Maximal [*or Maximum*] [*Medicine*] .... M
Maximal Acceptable Load (PDAA) .... MAL
Maximal Aerobic Power [*Laboratory*] (DAVI) .... MAP
Maximal Compatible Set (PDAA) .... MCS
Maximal Contraction Force [*Myology*] .... MCF
Maximal Credible Accident [*Nuclear technology*] .... MCA
Maximal Electroconvulsive Seizure [*Neurophysiology*] .... MECS
Maximal Electroshock [*Physiology*] .... MES
Maximal Esophageal Pressure [*Medicine*] (MAE) .... Max EP
Maximal Exercise Testing .... MEXT
Maximal Expiratory Flow [*Medicine*] .... MEF
Maximal Expiratory Flow Static Recoil Curve [*Medicine*] (MAE) .... MEFSR
Maximal Expiratory Flow Volume [*Medicine*] (AAMN) .... MEFV
Maximal Forced Expiratory Maneuver [*Medicine*] (DAVI) .... MFEM
Maximal Glucose Disposal [*Medicine*] (DMAA) .... MGD
Maximal Inspiratory Flow [*Medicine*] .... MIF
Maximal Inspiratory Flow Rate [*Medicine*] .... MIFR
Maximal left Atrial [*Dimension*] [*Cardiology*] (DAVI) .... LA-MAX
Maximal Midexpiratory Flow [*Also, MMF*] [*Medicine*] .... MMEF
Maximal Midexpiratory Flow Rate [*Medicine*] .... MMEFR
Maximal Midflow Rate [*Medicine*] (MAE) .... MMFR
Maximal Permitted Intake [*Medicine*] .... MPI
Maximal Principle Least Squares .... MPLS
Maximal Relative Error [*Mathematical statistics*] .... MRE
Maximal Relaxation Rate [*Medicine*] .... MRR
Maximal Renal Tubular Excretory Capacity [*Medicine*] (DAVI) .... Tm
Maximal Response .... MR
Maximal Sustained Level of Ventilation [*Medicine*] .... MSV
Maximal Temperature of the Synthesis Reaction [*Chemical engineering*] .... MTSR
Maximal Therapy [*Medicine*] .... MT
Maximal Treadmill Exercise Test .... MTET
Maximal Treadmill Test (CPH) .... MTT
Maximal Ventilation Time [*Medicine*] (DAVI) .... MVT
Maximal Ventilatory Volume (MAE) .... MVV_1
Maximal Voluntary Contraction .... MVC
Maximally Exposed Individual .... MEI
Maximally Flat Magnitude .... MFM
Maximally Restrictive Verifiable Test Ban [*For nuclear bombs*] .... MRVTB
Maximilian Numismatic and Historical Society (EA) .... MAX
Maximinus [*of Scriptores Historiae Augustae*] [*Classical studies*] (OCD) .... Max
Maximization of Expected Maximum Profit [*Econometrics*] .... MEMP
Maximize Indefinite Delivery Contracts (AFM) .... MAXID
Maximized LOD [*Logarithm of the Odds*] **Score** [*Statistics*] .... MLS
Maximized Relative Likelihood (PDAA) .... MRL
Maxims Appended to Lofft's Reports [*A publication*] (DLA) .... Lofft Max
Maxims of the Laws of England, by William Noye [*A publication*] (DLA) .... Noye's Max
Maximum .... MAX
Maximum (WDMC) .... max
Maximum (ADA) .... MXM
Maximum A Posteriori [*Statistics*] .... MAP
Maximum Absolute Percentage Error [*Statistics*] .... MAPE
Maximum Acceptable Deviation .... MAD
Maximum Acceptable Tolerance Concentration (GNE) .... MATC
Maximum Acceptable Toxicant Concentration .... MATC
Maximum Acceptance Quantity .... MAQ
Maximum Achievable Body Burden (PDAA) .... MABB
Maximum Achievable [*or Available*] **Control Technology** [*Environmental chemistry*] .... MACT
Maximum Acid Concentration [*Clinical chemistry*] .... MAC
Maximum Acid Output [*Biochemistry*] (DAVI) .... MAD
Maximum [*or Minimum*] **Acid Output** [*Clinical chemistry*] .... MAO
Maximum Admissible [*or Allowable*] **Concentration** .... MAC
Maximum Aerobic Speed [*Biology*] .... MAS
Maximum Aggregate Student Number [*Higher Education Funding Council*] (AIE) .... MASN
Maximum Allowable Actual Charge [*Medicare*] .... MAAC
Maximum Allowable Concentration [*Toxicology*] .... MAC
Maximum Allowable Cost [*Medicare, Medicaid*] .... MAC
Maximum Allowable Emission Rate [*Environmental Protection Agency*] (ERG) .... MAER
Maximum Allowable Housing Cost [*Army*] (AABC) .... MAHC
Maximum Allowable Increase [*Environmental Protection Agency*] .... MAI
Maximum Allowable Operating Pressure [*In pipelines*] .... MAOP
Maximum Allowable Operating Time (NASA) .... MAOT
Maximum Allowable Percent Defective (PDAA) .... MAPD
Maximum Allowable Pevailing Charge [*Medicine*] .... MAPC
Maximum Allowable Variation [*Net weight labeling*] .... MAV
Maximum Allowable Weight [*Military*] (INF) .... MAW
Maximum Allowable Working Pressure (PDAA) .... MAWP
Maximum Alternate Gross Weight .... MAGW
Maximum Amplitude Filter .... MAF
Maximum and Minimum (KSC) .... M/M
Maximum Androgen Blockade [*Oncology*] .... MAB
Maximum Annual Rate of Return [*Finance*] .... MARR
Maximum Applicable Dose [*Environmental chemistry*] .... MAD
Maximum Approximate Conditional Likelihood [*Statistics*] .... MACL
Maximum Asset Return Strategy [*Allingham, Anderson, Roll & Ross*] [*British*] (ECON) .... MARS
Maximum Atmospheric Concentration .... MAC
Maximum Authorized Altitude [*Aviation*] .... MAA
Maximum Authorized for Repair Parts (DNAB) .... MARP
Maximum Available Gain (IAA) .... MAG
Maximum Available Power Gain (MSA) .... MAPG
Maximum Average Planar Linear Heat-Generation Rate [*Nuclear energy*] (NRCH) .... MAPLHGR
Maximum Average Planar Linear Heat-Generator [*Nuclear energy*] (IAA) .... MAPLHGN
Maximum Average Price .... MAP
Maximum Base Rent .... MBR
Maximum Beam [*IOR*] .... BMAX
Maximum Benefit Amount [*Unemployment insurance*] .... MBA
Maximum Benefit Level [*Health insurance*] (GHCT) .... MBL
Maximum Boiling Point .... MBP
Maximum Breathing Capacity .... MBC

Maximum Calling Area Indicator (DNAB) .... MCAI
Maximum Capability Envelope .... MCE
Maximum Capacitance (IDOE) .... C_{max}
Maximum Card Study Unit (EA) .... MCSU
Maximum Care Unit [*Medicine*] .... MCU
Maximum Ceiling Absolute [*Aerospace*] (AAG) .... MCA
Maximum Certificated Gross Weight (MCD) .... MCGW
Maximum Clearance (AAMN) .... Cm
Maximum Climb Thrust (NASA) .... MCT
Maximum Column [*Computer science*] (PCM) .... MAXCOL
Maximum Combat Readiness [*Military*] .... MCR
Maximum Concentration .... MC
Maximum Contaminant Level .... MCL
Maximum Contaminant Level Goal [*Environmental Protection Agency*] .... MCLG
Maximum Contaminant Levels .... MCL
Maximum Continuous Power .... MCP
Maximum Continuous Rating [*Also, MC(S)R*] [*Mechanical engineering*] .... MCR
Maximum Continuous (Service) Rating [*Also, MCR*] [*Mechanical engineering*] .... MC(S)R
Maximum Continuous Thrust [*Aviation*] .... MCT
Maximum Count Output (IAA) .... MC
Maximum Credible Accident [*Nuclear energy*] (NRCH) .... MCA
Maximum Critical Power Ratio [*Nuclear energy*] (NRCH) .... MCPR
Maximum Crossing Altitude (MCD) .... MCA
Maximum Crossing Altitude .... MCA
Maximum Cruise Level Thrust (MCD) .... MCLT
Maximum Deductible Contribution [*Superannuation*] .... MDC
Maximum Deficit Amount [*Office of Management and Budget*] (GFGA) .... MDA
Maximum Degree Allowed to Fit .... MD
Maximum Degree of Emissions Reduction Deemed Achievable [*Environmental Protection Agency*] .... MDERDA
Maximum Demand (IAA) .... MD
Maximum Demographic Appeal [*Objective of commercial television programming*] .... MDA
Maximum Density Fuming Nitric Acid .... MDFNA
Maximum Density Nitric Acid .... MDNA
Maximum Dependable Capacity [*Nuclear energy*] (NRCH) .... MDC
Maximum Depth (NOAA) .... MXDTH
Maximum Depth of Colonization [*Botany*] .... MDC
Maximum Design Meter .... MD
Maximum Design Meter (MSA) .... MDM
Maximum Design Operating Pressure [*NASA*] .... MDOP
Maximum Detachable Activity [*Nuclear energy*] (NUCP) .... MDA
Maximum Diameter Heat [*Nuclear science*] (OA) .... MDH
Maximum Diastolic Potential [*Physiology*] .... MDP
Maximum Disclosure / Minimum Delay (DNAB) .... MAX/MIN
Maximum Dissolved Solids Nebulizer [*Product of Applied Research Laboratories*] .... MDSN
Maximum Dive Time .... MDT
Maximum Dynamic Pressure (NASA) .... MAXCO
Maximum Economic Finding Cost .... MEFC
Maximum Economic Justification .... MEJ
Maximum Economic Potential .... MEP
Maximum Economic Yield [*Fishery management*] (MSC) .... MEY
Maximum Effective Echo Ranging Speed (NVT) .... MEERS
Maximum Effective Range .... MER
Maximum Effective SONAR Speed (NVT) .... MESS
Maximum Efficiency Structural System (IAA) .... MESS
Maximum Efficient Rate [*Oil*] .... MER
Maximum Effort .... ME
Maximum Electroshock Seizure [*Medicine*] .... MES
Maximum Endurable Concentration (NATG) .... MEC
Maximum Energy .... ME
Maximum Energy Distribution Function .... MEDF
Maximum Energy Recovery [*Chemical engineering*] .... MER
Maximum Engagement Line [*Military*] (INF) .... MEL
Maximum Engine Operating Pressure .... MEOP
Maximum Engine Takeoff [*Power*] [*Air Force*] .... METO
Maximum Engine Thrust for Two-Engine Climb (GAVI) .... MAX CLB
Maximum Engine Thrust for Two-Engine Cruise (GAVI) .... MAX CRZ
Maximum Entropy Method [*Geomagnetism*] [*Computer science*] .... MEM
Maximum Entropy Noise Deconvolution [*Statistics*] .... MEND
Maximum Entropy Principle (PDAA) .... MEP
Maximum Entropy Spectrum Analysis .... MESA
Maximum Escape Performance [*Ejection seat*] (MCD) .... MEP
Maximum Except during Takeoff .... METO
Maximum Excess Loss .... MEL
Maximum Expected Operating Pressure .... MEOP
Maximum Expected Operating Value [*FCC*] .... MEOV
Maximum Expected Takeoff Power (AFM) .... METOP
Maximum Expenditure Limit (MCD) .... MEL
Maximum Experimental Safe Gap (IEEE) .... MESG
Maximum Expiratory Flow Rate [*Medicine*] .... MEFR
Maximum Exposed Individual [*Health risk assessment*] [*Environmental Protection Agency*] .... MEI
Maximum Exposed Individual (GNE) .... MEI
Maximum Exposure Limit [*Hazardous material control*] .... MEL
Maximum Flat Control System .... MFCS
Maximum Flat Envelope Delay .... MFED
Maximum Flight Rate (NASA) .... MFR
Maximum Flow Per Unit of Time [*Respiratory*] (DAVI) .... V_{Emax}
Maximum Flowering Day [*Botany*] .... MF
Maximum Flowering Period [*Botany*] .... MP
Maximum Fluoride Protection [*Colgate-Palmolive Co.*] .... MFP
Maximum Foreseeable Loss [*Insurance*] .... MFL
Maximum Forward Voltage Drop .... MFVD
Maximum Freezing Point .... MFP
Maximum Frequency Difference [*Statistics*] .... MFD
Maximum Gapless Coverage Distance (NG) .... MGCD
Maximum Girth [*Pisciculture*] .... MAXG
Maximum Gross Weight (WDAA) .... MGW
Maximum Heart Rate .... MHR
Maximum Height [*Ballistics*] .... MH
Maximum Histalog Stimulation [*Gastroenterology*] (DAVI) .... MHS
Maximum Hospital Benefit [*Medicine*] (DMAA) .... MHB
Maximum Hypothetical Accident [*Nuclear energy*] (IEEE) .... MHA
Maximum Hypothetical Fission Product Release [*Nuclear energy*] (NRCH) .... MHFPR
Maximum Hypothetical Fission Product Release [*Nuclear energy*] (NRCH) .... MHFR
Maximum Improvement in Electronics Effectiveness through Advanced Techniques .... MEETA
Maximum Improvement in Electronics Effectiveness through Advanced Techniques .... MEETAT
Maximum Incremental Reactivity [*Exhaust emissions*] [*Automotive engineering*] .... MIR
Maximum Individual Risk [*Environmental science*] (FFDE) .... MIR
Maximum Inhibiting Dilution [*Medicine*] (MAE) .... MID
Maximum Inhibiting Duration [*Medicine*] (DAVI) .... MID
Maximum Inscribed Circle [*Manufacturing term*] .... MIC
Maximum Inspiratory Pressure [*Medicine*] .... MIP
Maximum Interchange of the Latest Logistic Information Is Essential .... MILLIE
Maximum Interference Threshold [*Telecommunications*] (TEL) .... MAXIT
Maximum Isothermal System Temperature [*Nuclear energy*] (NRCH) .... MIST
Maximum Junction Field (IDOE) .... E_m
Maximum Landing Gear of Operating Speed (GAVI) .... VLO
Maximum Landing Gear Operating Speed [*Aviation code*] (AIA) .... VLG
Maximum Landing Gross Weight .... MLGW
Maximum Landing Weight [*Aviation*] (DA) .... Mlnd
Maximum Landing Weight [*Aviation*] .... MLW
Maximum Landing Weight Authorized [*Aviation*] (DA) .... MLWA
Maximum Lateral Damage (PDAA) .... MLD
Maximum Left Ventricular Developed Pressure [*Cardiology*] (DMAA) .... MLVDP
Maximum Lethal Time [*of radiation exposure*] (DEN) .... MLT
Maximum Life-Span .... MLS
Maximum Likelihood [*Statistics*] .... ML
Maximum Likelihood Detection (MCD) .... MLD
Maximum Likelihood Estimate [*or Estimator*] [*Statistics*] .... MLE
Maximum Likelihood Estimator Deconvolution [*Statistics*] .... MLED
Maximum Likelihood Method [*Statistics*] .... MLM
Maximum Likelihood Predictive Density [*Statistics*] .... MLPD
Maximum Likelihood Program .... MLP
Maximum Linear Heat Generation Ratio (NRCH) .... MLHGR
Maximum Load Factor .... MLF
Maximum Loss Expectancy [*Insurance*] .... MLE
Maximum Lung Volume [*Physiology*] .... MLV
Maximum Maintenance Effort [*Military*] (AFM) .... MME
Maximum Material Condition .... MMC
Maximum Metal Concept .... MMC
Maximum Metal Condition (IEEE) .... MMC
Maximum Midexpiratory Flow [*Also, MMEF*] [*Medicine*] .... MMF
Maximum Midexpiratory Flow Rate [*Medicine*] (DAVI) .... MEFR
Maximum Midexpiratory Flow Rate [*Physiology*] .... MMFR
Maximum Minimum Temperature System .... MMTS
Maximum Miscibility Composition [*Physical chemistry*] .... MMC
Maximum Mixing Depths [*Meteorology*] .... MMD
Maximum Mobile Army .... MAXMAR
Maximum Negative Pressure [*Nuclear energy*] (NRCH) .... MNP
Maximum Noise Area .... MNA
Maximum Number of Records (MHDB) .... MNR
Maximum Number of Runs (MCD) .... MAXNOR
Maximum Observed Frequency [*Radio*] .... MOF
Maximum Observed Frequency (AD) .... mof
Maximum Obtainable Irradiance (AD) .... moi
Maximum Obtainable Irradiance .... MOI
Maximum Operating Frequency .... MOF
Maximum Operating Hours (MCD) .... MOH
Maximum Operating Hours (AD) .... moh
Maximum Operating Level .... MOL
Maximum Operating Mach Number [*Aviation*] (DA) .... M_{mo}
Maximum Operating Pressure Differential (ECII) .... MOPD
Maximum Operating Speed (MCD) .... VMO
Maximum Operating Time (NG) .... MOT
Maximum Operational Capacity [*Chemical engineering*] .... MOC
Maximum Order Limitation (AAGC) .... MOL
Maximum Output Entropy (PDAA) .... MOE
Maximum [*Rate*] **Output Initiator** .... MOPI
Maximum Output Level .... MOL
Maximum Output Level (AD) .... mol
Maximum Overall Length (DAC) .... MOL
Maximum Oxygen Consumption .... MOC
Maximum Oxygen Uptake .... MOU
Maximum Ozone Incremental Reactivity [*Environmental science*] .... MOIR
Maximum Ozone Reactivity [*Exhaust emissions*] [*Automotive engineering*] .... MOR
Maximum Packing Depth (NG) .... MPD
Maximum Pain Intensity Difference [*Medicine*] .... MAXPID
Maximum Pain Relief [*Medicine*] .... MAXPAR
Maximum Participation Base (IIA) .... MPB
Maximum Payload (AD) .... m payl
Maximum Payload (AD) .... mpl

Maximum Penalized-Likelihood [*Statistics*] ..... MPL
Maximum Penalty ..... MAXPEN
Maximum Performance [*Automotive engineering*] ..... M/P
Maximum Performance Ejection Seat [*Navy*] ..... MPES
Maximum Performance Escape System (MCD) ..... MPS
Maximum Perfusion Pressure [*Cardiology*] (DAVI) ..... MPP
Maximum Permissible Accumulated Dose [*of radiation*] (ADA) ..... MPAD
Maximum Permissible Annual Dose (AD) ..... mpad
Maximum Permissible Annual Intake (AD) ..... mpai
Maximum Permissible Annual Intake [*Radiation*] (NRCH) ..... MPAI
Maximum Permissible Body Burden [*Radiation*] ..... MPBB
Maximum Permissible Body Burden [*of Radiation*] (AD) ..... mpbb
Maximum Permissible Concentration (AD) ..... mpc
Maximum Permissible Concentration [*Later, RCG*] [*Radiation*] ..... MPC
Maximum Permissible Concentration of Unidentified Radionuclides (AD) ..... mpcur
Maximum Permissible Concentration of Unidentified Radionuclides in Water ..... MPCU
Maximum Permissible Contaminent Level (Goal) (GNE) ..... MPCL(G)
Maximum Permissible Dose [*Radiation*] ..... MPD
Maximum Permissible Dose (AD) ..... mpd
Maximum Permissible Dose Equivalent (ERG) ..... MPDE
Maximum Permissible Exposure [*Radiation*] ..... MPE
Maximum Permissible Exposure [*to Radiation*] (AD) ..... mpe
Maximum Permissible Exposure Levels [*Radiation*] ..... MPEL
Maximum Permissible Language (AD) ..... mpl
Maximum Permissible Level (AD) ..... mpl
Maximum Permissible Level [*Radiation*] (DEN) ..... MPL
Maximum Permissible Lung Burden [*Industrial hygiene*] ..... MPLB
Maximum Permitted Mileage [*Airlines*] ..... MPM
Maximum Pionization Method (OA) ..... MPM
Maximum Point of Impulse ..... MPI
Maximum Point of Impulse (AD) ..... mpi
Maximum Positive Pressure [*Nuclear energy*] (NRCH) ..... MPP
Maximum Possible Error ..... MPE
Maximum Possible Storm (NOAA) ..... MXPST
Maximum Potential Representation (MUGU) ..... MPR
Maximum Power Output ..... MPO
Maximum Power Point Tracking [*Power system*] ..... MPPT
Maximum Power Ratio (IEEE) ..... MAPRAT
Maximum Power Transfer (IDOE) ..... MPT
Maximum Practical Rate [*Aviation*] ..... MPR
Maximum Precipitation Intensity [*Meteorology*] (PDAA) ..... MPI
Maximum Predicted Heart Rate [*Cardiology*] ..... MPHR
Maximum Probability Ratio Sequential Test (PDAA) ..... MPRST
Maximum Probable Loss [*Insurance*] ..... MPL
Maximum Probable Property Damage [*Hazard analysis*] ..... MPPD
Maximum Procurement Level (AFIT) ..... MPL
Maximum Rainfall (NOAA) ..... MXRAN
Maximum Range (IAA) ..... MR
Maximum Rate of Rise [*Biometrics*] ..... MRR
Maximum Rate Output Initiator (NASA) ..... MOPI
Maximum Rated Power ..... MRP
Maximum Rated Standard Deviation [*Statistics*] ..... MRSD
Maximum Rated Thrust (MCD) ..... MRT
Maximum Recoil Pressure [*Medicine*] (DAVI) ..... TLC
Maximum Recommended Daily Human Dose (AD) ..... mrdhd
Maximum Recording Level ..... MRL
Maximum Release Quantity [*DoD*] ..... MRQ
Maximum Rendezvous Altitude ..... MRA
Maximum Repair Time (PDAA) ..... MRT
Maximum Residue Limit (PDAA) ..... MRL
Maximum Resolving Power ..... MRP
Maximum Resolving Power (AD) ..... mrp
Maximum Retail Price (AD) ..... mrp
Maximum Retail Price [*British*] ..... MRP
Maximum Retarding Force (NASA) ..... MRF
Maximum Reverse Current ..... MRC
Maximum Safe Sampling Volume [*Analytical chemistry*] ..... MSSV
Maximum Security Communications (IAA) ..... MAXSECOM
Maximum Security Communications ..... MAXSECON
Maximum Service Life [*or Limit*] (AAG) ..... MSL
Maximum Service Telecasters ..... MST
Maximum Shear Force ..... MSF
Maximum Shipping Weight [*MTMC*] (TAG) ..... MSW
Maximum Silo Price [*Farming terminology*] ..... MSP
Maximum Solute Concentration [*Chemistry*] (DAVI) ..... Umax
Maximum Sound Pressure ..... MSP
Maximum Space Charge Limited Emission (IAA) ..... MSCLE
Maximum Speed ..... MSPD
Maximum Speed Indicator ..... MSI
Maximum Speed to Extend or Retract Landing Gear [*Aviation code*] (AIA) ..... VLO
Maximum Stable Gain (IAA) ..... MSG
Maximum Steam Rate [*Nuclear energy*] (NRCH) ..... MSR
Maximum Stillwater Level [*Nuclear energy*] (NRCH) ..... MSL
Maximum Storage Bus Rate ..... MSBR
Maximum Stress ..... MS
Maximum Stress (AD) ..... ms
Maximum Structural Cruising Speed (GAVI) ..... VNO
Maximum Summer Temperature [*Climatology*] ..... MST
Maximum Sustainable Yield ..... MSY
Maximum System Operational Range ..... MSOR
Maximum Takeoff Gross Weight [*Aviation*] (MCD) ..... MTOGW
Maximum Takeoff Weight [*Aviation*] (MCD) ..... MTOW
Maximum Taxi Weight [*Aviation*] ..... MTW
Maximum Temperature (NOAA) ..... MXTMP
Maximum Temperature Engine ..... MTE
Maximum Temperature of Previous Heating [*Archaeology*] ..... MTPH
Maximum Terminal Flow (MAE) ..... MTF
Maximum Theoretical Bandwidth (MHDI) ..... MTB
Maximum Time [*Telecommunications*] (TEL) ..... TMAX
Maximum Time Out (MCD) ..... MTO
Maximum Time to Repair [*Navy*] (CAAL) ..... MAXTTR
Maximum Time to Repair (MCD) ..... MTTR
Maximum Time to Replace [*Navy*] (IAA) ..... MTTR
Maximum Tire Pressure (ADA) ..... MTP
Maximum Tolerable Concentration [*Toxicology*] ..... MTC
Maximum Tolerable Exposure Level [*Toxicology*] ..... MTEL
Maximum Tolerable Insecurity Level (OA) ..... MTIL
Maximum Tolerated Dose [*Medicine*] ..... MTD
Maximum Torque ..... MT
Maximum Torque ..... MTORQ
Maximum Total Duration Penalty ..... MAXTOP
Maximum Total Gross Weight (MCD) ..... MTGW
Maximum Total Peaking Factor [*Nuclear energy*] (NRCH) ..... MTPF
Maximum Total Trihalomethane Potential (EG) ..... MTP
Maximum Total Trihalomethane Potential (FFDE) ..... MTTP
Maximum Total Weight Authorized [*Aviation*] (AIA) ..... MTWA
Maximum Total Work Content ..... MAXTWK
Maximum Touch Temperature (MCD) ..... MTT
Maximum Toxic Concentration [*Medicine*] ..... MTC
Maximum Track Capacity ..... MTC
Maximum Tracking Error ..... MTE
Maximum Tracking Range ..... MTR
Maximum Undistorted Output ..... MUO
Maximum Undistorted Power Output (IAA) ..... MAXUPO
Maximum Undistorted Power Output ..... MUPO
Maximum Unilateral Gain (IAA) ..... MUG
Maximum Urinary Concentration [*Medicine*] ..... MUC
Maximum Usable Altitude [*Aviation*] ..... MUA
Maximum Usable Frequency [*Signal transmission*] ..... MUF
Maximum Usable Gain [*Bell System*] ..... MUG
Maximum Useful Magnification (MCD) ..... MUM
Maximum Utilization of Skills and Training [*Civil Service Commission*] ..... MUST
Maximum Value [*Electronics*] ..... M
Maximum Velocity ..... VMAX
Maximum Venous Outflow [*Medicine*] ..... MVO
Maximum Ventilation Rate [*Medicine*] (DAVI) ..... MVR
Maximum Viscous Response [*Medicine*] ..... VCmax
Maximum Visual Impact (DNAB) ..... MVI
Maximum Vital Capacity [*Medicine*] (DAVI) ..... MVC
Maximum Voltage (IDOE) ..... E_m
Maximum Volt-Ampere Utilization [*Electronics*] ..... MVAU
Maximum Voluntary Isometric Strength ..... MVIS
Maximum Voluntary Ventilation ..... MVV
Maximum Voluntary Volume [*Medicine*] (DAVI) ..... MVV
Maximum Winch Launching Speed [*Gliders*] (AIA) ..... Vw
Maximum Wind (NOAA) ..... MXWND
Maximum Wind Speed ..... MWS
Maximum Working Pressure ..... MWP
Maximum Working Voltage [*Electronics*] ..... MWV
Maximum Yield Research [*Agricultural technology*] ..... MYR
Maximum Zero Fuel Weight [*Aviation*] (MCD) ..... MZFW
Maxis, Inc. [*Associated Press*] (SAG) ..... Maxis
Maxis, Inc. [*NASDAQ symbol*] (SAG) ..... MXIS
Maxon Computer Systems, Inc. [*Toronto Stock Exchange symbol*] ..... MXC
Max-Planck Institute for Meteorology [*Marine science*] [*Germany*] (OSRA) ..... MPI
Max-Planck-Gesellschaft [*West German research organization*] ..... MPG
Max-Planck-Institut ..... MPI
Max-Planck-Institut fuer Astronomie [*Max Planck Institute for Astronomy*] [*Germany*] ..... MPI
Max-Planck-Institut fuer Astronomie [*Max Planck Institute for Astronomy*] [*Germany*] ..... MPIA
Max-Planck-Institut fuer Medizinisch Forschung, Heidelberg, Germany [*Library symbol Library of Congress*] (LCLS) ..... GyHeM
Max-Planck-Institut fur Aeronomie [*An association*] ..... MPAE
Max-Planck-Institut fur Extraterrestrische Physik [*Germany*] ..... MPE
Max-Planck-Institut fur Meteorologie (USDC) ..... MPIM
Max-Planck-Institute fuer Meteorologie [*Marine science*] [*Germany*] (OSRA) ..... MPIM
Maxserv, Inc. [*Associated Press*] (SAG) ..... Maxserv
Maxserv, Inc. [*NASDAQ symbol*] (SAG) ..... MXSV
Maxton, NC [*Location identifier FAA*] (FAAL) ..... MEB
Maxton, NC [*Location identifier FAA*] (FAAL) ..... RKX
Maxtor Corp. [*Associated Press*] (SAG) ..... Maxtor
Maxtor Corp. [*NASDAQ symbol*] (NQ) ..... MXTR
Maxus Energy [*Associated Press*] (SAG) ..... Maxus
Maxus Energy [*NASDAQ symbol*] (SAG) ..... MXSBP
Maxus Energy $4 Cv Pfd [*NASDAQ symbol*] (TTSB) ..... MXSBP
Maxus Energy $2.50 Pfd [*NYSE symbol*] (TTSB) ..... MXSPrA
Maxus Energy Corp. [*Associated Press*] (SAG) ..... Maxu
Maxus Energy Corp. [*NYSE symbol*] (SPSG) ..... MXS
Maxville Branch, Stormount, Dundas, and Glengarry County Public Library, Ontario [*Library symbol National Library of Canada*] (NLC) ..... OMSDG
Maxwell [*Electronics*] (DEN) ..... M
Maxwell [*Unit of Magnetic Flux*] [*Electronics*] (IAA) ..... MAX
Maxwell [*Unit of magnetic flux*] [*Also, abWb*] ..... Mx
Maxwell, CA [*Location identifier FAA*] (FAAL) ..... MXW
Maxwell Color Triangle ..... MCT
Maxwell Communication Corp. [*Formerly, BPCC*] [*British*] ..... MCC

Maxwell Communication Corp. [Toronto Stock Exchange symbol] ...... MWC
Maxwell Electronic Publishing [Information service or system] (IID) ...... MEP
Maxwell House Coffee Package [Vendor-machine system for Maxwell House coffee] ...... MAXPAX
Maxwell International Development Simulation ...... MIDSIM
Maxwell International Microforms Corporation, Fairview Park, Elmsford, NY [Library symbol Library of Congress] (LCLS) ...... MimC
Maxwell International Subscription Agency ...... MISA
Maxwell Laboratories, Inc. [Associated Press] (SAG) ...... Maxwel
Maxwell Laboratories, Inc. [NASDAQ symbol] (NQ) ...... MXWL
Maxwell Labs [NASDAQ symbol] (TTSB) ...... MXWL
Maxwell Library Systems [Information service or system] (IID) ...... MLS
Maxwell on the Interpretation of Statutes [A publication] (DLA) ...... Max Int Stat
Maxwell on the Interpretation of Statutes [A publication] (DLA) ...... Maxw Interp St
Maxwell on the Interpretation of Statutes [A publication] (DLA) ...... Maxwell
Maxwell Scientific International [Inc.] ...... MSI
Maxwell Shoe Company, Inc. [NASDAQ symbol] (SAG) ...... MAXS
Maxwell Shoe Co., Inc. [Associated Press] (SAG) ...... MaxwllSh
Maxwell Shoe 'A' [NASDAQ symbol] (TTSB) ...... MAXS
Maxwell Technologies, Inc. [Associated Press] (SAG) ...... MaxwllT
Maxwell Technologies, Inc. [NASDAQ symbol] (SAG) ...... MXWL
Maxwellian Averaged Cross Section Reactor Physics Computer Code [Electronics] (IAA) ...... MACSRRPCC
Maxwell's Law Dictionary [A publication] (DLA) ...... Max LD
Maxwell's Marine Law [A publication] (DLA) ...... Max Mar L
Maxwell's Nebraska Digest [A publication] (DLA) ...... Max Dig
Maxwell's Treatise on Criminal Procedure [A publication] (DLA) ...... Maxw Cr Proc
Maxwell-Wagner Mechanism [Physics] ...... MWM
Maxwell-Wien Bridge [Electronics] ...... MWB
Maxxam Corp. [Associated Press] (SAG) ...... Maxam
MAXXAM, Inc. [AMEX symbol] (SPSG) ...... MXM
Maxxim Medical [NYSE symbol] (TTSB) ...... MAM
Maxxim Medical, Inc. [NYSE symbol] (SPSG) ...... MAM
Maxxim Medical, Inc. [Associated Press] (SAG) ...... Maxxim
.... EDAP
May [Germany ICAO location identifier] (ICLI) ...... M
May ...... MA
May ...... MY
May ...... MW
May Air Xpress, Inc. [ICAO designator] (FAAC) ...... MXP
May & Baker Ltd. [Great Britain] [Research code symbol] ...... MB
May and November [Denotes semiannual payments of interest or dividends in these months] [Business term] ...... M & N
May & Speh, Inc. [Associated Press] (SAG) ...... MaySpeh
May & Speh Inc. [NASDAQ symbol] (TTSB) ...... SPEH
May, August, November, and February [Denotes quarterly payments of interest or dividends in these months] [Business term] ...... MANF
May Be Elevated [Medicine] (DAVI) ...... MBE
May Be Issued ...... MBI
May Be Retained until Unserviceable ...... MBRUU
May Creek [Alaska] [Airport symbol] (OAG) ...... MYK
May Creek, AK [Location identifier FAA] (FAAL) ...... MYK
May Department Stores Co. [NYSE symbol] (SPSG) ...... MA
May Department Stores Co. [Associated Press] (SAG) ...... MayDS
May Department Stores Co., Corporate Information Center, St. Louis, MO [OCLC symbol] (OCLC) ...... MAY
May Dept Stores [NYSE symbol] (TTSB) ...... MA
May God Rest His Soul ...... MGRHS
May His Departed Soul Rest in Peace (BJA) ...... MHDSRIP
May Institute of Medical Research ...... MIMR
May on Insurance [A publication] (DLA) ...... May Ins
May Polarization Experiment [RADAR storm sensing] ...... MAYPOLE
May Repeat [Medicine] ...... MR
May Second Movement [1960s Yale University war protest] (VNW) M2M
Maya Airways [ICAO designator] (AD) ...... MW
Maya Airways Ltd. [Belize] [ICAO designator] (FAAC) ...... MAY
Maya Carga Internacional SA de CV [Mexico ICAO designator] (FAAC) ...... MCI
Mayaguana [Bahamas] [Airport symbol] (OAG) ...... MYG
Mayaguana Auxiliary Air Force Base, Mayaguana Island [Bahamas] [ICAO location identifier] (ICLI) ...... MYMM
Mayaguez [Puerto Rico] [Airport symbol] (OAG) ...... MAZ
Mayaguez [Diocesan abbreviation] [Puerto Rico] (TOCD) ...... MGZ
Mayaguez [Puerto Rico] [Seismograph station code, US Geological Survey] (SEIS) ...... MPR
Mayaguez [Puerto Rico] [ICAO location identifier] (ICLI) ...... TJMZ
Mayaguez, PR [AM radio station call letters] ...... WAEL
Mayaguez, PR [FM radio station call letters] ...... WIOB
Mayaguez, PR [Television station call letters] ...... WIPM
Mayaguez, PR [AM radio station call letters] ...... WKJB
Mayaguez, PR [FM radio station call letters] ...... WKJB-FM
Mayaguez, PR [Television station call letters] ...... WNJX
Mayaguez, PR [AM radio station call letters] ...... WORA
Mayaguez, PR [Television station call letters] ...... WORA-TV
Mayaguez, PR [FM radio station call letters] ...... WOYE
Mayaguez, PR [AM radio station call letters] ...... WPRA
Mayaguez, PR [FM radio station call letters] ...... WTIL
Mayaguez, PR [Television station call letters] ...... WTRA
Mayajigua [Cuba] [Airport symbol] (AD) ...... MJG
Mayajigua [Cuba ICAO location identifier] (ICLI) ...... MUMJ
Mayan [MARC language code Library of Congress] (LCCP) ...... myn
Mayan Energy, Inc. [Vancouver Stock Exchange symbol] ...... MYN
Maybell Public Library, Maybell, CO [Library symbol Library of Congress] (LCLS) ...... CoMay
Maybelline, Inc. [NYSE symbol] (SPSG) ...... MAY
Maybelline, Inc. [Associated Press] (SAG) ...... Maybel
Mayer [A unit of heat capacity] ...... my

Mayer, Brown & Platt Law Library, Chicago, IL [Library symbol Library of Congress] (LCLS) ...... ICMBP
Mayer's Ganz Mispocheh [Mayer's Whole Family] [A Yiddish nickname for Metro-Goldwyn-Mayer, it reflects the tendency of early studio chiefs to hire their relatives and friends] ...... MGM
Mayerthorpe Public Library, Alberta [Library symbol National Library of Canada] (NLC) ...... AMA
Mayfair College, Chicago, IL [Library symbol Library of Congress] (LCLS) ...... ICMay
Mayfield [Washington] [Seismograph station code, US Geological Survey Closed] (SEIS) ...... MAY
Mayfield, KY [AM radio station call letters] ...... WNGO
Mayfield, KY [FM radio station call letters] ...... WXID
Mayfield, KY [AM radio station call letters] ...... WYMC
Mayflower Co-Operative Bank [Associated Press] (SAG) ...... MayflCo
Mayflower Co-Operative Bank [NASDAQ symbol] (NQ) ...... MFLR
Mayflower Cooperative Bank [NASDAQ symbol] (TTSB) ...... MFLR
Mayflower Warehousemen's Association (EA) ...... MWA
May-Gruenwald-Giemsa [A stain] [Hematology] ...... MGG
Mayhew on Merger [1861] [A publication] (DLA) ...... May Merg
Mayhew's Action at Law [1828] [A publication] (DLA) ...... May Act
Mayland Technical Institute, Spruce Pine, NC [Library symbol Library of Congress] (LCLS) ...... NcSppM
Maymac Petroleum Corp. [Vancouver Stock Exchange symbol] ...... MMA
Maynard Community Library, Maynard, IA [Library symbol Library of Congress] (LCLS) ...... IaMay
Maynard Energy, Inc. [Toronto Stock Exchange symbol] ...... MAY
Maynard Listener Library [Defunct] (EA) ...... MLL
Maynard, MA [FM radio station call letters] ...... WAVM
Maynard Oil [NASDAQ symbol] (TTSB) ...... MOIL
Maynard Oil Co. [Associated Press] (SAG) ...... MaynOl
Maynard Oil Co. [NASDAQ symbol] (NQ) ...... MOIL
Maynard Public Library, Maynard, MN [Library symbol] [Library of Congress] (LCLS) ...... MnMay
Maynard Public Schools, Maynard, MN [Library symbol] [Library of Congress] (LCLS) ...... MnMayPS
Maynard's English Reports, Exchequer Memoranda of Edward I, and Year Books of Edward II [A publication] (DLA) ...... Mayn
Mayne Island Museum, British Columbia [Library symbol National Library of Canada] (NLC) ...... BMIM
Mayne Island Museum, Mayne Island, BC, Canada [Library symbol [Library of Congress] (LCLS) ...... CaBMIM
Mayne on the Law of Damages [A publication] (DLA) ...... May Dam
Mayo [Canada] [Airport symbol] (OAG) ...... YMA
Mayo and Moulton's Pension Laws [A publication] (DLA) ...... Mayo & Moul
Mayo Biotechnology Research Computer Facility [Mayo Clinic] [Research center] (RCD) ...... MRCF
Mayo Clinic Health Letter [A publication] ...... MCHL
Mayo Clinic Library, Rochester, MN [OCLC symbol] (OCLC) ...... OMC
Mayo Clinic, Rochester, MN [Library symbol Library of Congress] (LCLS) ...... MnRM
Mayo, FL [FM radio station call letters] ...... WGSG
Mayo Medicine School (GAGS) ...... Mayo Med Sch
Mayo Research Foundation (AD) ...... MRF
Mayo Research Foundation (NADA) ...... MRF
Mayo Smith Society (EA) ...... MSS
Mayo, YT [ICAO location identifier] (ICLI) ...... CYMA
Mayodan, NC [AM radio station call letters] ...... WMYN
Mayodan Public Library, Mayodan, NC [Library symbol] [Library of Congress] (LCLS) ...... NcEdR-M
Mayoko [Gabon] [Airport symbol] (AD) ...... MYZ
Mayoko/Legala [Congo] [ICAO location identifier] (ICLI) ...... FCMY
Mayonnaise and Salad Dressings Institute [Later, Association for Dressings and Sauces] (EA) ...... MSDI
Mayor (ROG) ...... MAY
Mayor ...... MC
Mayor's Court (DLA) ...... MOMR
Mayor's Office of Manpower Resources (AD) ...... MOMR
Mayo's Justice [A publication] (DLA) ...... May Just
Mayo's Justice [A publication] (DLA) ...... Mayo Just
Mayotte [ANSI two-letter standard code] (CNC) ...... YO
Mayoumba [Gabon] [Airport symbol] (OAG) ...... MYB
Mayport, FL [Location identifier FAA] (FAAL) ...... NRB
Mayport/Mayport Naval Station [Florida] [ICAO location identifier] (ICLI) ...... KNRB
May's Constitutional History of England [A publication] (DLA) ...... May Const Hist
May's Criminal Law [A publication] (DLA) ...... May Crim Law
May's Fraudulent Conveyances [3rd ed.] [1908] [A publication] (DLA) ...... May Fr Conv
Mays [J. W.], Inc. [NASDAQ symbol] (NQ) ...... MAYS
Mays [J. W.], Inc. [Associated Press] (SAG) ...... MaysJ
Mays (JW) [NASDAQ symbol] (TTSB) ...... MAYS
May's Parliamentary Law [A publication] (DLA) ...... May Parl Law
May's Parliamentary Practice [A publication] (ILCA) ...... May Parl
May's Parliamentary Practice [A publication] (DLA) ...... May Parl Pr
May's Parliamentary Practice [A publication] (DLA) ...... May PL
Maysville Community College, Maysville, KY [Library symbol] [Library of Congress] (LCLS) ...... KyMyC
Maysville, KY [AM radio station call letters] ...... WFTM
Maysville, KY [FM radio station call letters] ...... WFTM-FM
Maytag [NYSE symbol] (SAG) ...... MYG
Maytag Corp. [Associated Press] (SAG) ...... Maytag
Maytag Corp. [NYSE symbol] (TTSB) ...... MYG
Mayumba [Gabon] [ICAO location identifier] (ICLI) ...... FOOY
Mayurbhani Law Report [India] [A publication] (DLA) ...... May LR
Mayview State Hospital, Bridgeville, PA [OCLC symbol] (OCLC) ...... PHM
Mayville District Public Library, Mayville, MI [Library symbol Library of Congress] (LCLS) ...... MiMay

Mayville, ND [AM radio station call letters] .... KMAV
Mayville, ND [FM radio station call letters] .... KMAV-FM
Mayville State College, Mayville, ND [Library symbol Library of Congress]
  (LCLS) .... NdMayS
Mayville State College, Mayville, ND [OCLC symbol] (OCLC) .... NMY
Mayville, WI [Television station call letters] .... WWRS
Maywood & Sugar Creek [AAR code] .... MAYW
Maywood Public Library, Maywood, IL [Library symbol Library of Congress]
  (LCLS) .... IMay
Mazabuka [Zambia] [ICAO location identifier] (ICLI) .... FLMZ
Mazar-I-Sharif [Afghanistan] [Airport symbol] (OAG) .... MZR
Mazar-I-Sharif [Afghanistan] [ICAO location identifier] (ICLI) .... OAMS
Mazaruca [Argentina ICAO location identifier] (ICLI) .... SAAM
Mazatlan [Mexico] [Seismograph station code, US Geological Survey]
  (SEIS) .... MAZ
Mazatlan [Mexico ICAO location identifier] (ICLI) .... MMZT
Mazatlan [Mexico] [Airport symbol] (OAG) .... MZT
Mazatlan/General Rafael Buelna [Mexico ICAO location identifier] (ICLI) ..... MMMZ
Mazda Motor Corp. .... MMC
Mazda Motor Manufacturing USA Corp. .... MMUC
Mazda Motors of America .... MMA
Mazda Research & Development of North America .... MRA
Mazda Research of Europe [Automobile manufacturer operations] .... MRE
Mazdaznan Association (EA) .... MA
Mazel Stores, Inc. [Associated Press] (SAG) .... MazelSt
Mazel Stores, Inc. [NASDAQ symbol] (SAG) .... MAZL
Maze-Running Time [Psychology] .... MRT
Mazie Landing [Oklahoma] [Seismograph station code, US Geological Survey] (SEIS) .... MZO
Mazirat [France] [Seismograph station code, US Geological Survey] (SEIS) ... MZF
Mazuffarpur [India] [ICAO location identifier] (ICLI) .... VEMZ
Mazzite [A zeolite] .... MAZ
MB Brand Present [Cardiology] (DAVI) .... MBP
Mbabane [Swaziland] [ICAO location identifier] (ICLI) .... FDMB
Mbai [Indonesia] [ICAO location identifier] (ICLI) .... WRKI
Mbala [Zambia] [Airport symbol] (AD) .... ACN
Mbambanakira [Solomon Islands] [Airport symbol] (OAG) .... MBU
Mbandaka [Zaire] [ICAO location identifier] (ICLI) .... FZEA
Mbandaka [Zaire] [Airport symbol] (OAG) .... MDK
M'Banza Congo [Angola] [Airport symbol] (OAG) .... SSY
M'Banza-Congo [Angola] [ICAO location identifier] (ICLI) .... FNBC
Mbarara [Uganda] [Airport symbol] (OAG) .... MBQ
Mbarara/Obote [Uganda] [ICAO location identifier] (ICLI) .... HUMA
M'Baya [Congo] [ICAO location identifier] (ICLI) .... FCPM
MBB [Messerschmidt, Boelkow, Blohm] Raytheon-Thompson .... MRT
MBB-UV [Messerschmitt-Boelkow-Blohm] [Germany ICAO aircraft manufacturer identifier] (ICAO) .... BO
MBB-UV, MBB-UD [Messerschmitt-Boelkow-Blohm], und Pneuma-Technik [Germany ICAO aircraft manufacturer identifier] (ICAO) .... MB
Mbeya [Tanzania] [ICAO location identifier] (ICLI) .... HTMB
Mbeya [Tanzania] [Airport symbol Obsolete] (OAG) .... MBI
MBF USA, Inc. [Associated Press] (SAG) .... MBF
MBF USA, Inc. [NASDAQ symbol] (SAG) .... MBFA
MBF USA, Inc. [Associated Press] (SAG) .... MBFUSA
MBIA, Inc. [NYSE symbol] (SPSG) .... MBI
MBIA, Inc. [Associated Press] (SAG) .... MBIA
Mbigou [Gabon] [ICAO location identifier] (ICLI) .... FOGG
M'Bigou [Gabon] [Airport symbol] (OAG) .... MBC
MBLA Financial [NASDAQ symbol] (TTSB) .... MBLF
MBLA Financial Corp. [Associated Press] (SAG) .... MBLA
MBLA Financial Corp. [NASDAQ symbol] (SAG) .... MBLF
MBNA Corp. [NYSE symbol] (SPSG) .... KRB
MBNA Corp. [Associated Press] (SAG) .... MBNA
MBNA Corp. 7.50% Sr'A'Pfd [NYSE symbol] (TTSB) .... KRBPrA
Mboi [Zaire] [ICAO location identifier] (ICLI) .... FZUI
M'Bour [Senegal] [Seismograph station code, US Geological Survey] (SEIS) .... MBO
M'Bout [Mauritania] [ICAO location identifier] (ICLI) .... GQNU
Mbout [Mauritania] [Airport symbol] (OAG) .... MBR
MBPXL Corp. [Formerly, Missouri Beef Packers - Kansas Beef Industries] .... MBPXL
Mbuji-Mayi [Zaire] [ICAO location identifier] (ICLI) .... FZWA
Mbuji-Mayi [Zaire] [Airport symbol] (OAG) .... MJM
MC Beverages [Vancouver Stock Exchange symbol] .... MCB
MC Shipping [AMEX symbol] (TTSB) .... MCX
MC Shipping, Inc. [Associated Press] (SAG) .... MC Shp
MC Shipping, Inc. [AMEX symbol] (SPSG) .... MCX
McAdam on Landlord and Tenant [A publication] (DLA) .... McA L & Ten
McAdam on Landlord and Tenant [A publication] (DLA) .... McAdam Landl & T
McAdam Resources, Inc. [Toronto Stock Exchange symbol] .... MMM
McAdam's Marine Court Practice [A publication] (DLA) .... McA Mar Ct
McAfee Associates [NASDAQ symbol] (SAG) .... MCAF
McAfee Associates [Associated Press] (SAG) .... McAfee
McAlester [Oklahoma] [Airport symbol] (OAG) .... MLC
McAlester Army Ammunition Plant [Oklahoma] (AABC) .... MCAAP
McAlester/Municipal [Oklahoma] [ICAO location identifier] (ICLI) .... KMLC
McAlester, OK [FM radio station call letters] .... KMCO
McAlester, OK [AM radio station call letters] .... KNED
McAlester, OK [AM radio station call letters] .... KTMC
McAlester, OK [FM radio station call letters] .... KTMC-FM
McAlester, OK [Location identifier FAA] (FAAL) .... MLC
McAllen [Texas] [Airport symbol] (OAG) .... MFE
McAllen Memorial Library, McAllen, TX [Library symbol Library of Congress] (LCLS) .... TxMCa
McAllen/Miller International [Texas] [ICAO location identifier] (ICLI) .... KMFE
McAllen, TX [FM radio station call letters] .... KHID

McAllen, TX [Television station call letters] .... KNVO
McAllen, TX [FM radio station call letters] .... KQXX
McAllen, TX [AM radio station call letters] .... KRIO
McAllen, TX [FM radio station call letters] .... KVMV
McAllen, TX [Location identifier FAA] (FAAL) .... MFE
McAllister's United States Circuit Court Reports [A publication] (DLA) .... McAl
McAllister's United States Circuit Court Reports [A publication] (DLA) .... McAll
McAllister's United States Circuit Court Reports [California] [A publication] (DLA) .... McAll (Cal)
McAllister's United States Circuit Court Reports [A publication] (DLA) .... McAllister US Circ Court R
McAlpine Aviation Ltd. [British ICAO designator] (FAAC) .... MAL
McAlpine Helicopters Ltd. [British ICAO designator] (FAAC) .... MCH
McArthur College of Education, Queen's University, Kingston, Ontario [Library symbol National Library of Canada] (NLC) .... OKQM
McArthur, OH [Location identifier FAA] (FAAL) .... MPG
McArthur, OH [FM radio station call letters] .... WJTD
McArthur's District of Columbia Reports [A publication] (DLA) .... McAr
McBride Public Library, British Columbia [Library symbol National Library of Canada] (NLC) .... BMB
McBride's Reports [1 Missouri] [A publication] (DLA) .... McBride
McBurney's [Point] [Medicine] .... McB
McBurney's Point [Medicine] (CPH) .... McB Pt
McCahon's Kansas Reports [1858-68] [A publication] (DLA) .... McCah
McCahon's Kansas Reports [1858-68] [A publication] (DLA) .... McCahon
McCain Hospital, Medical Library, McCain, NC [Library symbol Library of Congress] (LCLS) .... NcMccH
McCall, ID [FM radio station call letters] .... KBSM
McCall, ID [AM radio station call letters] .... KMCL
McCall, ID [FM radio station call letters] .... KMCL-FM
McCall, ID [Location identifier FAA] (FAAL) .... MYL
McCall Information Systems Co. .... MISCO
McCall Public Library, McCall, ID [Library symbol] [Library of Congress] (LCLS) .... IdMcP
McCall's Clerk's Assistant [A publication] (DLA) .... McC Cl Ass
McCall's Forms [A publication] (DLA) .... McC F
McCall's Needlework [A publication] (BRI) .... McCall Nee
McCall's New York Justice [A publication] (DLA) .... McC Just
McCall's Precedents [A publication] (DLA) .... McCall Pr
McCanless' Tennessee Reports [A publication] (DLA) .... McCanless
McCarran International Airport [FAA] (TAG) .... LAS
McCarron-Dial Street Survival Skills Questionnaire [Occupational therapy] .... SSSQ
McCarter's New Jersey Chancery Reports [A publication] (DLA) .... McCarter
McCarter's New Jersey Equity Reports [A publication] (DLA) .... McCar
McCarter's New Jersey Equity Reports [A publication] (DLA) .... McCart
McCarthy [Panendoscope] [Medicine] (BABM) .... McC
McCarthy [Alaska] [Airport symbol] (OAG) .... MXY
McCarthy, AK [FM radio station call letters] (RBYB) .... KXKM
McCarthy, AK [Location identifier FAA] (FAAL) .... MXY
McCarthy & McCarthy, Barristers and Solicitors, Toronto, ON, Canada [Library symbol Library of Congress] (LCLS) .... CaOTMM
McCarthy & McCarthy, Barristers & Solicitors, Toronto, Ontario [Library symbol National Library of Canada] (NLC) .... OTMM
McCarthy, Crisanti & Maffei, Inc. [Information service or system] (IID) .... MCM
McCarthy Scales of Children's Abilities [Education] .... MSCA
McCarty's New York Civil Procedure Reports [A publication] (DLA) .... McCart
McCarty's New York Civil Procedure Reports [A publication] (DLA) .... McCartney
McCarty's New York Civil Procedure Reports [A publication] (DLA) .... McCarty
McCarty's New York Civil Procedure Reports [A publication] (DLA) .... McCarty Civ Proc
McCarver Sisters Fan Club (EA) .... MSFC
McCelland Engineers, Inc., Houston, TX [Library symbol] [Library of Congress] (LCLS) .... TxHMcE
McChip Resources, Inc. [Toronto Stock Exchange symbol] .... MCS
McChord Air Force Base, Base Library, McChord Air Force Base, WA [Library symbol] [Library of Congress] (LCLS) .... WaMcA
McClain Industries [NASDAQ symbol] (TTSB) .... MCCL
McClain Industries, Inc. [NASDAQ symbol] (NQ) .... MCCL
McClain Industries, Inc. [Associated Press] (SAG) .... McCln
McClain's Annotated Code and Statutes [Iowa] [A publication] (DLA) .... McClain's Code
McClain's Criminal Law [A publication] (DLA) .... McClain Cr Law
McClain's Iowa Code [A publication] (DLA) .... McCl IA Co
McClatchy Newspapers [Associated Press] (SAG) .... McClatN
McClatchy Newspapers, Inc. [Associated Press] (SAG) .... McClat
McClatchy Newspapers, Inc. [NYSE symbol] (SPSG) .... MNI
McClatchy Newspapers'A' [NYSE symbol] (TTSB) .... MNI
McCleary, WA [FM radio station call letters] .... KGY-FM
McClellan Central Laboratory (MCD) .... MCL
McClelland & Stewart [Canadian publisher] .... M & S
McClelland and Younge's English Exchequer Reports [1824-25] [A publication] (DLA) .... McCl & Y
McClelland and Younge's English Exchequer Reports [1824-25] [A publication] (DLA) .... McCle & Yo
McClelland and Younge's English Exchequer Reports [1824-25] [A publication] (DLA) .... McClell & Y
McClelland and Younge's English Exchequer Reports [1824-25] [A publication] (DLA) .... M'Cl & Y
McClelland Engineers, Inc., Houston, TX [Library symbol Library of Congress] (LCLS) .... TxHMc
McClelland on Civil Malpractice [A publication] (DLA) .... McCl Mal
McClelland's English Exchequer Reports [A publication] (DLA) .... McCl
McClelland's English Exchequer Reports [A publication] (DLA) .... McCle
McClelland's English Exchequer Reports [A publication] (DLA) .... McClel

McClelland's English Exchequer Reports [A publication] (DLA) ...... McClell
McClelland's English Exchequer Reports [A publication] (DLA) ...... M'Cl
McClelland's English Exchequer Reports [A publication] (DLA) .... M'Clel (Eng)
McClellan's Digest of Laws [Florida] [A publication] (DLA) ...... McClel Dig
McClellan's Florida Digest [A publication] (DLA) ...... McCl Dig
McClellan's Manual for Executors [A publication] (DLA) ...... McCl Ex
McClellan's Probate Practice [A publication] (DLA) ...... McCl Pr
McClellanville, SC [FM radio station call letters] (RBYB) ...... WWBZ
McClennan Community College, Waco, TX [Library symbol Library of Congress] (LCLS) ...... TxWM
McCloud Flat South [California] [Seismograph station code, US Geological Survey] (SEIS) ...... MFS
McCloud River [Railroad] (MHDW) ...... MR
McCloud River Railroad Co. [AAR code] ...... MCR
McComb, MS [Location identifier FAA] (FAAL) ...... MCB
McComb, MS [FM radio station call letters] ...... WAKH
McComb, MS [AM radio station call letters] ...... WAKK
McComb, MS [AM radio station call letters] ...... WAPF
McComb, MS [AM radio station call letters] ...... WHNY
McConnell Air Force Base [Kansas] ...... MCAFB
McConnell Peel Resources [Vancouver Stock Exchange symbol] ...... MNL
McConnellsburg, PA [AM radio station call letters] ...... WVFC
McConnelsville, OH [FM radio station call letters] ...... WJAW
McCook [Nebraska] [Airport symbol] (OAG) ...... MCK
McCook Community College, McCook, NE [Library symbol Library of Congress] (LCLS) ...... NbMC
McCook, NE [AM radio station call letters] ...... KBRL
McCook, NE [FM radio station call letters] ...... KICX
McCook, NE [FM radio station call letters] ...... KKYT
McCook, NE [AM radio station call letters] ...... KNGN
McCook, NE [Television station call letters] ...... KSNK
McCook, NE [Location identifier FAA] (FAAL) ...... MCK
McCook Public Library District, McCook, IL [Library symbol Library of Congress] (LCLS) ...... IMcc
McCook's Reports [1 Ohio] [A publication] (DLA) ...... McCook
McCook Public Library, McCook, NE [Library symbol Library of Congress] (LCLS) ...... NbM
McCook Public Library, McCook, NE [Library symbol] [Library of Congress] (LCLS) ...... NbML
McCord Museum, McGill University, Montreal, Quebec [Library symbol National Library of Canada] (NLC) ...... QMMMCM
McCord's South Carolina Chancery Reports [1825-27] [A publication] (DLA) ...... McCord Eq
McCord's South Carolina Equity Reports [1825-27] [A publication] (DLA) ...... McCord Ch
McCord's South Carolina Law Reports [1821-28] [A publication] (DLA) .... McCord
McCorkle's Reports [65 North Carolina] [A publication] (DLA) ...... McCork
McCorkle's Reports [65 North Carolina] [A publication] (DLA) ...... McCorkle
McCormack & Dodge (NITA) ...... M & D
McCormick Affective Assessment Technique [Teacher evaluation test] ...... MAAT
McCormick & Co. [NASDAQ symbol] (TTSB) ...... MCCRK
McCormick & Co., Inc. [Associated Press] (SAG) ...... McCor
McCormick & Co., Inc. [NASDAQ symbol] (NQ) ...... MCCRK
McCormick County Library, McCormick, SC [Library symbol] [Library of Congress] (LCLS) ...... ScMc
McCormick Theological Seminary, Chicago, IL [Library symbol Library of Congress] (LCLS) ...... ICMcC
McCowan Memorial Library, Pitman, NJ [Library symbol Library of Congress] (LCLS) ...... NjPi
McCowan Memorial Library, Pitman, NJ [Library symbol] [Library of Congress] (LCLS) ...... NjPiM
McCoy [Antibodies] [Immunology] ...... McC
McCrary's American Law of Elections [A publication] (DLA) ...... McCr Elect
McCrary's American Law of Elections [A publication] (DLA) ...... McCrary Elect
McCrary's United States Circuit Court Reports [A publication] (DLA) ...... McCr
McCrary's United States Circuit Court Reports [A publication] (DLA) ...... McCrary
McCrary's United States Circuit Court Reports [A publication] (DLA) ...... McCrary's Rep
McCulloch House, Pictou, Nova Scotia [Library symbol National Library of Canada] (NLC) ...... NSPMH
McCulloch House, Pictou, NS, Canada [Library symbol] [Library of Congress] (LCLS) ...... CaNSPMH
McCulloch International Airlines [Air carrier designation symbol] ...... MIAX
McCulloch's Political Economy [A publication] (DLA) ...... McCul Pol Econ
McCullough's Commercial Dictionary [A publication] (DLA) ...... McCul Dict
McDaniels, KY [FM radio station call letters] ...... WBFI
McDermot's Irish Land Laws [A publication] (DLA) ...... McDer Land L
McDermott Inc $2.20 cm Cv A Pfd [NYSE symbol] (TTSB) ...... MDEPrA
McDermott, Inc. [Associated Press] (SAG) ...... McDr
McDermott, Inc. [Formerly, Offshore Pipelines] [NYSE symbol] (SAG) ...... MDE
McDermott Inc. $2.60 cm Pfd [NYSE symbol] (TTSB) ...... MDEPrB
McDermott International, Inc. [Associated Press] (SAG) ...... McDerI
McDermott International, Inc. [NYSE symbol] (SPSG) ...... MDR
McDermott Intl. [NYSE symbol] (TTSB) ...... MDR
McDermott [J. Ray] SA [NYSE symbol] (SAG) ...... JRM
McDermott [J. Ray] SA [Associated Press] (SAG) ...... McDerJ
McDermott, Will & Emory, Chicago, IL [Library symbol] [Library of Congress] (LCLS) ...... ICMcDW
McDevitt's Irish Land Commissioner's Reports [A publication] (DLA) ...... McDevitt
McDonald & Co. Invest [NYSE symbol] (TTSB) ...... MDD
McDonald & Co. Investment, Inc. [Associated Press] (SAG) ...... McDInv
McDonald & Co. Investments, Inc. [NYSE symbol] (SPSG) ...... MDD
McDonald' Corp. 8.35% 'QUIDS' [NYSE symbol] (TTSB) ...... MCZ
McDonald Deep Test of Articulation [Speech and language therapy] (DAVI) ...... MDTA

McDonald Laser Ranging System [For observations] ...... MLRS
McDonald Observatory [Texas] [Seismograph station code, US Geological Survey] (SEIS) ...... MOT
McDonald's Corp. [NYSE symbol Toronto Stock Exchange symbol] (SPSG) .... MCD
McDonald's Corp. [Associated Press] (SAG) ...... McDn
McDonalds Corp. [Associated Press] (SAG) McDn25
McDonalds Corp. [Associated Press] (SAG) McDn36
McDonalds Corp. [Associated Press] (SAG) ...... McDnlds
McDonalds Corp. [NYSE symbol] (SAG) ...... MCW
McDonalds Corp. [NYSE symbol] (SAG) ...... MCZ
McDonald's Corp. 7.72% Dep Pfd [NYSE symbol] (TTSB) ...... MCDPrE
McDonald's Justice [A publication] (DLA) ...... McDon Jus
McDonald's Operators' Association (EA) ...... MOA
McDonnell Airborne Evaluator [McDonnell Douglas Corp.] (MCD) ...... MAE
McDonnell Airborne Sidewinder Evaluator [McDonnell Douglas Corp.] (MCD) ...... MASE
McDonnell Airborne Trainer and Evaluator [McDonnell Douglas Corp.] (MCD) ...... MATE
McDonnell Aircraft Co. [Later, McDonnell Douglas Corp.] (MCD) ...... MAC
McDonnell Aircraft Co. [Later, McDonnell Douglas Corp.] ...... MCAIR
McDonnell Automatic Checkout System [McDonnell Douglas Corp.] ...... MACS
McDonnell Douglas [NYSE symbol] (TTSB) ...... MD
McDonnell Douglas Aerospace Information Services [Formerly, MCATO] (MCD) ...... MDAIS
McDonnell Douglas Aircraft Corp. ...... MDAC
McDonnell Douglas Astronautics Co., Western Division, Huntington Beach, CA [Library symbol Library of Congress] (LCLS) ...... CHuMD
McDonnell Douglas Automated Voice Information System (MCD) ...... MAVIS
McDonnell Douglas Automation Co. [Robotics] ...... MCAUTO
McDonnell Douglas Automation Co., McAuto Campus Library, St. Louis, MO [OCLC symbol] (OCLC) ...... MCA
McDonnell Douglas Automation Co., St. Louis, MO [Library symbol Library of Congress] (LCLS) ...... MoSMcA
McDonnell Douglas Computer Systems Co. [Formerly, MICRODATA] (MCD) ...... MDCSC
McDonnell Douglas Corp. [ICAO designator] (FAAC) ...... DAC
McDonnell Douglas Corp. (KSC) ...... MACDAC
McDonnell Douglas Corp. ...... MCD
McDonnell Douglas Corp. ...... MCDC
McDonnell Douglas Corp. [Associated Press] (SAG) ...... McDnD
McDonnell Douglas Corp. [NYSE symbol] (SPSG) ...... MD
McDonnell Douglas Corp. (MCD) ...... MDC
McDonnell Douglas Corp., Corporate Library, St. Louis, MO [Library symbol Library of Congress] (LCLS) ...... MoSMc
McDonnell Douglas Finance Corp. Ltd. [British] ...... MDFC
McDonnell Douglas Helicopter Co. [Formerly, HHI] (MCD) ...... MDHC
McDonnell Douglas Helicopter Systems ...... MDHS
McDonnell Douglas Industrial Control Products (MCD) ...... MDICP
McDonnell Douglas Information Services ...... MDIS
McDonnell Douglas International Sales Corp. (MCD) ...... MDISC
McDonnell Douglas International Sales Corp. (MCD) ...... MDSS
McDonnell Douglas Support Services ...... MDSS
McDonnell Launch Vehicle [McDonnell Douglas Corp.] (MCD) ...... MLV
McDonnell Scrap Tool System [McDonnell Douglas Corp.] (MCD) ...... MSTS
McDonnell Simulator Recorder [McDonnell Douglas Corp.] (MCD) ...... MSR
McDonnell-Designed Assembly ...... MDA
McDonnell-Douglas Aerospace (GAVI) ...... MDA
McDonnell-Douglas Aircraft Co., Inc. [ICAO aircraft manufacturer identifier] (ICAO) ...... DC
McDonnell's Sierra Leone Reports [A publication] (DLA) ...... McDonnell
McDonough Feline Sarcoma Virus [Veterinary medicine] (MEDA) ...... sm-FeSV
McDonough, GA [AM radio station call letters] ...... WKKP
McDowall's Institutes of the Law of Scotland [A publication] (DLA) .... McDow Inst
McDowell County Public Library, Marion, NC [Library symbol Library of Congress] (LCLS) ...... NcMaMC
McDowell Technical Institute, Marion, NC [Library symbol Library of Congress] (LCLS) ...... NcMaM
McElhanney Engineering, Vancouver, BC, Canada [Library symbol] [Library of Congress] (LCLS) ...... CaBVaME
McElhanney Engineering, Vancouver, British Columbia [Library symbol National Library of Canada] (NLC) ...... BVAME
McFarland, CA [AM radio station call letters] ...... KJAZ
McFarland, CA [FM radio station call letters] ...... KSUV-FM
McFarland Energy [NASDAQ symbol] (TTSB) ...... MCFE
McFarland Energy, Inc. [Associated Press] (SAG) ...... McFarI
McFarland Energy, Inc. [NASDAQ symbol] (NQ) ...... MCFE
McFarlane's Jury Court Reports [Scotland] [A publication] (DLA) ...... McFar
McFinley Red Lake Mines Ltd. [Toronto Stock Exchange symbol] ...... MCF
McGarry Public Library, Virginiatown, Ontario [Library symbol National Library of Canada] (BIB) ...... OVM
McGehee, AR [AM radio station call letters] ...... KVSA
McGeorge School of Law, University of the Pacific, Sacramento, CA [Library symbol Library of Congress] (LCLS) ...... CSM
McGhee Tyson Airport [FAA] (TAG) ...... TYS
McGill Action Planning System ...... MAPS
McGill Pain Questionnaire [Dentistry] ...... MPQ
McGill University, Allan Memorial Institute of Psychiatry, Montreal, PQ, Canada [Library symbol Library of Congress] (LCLS) ...... CaQMAM
McGill University, Blackader/Lauterman Library of Architecture and Art, Montreal, PQ, Canada [Library symbol Library of Congress] (LCLS) .... CaQMMB
McGill University, Blacker-Wood Library, Montreal, PQ, Canada [Library symbol Library of Congress] (LCLS) ...... CaQMMBZ
McGill University, Botany-Genetics Library, Montreal, PQ, Canada [Library symbol Library of Congress] (LCLS) ...... CaQMMBG
McGill University, Dentistry Library, Montreal, PQ, Canada [Library symbol Library of Congress] (LCLS) ...... CaQMMFD

McGill University, Department of Geography, University Map Collection, Montreal,PQ, Canada [*Library symbol Library of Congress*] (LCLS) ..... CaQMMG
McGill University, Department of Geological Sciences, Montreal, PQ, Canada [*Library symbol Library of Congress*] (LCLS) ..... CaQMMGS
McGill University, Department of Rare Books and Special Collections, Montreal, PQ, Canada [*Library symbol Library of Congress*] (LCLS) ..... CaQMMRB
McGill University, Engineering Library, Montreal, PQ, Canada [*Library symbol Library of Congress*] (LCLS) ..... CaQMME
McGill University, Graduate School of Library Science, Montreal, PQ, Canada [*Library symbol Library of Congress*] (LCLS) ..... CaQMMLS
McGill University, Graduate School of Library Science, Montreal, PQ, Canada [*OCLC symbol*] (OCLC) ..... MCG
McGill University, Howard Ross Library of Management, Montreal, PQ, Canada [*Library symbol Library of Congress*] (LCLS) ..... CaQMMSC
McGill University, Institute of Islamic Studies, Montreal, PQ, Canada [*Library symbol Library of Congress*] (LCLS) ..... CaQMIIS
McGill University, Law Library [*UTLAS symbol*] ..... GLF
McGill University, Law Library, Montreal, PQ, Canada [*Library symbol Library of Congress*] (LCLS) ..... CaQMML
McGill University Library [*UTLAS symbol*] ..... GLL
McGill University, Macdonald College, Institute of Parasitology, Montreal, PQ, Canada [*Library symbol Library of Congress*] (LCLS) ..... CaQMIP
McGill University, Macdonald College, Montreal, PQ, Canada [*Library symbol Library of Congress*] (LCLS) ..... CaQMaC
McGill University, Map Collection, Montreal, PQ, Canada [*Library symbol Library of Congress*] (LCLS) ..... CaQMMMa
McGill University, McCord Museum, Montreal, PQ, Canada [*Library symbol Library of Congress*] (LCLS) ..... CaQMMMcM
McGill University, Medical Library [*UTLAS symbol*] ..... GLM
McGill University, Medical Library, Montreal, PQ, Canada [*Library symbol Library of Congress*] (LCLS) ..... CaQMMM
McGill University, Montreal, PQ, Canada [*Library symbol Library of Congress*] (LCLS) ..... CaQMM
McGill University, Northern Studies Library, Montreal, PQ, Canada [*Library symbol Library of Congress*] (LCLS) ..... CaQMMNS
McGill University, Nursing Library, Montreal, PQ, Canada [*Library symbol Library of Congress*] (LCLS) ..... CaQMMN
McGill University, Osler Collection, Montreal, PQ, Canada [*Library symbol Library of Congress*] (LCLS) ..... CaQMMO
McGill University, Physical Sciences Centre, Montreal, PQ, Canada [*Library symbol Library of Congress*] (LCLS) ..... CaQMMPS
McGill University Rare Books [*UTLAS symbol*] ..... GLR
McGill University RECON [*UTLAS symbol*] ..... GLX
McGill University, Religious Studies Library, Montreal, PQ, Canada [*Library symbol Library of Congress*] (LCLS) ..... CaQMMD
McGill University Savanna Research Project (MCD) ..... MUSRP
McGill University, Social Work Library, Montreal, PQ, Canada [*Library symbol Library of Congress*] (LCLS) ..... CaQMMS
McGill University System for Interactive Computing ..... MUSIC
McGill-Melzack Pain Index [*Questionnaire and Home Life Change Index*] (DAVI) ..... MMPI
McGill's Manuscript Decisions, Scotch Court of Session [*A publication*] (DLA) ..... McGill
McGlashan. Aliment [*Scotland*] [*A publication*] (DLA) ..... McGl Al
McGlashan's Sheriff Court Practice [*Scotland*] [*A publication*] (DLA) ..... McGl Sh
McGloin's Louisiana Court of Appeal Reports [*A publication*] (DLA) ..... McG
McGloin's Louisiana Courts of Appeal Reports [*A publication*] (DLA) ..... McGl
McGloin's Louisiana Courts of Appeal Reports [*A publication*] (DLA) ..... McGl (LA)
McGloin's Louisiana Courts of Appeal Reports [*A publication*] (DLA) ..... McGloin
McGloin's Louisiana Courts of Appeal Reports [*A publication*] (DLA) ..... McGloin Rep (LA)
McGrath [*Alaska*] [*Airport symbol*] (OAG) ..... MCG
McGrath [*Alaska*] [*ICAO location identifier*] (ICLI) ..... PAMC
McGrath, AK [*AM radio station call letters*] ..... KSKO
McGrath, AK [*Location identifier FAA*] (FAAL) ..... MCG
McGrath, AK [*Location identifier FAA*] (FAAL) ..... VTR
McGrath Elementary School, McGrath, MN [*Library symbol*] [*Library of Congress*] (LCLS) ..... MnMcgE
McGrath Rent Corp. [*Associated Press*] (SAG) ..... McGrth
McGrath RentCorp [*NASDAQ symbol*] (NQ) ..... MGRC
McGrath's Mandamus Cases [*Michigan*] [*A publication*] (DLA) ..... McGrath
McGraw-Hill (NITA) ..... M-H
McGraw-Hill Companies [*NYSE symbol*] (TTSB) ..... MHP
McGraw-Hill, Inc. [*Associated Press*] (SAG) ..... McGrH
McGraw-Hill, Inc. [*NYSE symbol*] (SPSG) ..... MHP
McGraw-Hill, Inc., New York, NY [*Library symbol Library of Congress*] (LCLS) ..... NNMcGraw
McGraw-Hill Information Exchange for Educators ..... MIX
McGraw-Hill Information Management Co. [*Database producer*] (IID) ..... MIMCO
McGraw-Hill Learning Architecture ..... MHLA
McGraw-Hill News [*Database*] (IT) ..... MHN
McGraw-Hill Ryerson Ltd. [*Toronto Stock Exchange symbol*] ..... MHR
McGregor Historical Society, McGregor, IA [*Library symbol Library of Congress*] (LCLS) ..... IaMcgHi
McGregor Point, HI [*Location identifier FAA*] (FAAL) ..... MPH
McGregor Public Library, Highland Park, MI [*Library symbol Library of Congress*] (LCLS) ..... MiHp
McGregor Public Library, McGregor, IA [*Library symbol Library of Congress*] (LCLS) ..... IaMcg
McGregor Public Library, McGregor, MN [*Library symbol*] [*Library of Congress*] (LCLS) ..... MnMcgr
McGregor School, McGregor, MN [*Library symbol*] [*Library of Congress*] (LCLS) ..... MnMcgrS
McGuire Nuclear Station (NRCH) ..... MNS
McGuire Safe Driver Interview Guide (AEBS) ..... MSDIG
McGuire Safe Driver Scale (AEBS) ..... MSDS
McHenry Museum, Modesto, CA [*Library symbol Library of Congress*] (LCLS) ..... CMMM
Mchinji [*Malawi*] [*ICAO location identifier*] (ICLI) ..... FWMC
M-Chlorophenylpiperazine [*Organic chemistry*] ..... mCPP
MCI Communications [*NASDAQ symbol*] (TTSB) ..... MCIC
MCI Communications Corp. [*Associated Press*] (SAG) ..... MCI
MCI Communications Corp. [*NASDAQ symbol*] (NQ) ..... MCIC
Mclnotosh Public Library, McIntosh, MN [*Library symbol*] [*Library of Congress*] (LCLS) ..... MnMci
McIntire Public Library, Charlottesville, VA [*Library symbol Library of Congress*] (LCLS) ViC
McIntosh Elementary School, McIntosh, MN [*Library symbol*] [*Library of Congress*] (LCLS) ..... MnMciE
McIntosh Elementary School, Rockford,IL [*Library symbol*] [*Library of Congress*] (LCLS) ..... IRoMcE
McIntosh Music [*Record label*] ..... McInt
McIntosh-Winger High School, McIntosh, MN [*Library symbol*] [*Library of Congress*] (LCLS) ..... MnMciH
McIntyre and Evans' Judicature Practice [*A publication*] (DLA) ..... McIn & E Jud Pr
McIntyre-Falconbridge Library, Toronto, ON, Canada [*Library symbol Library of Congress*] (LCLS) ..... CaOTMF
McIntyre-Falconbridge Library, Toronto, Ontario [*Library symbol National Library of Canada*] (NLC) ..... OTMF
McKee, KY [*FM radio station call letters*] ..... WWAG
McKeesport Connecting Railroad Co. [*AAR code*] ..... MKC
McKeesport, PA [*Location identifier FAA*] (FAAL) ..... MKP
McKeesport, PA [*AM radio station call letters*] ..... WEDO
McKeesport, PA [*AM radio station call letters*] ..... WIXZ
McKellar General Hospital, Medical Library, Thunder Bay, ON, Canada [*Library symbol*] [*Library of Congress*] (LCLS) ..... CaOTBMC
McKellar Township Public Library, Ontario [*Library symbol National Library of Canada*] (NLC) ..... OMT
McKelvey on Evidence [*A publication*] (DLA) ..... McKelvey Ev
McKendree College, Lebanon, IL [*OCLC symbol*] (OCLC) ..... ICJ
McKendree College, Lebanon, IL [*Library symbol Library of Congress*] (LCLS) ..... ILebM
McKenzie, TN [*AM radio station call letters*] ..... WHDM
McKenzie, TN [*FM radio station call letters*] ..... WWYN
McKesson Corp. [*Formerly, SP Ventures*] [*NYSE symbol*] (SPSG) ..... MCK
McKesson Corp. [*Associated Press*] (SAG) ..... McKesson
McKinley [*Alaska*] [*Seismograph station code, US Geological Survey*] (SEIS) ..... MCK
McKinley Elementary School, Fergus Falls, MN [*Library symbol*] [*Library of Congress*] (LCLS) ..... MnFfME
McKinley Elementary School, St. Cloud, MN [*Library symbol*] [*Library of Congress*] (LCLS) ..... MnStclMc
McKinley Memorial Library, Niles, OH [*OCLC symbol*] (OCLC) ..... MML
McKinley Memorial Library, Niles, OH [*Library symbol Library of Congress*] (LCLS) ..... ON
McKinley Park [*Alaska*] [*Airport symbol*] (AD) ..... MPK
McKinley Public Library, McKinley, MN [*Library symbol*] [*Library of Congress*] (LCLS) ..... MnMck
McKinney Memorial Public Library, McKinney, TX [*Library symbol Library of Congress*] (LCLS) ..... TxMck
McKinney, TX [*FM radio station call letters*] ..... KRVA
McKinney, TX [*Location identifier FAA*] (FAAL) ..... TKI
McKinney's Consolidated Laws of New York [*A publication*] (DLA) ..... McK Consol Laws
McKinney's Consolidated Laws of New York [*A publication*] (DLA) ..... NY Law (McKinney)
McKinney's Justice [*A publication*] (DLA) ..... McKin Jus
McKinnon, TN [*FM radio station call letters*] (RBYB) ..... WTPR-FM
McKinnon, TN [*FM radio station call letters*] ..... WTWL
McKinnon's Philosophy of Evidence [*A publication*] (DLA) ..... McKin Phil Ev
McKune Memorial Library, Chelsea, MI [*Library symbol Library of Congress*] (LCLS) ..... MiChel
McLain, MS [*FM radio station call letters*] ..... WXAB
McLaren Micropublishing, Toronto, ON, Canada [*Library symbol Library of Congress*] (LCLS) ..... McL
McLaren's Law of Wills [*Scotland*] [*A publication*] (DLA) ..... McLar W
McLaren's Trusts in Scotland [*A publication*] (DLA) ..... McLar Tr
McLaughlin-Buick Club of Canada (EAIO) ..... MBC
McLaughlin-Buick Club of Canada (EA) ..... MBCC
McLean and Robinson's Scotch Appeal Cases [*1839*] [*A publication*] (DLA) ..... McL & R
McLean County Historical Society, Bloomington, IL [*Library symbol Library of Congress*] (LCLS) ..... IBloHi
McLean Hospital, Belmont, MA [*Library symbol Library of Congress*] (LCLS) ..... MBelmM
McLean's United States Circuit Court Reports [*A publication*] (DLA) ..... Mc L
McLean's United States Circuit Court Reports [*A publication*] (DLA) ..... McLean
McLean's United States Circuit Court Reports [*A publication*] (DLA) ..... McLean's CCR
McLean's United States Circuit Court Reports [*A publication*] (DLA) ..... McLean's Rep
McLean's United States Circuit Court Reports [*A publication*] (DLA)..... M'Lean's R
McLeansboro, IL [*AM radio station call letters*] ..... WMCL
M'Clelland and Younge's English Exchequer Reports [*148 English Reprint*] [*A publication*] (DLA) ..... M'Cl & Yo
M'Clelland and Younge's English Exchequer Reports [*148 English Reprint*] [*A publication*] (DLA) ..... M'Cle & Yo
M'Clelland and Younge's English Exchequer Reports [*148 English Reprint*] [*A publication*] (DLA) ..... M'Clel & Y

M'Clelland and Younge's English Exchequer Reports [*148 English Reprint*] [*A publication*] (DLA) .... M'Clel & Y (Eng)
M'Clelland's English Exchequer Reports [*148 English Reprint*] [*A publication*] (DLA) .... M'Cle
M'Clelland's English Exchequer Reports [*148 English Reprint*] [*A publication*] (DLA) .... M'Clel
McLennan Library, McGill University, Montreal, Quebec [*Library symbol National Library of Canada*] (NLC) .... QMM
McLennan Municipal Library, Alberta [*Library symbol National Library of Canada*] (NLC) .... AMLM
McLennan Municipal Library, McLennan, AB, Canada [*Library symbol*] [*Library of Congress*] (LCLS) .... CaAMLM
McLeod Aerating Cardiac .... MAC
MCM Corp. [*Associated Press*] (SAG) .... MCM Cp
MCM Corp. [*NASDAQ symbol*] (NQ) .... MCMC
McM Corp. [*NASDAQ symbol*] (TTSB) .... MCMC
McMain Magnet Secondary School, New Orleans, LA [*Library symbol*] [*Library of Congress*] (LCLS) .... LNMMS
McMaster Institute for Polymer Production Technology [*McMaster University*] [*Canada*] (IRC) .... MiPPT
McMaster Nuclear Reactor [*Canada*] .... MNR
McMaster University [*Hamilton, ON*] (DSUE) .... MAC
McMaster University, Archives and Special Collections Division, Hamilton, ON, Canada [*Library symbol Library of Congress*] (LCLS) .... CaOHMA
McMaster University, Biomedical Library, Hamilton, ON, Canada [*Library symbol Library of Congress*] (LCLS) .... CaOHMB
McMaster University, Hamilton, ON, Canada [*Library symbol Library of Congress*] (LCLS) .... CaOHM
McMaster University, Hamilton, Ontario [*Library symbol National Library of Canada*] (NLC) .... OHM
McMaster University Health Sciences Library [*UTLAS symbol*] .... MHS
McMaster University Library [*UTLAS symbol*] .... MAS
McMaster University, Map Library, Hamilton, ON, Canada [*Library symbol Library of Congress*] (LCLS) .... CaOHMM
McMaster University, McMaster Divinity College, Canadian Baptist Archives, Hamilton, ON, Canada [*Library symbol*] [*Library of Congress*] (LCLS) .... CaOHMDBA
McMaster's Commercial Decisions [*A publication*] (DLA) .... McM Com Dec
McMasters Elementary School, Pasadena, TX [*Library symbol*] [*Library of Congress*] (LCLS) .... TxPME
McMaster's New York Railroad Laws [*A publication*] (DLA) .... McMas RR
McMaster's United States Commercial Cases [*A publication*] (DLA) .... McM Com Cas
McMechen Public Library, McMechen, WV [*Library symbol Library of Congress*] (LCLS) .... WvMc
McMichael Canadian Collection, Kleinburg, ON, Canada [*Library symbol Library of Congress*] (LCLS) .... CaOKleM
McMichael Canadian Collection, Kleinburg, Ontario [*Library symbol National Library of Canada*] (NLC) .... OKLEM
McMillan, Binch, Toronto, Ontario [*Library symbol National Library of Canada*] (NLC) .... OTMB
McMillan Memorial Library, Wisconsin Rapids, WI [*Library symbol Library of Congress*] (LCLS) .... WWr
McMillan Township Library, Ewen, MI [*Library symbol Library of Congress*] (LCLS) .... MiEw
McMillen Birch, Toronto, ON, Canada [*Library symbol Library of Congress*] (LCLS) .... CaOTMB
McMinnville, OR [*AM radio station call letters*] .... KLYC
McMinnville, OR [*FM radio station call letters*] .... KSLC
McMinnville, OR [*Location identifier FAA*] (FAAL) .... MMV
McMinnville Public Library, McMinnville, OR [*Library symbol Library of Congress*] (LCLS) .... OrMc
McMinnville, TN [*Location identifier FAA*] (FAAL) .... RNC
McMinnville, TN [*AM radio station call letters*] .... WAKI
McMinnville, TN [*AM radio station call letters*] .... WBMC
McMinnville, TN [*FM radio station call letters*] .... WTRZ
McMoRan Oil & Gas [*NASDAQ symbol*] (TTSB) .... MOXY
McMoRan Oil and Gas Co. [*Associated Press*] (SAG) .... McMoRn
McMoRan Oil and Gas Co. [*NASDAQ symbol*] (SAG) .... MOXY
McMullan's South Carolina Equity Reports [*A publication*] (DLA) .... McMul Eq
McMullan's South Carolina Equity Reports [*A publication*] (DLA) .... McMull Eq (SC)
McMullan's South Carolina Law Reports [*A publication*] (DLA) .... McMul
McMullan's South Carolina Law Reports [*A publication*] (DLA) .... McMull L (SC)
McMurdo Sound [*Antarctica*] [*Seismograph station code, US Geological Survey Closed*] (SEIS) .... MCM
McMurdo Sound, Antarctica [*New Zealand*] [*ICAO location identifier*] (ICLI) .... NZCM
McMurry College, Abilene, TX [*Library symbol Library of Congress*] (LCLS) .... TxAbM
McMurry College, Abilene, TX [*OCLC symbol*] (OCLC) .... TXD
MCN Corp. [*NYSE symbol*] (SAG) .... MCE
MCN Corp. [*Formerly, Michigan Consolidated Gas Co.*] [*Associated Press*] (SAG) .... MCN
MCN Corp. 8.75%'PRIDE' [*NYSE symbol*] (TTSB) .... MCE
MCN Financing [*NYSE symbol*] (SAG) .... MCN
MCN Financing [*Associated Press*] (SAG) .... MCN F
MCN Mich L.P.9.375% Pfd [*NYSE symbol*] (TTSB) .... MCNPrT
MCN Michigan Ltd. [*Associated Press*] (SAG) .... MCNMI
MCN Michigan LP [*NYSE symbol*] (SAG) .... MCN
McNamara-O'Hara Service Contract Act of 1965 (WYGK) .... MOSCA
McNaney Spectroelectric Device .... MSD
McNeese State University (GAGS) .... McNeese St U
McNeese State University, Lake Charles, LA [*OCLC symbol*] (OCLC) .... LHA
McNeese State University, Lake Charles, LA [*Library symbol Library of Congress*] (LCLS) .... LLcM
McNeil Island Correction Center, Steilacoom, WA [*Library symbol Library of Congress*] (LCLS) .... WaSteM
McNeil Laboratories (Canada) Ltd., Stouffville, ON, Canada [*Library symbol Library of Congress*] (LCLS) .... CaOSML
McNeil Laboratories (Canada) Ltd., Stouffville, Ontario [*Library symbol National Library of Canada*] (NLC) .... OSML
McNeil Laboratories, Inc. [*Research code symbol*] .... McN
McNeil Laboratories, Inc. [*Research code symbol*] .... McN-JR
McNeil Mantha, Inc. [*Toronto Stock Exchange symbol*] .... MCN
McNeil River [*Alaska*] [*Seismograph station code, US Geological Survey*] (SEIS) .... MCL
McNellen Resources, Inc. [*Vancouver Stock Exchange symbol Toronto Stock Exchange symbol*] .... MNR
M'Cord's South Carolina Equity Reports [*A publication*] (DLA) .... M'Cord Eq (SC)
M'Cord's South Carolina Law Reports [*A publication*] (DLA) .... M'Cord L (SC)
M-Corp Inc. [*Formerly, Mike's Submarines*] [*Toronto Stock Exchange symbol*] .... MKI
McPherson College, McPherson, KS [*Library symbol Library of Congress*] (LCLS) .... KMcpC
McPherson, KS [*FM radio station call letters*] .... KBBE
McPherson, KS [*AM radio station call letters*] .... KNGL
McPherson, KS [*Location identifier FAA*] (FAAL) .... MPR
McPherson, Lee, and Bell's Scotch Session Cases [*A publication*] (DLA) .... McPherson
McQuaid Jesuit High School Library, Rochester, NY [*OCLC symbol*] (OCLC) .... RWZ
McQuillin on Municipal Corporations [*A publication*] (DLA) .... McQuillin Mun Corp
McRae, GA [*Location identifier FAA*] (FAAL) .... MQW
McRae, GA [*AM radio station call letters*] .... WYIS
McRae, GA [*FM radio station call letters*] .... WYSC
McRae Indus Cv 'B' [*AMEX symbol*] (TTSB) .... MRI.B
McRae Indus'A' [*AMEX symbol*] (TTSB) .... MRI.A
McRae Industries, Inc. [*Associated Press*] (SAG) .... McRae
McRae Industries, Inc. [*AMEX symbol*] (SPSG) .... MRI
McUrtain County High Education Program, Idabel, OK [*Library symbol*] [*Library of Congress*] (LCLS) .... OkIM
McVey Elementary School, East Meadow, NY [*Library symbol Library of Congress*] (LCLS) .... NEmMcE
McVey's Ohio Digest [*A publication*] (DLA) .... McVey Dig
McWhorter Technologies, Inc. [*Associated Press*] (SAG) .... McWhrtr
McWhorter Technologies, Inc. [*NYSE symbol*] (SAG) .... MWT
McWillie's Reports [*73-76 Mississippi*] [*A publication*] (DLA) .... McWillie
MD Review [*Social Security Administration*] (OICC) .... MDR
M-Day Force Materiel Requirement .... MDFMR
M-Day Materiel Assets (AFIT) .... MDMA
M-Day Materiel Requirement (AFIT) .... MDMR
M-Day Mobilization Requirement .... MDMR
MDC Communication Cl'A' [*AMEX symbol*] (TTSB) .... MDQ
MDC Corp. [*Associated Press*] (SAG) .... MDC
MDC Corp. [*AMEX symbol*] (SAG) .... MDQ
MDC Corp. [*Toronto Stock Exchange symbol*] .... MDZ
MDC Financial, Inc. [*Vancouver Stock Exchange symbol*] .... MFN
M.D.C Hldgs [*NYSE symbol*] (TTSB) .... MDC
MDC Holdings, Inc. [*NYSE symbol*] (SPSG) .... MDC
MDC Holdings, Inc. (MCD) .... MDCH
MDC Library, Manitoba Developmental Centre, Portage La Prairie [*Library symbol National Library of Canada*] (BIB) .... MPLPDC
MDE Explorations [*Vancouver Stock Exchange symbol*] .... MDQ
MDI Mobile Data International, Inc. [*Toronto Stock Exchange symbol Vancouver Stock Exchange symbol*] .... MDB
MDL Information Sys [*NASDAQ symbol*] (TTSB) .... MDLI
MDL Information Systems, Inc. [*Associated Press*] (SAG) .... MDL Info
MDL Information Systems, Inc. [*NASDAQ symbol*] (SAG) .... MDLI
MDM [*Manipulator Deployment Mechanism*] **Flight Forward** [*NASA*] (GFGA) .... MFF
MDM [*Manipulator Deployment Mechanism*] **Launch Aft** [*NASA*] .... MLA
MDM [*Manipulator Deployment Mechanism*] **Launch Forward** [*NASA*] .... MLF
MDM [*Manipulator Deployment Mechanism*] **Launch Left** [*NASA*] .... MLL
MDM [*Manipulator Deployment Mechanism*] **Launch Right** [*NASA*] .... MLR
MDS Health Group Ltd. [*Toronto Stock Exchange symbol*] .... MHG
MDS [*Multipoint Distribution System*] **Industry Association** [*Telecommunications*] (EA) .... MDSIA
MDT Corp. [*Associated Press*] (SAG) .... MDT Cp
MDT Corp. [*NASDAQ symbol*] (NQ) .... MDTC
MDU Resources Group [*NYSE symbol*] (TTSB) .... MDU
MDU Resources Group, Inc. [*NYSE symbol*] (SPSG) .... MDU
ME Compu Software, Inc. [*Vancouver Stock Exchange symbol*] .... CPU
Meacham Bridge Oscillator [*Electronics*] .... MBO
Meacham, OR [*Location identifier FAA*] (FAAL) .... MEH
Meaconing, Intrusion, Jamming, Interference [*Military*] (NVT) .... MIJI
Mead Access Systems Co. .... MASCO
[*The*] **Mead Corp.** [*NYSE symbol*] (SPSG) .... MEA
[*The*] **Mead Corp.** [*Associated Press*] (SAG) .... Mead
Mead Corp., Dayton, OH [*Library symbol Library of Congress*] (LCLS) .... ODaMCo
Mead Data Central, Inc. [*Dayton, OH*] .... MDC
Mead Data Control (NITA) .... MDC
Mead Imaging, Miamisburg, OH [*Library symbol*] [*Library of Congress*] (LCLS) .... OMiabMI
Mead Johnson [*Commercial firm*] [*Pharmacology*] (DAVI) .... Mead-J
Mead Johnson & Co. [*Research code symbol*] .... MJ
Mead Johnson & Co., Research Library, Evansville, IN [*OCLC symbol*] (OCLC) .... IMG
Mead Johnson Research Center, Evansville, IN [*Library symbol Library of Congress*] (LCLS) .... InEM

Mead Johnson Tube [*Medicine*] (DMAA) ... MJT
Mead Public Library, Sheboygan, WI [*Library symbol Library of Congress*] (LCLS) ... WShe
Meade, KS [*Location identifier FAA*] (FAAL) ... MEJ
Meador Elementary School, Houston, TX [*Library symbol*] [*Library of Congress*] (LCLS) ... TxHME
Meadow ... MDW
Meadow [*Postal Service standard*] (OPSA) ... MDW
Meadow [*Commonly used*] (OPSA) ... MEADOW
Meadow Drive Elementary School, Albertson, NY [*Library symbol*] [*Library of Congress*] (LCLS) ... NAlbME
Meadow Elementary School, Baldwin, NY [*Library symbol Library of Congress*] (LCLS) ... NBaldME
Meadow Elementary School, Mineola, NY [*Library symbol Library of Congress*] (LCLS) ... NMinME
Meadow Lake [*Canada*] [*Airport symbol Obsolete*] (OAG) ... YLJ
Meadow Lake, SK [*AM radio station call letters*] ... CJNS
Meadow Lake, SK [*ICAO location identifier*] (ICLI) ... CYLJ
Meadow Mountain [*Vancouver Stock Exchange symbol*] ... MDW
Meadow Valley [*NASDAQ symbol*] (TTSB) ... MVCO
Meadow Valley Corp. [*Associated Press*] (SAG) ... MeaVlly
Meadow Valley Corp. [*Associated Press*] (SAG) ... MeaVly
Meadow Valley Corp. [*NASDAQ symbol*] (SAG) ... MVCO
Meadow Valley Wrrt [*NASDAQ symbol*] (TTSB) ... MVCOW
Meadow View School, Sauk Centre, MN [*Library symbol*] [*Library of Congress*] (LCLS) ... MnScM
Meadowbrook Elementary School, East Meadow, NY [*Library symbol Library of Congress*] (LCLS) ... NEmME
Meadowbrook Hospital, East Meadow, NY [*Library symbol Library of Congress*] (LCLS) ... NEmH
Meadowbrook Insurance Group [*Associated Press*] (SAG) ... MdbkIns
Meadowbrook Insurance Group [*NYSE symbol*] (SAG) ... MIG
Meadowbrook Insurance Grp [*NYSE symbol*] (TTSB) ... MIG
Meadowbrook Rehab Grp'A' [*NASDAQ symbol*] (TTSB) ... MBRK
Meadowbrook Rehabilitation Group [*NASDAQ symbol*] (SAG) ... MBRK
Meadowbrook Rehabilitation Group [*Associated Press*] (SAG) ... MdbrkRe
Meadowlane Community Library, Melbourne, FL [*Library symbol Library of Congress*] (LCLS) ... FMeM
Meadowood Manor Personal Care Home, Winnipeg, Manitoba [*Library symbol National Library of Canada*] (NLC) ... MWMMP
Meadowood Manor Personal Care Home, Winnipeg, MB, Canada [*Library symbol Library of Congress*] (LCLS) ... CaMWMMP
Meadows (MCD) ... MDWS
Meadows ... MDWS
Meadows [*Commonly used*] (OPSA) ... MEADOWS
Meadows [*Commonly used*] (OPSA) ... MEDOWS
Meadows Valley Community Library, New Meadows, ID [*Library symbol*] [*Library of Congress*] (LCLS) ... IdNm
Meadowview School, Long Prairie, MN [*Library symbol*] [*Library of Congress*] (LCLS) ... MnLpM
Meadville, PA [*Location identifier FAA*] (FAAL) ... GKJ
Meadville, PA [*FM radio station call letters*] ... WARC
Meadville, PA [*AM radio station call letters*] ... WMGW
Meadville, PA [*FM radio station call letters*] ... WZPR
Meadville Theological School, Chicago, IL [*Library symbol Library of Congress*] (LCLS) ... ICMe
Meadville Theological School, Chicago, IL [*OCLC symbol*] (OCLC) ... IDH
Meaford Public Library, Ontario [*Library symbol National Library of Canada*] (NLC) ... OMEA
Meal ... ME
Meal Card Number Recording System (MCD) ... MCNRS
Meal, Combat, Individual [*Military*] (AABC) ... MCI
Meal, Ordered Ready-to-Eat [*Army*] (RDA) ... MORE
Meal Ready to Eat (AD) ... mre
Meal, Ready-to-Eat [*Army rations designation, replaces C-rations*] ... MRE
Meal Semiconductor Metal (IAA) ... MSM
Meal Tickets Authorized and Issued [*Army*] (AABC) ... MTAI
Meals for Millions Foundation [*Later, MFM/FFH*] (EA) ... MFM
Meals for Millions/Freedom from Hunger Foundation (EA) ... MFM/FFH
Meals on Wheels ... MOW
Meals Rejected by Everyone ... MRE
Meals-on-Wheels America [*An association*] ... MOWA
Mean [*Arithmetic average*] ... M
Mean Absolute Deviation [*Statistics*] ... MAD
Mean Absolute Error ... MAE
Mean Absolute Percentage Error [*Statistics*] ... MAPE
Mean Absolute Value [*Statistics*] ... MAV
Mean Active Maintenance Downtime [*Computer science*] ... M
Mean Active Maintenance Time (MCD) ... MAMT
Mean Active Repair Time (IEEE) ... MART
Mean Administrative and Logistics Downtime [*Quality control*] (MCD) ... MALDT
Mean Administrative Delay Time ... MADT
Mean Aerodynamic Center ... MAC
Mean Aerodynamic Chord ... MAC
Mean Airway Pressure [*Medicine*] (DMAA) ... MAP
Mean Alveolar Nitrous Oxide Tension [*Medicine*] (DAVI) ... PA_{N2O}
Mean Ambient Flow Vector [*Geology*] ... MAFV
Mean and Standard Deviation ... MANDSD
Mean Annual Increment ... MAI
Mean Annual Temperature [*Climatology*] ... MAT
Mean Aortic Pressure [*Medicine*] ... MAP
Mean Area of Effectiveness (CINC) ... MAE
Mean Arterial Blood Pressure [*Medicine*] (MAE) ... MA
Mean Arterial Blood Pressure [*Medicine*] ... MABP
Mean Arterial Pressure [*Medicine*] ... MAP
Mean Barometric Pressure [*Symbol*] ... B
Mean Blood Pressure [*Medicine*] ... MBP
Mean Body Mass Index ... MBMI
Mean Body Temperature (WDAA) ... MBT
Mean Body Weight ... MBW
Mean Brachial Artery [*Pressure*] [*Cardiology*] (DAVI) ... BAm
Mean Brachial Artery Pressure [*Medicine*] ... MBP
Mean Cardiac Index ... MCI
Mean Carrier Frequency [*Radio*] (IAA) ... MCF
Mean Cell [*or Corpuscular*] **Diameter** [*Hematology*] ... MCD
Mean Cell [*or Corpuscular*] **Hemoglobin** [*Hematology*] ... MCH
Mean Cell [*or Corpuscular*] **Hemoglobin Concentration** [*Hematology*] ... MCC
Mean Cell [*or Corpuscular*] **Hemoglobin Concentration** [*Hematology*] ... MCHC
Mean Cell Retention Time (GNE) ... MCRT
Mean Cell [*or Corpuscular*] **Thickness** [*Hematology*] ... MCT
Mean Cell [*or Corpuscular*] **Threshold** [*Hematology*] (MAE) ... MCT
Mean Cell [*or Corpuscular*] **Volume** [*Hematology*] ... MCV
Mean Chance Expectation [*Parapsychology*] ... MCE
Mean Circulation Time [*Medicine*] ... MCT
Mean Clinical Value (AAMN) ... MCV
Mean Corpuscular Hemoglobin [*Hematology*] (DAVI) ... MCHb
Mean Corpuscular Hemoglobin [*Hematology*] (DAVI) ... MCHg
Mean Corpuscular Hemoglobin [*Count*] [*Hematology*] (DAVI) ... MCHL
Mean Corpuscular Hemoglobin and Red Cell Indices [*Hematology*] (DAVI) ... MCH
Mean Corpuscular Hemoglobin Concentration [*Hematology*] (DAVI) ... MCHbC
Mean Corpuscular Hemoglobin Concentration and Red Cell Indices [*Hematology*] (DAVI) ... MCHC
Mean Corpuscular Hemoglobin Count [*Hematology*] (DAVI) ... MCHbC
Mean Corpuscular Hemoglobin Count [*Hematology*] (DAVI) ... MCHC
Mean Corpuscular Hemogobin [*Hematology*] (DAVI) ... MCHgb
Mean Corpuscular Thickness [*Hematology*] (CPH) ... MCT
Mean Corpuscular Volume [*Physiology*] ... MCV
Mean Corpusculsar Hemoglobin Concentration [*Physiology*] ... MCHC
Mean Correct Time ... MCT
Mean Corrective Downtime [*Computer science*] ... MCDT
Mean Corrective-Maintenance Time (MCD) ... MCT
Mean Countdown Between Failures ... MCBF
Mean Crew Size (MCD) ... MCS
Mean Cycles between Failures [*Quality control*] ... MCBF
Mean Cycles between Operational Mission Failures [*Quality control*] ... MCBOMF
Mean Cycles between Premature Removals [*Quality control*] (MCD) ... MCBP
Mean Daily Difference [*Medicine*] ... MDD
Mean Daily Dose ... MDD
Mean Daily Nitrogen Balance [*Medicine*] ... MDNB
Mean Datum Plane ... MDP
Mean Days between Injuries ... MDBI
Mean Death Time ... MDT
Mean Delay Time (CAAL) ... MDT
Mean Designation Point (CAAL) ... MDP
Mean Detonating Time (NASA) ... MDT
Mean Deviation ... MD
Mean Diameter-Thickness Ratio (MAE) ... MDTR
Mean Distance between Failures [*Quality control*] (MCD) ... MDBF
Mean Diurnal High-Water Inequality ... DHQ
Mean Diurnal Low-Water Inequality ... DLQ
Mean Dominant Frequency (MAE) ... MDF
Mean Dominant Height ... MDH
Mean Dose [*Pharmacology*] (DAVI) ... D
Mean Dose Per Unit Cumulated Activity (DAVI) ... S
Mean Downtime [*Computer science*] ... MDT
Mean Ear Location [*Automotive engineering*] ... MEL
Mean Effective Horsepower (IAA) ... MEHP
Mean Effective Injection Pressure [*Diesel engines*] ... MEIP
Mean Effective Pressure ... MEP
Mean Effective Temperature Difference [*Refrigeration*] ... METD
Mean Ejection Rate [*Medicine*] ... MER
Mean Elapsed Downtime [*Computer science*] (MCD) ... MEDT
Mean Elapsed Time (MCD) ... MET
Mean Engine Operating Time between Failures [*Quality control*] ... MEOTBF
Mean Equivalent Wind [*Meteorology*] (DA) ... MEW
Mean Fault Location Time (DNAB) ... MFLT
Mean Fibre Extent (PDAA) ... MFE
Mean Firing Rate [*Neurophysiology*] ... MFR
Mean First Lesions Time [*Immunochemistry*] ... MFLT
Mean First-Passage Time [*Biochemistry*] ... MFPT
Mean Flight Hour between Unscheduled Maintenance Actions [*Quality control*] (MCD) ... MFHBUMA
Mean Flight Hours between Failures [*Quality control*] (MCD) ... MFHBF
Mean Flight Hours between Maintenance Actions [*Quality control*] (NVT) ... MFHBMA
Mean Flight Time (KSC) ... MFT
Mean Flight Time ... MFT
Mean Flights between Failures [*Military*] (CAAL) ... MFBF
Mean Flourescence Intensity [*Biochemistry*] ... MFI
Mean Forced Outage Time (PDAA) ... MFOT
Mean Free Path [*Symbol*] [*IUPAC*] ... l
Mean Free Path ... MFP
Mean Free Time ... MFT
Mean Gain Deviation (IEEE) ... MGD
Mean Hemispherical Candlepower ... MHSCP
Mean Hemolytic Dose [*Pharmacology*] (MAE) ... MHD
Mean High Tide [*Tides and currents*] ... MHT
Mean High Water [*Tides and currents*] ... MHW
Mean Higher High Water [*Tides and currents*] ... MHHW

Mean Higher High-Water Springs [*Tides and currents*]	MHHWS
Mean Higher Low Water [*Tides and currents*]	MHLW
Mean High-Water Lunitidal Interval [*Tides and currents*]	MHWI
Mean High-Water Neap [*Tides and currents*]	MHWN
Mean High-Water Springs [*Tides and currents*]	MHWS
Mean Hook Extent (PDAA)	MHE
Mean Horizontal Acceleration	MHA
Mean Horizontal Candle [*Aerospace*]	MHC
Mean Horizontal Candlepower	MHCP
Mean Horizontal Velocity	MHV
Mean Indicated Pressure	MIP
Mean Integral Square Error (PDAA)	MISER
Mean Interarrival Time (MHDB)	MIAT
Mean Intravascular Pressure [*Cardiology*] (MAE)	MIP
Mean Job Mill Time [*Quality control*] (MHDB)	MJMT
Mean Kilometers between Failures	MKBF
Mean Latitude	MLAT
Mean Left Atrial Pressure [*Cardiology*]	MLAP
Mean Length of Utterance [*Linguistics*]	MLU
Mean Length per Turn	MLT
Mean Lesion Length [*Pathology*]	MLL
Mean Lethal Radius	MLR
Mean Level	ML
Mean Life Time (NATG)	MLT
Mean Lifespan (AAMN)	MLS
Mean Line of Advance [*Military*] (NVT)	MLA
Mean Linear Intercept	MLI
Mean Logistic Delay Time [*Military*] (CAAL)	MLDT
Mean Logistic Down Time	MLDT
Mean Logistical Time (IEEE)	MLT
Mean Low Tide [*Tides and currents*]	MLT
Mean Low Water [*Tides and currents*]	MLW
Mean Lower Hemispherical Candlepower (IAA)	MLHCP
Mean Lower High Water [*Tides and currents*]	MLHW
Mean Lower Low Water [*Tides and currents*]	MLLW
Mean Lower Low Water Line [*Tides and currents*] (PDAA)	MLLWL
Mean Lower Low-Water Springs [*Tides and currents*]	MLLWS
Mean Low-Water Datum [*Nuclear energy*] (NRCH)	MLD
Mean Low-Water Lunitidal Interval [*Tides and currents*]	MLWI
Mean Low-Water Neap [*Tides and currents*]	MLWN
Mean Low-Water Spring [*Tides and currents*]	MLWS
Mean Manhours per Maintenance Action	MMH/MA
Mean Mass Density	MMD
Mean Mass Diameter	MMD
Mean Maternal Glucose [*Clinical chemistry*]	MMG
Mean Maximum Flow [*Medicine*]	MMW
Mean Maximum Weight	MMW
Mean Measure of Divergence [*Statistics*]	MMD
Mean Meridional Circulation [*Climatology*]	MMC
Mean Miles between Essential Maintenance Demand [*Quality control*]	MMBEMD
Mean Miles between Failures [*Quality control*]	MMBF
Mean Miles between Mission Failures [*Quality control*] (MCD)	MMBMF
Mean Miles between Operational Mission Failures [*Quality control*] (MCD)	MMBOMF
Mean Miles between Removals [*Quality control*] (MCD)	MMBR
Mean Miles between System Failures [*Quality control*] (MCD)	MMBSF
Mean Miles between Unscheduled Maintenance Actions [*Quality control*] (MCD)	MMBUMA
Mean Missile [*or Mission*] Duration (KSC)	MMD
Mean Motility Index [*For intestine*]	MMI
Mean Motion Resonance [*Astrophysics*]	MMR
Mean Narrow Dose [*Radiation therapy*] (DAVI)	MND
Mean Neap [*Tide*] Rise [*Tides and currents*]	MNR
Mean Neap Rise (AD)	mnr
Mean Neap Tide (AD)	mnt
Mean Normalized Systolic Ejection Rate [*Cardiology*]	MNSER
Mean of 1950 [*Coordinate system*] [*NASA*] (NASA)	M50
Mean of Consecutive Differences (MAE)	MCD
Mean One Way Propagation Time [*Telecommunications*] (TEL)	MOPT
Mean Operating Time	MOT
Mean Operating Time (AD)	mot
Mean Operational Delay Time	MODT
Mean Opinion Score	MOS
Mean Overhaul Cycle Time [*Quality control*] (MCD)	MOCT
Mean Personnel Quantity per Task (MCD)	MPQ/T
Mean Phenetic Distance	MPD
Mean Photon Flux Density	MPD
Mean Planned Outage Duration [*Electronics*] (IEEE)	MPOD
Mean Platelet Volume [*Hematology*]	MPV
Mean Point of Impact [*Air Force*]	MPI
Mean Point of Impact (AD)	mpi
Mean Population Doubling [*Cytology*]	MPD
Mean Power Frequency [*of myoelectric signals*]	MPF
Mean Pressure (MAE)	MP
Mean Pressure Suction Head (AAG)	MPSH
Mean Pressure Suction Head (AD)	mpsh
Mean Preventive Downtime [*Computer science*]	MPDT
Mean Preventive Maintenance Hours	MPMH
Mean Preventive Maintenance Time (MCD)	MPMT
Mean Preventive Maintenance Time (MCD)	MPT
Mean Probable Number (MCD)	MPN
Mean Pulmonary Artery Pressure [*Cardiology*]	MPAP
Mean Pulmonary Venous Pressure [*Cardiology*]	MPVP
Mean Pulse Time	MPT

Mean Radial Error	MRE
Mean Radial Error (AD)	mre
Mean Radiant Temperature (AD)	mrt
Mean Radiant Temperature	MRT
Mean Radiative-Transfer [*Meteorology*]	MRT
Mean Radius (MCD)	MR
Mean Range [*Difference in height between mean high water and mean low water*] [*Tides and currents*]	Mn
Mean Ready Time (MCD)	MRT
Mean Reciprocal Detection Latency	MRDL
Mean Reference Axis (MCD)	MRA
Mean Re-Initialization Time	MRIT
Mean Relative Growth Rate [*Physiology*]	MRGR
Mean Renal Blood Flow [*Nephrology*]	MRBF
Mean Repair Time	MRT
Mean Residence Time [*Kinetics*]	MRT
Mean Retention Time [*Physiology*]	MRT
Mean Right Atrial [*Cardiology*]	MRA
Mean Right Atrial Pressure [*Cardiology*]	MRAP
Mean Right Ventricular Pressure [*Cardiology*]	MRVP
Mean Rise Interval [*Tides and currents*]	MRI
Mean Rise Interval (AD)	mri
Mean Rounds between Corrective Maintenance Actions [*Quality control*] (MCD)	MRBCMA
Mean Rounds between Failures [*Military*] (CAAL)	MRBF
Mean Rounds between Operational Mission Failures [*Quality control*] (MCD)	MRBOMF
Mean Rounds between Stoppages [*Quality control*] (MCD)	MRBS
Mean Rounds to First Maintenance [*Army*]	MRTFM
Mean Sea Level	MSL
Mean Sea Level	MSL
Mean Sea Surface Temperature	MSST
Mean Sea Water	MSW
Mean Selected Temperature	MST
Mean Shallow Water	MSW
Mean Solar Day	MSD
Mean Solar Second (IAA)	MSS
Mean Solar Time	MST
Mean Sorties between Flights (MCD)	MSBF
Mean Sound Absorption [*Symbol*] [*Aerospace*]	a
Mean Spherical Approximation [*Physical chemistry*]	MSA
Mean Spherical Candlepower [*Computer science*] (IAA)	MSC
Mean Spherical Candlepower	MSCP
Mean Spleen Index	MSI
Mean Spring Rise [*Tides and currents*]	M
Mean Square	MS
Mean Square	MS
Mean Square (AD)	ms
Mean Square Deviation [*or Difference*]	MSD
Mean Square Error [*Statistics*]	MSE
Mean Square Error Efficiency [*Statistics*]	MSEE
Mean Square Error Inefficiency [*Statistics*]	MSEI
Mean Square Error of Prediction [*Statistics*] (PDAA)	MSEP
Mean Square Relative Displacement [*Spectra*]	MSRD
Mean Square Root (IAA)	MSR
Mean Square Signal-to-Noise (IAA)	MSSN
Mean Square Velocity	MSV
Mean Square Voltage (NRCH)	MSV
Mean Square Weighted Deviation [*Statistics*]	MSWD
Mean Squared Distance [*Data analysis*]	MSD
Mean Squared Distance Between Pairs [*Statistics*] (PDAA)	MSDBP
Mean Standard Toxicity Score (MCD)	MSTS
Mean Supply Downtime (CAAL)	MSDT
Mean Supply Response Time	MSRT
Mean Survival Time	MST
Mean Swell Time [*Botulism test*] [*Food analysis*]	MST
Mean Systemic Arterial Pressure [*Cardiology*]	MSAP
Mean Systolic Ejection Rate [*Cardiology*]	MSER
Mean Temperature Difference	MTD
Mean Therapeutic Dose [*Medicine*]	MTD
Mean Tide [*Tides and currents*]	MT
Mean Tide Level [*Tides and currents*]	MTL
Mean Time	MT
Mean Time Before Obsolescence [*Navy*] (DOMA)	MTBO
Mean Time between Any Maintenance Actions [*Quality control*] (MCD)	MTBAMA
Mean Time Between Confirmed Defects [*Quality control*] (MHDI)	MTBCD
Mean Time between Confirmed Failures [*Quality control*]	MTBCF
Mean Time between Corrective Action (MCD)	MTBCA
Mean Time between Corrective Maintenance Events [*Quality control*] (CAAL)	MTBCME
Mean Time between Corrective Maintenance Interrupts [*Quality control*] (CAAL)	MTBCMI
Mean Time between Defects [*Quality control*] (PDAA)	MTBD
Mean Time between Degradations [*Quality control*] [*Telecommunications*] (TEL)	MTBD
Mean Time between Demands [*Quality control*] (MCD)	MTBD
Mean Time between Depot Repair [*Quality control*] (PDAA)	MTBDR
Mean Time between Discrepancies [*Quality control*]	MTBD
Mean Time between Downing Events [*Quality control*]	MTBDE
Mean Time between Engine Removal [*Quality control*] (DNAB)	MTBER
Mean Time between Errors [*Quality control*]	MTBE
Mean Time between Essential Maintenance Actions [*Quality control*]	MTBEMA
Mean Time between Essential Replacement Actions [*Quality control*]	MTBE
Mean Time between Events [*Quality control*]	MTBE

Mean Time between [*or before*] **Failures** [*Quality control*] ..... MTBF
Mean Time between Failures, Critical [*Military*] ..... MTBFC
Mean Time between Failures Requiring Overhaul [*Quality control*] ..... MTBFRO
Mean Time between False Alarms [*Quality control*] (AABC) ..... MTBFA
Mean Time between Flight Cancellations [*Quality control*] ..... MTBFC
Mean Time between Function Loss [*Quality control*] ..... MTBFL
Mean Time between Interrupts [*Quality control*] ..... MTBI
Mean Time between Maintenance [*Quality control*] (AFM) ..... MTBM
Mean Time between Maintenance Actions [*Quality control*] ..... MTBMA
Mean Time between Malfunction Events [*Quality control*] (CAAL) ..... MTBME
Mean Time between Malfunctions [*Quality control*] ..... MTBM
Mean Time between Mission Affecting Failures [*Quality control*] ..... MTBMAF
Mean Time between Mission Critical Failure [*Quality control*] ..... MTBMCF
Mean Time between Operational Failures [*Quality control*] ..... MTBOF
Mean Time between Operational Mission Failures [*Quality control*] (MCD) ..... MTBOMF
Mean Time between Outages [*Quality control*] [*Telecommunications*] (TEL) ..... MTBO
Mean Time between Overhauls [*Quality control*] (MCD) ..... MTBO
Mean Time between Permanent Engine Removal [*Quality control*] (DNAB) ..... MTBPER
Mean Time Between Planned Maintenance [*Engineering*] ..... MTBPM
Mean Time between Removal [*or Repair or Replacement*] [*Quality control*] ..... MTBR
Mean Time between Removal for Depot Repair [*Quality control*] (MCD) ..... MTBRDR
Mean Time Between Replacement ..... MTBR
Mean Time between Service [*Quality control*] (MCD) ..... MTBS
Mean Time Between Software Errors [*Quality control*] (MHDI) ..... MTBSE
Mean Time between Software Failures [*Quality control*] (CAAL) ..... MTBSF
Mean Time Between Stops [*Quality control*] (IAA) ..... MTBS
Mean Time between Supply Demands [*Quality control*] (MCD) ..... MTBSD
Mean Time between System Failures [*Quality control*] ..... MTBSF
Mean Time between System Hardware Failures [*Quality control*] (MCD) ..... MTBSHF
Mean Time between System Operational Failures [*Quality control*] (MCD) ..... MTBSOF
Mean Time between Testable Failures [*Quality control*] ..... MTBTF
Mean Time Between Undetected Failures [*Quality control*] (IAA) ..... MTBUF
Mean Time Between Unscheduled Maintenance [*Quality control*] (MHDI) ..... MTBUM
Mean Time between Unscheduled Maintenance Actions ..... MBUMA
Mean Time between Unscheduled Maintenance Actions [*Quality control*] ..... MTBUMA
Mean Time between Unscheduled Removals [*or Replacements*] [*Quality control*] ..... MTBUR
Mean Time between Unscheduled Removals [*or Replacements*] [*Quality control*] (IIA) ..... MTUR
Mean Time for Repair [*Quality control*] (IAA) ..... MTFR
Mean Time in Shop [*Quality control*] (MCD) ..... MTIS
Mean Time Level ..... MTL
Mean Time Measurement ..... MTM
Mean Time to Accomplish [*Quality control*] (NASA) ..... MTTA
Mean Time to Bench [*Repair*] [*Quality control*] ..... MTTB
Mean Time to Catastrophic Failure [*Quality control*] ..... MTCF
Mean Time to Change Parts [*Quality control*] (MCD) ..... MTTC
Mean Time to Detect [*Quality control*] (MCD) ..... MTTD
Mean Time to Diagnosis [*Quality control*] (BUR) ..... MTTD
Mean Time to Exchange [*Quality control*] (MCD) ..... MTTE
Mean Time to Failure [*Quality control*] ..... MTF
Mean Time to Failure [*Quality control*] ..... MTTF
Mean Time to Fault Locate [*Quality control*] (CAAL) ..... MTFL
Mean Time to First Failure [*Quality control*] (AAG) ..... MTFF
Mean Time to First Failure [*Quality control*] ..... MTTFF
Mean Time to First System Failure [*Quality control*] (PDAA) ..... MTTFSF
Mean Time to First System Repair [*Quality control*] (PDAA) ..... MTTFSR
Mean Time to Inspect [*Quality control*] (CAAL) ..... MTTI
Mean Time to Maintain [*Quality control*] (CMD) ..... MTTM
Mean Time to Planned Outage (IEEE) ..... MTTPO
Mean Time to Provide Manpower (DNAB) ..... MTPM
Mean Time to Removal [*Quality control*] ..... MTR
Mean Time to Removal [*Quality control*] ..... MTTR
Mean Time to Repair [*Quality control*] (CAAL) ..... MTTR
Mean Time to Replacement [*Quality control*] ..... MTTR
Mean Time to Restore [*Quality control*] (IAA) ..... MTR
Mean Time to Restore [*Quality control*] (IEEE) ..... MTTR
Mean Time to Restore Software [*Quality control*] (CAAL) ..... MTTRS
Mean Time to Restore System [*Quality control*] ..... MTTRS
Mean Time to Service [*Quality control*] ..... MTTS
Mean Time to Service Restoral [*Quality control*] [*Telecommunications*] (TEL) ..... MTSR
Mean Time to System Failure [*Quality control*] (PDAA) ..... MTSF
Mean Time to System Failure [*Quality control*] (PDAA) ..... MTTSF
Mean Time to Test (MCD) ..... MTTT
Mean Time to Unplanned Outage (IEEE) ..... MTTUO
Mean Time to Unscheduled Replacement [*Quality control*] (PDAA) ..... MTUR
Mean Time to Wait for Parts [*Quality control*] (MCD) ..... MTTW
Mean Tolerated Dose [*Medicine*] ..... MTD
Mean Total Dose [*Medicine*] (DMAA) ..... MTD
Mean Transformed Value ..... MTV
Mean Transit Time ..... MTT
Mean Transit Time [*Radiology*] (DAVI) ..... tp
Mean Transverse Emmission Energy (PDAA) ..... MTEE
Mean Tryptic Activity (PDAA) ..... MTA
Mean Tubular Diameter ..... MTD
Mean Turn-Around Time [*Quality control*] ..... MTAT
Mean Units between Replacement [*Quality control*] ..... MUBR
Mean Unplanned Outage Duration (IEEE) ..... MUOD
Mean Up Time [*NASA*] (KSC) ..... MUT
Mean Value ..... MV
Mean Value Reference [*Mathematics*] ..... MVR
Mean Variation ..... MV
Mean Vertical Acceleration ..... MVA
Mean Vertical Velocity ..... MVV
Mean Voltage (IAA) ..... MV
Mean Waiting Time for Supply Replacement (DNAB) ..... MWTR
Mean Water Level ..... MWL
Mean Water Temperature ..... MWT
Mean Weighted Skin Temperature ..... MWST
Mean Width Ratio ..... MWR
Mean Wildlife Index Value [*Statistics*] (PDAA) ..... MWIV
Mean Year (IAA) ..... MY
Mean Yield [*Agriculture*] ..... MY
Mean Yield/Plants [*Agriculture*] ..... MY/P
Mean Zonal Candlepower (IAA) ..... MZCP
Meander Belt Deposit [*Geology*] ..... MBD
Meander Channels Plasma Display Panel (IAA) ..... MCPDP
Meander Electrodes Plasma Display Panel (IAA) ..... MEPDP
Meander Inverted Autocorrelated Function ..... MIACF
Mean-Family Replacement Factor ..... MFRF
Meaning (ABBR) ..... MENG
Meaning (ROG) ..... MG
Meaning ..... mng
Meaning Extraction [*Programming language*] [*1971*] (CSR) ..... MEANINGEX
Meaning of Energy Growth: An Assessment of Systems, Technologies, and Requirements [*NASA*] ..... MEGASTAR
Meaningful (ABBR) ..... MENGF
Meaningful Assistance in the Neighborhood [*of Legal Aid Bureau of George Washington University Law School*] (EA) ..... MAN
Meaningfully (ABBR) ..... MENGFY
Meaningfulness [*Psychology*] ..... M
Meaningless (ABBR) ..... MENGLS
Meaninglessly (ABBR) ..... MENGLSY
Meaning-Representation Language [*Computer science*] ..... MRL
Mean-Maintenance-Man-Hours to Repair (MCD) ..... MMTR
Meanness (ABBR) ..... MENNS
Meanook [*Canada*] [*Geomagnetic observatory code*] ..... MEA
Mean's Kansas Reports [*A publication*] (DLA) ..... Means
Means of Testing [*Telecommunications*] (OSI) ..... MOT
Means-End Problem-Solving Procedure [*or Test*] [*Psychology*] ..... MEPS
Mean-Square Displacement [*Statistical graphing*] ..... MSD
Mears' Edition of Justinian and Gaius [*A publication*] (DLA) ..... Mears Just
Measa Royalty Trust [*NYSE symbol*] (SAG) ..... MTR
Measles Immune Globulin [*Immunology*] ..... MIG
Measles, Rubella [*Immunology*] ..... MR
Measles Virus ..... MV
Measles-Containing Vaccine ..... MCV
Measles-Mumps-Rubella [*Immunology*] ..... MMR
Measurable Undesirable Respiratory Contaminants [*Pollution index*] [*Superseded by PSI*] ..... MURC
Measure [*Music*] ..... M
Measure (AABC) ..... MEAS
Measure and Inspection Masks for Integrated Circuits (MCD) ..... MIMIC
Measure and Record ..... M & R
Measure and Record Intake and Output [*Fluid measurement*] [*Medicine*] (CPH) ..... M & R I & O
Measure Calibrate (IAA) ..... MEASCAL
Measure Code (NITA) ..... MC
Measure for Measure [*Shakespearean work*] ..... MM
Measure of Academic Progress [*Educational test*] ..... MAP
Measure of Adult English Proficiency (EDAC) ..... MAEP
Measure of Economic Welfare ..... MEW
Measure of Effectiveness ..... MOE
Measure of Effectiveness (AD) ..... moe
Measure of Elementary Communication Apprehension (EDAC) ..... MECA
Measure of Intellectual Development (EDAC) ..... MID
Measure of Language Proficiency (EDAC) ..... MELP
Measure of Merit (MCD) ..... MOM
Measure of Mission Success [*Military*] (CAAL) ..... MOMS
Measure of Potential Training Effectiveness [*Army*] ..... MOPTE
Measure of Sampling Adequacy Index (EDAC) ..... MSA
Measure of Soil Absorption (GNE) ..... Koc
Measure of Suitability (CAAL) ..... MOS
Measure of Training Effectiveness [*Military*] ..... MOTE
Measure Specific Performance Guarantee [*Calculation*] (AAGC) ..... MSPG
Measured Blood Loss [*Physiology*] ..... MBL
Measured Ceiling [*Aviation*] ..... M
Measured Colloidal Osmotic Pressure [*Clinical chemistry*] ..... mCOP
Measured Daywork [*Payment system*] ..... MDW
Measured Depth [*Diamonds*] ..... MD
Measured Discard [*Nuclear energy*] (NRCH) ..... MD
Measured Drilling [*Diamonds*] ..... MD
Measured Rate of Time (PDAA) ..... MRT
Measured Rating [*IOR*] [*Yacht racing*] ..... MR
Measured Service Pricing [*Telecommunications*] (TEL) ..... MS
Measured Time ..... MT
Measured Tons Discharged or Loaded [*Shipping*] ..... METON
Measured Value ..... MV
Measured Workload Index [*Aviation*] ..... MWI
Measurement (ROG) ..... MEAS

Measurement (DS) .... met
Measurement (KSC) .... MSMT
Measurement .... MSRMNT
Measurement .... MST
Measurement .... MT
Measurement (IAA) .... MA
Measurement Accuracy .... MAC
Measurement and Analysis Center [*Telecommunications*] (TEL) .... MAC
Measurement and Control [*A publication*] (IAA) .... M&C
Measurement and Control [*The Journal of InstMC*] (ACII) .... M&C
Measurement and Control (1962-64) [*A publication*] .... Meas Control (1962-64)
Measurement and Control BASIC [*Programming language developed by Analog Devices*] .... MACBASIC
Measurement and Control System (MHDB) .... MACSYM
Measurement and Instrumentation Technology Panel (ACII) .... MITP
Measurement and Signature Data Requirements (MCD) .... MASDR
Measurement and Signature Intelligence (MCD) .... MASINT
Measurement and Stimuli System (SSD) .... MAST
Measurement and Test Equipment (KSC) .... M & TE
Measurement Assurance Program [*National Institute of Standards and Technology*] .... MAP
Measurement Base [*Military*] .... MB
Measurement, Command, and Control (NASA) .... MC & C
Measurement Compensation Factor (PDAA) .... MCF
Measurement, Control, LEID [*Limit of Error of the Inventory Difference*], and MUF Inventory Difference Simulation [*Material Unaccounted For*] [*Nuclear energy*] (NRCH) .... MCLAMS
Measurement, Control Regulation, and Automation (IEEE) .... MESUCORA
[*Association for*] **Measurement, Control, Regulation and Automation** (ECII) .... MESUCORA
Measurement Control Unit (IAA) .... MCU
Measurement, Decision, and Actuation [*Computer science*] .... MDA
Measurement Descriptor Table (NASA) .... MDT
Measurement Engine (IAA) .... ME
Measurement Facility [*Computer science*] (IBMDP) .... MF
Measurement for Assessing the Effects of Stratospheric Aircraft [*Marine science*] (OSRA) .... MAESA
Measurement Frequency/1 [*IBM*] (NITA) MF/1
Measurement Handicap Rule [*Sailing*] .... MHR
Measurement Handicapping System [*Yacht racing*] .... MHS
Measurement Information Data Analysis System [*or Subsystem*] (IEEE) .... MIDAS
Measurement Laboratory Information Service [*Battelle Memorial Institute*] .... MLIS
Measurement Name (NITA) .... MN
Measurement of Air Pollution from Satellites .... MAPS
Measurement of Air [*or Atmospheric*] **Pollution from Satellites** .... MAPS
Measurement of Atmospheric Turbulence .... MAT
Measurement of Gains and Losses (DICI) .... MG & L
Measurement of Haze and Visual Effects [*Study*] [*Marine science*] (OSRA) .... MOHAVE
Measurement of Haze and Visual Effects [*Study*] (USDC) .... MOHAVE
Measurement of Instantaneous Kinetic Energy (IEEE) .... MIKE
Measurement of Self Concept in Kindergarten Children [*Psychology*] .... MSCKC
Measurement of Skill (AEBS) .... MOS
Measurement Pipette .... MP
Measurement Pragmatic [*Computer science*] (OA) .... MP
Measurement Requirement Change Request [*NASA*] (KSC) .... MRCR
Measurement Requirements and Interface (MCD) .... MRI
Measurement Requirements Committee [*NASA*] (NASA) .... MRC
Measurement Research Center [*University of Iowa*] .... MRC
Measurement Sensitive Products (DICI) .... MSP
Measurement Specialities, Inc. [*Associated Press*] (SAG) .... Meas Spcl
Measurement Specialities, Inc. [*AMEX symbol*] (SAG) .... MSS
Measurement Specialties [*AMEX symbol*] (TTSB) .... MSS
Measurement Standard Sensitivity (DICI) .... MSS
Measurement Standards Laboratory .... MSL
Measurement Status Table (NASA) .... MST
Measurement Stimulation Identification (MCD) .... MSID
Measurement Stimuli (NASA) .... M/S
Measurement/Stimuli Change Request (MCD) .... MSCR
Measurement System Laboratory (MCD) .... MSL
Measurement System Operating Procedure (NG) .... MSOP
Measurement Ton (MUGU) .... MT
Measurement Ton .... MTON
Measurement Unit .... MU
Measurement while Drilling .... MWD
Measurements (NATG) .... MEA
Measurements Calibration System (KSC) .... MCS
Measurements Control Procedure (KSC) .... MCP
Measurements for Assessing the Effects of Stratospheric Aircraft (USDC) .... MAESA
Measurements Group, Inc., Raleigh, NC [*Library symbol Library of Congress*] (LCLS) .... NcRMG
Measurements of Earth Data for Environmental Analysis [*Marine science*] (OSRA) .... MEDEA
Measurements of Pollution in the Troposphere .... MOPITT
Measurements/Stimuli Request Form [*NASA*] (NASA) .... MRF
Measurement-While Drilling [*Drilling technology*] .... MWD
Measures for Air Quality [*Program*] [*National Institute of Standards and Technology*] .... MAQ
Measures for Encouraging the Development of the Audiovisual Production Industry [*EC*] (ECED) .... MEDIA
Measures of Effectiveness, Development, and Application (MCD) .... MOEDA
Measures of Performance (MCD) .... MOP
Measurex Corp. [*Associated Press*] (SAG) .... Mesrx
Measurex Corp. [*NYSE symbol*] (SPSG) .... MX
Measuring .... MEAS
Measuring Accuracy and Repeatability Study .... MARS
Measuring Air Pollution from Space [*Marine science*] (OSRA) .... MAPS
Measuring Air Pollution from Space (USDC) .... MAPS
Measuring and Confusing (DNAB) .... MEACONING
Measuring and Stimuli Equipment (NASA) .... MSE
Measuring and Stimuli Equipment .... MSE
Measuring and Test Equipment (IEEE) .... MATE
Measuring Element .... ME
Measuring Improved Capability [*Army*] .... MICAP
Measuring Improved Capability of Army Forces .... MICAF
Measuring Monitoring Module (KSC) .... MMM
Measuring Point (NASA) .... MP
Measuring Set .... MS
Measuring Stimuli Units (NASA) .... MSU
Measuring System .... MS
Measuring Transformer (IAA) .... MT
Meat and Bone Meal .... MBM
Meat and Livestock Commission [*British*] (ARC) .... MLC
Meat and Poultry Export Association .... MPEA
Meat and Poultry Inspection Program [*Department of Agriculture*] .... MPIP
Meat Base Formula [*Medicine*] (MEDA) .... MBF
Meat Export Research Center [*Iowa State University*] [*Research center*] (RCD) .... MERC
Meat Exporters' Association of Tasmania [*Australia*] .... MEAT
Meat Exporters' Association of the Northern Territory [*Australia*] .... MEANT
Meat Exporters' Association of Victoria [*Australia*] .... MEAV
Meat Extract Agar [*Microbiology*] .... MEA
Meat, Fish and Poultry .... MFP
Meat Free [*Diet*] .... MF
Meat Hygiene Authority [*Australia*] .... MHA
Meat Importers' Council [*Later, MICA*] (EA) .... MIC
Meat Importers' Council of America (EA) .... MICA
Meat Industries Employers' Association of Western Australia .... MIEAWA
Meat Industry Council [*Australia*] .... MIC
Meat Industry Research Institute of New Zealand .... MIRINZ
Meat Industry Suppliers Association (EA) .... MISA
Meat Industry Supply and Equipment Association [*Later, MISA*] (EA) .... MISEA
Meat Industry Training Organisation (AIE) .... MITO
Meat Innovation Grant .... MIG
Meat Inspection Division [*of ARS, Department of Agriculture*] .... MI
Meat Inspection Division [*of ARS, Department of Agriculture*] .... MID
Meat Inspectors' Association (Australian Public Service) .... MIA(APS)
Meat Machinery Manufacturers Institute (EA) .... MMMI
Meat Packing House (AD) .... MPH
Meat Promotion Executive [*British*] .... MPE
Meat Research Institute [*British*] .... MRI
Meat Research Institute of New Zealand (AD) .... MRINZ
Meat-and-Vegetable [*A canned ration*] [*Military*] .... M and V
Meath [*County in Ireland*] (ROG) .... MEA
Meath [*County in Ireland*] (ROG) .... MTH
Meaux/Esbly [*France ICAO location identifier*] (ICLI) .... LFPE
Mebane, NC [*AM radio station call letters*] .... WGSB
Mebstetten [*Germany ICAO location identifier*] (ICLI) .... EDSV
Mebyon Kernow [*Sons of Cornwall*] [*National liberation party*] [*Political party*] .... MK
Mecanorma [*Graphic artist products*] [*British*] .... MN
Mecca Minerals Ltd. [*Vancouver Stock Exchange symbol*] .... MAA
MeCCNU [*Semustine*], Adriamycin [*Antineoplastic drug regimen*] .... MAD
MeCCNU [*Semustine*], Adriamycin, Vincristine [*Antineoplastic drug regimen*] .... MAV
MeCCNU [*Semustine*], Oncovin , Fluorouracil [*Vincristine*] [*Antineoplastic drug regimen*] .... MOF
MeCCNU [*Semustine*], Oncovin , Fluorouracil, Streptozotocin [*Vincristine*] [*Antineoplastic drug regimen*] .... MOF-STREP
Mecdet MPC Corp. [*NASDAQ symbol*] (SAG) .... MMRX
Mechanic [*or Mechanics*] (AFM) .... MECH
Mechanic .... MECH
Mechanic Badge .... MECHBAD
Mechanic in Charge (DCTA) .... MECH I/C
Mechanica [*of Aristotle*] [*Classical studies*] (OCD) .... Mech
Mechanical .... M
Mechanical (DD) .... mech
Mechanical .... MECHL
Mechanical .... MECHNL
Mechanical Accessories (MCD) .... MA
Mechanical Accessory Repair Shop (MCD) .... MARS
Mechanical Accounting for Telephone Service (IAA) .... MATS
Mechanical Advantage .... MA
Mechanical Advantage Changer .... MAC
Mechanical Aerospace Ground Equipment (TEL) .... MAGE
Mechanical Aids for the Individual Soldier [*Army*] .... MAIS
Mechanical Ambush (VNW) .... MA
Mechanical Analog Computer (DEN) .... MAC
Mechanical and Electrical (IAA) .... MAE
Mechanical and Electrical Room (AAG) .... M & E
Mechanical and Electrical Room (AAG) .... M & ER
Mechanical and Electrical Room (IAA) .... MAER
Mechanical and Numerical Integrator and Computer (IEEE) .... MANIAC
Mechanical and Structural Subsystems (MCD) .... MSS
Mechanical and Structural Testing and Referral Service [*National Institute of Standards and Technology*] .... MASTARS
Mechanical Antenna Control Electronics (MCD) .... MACE
Mechanical Anti-Theft System [*Automotive engineering*] .... MATS
Mechanical Aptitude Test .... MAT
Mechanical Arm Assembly (NASA) .... MAA
Mechanical Arm Assembly .... MAA

Mechanical Assembly Technique (IAA) ... MAT
Mechanical Automation Breadboard (KSC) ... MAB
Mechanical Auxiliary Ventricle (PDAA) ... MAV
Mechanical Bag Retriever [*Garbage collector*] ... MBR
Mechanical Balance Package (OA) ... MBP
Mechanical Bank Collectors of America (EA) ... MBCA
Mechanical Bathythermograph ... MBT
Mechanical Booster Pump ... MBP
Mechanical Booster Pump System ... MBPS
Mechanical Booster Vacuum Pump ... MBVP
Mechanical Booster Vacuum Pump System ... MBVPS
Mechanical Boundary Layer [*Geology*] ... MBL
Mechanical Buffer Register [*Computer science*] ... MBR
Mechanical Chemical Codes ... MCC
Mechanical Circulatory Support System ... MCSS
Mechanical Compatibility Control Drawing (MCD) ... MCCD
Mechanical Comprehension Test ... MCT
Mechanical Computer-Aided Design ... MCAD
Mechanical Computer-Aided Engineering ... MCAE
Mechanical Computer-Aided Engineering ... MCAE
Mechanical Contractors Association of America ... MCA
Mechanical Contractors Association of America (EA) ... MCAA
Mechanical Control System [*Aviation*] ... MCS
Mechanical Copyright Protection Society [*British*] ... MCPS
Mechanical Council (EA) ... MC
Mechanical Current Meter [*Marine science*] (OSRA) ... MCM
Mechanical Design Environment ... MDE
Mechanical Development Report (MCD) ... MDR
Mechanical Diode [*Mechanical power transmission*] ... MD
Mechanical Disconnect Kit ... MDK
Mechanical Draft Cooling Tower [*Nuclear energy*] (NRCH) ... MDCT
Mechanical Drafting/Numerical Control (IEEE) ... MD/NC
Mechanical Dynamics [*NASDAQ symbol*] (TTSB) ... MDII
Mechanical Dynamics Inc. (NITA) ... MDI
Mechanical Dynamics, Inc. [*NASDAQ symbol*] (SAG) ... MDII
Mechanical Dynamics, Inc. [*Associated Press*] (SAG) ... MechDy
Mechanical Efficiency ... ME
Mechanical Electric Kong [*Robot*] ... MELKONG
Mechanical/Electrical (AAG) ... M/E
Mechanical, Electrical, and Electronic (MCD) ... MEE
Mechanical/Electrical Equipment Room (MCD) ... MEER
Mechanical Electronic Subassembly Simulator ... MESS
Mechanical Engineer ... M Eng
Mechanical Engineer [*or Engineering*] ... ME
Mechanical Engineer (PGP) ... Mech E
Mechanical Engineer ... Mech Eng
Mechanical Engineer ... MECHENGR
Mechanical Engineer and Electrical Engineer [*Academic degree*] ... ME-EE
Mechanical Engineering (NITA) ... MECHEN
Mechanical Engineering Bulletin [*A publication*] (GFGA) ... MEB
Mechanical Engineering Laboratory [*NASA*] (KSC) ... MELAB
Mechanical Engineering Research and Development Organisation ... MERADO
Mechanical Engineering Technician ... MET
Mechanical Equipment ... ME
Mechanical Equipment Design ... MED
Mechanical Equipment Manufacturers Representatives Association (EA) ... MEMRA
Mechanical Equipment Room (DAC) ... MER
Mechanical Equivalent of Heat [*Symbol*] ... J
Mechanical Evaluation Equipment ... MEE
Mechanical Facilities and Equipment (SAA) ... MFEQ
Mechanical Failures Prevention Group ... MFPG
Mechanical Fit Test Vehicle ... MFTV
Mechanical Flap [*Aviation*] ... MF
Mechanical Front Wheel Drive [*Off-highway equipment*] ... MFWD
Mechanical Ground Support Equipment ... MGSE
Mechanical Handling [*Describes type of produce; for example, MH-1 refers to a kind of tomato*] ... MH
Mechanical Handling Engineers' Association [*British*] (BI) ... MHEA
Mechanical Handling Equipment (MCD) ... MHE
Mechanical Handling System ... MHS
Mechanical/Hydraulic ... MECH/HYD
Mechanical Impact System [*Aerospace*] ... MIS
Mechanical Impact System Design for Advanced Spacecraft (IEEE) ... MISDAS
Mechanical Impedance ... MI
Mechanical Impulse (KSC) ... M/I
Mechanical, Instrument, and Electrical Engineering [*Department of Employment*] [*British*] ... MIEE
Mechanical Instrument Repair and Calibration Shop (DNAB) ... MIRCS
Mechanical Interruption Statistical Summary (IEEE) ... MISS
Mechanical Interruption Summary [*FAA*] ... MIS
Mechanical Jack Manufacturers Association [*Defunct*] (EA) ... MJMA
Mechanical Joint (NASA) ... MJ
Mechanical Launch Support Equipment [*NASA*] (KSC) ... MLSE
Mechanical Limit Stop ... MLS
Mechanical Limit Switch ... MLS
Mechanical Lubricator Association ... MLA
Mechanical Machine-Finished Paper (DGA) ... MMF
Mechanical Maintenance ... MM
Mechanical Maintenance Test Equipment (NASA) ... MTEM
Mechanical Neutral Start [*Automotive engineering*] ... MNS
Mechanical Oblique Sketcher ... MOS
Mechanical Off-Machine Coated Paper (DGA) ... MOC
Mechanical Operability Test ... MOT
Mechanical Operability Test (AD) ... mot
Mechanical Packing Association [*Later, Fluid Sealing Association*] (EA) ... MPA
Mechanical Paper ... MP
Mechanical Part ... MP
Mechanical Parts List (NASA) ... MPL
Mechanical Phase Shifter ... MPS
Mechanical Positioning Control ... MPC
Mechanical Power Systems ... MPS
Mechanical Power Transmission ... MPT
Mechanical Power Transmission Association (EA) ... MPTA
Mechanical Power Transmission Equipment Distributors Association [*Later, Power Transmission Distributors Association*] (EA) ... MPTEDA
Mechanical Pressure Regulator (NRCH) ... MPR
Mechanical Printer ... MP
Mechanical Properties Data Center [*Defense Logistics Agency*] [*Information service or system*] ... MPDC
Mechanical Properties Loop [*Nuclear energy*] (NRCH) ... MPL
Mechanical Properties of Materials Information Center (MCD) ... MPMIC
Mechanical Provisioning Data System ... MPDS
Mechanical Readiness Assessment (NASA) ... MRA
Mechanical Readiness Assessment ... MRA
Mechanical Recording Head ... MRH
Mechanical Reliability Report [*FAA*] ... MRR
Mechanical Reliability Research Center ... MRRC
Mechanical Remote Fuze Disassembly Kit [*Military*] (CAAL) ... MRFDK
Mechanical Research Report ... MRR
Mechanical Response Tissue Analyzer [*For measuring bone strength*] ... MRTA
Mechanical Restraint [*for mental patients*] [*British*] ... MR
Mechanical Road Transport Driver [*British military*] (DMA) ... MTD
Mechanical Road Transport Mechanic [*British military*] (DMA) ... MTM
Mechanical Seal ... MS
Mechanical Setting Device ... MSD
Mechanical Signature Analysis ... MSA
Mechanical Simulation [*of a computer-based directory assistance system*] ... MECHSIM
Mechanical Speed Switch ... MSS
Mechanical Stress Improvement Process [*Nuclear energy*] (NUCP) ... MSIP
Mechanical Subsystem Group [*NASA*] (NASA) ... MSG
Mechanical Super-Calendered Paper (DGA) ... MSC
Mechanical Support Equipment (KSC) ... MSE
Mechanical Support System (MCD) ... MSS
Mechanical Systems Laboratory [*NASA*] (NASA) ... MSL
Mechanical Technician (KSC) ... MT
Mechanical Technology, Inc. ... MTI
Mechanical Test (MCD) ... MT
Mechanical Test Model ... MTM
Mechanical, Thermal, and Optical Interface Control Document (MCD) ... MICD
Mechanical Thermal Pulse (IEEE) ... MTP
Mechanical Time [*Fuse*] (AABC) ... MT
Mechanical Time Base ... MTB
Mechanical Time Fuze ... MTF
Mechanical Time Keeping (NASA) ... MTK
Mechanical Time, Superquick [*Fuse*] [*Weaponry*] ... MTSQ
Mechanical Time, Superquick Fuze [*Weaponry*] (MCD) ... MTSQF
Mechanical Tolerance Index [*Food technology*] ... MTI
Mechanical Torpedo Countermeasure [*Military*] (CAAL) ... MTC
Mechanical Traction [*British military*] (DMA) ... MT
Mechanical Translation [*Computer science*] ... MT
Mechanical Transport ... MT
Mechanical Transport Corps ... MTC
Mechanical Transport Gasoline [*Military British*] ... MTGAS
Mechanical Vacuum Booster ... MVB
Mechanical Vacuum Pump ... MVP
Mechanical Vacuum Pump System ... MVPS
Mechanical Vapor Compressor [*Engineering*] ... MVC
Mechanical Vapor Recompression [*For evaporators*] ... MVR
Mechanical Vapor Recovery System [*Engineering*] ... MVRS
Mechanical Ventilation [*Medicine*] ... MV
Mechanical Vibrating Screen Manufacturers Association [*Later, Vibrating Screen Manufacturers Association*] (EA) ... MVSMA
Mechanical Vibration System ... MVS
Mechanical Wood Pulp [*Paper*] ... MWP
Mechanical Work of Breathing [*Medicine*] (DAVI) ... W
Mechanical-Front-Drive [*Tractor*] ... MFD
Mechanical-Hydraulic Control [*Nuclear energy*] (NRCH) ... MHC
Mechanically Accelerated Sabot System [*Generation of high-density molecular beams*] ... MASS
Mechanically Agitated Tank [*Engineering*] ... MAT
Mechanically Aimed Warhead ... MAW
Mechanically Alloyed [*Metallurgy*] ... MA
Mechanically Compensated Crystal ... MCC
Mechanically Controllable Break [*Junction*] [*In microstructures*] ... MCB
Mechanically Cooled ... MCHCL
Mechanically Deboned Broiler Product [*Food technology*] ... MDBP
Mechanically Deboned Chicken [*Food technology*] ... MDC
Mechanically Deboned Meat [*Food technology*] ... MDM
Mechanically Deboned Poultry [*Food technology*] ... MDP
Mechanically Deboned Poultry Meat [*Food technology*] ... MDPM
Mechanically Deboned Turkey [*Food technology*] ... MDT
Mechanically Deboned Turkey Meat [*Food technology*] ... MDTM
Mechanically Despun Antenna (KSC) ... MDA
Mechanically Induced Stress [*Agriculture*] ... MIS
Mechanically Operated Inlet Valve (ADA) ... MOIV
Mechanically Operated Inlet Valve (AD) ... moiv
Mechanically Processed Beef [*Food technology*] ... MPB
Mechanically Processed Beef Product [*Food technology*] ... MPBP

Mechanically Processed Pork Product [*Food technology*] ... MPPP
Mechanically Processed (Species) Product (DICI) ... MP(S)P
Mechanically Recovered Meat (AD) ... mrm
Mechanically Refrigerated ... MCHRF
Mechanically Removed Meat ... MRM
Mechanically Separated Meat [*Food technology*] ... MSM
Mechanically Separated Spleen [*Food technology*] ... MSS
Mechanically-Alterable Nondestructive Read Out [*Computer science*] (IAA) ... MANDRO
Mechanically-Guided Vehicle ... MGV
Mechanician [*Navy British*] ... MECHN
Mechanician Apprentice [*British military*] (DMA) ... MA
Mechanics' Assistants' and Dry Dock Workers' Union [*British*] ... MADDWU
Mechanics Educational Society of America (EA) ... MESA
Mechanics, Electrical, and Radio (MCD) ... MER
Mechanics Friendly Union Institution [*British*] ... MFUI
Mechanics Institute, San Francisco, CA [*Library symbol Library of Congress*] (LCLS) ... CSfMI
Mechanic's Lien [*Legal term*] (DLA) ... MECH L
Mechanics of Granular Materials ... MGM
Mechanics Savings Bank [*NASDAQ symbol*] (SAG) ... MECH
Mechanics Savings Bank [*Associated Press*] (SAG) ... MechSv
Mechanics Support Team [*Military*] (GFGA) ... MST
Mechanicsburg Defense Depot Activity [*AEC*] ... MDDA
Mechanicsburg, PA [*FM radio station call letters*] ... WTPA
Mechanicsville, MD [*FM radio station call letters*] ... WSMD
Mechanicsville, VA [*FM radio station call letters*] ... WCDX
Mechanicville, NY [*AM radio station call letters*] ... WMVI
Mechanicville, NY [*FM radio station call letters*] ... WXLE
Mechanised Combat Vehicle [*British military*] (DMA) ... MCV
Mechanised Transport Training Corps [*British military*] (DMA) ... MTTC
Mechanised Warfare Experimental Establishment [*British military*] (DMA) ... MWEE
Mechanism ... MCHSM
Mechanism [*Automotive engineering*] ... MECH
Mechanism ... MECHSM
Mechanism Integration Design and Analysis System [*Computer-assisted engineering*] ... MIDAS
Mechanism of Action [*Medicine*] (DAVI) ... MOA
Mechanization Control Area (AAG) ... MCA
Mechanization of Algebraic Operations (PDAA) ... MAO
Mechanization of Contract Administration Service (MCD) ... MOCAS
Mechanization of Defense Industrial Security Clearance Office [*DoD*] ... MODISCO
Mechanization of Freight and Shipping Terminal [*DoD*] ... MOFAST
Mechanization of Selected Transportation Movement ... MECHTRAM
Mechanization of Warehousing and Shipment Procedures [*or Processing*] [*Defense Supply Agency*] ... MOWASP
Mechanization of Warehousing and Shipment Processing (AD) ... mowasp
Mechanization Outside Plant Scheduling System (MHDB) ... MOPS
Mechanize (AAG) ... MECZ
Mechanized (VNW) ... Mech
Mechanized (DOMA) ... MECH
Mechanized Accounting Reserve Pay System ... MARPS
Mechanized Ammunition Recording and Reporting System ... MARRS
Mechanized and Army Combat Operations Vietnam (AABC) ... MACOV
Mechanized Artillery Transport [*Navy symbol Obsolete*] ... APM
Mechanized Assignment and Record Keeping [*Database management system*] ... MARK
Mechanized Battalion [*Army*] ... MB
Mechanized Battalion [*Army*] ... MECHBAT
Mechanized Calling Card Service [*Formerly, ABC*] [*Telecommunications*] ... MCCS
Mechanized Catalog (IEEE) ... MECCA
Mechanized Characteristics Screening ... MCS
Mechanized Cost Distribution and Reporting System (MCD) ... MCDARS
Mechanized Customer Trouble Report Analysis Plan [*Telecommunications*] (TEL) ... MCTRAP
Mechanized Defense Decision Anticipation [*AFSC*] ... MEDDA
Mechanized Desert Operations [*Military*] (MCD) ... MDO
Mechanized Design and Integrated Control ... MEDIC
Mechanized Directory Assistance [*Telecommunications*] (TEL) ... MDA
Mechanized Documentation System ... MDS
Mechanized Embarkation Data System [*Military*] (NVT) ... MEDS
Mechanized Engineering File ... MEF
Mechanized Equipment Assignment [*AT & T*] ... MEQA
Mechanized Export Traffic System [*Army*] (AABC) ... METS
Mechanized Flame Thrower ... MFT
Mechanized Hebrew Dictionary [*A publication*] (BJA) ... MHD
Mechanized Infantry [*Army*] ... MECHINF
Mechanized Infantry Battalion (MCD) ... MIB
Mechanized Infantry Combat Vehicle [*Army*] ... MICV
Mechanized Infantry Combat Vehicle - Firing Port Weapon (MCD) ... MICV-FPW
Mechanized Infantry Combat Vehicle Systems [*Army*] (RDA) ... MICVS
Mechanized Infantry in a Smoke Environment (MCD) ... MISE
Mechanized Infantry Program [*United States Army, Europe*] (MCD) ... MIP
Mechanized Infantry Squad Proficiency Course [*Army*] ... MISPC
Mechanized Information Center [*Information service or system*] ... MIC
Mechanized Integrated Financial Accounting System [*Department of State*] ... MIFAS
Mechanized Letter Office (DCTA) ... MLO
Mechanized Letter Sorting System [*Hong Kong Post Office*] ... MLSS
Mechanized Line Records [*Later, LMOS*] [*Bell System*] ... MLR
Mechanized Line Testing [*Telecommunications*] (TEL) ... MLT
Mechanized Loop Testing (MCD) ... MLT
Mechanized Manufacturing Information ... MMI
Mechanized Market Programming Procedures [*Computer science*] (TEL) ... MMPP
Mechanized Materials Handling System [*Air Force*] ... MMHS
Mechanized Outdoor Planning System ... MOPS
Mechanized Production Control ... MPC
Mechanized Production of Electronics ... MPE
Mechanized RADAR Observer ... MRO
Mechanized Retrieval for Greater Efficiency [*Computer science*] ... MERGE
Mechanized Sales Office Record System [*Telecommunications*] (TEL) ... MSORS
Mechanized Sandbag Filler and Sealer (MCD) ... MECHSFIL
Mechanized Scheduling [*Telecommunications*] (TEL) ... MS
Mechanized Storage and Retrieval [*Computer science*] ... MSR
Mechanized Teletypewriter Exchange (TEL) ... MTWX
Mechanized Unit Property System [*Telecommunications*] (TEL) ... MUPS
Mechanized Utility Vehicle (MCD) ... MUV
Mechanized Wire Centering/Cross Section [*AT & T*] [*Telecommunications*] (TEL) ... MWC/CS
Mechanoacoustic ... MA
Mechanomyography [*Medicine*] ... MMG
Mechanoreceptor Cueing Subsystem (MCD) ... MRCS
Mechanotherapy [*Physical therapy*] (DAVI) ... Mecano
Mechem on Agency [*A publication*] (DLA) ... Mechem
Mechem on Agency [*A publication*] (DLA) ... Mechem Ag
Mechem on Partnership [*A publication*] (DLA) ... Mechem
Mechem on Public Offices and Officers [*A publication*] (DLA) ... Mechem Pub Off
Mecheria [*Algeria*] [*ICAO location identifier*] (ICLI) ... DAAY
Mechernich [*Federal Republic of Germany*] [*Seismograph station code, US Geological Survey Closed*] (SEIS) ... MEC
Mechlorethamine [*Nitrogen mustard*] (MEDA) ... HN_2
Mechlorethamine [*Also, HN, HN2, MBA, NM*] [*Mustargen, nitrogen mustard*] [*Antineoplastic drug*] ... M
Mechlorethamine, Oncovin, Procarbazine, Prednisone [*Medicine*] (MEDA) ... MOPP
Mechlorethamine, Oncovin [*Vincristine*] **Procarbazine, Prednisone, Doxo rubicin, Bleomycin, Vinblastine, Dacarbazine** [*Antineoplastic drug regimen*] (DAVI) ... MOPP/ABVD
Mechlorethamine [*Vincristine*] **Procarbazine, Prednisone, Bleomycin** [*Antineoplastic drug regimen*] (DAVI) ... MOPP-LO BLEO
Mechlorethamine, Vincristine, Procarbazine, Prednisone [*Medicine*] (AD) ... moop
Meck Island Control Building [*Army*] (AABC) ... MICB
Meckel Syndrome [*Medicine*] (DMAA) ... MS
Mecklenburg County Medical Society, Charlotte, NC [*Library symbol Library of Congress*] (LCLS) ... NcCM
Mecklermedia Corp. [*NASDAQ symbol*] (SAG) ... MECK
Mecklermedia Corp. [*Associated Press*] (SAG) ... Mecklm
Meclofenamate [*Organic chemistry*] ... MF
Mecon Inc. [*NASDAQ symbol*] (TTSB) ... MECN
Meconium [*Gynecology*] ... MEC
Meconium Aspiration Syndrome [*Medicine*] ... MAS
Meconium Ileus [*Medicine*] ... Mel
Meconium Ileus [*Medicine*] ... MI
Meconium Stained Amniotic Fluid [*Neonatology*] (DAVI) ... MSAF
Mecoprop [*Herbicide*] ... MCPP
Mecury All Position (IAA) ... MAP
Med Mera [*And So Forth*] [*Latin*] (ILCA) ... MM
Med Waste [*Associated Press*] (SAG) ... MdWst
Med Waste [*NASDAQ symbol*] (SAG) ... MWDS
Med/Waste Inc. [*NASDAQ symbol*] (TTSB) ... MWDS
Med/Waste Inc. Wrrt'A' [*NASDAQ symbol*] (TTSB) ... MWDSW
Medaille College, Buffalo, NY [*Library symbol Library of Congress*] (LCLS) ... NBuM
Medal (ADA) ... M
Medal [*Numismatics*] ... MED
Medal (VRA) ... med
Medal Field Service [*Canada*] ... MFS
Medal for Gallantry ... MG
Medal for Humane Action [*Berlin Airlift, 1948-9*] [*Military decoration*] ... MFHA
Medal for Humane Action [*Berlin Airlift, 1948-9*] [*Military decoration*] ... MHA
Medal for Merit [*Military decoration*] ... MM
Medal of Bravery ... MB
Medal of Freedom [*Military decoration*] ... MF
Medal of Honor [*Often erroneously called Congressional Medal of Honor*] [*Military decoration*] ... MH
Medal of Honor [*Often erroneously called Congressional Medal of Honor*] [*Military decoration*] ... MOH
Medal of Honor Historical Society (EA) ... MHHS
Medal of Service of the Order of Canada ... SM
Medalist Indus [*NASDAQ symbol*] (TTSB) ... MDIN
Medalist Industries, Inc. [*NASDAQ symbol*] (NQ) ... MDIN
Medalist Industries, Inc. [*Associated Press*] (SAG) ... Medalst
Medallion [*Automotive engineering*] ... MEDAL
Medallion (VRA) ... medln
Medallion Books Ltd. [*Vancouver Stock Exchange symbol*] ... MLB
Medallion Explorations Ltd. [*Vancouver Stock Exchange symbol*] ... MED
Medallion Financial [*NASDAQ symbol*] (TTSB) ... TAXI
Medallist [*British*] (ROG) ... MED
Medals, Muscles, Master's Degrees, and Marathons [*Means to advancement in the armed forces*] ... 4M's
Medamicus, Inc. [*Associated Press*] (SAG) ... Medamic
Medamicus, Inc. [*NASDAQ symbol*] (SAG) ... MEDM
Medan [*Sumatra*] [*Seismograph station code, US Geological Survey Closed*] (SEIS) ... MED
Medan [*Indonesia*] [*Airport symbol*] (OAG) ... MES
Medan/Polonia [*Indonesia*] [*ICAO location identifier*] (ICLI) ... WIMM

Medan Sector [*Indonesia*] [*ICAO location identifier*] (ICLI) ... WIMZ
Medaphis Corp. [*NASDAQ symbol*] (SPSG) ... MEDA
Medaphis Corp. [*Associated Press*] (SAG) ... Medaph
Medar, Inc. [*NASDAQ symbol*] (NQ) ... MDXR
Medar, Inc. [*Associated Press*] (SAG) ... Medar
Medarex, Inc. [*Associated Press*] (SAG) ... Medarex
Medarex, Inc. [*Associated Press*] (SAG) ... Medarx
Medarex, Inc. [*NASDAQ symbol*] (SPSG) ... MEDX
Medarex Inc. Wrrt [*NASDAQ symbol*] (TTSB) ... MEDXW
Medborgerlig Samling [*Citizens Rally*] [*Sweden Political party*] (PPE) ... MBS
MedCath, Inc. [*NASDAQ symbol*] (SAG) ... MCTH
MedCath, Inc. [*Associated Press*] (SAG) ... MedCath
Medco Research [*AMEX symbol*] (TTSB) ... MRE
Medco Research, Inc. [*Associated Press*] (SAG) ... MedcR
Medco Research, Inc. [*AMEX symbol*] (SAG) ... MRE
Medcross, Inc. [*NASDAQ symbol*] (NQ) ... MDCR
Medcross, Inc. [*Associated Press*] (SAG) ... Medcross
Meddaugh's Reports [*13 Michigan*] [*A publication*] (DLA) ... Medd
Meddaugh's Reports [*13 Michigan*] [*A publication*] (DLA) ... Meddaugh
[*The*] **Med-Design Corp.** [*NASDAQ symbol*] (SAG) ... MEDC
[*The*] **Med-Design Corp.** [*Associated Press*] (SAG) ... MedDsg
Medea [*of Euripides*] [*Classical studies*] (OCD) ... Med
Medecin Extension [*Doctors' Aides, or Medics*] [*French*] ... MEDEX
Medecins sans Frontieres [*Doctors without Borders - DWB*] [*France*] (EAIO) ... MSF
Mededelingen Spinozahuis [*A publication*] (BJA) ... MSP
Medeea Ltd. [*Romania*] [*FAA designator*] (FAAC) ... MDE
Medellin [*Colombia*] [*Airport symbol*] (OAG) ... MDE
Medellin, Cebu [*Philippines*] [*ICAO location identifier*] (ICLI) ... RPVN
Medem Jewish Socialist Group [*Defunct*] (EA) ... MJSG
Medesto & Empire Traction Co. (MHDB) ... METC
Medeva [*AMEX symbol*] (SPSG) ... MDV
Medeva ADR [*AMEX symbol*] (TTSB) ... MDV
Medeva Ltd. [*Associated Press*] (SAG) ... Medeva
Medeva plc [*LO, exchange symbol*] (TTSB) ... MDVL
Medex, Inc. [*NASDAQ symbol*] (NQ) ... MDEX
Medex, Inc. [*Associated Press*] (SAG) ... Medex
Medford [*Oregon*] [*Airport symbol*] (OAG) ... MFR
Medford Free Public Library, Medford, WI [*Library symbol*] [*Library of Congress*] (LCLS) ... WMed
Medford, MA [*FM radio station call letters*] ... WMFO
Medford, MA [*AM radio station call letters*] ... WXKS
Medford, MA [*FM radio station call letters*] ... WXKS-FM
Medford, OK [*Location identifier FAA*] (FAAL) ... XED
Medford, OR [*FM radio station call letters*] ... KBOY
Medford, OR [*FM radio station call letters*] ... KCIA
Medford, OR [*FM radio station call letters*] (RBYB) ... KDOV
Medford, OR [*Television station call letters*] ... KDRV
Medford, OR [*AM radio station call letters*] ... KMED
Medford, OR [*Television station call letters*] ... KMVU
Medford, OR [*Television station call letters*] ... KOBI
Medford, OR [*FM radio station call letters*] ... KOPE
Medford, OR [*AM radio station call letters*] (RBYB) ... KRTA
Medford, OR [*AM radio station call letters*] ... KRVC
Medford, OR [*Television station call letters*] ... KSYS
Medford, OR [*FM radio station call letters*] ... KTMT
Medford, OR [*Television station call letters*] ... KTVL
Medford, OR [*Location identifier FAA*] (FAAL) ... MFR
Medford Public Library, Medford, MA [*Library symbol Library of Congress*] (LCLS) ... MMe
Medford Savings Bank [*NASDAQ symbol*] (SAG) ... MDBK
Medford Savings Bank [*Associated Press*] (SAG) ... MedfdSv
Medford, WI [*Location identifier FAA*] (FAAL) ... MDZ
Medford, WI [*AM radio station call letters*] ... WIGM
Medford, WI [*FM radio station call letters*] ... WIGM-FM
Medfra, AK [*Location identifier FAA*] (FAAL) ... MDR
Medgar Evers College of the City University of New York, Brooklyn, NY [*Library symbol Library of Congress*] (LCLS) ... NBME
Medgar Evers College of the City University of New York, Brooklyn, NY [*OCLC symbol*] (OCLC) ... XME
Medgroup Inc. Calif [*NASDAQ symbol*] (TTSB) ... MDGP
Media [*Laboratory*] (AAMN) ... M
Media ... MED
Media (VRA) ... medi
Media Access Control [*Telecommunications*] ... MAC
Media Access Control Logical Link Control [*Computer science*] ... MAC LLC
Media Access Device [*Telecommunications*] ... MAD
Media Access Project (EA) ... MAP
Media Access Unit [*Telecommunications*] ... MAU
Media Account Control System (PDAA) ... MACS
Media Action Coalition [*Defunct*] (EA) ... MAC
Media Action Research Center (EA) ... MARC
Media Advisory Service [*British*] ... MAS
Media Alert and Response System [*Public relations project devised by Pharmaceutical Manufacturers Association*] ... MARS
Media Alliance (EA) ... MA
Media Analysis Project (EA) ... MAP
Media and Adult Learning Section of the American Association for Adult and Continuing Education (EA) ... MAL-AAACE
Media and Information Services [*Queensland, Australia*] ... MIS
Media and Information Services, Quadraplegic Communications Group, Inc., Winnipeg, Manitoba [*Library symbol National Library of Canada*] (NLC) ... MWQCG
Media and Methods [*A publication*] (BRI) ... Media M
Media and People [*Information service or system*] (IID) ... MAP
Media and Status [*Code*] [*DoD*] ... M & S
Media Arts Group [*NASDAQ symbol*] (TTSB) ... ARTS
Media Arts Group, Inc. [*NASDAQ symbol*] (SAG) ... ARTS
Media Arts Group, Inc. [*Associated Press*] (SAG) ... MediaArt
Media Assistance Center (DNAB) ... MAC
Media Associates International [*An association*] (EA) ... MAI
Media Center, Audio Visual Library, University of Toronto [*UTLAS symbol*] ... KME
Media Center for Children (EA) ... MCC
Media Club of Canada [*Formerly, Canadian Women's Press Club*] ... MCC
Media Coalition [*Later, MC/ACF*] (EA) ... MC
Media Coalition/Americans for Constitutional Freedom (EA) ... MC/ACF
Media Commentary Council [*Defunct*] (EA) ... MCC
Media Control Interface ... MCI
Media Conversion Center [*Space Flight Operations Facility, NASA*] ... MCC
Media Conversion Computer Assembly [*Space Flight Operations Facility, NASA*] ... MCCA
Media Conversion Equipment [*Space Flight Operations Facility, NASA*] ... MCE
Media Conversion Program Generator ... MCPG
Media Credit Association (EA) ... MCA
Media Development Project for the Hearing Impaired (NITA) ... MDPHI
Media Directions, Inc. ... MDI
Media Expenditure Analysis Ltd. [*Database producer*] ... MEAL
Media Filter (ACRL) ... MF
Media Forum (EA) ... MF
Media Fund for Human Rights (EA) ... MFHR
Media General Financial Services [*Information retrieval*] ... MG
Media General Financial Services, Inc. [*Information service or system*] (IID) ... MGFS
Media General, Inc. [*Associated Press*] (SAG) ... Media
Media General, Inc. [*AMEX symbol*] (SPSG) ... MEG
Media Generated (VRA) ... medi gen
Media Industry Newsletter [*A publication*] ... MIN
Media Insertion Schedule Evaluation Report [*Advertising*] ... MISER
[*The*] **Media Institute** (EA) ... TMI
Media Institutes for Institute Directors ... MIID
Media Integration [*Computer science*] ... MINT
Media Language and Format (CET) ... MLF
Media Law and Practice [*1980*] [*A publication*] (DLA) ... Med L & P
Media Law and Practice [*A publication*] (DLA) ... Media L & P
Media Law Reporter [*A publication*] (NTCM) ... Med L Rptr
Media Liaison Officer ... MLO
Media Logic, Inc. [*Associated Press*] (SAG) ... MediaLog
Media Logic, Inc. [*AMEX symbol*] (SPSG) ... TST
Media/Medicine (NITA) ... MEDIA/M
Media Network (EA) ... MN
Media, PA [*FM radio station call letters*] ... WPLY
Media Processor [*Computer science*] (BUR) ... MP
Media Project (EA) ... MP
Media Quality Unit [*Communications*] ... MQU
Media Recognition System [*Computer science*] (PCM) ... MRS
Media Reference and Referral Center [*Library network*] ... BCL
[*The*] **Media Report** [*A publication*] (NTCM) ... MR
Media Report Service (NITA) ... MRS
Media Research Directors Association (EA) ... MRDA
Media Resource Center [*Adelaide, Australia*] ... MRC
Media Resource Centre, Access Network, Calgary, Alberta [*Library symbol National Library of Canada*] (NLC) ... ACAN
Media Resource Centre, Vanier College, Montreal, Quebec [*Library symbol National Library of Canada*] (NLC) ... QMVC
Media Resource Service [*Scientists' Institute for Public Information*] [*Information service or system*] (IID) ... MRS
Media Resources Officer (AIE) ... MRO
Media Society [*British*] (DBA) ... MS
Media Studies Association [*British*] ... MSA
Media Suite Pro [*Computer software*] (CDE) ... MSP
Media Systems Technology (HGAA) ... MST
Media Task Group [*Environmental Protection Agency*] (GFGA) ... MTG
Media Technology Associates Ltd. [*Bethesda, MD*] [*Telecommunications service*] (TSSD) ... MTA
Media Technology International [*British*] ... MTI
Media Transforming Virus [*Alleged virus causing immunodeficiency disease*] ... MTV
Media Videotex [*Vancouver Stock Exchange symbol*] ... MVX
Media Watch [*An association*] (EA) ... MW
Media Women's Association ... MWA
Media-Advertising Partnership for a Drug-Free America [*Later, DFA*] (EA) ... MAPDFA
Mediaeval Academy of America (EA) ... MAA
Mediaeval Towns [*A publication*] ... MT
Medial (DAVI) ... M
Medial [*Medicine*] ... med
Medial Ankle Orthosis [*Orthopedics*] (DAVI) ... MAO
Medial Axes Transformation (MHDI) ... MAT
Medial Axis Transformation (MHDB) ... MAT
Medial Bilateral (Neuron) [*Neuroanatomy*] ... MB
Medial Collateral Ligament [*Anatomy*] ... MCL
Medial Cruciate Ligament [*Anatomy*] ... MCL
Medial Dynamics [*NASDAQ symbol*] (TTSB) ... MEDY
Medial Efferent Bundle [*Neuroanatomy*] ... MEB
Medial Epicondyle [*Medicine*] ... ME
Medial Femorotibial Space [*Anatomy*] ... MFTS
Medial Forebrain Bundle [*Medicine*] ... MFB
Medial Gastrocnemius [*Anatomy*] ... MG
Medial Geniculate Nucleus [*Medicine*] ... MGN

Medial Giant Interneuron [Neurobiology]	MGI
Medial Habenular [Neuroanatomy]	MHb
Medial Heel Wedge [Orthopedics] (DAVI)	MHW
Medial Inferior Geniculate Artery [Anatomy]	MIG
Medial Interlaminar Nucleus [Neurology] (DAVI)	MN
Medial Joint Line [Orthopedics] (DAVI)	MJL
Medial Left Abdomen [Injection site]	MLA
Medial Lemniscus [Neuroanatomy]	ML
Medial Lethal Dose [Genetics] (DOG)	MLD
Medial Longitudinal Fasciculus [Medicine]	MLF
Medial Malleolus [Anatomy] (AAMN)	MM
Medial Meniscectomy [orthopedics] (DAVI)	med men
Medial Meniscus [Orthopedics] (DAVI)	med men
Medial Meniscus [Anatomy]	MM
Medial Muscle Motoneuron [Neuroanatomy]	MMN
Medial Nuclear Division [Cytology]	MND
Medial Nucleus of Trapezoid Body [Neuroanatomy]	MNTB
Medial Nucleus Tractus Solitarius [Neuroanatomy]	MNTS
Medial Oblique [View] [Radiology] (DAVI)	MO
Medial Olfactory Tract [Anatomy]	MOT
Medial Pallium [Neuroanatomy]	MP
Medial Preoptic [Brain anatomy]	MPO
Medial Preoptic Area [Medicine]	MPOA
Medial Preoptic Nucleus [Brain anatomy]	MPN
Medial Preoptic-Anterior Hypothalamic [Brain anatomy]	MPOAH
Medial Rectus [Eye anatomy]	MR
Medial Right Abdomen [Injection site]	MRA
Medial Septum [Anatomy]	MS
Medial Superior Olive [Brain anatomy]	MSO
Medial Superior Temporal [Brain Anatomy]	MST
Medial Temporal Lobe [Brain anatomy]	MTL
Medial Triceps Brachii [Medicine]	MT
Medial Vascularized Patellar Tendon Graft [Sports medicine]	MVPTG
Medial Vestibular Nucleus [Neuroanatomy]	MV
Mediamark Research, Inc. [Database producer and database] [Information service or system] (IID)	MRI
	(M)
Median	Md
Median	MDN
Median (MSA)	Me
Median	MED
Median (AFM)	MAD
Median Absolute Deviation [Statistics]	MPF
Median and Paired Fins [Ichthyology]	MB
Median Bundle [Botany]	MCD
Median Control Death	MCU
Median Control Unit (WDAA)	MDCT
Median Corrective Maintenance Time (MCD)	CD/50
Median Curative Dose [Medicine]	MDF
Median Demagnetizing Field [Geophysics]	MDR
Median Detection Range (NVT)	MDT
Median Detection Threshold (MAE)	MdD
Median Deviation [Statistics]	MDT
Median Dorsal Tract [Anatomy]	MDD
Median Droplet Diameter	MED
Median Effective Dose [Medicine]	ME
Median Eminence [of hypothalamus] [Anatomy]	MEF
Median Energy of Fission (NRCH)	MED
Median Erythrocyte Diameter [Medicine]	FD_5
Median Fatal Dose [Medicine] (MAE)	MFC
Median Femoral Condyle [Anatomy]	MID
Median Infective Dose [Bacteriology]	MIS
Median Iris Society (EA)	MLD
Median Lethal Dose [Also, LD_{50}] [Lethal for 50%] [Medicine]	MLT
Median Lethal Time [of radiation exposure]	MLS
Median Life Span [Oncology] (DAVI)	MLS
Median Longitudinal Section	MM
Median Method [Mathematics]	MN
Median Nerve [Anatomy]	MnSSEP
Median Nerve Somatosensory Evoked Potential [Neurology] (DAVI)	MnSSEP
Median Neuroblast [Cytology]	MNB
Median Normalized RADAR Cross Section	MNRCS
Median Period of Survival	MPS
Median Pontine Reticular Formation [Neurophysiology]	mPRF
Median Preoptic Area [Brain anatomy]	MNPO
Median Preventive Maintenance Time (MCD)	MDPT
Median Raphe Nucleus [Medicine]	MRN
Median Recognition Threshold (MAE)	MRT
Median Sample Number (PDAA)	MSN
Median Sternotomy (CPH)	med stern
Median Survival Time	MST
Median Tissue Culture Infective Dose [Laboratory science] (DAVI)	$TCID_{50}$
Median Tolerance Limit [Toxicity]	MTL
Median Tolerance Limit (GNE)	TL_{50}
Median Tolerance Limit (GNE)	TLM
Median Toxic Dose [Pharmacology] [Radiation therapy] (DAVI)	TD_{50}
Median Ventricular Nerve [Medicine]	MVN
Mediapolis Public Library, Mediapolis, IA [Library symbol Library of Congress] (LCLS)	IaMedi
Media-Service GmbH [Database producer] (IID)	MS
Mediastinal Diffuse Large-Cell Lymphoma with Sclerosis [Oncology]	MDLLS
MediaTel [Database] [British]	MT
Mediator	M
Mediator [Legal term] (DLA)	Med
Mediator Release Inhibitor [Biochemistry]	MRI
Medic Alert Foundation International [Also known as Medic Alert] (EA)	MAFI

Medic Alert Organ Donor Program (EA)	MAODP
Medic Computer Systems [NASDAQ symbol] (TTSB)	MCSY
Medic Computer Systems, Inc. [NASDAQ symbol] (SAG)	MCSY
Medic Computer Systems, Inc. [Associated Press] (SAG)	MedCmp
Medica Judaica [A publication] (BJA)	MJu
Medicaid (DLA)	MA
Medicaid Antidiscriminatory Drug Pricing [and Patient Benefit Restoration]Act	MADPA
Medicaid Eligibility Quality Control (GFGA)	MEQC
Medicaid Interim Payments	MIP
Medicaid Management Information System [HEW]	MMIS
Medicaid/Medicare Automated Certification System (GFGA)	MMACS
Medicaid Statistical Reporting and Analysis System (GFGA)	MEDSTAT
Medical	M
Medical (AFM)	MED
Medical	MED
Medical	MEDCL
Medical	MEDL
Medical	MA
Medical Abbreviation (AAMN)	MA
Medical Accessories Kit [Apollo] [NASA]	MAK
Medical Accounting [and Billing Process]	MEDAC
Medical Acronyms, Symbols & Abbreviations [A publication]	MASA
Medical Action Industries [NASDAQ symbol] (TTSB)	MDCI
Medical Action Industries, Inc. [NASDAQ symbol] (NQ)	MDCI
Medical Action Industries, Inc. [Associated Press] (SAG)	MedAct
Medical Administration and Miscellaneous Operating Expenses [Veterans Administration]	MAMOE
Medical Administrative Assistant (DAVI)	MAA
Medical Administrative Control System (IAA)	MEDACS
Medical Administrative Corps [Army World War II]	MAC
Medical Administrative Corps [Army World War II]	Med Adm C
Medical Administrative Management System	MAMS
Medical Administrative Service (DAVI)	MAS
Medical Advanced Technology Management Office	MATMO
Medical Advisory Board	MAB
Medical Advisory Committee [IATA] (DS)	MAC
Medical Advisory Service [British]	MAS
Medical Advisory Services for Travellers Abroad [London School of Hygiene andTropical Medicine] [Information service or system] (IID)	MASTA
Medical Aid [Federal program providing financial assistance for medical expenses of individual needy citizens]	MEDICAID
Medical Aid for El Salvador (EA)	MAES
Medical Aid for Indochina [An association] (EA)	MAI
Medical Aid for Iraq	MAI
Medical Aid for Sick Hippies [Volunteer medical group]	MASH
Medical Aid Post	MAP
Medical Air Evacuation	MAE
Medical Air Evacuation Transport Squadron [Army World War II]	MAETS
Medical Alert Center	MAC
Medical Analysis of Days of Care [Report]	MADOC
Medical and Chirurgical Faculty of the State of Maryland, Baltimore, MD [Library symbol Library of Congress] (LCLS)	MdBM
Medical and Dental Supply Office [Military]	MDSO
Medical and Health Information Directory [A publication]	MHID
Medical and Health Related Sciences Thesaurus [A publication] (IEEE)	MHRST
Medical and Hospital Department, Army	M & HDA
Medical and Nursing [Red Cross Disaster Services]	M & N
Medical and Occupational Radiation Program [HEW]	MORP
Medical and Osteopathic Scholarship Program (DNAB)	MOSP
Medical and Psychological Previews [Database] [BRS Information Technologies] [Information service or system] (IID)	PREV
Medical and Scientific Equipment	MASE
Medical and Sports Music Institute of America (EA)	MSMIA
Medical and Surgical (AD)	M&S
Medical and Surgical Relief Committee [Defunct] (EA)	MSRC
Medical and Technical Assistant	MTA
Medical Anti-Shock Trousers [Military]	MAST
Medical Architecture Research Unit [Polytechnic of North London] [British] (IRC)	MARU
Medical Artists Association of Great Britain (PDAA)	MAA
Medical Artists Association of Great Britain (DAVI)	MAAGB
Medical Assessment Tribunal [Queensland, Australia]	MAT
Medical Assistance [HEW]	MA
Medical Assistance for the Aged	MAA
Medical Assistance Only (GFGA)	MAO
Medical Assistance Unit [HEW]	MAU
Medical Assistant (DAVI)	MA
Medical Assistants Advisory Council (DAVI)	MAAC
Medical Association for the Prevention of War [British] (DBA)	MAPW
Medical Association of Georgia (SRA)	MAG
Medical Audit (MAE)	MA
Medical Audit Program [Computerized system of abstracted medical record information]	MAP
Medical Audit Statistics (PDAA)	MAS
Medical Audit Study (HCT)	MAS
Medical Augmentation (MCD)	MEDAUG
Medical Authority	MA
Medical Authorization (DAVI)	MA
Medical Automation Intelligence [System]	MAIN
Medical Aviation Services Ltd. [British ICAO designator] (FAAC)	MCL
Medical Awareness Foundation [Commercial firm] (EA)	MAF
Medical Badge	MBAD
Medical Badge	MEDBAD
Medical Battalion [Marine Corps]	MEDBN

Medical Benefits Consultative Committee ... MBCC
Medical Benefits (Dental Practitioners) Advisory Committee ... MB(DP)AC
Medical Benevolent Association of New South Wales [*Australia*] ... MBANSW
Medical Benevolent Association of South Australia ... MBASA
Medical Bioengineering Research and Development Command [*Army*] (PDAA) ... MBRDC
Medical Bioengineering Research and Development Laboratory [*Army*] (MCD) ... MBRDL
Medical Board ... MB
Medical Board ... MEB
Medical Board of Queensland [*Australia*] ... MBQ
Medical Board of South Australia ... MBSA
Medical Board of the Australian Capital Territory ... MBACT
Medical Board of Victoria [*Australia*] ... MBV
Medical Branch ... MEDBR
Medical Bulletin ... MB
Medical Campaign against Nuclear Weapons (PDAA) ... MCANW
Medical Care [*Federal program providing financial assistance for medical expenses of individual senior citizens*] ... MEDICARE
Medical Care, Civilian Source (DNAB) ... MC
Medical Care Development, Inc. [*Augusta, ME*] (TSSD) ... MCD
Medical Care Evaluation ... MCE
Medical Care Evaluation Study (HCT) ... MCES
Medical Care Insurance Commission [*Canada*] ... MCIC
Medical Care Research Unit [*University of Sheffield*] [*British*] (ECON) ... MCRU
Medical Care Support Equipment (AABC) ... MEDCASE
Medical Center ... MC
Medical Center [*Army*] (AABC) ... MEDCEN
Medical Center at Princeton, Princeton, NJ [*Library symbol Library of Congress*] (LCLS) ... NjPMC
Medical Center of Virginia [*University of Virginia*] ... MCV
Medical Certificate (ADA) ... MC
Medical Civic Action Teams ... MEDCAT
Medical College Admission [*or Aptitude*] **Test** ... MCAT
Medical College Admissions Test (GAGS) ... MCAT
Medical College of Georgia [*Augusta*] ... MCG
Medical College of Georgia (GAGS) ... Med C Georgia
Medical College of Georgia, Augusta, GA [*Library symbol Library of Congress*] (LCLS) ... GAuM
Medical College of Georgia, Augusta, GA [*OCLC symbol*] (OCLC) ... GXM
Medical College of Ohio at Toledo (GAGS) ... Med C Ohio
Medical College of Ohio at Toledo, Toledo, OH [*OCLC symbol*] (OCLC) ... MCL
Medical College of Ohio at Toledo, Toledo, OH [*Library symbol Library of Congress*] (LCLS) ... OTMC
Medical College of Pennsylvania ... MCP
Medical College of Pennsylvania, Philadelphia, PA [*Library symbol Library of Congress*] (LCLS) ... PPWM
Medical College of South Carolina ... MCSC
Medical College of Wisconsin ... MCOW
Medical College of Wisconsin, Medical-Dental Library, Milwaukee, WI [*Library symbol Library of Congress*] (LCLS) ... WMMCW
Medical College of Wisconsin, Milwaukee, WI [*OCLC symbol*] (OCLC) ... WIC
Medical Command (MCD) ... MEDCOM
Medical Commission on Accident Prevention (PDAA) ... MCAP
Medical Committee for Civil Rights [*Defunct*] (EA) ... MCCR
Medical Committee for Human Rights [*Defunct*] ... MCHR
Medical Committee Under the Poisons Act [*Australia*] ... MCUPA
Medical Communications ... MEDICOM
Medical Computer Services (IEEE) ... MCS
Medical Construction Liaison Office [*or Officer*] [*Air Force*] (AFM) ... MCLO
Medical Consultant [*Social Security Administration*] (OICC) ... MC
Medical Consultant Staff [*Social Security Administration*] (OICC) ... MCS
Medical Consumer Price Index (DHSM) ... MCPI
Medical Consumers' Association of New South Wales [*Australia*] ... MCANSW
Medical Contact Lens Association [*British*] ... MCLA
Medical Contingency Report [*Air Force*] ... MEDCON
Medical Continuation Pay [*Military*] (AABC) ... MCP
Medical Continuity of Operations Plan [*Army*] (AABC) ... MEDCOOP
Medical Contol [*Associated Press*] (SAG) ... MedCtrl
Medical Control [*NASDAQ symbol*] (SAG) ... MDCL
Medical Control [*Associated Press*] (SAG) ... MdCtr
Medical Corps [*Navy*] ... MC
Medical Corps [*Air Force*] ... MEDCORPS
Medical Corps, General Service [*USNR officer designation*] ... MCR
Medical Corps, Merchant Marine [*USNR officer designation*] ... MCM
Medical Corps, Merchant Marine, General Service [*USNR officer designation*] ... MCMR
Medical Corps, Merchant Marine, Special Service [*USNR officer designation*] ... MCMS
Medical Corps Reserve [*Military*] (DAVI) ... MCR
Medical Corps, Special Service [*USNR officer designation*] ... MCS
Medical Corps, Women's Reserve [*USNR officer designation*] ... MCW
Medical Correctional Association [*Defunct*] (EA) ... MCA
Medical Council of Canada ... MCC
Medical Council of Canada's Qualifying Examination ... MCCQE
Medical Council on Alcoholism [*British*] ... MCA
Medical Crew Director ... MCD
Medical Cybernetics Foundation (EA) ... MCF
Medical Data Acquisition System ... MDAC
Medical Data Acquisition System (KSC) ... MDAS
Medical Data Base Management System (SSD) ... MDBMS
Medical Data Exchange [*Los Altos, CA*] [*Commercial firm*] ... MDX
Medical Data Specialist (AABC) ... MEDDS
Medical Defence Union Ltd. [*British*] (BI) ... MDU
Medical Dental Division [*Air Force*] ... MED-DENT
Medical Department [*Army*] ... MD
Medical Department Activity [*Army*] (AABC) ... MEDDAC
Medical Department Personnel Support Agency [*Army*] (MCD) ... MEDDPERSA
Medical Device Register, Inc. (IID) ... MDR
Medical Device Reporting System ... MDR
Medical Device Technol [*NASDAQ symbol*] (TTSB) ... MEDD
Medical Device Technologies, Inc. [*NASDAQ symbol*] (SAG) ... MEDD
Medical Device Technologies, Inc. [*Associated Press*] (SAG) ... MedDevT
Medical Device Technologies, Inc. [*Associated Press*] (SAG) ... MedDv
Medical Device Technologies, Inc. [*Associated Press*] (SAG) ... MedDvt
Medical Devices Adverse Experience Reporting Project ... MDAERP
Medical Devices Reports (Commerce Clearing House) [*A publication*] (DLA) ... Med Devices Rep (CCH)
Medical Digital Imaging Support (RDA) ... MDIS
Medical Director ... MDPD
Medical Director-General [*Navy British*] ... MDG
Medical Director-General (Navy) [*British*] ... MDG(N)
Medical Discharge [*from military service*] ... MD
Medical Display Analysis and Recording System ... MEDDARS
Medical District Initiated Peer Review Organization [*Veterans Administration*] (GFGA) ... MEDIPRO
Medical District Initiated Program Planning [*Veterans Administration*] ... MEDIPP
Medical Documentation Service [*College of Physicians of Philadelphia*] [*Information service or system*] (IID) ... MDS
Medical Documentation Systems [*Eli Lilly & Co.*] [*Information service or system*] (IID) ... MEDDOC
Medical Documents [*Eccles Health Sciences Library - University of Utah*] [*Salt Lake City, UT Bibliographic database*] ... MEDOC
Medical Dressing Station ... MDS
Medical Dynamics, Inc. [*Associated Press*] (SAG) ... MedDyn
Medical Dynamics, Inc. [*NASDAQ symbol*] (NQ) ... MEDYN
Medical Early Direct Commissioning Program (MCD) ... MEDCOMP
Medical Education (MAE) ... ME
Medical Education for National Defense ... MEND
Medical Education for South African Blacks [*An association*] (EA) ... MESAB
Medical Education Program [*Air Force*] ... MEP
Medical Education Research and Information Database ... MERI
Medical Education Research Foundation [*San Diego*] ... MERF
Medical Education Resources Program (MEDA) ... MEDPRO
Medical Education Technologies, Inc. ... METI
Medical Electronic Data Aquisition and Control ... MEDAC
Medical Electronic Data Interpretation and Correlation (IAA) ... MEDIC
Medical Electronics and Data Society [*Later, MES*] (EA) ... MEDS
Medical Electronics Society [*Defunct*] (EA) ... MES
Medical Embarkment and Hospital Distribution Headquarters [*World War II*] ... MEHDHQ
Medical Emergencies [*Computerized management course*] ... MEDEMG
Medical Emergency Calling Aid (MCD) ... MECA
Medical Emergency Decisions Assistance System (MCD) ... MEDAS
Medical Emergency Officer (DAVI) ... MEO
Medical Emergency Relief Care for Youth ... MERCY
Medical Emergency Report [*Air Force*] ... MEDMER
Medical Engineering Development (IIA) ... MED
Medical Equestrian Association [*British*] (DBA) ... MEA
Medical Equipment Display and Conference (IAA) ... MEDAC
Medical Equipment Management Office [*Air Force*] (AFM) ... MEMO
Medical Equipment Reporting System [*Veterans Administration*] ... MERS
Medical Equipment Research and Development Laboratory [*Army*] ... MERDL
Medical Equipment Test and Evaluation [*Army Medical Material Agency*] (PDAA) ... MET & E
Medical Evacuation Team [*Army*] ... MEDEVAC
Medical Evacuation Vehicle (MCD) ... MEV
Medical Evaluation [*Military*] (AABC) ... MEDEVAL
Medical Evaluation Board [*Military*] (DAVI) ... MEB
Medical Evaluation Board [*Military*] (GFGA) ... MEBD
Medical Evaluation Data System (IEEE) ... MEDS
Medical Evidence Disaggregated Direct Input of Costs Database [*Social Security Administration*] (GFGA) ... MEDDIC
Medical Evidence (Medical Report or Record) (OICC) ... ME (MR)
Medical Examination Centre [*British World War II*] ... MEC
Medical Examiner ... ME
Medical Examiners and Coroners Alert Program [*Consumer Product Safety Commission*] ... MECAP
Medical Examiniation and Review Board [*DoD*] (DAVI) ... MERB
Medical Exhibitors Association [*Later, HCEA*] (EA) ... MEA
Medical Expense and Performance Reporting System/Dental Data System [*Air Force*] (GFGA) ... MEPRS/DDS
Medical Eye Centre Association [*British*] (DBA) ... MECAssn
Medical Field Service School [*Army*] ... MFSS
Medical Field Service School, Fort Sam Houston, TX [*Library symbol Library of Congress*] (LCLS) ... TxFshM
Medical Field Service Technician (BABM) ... MFST
Medical Field Service Technician [*Navy*] ... MFT
Medical Follow-Up Agency [*National Research Council*] ... MFUA
Medical Force 2000 [*Army*] (DOMA) ... MF^2K
Medical Foundation [*Australia*] ... MF
Medical Function Control System (PDAA) ... MFCS
Medical Functional Requirements Group (MCD) ... MFRG
Medical Graphics [*NASDAQ symbol*] (TTSB) ... MGCC
Medical Graphics Corp. [*Associated Press*] (SAG) ... MedGr
Medical Graphics Corp. [*NASDAQ symbol*] (NQ) ... MGCC
Medical Group [*Air Force*] ... MEDGP
Medical Group Management Association (EA) ... MGMA
Medical Group Management Association, Information Reference Service, Denver, CO [*Library symbol Library of Congress*] (LCLS) ... CoDMG

Medical Group Management Information Service [*Medical Group Management Association*] (DHSM) .... MGMIS
Medical Group Missions of the Christian Medical and Dental Society (EA) .... MGM
Medical Hemodialysis Unit [*Nephrology*] (DAVI) .... MHDU
Medical History (MAE) .... M Hx
Medical History .... MH
Medical Holding Detachment .... MHD
Medical Humanities Review [*A publication*] (BRI) .... MHR
Medical Illustration Service for Museum Design [*Armed Forces Institute of Pathology*] (RDA) .... MISMD
Medical Illustrator .... MI
Medical Impairment Bureau [*Insurance*] .... MIB
Medical Improvement [*Social Security Administration*] .... MI
Medical Incident Report .... MIR
Medical Indemnity of America, Inc. (DHSM) .... MIA
Medical Industrial Complex .... MIC
Medical Industries of America [*Associated Press*] (SAG) .... MedInd
Medical Industries of America [*Associated Press*] (SAG) .... MedIndA
Medical Industries of America [*NASDAQ symbol*] (SAG) .... MIOA
Medical Industry Association of Australia .... MIAA
Medical Informatics .... MEDINFO
Medical Information and Career Service [*British*] (DAVI) .... MEDICS
Medical Information and Communications System (NITA) .... MEDICS
Medical Information Bureau [*Databank*] .... MIB
Medical Information Centre (NITA) .... MIC
Medical Information Computer System (NASA) .... MEDICS
Medical Information Cooperation (DAVI) .... MEDICO
Medical Information Dissemination Using ASSASSIN (NITA) .... MIDAS
Medical Information Form [*British*] .... MEDIF
Medical Information Management System [*NASA*] .... MIMS
Medical Information Management System .... MIMS
Medical Information Network [*GTE Telenet Communications Corp.*] [*Telecommunications*] .... MEDINET
Medical Information Network [*GTE Telenet Communications Corp.*] [*Reston, VA*] [*Telecommunications*] .... MINET
Medical Information Online (NITA) .... MEDLINE
Medical Information Retrieval Service (NITA) .... MIRS
Medical Information Science .... MIS
Medical Information Science Section [*National Institutes of Health*] [*Information service or system*] (IID) .... MISS
Medical Information Services, Toronto, Ontario [*Library symbol National Library of Canada*] (BIB) .... OTMIS
Medical Information System via Telephone [*University of Alabama*] .... MIST
Medical Information Systems Program [*Computer science*] (BUR) .... MISP
Medical Injury Compensation Reform Act .... MICRA
Medical Innovations [*NASDAQ symbol*] (TTSB) .... MIXX
Medical Innovations, Inc. [*Associated Press*] (SAG) .... MedInn
Medical Innovations, Inc. [*NASDAQ symbol*] (NQ) .... MIXX
Medical Inspection [*Military*] (NVT) .... MEDINSP
Medical Inspection .... MI
Medical Institutions' Financial Accounting System .... MIFACS
Medical Instrument Calibration System (PDAA) .... MICS
Medical Intelligence (MCD) .... MEDINT
Medical Intelligence and Information Agency [*Formerly, MIO*] [*DoD*] .... MIIA
Medical Intelligence Office [*Later, MIIA*] [*DoD*] .... MIO
Medical Intelligence Production Requirements (MCD) .... MIPR
Medical Intensive Care .... MIC
Medical Intensive Care Nurse (DAVI) .... MICN
Medical Intensive Care Unit [*Medicine*] .... MICU
Medical Interfraternity Conference (EA) .... MIC
Medical Internal Radiation Dose [*Committee*] [*Society of Nuclear Medicine*] .... MIRD
Medical International Cooperation .... MEDICO
Medical Inventory Management System .... MIMS
Medical Journalists Association [*British*] (DBA) .... MJA
Medical Jurisprudence (ADA) .... MED JUR
Medical Laboratories Army Chemical Center [*Maryland*] .... MLCR
Medical Laboratory Contract Reports [*Army*] (MCD) .... MLCR
Medical Laboratory Technician [*or Technologist*] .... MLT
Medical Laboratory Technician (American Medical Technologists) (DAVI) .... MLT (AMT)
Medical Laboratory Technician (American Society of Clinical Pathologists) (DMAA) .... MLT(ASCP)
Medical Laboratory Technology-Associate Degree .... MLT-AD
Medical Lake, WA [*FM radio station call letters*] .... KTSL
Medical Letter (EA) .... ML
Medical Liability Commission [*Defunct*] (EA) .... MLC
Medical Liberation Front (EA) .... MLF
Medical Library Assistance Act [*1965*] .... MLAA
Medical Library Association (EA) .... MLA
Medical Library Association, Section on Mental Health Libraries (EA) .... MLA-SMHL
Medical Library, Bristol-Myers Pharmaceutical Group, Ottawa, Ontario [*Library symbol National Library of Canada*] (NLC) .... OOBMM
Medical Library Center (DIT) .... MLC
Medical Library Center of New York [*Information service or system*] (IID) .... MLCNY
Medical Library Center of New York, New York, NY [*Library symbol Library of Congress*] (LCLS) .... NNMLC
Medical Library Center of New York, New York, NY [*OCLC symbol*] (OCLC) .... VVZ
Medical Library Center of New York, Standardized Cataloging Service, New York, NY [*OCLC symbol*] (OCLC) .... ZML

Medical Library, Hoechst Canada, Inc., Montreal, Quebec [*Library symbol National Library of Canada*] (BIB) .... QMHC
Medical Library, Hotel-Dieu of St. Joseph Hospital, Windsor, Ontario [*Library symbol National Library of Canada*] (NLC) .... OWHD
Medical Library, Laurentian Hospital, Sudbury, Ontario [*Library symbol National Library of Canada*] (BIB) .... OSULH
Medical Library, McGill University, Montreal, Quebec [*Library symbol National Library of Canada*] (NLC) .... QMMM
Medical Library, McKellar General Hospital, Thunder Bay, Ontario [*Library symbol National Library of Canada*] (BIB) .... OTBMC
Medical Library, Melville Hospital, Goose-Bay, Newfoundland [*Library symbol National Library of Canada*] (BIB) .... NFGBM
Medical Library of Mecklenburg County, Inc., Charlotte, NC [*Library symbol Library of Congress*] (LCLS) .... NcCML
Medical Library, Pfizer Canada, Inc., Kirkland, Quebec [*Library symbol National Library of Canada*] (NLC) .... QKPC
Medical Library, Ross Memorial Hospital, Lindsay, Ontario [*Library symbol National Library of Canada*] (BIB) .... OLRM
Medical Library, Sir Thomas Roddick Hospital, Stephenville, Newfoundland [*Library symbol National Library of Canada*] (NLC) .... NFSTR
Medical Library, South Street Campus, Victoria Hospital Corp., London, Ontario [*Library symbol National Library of Canada*] (NLC) .... OLVH
Medical Library, Syntex, Inc., Mississauga, Ontario [*Library symbol National Library of Canada*] (NLC) .... OMSM
Medical Library, Tom Baker Cancer Center, Calgary, Alberta [*Library symbol National Library of Canada*] (NLC) .... ACTBC
Medical Library, University of Calgary, Alberta [*Library symbol National Library of Canada*] (NLC) .... ACUM
Medical Library, University of Manitoba, Winnipeg, Manitoba [*Library symbol National Library of Canada*] (NLC) .... MWM
Medical Library, University of Saskatchewan, Saskatoon, Saskatchewan [*Library symbol National Library of Canada*] (NLC) .... SSUM
Medical Library, Women's College Hospital, Toronto, Ontario [*Library symbol National Library of Canada*] (NLC) .... OTWCH
Medical Library, Wyeth Ltd., Downsview, Ontario [*Library symbol National Library of Canada*] (BIB) .... OTWY
Medical Library, Yarmouth Regional Hospital, Nova Scotia [*Library symbol National Library of Canada*] (BIB) .... NSYR
Medical Literature Analysis and Retrieval System [*National Library of Medicine*] [*Bethesda, MD Database*] .... MEDLARS
Medical Literature Training File (NITA) .... MEDTRAIN
Medical Maintenance Unit [*Army World War II*] .... MMU
Medical Malpractice Insurance Association .... MMIA
Medical Malpractice Lawsuit Filings [*Medical Malpractice Verdicts, Settlements & Experts*] [*Information service or system*] (CRD) .... MEDMAL
Medical Man (ROG) .... MM
Medical Management Analysis System (HCT) .... MMA
Medical Management, Inc. [*Associated Press*] (SAG) .... MedMgt
Medical Management, Inc. [*NASDAQ symbol*] (SAG) .... MMGT
Medical Management Information System [*Army*] .... MEDMIS
Medical Manpower and Training Information Service [*British*] (DAVI) .... MATRIS
Medical Material Mission Reserve [*Military*] (AABC) .... MMMR
Medical Materiel Account [*Military*] (AABC) .... MMA
Medical Materiel Advice Code [*Military*] (AFM) .... MMAC
Medical Materiel Management Center [*Military*] (AABC) .... MMMC
Medical Materiel Management System [*Army*] .... MEDMATS
Medical Materiel Management System-On Line [*Air Force*] (GFGA) .... MMMS-OL
Medical Materiel Manager [*Military*] .... MMM
Medical Materiel Program for Defense Against Biological and Chemical Agents [*Army*] (AABC) .... MMPDABC
Medical Materiel Program for Nuclear Casualties [*Army*] (AABC) .... MMPNC
Medical Media Production Service [*Commercial firm*] (DAVI) .... MMPS
Medical Microbiology Interdisciplinary Committee [*International Council of Scientific Unions*] .... MEMIC
Medical Mission Sisters (EA) .... MMS
Medical Mission Sisters (TOCD) .... SCMM
Medical Missionaries of Mary [*Roman Catholic women's religious order*] .... MMM
Medical Mobilization for Soviet Jewry (EA) .... MMSJ
Medical Monitor (MCD) .... MDM
Medical Mutual Aid (GNE) .... MMA
Medical Mycological Society of the Americas (EA) .... MMSA
Medical Network for Missing Children (EA) .... MNMC
Medical Neuropsychiatric Research Unit (AD) .... MNRU
Medical Nutrition Laboratory [*Army*] .... MNL
Medical Office Building (MEDA) .... MOB
Medical Office Building (DAVI) .... MOB
Medical Officer [*Military*] .... MO
Medical Officer in Command (AD) .... MOIC
Medical Officer of Health [*British*] .... MOH
Medical Officer of Health (Local Health Authority) [*British*] .... MOH(LHA)
Medical Officer of Schools (DAVI) .... SMO
Medical Officer of the Day [*Military*] .... MOD
Medical Officer of the Watch .... MOOW
Medical Officer on Duty (DAVI) .... MOD
Medical Officer Report [*Navy*] (NG) .... MOR
Medical Officer Training Plan [*Canada*] .... MOTP
Medical Officer-in-Charge [*Military*] .... MOIC
Medical Officer-in-Command [*Military*] .... MEDOFCOM
Medical Officers of Schools Associations [*British*] .... MOSA
Medical Officers (Qualified for General Detail) [*USNR designation*] .... MC-V(G)
Medical Officers (Qualified for Specialist Duties) [*USNR designation*] .... MC-V(S)
Medical Officers' Reserve Corps .... MORC
Medical Oncology Group .... MOG
Medical Operations Requirements Document (MCD) .... MORD
Medical Outpatient .... MOP

Medical Outpatient (AD) ... mop
Medical Outreach for Armenians (EA) ... MOA
Medical Passport Foundation [*Defunct*] (EA) ... MPF
Medical Pay Date ... MPD
Medical Payment [*Insurance*] ... MP
Medical Personnel Pool ... MPP
Medical Personnel (Priority) Committee [*World War II*] ... MPPC
Medical Photography Technician [*Navy*] ... PMT
Medical Planning and Execution System (DOMA) ... MEPES
Medical Planning and Execution System (DOMA) ... MPES
Medical Planning and Execution System (Model) ... MEPES
Medical Planning Module (DOMA) ... MPM
Medical Pocket-Book Series [*A publication*] ... MPBS
Medical Polymers Tech [*VS, exchange symbol*] (TTSB) ... MPS
Medical Practice Study ... MPS
Medical Practitioners' Union [*Later, Medical Practitioners' Section - MPS*] [*British*] (DCTA) ... MPU
Medical Procurement Agency ... MPA
Medical Program Review Committee [*DoD Washington, DC*] (EGAO) ... MPRC
Medical Protection Society [*British*] (DBA) ... MPS
Medical Provider Survey [*Department of Health and Human Services*] (GFGA) ... MPS
Medical Quality Assurance (AD) ... MQA
Medical Quality Assurance Board (AD) ... MQAB
Medical Readiness Assemblage Medical System [*Air Force*] (GFGA) ... MEDRAMS
Medical Readiness Exercise (MCD) ... MEDREX
Medical Readiness Training Exercises [*Army*] ... MEDRETES
Medical Receiving Station ... MRS
Medical Reception Station [*Military*] ... MRS
Medical Record ... MR
Medical Record Administrator ... MRA
Medical Record Analyst (HCT) ... MRA
Medical Record Librarian ... MRL
Medical Record Manager ... MRM
Medical Record Practitioner [*Medicare*] (DHSM) ... MRP
Medical Record Technician (HCT) ... MRT
Medical Records Department (DAVI) ... MRD
Medical Records Index (AD) ... MRI
Medical Records Library (AD) ... MRL
Medical Records Technician (DAVI) ... MRT
Medical Rectus [*Muscle*] [*Anatomy*] ... MR
Medical Reference Department (AD) ... MRD
Medical Registration Council [*British*] (DAVI) ... MRC
Medical Registration Council of Ireland (DAVI) ... MRCi
Medical Registration Council of Ireland (AD) ... MRCI
Medical Regulating Office [*or Officer*] [*Army*] (AABC) ... MRO
Medical Rehabilitation Unit (AD) ... MRU
Medical Reimbursement Plan ... MRP
Medical Remedial Enlistment Program (DNAB) ... MREP
Medical Repair Technician [*Navy*] ... MRM
Medical Report ... MR
Medical Research and Development Command [*Army*] (AD) ... MR & DC
Medical Research and Development Command [*Frederick, MD*] [*Army*] ... MRDC
Medical Research and Nutrition Laboratory [*Army*] (MCD) ... MRNL
Medical Research and Operations Directorate [*NASA*] (KSC) ... MROD
Medical Research Committee ... MRC
Medical Research Council (NADA) ... MEDRESCO
Medical Research Council [*Research center British*] (IRC) ... MRC
Medical Research Council, Collaborative Centre [*British*] (CB) ... MRCCC
Medical Research Council of Canada (BARN) ... MRCC
Medical Research Council of Ireland (SLS) ... MRCI
Medical Research Council Trial in Older Adults ... MRCOA
Medical Research Division ... MRD
Medical Research Endowment Fund ... MREF
Medical Research Ethics Committee ... MREC
Medical Research Information System [*Veterans Administration*] ... MRIS
Medical Research Institute [*Florida Institute of Technology*] [*Research center*] (RCD) ... MRI
Medical Research Institute of Chemical Defense (RDA) ... MRICD
Medical Research Institute of Infectious Diseases [*Army*] (RDA) ... MRIID
Medical Research Laboratory [*Navy and Air Force*] (MCD) ... MRL
Medical Research Library of Brooklyn, Brooklyn, NY [*Library symbol Library of Congress*] (LCLS) ... NBM
Medical Research Modernization Committee (EA) ... MRMC
Medical Research Organization [*Generic term*] ... MRO
Medical Research Reactor ... MRR
Medical Research Reactor (AD) ... mrr
Medical Research Society [*British*] ... MRS
Medical Reserve Corps [*Military*] (WDAA) ... MEDRC
Medical Reserve Corps ... MRC
Medical Resident Admitting Note (MEDA) ... MRAN
Medical Resident Admitting Note (DAVI) ... MRAn
Medical Resource Companies of America [*Associated Press*] (SAG) ... MedRA
Medical Resource Co. of America [*AMEX symbol*] (SPSG) ... MRA
Medical Resources [*NASDAQ symbol*] (TTSB) ... MRII
Medical Resources Consortium of Central New Jersey [*Library network*] ... MEDCORE
Medical Resources, Inc. [*Associated Press*] (SAG) ... MedResc
Medical Resources, Inc. [*NASDAQ symbol*] (SAG) ... MRII
Medical Review Officer (GFGA) ... MRO
Medical Savings Account ... MSA
Medical Savings Account ... MSA
Medical Savings Account ... MSA
Medical School (ADA) ... MEDSCH
Medical School Environmental Stress ... MSES
Medical Schools of the University of London (DAS) ... MSUL
Medical Science (DAVI) ... MS
Medical Sciences History Society [*British*] (DBA) ... MSHS
Medical Sciences Knowledge Profile (DAVI) ... MSKP
Medical Scientist Training Program [*National Institutes of Health*] ... MSTP
Medical Scientists' Association [*Australia*] ... MSA
Medical Scientists' Association of Victoria [*Australia*] ... MSAV
Medical Self-Help [*Defunct*] ... MSH
Medical Seminars International (EA) ... MSI
Medical Service Activity [*Army*] (AABC) ... MEDSAC
Medical Service Agency (WYGK) ... MSA
Medical Service Commission [*Canada*] ... MSC
Medical Service Corps [*Military*] (MCD) ... MEDSERV
Medical Service Corps [*Military*] ... MEDSERVC
Medical Service Corps [*Military*] ... MSC
Medical Service Corps, Office of the Surgeon General ... MSCOTSG
Medical Service Group [*Military*] ... MSEG
Medical Service Liaison Officer [*Air Force*] ... MSLO
Medical Service School [*Air Force*] (AFM) ... MSS
Medical Service Squadron [*Military*] ... MSES
Medical Service Unit [*Air Force*] (AFM) ... MSU
Medical Service Warrant ... MEDSERWRNT
Medical Service Wing [*Military*] ... MSEW
Medical Services [*Navy British*] ... MS
Medical Services Account ... MSA
Medical Services Accountable Officer ... MSAO
Medical Services Administration [*HEW*] ... MSA
Medical Sisters of St. Joseph (TOCD) ... MSJ
Medical Social Coordinator ... MSC
Medical Social Services ... MSS
Medical Social Worker [*British*] ... MSW
Medical Society Executives Association [*Later, AAMSE*] (EA) ... MSEA
Medical Society for the Study of Radiesthesia (EA) ... MSSR
Medical Society for the Study of Venereal Diseases [*Leeds, England*] (EAIO) ... MSSVD
Medical Society of the City and County of Denver, Denver, CO [*Library symbol Library of Congress*] (LCLS) ... CoDM
Medical Society of the County of Queens, Forest Hills, NY [*Library symbol Library of Congress*] (LCLS) ... NFhM
Medical Society of the State of New York, Lake Success, NY [*Library symbol Library of Congress*] (LCLS) ... NLsM
Medical Society of the United States and Mexico (EA) ... MSUSM
Medical Specialist ... MSP
Medical Specialist Corps [*Military*] ... MEDSPECC
Medical Specialist Corps [*Military*] ... MSC
Medical Specialist Corps [*Military*] ... MSPC
Medical Specialist Preference Blank ... MSPB
Medical Staff [*British military*] (DMA) ... MS
Medical Staff Corps [*British*] ... MSC
Medical Staff Organization (HCT) ... MSO
Medical Staffing and Training to Augment Readiness (MCD) ... MEDSTAR
Medical Stock Control System [*Army*] ... MEDSTOC
Medical Student (DAVI) ... MS
Medical Students for Choice ... MSFC
Medical Studies Unit (DAVI) ... MSU
Medical Subject Headings (NITA) ... MESH
Medical Subject Headings Vocabulary File [*National Library of Medicine*] [*Information service or system*] (CRD) ... MeSH
Medical Subjects Unit [*American Topical Association*] (EA) ... MSU
Medical Superintendents' Society (DAVI) ... MSS
Medical Supplies [*Military*] ... MS
Medical Supply Depot ... MEDSUPDEP
Medical Supply, Optical, and Maintenance [*Army*] (RDA) ... MEDSOM
Medical Support Equipment (NASA) ... MSE
Medical Survey [*Navy*] ... MS
Medical System Program Review [*Army*] (RDA) ... MSPR
Medical Systems Integration Office [*Army*] (RDA) ... MSIO
Medical Technician [*or Technologist*] (AAMN) ... med tech
Medical Technician [*British military*] (DMA) ... MT
Medical Technician, Acting, 4th Class [*British military*] (DMA) ... MTA 4
Medical Technologist ... MT
Medical Technologist (American Medical Technologists) (DAVI) ... MT(AMT)
Medical Technologist (American Society of Clinical Pathologists) Specialist in Blood Bank [*Technology*] (DAVI) ... MT(ASCP)SBB
Medical Technology (DAVI) ... Med Tech
Medical Technology Systems, Inc. [*Associated Press*] (SAG) ... MedT
Medical Technology Systems, Inc. [*Associated Press*] (SAG) ... MedTech
Medical Technology Systems, Inc. [*NASDAQ symbol*] (NQ) ... MSYS
Medical Television Network (BARN) ... MTN
Medical Test Cabinet ... MTC
Medical Testing Systems [*Commercial firm*] ... MTS
Medical Training Center [*Later, Academy of Health Sciences*] [*Army*] ... MTC
Medical Transcriptionist (DAVI) ... MT
Medical Transport Officer [*Navy*] ... MTO
Medical Treatment Facility (AABC) ... MTF
Medical Treatment Faculty (DAVI) ... MTF
Medical Ultrasound, Three-Dimensional and Portabel with Advanced Communications [*An imaging device*] (INF) ... MUSTPAC-1
Medical Unit Readiness Report [*Air Force*] ... MEDRED
Medical Unit Self-Contained Transportable [*Field hospital*] [*Army*] ... MUST
Medical University of South Carolina (GAGS) ... Med U So Car
Medical University of South Carolina ... MUSC
Medical University of South Carolina, Charleston, SC [*Library symbol Library of Congress*] (LCLS) ... ScCM

Medical University of South Carolina Library, Charleston, SC [OCLC symbol] (OCLC) .... SMC
Medical Urethral System for Erection .... MUSE
Medical Use of Simulation Electronics .... MUSE
Medical Waste Tracking Act [1988] (FFDE) .... MWTA
Medical Waste Treatment Act .... MWF
Medical Women's Federation [British] (DAS) .... MWIA
Medical Women's International Association [See also AIFM] [Cologne, Federal Republic of Germany] (EAIO) .... MWF
Medical Working File (DOMA) .... MDCL
MedicalControl Inc [NASDAQ symbol] (TTSB) .... MDCLW
MedicalControl Wrrt [NASDAQ symbol] (TTSB) .... MDCEF
Medical-Dental Committee on Evaluation of Fluoridation [Defunct] (EA) .... MDCEF
Medical-Dental-Hospital Bureaus of America (EA) .... MDHBA
Medically Indigent Adult (MEDA) .... MIA
Medically Indigent Adult (DAVI) .... MIA
Medically Oriented Data System (MCD) .... MODS
Medically Oriented Language .... MEDOL
Medical-Surgical Manufacturers Association [Later, HIMA] .... MSMA
Medicament .... MEDCMNT
Medicamenta [Medicaments] [Pharmacy] (ROG) .... MED
Medicamina Faciei [of Ovid] [Classical studies] (OCD) .... Medic
Medicare Administrative Reform Initiative [Health Care Financing Administration] .... MARI
Medicare Advocacy Project .... MAP
Medicare and Medicaid Patient and Program Protection Act .... MMPPPA
Medicare and Medicaid Statistical Systems (GFGA) .... M/MSS
Medicare Bureau [Health Care Financing Administration - Social Security Administration] .... MB
 .... MCO
Medicare Carve-Out [Insurance] (WYGK) .... MCCA
Medicare Catastrophic Coverage Act [1988] .... MCCRA
Medicare Catastrophic Coverage Repeal Act of 1989 (WYGK) .... MCE
Medicare Code Editor (MEDA) .... MEI
Medicare Economic Index .... MFS
Medicare Fee Schedule .... MGCRB
Medicare Geographic Classification Review Board .... MIG
Medicare Insured Group (HCT) .... MIG
Medicare, Medicaid, Education and the Environment [President Clinton political agenda] .... MMEE
Medicare Payment Advisory Commission .... MedPAC
Medicare Prospective Payment System .... MPPS
Medicare Provider Analysis and Review (GFGA) .... MEDPAR
Medicare Volume Performance Standard .... MVPS
Medicated Face Conditioner [Brand manufactured by Mennen] .... MED
Medication .... MAR
Medication Administration Record [Medicine] .... MILS
Medication Information Leaflet for Seniors [Medicine] (DMAA) .... Meds
Medications [or Medicines] .... MBK
Medications and Bandage Kit (MCD) .... M
Medicinae [Of Medicine] [Latin] .... MB
Medicinae Baccalaureus [Bachelor of Medicine] [Latin] .... MD
Medicinae Doctor [Doctor of Medicine] [Latin] .... M
Medicinae Doctor Chirurgia Magister [Doctor of Medicine and Master of Surgery] .... M
Medicine .... MED
Medicine (AABC) .... MEDCN
Medicine .... MEDI
Medicine (DSUE) .... MEDI
Medicine and Duty [Marked on a medical report and implying a suspicion of malingering] [Military British] .... M & D
 .... M & S
Medicine and Surgery (AD) .... MS
Medicine and Surgery (DAVI) .... MedSurg
Medicine and Surgery [Navy] (IEEE) .... MS
Medicine Bow, WY [Location identifier FAA] (FAAL) .... MBW
Medicine Cabinet [Technical drawings] (NFPA) .... MC
Medicine Cabinet Manufacturers Council (EA) .... MCMC
Medicine College of Pennsylvania (GAGS) .... Med C Penn
Medicine College of Wisconsin (GAGS) .... Med C Wis
Medicine Hat [Canada] [Airport symbol] (OAG) .... YXH
Medicine Hat, AB [Television station call letters] CFCN-TV-8
Medicine Hat, AB [AM radio station call letters] .... CHAT
Medicine Hat, AB [Television station call letters] .... CHAT-TV
Medicine Hat, AB [AM radio station call letters] .... CJCY
Medicine Hat, AB [FM radio station call letters] CKUA-3
Medicine Hat, AB [ICAO location identifier] (ICLI) .... CYXH
Medicine Hat College, Alberta [Library symbol National Library of Canada] (NLC) .... AMM
Medicine Hat College, Medicine Hat, AB, Canada [Library symbol Library of Congress] (LCLS) .... CaAMM
Medicine Hat General Hospital, Alberta [Library symbol National Library of Canada] (NLC) .... AMG
Medicine Hat General Hospital, Medicine Hat, AB, Canada [Library symbol Library of Congress] (LCLS) .... CaAMG
Medicine Hat High School, Alberta [Library symbol National Library of Canada] (NLC) .... AMHS
Medicine Hat High School, Medicine Hat, AB, Canada [Library symbol Library of Congress] (LCLS) .... CaAMHS
Medicine Hat Public Library, Alberta [Library symbol National Library of Canada] (NLC) .... AMP
Medicine Hat Public Library, Medicine Hat, AB, Canada [Library symbol Library of Congress] (LCLS) .... CaAMP
Medicine in the Public Interest (EA) .... MIPI
Medicine in the Public Interest (AD) .... MPI
Medicine, Law, and Public Policy [A publication] (DLA) .... Med L & Pub Pol

Medicine Lodge, KS [FM radio station call letters] .... KREJ
Medicine, Osteopathy, and Dentistry [HEW program] .... MOD
Medicines Control Agency [British] (ECON) .... MCA
Medicines/Drugs .... M/D
Medicines Evaluation Committee [Australia] .... MEC
Medicis Pharmaceutical 'A' [NASDAQ symbol] (TTSB) .... MDRX
Medicis Pharmaceutical Corp. [NASDAQ symbol] (SAG) .... MDRX
Medicis Pharmaceutical Corp. [Associated Press] (SAG) .... Medicis
Medicl Relief International (NADA) .... MERIT
Medico-Chirurgical .... M-C
Medico-Legal Journal [A publication] (DLA) .... Med-Legal J
Medico-Legal News [A publication] (DLA) .... Med LN
Medico-Legal Papers [A publication] (DLA) .... Med Leg Pap
Medico-Legal Papers [A publication] (DLA) .... Med LP
Medico-Legal Society of Tasmania [Australia] .... MLST
Medico-Legal Society of Victoria. Proceedings [A publication] ..... Med Leg Vic Proc
Medico-Legal Society of Victoria. Proceedings [A publication] .... Proc Med-Leg Soc Vic
Medico-Legal Society. Transactions [A publication] (DLA) .... Med-Legal Soc'y Trans
Medicore, Inc. [Associated Press] (SAG) .... Mdcore
Medicore, Inc. [AMEX symbol] (SPSG) .... MDK
Medicus Mundi Internationalis [International Organization for Cooperation in Health Care - IOCHC] [Nijmegen, Netherlands] (EAIO) .... MMI
Medicus Systems Corp. [NASDAQ symbol] (SAG) .... MECS
Medicus Systems Corp. [Associated Press] (SAG) .... Medicus
Medicus Systems Softwr [NASDAQ symbol] (TTSB) .... MECS
Medicus Veterinarius [Veterinary Physician] .... MV
Medicus Veterinarius Doctor [Doctor of Veterinary Medicine] .... MVDr
Medieval .... M
Medieval (VRA) .... mdvl
Medieval .... MED
Medieval .... MEDIEV
Medieval and Early Modern Data Bank [Information service or system] (IID) .... MEMDB
Medieval Greek [Language, etc.] .... MGR
Medieval Jewish Chronicles [A publication] (BJA) .... MJC
Medieval Latin [Language] .... Med Lat
Medieval Latin [Language, etc.] .... ML
Medieval Settlement Research Group [British] (DBA) .... MSRG
Medieval Village Research Group (EA) .... MVRG
Medieval Warm Period [Geoscience] .... MWP
MedImmune, Inc. [NASDAQ symbol] (SPSG) .... MEDI
MedImmune, Inc. [Associated Press] (SAG) .... MedImun
Medina [Saudi Arabia] [Airport symbol] (OAG) .... MED
Medina Memorial Hospital, Medina, NY [Library symbol Library of Congress] (LCLS) .... NMedH
Medina, OH [Location identifier FAA] (FAAL) .... MIF
Medina, OH [FM radio station call letters] .... WQMX
Medio Mundo [Nicaragua] [Seismograph station code, US Geological Survey] (SEIS) .... MMO
Mediobasal Hypothalamus [Brain anatomy] .... MBH
Mediocris [Middling] [Pharmacy] (ROG) .... MEDIOC
Mediodorsal [Anatomy] .... MD
Mediolanum [Milan] [Imprint] (ROG) .... MEDIOL
Medi-Physica, Inc. (DAVI) .... MPI
MEDIQ, Inc. [AMEX symbol] (SPSG) .... MED
Mediq, Inc. [Associated Press] (SAG) .... Mediq
MEDIQ Inc. Cv Pfd [AMEX symbol] (TTSB) .... MEDPr
Medis E Ltd. [NASDAQ symbol] (SAG) .... MDSL
Medis E Ltd. [Associated Press] (SAG) .... MedisE
Medis El Ltd [NASDAQ symbol] (TTSB) .... MDSLF
Medisave-cum-Subsidized Outpatient Scheme [Medical benefit program] [Singapore] .... MSO
MediSense, Inc. [Associated Press] (SAG) .... MediSens
MediSense, Inc. [NASDAQ symbol] (SAG) .... MSNS
Medi-Sota Library Consortium [Library network] .... MEDI-SOTA LIBR
Meditation (ROG) .... MED
Mediterranean (AFM) .... MED
Mediterranean .... MEDIT
Mediterranean/Adriatic [Shipping] (DS) .... M/A
Mediterranean Air Ambulance, SL [Spain] [FAA designator] (FAAC) .... MEM
Mediterranean Air Command [Military] .... MAC
Mediterranean Air Transport Service .... MATS
Mediterranean Airlines SA [Greece] [ICAO designator] (FAAC) .... MAX
Mediterranean Algeria-Sahara Zone [NATO] (NATG) .... MEDALSA
Mediterranean Allied Air Force .... MAAF
Mediterranean Allied Coastal Air Forces .... MACAF
Mediterranean Allied Photographic Reconnaissance Command .... MAPRC
Mediterranean Allied Strategic Air Force .... MASAF
Mediterranean Allied Tactical Air Force .... MATAF
Mediterranean Amphibious Ready Group (MCD) .... MARG
Mediterranean Area .... MA
Mediterranean Area Airlift Command Post (AFM) .... MAACP
Mediterranean Area Fighter Operations Grid .... MAFOG
Mediterranean Army Air Forces .... MAAF
Mediterranean Association for Marine Biology and Oceanology [ICSU] (EAIO) .... MAMBO
Mediterranean Association of International Schools (EA) .... MAIS
Mediterranean Base Section [Army World War II] .... MBS
Mediterranean Bombardment Code .... MBC
Mediterranean Chiefs of Staff [British World War II] .... MEDCOS
Mediterranean Coastal Air Force Headquarters .... MCAF
Mediterranean Communications [Military] (AFM) .... MEDCOM
Mediterranean Communications Plans [NATO] (NATG) .... MEDCOMPLAN
Mediterranean Communications Region [Air Force] (MCD) .... MCR

Mediterranean Contingency Target List (MCD) ... MCTL
Mediterranean Coordination Unit (GNE) ... MCU
Mediterranean Eddy [*Oceanography*] ... MEDDY
Mediterranean Engineer Division [*Army Engineers*] ... MED
Mediterranean Expeditionary Force [*World War I*] [*British*] ... MEF
Mediterranean Fruit Fly ... MEDFLY
Mediterranean Instructions to Convoys [*World War II*] ... MEDICOS
Mediterranean Joint Air Orders ... MJAO
Mediterranean Lines of Communication [*Military*] (IAA) ... MEDLOC
Mediterranean Location [*Navy*] ... MEDLOC
Mediterranean Mail Coordinating Office (DNAB) ... MEDMAILCOORD
Mediterranean Marine Sorting Center ... MMSC
Mediterranean Maritime Surveillance and Reconnaissance Center (DNAB) ... MMSRC
Mediterranean Medical Entente (EAIO) ... MME
Mediterranean, Mediterranean Littoral, and/or Middle East ... MMLME
Mediterranean Near-Term Prepositioned Ship ... MEDNTPS
Mediterranean Oceanographic Project [*1969*] ... MEDOC
Mediterranean Sea and Area [*MARC geographic area code Library of Congress*] (LCCP) ... mm----
Mediterranean Secret Convoy Instructions [*World War II*] ... MSCI
Mediterranean Secret General Orders ... MSGO
Mediterranean Shipping Board [*World War II*] ... MEDBO
Mediterranean Shipping Board [*World War II*] ... MSB
Mediterranean Shipping Group [*NATO*] (NATG) ... MESG
Mediterranean Society of Chemotherapy (EAIO) ... MSC
Mediterranean Sub-Commission [*Silva Mediterranea*] [*FAO*] ... MSC
Mediterranean Tactical Air Force Headquarters ... MTAF
Mediterranean Theater of Operations, United States Army [*Shortened form of MTOUSA*] [*World War II*] ... MTO
Mediterranean Theater of Operations, United States Army [*Sometimes shortened to MTO*] [*World War II*] ... MTOUSA
Mediterranean Tours and Travel [*Egypt*] ... MTT
Meditrust [*Associated Press*] (SAG) ... Meditr
Meditrust SBI [*NYSE symbol*] (SPSG) ... MT
Medium [*Women's shoe width*] ... B
Medium [*Standard & Poor's bond rating*] [*Investment term*] ... BBB
Medium [*Men's shoe width*] ... D
Medium [*Size designation for clothing, etc.*] ... M
Medium [*Spectral*] ... m
Medium (AABC) ... MDM
Medium (AFM) ... MED
Medium ... MEDM
Medium Access Control [*Telecommunications*] ... MAC
Medium Access Unit [*Computer science*] (BYTE) ... MAU
Medium Active Solid Waste Encapsulation Plant [*Nuclear energy*] (NUCP) ... MASWEP
Medium Active Waste [*Nuclear energy*] ... MAW
Medium Altitude Clear-Air Turbulence (MCD) ... MEDCAT
Medium Altitude Endurance (RDA) ... MAE
Medium and Heavy Patrol Bomber Squadron [*Land based and seaplane*] [*Navy symbol*] ... VPB
Medium- and High-Frequency Direction-Finding Station ... MHDF
Medium- and Very-High-Frequency Direction-Finding Station ... MVDF
Medium Antiaircraft Missile ... MAAM
Medium Antiaircraft Weapon (NATG) ... MAA
Medium Antiarmor Weapon (INF) ... MAW
Medium Antitank Assault Weapon ... MAAW
Medium Antitank Weapon ... MAW
Medium Aperture Optical Telescope (PDAA) ... MAOT
Medium Artillery ... MA
Medium Artillery Delivered Sensor [*Army*] ... MARDS
Medium Artillery Terminal Homing Projectile ... MATHP
Medium Artillery Tractor [*British military*] (DMA) ... MAT
Medium Assault Transport (MCD) ... MAT
Medium Assault Weapon ... MAW
Medium Atomic Demolition Munition [*Military*] (AABC) ... MADM
Medium Attachment Unit [*Computer science*] (TNIG) ... MAU
Medium Attack Advanced Readiness Program [*Navy*] (DOMA) ... MAARP
Medium Attack Aircraft [*Navy symbol*] (NVT) ... VAM
Medium Attack Tactical Employment School [*Military*] (CAAL) ... MATES
Medium Attack Wing (NVT) ... MATWING
Medium Automotive Maintenance ... MAM
Medium Auxiliary Repair Dry Dock [*Navy symbol*] ... ARDM
Medium Bandwidth Compression System ... MBCS
Medium Black and White [*Film*] (KSC) ... MBW
Medium Bomber ... MB
Medium Bomber Strike (NATG) ... MBS
Medium Bronze [*Numismatics*] ... MB
Medium Brown Loose [*Stool*] [*Gastroenterology*] (DAVI) ... MBL
Medium Caliber Antiarmor Automatic Cannon ... MCAAAC
Medium Caliber Antiarmor Automatic Cannon (MCD) ... MCAAC
Medium Capacity [*or Charge*] [*Bomb*] ... MC
Medium Capacity Bomb with Temporary Delay Fuse [*British military*] (DMA) ... MCTD
Medium Close Shot [*Photography*] (ADA) ... MCS
Medium Close Up [*A photograph or motion picture sequence taken from a relatively short distance*] ... MCU
Medium Corpuscular Density [*Cardiology*] (DAVI) ... MCD
Medium Corpuscular Fragility [*Hematology*] ... MCF
Medium Curing [*Asphalt grade*] ... MC
Medium Data Rate (DOMA) ... MDR
Medium Data Technique [*Computer science*] (IAA) ... MDT
Medium Deep Recess [*Automotive engineering*] ... MDR
Medium Density Fiberboard ... MDF
Medium Density Overlay [*Plywood*] ... MDO
Medium Dependent Interface [*Computer science*] (CDE) ... MDI
Medium Dosage [*Pharmacology*] (MAE) ... MD
Medium Duty ... MD
Medium Earth Orbit (SSD) ... MEO
Medium Earth Orbit Satellites (ACRL) ... MEOS
Medium Electroendosmosis [*Analytical biochemistry*] ... ME
Medium Endurance Cutter [*Coast Guard*] (NVT) ... WMEC
Medium Energy ... ME
Medium Energy Ion Scattering (MCD) ... MEIS
Medium Energy Source Program [*Air Force*] ... MES
Medium Equipment Transporter (MCD) ... MET
Medium [*Range*] **Extended Air Defense System** [*USA-Europe*] ... MEADS
Medium Frequency [*300-3000 Kilohertz*] ... MF
Medium Frequency [*Radio electronics*] ... MF
Medium Frequency (WDMC) ... mf
Medium Grain [*Lumber*] ... MG
Medium Harbor Tug [*Self-propelled*] [*Navy symbol*] ... YTM
Medium Hard Drawn (MSA) ... MHD
Medium Heavy-Duty Diesel Engine [*Motor vehicle specifications*] ... MHDDE
Medium-, High-, and Very-High-Frequency Direction-Finding Station ... MHVDF
Medium Industry Bank [*South Korea*] (IMH) ... MIB
Medium Intensity (MSA) ... MI
Medium Intensity Approach Light System [*Aviation*] (DA) ... MIALS
Medium Intensity Approach Light System with Rail [*FAA*] (TAG) ... MALSR
Medium Intensity Approach Light System with Sequenced Flashing Lights [*FAA*] (TAG) ... MALSF
Medium Intensity Runway Edge Lights [*FAA*] (TAG) ... MIRL
Medium Intensity Runway Edge Lights [*Aviation*] (FAAC) ... MIRL
Medium Interface Connector [*Optics*] (CDE) ... MIC
Medium Intermediate-Range Ballistic Missile (MCD) ... MIRBM
Medium Internal Radiation Dose (WDAA) ... MIRD
Medium Intertheater Transport (MCD) ... MIT
Medium Large Local Exchange [*Telecommunications*] (TEL) ... MLLE
Medium Launch Vehicle ... MLV
Medium Level Liquid Waste [*Nuclear energy*] (NUCP) ... MLLW
Medium Level Tripod [*British military*] (DMA) ... MLT
Medium Life Span ... MLS
Medium Lift Helicopter (MCD) ... MLH
Medium Local Exchange [*Telecommunications*] (TEL) ... MLE
Medium Long Shot [*A photograph or motion picture sequence taken from a relatively great distance*] ... MLS
Medium Lorry [*British*] ... ML
Medium/Low Frequency (NATG) ... M/LF
Medium Low-BIT [*Binary Digit*] **Rate** [*Computer science*] ... MLBR
Medium Machine Gun ... MMG
Medium Machine Oil (BARN) ... MMO
Medium Maintenance ... MM
Medium Minesweeper (NATG) ... MSM
Medium Narrow [*Men's shoe width*] ... C
Medium Observation Aircraft ... MOA
Medium Observation Aircraft (AD) ... moa
Medium Ocean Data Station ... MODS
Medium Oocyte ... MO
Medium Operating Speed Automatic Weapon [*Military*] ... MOSAW
Medium Orbiting Earth Resources Observatory (IEEE) ... MOERO
Medium [*or 2-engine*] **Plane** ... M
Medium Port ... MEDP
Medium Power Loop Range ... MPLR
Medium Power RADAR (NATG) ... MPR
Medium Power Reactor Experiment ... MPRE
Medium Power Traveling Wave Tube ... MPTWT
Medium Power-Switching Application (IAA) ... MESA
Medium Pressure ... MP
Medium Pressure (AD) ... mp
Medium Pressure (AD) ... mpress
Medium Pressure ... MPRESS
Medium Processing Channel [*Carbon*] (DICI) ... MPC
Medium Pulse Recurrence Frequency (MCD) ... MPRF
Medium Range ... MR
Medium Range (AD) ... mr
Medium Range ... MRG
Medium [*or Mid*]-Range Ballistic Missile ... MRBM
Medium Range Search ... MRS
Medium Range Surveillance Aircraft [*Military*] (PDAA) ... MRSA
Medium Range Truck [*Military*] ... MRT
Medium Reduction (NITA) ... MR
Medium Resolution ... MR
Medium Resolution Camera System (MCD) ... MRCS
Medium Resolution Imaging Spectrometer (SSD) ... MERIS
Medium Resolution Infrared (AD) ... mrir
Medium Scale Hybrid Integration [*Computer science*] (IAA) ... MSHI
Medium SEAL [*Sea, Air, and Land*] **Support Craft** [*Navy symbol*] ... MSSC
Medium Setting [*Asphalt grade*] ... MS
Medium Shot [*Refers to distance from which a photograph or motion picture sequence is taken*] ... MS
Medium Shot (AD) ... ms
Medium Side Prong [*Lamp base type*] (NTCM) ... MSP
Medium Soft (IAA) ... MS
Medium Standard Frequency (DEN) ... MSF
Medium Steel ... MS
Medium Steel (AD) ... ms
Medium Stocking Rate [*Agriculture*] (OA) ... MSR
Medium STOL [*Short Takeoff and Landing*] **Transport** [*Aircraft*] ... MST
Medium Stressed Platform ... MSP

Medium Surface-to-Air Missile [*Army*] ... M-SAM
Medium Survey Ship [*Marine science*] (MSC) ... MSS
Medium Tactical Transport [*Army*] ... MTT
Medium Tactical Transport Aircraft [*Military*] ... METAC
Medium Tactical Truck [*Army*] (RDA) ... MTT
Medium Tactical Vehicle [*Army*] (RDA) ... MTV
Medium Tactical Vehicle ... MTV
Medium Tank ... MTK
Medium Tank Battalion ... MTB
Medium Term Defense Plan (NATG) ... MTDP
Medium Term Development Plan [*Economics*] (FEA) ... MTDP
Medium Term Loan (DCTA) ... MTL
Medium Terminal Complexes (MCD) ... MTC
Medium Truck [*British*] ... MT
Medium Value Item (NATG) ... MVI
Medium Viscosity Index (PDAA) ... MVI
Medium Viscosity Index-Naphthenic (PDAA) ... MVIN
Medium Viscosity Index-Paraffinic (PDAA) ... MVIP
Medium Voltage ... MV
Medium Volume ... MV
Medium Wall ... MW
Medium Wave Band ... MW
Medium Weight Coated Offset Paper (DGA) ... MWCO
Medium Weight Coated Paper (DGA) ... MWC
Medium Wide [*Women's shoe width*] ... C
Medium Wide [*Men's shoe width*] [*More than one "E" indicates increasing wideness, up to EEEE*] ... E
Medium Wide Shot [*Photography*] ... MWS
Medium-Accuracy Gyro Assembly ... MAGA
Medium-Altitude Communications Satellite ... MACS
Medium-Altitude Communications Satellite System ... MACSS
Medium-Altitude Critical Atmospheric Turbulence (MCD) ... MEDCAT
Medium-Altitude Gravity Gradient Experiment ... MAGGE
Medium-Altitude Missile (MCD) ... MAM
Medium-Chain [*Triglycerides*] [*Biochemistry*] (MAE) ... MC
Medium-Chain Fatty Acids [*Organic chemistry*] ... MCFA
Medium-Chain Triglyceride [*Biochemistry*] ... MCT
Medium-Depth Mine (MCD) ... MDM
Medium-Dollar Value ... MDV
Medium-Energy Electron Diffraction ... MEED
Medium-Energy Intense Neutron ... MEIN
Medium-Energy Particle Spectrometer (MCD) ... MEPS
Medium-Energy Proton and Electron Detector ... MEPED
Medium-Energy Reactor Light-Water Industrial Neutron [*British*] (DEN) ... MERLIN
Medium-Frequency Direction Finder [*or Finding*] ... MDF
Medium-Frequency Direction Finder [*or Finding*] (NVT) ... MF/DF
Medium-Gain Antenna ... MGA
Medium-Gain Autotrack Antenna ... MGAA
Medium-Girder Bridge (RDA) ... MGB
Medium-High Frequency ... MHF
Medium-High Pressure (MSA) ... MHP
Medium-Intensity Approach Lighting System [*Aviation*] ... MALS
Medium-Intensity Approach Lighting System with Runway Alignment Indicator Lights [*Aviation*] ... MALSR
Medium-Intensity Approach Lighting System with Sequenced Flashers [*Aviation*] ... MALSF
Medium-Intensity Conflict [*Military*] ... MIC
Medium-Level Radioactive Waste (NUCP) ... MLW
Medium-Lift Requirement [*Helicopter/VSTOL*] [*Marine Corps*] (DOMA) ... MLR
Medium-Power Diode-Transistor Logic (ECII) ... MPDTL
Medium-Power RADAR (AD) ... mpr
Medium-Powered Radio Range (AD) ... mra
Medium-Powered Radio Range (AD) ... mrl
Medium-Powered Radio Range [*Loop radiators*] ... MRL
Medium-Powered Radio Range (Adcock) ... MRA
Medium-Pressure Liquid Chromatography ... MPLC
Medium-Processing Channel Black (AD) ... mpc black
Medium-Range Air-to-Air Missile [*Military*] (AD) ... mraam
Medium-Range Air-to-Air Missile (MCD) ... MRAAM
Medium-Range Air-to-Surface Missile (MCD) ... MRASM
Medium-Range Air-to-Surface Missile [*Military*] (AD) ... mrasm
Medium-Range and Intermediate-Range Ballistic Missile (MCD) ... MRIRBM
Medium-Range Antisubmarine Torpedo Carrying Helicopter (NATG) ... MATCH
Medium-Range Applied Technology (AD) ... mrat
Medium-Range Ballistic Missile [*Military*] (AD) ... mrbm
Medium-Range Forecast [*Model*] [*Marine science*] (OSRA) ... MRF
Medium-Range Forecast [*Model*] (USDC) ... MRF
Medium-Range Interceptor (AD) ... mri
Medium-Range Interceptor ... MRI
Medium-Range Missile (MCD) ... MRM
Medium-Range Missile Launcher ... MRML
Medium-Range Planes [*Navy*] ... MR
Medium-Range RADAR (NG) ... MRR
Medium-Range Recovery ... MRR
Medium-Range SOF [*Special Operations Forces*] **Insertion** (DOMA) ... MRSI
Medium-Range SONAR (NVT) ... MRS
Medium-Range Surveillance Aircraft (AD) ... mrsa
Medium-Range Typhon [*Missile*] (NG) ... MRT
Medium-Range Unmanned Aerial Surveillance and Target Acquisition System (NATG) ... MRUASTAS
Medium-Resolution Infrared Radiometer [*NASA*] ... MRIR
Medium-Round Nose [*Diamond drilling*] ... MRN
Medium-Scale (IAA) ... MS
Medium-Scale Computer (IAA) ... MSC
Medium-Scale Integration [*Circuit packaging*] ... MSI
Medium-Scale Integration Device [*Circuit packaging*] ... MSID
Medium-Scale Technology ... MST
Medium-Sized Libraries/OCLC [*Online Computer Library Center*] **Users Group** ... MSLOUG
Medium-Sized Orbital Research Laboratory (SAA) ... MORL
Medium-Slow Takeoff and Landing ... MSTOL
Medium-Speed (IAA) ... MS
Medium-Speed DynaBIT [*Binary Digit*] **Memory** [*Computer science*] ... MSDM
Medium-Speed Printer (AABC) ... MSP
Medium-Term Energy Policy Model ... MEPM
Medium-Term Financial Assistance ... MTFA
Medium-Term Financial Strategy ... MTFS
Medium-Term Note [*Finance*] ... MTN
Medium-Voltage Mode ... MVM
Medium-Voltage Power Supply (IAA) ... MVPS
Medium-Wavelength Infrared ... MWIR
MediVators, Inc. [*Associated Press*] (SAG) ... MedVat
MediVators, Inc. [*NASDAQ symbol*] (SAG) ... MVAT
Mediware Information Sys [*NASDAQ symbol*] (TTSB) ... MEDW
Mediware Information Systems, Inc. [*Associated Press*] (SAG) ... Mediwre
Mediware Information Systems, Inc. [*NASDAQ symbol*] (SAG) ... MEDW
Medizinische Hochschule, Karl Wiechert, Hannover-Kleefeld, Germany [*Library symbol Library of Congress*] (LCLS) ... GyHanM
Medjet International, Inc. [*ICAO designator*] (FAAC) ... MEJ
Medjunarodni Institut za Kucnu Knjizevnost [*International Institute for Home Literature - IIHL*] [*Belgrade, Yugoslavia*] (EAIO) ... MIKK
MEDLARS [*Medical Literature Analysis and Retrieval System*] **On-Line** [*National Library of Medicine*] [*Bibliographic database*] ... MEDLINE
Medley Memorial Library, Christ Church Cathedral, Fredericton, NB, Canada [*Library symbol Library of Congress*] (LCLS) ... CaNBFMM
Medley Memorial Library, Christ Church Cathedral, Fredericton, New Brunswick [*Library symbol National Library of Canada*] (NLC) ... NBFMM
Medley Public Library, Alberta [*Library symbol National Library of Canada*] (NLC) ... AME
Medley Public Library, Medley, AB, Canada [*Library symbol Library of Congress*] (LCLS) ... CaAMe
Medmarco, Inc. [*Associated Press*] (SAG) ... Mdmarco
Medmarco, Inc. [*NASDAQ symbol*] (SAG) ... MDMC
Medmarco, Inc. [*Associated Press*] (SAG) ... Medm
Medmarco Inc. Wrrt'A' [*NASDAQ symbol*] (TTSB) ... MDMCW
Medmarco Inc. Wrrt'B' [*NASDAQ symbol*] (TTSB) ... MDMCZ
Mednet MPC [*NASDAQ symbol*] (TTSB) ... MMRX
Mednet MPC Corp. [*Associated Press*] (SAG) ... Mednet
Mednet MPC Corp. [*NASDAQ symbol*] (SAG) ... MMRX
Medouneu [*Gabon*] [*Airport symbol*] (OAG) ... MDV
MedPartners, Inc. [*Associated Press*] (SAG) ... MedPart
MedPartners, Inc. [*NASDAQ symbol*] (SAG) ... MPTR
MedPartners/Mullikin [*NYSE symbol*] (TTSB) ... MDM
MedPlus, Inc. [*NASDAQ symbol*] (SAG) ... MEDP
MedPlus, Inc. [*Associated Press*] (SAG) ... MedPlus
MedQuist, Inc. [*AMEX symbol*] (SAG) ... MBS
MedQuist Inc. [*NASDAQ symbol*] (TTSB) ... MEDQ
MedQuist, Inc. [*Associated Press*] (SAG) ... MedQst
Medroxyprogesterone [*Medicine*] (AD) ... MPA
Medroxyprogesterone Acetate [*Also, MAP*] [*Endocrinology*] ... MPA
Medsource Systems, Inc. [*Vancouver Stock Exchange symbol*] ... MES
Medstone International, Inc. [*NASDAQ symbol*] (SAG) ... MEDS
Medstone International, Inc. [*Associated Press*] (SAG) ... Medstone
Medstone Intl. [*NASDAQ symbol*] (TTSB) ... MEDS
Med-Tech Systems, Inc. [*Vancouver Stock Exchange symbol*] ... MDT
Med-Trans of Florida, Inc. [*ICAO designator*] (FAAC) ... MEK
Medtronic, Inc. [*NYSE symbol*] (SPSG) ... MDT
Medtronic, Inc. [*Associated Press*] (SAG) ... Medtrnc
Medtronic, Inc., Minneapolis, MN [*Library symbol Library of Congress*] (LCLS) ... MnMMe
Medugorje Information Center (EA) ... MIC
Medullary Cancer of the Thyroid [*Medicine*] ... MCT
Medullary Carcinoma of the Thyroid [*Medicine*] (AAMN) ... MCT
Medullary Collecting Tubules [*Anatomy*] ... MCT
Medullary Cystic Disease [*Medicine*] (AAMN) ... MC
Medullary Cystic Disease [*Medicine*] (MAE) ... MCD
Medullary Dorsal Horn [*Anatomy*] ... MDH
Medullary Ray [*Botany*] (BARN) ... MR
Medullary Sponge Kidney [*Anatomy*] (MAE) ... MSK
Medullary Thick Ascending Limb [*Anatomy*] ... MAL
Medullary Thick Ascending Limb [*Anatomy*] ... mTAL
Medullary Thyroid Carcinoma [*Medicine*] ... MTC
Medulloblastoma [*A type of brain cancer*] (CDI) ... MDL
Medusa Corp. [*Associated Press*] (SAG) ... Medusa
Medusa Corp. [*NYSE symbol*] (CTT) ... MSA
Medvedev, Sponheuer, Karnick [*Earthquake intensity scale*] ... MSK
Medwave, Inc. [*NASDAQ symbol*] (SAG) ... MDWV
Medwave, Inc. [*Associated Press*] (SAG) ... Medwve
Meecham Verbal Language Scale (DAVI) ... MVLS
MEECN [*Minimum Essential Emergency Communications Network*] **Communication Plan** (MCD) ... MCP
MEECN Message Processing System [*Military*] ... MMPS
Meekatharra [*Australia ICAO location identifier*] (ICLI) ... APMR
Meekatharra [*Australia Seismograph station code, US Geological Survey*] (SEIS) ... MEK
Meekatharra [*Australia Airport symbol*] (OAG) ... MKR
Meeker, CO [*Location identifier FAA*] (FAAL) ... EKR
Meeker Public Library, Meeker, CO [*Library symbol Library of Congress*] (LCLS) ... CoMe

Meerblick, SA [Spain] [FAA designator] (FAAC) .... MIK
Meersk Air [ICAO designator] (AD) .... DM
Meerut [India] [Seismograph station code, US Geological Survey Closed]
 (SEIS) .... MEE
Meerwein-Ponndorf-Verley [Organic chemistry] .... MPV
Meeson and Roscoe's English Exchequer Reports [A publication]
 (DLA) .... Mees & Ros
Meeson and Welsby's English Exchequer Reports [A publication]
 (DLA) .... M & W
Meeson and Welsby's English Exchequer Reports [A publication]
 (DLA) .... Mees & W
Meeson and Welsby's English Exchequer Reports [A publication]
 (DLA) .... Mees & Wels
Meester [Master] [Dutch] (AD) .... mr
Meet Me Conference [Telecommunications] (DOM) .... MMC
Meet the Composer (EA) .... MTC
Meet-a-Mum Association [British] (DI) .... MAMA
Meeting (AFM) .... MTG
Meeting (AFM) .... MTG
Meeting Individual Needs [Educational publishing] .... MIN
Meeting Number (NITA) .... MN
Meeting of Consultation of Ministers of Foreign Affairs .... MCMFA
Meeting of Signatories [INTELSAT] .... MS
Meeting Our Operational Needs .... MOON
Meeting Planners Expo (ITD) .... MPE
Meeting Planners International (EA) .... MPI
Meeting Point [Military] .... MP
Meeting Point (AD) .... mp
Meeting Series [Online database field identifier] .... MS
Meeting Street School Screening Test [Used to detect learning
 disabilities] .... MSSST
Meeting Updates in Skill Training [International Labor Organization]
 [Information service or system United Nations] (DUND) .... MUST
Meetings and Incentive Travel Exposition [Trade show] .... MITE
Meetings Industry Association of Australia .... MIAA
Meetings Industry Microcomputer Users Group [Defunct] (EA) .... MIMUG
Meetings Name (NITA) .... MN
Meetings Word (NITA) .... MW
Mega [A prefix meaning multiplied by one million] [Symbol] .... M
Mega [A prefix meaning multiplied by one million] .... MA
Mega [A prefix meaning multiplied by one million] (AAG) .... MEG
Mega Cisterna Magna [Medicine] .... MCM
Mega [or Million] Electron Volts .... MEV
Mega Floating-Point Operations per Second [Computer science] .... MFLOP
Mega Gold Resources Ltd. [Vancouver Stock Exchange symbol] .... MGG
Mega Society (EA) .... MS
Mega Symbols per Second (MCD) .... MSPS
Megaampere (IAA) .... MEGA
Mega-Ampere Generator for Plasma Implosion Experiments [Astrophysics]
 (ECON) .... MAGPIE
Megaannum (DOG) .... Ma
Megabar .... MB
Megabar Diamond Cell [For high-pressure measurements] .... MBC
Megabase [A unit of molecular size] .... Mb
Megabit [Binary Digit] [Computer science] .... MB
Megabit [Computer science] (WDMC) .... Mb
Megabit [Marine science] (OSRA) .... Mb
MegaBIT [Binary Digit] [Computer science] (MDG) .... MBIT
MegaBIT [Binary Digit] Digital Troposcatter Subsystem [Communications]
 (MCD) .... MDTS
MegaBITS [Binary Digits] per Second [Transmission rate] [Computer
 science] .... MB/S
Megabits per Second .... MB/S
MegaBITS [Binary Digits] per Second [Transmission rate] [Computer
 science] .... MBPS
Megabits Per Second (NITA) .... MBS
MegaBITS [Binary Digits] per Second [Transmission rate] [Computer
 science] (MCD) .... MPS
Megabuck [Defense industry colloquialism for one million dollars] (AAG) .... MB
Megabyte [Data storage capacity] [Computer science] .... M
Megabyte [Data storage capacity] [Computer science] .... MB
Megabytes Per Second (NITA) .... MBS
Megacards Inc. [NASDAQ symbol] (TTSB) .... MEGX
Megachannel Extraterrestrial Array [For receiving possible radio signals from
 non-earth civilizations] .... META
Megachips per Second (MCD) .... MCPS
Megacurie .... Mc
Megacurie .... MCi
Megacycle .... Mc
Megacycle (IDOE) .... mc
Megacycle (IAA) .... ME
Megacycle (NTCM) .... MEG
Megacycle (IAA) .... MEGC
Megacycle (ABBR) .... MGCYL
Megacycle per Second [Megahertz] (IAA) .... MEGC
Megacycles per Second (IAA) .... MC
Megacycles per Second [Megahertz] [See also MC/S, MCS, MH, MHz] .... MCPS
Megacycles per Second [Megahertz] [See also MCPS, MH, MHz] .... MCS
Megacycles per Second (AD) .... mps
Megacyles [Also, MCPS] (WDAA) .... MPS
Megacystis-Microcolon-Intestinal Hypoperistalsis Syndrome [Medicine]
 (DMAA) .... MMIHS
Megadalton .... MD
Megadata Corp. (MHDW) .... MSHK
Mega-Dyne Industrial Corp. [Vancouver Stock Exchange symbol] .... MGY

Megaelectronvolt (IDOE) .... MeV
Mega-Electronvolt (ODBW) .... MeV
Mega-Floating Point Operation .... MFLOP
Megagauss-Oersted [Magnetic field strength] .... MGO
Megagauss-Oersted [Also, MGO] [Magnetic field strength] .... MGOe
Megagram .... MG
Megagrams per Cubic Meter .... MG/M³
Megagrams per Day .... MG/D
Megagrams per Square Meter .... MG/M²
Megahertz [Megacycles per second] [See also MCPS, MCS, MC/S, MHZ]
 (NATG) .... MH
Megahertz [Megacycles per Second] [See also MCPS, MCS, MC/S, MH] .... MHz
Megahertz [Megacycles per Second] .... MHz
Megajoule .... MJ
Megakaryoblast [Hematology] .... MKB
Megakaryocyte [Hematology] .... Meg
Megakaryocyte [Hematology] (DAVI) .... MEGA
Megakaryocyte Growth-Promoting Activity [Hematology] .... Meg-GPA
Megakaryocytic Leukemia [Hematology] .... MKL
Megaline Resources [Vancouver Stock Exchange symbol] .... MGA
Megaliter .... ML
Megaloblastic [Cytology] (AAMN) .... meg
Megaloblastic Anemia of Pregnancy [Obstetrics] (MAE) .... MAP
Megalomania (ABBR) .... MGLMNA
Megalomaniac (ABBR) .... MGLMNAC
Megalopolis (ABBR) .... MGLPS
Megamega [A prefix meaning multiplied by one trillion] (DEN) .... MM
Megameter .... MM
Megampere (IEEE) .... MA
Meganewton .... MN
Megaparsec .... MPC
Megapascal .... MPa
Megapascal (AD) .... mpa
Megaphone (ABBR) .... MGPHN
Megapounds per Square Inch .... MSI
Megara [Greece] [ICAO location identifier] (ICLI) .... LGMG
Megarad (AD) .... mrad
Megarayleigh [Optics] .... MR
Megaron (VRA) .... meg
Megarry's The Rent Acts [A publication] (DLA) .... Megarry
Megasample per Second (IAA) .... MSPS
Megasample per Second (IAA) .... MSS
MegaSamples per Second (CDE) .... MSa/s
Megasecond (AAG) .... MEGS
Megasecond (IAA) .... MS
Megasporocyte [Botany] .... MS
Megastar Ventures [Vancouver Stock Exchange symbol] .... MVS
Megatest Corp. [Associated Press] (SAG) .... Megatest
Megatest Corp. [NASDAQ symbol] (SAG) .... MEGT
Megaton (WDAA) .... MEG
Megaton [Nuclear equivalent of one million tons of high explosive] (AAG) .... MEGT
Megaton [Nuclear equivalent of one million tons of high explosive] (AAG) .... MGT
Megaton [Nuclear equivalent of one million tons of high explosive] (AFM) .... MT
Megatron (CET) .... MT
Megavar .... MVAR
Megavar-Hour .... MVARH
Megavolt (AAG) .... MEGV
Megavolt .... MV
Megavolt Direct Current [Nuclear energy] (IAA) .... MVDC
Megavolt-Ampere .... MVA
Megavolt-Ampere Reactive [Nuclear energy] (IAA) .... MVAR
Megawatt (WDAA) .... MEG
Megawatt [Also, MW] .... MEGW
Megawatt [Also, MEGW] .... MW
Megawatt Air-to-Ground Illumination System (MCD) .... MAGIS
Megawatt Cassegrain Diplexer .... MCD
Megawatt Cassegrain Monopulse .... MCM
Megawatt Demand Setter (NRCH) .... MDS
Megawatt Electric (IAA) .... MWE
Megawatt Hour .... Mwh
Megawatt Receiver Filter .... MRF
Megawatt Thermal [Nuclear energy] (NRCH) .... MWT
Megawatt Transmitter Filter .... MTF
Megawatt Waveguide Switch .... MWS
Megawatt Year of Electricity (IAA) .... MWYE
Megawatt-Day .... MWD
Megawatt-Days per Metric Ton of Uranium .... MWD/MTU
Megawatt-Days per Ton .... MWD/T
Megawatt-Hour .... MEGWH
Megawatt-Hour (MCD) .... MWh
Megawatts [Heat] (IEEE) .... MW(H)
Megawatts of Electric Power .... MWe
Megawatts [Thermal] .... MW(th)
Megaword .... MWD
Megestrol Acetate [Antineoplastic drug] .... MEGACE
Megeve [France ICAO location identifier] (ICLI) .... LFHM
Meggison's Assets in Equity [1832] [A publication] (DLA) .... Megg Ass
Meghauli [Nepal] [Airport symbol] (OAG) .... MEY
Meghauli [Nepal] [ICAO location identifier] (ICLI) .... VNMG
Megiddo (BJA) .... Meg
Megillah (BJA) .... MEG
Megillat Ta'anit (BJA) .... MegTa'an
Megilot Genuzot [E. L. Sukenik] [A publication] (BJA) .... SMG
Megis Local School District Public Library, Middleport Branch, Middleport,
 OH [Library symbol Library of Congress] (LCLS) .... OMiM

Megis Local School District Public Library, Pomeroy, OH [*Library symbol Library of Congress*] (LCLS) .... OPo

Mego Financial [*NASDAQ symbol*] (TTSB) .... MEGO

Mego Financial [*Associated Press*] (SAG) .... MegoFinl

Mego Financial Corp. [*NASDAQ symbol*] (SAG) .... MEGO

Mego Financial Corp. [*Associated Press*] (SAG) .... MegoFin

Mego Mortgage Corp. [*Associated Press*] (SAG) .... MegoMrt

Mego Mortgage Corp. [*NASDAQ symbol*] (SAG) .... MMGC

Megohm (AAG) .... M

Megohm (AAG) .... MEG

Megohm (IDOE) .... meg

Megohm .... MEG

Megohm (MSA) .... MEGO

Megone's Companies Acts Cases [*1888-90*] [*England*] [*A publication*] (DLA) .... Meg

Megone's Companies Acts Cases [*1888-90*] [*England*] [*A publication*] (DLA) .... Megone

Mehamn [*Norway ICAO location identifier*] (ICLI) .... ENMH

Mehamn [*Norway*] [*Airport symbol*] (OAG) .... MEH

Meharry Medical College, Nashville, TN [*OCLC symbol*] (OCLC) .... TMD

Meharry Medical College, Nashville, TN [*Library symbol Library of Congress*] (LCLS) .... TNM

Meharry Medicine College (GAGS) .... Meharry Med C

Mehl Biophile International Corp. [*NASDAQ symbol*] (SAG) .... MEHL

Mehl Biophile International Corp. [*Associated Press*] (SAG) .... MehlBio

Mehran [*Iran*] [*ICAO location identifier*] (ICLI) .... OICM

Mehri (BJA) .... Mh

Mehriz [*Iran*] [*ICAO location identifier*] (ICLI) .... OIYM

Mehrzweck Forschungs [*Reactor*] [*Germany*] (NRCH) .... MZFR

Meiganga [*Cameroon*] [*ICAO location identifier*] (ICLI) .... FKAM

Meigs' Digest of Decisions of the Courts of Tennessee [*A publication*] (DLA) .... Meigs Dig

Meigs' Tennessee Reports [*A publication*] (DLA) .... Meigs' R

Meigs' Tennessee Supreme Court Reports [*1838-39*] [*A publication*] (DLA) .... Meigs

Meiji Seika Kaisha Ltd. [*Japan*] .... Mei

Meiji Seika Kaisha Ltd. [*Japan*] [*Research code symbol*] .... SF

Meiji University, Maruzen Co. Ltd. [*UTLAS symbol*] .... ULM

Meiklejohn Civil Liberties Institute (EA) .... MCLI

Meiktila [*Myanmar*] [*ICAO location identifier*] (ICLI) .... VBML

Me'ilah (BJA) .... Me

Me'ilah (BJA) .... Me'il

Mein Gott, Fueg Es zum Besten [*My God, Order It for the Best*] [*Motto of Sophie, consort of Georg Friedrich, Margrave of Brandenburg-Anspach (1563-1639)*] [*German*] .... MGFZB

Mein Verlangen zu Gott [*My Desires (I Give) to God*] [*Motto of Anna Marie, Margravine of Brandenburg (1609-80)*] [*German*] .... MVZG

Mein Vertrauen Steht zu Gott Allein [*My Trust Is in God Alone*] [*Motto of Johann Adolf II, Duke of Saxony-Weissenfels (1649-97)*] [*German*] .... MVSZGA

Meinerzhagen [*Germany ICAO location identifier*] (ICLI) .... EDKZ

Meinicke Turbidity Reaction [*Obsolete test for syphilis*] .... MTR

Meiosis-Activating Sterol [*Cytology*] .... MAS

Meiosis-Preventing Substance [*Cyctology*] .... MPS

Meishan [*Republic of China*] [*Seismograph station code, US Geological Survey*] (SEIS) .... TWO

Meitnerium [*Proposed name and symbol for recently-discovered element*] .... Mt

Mejdunarodna Fondatzia Lyudmila Zhivkova [*Lyudmila Zhivkova International Foundation*] (EAIO) .... MFLZ

Mejit [*Marshall Islands*] [*Airport symbol*] (OAG) .... MJB

Mekambo [*Gabon*] [*ICAO location identifier*] (ICLI) .... FOOE

Mekambo [*Gabon*] [*Airport symbol*] (OAG) .... MKB

Mekane [*Ethiopia*] [*Airport symbol*] (OAG) .... MKS

Mekhilta (BJA) .... Mek

Mekhilta (BJA) .... MeKh

Mekhilta Exodus (BJA) .... MEx

Mekhitarist Fathers (TOCD) .... cmvd

Mekhitarist Order of Vienna [*Roman Catholic men's religious order*] .... CMVd

Mekhon ha-Tekanim ha-Yisre'eli (BJA) .... MTY

Meknes [*Morocco*] [*Airport symbol*] (AD) .... MEK

Meknes/Bassatine [*Morocco*] [*ICAO location identifier*] (ICLI) .... GMFM

Mekong Delta Mobile Afloat Force [*Vietnam*] .... MDMAF

Mekong Delta Mobile Afloat Force [*Vietnam*] [*Military*] (VNW) .... MEDMAF

Mekong Delta Riverine Assault Force [*Vietnam*] .... MDRAF

Mekong River and Basin [*MARC geographic area code Library of Congress*] (LCCP) .... ag----

Mekong River Commission [*Thailand*] .... MRC

Mekoryuk [*Alaska*] [*Airport symbol*] (OAG) .... MYU

Mekoryuk, AK [*Location identifier FAA*] (FAAL) .... AIX

Mel Anderson Fan Club [*Defunct*] (EA) .... MAFC

[*The*] Mel Gibson Fan Club [*Defunct*] (EA) .... TMGFC

Mel Tillis National Fan Club (EA) .... MTNFC

Melamine .... MEL

Melamine Chemicals [*NASDAQ symbol*] (TTSB) .... MTWO

Melamine Chemicals, Inc. [*Associated Press*] (SAG) .... Melami

Melamine Chemicals, Inc. [*NASDAQ symbol*] (NQ) .... MTWO

Melamine Council [*Defunct*] (EA) .... MC

Melamine Paper Laminate (PDAA) .... MPLAW

Melamine Tableware Association (EA) .... MTA

Melamine-Formaldehyde [*Plastics technology*] .... MF

Melandrium Yellow Fleck Virus [*Plant pathology*] .... MYFV

Melanesia (ROG) .... MELAN

Melanesia [*MARC geographic area code Library of Congress*] (LCCP) .... pome--

Melanesian Alliance [*Papua New Guinea*] [*Political party*] (FEA) .... MELC

Melanesian Progressive Parti [*Vanuatu*] [*Political party*] (EY) .... MPP

Melange .... MLNG

Melanges d'Archeologie et d'Histoire. Ecole Francaise de Rome [*A publication*] (OCD) .... Melanges d'Arch

Melanges Maspero [*A publication*] (OCD) .... Mel Masp

Melangguane [*Indonesia*] [*ICAO location identifier*] (ICLI) .... WAMN

Melanguane [*Indonesia*] [*Airport symbol*] (OAG) .... MNA

Melanin [*Pigmentation*] (DAVI) .... MELAN

Melanin-Concentrating Hormone [*Endocrinology*] .... MCH

Melanin-Producing Cell Autoantibody [*Endocrinology*] .... MPCA

Melanocortin Receptor [*Biochemistry*] .... MCR

Melanocyte-Inhibiting Factor [*Endocrinology*] .... MIF

Melanocyte-Releasing Hormone [*Endocrinology*] .... MRH

Melanocyte-Stimulating Hormone [*Also, MH*] [*Endocrinology*] .... MSH

Melanocyte-Stimulating Hormone Releasing Factor [*Endocrinology*] .... MRF

Melanocyte-Stimulating Hormone-Inhibiting Factor [*Endocrinology*] (MAE) .... MSH-IF

Melanocyte-Stimulating Hormone-Inhibitory Hormone [*Endocrinology*] (DAVI) .... MIH

Melanocyte-Stimulating Hormone-Release-Inhibiting Hormone [*Endocrinology*] (MAE) .... MRIH

Melanocyte-Stimulating-Hormone Release Inhibiting Factor [*Also, MRIF*] [*Endocrinology*] .... MIF

Melanocyte-Stimulating-Hormone Release Inhibiting Factor [*Also, MIF*] [*Endocrinology*] .... MRIF

Melanoma [*Oncology*] .... MEL

Melanoma Growth Stimulatory Activity [*Biochemistry*] .... MGSA

Melanoma-Associated Antigen [*Oncology*] .... MAA

Melanophore Hormone [*Also, MSH*] [*Endocrinology*] .... MH

Melanophore Index [*Biology*] .... MI

Melanophore-Stimulating Hormone [*Endocrinology*] (AAMN) .... MSH

Melanophore-Stimulating Hormone [*Intermedin*] Inhibiting Factor [*Laboratory science*] (DAVI) .... MSH-IF

Melanotropin Inhibiting Factor [*Biochemistry*] .... MIF

Melanotropin Releasing Factor [*Biochemistry*] .... MRF

Melatonin .... MLT

Melaveh Malka (BJA) .... MM

Melbourne [*Australia ICAO location identifier*] (ICLI) .... AMHS

Melbourne [*Australia ICAO location identifier*] (ICLI) .... AMMC

Melbourne [*Australia ICAO location identifier*] (ICLI) .... AMML

Melbourne [*Australia ICAO location identifier*] (ICLI) .... AMMM

Melbourne [*Australia ICAO location identifier*] (ICLI) .... AMMR

Melbourne [*Australia ICAO location identifier*] (ICLI) .... AMMX

Melbourne [*Australia ICAO location identifier*] (ICLI) .... AMRF

Melbourne [*Australia ICAO location identifier*] (ICLI) .... AMTU

Melbourne [*Australia Airport symbol*] (OAG) .... MEB

Melbourne [*Australia Airport symbol*] (OAG) .... MEL

Melbourne [*Australia Seismograph station code, US Geological Survey*] (SEIS) .... MEL

Melbourne [*Later, TOO*] [*Australia Geomagnetic observatory code*] .... MEL

Melbourne [*Florida*] [*Airport symbol*] (OAG) .... MLB

Melbourne Business Information Guide [*A publication*] (APTA) .... BIG

Melbourne/Cape Kennedy Regional [*Florida*] [*ICAO location identifier*] (ICLI) .... KMLB

Melbourne Corn Exchange [*Australia*] .... MCE

Melbourne/Essendon [*Australia ICAO location identifier*] (ICLI) .... AMEN

Melbourne Film Festival [*Australia*] .... MFF

Melbourne, FL [*Location identifier FAA*] (FAAL) .... SQT

Melbourne, FL [*FM radio station call letters*] .... WAOA

Melbourne, FL [*Television station call letters*] .... WBSF

Melbourne, FL [*FM radio station call letters*] .... WCIF

Melbourne, FL [*FM radio station call letters*] .... WFIT

Melbourne, FL [*FM radio station call letters*] .... WGGD

Melbourne, FL [*Television station call letters*] .... WIRB

Melbourne, FL [*AM radio station call letters*] .... WMEL

Melbourne, FL [*AM radio station call letters*] .... WMMB

Melbourne, FL [*AM radio station call letters*] .... WTAI

Melbourne Greyhound Racing Club [*Australia*] .... MGRC

Melbourne Institute of Applied Economic and Social Research [*Australia*] .... MIAESR

Melbourne International Festival [*Australia*] .... MIF

Melbourne Junior Chamber of Commerce [*Australia*] .... MJCC

Melbourne Magistrates Court [*Australia*] .... MMC

Melbourne Marathon [*Australia*] .... MM

Melbourne/Moorabbin [*Australia ICAO location identifier*] (ICLI) .... AMMB

Melbourne Public Library, Melbourne, FL [*Library symbol Library of Congress*] (LCLS) .... FMe

Melbourne Record, Melbourne, IA [*Library symbol Library of Congress*] (LCLS) .... IaMelbR

Melbourne Report [*A publication*] .... Melb Rpt

Melbourne Screen and Theatre Guild [*Australia*] .... MSTG

Melbourne Studies in Education [*A publication*] .... Melb Stud Ed

Melbourne Tenpin Bowling Association [*Australia*] .... MTBA

Melbourne Theatre Cooperative Society [*Australia*] .... MTCS

Melbourne Walking Club [*Australia*] .... MWC

Melbourne Western Region Commission [*Australia*] .... MWRC

Melchor De Mencos [*Guatemala*] [*ICAO location identifier*] (ICLI) .... MGMM

Melchor Developments Ltd. [*Toronto Stock Exchange symbol*] .... MP

Melcom All Round Adaptive Consolidated Software [*Japan*] .... MARCS

MELCOM All Round Adaptive Consolidated Software (NITA) .... MARCS

Melcom Optical Software Applications for Integrated Commercial Systems (PDAA) .... MOSAICS

Melcombe [*England*] .... MELC

Melcor Developments Ltd. [*Toronto Stock Exchange symbol*] .... MRD

Meldesammelstelle [*Message Center*] [*German military - World War II*] .... MSST

Melena [*Gastroenterology*] (DAVI) .... mel

Melendus [*Flourished, 1188-1209*] [*Authority cited in pre-1607 legal work*] (DSA) ... M
Melendus [*Flourished, 1188-1209*] [*Authority cited in pre-1607 legal work*] (DSA) ... Me
Melendus [*Flourished, 1188-1209*] [*Authority cited in pre-1607 legal work*] (DSA) ... Mel
Melengestrol Acetate [*Endocrinology*] ... MGA
Melfa, VA [*Location identifier FAA*] (FAAL) ... MFV
Melfi [*Chad*] [*Airport symbol*] (AD) ... MEF
Melfort, SK [*AM radio station call letters*] ... CJVR
Melfort, SK [*Television station call letters*] ... CKBQ
Melilla [*Spain ICAO location identifier*] (ICLI) ... GEML
Melilla [*Spain*] [*Airport symbol*] (OAG) ... MLN
Melilotus Latent Virus [*Plant pathology*] ... MELV
Melinga Resources Ltd. [*Vancouver Stock Exchange symbol*] ... MNA
Melioidosis [*Dermatology*] (DAVI) ... MELDOS
Melissa Resources, Inc. [*Vancouver Stock Exchange symbol*] ... MRE
Melitensis, Bovine, Porcine [*Antigen*] (AAMN) ... MBP
Melittin [*Bee venom*] ... M
Melkersson-Rosenthal Syndrome [*Medicine*] (DMAA) ... MRS
Melkite Laymen's Association of North America (EA) ... MLANA
Mellinger Memorial Library, Morning Sun, IA [*Library symbol Library of Congress*] (LCLS) ... IaMorn
Mellis [*Of Honey*] [*Pharmacy*] (ROG) ... MEL
Mellis [*Of Honey*] [*Pharmacy*] (ROG) ... MELL
Mellon Bank Corp. [*NYSE symbol*] (SPSG) ... MEL
Mellon Bank Corp. [*Associated Press*] (SAG) ... MellonBk
Mellon Bank Corp. [*Associated Press*] (SAG) ... Meln
Mellon Bank Corp. [*Associated Press*] (SAG) ... Melon
Mellon Bk 8.20% 'K' Pfd [*NYSE symbol*] (TTSB) ... MELPrK
Mellon Bk 8.50% 'J'Pfd [*NYSE symbol*] (TTSB) ... MELPrJ
Mellon Bk 9.60% 'I' Pfd [*NYSE symbol*] (TTSB) ... MELPrI
Mellon Institute [*Carnegie-Mellon University*] [*Research center*] (RCD) ... MI
Mellon InvestData Corp. [*New York, NY Information service or system*] (IID) ... MIC
Mellon Participating Mortgage Trust Commercial Properties Series [*NASDAQ symbol*] (NQ) ... MPMT
Mellon Participating Mortgage Trust Commercial Property Series [*Associated Press*] (SAG) ... MellonP
Mellonics Information Center [*Information service or system*] (IID) ... MIC
Mell's Parliamentary Practice [*A publication*] (DLA) ... Mell Parl Pr
Melo [*Uruguay*] [*Airport symbol*] (OAG) ... MLZ
Melo/Aeropuerto Deptal de Cerro Largo [*Uruguay*] [*ICAO location identifier*] (ICLI) ... SUMO
Melodic Dictation Computerized Instruction (EDAC) ... MEDICI
Melodious Accord (EA) ... MA
Melody ... MEL
Melodyland School of Theology, Anaheim, CA [*Inactive*] [*OCLC symbol*] (OCLC) ... CMS
Meloidogyne incognita [*A nematode*] ... MI
Melomanes Francais [*Record label*] [*France*] ... MF
Melomanes Francais [*Record label*] [*France*] ... MFr
Melphalan [*Also, A, L-PAM, MPH, MPL*] [*Antineoplastic drug*] ... M
Melphalan [*Antineoplastic drug*] (DAVI) ... Mel
Melphalan [*Also, A, L-PAM, M, MPL*] [*Antineoplastic drug*] ... MPH
Melphalan [*Also, A, L-PAM, M, MPH*] [*Antineoplastic drug*] ... MPL
Melphalan, Adriamycin, Prednisone [*Antineoplastic drug regimen*] ... MAP
Melphalan and Prednisone [*Antineoplastic drug regimen*] (DAVI) ... MPL + PRED
Melphalan and Prednisone [*Antineoplastic drug regimen*] (DAVI) ... MPL + PRED(MP)
Melphalan, Cyclophosphamide, BCNU [*Carmustine*], Prednisone [*Antineoplastic drug regimen*] ... MCBP
Melphalan, Cyclophosphamide, Prednisone [*Antineoplastic drug regimen*] ... MCP
Melphalan, Fluorouracil, Farlutal (Medroxyprogesterone acetate) [*Antineoplastic drug regimen*] ... MFP
Melphalan, Prednisone [*Antineoplastic drug regimen*] ... MP
Melphalan, Prednisone [*Antineoplastic drug*] (CDI) ... MP
Melphalan, Prednisone, Procarbazine [*Antineoplastic drug regimen*] ... MPP
Melpomene Institute for Women's Health Research (EA) ... MIWHR
Melrose High School, Melrose, MN [*Library symbol*] [*Library of Congress*] (LCLS) ... MnMeH
Melrose Junior High School, Melrose, MN [*Library symbol*] [*Library of Congress*] (LCLS) ... MnMeJ
Melrose, New Munich, Spring Hill Elementary School, Melrose, MN [*Library symbol*] [*Library of Congress*] (LCLS) ... MnMeE
Melrose Park Public Library, Melrose Park, IL [*Library symbol Library of Congress*] (LCLS) ... IMelp
Melrose Public Library, Melrose, MA [*Library symbol Library of Congress*] (LCLS) ... MMel
Melrose Public Library, Melrose, MN [*Library symbol*] [*Library of Congress*] (LCLS) ... MnMe
Melrose Resources Ltd. [*Vancouver Stock Exchange symbol*] ... MEL
Melrose Township Public Library, Walloon Lake, MI [*Library symbol Library of Congress*] (LCLS) ... MiWal
Melsbroek [*Belgium ICAO location identifier*] (ICLI) ... EBMB
Melt Back ... MB
Melt Inclusions [*Geology*] ... MI
Melt Through [*Nuclear energy*] (NRCH) ... MT
Melt Volume Index [*Materials science*] ... MVI
Melt-Down Accident Response Characteristics [*Nuclear energy*] (NRCH) ... MARCH
Melt-Flow Index [*of plastics*] ... MFI
Melt-Flow Rate [*of plastics*] ... MFR
Melting ... MLTG
Melting Level [*NWS*] (FAAC) ... MLTLVL
Melting Point (ROG) ... M PT
Melting Point ... MP
Melting Point (AD) ... mp
Melting Point (AD) ... mpt
Melting Pot ... MP
Melting-Assimilation-Storage-Homogenization [*Geology*] ... MASH
Melton Public Library, French Lick, IN [*Library symbol Library of Congress*] (LCLS) ... InFren
Melt-Powder Melt-Growth [*Materials Science*] ... MPMG
Melt-Processible Fluoropolymers [*Plastics technology*] ... MPFP
Melts At ____ [*Followed by a temperature*] ... M
Melt-Textured Growth [*Chemistry*] ... MTG
Melun/Villaroche [*France ICAO location identifier*] (ICLI) ... LFPM
Melvil Dewey [*Public access online catalog, University of California*] (NITA) ... MELVYL
Melvil Dui Chowder and Marching Association [*Later, MDMCA*] (EA) ... MDCMA
Melvil Dui Marching and Chowder Association (EA) ... MDMCA
Melville Corp. [*Formerly, Melville Shoe Corp.*] [*Associated Press*] (SAG) ... Melvile
Melville Corp. [*Formerly, Melville Shoe Corp.*] [*NYSE symbol*] (SPSG) ... MES
Melville Society (EA) ... MS
Melvill's Trial (Impeachment) [*London*] [*A publication*] (DLA) ... Melv Tr
Melvin News, Ocheyedan, IA [*Library symbol Library of Congress*] (LCLS) ... IaOchMH
Melvin News, Ocheyedan, IA [*Library symbol*] [*Library of Congress*] (LCLS) ... IaOchMN
Melvin Public Library, Melvin, IA [*Library symbol Library of Congress*] (LCLS) ... IaMel
Melvin Public Library, Melvin, IL [*Library symbol Library of Congress*] (LCLS) ... IMel
Melvin-Sibley Community Unit School District, Melvin, IL [*Library symbol*] [*Library of Congress*] (LCLS) ... IMelSD
MEM Co. [*AMEX symbol*] (TTSB) ... MEM
MEM Co., Inc. [*AMEX symbol*] (SPSG) ... MEM
Memanbetsu [*Japan*] [*Geomagnetic observatory code*] ... MMB
Memanbetsu [*Japan*] [*Airport symbol*] (OAG) ... MMB
Membach [*Belgium*] [*Seismograph station code, US Geological Survey*] (SEIS) ... MEM
Member ... M
Member ... MBER
Member (AFM) ... MBR
Member (DD) ... mbr
Member ... MBR
Member (WDMC) ... mem
Member (EY) ... MEM
Member ... MEMB
Member, Advisory Board ... MAB
Member, Appraisal Institute [*American Institute of Real Estate Appraisers of the National Association of Realtors*] [*Designation awarded by*] ... MAI
Member, Association of Occupational Therapists [*British*] ... MAOT
Member Budget Information System [*for House of Representatives*] ... MEMBIS
Member Canadian Institute of Mining and Metallurgy (DD) ... MCIM
Member, Fundraising Institute-Australia, Inc. (NFD) ... MFIA
Member Get a Member [*Prodigy Services Co.*] ... MGAM
Member Information Exchange [*American Society for Training and Development - ASTD*] [*Alexandria, VA*] [*Information service or system*] (IID) ... MIX
Member Information Network [*for House of Representatives*] ... MIN
Member Institution of Sewage Purification (BABM) ... MInstSP
Member Institution of Sewage Purification [*Ecology*] (DAVI) ... MInstSP
Member Library [*OCLC or RLIN*] ... ML
Member of APSAS [*Association of Public Service Administrative Staff*] [*British*] ... MAPSAS
Member of Congress ... MC
Member of Council ... MC
Member of Executive Council [*British*] ... MEC
Member of House of Assembly [*British*] ... MHA
Member of Knesset (BJA) ... MK
Member of Our Tribe [*Jewish slang*] ... MOT
Member of Our Tribe (AD) ... mot
Member of Parliament [*British*] (AD) ... M o P
Member of Parliament [*British*] ... MOP
Member of Parliament [*British*] ... MP
Member of Parliament of Canada ... MPC
Member of Police ... MP
Member of Provincial Parliament [*British*] ... MPP
Member of Royal Australasian College of Physicians ... MRACP
Member of Technical College [*British*] (DI) ... MTC
Member of the Accountants' Society (South Africa) ... CA(SA)
Member of the Acupuncture Association [*British*] ... MAcA
Member of the American Academy of Actuaries ... MAAA
Member of the American Chemical Society ... MACS
Member of the American College of Radiology ... MACR
Member of the American Concrete Institute ... MACI
Member of the American Electrical Railway Engineering Association ... MEREA
Member of the American Institute of Aeronautics and Astronautics [*Formerly, MIAS*] ... MAIAA
Member of the American Institute of Appraisers ... MAIA
Member of the American Institute of Chemical Engineers ... MAIChE
Member of the American Institute of Consulting Engineers ... MAICE
Member of the American Institute of Electrical Engineers ... MAIEE
Member of the American Institute of Mining and Metallurgical Engineers ... M Am IMME
Member of the American Institute of Mining and Metallurgical Engineers ... MAIME
Member of the American Ornithologists' Union ... MAOU

Member of the American Railway Engineering Association ... MAREA
Member of the American Society of Agricultural Engineering ... MASAE
Member of the American Society of Civil Engineers ... M Am Soc CE
Member of the American Society of Civil Engineers ... MASCE
Member of the American Society of Mechanical Engineers ... MASME
Member of the Anthropological Institute [*British*] ... MAI
Member of the Appropriate Sex (NHD) ... MOTAS
Member of the Architectural Institute of British Columbia [*Canada*] (DD) ... MAIBC
Member of the Arundel Society [*British*] ... MAS
Member of the Association for Promoting the Unity of Christendom [*British*] ... MAPUC
Member of the Association of Accounting Technicians [*British*] (DCTA) ... MAAT
Member of the Association of Business and Administrative Computing [*British*] (DBQ) ... MABAC
Member of the Association of Business Executives (DCTA) ... MABE
Member of the Association of Conference Executives [*British*] (DBQ) ... MACE
Member of the Association of Consulting Engineers [*British*] (EY) ... MConsE
Member of the Association of Hypnotists and Physiotherapists [*British*] ... MAHP
Member of the Association of Medical Secretaries, Practice Administrators, and Receptionists [*British*] (DBQ) ... MAMS
Member of the Association of Medical Secretaries, Practice Administrators, and Receptionists [*British*] (DI) ... MAMSPAR
Member of the Association of Supervisory and Executive Engineers [*British*] (DBQ) ... MASEE
Member of the Astronomical Society ... MAstS
Member of the Australasian Institute for Fundraising (NFD) ... MTAIF
Member of the Austrlaian Institute of Welfare Officers ... MAIWO
Member of the Bibliographical Society (ROG) ... MBS
Member of the Boot and Shoe Industry [*British*] (DAS) ... MBSI
Member of the British Association of Chemists (DAS) ... MBAC
Member of the British Association of Electrolysis (DI) ... MBAE
Member of the British Association of Industrial Editors (DBQ) ... MAIE
Member of the British Association of Occupational Therapists (DI) ... MBAOT
Member of the British Association of Social Workers ... MBASW
Member of the British College of Obstetricians and Gynaecologists (DAS) ... MCOG
Member of the British College of Ophthalmic Opticians [*British*] (DBQ) ... MBCO
Member of the British Computer Society (DCTA) ... MBCS
Member of the [*Order of the*] **British Empire** [*Facetious translation: "My Bloody Efforts"*] ... MBE
Member of the British Horological Institute (DBQ) ... MBHI
Member of the British Horological Institute (ROG) ... MBHINST
Member of the British Hypnotherapy Association (DBQ) ... MBHA
Member of the British Institute of Embalmers (DBQ) ... MBIE
Member of the British Institute of Interior Design (DBQ) ... MBID
Member of the British Institute of Management [*Formerly, MIIA*] ... MBIM
Member of the British Institute of Non-Destructive Testing (DBQ) ... MInstNDT
Member of the British Institution of Radio Engineers [*Later, MIERE*] ... M Brit IRE
Member of the British Naturopathic and Osteopathic Association ... MBNOA
Member of the British Ornithologists Union (EY) ... MBOU
Member of the Bureau of Engineer Surveyors [*British*] (DBQ) ... MBES
Member of the Cambridge Philosophical Society (ROG) ... MCPS
Member of the Canadian Institute of Forestry ... MCIF
Member of the Canadian Institute of Mining ... MCIM
Member of the Canadian Institute of Mining and Metallurgy ... MCIMM
Member of the Canadian Psychological Association ... MCPA
Member of the Canadian Society of Electrical Engineers (DI) ... MCSEE
Member of the Certified Bailiffs Association [*British*] (DI) ... MCBA
Member of the Chartered Institute of Building [*British*] (DBQ) ... MCIOB
Member of the Chartered Institute of Public Finance and Accountancy [*British*] ... IPFA
Member of the Chartered Institute of Transport [*British*] (DCTA) ... MCIT
Member of the Chartered Institution of Building Services [*British*] (DBQ) ... MCIBS
Member of the Chartered Society of Physiotherapists [*British*] ... MCSP
Member of the Chemical Institute of Canada ... MCIC
Member of the Civil and Mechanical Engineering Society ... MCMES
Member of the College of Craft Education [*British*] (DI) ... MCCEd
Member of the College of Dentists [*British*] ... MCD
Member of the College of Family Physicians [*British*] ... MCFP
Member of the College of General Practitioners [*British*] ... MCGP
Member of the College of Musicians [*British*] ... MCM
Member of the College of Pathologists [*British*] ... MC Path
Member of the College of Pathologists Australasia ... MCPA
Member of the College of Physicians and Surgeons [*British*] ... MCPS
Member of the College of Preceptors [*British*] (DBQ) ... MCollP
Member of the College of Preceptors [*British*] ... MCP
Member of the College of Radiologists Australasia ... MCRA
Member of the College of Speech Therapists [*British*] ... MCST
Member of the Colonial Parliament [*British*] ... MCP
Member of the Communication, Advertising, and Marketing Education Foundation [*British*] (DBQ) ... MCAM
Member of the Confederation of Professional Management [*British*] (DBQ) ... MCPM
Member of the Construction Surveyors' Institute [*British*] (DBQ) ... MCSI
Member of the County Council [*British*] ... MCC
Member of the Credit Institute ... MCI
Member of the Engineering Institute of Canada ... MEIC
Member of the English Church Union ... MECU
Member of the European Osteopathic Register ... MEOER
Member of the European Parliament ... MEP
Member of the Faculty of Community Medicine [*British*] ... MFCM
Member of the Faculty of Dispensing Opticians [*British*] (DBQ) ... MFDO
Member of the Faculty of Homoeopathy [*British*] ... MF Hom
Member of the Faculty of Physiatrists [*British*] ... MFPhys
Member of the Faculty of Physicians and Surgeons [*Glasgow*] ... MFPS
Member of the Faculty of Physiotherapists [*British*] ... MFPh
Member of the Faculty of Teachers in Commerce [*British*] (DBQ) ... MFTCom
Member of the Force (LAIN) ... MOF
Member of the Gas Institute [*British*] ... MGI
Member of the Gymnastic Teachers' Institute [*British*] (ROG) ... MGTI
Member of the Highway and Traffic Technicians Association [*British*] (DBQ) ... MHTTA
Member of the Historical Society ... MHS
Member of the Hotel, Catering, and Institutional Management Association [*British*] (DBQ) ... MHCIMA
Member of the House of Keys [*Isle Of Man*] [*British*] ... MHK
Member of the House of Representatives ... MHR
Member of the Incorporated Advertising Managers' Association [*British*] (DAS) ... MIAMA
Member of the Incorporated Association of Architects and Surveyors [*British*] (DBQ) ... MIAA
Member of the Incorporated Association of Architects and Surveyors [*British*] (DBQ) ... MIAS
Member of the Incorporated Law Society [*British*] ... MILS
Member of the Incorporated Sales Managers Association [*British*] (DAS) ... MISMA
Member of the Incorporated Society of Advertisement Consultants [*British*] (DAS) ... MISAC
Member of the Industrial Transport Association [*British*] ... MITA
Member of the Institute of Accredited Public Accountants [*Canada*] (DD) ... APA
Member of the Institute of Administrative Management [*British*] (DCTA) ... M Inst AM
Member of the Institute of Aeronautical Engineers [*British*] ... MI Ae E
Member of the Institute of Aeronautical Science [*Later, MIAAA*] ... MIAS
Member of the Institute of Aeronautical Sciences ... MIAeS
Member of the Institute of Affiliate Accountants (ADA) ... MIAA
Member of the Institute of Arbitrators [*British*] ... MIA
Member of the Institute of Asphalt Technology [*British*] (DBQ) ... MIAT
Member of the Institute of Automobile Assessors [*British*] ... MIAA
Member of the Institute of Automotive Engineer Assessors [*British*] (DBQ) ... MIAEA
Member of the Institute of Automotive Engineer Assessors [*British*] (DBQ) ... MInstAEA
Member of the Institute of Automotive Mechanical Engineers (ADA) ... MIAME
Member of the Institute of Baths and Recreation Management [*British*] (DBQ) ... MInstBRM
Member of the Institute of Biology [*British*] (EY) ... MI Biol
Member of the Institute of Body Engineers [*British*] (DBQ) ... MBEI
Member of the Institute of British Architects (ROG) ... MIBA
Member of the Institute of British Bakers (DBQ) ... MInstBB
Member of the Institute of British Engineers (EY) ... MIBritE
Member of the Institute of British Engineers ... MIBritishE
Member of the Institute of British Foundrymen ... MIBF
Member of the Institute of Building [*British*] ... MIOB
Member of the Institute of Burial and Cremation Administration [*British*] (DBQ) ... MInstBCA
Member of the Institute of Business and Technical Management [*British*] (DBQ) ... MInstBTM
Member of the Institute of Careers Officers [*British*] (DBQ) ... MICO
Member of the Institute of Certificated Grocers [*British*] ... MGI
Member of the Institute of Clerks of Works of Great Britain, Inc. (DBQ) ... MICW
Member of the Institute of Commerce [*British*] (DBQ) ... MCI
Member of the Institute of Commercial Management [*British*] (DCTA) ... M Inst CM
Member of the Institute of Corrosion Science and Technology [*British*] (DBQ) ... MICorrST
Member of the Institute of Data Processing Management [*British*] (DCTA) ... MIDPM
Member of the Institute of Directors [*British*] (DI) ... MInstD
Member of the Institute of Electrical and Electronic Engineers ... MIEEE
Member of the Institute of Employment Consultants [*British*] (DBQ) ... MECI
Member of the Institute of Energy [*British*] (DBQ) ... MInstE
Member of the Institute of Executive Engineers and Officers [*British*] (DBQ) ... MIExE
Member of the Institute of Explosives Engineers [*British*] (DBQ) ... MIExpE
Member of the Institute of Export [*British*] ... MI Ex
Member of the Institute of Export [*British*] (DBQ) ... MIEx(Grad)
Member of the Institute of Freight Forwarders [*British*] (ODBW) ... MIFF
Member of the Institute of Freight Forwarders [*British*] (DBQ) ... MInstFF
Member of the Institute of Fuel [*British*] ... MInstF
Member of the Institute of Grocery Distribution [*British*] (DBQ) ... MIGD
Member of the Institute of Health Education [*British*] ... MIHE
Member of the Institute of Home Economics [*British*] (DBQ) ... MIHEc
Member of the Institute of Housing [*British*] (DBQ) ... MIH
Member of the Institute of Hygiene [*British*] ... MIH
Member of the Institute of Industrial Administration [*Later, MBIM*] [*British*] ... MIIA
Member of the Institute of Industrial Security [*British*] (DBQ) ... MIISec
Member of the Institute of Information Scientists [*British*] ... MI Inf Sc
Member of the Institute of Journalists [*British*] (DGA) ... M INST J
Member of the Institute of Journalists [*British*] (ROG) ... M Inst Jour
Member of the Institute of Linguists [*British*] ... MIL
Member of the Institute of Local Government Administrators [*British*] (ODBW) ... MILGA
Member of the Institute of Management (DD) ... MIM
Member of the Institute of Management Consultants ... MIMC

Member of the Institute of Management Services [*British*] (DBQ) .... MMS
Member of the Institute of Management Specialists [*British*] (DBQ) .... MIMS
Member of the Institute of Manufacturing [*British*] (DBQ) .... MIManf
Member of the Institute of Marine Engineers [*British*] (EY) .... MIMarE
Member of the Institute of Market Officers [*British*] (DI) .... MInstMO
Member of the Institute of Marketing [*British*] .... MInstM
Member of the Institute of Materials Handling [*British*] (DBQ) .... MIMH
Member of the Institute of Measurement and Control [*British*] (DBQ) .... MInstMC
Member of the Institute of Metal Finishing [*British*] (DBQ) .... MIMF
Member of the Institute of Metals [*British*] .... MInstMet
Member of the Institute of Mining and Metallurgy [*British*] (EY) .... MIMM
Member of the Institute of Mining Engineers .... MIME
Member of the Institute of Motor Industry [*British*] .... MIMI
Member of the Institute of Municipal Building Management [*British*] (DBQ) .... MIMBM
Member of the Institute of Municipal Engineers [*British*] (EY) .... MIMunE
Member of the Institute of Music Teachers (ADA) .... MIMT
Member of the Institute of Musical Instrument Technology [*British*] (DBQ) .... MIMIT
Member of the Institute of Navigation [*British*] .... MIN
Member of the Institute of Operating Theatre Technicians [*British*] .... MIOT
Member of the Institute of Osteopathy and Physiotherapy [*British*] .... MIOP
Member of the Institute of Packaging [*British*] (DI) .... MInstPkg
Member of the Institute of Patentees and Inventors [*British*] (EY) .... MInstPI
Member of the Institute of Personnel Management [*British*] .... MIPM
Member of the Institute of Petroleum [*British*] (EY) .... MInstPet
Member of the Institute of Petroleum Engineers (ADA) .... MInstPE
Member of the Institute of Physics (ADA) .... MInstP
Member of the Institute of Plumbing [*British*] (DBQ) .... MIP
Member of the Institute of Population Registration [*British*] (DBQ) .... MIR
Member of the Institute of Practitioners in Advertising [*British*] .... MIPA
Member of the Institute of Printing [*British*] (DBQ) .... MIOP
Member of the Institute of Printing Management [*British*] (DGA) .... MI PTG M
Member of the Institute of Production Control [*British*] (DBQ) .... MIPC
Member of the Institute of Professional Investigators [*British*] (DBQ) .... MIPI
Member of the Institute of Psionic Medicine [*British*] .... MIPsiMed
Member of the Institute of Public Administration (ADA) .... MIPA
Member of the Institute of Public Health Engineers [*British*] (DBQ) .... MIPHE
Member of the Institute of Public Relations [*British*] .... MIPR
Member of the Institute of Purchasing and Supply [*British*] (DCTA) .... M Inst PS
Member of the Institute of Purchasing and Supply Management (ADA) .... MIPSM
Member of the Institute of Qualified Private Secretaries [*British*] (DI) .... MIQPS
Member of the Institute of Quality Assurance [*British*] (DBQ) .... MIQA
Member of the Institute of Quarrying [*British*] (DBQ) .... MIQ
Member of the Institute of Refrigeration [*British*] (DBQ) .... MInstR
Member of the Institute of Registered Architects [*British*] .... MInstRA
Member of the Institute of Road Transport Engineering [*British*] (DBQ) .... MIRTE
Member of the Institute of Sales and Marketing Management [*British*] (DBQ) .... MInstSMM
Member of the Institute of Sales Promotion [*British*] (DI) .... MISP
Member of the Institute of Sales Technology and Management [*British*] (DBQ) .... MISTM
Member of the Institute of Science Technology [*British*] (DBQ) .... MIST
Member of the Institute of Scientific and Technical Communicators [*British*] (DBQ) .... MISTC
Member of the Institute of Social Welfare [*British*] (DBQ) .... MISW
Member of the Institute of Solid Waste Management [*British*] (DI) .... MInstSWM
Member of the Institute of Statisticians [*Formerly, AIS*] [*British*] .... MIS
Member of the Institute of Supervisory Management [*British*] (DBQ) .... MISM
Member of the Institute of Surveyors (ADA) .... MIS
Member of the Institute of Technical Journalists [*British*] (DGA) .... MITJ
Member of the Institute of Technology [*British*] (EY) .... MInstT
Member of the Institute of Trade Mark Agents [*British*] .... MITMA
Member of the Institute of Trading Standards Administration [*British*] (DBQ) .... MITSA
Member of the Institute of Training and Development [*British*] (DBQ) .... MITD
Member of the Institute of Training Officers [*International Institute of Social Economics*] [*British*] (DI) .... MITO
Member of the Institute of Transport [*British*] .... MInstT
Member of the Institute of Transport Administration [*British*] (DCTA) .... M Inst TA
Member of the Institute of Travel Agents [*British*] .... MTAI
Member of the Institute of Travel and Tourism [*British*] (ODBW) .... MITT
Member of the Institute of Travel Managers in Industry and Commerce [*British*] (ODBW) .... MInstTM
Member of the Institute of Water Pollution Control [*British*] .... MIWPC
Member of the Institute of Weights and Measures Administration [*British*] .... MIWMA
Member of the Institute of Welding [*British*] .... MInstW
Member of the Institute of Wireless Technology [*British*] .... MIWT
Member of the Institute of Work Study Practitioners [*British*] .... MIWSP
Member of the Institute of Works and Highways Superintendents [*British*] (DI) .... MInstWHS
Member of the Institution of Agricultural Engineers [*British*] .... MIAgrE
Member of the Institution of Analysts and Programmers [*British*] (DBQ) .... MIAP
Member of the Institution of Automobile Engineers [*British*] .... MIAE
Member of the Institution of British Engineers .... MInstBE
Member of the Institution of Building Control Officers [*British*] (DBQ) .... MIBCO
Member of the Institution of Chemical Engineers [*British*] (EY) .... MIChemE
Member of the Institution of Civil Engineers [*Formerly, AMICE*] [*British*] .... MICE
Member of the Institution of Civil Engineers [*Later, MICE*] [*British*] (EY) .... MInstCE
Member of the Institution of Civil Engineers of Ireland .... MICEI
Member of the Institution of Electrical Engineers [*Formerly, AMIEE*] [*British*] (EY) .... MIEE
Member of the Institution of Electronic and Radio Engineers [*Formerly, M Brit IRE*] [*British*] .... MIERE
Member of the Institution of Engineering Designers [*British*] (DBQ) .... MIED
Member of the Institution of Engineering Inspection [*British*] .... MIEI
Member of the Institution of Engineers [*British*] (EY) .... MInstE
Member of the Institution of Engineers and Shipbuilders, Scotland .... MIES
Member of the Institution of Engineers Australia .... MEIA
Member of the Institution of Engineers, India .... MIE(Ind)
Member of the Institution of Fire Engineers [*British*] (DCTA) .... MIFirE
Member of the Institution of Fire Engineers [*British*] (EY) .... MIFireE
Member of the Institution of Gas Engineers [*British*] .... MIGasE
Member of the Institution of Gas Engineers [*British*] (EY) .... MInstGasE
Member of the Institution of Geologists [*British*] (DBQ) .... MIGeol
Member of the Institution of Heating and Ventilating Engineers [*British*] .... MIHVE
Member of the Institution of Highway Engineers [*British*] .... MInstHE
Member of the Institution of Highways and Transportation [*British*] (DBQ) .... MIHT
Member of the Institution of Industrial Managers [*British*] (DCTA) .... MIIM
Member of the Institution of Journalists .... MIJ
Member of the Institution of Locomotive Engineers [*British*] (EY) .... MILocoE
Member of the Institution of Mechanical Engineers [*Formerly, AMIMechE*] [*British*] .... MIME
Member of the Institution of Mechanical Engineers [*Formerly, AMIMechE*] [*British*] (EY) .... MIMechE
Member of the Institution of Mechanical Engineers and General Technician Engineers [*British*] (DBQ) .... MIMGTechE
Member of the Institution of Metallurgists [*British*] (DBQ) .... MIM
Member of the Institution of Mining and Metallurgy [*British*] .... MInstMM
Member of the Institution of Mining Engineers [*British*] (EY) .... MIMinE
Member of the Institution of Mining Engineers [*British*] .... MInstME
Member of the Institution of Naval Architects [*British*] .... MINA
Member of the Institution of Naval Architects [*British*] (EY) .... MInstNA
Member of the Institution of Nuclear Engineers [*British*] .... MI Nucl E
Member of the Institution of Nuclear Engineers [*British*] .... MINucE
Member of the Institution of Occupational Safety and Health [*British*] (DCTA) .... MIOSH
Member of the Institution of Plant Engineers [*British*] .... MIPlantE
Member of the Institution of Production Engineers [*British*] (DAS) .... MIPE
Member of the Institution of Production Engineers [*British*] (EY) .... MIProdE
Member of the Institution of Radio Engineers [*British*] (EY) .... MIRE
Member of the Institution of Railway Signal Engineers [*British*] (DBQ) .... MIRSE
Member of the Institution of Structural Engineers (ADA) .... MInstStructE
Member of the Institution of Structural Engineers [*British*] (EY) .... MIStructE
Member of the Institution of Surveyors of India .... MIS(India)
Member of the Institution of Water Engineers [*British*] .... MInstWE
Member of the Institution of Water Engineers [*British*] (EY) .... MIWE
Member of the Institution of Water Engineers and Scientists [*British*] (DI) .... MIWES
Member of the Institution of Water Pollution Control [*British*] (DI) .... MInstWPC
Member of the Institution of Works and Highways Technician Engineers [*British*] (DBQ) .... MIWHTE
Member of the Institution of Works Managers [*British*] .... MIWM
Member of the International Dance Teachers' Association [*British*] (DBQ) .... MIDTA
Member of the International Institute of Social Economics [*British*] (DBQ) .... MIISE
Member of the Iron and Steel Institute [*British*] .... MISI
Member of the Japan Society .... MJS
Member of the Journalists Institute .... MJI
Member of the Junior Institute of Engineers [*British*] .... MJIE
Member of the King's and Queen's College of Physicians [*Ireland*] .... MKQCP
Member of the Legislative Assembly .... MLA
Member of the Legislative Council .... MLC
Member of the Library Association [*British*] (ROG) .... MLA
Member of the Library Association, United Kingdom (ROG) .... MLAUK
Member of the London College of Osteopathic Medicine [*British*] (DBQ) .... MLCOM
Member of the London College of Osteopathy [*British*] (DI) .... MLCO
Member of the London Mathematical Society .... MLMS
Member of the London School Board .... MLSB
Member of the London Society of Compositors .... MLSC
Member of the Medical Faculty .... MMF
Member of the Mining and Metallurgical Society of America .... MM & M Soc of Am
Member of the Mining, Geological, and Metallurgical Institute of India .... MMGI
Member of the National Academy of Sciences .... MNAS
Member of the National Assembly [*British*] .... MNA
Member of the National Assembly [*Quebec*] [*Canada*] (BARN) .... MNA
Member of the National Association of Estate Agents [*British*] (DBQ) .... MNAEA
Member of the National Institute of Accountants [*Australia*] .... MNIA
Member of the National Institute of Hardware [*British*] (DBQ) .... MNIH
Member of the National Institute of Medical Herbalists [*British*] .... MNIMH
Member of the Nautical Institute [*British*] .... MNI
Member of the Non-Destructive Testing Society of Great Britain .... MNDTS
Member of the Numismatical Society [*British*] .... MNS
Member of the Opposite Sex [*Electronic mail language*] .... MOTOS
Member of the Order of Canada .... CM
Member of the Order of Merit [*Canada*] (DD) .... OM
Member of the Order of Military Merit [*Canada*] (DD) .... MMM
Member of the Order of Military Merit .... MMM
Member of the Order of the Niger [*Nigeria*] .... MON
Member of the Organisation and Methods Society [*British*] (DI) .... MOMS
Member of the Pharmaceutical Society [*British*] .... MPS
Member of the Philological Society [*British*] .... MPS

Member of the Phonographic Society [British] (ROG) .... MIPS
Member of the Physical Society [British] .... MPS
Member of the Physiotherapists' Association [British] .... M Phys A
Member of the Plastics and Rubber Institute [British] (DBQ) ...... MPRI
Member of the Police Force (AD) .... mof
Member of the Post Office [British] .... MPO
Member of the Profession of Journalism [British] (DGA) .... MPJ
Member of the Radionic Association [British] .... MRadA
Member of the Rating and Valuation Association [British] (DI) ...... MRVA
Member of the Register of Osteopaths [British] .... MRO
Member of the Royal Academy of Music [British] .... MRAM
Member of the Royal Academy of Science [British] .... MRAS
Member of the Royal Aeronautical Society [British] (ADA) ..... MRAeS
Member of the Royal Agricultural College [British] .... MRAC
Member of the Royal Agricultural Society of England .... MRASE
Member of the Royal Architectural Institute of Canada .... MRAIC
Member of the Royal Asiatic Society [British] .... MRAS
Member of the Royal Asiatic Society of Bengal .... MRASB
Member of the Royal Astronomical Society [British] (DI) .... MRAS
Member of the Royal Australasian College of General Practice
   (BABM) .... MRACGP
Member of the Royal Australasian College of Ophthalmologists [British]
   (BABM) .... MRACO
Member of the Royal Australasian College of Radiologists [British]
   (BABM) .... MRACR
Member of the Royal Australian and New Zealand College of Psychiatrists
   [British] (BABM) .... MRANZCP
Member of the Royal British Nursing Association (ROG) ..... MRBNA
Member of the Royal College of Chemistry [British] .... MRCC
Member of the Royal College of General Practitioners [British] ...... MRCGP
Member of the Royal College of Obstetricians and Gynaecologists
   [British] .... MRCOG
Member of the Royal College of Organists [British] .... MRCO
Member of the Royal College of Pathologists [British] ...... MRC Path
Member of the Royal College of Physicians [British] .... MRCP
Member of the Royal College of Physicians and Surgeons of Glasgow
   (AAMN) .... MRCP (Glasg)
Member of the Royal College of Physicians, Edinburgh ...... MRCPE
Member of the Royal College of Physicians of Edinburgh ... MRCP Edin
Member of the Royal College of Physicians of Edinburgh ...... MRCPEd
Member of the Royal College of Physicians of Glasgow ...... MRCP Glasg
Member of the Royal College of Physicians of Glasgow ...... MRCPGlas
Member of the Royal College of Physicians of Ireland .... MRCP Irel
Member of the Royal College of Physicians of Ireland .... MRCPI
Member of the Royal College of Physicians of the United Kingdom
   [British] (AD) .... MRCPUK
Member of the Royal College of Preceptors [British] .... MRCP
Member of the Royal College of Psychiatrists [British] ..... MRC Psych
Member of the Royal College of Surgeons [British] .... MRCS
Member of the Royal College of Surgeons, Edinburgh .... MRCSE
Member of the Royal College of Surgeons, Ireland (ROG) .... MRCSI
Member of the Royal College of Veterinary Surgeons [British] (EY) ...... MRCVS
Member of the Royal Colleges of Physicians of the United
Kingdom .... MRCP UK
Member of the Royal Drawing Society [British] (ROG) .... MRDS
Member of the Royal Empire Society [British] .... MREmpS
Member of the Royal Entomological Society [British] (ROG) ...... MRES
Member of the Royal Environmental Health Institute of Scotland
   (DBQ) .... MREHIS
Member of the Royal Geographical Society [British] .... MRGS
Member of the Royal Historical Society [British] (ROG) ...... MRHS
Member of the Royal Household [British] (AD) .... MRH
Member of the Royal Institute of British Architects (ROG) ...... MRIBA
Member of the Royal Institute of Chemistry [British] .... MRIC
Member of the Royal Institute of Navigation [British] (DBQ) ...... MRIN
Member of the Royal Institute of Oil Painters [British] .... ROI
Member of the Royal Institute of Painters in Water Colours [British]
   (ROG) .... MRIPWC
Member of the Royal Institute of Painters in Water Colours [British] ...... RI
Member of the Royal Institute of Public Administration (ADA) ...... MRIPA
Member of the Royal Institute of Public Health and Hygiene [British] ..... MRIPHH
Member of the Royal Institute of the Architects of Ireland ...... MRIAI
Member of the Royal Institution [British] .... MRI
Member of the Royal Institution of Chartered Surveyors [British] ...... MRICS
Member of the Royal Institution of Naval Architects [British] ...... MRINA
Member of the Royal Irish Academy (EY) .... MRIA
Member of the Royal Pharmaceutical Society [Canada] (DD) ...... MPPhS
Member of the Royal Pharmaceutical Society [Canada] (DD) ...... MRPhS
Member of the Royal Sanitary Association [British] (AD) ..... MR San Asn
Member of the Royal Sanitary Association of Scotland .... MR San A
Member of the Royal Sanitary Institute [British] (ROG) .... MRSI
Member of the Royal Society of Arts [British] .... MRSA
Member of the Royal Society of Canada .... MRSC
Member of the Royal Society of Chemistry [British] (DBQ) .... MRSC
Member of the Royal Society of Health [British] .... MRSH
Member of the Royal Society of Literature [British] .... MRSL
Member of the Royal Society of Marine Artists [British] (DI) ...... MRSMA
Member of the Royal Society of Medicine [British] (DI) .... MRSM
Member of the Royal Society of Miniature Painters [British] (DI) ...... MRSMP
Member of the Royal Society of Musicians [British] (DI) .... MRSM
Member of the Royal Society of Musicians of Great Britian (AD) ...... MRSMGB
Member of the Royal Society of Painters and Etchers [British] (DI) ...... MRSPE
Member of the Royal Society of Painters in Water Colours [British] ...... MRSPWC
Member of the Royal Society of Scottish Painters and Watercolours
   [British] (DAS) .... MRSW

Member of the Royal Society of Teachers [British] .... MRST
Member of the Royal Town Planning Institute [British] .... MRTPI
Member of the Royal United Service Institution [British] ...... MRUSI
Member of the Royal Veterinary College [British] .... MRVC
Member of the Royal Victorian Order [British] .... MVO
Member of the Same Sex [Electronic mail language] .... MOTSS
Member of the Sanitary Institute [British] (ROG) .... MSI
Member of the School Board [British] (ROG) .... MSB
Member of the School Board, London [Defunct British] (ROG) ...... MSBL
Member of the Society of Apothecaries [British] .... MSA
Member of the Society of Architects [British] (DAS) .... MSA
Member of the Society of Architectural and Allied Technicians [British]
   (DI) .... MSAAT
Member of the Society of Arts [British] .... MSA
Member of the Society of Automobile Engineers [British] ...... MSAutE
Member of the Society of Automotive Engineers .... MSAE
Member of the Society of Cardiological Technicians [British] ...... MSCT
Member of the Society of Certified Professionals [British] (DBQ) ...... MSCP
Member of the Society of Chiropodists .... MChS
Member of the Society of Electronic and Radio Technicians [British]
   (DBQ) .... MSERT
Member of the Society of Engineers [British] .... M Soc E
Member of the Society of Engineers [British] .... MSE
Member of the Society of Floristry [British] (DI) .... MSF
Member of the Society of Health and Beauty Therapists [British]
   (DBQ) .... MSBTh
Member of the Society of Hearing Aid Audiologists [British] (DBQ) ...... MSHAA
Member of the Society of Industrial Artists [British] .... MSIA
Member of the Society of Industrial Artists and Designers [British]
   (DBQ) .... MSIAD
Member of the Society of Instrument Technology [British] ...... MSIT
Member of the Society of Licensed Aircraft Engineers and Technologists
   [British] (DBQ) .... MSLAET
Member of the Society of Osteopaths [British] .... MSO
Member of the Society of Radiographers [British] .... MSR
Member of the Society of Radiographers (Radiography) [British] ...... MSR (R)
Member of the Society of Radiographers (Radiotherapy) [British] ...... MSR (T)
Member of the Society of Remedial Gymnasts [British] ...... MSRG
Member of the Society of Surveying Technicians [British] (DBQ) ...... MSST
Member of the Society of Telegraph Engineers, London [British]
   (ROG) .... MSTEL
Member of the Society of Thoracic and Cardiovascular Surgeons (Great
Britain) .... MSTCS(GB)
Member of the Society of Typographic Designers (DGA) ...... MSTD
Member of the South African Institute of Mining and Metallugy ...... MSAInstMM
Member of the South African Institution of Civil Engineers ...... MSAICE
Member of the Spectacle Makers Co. [British] (ROG) .... MSMC
Member of the Statistical Society [British] (ROG) .... MSS
Member of the Surveyors' Institute of New Zealand .... MSINZ
Member of the Surveyors' Institution [British] (ROG) .... MSI
Member of the Swimming Teachers' Association [British] (DBQ) ...... MSTA
Member of the Technical Staff [A generic term] .... MTS
Member of the Telegraph Engineers [British] (ROG) .... MTE
Member of the Town Planning Institute [British] .... MTPI
Member of the Trust Companies Institute (DD) .... MTCI
Member of the Trust Institute (DD) .... MTI
Member of the Welding Institute [British] (DBQ) .... MWeldI
Member of the Wernerian Society [British] (ROG) .... MWS
Member of the Women's Engineering Society [British] (DBQ) ...... MWES
Member Organisation (ACII) .... MO
Member Pickwick Club [From "The Pickwick Papers" by Charles Dickens] ...... MPC
Member, Royal Nurses Pension Fund [British] (ROG) .... MRNPF
Member, Society of Pension Actuaries [American Society of Pension Actuari
   es] [Designation awarded by] .... MSPA
Member State (DCTA) .... M/S
Member-Get-a-Member [Marketing] (WDMC) .... MGM
Member's Liability [Health insurance] (GHCT) .... ML
Members of an Amalgamated Society [Slang British] (DSUE) ...... MALS
Members of Anything Bill [Clinton] Was Ever Part Of [Pronounced "Mo-ab-
   wee-po"] .... MOABWEPO
Members of Congress for Peace through Law [An association] ...... MCPL
Members of New England Regional Art Museum .... MNERAM
Members of the European Parliament (ECON) .... MEPS
Members Retirement Plan [of the American Medical Association] (DAVI) ...... MRP
Membership .... MBRSHP
Membership in General Dental Surgery, Royal College of Surgeons of
England [British] (DBQ) .... MGDSRCS Eng
Membership Information Processing System [AARP] .... MIPS
Membership Section for Health Care Systems [An association] (EA) ...... HCS
Membership Section for Multihospital Systems [Later, HCS] (EA) ...... MSMS
MemberWorks, Inc. [NASDAQ symbol] (SAG) .... MBRS
MemberWorks, Inc. [Associated Press] (SAG) .... MemWks
Membrana [Membrane] [Anatomy] .... M
Membrana Flaccida [Flaccid Membrane] [Latin Medicine] (MAE) ...... m flac
Membrana Tympani [Anatomy] .... MT
Membranaceous Vellum [Manuscripts] (ROG) .... MEMB
Membrane .... MBRM
Membrane (MSA) .... MEMB
Membrane [Medicine] .... MMB
Membrane Affinity Chromatography .... MAC
Membrane Affinity Separation System .... MASS
Membrane Antigen [Immunology] .... MA
Membrane Applications Centre [University of Bath] [British] (CB) ...... MAC
Membrane Attack Complex [Biochemistry] .... MAC
Membrane Bioreactor [Chemical engineering] .... MBR

Membrane Cofactor Protein [*Biochemistry*] ... MCP
Membrane Component of Diffusion [*Cytology*] (MAE) ... Dm
Membrane Fecal Coliform (PDAA) ... MFC
Membrane Filter ... MF
Membrane Form of Variant Surface Glycoprotein [*Biochemistry*] ... mfVSG
Membrane Immunofluorescence [*Analytical biochemistry*] ... MIF
Membrane Immunoglobulin [*Immunology*] ... M-Ig
Membrane Isolation Process [*Food technology*] ... MIP
Membrane Light Modulator (PDAA) ... MLM
Membrane Light Valve [*Optics*] ... MLV
Membrane Polarographic Detector [*Instrumentation*] ... MPD
Membrane Potential Difference [*Medicine*] (DMAA) ... MPD
Membrane Production (SSD) ... MP
Membrane Protein Complex [*Cytology*] ... MPC
Membrane Structures Association of Australasia ... MSAA
Membrane Surface Area [*Cytology*] ... MSA
Membrane Waterproofing ... MWP
Membrane-Bound Ribosomes [*Cytology*] ... MBR
Membrane-Covered Mercury Film Electrode [*Electrochemistry*] ... MCMFE
Membrane-Derived Oligosaccharide [*Biochemistry*] ... MDO
Membrane-Enveloped Soil Layer ... MESL
Membrane-Filtered Sea Water ... MFSW
Membrane-Free Hemolystate [*Hematology*] (DAVI) ... MFH
Membrane-Intercalated Particles [*Cytology*] ... MIP
Membranes [*Leaves of parchment*] (ROG) ... MM
Membrane-Spanning Region [*Cytology*] ... MSR
Membrane-Stabilizing Activity [*Cardiology*] ... MSA
Membrano Proliferative Glomerulonephritis [*Medicine*] (AD) ... mpgn
Membranoproliferative Glomerulonephritis [*Nephrology*] ... MPGN
Membranous Cytoplasmic Body ... MCB
Membranous Glomerulonephritis [*Nephrology*] ... MGN
Membranous Glomerulopathy [*Nephrology*] ... MG
Membre de l'Ordre des Chimistes du Quebec [*Canada*] (DD) ... OCQ
MEMC Electronic Materials [*NYSE symbol*] (TTSB) ... WFR
MEMC Electronic Materials, Inc. [*Associated Press*] (SAG) ... MEMC
MEMC Electronic Materials, Inc. [*NYSE symbol*] (SAG) ... WFR
Memco Software Ltd. [*NASDAQ symbol*] (SAG) ... MEMC
Memco Software Ltd. [*Associated Press*] (SAG) ... MemcoSf
Memento ... MEM
Memmingen [*Germany ICAO location identifier*] (ICLI) ... EDSM
Memo Routing Slip ... MRS
Memo to Management [*Australian Institute of Management, Queensland Division*] [*A publication*] ... Memo Mgmt
Memoir ... MEM
Memoir (WDMC) ... mem
Memoires. Delegation Archeologique Francaise [*A publication*] (BJA) ... MDAF
Memoirs. American Academy at Rome [*A publication*] (OCD) ... Amer Acad Rome
Memoirs. American Folklore Society [*A publication*] ... MAFS
Memoirs. Commonwealth Solar Observatory. Australia [*A publication*] ... Mem Comm Solar Observ Aust
Memoirs. Geological Survey of Victoria [*Australia A publication*] ... Mem Geol Survey Vic
Memorabilia [*of Xenophon*] [*Classical studies*] (OCD) ... Mem
Memorable (ROG) ... MEMBLE
Memoranda (ROG) ... MEMDA
Memorandum ... M
Memorandum ... MEM
Memorandum (WDMC) ... mem
Memorandum (ROG) ... MEMDUM
Memorandum (AFM) ... MEMO
Memorandum (WDMC) ... memo
Memorandum ... MEMO
Memorandum Accounts Statement System (DCTA) ... MASS
Memorandum Book (ROG) ... MB
Memorandum by the Director, Joint Staff for the Joint Chiefs of Staff (MCD) ... MDJCS
Memorandum Club [*Defunct*] (EA) ... MC
Memorandum for Record [*Military*] ... MFR
Memorandum for Record [*Military*] (AFM) ... MR
Memorandum for Regional Directors (AAGC) ... MRD
Memorandum for the Joint Chiefs of Staff (MCD) ... MJCS
Memorandum of Agreement (AD) ... M o A
Memorandum of Agreement ... MOA
Memorandum of Assistance ... MOA
Memorandum of Conditions ... MC
Memorandum of Conditions ... MOC
Memorandum of Conversation ... MEMCON
Memorandum of Deposit [*Business term*] ... MD
Memorandum of Instruction (INF) ... MOI
Memorandum of Interest (MCD) ... MOI
Memorandum of Negotiation (MCD) ... MON
Memorandum of Partnership [*Business term*] ... M/P
Memorandum of Policy ... MOP
Memorandum of Understanding ... MOU
Memorandum of Understanding (AD) ... mou
Memorandum of Understanding (AD) ... MoU
Memorandum of Understanding and Agreement ... MUA
Memorandum Opinion and Order (NTCM) ... MO & O
Memorandum Opinion of the United States Tax Court (AAGC) ... TC Memo
Memorandum Program Change Request [*Military*] (CAAL) ... MPCR
Memorandum Purchase Order (AD) ... MPO
Memorandum Receipt [*Military*] (MUGU) ... MR
Memorandum Report ... MR
Memorandum Slip [*for informal interoffice communications*] ... M/S
Memore [*Bolivia*] [*ICAO location identifier*] (ICLI) ... SLMR
Memorex (NITA) ... MRX
Memorex Corp. (IAA) ... MRX
Memorex Corp., Memorex Technical Information Library, Santa Clara, CA [*OCLC symbol*] (OCLC) ... MEX
Memorex Corp., Santa Clara, CA [*Library symbol Library of Congress*] (LCLS) ... CStclM
Memorex Tape Management System [*Computer science*] (IAA) ... MTMS
Memorex Telex ADS [*NASDAQ symbol*] (TTSB) ... MEMXY
Memorex Telex NV [*Associated Press*] (SAG) ... Memorex
Memorex Telex NV [*NASDAQ symbol*] (SAG) ... MEMX
Memoria [*Memory*] [*Latin*] ... M
Memoriae Sacrum [*Sacred to the Memory Of*] [*Latin*] ... MS
Memorial ... MEM
Memorial (WDMC) ... mem
Memorial ... MEML
Memorial (FAAC) ... MEML
Memorial (VRA) ... memrl
Memorial Activities [*Military*] (AABC) ... MEMLACTV
Memorial Advisory Bureau [*British*] (CB) ... MAB
Memorial Baptist Hospital, Lillie Jolly School of Nursing, Houston, TX [*Library symbol Library of Congress*] (LCLS) ... TxHLJ
Memorial Commission [*Federal body*] ... MC
Memorial Dose Distribution Computation Service [*Memorial Sloan-Kettering Cancer Center*] [*Information service or system*] (IID) ... MDDCS
Memorial Foundation for Jewish Culture (EA) ... MFJC
Memorial High School, Sidney Mines, NS, Canada [*Library symbol Library of Congress*] (LCLS) ... CaNSSmM
Memorial High School Sidney Mines, NS, Canada [*Library symbol*] [*Library of Congress*] (LCLS) ... CaNSSmMM
Memorial High School, Sydney Mines, Nova Scotia [*Library symbol National Library of Canada*] (NLC) ... NSSMM
Memorial Hospital and Nursing Home, Menomonie, WI [*Library symbol Library of Congress*] (LCLS) ... WMenM
Memorial Hospital Association, Modesto, CA [*Library symbol Library of Congress*] (LCLS) ... CMMH
Memorial Hospital at Oconomowoc, Oconomowoc, WI [*Library symbol Library of Congress*] (LCLS) ... WOccM
Memorial Hospital, Chattanooga, TN [*Library symbol Library of Congress*] (LCLS) ... TCMH
Memorial Hospital District Library, Mattoon, IL [*Library symbol Library of Congress*] (LCLS) ... IMatH
Memorial Hospital, Medical Library, Albany, NY [*Library symbol Library of Congress*] (LCLS) ... NAlMem
Memorial Inscription ... MI
Memorial; Journal Officiel du Grand Duche de Luxembourg [*A publication*] (ILCA) ... M
Memorial Junior High School, Huntington Station, NY [*Library symbol*] [*Library of Congress*] (LCLS) ... NHsMJ
Memorial Junior High School, Huntington Station, NY [*Library symbol Library of Congress*] (LCLS) ... NHusMJ
Memorial Junior High School, Valley Stream, NY [*Library symbol Library of Congress*] (LCLS) ... NVsMJH
Memorial Junior/Senior High School, Ely, MN [*Library symbol*] [*Library of Congress*] (LCLS) ... MnElyJS
Memorial Medical Center, Health Sciences Library, Ashland, WI [*Library symbol Library of Congress*] (LCLS) ... WAsM
[*The*] **Memorial of Moses on Mount Nebo** [*A publication*] (BJA) ... MMMN
Memorial Research Center [*University of Tennessee*] [*Research center*] (RCD) ... MRC
Memorial Sloan-Kettering Cancer Center [*Research center*] (RCD) ... MSKC
Memorial Sloan-Kettering Cancer Center [*New York*] ... MSKCC
Memorial Sloan-Kettering Cancer Center, New York, NY [*Library symbol Library of Congress*] (LCLS) ... NNMSK
Memorial Sloan-Kettering Cancer Center, New York, NY [*OCLC symbol*] (OCLC) ... VVM
Memorial University, Education Library, Curriculum Materials Centre, St. John's,NF, Canada [*Library symbol Library of Congress*] (LCLS) ... CaNfSMEC
Memorial University, Education Library, St. John's, NF, Canada [*Library symbol Library of Congress*] (LCLS) ... CaNfSMEd
Memorial University, Ocean Engineering Centre, St. John's, NF, Canada [*Library symbol Library of Congress*] (LCLS) ... CaNfSMO
Memorial University of Newfoundland [*Marine science*] (MSC) ... MUN
Memorial University of Newfoundland, Department of Geography, St. John's, NF, Canada [*Library symbol Library of Congress*] (LCLS) ... CaNfMG
Memorial University of Newfoundland, Faculty of Medicine Library, St. John's, NF, Canada [*Library symbol Library of Congress*] (LCLS) ... CaNfSMM
Memorial University of Newfoundland Folklore and Language Archive [*Research center Canada*] (RCD) ... MUNFLA
Memorial University of Newfoundland, Health Sciences Library [*UTLAS symbol*] ... MUH
Memorial University of Newfoundland Library [*UTLAS symbol*] ... MUN
Memorial University of Newfoundland, St. John's, NF, Canada [*Library symbol Library of Congress*] (LCLS) ... CaNfSM
Memorial University Regional College at Corner Brook, Corner Brook, NF, Canada [*Library symbol Library of Congress*] (LCLS) ... CaNfCBM
Memorial University, St. John's, Newfoundland [*Library symbol National Library of Canada*] (NLC) ... NFSM
Memorialization (ABBR) ... MEMLZN
Memorialize (ABBR) ... MEMLZ
Memorialized (ABBR) ... MEMLZD
Memorializer (ABBR) ... MEMLZR
Memorializing (ABBR) ... MEMLZG
Memory ... M
Memory (MSA) ... MEM
Memory ... MEM

Memory (ROG) ... MEMY
Memory Access Command [*Computer science*] (IAA) ... MAC
Memory Access Controller ... MAC
Memory Access Director [*Computer science*] (IAA) ... MAD
Memory Access Logic ... MAL
Memory Access Multiplexer (NITA) ... MAM
Memory Access Table [*Computer science*] ... MAT
Memory Access Unit ... MAU
Memory Address [*Computer science*] ... MA
Memory Address Register (NITA) ... MAE
Memory Address Translator (NITA) ... MAT
Memory Allocation and Protection ... MAP
Memory Allocation and Protection Unit (MSA) ... MAPU
Memory Allocation Manager ... MAM
Memory Allocation Processor (NITA) ... MAP
Memory Analysis, Response Generation, and Interference in English ... MARGIE
Memory and Auxiliary Storage Subsystem [*Space Flight Operations Facility, NASA*] ... MAS
Memory and Electronic Components [*Commercial firm British*] ... MEMEC
Memory Available [*Computer science*] (IAA) ... MA
Memory Bank ... MB
Memory Bank Interface ... MBI
Memory Base Register ... MBR
Memory Block Table [*Computer science*] (HGAA) ... MBT
Memory Buffer [*Computer science*] ... MB
Memory Buffer Register [*Computer science*] ... MBR
Memory Buffer Register, Even [*Computer science*] ... MBRE
Memory Buffer Register, Odd [*Computer science*] ... MBRO
Memory Buffer Unit [*Computer science*] ... MBU
Memory Bus [*Digital Equipment Corp.*] ... MASSBUS
Memory Bus ... MB
Memory Bus Controller ... MBC
Memory Call Queue [*Computer science*] (IAA) ... MCQ
Memory Card Writer [*Telecommunications*] (TEL) ... MCW
Memory Channel ... M-Ch
Memory Character Generator ... MCG
Memory Character Vector Generator ... MCVG
Memory Charts ... MC
Memory Clear [*Computer science*] (PCM) ... MC
Memory Clock Pulse Amplifier ... MCPA
Memory Configuration [*Computer science*] (MCD) ... MC
Memory Control [*Unit*] [*Computer science*] ... MC
Memory Control and Logging [*Hewlett-Packard Co.*] ... MCL
Memory Control Circuit [*Computer science*] (IAA) ... MCC
Memory Control Data ... MCD
Memory Control J Bus ... MCJ
Memory Control Module ... MCM
Memory Control Register ... MCR
Memory Control Unit ... MCU
Memory Control Unit Special Register [*Computer science*] (MHDB) ... MCUSR
Memory Controller Gate Array [*Computer science*] ... MCGA
Memory Controller Group (DWSG) ... MCG
Memory Cycle Time [*Computer science*] (MCD) ... MCT
Memory Data Capture Cash and Credit Register [*Datacap Systems, Inc.*] ... MCCR
Memory Data Register (DNAB) ... MD
Memory Decrement (MHDB) ... MD
Memory Disk Controller ... MDC
Memory Disk System [*Computer science*] (IEEE) ... MDS
Memory Element [*Computer science*] ... ME
Memory Error (WDAA) ... ME
Memory Error [*Information retrieval*] ... MEM ERR
Memory Excellence [*Brand name*] ... MEMOREX
Memory Expansion Unit ... MEU
Memory for Sequence Subtest of the Goldman-Fristoe-Woodcock Auditory Skills TestBattery (EDAC) ... MS-GFW
Memory Gate Generator [*Computer science*] ... MGG
Memory Implemented Data Acquisition Systems ... MIDAS
Memory Input Register [*Computer science*] ... MIR
Memory Inspection Ending Address (MHDB) ... MEA
Memory Interface ... MI
Memory Interface Connection [*Computer science*] ... MIC
Memory Loader Verifier (DWSG) ... MLV
Memory Loading Unit [*of FADAC*] [*Military*] ... MLU
Memory Location [*Computer science*] ... ML
Memory Lockout Register [*Computer science*] ... MLR
Memory Logic Unit [*Computer science*] ... MLU
Memory Management Controller (IEEE) ... MMC
Memory Management System ... MMS
Memory Management Unit [*Computer chip*] ... MMU
Memory Manager and Protect Unit (IEEE) ... MMPU
Memory Mapping Unit (NITA) ... MMU
Memory Module (IAA) ... MEMMDLE
Memory Module (MCD) ... MM
Memory Multiplexer [*Computer science*] (MDG) ... MM
Memory Multiplexer [*Computer science*] ... MMX
Memory Operating Characteristic [*Computer science*] (IEEE) ... MOC
Memory Operating Software [*Computer science*] ... MOS
Memory Operation ... MO
Memory Organization Packet [*Artificial intelligence*] ... MOP
Memory Output [*Computer science*] ... MO
Memory Output Register [*Computer science*] ... MOR
Memory Parity and Protect (NITA) ... MPP
Memory Parity Error ... MPE
Memory Point ... MEMPT
Memory Printout [*Computer science*] ... MPO
Memory Printout (AD) ... mpo
Memory Processing Time ... MPT
Memory Processor Switch ... MPS
Memory Protect Override ... MPO
Memory Protection Check (MCD) ... MPC
Memory Protection Unit ... MPU
Memory Quotient (AD) ... mq
Memory Quotient ... MQ
Memory Raster Colour Display (PDAA) ... MRCD
Memory Raster Display [*Computer science*] ... MRD
Memory Read [*Computer science*] (MHDI) ... MEMR
Memory Read [*Computer science*] ... MR
Memory Read [*Computer science*] (MHDI) ... MRD
Memory Recall [*Computer science*] (PCM) ... MR
Memory Reclaimer ... MR
Memory Reference Instruction ... MRI
Memory Register [*Computer science*] ... MR
Memory Register Exponent [*Computer science*] (MHDI) ... MRE
Memory Request Controller ... MRC
Memory Resistor (DEN) ... MEMISTOR
Memory Select [*Computer science*] (MHDI) ... MEMSEL
Memory Select Register (NITA) ... MSR
Memory Service Unit [*Computer science*] ... MSU
Memory Storage Buffer [*Computer science*] (CAAL) ... MSB
Memory Storage Control [*Computer science*] ... MSC
Memory Storage Module ... MSM
Memory Store [*Computer science*] (PCM) ... MS
Memory System ... MS
Memory System Security [*Computer science*] (ECII) ... MSS
Memory Test Computer [*SAGE*] ... MTC
Memory Test System ... MTS
Memory Transfer Unit (NITA) ... MTU
Memory Unit [*Computer science*] (MCD) ... MU
Memory Unit Drum [*Computer science*] ... MUD
Memory Write [*Computer science*] (MHDB) ... MEMW
Memory Write [*Computer science*] (MHDI) ... MRMW
Memory Write [*Computer science*] ... MW
Memory-Address Counter [*Computer science*] (IAA) ... MAC
Memory-Address Register [*Computer science*] ... MAR
Memory-Address Register Storage [*Computer science*] ... MARS
Memory-Address Select Register [*Computer science*] (IAA) ... MASR
Memory-Address Test ... MAT
Memory-Aided Antiradiation Missile (MCD) ... MAARM
Memory-Assisted Terminal Equipment (PDAA) ... MATE
Memory-Centered Processing [*or Processor*] [*System*] [*Computer science*] ... MCP
Memory-Constrained [*Computer science*] ... MC
Memory-Data Bank ... MDB
Memory-Data Register ... MDR
Memory-for-Designs [*Test*] [*Psychology*] ... MFD
Memory-for-Designs Test [*Psychology*] ... MFDT
Memory-Information Register [*Computer science*] ... MIR
Memory-Oriented System ... MOS
Memory-Segment [*Computer science*] ... MSEG
Memory-to-Memory Adapter [*Computer science*] ... MMA
Memotec Data, Inc. [*Toronto Stock Exchange symbol*] ... MDI
Memotron Storage Tube ... MST
Memphis [*Tennessee*] [*ICAO location identifier*] (ICLI) ... KZME
Memphis [*Tennessee*] [*Airport symbol*] (OAG) ... MEM
Memphis [*Tennessee*] [*Seismograph station code, US Geological Survey*] (SEIS) ... MET
Memphis Academy of Arts, Memphis, TN [*Library symbol Library of Congress*] (LCLS) ... TMA
Memphis and Shelby County Bar Association, Memphis, TN [*Library symbol Library of Congress*] (LCLS) ... TMSB
Memphis and Shelby County Health Department, Memphis, TN [*Library symbol Library of Congress*] (LCLS) ... TMSCH
Memphis and Shelby County Public Library and Information Center, Memphis, TN [*OCLC symbol*] (OCLC) ... TMN
Memphis and Shelby County Safety Council, Memphis, TN [*Library symbol Library of Congress*] (LCLS) ... TMSCS
Memphis Army Depot (AABC) ... MEAD
Memphis City Schools Professional Library, Memphis, TN [*Library symbol Library of Congress*] (LCLS) ... TMCS
Memphis Cotton Exchange (EA) ... MCE
Memphis Eye and Ear Hospital, Memphis, TN [*Library symbol Library of Congress*] (LCLS) ... TMMEE
Memphis Group [*In name of singing group "Booker T and the MG's"*] ... MG's
Memphis Housing Authority, Memphis, TN [*Library symbol Library of Congress*] (LCLS) ... TMHA
Memphis/International [*Tennessee*] [*ICAO location identifier*] (ICLI) ... KMEM
Memphis Law Journal [*Tennessee*] [*A publication*] (DLA) ... Mem LJ
Memphis Law Journal [*Tennessee*] [*A publication*] (DLA) ... Memp LJ
Memphis Law Journal [*Tennessee*] [*A publication*] (DLA) ... Memphis LJ
Memphis Law Journal [*A publication*] (DLA) ... MLJ
Memphis Library Council [*Library network*] ... MLC
Memphis Light, Gas, and Water Division Library, Memphis, TN [*Library symbol Library of Congress*] (LCLS) ... TMLG
Memphis, MO [*FM radio station call letters*] ... KMEM
Memphis Planning Commission, Memphis, TN [*Library symbol Library of Congress*] (LCLS) ... TMPC
Memphis Power Boat Club [*Tennessee*] (AD) ... MPBC
Memphis Public Library (AD) ... MPL
Memphis Service Center [*IRS*] ... MSC
Memphis State University (GAGS) ... Memphis St U

Memphis State University [*Tennessee*] .... MSU
Memphis State University, Bureau of Business Research Library, Memphis, TN [*Library symbol Library of Congress*] (LCLS) .... TMM-B
Memphis State University, Engineering Library, Memphis, TN [*Library symbol Library of Congress*] (LCLS) .... TMM-E
Memphis State University. Law Review [*A publication*] (DLA) .... Mem St UL Rev
Memphis State University, Memphis, TN [*OCLC symbol*] (OCLC) .... TMA
Memphis State University, Memphis, TN [*Library symbol Library of Congress*] (LCLS) .... TMM
Memphis State University, School of Law, Memphis, TN [*Library symbol Library of Congress*] (LCLS) .... TMM-L
Memphis State University, Speech and Hearing Center, Memphis, TN [*Library symbol Library of Congress*] (LCLS) .... TMM-SH
Memphis Theological Seminary of the Cumberland Presbyterian Church, Memphis, TN [*Library symbol Library of Congress*] (LCLS) .... TMTS
Memphis, TN [*Location identifier FAA*] (FAAL) .... JIM
Memphis, TN [*FM radio station call letters*] .... KJMS
Memphis, TN [*AM radio station call letters*] .... KWAM
Memphis, TN [*Location identifier FAA*] (FAAL) .... NQA
Memphis, TN [*Location identifier FAA*] (FAAL) .... OHN
Memphis, TN [*Location identifier FAA*] (FAAL) .... OOI
Memphis, TN [*Location identifier FAA*] (FAAL) .... SDU
Memphis, TN [*Location identifier FAA*] (FAAL) .... SPQ
Memphis, TN [*Location identifier FAA*] (FAAL) .... TSE
Memphis, TN [*AM radio station call letters*] .... WBBP
Memphis, TN [*AM radio station call letters*] .... WDIA
Memphis, TN [*FM radio station call letters*] .... WEGR
Memphis, TN [*FM radio station call letters*] .... WEVL
Memphis, TN [*Television station call letters*] .... WFBI
Memphis, TN [*FM radio station call letters*] .... WGKX
Memphis, TN [*AM radio station call letters*] .... WHBQ
Memphis, TN [*Television station call letters*] .... WHBQ-TV
Memphis, TN [*FM radio station call letters*] .... WHRK
Memphis, TN [*AM radio station call letters*] .... WJCE
Memphis, TN [*FM radio station call letters*] .... WKNO
Memphis, TN [*Television station call letters*] .... WKNO-TV
Memphis, TN [*Television station call letters*] .... WLMT
Memphis, TN [*AM radio station call letters*] .... WLOK
Memphis, TN [*AM radio station call letters*] .... WMC
Memphis, TN [*FM radio station call letters*] .... WMC-FM
Memphis, TN [*Television station call letters*] .... WMC-TV
Memphis, TN [*Television station call letters*] .... WPTY
Memphis, TN [*FM radio station call letters*] .... WQOX
Memphis, TN [*AM radio station call letters*] .... WREC
Memphis, TN [*Television station call letters*] .... WREG
Memphis, TN [*FM radio station call letters*] .... WRVR
Memphis, TN [*AM radio station call letters*] (RBYB) .... WSFZ-AM
Memphis, TN [*FM radio station call letters*] .... WUMR
Memphis, TN [*AM radio station call letters*] .... WXSS
Memphis, TN [*FM radio station call letters*] .... WYPL
Memphis, TN [*Location identifier FAA*] (FAAL) .... ZME
Memphis, TX [*AM radio station call letters*] .... KLSR
Memphis, TX [*FM radio station call letters*] .... KLSR-FM
Memphis Union Station Co. [*AAR code*] .... MUSC
Memphis University School, Hyde Library, Memphis, TN [*OCLC symbol*] (OCLC) .... TEM
Memphis-Shelby County Public Library and Information Center, Memphis, TN [*Library symbol Library of Congress*] (LCLS) .... TM
Memrykord Ltd. [*British ICAO designator*] (FAAC) .... JPN
Memtec Ltd. [*Associated Press*] (SAG) .... Memtec
Memtec Ltd. [*NASDAQ symbol*] (SAG) .... MMTC
Memtec Ltd ADS [*NASDAQ symbol*] (TTSB) .... MMTCY
Men after Christ Band [*R & B recording group*] .... MAC
Men Against Sexual Assault [*Australia*] .... MASA
Men Against the Maxi-Midi Atrocity [*Klosters, Switzerland, group opposing below-the-knee fashions introduced in 1970*] .... MAMMA
Men for Missions International (EA) .... MFMI
Men in Black [*UFO mythology*] .... MIB
Men of the Sacred Hearts (EA) .... MSH
Men of the Stones (EA) .... MS
Men of the Trees [*Australia An association*] .... MOT
Men Organized to X-press Indignant Exasperation [*Seattle group opposing below-the-knee fashions introduced in 1970*] .... MOXIE
Men Our Masters/Women Our Wonders [*Antifeminist group*] (EA) .... MOM/WOW
Men to End Spouse Abuse (EA) .... MESA
Men Who Have Sex with Men [*Australia An association*] .... MSM
Men Who Have Sex With Men [*AIDS transmission group*] .... MSWM
Mena [*Indonesia*] [*ICAO location identifier*] (ICLI) .... WRKJ
Mena, AR [*AM radio station call letters*] .... KENA
Mena, AR [*FM radio station call letters*] .... KENA-FM
Mena, AR [*FM radio station call letters*] (RBYB) .... KTTG
Mena, AR [*Location identifier FAA*] (FAAL) .... MEZ
Menadiol Sodium Diphosphate [*Vitamin K_4*] (DAVI) .... K_4
Menadione [*Vitamin K_3*] (DAVI) .... K_3
Menado [*Indonesia*] [*Airport symbol*] (OAG) .... MDC
Menado Sector [*Indonesia*] [*ICAO location identifier*] (ICLI) .... WAMZ
Menaechmi [*of Plautus*] [*Classical studies*] (OCD) .... Men
Menagha High School, Menagha, MN [*Library symbol*] [*Library of Congress*] (LCLS) .... MnMenH
Menahga Elementary School, Menagha, MN [*Library symbol*] [*Library of Congress*] (LCLS) .... MnMenE
Menahot (BJA) .... Men
Menaka [*Mali*] [*ICAO location identifier*] (ICLI) .... GAMK
Menan Buttes [*Idaho*] [*Seismograph station code, US Geological Survey Closed*] (SEIS) .... MBI
Menander [*Fourth century BC*] [*Classical studies*] (OCD) .... Men
Menandri Reliquiae [*A publication*] (OCD) .... Men Rel
Menaquinone [*Vitamin K*] [*Also, MQ*] [*Biochemistry*] .... MK
Menaquinone [*Vitamin K*] [*Also, MK*] [*Biochemistry*] .... MQ
Mence's Law of Libel [*1824*] [*A publication*] (DLA) .... Mence Lib
Mencken Society (EA) .... MS
Mend Our Tongues Society (EA) .... MOTS
Mende [*MARC language code Library of Congress*] (LCCP) .... men
Mende/Brenoux [*France ICAO location identifier*] (ICLI) .... LFNB
Mended Hearts (EA) .... MH
Mendelevium [*Preferred form, but also see Mv*] [*Chemical element*] .... Md
Mendelevium [*Symbol is Md*] [*Chemical element*] .... Mv
Mendelian Inheritance in Man [*Genetics*] .... MIM
Mendelism .... MEND
Mendelsohn Rosentzveig Schacter, Montreal, PQ, Canada [*Library symbol*] [*Library of Congress*] (LCLS) .... CaQMMRS
Mendelsohn Rosentzveig Shacter, Montreal, Quebec [*Library symbol National Library of Canada*] (BIB) .... QMMRS
Mendenhall, AK [*Location identifier FAA*] (FAAL) .... MND
Mendes (AD) .... Ms
Mendham Public Library, Mendham, NJ [*Library symbol Library of Congress*] (LCLS) .... NjMen
Mendham Township Library, Brookside, NJ [*Library symbol Library of Congress*] (LCLS) .... NjBro
Mendi [*Ethiopia*] [*ICAO location identifier*] (ICLI) .... HAMN
Mendi [*Papua New Guinea*] [*Airport symbol*] (OAG) .... MDU
Mendial Geniculate Nucleus (PDAA) .... MGN
Mendig [*Germany ICAO location identifier*] (ICLI) .... EDPN
Mendocino, CA [*FM radio station call letters*] (RBYB) .... KAKX
Mendocino, CA [*FM radio station call letters*] .... KMFB
Mendocino, CA [*AM radio station call letters*] .... KPMO
Mendocino County Historical Society, Held-Poage Memorial Home and Research Library, Ukiah, CA [*Library symbol*] [*Library of Congress*] (LCLS) .... CUkHi
Mendon Township Library, Mendon, MI [*Library symbol Library of Congress*] (LCLS) .... MiMen
Mendota High School, Mendota, IL [*Library symbol Library of Congress*] (LCLS) .... IMenHS
Mendota, IL [*AM radio station call letters*] .... WGLC
Mendota, IL [*FM radio station call letters*] .... WGLC-FM
Mendota Mental Health Institute, Madison, WI [*Library symbol Library of Congress*] (LCLS) .... WMaMS
Mendoza [*Argentina*] [*Airport symbol*] (OAG) .... MDZ
Mendoza [*Argentina*] [*Seismograph station code, US Geological Survey*] (SEIS) .... MDZ
Mendoza [*Argentina*] [*Seismograph station code, US Geological Survey Closed*] (SEIS) .... MEN
Mendoza [*Argentina ICAO location identifier*] (ICLI) .... SAMF
Mendoza [*Argentina ICAO location identifier*] (ICLI) .... SAMV
Mendoza Aeroparque [*Argentina ICAO location identifier*] (ICLI) .... SAMQ
Mendoza/El Plumerillo [*Argentina ICAO location identifier*] (ICLI) .... SAME
Menevensis [*Signature of the Bishops of St. David's*] [*British*] (ROG) .... MENEV
Menexemus [*of Plato*] [*Classical studies*] (OCD) .... Menex
Mengen [*Germany ICAO location identifier*] (ICLI) .... EDTM
Mengen [*Turkey*] [*Seismograph station code, US Geological Survey*] (SEIS) .... MGN
Mengenverbrauchsguttern [*Mass Consumption Goods*] [*German*] .... MVG
Menggala/Astrakestra [*Indonesia*] [*ICAO location identifier*] (ICLI) .... WIAG
Meniere's Disease [*Medicine*] (DMAA) .... MD
Meniere's Network [*An association*] (EA) .... MN
Menika Mining Ltd. [*Vancouver Stock Exchange symbol*] .... MML
Meningitis [*Medicine*] (MAE) .... mgtis
Meningopneumonitis [*Medicine*] .... MN
Menken's Civil Procedure Reports [*30 New York*] [*A publication*] (DLA) .... Menken
Menkijarvi [*Finland ICAO location identifier*] (ICLI) .... EFME
Menley & James, Inc. [*NASDAQ symbol*] (SPSG) .... MENJ
Menley & James, Inc. [*Associated Press*] (SAG) .... MenleyJ
Menlo Park [*California*] [*Seismograph station code, US Geological Survey*] (SEIS) .... MOB
Menlo Park Applications Development [*IBM Corp.*] .... MPAD
Menlo Park Public Library, Menlo Park, CA [*Library symbol Library of Congress*] (LCLS) .... CMen
Menlo School and College, Menlo Park, CA [*Library symbol Library of Congress*] (LCLS) .... CMenC
Menningar- og Fraedslusamband Althydu [*Workers' Educational Association*] [*Iceland*] (EY) .... MFA
Menninger [*Karl Augustus*] [*American psychiatrist*] (DAVI) .... Menn
Menninger Clinic Library, Topeka, KS [*Library symbol Library of Congress*] (LCLS) .... KTM
Menno Public School Library, Menno, SD [*Library symbol Library of Congress*] (LCLS) .... SdMeS
Menno Simons Community School, Cleardale, Alberta [*Library symbol National Library of Canada*] (BIB) .... ACLMS
Mennonite (ABBR) .... MEN
Mennonite .... MENIT
Mennonite (ABBR) .... MENNON
Mennonite Biblical Seminary, Elkhart, IN [*Library symbol Library of Congress*] (LCLS) .... InElkB
Mennonite Biblical Seminary Library, Elkhart, IN [*OCLC symbol*] (OCLC) .... IME
Mennonite Board of Education (EA) .... MBE
Mennonite Brethren Bible College, Winnipeg, Manitoba [*Library symbol National Library of Canada*] (NLC) .... MWMBC
Mennonite Brethren Biblical Seminary, Fresno, CA [*Library symbol Library of Congress*] (LCLS) .... CFMen
Mennonite Brethren College, Winnipeg, MB, Canada [*Library symbol Library of Congress*] (LCLS) .... CaMWMBC

Mennonite Central Committee (EA) .... MCC
Mennonite Central Committee Overseas Peace Office (EA) .... MCCOPO
Mennonite Disaster Service (EA) .... MDS
Mennonite Economic Development Associates (EA) .... MEDA
Mennonite Health Association (EA) .... MHA
Mennonite Heritage Centre, Winnipeg, Manitoba [*Library symbol National Library of Canada*] (NLC) .... MWMHC
Mennonite Historical Library, Goshen College, Goshen, IN [*OCLC symbol*] (OCLC) .... IMH
Mennonite Historical Library, Goshen College, Goshen, IN [*Library symbol Library of Congress*] (LCLS) .... InGoM
Mennonite Historical Society, Newton, KS [*Library symbol Library of Congress*] (LCLS) .... KNM
Mennonite Hospital Association, Medical-Nursing Library, Bloomington, IL [*Library symbol Library of Congress*] (LCLS) .... IBloMH
Mennonite Hospital, Health Sciences Library, Bloomington, IL [*OCLC symbol*] (OCLC) .... JAT
Mennonite Publishing House, Scottsdale, PA [*Library symbol Library of Congress*] (LCLS) .... PSdM
Mennonite Urban Professional [*Lifestyle classification*] .... Muppie
Mennonite Village Museum, Steinbach, Manitoba [*Library symbol National Library of Canada*] (NLC) .... MSTM
Mennonite Village Museum, Steinbach, MB, Canada [*Library symbol Library of Congress*] (LCLS) .... CaMSteM
Mennonite Voluntary Service .... MVS
Meno [*Slower*] [*Music*] .... MEN
Menology .... MEN
Menominee [*Michigan*] [*Airport symbol*] (OAG) .... MNM
Menominee County Library, Stephenson, MI [*Library symbol Library of Congress*] (LCLS) .... MiStep
Menominee, MI [*AM radio station call letters*] .... WAGN
Menominee, MI [*FM radio station call letters*] .... WHYB
Menomonee Falls, WI [*FM radio station call letters*] .... WFMR
Menomonie, WI [*FM radio station call letters*] .... WHWC
Menomonie, WI [*Television station call letters*] .... WHWC-TV
Menomonie, WI [*AM radio station call letters*] .... WMEQ
Menomonie, WI [*FM radio station call letters*] .... WMEQ-FM
Menomonie, WI [*FM radio station call letters*] .... WVSS
Menongue [*Angola*] [*ICAO location identifier*] (ICLI) .... FNME
Menongue [*Angola*] [*Airport symbol*] (OAG) .... SPP
Menopausal (ABBR) .... MENPL
Menopausal Gonadotropin [*Endocrinology*] .... MG
Menopause (DSUE) .... MENO
Menopause (ABBR) .... MENP
Menorah Association [*Defunct*] (EA) .... MA
Menorah: Australian Journal of Jewish Studies [*A publication*] (APTA) .... Men
Menorah Book Service (BJA) .... MBS
Menorah Medical Center, Kansas City, MO [*Library symbol Library of Congress*] (LCLS) .... MoKMM
Menorrhoea (ABBR) .... MENO
Men's Apparel Club of New York City (EA) .... MACNYC
Men's Equality Now International (EA) .... MEN
Men's Fashion Association of America (EA) .... MFA
Men's Garden Clubs of America (EA) .... MGCA
Men's Hat Linings and Trimmings Association [*Defunct*] (EA) .... MHLTA
Men's International Professional Tennis Council [*Defunct*] (EA) .... MIPTC
Men's International Squash Tournament Council [*Cardiff, Wales*] (EAIO) .... MISTC
Men's Journal [*A publication*] (BRI) .... Men's J
Men's Neckwear Manufacturers Association of New York [*Defunct*] (EA) .... MNMANY
Men's Neckwear Manufacturers Institute of America (EA) .... MNMIA
Men's Republican Club [*Political party*] (AD) .... MRC
Men's Republican Club (NADA) .... MRC
Men's Resource Center (EA) .... MRC
Men's Resource Connection [*An association*] (EA) .... MRC
Men's Rights Association (EA) .... MRA
Men's Rights, Inc. (EA) .... MR INC
Men's Social Services [*Salvation Army*] .... MSS
Men's Tie Foundation [*Later, NAA*] (EA) .... MTF
Mens Warehouse [*Associated Press*] (SAG) .... MenWre
Mens Warehouse [*NASDAQ symbol*] (SAG) .... SUIT
Mensa [*Constellation*] .... Men
Mensa [*Constellation*] .... Mens
Mensa International [*British*] (EAIO) .... MI
Mensa International [*British*] (EAIO) .... MIL
Mense [*or Menses*] (ABBR) .... MEN
Mensis [*Month*] [*Latin*] .... MENS
Menstrual [*or Menstruate*] (AAMN) .... menst
Menstrual (ABBR) .... MENSTL
Menstrual Age [*Medicine*] .... MA
Menstrual Blood Loss [*Medicine*] .... MBL
Menstrual History [*Medicine*] .... MH
Menstrual Induction [*Medicine*] .... MI
Menstrual Period [*Medicine*] .... MP
Menstruated (ABBR) .... MENSTD
Menstruating (ABBR) .... MENSTG
Menstruation (ABBR) .... MEN
Menstruation (ABBR) .... MENSTN
Menstruation Pill [*Medicine*] (AD) .... M-pill
Mensura [*By Measure*] [*Pharmacy*] (ROG) .... M
Mensura [*By Measure*] [*Pharmacy*] (ROG) .... MENS
Mensuration (ABBR) .... MEN
Mensuration (ROG) .... MENSUR
Menswear Association of Britain (PDAA) .... MAB

Menswear Retailers of America (EA) .... MRA
Mental .... MENT
Mental .... MENTL
Mental .... MNTL
Mental After Care Association [*British*] (EAIO) .... MACA
Mental Age [*Psychology*] .... MA
Mental and Physical Disability Law Reporter [*A publication*] (DLA) .... Mental & Physical Disab L Rep
Mental Development Index [*Bayley Scales of Infant Development*] [*Psychometrics*] .... MDI
Mental Disability Legal Resource Center [*Later, MPDLRSDB*] (EA) .... MDLRC
Mental Handicap Staff Training Board [*British*] .... MHSTB
Mental Health .... MH
Mental Health Abstracts [*Database*] [*IFI/Plenum Data Co.*] [*Information service or system*] (CRD) .... MHA
Mental Health Administration [*Later, ADAMHA*] (EA) .... MHA
Mental Health Analysis [*Psychology*] (AEBS) .... MHA
Mental Health and Mental Retardation (DAVI) .... MH/MR
Mental Health Association [*Later, NMHA*] (EA) .... MHA
Mental Health Authority (NADA) .... MHA
Mental Health Care [*British*] (DAVI) .... MHC
Mental Health Care Unit [*Medicine*] .... MHCU
Mental Health Center (MEDA) .... MHC
Mental Health Centre, Penetanguishene, ON, Canada [*Library symbol Library of Congress*] (LCLS) .... CaOPenM
Mental Health Centre, Penetanguishene, Ontario [*Library symbol National Library of Canada*] (NLC) .... OPENM
Mental Health Clinic (DAVI) .... MHC
Mental Health Course [*British*] .... MHC
Mental Health Department [*Medicine*] .... MHD
Mental Health Digest .... MHD
Mental Health Enquiry [*Medical/computing registers*] [*British*] .... MHE
Mental Health Fieldwork Performance Report [*Occupational therapy*] .... MHFWPR
Mental Health Film Board (EA) .... MHFB
Mental Health Foundation (Victoria) [*Australia*] .... MHF(V)
Mental Health in Australia [*A publication*] .... Ment Hlth Aust
Mental Health Institute (OICC) .... MHI
Mental Health Law Project (EA) .... MHLP
Mental Health Management [*AMEX symbol*] (SPSG) .... MHM
Mental Health Management, Inc. [*Associated Press*] (SAG) .... MentlHlt
Mental Health Materials Center (EA) .... MHMC
Mental Health Project .... MHP
Mental Health Research Institute [*University of Michigan*] [*Research center*] .... MHRI
Mental Health Review Board [*Victoria, Australia*] .... MHRB
Mental Health Review Tribunal [*British*] .... MHRT
Mental Health Services for Clark County, Springfield, OH [*Library symbol*] [*Library of Congress*] (LCLS) .... OSM
Mental Health Services for Clark County, Springfield, OH [*Library symbol Library of Congress*] (LCLS) .... OSpM
Mental Health Services for the Homeless [*Department of Health and Human Services*] (GFGA) .... MHSH
Mental Health Special Interest Section [*American Occupational Therapy Association*] .... MHSS
Mental Health Statistics Improvement Program [*Department of Health and Human Services*] (GFGA) .... MHSIP
Mental Health Study Center [*National Institute of Mental Health*] (GRD) .... MHSC
Mental Hygiene Consultation Service .... MHCS
Mental Hygiene Institute, Montreal, PQ, Canada [*Library symbol Library of Congress*] (LCLS) .... CaQMMH
Mental Hygiene Istitute [*Institut de l'Hygiene Mentale*] Montreal, Quebec [*Library symbol National Library of Canada*] (NLC) .... QMMH
Mental Illness .... MI
Mental Illness Nervous Disorders Society [*Australia*] .... MINDS
Mental Illness Research, Education, and Clinical Center [*Department of Veterans Affairs*] .... MIRECC
Mental Measurements Yearbook [*Psychology A publication*] .... MMY
Mental Measurements Yearbook Database [*University of Nebraska, Lincoln*] [*Database*] .... MMYD
Mental Nurses' Cooperation (ROG) .... MNC
Mental Parents Union (AD) .... MPU
Mental Patient Civil Liberties Project (EA) .... MPCLP
Mental Patients Liberation Projects .... MPLP
Mental Process [*Work-factor system*] .... MP
Mental Research Institute (EA) .... MRI
Mental Residual Functional Capacity Assessment [*Social Security Administration*] .... MRFCA
Mental Retardation .... MR
Mental Retardation and Developmental Disabilities [*National Institutes of Health*] .... MRDD
Mental Retardation Association of America (EA) .... MRAA
Mental Retardation Facility .... MRF
Mental Retardation Research Center .... MMRC
Mental Retardation Research Center [*University of California, Los Angeles*] [*Research center*] (RCD) .... MRRC
Mental Status [*Psychology*] .... MS
Mental Status Examination [*Neurology*] (DAVI) .... MSE
Mental Status Schedule [*Psychology*] .... MSS
Mental Treatment Rules [*British*] .... MTR
Mental Units of Growth [*Psychology*] .... MU
Mental Welfare Commission for Scotland .... MWCS
Mental Welfare Officer [*British*] .... MWO
Mentalis (ABBR) .... MENT
Mentality (ABBR) .... MENTT
Mentally .... MENTLY

Mentally (ABBR) ... MENTY
Mentally and Physically Handicapped (OICC) ... MPH
Mentally Deficient ... MD
Mentally Disabled (OICC) ... MD
Mentally Disordered Sex Offender ... MDSO
Mentally Handicapped (AIE) ... MH
Mentally Ill Chemical Abuser ... MICA
Mentally Retarded (AD) ... mr
Mentally Retarded and Developmentally Disabled ... MR/DD
Mentha [*Mint*] [*Pharmacy*] (ROG) ... MENTH
Menthanediamine [*Organic chemistry*] ... MDA
Menthoxyacetic Acid [*Organic chemistry*] ... MAA
Menthyldiphenyphosphine [*Organic chemistry*] ... MDP
Mention ... MEN
Mention (ROG) ... MENTN
Mentionable (ABBR) ... MENTNB
Mentioned ... MENT
Mentioned ... MENTD
Mentioned (ABBR) ... MENTND
Mentioned in Dispatches (ADA) ... MID
Mentioner (ABBR) ... MENTNR
Mentioning (ABBR) ... MENTNG
Mento-Dextra Anterior [*A fetal position*] [*Obstetrics*] ... MDA
Mento-Dextra Posterior [*A fetal position*] [*Obstetrics*] ... MDP
Mento-Dextra Transversa [*A fetal position*] [*Obstetrics*] ... MDT
Mentolaeva Transverse [*A fetal position*] [*Obstetrics*] (AAMN) ... MLT
Mento-Laeval Anterior [*A fetal position*] [*Obstetrics*] ... MLA
Mentole [*Zaire*] [*ICAO location identifier*] (ICLI) ... FZEP
Mentoleva Posterior [*A fetal position*] [*Obstetrics*] ... MLP
Mentone [*France*] [*Airport symbol*] (AD) ... MNE
Mentor Corp. [*Associated Press*] (SAG) ... Mentor
Mentor Corp. [*NASDAQ symbol*] (NQ) ... MNTR
Mentor Exploration & Development Co. Ltd. [*Toronto Stock Exchange symbol*] ... MV
Mentor Graphics [*NASDAQ symbol*] (TTSB) ... MENT
Mentor Graphics Corp. [*NASDAQ symbol*] (NQ) ... MENT
Mentor Graphics Corp. [*Associated Press*] (SAG) ... MentGr
Mentor Income Fund [*Associated Press*] (SAG) ... MentInc
Mentor Income Fund [*Formerly, RAC Income Fund*] [*NYSE symbol*] (SPSG) ... MRF
Mentor Income Fund [*NYSE symbol*] (TTSB) ... MRF
Mentum [*Chin*] ... M
Mentum Anterior [*In reference to the chin*] ... MA
Mentum Posterior [*In reference to the chin*] ... MP
MENU - the International Software Database [*Menu the International Software Database Corp.*] [*Information service or system*] (CRD) ... ISD
Menxel Bouzelfa [*Tunisia*] [*Seismograph station code, US Geological Survey*] (SEIS) ... MBZ
Menyamya [*Papua New Guinea*] [*Airport symbol*] (OAG) ... MYX
Menzies' Cape Colony Supreme Court Reports [*A publication*] (DLA) ... M
Menzies' Cape Of Good Hope Reports [*1828-49*] [*A publication*] (DLA) ... Men
Menzies' Cape Of Good Hope Reports [*1828-49*] [*A publication*] (DLA) ... Menz
Menzies' Cape Of Good Hope Reports [*1828-49*] [*A publication*] (DLA) ... Menzies
Menzies' Conveyancing [*A publication*] (DLA) ... Menz Conv
MEPC International Capital LP [*Associated Press*] (SAG) ... MEPC
MEPC International Capital LP [*NYSE symbol*] (SAG) ... MUK
MEPC Intl Cap 9.125%'QUIPS' [*NYSE symbol*] (TTSB) ... MUKPrA
Meperidine [*Also, MEP*] [*An analgesic*] ... M
Meperidine [*Also, M*] [*An analgesic*] ... MEP
Meperidine, Promethazine, and Chlorpromazine [*Drug regime*] ... MPC
Mephistopheles [*Foreman*] [*Slang British*] (DSUE) ... MEPHISTO
Mephobarbital [*Antiepileptic drug*] ... MPB
Mephobarital [*A sedative and anticonvulsant*] [*Pharmacology*] (DAVI) ... MEPH
Meprobamate [*Mythyl propyltrimethylene carbamate*] [*Tranquilizer*] (DAVI) ... MEPROB
MERADCOM [*Mobility Equipment Research and Development Command*] **Technical Library, Fort Belvoir, VA** [*OCLC symbol*] (OCLC) ... AME
Merapi [*Java*] [*Seismograph station code, US Geological Survey Closed*] (SEIS) ... MRP
Merauke [*Indonesia*] [*Airport symbol*] (OAG) ... MKQ
Merauke/Mopah [*Indonesia*] [*ICAO location identifier*] (ICLI) ... WAKK
Mercado Comune Europeo [*European Common Market*] [*Spanish*] (DLA) ... MEC
Mercantile ... MER
Mercantile (ROG) ... MERC
Mercantile ... MERCTL
Mercantile Adjuster and Lawyer and Credit Man [*A publication*] (DLA) ... Merc Ad & Law & Credit Man
Mercantile Adjuster and the Lawyer and Credit Man [*A publication*] (DLA) ... MALCM
Mercantile Atlantic Coastal Routing Instructions ... MACRI
Mercantile Atlantic Routing Instructions ... MARI
Mercantile Bancorp [*Associated Press*] (SAG) ... MercBcp
Mercantile Bancorp [*NYSE symbol*] (TTSB) ... MTL
Mercantile Bancorp, Inc. [*NYSE symbol*] (SPSG) ... MTL
Mercantile Bank of Canada [*Toronto Stock Exchange symbol Vancouver Stock Exchange symbol*] ... MBC
Mercantile Bankshares [*NASDAQ symbol*] (TTSB) ... MRBK
Mercantile Bankshares Corp. [*Associated Press*] (SAG) ... MerctlBk
Mercantile Bankshares Corp. [*NASDAQ symbol*] (NQ) ... MRBK
Mercantile Cases [*A publication*] (DLA) ... Merc Cas
Mercantile Communications [*Shipping*] ... MERCO
Mercantile Fleet Auxiliary [*British*] ... MFA
Mercantile Gold [*Vancouver Stock Exchange symbol*] ... MGA
Mercantile Law Journal [*Madras, India*] [*A publication*] (DLA) ... Mer LJ
Mercantile Law Journal [*New York or Madras*] [*A publication*] (DLA) ... Merc LJ
Mercantile Library Association, New York, NY [*Library symbol Library of Congress*] (LCLS) ... NNMer
Mercantile Library, Philadelphia, PA [*Library symbol Library of Congress Obsolete*] (LCLS) ... PPM
Mercantile Marine ... MM
Mercantile Marine Office [*or Officer*] [*British*] ... MMO
Mercantile Marine Service Association [*British*] ... MMSA
Mercantile Marine Trawlermen's Association [*A union*] [*British*] ... MMTA
Mercantile Open Stock ... MOS
Mercantile Pacific Coastal Routing Instructions ... MPCRI
Mercantile Stores [*NYSE symbol*] (TTSB) ... MST
Mercantile Stores Co., Inc. [*Associated Press*] (SAG) ... MercSt
Mercantile Stores Co., Inc. [*NYSE symbol*] (SPSG) ... MST
Mercantilism (ABBR) ... MERCM
Mercantilist (ABBR) ... MERCT
Mercaptobenzothiazole [*Organic chemistry*] ... MBT
Mercaptobenzothiazole Disulfide [*Organic chemistry*] ... MBTS
Mercaptoethanol [*Biochemistry*] ... ME
Mercaptoethanol [*Organic chemistry*] ... Meth
Mercaptoethylamine [*Pharmacology*] ... MEA
(Mercaptoethyl)dimethylammonium Chloride [*Organic chemistry*] ... MEDA
Mercaptoethylguanidine [*Biochemistry*] (AAMN) ... MEG
(Mercaptoethyl)trimethylammonium Iodide [*Pharmacology*] ... MI
Mercaptoimidazole [*Organic chemistry*] (MAE) ... MI
Mercaptomerin [*Pharmacology*] (DAVI) ... MT6
Mercaptomethyl Uracil [*Pharmacology*] (MAE) ... MMU
Mercaptopropionic Acid [*Organic chemistry*] ... MPA
Mercaptopurine [*Purinethol*] [*Also, MP, P*] [*Antineoplastic drug*] ... M
Mercaptopurine [*Purinethol*] [*Also, M, P Antineoplastic drug*] ... MP
Mercaptopurine Ribonucleoside [*Antineoplastic drug*] ... MPR
Mercaptopurine Ribonucleotide [*Antineoplastic drug*] ... MPRP
Mercaptopyrazidopyrimidine [*Antineoplastic drug*] (MAE) ... MPP
Mercaptoundecanol [*Organic chemistry*] ... MUD
Mercaptoundecanol [*Organic chemistry*] ... MUD
Mercapturic Acid Pathway [*Biochemistry*] ... MAP
Mercator [*of Plautus*] [*Classical studies*] (OCD) ... Merc
Mercator's Projection (BARN) ... MP
Merced [*California*] [*Airport symbol*] (AD) ... MCE
Merced, CA [*Location identifier FAA*] (FAAL) ... AWZ
Merced, CA [*FM radio station call letters*] ... KABX
Merced, CA [*FM radio station call letters*] ... KAMB
Merced, CA [*FM radio station call letters*] ... KFIE
Merced, CA [*FM radio station call letters*] (RBYB) ... KIBG-FM
Merced, CA [*AM radio station call letters*] ... KLOQ
Merced, CA [*Television station call letters*] ... KNSO
Merced, CA [*FM radio station call letters*] ... KYAJ
Merced, CA [*AM radio station call letters*] ... KYOS
Merced, CA [*FM radio station call letters*] (RBYB) ... KZFT
Merced, CA [*Location identifier FAA*] (FAAL) ... MCE
Merced, CA [*Location identifier FAA*] (FAAL) ... MER
Merced/Castle Air Force Base [*California*] [*ICAO location identifier*] (ICLI) ... KMER
Merced Community College, Merced, CA [*Library symbol Library of Congress*] (LCLS) ... CMerCC
Merced County Bar Association Law Library, Merced, CA [*Library symbol Library of Congress*] (LCLS) ... CMerCL
Merced County Free Library, Merced, CA [*Library symbol Library of Congress*] (LCLS) ... CMerC
Merced County Free Library, Merced, CA [*OCLC symbol*] (OCLC) ... MCF
Merced National Wildlife Refuge [*California*] (AD) ... MNWR
Mercedarian Missionaries of Berriz [*Also, OMerc*] [*Roman Catholic women's religious order*] ... MMB
Mercedarian Sisters (TOCD) ... RMM
Mercedarios Descalzos (TOCD) ... MDes
Mercedarious Descalzos (TOCD) ... md
Mercedes [*Argentina*] [*Airport symbol*] (OAG) ... MDX
Mercedes [*Automobile*] (DSUE) ... MERC
Mercedes [*Automobile*] (DSUE) ... MERCE
Mercedes [*Argentina ICAO location identifier*] (ICLI) ... SATM
Mercedes Benz of North America ... MBNA
Mercedes/Ricardo de Tomasi [*Uruguay*] [*ICAO location identifier*] (ICLI) ... SUME
Mercedes, TX [*FM radio station call letters*] ... KTJN
Mercedes-Benz [*Automobile*] ... MB
Mercedes-Benz Club of America (EA) ... MBCA
Mercedes-Benz Model Car Club ... MBMCC
Mercedes-Benz Truck Co. ... MBTC
Mercedes-Benz (United Kingdom) ... MBUK
[*A*] **Mercenary** ... MERC
Mercenary Association (EA) ... MA
Mercer [*Alaska*] [*Seismograph station code, US Geological Survey Closed*] (SEIS) ... MCR
Mercer Associates (EA) ... MA
Mercer Beasley Law Review [*A publication*] (DLA) ... Mercer Beasley L Rev
Mercer Beasley Law Review [*A publication*] (DLA) ... Mercer BL Rev
Mercer County Community College, Trenton, NJ [*Library symbol Library of Congress*] (LCLS) ... NjTMC
Mercer County Law Journal [*Pennsylvania*] [*A publication*] (DLA) ... Mercer
Mercer Enterprises [*Air carrier designation symbol*] ... MERX
Mercer Free Library, Mercer, PA [*Library symbol Library of Congress*] (LCLS) ... PMer
Mercer International [*Associated Press*] (SAG) ... Mercer
Mercer International SBI [*NASDAQ symbol*] (SPSG) ... MERCS
Mercer Intl. SBI [*NASDAQ symbol*] (TTSB) ... MERCS
Mercer Island, WA [*FM radio station call letters*] ... KMIH
Mercer Island-Seattle, WA [*AM radio station call letters*] ... KIXI
Mercer, PA [*FM radio station call letters*] ... WLLF

Mercer, PA [*FM radio station call letters*] ... WWIZ
Mercer University (GAGS) ... Mercer U
Mercer University, Atlanta, GA [*Library symbol Library of Congress*] (LCLS) ... GAMU
Mercer University, Law Library, Macon, GA [*OCLC symbol*] (OCLC) ... GML
Mercer University, Macon, GA [*Library symbol Library of Congress*] (LCLS) ... GMM
Mercer University, Macon, GA [*OCLC symbol*] (OCLC) ... GMU
Mercer University, School of Law, Macon, GA [*Library symbol Library of Congress*] (LCLS) ... GMM-L
Mercer University, School of Medicine, Macon, GA [*OCLC symbol*] (OCLC) ... GMM
Mercer University, Southern School of Pharmacy, Atlanta, GA [*Library symbol Library of Congress*] (LCLS) ... GAMU-P
Mercer University, Southern School of Pharmacy, Atlanta, GA [*OCLC symbol*] (OCLC) ... MWU
Mercersburg, PA [*FM radio station call letters*] ... WSRT
Merces [*Brazil*] [*Airport symbol*] (AD) ... MEZ
Merchandise ... MDISE
Merchandise (AFM) ... MDSE
Merchandise (DD) ... mdse
Merchandise ... MDSE
Merchandise (ADA) ... MER
Merchandise Information System (PDAA) ... MIS
Merchandise Marks Act (ROG) ... MMA
Merchandise Mart Apparel Association [*Defunct*] ... MMAA
Merchandise Ordering Processing System (AD) ... MOPS
Merchandises (ROG) ... MISES
Merchandising ... MDSG
Merchandising (DD) ... mdsg
Merchandising ... MDSNG
Merchandising and Operating Results ... MOR
Merchang Mariner's Document [*Navy*] ... MMD
Merchant ... MCHT
Merchant (AFM) ... MER
Merchant ... MERCHT
Merchant ... MRCHNT
Merchant Aircraft Carrier [*A ship carrying a cargo of oil or grain and provided with a flight deck for the operation of antisubmarine aircraft*] [*British World War II*] ... MAC
Merchant Airship Cargo Satellite (PDAA) ... MACS
Merchant Bank ... MB
Merchant Bank of Central Africa Ltd. ... MBCA
Merchant Coastal Transport, Small [*Ship symbol*] ... XAPC
Merchant Codes [*Shipping*] ... MERCOS
Merchant Deposit Transmittal ... MDT
Merchant Express Aviation [*Nigeria*] [*ICAO designator*] (FAAC) ... MXX
Merchant Intelligence Report [*Navy*] ... MERINT
Merchant Jewellers' Association Ltd. [*British*] (BI) ... MJA
Merchant Management System [*Forman Interactive*] [*Computer science*] ... MMS
Merchant Marine ... MM
Merchant Marine and Fisheries Committee [*Congressional committee*] (MSC) ... MM & F
Merchant Marine Communications System (DNAB) ... MERCOMMS
Merchant Marine Council [*Coast Guard*] ... MMC
Merchant Marine Detail ... MMD
Merchant Marine Officers Guild [*Defunct*] (EA) ... MMOG
Merchant Marine Personnel Division [*Coast Guard*] ... MMP
Merchant Marine Reserve (DNAB) ... MMR
Merchant Marine Safety ... MMS
Merchant Marine Technical Division [*Coast Guard*] ... MMT
Merchant Mariners Documentation [*BTS*] (TAG) ... MMDOC
Merchant Mariners Licensing and Documentation [*BTS*] (TAG) ... MMLD
Merchant Navy ... MN
Merchant Navy and Air Line Officers' Association [*A union*] [*British*] (DS) ... MN & ALOA
Merchant Navy and Air Line Officers' Association [*A union*] [*British*] (DCTA) ... MNAOA
Merchant Navy Discipline Organisation [*British*] (DS) ... MNDO
Merchant Navy Establishment [*British*] (DS) ... MNE
Merchant Navy Establishment Administration [*British*] (DS) ... MNEA
Merchant Navy Officers' Pension Fund [*British*] (DS) ... MNOPF
Merchant Navy Training Board [*British*] (DS) ... MNTB
Merchant Navy War Service League [*Australia*] ... MNWSL
[*The*] **Merchant of Venice** [*Shakespearean work*] ... M of V
[*The*] **Merchant of Venice** [*Shakespearean work*] (BARN) ... Merch V
Merchant Oriented Data Entry ... MODE
Merchant Pacific Routing Instructions [*Shipping*] ... MPRI
Merchant Service Fighter Unit [*Air Force British*] ... MSFU
Merchant Service Guild of Australia ... MSGA
Merchant Ship [*Navy*] (NVT) ... MERSHIP
Merchant Ship Arrival and/or Departure Intermediate Report (NATG) ... MERINTREP
Merchant Ship Arrival and/or Departure Report (NATG) ... MEREP
Merchant Ship Auxiliary Program (DNAB) ... MERSAP
Merchant Ship Broadcast [*Navy*] ... MERCAST
Merchant Ship Casualty Report [*Navy*] (NVT) ... MERCASREP
Merchant Ship Casualty Summary [*Navy*] (NVT) ... MERCASUM
Merchant Ship Code Systems [*NATO*] (NATG) ... MERSEX
Merchant Ship Communications Formatted (MCD) ... MERCOFORM
Merchant Ship Control [*Navy*] ... MERCO
Merchant Ship Control Service [*Navy*] ... MSCS
Merchant Ship Converted to a Minesweeper [*Navy symbol Obsolete*] ... XAM
Merchant Ship Intelligence (NVT) ... MERINT
Merchant Ship Naval Augmentation Program [*Navy*] ... MSNAP
Merchant Ship Reactor [*Navy*] ... MSR
Merchant Ship Report [*Navy*] ... MEREP
Merchant Ship Search and Rescue (PDAA) ... MERSAR
Merchant Shipbuilding and Repairs ... MS & R
Merchant Shipping ... MS
Merchant Shipping Act ... MSA
Merchant Shipping Control Zone [*NATO*] (NATG) ... MERZONE
Merchant Signals [*Shipping*] ... MERSIGS
Merchant Token Collectors Association (EA) ... METCA
Merchant Transport [*Ship symbol*] ... XAP
Merchant Vessel ... MV
Merchant Vessel Inspection Division [*Coast Guard*] ... MVI
Merchantable ... MERCH
Merchants and Manufacturers Association (EA) ... M & M
Merchants and Manufacturers Association ... MMA
Merchants Banchares, Inc. [*NASDAQ symbol*] (NQ) ... MBVT
Merchants Bancorp [*NASDAQ symbol*] (SAG) ... MBIA
Merchants Bancshares [*NASDAQ symbol*] (SAG) ... MBVT
Merchants Bancshares [*Associated Press*] (SAG) ... MrcBnc
Merchants Bancshares, Inc. [*Associated Press*] (SAG) ... MrchBnc
Merchants Bancshares (VT) [*NASDAQ symbol*] (TTSB) ... MBVT
Merchants Bank of New York [*NASDAQ symbol*] (NQ) ... MBNY
Merchants Bcp. [*Associated Press*] (SAG) ... MrchBcp
Merchants' Dictionary [*A publication*] (DLA) ... Merch Dict
Merchants' Exchange of St. Louis (EA) ... MESL
Merchants Group [*AMEX symbol*] (TTSB) ... MGP
Merchants Group, Inc. [*AMEX symbol*] (SPSG) ... MGP
Merchants Group, Inc. [*Associated Press*] (SAG) ... MrchGp
Merchants Haulage (DS) ... MH
Merchants Instant Response Authorization (SAA) ... MIRA
Merchants New York Bancorp [*NASDAQ symbol*] (SAG) ... MBNY
Merchants New York Bancorp [*Associated Press*] (SAG) ... MerBkNY
Merchants New York Bancorp [*Associated Press*] (SAG) ... MerBNY
Merchants NY Bancorp [*NASDAQ symbol*] (TTSB) ... MBNY
Merck & Co. [*NYSE symbol*] (TTSB) ... MRK
Merck & Co., Inc. [*Research code symbol*] ... L
Merck & Co., Inc. [*Associated Press*] (SAG) ... Merck
Merck & Co., Inc. [*Research code symbol*] ... MK
Merck & Co., Inc. [*NYSE symbol*] (SPSG) ... MRK
Merck & Co., Inc., Stonewall Process Development Library, Elkton, VA [*Library symbol Library of Congress*] (LCLS) ... ViElM
Merck Frosst Laboratories [*Canada*] ... MF
Merck Frosst Laboratories [*Laboratoires Merck Frosst*] **Montreal, Quebec** [*Library symbol National Library of Canada*] (NLC) ... QMCF
Merck Infrared Spectral Interpretation Package [*For minicomputers*] [*Analytical chemistry*] ... MISIP
Merck, Sharp & Dohme [*Later, Merck & Co., Inc.*] ... MSD
Merck, Sharp & Dohme [*Later, Merck & Co., Inc.*] **Research Laboratories, Library Services, West Point, PA** [*Library symbol Library of Congress*] (LCLS) ... PWpM
Merck, Sharp & Dohme [*Later, Merck & Co., Inc.*] **Research Laboratory, Rahway , NJ** [*OCLC symbol*] (OCLC) ... MSE
Merck, Sharp & Dohme [*Later, Merck & Co., Inc.*] **Research Laboratory, Research Library, Rahway, NJ** [*Library symbol Library of Congress*] (LCLS) ... NjRahM
Merck, Sharp & Dohme [*Later, Merck & Co., Inc.*] **Research Laboratory, West Point, PA** [*OCLC symbol*] (OCLC) ... MSD
Mercurial (WDAA) ... MER
Mercurial (ABBR) ... MERC
Mercurial ... MRCL
Mercuric Ion Receptor [*Biochemistry*] ... MerR
Mercurihematoporphyrin [*Pharmacology*] ... MH
Mercurihydroxypropane [*Clinical chemistry*] ... MHP
Mercury [*Record label*] [*Great Britain*] ... EMer
Mercury [*Chemical*] (EERA) ... Hg
Mercury [*Chemical element*] (DOG) ... Hg
Mercury [*Chemical symbol is Hg*] (KSC) ... M
Mercury ... M
Mercury [*Nevada*] [*Seismograph station code, US Geological Survey Closed*] (SEIS) ... MCN
Mercury [*Nevada*] [*Seismograph station code, US Geological Survey*] (SEIS) ... MCV
Mercury (ADA) ... MER
Mercury [*Record label*] ... Mer
Mercury ... MERC
Mercury ... MERC
Mercury [*Chemistry*] (DAVI) ... MERCRy
Mercury Abort Sensing Instrumentation System [*NASA*] (AAG) ... MASIS
Mercury Air Group [*AMEX symbol*] (TTSB) ... MAX
Mercury Air Group, Inc. [*AMEX symbol*] (SPSG) ... MAX
Mercury Air Group, Inc. [*Associated Press*] (SAG) ... MercAir
Mercury Aircourier Service [*ICAO designator*] (FAAC) ... MEC
Mercury Amalgamation Trap [*Analytical chemistry*] ... MAT
Mercury Analyzer System [*Perkin-Elmer Co. instrument designation*] ... MAS
Mercury Arc (MSA) ... MA
Mercury Arc Lamp ... MAL
Mercury Arc Rectifier (IAA) ... MAR
Mercury Asset Management [*Commercial firm British*] ... MAM
Mercury Bombardment Thrustor ... MBT
Mercury Cadmium Telluride [*Photodetector*] ... MCT
Mercury Club [*Defunct*] (EA) ... MC
Mercury Contact (IAA) ... MC
Mercury Control Center ... MCC
Mercury Delay Line ... MDL
Mercury Doped Germanium Detector ... MDGD

Mercury Dynamic Test .... MDT
Mercury Electron Bombardment .... MEB
Mercury Enthusiast Restorer Custom Performance Auto Club (EA) .... MERCPAC
Mercury Evaporation and Condensation Analysis [*NASA*] .... MECA
Mercury Feed System .... MFS
Mercury Film Electrode [*Electrochemistry*] .... MFE
Mercury Finance [*NYSE symbol*] (TTSB) .... MFN
Mercury Finance Co. [*Associated Press*] (SAG) .... MercFn
Mercury Finance Co. [*NYSE symbol*] (SPSG) .... MFN
Mercury General [*NYSE symbol*] (SAG) .... MCY
Mercury General [*NASDAQ symbol*] (TTSB) .... MRCY
Mercury General Corp. [*Associated Press*] (SAG) .... MercGn
Mercury General Corp. [*NASDAQ symbol*] (NQ) .... MRCY
Mercury Germanium Detector .... MGD
Mercury (Hobart) [*A publication*] .... Merc (Hob)
Mercury Integrated Test .... MIT
Mercury Interactive [*NASDAQ symbol*] (TTSB) .... MERQ
Mercury Interactive Corp. [*Associated Press*] (SAG) .... MercInt
Mercury Interactive Corp. [*NASDAQ symbol*] (SAG) .... MERQ
Mercury Iodide Crystal Growth .... MICG
Mercury Ion Thruster .... MIT
Mercury Marine, Fond Du Lac, WI [*Library symbol Library of Congress*] (LCLS) .... WFonMM
Mercury Network Test Vehicle (MUGU) .... MNTV
Mercury, NV [*Location identifier FAA*] (FAAL) .... DRA
Mercury, NV [*Location identifier FAA*] (FAAL) .... MCY
Mercury Plunger Relay .... MPR
Mercury Procedures Simulator [*NASA*] .... MPS
Mercury Procedures Trainer .... MPT
Mercury Project [*NASA*] (KSC) .... MERC
Mercury Project Office [*NASA*] (SAA) .... MPO
Mercury Rankine Power Conversion [*Nuclear energy*] .... MRPC
Mercury Recovery Control Center .... MRCC
Mercury Rectifier (IAA) .... MERRECT
Mercury Scientific Experiment Panel .... MSEP
Mercury Singapore Airlines .... MSA
Mercury Specialist Management [*Commercial firm British*] .... MSM
Mercury Substitution and Nucleonic Detection (PDAA) .... MSND
Mercury Support Planning Office (MUGU) .... MSPO
Mercury System Test [*NASA*] .... MST
Mercury Thin Film Electrode [*Electrochemistry*] .... MTFE
Mercury Tube Nutation Damper .... MTND
Mercury Unit Test .... MUT
Mercury Vapor .... MV
Mercury Vapor Isolator .... MVI
Mercury Vapor Lamp .... MVL
Mercury, Venus, Earth, Mars, Jupiter (PDAA) .... MeVEMsJ
Mercury Volatilizing Activity .... MVA
Mercury Xenon Arc Lamp .... MXAL
Mercury-Atlas [*Spacecraft*] [*NASA*] .... MA
Mercury-Redstone [*NASA*] .... MR
Mercury-Redstone Booster Development [*Spacecraft*] [*NASA*] .... MR-BD
Mercury-Scout [*Spacecraft*] [*NASA*] .... MS
Mercury-Wetted Contact Relay .... MWCR
Mercy College, Dobbs Ferry, NY [*Library symbol Library of Congress*] (LCLS) .... NDfM
Mercy College, Dobbs Ferry, NY [*OCLC symbol*] (OCLC) .... VZE
Mercy College of Detroit [*Michigan*] .... MCD
Mercy College of Detroit, Detroit, MI [*OCLC symbol*] (OCLC) .... EYY
Mercy College of Detroit, Detroit, MI [*Library symbol Library of Congress*] (LCLS) .... MiDMC
Mercy Hospital and Medical Center, Chicago, IL [*Library symbol Library of Congress*] (LCLS) .... ICMH
Mercy Hospital, Devils Lake, ND [*Library symbol Library of Congress*] (LCLS) .... NdDeH
Mercy Hospital, Health Science Library, Hamilton, OH [*Library symbol Library of Congress*] (LCLS) .... OHaMH
Mercy Hospital, Janesville, WI [*Library symbol Library of Congress*] (LCLS) .... WJaM
Mercy Hospital, Library and Media Resources Center, Denver, CO [*Library symbol Library of Congress*] (LCLS) .... CoDMH
Mercy Hospital, Library, Watertown, NY [*OCLC symbol*] (OCLC) .... VNA
Mercy Hospital, McGlannan Memorial Library, Baltimore, MD [*Library symbol Library of Congress*] (LCLS) .... MdBMH
Mercy Hospital, Nursing Library, Oshkosh, WI [*Library symbol Library of Congress*] (LCLS) .... WOshM
Mercy Hospital of Watertown, Watertown, NY [*Library symbol Library of Congress*] (LCLS) .... NWattMH
Mercy Hospital, Rockville Centre, NY [*Library symbol Library of Congress*] (LCLS) .... NRockH
Mercy Hospital, School of Nursing, Baltimore, MD [*Library symbol Library of Congress*] (LCLS) .... MdBMH-N
Mercy Hospital, Urbana, IL [*Library symbol Library of Congress*] (LCLS) .... IUrH
Mercy Hospital-School of Nursing, Library, Denver, CO [*Library symbol Library of Congress*] (LCLS) .... CoDMH-M
Mercy Junior College [*Missouri*] [*Closed, 1971*] .... MJC
Mercy Medical Airlift (EA) .... MMA
Mercy Medical Center, Coon Rapids, MN [*Library symbol Library of Congress*] (LCLS) .... MnCrpM
Mercy Medical Center, Medical Library, Nampa, ID [*Library symbol*] [*Library of Congress*] (LCLS) .... IdNMH
Mercy Medical Center, Medical Library, Oshkosh, WI [*Library symbol Library of Congress*] (LCLS) .... WOshM-M
Mercy Medical Center, Roseburg, OR [*Library symbol Library of Congress*] (LCLS) .... OrRoMM
Mercy Medical Center, Springfield, OH [*Library symbol Library of Congress*] (LCLS) .... OSMM
Mercyhurst College, Erie, PA [*Library symbol Library of Congress*] (LCLS) .... PErMC
Merdei [*Indonesia*] [*ICAO location identifier*] (ICLI) .... WASM
Meredith College, Raleigh, NC [*Library symbol Library of Congress*] (LCLS) .... NcRM
Meredith College, Raleigh, NC [*Library symbol*] [*Library of Congress*] (LCLS) .... NcRMC
Meredith College, Raleigh, NC [*OCLC symbol*] (OCLC) .... NMC
Meredith Corp. [*NYSE symbol*] (SPSG) .... MDP
Meredith Corp. [*Associated Press*] (SAG) .... Merdth
Meredith, NH [*FM radio station call letters*] .... WBHG
Meredosia-Chambersburg River Valley Public Library District, Meredosia, IL [*Library symbol Library of Congress*] (LCLS) .... IMerD
Merehurst [*Publisher*] [*British*] .... M
Meres et Enfants Internationale [*Switzerland*] (EAIO) .... MEI
Merewether and Stephen's Municipal Corporations [*A publication*] (DLA) .... Mer & St Corp
Merfin Hygienic [*Vancouver Stock Exchange symbol*] .... MIP
Merfin Resources Ltd. [*Vancouver Stock Exchange symbol*] .... MRF
Merge [*Computer science*] (IBMDP) .... M
Merge [*Computer science*] .... MRG
Merge and Correlate Recorded Output [*Computer science*] (NASA) .... MACRO
Merged Accountability and Fund Reporting [*Air Force*] (AFM) .... MAFR
Merged Accounts (AAGC) .... M-Accounts
Merged Area Schools (OICC) .... MAS
Merged Area Schools Administrators Association (OICC) .... MASA
Merged Charge Memory [*Computer science*] (IAA) .... MCM
Merged-Transistor Logic .... MTL
Merger Acquisition Improved Decision [*Computer science*] .... MAID
Mergers and Acquisitions .... M & A
Mergers and Acquisitions (TDOB) .... M&A
Mergers & Acquisitions Data Base [*MLR Publishing Co.*] [*Information service or system*] (CRD) .... M & A
Mergers and Divestures .... M & D
Merging (FAAC) .... MEGG
Mergui [*Myanmar*] [*Airport symbol*] (OAG) .... MGZ
Mergui [*Myanmar*] [*ICAO location identifier*] (ICLI) .... VBRN
Merida [*Mexico*] [*Seismograph station code, US Geological Survey*] (SEIS) .... MER
Merida [*Mexico*] [*Airport symbol*] (OAG) .... MID
Merida [*Mexico ICAO location identifier*] (ICLI) .... MMID
Merida [*Venezuela*] [*Airport symbol*] (OAG) .... MRD
Merida/Alberto Carnevalli, Merida [*Venezuela ICAO location identifier*] (ICLI) .... SVMD
Merida/Lic. Manuel Crecencio Rejon Internacional [*Mexico ICAO location identifier*] (ICLI) .... MMMD
Meridan Natl [*NASDAQ symbol*] (TTSB) .... MRCO
Meridan Natl $3.75 Cv'B'Pfd [*NASDAQ symbol*] (TTSB) .... MRCOP
Meriden, CT [*Location identifier FAA*] (FAAL) .... MMK
Meriden, CT [*AM radio station call letters*] .... WMMW
Meriden, CT [*FM radio station call letters*] .... WPKT
Merides [*Latin*] [*Noon*] (WDMC) .... M
Meridian [*Mississippi*] [*Airport symbol*] (OAG) .... MEI
Meridian (KSC) .... MER
Meridian .... MER
Meridian (ABBR) .... MERID
Meridian [*A publication*] .... Meridn
Meridian Air Cargo, Inc. [*ICAO designator*] (FAAC) .... MRD
Meridian Altitude [*Navigation*] .... MERALT
Meridian & Bigbee Railroad Co. [*Later, MBRR*] [*AAR code*] .... MB
Meridian & Bigbee Railroad Co. [*Formerly, MB*] [*AAR code*] .... MBRR
Meridian & Bigbee River Railroad Co. (IIA) .... M & BR
Meridian Angle .... T
Meridian Bancorp, Inc. [*NASDAQ symbol*] (NQ) .... MRDN
Meridian Bancorp, Inc. [*Associated Press*] (SAG) .... MrdnBc
Meridian Control Integrator .... MCI
Meridian Control Signal .... MCS
Meridian Data [*NASDAQ symbol*] (TTSB) .... MDCD
Meridian Data, Inc. [*NASDAQ symbol*] (SAG) .... MDCD
Meridian Data, Inc. [*Associated Press*] (SAG) .... MeridDta
Meridian Diagnostics [*NASDAQ symbol*] (TTSB) .... KITS
Meridian Diagnostics, Inc. .... MDI
Meridian Diagnostics, Inc. [*Associated Press*] (SAG) .... MeridDia
Meridian Difference .... MERDIFF
Meridian House Foundation [*Later, MHI*] .... MHF
Meridian House International (EA) .... MHI
Meridian Indl Tr Wrrt [*AMEX symbol*] (TTSB) .... MDN.WS
Meridian Industrial Trust [*NYSE symbol*] (TTSB) .... MDN
Meridian Industrial Trust, Inc. [*AMEX symbol*] (SAG) .... MDN
Meridian Industrial Trust, Inc. [*Associated Press*] (SAG) .... Meridl
Meridian Insrance Gp [*NASDAQ symbol*] (TTSB) .... MIGI
Meridian Insurance Group, Inc. [*Associated Press*] (SAG) .... MerdIns
Meridian Insurance Group, Inc. [*NASDAQ symbol*] (NQ) .... MIGI
Meridian Junior College, Meridian, MS [*Library symbol Library of Congress*] (LCLS) .... MsMM
Meridian Library District, Meridian, ID [*Library symbol*] [*Library of Congress*] (LCLS) .... IdMe
Meridian (Lower Branch) .... m
Meridian, MS [*Location identifier FAA*] (FAAL) .... MEI
Meridian, MS [*Location identifier FAA*] (FAAL) .... NMM
Meridian, MS [*AM radio station call letters*] .... WALT
Meridian, MS [*Television station call letters*] .... WGBC
Meridian, MS [*FM radio station call letters*] .... WJDQ
Meridian, MS [*FM radio station call letters*] .... WMAW

Meridian, MS [*Television station call letters*] .... WMAW-TV
Meridian, MS [*Television station call letters*] .... WMDN
Meridian, MS [*AM radio station call letters*] .... WMER
Meridian, MS [*AM radio station call letters*] .... WMGP
Meridian, MS [*AM radio station call letters*] .... WMOX
Meridian, MS [*AM radio station call letters*] .... WNBN
Meridian, MS [*FM radio station call letters*] .... WOKK
Meridian, MS [*Television station call letters*] .... WTOK
Meridian, MS [*FM radio station call letters*] .... WTUX
Meridian Municipal Junior College [*Mississippi*] .... MMJC
Meridian National Corp. [*Associated Press*] (SAG) .... MerdrNt
Meridian National Corp. [*NASDAQ symbol*] (NQ) .... MRCO
Meridian National Corp. [*Associated Press*] (SAG) .... MrdN
Meridian National Corp. [*Associated Press*] (SAG) .... MrdN 99
Meridian Natl Wrrt [*NASDAQ symbol*] (TTSB) .... MRCOZ
Meridian Natl Wrrt'A' [*NASDAQ symbol*] (TTSB) .... MRCOL
Meridian Park Hospital, Medical Library, Tualatin, OR [*Library symbol Library of Congress*] (LCLS) .... OrTuaM
Meridian Passage [*Navigation*] .... MERPASS
Meridian Point Realty [*AMEX symbol*] (SPSG) .... MPH
Meridian Point Realty IV [*AMEX symbol*] (SPSG) .... MPD
Meridian Point Realty Trust [*NASDAQ symbol*] (SAG) .... MPTB
Meridian Point Realty Trust 1983 [*Associated Press*] (SAG) MerPt83
Meridian Point Realty Trust IV [*Associated Press*] (SAG) MerPt4
Meridian Point Realty Trust VI [*Associated Press*] (SAG) MerPt6
Meridian Point Realty Trust VI Co. [*Associated Press*] (SAG) MerP6
Meridian Point Realty Trust VII [*Associated Press*] (SAG) MerPnt7
Meridian Point Realty Trust VIII [*Associated Press*] (SAG) .... MerPnt 8
Meridian Point Realty Trust VIII Co. [*Associated Press*] (SAG) .... MerPt 8
Meridian Point Realty VI [*AMEX symbol*] (SPSG) .... MPF
Meridian Point Realty VII [*AMEX symbol*] (SPSG) .... MPG
Meridian Point Rity Tr 83 [*NASDAQ symbol*] (TTSB) .... MPTBS
Meridian Point Rlty VIII [*AMEX symbol*] (TTSB) .... MPH
Meridian Point Rlty VIII Pfd [*AMEX symbol*] (TTSB) .... MPHPr
Meridian Public Library, Meridian, MS [*Library symbol Library of Congress*] (LCLS) .... MsM
Meridian Sports [*NASDAQ symbol*] (TTSB) .... MSPO
Meridian Sports, Inc. [*Associated Press*] (SAG) .... MeridSpt
Meridian Sports, Inc. [*NASDAQ symbol*] (SAG) .... MSPO
Meridian Technologies [*TS, exchange symbol*] (TTSB) .... MNI
Meridian Technologies, Inc. [*Toronto Stock Exchange symbol*] .... MNI
Meridian Telecommunication Services [*Indianapolis, IN*] (TSSD) .... M
Meridian (Upper Branch) .... MTS
Meridiana SpA [*Italy ICAO designator*] (FAAC) .... ISS
Meridianville, AL [*FM radio station call letters*] (RBYB) .... WXQW-FM
Meridies [*Noon*] [*Latin*] .... M
Meridional [*Geology*] .... MER
Meridional .... MRDNL
Meridional Elementary Circulation Mechanism .... MECM
Meridional Part [*Navigation*] .... M
Meridional Part [*Navigation*] .... MP
Meridional Ray Trace .... MRT
Meridor Resources Ltd. [*Vancouver Stock Exchange symbol*] .... MRO
Meriline Branch, Canada Post [*Postes Canada*], Ottawa, Ontario [*Library symbol National Library of Canada*] (BIB) .... OOPOM
Merimbula [*Australia Airport symbol*] (OAG) .... MIM
Merion Bluegrass Association [*Defunct*] (EA) .... MBA
Merionethshire [*County in Wales*] .... MERIONS
Meris Laboratories [*NASDAQ symbol*] (SPSG) .... MERS
Meris Laboratories, Inc. [*Associated Press*] (SAG) .... MerisL
Merisel, Inc. [*Associated Press*] (SAG) .... Merisel
Merisel, Inc. [*NASDAQ symbol*] (SPSG) .... MSEL
Meristem Height [*Botany*] .... MH
Merit [*Record label*] .... Mrt
Merit Holding [*NASDAQ symbol*] (TTSB) .... MRET
Merit Holding Corp. [*Associated Press*] (SAG) .... MeritH
Merit Holding Corp. [*NASDAQ symbol*] (SAG) .... MRET
Merit Increase (MHDW) .... MI
Merit Medical Systems [*NASDAQ symbol*] (TTSB) .... MMSI
Merit Medical Systems, Inc. [*Associated Press*] (SAG) .... MertMd
Merit Medical Systems, Inc. [*NASDAQ symbol*] (SAG) .... MMSI
Merit of a Coil or Capacitor [*Electronics*] .... Q
Merit Pay System (MCD) .... MPS
Merit Promotion Bulletin [*Military*] .... MPB
Merit Promotion Plan [*or Program*] [*NASA*] (NASA) .... MPP
Merit Quotient .... MQ
Merit Shop Foundation [*Washington, DC*] (EA) .... MSF
Merit Software, Inc. [*NASDAQ symbol*] (SAG) .... MRIT
Merit Students Encyclopedia [*A publication*] .... MSE
Merit System (OICC) .... MS
Merit System Protection Plan .... MSPP
Merit Systems Protection Board [*Formerly, Civil Service Commission*] .... MSPB
Merit Technologies Ltd. [*Vancouver Stock Exchange symbol*] .... MTE
Meritocracy (ABBR) .... MERITOC
Meritocrat (ABBR) .... MERITOC
Meritorious Civilian Service Award .... MCSA
Meritorious Service Medal [*Military decoration*] .... MSM
Meritorious Service Medal [*Military decoration*] .... MUC
Meritorious Unit Citation [*Military decoration*] .... MUC
Meritorious Unit Commendation [*Military decoration*] (AFM) .... MUC
Meritorious Unit Emblem [*Military decoration*] .... MUE
Meritrust Fed Svg Bk Morgan [*NASDAQ symbol*] (TTSB) .... MERI
Meritrust Federal Savings Bank [*NASDAQ symbol*] (SAG) .... MERI
Meritrust Federal Savings Bank [*Associated Press*] (SAG) .... MeriFdl
Merivale High School, Ottawa, ON, Canada [*Library symbol Library of Congress*] (LCLS) .... CaOOMHS

Merivale High School, Ottawa, Ontario [*Library symbol National Library of Canada*] (NLC) .... OOMHS
Merivale Road Branch, Nepean Public Library, Ontario [*Library symbol National Library of Canada*] (BIB) .... ONMB
Merivale's English Chancery Reports [*A publication*] (DLA) .... Mer
Merivale's English Chancery Reports [*A publication*] (DLA) .... Meriv
Merivale's English Chancery Reports [*A publication*] (DLA) .... Meriv (Eng)
Merix Corp. [*Associated Press*] (SAG) .... Merix Cp
Merix Corp. [*NASDAQ symbol*] (SAG) .... MERX
Merkel Cell [*Anatomy*] .... MC
Merkel, TX [*FM radio station call letters*] .... KCWS
Merkel, TX [*AM radio station call letters*] .... KMXO
Merland Explorations Ltd. [*Toronto Stock Exchange symbol*] .... MOC
Merle Haggard Fan Club (EA) .... MHFC
Merle West Medical Center Library, Klamath Falls, OR [*Library symbol*] [*Library of Congress*] (LCLS) .... OrKM
Merleau-Ponty Circle (EA) .... MPC
Merlin Executive Aviation Group Ltd. [*British ICAO designator*] (FAAC) .... WIZ
Merlin Express, Inc. [*FAA designator*] (FAAC) .... FAE
Merlin Resources Ltd. [*Vancouver Stock Exchange symbol*] .... MLH
Merlinoite [*A zeolite*] .... MER
Merlo [*Argentina ICAO location identifier*] (ICLI) .... SADR
Mermaid Series [*A publication*] .... MSA
Merowe [*Sudan*] [*ICAO location identifier*] (ICLI) .... HSMR
Merowe [*Sudan*] [*Airport symbol*] (OAG) .... MWE
Merozoite Surface Protein [*Of protozoa*] .... MSP
Merpati Nusantara Airlines PT [*Indonesia*] [*ICAO designator*] (FAAC) .... MNA
Merpati Nusatnara Airlines [*ICAO designator*] (AD) .... MZ
Merrell-National [*Commercial firm*] (DAVI) .... M-N
Merrell-National Laboratories [*Research code symbol*] .... MER
Merrell-National Laboratories [*Research code symbol*] .... MRL
Merrell-National Laboratories [*Research code symbol*] .... RMI
Merrell-National Laboratories, Cincinnati, OH [*Library symbol Library of Congress*] (LCLS) .... OCMN
Merrell's Fan Club (EA) .... MFC
Merriam-Webster [*Publisher*] .... M-W
Merrick Avenue Junior High School, Merrick, NY [*Library symbol*] [*Library of Congress*] (LCLS) .... NMerkMJ
Merrick Public Library, Merrick, NY [*Library symbol Library of Congress*] (LCLS) .... NMerk
Merrickville Public Library, Ontario [*Library symbol National Library of Canada*] (NLC) .... OMER
Merrifield on Attorneys [*1830*] [*A publication*] (DLA) .... Merr Att
Merrifield's Law of Costs [*A publication*] (DLA) .... Merr Costs
Merrill Corp. [*Associated Press*] (SAG) .... MerilCp
Merrill Corp. [*NASDAQ symbol*] (NQ) .... MRLL
Merrill Corp. [*NASDAQ symbol*] (TTSB) .... MRLL
Merrill District Library, Merrill, MI [*Library symbol Library of Congress*] (LCLS) .... MiMer
Merrill Language Screening Test [*Educational test*] .... MLST
Merrill Lyn 6.00%'STRYPES' [*NYSE symbol*] (TTSB) .... MCO
Merrill Lyn 6.50%'STRYPES' [*NYSE symbol*] (TTSB) .... MML
Merrill Lyn Gl'MITTS'98 [*NYSE symbol*] (TTSB) .... MLC
Merrill Lynch [*NYSE symbol*] (TTSB) .... MER
Merrill Lynch 9% Sr'A'Dep Pfd [*NYSE symbol*] (TTSB) .... MERPrA
Merrill Lynch & Co'MITTS' 2001 [*NASDAQ symbol*] (TTSB) .... MIT
Merrill Lynch & Co'MITTS' 2001 [*NYSE symbol*] (TTSB) .... MIX
Merrill Lynch & Co'MITTS'98 [*NYSE symbol*] (TTSB) .... MIE
Merrill Lynch & Co. [*AMEX symbol*] (SAG) .... DMY
Merrill Lynch & Co. [*NYSE symbol*] (SAG) .... IML
Merrill Lynch & Co. [*NYSE symbol*] (SAG) .... MCO
Merrill Lynch & Co. [*NYSE symbol*] (SAG) .... MER
Merrill Lynch & Co. [*AMEX symbol*] (SAG) .... MHW
Merrill Lynch & Co. [*NYSE symbol*] (SAG) .... MIX
Merrill Lynch & Co. [*Associated Press*] (SAG) .... ML SAI99
Merrill Lynch & Co. [*Associated Press*] (SAG) .... ML SYP98
Merrill Lynch & Co. [*Associated Press*] (SAG) .... ML Tech01
Merrill Lynch & Co. [*NYSE symbol*] (SAG) .... MLB
Merrill Lynch & Co. [*Associated Press*] (SAG) MLCox99n
Merrill Lynch & Co. [*Associated Press*] (SAG) .... MLCur
Merrill Lynch & Co. [*Associated Press*] (SAG) .... MLHK
Merrill Lynch & Co. [*Associated Press*] (SAG) MLIGL01
Merrill Lynch & Co. [*Associated Press*] (SAG) MLMGIC98
Merrill Lynch & Co. [*Associated Press*] (SAG) .... MLNik 97
Merrill Lynch & Co. [*Associated Press*] (SAG) MLRus98
Merrill Lynch & Co. [*Associated Press*] (SAG) .... MLUS
Merrill Lynch & Co. [*NYSE symbol*] (SAG) .... MML
Merrill Lynch & Co. [*AMEX symbol*] (SAG) .... NKC
Merrill Lynch & Co. [*AMEX symbol*] (SAG) .... RIM
Merrill Lynch & Co. [*NYSE symbol*] (SAG) .... TKM
Merrill Lynch & Co. [*AMEX symbol*] (SAG) .... YIX
Merrill Lynch & Co., Inc. [*NYSE symbol*] (SAG) .... MEE
Merrill Lynch & Co., Inc. [*Associated Press*] (SAG) .... MerL
Merrill Lynch & Co., Inc. [*Associated Press*] (SAG) .... MerLEur
Merrill Lynch & Co., Inc. [*Associated Press*] (SAG) .... MerrLyn
Merrill Lynch & Co., Inc. [*NYSE symbol*] (SPSG) .... MIT
Merrill Lynch & Co., Inc. [*NYSE symbol*] (SAG) .... MLC
Merrill Lynch & Co., Inc. [*Associated Press*] (SAG) MLGT98
Merrill Lynch & Co., Inc. [*Associated Press*] (SAG) MLSP97
Merrill Lynch & Co., Inc. [*Associated Press*] (SAG) MLSP98
Merrill Lynch & Co. "MITTS" 98 [*NYSE symbol*] (SPSG) .... MIE
Merrill Lynch & Co. Preferred Capital Trust I [*NYSE symbol*] (SAG) .... MER
Merrill Lynch & Co. Preferred Capital Trust I [*Associated Press*] (SAG) .... MerL
Merrill Lynch Economics (NITA) .... MLE
Merrill Lynch Financial Advantage .... MLFA

Merrill Lynch, Pierce, Fenner & Smith [of Merrill Lynch & Co., Inc.]
[Stockbrokers Wall Street slang name: "Thundering Herd"] ...... MLPFS
Merrill Public Library, Merrill, IA [Library symbol Library of Congress]
(LCLS) ...... IaMer
Merrill, WI [Location identifier FAA] (FAAL) ...... RRL
Merrill, WI [AM radio station call letters] ...... WJMT
Merrill, WI [FM radio station call letters] ...... WMZK
Merrill-Demos DD Scale [Drug abuse and delinquent behavior test] ...... MDDD
Merrill-Palmer Institute, Detroit, MI [Library symbol Library of Congress]
(LCLS) ...... MiDMP
Merrill-Palmer Scale of Mental Tests [Psychology] (DAVI) ...... MPSMT
Merrill's Marauders Association (EA) ...... MMA
Merrimac Industries [AMEX symbol] (TTSB) ...... MRM
Merrimac Industries, Inc. [Associated Press] (SAG) ...... Mermic
Merrimac Industries, Inc. [AMEX symbol] (SPSG) ...... MRM
Merrimack College, McQuade Library, North Andover, MA [OCLC symbol]
(OCLC) ...... MRK
Merrimack College, North Andover, MA [Library symbol Library of
Congress] (LCLS) ...... MNoanM
Merrimack Education Center [Chelmsford, MA] [Information service or
system] ...... MEC
Merrimack, NH [Television station call letters] ...... WGOT
Merrimack Valley College Library, Manchester, NH [OCLC symbol]
(OCLC) ...... MVA
Merrimack Valley Textile Museum, North Andover, MA [Library symbol
Library of Congress] (LCLS) ...... MNoanMV
Merriman, NE [FM radio station call letters] ...... KRNE
Merriman, NE [Television station call letters] ...... KRNE-TV
Merritech Development [Vancouver Stock Exchange symbol] ...... MDX
Merritt and Miller's Own Block Structured Simulation Language,
Unpronounceable Acronym For [1969] [Computer science]
(CSR) ...... MOBSSL-UAF
Merritt, BC [FM radio station call letters] ...... CFJC
Merritt, BC [AM radio station call letters] ...... CJNL
Merritt College, Oakland, CA [Library symbol Library of Congress] (LCLS) ..... COM
Merritt Elementary School, Duluth, MN [Library symbol] [Library of
Congress] (LCLS) ...... MnDuME
Merritt Elementary School, Mt. Iron, MN [Library symbol] [Library of
Congress] (LCLS) ...... MnMtiE
Merritt Island [Florida] [NASA] (KSC) ...... MI
Merritt Island, Florida [Spaceflight Tracking and Data Network] [NASA] ...... MLX
Merritt Island Industrial Area [NASA] (KSC) ...... MIIA
Merritt Island Launch Area [NASA] ...... MILA
Merritt Island Press Site [NASA] (NASA) ...... MIPS
Merritt Island Public Library, Merritt Island, FL [Library symbol Library of
Congress] (LCLS) ...... FMi
Merritt Island Tracking Station [Florida] ...... MIL
Merritt Island Tracking Station [Florida] ...... MLA
Merrix Air Ltd. [British ICAO designator] (FAAC) ...... MXR
Merry Island, BC [ICAO location identifier] (ICLI) ...... CYMR
Merry Land & Inv Sr'A'Cv Pfd [NYSE symbol] (TTSB) ...... MRYPr
Merry Land & Inv Sr'C'Cv Pfd [NYSE symbol] (TTSB) ...... MRYPrC
Merry Land & Invest [NYSE symbol] (TTSB) ...... MRY
Merry Land & Investment [NYSE symbol] (SAG) ...... MRY
Merry Land & Investment Co., Inc. [Associated Press] (SAG) ...... MeryL
Merry Land & Investment Co., Inc. [Associated Press] (SAG) ...... MeryLd
[The] Merry Wives of Windsor [Shakespearean work] (BARN) ...... Merry W
[The] Merry Wives of Windsor [Shakespearean work] (BARN) ...... MWW
[The] Merry Wives of Windsor [Shakespearean work] ...... Wiv
Mersa Matruh [Egypt] [Airport symbol] (AD) ...... MUH
Mersa-Matruh [Egypt] [ICAO location identifier] (ICLI) ...... HEMM
Mersey Dock Board [British] (DAS) ...... MDB
Mersey Docks and Harbour Co. [British] ...... MDHC
Merseyside [County in England] (WGA) ...... Mersey
Merseyside and North Wales Electricity Board [British] (AD) ...... MNWEB
Merseyside Aviation Society [British] (DBA) ...... MAS
Merseyside Innovation Centre Ltd. [Research center British] (CB) ...... MIC
Mersing [Malaysia] [Airport symbol] (OAG) ...... MEP
Mersing [Malaysia] [ICAO location identifier] (ICLI) ...... WMAU
Merten's Law of Federal Income Taxation [A publication] (DLA) ...... Mert
Merthiolate-Formaldehyde [Solution] ...... MF
Merthiolate-Formaldehyde [Stock] Solution (BABM) ...... MF SOL
Merthiolate-Iodine Formalin Concentration ...... MIFC
Merthiolate-Iodine-Formaldehyde [Technique] ...... MIF
Merthyr [Cardiff] [Welsh depot code] ...... MTHR
Merton College [Oxford University] (ROG) ...... MERT
Merty [Australia Airport symbol Obsolete] (OAG) ...... RTY
Meru National Park [Equatorial Kenya] (AD) ...... MNP
Mervaerdiomsaetningsskat [Value-Added Tax] [Danish] (AD) ...... moms
Merville/Calonne [France ICAO location identifier] (ICLI) ...... LFQT
Mervyn Peake Society (EA) ...... MPS
Merzifon [Turkey ICAO location identifier] (ICLI) ...... LTAP
Mesa [Type of transistor] (MDG) ...... MS
Mesa [Arizona] [Airport symbol Obsolete] (OAG) ...... MSC
Mesa Air Group [NASDAQ symbol] (TTSB) ...... MESA
Mesa Air Group, Inc. [NASDAQ symbol] (SAG) ...... MESA
Mesa Air Group, Inc. [Associated Press] (SAG) ...... MesaAir
Mesa Airlines, Inc. [ICAO designator] (FAAC) ...... ASH
Mesa Airlines, Inc. [NASDAQ symbol] (NQ) ...... MESA
Mesa Airlines, Inc. [Associated Press] (SAG) ...... MesaAr
Mesa Aviation [ICAO designator] (AD) ...... YV
Mesa, AZ [FM radio station call letters] (RBYB) ...... KDKB-FM
Mesa, AZ [AM radio station call letters] ...... KFNN
Mesa, AZ [Television station call letters] ...... KPNX-TV
Mesa, AZ [FM radio station call letters] ...... KVRY

Mesa, AZ [AM radio station call letters] ...... KXAM
Mesa College, Grand Junction, CO [Library symbol Library of Congress]
(LCLS) ...... CoGjM
Mesa College, Grand Junction, CO [OCLC symbol] (OCLC) ...... COM
Mesa Community College, Mesa, AZ [Library symbol Library of Congress]
(LCLS) ...... AzMC
Mesa County Public Library, Grand Junction, CO [Library symbol Library of
Congress] (LCLS) ...... CoGj
Mesa, Inc. [Associated Press] (SAG) ...... MesaInc
Mesa, Inc. [NYSE symbol] (SAG) ...... MXP
Mesa Laboratories [NASDAQ symbol] (TTSB) ...... MLAB
Mesa Laboratories, Inc. [Associated Press] (SAG) ...... MesaLb
Mesa Laboratories, Inc. [NASDAQ symbol] (SAG) ...... MLAB
Mesa Lucera [New Mexico] [Seismograph station code, US Geological
Survey] (SEIS) ...... MLM
Mesa Public Library, Los Alamos, NM [OCLC symbol] (OCLC) ...... LAN
Mesa Public Library, Los Alamos, NM [Library symbol Library of Congress]
(LCLS) ...... NmLa
Mesa Public Library, Mesa, AZ [Library symbol Library of Congress]
(LCLS) ...... AzM
Mesa Public Library, Mesa, AZ [OCLC symbol] (OCLC) ...... MSA
Mesa Royalty Trust [Associated Press] (SAG) ...... MesaR
Mesa Royaty Tr UBI [NYSE symbol] (TTSB) ...... MTR
Mesa Verde Community Library, Mesa Verde National Park, CO [Library
symbol Library of Congress] (LCLS) ...... CoMes
Mesa Verde National Park ...... MEVE
Mesa View Elementary School Library, Grand Junction, CO [Library symbol
Library of Congress] (LCLS) ...... CoGjME
Mesaba Aviation [ICAO designator] (FAAC) ...... MES
Mesaba Aviation [ICAO designator] (AD) ...... XJ
Mesaba Holdings [NASDAQ symbol] (TTSB) ...... MAIR
Mesaba Holdings, Inc. [NASDAQ symbol] (SAG) ...... MAIR
Mesaba Holdings, Inc. [Associated Press] (SAG) ...... Mesaba
Mesaba Holdings, Inc. [Associated Press] (SAG) ...... MesabaH
Mesabi Community College, Virginia, MN [OCLC symbol] (OCLC) ...... MCV
Mesabi Community College, Virginia, MN [Library symbol Library of
Congress] (LCLS) ...... MnVM
Mesabi East High School, Aurora, MN [Library symbol] [Library of Congress]
(LCLS) ...... MnAurH
Mesabi Tr Ctfs SBI [NYSE symbol] (TTSB) ...... MSB
Mesabi Trust [Associated Press] (SAG) ...... Mesab
Mesabi Trust [NYSE symbol] (SAG) ...... MSB
Mesangial Proliferative Glomerulonephritis [Nephrology] (DMAA) ...... MesPGN
Mesangial Proliferative Glomerulonephritis [Nephrology] ...... MSPGN
Mesangiocapillary Glomerulonephritis [Medicine] (AAMN) ...... MCGN
Mesangioproliferative Glomerulonephritis [Nephrology] (DAVI) ...... MPGN
Mesangium [Anatomy] ...... M
Mescaline ...... MESC
Meschede/Schuren [Germany ICAO location identifier] (ICLI) ...... EDKM
Mesdames [Plural of Mrs.] [France] ...... MESD
Mesdames [Ladies] [French] ...... Mmes
Mesdemoiselles [Misses] [French] ...... Mlles
Mesencephalic [or Midbrain] Reticular Formation [Anatomy] ...... MRF
Mesenterial Arterial Pressure [Medicine] ...... MAP
Mesenteric Collateral [Cardiology] (DAVI) ...... MC
Mesenteric Node Lymphocyte ...... MNL
Mesenteric Traction [Medicine] ...... MT
Mesh ...... M
MeSH Heading [Online database field identifier] ...... MH
Mesh Level Control ...... MLC
Mesha Inscription (BJA) ...... MI
Meshed [Iran] [Airport symbol] (AD) ...... MHD
Meshgin Shahr [Iran] [ICAO location identifier] (ICLI) ...... OITN
Meshing ...... MSHG
Meshless Storage Display Tube ...... MSDT
Mesial [Dentistry] ...... M
Mesial, Occlusal, and Distal [Describes location of openings in a carious
tooth] [Dentistry] ...... MOD
Mesial Temporal Lobe Seizure [Medicine] ...... MTLS
Mesial-Occlusal-Distal [Dentistry] (AD) ...... m-o-d
Mesial-Occlusal-Distal [Dentistry] ...... mods
Mesial-Occlusal-Distal-Buccal [Dentistry] (AD) ...... m-o-d-b
Mesick Public Library, Mesick, MI [Library symbol Library of Congress]
(LCLS) ...... MiMes
Mesifta Tifereth Jerusalem (BJA) ...... MTJ
Mesilla Park, NM [FM radio station call letters] ...... KMVR
Mesiobuccal [Dentistry] ...... MB
Mesiobucco-Occlusal [Dentistry] ...... MBO
Mesiobuccopulpal [Dentistry] ...... MBP
Mesiocervical [Dentistry] ...... MC
Mesiodistal [Dentistry] ...... MD
Mesiogingival [Dentistry] ...... MG
Mesioincisal [Dentistry] ...... MI
Mesioincisodistal [Dentistry] ...... MID
Mesiolabial [Dentistry] ...... MLA
Mesiolabioincisal [Dentistry] ...... MLAI
Mesiolabioincisal [Medicine] (MEDA) ...... MLaI
Mesiolabiopulpal [Dentistry] ...... MLaP
Mesiolingual [Dentistry] ...... ML
Mesiolinguoincisal [Dentistry] ...... MLI
Mesiolinguo-Occlusal [Dentistry] ...... MLO
Mesiolinguopulpal [Dentistry] ...... MLP
Mesio-Occlusal [Dentistry] ...... MO
Mesiopulpal [Dentistry] ...... MP
Mesiopulpolabial [Dentistry] (MAE) ...... MPLa

Mesiopulpolingual [*Dentistry*] (MAE) .... MPL
Mesityl Oxide [*Also, MSO*] [*Organic chemistry*] .... MO
Mesityl Oxide [*Also, MO*] [*Organic chemistry*] .... MSO
Mesitylenesulfonyl Chloride [*Biochemistry*] .... MSC
(Mesitylenesulfonyl)nitroimidazole [*Organic chemistry*] .... MSNI
(Mesitylenesulfonyl)nitrotriazolide [*Biochemistry*] .... MSNT
Mesna, Ifosfamide, Mitoxantrone, Etoposide [*Antineoplastic drug*] (CDI) .... MINE
Meso American (VRA) .... MesoAm
Mesoamerican Archaeology Study Unit [*American Topical Association*] (EA) .... MASU
Mesoatrial Shunt [*Medicine*] (DMAA) .... MAS
Mesocale and Microscale Meteorology (GNE) .... MMM
Mesocaval Shunt [*Medicine*] (DMAA) .... MCS
Mesocyclone Detection Algorithm [*Marine science*] (OSRA) .... MDA
Mesocyclone Detection Algorithm (USDC) .... MDA
Mesoderm [*Botany*] .... Md
Mesoderm-Inducing Factor [*Embryology*] .... MIF
Meso-Inositol [*or Myoinositol*] [*Organic chemistry*] .... MI
Mesolithic (VRA) .... Mesol
Mesomeric [*Organic chemistry*] .... M
Meson Field Theory .... MFT
Mesophyll [*Botany*] .... M
Mesopotamia .... MESOP
Mesopotamia (VRA) .... Mesop
Mesopotamia (DSUE) .... MESPOT
Mesopotamian Expeditionary Force [*British*] .... MEF
Mesoscale Air Pollution Simulation Model [*Environmental Protection Agency*] (GFGA) .... MAPSIM
Mesoscale Analysis and Prediction System [*Marine science*] (OSRA) .... MAPS
Mesoscale Analysis and Prediction System (USDC) .... MAPS
Mesoscale Atmospheric Processes Research Program [*National Oceanic and Atmospheric Administration*] .... MAPRP
Mesoscale Convective Complex [*Meteorology*] .... MCC
Mesoscale Convective System [*Meteorology*] .... MCS
Mesoscale Convectively-Generated Vortices [*Marine science*] (OSRA) .... MCV
Mesoscale Convectively-Generated Vortices (USDC) .... MCV
Mesoscale Evolution Project-1991 (USDC) MEP-91
Mesoscale Evolution Project-1991 [*Marine science*] (OSRA) MEP-91
Mesoscale Meteorological Model-Version 4 [*Marine science*] (OSRA) MM4
Mesoscale Meteorological Model-Version 4 (USDC) MM4
Mesoscale Model (USDC) .... MM
Mesoscale Model [*Marine science*] (OSRA) .... MM
Mesoscale Model Version 5 [*Marine science*] [*Pennsylvania State University*] (OSRA) MM5
Mesoscale Research Division [*Marine science*] (OSRA) .... MRD
Mesoscale Research Division [*National Severe Storms Laboratory*] (USDC) .... MRD
Mesoscale Transport Diffusion and Deposition Model for Industrial Sources [*Environmental Protection Agency*] (GFGA) .... MTDDIS
Mesosphere-Stratosphere-Troposhere (USDC) .... MST
Mesosphere-Stratosphere-Troposphere [*Marine science*] (OSRA) .... MST
Mesothorium (AD) .... Ms
Mesothorium [*Radioelement*] .... MSTh
Mesotocin [*Endocrinology*] .... MT
Mesozoic [*Period, era, or system*] [*Geology*] .... MES
Mesquite Public Library, Mesquite, TX [*Library symbol Library of Congress*] (LCLS) .... TxMe
Mesquite, TX [*Location identifier FAA*] (FAAL) .... HUZ
Mesquite, TX [*FM radio station call letters*] .... KEOM
Mess Attendant .... M/A
Mess Call [*Military*] .... MC
Mess Corporal [*Marine Corps*] .... MESCPL
Mess Corporal [*Marine Corps*] .... MESSCPL
Mess Deck [*Naval*] .... MD
Mess Deck Master-at-Arms (DNAB) .... MDMAA
Mess Management Specialist, First Class [*Navy rating*] (DNAB) MS1
Mess Management Specialist, Second Class [*Navy rating*] (DNAB) MS2
Mess Management Specialist, Third Class [*Navy rating*] (DNAB) MS3
Mess Sergeant [*Marine Corps*] .... MESSSGT
Message (ABBR) .... MESGE
Message (ADA) .... MGE
Message (AFM) .... MSG
Message (IDOE) .... msg
Message .... MSSG
Message Acceptance Pulse [*Aerospace communications*] .... MAP
Message Access Method [*Honeywell, Inc.*] .... MAM
Message Act Concellation (DA) .... MAC
Message Assembler .... MA
Message Authentication Code .... MAC
Message Authenticity Check [*Computer science*] .... MAC
Message Buffer (ACRL) .... MB
Message Business .... MB
Message Center .... MC
Message Center .... MCTR
Message Center .... MSGCEN
Message Center [*Aviation*] (FAAC) .... MSGCTR
Message Change (MCD) .... MC
Message Competition Ratio (MAE) .... MCR
Message Composer [*Communications, data processing*] .... MC
Message Construction Unit .... MCU
Message Control Block [*Computer science*] (CET) .... MCB
Message Control Language [*Computer science*] .... MCL
Message Control Program [*Computer science*] .... MCP
Message Control Supervisor [*Computer science*] (MHDI) .... MCS
Message Control System [*Burroughs Corp.*] [*Computer science*] (BUR) .... MCS
Message Control Task [*Computer science*] .... MCT
Message Cryptographic Check Digits .... MCCD
Message Data .... MD
Message Data Exchange Terminal (MCD) .... MEDAX
Message Database (MCD) .... MDB
Message Decoder Unit .... MDU
Message Detail Recording [*Later, SMDR*] [*Telecommunications*] .... MDR
Message Digest (ACRL) .... MD
Message Digest Signature Block (HGAA) .... MDSB
Message Direction Table (MCD) .... MDT
Message Discrimination Process [*Telecommunications*] (TEL) .... MDP
Message Display Console (MCD) .... MDC
Message Display Terminal (MCD) .... MDT
Message Distribution Center (NATG) .... MDC
Message Distribution Systems .... MDS
Message Diversion Relay System (IAA) .... MEDIS
Message Editing and Processing System (MCD) .... MEPS
Message Electronic Switching Computer (IAA) .... MESCO
Message Element [*Telecommunications*] (TEL) .... ME
Message Encoder Unit .... MEU
Message Entry Device .... MED
Message Entry Generator (NVT) .... MEG
Message Entry System (MCD) .... MES
Message Exchange Terminal .... MXT
Message Expediting Group (IEEE) .... MEG
Message Field [*Computer science*] .... MFLD
Message Flag [*Computer science*] (MHDI) .... MSGFLG
Message Flow Graph .... MFG
Message Form (MUGU) .... MSGFM
Message Format (ECII) .... MF
Message Format Designator .... MFD
Message Format Service .... MFS
Message from Base .... MFB
Message from Multiple Media Maximizes [*Communications*] (WDMC) M4
Message Generator .... MG
Message Generator (MSA) .... MSGG
Message Handler [*Computer science*] .... MH
Message Handling Processor .... MHP
Message Handling Service [*Telecommunications*] (PCM) .... MHS
Message Handling System [*Computer science*] .... MHS
Message Handling System Service (NITA) .... MHSS
Message Has Been Misrouted [*Communications*] .... MSR
Message Header Generator (PDAA) .... MHG
Message Identification [*Computer science*] .... MID
Message Identification Code [*Computer science*] (BUR) .... MIC
Message Identifier (ACRL) .... MID
Message Identifier .... MSGID
Message Input Description .... MID
Message Input Device (AABC) .... MID
Message Input Module [*Telecommunications*] (TEL) .... MIM
Message Input Processor .... MIP
Message Input-Output Devices (MCD) .... MIOD
Message Interchange Distributed Application [*Telecommunications*] (OSI) .... MIDA
Message Interface Unit (CAAL) .... MIU
Message Level Interface (NITA) .... MLI
Message Level Interface Port (NITA) .... MLIP
Message Multiplexer Operating System .... MMOS
Message of Operational Intent (NVT) .... MOI
Message Oriented Text Interchange [*Telecommunications*] (OSI) .... MOTI
Message Oriented Text Interchange System [*Telecommunications*] (OSI) .... MOTIS
Message Output Description [*Computer science*] .... MOD
Message Output Module [*Telecommunications*] (TEL) .... MOM
Message Output Processing .... MOP
Message Passing Interface [*Software program conducted at Mississippi State University*] .... MPI
Message Passing Interface Forum [*Marine science*] (OSRA) .... MPIF
Message Passing Interface Forum (USDC) .... MPIF
Message Pattern Indicator .... MPI
Message Picking-Up .... MPU
Message Processing and Distributing System [*Navy*] (NVT) .... MPDS
Message Processing Center .... MPC
Message Processing Interactive (MCD) .... MPI
Message Processing Interrupt Count .... MPIC
Message Processing Language [*Burroughs Corp.*] .... MPL
Message Processing Language [*Computer science*] (AD) .... mpl
Message Processing Modules (MCD) .... MPM
Message Processing Program [*Computer science*] .... MPP
Message Processing Region [*IBM Corp.*] .... MPR
Message Processing System (NVT) .... MPS
Message Processing Systems, Inc. [*Charlotte, NC*] [*Telecommunications service*] (TSSD) .... MPSI
Message Processing Task [*Computer science*] (ECII) .... MPT
Message Processor .... MP
Message Protocol Data Unit [*Telecommunications*] (OSI) .... MPDU
Message Queue Element [*Computer science*] .... MQE
Message Queue Manager [*Computer science*] (MCD) .... MQM
Message Ready [*Computer science*] (MHDI) .... MRDY
Message Refusal [*Telecommunications*] (TEL) .... MRF
Message Register (AAG) .... MR
Message Releasing Officer .... MRO
Message Repeat .... MR
Message Reproduction and Distribution System [*Military*] (CAAL) .... MRDIS
Message Reproduction and Distribution System [*Military*] (MCD) .... MRDS

Message Retransmission Unit .... MRU
Message Review Officer (MCD) .... MRO
Message Routing Process [Telecommunications] (TEL) .... MRP
Message Sequence Chart [Telecommunications] (TEL) .... MSC
Message Sequence Number (CAAL) .... MSN
Message Status Table (MCD) .... MST
Message Store [Telecommunications] (OSI) .... MS
Message Support Subsystem (MCD) .... MSS
Message Switched Line (MCD) .... MSL
Message Switching [Telecommunications] (IAA) .... MS
Message Switching Center [Telecommunications] .... MSC
Message Switching Computer [Telecommunications] (TEL) .... MSC
Message Switching Concentration .... MSC
Message Switching Data Service .... MSDS
Message Switching Station [Telecommunications] (CET) .... MSS
Message Switching System .... MSS
Message Switching Unit .... MSU
Message Table [Computer science] (OA) .... MT
Message Table of Contents (MCD) .... MTC
Message Telecommunications Service .... MTS
Message Telephone Service (NITA) .... MTS
Message Terminal Area (MCD) .... MTA
Message Terminal Operation [Military] (CAAL) .... MTO
Message Text Formatting .... MTF
Message Text Formatting Reporting .... MTFR
Message to Base .... MTB
Message Toll Service [Communications] .... MTS
Message Traffic Study .... MTS
Message Transfer Agent [Telecommunications] (PCM) .... MTA
Message Transfer Agent Entity [Telecommunications] (OSI) .... MTAE
Message Transfer Facility [Telecommunications] (OSI) .... MTF
Message Transfer Layer [Telecommunications] (OSI) .... MTL
Message Transfer Protocol [Telecommunications] (OSI) .... MTP
Message Transfer Service .... MTS
Message Transfer Sublayer [Telecommunications] (OSI) .... MTSL
Message Transfer System [Telecommunications] (OSI) .... MTS
Message Transfer Time (NITA) .... MTT
Message Transmission Controller .... MTC
Message Transmission Part [Telecommunications] (TEL) .... MTP
Message Transmission Subsystem [Telecommunications] (TEL) .... MTS
Message Transport Agent [Telecommunications] (PCM) .... MTA
Message Unit [Telecommunications] .... MU
Message User Service Transcriber (IAA) .... MUST
Message Waiting (MDG) .... MSG/WTG
Message Waiting .... MW
Message check (EA) .... MC
Message-Drop and Pick-Up [Military] (IAA) .... MSGDPU
Message-Dropping [Military] .... MD
Message-Dropping Station [Military] (IAA) .... MDS
Message-Oriented Middleware [Computer science] .... MOM
Messageries Maritimes [Forwarding agents] [French] .... MM
Messages of the Bible [A publication] .... MB
Messages per Day .... MD
Message-Waiting Indicator .... MWI
Messaging API [Application Programming Interface] [Computer science] .... MAPI
Messenger (ABBR) .... MESGER
Messenger (MSA) .... MESS
Messenger (AFM) .... MSGR
Messenger (ADA) .... MSNGR
Messenger Courier Association of America (EA) .... MCAA
Messenger Transport Organizer [Developmental biology] .... METRO
Messensch Afteliche Autonome Experiment Unter Schewerelosigkeit .... MAUS
Messerschmitt [German fighter aircraft] (DSUE) .... MESS
Messerschmitt [German fighter aircraft] (DSUE) .... MESSER
Messerschmitt AG [Germany ICAO aircraft manufacturer identifier] (ICAO) .... ME
Messerschmitt Owners Club (EA) .... MOC
Messerschmitt-Boelkow-Blohm [Germany ICAO aircraft manufacturer identifier] (ICAO) .... HF
Messerschmitt-Boelkow-Blohm GmbH [West German aircraft company] .... MBB
Messiah College, Grantham, PA [Library symbol Library of Congress] (LCLS) .... PGraM
Messiah College Learning Center, Grantham, PA [OCLC symbol] (OCLC) .... PGM
Messianic Jewish Alliance of America (EA) .... MJAA
Messianic Jewish Movement International (EA) .... MJMI
[A] Messianic Jewish Perspective (EA) .... AMJP
Messies Anonymous [Commercial firm] (EA) .... MA
Messieurs [Plural of Mister] [French] .... MESSRS
Messieurs [Plural of Mister] [French] .... MM
Messina [South Africa] [ICAO location identifier] (ICLI) .... FAMS
Messina [Italy ICAO location identifier] (ICLI) .... LICF
Messina [Italy] [Seismograph station code, US Geological Survey] (SEIS) .... MES
Messina ING [Istituto Nazionale Geodetico] [Sicily] [Seismograph station code, US Geological Survey] (SEIS) .... MSI
Messing Allowance [British military] (DMA) .... MA
Messinian Benevolent Association "Aristomenis" (EA) .... MBAA
Messman .... MSM
Messtechnik, Regelungstechnik, Automatik [Hoppenstedt Wirtschaftsdatenbank GmbH] [Germany Information service or system] (CRD) .... MRA
Messtetten [Federal Republic of Germany] [Seismograph station code, US Geological Survey] (SEIS) .... MSS
Messuage (ROG) .... MESSE
Mestek, Inc. [NYSE symbol] (SPSG) .... MCC
Mestek, Inc. [Associated Press] (SAG) .... Mestek
Mesters Vig [Greenland] [ICAO location identifier] (ICLI) .... BGMV

Mesters Vig [Greenland] [Airport symbol] (AD) .... MRG
Mestizo (ABBR) .... MEST
Mestome Sheath [Botany] .... MS
Meston Lake Resources, Inc. [Toronto Stock Exchange symbol Vancouver Stock Exchange symbol] .... MLR
Mesyl [Organic chemistry] .... Ms
Mesylate [Organic chemistry] .... MES
Met Coil Systems Corp. [Associated Press] (SAG) .... MetCoil
MET Databank [ICAO designator] (ICDA) .... YZ
Meta [Chemistry] .... m
Meta Assembly Language .... MAL
Meta Aviotransport-Macedonia [Yugoslavia] [ICAO designator] (FAAC) .... MAM
Meta Biosystems [NASDAQ symbol] (SAG) .... MTRA
Meta Communications Group, Inc. [Toronto Stock Exchange symbol] .... MTA
Meta Content File [Netscape] [Computer science] .... MCF
META Group [NASDAQ symbol] (TTSB) .... METG
Meta Group, Inc. [Associated Press] (SAG) .... MetaGp
Meta Group, Inc. [NASDAQ symbol] (SAG) .... METG
Meta LISP [List Processor] [Programming language] [Computer science] (CSR) .... MLISP
Meta Postprocessor [Software program] [Symbolic Control, Inc.] .... MPP
Meta-Aminobenzoic Acid [Organic chemistry] .... MABA
Meta-Aminophenol [Organic chemistry] .... MAP
Meta-Aminopyrimethamine [Biochemistry] .... MAP
Meta-Assembler (NITA) .... MASM
Meta-Assembler Language [Sperry UNIVAC computer language] .... MASM
Meta-Azidopyrimethamine [Biochemistry] .... MZP
Metabaru [Japan ICAO location identifier] (ICLI) .... RJDM
Metabisulfite [Inorganic chemistry] .... MB
Metabolic (ABBR) .... METABC
Metabolic Activity .... MA
Metabolic Analyzer .... MA
Metabolic and Analytical Chemistry .... MAC
Metabolic and Electrolyte Disorders [Medicine] (MEDA) .... ME
Metabolic Clearance Rate .... MCR
Metabolic Control Theory [Biochemistry] .... MCT
Metabolic Coronary Dilation [Medicine] (AAMN) .... MCD
Metabolic Equivalent [Medicine] .... MET
Metabolic Equivalent Level [Medicine] .... MEL
Metabolic Fecal Nitrogen (PDAA) .... MFN
Metabolic Heat Load Simulator .... MHLS
Metabolic Heat Production [Physiology] .... MHP
Metabolic Index .... MI
Metabolic Laboratory [Colorado State University] (RCD) .... Met Lab
Metabolic Loss [Physiology] .... ML
Metabolic Measurement Cart [Beckman Instruments, Inc.] .... MMC
Metabolic Monitoring System .... MMS
Metabolic Profile 1 [Biochemistry] (DAVI) .... META 1
Metabolic Rate .... MR
Metabolic Rate (AD) .... mr
Metabolic Rate Measuring System .... MRMS
Metabolic Rate Monitor [Trademark] .... MRM
Metabolic Toxemia of Late Pregnancy [Medicine] .... MTLP
Metabolic Waste Production .... MWP
Metabolism .... METAB
Metabolism and Radiation Research Laboratory [North Dakota State University] [Research center] (RCD) .... MRRL
Metabolite .... M
Metabolizable Energy .... ME
Metabolize (ABBR) .... METABZ
Metabolized (ABBR) .... METABZD
Metabolizing (ABBR) .... METABZG
Metacaine Methanesulfonate [Local anesthetic] .... MMS
Metacarpal [or Metacarpus] [Anatomy] .... MC
Metacarpal [Anatomy] (DAVI) .... meta
Metacarpal Ash per Centimeter .... MAC
Metacarpal Cortical Density [Anatomy] .... MCD
Metacarpal Total Density [Anatomy] .... MTD
Metacarpophalangeal [Anatomy] .... MCP
Metacarpophalangeal [Anatomy] .... MCPH
Metacarpophalangeal [Anatomy] .... MP
Metacarpophalangeal Joint [Anatomy] .... MPJ
Metacenter .... M
Metacentric Height [Naval architecture] .... GM
Metacerebral Cell [Neurobiology] .... MCC
Metacerebral Giant Cell [Cytology] .... MGC
Meta-Chloroperoxybenzoic Acid [Organic chemistry] .... MCPBA
Meta-Chlorophenylpiperazine [Biochemistry] .... MCCP
Meta-Chlorotoluene [Organic chemistry] .... MCT
Metachromatic Leukodystrophy [Medicine] .... MLD
Metachrondral Wave [Physiology] .... MW
Metaclad Corp. [Associated Press] (SAG) .... MetalCld
Meta-Cresol Purple [Organic chemistry] .... MCP
Metacyclic Variant Antigen Type [Immunology] .... MVAT
Meta-Dinitrobenzene [Organic chemistry] .... MDNB
Meta-Iodobenzylguanidine [Biochemistry] .... MIBG
Metal .... M
Metal [or Metallic] (AAG) .... MET
Metal .... METL
Metal .... METL
Metal (AAG) .... MTL
Metal Abstracts Index Data Base [Bibliographic database] [British] (IID) .... METADEX
Metal Alkyl Vapor-Phase Epitaxy [Semiconductor technology] .... MAVPE
Metal Alloy Separation Unit .... MASU

Metal Anchor (AAG) ... MA
Metal Anchor Slots [*Technical drawings*] ... MAS
Metal Arc Cutting [*Welding*] ... MAC
Metal Awning Type Window ... MATW
Metal Base ... METB
Metal Belt Institute [*Defunct*] (EA) ... MBI
Metal Bond Tape ... MBT
Metal Box [*Commercial firm British*] ... MB
Metal Building Component Manufacturers' Association (EA) ... MBCMA
Metal Building Dealers Association [*Later, Systems Builders Association*] (EA) ... MBDA
Metal Building Manufacturers Association (EA) ... MBMA
Metal Building News [*A publication*] (APTA) ... MBN
Metal Bulletin Research [*Commercial firm British*] (ECON) ... MBR
Metal Carbide ... MC
Metal Case [*Bullet*] (DICI) ... MC
Metal Case Profile [*Ammunition*] ... MCP
Metal Casement Window [*Technical drawings*] ... MCW
Metal Casting Pattern (MSA) ... MCP
Metal Catalyzed Oxidation [*Chemistry*] ... MCO
Metal Clad (IAA) ... MC
Metal Construction Association (EA) ... MCA
Metal Cookware Manufacturers Association [*Later, CMA*] (EA) ... MCMA
Metal Corner Bead [*Technical drawings*] ... MCB
Metal Crystal Lattice ... MCL
Metal Curb (AAG) ... METC
Metal Cutting Knife Association (EA) ... MCKA
Metal Cutting Tool Institute (EA) ... MCTI
Metal Deactivator ... MD
Metal Deactivator [*Fuel technology*] ... MDA
Metal Density Gauge ... MDG
Metal Disintegration Machining [*Nuclear energy*] (NRCH) ... MDM
Metal Dome [*Watchmaking*] (ROG) ... MD
Metal Door ... METD
Metal Edge Amplifier (MCD) ... MEA
Metal Electrode Face Bonding (IAA) ... MELF
Metal Etch Resist ... MER
Metal Etching and Fabricating Association [*Later, National Association of Name Plate Manufacturers*] (EA) ... MEFA
Metal Evaporated [*Videotape*] ... ME
Metal Evaporated Resistor ... MER
Metal Fabricating Institute (EA) ... MFI
Metal Factor [*Geophysical measurement*] ... MF
Metal Film Resistor ... MFT
Metal Findings Manufacturers Association (EA) ... MFMA
Metal Finishing Association [*British*] (DBA) ... MFA
Metal Finishing Suppliers' Association (EA) ... MFSA
Metal Flashing ... METF
Metal Floor Deck [*Technical drawings*] ... MFD
Metal Framing Manufacturers Association (EA) ... MFMA
Metal Furring [*Technical drawings*] ... MTFR
Metal Glass (IAA) ... MG
Metal Glaze Resistor ... MGR
Metal Goods [*Department of Employment*] [*British*] ... MG
Metal Goods Not Elsewhere Specified [*Department of Employment*] [*British*] ... MGNES
Metal Grating Institute [*Defunct*] ... MGI
Metal Gravel Stop ... MGS
Metal Grill ... METG
Metal Halide (MCD) ... MH
Metal Impact Monitoring System [*Nuclear energy*] (NRCH) ... MIMS
Metal Injection Molding [*Metal fabrication*] ... MIM
Metal Insulated Structure ... MIS
Metal Insulator Junction ... MIJ
Metal Insulator Metal [*Light detector*] ... MIM
Metal Insulator - Metal Junction ... MIMJ
Metal Insulator Silicon Field-Effect Transistor [*Also, MISFET*] (EECA) ... MIST
Metal Interconnect Cascade Cell [*Photovoltaic energy systems*] ... MICC
Metal Interface Amplifier ... MIA
Metal Ion Liquid Chromatography ... MILC
Metal Jalousie ... METJ
Metal Ladder Manufacturers Association (EA) ... MLMA
Metal Lath and Plaster [*Technical drawings*] ... MLP
Metal Lath Association [*Later, ML/SFA*] (EA) ... MLA
Metal Lath Manufacturers Association [*Later, ML/SFA*] ... MLMA
Metal Lath/Steel Framing Association Division of National Association of Architectural Metal Manufactureres (EA) ... ML/SFA
Metal Management [*NASDAQ symbol*] (TTSB) ... MTLM
Metal Manufacture [*Department of Employment*] [*British*] ... MM
Metal Matrix Composite Analyzer [*Organic chemistry*] ... METCAN
Metal Matrix Composites Information Analysis Center [*DoD Information service or system*] (IID) ... MMCIAC
Metal Mold ... METM
Metal Mount ... MMT
Metal Nonmetal [*Materials science*] ... MNM
Metal or Plastic (AAG) ... M-P
Metal Oxide Film (AD) ... mof
Metal Oxide on a Substrate (MCD) ... MOS
Metal Oxide Semiconductor Analogue Shift Register [*Electronics*] (PDAA) ... MOSASR
Metal Oxide Semiconductor Field Effect Transformer (NITA) ... MOSFET
Metal Oxide Silicon/Large Scale Integration [*Electronics*] ... MOS/LSI
Metal Oxide Substrate Field Effect Transistor ... MOSFETS
Metal Oxide Threshold Switches (MCD) ... MOTS
Metal Packaging Manufacturers Association [*British*] (DBA) ... MPMA
Metal Partition ... METP
Metal Parts (AABC) ... MPTS
Metal Parts Furnace (MCD) ... MPF
Metal Polishers, Buffers, Platers, and Allied Workers International Union (EA) ... MPBP
Metal Portion ... METP
Metal Powder Association [*Later, MPIF*] ... MPA
Metal Powder Industries Federation ... MPI
Metal Powder Industries Federation (EA) ... MPIF
Metal Powder Producers Association (EA) ... MPPA
Metal RADAR ... METRA
Metal Regulatory Element [*Genetics*] ... MRE
Metal Regulatory Factor [*Genetics*] ... MRF
Metal Removal Rate ... MRR
Metal Re-Radiation RADAR [*Mine detection system*] [*Army*] (RDA) ... METRRA
Metal Rolling Door [*Technical drawings*] ... MRD
Metal Rolling Door (AD) ... mrd
Metal Roof ... METR
Metal Roof Deck [*Technical drawings*] ... MRD
Metal Roof Deck (AD) ... mrd
Metal Roof Deck Technical Institute [*Later, Steel Deck Institute*] (EA) ... MRDTI
Metal Schottky Gate Field Effect Transistor [*Electronics*] (IAA) ... MSFET
Metal Seal Ring ... MSR
Metal Sensor Detection ... MSD
Metal Shank (AD) ... m/s
Metal Shielded Cabinet ... MSC
Metal Sink Manufacturers Association [*British*] (DBA) ... MSMA
Metal Slitting ... MLS
Metal Space-Frame (MCD) ... MSF
Metal Splash Pan (AAG) ... MSP
Metal Spring Seal ... MSS
Metal Stamping ... MS
Metal Strip ... METS
Metal Support Interaction [*Catalysis*] ... MSI
Metal Threshold (AAG) ... MT
Metal Thru-Wall Flashing [*Technical drawings*] ... MTWF
Metal Trades Department, AFL-CIO [*American Federation of Labor and Congress of Industrial Organizations*] (EA) ... MTD
Metal Trades Employers Association (NADA) ... MTEA
Metal Trades Federation (NADA) ... MTF
Metal Trades Industry Association (NADA) ... MTIA
Metal Trades Industry Association of Australia ... MTIAA
Metal Trades Journal [*A publication*] ... Met Tr J
Metal Treating Institute (EA) ... MTI
Metal Tube Packaging Council of North America [*Later, TCNA*] (EA) ... MTPC
Metal Tube Packaging Council of North America [*Later, TCNA*] ... MTPCNA
Metal/Tunnelling-Nitride Polysilicon Gate FET (NITA) ... MTP FET
Metal Vapor LASER ... MVL
Metal Vapour Synthesis [*Chemistry*] ... MVS
Metal Ventilator Institute (EA) ... MVI
Metal Whisker Reinforcement ... MWR
Metal-Alumina Semiconductor (IAA) ... MAS
Metal-Alumina-Oxide Semiconductor [*Computer science*] (IAA) ... MAOS
Metal-Alumina-Silicon (IEEE) ... MAS
Metal-Alumina-Silicon Field Effect Transistor (IAA) ... MASFET
Metal-Aluminum-Oxide Silicon (MSA) ... MAOS
Metalanguage Symbol ... METASYMBOL
Metal-Barrier-Metal (IEEE) ... MBM
Metal-Base Transistor [*Electronics*] (IEEE) ... MBT
Metal-Ceramic Transmitting Tube ... MCTT
Metalclad Corp. [*Associated Press*] (SAG) ... Metalcld
Metalclad Corp. [*NASDAQ symbol*] (SAG) ... MTLC
Metal-Covered Door [*Technical drawings*] ... MCD
Metal-Dielectric Semiconductor [*Electronics*] (PDAA) ... MDS
Metal-Dielectric-Metal [*Filter*] ... MDM
Metal-Dielectric-Semiconductor Integrated Circuit [*Electronics*] (PDAA) ... MDSIC
Metal-Engraver [*MARC relator code*] [*Library of Congress*] (LCCP) ... mte
Metal-Finishing Category (GNE) ... MFC
Metal-Finishing Industy ... MFI
Metalforming Machinery Makers Association [*British*] (DBA) ... MMMA
Metalgesellschaft Canada Investment [*Toronto Stock Exchange symbol*] ... MLG
Metal-Glass-Oxide-Silicon (PDAA) ... MGOS
Metal-Hydrogen-Metal [*Chemical bond*] ... MHM
Metal-Inert-Gas [*Underwater welding*] ... MIG
Metaling Clause [*Marine insurance*] ... MC
Metal-Insulator-Semiconductor (MCD) ... MIS
Metal-Insulator-Semiconductor Field-Effect Transistor ... MISFET
Metal-Insulator-Semiconductor Insulator Metal (MCD) ... MISIM
Metal-Insulator-Semiconductor Inversion Layer [*Photovoltaic energy systems*] ... MIS/IL
Metal-Insulator-Semiconductor Metal (MCD) ... MISM
Metall Mining Corp. [*Toronto Stock Exchange symbol*] ... MLM
Metallgesellschaft [*German commodities and futures contractor*] (ECON) ... MG
Metallgesellschaft Refining & Marketing [*American subsidiary of the German commodities and futures contractor*] (ECON) ... MGRM
Metallic [*Automotive advertising*] ... MET
Metallic [*Referring to breath sounds*] [*Medicine*] (DAVI) ... met
Metallic ... METLC
Metallic (MSA) ... MTLC
Metallic Currency (ROG) ... M/C
Metallic Facility Terminal [*Telecommunications*] (TEL) ... MFT
Metallic Film ... MF
Metallic Foreign Body ... MFB
Metallic Link Belt (AABC) ... MLB
Metallic Nitrogen-Oxide Semiconductor (AD) ... mnos

Metallic Yarns Institute [*Defunct*] ... MYI
Metallica Resources, Inc. [*Associated Press*] (SAG) ... MetalR
Metallica Resources, Inc. [*NASDAQ symbol*] (SAG) ... METL
Metallic-Longitudinal (IEEE) ... M-L
Metal-Liquid-Insulator Semiconductor [*Electronics*] (PDAA) ... MLIS
Metallize (MSA) ... MTLZ
Metallized Glass Coil ... MGC
Metallizing ... MTLNG
Metallo-Carbohedrene [*Organic chemistry*] ... MET-CAR
Metallography (DGA) ... METALLOG
Metallo-Organic Deposition [*Materials technology*] ... MOD
Metallo-Organic LASER ... MOL
Metallo-Organic Liquid LASER ... MOLL
Metallo-Organic Liquid LASER (AD) ... moll
Metallo-Organic Molecular Beam Epitaxy [*Solid state physics*] ... MOMBE
Metallo-Organic Petroleum-Based Coating [*Materials science*] ... MOPB
Metallophthalocyanine [*Organic chemistry*] ... MPc
Metallothionein [*Biochemistry*] ... MT
Metallothionein-Human Growth Hormone [*Endocrinology*] ... MThGH
Metallurgical ... MET
Metallurgical ... METLLRGCL
Metallurgical and Thermochemical Data Service [*Department of Trade and Industry*] [*Information service or system*] (IID) ... MTDS
Metallurgical Engineer ... Met E
Metallurgical Engineering (DD) ... MetEng
Metallurgical Grade ... MG
Metallurgical Laboratory, Falconbridge Nickel Mines Ltd., Thornhill, Ontario [*Library symbol National Library of Canada*] (NLC) ... OTHORF
Metallurgical Plantmakers Federation (AD) ... MPF
Metallurgical Quenching Dilatometry ... MQD
Metallurgical Research Library, Falconbridge Nickel Mines Ltd., Falconbridge, Ontario [*Library symbol National Library of Canada*] (NLC) ... OFAF
[*The*] **Metallurgical Society** [*Later, TMS*] ... MS
Metallurgical Society (NADA) ... MS
Metallurgist ... METLLRGST
Metallurgistes Unis d'Amerique [*United Steelworkers of America*] (EAIO) ... MA
Metallurgistes Unis d'Amerique [*United Steelworkers of America - USWA*] ... MUA
Metallurgy ... METAL
Metallurgy ... METALL
Metallurgy ... MTLGY
[*The*] **Metallurgy Society** [*Formerly, MS*] (IAA) ... TMS
Metal-Matrix Composite ... MMC
Metal-Metal Laminate ... MML
Metal-Nitride Oxide Semiconductor / Silicon-on-Sapphire ... MNOS/SOS
Metal-Nitride-Oxide Silicon [*or Semiconductor*] ... MNOS
Metal-Nitride-Oxide-Semiconductor Field-Effect Transistor ... MNOSFET
Metal-Nitride-Semiconductor (AD) ... mns
Metal-on-Silicon Field-Effect Transistor [*Electronics*] (IAA) ... MSFET
Metalore Resources Ltd. [*Toronto Stock Exchange symbol*] ... MET
Metal-Organic Chemical Vapor Deposition [*Also, MO-VPE, OM-CVD, OM-VPE*] [*Semiconductor technology*] ... MO-CVD
Metal-Organic Vapor Phase Epitaxy [*Also, MO-CVD, OM-CVD, OM-VPE*] [*Semiconductor technology*] ... MO-VPE
Metal-Oxide Film ... MOF
Metal-Oxide Metal (MCD) ... MOM
Metal-Oxide Semiconductor ... MOS
Metal-Oxide Semiconductor (AD) ... mos
Metal-Oxide Semiconductor Field-Effect Transistor (AD) ... mosfet
Metal-Oxide Semiconductor Random-Access Memory (EECA) ... MOSRAM
Metal-Oxide Semiconductor Read-Only Memory (MHDB) ... MOS ROM
Metal-Oxide Semiconductor Transistor (AD) ... most
Metal-Oxide Semiconductor Transistor Logic (AD) ... mostl
Metal-Oxide Semimetal (IEEE) ... MOSM
Metal-Oxide Silicon (AD) ... mos
Metal-Oxide Varistor ... MOV
Metal-Oxide-Semiconductor Advanced Integrated Circuit [*Electronics*] (IEEE) ... MOSAIC
Metal-Oxide-Semiconductor [*or Silicon*] **Field-Effect Transistor** ... MOSFET
Metal-Oxide-Semiconductor Integrated Circuit (AD) ... mosic
Metal-Oxide-Semiconductor Transistor ... MOST
Metal-Oxide-Semiconductor Transistor Logic (CET) ... MOSTL
Metal-Oxide-Silicon [*Integrated circuit*] [*Electronics*] ... MOS
Metal-Oxide-Silicon Field-Effect Transistor (IDOE) ... MOSFET
Metal-Oxide-Silicon Read-Only Memory (IDOE) ... MOSROM
Metal-Oxide-Silicon Transistor (IDOE) ... MOST
Metal-Oxygen Cluster Compounds [*Chemistry*] ... MOCC
Metal-Phthalocyanine Tetramine [*Organic chemistry*] ... MPT
Metal-Plastic Metal [*Automotive engineering*] ... MPM
Metalpoint (VRA) ... metpt
Metal-Point (AD) ... m-p
Metal-Powder [*Videotape*] ... MP
Metal-Responsive Element [*Genetics*] ... MRE
Metals Abstracts Inex (NITA) ... METADEX
Metals and Ceramics Division [*Air Force*] ... MCD
Metals and Ceramics Information Center [*Battelle Memorial Institute*] [*DoD Information service or system*] (IID) ... MCIC
Metals and Minerals Research Services [*British*] ... M & M
Metals and Minerals Shippers Association of Australia ... MMSAA
Metals Crystallographic Data File [*Canada Institute for Scientific and Technical Information*] [*Information service or system*] (CRD) ... CRYSTMET
Metals Data File/1 (NITA) ... MDF/1
Metals Datafile [*Materials Information*] [*Information service or system*] (IID) ... MDF
Metals Disintegrating ... MD
Metals Engineering Institute (EA) ... MEI
Metals Information Analysis Center (IID) ... MIAC
Metals Processing Laboratory [*MIT*] (MCD) ... MPL
Metals Removal System [*Petroleum refining*] ... MRS
Metals Research and Development Foundation [*Defunct*] (EA) ... MRDF
Metals Reserve Board [*of the Reconstruction Finance Corp.*] ... MRB
Metals Reserve Co. [*World War II*] ... MRC
Metals Society [*Later, IOM*] (EAIO) ... MS
Metals-Based Engineering ... MBE
Metals-Based Engineering Program ... MBEP
Metal-Semiconductor Field-Effect Transistor ... MESFET
Metal-Semiconductor-Metal (IEEE) ... MSM
Metal-Skinned, Paper-Honeycomb Cored (PDAA) ... MPHC
Metalsmith [*Navy*] ... M
Metalsmith [*Navy*] ... ME
Metalsmith [*Navy*] ... MSMTH
Metalsmith, Ship Repair [*Navy*] ... MSR
Metalsmith, Ship Repair, Blacksmith [*Navy*] ... MSRB
Metalsmith, Ship Repair, Coppersmith [*Navy*] ... MSRC
Metalsmith, Ship Repair, Forger-Anglesmith [*Navy*] ... MSRF
Metalsmith, Ship Repair, Sheet Metal Worker [*Navy*] ... MSRS
Metal-Thick Nitride Semiconductor (IAA) ... MTNS
Metal-Thick Nitride-Silicon (IAA) ... MTNS
Metal-Thick Oxide Semiconductor (IAA) ... MTOS
Metal-Thick Oxide Semiconductor Field Effect Transistor (IAA) ... MTOSFET
Metal-Thick Oxide-Nitride-Silicon ... MTNS
Metal-Thick Oxide-Nitride-Silicon (MSA) ... MTONS
Metal-Thick Oxide-Silicon ... MTOS
Metal-to-Glass Seal ... MTGS
Metal-to-Insulator [*Transition*] ... MI
Metal-to-Ligand Charge Transfer [*Physical chemistry*] ... MLCT
Metal-to-Metal Charge Transfer [*Physical chemistry*] ... MMCT
Metal-to-Metal Seal ... MTMS
Metalwork (VRA) ... metwk
Metalworker [*British military*] (DMA) ... MW
Metalworking Fair Trade Coalition [*Later, MTC*] (EA) ... MFTC
Metal-Working Machine and Robot ... MWM & R
Metal-Working Machine Tool ... MWMT
Metalworking Processes and Equipment Program ... MPEP
Metalworking under Pressure (PDAA) ... MUP
Meta-Methoxyhydroquinone [*Organic chemistry*] ... MMHQ
Metamorphic Core Complex [*Geology*] ... MCC
Metamorphoses [*of Apuleius*] [*Classical studies*] (OCD) ... Met
Metamorphoses [*of Ovid*] [*Classical studies*] (OCD) ... Met
Metamorphosis [*Phylogeny*] ... M
Metamorphosizing [*Video technology*] ... Morphing
metamyelocyte [*Hematology*] (DAVI) ... META
Metanephrine [*Medicine*] (DMAA) ... MN
Meta-Nitride Semiconductor (MCD) ... MNS
Meta-Nitroaniline [*Organic chemistry*] ... MNA
Meta-Nitrobenzenediazonium Tetrafluoroborate [*Organic chemistry*] ... MNBDF
Meta-Nitro-para-toluidine [*Organic chemistry*] ... MNPT
Meta-Nitrophenol [*Organic chemistry*] ... MNP
Metaphenoxylene [*Analytical chemistry*] ... MPE
Meta-Phenylenediamine [*Organic chemistry*] ... MPD
Metaphloem Sieve Element [*Botany*] ... MSE
Metaphor ... MET
Metaphorical (ROG) ... METAPH
Metaphors Dictionary [*A publication*] ... MD
Metaphyseal Chondrodysplasia [*Medicine*] ... MCD
Metaphysic (ABBR) ... METAPHYS
Metaphysica [*of Aristotle*] [*Classical studies*] (OCD) ... Metaph
Metaphysical [*or Metaphysics*] (ROG) ... METAPH
Metaphysical Magazine [*A publication*] (ROG) ... META M
Metaphysical Society of America (EA) ... MSA
Metaphysician (ABBR) ... METAPH
Metaphysics ... MET
Metaphysics [*Parapsychology*] (DAVI) ... metaph
Metaproterenol [*Pharmacology*] ... M
Metarrithmistikon Komma [*Reformist Party*] [*Greece*] [*Political party*] (PPE) ... MK
MetaScience Foundation (EA) ... MSF
Meta-Software [*NASDAQ symbol*] (TTSB) ... MESW
Meta-Software, Inc. [*NASDAQ symbol*] (SAG) ... MESW
Meta-Software, Inc. [*Associated Press*] (SAG) ... MetaSft
Metastable Atomic State ... MAS
Metastable Electron Emission Microscopy ... MEEM
Metastable Helium (MCD) ... MSH
Metastable Helium Level ... MHL
Metastable Metal Surface [*Catalyst science*] ... MMS
Metastable Reaction Monitoring [*Analytical chemistry*] ... MRM
Metastable State (IAA) ... MSS
Metastable Time of Flight ... MTF
Metastable Transfer Emission Spectroscopy ... MTES
Metastable-Atom De-excitation Spectroscopy ... MDS
Metastases below the Head and Neck [*Oncology*] ... MI
Metastasis [*Oncology*] ... M
Metastasis [*Medicine*] ... MET
Metastasis [*Oncology*] (MAE) ... Mets
Metastasis-Stimulating Factor [*Immunosuppressant*] ... MSF
Metastasize [*Medicine*] ... METAS
Metastatic Breast Cancer [*Medicine*] ... MBC
Metastatic Disease [*Oncology*] ... METD
Metastatic Trophoblastic Disease [*Medicine*] (AAMN) ... MTD
Metasystems Design Group, Inc. [*Arlington, VA*] [*Telecommunications service*] (TSSD) ... MDG
Metatarsal [*Anatomy*] (DAVI) ... meta

Metatarsal [*Anatomy*] ... MT
Metatarsocuneiform [*Orthopedics*] (DAVI) ... MC
Metatarsophalangeal [*Anatomy*] ... MP
Metatarsophalangeal [*Anatomy*] ... MTP
Metatarsus [*Flamenco dance term*] ... MET
Metatarsus Adductus [*Anatomy*] (DAVI) ... MTA
Metatarsus Primus Varus [*Orthopedics*] (DAVI) ... MPV
Metatarsus Varus [*Anatomy*] (DAVI) ... MTV
Metatec Corp. [*NASDAQ symbol*] (SAG) ... META
Metatec Corp. [*Associated Press*] (SAG) ... Metatec
MetaTechnologies Associates [*Oakland, CA*] [*Telecommunications service*] (TSSD) ... MTA
Metathesis ... METATH
Meta-Toluenediamine [*Organic chemistry*] ... MTD
Metatolylnitrile [*Organic chemistry*] ... MTN
MetaTools Inc. [*NASDAQ symbol*] (TTSB) ... MTLS
Meta-Trifluoromethylphenylpiperazine [*Biochemistry*] ... MTFMPP
Metaxylene ... MX
Meta-Xylenediamine [*Organic chemistry*] ... MXDA
Metcalf & Eddy, Inc., Boston, MA [*Library symbol Library of Congress*] (LCLS) ... MBMetE
Metcalf on the Law of Contracts [*A publication*] (DLA) ... Metc Cont
Metcalfe Branch, Osgoode Township Library, Ontario [*Library symbol National Library of Canada*] (BIB) ... OMOT
Metcalfe's Reports [*58-61 Kentucky*] [*A publication*] (DLA) ... Met
Metcalfe's Reports [*58-61 Kentucky*] [*A publication*] (DLA) ... Metc
Metcalfe's Reports [*58-61 Kentucky*] [*A publication*] (DLA) ... Metc KY
Metcalf's Edition of Yelverton [*A publication*] (DLA) ... Metc Yelv
Metcalf's Reports [*Rhode Island*] [*A publication*] (DLA) ... Met
Metcalf's Reports [*Massachusetts*] [*A publication*] (DLA) ... Met
Metcalf's Reports [*Rhode Island*] [*A publication*] (DLA) ... Metc
Metcalf's Reports [*Massachusetts*] [*A publication*] (DLA) ... Metc
Metcalf's Reports [*Massachusetts*] [*A publication*] (DLA) ... Metc Mass
Metco, Inc., Westbury, NY [*Library symbol Library of Congress*] (LCLS) ... NWeM
Met-Coil Systems [*NASDAQ symbol*] (TTSB) ... METS
Met-Coil Systems Corp. [*NASDAQ symbol*] (NQ) ... METS
Meteacarpophalangeal [*Joint*] [*Anatomy*] (DAVI) ... MCP
Met-Ed Capital L.P.'MIPS' [*NYSE symbol*] (TTSB) ... MTTPrZ
Metega [*Libya*] [*ICAO location identifier*] (ICLI) ... HLLO
Metekel [*Ethiopia*] [*Airport symbol*] (AD) ... MXK
Metema [*Ethiopia*] [*ICAO location identifier*] (ICLI) ... HAMM
Metemma [*Ethiopia*] [*Airport symbol*] (OAG) ... ETE
Meteor Burst Communication System ... MBCS
Meteor Burst Communications [*Military*] ... MBC
Meteor Construzioni Aeronautiche & Elettroniche SpA [*Italy ICAO aircraft manufacturer identifier*] (ICAO) ... MT
Meteor Ionizing Efficiency ... MIE
Meteor Scatter (PDAA) ... MS
Meteor Simulation Vehicle (SAA) ... MSV
Meteor Trail Communications System ... MTCS
Meteoric Water Line [*Geology*] ... MWL
Meteorite Observation and Recovery Project [*Canada*] ... MORP
Meteoritic Impact Origin (AAG) ... MIO
Meteoritical ... METEORIT
Meteoritical Society (EA) ... MS
Meteor-Kilogram ... M-KG
Meteoroid Detection Experiment (KSC) ... MDE
Meteoroid Detection Satellite [*NASA*] ... MDS
Meteoroid Detector-Analyzer ... MDA
Meteoroid Exposure Module (MCD) ... MEM
Meteoroid Shield (KSC) ... MS
Meteoroid Shield Release System (MCD) ... MSRS
Meteoroid Technology [*Satellite*] [*NASA*] ... METEC
Meteoroid Technology Satellite [*NASA*] ... MTS
Meteorologica [*of Aristotle*] [*Classical studies*] (OCD) ... Mete
Meteorological [*JETDS nomenclature*] ... M
Meteorological (WGA) ... METGL
Meteorological Acquisition and Display System (PDAA) ... METADS
Meteorological Advisory Group [*ICAO*] (DA) ... METAG
Meteorological Aids Station [*ITU designation*] ... SM
Meteorological Airborne Data System ... MADS
Meteorological Analog Test and Evaluation (PDAA) ... MATE
Meteorological and Environmental Data Services (USDC) ... MEDS
Meteorological and Geoastrophysical Titles ... MGT
Meteorological and Lighting Data Acquisition System [*NASA*] (KSC) ... MLDAS
Meteorological and Oceanographic Analyst/Forecaster [*Course*] (DNAB) ... MOAF
Meteorological and Oceanographic Equipment Maintenance Course (DNAB) ... MOCEM
Meteorological and Oceanographic Equipment Program (NG) ... MOEP
Meteorological and Oceanographic Equipment Technical Liaison Officer ... MOETLO
Meteorological and Oceanographic Measurements System [*Chevron Oil Co.*] ... MOMS
Meteorological Applications [*Branch*] [*Marine science*] (OSRA) ... MA
Meteorological Applications [*Branch*] [*Forecast Systems Laboratory*] (USDC) ... MA
Meteorological Applied Problem Solving ... MAPS
Meteorological Aspects of Ocean Affairs [*Marine science*] (MSC) ... MAOA
Meteorological Atmospheric Turbulence (MCD) ... MAT
Meteorological Automatic Reporting Station [*Canada*] ... MARS
Meteorological Auxiliary Sea Current Observation Transmitter ... MASCOT
Meteorological Balloon Tracking System ... MBTS
Meteorological Broadcast (IAA) ... MET
Meteorological Coordination Officer (MUGU) ... METCO
Meteorological Data Acquisition System [*NASA*] (KSC) ... MDAS
Meteorological Data Acquisition System ... MDAS
Meteorological Data Acquisition System [*NASA*] (KSC) ... MEDAS
Meteorological Data Bank [*FAA designator*] (FAAC) ... YZY
Meteorological Data Collection ... MDC
Meteorological Data Collection and Reporting System [*FAA*] (TAG) ... MDCRS
Meteorological Data Distribution ... MDD
Meteorological Data Sounding System (IEEE) ... MDSS
Meteorological Data System ... MDS
Meteorological Datum Plane ... MDP
Meteorological Devices [*JETDS nomenclature*] [*Military*] (CET) ... ML
Meteorological Environmental Data Services [*Marine science*] (OSRA) ... MEDS
Meteorological Equipment Change (MCD) ... MEC
Meteorological Equipment Improvement Program (NG) ... METIMP
Meteorological Equipment Terminal and Representative Observation (MCD) ... METRO
Meteorological Group [*Range Commanders Council*] [*White Sands Missile Range, NM*] ... MG
Meteorological Impact Statement [*FAA*] (TAG) ... MIS
Meteorological Information and Dose Acquisition System [*Nuclear energy*] (NRCH) ... MIDAS
Meteorological Information Committee [*NATO*] (NATG) ... MIC
Meteorological Information Extraction Center ... MIEC
Meteorological Information for Aircraft in Flight ... MIAIF
Meteorological Information for Aircraft in Flight [*ICAO*] (FAAC) ... VOLMET
Meteorological Institute of the University of Uppsala [*Sweden*] (USDC) ... MIUU
Meteorological Integrating Data Acquisition System [*Marine science*] (MSC) ... MIDAS
Meteorological Measuring System ... MMS
Meteorological Office [*British*] (DSUE) ... MET
Meteorological Office [*British*] (AIA) ... Met Off
Meteorological Office [*or Officer*] [*Air Force*] ... METO
Meteorological Office ... METOF
Meteorological Office [*British*] ... MO
Meteorological Office [*ICAO designator*] (ICDA) ... YM
Meteorological Office [*FAA designator*] (FAAC) ... YMY
Meteorological Office Computer [*British*] (DEN) ... COMET
Meteorological Office Joint Meteorological Radio Propagation (IAA) ... MOJMRP
Meteorological Office Library Accessions and Retrieval System (NITA) ... MOLARS
Meteorological Office Weather Observing System (PDAA) ... MOWOS
Meteorological Operational Telecommunication Network in Europe, Regional Planning Group [*ICAO*] (PDAA) ... MOTNEG
Meteorological Operational Telecommunications Network Europe ... MOTNE
Meteorological Operational Telecommunications Network Europe [*ICAO designator*] (ICDA) ... YB
Meteorological Optic Measuring System (MCD) ... MOMS
Meteorological Optical Range (PDAA) ... MOR
Meteorological Penetration Detection Development ... MPDD
Meteorological Prediction Center (KSC) ... MPC
Meteorological RADAR Station [*ITU designation*] (CET) ... WXD
Meteorological Real-Time System [*Computer science*] (KSC) ... MRTS
Meteorological Research Committee [*British*] ... MRC
Meteorological Research Flight [*British ICAO designator*] (FAAC) ... MET
Meteorological Research Flight (AD) ... mr flight
Meteorological Research Institute (AD) ... MRI
Meteorological Rocket ... METROC
Meteorological Rocket Facility ... MRF
Meteorological Rocket Network [*NASA*] ... MRN
Meteorological Rocket Network Committee [*NASA*] (SAA) ... MRNC
Meteorological Satellite ... MET/SAT
Meteorological Satellite [*Former USSR*] ... METEOR
Meteorological Satellite [*European Space Agency*] ... METEOSAT
Meteorological Satellite ... METSAAT
Meteorological Satellite (USDC) ... METSAT
Meteorological Satellite [*Marine science*] (OSRA) ... METSATT
Meteorological Satellite Activity (IAA) ... MSA
Meteorological Satellite Center [*Aerospace*] (IAA) ... MSC
Meteorological Satellite Laboratory ... MSL
Meteorological Satellite Program Review Board [*NOAA and NASA*] ... MSPRB
Meteorological Satellite Section ... MSS
Meteorological Service [*Israel*] [*ICAO location identifier*] (ICLI) ... LLBD
Meteorological Services to Marine Activities [*WMO*] (MSC) ... MSMA
Meteorological Sounding Rocket ... MSR
Meteorological Sounding Rocket Program [*NASA*] ... MSRP
Meteorological Sounding Rocket, Ramjet-Powered [*NASA*] (SAA) ... METJET
Meteorological Support Activity [*Army Electronics Command*] ... MSA
Meteorological Systems Management Section ... MSMS
Meteorological Task Force (MCD) ... MTF
Meteorological Terminal Aviation Routine Weather Report [*FAA*] (TAG) ... METAR
Meteorological Terminal Aviation Weather Forecast [*FAA*] (TAG) ... METAF
Meteorological Training Center ... MTC
Meteorological Watch Advisory ... MWA
Meteorological Weather Processor (GAVI) ... MWP
Meteorological Working Group ... MWG
Meteorologist ... METRLGST
Meteorologist Observation (NOAA) ... METOB
Meteorologist Technician (NOAA) ... METEC
Meteorologist Weather Processor [*FAA*] (TAG) ... MWP
Meteorologist-In-Charge [*Marine science*] (OSRA) ... MIC
Meteorologist-in-Charge (USDC) ... MIC
Meteorology (AFM) ... MET
Meteorology ... METEOR
Meteorology ... METEOROL
Meteorology (ABBR) ... METEOROLO
Meteorology (NG) ... METR

Meteorology (NG) ... METRL
Meteorology ... METRO
Meteorology ... METRO
Meteorology and Earth Observation Satellite (NASA) ... MERSAT
Meteorology Department [*Navy*] ... MD
Meteorology Engineering Center [*Navy*] (MCD) ... MEC
Meteorology Laboratory (GNE) ... ML
Meteorology Officer (MUGU) ... MO
Meteorology on Stamps Study Unit [*American Topical Association*] (EA) ... MSSU
Meteorology on Stamps Study Unit [*American Topical Association*] (EA) ... MSU
Meteorology Panel (MCD) ... MP
Meteosat Ground Computer System [*Aviation*] (DA) ... MGCS
Meter [*SI unit of length*] ... m
Meter (WDMC) ... M
Meter ... MR
Meter (MCD) ... MT
Meter [*or Metering*] (AAG) ... MTR
Meter (IDOE) ... mtr
Meter Amplifier ... MA
Meter Angle ... MA
Meter Fix Time [*Aviation*] (FAAC) ... MFXT
Meter Fix Time/Slot Time [*FAA*] (TAG) ... MFT
Meter Gauge Rolling-Stock [*British*] ... MGRS
Meter Heading Differential ... MHD
Meter List Display Interval [*FAA*] (TAG) ... MLDI
Meter Manufacturers' Association (IAA) ... MMA
Meter Resistance (IDOE) ... R_m
Meter Stamp Society (EA) ... MSS
Meter-Candle ... MC
Meter-Candle (IDOE) ... mc
Meter-Candle Second ... MCS
Metered Dose Inhaler [*Medicine*] ... MDI
Metered Market Service [*A. C. Nielsen Co.*] (NTCM) ... MM
Metered Message Unit [*Telecommunications*] (TEL) ... MMU
Metering (MSA) ... MTRG
Metering and Accounting System (NITA) ... MACS
Metering and Directional Control System ... MDCS
Metering and Traffic Recording with Offline Processing (PDAA) ... METRO
Metering Information System [*Telecommunications*] (OA) ... MIS
Metering over Junction [*Network administration*] [*Telecommunications*] (TEL) ... MOJ
Metering Pumps Limited ... MPL
Metering Research Facility [*Research center*] (RCD) ... MRF
Metering Suction Differential (NG) ... MSD
Metering Valve Sensor [*Automotive engineering*] ... MVS
Metering Water Dispenser [*Apollo*] [*NASA*] ... MWD
Meter-Kilogram (KSC) ... M-KG
Meter-Kilogram-Second [*System of units*] ... MKS
Meter-Kilogram-Second (IDOE) ... mks
Meter-Kilogram-Second-Ampere [*System of units*] ... MKSA
Meter-Newton ... m-N
Meterorological Institute of the University of Uppsala, Sweden [*Marine science*] (OSRA) ... MIUU
Meter-Reading Access Circuit [*Bell Laboratories*] ... MRAC
Meters [*JETDS nomenclature*] [*Military*] (CET) ... ME
Meters above Sea Level ... masl
Meters of Seawater [*Deep-sea diving*] ... MSW
Meters of Water Equivalent ... MWE
Meters per Day ... M/D
Meters per Hour ... M/H
Meters per Minute ... MPM
Meters Per Minute (AD) ... mpm
Meters per Second ... M/S
Meters per Second ... MPS
Meters per Second (AD) ... mps
Meters per Second (IDOE) ... mps
Meters per Second (AD) ... ms
Meters per Second Squared ... M/S^2
Meters per Year ... M/A
Meters Water Depth ... MWD
Methacholine [*A cholinergic*] ... MCH
Methacholine Challenge [*Medicine*] ... MC
Methacholine Response [*Medicine*] ... MR
Methacrolein [*Also, MAL*] [*Organic chemistry*] ... MACR
Methacrolein [*Also, MACR*] [*Organic chemistry*] ... MAL
Methacrylamidopropyltrimethylammonium Chloride [*Organic chemistry*] ... MAPTAC
Methacrylate Butadiene Styrene [*Plastics technology*] ... MBS
Methacrylate Producers Association (EA) ... MPA
Methacrylate Structural Adhesive ... MSA
Methacrylic Acid [*Organic chemistry*] ... MAA
Methacryloyloxyethyltrimethylammonium Chloride [*Organic chemistry*] ... METAC
Methadone (ABBR) ... METH
Methadone Maintenance and Aftercare Treatment Program [*Medicine*] (DMAA) ... MMATP
Methadone Maintenance Program ... MMP
Methadone Maintenance Treatment Program (AAMN) ... MMTP
Methadone Treatment Quality Assurance System [*National Institute on Drug Abuse*] ... MTQAS
Methallyloxyphenol ... MOP
Methamphetamine [*Pharmacology*] ... MA
Methamphetamine (ABBR) ... METH
Methane [*BTS*] (TAG) ... CH4
Methane (AAG) ... METH
Methane Inert Gas (MCD) ... MIG
Methane Monooxygenase [*An enzyme*] ... MMO
Methane Phophonyl Dichloride [*Nerve gas intermediate*] [*Organic chemistry*] ... MPD
Methane Rich Gas ... MRG
Methane Sulfonyl Chloride [*Organic chemistry*] ... MSC
Methanearsonic Acid [*Organic chemistry*] ... MAA
Methane-Powered Vehicle ... MPV
Methane-Rich Gas (AD) ... mrg
Methanesulfonic Acid [*Organic chemistry*] ... MSA
Methanesulfonyl Fluoride [*Organic chemistry*] ... MSF
Methanethiosulphonate Spin Label [*Analytical chemistry*] ... MTSSL
Methanex Corp. [*NASDAQ symbol*] (SAG) ... MEOH
Methanex Corp. [*NASDAQ symbol*] (TTSB) ... MEOHF
Methanex Corp. [*Associated Press*] (SAG) ... Methanx
Methanol [*DOE*] (TAG) ... CH3OH
Methanol Environmental Performance [*Automotive engineering*] ... MEP
Methanol Extraction [*or Extruded*] **Residue** [*Immunology*] ... MER
Methanol/Water ... M/W
Methanol-Fueled Vehicle [*Automotive engineering*] ... MFV
Methanol-to-Gasoline [*Process*] [*Mobil Oil Corp.*] ... MTG
Methanol-to-Olefin [*Process*] ... MTO
Methantheline [*or Methanthine*] **Bromide** [*Pharmacology*] ... MTB
Methaphetamine Hydrochloride [*An amphetamine, commonly known as speed*] (VNW) ... Meth
Methaqualone [*or Methyltolylquinazolone, or Metolquizolone*] [*Sedative*] ... MTQ
Metharbital [*An anticonvulsant*] [*Pharmacology*] (DAVI) ... MTH
Methedrine [*Stimulant*] ... Meth
Methemalbumin [*Medicine*] (MAE) ... MHA
Methemoglobin [*Symbol*] [*Medicine*] ... Hi
Methemoglobin [*Biochemistry*] (DAVI) ... met hgh
Methemoglobin [*Biochemistry, medicine*] ... MetHb
Methemoglobin [*Biochemistry, medicine*] ... MHb
Methemoglobin [*Immunochemistry*] (DAVI) ... MHB
Methemoglobin Reductase [*Hematology and laboratory*] (DAVI) ... MHR
Methemoglobin Reductase [*An enzyme*] (MAE) ... MR-E
Methemoglobin-Sulfhemoglobin [*Hematology*] (DAVI) ... HGBS
Methicillin [*An antibiotic*] ... METH
Methicillin-Resistant Staphylococcus [*Qureus*] [*Medicine*] (DAVI) ... MRS
Methicillin-Resistant Staphylococcus Aureus [*Antimicrobial therapy*] (MEDA) ... MRS
Methicillin-Resistant Staphylococcus Aureus [*Antimicrobial therapy*] ... MRSA
Methidiumpropyl Ethylenediaminetetraacetic Acid [*Analytical biochemistry*] ... MPE
Methionine [*One-letter symbol; see Met*] ... M
Methionine [*Also, M*] [*An amino acid*] ... Met
Methionine [*An amino acid*] (DOG) ... met
Methionine Adenosyltransferase [*An enzyme*] ... MAT
Methionine Enkephalin [*Biochemistry*] ... ME
Methionine Hydroxy Analog [*Poultry feed*] ... MHA
Methionine Sulfoxime [*Biochemistry*] ... MSO
Methionine Synthase [*An enzyme*] ... MS
Methionyl Aminopeptidase [*An enzyme*] ... MAP
Methionyl Bovine Somatotropin [*Biochemistry*] ... MBS
Methionyl-Transfer Ribonucleic Acid Synthetase [*An enzyme*] ... MetRS
Method ... M
Method (ROG) ... METH
Method ... METH
Method (MSA) ... MTHD
Method 1 (NITA) ... M/1
Method Detection Limit [*Analytical chemistry*] ... MDL
Method for Analysis of Fleet Tactical Effectiveness Performance [*Navy*] (PDAA) ... MAFTEP
Method for Asynchronous Graphics Integral Control [*Computer science*] (PDAA) ... MAGIC
Method Improvement Request (MCD) ... MIR
Method in Natural Development [*Mental diet plan*] ... MIND
Method Index [*British police term*] ... MI
Method, Meat, and Morality [*Cure for insanity, according to Victorian medical theory*] ... 3M's
Method of Accomplishment (AFIT) ... MOA
Method of Adjustment [*Aviation*] ... MOA
Method of Characteristics [*Equilibrium flow*] ... MOC
Method of Composition Velocity [*Physical chemistry*] ... MCV
Method of Constant Stimuli [*Psychophysics*] ... MCS
Method of Delivery ... MOD
Method of Designing Instructional Alternatives (PDAA) ... MODIA
Method of Ensemble Average of Periodic Systems ... MEAPS
Method of Generated Responses [*Psychology*] ... MGR
Method of Implicit Nonstationary Iteration (PDAA) ... MINI
Method of Integral Relations ... MIR
Method of Lines [*Mathematics*] ... MOL
Method of Mass Balance [*Physical chemistry*] ... MMB
Method of Micromolding in Capillaries [*Materials science*] ... MIMIC
Method of Mixed Ranges (PDAA) ... MMR
Method of Operation ... MO
Method of Operation (AD) ... mo
Method of Personnel Evaluation ... MOPE
Method of Sale ... MS
Method of Scenic Alternative Impacts by Computer (PDAA) ... MOSAIC
Method of Standard Addition [*Statistics*] ... MOSA
Method of Standard Additions ... MSA
Method of Steepest Descent ... MSD
Method of Testing (MCD) ... MOT
Method of Unweighted Means [*Statistics*] ... MUM
Method of Validation ... MOV

Method of Weighted Residual ... MWR
Method to Extend Research in Time [*National Institutes of Health*] ... MERIT
Methode Electronics, Inc. [*NASDAQ symbol*] (NQ) ... METH
Methode Electronics, Inc. [*Associated Press*] (SAG) ... Methd
Methode Electronics'A' [*NASDAQ symbol*] (TTSB) ... METHA
Methode Electronics'B' [*NASDAQ symbol*] (TTSB) ... METHB
Methodic (ABBR) ... METHC
Methodist ... M
Methodist ... ME
Methodist ... METH
Methodist ... METHDST
Methodist Archives and Research Centre [*John Rylands University Library of Manchester*] [*British*] (CB) ... MARC
Methodist Association of Youth Clubs [*British*] (BI) ... MAYC
Methodist Board of Missions, New York, NY [*Library symbol Library of Congress*] (LCLS) ... NNMB
Methodist Boys' School ... MBS
Methodist Chaplain ... MC
Methodist Chaplain [*Navy British*] ... MethCh
Methodist Church (WDAA) ... MC
Methodist College, Belfast [*Northern Ireland*] ... MCB
Methodist College, Fayetteville, NC [*Library symbol Library of Congress*] (LCLS) ... NcFayM
Methodist Committee for Overseas Relief [*Later, UMCOR*] (EA) ... MCOR
Methodist Episcopal ... ME
Methodist Episcopal Church ... MEC
Methodist Episcopal Church ... MECH
Methodist Episcopal, South ... ME(S)
Methodist Federation for Social Action (EA) ... MFSA
Methodist Historical Society, South Carolina Conference of the Methodist Church,Wofford College, Spartanburg, SC [*Library symbol Library of Congress*] (LCLS) ... ScSpW-MHi
Methodist Homes for the Aged [*British*] (BI) ... MHA
Methodist Hospital, Lubbock, TX [*Library symbol Library of Congress*] (LCLS) ... TxLMH
Methodist Hospital, Minneapolis, MN [*Library symbol Library of Congress*] (LCLS) ... MnMMeH
Methodist Hospital of Central Illinois, Peoria, IL [*Library symbol Library of Congress*] (LCLS) ... IPMH
Methodist Hospital, Pathology Library, Memphis, TN [*Library symbol Library of Congress*] (LCLS) ... TMMH-P
Methodist Hospital School of Nursing, Madison, WI [*Library symbol Library of Congress*] (LCLS) ... WMaM
Methodist Hospital, Stratton Medical Library, Memphis, TN [*Library symbol Library of Congress*] (LCLS) ... TMMH
Methodist Medical Center of Illinois, Medical Library, Peoria, IL [*Library symbol Library of Congress*] (LCLS) ... IPMH-M
Methodist Medical Center of Illinois, Peoria, IL [*OCLC symbol*] (OCLC) ... ISR
Methodist Medical Center, St. Joseph, MO [*Library symbol Library of Congress*] (LCLS) ... MoStjM
Methodist Missionary Society [*British*] ... MMS
Methodist Peace Fellowship [*Defunct*] (EA) ... MPF
Methodist Philatelic Society (EA) ... MPS
Methodist Protestant ... MP
Methodist Protestant Church ... MPCH
Methodist Publishing House (DGA) ... MPH
Methodist Publishing House Library, Nashville, TN [*Library symbol Library of Congress*] (LCLS) ... TNMPH
Methodist Relief Fund [*British*] ... MRF
Methodist Theological School in Ohio, Delaware, OH [*Library symbol Library of Congress*] (LCLS) ... ODM
Methodist Theological School in Ohio, Delaware, OH [*OCLC symbol*] (OCLC) ... TSM
Methodist Youth Fellowship ... MYF
Methodists Associated Representing the Cause of Hispanic Americans [*An association*] ... MARCHA
Methodists for Church Renewal ... MCR
Methodists for Life [*Defunct*] (EA) ... MFL
Methodize (ABBR) ... METHZ
Methodized (ABBR) ... METHZD
Methodological (ABBR) ... METHOGL
Methodology ... METDLGY
Methodology (ABBR) ... METHO
Methodology (ABBR) ... METHOG
Methodology Approach to Planning and Programming Air Force Operational Requirements, Research and Development (IEEE) ... MAPORD
Methodology for Assessing Radiological Consequences (PDAA) ... MARC
Methodology for Total Force Concept [*Military*] ... METOFOR
Methodology for Unmanned Manufacture [*Robotics project*] [*Japan*] ... MUM
Methodology Investigation Proposal (MCD) ... MIP
Methods and Materials Standards Association (EA) ... MMSA
Methods and Procedures Technical Orders ... MPTO
Methods and Standards ... M & S
Methods and Standards (MCD) ... MAS
Methods Development Survey [*Bureau of the Census*] (GFGA) ... MDS
Methods Engineering (NG) ... ME
Methods Engineering Program [*Navy*] (NVT) ... MEP
Methods for Chemical Analysis of Water and Wastes [*Environmental Protection Agency*] ... MCAWW
Methods Improvement Program [*IBM Corp.*] ... MIP
Methods in Molecular and Cellular Biology [*A publication*] ... MMCB
Methods Instruction (DNAB) ... MI
Methods of Administration [*Department of Education*] (OICC) ... MOA
Methods of Air Sampling and Analysis [*Air Pollution Control Association*] ... MAS
Methods of Appraisal and Test (MHDB) ... MOAT
Methods of Defeating Advanced RADAR Threats (NASA) ... MODART
Methods of Extracting Text Automatically [*Programming language*] [*General Electric Co.*] [*Computer science*] (IEEE) ... META
Methods of Extracting Text Automatically Programming - Language [*General Electric Co.*] [*Computer science*] (IEEE) ... METAPLAN
Methods of Instruction ... MOI
Methods of Intellectual Development [*National Association of Manufacturers*] ... MIND
Methods of Limits (IEEE) ... ML
Methods of Moderation [*An association*] (EA) ... MOM
Methods Research Corp. (AD) ... MRC
Methods Test Panel [*Bureau of the Census*] (GFGA) ... MTP
Methods Time Measurement and General Purpose Data (PDAA) ... MTM-GPD
Methods Time-Measurement Association (IAA) ... MTMA
Methods-Time Analysis [*Industrial engineering*] ... MTA
Methods-Time Measurement [*Industrial engineering*] ... MTM
Methods-Time Study [*Industrial engineering*] ... MTS
Method-Times Measurement (DICI) ... MTM
Methohexital [*A barbiturate*] [*Pharmacology*] (DAVI) ... HEXL
Methohexital [*An anesthetic*] ... MHEX
Methotrexate [*Antineoplastic drug*] ... M
Methotrexate [*Antineoplastic drug*] ... MTX
Methotrexate [*Antineoplastic drug*] (CDI) ... MYX
Methotrexate, 6-Thioguanine, Oncovin, Prednisone [*Antineoplastic drug regimen*] (DAVI) ... T-MOP
Methotrexate, Actinomycin D, Cyclophosphamide [*Antineoplastic drug regimen*] ... MAC
Methotrexate, Adriamycin, Cyclophosphamide, CCNU [*Lomustine*] [*Antineoplastic drug regimen*] ... MACC
Methotrexate, Adriamycin [*Doxorubicin*], Cyclophosphamide [*Cytoxan*], CCNU [*Lomustine*] (DAVI) ... MACC
Methotrexate, Adriamycin, Cytoxan, CCNU [*Lomustine*] [*Antineoplastic drug*] (CDI) ... MACC
Methotrexate and Cytosine Arabinoside [*Antineoplastic drug regimen*] (DAVI) ... MAIT
Methotrexate and Mercaptopurine [*Antineoplastic drug regimen*] (DAVI) ... MTX + MP
Methotrexate, Ara-C, Cyclophosphamide, Oncovin [*Vincristine*], Prednisone [*Antineoplastic drug regimen*] ... MACOP
Methotrexate, Bleomycin, Cisplatin [*Antineoplastic drug*] (CDI) ... MBC
Methotrexate, Bleomycin, Diamminedichloroplatinum [*Cisplatin*] [*Antineoplastic drug regimen*] ... MBD
Methotrexate, Cyclophosphamide [*Antineoplastic drug regimen*] ... MECY
Methotrexate, Fluorourcil, Calcium Leucovorin Rescue [*Antineoplastic drug*] (CDI) ... MF
Methotrexate (High-Dose) (with Citrovorum Factor Rescue), Bleomycin, Adriamycin,Cyclophosphamide, Oncovin [*Vincristine*], Dexamethasone [*Antineoplastic drug regimen*] ... M-BACOD
Methotrexate, Mercaptopurine, and Cytoxan [*Cyclophosphamide*] [*Antineoplastic drug regimen*] (DAVI) ... MTX + MP + CTX
Methotrexate, Oncomycin, Prednisone, Procarbazine [*Antineoplastic drug regimen*] (DAVI) ... MOPP
Methotrexate, Oncovin [*Vincristine*] **5-Fluorouracil** [*Antineoplastic drug regimen*] (DAVI) ... MOF
Methotrexate, Oncovin [*Vineristine*], Bleomycin [*Antineoplastic drug regimen*] (DAVI) ... MOB-III
Methotrexate, Oncovin [*Vincristine*], Cyclophosphamide, Adriamycin [*Antineoplastic drug regimen*] ... MOCA
Methotrexate, Oncovin [*Vincristine*] **L-asparaginase, Dexamethasone** [*Antineoplastic drug regimen*] (DAVI) ... MOAD
Methotrexate, Vinblastine, Adriamiacin [*Doxorubicin*] **Cisplatin** [*Antineoplastic drug regimen*] (DAVI) ... M-VAC
Methotrexate, Vinblastine, Adriamycin, Cisplatin [*Antineoplastic drug*] (CDI) ... MVAC
Methotrexate, VP-16 Hyxamethylmelamine [*Antineoplastic drug regimen*] (DAVI) ... MVH
Methotrexate with Citrovorum Factor Rescue [*Antineoplastic drug regimen*] ... MTX-CF
Methow Aviation, Inc. [*ICAO designator*] (FAAC) ... MER
Methoxime [*Organic chemistry*] ... MO
Methoxybenzoxazolinone [*Biochemistry*] ... MBOA
Methoxybenzylaminonitrobenzoxadiazole [*Fluorescent probe*] [*Biochemistry*] ... MBD
Methoxybenzylidene Butylaniline [*Organic chemistry*] ... MBBA
Methoxychlor [*An insecticide*] (DAVI) ... DMDT
Methoxy(diphenyl)furanone [*Organic chemistry*] ... MDPF
Methoxyethanol [*Organic chemistry*] ... ME
Methoxyethoxymethyl [*Organic chemistry*] ... MEM
Methoxyethylmercuric Chloride ... MEMC
Methoxyflurane [*Anesthetic*] (AAMN) ... MOF
Methoxyhydropheny Gylcol Conjugate [*Organic chemistry*] (DAVI) ... MHPG Conj
Methoxyhydroxymandelic Acid [*Organic chemistry*] ... MOMA
Methoxy-Hydroxyphenylacetic Acid [*Chemistry*] (DAVI) ... HVA
Methoxyhydroxyphenylacetic Acid [*Organic chemistry*] ... MOPAC
Methoxy-Hydroxyphenylethanol [*Organic chemistry*] (MAH) ... MHPE
Methoxyhydroxyphenylethanol [*Organic chemistry*] ... MOPET
Methoxy-Hydroxyphenylethanol Conjugate [*Organic chemistry*] (DAVI) ... MHPE Conj
(Methoxyhydroxyphenyl)ethyleneglycol [*Also, MOPEG*] [*Organic chemistry*] ... MHPG
(Methoxyhydroxyphenyl)ethyleneglycol [*Also, MHPG*] [*Organic chemistry*] ... MOPEG
Methoxylamine [*Organic chemistry*] ... MA
Methoxy-Meta-Phenylenediamine [*Organic chemistry*] ... MMPD
Methoxy-Meta-Phenylenediamine Sulfate [*Organic chemistry*] ... MMPDS

Methoxymethyl [*Organic chemistry*] ... MOM
(Methoxy)methylenedioxyamphetamine [*A hallucinogen*] ... MMDA
Methoxynaphthylamine [*Organic chemistry*] ... MNA
Methoxy(O-desmethyl)encainide [*Biochemistry*] ... MODE
Methoxyphenylacetic Acid [*Herbicide*] ... MOPA
Methoxyphenylazobenzyloxycarbonyl [*Biochemistry*] ... Mz
Methoxypolyethylene Glycol [*Organic chemistry*] ... MPEG
Methoxypropionitrile [*Organic chemistry*] ... MOPN
Methoxypropylamine [*Organic chemistry*] ... MOPA
Methoxypropylamine [*Organic chemistry*] ... MPA
Methoxypsoralen [*Also, MP*] [*Pharmacology*] ... MOP
Methoxypsoralen [*Also, MOP*] [*Pharmacology*] ... MP
Methoxy(trifluoromethyl)butyrophenone [*Biochemistry*] ... MTB
(Methoxy)trifluoromethylphenylacetic Acid [*Organic chemistry*] ... MTPA
Methoxytriglycol [*Organic chemistry*] ... MTG
Methoxytryptamine [*Biochemistry*] ... MT
Methoxytyramine [*Biochemistry*] ... MT
methoxytyramine [*Chemistry*] (DAVI) ... MT
(Methozybenzylidene)butylaniline [*Organic chemistry*] ... MBBA
Methuen's Commercial Series [*A publication*] ... MCSA
Methuen's Standard Library [*A publication*] ... MSL
Methuen's Text-Books of Science [*A publication*] ... MTBS
Methycarboxyphenglycine [*Biochemistry*] ... MCPG
Methyl [*As substituent on nucleoside*] [*Biochemistry*] ... m
Methyl [*Organic chemistry*] ... Me
Methyl [*Organic chemistry*] (DAVI) ... meth
Methyl Acceptor Protein [*Biochemistry*] (DAVI) ... MAP
Methyl Acetamido Cinnamate [*Organic chemistry*] ... MAC
Methyl Acetoacetate [*Organic chemistry*] ... MAA
Methyl Acetyl Propadrine and Propane (MCD) ... MAPP
Methyl Acrylate [*Organic chemistry*] ... MA
Methyl Alcohol ... MEOH
Methyl Allyl Chloride [*Organic chemistry*] ... MAC
Methyl Aluminoxane Cocatalyst ... MAO
Methyl Amyl Ketone [*Organic chemistry*] ... MAK
Methyl Anthranilate [*Organic chemistry*] ... MA
Methyl Benzimidazolecarbamate [*Organic chemistry*] ... MBC
Methyl Benzyl Alcohol [*Organic chemistry*] ... MBA
Methyl Bromide [*Organic chemistry*] ... MB
Methyl Butyl Ketone [*Organic chemistry*] ... MBK
Methyl Cap. Isobutyl Carbinol [*Also, MIC*] [*Organic chemistry*] ... MIBC
Methyl Carbamate [*Organic chemistry*] ... MC
Methyl Cation Affinity [*Physical chemistry*] ... MCA
Methyl Chloride Industry Association (EA) ... MCIA
Methyl Cyanoacrylate [*Organic chemistry*] ... MCA
Methyl Diamphetamine ... MDA
Methyl Dihydrojasmonate [*Organic chemistry*] ... MDHJ
Methyl Dihydroretinoate [*Biochemistry*] ... MDHR
Methyl Dimethyldihydropyrancarboxylate [*Organic chemistry*] ... MDDPC
Methyl Dinitropentanoate [*An explosive*] ... MDNP
Methyl Ethyl Ether [*Organic chemistry*] ... MEE
Methyl Ethyl Ketone [*Organic chemistry*] ... MEK
Methyl Ethyl Ketone Peroxide [*Organic chemistry*] ... MEKP
Methyl Ethyl Ketoxime [*Organic chemistry*] ... MEKO
Methyl Farnesoate [*Organic chemistry*] ... MF
Methyl Fluoracetate [*Organic chemistry*] ... MFA
Methyl Formate [*Organic chemistry*] ... MF
Methyl Green [*A dye*] ... MG
Methyl Green Pyronine [*A stain*] ... MGP
Methyl Isatin-beta-thiosemicarbazone ... MIBT
Methyl Isoamyl Ketone [*Organic chemistry*] ... MIAK
Methyl Isobutyl Ketone [*Also, MIK*] [*Organic chemistry*] ... MIBK
Methyl Isobutyl Ketone [*Also, MIBK*] [*Organic chemistry*] ... MIK
Methyl Isocyanate [*Organic chemistry*] ... MIC
Methyl Isopropyl Ketone [*Organic chemistry*] ... MIPK
Methyl Mercaptan [*Organic chemistry*] ... MM
Methyl Methacrylate [*Also, MMA*] [*Organic chemistry*] ... MM
Methyl Methacrylate [*Also, MM*] [*Organic chemistry*] ... MMA
Methyl Methanesulfonate [*Experimental mutagen*] ... MMS
Methyl Methanethiolsulfonate [*Organic chemistry*] ... MMTS
Methyl Monochloroacetate [*Organic chemistry*] ... MMCA
Methyl Orange [*Organic chemistry*] ... MO
Methyl Palmoxirate [*Organic chemistry*] ... MP
Methyl Parathion [*Also, MP, MPN*] [*Pesticide*] ... MEP
Methyl Parathion [*Also, MEP, MPN*] [*Pesticide*] ... MP
Methyl Parathion [*Also, MEP, MP*] [*Pesticide*] ... MPN
Methyl Phenyl Sulfide [*Organic chemistry*] ... MPS
Methyl Propyltrimethylene Carbamate [*Tranquilizer*] ... MEPROBAMATE
Methyl Red [*A dye*] ... MR
Methyl Red (AD) ... mr
Methyl Red Voges-Proskauer [*Bacteriology*] (AD) ... mrV-P
Methyl Reductase [*An enzyme*] ... MR
Methyl Salicylate [*Organic chemistry*] ... MS
Methyl Sulfonylmethane [*Biochemistry*] ... MSM
Methyl Tertiary Butyl Ether [*Fuel additive*] ... MTBE
Methyl Tertiary Butyl Ether Task Force (EA) ... MTBETF
Methyl Tetradecylglycidate [*Biochemistry*] ... MTG
Methyl Trimethylsilyl Dimethylketene Acetal [*Organic chemistry*] ... MTDA
Methyl Vinyl Ether [*Organic chemistry*] ... MVE
Methyl Vinyl Ketone [*Organic chemistry*] ... MVK
Methyl Violet [*A dye*] ... MV
Methyl Viologen [*Organic chemistry*] ... MV
Methyl-1-(2-chloroethyl)-3-cyclohexyl-1 Nitrosourea [*Antineoplastic drug regimen*] (DAVI) ... methyl-CCNU
Methyl-Accepting Chemotaxis Proteins [*Biochemistry*] ... MCP
Methylacetoxyprogesterone [*Also, MPA*] [*Endocrinology*] ... MAP
Methylacetylene Propadiene [*Organic chemistry*] ... MAP
Methyl(acetylenyl)putrescine [*Biochemistry*] ... MAP
Methylacridone [*Organic chemistry*] ... MAD
Methylallyl Nitrophenyl Ether [*Organic chemistry*] ... MNE
Methylaluminoxane [*Organic chemistry*] ... MAO
Methylaluminum Sesquichloride [*Organic chemistry*] ... MASC
Methylamine Dehydrogenase [*An enzyme*] ... MADH
(Methylamino) Benzoic Acid [*Organic chemistry*] ... MABA
Methylaminoacetaldehyde Dimethyl Acetal [*Organic chemistry*] ... MAADMA
Methylaminoazobenzene [*Organic chemistry*] ... MAB
Methylamino(chloro)benzophenone [*Organic chemistry*] ... MCB
Methylaminodeoxyuridine [*Pharmacology*] ... MADU
(Methylamino)ethanol [*Organic chemistry*] ... MAE
(Methylamino)isobutyric Acid [*Biochemistry*] ... MeAIB
Methyl(amino)propanediol [*Organic chemistry*] ... MAP
Methylaminopurine (MAE) ... MAP
Methylandrostenediol [*Methandriol*] [*Endocrinology*] ... MAD
Methylanthranilic Acid ... MA
Methylated (ADA) ... METH
Methylated Albumin Kieselguhr [*Chromatography*] ... MAK
Methylated Albumin-Nitrocelluse Membrane [*Analytical biochemistry*] ... MANM
Methylated Bovine Serum Albumin ... MBSA
Methylated Bovine Serum Albumin [*Biochemistry*] ... MeBSA
Methylated Low-Density Lipoprotein [*Biochemistry*] ... MeLDL
Methylated Spirit (DSUE) ... METH
Methylated Spirits (ADA) ... METHS
Methylazoxymethanol Acetate [*Organic chemistry*] ... MAM
Methylazoxymethanol Acetate [*Organic chemistry*] (DMAA) ... MAM Ac
Methylbenzothiazolinone Hydrazone [*Organic chemistry*] ... MBTH
Methyl(benzylideneamino)mercaptotriazole [*Reagent*] ... MBAMT
Methylbenzyllinoleic Acid [*Organic chemistry*] ... MBLA
Methylbenzylnitrosamine [*Organic chemistry*] ... MBN
Methylbis(beta-chloroethyl)amine [*Nitrogen mustard*] [*Also, HN, NM Antineoplastic; war-gas base*] ... MBA
Methylbistrifluoroacetamide [*Organic chemistry*] ... MBTFA
Methylbutenedial [*Organic chemistry*] ... MBD
Methyl(butyl)nitrosamine [*Organic chemistry*] ... MBNA
Methyl-CCNU 5-Fluorouracil, Adriamycin [*Antineoplastic drug regimen*] (DAVI) ... MEFA
Methyl-CCNU, Cytoxan, Prednisone [*Antineoplastic drug*] (CDI) ... MeCP
Methylcellulose [*Organic chemistry*] ... MC
Methylchlorobiphenyl [*Organic chemistry*] ... MCBP
Methyl-(Chloroethyl)-Cyclohexyl-Nitrosourea [*Antineoplastic drug regimen*] (DAVI) ... MCCNU
Methyl(chloroethyl)cyclohexylnitrosourea [*Semustine*] [*Antineoplastic drug*] ... MeCCNU
Methylchloroform [*Organic chemistry*] ... MC
Methylchloroform Chloroacetophenone [*Riot-control gas*] ... MACE
Methylchlorophenoxyacetic Acid [*Also, MCPA*] [*Herbicide*] ... MCP
Methylchlorophenoxyacetic Acid [*Also, MCP*] [*Herbicide*] ... MCPA
Methylcholanthrene [*Also, MCA*] [*Organic chemistry*] ... MC
Methylcholanthrene [*Also, MC*] [*Biochemistry*] ... MCA
Methyl(ciethylamino)coumarin [*Organic chemistry*] ... MDAC
(Methylcinnamylhydrazono)propionate [*Biochemistry*] ... MCHP
Methylcyclohexane [*Organic chemistry*] ... MCH
Methylcyclohexanol [*Organic chemistry*] ... MCH
Methylcyclohexenone [*Organic chemistry*] ... MCH
Methylcyclopentadienyl Manganese Tricarbonyl [*Organic chemistry*] ... MMT
Methylcyclopentane [*Organic chemistry*] ... MCP
Methylcystyosine [*Biochemistry*] ... MC
Methyl(deazaisoalloxazine)propanesulfonic Acid [*Organic chemistry*] ... MAPS
Methyldichloroarsine [*Poison gas*] ... MD
Methyldichlorophosphine [*Organic chemistry*] ... MDP
Methyldiethanolamine [*Organic chemistry*] ... MDEA
Methyl-D-Mannopyranoside [*Organic chemistry*] ... MMP
Methyldopa [*Also, AMD*] [*Antihypertensive compound*] ... MD
Methyldopamine [*Biochemistry*] ... MDA
Methyldopamine [*Biochemistry*] ... MDOPA
Methylene Bisacrylamide (PDAA) ... MBAA
Methylene Blue [*Organic chemistry*] ... MB
Methylene Blue [*Organic chemistry*] ... MeB
Methylene Blue Active Substance [*Organic chemistry*] ... MBAS
Methylene Blue Dye [*Organic chemistry*] (MAE) ... MBD
Methylene Blue Installation [*Medicine*] (DAVI) ... MBI
Methylene Blue Reduced ... MBR
Methylene Blue Reduction Time ... MBRT
Methylene Blue Test [*Analytical chemistry*] ... MBT
Methylene Chloride [*Organic chemistry*] ... MC
Methylene Diisocyanate [*Organic chemistry*] ... MDI
Methylene Diphenyl Diisocyanate [*Organic chemistry*] ... MDI
Methylene Diphosphonate [*Organic chemistry*] ... MDP
Methylene Glutamine ... MG
Methylene Unit ... MU
Methyleneaminoacetonitrile [*Organic chemistry*] ... MAAN
Methylenebis (Phenylisocyanate) (GNE) ... MDI
Methylenebisacrylamide [*Organic chemistry*] ... MBA
Methylene-bis-(aminothiadiazole) [*Pesticide*] ... MATDA
Methylenebis(ortho-chloroaniline) [*Also, MOCA*] [*Organic chemistry*] ... MBOCA
Methylenebis(ortho-chloroaniline) [*Also, MBOCA*] [*Organic chemistry*] ... MOCA
Methylenebisthiocyanate [*Antimicrobial agent*] ... MBT
Methylenecyclohexadiene [*Organic chemistry*] ... MCH
Methylenecyclopropylacetic Acid [*Organic chemistry*] ... MCPA
Methylenedianiline [*Also, DAPM, DDM*] [*Organic chemistry*] ... MDA
Methylenedioxyamphetamine [*Biochemistry*] ... MDA

Methylenedioxybenzene [Organic chemistry] .... MDB
Methylenedioxyethamphetamine [Biochemistry] .... MDEA
Methylenedioxymethamphetamine [A hallucinogenic drug, also known as "Ecstasy," banned in 1985] [Also, MDMA] .... MDM
Methylenedioxymethamphetamine [A hallucinogenic drug, also known as "Ecstasy," banned in 1985] [Also, MDM] .... MDMA
Methylenedioxyphenyl [Organic chemistry] .... MDO
Methylenediphenyl Isocyanate [Organic chemistry] .... MDI
Methylenediphosphonic Acid [Organic chemistry] .... MDP
Methyl(ethyl)glycine [Biochemistry] .... MEG
Methyl(ethyl)pyridine [Organic chemistry] .... MEP
Methylfuran [Organic chemistry] .... MF
Methylglucose Lipopolysaccharide [Biochemistry] .... MGLP
Methylglucose Polysaccharide [Biochemistry] .... MGP
Methylglucoside [Organic chemistry] .... MG
Methylglyoxal [Also, MGLY] [Organic chemistry] .... MG
Methylglyoxal [Also, MG] [Organic chemistry] .... MGLY
methyl-Glyoxal Bisguanylhydrazone [Antineoplastic drug] (DAVI) .... methyl-GAG
Methylglyoxal Guanylhydrazone [Antineoplastic drug] (MAE) .... MGGH
Methylglyoxalbis(guanylhydrazone) [Mitoguazone] [Also, MGBG] [Antineoplastic drug] .... Me-GAG
Methylglyoxal-bis-guanylhydrazone [Antineoplastic drug] (CDI) .... Methyl-GAG
Methylglyoxalbis(guanylhydrazone) [Mitoguazone] [Also, Me-GAG] [Antineoplastic drug] .... MGBG
Methylhexahydrophthalic Anhydride [Organic chemistry] .... MHHPA
Methylhydrazine Sulfate [Organic chemistry] .... MHS
Methyl(hydroxyethyl)thiazole [Organic chemistry] .... MHT
Methyl(hydroxylnaphthalamino)mercaptotriazole [Organic chemistry] .... MHNAMT
Methyliminobispropylamine [Organic chemistry] .... MIBPA
Methylindole [Organic chemistry] .... MI
Methylisatoic Anhydride [Organic chemistry] .... MIA
Methylisobutyl Carbinol [Also, MIBC] [Organic chemistry] .... MIC
Methylisobutylxanthine [Also, IBMX] [Biochemistry] .... MIX
Methylisopropylaniline [Organic chemistry] .... MIPA
Methylisothiocyanate [Pesticide] .... MITC
Methylisourea [Organic chemistry] .... MIU
Methylmalonic Acid [Organic chemistry] .... MMA
Methylmalonic Acidemia [Medicine] .... MMA
Methylmalonyl-CoA Mutase [An enzyme] .... MM
Methylmercaptoimidazole [Also, MMI] [Thyroid inhibitor] .... METHIMAZOLE
Methylmercaptoimidazole [Also, METHIMAZOLE] [Thyroid inhibitor] .... MMI
Methylmercaptopurine Ribose [Biochemistry] .... MMPR
Methylmercuric Hydroxide [Organic chemistry] .... MMH
Methylmercury Bromide [Organic chemistry] .... MMB
Methylmeth (ABBR) .... METH
Methylmethacrylate [Organic chemistry] .... MME
Methyl(methionine)sulfonium Bromide [Organic chemistry] .... MMSB
Methyl-methoxy-nitrostilbene [Organic chemistry] .... MMONS
Methyl(methylthio)phenol [Organic chemistry] .... MMTP
Methylnadic Anhydride [Organic chemistry] .... MNA
Methylnaphthoquinone [Organic chemistry] .... MNQ
Methylnitroaniline [Organic chemistry] .... MNA
Methylnitronitrosoguanidine [Biochemistry] .... MNNG
Methyl(Nitroso) Toluenesulphonamide [Organic chemistry] .... MNTS
Methylnitrosothiazolidine [Organic chemistry] .... MNTHZ
Methylnitrosourea [Also, NMU] [Organic chemistry] .... MNU
Methylnitrosourethane [Organic chemistry] .... MNUT
Methylnorepinephrine [Also, Normetanephrine] [Biochemistry] .... MNE
Methylnorlaudanosolinecarboxylic Acid [Biochemistry] .... MNLCA
Methylo-CCNU, Vineristine, Fluorouracil [Antineoplastic drug regimen] (DAVI) .... MOF
Methylol Dimethylhydantoin [Organic chemistry] .... MDMH
Methyl-para-Tyrosine [Biochemistry] .... MPT
Methylpentanediol [Organic chemistry] .... MPD
Methylphenidate [Central Nervous system stimulant] .... MP
Methylphenidate [Pharmacology] (DAVI) .... MPH
Methylphenothiazine [Organic chemistry] .... MPTH
Methyl(phenyl)(butyl)barbituric (Acid) [Biochemistry] .... MPBB
Methylphenylethylhydantoin [Organic chemistry] (MAE) .... MPEH
(Methylphenyl)phenylhydantoin [Organic chemistry] .... MPPH
Methyl(phenyl)(propionoxy)piperidine [Organic chemistry] .... MPPP
Methyl(phenyl)(propyl)barbituric (Acid) [Biochemistry] .... MPPB
Methyl(phenyl)pyridine [Biochemistry] .... MPP
Methyl(phenyl)tetrahydropyridine [Organic chemistry] .... MPTP
Methylphorbol Myristate Acetate [Organic chemistry] .... MPMA
Methylphosphonic Diamide [Flame retardant] [Organic chemistry] .... MPD
Methylphosphonous Dichloride [Toxic compound] [Army symbol] .... SW
Methylphosphoric Acid [Organic chemistry] .... MPA
Methylpiperazine [Organic chemistry] .... MPP
(Methylpiperidyl)methylphenothiazine [Sedative] .... MPMP
Methylprednisolone [Endocrinology] .... MP
Methylprednisolone Acetate [A glucocorticoid] (MAE) .... MPA
Methylprednisolone Pulse Therapy [Medicine] .... MPPT
Methylprednisolone Sodium Succinate [Medicine] (DAVI) .... MP
Methylprednisolone Sodium Succinate [Antirheumatoid compound] .... MSS
Methylpurine [Organic chemistry] .... MP
Methyl-Red, Voges-Proskauer [Medium] [Bacteriology] .... MRVP
Methylrhodamine Isothiocyanate [Organic chemistry] .... MRITC
Methylrosaniline Chloride [Also, GV] [A dye] .... MRC
Methylstyrylbenzene [Fluorescent compound] .... MSB
Methyl-tert-butylaniline [Organic chemistry] .... MTBA
Methyltetrahydrocarbolinecarboxylic Acid [Organic chemistry] .... MTCA
Methyltetrahydrofolate [or Methyltetrahydrofolic] [Biochemistry] .... MTHF
Methyltetrahydrofolic Acid [Biochemistry] .... MeTHF
Methyltetrahydrofuran [Organic chemistry] .... MTHF

Methyltetrahydrohomofolate [Biochemistry] .... MTHHF
Methyltetrahydrophthalic Anhydride [Organic chemistry] .... MTHPA
Methylthiazolidinecarboxylic Acid [Organic chemistry] .... MTCA
Methylthioadenosine Phosphorylase [An enzyme] .... MTAP
Methylthiocarbamoyl [Biochemistry] .... Mtc
Methylthiocholine [Biochemistry] .... MeThCh
(Methylthio)ethyl Acetoacetate [Organic chemistry] .... MTEAA
(Methyl)thiogalactoside [Biochemistry] .... MTG
Methylthiohydantoin [Organic chemistry] .... MTH
Methylthioinosine [Biochemistry] .... MTI
(Methylthio)-meta-Cresol [Organic chemistry] .... MTMC
Methylthiomethyl [Organic chemistry] .... MTM
Methylthionadenosine [Biochemistry] .... MTA
(Methylthio)phenol [Organic chemistry] .... MTP
Methylthioribose [Biochemistry] .... MTR
Methyl(thio)tetrazole [Biochemistry] .... MTT
Methylthiouracil [Pharmacology] .... MTU
Methylthymol Blue [An indicator] [Chemistry] .... MTB
Methylthymol Blue Complex (BABM) .... MBC
Methyltransferase [An enzyme] .... MTase
Methyltransferase I [An enzyme] .... MTI
Methyl(triazabicyclo)decene [Organic chemistry] .... MTBD
Methyltriazolinedione [Organic chemistry] .... MTD
Methyltrichlorodibenzofuran [Organic chemistry] .... MCDF
Methyltrichlorosilane [Organic chemistry] .... MTS
Methyltriethoxysilane [Organic chemistry] .... MTES
Methyltriethyllead [Organic chemistry] .... MTEL
Methyltrimethoxysilane [Organic chemistry] .... MTMS
Methyltrimethylsilylacetamide [Organic chemistry] .... MSA
(Methyl)trimethylsilyltrifluoroacetamide [Organic chemistry] .... MSTFA
Methyltryptophan [Biochemistry] .... MT
Methyltyrosine [Biochemistry] .... MT
Methylumbelliferone [Biochemistry] .... MEU
Methylumbelliferone [Biochemistry] .... MU
Methylumbelliferone Sulfate [Biochemistry] .... MUS
Methylumbelliferyl [Biochemistry] .... MeUmb
Methylumbelliferyl Guanidinobenzoate [Biochemistry] .... MUGB
Methylumbelliferyl-B-Galactosidase [Biochemistry] (MAE) .... MU-GAL
Methylumbelliferylglucuronide [Biochemistry] .... MUG
Methylurea [Organic chemistry] .... MU
Methylvinylpyridine [Organic chemistry] .... MVP
Methyl-Violet Paper (MSA) .... MVP
Methyprylon (ABBR) .... METH
Methysergide [A serotonin antagonist] [Pharmacology] (DAVI) .... MSG
Metical (ODBW) .... Mt
Meticulous (ABBR) .... METIC
Metina Development [Vancouver Stock Exchange symbol] .... MDE
Metlakatla [Alaska] [Airport symbol] (OAG) .... MTM
Metlakatla, AK [Location identifier FAA] (FAAL) .... ICK
Metlakatla, AK [Location identifier FAA] (FAAL) .... MTM
Metmyoglobin [Medicine] (MEDA) .... metMb
Metoclopramide [An antiemetic] .... M
Metocurine [A muscle relaxant] .... MTC
Metol-Quinol [Developer] [Photography] (ROG) .... MQ
Metol-Quinol [Medicine] (AD) .... mq
Metol-Quinone [Medicine] (AD) .... MQ
Metol-Quinone [Medicine] (AD) .... mq
Metonymy .... METON
Metopon Ethnikis Adadimiourgias [National Regeneration Front] [Greece] [Political party] (PPE) .... MEA
Metoprolol in Acute Myocardial Infarction [Cardiology study] .... MIAMI
Met-Pro Corp. [Associated Press] (SAG) .... MetPro
Met-Pro Corp. [AMEX symbol] (SPSG) .... MPR
Metra Biosystems [Associated Press] (SAG) .... MetraB
Metra Biosystems [NASDAQ symbol] (SAG) .... MTRA
Metra Potential (NITA) .... MP
Metra-Potential Method [Graph theory] .... MPM
Metre-Gram-Second .... MGS
Metres of Fresh Water .... MFW
Metres of Salt Water .... MSW
Metric .... MTRC
Metric Association [Later, USMA] (EA) .... MA
Metric Board (OICC) .... MB
Metric Carat [200 milligrams] (ADA) .... CM
Metric Carat [200 milligrams] (ADA) .... MC
Metric Color Tag [Computer science] (PCM) .... MCT
Metric Commission Reference Unit, Ottawa, ON, Canada [Library symbol Library of Congress] (LCLS) .... CaOOMC
Metric Conversion Board (NADA) .... MCB
Metric Conversion Bureau (NADA) .... MCB
Metric Coordinating Group (MCD) .... MCG
Metric Data Facility (MCD) .... MDF
Metric Data Processing System [Air Force] .... MDPS
Metric Information Office [National Institute of Standards and Technology] .... MIO
Metric Paper Sizer of Standard Heights for Stationery and Printing [International organization for standardization] (BARN) .... A
Metric Size (IAA) .... MS
Metric System .... MS
Metric System (AD) .... ms
Metric System - Conversion (NATG) .... MSC
Metric Time System (NASA) .... MTS
Metric Time System .... MTS
Metric Ton [1,000 kilograms] .... MT
Metric Ton .... t
Metric Ton of Heavy Metal (NUCP) .... MTHM

Metric Ton Unit ... MTU
Metric Tons Energy Consumption ... MTec
Metric Tons Initial Heavy Metal (GAAI) ... MTIHM
Metric Tons of Uranium ... MTU
Metric Tons per Annum ... MTA
Metric Tons per Cubic Meter ... T/M^3
Metric Tons per Square Meter ... T/M^2
Metric Units (DFIT) ... MTU
Metrication Board [*British*] ... MB
Metrication Days [*Sponsored by the Metrication Board to educate merchants and public on metric system*] [*British*] ... M (Days)
Metricom, Inc. [*NASDAQ symbol*] (SAG) ... MCOM
Metricom, Inc. [*Associated Press*] (SAG) ... Metrcm
Metrics Research Corp. [*Information service or system*] (IID) ... MRC
Metris Companies, Inc. [*Associated Press*] (SAG) ... MetrisCo
Metris Companies, Inc. [*NASDAQ symbol*] (SAG) ... MTRS
Metrizamide Computed Tomography ... MCT
Metrizamide Computed Tomography Cisternography [*Medicine*] (DMAA) ... MCTC
Metro Airlines [*ICAO designator*] (AD) ... HY
Metro Canada Ltd., Kingston, ON, Canada [*Library symbol*] [*Library of Congress*] (LCLS) ... CaOKME
Metro Canada Ltd., Kingston, Ontario [*Library symbol National Library of Canada*] (NLC) ... OKME
Metro Capital Corp. [*NASDAQ symbol*] (SAG) ... METO
Metro Capital Corp. [*Associated Press*] (SAG) ... MetrCap
Metro Express II, Inc. [*ICAO designator*] (FAAC) ... MEX
Metro Express, Inc. [*ICAO designator*] (FAAC) ... EME
Metro Financial Corp. [*Associated Press*] (SAG) ... MetroFn
Metro Financial Corp. [*NASDAQ symbol*] (SAG) ... MFIN
Metro General Hospital, Nashville, TN [*Library symbol Library of Congress*] (LCLS) ... TNMH
Metro Global Media [*NASDAQ symbol*] (TTSB) ... MGMA
Metro Global Media, Inc. [*Associated Press*] (SAG) ... MetGlob
Metro Global Media, Inc. [*NASDAQ symbol*] (SAG) ... MGMA
Metro Industrial [*Vancouver Stock Exchange symbol*] ... MIC
Metro Manila Airways International, Inc. [*Philippines*] [*ICAO designator*] (FAAC) ... MMA
Metro Networks, Inc. [*Associated Press*] (SAG) ... MetrNet
Metro Networks, Inc. [*NASDAQ symbol*] (SAG) ... MTNT
Metro One Telecommunications, Inc. [*NASDAQ symbol*] (SAG) ... MTON
Metro One Telecommunications, Inc. [*Associated Press*] (SAG) ... MtroOne
Metro Prop-Jet [*Airplane code*] ... Swm
Metro Rating Area [*Arbitron television ratings*] (NTCM) ... MRA
Metro Rating Area (AD) ... mra
Metro Tel Corp. [*NASDAQ symbol*] (TTSB) ... MTRO
MetroBanCorp [*NASDAQ symbol*] (SAG) ... METB
MetroBancorp [*Associated Press*] (SAG) ... MetrBcp
Metrobank NA [*AMEX symbol*] (SPSG) ... MBN
Metrobank North America [*Associated Press*] (SAG) ... Metrbk
Metrocall, Inc. [*NASDAQ symbol*] (SAG) ... MCLL
Metrocall, Inc. [*Associated Press*] (SAG) ... Metrocall
Metro-Cammell Weymaua Ltd. [*British*] (DCTA) ... MCW
Metrofiber Multi-Megabit Data Service [*Metropolitan Fiber Systems, Inc.*] ... MDS
Metroflight Airlines and Great Plains Airline [*ICAO designator*] (AD) ... FY
Metroflight, Inc. [*ICAO designator*] (FAAC) ... MTR
Metrogas SA [*Associated Press*] (SAG) ... Metrogs
Metrogas SA [*NYSE symbol*] (SAG) ... MGS
MetroGas S.A. Cl'B'ADS [*NYSE symbol*] (TTSB) ... MGS
Metro-Goldwyn-Mayer (WDMC) ... Metro
Metro-Goldwyn-Mayer [*Record label*] [*USA, Great Britain, etc.*] ... MGM
Metro-Goldwyn-Mayer, Research Department, Culver City, CA [*Library symbol Library of Congress*] (LCLS) ... CCuM
Metro-International Program Services of New York (EA) ... M-I
Metro-International Program Services of New York (EA) ... MIPSNY
Metrolina Educational Consortium [*North Carolina*] (EDAC) ... MEC
Metrolina Library Association [*Library network*] ... MLA
Metrologic Instruments [*NASDAQ symbol*] (TTSB) ... MTLG
Metrologic Instruments, Inc. [*Associated Press*] (SAG) ... Metrolog
Metrologic Instruments, Inc. [*NASDAQ symbol*] (SAG) ... MTLG
Metrological Equipment and Technical Liaison Officer [*Navy*] (NG) ... METLO
Metrology ... METROL
Metrology and Calibration [*Air Force*] (AFIT) ... METCAL
Metrology and Calibration Center [*Army*] (MCD) ... MCC
Metrology Automated System for Uniform Recall and Reporting [*Navy*] ... MEASURE
Metrology Data Bank [*GIDEP*] ... MDB
Metrology Information Service [*GIDEP*] ... MIS
Metrology Requirements List [*DoD*] ... METRL
Metrology Standards Requirements Board (ACII) ... MSRB
Metromail Corp. [*Associated Press*] (SAG) ... Metmail
Metromail Corp. [*NYSE symbol*] (SAG) ... ML
Metromedia International Group [*Associated Press*] (SAG) ... Metromda
Metromedia International Group [*AMEX symbol*] (SAG) ... MMG
Metromedia Intl Grp [*AMEX symbol*] (TTSB) ... MMG
Metromedia Producers Corp. ... MPC
Metronome ... M
Metronome [*Music*] ... MET
Metronome [*Record label*] [*Scandinavia, Germany, etc.*] ... Mtr
Metronome Mark (ROG) ... MM
Metronome-Conditioned Relaxation ... MCR
Metroplex Control Facility [*FAA*] (TAG) ... MCF
Metropol (WDAA) ... METROP
Metropol Ed 3.90% cm Pfd [*NYSE symbol*] (TTSB) ... MTTPrC
Metropolis (ROG) ... MET
Metropolis (ADA) ... METROP
Metropolis [*or Metropolitan*] (ABBR) ... METROPOL
Metropolis, IL [*Location identifier FAA*] (FAAL) ... MIX
Metropolis, IL [*AM radio station call letters*] ... WMOK
Metropolis, IL [*FM radio station call letters*] ... WREZ
Metropolis, IL [*FM radio station call letters*] ... WRIK
Metropolitan ... M
Metropolitan (AAG) ... MET
Metropolitan ... METR
Metropolitan [*Subway system*] (DSUE) ... METRO
Metropolitan ... METRO
Metropolitan ... METROP
Metropolitan Academic Consultants Sales Corp. ... MACSCO
Metropolitan Achievement Test ... MAT
Metropolitan Action Institute [*Formerly, SAI*] (EA) ... MAI
Metropolitan Administration for Review and Comment [*Program using regional councils of government to serve as clearinghouses for Federal grants*] ... MARC
Metropolitan Air Post Society (EA) ... MAPS
Metropolitan Applied Research Center (BARN) ... MARC
Metropolitan Architectural Consortium for Education (AIE) ... MACE
Metropolitan Area Apparel Association (EA) ... MAAA
Metropolitan Area Digital Network (NTCM) ... MADN
Metropolitan Area Exchange [*Telecommunications*] (ACRL) ... MAE
Metropolitan Area Express [*Railway*] [*Portland, OR*] (ECON) ... MAX
Metropolitan Area Network [*Telecommunications*] ... MAN
Metropolitan Area Trunk [*Telecommunications*] (TEL) ... MAT
Metropolitan Association of Handwriting Analysts (EA) ... MAHA
Metropolitan Association of Urban Designers and Environmental Planners (EA) ... MAUDEP
Metropolitan Asylums Board [*British*] ... MAB
Metropolitan Atlanta Rapid Transit Authority [*FTA*] (TAG) ... MARTA
Metropolitan Atlanta Rapid Transit Authority, Atlanta, GA [*Library symbol Library of Congress*] (LCLS) ... GAMARTA
Metropolitan Bag and Paper Distributors Association (EA) ... MBPDA
Metropolitan Ballet Theatre [*Detroit*] ... MBT
Metropolitan Bancorp [*Associated Press*] (SAG) ... MetroBcp
Metropolitan Bancorp [*NASDAQ symbol*] (TTSB) ... MSEA
Metropolitan Bancorp Seattle [*NASDAQ symbol*] (SAG) ... MSEA
Metropolitan Board of Works [*British*] ... MBW
Metropolitan Borough ... METB
Metropolitan Borough Council [*British*] ... MBC
Metropolitan Boston Transit Authority (BARN) ... MBTA
Metropolitan Cemeteries Board [*Western Australia*] ... MCB
Metropolitan Centrex [*Telephone network*] ... METREX
Metropolitan Church Schoolmasters' Association [*A union*] [*British*] ... MCSA
Metropolitan Cities Drug Association Secretaries (EA) ... MCDAS
Metropolitan Club of America (EA) ... MCA
Metropolitan Club, Washington, DC [*Library symbol Library of Congress*] (LCLS) ... DMC
Metropolitan Club, Washington, DC [*Library symbol*] [*Library of Congress*] (LCLS) ... DMCu
Metropolitan College Mental Health Association (EA) ... MCMHA
Metropolitan Collegiate Athletic Conference (EA) ... METRO
Metropolitan Communications Squadron [*British military*] (DMA) ... MCS
Metropolitan Commuter Transportation Authority [*Greater New York City*] [*Later, Metropolitan Transportation Authority*] ... MCTA
Metropolitan Consortium for Minorities in Science and Engineering (USDC) ... METCON
Metropolitan Cooperative Library System [*Library network*] ... MCLS
Metropolitan Cooperative Library System, Pasadena, CA [*OCLC symbol*] (OCLC) ... MSH
Metropolitan Council for Educational Opportunity (EA) ... METCO
Metropolitan Counties [*British*] ... MC
Metropolitan County Council [*British*] ... MCC
Metropolitan Dairymen's Society [*British*] (BI) ... MDS
Metropolitan District [*British*] ... MD
Metropolitan District Commission ... MDC
Metropolitan District Council [*British*] ... MDC
Metropolitan District Railway [*London*] ... MDR
Metropolitan Economic Area ... MEA
Metropolitan Edison Capital Ltd. [*Associated Press*] (SAG) ... MetEC
Metropolitan Edison Co. [*Associated Press*] (SAG) ... MtE
Metropolitan Edison Co. [*NYSE symbol*] (SPSG) ... MTT
Metropolitan Educational Television Association [*Canada*] ... META
Metropolitan Electric Tramways [*British*] (ROG) ... MET
Metropolitan Engineers Council on Air Resources ... MECAR
Metropolitan Entertainers' Association [*British*] (BI) ... MEA
Metropolitan Fiber Systems, Inc. ... MFS
Metropolitan Fire Brigade [*British*] ... MFB
Metropolitan Information Network ... MINET
Metropolitan Information Processing Conference (MCD) ... MIPC
Metropolitan Instructional Support Laboratory, Portland State University, Portland, OR [*Library symbol*] [*Library of Congress*] (LCLS) ... OrPS-MI
Metropolitan Intercollegiate Basketball Association (EA) ... MIBA
Metropolitan Interlibrary Cooperative System [*New York Public Library*] [*Information service or system*] ... MILCS
Metropolitan Libraries Section [*Public Library Association*] ... MLS
Metropolitan Library Network [*Library network*] ... MLN
Metropolitan Library Service Agency [*Library network*] ... MELSA
Metropolitan Library System, Capitol Hill Branch, Oklahoma City, OK [*OCLC symbol*] (OCLC) ... OKE
Metropolitan Life Insurance Co. Financial and Administrative Customer Services System (HGAA) ... MetFACS
Metropolitan Life Insurance Co., New York, NY [*Library symbol Library of Congress*] (LCLS) ... NNML

Metropolitan Life Insurance Co., Ottawa, ON, Canada [*Library symbol Library of Congress*] (LCLS) ... CaOOML
Metropolitan Life Insurance Co., Ottawa, Ontario [*Library symbol National Library of Canada*] (NLC) ... OOML
Metropolitan Life Insurance Co., San Francisco, CA [*Library symbol Library of Congress*] (LCLS) ... CSfMetL
Metropolitan Magazine Association [*Later, Magazine Publishers Association*] (EA) ... MMA
Metropolitan Map Series [*Bureau of the Census*] (GFGA) ... MMS
Metropolitan Medical Center, Hospital Services Library, Minneapolis, MN [*Library symbol Library of Congress*] (LCLS) ... MnMMet-H
Metropolitan Medical Center, Medical Library, Minneapolis, MN [*Library symbol Library of Congress*] (LCLS) ... MnMMet
Metropolitan Meteorological Experiment ... METROMEX
Metropolitan Milk Board [*South Australia*] ... MMB
Metropolitan Motor Carriers Conference Inc., Dover NJ [*STAC*] ... MMC
Metropolitan Museum of Art [*New York*] (BJA) ... MMA
Metropolitan Museum of Art, Costume Institute, New York, NY [*Library symbol Library of Congress*] (LCLS) ... NNMM-CI
Metropolitan Museum of Art, New York, NY [*Library symbol Library of Congress*] (LCLS) ... NNMM
Metropolitan Museum of Art, The Cloisters Library, New York, NY [*Library symbol*] [*Library of Congress*] (LCLS) ... NNMM-C
Metropolitan Music Hall [*London*] [*British*] (DSUE) ... MET
Metropolitan Mutual Housing Association [*Defunct*] (EA) ... MMHA
Metropolitan Opera Association (EA) ... Metopera
Metropolitan Opera Association (AD) ... MOA
Metropolitan Opera Association (NADA) ... MOA
Metropolitan Opera Auditions (AD) ... MOA
Metropolitan Opera Guild (EA) ... MOG
[*New York*] **Metropolitan Opera House** ... Met
Metropolitan Opera National Council ... MONC
Metropolitan Owners' Club [*Woking, Surrey, England*] (EAIO) ... MOC
Metropolitan Owners Club of North America (EA) ... MOCNA
Metropolitan Park District (AD) ... MPD
Metropolitan Pensions Associations (AD) ... MPA
Metropolitan Pharmaceutical Secretaries Association (EA) ... MPSA
Metropolitan Planning Organization [*FHWA*] [*MTMC*] (TAG) ... MPO
Metropolitan Planning Organization ... MPO
Metropolitan Police ... MP
Metropolitan Police College (AD) ... MPC
Metropolitan Police Commissioner (AD) ... MPC
Metropolitan Police Department (AD) ... MPD
Metropolitan Police District [*London*] ... MPD
Metropolitan Police Force [*Scotland Yard*] [*London, England*] ... MPF
Metropolitan Police Laboratory (AD) ... MPL
Metropolitan Police Missing Persons Register [*British*] ... MPMPR
Metropolitan Police Office [*Familiarly called "Scotland Yard" from its site at New Scotland Yard*] [*British*] ... MPO
Metropolitan Police Officers [*British*] ... MEPOL
Metropolitan Post Card Collectors Club (EA) ... MPCCC
Metropolitan Public Gardens Association [*British*] (BI) ... MPGA
Metropolitan Public Libraries Association [*New South Wales, Australia*] ... MPLA
[*The*] **Metropolitan Railway** [*British*] (ROG) ... MET
Metropolitan Railway [*British*] ... MetR
Metropolitan Railway [*British*] ... MR
Metropolitan Readiness Test ... MRT
Metropolitan Realty [*AMEX symbol*] (TTSB) ... MET
Metropolitan Realty Corp. [*AMEX symbol*] (CTT) ... MET
Metropolitan Realty Corp. [*Associated Press*] (SAG) ... MetRlt
Metropolitan Refuse Disposal Consultative Committee [*Melbourne, Australia*] ... MRDCC
Metropolitan Region Planning Authority (AD) ... MRPA
Metropolitan Sanitary District of Greater Chicago, Chicago, IL [*Library symbol Library of Congress*] (LCLS) ... ICSD
Metropolitan School Study Council [*Columbia University*] (AEE) ... MSSC
Metropolitan Separate School Board [*UTLAS symbol*] ... MSB
Metropolitan Separate School Board, Professional Library, Willowdale, ON, Canada [*Library symbol*] [*Library of Congress*] (LCLS) ... CaOTMSS
Metropolitan Service Area [*Telecommunications*] (TSSD) ... MSA
Metropolitan Sewer District (GNE) ... MSD
Metropolitan Speleological Society [*Australia*] ... MSS
Metropolitan State College [*Denver, CO*] ... MSC
Metropolitan State Community College, Minneapolis, MN [*Library symbol Library of Congress*] (LCLS) ... MnMMC
Metropolitan State Junior College, Minneapolis, MN [*Library symbol Library of Congress*] (LCLS) ... MnMMetS
Metropolitan Statistical Area [*Census Bureau*] ... MSA
Metropolitan Symphony Managers Association (EA) ... MSMA
Metropolitan Taxicab Board (NADA) ... MTCB
Metropolitan Technical Community College, Omaha, NE [*Library symbol Library of Congress*] (LCLS) ... NbOMC
Metropolitan Technical Community College, Omaha, NE [*OCLC symbol*] (OCLC) ... NEM
Metropolitan Toronto Central Library, Baldwin Room, Toronto, ON, Canada [*Library symbol Library of Congress*] (LCLS) ... CaOTPB
Metropolitan Toronto Central Library, History Section, Toronto, ON, Canada [*Library symbol Library of Congress*] (LCLS) ... CaOTPH
Metropolitan Toronto Central Library, Toronto, ON, Canada [*Library symbol Library of Congress Obsolete*] (LCLS) ... CaOTMCL
Metropolitan Toronto Library Board, Cataloguing Department [*UTLAS symbol*] ... MLC
Metropolitan Toronto Library Board, Systems Unit [*UTLAS symbol*] ... MLB
Metropolitan Toronto Library, Multilanguage Service [*UTLAS symbol*] ... OMT
Metropolitan Toronto Library, Ontario [*Library symbol National Library of Canada*] (NLC) ... OTMCL
Metropolitan Toronto School Board, Ontario [*Library symbol National Library of Canada*] (NLC) ... OTMTS
Metropolitan Toronto School Board, Secondary Schools, Toronto, ON, Canada [*Library symbol*] [*Library of Congress*] (LCLS) ... CaOTMTSS
Metropolitan Toronto School Board, Toronto, ON, Canada [*Library symbol Library of Congress*] (LCLS) ... CaOTMTS
Metropolitan Transit Authority [*Later, MBTA*] [*Initialism also title of folk song about Boston's transit system*] ... MTA
Metropolitan Transit Development Board (NADA) ... MTDB
Metropolitan Transportation Authority [*Greater New York City*] ... MTA
Metropolitan Travel Agents [*Inactive*] (EA) ... MTA
Metropolitan Tree Improvement Alliance (EA) ... METRIA
Metropolitan Visiting and Relief Association [*British*] ... MVRA
Metropolitan Waste Management Council [*Melbourne, Australia*] ... MWMC
Metropolitan Water Board [*British*] ... MWB
Metropolitan Water District ... MWD
Metropolitan Water District of Southern California, Los Angeles, CA [*Library symbol Library of Congress*] (LCLS) ... CLMeW
Metropolitan Waterworks and Sewerage System [*Philippines*] ... MWSS
Metropolitian Museum of Art, Uris Library and Resources Center, New York, NY [*Library symbol*] [*Library of Congress*] (LCLS) ... NNMMA-U
Metro-Tel Corp. [*Associated Press*] (SAG) ... MetrTl
Metro-Tel Corp. [*NASDAQ symbol*] (NQ) ... MTRO
Metrotrans Corp. [*Associated Press*] (SAG) ... Metrotrn
Metrotrans Corp. [*NASDAQ symbol*] (SAG) ... MTRN
metrotrexate, Citrovorum Factor, VM-26, Procarbazine, Dexamethasone [*Antineoplastic drug regimen*] (DAVI) ... MVPD-26
MetroVision of North America, Inc. [*Associated Press*] (SAG) ... MetroV
MetroVision of North America, Inc. [*Associated Press*] (SAG) ... MetrV
MetroVision of North America, Inc. [*NASDAQ symbol*] (SAG) ... MVTV
Metter, GA [*FM radio station call letters*] ... WHCG
Metter, GA [*AM radio station call letters*] ... WMAC
Metuchen [*Diocesan abbreviation*] [*New Jersey*] (TOCD) ... MET
Metwork Six [*NASDAQ symbol*] (TTSB) ... MWSS
Metz [*France*] [*Airport symbol*] (OAG) ... MZM
Metz/Frescaty [*France ICAO location identifier*] (ICLI) ... LFSF
Metz Owners Club Library (EA) ... MOCL
Metz Owners Club Register (EA) ... MOCR
Metzada/I. Bar Yehuda [*Israel*] [*ICAO location identifier*] (ICLI) ... LLMZ
Metzenbaum [*Instruments*] [*Surgery*] (DAVI) ... Metz
Meulaboh/Cut Nyak Dien [*Indonesia*] [*ICAO location identifier*] (ICLI) ... WITC
Mevalonic Acid [*Organic chemistry*] ... MVA
Mevinolin Atherosclerosis Regression Study (MEDA) ... MARS
Mewar Bhil Corps [*British military*] (DMA) ... MBC
Mews ... M
Mews [*Postal Service standard*] (OPSA) ... MEWS
Mews' Digest of English Case Law [*A publication*] (DLA) ... Mews
Mews' Digest of English Case Law [*A publication*] (DLA) ... Mews Dig
Mexair SA [*Switzerland ICAO designator*] (FAAC) ... MXC
Mexia, TX [*AM radio station call letters*] ... KRQX
Mexia, TX [*FM radio station call letters*] ... KYCX
Mexia, TX [*Location identifier FAA*] (FAAL) ... LXY
Mexicali [*Mexico*] [*Airport symbol*] (OAG) ... MXL
Mexicali/General Rodolfo Sanchez Taboada Internacional [*Mexico ICAO location identifier*] (ICLI) ... MMML
Mexican (ROG) ... MEX
Mexican ... MEX
Mexican American Legal Defense and Educational Fund (EA) ... MALDEF
Mexican American State Legislators Policy Institute (CROSS) ... MASLPI
Mexican American Studies and Research Center [*University of Arizona*] [*Research center*] (RCD) ... MASRC
Mexican American Women's National Association (EA) ... MANA
Mexican American Workers Importation Act ... MAWIA
Mexican Border Service Medal ... MBSM
Mexican Border Veterans (EA) ... MBV
Mexican Chamber of Commerce of US ... MCCM
Mexican Coffee Institute (EA) ... MCI
Mexican Epigraphic Society (EA) ... MES
Mexican Food and Beverage Board (EA) ... MFBB
Mexican Government Tourism Office (EA) ... MGTO
Mexican Investment Board [*Public relations and investor assistance*] [*Mexico*] (CROSS) ... MIB
Mexican L & P Co. Ltd. [*Toronto Stock Exchange symbol*] ... MX
Mexican League [*Baseball*] ... ML
Mexican Meteorological Service ... MMS
Mexican National Tourist Council (EA) ... MNTC
Mexican Passionist Sisters (TOCD) ... CFP
Mexican Peso [*Monetary unit*] ... MP
Mexican Pharmacopoeia [*A publication*] ... MexP
Mexican Stock Exchange (MHDW) ... MSE
Mexican War Veteran ... MWV
Mexican Water Plan [*Land use*] ... MWP
Mexicana [*Airline*] (DS) ... MX
Mexicana de Aviacion [*ICAO designator*] (AD) ... MX
Mexican-American ... MA
Mexican-American Affairs Unit [*Office of Education*] ... MAAU
Mexican-American Correctional Association (OICC) ... MACA
Mexican-American Documentation and Educational Research Institute ... MADERI
Mexican-American Engineering Society (EA) ... MAES
Mexican-American Opportunity Foundation (EA) ... MAOF
Mexican-American Political Association ... MAPA

Mexican-Chicano Cooperative Programs on Mexican-US-Chicano Futures
(EA) .... PROCOMEXCHI
Mexican-Spanish Speaking (OICC) .... MSS
Mexico [ANSI three-letter standard code] (CNC) .... MEX
Mexico (VRA) .... Mex
Mexico [Mexico ICAO location identifier] (ICLI) .... MMEX
Mexico [ANSI two-letter standard code] (CNC) .... MX
Mexico [IYRU nationality code] [MARC country of publication code Library of
Congress] (LCCP) .... mx
Mexico [MARC geographic area code Library of Congress] (LCCP) .... n-mx--
Mexico [International civil aircraft marking] (ODBW) XC
Mexico Beach, FL [FM radio station call letters] .... WEBZ
Mexico Beach, FL [FM radio station call letters] (RBYB) .... WSHF-FM
Mexico City [Mexico] [Later, TEO] [Geomagnetic observatory code] .... MEX
Mexico City [Mexico] [Airport symbol] (OAG) .... MEX
Mexico Eqty & Income Fd [NYSE symbol] (TTSB) .... MXE
Mexico Equity & Income Fund [Associated Press] (SAG) .... MexEqt
Mexico Equity & Income Fund [NYSE symbol] (SPSG) .... MXE
Mexico Fund [NYSE symbol] (TTSB) .... MXF
[The] Mexico Fund, Inc. [Associated Press] (SAG) .... MexFd
[The] Mexico Fund, Inc. [NYSE symbol] (SPSG) .... MXF
Mexico/Lic. Benito Juarez Internacional [Mexico ICAO location identifier]
(ICLI) .... MMMX
Mexico, ME [FM radio station call letters] .... WTBM
Mexico, MO [FM radio station call letters] .... KJAB
Mexico, MO [FM radio station call letters] .... KWWR
Mexico, MO [AM radio station call letters] .... KXEO
Mexico, NY [FM radio station call letters] (RBYB) .... WUPN
Mexico, PA [AM radio station call letters] .... WJUN
Mexico, PA [FM radio station call letters] .... WJUN-FM
Mexico Pilgrims Foundation (EA) .... MPF
Mexico-Albania Friendship Society (EAIO) .... MAFS
Mexico-Audrain County Library, Mexico, MO [Library symbol Library of
Congress] (LCLS) .... MoMex
Mexico-Elmhurst Philatelic Society, International (EA) .... MEPSI
Mexico-United States Institute (EA) .... MUSI
Meyer Ammunition Module - Emerson Electric .... MAMEE
Meyer, Hendricks, Victor, Osborn & Maledon, P.A., Phoenix, AZ [Library
symbol] [Library of Congress] (LCLS) .... AzPhMH
Meyer Hydraulic Theory .... MHT
Meyer [Fred], Inc. [NYSE symbol] (SPSG) .... FMY
Meyer [Fred], Inc. [Associated Press] (SAG) .... FrMeyer
Meyer, Jr., L. Agnew, Washington DC [STAC] .... MJL
Meyer-Kendall Assessment Survey [Interpersonal skills and attitudes
test] .... MKAS
Meyers Aircraft Owners Association (EA) .... MAOA
Meyer's Des Institutiones Judiciares [A publication]
(DLA) .... Meyer Des Inst Judiciares
Meyersdale, PA [FM radio station call letters] .... WQZS
Meyerson [M.H.] & Co. [Associated Press] (SAG) .... MHMey
Meyerson [M.H.] & Co. [Associated Press] (SAG) .... MHMeyer
Meyerson [M.H.] & Co. [NASDAQ symbol] (SAG) .... MHMY
Meyerton [South Africa] [ICAO location identifier] (ICLI) .... FAMT
Meymeh [Iran] [ICAO location identifier] (ICLI) .... OIFY
Mezhdunarodnaja Assotsiatsija Professorov Russkogo Jazyka i Literatury
[International Association of Teachers of Russian Language and
Literature] (EAIO) .... MAPRIAL
Mezhdunarodnaya Assotsiatsiya Sudovladeltsev [International Shipowners'
Association] [Poland] (EAIO) .... MAS
Mezhdunarodnaya Organizacia Zhurnalistov [International Organization of
Journalists] [Russian] (EAIO) .... MOZ
Mezhdunarodnoe Obshchestvo po Mashinam dlja Ovoshchevodstva,
Sadovodstva, i Vinogradstva [International Association for Vine, Fruit, and
Vegetable-Growing Mechanization] (EAIO) .... AGROMASH
Mezhdunarodnyi Bank Ekonomicheskovo Sotrudnichestva [International
Bank for Economic Co-Operation - IBEC] [Moscow, USSR] (EAIO) .... MBES
Mezhdunarodnyi Investitsionnyi Bank [International Investment Bank - IIB]
[Moscow, USSR] (EAIO) .... MIB
Mezhotraslevoi Naucho-Tekhni-Cheskii Kompleks [Interdisciplinary Scientific-
Technological Complex] [Russian] .... MNTK
Mezuzah (BJA) .... Mez
Mezza Voce [Half the Power of the Voice] [Music] .... MV
Mezzanine (ABBR) .... MEZN
Mezzanine (VRA) .... mezn
Mezzanine (KSC) .... MEZZ
Mezzo [Moderate] [Music] .... M
Mezzo [Moderate] [Music] .... MEZ
Mezzo [Moderate] [Music] (ROG) .... MZ
Mezzo Forte [Moderately Loud] [Music] (ROG) .... MF
Mezzo Fortissimo [Rather Loud] [Music] (ADA) .... MFF
Mezzo Forzando [Music] .... MFZ
Mezzo Piano [Moderately Soft] [Music] .... MP
Mezzo Soprano [Music] .... M Sopr
Mezzo Soprano [Music] (ROG) .... MS
Mezzo Soprano [Music] .... MSOP
Mezzo-Piano [Moderately Soft] [Italian] (AD) .... mp
Mezzosoprano (ABBR) .... MEZZO
Mezzotint (VRA) .... mez
Mezzotint [Printing] (ABBR) .... MEZT
Mezzotint [Printing] (ABBR) .... MEZZ
Mezzotint [Printing] (ROG) .... MEZZO
Mezzotinto [Medium Tint, Half Tone] [Engraving] (ROG) .... MEZ
MFB Corp. [Associated Press] (SAG) .... MFB Cp
MFB Corp. [NASDAQ symbol] (SAG) .... MFBC

MFB Mutual Insurance Co. [from Manufacturers Mutual Fire Insurance Co.,
Firemen's Mutual Insurance Co., Blackstone Mutual Insurance Co.] .... MFB
MFC Mining Finance Corp. [Toronto Stock Exchange symbol Vancouver Stock
Exchange symbol] .... MFM
MFRI, Inc. [NASDAQ symbol] (SPSG) .... MFRI
MFS Charter Income Tr [NYSE symbol] (TTSB) .... MCR
MFS Charter Income Trust [NYSE symbol] (SPSG) .... MCR
MFS Commun 8% Cv Dep'A'Pfd [NASDAQ symbol] (TTSB) .... MFSTP
MFS Communiations [NASDAQ symbol] (TTSB) .... MFST
MFS Communication Co. [Associated Press] (SAG) .... MFS C
MFS Communication Co. [Associated Press] (SAG) .... MFS Cm
MFS Communication Co. [NASDAQ symbol] (SAG) .... MFST
MFS Government Markets Income Trust [NYSE symbol] (SPSG) .... MGF
MFS Gvt Mkts Income Tr [NYSE symbol] (TTSB) .... MGF
MFS Interm Incme SBI [NYSE symbol] (TTSB) .... MIN
MFS Intermediate Income SBI [NYSE symbol] (SPSG) .... MIN
MFS Intermediate Income Trust [Associated Press] (SAG) .... MIN
MFS Multimarket Income [NYSE symbol] (SPSG) .... MMT
MFS Multimarket Income Trust [Associated Press] (SAG) .... MMT
MFS Multimkt Income [NYSE symbol] (TTSB) .... MMT
MFS Municipal Income Trust [NYSE symbol] (SPSG) .... MFM
MFS Municipal Inc. Tr [NYSE symbol] (TTSB) .... MFM
MFS Special Value Trust [NYSE symbol] (SPSG) .... MFV
Mfuwe [Zambia] [ICAO location identifier] (ICLI) .... FLMF
Mfuwe [Zambia] [Airport symbol] (OAG) .... MFU
MG Car Club (EA) .... MG
MG [Morris Garage]Car Club .... MGCC
MG Octagon Car Club [Formerly, Octagon Car Club] (EA) .... MOCC
M.G. Products [NASDAQ symbol] (TTSB) .... MGPR
MG Products, Inc. [Associated Press] (SAG) .... MG Prod
MG Products, Inc. [NASDAQ symbol] (SAG) .... MGPR
Mgahinga and Bwindi Inpenetrable Forest Conservation Trust
(ECON) .... MBIFCT
MGI PHARMA, Inc. [Associated Press] (SAG) .... MGI Phr
MGI PHARMA, Inc. [NASDAQ symbol] (NQ) .... MOGN
MGI Properties [NYSE symbol] (SPSG) .... MGI
MGI Properties [Associated Press] (SAG) .... MGI Prp
MGIC Investment [NYSE symbol] (TTSB) .... MTG
MGIC Investment Co. [Associated Press] (SAG) .... MGIC
MGIC Investment Co. [NYSE symbol] (SPSG) .... MTG
MGIC Investment Corp., Milwaukee, WI [Library symbol Library of Congress]
(LCLS) .... WMMGIC
MGM Grand [NYSE symbol] (TTSB) .... MGG
MGM Grand Air [ICAO designator] (AD) .... MG
MGM Grand Air, Inc. [ICAO designator] (FAAC) .... MGM
MGM Grand, Inc. [NYSE symbol] (SPSG) .... MGG
MGM Grand, Inc. [Associated Press] (SAG) .... MGMG
MGM Resources Corp. [Vancouver Stock Exchange symbol] .... MGU
M.H. Meyerson & Co. [NASDAQ symbol] (TTSB) .... MHMY
Mhic Easmuinn Baldonnel, County Dublin [Ireland] [ICAO location
identifier] (ICLI) .... EIME
Mhlume [Swaziland] [ICAO location identifier] (ICLI) .... FDMH
MHM Services [AMEX symbol] (SAG) .... MHM
MHM Services [AMEX symbol] (TTSB) .... MHM
MHM Services [Associated Press] (SAG) .... MHM Serv
Mi Favor [My Favor] [Spanish] .... MF
Mi Orden [My Order] [Spanish] (AD) .... m/o
Mi Remesa [My Remittance] [Spanish Business term] .... MR
MI Software Co. [Vancouver Stock Exchange symbol] .... MSW
Miami [Florida] [ICAO location identifier] (ICLI) .... KZMA
Miami [Florida] [Seismograph station code, US Geological Survey Closed]
(SEIS) .... MIA
Miami [Florida] [Airport symbol] (OAG) .... MIA
Miami Air Charter [ICAO designator] (FAAC) .... HUR
Miami Air International, Inc. [ICAO designator] (FAAC) .... BSK
Miami, AZ [AM radio station call letters] .... KIKO
Miami, AZ [FM radio station call letters] .... KQSS
Miami Beach, FL [FM radio station call letters] .... WLVE
Miami Beach, FL [AM radio station call letters] (RBYB) .... WMBM
Miami Beach, FL [FM radio station call letters] .... WZTA
Miami City Ballet .... MCB
Miami Computer Supply Corp. [NASDAQ symbol] (SAG) .... MCSC
Miami Computer Supply Corp. [Associated Press] (SAG) .... MiamiCm
Miami County Historical Museum, Peru, IN [Library symbol Library of
Congress] (LCLS) .... InPerM
Miami/Dade-Collier Training and Transition Airport [Florida] [ICAO location
identifier] (ICLI) .... KTNT
Miami, FL [Location identifier FAA] (FAAL) .... BUL
Miami, FL [Location identifier FAA] (FAAL) .... CKK
Miami, FL [Location identifier FAA] (FAAL) .... DCX
Miami, FL [Location identifier FAA] (FAAL) .... GEM
Miami, FL [Location identifier FAA] (FAAL) .... MFA
Miami, FL [Location identifier FAA] (FAAL) .... MMN
Miami, FL [Location identifier FAA] (FAAL) .... NMA
Miami, FL [Location identifier FAA] (FAAL) .... OPF
Miami, FL [Location identifier FAA] (FAAL) .... TMB
Miami, FL [Location identifier FAA] (FAAL) .... TNT
Miami, FL [Location identifier FAA] (FAAL) .... VIN
Miami, FL [FM radio station call letters] (RBYB) .... WAMR-FM
Miami, FL [AM radio station call letters] .... WAQI
Miami, FL [Television station call letters] .... WBFS
Miami, FL [Television station call letters] .... WCTD
Miami, FL [FM radio station call letters] .... WDNA
Miami, FL [Television station call letters] .... WDZL
Miami, FL [FM radio station call letters] .... WEDR

Miami, FL [*AM radio station call letters*] .... WFBA
Miami, FL [*FM radio station call letters*] .... WFLC
Miami, FL [*Television station call letters*] (RBYB) .... WFOR-TV
Miami, FL [*Television station call letters*] .... WHFT
Miami, FL [*Television station call letters*] .... WINZ
Miami, FL [*AM radio station call letters*] .... WIOD
Miami, FL [*FM radio station call letters*] .... WLRN
Miami, FL [*FM radio station call letters*] .... WLRN-TV
Miami, FL [*Television station call letters*] .... WLTV
Miami, FL [*FM radio station call letters*] .... WLYF
Miami, FL [*FM radio station call letters*] .... WMCU
Miami, FL [*FM radio station call letters*] .... WOCN
Miami, FL [*AM radio station call letters*] .... WPBT
Miami, FL [*Television station call letters*] .... WPLG
Miami, FL [*Television station call letters*] .... WPOW
Miami, FL [*FM radio station call letters*] .... WQAM
Miami, FL [*AM radio station call letters*] .... WQBA
Miami, FL [*AM radio station call letters*] .... WSUA
Miami, FL [*AM radio station call letters*] .... WSVN
Miami, FL [*Television station call letters*] .... WTMI
Miami, FL [*FM radio station call letters*] .... WTVJ
Miami, FL [*Television station call letters*] .... WWFE
Miami, FL [*AM radio station call letters*] .... ZMA
Miami, FL [*Location identifier FAA*] (FAAL) .... ZMA
Miami/International [*Florida*] [*ICAO location identifier*] (ICLI) .... KMIA
Miami International Boat Show and Sailboat Show (ITD) .... MIBS
Miami Law Quarterly [*A publication*] (DLA) .... Miami LQ
Miami Law Review [*Florida*] [*A publication*] (DLA) .... Miami L Rev
Miami Memorial-Gila County Library, Miami, AZ [*Library symbol Library of
Congress*] (LCLS) .... AzMi
Miami/New Tamiami [*Florida*] [*ICAO location identifier*] (ICLI) .... KTMB
Miami, OK [*FM radio station call letters*] .... KGLC
Miami, OK [*AM radio station call letters*] .... KVIS
Miami, OK [*Location identifier FAA*] (FAAL) .... MIO
Miami, OK [*Location identifier FAA*] (FAAL) .... MMW
Miami/Opa Locka [*Florida*] [*ICAO location identifier*] (ICLI) .... KOPF
Miami Philharmonic Orchestra (AD) .... MPO
Miami Pornography [*FBI undercover investigation, 1977-80*] .... MIPORN
Miami Public Library (AD) .... MPL
Miami [*Florida*] Public Seaplane Base [*Airport symbol*] (OAG) .... MPB
Miami Springs, FL [*AM radio station call letters*] .... WCMQ
Miami Subs [*NASDAQ symbol*] (TTSB) .... MiamSb
Miami Subs Corp. [*Associated Press*] (SAG) .... MiamSb
Miami Subs Corp. [*NASDAQ symbol*] (SAG) .... SUBS
Miami University, Hamilton Campus, Hamilton, OH [*Library symbol Library of
Congress*] (LCLS) .... OHaU
Miami University, Hamilton Campus, Hamilton, OH [*OCLC symbol*]
(OCLC) .... OHM
Miami University, Middletown Campus, Middletown, OH [*Library symbol
Library of Congress*] (LCLS) .... OMidU
Miami University, Middletown Campus, Middletown, OH [*OCLC symbol*]
(OCLC) .... OMM
Miami University (Ohio) (GAGS) .... Miami U (Ohio)
Miami University, Oxford, OH [*OCLC symbol*] (OCLC) .... MIA
Miami University, Oxford, OH [*Library symbol Library of Congress*]
(LCLS) .... OOxM
Miami University, Scripps Foundation for Research in Population
Problems, Oxford, OH [*Library symbol Library of Congress*] (LCLS) ..... OOxM-S
Miami Valley Hospital, Dayton, OH [*Library symbol Library of Congress*]
(LCLS) .... ODaMVH
Miami Valley Library Organization [*Library network*] .... MILO
Miami, WV [*FM radio station call letters*] .... WKAZ
Miami-Dade Community College, Miami, FL [*Library symbol Library of
Congress*] (LCLS) .... FMMD
Miami-Dade Community College, Miami, FL [*OCLC symbol*] (OCLC) .... FYM
Miami-Dade Public Library, Miami, FL [*Library symbol Library of Congress*]
(LCLS) .... FM
Miami-Dade Public Library System, Miami, FL [*OCLC symbol*] (OCLC) ...... DZM
Miami-Jacobs College [*Ohio*] .... MJC
Miamisburg, OH [*FM radio station call letters*] .... WFCJ
Mian Do Ab [*Iran*] [*ICAO location identifier*] (ICLI) .... OITO
Miandrivazo [*Madagascar*] [*ICAO location identifier*] (ICLI) .... FMMN
Miandrivazo [*Madagascar*] [*Airport symbol*] (OAG) .... ZVA
Mianeh [*Iran*] [*ICAO location identifier*] (ICLI) .... OITI
Mianwali [*Pakistan*] [*ICAO location identifier*] (ICLI) .... OPMI
Mianwali [*Pakistan*] [*ICAO location identifier*] (ICLI) .... OPMW
Mi-Avia [*Russian Federation*] [*ICAO designator*] (FAAC) .... MIV
Mica [*A mineral*] .... Mi
Mica and Chessy [*Acronym is name of interior decorating firm and is taken
from first names of owners Mica Ertegun and Chessy Rayner*] .... MAC II
Mica Creek [*British Columbia*] [*Seismograph station code, US Geological
Survey Closed*] (SEIS) .... MCC
Mica Industry Association [*Defunct*] (EA) .... MIA
Mica Panis [*Crumb of Bread*] [*Pharmacy*] .... MIC PAN
Mica-Amphibole-Rutile-Ilmenite-Diopside [*Geology*] .... Mi
Micah [*Old Testament book*] .... Mic
Micah [*Old Testament book*] .... Mi
Micanite and Insulators (IAA) .... MAI
Micanopy, FL [*FM radio station call letters*] .... WRRX
MICAP [*Mission Critical Parts*] Asset Sourcing System (DOMA) .... MASS
MICC Investments Ltd. [*Toronto Stock Exchange symbol*] .... MIV
Micellar Electrokinetic Capillary Chromatography .... MECC
Micellar Electrokinetic Capillary Electrophoresis [*Analytical chemistry*] ...... MECE
Micellar Electrokinetic Chromatography .... MEKC
Micellar Liquid Chromatography .... MLC
Micellar Polymer Flooding [*Petroleum technology*] .... MPF

Micellar-Enhanced Ultrafiltration [*Chemical engineering*] .... MEUF
Micelle-Stabilized Room-Temperature Phosphorescence .... MS-RTP
Michael A. Dagg Associates, Ottawa, ON, Canada [*Library symbol*] [*Library of
Congress*] (LCLS) .... CaOOMAD
Michael A. Dagg Associates [*Michael A. Dagg Associes*], Ottawa, Ontario
[*Library symbol National Library of Canada*] (NLC) .... OOMAD
Michael Anthony Jewelers [*AMEX symbol*] (TTSB) .... MAJ
Michael Anthony Jewelers, Inc. [*AMEX symbol*] (SPSG) .... MAJ
Michael Anthony Jewelers, Inc. [*Associated Press*] (SAG) .... MichAnt
Michael Army Air Field (MCD) .... MAAF
Michael Calidonius [*Flourished, 16th century*] [*Authority cited in pre-1607 legal
work*] (DSA) .... Mich Calidon
Michael E. DeBakey International Cardiovascular Society [*Later, MEDISS*]
(EA) .... MEDICS
Michael E. DeBakey International Surgical Society (EA) .... MEDISS
Michael F. Stokes Elementary School, Levittown, NY [*Library symbol*]
[*Library of Congress*] (LCLS) .... NLevMSE
Michael Foods [*NASDAQ symbol*] (TTSB) .... MIKL
Michael Foods, Inc. [*Associated Press*] (SAG) .... MichIF
Michael Foods, Inc. [*NASDAQ symbol*] (NQ) .... MIKL
Michael Fund (International Foundation for Genetic Research) (EA) ..... MF-IFGR
Michael Harding International Fan Club (EA) .... MHIFC
Michael Joseph [*Commercial firm British*] .... MJ
Michael Murphy Fan Club (EA) .... MMFC
Michael O'Leary Fan Club [*Defunct*] (EA) .... MOFC
Michael Reese Hospital and Medical Center (AD) .... MRHMC
Michael Reese Hospital and Medical Center, Lillian W. Florsheim Memorial
Library, Chicago, IL [*Library symbol Library of Congress*] (LCLS) .... ICRH
Michael Resources Ltd. [*Vancouver Stock Exchange symbol*] .... MR
Michael Stanley Band [*Musical group*] .... MSB
Michael Stores [*Associated Press*] (SAG) .... MichStr
Michael Stores [*NASDAQ symbol*] (SAG) .... MIKE
Michael-Initiated Ring Closure [*Organic chemistry*] .... MIRC
Michaelis-Gutmann Bodies (MAE) .... MG
Michaelis-Menten Dissociation Constnat (DAVI) .... Km
Michaelmas [*Feast of St. Michael the Archangel, September 29*] (ROG) .... MCHMAS
Michaelmas [*Feast of St. Michael the Archangel, September 29*] .... MICH
Michaelmas [*Feast of St. Michael the Archangel, September 29*] .... MICHS
Michaelmas Term [*British Legal term*] (ILCA) .... Mich
Michaelmas Term [*British Legal term*] (DLA) .... Mich T
Michaelmas Term [*British Legal term*] (DLA) .... MT
Michaelmas Term [*British Legal term*] (ROG) .... MT
Michaelmas Vacation [*British Legal term*] (DLA) .... Mich Vac
Michaels [*J.*], Inc. [*NASDAQ symbol*] (NQ) .... MICH
Michaels [*J.*], Inc. [*Associated Press*] (SAG) .... MichJ
Michaels J [*NASDAQ symbol*] (TTSB) .... MICH
Micham Explorations, Inc. [*Vancouver Stock Exchange symbol*] .... MCH
Micheas [*Old Testament book*] [*Douay version*] .... MICH
Michele Gold Mountain Ltd. [*Vancouver Stock Exchange symbol*] .... MGK
Michele Lee Fan Club (EA) .... MLFC
Michelin Capital Ltd. [*Toronto Stock Exchange symbol*] .... MCX
Michelin Tire Monitor [*System*] [*Automotive engineering*] .... MTM
Michelle Lynn International Fan Club (EA) .... MLIFC
Michelson Doppler Imager [*Biochemistry*] .... MDI
Michelson Doppler Imager [*Instrumentation*] .... MDI
Michelson Interferometer (PDAA) .... MI
Michelson Polarizing Interferometer [*Instrumentation*] .... MPI
Michelson Rotating Mirror .... MRM
Michelstadt [*Germany ICAO location identifier*] (ICLI) .... EDFO
Michener Centre Library, Red Deer, Alberta [*Library symbol National Library
of Canada*] (NLC) .... ARDMC
Michener Centre, Red Deer, AB, Canada [*Library symbol Library of
Congress*] (LCLS) .... CaARDMC
Michie's Jurisprudence of Virginia and West Virginia [*A publication*]
(DLA) .... Michie's Jur
Michigan [*Postal code*] .... MI
Michigan .... MICH
Michigan (ODBW) .... Mich
Michigan [*MARC country of publication code Library of Congress*] (LCCP) .... miu
Michigan [*Obsolete*] (ROG) .... MN
Michigan [*MARC geographic area code Library of Congress*] (LCCP) .... n-us-mi
Michigan Academy of Science, Arts, and Letters .... MASAL
Michigan Accident Location Index [*Michigan State Police*] [*Information
service or system*] (IID) .... MALI
Michigan Administrative Code (AAGC) .... AC
Michigan Administrative Code [*A publication*] (DLA) .... Mich Admin Code
Michigan Administrative Code Annual Supplement [*A publication*]
(AAGC) .... AACS
Michigan Agricultural Experiment Station [*Michigan State University*]
[*Research center*] (RCD) .... MAES
Michigan Airways [*ICAO designator*] (AD) .... QQ
Michigan Airways, Inc. [*ICAO designator*] (FAAC) .... DRE
Michigan Alcoholism Screening Test .... MAST
Michigan Algorithmic Decoder [*IBM Corp.*] [*University of Michigan
Programming language 1961*] .... MAD
Michigan Amber [*Variety of wheat*] .... MA
Michigan Apple Committee (EA) .... MAC
Michigan Area Serial Holdings Consortium [*Library network*] .... MASH
Michigan Army Missile Plant (MCD) .... MAMP
Michigan Association for Computer Users in Learning (EDAC) .... MACUL
Michigan Association of Ambulance Services (SRA) .... MAAS
Michigan Association of Certified Public Accountants (SRA) .... MACPA
Michigan Association of Cherry Producers (EA) .... MACP
Michigan Association of Chiefs of Police (SRA) .... MACP
Michigan Association of Children's Alliances (SRA) .... MACA

Michigan Association of Christian Schools (SRA) .... MACS
Michigan Association of Convenience Stores (SRA) .... MACS
Michigan Association of Insurance Companies (SRA) .... MAIC
Michigan Association of Life Underwriters (SRA) .... MALU
Michigan Association of Single Adoptive Parents (EA) .... MASAP
Michigan Automated Clearing House Association .... MACHA
Michigan Automatic General Integrated Computation (MCD) ... MAGIC
Michigan Automatic Scanning System (IEEE) .... MASS
Michigan Bigfoot Information Center [Later, MCBIC] (EA) .... MBIC
Michigan Biotechnology Institute [Michigan State University] [Research
  center] (RCD) .... MBI
Michigan Brewery, Inc. [NASDAQ symbol] (SAG) .... BBUC
Michigan Brewery, Inc. [Associated Press] (SAG) .... MichBr
Michigan Brewery, Inc. [Associated Press] (SAG) .... MichBrw
Michigan/Canadian Bigfoot Information Center (EA) .... MCBIC
Michigan Cancer Foundation - Seventh Sample [Strain of rapid-growing
  breast cancer cells used world-wide in cancer research] MCF-7
Michigan Central Railroad [Absorbed into Consolidated Rail Corp.] [AAR
  code] .... MC
Michigan Chemical Corp. .... MC
Michigan Circuit Court Reporter [A publication] (DLA) ...... Mich CCR
Michigan Circuit Court Reporter [A publication] (DLA) .... Mich Cr Ct Rep
Michigan City [Indiana] [Airport symbol] (OAG) .... MGC
Michigan City, IN [Location identifier FAA] (FAAL) .... MGC
Michigan City, IN [FM radio station call letters] .... WEFM
Michigan City, IN [AM radio station call letters] .... WIMS
Michigan City News-Dispatch, Michigan City, IN [Library symbol Library of
  Congress] (LCLS) .... InMicND
Michigan City Public Library, Michigan City, IN [OCLC symbol] (OCLC) .... IMY
Michigan City Public Library, Michigan City, IN [Library symbol Library of
  Congress] (LCLS) .... InMic
Michigan Civil Jurisprudence [A publication] (DLA) .... MCJ
Michigan Coalition for Clean Forests .... MCCF
Michigan Community College Occupational Education Evaluation System
  (EDAC) .... MCCOEES
Michigan Compiled Laws (AAGC) .... MCL
Michigan Compiled Laws [A publication] (DLA) .... Mich Comp Laws
Michigan Compiled Laws, Annotated [A publication] (DLA) ...... MCLA
Michigan Compiled Laws, Annotated [A publication] (DLA) ... Mich Comp L Ann
Michigan Compiled Laws Annotated [West] [A publication]
  (AAGC) .... Mich Comp Laws
Michigan Compiled Laws, Annotated [A publication] (DLA) .... Mich Comp Laws Ann
Michigan Consolidated Gas Co. [Associated Press] (SAG) .... MCGC
Michigan Contractor & Builder [A publication] .... MC & B
Michigan Court of Appeals Reports [A publication] (DLA) ..... Mich App
Michigan Court of Claims (AAGC) .... Mich Ct Cl
Michigan Court of Claims Reports [A publication] (DLA) ..... Mich Ct Cl
Michigan Department of Education, State Library Services, Blind and
  Physically Handicapped Library, Lansing, MI [Library symbol Library of
  Congress] (LCLS) .... Mi-BPH
Michigan Department of Transportation .... MDOT
Michigan [University of] Digital Automatic Computer .... MIDAC
Michigan Education Resources Information Center [Michigan State Library]
  [Information service or system Defunct] (IID) .... MERIC
Michigan Educational Assessment Program .... MEAP
Michigan Educational Research Information Triad, Inc. .... MERIT
Michigan Effectuation, Training, and Research Organization [Computer-
  programmed simulation game] .... METRO
Michigan English Language Assessment Battery (GAGS) ...... MELAB
Michigan Environmental Science Board .... MESB
Michigan Financial Corp. [NASDAQ symbol] (SAG) .... MFCB
Michigan Financial Corp. [Associated Press] (SAG) .... MichFncl
Michigan Finl Corp. [NASDAQ symbol] (TTSB) .... MFCB
Michigan Health and Social Security Research Institute [Detroit, MI]
  [Research center] (RCD) .... MHSSRI
Michigan Historical Commission, State Archives Library, Lansing, MI
  [Library symbol Library of Congress] (LCLS) .... Mi-HC
Michigan Industrial Accident Board, Workmen's Compensation Cases
  [A publication] (DLA) .... Mich WCC
Michigan Information Center [Michigan State Department of Management and
  Budget] [Information service or system] (IID) .... MIC
Michigan Information Transfer Source [University of Michigan] (IID) .... MITS
Michigan Instructional Computer .... MIC
Michigan Interorganizational Committee on Continuing Library Education
  (EDAC) .... MICCLE
Michigan Intra-State Motor Tariff Bureau Inc., Lansing MI [STAC] .... MIB
Michigan Jurisprudence [A publication] (DLA) .... Mich Jur
Michigan Law and Practice [A publication] (DLA) .... MLP
Michigan Law Journal [A publication] (DLA) .... Mich LJ
Michigan Lawyer [A publication] (DLA) .... Mich L
Michigan Legal News [A publication] (DLA) .... Mich Leg News
Michigan Legislative Service [A publication] (DLA) ...... Mich Legis Serv
Michigan Library Consortium [Lansing, MI] [Library network] ...... MLC
Michigan Library Consortium, Detroit, MI [OCLC symbol] (OCLC) ...... TQE
Michigan Library Consortium, Detroit, MI [OCLC symbol] (OCLC) ...... TQF
Michigan Library Consortium, Wayne State University, Detroit, MI [OCLC
  symbol] (OCLC) .... EYC
Michigan Library Consortium, Wayne State University, Detroit, MI [Library
  symbol Library of Congress] (LCLS) .... MiDL
Michigan Library Film Circuit [Library network] .... MLFC
Michigan Lutheran Seminary, Saginaw, MI [Library symbol Library of
  Congress] (LCLS) .... MiSM
Michigan Metropolitan Information Center/Center for Urban Studies [Wayne
  State University] [Information service or system] (IID) .... MIMIC/CUS

Michigan Molecular Institute, Inc. [Formerly, Midland Macromolecular
  Institute] [Research center] (RCD) .... MMI
Michigan Multispectral Scanner .... MMS
Michigan Natural Features Inventory [Michigan State Department of Natural
  Resources] [Information service or system] (IID) .... MNFI
Michigan North Processing Center, Cadillac, MI [OCLC symbol] (OCLC) .... EZZ
Michigan Northern Railway Co., Inc. [AAR code] .... MIGN
Michigan Occupational Information System [Michigan State Department of
  Education] [Lansing] [Information service or system] (IID) ...... MOIS
Michigan Ohio Telecommunications Association (TSSD) .... MOTA
Michigan Opportunities and Skills Training (AD) .... MOST
Michigan Ordnance Missile Plant [Army] .... MOMP
Michigan Personnel and Guidance Association (AD) .... MPGA
Michigan Picture Language Inventory (EDAC) .... MPLI
Michigan Picture Stories [Psychology] (DAVI) .... MPS
Michigan Picture Test [Psychology] .... MPT
Michigan Products Information Exchange [Interchange Plus, Inc.]
  [Information service or system] (IID) .... MIPIE
Michigan Project for Computer-Assisted Biblical Studies [University of
  Michigan] [Information service or system] (IID) .... MPCABS
Michigan Public Utilities Commission Orders and Opinions [A publication]
  (DLA) .... Mich PUC Ops
Michigan Pure Water Council (EA) .... MPWC
Michigan Quarterly Economic Model (NITA) .... MQEM
Michigan Quarterly Review [A publication] (BRI) .... MQR
Michigan Railroad Commission Decisions [A publication] (DLA) ...... Mich RC Dec
Michigan Reformatory (AD) .... MR
Michigan Regional Libraries Film Program at Cadillac [Library network] ..... MMLL
Michigan Regional Libraries Film Program at Monroe [Library
  network] .... SEMRFL
Michigan Reports [A publication] (DLA) .... Mch
Michigan Reports [A publication] (DLA) .... MI
Michigan Reports [A publication] (DLA) .... Mich R
Michigan Reports [A publication] (DLA) .... Mich Supr Ct Rep
Michigan Reports Advanced Sheets [A publication] (DLA) ..... Mich Adv
Michigan Screening Profile of Parenting [Psychology] .... MSPP
Michigan Southern & Northern Indiana Railroad .... MS & NI
Michigan State Bar Association. Journal [A publication] (DLA) ...... Mich SBA Jo
Michigan State Integral Computer .... MISTIC
Michigan State Library, Escanaba Branch, Escanaba, MI [Library symbol
  Library of Congress] (LCLS) .... Mi-E
Michigan State Library, Lansing, MI [Library symbol Library of Congress]
  (LCLS) .... Mi
Michigan State Library Services, Lansing, MI [OCLC symbol] (OCLC) ...... EEX
Michigan State University (GAGS) .... Mich St U
Michigan State University [East Lansing] .... MSU
Michigan State University Advisory Group [Contracted with the Government
  of South Vietnam to provide-civilian training] (VNW) .... MSUAG
Michigan State University Business Topics [A publication]
  (DLA) .... MSU Business Topics
Michigan State University Discrete Computer .... MSUDC
Michigan State University, East Lansing, MI [OCLC symbol] (OCLC) ...... EEM
Michigan State University, East Lansing, MI [Library symbol Library of
  Congress] (LCLS) .... MiEM
Michigan State University of Agriculture and Applied Sciences (AD) ...... MS
Michigan Statutes, Annotated [A publication] (DLA) ...... Mich Stat Ann
Michigan Statutes Annotated [A publication] (AAGC) .... MSA
Michigan Supreme Court Reports [A publication] (DLA) .... Mich
Michigan Technological University (GAGS) .... Mich Tech U
Michigan Technological University [Houghton] .... MTU
Michigan Technological University, Houghton, MI [OCLC symbol] (OCLC) .... EZT
Michigan Technological University, Houghton, MI [Library symbol Library of
  Congress] (LCLS) .... MiHM
Michigan Terminal System [Computer science] .... MTS
Michigan Travel System .... MITS
Michigan Travel Trade Information Service .... MITTINS
Michigan United Conservation Clubs .... MUCC
Michigan Wild Turkey Hunters Association .... MWTHA
Michigan Wildlife Habitat Foundation .... MWHF
Michigan Women for Medical Control of Abortion (EA) .... MWMCA
Michigan Youth Hunter Education Challenge .... MYHEC
Michigan-Dartmouth-Massachusetts Institute of Technology
  [Observatory] .... MDM
Michigan-Ohio Regional Educational Laboratory .... MOREL
Michilla [Chile] [Seismograph station code, US Geological Survey] (SEIS) .... MIC
Michipicoten Township Public Library, Wawa, Ontario [Library symbol
  National Library of Canada] (NLC) .... OWMT
Michoacan Information Center on the Mexico-US Future (EA) ...... CEMICH
Michoud Assembly Facility [NASA] (MCD) .... MAF
Michoud Operations Facility [NASA] (AAG) .... MOF
Michoud Plant [NASA] (MCD) .... MP
Mickey Gilley Fan Club [Defunct] (EA) .... MGFC
Mickey Thompson Entertainment Group [Auto racing] .... MTEG
Micks External Compression Fixator [Instrumentation] .... MECF
"Micky the D" Show [Later, MDS/MMFC] [An association] (EA) ...... MDS
"Micky the D" Show/Metal Micky Fan Club (EA) .... MDS/MMFC
Micmac [MARC language code Library of Congress] (LCCP) .... mic
MICOM [Missile Command] Automated Test Equipment .... MATE
MICOM Communications [NASDAQ symbol] (TTSB) .... MICM
Micom Communications Corp. [NASDAQ symbol] (SAG) .... MICM
Micom Communications Corp. [Associated Press] (SAG) ..... MicomC
MICOM [Missile Command] Specification [Army] .... MIS
Micrecord Sales Corp., Chicago, IL [Library symbol Library of Congress]
  (LCLS) .... McR

Micrecord Sales Corp., Lombard, IL [Library symbol] [Library of Congress]
(LCLS) .... McRe
Micrel, Inc. [NASDAQ symbol] (SAG) .... MCRL
Micrel, Inc. [Associated Press] (SAG) .... Micrel
Micrion Corp. [NASDAQ symbol] (SAG) .... MICN
Micrion Corp. [Associated Press] (SAG) .... Micrion
Micro (WGA) .... m
Micro .... MCR
Micro [One millionth] (WDAA) .... MU
Micro (IDOE) .... u
Micro Aided Engineering (NITA) .... MAE
Micro Archives and Records Online [Developed by AirS, Inc.] .... MARCON
Micro Area Electron Diffraction [Surface analysis] .... MAED
Micro Asynchronous Communications Controller (MHDI) .... MACC
Micro Automation System .... MAS
Micro Bio-Medics [NASDAQ symbol] (TTSB) .... MBMI
Micro Bio-Medics, Inc. [NASDAQ symbol] (NQ) .... MBMI
Micro Bio-Medics, Inc. [Associated Press] (SAG) .... MicrBi
Micro Business Systems (NITA) .... MBS
Micro Camera (NITA) .... MICAM
Micro Cellular Network [Computer science] .... MCN
Micro Channel [Computer science] (CDE) .... MCA
Micro Channel Architecture [Computer hardware] .... MCA
Micro Component Tech [NASDAQ symbol] (TTSB) .... MCTI
Micro Component Technology Inc. (NITA) .... MCT
Micro Component Technology, Inc. [NASDAQ symbol] (SAG) .... MCTI
Micro Component Technology, Inc. [Associated Press] (SAG) .... MicroCT
Micro Computer Business Services .... MCBS
Micro Data Base Systems (NITA) .... MDBS
Micro Defect Free .... MDF
Micro Education Corp. of America .... MECA
Micro Electro Mechanical Systems .... MEMS
Micro Focus Group Ltd. [NASDAQ symbol] (SAG) .... MIFG
Micro Focus Group PLC [Associated Press] (SAG) .... MicFocu
Micro Focus Grp ADS [NASDAQ symbol] (TTSB) .... MIFGY
Micro General [NASDAQ symbol] (TTSB) .... MGEN
Micro General Corp. [NASDAQ symbol] (NQ) .... MGEN
Micro General Corp. [Associated Press] (SAG) .... MicrGn
Micro Graphic Corp., Garfield, NJ [Library symbol] [Library of Congress]
(LCLS) .... McGC
Micro Image Relative Position Formula [Computer science] .... MIRPF
Micro Industrial Corp., Bayville, NJ [Library symbol] [Library of Congress]
(LCLS) .... McIC
Micro Instrumentation and Telemetry Systems (NITA) .... MITS
Micro Integrated Storm Information System [Marine science] (OSRA) .... MISIS
Micro Interpreter for Knowledge Engineering [Computer science] .... MIKE
Micro Library Canisianum, Maastricht, Holland [Library symbol Library of
Congress] (LCLS) .... McC
Micro Linear [NASDAQ symbol] (TTSB) .... MLIN
Micro Linear Corp. [Associated Press] (SAG) .... MicroLin
Micro Linear Corp. [NASDAQ symbol] (SAG) .... MLIN
Micro Measurement System [3D Digital Design & Development Ltd.] [Software
package] (NCC) .... MMS
Micro Memory Systems (NITA) .... MMS
Micro Miniature Compact Harness (MCD) .... MIMI
Micro OnLine Library Information [Nichols Advanced Technologies, Inc.] .... MOLLI
Micro Photo Division, Bell & Howell Co., Wooster, OH [Library symbol
Library of Congress] (LCLS) .... McP
Micro Power Light [Automotive lighting] .... MPL
Micro Professor (NITA) .... MPF
Micro Reflective Structure [Computer science] .... MRS
Micro Support Resource Corp. [Atlanta, GA] .... MSR
Micro Surface Mapping [Software package] (NCC) .... MSM
Micro Touch Systems [NASDAQ symbol] (TTSB) .... MTSI
Micro Ventures Ltd. [Vancouver Stock Exchange symbol] .... MVC
Micro Warehouse [NASDAQ symbol] (TTSB) .... MWHS
Micro Warehouse, Inc. [Associated Press] (SAG) .... MicroWre
Micro Warehouse, Inc. [NASDAQ symbol] (SAG) .... MWHS
Microabrasion Foil Experiment [For cosmic dust retrieval] .... MFE
Microactivity Testing [Catalysis technology] .... MAT
Microaddress Register [Computer science] (MHDI) .... MIAR
Microaerophilus Stationary Phase [Biochemistry] (DAVI) .... MASP
MicroAge, Inc. [NASDAQ symbol] (SAG) .... MICA
MicroAge, Inc., [Associated Press] (SAG) .... MicroAge
Microagglutination [Immunochemistry] (DAVI) .... MA
Micro-Aided Engineering 3D Visualisation [Micro-Aided Engineering Ltd. and
Micro-Aided Engineering Digital Microsystems Ltd.] [Software package]
(NCC) .... MAEVIS
Micro-Aided Engineering/Computer Aided Manufacturing [Micro-Aided
Engineering Ltd. and Digital Microsystems Ltd.] [Software package]
(NCC) .... MAECAM
Micro-Aided Engineering/Drawing Office System [Micro-Aided Engineering
Ltd.] [Software package] (NCC) .... MAEDOS
Microalgae International Union (EA) .... MIU
Microalloy .... MA
Microalloy Diffused .... MD
Micro-Alloy Diffused Base Transistor (NITA) .... MADT
Microalloy Diffused Electrode .... MADE
Microalloy Diffused Transistor (MUGU) .... MADT
Microalloy Transistor .... MAT
Micro-Alloyed Steel [Metallurgical engineering] .... MAS
Microammeter [Electronics] .... MICAM
Microampere (WDAA) .... MU A
Micro-Analytic Simulation of Households (PDAA) .... MASH
Microanalytical Reagent .... MAR

Microangiopathic Hemolytic Anemia [Medicine] .... MAHA
Microangiopathic Hemolytic Anemia [Medicine] .... MHA
Microatomized Protein Food (MAE) .... MAPF
Microbalance Inverted Knudsen Effusion Recoil .... MIKER
Microband National System, Inc. [New York, NY] [Telecommunications]
(TSSD) .... MNS
Microbar (WDAA) .... MU BAR
Microbeam [Physics] .... MB
Microbeam Analysis Society (EA) .... MAS
Microbial Check Valve (PDAA) .... MCV
Microbial Coal Desulfurization .... MCD
Microbial Culture Information Service [Department of Trade and Industry]
[British Information service or system] .... MICIS
Microbial Ecological Monitoring System [Apollo] [NASA] .... MEMS
Microbial Ecology Evaluation Device [NASA] (KSC) .... MEED
Microbial Enhanced Oil Recovery [Petroleum technology] .... MEOR
Microbial Evaluation Analysis Device (PDAA) .... MEAD
Microbial Exchanges and Coupling in Coastal Atlantic Systems .... MECCAS
Microbial Information Network Europe [EEC] .... MINE
Microbial Load Monitor (MCD) .... MLM
Microbial Oil Recovery Enhancement [Petroleum technology] .... MORE
Microbial Profile System [Microbiology] .... MPS
Microbial Strain Data Network [Information service or system] (IID) .... MSDN
MicroBilt Applications Network [MicroBuilt Corp.] [Telecommunications
service] (TSSD) .... APPNET
Microbiological [or Microbiology] .... MICROBIOL
Microbiological Assay [Biochemistry] (DAVI) .... MB
Microbiological Associates, Inc. .... MBA
Microbiological Inputs [Canning] (DICI) .... MI
Microbiological Research Department (AD) .... MRD
Microbiological Research Establishment [British] .... MRE
Microbiological Resource Center [UNESCO] .... MIRCEN
Microbiological Warfare .... MBW
Microbiologically Influenced Corrosion .... MIC
Microbiologically-Influenced Corrosion [Metallurgical engineering] .... MIC
Microbiology .... MCRBIO
Microbiology .... MCRBLGY
Microbiology and Infectious Diseases Program [Bethesda, MD] [National
Institute of Allergy and Infectious Diseases] [Department of Health and
Human Services] (GRD) .... MIDP
Microbiology Data Management System .... MDMS
Microbody .... MB
Microbore Liquid Chromatography .... MBLC
Microbursts in Severe Thunderstorms .... MIST
[The] MicroCap Fund [NASDAQ symbol] (SAG) .... MCAP
[The] MicroCap Fund [Associated Press] (SAG) .... MicroCap
Microcarbon Residue [Petroleum analysis] .... MCR
Microcard Editions, Inc., Englewood, CO [Library symbol Library of
Congress] (LCLS) .... McE
Microcarrier [Cell culture technology] .... MC
Micro-Catalogue (NITA) .... MICROCAT
Microcell-Mediated Chromosome Transfer [Genetics] .... MMCT
Microcentrifugal Analyzer [Instrumentation] .... MCA
Microcephaly [Medicine] (AAMN) .... MC
Microchannel Analyzer [Instrumentation] .... MCA
Microchannel Plate [Computer science] .... MCP
Microchannel Spatial Light Modulator [Electronics] .... MSLM
Microchip Module .... MCM
Microchip Technology [NASDAQ symbol] (TTSB) .... MCHP
Microchip Technology, Inc. [NASDAQ symbol] (SAG) .... MCHP
Microchip Technology, Inc. [Associated Press] (SAG) .... Microchip
Microchromatographic .... MC
Microcide Pharmaceuticals [NASDAQ symbol] (TTSB) .... MCDE
Microcide Pharmaceuticals, Inc. [NASDAQ symbol] (SAG) .... MCDE
Microcide Pharmaceuticals, Inc. [Associated Press] (SAG) .... MicroPh
Microcircuit Emulation Program .... MEP
Microcircuit Module .... MCM
Microcircuit Module, Driver/Receiver .... MMDR
Microcircuit Power Converter .... MPC
Microcircuit Reliability Bibliography (NITA) .... MRB
Microcircuit Technology in Logistics Applications [Defense Logistics
Agency] .... MITLA
Microcirculation Research Institute [Texas A & M University] [Research
center] (RCD) .... MCRI
Microcirculatory Society (EA) .... MS
Microclimate Conditioning / Power Subsystem [Army] (RDA) .... MCC/PS
Microclimatic Conditioning .... MCC
Microclimatic Cooling System [Army] .... MCC
Microclimatic Cooling System [Army] (DWSG) .... MCS
Micrococcal Nuclease [Also, MN] [An enzyme] .... MCN
Micrococcal Nuclease [Also, MCN] [An enzyme] .... MN
Micrococcus [Genus of bacteria] .... M
Microcoded Communications Line Adapter .... MCLA
Micro-Coded Communications Link Adaptor (NITA) .... MCLA
Microcom, Inc. [Associated Press] (SAG) .... Microcm
Microcom, Inc. [NASDAQ symbol] (NQ) .... MNPI
Microcom Networking Protocol [Telecommunications] (ACRL) .... MNP
Microcomfax, Incorporated, Camp Hill, PA [Library symbol Library of
Congress] (LCLS) .... McInc
Microcomplement Fixation [Immunochemistry] .... MCF
Microcomputer (IAA) .... MC
Microcomputer .... MCRRCMPTR
Microcomputer (MSA) .... MICMPTR
Microcomputer .... MICRO
Microcomputer Advice and Selection Expert System (PDAA) .... MASES

Microcomputer Based Services for Retrospective Conversions (NITA) ... MICROCON
Microcomputer Board ... MCB
Microcomputer Bus Users' Show and Conference [*MultiDynamics, Inc.*] (TSPED) ... BUSCON
Microcomputer Center and Library [*Wisconsin State Department of Public Instruction*] [*Information service or system*] (IID) ... MCL
Microcomputer Control Unit ... MCU
Microcomputer Development Facilities (IEEE) ... MDF
Microcomputer Development System (IAA) ... MDS
Microcomputer Education Application Network [*Commercial firm*] (EA) ... MEAN
Microcomputer Electronic Information Exchange [*Institute for Computer Science and Technology*] ... MEIE
Microcomputer Graphic System ... MGS
Microcomputer Index [*Information service or system*] (IID) ... MIC
Microcomputer Industry Trade Association ... MITA
Microcomputer Information Support Tools [*2B Enterprises*] [*Washington, DC*] (TSSD) ... MIST+
Microcomputer Integrated Library System ... MILS
MicroComputer Investors Association [*Database producer*] (EA) ... MCIA
Microcomputer Language [*Computer science*] (ECII) ... MCL
Microcomputer Machine (IAA) ... MCM
Microcomputer Managers Association (HGAA) ... MMA
Microcomputer Marketing Council [*Direct Marketing Association*] (PCM) ... MMC
Microcomputer Network (NITA) ... MICRONET
Microcomputer Networking Protocol ... MNP
Microcomputer Numerical Control (IAA) ... MCNC
Microcomputer Numerical Control (MCD) ... MNC
Microcomputer Printed Subject Indexes (NITA) ... MICROPSI
Microcomputer Sales and Leasing, Inc. ... MSL
Microcomputer Software and Information for Teachers [*Northwest Regional Educational Laboratory*] [*Information service or system*] (IID) ... MicroSIFT
Microcomputer Software Association (EA) ... MSA
Microcomputer Software Association - of ADAPSO [*Association of Data Processing Service Organizations*] (EA) ... MCSA
Microcomputer Support Group ... MSG
Microcomputer System ... MCS
Microcomputer Users in Education (AIE) ... MUE
Microcomputer Users in Education ... MUSE
Microcomputer Vocational Education Reporting System (EDAC) ... MICRO-VERS
Microcomputer-Assisted Instruction (NITA) ... MCAI
Microcomputer-Controlled Electroanalysis System [*Interactive Microwave*] ... MiCES
Microcomputer-Interfaced Data Acquisition System [*Computer science*] ... MIDAS
Microcomputers and Primary Education ... MAPE
Microcomputers in Human Resource Management [*Advanced Personnel Systems*] [*Information service or system*] (CRD) ... MHRM
Microcomputers in Mathematics Education (AIE) ... MIME
Microcomputer-Videodisc ... MICRO-DISC
Microcone Networking Protocol ... MNP
Microconfined Bed Unit [*Chemical engineering*] ... MCBU
Micro-Connection Assembly Method ... MICAM
Microcontrol ... MC
Micro-Control Unit (NITA) ... MCU
Microcontroller Unit (CDE) ... MCU
Micro-Copy, Inc., Rochester, NY [*Library symbol*] [*Library of Congress*] (LCLS) ... McCl
Microcrystalline (BARN) ... microcryst
Microcrystalline Cellulose [*Organic chemistry*] ... MCC
Microcrystalline Chitin ... MCC
Microcrystalline Polymer [*Plastics technology*] ... MCP
Microculture and Sensitivity [*Laboratory*] (DAVI) ... M & S
Microculture and Sensitivity [*Microbiology*] (DAVI) ... MCS
Microcystic Adnexal Carcinoma [*Oncology*] ... MAC
Microcytic/Hypochromic [*Anemia*] [*Hematology*] (DAVI) ... M/H
Microcytic/Normochromic [*Anemia*] [*Hematology*] (DAVI) ... M/N
Microcytosis [*Biochemistry*] (DAVI) ... MIC
Microdata ... MCRDT
Microdata Software Development (MCD) ... MSD
Microdensitometer (IAA) ... MDM
Micro-Diagnostics for Analysis and Repair (NITA) ... MIDAS
Micro-Dose-Focusing [*Electron microscopy*] ... MDF
Microdosimetric Instrumentation ... MDI
Microdot (KSC) ... MD
Microdot ... MD
Microdynamic Angle and Rate Monitoring System ... MIDARM
Microdyne Corp. [*NASDAQ symbol*] (NQ) ... MCDY
Microdyne Corp. [*Associated Press*] (SAG) ... Micrdy
Microeditions Hachette, Paris, France [*Library symbol Library of Congress*] (LCLS) ... McH
Microelectric Logic Circuit ... MLC
Microelectromechanical System [*Materials science and technology*] ... MEMS
Micro-Electro-Mechanical Systems ... MEMS
Microelectronic ... MCRELCTRNC
Microelectronic ... ME
Microelectronic Circuits Division (AAGC) ... MCD
Microelectronic Device ... MED
Microelectronic Indicator for RADAR Ground Equipment (MCD) ... MIRAGE
Microelectronic Integrated Checkout Equipment ... MICE
Microelectronic Integrated Circuit (MCD) ... MIC
Microelectronic Integrated Circuit Package (MCD) ... MICPAC
Microelectronic Integrated Processing [*Symposium*] ... MIP
Microelectronic Integrated Test Equipment ... MITE
Microelectronic Modular Assembly ... MEMA
Microelectronic Noise Jammer ... MNJ
Microelectronic Packaging [*NASDAQ symbol*] (TTSB) ... MPIX
Microelectronic Packaging, Inc. [*Associated Press*] (SAG) ... MicrPck
Microelectronic Packaging, Inc. [*NASDAQ symbol*] (SAG) ... MPIX
Microelectronic Radio Receiver ... MRR
Microelectronic Replacement Assembly (NG) ... MCIRA
Micro-Electronic Technology (ADA) ... MET
Microelectronic Test Laboratory (IAA) ... MTL
Microelectronic Weld Tester ... MEWT
Microelectronics (IEEE) ... MELEC
Microelectronics and Computer Technology Corp. ... MCC
Microelectronics Application Programme (AIE) ... MAP
Microelectronics Application Project [*British*] (DCTA) ... MAP
Microelectronics Applications Research Institute [*Newcastle-Upon-Tyne, England*] ... MARI
Microelectronics Bibliography [*A publication*] ... MB
Microelectronics Center ... MEC
Microelectronics Center Library, Durham, NC [*Library symbol*] [*Library of Congress*] (LCLS) ... NcDurMi
Microelectronics Center of North Carolina [*Research center*] (RCD) ... MCNC
Micro-Electronics Education Programme (NITA) ... MEP
Microelectronics Educational Development Centre [*Paisley College*] [*British*] (CB) ... MEDC
Microelectronics for All Kit (NITA) ... MFA
Microelectronics for RADAR Application (MCD) ... MERA
Microelectronics Industry Support Programme (NITA) ... MISP
Microelectronics Innovation and Computer Science Research Program [*University of California*] [*Research center*] (RCD) ... MICRO
Microelectronics Manufacturing Facility [*Philco-Ford Corp.*] (MCD) ... MMF
Microelectronics Programme [*British*] ... MEP
Microelectronics Support Unit [*for the Microelectronics Education Programme*] [*British*] ... MESU
Microelectronics Support Unit [*Department of Education and Science*] (NITA) ... MSU
Microelectronics Test and Evaluation [*Raytheon Co.*] ... MITE
Microelectrostatic Gyro ... MESG
Microelectrostatic Gyro-Accelerometer ... MESGA
Microelement (IEEE) ... MELEM
Microencapsulated ... M-E
Microencapsulation [*Chemical engineering*] ... MEC
Microenergy, Inc. [*NASDAQ symbol*] (SAG) ... MICR
Microenergy, Inc. [*Associated Press*] (SAG) ... Micrenr
Microenergy Logic (IAA) ... MEL
Microfabrication Laboratory [*University of California, Berkeley*] [*Research center*] (RCD) ... MICROLAB
Microfarad ... MF
Microfarad ... MFD
Microfarad (WDAA) ... MU F
Microfax, Universal Information System, Paramus, NJ [*Library symbol*] [*Library of Congress*] (LCLS) ... McFx
Microfibrillar Collagen Hemostat [*Medicine*] (MEDA) ... MCH
Microfibrillar-Associated Glycoprotein [*Biochemistry*] ... MAGP
Microfiche ... MCRFCH
Microfiche [*Sheet microfilm*] ... MF
Microfiche File Update System [*Computer science*] (PDAA) ... MFUSYS
Microfiche Image Transmission System (MCD) ... MITS
Microfiche Management System ... MMS
Microfiche (Positive) ... MF(P)
Microfield Graphics [*NASDAQ symbol*] (TTSB) ... MICG
Microfield Graphics, Inc. [*NASDAQ symbol*] (SAG) ... MICG
Microfield Graphics, Inc. [*Associated Press*] (SAG) ... Microfd
Microfield Graphics, Inc. [*Associated Press*] (SAG) ... MicrofdG
Microfield Virtual Device Interface [*Computer science*] (HGAA) ... MVDI
Microfilariae ... Mf
Microfile Enlarger Printer (NITA) ... MEP
Microfile (Pty.) Ltd., Johannesburg, South Africa [*Library symbol Library of Congress*] (LCLS) ... MfL
Microfilm ... MCFIM
Microfilm (AAG) ... MCFLM
Microfilm ... MF
Microfilm ... MM
Microfilm Address (NITA) ... MA
Microfilm Advisory Service of the Public Archives of Canada (PDAA) ... MASPAC
Microfilm Alpha Index System ... MAIS
Microfilm and Information Technology Center ... MITC
Microfilm Aperture Card ... MAC
Microfilm Aperture Card Automated Retrieval System ... MACARS
Microfilm Association of Great Britain ... MAGB
Microfilm Center, Incorporated, Dallas, Texas [*Library symbol Library of Congress*] (LCLS) ... McI
Microfilm Corporation of America (NITA) ... MCA
Microfilm Corp. of Pennsylvania, Pittsburgh, PA [*Library symbol Library of Congress*] (LCLS) ... McPA
Microfilm Enhanced Data System (PDAA) ... MEDAS
Microfilm Frame Card ... MFC
Microfilm Information and Retrieval System (DNAB) ... MIARS
Microfilm Information Master Image Converter (PDAA) ... MIMIC
Microfilm Information Retrieval Access Code ... MIRACODE
Microfilm Information Storage and Retrieval (MCD) ... MISAR
Microfilm (Positive) ... M(P)
Microfilm Printer/Plotter ... MPP
Microfilm Reader Recorder ... MRR
Microfilm Recording Co., Weston, ON, Canada [*Library symbol Library of Congress*] (LCLS) ... McRC
Microfilm Recording Unit ... MRU

Microfilm Records System, Inc., Mamaroneck, NY [*Library symbol*] [*Library of Congress*] (LCLS) .... MrS
Microfilm Replacement System [*Computer science*] .... MRS
Microfilm Research Centers Project [*Defunct*] (EA) .... MRCP
Microfilm Sequential Coding System [*Bell System*] .... MICROSECS
Microfilm Services Ltd., Auckland, New Zealand [*Library symbol Library of Congress*] (LCLS) .... MsLi
Microfilm Sorter [*Electronics*] .... FILMSORT
Microfilm Systems, Colorado Springs, CO [*Library symbol Library of Congress*] (LCLS) .... MfS
Microfilm Viewer .... MFV
Microfilmed Abstract System for Technical Information Retrieval [*Illinois Institute of Technology*] (IID) .... MASTIR
Microfilmed Reports and Accounts (PDAA) .... MIRAC
Microfilming Corp. of America [*Information service or system*] (IID) .... MCA
Microfilming Corp. of America, Glen Rock, NJ [*Library symbol Library of Congress*] (LCLS) .... McA
Microfilming Executors & Methods Organization Ltd., Dublin, Ireland [*Library symbol Library of Congress*] (LCLS) .... McEM
Microfilm-Output Device .... MOD
Microfiltration .... MF
Microfische .... MCFSHE
Microflocculation [*Biochemistry*] (DAVI) .... MF
Microfluidics International [*NASDAQ symbol*] (TTSB) .... MFIC
Microfluidics International Corp. [*NASDAQ symbol*] (SAG) .... MFIC
Microfluidics International Corp. [*Associated Press*] (SAG) .... Microflu
Microform .... MF
Microform Document of Information System (MCD) .... MICRODIS
Microform Personnel Records System (NVT) .... MPRS
Microform Review, Inc., Weston, CT [*Library symbol Library of Congress*] (LCLS) .... MfR
Microforms in Print [*Database*] .... MFIP
Microforms International Marketing Corp. [*Pergamon*] .... MIMC
Microframe, Inc. [*NASDAQ symbol*] (SAG) .... MCFR
Microframe, Inc. [*Associated Press*] (SAG) .... Micfrm
Microfuel Systems [*Vancouver Stock Exchange symbol*] .... MFS
Microfunctional Circuit .... MFC
Micro-G Physics and Chemistry Experiments Group [*NASA*] (SSD) .... MGP
Micrografx, Inc. [*NASDAQ symbol*] (SAG) .... MGXI
Micrografx, Inc. [*Associated Press*] (SAG) .... Micrgfx
Micrograin (ABBR) .... MGN
Micro-Grain Array Processor [*Electronics*] .... MGAP
Microgram [*One millionth of a gram*] .... MCG
Microgram (DAVI) .... mg
Microgram [*One millionth of a gram*] .... MICROG
Microgram (WDAA) .... MU G
Micrograms per Gram .... MPG
Micrographic Catalog Retrieval .... MCR
Micrographic Catalog Retrieval System .... MCRS
Micro-Graphic Reporting (PDAA) .... MGR
Micrographics Management Officer (MCD) .... MMO
Microgravity and Materials Processing Facility .... MMPF
Microgravity Materials Science Laboratory [*NASA*] .... MMSL
Microgravity Research Associates .... MRA
Microgravity Science and Applications .... MSA
Microgravity Science Laboratory [*NASA*] .... MSL
Microhemagglutination [*Test for Syphilis*] [*Immunochemistry*] (DAVI) .... MHA
Microhemagglutination Assay Treponema Pallidum [*Immunochemistry*] .... MHA-TP
Microhematocrit [*Clinical chemistry*] .... M/hct
Microhematuria [*Medicine*] .... MH
Microhenry (WDAA) .... MU H
Microimaged Data Addition System [*CAPS Equipment Ltd.*] .... MIDAS
Microimplementation Language [*Burroughs Corp.*] .... MIL
Microinch (IAA) .... MI
Microinch (BARN) .... min
Microinch (WDAA) .... MU IN
Microinches per Inch (KSC) .... MI/I
Microinstruction [*Computer science*] .... MI
Microinstruction Bus [*Computer science*] .... MIB
Microinstruction Read-Only Memory [*Computer science*] .... MICROM
Microinstruction Register .... MIR
Microinstruction Register (MHDI) .... MUIR
Microinstruction Simulator [*Computer science*] (MHDI) .... MICROSIM
Microinstruction Word .... MIW
Micro-Integration [*NASDAQ symbol*] (TTSB) .... MINT
Micro-Integration Corp. [*Associated Press*] (SAG) .... MicroIntg
Micro-Integration Corp. [*NASDAQ symbol*] (SAG) .... MINT
Micro-Interactive Retrieval System (DNAB) .... MIRS
Microion Mill .... MIM
Microlayer Transistor .... MLT
Microleague Multimedia [*NASDAQ symbol*] (TTSB) .... MLMI
Microleague Multimedia, Inc. [*Associated Press*] (SAG) .... Micrl
Microleague Multimedia, Inc. [*Associated Press*] (SAG) .... Micrleag
Microleague Multimedia, Inc. [*NASDAQ symbol*] (SAG) .... MLMI
Microleague Multimedia Wrrt [*NASDAQ symbol*] (TTSB) .... MLMIW
Microlight Aircrafts Association [*British*] (DI) .... MAA
Microliters of Carbon Dioxide Given Off per Milligram of Tissue per Hour [*Medicine*] (DAVI) .... QCO$_2$
Microlog Corp. [*Associated Press*] (SAG) .... Microlg
Microlog Corp. [*NASDAQ symbol*] (NQ) .... MLOG
Micromagnetic Industries .... MMI
Micromanipulator [*Instrumentation*] .... MM
Micro-Master Control Processor (NITA) .... MMCP
Micromation Microfilm .... MMF

Micromation Online Microfilmer .... MOM
Micromation Online Microfilmer [*Computer science*] (AD) .... mom
Micromation Systems, Inc., Feasterville, PA [*Library symbol Library of Congress*] (LCLS) .... McS
Micromechanized Engineering Data for Automated Logistics .... MEDAL
Micromedia Ltd. [*ACCORD*] [*UTLAS symbol*] .... MML
Micromedia Ltd., Toronto, ON, Canada [*Library symbol*] [*Library of Congress*] (LCLS) .... CaOTMML
Micromedia Ltd., Toronto, ON, Canada [*Library symbol Library of Congress*] (LCLS) .... McM
Micromedia Ltd., Toronto, ON, Canada [*Library symbol Library of Congress*] (LCLS) .... McMdL
Micromedia Ltd., Toronto, Ontario [*Library symbol National Library of Canada*] (NLC) .... OTMML
Micromedia Ltee., Hull, Quebec [*Library symbol National Library of Canada*] (BIB) .... QHMML
Micromembrane Filter .... MMF
Micromembrane Suppressor [*Ion chromatography*] .... MMS
Micrometeoric Erosion (AAG) .... MME
Micrometeoroid Capsule (OA) .... MMC
Micrometeoroid Explorer [*Satellite*] .... ME
Micrometer .... M
Micrometer [*A "mike"*] .... MIC
Micrometer (WDMC) .... mic
Micrometer Frequency Meter .... MFM
Micrometer Low-Approach System .... MILAS
Micromicrofarad (MUGU) .... MMF
Micromicrofarad (IDOE) .... mmf
Micromicrofarad (GPO) .... MMFD
Micromillimeter (WGA) .... mmm
Microminiature (IEEE) .... MICROMIN
Microminiature Automatic Checkout Equipment .... MICROACE
Microminiature Circuit (IAA) .... MC
Microminiature Delay Line .... MMDL
Microminiature Individual Components Reliable Assembled Modules .... MICRAM
Microminiature Mixer Amplifier .... MMA
Microminiature Relay .... MR
Microminiaturized Autonetics Telemetry .... MAUTEL
Micromodule (AAG) .... MM
Micromodule (IEEE) .... MMOD
Micromodule Data Processor and Computer (IEEE) .... MICROPAC
Micromodule Microprogrammed Computer System (PDAA) .... MIMICS
Micromoulding in Capillaries [*Plastics technology*] .... MIMIC
Micron [*Micrometer*] (AAMN) .... mu
Micron (DAVI) .... u
Micron (DAVI) .... um
Micron Electronics [*NASDAQ symbol*] (TTSB) .... MUEI
Micron Electronics, Inc. [*Associated Press*] (SAG) .... MicronEl
Micron Electronics, Inc. [*NASDAQ symbol*] (SAG) .... MUEI
Micron Industries Ltd. [*Vancouver Stock Exchange symbol*] .... MCR
Micron Technology [*Associated Press*] (SAG) .... MicrnT
Micron Technology [*NYSE symbol*] (TTSB) .... MU
Micron Technology, Inc. [*NYSE symbol*] (SPSG) .... MU
Micronavigator [*Air Force*] .... MICRON
Micronesia Coalition [*Defunct*] (EA) .... MC
Micronesia Support Committee [*Later, MC*] (EA) .... MSC
Micronesian Area Research Center [*University of Guam*] [*Research center*] (RCD) .... MARC
Micronesian Legal Services Corp. (EA) .... MLSC
Micronesian Minerals [*Vancouver Stock Exchange symbol*] .... MMC
MicroNet Apple User's Group [*CompuServe*] [*Database*] .... MAUG
Micronetics, Inc. [*Associated Press*] (SAG) .... Micront
Micronetics, Inc. [*NASDAQ symbol*] (NQ) .... NOIZ
Micronetics Wireless [*NASDAQ symbol*] (TTSB) .... NOIZ
Microneurography Society (EA) .... MNS
Microneutralization [*Chemistry*] .... MN
Micronics Computers [*NASDAQ symbol*] (SPSG) .... MCRN
Micronics Computers, Inc. [*Associated Press*] (SAG) .... Micrnics
Micronized Progesterone [*A natural hormone*] .... MP
Micronized Progesterone .... MP
Micron's Millenia XKU [*Computer science*] .... MMX
Micro-Opaque .... MO
Microoperation (MHDB) .... mo
Micro-Optic Gyroscope .... MOG
Micro-Opto-Mechanical Systems .... MOMS
Micro-Osmometer .... MO
Microparticle Concentration [*Analytical chemistry*] .... MPC
Microparticle Enzyme Immunoassay .... MEIA
Microphone (AABC) .... MIC
Microphone (WDMC) .... mic
Microphone (IDOE) .... mike
Microphone (CET) .... MIKE
Microphone (MDG) .... MK
Microphone Amplifier .... MA
Microphone Element (IEEE) .... MICELEM
Microphone Power Supply .... MPS
Microphone Probe Kit .... MPK
Microphones [*JETDS nomenclature*] [*Military*] (CET) .... M
Micro-Phonics Technology International Corp. [*Vancouver Stock Exchange symbol*] .... MPH
Microplate Reader [*Computer science*] .... MR
Microplex, Inc., Dallas, TX [*Library symbol of Congress*] (LCLS) .... Mcl
Micropolis Corp. [*Associated Press*] (SAG) .... Microp
Micropolis Corp. [*NASDAQ symbol*] (NQ) .... MLIS
Micropound Extended Range Thrust Stand [*NASA*] .... MERTS

Micropower Impulse RADAR [*For fluid level sensing*] ... MIR
Micropower/St. Joseph's High School, Islington, ON, Canada [*Library symbol*] [*Library of Congress*] (LCLS) ... CaOIsMSJ
Micropower/St. Joseph's High School, Islington, Ontario [*Library symbol National Library of Canada*] (NLC) ... OIMSJ
Microprint ... MP
Microprobe Analysis Generalized Intensity Corrections ... MAGIC
Microprocedure Call [*Computer science*] (MHDB) ... MICALL
Microprocedure Definition ... MIDEF
Microprocessed Sensing and Automatic Regulation [*Engine control system*] [*Automotive industry*] ... MISAR
Microprocessing Programmable Terminal [*Computer science*] (AD) ... mpt
Microprocessor ... M
Microprocessor ... MICRO
Microprocessor (MSA) ... MIPRCS
Microprocessor [*Instrumentation*] ... MP
Microprocessor [*Computer science*] [*Unit*] (ECII) ... MPC
Microprocessor Application of Graphic with Interactive Communication ... MAGIC
Microprocessor Application Project [*In manufacturing industry*] [*Department of the Interior*] ... MAP
Microprocessor Application to Control-Firmware Translator [*Computer science*] (MHDI) ... MPACT
Microprocessor Applications Consultancy (NITA) ... MAPCON
Microprocessor Arithmetic Model ... MARM
Microprocessor Automatic Testing [*ASMAP Electronics Ltd.*] [*Software package*] (NCC) ... MATE
Microprocessor Communications System (MCD) ... MCS
Microprocessor Control Unit ... MCU
Microprocessor Data Analyzer [*Instrumentation*] ... MIDAN
Microprocessor Data Extraction System [*Military*] (CAAL) ... MPDES
Microprocessor Debugging Program [*Computer science*] (IAA) ... MDP
Microprocessor Development Aid ... MDA
Microprocessor Development Center [*American Microsystems Inc. US*] (NITA) ... MDC
Microprocessor Development Lab (MHDI) ... MDL
Microprocessor Development Support System ... MDSS
Microprocessor Development System [*Motorola, Inc.*] ... MDS
Microprocessor Developments (NITA) ... MPD
Microprocessor Exchange [*Computer science*] ... MPX
Microprocessor Flight Control System (DOMA) ... MFCS
Microprocessor Host Loader [*Electronics*] ... MHL
Microprocessor Industrial Terminal [*Computer science*] (MHDB) ... MITE
Microprocessor Industry Support Programme [*British*] (DCTA) ... MISP
Microprocessor Inertia and Communication System ... MICS
Microprocessor Interface ... MPI
Microprocessor Language Assembler [*Computer science*] ... MLA
Microprocessor Language Editor [*Computer science*] ... MLE
Microprocessor Optimized Vehicle Actuation ... MOVA
Microprocessor [*or Motorola's*] **Programming Language** [*1975*] [*Computer science*] (CSR) ... MPL
Microprocessor Series [*or System*] (MDG) ... MPS
Microprocessor Spark Timing System ... MSTS
Microprocessor Training System [*Integrated Computer Systems*] (NITA) ... MTS
Microprocessor Unit [*CPU of microcomputer*] [*Computer science*] ... MPU
Microprocessor Unit (AD) ... mpu
Microprocessor Universal Asynchronous Receiver Transmitter (IAA) ... MUART
Microprocessor Without Interlocked Pipeline Stages (NITA) ... MIPS
Microprocessor-Based Audio Visual Information System (PDAA) ... MAVIS
Microprocessor-Controlled Crystal Oscillator [*Hughes Aircraft Co.*] (ECON) ... MCXO
Microprogram ... MP
Microprogram Address Register ... MADR
Microprogram Address Register ... MAR
Microprogram Address Register ... MPAR
Microprogram Automation System [*Computer science*] (IAA) ... MAS
Microprogram Certification System (MHDB) ... MCS
Microprogram Control ... MPC
Microprogram Control Logic [*Computer science*] (MDG) ... MCL
Microprogram Control Memory ... MPCM
Microprogram Control Unit (NITA) ... MCU
Microprogram Count Register [*Computer science*] (MHDB) ... MPCR
Microprogram Design Description Language [*1977*] [*Computer science*] (CSR) ... MIDDLE
Microprogram Generating System ... MPGS
Microprogram Location Counter ... MLC
Microprogram Memory ... MPM
Microprogram Memory Control (NITA) ... MPMC
Microprogram Operating System ... MOS
Microprogram Optimization Technique Considering Resource Occupancy and Instruction Formats (MHDB) ... MORIF
Microprogram Register (MHDI) ... MPR
Microprogram Storage [*Computer science*] (MDG) ... MS
Microprogramable Arithmetic Processor System (PDAA) ... MAPS
Microprogrammable Block Input/Output ... MBIO
Microprogrammable Communications Controller [*Computer science*] (MHDI) ... MPCC
Microprogrammable Computer Operating System ... MCOS
Microprogrammable Integrated Data Acquisition System ... MIDAS
Microprogrammable Multiprocessor (MCD) ... MMP
Microprogrammable Processor (MCD) ... MPP
Microprogrammed and Simulated Computer Organization ... MASCO
Microprogrammed Array Processor ... MAP
Microprogrammed Communication Data Processor (MCD) ... MCDP
Microprogrammed Control Unit [*Navy*] ... MCU
Microprogrammed Experimental Machine with a Basic Executive for Real-Time Systems (PDAA) ... MEMBERS
Microprogramming Design Aided System [*RCA*] ... MIDAS
Microprogramming Generating System (NITA) ... MPGS
Microprogramming Language ... ML
Microprogramming Language (NITA) ... MPL
Microprogramming Technique ... MPT
Microptic Theodolite ... MT
Microptic Theodolite ... MTH
Micropublishers' Trade List Annual [*A publication*] ... MTLA
Micropurulent Cervicitis [*Medicine*] ... MPC
Microreciprocal Degrees ... MIRED
Microrocket Engine ... MRE
Micros Systems, Inc. [*NASDAQ symbol*] (NQ) ... MCRS
Micros Systems, Inc. [*Associated Press*] (SAG) ... Micros
Micros To Mainframes [*NASDAQ symbol*] (TTSB) ... MTMC
Microsatelite Mutator Phenotype [*Oncology*] ... MMP
Microsatellite Mutator Phenotype [*Cytology*] ... MMP
Microscale Cloud [*Module*] [*Air Force*] ... MSC
Microscheduler (MHDI) ... msch
Microscope (MSA) ... MICR
Microscope and X-Ray Inspection ... M & X
Microscope Slide (DMAA) ... MS
Microscope-Photometer ... MPM
Microscopic (DAVI) ... MIC
Microscopic ... micro
Microscopic (DAVI) ... SCOPE
Microscopic Agglutination [*Medicine*] (DMAA) ... MA
Microscopic Camera Subsystem (KSC) ... MCSS
Microscopic Factor ... MF
Microscopic Findings in Centrifugal Urinary Sediment [*Biochemistry*] (DAVI) ... MIC
Microscopic Image Digital Acquisition System (PDAA) ... MIDAS
Microscopic System ... MS
Microscopically Controlled Excision [*Medicine*] ... MCE
Microscopium [*Constellation*] ... Mic
Microscopium [*Constellation*] ... Micr
Microscopy ... MCROSCPY
Microscopy ... MIC
Microscopy ... MICROS
Microsecond (WDAA) ... MU S
Microsecond Trip ... MST
Microseismic (AD) ... ms
Microsemi Corp. [*Associated Press*] (SAG) ... MicSem
Microsemi Corp. [*NASDAQ symbol*] (NQ) ... MSCC
MicroServe Information Systems ... MIS
Micro-Set System 2 (NITA) ... MS2
Microsillon et Haute-Fidelite [*Record label*] [*France*] ... MHF
Microsoft [*Software manufacturer*] ... MS
Microsoft Access Script Command [*Computer language*] ... MASC
Microsoft Active Accessibility [*Computer science*] ... MSAA
Microsoft and First Data Corp. ... MSFDC
Microsoft Anti-Virus [*Microsoft Corp.*] [*Computer science*] (PCM) ... MSAV
Microsoft At Work [*Computer software*] (PCM) ... MAW
Microsoft Clustering Server [*Computer science*] ... MSCS
Microsoft Compact Disc Extension [*Computer science*] (DOM) ... MSCDEX
Microsoft Consulting Services (CDE) ... MCS
Microsoft Corp. [*Associated Press*] (SAG) ... Microsft
Microsoft Corp. [*Associated Press*] (SAG) ... Microsoft
Microsoft Corp. [*Associated Press*] (SAG) ... Micsft
Microsoft Corporation (WDMC) ... MS
Microsoft Corp. [*NASDAQ symbol*] (NQ) ... MSFT
Microsoft Corp. National Broadcasting Co. [*Cable news channel*] ... MSNBC
Microsoft Developer Network [*Computer software*] (PCM) ... MSDN
Microsoft Developer Network [*Computer science*] ... MSDN
Microsoft Developer's Network [*Computer science*] (PCM) ... MSDN
Microsoft Diagnostics [*Microsoft Corp.*] [*Computer science*] (PCM) ... MSD
Microsoft Disk Operating System [*IBM Corp.*] [*Computer science*] ... MS-DOS
Microsoft DoubleSpace [*Computer science*] (PCM) ... MD
Microsoft DoubleSpace BIOS [*Basic Input-Output System*] **Parameter Block** [*Computer science*] (PCM) ... MDBPB
Microsoft DoubleSpace File Allocation Table (PCM) ... MDFAT
Microsoft Editor [*Computer program*] (PCM) ... ME
Microsoft Extended Basic (NITA) ... MSX
Microsoft Foundation Class Library [*Computer science*] (PCM) ... MFC
Microsoft Foundation Classes [*Computer science*] (PCM) ... MFC
Microsoft Knowledge Base [*Computer science*] (PCM) ... MSKB
Microsoft Network [*Online information service launched in 1995*] (WDMC) ... MSN
Microsoft Network [*Microsoft Corp.*] ... MSN
Microsoft Network [*Computer science*] [*Also, MSN*] (CDE) ... MS-Net
Microsoft Network [*Computer science*] (HGAA) ... MSNET
Microsoft Office Manager [*Microsoft Corp. computer program*] (PCM) ... MOM
Microsoft Paint [*Computer science*] (CDE) ... MSP
Microsoft Point to Point Compression [*Microsoft Corp.*] [*Computer science*] (PCM) ... MPPC
Microsoft Press Computer Dictionary ... MPCI
Microsoft Real-Time Compression Format [*Microsoft Corp.*] (PCM) ... MRCF
Microsoft Real-Time Compression Interface [*Microsoft Corp.*] (PCM) ... MRCI
Microsoft Solution Provider [*Computer science*] (CDE) ... MSP
Microsoft Tape Format [*Computer science*] ... MTF
Microsoft Tape Format [*Microsoft Corp.*] [*Computer science*] (PCM) ... MTF
Microsoft Transaction Server [*Computer science*] ... MTS
Microsomal Antibody ... MSA
Microsomal Ethanol-Oxidizing System [*Biochemistry*] ... MEOS
Microsomal Lipoprotein [*Immunochemistry*] ... MLP

Microsomal Triglyceride Transfer Protein [*Biochemistry*] ... MTP
Microspectrophotometry ... MSP
Microsphere ... MS
Microsporum [*Genus of fungi*] ... M
Microstar Software Ltd. [*Nepean, ON*] [*Telecommunications*] (TSSD) ... MSL
Microstat Development Corp. [*Vancouver Stock Exchange symbol*] ... MCT
MicroStation Customer Support Library [*Intergraph Corp.*] (PCM) ... MicroCSI
MicroStation Development Language [*Intergraph Corp.*] (PCM) ... MDL
Microstation Development Language ... MDL
Micros-To Mainframe, Inc. [*Associated Press*] (SAG) ... MicrosTo
Micros-To Mainframe, Inc. [*Associated Press*] (SAG) ... MicroTo
Micros-To Mainframe, Inc. [*NASDAQ symbol*] (SAG) ... MTMC
Microsurgery Drill System (DAVI) ... MDS
Microsurgical Epididymal Sperm Aspiration ... MESA
Microsuspension Seeded Polymerization (DICI) ... MSP
Microswitch (KSC) ... MSW
Microswitch ... MSW
Microsyn Torque Generator (SAA) ... MTG
Microsyn Torquer (SAA) ... MT
Microsystems Centre (NITA) ... MSC
Microtec Research, Inc. [*Associated Press*] (SAG) ... MicrtcRs
Microtec Research, Inc. [*NASDAQ symbol*] (SAG) ... MTEC
Micro-Technology, Inc., Cedar Rapids, IA [*Library symbol Library of Congress*] (LCLS) ... IaCrMT
Microtek Medical [*NASDAQ symbol*] (TTSB) ... MTMI
Microtek Medical, Inc. [*Associated Press*] (SAG) ... Micrtek
Microtek Medical, Inc. [*NASDAQ symbol*] (SAG) ... MTMI
Microtel Franchise & Development Corp. [*NASDAQ symbol*] (NQ) ... MCTL
Microtel Franchise & Development Corp. [*Associated Press*] (SAG) ... Microtl
Microtel Franchise&Development [*NASDAQ symbol*] (TTSB) ... MCTL
Microtel International, Inc. [*NASDAQ symbol*] (SAG) ... MCTL
Microtel International, Inc. [*Associated Press*] (SAG) ... Microtel
Microtel International, Inc. [*AMEX symbol*] (SAG) ... MOL
Microtel Intl [*AMEX symbol*] (TTSB) ... MOL
Microtel Pacific Research Ltd., Ottawa, Ontario [*Library symbol National Library of Canada*] (NLC) ... OOMPR
Microtest, Inc. [*Associated Press*] (SAG) ... Micrtest
Microtest, Inc. [*NASDAQ symbol*] (SAG) ... MTST
Microthrombus [*Hematology*] ... MT
Microthrust Ion Engine ... MTIE
Microtome [*Instrumentation*] ... MT
Microtome Manufacturers Association [*British*] (DBA) ... MMA
Microtouch Systems, Inc. [*Associated Press*] (SAG) ... MictchS
Microtouch Systems, Inc. [*Associated Press*] (SAG) ... MictchSy
Microtouch Systems, Inc. [*NASDAQ symbol*] (SAG) ... MTSI
Microtray Agglutination Test [*Clinical chemistry*] ... MAT
Microtubular Organizing Complex [*Physiology*] ... MTOC
Microtubule [*Cytology*] ... M
Microtubule [*Cytology*] ... MT
Microtubule Organizing Center [*Cytology*] ... MTOC
Microtubule Organizing Centers (DOG) ... MTOCs
Microtubule Protein [*Cytology*] ... MTP
Microtubule-Associated Protein [*Cytology*] ... MAP
Microtubule-Stabilizing Solution [*Cytology*] ... MTS
Microtunneling Boring Machine (RDA) ... MTBM
Microturbo [*France ICAO aircraft manufacturer identifier*] (ICAO) ... MJ
Microunit ... mcU
Microvilli [*Cytology*] ... MV
Microvillous Membrane [*Cytology*] (MAE) ... MVM
Microvision, Inc. [*Associated Press*] (SAG) ... Mcrvsn
Microvision, Inc. [*Associated Press*] (SAG) ... Micrvisn
Microvision, Inc. [*NASDAQ symbol*] (SAG) ... MVIS
Microvolt (WDAA) ... MU V
Microvolume Thermal Conductivity Detector [*Instrumentation*] ... MTCD
Microware Systems Corp. [*Associated Press*] (SAG) ... Micware
Microware Systems Corp. [*NASDAQ symbol*] (SAG) ... MWAR
Microwatt (WDAA) ... MU W
Microwatt (IAA) ... W
Microwave (AAG) ... MCRWV
Microwave ... MCRWV
Microwave [*Physics*] (DAVI) ... MV
Microwave ... MW
Microwave ... MWAVE
Microwave Accurate Surface Antenna Reflector (PDAA) ... MASAR
Microwave Acoustic Delay Line ... MADL
Microwave Aeropace Terminal Control [*Air Force*] (IAA) ... MTCON
Microwave Aerospace Navigation ... MAN
Microwave Aerospace Terminal Control [*Air Force*] ... MATCON
Microwave Airborne Communications Relay (IEEE) ... MARCOM
Microwave Aircraft Digital Guidance Equipment [*Helicopters*] ... MADGE
Microwave [*or Molecular*] **Amplification by Stimulated Emission of Radiation** ... MASER
Microwave Amplification by Stimulated Emission of Radiation (WDMC) ... maser
Microwave Amplification by Variable Reactance (IAA) ... MAVAR
Microwave Amplifier Electron Tube ... MAET
Microwave Analysis Threat Indication and Launch Direction Apparatus [*Military*] ... MATILDA
Microwave and Electronic System (IAA) ... MELS
Microwave and Millimeter-Wave Monolithic Integrated Circuits Project [*DoD*] ... MIMIC
Microwave and Optical Generation and Amplification (MCD) ... MOGA
Microwave Anisotropy Probe [*NASA*] ... MAP
Microwave Anisotropy Probe [*NASA*] ... MAP
Microwave Antenna Tower ... MAT
Microwave Associates, Inc. [*Later, M/A-Com*] (AAG) ... MA
Microwave Atmosphere Sounding Radiometer (PDAA) ... MASR
Microwave Attenuator Monitor (IAA) ... MAM
Microwave Attitude Control Sensor ... MACS
Microwave Automatic Vehicle Identification (MCD) ... MAVI
Microwave Background Radiation [*Physics*] ... MBR
Microwave Backward Wave Oscillator ... MBWO
Microwave Carrier Supply ... MCS
Microwave Cavity Laboratory (IAA) ... MCL
Microwave Ceramic Triode ... MCT
Microwave Circuit Analysis Package (PDAA) ... MCAP
Microwave Circuit Control Program [*Computer science*] ... MCCP
Microwave Circuit Module [*Computer science*] (IAA) ... MCM
Microwave Command Guidance ... MCG
Microwave Command Guidance System [*RADC*] ... MCGS
Microwave Communication System ... MCS
Microwave Communications Association (EA) ... MCA
Microwave Communications Inc. (NITA) ... MCI
Microwave Communications of America, Inc. ... MCI
Microwave Control Assembly ... MCA
Microwave Coupled Plasma [*Spectroscopy*] ... MCP
Microwave Delay Line ... MDL
Microwave Desorber [*Instrumentation*] ... MD
Microwave Detection and Ranging ... MIDAR
Microwave Development Laboratories ... MDL
Microwave Device Reliability (MCD) ... MDR
Microwave Diathermy [*Physical therapy*] (DAVI) ... MWD
Microwave Dielectric Integrated Circuit (IEEE) ... MDIC
Microwave Doppler Speed [*Electronic engineering*] ... MDS
Microwave Early Warning [*Radio*] [*Air Force*] ... MEW
Microwave Electronic Systems Ltd. ... MESL
Microwave Electronic Warfare System ... MEWS
Microwave Electronics Corp. ... MEC
Microwave Emission Detector [*Instrumentation*] ... MED
Microwave Energy Transmission Test (SSD) ... METT
Microwave Engineering Laboratories, Inc. (MCD) ... MELABS
Microwave Filter [*NASDAQ symbol*] (TTSB) ... MFCO
Microwave Filter Co., Inc. [*NASDAQ symbol*] (NQ) ... MFCO
Microwave Filter Co., Inc. [*Associated Press*] (SAG) ... MicrFlt
Microwave Frequency Measurement Module ... MFMM
Microwave Frequency Modulation Transmitter ... MFMT
Microwave Generator ... MG
Microwave Hologram RADAR ... MHR
Microwave Hybrid Junction ... MHJ
Microwave Ice Accretion Measurement Instrument (MCD) ... MIAMI
Microwave Identification Railroad Encoding Reflector (DNAB) ... MIRRER
Microwave Imager Sensor Study (MCD) ... MISS
Microwave Instantaneous Frequency Indication Receiver (MCD) ... MIFIR
Microwave Instrument Landing System ... MILS
Microwave Insular Line Integrated Circuit (IEEE) ... MILIC
Microwave Integrated Circuitry ... MIC
Microwave Integrated Circuits (NITA) ... MIC
Microwave Interface Module ... MIM
Microwave Interference Coordination ... MIC
Microwave Interference Protection ... MIP
Microwave Keying Switch ... MKS
Microwave Keying Switching Station ... MKSS
Microwave Laboratory [*Stanford University*] (MCD) ... ML
Microwave Landing Guidance System [*FAA*] ... MLGS
Microwave Landing System [*Aviation*] ... MLS
Microwave Landing System / Curved Path [*Aviation*] ... MLS/CP
Microwave Limb Sounder ... MLS
Microwave Line Stretcher ... MLS
Microwave Linear Accelerator ... MLA
Microwave Microminiature Communications System for Aircraft (DNAB) ... MMCSA
Microwave Mixer Diode ... MMD
Microwave Monolithic Integrated Circuit [*Used in wireless communication*] ... MIMIC
Microwave Multi-Application Payload [*NASA*] (PDAA) ... MMAP
Microwave Multipoint Distribution Systems (EDAC) ... MDS
Microwave Negative Grid ... MNG
Microwave Optical Double Resonance (PDAA) ... MODR
Microwave Optical-Photoselection Microscopy ... MOPS
Microwave Oscillating Diode (MCD) ... MOD
Microwave Oven (PDAA) ... MO
Microwave Phase Shifter ... MPS
Microwave Plasma Detector [*Instrumentation*] ... MPD
Microwave Position-Fixing System (NOAA) ... MPFS
Microwave Power Amplifier ... MPA
Microwave Power Devices [*NASDAQ symbol*] (TTSB) ... MPDI
Microwave Power Devices, Inc. [*Associated Press*] (SAG) ... MicPwr
Microwave Power Devices, Inc. [*NASDAQ symbol*] (SAG) ... MPDI
Microwave Power Meter ... MPM
Microwave Pressure Sounder (MCD) ... MPS
Microwave Pulse Generator ... MPG
Microwave Pulse Shaping Network ... MPSN
Microwave Pulse Source ... MPS
Microwave Pulse Storage System [*or Subsystem*] (MCD) ... MIPS
Microwave Radiation System (PDAA) ... MICRADS
Microwave Radiometer, Scatterometer, and Altimeter (MCD) ... MRSA
Microwave Radiometry (MCD) ... MICRAD
Microwave Relay Unit ... MRU
Microwave Remote Area Instrument Landing System (IAA) ... MWRAILS
Microwave Repeater Test Set (DA) ... MRTS
Microwave Research Institute [*Polytechnic Institute of Brooklyn*] (MCD) ... MRI

Microwave Rotary Joint ... MRJ
Microwave Satellite Technologies, Inc. [*Wellington, NJ*] (TSSD) ... MST
Microwave Scanner [*Marine science*] (OSRA) ... MS
Microwave Scanning Beam Land Station [*NASA*] ... MSBLS
Microwave Scanning Beam Landing Station [*or System*] [*NASA*] (NASA) ... MSBLS
Microwave Scanning Beam Landing System Ground Station [*NASA*] (NASA) ... MSBLS-GS
Microwave Scanning Beam Landing System Ground Station [*NASA*] ... MSBLS-GS
Microwave Scatterometer [*Telecommunications*] (TEL) ... MWS
Microwave Sensitivity Time Control [*Circuit*] ... MSTC
Microwave Services International, Inc. [*Denville, NJ*] [*Telecommunications*] (TSSD) ... MSI
Microwave Signal Generator ... MSG
Microwave Signature Acquisition System (MCD) ... MSAS
Microwave Sounding Unit [*Telecommunications*] (TEL) ... MSU
Microwave Space Electronics Relay ... MISER
Microwave Space Relay [*Electronics*] ... MISRE
Microwave Space Research Facility ... MSRF
Microwave Spectra Data Center [*National Institute of Standards and Technology*] ... MSDC
Microwave Spectrometer (TEL) ... MSW
Microwave Spectrum ... MS
Microwave Station ... MWS
Microwave Steerable Null Antenna Processor (MCD) ... MSNAP
Microwave Stripline-Circuit (PDAA) ... MSC
Microwave Switch Control Assembly ... MSCA
Microwave Switch Matrix (LAIN) ... MSM
Microwave Switching Station ... MSS
Microwave Systems [*NASDAQ symbol*] (TTSB) ... MWAR
Microwave Target Designator ... MTD
Microwave Technology as Applied to Air Navigation (ADA) ... MITAN
Microwave Test Equipment ... MTE
Microwave Test Facility ... MTF
Microwave Test Set (MCD) ... MTS
Microwave Theory and Technique (MCD) ... MTT
Microwave Thermograph [*Medical instrumentation*] ... MT
Microwave TOKAMAK [*Toroidal Kamera Magnetic*] **Experiment** [*Plasma physics*] ... MTX
Microwave Tower [*Nautical charts*] ... MICRO TR
Microwave Ultrasonic Delay Line ... MUDL
Microwave Vacuum [*Dryer*] (MCD) ... MIVAC
Microwave Water Substance Radiometer [*Marine science*] (OSRA) ... MWSR
Microwave Water Substance Radiometer (USDC) ... MWSR
Microwave Wind Spectrometer ... MWS
Microwave Window Failure Mechanism ... MWFM
Microwave Zone Position Indicator (IAA) ... MZPI
Microwave-Assisted Chemical Vapor Deposition [*Coating technology*] ... MACVD
Microwave-Assisted Curing [*Chemical engineering*] ... MAC
Microwave-Induced Helium Plasma Emission Detection (NATG) ... MIHPED
Microwave-Induced Nitrogen Discharge at Atmospheric Pressure [*Spectrometry*] ... MINDAP
Microwave-Induced Optical Nuclear Polarization [*Physics*] ... MIONP
Microwave-Induced Plasma [*Spectrometry*] ... MIP
Microwave-Induced Plasma Mass Spectrometry ... MIPMS
Microwave-Induced Plasma-Atomic Emission Spectroscopy ... MIP-AES
Micru International (EA) ... MI
MICRU International (EA) ... MICRU
Micturating Cystourethrography [*Medicine*] (DMAA) ... MCU
Mid Airways [*France*] [*FAA designator*] (FAAC) ... MID
Mid Am $1.8125 Cv'A'Pfd [*NASDAQ symbol*] (TTSB) ... MIAMP
MID Am Inc. [*NASDAQ symbol*] (TTSB) ... MIAM
Mid America Apartment Communities [*Associated Press*] (SAG) ... MidAp
Mid America Apartment Communities, Inc. [*Associated Press*] (SAG) ... MidAApt
Mid America Crop Protection Association (SRA) ... MACPA
Mid America Realty, Inc. [*Formerly, Dial REIT*] [*NYSE symbol*] (SAG) ... MDI
Mid America Realty, Inc. [*Formerly, Dial REIT*] [*Associated Press*] (SAG) ... MidAmR
Mid American Baptist Theological Seminary, Memphis, TN [*OCLC symbol*] (OCLC) ... TBT
Mid American Energy Co. [*NYSE symbol*] (SAG) ... MEC
Mid American Energy Co. [*Associated Press*] (SAG) ... MidAE
Mid American Energy Co. [*Associated Press*] (SAG) ... MidAmEn
Mid- and South Staffordshire Libraries in Cooperation (NITA) ... MISLIC
Mid Atlantic Medical Svcs [*NYSE symbol*] (TTSB) ... MME
Mid Continent Bancshares [*NASDAQ symbol*] (TTSB) ... MCBS
Mid Continent Bancshares, Inc. [*NASDAQ symbol*] (SAG) ... MCBS
Mid Continent Bancshares, Inc. [*Associated Press*] (SAG) ... MidContB
Mid Continent Wildcatters Association [*Defunct*] (EA) ... MCWA
Mid Fuselage ... MF
Mid Glamorgan [*County in Wales*] ... M GLAM
Mid Iowa Financial Corp. [*Associated Press*] (SAG) ... MidIwa
Mid Iowa Financial Corp. [*NASDAQ symbol*] (SAG) ... MIFC
Mid Mountain Mining [*Vancouver Stock Exchange symbol*] ... MIM
Mid Ocean Ltd. [*Associated Press*] (SAG) ... MidOcn
Mid Ocean Limited [*NYSE symbol*] (SAG) ... MOC
Mid Ocean Ltd. [*NASDAQ symbol*] (SAG) ... MOCN
Mid Ocean Ltd [*NYSE symbol*] (TTSB) ... MOC
Mid Pacific Air Corp. [*ICAO designator*] (FAAC) ... MPA
Mid Plate Gyre [*Nuclear energy*] (NUCP) ... MPG
Mid Upper Arm Circumference [*Anatomy*] ... MUAC
Midair Collision (IIA) ... MAC
Midair Recovery [*or Retrieval*] **System** [*Rescue by helicopter*] [*Military*] ... MARS
Mid-Air Retrieval (MCD) ... MAR
Mid-Am Antique Appraisers Association (EA) ... MAAAA
Mid-Am, Inc. [*NASDAQ symbol*] (NQ) ... MIAM
Mid-Am, Inc. [*Associated Press*] (SAG) ... MidAm
Mid-Am, Inc. [*Associated Press*] (SAG) ... MidAmIn
Mid-Amer Apart Communities [*NYSE symbol*] (TTSB) ... MAA
MidAmer Energy $1.7375 Pfd [*NYSE symbol*] (TTSB) ... MECPr
Mid-America: An Historical Review [*A publication*] (BRI) ... Mid-Am
[*The*] **Mid-America Apartment Communities** [*NYSE symbol*] (SPSG) ... MAA
Mid-America Bancorp [*AMEX symbol*] (SPSG) ... MAB
Mid-America Bancorp [*Associated Press*] (SAG) ... MidABc
Mid-America Baptist Theological Seminary, Memphis, TN [*Library symbol Library of Congress*] (LCLS) ... TMMAB
Mid-America Bible College, Oklahoma City, OK [*Library symbol*] [*Library of Congress*] (LCLS) ... OkOkM
Mid-America Commodity Exchange [*Chicago, IL*] ... MACE
Midamerica Commodity Exchange (EA) ... MIDAM
Mid-America Dance Company [*St. Louis, MO*] ... MAD/CO
Mid-America Dance Network [*Kansas City, MO*] ... MAD-N
Mid-America Electronics Conference ... MAECON
Mid-America Food Processors Association (SRA) ... MAFPA
Mid-America Interconnected Network [*Regional power council*] ... MAIN
Mid-America Interlibrary Services [*Library network*] ... MAILS
Mid-America International Agricultural Consortium ... MAIC
Mid-America International Agri-Trade Council ... MIATCO
Mid-America Nazarene College, Olathe, KS [*Library symbol Library of Congress*] (LCLS) ... KOlMN
Mid-America Payment Exchange ... MAPEX
Mid-America Periodical Distributors Association ... MAPDA
Mid-America Periodical Distributors Association (EA) ... MARPDA
Mid-America Realty Inv [*NYSE symbol*] (TTSB) ... MDI
Mid-America Reformed Seminary, Orange City, IA [*Library symbol*] [*Library of Congress*] (LCLS) ... IaOcM
Mid-America Regional Bargaining Association ... MARBA
Mid-America Regional Council [*Information service or system*] (IID) ... MARC
Mid-America State Universities Association [*Defunct*] (EA) ... MASUA
MidAmerica Vocational Curriculum Consortium (OICC) ... MAVCC
MidAmerican Communications Corp. [*Telecommunications service*] (TSSD) ... MACC
Mid-American Conference [*College football*] ... MAC
Mid-American Dance Network ... MADN
MidAmerican Energy [*NYSE symbol*] (TTSB) ... MEC
Mid-American International Development Association [*Nigeria*] ... MIDA
Mid-American Pipeline Co. ... MAPCO
Mid-American Reformed Seminary, Orange City, IA [*Library symbol Library of Congress*] (LCLS) ... IaOrM
Mid-American Research Corp. ... MARCO
Mid-American Waste Sys [*NYSE symbol*] (TTSB) ... MAW
Mid-American Waste Systems, Inc. [*NYSE symbol*] (SPSG) ... MAW
Mid-American Waste Systems, Inc. [*Associated Press*] (SAG) ... MAWste
Mid-Arkansas Regional Library [*Library network*] ... MID-ARK
Mid-Arkansas Regional Library, Malvern, AR [*Library symbol*] [*Library of Congress*] (LCLS) ... ArMalM
Midarm Circumference ... MAC
Midarm Muscle Circumference [*Myology*] ... MAMC
Midas Commuter Airlines CA [*Venezuela*] [*ICAO designator*] (FAAC) ... MIO
Midas Minerals, Inc. [*Toronto Stock Exchange symbol*] ... MDM
Mid-Atlantic (DNAB) ... MIDATL
Mid-Atlantic Area Council [*Regional power council*] ... MAAC
Mid-Atlantic Clearinghouse Association [*Maryland, Virginia, and Washington, DC*] ... MACHA
Mid-Atlantic Continental Shelf ... MACONS
Mid-Atlantic Electrical Exhibition (ITD) ... MAEE
Mid-Atlantic Independent Power Producers (SRA) ... MAIPP
Mid-Atlantic Medical Services, Inc. [*Associated Press*] (SAG) ... MidAtlan
Mid-Atlantic Medical Services, Inc. [*NYSE symbol*] (SAG) ... MME
Midatlantic Realty Trust [*Associated Press*] (SAG) ... MidatRty
Mid-Atlantic Realty Trust [*AMEX symbol*] (SPSG) ... MRR
Mid-Atlantic Regional Medical Library Program [*Library network*] ... RML IV
Mid-Atlantic Ridge [*of sea floor*] ... MAR
Mid-Atlantic Ridge Kane ... MARK
Mid-Atlantic Technology Applications Center [*University of Pittsburgh*] [*Research center*] (RCD) ... MTAC
Midaxillary Line [*Medicine*] ... MAL
Midazolan [*An anesthetic*] ... M
Mid-Bergen Federation of Public Libraries [*Library network*] ... MBFL
Midblastula Stage [*Embryology*] ... MBT
Mid-Blastula Transition [*Developmental biology*] ... MBT
Midbody ... MB
Midbody (NASA) ... MID
Midbody ... MID
Midbody Jettison Control Assembly ... MJCA
Midbody Jettison Control Assembly (NASA) ... MJCA
Midbody Motor Control Assembly (NASA) ... MMCA
Midbody Motor Control Assembly ... MMCA
Midbody Pyro Controller (NASA) ... MPC
Mid-Boiling Point ... MBP
Midbrain Central Gray [*Brain anatomy*] ... MCG
Midbrain Reticular Formation [*Anatomy*] ... MBRF
Midbrain Reticular Formation [*Medicine*] (DMAA) ... MRF
Midbrain Reticular Formation [*Brain anatomy*] ... MRF
Mid-Canada Gold & Copper [*Vancouver Stock Exchange symbol*] ... MCG
Mid-Canada Identification Zone ... MIDIZ
Mid-Canada Line [*RADAR warning chain of fence across Canada; sometimes called the McGill Fence*] ... MCL
Midcavity Forcep [*Medicine*] (DMAA) ... MF

Mid-Central Air Procurement District .... MIAPD
Mid-Central District [*ATSC*] .... MCD
Mid-Century Mercury Car Club (EA) .... MMCC
Midclavicular Line [*Medicine*] .... MCL
Mid-Coast Bancorp [*NASDAQ symbol*] (TTSB) .... MCBN
Mid-Coast Bancorp, Inc. [*NASDAQ symbol*] (NQ) .... MCBN
Mid-Coast Bancorp, Inc. [*Associated Press*] (SAG) .... MidCst
Midcoast Energy Resources, Inc. [*Associated Press*] (SAG) .... MidcstE
Midcoast Energy Resources, Inc. [*AMEX symbol*] (SAG) .... MRS
Mid-Columbia Mental Health Center, Richland, WA [*Library symbol Library of Congress*] (LCLS) .... WaRiMC
Mid-Columbia Regional Library, Kennewick, WA [*Library symbol Library of Congress*] (LCLS) .... WaKeM
MIDCOM Communications [*NASDAQ symbol*] (TTSB) .... MCCI
Midcom Communications, Inc. [*NASDAQ symbol*] (SAG) .... MCCI
Midcom Communications, Inc. [*Associated Press*] (SAG) .... Midcom
MidCon Corp., Lombard, IL [*Library symbol*] [*Library of Congress*] (LCLS) ..... ILoM
Midcon Oil & Gas Ltd. [*Toronto Stock Exchange symbol*] .... MID
Mid-Conn Bank [*Associated Press*] (SAG) .... MdConn
MidConn Bank [*NASDAQ symbol*] (NQ) .... MIDC
Midcontinent Airlines, Inc. [*ICAO designator*] (FAAC) .... MCA
Mid-Continent Area Power Pool [*Electric power*] .... MAPP
Mid-Continent Area Reliability Coordination Agreement [*Regional power council*] .... MARCA
Mid-Continent Association of the Pet Industry .... MCAPI
Mid-Continent Oil and Gas Association (EA) .... MCOGA
Mid-Continent Petroleum [*Stock exchange symbol*] (AD) .... MPZ
Mid-Continent Public Library Service, Independence, MO [*Library symbol Library of Congress*] (LCLS) .... MoIM
Mid-Continent Railway Historical Society (EA) .... MCRHS
Mid-Continent Regional Educational Laboratory [*Aurora, CO*] [*Department of Education*] .... MCREL
Mid-Continental Airlines .... MCA
Midcontinental Regional Medical Library Program [*University of Nebraska*] [*Library network*] (IID) .... MCRML
Midcontinental Regional Medical Library Program [*McGoogan Library of Medicine*] [*Information service or system*] (IID) .... MCRMLP
Midcostal Line [*Medicine*] .... MCL
Midcourse .... MC
Midcourse Active System (MCD) .... MAS
Midcourse Airborne Target Signature [*Military*] (PDAA) .... MATS
Midcourse and Terminal Guidance System [*NASA*] .... MTGS
Midcourse Correction (SAA) .... MC
Midcourse Correction .... MCC
Midcourse Fix and Terminal Guidance System (MCD) .... MFTGS
Midcourse Guidance [*Navy*] (CAAL) .... MCG
Midcourse Guidance and Control .... MGC
Midcourse Guidance Unit [*Navy*] (CAAL) .... MGU
Midcourse Maneuvering Unit [*Aerospace*] (MCD) .... MMU
Midcourse Measurement Correction .... MMC
Midcourse Measurement Unit [*Aerospace*] (KSC) .... MMU
Midcourse Mode [*Navy*] (CAAL) .... MM
Midcourse Navigation [*Navy*] (IAA) .... MCN
Midcourse Space Experiment (MCD) .... MSX
Mid-Course Surveillance System (MCD) .... MISS
Midcourse Surveillance System (MCD) .... MSS
Mid-Cycle Test [*Army training*] (INF) .... MCT
Midday (ADA) .... M
Middeck Act .... MA
Middeck Aft (MCD) .... MA
Middeck Assembly (MCD) .... MDA
Middeck Forward (MCD) .... MF
Middeck Left (MCD) .... ML
Middeck Overhead (MCD) .... MO
Middelburg [*South Africa*] [*ICAO location identifier*] (ICLI) .... FAMB
Middelburg [*South Africa*] [*ICAO location identifier*] (ICLI) .... FAMC
Middelburg/Midden Zeeland [*Netherlands ICAO location identifier*] (ICLI) ..... EHMZ
Mid-Diastolic Murmur [*Medicine*] .... MDM
Middle .... M
Middle .... M
Middle (MSA) .... MDL
Middle (AFM) .... MID
Middle (VRA) .... mid
Middle .... MID
Middle Ages .... MA
Middle Air Space (PDAA) .... MAS
Middle Airspace RADAR Advisory Service [*Military*] (DA) .... MARAS
Middle America [*MARC geographic area code Library of Congress*] (LCCP) .... cm----
Middle America Research Unit .... MARU
Middle Assyrian [*Language, etc.*] (BJA) .... MA
Middle Assyrian [*Language, etc.*] (BJA) .... MAss
Middle Assyrian Laws (BJA) .... MAL
Middle Atlantic .... MATL
Middle Atlantic Association of Colleges of Business Administration ..... MAACBA
Middle Atlantic Association of Women Sailors .... MAAWS
Middle Atlantic Conference, East Riverdale MD [*STAC*] .... MAC
Middle Atlantic Fisheries Association (EA) .... MAFA
Middle Atlantic Fisheries Research Center [*National Oceanic and Atmospheric Administration*] .... MAFRC
Middle Atlantic Intercollegiate Sailing Association .... MAISA
Middle Atlantic Lawn Tennis Association .... MALTA
Middle Atlantic Planetarium Society (EA) .... MAPS
Middle Atlantic Regional Information Network .... MARLIN
Middle Atlantic Regional Meeting [*of American Chemical Society*] .... MARM
Middle Atlantic States [*MARC geographic area code Library of Congress*] (LCCP) .... n-usl-
Middle Atmosphere Programme [*International Council of Scientific Unions*] .... MAP
Middle Babylonian [*Language, etc.*] (BJA) .... MB
Middle Babylonian [*Language, etc.*] (BJA) .... MBab
Middle Bay Oil [*NASDAQ symbol*] (TTSB) .... MBOC
Middle Bay Oil Co., Inc. [*NASDAQ symbol*] (SAG) .... MBOC
Middle Bay Oil Co., Inc. [*Associated Press*] (SAG) .... MidBay
Middle Border Zone [*Geology*] .... MBZ
Middle Breton [*Language, etc.*] .... MBRET
Middle Bronze Age (BJA) .... MB
Middle Bronze I [*Age*] .... MBI
Middle Caicos [*Turks and Caicos Islands*] [*ICAO location identifier*] (ICLI) .... MBMC
Middle Caicos [*British West Indies*] [*Airport symbol*] (OAG) .... MDS
Middle Cape [*Alaska*] [*Seismograph station code, US Geological Survey*] (SEIS) .... MMC
Middle Cerebral Aneurysm [*Cardiology*] [*Neurology*] (DAVI) .... MCA
Middle Cerebral Artery [*Anatomy*] .... MCA
Middle Chamber [*Freemasonry*] .... MC
Middle Class, Intelligent, Nice Girl [*Lifestyle classification*] .... MING
Middle Country Public Library, Centereach, NY [*Library symbol Library of Congress*] (LCLS) .... NCe
Middle Country Public Library, Selden Branch, Selden, NY [*Library symbol Library of Congress*] (LCLS) .... NSel
Middle Creek Railroad (IIA) .... MC
Middle Deltoid [*Myology*] .... MD
Middle Distance Swimmer .... MDS
Middle Distillate [*Fuel technology*] .... MD
Middle District (DLA) .... MD
Middle Door [*Theater*] .... MD
Middle Dutch [*Language, etc.*] .... MD
Middle Dutch [*Language, etc.*] .... MDU
Middle Ear .... ME
Middle Ear Cell (BABM) .... MEC
Middle Ear Effusion [*Medicine*] .... MEE
Middle Ear Fluid .... MEF
Middle East [*or Middle Eastern*] .... ME
Middle East Air Force [*British*] .... MEAF
Middle East Airlines [*ICAO designator*] (AD) .... ME
Middle East Airlines - Air Liban [*Lebanon*] .... MEA
Middle East and North Africa [*A publication*] .... MENA
Middle East/Asia Region [*USTTA*] (TAG) .... MID/ASIA
Middle East Association [*British*] (EAIO) .... MEA
Middle East Basic Encyclopedia [*A publication*] (MCD) .... MEBE
Middle East Center for Arab Studies .... MECAS
Middle East Centre [*University of Cambridge*] [*British*] (CB) .... MEC
Middle East Civil Aviation Conference (PDAA) .... MECACON
Middle East Command [*Military*] .... MEC
Middle East Command [*Military*] .... MECOM
Middle East Committee for the Welfare of the Blind (EA) .... MECWB
Middle East Council of Churches (EA) .... MECC
Middle East Database (IID) .... MEDAB
Middle East Defense Organization (NATG) .... MEDO
Middle East Economic Survey [*A publication*] .... MEES
Middle East Electronic Communications Show and Conference [*Arabian Exhibition Management WLL*] [*Manama, Bahrain*] .... MECOM
Middle East Food and Equipment Exhibition [*Arabian Exhibition Management*] .... MEFEX
Middle East Force [*Military*] (AABC) .... MIDEASTFOR
Middle East Force (DOMA) .... MIDEASTFOR
Middle East Force Target List (MCD) .... MEFTL
Middle East Forces [*British*] .... MEF
Middle East Forum [*Lebanon*] (BJA) .... MEF
Middle East Information Service (BJA) .... MEI
Middle East Information Service (BJA) .... MEIS
Middle East Institute (EA) .... MEI
Middle East Intelligence Center [*World War II*] .... MEIC
Middle East Interpretation Unit [*British*] .... MEIU
Middle East Journal [*A publication*] (BRI) .... MEJ
Middle East Land Forces [*British*] (NATG) .... MELF
Middle East Law Review [*A publication*] (DLA) .... Mid East L Rev
Middle East Liaison Group [*Military*] (AABC) .... MELG
Middle East Librarians' Association (EA) .... MELA
Middle East Libraries Committee .... MELCOM
Middle East Lutheran Ministry [*Lebanon*] (EAIO) .... MELM
Middle East Medical Advisory Committee [*World War II*] .... MEMAC
Middle East Money [*London-Beirut*] (BJA) .... MEMO
Middle East Neurosurgical Society (EAIO) .... MENS
Middle East News Agency .... MENA
Middle East Peace and Stability Act [*1957*] .... MEPSA
Middle East Peace Project (EA) .... MEPP
Middle East Policy [*A publication*] (BRI) .... MEP
Middle East Policy and Research Center (EA) .... MEPARC
Middle East Quarterly [*A publication*] (BRI) .... MEQ
Middle East Record [*A publication*] (BJA) .... MER
Middle East Relief and Rehabilitation Administration [*World War II*] .... MERRA
Middle East Research and Information Project (EA) .... MERIP
Middle East Resource Center [*Defunct*] (EA) .... MERC
Middle East Section of the War Cabinet [*British World War II*] .... MEWC
Middle East Service Command [*Army World War II*] .... MESC
Middle East/Southern Asia .... ME/SA
Middle East/Southern Asia and Africa South of the Sahara [*Military*] ..... MEAFSA
Middle East Special Requirement Fund .... MESRF
Middle East Studies Association of North America (EA) .... MESA

Middle East Supercomputer Centre [Bahrain Centre for Studies and Research] (ECON) .... MESC
Middle East Supply Center [World War II] .... MESC
Middle East Supply Committee (Washington) [World War II] .... MESC(W)
Middle East Supply Council [World War II] .... MESC
Middle East Task Group (DNAB) .... METG
Middle East Treaty Organization .... METO
Middle East War Council [British military] (DMA) .... MEWC
Middle East Watch [An association] (EA) .... MEW
Middle Eastern Regional Radioisotope Centre for the Arab Countries [Cairo, Egypt] (WND) .... MERRC
Middle English [Language, etc.] .... ME
Middle Flemish [Language] (BARN) .... MFlem
Middle Fork [AAR code] .... MF
Middle Free Path .... MFP
Middle French [Language, etc.] .... MF
Middle French [Language, etc.] .... MFR
Middle Georgia College [Cochran] .... MGC
Middle Georgia College, Cochran, GA [Library symbol Library of Congress] (LCLS) .... GCocM
Middle Georgia College, Cochran, GA [OCLC symbol] (OCLC) .... GMC
Middle Gimbal .... MG
Middle Gimbal [Yaw] .... MG
Middle Gimbal Angle (NASA) .... MGA
Middle Gimbal Assembly (KSC) .... MGA
Middle Gimbal Axis (KSC) .... MGA
Middle Greek [Language, etc.] (ROG) .... M GR
Middle Greek [Language] (BARN) .... MGk
Middle Hebrew [Language, etc.] (BJA) .... MHeb
Middle High German [Language, etc.] .... MHG
Middle Income Country [Category of developing country] .... MIC
Middle Income Student Assistance Act [1978] .... MISAA
Middle Initial .... MI
Middle Interphalangeal Joint [Anatomy] (DAVI) .... MIP
Middle Irish [Language, etc.] .... MIR
Middle Iron Age (BJA) .... MI
Middle Island Central Public Library, Yaphank, NY [Library symbol Library of Congress] (LCLS) .... NYap
Middle Italian [Language, etc.] .... MIT
Middle Kingdom [Egyptology] (ROG) .... MK
Middle Landing .... MLD
Middle Latency Response [Medicine] .... MLR
Middle Latin [Language, etc.] .... ML
Middle Latitude [Navigation] .... LM
Middle Latitude [Navigation] .... MIDLAT
Middle Leaf Area [Botany] .... MAREA
Middle Left (WDAA) .... ML
Middle Linebacker [Football] .... MLB
Middle Lobe [Of lung] .... ML
Middle Low German [Language, etc.] .... MLG
Middle Management Development .... MMD
Middle Management Development Initiative .... MMDI
Middle Management Development Program .... MMDP
Middle Management Institute [Special Libraries Association] .... MMI
Middle Management Module .... MMM
Middle Manager .... MM
Middle Marker [in an instrument landing system] .... MM
Middle Marker [in an instrument landing system] .... MMKR
Middle Meningeal Artery [Neuroanatomy] .... MMA
Middle Meningeal System [Neuroanatomy] .... MMS
Middle Minoan [Archaeology] (BJA) .... MM
Middle Name Unknown (MCD) .... MNU
Middle of Bow [Music] (ROG) .... MB
Middle of Month (AD) .... m-o-m
Middle of Target (AD) .... mot
Middle of the Month .... MOM
Middle of the Road [Broadcasting] .... MOR
Middle of the Road (AD) .... mor
Middle Persian (AD) .... MPers
Middle phalanx [Anatomy] (DAVI) .... MP
Middle Point .... MP
Middle Repetitive [Genetics] .... MR
Middle Right (AD) .... m/r
Middle River School, Middle River, MN [Library symbol] [Library of Congress] (LCLS) .... MnMirS
Middle School [British] .... M
Middle States Association (NADA) .... MSA
Middle States Association of Colleges and Schools (EA) .... MSA
Middle States Regatta Association (EA) .... MSRA
Middle Stone Age [Anthropology] .... MSA
Middle Temple [London] [One of the Inns of Court] .... MT
Middle Temporal [Anatomy] .... MT
Middle Temporal Lobe [of the brain] .... MT
Middle Tennessee State University (GAGS) .... Mid Tenn St U
Middle Tennessee State University .... MTSU
Middle Tennessee State University, Murfreesboro, TN [Library symbol Library of Congress] (LCLS) .... TMurS
Middle Tennessee State University, Murfreesboro, TN [OCLC symbol] (OCLC) .... TXM
Middle Term of a Syllogism [Logistics] (WDAA) .... MT
Middle Third [of long bones] [Orthopedics] (DAVI) M/3
Middle Turbinate [Otorhinolaryngology] (DAVI) .... MT
Middle Ultraviolet .... MUV
Middle, Up, Down [in game of bridge] .... MUD
Middle Valve Select (MCD) .... MVS

Middle Wallop [British ICAO location identifier] (ICLI) .... EGVP
Middle Welsh [Language, etc.] .... MW
Middle Zero (IAA) .... MDZ
Middle-Aged Affluent Folks [Lifestyle Classification] .... Maffies
Middle-Aged, Overstressed, Semiaffluent Suburbanite [Lifestyle classification] .... MOSS
Middle-Aged, Overstressed Semiaffluent Suburbanites [Lifestyle Classification] .... Mossies
Middle-Aged Rural Professional [Lifestyle classification] .... Marpie
Middle-Aged Urban Pinhead [Lifestyle classification] .... Muppie
Middle-Aged Urban Professional [Lifestyle classification] .... Muppie
Middle-Atlantic Educational and Research Center .... MERC
Middleboro, MA [AM radio station call letters] .... WCEG
Middlebury [Vermont] [Seismograph station code, US Geological Survey] (SEIS) .... MDV
Middlebury College (GAGS) .... Middlebury C
Middlebury College, Middlebury, VT [OCLC symbol] (OCLC) .... MDY
Middlebury College, Middlebury, VT [Library symbol Library of Congress] (LCLS) .... VtMiM
Middlebury Independent, Middlebury, IN [Library symbol Library of Congress] (LCLS) .... InMidbI
Middlebury Public Library, Middlebury, IN [Library symbol Library of Congress] (LCLS) .... InMidb
Middlebury, VT [AM radio station call letters] .... WFAD
Middlebury, VT [FM radio station call letters] .... WGTK
Middlebury, VT [FM radio station call letters] .... WRMC
Middleby Corp. [AMEX symbol] (SPSG) .... MBY
Middleby Corp. [NASDAQ symbol] (TTSB) .... MIDD
Middleby Corp. [Associated Press] (SAG) .... Midlby
Middle-Ear Muscle [Anatomy] .... MEM
Middle-Ear Muscle Activity .... MEMA
Middlegate Resources, Inc. [Vancouver Stock Exchange symbol] .... MGR
Middleground (VRA) .... mgrd
Middlemount [Australia Airport symbol] (OAG) .... MMM
Middleport Free Library, Middleport, NY [Library symbol Library of Congress] (LCLS) .... NMidp
Middleport-Pomeroy, OH [AM radio station call letters] .... WMPO
Middleport-Pomeroy, OH [FM radio station call letters] .... WMPO-FM
Middlesboro, KY [AM radio station call letters] .... WFXY
Middlesboro, KY [AM radio station call letters] .... WMIK
Middlesboro, KY [FM radio station call letters] .... WMIK-FM
Middlesborough [England] [Airport symbol] (AD) .... MME
Middle-Scale Integration [Computer science] (IAA) .... MSI
Middlesex [Region of London] .... MDDX
Middlesex [County in England] .... MDX
Middlesex [County in England] .... MIDDX
Middlesex [County in England] (ODBW) .... Middx
Middlesex [Region of London] .... MX
Middlesex Community College [Bedford, MA] .... MCC
Middlesex Community College, Bedford, MA [Library symbol Library of Congress] (LCLS) .... MBdM
Middlesex County College, Edison, NJ [Library symbol Library of Congress] (LCLS) .... NjEdM
Middlesex County Public Library, Arva, ON, Canada [Library symbol Library of Congress] (LCLS) .... CaOArM
Middlesex County Public Library, Arva, Ontario [Library symbol National Library of Canada] (NLC) .... OARM
Middlesex, Duke of Cambridge's Hussars [Military unit] [British] .... MDCH
Middlesex General Hospital, New Brunswick, NJ [Library symbol Library of Congress] (LCLS) .... NjNbM
Middlesex Hussars (Duke of Cambridge's) [British military] (DMA) .... MH
Middlesex Public Library, Middlesex, NJ [Library symbol Library of Congress] (LCLS) .... NjMid
[The] Middlesex Regiment [British] .... MR
Middlesex Rifle Volunteers [Military British] (ROG) .... MRV
Middlesex Rifle Volunteers [Military British] (DMA) .... MXRV
Middlesex Volunteer Rifle Corps [British military] (DMA) .... MXVRC
Middlesex Water [NASDAQ symbol] (TTSB) .... MSEX
Middlesex Water Co. [Associated Press] (SAG) .... MdsxWat
Middlesex Water Co. [NASDAQ symbol] (NQ) .... MSEX
Middlesex Yeomanry Cavalry [British military] (DMA) .... MYC
Middleton Gardens [South Carolina] [Seismograph station code, US Geological Survey] (SEIS) .... MGS
Middleton Island [Alaska] [Seismograph station code, US Geological Survey] (SEIS) .... MID
Middleton Island, AK [Location identifier FAA] (FAAL) .... ESS
Middleton Island, AK [Location identifier FAA] (FAAL) .... MDO
Middleton, NS [AM radio station call letters] .... CKAD
Middleton Place, Charleston, SC [Library symbol Library of Congress] (LCLS) .... ScCMP
Middleton Public Library, Middleton, ID [Library symbol] [Library of Congress] (LCLS) .... IdMi
Middleton, WI [FM radio station call letters] .... WWQM
Middletown Air Materiel Area (SAA) .... MAAMA
Middletown Air Materiel Area [Air Force] .... MAMA
Middletown Air Service Command [Air Force] .... MASC
Middletown Air Technical Service Command [Air Force] .... MATSC
Middletown & Hummelstown Railroad Co. [AAR code] .... MIDH
Middletown & New Jersey Railway Co., Inc. [AAR code] .... MNJ
Middletown & Unionville Railroad [Nickname: Miserable and Useless] .... M & U
Middletown, CA [FM radio station call letters] .... KRSH
Middletown, CT [AM radio station call letters] .... WCNX
Middletown, CT [FM radio station call letters] .... WESU
Middletown, CT [FM radio station call letters] .... WIHS
Middletown, CT [AM radio station call letters] (RBYB) .... WMRD-AM

Middletown/Harrisburg International-Olmsted Field [*Pennsylvania*] [*ICAO location identifier*] (ICLI) .... KMDT
Middletown Hospital Association, Ada Leonard Memorial Library, Middletown, OH [*Library symbol*] [*Library of Congress*] (LCLS) .... OMidH
Middletown Library, Middletown, CA [*Library symbol Library of Congress*] (LCLS) .... CMid
Middletown, MD [*FM radio station call letters*] .... WAFY
Middletown News, Middletown, IN [*Library symbol Library of Congress*] (LCLS) .... InMidN
Middletown, NY [*AM radio station call letters*] .... WALL
Middletown, NY [*FM radio station call letters*] .... WOSR
Middletown, NY [*FM radio station call letters*] (RBYB) .... WRRV
Middletown, OH [*Location identifier FAA*] (FAAL) .... HKF
Middletown, OH [*Location identifier FAA*] (FAAL) .... MWO
Middletown, OH [*AM radio station call letters*] .... WPFB
Middletown, OH [*FM radio station call letters*] .... WPFB-FM
Middletown, PA [*Location identifier FAA*] (FAAL) .... HQA
Middletown, PA [*Location identifier FAA*] (FAAL) .... MDT
Middletown, PA [*FM radio station call letters*] .... WMSS
Middletown Public Library, Middletown, IN [*Library symbol*] [*Library of Congress*] (LCLS) .... InMid
Middletown Public Library, Middletown, OH [*OCLC symbol*] (OCLC) .... OMI
Middletown Public Library, Middletown, OH [*Library symbol Library of Congress*] (LCLS) .... OMid
Middletown, RI [*FM radio station call letters*] (RBYB) .... WDGF-FM
Middletown, RI [*FM radio station call letters*] .... WOTB
Middletown Township Free Public Library, Middletown, NJ [*Library symbol Library of Congress*] (LCLS) .... NjMi
Middletown Township Public Library, Middletown, NJ [*Library symbol*] [*Library of Congress*] (LCLS) .... NjMiP
Middlewest Motor Freight Bureau .... MWMFB
Middlewest Motor Freight Bureau, Kansas City MO [*STAC*] .... MWB
Middling Fair (IAA) .... MF
Middling Space [*Typesetting*] (DGA) .... MID
Middoth (BJA) .... Mid
Mideast File [*Tel-Aviv University*] [*Israel*] [*Information service or system*] (IID) .... MEF
Mideast Information Resource (BJA) .... MEIR
Mid-Eastern Athletic Conference .... MEAC
Mideastern Michigan Library Cooperative [*Library network*] .... MIDEAST MI LIB
Mideastern Ohio Library Organization [*Library network*] .... MOLO
Mid-Eastern Regional Medical Library Service [*Library network*] .... MERMLS
Mid-Engine [*Automotive engineering*] .... ME
Mid-Engine, Rear-Drive [*Automotive engineering*] .... MR
Mid-European Law Project .... MELP
Mid-European Studies Center, New York, NY [*Library symbol Library of Congress*] (LCLS) .... NNME
Midexpiratory Dynamic Flow Rate [*Medicine*] (DAVI) .... MEDF
Midexpiratory Flow [*Medicine*] (DMAA) .... MEF
Midexpiratory Time [*Medicine*] .... MET
Midfield [*Men's lacrosse position*] .... M
Midforceps Delivery [*Obstetrics*] .... MFD
Mid-Forceps Rotation [*Obstetrics*] (DAVI) .... MFR
Mid-Frequency (IDOE) .... mf
Mid-Frequency Execution .... MFE
Mid-Frequency Executive (NASA) .... MFE
Mid-Function Integral Control Alarm Module [*Electronics systems*] [*Automotive engineering*] .... MICAM
Midfuselage (NASA) .... MF
Midget (MSA) .... MDGT
Midget Auto Racing Association [*Sanctioning organization*] .... MARA
Midget Ocean Racing Class [*or Club*] .... MORC
Midget Submarine [*Navy symbol*] .... SSM
Mid-Hudson Libraries, Poughkeepsie, NY [*Library symbol Library of Congress*] (LCLS) .... NPMH
Mid-Hudson Library System [*Library network*] .... MHLS
Midhurst Branch Library, Ontario [*Library symbol National Library of Canada*] (NLC) .... OMB
MIDI [*Musical Instrument Digital Interface*] Processing Unit [*Computer technology*] .... MPU
MIDI [*Musical Instrument Digital Interface*] Time Code .... MTC
MIDI [*Musical Instrument Digital Interface*] Users Sequencer/Editor [*Roland International Corp.*] .... MUSE
Mid-Infrared Advanced Chemical LASER .... MIRACL
Mid-Infrared Spectrum [*Spectroscopy*] .... MIR
Midinspiratory Flow [*Medicine*] (DMAA) .... MIF
Mid-Intensity Conflict [*Military*] (INF) .... MIC
Mid-Iowa Finl [*NASDAQ symbol*] (TTSB) .... MIFC
Mid-Island Hospital, Bethpage, NY [*Library symbol Library of Congress*] (LCLS) .... NBetH
Midisoft Corp. [*NASDAQ symbol*] (SAG) .... MIDI
Midisoft Corp. [*Associated Press*] (SAG) .... Midisoft
Midivariant [*Genetics*] .... MDV
Midland .... MDLND
Midland [*Topography*] (ROG) .... MID
Midland [*English dialect*] (ROG) .... MIDL
Midland [*AAR code*] .... MLD
Midland and Great Northern Joint Line [*Railway*] [*British*] (ROG) .... M & GN
Midland & International Banks Ltd. [*British*] .... MAIBL
Midland and South Western Junction Railway [*British*] .... MSWJ
Midland Bancorp [*NYSE symbol*] (SPSG) .... MIB
Midland Bank A1/A2 Unit ADS [*NYSE symbol*] (TTSB) .... MIBPrA
Midland Bank B1/B2 Unit ADS (TTSB) .... MIBPrB
Midland Bank C1/C2 Unit ADS [*NYSE symbol*] (TTSB) .... MIBPrC
Midland Bank PLC [*NYSE symbol*] (SAG) .... MIB

Midland Bank PLC [*Associated Press*] (SAG) .... MidBk
Midland Bank PLC [*Associated Press*] (SAG) .... MidlBk
Midland Co. [*Associated Press*] (SAG) .... MidInd
Midland Co. [*AMEX symbol*] (SPSG) .... MLA
Midland Continental R. R. [*AAR code Obsolete*] .... MICO
Midland County Public Library, Midland, TX [*Library symbol Library of Congress*] (LCLS) .... TxMM
Midland Doherty Financial Corp. [*Toronto Stock Exchange symbol*] .... MDF
Midland Financial Group [*NASDAQ symbol*] (SAG) .... MDLD
Midland Financial Group [*Associated Press*] (SAG) .... MidlFn
Midland Gold Corp. [*Formerly, Midland Energy Corp.*] [*Vancouver Stock Exchange symbol*] .... MDY
Midland Great Western Railway [*British*] (ROG) .... MGWR
Midland Lutheran College, Fremont, NE [*Library symbol Library of Congress*] (LCLS) .... NbFrM
Midland Lutheran College, Fremont, NE [*OCLC symbol*] (OCLC) .... NFM
Midland Macromolecular Institute [*Midland, MI*] .... MMI
Midland, MI [*FM radio station call letters*] .... WKQZ
Midland, MI [*AM radio station call letters*] .... WMPX
Midland, MI [*FM radio station call letters*] .... WUGN
Midland Network (NITA) .... MIDNET
Midland Nuclear Power Plant (NRCH) .... MNPP
Midland/Odessa [*Texas*] [*Airport symbol*] (OAG) .... MAF
Midland, ON [*FM radio station call letters*] .... CICZ
Midland, ON [*Television station call letters*] CIII-7
Midland Operational Research Society (AD) .... MORS
Midland Plant [*Nuclear energy*] (NRCH) .... MP
Midland Public Library, Midland, ON, Canada [*Library symbol Library of Congress*] (LCLS) .... CaOMi
Midland Public Library, Ontario [*Library symbol National Library of Canada*] (NLC) .... OMI
Midland Railway [*British*] .... MR
Midland Railway Company of Western Australia (AD) .... MRCWA
Midland Railway of Western Australia (AD) .... MRWA
Midland/Regional Air Terminal [*Texas*] [*ICAO location identifier*] (ICLI) .... KMAF
Midland Res Inc. Wrrt [*NASDAQ symbol*] (TTSB) .... MRIXZ
Midland Resources [*NASDAQ symbol*] (SPSG) .... MRIX
Midland Resources, Inc. [*Associated Press*] (SAG) .... MidlRs
Midland Resources, Inc. [*Associated Press*] (SAG) .... MidR
Midland Steel Stockholders Association [*British*] (DBA) .... MSSA
Midland Technical College, Airport Campus, Library and Information Center, Columbia, SC [*Library symbol*] [*Library of Congress*] (LCLS) .... ScCoM-A
Midland Terminal Railroad (IIA) .... MT
Midland, TX [*FM radio station call letters*] .... KBAT
Midland, TX [*FM radio station call letters*] .... KCHX
Midland, TX [*AM radio station call letters*] .... KCRS
Midland, TX [*FM radio station call letters*] .... KCRS-FM
Midland, TX [*AM radio station call letters*] .... KJBC
Midland, TX [*Television station call letters*] .... KMID
Midland, TX [*FM radio station call letters*] .... KMND
Midland, TX [*FM radio station call letters*] .... KNFM
Midland, TX [*FM radio station call letters*] .... KQRX
Midland, TX [*AM radio station call letters*] .... KWEL
Midland, TX [*Location identifier FAA*] (FAAL) .... MDD
Midland Valley R. R. [*AAR code*] .... MV
Midland-Odessa Symphony and Chorale (AD) .... MOSC
Midland-Ross Corp., Library, Cleveland, OH [*OCLC symbol*] (OCLC) .... OMR
Midlands Asthma and Allergy Research Association [*British*] (DBA) .... MAARA
Midlands Electricity Board [*British*] .... MEB
Midlands Examining Group [*British*] (AIE) .... MEG
Midlands Technical College, Beltline Campus, Columbia, SC [*Library symbol*] [*Library of Congress*] (LCLS) .... ScCoM-B
Midlands Technical College, Columbia, SC [*Library symbol*] [*Library of Congress*] (LCLS) .... ScCoM
Midlantic Corp. [*NASDAQ symbol*] (NQ) .... MIDL
Midlantic Corp. [*Associated Press*] (SAG) .... MidlCp
Mid-Lateral Nerve .... MLN
Midlevel Positions in Administrative, Staff, and Technical Services [*Civil Service Commission*] .... MAST
Midlife (DAVI) .... ML
Midlife Conversion .... MLC
Mid-Life Update .... MLU
Midline .... M
Midline .... ML
Midline Episiotomy [*Obstetrics*] (DAVI) .... MLE
Midline Malignant Reticulosis [*Hematology*] (DAVI) .... MMR
Midline Precursor [*Cytology*] .... MP
MIDLNET [*Midwest Regional Library Network*], St. Louis, MO [*OCLC symbol*] (OCLC) .... MID
MIDLNET [*Midwest Regional Library Network*], St. Louis, MO [*OCLC symbol*] (OCLC) .... TQG
MIDLNET [*Midwest Regional Library Network*], St. Louis, MO [*OCLC symbol*] (OCLC) .... TQH
Midlothian Public Library, Midlothian, IL [*Library symbol Library of Congress*] (LCLS) .... IMid
Midmarch Associates (EA) .... MA
Mid-Michigan Community College, Harrison, MI [*Library symbol Library of Congress*] (LCLS) .... MiHarsM
Mid-Michigan Library League, Cadillac, MI [*Library symbol Library of Congress*] (LCLS) .... MiCadM
Mid-Mississippi Regional Library, Kosciusko, MS [*Library symbol Library of Congress*] (LCLS) .... MsK
Mid-Molecule Parathyroid Hormone [*Endocrinology*] (DAVI) .... mm-PTH

Mid-Month [*Amount of pay to be received by payee on the 15th day of the month*] (AABC) .... MID-MO
Mid-Murray Citrus Growers [*Australia*] .... MMCG
Midnapore (1979) Resources, Inc. [*Vancouver Stock Exchange symbol*] .... MNP
Midnight (ROG) .... M
Midnight .... MDNT
Midnight .... MID
Midnight (DAVI) .... midnoc
Midnight .... MN
Midnight Dumping (MHDW) .... MD
Midnight Rations [*Navy*] .... MID-RATS
Mid-North Resources [*Vancouver Stock Exchange symbol*] .... MDU
Mid-Ocean Dynamics Experiment [*National Science Foundation*] .... MODE
Mid-Ocean Meeting Place .... MOMP
Mid-Ocean Ridge Basalt [*Geology*] .... MORB
Mid-Ocean Ridge Peridotite [*Geology*] .... MORP
Mid-Ocean Target Array (AAG) .... MOTA
Mid-Oceanic Ridge .... MOR
Mid-Oxygen [*Beta-alumina crystallography*] .... mO
Mid-Pacific .... MIDPAC
Mid-Pacific Marine Laboratory (MSC) .... MPML
Mid-Pacific Mountains [*Geology*] .... MPM
Mid-Peninsula Conversion Project [*Later, CEC*] (EA) .... MPCP
Mid-Peninsula Library Cooperative [*Library network*] .... MPLC
Mid-Peninsula Library Cooperative, Iron Mountain, MI [*OCLC symbol*] (OCLC) .... EZI
Mid-Peninsula Library Federation Headquarters, Iron Mountain, MI [*Library symbol Library of Congress*] (LCLS) .... MilrmM
Mid-Phase .... MP
Mid-Plains Community College, North Platte, NE [*Library symbol Library of Congress*] (LCLS) .... NbNpM
Midpoint (FAAC) .... MIDPT
Midpoint (AD) .... mpt
Mid-Range Estimate .... MRE
Mid-Range Force Study [*DoD*] .... MRFS
Mid-Range Objectives .... MRO
Mid-Range Plan [*1969-70*] [*Military*] .... MRP
Mid-Range Trajectory (AD) .... mrt
Midrash [*Interpretation of Old Testament writings*] (BJA) .... Mid
Midrash [*Interpretation of Old Testament writings*] (BJA) .... Midr
Midrash Aggadah (BJA) .... MidAg
Midrash ha-Gadol (BJA) .... MHG
Midrash ha-Gadol (BJA) .... MidHag
Midrash Job (BJA) .... MidJob
Midrash Jonah (BJA) .... MidJonah
Midrash Lekah Tov (BJA) .... MidLekTov
Midrash Proverbs (BJA) .... MidProv
Midrash Rabbah (BJA) .... MidR
Midrash Rabbah [*H. Freedman and Maurice Simon*] [*A publication*] (BJA) .... SMR
Midrash Samuel (BJA) .... MidSam
Midrash Tanna'im (BJA) .... MT
Midrash Tanna'im on Deuteronomy (BJA) .... MidTan
Midrash Tehillim [*or The Midrash on Psalms*] (BJA) .... MidPs
Midrash Tehillim [*or The Midrash on Psalms*] (BJA) .... Mid'Tehil
Midrash to the Song of Songs (BJA) .... MidrSong
Midrasha College of Jewish Studies, Southfield, MI [*Library symbol Library of Congress*] (LCLS) .... MiSfM
Midrib [*Botany*] .... MR
Mid-Roll Interchange [*Advanced photo system*] .... MRC
Midsagittal [*Medicine*] .... Midsag
Midship [*Shipping*] (DS) .... m
Midship Deep Tank .... MT
Midshipman .... MDPN
Midshipman .... MDSHPMN
Midshipman [*Navy*] .... MID
Midshipman [*Navy*] .... MIDN
Midshipman Cruise [*Navy*] (NVT) .... MIDCRU
Midshipman Embarkation Team [*Navy*] .... MET
Midshipman Training Squadron [*Navy*] (NVT) .... MIDTRARON
Mid-Shot .... MS
Mid-Small Bowel [*Gastroenterology*] (DAVI) .... MSB
Mid-Song Element [*Ornithology*] .... MSE
Mid-South Automated Clearing House Association .... MSACHA
MidSouth Bancorp [*AMEX symbol*] (TTSB) .... MSL
Midsouth Bancorp, Inc. [*Associated Press*] (SAG) .... Midsth
Midsouth Bancorp, Inc. [*Associated Press*] (SAG) .... MidsthB
Midsouth Bancorp, Inc. [*AMEX symbol*] (SAG) .... MSL
MidSouth Bancorp Sr'A'Cv Pfd [*AMEX symbol*] (TTSB) .... MSLPr
Mid-South Bible College, Memphis, TN [*Library symbol Library of Congress*] (LCLS) .... TMMBC
Mid-South Commuter Airlines [*ICAO designator*] (AD) VL
Mid-South Insurance Co. [*NASDAQ symbol*] (NQ) .... MIDS
Mid-South Insurance Co. [*Associated Press*] (SAG) .... MidSou
Midstate Airlines [*ICAO designator*] (AD) .... IU
Midstate Airlines, Inc. [*ICAO designator*] (FAAC) .... MIS
Mid-State Educational Cooperative, Little Falls, MN [*Library symbol*] [*Library of Congress*] (LCLS) .... MnLfMS
Midstates Jeepster Association (EA) .... MJA
Mid-States PLC [*Associated Press*] (SAG) .... MidStat
Mid-States plc ADS [*NASDAQ symbol*] (TTSB) .... MSADY
Midsternal Line .... MSL
Midstream Clean Catch [*Urine Sample*] (DAVI) .... MSCC
Midstream Specimen of Urine [*Medicine*] .... MSSU
Midstream Specimen of Urine [*Medicine*] .... MSU
Midsummer (ROG) .... MIDSR

[*A*] Midsummer Night's Dream [*Shakespearean work*] (BARN) .... Mids ND
Midsummer Night's Dream [*Shakespearean work*] .... MND
Midsummer Time .... MST
Midtarsal Joint [*Anatomy*] (DAVI) .... MTJ
Midterm Availability .... MTA
Midterm Energy Forecasting System [*Department of Energy*] (GFGA) .... MEFS
Mid-Term Review .... MTR
Mid-Term Status Reports .... MTSR
Midtfly Aps [*Denmark ICAO designator*] (FAAC) .... MDF
Midtown .... MDTWN
Mid-Upper [*Turret*] Air Gunner [*British military*] (DMA) .... MU/AG
Midvale District Library, Midvale, ID [*Library symbol*] [*Library of Congress*] (LCLS) .... IdMid
Midvale, UT [*FM radio station call letters*] (RBYB) .... KQMB-FM
Mid-Valley Genealogical Society, Corvallis, OR [*Library symbol Library of Congress*] (LCLS) .... OrCMG
Midwave Infrared Sensor (MCD) .... MWIR
Midway [*Washington*] [*Seismograph station code, US Geological Survey*] (SEIS) .... MDW
Midway .... MDWY
Midway [*Midway Islands*] [*Seismograph station code, US Geological Survey Closed*] (SEIS) .... MDY
Midway Aviation, Inc. [*ICAO designator*] (FAAC) .... MDW
Midway, FL [*FM radio station call letters*] (RBYB) .... WJZT-FM
Midway, GA [*FM radio station call letters*] .... WGCO
Midway Games, Inc. [*Associated Press*] (SAG) .... MidwGm
Midway Games, Inc. [*NYSE symbol*] (SAG) .... MWY
Midway/Henderson Naval Station, HI [*Location identifier FAA*] (FAAL) .... NQM
Midway Islands [*MARC geographic area code Library of Congress*] (LCCP) .... poxf--
Midway Islands [*MARC country of publication code Library of Congress*] (LCCP) .... xf
Midway Junior College [*Kentucky*] .... MJC
Midway Junior College and Pinkerton High School, Midway, KY [*Library symbol Library of Congress*] (LCLS) .... KyMdC
Midway Naval Station [*Henderson Field*], Sand Island [*Midway Islands*] [*ICAO location identifier*] (ICLI) .... PMDY
Midway Railroad Co. [*AAR code*] .... MID
Midweek Travel [*Airline fare code*] X
Midwest .... MDWST
Midwest Academy (EA) .... MA
Midwest Agri Industries Expo [*Illinois Fertilizer and Chemical Association*] (TSPED) .... MAGIE
Midwest Agribusiness Trade Research and Information Center [*Iowa State University of Science and Technology*] [*Research center*] (RCD) .... MATRIC
Midwest Air Freighters, Inc. [*ICAO designator*] (FAAC) .... FAX
Midwest Alliance in Nursing (SRA) .... MAIN
Midwest Archeological Center [*National Park Service*] (GRD) .... MWAC
Midwest Archives Conference (EA) .... MAC
Midwest Assisted Housing Management Association (SRA) .... MAHMA
Midwest Association of Student Employment Administrators [*Formerly, MAUSED*] (EA) .... MASEA
Midwest Association of University Student Employment Directors [*Later, MASEA*] (EA) .... MAUSED
Midwest Automated Clearing House Association .... MACHA
Midwest Automated Technical Services Systems [*Information service or system*] (IID) .... MATSS
Midwest Aviation [*Southwest Aviation, Inc.*] [*ICAO designator*] (FAAC) .... MWT
Midwest Aviation [*ICAO designator*] (AD) .... WV
Midwest Aviation Corp. [*ICAO designator*] (FAAC) .... NIT
Midwest Bacshares Del [*NASDAQ symbol*] (TTSB) .... MWBI
Midwest Bancshares [*Associated Press*] (SAG) .... MidwBn
Midwest Bancshares [*NASDAQ symbol*] (SAG) .... MWBI
Midwest Cable & Satellite, Inc. [*Minneapolis, MN*] [*Telecommunications*] (TSSD) .... MWCS
Midwest Center for Labor Research (EA) .... MCLR
Midwest Center for Mass Spectrometry [*University of Nebraska - Lincoln*] [*Research center*] (RCD) .... MCMS
Midwest City, OK [*AM radio station call letters*] .... KTLV
Midwest Climate Center [*Marine science*] (OSRA) .... MCC
Midwest Climate Center (USDC) .... MCC
Midwest College of Medical Assistants, Kansas City, MO [*Library symbol Library of Congress*] (LCLS) .... MoKMC
Midwest College Placement Association .... MCPA
Midwest Collegiate Sailing Association .... MCSA
Midwest Committee for Military Counseling (EA) .... MCMC
Mid-West Compensation Association [*Superseded by ACA*] (EA) .... MCA
Midwest Continuing Education Professional Nurses (DHSM) .... MCEPEN
Midwest Council of Sports Car Clubs .... MWCSCC
Midwest Council on Airborne Television .... MCAT
Midwest Curling Association [*Defunct*] (EA) .... MCA
Midwest Curriculum Coordination Network (OICC) .... MCCN
Midwest Decoy Collectors Association (EA) .... MWDCA
Midwest Division Naval Facilities Engineering Command ...... DIRMIDWESTDOCKS
Midwest Division Naval Facilities Engineering Command .... MIDWESTNAVFACENGCOM
Midwest Express Airlines [*ICAO designator*] (AD) .... YX
Midwest Express Airlines, Inc. [*ICAO designator*] (FAAC) .... MEP
Midwest Express Holdings [*NYSE symbol*] (SAG) .... MEH
Midwest Exprss Holding [*Associated Press*] (SAG) .... MdwEx
Midwest Fed Finl [*NASDAQ symbol*] (TTSB) .... MWFD
Midwest Federal Financial [*Associated Press*] (SAG) .... MdwFdl
Midwest Federal Financial [*NASDAQ symbol*] (SAG) .... MWFD
Midwest Federation of Library Associations .... MFLA
Midwest Feed Manufacturers Association [*Later, AFMA*] (EA) .... MFMA

Midwest Fuel Recovery Plant [*AEC*] .... MFRP
Midwest Grain Products [*NASDAQ symbol*] (TTSB) .... MWGP
Midwest Grain Products, Inc. [*Associated Press*] (SAG) .... MidwGr
Midwest Grain Products, Inc. [*NASDAQ symbol*] (CTT) .... MWGP
Midwest Health Science Library Network [*Library network*] .... MHSLN
Midwest Integrated Systems Laboratories, Inc. [*Watertown, WI*] (TSSD) .... MIS LABS
Midwest Interlibrary Center [*Later, CRL*] .... MILC
Midwest Interstate Sulfur Transformation and Transport [*Meteorology*] .... MISTT
Midwest Job Galvanizers Association [*Defunct*] (EA) .... MJGA
Midwest Medical Union Catalog .... MMUC
Midwest Microfilm Service, Co., Springfield, IL [*Library symbol*] [*Library of Congress*] (LCLS) .... MwMC
Midwest Migrant Health Information Office (EA) .... MMHIO
Midwest Modern Language Association (BARN) .... MMLA
Midwest Motor Carriers Bureau, Inc. .... MMCB
Midwest Motor Carriers Bureau, Inc., Oklahoma City OK [*STAC*] .... MMB
[*The*] **Midwest Network** [*Computer science*] (TNIG) .... MIDnet
Midwest Old Settlers and Threshers Association (EA) .... MOSTA
Midwest Open Land Association (EA) .... MOLA
Midwest Organization for Research in Education (AEBS) .... MORE
Midwest Parentcraft Center (EA) .... MPC
Midwest Presenters Directory [*Information service or system*] (IID) .... MPD
Midwest Professional Needlework Association [*Later, APNRA*] (EA) .... MPNA
Midwest Program for Airborne Television Instruction [*Defunct*] .... MPATI
Midwest Railway Historical Society (EA) .... MRHS
Midwest Real Estate Shopping Centers Ltd. [*NYSE symbol*] (SAG) .... EQM
Midwest Real Estate Shopping Centers Ltd. [*Associated Press*] (SAG) .... MidwRE
Midwest Regional Library Network .... MIDLNET
Midwest Research Institute .... MRI
Midwest Research Institute, Kansas City, MO [*Library symbol Library of Congress*] (LCLS) .... MoKMR
Midwest R.E.Shop'g Ctr L.P. [*NYSE symbol*] (TTSB) .... EQM
Midwest Resources Association [*Defunct*] .... MRA
Midwest Securities Trust Co. .... MSTC
Midwest Ski Representatives Association (EA) .... MSRA
Midwest Sociological Society (AEBS) .... MSS
Mid-West Spring Manufacturing Co. [*Associated Press*] (SAG) .... MW Sprg
Mid-West Spring Manufacturing Co. [*NASDAQ symbol*] (SAG) .... MWSS
Mid-West Spring Mfg [*NASDAQ symbol*] (TTSB) .... MWSSE
Midwest Stock Exchange [*Chicago, IL*] .... M
Midwest Stock Exchange [*Chicago, IL*] (CDAI) .... MID
Midwest Stock Exchange [*Chicago, IL*] (EA) .... MSE
Midwest Stock Exchange, Inc. (HGAA) .... MWSE
Midwest Sunbeam Registry (EA) .... MSR
Mid-West Truckers Association (EA) .... MTA
Midwest Universities Consortium for International Activities [*University of Indiana*] .... MUCIA
Midwest Women's Legal Group (EA) .... MWLG
Midwestern .... MDWSTRN
Midwestern (AFM) .... MIDW
Midwestern Association for Latin American Studies .... MALAS
Midwestern Baptist Theological Seminary, Kansas City, MO [*OCLC symbol*] (OCLC) .... LOS
Midwestern Baptist Theological Seminary, Kansas City, MO [*Library symbol Library of Congress*] (LCLS) .... MoKMB
Midwestern Climate Information System [*Marine science*] (OSRA) .... MICIS
Midwestern Climate Information System (USDC) .... MICIS
Midwestern Gilbert and Sullivan Society (EA) .... MGS
Midwestern Governors Conference .... MWGC
Midwestern Psychological Association (MCD) .... MPA
Midwestern Regional Library, Kitchener, ON, Canada [*Library symbol Library of Congress*] (LCLS) .... CaOKitM
Midwestern Relay Co. [*Milwaukee, WI*] [*Telecommunications*] (TSSD) .... MRC
Midwestern Signal Corps School .... MWSCS
Midwestern Simulation Council .... MSC
Midwestern Simulation Council .... MWSC
Midwestern State University (GAGS) .... Midwest S U
Midwestern State University, George Moffett Library, Wichita Falls, TX [*OCLC symbol*] (OCLC) .... TMI
Midwestern State University, Wichita Falls, TX [*Library symbol Library of Congress*] (LCLS) .... TxWicM
Midwestern Universities Research Association .... MURA
Midwife .... MDWF
Midwife Teacher's Diploma [*British*] .... MTD
Midwifery .... MDWFY
Midwifery (ROG) .... MID
Midwing [*Aviation*] (AIA) .... MW
Mid-Wisconsin Federated Library System, Fond Du Lac, WI [*OCLC symbol*] (OCLC) .... WIF
Midwives Alliance of North America (EA) .... MANA
Midwives Information and Resource Service [*British*] (EAIO) .... MIDIRS
Mid-York Library System [*Library network*] .... MYLS
Mid-York Library System, Utica, NY [*Library symbol Library of Congress*] (LCLS) .... NUtMY
Mid-York Library System, Utica, NY [*OCLC symbol*] (OCLC) .... ZTM
Midzone Phenomenon [*Immunology*] .... MZ
Miedzynarodowe Stowarzyszenie Przyjaciele Angkor Wat [*International Association of Friends of Angkor Wat*] [*Multinational association based in Poland*] (EAIO) .... MSPAW
Miehle-Goss-Dexter [*Rockwell International Corp.*] .... MGD
Miele Mimbale [*Gabon*] [*Airport symbol*] (AD) .... GIM
Miesau-West [*Germany ICAO location identifier*] (ICLI) .... EDEI
Miesiecznik Zydowski (BJA) .... MZ
Mieso [*Ethiopia*] [*ICAO location identifier*] (ICLI) .... HAME
Mifflin County Legal Journal [*Pennsylvania*] [*A publication*] (DLA) .... MCLJ
Mifflinburg, PA [*FM radio station call letters*] .... WWBE
Mifflintown, PA [*FM radio station call letters*] .... WQJU
Mifleget Po'alei Eretz-Yisrael (BJA) .... MAPAI
Mifleget Po'alim Me'uhedet (BJA) .... MAPAM
MIG [*Mikoyan and Gurevich*] **Combat Air Patrol** (DNAB) .... MIGCAP
MIG Operational Fighter Training Unit [*India*] [*Air Force*] .... MOFTU
Migent Software [*Vancouver Stock Exchange symbol*] .... MSC
Might .... MT
Mightier (ABBR) .... MGTIR
Mightiest (ABBR) .... MGTIST
Mightiness (ABBR) .... MGTNS
Mighty (ABBR) .... MGTY
Migne Series [*Latina*] [*A publication*] (BJA) .... ML
Mignon [*Horticulture*] .... Mig
Migraine with Interparoxysmal Headache [*Neurology*] (DAVI) .... MIH
Migrant (ABBR) .... MGRT
Migrant Action Program (OICC) .... MAP
Migrant Advisory Committee .... MACS
Migrant and Seasonal Agricultural Worker Act of 1983 (WYGK) .... MSAWA
Migrant and Seasonal Farmworkers .... MSFW
Migrant and Seasonal Farmworkers Program [*Title III*] (OICC) .... MSFP
Migrant Children's Fund [*Absorbed by NCEMC*] .... MCF
Migrant Dropout Reconnection Program [*Board of Cooperative Educational Services Geneseo Migrant Center*] (EA) .... MDRP
Migrant Farm Worker (OICC) .... MFW
Migrant Health Education Officer [*Australia*] .... MHEO
Migrant Legal Action Program (EA) .... MLAP
Migrant Opportunity Program [*Department of Labor*] .... MOP
Migrant Resource Center of South Australia .... MRCSA
Migrant Student Records Transfer System (GFGA) .... MSRTS
Migrant Studies and Media Center [*Australia*] .... MSMC
Migrant with English Language Difficulty .... MD
Migrate (ABBR) .... MGRA
Migrated (ABBR) .... MGRAD
Migrating (ABBR) .... MGRAG
Migrating Action Potential Complex [*Electrophysiology*] .... MAPC
Migrating Combustion Chamber [*Increases fuel efficiency*] .... MCC
Migrating Myoelectric Complex [*Physiology*] .... MMEC
Migrating Myoelectric Complexes [*Electrophysiology*] .... MMC
Migrating Neuron [*Neuroanatomy*] .... MN
Migration (ABBR) .... MGRAN
Migration (ABBR) .... MGRN
Migration Agents' Registration Scheme [*Australia*] .... MARS
Migration and Refugee Services (EA) .... MRS
Migration Enhancement Factor [*Biochemistry*] .... MEF
Migration Index [*Immunology*] .... MI
Migration Inhibition [*Cytology*] .... MI
Migration Inhibition [*or Inhibitory*] **Factor** [*Cytology*] .... MIF
Migration Ratio (DNAB) .... MR
Migration Stimulating Factor [*Cytology*] .... MSF
Migration Traffic Rate (OA) .... MTR
Migrational (ABBR) .... MGRNL
Migrator (ABBR) .... MGRATR
Migratory (ABBR) .... MGRATRY
Migratory (ABBR) .... MGRTY
Migratory Animal Pathological Survey (PDAA) .... MAPS
Migratory Bird Act .... MBA
Migratory Bird Conservation Commission [*A federal government body*] .... MBCC
Migratory Bird Treaty Act (GNE) .... MBTA
Migratory Fish Research Institute [*University of Maine*] [*Research center*] (RCD) .... MFRI
Migratory Trout .... MT
Migratory Worker (OICC) .... MW
Miho [*Japan ICAO location identifier*] (ICLI) .... RJOH
Mijnherr [*Mr.*] [*Dutch*] (AD) .... Mnr
Mikado Resources Ltd. [*Vancouver Stock Exchange symbol*] .... MKO
Mikasa, Inc. [*Associated Press*] (SAG) .... Mikasa
Mikasa, Inc. [*NYSE symbol*] (SAG) .... MKS
Mikawa [*Japan*] [*Seismograph station code, US Geological Survey*] (SEIS) .... MKW
Mike [*Phonetic alphabet*] [*International*] [*World War II*] (DSUE) .... M
Mike Amplifier (NASA) .... MA
Mike Amplifier .... MA
Mike and Kathy Yager Fan Club [*Later, MYFC*] (EA) .... MKYFC
Mike and Terry's Lawnmowers [*Commercial firm*] [*canada*] .... MITEL
Mike Force [*Indigenous personnel trained and commanded jointly by US and Vietnamese forces, and used as a reaction and/or reinforcing unit*] .... MF
Mike Lunsford Fan Club (EA) .... MLFC
Mike Monroney Aeronautical Center [*FAA*] (TAG) .... AAC
Mikes of America (EA) .... MA
Mikheyev-Smirnov-Wolfenstein Theory [*Oscillation effect*] [*Particle physics*] .... MSW
Mikity-Wilson Syndrome [*Neonatology*] (DAVI) .... MWS
Mikkeli [*Finland ICAO location identifier*] (ICLI) .... EFMI
Mikkeli [*Finland*] [*Airport symbol*] (OAG) .... MIK
Mikma Ltd. [*Moldova*] [*FAA designator*] (FAAC) .... ITL
Mikohn Gaming [*NASDAQ symbol*] (TTSB) .... MIKN
Mikohn Gaming Corp. [*NASDAQ symbol*] (SAG) .... MIKN
Mikohn Gaming Corp. [*Associated Press*] (SAG) .... Mikohn
Mikonos [*Greece*] [*Airport symbol*] (OAG) .... JMK
Mikonos [*Greece*] [*ICAO location identifier*] (ICLI) .... LGMK
Mikoyan and Gurevich [*Acronym used as designation for a Russian aircraft and is formed from the names of the aircraft's designers*] .... MIG
Mikra'ot Gedolot (BJA) .... MikGed

Mikrofilmarchiv der Deutschsparchigen Presse e.V., Dortmund, Germany [*Library symbol Library of Congress*] (LCLS) .... GyDMA
Mikromatika Air Cargo Ltd. [*Hungary ICAO designator*] (FAAC) ...... MMH
Mikron Instr [*NASDAQ symbol*] (TTSB) .... MIKR
Mikron Instrument Co., Inc. [*NASDAQ symbol*] (NQ) .... MIKR
Mikron Instrument Co., Inc. [*Associated Press*] (SAG) .... Mikron
Mikropress GmbH, Bonn, Germany [*Library symbol Library of Congress*] (LCLS) .... MkP
Mikumi [*Tanzania*] [*ICAO location identifier*] (ICLI) .... HTMK
Mikumi National Park [*Tanzania*] (AD) .... MNP
Mikva'ot (BJA) .... Mik
Mikva'ot (BJA) .... Mikv
Mil [*Monetary unit*] [*Cyprus*] .... M
Mil[*thousand*] (DAVI) .... m
Mil [*Former USSR ICAO aircraft manufacturer identifier*] (ICAO) .... MI
MIL Systems Engineering, Inc., Ottawa, Ontario [*Library symbol National Library of Canada*] (BIB) .... OOMIL
Milaca Elementary School, Milaca, MN [*Library symbol*] [*Library of Congress*] (LCLS) .... MnMiE
Milaca High School, Milaca, MN [*Library symbol*] [*Library of Congress*] (LCLS) .... MnMiH
Milaca Middle School, Milaca, MN [*Library symbol*] [*Library of Congress*] (LCLS) .... MnMiM
Milagra Ridge [*California*] [*Seismograph station code, US Geological Survey*] (SEIS) .... MGA
Milan [*Italy*] [*Seismograph station code, US Geological Survey Closed*] (SEIS) .... MIL
Milan [*Italy*] [*Airport symbol*] (OAG) .... MIL
Milan Army Ammunition Plant (AABC) .... MAAP
Milan Elementary School, Milan, MN [*Library symbol*] [*Library of Congress*] (LCLS) .... MnMlnES
Milan [*Italy*] Forlanini-Linate [*Airport symbol*] (OAG) .... LIN
Milan, GA [*FM radio station call letters*] .... WMCG
Milan [*Italy*] Malpensa Airport [*Airport symbol*] (OAG) .... MXP
Milan, NM [*AM radio station call letters*] (RBYB) .... KCIB
Milan Public Library, Milan, MI [*Library symbol Library of Congress*] (LCLS) .... MiMil
Milan Public Library, Milan, MN [*Library symbol*] [*Library of Congress*] (LCLS) .... MnMln
Milan Resources & Development [*Vancouver Stock Exchange symbol*] .... MLN
Milan, TN [*AM radio station call letters*] .... WKBJ
Milan, TN [*FM radio station call letters*] .... WYNU
Milano [*Italy ICAO location identifier*] (ICLI) .... LIMM
Milano/Bresso [*Italy ICAO location identifier*] (ICLI) .... LIMB
Milano/Linate [*Italy ICAO location identifier*] (ICLI) .... LIML
Milano/Malpensa [*Italy ICAO location identifier*] (ICLI) .... LIMC
Milastar Corp. [*NASDAQ symbol*] (NQ) .... MILAA
Milbank Carnegie Library, Milbank, SD [*Library symbol Library of Congress*] (LCLS) .... SdMil
Milbank, SD [*AM radio station call letters*] .... KMSD
Milbank, SD [*FM radio station call letters*] .... KPHR
Milburn Elementary School, Baldwin, NY [*Library symbol Library of Congress*] (LCLS) .... NBaldMiE
Milchemet, the War of the Sons of Light and the Sons of Darkness from Qumran. C ave One (BJA) 1QM
Mild (DAVI) .... M
Mild (WGA) .... MLD
Mild and Bitter [*Beer*] .... M & B
Mild Detonating Cord (MCD) .... MDC
Mild Detonating Fuse .... MDF
Mild General Learning Disability .... MGLD
Mild Heat Treatment (IEEE) .... MHT
Mild Hydrocracking [*Petroleum technology*] .... MHC
Mild [*or Minimal*] Memory Impairment [*Medicine*] .... MMI
Mild Resid Hydrocracking [*M. W. Kellogg Co. process*] .... MRH
Mild Sickle Cell Disease (AAMN) .... MSD
Mild Steel .... MS
Mild Steel (AD) .... ms
Mild Steel, Black Finish (IAA) .... MSBLK
Mild Steel, Bright Finish (IAA) .... MSBRT
Mild Upper Respiratory Illness [*Virus*] [*Obsolete usage*] .... MURI
Mildenhall [*British ICAO location identifier*] (ICLI) .... EGUN
Mildew-Induced Defacement of Organic Coatings .... MIDOC
Mildew-Resistant Thread .... MRT
Mildew-Resistant Thread (AD) .... mrt
Mildly Context-Sensitive Grammar [*Artificial intelligence*] .... MCSG
Mildly Diabetic .... MD
Mildly Subnormal [*Medicine*] (MAE) .... MSN
Mildmay Branch, Bruce County Public Library, Ontario [*Library symbol National Library of Canada*] (NLC) .... OMILD
Mildura [*Australia ICAO location identifier*] (ICLI) .... AMMI
Mildura [*Australia Airport symbol*] (OAG) .... MQL
Mile (WDMC) .... M
mile (WDMC) .... m
Mile .... MI
Mile .... mi
Mile .... MI
Mile (IDOE) .... ml
Mile .... MLE
Mile of Standard Cable .... MSC
Mileage .... MIL
Mileage Accumulation Dynamometer .... MAD
Mileage Allowance .... MA
Mileage Rationing Board [*World War II*] .... MRB
Mile-Post .... MP

Milepost (AD) .... mp
Miles .... M
MILES [*Multiple Integrated LASER Engagement System*] Action Item Log [*Army*] .... MAIL
Miles City [*Montana*] [*Airport symbol*] (OAG) .... MLS
Miles City, MT [*Location identifier FAA*] (FAAL) .... HTN
Miles City, MT [*AM radio station call letters*] .... KATL
Miles City, MT [*FM radio station call letters*] .... KECC
Miles City, MT [*FM radio station call letters*] .... KMCM
Miles City, MT [*AM radio station call letters*] .... KMTA
Miles City, MT [*Television station call letters*] .... KYUS
Miles City, MT [*Location identifier FAA*] (FAAL) .... MLS
Miles City Public Library, Miles City, MT [*Library symbol Library of Congress*] (LCLS) .... MtMc
Miles College, Birmingham, AL [*Library symbol Library of Congress*] (LCLS) .... ABM
Miles College, Birmingham, AL [*OCLC symbol*] (OCLC) .... MLC
Miles Community College, Miles City, MT [*Library symbol Library of Congress*] (LCLS) .... MtMcC
Miles' District Court Reports [*1825-41*] [*Philadelphia, PA*] [*A publication*] (DLA) .... Miles
Miles [*Multiple Integrated Laser Engagement System*] Gunnery Skills Test [*USA*] .... MGST
Miles Homes [*NASDAQ symbol*] (TTSB) .... MIHO
Miles Homes, Inc. [*NASDAQ symbol*] (SAG) .... MIHO
Miles Homes, Inc. [*Associated Press*] (SAG) .... MileH
Miles Homes, Inc. [*Associated Press*] (SAG) .... MileHme
Miles in the Hour [*Rate of military march*] .... MIH
Miles in Trail [*Aviation*] (FAAC) .... MIT
Miles in-Trail [*FAA*] (TAG) .... MIT
Miles Laboratories, Inc. [*Research code symbol*] .... MA
Miles Laboratories, Inc., Elkhart, IN [*Library symbol Library of Congress*] (LCLS) .... InElkM
Miles Laboratories, Inc., Library Resources and Services, Elkhart, IN [*OCLC symbol*] (OCLC) .... IML
Miles Laboratories, Inc., Miles Pharmaceutical Division, West Haven, CT [*OCLC symbol*] (OCLC) .... XML
Miles Laboratories, Inc., Miles Pharmaceutical, West Haven, CT [*Library symbol Library of Congress*] (LCLS) .... CtWehavM
Miles Laboratories, Inc., Miles Pharmaceutical, West Haven, CT [*Library symbol*] [*Library of Congress*] (LCLS) .... CtWhvM
Miles of Relative Movement [*Navigation*] .... MRM
Miles of Relative Movement (AD) .... mrm
Miles on Course .... MC
Miles' Pennsylvania Reports [*A publication*] (DLA) .... M
Miles' Pennsylvania Reports [*A publication*] (DLA) .... Mil
Miles' Pennsylvania Reports [*A publication*] (DLA) .... Miles (PA)
Miles' Pennsylvania Reports [*A publication*] (DLA) .... Miles R
Miles' Pennsylvania Reports [*A publication*] (DLA) .... Miles Rep
Miles per Gallon .... M/G
Miles per Gallon (WDAA) .... MI/GAL
Miles per Gallon .... MPG
Miles per Hour [*Also, MPH*] .... M/H
Miles per Hour [*Also, M/H*] .... MPH
Miles per Hour (IDOE) .... mph
Miles per Hour per Second .... M/H/S
Miles per Hour per Second .... MPHPS
Miles Per Hour Per Second (AD) .... mphps
Miles per Minute (WDAA) .... MI MIN
Miles per Minute .... MPM
Miles per Pound [*NASA*] (KSC) .... MPP
Miles per Second .... MPS
Miles per Second (IDOE) .... mps
Miles per Tankful (AD) .... MPT
Miles per Tankful (AD) .... mpt
Miles' Rules and Orders [*A publication*] (DLA) .... Miles R & O
Milestone (AD) .... m/s
Milestone (KSC) .... MS
Milestone Analysis Procedure .... MAP
Milestone Car Society (EA) .... MCS
Milestone Decision Authority .... MDA
Milestone Decision Review (MCD) .... MDR
Milestone Planning Meeting (MCD) .... MPM
Milestone Properties [*Associated Press*] (SAG) .... MilePr
Milestone Properties [*Associated Press*] (SAG) .... MilPr
Milestone Properties [*NYSE symbol*] (SPSG) .... MPI
Milestone Properties Cv $0.78Pfd [*NYSE symbol*] (TTSB) .... MPIPrA
Milestone Readiness Review [*NASA*] (KSC) .... MRR
Milestone Reference File [*Military*] (CAAL) .... MRF
Milestone Review Documentation [*Army*] .... MRD
Milestone Schedule Charts (MCD) .... MSC
Milestone Scientific, Inc. [*Associated Press*] (SAG) .... MilestnSci
Milestone Scientific, Inc. [*NASDAQ symbol*] (SAG) .... WAND
Milestone Status Report [*Military*] (AFIT) .... MSR
Milestones Reporting Techniques .... MRT
Mileto [*Italy*] [*Seismograph station code, US Geological Survey Closed*] (SEIS) .... MLE
Milford [*Ohio*] [*Seismograph station code, US Geological Survey*] (SEIS) .... MLF
Milford [*Kansas*] [*Seismograph station code, US Geological Survey*] (SEIS) .... MLK
Milford, CT [*AM radio station call letters*] .... WFIF
Milford, DE [*FM radio station call letters*] .... WAFL
Milford, DE [*FM radio station call letters*] .... WXPZ
Milford, DE [*AM radio station call letters*] .... WYUS
Milford Docks Air Services Ltd. [*British ICAO designator*] (FAAC) .... MDS
Milford Haven [*Wales*] [*Airport symbol*] (AD) .... ILF

Milford, IA [*FM radio station call letters*] (RBYB) .... KUQQ-FM
Milford, MA [*AM radio station call letters*] .... WMRC
Milford Mail, Milford, IA [*Library symbol Library of Congress*] (LCLS) .... IaMilfM
Milford Mail-Journal, Millford, IN [*Library symbol Library of Congress*] (LCLS) .... InMilMJ
Milford Memorial Library, Milford, IA [*Library symbol Library of Congress*] (LCLS) .... IaMilf
Milford, NE [*FM radio station call letters*] .... KUHG
Milford News, Milford, IA [*Library symbol Library of Congress*] (LCLS) .... IaMilfN
Milford North [*Utah*] [*Seismograph station code, US Geological Survey*] (SEIS) .... MNU
Milford, OH [*FM radio station call letters*] .... WAQZ
Milford Public Library, Milford, IN [*Library symbol Library of Congress*] (LCLS) .... InMil
Milford Public Library, Milford, NE [*Library symbol Library of Congress*] (LCLS) .... NbMi
Milford Sound [*New Zealand*] [*Airport symbol*] (OAG) .... MFN
Milford Sound [*New Zealand*] [*Seismograph station code, US Geological Survey*] (SEIS) .... MSZ
Milford Sound [*New Zealand*] [*ICAO location identifier*] (ICLI) .... NZMF
Milford Township Public Library, Milford, IL [*Library symbol Library of Congress*] (LCLS) .... IMil
Milford, UT [*Location identifier FAA*] (FAAL) .... MLF
Milgarra [*Queensland*] [*Airport symbol*] (AD) .... MQG
Milgray Electronics [*NASDAQ symbol*] (TTSB) .... MGRY
Milgray Electronics, Inc. [*NASDAQ symbol*] (NQ) .... MGRY
Milgray Electronics, Inc. [*Associated Press*] (SAG) .... Milgray
Mili [*Marshall Islands*] [*Airport symbol*] (OAG) .... MIJ
Milicias Obreras Guatemaltecas [*Guatemalan Workers' Militia*] (PD) ...... MOG
Milieu .... ML
Milieu Information Service (EA) .... MIS
Militant Society for the Eradication of Rounds [*British*] (DI) ...... MISER
Militarily Critical Technology List [*DoD*] .... MCTL
Militarily Significant Emergent Technologies Awareness List [*Proposed*] [*DoD*] .... METAL
Militarischer Abschirmdienst [*Military counterintelligence*] [*Germany*] .... MAD
Militarism Resource Project (EA) .... MRP
Militarized Digital Element Tester (MCD) .... MDET
Militarized Universal Digital Element Tester (MCD) .... MUDET
Military .... M
Military (EY) .... MIL
Military .... MILIT
Military .... MLTRY
Military (MDG) .... MLTY
Military Academy .... MA
Military Accepts Responsibility for Separation of Aircraft (AFM) ...... MARSA
Military Accessories Service Association (EA) .... MASA
Military Accountant [*British military*] (DMA) .... MA
Military Acquisition Management Branch [*Army*] (RDA) .... MAMB
Military Acquisition Position List (RDA) .... MAPL
Military Adaptation of Command [*or Commercial*] Items [*DoD*] (AABC) .... MACI
Military Administration .... MA
Military Advanced Technology Management Office (RDA) .... MATMO
Military Adviser's Language Text .... MALT
Military Advisor [*SEATO or ANZUS Council*] (CINC) .... MILAD
Military Advisors Representative (CINC) .... MILADREP
Military Advisory Government .... MILADGOVT
Military Advisory Group .... MAG
Military Advisory Group .... MILADGRU
Military Advisory Group, Government of the Republic of China, Vietnam .... MAGROCV
Military Advisory Mission, Brazil .... MAMB
Military Aerodrome Traffic Zone .... MATZ
Military Aeronautical Communications Service .... MACS
Military Aeronautical Research and Development (PDAA) ...... MARD
Military Aerospace Vehicle .... MAV
Military Affairs Division, Office of Judge Advocate General, United States Army (DLA) .... CSJAGA
Military Affairs Division, Office of Judge Advocate General, United States Army (DLA) .... JAGA
Military Affiliate Radio System Repeater System (DNAB) ...... MARSREPSYS
Military Affiliate Radio System Teletypewriter Relay System (DNAB) .... MARSTELSYS
Military Affiliated Radio System [*or Stations*] [*Amateur-operated radio stations*] .... MARS
Military Agency for Standardization [*Brussels, Belgium*] [*NATO*] .... MAS
Military Agency for Standardization [*NATO*] .... MILSTAN
Military Aid to Civil Community [*British*] .... MACC
Military Aid to Civil Ministries [*British military*] (DMA) ...... MACM
Military Aid to the Civil Power [*British military*] (DMA) .... MACP
Military Aid to the Community [*British military*] (DMA) .... MAC
Military Air Cargo Export [*Subsystem*] .... MACE
Military Air Command Hunter [*In MACH 3, a video game by Mylstar Electronics*] .... MACH
Military Air Defense Identification Zone (MCD) .... MADIZ
Military Air Defense Warning Network .... MADW
Military Air Defense Warning Network (IAA) .... MADWN
Military Air Distress (LAIN) .... MAD
Military Air Integrated Reporting System (MCD) .... MAIRS
Military Air Movement .... MAM
Military Air Traffic Control System .... MATRAC
Military Air Traffic Coordinating Office [*or Officer*] [*Air Force*] (AFM) .... MATCO
Military Air Traffic Coordinating Unit [*MTMC*] (TAG) .... MATCU
Military Air Traffic Operations [*British military*] (DMA) ...... MATO
Military Air Transport .... MAT

Military Air Transport Board .... MATB
Military Air Transport Command [*France*] .... COTAM
Military Air Transport Command (MUGU) .... MATC
Military Air Transport Service [*Later, Military Airlift Command*] ...... MATS
Military Air Transport Service [*later, Military Airlift Command*] Regulation .... MATSR
Military Air Transport Service [*later, Military Airlift Command*] TransportControl Center .... MTCC
Military Airborne RADAR System [*Air Force*] (IAA) .... MARS
Military Aircraft .... MA
Military Aircraft Command [*Airline call sign*] .... Mac
Military Aircraft Marshaling System .... MAMS
Military Aircraft Storage and Disposition Center .... MASDC
Military Aircraft Types .... MAT
Military Aircraft Voice Weather Code (NATG) .... MAVWC
Military Airlift Capability Estimator .... MACE
Military Airlift Center, Europe (MCD) .... MACE
Military Airlift Clearance Authority (AABC) .... MACA
Military Airlift Combat Operations Staff .... MACOS
Military Airlift Command [*Formerly, Military Air Transport Service*] ...... MAC
Military Airlift Command Airlift Operations Report .... MACAL
Military Airlift Command Automated Management .... MACAM
Military Airlift Command Integrated Management System ...... MACIMS
Military Airlift Command Operational Phone System (AFM) ...... MACOPS
Military Airlift Command Service (NATG) .... MACS
Military Airlift Command Teletype Network (SAA) .... MACOMTELNET
Military Airlift Command Teletype Network (AFM) .... MACTELNET
Military Airlift Command Traffic Reporting and Control System .... MACTRAC
Military Airlift Group [*Air Force*] .... MAG
Military Airlift Group [*Air Force*] (AFM) .... MAGp
Military Airlift Special Squadron [*Air Force*] .... MASPSq
Military Airlift Squadron [*Air Force*] (CINC) .... MAS
Military Airlift Squadron [*Air Force*] (AFM) .... MASq
Military Airlift Support Group [*Air Force*] .... MASG
Military Airlift Support Group [*Air Force*] .... MASGP
Military Airlift Support Squadron [*Air Force*] .... MASPTSq
Military Airlift Support Squadron [*Air Force*] .... MASS
Military Airlift Support Squadron [*Air Force*] (AFM) .... MASSq
Military Airlift Support Wing [*Air Force*] .... MASW
Military Airlift Support Wing [*Air Force*] (AFM) .... MASWg
Military Airlift Training Squadron [*Air Force*] .... MATRS
Military Airlift Training Wing [*Air Force*] .... MATRW
Military Airlift Wing [*Air Force*] (MCD) .... MAW
Military Airlift Wing [*Air Force*] (AFM) .... MAWg
Military Airport Plan [*FAA*] (TAG) .... MAP
Military Air-Transportable Satellite Communications Terminal .... MASCOT
Military/Allied Commission [*World War II*] .... MAC
Military Amateur Radio System (IAA) .... MARS
Military Amphibious Reconnaissance System (RDA) .... MARS
Military and Aerospace Connector Manufacturers Association (EA) ...... MACMA
Military and Air Force Police [*British military*] (DMA) .... MAFP
Military and Federal Specifications and Standards [*Information Handling Services*] [*Information service or system*] (CRD) .... MLSS
Military and Government Fiber Optics and Communications [*Conference*] (TSSD) .... MFOC
Military and Orchestral Musical Instrument Makers' Trade Society [*A union*] [*British*] (DCTA) .... MOMIMTS
Military and Sporting Gun Workers' Association [*A union*] [*British*] .... MSGWA
Military and Veterans Code [*A publication*] (DLA) .... Mil & Vet C
Military Antishock Trousers [*Medicine*] .... MAST
Military Application Division of the Atomic Energy Commission .... MADAEC
Military Applications of Photovoltaic Systems .... MAPS
Military Armistice Commission (KSC) .... MAC
Military Armistice Commission Headquarters Area (INF) ...... MACHA
Military Armistice Commission (Korea) .... MAC(K)
Military Articles and Services List .... MASL
Military Articles Pacific Excesses (AFIT) .... MAPEX
Military Assistance [*or Assistant*] .... MA
Military Assistance Advisory Command (DOMA) .... MAAC
Military Assistance Advisory Group [*Merged with US Military Assistance Command*] .... MAAG
Military Assistance Advisory Group, Army Branch, Logistics-Medical (CINC) .... MAGARLM
Military Assistance Advisory Group, Indochina [*Later, MAAGV*] (VNW) .... MAAGI
Military Assistance Advisory Group, Vietnam [*Formerly, MAAGI*] (VNW) .... MAAGV
Military Assistance and Sales Manual (AFIT) .... MASM
Military Assistance Article and Service List (AFIT) .... MAASL
Military Assistance Article and Service List (MCD) .... MASL
Military Assistance Basic Planning Document (CINC) .... MABPD
Military Assistance Command (CINC) .... MAC
Military Assistance Command Director of Construction ...... MACDC
Military Assistance Command, Southeast Asia .... MACSEA
Military Assistance Command Studies and Observation Group (CINC) .... MACSOG
Military Assistance Command, Thailand (VNW) .... MACT
Military Assistance Command, Vietnam .... MACV
Military Assistance Command, Vietnam Naval Advisory Group (VNW) .... MACVNAG
Military Assistance Command Vietnam Special Operations Group (INF) .... MACVSOG
Military Assistance Command, Vietnam Studies and Observations Group (VNW) .... MACV-SOG
Military Assistance Institute [*Air Force*] .... MAI
Military Assistance Language Training .... MALT

Military Assistance Manual (AFM)	MAM
Military Assistance Observer Team	MAOT
Military Assistance Officer [Army]	MAO
Military Assistance Program [DoD]	MAP
Military Assistance Program Address Directory	MAPAD
Military Assistance Program Address File	MAPAF
Military Assistance Program Advisory Group	MAPAG
Military Assistance Program/Common Item Order	MAP/CIO
Military Assistance Program Country Code (AFM)	MAPCC
Military Assistance Program Evaluation Team, Thailand (CINC)	MAPETT
Military Assistance Program - Grant Aid	MAP-GA
Military Assistance Program Logistics Agency [Merged with Defense Supply Agency]	MAPLA
Military Assistance Program Offshore Procurement (DNAB)	MAP/OSP
Military Assistance Program Order Amendment (AFM)	MOA
Military Assistance Program Owned Materiel (AFM)	MAPOM
Military Assistance Program Training (AFM)	MAPT
Military Assistance Program Transfer (AFM)	MAPT
Military Assistance Property Sales and Disposal (AFM)	MAPSAD
Military Assistance Sales (MCD)	MAS
Military Assistance Sales Order (CINC)	MASO
Military Assistance Service Fund (AAGC)	MASE
Military Assistance Service Funded	MASF
Military Assistance to Safety and Traffic [Project] [Army] (RDA)	MAST
Military Assistance Training Advisor	MATA
Military Assistance Training Program (AABC)	MATP
Military Assistant to the Civil Community	MACC
Military Association of Podiatrists [Later, FSPMA] (EA)	MAP
Military Attache [Diplomacy]	MA
Military Audit Project	MAP
Military Authorization Identification Number	MAIN
Military Automotive Supply Agency	MASA
Military Automotive Supply Center (MCD)	MASC
Military Aviation Notice [Air Force]	MAN
Military Aviation Preservation Society (EA)	MAPS
Military Aviator	MA
Military Aviator [Army]	Mil Av
Military Awards Profile [Information service or system] (IID)	MAP
Military Banking Facility	MBF
Military Base Agreement (CINC)	MBA
Military Base Agreement (CINC)	MILBA
Military Benefit Association (EA)	MBA
Military Benefit Base Amounts	MBBA
Military Blood Program Agency (AABC)	MBPA
Military Blood Program Office (AABC)	MBPO
Military Board Instruction	MBI
Military Boot Manufacturers Association (EA)	MBMA
Military Budget Committee [NATO] (NATG)	MBC
Military Chaplains Association of the USA (EA)	MCA
Military Characteristics	MC
Military Characteristics [Technical specification document for nuclear bombs and warheads]	MC's
Military Characteristics	MILC
Military Characteristics Equipment	MCE
Military Characteristics Motor Vehicles	MCM
Military Characteristics Requirement (MCD)	MCR
Military Citizen of the Year (DNAB)	MCOY
Military City Online [Computer program]	MCO
Military Civic Action (DOMA)	MCA
Military Civic Action Program	MILCAP
Military Civil Affairs Administration (NADA)	MCAA
Military Climb Corridor [Aviation]	MCC
Military Clothing and Textile Supply Agency [Merged with Defense Supply Agency] [Army]	MCTSA
Military Clothing Sales Store	MCSS
Military Code of Conduct (VNW)	MCC
Military College [British] (ROG)	MC
Military College of Science [British military] (DMA)	MCoS
Military Colonization Company [British ranch in the Calgary area of Canada]	MCC
Military Command (DNAB)	MILCOM
Military Command, Control, and Information Systems Working Group (NATG)	MCCISWG
Military Command Region (MCD)	MCR
Military Command Technology (AAG)	MCT
Military/Commercial Transport Aircraft Simulation (PDAA)	MCTAS
Military Committee [NATO]	MC
Military Committee Communication [NATO]	MILCOM
Military Committee in Chiefs of Staff Session [NATO] (NATG)	MCCS
Military Committee in Permanent Session [NATO] (NATG)	MCPS
Military Committee Memorandum [NATO] (NATG)	MCM
Military Committee Meteorological Group [NATO] (NATG)	MCMG
Military Committee of National Liberation [Mali] [Political party] (PPW)	MCNL
Military Committee of Western European Union (NATG)	MCWU
Military Committee Representative [to the North Atlantic Council] (AABC)	MCREP
Military Committee Representative Communication to the Private Office of the NATO Secretary General (NATG)	MCPO
Military Committee Representative Liaison Paper to the International Staff [North Atlantic Council] (NATG)	MCLP
Military Committee Special Study Group [NATO] (NATG)	MCSSG
Military Committee Standing Group Distribution and Accounting Agency, NATO	DACAN
Military Committee Working Memorandum (NATG)	MCWM
Military Common Area Control	MCAC
Military Communications Center, Inc. [Minneapolis, MN] (TSSD)	MCC
Military Communications Electronic Systems Technology (MCD)	MILCEST
Military Communications Satellite	MILCOMSAT
Military Communications Satellite System	MCSS
Military Communications Stations	MCS
Military Communications System Technical Standards Committee [Army] (AABC)	MCSTSC
Military Communications-Electronics Board [DoD Washington, DC]	MCEB
Military Community Oral Health Managers [Army]	MCOHM
Military Compact Reactor	MCR
Military Comptrollership Course (MCD)	MCC
Military Computer (IEEE)	MC
Military Computer	MILCOMP
Military Computer Basic Environment for Test Handling	MCBETH
Military Computer Family (MCD)	MCF
Military Computers Users Group	MCUG
Military Confinement	MILCONF
Military Construction (AFM)	MC
Military Construction	MCON
Military Construction	MILCON
Military Construction, Air Force	MCAF
Military Construction Appropriation [or Authorization] (AFM)	MCA
Military Construction Appropriations Act (AAGC)	MCAA
Military Construction Army (AFIT)	MCA
Military Construction, Army / Five Year Plan	MCA/FYP
Military Construction, Army National Guard (AABC)	MCARNG
Military Construction, Army Reserve (AABC)	MCAR
Military Construction Authorized Program	MCAP
Military Construction, Defense Agencies	MILCON-DA
Military Construction, Marine Corps (DNAB)	MCMC
Military Construction, National Guard	MCNG
Military Construction, Naval Reserve Facilities	MCNRF
Military Construction, Naval Reserves	MCNR
Military Construction, Navy	MCN
Military Construction Plan	MCP
Military Construction Program (AFIT)	MCP
Military Construction Program (MUGU)	MICON
Military Construction Programs Advisory Committee (AFM)	MCPAC
Military Construction Supply Agency [Later, Defense Construction Supply Center]	MCSA
Military Contracts Administration Department	MCAD
Military Contracts Department	MCD
Military Cooperation Committee [US-Canada]	MCC
Military Coordinating Activity (MCD)	MCA
Military Coordinating Committee	MCC
Military Coordinating Committee, United States Element, Canada-United States Regional Planning Group (AABC)	MCCUSCUSRPG
Military Coordination [British]	MC
Military Coordination Detachment (NATG)	MCD
Military Corrective Establishment	MCE
Military Cost Review Board (MCD)	MCRB
Military Cross [World War I nickname: Maconochie Cross] [British]	MC
Military Damage Assessment	MDA
Military Damage Assessment Reporting System (MCD)	MDARS
Military Damage Assessment Team (AABC)	MILDAT
Military Damage Expectancy	MDE
Military Decision (NATG)	MILDEC
Military Decision Items (AFIT)	MDI
Military Defence Works [British]	MDW
Military Defense Readiness (SAA)	MDR
Military Demarcation Line (CINC)	MDL
Military Demarkation Line Extended (MCD)	MDLX
Military Department	MILDEPT
Military Departments (AABC)	MILDEPS
Military Detachment	MILDET
Military District [Former USSR] (NATG)	MD
Military District Commander	MDC
Military District of Washington [DC]	MDW
Military Document (AAGC)	MILDOC
Military Early Bird	MEB
Military Economic Advisory Panel (MCD)	MEAP
Military Education Level (INF)	MEL
Military Educators and Counselors Association (EA)	MECA
Military Effectiveness in a Toxin Environment (AABC)	METOXI
Military Electronic Conference	MIL-E-CON
Military Electronic Data Advisory Committee [NATO] (NATG)	MEDAC
Military [or Miniaturized] Electronic Information Delivery System (MCD)	MEIDS
Military Electronic Light Valve	MELVA
Military Electronics (MCD)	ME
Military Emergency Diversion Aerodrome (DA)	MEDA
Military Emergency Travel Warrant [MTMC] (TAG)	METW
Military Energy Depot (SAA)	MED
Military Engineer	ME
Military Engineer Services [British]	MES
Military Engineering Applications of Commercial Explosives [Army] (PDAA)	MEACE
Military Engineering Experimental Establishment [British]	MEX
Military Engineering Experimental Establishment [British]	MEXE
Military Engineering Item (MCD)	MEI
Military Enlistment Processing Command [DoD]	MEPCOM
Military Entomology Information Service	MEIS
Military Entrance and Processing Station	MEPS
Military Entrance Physical Strength Capacity Test (INF)	MEPSCAT
Military Entrant-Processing and Reporting System (GFGA)	MEPRS
Military Equal Opportunity (MCD)	MEO

Military Equipment Characteristics Document (RDA) ... MECD
Military Equipment Code (DNAB) ... MEC
Military Equipment Delivery Team ... MEDT
Military Equipment Delivery Team Cambodia (VNW) ... MEDTC
Military Equipment Test Center (CAAL) ... METC
Military Essential Equipment (CINC) ... MEE
Military Essentiality Class [*or Code*] ... MEC
Military Essentiality through Readiness Indices ... METRI
Military Evaluation of Geographic Areas ... MEGA
Military Exchange ... MEX
Military Experience Directed into Health Careers [*DoD/HEW project*] ... MEDIHC
Military Export Cargo Offering and Booking Office ... MECOBO
Military Family Housing (AFM) ... MFH
Military Field Representative (SAA) ... MFR
Military Financial Instruction ... MFI
Military Flight Information Center ... MFIC
Military Flight Operational Control Center [*ICAO designator*] (ICDA) ... YW
Military Flight Operational Control Centre [*FAA designator*] (FAAC) ... YWY
Military Flight Service ... MFS
Military Flight Vehicles ... MFV
Military Flying Area [*Canadian*] ... MFA
Military Forwarding Depot [*British military*] (DMA) ... MFD
Military Forwarding Officer ... MFO
Military Forwarding Organization ... MFO
Military Foul-Up [*Bowdlerized version*] (DSUE) ... MFU
Military Free Fall [*Parachute jump*] (MCD) ... MFF
Military Free Fall / High Altitude Low Opening Parachute ... MFF/HALO
Military Frequency Changer ... MFC
Military Functions Appropriation (AABC) ... MFA
Military Gamma Irradiator ... MAGI
Military General Supply Agency [*Merged with Defense General Supply Center*] ... MGSA
Military Geographic Documentation (AABC) ... MGD
Military Geographic Information [*or Intelligence*] (MCD) ... MGI
Military Geographic Information and Documentation (AABC) ... MGID
Military Geography Specialist Team ... MGST
Military Government [*or Governor*] ... MG
Military Government Association ... MGA
Military Government Officer ... MGO
Military Government Section [*World War II*] ... MGS
Military Government Unit ... MGU
Military Grid Reference System (AABC) ... MGRS
Military Group ... MILGP
Military Group (DNAB) ... MILGRP
Military Group (DNAB) ... MILGRU
Military Handbook ... MIL-HDBK
Military Health Affairs (DOMA) ... MHA
Military Health Institute ... MHI
Military Health Plan [*DoD*] ... MHP
Military Health Service System ... MHSS
Military Historical Society [*Defunct*] (EA) ... MHS
Military History (AABC) ... MH
Military History Branch [*USMACV*] ... MHB
Military History Detachment ... MHD
Military History Institute [*Army*] (MCD) ... MHI
Military History of Korea ... MHK
Military Hospital (ADA) ... MH
[*The*] **Military Housing Association** ... TMHA
Military Implications of LASER Employment by the Soviets ... MILES
Military Improvement Program ... MIP
Military in Transition Database [*Information service or system*] (IID) ... MILITRAN
Military Incentive Analysis Program (MCD) ... MIAP
Military Incident Report (MCD) ... MILINREP
Military Indoctrination Center ... MIC
Military Industrial Commission [*Soviet-Russian*] (DOMA) ... VPK
Military Information Center [*Defunct*] (EA) ... MIC
Military Information Control Committee (CINC) ... MICC
Military Information Processing System ... MIPS
Military Information Program ... MIP
Military Inspection Agency (NATG) ... MIA
Military Institute ... MI
Military Instruction (AAGC) ... MIL-I
Military Instrumentation List ... MIL
Military Integrated Communications System (CINC) ... MICS
Military Intelligence [*Army*] ... MI
Military Intelligence [*State security*] [*British*] (ODBW) ... MI5
Military Intelligence [*Espionage*] [*British*] (ODBW) ... MI6
Military Intelligence Agency (MCD) ... MIA
Military Intelligence Battalion (MCD) ... MIB
Military Intelligence Battalion Aerial Reconnaissance and Support [*Army*] (AFM) ... MIBARS
Military Intelligence Board (MCD) ... MIB
Military Intelligence Board Working Group ... MIBWG
Military Intelligence Co., Aerial Surveillance (MCD) ... MICAS
Military Intelligence Detachment (AABC) ... MID
Military Intelligence Division [*War Department*] [*World War II*] ... MID
Military Intelligence Exchange Center (CINC) ... MIEC
Military Intelligence Group (MCD) ... MIG
Military Intelligence Guide (MCD) ... MIG
Military Intelligence Interpreter ... MII
Military Intelligence Interrogation ... MII
Military Intelligence Officer [*British military*] (DMA) ... MIO
Military Intelligence Officer Advanced Course (DOMA) ... MIOAC
Military Intelligence, Research [*World War II*] ... MIR
Military Intelligence Research Section [*Navy*] ... MIRS
Military Intelligence Section [*of an Army or Marine Corps division general staff, or Marine brigade or aircraft wing general staff; also, the officer in charge of this section*] ... G-2
Military Intelligence Section [*South Africa*] ... MIS
Military Intelligence Service Organization (NADA) ... MISO
Military Intelligence Services [*Army*] ... MIS
Military Intelligence Special Training Element (DOMA) ... MISTE
Military Intelligence Summary [*Defense Intelligence Agency*] ... MIS
Military Intelligence Translator ... MIT
Military Intelligence Unit Training Center (AABC) ... MIUTC
Military Interdepartmental Procurement [*or Purchase*] **Request** ... MIPR
Military Interdepartmental Purchase ... MIP
Military Intergovernmental Purchase Request (NASA) ... MIPR
Military Intergovernmental Purchase Request ... MIPR
Military Interim Specification [*Army*] (MCD) ... MIS
Military Internee ... MI
Military Introductory Letter ... MIC
Military Inventory Control Point (MCD) ... MICP
Military Iranian Mission [*World War II*] ... MIM
Military Item ... MI
Military Judge (AFM) ... MJ
Military Junior College (AABC) ... MJC
Military Jurisprudence, Cases and Materials [*A publication*] (DLA) ... Mil Jur Cas & Mat
Military Justice Docket File (DNAB) ... MILJUSDOCFILE
Military Justice Reporter (West) [*A publication*] (DLA) ... MJ
Military Knight of Windsor [*British*] ... MKW
Military Labor Service ... MLS
Military Landing Craft ... MLC
Military Landing Officer ... MLO
Military Law ... ML
Military Law Journal [*A publication*] (DLA) ... Military LJ
Military Law Task Force (EA) ... MLTF
Military Leave (GFGA) ... ML
Military Liaison ... ML
Military Liaison Assistant (DOMA) ... MLA
Military Liaison Committee [*Energy Research and Development Administration*] ... MLC
Military Liaison Committee to the Atomic Energy Commission (IEEE) ... MLCAEC
Military Liaison Mission [*Germany*] ... MLM
Military Liaison Officer [*British*] ... MLO
Military Load Class (RDA) ... MLC
Military Load Classification [*BTS*] (TAG) ... MLC
Military Mail Terminal (AFM) ... MMT
Military Maintenance Technician ... MMT
Military Manpower Claimant Code (DNAB) ... MMCC
Military Manpower Management Evaluation Project (NG) ... MMMEP
Military Manpower Models ... M3
Military Manpower Models Airborne Personnel Detector [*Device used to collect and test air samples to identify enemy sites*] [*Vietnam*] (VNW) ... M-3 APD
Military Manpower Models Toxicological Agents Protective Suit [*Provided protection from chemical agents*] (VNW) ... M-3 TAP
Military Manpower Requirements Report (MCD) ... MMRR
Military Manpower Task Force ... MMTF
Military Manpower Training Report (MCD) ... MMTR
Military Manual (MCD) ... MIL-M
Military Man-Years (AABC) ... MMY
Military Medal [*World War I nickname: Maconochie Medal*] [*British*] ... MM
Military Media Review [*A publication*] (DNAB) ... MMR
Military Medical Academy [*Armed forces medical college*] ... MMA
Military Medical Benefits Property (AABC) ... MMBP
Military Medical Research and Services Program (CINC) ... MMR & S
Military Medical Supply Agency [*Later, Defense Medical Supply Center*] ... MMSA
Military Medicine ... MM
Military Medicine Education Institute [*DoD*] (DOMA) ... MMEI
Military Message Service [*British military*] (DMA) ... MMS
Military Microwave Landing System (MCD) ... MMLS
Military Microwave Landing System, Avionics (DWSG) ... MMLSA
Military Mission of Liaison Administration [*World War II*] ... MMLA
Military Mission to the Italian Army [*World War II*] ... MMIA
Military Mobilization Working Group ... MMWG
Military Money Order Branch (AFM) ... MMOB
Military Morale Division [*Coast Guard*] ... PMM
Military Motorcycle [*Army*] (INF) ... MILMO
Military Mounted Police ... MMP
Military Necessity ... MINEC
Military Necessity Modification ... MNM
Military Network ... MILNET
Military North African Mission [*World War II*] ... MNAM
Military Obligation Designator ... MOD
Military Observer (WDAA) ... MO
Military Occupation Code (MCD) ... MOC
Military Occupational Data Bank [*Later, AOSP*] (AABC) ... MODB
Military Occupational Information (AABC) ... MOI
Military Occupational Information (AD) ... moi
Military Occupational Information Data Bank ... MOIDE
Military Occupational Specialty [*Army*] ... MOS
Military Occupational Specialty (AD) ... mos
Military Occupational Specialty Code (AABC) ... MOSC
Military Occupational Specialty Level System ... MOSLS
Military Occupational Specification Serial Number [*British World War II*] ... MOS
Military Ocean Terminal (AABC) ... MOT
Military Ocean Terminal, Bay Area [*Oakland, CA*] (AABC) ... MOTBA

Military Ocean Terminal, Bayonne (AABC) ... MOTBY
Military Ocean Terminal, King's Bay (AABC) ... MOTKI
Military Ocean Terminal, Sunny Point (AABC) ... MOTSU
Military Oceanographic Information Center (NATG) ... MOIC
Military Oceanography (PDAA) ... MILOC
Military Oceanography Subcommittee [*Marine science*] (OSRA) ... MOS
Military Oceanography Subcommittee [*National Security Industrial Association*] (USDC) ... MOS
Military Officer Record Examination ... MORE
Military Official Mail (AABC) ... MOM
Military Oil Subcommittee [*of North African Economic Board*] [*World War II*] ... MOSC
Military Operation (GFGA) ... MOP
Military Operation Phone System ... MOPS
Military Operational Protective Posture [*Chemical warfare*] (RDA) ... MOPP
Military Operations [*USCG*] (TAG) ... MIL OPS
Military Operations [*British military*] (DMA) ... MO
Military Operations and Intelligence ... MOI
Military Operations Area (AD) ... MOA
Military Operations Area [*FAA*] (TAG) ... MOA
Military Operations in Built-Up Areas ... MOBA
Military Operations on Urbanized Terrain (MCD) ... MOUT
Military Operations Other than War (RDA) ... MOOTW
Military Operations Research ... MOR
Military Operations Research Department ... MORD
Military Operations Research Society (EA) ... MORS
Military Operations Research Symposia (MCD) ... MORS
Military Orbital Development System [*See also MODS, MOSS, MTSS*] [*Air Force/NASA*] ... MOD
Military Orbital Development System [*See also MOD, MOSS, MTSS*] [*Air Force/NASA*] ... MODS
Military Orbital Space System [*See also MOD, MODS, MTSS*] [*Air Force/NASA*] ... MOSS
Military Order, Devil Dog Fleas (EA) ... DDF
Military Order, Devil Dog Fleas (EA) ... MODDF
Military Order of Columbia's Shield (EA) ... MOCS
Military Order of Devil Dogs (EA) ... MODD
Military Order of Foreign Wars of the United States (EA) ... MOFW
Military Order of the Carabao (EA) ... MOC
Military Order of the Loyal Legion of the United States (EA) ... MOLLUS
Military Order of the Loyal Legion of the United States, [*Civil*] **War Library and Museum, Philadelphia, PA** [*Library symbol Library of Congress*] (LCLS) ... PPLL
Military Order of the Loyal Legion of the USA (AD) ... MOLLUSA
Military Order of the Purple Heart of the United States of America (EA) ... MOPH
Military Order of the Stars and Bars (EA) ... MOSB
Military Order of the World Wars (EA) ... MOWW
Military Order of the Zouave Legion of the United States (EA) ... MOZL
Military Order of the Zouave Legion of the US (EA) ... MOZLUS
Military Orders Issued by the President as Commander in Chief of the Armed Forces [*A publication*] (DLA) ... MO
Military Ordinary Mail (AABC) ... MOM
Military Ordinary Mail (AD) ... mom
Military/Ordnance Specification (MCD) ... MIL/OS
Military Overseas Mail [*An association*] (EA) ... MOM
Military Overseas Shelter Survey [*Civil Defense*] ... MOSS
Military Overseas Supply [*British*] ... MOS
Military Parts Control Advisory Group [*DoD*] ... MPCAG
Military Pay (AFM) ... MP
Military Pay Account ... MPA
Military Pay and Allowance ... MPA
Military Pay and Allowance Committee (AFM) ... MPAC
Military Pay Area (AFM) ... MPA
Military Pay Division (AD) ... MPD
Military Pay Division, Finance Center, US Army ... MPD
Military Pay, Navy [*An appropriation*] ... MPN
Military Pay Order ... MPO
Military Pay Procedure Committee ... MPPC
Military Pay Procedures ... MPP
Military Pay Record ... MPR
Military Pay Voucher ... MPV
Military Pay Voucher Summary and Certification Sheet ... MPVSCS
Military Payment Certificate ... MPC
Military Payment Certificate (AD) ... mpc
Military Payroll Money List ... ML
Military Permit Office [*or Officer*] ... MPO
Military Personnel ... MILPERS
Military Personnel Accounting Activity [*Army*] (AABC) ... MILPAC
Military Personnel and Transportation Assistance Office (MCD) ... MPTAO
Military Personnel Appropriation (AFM) ... MPA
Military Personnel, Army ... MPA
Military Personnel Center [*Alexandria, VA*] [*Army*] (AABC) ... MILPERCEN
Military Personnel Center (AFM) ... MPC
Military Personnel/Civilian Personnel ... MP/CP
Military Personnel Information Subsystem (MCD) ... MILPERSIS
Military Personnel Information System ... MILPERSINS
Military Personnel Instructions (MCD) ... MILPERSINST
Military Personnel, Marine Corps ... MPMC
Military Personnel, Navy ... MPN
Military Personnel Office (AABC) ... MILPO
Military Personnel Office ... MPO
Military Personnel Procurement Manual ... MPPM
Military Personnel Record (AFM) ... MPR
Military Personnel Records Center (MCD) ... MPRC
Military Personnel Records Jacket [*Army*] (AABC) ... MPRJ
Military Personnel Security Committee ... MPSC
Military Personnel Security Program ... MPSP
Military Petroleum Advisory Board ... MPAB
Military Petroleum Supply Agency [*Later, Defense Petroleum Supply Center*] ... MPSA
Military Photo-Reconnaissance (PDAA) ... MPR
Military Physics Research Laboratory [*University of Texas*] (MCD) ... MPRL
Military Pioneer Corps [*British*] ... MPC
Military Planning Office [*SEATO*] (CINC) ... MPO
Military Planning Staff (CINC) ... MPS
Military Plans and Operations Staff ... MPOS
Military Police [*Army*] ... MP
Military Police Association [*Defunct*] (EA) ... MPA
Military Police Battalion ... MPBN
Military Police Commanding Officer (MCD) ... MPCO
Military Police Company ... MPCO
Military Police Corps ... MPC
Military Police Criminal Investigation ... MPCI
Military Police Criminal Investigation Detachment ... MPCID
Military Police Escort Guard ... MPEG
Military Police Force (AD) ... MPC
Military Police Functional Automation System for the Army in the Field (MCD) ... MPFASAF
Military Police Information System (DNAB) ... MILPINS
Military Police Investigator [*or Investigation*] (AABC) ... MPI
Military Police Management Information System ... MPMIS
Military Police Operations and Information System [*Army*] (MCD) ... MPOIS
Military Police Platoon (DNAB) ... MPPLT
Military Police Prisoner of War Command (AABC) ... MPPWCOM
Military Police Regimental Association (EA) ... MPRA
Military Police Special Weapons and Tactics Team (VNW) ... MP SWAT
Military Police Tripartite Standing Working Group (AABC) ... MP(TSWG)
Military Position Description ... MPD
Military Post ... Mil P
Military Post Office ... MPO
Military Post Office Location List (AFM) ... MPOLL
Military Postal Clerk (AFM) ... MPC
Military Postal Liaison Office ... MPLO
Military Postal Service (AFM) ... MPS
Military Postal Service Agency ... MPSA
Military Potential Test (AABC) ... MPT
Military Primary Radar [*FAA*] (TAG) ... FPS
Military Priority Date ... MPD
Military Prisons Department [*British military*] (DMA) ... MPD
Military Procurement Instruction ... MPI
Military Procurement, Navy (MCD) ... MPN
Military Production Master Urgency List ... MPMUL
Military Production Specifications ... MPS
Military Production Urgencies List (NG) ... MPUL
Military Production Urgencies System ... MPUS
Military Products Group ... MPG
Military Prohibitionist [*Slang*] ... MP
Military Property (MCD) ... MP
Military Property Custodian (AFIT) ... MPC
Military Proposal and Analysis ... MPA
Military Provincial Health Assistance Program (AABC) ... MILPHAP
Military Provost Staff Corps [*British*] ... MPSC
Military Qualification Program (NG) ... MQP
Military Qualification Standard ... MQS
Military Qualification Test (NG) ... MQT
Military RADAR Service Area [*Aviation*] (AIA) ... MRSA
Military RADAR Unit [*Aviation*] (FAAC) ... MRU
Military Railroad (AD) ... MR
Military Railway Service [*Army*] ... MRS
Military Railway Service Veterans (EA) ... MRSV
Military Rated Power (NG) ... MRP
Military Rated Thrust (NG) ... MRT
Military Readiness ... MR
Military Real-Time Computer (AAG) ... MRTC
Military Reconnaissance Force [*British military*] (DMA) ... MRF
Military Reference Data ... MRD
Military Reform Caucus (EA) ... MRC
Military Reform Institute (AD) ... MRI
Military Region [*Viet Cong term*] ... MR
Military Region Command (MCD) ... MRC
Military Regulation ... MR
Military Release Orders ... MRO
Military Reliable Tube Program ... MRTP
Military Renegotiation Regulation ... MRR
Military Representative (NATG) ... MILREP
Military Representative (NATG) ... MR
Military Representatives Committee [*NATO*] (NATG) ... MRC
Military Representatives of Associated Pacific Powers [*World War II*] ... MRP
Military Requirement ... MR
Military Requirement and Development Committee (NATG) ... MRDC
Military Requirements Determination ... MRD
Military Requirements Estimation System ... MRES
Military Requirements Plan (NATG) ... MRP
Military Requirements Study (AAGC) ... MRS
Military Research and Development Center [*US-Thailand*] ... MRDC
Military Reserve (CINC) ... M/R
Military Reserve Technician (GFGA) ... MRT
Military Retirement Reform Act ... MRRA
Military Retirement System ... MRS

Military Reunions Council (EA) ... MRC
Military Review [*A publication*] (BRI) ... Mil Rev
Military Review (MCD) ... MR
Military Review Team (AD) ... MRT
Military Revolutionary Council (CINC) ... MRC
Military Routing Identifier System ... MILRIS
Military Sales Department ... MSD
Military Satellite ... MILSAT
Military Satellite Communications [*Systems*] ... MILSATCOM
Military Satellite Organization ... MSO
Military School Band Association (EA) ... MSBA
Military Science (AABC) ... MS
Military Science Training ... MST
Military Scout Car [*British*] ... MSC
Military Sea Transport Service, Far East ... MSTSFE
Military Sea Transport Union ... MSTU
Military Sea Transportation Service [*Later, MSC*] [*Navy*] ... MSTS
Military Sea Transportation Service Office [*Obsolete*] ... MSTSO
Military Sealift Command ... MLS
Military Sealift Command [*Formerly, MSTS, NTS*] [*Navy*] (NOAA) ... MSC
Military Sealift Command, Atlantic (DNAB) ... MSCLANT
Military Sealift Command, Atlantic Detachment (DNAB) ... MSCLANTDET
Military Sealift Command, Eastern Atlantic and Mediterranean (DNAB) ... MSCELM
Military Sealift Command, Far East (DNAB) ... MSCFE
Military Sealift Command, Pacific (DNAB) ... MSCPAC
Military Sealift Command Representative (DNAB) ... MSCREP
Military Sealift Command Service Office - Maintenance and Repair (DNAB) ... MSCSO-M & R
Military Sealift Command Service Office - Operations Cargo Passenger Office (DNAB) ... MSCSO-OCPO
Military Sealift Command Service Office - Supply Assistant (DNAB) ... MSCSO-SA
Military Sealift Command Ship [*When precedes vessel classification*] [*Navy symbol*] ... T
Military Sealift Command Transportation Unit (DNAB) ... MSCTRANSU
Military Sealift Command Unit (DNAB) ... MSCU
Military Sealift Command, Washington, DC [*OCLC symbol*] (OCLC) ... NSN
Military Secretary [*British*] ... MS
Military Security Assistance Projection [*Military*] ... MSAP
Military Security Board ... MSB
Military Security Service [*RVNAF*] ... MSS
Military Selective Service Act (OICC) ... MSSA
Military Serial Number ... MSN
Military Service ... MS
Military Service [*FAA designator*] (FAAC) ... YXY
Military Service Act [*British*] ... MS
Military Service Act [*British*] (DMA) ... MSA
Military Service Branch [*World War I*] [*Canada*] ... MSB
Military Service Indicator (MCD) ... MSI
Military Service Number ... MSN
Military Service Number / Social Security Number (DNAB) ... MSN/SSN
Military Service Obligation (AFM) ... MSO
Military Service Obligation Date (AFM) ... MSOD
Military Service or Organization [*ICAO designator*] (ICDA) ... YX
Military Services ... MILSVC
Military Services [*Diocesan abbreviation*] [*Maryland*] (TOCD) ... MO
Military Services Ammunition Allocation Board (AABC) ... MSAAB
Military Shipping Label ... MSL
Military Shipping Tag ... MST
Military Side Loader [*Air transport*] [*British*] ... MSL
Military Solid Logic Technology (IAA) ... MSLT
Military Space Program (AAG) ... MSP
Military Space Surveillance Control Center (IAA) ... MSCC
Military Space Surveillance Control Center (MUGU) ... MSSCC
Military Space Systems Technology Model (MCD) ... MSSTM
Military Specification [*Followed by a single capital letter and numbers*] (IEEE) ... MIL
Military Specification ... MILSPEC
Military Specification (AAG) ... MS
Military Specification Exception (RDA) ... MSE
Military Specification on Interference (IEEE) ... MIL-I
Military Specifications (GAVI) ... MILSPEC
Military Spending Research Services, Inc. [*Information service or system*] (IID) ... MSRS
Military Staff [*British military*] (DMA) ... MS
Military Staff Committee [*United Nations*] (DLA) ... MSC
Military Staff Committee of the United Nations ... MSC(UN)
Military Staff Communication (NATG) ... MILSTAC
Military Staffing Standards System ... MS-3
Military Standard ... MILSTD
Military Standard ... MS
Military Standard [*Parts designation*] ... MS
Military Standard Activity Address Directory ... MILSTAAD
Military Standard and Specification Committee ... MSSC
Military Standard Billing System ... MILSBILLS
Military Standard Contract Administration Procedures [*DoD*] ... MILCAP
Military Standard Contract Administration Procedures [*DoD*] ... MILSCAP
Military Standard Engines ... MSE
Military Standard Evaluation Procedure ... MILSTEP
Military Standard Evaluation Program ... MSEP
Military Standard for Providing Research and Exploratory Development Data ... MILSPRED
Military Standard Inventory Management System ... MILSIMS
Military Standard Item (MCD) ... MSI
Military Standard Item Characteristics Coding ... MILSTICC
Military Standard Item Characteristics Coding Structure (SAA) ... MILSICCS
Military Standard Item Characteristics Coding Structure ... MILSTICCS
Military Standard Item Identification Coding System ... MILSTIICS
Military Standard Item Management Data System ... MILSIMDS
Military Standard Logistics System (MCD) ... MILS
Military Standard Logistics Systems Office [*DoD*] (MCD) ... MILSO
Military Standard Petroleum System (MCD) ... MILSPETS
Military Standard Procurement Operations Technique ... MIL SPOT
Military Standard Purchase Operating Technique ... MILSPOT
Military Standard Requisition and Accounting Procedures (MCD) ... MILSTRAP
Military Standard Requisitioning and Issue Procedure ... MILSTRIP
Military Standard Transaction Reporting and Accounting Procedures ... MILSTRAP
Military Standard Transportation Action Report and Accounting Procedures (MCD) ... MILSTARAP
Military Standard Transportation and Movement Procedure ... MILSTAMP
Military Standard Transportation and Movement Procedure ... MILSTRAMP
Military Standardization Agreement (CINC) ... MILSTAG
Military Static Inverter ... MSI
Military Store Department [*British military*] (DMA) ... MSD
Military Store Staff Corps [*British military*] (DMA) ... MSSC
Military Strategic and Tactical Relay System [*Satellite communications*] ... MILSTAR
Military Strength Balance Report (AFM) ... MSBR
Military Studies and Operational Analysis (ADA) ... MSOA
Military Studies Center (EA) ... MSC
Military Subsistence Agency [*Merged with Defense Supply Agency*] ... MSA
Military Subsistence Market Center (MUGU) ... MSMC
Military Subsistence Supply Agency [*Later, Defense Subsistence Supply Center*] ... MSSA
Military Subvention Type Lorry [*British*] ... MSTL
Military Supply and Transportation Evaluation Procedures (AFM) ... MILSTEP
Military Supply Officer (AFM) ... MSO
Military Supply Standards [*DoD*] (MCD) ... MSS
Military Support Division [*of Materiel Testing Directorate*] (RDA) ... MSD
Military Support Fund (MCD) ... MSF
Military Support List (MCD) ... MSL
Military Support of Civil Defense (AABC) ... MSCD
Military Support Planning Officer [*Civil Defense*] ... MSPO
Military Support to Civil Authorities (AABC) ... MSCA
Military Survivors (EA) ... MS
Military System Training Organization (SAA) ... MSTO
Military Tactical Computer (MCD) ... MTC
Military Tanker [*British*] ... MT
Military Technical Acceptance Board (MCD) ... MTAB
Military Technical Advisor (DNAB) ... MTA
Military Technical Assistance Group ... MILTAG
Military Technical Revolution (DOMA) ... MTR
Military Technician ... MT
Military Telecommunications ... MILTELCOMM
Military Temperature Range ... MTR
Military Terminal Control Area ... MTCA
Military Terminal Major Aerodromes (NATG) ... MTMA
Military Test Directorate [*Program*] [*Army*] (RDA) ... MTD
Military Test Satellite ... MTS
Military Test Space Station [*See also MOD, MODS, MOSS*] [*Air Force/NASA*] ... MTSS
Military Testing Association (MCD) ... MTA
Military Tractor [*British*] ... MT
Military Traffic Expediting Service (AABC) ... MTX
Military Traffic Management Agency [*Later, DTMS*] ... MITMA
Military Traffic Management Agency [*Later, DTMS*] ... MTMA
Military Traffic Management and Terminal Service [*Later, MTMC*] [*Army*] ... MTMTS
Military Traffic Management and Terminal Service Transportation Strike Plan (DNAB) ... MTMTS-TSP
Military Traffic Management Bulletin (SAA) ... MTMB
Military Traffic Management Command [*DoD*] ... MTMC
Military Traffic Management Command, Eastern Area [*Bayonne, NJ*] ... MTMCEA
Military Traffic Management Command Operations Analysis Division [*Newport News, VA*] ... MTMC-OA
Military Traffic Management Command Transportation Engineering Agency (AABC) ... MTMCTEA
Military Traffic Management Command Transportation Terminal Command, Europe [*MTMC*] (TAG) ... MTMCTTC
Military Traffic Management Command Transportation Terminal Unit (AABC) ... MTMCTTU
Military Traffic Management Command, Western Area [*Oakland, CA*] ... MTMCWA
Military Traffic Management Regulation ... MTMR
Military Traffic Management Service (MCD) ... MTMS
Military Train [*British military*] (DMA) ... MT
Military Training [*USCG*] (TAG) ... MIL TRA
Military Training ... MT
Military Training Airspace (NATG) ... MTA
Military Training Area (DA) ... MTA
Military Training Cadets [*A boys' World War II organization*] ... MTC
Military Training Instructor (AFM) ... MTI
Military Training Route [*Aviation*] (FAAC) ... MTR
Military Training Routes [*FAA*] (TAG) ... MTR
Military Training Standard (AFM) ... MTS
Military Training Team (MCD) ... MTT
Military Transmission Systems Department [*NORAD*] ... MTSD
Military Transport ... MT
Military Transport Wagon [*British*] ... MTW

Military Transportation Authorization [*Air Force*]	MTA
Military Transportation Command	MTC
Military Transportation Committee [*NATO*] (NATG)	MTC
Military Transportation of Small Shipments (NVT)	MILTOSS
Military Treatment Facility [*DoD*]	MTF
Military Type Property	MTP
Military Upper Traffic Control Area (DA)	MUTA
Military Urgency Planning List (NG)	MUPL
Military Utility Tactical Transport	MUTT
Military Utility Tactical Truck	MUTT
Military Van (MCD)	MILVAN
Military Vehicle	MV
Military Vehicle Collectors Club [*Later, MVPA*] (EA)	MVCC
Military Vehicle Historical Society of British Columbia and Museum, Vancouver, British Columbia [*Library symbol National Library of Canada*] (NLC)	BVAMV
Military Vehicle Preservation Association (EA)	MVPA
Military Vehicles and Engineering Establishment [*Research center British*]	MVEE
Military Vehicles Operation [*of General Motors Corp.*]	MVO
Military Vigilance (NATG)	MV
Military Weather Warning Center (NOAA)	MWWC
Military Working Dog (DOMA)	MWD
Military-Industrial Complex	M-IC
Military-Industrial Supply Agency	MISA
Military-Industry Logistics Data Development Unit	MILDDU
Military-Industry Logistics Data Interchange Procedures	MILDIP
Military-Industry Logistics Data Interchange System	MILDIS
Military-Industry Technical Manual	MITM
Military-Industry Technical Manual Specifications	MITMS
Military-Owned Vehicle	MOV
Military-Owned Vehicle Plan (AFM)	MOVP
Military-Owned Vehicle Service (AABC)	MOVS
Military-Rated Thrust (AD)	mrt
Militia	M
Militia	MIL
Militia [*British military*] (DMA)	Mila
Militia Bureau [*Superseded in 1933 by National Guard Bureau*]	MB
Militia Career Program [*DoD*]	MCP
Militia Mariae Immaculatae [*Militia of the Immaculate*] (EAIO)	MI
Militia Mea Multiplex [*Pseudonym used by William Tooke*]	MMM
Militia Reporter [*Boston*] [*A publication*] (DLA)	Mil Rep
Militia Reserve [*British military*] (DMA)	MR
Militia Royal Engineers [*British military*] (DMA)	MRE
Milk (ROG)	M
Milk and Molasses [*Enema*] [*Medicine*]	M & M
Milk Bars Association of Great Britain and Ireland Ltd. (BI)	MBA
Milk Bottle Crate Manufacturers Council [*Defunct*] (EA)	MBCMC
Milk Bottlers Federation	MBF
Milk Can Institute [*Defunct*]	MCI
Milk Carton Quality Performing Council (EA)	MCQP
Milk Distribution Trade Board [*British*] (DAS)	MDTB
Milk Drinker's Syndrome [*Medicine*] (DMAA)	MDS
Milk Fat Globule	MFG
Milk Fat Globule Membrane	MFGM
Milk Foundation [*National Dairy Council*] (EA)	MF
Milk in First [*Tea-pouring procedure*]	MIF
Milk Indemnity Payment Program	MIPP
Milk Industry Foundation (EA)	MIF
Milk Ingredient Water (OA)	MIW
Milk Marketing Board (NADA)	MMB
Milk Marketing Board for England and Wales	MMB
Milk Marketing (New South Wales) [*Australia*]	MM(NSW)
Milk of Magnesia	MOM
Milk of Magnesia (AD)	mom
Milk Pasteurization Tribunal [*Australia*]	MPT
Milk/Plasma [*Ratio*] [*Physiology*]	M/P
Milk Powder (AD)	m/p
Milk Products Advertising-Merchandising Association (EA)	MPAMA
Milk Protein Hydrolysate [*Biochemistry*] (DAVI)	MPG
Milk Protein Hydrolysate (BABM)	MPH
Milk Ring Test (PDAA)	MRT
Milk River Public Library, Alberta [*Library symbol National Library of Canada*] (NLC)	AMR
Milk Solids - Not Fat [*Food industry*]	MSNF
Milk-Alkali Syndrome [*Medicine*] (DMAA)	MAS
Milkbottles Only Organization (EA)	MOO
Milking Machine Manufacturers Association [*British*] (DBA)	MMMA
Milking Machine Manufacturers Council (EA)	MMMC
Milk-of-Magnesia in the Morning if No Bowel Movement by Evening [*Medicine*] (AD)	m-o-m in am if no bm by pm
Milk-Ring [*Test*] [*Medicine*] (MEDA)	MR
Milk-Sensitive Enteropathy [*Medicine*]	MSE
Milkweed Virus	MWV
Milky [*Philately*]	miky
Mill	M
Mill	MI
Mill [*Commonly used*] (OPSA)	MILL
Mill	ML
Mill	ML
Mill Annealed	MA
Mill Arbor	MLAR
Mill Culls Out [*Lumber*]	MCO
Mill Cutter [*Tool*] (MCD)	MC
Mill Cutter [*Tool*]	MLCU

Mill Edge (ADA)	ME
Mill Finish	MF
Mill Fixture (MCD)	MF
Mill Fixture [*Tool*]	MF
Mill Fixture Base (MCD)	MLFX
Mill Fixture Base (MCD)	MFB
Mill Fixture Key [*Tool*]	MFK
Mill Glazed [*Paper*]	MG
Mill Hall, PA [*FM radio station call letters*] (RBYB)	WZRZ-FM
Mill Hill Missionaries (TOCD)	mhm
Mill Hill Missionaries [*Roman Catholic men's religious order*]	MHM
Mill Hill Sisters (TOCD)	FMSJ
Mill Mutual Fire Prevention Bureau [*Defunct*] (EA)	MMFPB
Mill Run [*Unselected lot of a manufactured product*]	MR
Mill Run (AD)	mr
Mill Sawyers' Union [*British*]	MSU
Mill Valley Public Library, Mill Valley, CA [*Library symbol Library of Congress*] (LCLS)	CMI
Mill Vise	MLVS
Mill Work [*Technical drawings*]	MWK
Milla Wa-Milla (BJA)	MM
Milladore, WI [*FM radio station call letters*]	WGNV
Millampere [*or Milliamperage*] (IAA)	MAMP
Millard Fillmore National Society [*Defunct*] (EA)	MFNS
Millard Fillmore Suburban Hospital, Williamsville, NY [*Library symbol*] [*Library of Congress*] (LCLS)	NWvH
Millard Filmore [*US president, 1800-1874*]	MF
Millardair Ltd. [*Canada ICAO designator*] (FAAC)	MAB
Millarville Community Library, Alberta [*Library symbol National Library of Canada*] (NLC)	AMC
Millarville Community Library, Millarville, AB, Canada [*Library symbol Library of Congress*] (LCLS)	CaAMiC
Millau/Larzac [*France ICAO location identifier*] (ICLI)	LFCM
Millbrook, AL [*FM radio station call letters*]	WMCZ
Millbrook Library, Millbrook, NY [*Library symbol*] [*Library of Congress*] (LCLS)	NMbr
Millbrook Public Library, Ontario [*Library symbol National Library of Canada*] (BIB)	OMILL
Millburn Free Public Library, Millburn, NJ [*Library symbol Library of Congress*] (LCLS)	NjMil
Mille [*Thousand*] [*Roman numeral*]	M
Mille Iacs Lake Community Library, Isle, MN [*Library symbol*] [*Library of Congress*] (LCLS)	Mnl
Mille Pasuum [*Thousand Paces*] [*Latin*] (AD)	mp
Milled Carbon Fiber	MCF
Milled in Transit [*Commodities*]	MIT
Milledgeville, GA [*Location identifier FAA*] (FAAL)	MLJ
Milledgeville, GA [*AM radio station call letters*]	WKGQ
Milledgeville, GA [*FM radio station call letters*]	WKZR
Milledgeville, GA [*FM radio station call letters*]	WLRR
Milledgeville, GA [*AM radio station call letters*]	WMVG
Milledgeville, GA [*FM radio station call letters*]	WXGC
Milled-Wood Lignin	MWL
Millen, GA [*FM radio station call letters*]	WHKN
Millenia, Inc. [*AMEX symbol*] (SAG)	IA
Millenia, Inc. [*Associated Press*] (SAG)	Millenia
Millenium Chemicals, Inc. [*NYSE symbol*] (SAG)	MCH
Millenium Chemicals, Inc. [*Associated Press*] (SAG)	MillenCh
Millenium Film Workshop, New York, NY [*Library symbol Library of Congress*] (LCLS)	NNMi
Millennium Guild (EA)	MG
Millennium Pharmaceuticals [*NASDAQ symbol*] (TTSB)	MLNM
Millennium Pharmaceuticals, Inc. [*Associated Press*] (SAG)	MillPhar
Millennium Pharmaceuticals, Inc. [*NASDAQ symbol*] (SAG)	MLNM
Millennium Society (EA)	MS
Miller Air Transporters [*ICAO designator*] (FAAC)	MIT
Miller Analogies Test [*Psychology*]	MAT
Miller Analogies Test (GAGS)	MAT
Miller and Collier on Bills of Sale [*A publication*] (DLA)	M & C Bills
Miller and Collier on Bills of Sale [*A publication*] (DLA)	Mill & C Bills
Miller and Field's Federal Practice [*A publication*] (DLA)	Mill & F Pr
Miller Assessment for Preschoolers	MAP
Miller Brewing Co., Research Library, Milwaukee, WI [*Library symbol Library of Congress*] (LCLS)	WMMBC
Miller Building Sys [*NASDAQ symbol*] (TTSB)	MTIK
Miller Building Systems, Inc. [*Associated Press*] (SAG)	MilrBld
Miller Building Systems, Inc. [*NASDAQ symbol*] (NQ)	MTIK
Miller Communications Systems Ltd. [*Telecommunications service*] (TSSD)	MCS
Miller Communications Systems Ltd., Kanata, ON, Canada [*Library symbol Library of Congress*] (LCLS)	CaOKanMC
Miller Communications Systems Ltd., Kanata, Ontario [*Library symbol National Library of Canada*] (NLC)	OKMC
Miller Flying Services, Inc. [*ICAO designator*] (FAAC)	MFS
Miller (Herman) [*NASDAQ symbol*] (TTSB)	MLHR
Miller [*Herman*], Inc. [*Associated Press*] (SAG)	MillrHr
Miller [*Herman*], Inc. [*NASDAQ symbol*] (NQ)	MLHR
Miller Indusries, Inc. [*Associated Press*] (SAG)	MillerIn
Miller Industries [*NYSE symbol*] (SAG)	MLR
Miller Industries [*NYSE symbol*] (TTSB)	MLR
Miller Industries, Inc. [*NASDAQ symbol*] (SAG)	MILL
Miller Integrator	MI
Miller Intermediate School, Pasadena, TX [*Library symbol*] [*Library of Congress*] (LCLS)	TxPMI
Miller on Partition [*A publication*] (DLA)	Mill Part

Miller on the Constitution of the United States [*A publication*]
(DLA) .... Miller Const

Miller, SD [*Location identifier FAA*] (FAAL) .... MKA

Miller Township Consolidated Community, School District 210, Marseilles, IL [*Library symbol Library of Congress*] (LCLS) .... IMarseMSD

Miller Township Consolidated Community, School District 210, Seneca, IL [*Library symbol*] [*Library of Congress*] (LCLS) .... ISenMS

Miller-Abbot (Tube) [*Medicine*] .... MA

Miller-Abbott Tube [*Surgery*] [*Medicine*] (DAVI) .... MAT

Miller-Dawn Hospital and Medical Center, Duluth, MN [*Library symbol Library of Congress*] (LCLS) .... MnDuM

Miller-Dieker Chromosomal Region [*Genetics*] .... MDCR

Miller-Dieker Lissencephaly Syndrome [*Medicine*] .... MDS

Miller-Dieker Syndrome [*Medicine*] (DMAA) .... MDS

Miller-Motte Business College, Wilmington, NC [*Library symbol*] [*Library of Congress*] (LCLS) .... NcWMM

Miller's Circuit Court Decisions (Woolworth) [*United States*] [*A publication*] (DLA) .... Mill Dec

Miller's Circuit Court Decisions (Woolworth) [*United States*] [*A publication*] (DLA) .... Mill Op

Miller's Civil Law of England [*1825*] [*A publication*] (DLA) .... Mill Civ L

Miller's Elements of the Law of Insurances [*A publication*] (DLA) .... Mill El

Miller's Elements of the Law of Insurances [*A publication*] (DLA) .... Mill Ins

Miller's Equitable Mortgages [*1844*] [*A publication*] (DLA) .... Mill Eq M

Miller's Iowa Code [*A publication*] (DLA) .... Mill Code

Miller's Iowa Pleading and Practice [*A publication*] (DLA) .... Mill Pl & Pr

Millers' National Federation (EA) .... MNF

Miller's Reports [*1-5 Louisiana*] [*A publication*] (DLA) .... Mil

Miller's Reports [*3-18 Maryland*] [*A publication*] (DLA) .... Mil

Miller's Reports [*1-5 Louisiana*] [*A publication*] (DLA) .... Mill

Miller's Reports [*3-18 Maryland*] [*A publication*] (DLA) .... Mill

Miller's Reports [*1-5 Louisiana*] [*A publication*] (DLA) .... Mill LA

Miller's Reports [*3-18 Maryland*] [*A publication*] (DLA) .... Mill MD

Miller's Reports [*1-5 Louisiana*] [*A publication*] (DLA) .... Miller

Miller's Reports [*3-18 Maryland*] [*A publication*] (DLA) .... Miller

Miller's Revised and Annotated Code [*Iowa*] [*A publication*] (DLA) .... Miller's Code

Miller's United States Supreme Court Decisions [*Condensed, Continuation of Curtis*] [*A publication*] (DLA) .... Mill Dec

Millersburg, OH [*Location identifier FAA*] (FAAL) .... MLR

Millersburg, OH [*FM radio station call letters*] .... WKLM

Millersburg, OH [*FM radio station call letters*] .... WQLV

Millersburg, PA [*FM radio station call letters*] .... WIXQ

Millersville, PA [*FM radio station call letters*] .... MVS

Millersville State College, Millersville, PA [*OCLC symbol*] (OCLC) .... PMilS

Millersville State College, Millersville, PA [*Library symbol Library of Congress*] (LCLS) .... Millersville U

Millersville University of Pennsylvania (GAGS) .... NMil

Millerton Free Library, Millerton, NY [*Library symbol Library of Congress*] (LCLS) .... MY

Miller-Yoder Language Comprehension Test .... MY

Miller-Yoder Test of Grammatical Comprehension [*Speech and lanaguage therapy*] (DAVI) .... MYTGC

Millet Public Library, Alberta [*Library symbol National Library of Canada*] (NLC) .... AMI

Millhaven Fibers Ltd., Kingston, ON, Canada [*Library symbol Library of Congress*] (LCLS) .... CaOKCIL

Millhouse Developments Ltd. [*British ICAO designator*] (FAAC) .... MHO

Milli- [*A prefix meaning divided by 1000*] [*SI symbol*] .... m

Milli (DFIT) .... MCM

Milli Circular Mil (IAA) .... MCM

Milli Hedef Partisi [*National Goal Party*] [*Turkish Cyprus*] [*Political party*] (PPE) .... MHP

Milli Kutuphane [*National Library*], Ankara, Turkey [*Library symbol Library of Congress*] (LCLS) .... Tk

Millia Passuum [*1,000 Paces; the Roman mile*] .... MP

Milliabsorbance Unit [*Spectroscopy*] .... mAU

Milliammeter (IAA) .... MA

Milliammeter .... MAM

Milliammeter .... MAMTR

Milliammeter (IAA) .... MTR

Milliampere [*or Milliamperage*] .... mA

Milliampere .... MA

Milliampere Alternating Current (IAA) .... MAAC

Milliampere Direct Current [*Electronics*] (IAA) .... MADC

Milliampere Hour .... mAH

Milliampere Minutes .... MAM

Milliampere-Minute .... Ma-Min

Milliampere-Minute .... MA/CM

Milliamperes per Centimeter .... mA/V

Milliamperes per Volt (DEN) .... mAs

Milliampere-Second .... MA

Milliangstrom [*Unit of wavelength of light*] (WGA) .... mb

Millibar [*Unit of pressure*] .... MB

Millibar .... mbar

Millibar [*Unit of pressure*] .... mb

Millibarn [*Area of nuclear cross-section*] .... mb

Millibyte [*Computer science*] .... MCD

Millicandela .... MFai

Millicent Library, Fairhaven, MA [*Library symbol Library of Congress*] (LCLS) .... MFai

Millicm International Cellular S.A. [*Commercial firm*] [*Luxembourg*] .... MIC

Millicom International Cellular [*NASDAQ symbol*] (SAG) .... MICC

Millicom International Cellular [*Associated Press*] (SAG) .... MilcmIn

Millicom Intl Cellular S.A. [*NASDAQ symbol*] (TTSB) .... MICCF

Millicoulomb (MAE) .... mC

Millicoulomb .... Mcoul

Millicurie [*Also, mCi*] .... mC

Millicurie (IDOE) .... mc

Millicurie [*Also, mC*] .... mCi

Millicurie [*Also, mC, mCI*] (IAA) .... MCU

Millicurie Hour .... mch

Millicurie Hour (MAE) .... mchr

Millicurie Hour (MAE) .... mCihr

Millicurie-Destroyed .... mcD

Millicycle [*Also, as millihertz*] (WGA) .... MC

Millidarcy .... mD

Milliearth Rate Unit [*NASA*] (KSC) .... MERU

Millieme [*Monetary unit*] [*Egypt, Sudan*] .... MIL

Milliequivalent [*or Milligram Equivalent*] [*Also, MEQ*] .... ME

Milliequivalent [*or Milligram Equivalent*] [*Also, ME*] .... MEQ

Milliequivalent [*Gram equivalent weight*] (DOG) .... meq

Milliequivalent per Liter .... MEQ/L

Millifarad (GPO) .... MF

Millifarad (IDOE) .... mF

Millifarad (MCD) .... MFD

Millifoot Lamberts (DEN) .... MFT L

Milligal [*Unit of acceleration*] .... mgal

Milligals (ABBR) .... MGALS

Milligan College, Milligan College, TN [*Library symbol Library of Congress*] (LCLS) .... TMilM

Milligauss (ABBR) .... MG

Milligram .... mg

Milligram .... mg

Milligram .... mgm

Milligram (DFIT) .... MGM

Milligram (ROG) .... MGRM

Milligram Hour [*Pharmacy*] .... mgh

Milligram-Element (MAE) .... mg-el

Milligrams of Material per Cubic Meter of Air (GNE) .... mg/m_3

Milligrams per Deciliter .... mg/d

Milligrams per Kilogram (AAMN) .... mg/kg

Milligrams per Liter (GNE) .... $Mg/_1$

Milligrams per Liter .... MG/L

Milligrams per Square Decimeter per Day .... MDD

Millihenry (GPO) .... mH

Millihertz (WDAA) .... MHZ

Millihour [*One-thousandth of an hour*] (AAG) .... mH

Milli-Inch .... mil

Milli-Inches per Year [*Corrosion technology*] .... m/yr

Milli-Inches per Year [*Corrosion technology*] .... MPY

Milli-International Unit .... mIU

Milli-International Unit per Milliliter (DAVI) .... milli IU/ml

Millikelvin .... mK

Milliken and Vertrees' Tennessee Code [*A publication*] (DLA) .... Mill & V Code

Milliken Research Corp., Research Library, Spartanburg, SC [*Library symbol Library of Congress*] (LCLS) .... ScSpM

Millikin University, Decatur, IL [*OCLC symbol*] (OCLC) .... ICK

Millilambert .... mL

Millilambert .... MIL

Milliliter .... mL

Milliliter .... mL

Milliliter (IDOE) .... ml

Milliliters per Liter (EG) .... ML/L

Milliliters per Minute per Square Meter (CPH) .... $ml/min/m^2$

Milliliters per Second .... ML/S

Millimass Unit (IAA) .... MMAU

Millimass Unit (DEN) .... MMU

Millime [*Monetary unit*] [*Tunisia*] .... M

Millimeter [*Metric*] .... mm

Millimeter .... MM

Millimeter (DFIT) .... MSM

Millimeter and Submillimeter Conference (MCD) .... MSM

Millimeter Array [*Astronomy*] .... MMA

Millimeter Insular Line Integrated Circuit (PDAA) .... MILIC

Millimeter/Microwave Integrated Circuit .... MMIC

Millimeter RADAR (MCD) .... MILIRAD

Millimeter Wave .... MMW

Millimeter Wave Amplification by Resonance Saturation (IAA) .... MARS

Millimeter Wave Communications Experiment .... MWCE

Millimeter Wave Contrast Guidance [*Munitions*] (MCD) .... MCG

Millimeter Wave Contrast Seeker (MCD) .... MWCS

Millimeter Wave Device .... MWD

Millimeter Wave Experiment .... MMWE

Millimeter Wave Experiment .... MWE

Millimeter Wave Large Antenna Experiment [*NASA*] (PDAA) .... MWLAE

Millimeter Wave Mixer .... MWM

Millimeter Wave Observatory [*University of Texas at Austin*] [*Research center*] (RCD) .... MWO

Millimeter Wave Propagation .... MWP

Millimeter Wave RADAR Fuze (MCD) .... MILIRAD

Millimeter Wave Radio System (MCD) .... MWRS

Millimeter Wave Seeker Feasibility Demonstration .... MSFD

Millimeter Wave Tube .... MWT

Millimeter Wavelength Oscillator .... MWO

Millimeters of Mercury [*A measurement of pressure*] (MAE) .... mHg

Millimeters of Mercury [*A measurement of pressure*] (KSC) .... mHg

Millimeters Partial Pressure .... mmpp

Millimeters per Hour .... MM/H

Millimeters per Second .... MM/S

Millimeter-Wave Radar (DOMA) .... MWR

Millimicro- [*Now nano*] (IDOE) .... mu

Millimicrometer (IAA) .... M

Millimicron (IAA) .... M

Millimicron [*Microscopy*] (CPH) .... mmm

Millimicron (AAG)	Mu
Millimicron [Nanometer] (IDOE)	mu
Millimole [Mass]	mM
Millimole [Mass]	mmol
Millimole/Liter [Chemistry]	mM/L
Millimole per Liter [Measurement] (DAVI)	mmol/l
Milliner (WGA)	MLNR
Millinery	MILNRY
Millinery	MILNRY
Millinery Credit Association [Defunct] (EA)	MCA
Millinery Distributors Association [British] (BI)	MDA
Millinery Information Bureau (EA)	MIB
Millinery Institute of America [Later, MIB] (EA)	MIA
Millinery Institute of Great Britain (BI)	MIGB
Milling	MIL
Milling [Freight]	MLG
Milling and Baking Division of American Association of Cereal Chemists (EA)	MBDAACC
Millingimbi [Airport symbol]	MGT
Millington, TN [Location identifier FAA] (FAAL)	MIG
Millington, TN [AM radio station call letters]	WMPS
Millington, TN [FM radio station call letters] (RBYB)	WSRR-FM
Millington Township Library, Millington, MI [Library symbol Library of Congress] (LCLS)	MiMill
Millinocket, ME [Location identifier FAA] (FAAL)	LNT
Millinocket, ME [Location identifier FAA] (FAAL)	MLT
Millinocket, ME [AM radio station call letters]	WSYY
Millinocket, ME [FM radio station call letters]	WSYY-FM
Millinocket Memorial Library, Millinocket, ME [Library symbol Library of Congress] (LCLS)	MeMi
Millinocket/Millinocke [Maine] [ICAO location identifier] (ICLI)	KMLT
Millinormal [One one-thousandth of normal]	mN
Milliohms (WDAA)	MOHMS
Milliohms (AD)	mohms
Million	M
Million	MIL
Million	MILL
Million (WDMC)	mm
Million (10^6) Transitions Per Second [Of magnetic storage] (NITA)	MTS
Million (10^6) Words (NITA)	MW
Million Accounting Units (NASA)	MAU
Million Acre Feet [Hydrology]	MAF
Million Adds per Second	MAPS
Million Air, Inc. [ICAO designator] (FAAC)	OXO
Million Ampere Generator [British] (DEN)	MAGGI
Million Barrels	MMB
Million Barrels Daily	MBD
Million Barrels per Day	MBPD
Million Barrels per Day	MMB/D
Million Barrels per Day Oil Equivalent (MHDB)	MBDOE
Million BITs [Binary Digits] per Second [Data transmission speed] [Computer science] (NASA)	MBPS
Million British Thermal Units	MBtu
Million British Thermal Units (MENA)	MMBTU
Million Bytes [Computer science] (BUR)	MB
Million Centimeters (MCD)	MCM
Million Cubic Feet	MCF
Million Cubic Feet	MMCF
Million Cubic Feet a Day	MMCFD
Million Dollar Contract [File] [Military]	MDC
Million Dollar Directory [Dun's Marketing Services] [Parsippany, NJ Database]	MDD
Million Dollar Round Table [Des Plaines, IL] (EA)	MDRT
Million Electron Volts (MCD)	MEV
Million European Units of Account (PDAA)	MEUA
Million Floating-Point Operations per Second [Processing power units] [Computer science]	MFLOPS
Million Floating-Point Operations per Second [Computer science] (ODBW)	Mflops
Million Gallons per Day	MGAL/D
Million Gallons per Day	MGD
Million Gauss Oersted [Unit of energy density]	MGO
Million Instructions per Second	MIP
Million Instructions Per Second [Computer science] (WDMC)	mips
Million Market Edition [US News and World Report]	MME
Million Metric Tons (IMH)	MMT
Million Metric Tons of Standard Fuel	MMTSF
Million Monetary Units (PDAA)	MMU
Million Nighttime Vehicle Mile	MNVM
Million of Kilowatt Hours (MCD)	MKH
Million Operations per Second [Processing power units] [Computer science]	MOPS
Million Pair Feet [Telecommunications] (TEL)	MPF
Million Parsecs [Interstellar space measure]	Mpc
Million Particles per Cubic Foot [in air]	MPPCF
Million Pulses per Second (AD)	mpps
Million Standard Cubic Feet per Day	MMSCFD
Million Theoretical Operations per Second [Computer science]	MTOPS
Million Ton Miles	MTM
Million Ton Miles/Day (MCD)	MTM/D
Million Tons Heavy Metal	MTHM
Million Tons of Coal Equivalent [A comparative unit of energy content widely used in the oil industry]	MTCE
Million Tons of Oil Equivalent	MTOE
Million Tons per Year	MTY
Million Train Miles	MTM
Million Units	MU
Million US Gallons per Day [AEC, OSW]	M-GPD
Million Vehicle Miles	MVM
Million Volt Amperes	MVA
Million Volts	MV
Million Years	MY
Million Years [Also, MY]	MYR
Million Years Ago	Ma
Million Years Ago	MYA
Million Years before Present [Geology]	MYBP
Million-Dollar Deal	MDD
Millions (10^6) (IDOE)	mega-
Millions of Floating Point Operations per Second (PDAA)	MEGAFLOPS
Millions of Floating Point Operations Per Second [Telecommunications] (ACRL)	MFLOPS
Millions of Instructions per Second [Facetious translations: "Meaningless Indication of Performance"; "Meaningless Instructions per Second"; "Meaningless Indicator of Processor Speed"] [Computer science]	MIPS
Millions of Octane-Barrels per Calendar Day [Petroleum industry]	MMOBCD
Millions of Particles per Cubic Foot (PDAA)	MPCF
Millions of Particles per Cubic Foot of Air (AD)	mppcf
Millions of Standard Cubic Feet (AAG)	MSCF
Millions of Tons per Year [of solids, e.g., coal]	MTPY
Millions of Unusual Small Creatures Lurking Everywhere [Toy by Mattel, Inc.]	MUSCLE
Milliosmol [or Milliosmole] [Chemistry]	mOsm
Milliosmol	mosm
Milliosmole [or Milliosmolar] (AAMN)	mOs
Milliosmole [Measurement] (DAVI)	mOsmol
Millipascal [Unit of pressure]	mPa
Millipascal Second (AD)	mpas
Millipore Corp. [Bedford, MA]	MC
Millipore Corp. [NYSE symbol] (SPSG)	MIL
Millipore Corp. [Associated Press] (SAG)	Millipore
Millipore Corp. [Associated Press] (SAG)	Millipre
Millipore Corp., Bedford, MA [OCLC symbol] (OCLC)	MLP
Millipore Filter [Intravenous therapy] (CPH)	MF
Millirad (AD)	mrad
Milliradian (DEN)	MR
Milliradian (IDOE)	mrad
Milliradians (KSC)	MILS
Milliradians (KSC)	MRAD
Milliradians per Inch	MRAD/IN
Millirem (DEN)	MR
Millirem per Hour (DS)	mrem/h
Milliroentgen	mr
Milliroentgen (AD)	mR
Milliroentgen Equivalent Man (AD)	mrem
Milliroentgen Equivalent Man [Radiation measurement]	MREM
Milliroentgen Equivalent Physical (MAE)	mrep
Milliroentgens per Hour (DS)	mr/h
Milliroentgens per Hour	mr/hr
Milliroentgens per Hour at One Meter	mrhm
Millirutherford	mrd
Millisecond	millisec
Millisecond	ms
Millisecond (WGA)	msc
Millisecond	msec
Milli-Second Delay Detonator [Military] (PDAA)	MSDD
Millisecond Pulsar [Astronomy]	MSP
Millisiemens	mS
Millisievert [Radiation dose]	mSv
Millitesla	mT
Milliunit (AAMN)	mU
Millivolt	mV
Millivolt Ampere [Nuclear energy] (IAA)	MVA
Millivolt Analog-Digital Instrumentation System	MADIS
Millivolt Direct Current [Nuclear energy] (IAA)	MVDC
Millivolt per Centimeter [Nuclear energy] (IAA)	MVCM
Millivolt Potentiometer (IDOE)	MVP
Millivolt to Current [Converter] [Nuclear energy] (NRCH)	MV/I
Millivolts per Meter (DEN)	mV/m
Milliwatt	mW
Milliwatt	mW
Milliwatt Hour	MWH
Milliwatt Logic	mWL
Milliwatt Motorola Resistor Transistor Logic (IAA)	MWMRTL
Milliwatt per Square Centimeter (IAA)	MWCM
Milliwatt Resistor-Transistor Logic (IDOE)	mWRTL
Milliwatts per Square Centimeter	MSC
Milliyetci Demokrasi Partisi [Nationalist Democracy Party] [Turkey Political party] (EY)	MDP
Millon Adolescent Personality Inventory [Personality development test] [Psychology]	MAPI
Millon Behavioral Health Inventory [Personality development test] [Psychology]	MBHI
Millon Clinical Multiaxial Inventory [Psychology]	MCMI
Millrock Development Corp. [Vancouver Stock Exchange symbol]	MRK
Mills [Commonly used] (OPSA)	MILLS
Mills	MLS
Mills (MCD)	MLS
Mills' Annotated Statutes [Colorado] [A publication] (DLA)	Mills Ann St
Mills, Clarence W., Laurel MD [STAC]	MCW

Mills College (GAGS) ... Mills C
Mills College, Oakland, CA [*Library symbol Library of Congress*] (LCLS) ... COMC
Mills Corp. [*Associated Press*] (SAG) ... MillsCp
Mills Corp. [*NYSE symbol*] (SAG) ... MLS
Mill's Logic [*A publication*] (DLA) ... Mill Log
Mills' New York Surrogate's Court Reports [*A publication*] (DLA) ... Mil
Mills' New York Surrogate's Court Reports [*A publication*] (DLA) ... Mill
Mills' New York Surrogate's Court Reports [*A publication*] (DLA) ... Mills
Mills' New York Surrogate's Court Reports [*A publication*] (DLA) ... Mills (NY)
Mills' New York Surrogate's Court Reports [*A publication*] (DLA) ... Mills' Surr Ct
Mills on Eminent Domain [*A publication*] (DLA) ... Mills Em D
Mills on Eminent Domain [*A publication*] (DLA) ... Mills Em Dom
Mill's South Carolina Constitutional Reports [*A publication*] (DLA) ... Mil
Mill's South Carolina Constitutional Reports [*A publication*] (DLA) ... Mill
Mill's South Carolina Constitutional Reports [*A publication*] (DLA) ... Mill Const
Mill's South Carolina Constitutional Reports [*A publication*] (DLA) ... Mill Const (SC)
Millsaps College, Jackson, MS [*OCLC symbol*] (OCLC) ... MMC
Millsaps College, Jackson, MS [*Library symbol Library of Congress*] (LCLS) ... MsJMC
Millstadt Community Consolidated School District 160, Millstadt, IL [*Library symbol Library of Congress*] (LCLS) ... IMilsSD
Millstone Nuclear Power Station (NRCH) ... MNPS
Milltown Public Library, Milltown, NJ [*Library symbol Library of Congress*] (LCLS) ... NjMilt
Millville Daily, Millville, NJ [*Library symbol Library of Congress*] (LCLS) ... NjMilvM
Millville/Millville [*New Jersey*] [*ICAO location identifier*] (ICLI) ... KMIV
Millville, NJ [*Location identifier FAA*] (FAAL) ... MIV
Millville, NJ [*Location identifier FAA*] (FAAL) ... RNB
Millville, NJ [*Location identifier FAA*] (FAAL) ... VCN
Millville, NJ [*FM radio station call letters*] ... WBSS
Millville, NJ [*AM radio station call letters*] ... WREY
Millville Public Library, Millville, NJ [*Library symbol Library of Congress*] (LCLS) ... NjMilv
Millwall Dock [*British*] ... MD
Millwork ... MLLWK
Millwork Cost Bureau [*Later, AWI*] ... MCB
Millwright Group (EA) ... MG
Milner & Steer, Edmonton, Alberta [*Library symbol National Library of Canada*] (BIB) ... AEMS
Milner. Questions de Droit [*A publication*] (DLA) ... MQD
Milo [*Maine*] [*Seismograph station code, US Geological Survey*] (SEIS) ... MIM
Milo Municipal Library, Alberta [*Library symbol National Library of Canada*] (NLC) ... AMILM
Milo Public Library, Milo, IA [*Library symbol Library of Congress*] (LCLS) ... IaMil
Milos [*Greece*] [*ICAO location identifier*] (ICLI) ... LGML
Milos [*Greece*] [*Airport symbol*] (OAG) ... MLO
MILPERCEN Initial Recruiting and Training Plan (MCD) ... MIRAT
Milrinone [*Biochemistry*] ... MR
Milroy Public Schools, Milan, MN [*Library symbol*] [*Library of Congress*] (LCLS) ... MnMlyPS
MILSTAR [*Military Strategic and Tactical Relay System*] **Mobile Consolidation and Control Station** (DWSG) ... MMCCS
Milstead [*AAR code*] ... MLST
Milstep Central Data Collection Point [*McClellan Air Force Base*] ... CDCP
MILSTRIP [*Military Standard Requisitioning and Issue Procedure*] **Routing Identifier** (AFM) ... MRI
Milstrip Routing Identifier (AD) ... mri
Miltarpsykologiska Institutet [*Military Psychology Institute*] [*Sweden*] (PDAA) ... MPI
Milton [*England*] ... MILT
Milton Bradley Ltd. [*British*] ... MB
Milton Central Library, Milton, ON, Canada [*Library symbol Library of Congress*] (LCLS) ... CaOMil
Milton Clinical Multi-Axial Inventory [*Psychology*] (DAVI) ... MCMAI
Milton College, Milton, WI [*Library symbol Library of Congress*] (LCLS) ... WMiltM
Milton Elementary School, Custar, OH [*Library symbol*] [*Library of Congress*] (LCLS) ... OCuME
Milton Federal Financial [*NASDAQ symbol*] (TTSB) ... MFFC
Milton Federal Financial Corp. [*NASDAQ symbol*] (SAG) ... MFFC
Milton Federal Financial Corp. [*Associated Press*] (SAG) ... MiltonF
Milton, FL [*Location identifier FAA*] (FAAL) ... NDZ
Milton, FL [*Location identifier FAA*] (FAAL) ... NFJ
Milton, FL [*Location identifier FAA*] (FAAL) ... NSE
Milton, FL [*Location identifier FAA*] (FAAL) ... NVK
Milton, FL [*Location identifier FAA*] (FAAL) ... NXN
Milton, FL [*AM radio station call letters*] ... WEBY
Milton, FL [*AM radio station call letters*] ... WECM
Milton, FL [*FM radio station call letters*] ... WEGS
Milton, FL [*FM radio station call letters*] ... WTGF
Milton, FL [*FM radio station call letters*] ... WXBM
Milton H. Erickson Foundation (EA) ... MHEF
Milton Helpern Institute of Forensic Medicine (EA) ... MHIFM
Milton Historical Society, Milton, MA [*Library symbol Library of Congress*] (LCLS) ... MMHi
Milton Keynes [*Russian city*] ... MK
Milton, MA [*FM radio station call letters*] ... WMLN
Milton Memorial Library, Milton, WA [*Library symbol*] [*Library of Congress*] (LCLS) ... WaMil
Milton Olive Middle School, Wyandanch, NY [*Library symbol*] [*Library of Congress*] (LCLS) ... NWyaOMS
Milton, PA [*Location identifier FAA*] (FAAL) ... MIP
Milton, PA [*AM radio station call letters*] ... WMLP
Milton, PA [*FM radio station call letters*] ... WVLY
Milton Public Library, Milton, MA [*Library symbol Library of Congress*] (LCLS) ... MMilt
Milton Public Library, Milton, PA [*Library symbol Library of Congress*] (LCLS) ... PMi
Milton Public Library, Ontario [*Library symbol National Library of Canada*] (NLC) ... OMIL
Milton Society of America (EA) ... MSA
Milton, WV [*FM radio station call letters*] (RBYB) ... WFXN
Milton, WV [*FM radio station call letters*] ... WZZW
Miltona Elementary School, Miltona, MN [*Library symbol*] [*Library of Congress*] (LCLS) ... MnMilE
Milton-Freewater [*Oregon*] [*Seismograph station code, US Geological Survey*] (SEIS) ... MFW
Milton-Freewater, OR [*AM radio station call letters*] ... KLKY
Milton-Freewater, OR [*FM radio station call letters*] (RBYB) ... KLKY-FM
Milton-Freewater Public Library, Milton-Freewater, OR [*Library symbol Library of Congress*] (LCLS) ... OrMf
Miltonvale Wesleyan College [*Kansas*] ... MWC
Miltope Group [*NASDAQ symbol*] (TTSB) ... MILT
Miltope Group, Inc. [*NASDAQ symbol*] (NQ) ... MILT
Miltope Group, Inc. [*Associated Press*] (SAG) ... Miltope
Milverton Public Library, Milverton, ON, Canada [*Library symbol*] [*Library of Congress*] (LCLS) ... CaOMILV
Milverton Public Library, Ontario [*Library symbol National Library of Canada*] (NLC) ... OMILV
Milward's Irish Ecclesiastical Reports [*1819-43*] [*A publication*] (DLA) ... Milw
Milward's Irish Ecclesiastical Reports [*1819-43*] [*A publication*] (DLA) ... Milw Ir Ecc Rep
Milwaukee [*Wisconsin*] ... MIL
Milwaukee [*Wisconsin*] ... Milw
Milwaukee [*Wisconsin*] [*Airport symbol*] (OAG) ... MKE
Milwaukee [*Wisconsin*] [*Seismograph station code, US Geological Survey Closed*] (SEIS) ... MLW
Milwaukee and Greatlakes MG [*Morris Garage*] **Motorcar Group** ... MGMGMG
Milwaukee & St. Paul Railway ... M & StP
Milwaukee & Superior Railroad ... M & S
Milwaukee Area Technical College (PCM) ... MATC
Milwaukee Area Technical College, North Campus Center Library, Mequon, WI [*Library symbol Library of Congress*] (LCLS) ... WMTC-N
Milwaukee Area Technical College, South Campus Center Library, Oak Creek, WI [*Library symbol Library of Congress*] (LCLS) ... WMTC-S
Milwaukee Area Technical College, West Campus Center Library, West Allis, WI [*Library symbol Library of Congress*] (LCLS) ... WMTC-W
Milwaukee Blood Center, Inc., Milwaukee, WI [*Library symbol Library of Congress*] (LCLS) ... WMMB
Milwaukee Children's Hospital, Milwaukee, WI [*Library symbol Library of Congress*] (LCLS) ... WMMC
Milwaukee Contract Management District (SAA) ... MICMD
Milwaukee County General Hospital, Milwaukee, WI [*Library symbol Library of Congress*] (LCLS) ... WMCG
Milwaukee County Historical Society, Milwaukee, WI [*Library symbol Library of Congress*] (LCLS) ... WMCHi
Milwaukee County Institutions, Mental Health Centers Libraries, Milwaukee, WI [*Library symbol Library of Congress*] (LCLS) ... WMCM
Milwaukee Electric Railway & Transport Co. [*AAR code*] ... MERT
Milwaukee Exposition and Convention Center and Arena ... MECCA
Milwaukee/General Mitchell Field [*Wisconsin*] [*ICAO location identifier*] (ICLI) ... KMKE
Milwaukee Grain Exchange [*Defunct*] ... MGE
Milwaukee Institute of Technology [*Wisconsin*] ... MIT
Milwaukee Journal [*A newspaper*] ... MJ
Milwaukee Land [*AMEX symbol*] (TTSB) ... MWK
Milwaukee Land Co. [*Associated Press*] (SAG) ... MilwLnd
Milwaukee Land Co. [*AMEX symbol*] (SPSG) ... MWK
Milwaukee Lawyer [*A publication*] (DLA) ... Milwaukee Law
Milwaukee Psychiatric Hospital, Wauwatosa, WI [*Library symbol Library of Congress*] (LCLS) ... WWaMP
Milwaukee Public Library (AD) ... MPL
Milwaukee Public Library, Milwaukee, WI [*OCLC symbol*] (OCLC) ... GZD
Milwaukee Public Library, Milwaukee, WI [*Library symbol Library of Congress*] (LCLS) ... WM
Milwaukee Public Museum (AD) ... MPM
Milwaukee Public Museum (AD) ... MPS
Milwaukee Public Museum, Reference Library, Milwaukee, WI [*Library symbol Library of Congress*] (LCLS) ... WMMus
Milwaukee School of Engineering (GAGS) ... Milwau Sch Eng
Milwaukee School of Engineering [*Wisconsin*] ... MSE
Milwaukee School of Engineering [*Wisconsin*] ... MSOE
Milwaukee School of Engineering, Walter Schroeder Library, Milwaukee, WI [*Library symbol Library of Congress*] (LCLS) ... WMSE
Milwaukee Technical College, Milwaukee, WI [*Library symbol Library of Congress*] (LCLS) ... WMTC
Milwaukee, WI [*Location identifier FAA*] (FAAL) ... BAE
Milwaukee, WI [*Location identifier FAA*] (FAAL) ... BLY
Milwaukee, WI [*Location identifier FAA*] (FAAL) ... GMF
Milwaukee, WI [*Location identifier FAA*] (FAAL) ... MWC
Milwaukee, WI [*Location identifier FAA*] (FAAL) ... PXY
Milwaukee, WI [*Television station call letters*] ... WCGV
Milwaukee, WI [*Television station call letters*] ... WDJT
Milwaukee, WI [*AM radio station call letters*] ... WEMP
Milwaukee, WI [*AM radio station call letters*] ... WISN
Milwaukee, WI [*Television station call letters*] ... WISN-TV
Milwaukee, WI [*Television station call letters*] ... WITI
Milwaukee, WI [*FM radio station call letters*] (RBYB) ... WJZI-FM
Milwaukee, WI [*FM radio station call letters*] ... WKLH

Milwaukee, WI [*FM radio station call letters*] ... WKTI
Milwaukee, WI [*FM radio station call letters*] ... WLTQ
Milwaukee, WI [*FM radio station call letters*] ... WLUM
Milwaukee, WI [*AM radio station call letters*] ... WLZR
Milwaukee, WI [*FM radio station call letters*] ... WLZR-FM
Milwaukee, WI [*FM radio station call letters*] ... WMSE
Milwaukee, WI [*Television station call letters*] ... WMVS
Milwaukee, WI [*Television station call letters*] ... WMVT
Milwaukee, WI [*FM radio station call letters*] ... WMWK
Milwaukee, WI [*FM radio station call letters*] ... WMYX
Milwaukee, WI [*AM radio station call letters*] ... WNOV
Milwaukee, WI [*AM radio station call letters*] ... WOKY
Milwaukee, WI [*FM radio station call letters*] ... WQFM
Milwaukee, WI [*AM radio station call letters*] ... WTMJ
Milwaukee, WI [*Television station call letters*] ... WTMJ-TV
Milwaukee, WI [*FM radio station call letters*] ... WUWM
Milwaukee, WI [*FM radio station call letters*] ... WVCY
Milwaukee, WI [*Television station call letters*] ... WVCY-TV
Milwaukee, WI [*Television station call letters*] ... WVTV
Milwaukee, WI [*FM radio station call letters*] ... WYMS
Milwaukee, WI [*FM radio station call letters*] ... WZTR
Milwaukee, WI [*Location identifier FAA*] (FAAL) ... XJN
Milwaukee-Downer College [*Later, Lawrence University*] [*Wisconsin*] ... MDC
Milwaukie High School, Milwaukie, OR [*Library symbol Library of Congress*] (LCLS) ... OrMiHS
Milwaukie, OR [*AM radio station call letters*] ... KXYQ
Milwaukie Public Library, Milwaukie, OR [*Library symbol Library of Congress*] (LCLS) ... OrMi
Milwhite Co., Houston, TX [*Library symbol Library of Congress*] (LCLS) ... TxHMM
Mimeograph (AAGC) ... Mim
Mimeographed (ADA) ... MIM
Mimeographed (ADA) ... MIMEO
Mimimum Distance Decoding Rule (IAA) ... MDDR
Mimimum Off-Route Altitude [*Aviation*] (DA) ... MORA
Mimino [*Former USSR*] [*FAA designator*] (FAAC) ... MIM
Mimizan [*France ICAO location identifier*] (ICLI) ... LFCZ
Mims, FL [*AM radio station call letters*] ... WPGS
Mina [*Nevada*] [*Seismograph station code, US Geological Survey*] (SEIS) ... MNA
Mina [*Nevada*] [*Seismograph station code, US Geological Survey*] (SEIS) ... MNV
Mina Airline Company [*Egypt*] [*FAA designator*] (FAAC) ... NAB
Mina, NV [*Location identifier FAA*] (FAAL) ... MVA
Minab [*Iran*] [*ICAO location identifier*] (ICLI) ... OIKO
Minaean [*or Minean*] (BJA) ... Min
Minami Daito Jima [*Volcano Islands*] [*Airport symbol*] (OAG) ... MMD
Minami Daito Jima [*Volcano Islands*] [*Seismograph station code, US Geological Survey*] (SEIS) ... MVI
Minami Daito Jima [*Ryukyu Islands*] [*ICAO location identifier*] (ICLI) ... ROMD
Minamitorishima [*Japan ICAO location identifier*] (ICLI) ... RJAM
Minard, Bryant H., Pennsauken NJ [*STAC*] ... MBH
Minaret (VRA) ... mnrt
Minatitlan [*Mexico ICAO location identifier*] (ICLI) ... MMMT
Minatitlan [*Mexico*] [*Airport symbol*] (OAG) ... MTT
Minced Fish Meat [*Food technology*] ... MFM
Minchumina, AK [*Location identifier FAA*] (FAAL) ... MHM
Mind Association (EA) ... MA
Mind/Body Medical Institute ... MBMI
Mind Development and Control Association (EA) ... MDCA
Mind Extension University [*Cable television channel*] ... MEU
Mind Freedom ... MF
Mind Science Foundation (EA) ... MSF
Mind Your Own Business [*Slang*] ... MYOB
Mind Your Own Business, Buster [*Slang*] ... MYOBB
Mind-Altering Drug ... MAD
Mindanao Independence Movement [*Philippines*] [*Political party*] ... MIM
Minden, LA [*AM radio station call letters*] ... KASO
Minden, LA [*FM radio station call letters*] ... KASO-FM
Minden, LA [*Location identifier FAA*] (FAAL) ... MNE
Minden, NV [*Location identifier FAA*] (FAAL) ... MEV
Mindiptana [*Indonesia*] [*Airport symbol*] (OAG) ... MDP
Mindiptana [*Indonesia*] [*ICAO location identifier*] (ICLI) ... WAKD
Mindless Operative of the Devil [*Mods - Facetious translation referring to Moderate Republicians*] ... Mod
Mind-Machine Interaction Research Center [*University of Florida*] [*Research center*] (RCD) ... MMIRC
MindSpring Enterprises [*NASDAQ symbol*] (TTSB) ... MSPG
MindSpring Enterprises, Inc. [*Associated Press*] (SAG) ... MindSpr
MindSpring Enterprises, Inc. [*NASDAQ symbol*] (SAG) ... MSPG
Mindy Explorations Ltd. [*Vancouver Stock Exchange symbol*] ... MDE
Mine ... M
Mine [*or Minecraft*] [*Navy*] ... MIN
Mine Advisory Committee [*NAS-NRC*] (MCD) ... MAC
Mine and Torpedo Detector [*SONAR*] [*Navy*] ... MATD
Mine Assembly Depot [*Navy*] ... MAD
Mine Assembly Facilities ... MINEASYFAC
Mine Assembly Team [*Navy*] (NVT) ... MAT
Mine Clearance [*British military*] (DMA) ... MC
Mine Clearing Line Charge [*Army*] ... MCLC
Mine Clearing Line Charge [*Army*] (INF) ... MICLIC
Mine Clearing Roller [*Military*] (INF) ... MCR
Mine Countermeasure Station [*Military*] ... MINECTRMEASSTA
Mine Countermeasure Support [*Obsolete Military*] ... MCS
Mine Countermeasure Support Ship [*Military*] (PDAA) ... MCSS
Mine Countermeasure Tender [*Navy symbol*] ... AM
Mine Counter-Measure Vessel ... MCMV
Mine Countermeasures (NG) ... MCM
Mine Countermeasures Catamaran [*Military*] ... MCMCAT
Mine Countermeasures Command and Support Ship [*Navy*] ... MCC
Mine Countermeasures Helicopter Controller (MCD) ... MCMHC
Mine Counter-Measures Hovercraft [*Military*] (PDAA) ... MCMH
Mine Countermeasures Operations [*Military*] (NVT) ... MCMOPS
Mine Countermeasures Ship [*Navy symbol*] ... MCS
Mine Countermeasures Station [*Military*] (DNAB) ... MINECTRMEASTA
Mine Countermeasures Vessel [*or Vehicle*] (NATG) ... MCMV
Mine/Countermine Casualty Assessment Producing System (MCD) ... MICAPS
Mine Defense Laboratory [*Panama City, Florida*] [*Navy*] ... MDL
Mine Defense Laboratory [*Navy*] ... MINEDEFLAB
Mine Depot [*Naval*] ... MD
Mine Detection and Avoidance System (MCD) ... MIDAS
Mine Detection Set ... MDS
Mine Dispatch Control ... MDC
Mine Disposal ... MD
Mine Disposal Unit ... MDU
Mine Disposal Weapon (NATG) ... MDW
Mine Division [*Navy*] ... MINDIV
Mine Firing Mechanism ... MFM
Mine Flotilla [*Navy*] ... MINFLOT
Mine Force, Pacific Fleet, Support Group Unit (DNAB) ... MINEPACSUPPGRU
Mine Fuse Train ... MFT
Mine Health Research Advisory Committee [*National Institute for Occupational Safety and Health*] [*Morgantown, WV*] (EGAO) ... MHRAC
Mine Hunter Experimental ... MHX
Mine Identification and Neutralization (PDAA) ... MIN
Mine Inspectors' Institute of America (EA) ... MIIA
Mine Issuing Ship ... MIS
Mine Layer (WDAA) ... ML
Mine Neutralization System [*Military*] (CAAL) ... MNS
Mine Operating System (PDAA) ... MINOS
Mine Planter (NATG) ... MPL
Mine Production Report ... MPR
Mine Radiographic Outfit [*Military*] (PDAA) ... MRO
Mine Rake (DWSG) ... MR
Mine Readiness/Certification Inspection (MCD) ... MRCI
Mine Run (AD) ... mr
Mine Safety and Health Administration [*Department of Labor*] ... MSHA
Mine Safety and Health Administration, Denver, Denver, CO [*OCLC symbol*] (OCLC) ... ULM
Mine Safety Appl [*NASDAQ symbol*] (TTSB) ... MNES
Mine Safety Appliance ... MSA
Mine Safety Appliances Co. [*Associated Press*] (SAG) ... MineSf
Mine Safety Appliances Co. [*NASDAQ symbol*] (NQ) ... MNES
Mine Safety Appliances Co., Pittsburgh, PA [*Library symbol Library of Congress*] (LCLS) ... PPiMS
Mine Search System [*Navy*] (DOMA) ... MSS
Mine Smelter and Refinery Databank [*Commodities Research Unit Ltd.*] [*Information service or system*] (CRD) ... MSR
Mine Squadron [*Navy*] ... MINRON
Mine Subsidence Board [*New South Wales, Australia*] ... MSB
Mine Ventilation System [*Engineering*] ... MVS
Mine Warfare (NVT) ... MIW
Mine Warfare ... MW
Mine Warfare and Clearance Diving [*Navy British*] ... MCD
Mine Warfare Evaluation Detachment ... MINEVDET
Mine Warfare Evaluation Model ... MWEM
Mine Warfare Exercise (NVT) ... MINEX
Mine Warfare Forces, Atlantic [*Navy*] ... MINLANT
Mine Warfare Forces, Pacific [*Navy*] ... MINPAC
Mine Warfare Operations (NVT) ... MWFOPS
Mine Warfare Project Office [*Naval Material Command*] ... MWPO
Mine Warfare Technician [*Navy*] (DNAB) ... MINWARTECH
Mine Warning (NATG) ... MW
Mine Watching RADAR (NATG) ... MWR
Mine Workers Union [*South Africa*] (IMH) ... MWU
Mine-Clearing Blade System [*Military*] (INF) ... MCBS
Minecraft Battle Force, Pacific Fleet ... MINBATFOR
Mined Land Conservation Conference [*Later, BCR*] ... MLCC
Mine-Dispensing Vehicle [*Army*] ... MDV
Minefield Planning Folder [*Navy*] (DOMA) ... MFPF
Minefield Reconnaissance and Detector System [*Army*] ... MIRADOR
Mine-Hauling Bogie [*Mining engineering*] ... MHB
Minehunter, Auxiliary [*Navy symbol Obsolete*] ... MHA
Minehunter Catamaran [*Military*] ... MHCAT
Minehunter, Coastal [*Navy symbol*] ... MHC
Minehunter Ocean [*Navy*] (ANA) ... MHO
Minehunter Sweeper Ocean [*Navy*] (ANA) ... MHSO
Mine-Hunting Control Officer (NATG) ... MHCO
[*A*] **Minehunting SONAR** (MCD) ... AMS
Mineiros [*Brazil*] [*Airport symbol*] (AD) ... MRX
Minelayer [*Navy symbol NATO*] ... CM
Minelayer [*or Minelaying*] ... ML
Minelayer Auxiliary Ship [*Navy symbol Obsolete*] ... MMA
Minelayer, Coastal [*Navy symbol Obsolete*] ... MMC
Minelayer, Fast [*Navy symbol*] ... MMD
Minelayer Fleet [*Navy symbol Obsolete*] ... MM
Minelayer, Fleet [*Navy symbol Obsolete*] ... MMF
Minelaying, Minesweeping, and Mine-Hunting Exercise [*NATO*] (NATG) ... MINEX
Minelaying Submarine [*Navy symbol*] ... APS
Mineman [*Navy rating*] ... MN
Mineman, Chief [*Navy rating*] ... MNC
Mineman, First Class [*Navy rating*] ... MN1
Mineman, Master Chief [*Navy rating*] ... MNCM

Mineman, Second Class [*Navy rating*] ... MN2
Mineman, Senior Chief [*Navy rating*] ... MNCS
Mineman, Third Class [*Navy rating*] ... MN3
Mine-Neutralization Vehicle [*Military*] (MCD) ... MNV
Mineo [*Sicily*] [*Seismograph station code, US Geological Survey Closed*] (SEIS) ... MNE
Mineola High School, Garden City Park, NY [*Library symbol Library of Congress*] (LCLS) ... NGcMH
Mineola High School, Garden City Park, NY [*Library symbol*] [*Library of Congress*] (LCLS) ... NGcpMH
Mineola Junior High School, Mineola, NY [*Library symbol Library of Congress*] (LCLS) ... NMinMJ
Mineola Memorial Library, Mineola, NY [*Library symbol Library of Congress*] (LCLS) ... NMin
Mineola Middle School, Mineola, NY [*Library symbol*] [*Library of Congress*] (LCLS) ... NMinMS
Mineola, NY [*AM radio station call letters*] ... WTHE
Mineola, TX [*FM radio station call letters*] ... KMOO-FM
Mineola, TX [*AM radio station call letters*] ... KVCI
Miner Sentence Completion Scale [*Psychology*] ... MSCS
Minerais LAC Ltee., Malartic, Quebec [*Library symbol National Library of Canada*] (NLC) ... QMAMI
Mineral [*California*] [*Seismograph station code, US Geological Survey*] (SEIS) ... MIN
Mineral ... MIN
Mineral ... MINRL
Mineral (MSA) ... MNRL
Mineral (VRA) ... mnrl
Mineral ... MNRL
Mineral Basal Medium [*Microbiology*] ... MBM
Mineral Constitution Laboratories [*Pennsylvania State University*] [*Research center*] (RCD) ... MCL
Mineral County Public Library, Superior, MT [*Library symbol*] [*Library of Congress*] (LCLS) ... MtSu
Mineral Deposit Inventory Database [*Ontario Geological Survey*] [*Information service or system Canada*] (CRD) ... MDI
Mineral Dust Airway Disease [*Medicine*] (DMAA) ... MDAD
Mineral Economics and Management Society ... MEMS
Mineral Engineer ... Min E
Mineral Engineer (PGP) ... Minl E
Mineral Exploration Research Institute [*See also IREM*] [*Canada Research center*] (RCD) ... MERI
Mineral Fiber Products Bureau ... MFPB
Mineral Industries Census ... MIC
Mineral Industry Location System [*Bureau of Mines*] [*Information service or system*] (IID) ... MILS
Mineral Industry Research Laboratory ... MIRL
Mineral Industry Research Organisation [*British*] (DBA) ... MIRO
Mineral Industry Survey [*Department of Commerce*] (GFGA) ... MIS
Mineral Information Institute (EA) ... MII
Mineral Information Section [*Natural Environment Research Council*] (IID) ... MIS
Mineral Insulated [*Cable*] (NRCH) ... MI
Mineral Insulated, Copper Covered [*Cable*] ... MICC
Mineral Insulated, Metal Sheathed [*Cable*] ... MIMS
Mineral Insulation Manufacturers Association (EA) ... MIMA
Mineral Lease (ADA) ... ML
Mineral Nyye Vody [*Former USSR Airport symbol*] (OAG) ... MRV
Mineral Oil ... MO
Mineral Order [*Defense Minerals Exploration Administration*] [*Department of the Interior A publication*] (DLA) ... MO
Mineral Point, WI [*Location identifier FAA*] (FAAL) ... MRJ
Mineral Policy Center (EA) ... MPC
Mineral Processing Technology [*Canada Department of Energy, Mines, and Resources*] [*Information service or system*] (CRD) ... MINPROC
Mineral Range Railroad (IIA) ... MR
Mineral Resource Simulation Model (PDAA) ... MIRSIM
Mineral Resources Data System [*US Geological Survey*] [*Information service or system*] (IID) ... MRDS
Mineral Resources Institute [*University of Alabama*] [*Research center*] (RCD) ... MRI
Mineral Resources International Ltd. [*Toronto Stock Exchange symbol*] ... MRI
Mineral Respurces Development Laboratory [*Australia*] ... MRDL
Mineral Rubber ... MR
Mineral Rubber (AD) ... mr
Mineral Salts Medium [*Medicine*] (DMAA) ... MSM
Mineral Water Co. of Canada (ECON) ... MWCC
Mineral Wells [*Texas*] [*ICAO location identifier*] (ICLI) ... KMWL
Mineral Wells [*Texas*] [*Airport symbol*] (AD) ... MWL
Mineral Wells, TX [*AM radio station call letters*] ... KJSA
Mineral Wells, TX [*FM radio station call letters*] ... KYXS
Mineral Wells, TX [*Location identifier FAA*] (FAAL) ... MQP
Mineral Wells, TX [*Location identifier FAA*] (FAAL) ... MWL
Mineral Workings Act [*Town planning*] [*British*] ... MWA
Mineral-Insulated Copper-Sheathed [*Cable*] (IEEE) ... MICS
Mineralny Vody Department of Cibil Aviation [*Former USSR*] [*FAA designator*] (FAAC) ... MVD
Mineralnye Vody [*Former USSR ICAO location identifier*] (ICLI) ... URMM
Mineralo-Corticoid [*Endocrinology*] ... M-C
Mineralo-Corticoid Receptor [*Endocrinology*] ... MR
Mineralogical ... MINERALOG
Mineralogical Association of Canada ... MAC
Mineralogical Society of America (EA) ... MSA
Mineralogical Society of Great Britain and Ireland (EAIO) ... MSGBI
Mineralogy ... MIN
Mineralogy ... MINERAL
Mineralogy (ROG) ... MINY
Mineralogy Laboratory, Iron Ore Co., Sept-Iles, Quebec [*Library symbol National Library of Canada*] (NLC) ... QSIIOM
Mineral-Oil Tolerance [*of resin solutions*] ... MOT
Minerals and Materials Research Programs [*North Carolina State University*] [*Research center*] (RCD) ... MMRP
Minerals Availability System [*Bureau of Mines*] [*Information service or system*] (IID) ... MASNC
Minerals Availability System/Minerals Industry Location Subsystem [*Bureau of Mines*] [*Database*] ... MAS/MILS
Minerals Data Base [*of the Law of the Sea*] (GNE) ... MINDAT
Minerals Data System [*Database*] ... MDS
Minerals Engineering Society [*British*] ... MES
Minerals Management Service [*Department of the Interior Washington, DC*] ... MMS
Minerals, Metals, and Materials Society (EA) ... MMMS
Minerals, Metals, and Materials Society (EA) ... TMS
Minerals, Mining, and Metallurgy ... MM & M
Minerals, Oils, and Resources Shares Fund [*British*] ... MORES
Minerals Research Laboratory (MCD) ... MRL
Minerals Technologies [*NYSE symbol*] (SPSG) ... MTX
Minerals Technologies, Inc. [*Associated Press*] (SAG) ... MinTch
Mineral-Surface Roof [*Technical drawings*] ... MSR
Minerex Resources Ltd. [*Vancouver Stock Exchange symbol Toronto Stock Exchange symbol*] ... MAX
Minerology (DD) ... miner
Miners' Federation of Great Britain (DAS) ... MFed
Miners' International Federation [*See also FIM*] [*Brussels, Belgium*] (EAIO) ... MIF
Miners' Lamp Manufacturers' Association [*British*] (BI) ... MLMA
Miner's Legal Defense Committee [*Defunct*] (EA) ... MLDC
Mine-Run ... MR
Minerva Library [*A publication*] ... ML
Minerva Mikrofilm A/S, Hellerup, Denmark [*Library symbol Library of Congress*] (LCLS) ... MmAS
Mines ... MNS
Mines (AD) ... Mns
Mines Air Service Zambia Ltd. [*ICAO designator*] (FAAC) ... MAZ
Mines and Countermeasures Technical Unit [*Navy*] ... MACTU
Mines and Quarries (AD) ... M&Q
Mines, Countermines, and Demolitions [*Military*] (RDA) ... MCD
Mines Library, Ontario Ministry of Natural Resources, Toronto, Ontario [*Library symbol National Library of Canada*] (NLC) ... OTDM
Mines Road [*California*] [*Seismograph station code, US Geological Survey*] (SEIS) ... MNR
Mines Safety Appliance Research (IEEE) ... MSAR
Minesing Branch, Vespra Township Public Library, Ontario [*Library symbol National Library of Canada*] (BIB) ... OMBVT
Minesweeper [*Navy*] ... M
Minesweeper [*or Minesweeping*] ... MS
Minesweeper, Auxiliary [*Navy symbol Obsolete*] ... MSA
Minesweeper Catamaran [*Military*] ... MSCAT
Minesweeper, Coastal [*Nonmagnetic*] [*Navy symbol*] ... MSC
Minesweeper, Coastal (Old) [*Navy symbol*] ... MSC(O)
Minesweeper, Coastal (Underwater Locator) [*Navy symbol*] ... AMC(U)
Minesweeper, Drone [*Navy symbol*] ... MSD
Minesweeper, Experimental [*Navy symbol*] ... MSX
Minesweeper, Fleet [*Steel hull*] [*Navy symbol*] ... MSF
Minesweeper, Harbor [*Navy symbol Obsolete*] ... AMB
Minesweeper Hunter Vessel ... MSH
Minesweeper, Inshore [*Navy symbol*] ... MSI
Minesweeper, Ocean [*Nonmagnetic*] [*Navy symbol*] ... MSO
Minesweeper, Patrol [*Navy*] (DNAB) ... MSP
Minesweeper, Patrol [*Navy symbol Obsolete*] ... MSR
Minesweeper Refresher Training [*Navy*] (NVT) ... MSRFT
Minesweeper, River [*Navy symbol*] (VNW) ... MLM
Minesweeper, River [*Navy symbol Obsolete*] ... MSM
Minesweeper River [*Navy symbol*] (VNW) ... MSR
Minesweeper, Special [*Device*] [*Navy symbol*] ... MSS
Minesweeping Boat [*Navy symbol*] ... MSB
Minesweeping Launch [*Navy ship symbol*] ... MSL
Minesweeping Motorlaunch [*Navy*] ... MSML
Mineta Resources Ltd. [*Vancouver Stock Exchange symbol*] ... MIR
Ming Mines Ltd. [*Vancouver Stock Exchange symbol*] ... MIG
Mingan [*Canada*] [*Airport symbol Obsolete*] (OAG) ... YLP
Mingle (ABBR) ... MGL
Mingled (ABBR) ... MGLD
Mingling (ABBR) ... MGLG
Mingo National Wildlife Refuge [*Missouri*] (AD) ... MNWR
Minha Carta [*My Respects*] [*Correspondence*] [*Portuguese*] ... m/c
Minha Conta [*My Regards*] [*Correspondence*] [*Portuguese*] ... m/c
Mini Air Passenger Reservation System ... MAPRES
Mini Armored Troop Carrier [*Navy symbol*] ... ATC
Mini Badge Reader (IAA) ... MBR
Mini Bike Association of America (EA) ... MBAA
Mini Car Club of New South Wales [*Australia*] ... MCCNSW
Mini Car Club, USA (EA) ... MCC
Mini Circuits Laboratory (IAA) ... MCL
Mini Computer Systems (NITA) ... MICOS
Mini Conference System (PDAA) ... MCS
Mini Core Processing Subsystem (TEL) ... MCPS
Mini Disc Terminal [*Computer science*] (DGA) ... MDT
Mini Disk [*Audio/video technology*] ... MD
Mini Disk Operating System (IDOE) ... MINIDOS
Mini Instant Keyboard Assembler, Debug, and Operating System [*Computer science*] (MHDI) ... MIKADOS

Mini Landbridge [*MARAD*] (TAG) ... MLB
Mini Lop Rabbit Club of America (EA) ... MLRCA
Mini Mobile Target [*Military*] (CAAL) ... MMT
[*The*] **Mini Page** [*A newspaper supplement*] ... MP
Mini Registry (EA) ... MR
Mini Web Reel (DGA) ... MWR
Mini Workstation (SSD) ... MWS
Mini-Accommodation Center [*In MAC-1, a low-cost, plastic sleeping module promoted by Texas businessman Charles McLaren*] ... MAC
Mini-America's Cup Association (EA) ... MACA
Mini-Attack Drone ... MAD
Miniature [*Horticulture*] ... M
Miniature ... MIN
Miniature ... MINAT
Miniature (VRA) ... minat
Miniature (KSC) ... MINI
Miniature ... MINI
Miniature (MSA) ... MINTR
Miniature Accessory Power Supply ... MINIAPS
Miniature Air Pilot System ... MAPS
Miniature Airborne Telemetry Receiving Station ... MATRS
Miniature Armoured Fighting Vehicle Association (EA) ... MAFVA
Miniature Arms Collectors/Makers Society (EA) ... MACMS
Miniature Attitude Reference System ... MARS
Miniature Autonetics Baseline Equipment ... MABLE
Miniature Ball [*Horticulture*] ... MBa
Miniature Bayonet Cap ... MBC
Miniature Book Society (EA) ... MBS
Miniature Brushless Blower ... MBB
Miniature Bull Terrier Club of America (EA) ... MBTCA
Miniature Button Light ... MBL
Miniature Cartridge Light ... MCL
Miniature Center Cap ... MCC
Miniature Circuit Breaker ... MCB
Miniature Command Unit ... MCU
Miniature Compact (MCD) ... MINI COMP
Miniature Data Acquisition System ... MDAS
Miniature Data Acquisition System ... MIDAS
Miniature Detonating Cord (MCD) ... MDC
Miniature Display Light ... MDL
Miniature Donkey Registry of the United States (EA) ... MDRUS
Miniature Edison Screw ... MES
Miniature Electronic Auto-Collimator ... MINEAC
Miniature Electronic Component (WDAA) ... MINELCO
Miniature Electronic Repair Program (DNAB) ... MERP
Miniature Electrostatic Gyro ... MEG
Miniature Electrostatically Suspended Accelerometer (MCD) ... MESA
Miniature End Plate Current ... MEPC
Miniature End Plate Potential ... MEPP
Miniature Excitatory Junction Potential [*Neurophysiology*] ... MEJC
Miniature Excitatory Postsynaptic Potential [*Neurophysiology*] ... MEPSP
Miniature Excitatory Synaptic Current [*Neurophysiology*] ... MESC
Miniature Excitory Postsynaptic Currents [*Neurobiology*] ... mEPSC
Miniature Eyesafe LASER Infrared Observation Set [*A rangefinder*] ... MELIOS
Miniature Figure Collectors of America (EA) ... MFCA
Miniature Fluxgate Magnetometer ... MFM
Miniature Gate Valve ... MGV
Miniature Golf Association of America (EA) ... MGAA
Miniature Helium Refrigerator ... MHR
Miniature Homing Vehicle [*Missile*] ... MHV
Miniature Hydrogen Generator ... MHG
Miniature Implantable Power System ... MIPS
Miniature, Indicating and Sampling Electronic Respirometer (PDAA) ... MISER
Miniature Individual Transmitter-Receiver Equipment (MCD) ... MITRE
Miniature Inertial Navigation System ... MINS
Miniature Information Storage and Retrieval (PDAA) ... MISAR
Miniature Infrared Alarm ... MIRA
Miniature Infrared Analyzer [*Spectrometer*] ... MIRAN
Miniature Infrared Guidance Sensor ... MIGS
Miniature Insulated Contact Range (PDAA) ... MICRA
Miniature Integrated Data System (MCD) ... MIDS
Miniature Integrating Gyroscope ... MIG
Miniature Interface General-Purpose Economy Terminal [*Computer science*] (MHDB) ... MIGET
Miniature International Racing Association ... MINRA
Miniature Kill Vehicle [*Military*] (SDI) ... MKV
Miniature LASER Weapon Simulator (MCD) ... MLWS
Miniature Linguistic Systems ... MLS
Miniature Low Pass Filter ... MLPF
Miniature Micropower Resistor ... MMR
Miniature Microwave Integrated Circuit ... MMIC
Miniature Moving Target (MCD) ... MMT
Miniature Multipurpose RADIAC Device (MCD) ... MMRD
Miniature Navigation Airborne Computer ... MINAC
Miniature Pendulum Accelerometer (SAA) ... MPA
Miniature Photocell Activator ... MPA
Miniature Piano Enthusiast Club (EA) ... MPEC
Miniature Pinscher Club of America (EA) ... MPCA
Miniature Piston Actuator (MCD) ... MPA
Miniature Portable Unit ... MPU
Miniature Precision Bearing, Inc. ... MPB
Miniature Precision Bearings (AD) ... MPB
Miniature Precision Gyrocompass (IEEE) ... MPG
Miniature Precision Inertial Platform (OA) ... MPIP
Miniature Protector Connector [*Telecommunications*] (TEL) ... MPC
Miniature Quartz Incandescent Lamp ... MQIL
Miniature Quartz Incandescent Lamp (AD) ... mqil
Miniature Quartz Lamp (AD) ... mql
Miniature Quartz Lamp ... MQL
Miniature RADAR Illumination Detector (MCD) ... MIRID
Miniature Radio-Controlled Aerial Target (MCD) ... MRCAT
Miniature Receiver Terminal ... MRT
Miniature Reed Relay ... MRR
Miniature Revolving Joint ... MRJ
Miniature Sample (AAG) ... MISE
Miniature Screw [*Lamp base*] (NTCM) ... MS
Miniature Seismic Intrusion Detector [*DoD*] ... MINISID
Miniature Sensor Technology Integration [*Orbital satellites*] ... MSTI
Miniature Series of Painters [*A publication*] ... MSP
Miniature Sheet of Stamps (AD) ... m/s
Miniature Ship Inertial Navigation System (MCD) ... MINISINS
Miniature Signaling System [*Railway term*] (DCTA) ... MSS
Miniature Situations Test (EDAC) ... MST
Miniature SOFAR [*Sound Fixing and Ranging*] **System** ... MISS
Miniature Solenoid Valve ... MSV
Miniature Stepping Switch ... MSS
Miniature Submarine Laboratory ... MINI-SUBLAB
Miniature Synaptic Calcium Transient [*Neurophysiology*] ... MSCT
Miniature Temperature Pressure Recorder [*Marine science*] (OSRA) ... MTPR
Miniature Temperature Pressure Recorder (USDC) ... MTPR
Miniature Temperature Recorder (USDC) ... MTR
Miniature Template [*Tool*] ... MITP
Miniature Thermal Bar Torch [*Army*] (RDA) ... MTBT
Miniature Trimmer Potentiometer ... MTP
Miniature Truck Association [*Defunct*] (EA) ... MTA
Miniature True Airspeed Computer ... MINITAS
Miniature Tube (NTCM) ... MT
Miniature Variable Inductor ... MVI
Miniature Vehicle (MCD) ... MV
Miniatures Industry Association of America (EA) ... MIAA
Miniaturization of Federal Catalog System Publications ... MINICATS
Miniaturized Ballistic Computer ... MBC
Miniaturized Cassegranian Concentration [*Instrumentation*] ... MCC
Miniaturized Communications [*Navy*] (DNAB) ... MINCOM
Miniaturized Instrumentation (MCD) ... MI
Miniaturized Integrated Telephone Equipment ... MITE
Miniaturized Multiplexes (MCD) ... MINI MUX
Miniaturized Pointing Mount [*Spacelab*] [*NASA*] ... MPM
Miniaturized Sink-Rate Telemetering RADAR ... MASTER
Minicar and Microcar Club (EA) ... MMC
Mini-Channel Communications Control (NITA) ... MCC
Minichromosome Maintenance [*Cytology*] ... MCM
Minicomputer ... MINC
Minicomputer (MSA) ... MNCMPTR
Minicomputer Industry National Interchange [*An association*] (EA) ... MINI
Minicomputer Interfacing Support System [*Computer science*] ... MISS
Mini-Computer Systems Inc. (NITA) ... MCS
Minicomputer Unit (IAA) ... MCU
Minicomputer Users Interest Group [*Later, Mini/Micro Special Interest Group*] (EA) ... MUIG
Minicomputer-Operated Retrieval (Partially Heuristic) System [*Computer science*] ... MORPHS
MINICS Periodicals Data System (NITA) ... MINICS/PDS
Minicube System, Inc., Carlisle PA [*STAC*] ... MIS
Mini-Decay Heat Removal [*Nuclear energy*] (NRCH) ... MDHR
Minidoka Memorial Hospital, Medical Library, Rupert, ID [*Library symbol*] [*Library of Congress*] ... IdRuH
Minidoka National Wildlife Refuge [*Idaho*] (AD) ... MNWR
Minidoka-Acequia District Library, Minidoka, ID [*Library symbol*] [*Library of Congress*] (LCLS) ... IdMin
Mini-Emitter Location System (MCD) ... MINI-ELS
Miniere de Bakwanga [*Zaire*] ... MIBA
Minilab ... ML
Miniliner SRL [*Italy ICAO designator*] (FAAC) ... MNL
Minim ... M
Minim ... MIN
Minim Daughters of Mary Immaculate (TOCD) ... CFMM
Minim Fathers (TOCD) ... OM
Minim Fathers (TOCD) ... om
Mini-Macroeconomic Personal Computer Model [*Department of Energy*] (GFGA) ... MINMAC-PC
Minimal Alveolar Concentration [*Anesthesiology*] ... MAC
Minimal Angle Resolution ... MAR
Minimal APSE [*Ada Program Support Environment*] [*Computer science*] ... MAPSE
Minimal Attended RADAR Station Display (DWSG) ... MARSD
Minimal Auditory Capability Test [*Medicine*] ... MAC
Minimal Aural Dose ... MAD
Minimal Aversion Threshold [*to noise*] ... MAT
Minimal Bactericidal Level ... MBL
Minimal Baryonic Isocurvature [*Galactic science*] ... MBI
Minimal Brain Damage [*or Dysfunction*] ... MBD
Minimal Brain Dysfunction ... MBD
Minimal Brain Dysfunction [*Neurology*] (DAVI) ... MBD
Minimal Cerebral Dysfunction ... MCD
Minimal Change Disease [*Nephrology*] ... MCD
Minimal Change Idiopathic Nephrotic Syndrome [*Medicine*] (DMAA) ... MCINS
Minimal Change Nephropathy [*Medicine*] (DMAA) ... MCN
Minimal Change Nephrotic Syndrome [*Medicine*] (DMAA) ... MCNS
Minimal Computer Load ... MCL
Minimal Cross-Sectional Area [*Radiology*] (DAVI) ... MCSA

Minimal Cut Set [Engineering]	MCS
Minimal Disjunctive Normal Form (MHDB)	MDNF
Minimal Effective Dose [Medicine]	MED
Minimal Erythema Dose [Medicine]	MED
Minimal Flight Forecasting Charts [Air Force]	MFC
Minimal Flight Path	MFP
Minimal Flight Planning Charts [Air Force]	MPC
Minimal Glomerular Change [Nephrology]	MGC
Minimal Identifiable Odor	MIO
Minimal Inhibiting Dose [Medicine]	MID
Minimal Inhibitor Mole Ratio [Biochemistry]	MIMR
Minimal [or Minimum] Inhibitory Concentration	MIC
Minimal Intermittent [Dosage of] Heparin [Pharmacology] (DAVI)	MIH
Minimal Isorrheic Concentration [Medicine]	MIC
Minimal Lactose-Arabinose [Culture medium]	MLA
Minimal Lesion Disease	MLD
Minimal Lesion Glomerulonephritis [Medicine] (DMAA)	MLGN
Minimal Medium [Microbiology]	MM
Minimal Medullary Concentration [Medicine] (MAE)	MMC
Minimal Morbidostatic Dose [Medicine] (MAE)	MMD
Minimal Oxygen Consumption	MOC
Minimal Recognizable Odor [Medicine] (DMAA)	MRO
Minimal Reproductive Unit (AD)	mru
Minimal Reproductive Units [Bacteriology]	MRU
Minimal Residual Disease [Medicine]	MRD
Minimal Response Level [Audiometry]	MRL
Minimal Shift Keying (NITA)	MSK
Minimal Spanning Tree [Computer science]	MST
Minimal Steric Difference [Organic chemistry]	MSD
Minimal Support (DAVI)	MS
Minimal Terminal Communications System (NVT)	MTCS
Minimal Total Processing Time (NITA)	MTPC
Minimal Total Processing Time (IEEE)	MTPT
Minimal Toxic Dose (IEEE)	MTD
Minimal Variant (IAA)	MV
Minimal-Change Glomerular Nephritis [Minimal-change glomerulonephritis] [Nephrology] (DAVI)	MCGN
Minimal-Input Cataloguing System [Loughborough University of Technology]	MINICS
Minimally Attended RADAR (MCD)	MAR
Minimally Distinct Border [Color perception]	MDB
Minimally-Cleaned, Coal-Derived Gas	MCG
Mini-Manned Aircraft System (PDAA)	MMAS
MiniMed, Inc. [Associated Press] (SAG)	MiniMd
MiniMed, Inc. [NASDAQ symbol]	MNMD
MiniMed Inc. [NASDAQ symbol] (TTSB)	MMS
Mini-Mental State [Psychometric testing]	MMS
Mini-Mental State Examination [Psychometrics]	MMSE
Minimization of Earthworks for Vertical Alignment (PDAA)	MINERVA
Minimize Communications	MCOMM
Minimize Individually Negotiated Instruments (AFM)	MINI
Minimobile Data Center [Military]	MDC
Mini-Module Drive (PDAA)	MMD
Minimum (ADA)	M
Minimum (DA)	MIM
Minimum (AFM)	MIN
Minimum (DFIT)	Min
Minimum [A minim measurement] (DAVI)	min
Minimum (DSUE)	MINI
Minimum	MNM
Minimum (AD)	mnm
Minimum Abbreviations [of MAST]	MINABB
Minimum Abbreviations of Serial Titles [A publication]	MAST
Minimum Absolute Deviation [Statistics]	MAD
Minimum Acceptable Compliance Level (IAA)	MACL
Minimum Acceptable Performance [Telecommunications] (TEL)	MAP
Minimum Acceptable Rate of Return (MHDW)	MAR
Minimum Acceptable Reliability	MAR
Minimum Acceptable Value (MCD)	MAV
Minimum Accepted Level of Fill [Military]	MALOF
Minimum Acquisition Flux Density	MAFD
Minimum Acquisition Tracking System (MUGU)	MINIACT
Minimum Additive Waste Stabilization System [Department of Energy]	MAWS
Minimum Adverse Effect Concentration [Pollution technology]	MAEC
Minimum Air Low Noise (PDAA)	MALN
Minimum Airborne Digital Equipment	MADE
Minimum Aircraft [Powered hang gliders, replicas of early flying machines, etc.] [British]	MA
Minimum Airfield Operating Surface [Military]	MAOS
Minimum Allowable Threshold [Chemistry]	MAT
Minimum Altitude at Glide Slope Intersection Inbound [Aviation] (FAAC)	MAGSI
Minimum Altitude over FAcility on Final Approach Course [Aviation] (FAAC)	MAFAP
Minimum Alveolar Concentration [Physiology]	MAC
Minimum Angle of Resolution (MCD)	MAR
Minimum Annual Income (WDAA)	MAI
Minimum Annual Premium (MHDW)	MAP
Minimum Approach Distance (SAA)	MAD
Minimum Association Price (WDAA)	MAP
Minimum Attack Parameter [Military]	MAP
Minimum Attractive Rate of Return [Economics]	MARR
Minimum Audible Field	MAF
Minimum Audible Pressure	MAP
Minimum Autoignition Temperature	MAIT

Minimum AUTOLAND [Automatic Landing] Entry Point (NASA)	MAEP
Minimum Automatic Computer (IEEE)	MIAC
Minimum Automatic Machine for Interpolation and Extrapolation	MAMIE
Minimum Aviation System Performance Standards [FAA] (TAG)	MASPS
Minimum Bactericidal Concentration	MBC
Minimum Best Torque	MBT
Minimum Bid [Philately]	MB
Minimum Bill of Lading (DS)	Min B/L
Minimum Breakdown Voltage	MBV
Minimum Break-Off Height	MBOH
Minimum Burst Altitude (AABC)	MBA
Minimum Call [Television studio on standby]	MC
Minimum Capacitance (IDOE)	C_{min}
Minimum Cell Rate [Telecommunications] (ACRL)	MCR
Minimum Change/Minimum Risk [Mask design concept] [Army] (INF)	MC/MR
Minimum Chi-Square	MCS
Minimum Circumscribed Circle [Manufacturing term]	MCC
Minimum Communications	MINICOM
Minimum Competency Test [Education]	MCT
Minimum Complete-Killing Concentration (MAE)	MCC
Minimum Concentration of Bilirubin [Medicine] (MAE)	MCBR
Minimum Connecting Time [Travel industry]	MCT
Minimum Control Speed for the Landing Approach [Aviation code] (AIA)	Vmcl
Minimum Control Speed in Air [Aviation code] (AIA)	Vmca
Minimum Control Speed on the Ground [Aviation code] (AIA)	Vmcg
Minimum Control Speed with Critical Engine Out (GAVI)	VMC
Minimum Cost Design (MCD)	MCD
Minimum Cost Design Booster (KSC)	MCDB
Minimum Cost Design/Space Launch Vehicle [NASA] (KSC)	MCD/SLV
Minimum Critical Heat Flux Rates [Nuclear energy] (NRCH)	MCHFR
Minimum Critical Heat Flux Ratio [Nuclear energy] (NRCH)	MCHFR
Minimum Critical Leaching Rate	MCLR
Minimum Critical Power Ratio [Nuclear energy] (NRCH)	MCPR
Minimum Critical Size of Ecosystem [Project]	MCSE
Minimum Crossing Altitude [Aviation]	MCA
Minimum Daily Adult Requirement	MDAR
Minimum Daily Requirement [of a vitamin, etc.] [Later, Recommended Daily Requirement FDA]	MDR
Minimum Data Set [Computer science]	MDS
Minimum Decision Altitude (SAA)	MDA
Minimum Delay Data Format (MCD)	MDDF
Minimum Depth (NOAA)	MNDTH
Minimum Descent Altitude [Aviation]	MDA
Minimum Descent Height [Aviation] (FAAC)	MDH
Minimum Detectable Activity [Nuclear energy] (NRCH)	MDA
Minimum Detectable Amount [of radiation] [Analytical chemistry]	MDA
Minimum Detectable Concentration [Analytical chemistry]	MDC
Minimum Detectable Quantity	MDQ
Minimum Detectable Signal	MDS
Minimum Detectable Velocity [Physics]	MDV
Minimum Detection Limit [Chemistry]	MDL
Minimum Discernable System	MDS
Minimum Discernible Pulse (MCD)	MDP
Minimum Discernible Signal [Radio]	MDS
Minimum Discernible System (NASA)	MDS
Minimum Discrimination Information [Statistics]	MDI
Minimum Distribution Incidental Benefit [Finance]	MDIB
Minimum Domian Velocity (IAA)	MDV
Minimum Dosage [Medicine]	MD
Minimum Dose Causing Malformation or Death of 100 Percent of Fetuses [Radiation therapy] (DAVI)	T/LD_{100}
Minimum Due Date per Order	MINDD
Minimum Earnings Level	MEL
Minimum Effect [Pharmacology]	MiE
Minimum Effective Concentration [Medicine]	MEC
Minimum Efficiency Scale	MES
Minimum Electrical Resistance Condition (PDAA)	MERC
Minimum en Route IFR Altitude [FAA] (TAG)	MEA
Minimum Energy Absorbed	MEC
Minimum Energy Curve (IAA)	MEC
Minimum Energy Path [Physical chemistry]	MEP
Minimum Energy Requirements	MER
Minimum Energy Trajectory	MET
Minimum Energy Trajectory Model [Army] (AABC)	MINUET
Minimum Engineered Safety Features (NRCH)	MESF
Minimum Engineering Development (MCD)	MED
Minimum Enroute Altitude	MEA
Minimum Entry Point (MCD)	MEP
Minimum Envelope Weight (MCD)	MEW
Minimum Equipment Level for Training (MCD)	MELT
Minimum Equipment List	MEL
Minimum Equipment List Index (NASA)	MELI
Minimum Equipment List Manual	MELM
Minimum Essential Criteria (MCD)	MEC
Minimum Essential Emergency Communications Network [Military]	MEECN
Minimum Essential Equipment	MEE
Minimum Essential Equipment for Training	MEET
Minimum Essential Force (CINC)	MEF
Minimum Essential Improvement in System Reliability (MCD)	MEISR
Minimum Essential Medium [Culture medium]	MEM
Minimum Essential Support Analysis (MCD)	MESA
Minimum Essential Training Requirements	METR
Minimum Essentials Test [Educational test]	MET
Minimum Expected Loss [Statistics]	MELO
Minimum Explosive Concentration [Safety]	MEC

Minimum Exposure Time	MET
Minimum Eye Height over Threshold [Aviation] (FAAC)	MEHT
Minimum Fatal Dose	MFD
Minimum Film Boiling Flux	MFBF
Minimum Film Formation Temperature [Coating technology]	MFFT
Minimum Film-Forming Temperature [Wax polishes]	MFT
Minimum Final Prediction Error (MHDI)	MFPE
Minimum Flight Altitude [Aviation] (DA)	MFA
Minimum Focusing Distance [Optics]	MFD
Minimum Functional Combat Capability	MFCC
Minimum Gelling Concentration [Hematology]	MGC
Minimum Ground Support Equipment Concept (MCD)	MINGSE
Minimum Hamming Distance [Computer science]	MHD
Minimum Hardware Modification [Aircraft landing]	MHM
Minimum Helium Loss [System]	MHL
Minimum Hemolytic Dose	MHD
Minimum Holding Altitude [Aviation]	MHA
Minimum Identifiable Quantity [Analytical chemistry]	MIQ
Minimum IFR Altitude [FAA] (TAG)	MIA
Minimum Ignition Current (IEEE)	MIC
Minimum Ignition Energy	MIE
Minimum Implementation ADA Programming Support Environment (NITA)	MAPSE
Minimum Import Prices [Economics]	MIP
Minimum Impulse (KSC)	M/I
Minimum Impulse BIT [Binary Digit] [Computer science] (MCD)	MIB
Minimum Impulse Pulse	MIP
Minimum Impulse Pulse	MIP
Minimum Income Requirements (OICC)	MIR
Minimum Independent Failure Element	MIFE
Minimum Individual Training	MIT
Minimum Industrial Sustaining Role (NG)	MISR
Minimum Infective Dose [Bacteriology]	MID
Minimum Inhibitory Concentration [Bactericidal characteristic]	MIC
Minimum Instrument Altitude [Aviation] (AFM)	MIA
Minimum Interference Threshold [Telecommunications] (TEL)	MINIT
Minimum Interval Takeoff	MITO
Minimum Investment [Finance]	MIN INVEST
Minimum Latency Programming	MLP
Minimum Latency Routine	MLR
Minimum Launch Speed [British military] (DMA)	MLS
Minimum Legal Size [Pisciculture]	MLS
Minimum Lending Rate	MLR
Minimum Lethal Concentration	MLC
Minimum Lethal Dose	MLD
Minimum Level Water Stand (NATG)	MLWS
Minimum Line of Detection [Air Force]	MLD
Minimum Line of Interception [Air Force]	MLI
Minimum List Heading [Standard Industrial Classification] (PDAA)	MLH
Minimum Manufacturing Quality	MMQ
Minimum Marginal Return	MMR
Minimum Material Condition [Computer science]	MIN MC
Minimum/Maximum	M/M
Minimum Mean Estimate	MME
Minimum Mean Square (PDAA)	MMS
Minimum Mean Square Error	MMSE
Minimum Mean Squared Error	MMSE
Minimum Miscibility Pressure [Physical chemistry]	MMP
Minimum Modified Chi-Squared [Statistics]	MMCS
Minimum Monthly Balance [Finance]	MMB
Minimum Monthly Maintenance Charge (MHDW)	MMMC
Minimum Mycoplasmacidal Concentration [Medicine] (MAE)	MPC
Minimum Navigation Performance Specification [Aviation] (FAAC)	MNPS
Minimum Navigation Performance Specification Airspace [Aviation] (FAAC)	MNPSA
Minimum Necrosing Dose	MND
Minimum Noise Routes	MNR
Minimum Norm Quadratic Unbiased [Statistics]	MINQU
Minimum Norm Quadratic Unbiased Estimation [Statistics] (PDAA)	MINQUE
Minimum Normal Burst Altitude	MNBA
Minimum Number of Animals Known Alive [Ecology]	MNKA
Minimum Number of Elements	MNE
Minimum Number of Individuals [Statistics]	MNI
Minimum Number of Units [Chemical engineering]	MNU
Minimum Obstacle Clearance [Aviation] (FAAC)	MOC
Minimum Obstruction Clearance Altitude [Aviation]	MOCA
Minimum Obstruction Clearance Altitude (AD)	moca
Minimum Operating Inventory [Business term]	MOI
Minimum Operating System [Sperry Univac] (NITA)	MOS
Minimum Operational Characteristics	MOC
Minimum Operational Performance Standard [Aviation] (DA)	MOPS
Minimum Operational Safe Altitude (DOMA)	MOSA
Minimum Orbital Unmanned Satellite (AD)	MOUSE
Minimum Orbital Unmanned Satellite of the Earth	MOUSE
Minimum Order Quantity (MCD)	MOQ
Minimum Ordered Partition	MOP
Minimum Oxidizer (KSC)	MINOX
Minimum Oxygen Concentration [at which ignition occurs]	MOL
Minimum Perceptible Color Difference	MPCD
Minimum Perceptible Erythema [Dermatology]	MPE
Minimum Performance Envelope (MCD)	MPE
Minimum Performance Specification (DA)	MPS
Minimum Performance Standard Test [Military] (CAAL)	MPST
Minimum Permissible Dose	MPD
Minimum Phase (IEEE)	MP
Minimum Piecework Standard [British]	MPS
Minimum Planned Start Date per Operation	MINSD
Minimum Planning Chart (AD)	mpc
Minimum Potential Energy [Fission]	MPE
Minimum Power Level (KSC)	MPL
Minimum Premarket [Health and Safety] Data [OEEC]	MPD
Minimum Premium [Insurance]	MP
Minimum Premium Plans [Insurance]	MPP
Minimum Pressurization Temperature [Nuclear energy] (NRCH)	MPT
Minimum Process Time	MPT
Minimum Processing Requirement	MPR
Minimum Processing Time per Operation	MINPRT
Minimum Property Standards [FHA]	MPS
Minimum Protozoacidal Concentration	MPC
Minimum Pure Radium Equivalent (MCD)	MPRE
Minimum Quantity Yards per Color (AD)	mqyco
Minimum Quantity Yards per Design (AD)	mqyds
Minimum R Factor [Spectrometry]	MINR
Minimum Radial Separation [Manufacturing term]	MRS
Minimum Radiation (CAAL)	MINIRAD
Minimum Radiation (MCD)	MINIRAD
Minimum Radiation Requirements [Missiles] (IEEE)	MINIRAR
Minimum Range to Avoid Plumb Impingement (MCD)	RIMP
Minimum Reacting Dose	MRD
Minimum Reacting Dose (AD)	mrd
Minimum Reaction Posture (NVT)	MRP
Minimum Real Time Operating System (NITA)	MIRTOS
Minimum Reception Altitude [Aviation]	MRA
Minimum Reception Altitude (AD)	mra
Minimum Rediscount Rate	MRR
Minimum Rejection Number	MRN
Minimum Release Interval (DNAB)	MRI
Minimum Remaining Slack Time (PDAA)	MRST
Minimum Replacement Unit	MRU
Minimum Reporting Requirement [NASA] (KSC)	MRR
Minimum Reporting Standard [Broadcasting] (NTCM)	MRS
Minimum Required	MR
Minimum Required Logistics Augmentation Europe (MCD)	MRLOGAEUR
Minimum Requirements Specified	MIREQ
Minimum Reserve Authorization	MRA
Minimum Residue Level	MRL
Minimum Resolvable Angle	MRA
Minimum Resolvable Object Length	MROL
Minimum Resolvable Temperature (MCD)	MRT
Minimum Resolvable Temperature Difference (PDAA)	MRTD
Minimum Retirement Age (GFGA)	MRA
Minimum Risk Route (MCD)	MRR
Minimum Safe Air Travel (SAA)	MINSAT
Minimum Safe Altitude [Aviation]	MSA
Minimum Safe Altitude Warning [Aviation]	MSAW
Minimum Safe Distance (AABC)	MSD
Minimum Safe Height of Burst [Military]	MSHB
Minimum Sales Responsibility [Automotive sales quotas]	MSR
Minimum Security Requirement	MSR
Minimum Seed-Bearing Age [Botany]	MINAGE
Minimum Shift Keyed Modulation (NITA)	MSKM
Minimum Shift Keying	MSK
Minimum Shuffle Control Cell Core [Nuclear energy] (NUCP)	MSCCC
Minimum Signal Element Duration [Telecommunications] (TEL)	MSED
Minimum Size Executive Routines	MISER
Minimum Size Limit [Pisciculture]	MSL
Minimum Slack Time per Operation	MINSOP
Minimum Social Behavior Scale [Psychology]	MSBS
Minimum Spawning Time [Pisciculture]	MST
Minimum Speed in a Stall [Aviation code] (AIA)	Vmsl
Minimum Speed in a Stall, Flaps Down [Aviation code] (AIA)	Vmso
Minimum Squares [Mathematical statistics]	MINSQ
Minimum Stress (AD)	ms
Minimum Structure Module	MIST
Minimum Surface Area (KSC)	MSA
Minimum Sustainable Yield [Pisciculture]	MSY
Minimum Sustaining Field [Atomic reactor]	MSF
Minimum Sustaining Power	MSP
Minimum Sustaining Rate (MCD)	MSR
Minimum Target Elevation Angle (MCD)	MTEA
Minimum Tax Credit Net Operating Loss Deduction [Business term]	MTCNOLD
Minimum Technological Requirement	MTR
Minimum Teleprocessing Commmunications System	MTCS
Minimum Temperature (NOAA)	MNTMP
Minimum Temperature (AD)	mntmp
Minimum Temperature (DS)	MT
Minimum Terms Agreement	MTA
Minimum Terrain-Clearance Altitude [Aviation]	MTA
Minimum Terrain-Clearance Altitude [Aviation]	MTCA
Minimum Test Instrumentation Equipment	MINTIE
Minimum Time [Telecommunications] (TEL)	TMIN
Minimum Time before Overhaul [Quality control]	MTBO
Minimum Time Interval [Medicine]	MTI
Minimum Time Limit	MTL
Minimum Time Path (OA)	MTP
Minimum Time Rate	MTR
Minimum Total Work Content	MINTWK
Minimum Tracking Flux Density	MTFD
Minimum Transfer (DCTA)	MT
Minimum Triggering Level [Aviation] (DA)	MTL

Minimum Universal Pension System [*Proposed to reform pension coverage*] .... MUPS

Minimum Unstick Speed [*Aviation code*] (AIA) .... Vmu

Minimum Use of Force Tactical Intervention [*British police*] .... MUFTI

Minimum Variance Linear Unbiased [*Statistics*] .... MVLU

Minimum Variance Linear Unbiased Estimator [*Statistics*] (OA) .... MVLUE

Minimum Variance Orbit Determination (MCD) .... MINIVAR

Minimum Variance Unbiased [*Statistics*] .... MVU

Minimum Variance Unbiased Estimate [*Statistics*] .... MVUE

Minimum Variance Unbiased Linear Estimator [*Statistics*] .... MVULE

Minimum Vectoring Altitude [*FAA*] (TAG) .... MVA

Minimum Viable Population [*Demographics*] .... MVP

Minimum Virtual Memory .... MVM

Minimum Viscosity .... MV

Minimum Visual Signal .... MVS

Minimum Wage Coalition to Save Jobs [*Defunct*] (EA) .... MWCSJ

Minimum Wage Laws (OICC) .... MWL

Minimum Weapon Radius (SAA) .... MINWR

Minimum Weight (WDAA) .... MIN WT

Minimum When Control Zone Effective (FAAC) .... MCZNE

Minimum-Altitude Release and Strafe (MCD) .... MARS

Minimum-Approach Lighting System with Runway Alignment Indicator Lights [*Aviation*] (DNAB) .... MALS/RAIL

Minimum-Cost Expediting .... MCX

Minimum-Gradient Reaction Path [*Chemical kinetics*] .... MGRP

Minimum-Speed Wind Tunnel (MCD) .... MSWT

Minimum-Variance Deconvolution (MCD) .... MVD

Minimum-Variance Reduced-Order [*Statistics*] (PDAA) .... MVRO

Minimum-Weight Tracking [*System*] (MUGU) .... MINITRACK

Minimum-Weighted Mean Square Error (IAA) .... MWMSE

Minimum-Weighted-Absolute Error [*Statistics*] (PDAA) .... MWAE

Mining .... MIN

Mining (DD) .... min

Mining .... MIN

Mining and Chemical Engineering Review [*A publication*] .... Mining Chem Engng Rev

Mining and Engineering Review [*A publication*] .... Mining Engng Rev

Mining and Excavation Research Institute [*Research center*] (RCD) .... MERI

Mining and Logging [*Tires*] .... ML

Mining and Materials Processing Institute of Japan .... MMIJ

Mining and Metallurgical Society of America (EA) .... MMSA

Mining & Metallurgy Divisions (ACII) .... M&M

Mining and Quarrying [*Department of Employment*] [*British*] .... MQ

Mining and Reclamation Council of America (EA) .... MARC

Mining and Water Cases, Annotated [*United States*] [*A publication*] (DLA) .... M & W Cas

Mining Association of Canada .... MAC

Mining Club (EA) .... MC

Mining Club of the Southwest (EA) .... MCSW

Mining Commissioner's Cases [*Canada*] [*A publication*] (DLA) .... MCC

Mining, Construction, and Agricultural Equipment .... MCAE

Mining Electromechanical Maintenance Association (IAA) .... MEMMA

Mining Enforcement and Safety Administration [*Terminated, 1978; functions transferred to Mine Safety and Health Administration, Department of Labor*] .... MESA

Mining Engineer (PGP) .... EM

Mining Engineer .... ME

Mining Engineer .... Min E

Mining Engineer in Geology .... EM in Geol

Mining Engineering Officer [*British military*] (DMA) .... MEO

Mining Industry Research Organisation [*British*] .... MIRO

Mining Item Name Directory [*A publication*] .... MIND

Mining Lease Application .... MLA

Mining Library, Falconbridge Ltd., Onaping, Ontario [*Library symbol National Library of Canada*] (NLC) .... OOFM

Mining Permit (AD) .... MP

Mining Qualifications Board [*British*] (BI) .... MQB

Mining Reports, Edited by R. S. Morrison [*Chicago*] [*A publication*] (DLA) .... MR

Mining Research and Development Establishment [*National Coal Board*] [*British*] .... MRDE

Mining Review [*A publication*] .... MR

Mining Rock-Mass Rating [*Mining technology*] .... MRMR

Mining Services International Corp. [*Associated Press*] (SAG) .... MiningS

Mining Services International Corp. [*NASDAQ symbol*] (NQ) .... MSIX

Mining Svcs Intl [*NASDAQ symbol*] (TTSB) .... MSIX

Mining Technology Abstracts [*Canada Centre for Mineral and Energy Technology*] [*Information service or system*] (CRD) .... MINTEC

Mining Technology Clearing House [*British Information service or system*] (IID) .... MIN

Minion [*Typography*] (DGA) .... MIN

Mini-Pressurized Logistic Modules [*Space technology*] .... MPLM

Mini-Reconstruction System (MCD) .... MRS

Mini-Remote Control Unit (MHDI) .... MRCU

Mini-Remotely Piloted Vehicle (PDAA) .... MRPV

Mini-Rotary Viscometer [*Mechanical engineering*] .... MRV

Minisatellite Variant Repeat [*Genetics*] .... MNSCL

Miniscule .... MNSCL

Ministe de la Main-d'Oeuvre et de la Securite du Revenu du Quebec, Centre de Documentation, Montreal, PQ, Canada [*Library symbol*] [*Library of Congress*] (LCLS) .... CaQMMSR

Minister [*or Ministry*] (ODBW) .... Min

Minister [*or Ministry*] .... MIN

Minister .... MINSTR

Minister, External Affairs (CINC) .... MEA

Minister for Foreign Affairs [*British*] .... MFA

Minister for [*or Ministry of*] War Communications [*British World War II*] .... MWC

Minister of Armed Forces (NATG) .... MAF

Minister [*or Ministry*] of Food [*British*] .... MF

Minister of Labour [*British*] (AD) .... M o L

Minister of Munitions [*British World War II*] .... MM

Minister of National Defence [*Canada*] .... MND

Minister of Pensions [*British*] (AD) .... M o P

Minister of Pensions [*British*] (AD) .... M Pen

Minister of Power [*British*] (AD) .... M o P

Minister of Production [*British*] (AD) .... M o P

Minister of Public Security [*British*] .... MPS

Minister of Reconstruction [*British*] (AD) .... M of R

Minister of State [*British*] .... MS

Minister of Transport [*British*] (AD) .... M o T

Minister of War Transport [*British*] (AD) .... M o WT

Minister of Works [*British*] (AD) .... M o W

Minister Plenipotentiary (WDAA) .... MIN PLEN

Minister Plenipotentiary .... MP

Minister Provincial (AD) .... MP

Ministere de la Defense Nationale [*Department of National Defense*] [*Canada*] .... MDN

Ministere de la Fonction Publique, Direction de la Classification et de l'Evaluation des Emplois, Quebec, PQ, Canada [*Library symbol Library of Congress*] (LCLS) .... CaQQFPCE

Ministere de la Justice, Commission des Services Juridiques, Montreal, PQ, Canada [*Library symbol Library of Congress*] (LCLS) .... CaQMJSJ

Ministere de la Justice du Quebec, Ste.-Foy, PQ, Canada [*Library symbol Library of Congress*] (LCLS) .... CaQQJ

Ministere de la Justice du Quebec, Ste-Foy, Quebec [*Library symbol National Library of Canada*] (NLC) .... QQJ

Ministere de la Main-d'Oeuvre et de la Securite du Revenu, Direction du Developpement du Systeme, Centre de Documentation, Quebec, PQ, Canada [*Library symbol*] [*Library of Congress*] (LCLS) .... CaQQMSRD

Ministere de la Qualite de la Vie [*Ministry of the Quality of Life*] [*France*] (AD) .... MQV

Ministere de la Recherche et de la Technologie (USDC) .... MRT

Ministere de l'Agriculture, des Pecheries, et de l'Alimentation, Centre de Documentation en Peches Maritimes, Gaspe, PQ, Canada [*Library symbol*] [*Library of Congress*] (LCLS) .... CaQGaP

Ministere de l'Agriculture, des Pecheries et de l'Alimentation, Chateauguay, Quebec [*Library symbol National Library of Canada*] (NLC) .... QCAG

Ministere de l'Agriculture, des Percheries et de l'Alimentation, Chateauguay, PQ, Canada [*Library symbol*] [*Library of Congress*] (LCLS) .... CaQChaAG

Ministere de l'Agriculture et de la Colonisation, Quebec, PQ, Canada [*Library symbol Library of Congress*] (LCLS) .... CaQQAg

Ministere de l'Education, Office des Professions du Quebec, Quebec, PQ, Canada [*Library symbol Library of Congress*] (LCLS) .... CaQQEDOP

Ministere de l'Energie et des Ressources du Quebec, Quebec, PQ, Canada [*Library symbol Library of Congress*] (LCLS) .... CaQQER

Ministere de l'Energie et des Ressources du Quebec, Trois-Rivieres, Quebec [*Library symbol National Library of Canada*] (BIB) .... QTME

Ministere de l'Energie et des Ressources, Secteur Energie, Centre de Documentation et de Renseignements, Quebec, PQ, Canada [*Library symbol Library of Congress*] (LCLS) .... CaQQERE

Ministere de l'Environnement, Montreal, PQ, Canada [*Library symbol Library of Congress*] (LCLS) .... CaQMEN

Ministere de l'Environnement, Montreal, Quebec [*Library symbol National Library of Canada*] (NLC) .... QMEN

Ministere de l'Environnement, Ste-Foy, Quebec [*Library symbol National Library of Canada*] (NLC) .... QQEN

Ministere de l'Industrie, du Commerce, et du Tourisme, Centre de Recherche Industrielle du Quebec, Complexe Scientifique, Ste.-Foy, PQ, Canada [*Library symbol Library of Congress*] (LCLS) .... CaQSFCR

Ministere de l'Industrie, du Commerce et du Tourisme, Quebec, Quebec [*Library symbol National Library of Canada*] (NLC) .... QQIC

Ministere de l'Industrie et du Commerce du Quebec, Quebec, PQ, Canada [*Library symbol Library of Congress*] (LCLS) .... CaQQIC

Ministere des Affaires Culturelles du Quebec, Quebec, Quebec [*Library symbol National Library of Canada*] (NLC) .... QQAC

Ministere des Affaires Indiennes et du Nord Canadien [*Department of Indian Affairs and Northern Development*] [*Canada*] .... AINC

Ministere des Affaires Municipales, Centre de Documentation, PQ, Canada [*Library symbol Library of Congress*] (LCLS) .... CaQQAM

Ministere des Affaires Sociales, Informatheque-Laboratoires, Ste.-Anne-De-Bellevue, PQ, Canada [*Library symbol Library of Congress*] (LCLS) .... CaQMASI

Ministere des Affaires Sociales, Informatheque-Laboratoires, Ste.-Anne-De-Bellevue, PQ, Canada [*Library symbol Library of Congress*] (LCLS) .... CaQSTAIAS

Ministere des Communautes Culturelles et de l'Immigration, Montreal, Quebec [*Library symbol National Library of Canada*] (NLC) .... QMIMM

Ministere des Communications [*Department of Communications*] [*Canada*] .... MDC

Ministere des Communications du Quebec, Bibliotheque Administrative, Quebec, PQ, Canada [*Library symbol Library of Congress*] (LCLS) .... CaQQBQ

Ministere des Communications du Quebec, Bibliotheque Administrative, Quebec, PQ, Canada [*Library symbol Library of Congress*] (LCLS) .... CaQQMC

Ministere des Communications du Quebec, Direction Generale du Cinema et de l'Audiovisuel, Montreal, PQ, Canada [*Library symbol Library of Congress*] (LCLS) .... CaQMCAV

Ministere des Finances, Service du Traitement de l'Information, Duberger, PQ, Canada [*Library symbol Library of Congress*] (LCLS) .... CaQQDTI

Ministere des Finances, Service du Traitement de l'Information, Duberger, PQ, Canada [*Library symbol Library of Congress*] (LCLS) .... CaQQFTI

Ministere des Institutions Financieres, Compagnies, et Cooperatives, Quebec, PQ,Canada [*Library symbol Library of Congress*] (LCLS) .... CaQQIF
Ministere des Pecheries et de la Chasse, Office de Biologie, Montreal, PQ, Canada [*Library symbol Library of Congress*] (LCLS) .... CaQMOB
Ministere des Richesses Naturelles du Quebec, Quebec, PQ, Canada [*Library symbol Library of Congress*] (LCLS) .... CaQQRN
Ministere des Terres et Forets du Quebec, Quebec, PQ, Canada [*Library symbol Library of Congress*] (LCLS) .... CaQQT
Ministere des Transports, Quebec, PQ, Canada [*Library symbol Library of Congress*] (LCLS) .... CaQQTR
Ministere des Transports, Quebec, Quebec [*Library symbol National Library of Canada*] (NLC) .... QQTR
Ministere des Trasports-Rue Dorchester, Centre de Documentation, Quebec, PQ, Canada [*Library symbol*] [*Library of Congress*] (LCLS) .... CaQQTRD
Ministere d'Etat, Sciences et Technologie [*Ministry of State for Science and Technology - MOSST*] [*Canada*] .... MEST
Ministere du Loisir de la Chasse et de la Peche du Quebec, Bibliotheque de la Faune, Montreal, PQ, Canada [*Library symbol Library of Congress*] (LCLS) .... CaQMFLCP
Ministere du Loisir de la Chasse et de la Peche, Quebec, PQ, Canada [*Library symbol Library of Congress*] (LCLS) .... CaQQLCP
Ministere du Loisir, de la Chasse et de la Peche, Quebec, Quebec [*Library symbol National Library of Canada*] (NLC) .... QQLCP
Ministere du Revenu, Ste.-Foy, PQ, Canada [*Library symbol Library of Congress*] (LCLS) .... CaQQRE
Ministere du Revenu, Ste.-Foy, Quebec [*Library symbol National Library of Canada*] (NLC) .... QQRE
Ministere du Tourisme, de la Chasse, et de la Peche, Orsainville, PQ, Canada [*Library symbol Library of Congress*] (LCLS) .... CaQOTCP
Ministere du Tourisme du Quebec, Quebec [*Library symbol National Library of Canada*] (NLC) .... QQTO
Ministere du Tourisme du Quebec, Quebec, PQ, Canada [*Library symbol*] [*Library of Congress*] (LCLS) .... CaQQTO
Ministere du Travaile et de la Main-D'Oeuvre, Montreal, PQ, Canada [*Library symbol Library of Congress*] (LCLS) .... CaQMTMO
Ministere Federal de l'Expansion Industrielle Regionale [*Department of Regional Industrial Expansion - DRIE*] [*Canada*] .... MEIR
Ministerial Committee on Military Coordination [*British World War II*] .... MCC
Ministerial Committee on Science and Technology [*South Africa*] .... MCST
Ministerial Conference of West and Central African States on Maritime Transport [*Ivory Coast*] (EAIO) .... MINCONMAR
Ministerial Conference of West and Central African States on Maritime Transportation [*See also CMEAOC*] [*Abidjan, Ivory Coast*] (EAIO) .... MCWCS
Ministerial Consultative Committee on Curriculum [*Queensland, Australia*] .... MCCC
Ministerial Correspondence Tracking System [*Australia*] .... MCTS
Ministerial Council for Corporations [*Australia*] .... MCC
Ministerial Council on Common Services Provision [*Australia*] .... MCCSP
Ministerial Group on the Misuse of Drugs [*British*] .... MGMD
Ministerial Libraries and Information Centers .... MILIC
Ministerial Nomination Committee [*Australia*] .... MNC
Ministerial Task Force on Soil Conservation [*Australia*] .... MTFSC
Ministering Children's League [*Australia*] .... MCL
Ministerio de Obras Publicas [*Ministry of Public Works*] [*Spanish*] (AD) .... MOP
Ministerio do Interior [*Ministry of the Interior*] [*Information service or system*] (IID) .... MINTER
Ministerium fuer Aussenhandel und Innerdeutschen Handel [*Ministry for Foreign Trade and Domestic German Trade*] [*See also MfAI*] .... MAI
Ministerium fuer Staatssicherheit [*Ministry for State Security*] [*See also MISTAI, MSS*] [*Germany*] (EG) .... MfS
Minister-Residentiary [*Diplomacy*] .... MR
Ministers Leadership Training Program [*Defunct*] (EA) .... MLTP
Ministerstvo Gosudarstvennoy Bezopasnosti [*Ministry of State Security*] [*Former USSR*] (LAIN) .... MGB
Ministerstvo Inostrannykh Del [*Ministry of Foreign Affairs*] [*Former USSR*] .... MID
Ministerstvo Oborony [*Ministry of Defense*] [*Former USSR*] .... MO
Ministerstvo Okhrany Obshchestvennogo Poryadka [*Ministry for Maintenance of Public Order*] [*Former USSR*] (LAIN) .... MOOP
Ministerstvo Vnutrennikh Del-Ministerstvo Gosudarstvennoe Bezopasnosti [*Later, KGB*] .... MVD-MGB
Ministerstvo Voenno-Morskogo Flota [*Ministry of the Navy*] [*1950-53; merged into the MO*] [*Former USSR*] .... MVMF
Ministerstvo Vooruzhennykh Sil [*Ministry of the Armed Forces*] [*1946-50; superseded by VM, MVMF*] [*Former USSR*] .... MVS
Ministerstwo Opieki Spotecznes [*Ministry of Social Welfare*] [*Poland*] (AD) .... MOS Poland
Ministic Air [*Canada ICAO designator*] (FAAC) .... MNS
Ministries to Blacks in Higher Education (EA) .... MBHE
Ministry .... M
Ministry .... MNSTRY
Ministry for Environment and Forests [*India*] .... MEF
Ministry Library, Ministry of Municipal Affairs, Recreation, and Culture, Victoria, British Columbia [*Library symbol National Library of Canada*] (NLC) .... BVIHCR
Ministry of Agriculture [*British*] (AD) .... MoA
Ministry of Agriculture and Fisheries [*British*] .... MAF
Ministry of Agriculture, Fisheries, and Food [*British*] .... MAFF
Ministry of Agriculture Fisheries and Food [*British ICAO designator*] (FAAC) .... WDG
Ministry of Agriculture, Forestry and Fisheries [*Japan*] (ECON) .... MAFF
Ministry of Aircraft Production [*British*] .... MAP
Ministry of Aircraft Uranium Development [*British World War II*] .... MAUD
Ministry of Aviation [*British*] .... MA
Ministry of Aviation [*British*] .... MOA

Ministry of Aviation Supply [*British*] .... MAS
Ministry of Civil Aviation [*Later, MTCA*] [*British*] .... MCA
Ministry of Commerce and Industry [*Korea*] .... MCI
Ministry of Commerce and Industry [*British*] (AD) .... MOCI
Ministry of Communications (CINC) .... MOC
Ministry of Community and Social Services, Rideau Regional Centre, Smith Falls, ON, Canada [*Library symbol*] [*Library of Congress*] (LCLS) .... CaOSFCSR
Ministry of Concern for Public Health (EA) .... MCPH
Ministry of Consumer and Commercial Relations, Technical Standards Division, Toronto, ON, Canada [*Library symbol Library of Congress*] (LCLS) .... CaOTCCRT
Ministry of Defence [*British*] (AD) .... M o D
Ministry of Defence [*British*] .... M of D
Ministry of Defence [*British*] .... MIN-DEF
Ministry of Defence [*British*] .... MOD
Ministry of Defence (Army Department) [*British*] .... MOD(AD)
Ministry of Defence (Navy) [*British*] .... MOD(N)
Ministry of Defence (Procurement Executive) [*British*] .... MOD(PE)
Ministry of Defence, United Kingdom [*ICAO location identifier*] (ICLI) .... EGWB
Ministry of Defense and Aviation (MCD) .... MODA
Ministry of Economic Affairs [*British*] (AD) .... MOEA
Ministry of Economic Warfare [*British*] .... MEW
Ministry of Education [*British*] .... M of E
Ministry of Education [*British*] (DAS) .... MOE
Ministry of Education [*British*] (AD) .... MoE
Ministry of Education, Information Centre [*Ontario*] [*UTLAS symbol*] .... EDU
Ministry of Education (Northern Ireland) .... ME(NI)
Ministry of Education, Western Australia .... MEWA
[*The*] Ministry of Electronics Industry [*China*] .... MEI
Ministry of Energy [*British*] (AD) .... M o E
Ministry of Environment [*Canada*] .... MOE
Ministry of External Affairs, Government Documents [*UTLAS symbol*] .... EAG
Ministry of External Affairs, Library Services Division [*UTLAS symbol*] .... MEA
Ministry of Finance [*Japan*] (ECON) .... MOF
Ministry of Finance [*British*] (AD) .... MoF
Ministry of Food [*British*] .... MOF
Ministry of Food Education and Information Practice [*British*] .... MFEIP
Ministry of Foreign Economic Relations and Trade [*China*] .... MOFERT
Ministry of Foreign Trade & Economic Cooperation [*China*] .... MOFTEC
Ministry of Fuel and Power [*British*] .... MFP
Ministry of Fuel and Power [*British*] .... MOFAP
Ministry of Geology and Mineral Resources [*China*] .... MGMR
Ministry of Health [*British*] (AD) .... M o H
Ministry of Health [*British*] .... MH
Ministry of Health [*British*] .... MOH
Ministry of Health and Social Services (Northern Ireland) .... MHSS(NI)
Ministry of Health and Welfare [*Japan*] (ECON) .... MHW
Ministry of Home Security [*British*] .... MHS
Ministry of Housing and Local Government [*British*] (AD) .... MOHLG
Ministry of Industry and Trade [*Israel*] .... MIT
Ministry of Information [*British World War II*] .... MI
Ministry of Information [*British World War II*] .... MOI
Ministry of Information Middle East [*British World War II*] .... MIME
Ministry of International Trade and Industry [*Japan*] .... MITI
Ministry of Jute [*Bangladesh*] .... MOJ
Ministry of Labour [*Later, DE*] [*British*] .... MOL
Ministry of Labour and National Service [*British World War II*] .... MLNS
Ministry of Labour and National Service [*World War II British*] (DAS) .... MOLNS
Ministry of Labour Occupational Classification [*Later, CODOT*] [*British*] .... MOLOC
Ministry of Labour Staff Association [*British*] .... MLSA
Ministry of Love [*From George Orwell's novel, "1984"*] .... Miniluv
Ministry of Mines [*British*] (DAS) .... MM
Ministry of National Defence [*British*] (MCD) .... MND
Ministry of National Insurance [*British*] .... MNI
Ministry of National Service [*World War I*] [*British*] .... MNS
Ministry of Natural Resources Development and Environmental Protection [*Ethiopia*] (ECON) .... MoNRDEP
Ministry of Overseas Development [*British*] (ILCA) .... MOD
Ministry of Peace [*From George Orwell's novel, "1984"*] .... Minipax
Ministry of Pensions [*British*] (AD) .... M Pen
Ministry of Pensions [*British*] .... MOP
Ministry of Pensions and National Insurance [*Later, MSS*] [*British*] .... MPNI
Ministry of Planning and Economic Development [*Ethiopia*] (ECON) .... MPED
Ministry of Plenty [*From George Orwell's novel, "1984"*] .... Miniplenty
Ministry of Population Welfare [*Pakistan*] (ECON) .... MOPW
Ministry of Posts and Telecommunications [*People's Republic of China*] (ECON) .... MPT
Ministry of Posts and Telecommunications .... MPT
Ministry of Posts and Telecommunictions [*China*] (ECON) .... MPT
Ministry of Power [*British*] .... MOP
Ministry of Production [*British*] .... MOP
Ministry of Public Building and Works [*Later, DOE*] [*British*] .... MPBW
Ministry of Reconstruction [*British*] (AD) .... M o R
Ministry of Reconstruction [*World War I*] [*British*] .... MR
Ministry of Recreation and Sport [*British*] (AD) .... MRS
Ministry of Revolutionary Development [*Vietnam*] .... MORD
Ministry of Science and Arts [*US and Israel*] .... MOSA
Ministry of Shipping [*British*] .... MS
Ministry of Social Security [*British*] .... MSS
Ministry of Solicitor General [*Canada*] .... MSG
Ministry of State [*British*] .... MOS
Ministry of State for Economic and Regional Development [*Canada*] .... MSERD
Ministry of State for Economic Development [*Canada*] .... MSED

Ministry of State for Economic Development, Ottawa, ON, Canada [*Library symbol Library of Congress*] (LCLS) .... CaOOED
Ministry of State for Science and Technology [*Canada*] .... MOSST
Ministry of State for Science and Technology [*Canada*] .... MSST
Ministry of State for Science and Technology [*Ministere d'Etat pour les Sciences et la Technologie*], Ottawa, Ontario [*Library symbol National Library of Canada*] (NLC) .... OOMSS
Ministry of State for Social Development, Ottawa, ON, Canada [*Library symbol Library of Congress*] (LCLS) .... CaOOMSD
Ministry of State for Social Development [*Ministere d'Etat au Developpement Social*] Ottawa, Ontario [*Library symbol National Library of Canada*] (NLC) .... OOMSD
Ministry of State for Urban Affairs [*Canada*] .... MUA
Ministry of Supply [*Also, MS*] [*British*] .... MOS
Ministry of Supply [*Also, MOS*] [*British*] .... MS
Ministry of Supply Automatic Integrator and Computer [*British*] (DEN).... MOSAIC
Ministry of Supply Inspection Department [*British*] (AD) .... MOSID
Ministry of Technology [*British*] .... MINTECH
Ministry of the Interior [*British*] (AD) .... MoI
Ministry of the Provincial Secretary and Government Services, Library Services Branch, Victoria, BC, Canada [*Library symbol Library of Congress*] (LCLS) .... CaBViLSB
Ministry of the Solicitor General Library [*UTLAS symbol*] .... MSG
Ministry of the Solicitor General [*Ministere du Solliciteur General*] Ottawa, Ontario [*Library symbol National Library of Canada*] (NLC) .... OOSG
Ministry of Tourism [*Philippines*] (DS) .... MOT
Ministry of Town and Country Planning [*British*] (AD) .... M o TCP
Ministry of Town and Country Planning [*British*] (DAS) .... MOTCP
Ministry of Town and Country Planning [*British*] .... MTCP
Ministry of Trade and Industry [*Canada*] .... MTI
Ministry of Transit and Communications [*Philippines*] (AD) .... MOTC
Ministry of Transport [*Israel*] [*ICAO location identifier*] (ICLI) .... LLJM
Ministry of Transport [*British or Canadian*] .... MOT
Ministry of Transport [*Later, DOE*] [*British*] .... MT
Ministry of Transport, Airports and Construction Services, Ottawa, ON, Canada [*Library symbol Library of Congress*] (LCLS) .... CaOOTAC
Ministry of Transport and Civil Aviation [*Later, MT*] [*British*] (MCD) .... MTCA
Ministry of Transport, Aviation Safety Bureau, Ottawa, ON, Canada [*Library symbol Library of Congress*] (LCLS) .... CaOOTAS
Ministry of Transport, Canadian Air Transportation Administration, Civil Aviation Branch, Edmonton, AB, Canada [*Library symbol*] [*Library of Congress*] (LCLS) .... CaAEMTCA
Ministry of Transport, Canadian Air Transportation Administration, Construction Branch, Edmonton, AB, Canada [*Library symbol*] [*Library of Congress*] (LCLS) .... CaAEMTC
Ministry of Transport, Canadian Air Transportation Administration, Edmonton, AB,Canada [*Library symbol Library of Congress*] (LCLS) .... CaAEMT
Ministry of Transport, Ottawa, ON, Canada [*Library symbol Library of Congress*] (LCLS) .... CaOOT
Ministry of Transport, Railway Transportation Directorate, Ottawa, ON, Canada [*Library symbol Library of Congress*] (LCLS) .... CaOOTRT
Ministry of Transport, Telecommunications and Electronics Directorate, Ottawa, ON, Canada [*Library symbol Library of Congress*] (LCLS) .... CaOOTTE
Ministry of Truth [*From George Orwell's novel, "1984"*] .... Minitrue
Ministry of Useless Gestures [*Organization to increase number of voters*] [*British*] .... MUG
Ministry of War Time Communications [*British World War II*] .... MWTC
Ministry of War Transport [*Terminated, 1956*] [*British*] .... MOWT
Ministry of War Transport [*Terminated, 1956*] [*British*] .... MWT
Ministry of Works [*British*] (MCD) .... MOW
Ministry of Works [*British*] .... MW
Ministry of Works and Buildings [*British*] .... MOWB
Ministry of Works and Buildings [*British*] .... MWB
Ministry of Works and Development [*British*] (AD) .... MoWD
Ministry of Works and Planning [*British*] .... MWP
Ministry, Society, and Theology [*A publication*] (APTA) .... MST
MINITEX [*Minnesota Interlibrary Teletype Exchange*], Minneapolis, MN [*OCLC symbol*] (OCLC) .... TQI
MINITEX [*Minnesota Interlibrary Teletype Exchange*], Minneapolis, MN [*OCLC symbol*] (OCLC) .... TQJ
Minitrack [*Alaska*] [*Seismograph station code, US Geological Survey Closed*] (SEIS) .... MIK
Minitrack (KSC) .... MTRK
Minitrack Optical Tracking Station [*or System*] [*NASA*] .... MOTS
Minitrack Optical Tracking System (AD) .... mots
Minj [*New Guinea*] [*Airport symbol*] (AD) .... MZN
Mink Cell Focus-Inducing [*Virus*] .... MCF
Mink Minerals Resources, Inc. [*Vancouver Stock Exchange symbol*] .... MKM
Minlaton [*Australia Airport symbol Obsolete*] (OAG) .... XML
Minn Pwr & Lt 5% cm Pfd [*AMEX symbol*] (TTSB) .... MPLPrA
Minneapolis [*Branch in the Federal Reserve regional banking system*] (BARN) I
Minneapolis [*Minnesota*] [*Seismograph station code, US Geological Survey*] (SEIS) .... MNM
Minneapolis [*Minnesota*] [*Seismograph station code, US Geological Survey*] (SEIS) .... MNN
Minneapolis (AD) .... Mpls
Minneapolis & St. Louis [*Railroad*] (MHDB) .... MSL
Minneapolis & St. Louis Railway Co. [*Later, MSL Industries, Inc.*] [*AAR code*] .... MSTL
Minneapolis, Anoka & Cuyuna Range Railroad Co. [*AAR code*] .... MACR
Minneapolis Center for Microbiological Investigations [*Public Health Service*] (GRD) .... MCMI
Minneapolis College of Art and Design .... MCAD
Minneapolis College of Art and Design, Minneapolis, MN [*Library symbol Library of Congress*] (LCLS) .... MnMCA

Minneapolis College of Music .... MCM
Minneapolis Community College, Minneapolis, MN [*OCLC symbol*] (OCLC) .... MCO
Minneapolis Community College, Minneapolis, MN [*Library symbol Library of Congress*] (LCLS) .... MnMCC
Minneapolis Eastern Railway .... ME
Minneapolis Eastern Railway Co. [*AAR code*] .... MINE
Minneapolis, Farmington [*Minnesota*] [*ICAO location identifier*] (ICLI) .... KZMP
Minneapolis Grain Exchange (EA) .... MGE
Minneapolis Industrial Railway Co. [*AAR code*] .... MIR
Minneapolis, KS [*FM radio station call letters*] .... KILS
Minneapolis/Minneapolis-St. Paul International [*Minnesota*] [*ICAO location identifier*] (ICLI) .... KMSP
Minneapolis, MN [*Location identifier FAA*] (FAAL) .... ANE
Minneapolis, MN [*Location identifier FAA*] (FAAL) .... APL
Minneapolis, MN [*Location identifier FAA*] (FAAL) .... FCM
Minneapolis, MN [*Location identifier FAA*] (FAAL) .... GEP
Minneapolis, MN [*Location identifier FAA*] (FAAL) .... HKZ
Minneapolis, MN [*Location identifier FAA*] (FAAL) .... HNP
Minneapolis, MN [*Location identifier FAA*] (FAAL) .... INN
Minneapolis, MN [*Location identifier FAA*] (FAAL) .... JNS
Minneapolis, MN [*Television station call letters*] .... KARE
Minneapolis, MN [*FM radio station call letters*] .... KBEM
Minneapolis, MN [*FM radio station call letters*] .... KEGE-FM
Minneapolis, MN [*FM radio station call letters*] .... KFAI
Minneapolis, MN [*AM radio station call letters*] .... KFAN
Minneapolis, MN [*Television station call letters*] .... KLGT-TV
Minneapolis, MN [*FM radio station call letters*] .... KMOJ
Minneapolis, MN [*Television station call letters*] .... KMSP
Minneapolis, MN [*FM radio station call letters*] .... KSJN
Minneapolis, MN [*AM radio station call letters*] .... KTCJ
Minneapolis, MN [*FM radio station call letters*] .... KTCZ
Minneapolis, MN [*AM radio station call letters*] .... KTIS
Minneapolis, MN [*FM radio station call letters*] .... KTIS-FM
Minneapolis, MN [*AM radio station call letters*] .... KUOM
Minneapolis, MN [*Television station call letters*] .... KVBM
Minneapolis, MN [*Location identifier FAA*] (FAAL) .... MIC
Minneapolis, MN [*Location identifier FAA*] (FAAL) .... SIJ
Minneapolis, MN [*FM radio station call letters*] .... WBOB
Minneapolis, MN [*AM radio station call letters*] .... WCCO
Minneapolis, MN [*Television station call letters*] .... WCCO-TV
Minneapolis, MN [*Television station call letters*] (RBYB) .... WFTC
Minneapolis, MN [*FM radio station call letters*] .... WLTE
Minneapolis, MN [*AM radio station call letters*] (RBYB) .... WMNN
Minneapolis, MN [*AM radio station call letters*] .... WWTC
Minneapolis, MN [*Location identifier FAA*] (FAAL) .... ZMP
Minneapolis, Northfield & Southern Railway [*AAR code*] .... MNS
Minneapolis Public Library and Information Center, Minneapolis, MN [*Library symbol Library of Congress*] (LCLS) .... MnM
Minneapolis Public Library and Information Center, Minneapolis, MN [*OCLC symbol*] (OCLC) .... MPI
Minneapolis, St. Paul & Ashland Railway .... MStP & A
Minneapolis, St. Paul & Sault Ste. Marie Railway Co. (IIA) .... MSP & SSM
Minneapolis, St. Paul & Sault Ste. Marie Railway Co. .... MSTP & SSM
Minneapolis-Honeywell Library, Duarte, CA [*Library symbol Library of Congress*] (LCLS) .... CDuM
Minneapolis-Honeywell Regulator Co. [*Later, HON*] .... M-H
Minneapolis-Honeywell Regulator Co., Minneapolis, MN [*Library symbol Library of Congress*] (LCLS) .... MnMMH
Minneapolis-Moline [*Stock exchange symbol*] (AD) .... MPW
Minneapolis-St. Paul [*Minnesota*] [*Seismograph station code, US Geological Survey*] (SEIS) .... MFM
Minneapolis-St. Paul [*Minnesota*] [*Airport symbol*] .... MSP
Minneapolis-St. Paul, MN [*FM radio station call letters*] .... KNOW-FM
Minnedosa, MB [*Television station call letters*] CKND-2
Minnedosa Regional Library, Minnedosa, Manitoba [*Library symbol National Library of Canada*] (NLC) .... MMR
Minnedosa Regional Library, Minnedosa, MB, Canada [*Library symbol Library of Congress*] (LCLS) .... CaMMiR
Minnehaha County Rural Library, Hartford, SD [*Library symbol Library of Congress*] (LCLS) .... SdHM
Minnehaha Middle School, Two Harbors, MN [*Library symbol*] [*Library of Congress*] (LCLS) .... MnThM
Minneota Public Schools, Minneota, MN [*Library symbol*] [*Library of Congress*] (LCLS) .... MnMinPS
Minnesota [*Obsolete*] (ROG) .... MA
Minnesota (AFM) .... MINN
Minnesota (ODBW) .... Minn
Minnesota [*Postal code*] .... MN
Minnesota [*MARC country of publication code Library of Congress*] (LCCP) .... mnu
Minnesota [*MARC geographic area code Library of Congress*] (LCCP) .... n-us-mn
Minnesota Academy of Science .... MAS
Minnesota Adaptive Instructional System (EDAC) .... MAIS
Minnesota Analysis and Planning System [*University of Minnesota*] [*Research center*] (RCD) .... MAPS
Minnesota & International Railway .... M & I
Minnesota & Northwestern Railroad .... M & NW
Minnesota and Ontario Paper [*Stock exchange symbol*] (AD) .... MNT
Minnesota Association of Farm Mutual Insurance Companies (SRA) .... MAFMIC
Minnesota Association of Law Libraries [*Library network*] .... MALL
Minnesota Attorney General's Office, St. Paul, MN [*OCLC symbol*] (OCLC) .... MAG
Minnesota Attorney General's Office, St. Paul, MN [*Library symbol Library of Congress*] (LCLS) .... MnSAG
Minnesota Bible College [*Rochester*] .... MBC

Minnesota Brewing [*NASDAQ symbol*] (TTSB) .... MBRW
Minnesota Brewing Co. [*NASDAQ symbol*] (SAG) .... MBRW
Minnesota Brewing Co. [*Associated Press*] (SAG) .... MinnBrw
Minnesota Business Educators, Inc (EDAC) .... MBEI
Minnesota Business Utility Users Council [*An association*] (TSSD) .... MBUUC
Minnesota Center for Twin and Adoption Research (ECON) .... MICTAR
Minnesota Child Development Inventory [*Child development test*]
  [*Psychology*] .... MCDI
Minnesota Clerical Test .... MCT
Minnesota Code, Annotated [*A publication*] (DLA) .... Minn Code Ann
Minnesota Code of Agency Rules [*A publication*] .... MCAR
Minnesota Code of Agency Rules [*A publication*] (DLA) .... Minn Code Agency
Minnesota Computer Literacy and Awareness Assessment (EDAC) .... MCLAA
Minnesota Computer-Aided Library System [*University of Minnesota*] .... MCALS
Minnesota Corrections Facility Library, St. Cloud, MN [*Library symbol*]
  [*Library of Congress*] (LCLS) .... MnStClCF
Minnesota Council on the Teaching of Foreign Languages (EDAC) .... MCTFL
Minnesota Counseling Inventory [*Psychology*] .... MCI
Minnesota Court Reporter [*A publication*] (DLA) .... Minn Ct Rep
Minnesota, Dakota & Western Railway Co. [*AAR code*] .... MDW
Minnesota Dance Theatre .... MDT
Minnesota Department of Agriculture, St. Paul, MN [*OCLC symbol*]
  (OCLC) .... MDA
Minnesota Department of Agriculture, St. Paul, MN [*Library symbol Library of Congress*] (LCLS) .... Mn-Ag
Minnesota Department of Labor and Industries. Compilation of Court
  Decisions [*A publication*] (DLA) .... Minn DL & I Comp
Minnesota Department of Natural Resources .... MDNR
Minnesota Department of Public Welfare Library Consortium [*Library network*] .... MINN DPW LIB
Minnesota Educational Computing Corp. [*NASDAQ symbol*] (SAG) .... MECC
Minnesota Educational Computing Corp. [*Associated Press*] (SAG) .... MinnEd
Minnesota Educational Media Organization (EDAC) .... MEMO
Minnesota Energy Agency, St. Paul, MN [*Library symbol Library of Congress*] (LCLS) .... MnSEA
Minnesota Follow-Up Study Rehabilitation Rating Scale .... MFS
Minnesota General Laws [*A publication*] (DLA) .... Minn Gen Laws
Minnesota Governor's Commission on Crime Prevention and Control, St.
  Paul, MN [*Library symbol Library of Congress*] (LCLS) .... MnSGC
Minnesota Groundswell (EA) .... MG
minnesota Historical Society, Division of Archives and Manuscripts, St.
  Paul, MN [*Library symbol*] [*Library of Congress*] (LCLS) .... MnHi-Ar
Minnesota Historical Society, St. Paul, MN [*OCLC symbol*] (OCLC) .... MHS
Minnesota Historical Society, St. Paul, MN [*Library symbol Library of Congress*] (LCLS) .... MnHi
Minnesota Importance Questionnaire [*Vocational test*] .... MIQ
Minnesota Infant Development Inventory [*Child development test*]
  [*Psychology*] .... MIDI
Minnesota Instructional Language [*Computer science*] (CSR) .... MIL
Minnesota Interlibrary Telecommunications Exchange [*Library cooperative*]
  [*Minnesota Higher Education Coordinating Board Minneapolis, MN*] .... MINITEX
Minnesota Interlibrary Telecommunications Exchange, Minneapolis, MN
  [*OCLC symbol*] (OCLC) .... MII
Minnesota Job Description Questionnaire [*Research test*] .... MJDQ
Minnesota Law Journal [*A publication*] (DLA) .... Minn Law J
Minnesota Law Journal [*St. Paul*] [*A publication*] (DLA) .... Minn LJ
Minnesota Legislative Reference Library, St. Paul, MN [*OCLC symbol*]
  (OCLC) .... MLR
Minnesota Metropolitan State College .... MMSC
Minnesota Min'g/Mfg [*NYSE symbol*] (TTSB) .... MMM
Minnesota Mining & Manufacturing Co. [*Also, MMM*] 3M
Minnesota Mining & Manufacturing Co. [*Also known as 3M Co.*] [*NYSE symbol*] (SPSG) .... MMM
Minnesota Mining & Manufacturing Co. [*Also known as 3M Co.*] [*Associated Press*] (SAG) .... MMM
Minnesota Mining & Manufacturing Co., St. Paul, MN [*OCLC symbol*]
  (OCLC) .... MMI
Minnesota Mining & Manufacturing Co., Technical Library, St. Paul, MN
  [*Library symbol Library of Congress Obsolete*] (LCLS) .... MnSMMfg
Minnesota Multiphasic Personality Inventory [*Psychology*] .... MMPI
Minnesota Muni Inc. Portfolio [*AMEX symbol*] (TTSB) .... MXA
Minnesota Muni Term Tr-II [*AMEX symbol*] (TTSB) .... MNB
Minnesota Muni Term Trust [*NYSE symbol*] (TTSB) .... MNA
Minnesota Municipal Income Portfolio [*AMEX symbol*] (SPSG) .... MXA
Minnesota Municipal Income Trust [*Associated Press*] (SAG) .... MinnMul
Minnesota Municipal Term Trust [*Associated Press*] (SAG) .... MinnMuT
Minnesota Municipal Term Trust [*NYSE symbol*] (SPSG) .... MNA
Minnesota National Laboratory .... MNL
Minnesota North Stars Booster Club (EA) .... MNSBC
Minnesota Occupational Information System (AD) .... MOIS
Minnesota Office of Economic Opportunity, St. Paul, MN [*Library symbol Library of Congress*] (LCLS) .... MnSOEO
Minnesota Orchestral Association (AD) .... MOA
Minnesota Perception Diagnostic Test (AD) .... MPDT
Minnesota Percepto-Diagnostic Test .... MPD
Minnesota Percepto-Diagnostic Test [*Psychology*] .... MPDT
Minnesota Personnel and Guidance Association (AD) .... MPGA
Minnesota Power & Light Co. [*Associated Press*] (SAG) .... MinnPL
Minnesota Power & Light Co. [*Associated Press*] (SAG) .... MinP
Minnesota Power & Light Co. [*AMEX symbol*] (SAG) .... MPL
Minnesota Power & Light Co. [*NYSE symbol*] (SPSG) .... MPL
Minnesota Preschool Inventory [*Child development test*] .... MPI
Minnesota Private College Council (AD) .... MPCC
Minnesota Pwr & Lt [*NYSE symbol*] (TTSB) .... MPL

Minnesota Railroad and Warehouse Commission. Auto Transportation Co.
  Division Reports [*A publication*] (DLA) .... Minn R & WCAT Div
[*The*] Minnesota Regional Network [*Computer science*] (TNIG) .... MRNet
Minnesota Register [*A publication*] (AAGC) .... Minn Reg
Minnesota Reports [*A publication*] (DLA) .... Min
Minnesota Reports [*A publication*] (DLA) .... Min R
Minnesota Reports [*A publication*] (DLA) .... Min Rep
Minnesota Reports [*A publication*] (DLA) .... Minn Rep
Minnesota Reports [*A publication*] (DLA) .... Minn Reps
Minnesota Reports (Gilfillan Edition) [*A publication*] (DLA) .... Minn (Gil)
Minnesota Reports (Gilfillan Edition) [*A publication*] (DLA) .... Minn (Gill)
Minnesota Restitution Center (AD) .... MRC
Minnesota Review [*A publication*] (BRI) .... MR
Minnesota Satisfaction Questionnaire .... MSQ
Minnesota Satisfactoriness Scale [*Job performance test*] .... MSS
Minnesota Scholastic Aptitude Test .... MSAT
Minnesota School Attitude Survey [*Educational test*] .... MSAS
Minnesota School Mathematics and Science Teaching Project [*University of Minnesota*] (AEE) .... MINNEMAST
Minnesota School of Professional Psychology, Minneapolis, MN [*Library symbol*] [*Library of Congress*] (LCLS) .... MnMMSP
Minnesota Session Law Service (West) [*A publication*]
  (DLA) .... Minn Sess Law Serv (West)
Minnesota Short Lines Co. [*AAR code*] .... MSLC
Minnesota State Association of Life Underwriters (SRA) .... MALU
Minnesota State Department of Administration, Budget Library, St. Paul,
  MN [*Library symbol Library of Congress*] (LCLS) .... Mn-Ad
Minnesota State Department of Corrections, St. Paul, MN [*Library symbol Library of Congress*] (LCLS) .... Mn-C
Minnesota State Department of Education, Professional Library, St. Paul,
  MN [*OCLC symbol*] (OCLC) .... MDE
Minnesota State Department of Education, St. Paul, MN [*Library symbol Library of Congress*] (LCLS) .... Mn-E
Minnesota State Department of Health, St. Paul, MN [*Library symbol Library of Congress*] (LCLS) .... Mn-H
Minnesota State Department of Natural Resources, St. Paul, MN [*Library symbol Library of Congress*] (LCLS) .... Mn-N
Minnesota State Department of Planning, St. Paul, MN [*Library symbol Library of Congress*] (LCLS) .... Mn-P
Minnesota State Department of Public Welfare, St. Paul, MN [*Library symbol Library of Congress*] (LCLS) .... Mn-W
Minnesota State Department of Taxation, St. Paul, MN [*Library symbol Library of Congress*] (LCLS) .... Mn-T
Minnesota State Department of Transportation, St. Paul, MN [*Library symbol Library of Congress*] (LCLS) .... Mn-Hw
Minnesota State Drafting Advisory Committee (EDAC) .... MSDAC
Minnesota State Law Library, St. Paul, MN [*Library symbol Library of Congress*] (LCLS) .... Mn
Minnesota State Law Library, St. Paul, MN [*OCLC symbol*] (OCLC) .... MSL
Minnesota State Legislative Library, St. Paul, MN [*Library symbol Library of Congress*] (LCLS) .... Mn-Leg
Minnesota State Pollution Control Agency, Roseville, MN [*Library symbol Library of Congress*] (LCLS) .... MnRoP
Minnesota State Register [*A publication*] (DLA) .... Minn Admin Reg
Minnesota State Universities System Project for Automated Library
  Systems [*Mankato State University Library*] [*Mankato, MN*] [*Information service or system*] .... MSUS/PALS
Minnesota State Vocational Rehabilitation Library, St. Paul, MN [*Library symbol Library of Congress*] (LCLS) .... Mn-V
Minnesota Statutes [*A publication*] (AAGC) .... Minn Stat
Minnesota Statutes, Annotated [*A publication*] (DLA) .... Minn Stat Ann
Minnesota Statutes, Annotated [*A publication*] (DLA) .... MSA
Minnesota Study of Twins Reared Apart .... MISTRA
Minnesota Supreme Court Reports [*A publication*] (DLA) .... Minn
Minnesota Teacher Attitude Inventory .... MTAI
Minnesota Term Trust, Inc. II [*Associated Press*] (SAG) MinnTr2
Minnesota Term Trust, Inc. II [*AMEX symbol*] (SAG) .... MNB
Minnesota Test for Differential Diagnosis of Aphasia [*Psychology*] .... MTDDA
[*The*] Minnesota Transfer Railway Co. [*AAR code*] .... MTFR
Minnesota Valley Regional Library, Mankato, MN [*Library symbol Library of Congress*] (LCLS) .... MnManM
Minnesota Vocational Interest Inventory .... MVII
Minnesota Western Railroad (IIA) .... MW
Minnesota Workmen's Compensation Decisions [*A publication*]
  (DLA) .... Minn WCD
Minnesota Zoological Garden, Apple Valley, MN [*Library symbol Library of Congress*] (LCLS) .... MnAvZ
Minnesota Zoological Garden, Apple Valley, MN [*OCLC symbol*] (OCLC) .... ZOO
Minnetrista Cultural Center, Muncie, IN [*Library symbol*] [*Library of Congress*] (LCLS) .... InMuMC
Minnova, Inc. [*Toronto Stock Exchange symbol*] (SPSG) .... MVA
Minntech Corp. [*Associated Press*] (SAG) .... Minntc
Minntech Corp. [*NASDAQ symbol*] (NQ) .... MNTX
Minocqua, WI [*AM radio station call letters*] .... WMQA
Minocqua, WI [*FM radio station call letters*] .... WMQA-FM
Minocqua/Woodruff, WI [*Location identifier FAA*] (FAAL) .... ARV
Minocqua-Woodruff, WI [*Location identifier FAA*] (FAAL) .... RUF
Minocycline [*Antibiotic compound*] (AAMN) .... MiC
Minolta Automatic Retrieval System (NITA) .... MARS
Minolta Integrated Information and Image Management System [*Optical disc*] (IT) .... MI^{3}MS
Minoo Dasht [*Iran*] [*ICAO location identifier*] (ICLI) .... OIND
Minor .... M
Minor (ROG) .... MI
Minor .... MIN

Minor Assist Work ..... MAW
Minor Atomic Prolonged Life Equipment (PDAA) ..... MAPLE
Minor Basic Allergens [*Immunology*] ..... MBA
Minor Care Clinic [*Medicine*] ..... MIC
Minor Civil Division [*Bureau of Census*] ..... MCD
Minor Construction (AFIT) ..... MC
Minor Counties Cricket Association [*British*] (DBA) ..... MCCA
Minor Determinant Mixture [*Medicine*] ..... MDM
Minor Discrepancy Repair [*NASA*] (KSC) ..... MDR
Minor Discrepancy Review [*NASA*] (GFGA) ..... MDR
Minor Equipment Relocations, Replacements (DNAB) ..... MERR
Minor Expendable Tool (MCD) ..... MET
Minor Hill, TN [*FM radio station call letters*] ..... WEUP
Minor Irregularities and Deficiencies ..... MIRD
Minor Isotopes Safeguards Techniques [*Nuclear energy*] ..... MIST
Minor Karyotypic Abnormalities [*Medicine*] ..... MIKA
Minor League Research Committee (EA) ..... MLRC
Minor Lymphocyte Stimulating [*Genetics*] ..... MLS
Minor Machine Accessory (MCD) ..... MIMA
Minor Machine Equipment (MCD) ..... MIME
Minor Metals Traders' Association [*British*] ..... MMTA
Minor Military Construction, Army ..... MMCA
Minor Neurological Dysfunction ..... MND
Minor Planet Center [*Smithsonian Institution*] ..... MPC
Minor Repair (MCD) ..... MR
Minor Restricted Activity Day [*Environmental medicine*] ..... MRAD
Minor Subcontractor or IDWA [*Interdivisional Work Authorization*] **Notification** [*NASA*] (NASA) ..... MSOIN
Minor Subcontractor Or Iowa [*Interdivisional Work Authorization*] **Notification** ..... MSOIN
Minor Subject Descriptor [*Online database field identifier*] ..... MN
Minor Suma Corp. [*Kansas City, MO*] (TSSD) ..... MSC
Minor Support (KSC) ..... M/S
Minor Surgery Suite [*Medicine*] (DAVI) ..... MSS
Minor Task Authorization [*Navy*] ..... MTA
Minorco [*Formerly, Minerals & Resources Corp. Ltd.*] [*Associated Press*] (SAG) ..... Minorc
Minorco [*Formerly, Minerals & Resources Corp. Ltd.*] [*NASDAQ symbol*] (NQ) ..... MNRC
Minorco ADR [*NASDAQ symbol*] (TTSB) ..... MNRCY
Minorco Canada Ltd. [*Toronto Stock Exchange symbol*] ..... MRC
Minorities Advancement Plan ..... MAP
Minorities Caucus of Family Service Association of America [*Later, MCFSA*] (EA) ..... MCFSAA
Minorities/Females ..... M/F
Minorities in Cable [*Defunct*] (EA) ..... MC
Minorities in Media (EA) ..... MIM
Minorities in Medicine [*Eastern Michigan University Macy Scholarship*] ..... MIM
Minorities International Network for Trade (EA) ..... MINT
Minorities Research Group (AD) ..... MRG
Minority ..... MIN
Minority ..... MINRTY
Minority (ROG) ..... MINY
Minority Access to Research Careers [*Program*] [*Public Health Service Bethesda, MD*] ..... MARC
Minority Advisory Committee on Energy [*Terminated, 1982*] (EGAO) ..... MACE
Minority Affairs Task Group (DNAB) ..... MITAG
Minority Bank Deposit Program [*Treasury Department*] ..... MBDP
Minority Biomedical Research Support Program [*Bethesda, MD*] [*National Institutes of Health*] (GRD) ..... MBRS
Minority Business Development Agency [*Formerly, OMBE*] [*Department of Commerce*] ..... MBDA
Minority Business Development Center [*Minority Business Development Administration*] ..... MBDC
Minority Business Enterprise (MCD) ..... MBE
Minority Business Enterprise Legal Defense and Education Fund (EA) ..... MBELDEF
Minority Business Information Institute [*Defunct*] (EA) ..... MBII
Minority Business Opportunity Committee [*Federal interagency group*] ..... MBOC
Minority Carrier Lifetime [*Solar cell technology*] ..... MCL
Minority Caucus of Family Service America (EA) ..... MCFSA
Minority Centers of Influence (DNAB) ..... MCOI
Minority Contractors Assistance Project [*Jamaica, NY*] (EA) ..... MCAP
Minority Economic Resource Center [*Howard University, Washington, DC*] ..... MERC
Minority Educational Institution ..... MEI
Minority Engineering Education Effort [*Later, NACME*] ME3
Minority Enterprise Development ..... MED
Minority Enterprise Small Business Investment Company ..... MESBIC
Minority Entrepreneurship Program [*Small Business Administration*] ..... MEP
Minority Graphic Arts Organization (EA) ..... MGAO
Minority Group ..... MG
Minority Group Designator [*Office of Personnel Management*] (GFGA) ..... MGD
Minority Information Trade Annual [*A publication*] ..... MITA
Minority Institution ..... MI
Minority Institutions Science Improvement Program [*National Science Foundation*] ..... MISIP
Minority Interest [*Business term*] ..... MI
Minority Legislative Education Program ..... MLEP
Minority Officer Recruitment Effort ..... MORE
Minority Procurement Policy (AAGC) ..... MPP
Minority Recruiting Officer (DNAB) ..... MRO
Minority Research Institution [*Program*] [*National Science Foundation*] ..... MRI
Minority Rights Group (EAIO) ..... MRG
Minority Rights Group International [*British*] (EAIO) ..... MRGI
Minority Science Improvement Program [*Department of Education*] (GFGA) ..... MSIP
Minority Small Business (BARN) ..... MSB
Minority Small Business Investment Company (AAGC) ..... MSBIC
Minority Small Business-Capital Ownership Development Program [*Small Business Administration*] ..... MSB-COD
Minority Stockholder ..... MS
Minority Undergraduate Research Support ..... MURS
Minority Vendor Information Service [*National Minority Supplier Development Council, Inc.*] (IID) ..... VIS
Minority Vendors Program ..... MVP
Minor's Alabama Reports [*A publication*] (DLA) ..... Min
Minor's Alabama Reports [*A publication*] (DLA) ..... Minor (Ala)
Minor's Alabama Reports [*A publication*] (DLA) ..... Minor's Ala R
Minor's Alabama Reports [*A publication*] (DLA) ..... Minor's Ala Rep
Minor's Alabama Reports [*A publication*] (DLA) ..... Minor's Alabama Rep
Minor's Alabama Reports [*A publication*] (DLA) ..... Minor's R
Minor's Alabama Reports [*A publication*] (DLA) ..... Minor's Rep
Minor's Alabama Supreme Court Reports [*1820-26*] [*A publication*] (DLA) ..... Minor
Minors in Need of Supervision [*Classification for delinquent children*] ..... MINS
Minor's Institutes [*A publication*] (DLA) ..... Minor
Minor's Institutes [*Alabama*] [*A publication*] (DLA) ..... Minor (Ala)
Minor's Institutes of Common and Statute Law [*A publication*] (DLA) ..... Min Inst
Minor's Institutes of Common and Statute Law [*A publication*] (DLA) ..... Minor Inst
Minot [*North Dakota*] [*Airport symbol*] (OAG) ..... MOT
Minot Air Defense Sector [*ADC*] ..... MIADS
Minot/International [*North Dakota*] [*ICAO location identifier*] (ICLI) ..... KMOT
Minot/Minot Air Force Base [*North Dakota*] [*ICAO location identifier*] (ICLI) ..... KMIB
Minot, ND [*Location identifier FAA*] (FAAL) ..... DDQ
Minot, ND [*FM radio station call letters*] ..... KBQQ
Minot, ND [*AM radio station call letters*] ..... KCJB
Minot, ND [*AM radio station call letters*] ..... KHRT
Minot, ND [*FM radio station call letters*] ..... KIZZ
Minot, ND [*Television station call letters*] ..... KMCY
Minot, ND [*Television station call letters*] ..... KMOT
Minot, ND [*FM radio station call letters*] ..... KMPR
Minot, ND [*FM radio station call letters*] (RBYB) ..... KMXA-FM
Minot, ND [*AM radio station call letters*] ..... KRRZ
Minot, ND [*Television station call letters*] ..... KSRE
Minot, ND [*AM radio station call letters*] ..... KTYN
Minot, ND [*Television station call letters*] ..... KXMC
Minot, ND [*FM radio station call letters*] ..... KYYX
Minot, ND [*FM radio station call letters*] ..... KZPR
Minot, ND [*Location identifier FAA*] (FAAL) ..... MIB
Minot Public Library, Minot, ND [*Library symbol Library of Congress*] (LCLS) ..... NdMin
Minot State College, Minot, ND [*Library symbol Library of Congress*] (LCLS) ..... NdMinS
Minot State College, Minot, ND [*OCLC symbol*] (OCLC) ..... NMI
Minot State University (GAGS) ..... Minot St U
Minot's Digest [*Massachusetts*] [*A publication*] (DLA) ..... Min Dig
Minsk [*Former USSR Airport symbol*] (OAG) ..... MSQ
Minsk/Loshitsa [*Former USSR ICAO location identifier*] (ICLI) ..... UMMM
Minskoff, Wiseman, Minskoff [*Program for the development of language abilities*] ..... MWM
Minson Aviation, Inc. [*ICAO designator*] (FAAC) ..... CSL
Minstrel Instruction Service (NADA) ..... MIS
Mint [*Condition*] [*Numismatics, etc.*] ..... M
Mint Hill, NC [*AM radio station call letters*] ..... WNOW
Mint in Package [*Doll collecting*] ..... MIP
Mint in the Box [*Doll collecting*] ..... MIB
Mint Mark [*Numismatics*] ..... MM
Mint Never Hinged [*Philately*] ..... MNH
Mint No Box [*Doll collecting*] ..... MNB
Mint State ..... MS
Mint State (AD) ..... ms
Mintek Resources [*Vancouver Stock Exchange symbol*] ..... MTK
Mintel International Development Corp. [*Vancouver Stock Exchange symbol*] ..... MTD
Minto [*Alaska*] [*Airport symbol*] (OAG) ..... MNT
Minto Coal Museum, Minto, NB, Canada [*Library symbol*] [*Library of Congress*] (LCLS) ..... CaNBMCM
Minto Coal Museum, New Brunswick [*Library symbol National Library of Canada*] (NLC) ..... NBMCM
Minto Resources [*Vancouver Stock Exchange symbol*] ..... MIN
Minuetto [*Slow Air*] [*Music*] (ROG) ..... MTTO
Minus ..... M
Minus ..... MS
Minus Optical Sound [*Film industry*] ..... MOS
Minus Sense (SAA) ..... MSE
Minus Zero (IAA) ..... MZ
Minute ..... M
Minute (ADA) ..... MI
Minute (AFM) ..... MIN
Minute (IDOE) ..... min
Minute (ODBW) ..... min
Minute ..... min
Minute [*Angle*] ..... MNT
Minute Alveolar Volume [*Medicine*] (DAVI) ..... MAV
Minute Difference ..... MD
Minute Man National Historical Park ..... MIMA
Minute Men of America (NADA) ..... NMA
Minute of Angle (AD) ..... moa

Minute of Angle .... MOA
Minute of Program [Broadcasting] (NTCM) .... MOP
Minute Output [Of heart] .... MO
Minute Respiratory Volume .... MRV
Minute Ventilation [Medicine] .... MV
Minute Ventilation [Medicine] (DAVI) .... VE
Minute Virus of Mice .... MVM
Minute Volume [Medicine] .... MV
Minute Volume [Laboratory science] (DAVI) V
Minute Women of the United States of America (EA) .... MWUSA
Minuteman [Missile] (AABC) .... MM
Minuteman Action Committee (SAA) .... MINAC
Minuteman Assembly-Maintenance Building, Ogden (SAA) ... MAMBO
Minuteman Change Committee [Air Force] (IAA) .... MCC
Minuteman Change Request [Air Force] (IAA) .... MCR
Minuteman Configuration Accountability System [Air Force] (IAA) ... MCAS
Minuteman Defense Study [DoD] .... MDS
Minuteman Defense System [DoD] .... MDS
Minuteman Education Program [Air Force] (AFM) .... MEP
Minuteman Education Program [Air Force] (AFM) .... MMEP
Minuteman Engineering Instruction Manual (SAA) .... MEIM
Minuteman Extended Survivable Power (DWSG) .... MESP
Minuteman Integrated Command and Control System [Missiles] ... MICCS
Minuteman Integrated Life Extension [Telecommunications] (LAIN) ... MILE
Minuteman Integrated Schedules Status and Data Systems [Missiles] ... MISS-D
Minuteman International [Associated Press] (SAG) .... MinutInt
Minuteman International [NASDAQ symbol] (SAG) .... MMAN
Minuteman Int'l [NASDAQ symbol] (TTSB) .... MMAN
Minuteman Library Network [Information service or system] (IT) ... MLN
Minuteman Long Range Plan [Telecommunications] (LAIN) ... MLRP
Minuteman Operating Directive (SAA) .... MOD
Minuteman Ordnance (SAA) .... MMO
Minuteman Parts Control Board [Missiles] .... MPCB
Minuteman Parts Working Group [Missiles] .... MPWG
Minuteman Platform .... MP
Minuteman Production Quality Assurance (MCD) .... MPQA
Minuteman Requirement Control Number (SAA) .... MRCN
Minute-of-Angle (NASA) .... MOA
Minutes [International telex abbreviation] (WDMC) .... MNS
Minutes (AAG) .... MS
Minutes of Evidence .... M of E
Minutes of Evidence [Legal term] (DLA) .... MIN EV
Minutes of Meeting .... MOM
Minutes of Telecommunications Traffic [Measure of voice, fax, and data transmission] ... MITTS
Minutes per Unit .... MPU
Minutes Played [Hockey] .... MP
Minutes Zero Zero Seconds [Aerospace] (AAG) M/0/0/S
Minven Gold Corp. [Toronto Stock Exchange symbol] ..... MVG
Minven Gold Corp. [Vancouver Stock Exchange symbol] ... MVG
Minvoul [Gabon] [ICAO location identifier] (ICLI) .... FOGV
Minvoul [Gabon] [Airport symbol] (OAG) .... MVX
Mio, MI [FM radio station call letters] .... WCLX
Miotic [Biology] .... M
MIPR [Military Interdepartmental Purchase Request] Management Office (AFIT) ... MMO
Miquelon [France ICAO location identifier] (ICLI) .... LFVM
Miqva'ot [or Miqwa'ot] (BJA) .... Miq
Mir Pur Khas [Pakistan] [ICAO location identifier] (ICLI) ... OPMK
Mira [A star] [Astronomy] (OA) .... M
MIRA [Multifunctional Inertial Reference Assembly] Basic Unit [Air Force] (MCD) ... MBU
MIRA [Multifunctional Inertial Reference Assembly] Basic Unit Mounting Rack [Air Force] (MCD) ... MBUMR
MIRA [Multifunctional Inertial Reference Assembly] Fighter Unit [Air Force] (MCD) ... MFU
MIRA [Multifunctional Inertial Reference Assembly] Fighter Unit Mounting Rack [Air Force] (MCD) ... MFUMR
MIRA [Multifunctional Inertial Reference Assembly] Transport Unit [Air Force] (MCD) ... MTU
MIRA [Multifunctional Inertial Reference Assembly] Transport Unit MountingRack [Air Force] (MCD) ... MTUMR
Mirabilis Mosaic Virus [Plant pathology] .... MIMV
Miracema do Norte [Brazil] [Airport symbol] (AD) .... MMX
Miracidal Immobilization Test [Parasitology] .... MIT
Miracle of Grace [Pseudonym used by William Smith] ..... MG
MiraCosta Community College, Oceanside, CA [Library symbol] [Library of Congress] (LCLS) ... COcM
Miraflores [Colombia] [Airport symbol] (OAG) .... MFS
Miraflores [Peru] [Seismograph station code, US Geological Survey] (SEIS) ... MRF
Mirage Resorts [NYSE symbol] (SPSG) .... MIR
Mirage Resorts [Associated Press] (SAG) .... MirRsrt
Miraloma, CA [Location identifier FAA] (FAAL) .... LKA
Miramar Beach, FL [FM radio station call letters] (RBYB) ... WSBZ
Miramar Energy Corp. [Vancouver Stock Exchange symbol] ... MAE
Miramar Mining [NASDAQ symbol] (TTSB) .... MAENF
Miramar Mining Corp. [NASDAQ symbol] (SAG) .... MAENF
Miramar Mining Corp. [Associated Press] (SAG) .... Miramr
Miramar Naval Air Station [California] [ICAO location identifier] (ICLI) ... KNKX
Miramichi Air Services Ltd. [Canada ICAO designator] (FAAC) ... MIR
Miramichi Campus, New Brunswick Community College [Campus Miramichi, College Communautaire du Nouveau-Brunswick], Chatham, New Brunswick [Library symbol National Library of Canada] (NLC) ... NBCCC
Miramichi Historical Society Archives, Newcastle, NB, Canada [Library symbol Library of Congress] (LCLS) ... CaNBNAM

Miramichi Natural History Society, Chatham, NB, Canada [Library symbol] [Library of Congress] (LCLS) ... CaNBChM
Miramichi Natural History Society, Chatham, New Brunswick [Library symbol National Library of Canada] (NLC) ... NBCM
Miramichi, NB [AM radio station call letters] .... CFAN
Miramichi Salmon Museum, Inc., Doaktown, New Brunswick [Library symbol National Library of Canada] (NLC) ... NBDM
Miranda Downs [Australia Airport symbol Obsolete] (OAG) ... MWY
Mirandela [Portugal ICAO location identifier] (ICLI) .... LPMI
Mirando City, TX [FM radio station call letters] .... KBDR
Miranshah [Pakistan] [ICAO location identifier] (ICLI) ..... OPMN
Miranshah [Pakistan] [ICAO location identifier] (ICLI) ..... OPMS
Miravant [NASDAQ symbol] .... MRVT
Miravant Medical Technologies .... MRVT
Miravia Ltd. [Romania] [FAA designator] (FAAC) .... MRV
Mirchall's Doctor and Student [A publication] (DLA) ...... Mirch D & S
MIRCOM [Missile Material Readiness Command] Automated Microfilm System [Army] (IID) ... MAMS
Mired (IAA) .... M
Mirehouse on Advowsons [1824] [A publication] (DLA) ... Mireh Advow
Mirehouse on Tithes [2nd ed.] [1822] [A publication] (DLA) ... Mireh Ti
Miri [Malaysia] [Airport symbol] (AD) .... LUT
Miri [Malaysia] [Airport symbol] (OAG) .... MYY
Miri [Indonesia] [ICAO location identifier] (ICLI) .... WBGR
Miriadair [France ICAO designator] (FAAC) .... MYR
Mirinda's Friendship Club (EA) .... MFC
Mirjaveh [Iran] [ICAO location identifier] (ICLI) .... OIZM
MIRLYN [Michigan Research Library Network] .... MIR
Mirny [Antarctica] [Seismograph station code, US Geological Survey] (SEIS) ... MIR
Miron Co. Ltd., Montreal, PQ, Canada [Library symbol Library of Congress] (LCLS) ... CaQMMC
Miron Co. Ltd., Montreal, Quebec [Library symbol National Library of Canada] (NLC) ... QMMC
Mirrer Yeshiva Central Institute (EA) .... MYCI
Mirror (KSC) .... MIR
Mirror .... MIR
Mirror .... MIR
Mirror (VRA) .... mirr
Mirror Advanced Reactor Study (MCD) .... MARS
Mirror Coil (MCD) .... MC
Mirror, Digby, Nova Scotia [Library symbol National Library of Canada] (NLC) ... NSDM
Mirror, Digby, NS, Canada [Library symbol] [Library of Congress] (LCLS) ... CaNSDiM
Mirror Electron Microscope (PDAA) .... MEM
Mirror Fusion Experiment [Nuclear energy] .... MFX
Mirror Fusion Test Facility [For study of new energy source] ... MFTF
Mirror Group Newspapers [British] .... MGN
Mirror Landing Procedures (MCD) .... MLP
Mirror Manufacturers Association .... MMA
Mirror Mode (MCD) .... MMODE
Mirror of Parliament, London [A publication] (DLA) .... Mir Parl
Mirror of the Patent Office [Washington, DC] [A publication] (DLA) ... Mir Pat Off
Mirror Optional Landing System [Aviation] (NG) .... MOLS
Mirror Public Library, Alberta [Library symbol National Library of Canada] (NLC) ... AMIR
Mirror Sign Convention .... MSC
Mirror Streak Camera .... MSC
Mirrored Ions Closed-Loop Electrons (MCD) .... MIRICLE
Mirtone International, Inc. [Toronto Stock Exchange symbol] ... MTN
MIS Division, Turnelle Productions Ltd., Gloucester, Ontario [Library symbol National Library of Canada] (BIB) ... OGT
Misaki [Japan] [Seismograph station code, US Geological Survey Closed] (SEIS) ... MSK
Misalignment Estimation Software System (MCD) .... MESS
Misallat [Egypt] [Geomagnetic observatory code] .... MLT
Misappropriation, Interference and Misrepresentation ..... MIM
Misawa [Japan] [Airport symbol] (OAG) .... MSJ
Misawa [Japan ICAO location identifier] (ICLI) .... RJSM
Misay [Zaire] [ICAO location identifier] (ICLI) .... FZDY
Miscarriage [Obstetrics] (DAVI) .... MC
Miscarriage (DSUE) .... MIS
Miscarriage [Medicine] .... MISC
Miscarriage Infant Death Stillbirth Support Group .... MIDS
Misce [Mix] [Pharmacy] .... M
Misce Accuratissime [Mix Thoroughly] [Pharmacy] .... M ACCUR
Misce Bene [Mix Well] [Pharmacy] .... MB
Misce Caute [Mix Cautiously] [Pharmacy] .... M CAUTE
Misce et Signa [Mix and Label] [Pharmacy] .... M et Sig
Misce et Signa [Mix and write a label] [Latin] [Pharmacy] (DAVI) ... m et sig
Misce Fiat Mistura [Mix to Make a Mixture] [Pharmacy] ... M FT M
Misce Secundum Artem [Mix Pharmaceutically] [Latin] ... MSA
Misce, Signa, Da [Mix, Write (the Directions), and Give (to the Patient)] [Pharmacy] (ROG) ... MSD
Miscellaneous .... M
Miscellaneous [MARC language code Library of Congress] (LCCP) ... mis
Miscellaneous (NATG) .... MIS
Miscellaneous (AFM) .... MISC
Miscellaneous (DFIT) .... Misc
Miscellaneous .... MISC
Miscellaneous (WDMC) .... misc
Miscellaneous .... MISCL
Miscellaneous .... MS
Miscellaneous (ADA) .... MSC
Miscellaneous and Other Operations [USCG] (TAG) ...... MISC

Miscellaneous Apparatus Rack (IAA) ... MAR
Miscellaneous Armament Unit ... MAU
Miscellaneous at Anchor [*Navy*] (NVT) ... MA
Miscellaneous Auxiliary [*Self-propelled*] [*Navy ship symbol*] ... YAG
Miscellaneous Auxiliary Ship [*Navy ship symbol*] ... AG
Miscellaneous Babylonian Inscriptions [*A publication*] (BJA) ... MBI
Miscellaneous Branch, Internal Revenue Bureau [*United States*] (DLA) ... MB
Miscellaneous Charges Order [*Business term*] ... MCO
Miscellaneous Command Ship [*Navy symbol*] ... AGF
Miscellaneous Common Carrier ... MCC
Miscellaneous Contract Material ... MCM
Miscellaneous Defense Activities (AAGC) ... MDA
Miscellaneous Direct (MCD) ... MD
Miscellaneous Document ... MD
Miscellaneous Document [*US. House of Representatives of Senate*] (BARN) ... Misc Doc
Miscellaneous Equipment (KSC) ... ME
Miscellaneous Equipment Specification (HGAA) ... MES
Miscellaneous Exercise [*Military*] (NVT) ... MISCEX
Miscellaneous Hardware ... MH
Miscellaneous Income (MHDW) ... MI
Miscellaneous Information Listing Program Apollo Spacecraft [*NASA*] (KSC) ... MILPAS
Miscellaneous Inputs Information Subsystem [*Computer science*] ... MIIS
Miscellaneous Kits [*JETDS nomenclature*] [*Military*] (CET) ... MK
Miscellaneous Liquid Waste Management System (NRCH) ... MLWMS
Miscellaneous Live Unit [*Military*] (AFM) ... MLU
Miscellaneous New York Reports [*A publication*] (AAGC) ... Misc New York
Miscellaneous Obligation Document ... MOD
Miscellaneous Operation (MUGU) ... MO
Miscellaneous Paper [*or Publication*] ... MP
Miscellaneous Personal Property [*Legal term*] (DLA) ... MPP
Miscellaneous Proposal (AD) ... MP
Miscellaneous Quote Request (MCD) ... MQR
Miscellaneous RADAR Input ... MRI
Miscellaneous Radioactive Material (GAAI) ... MRM
Miscellaneous Reference Tool (AD) ... mrto
Miscellaneous Relay Panel (MCD) ... MRP
Miscellaneous Report ... MR
Miscellaneous Reports [*New York*] [*A publication*] (DLA) ... Misc
Miscellaneous Reports [*New York*] [*A publication*] (DLA) ... Misc (NY)
Miscellaneous Reports [*New York*] [*A publication*] (DLA) ... Misc Rep
Miscellaneous Reports [*New York*] [*A publication*] (DLA) ... Miscel
Miscellaneous Reports, Second Series [*New York*] [*A publication*] (DLA) ... Misc 2d
Miscellaneous Services [*Department of Employment*] [*British*] ... MS
Miscellaneous Simulation Generator ... MSG
Miscellaneous Small Parts ... MSP
Miscellaneous Small Special Projects (AAG) ... MSSP
Miscellaneous Tax Ruling [*IRS*] (AAGC) ... MTR
Miscellaneous Tax Rulings [*Australia A publication*] ... MT Rulings
Miscellaneous Tool (SAA) ... MIT
Miscellaneous Vector Table ... MVT
Miscellaneous Waste Holdup Tank [*Nuclear energy*] (NRCH) ... MWHT
Miscellaneous Waste Storage Tank [*Nuclear energy*] (NRCH) ... MWST
Miscendus [*To Be Mixed*] [*Pharmacy*] ... MISCEND
Misch Metal [*A commercial mixture of rare earth metals*] ... Mm
Mischief Enterprises Ltd. [*Vancouver Stock Exchange symbol*] ... MFE
Miscible ... M
Misconduct ... MISCON
Misconduct Policy Officer [*National Institutes of Health*] ... MPO
Misdemeanor [*FBI standardized term*] ... MISD
Misdemeanor [*Legal shorthand*] (LWAP) ... MISDM
Misdemeanor (ROG) ... MISDMR
Misdemeanor and Cure [*Legal shorthand*] (LWAP) ... MISDM
Miserable (DSUE) ... MIS
Misericorde Sisters [*Roman Catholic religious order*] ... SM
Misericordia General Hospital, Winnipeg, Manitoba [*Library symbol National Library of Canada*] (NLC) ... MWMG
Misericordia General Hospital, Winnipeg, MB, Canada [*Library symbol Library of Congress*] (LCLS) ... CaMWMG
Misericordia Hospital, Edmonton, AB, Canada [*Library symbol*] [*Library of Congress*] (LCLS) ... CaAEMH
Misericordia Hospital, Edmonton, Alberta [*Library symbol National Library of Canada*] (NLC) ... AEMH
Misericordia Hospital, Medical Library, Bronx, NY [*OCLC symbol*] (OCLC) ... VMH
Misericordia Hospital, Milwaukee, WI [*Library symbol Library of Congress*] (LCLS) ... WMMH
Misericordia Hospital, Philadelphia, PA [*Library symbol Library of Congress Obsolete*] (LCLS) ... PPMis
Misery, Famine, Misery [*Said to be "earth's song," in theory that all planets emit musical sounds governed by their paths around the sun*] ... MI-FA-MI
Mishap Investigation Report (MCD) ... MIR
Mishawaka Enterprise-Record, Mishawaka, IN [*Library symbol Library of Congress*] (LCLS) ... InMisER
Mishawaka Public Library, Mishawaka, IN [*OCLC symbol*] (OCLC) ... IMP
Mishawaka Public Library, Mishawaka, IN [*Library symbol Library of Congress*] (LCLS) ... InMis
Mishibishu Resources [*Vancouver Stock Exchange symbol*] ... MSH
Mishicot, WI [*FM radio station call letters*] ... WGBM
Mishima [*Japan*] [*Seismograph station code, US Geological Survey*] (SEIS) ... MIS
Mishnah [*Basis of the Talmud*] (BJA) ... M
Mishnah [*Basis of the Talmud*] (BJA) ... Mi
Mishnah [*Basis of the Talmud*] (BJA) ... Mish
Mishnaic Hebrew [*Language, etc.*] (BJA) ... MH
Mishneh Torah [*Maimonides*] (BJA) ... MT
Misima [*Papua New Guinea*] [*Airport symbol*] (OAG) ... MIS
Misionaras Clarisas [*Poor Clare Missionary Sisters*] [*Roman Catholic religious order*] ... MC
Misioneras del Perpetual Socorro (TOCD) ... MPS
Misioneros de Guadalupe [*Missionaries of Guadelupe*] [*Mexico*] (EAIO) ... MG
Misioneros del Espiritu Santo [*Missionaries of the Holy Spirit*] [*Mexico*] (EAIO) ... MSpS
Miskito, Sumo, and Rama [*Nicaraguan Indian coalition*] ... MISURA
Miskito, Sumo, and Rama [*Nicaraguan Indian coalition*] ... MISURASATA
Mismatch Negativity [*Neurophysiology*] ... MMN
Mismatch Repair [*Genetics*] ... MMR
Mismated [*Merchandising slang*] ... MM
Misnumbered (WGA) ... MISN
Misonidazole [*Azomycin*] [*Oncology, Radiosensitizer*] ... MISO
Misonix, Inc. [*Associated Press*] (SAG) ... Misonix
Misonix, Inc. [*Associated Press*] (SAG) ... Misonx
Misonix, Inc. [*NASDAQ symbol*] (SAG) ... MSON
Misonix Inc. Wrrt [*NASDAQ symbol*] (TTSB) ... MSONW
Misopogon [*of Julian*] [*Classical studies*] (OCD) ... Mis
Misr Iran Development Bank ... MIDB
Misr Overseas Airways [*Egypt*] ... MOA
MISR Overseas Airways [*Egypt*] [*ICAO designator*] (FAAC) ... MOS
Misrad Isre'eli Li-tevi'ot Mi-Germanyah (BJA) ... MILTAM
Misrair [*ICAO designator*] (AD) ... MU
Misrepresentation [*Legal shorthand*] (LWAP) ... MISREP
Misroute ... MSRTE
Miss Angle ... MA
Miss Distance [*Military*] ... MD
Miss Distance Indicator (MCD) ... MIDI
Miss Distance Optical Recorder [*Military*] (PDAA) ... MIDOR
Miss or Mrs. [*Pronounced "Miz"*] ... MS
Miss Porter's School [*Farmington, CT*] ... MPS
Miss Porter's School, Farmington, CT [*Library symbol*] [*Library of Congress*] (LCLS) ... CtFP
Missabe Southern Railroad ... MSO
Missaukee County Library, Lake City, MI [*Library symbol Library of Congress*] (LCLS) ... MiLac
Miss-Distance Indicator [*Missiles*] (MUGU) ... MDI
Miss-Distance Measuring System ... MDMS
Miss-Distance-Indicator Radioactive Tests [*Missiles*] (MUGU) ... M-DIRT
Missed Appointment ... MA
Missed Approach ... MA
Missed Approach Azimuth [*Aviation*] ... MAZ
Missed Approach Point [*Aviation*] (AFM) ... MAP
Missed Approach Point [*Aviation*] (FAAC) ... MAPT
Missed Approach Procedure [*Aviation*] ... MAP
Missed Byte [*Computer science*] (ECII) ... MB
Missed Contact Rate (CAAL) ... MCR
Missed Interception [*Military*] ... MI
Missed Interception Due to Airborne Equipment Failure [*Air Force*] ... MIAEF
Missed Message Rate (CAAL) ... MMR
Missed Recognition (SAA) ... MR
Missile [*Air Force*] ... M
Missile (CINC) ... MI
Missile ... MIS
Missile ... MIS
Missile ... MISL
Missile (AFM) ... MSL
Missile Acceptance Team (AAG) ... MAT
Missile Acceptance Test ... MAT
Missile Accident Emergency Team (AFM) ... MAET
Missile Acquisition and Track ... MAT
Missile Activation Building [*NWA*] ... MAB
Missile Activation Circuit ... MAC
Missile Adapter Tester ... MAT
Missile Advisory Committee [*Pacific Missile Range*] (MUGU) ... MAC
Missile Airborne Equipment (IAA) ... MAE
Missile Air-Conditioning System ... MACS
Missile/Aircraft Test Equipment ... MATE
Missile Airframe (AAG) ... MA
Missile Airframe Technology (MCD) ... MAT
Missile Alarm Monitor ... MAM
Missile Alignment Set ... MAS
Missile Altitude Measurement System ... MAMS
Missile and Munitions Center and School [*Army*] (RDA) ... MMCS
Missile and Munitions Evaluation (MCD) ... MAME
Missile and Munitions Materiel Center (MCD) ... MISMAC
Missile and Nuclear Programming Data (AABC) ... MNPD
Missile and Package Tester ... MAP
Missile and Rockets Inventory Control Center [*Army*] ... MRICC
Missile and Space Council [*Defunct*] (EA) ... M & SC
Missile and Space Council [*Defunct*] (AAG) ... MSC
Missile and Space Intelligence Center [*DoD*] ... MSIC
Missile and Space Summary (MCD) ... MASS
Missile and Space Vehicle Department [*NASA*] (KSC) ... MSVD
Missile and Space Vehicle Office [*NASA*] (IAA) ... MSVO
Missile and Warhead Magazines ... M & WH
Missile and Weapons Systems Division [*Military*] (IAA) ... MWSD
Missile Antiradiation Television [*Military*] (CAAL) ... MARTEL
Missile Antitank ... MAT
Missile Application Propulsion ... MAP
Missile Application Propulsion Study ... MAPS
Missile Approach Warning System (DOMA) ... MAWS

Missile Assembly and Maintenance [*NASA*] (IAA) .... MAM
Missile Assembly and Maintenance Building [*NASA*] (IAA) ...... MAMB
Missile Assembly and Maintenance Shop [*NASA*] .... MAMS
Missile Assembly and Test [*Building*] (NATG) .... MA and T
Missile Assembly Building (MCD) .... MAB
Missile Assembly Control Building .... MACB
Missile Assembly Data .... MAD
Missile Assembly Equipment (IAA) .... MAE
Missile Assembly Facility .... MAF
Missile Assembly Site (NATG) .... MAS
Missile Assigned Switch .... MAS
Missile Assignment Program (SAA) .... MAP
Missile Assistance Maintenance Structure (IAA) .... MAMS
Missile ASW [*Antisubmarine Warfare*] Torpedo Target (MCD) ...... MATT
Missile Attack Emergency Conference (MCD) .... MAEC
Missile Attack Warning and Assessment [*Military*] (PDAA) ...... MAWA
Missile Attitude Determination System [*LASER device*] [*Air Force*] ...... MADS
Missile Automatic Supply Technique .... MAST
Missile Automation Radiation Test (IAA) .... MART
Missile Auxiliaries System .... MAS
Missile Auxiliaries Test Console .... MATC
Missile Auxiliaries Test Set .... MATS
Missile Auxiliary Output Tester .... MAOT
Missile Auxiliary Signal Generator .... MASG
Missile Auxiliary Test Bench .... MATB
Missile Auxiliary Test Position .... MATP
Missile Away .... MA
Missile Azimuth Heading [*Air Force*] .... MAZH
Missile Azimuth Orientation [*Air Force*] (IAA) .... MAZO
Missile Base [*Military*] .... MB
Missile Base Operations Supervisor [*Air Force*] (IAA) ...... MBOS
Missile Baseline .... MBL
Missile Battery Data Link (MCD) .... MBDL
Missile Battery Status Indicator .... MBSI
Missile Battery Test Set [*Military*] (IAA) .... MBTS
Missile Beacon Filter .... MBF
Missile Body .... MB
Missile Bomber .... MB
Missile Calibration Station .... MCS
Missile Capability Console (MCD) .... MCC
Missile Car (SAA) .... MC
Missile Carrier Aircraft [*Designation for all US military aircraft*] ...... M
Missile Carrying Missile (AAG) .... MCM
Missile Change Committed (SAA) .... MCC
Missile Checkout .... MC
Missile Checkout (NG) .... MCO
Missile Checkout Console (SAA) .... MCC
Missile Checkout Set (AAG) .... MCS
Missile Checkout Station .... MCS
Missile Checkout System Selector .... MCSS
Missile Checkout Trailer .... MCOT
Missile Clock Receiver .... MCR
Missile Code (MUGU) .... MC
Missile Combat Crew (AAG) .... MCC
Missile Combat Crew Commander .... MCCC
Missile Command [*Army*] .... MC
Missile Command [*Army*] (MCD) .... MCOM
Missile Command [*Redstone Arsenal, AL*] [*Army*] .... MICOM
Missile Command [*Army*] .... MSLCOMD
Missile Command Coder (AAG) .... MCC
Missile Command Research, Development, and Engineering Center
[*Army*] (RDA) .... MICOM-RDEC
Missile Commit Sequence (AAG) .... MCS
Missile Compartment .... MC
Missile Compartment, Lower Level .... MCLL
Missile Compartment, Middle Level .... MCML
Missile Compartment, Upper Level .... MCUL
Missile Compensating Control .... MCC
Missile Compensating Equipment .... MCE
Missile Compensating System .... MCS
Missile Compensating Tank .... MCT
Missile Computer Room .... MCR
Missile Container .... MC
Missile Continuity Loop (MCD) .... MCL
Missile Control .... MC
Missile Control Center [*Air Force*] .... MCC
Missile Control Console .... MCC
Missile Control Module (NVT) .... MCM
Missile Control Officer .... MCO
Missile Control Officer, Trainer (NG) .... MCOT
Missile Control Panel .... MCP
Missile Control Point (NATG) .... MCP
Missile Control System .... MCS
Missile Control Test Panel .... MCTP
Missile Controller Set .... MCS
Missile Countermeasure Device (DWSG) .... MCD
Missile Critical Circuit Simulator .... MCCS
Missile Danger Zone (NVT) .... MDZ
Missile Data Processor (OA) .... MDP
Missile Defense Alarm [*or Alert*] System [*Air Force*] ...... MIDAS
Missile Defense [*or Alert*] System Control and Display Facility [*Air Force*]
(IAA) .... MCDF
Missile Design Unit (SAA) .... MDU
Missile Detection and Alarm System [*Army*] (AABC) ...... MIDAS
Missile Detection and Surveillance (CAAL) .... MIDAS

Missile Detection System .... MIDES
Missile Development Center [*Air Force*] .... MDC
Missile Deviation Report (AAG) .... MDR
Missile d'Infanterie Leger Antichar .... MILAN
Missile Direction Center .... MDC
Missile Director Train Indicator .... MDTI
Missile Display Equipment .... MDE
Missile Division (AAG) .... MD
Missile Doppler .... MIDOP
Missile Driver .... MD
Missile Early Warning Station (AFM) .... MEWS
Missile Electric System Test Set [*Military*] (PDAA) ...... MESTS
Missile Electrical Simulator .... MES
Missile Electrical System Test (NG) .... MEST
Missile Electrical Technician [*Aerospace*] (IAA) .... MET
Missile Electrical Technician/Specialist (AAG) .... MET/S
Missile Electrician .... ME
Missile Electronic Warfare Division [*White Sands Missile Range*] (AAG) .... MEWD
Missile Electronic Warfare System [*Army*] .... MEWS
Missile Electronic Warfare Technical Area [*White Sands Missile Range*]
(AABC) .... MEWTA
Missile Electronics and Computer Assembly [*Military*] (PDAA) ...... MECA
Missile Element Need Statement .... MENS
Missile Elevation Heading (IAA) .... MELH
Missile End-Game Scoring System (DWSG) .... MEGS
Missile Engagement Console [*Military*] (CAAL) .... MEC
Missile Engagement Controller [*Military*] (CAAL) .... MEC
Missile Engagement Mechanism (MCD) .... MEM
Missile Engagement Zone (NVT) .... MEZ
Missile Engine Technician/Mechanic (AAG) .... MET/M
Missile Engineering Station .... MES
Missile Environment Computer Control Analysis (MCD) ...... MECCA
Missile Environmental Testing Study .... METS
Missile Equipment Code .... MEC
Missile Equipment Maintenance Sets (MUGU) .... MEMS
Missile Era Data Integration Analysis .... MEDIA
Missile Era Data Integration - Ultimate Method .... MEDIUM
Missile Error Data Integration [*Military*] (IAA) .... MEDI
Missile Escort Team [*Air Force*] (AFM) .... MET
Missile Exercise (DOMA) .... MSLEX
Missile Exhaust Gas Ingestion (MCD) .... MEGI
Missile, Experimental .... MX
Missile Explosive Ordnance Safety Advisory Board [*Pacific Missile Range*]
(MUGU) .... MEOSAB
Missile Facilities Technician/Specialist (AAG) .... MFT/S
Missile Failure (AAG) .... MF
Missile Farm Monitor [*Army*] (AABC) .... MFM
Missile Fatigue Monitor .... MFM
Missile Field Office (AAG) .... MFO
Missile Fire Control (MCD) .... MFC
Missile Fire Control Computer [*Military*] (CAAL) .... MFCC
Missile Fire Control System (NG) .... MFCS
Missile Firing Exercise (NVT) .... MISSILEX
Missile Firing Laboratory (KSC) .... MFL
Missile Firing Order .... MFO
Missile Firing Order Normal [*Military*] (CAAL) .... MFON
Missile Firing Order Patch Panel .... MFOPP
Missile Firing Range (AAG) .... MFR
Missile Firing Safety Group (MUGU) .... MFSG
Missile Firing Simulator (NATG) .... MFS
Missile Firing Station [*Army*] .... MFS
Missile Firing Zone .... MFZ
Missile Flight Caution Corridor (AFM) .... MFCC
Missile Flight Hazard Corridor (AFM) .... MFHC
Missile Flight Safety Center [*Pacific Missile Range*] (MUGU) ...... MFSC
Missile Flight Safety Officer .... MFSO
Missile Flight Safety Officer Assistant (MUGU) .... MFSOA
Missile Flight Safety Officer Console (MUGU) .... MFSOC
Missile Flight Safety Operations Plan .... MFSOP
Missile Flight Safety System (AAG) .... MFSS
Missile Flight Time .... MFT
Missile Fuse Set Servo .... MFS
Missile Gas .... MG
Missile Ground Power Control Unit (AAG) .... MGPCU
Missile Ground Support Equipment .... MGSE
Missile Guidance .... MG
Missile Guidance and Control .... MGC
Missile Guidance and Control Computer .... MGCC
Missile Guidance and Control System (MCD) .... MGCS
Missile Guidance Computer (MCD) .... MGC
Missile Guidance Cooling System (DWSG) .... MGCS
Missile Guidance Element .... MGE
Missile Guidance Group .... MGG
Missile Guidance Section [*or Set, or System*] .... MGS
Missile Guidance Set Control .... MGSC
Missile Handling Equipment .... MHE
Missile Handling Trailer (AAG) .... MHT
Missile Hazard Report (AFM) .... MHR
Missile Hazard Space (AFM) .... MHS
Missile Homing Improvement Program (DWSG) .... MHIP
Missile Identification Code [*Military*] (CAAL) .... MIC
Missile Identification Module [*Military*] (CAAL) .... MIM
Missile Identification Record .... MIR
Missile Ignition and Destruct Simulator .... MIDS
Missile Ignition Test Simulator .... MITS

Missile Impact Locating [*or Location*] **System** ..... MILS
Missile Impact Location System, Pacific (SAA) ..... MILS/PAC
Missile Impact Prediction System ..... MIPS
Missile Impact Predictor [*Air Force*] ..... MIP
Missile in Place/Missile Away ..... MIP/MA
Missile In-Commission Level ..... MICL
Missile Industry (AAG) ..... MI
Missile Industry Liaison (SAA) ..... MIL
Missile, Infantry Light Antiarmor [*Antitank system*] (INF) ..... MILAN
Missile In-Flight Indicator ..... MIFI
Missile In-Flight Safety Approval (MUGU) ..... MIFSA
Missile Information Processing System (MCD) ..... MIPS
Missile Infrared Tracking System (DNAB) ..... MIRTRAC
Missile Inspection Completion Sheet (MCD) ..... MICS
Missile Instrumentation Package [*Military*] (CAAL) ..... MIP
Missile Integration Terminal Equipment [*Computer science*] ..... MITE
Missile Intelligence Agency (AABC) ..... MIA
Missile Intelligence Directorate [*Army*] (AABC) ..... MID
Missile Intelligence Directory ..... MID
Missile Intelligence Report ..... MIR
Missile Intercept Data Acquisition System ..... MIDAS
Missile Intercept Simulation System ..... MISS
Missile Interception Zone [*Military*] ..... MIZ
Missile Interface Test Bench ..... MITB
Missile Interface Test Set ..... MITS
Missile Interface Unit ..... MIU
Missile Interim Specification [*Army*] ..... MIS
Missile Interior Intrusion Detection System (DWSG) ..... MIIDS
Missile Joint Optimization ..... MIJO
Missile Junction Box ..... MJB
Missile Launch Control Blockhouse ..... MLCB
Missile Launch Detector (MCD) ..... MLD
Missile Launch Envelope ..... MLE
Missile Launch Officer (AAG) ..... MLO
Missile Launch Response [*Navy*] (CAAL) ..... MLR
Missile Launch Tube Group ..... MLTG
Missile Launcher ..... ML
Missile Launcher Control Group ..... MLCG
Missile Layout ..... ML
Missile Lethality [*Military*] ..... ML
Missile Lift System (AAG) ..... MLS
Missile Lift-Off (AAG) ..... MLO
Missile Liner ..... ML
Missile Loading Alignment Fixture ..... MLAF
Missile Location System (IEEE) ..... MLS
Missile Logistics Center [*Army*] ..... MLC
Missile Loop Test Unit ..... MLTU
Missile Maintenance Area (AAG) ..... MMA
Missile Maintenance Crew (AFM) ..... MMC
Missile Maintenance Equipment (AABC) ..... MME
Missile Maintenance Squadron [*Air Force*] ..... MIMS
Missile Maintenance Squadron [*Air Force*] (AFM) ..... MIMSq
Missile Maintenance Squadron (SAA) ..... MMS
Missile Maintenance Squadron [*Air Force*] ..... MSLMAINTSq
Missile Maintenance Technician (AABC) ..... MMT
Missile Maintenance Technician/Mechanic (AAG) ..... MMT/M
Missile Manufacturer's Planning Report ..... MMPR
Missile Master [*Fire direction and coordination system*] ..... MM
Missile Master Replacement Program ..... MMRP
Missile Mate Test ..... MMT
Missile Materiel Readiness Command [*Army*] ..... MIRCOM
Missile Measurements Center ..... MMC
Missile Minder (MCD) ..... MM
Missile Miss Distance [*Military*] (CAAL) ..... MMD
Missile Mix Study [*NAVAIR*] (NG) ..... MMS
Missile Mode Panel (MCD) ..... MMP
Missile Monitor System [*Army*] ..... MMS
Missile Motion ..... MM
Missile Motion Computer ..... MMC
Missile Motion Subsystem ..... MMSS
Missile Motion Unit ..... MMU
Missile Not Fully Equipped (AAG) ..... MNFE
Missile Not Operationally Ready [*Air Force*] (SAA) ..... MNOR
Missile Not Operationally Ready - Maintenance [*Air Force*] ..... MNORM
Missile Not Operationally Ready - Parts [*Air Force*] ..... MNORP
Missile Offense/Defense System ..... MODS
Missile Officer (AAG) ..... MO
Missile on Aircraft Test ..... MOAT
Missile on Internal Power ..... MOIP
Missile on Internal Power [*Military*] (AD) ..... moip
Missile On Stand (AD) ..... mos
Missile on Stand ..... MOS
Missile on Stand Timing Simulator (MCD) ..... MOTIS
Missile Onloading Prism Fixture ..... MOPF
Missile Onloading Prism Fixture (AD) ..... mopf
Missile Operability Test (MCD) ..... MOT
Missile Operability Test Station (MCD) ..... MOTS
Missile Operate Mode Simulator ..... MOMS
Missile Operate Mode Simulator (AD) ..... moms
Missile Operation Center [*Air Force*] ..... MOC
Missile Operation [*or Ordnance*] **Readiness Test** [*or Testing*] ..... MORT
Missile Operationally Ready [*Air Force*] ..... MOR
Missile Operations ..... MOPS
Missile Operations Control Officer (AAG) ..... MOCO
Missile Operations Manager (MUGU) ..... MOM

Missile Operations Officer [*NASA*] (KSC) ..... MOO
Missile Operations Paging [*or Phone*] System [*NASA*] ..... MOPS
Missile Operations Station ..... MOS
Missile Operations System (AD) ..... MOPS
Missile Optical Alignment (AD) ..... moa
Missile Optical Alignment ..... MOA
Missile Optical Destruction Technique ..... MODEST
Missile Order of Battle (AFM) ..... MOB
Missile Out of Commission for Maintenance (MUGU) ..... MOCM
Missile Out of Commission for Parts (AFM) ..... MOCP
Missile Out of Commission for Parts [*Military*] (AD) ..... mocp
Missile Out of Order for Parts (MCD) ..... MOOP
Missile Performance Measuring System (MCD) ..... MPMS
Missile Periodic Inspection (AAG) ..... MPI
Missile Piercing Discarding Sabot (PDAA) ..... MPDS
Missile Platform ..... MP
Missile Pneudraulic Repair Technician/Repairman (AAG) ..... MPRT/R
Missile Positioning ..... MP
Missile Positioning Equipment (KSC) ..... MPE
Missile Possessed (SAA) ..... MP
Missile Power Control Panel (AAG) ..... MPCP
Missile Power Control Panel (AD) ..... mpcp
Missile Power Monitor (AD) ..... mpm
Missile Power Monitor (AAG) ..... MPM
Missile Power Panel (AAG) ..... MPP
Missile Power Unit (DNAB) ..... MPU
Missile Precision Instrumentation RADAR ..... MIPIR
Missile Precision Instrumentation RADAR (MSA) ..... MPIR
Missile Preflight Tester ..... MPT
Missile Prelaunch Data Computer (MCD) ..... MPDC
Missile Pressure Fuel ..... MPF
Missile Pressure Status Unit (AAG) ..... MPSU
Missile Procedure Trainer ..... MPT
Missile Processing Operation (MCD) ..... MPO
Missile Procurement, Army (AABC) ..... MIPA
Missile Procurement, Army (AABC) ..... MPA
Missile Procurement Fund (AAGC) ..... MPF
Missile Purchase Description [*Army*] ..... MPD
Missile Purchase Description (AD) ..... mpd
Missile RADAR [*Military*] (CAAL) ..... MR
Missile RADAR Altimeter (MCD) ..... MRA
Missile Range ..... MISRAN
Missile Range Calibration Satellite ..... MRCS
Missile Range Index ..... MRI
Missile Range Instrumentation Ship [*Navy symbol*] ..... AGM
Missile Ranging ..... MIRAN
Missile Ready for Test (MCD) ..... MRFT
Missile Receiver ..... MR
Missile Recertification Equipment ..... MRE
Missile Reconstitution Force [*Air Force*] (DOMA) ..... MRF
Missile Recovery Vessel (AD) ..... MRV
Missile Recycle Equipment (SAA) ..... MRE
Missile Recycle Facility (SAA) ..... MRCF
Missile Reentry Systems (AFIT) ..... MRS
Missile Re-Entry Vehicle (AD) ..... mrv
Missile Reference ..... MR
Missile Research and Development Command [*Army*] ..... MIRADCOM
Missile Research and Development Command [*Army*] (MCD) ..... MRDC
Missile Research Corp. ..... MRC
Missile Research Development and Engineering Center [*Formerly, Army Missile Laboratory*] (RDA) ..... MRDEC
Missile Response Simulation Software ..... MRSS
Missile Restraint Release ..... MRR
Missile Round Assembly Facility ..... MRAF
Missile Round Cable Test System ..... MRCTS
Missile Round Interface Unit ..... MRIU
Missile Round Simulator ..... MRS
Missile Round Test Equipment ..... MRTE
Missile Round Test Set ..... MRTS
Missile Round Trainer (MCD) ..... MRT
Missile Round Transporter (MCD) ..... MRT
Missile Rounds (MCD) ..... MR
Missile Safety Officer (AFM) ..... MSO
Missile Safety Set (IAA) ..... MSS
Missile Scoring Reliability (MCD) ..... MSR
Missile Sea Level ..... MSL
Missile Security Squadron ..... MSS
Missile Select Switch ..... MSS
Missile Sequence Charts (AAG) ..... MSC
Missile Service Test Model [*Military*] (IAA) ..... MSTM
Missile Servicing and Storage Building [*Military*] (IAA) ..... MSSB
Missile Setting Panel [*Military*] (CAAL) ..... MSP
Missile Ship Qualification Test [*Navy*] (NVT) ..... MSQT
Missile Sight System [*Army*] ..... MSS
Missile Sight Video Camera Systems (MCD) ..... MSVCS
Missile Simulator Plug ..... MSP
Missile Simulator Test Set (MCD) ..... MSTS
Missile Site Activation Task Force (SAA) ..... MSATF
Missile Site Construction Agency [*Army*] ..... MSCA
Missile Site Control Building (AABC) ..... MSCB
Missile Site Control Center (MCD) ..... MSCC
Missile Site Data Processing Subsystem (AABC) ..... MSDPSS
Missile Site Data Processing System (AABC) ..... MSDPS
Missile Site Data Processor (AABC) ..... MSDP
Missile Site Load (MCD) ..... MSL

Missile Site Location System (MCD)	MSLS
Missile Site RADAR [Army] (MCD)	MSR
Missile Site RADAR Simulation [Missile system evaluation] (RDA)	MSRSIM
Missile Site Range	MSR
Missile Sites Labor Commission [A federal government body] [Abolished 1967; functions transferred to Federal Mediation and Conciliation Service]	MSLC
Missile, Space and Range Pioneers (EA)	MSRP
Missile Specification	MIS
Missile Stability and Frequency Response	MS & FR
Missile Stabilization System	MSS
Missile Standards Manual [Military] (IAA)	MSM
Missile Static Development Site (AAG)	MSDS
Missile Static Test Site [Air Force]	MSTS
Missile Station (AAG)	MS
Missile Station Select	MSS
Missile Station Test Set (MCD)	MSTS
Missile Status Control Indicator [Military] (CAAL)	MSCI
Missile Status Indicator	MSI
Missile Storage Building (NATG)	MSB
Missile Strike Reporting System	MSRS
Missile Subsystem	MSS
Missile Subsystem Integration (SAA)	MSI
Missile Subsystem Test Set [Military] (CAAL)	MSTS
Missile Support Activity (MCD)	MSA
Missile Support Base (SAA)	MSB
Missile Support Co. [Army]	MSC
Missile Support Days (AAG)	MSD
Missile Support Element (AABC)	MSE
Missile Support Equipment	MSE
Missile Support Equipment Manufacturers Planning Reports (MCD)	MSEMPR
Missile Support Plan	MSP
Missile Support Ship (NATG)	AEM
Missile Support Stand (MCD)	MSS
Missile Surface RADAR (MCD)	MSR
Missile Surveillance Technology (MCD)	MST
Missile System	MS
Missile System Analyst (SAA)	MSA
Missile System Analyst Console (AAG)	MSAC
Missile System Analyst Technician (SAA)	MSAT
Missile System Availability (MCD)	MSA
Missile System Checkout (AAG)	MSC
Missile System Development and Evaluation Facility (MCD)	MSDEF
Missile System Development Stand (AAG)	MSDS
Missile System Evaluation Flight (MUGU)	MSEF
Missile System Installation Interrupted for Parts (NVT)	MSIIP
Missile System Readiness Test (IEEE)	MSRT
Missile System Requirements Outline (MCD)	MSRO
Missile System Software Center	MSSC
Missile System Stockage List (AFIT)	MSSL
Missile System Supervisor/Engagement Controller [Military] (CAAL)	MSS/EC
Missile System Support Equipment	MSSE
Missile System Target Illuminator Controlled (MCD)	MISTIC
Missile System Test	MST
Missile Systems Checkout Program [Aerospace] (IAA)	MSCOP
Missile Systems Checkout Programmer [Aerospace] (IAA)	MSCP
Missile Systems Development (AAG)	MSD
Missile Systems Evaluation Group (CINC)	MSEG
Missile Systems Group [of General Motors Corp.]	MSG
Missile Systems Operational Report [Military] (IAA)	MSOR
Missile Tank Pressurization Unit (AAG)	MTPU
Missile Target Tracking RADAR (MCD)	MTTR
Missile Technical Operations Communications System (MCD)	MITOCS
Missile Technician [Navy rating]	MT
Missile Technician, Chief [Navy rating]	MTC
Missile Technician, First Class [Navy rating]	MT1
Missile Technician, Master Chief [Navy rating]	MTCM
Missile Technician, Second Class [Navy rating]	MT2
Missile Technician, Senior Chief [Navy rating]	MTCS
Missile Technician, Third Class [Navy rating]	MT3
Missile Technology Control Regime [US, Canada, Britain, France, West Germany, Japan]	MTCR
Missile Test	MT
Missile Test and Checkout Equipment	MT & CE
Missile Test and Readiness Equipment	MTRE
Missile Test and Readiness Evaluation [Military] (IAA)	MTRE
Missile Test Center	MTC
Missile Test Engineer (MUGU)	MTE
Missile Test Installation Kit	MTIK
Missile Test Operator (SAA)	MTO
Missile Test Range Instrumentation	MTRI
Missile Test Set	MTS
Missile Test Stand	MTS
Missile Test Station	MTS
Missile Test Vehicle	MTV
Missile Tilt	MT
Missile Tilt and Azimuth Error Test Fixture	MT & AETF
Missile Track Jamming [Military] (CAAL)	MTJ
Missile Track [or Tracking] RADAR [Air Force]	MTR
Missile Tracking Station [DoD]	MTS
Missile Tracking System (IEEE)	MTS
Missile Tracking Unit (MCD)	MTU
Missile Training Installation (NATG)	MTI
Missile Training Squadron	MTS
Missile Training Unit [Air Force]	MTU

Missile Training Vehicle	MTV
Missile Trajectory Data System (MUGU)	MTDS
Missile Trajectory Measurement [Air Force]	MISTRAM
Missile Transfer Area (IAA)	MTA
Missile Transfer Car	MTC
Missile Transfer Panel (AAG)	MTP
Missile Tube Air	MTA
Missile Tube Comparator Fixture	MTCF
Missile Tube Control	MTC
Missile Tube Pressurization	MTP
Missile Tube Supply	MTS
Missile Unit Simulated Combat Mission (SAA)	MUSCM
Missile Unit Support System	MUSS
Missile Velocity Servo	MVS
Missile Verification Firing	MVF
Missile Viewing Window	MVW
Missile Viewing Window Deicing Unit	MVWDU
Missile Warning and Display System [or Subsystem] (MCD)	MWDS
Missile Warning/Attack Assessment (MCD)	MW/AA
Missile Warning Bypass (DWSG)	MWBP
Missile Warning Position (MCD)	MWP
Missile Warning Squadron [Air Force]	MSLWARNINGSq
Missile Warning Squadron	MWS
Missile Warning System Test (MCD)	MWST
Missile Weapon System [Military] (CAAL)	MWS
Missile Weapons Control (MCD)	MWC
Missile Weapons Control System (MCD)	MWCS
Missile Weapons System Training Unit, Atlantic (DNAB)	MISTRAULANT
Missile Weapons System Training Unit, Pacific (DNAB)	MISTRAUPAC
Missile X/Minuteman Missile	MX/MM
Missile X [Deploy In] Multiple Protective Shelters	MX/MPS
Missile-Borne Equipment	MBE
Missile-Borne Guidance Equipment (AFM)	MBGE
Missile-Borne Guidance Set (MCD)	MBGS
Missile-Borne Guidance Test Set (AABC)	MBGTS
Missile-in-Flight	MIF
Missile-in-Range Computer (MCD)	MIRC
Missile-Launching System (NG)	MLS
Missile-Lift [Aerospace] (AAG)	M/L
Missile-on-Aircraft Testing [Military] (AD)	moat
Missiles/Ammunition System Study	MASS
Missiles and Rockets [A publication]	M/R
Missiles and Space Division [NASA] (KSC)	MSD
Missiles High-Speed Assembly Program	MISHAP
Missiles Made to Order [Military] (RDA)	MMTO
Missile-Supersonic Transport	MISST
Missile-to-Target Patch Panel	MTPP
Missile-Warning Group [Military]	MWG
Missile-Warning Receiver (MCD)	MWR
Missilized Driver Assembly (MCD)	MDA
Missing [Data]	M
Missing (AABC)	MIS
Missing [Military]	MSG
Missing Air Crew Report	MACR
Missing, Believed Killed (ADA)	MBK
Missing Cargo (DS)	msca
Missing Children Network [Defunct] (EA)	MCN
Missing Children of America (EA)	MCA
Missing Children...Help Center (EA)	MCHC
Missing Data Report (NASA)	MDR
Missing/Embryo Fetus Syndrome	ME/FS
Missing from Shelf (ADA)	MFS
Missing in Action [Military]	MIA
Missing in Colon Cancer [Genetics]	MCC
Missing Interruption Character (NITA)	MIC
Missing Interruption Checker (MCD)	MIC
Missing Interruption Handler [Computer science] (IBMDP)	MIH
Missing, Lost, Stolen, or Recovered [Government property] (DNAB)	M-L-S-R
Missing, Not Enemy Action	MNA
Missing Perforation [Philately]	MP
Missing Person	MP
Missing Persons Bureau	MPB
Missing Persons International (EA)	MPI
Missing Persons Unit (AD)	MPU
Missing Pulse Detector (MHDI)	MPD
Missing Volume Report	MVR
Missing (Weather Reports Only) [NWS] (FAAC)	M
Mission	M
Mission [NASA] (KSC)	MISS
Mission	MISS
Mission [Commonly used] (OPSA)	MISSION
Mission [Commonly used] (OPSA)	MISSN
Mission	MSN
Mission (AFM)	MSN
Mission	MSSN
Mission	MSSN
Mission Accomplished [Air Force]	MA
Mission Accomplished [Military] (AABC)	MSNA
Mission Accomplishment Estimate [DoD]	MAE
Mission Adaptive Wing (MCD)	MAW
Mission Air Ministries [Defunct] (EA)	MAM
Mission Analysis (MCD)	MA
Mission Analysis and Design	MA & D
Mission Analysis and Engineering [NASA]	MA & E
Mission Analysis and Performance Program	MAPP

Mission Analysis and Planning System (MCD) .... MAPS
Mission Analysis and Systems Acquisition Division (AAGC) ... MASAD
Mission Analysis and Trajectory Simulation (MCD) .... MATS
Mission Analysis Branch [Manned Spacecraft Center] .... MAB
Mission Analysis Computer Program .... MACP
Mission Analysis Division [NASA] (KSC) .... MAD
Mission Analysis Evaluation and Space Trajectory Operations
  [NASA] .... MAESTRO
Mission Analysis Program for Solar Electric Propulsion [Computer science
  NASA] .... MAPSEP
Mission Analysis Representative .... MAR
Mission Analysis Technique for Experiments .... MATE
Mission and Data Operations Directorate (MCD) .... M & DOD
Mission and Data Operations Directorate Network (MCD) .... MNET
Mission and Payload Integration Office [NASA] .... MPIO
Mission and Performance Envelope .... MPE
Mission and System Requirements Review [NASA] .... MSRR
Mission and Test Computer .... MTC
Mission and Traffic Control .... MTC
Mission Application Program (NASA) .... MAP
Mission Area Analysis (MCD) .... MAA
Mission Area Analysis Test Advisory Group [Army] .... MAATAG
Mission Area Deficiency [Army] .... MAD
Mission Area Deficiency Statement [Army] (RDA) .... MADS
Mission Area Development Plan [DoD] .... MADP
Mission Area Manager [Army] .... MAM
Mission Area Materiel Plan [Army] .... MAMP
Mission Assignment Code (NATG) .... MAC
Mission Aviation Fellowship [Indonesia] [ICAO designator] (FAAC) .... MAF
Mission Baseline Description [NASA] (KSC) .... MBD
Mission Briefing Room [NASA] (KSC) .... MBR
Mission Briefing Unit .... MBU
Mission Budget Statement [Army] .... MBS
Mission Capability [NASA] (NASA) .... MC
Mission Capability .... MICAP
Mission Capability Statement (MCD) .... MISCAP
Mission Capital 8.50% 'MIPS' [NYSE symbol] (TTSB) .... MEPrB
Mission Capital 9.875% 'MIPS' [NYSE symbol] (TTSB) .... MEPrA
Mission Capital Ltd. [NYSE symbol] (SAG) .... ME
Mission Capital Ltd. [Associated Press] (SAG) .... MisCa
Mission Change Indicator [Air Force] (AFIT) .... MCI
Mission Chapel [Church of England] .... MCH
Mission College, Santa Clara, CA [OCLC symbol] (OCLC) .... MIS
Mission Commander, Fleet Air Reconnaissance Squadron
  (DNAB) .... MSNCDRFAIRECONRON
Mission Communication Display (MCD) .... MCD
Mission/Communication Keyboard (MCD) .... MCK
Mission Communications Manager (SSD) .... MCM
Mission Completion (MCD) .... MC
Mission Completion Success Probability (MCD) .... MCSP
Mission Computer (MCD) .... MC
Mission Concept Paper (MCD) .... MCP
Mission Continuation (MCD) .... MC
Mission Control [NASA] .... MC
Mission Control and Computing Center [NASA] (NASA) .... MCCC
Mission Control and Interface Unit [NASA] (NASA) .... MCIU
Mission Control and Interface Unit .... MCIU
Mission Control Center [NASA] (NASA) .... MCC
Mission Control Center - Cape Kennedy [NASA] (KSC) .... MCC-K
Mission Control Center - Department of Defense [NASA] (NASA) .... MCC-DoD
Mission Control Center - Houston [NASA] (MCD) .... MCC-H
Mission Control Center - National Aeronautics and Space Administration
  (NASA) .... MCC-NASA
Mission Control Center Simulation [NASA] (NASA) .... MCCS
Mission Control Complex [Air Force] .... MCC
Mission Control Computer Program [NASA] .... MCCP
Mission Control Directorate [NASA] .... MCD
Mission Control/Electronic Display System (MCD) .... MC/EDS
Mission Control Equipment [NASA] .... MCE
Mission Control Facility (MCD) .... MCF
Mission Control Module .... MCM
Mission Control Operation [NASA] .... MCO
Mission Control Operations Panel [NASA] (KSC) .... MCOP
Mission Control Programmer [NASA] (KSC) .... MCP
Mission Control Room [Space Flight Operations Facility, NASA] .... MCR
Mission Control Routine [NASA] .... MCR
Mission Control Segment (SSD) .... MCS
Mission Control Table (MCD) .... MCT
Mission Control Unit (MCD) .... MCU
Mission Creek Youth Camp, Resident Library, Belfair, WA [Library symbol
  Library of Congress] (LCLS) .... WaBfM-R
Mission Creek Youth Camp, Staff Library, Belfair, WA [Library symbol
  Library of Congress] (LCLS) .... WaBfM
Mission Critical Computer System (DOMA) .... MCCS
Mission Data Acquisition System [NASA] (NASA) .... MDAS
Mission Data Book [NASA] (NASA) .... MDB
Mission Data Collection Sheets (CINC) .... MDCS
Mission Data Display .... MDD
Mission Data Formats Project [NASA] (SSD) .... MDFP
Mission Data Preparation System [Military] (CAAL) .... MDPS
Mission Data Reduction .... MDR
Mission Data Requirements Document [NASA] (KSC) .... MDRD
Mission Data Retrieval System [NASA] .... MDRS
Mission Data Support System [NASA] (KSC) .... MDSS
Mission Day .... MD

Mission de Ras Shamra [A publication] (BJA) .... MRS
Mission Debrief Forms (CINC) .... MIDEFO
Mission Defendent Experiment .... MDE
Mission Defendent Experiment .... MD
Mission Dependent .... MD
Mission Dependent Elements [NASA] (KSC) .... MDE
Mission Dependent Equipment [NASA] (KSC) .... MDE
Mission Dependent Experiment [NASA] (NASA) .... MDE
Mission Dependent Interface .... MDI
Mission Description Document (SSD) .... MDD
Mission Design and Series [Military] (AFM) .... MDS
Mission Design Requirements, Objectives, and Constraints .... MDROC
Mission Development Simulator [NASA] (NASA) .... MDS
Mission Deviation (MCD) .... MD
Mission Director [NASA] (KSC) .... MD
Mission Director Center [NASA] (KSC) .... MDC
Mission Directors Flight Readiness Review [NASA] (KSC) .... MDFRR
Mission Display Board Assembly [Space Flight Operations Facility,
  NASA] .... MDB
Mission Display Equipment .... MDE
Mission Display System [Navy] (DOMA) .... MDS
Mission Doctors Association (EA) .... MDA
Mission Duration, Average (MCD) .... MDAVG
Mission Duty Cycle [NASA] (KSC) .... MDC
Mission Effective Information Transmission System .... MEITS
Mission Effects Projector [Lunar exploration] .... MEP
Mission Elapsed Time [NASA] (KSC) .... MET
Mission Element Need Analysis (MCD) .... MENA
Mission Element Needs Statement (MCD) .... MENS
Mission Endurance Cycle Test .... MECT
Mission, Enemy, Terrain and Weather, Troops and Firepower Available .... METT
Mission, Enemy, Terrain and Weather, Troops and Firepower Available,
  and Maneuver Space (MCD) .... METTM
Mission, Enemy, Terrain and Weather, Troops and Firepower Available and
  Time (INF) .... METT-T
Mission, Enemy, Terrain, Tactics, Weather [Criteria for establishing military
  strategy] [Army] (VNW) .... METTW
Mission Enhancement-Little Bird [Military] (RDA) .... MELB
Mission Entry Time .... MET
Mission Envelope (AAG) .... ME
Mission Environment Tape .... MET
Mission Equipment Essentiality List .... MEEL
Mission Equipment Facility (MCD) .... MEF
Mission Equipment Package .... MEP
Mission Essential Backup (MCD) .... MEBU
Mission Essential Bare Base Augmentation Sets [Air Force] .... MEBBAS
Mission Essential Contingency Item [Military] .... MECI
Mission Essential Equipment [NASA] (KSC) .... MEE
Mission Essential Item [Army] .... MEI
Mission Essential Maintenance Only (MCD) .... MEMO
Mission Essential Maintenance Operation (MCD) .... MEMO
Mission Essential Material Readiness and Condition (MCD) .... MEMRAC
Mission Essential Repair Parts List (MCD) .... MERPL
Mission Essential Subsystem Inoperative Maintenance .... MESIM
Mission Essential Subsystem Matrix [Navy] (ANA) .... MESM
Mission Essential Subsystems List (NVT) .... MESL
Mission Essential Task List [Army] (INF) .... METL
Mission Essential Weapon System [Military] (CAAL) .... MEWS
Mission Evaluation Room [NASA] .... MER
Mission Event Timer [NASA] (KSC) .... MET
Mission Events Controller [NASA] (MCD) .... MEC
Mission Events Sequence (MCD) .... MES
Mission Events Sequence Controller [NASA] (KSC) .... MESC
Mission Flight Trainer [Navy] .... MFT
Mission for Deep Sea Fishermen [British] (DI) .... MDSF
Mission for Outreach, Renewal, and Evangelism (AD) .... MORE
Mission Gross Weight .... MGW
Mission Ground Station (MCD) .... MGS
Mission Helpers of the Sacred Heart [Roman Catholic women's religious
  order] .... MHSH
Mission House Theological Seminary, Plymouth, WI [Library symbol Library
  of Congress] (LCLS) .... WPlyM
Mission Incapable, Awaiting Parts (MCD) .... MICAP
Mission Independent [NASA] .... MI
Mission Information System [or Subsystem] .... MIS
Mission Inherent Reliability .... MIR
Mission Integration Panel [NASA] (SSD) .... MIP
Mission Interministerielle de l'Information Scientifique et Technique
  [Interministerial Mission for Scientific and Technical Information] [France
  Information service or system] (IID) .... MIDIST
Mission Kit Technical Instruction (NASA) .... MKTI
Mission Kit Technical Instruction .... MKTI
Mission, KS [AM radio station call letters] (RBYB) .... KCAZ
Mission Liaison Group [Military] .... MLG
Mission Life [Aerospace] .... ML
Mission Load (AABC) .... ML
Mission Maintenance and Reliability Simulation (MCD) .... MARS
Mission Management and Dissemination (MCD) .... MMD
Mission Management Center [NASA] (NASA) .... MMC
Mission Manager (NASA) .... MM
Mission Manager [NASA/USAF] .... MM
Mission Mode Data File .... MMDF
Mission Model Data File [NASA] (NASA) .... MMDF
Mission Modes and Space Analysis (NASA) .... MIMOSA
Mission Modular Spacecraft (MCD) .... MMS
Mission Module .... MM

Mission Module Simulation Equipment (MCD) .... MMSE
Mission Monitor (MCD) .... MM
Mission Monitoring Center [*Army*] .... MMC
Mission Monitoring Direction .... MON/DIR
Mission Museum and Archives, British Columbia [*Library symbol National Library of Canada*] (NLC) .... BMM
Mission Need .... MN
Mission Need Determination (DOMA) .... MND
Mission Need Document [*DoD*] .... MND
Mission Needs Statement [*Army*] (RDA) .... MNS
Mission Non-Delivery (MCD) .... MND
Mission Nonessential Equipment [*NASA*] (KSC) .... MNEE
Mission Objectives Document (MCD) .... MOD
Mission of Economic Affairs in London [*World War II*] .... MEA(L)
Mission Operation Computer .... MOC
Mission Operation Control Room (AD) .... mocr
Mission Operation Wing [*NASA*] (KSC) .... MOW
Mission Operations [*NASA*] .... MO
Mission Operations and Data Systems Directorate (SSD) .... MO & DSD
Mission Operations Complex [*NASA*] (KSC) .... MOC
Mission Operations Computational Facilities [*NASA*] (NASA) .... MOCF
Mission Operations Computer (AD) .... moc
Mission Operations Control Center (SSD) .... MOCC
Mission Operations Control Room .... MOCR
Mission Operations Design Support .... MODS
Mission Operations Director [*NASA*] (KSC) .... MOD
Mission Operations Facility [*NASA*] (KSC) .... MOF
Mission Operations Intercommunication System [*NASA*] .... MOIS
Mission Operations Plan (MCD) .... MOP
Mission Operations Planning Review [*NASA*] (NASA) .... MOPR
Mission Operations Planning Review .... MOPR
Mission Operations Planning Room (MCD) .... MOPR
Mission Operations Planning System [*NASA*] (KSC) .... MOPS
Mission Operations Requirements Document [*NASA*] (NASA) .... MORD
Mission Operations Room (MCD) .... MOR
Mission Operations Strategy [*NASA*] .... MOS
Mission Operations System [*NASA*] .... MOS
Mission Operations System Manager [*NASA*] .... MOSM
Mission Oriented .... MO
Mission Oriented Protective Posture [*Gear*] [*USA*] .... MOPP
Mission Oriented System Tape [*Military*] (CAAL) .... MOST
Mission Oriented Unit Training by Echelon [*Military*] (INF) .... MOUTRE
Mission Parcels Society [*British*] .... MPS
Mission Payload (MCD) .... MP
Mission Payload Assessment [*Air Force*] (DOMA) .... MPA
Mission Payload Integration (MCD) .... MPI
Mission Payload System Segment .... MPSS
Mission Peculiar Experiment Support Structure .... MPESS
Mission Performance Assessment [*NASA*] (KSC) .... MPA
Mission Phase Analysis .... MPA
Mission Planner (MCD) .... MP
Mission Planning and Analysis Division [*NASA*] .... MPAD
Mission Planning Center (MCD) .... MPC
Mission Planning Debriefing Station (MCD) .... MPDS
Mission Planning Forecast .... MPF
Mission Planning Laboratory [*NASA*] (KSC) .... MPL
Mission Planning System Test Working Group [*Military*] (CAAL) .... MPSTWG
Mission Planning Table [*NASA*] (KSC) .... MPT
Mission Planning Task Force (KSC) .... MPTF
Mission Planning Terminal (MCD) .... MPT
Mission Prediction and Performance Module [*Aerospace*] .... MPPM
Mission Preparation Sheet .... MPS
Mission Profile (MCD) .... MP
Mission Profile Analysis .... MPA
Mission Profile Course (MCD) .... MPC
Mission Profile Development List .... MPDL
Mission Profile Simulator [*NASA*] .... MPS
Mission Profile Storage and Retrieval [*NASA*] (NASA) .... MPSR
Mission Qualification Training .... MQT
Mission Radius (MCD) .... MR
Mission Readiness Flying .... MRF
Mission Readiness Tester (AD) .... mrt
Mission Ready [*Aircraft*] .... MR
Mission Reconfiguration Request (MCD) .... MRR
Mission Recorder Display Set (MCD) .... MRDS
Mission Reliability .... MR
Mission Reliability Factor [*Military*] (AABC) .... MRF
Mission Report [*Air Force*] (AFM) .... MISREP
Mission Report [*NASA*] .... MR
Mission Requirements Change [*NASA*] (KSC) .... MRC
Mission Requirements Data Base [*NASA*] (SSD) .... MRDB
Mission Requirements Document [*NASA*] (KSC) .... MRD
Mission Requirements on System Design [*NASA*] .... MRSD
Mission Resources Center [*Sydney, Australia*] .... MRC
Mission Review Board [*NASA*] .... MRB
Mission Rules Guidelines [*NASA*] (KSC) .... MRG
Mission/Safety Critical Item [*NASA*] (NASA) .... M/SCI
Mission San Jose [*California*] [*Seismograph station code, US Geological Survey*] (SEIS) .... MSJ
Mission Scientifique en Perse (BJA) .... MSP
Mission Sequence/Electromagnetic Interference .... MS/EMI
Mission Sequencer (SAA) .... MS
Mission Services Association (EA) .... MSA
Mission Simulation Model .... MSM
Mission Simulator .... MS
Mission Simulator and Training Building .... MSTB
Mission Simulator Building (MCD) .... MSB
Mission Simulator Facility .... MSF
Mission Simulator System .... MSS
Mission Simulator Test (MCD) .... MST
Mission Sisters of the Holy Spirit [*Roman Catholic religious order*] .... MSSp
Mission Society for United Methodists (EA) .... MSUM
Mission Specialist (MCD) .... MS
Mission Specialist Station [*NASA*] (NASA) .... MSS
Mission Staff Engineer (MCD) .... MSE
Mission Station (MCD) .... MS
Mission Status and Evaluation Module .... MSEM
Mission Status Summary (MCD) .... MSS
Mission Success Indicator (MCD) .... MSI
Mission Success Ratio [*Military*] (CAAL) .... MSR
Mission Support .... MS
Mission Support Area [*NASA*] .... MSA
Mission Support Element (MCD) .... MSE
Mission Support Groups (MCD) .... MSG
Mission Support Kit .... MSK
Mission Support Plan (MCD) .... MSP
Mission Support Real Property [*NASA*] (KSC) .... MSRP
Mission Support Recording [*Deep Space Instrumentation Facility, NASA*] .... MSR
Mission Support Room [*NASA*] (KSC) .... MSR
Mission Support Site [*Army*] .... MSS
Mission Support Squadron .... MSSQ
Mission Support Team (MCD) .... MST
Mission System Project Office [*Military*] (CAAL) .... MSPO
Mission System Simulator (MCD) .... MSS
Mission Systems Data (SAA) .... MSD
Mission Tailored Product .... MTP
Mission, Task, Objective .... MTO
Mission Template Expert (SSD) .... MTEX
Mission Test and Video System .... MTVS
Mission Test Module (IAA) .... MTM
Mission Test Plan (KSC) .... MTP
Mission Time (MCD) .... MT
Mission Time between Critical Failures .... MTBCF
Mission Time Extreme Environment [*NASA*] (KSC) .... MTEE
Mission Time to Restore Function .... MTTRF
Mission to Planet Earth [*Marine science*] (OSRA) .... MPE
Mission to Planet Earth (USDC) .... MPE
Mission to Planet Earth [*Proposed NASA satellite*] .... MTPE
Mission to the Deaf, International (EA) .... MDI
Mission to the World (EA) .... MTW
Mission Training Plan [*Military*] (INF) .... MTP
Mission Trajectory (MCD) .... MT
Mission, TX [*AM radio station call letters*] .... KIRT
Mission, TX [*FM radio station call letters*] .... KTJX
Mission Type Order (DOMA) .... MTO
Mission Variation Drawing (MCD) .... MVD
Mission Verification Test [*NASA*] (NASA) .... MVT
Mission Verification Test .... MVT
Mission Video System [*NASA*] .... MVS
Mission Viejo, CA [*FM radio station call letters*] .... KSBR
Mission West Prop [*AMEX symbol*] (TTSB) .... MSW
Mission West Properties [*Associated Press*] (SAG) .... MissnW
Mission West Properties [*AMEX symbol*] (SPSG) .... MSW
Missionaries of Africa (TOCD) .... mafr
Missionaries of Africa (TOCD) .... MAfr
Missionaries of Charity (TOCD) .... MC
Missionaries of Charity [*Roman Catholic women's religious order*] .... MC
Missionaries of Charity [*Australia*] .... MOC
Missionaries of Jesus, Mary, and Joseph [*Roman Catholic women's religious order*] .... MJMJ
[*The*] **Missionaries of Our Lady La Salette** (TOCD) .... ms
Missionaries of Our Lady of LaSalette [*Roman Catholic religious order*] .... MS
Missionaries of St. Charles-Scalabrinians (TOCD) .... CS
Missionaries of St. Charles-Scalabrinians (TOCD) .... cs
Missionaries of St. Francis of Sales [*Roman Catholic religious order*] .... MSFS
Missionaries of St. Joseph (TOCD) .... mj
Missionaries of St. Joseph (Mexico) (TOCD) .... MJ
Missionaries of St. Paul (TOCD) .... MSP
Missionaries of St. Paul (TOCD) .... msp
Missionaries of the Eternal Word [*Formerly, CFMA*] (EA) .... MEW
Missionaries of the Holy Apostles [*Roman Catholic men's religious order*] .... MSsA
Missionaries of the Holy Apostles (TOCD) .... mssa
Missionaries of the Holy Spirit (TOCD) .... msps
Missionaries of the Holy Spirit (TOCD) .... MSpS
Missionaries of the Kingship of Christ (TOCD) .... SIM
Missionaries of the Sacred Heart (TOCD) .... MSC
Missionaries of the Sacred Heart (TOCD) .... msc
Missionaries of the Sacred Heart [*Roman Catholic men's religious order*] .... MSH
Missionaries of the Sacred Heart of Jesus and of Our Lady of Guadalupe (TOCD) .... MSCGpe
Missionaries of the Sacred Hearts of Jesus and Mary (TOCD) .... mssc
Missionaries of the Sacred Hearts of Jesus and Mary (TOCD) .... MSSCC
Missionaries of the Third Order of St. Francis of Our Lady of the Prairies [*Roman Catholic women's religious order*] .... OLP
Missionarii a Sacris Cordibus Jesus et Mariae [*Missionaries of the Sacred Hearts of Jesus and Mary*] [*Roman Catholic men's religious order*] .... MSSCC
Missionarii Sacratissimi Cordis [*Missionaries of the Most Sacred Heart*] [*Roman Catholic men's religious order*] .... MSC

Missionarii Sancti Caroli [*Missionaries of St. Charles*] [*Roman Catholic men's religious order*] .... MSC
Missionarii Servi Sanctissimae Trinitatis [*Missionary Servants of the Most Holy Trinity*] [*Roman Catholic men's religious order*] .... ST
Missionarius Apostolicus [*Missionary Apostolic*] [*Latin*] .... MA
Missionarius Rector [*Missionary Rector*] [*Latin*] .... MR
Missionary .... miss
Missionary .... MISSY
Missionary .... MSSNRY
Missionary and Ecumenical Council of the Church Assembly [*Church of England*] .... MECCA
Missionary Association of Catholic Women [*Defunct*] (EA) .... MACW
Missionary Benedictine Sisters (TOCD) .... OSB
Missionary Catechists of Divine Providence [*Roman Catholic women's religious order*] .... MCDP
Missionary Catechists of Divine Providence, San Antonio, TX (TOCD) .... MCDP
Missionary Catechists of the Sacred Hearts of Jesus and Mary [*Violetas*] [*Roman Catholic women's religious order*] .... MC
Missionary Catechists of the Sacred Hearts of Jesus and Mary (TOCD) .... MCSSCCJM
Missionary Church (EA) .... MC
Missionary Congregation of the Blessed Sacrament (TOCD) .... MCBS
Missionary Congregation of the Blessed Sacrament (TOCD) .... mcbs
Missionary Daughters of the Most Pure Virgin Mary (TOCD) .... MDPVM
Missionary Ecumenical (Rome) (TOCD) .... ME
Missionary Evangelical Alliance [*See also AME*] [*Switzerland*] (EAIO) .... MEA
Missionary Flight Training Foundation [*Defunct*] .... MFTF
Missionary Franciscan Sisters of the Immaculate Conception (TOCD) .... OSF
Missionary Fraternity of Mary (TOCD) .... FMM
Missionary Gospel Fellowship (EA) .... MGF
Missionary Information Bureau .... MIB
Missionary Internship [*An association*] (EA) .... MI
Missionary Pilots Association [*Defunct*] (EA) .... MPA
Missionary Research Library (EA) .... MRL
Missionary Research Library, New York, NY [*Library symbol Library of Congress*] (LCLS) .... NNMR
Missionary Servants of Christ (TOCD) .... msc
Missionary Servants of St. Anthony [*Roman Catholic women's religious order*] .... MSSA
Missionary Servants of St. Joseph [*Roman Catholic women's religious order*] .... MSSJ
Missionary Servants of the Most Blessed Trinity [*Roman Catholic women's religious order*] .... MSBT
Missionary Servants of the Most Holy Trinity [*Roman Catholic men's religious order*] .... MSST
Missionary Servants of the Most Holy Trinity (TOCD) .... st
Missionary Service With .... Miss Serv W
Missionary Sisters of Christ the King (TOCD) .... MSCK
Missionary Sisters of Christ the King of Polonia (TOCD) .... MSKCP
Missionary Sisters of Jesus (TOCD) .... MJ
Missionary Sisters of Notre Dame des Anges [*Roman Catholic religious order*] .... MNDA
Missionary Sisters of Our Lady of Africa [*White Sisters*] [*Roman Catholic religious order*] .... MS
Missionary Sisters of Our Lady of Africa (TOCD) .... MSOLA
Missionary Sisters of Our Lady of Africa [*White Sisters*] [*Roman Catholic religious order*] .... SA
Missionary Sisters of Our Lady of Mercy [*Roman Catholic religious order*] .... MOM
Missionary Sisters of Our Lady of Perpetual Help (TOCD) .... MPH
Missionary Sisters of Our Lady of Perpetual Help (TOCD) .... MPS
Missionary Sisters of Our Lady of the Angels [*Lennoxville, PQ*] (EAIO) .... MSLA
Missionary Sisters of Our Lady of the Holy Rosary [*Roman Catholic religious order*] .... HRS
Missionary Sisters of Our Lady of the Holy Rosary [*Blackrock, County Dublin, Republic of Ireland*] (EAIO) .... MSHR
Missionary Sisters of St. Charles Borromeo (TOCD) .... MSSCB
Missionary Sisters of St. Columban [*Roman Catholic religious order*] .... SSC
Missionary Sisters of St. Peter Claver (EA) .... MSSPC
Missionary Sisters of St. Peter Claver (TOCD) .... SSPC
Missionary Sisters of the Assumption [*Roman Catholic religious order*] .... MSA
Missionary Sisters of the Holy Family (TOCD) .... MSF
Missionary Sisters of the Holy Family (Poland) (TOCD) .... MSHP
Missionary Sisters of the Immaculate Conception [*Roman Catholic religious order*] .... MIC
Missionary Sisters of the Immaculate Conception (Canada) (TOCD) .... MIC
Missionary Sisters of the Immaculate Conception of the Mother of God [*Roman Catholic religious order*] .... SMIC
Missionary Sisters of the Immaculate Heart of Mary (TOCD) .... ICM
Missionary Sisters of the Most Blessed Sacrament (TOCD) .... MSSS
Missionary Sisters of the Most Blessed Sacrament [*Roman Catholic religious order*] .... MSSS
Missionary Sisters of the Most Sacred Heart of Jesus [*Roman Catholic religious order*] .... MSC
Missionary Sisters of the Most Sacred Heart of Jesus of Hiltrup (TOCD) .... MSC
Missionary Sisters of the Mother of God [*Roman Catholic religious order*] .... MSMG
Missionary Sisters of the Precious Blood [*Italy*] .... CPS
Missionary Sisters of the Precious Blood (TOCD) .... CPS
Missionary Sisters of the Sacred Heart [*Cabrini Sisters*] [*Roman Catholic religious order*] .... MSC
Missionary Sisters of the Sacred Side (TOCD) .... MCS
Missionary Sisters of the Society of Mary [*Italy*] (EAIO) .... MSSM
Missionary Sisters of the Society of Saint Mary - Marist Missionary Sisters (EA) .... MSSSM-MMS

Missionary Sisters of Verona [*Roman Catholic religious order*] .... MSV
Missionary Sisters Servants of the Holy Spirit (TOCD) .... SSpS
Missionary Society [*British*] .... MS
Missionary Society of St. Columban (EAIO) .... MSSC
Missionary Society of Saint Paul [*Australia*] .... MSSP
Missionary Society of St. Paul the Apostle (EA) .... MSSPA
Missionary Society of St. Thomas the Apostle (TOCD) .... SST
Missionary Society of St. Thomas the Apostle (TOCD) .... sst
Missionary Tech Team (EA) .... MTT
Missionary Union of the Clergy [*British*] (BI) .... MUC
Missionary Union of the Clergy in the United States of America [*Later, PMUPR*] (EA) .... MUCUSA
Missionary Vehicle Association of America (EA) .... MIVA-America
Missionary Women International (EA) .... MWI
Missionary Zelatrices of the Sacred Heart [*Roman Catholic women's religious order*] .... MZSH
Mission-Critical Computer Resource [*Computer science*] .... MCCR
Mission-Critical Defense System [*Army*] .... MCDS
Mission-Critical Function (PDAA) .... MCF
Missioner (ROG) .... MISSR
Missioneras Catequestas de los Pobres (TOCD) .... MCP
Missionhurst Congregation of the Immaculate Heart of Mary (TOCD) .... CICM
Missionhurst Congregation of the Immaculate Heart of Mary (TOCD) .... cicm
Mission-Independent Area [*NASA*] .... MIA
Mission-Independent Equipment [*NASA*] .... MIE
Mission-Oriented Equipment .... MOE
Mission-Oriented Protection Posture [*Army*] (AABC) .... MOPP
Mission-Peculiar Equipment .... MPE
Mission-Peculiar Experiment Support Structure (NASA) .... MPESS
Mission-Planning Program [*Gerospace*] (BARN) .... MPP
Mission-Processing Subsystem (MCD) .... MPS
Mission-Related Hardware .... MRH
Mission-Related Software .... MRS
Missions Advanced Research and Communication Center (EA) .... MARC
Missions Gouvernementales Francaises [*France ICAO designator*] (FAAC) .... MRN
Missions Operations Report [*NASA*] (KSC) .... MOR
Missions to Seamen (EA) .... MS
Missions to Seamen [*British*] .... MTS
Missisquoi Historical Society [*Societe d'Histoire de Missisquoi*] **Stanbridge-East, Quebec** [*Library symbol National Library of Canada*] (NLC) .... QSEMH
Mississauga, ON [*FM radio station call letters*] CFMX-FM-1
Mississauga, ON [*AM radio station call letters*] .... CJMR
Mississauga Public Library [*UTLAS symbol*] .... MSS
Mississauga Public Library, Mississauga, ON, Canada [*Library symbol Library of Congress*] (LCLS) .... CaOM
Mississauga Public Library, Ontario [*Library symbol National Library of Canada*] (NLC) .... OM
Mississauga Reserve Library, Blind River, Ontario [*Library symbol National Library of Canada*] (NLC) .... OBRMR
Mississippi [*Obsolete*] (ROG) .... MI
Mississippi (AFM) .... MISS
Mississippi (ODBW) .... Miss
Mississippi [*Postal code*] .... MS
Mississippi [*MARC country of publication code Library of Congress*] (LCCP) .... msu
Mississippi [*MARC geographic area code Library of Congress*] (LCCP) .... n-us-ms
Mississippi Aerophysics Research Vehicle with Extended Latitude .... MARVEL
Mississippi Agricultural and Forestry Experiment Station [*Mississippi State University*] [*Research center*] (RCD) .... MAFES
Mississippi Air National Guard [*FAA designator*] (FAAC) .... MAG
Mississippi, Alabama, and Florida [*Oil industry*] .... MAFLA
Mississippi & Alabama Railroad (IIA) .... M & A
Mississippi & Skuna Valley Railroad Co. [*AAR code*] .... MSV
Mississippi Army Ammunition Plant (AABC) .... MSAAP
Mississippi Association of Convenience Stores (SRA) .... MACS
Mississippi Association of Educators (SRA) .... MAE
Mississippi Association of Life Underwriters (SRA) .... MALU
Mississippi Automated Interlibrary Loan System [*Mississippi State Library Commission*] [*Information service or system*] (IID) .... MAILS
Mississippi Baptist Historical Society, Clinton, MS [*Library symbol Library of Congress*] (LCLS) .... MsCliBHi
Mississippi Bureau of Geology, Jackson, MS [*Library symbol*] [*Library of Congress*] (LCLS) .... MsJG
Mississippi Burning [*Code name of FBI investigation*] .... MIBURN
Mississippi Central [*Railroad*] (MHDB) .... MC
Mississippi Central R. R. [*AAR code*] .... MSC
Mississippi Central Railroad (IIA) .... MC
Mississippi Chemical [*NASDAQ symbol*] (TTSB) .... MISS
Mississippi Chemical Corp. [*NASDAQ symbol*] (SAG) .... MISS
Mississippi Chemical Corp. [*Associated Press*] (SAG) .... MissChm
Mississippi Code, Annotated [*A publication*] (DLA) .... MCA
Mississippi Code, Annotated [*A publication*] (DLA) .... Miss Code Ann
Mississippi College (GAGS) .... Miss C
Mississippi College, Clinton, MS [*OCLC symbol*] (OCLC) .... MCM
Mississippi College, Clinton, MS [*Library symbol Library of Congress*] (LCLS) .... MsCliM
Mississippi College, Law Library, Clinton, MS [*OCLC symbol*] (OCLC) .... MCC
Mississippi County Community College Library, Blytheville, AR [*OCLC symbol*] (OCLC) .... MMS
Mississippi County Library System, Blytheville, AR [*Library symbol Library of Congress*] (LCLS) .... ArBIM
Mississippi County Library System, Blytheville, AR [*Inactive*] [*OCLC symbol*] (OCLC) .... MLS
Mississippi Decisions [*A publication*] (DLA) .... Miss Dec

Mississippi Department of Archives and History, Jackson, MS [*Library symbol Library of Congress*] (LCLS) .... Ms-Ar
Mississippi Export Railroad (IIA) .... MEX
Mississippi Export Railroad Co. [*AAR code*] .... MSE
Mississippi Forest Products Utilization Laboratory [*Mississippi State University*] [*Research center*] (RCD) .... MFPUL
Mississippi Freedom Democratic Party .... MFDP
Mississippi Gulf Coast Junior College, Perkinston, MS [*Library symbol Library of Congress*] (LCLS) .... MsPeM
Mississippi, Hill City & Western Railroad .... MHC & W
Mississippi Industrial College [*Holly Springs*] .... MIC
Mississippi Law Review [*A publication*] (DLA) .... Miss L Rev
Mississippi Law Review [*A publication*] (DLA) .... Miss Law Rev
Mississippi Lawyer [*A publication*] (DLA) .... Miss Law
Mississippi Lawyer [*A publication*] (DLA) .... Miss Lawyer
Mississippi Library Commission, Jackson, MS [*OCLC symbol*] (OCLC) .... MPC
Mississippi Library Commission, Jackson, MS [*Library symbol Library of Congress*] (LCLS) .... Ms-C
Mississippi Library Commission, Services for the Handicapped, Jackson, MS [*Library symbol Library of Congress*] (LCLS) .... Ms-BPH
Mississippi Mineral Resources Institute [*University of Mississippi*] [*Research center*] (RCD) .... MMRI
Mississippi Natural Heritage Program [*Mississippi State Department of Wildlife Conservation*] [*Jackson, MS*] [*Information service or system*] (IID) .... MSNHP
Mississippi Power Co. [*Associated Press*] (SAG) .... MissPw
Mississippi Power Co. [*NYSE symbol*] (SPSG) .... MP
Mississippi Power Co. [*Associated Press*] (SAG) .... MS Pw
Mississippi Pwr 6.32% Dep Pfd [*NYSE symbol*] (TTSB) .... MPPrC
Mississippi Pwr 6.65% Dep Pfd [*NYSE symbol*] (TTSB) .... MPPrB
Mississippi Pwr 7.25% Dep Pfd [*NYSE symbol*] (TTSB) .... MPPrA
Mississippi Railroad Commission Reports [*A publication*] (DLA) .... Miss RC
Mississippi Register [*A publication*] (AAGC) .... Miss Reg
Mississippi Remote Sensing Center [*Mississippi State University*] [*Research center*] (RCD) .... MRSC
Mississippi Reports [*A publication*] (DLA) .... Mis
Mississippi Reports [*A publication*] (DLA) .... Miss R
Mississippi Reports [*A publication*] (DLA) .... Miss Rep
Mississippi River and Basin [*MARC geographic area code Library of Congress*] (LCCP) .... n-usm-
Mississippi River and Tributaries [*Flood-control project*] .... MR & T
Mississippi River Bridge Authority (AD) .... MRBA
Mississippi River Commission [*Vicksburg, MS*] [*Army*] .... MRC
Mississippi River Division [*Army Corps of Engineers*] .... MRD
Mississippi River Gulf Outflow (AD) .... MRGO
Mississippi River Plume [*Marine science*] (OSRA) .... MRP
Mississippi River Plume (USDC) .... MRP
Mississippi River Suspended Matter .... MRSM
Mississippi River-Gulf Outlet .... MR-GO
Mississippi Southern College .... MSC
Mississippi State Board of Health, Jackson, MS [*Library symbol Library of Congress*] (LCLS) .... Ms-H
Mississippi State Chemical Laboratory [*Mississippi State University*] [*Research center*] (RCD) .... MSCL
Mississippi State College for Women [*Columbus*] .... MSCW
Mississippi State College for Women, Columbus, MS [*Library symbol Library of Congress*] (LCLS) .... MsColS
Mississippi State Library Commission [*Information service or system*] (IID) .... MLC
Mississippi State Library, Jackson, MS [*Library symbol Library of Congress*] (LCLS) .... Ms
Mississippi State, MS [*FM radio station call letters*] .... WMAB
Mississippi State, MS [*Television station call letters*] .... WMAB-TV
Mississippi State University (GAGS) .... Miss St U
Mississippi State University (PDAA) .... MSSU
Mississippi State University for Women (GAGS) .... Miss St U Women
Mississippi State University, Meridian Branch, Meridian, MS [*Library symbol Library of Congress*] (LCLS) .... MsMU
Mississippi State University, Mississippi State, MS [*OCLC symbol*] (OCLC) .... MFM
Mississippi State University, State College, MS [*Library symbol Library of Congress*] (LCLS) .... MsSM
Mississippi Student Information System (EDAC) .... MISSIS
Mississippi Supreme Court Reports [*A publication*] (DLA) .... Miss
Mississippi Test Area [*Aerospace*] (AAG) .... MTA
Mississippi Test Facility [*Later, NSTL*] [*NASA*] .... MTF
Mississippi Test Operations [*NASA*] .... MTO
Mississippi Test Site [*Aerospace*] (AAG) .... MTS
Mississippi Valley Airlines, Inc. [*ICAO designator*] (FAAC) .... MVA
Mississippi Valley Airways [*ICAO designator*] (AD) XV
Mississippi Valley Bancshares [*NASDAQ symbol*] (TTSB) .... MVBI
Mississippi Valley Bancshares, Inc. [*Associated Press*] (SAG) .... MissVly
Mississippi Valley Bancshares, Inc. [*NASDAQ symbol*] (SAG) .... MVBI
Mississippi Valley Motor Freight Bureau .... MVMFB
Mississippi Valley Motor Freight Bureau, Saint Louis MO [*STAC*] .... MVB
Mississippi Valley State College, Itta Bena, MS [*Library symbol Library of Congress*] (LCLS) .... MsIbM
Mississippi Valley Type [*Ore deposits*] [*Geology*] .... MVT
Mississippi View Holding [*NASDAQ symbol*] (TTSB) .... MIVI
Mississippi View Holding Co. [*Associated Press*] (SAG) .... MissVw
Mississippi View Holding Co. [*NASDAQ symbol*] (SAG) .... MIVI
Mississippi Vocational College .... MVC
Mississippi-Alabama Sea Grant Consortium [*Sea Grant College*] [*Research center*] (RCD) .... MASGC
Mississippian [*Period, era, or system*] [*Geology*] .... MISS
Mississippian [*Railway*] [*AAR code*] .... MISS
Mississippi-Atchafalaya River [*Marine science*] (OSRA) .... MAR
Mississippi-Atchafalaya River [*System*] (USDC) .... MAR
Missisquoi National Wildlife Refuge [*Vermont*] (AD) .... MNWR
Missoula [*Montana*] [*Airport symbol*] (OAG) .... MSO
Missoula [*Montana*] [*Seismograph station code, US Geological Survey*] (SEIS) .... MSO
Missoula, MT [*Location identifier FAA*] (FAAL) .... DST
Missoula, MT [*Location identifier FAA*] (FAAL) .... INE
Missoula, MT [*FM radio station call letters*] (RBYB) .... KBGA-FM
Missoula, MT [*Television station call letters*] .... KECI
Missoula, MT [*FM radio station call letters*] (RBYB) .... KGGL
Missoula, MT [*AM radio station call letters*] .... KGRZ
Missoula, MT [*AM radio station call letters*] .... KGVO
Missoula, MT [*FM radio station call letters*] .... KMSO
Missoula, MT [*Television station call letters*] .... KPAX
Missoula, MT [*Television station call letters*] .... KTMF
Missoula, MT [*FM radio station call letters*] .... KUFM
Missoula, MT [*Television station call letters*] .... KUFM-TV
Missoula, MT [*AM radio station call letters*] .... KYLT
Missoula, MT [*FM radio station call letters*] .... KYSS-FM
Missoula, MT [*FM radio station call letters*] .... KZOQ
Missoula Public and Missoula County Free Library, Missoula, MT [*Library symbol Library of Congress*] (LCLS) .... MtMis
Missouri .... MIS
Missouri [*Postal code*] (AFM) .... MO
Missouri [*MARC country of publication code Library of Congress*] (LCCP) .... mou
Missouri [*MARC geographic area code Library of Congress*] (LCCP) .... n-us-mo
Missouri Agricultural Experiment Station [*University of Missouri - Columbia*] [*Research center*] (RCD) .... AES
Missouri & Arkansas Railway Co. .... M & A
Missouri & Illinois Bridge & Belt Railroad [*AAR code Terminated*] .... MIBB
Missouri & North Arkansas Railroad [*Nickname: May Never Arrive*] .... M & NA
Missouri Appeal Reports [*A publication*] (DLA) .... MA
Missouri Appeal Reports [*A publication*] (DLA) .... MO Ap
Missouri Appeal Reports [*A publication*] (DLA) .... MO App
Missouri Appeal Reports [*Kansas City*] [*A publication*] (DLA) .... MO App (KC)
Missouri Appeal Reports [*A publication*] (DLA) .... MO App Rep
Missouri Appeal Reports [*St. Louis*] [*A publication*] (DLA) .... MO App (St L)
Missouri Appeal Reports [*A publication*] (DLA) .... MO Appeals
Missouri Appeal Reports [*A publication*] (DLA) .... MO Apps
Missouri Appellate Reporter [*A publication*] (DLA) .... MO AR
Missouri Aptitude and Career Information Inventory [*Vocational guidance test*] .... MACII
Missouri Associated Migrant Opportunities Services (EA) .... MAMOS
Missouri Association of Life Underwriters (SRA) .... MALU
Missouri Basin Inter-Agency Committee .... MBIAC
Missouri Botanical Garden .... MBG
Missouri Botanical Garden, St. Louis, MO [*OCLC symbol*] (OCLC) .... MOA
Missouri Botanical Garden, St. Louis, MO [*Library symbol Library of Congress*] (LCLS) .... MoSB
Missouri Business Education Association (EDAC) .... MBEA
Missouri Children's Picture Series [*Child development test*] [*Psychology*] .... MCPS
Missouri Code of State Regulations [*A publication*] (DLA) .... MO Admin Code
Missouri Concert Ballet .... MCB
Missouri Decisions [*A publication*] (DLA) .... MO Dec
Missouri Department of Conservation .... MDOC
Missouri Department of Natural Resources (DOGT) .... MDNR
Missouri Division of Geology and Land Survey [*State of Missouri Department of Natural Resources*] [*Research center*] (RCD) .... DGLS
Missouri Followback Survey [*Department of Health and Human Services*] (GFGA) .... MFS
Missouri Fox Trotting Horse Breed Association (EA) .... MFTHBA
Missouri Gravity Low [*Geology*] .... MGL
Missouri Historical Society, St. Louis, MO [*Library symbol Library of Congress*] (LCLS) .... MoSHi
Missouri Institute of Psychiatry Library, St. Louis, MO [*OCLC symbol*] (OCLC) .... MIP
Missouri Institute of Psychiatry, St. Louis, MO [*Library symbol Library of Congress*] (LCLS) .... MoSIP
Missouri Institute of Technology, Kansas City, MO [*Library symbol Library of Congress*] (LCLS) .... MoKMI
Missouri Legislative Service (Vernon) [*A publication*] (DLA) .... MO Legis Serv (Vernon)
Missouri Library Network Corp. [*Information service or system*] (IID) .... MLNC
Missouri Mathematics Effectiveness Project (EDAC) .... MMEP
Missouri Natural Heritage Inventory [*Missouri State Department of Conservation*] [*Information service or system*] (IID) .... MoNHI
Missouri Pacific Lines (AD) .... MPL
Missouri Pacific Railroad Co. .... MOPAC
Missouri Pacific Railroad Co. [*AAR code*] .... MP
Missouri Pacific - Texas & Pacific (AD) .... MoPac
Missouri Personnel and Guidance Association (AD) .... MPGA
Missouri Public Service Commission Reports [*A publication*] (DLA) .... MO PSC
Missouri Public Service Commission Reports [*A publication*] (DLA) .... MO PSCR
Missouri Public Service Commission Reports (New Series) [*A publication*] (DLA) .... MO PSC (NS)
Missouri Public Utility Reports [*A publication*] (DLA) .... MO PUR
Missouri Register [*A publication*] (DLA) .... MO Admin Reg
Missouri Reports [*A publication*] (DLA) .... Mis
Missouri Reports [*A publication*] (DLA) .... Mis R
Missouri Reports [*A publication*] (DLA) .... Mis Rep
Missouri Reports [*A publication*] (DLA) .... Misso
Missouri Reports [*A publication*] (DLA) .... Misso R
Missouri Reports [*A publication*] (DLA) .... Misso Rep

Missouri Reports [*A publication*] (DLA) ... Missour Rep
Missouri Reports [*A publication*] (DLA) ... Missouri
Missouri Reports [*A publication*] (DLA) ... Missouri R
Missouri Reports [*A publication*] (DLA) ... Missouri Rep
Missouri Reports [*A publication*] (AAGC) ... Mo
Missouri Reports [*A publication*] (DLA) ... MO R
Missouri Reports [*A publication*] (DLA) ... MO Rep
Missouri Research and Education Network ... MORENET
Missouri Revised Statutes [*A publication*] (DLA) ... MO Rev Stat
Missouri Revised Statutes [*1855*] [*A publication*] (DLA) ... RC
Missouri River and Basin [*MARC geographic area code Library of Congress*] (LCCP) ... n-uss-
Missouri River Basin Commission ... MRBC
Missouri River Basin Project ... MRBP
Missouri River Division [*Army Corps of Engineers*] ... MRD
Missouri River Division Laboratory [*Army Corps of Engineers*] ... MRDL
Missouri School of Mines ... MSM
Missouri School of Mines Reactor ... MSMR
Missouri Sexual Offender Program (AD) ... MOSOP
Missouri Southern State College, Joplin, MO [*Library symbol Library of Congress*] (LCLS) ... MoJoM
Missouri Southern State College, Library, Joplin, MO [*OCLC symbol*] (OCLC) ... MOZ
Missouri State Census Data Center [*Information service or system*] (IID) ... MSCDC
Missouri State Historical Society, Columbia, MO [*Library symbol Library of Congress*] (LCLS) ... MoHi
Missouri State Library, Jefferson City, MO [*Library symbol Library of Congress*] (LCLS) ... Mo
Missouri State Library, Jefferson City, MO [*OCLC symbol*] (OCLC) ... MOL
Missouri State University Continuing Legal Education (DLA) ... MSUCLE
Missouri Statutes, Annotated [*A publication*] (DLA) ... MO St Ann
Missouri Supreme Court Reports [*1821-1956*] [*A publication*] (DLA) ... MO
Missouri Union List of Serial Publications [*St. Louis Public Library*] [*Missouri*] [*Information service or system*] (IID) ... MULSP
Missouri Valley Authority ... MVA
Missouri Valley College ... MVC
Missouri Valley College, Marshall, MO [*Library symbol Library of Congress*] (LCLS) ... MoMM
Missouri Valley College, Marshall, MO [*Inactive*] [*OCLC symbol*] (OCLC) ... MON
Missouri Valley Conference [*Sports*] ... MVC
Missouri Valley Public Library, Missouri Valley, IA [*Library symbol Library of Congress*] (LCLS) ... IaMisv
Missouri Valley Times-News, Missouri Valley, IA [*Library symbol Library of Congress*] (LCLS) ... IaMisvTN
Missouri Western State College, St. Joseph, MO [*Library symbol Library of Congress*] (LCLS) ... MoStjMW
Missouri Western State College, St. Joseph, MO [*OCLC symbol*] (OCLC) ... MWS
Missourian (AD) ... Mo
Missouri-Illinois Railroad Co. [*AAR code*] ... MI
Missouri-Illinois Traffic Service ... MITS
Missouri-Illinois Traffic Service, East Saint Louis IL [*STAC*] ... MIT
Missouri-Iowa-Nebraska-Kansas League [*Old baseball league*] ... MINK
Missouri-Kansas-Texas Railroad Co. [*AAR code*] ... MKT
Missouri-Kansas-Texas Railroad Co. (of Texas) [*AAR code*] ... MKTT
Missus (AD) ... Mrs
Mist [*Meteorology*] ... M
Mist Therapy Unit [*Medicine*] ... MTU
Mistake [*or Error*] [*Symbol*] ... X
Mistassinity School, Desmarais, Alberta [*Library symbol National Library of Canada*] (BIB) ... ADESMS
Mister ... MR
Mister ... MR
Mister Build Industry, Inc. [*Vancouver Stock Exchange symbol*] ... MRB
Mister Ed Fan Club (EA) ... MEFC
Mister Jax Fashions, Inc. [*Toronto Stock Exchange symbol*] ... JAX
Mister Jay Fashions International, Inc. [*Associated Press*] (SAG) ... MistrJay
Mister Jay Fashions International, Inc. [*NASDAQ symbol*] (SAG) ... MRJY
Mister or Mrs. [*In addresses*] [*Correspondence*] ... M/M
Mistico [*Ship's rigging*] (ROG) ... MIS
Mistozen Electronic Nebulizer ... MEN
Mistral Air SRL [*Italy ICAO designator*] (FAAC) ... MSA
Mistral Class Association (EA) ... MCA
Mistral Resources Ltd. [*Vancouver Stock Exchange symbol*] ... MST
Mistranslation (ADA) ... MISTRANS
Mistress (AD) ... Mrs
Mistress (DAVI) ... MRS
Mistress (DAVI) ... Ms
Mistress of Arts ... AM
Mistress of English ... ME
Mistress of English Literature ... MEL
Mistress of Liberal Arts ... MLA
Mistress of Liberal Learning ... MLL
Mistress of Music ... Mis Mus
Mistress of Music ... MM
Mistress of Philosophy ... M Ph
Mistress of Philosophy ... MP
Mistress of Polite Literature ... MPL
Mistress of Science ... B Sc
Mistresses Anonymous (EA) ... MA
Mistura [*Mixture*] [*Pharmacy*] ... M
Mistura [*Mixture*] [*Pharmacy*] ... MIST
Mistura [*Mixture*] [*Pharmacy*] (ROG) ... MR
Mistura Fiat [*Let a Mixture Be Made*] [*Pharmacy*] ... M FT
Misty Mountain Gold Ltd. [*NASDAQ symbol*] (SAG) ... MGLC
Misty Mountain Gold Ltd. [*Associated Press*] (SAG) ... MistyM
Misurata [*Libya*] [*Airport symbol*] (OAG) ... MRA
MIT Airlines Ltd. [*ICAO designator*] (FAAC) ... MNC
Mit Beschraenkter Haftung [*With Limited Liability*] [*German*] (EG) ... mbH
MIT [*Massachusetts Institute of Technology*] **Cell Culture Center** [*Research center*] (RCD) ... CCC
MIT [*Massachusetts Institute of Technology*]-Industry Composites and Polymer Processing Program [*Research center*] (RCD) ... CP3
Mit Kappe [*With Cap*] [*German military - World War II*] ... MK
Mit Kern [*With Core*] [*German military - World War II*] ... MK
Mit Out Sound [*i.e., "without sound"*] [*Film industry*] ... MOS
Mitaka [*Japan*] [*Seismograph station code, US Geological Survey Closed*] (SEIS) ... MTK
Mitannian (BJA) ... Mit
Mitcham Indus [*NASDAQ symbol*] (TTSB) ... MIND
Mitcham Industries [*NASDAQ symbol*] (SAG) ... MIND
Mitcham Industries [*Associated Press*] (SAG) ... Mitch
Mitcham Industries [*Associated Press*] (SAG) ... Mitcham
Mitchell [*South Dakota*] [*Airport symbol*] (OAG) ... MHE
Mitchell [*Australia Airport symbol*] (OAG) ... MTQ
Mitchell Aero, Inc. [*ICAO designator*] (FAAC) ... MTA
Mitchell Air Force Base ... MAFB
Mitchell Bancorp, Inc. [*NASDAQ symbol*] (SAG) ... MBSP
Mitchell Bancorp, Inc. [*Associated Press*] (SAG) ... MtchBnc
Mitchell Carnegie Public Library, Harrisburg, IL [*Library symbol*] [*Library of Congress*] (LCLS) ... IHar
Mitchell College, Statesville, NC [*Library symbol Library of Congress*] (LCLS) ... NcStMC
Mitchell Community Public Library, Mitchell, IN [*Library symbol Library of Congress*] (LCLS) ... InMit
Mitchell County Courthouse, Osage, IA [*Library symbol Library of Congress*] (LCLS) ... IaOsaCoC
Mitchell County Library, Bakersville, NC [*Library symbol Library of Congress*] (LCLS) ... NcBa
Mitchell County Press-News, Osage, IA [*Library symbol Library of Congress*] (LCLS) ... IaOsaP
Mitchell Energy & Development Corp. [*NYSE symbol*] (SAG) ... MND
Mitchell Energy & Development Corp. [*Associated Press*] (SAG) ... MtchlE
Mitchell Energy/Dev'A' [*NYSE symbol*] (TTSB) ... MND A
Mitchell Energy/Dev'B' [*NYSE symbol*] (TTSB) ... MND B
Mitchell Field [*Alaska*] [*Seismograph station code, US Geological Survey Closed*] (SEIS) ... MFA
Mitchell, IN [*FM radio station call letters*] ... WWEG
Mitchell Library, Glasgow, United Kingdom [*Library symbol Library of Congress*] (LCLS) ... UkGM
Mitchell on Bills, Notes, Etc. [*1829*] [*A publication*] (DLA) ... Mitch B & N
Mitchell Public Library, Hillsdale, MI [*Library symbol Library of Congress*] (LCLS) ... MiHil
Mitchell Public Library, Mitchell, ON, Canada [*Library symbol*] [*Library of Congress*] (LCLS) ... CaOMIT
Mitchell Public Library, Mitchell, SD [*Library symbol Library of Congress*] (LCLS) ... SdM
Mitchell Public Library, Ontario [*Library symbol National Library of Canada*] (NLC) ... OMIT
Mitchell, SD [*Television station call letters*] ... KDLT
Mitchell, SD [*FM radio station call letters*] ... KMIT
Mitchell, SD [*AM radio station call letters*] ... KORN
Mitchell, SD [*FM radio station call letters*] ... KQRN
Mitchell, SD [*Location identifier FAA*] (FAAL) ... MHE
Mitchell's Maritime Register [*England*] [*A publication*] (DLA) ... Mar Reg
Mitchell's Maritime Register [*England*] [*A publication*] (ILCA) ... Mit MR
Mitchell's Maritime Register [*England*] [*A publication*] (DLA) ... Mitch MR
Mitchell's Maritime Register [*England*] [*A publication*] (DLA) ... Mitchell's Mar Reg
Mitchell's Maritime Register [*England*] [*A publication*] (DLA) ... MMR
Mitchell's Modern Geography [*A publication*] (DLA) ... Mitch Mod Geog
Mitek Systems [*NASDAQ symbol*] (TTSB) ... MITK
Mitek Systems, Inc. [*Associated Press*] (SAG) ... MitekS
Mitek Systems Inc. [*NASDAQ symbol*] (SAG) ... MITK
Mitel Corp. [*Associated Press*] (SAG) ... Mitel
Mitel Corp. [*NYSE symbol Toronto Stock Exchange symbol*] (SPSG) ... MLT
Mitel Corp., Digital Systems, Kanata, ON, Canada [*Library symbol Library of Congress*] (LCLS) ... CaOKanMD
Mitel Corp., Kanata, ON, Canada [*Library symbol*] [*Library of Congress*] (LCLS) ... CaOKanM
Mitel Corp., Kanata, Ontario [*Library symbol National Library of Canada*] (NLC) ... OKM
Mitel Semiconductor, Bromont, PQ, Canada [*Library symbol*] [*Library of Congress*] (LCLS) ... CaQBrMS
Mitel Semiconductor, Bromont, Quebec [*Library symbol National Library of Canada*] (NLC) ... QBMS
Miter ... MIT
Miter End [*Technical drawings*] ... ME
Mitford on Equity Pleading [*A publication*] (DLA) ... Mit Ch Pl
Mitford on Equity Pleading [*A publication*] (DLA) ... Mitf Eq Pl
Mitglied des Deutschen Bundestages [*Member of the German Federal Parliament*] ... MDB
Mithracin [*Antineoplastic drug*] (CDI) ... MITH
Mithramycin [*Antineoplastic drug*] (DAVI) ... Mith
Mithramycin (Aureolic acid, mithracin) [*Antineoplastic drug*] ... MTH
Mitiaro [*Cook Islands*] [*Airport symbol*] (OAG) ... MOI
Mitic Subgroup [*Magnetite, chromite, hematite, ilmenite, titanite, perofskite, rutile*] [*CIPW classification Geology*] ... M
Mitigate ... MIT
Mitilini [*Greece*] [*ICAO location identifier*] (ICLI) ... LGMT
Mito [*Japan*] [*Seismograph station code, US Geological Survey*] (SEIS) ... MIT

Mitochondria Lipid Glucogen [*Cytology*] (AAMN) .... MLG
Mitochondrial Capsule Selenoprotein [*Biochemistry*] .... MCS
Mitochondrial Complementation .... MC
Mitochondrial DNA [*Deoxyribonucleic acid*] (USDC) .... mtDNA
Mitochondrial Import Receptor [*Biochemistry*] .... MIR
Mitochondrial Messenger RNA[*Ribonucleic Acid*] [*Genetics*] (DOG) .... mt mRNA
Mitochondrial Myopathy [*Medicine*] .... MM
Mitochondrial Myopathy, Encephalopathy, Lactic Acidosis, and Stroke-Like Episod es [*Medicine*] .... MELAS
Mitochondrial Outer-Membrane [*Biochemistry*] .... MOM
Mitochondrial Processing Peptidase [*Biochemistry*] .... MPP
Mitochondrial Ribosomal RNA[*Ribonucleic Acid*] [*Genetics*] (DOG) .... mtrRNA
Mitochondrial RNA [*Ribonucleic Acid*] **Processing** [*Cytology*] .... MRP
Mitochondrial Transfer RNA[*Ribonucleic Acid*] [*Genetics*] (DOG) .... mttRNA
Mitochondriarich [*Cytology*] .... MR
Mitochondrion [*Cytology*] .... M
Mitogen Activated Protein Kinase [*An enzyme*] .... MAPK
Mitogen-Activated Protein [*Biochemistry*] .... MAP
Mitogenic Factor [*Cytology*] .... MF
Mitomycin [*Also, MC, MT*] [*Antineoplastic drug*] .... M
Mitomycin [*Also, M, MT*] [*Antineoplastic drug*] .... MC
Mitomycin [*Medicine*] (DMAA) .... MIT
Mitomycin [*Also, M, MC*] [*Antineoplastic drug*] .... MT
Mitomycin A [*Antineoplastic drug*] .... MMA
Mitomycin C [*Also, MMC, MTC*] [*Antineoplastic drug*] .... Mi
Mitomycin C [*Mutamycin*] [*Also, Mi, MTC*] [*Antineoplastic drug*] .... MMC
Mitomycin C [*Mutamycin*] [*Also, Mi, MMC*] [*Antineoplastic drug*] .... MTC
Mitomycin C, Adriamycin, Cyclophosphamide [*Antineoplastic drug regimen*] .... MAC
Mitomycin C, Fluorouracil, Adriamycin [*Antineoplastic drug regimen*] .... MIFA
Mitomycin C, Oncovin [*Vincristine*], Bleomycin, Cisplatin [*Antineoplastic drug regimen*] .... MOB-III
Mitomycin C Resistance Protein A .... MCRA
Mitomycin, Fluorouracil [*Antineoplastic drug regimen*] .... MF
Mitomycin-C [*Antineoplastic drug*] (DAVI) .... Mito
Mitomycin-C [*Antineoplastic drug*] (DAVI) .... MITO-C
Mitomycin-C and Adriamycin [*Antineoplastic drug regimen*] (DAVI) .... MA
Mitosis [*Cytology*] .... M
Mitosis with Unreplicated Genome [*Cytology*] .... MUG
Mitosis-Promoting Factor [*Cytology*] .... MPF
Mitotic Apparatus [*Cytology*] .... MA
Mitotic Arrest-Deficient [*Cytology*] .... MAD
Mitotic Cycle [*Biochemistry*] (DAVI) .... MC
Mitotic Figure [*Genetics*] .... MF
Mitotic Indices [*Cytology*] .... MI
Mitotic Kinesin-Like Protein [*Biochemistry*] .... MKLP
Mitotic Organizing Center [*Cytology*] .... MTOC
Mitotic-Control Protein [*Cytology*] (MAE) .... MCP
Mit-Out Sound (AD) .... mos
Mitoxantrone, Cytarabine [*Antineoplastic drug*] (CDI) .... MC
Mitoxantrone, VePesid [*Antineoplastic drug*] (CDI) .... MV
Mitral [*Valve*] [*Cardiology*] .... MT
Mitral Annular Calcification [*Cardiology*] .... MAC
Mitral Annulus [*Cardiology*] (DAVI) .... MA
Mitral Disease [*Medicine*] .... MD
Mitral First Sound [*Cardiology*] .... M_1
Mitral First Sound [*Cardiology*] (CPH) .... MFS
Mitral Incompetence [*Cardiology*] .... MI
Mitral Insufficiency [*Cardiology*] .... MI
Mitral Insufficiency [*Cardiology*] (DAVI) .... MI insuf
Mitral Insufficiency [*Cardiology*] .... Mit Insuf
Mitral Opening Sound [*Cardiology*] .... MOS
Mitral Reflux [*Cardiology*] (MAE) .... MR
Mitral Regurgitant Flow [*Medicine*] .... MRF
Mitral Regurgitation [*Cardiology*] .... MR
Mitral Second Heart Sound [*Cardiology*] (DAVI) .... M_2
Mitral Stenosis [*Cardiology*] .... MS
Mitral Stenosis (AD) .... ms
Mitral Valve [*Cardiology*] .... MV
Mitral Valve Area [*Cardiology*] .... MVA
Mitral Valve Closure [*Cardiology*] .... MC
Mitral Valve Disease [*Cardiology*] .... MVD
Mitral Valve Echogram [*Cardiology*] .... MVE
Mitral Valve Gradient [*Cardiology*] (MAE) .... MV Grad
Mitral Valve Opening [*Cardiology*] .... MO
Mitral Valve Orifice Area [*Cardiology*] (DMAA) .... MVOA
Mitral Valve Prolapse [*Cardiology*] .... MVP
Mitral Valve Prolapse Syndrome [*Cardiology*] .... MVPS
Mitral Valve Regurgitation [*Cardiology*] (DAVI) .... MVR
Mitral Valve Replacement [*Cardiology*] .... MVR
Mitral Valve Stenosis [*Cardiology*] (DAVI) .... MVS
Mitre Corp., Bedford Operations Library, Bedford, MA [*OCLC symbol*] (OCLC) .... MTE
MITRE Corp., Library Department, McLean, VA [*OCLC symbol*] (OCLC) .... MTR
Mitre Corps., Bedford, MA [*Library symbol Library of Congress*] (LCLS) .... MBdMi
Mitrol Industrial Management System [*Mitrol, Inc.*] [*Information service or system*] (IID) .... MIMS
Mitropolia Ardealului [*Sibiu, Rumania*] (BJA) .... MitrArd
Mitropolia Banatului [*Timisoara, Rumania*] (BJA) .... MitrBan
Mitropolia Moldovei si Sucevei [*Jassy, Rumania*] (BJA) .... MitrMoldSuc
Mi-Tsiyon Tetse Torah [*Tel Aviv*] (BJA) .... MTT
Mitsubishi Atomic Power Industries (IAA) .... MAPI
Mitsubishi Bank Ltd. [*Associated Press*] (SAG) .... MitsbBk
Mitsubishi Bank Ltd. ADS [*NYSE symbol*] (SPSG) .... MBK
Mitsubishi Caterpillar Forklift America .... MCFA
Mitsubishi Clean Air [*Automotive engineering*] .... MCA
Mitsubishi Electric Corp. [*Japan*] .... MELCO
Mitsubishi Electric Corporation (NITA) .... MIT
Mitsubishi Electric Corp. Literature and Information Search Service .... MELISS
Mitsubishi Electric Corp. Multiterm Out-of-Context System .... MEMOCS
Mitsubishi Engine North America .... MENA
Mitsubishi Engine North America, Inc. .... MENA
Mitsubishi Heavy Industries .... MHI
Mitsubishi Heavy Industries America, Inc. .... MHIA
Mitsubishi Heavy Industries Ltd. [*Japan ICAO aircraft manufacturer identifier*] (ICAO) .... MH
Mitsubishi Heavy Industries Ltd. .... MHI
Mitsubishi Innovative Valve Timing and Lift Electronic Control System [*Automotive engineering*] (PS) .... MIVEC
Mitsubishi Intelligent Cockpit System [*Automotive engineering*] .... MICS
Mitsubishi Motor Sales of America, Inc. .... MMSA
Mitsubishi Motors Corp. .... MMC
Mitsubishi Multi-Communication System [*Driver information system*] .... MMCS
Mitsubishi Owner's Club of America .... MOCA
Mitsubishi Plastics [*Japan*] (PDAA) .... MP
Mitsubishi Research Reactor [*Japan*] .... MIRR
Mitsubishi Transfer-Line Heat Exchanger .... M-TLX
Mitsubishi Variable Intake System [*Automotive engine design*] .... MVIC
Mitsubishi Vertical Vortex [*Automotive engineering*] .... MVV
Mitsui & Co ADR [*NASDAQ symbol*] (TTSB) .... MITSY
Mitsui & Co. Ltd. [*NASDAQ symbol*] (NQ) .... MITS
Mitsui & Co. Ltd. [*Associated Press*] (SAG) .... Mitsui
Mitsui Petrochemical Industries (AD) .... MPI
Mitsui Toatsu Chemicals, Inc. [*Japan*] .... MTC
Mittatur [*Let Be Sent*] [*Pharmacy*] (ROG) .... MITTAT
Mitte [*Send*] [*Latin*] .... M
Mitte [*Send*] [*Latin*] .... MIT
Mitte [*Send*] [*Latin*] .... MITT
Mitte Sanguinem [*Take Away Blood*] [*Latin*] (MAE) .... mit sang
Mitte Sanguinem [*Bleed*] [*Pharmacy*] (BABM) .... Mitte Sang
Mitte Sanguinem ad Uncias ___ Saltem [*Take Away ___ Ounces of Blood at Least*] [*Pharmacy*] (ROG) .... MITT SANG ad UNC SALTEM
Mitte Sanguineum [*Bleed*] [*Latin*] (DAVI) .... mitte sang
Mitte Tales [*Send Such*] [*Pharmacy*] .... MITT TAL
Mitte Tales Doses [*Send Such Doses*] [*Pharmacy*] .... MTD
Mitteilung [*Report*] [*German*] (BJA) .... Mtlg
Mittel Europaeische Zeit [*Central European Time*] [*German*] .... MEZ
Mittelassyrisches Gesetz (BJA) .... MAG
Mitteldeutschen Brunkohle (ECON) .... MIBRAG
Mitteleuropaeisches Reisebuero [*Middle European Travel Bureau*] [*German*] .... MER
Mittelsatz [*Middle Movement*] [*Music*] .... MS
Mittenwald-Luttensee [*Germany ICAO location identifier*] (ICLI) .... EDZA
Mittermaier's Effect of Drunkenness on Criminal Responsibilty [*A publication*] (DLA) .... Mit Drunk
Mitte-Seite [*Stereo*] (IEEE) .... M-S
Mittleres Reich in Aegypten [*A publication*] (BJA) .... MR
Mitu [*Colombia*] [*Airport symbol*] (OAG) .... MVP
Mitu/Mitu [*Colorado ICAO location identifier*] (ICLI) .... SKMU
Mitwaba [*Zaire*] [*ICAO location identifier*] (ICLI) .... FZQV
Mity Lite, Inc. [*NASDAQ symbol*] (SAG) .... MITY
Mity Lite, Inc. [*Associated Press*] (SAG) .... MityLite
Mity-Lite Inc. [*NASDAQ symbol*] (TTSB) .... MITY
Mitzic [*Gabon*] [*ICAO location identifier*] (ICLI) .... FOOM
Mitzic [*Gabon*] [*Airport symbol*] (OAG) .... MZC
Mitzpe-Ramon [*Israel*] [*ICAO location identifier*] (ICLI) .... LLMR
MIUS [*Modular Integrated Utility Systems*] **Integration and Subsystems Test** (MCD) .... MIST
MIUW [*Mobile Inshore Undersea Warfare*] **Attack Craft** [*Navy symbol*] .... MAC
Mix [*or Mixture*] .... M
Mix .... MX
Mix Canyon Road [*California*] [*Seismograph station code, US Geological Survey*] (SEIS) .... MIX
Mixed .... MXD
Mixed .... MXD
Mixed Air Battle Simulation .... MABS
Mixed Amine Fuel .... MAF
Mixed Analog and Digital [*Telecommunications*] (TEL) .... MAD
Mixed Aniline Point .... MAP
Mixed Armistice Commission [*Arab-Israel borders*] (BJA) .... MAC
Mixed Artillery [*Military*] (VNW) .... MXD
Mixed Astigmatism [*Ophthalmology*] (DAVI) .... Mis Astig
Mixed Astigmatism with Exceeding Myopia [*Ophthalmology*] .... AMH
Mixed Astigmatism with Myopia Predominating [*Ophthalmology*] (DAVI) .... Amh
Mixed Bacterial Toxin .... MBT
Mixed Base Notation .... MBN
Mixed Bed [*Nuclear energy*] (NRCH) .... MB
Mixed Carload [*Freight*] .... MXD CL
Mixed Cell [*Lymphoma classification*] .... MC
Mixed Cell Agglutination Reaction [*Immunology*] .... MCAR
Mixed Cellularity [*Biochemistry*] (DAVI) .... MC
Mixed Cellulose Ester Filter (GNE) .... MCEF
Mixed Cellulose Esters Membrane Filters .... MCE
Mixed Condition [*Deltiology*] .... MC
Mixed Connective Tissue Disease [*Medicine*] .... MCTD
Mixed Cryoglobulinemia [*Medicine*] .... MC
Mixed Cryoglobulinemia-Associated Glomerulonephritis [*Medicine*] .... MCGN
Mixed Dark Matter [*Cosmology*] .... MDM
Mixed Diet (DMAA) .... MD
Mixed Dipterocarp Forest .... MDF

Mixed Distribution Analysis [Mathematics] .... MDA
Mixed Evolutionarily Stable Strategy [Breeding selection] ... MESS
Mixed Expired Carbon Dioxide Tension [Medicine] (DAVI) ...... $PECO_2$
Mixed Fission Products [Nuclear energy] .... MFP
Mixed Fission Products Generator [Nuclear energy] .... MFPG
Mixed Flow (AAG) .... MF
Mixed Flow .... MXFL
Mixed Functional Block (IEEE) .... MFB
Mixed Gas Rebreather .... MGR
Mixed Gonadal Dysgenesis [Medicine] .... MGD
Mixed Grain .... MG
Mixed Hemadsorption Assay [Clinical chemistry] .... MHA
Mixed Hydrazine Fuel .... MHF
Mixed Immunofluorescence [Medicine] (MAE) .... MIF
Mixed Income .... MI
Mixed Integer and Linear Programming Open Deck (PDAA) ...... MILPOD
Mixed Integer Linear Program [Statistics] .... MILP
Mixed Integer Operational Scheduling (PDAA) .... MINOS
Mixed Integer Programming [Computer science] .... MIP
Mixed Ionic and Electronic Conducting [Polymers] .... MIEC
Mixed Language System (PDAA) .... MLS
Mixed Layer Depth (MCD) .... MLD
Mixed Lead Alkyl [Organic chemistry] .... ML
Mixed Lengths .... MLC
Mixed Leukocyte Culture [Hematology] .... MLC
Mixed Leukocyte Reaction [Analytical biochemistry] .... MLR
Mixed Level Matrix .... MLM
Mixed Low-Level Waste (GAAI) .... MLLW
Mixed Lymphocyte Culture [Hematology] .... MLC
Mixed Lymphocyte Culture Reaction [Hematology] (AAMN) ...... MLCR
Mixed Lymphocyte Interaction [Immunology] .... MLI
Mixed Lymphocyte [or Leukocyte] Reaction [or Response] [Immunology] ...... MLR
Mixed Lymphocyte-Tumor Culture [Immunology] .... MLTC
Mixed Lymphocyte-Tumor [Cell] Interaction [Immunology] ..... MLTI
Mixed Media (VRA) .... mm
Mixed Melting Point [Chemistry] .... mmp
Mixed Monitor [Obstetrics] (DAVI) .... mix mon
Mixed Monitor [External Tocotransducer and internal scalp exectrode]
  [Neonatology] [Obstetrics] (DAVI) .... MM
Mixed Motor and Sensory Deficits [Neurology] .... MMSD
Mixed Municipal Refuse .... MMR
Mixed Object Document Content Architecture [Computer science]
  (BTTJ) .... MODCA
Mixed Object: Document Content Architecure [Computer science]
  (CDE) .... MO:DCA
Mixed Oligonucleotide Primed Amplification of cDNA [Biochemistry] ...... MOPAC
Mixed Oxide (NRCH) .... MO
Mixed Oxide [Fuel] .... MOX
Mixed Oxides .... MO_2
Mixed Oxides (AD) .... mox
Mixed Oxides of Nitrogen .... MON
Mixed Parotid Gland Tumor [Oncology] .... MPT
Mixed Pattern .... MP
Mixed Population .... MP
Mixed Potential System (PDAA) .... MPS
Mixed Refrigerant Autocascade [Cryogenic system] .... MRA
Mixed Reproductive Strategy [Avian biology] .... MRS
Mixed Respiratory Vaccine .... MRV
Mixed Respiratory Vaccine [Medicine] (AD) .... mrv
Mixed School [British] .... M
Mixed Services Organisation [British Armed Services] .... MSO
Mixed Skin Cell-Leukocyte Reaction [Medicine] (DMAA) .... MSLR
Mixed Spectrum Critical Assembly [Nuclear energy] .... MSCA
Mixed Spectrum Superheat Reactor .... MSSR
Mixed Spectrum Superheater [Nuclear energy] .... MSS
Mixed Spectrum Superheater Critical Experiment [Nuclear energy] ...... MSSCE
Mixed Transuranic Waste (GAAI) .... MTRUW
Mixed Underachievers [Education] .... MUA
Mixed Vaccine, Respiratory Infection [Medicine] .... MVRI
Mixed Venous [Blood] .... MV
Mixed Venous Blood [Medicine] .... MVB
Mixed Venous Blood [Medicine] (DAVI) v
Mixed Vespid Venom [Pharmacology] (DAVI) .... MVV
Mixed Waste Integrated Program [Department of Energy] ...... MWIP
Mixed Waste Integrated Program (DOGT) .... MWIP
Mixed Waste Inventory Report (DOGT) .... MWIR
Mixed Waste Inventory Report [Department of Energy] .... MWIR
Mixed Waste Inventory Report [Department of Energy] (GAAI) .. MWIR
Mixed Waste Office Paper [Pulp and paper technology] .... MWOP
Mixed Waste Treatment Project .... MWTP
Mixed Widths .... MW
Mixed Workload [Computer science] (PCM) .... MXL
Mixed-Function Oxidase [Biochemistry] .... MFO
Mixed-Function Oxidase Enzyme System .... MFOE
Mixed-Integer Nonlinear Program [Computer science] .... MINLP
Mixed-Liquor Suspended Solid [Water pollution] .... MLSS
Mixed-Liquor Volatile Suspended Solids [Chemical engineering] .... MLVSS
Mixed-Signal Integrated Circuit [Electronics] .... MSIC
Mixed-Suspension, Classified-Product Removal [Crystallizer] [Chemical
  engineering] .... MSCPR
Mixed-Suspension, Mixed-Product Removal [Crystallizer] [Chemical
  engineering] .... MSMPR
Mixer (MSA) .... MXR
Mixer Amplification by Variable Reactance (IAA) .... MAVAR
Mixer Manufacturers Bureau [Defunct] (EA) .... MMB

Mixer/Power Amplifier [Telecommunications] .... MPA
Mixing .... MIX
Mixing (MSA) .... MXG
Mixing and Pumping Unit [Bulk explosives] (MCD) .... MPU
Mixing Box (OA) .... MB
Mixing Chamber .... MC
Mixing Cross-Bar Connector [Telecommunications] (OA) .... MCC
Mixing Equipment Co., Library, Rochester, NY [OCLC symbol] (OCLC) .... VQQ
Mixing Smoke Chamber (MCD) .... MSC
Mixing-Length Theory [Physics of convection] [Chemical engineering] ...... MLT
Mixtura [Mixture] [Pharmacy] .... MIXT
Mixture (KSC) .... MIX
Mixture .... MXT
Mixture Control [Automobile fuel technology] .... M/C
Mixture Control Solenoid [Automotive engineering] .... MCS
Mixture Ratio [Fuel to oxidizer] .... M/R
Mixture Ratio (KSC) .... MR
Mixture Ratio Control Valve (KSC) .... MRCV
Miyadu [Japan] [Seismograph station code, US Geological Survey Closed]
  (SEIS) .... MYD
Miyake Jima [Japan] [Airport symbol] (OAG) .... MYE
Miyakejima [Japan ICAO location identifier] (ICLI) .... RJTQ
Miyako [Japan] [Seismograph station code, US Geological Survey] (SEIS) ...... MIY
Miyako [Ryukyu Islands] [ICAO location identifier] (ICLI) .. ROMY
Miyakojima [Japan] [Airport symbol] (OAG) .... MMY
Miyakojima [Ryukyu Islands] [Seismograph station code, US Geological
  Survey] (SEIS) .... MYK
Miyazaki [Japan] [Airport symbol] (OAG) .... KMI
Miyazaki [Japan] [Seismograph station code, US Geological Survey] (SEIS) ... MYZ
Miyazaki [Japan ICAO location identifier] (ICLI) .... RJFM
Mizan Teferi [Ethiopia] [ICAO location identifier] (ICLI) .. HAMT
Mizan Teferi [Ethiopia] [Airport symbol Obsolete] (OAG) .... MTF
Mizar, Inc. [Associated Press] (SAG) .... Mizar
Mizar, Inc. [NASDAQ symbol] (SAG) .... MIZR
Mizlou Television Network .... MTN
Mizo National Front [India] (PD) .... MNF
Mizrachi [or Mizrahi] (BJA) .... Miz
Mizrachi Palestine Fund (EA) .... MPF
Mizrachi Women's Organization of America [Later, AMW] (EA) . MWOA
Mizusawa [Japan] [Seismograph station code, US Geological Survey] (SEIS) .... MIZ
MK Aircargo [British ICAO designator] (FAAC) .... MKA
MK Burundi Air Cargo [ICAO designator] (FAAC) .... BUC
MK Gold [NASDAQ symbol] (TTSB) .... MKAU
MK Gold Co. [Associated Press] (SAG) .... MK Gold
MK Gold Co. [NASDAQ symbol] (SAG) .... MKAU
MK Rail [NASDAQ symbol] (TTSB) .... MKRL
MK Rail Corp. [Associated Press] (SAG) .... MK Rail
MK Rail Corp. [NASDAQ symbol] (SAG) .... MKRL
Mkushi [Zambia] [ICAO location identifier] (ICLI) .... FLMK
ML Bancorp, Inc. [Associated Press] (SAG) .... ML Bncp
ML Bancorp, Inc. [NASDAQ symbol] (SAG) .... MLBC
ML Direct, Inc. [Associated Press] (SAG) .... ML Dirct
ML Direct, Inc. [NASDAQ symbol] (SAG) .... MLDR
M'Laurin's Scotch Judiciary Cases [1774] [A publication] (DLA) ...... M'Laur
MLC Holdings, Inc. [Associated Press] (SAG) .... MLC Hld
MLC Holdings, Inc. [NASDAQ symbol] (SAG) .... MLCH
MLF Bancorp [NASDAQ symbol] (TTSB) .... MLFB
MLF Bancorp, Inc. [Associated Press] (SAG) .... MLF Bc
MLF Bancorp, Inc. [NASDAQ symbol] (SAG) .... MLFB
MLM Groundwater Engineering, St. Albert, AB, Canada [Library symbol
  Library of Congress] (LCLS) .... CaASAMLM
MLM Groundwater Engineering, St. Albert, Alberta [Library symbol National
  Library of Canada] (NLC) .... ASAMLM
MLN (Modern Language Notes) [A publication] (BRI) .... MLN
MLRS [Multiple Launch Rocket System] Smart Tactical Rocket [USA] .... MSTAR
MLV Integration and Checkout (MCD) .... MICO
MLX Corp. [Associated Press] (SAG) .... MLX
MLX Corp. [NASDAQ symbol] (SAG) .... MLXR
Mmabatho International [South Africa] [ICAO location identifier] (ICLI) .... FAMM
MMC Video One Canada Ltd. [Toronto Stock Exchange symbol Vancouver
  Stock Exchange symbol] .... MVO
MMI Companies [NYSE symbol] (SPSG) .... MMI
MMI Companies [Associated Press] (SAG) .... MMI CoS
MMICS Administration Subsystem (AFIT) .... MAS
MMT Resources [Vancouver Stock Exchange symbol] .... MMO
MMU [Manned Maneuvering Unit] Integration Plan [NASA] (GFGA) ...... MIP
M'Mullan's South Carolina Equity Reports [1840-42] [A publication]
  (DLA) .... M'Mul Ch SC
M'Mullan's South Carolina Law Reports [1840-42] [A publication]
  (DLA) .... M'Mul LSC
MNB Bancshares [Associated Press] (SAG) .... MNB Bn
MNB Bancshares [NASDAQ symbol] (SAG) .... MNBB
Mnemonic .... MN
Mnemonic (AD) .... mnm
Mnemonic Assembly Language Translator [Computer science] (IEEE) .... MALT
Mnemonic Code (AAG) .... MC
Mnemosyne [A publication] (OCD) .... Mnemos
Mo I Rana/Rossvoll [Norway ICAO location identifier] (ICLI) . ENRA
Mo Time [An association] (EA) .... MT
Moa [Cuba] [Airport symbol] (OAG) .... MOA
Moa [Cuba ICAO location identifier] (ICLI) .... MUMO
Moab [Utah] [Airport symbol] (OAG) .... CNY
Moab, UT [Location identifier FAA] (FAAL) .... CNY
Moab, UT [FM radio station call letters] (RBYB) .... KCYN-FM
Moab, UT [FM radio station call letters] .... KZMU

Moab, UT [Location identifier FAA] (FAAL) .... OAB
Moabi [Gabon] [ICAO location identifier] (ICLI) .... FOGI
Moabi [Gabon] [Airport symbol] (OAG) .... MGX
Moak's Edition of Underhill on Torts [A publication] .... Moak Und
Moak's Edition of Underhill on Torts [A publication] (DLA) ..... Moak Underh Torts
Moak's Edition of Van Santvoord's Equity Pleading [A publication] (DLA) .... Moak Van S Pl
Moak's English Reports [A publication] (DLA) .... Moak
Moak's English Reports [A publication] (DLA) .... Moak (Eng)
Moak's English Reports [A publication] (DLA) .... Moak Eng Rep
Moala [Fiji] [Airport symbol] (OAG) .... MFJ
Moanamani [Indonesia] [Airport symbol] (OAG) .... ONI
Moanamani [Indonesia] [ICAO location identifier] (ICLI) .... WABD
Moanda [Gabon] [ICAO location identifier] (ICLI) .... FOOD
Moanda [Zaire] [ICAO location identifier] (ICLI) .... FZDO
Moanda [Gabon] [Airport symbol] (OAG) .... MFF
Moanda [Zaire] [Airport symbol] (OAG) .... MNB
Moated Sites Research Group (EA) .... MSRG
Moba [Zaire] [ICAO location identifier] (ICLI) .... FZRB
Mobay Chemical Corp., Kansas City, MO [Library symbol] [Library of Congress] (LCLS) .... MoKMoC
Mobay Chemical Corp., Research Library, New Martinsville, WV [Library symbol Library of Congress] (LCLS) .... WvNmM
Moberly Junior College [Missouri] .... MJC
Moberly, MO [FM radio station call letters] .... KRES
Moberly, MO [AM radio station call letters] .... KWIX
Moberly, MO [FM radio station call letters] .... KZZT
Moberly, MO [Location identifier FAA] (FAAL) .... MBY
Mobil Chemical Co., Industrial Chemicals Division, Ashland, VA [Library symbol Library of Congress] (LCLS) .... ViAsM
Mobil Chemical Co., Plastics Division, Research Library, Macedon, NY [OCLC symbol] (OCLC) .... VQS
Mobil Chemical Co., Research and Development Laboratory, Beaumont, TX [Library symbol Library of Congress] (LCLS) .... TxBeaMC
Mobil Corp. [NYSE symbol Toronto Stock Exchange symbol] (SPSG) .... MOB
Mobil Corp. [Associated Press] (SAG) .... Mobil
Mobil Exploration & Producing Services, Inc., Dallas, TX [OCLC symbol] (OCLC) .... MEP
Mobil Exploration & Producing Services, Inc., Dallas, TX [Library symbol Library of Congress] (LCLS) .... TxDaME
Mobil Exploration and Producing U.S., Inc., New Orleans, LA [Library symbol] [Library of Congress] (LCLS) .... LNME
Mobil Oil Canada Ltd., Calgary, Alberta [Library symbol National Library of Canada] (NLC) .... ACM
Mobil Oil Canada Ltd., Exploration Library, Calgary, AB, Canada [Library symbol Library of Congress] (LCLS) .... CaACM
Mobil Oil Canada Ltd., Halifax, Nova Scotia [Library symbol National Library of Canada] (NLC) .... NSHMO
Mobil Oil Corp., Exploration and Producing Division, Denver, CO [Library symbol Library of Congress] (LCLS) .... CoDMO
Mobil Oil Corp., Secretariat Library, New York, NY [Library symbol] [Library of Congress] (LCLS) .... NNMO
Mobil Oil Corp., Toxicology Division, Information Center, Princeton, NJ [OCLC symbol] (OCLC) .... MRX
Mobil Oil Direct Oxidation Process [Gas desulfurization process] .... MODOP
Mobil Oil Estates Ltd., Vancouver, BC, Canada [Library symbol Library of Congress] (LCLS) .... CaBVaMOE
Mobil Oil Estates Ltd., Vancouver, British Columbia [Library symbol National Library of Canada] (NLC) .... BVAMOE
Mobil Oil Ltd. [Canada ICAO designator] (FAAC) .... MBO
Mobil Producing TX & NM, Inc., Houston, TX [OCLC symbol] (OCLC) .... MTN
Mobil Research & Development Corp., Central Research Division Library, Princeton, NJ [Library symbol Library of Congress] (LCLS) .... NjPM
Mobil Research & Development Corp., Dallas, TX [OCLC symbol] (OCLC) .... FRL
Mobil Research & Development Corp., Dallas, TX [Library symbol Library of Congress] (LCLS) .... TxDaSM
Mobil Research & Development Corp., Engineering Information Center, Princeton, NJ [OCLC symbol] (OCLC) .... MRD
Mobil Research & Development Corp., Paulsboro, NJ [OCLC symbol] (OCLC) .... MRE
Mobil Research & Development Corp., Paulsboro, NJ [Library symbol Library of Congress] (LCLS) .... NjPauS
Mobil Showcase Network [Television] .... MSN
Mobil Tyco Solar Energy Corp., Waltham, MA [Library symbol Library of Congress] (LCLS) .... MWalMT
Mobile [Missile launch environment symbol] [Biology] .... M
Mobile (AFM) .... MBL
Mobile .... MBL
Mobile [Alabama] [Airport symbol] .... MOB
Mobile (AD) .... mob
Mobile Acoustic Communications System .... MACS
Mobile Acoustic Recording Vehicle (MCD) .... MARV
Mobile Acoustic Torpedo Target (NG) .... MATT
Mobile Acoustics Research Laboratory (MCD) .... MARL
Mobile Advance Tactical Support Base [Navy] (VNW) .... MATSB
Mobile Advisor Team [Vietnamese team trained by US Army advisors] (VNW) .... MAT
Mobile Aerial Port Flight [Air Force] .... MAPF
Mobile Aerial Port Squadron [Air Force] .... MAPS
Mobile Aerial Port Squadron [Air Force] .... MAPSq
Mobile Aerial Target (AAG) .... MAT
Mobile Aerobee Launch Facility .... MALF
Mobile Aeromedical Staging Facility .... MASF
Mobile/Aerospace [Alabama] [ICAO location identifier] (ICLI) .... KBFM
Mobile Air and Space Defense [Air Force] .... MASD

Mobile Air Conditioning Society (EA) .... MACS
Mobile Air Defense System .... MADS
Mobile Air Force (NATG) .... MAF
Mobile Air Logistics Center [Air Force] .... MOALC
Mobile Air Materiel Area .... MOAMA
Mobile Air Operations Team [Military] .... MAOT
Mobile Air Research Laboratory (PDAA) .... MARLAB
Mobile Air Traffic Control and All-Weather Landing System (MCD) ...... MATCALS
Mobile Air Traffic Control Vehicle [Military] .... MATCV
Mobile Air Weapons Control System [ESD] .... MAWCS
Mobile Airborne Defense Station Concept [Air Force] .... MADS
Mobile Aircraft Instrument Repair Unit .... MAIRU
Mobile Aircraft Torpedo Maintenance Unit .... MATMU
Mobile Aircraft Weighing System (OA) .... MAWS
Mobile Airlock (MCD) .... MA
Mobile Airlock (MCD) .... MAL
Mobile, Air-Transportable Hospital [Military] .... MATH
Mobile Air-Transportable Satellite Communications Terminal [Military] (IAA) .... MASCOT
Mobile, AL [Location identifier FAA] (FAAL) .... ATE
Mobile, AL [Location identifier FAA] (FAAL) .... BFM
Mobile, AL [Location identifier FAA] (FAAL) .... SJI
Mobile, AL [AM radio station call letters] .... WABB
Mobile, AL [FM radio station call letters] .... WABB-FM
Mobile, AL [Television station call letters] .... WALA
Mobile, AL [FM radio station call letters] .... WBHY
Mobile, AL [FM radio station call letters] .... WBHY-FM
Mobile, AL [FM radio station call letters] .... WBLX
Mobile, AL [Television station call letters] .... WEIQ
Mobile, AL [FM radio station call letters] .... WGOK
Mobile, AL [FM radio station call letters] .... WHIL
Mobile, AL [Television station call letters] .... WKRG
Mobile, AL [FM radio station call letters] .... WKSJ
Mobile, AL [AM radio station call letters] .... WLVV
Mobile, AL [AM radio station call letters] .... WMOB
Mobile, AL [Television station call letters] .... WMPV
Mobile, AL [FM radio station call letters] .... WMXC
Mobile, AL [FM radio station call letters] .... WMYC
Mobile, AL [AM radio station call letters] .... WNTM
Mobile, AL [Television station call letters] .... WPMI
Mobile, AL [FM radio station call letters] (RBYB) .... WRKH-FM
Mobile, AL [FM radio station call letters] .... WTOH
Mobile, Alabama [Maritime abbreviation] (AD) .... Mob
Mobile America [NASDAQ symbol] (TTSB) .... MAME
Mobile America Corp. [NASDAQ symbol] (NQ) .... MAME
Mobile America Corp. [Associated Press] (SAG) .... MoblAm
Mobile Ammunition and Reconditioning Unit [Military] .... MAER
Mobile Ammunition Evaluation .... MAE
Mobile Ammunition Evaluation and Reconditioning Unit .... MAERU
[The] Mobile & Gulf Railroad Co. [Formerly, MGU] [AAR code] .... MG
[The] Mobile & Gulf Railroad Co. [Later, MG] [AAR code] .... MGU
Mobile & Ohio Railroad .... M & O
Mobile and Three-Dimensional Air Defense Operations RADAR [Military] (PDAA) .... MATADOR
Mobile Antiaircraft Training Center .... MAATC
Mobile Antisubmarine Training Unit [British] .... MASTU
Mobile Antisubmarine Warfare Target (MCD) .... MASWT
Mobile Arm Support [Orthopedics] (DAVI) .... MAS
Mobile Arming Tower (KSC) .... MAT
Mobile Armored Reconnaissance/Operational Vehicle (MCD) .... MARV
Mobile Armored Strike Kommand [Game] .... MASK
Mobile Armored Vehicle Indigo System [Radio-controlled tank] .... MAVIS
Mobile Army Ground Imagery Interpretation Center (MCD) .... MAGIIC
Mobile Army Sensor System Test, Evaluation, and Review .... MASSTER
Mobile Army Surgical Hospital [Acronym also used as title of a satirical film, 1970, and a TV series] .... MASH
Mobile Army Surgical Unit .... MASU
Mobile Arresting Gear [Navy] .... MOREST
Mobile Assault Bridge [Army] .... MAB
Mobile Assault Bridge Equipment (SAA) .... MABE
Mobile Assault Bridge/Ferry [Army] (RDA) .... MABF
Mobile Assault Ferry [Army] .... MAF
Mobile Assembly Sterilizer for Testing .... MAST
Mobile Assistance Team [Federal disaster planning] .... MAT
Mobile Atlantic Range Stations [Tracking stations] (MUGU) .... MARS
Mobile Atmospheric Spectrometer [Marine science] (OSRA) .... MAS
Mobile Atmospheric Spectrometer (USDC) .... MAS
Mobile Automated Field Instrumentation System [TRADOC] (RDA) .... MAFIS
Mobile Automated Instrumentation Suite (DWSG) .... MAIS
Mobile Automated Metabolic Analyzer [Aerospace] .... MAMA
Mobile Automated Microwave Test Facility (PDAA) .... MAMTF
Mobile Automated Scanner .... MAUS
Mobile Automatic Exchange [Telecommunications] (NITA) .... MAX
Mobile Automatic Programmed Checkout Equipment .... MAPCHE
Mobile Automatic Radiation Tester .... MART
Mobile Automatic Radio Telephone System (MCD) .... MARTS
Mobile Automatic Reporting System (MCD) .... MARS
Mobile Automatic Telephone System [Telecommunications] .... MATS
Mobile Automatic Test Set (MCD) .... MATS
Mobile Automatic X-Ray (PDAA) .... MAX
Mobile Base (DEN) .... MB
Mobile Base Maintenance Unit .... MBMU
Mobile/Bates Field [Alabama] [ICAO location identifier] (ICLI) .... KMOB
Mobile Battalion Antitank Gun [British military] (DMA) .... MOBAT
Mobile Bay, Alabama [Montego Bay, Jamaica] (AD) .... Mo' Bay

Mobile Boarding Detachment [*Coast Guard*] ... MBDET
Mobile Boarding Team ... MBT
Mobile Bombardment Communications Unit [*Military*] (IAA) ... MBCU
Mobile Branch Librarian (AD) ... Mobilarian
Mobile Calibration Facility ... MCF
Mobile Calibration Station (IAA) ... MCS
Mobile Care Unit [*Emergency medicine*] (DAVI) ... MCU
Mobile Checkout and Maintenance (AAG) ... MOCAM
Mobile Checkout Station (AAG) ... MCS
Mobile Cinetheodolite Mounts (SAA) ... MCM
Mobile Civil Emergency Unit ... MCEU
Mobile CLASS [*Cross-Chain Long-Range Navigation Atmospheric Sounding System*] (USDC) ... M-CLASS
Mobile Coastal Defense System (MCD) ... MOCODES
Mobile College, Mobile, AL [*Library symbol*] [*Library of Congress*] (LCLS) ... AMobC
Mobile Combat Service Support Detachment (DOMA) ... MCSSD
Mobile Combustion Diagnostic Fixture (MCD) ... MCDF
Mobile Command [*Canada*] (AD) ... MOBCOM
Mobile Command (AD) ... MoCom
Mobile Command and Control System (MCD) ... MCCS
Mobile Command Center ... MCC
Mobile Command Element (NATG) ... MCE
Mobile Command Guidance ... MCG
Mobile Communication Terminal ... MCT
Mobile Communication Terminal ... MCT
Mobile Communications ... MOBCOM
Mobile Communications (AD) ... mobcom
Mobile Communications Group [*Air Force*] (MCD) ... MCG
Mobile Communications Group [*Air Force*] (AFM) ... MCGp
Mobile Communications System (MCD) ... MCS
Mobile Computer System ... MCS
Mobile Conduct of Fire Trainer [*Combat simulator*] ... M-COFT
Mobile Construction Battalion [*Navy*] ... MCB
Mobile Construction Battalion [*Navy*] (DNAB) ... MOBCONBAT
Mobile Contact Teams [*Military*] (AABC) ... MCT
Mobile Control (DEN) ... MC
Mobile Control and Reporting Unit (IAA) ... MCRU
Mobile Control Room (DEN) ... MCR
Mobile Coronary Care Unit [*Medicine*] ... MCCU
Mobile Crane (DCTA) ... MC
Mobile Cryptologic Support Facility (DOMA) ... MCSF
Mobile Data Acquisition System (MCD) ... MOBIDA
Mobile Data Acquisition System ... MOBIDAC
Mobile Data Acquisition System (AD) ... MOBIDACS
Mobile Data Service (DA) ... MDS
Mobile Data Terminal (MCD) ... MDT
Mobile Database Station [*Telecommunications*] (ACRL) ... MDBS
Mobile Defence Corps [*British military*] (DMA) ... MDC
Mobile Demonstration Unit ... MDU
Mobile Dental Detachment [*Coast Guard*] ... MDENDET
Mobile Dental Services ... MDS
Mobile Depot [*Air Force*] (MCD) ... MD
Mobile Depot Activities [*Air Force*] ... MDA
Mobile Depot Maintenance [*Air Force*] (AFM) ... MDM
Mobile Detection, Assessment, and Response System ... MDARS
Mobile Detection Assessment Response System [*USA*] ... MDAR
Mobile Development Unit [*Military*] (GFGA) ... MDU
Mobile Digital Computer ... MOBDIC
Mobile Digital Computer [*Sylvania Electric Products Co.*] ... MOBIDIC
Mobile Digital Computer (AD) ... mobidic
Mobile Display Terminal [*Vehicle navigation systems*] ... MDT
Mobile Distress Call ... MDC
Mobile Distribution System (AFM) ... MDS
Mobile District Engineer (AAG) ... MDE
Mobile District Office [*Army Corps of Engineers*] ... MDO
Mobile Dockside Transfer Unit ... MDTU
Mobile Doppler Tracking Station ... MDTS
Mobile Drydock Launch Facility ... MDLF
Mobile Dryer Loan Program ... MDLP
Mobile Dynamic Checkout Unit (AAG) ... MDCU
Mobile Dynamic Unit (AAG) ... MDU
Mobile Early Warning ... MEW
Mobile Earth Station (DA) ... MES
Mobile Earth Station Facility ... MESF
Mobile Education Demonstration ... MOBED
Mobile Electric Power (NG) ... MEP
Mobile Electric Power Generator Set (MCD) ... MEPGS
Mobile Electric Power Plant (NG) ... MEPP
Mobile Electrical Network Testing, Observation, and Recording (PDAA) ... MENTOR
Mobile Electronic Robot Manipulator and Underwater Television (IEEE) ... MERMUT
Mobile Electronic Test Set (MCD) ... METS
Mobile Electronic Warfare Simulator (MCD) ... MEWS
Mobile Electronic Warfare Support System [*Military*] (LAIN) ... MEWSS
Mobile Electronics Technical Unit ... METU
Mobile Electronics Training Unit ... METU
Mobile Eletromagnetic Incompatibility (PDAA) ... MEMIC
Mobile Emergency Response Support ... MERS
Mobile Emergency Unit (NOAA) ... MOBEU
Mobile Emergency Unit (AD) ... mobeu
Mobile End System (ACRL) ... M-ES
Mobile Energy Depot ... MED
Mobile Engine Test Stand ... METS
Mobile Engine Tester, Computer-Operated (DNAB) ... METCO
Mobile Engineering Team [*Navy*] ... MET
Mobile Entertainments, Southern Area [*British military*] (DMA) ... MESA
Mobile Equipment Allowance List (MCD) ... MEAL
Mobile Equipment Employment File [*Air Force*] (AFM) ... MEEF
Mobile Equipment Information File [*Air Force*] (AFM) ... MEIF
Mobile Equipment Replacement Cask [*Nuclear energy*] (NUCP) ... MERC
Mobile Equipment Transporter [*NASA*] ... MET
Mobile Erector Launcher [*Military*] ... MEL
Mobile Examination Center [*Department of Health and Human Services*] (GFGA) ... MEC
Mobile Excursion (MCD) ... MOBEX
Mobile Exercise ... MEX
Mobile Exercise Area [*Military*] (NVT) ... MXA
Mobile Exhibition Unit (NITA) ... MXU
Mobile Exploration [*NASA*] ... MOBEX
Mobile Explosives Investigation Unit ... MEIU
Mobile Facility (MCD) ... MF
Mobile Field Hospital ... MFH
Mobile Field Kitchen Trailer (MCD) ... MFKT
Mobile Field Laboratory ... MFL
Mobile Field Laundry [*Military*] ... MFL
Mobile Field Photographic Section (NATG) ... MFPS
Mobile Field Service Unit ... MFSU
Mobile Field Training Detachment [*Military*] (AFM) ... MFTD
Mobile Fire Safety Team ... MFST
Mobile Floating Assault Bridge-Ferry [*Military*] ... MFAB-F
Mobile Floating Assault Bridge-Ferry [*Military*] (MCD) ... MOFAB
Mobile Flux Platform [*Marine science*] (OSRA) ... MFP
Mobile Flux Platform (USDC) ... MFP
Mobile Foot Restraint (SSD) ... MFT
Mobile Fuel Irradiator (IEEE) ... MFI
Mobile Gamma Irradiator [*Nuclear energy*] ... MGI
Mobile Garbage Bin ... MGB
Mobile Gas Service [*NASDAQ symbol*] (TTSB) ... MBLE
Mobile Gas Service Corp. [*NASDAQ symbol*] (NQ) ... MBLE
Mobile Gas Service Corp. [*Associated Press*] (SAG) ... MoblGs
Mobile Generator (KSC) ... MG
Mobile Ground Radio Installation ... MGRI
Mobile Ground Support Equipment ... MGSE
Mobile Ground System ... MGS
Mobile [*Truck-Mounted*] **Ground Terminal** ... MGT
Mobile Ground-Controlled Approach [*Aviation*] ... MGCA
Mobile Guerrilla Force [*Vietnam*] ... MGF
Mobile High-Power [*Reactor*] [*Proposed*] (NRCH) ... MH
Mobile Home (WGA) ... MH
Mobile Home Dealers National Association [*Defunct*] ... MHDNA
Mobile Home Landscapers and Landscape Designers Association (EA) ... MHLLDA
Mobile Home Manufacturers Association [*Later, Manufactured Housing Institute*] ... MHMA
Mobile Home Owners Federation [*NFMHO*] [*Superseded by*] (EA) ... MHOF
Mobile Hospitals [*Military slang*] ... MOBS
Mobile Hostile Weapon Locating RADAR (NATG) ... MHWLR
Mobile Housing Carriers Conference [*Defunct*] (EA) ... MHCC
Mobile Housing Carriers Conference Inc., Arlington VA [*STAC*] ... MHC
Mobile Identification Number (ACRL) ... MIN
Mobile IGOR [*Intercept Ground Optical Recorder*] **Tracking Telescope System** [*Air Force*] ... MITTS
Mobile Imagery Transmission Terminal (DOMA) ... MITT
Mobile Independent Target System (INF) ... MITS
Mobile Industrial Caterers' Association (EA) ... MICA
Mobile Information Center [*An association*] ... MIC
Mobile Inshore Undersea War Group [*Navy*] (VNW) ... MIUWG
Mobile Inshore Undersea Warfare [*Navy*] (NG) ... MIUW
Mobile Inshore Undersea Warfare Attack Craft [*Navy*] (MCD) ... MAC
Mobile Inshore Undersea Warfare Surveillance [*Navy*] (NVT) ... MIUWS
Mobile Inshore Undersea Warfare Surveillance Unit [*Navy*] (CINC) ... MIUWSU
Mobile Inspection Equipment (SAA) ... MIE
Mobile Inspection Unit [*Military*] (AFM) ... MIU
Mobile Inspection Unit / Functional Checkout (SAA) ... MIU/FCO
Mobile Instructor Team (MCD) ... MIT
Mobile Instructor Training [*Army*] ... MIT
Mobile Instrument Facility ... MIF
Mobile Instrument Investigation Unit ... MINU
Mobile Instrumentation Support System ... MISS
Mobile Instrumentation Van (KSC) ... MIV
Mobile Integrated Support System (MCD) ... MISS
Mobile Integrated System Trainer, Evaluator, and Recorder [*Navy*] ... MISTER
Mobile Integrated Tactical Terminal (DOMA) ... MITT
Mobile Intelligence Processing Element (DOMA) ... MIPE
Mobile Intensive Care [*Medicine*] (DHSM) ... MIC
Mobile Intensive Care Nurse [*Emergency Medicine*] (DAVI) ... MICN
Mobile Intensive Care Registered Nurse [*Emergency medicine*] (DAVI) ... MIC-RN
Mobile Intensive Care Unit [*Medicine*] ... MICU
Mobile Intensive Care Unit [*or Nurse*] (GNE) ... MICU(N)
Mobile Intercontinental Ballistic Missile ... MICBM
Mobile Ionospheric Observatory [*Boston University*] ... MIO
Mobile Issuing Office [*Navy*] ... MIO
Mobile Kitchen Trailer [*Military*] (INF) ... MKT
Mobile Laboratory [*NASA*] ... MOLAB
Mobile Laboratory (AD) ... molab
Mobile Laboratory Table ... MLT
Mobile Land Command Post (AABC) ... MLCP
Mobile Land Force (NATG) ... MLF

Mobile Landing Craft Advanced Base ... MOLCAB
Mobile LASER Satellite Tracking Station (AD) ... moblas
Mobile Launch Center ... MLC
Mobile Launch Tower ... MLT
Mobile Launch Vehicle [*Air Force*] ... MLV
Mobile Launch Vehicle Transporter [*Air Force*] ... MLVT
Mobile Launcher [*NASA*] (KSC) ... ML
Mobile Launcher Computer [*NASA*] (NASA) ... MLC
Mobile Launcher Equipment [*NASA*] (SAA) ... MLE
Mobile Launcher Facility [*NASA*] (KSC) ... MLF
Mobile Launcher Pedestal [*NASA*] (NASA) ... MLPED
Mobile Launcher Platform [*NASA*] (NASA) ... MLP
Mobile Laundry and Bath Unit [*Military British*] ... MLBU
Mobile Laundry Unit ... MLU
Mobile Librarian (AD) ... mob lib
Mobile Library (AD) ... mobilary
Mobile Library Service [*British*] ... MLS
Mobile Living Unit [*Mobile home*] ... MLU
Mobile Logistic Support (CINC) ... MLS
Mobile Logistic Support Forces (MCD) ... MLSF
Mobile Logistics Support Base (NVT) ... MLB
Mobile Logistics Support Group (NVT) ... MLSG
Mobile Low-Power [*Reactor*] (NRCH) ... ML
Mobile Low-Power Nuclear Power Plant ... MLPNPP
Mobile Lunar Excursion Module [*NASA*] (PDAA) ... MOLEM
Mobile Lunar Laboratory (AD) ... MOLAB
Mobile Magnetic Field ... MMF
Mobile Maintenance Contact Team (MCD) ... MMCT
Mobile Maintenance Team (MCD) ... MMT
Mobile Mass X-Ray (MAE) ... MMR
Mobile Medical Augmentation Readiness Team (DNAB) ... MMART
Mobile Medium-Range Ballistic Missile [*Air Force*] ... MMRBM
Mobile Micrometeorological Observation System ... MMMOS
Mobile Micrometeorological Observation System (KSC) ... MMOS
Mobile Mine Assembly Group [*Military*] (CAAL) ... MOMAG
Mobile Mine Assembly Group Detachment (DNAB) ... MOMAGDET
Mobile Mine Assembly Group Unit (DNAB) ... MOMAGU
Mobile Mine Assembly Team ... MAT
Mobile Mine Assembly Team (NG) ... MMAT
Mobile Mine Assembly Team ... MOMAT
Mobile Mine Assembly Team, Atlantic (DNAB) ... MOMATLANT
Mobile Mine Assembly Team, Pacific (DNAB) ... MOMATPAC
Mobile Mine Assembly Unit (NVT) ... MOMAU
Mobile Mine Assembly Unit (AD) ... momau
Mobile Mine Assembly Unit, Atlantic (DNAB) ... MOMAULANT
Mobile Mine Assembly Unit, Atlantic, Keflavik Detachment (DNAB) ... MOMAULANTDETKEF
Mobile Mine Assembly Unit, Pacific (DNAB) ... MOMAUPAC
Mobile Mine Countermeasures Command (DNAB) ... MOMCOMS
Mobile Mini [*NASDAQ symbol*] (TTSB) ... MINI
Mobile Mini, Inc. [*NASDAQ symbol*] (SAG) ... MINI
Mobile Mini, Inc. [*Associated Press*] (SAG) ... MoblM
Mobile Mini, Inc. [*Associated Press*] (SAG) ... MoblMin
Mobile Mini Wrrt [*NASDAQ symbol*] (TTSB) ... MINIW
Mobile Minuteman Train Test (SAA) ... MMTT
Mobile Missile Facility (MCD) ... MMF
Mobile, Missile Maintenance Unit (DNAB) ... MOMISMAINTU
Mobile Mixed Deployment Minuteman (SAA) ... MMDM
Mobile Modular Office Association (EA) ... MMOA
Mobile Module [*Computer science*] ... MMO
Mobile Monitoring Station ... MMS
Mobile Monitoring Unit ... MMU
Mobile National Emergency Command Post [*Air Force*] ... MNECP
Mobile Naval Advanced Base [*British military*] (DMA) ... MONAB
Mobile Naval Airfield Organization ... MNAO
Mobile Naval Airfield Unit ... MNAU
Mobile Naval Base [*British military*] (DMA) ... MNB
Mobile Naval Base Defence Organization [*British World War II*] ... MNBDO
Mobile Navy Post Office ... MNPO
Mobile Networks Integration [*Telecommunications*] ... MONET
Mobile Neutron Radiographic System ... MNRS
Mobile Noise Analysis Barge ... MONAB
Mobile Noise Barge ... MONOB
Mobile Noise Barge (AD) ... monob
Mobile Nondestructive Assay Laboratory [*AEC*] ... MONAL
Mobile Non-Destructive Inspection Laboratory (DNAB) ... MONIL
Mobile Non-Director Exchange [*Telecommunications*] (NITA) ... MNDX
Mobile Nuclear Ordnance Maintenance Unit (MCD) ... MNOMU
Mobile Object [*Telecommunications*] (OA) ... MO
Mobile Object Location System ... MOLS
Mobile Obstacle Detachment (MCD) ... MOD
Mobile Ocean Basing System (PDAA) ... MOBS
Mobile Offshore Drilling Unit ... MODU
Mobile Oil Cooler ... MOC
Mobile Operating Naval Air Base ... MONAB
Mobile Operational Training Unit (MCD) ... MOTU
Mobile Operations Center [*Air Force*] (DOMA) ... MOC
Mobile Operations Command Center (DOMA) ... MOCC
Mobile Optical Propagation Facility ... MOPF
Mobile Optical Surveillance Tracker ... MOST
Mobile Optical Tracking System ... MOTS
Mobile Optical Tracking Unit (MCD) ... MOTU
Mobile Ordnance Service Unit ... MOSU
Mobile Ordnance Technical Unit [*Military*] (CAAL) ... MOTU
Mobile Ordnance Technical Unit Detachment (DNAB) ... MOTUDET
Mobile Oriented Triangulation of Reentry ... MOTOR
Mobile Overland Hauling and Transport System [*Air Force*] ... MOHATS
Mobile Overpass Roadway-Repair Vehicle ... MORV
Mobile Oversnow Transport ... MOST
Mobile Payload Ground Handling Mechanism (MCD) ... MPGHM
Mobile Petrol Filling Centre [*British military*] (DMA) ... MPFC
Mobile Phase Ion Chromatography ... MPIC
Mobile Photographic Tracking Station (IEEE) ... MOPTS
Mobile Photographic Tracking Station ... MPTS
Mobile Position Tracking RADAR ... MPTR
Mobile Positioning Ship (DNAB) ... MPS
Mobile Post Office ... MPO
Mobile Post Office Society (EA) ... MPOS
Mobile Power Distribution Unit (DWSG) ... MPDU
Mobile Press Association (EA) ... MPA
Mobile Printing Office (AD) ... MPO
Mobile Processing Center (MCD) ... MPC
Mobile Production Unit [*On-site television recording*] (NTCM) ... MPU
Mobile Protected Gun [*Army*] (RDA) ... MPG
Mobile Protected Gun System [*Army*] (MCD) ... MPGS
Mobile Protected Weapon System (RDA) ... MPWS
Mobile Psychological Operations Transmitter (DOMA) ... M-POTS
Mobile Public Library, Mobile, AL [*Library symbol Library of Congress*] (LCLS) ... AMob
Mobile Public Library, Mobile, AL [*OCLC symbol*] (OCLC) ... AMP
Mobile Quality Services (AD) ... MQS
Mobile Quarantine Facility (AD) ... mqf
Mobile Quarantine Facility [*NASA*] ... MQF
Mobile RADAR Approach Control (AFM) ... MRAPCON
Mobile RADAR Control Post ... MRCP
Mobile RADAR Post ... MRP
Mobile RADAR Target ... MRT
Mobile RADAR Weather System (DNAB) ... MRWS
Mobile Radiation Tester (IAA) ... MRAT
Mobile Radio Communications ... MRC
Mobile Radio Service (DA) ... MRS
Mobile Radio Unit [*Air Force*] ... MRU
Mobile Radio Unit (AD) ... mru
Mobile Radio Users' Association (IAA) ... MRUA
Mobile Radiological Measuring Unit ... MRMU
Mobile Rail Repair Shop (MCD) ... MRRS
Mobile Range Instrumentation System ... MRIS
Mobile Range Operation Center (NVT) ... MROC
Mobile Refrigeration Unit (KSC) ... MRU
Mobile Remote Handler ... MRH
Mobile Remote Manipulating Unit [*Air Force*] ... MRMU
Mobile Remote Manipulator System (MCD) ... MRMS
Mobile Remote Servicer (SSD) ... MRS
Mobile Remote Unit [*From computer game "Hacker II"*] ... MRU
Mobile Remote-Controlled Robot ... MOBOT
Mobile Repair Parts Container ... MOCON
Mobile Repair Party (MCD) ... MRP
Mobile Replenishment List (AFIT) ... MRL
Mobile Revertant [*Bacteriology*] ... Mr
Mobile River Group [*Navy*] (VNW) ... MRG
Mobile Riverine Base [*Navy*] ... MRB
Mobile Riverine Force [*Navy*] (NVT) ... MRF
Mobile Robot (AD) ... mobot
Mobile Satellite Corp. [*King Of Prussia, PA*] [*Telecommunications*] (TSSD) ... MOBILESAT
Mobile Satellite Experiment (MCD) ... MSAT-X
Mobile Satellite Photometric Observatory [*NASA*] (NASA) ... MOSPO
Mobile Satellite Service ... MSS
Mobile Satellite System (DA) ... MSS
Mobile Sea Range (NVT) ... MSR
Mobile Searchlight [*British*] ... MS
Mobile Secondary Reference Laboratory ... MSRL
Mobile Service [*Telecommunications*] (TEL) ... MS
Mobile Service Structure (KSC) ... MSS
Mobile Service Structure Test Conductor (KSC) ... MSSTC
Mobile Service Switching Center ... MSSC
Mobile Service Tower [*Aerospace*] ... MST
Mobile Servicing and Repair Detachment [*Military British*] ... MSRD
Mobile Servicing Center [*Canada*] ... MSC
Mobile Servicing Center, Maintenance Department [*Canada*] ... MMD
Mobile Servicing System [*For space station*] ... MSS
Mobile Signals Unit [*British military*] (DMA) ... MSU
Mobile SONAR Technology [*Marine science*] (MSC) ... MOST
Mobile SONAR Technology/Technical Document Information System [*Marine science*] (MSC) ... MOST/TDIS
Mobile Source Control Division ... MSCD
Mobile Source Enforcement Division [*Environmental Protection Agency*] ... MSED
Mobile Source Operations Division ... MSOD
Mobile Source Pollution Control Program [*Environmental Protection Agency*] ... MSPCP
Mobile Spectrum Monitoring Unit ... MSMU
Mobile Spectrum Search System ... MSSS
Mobile Station [*Air Force*] ... MO
Mobile Status Entry System ... MSES
Mobile Strike Force Command [*Military*] (VNW) ... MSFC
Mobile Strike Team ... MST
Mobile Striking Force [*Military*] ... MSF
Mobile Submarine Simulator (NVT) ... MOSS
Mobile Submarine Simulator System (DWSG) ... MSSS
Mobile Subscriber Access (MCD) ... MSA

Mobile Subscriber Equipment [*Military*] ... MSE
Mobile Subscriber Equipment [*Army*] (DOMA) ... MSE
Mobile Subscriber Equipment Tactical Packet Network [*Computer science Military*] (RDA) ... MSE TPN
Mobile Subscriber Radio Terminal [*Army*] ... MSRT
Mobile Support Base (DNAB) ... MSB
Mobile Support Group [*Military*] (DNAB) ... MOBSUPPGRU
Mobile Support Group [*Military*] (NVT) ... MSG
Mobile Support Group [*Military*] ... MSGP
Mobile Support Group [*Military*] ... MSGR
Mobile Support Package (MCD) ... MSP
Mobile Support Team (NVT) ... MST
Mobile Support Unit (DNAB) ... MOSUPPU
Mobile Surface Contamination Monitor ... MSCM
Mobile Surface Vehicle (AAG) ... MSV
Mobile Surface-to-Air Missile ... MSAM
Mobile Surface-to-Air Missile System (MCD) ... MSAMS
Mobile Surface-to-Air Weapon System (MCD) ... MSAWS
Mobile Surgery [*British*] ... MS
Mobile Switching Center (ACRL) ... MSC
Mobile Switching Office [*Bell System*] ... MSO
Mobile System for Accurate ICBM Control (MCD) ... MOSAIC
Mobile Tactical Computer (PDAA) ... MTC
Mobile Tactical Early Warning System for Air Defense [*NATO*] ... MTEWS/AD
Mobile Tactical Exercise Control System (DNAB) ... MOTECS
Mobile Tank Depermer Facility (DWSG) ... MTDF
Mobile Target Carrier ... MTC
Mobile Target Division [*Mine Force*] [*Navy*] ... MOTARDIV
Mobile Target Division [*Mine Force*] [*Navy*] ... MTD
Mobile Target Tracking System ... MTTS
Mobile Team ... MT
Mobile Technical Unit (NG) ... MOTU
Mobile Technical Unit (MCD) ... MTU
Mobile Telecommun Tech [*NASDAQ symbol*] (TTSB) ... MTEL
Mobile Telecommunications & Technology Corp. [*Associated Press*] (SAG) ... MblTel
Mobile Telecommunications & Technology Corp. [*NASDAQ symbol*] (SAG) ... MTEL
Mobile Telemetering Station [*ITU designation*] (DEN) ... MDE
Mobile Telephone Exchange [*Nordic Mobile Telephone*] ... MTE
Mobile Telephone Service ... MTS
Mobile Telephone Switching Office [*Telecommunications*] ... MTSO
Mobile Terminal (DA) ... MT
Mobile Terminal System [*IBM Corp.*] ... MTS
Mobile Test Unit [*Army*] (RDA) ... MTU
Mobile/Tracked Remote Manipulator System (SSD) ... MRMS
Mobile Tracking Range [*Military*] (CAAL) ... MTR
Mobile Tracking Station [*NASA*] ... MTS
Mobile Trainer ... MOBTR
Mobile Training Assistance (CINC) ... MTA
Mobile Training Detachment ... MTD
Mobile Training Institute [*Klamath Falls, OR*] [*Telecommunications service*] (TSSD) ... MTI
Mobile Training Set (AFM) ... MTS
Mobile Training Team ... MTT
Mobile Training Unit ... MTU
Mobile Training Units Out for Parts ... MTUOP
Mobile Training Wing [*Air Force*] ... MTW
Mobile Transfer Method (AAG) ... MTM
Mobile Transponder Performance Analyzer [*Aviation*] (DA) ... MTPA
Mobile Transportation Ground Command Facility (MCD) ... MTGCF
Mobile Travel Team (MCD) ... MTT
Mobile Traveler [*Recreational vehicle*] ... MT
Mobile Treatment Unit [*Environmental Protection Agency*] (GFGA) ... MTU
Mobile Underwater Acoustic Unit (NATG) ... MUAT
Mobile Underwater Surveillance Team (MCD) ... MUST
Mobile Underwater Vehicle ... MUV
Mobile Unit ... MU
Mobile Unit Launch Site (IAA) ... MULS
Mobile Unit Sanitation Trailer ... MUST
Mobile Unit Support Base (AAG) ... MUSB
Mobile Unit Support System (IAA) ... MUSS
Mobile Universal Test Equipment (PDAA) ... MUTE
Mobile Utilities Support Equipment [*Navy*] (NG) ... MUSE
Mobile Utilities Support Equipment Detachment [*Navy*] (DNAB) ... MUSEDET
Mobile Utility Module System (IEEE) ... MUMS
Mobile Utility Transfer Tank [*To collect used oils*] ... MUTT
Mobile Video Services Ltd. [*Washington, DC*] [*Telecommunications*] (TSSD) ... MVS
Mobile Vocational Evaluation [*Vocational guidance test*] ... MVE
Mobile Vulgus [*Disorderly Group of People*] [*Latin*] (AD) ... mob
Mobile Water Mine (MCD) ... MOWAM
Mobile Weapon System ... MWS
Mobile Weapons Control System ... MWCS
Mobile Window Thermal Test Facility [*Berkeley, CA*] [*Lawrence Berkeley Laboratory*] [*Department of Energy*] (GRD) ... MoWitt
Mobile Wing Reconnaissance Technical [*Squadron*] ... MWRT
Mobile Workshop [*British*] ... MW
Mobile-Base Simulator (PDAA) ... MBS
Mobilehome Dealers National Association (EA) ... MDNA
Mobile-Launched Ground-Attack Missile ... MGM
Mobile-Launched Ground-Attack Rocket ... MGR
Mobile-Launched Interceptor Missile ... MIM
MobileMedia Corp. [*NASDAQ symbol*] (SAG) ... MBLM
MobileMedia Corp. [*Associated Press*] (SAG) ... MobMda
Mobile-Moored Undersea Laboratory ... MUL
Mobilisation pour le Developpement National [*Haiti*] [*Political party*] (EY) ... MDN
Mobility [*MTMC*] (TAG) ... MOB
Mobility ... MOBIL
Mobility (AD) ... mobil
Mobility Analysis Planning System (MCD) ... MAPS
Mobility Analysis Support System [*Air Force*] ... MASS
Mobility Command [*AMC*] ... MOCOM
Mobility, Countermobility, and Survivability ... M-CM-S
Mobility Environmental Research Studies ... MERS
Mobility Equipment [*Military*] (AFM) ... ME
Mobility Equipment Command [*Later, TROSCOM*] [*Army*] ... MEC
Mobility Equipment Command [*Later, TROSCOM*] [*Army*] ... MECOM
Mobility Equipment Command Scientific Advisory Group (MCD) ... MECOMSAG
Mobility Equipment Research and Development Center [*Army*] (MCD) ... MERDC
Mobility Equipment Research and Development Command [*Army*] ... MERADCOM
Mobility Haiti (EA) ... MH
Mobility Impairment (NVT) ... MI
Mobility Information Service [*British*] ... MIS
Mobility International (EA) ... MI
Mobility International USA (EA) ... MIUSA
Mobility Maintenance Facility (NVT) ... MMF
Mobility Operating Procedure [*Military*] (AFM) ... MOP
Mobility Opportunity and Development ... MOD
Mobility Required [*Civil Service*] ... MR
Mobility Requirements Study [*DoD*] ... MRS
Mobility Subsystem (KSC) ... MSS
Mobility Support Flight [*Military*] ... MOBSF
Mobility Support Forces [*Military*] ... MSF
Mobility Support Kit ... MSK
Mobility Support Set [*or System*] [*for aircraft*] (MCD) ... MOSS
Mobility Support Squadron [*Air Force*] ... MOBSS
Mobility Support Squadron [*Air Force*] ... MOBSSq
Mobility, Survivability, Sizing Recommendations (MCD) ... MSSR
Mobility Test Article [*Lunar-surface rover*] [*NASA*] ... MTA
Mobility Test Exercise [*Military*] ... MOBEX
Mobility-Affect-Cooperation-Communication [*Psychiatry*] ... MACC
Mobility-Planning Data System [*Military*] (GFGA) ... MODS
Mobilizacion Republicana [*Republican Mobilization*] [*Nicaragua*] [*Political party*] (AD) ... MR
Mobilization [*as in M-Day*] [*Military*] (AABC) ... M
Mobilization [*or Mobilize*] (AFM) ... MOB
Mobilization Against the Draft and Student Peace Mobilization [*An association*] (EA) ... MADSPM
Mobilization Air Force Specialty ... MAFS
Mobilization Air Force Specialty Code ... MAFSC
Mobilization and Deployment Capability Assurance Concept [*Military*] ... MADCAP
Mobilization and Deployment Planning System [*Army*] ... MDPS
Mobilization and Training Equipment (MCD) ... MATE
Mobilization and Training Equipment Site [*Military*] (AABC) ... MATES
Mobilization Army Training Center ... MATC
Mobilization Asset Planning System [*Army*] ... MAPS
Mobilization Assignment Reserve Section [*Military*] ... MOARS
Mobilization Augmentee [*Military*] (AFM) ... MA
Mobilization Augmentee/Reserve Supplement Officer [*Air Force*] (AFM) ... MA/RSO
Mobilization Augmentee Revitalization Program [*Military*] ... MARP
Mobilization Automation Appraisal (MCD) ... MAA
Mobilization Base Units ... MOBU
Mobilization Center (DNAB) ... MOBCTR
Mobilization Concepts Development Center [*Washington, DC DoD*] (MCD) ... MCDC
Mobilization Construction Plan [*Military*] (NVT) ... MOBCON
Mobilization Contracting Requirement (AFIT) ... MCR
Mobilization Day [*Military*] (AFM) ... M (Day)
Mobilization Day Increment [*Military*] ... MDI
Mobilization Day Index [*Military*] (NG) ... MDI
Mobilization Deployment Exercise (MCD) ... MODEX
Mobilization Designation [*or Designee*] ... MOBDES
Mobilization Designation Reserve Section ... MDRS
Mobilization Equipment Redistribution System ... MOBERS
Mobilization for Animals [*Defunct*] (EA) ... MA
Mobilization for Animals (EA) ... MFA
Mobilization for Youth ... MFY
Mobilization Identification Number [*Military*] ... MIN
Mobilization Improvement Program [*MTMC*] (TAG) ... MIP
Mobilization Manpower Allocations/Requirements Plan [*Military*] ... M-MARP
Mobilization Manpower Planning System [*DoD*] ... MOBMAN
Mobilization Manpower Policy Analysis [*Military*] ... MMPAS
Mobilization Master Data Record [*Army*] ... MOBMDR
Mobilization Material Procurement Capability ... MMPC
Mobilization Materiel Management Task Force ... MMMTF
Mobilization Materiel Requirement [*Military*] ... MMR
Mobilization Materiel Requirement Adjustment [*Military*] (NG) ... MMRA
Mobilization, Military and Civilian Manpower Program (AABC) ... MMCMP
Mobilization Movement Control [*MTMC*] (TAG) ... MOBCON
Mobilization on Development, Trade, Labor, and Environment [*An association*] ... MODTLE
Mobilization Operational Readiness Deployment Test [*DoD*] ... MORDT
Mobilization Personnel Structure and Composition System [*DoD*] ... MOBPERSACS
Mobilization Plan ... MP
Mobilization Production Planning Requirements [*Military*] ... MPPR
Mobilization Regulation [*Army*] ... MR

Mobilization Requirement Study ..... MRS
Mobilization Requirements in Support of the Army Strategic Objectives Plan ..... MOBRASOP
Mobilization Requirements, Secondary Items ..... MRSI
Mobilization Reserve Acquisition Objective [Military] ..... MRAO
Mobilization Reserve Components Program of the Army (AABC) ..... MRCPA
Mobilization Reserve for Retention [Military] ..... MRFR
Mobilization Reserve Materiel Objective [Army] ..... MRMO
Mobilization Reserve Materiel Objective - Acquisition [Army] (AFIT) ..... MRMO-A
Mobilization Reserve Materiel Procurement Objective [Army] ..... MRMPO
Mobilization Reserve Materiel Requirement [Army] ..... MRMR
Mobilization Reserve Stockage List [Army] (AABC) ..... MORSL
Mobilization Reserve Stockage Objective [Army] ..... MRSO
Mobilization Reserve Stocks [Army] ..... MRS
Mobilization Shipments Configured for Operation Planning and Execution [MTMC] (TAG) ..... MOBSCOPE
Mobilization Station [DoD] ..... MS
Mobilization Station Planning System [MTMC] (TAG) ..... MSPS
Mobilization Support System [MTMC] (TAG) ..... MOBSS
Mobilization Table of Allowance Listing [Military] (DNAB) ..... MTOAL
Mobilization Table of Distribution [Military] ..... MTD
Mobilization Table of Distribution and Allowances (AD) ..... MOBTA
Mobilization Table of Distribution and Allowances [Military] (AABC) ..... MOBTDA
Mobilization Training Loss [Military] ..... MTL
Mobilization Training Management System [DoD] ..... MTMS
Mobilization Training Program [Military] ..... MTP
Mobilization Troop Basic Stationing Plan (MCD) ..... MTBSP
Mobilization Troop Basis [Army] (AABC) ..... MOBTB
Mobilization Troop Program [Army] ..... MTP
Mobiltherm Light (NRCH) ..... MTL
Mobil-Trac System [MTMC] (TAG) ..... MTS
Mobley Environmental Services [NASDAQ symbol] (SPSG) ..... MBLY
Mobley Environmental Services [Associated Press] (SAG) ..... Mobley
Mobley's Contested Election Cases, United States House of Representatives [1882-89] [A publication] (DLA) ..... Mob
Mobley's Contested Election Cases, United States House of Representatives [1882-89] [A publication] (DLA) ..... Mobl
Mobridge, SD [AM radio station call letters] ..... KOLY
Mobridge, SD [FM radio station call letters] ..... KOLY-FM
Mobridge, SD [Location identifier FAA] (FAAL) ..... MBG
Moca [Puerto Rico] [Seismograph station code, US Geological Survey] (SEIS) ..... MCP
Moca [Fernando Poo] [Equatorial Guinea] [Seismograph station code, US Geological Survey] (SEIS) ..... MFP
Moca, PR [AM radio station call letters] ..... WZNA
Mocassin (AD) ..... moc
Moccasin ..... MOC
Moccasin Bend Mental Health Institute, Chattanooga, TN [Library symbol Library of Congress] (LCLS) ..... TCMI
Mochaware (VRA) ..... mochwr
Moche Resources, Inc. [Vancouver Stock Exchange symbol] ..... MOH
Mocimboa Da Praia [Mozambique] [ICAO location identifier] (ICLI) ..... FQMP
Mocimboa da Praia [Mozambique] [Airport symbol] (AD) ..... MZB
Mocksville, NC [Location identifier FAA] (FAAL) ..... DVZ
Mocksville, NC [AM radio station call letters] ..... WDSL
Mockup ..... M/U
Mock-Up ..... MKU
Mock-Up (AAG) ..... MU
Mock-Up Board [Navy] (AFIT) ..... MOB
Mock-Up Discrepancy Report [Aerospace] (AAG) ..... MDR
Mock-Up Planning ..... MUPL
Mock-Up Purchase Request [NASA] (NASA) ..... MPR
Mock-Up Reactor [NASA] ..... MUR
Mock-Up Release ..... MURL
Mock-Up Spallation Target Assembly (PDAA) ..... MUSTA
Mock-Up Template ..... MUT
Mock-Up Test Facility (MCD) ..... MTF
Mocoro/Dix-Sept Rosado [Brazil ICAO location identifier] (ICLI) ..... SBMS
MOD [Maintenance of Deception] Personnel Interceptor Assembly/Disassembly ..... MPIAD
ModaCad, Inc. [Associated Press] (SAG) ..... MdaCad
ModaCad, Inc. [Associated Press] (SAG) ..... MdaCd
ModaCad, Inc. [NASDAQ symbol] (SAG) ..... MODA
ModaCad Inc. [NASDAQ symbol] (TTSB) ..... MODA
ModaCAD Inc. Wrrt [NASDAQ symbol] (TTSB) ..... MODAW
Modal Acoustic Transmission Loss (MCD) ..... MOATL
Modal Data Acquisition and Processing System ..... MODAPS
Modal Sensation [Psychology] ..... MS
Modal Sensitivity [Medicine] ..... MS
Modal Stamen Number per Flower [Botany] ..... MSTAN
Modal Suppression Augmentation System [Aerospace] ..... MSAS
Modal Survey Test (MCD) ..... MST
Modal (Verb) [Linguistics] ..... M
Modal (Verb) [Linguistics] ..... MOD
modality [Physical therapy] (DAVI) ..... mod
Modatech Systems, Inc. [Vancouver Stock Exchange symbol] ..... MOD
Mode ..... M
Mode [Grammar] (ROG) ..... MD
Mode [Statistics] ..... Mo
Mode and Power Control [Aviation] ..... MPC
Mode Annunciator and Logic Unit (PDAA) ..... MALU
Mode Change (CET) ..... MC
Mode Change Flag ..... MCF
Mode Code ..... MC
Mode Control (IAA) ..... MC
Mode Control Message (MCD) ..... MCM
Mode Control Panel ..... MCP
Mode Counter ..... MC
Mode Coupling Theory [Physics] ..... MCT
Mode/Energy Offset ..... MEOS
Mode Indicator (HGAA) ..... MI
Mode of Operation ..... MOP
Mode Products, Inc. [Vancouver Stock Exchange symbol] ..... MDP
Mode Select Panel (IAA) ..... MSP
Mode Selection Switch (KSC) ..... MSS
Mode Selector Controller (MCD) ..... MSC
Mode Selector Unit ..... MSU
Mode Shape Display [Module] ..... MODIS
Mode Sickness Susceptibility (KSC) ..... MSS
Mode Status Register (IAA) ..... MSR
Mode Suppressor (KSC) ..... MDSPR
Mode Switch Chassis ..... MSCH
Mode Transducer (KSC) ..... MDXDCR
Mode Transducer ..... MT
Mode Transducer (MSA) ..... MXDCR
Mode-Independent Unnumbered Information ..... MUI
Model [in military nomenclature] ..... M
Model (ADA) ..... MDL
Model ..... MDL
Model (KSC) ..... MOD
Model (AD) ..... mod
Model A Drivers (EA) ..... MAD
Model A Ford Cabriolet Club (EA) ..... MAFCC
Model A Ford Club of America (EA) ..... MAFCA
Model "A" Restorers Club (EA) ..... MARC
Model Adoption Exchange Payment System (EDAC) ..... MAEPS
Model Air Jet ..... MAJ
Model Aircraft Target System [British military] (DMA) ..... MATS
Model Airplane Club ..... MAC
Model Algorithmic Control [Chemical engineering] [Computer science] ..... MAC
Model and Program [Computer science] ..... MAP
Model and Series (AAG) ..... M & S
Model and Series (AD) ..... m & s
Model Annotation Search and Retrieval System [Geological program] ..... MARS
Model Assembly Sterilizer for Testing [NASA] ..... MAST
Model Assignment Sheet (MCD) ..... MAS
Model Base Management Software [Computer science] (IAA) ..... MBMS
Model Basin ..... MOBAS
Model Block (MSA) ..... MB
Model Boiler-Two [Nuclear energy] (GFGA) MB-2
Model Breakdown List ..... MBL
Model Building Language [Programming language] (IEEE) ..... MOBULA
Model Car Collectors Association (EA) ..... MCCA
Model Car Journal Association [Publishing company] (EA) ..... MCJ
Model Change Training Guide ..... MCTG
Model Cities (OICC) ..... MC
Model Cities Administration [HUD] ..... MCA
Model Cities Program ..... MCP
Model Codes Standardization Council [Defunct] ..... MCSC
Model Data Set Control Block (NITA) ..... MDSCB
Model Designation and Series [Military] (AFIT) ..... MDS
Model Emission Model [Environmental Protection Agency] (GFGA) ..... MEM
Model Engineering Trade Association [British] (BI) ..... META
Model Experiment in Drug Indexing by Computer [Rutgers University] ..... MEDICO
Model Experimental Systems Analysis [In-depth study of sewage outfall in the New York Bight] [Inactive] (OSRA) ..... MESA
Model Experimental Systems Analysis [An in-depth study of sewage outfall in the New York Bight] [Defunct] (USDC) ..... MESA
Model for Articulated Vocational Education (EDAC) ..... MAVE
Model for Evaluating Missile Observation ..... MEMO
Model for Interheater Deployment by Air and Sea [DoD] ..... MIDAS
Model for Spare Optimization (MCD) ..... MSO
Model Form and Record ..... MFR
Model Immune Complex [Medicine] (DMAA) ..... MIC
Model Imperial, Inc. [Associated Press] (SAG) ..... ModelImp
Model Imperial, Inc. [NASDAQ symbol] (SAG) ..... MODL
Model Implementation Plan ..... MIP
Model Improvement Experiment (MCD) ..... MIPEX
Model Improvements Program [TRADOC] (MCD) ..... MIP
Model Incident Report [Telecommunications] (TEL) ..... MIR
Model Inner City Community Organization [Washington, DC] ..... MICCO
Model Installation Program (AAGC) ..... MIP
Model Interface Unit (NITA) ..... MIU
Model Interstate Scientific and Technical Information Clearinghouse ..... MISTIC
Model of Advection, Diffusion, and Chemistry for Air Pollution [Environmental Protection Agency] (GFGA) ..... MADCAP
Model of International Relations in Agriculture (PDAA) ..... MOIRA
Model of Light Diode ..... MOLD
Model of the Global Universal Tracer Transport in the Atmosphere [Marine science] (OSRA) ..... MOGUNTIA
Model Office Project ..... MOP
Model Operational Environment (SAA) ..... MOE
Model Operational Plan ..... MOP
Model Output Statistics [Meteorology] ..... MOS
Model Penal Code (AD) ..... MPC
Model Performance Evaluation Program [Centers for Disease Control] ..... MPEP
Model Potential [Physics] ..... MODPOT
Model Power Boat Association [British] (DBA) ..... MPBA
Model Predictive Control [Chemical engineering] ..... MPC
Model Procurement Code [for State and Local Governments] (AAGC) ..... MPC

Model Qualification Test ... MQT
Model Railroad Industry Association (EA) ... MRIA
Model Railroader [*A publication*] ... Model R
Model Railway Club [*British*] ... MRC
Model Reference Adaptive System (PDAA) ... MRAS
Model Reporting Area [*for Blindness Statistics*] [*HEW*] ... MRA
Model Seafood Surveillance Project [*National Marine Fisheries Service*] ... MSSP
Model Secondary School for the Deaf (EA) ... MSSD
Model Skin Surface [*Artificial skin*] ... MSS
Model State Information System [*Environmental Protection Agency*] (GFGA) ... MSIS
Model State Packaging Regulation [*National Institute of Standards and Technology*] ... MSPR
Model Station ... MS
Model T Ford Club International (EA) ... MTFCI
Model "T" Ford Club of America (EA) ... MTFCA
Model to Evaluate Maintenance Support Concepts (MCD) ... MASC
Model to Understand Simple English (PDAA) ... MUSE
Model Urban Neighborhood Demonstration ... MUND
Model Wave Height ... MWH
Model Work Group [*Environmental Protection Agency*] (GFGA) ... MWG
Model X-Y [*AEC computer code*] ... MOXY
Model Yacht Racing Association of America (EA) ... MYRAA
Model Yachting Association [*British*] (DBA) ... MYA
Model Year [*Automotive industry*] ... MY
Model Year to Date ... MYTD
Model-Based System Analysis (PDAA) ... MBSA
Model-Building Language (AD) ... mobula
Model-Controlled System [*NASA*] ... MCS
Modeling and Simulation ... M & S
Modeling and Simulation Investment Plan [*Army*] ... MSIP
Modeling and Simulation Master Plan [*Army*] ... MSMP
Modeling and Simulation Working Group ... MSWG
Modeling Association of America [*Later, MAAI*] ... MAA
Modeling Association of America International (EA) ... MAAI
Modeling Laboratory [*Programming language*] [*1970*] (CSR) ... MLAB
Modeling Paste (VRA) ... mod pst
Modelling and Simulation Studies [*Marine science*] (MSC) ... MSS
Modelling Research Group [*University of Southern California*] [*Research center*] (RCD) ... MRG
Modelling Systems [*Moss Systems Ltd.*] [*Software package*] (NCC) ... MOSS
Model-Modes-Loads-Stresses (NASA) ... M-M-L-S
Model-Modes-Loads-Stresses ... MMLS
Mode-Locked [*Laser technology*] ... ML
Mode-Locked Surface-Acoustic Wave Oscillator [*Telecommunications*] (TEL) ... MLSO
Models (MCD) ... MODS
Models and Photographers of America (EA) ... MPA
Models for Organizational Design and Staffing (DNAB) ... MODS
Models of the [*US*] **Army Worldwide Logistics System** (AABC) ... MAWLOGS
Model-View-Controller [*Computer science*] ... MVC
MODEM [*Computer science*] ... M
MODEM and Radio [*Telecommunications*] ... Modio
Modem Controller [*Telecommunications*] (IAA) ... MC
Modem Equivalent Device (ACRL) ... MED
Modem Evaluation Board (NITA) ... MEB
MODEM Executive [*Computer telecommunications program*] ... MEX
MODEM Interface Modules [*Computer science*] ... MIM
MODEM Pooling Service Module [*Telecommunications*] ... MPSM
MODEM Ready [*Computer science*] ... MR
MODEM Sharing Device ... MSD
Modem Test Set (NITA) ... MTS
Mode-Media Interaction (MCD) ... MMI
MODEM-Sharing Unit [*Telecommunications*] (TSSD) ... MSU
Modena, PA [*Location identifier FAA*] (FAAL) ... MXE
Mode-Power Distribution [*Electronics*] ... MPD
Moderata Samlingspartiet [*Moderate Unity Party*] [*Sweden Political party*] (PPE) ... MSP
Moderate ... M
Moderate (AFM) ... MDT
Moderate [*or Moderator*] (AABC) ... MOD
Moderate (AD) ... mod
Moderate Angle of Attack ... MAA
Moderate Dose [*Medicine*] ... MD
Moderate Environment Buoy [*Marine science*] (MSC) ... MEB
Moderate Learning Difficulties (AIE) ... MLD
Moderate Load service [*Automotive engineering*] ... ML
Moderate Renal Insufficiency [*Medicine*] ... MRI
Moderate Room Rate Desired (AD) ... modr
Moderate Scale Integration [*Electronics*] ... MSI
Moderate Sea or Swell [*Meteorology*] ... M
Moderate Speed Digital Subscriber Line [*Telecommunications*] (ACRL) ... MDSL
Moderate Tactile Stimulus [*Neurology*] (DAVI) ... MTS
Moderately Advanced (MAE) ... MA
Moderately Advanced Data Management [*Computer science*] ... MADAM
Moderately Differentiated ... MD
Moderately Included [*Colored gemstone grade*] ... MI
Moderately Lightly Doped Drains (NITA) ... MLDD
Moderately Long [*Botany*] ... ML
Moderately Repressive Authoritarian Government ... M-RAG
Moderately Resistant [*Plant pathology*] ... MR
Moderately Severe Aplastic Anemia [*Hematology*] ... MSAA
Moderately Susceptible [*Plant pathology*] ... MS
Moderate-Resolution Imaging Spectrometer (MCD) ... MODIS
Moderates [*Reference to political philosophy of some members of the Republican party*] ... Mods
Moderation Management ... MM
Moderations [*First public Oxford examination*] (ROG) ... MODS
Moderato [*Moderate Speed*] [*Music*] (ADA) ... MO
Moderato [*Moderate Speed*] [*Music*] ... MOD
Moderato [*Moderate Speed*] [*Music*] (ROG) ... MODO
Moderato [*Moderately*] [*Italian*] (AD) ... modo
Moderato [*Moderately*] [*Italian*] (AD) ... modto
Moderato [*Moderate Speed*] [*Music*] ... MODTO
Moderator ... MO
Moderator Temperature Coefficient (NRCH) ... MTC
Modern [*Post-1920*] [*Deltiology*] ... M
Modern [*Linguistics*] ... Mn
Modern ... MOD
Modern (AD) ... Mod
Modern (AD) ... mod
Modern ... MOD
Modern Accounts Payable System (MHDW) ... MAPS
Modern Age [*A publication*] (BRI) ... MA
Modern Aids to Planning Program [*Military*] (GFGA) ... MAPP
Modern Air Transport [*Air carrier designation symbol*] ... MDNX
Modern American Law [*A publication*] (DLA) ... MAL
Modern American Law [*A publication*] (DLA) ... Mod Am Law
Modern American Usage [*A publication*] ... MAU
Modern Analytical Generator of Improved Circuits [*Computer science*] ... MAGIC
Modern Approach to Software Construction, Operation and Test [*Ministry of Defence*] [*British*] ... MASCOT
Modern Army Logistics Data Exchange System ... MALODES
Modern Army Maintenance System ... MAMS
Modern Army Record Keeping System (INF) ... MARKS
Modern Army Selected System Test, Evaluation, and Review ... MASSTER
Modern Army Supply ... MAS
Modern Army Supply System ... MASS
Modern Army System ... MAS
Modern Arts Criticism [*A publication*] ... MAC
Modern Authors Checklist [*Publication series*] ... MAC
Modern Black Men [*Johnson Publishing Co., Inc.*] [*A publication*] ... MBM
Modern Cases [*6 Modern Reports*] [*1702-45*] [*A publication*] (DLA) ... Mod Cas
Modern Cases at Law and Equity [*8, 9 Modern Reports*] [*1721-55*] [*A publication*] (DLA) ... Mod Cas L & Eq
Modern Cases Tempore Holt, by Farresley [*7 Modern Reports*] [*A publication*] (DLA) ... Mod Cas per Far
Modern Cases Tempore Holt, by Farresley [*7 Modern Reports*] [*A publication*] (DLA) ... Mod Cas T Holt
Modern Cereal Chemistry (OA) ... MCC
Modern Churchmen's Union [*British*] ... MCU
Modern Controls [*NASDAQ symbol*] (TTSB) ... MOCO
Modern Controls, Inc. [*Associated Press*] (SAG) ... MOCN
Modern Controls, Inc. [*NASDAQ symbol*] (NQ) ... MOCO
Modern Convenience (DSUE) ... MOD CON
Modern Conveniences (AD) ... mod cons
Modern Data Systems (IEEE) ... MDS
Modern Drug Encyclopedia [*A publication*] ... MDE
Modern English [*Language, etc.*] ... MNE
Modern English (AD) ... ModE
Modern English Usage (WDAA) ... MEU
Modern English Writers [*A publication*] ... MEW
Modern Entries [*Legal term*] (DLA) ... MOD ENT
Modern Federal Practice Digest [*A publication*] (DLA) ... MFPD
Modern Fiction ... MF
Modern Fiction Studies [*A publication*] (BRI) ... MFS
Modern Foods Council [*Defunct*] (EA) ... MFC
Modern Foreign Language ... MFL
Modern Free and Accepted Masons of the World (EA) ... MFAMW
Modern Greek [*Language, etc.*] ... MGK
Modern Greek [*Language*] ... ModGr
Modern Greek Studies Association (EA) ... MGSA
Modern Greek Teachers' Association of Victoria [*Australia*] ... MGTAV
Modern Gun Effectiveness Model (MCD) ... MGEM
Modern Heavy Ballistic Missile (ADA) ... MHBM
Modern Hebrew (AD) ... ModHeb
Modern High German [*Language, etc.*] (ROG) ... MHG
Modern Humanities Research Association, American Branch [*Defunct*] (EA) ... MHRA
Modern Investment Theory [*Finance*] (MHDB) ... MIT
Modern Irish Printer [*A publication British*] (DGA) ... MIP
Modern Jazz Quartet [*Musical group*] ... MJQ
Modern Language Aptitude Test [*Military*] (AFM) ... MLAT
Modern Language Aptitude Test-Elementary [*Education*] (AEE) ... EMLAT
Modern Language Association (NADA) ... MLA
Modern Language Association, New York, NY [*Library symbol Library of Congress*] (LCLS) ... ModLA
Modern Language Association of America (EA) ... MLA
Modern Language Association of America (NADA) ... MLLAA
Modern Language Association Research in Progress Program, New York NY [*Library symbol*] [*Library of Congress*] (LCLS) ... ModLA-R
Modern Language Caucus [*of New University Conference*] ... MLC
Modern Language Centre [*Ontario Institute for Studies in Education*] [*Canada*] (IRC) ... MLC
Modern Language Journal [*A publication*] (BRI) ... MLJ
Modern Language Review [*A publication*] (BRI) ... MLR
Modern Languages (AIE) ... ML
Modern Languages Working Group (AIE) ... MLWG
Modern Large Ballistic Missile ... MLBM

Modern Latin [*Language*] ..... ModL
Modern Law and Society [*A publication*] (DLA) ..... Mod L & Soc'y
Modern Library (AD) ..... Modern Lib
Modern Lithographer [*A publication*] (DGA) ..... ML
Modern Lithographer [*A publication*] (DGA) ..... MOD LITH
Modern Med Modalities Wrr'B' [*NASDAQ symbol*] (TTSB) ..... MODMZ
Modern Med Modalities Wrrt'A' [*NASDAQ symbol*] (TTSB) ..... MODMW
Modern Medical Modalities Corp. [*Associated Press*] (SAG) ..... Modd
Modern Medical Modalities Corp. [*NASDAQ symbol*] (SAG) ..... MODM
Modern Medical Modalities Corp. [*Associated Press*] (SAG) ..... ModMd
Modern Medical Modalities Corp. [*Associated Press*] (SAG) ..... ModMed
Modern Medicine of Australia [*A publication*] ..... Mod Med Aust
Modern Medl Modalities [*NASDAQ symbol*] (TTSB) ..... MODM
Modern Mobile Army [*Military*] ..... MOMAR
Modern Mobile Army (AD) ..... momar
Modern Motor [*A publication*] ..... MM
Modern Music Masters Society ..... MMM
Modern Network Theory [*Electrical engineering computer*] ..... MNT
Modern Office and Data Management [*A publication*] ..... Mod Off Dat Man
Modern Office and Data Management [*A publication*] ..... Mod Office Data Mgmt
Modern Operating Agreement [*Labor negotiations*] ..... MOA
Modern Operating Contract [*Automibile industry labor relations*] ..... MOC
Modern Orthodox (BJA) ..... MO
Modern Pentathlon Association of Great Britain (DBA) ..... MPAGB
Modern Philology [*A publication*] (BRI) ..... MP
Modern Poetry Association (EA) ..... MPA
Modern Portfolio Theory [*Finance*] ..... MPT
Modern Practice Commentator [*A publication*] (DLA) ..... Mod Pract Comm
Modern Practice of the Exchequer [*A publication*] (DLA) ..... MP Ex
Modern Programming Practice ..... MODP
Modern Programming Practice ..... MPP
Modern Railroad Club (AD) ..... MRC
Modern Ramjet Engine (MCD) ..... MRE
Modern Ramjet System Synthesis (MCD) ..... MORASS
[*The*] **Modern Reader's Bible (1907)** [*A publication*] (BJA) ..... MR
Modern Religious Problems [*A publication*] ..... MRP
Modern Reports [*England*] [*A publication*] (DLA) ..... Mo
Modern Reports [*England*] [*A publication*] (DLA) ..... Mod
Modern Reports [*England*] [*A publication*] (DLA) ..... Mod Rep
Modern Rythmic Gynmastics (EDAC) ..... MRG
Modern Satellite Network [*Cable-television system*] ..... MSN
Modern Satellite Systems, Inc. [*Whitehouse Station, NJ*] [*Telecommunications*] (TSSD) ..... MSS
Modern Science [*A publication*] ..... MS
Modern Sharing Unit [*Computer science*] (OA) ..... MSU
Modern Ship Equivalent ..... MSE
Modern Studies Association [*British*] (DBA) ..... MSA
Modern Talking Picture Service, Inc. [*Funded by U.S. Department of Education*] (PAZ) ..... MTPS
Modern Technology Demonstration Engine ..... MTDE
Modern Technology Engine ..... MTE
Modern Telecommunications, Inc. [*New York, NY*] (TSSD) ..... MTI
Modern Transport Technical and Historical Society [*Later, SFCH*] (EA) ..... MTTHS
Modern Unionist [*A publication*] ..... Mod Un
Modern Unionist [*A publication*] ..... Mod Unionist
Modern Uses of Logic in Law ..... MULL
Modern Varieties [*Agriculture*] ..... MV
Modern Volunteer Army ..... MVA
Modern Volunteer Army Program (AABC) ..... MVAP
Modern Weapons Training Exercises (MCD) ..... MWTE
Modern Woodmen of America (EA) ..... MWA
Modern-Construction Houses (AD) ..... mod-cons
Modernity Commercialized (AD) ..... modcom
Modernization and Improvement (AABC) ..... M & I
Modernization Management and Control System [*Social Security Administration*] ..... MMCS
Modernization Management Plan ..... MMP
Modernization Management Team [*Military*] (CAAL) ..... MMT
Modernization of Land Data Systems [*North American Institute for the Modernization of Land Data Systems*] [*Falls Church, VA*] ..... MOLDS
Modernization of Logistics 1977 [*Army*] ..... MODLOG 77
Modernization Resource Information Submission [*Army*] (RDA) ..... MRIS
Modernization through Spares [*Army program*] ..... MTS
Modernization through Spares ..... MTS
Modernized Army Research and Development Information System ..... MARDIS
Modernized Fleet Accounting and Reporting ..... MFAR
Modernized Imagery Exploitation and Reporting System (MCD) ..... MIERS
Modernized National Military Intelligence Center ..... MNMIC
Modernized NMIC [*National Military Intelligence Center*] (MCD) ..... MNMIC
Modernized Systems Operations Manual [*Computer science*] ..... MSOM
Modernized Weather Teletypewriter Communications System (FAAC) ..... MWTCS
Modes in Math Project [*National Science Foundation*] ..... MMP
Modest Improvement Program [*Military*] (NVT) ..... MIP
Modest Petrovich Mussorgsky [*1839-1881*] (AD) ..... MPM
Modestinus Pistoris [*Deceased, 1565*] [*Authority cited in pre-1607 legal work*] (DSA) ..... Modest Pistor
Modesto [*California*] [*Airport symbol*] (OAG) ..... MOD
Modesto & Empire Traction Co. [*Formerly, METC*] [*AAR code*] ..... MET
Modesto & Empire Traction Co. [*Later, MET*] [*AAR code*] ..... METC
Modesto Bee, Modesto, CA [*Library symbol Library of Congress*] (LCLS) ..... CMB
Modesto, CA [*FM radio station call letters*] ..... KADV
Modesto, CA [*FM radio station call letters*] ..... KATM
Modesto, CA [*AM radio station call letters*] ..... KBEE
Modesto, CA [*Television station call letters*] ..... KCSO
Modesto, CA [*FM radio station call letters*] (RBYB) ..... KEJC
Modesto, CA [*AM radio station call letters*] ..... KFIV
Modesto, CA [*FM radio station call letters*] (RBYB) ..... KHKK-FM
Modesto, CA [*FM radio station call letters*] ..... KHOP
Modesto, CA [*FM radio station call letters*] ..... KJSN
Modesto, CA [*FM radio station call letters*] ..... KMPO
Modesto, CA [*AM radio station call letters*] ..... KTRB
Modesto Junior College [*California*] ..... MJC
Modesto Junior College, Modesto, CA [*OCLC symbol*] (OCLC) ..... CCM
Modesto Junior College, Modesto, CA [*Library symbol Library of Congress*] (LCLS) ..... CMJ
Modesto State Hospital, Staff Library, Modesto, CA [*Library symbol Library of Congress*] (LCLS) ..... CMH
Mode-Woche-Muenchen [*Munich Fashion Week - International Fashion Fair*] [*Germany*] (TSPED) ..... MWM
Modification [*FCC*] (NTCM) ..... M
Modification [*or Modify*] (AFM) ..... MOD
Modification (AD) ..... mod
Modification (IDOE) ..... mod
Modification (AD) ..... modf
Modification (AAG) ..... MODFN
Modification (KSC) ..... MODIF
Modification and Installation (KSC) ..... M & I
Modification and Repair Order and Acceptance Record (AD) ..... MROAR
Modification and Restriction [*of DNA*] [*Biochemistry, genetics*] ..... M-R
Modification Application Plan [*Army*] ..... MAP
Modification Change Kit ..... MCK
Modification Detection Code (HGAA) ..... MDC
Modification Document (MCD) ..... MD
Modification/Inspection and Repair as Necessary ..... MOD/IRAN
Modification, Inspection, and Repair as Necessary (AD) ..... mod/iran
Modification Instruction Package (KSC) ..... MIP
Modification Instructions (KSC) ..... MI
Modification Kit (AAG) ..... MK
Modification Kit Order ..... MKO
Modification of Benefits [*Health insurance*] (GHCT) ..... MOB
Modification of Contract Documents (AAGC) ..... MCD
Modification of Special Service Authorization [*FCC*] (NTCM) ..... MSSA
Modification or Maintenance [*Aircraft*] ..... MM
Modification Order (AFIT) ..... MO
Modification Package ..... MP
Modification Procurement Instrument Identification Number [*NASA*] (NASA) ..... MPIIN
Modification Program Directive (AFIT) ..... MPD
Modification Program Management Plan (MCD) ..... MPMP
Modification Program Progress Report (AFIT) ..... MPPR
Modification Proposal and Analysis (MCD) ..... MPA
Modification Record Sheet [*NASA*] (KSC) ..... MRS
Modification Request [*or Requirement*] ..... MR
Modification Requirements Board [*NASA*] (KSC) ..... MRB
Modification Review Board (AFM) ..... MRB
Modification Status Report (KSC) ..... MSR
Modification Table of Distribution and Allowances [*Army*] (AABC) ..... MTDA
Modification Table of Organization and Equipment [*Army*] (AABC) ..... MTOE
Modification Task Outline (KSC) ..... MTO
Modification Traceability Record (MCD) ..... MTR
Modification Work Order ..... MWO
Modification Work Order Fielding Plan ..... MWOFP
Modification Work Order Report Status ..... MODWORS
Modifications ..... MODS
Modified [*Regulation or order modified*] [*Used in Shepard's Citations*] [*Legal term*] (DLA) ..... m
Modified Accelerated Cost Recovery System [*IRS*] ..... MACRS
Modified Action Generated Input Control ..... MAGIC
Modified Advanced Forward-Looking Infrared ..... MAFLIR
Modified Advanced Research Environmental Test Satellite [*Air Force*] ..... MARENTS
Modified Advanced Underwater Weapons (MCD) ..... MAUW
Modified Air Control Center [*Air Force*] (DOMA) ..... MACC
Modified Alternate Mark Inversion [*Telecommunications*] (TEL) ..... MAMI
Modified American Plan [*Travel*] ..... MAP
Modified Ames Assay [*For toxicology*] ..... MAA
Modified Anarchy Flood Routing (PDAA) ..... MAFR
Modified Anglia Engine [*Cosworth racing engines*] ..... MAE
Modified Apollo [*NASA*] (MCD) ..... MODAP
Modified Area Production Urgency Committee [*World War II*] ..... MAPUC
Modified Atlantic Naval Intelligence Summary ..... MANIS
Modified Atlantic Naval Intelligence Summary (MCD) ..... MLNIS
Modified Atmosphere [*Food technology*] ..... MA
Modified Atmospheric Packaging [*Food industry*] ..... MAP
Modified Azimuth RADAR Correlator ..... MARC
Modified Binary-Coded Decimal ..... MBCD
Modified Biquinary Code [*Computer science*] ..... MBQ
Modified Bitumen, Reinforced ..... MBR
Modified Boiling Test (PDAA) ..... MBT
Modified Brequet Cruise [*SST*] ..... MBC
Modified Central Computer Display Set (DNAB) ..... MCCDS
Modified Chemical Vapor Deposition [*Telecommunications*] ..... MCVD
Modified Chest Lead [*Medicine*] ..... MCL
Modified Clinical Technique [*Medicine*] ..... MCT
Modified Close Control [*Air Force*] ..... MCC
Modified Combat System Ship Qualification Trial [*Navy*] (CAAL) ..... MCSSQT
Modified Community Rating ..... MCR
Modified Construction Permit [*FCC*] (NTCM) ..... MP
Modified Construction Permit and License [*FCC*] (NTCM) ..... MP/L

Modified Construction Permit and Modified License [*FCC*] (NTCM) .... MP/ML
Modified Continuous Cooking [*Pulp and paper technology*] .... MCC
Modified Continuous Wave [*Telecommunications*] (IAA) .... MCW
Modified Cost Approach Document [*Department of Housing and Urban Development*] .... MCA
Modified Current Expendable Launch Vehicle [*NASA*] (KSC) .... MCEN
Modified Data Tag [*Computer science*] (IAA) .... MDT
Modified Design [*Cordite*] [*British military*] (DMA) .... MD
Modified Diffusion Approximation (PDAA) .... MDA
Modified Diffusion Method (NRCH) .... MDM
Modified Diode Transistor Logic [*Electronics*] (IAA) .... MDTL
Modified Distribution .... MODI
Modified Effective-Range Theory (PDAA) .... MERT
Modified Engineered Time Standards .... METS
Modified, Exclusive, Shared, and Invalid Data (PCM) .... MESI
Modified Expansion Tube (IEEE) .... MET
Modified Federal Test Procedure [*EPA engine test*] .... MFTP
Modified Field Fire Range (MCD) .... MFFR
Modified Filing System [*Computer science*] (PCM) .... MFS
Modified Final Judgment [*Telecommunications*] .... MFJ
Modified Flight Intersection Tape (SAA) .... MFIT
Modified Fluid in Cell [*Automotive engine combustion analysis*] .... MFLIC
Modified Frequency Modulation [*Electronics*] .... MFM
Modified Full Spray .... MFS
Modified Gain Ratio [*Medicine*] (MAE) .... MGR
Modified Granular Diffusion Flame [*Propellant*] .... MGDF
Modified Guaranteed [*Securities trading*] .... MG
Modified Handling Authorized [*Air Force*] .... MHA
Modified Hank's Balanced Salt Solution [*Cell culture*] .... MHBSS
Modified Hatrack [*Cyclone forecasting*] [*Navy*] .... MODHATR
Modified Heat-Degraded Gelatin [*Medicine*] (MEDA) .... MFG
Modified High-Density Acid (MCD) .... MHDA
Modified Hodges-Lehmann Estimator [*Statistics*] .... MDHL
Modified Huffman Coding (NITA) .... MHC
Modified in Situ [*Experimental technique for converting shale into oil*] .... MIS
Modified Index Method (IEEE) .... MIM
Modified Infrared Interferometer Spectrometer .... MIRIS
Modified Input - Modified Output [*Computer science*] .... MIMO
Modified Inside Vapor Phase Oxidation (EECA) .... MIVPO
Modified Integration Digital Analog Simulator [*Computer science*] (MCD) .... MIDAS
Modified Intermediate Neglect of Differential Overlap [*Quantum mechanics*] .... MINDO
Modified Ionization Detector (MCD) .... MID
Modified Julian Date [*Astronomy*] (TEL) .... MJD
Modified Krebs-Ringer Bicarbonate [*Solution*] .... mKRB
Modified Lensless Fourier Transform (PDAA) .... MLLFT
Modified License [*FCC*] (NTCM) .... ML
Modified Link Pack Area (MCD) .... MLPA
Modified Location .... MODLOC
Modified Longest Path .... MLP
Modified Maximum Likelihood [*Statistics*] .... MDML
Modified Maximum Likelihood Estimates [*Statistics*] .... MMLE
Modified Melin-Norkram's Agar [*Microbiology*] .... MMN
Modified Mercalli [*Scale measuring earthquake intensity*] [*Seismology*] .... MM
Modified Mercalli Intensity [*Earthquake magnitude*] [*Seismology*] .... MMI
Modified Military Pay Voucher System (AABC) .... MMPVS
Modified Modified Frequency Modulation M2FM
Modified Modified Frequency Modulation (NITA) .... MMFM
Modified Motorcycle Association .... MMA
Modified Nearly Best Linear Estimator [*Statistics*] .... MNBLE
Modified Need Satisfaction Schedule .... MNSS
Modified Neglect of Differential Overlap [*Quantum mechanics*] .... MNDO
Modified New Haven Schizophrenic Scale .... M-NHSS
Modified New Least Square (PDAA) .... MNLS
Modified OECD [*Organization for Economic Cooperation and Development*] **Screening Test** [*Biodegradability Test*] .... MOST
Modified Operational Missile .... MOM
Modified Operational Missile System (DNAB) .... MOMS
Modified Operational Propulsion Plan Examination [*Navy*] (NVT) .... MOPPE
Modified Owners and Drivers Corp. for the Advancement of Racing (EA) .... MODCAR
Modified Plane Wave (IEEE) .... MPW
Modified Polyphenylene Oxide [*Plastics technology*] .... MPPO
Modified Posterior Mean [*Statistics*] .... MDMN
Modified Programmers Language [*Computer science*] (PDAA) .... MPLAW
Modified Protamine Zinc [*Insulin*] .... MPZ
Modified Quadratic Residue Number System (MCD) .... MQRNS
Modified Random Network [*Crystallography*] .... MRN
Modified Random Phase Approximation .... MRPA
Modified Rapid Fermentation Test .... MRFT
Modified Redlich-Kwong [*Chemical equation*] .... MRK
Modified Refresher Training [*Navy*] (NVT) .... MODREFTRA
Modified Rhyme Test .... MRT
Modified Road Brigade Slice (MCD) .... MRBS
Modified Rydberg Intermediate Neglect of Differential Overlap [*Physics*] .... MRINDO
Modified Scram System [*Nuclear energy*] (NRCH) .... MSS
Modified Seawater Yeast Extract [*Agar*] [*Microbiology*] (DAVI) .... MSWYE
Modified Service Contract and Procedures [*DoD*] .... MOSCAP
Modified Ship Plan Index .... MSPI
Modified Ship Qualification Test .... MSQT
Modified Sodium Polyacrylate [*Organic chemistry*] .... MSPA
Modified Source Multiplication (NRCH) .... MSM
Modified Tape Armor [*Telecommunications*] (TEL) .... MT
Modified Tape Armor [*Telecommunications*] (IAA) .... MTA
Modified Tension Time Index [*Cardiology*] .... MTTI
Modified Thayer-Martin [*Medium*] [*Microbiology*] .... MTM
Modified Tone Decay Test (MAE) .... MTDT
Modified Total Direct Costs [*Economics*] .... MTDC
Modified Tyrode's Buffer [*Clinical chemistry*] .... MTB
Modified Ultrapherical Polynominal Filter (IAA) .... MUPF
Modified Universal Soil Loss Equation [*Agricultural Research Service*] .... MUSLE
Modified Variable-Threshold Logic [*Computer science*] .... MVTL
Modified Warhead Section (MCD) .... MWHS
Modified Wohlgemuth Unit [*Of hydrolytic enzyme activity*] .... MWU
Modified-Adopted-Fernald Technique (EDAC) .... MAFT
Modifier [*Linguistics*] .... MOD
Modifier (AAG) .... MODFR
Modify .... MDF
Modify (AAG) .... MODF
Modify Address (IEEE) .... MA
Modifying [*Legal term*] (DLA) .... Mod'g
Modifying Factor [*Toxicology*] .... MF
Modigliani-Miller Propositions [*Corporate finance*] (ECON) .... MM
Modiim [*Israel*] [*Later, AMT*] [*Geomagnetic observatory code*] .... MOD
Modine Manufacturing Co. [*NASDAQ symbol*] (NQ) .... MODI
Modine Manufacturing Co. [*Associated Press*] (SAG) .... Modine
Modine Mfg [*NASDAQ symbol*] (TTSB) .... MODI
Moding Sequencing and Control (MCD) .... MSC
Modo Praescripto [*In the manner prescribed*] [*Latin*] [*Pharmacy*] (BARN) .... mod praes
Modo Praescripto [*In the Manner Prescribed*] [*Latin Pharmacy*] (MAH) .... MOD PRAESC
Modo Praescripto [*In the Manner Prescribed*] [*Pharmacy*] .... MOD PRAESCRIPT
Modo Praescripto [*In the Manner Prescribed*] [*Pharmacy*] (ROG) .... MOD PRESCR
Modo Praescripto [*In the Manner Prescribed*] [*Pharmacy*] .... MP
Modo Prescripto [*In the Manner Prescribed*] [*Latin*] (AD) .... mod pres
Modoc County Free Library, Alturas, CA [*Library symbol Library of Congress*] (LCLS) .... CAltu
Modoc National Wildlife Refuge [*California*] (AD) .... MNWR
Modtech, Inc. [*NASDAQ symbol*] (SAG) .... MODT
Modtech, Inc. [*Associated Press*] (SAG) .... Modtec
Modular (AD) .... mod
Modular 8mm Video System [*Eastman Kodak Co.*] .... MVS
Modular Accounting System [*Computer science*] (IAA) .... MAS
Modular Acoustic Panel .... MAP
Modular Acoustic Processing System (MCD) .... MAPS
Modular, Adaptable, Expandable, Intelligent Terminal [*Link Technologies, Inc.*] (PCM) .... MAX/IT
Modular Adaptive Signal Sorter .... MASS
Modular Advanced Graphics Generation System (IEEE) .... MAGGS
Modular Air Defense System (MCD) .... MADS
Modular Airborne Fire Fighting System [*Air Force*] .... MAFFS
Modular Airborne Intercept RADAR (IAA) .... MAIR
Modular Airborne Recorder System (MCD) .... MARS
Modular Air-to-Surface Missile (MCD) .... MODASM
Modular Air-to-Surface Missile [*Military*] (AD) .... modasm
Modular Allocation Technique (PDAA) .... MAT
Modular Alphanumeric Graphics Generator (IEEE) .... MAGG
Modular Alter and Compose Console [*Computer science*] .... MACC
Modular Analysis of Learning Difficulties (OICC) .... MALD
Modular Analysis Processor [*Applied Data Research, Inc.*] .... MAP
Modular Analysis, Speedup, Sampling, and Data Reduction .... MASSDAR
Modular Application Executive for Computer Networks (PDAA) .... MAXNET
Modular Application System [*Computer science*] .... MAP
Modular Application Systems [*Martin Marietta Data Systems*] .... MAS
Modular Applications Executive [*Modular Computer Systems*] .... MAX
Modular Applications Executive for Communications [*Modular Computer Systems*] .... MAXCOM
Modular Applications Executive Network (NITA) .... MAXNET
Modular Approach to Software Construction Operation and Test (NITA) .... MASCOT
Modular Approach to System Construction Operation and Test (MCD) .... MASCOT
Modular Area Graphics Illustrations Composition (DGA) .... MAGIC
Modular Army Demonstration System (MCD) .... MADS
Modular Arrangement of Predetermined Time Standards .... MODAPTS
Modular Assembly Prosthesis [*Medicine*] .... MAP
Modular Assembly Technique (IAA) .... MAT
Modular Atmosphere Simulation Program [*NASA*] (KSC) .... MASP
Modular Attack RADAR System (MCD) .... MARS
Modular Audio Visual Unit (PDAA) .... MAVU
Modular Automated Container Handling [*Shipping*] (DS) .... MACH
Modular Automated Integrated Systems / Interoperability Test and Evaluation (PDAA) .... MAINSITE
Modular Automated System to Identify Friend from Foe [*Military*] (PDAA) .... MASTIFF
Modular Automated Weather System .... MAWS
Modular Automatic Test Equipment .... MATE
Modular Auxiliary Data System .... MADS
Modular Auxiliary Data Systems (NASA) .... MADS
Modular Avionics Systems Architecture (MCD) .... MASA
Modular Azimuth Position System [*Army*] (RDA) .... MAPS
Modular Banking System (PDAA) .... MBS
Modular Building Distribution System [*Telecommunications*] (TEL) .... MBDS
Modular Building Standards Association (EA) .... MBSA
Modular Building Systems Council (EA) .... MBSC
Modular Cargo Delivery System [*MARAD*] (TAG) .... MCDS
Modular Chaff/Flare Dispenser (PDAA) .... MCFD

Modular Clinical Laboratory [*Military*] (CAAL) ... MODULAB
Modular Collective Protection Equipment (RDA) ... MCPE
Modular Combustion Facility (SSD) ... MCF
Modular Composition System [*Diskettes*] ... MCS
Modular Computer ... MC
Modular Computer System (IEEE) ... MCS
Modular Computer System ... MODCOM
Modular Computer Systems Inc. (NITA) ... MODCOMP
Modular Concept Unit (DA) ... MCU
Modular Containerless Processing Facility (SSD) ... MCPF
Modular Control Element (MCD) ... MCE
Modular Control Equipment [*DoD*] ... MCE
Modular Controllable Booster (MCD) ... MCB
Modular Data Acquisition and Control System [*or Subsystem*] [*Modular Computing Systems, Inc.*] ... MODACS
Modular Data Acquisition System (NITA) ... MDAS
Modular Data Module (HGAA) ... MDM
Modular Data System ... MDS
Modular Data Transaction System ... MDTS
Modular Decontamination System (DWSG) ... MDS
Modular Design ... MD
Modular Design Language [*Computer science*] (CSR) ... MDL
Modular Design of Electronics (MCD) ... MDE
Modular Digital Image Generation [*Computer science*] ... MODIG
Modular Digital Output Timer ... MDOT
Modular Digital Scan Converter (MCD) ... MDSC
Modular Digital Simulation (MCD) ... MODIGSI
Modular Disc Storage (NITA) ... MDS
Modular Display Electronics (MCD) ... MDE
Modular Display Tactical ... MDT
Modular Distribution System ... MDS
Modular Dummy Load ... MDL
Modular Electrical Power Station ... MEPS
Modular Electron Column Control and Automation ... MECCA
Modular Electronic Digital Instrumentation Assemblies (PDAA) ... MEDIA
Modular Electronic Kay Telephone System (IAA) ... MEKTS
Modular Electronic Solid-State Aerospace Ground Equipment ... MESSAGE
Modular Electronic Warfare Simulator [*Navy*] ... MEWS
Modular Electronics (IAA) ... ME
Modular Engine Analyzer [*Automotive engineering*] ... MEA
Modular Engine Management System [*Automotive engineering*] ... MEMS
Modular Engine Test System (MCD) ... METS
Modular Engineering Drafting and Library System (IAA) ... MEDALS
Modular Equipment Transporter [*NASA*] ... MET
Modular Evolutionary Development (MCD) ... MED
Modular Flare Chaff Dispenser [*Military*] (PDAA) ... MFCD
Modular Flexible Scheduling [*Education*] ... MFS
Modular Force Planning System (MCD) ... MFPS
Modular Forward-Looking Infrared Seeker ... MODFLIR
Modular Fuel Delivery Station [*Shipboard installation*] [*Navy*] (DOMA) ... MFDS
Modular Gas-Cooled Reactor [*Developed by MIT*] [*Nuclear energy*] ... MGR
Modular Gas-Cooled Reactor Gas Turbine [*Developed by MIT*] [*Nuclear energy*] ... MGRGT
Modular Geographic Environment ... MGE
Modular Guided Glide Bomb (MCD) ... MGGB
Modular Guided Weapon System (MCD) ... MGWS
Modular Handling and Transport ... MOHAT
Modular High-Temperature Gas Reactor [*Nuclear energy*] ... MHTGR
Modular Hydrologic Modeling System [*Marine science*] (OSRA) ... MHMS
Modular Hydrologic Modeling System (USDC) ... MHMS
Modular Industrial Solar Retrofit Program [*Department of Energy*] ... MISR
Modular Industrial Terminal ... MIT
Modular Information Processing Equipment ... MIPE
Modular Input/Output [*Telecommunications*] ... MIO
Modular Input/Output System ... MINOS
Modular Input-Output System [*Telecommunications*] (TEL) ... MIOS
Modular Installation of Telecommunications Equipment Racks (TEL) ... MITER
Modular Instrument Landing System ... MODILS
Modular Instrumentation Package System (MCD) ... MIPS
Modular Integrated Circuit Package ... MICPAK
Modular Integrated Communications and Navigation System (RDA) ... MICNS
Modular Integrated Design Automated System ... MIDAS
Modular Integrated Pallet System [*Tank monitoring*] [*Army*] (RDA) ... MIPS
Modular Integrated Rack (MCD) ... MIR
Modular Integrated Utility System [*HUD*] ... MIUS
Modular Integrated Utility Systems (MCD) ... MINUS
Modular Intelligent Terminal ... MIT
Modular Interactive Data Acquisition System [*National Institute of Standards and Technology*] ... MIDAS
Modular Interactive Network Designer ... MIND
Modular Interchangeable Ambulance Body [*Military British*] ... MIAB
Modular International Dealing and Accounting System (NITA) ... MIDAS
Modular Isodrive Memory Series ... MIMS
Modular Magnetic Tape Transport Units (MCD) ... MMTTU
Modular Maneuvering Unit [*Aerospace*] ... MMU
Modular Measuring System ... MMS
Modular Midcourse Package [*DoD*] ... MMP
Modular Modeling System ... MMS
Modular Multiband Radiometer ... MMR
Modular Multiband Scanner (MCD) ... MMS
Modular Multimission Spacecraft [*NASA*] ... MMS
Modular Multispectral Scanner ... MMS
Modular Navigation [*Aviation*] ... MONA
Modular Nuclear Vehicle ... MNV
Modular Observation Device (RDA) ... MOD
Modular Ocean Model [*Marine science*] (OSRA) ... MOM
Modular Ocean Model (USDC) ... MOM
Modular Ocean Observation System [*Marine science*] (MSC) ... MOOS
Modular One Dynamic User System [*Computer science*] (MHDI) ... MODUS
Modular Operating Procedure (MUGU) ... MOP
Modular Operating Procedure (MUGU) ... MOPP
Modular Operating System (BUR) ... MOS
Modular Optical Digital Interface ... MODI
Modular Optoelectronic Multispectral Scanner (MCD) ... MOMS
Modular Organization Charting (PDAA) ... MOC
Modular Oriented Direct Support (MCD) ... MODS
Modular Output Unit for Talking to Humans ... MOUTH
Modular Pack Mine System (RDA) ... MOPMS
Modular Peripheral Interface Converter ... MPC
Modular Personnel Office (SSD) ... MPO
Modular Power System (MCD) ... MPS
Modular Processing and Support System ... MPASS
Modular Processor System [*Computer science*] (PCM) ... MPS
Modular Programming Language (CSR) ... MODULA
Modular Record Traffic Terminal [*Formerly, COED*] [*Army*] (MCD) ... MRTT
Modular Redundancy ... MR
Modular Responsive Defense System ... MRDS
Modular Restraint, Recovery, and Survival Package ... MODPAC
Modular Reusable Nuclear Shuttle ... MRNS
Modular Rigid Frame (PDAA) ... MRF
Modular Robot ... MOBOT
Modular Semi-Automatic Forces ... MODSAF
Modular Shift Register Generator ... MSRG
Modular Space Electrical Power Station ... MSEPS
Modular Space Power Station ... MSPS
Modular Space Station ... MSS
Modular Stability [*Derivative program*] ... MOSTAB
Modular Standoff Weapon [*Ballistic missile*] ... MSOW
Modular Steam Generator (NRCH) ... MSG
Modular Store Control Unit ... MSCU
Modular System Programs [*IBM Corp.*] ... MSP
Modular Systems Interface Bus (NITA) ... MSIB
Modular Tactical Communications Center ... MTCC
Modular Television System [*Telecommunications*] (CDE) ... MTS
Modular Terminal Processor (NITA) ... MTP
Modular Terminal System (NITA) ... MTS
Modular Thermal Analyzer Routine [*Computer science*] ... MOTAR
Modular Threat Emitter (DWSG) ... MTE
Modular Timing Terminal Unit ... MTTU
Modular Torque Motor ... MTM
Modular Toxic Environment Protective Suit [*NASA*] ... MODTEPS
Modular Training Field Option (NASA) ... MTFO
Modular Tree Representation (MHDI) ... MTR
Modular Unit (IAA) ... MU
Modular Universal LASER Equipment (MCD) ... MULE
Modular Universal Terminal (IAA) ... MUT
Modular Utilities for Systems Education (IAA) ... MUSE
Modular Vault Dry Store [*Nuclear energy*] (NUCP) ... MVDS
Modular Video Data System [*Sperry UNIVAC*] ... MVDS
Modular Weapons System (MCD) ... MWS
Modular X-Ray Quantometer ... MXQ
Modular-Dispersed-Control ... MODICON
Modularized Equipment Storage [*or Stowage*] **Area** [*or Assembly*] [*Apollo*] [*NASA*] ... MESA
Modularized Equipment Transport System [*NASA*] ... METS
Modularized Vehicle Stimulation [*Program*] ... MVS
Modulate/Demodulate [*or Modulation/Demodulation or Modulator-Demodulator*] [*Computer science*] ... MODEM
Modulate Open [*Nuclear energy*] (NRCH) ... MO
Modulated Bayard-Alpert Gauge ... MBAG
Modulated Carrier Wave [*Telecommunications*] (IAA) ... MCW
Modulated Continuous Wave [*Radio signal transmission*] ... MCW
Modulated Frequency Radio Telephone (PDAA) ... MFRT
Modulated Interframe Plan ... MIP
Modulated Lapped Transform [*Telecommunications*] ... MLT
Modulated Noise Generator (PDAA) ... MNG
Modulated Noise Reference Unit [*Telecommunications*] (TEL) ... MNRU
Modulated Pulse Amplifier [*Telecommunications*] (IAA) ... MPA
Modulated Throat-Rocket Motor (MCD) ... MTRM
Modulated Throttle Valve [*Automotive engineering*] ... MTV
Modulated/Unmodulated (SSD) ... MOD/UM
Modulated Wave (IAA) ... MW
Modulated Wavy Vortex [*Fluid mechanics*] ... MWV
Modulated Zone Plate (PDAA) ... MZP
Modulate-Demodulate (AD) ... mod/demod
Modulate-Demodulate Subsystem ... MDS
Modulating Amplifier Using Variable Resistance ... MAVAR
Modulating Flow Control Valve (MCD) ... MFCV
Modulating-Demodulating (AD) ... modem
Modulation [*Telecommunications*] (KSC) ... MOD
Modulation ... MOD
Modulation Coefficient (IDOE) ... m
Modulation, Demodulation, Terminal, and Associated Equipment ... MDTA
Modulation Depth [*Broadcasting*] ... M
Modulation Efficiency ... ME
Modulation Factor ... MF
Modulation Frequency (IDOE) ... f_m
Modulation Inducing Reactive Retrodirective Optical System [*NASA*] ... MIRROS
Modulation Inducing Retrodirective Optical System [*NASA*] ... MIROS
Modulation on the Pulse (NG) ... MOP

Modulation Response ... MR
Modulation Scan Array RADAR [*or Receiver*] ... MOSAR
Modulation Sensitivity ... MS
Modulation Signal Generator (NITA) ... MSG
Modulation Transfer Curve (OA) ... MTC
Modulation Transfer Function [*Resolution measure*] ... MTF
Modulation Transfer Function Analyzer ... MTFA
Modulation with Constant Control ... MCC
Modulation-Controlled Synchronization (IAA) ... MCS
Modulation-Demodulation (HGAA) ... M-D
Modulation-Doped Field-Effect Transistor [*Solid-state physics*] ... MODFET
Modulator (IAA) ... M
Modulator (CET) ... MOD
Modulator (IDOE) ... mod
Modulator Band Filter (IAA) ... MBF
Modulator/Demodulator [*Computer science*] (WDMC) ... modem
Modulator Isolation Diagnostic Analysis System (IEEE) ... MIDAS
Modulator-Demodulator [*Telecommunications*] (CET) ... M/D
Modulator-Demodulator [*Telecommunications*] (MCD) ... MOD
Modulator-Demodulator (AD) ... moddem
Modulators [*JETDS nomenclature*] [*Military*] (CET) ... MD
Module (MSA) ... MDL
Module [*or Modular or Modulation*] (KSC) ... MOD
Module ... MOD
Module ... MB
Module Balance [*Computer science*] ... MCB
Module Control Block (KSC) ... MCB
Module Exchange Mechanism [*NASA*] (NASA) ... MEM
Module Experimental Process System Development Unit [*Photovoltaic energy systems*] ... MEPSDU
Module for Automatic Dock and Detumble [*Orbital rescue*] [*NASA*] ... MADD
Module Generator Assembly (DWSG) ... MGA
Module Integration Facility (SSD) ... MIF
Module Interconnection Language ... MIL
Module Maintenance Facility ... MMF
Module Rack Assembly ... MRA
Module RADAR Display Console ... MRDC
Module Repair Calibration Facility ... MRCF
Module Repair Facility (DNAB) ... MRF
Module Resources, Inc. [*Vancouver Stock Exchange symbol*] ... MLE
Module Service Tool (NASA) ... MST
Module Service Tool ... MST
Module Support Rack ... MSR
Module Support Rack (NASA) ... MSR
Module Table Entry [*Computer science*] (BYTE) ... MTE
Module Test Bed [*Military*] (CAAL) ... MTB
Module Test Set ... MOTS
Module Test Set (MCD) ... MTS
Module Test Set / Guided Missile System (DWSG) ... MTS/GMS
Module Test System (IAA) ... MTS
Module Test Unit [*Nuclear energy*] (NRCH) ... MTU
Module Thruster Valve Unit ... MTVU
Module Tracking System (NRCH) ... MTS
Module under Test ... MUT
Module Utility Support Structure (NASA) ... MUSS
Modulo [*Mathematics*] (CDE) ... mod
Modulus ... M
Modulus ... MOD
Modulus ... mod
Modulus (IDOE) ... mod
Modulus 10 Check Digit [*Computer science*] ... MOD10
Modulus of Elasticity [*Mechanics*] ... E
Modulus of Elasticity [*Mechanics*] ... MOE
Modulus of Rupture [*Mechanics*] ... MOR
Modulus of Rupture Test (AD) ... MRT
Modus Operandi [*Police term for distinctive techniques used by criminals*] ... MO
Modus Operandi - Personal Appearance [*FBI computer procedure*] ... MOPA
Modus Ponens [*Rule of inference*] [*Logic*] [*Latin*] ... MP
Modus Tolens [*Rule of inference*] [*Logic*] [*Latin*] ... MT
Modus Vivendi [*Way of Living*] [*Latin*] ... MV
Moe Bandy Fan Club (EA) ... MBFC
Mo'ed Katan (BJA) ... MK
Mo'ed Qatan [*or Qattan*] (BJA) ... MQ
Moenchengladbach [*Germany ICAO location identifier*] (ICLI) ... EDLN
Moengo [*Surinam*] [*ICAO location identifier*] (ICLI) ... SMMO
Moenjodaro [*Pakistan*] [*ICAO location identifier*] (ICLI) ... OPMJ
Moersch-Woltman Syndrome [*Medicine*] (DMAA) ... MWS
Moeso-Gothic [*Language, etc.*] (ROG) ... M GOTH
Moeso-Gothic [*Language, etc.*] (ROG) ... MG
Moessbauer Effect (OA) ... ME
Moessbauer Effect Data Center [*University of North Carolina*] [*Information service or system*] (IID) ... MEDC
Moessbauer Effect Data Index ... MEDI
Moessbauer Emission Spectroscopy ... MES
Moessbauer Isotopic Resonant Absorption of Gamma Emission [*Physics*] ... MIRAGE
Moessbauer Spectroscopy ... MS
Moessingen [*Federal Republic of Germany*] [*Seismograph station code, US Geological Survey*] (SEIS) ... MSG
Moewe Flugzeugbau, Heini Dittmar [*Germany ICAO aircraft manufacturer identifier*] (ICAO) ... MW
Mofaz Air [*Malawi*] [*FAA designator*] (FAAC) ... MFZ
Moffat Communications Ltd. [*Toronto Stock Exchange symbol*] ... MOF
Moffat Library Association, Washingtonville, NY [*Library symbol Library of Congress*] (LCLS) ... NWas
Moffatt New Testament Commentary [*A publication*] (BJA) ... MNT
Moffatt New Testament Commentary [*A publication*] (BJA) ... MNTC
Moga [*Zaire*] [*ICAO location identifier*] (ICLI) ... FZOH
Moga [*India*] [*ICAO location identifier*] (ICLI) ... VIMG
Moga Stan Fin 7.80% Cp Uts [*NYSE symbol*] (TTSB) ... MSZ
Mogadishu [*Somalia*] [*ICAO location identifier*] (ICLI) ... HCMM
Mogadishu [*Somalia*] [*ICAO location identifier*] (ICLI) ... HCSM
Mogadishu [*Somalia*] [*Airport symbol*] (OAG) ... MGQ
Mogadishu [*Somalia*] [*Seismograph station code, US Geological Survey Closed*] (SEIS) ... MOG
Mogul ... MGL
Mogul End Prong [*Lamp base*] (NTCM) ... MEP
Mohair Council of America (EA) ... MCA
Mohajir Qami Movement [*Pakistan*] [*Political party*] ... MQM
Mohales'Hoek [*Lesotho*] [*ICAO location identifier*] (ICLI) ... FXMH
Mohammedan (ROG) ... MOHAM
Mohammedan (AD) ... Moham
Mohanbari [*India*] [*Airport symbol*] (AD) ... MHO
Mohanbari [*India*] [*ICAO location identifier*] (ICLI) ... VEMN
Mohasco Corp., Corporate Planning Library, Amsterdam, NY [*Library symbol Library of Congress*] (LCLS) ... NAmsM
Mohave Community College, Resource Center, Kingman, AZ [*Library symbol Library of Congress*] (LCLS) ... AzKiMC
Mohave Gold, Inc. [*Vancouver Stock Exchange symbol*] ... MVH
Mohawk [*MARC language code Library of Congress*] (LCCP) ... moh
Mohawk Aerial Surveillance/Flight Simulator (MCD) ... MAS/FS
Mohawk Airlines [*ICAO designator*] (FAAC) ... MOW
Mohawk Airlines, Inc. [*Obsolete*] ... MO
Mohawk Airlines, Inc. [*Obsolete*] ... MOH
Mohawk Business-Oriented Language [*Mohawk Data Systems*] ... MOBOL
Mohawk Carpet Mills [*Stock exchange symbol*] (AD) ... MOK
Mohawk College of Applied Arts and Technology, Hamilton, ON, Canada [*Library symbol Library of Congress*] (LCLS) ... CaOHMC
Mohawk College of Applied Arts and Technology, Hamilton, Ontario [*Library symbol National Library of Canada*] (NLC) ... OHMC
Mohawk College of Applied Arts and Technology, Library Technician Program, Hamilton, ON, Canada [*Library symbol*] [*Library of Congress*] (LCLS) ... CaOHMCL
Mohawk Data Sciences [*Computer science*] (IAA) ... MDS
Mohawk Data Systems Corporation (NITA) ... MDS
Mohawk Data Transmission System (MCD) ... MODATS
Mohawk Industries [*NASDAQ symbol*] (SAG) ... MOHK
Mohawk Industries, Inc. [*Associated Press*] (SAG) ... Mohawk
Mohawk Synchronous Communication Data Recorder [*Military*] (PDAA) ... MSCDR
Mohawk Valley (FAAC) ... MHKVLY
Mohawk Valley Community College, Utica, NY [*Library symbol Library of Congress*] (LCLS) ... NUtMV
Mohawk Valley Community College, Utica, NY [*OCLC symbol*] (OCLC) ... ZVM
Mohawk Valley Learning Resource Center, Utica Library, Utica, NY [*OCLC symbol*] (OCLC) ... ZUX
Mohawk Valley Learning Resource Center, Utica Psychiatric Center, Utica, NY [*Library symbol Library of Congress*] (LCLS) ... NUtMVL
Mohawk Valley Library Association, Schenectady County Public Library, Schenect ady, NY [*OCLC symbol*] (OCLC) ... VML
Mohawk Valley Library Association, Schenectady, NY [*Library symbol Library of Congress*] (LCLS) ... NSchM
Mohed [*Sweden ICAO location identifier*] (ICLI) ... ESUM
Mohelbuch (BJA) ... MB
Moheli [*Comoro Islands*] [*Airport symbol*] (OAG) ... NWA
Moheli/Bandaressalam [*Comoros*] [*ICAO location identifier*] (ICLI) ... FMCI
Mohenjo Daro [*Pakistan*] [*Airport symbol*] (OAG) ... MJD
Mohlanapeng [*Lesotho*] [*ICAO location identifier*] (ICLI) ... FXMP
Moholm [*Sweden ICAO location identifier*] (ICLI) ... ESFM
Mohorovicic Discontinuity [*Geology*] ... MOHO
Mohorovicic Discontinuity [*Geology*] (AD) ... moho
Mohs' Micrographic Surgery ... MMS
Moile's Precedents [*A publication*] (DLA) ... Mo Prec
Moir on Capital Punishment [*A publication*] (DLA) ... Moir Cap Pun
Moire Fringe Effect (PDAA) ... MFE
Mois Maconnique [*Masonic Month*] [*Freemasonry*] [*French*] ... MM
Moise Memorial Library, Santa Rosa, NM [*Library symbol Library of Congress*] (LCLS) ... NmSr
Moises (AD) ... Mose
Moishe (AD) ... Moish
Moist Burn Ointment [*Medicine*] ... MBO
Moisture ... M
Moisture ... MOISTR
Moisture [*NWS*] (FAAC) ... MSTR
Moisture (MSA) ... MSTRE
Moisture and Ash Free ... MAF
Moisture and Impurities [*In fats*] ... M & I
Moisture Balance ... MB
Moisture Content ... MC
Moisture Detector Control Box ... MDCB
Moisture Evaluation Analysis (PDAA) ... MEA
Moisture Free Basis ... MFB
Moisture Holding Capacity ... MHC
Moisture, Insolubles, and Unsaponifiables [*Fat analysis*] ... MIU
Moisture Resistant (IEEE) ... MR
Moisture Seekers Foundation [*Later, Sjogren's Syndrome Foundation - SSF*] (EA) ... MSF
Moisture Separator Reheater (NRCH) ... MSR
Moisture Vapor Transmission Rate ... MVT
Moisture Vapor Transmission Rate ... MVTR
Moisture Volume Fraction (PDAA) ... MVF
Moisture-Proof Heat-Sealing Transparent [*Flexography*] (DGA) ... MST

Mojave, CA [FM radio station call letters] .... KAVS
Mojave, CA [AM radio station call letters] .... KVOY
Mojave, CA [Location identifier FAA] (FAAL) .... MHV
Mojave Desert Block [Geology] .... MDB
Mojica [Costa Rica] [ICAO location identifier] (ICLI) .... MRMJ
Mojo Nixon World Headquarters (EA) .... MNWH
Mokapu [Hawaii] [Seismograph station code, US Geological Survey] (SEIS) .... MOK
Mokaria-Yamoleta [Zaire] [ICAO location identifier] (ICLI) .... FZFH
Mokha [Yemen] [ICAO location identifier] (ICLI) .... OYMC
Mokhotlong [Lesotho] [ICAO location identifier] (ICLI) .... FXMK
Mokhotlong [Lesotho] [Airport symbol] (OAG) .... MKH
Mokpo (AD) .... Mok
Mokpo [South Korea ICAO location identifier] (ICLI) .... RKJM
Mokuaweoweo [Hawaii] [Seismograph station code, US Geological Survey]
  (SEIS) .... MWH
Mokuleia, HI [Location identifier FAA] (FAAL) .... HDH
Mokuleia, Oahu, HI [Location identifier FAA] (FAAL) .... DHM
Mokum Industrial Research Automatic Calculator for Laboratory and
  Engineering .... MIRACLE
Mol [or Mole] [Measurement] (DAVI) .... M
MOL [Manned Orbiting Laboratory] Environmental Shelter .... MES
MOL [Manned Orbiting Laboratory] Launch Complex (MCD) .... MLC
MOL [Manned Orbiting Laboratory] Launch Facilities (MCD) .... MLF
MOL [Manned Orbiting Laboratory] Launch Facilities Acceptance Team
  (MCD) .... MLFAT
MOL [Manned Orbiting Laboratory] Launch Site (MCD) .... MLS
Molal [Solute concentration by weight] [Chemistry] .... m
Molalla Mid-High School, Molalla, OR [Library symbol] [Library of Congress]
  (LCLS) .... OrMolMS
Molalla Public Library, Molalla, OR [Library symbol Library of Congress]
  (LCLS) .... OrMol
Molalla Senior High School, Molalla, OR [Library symbol Library of
  Congress] (LCLS) .... OrMolHS
Molar [Tooth, deciduous] [Dentistry] (DAVI) .... m
Molar [Permanent] [Dentistry] .... M
Molar [Solute concentration by volume] [Chemistry] .... M
Molar Concentration [Chemistry] (MAE) .... molc
Molar Degree of Substitution [Organic chemistry] .... MS
Molar Gas Constant [Symbol] [IUPAC] (NASA) .... R
Molar Mass [Symbol] [IUPAC] .... M
Molar Refraction .... MR
Molar Solution [Dentistry] .... MS
Molar Volume [Chemistry] .... MV
Molasses [Freight] .... MLASES
Molasses Information Network (EA) .... MIN
Molco Industries [Vancouver Stock Exchange symbol] .... MOI
Mold (VRA) .... mld
Mold Line [Technical drawings] .... ML
Moldavia (AD) .... Moldv
Moldavian [MARC language code Library of Congress] (LCCP) .... mol
Moldavian Airlines [Macedonia] [FAA designator] (FAAC) .... MDV
Moldavian Soviet Socialist Republic [MARC geographic area code Library of
  Congress] (LCCP) .... e-ur-mv
Moldavian Soviet Socialist Republic [MARC country of publication code
  Library of Congress] (LCCP) .... mvr
Molde [Norway] [Airport symbol] (OAG) .... MOL
Molde/Aro [Norway ICAO location identifier] (ICLI) .... ENML
Molded (KSC) .... MLD
Molded .... MLD
Molded [Construction] .... MO
Molded Case Circuit Breaker .... MCCR
Molded Components (IEEE) .... MC
Molded Fiberglass .... MFG
Molded Nylon Screw .... MNS
Molded Plastic Insulation .... MPI
Molded Rubber Blended Cover .... MRBC
Molded Rubber Coupling Cushion .... MRCC
Molded Rubber Duct System .... MRDS
Molded Urea Plastics .... MUP
Molder [Navy rating] .... ML
Molder (ADA) .... MLDR
Molder, Chief [Navy rating] .... MLC
Molder, First Class [Navy rating] ML1
Molder, Master Chief [Navy rating] .... MLCM
Molder, Second Class [Navy rating] ML2
Molder, Senior Chief [Navy rating] .... MLCS
Molder, Ship Repair [Navy rating] .... MLSR
Molder, Ship Repair, Cupola Tender [Navy rating] .... MLSRC
Molder, Ship Repair, Foundryman [Navy rating] .... MLSRF
Molder, Ship Repair, Molder [Navy rating] .... MLSRM
Molder, Third Class [Navy rating] ML3
Molding [Technical drawings] .... MLD
Molding (KSC) .... MLDG
Molding .... MLDG
Mole .... M
Mole [Amount of substance] [SI unit] .... mol
Mole Fraction [Chemistry] .... MF
Mole Fraction [Chemistry] (DMAA) .... molfr
Molecular (AD) .... mol
Molecular (AD) .... mole
Molecular .... MOLEC
Molecular Access System [Computer program] .... MACCS
Molecular Airborne Intercept RADAR .... MAIR
Molecular Analysis [by a computer graphics system] [Chemistry] .... MOLY
Molecular Analysis Team .... MAT

Molecular Anatomy .... MAN
Molecular and Cellular Neuroscience [A publication] .... MCN
Molecular and Genetic Medicine .... MGM
Molecular Application by Stimulated Emission of Radiation [Organic
  chemistry] (DAVI) .... MASER
Molecular Beam Electric Resonance [Physics] .... MBER
Molecular Beam Epitaxy [Crystallography] .... MBE
Molecular Beam Facility [NASA] .... MBF
Molecular Biosystems [NYSE symbol] (TTSB) .... MB
Molecular Biosystems, Inc. [NYSE symbol] (SPSG) .... MB
Molecular Biosystems, Inc. .... MBI
Molecular Biosystems, Inc. [Associated Press] (SAG) .... MolBio
Molecular Cellular, and Developmental Biology [A discipline division] .... MCDB
Molecular Contamination [of Clean rooms] .... MC
Molecular Crystals and Liquid Crystals (AD) .... Mol Crys Liq Crys
Molecular Devices [NASDAQ symbol] (TTSB) .... MDCC
Molecular Devices Corp. [NASDAQ symbol] (SAG) .... MDCC
Molecular Devices Corp. [Associated Press] (SAG) .... MolecDev
Molecular Diameter .... MD
Molecular Drag Gauge [Instrumentation] .... MDG
Molecular Dynamics .... MD
Molecular Dynamics, Inc. [NASDAQ symbol] (SAG) .... MDYN
Molecular Dynamics, Inc. [Associated Press] (SAG) .... MolecDy
Molecular Electron Density Lego Assembler [Modeling technique] [Organic
  chemistry] .... MEDLA
Molecular Electronic Device .... MED
Molecular Electronic Technique .... MET
Molecular Electronics .... ME
Molecular Electronics .... MOLETRONICS
Molecular Electronics for RADAR Applications (IEEE) .... MERA
Molecular Electrostatic Potentials [Physical chemistry] .... MEP
Molecular Emission Cavity Analysis [Flame spectrophotometry] .... MECA
Molecular Engineering and Materials Laboratory [MIT] (MCD) .... MEML
Molecular Evolutionary Genetics Analysis [Computer software] .... MEGA
Molecular Exciton Microscopy .... MEM
Molecular Exclusion Chromatography .... MEC
Molecular Executive [Graphic substructure chemical search system] .... MOLEX
Molecular Field Theory [Physical chemistry] .... MFT
Molecular Formula (NITA) .... MF
Molecular Free Path .... MFP
Molecular Genetics [Program] [Computer science] .... MOLGEN
Molecular Genetics, Inc. (MHDW) .... MOGN
Molecular Infrared Track (IEEE) .... MIRT
Molecular Kinetic Energy .... MKE
Molecular LASER Isotope Separation .... MLIS
Molecular Layer [of the hippocampus] [Neurology] .... ML
Molecular Layer .... MOL
Molecular Layer Epitaxy [Coating technology] .... MLE
Molecular Marine Biology and Biotechnology [A publication] .... MMBB
Molecular Mass Distribution [Organic chemistry] .... MMD
Molecular Mechanics [Physical chemistry] .... MM
Molecular Neurobiology Laboratory [Salk Institute for Biological Studies] ...... MNL
Molecular Neutron Activation Analysis .... MNAA
Molecular Nitrogen [Chemistry] (DAVI) .... N_2
Molecular Nonthermal Excitation Spectrometry .... MONES
Molecular Optics LASER Examiner [Spectrometry] .... MOLE
Molecular Orbital [Atomic physics] .... MO
Molecular Orbital (AD) .... mo
Molecular Orbital Constraint of Interaction Coordinates [Atomic
  physics] .... MOCIC
Molecular Orbital Energy Diagram .... MOED
Molecular Orbital Self-Consistent Energy System (PDAA) .... MOSES
Molecular Pair [Physical Chemistry] .... MP
Molecular Parameter Index .... MPI
Molecular Photoemission Spectroscopy .... MPS
Molecular Physics (AD) .... Mol Phys
Molecular Presentation Graphics [Software program] .... MPG
Molecular Replacement [Crystallography] .... MR
Molecular Rotational Resonance .... MRR
Molecular Sciences Institute .... MSI
Molecular Sieve (MCD) .... MS
Molecular Sieve Oxygen Generating (PDAA) .... MSOG
Molecular Sink of Outer Space [Vacuum testing chamber for spacecraft
  systems] .... MOLSINK
Molecular Size Distribution [Chemistry] .... MSD
Molecular Solution Volume .... MSV
Molecular Spectroscopy Laboratory [Fisk University] [Research center]
  (RCD) .... MSL
Molecular Staffing [Optics] (EECA) .... MS
Molecular Structures and Dimensions [A publication] .... MSD
Molecular Surface Ionization .... MSI
Molecular Total Overlap Population (IEEE) .... MTOP
Molecular Weight [Also, MOL WT, MW] .... M
Molecular Weight [Also, M, MW] .... MOL WT
Molecular Weight (AD) .... mol wt
Molecular Weight [Also, M, MOL WT] .... MW
Molecular Weight [Also, M, MOL WT, MW] (AAMN) .... MWt
Molecular Weight Cutoff [Chemistry] .... MWCO
Molecular Weight Cut-Off [Metallurgy] .... MWCU
Molecular Weight Distribution .... MWD
Molecularized Computer (AD) .... molecom
Molecularized Digital Computer .... MOLECOM
Molecularized Doppler RADAR .... MODOR
Molecularly Engineered Layered Structure .... MELS
Molecular-Orbital Theory [Physical chemistry] .... MOT

Molecule [*or Molecular*] (AAG) ... MOL
Molecule ... MOL
Molecule-Induced Homolysis [*Chemistry*] ... MIH
Molecules per Liter (MAE) ... mol/l
Molecules per Liter [*Measurement*] (DAVI) ... mol/l
Mole-Percent Metal (AD) ... mpm
Molepolole [*Botswana*] [*ICAO location identifier*] (ICLI) ... FBML
Moles per Cubic Meter ... MOL/M^3
Molesters Anonymous (EA) ... MAN
Molesting [*FBI standardized term*] ... MOL
Molex Inc'A' [*NASDAQ symbol*] (TTSB) ... MOLXA
Molex, Inc. [*Associated Press*] (SAG) ... Molex
Molex, Inc. [*NASDAQ symbol*] (NQ) ... MOLX
Moli Energy Ltd. [*Toronto Stock Exchange symbol Vancouver Stock Exchange symbol*] ... MOE
Moliere [*Pseudonym of French actor and dramatist Jean Baptiste Poquelin, 1622-1673*] (ROG) ... MOL
Moline [*Illinois*] [*Airport symbol*] (OAG) ... MLI
Moline, IL [*Location identifier FAA*] (FAAL) ... GEQ
Moline, IL [*Location identifier FAA*] (FAAL) ... MLI
Moline, IL [*Location identifier FAA*] (FAAL) ... MZV
Moline, IL [*AM radio station call letters*] ... WLLR
Moline, IL [*Television station call letters*] ... WQAD
Moline, IL [*Television station call letters*] ... WQPT
Moline, IL [*FM radio station call letters*] ... WXLP
Moline Public Library, Moline, IL [*Library symbol Library of Congress*] (LCLS) ... IMol
Molinia Streak Virus ... MSV
Mollendo (AD) ... Mol
Mollendo [*Peru*] [*ICAO location identifier*] (ICLI) ... SPDO
Moller Organ Co. [*Record label*] ... Moll
Moller-Plesset Perturbation Theory [*Physical chemistry*] ... MPPT
Mollie Gibson Mines [*Vancouver Stock Exchange symbol*] ... MLI
Mollienisia (AD) ... mollie
Mollis [*Soft*] [*Latin*] (AD) ... mol
Mollis [*Soft*] [*Pharmacy*] ... MOLL
Molln [*Austria*] [*Seismograph station code, US Geological Survey*] (SEIS) ... MOA
Molloy College, Rockville Centre, NY [*Library symbol Library of Congress*] (LCLS) ... NRockM
Molloy College, Rockville Centre, NY [*OCLC symbol*] (OCLC) ... VYA
Molloy's De Jure Maritimo [*A publication*] (DLA) ... Jur Mar
Molloy's De Jure Maritimo [*A publication*] (DLA) ... Mol
Molloy's De Jure Maritimo [*A publication*] (DLA) ... Moll
Molloy's De Jure Maritimo et Navali [*A publication*] (DLA) ... Mol De Jure Mar
Molloy's De Jure Maritimo et Navali [*A publication*] (DLA) ... Mol JM
Molloy's Irish Chancery Reports [*1827-31*] [*A publication*] (DLA) ... Mol
Molloy's Irish Chancery Reports [*1827-31*] [*A publication*] (DLA) ... Moll
Mollusca (AD) ... Mollus
Molluscum Contagiosum Virus ... MCV
Molodezhnaya [*Former USSR Geomagnetic observatory code*] ... MOL
Molokai/Kaunakakai [*Hawaii*] [*Airport symbol*] (OAG) ... MKK
Molokai, Molokai Island [*Hawaii*] [*ICAO location identifier*] (ICLI) ... PHMK
Moloney Cell Surface Antigen [*Medicine*] (DMAA) ... MCSA
Moloney Leukemia Virus [*Also, MLV(M)*] ... MLV
Moloney Mouse Sarcoma Virus ... MoMSV
Moloney Murine Leukaemia Virus [*Medicine*] (BABM) ... MMLV
Moloney Murine Leukemia Virus ... M-MLV
Moloney Murine Leukemia Virus [*of micel*] [*Veterinary medicine*] (DAVI) ... MMLV
Moloney Murine Leukemia Virus [*Medicine*] (DMAA) ... MMuLV
Moloney Murine Leukemia Virus [*Also, MLV*] ... MoMuLV
Moloney Murine Luekemia Virus [*Used for gene transfer protocols*] (DOG) ... MoMLV
Moloney Sarcoma Virus (AAMN) ... MSV
Molonglo Observatory Synthesis Telescope ... MOST
Molson Breweries of Canada Ltd., Montreal, Quebec [*Library symbol Obsolete National Library of Canada*] (NLC) ... QMMBC
Molson Companies Ltd. [*Toronto Stock Exchange symbol Vancouver Stock Exchange symbol*] ... MOL
Molt Inhibitory Hormone ... MIH
Molten ... MOLT
Molten (AD) ... molt
Molten Carbonate Fuel Cell [*Energy source*] ... MCFC
Molten Fuel Coolant Interaction [*Nuclear energy*] (NRCH) ... MFCI
Molten High-Temperature Alloy ... MHTA
Molten Metal Technology [*NASDAQ symbol*] (TTSB) ... MLTN
Molten Metal Technology [*Waste management*] (ECON) ... MMT
Molten Metal Technology, Inc. [*NASDAQ symbol*] (SAG) ... MLTN
Molten Metal Technology, Inc. [*Associated Press*] (SAG) ... MoltenM
Molten Plutonium Burn-Up Experiment [*Nuclear energy*] (IEEE) ... MPBE
Molten Salt Destruction [*Incineration process*] ... MSD
Molten Salt Reactor Experiment ... MSRE
Molten Salts Data Center [*Rensselaer Polytechnic Institute*] [*National Institute of Standards and Technology Research center*] (IID) ... MSDC
Molten Steel Coolant Interaction (NRCH) ... MSCI
Molten-Caustic-Leaching [*Coal technology*] ... MCL
Molten-Salt Breeder Experiment [*Nuclear energy*] ... MSBE
Molten-Salt Breeder Reactor ... MSBR
Molten-Salt Epithermal Reactor ... MOSEL
Molten-Salt Reactor ... MSR
Molten-Salt Reactor Information System ... MSRIS
Molting Hormone [*Endocrinology, entomology*] ... MH
Moly Mite Resources [*Vancouver Stock Exchange symbol*] ... MLY
Molybdate-Reactive Phosphorus [*Analytical chemistry*] ... MRP
Molybdenum [*Chemical element*] (ROG) ... MB
Molybdenum [*Chemical element*] ... Mo
Molybdenum (AD) ... moly
Molybdenum Corp. of America, Louviers, CO [*Library symbol Library of Congress*] (LCLS) ... CoLvM
Molybdenum Disulfide [*Inorganic chemistry*] ... MDS
Molybdeophosphoric Acid [*Inorganic chemistry*] ... MPA
Molybdopterin Guanine Dinucleotide [*Biochemistry*] ... MGD
Molydopterin [*Biochemistry*] ... MPT
Molyneaux's Reports. English Courts, Tempore Car. I [*A publication*] (DLA) ... Moly
Molypermalloy Powder [*Metallurgy*] (EECA) ... MPP
Moma [*Zaire*] [*ICAO location identifier*] (ICLI) ... FZUH
Mombasa [*Kenya*] [*Airport symbol*] (OAG) ... MBA
Mombasa [*Island near Kenya*] (ROG) ... MOMB
Mombasa/Moi International [*Kenya*] [*ICAO location identifier*] (ICLI) ... HKMO
Mombo [*Tanzania*] [*ICAO location identifier*] (ICLI) ... HTMO
Mombo [*Tanzania*] [*Airport symbol*] (AD) ... MBN
Momeik [*Myanmar*] [*Airport symbol*] (OAG) ... MOE
Momeik [*Myanmar*] [*ICAO location identifier*] (ICLI) ... VBMO
Moment ... M
Moment (DSUE) ... MO
Moment (AD) ... mo
Moment ... MOM
Moment Connections [*Computer Services Consultants Ltd.*] [*Software package*] (NCC) ... MCON
Moment Estimator (PDAA) ... ME
Moment Gyro System ... MGS
Moment of Area (BARN) ... Q
Moment of Force [*Symbol*] [*IUPAC*] ... M
Moment of Inertia [*Symbol*] [*IUPAC*] ... I
Moment of Inertia ... M of I
Moment of Inertia ... MI
Moment of Inertia ... MOI
Moment of Resistance ... MR
Moment to Change Trim (DS) ... MCT
Momentary (MSA) ... MOM
Momentary (FAAC) ... MTRY
Momentary Contact [*Electronics*] ... MC
Moment-Generating Function [*Mathematics*] ... MGF
Moment-Generating Function Estimator ... MGFE
Moments with Meredith - Meredith Baxter-Birney Fan Club [*Defunct*] (EA) ... MWM
Momentum [*Measurement*] ... H
Momentum ... MOM
Momentum [*Symbol*] [*IUPAC*] ... p
Momentum/Energy Integral Technique (MCD) ... MEIT
Momentum Management Program [*NASA*] (KSC) ... MMP
Momentum Management System [*NASA*] (SSD) ... MMS
Momentum-Wheel Assembly ... MWA
Momma (AD) ... Mom
Momote [*Admiralty Islands*] [*Seismograph station code, US Geological Survey*] (SEIS) ... MOM
Mompos [*Colombia*] [*Airport symbol*] (OAG) ... MMP
Moms in Touch International (EA) ... MITI
Mon National Liberation Army [*Myanmar*] [*Political party*] (EY) ... MNLA
Mon Repos Est au Ciel [*My Rest Is in Heaven*] [*Motto of Ludwig Philipp, Count of the Palatinate of Simmern (1602-1654)*] [*French*] ... MREAC
Mona [*British ICAO location identifier*] (ICLI) ... EGOQ
Mona Lisas and Mad Hatters [*Defunct*] (EA) ... MLAMH
Monacair-Agusta [*Monaco*] [*ICAO designator*] (FAAC) ... MCR
Monaco [*MARC geographic area code Library of Congress*] (LCCP) ... e-mc--
Monaco [*Monaco*] [*ICAO location identifier*] (ICLI) ... LNMC
Monaco [*MARC country of publication code Library of Congress*] (LCCP) ... mc
Monaco [*ANSI two-letter standard code*] (CNC) ... MC
Monaco [*ANSI three-letter standard code*] (CNC) ... MCO
Monaco [*IYRU nationality code*] (IYR) ... MO
Monaco [*Monaco*] [*Seismograph station code, US Geological Survey*] (SEIS) ... MON
Monaco (AD) ... Mon
Monaco (VRA) ... Mona
Monaco Coach [*NASDAQ symbol*] (TTSB) ... MCCO
Monaco Coach Corp. [*NASDAQ symbol*] (SAG) ... MCCO
Monaco Coach Corp. [*Associated Press*] (SAG) ... MonacoC
Monaco Finance [*Associated Press*] (SAG) ... Monac
Monaco Finance [*Associated Press*] (SAG) ... MonacoF
Monaco Finance [*NASDAQ symbol*] (SAG) ... MONF
Monaco Finance'A' [*NASDAQ symbol*] (TTSB) ... MONFA
Monaco Group, Inc. [*Toronto Stock Exchange symbol*] ... MAS
Monaco Oceanographic Institute ... MOI
Monagas Pipeline Crude [*Petrochemical engineering*] ... MPC
Monaghan [*County in Republic of Ireland*] (ROG) ... MON
Monaghan (AD) ... Monag
Monaghan [*County in Republic of Ireland*] (ROG) ... MONAGH
Monaghan [*County in Republic of Ireland*] ... MONAGN
Monaghan's Reports [*147-165 Pennsylvania*] [*A publication*] (DLA) ... Mona
Monaghan's Reports [*147-165 Pennsylvania*] [*A publication*] (DLA) ... Monag
Monaghan's Reports [*147-165 Pennsylvania*] [*A publication*] (DLA) ... Monaghan
Monaghan's Reports [*147-165 Pennsylvania*] [*A publication*] (DLA) ... Monaghan (PA)
Monaghan's Unreported Cases (Pennsylvania Superior Court) [*A publication*] (DLA) ... Mon
Monahan's Method of the Law [*1878*] [*A publication*] (DLA) ... Mon Meth
Monahans, TX [*FM radio station call letters*] ... KCDQ
Monahans, TX [*FM radio station call letters*] ... KGEE
Monahans, TX [*AM radio station call letters*] ... KLBO
Monair SA [*Switzerland ICAO designator*] (FAAC) ... MNR

Monaldus [*Flourished, 13th century*] [*Authority cited in pre-1607 legal work*] (DSA) .... Mo
Monalta Resources, Inc. [*Vancouver Stock Exchange symbol*] .... MOT
Monarch [*Record label*] [*British*] .... Mon
Monarch Airlines [*ICAO designator*] (FAAC) .... MNH
Monarch Airlines Ltd. [*British ICAO designator*] (FAAC) .... MON
Monarch Avalon [*NASDAQ symbol*] (TTSB) .... MAHI
Monarch Avalon, Inc. [*NASDAQ symbol*] (NQ) .... MAHI
Monarch Avalon, Inc. [*Associated Press*] (SAG) .... MonAvl
Monarch Casino & Resort [*NASDAQ symbol*] (SAG) .... MCRI
Monarch Casino & Resort [*Associated Press*] (SAG) .... MonCasn
Monarch Investments Ltd. [*Toronto Stock Exchange symbol*] .... MON
Monarch Mach Tool [*NYSE symbol*] (TTSB) .... MMO
Monarch Machine Tool Co. [*NYSE symbol*] (SPSG) .... MMO
Monarch Machine Tool Co. [*Associated Press*] (SAG) .... Monrch
Monarch Marking Systems, Pitney Bowes, Chemical Research and Development Library, Miamisburg, OH [*Library symbol Library of Congress*] (LCLS) .... OMiabMM
Monarch Peak [*California*] [*Seismograph station code, US Geological Survey*] (SEIS) .... MOP
Monarchist Alliance (EA) .... MA
Monarchist League [*Defunct*] (EA) .... ML
Monarchist League of Canada (EAIO) .... MLC
Monaro Conservation Society. Bulletin [*A publication*] .... Bull Monaro Conserv Soc
Monarticular Arthritis [*Medicine*] .... MA
Monarticular Arthritis [*Orthopedics*] (DAVI) .... MAA
Monash Asia Institute [*Monash University*] [*Australia*] .... MAI
Monash Timber Engineering Center [*Australia*] .... MTEC
Monash University Accident Research Center [*Australia*] .... MUARC
Monash University, Clayton, V, Australia [*Library symbol Library of Congress*] (LCLS) .... AuCIM
Monash University. Law Review [*A publication*] .... Mon ULR
Monash University. Law Review [*A publication*] .... Monash Univ Law Rev
Monash University Malaysian Students' Union [*Australia*] .... MUMSU
Monastere de Peres Redemptoristes, Sherbrooke, PQ, Canada [*Library symbol Library of Congress*] (LCLS) .... CaQSherM
Monastere des Peres Redemptoristes, Sherbrooke, Quebec [*Library symbol Obsolete National Library of Canada*] (NLC) .... QSHERM
Monastery .... M
Monastery .... MON
Monastery .... MONS
Monastery .... MONSTRY
Monastery (AD) .... Mony
Monastery of the Holy Ghost, Conyers, GA [*Library symbol Library of Congress*] (LCLS) .... GConT
Monastic (AD) .... Monas
Monasticon Anglicanum [*A publication*] (DLA) .... Mon Angl
Monastir [*Tunisia*] [*Airport symbol*] (OAG) .... MIR
Monastir [*Tunisia*] [*Airport symbol*] (AD) .... MIR
Monastir/Habib Bourgiba [*Tunisia*] [*ICAO location identifier*] (ICLI) .... DTMB
Monaural (KSC) .... MONO
Monaural Bifrequency Loudness Balance [*Audiology*] (MAE) .... MBFLB
Monaural Detection with Contralateral Cue (PDAA) .... MDCC
Monaural Loudness Balance [*Audiology*] .... MLB
Monbetsu [*Japan*] [*Airport symbol*] (OAG) .... MBE
Monbetsu [*Japan ICAO location identifier*] (ICLI) .... RJEB
Moncalcium Phosphate Monohydrate [*Inorganic chemistry*] .... MCPM
Moncalieri [*Italy*] [*Seismograph station code, US Geological Survey Closed*] (SEIS) .... MNC
Moncks Corner [*South Carolina*] [*Seismograph station code, US Geological Survey Closed*] (SEIS) .... MKC
Moncks Corner, SC [*Location identifier FAA*] (FAAL) .... MKS
Moncks Corner, SC [*AM radio station call letters*] .... WMCJ
Moncks Corner, SC [*FM radio station call letters*] (RBYB) .... WNST
Monclova [*Mexico*] [*Airport symbol*] (AD) .... LOV
Monclova [*Mexico ICAO location identifier*] (ICLI) .... MMMV
Monclova, MX [*Location identifier FAA*] (FAAL) .... MOV
Moncrieff's Liability of Innkeepers [*1874*] [*A publication*] (DLA) .... Monc Inn
Moncton [*Canada*] [*Airport symbol*] (OAG) .... YQM
Moncton Civic Museum, Moncton, NB, Canada [*Library symbol Library of Congress*] (LCLS) .... CaNBMoM
Moncton Flying Club [*Canada ICAO designator*] (FAAC) .... MFC
Moncton Museum, New Brunswick [*Library symbol National Library of Canada*] (NLC) .... NBMOM
Moncton, NB [*AM radio station call letters*] .... CBA
Moncton, NB [*FM radio station call letters*] .... CBAF-FM
Moncton, NB [*FM radio station call letters*] .... CBA-FM
Moncton, NB [*Television station call letters*] .... CBAFT
Moncton, NB [*FM radio station call letters*] .... CBAL
Moncton, NB [*Television station call letters*] CBAT-2
Moncton, NB [*FM radio station call letters*] .... CFQM
Moncton, NB [*FM radio station call letters*] .... CJMO
Moncton, NB [*AM radio station call letters*] .... CKCW
Moncton, NB [*Television station call letters*] .... CKCW-TV
Moncton, NB [*FM radio station call letters*] .... CKUM
Moncton, NB [*ICAO location identifier*] (ICLI) .... CYQM
Moncton, NB [*ICAO location identifier*] (ICLI) .... CZQM
Mond Excavation at Thebes [*London*] [*A publication*] (BJA) .... MET
Mondavi [*Robert*] [*NASDAQ symbol*] (SAG) .... MOND
Mondavi [*Robert*] [*Associated Press*] (SAG) .... Mondavi
Mondavi Resources Ltd. [*Vancouver Stock Exchange symbol*] .... MVR
Monday .... M
Monday (CDAI) .... Mo
Monday (AFM) .... MON
Monday (AD) .... Mon
Monday (ODBW) .... Mon
Monday (ROG) .... MOND
Monday through Friday (CDAI) .... M-F
Monday through Saturday (AD) .... M-S
Monday, Wednesday, Friday (BARN) .... MWF
Mondcivitan Republic [*Defunct*] (EAIO) .... MR
Mondombe [*Zaire*] [*ICAO location identifier*] (ICLI) .... FZGG
Mondpaca Esperantista Movado [*Esperantist Movement for World Peace - EMWP*] [*Tours, France*] (EAIO) .... MEM
Mondy [*Former USSR Seismograph station code, US Geological Survey*] (SEIS) .... MOY
Moneda Corriente [*Current Money*] [*Spanish*] .... MC
Moneda Legal [*Legal Tender*] [*Spanish Business term*] .... ML
Moneda Nacional [*National Money*] [*Spanish*] .... M/N
Monee, IL [*FM radio station call letters*] .... WGNR
Monegasque (AD) .... Mon
Monenco Consultants Ltd., Calgary, AB, Canada [*Library symbol*] [*Library of Congress*] (LCLS) .... CaACMO
Monenco Consultants Ltd., Calgary, Alberta [*Library symbol National Library of Canada*] (NLC) .... ACME
Monenco Consultants Ltd., Montreal, Quebec [*Library symbol National Library of Canada*] (NLC) .... QMEC
Monenco Consultants Ltd., St. Catharines, Ontario [*Library symbol National Library of Canada*] (NLC) .... OSTCMEC
Monenco Ltd. [*Toronto Stock Exchange symbol*] .... MNN
Monessen Public Library, Monessen, PA [*OCLC symbol*] (OCLC) .... MPL
Monessen Public Library, Monessen, PA [*Library symbol Library of Congress*] (LCLS) .... PMo
Moneta Porcupine Mines, Inc. [*Toronto Stock Exchange symbol*] .... ME
Moneta, VA [*AM radio station call letters*] .... WLQE
Monetary (AFM) .... MON
Monetary (AD) .... mon
Monetary .... MONET
Monetary Allowance .... M/A
Monetary Allowance in Lieu of Quarters .... MAQ
Monetary Allowance in Lieu of Subsistence .... MAS
Monetary Allowance in Lieu of Transportation [*DoD*] .... MALT
Monetary and Economic Council (NADA) .... MEC
Monetary and Payments System [*Committee*] [*American Bankers Association*] .... MAPS
Monetary Committee .... MC
Monetary Compensation Amount [*European Community*] .... MCA
Monetary Contact .... MC
Monetary Incentive .... MI
Monetary Policy .... MP
Monetary Policy Committee [*France*] (ECON) .... MPC
Monetary Ration Credit Allowance System [*Military*] (AFM) .... MRCAS
Monetary Ration Management System [*Military*] (AFM) .... MRMS
Monetary Times, Toronto, ON, Canada [*Library symbol Library of Congress*] (LCLS) .... CaOTMT
Monetary Times, Toronto, Ontario [*Library symbol National Library of Canada*] (NLC) .... OTMT
Monetary Unit (ADA) .... MU
Monetary Unit Sampling (ADA) .... MUS
Monetary Working Capital Adjustment [*British*] .... MWCA
Monethylcholine [*Biochemistry*] .... MEC
Monett, MO [*FM radio station call letters*] .... KKBL
Monett, MO [*AM radio station call letters*] .... KRMO
Monett, MO [*Location identifier FAA*] (FAAL) .... UMN
Monetta Fire Tower [*South Carolina*] [*Seismograph station code, US Geological Survey*] (SEIS) .... MTT
Money .... M
Money .... MNY
Money .... MOY
Money (AD) .... moy
Money and Advice .... M & A
Money and Real Estate [*Newspaper section*] (ADA) .... M & RE
Money Down .... MD
Money, Ideology, Compromise, Ego [*CIA acronym for possible explanations for spy defections*] .... MICE
Money List .... ML
Money Management Analytical Research Group .... MMAR
Money Management Council [*British*] .... MMC
Money Management Institute [*Commercial firm*] (EA) .... MMI
Money Management System .... MMS
Money Manager Profile Diskettes [*Investment Management Institute*] [*Information service or system*] (IID) .... MMPD
Money Market [*Investment term*] .... MM
Money Market (NITA) .... MNMKT
Money Market Certificate [*Investment term*] .... MMC
Money Market Deposit Account [*Investment term*] .... MMDA
Money Market Directories, Inc. [*Also, an information service or system*] (IID) .... MMD
Money Market Fund [*Investment term*] .... MMF
Money Market Monitor [*Financial Products Group*] [*Information service or system*] (IID) .... MMM
Money Market Mutual Fund [*Investment term*] .... MMMF
Money Market Mutual Fund Shares [*Investment term*] .... MMMFS
Money Market Preferred Stock [*Investment term*] .... MMP
Money Market Rates [*I. P. Sharp Associates*] [*Canada Information service or system*] (CRD) .... MRATE
Money Market Services, Inc. [*Belmont, CA*] [*Database producer*] .... MMS
Money, Opportunity, Responsibility, and Equality [*Of organization "MORE for Women"*] .... MORE
Money Order .... MO

Money Stock [British] (DCTA) .... MI
Money Store [NASDAQ symbol] (TTSB) .... MONE
[The] Money Store, Inc. [NASDAQ symbol] (SAG) .... MONE
[The] Money Store, Inc. [Associated Press] (SAG) .... MoneySt
Money Supply .... MS
Money Supply of a Country, Consisting of Currency and Demand Deposits
  [Economics] .... M_1
Money Supply of a Country, Including M_1 and Commercial Time Deposits
  [Economics] .... M_2
Money Supply of a Country, Including M_2, Savings and Loan Association
  Deposits, and Certificates of Deposit [Economics] .... M_3
Money Transfer System (IAA) .... MTS
Money Value Only (AFIT) .... MVO
Money Velocity [Economics] .... MV
Money Wages [Economics] .... MW
Moneygram Payment Systems [NYSE symbol] (SAG) .... MNE
Moneygram Payment Systems [Associated Press] (SAG) .... Moneygr
Money-Order Business .... MOB
Money-Order Department .... MOD
Money-Order Office .... MOO
Money-Purchase Pension Plan [Human resources] (WYGK) .... MPPP
Moneywise Resources [Vancouver Stock Exchange symbol] .... MNW
Monfortinho [Portugal ICAO location identifier] (ICLI) .... LPMF
Mong Pyin [Myanmar] [ICAO location identifier] (ICLI) .... VBMP
Mong Tong [Myanmar] [ICAO location identifier] (ICLI) .... VBMT
Mong-Hpayak [Myanmar] [ICAO location identifier] (ICLI) .... VBMH
Monghsat [Myanmar] [Airport symbol] (OAG) .... MOG
Mong-Hsat [Myanmar] [ICAO location identifier] (ICLI) .... VBMS
Mongo [Chad] [ICAO location identifier] (ICLI) .... FTTM
Mongo [Chad] [Airport symbol] (AD) .... MVO
Mongo Wa Kenda [Zaire] [ICAO location identifier] (ICLI) .... FZDN
Mongol [MARC language code Library of Congress] (LCCP) .... mon
Mongol (AD) .... Mon
Mongol [One affected with Down's syndrome] [Medicine] (DAVI) .... Mon
Mongol (AD) .... Mong
Mongol People's Party [Mongolia] [Political party] (FEA) .... MPP
Mongolia [MARC geographic area code Library of Congress] (LCCP) .... a-mp--
Mongolia [ANSI two-letter standard code] (CNC) .... MN
Mongolia [ANSI three-letter standard code] (CNC) .... MNG
Mongolia (VRA) .... Mongo
Mongolia [MARC country of publication code Library of Congress] (LCCP) .... mp
Mongolian (AABC) .... MON
Mongolian [Language, etc.] .... MONG
Mongolian Airlines [ICAO designator] (FAAC) .... MGL
Mongolian Peoples Republic .... MPR
Mongolian People's Revolutionary Party [Mongol Ardyn Khuv'sgalt Nam]
  [Political party] (PPW) .... MPRP
Mongolian Spot [Medicine] .... MS
Mongolisch [Mongolian] [German] (AD) .... mong
Mongoloid Development Council [Later, NADS] (EA) .... MDC
Mongolyn Tsahilgaan Medeeniy Agentlag [Press agency]
  [Mongolia] .... MONTSAME
Mongrel (ABBR) .... MGL
Mongrel (DSUE) .... MONG
Mongu [Zambia] [ICAO location identifier] (ICLI) .... FLMG
Mongu [Zambia] [Airport symbol] (OAG) .... MNR
Mongyai [Myanmar] [ICAO location identifier] (ICLI) .... VBMI
Monica Resources [Vancouver Stock Exchange symbol] .... MNC
Monida, MT [Location identifier FAA] (FAAL) .... MQM
Monieka [Zaire] [ICAO location identifier] (ICLI) .... FZEB
Monier-Williams Method (RDA) .... MW
Moniker (AD) .... monik
Moning [Tea trade] (ROG) .... MONG
Moniteur Belge [A publication] (ILCA) .... Mon
Monitor [Ship] [Navy] (MCD) .... BM
Monitor (MDG) .... M
Monitor .... M
Monitor .... MNT
Monitor (MDG) .... MNTR
Monitor (AD) .... mntr
Monitor (IDOE) .... mntr
Monitor (WDMC) .... mon
Monitor (AD) .... Mon
Monitor [Navy ship symbol] .... MON
Monitor (DEN) .... MON
Monitor .... MON
Monitor [Computer science] (BUR) .... MTR
Monitor, Access, and Control Interface (NASA) .... MACI
Monitor and Alarm Subsystem Group (MCD) .... MASG
Monitor and Alarm System (MCD) .... MAS
Monitor and Assembly System [or Subsystem] [Computer science]
  (BUR) .... MASS
Monitor and Control [Computer science] (IAA) .... MAC
Monitor and Control [Computer science] (BUR) .... MC
Monitor and Control Display System (MCD) .... MACDS
Monitor and Control Panel [Computer science] (NASA) .... M & C
Monitor and Control Software [FAA] (TAG) .... MCS
Monitor and Control Subsystem .... MCS
Monitor and Control Subsystem [Deep Space Instrumentation Facility,
  NASA] .... MCSS
Monitor and Control System [Deep Space Instrumentation Facility, NASA] .... MCS
Monitor and Control Unit [Aerospace] (AAG) .... M & CU
Monitor and Control Unit [Aerospace] (IAA) .... MACU
Monitor and Operations Control Software Subsystem [Space Flight
  Operations Facility, NASA] .... MOCSW

Monitor and Operations Control System [Space Flight Operations Facility,
  NASA] .... M & OC
Monitor and Replenisher System .... MARS
Monitor and Results Computer (IAA) .... MARC
Monitor and Switching Assembly .... MSA
Monitor and Test Control Area [NASA] (NASA) .... MTCA
Monitor Assembly [Ground Communications Facility, NASA] .... MONA
Monitor, Bridgetown, Nova Scotia [Library symbol National Library of
  Canada] (NLC) .... NSBM
Monitor, Bridgetown, NS, Canada [Library symbol] [Library of Congress]
  (LCLS) .... CaNSBrM
Monitor Call [Computer science] (IBMDP) .... MC
Monitor/Contractor [MARC relator code] [Library of Congress] (LCCP) .... mon
Monitor Control Console (CAAL) .... MCC
Monitor Criteria Data [Space Flight Operations Facility, NASA] .... MCD
Monitor Criteria Data Set Generation Processor Assembly [Space Flight
  Operations Facility, NASA] .... MCDG
Monitor Data Equipment .... MODE
Monitor Displays [Computer science] (BUR) .... MD
Monitor Distribution System [Television] .... MDS
Monitor Event Simulation System (IEEE) .... MESS
Monitor Execution Dump [Computer science] .... MED
Monitor Inspection (AFM) .... MI
Monitor International (ASF) .... MI
Monitor of Ultraviolet Solar Energy .... MUSE
Monitor Out of Service [Aviation communications] .... MONOS
Monitor Out of Service (AD) .... monos
Monitor Output .... MO
Monitor Output Signal Strength .... MOSS
Monitor Panel .... MP
Monitor Printer (CET) .... MP
Monitor Printing Unit [Computer science] .... MPU
Monitor Printing Unit (AD) .... mpu
Monitor Proportional Counter (MCD) .... MPC
Monitor Recorder .... MR
Monitor Research and Recovery Foundation .... MRRF
Monitor Resumed Normal Operation [Aviation communications] .... MONOK
Monitor Station .... MS
Monitor Station Reports .... MOREPS
Monitor Station Reports (AD) .... moreps
Monitor Table Generator Program (MCD) .... MTGP
Monitor Table Listing Program (NASA) .... MTLP
Monitor the Earth Rotation and Intercompare Techniques [by means of
  radio telescope measurements] .... MERIT
Monitor, Trenton, NJ [Library symbol Library of Congress] (LCLS) .... NjTM
Monitor Unit [Telecommunications] (TEL) .... M/U
Monitored and Modulated Periodontal Therapeutics [Dentistry] .... MMPT
Monitored Anesthesia Care [Medicine] (DAVI) .... MAC
Monitored Command Code [Marine Corps] .... MCC
Monitored International Frequency Register (NITA) .... MIFR
Monitored Retrievable Storage [of nuclear waste] .... MRS
Monitored Sine Vibration [Test] (MCD) .... MSV
Monitoring .... MNTRNG
Monitoring (AABC) .... MONTRG
Monitoring (AD) .... montrg
Monitoring Accounting Reporting and Statistical System [Aviation] .... MARS
Monitoring Agency .... MA
Monitoring and Assessment Research Centre [Marine science] (MSC) .... MARC
Monitoring and Control Assembly [NASA] (NASA) .... MCA
Monitoring and Control Assembly .... MCA
Monitoring and Control Panel (NASA) .... MCP
Monitoring and Control Station .... MACS
Monitoring and Data Analysis Division [Environmental Protection Agency]
  (GFGA) .... MDAD
Monitoring and Data Support Division [Environmental Protection Agency]
  (GFGA) .... MDSD
Monitoring and Evaluation (ECON) .... M & E
Monitoring and Evaluation of Drug Interactions in a Pharmacy-Oriented
  Reporting System [National Center for Health Services Research]
  (DHSM) .... MEDIPHOR
Monitoring and Risk Assessment Centre [British] .... MARC
Monitoring and Technical Support Laboratory [Environmental Protection
  Agency] (GFGA) .... MTSL
Monitoring and Test Subsystem .... MATS
Monitoring Attitudes of the Public [ACLI] .... MAP
Monitoring Direction (AD) .... mon/dir
Monitoring Energy Systems .... MES
Monitoring, Identification, and Correlation .... MIC
Monitoring Information (NITA) .... MI
Monitoring/Metering Panel [Telecommunications] (OA) .... MMP
Monitoring of Air Pollution by Satellites (KSC) .... MAPS
Monitoring of the Sun Earth Environment [International Council of Scientific
  Unions] (MCD) .... MONSEE
Monitoring of Trends and Determinants in Cardiovascular Disease .... MONICA
Monitoring Overseas Direct Employment (DNAB) .... MODE
Monitoring Transport of Ocean Currents [Project] [Marine science]
  (OSRA) .... MTOC
Monitor-Printer-Diskette Adapter .... MPDA
Monitor-Review, Stacyville, IA [Library symbol] [Library of Congress]
  (LCLS) .... IaStacM
Monjas Sur [Ecuador] [ICAO location identifier] (ICLI) .... SEMS
Monk .... MK
Monk Seal Morbillivirus .... MSMV
[The] Monkees, Boyce and Hart Photo Fan Club (EA) .... MBHPFC
Monkees Buttonmania Club [Defunct] (EA) .... MBC

Monkey [*Phonetic alphabet*] [*Royal Navy World War I Pre-World War II*] (DSUE) .... M
Monkey Bay [*Malawi*] [*ICAO location identifier*] (ICLI) .... FWMY
Monkey Bay [*Malawi*] [*Airport symbol*] (AD) .... ONB
Monkey Cells .... MC
Monkey Chorionic Gonadotrophin [*Endocrinology*] .... mCG
Monkey Complement [*Immunology*] .... MC
Monkey Immunoglobulin G [*Immunology*] .... MIgG
Monkey Intranuclear Inclusion Agent (MAE) .... MINIA
Monkey Kidney .... MK
Monkey Kidney [*Medicine*] (DMAA) .... MkK
Monkey Mountain [*Guyana*] [*Airport symbol*] (OAG) .... MYM
Monkey Mountain [*Guyana*] [*ICAO location identifier*] (ICLI) .... SYMM
Monkey Mountain Advisory Center [*Military*] (CINC) .... MOMAC
Monkey Placental Lactogen .... MPL
Monkey Red Blood Cells .... MRBC
Monkira [*Queensland*] [*Airport symbol*] (AD) .... ONR
Monky Aerotaxis SA [*Mexico ICAO designator*] (FAAC) .... MKY
Monmouth Airlines, Inc. [*ICAO designator*] (FAAC) .... VMA
Monmouth Antiquarian Society (EA) .... MAS
Monmouth Biomedical Information Consortium [*Library network*] .... MBIC
Monmouth Capital [*NASDAQ symbol*] (TTSB) .... MONM
Monmouth Capital Corp. [*Associated Press*] (SAG) .... MonCap
Monmouth Capital Corp. [*NASDAQ symbol*] (SAG) .... MONM
Monmouth College (GAGS) .... Monmouth C
Monmouth College, Monmouth, IL [*OCLC symbol*] (OCLC) ICL
Monmouth College, Monmouth, IL [*Library symbol Library of Congress*] (LCLS) .... IMonC
Monmouth College, West Long Beach, NJ [*Library symbol Library of Congress*] (LCLS) .... NjWIM
Monmouth County Historical Association, Freehold, NJ [*Library symbol Library of Congress*] (LCLS) .... NjFrHi
Monmouth County Library, Freehold, NJ [*Library symbol Library of Congress*] (LCLS) .... NjFrM
Monmouth, IL [*FM radio station call letters*] .... WMOI
Monmouth, IL [*AM radio station call letters*] .... WRAM
Monmouth Library, Monmouth, OR [*Library symbol Library of Congress*] (LCLS) .... OrMon
Monmouth R.E. Inv CL'A' [*NASDAQ symbol*] (TTSB) .... MNRTA
Monmouth Real Estate Investment Corp. [*Associated Press*] (SAG) .... MonRE
Monmouth Real Estate Investment Trust [*NASDAQ symbol*] (NQ) .... MNRT
Monmouths Nominal [*Software engineering cost model*] .... MMNOM
Monmouthshire [*County in Wales*] .... MON
Monmouthshire (AD) .... Mon
Monmouthshire [*County in Wales*] .... MONMS
Monmouthshire [*County in Wales*] .... MONS
Mono County Free Library, Bridgeport, CA [*Library symbol Library of Congress*] (LCLS) .... CBri
Mono Gold Mines, Inc. [*Vancouver Stock Exchange symbol*] .... MGL
Mono Island [*Solomon Islands*] [*Airport symbol*] (OAG) .... MNY
Mono Power Pack (HGAA) .... MPP
Monoacetoxylscirpenol [*Organic toxin*] .... MAS
Monoacetylmorphine [*Organic chemistry*] .... MAM
Monoalythic Design Automation (IAA) .... MDA
Monoamin Oxidase Inhibitors [*An antidepressant*] .... MAO
Monoamine [*Chemistry*] .... MA
Monoamine Oxidase [*An enzyme*] .... MAO
Monoamine Oxidase A [*An enzyme*] .... MAOA
Monoamine Oxidase B [*An enzyme*] .... MAO-B
Monoamine Oxidase Inhibitor [*Biochemistry*] .... MAOI
Monoamine Transporter [*Biochemistry*] .... MAT
Monoaminoguanidine Nitrate [*Organic chemistry*] .... MAGN
Monoammonium Glutamate [*Organic chemistry*] .... MAG
Monoammonium Methanearsonate .... MAMA
Monoammonium Phosphate [*Inorganic chemistry*] .... MAP
Monobasic (AD) .... monbas
Monobutyl Sulfate [*Organic chemistry*] .... MBS
Monocalcium Phosphate [*Inorganic chemistry*] [*Food additive*] .... MCP
Monoceros [*Constellation*] .... Mon
Monoceros [*Constellation*] .... Mono
Monochlorinated Biphenyl [*Organic chemistry*] .... MCB
Monochloroacetic Acid [*Also, MCAA*] [*Organic chemistry*] .... MCA
Monochloroacetic Acid [*Also, MCA*] [*Organic chemistry*] .... MCAA
Monochlorobenzene [*Organic chemistry*] .... MCB
Monochlorodimethyl Ether [*Organic chemistry*] .... MCDE
Monochlorodioxin [*Organic chemistry*] .... MCDD
Monochlorotriazine [*Organic chemistry*] .... MCT
Monochromatic Vision (WDAA) .... MV
Monochrome (IAA) .... M
Monochrome (VRA) .... monch
Monochrome (DSUE) .... MONO
Monochrome Display Adapter [*Computer technology*] .... MDA
Monochrome Electronic Prepress Systems (DGA) .... MEPS
Monochrome Graphics Adapter [*Hercules*] [*Computer science*] (PCM) .... MGA
Monochrome Graphics Printer [*Computer science*] (CDE) .... MGP
Monochrome Lens Assembly (MCD) .... MLA
Monochrome Video Graphics Array [*Computer science*] (CDE) .... MVGA
Monoclinic [*Crystallography*] .... M
Monoclinic .... MONOCL
Monoclinic (AD) .... monocl
Monoclinic Enstatite [*Geology*] .... CLEN
Monoclonal [*Biochemistry*] .... M
Monoclonal Antibodies [*Microbiology*] (DAVI) .... MCA
Monoclonal Antibodies, Inc. .... Mon
Monoclonal Antibody [*Medicine*] (DMAA) .... MA

Monoclonal Antibody [*Immunochemistry*] .... MAb
Monoclonal Antibody [*Immunochemistry*] .... MCAB
Monoclonal Antibody [*Immunochemistry*] .... MoAB
Monoclonal Antibody Production Rate .... MPR
Monoclonal Antibody Purification System .... MAPS
Monoclonal Antibody Resistant [*Immunochemistry*] .... MAR
Monoclonal Antimalignant Antibody [*Immunochemistry*] .... MAMA
Monoclonal Gammopathies of Undetermined Significance [*Medicine*] (DMAA) .... MGUS
Monoclonal Gammopathy [*Immunochemistry*] (DMAA) .... MCG
Monoclonal Gammopathy Identified [*Immunology*] (DAVI) .... MNCL
Monoclonal-Nonspecific Suppressor Factor [*Immunology*] .... MNSF
Monocomponent Highly Purified Port Insulin [*Endocrinology*] [*Pharmacology*] (DAVI) .... MC
Monocoque (MSA) .... MONOC
Monocotyledon [*Biology*] (BARN) .... monocot
Monocoupe Club (EA) .... MC
Monocular Deprivation [*Optics*] .... MD
Monocular Heads-Up Display [*Aviation*] .... MHUD
Monocycle Position Modulation .... MPM
Monocyte [*Hematology*] .... M
Monocyte [*Hematology*] .... MON
Monocyte [*Hematology*] .... mono
Monocyte Chemotactic Protein [*Biochemistry*] .... MCP
Monocyte-Lymphocyte [*Ratio*] [*Clinical chemistry*] .... M/L
Monocytic Leukemia, Acute (MAE) .... MLA
Monocyto-Angiotropin [*Biochemistry*] .... MAT
Monodehydroascorbate [*Biochemistry*] .... MDA
Monodesmethylchlorpromazine [*Biochemistry*] .... MDCPZ
Monodetail Drawing (MSA) .... MODR
Monodibutyl Phosphate [*Organic chemistry*] (NUCP) .... MBP
Monodisperse Aerosol Generation Interface [*Physics*] .... MAGIC
Monodisperse Latex Reactor .... MLR
Monodisperse Latex Reactor System .... MLRS
Monodisperse Polymer Particle .... MPP
Monod-Wyman-Changeux [*Model*] [*Enzymology*] .... MWC
Monoecious Sex Form .... MSF
Monoethanolamine [*Organic chemistry*] .... MEA
Monoethylamine [*Organic chemistry*] .... MEA
Monoethylene Glycol [*Chemicals*] .... MEG
Monoethylglycine Xylidide [*Biochemistry*] .... MEGX
Monoethylhexyl Phthalate [*Organic chemistry*] .... MEHP
Monofluoroacetate [*Organic chemistry*] .... MFA
Monofluoromethylhistidine [*Antineoplastic drug*] .... MFMH
Monofluorophosphate [*Inorganic chemistry*] .... MFP
Monofuel Emergency Power Unit .... MEPU
Monogahela Pwr 4.4% Pfd [*AMEX symbol*] (TTSB) .... MPNPrA
Monoglyceride [*An enzyme*] (MAE) .... MG
Monoglyceride Hydrolase [*An enzyme*] (MAE) .... MGH
Monogram .... MNGRM
Monogram [*Numismatics*] .... MON
Monogram [*Record label*] .... Mono
Monogram (AD) .... monog
Monogram Oil & Gas, Inc. [*Vancouver Stock Exchange symbol*] .... MGV
Monograph .... M
Monograph (BJA) .... mon
Monograph .... MONOG
Monograph (AD) .... monog
Monographs of the Peshitta Institute [*A publication*] (BJA) .... MPI
Monohexadecylphosphoric Acid [*Organic chemistry*] .... MHDPA
Monohydrogen (AD) .... mon-H
Monoiodoacetic Acid [*Organic chemistry*] .... MIA
Monoiodotyrosine [*Biochemistry*] .... MIT
Monoisonitrosoacetone [*Biochemistry*] .... MINA
Monoisopropylamine [*Organic chemistry*] .... MIPA
Monoisopropylbiphenyl (PDAA) .... MIPB
Monolayer [*Physical chemistry*] .... ML
Monolayer Formation Time [*Physical chemistry*] (OA) .... MFT
Monolithic .... ML
Monolithic Circuit Mask .... MCM
Monolithic Crystal Filter .... MCF
Monolithic Diode Matrix .... MDM
Monolithic Ferrite Memory Array .... MFMA
Monolithic Focal Plane Array (PDAA) .... MFPA
Monolithic Hot Electron Transistor (NITA) .... MHET
Monolithic Integrated Circuit .... MIC
Monolithic Integrated Circuit Mask .... MICM
Monolithic Memories, Inc. [*Computer science*] .... MMI
Monolithic Memory Unit .... MMU
Monolithic Memory Unit Diagnostic .... MMUD
Monolithic Microwave Integrated Circuit .... MMIC
Monolithic Mirror Telescope .... MMT
Monolithic Quad Device .... MQD
Monolithic Systems Technology .... MST
Monolithical Peltier Cooled LASER (MCD) .... MPCL
Monomer Reactivity Ratio (PDAA) .... MRR
Monomethoxytrityl [*As substituent on nucleoside*] [*Biochemistry*] .... mmt
Monomethyl Arsonic Acid [*Organic chemistry*] .... MMA
Monomethyl Ether of Hydroquinone [*Organic chemistry*] .... MEHQ
Monomethylamine [*Organic chemistry*] .... MMA
Monomethylarsonic Acid [*Organic chemistry*] .... MMAA
Monomethylhydrazine [*Organic chemistry*] .... MMH
Monomethylmetoxuron [*Organic chemistry*] .... MMM
Monomethylolrutin [*Organic chemistry*] .... MMR
Monomoy Surfboat [*Coast Guard*] (DNAB) .... MON

Monon [*Railroad*] (MHDW) ... MON
Monon News, Monon, IN [*Library symbol Library of Congress*] (LCLS) ... InMonN
Monon Railroad (AD) ... Monod
Monon Railroad (AD) ... MR
Monon Town and Township Library, Monon, IN [*Library symbol Library of Congress*] (LCLS) ... InMon
Monona Billboard, Monona, IA [*Library symbol Library of Congress*] (LCLS) ... IaMonoB
Monona County Courthouse, Onawa, IA [*Library symbol Library of Congress*] (LCLS) ... IaOnCoC
Monona Historical Society, Monona, IA [*Library symbol Library of Congress*] (LCLS) ... IaMonoHi
Monongah Power 4/50%cm C Pfd [*AMEX symbol*] (TTSB) ... MPNPrC
Monongahela (AD) ... Mon
[*The*] **Monongahela Connecting Railroad Co.** [*AAR code*] ... MCRR
Monongahela Power Co. [*Associated Press*] (SAG) ... MonP
Monongahela Power Co. [*Associated Press*] (SAG) ... MonP25
Monongahela Power Co. [*AMEX symbol*] (SPSG) ... MPN
Monongahela Power Co. [*NYSE symbol*] (SAG) ... WVQ
Monongahela Pwr 8% 'QUIDS' [*NYSE symbol*] (TTSB) ... WVQ
[*The*] **Monongahela Railway Co.** [*AAR code*] ... MGA
Monongahela River (AD) ... Mon River
Mononitroiodophenyl [*Organic chemistry*] (DAVI) ... NIP
Mononitrosopiperazine [*Biochemistry*] ... MNPZ
Mononitrotoluene [*Organic chemistry*] ... MNT
Mono-N-methylacetoacetamide [*Organic chemistry*] ... MMAA
Mono-normal-butylamine [*Organic chemistry*] ... MNBA
Mono-normal-propylamine [*Organic chemistry*] ... MNPA
Mononuclear [*Hematology*] ... MN
Mononuclear Blood Cell [*Hematology*] ... MBC
Mononuclear Cell [*Clinical chemistry*] [*Also, MNC*] ... MC
Mononuclear Cell Factor [*Cytology*] ... MCF
Mononuclear Leukocyte [*Hematology*] ... MNL
Mononuclear Phagocyte System [*Hematology*] ... MPS
Mononucleated Cell [*Clinical chemistry*] [*Also, MC*] ... MNC
Mononucleosis [*Medicine*] ... MONO
Mononucleosis [*Medicine*] (AD) ... mono
Monooxygenase [*An enzyme*] ... MO
Monophage [*Biology*] ... M
Monophasic Action Potential [*Electrophysiology*] (AAMN) ... MAP
Monophonic ... MONO
Monophonic (AD) ... mono
Monophosphate [*Chemistry*] (MAE) ... MP
Monophosphate Tungsten Bronze [*Metallurgy*] ... MPTB
Monophosphoglycerate Mutase [*Biochemistry*] (DAVI) ... MPGM
Monophosphoryl Lipid [*Biochemistry*] ... MPL
Monophosphoryl Lipid A [*Biochemistry*] ... MPLA
Monoplane ... M
Monopole, Astrophysics and Cosmic Ray Observatory [*Italy*] ... MACRO
Monopolies and Mergers Commission [*British*] ... MMC
Monopolies Commission [*British*] (DCTA) ... MC
Monopolization (AD) ... mnpzn
Monopolize (AD) ... mnpz
Monopolized (AD) ... mnpzd
Monopolizing (AD) ... mnpzg
Monopoly (AD) ... mono
Monopoly [*Legal shorthand*] (LWAP) ... MONOP
Monopoly (AD) ... monpl
Monopoly Information and Data Analysis System ... MIDAS
Monoprint (VRA) ... monpr
Monopropellant (AD) ... mono
Monopropellant Accessory Power Supply [*Aerospace*] (AAG) ... MAPS
Monopropellant Gas Generator (PDAA) ... MGG
Monopropylene Glycol [*Chemicals*] ... MPG
Monopros Ltd., Toronto, Ontario [*Library symbol National Library of Canada*] (BIB) ... OTMO
Monopulse Antenna Kit ... MAK
Monopulse Display Improvement (IAA) ... MDI
Monopulse Interference Filter ... MIF
Monopulse RADAR (MSA) ... MPR
Monopulse Resolution Improvement ... MRI
Monopulse Resolution Improvement (AD) ... mri
Monopulse Secondary Surveillance RADAR (DA) ... MSSR
Monopulse Tracking Antenna ... MTA
Monopulse Tracking Receiver ... MTR
Monorail (WDAA) ... MONO
Monorail (AD) ... mono
Monorail and Suspension Device [*British*] ... MSD
Monorail Manufacturers Association (EA) ... MMA
Monorail Society (EA) ... MS
Monorail System ... MRS
Monos Arana [*Bolivia*] [*ICAO location identifier*] (ICLI) ... SLMX
Monosegmented Continuous Flow Analysis [*Analytical chemistry*] ... MCFA
Monosialoganglioside [*Chemistry*] ... GM
Monosodium Glutamate [*Food additive*] [*Pharmacology*] ... MSG
Monosodium Methyl Arsonate [*Herbicide*] ... MSMA
Monosodium Orthophosphate [*Inorganic chemistry*] ... MSP
Monosodium Salt of Methylarsonic Acid [*Agriculture*] ... MSMA
Monosodium Urate [*Organic chemistry*] ... MSU
Monosodium Urate Monohydrate [*Organic chemistry*] ... MSUM
Monostable (MSA) ... MNSTB
Monostable Blocking Oscillator [*Electronics*] ... MBO
Monostable Multivibrator [*Electronics*] (OA) ... MM
Monostable Multivibrator ... MMV
Monostable Multivibrator (IDOE) ... mmv
Monostable Multivibrator (MSA) ... MNSTBMV
Monostable Multivibrator ... MSMV
Monostable Relay Driver ... MRD
Monostatic Infrared Intrusion Detector (WDAA) ... MIRAD
Monostatic Infrared Intrusion Detector (PDAA) ... MIRID
Mono-Stereo Compatible (PDAA) ... MSC
Monosyllable, Trochee, Spondee Test [*Of speech discrimination*] (DAVI) ... MTS
Monosymptomatic Hypochondriasis [*Medicine*] (DMAA) ... MH
Mono-Tertiarybutylhydroquinone [*Also, TBHQ*] [*Organic chemistry*] ... MTBHQ
Monotetrazolium [*Medicine*] (MAE) ... MTT
Monotone (DOAD) ... MONO
Monotone Likelihood Ratio [*Statistics*] ... MLR
Monotonous (AD) ... monot
Monotype (DGA) ... M
Monotype (ADA) ... MONO
Monotype (AD) ... mono
Monotype (AD) ... monot
Monotype (VRA) ... montp
Monotype Caster (DGA) ... MC
Monotype Users' Association (NADA) ... MUA
Monovalent Metal Azide [*Inorganic chemistry*] ... MMA
Monovalent Oral Polio Vaccine [*Immunology*] ... MOPV
Monovinylacetylene [*Organic chemistry*] ... MVA
Monowai [*New Zealand*] [*Seismograph station code, US Geological Survey*] (SEIS) ... MNW
Monozygotic [*Genetics*] ... MZ
Monozygotic Twins Reared Apart [*Genetics*] ... MZA
Monozygotic Twins Reared Together [*Genetics*] ... MZT
Monro Muffler Brake, Inc. [*NASDAQ symbol*] (SAG) ... MNRO
Monro Muffler Brake, Inc. [*Associated Press*] (SAG) ... MonroM
Monroc, Inc. [*Associated Press*] (SAG) ... Monroc
Monroc, Inc. [*NASDAQ symbol*] (SAG) ... MROC
Monroe [*Louisiana*] [*Airport symbol*] (OAG) ... MLU
Monroe Automatic Internal Diagnosis [*Computer science*] ... MAID
Monroe City, MO [*FM radio station call letters*] ... KDAM
Monroe Clinic, Monroe, WI [*Library symbol Library of Congress*] (LCLS) ... WMoM
Monroe Community College, L. V. Good Library, Rochester, NY [*OCLC symbol*] (OCLC) ... VQT
Monroe Community College, Rochester, NY [*Library symbol Library of Congress*] (LCLS) ... NRMC
Monroe Community Hospital, Medical-Nursing Library, Rochester, NY [*OCLC symbol*] (OCLC) ... VQU
Monroe County Department of Health, Library, Rochester, NY [*OCLC symbol*] (OCLC) ... VQV
Monroe County Historical Museum, Archives, Monroe, MI [*Library symbol*] [*Library of Congress*] (LCLS) ... MiMoHi
Monroe County Historical Society, Albia, IA [*Library symbol Library of Congress*] (LCLS) ... IaAlbMHi
Monroe County Library System [*Library network*] ... MCLS
Monroe County Library System, Monroe, MI [*Library symbol Library of Congress*] (LCLS) ... MiMo
Monroe County Library System, Rochester, NY [*Library symbol Library of Congress*] (LCLS) ... NRML
Monroe County News, Albia, IA [*Library symbol Library of Congress*] (LCLS) ... IaAlbN
Monroe County Public Library, Bloomington, IN [*OCLC symbol*] (OCLC) ... IMR
Monroe County Public Library, Bloomington, IN [*Library symbol Library of Congress*] (LCLS) ... InBlo
Monroe County Public Library, Key West, FL [*Library symbol Library of Congress*] (LCLS) ... FKw
Monroe, CT [*FM radio station call letters*] ... WMNR
Monroe Development Center, Library, Rochester, NY [*OCLC symbol*] (OCLC) ... VQW
Monroe Doctrine ... MD
Monroe, GA [*Television station call letters*] ... WHSG
Monroe, GA [*AM radio station call letters*] ... WKUN
[*The*] **Monroe Institute** (EA) ... TMI
Monroe Institute of Applied Sciences [*Later, TMI*] (EA) ... MIAS
Monroe, LA [*FM radio station call letters*] ... KEDM
Monroe, LA [*FM radio station call letters*] ... KJLO
Monroe, LA [*AM radio station call letters*] ... KLIC
Monroe, LA [*FM radio station call letters*] ... KLIP
Monroe, LA [*Television station call letters*] ... KLTM
Monroe, LA [*AM radio station call letters*] ... KMLB
Monroe, LA [*FM radio station call letters*] ... KMYY
Monroe, LA [*FM radio station call letters*] ... KNLU
Monroe, LA [*AM radio station call letters*] ... KNOE
Monroe, LA [*FM radio station call letters*] ... KNOE-FM
Monroe, LA [*Television station call letters*] ... KNOE-TV
Monroe, LA [*FM radio station call letters*] ... KYFL
Monroe, LA [*Location identifier FAA*] (FAAL) ... MLU
Monroe, LA [*Location identifier FAA*] (FAAL) ... MZR
Monroe Legal Reporter [*Pennsylvania*] [*A publication*] (DLA) ... Mon Leg R (PA)
Monroe Legal Reporter [*Pennsylvania*] [*A publication*] (DLA) ... Monroe
Monroe Legal Reporter [*Pennsylvania*] [*A publication*] (DLA) ... Monroe LR
Monroe Mendelsohn Research, Inc. [*Information service or system*] (IID) ... MMR
Monroe, MI [*FM radio station call letters*] ... WEJY
Monroe, MI [*AM radio station call letters*] ... WHND
Monroe, MI [*FM radio station call letters*] ... WTWR
Monroe Mirror, Monroe, IA [*Library symbol Library of Congress*] (LCLS) ... IaMonM
Monroe/Monroe Municipal [*Louisiana*] [*ICAO location identifier*] (ICLI) ... KMLU
Monroe Muffler Brake [*NASDAQ symbol*] (SPSG) ... MNRO
Monroe, NC [*Location identifier FAA*] (FAAL) ... EQY
Monroe, NC [*AM radio station call letters*] ... WDEX
Monroe, NC [*AM radio station call letters*] ... WIXE

Monroe, NC [*AM radio station call letters*] ... WMAP
Monroe, NY [*FM radio station call letters*] ... WLJP
Monroe Tidal Drainage [*Medicine*] (DMAA) ... MT
Monroe Tidal Drainage [*Urology*] (DAVI) ... MTD
Monroe, WI [*AM radio station call letters*] ... WEKZ
Monroe, WI [*FM radio station call letters*] ... WEKZ-FM
Monroeville, AL [*Location identifier FAA*] (FAAL) ... MVC
Monroeville, AL [*AM radio station call letters*] ... WMFC
Monroeville, AL [*FM radio station call letters*] ... WMFC-FM
Monroeville, AL [*AM radio station call letters*] ... WYNI
Monroeville, PA [*AM radio station call letters*] ... WXVX
Monroeville Public Library, Monroeville, PA [*Library symbol Library of Congress*] (LCLS) ... PMv
Monro's Acta Cancellariae [*1545-1625*] [*A publication*] (DLA) ... Monro AC
Monrovia [*Liberia*] [*Airport symbol*] (OAG) ... MLW
Monrovia City [*Liberia*] [*ICAO location identifier*] (ICLI) ... GLMC
Monrovia Public Library, Monrovia, CA [*Library symbol Library of Congress*] (LCLS) ... CMon
Monrovia/Roberts International [*Liberia*] [*ICAO location identifier*] (ICLI) ... GLRB
Monrovia [*Liberia*] **Roberts International Airport** [*Airport symbol*] (OAG) ... ROB
Monrovia/Spriggs Payne [*Liberia*] [*ICAO location identifier*] (ICLI) ... GLMR
Monsanto Canada Ltd., Montreal, PQ, Canada [*Library symbol Library of Congress*] (LCLS) ... CaQMMoC
Monsanto Canada Ltd., Montreal, Quebec [*Library symbol National Library of Canada*] (NLC) ... QMMOC
Monsanto Chemical Co. [*Research code symbol*] ... ACL
Monsanto Chemical Co. [*Research code symbol*] ... CRD
Monsanto Chemical Co., Norfolk, VA [*Library symbol Library of Congress*] (LCLS) ... ViNMoN
Monsanto Chemical Co., St. Louis, MO [*Library symbol Library of Congress*] (LCLS) ... MoSMon
Monsanto Co. [*Associated Press*] (SAG) ... Monsan
Monsanto Co. [*NYSE symbol*] (SPSG) ... MTC
Monsanto Co., Houston, TX [*Library symbol Library of Congress*] (LCLS) ... TxHMon
Monsanto Co., Texas City, TX [*Library symbol Library of Congress*] (LCLS) ... TxTMC
Monsanto Research Corp., Dayton Laboratory, Dayton, OH [*Library symbol Library of Congress*] (LCLS) ... ODaMR
Monsanto Research Corp., Mound Laboratory, Miamisburg, OH [*Library symbol Library of Congress*] (LCLS) ... OMiabM
Monsanto Triangle Park Development Center, Durham, NC [*Library symbol Library of Congress*] (LCLS) ... NcDurM
Monseigneur [*My Lord*] [*French*] (AD) ... Monsig
Monseigneur ... MSGR
Monsieur [*Mister*] [*French*] ... M
Monsieur [*Mister*] [*French*] ... Mon
Monsieur [*In France this form is considered contemptuous*] [*Preferred form is M*] ... MONS
Monsieur [*Mister*] [*French*] (AD) ... Mons
Monsignor ... MGR
Monsignor (ODBW) ... Mgr
Monsignor ... MNGR
Monsignor (WGA) ... Mon
Monsignor [*Lord, Sir*] [*French*] ... MONSIG
Monsignor ... MSGR
Monsoon ... M
Monsoon (AD) ... mon
Monsoon Current (AD) ... Mons Cur
Monsoon Experiment (AD) ... monex
Monsoon Experiment [*Also, MONSOONEX*] ... MONEX
Monsoon Experiment [*Also, MONEX*] ... MONSOONEX
Monsoon Pollen Index [*Paleoceanography*] ... MPI
Monsoonal Upwelling Index [*Paleoceanography*] ... MUI
Monstrosity (AD) ... monstro
Mont [*Monte, etc.*] [*Italy and Sicily only*] ... M
Mont Pelerin Society (EA) ... MPS
Montadale Sheep Breeders Association (EA) ... MSB
Montag [*Monday*] [*German*] (AD) ... Mon
Montage (VRA) ... montg
Montagu and Ayrton's Bankrupt Laws [*A publication*] (DLA) ... M & ABL
Montagu and Ayrton's Bankrupt Laws [*A publication*] (DLA) ... Mont & Ayr BL
Montagu and Ayrton's English Bankruptcy Reports [*1833-38*] [*A publication*] (DLA) ... M & A
Montagu and Ayrton's English Bankruptcy Reports [*1833-38*] [*A publication*] (DLA) ... M & Ayr
Montagu and Ayrton's English Bankruptcy Reports [*1833-38*] [*A publication*] (DLA) ... Mont & A
Montagu and Ayrton's English Bankruptcy Reports [*1833-38*] [*A publication*] (DLA) ... Mont & Ayr
Montagu and Ayrton's English Bankruptcy Reports [*1833-38*] [*A publication*] (DLA) ... Mont & Ayr Bankr
Montagu and Ayrton's English Bankruptcy Reports [*1833-38*] [*A publication*] (DLA) ... Mont & Ayr Bankr (Eng)
Montagu and Bligh's English Bankruptcy Reports [*1832-33*] [*A publication*] (DLA) ... M & B
Montagu and Bligh's English Bankruptcy Reports [*1832-33*] [*A publication*] (DLA) ... Mont & B
Montagu and Bligh's English Bankruptcy Reports [*1832-33*] [*A publication*] (DLA) ... Mont & B Bankr
Montagu and Bligh's English Bankruptcy Reports [*1832-33*] [*A publication*] (DLA) ... Mont & B Bankr (Eng)
Montagu and Bligh's English Bankruptcy Reports [*1832-33*] [*A publication*] (DLA) ... Mont & Bl
Montagu and Chitty's English Bankruptcy Reports [*1838-40*] [*A publication*] (DLA) ... M & C
Montagu and Chitty's English Bankruptcy Reports [*1838-40*] [*A publication*] (DLA) ... M & Chit Bankr
Montagu and Chitty's English Bankruptcy Reports [*1838-40*] [*A publication*] (DLA) ... M & Cht Bankr
Montagu and Chitty's English Bankruptcy Reports [*1838-40*] [*A publication*] (DLA) ... Mont & C
Montagu and Chitty's English Bankruptcy Reports [*1838-40*] [*A publication*] (DLA) ... Mont & C Bankr
Montagu and Chitty's English Bankruptcy Reports [*1838-40*] [*A publication*] (DLA) ... Mont & C Bankr (Eng)
Montagu and Chitty's English Bankruptcy Reports [*1838-40*] [*A publication*] (DLA) ... Mont & Ch
Montagu and Chitty's English Bankruptcy Reports [*1838-40*] [*A publication*] (DLA) ... Mont & Chitt
Montagu and MacArthur's English Bankruptcy Reports [*A publication*] (DLA) ... M & M
Montagu and MacArthur's English Bankruptcy Reports [*A publication*] (DLA) ... M & M'A
Montagu and MacArthur's English Bankruptcy Reports [*A publication*] (DLA) ... M & McA
Montagu and MacArthur's English Bankruptcy Reports [*A publication*] (DLA) ... Mont & M
Montagu and MacArthur's English Bankruptcy Reports [*A publication*] (DLA) ... Mont & MacA
Montagu, Deacon, and De Gex's English Bankruptcy Reports [*1840-44*] [*A publication*] (DLA) ... MD & D
Montagu, Deacon, and De Gex's English Bankruptcy Reports [*1840-44*] [*A publication*] (DLA) ... MD & DeG
Montagu, Deacon, and De Gex's English Bankruptcy Reports [*1840-44*] [*A publication*] (DLA) ... Mont D & DeG
Montagu Investments Management [*Commercial firm British*] ... MIM
Montagu on Composition [*1823*] [*A publication*] (DLA) ... Mont Comp
Montagu on Liens [*A publication*] (DLA) ... Mont Liens
Montagu. Set-Off [*2nd ed.*] [*1828*] [*A publication*] (DLA) ... Mont SO
Montague and McArthur's English Bankruptcy Reports [*A publication*] (DLA) ... M McA
Montague, CA [*Location identifier FAA*] (FAAL) ... MOG
Montague, CA [*Location identifier FAA*] (FAAL) ... SIY
Montague Island [*Alaska*] [*Seismograph station code, US Geological Survey*] (SEIS) ... MTG
Montagu's Bankrupt Law [*4th ed.*] [*1827*] [*A publication*] (DLA) ... Mont Bk L
Montagu's Digest of Pleadings in Equity [*A publication*] (DLA) ... Mont Dig
Montagu's Digest of Pleadings in Equity [*A publication*] (DLA) ... Mont Eq Pl
Montagu's Digest of the Law of Partnership [*A publication*] (DLA) ... Mont Part
Montagu's English Bankruptcy Reports [*A publication*] (DLA) ... Mont
Montagu's English Bankruptcy Reports [*A publication*] (DLA) ... Mont Bank Rep
Montagu's English Bankruptcy Reports [*A publication*] (DLA) ... Mont Bankr (Eng)
Montagu's English Bankruptcy Reports [*A publication*] (DLA) ... Mont BC
Montaigu-Saint-Georges [*France ICAO location identifier*] (ICLI) ... LFFW
Montalvo [*Ecuador*] [*ICAO location identifier*] (ICLI) ... SEMO
Montana (DLA) ... M
Montana ... MON
Montana (AFM) ... MONT
Montana (AD) ... Mont
Montana (ODBW) ... Mont
Montana [*Postal code*] ... MT
Montana [*MARC country of publication code Library of Congress*] (LCCP) ... mtu
Montana [*MARC geographic area code Library of Congress*] (LCCP) ... n-us-mt
Montana Administrative Register [*A publication*] (AAGC) ... MAR
Montana Administrative Register [*A publication*] (DLA) ... Mont Admin Reg
Montana Agri-Trade Exposition [*Jerry Hanson and Associates, Inc.*] (TSPED) ... MATE
Montana Bureau of Mines and Geology [*Montana College of Mineral Science and Technology*] [*Research center*] (RCD) ... MBMG
Montana Census and Economic Information Center, Helena, MT [*Library symbol*] [*Library of Congress*] (LCLS) ... MtHCE
Montana Code, Annotated [*A publication*] (DLA) ... MCA
Montana Code, Annotated [*A publication*] (DLA) ... Mont Code Ann
Montana College of Mineral Science and Technology (GAGS) ... Mont CMS&T
Montana College of Mineral Science and Technology, Butte, MT [*Library symbol Library of Congress*] (LCLS) ... MtBuM
Montana Council for Computers in Education (EDAC) ... MCCE
Montana Energy and Magneto-Hydrodynamics Research Institute [*Later, Montana Energy Research and Development Institute*] [*Research center*] ... MERDI
Montana Energy Research and Development Institute, Butte, MT [*Library symbol Library of Congress*] (LCLS) ... MtBuE
Montana Historical Society, Helena, MT [*Library symbol Library of Congress*] (LCLS) ... MtHi
Montana Information Network Exchange [*Library network*] ... MINE
Montana Lawyer [*A publication*] (DLA) ... Mont Law
Montana Myotis Leukoencephalitis [*Virus*] ... MMI
Montana Natural Heritage Program [*Helena, MT*] [*Information service or system*] (IID) ... MTNHP
Montana Office of Public Instruction, Resource Center, Helena, MT [*Library symbol*] [*Library of Congress*] (LCLS) ... MtHPI
Montana Outfitters and Guides Association (EA) ... MOGA
Montana Power [*NYSE symbol*] (TTSB) ... MTP
Montana Power Co. [*Associated Press*] (SAG) ... MonPw
Montana Power Co. [*NYSE symbol*] (SPSG) ... MTP
Montana Reports [*A publication*] (DLA) ... Mon
Montana Reports [*A publication*] (DLA) ... MT
Montana Revised Code, Annotated [*A publication*] (DLA) ... Mont Rev Code Ann

Montana School of Mines .... MSM
Montana State College (MCD) .... MSC
Montana State Hospital, Patient Library, Warm Springs, MT [*Library symbol*]
   [*Library of Congress*] (LCLS) .... MtWs
Montana State Law Library, Helena, MT [*Library symbol Library of*
   Congress] (LCLS) .... Mt-L
Montana State Library, Helena, MT [*Library symbol Library of Congress*]
   (LCLS) .... Mt
Montana State Prison, Conley Lake, Deer Lodge, MT [*Library symbol*]
   [*Library of Congress*] (LCLS) .... MtDeSP
Montana State University (GAGS) .... Mont St U
Montana State University [*Bozeman*] .... MSU
Montana State University at Bozeman, Bozeman, MT [*Library symbol Library*
   of Congress] (LCLS) .... MtBC
Montana Supreme Court Reports [*A publication*] (DLA) .... Mon
Montana Supreme Court Reports [*A publication*] (DLA) .... Mont
Montana Territory .... MONT TER
Montana Utilities Reports [*A publication*] (DLA) .... MUR
Montana Water Resources Research Center [*Montana State University,*
   University ofMontana, and Montana College of Mineral Science and
   Technology] [*Research center*] (RCD) .... MWRRC
Montana Western Railway [*AAR code*] .... MOW
Montana Western Railway (IIA) .... MW
Montant de Soutien [*Amount of Support*] [*A trade negotiating plan EC*] .... MDS
Montargis/Vimory [*France ICAO location identifier*] (ICLI) ...... LFEM
Montauban [*France ICAO location identifier*] (ICLI) .... LFDB
Montauk Caribbbean Airways and Ocean Reef Airways [*ICAO designator*]
   (AD) .... YL
Montauk Caribbean Airways, Inc. [*ICAO designator*] (FAAC) ...... ORA
Montauk, NY [*FM radio station call letters*] .... WBEA
Montauk, NY [*FM radio station call letters*] .... WVZC
Montauk Point [*New York*] [*Airport symbol Obsolete*] (OAG) .... MTP
Montavit Co. [*Austria*] [*Research code symbol*] .... M
Montbeliard/Courcelles [*France ICAO location identifier*] (ICLI) .... LFSM
Montceau Les Mines/Pouilloux [*France ICAO location identifier*] (ICLI) .... LFGM
Montclair Free Public Library, Montclair, NJ [*Library symbol Library of*
   Congress] (LCLS) .... NjMon
Montclair, NJ [*Television station call letters*] .... WNJN
Montclair State College (GAGS) .... Montclair St C
Montclair State College, Upper Montclair, NJ [*OCLC symbol*] (OCLC) ...... NJM
Montclair State College, Upper Montclair, NJ [*Library symbol Library of*
   Congress] (LCLS) .... NjUpM
Montclair Times, Montclair, NJ [*Library symbol Library of Congress*]
   (LCLS) .... NjMonM
Mont-Dauphin/Saint-Crepin [*France ICAO location identifier*] (ICLI) ...... LFNC
Mont-De-Marsan [*France ICAO location identifier*] (ICLI) ...... LFBM
Mont-De-Marsan [*France ICAO location identifier*] (ICLI) ...... LFBW
Montdidier [*France ICAO location identifier*] (ICLI) .... LFAR
Monte Alegre [*Brazil*] [*Airport symbol*] (AD) .... MTE
Monte Argentario [*Italy ICAO location identifier*] (ICLI) ...... LIQO
Monte Bisbino [*Italy ICAO location identifier*] (ICLI) .... LIMO
Monte Capellino [*Italy*] [*Later, ROB*] [*Geomagnetic observatory code*] ...... MCP
Monte Carlo [*South Africa*] [*ICAO location identifier*] (ICLI) .... FACA
Monte Carlo [*Calculation technique*] [*Nuclear energy*] (NUCP) .... MC
Monte Carlo [*Monaco*] [*Airport symbol*] (OAG) .... MCM
Monte Carlo (AD) .... Monte
Monte Carlo Method [*Computer science*] .... MCM
Monte Carlo Particle Trajectory Model [*Physics*] .... MCPTM
Monte Carlo Resources [*Vancouver Stock Exchange symbol*] ...... MA
Monte Carlo Simulation [*Computer science*] (IAA) .... MCS
Monte Caseros [*Argentina*] [*Airport symbol*] (AD) .... MCS
Monte Caseros [*Argentina ICAO location identifier*] (ICLI) ..... SARM
Monte Cassino [*Italy*] [*Seismograph station code, US Geological Survey*
   Closed] (SEIS) .... MCI
Monte Cavo [*Italy ICAO location identifier*] (ICLI) .... LIQQ
Monte Cimone [*Italy ICAO location identifier*] (ICLI) LIVC
Monte Cristo Peak [*Utah*] [*Seismograph station code, US Geological Survey*]
   (SEIS) .... MCU
Monte Cristy [*Dominican Republic*] [*ICAO location identifier*] (ICLI) .... MDMC
Monte Grande [*Argentina ICAO location identifier*] (ICLI) ...... SADG
Monte Grappa [*Italy ICAO location identifier*] (ICLI) .... LIVG
Monte Libano [*Colombia*] [*Airport symbol*] (OAG) .... MTB
Monte Malanotte [*Italy ICAO location identifier*] (ICLI) .... LIMY
Monte Pirata [*Puerto Rico*] [*Seismograph station code, US Geological*
   Survey] (SEIS) .... MTP
Monte Quemado [*Argentina ICAO location identifier*] (ICLI) ..... SACQ
Monte Real [*Portugal ICAO location identifier*] (ICLI) .... LPMR
Monte Reale Valcellina [*Italy*] [*Seismograph station code, US Geological*
   Survey] (SEIS) .... MRVI
Monte Rio, CA [*FM radio station call letters*] .... KMGG
Monte S. Angelo [*Italy ICAO location identifier*] (ICLI) ...... LIBE
Monte Scuro [*Italy ICAO location identifier*] (ICLI) .... LIBQ
Monte Terminillo [*Italy ICAO location identifier*] (ICLI) ...... LIRK
Monte Venda [*Italy ICAO location identifier*] (ICLI) LIVV
Monte Verde [*Bolivia*] [*ICAO location identifier*] (ICLI) ...... SLMV
Monte Vettore [*Italy*] [*Seismograph station code, US Geological Survey*]
   (SEIS) .... MVT
Monte Vista, CO [*AM radio station call letters*] .... KSLV
Monte Vista, CO [*FM radio station call letters*] .... KSLV-FM
Monte Vista Public Library, Monte Vista, CO [*Library symbol Library of*
   Congress] (LCLS) .... CoMv
Monteagle [*Australia Seismograph station code, US Geological Survey*
   Closed] (SEIS) .... MEA
Monteagle, TN [*Location identifier FAA*] (FAAL) .... MGL
Monteagudo [*Bolivia*] [*ICAO location identifier*] (ICLI) ...... SLAG

Montealto [*Costa Rica*] [*ICAO location identifier*] (ICLI) ...... MRMA
Montebello Resources Ltd. [*Vancouver Stock Exchange symbol*] ...... MBR
Montebello, VA [*Location identifier FAA*] (FAAL) .... MOL
Montebianco (AD) .... Monte
Monte-Carlo Inelastic Scattering [*Code*] [*Computer science*] (NRCH) .... MIS
Montecito, CA [*FM radio station call letters*] .... KJEE
Montecito, CA [*AM radio station call letters*] .... KNZS
Montecito History Association, Santa Barbara, CA [*Library symbol*] [*Library*
   of Congress] (LCLS) .... CStbMHi
Montedison Bearer Svg Pfd ADS [*NYSE symbol*] (TTSB) ...... MNTPr
Montedison S p AADS [*NYSE symbol*] (TTSB) .... MNT
Montedison SpA [*NYSE symbol*] (SPSG) .... MNT
Montedison SpA [*Associated Press*] (SAG) .... Monted
Montefiore (AD) .... Monte
Montefiore Hospital, Bronx, NY [*OCLC symbol*] (OCLC) ...... VZY
Montefiore Hospital, New York, NY [*Library symbol Library of Congress*]
   (LCLS) .... NNMH
Montefiore-Morrisania Comprehensive Health Care Center [*Research*
   center] (RCD) .... CHCC
Montefiore's Synopsis of Mercantile Law [*A publication*] (DLA) ...... Mont Merc Law
Montego Bay [*Jamaica*] [*Airport symbol*] (OAG) .... MBJ
Montego Bay [*Jamaica*] [*ICAO location identifier*] (ICLI) ..... MKJM
Montego Bay/Sangster International [*Jamaica*] [*ICAO location identifier*]
   (ICLI) .... MKJS
Montelimar/Ancone [*France ICAO location identifier*] (ICLI) ...... LFLQ
Montelimar O Los Sitios [*Costa Rica*] [*ICAO location identifier*] (ICLI) ...... MRML
Montello Resources Ltd. [*Vancouver Stock Exchange symbol*] ...... MEO
Montendre/Marcillac [*France ICAO location identifier*] (ICLI) ...... LFDC
Montenegro .... Monten
Monterey [*California*] [*Airport symbol*] (OAG) .... MRY
Monterey Bay Aquarium Research Institute [*California*] ...... MBARI
Monterey Bay Area Cooperative Library System [*Library network*] ...... MOBAC
Monterey Bay Area Cooperative Library System, Salinas, CA [*OCLC*
   symbol] (OCLC) .... MBL
Monterey Bay Area Cooperative System, Salinas, CA [*Library symbol Library*
   of Congress] (LCLS) .... CSalM
Monterey Bay Bancorp [*NASDAQ symbol*] (TTSB) .... MBBC
Monterey Bay Bancorp, Inc. [*NASDAQ symbol*] (SAG) ...... MBBC
Monterey Bay Bancorp, Inc. [*Associated Press*] (SAG) ..... MontBB
Monterey, CA [*Television station call letters*] .... KCCN
Monterey, CA [*AM radio station call letters*] .... KIDD
Monterey, CA [*AM radio station call letters*] .... KNRY
Monterey, CA [*Television station call letters*] .... KSMS-TV
Monterey, CA [*FM radio station call letters*] .... KWAV
Monterey, CA [*Location identifier FAA*] (FAAL) .... MTB
Monterey County Library, Salinas, CA [*Library symbol Library of Congress*]
   (LCLS) .... CSalCL
Monterey/Fort Ord, CA [*Location identifier FAA*] (FAAL) ...... FTQ
Monterey/Fort Ord, CA [*Location identifier FAA*] (FAAL) ...... OAR
Monterey Homes Corp. [*Associated Press*] (SAG) .... MontryH
Monterey Homes Corp. [*NYSE symbol*] (SAG) .... MTH
Monterey Institute for Research in Astronomy .... MIRA
Monterey Institute of Foreign Studies (GAGS) .... Monterey Inst
Monterey Institute of Foreign Studies, Monterey, CA [*Library symbol Library*
   of Congress] (LCLS) .... CMontFS
Monterey Institute of International Studies (ECON) .... MIIS
Monterey Pasta [*Associated Press*] (SAG) .... MontPas
Monterey Pasta [*NASDAQ symbol*] (SAG) .... PSTA
Monterey Peninsula College [*California*] .... MPC
Monterey Peninsula College, Monterey, CA [*Library symbol Library of*
   Congress] (LCLS) .... CMontM
Monterey Public Library, Monterey, CA [*Library symbol Library of Congress*]
   (LCLS) .... CMont
Monterey Resources, Inc. [*Associated Press*] (SAG) ...... MontryR
Monterey Resources, Inc. [*NYSE symbol*] (SAG) .... MRC
Monterey, TN [*FM radio station call letters*] .... WKXD
Monterey, TN [*FM radio station call letters*] (RBYB) .... WLMQ
Monterey, VA [*FM radio station call letters*] .... WVLS
Monterey Wine Country Association (EA) .... MWCA
Monteria [*Colombia*] [*Airport symbol*] (OAG) .... MTR
Monteria/Los Garzones [*Colorado ICAO location identifier*] (ICLI) ...... SKMR
Monterrey [*Mexico ICAO location identifier*] (ICLI) .... MMTY
Monterrey (AD) .... Mont
Monterrey [*Colombia*] [*Airport symbol*] (AD) .... MOY
Monterrey [*California*] [*Seismograph station code, US Geological Survey*]
   (SEIS) .... MTR
Monterrey [*Mexico*] [*Airport symbol*] (OAG) .... MTY
Monterrey/General Mariano Escobedo Internacional [*Mexico ICAO location*
   identifier] (ICLI) .... MMMY
Monterrey-Tippecanoe Township Public Library Monterrey, IN [*Library*
   symbol Library of Congress] (LCLS) .... InMont
Montes Claros [*Brazil*] [*Airport symbol*] (OAG) .... MOC
Montes Claros [*Brazil ICAO location identifier*] (ICLI) .... SBMK
Montesquieu's Spirit of Laws [*A publication*] (DLA) ...... Mont Sp L
Montessori Center [*Education*] .... MC
Montessori School, Albuquerque, NM [*Library symbol Library of Congress*]
   (LCLS) .... NmAM
Montessori School, Washington, DC [*Library symbol Library of Congress*]
   (LCLS) .... DMon
Montessori World Educational Institute Australia .... MWEIA
Montevideo (AD) .... Mont
Montevideo (AD) .... Monte
Montevideo [*City in Uruguay*] (ROG) .... MV
Montevideo [*Uruguay*] [*Airport symbol*] (OAG) .... MVD
Montevideo [*Uruguay*] [*ICAO location identifier*] (ICLI) ...... SUEO

Montevideo/Angel S. Adami [*Uruguay*] [*ICAO location identifier*] (ICLI) .... SUAA
Montevideo/Carrasco Internacional [*Uruguay*] [*ICAO location identifier*] (ICLI) .... SUMU
Montevideo Middle School, Montevideo, MN [*Library symbol*] [*Library of Congress*] (LCLS) .... MnMovMS
Montevideo, MN [*AM radio station call letters*] .... KDMA
Montevideo, MN [*FM radio station call letters*] .... KMGM
Montevideo, MN [*Location identifier FAA*] (FAAL) .... MVE
Montevideo Senior High School, Montevideo, MN [*Library symbol*] [*Library of Congress*] (LCLS) .... MnMovSH
Montevideo Units [*Of uterine activity*] .... MU
Monteynard [*France*] [*Seismograph station code, US Geological Survey*] (SEIS) .... MNY
Montezuma [*Chile*] [*Seismograph station code, US Geological Survey Closed*] (SEIS) .... MTZ
Montezuma Castle National Monument .... MOCA
Montezuma, GA [*FM radio station call letters*] .... WLML
Montezuma, GA [*AM radio station call letters*] .... WMNZ
Montezuma National Wildlife Refuge [*New York*] (AD) .... MNWR
Montezuma Public Library, Montezuma, IN [*Library symbol Library of Congress*] (LCLS) .... InMotz
Montezuma Republican, Montezuma, IA [*Library symbol Library of Congress*] (LCLS) .... IaMonteR
Montezuma Seminary, Montezuma, NM [*Library symbol Library of Congress*] (LCLS) .... NmMS
Montford Point Marine Association (EA) .... MPMA
Montfort Hospital [*Hopital Montfort*] Ottawa, Ontario [*Library symbol National Library of Canada*] (NLC) .... OOSLM
Montfort Missionaries (TOCD) .... smm
Montfort Missionaries (TOCD) .... SMM
Montgomery [*Alabama*] [*Airport symbol*] (OAG) .... MGM
Montgomery [*Vermont*] [*Seismograph station code, US Geological Survey*] (SEIS) .... MGVT
Montgomery (AD) .... Mont
Montgomery (AD) .... Monte
Montgomery (AD) .... Monty
Montgomery [*Pakistan*] [*Airport symbol*] (AD) .... MYP
Montgomery Air Defense Sector [*of SAGE*] (MUGU) .... MOADS
Montgomery, AL [*Location identifier FAA*] (FAAL) .... DLV
Montgomery, AL [*Location identifier FAA*] (FAAL) .... GUN
Montgomery, AL [*Location identifier FAA*] (FAAL) .... MXF
Montgomery, AL [*AM radio station call letters*] .... WACV
Montgomery, AL [*Television station call letters*] .... WAIQ
Montgomery, AL [*FM radio station call letters*] .... WBAM
Montgomery, AL [*Television station call letters*] .... WCOV
Montgomery, AL [*AM radio station call letters*] .... WHHY
Montgomery, AL [*FM radio station call letters*] .... WHHY-FM
Montgomery, AL [*Television station call letters*] .... WHOA
Montgomery, AL [*FM radio station call letters*] (RBYB) .... WJCC-FM
Montgomery, AL [*FM radio station call letters*] .... WLBF
Montgomery, AL [*FM radio station call letters*] .... WLWI-FM
Montgomery, AL [*Television station call letters*] .... WMCF
Montgomery, AL [*AM radio station call letters*] .... WMGY
Montgomery, AL [*AM radio station call letters*] (RBYB) .... WMSP
Montgomery, AL [*FM radio station call letters*] .... WMXS
Montgomery, AL [*AM radio station call letters*] (RBYB) .... WNZZ-AM
Montgomery, AL [*FM radio station call letters*] (RBYB) .... WRWO
Montgomery, AL [*Television station call letters*] .... WSFA
Montgomery, AL [*AM radio station call letters*] .... WVAS
Montgomery, AL [*AM radio station call letters*] .... WXVI
Montgomery City, MO [*FM radio station call letters*] .... KMCR
Montgomery College, Germantown Campus, Germantown, MD [*Library symbol Library of Congress*] (LCLS) .... MdMC-G
Montgomery College, Rockville Campus, Rockville, MD [*Library symbol Library of Congress*] (LCLS) .... MdMC-R
Montgomery College, Takoma Park Campus, Takoma Park, MD [*Library symbol Library of Congress*] (LCLS) .... MdMC-T
Montgomery Cotton Exchange [*Defunct*] (EA) .... MCE
Montgomery County Community College, Blue Bell, PA [*OCLC symbol*] (OCLC) .... MGC
Montgomery County Community College, Blue Bell, PA [*Library symbol Library of Congress*] (LCLS) .... PBIbM
Montgomery County Department of Public Libraries, Rockville, MD [*Library symbol Library of Congress*] (LCLS) .... MdRMC
Montgomery County Memorial Library, Conroe, TX [*Library symbol Library of Congress*] (LCLS) .... TxConM
Montgomery County Public Library, Troy, NC [*Library symbol Library of Congress*] (LCLS) .... NcTr
Montgomery County-Norristown Public Library, Norristown, PA [*OCLC symbol*] (OCLC) .... MNL
Montgomery County-Norristown Public Library, Norristown, PA [*Library symbol Library of Congress*] (LCLS) .... PNo
Montgomery GI Bill (INF) .... MGIB
Montgomery Junior College [*Maryland*] .... MJC
Montgomery/Maxwell Air Force Base [*Alabama*] [*ICAO location identifier*] (ICLI) .... KMXF
Montgomery Medical and Psychological Institute (EA) .... MMPI
Montgomery Memorial Library, Jewell, IA [*Library symbol Library of Congress*] (LCLS) .... IaJew
Montgomery, NY [*Location identifier FAA*] (FAAL) .... MGJ
Montgomery Public Library, Montgomery, AL [*Library symbol Library of Congress*] (LCLS) .... AM
Montgomery St Inc. Sec [*NYSE symbol*] (TTSB) .... MTS
Montgomery Street Income Securities, Inc. [*Associated Press*] (SAG) .... MonSt
Montgomery Street Income Securities, Inc. [*NYSE symbol*] (SPSG) .... MTS

Montgomery Technical Institute, Troy, NC [*Library symbol Library of Congress*] (LCLS) .... NcTrM
Montgomery, WV [*AM radio station call letters*] .... WMON
Montgomery, WV [*FM radio station call letters*] .... WZKM
Montgomeryshire [*County in Wales*] .... MONT
Montgomeryshire [*County in Wales*] .... MONTG
Montgomeryshire [*County in Wales*] .... MONTGOM
Montgomeryshire [*England*] (AD) .... Montgom
Montgomeryshire Imperial Yeomanry [*British military*] (DMA) .... MIY
Montgomeryshire Yeomanry [*British military*] (DMA) .... MY
Montgomeryshire Yeomanry Cavalry [*British military*] (DMA) .... MYC
Month .... M
Month (WDMC) .... m
Month (WDMC) .... mo
Month (AFM) .... MO
Month .... MON
Month .... MTH
Month after Sight (AD) .... m/s
Month, Date, Year .... MDY
Month, Day, Year (HGAA) .... mmddyy
[*The*] Month in Parliament [*A publication British*] .... MP
Month Name (BJA) .... MN
Month of Detachment .... MOD
Month of Travel [*Military*] .... MOT
Month-Day-Hour [*Automotive manufacturing*] .... MDH
Month-in-Sample [*Bureau of the Census*] (GFGA) .... MIS
Monthly .... M
Monthly .... MNTHLY
Monthly (DLA) .... Mthly
Monthly [*Publishing*] (WDMC) .... mthy
Monthly Adjustment Acceptance List [*Military*] (AFIT) .... MAAL
Monthly Advance Retail Trade Survey [*Bureau of the Census*] (GFGA) ..... MARTS
Monthly Aerial Reconnaissance Summary (MCD) .... MARS
Monthly Associate Administrator's Review [*NASA*] (NASA) .... MAAR
Monthly Associate Administrator's Review [*NASA*] .... MAAR
Monthly Availability Charge (BUR) .... MAC
Monthly Breakdown [*Used in atmospheric studies*] .... MB
Monthly Bulk Petroleum Accounting Summary [*Army*] (AABC) .... MBPAS
Monthly Bulletin of Decisions of the High Court of Uganda [*A publication*] (DLA) .... MB
Monthly Debit Industrial [*Insurance*] .... MDI
Monthly Debit Ordinary [*Insurance*] .... MDO
Monthly Depot Space and Operating Report .... MDSOR
Monthly Digest of Tax Articles [*A publication*] (DLA) .... Month Dig Tax Articles
Monthly Director's Review [*NASA*] (NASA) .... MDR
Monthly Directors' Review [*NASA*] .... MDR
Monthly Energy Review [*Department of Energy*] [*Database*] .... MER
Monthly Estimate to Completion (MCD) .... METC
Monthly Evaluation Report [*Military*] .... MONEVAL
Monthly Index of Russian Accessions [*Library of Congress*] .... MIRA
Monthly Index to Reporters [*A publication*] (DLA) .... Mont Ind
Monthly Intelligence Production (MCD) .... MIP
Monthly Intelligence Production Listing (MCD) .... MIPL
Monthly Interim Progress Report .... MIPR
Monthly International Terrorist Summary (MCD) .... MITS
Monthly Inventory Report of Special Items .... MIRSI
Monthly Investment Plan [*Stock exchange term*] (SPSG) .... MIP
Monthly Journal of Law [*A publication*] (DLA) .... Month JL
Monthly Journal of Law [*Washington*] [*A publication*] (DLA) .... Month LJ
[*The*] Monthly Journal of the Institution of Mechanical Engineers [*A publication*] .... CME
Monthly Jurist [*A publication*] (DLA) .... Mo Jur
Monthly Jurist [*Bloomington, IL*] [*A publication*] (DLA) .... Month Jur
Monthly Labor Review [*A publication*] (BRI) .... M Lab R
Monthly Labor Review [*A publication*] (DLA) .... Monthly Lab Rev
Monthly Law Bulletin [*New York*] [*A publication*] (DLA) .... Month Law Bul
Monthly Law Bulletin (New York) [*A publication*] (DLA) .... Month L Bull (NY)
Monthly Law Digest and Reporter [*Canada*] [*A publication*] (DLA) .... ML Dig & R
Monthly Law Magazine [*London*] [*A publication*] (DLA) .... Mo L Mag
Monthly Law Magazine [*London*] [*A publication*] (DLA) .... Mon Law Mag
Monthly Law Magazine [*London*] [*A publication*] (DLA) .... Month LM
Monthly Law Reporter [*A publication*] (DLA) .... Mo Law Rep
Monthly Law Reporter [*A publication*] (DLA) .... Mon Law Rep
Monthly Law Reporter [*Boston*] [*A publication*] (DLA) .... Month L Rep
Monthly Law Reports [*Canada*] [*A publication*] (DLA) .... Month L Rep
Monthly Law Review [*A publication*] (DLA) .... Month L Rev
Monthly Legal Examiner [*New York*] [*A publication*] (DLA) .... Mo Leg Exam
Monthly Legal Examiner [*New York*] [*A publication*] (DLA) .... Month Leg Ex
Monthly Legal Examiner [*New York*] [*A publication*] (DLA) .... Month Leg Exam
Monthly Legal Examiner (New York) [*A publication*] (DLA) .... Month Leg Exam (NY)
[*A*] Monthly Lesson in Criminal Politics [*Center for Financial Freedom and Accuracy in Financial Reporting*] [*A publication*] .... AMLICP
Monthly Letter Report .... MLR
Monthly Materiel Status Report .... MMSR
Monthly Mean Temperature [*Meteorology*] .... MMT
Monthly Meetings [*Quakers*] .... MM
Monthly Meteorological Records (DNAB) .... MMR
Monthly Notes. Astronomical Society of Southern Africa [*A publication*] .... MNASSA
Monthly Notices. Royal Society of Tasmania [*A publication*] .... Mon Not Roy Soc Tas
Monthly Operating Report (IEEE) .... MOR
Monthly Operating Review [*Marine science*] (OSRA) .... MOR
Monthly Operating Review (USDC) .... MOR
Monthly Order [*Navy*] .... MO

Monthly Product Announcement [*Bureau of the Census*] (GFGA) .... MPA
Monthly Production Progress Reports (MCD) .... MPPR
Monthly Program Review (USDC) .... MPR
Monthly Progress Report .... MPR
Monthly Project Evaluation .... MPE
Monthly Project Report .... MPR
Monthly Report .... MOREP
Monthly Report .... MR
Monthly Report of Progress .... MRP
Monthly Report on the Labor Force (OICC) .... MRLF
Monthly Review .... MR
Monthly Review Report .... MRR
Monthly Status Report [*Navy*] .... MSR
Monthly Throughput Observation Report (DNAB) .... MOTOR
Monthly Treasury Statement [*Government*] (AFM) .... MTS
Monthly Vital Statistics Report [*A publication*] (DHSM) .... MVSR
Monthly Western Jurist [*A publication*] (DLA) .... Mo W Jur
Monthly Western Jurist [*A publication*] (DLA) .... Mon WJ
Monthly Western Jurist [*A publication*] (DLA) .... Month West Jur
Monthly Wholesale Trade Report [*A publication*] .... MWTR
Monthly Work Package Report [*NASA*] (NASA) .... MWPR
Months .... MOS
Months (AD) .... mos
Months (WDMC) .... mos
Months (WDMC) .... MA
Months After .... MAC
Months after Contract Award .... MD
Months after Date [*or Month's Date*] [*Business term*] .... MD
Months after Exercise of Option .... M/P
Months after Payment [*Business term*] .... MAEO
Months after Receipt of Delivery Order (MCD) .... MARDO
Months after Receipt of Equipment [*Navy*] .... MARE
Months after Receipt of Problem [*Navy*] (NG) .... MARP
Months after Sight [*or Month's Sight*] [*Business term*] .... MS
Months after Sight (AD) .... ms
Months Before .... MB
Months for Cyclical Dominance [*Economics*] .... MCD
Months in Service .... MIS
Months of Operational Flying (DNAB) .... MOF
Months Old (MEDA) .... MO
Months Old (AD) .... m-o
Month-Second-Foot [*Measurement*] .... MSF
Monticello [*Utah*] [*Airport symbol*] (OAG) .... MXC
Monticello, AR [*FM radio station call letters*] (RBYB) .... KGPQ-FM
Monticello, AR [*AM radio station call letters*] .... KHBM
Monticello, AR [*FM radio station call letters*] .... KHBM-FM
Monticello, AR [*Location identifier FAA*] (FAAL) .... MON
Monticello College, Godfrey, IL [*Library symbol Library of Congress*] (LCLS) .... IGoM
Monticello Community Unit School District, Monticello, IL [*Library symbol*] [*Library of Congress*] (LCLS) .... IMontSD
Monticello Express, Monticello, IA [*Library symbol Library of Congress*] (LCLS) .... IaMontE
Monticello, FL [*FM radio station call letters*] .... WJPH
Monticello, FL [*AM radio station call letters*] .... WMFL
Monticello, IA [*Location identifier FAA*] (FAAL) .... MXO
Monticello, IL [*FM radio station call letters*] .... WCZQ
Monticello, IN [*Location identifier FAA*] (FAAL) .... MCX
Monticello, IN [*FM radio station call letters*] .... WMRS
Monticello Junior High School, Monticello, MN [*Library symbol*] [*Library of Congress*] (LCLS) .... MnMcJ
Monticello, KY [*Location identifier FAA*] (FAAL) .... EKQ
Monticello, KY [*AM radio station call letters*] .... WFLW
Monticello, KY [*FM radio station call letters*] .... WKYM
Monticello, KY [*FM radio station call letters*] .... WMKZ
Monticello, ME [*AM radio station call letters*] (RBYB) .... WREM-AM
Monticello, MN [*AM radio station call letters*] .... KMOM
Monticello, MS [*AM radio station call letters*] .... WMLC
Monticello, MS [*FM radio station call letters*] .... WRQO
Monticello Nuclear Generating Plant (NRCH) .... MNGP
Monticello, NY [*Location identifier FAA*] (FAAL) .... MSV
Monticello, NY [*FM radio station call letters*] (RBYB) .... WJUX
Monticello, NY [*FM radio station call letters*] .... WSUL
Monticello Public Library, Monticello, IA [*Library symbol Library of Congress*] (LCLS) .... IaMont
Monticello Public Library, Monticello, MN [*Library symbol*] [*Library of Congress*] (LCLS) .... MnMc
Monticello Senior High School, Monticello, MN [*Library symbol*] [*Library of Congress*] (LCLS) .... MnMcS
Monticello Union Township Public Library, Monticello, IN [*Library symbol Library of Congress*] (LCLS) .... InMotc
Monticello-Big Lake Community Hospital Library, Monticello, MN [*Library symbol*] [*Library of Congress*] (LCLS) .... MnMcH
Montichiari [*Italy ICAO location identifier*] (ICLI) .... LIPO
Montijo [*Portugal ICAO location identifier*] (ICLI) .... LPMT
Montilla [*Record label*] [*USA, Spain, etc.*] .... Mont
Mont-Joli [*Canada*] [*Airport symbol*] (OAG) .... YYY
Mont-Joli, PQ [*ICAO location identifier*] (ICLI) .... CYYY
Mont-Laurier, PQ [*Television station call letters*] CBFT-2
Mont-Laurier, PQ [*FM radio station call letters*] (RBYB) .... CFLO
Mont-Louis-La-Quillane [*France ICAO location identifier*] (ICLI) .... LFNQ
Montlucon Air Service [*France ICAO designator*] (FAAC) .... MLU
Montlucon/Domerat [*France ICAO location identifier*] (ICLI) .... LFLT
Montlucon-Gueret [*France ICAO location identifier*] (ICLI) .... LFBK
Montmagny, PQ [*FM radio station call letters*] .... CFEL
Montmorency (AD) .... Monty

Montmorency County Public Library, Atlanta, MI [*Library symbol Library of Congress*] (LCLS) .... MiAt
Montmorillonite [*A mineral*] .... M
Montmorillonite [*Mineralogy*] .... MONT
Monto [*Australia Airport symbol*] (OAG) .... MNQ
Montoneros Patria Libre [*Guerrila group*] [*Ecuador*] (EY) .... MPL
Montoro Gold, Inc. [*Vancouver Stock Exchange symbol*] .... MNT
Montoro Resources [*Vancouver Stock Exchange symbol*] .... MNQ
Montour County Historical Society, Danville, PA [*Library symbol Library of Congress*] (LCLS) .... PDanMHi
Montour Falls, NY [*FM radio station call letters*] .... WNGZ
Montour Railroad Co. [*AAR code*] .... MTR
Montparnasse (AD) .... Montparno
Montpelier (AD) .... Mont
Montpelier [*Vermont*] [*Airport symbol*] (OAG) .... MPV
Montpelier [*Vermont*] [*Seismograph station code, US Geological Survey*] (SEIS) .... MPVT
Montpelier & Barre Railroad Co. [*AAR code*] .... MB
Montpelier & Barre Railroad Co. [*Later, MB*] [*AAR code*] .... MPB
Montpelier/Edward F. Knapp [*Vermont*] [*ICAO location identifier*] (ICLI) .... KMPV
Montpelier Herald, Montpelier, IN [*Library symbol Library of Congress*] (LCLS) .... InMopH
Montpelier, ID [*AM radio station call letters*] .... KVSI
Montpelier, OH [*FM radio station call letters*] .... WLZZ
Montpelier Public Library, Montpelier, IN [*Library symbol Library of Congress*] (LCLS) .... InMop
Montpelier, VT [*Location identifier FAA*] (FAAL) .... MWX
Montpelier, VT [*FM radio station call letters*] .... WNCS
Montpelier, VT [*AM radio station call letters*] .... WSKI
Montpellier [*France*] [*Airport symbol*] (OAG) .... MPL
Montpellier/Frejorgues [*France ICAO location identifier*] (ICLI) .... LFMT
Montpellier/L'Or [*France ICAO location identifier*] (ICLI) .... LFNG
Montreal [*Quebec*] [*Seismograph station code, US Geological Survey*] (SEIS) .... MNT
Montreal (AD) .... Mont
Montreal [*Canada*] (AD) .... Montr
Montreal [*Canada*] .... MONTR
Montreal [*Canada*] [*Airport symbol*] (OAG) .... YUL
Montreal Association for the Blind, Montreal, PQ, Canada [*Library symbol*] [*Library of Congress*] (LCLS) .... CaQMAB
Montreal Association for the Blind, Quebec [*Library symbol National Library of Canada*] (NLC) .... QMAB
Montreal Association for the Mentally Retarded, Montreal, PQ, Canada [*Library symbol Library of Congress*] (LCLS) .... CaQMDM
Montreal Association for the Mentally Retarded [*Association de Montreal pour les Deficients Mentaux*] Quebec [*Library symbol National Library of Canada*] (NLC) .... QMDM
Montreal Board of Trade, Montreal, PQ, Canada [*Library symbol Library of Congress*] (LCLS) .... CaQMBT
Montreal Board of Trade [*Chambre de Commerce du District de Montreal*] Quebec [*Library symbol National Library of Canada*] (NLC) .... QMBT
Montreal Branch, Pulp and Paper Research Institute of Canada [*Succursale de Montreal, Centre Canadien de Recherche sur les Pates et Papiers*], Quebec [*Library symbol National Library of Canada*] (BIB) .... QMPPM
Montreal/Cartierville, PQ [*ICAO location identifier*] (ICLI) .... CYCV
Montreal Chest Hospital Centre [*Centre Hospitalier Thoracique de Montreal*]Quebec [*Library symbol National Library of Canada*] (NLC) .... QMCHC
Montreal Chest Hospital, Montreal, PQ, Canada [*Library symbol Library of Congress*] (LCLS) .... CaQMCHC
Montreal Children's Hospital, Montreal, PQ, Canada [*Library symbol Library of Congress*] (LCLS) .... CaQMMCH
Montreal Children's Hospital, Quebec [*Library symbol National Library of Canada*] (NLC) .... QMMCH
Montreal City & District Savings Bank [*Toronto Stock Exchange symbol*] .... BEM
Montreal Condensed Reports [*A publication*] (DLA) .... MCR
Montreal Condensed Reports [*A publication*] (DLA) .... Mont Cond Rep
Montreal Condensed Reports [*A publication*] (DLA) .... Montr Cond Rep
Montreal Diocesan College [*Quebec*] .... MDC
Montreal/Dorval International, PQ [*ICAO location identifier*] (ICLI) .... CYUL
Montreal Engineering Co. Ltd., Calgary, AB, Canada [*Library symbol Library of Congress*] (LCLS) .... CaACEC
Montreal Engineering Co. Ltd., Monenco Library, Calgary, AB, Canada [*Library symbol Library of Congress*] (LCLS) .... CaACME
Montreal Engineering Co. Ltd., Montreal, PQ, Canada [*Library symbol Library of Congress*] (LCLS) .... CaQMEC
Montreal Engineering Co. Ltd., St. Catharines, ON, Canada [*Library symbol Library of Congress*] (LCLS) .... CaOStCMEC
Montreal Gazette, Montreal, PQ, Canada [*Library symbol Library of Congress*] (LCLS) .... CaQMGa
Montreal Gazette, Quebec [*Library symbol National Library of Canada*] (NLC) .... QMGA
Montreal General Hospital, Community Health Department, Montreal, PQ, Canada [*Library symbol*] [*Library of Congress*] (LCLS) .... CaQMGHC
Montreal General Hospital, Montreal, PQ, Canada [*Library symbol Library of Congress*] (LCLS) .... CaQMGH
Montreal General Hospital, Nurses' Library, Montreal, PQ, Canada [*Library symbol*] [*Library of Congress*] (LCLS) .... CaQMGHN
Montreal General Hospital [*Hopital General de Montreal*] Quebec [*Library symbol National Library of Canada*] (NLC) .... QMGH
Montreal International Book Fair .... MIBF
Montreal Lake Library, Saskatchewan [*Library symbol National Library of Canada*] (NLC) .... SML
Montreal Law Reports [*A publication*] (DLA) .... MLR
Montreal Law Reports, Queen's Bench [*A publication*] (DLA) .... MLRQB
Montreal Law Reports, Queen's Bench [*A publication*] (DLA) .... Mont LR

Montreal Law Reports, Queen's Bench [*A publication*] (DLA) ... Mont LRQB
Montreal Law Reports, Queen's Bench [*A publication*] (DLA) ... Montr QB
Montreal Law Reports, Queen's Bench [*Canada*] [*A publication*] (DLA) ... Montreal LQB (Can)
Montreal Law Reports, Queen's Bench [*Canada*] [*A publication*] (DLA) ... Montreal LRQB
Montreal Law Reports, Superior Court [*Canada*] [*A publication*] (DLA) ... MLR CS
Montreal Law Reports, Superior Court [*Canada*] [*A publication*] (DLA) ... MLRSC
Montreal Law Reports, Superior Court [*A publication*] (DLA) ... Mont LR
Montreal Law Reports, Superior Court [*A publication*] (DLA) ... Mont LRSC
Montreal Law Reports, Superior Court [*A publication*] (DLA) ... Mont Super
Montreal Law Reports, Superior Court [*A publication*] (DLA) ... Montr Super
Montreal Law Reports, Superior Court [*Canada*] [*A publication*] (DLA) ... Montreal LRSC
Montreal Law Reports, Superior Court [*Canada*] [*A publication*] (DLA) ... Montreal LSC (Can)
Montreal Legal News [*A publication*] (DLA) ... Mont Leg News
Montreal Legal News [*A publication*] (DLA) ... Montr Leg N
Montreal Military and Maritime Museum, Quebec [*Library symbol National Library of Canada*] (NLC) ... QMMMM
Montreal [*Canada*] **Mirabel International Airport** [*Airport symbol*] (OAG) ... YMX
Montreal/Mirabel International, PQ [*ICAO location identifier*] (ICLI) ... CYMX
Montreal Museum of Fine Arts, Montreal, PQ, Canada [*Library symbol Library of Congress*] (LCLS) ... CaQMFA
Montreal Museum of Fine Arts [*Musee des Beaux-Arts de Montreal*] **Quebec** [*Library symbol National Library of Canada*] (NLC) ... QMFA
Montreal Neurological Institute and Hospital, Montreal, PQ, Canada [*Library symbol Library of Congress*] (LCLS) ... CaQMNIH
Montreal Neurological Institute and Hospital [*Institut et Hopital Neurologiques de Montreal*] **Quebec** [*Library symbol National Library of Canada*] (NLC) ... QMNIH
Montreal Platelet Syndrome [*Medicine*] (DMAA) ... MPS
Montreal, PQ [*AM radio station call letters*] ... CBF
Montreal, PQ [*FM radio station call letters*] ... CBF-FM
Montreal, PQ [*Television station call letters*] ... CBFT
Montreal, PQ [*AM radio station call letters*] ... CBM
Montreal, PQ [*FM radio station call letters*] ... CBM-FM
Montreal, PQ [*Television station call letters*] ... CBMT
Montreal, PQ [*Television station call letters*] ... CFCF
Montreal, PQ [*Television station call letters*] ... CFJP
Montreal, PQ [*AM radio station call letters*] ... CFMB
Montreal, PQ [*FM radio station call letters*] ... CFQR
Montreal, PQ [*Television station call letters*] ... CFTM
Montreal, PQ [*Television station call letters*] ... CFTU
Montreal, PQ [*Radio station call letters*] [*1930's*] ... CHLP
Montreal, PQ [*FM radio station call letters*] ... CHOM
Montreal, PQ [*FM radio station call letters*] ... CIBL
Montreal, PQ [*FM radio station call letters*] ... CINQ
Montreal, PQ [*AM radio station call letters*] ... CIQC
Montreal, PQ [*FM radio station call letters*] (RBYB) ... CIRA
Montreal, PQ [*FM radio station call letters*] ... CISM
Montreal, PQ [*FM radio station call letters*] ... CITE
Montreal, PQ [*Television station call letters*] ... CIVM
Montreal, PQ [*AM radio station call letters*] ... CJAD
Montreal, PQ [*FM radio station call letters*] ... CJFM
Montreal, PQ [*TV station call letters*] (RBYB) ... CJNT-TV
Montreal, PQ [*AM radio station call letters*] ... CKAC
Montreal, PQ [*AM radio station call letters*] (RBYB) ... CKGM-AM
Montreal, PQ [*AM radio station call letters*] ... CKIS
Montreal, PQ [*FM radio station call letters*] ... CKMF
Montreal, PQ [*FM radio station call letters*] ... CKUT
Montreal, PQ [*ICAO location identifier*] (ICLI) ... CWAO
Montreal, PQ [*ICAO location identifier*] (ICLI) ... CWUL
Montreal, PQ [*ICAO location identifier*] (ICLI) ... CZUL
Montreal Presbyterian College ... MPC
Montreal Public Library [*Canada*] (AD) ... MPL
Montreal/St. Hubert, PQ [*ICAO location identifier*] (ICLI) ... CYHU
Montreal Star [*A publication*] (AD) ... Mont S
Montreal Star, Montreal, PQ, Canada [*Library symbol Library of Congress*] (LCLS) ... CaQMMoS
Montreal Star, Quebec [*Library symbol National Library of Canada*] (NLC) ... QMMOS
Montreal Stock Exchange ... M
Montreal Stock Exchange (CDAI) ... MSE
Montreal Tramways [*AAR code*] ... MOTC
Montreal Trust Co., Montreal, PQ, Canada [*Library symbol Library of Congress*] (LCLS) ... CaQMT
Montreal Trust Co., Quebec [*Library symbol National Library of Canada*] (NLC) ... QMT
Montreal Trustco, Inc. [*Toronto Stock Exchange symbol*] ... MTU
Montreat-Anderson College, Montreat, NC [*Library symbol Library of Congress*] (LCLS) ... NcMM
Montreux Development [*Vancouver Stock Exchange symbol*] ... MDC
Montreux-Oberland-Bernois [*Railway*] [*Canada*] (AD) ... MOB
Montricher [*Switzerland ICAO location identifier*] (ICLI) ... LSTR
Montriou's Bengal Reports [*A publication*] (DLA) ... Mont
Montriou's Bengal Reports [*A publication*] (DLA) ... Montr
Montriou's Cases in Hindoo Law [*A publication*] (DLA) ... Mont Cas
Montriou's Institutes of Jurisprudence [*A publication*] (DLA) ... Mont Inst
Montriou's Reports, Supreme Court [*1846*] [*Bengal, India*] [*A publication*] (DLA) ... Mont Rep
Montriou's Supplement to Morton's Reports [*A publication*] (DLA) ... Montr
Montrose [*Colorado*] [*Seismograph station code, US Geological Survey Closed*] (SEIS) ... MRC
Montrose [*Colorado*] [*Airport symbol*] (OAG) ... MTJ
Montrose, CO [*FM radio station call letters*] ... KKXK
Montrose, CO [*Television station call letters*] ... KREY
Montrose, CO [*FM radio station call letters*] ... KSTR
Montrose, CO [*AM radio station call letters*] ... KUBC
Montrose County Regional District Library, Montrose, CO [*Library symbol Library of Congress*] (LCLS) ... CoMo
Montrose Elementary School, Montrose, MN [*Library symbol*] [*Library of Congress*] (LCLS) ... MnMtE
Montrose Memorial Hospital, Montrose, CO [*Library symbol*] [*Library of Congress*] (LCLS) ... CoMoH
Montrose, PA [*AM radio station call letters*] ... WPEL
Montrose, PA [*FM radio station call letters*] ... WPEL-FM
Montserrat [*MARC country of publication code Library of Congress*] (LCCP) ... mj
Montserrat [*West Indies*] [*Airport symbol*] (OAG) ... MNI
Montserrat [*ANSI two-letter standard code*] (CNC) ... MS
Montserrat [*ANSI three-letter standard code*] (CNC) ... MSR
Montserrat [*West Indies*] [*Seismograph station code, US Geological Survey*] (SEIS) ... MWI
Montserrat [*MARC geographic area code Library of Congress*] (LCCP) ... nwmj--
Montserrat [*International civil aircraft marking*] (ODBW) ... VP-LMA
Montserrat Airways Ltd. [*Antigua and Barbuda*] [*ICAO designator*] (FAAC) ... MNT
Montserrat Progressive Society of New York (EA) ... MPSNY
Montvale Free Public Library, Montvale, NJ [*Library symbol Library of Congress*] (LCLS) ... NjMov
Monty Python Special Interest Group (EA) ... MPSIG
Monument [*Board on Geographic Names*] ... MNMT
Monument ... MNMT
Monument (AAG) ... MON
Monument (AD) ... Mon
Monument (AD) ... mon
Monument (VRA) ... mont
Monument Builders of America [*Later, MBNA*] ... MBA
Monument Builders of North America (EA) ... MBNA
Monument, CO [*AM radio station call letters*] ... KCBR
Monument Inscription [*Genealogy*] ... MI
Monument Resources [*Vancouver Stock Exchange symbol*] ... MMT
Monument Still Exists [*Genealogy*] (ROG) ... MON
Monument Valley High School Library, Kayenta, AZ [*Library symbol Library of Congress*] (LCLS) ... AzKaH
Monument Valley, UT [*Location identifier FAA*] (FAAL) ... MOV
Monumenta Biblica et Ecclesiastica [*Rome*] [*A publication*] (BJA) ... MBE
Monumenta Talmudica (BJA) ... MonTal
Monumental Brass Society (EA) ... MBS
Monumental Maintenance Requirements (MCD) ... MMR
Monuments, Fine Arts, and Archives [*SHAEF*] [*World War II*] ... MFA & A
Monumentum [*Monument*] [*Latin*] ... M
Monumentum Ancyranum [*Classical studies*] (OCD) ... Mon Anc
Monumentum Posuit [*Erected a Monument*] [*Latin*] ... MP
Monze [*Zambia*] [*ICAO location identifier*] (ICLI) ... FLMO
Mooamedes/Yuri Gagarin [*Angola*] [*ICAO location identifier*] (ICLI) ... FNMO
Mood [*Grammar*] (ROG) ... MD
Mood Adjective Check List [*Psychometrics*] ... MACL
Mood and/or Affect [*Psychology*] (DAVI) ... M/A
Mood, Orientation, Judgment, Affect, Content (AAMN) ... MOJAC
Moody, AL [*AM radio station call letters*] ... WURL
Moody and Malkin's English Nisi Prius Reports [*A publication*] (DLA) ... M & M
Moody and Malkin's English Nisi Prius Reports [*A publication*] (DLA) ... Moo & M
Moody and Malkin's English Nisi Prius Reports [*A publication*] (DLA) ... Moo & Mal
Moody and Malkin's English Nisi Prius Reports [*A publication*] (DLA) ... Mood & M
Moody and Malkin's English Nisi Prius Reports [*A publication*] (DLA) ... Mood & Malk
Moody and Malkin's English Nisi Prius Reports [*A publication*] (DLA) ... Moody & M
Moody and Malkin's English Nisi Prius Reports [*A publication*] (DLA) ... Moody & M (Eng)
Moody and Robinson's English Nisi Prius Reports [*1830-44*] [*A publication*] (DLA) ... M & R
Moody and Robinson's English Nisi Prius Reports [*A publication*] (DLA) ... M & Rob
Moody and Robinson's English Nisi Prius Reports [*A publication*] (DLA) ... Mo & R
Moody and Robinson's English Nisi Prius Reports [*A publication*] (DLA) ... Moo & R
Moody and Robinson's English Nisi Prius Reports [*A publication*] (DLA) ... Moo & Rob
Moody and Robinson's English Nisi Prius Reports [*A publication*] (DLA) ... Mood & R
Moody and Robinson's English Nisi Prius Reports [*A publication*] (DLA) ... Mood & Rob
Moody and Robinson's English Nisi Prius Reports [*A publication*] (DLA) ... Moody & R
Moody and Robinson's English Nisi Prius Reports [*A publication*] (DLA) ... Moody & R (Eng)
Moody Bible Institute, Chicago, IL [*Library symbol Library of Congress*] (LCLS) ... ICMB
Moody Institute of Science (EA) ... MIS
Moody Literature Ministries (EA) ... MLM
Moody's Bond Information Database Service [*Moody's Investors Service, Inc.*] [*Information service or system*] (CRD) ... BIDS
Moody's English Crown Cases [*168, 169 English Reprint*] [*A publication*] (DLA) ... Moo
Moody's English Crown Cases [*168, 169 English Reprint*] [*A publication*] (DLA) ... Moody

Moody's English Crown Cases [*168, 169 English Reprint*] [*A publication*] (DLA) ... Moody CC (Eng)
Moody's English Crown Cases [*168, 169 English Reprint*] [*A publication*] (DLA) ... Moody Cr C
Moody's English Crown Cases [*168, 169 English Reprint*] [*A publication*] (DLA) ... Moody Cr Cas
Moody's English Crown Cases Reserved [*1824-44*] [*A publication*] (DLA) ... MCC
Moody's English Crown Cases Reserved [*1824-44*] [*A publication*] (DLA) ... Moo CC
Moody's English Crown Cases Reserved [*1824-44*] [*A publication*] (DLA) ... Moo Cr C
Moody's English Crown Cases Reserved [*1824-44*] [*A publication*] (DLA) ... Mood
Moody's English Crown Cases Reserved [*1824-44*] [*A publication*] (DLA) ... Mood CC
Moody's Investment Grade ... MIG
Moody's Investment Grade (DFIT) ... MIG-1
Moody's Investor Service [*A publication*] (MHDW) ... MIS
Moog, Inc. [*AMEX symbol*] (SPSG) ... MOG
Moog, Inc. [*Associated Press*] (SAG) ... Moog
Moolawatana [*Australia Airport symbol Obsolete*] (OAG) ... MWT
Moomba [*Australia Airport symbol Obsolete*] (OAG) ... MOO
Moon ... M
Moon (ROG) ... MN
Moon Rise (DNAB) ... MR
Moon Signal Rejection Equipment (AFM) ... MSRE
Moon Sphere of Influence (KSC) ... MSI
Moonbeam Public Library, Ontario [*Library symbol National Library of Canada*] (BIB) ... OMO
Moon-Earth-Plane (SAA) ... MEP
Mooney Aircraft, Inc. [*ICAO aircraft manufacturer identifier*] (ICAO) ... MO
Mooney Aircraft Pilots Association (EA) ... MAPA
Mooney Problem Check List [*Psychology*] ... MPCL
Mooneyham Public Library, Forest City, NC [*Library symbol Library of Congress*] (LCLS) ... NcFc
Moongold Resources [*Vancouver Stock Exchange symbol*] ... MOO
Moonroof [*Automotive advertising*] ... MNRF
Moon's RADAR Coordinates ... MRC
Moon's Reports [*133-144 Indiana*] [*6-14 Indiana Appeals*] [*A publication*] (DLA) ... Moon
Moorabbin [*Airport symbol*] ... MBW
Mooraberrie [*Queensland*] [*Airport symbol*] (AD) ... OOR
Moore and Payne's English Common Pleas Reports [*A publication*] (DLA) ... M & P
Moore and Payne's English Common Pleas Reports [*A publication*] (DLA) ... Mo & P
Moore and Payne's English Common Pleas Reports [*A publication*] (DLA) ... Moo & P
Moore and Payne's English Common Pleas Reports [*A publication*] (DLA) ... Moo & Pay
Moore and Payne's English Common Pleas Reports [*A publication*] (DLA) ... Moore & P
Moore and Payne's English Common Pleas Reports [*A publication*] (DLA) ... Moore & P (Eng)
Moore and Scott's English Common Pleas Reports [*1831-34*] [*A publication*] (DLA) ... M & S
Moore and Scott's English Common Pleas Reports [*1831-34*] [*A publication*] (DLA) ... M & Sc
Moore and Scott's English Common Pleas Reports [*1831-34*] [*A publication*] (DLA) ... M & Scott
Moore and Scott's English Common Pleas Reports [*1831-34*] [*A publication*] (DLA) ... Mo & S
Moore and Scott's English Common Pleas Reports [*1831-34*] [*A publication*] (DLA) ... Mo & Sc
Moore and Scott's English Common Pleas Reports [*1831-34*] [*A publication*] (DLA) ... Moo & S
Moore and Scott's English Common Pleas Reports [*1831-34*] [*A publication*] (DLA) ... Moo & Sc
Moore and Scott's English Common Pleas Reports [*1831-34*] [*A publication*] (DLA) ... Moore & S
Moore and Scott's English Common Pleas Reports [*1831-34*] [*A publication*] (DLA) ... Moore & S (Eng)
Moore and Walker's Reports [*22-24 Texas*] [*A publication*] (DLA) ... Moore & W
Moore and Walker's Reports [*22-24 Texas*] [*A publication*] (DLA) ... Moore & Walker
Moore Automatic Remote Control ... MARC
Moore Business Forms, Niagara Falls, NY [*Library symbol Library of Congress*] (LCLS) ... NNiaM
Moore College of Art, Philadelphia, PA [*Library symbol Library of Congress*] (LCLS) ... PPMoI
Moore Corp. Ltd. [*NYSE symbol Toronto Stock Exchange symbol*] (SPSG) ... MCL
Moore Corp. Ltd. [*Associated Press*] (SAG) ... Moore
Moore County Library, Carthage, NC [*Library symbol Library of Congress*] (LCLS) ... NcCar
Moore Data Management Services [*Information service or system*] (IID) ... MDMS
Moore Elementary School, Houston, TX [*Library symbol*] [*Library of Congress*] (LCLS) ... TxHMoE
Moore Jig Borer ... MJB
Moore Jig Grinder ... MJG
Moore Medical Corp. [*AMEX symbol*] (SPSG) ... MMD
Moore Medical Corp. [*Associated Press*] (SAG) ... MMed
Moore Museum, Mooretown, Ontario [*Library symbol National Library of Canada*] (BIB) ... OMMM
Moore, OK [*FM radio station call letters*] ... KMSI
Moore, OK [*AM radio station call letters*] ... WWLS
Moore Products [*NASDAQ symbol*] (TTSB) ... MORP
Moore Products Co. [*NASDAQ symbol*] (NQ) ... MORP
Moore Products Corp. [*Associated Press*] (SAG) ... MooreP
Moore Public Library, Lexington, MI [*Library symbol Library of Congress*] (LCLS) ... MiLex
Moore School Air Space Simulation Effort (MCD) ... MASE
Moore School Information Systems Laboratory ... MSISL
Moore School of Automatic Computers [*University of Pennsylvania*] ... MSAC
Moorea Island [*French Polynesia*] [*Airport symbol*] (OAG) ... MOZ
Moorea/Temae [*French Polynesia*] [*ICAO location identifier*] (ICLI) ... NTTM
Moore-Cottrell Subscription Agencies, Inc., North Cohocton, NY [*Library symbol Library of Congress*] (LCLS) ... NNcoM
Moore-Cottrell Subscription Agencies, Inc., North Cohocton, NY [*OCLC symbol*] (OCLC) ... YMC
Moored Acoustic Buoy System [*Marine science*] (MSC) ... MABS
Moored Acoustic Vertical Array ... MAVA
Moored Alongside [*Navy*] (NVT) ... MA
Moored Limited Capability Buoy [*Marine science*] (MSC) ... MLCB
Moored Sonobuoy System (MCD) ... MSS
Moored Surveillance System [*To detect and destroy enemy submarines*] [*Navy*] ... MSS
Moore-Handley, Inc. [*Birmingham, AL*] [*NASDAQ symbol*] (NQ) ... MHCO
Moore-Handley, Inc. [*Associated Press*] (SAG) ... MooreHd
Mooreland, OK [*Location identifier FAA*] (FAAL) ... MDF
Moorepark Whey Protein Concentrate (OA) ... MWPC
Moore-Rott-Sears [*Theory*] ... MRS
Moore's Abstracts of Title [*6th ed.*] [*1925*] [*A publication*] (DLA) ... Moore Abs
Moores Creek National Military Park ... MOCR
Moore's Criminal Law and Procedure [*A publication*] (DLA) ... Moore Cr Law
Moore's Digest [*Legal term*] (AD) ... Moore's Dig
Moore's Digest of International Law [*A publication*] (DLA) ... Moore Int L
Moore's Divorce Trials [*A publication*] (DLA) ... Moo Tr
Moore's East Indian Appeals [*A publication*] (DLA) ... Moore EI
Moore's English Common Pleas Reports [*A publication*] (DLA) ... Moo CP
Moore's English Common Pleas Reports [*A publication*] (DLA) ... Moore
Moore's English Common Pleas Reports [*A publication*] (DLA) ... Moore CP
Moore's English King's Bench Reports (Arguments of Moore) [*A publication*] (DLA) ... Arg Mo
Moore's English Privy Council Cases [*A publication*] (DLA) ... Moo PCC
Moore's English Privy Council Cases [*A publication*] (DLA) ... Moore PCC
Moore's English Privy Council Cases [*A publication*] (DLA) ... Moore PCC (Eng)
Moore's English Privy Council Cases [*A publication*] (DLA) ... MPC
Moore's English Privy Council Cases, New Series [*A publication*] (DLA) ... Moo PC Cas NS
Moore's English Privy Council Cases, New Series [*A publication*] (DLA) ... Moo PC (NS)
Moore's English Privy Council Cases, New Series [*A publication*] (DLA) ... Moo PCC NS
Moore's English Privy Council Cases, New Series [*A publication*] (DLA) ... Moore PCC NS
Moore's English Privy Council Cases, New Series [*A publication*] (DLA) ... Moore PCC NS (Eng)
Moore's English Privy Council Cases, Old and New Series [*A publication*] (DLA) ... Moo PC
Moore's English Privy Council Reports [*1836-62*] [*A publication*] (DLA) ... Mo
Moore's English Privy Council Reports [*A publication*] (DLA) ... Mo PC
Moore's English Privy Council Reports [*A publication*] (DLA) ... Moore
Moore's English Privy Council Reports [*A publication*] (DLA) ... Moore PC
Moore's English Privy Council Reports, New Series [*A publication*] (DLA) ... Moore PC NS
Moore's English Queen's Bench Reports [*A publication*] (DLA) ... Moore QB
Moore's Federal Practice [*A publication*] (DLA) ... Moore Fed Practice
Moore's Gorham Case, English Privy Council [*A publication*] (DLA) ... Moo GC
Moore's Gorham Case, English Privy Council [*A publication*] (DLA) ... Moore GC
Moore's Indian Appeals [*A publication*] (DLA) ... MIA
Moore's Indian Appeals [*A publication*] (DLA) ... Mo
Moore's Indian Appeals [*A publication*] (DLA) ... Mo IA
Moore's Indian Appeals [*A publication*] (DLA) ... Moore Ind App
Moore's Indian Appeals [*England*] [*A publication*] (DLA) ... Moore Ind App (Eng)
Moore's Indian Appeals [*England*] [*A publication*] (DLA) ... Moore Indian App
Moore's International Adjudications [*Legal term*] (AD) ... Moore's Adj
Moore's International Arbitrations [*Legal term*] (AD) ... Moore's Arb
Moores Island, Abaco Island [*Bahamas*] [*ICAO location identifier*] (ICLI) ... MYAO
Moore's Presbyterian Digest [*A publication*] (DLA) ... Moore Presby Dig
Moore's Reports [*Bosanquet and Puller*] [*England*] [*A publication*] (DLA) ... A Moo
Moore's Reports [*England*] [*A publication*] (DLA) ... B Monr
Moore's Reports [*England*] [*A publication*] (DLA) ... BM
Moore's Reports [*Bosanquet and Puller*] [*England*] [*A publication*] (DLA) ... Moo A
Moore's Reports [*Alabama*] [*A publication*] (DLA) ... Moore
Moore's Reports [*Arkansas*] [*A publication*] (DLA) ... Moore
Moore's Reports [*Texas*] [*A publication*] (DLA) ... Moore
Moore's Reports [*Bosanquet and Puller*] [*England*] [*A publication*] (DLA) ... Moore A
Moore's Reports, Privy Council, Indian Appeals [*1836-72*] [*A publication*] (DLA) ... Moo Ind App
Moore's Separate Report of Westerton Versus Liddell [*A publication*] (DLA) ... Moo Sep Rep
Moorestown Free Library, Moorestown, NJ [*Library symbol Library of Congress*] (LCLS) ... NjMor
Mooresville, NC [*AM radio station call letters*] ... WHIP
Mooresville Public Library, Mooresville, IN [*Library symbol*] [*Library of Congress*] (LCLS) ... InMoo
Mooresville Public Library, Mooresville, NC [*Library symbol Library of Congress*] (LCLS) ... NcMv
Moorhead Junior High School, Moorhead, MN [*Library symbol*] [*Library of Congress*] (LCLS) ... MnMohJ

Moorhead, MN [*FM radio station call letters*] .... KCCD
Moorhead, MN [*FM radio station call letters*] .... KCCM
Moorhead, MN [*FM radio station call letters*] .... KQWB
Moorhead, MN [*AM radio station call letters*] .... KVOX
Moorhead, MN [*FM radio station call letters*] .... KVOX-FM
Moorhead Public Library, Moorhead, MN [*Library symbol*] [*Library of Congress*] (LCLS) .... MnMoh
Moorhead Public Schools System, Moorhead, MN [*Library symbol Library of Congress*] (LCLS) .... MnMohPS
Moorhead Senior High School, Moorhead, MN [*Library symbol*] [*Library of Congress*] (LCLS) .... MnMohSH
Moorhead State College [*Minnesota*] .... MSC
Moorhead State College, Moorhead, MN [*Library symbol Library of Congress*] (LCLS) .... MnMohS
Moorhead State University (GAGS) .... Moorhead St U
Mooring [*Freight*] .... MOORNG
Mooring (MSA) .... MRG
Mooring (AD) .... mrng
Mooring and Salvage Officer [*Navy British*] .... MSBO
Mooring Buoy .... MB
Mooring Dynamics Experiment [*Marine science*] (MSC) .... MDE
Mooring Leg Deployment Device (PDAA) .... MLDD
Mooring Line Data Line [*Environmental buoy cable*] .... MLDL
Mooring Pipe [*or Post*] (ADA) .... MP
Mooring Salvage and Boom Vessel (PDAA) .... MSBV
Moorish Divine and National Movement in North America (EA) .... MDNMNA
Moorlands [*Tasmania*] [*Seismograph station code, US Geological Survey*] (SEIS) .... MOO
Moorsele [*Belgium ICAO location identifier*] (ICLI) .... EBMO
Moose .... MSE
Moose Creek [*Alaska*] [*Seismograph station code, US Geological Survey Closed*] (SEIS) .... MCB
Moose Creek Branch, Stormount, Dundas, and Glengarry County Public Library, Ontario [*Library symbol National Library of Canada*] (NLC) .... OMCSDG
Moose Factory Library, Ontario [*Library symbol National Library of Canada*] (BIB) .... OMF
Moose, International (EAIO) .... MI
Moose Jaw Canadian Forces Base, SK [*ICAO location identifier*] (ICLI) .... CYMJ
Moose Jaw Public Library, Moose Jaw, SK, Canada [*Library symbol Library of Congress*] (LCLS) .... CaSMJ
Moose Jaw Public Library, Saskatchewan [*Library symbol National Library of Canada*] (NLC) .... SMJ
Moose Jaw, SK [*AM radio station call letters*] .... CHAB
Moose Lake Public Lake, Moose Lake, MN [*Library symbol*] [*Library of Congress*] (LCLS) .... MnMol
Moose Lake Public School, Moose Lake, MN [*Library symbol*] [*Library of Congress*] (LCLS) .... MnMolS
Moose Pass [*Alaska*] [*Seismograph station code, US Geological Survey*] (SEIS) .... MPA
Moosehorn National Wildlife Refuge [*Maine*] (AD) .... MNWR
Moosonee [*Canada*] [*Airport symbol*] (OAG) .... YMO
Moosonee, ON [*AM radio station call letters*] .... CHMO
Moosonee, ON [*ICAO location identifier*] (ICLI) .... CYMO
Moosonee Public Library, Ontario [*Library symbol National Library of Canada*] (BIB) .... OMOO
Moovies, Inc. [*NASDAQ symbol*] (SAG) .... MOOV
Moovies, Inc. [*Associated Press*] (SAG) .... Moovie
Mop Rack .... MOPR
Mop Rack (AD) .... mopr
Mopa [*Ecuador*] [*ICAO location identifier*] (ICLI) .... SEMP
Mopar Muscle Club International (EA) .... MMCI
MOPAR Scat Pack Club (EA) .... MSPC
Mopar Trans-Am Association [*Commercial firm*] (EA) .... MTAA
Moped Association of America [*Defunct*] (EA) .... MAA
Mopliert [*Furnished*] [*German*] (AD) .... mobl
Mopti [*Mali*] [*Airport symbol*] (OAG) .... MZI
Mopti/Barbe [*Mali*] [*ICAO location identifier*] (ICLI) .... GAMB
Moquegua [*Peru*] [*ICAO location identifier*] (ICLI) .... SPEQ
Mora [*Sweden*] [*Airport symbol*] (OAG) .... MXX
Mora Fairview Central Middle School, Mora, MN [*Library symbol*] [*Library of Congress*] (LCLS) .... MnMrMS
Mora High School, Mora, MN [*Library symbol*] [*Library of Congress*] (LCLS) .... MnMrH
Mora, MN [*FM radio station call letters*] .... KBEK
Mora/Siljan [*Sweden ICAO location identifier*] (ICLI) .... ESKM
Morab Horse Registry of America (EA) .... MHRA
Morafenobe [*Madagascar*] [*ICAO location identifier*] (ICLI) .... FMMR
Morafenobe [*Madagascar*] [*Airport symbol*] (OAG) .... TVA
Moraga, CA [*FM radio station call letters*] .... KSMC
Moraga Resources Ltd. [*Vancouver Stock Exchange symbol*] .... MGR
Moraine Valley Community College, Palos Hills, IL [*Library symbol Library of Congress*] (LCLS) .... IPhiM
Moraine Valley Community College, Palos Hills, IL [*OCLC symbol*] (OCLC) .... JAM
Moral (ROG) .... MOR
Moral Action Choice Test (EDAC) .... MACT
Moral Alternatives [*An association*] (EA) .... MA
Moral Development Unit [*Prisoner reform program*] .... MDU
[The] Moral Equivalent of War [*Phrase used by President Jimmy Carter to describe his energy bill*] .... MEOW
Moral Fiber (AD) .... mor fib
Moral Majority [*An association*] (EA) .... MM
Moral Majority (AD) .... Mor Maj
Moral Obligation (MHDW) .... MO
Moral Re-Armament (EA) .... MRA

Morale Branch [*Military*] .... MB
Morale, Recreation, and Welfare [*Military*] (AFM) .... MRW
Morale, Recreation, and Welfare (AD) .... mrw
Morale Support Activities [*Military*] (AABC) .... MSA
Morale Support Activities Office .... MSAO
Morale Support Detachment [*Army*] .... MSD
Morale Support Fund Council [*Military*] (AABC) .... MSFC
Morale Support Funds (MCD) .... MSF
Morale Support Officer [*Military*] (AABC) .... MSO
Morale Tendency Score (AEE) .... MTS
Morale, Welfare, and Recreation [*DoD*] .... MWR
Morale, Welfare, and Recreation Activity [*OCD*] (AFIT) .... MWRA
Moralia [*of Plutarch*] [*Classical studies*] (OCD) .... Mor
Morality in Media (EA) .... MIM
Morality in Media (EA) .... MM
Morally Obliged to Go [*British Slang*] .... MOTG
Morally Repugnant Elite [*Lifestyle classification*] (ECON) .... MRE
Moran Resources Corp. [*Vancouver Stock Exchange symbol*] .... MRN
Moranbah [*Australia Airport symbol*] (OAG) .... MOV
Moravia (AD) .... Morav
Moravia Union, Moravia, IA [*Library symbol Library of Congress*] (LCLS) .... IaMoraU
Moravian (AD) .... MO
Moravian Archives, Winston-Salem, NC [*Library symbol Library of Congress*] (LCLS) .... NcWsM
Moravian College and Theological Seminary, Bethlehem, PA [*Library symbol Library of Congress*] (LCLS) .... PBMC
Moravian College, Bethlehem, PA [*OCLC symbol*] (OCLC) .... MOR
Moravian College, Bethlehem, PA [*Library symbol Library of Congress*] (LCLS) .... PBMW
Moravian Historical Society (EA) .... MHS
Moravian Historical Society, Nazareth, PA [*Library symbol Library of Congress*] (LCLS) .... PNazMHi
Moravian Missionary Society .... MMS
Moravian Music Foundation (EA) .... MMF
Moravian Music Foundation, Winston-Salem, NC [*Library symbol Library of Congress*] (LCLS) .... NcWsMM
Morawetz on Private Corporations [*A publication*] (DLA) .... Mor Corp
Morawetz on Private Corporations [*A publication*] (DLA) .... Mor Priv Corp
Moray [*County in Scotland*] (ROG) .... MOR
Morbidity and Mortality [*Medicine*] (DMAA) .... MM
Morbidity Report .... MORBREPT
Morbidity Telegraphic Report .... MORBTGREPT
Morbihan (AD) .... Morb
Morbus Maculosus Neonatorum [*Medicine*] (DMAA) .... MMN
Mordechai (AD) .... Mordy
Mordechai Anielewicz Circle of Americans for Progressive Israel (EA) .... MAC-API
Mordehai (AD) .... Mord
Mordehai (AD) .... Mordhy
Morden & Helwig Group, Inc. [*Toronto Stock Exchange symbol*] .... MGH
Mordenite [*A zeolite*] .... MOR
Morden-Winkler Regional Library, Morden, Manitoba [*Library symbol National Library of Canada*] (NLC) .... MMOW
Morden-Winkler Regional Library, Morden, MB, Canada [*Library symbol Library of Congress*] (LCLS) .... CaMMoW
More Advanced Petrol Tractors [*Germany*] .... MAPT
More After Dark [*Screen-saver computer program from Berkeley Systems*] (PCM) .... MAD
More Better for Russia [*Facetious translation of MBFR - Mutual and Balanced Force Reduction*] .... MBFR
More Developed Country .... MDC
More Dicto [*As Directed*] [*Pharmacy*] .... M DICT
More Dicto [*As Directed*] [*Pharmacy*] .... MD
More Dicto [*As Directed*] [*Latin*] (AD) .... mor dict
More Dicto [*As Directed*] [*Pharmacy*] (ROG) .... MORE DICT
More Education - More Opportunities (DNAB) .... MEMO
More Effective Schools [*Program*] [*Defunct*] .... MES
More Follows [*Newspaper copy*] (DGA) .... MF
More Follows [*Copyediting*] (WDMC) .... mf
More Fragments (ACRL) .... MF
More Heart More Edge [*Screenwriter's lexicon*] .... MHME
More in the Kitchen [*Family dinner-table expression*] .... MIK
More Moderate Service [*Automotive engineering*] .... MM
More Nearly Perfect [*Microsoft Corp.*] [*Computer science*] .... MNP
More Significant [*Statistics*] .... MS
More Solito [*In the Usual Manner*] [*Latin*] (AD) .... mor sal
More Solito [*In the Usual Way*] [*Pharmacy*] .... MOR SOL
More Solito [*In the usual manner*] [*Latin*] [*Pharmacy*] (DAVI) .... mor sol
More Solito [*In the Usual Way*] [*Pharmacy*] (ROG) .... MORE SOL
More Than .... MT
More to Follow [*Copyediting*] (WDMC) .... mtf
Moreau-Lislet and Carleton's Laws of Las Siete Partidas in Force in Louisiana [*A publication*] (DLA) .... M & C Partidas
Moreau-Lislet and Carleton's Laws of Las Siete Partidas in Force in Louisiana [*A publication*] (DLA) .... Mor & Carl
Moreau-Lislet and Carleton's Laws of Las Siete Partidas in Force in Louisiana [*A publication*] (DLA) .... Moreau & Carleton's Partidas
Moreau-Lislet and Carleton's Laws of Las Siete Partidas in Force in Louisiana [*A publication*] (DLA) .... Partidas
Moreauville, LA [*FM radio station call letters*] .... KLIL
Moree [*Australia Airport symbol*] (OAG) .... MRZ
Moreh Nebukhim [*Maimonides*] (BJA) .... MN
Morehead [*Papua New Guinea*] [*Airport symbol*] (OAG) .... MHY

Morehead and Brown. Digest of Kentucky Statute Laws [*A publication*] (DLA) ... KY St Law
Morehead & North Fork R. R. [*AAR code*] ... MNF
Morehead City, NC [*Television station call letters*] ... WFXI
Morehead City, NC [*AM radio station call letters*] ... WMBL
Morehead City, NC [*FM radio station call letters*] ... WOTJ
Morehead City, NC [*FM radio station call letters*] ... WRHT
Morehead, KY [*Television station call letters*] ... WAOM
Morehead, KY [*FM radio station call letters*] ... WIKO
Morehead, KY [*Television station call letters*] ... WKMR
Morehead, KY [*FM radio station call letters*] ... WMKY
Morehead, KY [*AM radio station call letters*] ... WMOR
Morehead, KY [*FM radio station call letters*] ... WMOR-FM
Morehead State University (GAGS) ... Morehead St U
Morehead State University, Morehead, KY [*OCLC symbol*] (OCLC) ... KMM
Morehead State University, Morehead, KY [*Library symbol Library of Congress*] (LCLS) ... KyMoreU
Morehead's Practice [*A publication*] (DLA) ... Mor Pr
Morehouse College, Atlanta, GA [*Library symbol Library of Congress*] (LCLS) ... GAM
Morehouse College, School of Medicine, Atlanta, GA [*Library symbol Library of Congress*] (LCLS) ... GAM-M
Morehouse College, School of Medicine, Atlanta, GA [*OCLC symbol*] (OCLC) ... GMS
Morehouse Parish Library, Bastrop, LA [*Library symbol Library of Congress*] (LCLS) ... LBM
Morehouse School of Medicine (GAGS) ... Morehouse Sch of Med
Morehouse School of Medicine [*Atlanta, GA*] ... MSM
Morelia [*Mexico*] [*Airport symbol*] (OAG) ... MLM
Morelia [*Mexico ICAO location identifier*] (ICLI) ... MMMM
Morelia (AD) ... Mor
Morelos (AD) ... Mor
Morenci Public Library, Morenci, AZ [*Library symbol Library of Congress*] (LCLS) ... AzMo
Morendo [*Gradually Softer*] [*Music*] ... MOR
Morendo [*Dying Away*] [*Italian*] (AD) ... mor
Moreno Valley, CA [*AM radio station call letters*] ... KHPY
Moreover (AD) ... mrov
Mores Island [*Bahamas*] [*Airport symbol*] (AD) ... MIX
More's Lectures on the Law of Scotland [*A publication*] (DLA) ... More Lect
More's Notes on Stair's Institutes of Scotland [*A publication*] (ILCA) ... M St
More's Notes on Stair's Institutes of Scotland [*A publication*] (DLA) ... More St
Moreshet Archives [*Jerusalem*] (BJA) ... MA
Morestel [*France ICAO location identifier*] (ICLI) ... LFHI
Moret/Episy [*France ICAO location identifier*] (ICLI) ... LFPU
Moreton [*England*] ... MORET
Morewood Branch, Stormont, Dundas, and Glengarry County Public Library, Ontario [*Library symbol National Library of Canada*] (BIB) ... OMORSDG
Morey's Outlines of Roman Law [*A publication*] (DLA) ... Morey Out Rom Law
Morfee Wheel Manufacturing [*Vancouver Stock Exchange symbol*] ... MWM
Morgain Minerals, Inc. [*Vancouver Stock Exchange symbol*] ... MGM
Morgan [*George T.*] [*Designer's mark, when appearing on US coins*] ... M
Morgan [*Automobile*] ... MOG
Morgan and Arabian [*Type of horse developed from these two breeds*] [*Acronym is also said to stand for "Muscular, Outstanding, Refined, Athletic, Beautiful," the horse's distinguishing characteristics*] ... MORAB
Morgan and Chute on the Judicature Acts [*A publication*] (DLA) ... Morg & Ch Jud Acts
Morgan [*J. P.*] **& Co., Inc.** [*NYSE symbol*] (SPSG) ... JPM
Morgan [*J. P.*] **& Co., Inc.** [*Associated Press*] (SAG) ... Morgan
Morgan [*J. P.*] **& Co., Inc.** [*Associated Press*] (SAG) ... Morgn
Morgan and Williams' Law Journal [*London*] [*A publication*] (DLA) ... Law Jour (M & W)
Morgan and Williams' Law Journal [*London*] [*A publication*] (DLA) ... LJM & W
Morgan and Williams' Law Journal [*London*] [*A publication*] (DLA) ... Morg & WLJ
Morgan Aviation Services Ltd. [*Nigeria*] [*ICAO designator*] (FAAC) ... MGN
Morgan Car Club (EA) ... MCC
Morgan City, LA [*FM radio station call letters*] ... KFXY
Morgan City, LA [*AM radio station call letters*] ... KMRC
Morgan City/Patterson [*Louisiana*] [*Airport symbol*] (OAG) ... PTN
Morgan City Public Library, Morgan City, LA [*Library symbol Library of Congress*] (LCLS) ... LMc
Morgan County Community College, Fort Morgan, CO [*Library symbol Library of Congress*] (LCLS) ... CoFtmM
Morgan County Court House, Decatur, AL [*Library symbol*] [*Library of Congress*] (LCLS) ... ADeCC
Morgan County Public Library, Martinsville, IN [*Library symbol Library of Congress*] (LCLS) ... InMart
Morgan Financial Corp. [*Toronto Stock Exchange symbol*] ... MFI
Morgan Financial Corp. [*NASDAQ symbol*] (SAG) ... MORG
Morgan Financial Corp. [*Associated Press*] (SAG) ... MorgFn
Morgan Finl (Del) [*NASDAQ symbol*] (TTSB) ... MORG
Morgan Funshares [*NASDAQ symbol*] (TTSB) ... MFUN
Morgan Funshares, Inc. [*NASDAQ symbol*] (SAG) ... MFUN
Morgan Funshares, Inc. [*Associated Press*] (SAG) ... MorgFun
Morgan Grenfell Asset Management [*Investment management firm*] [*British*] ... MGAM
Morgan Grenfell Smallcap [*NYSE symbol*] (TTSB) ... MGC
Morgan Grenfell Smallcap Fund, Inc. [*NYSE symbol*] (SPSG) ... MGC
Morgan Grenfell Smallcap Fund, Inc. [*Associated Press*] (SAG) ... MorgGr
Morgan Group [*AMEX symbol*] (TTSB) ... MG
[*The*] **Morgan Group, Inc.** [*AMEX symbol*] (SAG) ... MG
Morgan, H. W., Los Angeles CA [*STAC*] ... MHW
Morgan Hill, CA [*FM radio station call letters*] ... KSQQ
Morgan Horse Breeders Association [*Defunct*] (EA) ... MHBA
Morgan Horse Club [*Later, American Morgan Horse Association*] (EA) ... MHC
Morgan Horse Development Institute [*Defunct*] (EA) ... MHDI
Morgan Hydrocarbons, Inc. [*Toronto Stock Exchange symbol*] ... MHI
Morgan Intertrades Ltd. [*Nigeria*] [*FAA designator*] (FAAC) ... INL
Morgan (J.P.) [*NYSE symbol*] (TTSB) ... JPM
Morgan Keegan [*Associated Press*] (SAG) ... MorgK
Morgan Keegan & Co., Inc. [*NYSE symbol*] (SPSG) ... MOR
Morgan Keegan & Co., Inc. [*Associated Press*] (SAG) ... MorgKeg
Morgan Keegan Inc. [*NYSE symbol*] (TTSB) ... MOR
Morgan Keenan [*System*] [*Astronomy*] ... MK
Morgan Keenan [*System for determining the luminosity of stars*] ... M-K
Morgan, Keenan, Kellman [*System*] [*Astronomy*] ... MKK
Morgan Library (AD) ... Mor Lib
Morgan, M. B., Glen Burnie MD [*STAC*] ... MOR
Morgan on the Law of Literature [*A publication*] (DLA) ... Morg Lit
Morgan on the United States Tariff [*A publication*] (DLA) ... Morg Tar
Morgan Owners Register (EA) ... MOR
Morgan Park Junior High School, Duluth, MN [*Library symbol*] [*Library of Congress*] (LCLS) ... MnDuMPJ
Morgan Plus Four Club (EA) ... MPFC
Morgan Products Ltd. [*NYSE symbol*] (SPSG) ... MGN
Morgan Products Ltd. [*Associated Press*] (SAG) ... MorgnP
Morgan Pubic Library, Morgan, MN [*Library symbol*] [*Library of Congress*] (LCLS) ... MnMnP
Morgan Sports Car Club (EA) ... MSCC
Morgan Stan Fin 9% Cp Uts [*NYSE symbol*] (TTSB) ... MSV
Morgan Stan Fin 7.82% Cp Uts [*NYSE symbol*] (TTSB) ... MSU
Morgan Stan Fin 8.20% Cp Uts [*NYSE symbol*] (TTSB) ... MSP
Morgan Stan Fin 8.40% Cp Uts [*NYSE symbol*] (TTSB) ... MSE
Morgan Stan Global Opt Bd Fd [*NYSE symbol*] (TTSB) ... MGB
Morgan StanGp 6% Telebras'PERQS' [*AMEX symbol*] (TTSB) ... TBM
Morgan StanGp 7%CiscoSy'PERQS' [*AMEX symbol*] (TTSB) ... XPC
Morgan StanGp 6.00% Tele'PERQS' [*AMEX symbol*] (TTSB) ... MXT
Morgan StanGp 6.50% IGT'PERQS' [*AMEX symbol*] (TTSB) ... IGS
Morgan Stanley 8.75% Dep Pfd [*NYSE symbol*] (TTSB) ... MSPrC
Morgan Stanley 8.88% Dep Pfd [*NYSE symbol*] (TTSB) ... MSPrB
Morgan Stanley 9.36% Pfd [*NYSE symbol*] (TTSB) ... MSPr
Morgan Stanley Africa Inv Fd [*NYSE symbol*] (TTSB) ... AFF
Morgan Stanley Africa Investment Fund [*NYSE symbol*] (SAG) ... AFF
Morgan Stanley Africa Investment Fund [*Associated Press*] (SAG) ... MSAfrica
Morgan Stanley Asia Pacific Fund [*NYSE symbol*] (SAG) ... APF
Morgan Stanley Asia Pacific Fund [*Associated Press*] (SAG) ... MSAsia
Morgan Stanley Asia-Pac Fund [*NYSE symbol*] (TTSB) ... APF
Morgan Stanley Asset Management [*Commercial firm*] ... MSAM
Morgan Stanley Capital International ... MSCI
Morgan Stanley Emer'g Mkt Debt [*NYSE symbol*] (TTSB) ... MSD
Morgan Stanley Emerging Market [*NYSE symbol*] (SPSG) ... MSF
Morgan Stanley Emerging Markets [*Associated Press*] (SAG) ... MorSEm
Morgan Stanley Emerging Markets Debt Fund, Inc. [*Associated Press*] (SAG) ... MS EMD
Morgan Stanley Emerging Markets Debt Fund, Inc. [*NYSE symbol*] (SAG) ... MSD
Morgan Stanley Emerging Mkt [*NYSE symbol*] (TTSB) ... MSF
Morgan Stanley European Emerging Markets Ltd. [*Associated Press*] (SAG) ... MSEuro
Morgan Stanley Finance Markets Ltd. Capital Unit [*NYSE symbol*] (SAG) ... MSZ
Morgan Stanley Finance Markets Ltd. Capital Units [*NYSE symbol*] (SAG) ... EEM
Morgan Stanley Finance Markets Ltd. Capital Units [*NYSE symbol*] (SAG) ... MSV
Morgan Stanley Finance PLC Capital Unit [*Associated Press*] (SAG) ... MS Fin
Morgan Stanley Finance PLC Capital Unit [*NYSE symbol*] (SAG) ... MSE
Morgan Stanley Finance PLC Capital Unit [*Associated Press*] (SAG) ... MSFn
Morgan Stanley Finance PLC Capital Unit [*NYSE symbol*] (SAG) ... MSP
Morgan Stanley Financial [*NYSE symbol*] (SPSG) ... MSU
Morgan Stanley Global Opportunities Bond Fund, Inc. [*NYSE symbol*] (SAG) ... MGB
Morgan Stanley Global Opportunities Bond Fund, Inc. [*Associated Press*] (SAG) ... MSGlobl
Morgan Stanley Group [*AMEX symbol*] (SAG) ... MPQ
Morgan Stanley Group [*NYSE symbol*] (TTSB) ... MS
Morgan Stanley Group [*Associated Press*] (SAG) ... MS TBR
Morgan Stanley Group [*Associated Press*] (SAG) ... MSPEQ
Morgan Stanley Group, Inc. [*AMEX symbol*] (SAG) ... DWC
Morgan Stanley Group, Inc. [*AMEX symbol*] (SAG) ... HKM
Morgan Stanley Group, Inc. [*AMEX symbol*] (SAG) ... IGS
Morgan Stanley Group, Inc. [*AMEX symbol*] (SAG) ... JIC
Morgan Stanley Group, Inc. [*AMEX symbol*] (SAG) ... JMS
Morgan Stanley Group, Inc. [*AMEX symbol*] (SAG) ... MHK
Morgan Stanley Group, Inc. [*Associated Press*] (SAG) ... MorgSt
Morgan Stanley Group, Inc. [*Associated Press*] (SAG) ... MrgS
Morgan Stanley Group, Inc. [*NYSE symbol*] (SPSG) ... MS
Morgan Stanley Group, Inc. [*Associated Press*] (SAG) ... MS CSCO
Morgan Stanley Group, Inc. [*Associated Press*] (SAG) ... MS IGT
Morgan Stanley Group, Inc. [*Associated Press*] (SAG) ... MS TMX
Morgan Stanley Group, Inc. [*Associated Press*] (SAG) ... MSDM
Morgan Stanley Group, Inc. [*Associated Press*] (SAG) ... MSHK
Morgan Stanley Group, Inc. [*Associated Press*] (SAG) ... MSJ96
Morgan Stanley Group, Inc. [*Associated Press*] (SAG) ... MSNik 97
Morgan Stanley Group, Inc. [*AMEX symbol*] (SAG) ... MXT
Morgan Stanley Group, Inc. [*AMEX symbol*] (SAG) ... XPC
Morgan Stanley Hi Yld Fd [*NYSE symbol*] (TTSB) ... MSY
MorgaN Stanley High Yield Fund [*Associated Press*] (SAG) ... MrgSHY
Morgan Stanley High Yield Fund [*NYSE symbol*] (SPSG) ... MSY
Morgan Stanley India Inv Fd [*NYSE symbol*] (TTSB) ... IIF

Morgan Stanley India Investment Fund [*NYSE symbol*] (SAG) ... IIF
Morgan Stanley India Investment Fund [*Associated Press*] (SAG) ... MS India
Morgan Stanley Russia & New Europe Fund, Inc. [*Associated Press*] (SAG) ... MS Russ
Morgan Stanley Russia & New Europe Fund, Inc. [*NYSE symbol*] (SAG) ... RNE
Morgan Stanly 7.375% Dep Pfd [*NYSE symbol*] (TTSB) ... MSPrD
Morgan State College [*Later, Morgan State University*] [*Baltimore, MD*] ... MSC
Morgan State College [*Later, Morgan State University*] **Baltimore, MD** [*Library symbol Library of Congress*] (LCLS) ... MdBMC
Morgan State University (GAGS) ... Morgan St U
Morgan State University, Baltimore, MD [*OCLC symbol*] (OCLC) ... MSU
Morgan Territory [*California*] [*Seismograph station code, US Geological Survey*] (SEIS) ... MTC
Morgan Three-Wheeler Club (EA) ... MTWC
Morganatic Marriage (AD) ... morg mar
Morganfield, KY [*AM radio station call letters*] ... WMSK
Morganfield, KY [*FM radio station call letters*] ... WMSK-FM
Morgan(JP) Adj Rt A Pfd [*NYSE symbol*] (TTSB) ... JPMPrA
Morgan(JP)6.625% Dep'H'Pfd [*NYSE symbol*] (TTSB) ... JPMPrH
Morgan's Chancery Acts and Orders [*6th ed.*] [*1885*] [*A publication*] (DLA) ... Mor Chy Acts
Morgan's Chancery Acts and Orders [*6th ed.*] [*1885*] [*A publication*] (DLA) ... Morg
Morgan's Chancery Acts and Orders [*6th ed.*] [*1885*] [*A publication*] (DLA) ... Morg Ch
Morgan's Digest [*Ceylon*] [*A publication*] (DLA) ... Morgan
Morgan's Food [*AMEX symbol*] (TTSB) ... MR
Morgan's Foods, Inc. [*Associated Press*] (SAG) ... MorgnF
Morgan's Foods, Inc. [*AMEX symbol*] (SPSG) ... MR
Morgan's Legal Miscellany [*Ceylon*] [*A publication*] (DLA) ... Morgan LM
Morgan-Stanley Capital International - Europe, Australia, Far East [*Free*] [*Index - Financial*] ... MSCI-EAFE
Morganton, NC [*Location identifier FAA*] (FAAL) ... FIQ
Morganton, NC [*Location identifier FAA*] (FAAL) ... MRN
Morganton, NC [*AM radio station call letters*] ... WCIS
Morganton, NC [*AM radio station call letters*] ... WMNC
Morganton-Burke Library, Inc., Morganton, NC [*Library symbol Library of Congress*] (LCLS) ... NcMoM
Morgantown [*West Virginia*] [*Airport symbol*] (OAG) ... MGW
Morgantown [*West Virginia*] [*Seismograph station code, US Geological Survey*] (SEIS) ... MRG
Morgantown Energy Technology Center [*Morgantown, WV*] [*Department of Energy*] (GRD) ... METC
Morgantown, KY [*AM radio station call letters*] ... WLBQ
Morgantown, NC [*FM radio station call letters*] ... WMNC-FM
Morgantown Public Library, Morgantown, WV [*Library symbol Library of Congress*] (LCLS) ... WvM
Morgantown, WV [*Location identifier FAA*] (FAAL) ... BBO
Morgantown, WV [*Location identifier FAA*] (FAAL) ... MGW
Morgantown, WV [*AM radio station call letters*] ... WAJR
Morgantown, WV [*AM radio station call letters*] ... WCLG
Morgantown, WV [*FM radio station call letters*] ... WCLG-FM
Morgantown, WV [*Television station call letters*] ... WNPB
Morgantown, WV [*FM radio station call letters*] ... WVAQ
Morgantown, WV [*FM radio station call letters*] ... WVPM
Morgantown, WV [*FM radio station call letters*] ... WWVU
Morgororo [*Tanzania*] [*ICAO location identifier*] (ICLI) ... HTMG
Mori [*Japan*] [*Seismograph station code, US Geological Survey Closed*] (SEIS) ... MOR
Morice's English and Roman Dutch Law [*A publication*] (DLA) ... Mor E & RD Law
Morinville Public Library, Alberta [*Library symbol National Library of Canada*] (NLC) ... AMO
Morinville Public Library, Morinville, AB, Canada [*Library symbol*] [*Library of Congress*] (LCLS) ... CaAMor
Morioka [*Japan*] [*Seismograph station code, US Geological Survey*] (SEIS) ... MRK
Morioka [*Japan*] [*Airport symbol*] (OAG) ... MRW
Morisco (AD) ... Mor
Morison's Dictionary of Decisions, Scotch Court of Session [*1540-1808*] [*A publication*] (DLA) ... M
Morison's Dictionary of Decisions, Scotch Court of Session [*1540-1808*] [*A publication*] (DLA) ... M Dict
Morison's Dictionary of Decisions, Scotch Court of Session [*1540-1808*] [*A publication*] (DLA) ... Mor
Morison's Dictionary of Decisions, Scotch Court of Session [*1540-1808*] [*A publication*] (DLA) ... Mor Dic
Morison's Dictionary of Decisions, Scotch Court of Session [*1540-1808*] [*A publication*] (DLA) ... Mor Dict
Morison's Dictionary of Decisions, Scotch Court of Session, Supplement [*1620-1768*] [*A publication*] (DLA) ... Mor Supp
Morison's Dictionary of Scotch Session Cases [*A publication*] (DLA) ... D
Morison's Synopsis, Scotch Session Cases [*1808-16*] [*A publication*] (DLA) ... Mor Syn
Moritz Community Hospital, Medical Library, Sun Valley, ID [*Library symbol*] [*Library of Congress*] (LCLS) ... IdSvH
Morjumiid-Pterocephalid Boundary [*Paleogeologic boundary*] ... M/P
Morlaix [*France*] [*Airport symbol*] (OAG) ... MXN
Morlaix/Ploujean [*France ICAO location identifier*] (ICLI) ... LFRU
Morley Library, Painesville, OH [*OCLC symbol*] (OCLC) ... MRP
Morley Library, Painesville, OH [*Library symbol Library of Congress*] (LCLS) ... OPa
Morley's Digest of the Indian Reports [*A publication*] (DLA) ... Mor Dig
Morley's East Indian Digest [*A publication*] (DLA) ... Morl Dig
Morley-Stanwood Community Library, Morley, MI [*Library symbol Library of Congress*] (LCLS) ... MiMory
Mormon (WDAA) ... MORM
Mormon (AD) ... Morm
Mormon History Association (EA) ... MHA
Mormon Mesa, NV [*Location identifier FAA*] (FAAL) ... MMM
Mormon Station State Park, Genoa, NV [*Library symbol Library of Congress*] (LCLS) ... NvGM
Mormons for ERA (EA) ... MERA
Morning ... M
Morning (WDMC) ... m
Morning ... MG
Morning ... MNG
Morning ... MO
Morning ... MORN
Morning (AD) ... morn
Morning (ROG) ... MRN
Morning ... MRNG
Morning (AD) ... mrng
Morning After (IIA) ... MA
Morning and Evening (WDMC) ... M & E
Morning and Night [*Medicine*] ... M & N
Morning Prayer (WGA) ... MP
Morning Readiness Check ... MRC
Morning Report [*Army*] ... MR
Morning Report Indicator Code [*Army*] (AABC) ... MRIC
Morning Star Co-Operative Society, London, United Kingdom [*Library symbol Library of Congress*] (LCLS) ... UkLMS
Morning Star Resources [*Vancouver Stock Exchange symbol*] ... MOR
Morning Sun News-Herald, Morning Sun, IA [*Library symbol Library of Congress*] (LCLS) ... IaMornN
Morning-After Call [*Sales*] ... MAC
Morningside College (GAGS) ... Morningside C
Morningside College, Sioux City, IA [*Library symbol Library of Congress*] (LCLS) ... IaScM
Morningside College, Sioux City, IA [*OCLC symbol*] (OCLC) ... IOM
Morningside, MD [*AM radio station call letters*] ... WPGC
Morningside, MD [*FM radio station call letters*] ... WPGC-FM
Morningstar Foundation (EA) ... MF
Morningstar Group [*Associated Press*] (SAG) ... MornGp
Morningstar Group [*NASDAQ symbol*] (SAG) ... MSTR
Mornington Island [*Australia Airport symbol*] (OAG) ... ONG
Moro Dicto [*As Directed*] [*Pharmacy*] ... MOR DICT
Moro Islamic Liberation Front [*Philippines*] [*Political party*] ... MILF
Moro National Liberation Front [*Philippines*] [*Political party*] (PD) ... MNLF
Morobe [*Papua New Guinea*] [*Airport symbol*] (OAG) ... OBM
Moroccan (AD) ... Mor
Moroccan (AD) ... Moroc
Moroccan National Tourist Office (AD) ... MNTO
Moroccan Party of Progress and Socialism [*Political party*] ... MPPS
Moroccan Sea Frontier [*Navy World War II*] ... MORSEAFRON
Moroccan Sea Frontier [*Navy World War II*] ... MSF
Morocco [*International civil aircraft marking*] (ODBW) ... CN
Morocco [*MARC geographic area code Library of Congress*] (LCCP) ... f-mr--
Morocco [*IYRU nationality code*] [*ANSI two-letter standard code*] (CNC) ... MA
Morocco [*ANSI three-letter standard code*] (CNC) ... MAR
Morocco ... MOR
Morocco (AD) ... mor
Morocco (VRA) ... Moro
Morocco [*MARC country of publication code Library of Congress*] (LCCP) ... mr
Morocco Explorations [*Vancouver Stock Exchange symbol*] ... MOQ
Morocco Leather [*Bookbinding*] (DGA) ... MCO
Morocco Leather [*Bookbinding*] (ROG) ... MOR
Morocco Leather [*Bookbinding*] (ROG) ... MORO
Morocco Lined [*Covers*] [*Bookbinding*] (ROG) ... ML
Morocco Spotted Horse Association of America [*Defunct*] (EA) ... MSHAA
Morocco-United States Liaison Office (AFM) ... MUSLO
Morombe [*Madagascar*] [*ICAO location identifier*] (ICLI) ... FMSR
Morombe [*Madagascar*] [*Airport symbol*] (OAG) ... MXM
Moron [*Argentina ICAO location identifier*] (ICLI) ... SADM
Morondava [*Madagascar*] [*ICAO location identifier*] (ICLI) ... FMMV
Morondava [*Madagascar*] [*Airport symbol*] (OAG) ... MOQ
Moroni [*Comoro Islands*] [*Airport symbol*] (OAG) ... YVA
Moroni/Hahaia [*Comoros*] [*ICAO location identifier*] (ICLI) ... FMCH
Moroni [*Comoro Islands*] **Hahaia Airport** [*Airport symbol*] (OAG) ... HAH
Moroni/Iconi [*Comoros*] [*ICAO location identifier*] (ICLI) ... FMCN
Morotai Island [*Indonesia*] [*Airport symbol*] (OAG) ... OTI
Morotai/Pitu [*Indonesia*] [*ICAO location identifier*] (ICLI) ... WAMR
Moroto [*Uganda*] [*ICAO location identifier*] (ICLI) ... HUMO
Morovis [*Puerto Rico*] [*Seismograph station code, US Geological Survey*] (SEIS) ... MOV
Morovis, PR [*AM radio station call letters*] ... WMTI
Morozovsk [*Former USSR ICAO location identifier*] (ICLI) ... URRM
Morpha [*Form*] [*Biology*] ... m
Morphine [*Slang*] ... M
Morphine [*A narcotic*] ... MOR
Morphine (WDAA) ... MORPH
Morphine (AD) ... morph
Morphine and Cocaine [*Mixture*] [*Slang*] ... M & C
Morphine Positive Control [*Epidemiology*] ... MPC
Morphine Provocative Test [*Gastroenterology*] (DAVI) ... MPT
Morphine Sulfate [*Narcotic*] ... MS
Morphine-Dependent Rate ... MDR
Morphine-Like Compound [*Immunology*] ... MLC
Morphine-Naive Rats ... MNR
Morphogenetic Furrow [*Cell differentiation*] ... MF
Morpholine [*Organic chemistry*] ... MOR
Morpholine-Based Sulfenamide [*Chemistry*] ... MBS

Morpholinodaunomycin [*Also, MRD*] [*Antineoplastic drug*] .... MoDNM
Morpholinodaunorubicin [*Also, MoDNM*] [*Antineoplastic drug*] .... MRD
Morpholinoethanesulfonic Acid [*A buffer*] .... MES
Morpholinoethylisocyanide [*Organic chemistry*] .... MEI
Morpholinoethylmethylphenylpyridazone [*An analgesic*] .... MEMPP
Morpholinomethyl Salicyclamide [*Analgesic compound*] .... MSAM
Morpholinopropanesulfonic Acid [*A buffer*] .... MOPS
(Morpholinylthio)benzothiazole [*Organic chemistry*] .... MTB
Morphologic Index [*Volume of trunk divided by length of limbs*] .... MI
Morphological Dictionary Adaptor Program (PDAA) .... MDAP
Morphological Rule [*Linguistics*] .... M
Morphology .... MORPH
Morphology .... morph
Morphology (AD) .... MORPHOL
Morphology Dependent Resonance [*Physics*] .... MDR
Morphology-Immunology-Cytogenetics [*Classification of Leukemias*] .... MIC
Morphometric Analysis [*Botany*] .... M
Morphophysiological (AD) .... morphophysio
Morquio-Brailsford Disease [*Medicine*] (DMAA) .... MBD
Morrell on the Law of Horses [*A publication*] (DLA) .... Mor Hors
Morrell on the Law of Wills [*A publication*] (DLA) .... Mor Wills
Morrell Tank Line [*AAR code*] .... MTX
Morrell's English Bankruptcy Cases [*A publication*] (DLA) .... Morr Bankr Cas
Morrell's English Bankruptcy Cases [*A publication*] (DLA) .... Morrell Bankr Cas
Morrell's English Bankruptcy Cases [*A publication*] (DLA) .... Morrell BC
Morrell's English Bankruptcy Cases [*A publication*] (DLA) .... Morrell (Eng)
Morrell's English Bankruptcy Reports [*A publication*] (DLA) .... MB
Morrell's English Bankruptcy Reports [*A publication*] (DLA) .... Morr
Morrell's English Bankruptcy Reports [*A publication*] (DLA) .... Morr BC
Morrill Memorial Library, Norwood, MA [*Library symbol Library of Congress*] (LCLS) .... MNr
Morrill Memorial Library, Norwood, MA [*Library symbol*] [*Library of Congress*] (LCLS) .... MNrL
Morrilton, AR [*AM radio station call letters*] .... KVOM
Morrilton, AR [*FM radio station call letters*] .... KVOM-FM
Morrilton, AR [*Location identifier FAA*] (FAAL) .... MPJ
Morrin Municipal Library, Alberta [*Library symbol National Library of Canada*] (NLC) .... AMOM
Morrin Municipal Library, Morrin, AB, Canada [*Library symbol Library of Congress*] (LCLS) .... CaAMoM
Morris Air Service [*ICAO designator*] (FAAC) .... MSS
Morris and Harrington's Reports [*Bombay, India*] [*A publication*] (DLA) .... Morris & Har
Morris Animal Foundation (EA) .... MAF
Morris Brown College [*Atlanta, GA*] .... MBC
Morris Brown College, Atlanta, GA [*Library symbol Library of Congress*] (LCLS) .... GAMB
Morris Brown College, Atlanta, GA [*OCLC symbol*] (OCLC) .... MBC
Morris College, Sumter, SC [*Inactive*] [*OCLC symbol*] (OCLC) .... MOC
Morris College, Sumter, SC [*Library symbol Library of Congress*] (LCLS) .... ScSuM
Morris County Clerk, Morristown, NJ [*Library symbol Library of Congress*] (LCLS) .... NjMoCoC
Morris County Free Library, Whippany, NJ [*Library symbol Library of Congress*] (LCLS) .... NjWhiM
Morris County Free Library, Whippany, NJ [*OCLC symbol*] (OCLC) .... NWM
Morris County News, Rockaway, NJ [*Library symbol Library of Congress*] (LCLS) .... NjRocM
Morris Dam Laboratory .... MDL
Morris Elementary School, Morris, MN [*Library symbol*] [*Library of Congress*] (LCLS) .... MnMoE
Morris Foundation [*British*] (DBA) .... MF
Morris Garage Octagon Car Club [*British*] (EAIO) .... MGOCC
Morris Garages [*British automobile manufacturer; initialism used as name of sports car it produces*] .... MG
Morris Harvey College [*West Virginia*] .... MHC
Morris Harvey College, Charleston, WV [*Library symbol Library of Congress*] (LCLS) .... WvCM
Morris High School, Morris, MN [*Library symbol*] [*Library of Congress*] (LCLS) .... MnMoMHS
Morris, IL [*FM radio station call letters*] .... WCFL
Morris, IL [*AM radio station call letters*] .... WCSJ
Morris, IL [*FM radio station call letters*] .... WJDK
Morris' Iowa Reports [*1839-46*] [*A publication*] (DLA) .... Mor IA
Morris' Iowa Reports [*1839-46*] [*A publication*] (DLA) .... Morr
Morris' Iowa Reports [*1839-46*] [*A publication*] (DLA) .... Morris
Morris' Iowa Reports [*1839-46*] [*A publication*] (DLA) .... Morris (IA)
Morris' Iowa Reports [*1839-46*] [*A publication*] (DLA) .... Morris (Iowa)
Morris' Jamaica Reports [*A publication*] (DLA) .... Morr
Morris' Jamaica Reports [*A publication*] (DLA) .... Morr Jam
Morris' Jamaica Reports [*A publication*] (DLA) .... Morris
Morris' Jamaica Reports [*A publication*] (DLA) .... Morris R
Morris' Law of Replevin [*A publication*] (DLA) .... Mor Rep
Morris' Law of Replevin [*A publication*] (DLA) .... Morr Repl
Morris Middle School, Morris, MN [*Library symbol*] [*Library of Congress*] (LCLS) .... MnMoM
Morris Minor Registry (EA) .... MMR
Morris' Mississippi State Cases [*1818-72*] [*A publication*] (DLA) .... Miss St Ca
Morris' Mississippi State Cases [*1818-72*] [*A publication*] (DLA) .... Miss St Cas
Morris' Mississippi State Cases [*1818-72*] [*A publication*] (DLA) .... Mor St Ca
Morris' Mississippi State Cases [*1818-72*] [*A publication*] (DLA) .... Mor St Cas
Morris' Mississippi State Cases [*1818-72*] [*A publication*] (DLA) .... Morr St Cas
Morris' Mississippi State Cases [*1818-72*] [*A publication*] (DLA) .... Morris St Cas
Morris, MN [*FM radio station call letters*] .... KKOK
Morris, MN [*AM radio station call letters*] .... KMRS
Morris, MN [*FM radio station call letters*] .... KUMM
Morris, MN [*Location identifier FAA*] (FAAL) .... MOX
Morris News-Bee, Morris Plains, NJ [*Library symbol Library of Congress*] (LCLS) .... NjMpN
Morris on Compensations [*A publication*] (DLA) .... Mor Comp
Morris on Dilapidations [*2nd ed.*] [*1871*] [*A publication*] (DLA) .... Mor Dil
Morris on Railway Compensations [*A publication*] (DLA) .... Mor Ry Com
Morris on Replevin [*A publication*] (DLA) .... Morris Repl
Morris on the Law of Easements [*A publication*] (DLA) .... Mor Eas
Morris Plains Public Library, Morris Plains, NJ [*Library symbol Library of Congress*] (LCLS) .... NjMp
Morris Pratt Institute Association (EA) .... MPI
Morris Public Library, Morris, CT [*Library symbol Library of Congress*] (LCLS) .... CtMor
Morris Public Library, Morris, MN [*Library symbol*] [*Library of Congress*] (LCLS) .... MnMo
Morris Register [*An association*] (EAIO) .... MR
Morris' Reports [*Jamaica*] [*A publication*] (ILCA) .... Mor
Morris' Reports [*Mississippi*] [*A publication*] (DLA) .... Mor Miss
Morris' Reports [*Oregon*] [*A publication*] (DLA) .... Morr
Morris' Reports [*California*] [*A publication*] (DLA) .... Morr
Morris' Reports [*Bombay, India*] [*A publication*] (DLA) .... Morr
Morris' Reports [*Bombay, India*] [*A publication*] (DLA) .... Morr Bomb
Morris' Reports [*California*] [*A publication*] (DLA) .... Morr Cal
Morris' Reports [*Mississippi*] [*A publication*] (DLA) .... Morr Miss
Morris' Reports [*Mississippi*] [*A publication*] (DLA) .... Morris
Morris' Reports [*Oregon*] [*A publication*] (DLA) .... Morris
Morris' Reports [*Bombay, India*] [*A publication*] (DLA) .... Morris
Morris' Reports [*California*] [*A publication*] (DLA) .... Morris
Morris Wolseley Group [*Automobile manufacturing organization*] .... MOWOG
Morrisburg Branch, Stormont, Dundas, and Glengarry County Public Library, Ontario [*Library symbol National Library of Canada*] (NLC) .... OMOSDG
Morrison and Mary Wiley Public Library, Elmwood, IL [*Library symbol Library of Congress*] (LCLS) .... IElw
Morrison and Mary Wiley Public Library, Elmwood, IL [*OCLC symbol*] (OCLC) .... IPM
Morrison, CO [*FM radio station call letters*] .... KWBI
Morrison Commemorative Stamp Committee (EA) .... MCC
Morrison Flying Service, Inc. [*ICAO designator*] (FAAC) .... MRO
Morrison Fresh Cooking [*NYSE symbol*] (TTSB) .... MFC
Morrison Fresh Cooking, Inc. [*NYSE symbol*] (SAG) .... MFC
Morrison Fresh Cooking, Inc. [*Associated Press*] (SAG) .... MorsnFr
Morrison Health Care [*NYSE symbol*] (TTSB) .... MHI
Morrison Health Care, Inc. [*NYSE symbol*] (SAG) .... MHI
Morrison Health Care, Inc. [*Associated Press*] (SAG) .... MorsnHI
Morrison Hershfield Ltd., Guelph, Ontario [*Library symbol National Library of Canada*] (NLC) .... OGMH
Morrison, IL [*FM radio station call letters*] .... WZZT
Morrison Knudsen [*NYSE symbol*] (TTSB) .... MRN
Morrison Knudsen Corp. [*Associated Press*] (SAG) .... MorrKn
Morrison Knudsen Corp. [*Associated Press*] (SAG) .... MorrKnud
Morrison Library Outpost, Severn Bridge, ON, Canada [*Library symbol Library of Congress*] (LCLS) .... CaOSbM
Morrison Library Outpost, Severn Bridge, Ontario [*Library symbol National Library of Canada*] (NLC) .... OSBM
Morrison Minerals Ltd. [*Toronto Stock Exchange symbol*] .... MSN
Morrison Petroleums Ltd. [*Toronto Stock Exchange symbol*] .... MRP
Morrison Restaurants, Inc. [*Associated Press*] (SAG) .... Morrison
Morrison Restaurants, Inc. [*NYSE symbol*] (SPSG) .... RI
Morrison-Grey Enterprises [*Vancouver Stock Exchange symbol*] .... MGP
Morrison-Knudsen Co., Inc. [*Boise, ID*] (TSSD) .... M-K
Morrison-Knudsen Co., Inc. [*Associated Press*] (SAG) .... MorKnd
Morrison-Knudsen Co., Inc. [*NYSE symbol*] (SPSG) .... MRN
Morrison-Knudsen Technologies, Inc. [*Boise, ID*] [*Telecommunications*] (TSSD) .... MKTI
Morrison-Krudsen Co., Inc., Records and Micrographics Center, Boise, ID [*Library symbol Library of Congress*] (LCLS) .... IdBMK
Morrison-Reeves Public Library, Richmond, IN [*Library symbol Library of Congress*] (LCLS) .... InRM
Morrison's Dictionary of Decisions, Scotch Court of Session [*A publication*] (DLA) .... M Dict
Morrison's Dictionary of Decisions, Scotch Court of Session [*A publication*] (DLA) .... Morr Dict
Morrison's Digest of Mining Decisions [*A publication*] (DLA) .... Morr Dig
Morrison's Digest of Mining Decisions [*A publication*] (DLA) .... Morr Mines
Morrison's Mining Reports [*A publication*] (DLA) .... Mor Min Rep
Morrison's Mining Reports [*United States*] [*A publication*] (DLA) .... Morr Min R
Morrison's Mining Reports [*A publication*] (DLA) .... Morr Min Rep
Morrison's Mining Reports [*United States*] [*A publication*] (DLA) .... Morr MR
Morrison's Mining Reports [*United States*] [*A publication*] (DLA) .... Morrison Min Rep
Morrison's New Hampshire Digest [*A publication*] (DLA) .... Mor Dig
Morrison's New Hampshire Digest [*A publication*] (DLA) .... Morr Dig
Morrison's Transcript of United States Supreme Court Decisions [*A publication*] (DLA) .... Mor Tran
Morrison's Transcript of United States Supreme Court Decisions [*A publication*] (DLA) .... Morr Trans
Morrison-Talbott Library, Waterloo, IL [*Library symbol Library of Congress*] (LCLS) .... IWatl
Morris-Oxford (AD) .... M-O
Morrissett's Reports [*80, 98 Alabama*] [*A publication*] (DLA) .... Morris
Morrissey, Fernie & Michel Railway [*AAR code*] .... MFM
Morrisson-Reeves Public Library, Richmond, IN [*OCLC symbol*] (OCLC) .... INR
Morristown & Erie Railroad Co. [*AAR code*] .... ME
Morristown Centennial Library, Morrisville, VT [*Library symbol Library of Congress*] (LCLS) .... VtMor

Morristown College, Morristown, TN [Library symbol Library of Congress] (LCLS) .... TMorM
Morristown Memorial Hospital, Morristown, NJ [Library symbol Library of Congress] (LCLS) .... NjMoH
Morristown, MN [Location identifier FAA] (FAAL) .... FOW
Morristown National Historical Park .... MORR
Morristown National Historical Park, Morristown, NJ [Library symbol Library of Congress] (LCLS) .... NjMoHP
Morristown, NJ [Location identifier FAA] (FAAL) .... MMU
Morristown, NJ [FM radio station call letters] .... WJSV
Morristown, NJ [AM radio station call letters] .... WMTR
Morristown, NY [FM radio station call letters] .... WNCQ
Morristown, TN [Location identifier FAA] (FAAL) .... JXT
Morristown, TN [Location identifier FAA] (FAAL) .... MOR
Morristown, TN [AM radio station call letters] .... WCRK
Morristown, TN [FM radio station call letters] .... WMTN
Morristown, TN [FM radio station call letters] .... WMXK
Morristown-Edison National Park Service Group .... MOED
Morrisville, VT [Location identifier FAA] (FAAL) .... MVL
Morrisville, VT [FM radio station call letters] .... WLVB
Morro Bay, CA [FM radio station call letters] (RBYB) .... KAGR
Morro Bay, CA [AM radio station call letters] .... KBAI
Morro Bay, CA [FM radio station call letters] .... KWWV
Morrow, GA [AM radio station call letters] .... WSSA
Morrow, OH [FM radio station call letters] .... WLMH
Morrow Snowboards [NASDAQ symbol] (TTSB) .... MRRW
Morrow Snowboards, Inc. [Associated Press] (SAG) .... MorrowSn
Morrow Snowboards, Inc. [NASDAQ symbol] (SAG) .... MRRW
Morse Automatic Decoder (IAA) .... MAD
Morse Automatic Decoder .... MAUDE
Morse Code .... MC
Morse Code - Barry Morse Fan Club (EA) .... MC
Morse Code Light [or Fog Signal] [Navigation signal] .... MO
Morse Junior College [Connecticut] .... MJC
Morse Key (DEN) .... MK
Morse Mission Trainer .... MMT
Morse on the Law of Arbitration and Award [A publication] (DLA) .... Morse Arb
Morse on the Law of Banks and Banking [A publication] (DLA) .... Morse Banks
Morse on the Law of Banks and Banking [A publication] (DLA) .... Morse Bk
Morse Tape (IAA) .... MS
Morse Taper (AD) .... mor t
Morse Taper .... MORT
Morse Taper (IAA) .... MT
Morse Telegraph Club (EA) .... MTC
Morse's Exchequer Reports [Canada] [A publication] (DLA) .... Morse Exch Rep
Morse's Famous Trials [A publication] (DLA) .... Morse Tr
Morso [Denmark ICAO location identifier] (ICLI) .... EKNM
Mort [Dead] [French] (ROG) .... M
Mortagne-Au-Perche [France ICAO location identifier] (ICLI) .... LFAX
Mortal (AD) .... mort
Mortality .... mort
Mortality (BABM) .... MORTAL
Mortality [Statistics] (DAVI) .... mortal
Mortality Enhancing Factors [Chemical and biological warfare] .... MEF
Mortality Odds Ratio .... MOR
Mortality Probability Models [Medicine] .... MPM
Mortality Rate Doubling Time .... MRDT
Mortality Rate to Double .... MRD
Mortality Rates .... MR
Mortality Ratio (MAE) .... MR
Mortar .... M
Mortar .... MOR
Mortar (AD) .... mor
Mortar (AD) .... mort
Mortar (AABC) .... MORT
Mortar [Technical drawings] (DAC) .... MRTR
Mortar Air Delivery System [Military] (VNW) .... MAD
Mortar and Artillery Location RADAR (RDA) .... MALOR
Mortar/Artillery Locating RADAR (PDAA) .... MALR
Mortar Ballistic Computer [Formerly, MFCC] [Army] (INF) .... MBC
Mortar Board (EA) .... MB
Mortar Bombing Report .... MORTREP
Mortar Box Assembly .... MBA
Mortar Carrier [British] .... MC
Mortar Detection .... MODET
Mortar Fire Control Calculator [Later, MBC] [Military] (INF) .... MFCC
Mortar Fire Control System [Military] (INF) .... MFCS
Mortar Fire Controller [British] .... MFC
Mortar Fire Direction Center Data Calculator [Army] .... MFCC
Mortar Howitzer (NATG) .... MORITZER
Mortar Howitzer (AD) .... moritzer
Mortar Locating RADAR (MCD) .... MLR
Mortar Master Plan [Military] (INF) .... MMP
Mortar Motor Carrier .... MMC
Mortar Package Assembly .... MPA
Mortar Producers Association [British] (DBA) .... MPA
Morte alla Francia Italia Anelo [Death to the French is Italy's Cry] [When used in reference to the secret society often associated with organized crime, "Mafia" is from the Sicilian word for boldness or lawlessness] .... MAFIA
Mortemart (AD) .... Mort
Mortgage .... M
Mortgage (ADA) .... MORT
Mortgage (AD) .... mort
Mortgage .... MORTG
Mortgage .... MRTG

Mortgage [Finance] (SPSG) .... MTG
Mortgage .... MTGE
Mortgage (DD) .... mtge
Mortgage Account Report Compiler (IAA) .... MARC
Mortgage and Rental Assistance Program [Australia] .... MRAP
Mortgage Bankers Association of America [Washington, DC] (EA) .... MBA
Mortgage Brokers' Association of Australia .... MBAA
Mortgage Collateralized Bond .... MCB
Mortgage Constant (DICI) .... MC
Mortgage Credit Certificate (EMRF) .... MCC
Mortgage Credit Condition (EMRF) .... MC
Mortgage Funding Corp. [British] .... MFC
Mortgage Guaranty Insurance Corp. [Subsidiary of MGIC Investment Corp.] .... MGIC
Mortgage Indemnity Fund [Veterans Administration] .... MIF
[The] Mortgage Index [Hale Systems, Inc.] [Information service or system] (CRD) .... MI
[The] Mortgage Index, Inc. [Remote Computing Corp.] [Information service or system] (IID) .... TMI
Mortgage Information Direct Access Network [FHLMC] (EMRF) .... MIDANET
Mortgage Insurance (EMRF) .... MI
Mortgage Insurance Certificate (EMRF) .... MIC
Mortgage Insurance Companies of America (EA) .... MICA
Mortgage Insurance Co. .... MIC
Mortgage Insurance Co. of Canada [Toronto Stock Exchange symbol] .... MGO
Mortgage Insurance Co. of Canada .... MICC
Mortgage Insurance Premium .... MIP
Mortgage Interest Differential .... MID
Mortgage Interest Relief at Source [British] (DCTA) .... MIRAS
Mortgage Interest Tax Relief [British] .... MITR
Mortgage Investments Plus, Inc. (MHDW) .... MIP
Mortgage Loan Partnership [Investment term] .... MLP
Mortgage Payment in Full .... MP
Mortgage Rate Protection Program [Canada] .... MRPP
Mortgage Revenue Bond .... MRB
Mortgage Secondary Market Board [Australia] .... MSMB
Mortgage-Backed Bonds .... MBB
Mortgage-Backed Securities Clearing Corp. (EMRF) .... MBSCC
Mortgage-Backed Securities Information Services [The Bond Buyer, Inc.] [New York, NY] [Information service or system] (IID) .... MBS
Mortgage-Backed Security (DFIT) .... MBS
Mortgage-Backed Security Program [Government National Mortgage Association] .... MBS
Mortgaged (ROG) .... MTGD
Mortgagee .... MTGEE
Mortgage-Participation Certificate [Investment term] .... MP
Mortgage-Participation Certificate [Investment term] (GFGA) .... MPC
Mortgage-Related Security (EMRF) .... MRS
Mortgagor .... MTGOR
Mortice Kern Systems, Inc. [Waterloo, ON Canada] [Commercial firm] (CDE) .... MKS
Mortician (AD) .... mort
Mortician .... MORT
Mortimer (AD) .... Mort
Mortis [Of Death] [Latin] .... M
Morton (AD) .... Mort
Morton Air Services Ltd. .... MOS
Morton Arboretum, Lisle, IL [Library symbol Library of Congress] (LCLS) .... ILMA
Morton College, Cicero, IL [Library symbol Library of Congress] (LCLS) .... ICicM
Morton F. Plant Hospital, Clearwater, FL [Library symbol Library of Congress] (LCLS) .... FCIM
Morton Grove Public Library, Morton Grove, IL [Library symbol Library of Congress] (LCLS) .... IMg
Morton Grove Public Library, Morton Grove, IL [OCLC symbol] (OCLC) .... IMT
Morton, IL [FM radio station call letters] .... WTAZ
Morton International [NYSE symbol] (TTSB) .... MII
Morton International, Inc. [NYSE symbol] (SPSG) .... MII
Morton International, Inc. [Associated Press] (SAG) .... Morton Int
Morton Junior College [Later, Morton College] [Cicero, IL] .... MJC
Morton Public Library, Morton, IL [Library symbol Library of Congress] (LCLS) .... IMort
Morton Public Library, Morton, IL [OCLC symbol] (OCLC) .... IST
Morton Township Library, Mecosta, MI [Library symbol Library of Congress] (LCLS) .... MiMec
Morton-James Public Library, Nebraska City, NE [Library symbol [Library of Congress] (LCLS) .... NbNcM
Morton's Reports, Calcutta Superior Court [India] [A publication] (DLA) .... Morton
Mortons Restaurant Group [Associated Press] (SAG) .... MortnRst
Mortons Restaurant Group [NYSE symbol] (SAG) .... MRG
Morton's Restaurant Group [NYSE symbol] (TTSB) .... MRG
Morton's Vendors and Purchasers [1837] [A publication] (DLA) .... Mort Vend
Morton's Vendors and Purchasers [1837] [A publication] (DLA) .... MV & P
Mortuary (ADA) .... MORT
Mortuary .... MRTRY
Mortuary Affairs [Army] (INF) .... MA
Mortuary Affairs Collection Point [Army] (INF) .... MACP
Mortuus sine Prole [Dead without Issue] [Latin] (WGA) .... msp
Moruya [Australia Airport identifier] (OAG) .... MYA
Morzen Mortar Fire Data Computer [Military British] (INF) .... MFDC
MOS Implementation Service (NITA) .... MOSIS
MOS [Military Occupational Specialty] Medical Retention Board [Army] .... MMRB
MOS [Military Occupational Specialty] Proficiency Training [DoD] .... MPT
MOS Timing Simulator Software (NITA) .... MOTIS
MOS [Military Occupation Specialty] Training Plan .... MTP
Mosaic .... MOS

Mosaic (VRA) ... mos
Mosaic ... MOSC
Mosaic Resources Ltd. [*Vancouver Stock Exchange symbol*] ... MAC
Mosaic Sensor Program (MCD) ... MSP
Mosbach-Lohrbach [*Germany ICAO location identifier*] (ICLI) ... EDGM
Mosca [*Moscow*] [*Italian*] (AD) ... Mos
Mosca Public Library, Mosca, CO [*Library symbol Library of Congress*] (LCLS) ... CoMos
Moscavia [*Former USSR*] [*FAA designator*] (FAAC) ... MAV
Moschus [*Musk*] [*Pharmacology*] (ROG) ... MOSCH
Moscom Corp. [*Associated Press*] (SAG) ... Moscom
MOSCOM Corp. [*NASDAQ symbol*] (NQ) ... MSCM
Moscou [*Moscow*] [*French*] (AD) ... Mos
Moscovici (AD) ... Mosk
Moscow [*Former USSR Airport symbol*] ... DME
Moscow [*Russia*] [*Seismograph station code, US Geological Survey*] (SEIS) ... MOS
Moscow (AD) ... Mos
Moscow [*Former USSR Airport symbol*] (OAG) ... MOW
Moscow Airways [*Russian Federation*] [*ICAO designator*] (FAAC) ... MSC
Moscow Basin (AD) ... Mosbas
Moscow, Camden & San Augustine Railroad [*AAR code*] ... MCSA
Moscow City Relay Network ... MCRN
Moscow Classical Ballet ... MCB
Moscow Commodity Exchange [*Russian Federation*] (EY) ... MCE
Moscow Domodedovo Airport [*Former USSR Airport symbol*] (OAG) ... DME
Moscow Exchange of Building Materials [*Russian Federation*] (EY) ... ALISA
Moscow High School, Moscow, ID [*Library symbol*] [*Library of Congress*] (LCLS) ... IdMHS
Moscow, ID [*FM radio station call letters*] ... KRFA
Moscow, ID [*AM radio station call letters*] ... KRPL
Moscow, ID [*Television station call letters*] ... KUID
Moscow, ID [*FM radio station call letters*] ... KUOI
Moscow, ID [*FM radio station call letters*] ... KZFN
Moscow Junior High School, Moscow, ID [*Library symbol*] [*Library of Congress*] (LCLS) ... IdMJH
Moscow Link (AD) ... Molink
Moscow Narodny Bank Ltd. [*Former USSR*] ... MNB
Moscow Sheremetyevo Airport [*Former USSR Airport symbol*] (OAG) ... SVO
Moscow Vnukovo Airport [*Former USSR Airport symbol*] (OAG) ... VKO
Moscow/Washington Emergency Communications Link (MCD) ... MOLINK
Moscowitz (AD) ... Mosk
Moscow-Latah County District Library, Deary Branch, Deary, ID [*Library symbol*] [*Library of Congress*] (LCLS) ... IdMC-D
Moscow-Latah County District Library, Genesee Branch, Genesee, ID [*Library symbol*] [*Library of Congress*] (LCLS) ... IdMC-G
Moscow-Latah County District Library, Juliaetta Branch, Juliaetta, ID [*Library symbol*] [*Library of Congress*] (LCLS) ... IdMC-J
Moscow-Latah County District Library, Potlatch Branch, Potlatch, ID [*Library symbol*] [*Library of Congress*] (LCLS) ... IdMC-P
Moscow-Latah County District Library, Troy Branch, Troy, ID [*Library symbol*] [*Library of Congress*] (LCLS) ... IdMC-T
Moscow-Latah County Library System, Moscow, ID [*Library symbol*] [*Library of Congress*] (LCLS) ... IdMC
Moscu [*Moscow*] [*Spanish*] (AD) ... Mos
Moseley (AD) ... Mose
Moseley's Contraband of War [*1861*] [*A publication*] (DLA) ... Mos Cont
Moseley's Elementary Law [*2nd ed.*] [*1878*] [*A publication*] (DLA) ... Mos El L
Moseley's English Chancery Reports [*25 English Reprint*] [*A publication*] (DLA) ... Mos
Moseley's English Chancery Reports [*25 English Reprint*] [*A publication*] (DLA) ... Moseley
Moseley's English Chancery Reports [*25 English Reprint*] [*A publication*] (DLA) ... Mosely (Eng)
Moseley's English Chancery Reports Tempore King [*A publication*] (DLA) ... Cas T K
Moseley's English Chancery Reports Tempore King [*A publication*] (DLA) ... Cas T King
Mosella [*of Ausonius*] [*Classical studies*] (OCD) ... Mos
Mosen (AD) ... Mose
Moser Bay [*Alaska*] [*Airport symbol*] (OAG) ... KMY
Moses (AD) ... Mose
Moses H. Cone Memorial Hospital, Medical Library, Greensboro, NC [*Library symbol Library of Congress*] (LCLS) ... NcGH
Moses Lake [*Washington*] [*Airport symbol*] (OAG) ... MWH
Moses Lake Flight Center [*Washington*] (SAA) ... MLFC
Moses Lake Public Library, Moses Lake, WA [*Library symbol Library of Congress*] (LCLS) ... WaMl
Moses Lake, WA [*AM radio station call letters*] ... KBSN
Moses Lake, WA [*FM radio station call letters*] ... KDRM
Moses Lake, WA [*FM radio station call letters*] (RBYB) ... KMLW
Moses Lake, WA [*AM radio station call letters*] ... KWIQ
Moses Lake, WA [*FM radio station call letters*] ... KWIQ-FM
Moses Maimonides [*Spanish Talmudist, 1135-1204*] (BJA) ... Maim
Moses on the Law of Mandamus [*A publication*] (DLA) ... Mos Man
Moses Point, AK [*Location identifier FAA*] (FAAL) ... MOS
Moses Point, AK [*Location identifier FAA*] (FAAL) ... OAY
Mosetse [*Botswana*] [*ICAO location identifier*] (ICLI) ... FBMS
Moshassuck Valley Railroad Co. [*AAR code*] ... MOV
Moshav [*or Moshava*] (BJA) ... Mosh
Moshe (AD) ... Mos
Moshi [*Tanzania*] [*ICAO location identifier*] (ICLI) ... HTMS
Moshi [*Tanzania*] [*Airport symbol*] (AD) ... MSI
Mosinee Paper [*NASDAQ symbol*] (TTSB) ... MOSI
Mosinee Paper Co. [*Associated Press*] (SAG) ... Mosine
Mosinee Paper Corp. [*NASDAQ symbol*] (NQ) ... MOSI
Mosinee, WI [*Location identifier FAA*] (FAAL) ... CWA
Mosinee, WI [*FM radio station call letters*] ... WOFM
Mosjoen/Kjaerstad [*Norway ICAO location identifier*] (ICLI) ... ENMS
Moskau [*Moscow*] [*German*] (AD) ... Mos
Moskou [*Moscow*] [*Dutch*] (AD) ... Mos
Moskovskiy Gosudarstvenniy Universitet [*Moscow State University*] [*Former USSR*] (MSC) ... MGU
Moskovsky Akademichesky Khoreografichesky Uchilishche ... MAKHU
Moskowitz (AD) ... Mosk
Moskva [*Former USSR ICAO location identifier*] (ICLI) ... UUUM
Moskva [*Former USSR ICAO location identifier*] (ICLI) ... UUUU
Moskva/Sheremetyevo [*Former USSR ICAO location identifier*] (ICLI) ... UUEE
Moskva/Vnukovo [*Former USSR ICAO location identifier*] (ICLI) ... UUWW
Moslem (AD) ... Mos
Moslem Democratic Party [*Philippines*] [*Political party*] (PPW) ... MDP
Moslem Electoral Lobby [*Australia*] ... MEL
Moslem Meal [*Airline notation*] (ADA) ... MOML
Moslem Meal (AD) ... Moml
Moslem Mosque (EA) ... MM
Moslem People's Republican Party [*Iran*] [*Political party*] (PPW) ... MPRP
Moslem People's Revolutionary Movement [*Iran*] [*Political party*] (PPW) ... JAMA
Mosler Information Storage and Retrieval System (MCD) ... MISR
Mosport Park Corp. [*Vancouver Stock Exchange symbol*] ... MOS
Mosque (AD) ... Mq
Mosque (BARN) ... mq
Mosquito Abatement District (DICI) ... MAD
[*The*] **Mosquito Association** (EA) ... TMA
Mosquito Biting Activity Index [*Canada*] ... MBAI
Mosquito Construction Gold [*Vancouver Stock Exchange symbol*] ... MSQ
Mosquito Conversion Unit [*British military*] (DMA) ... MCU
Mosquito Creek Gold Mining [*Vancouver Stock Exchange symbol*] ... MQO
Mosquito Data Bank of the University of Notre Dame ... MODABUND
Mosquito Training Unit [*British military*] (DMA) ... MTU
Moss Adams Information Center, Seattle, WA [*Library symbol*] [*Library of Congress*] (LCLS) ... WaSMA
Moss Landing Marine Laboratories [*San Jose State University*] [*Research center*] (RCD) ... MLML
Moss Landing Marine Laboratory, Moss Landing, CA [*Library symbol Library of Congress*] (LCLS) ... CMosM
Moss Memorial Library, Hayesville, NC [*Library symbol Library of Congress*] (LCLS) ... NcHay
Moss Point, MS [*FM radio station call letters*] (RBYB) ... WYOK
Moss Resources Ltd. [*Vancouver Stock Exchange symbol*] ... MSO
Mossamedes [*Angola*] [*Airport symbol*] (OAG) ... MSZ
Mossel Bay/Baai [*South Africa*] [*ICAO location identifier*] (ICLI) ... FAMO
Mossendjo [*Congo*] [*ICAO location identifier*] (ICLI) ... FCMM
Mossendjo [*Congo*] [*Airport symbol*] (OAG) ... MSX
Mossi [*MARC language code Library of Congress*] (LCCP) ... mos
Mossimo, Inc. [*NYSE symbol*] (SAG) ... MGX
Mossimo Inc. [*NYSE symbol*] (TTSB) ... MGX
Mossimo, Inc. [*Associated Press*] (SAG) ... Mossimo
Mossine Nagant Rifle ... MOSNAG
Mossoro [*Brazil*] [*Airport symbol*] (AD) ... MSD
Mossy Fiber [*Neuroanatomy*] ... MF
Most (WGA) ... MT
Most Advanced, Yet Acceptable [*Industrial design*] ... MAYA
Most Comfortable Level [*Referring to sound level*] [*Otorhinolaryngology*] (DAVI) ... MCL
Most Comfortable Loudness Level [*On audiometry*] [*Otorhinolaryngology*] (DAVI) ... MCLL
Most Comfortable Loudness Test [*Audiometry*] ... MCL
Most Demands to Be Traded [*Baseball*] ... MDT
Most Dispensable Program [*Television*] ... MDP
Most Distal Leaf [*Botany*] ... DL
Most Economical Rating ... MER
Most Economical Route Selection [*Also, ARS*] [*Bell System*] [*Telecommunications*] ... MERS
Most Efficient/Effective Method [*DoD*] ... MEM
Most Efficient/Effective Organization [*DoD*] ... MEO
Most Eminent [*Freemasonry*] (ROG) ... ME
Most Eminent Grand Master [*Freemasonry*] (ROG) ... MEGM
Most Excellent [*In titles*] ... ME
Most Excellent Companion [*Freemasonry*] (ROG) ... MEC
Most Excellent Grand High Priest [*Freemasonry*] ... MEGHP
Most Excellent Master [*Freemasonry*] ... MEM
Most Exposed Individual [*Environmental science*] (FFDE) ... MEI
Most High [*Freemasonry*] ... MH
Most Honorable ... MH
Most Important Person ... MIP
Most in Need Population ... MIN
Most Input for the Least Output [*Business term*] ... MILO
Most Probable Cost (AAGC) ... MPC
Most Probable Library User ... MPLU
Most Probable Number ... MPN
Most Probable Number (AD) ... mpn
Most Probable Position (AD) ... mpp
Most Probable Position [*Navigation*] ... MPP
Most Probable Total Contract Cost (AAGC) ... MPTCC
Most Puissant Sovereign Grand Commander [*United States*] [*Freemasonry*] (ROG) ... MP SOV GR COM
Most Recent Common Ancestor ... MRCA
Most Recently Used [*Computer science*] ... MRU
Most Recently Used Data [*Computer science*] (PCM) ... MRU
Most Recently Used Master [*Computer science*] ... MRM
Most Reverend ... M REV

Most Reverend (ROG) .... MT REVD
Most Seriously Affected [*Food-deficient nations*] .... MSA
Most Severe [*Automotive engineering*] .... MS
Most Significant .... MS
Most Significant (IAA) .... MSIG
Most Significant BIT [*Binary Digit*] [*Computer science*] .... MSB
Most Significant Byte [*Computer science*] .... MSBY
Most Significant Character [*Computer science*] (MDG) .... MSC
Most Significant Decade (IAA) .... MSD
Most Significant Digit [*Computer science*] .... MSD
Most Significant Position (CMD) .... MSP
Most Valuable Girl .... MVG
Most Valuable Player [*Athletics*] [*Facetious translation: "Most Volatile Player"*] .... MVP
Most Valuable Princess [*Princess Diana*] [*British Slang*] .... MVP
Most Valuable Product (PCM) .... MVP
Most Valued Supplier [*Mazda Motor Corp.*] .... MVS
Most Wise Sovereign [*Freemasonry*] .... MWS
Most Worshipful [*Freemasonry*] .... MW
Most Worshipful [*or Worthy*] **Grand Master** [*Freemasonry*] .... MWGM
Most Worshipful Scribe [*Freemasonry*] (ROG) .... MWS
Most Worthy .... MW
Most Worthy Grand Chief Patriarch .... MWGCP
Most Worthy Patriarch .... MWP
Mostar [*Former Yugoslavia*] [*ICAO location identifier*] (ICLI) .... LYMO
Mostar [*Yugoslavia*] [*Seismograph station code, US Geological Survey Closed*] (SEIS) .... MST
Mostar [*Yugoslavia*] [*Airport symbol*] (AD) .... OMO
Mosteiros [*Cape Verde Islands*] [*Airport symbol*] (OAG) .... MTI
Mosteiros, Fogo Island [*Cape Verde*] [*ICAO location identifier*] (ICLI) .... GVMT
Mostek Corporation (NITA) .... MSK
Mostellaria [*of Plautus*] [*Classical studies*] (OCD) .... Mostell
Most-Favorable Term (MHDW) .... MFT
Most-Favored Customer (AAGC) .... MFC
Most-Favored-Nation [*Trading status*] .... MFN
Mostly (MSA) .... MSLY
Mostly [*NWS*] (FAAC) .... MSTLY
Mostly Verbatim [*FAR clauses*] (AAGC) .... MV
Mosul [*Iraq*] [*ICAO location identifier*] (ICLI) .... ORBM
Mosul [*Iraq*] [*Airport symbol*] (AD) .... OSM
Mot a Mot [*Word for Word*] [*French*] .... MAM
Mota [*Ethiopia*] [*Airport symbol*] (AD) .... OTA
Mota Lava [*Vanuatu*] [*Airport symbol*] (OAG) .... MTV
Mote Marine Laboratory (NOAA) .... MML
Motel .... M
Motel .... MTL
Motel Association of America [*Later, National Innkeeping Association*] .... MAA
Motel Brokers Association of America [*Later, AHMB*] (EA) .... MBAA
Moth Eaten (AD) .... mo
Mother .... M
Mother .... MO
Mother (AD) .... moth
Mother (AD) .... Mr
Mother .... MTHR
Mother .... MTHR
Mother and Baby Care [*Red Cross Nursing Services*] .... MBC
Mother and Child International [*Switzerland*] (EAIO) .... MCI
Mother and Father .... M & F
Mother/Daughter [*Apartment*] (BARN) .... M/D
Mother Earth News, Hendersonville, NC [*Library symbol Library of Congress*] (LCLS) .... NcHvME
Mother, Father, Sister, Brother [*Musical group*] .... MFSB
Mother Fooler [*Bowdlerized version*] .... MF
Mother Guardian Allowance .... MGA
Mother Jones [*A publication*] (BRI) .... Moth Jones
Mother of Pearl (AD) .... mop
Mother of the Chapel [*Unions*] [*British*] (DI) .... MOC
Mother Symptom Inventory [*Psychology*] .... MSI
Mother Tongue and English Teaching (AIE) .... MOTET
Mother Tongue Project (AIE) .... MTP
Mother Whiteside Memorial Library, Grants, NM [*Library symbol Library of Congress*] (LCLS) .... NmGr
Motherboard (MSA) .... MTHBD
Mother-Child Relationship [*Psychology*] .... MCR
Mother-Child Relationship Evaluation [*Psychology*] .... MCRE
Mothercraft Certificate [*British*] (ADA) .... MC
Mother-Daughter Ionosphere Experiment .... MDIE
Mothering Quotient .... MQ
Mother-in-Law (AD) .... moth-in-law
Motherland Party [*Anatavan Partisi*] [*Turkey Political party*] (PPW) .... MP
Mother-of-Pearl .... MOP
Mother-of-Pearl (VRA) .... moprl
Mother-of-Pearl Clouds [*Meteorology*] (PDAA) .... MPC
Mothers Against Drunk Driving (EA) .... MADD
Mother's Aide [*Red Cross Nursing Services*] .... MA
Mothers and Midwives Action [*Australia An association*] .... MMA
Mothers Apart from Their Children [*British*] (DI) .... MATCH
Mothers Are People Too [*Defunct*] (EA) .... MAPT
Mothers at Home [*An association*] (PAZ) .... MAH
Mother's Breast Milk [*Neonatology*] (DAVI) .... MBM
Mother's Day Council (EA) .... MDC
Mothers Embracing Nuclear Disarmament [*An association*] (EA) .... MEND
Mothers for Decency in Action [*Group opposing sex education in schools*] .... MDA
Mothers for Moral Stability [*Group opposing sex education in schools*] .... MOMS
Mothers for Peace - UK (EAIO) .... MFP-UK
Mother's Grandmother (MAE) .... MGM
Mothers' Home Business Network (EA) .... MHBN
Mothers in Prison Projects (EA) .... MPP
Mothers Matter [*Commercial firm*] (EA) .... MM
Mothers of AIDS [*Acquired Immune Deficiency Syndrome*] **Patients** (EA) .... MAP
Mothers of Asthmatics (EA) .... MA
Mothers of Men in Service [*World War II*] .... MOMS
Mothers of Preschoolers International (PAZ) .... MOPS
Mothers of Sons in Service [*World War II*] .... MOSS
Mothers of Super Twins [*Military*] .... MOST
Mothers of the Helpless (TOCD) .... MD
Mothers of World War II .... MWWII
Mothers of Young Mongoloids [*Later, PODSC*] (EA) .... MYMS
Mother's Restaurants Ltd. [*Toronto Stock Exchange symbol*] .... MOM
Mothers Return to School .... MRS
Mothers' Sensory Developmental Expectation Questionnaire [*Occupational therapy*] .... MSDEQ
Mothers' Union [*Episcopalian*] .... MU
Mothers' Union in Australia .... MUA
Mothers United for Moral Support .... MUMS
Mothers without Custody (EA) .... MWOC
Mothers Work [*NASDAQ symbol*] (TTSB) .... MWRK
Mothers Work, Inc. [*Associated Press*] (SAG) .... MothrWk
Mothers Work, Inc. [*NASDAQ symbol*] (SAG) .... MWRK
Mothers-in-Law Club International (EA) .... MIL
Motherwell [*Postcode*] (ODBW) .... ML
Motherwell [*Scotland*] .... MTHWL
Motiers [*Switzerland ICAO location identifier*] (ICLI) .... LSTO
Motif .... MTF
Motile [*Sperm*] (MAE) .... m
Motile Sperm .... MS
Motilin [*Biochemistry*] .... MT
Motility Index [*Of intestine*] [*Gastroenterology*] .... MI
Motility Indol Ornithine [*Medium*] [*Medicine*] (BABM) .... MIO
Motility Indol Ornithine [*Medium*] [*Microbiology*] (DAVI) .... MIO
Motility Nitrate [*Medium*] [*Microbiology*] (DAVI) .... M-N
Motility Nitrate [*Medium*] [*Medicine*] (BABM) .... M-N
Motion .... MOT
Motion .... MOTN
Motion (MSA) .... MTN
Motion Aftereffect .... MAE
Motion Analysis Camera .... MAC
Motion Base Crew Station [*NASA*] (NASA) .... MBCS
Motion Base Simulator (MCD) .... MBS
Motion Compensation - Coherent on Receive .... MCCOR
Motion Detection Radar [*Hughes Electronics*] .... MDR
Motion Detection Unit [*Nuclear energy*] (NRCH) .... MDU
Motion Detector and Alarm [*Army*] .... MODA
Motion for a Finding of Not Guilty .... MFNG
Motion for Mandamus Granted [*Legal term*] (ILCA) .... MG
Motion for Mandamus Overruled [*Legal term*] (DLA) .... MO
Motion Icon [*Computer science*] (WDMC) .... micon
Motion Indicating RADAR (MCD) .... MIDAR
Motion Picture [*Army*] (AABC) .... MOPIC
Motion Picture [*Military*] (WDMC) .... mopic
Motion Picture .... MOTPICT
Motion Picture (NTCM) .... MP
Motion Picture (AD) .... mp
Motion Picture Alliance .... MPA
Motion Picture and Television Credit Association (EA) .... MPTCA
Motion Picture and Television Credit Managers Association [*Later, MPTCA*] (EA) .... MPTCMA
Motion Picture and Television Fund .... MP & TF
Motion Picture and Television Fund (EA) .... MPTF
Motion Picture Association of America (EA) .... MPAA
Motion Picture Association of America, Inc., Research Department Library, New York, NY [*Library symbol Library of Congress*] (LCLS) .... NNMP
Motion Picture Camera (MCD) .... MPC
Motion Picture Control Panel (MSA) .... MPC
Motion Picture Distributors Association (AD) .... MPDA
Motion Picture Distributors Association (NADA) .... MPDA
Motion Picture Distributors' Association of Australia .... MPDAA
Motion Picture Exhibitors Association (AD) .... MPEA
Motion Picture Experts Group .... MPEG
Motion Picture Experts Group [*Computer science*] .... mpeg
Motion Picture Export Association of America (EA) .... MPEAA
Motion Picture Film Editors [*Defunct*] (EA) .... MPFE
Motion Picture Industry Controllers (EA) .... MPIC
Motion Picture Industry Council (EA) .... MPIC
Motion Picture Institute of Canada .... MPIC
Motion Picture Laboratories [*Commercial firm*] .... MPL
Motion Picture Machine Operator [*A union*] (NTCM) .... MPMO
Motion Picture Museum Association [*British*] (BI) .... MPMA
Motion Picture Operator .... MPO
Motion Picture Phonographic Unit .... MPPH
Motion Picture Pioneers (EA) .... MPP
Motion Picture Production [*Navy*] .... MP
Motion Picture Projector (MSA) .... MPP
Motion Picture Relief Fund [*Later, MPTF*] (EA) .... MPRF
Motion Picture Research Council .... MPRC
Motion Picture Service [*Department of Agriculture*] .... MPS
Motion Picture Sound Editors (EA) .... MPSE
Motion Pictures .... MOPIX
Motion Reference Unit (MCD) .... MRU
Motion Sensitivity (KSC) .... MS

Motion Sickness Susceptibility (MCD)	MSS
Motion to Quash Subpoena (NRCH)	MQS
Motional Feedback	MFB
Motional Pickup Transducer (MCD)	MPT
Motion-Picture Film (AD)	mpf
Motion-Time Analysis	MTA
Motion-Time Standards [Industrial engineering]	MTS
Motivated Productivity Level [Quality control]	MPL
Motivation Analysis Test [Psychology]	MAT
Motivation and Potential for Adoptive Parenthood Scale [Psychology]	MPAPS
Motivation and Training Laboratory [Army] (RDA)	MTL
Motivation by Rotation	MBR
Motivation Indoctrination Program [Military]	MIP
Motivation Research	MR
Motivational Ability	M
Motivational Research (AD)	mr
Motivational Research (AD)	mr
Motivational Research [Psychology] (WDMC)	MARI
Motivator and Response Indicator	mp & rs
Motive Power and Rolling Stock (AD)	MCFC
Motley Crue Fan Club (EA)	
Motley School, Motley, MN [Library symbol] [Library of Congress] (LCLS)	MnMotS
Motne-Centre, Offenbach [Germany ICAO location identifier] (ICLI)	EDZO
Moto Club of Amer [NASDAQ symbol] (TTSB)	MOTR
Moto Morini Club of North America (EA)	MMCNA
Moto Morini Club of North America (EA)	MMNA
Moto Nave [Motor ship] [Latin] (IIA)	MN
Moto Photo [NQS] (TTSB)	MOTO
Moto Photo, Inc. [NASDAQ symbol] (NQ)	MOTO
Moto Photo, Inc. [Associated Press] (SAG)	MotoPh
Motocross (WGA)	MX
Motor	M
Motor (AAG)	MOT
Motor (AD)	mot
Motor	MOT
Motor	MTR
Motor (AABC)	MTR
Motor	MTR
Motor Accidents (Compensation) Appeal Tribunal [Northern Territory, Australia]	MA(C)AT
Motor Accidents Insurance Board [Tasmania, Australia]	MAIB
Motor Agents' Association [British]	MAA
Motor Ambulance Convoy	MAC
Motor Ambulance Trolley [British]	MAT
Motor Ambulance Van [British]	MAV
Motor and Equipment Manufacturers Association (EA)	MEMA
Motor and Equipment Manufacturers Association's Technical Training Council	MEMA/TTC
Motor and Equipment Wholesalers Association [Later, ASIA]	MEWA
Motor Antisubmarine Boat [Obsolete British]	MA/SB
Motor Assembly and Disassembly	MAD
Motor Barge (ADA)	MB
Motor Behavior Screening Test [Physical education]	MBST
Motor Belt Drive (MSA)	MBD
Motor Boat	MB
Motor Boat Subchaser [Navy symbol Obsolete]	PTC
Motor Burning Time	MBT
Motor Burnout (AABC)	MBO
Motor Burnout Locking (AABC)	MBOL
Motor Bus Society (EA)	MBS
Motor Cab Owner Drivers' Association [British] (BI)	MCODA
Motor Camp (AD)	mocamp
Motor Can	MOCAN
Motor Car (IAA)	MC
Motor Car Collectors of America (EA)	MCCA
Motor Car Traders' Licensing Authority [Victoria, Australia]	MCTLA
Motor Cargo Boat	MCB
Motor Cargo Boat (Large) [Coast Guard] (DNAB)	MCBL
Motor Carrier	MC
Motor Carrier Cases [ICC]	MCC
Motor Carrier Lawyers Association (EA)	MCLA
Motor Carrier Management Information System [BTS] [MM] (TAG)	MCMIS
Motor Carrier Rate Bureau	MCRB
Motor Carrier Regulation Information System [BTS] (TAG)	MCREGIS
Motor Carrier Safety Act of 1984 [FHWA] (TAG)	MCSA
Motor Carrier Safety Assistance Program [Department of Transportation]	MCSAP
Motor Carrier Safety Regulations [Department of Transportation]	MCSR
Motor Carriers Service Bureau	MCSB
Motor Carriers Service Tariff Bureau	MCSTB
Motor Carriers Tariff Association	MCTA
Motor Carriers Tariff Bureau (EA)	MCTB
Motor Carriers Tariff Bureau Inc., Cleveland OH [STAC]	MCB
Motor Carriers Tariff Service (EA)	MCTS
Motor Carriers Traffic Association	MCTA
Motor Carriers Traffic Association Inc., Greensboro NC [STAC]	MCA
Motor Chain	MC
Motor Circuit Switch	MCS
Motor Circuit Switch (MSA)	MCSW
Motor City Five [Rock music group]	MC5
Motor Club of America [Associated Press] (SAG)	MotClb
Motor Club of America [NASDAQ symbol] (NQ)	MOTR
Motor Coaches [Public-performance tariff class] [British]	MC
Motor Contact (WGA)	MC
Motor Control Assembly (MCD)	MCA
Motor Control Center	MCC
Motor Control Center [NASA]	MCC
Motor Converter (IAA)	MC
Motor Coordination [Neurology and orthopedics] (DAVI)	K
Motor Cortex [Neuroanatomy]	MC
Motor Cycle Club [British]	MCC
Motor Cycle Industry Association of Great Britain (EAIO)	MCA
Motor Dealers' Council [New South Wales, Australia]	MDC
Motor Dealers' Disputes Council [Australia]	MDDC
Motor Direct	MD
Motor Direct-Connected	MDC
Motor Discriminative Acuity [Psychology]	MDA
Motor Distal Latency [Medicine]	MDL
Motor Drive	MD
Motor Drive Amplifier	MDA
Motor Drive Cassette Support Unit	MD/CSU
Motor Driver [British military] (DMA)	MT
Motor Elevator [Mechanical lifting stand for arc lamps]	MOLEVATOR
Motor End Plate	MEP
Motor End Support	MES
Motor Explosive Boat [British military] (DMA)	MExB
Motor Factors Association [British] (BI)	MFA
Motor Field	MF
Motor Fishing Vessel [British military] (DMA)	MFV
Motor Freight	MF
Motor Freight Controller [National Accounting and Finance Council] [A publication]	MFC
Motor Freight Line	MFL
Motor Freight Tariff [Business term] (ADA)	MFT
Motor Freight Tariff Bureau	MFTB
Motor Freight Tariff Bureau, Springfield IL [STAC]	MFB
Motor Freight Terminal	MFT
Motor Fuel Licensing Board [Australia]	MFLB
Motor Gasoline [Military]	MGAS
Motor Gasoline [Military]	MOGAS
Motor Gasoline (AD)	mogas
Motor Gasoline [Military]	MOTOGAS
Motor Generator	MG
Motor Generator Set (CAAL)	MGS
Motor Glider Instructor Rating [Aviation] (DA)	MGIR
Motor Glider Private Pilot's Licence [British] (AIA)	MGPPL
Motor Gunboat [British]	MGB
Motor, Hearse, and Car Owners Association (EA)	MHCOA
Motor Hotel	MOTEL
Motor Impeller Unit	MIU
Motor Industry Development Program	MIDP
Motor Industry Research Association [British] (DCTA)	MIRA
Motor Inert Storage	MIS
Motor Inn, Motel and Accommodation Association [Australia]	MIMAA
Motor Inspection Building	MIB
Motor Insurance Anti-Fraud and Theft Register [Database] [British]	MIAFTR
Motor Insurance Repair Research Centre [British] (CB)	MIRRC
Motor Insurers' Bureau Ltd. [British] (ILCA)	MIB
Motor Launch	ML
Motor Launch, Auxiliary [NATO]	MLA
Motor Launch, Cabin	MLC
Motor Launch, Double Shelter	MLDS
Motor Launch, Fast [NATO]	MLF
Motor Lifeboat	MLB
Motor Load Control	MLC
Motor Machine Gun Battalion [British military] (DMA)	MMGB
Motor Machine Gun Corps [British military] (DMA)	MMG
Motor Machine Gun Service [British military] (DMA)	MMGS
Motor Machinist's Mate [Navy rating]	MOMM
Motor Machinist's Mate, Ship Repair [Navy rating]	MOMMSR
Motor Machinist's Mate, Ship Repair, Diesel Engineering Mechanic [Navy rating]	MOSRD
Motor Machinist's Mate, Ship Repair, Gasoline Engine Mechanic [Navy rating]	MOSRG
Motor Magnet	MM
Motor Maintenance [Army]	MM
Motor Maintenance Aptitude Area [Army]	MM
Motor Maintenance Company (DNAB)	MTMAINTCO
Motor Meal [Medicine] (MEDA)	MM
Motor Mechanic [British military] (DMA)	MM
Motor Mine Planter [Navy symbol]	YMP
Motor Minesweeper [Navy symbol Obsolete]	AMS
Motor Minesweeper	MMS
Motor Movement Latency	MML
Motor Nerve Conduction Velocity [Medicine]	MNCV
Motor Network Calculator	MONECA
Motor Neuron [Anatomy]	MN
Motor Neuron Disease [Medicine]	MND
Motor Neurone Disease Association [British] (DBA)	MNDA
Motor Neurone Disease Association of Western Australia	MNDAWA
Motor Neurone Society of Queensland [Australia]	MNSQ
Motor Neurone Society of South Australia	MNSSA
Motor Neurone Society of Tasmania [Australia]	MNST
Motor Neurone Society of Victoria [Australia]	MNSV
Motor Octane Number [Fuel technology]	MON
Motor Octane Number (AD)	mon
Motor Oil	MOIL
Motor Operated (MSA)	MO
Motor Operated (AD)	mo
Motor Operated (AD)	mot op

Motor Operated [*Freight*]	MTR OP
Motor Operating Time	MOT
Motor Optimization Design Evaluation Code (MCD)	MODEC
Motor, Pain, Touch, Reflex [*Neurology*] (DAVI)	MPTR
Motor Parts [*Chrysler Corp.*]	MOPAR
Motor Parts Stock (AD)	mps
Motor Patrol Boat [*Navy symbol Obsolete*]	SP
Motor/Pedal [*Motorized bicycle*]	MOPED
Motor Potential	MP
Motor Pressurization Unit	MPU
Motor Pump System (MCD)	MPS
Motor Qualification Program (NG)	MQP
Motor Qualification Test (NG)	MQT
Motor Racing Club (AD)	MRC
Motor Racing Club (NADA)	MRC
Motor Racing Developments	MRD
Motor Racing Network	MRN
Motor Racing Publications [*Publisher*] [*British*]	MRP
Motor Receiving Dolly	MRD
Motor Reduction	MR
Motor Refrigeration Lighter (ADA)	MRL
Motor Refrigerator Lighter (AD)	mrl
Motor Repair Insurance (AD)	MRI
Motor Rescue Boat	MRB
Motor Rotation Stand	MRS
Motor Routing Order	MRO
Motor Safe and Arm Device	MSAD
Motor Schools' Association of Great Britain (BI)	MSA
Motor Ship	MS
Motor Short-Circuit Protector (IAA)	MSCP
Motor Sich [*Ukraine*] [*FAA designator*] (FAAC)	MSI
Motor Skills Inventory [*Sensorimotor skills test*]	MSI
Motor Speed Changer (IAA)	MSC
Motor Speed Control	MSC
Motor Starting (IAA)	MS
Motor Starting Contractor	MSC
Motor Storage Dolly	MSD
Motor Submersible Canoe [*British Marines' Special Forces*] [*World War II*]	MSC
Motor Supports	MS
Motor Surfboat [*Coast Guard*] (DNAB)	MRB
Motor Surfboat	MSB
Motor Surveillance Service [*MTMC*] (TAG)	MSS
Motor Tanker	MT
Motor Tariff Bureau, Charleston WV [*STAC*]	MTB
Motor Tariff Bureau of West Virginia, Charleston WV [*STAC*]	MWV
Motor Tariff Service	MTS
Motor Terminal (IAA)	MT
Motor Test Vehicle (IAA)	MTV
Motor Threshold [*Medicine*]	MT
Motor Torpedo Boat	MTB
Motor Torpedo Boat [*Navy symbol Obsolete*]	PT
Motor Torpedo Boat Squadron [*Navy*]	MTBRON
Motor Torpedo Boat Squadrons Training Center [*Melville, RI*] [*Navy*]	MTBSTC
Motor Torpedo Boat Tender [*Navy symbol Obsolete*]	AGP
Motor Torpedo Vessel [*British*]	MTV
Motor Trade Association (NADA)	MTA
Motor Trade Association of South Australia	MTASA
Motor Trade Association of Western Australia	MTAWA
Motor Trades Association of New South Wales [*Australia*]	MTANSW
Motor Transport [*Military*]	MT
Motor Transport Corps [*Military*]	MTC
Motor Transport Officer [*Military*]	MTO
Motor Transport Volunteers [*Military unit*] [*British*]	MTV
Motor Transportation Battalion [*Military*]	MTBN
Motor Transportation Supervisor/Vehicle Operator (AAG)	MTS/VO
Motor Trend Magazine [*A publication*]	MT
Motor Truck, Bus, and Fire Engine Club [*Defunct*] (EA)	MTBFEC
Motor Truck Rate Bureau	MTRB
Motor Truck Rate Bureau Inc., Columbia SC [*STAC*]	MRB
Motor Tug [*Navy symbol*]	YMT
Motor Turbine Ship (IIA)	MTS
Motor Union	MU
Motor Unit	MU
Motor Unit Action Potential [*Physiology*]	MUAP
Motor Unit Potential	MUP
Motor V-Belt	MVB
Motor Vehicle (CDAI)	MV
Motor Vehicle Accident [*Medicine*] (AFM)	MVA
Motor Vehicle Air Pollution Control Act (GFGA)	MVAPCA
Motor Vehicle Allowance	MVA
Motor Vehicle Assembly [*Military World War II*]	MVA
Motor Vehicle Brake Fluid [*Automotive engineering*]	MVBF
Motor Vehicle Certification System	MVCS
Motor Vehicle Dealers Act	MVDA
Motor Vehicle Dealers' Licensing Board [*Western Australia*]	MVDLB
Motor Vehicle Department (DLA)	MVD
Motor Vehicle Distributing [*Military*]	MVD
Motor Vehicle Driver Selection Battery [*Army*]	MVD
Motor Vehicle Emission Laboratory [*Environmental Protection Agency*]	MVEL
Motor Vehicle Industry Joint Council [*British*] (DCTA)	MVIJC
Motor Vehicle Information and Cost Saving Act	MVICSA
Motor Vehicle Information and Cost Savings Act (EG)	MVICSA
Motor Vehicle Information Management System [*Bell System*]	MOVIMS
Motor Vehicle Inspection	MVI
Motor Vehicle Inspection/Maintenance (GFGA)	MVI/M

Motor Vehicle Maintenance Course	MVMC
Motor Vehicle Manufacturers Association (NADA)	MVMA
Motor Vehicle Manufacturers Association of the United States (EA)	MVMA
Motor Vehicle Mishap (DNAB)	MV
Motor Vehicle Plan Administration	MVPA
Motor Vehicle Pollution Control Board (NADA)	MVPCB
Motor Vehicle Post Crash Communications System (PDAA)	MVPCCS
Motor Vehicle Repair Disputes Committee [*New South Wales, Australia*]	MVRDC
Motor Vehicle Repair Industry Council [*New South Wales, Australia*]	MVRIC
Motor Vehicle Report	MVR
Motor Vehicle Safety Standard	MVSS
Motor Vehicle Storage Building	MVSB
Motor Vehicle Storage Shed [*Army*] (AABC)	MVSS
Motor Vehicle Theft Law Enforcement Act [*1984*]	MVTLEA
Motor Vehicle Title	MVT
Motor Vehicles Dismantlers Association [*British*] (BI)	MVDA
Motor Vessel	MV
Motor Vessel (ODBW)	mv
Motor Vessel Boat	MVB
Motor Voltage Drop (IAA)	MVD
Motor Volunteer Corps [*British military*] (DMA)	MVC
Motor Volunteers [*British military*] (DMA)	MV
Motor Wagon [*British*]	MW
Motor Water Lighter (ADA)	MWL
Motor Whale Boat	MWB
Motor Wheel and Flyer Club of America [*Defunct*] (EA)	MWFCA
Motor Yacht	MY
Motorboat Crew [*British military*] (DMA)	MBC
Motorcar Parts & Accesories, Inc. [*NASDAQ symbol*] (SAG)	MPAA
Motorcar Parts & Accessories [*NASDAQ symbol*] (TTSB)	MPAA
Motorcar Parts & Accessories, Inc. [*Associated Press*] (SAG)	MotrPrt
Motorcycle	MC
Motorcycle	MTCL
Motorcycle (AABC)	MTRCL
Motorcycle	MTRCYL
Motorcycle Accident (DAVI)	MCA
Motorcycle Action Group [*British*] (DBA)	MAG
Motorcycle and Allied Trades Association [*Later, MIC*] (EA)	MATA
Motorcycle Combination [*British*]	MCC
Motorcycle Cross (AD)	motorcross
Motorcycle Cross Country Race (AD)	motocross
Motorcycle Driver [*British military*] (DMA)	MC
Motorcycle Industry Association of Great Britain (EAIO)	MCI
Motorcycle Industry Association of South Australia	MIASA
Motorcycle Industry Council (EA)	MIC
Motorcycle Operator Skill Test	MOST
Motorcycle Retailers of America [*Later, NMRA*] (EA)	MRA
Motorcycle Safety Foundation (EA)	MSF
Motorcycle, Scooter, and Allied Trades Association [*Later, MIC*]	MSATA
Motorcycling Australia (Victoria) [*Australia An association*]	MA(V)
Motorcycling Doctors Association (EA)	MDA
Motorcyclist [*Army*]	Mtrclt
Motor-Driven	MTRDN
Motor-Driven Auxiliary Feedwater Pump (IEEE)	MDAFWP
Motor-Driven Emergency Feedwater Pump [*Nuclear energy*] (NRCH)	MDEFWP
Motor-Driven Relay [*or Roter*]	MDR
Motor-Evoked Potential (OA)	MEP
Motor-Free Test of Visual Perception [*Psychology*] (DAVI)	MFTVP
Motor-Free Visual Perception Test	MFVPT
Motor-Free Visual Perception Test	MVPT
Motor-Generator Flywheel (MCD)	MGF
Motorhome Travelers Association [*Defunct*] (EA)	MTA
Motorinen Turbo-Union [*Germany*]	MTU
Motoring Experience for the Disabled by Lions International [*British*]	MEDLI
Motoring in Miniature Association (EA)	MMA
Motoring Organisations Land Access and Rights Association [*British*] (DBA)	MOLARA
Motoring Press Association	MPA
Motorist Inclusive Tour [*British*] (DCTA)	MIT
Motorists Information, Inc. [*Defunct*] (EA)	MII
Motorists Information Services Association (EA)	MISA
Motorized	MOT
Motorized (AAG)	MTZ
Motorized Air Cycle Machine (MCD)	MACM
Motorized Antenna Switching Matrix	MASM
Motorized Bicycle Association [*Later, MAA*] (EA)	MBA
Motorized Flow Control	MFC
Motorized Microfilm Reader	MMR
Motorized Pedals (AD)	mopeds
Motorized Pontoon Bridge (MCD)	MPB
Motorized Rifle Battalion [*Former USSR*]	MRB
Motorized Rifle Co. (INF)	MRC
Motorized Rifle Division [*Former USSR*] (NATG)	MRD
Motorized Rifle Division [*Military*] (AD)	MRD
Motorized Rifle Regiment [*Former USSR*]	MRR
Motorized Set Point (IAA)	MSP
Motorized Skateboard (AD)	motoboard
Motorized Switching Matrix	MSM
Motorized Valve (KSC)	MV
Motorized-Vehicle Parade (AD)	motorcade
Motormannes Riksforbund [*Motorists' Association*] [*Swedish*] (AD)	MR
Motor-Motor Generator [*Nuclear energy*] (NRCH)	MMG
Motorola Aerial Remote Sensing [*Flying laboratory*]	MARS
Motorola Automatic Sequential Computer Operated Tester	MASCOT

Motorola Automatically Generated Integrated Circuits ... MAGIC
Motorola Communications Sector Library, Schaumburg, IL [*Library symbol*] [*Library of Congress*] (LCLS) ... ISbM
Motorola Complementary Metal-Oxide Semi-Conductor [*Electronics*] (IAA) ... MCMOS
Motorola Data Processor [*Computer science*] (IAA) ... MDP
Motorola Disk Operating System ... MDOS
Motorola Emitter-Coupled Logic (IEEE) ... MECL
Motorola Environmental Telemetry ... MET
Motorola High-Threshold Logic ... MHTL
Motorola, Inc. [*NYSE symbol*] (SPSG) ... MOT
Motorola, Inc. [*Associated Press*] (SAG) ... Motorola
Motorola, Inc., Semiconductor Products Division Library, Phoenix, AZ [*Library symbol Library of Congress*] (LCLS) ... AzPhMo
Motorola Interconnect [*Electronics*] ... MI
Motorola Processor Unit ... MPU
Motorola Transistor-Transistor Logic (IAA) ... MTTL
Motor-Operated Disconnect [*Nuclear energy*] (NRCH) ... MOD
Motor-Operated Sled Ejection System (MCD) ... MOSES
Motor-Operated Transfer Switch ... MTS
Motor-Operated Valve (NRCH) ... MOV
Motorship (DS) ... M
Motorskib [*Motorship*] [*Norwegian*] (AD) ... m/s
Motorsport Advanced Display [*Auto racing*] ... MAD
Motorsports Marketing Association [*Langhorne, PA*] [*Defunct*] (EA) ... MMA
Motorsports Technology Group [*General Motors Corp.*] ... MTG
Motorsteuerelectronik ... MSE
Motorsteuermonolith ... MSM
Motor-Switching Unit (MCD) ... MSU
Motor-Torque Generator ... MTG
MotorVac Technologies [*NASDAQ symbol*] (TTSB) ... MVAC
MotorVac Technologies, Inc. [*Associated Press*] (SAG) ... MtrVac
MotorVac Technologies, Inc. [*NASDAQ symbol*] (SAG) ... MVAC
Motorway [*Traffic sign*] [*British*] ... M
Motorway [*British*] ... M (Way)
Motorway [*Commonly used*] (OPSA) ... MOTORWAY
Motorway [*Postal Service standard*] (OPSA) ... MTWY
Motorway ... MTWY
Motorway [*British*] ... M-Way
Motor-Ways Inc., Des Moines IA [*STAC*] ... MWI
Motorways, Roads, and Road Programmes [*British*] ... MRRP
MOTS [*Module Test Set*] **Design Information Memorandum** ... MODIM
MOTS [*Module Test Set*] **Information Retrieval System** ... MIRS
Mott Center for Human Growth and Development (EA) ... MCHGD
Mott Public Library, Mott, ND [*Library symbol Library of Congress*] (LCLS) ... NdMo
Mott Scattering Formula [*Physics*] ... MSF
Motta [*Ethiopia*] [*ICAO location identifier*] (ICLI) ... HAMO
Mottled Cast Iron ... MCI
Mottled Edges [*Bookbinding*] (DGA) ... ME
Moudjeria/Letfotar [*Mauritania*] [*ICAO location identifier*] (ICLI) ... GQNL
Mouila [*Gabon*] [*ICAO location identifier*] (ICLI) ... FOGM
Mouila [*Gabon*] [*ICAO location identifier*] (ICLI) ... FOOA
Mouila [*Gabon*] [*Airport symbol*] (OAG) ... MJL
Moulage ... MLG
Mould Bay [*Northwest Territories*] [*Seismograph station code, US Geological Survey*] (SEIS) ... MBC
Mould Bay, NT [*ICAO location identifier*] (ICLI) ... CYMD
Mould Made Paper (DGA) ... MM
Moulded Fiber Technology ... MTF
Moulder [*Navy rating British*] ... M
Moulding ... MLDNG
Moulins/Avermes [*France ICAO location identifier*] (ICLI) ... LFHB
Moulins/Montbeugny [*France ICAO location identifier*] (ICLI) ... LFHY
Moulis [*France*] [*Seismograph station code, US Geological Survey*] (SEIS) ... MLS
Moulmein [*Myanmar*] [*Airport symbol*] (OAG) ... MNU
Moulmein [*Myanmar*] [*ICAO location identifier*] (ICLI) ... VBMM
Moulton, AL [*AM radio station call letters*] ... WHIY
Moulton, AL [*FM radio station call letters*] ... WXKI
Moulton Weekly Tribune, Moulton, IA [*Library symbol Library of Congress*] (LCLS) ... IaMouT
Moultonboro, NH [*Location identifier FAA*] (FAAL) ... ROY
Moultonborough, NH [*FM radio station call letters*] ... WSCY
Moulton's New York Chancery Practice [*A publication*] (DLA) ... Moult Ch
Moulton's New York Chancery Practice [*A publication*] (DLA) ... Moult Ch P
Moultrie, GA [*Location identifier FAA*] (FAAL) ... MGR
Moultrie, GA [*Location identifier FAA*] (FAAL) ... MUL
Moultrie, GA [*AM radio station call letters*] ... WMGA
Moultrie, GA [*AM radio station call letters*] ... WMTM
Moultrie, GA [*FM radio station call letters*] ... WMTM-FM
Moultrie/Thomasville [*Georgia*] [*Airport symbol*] (OAG) ... MGR
Mound (MSA) ... M
Mound ... MND
Mound Bayou, MS [*FM radio station call letters*] (RBYB) ... WZYQ
Mound City Group National Monument ... MOCI
Mound Laboratory, Miamisburg [*AEC*] (MCD) ... MLM
Mound Plant [*Department of Energy*] [*Miamisburg, OH*] (GAAI) ... MOUND
Moundou [*Chad*] [*ICAO location identifier*] (ICLI) ... FTTD
Moundou [*Chad*] [*Airport symbol*] (AD) ... MQQ
Mounds-Midway School of Nursing, St. Paul, MN [*Library symbol Library of Congress*] (LCLS) ... MnSMN
Moundsville, WV [*AM radio station call letters*] ... WMJT
Moundsville, WV [*FM radio station call letters*] ... WRKP
Mount (KSC) ... MNT
Mount [*Commonly used*] (OPSA) ... MOUNT
Mount ... MT
Mount (ODBW) ... Mt
Mount [*Maps and charts*] (KSC) ... MT
Mount Airy, NC [*Location identifier FAA*] (FAAL) ... AXI
Mount Airy, NC [*Location identifier FAA*] (FAAL) ... MWK
Mount Airy, NC [*AM radio station call letters*] ... WPAQ
Mount Airy, NC [*AM radio station call letters*] ... WSYD
Mount Airy Public Library, Mount Airy, NC [*Library symbol Library of Congress*] (LCLS) ... NcMta
Mount Allard Resources [*Vancouver Stock Exchange symbol*] ... MTQ
Mount Allison University [*New Brunswick, Canada*] ... MAU
Mount Allison University Library [*UTLAS symbol*] ... MTA
Mount Allison University, Sackville, NB, Canada [*Library symbol Library of Congress*] (LCLS) ... CaNBSaM
Mount Allison University, Sackville, New Brunswick [*Library symbol National Library of Canada*] (NLC) ... NBSAM
Mount Aloysius Junior College [*Pennsylvania*] ... MAJC
Mount Alvernia Friary, Wappingers Falls, NY [*Inactive*] [*OCLC symbol*] (OCLC) ... TDM
Mount Alvernia Seminary, Wappingers Falls, NY [*Library symbol*] [*Library of Congress*] (LCLS) ... NWapA
Mount Angel College, Mount Angel Abbey, St. Benedict, OR [*Library symbol Library of Congress*] (LCLS) ... OrStbM
Mount Angel College [*Later, Cesar Chavez College*], Mount Angel, OR [*Library symbol Library of Congress*] (LCLS) ... OrMtaC
Mount Angel Public Library, Mount Angel, OR [*Library symbol Library of Congress*] (LCLS) ... OrMta
Mount Angel Seminary [*Oregon*] ... MAS
Mount Auburn Hospital, Cambridge, MA [*OCLC symbol*] (OCLC) ... MTA
Mount Ayr Public Library, Mount Ayr, IA [*Library symbol Library of Congress*] (LCLS) ... IaMayr
Mount Baker [*Washington*] [*Seismograph station code, US Geological Survey*] (SEIS) ... MBW
Mt. Bethany Christian School, Mountain Lake, MN [*Library symbol*] [*Library of Congress*] (LCLS) ... MnMnlMB
Mount Bingar [*Australia Seismograph station code, US Geological Survey Closed*] (SEIS) ... MBA
Mount Bullion, CA [*FM radio station call letters*] ... KCIV
Mount Calvery Resources Ltd. [*Vancouver Stock Exchange symbol*] ... MCY
Mount Carmel Community Unit School District No. 348, Mt. Carmel, IL [*Library symbol Library of Congress*] (LCLS) ... IMtcaSD
Mt. Carmel, IL [*FM radio station call letters*] ... WRBT
Mount Carmel, IL [*FM radio station call letters*] (RBYB) ... WTRI-FM
Mount Carmel, IL [*FM radio station call letters*] ... WVJC
Mount Carmel, IL [*AM radio station call letters*] ... WYER
Mount Carmel Mercy Hospital, Medical Library, Detroit, MI [*Library symbol Library of Congress*] (LCLS) ... MiDMtC
Mount Carmel, PA [*AM radio station call letters*] (RBYB) ... WMIM
Mount Carmel, PA [*FM radio station call letters*] ... WSPI
Mount Carmel Public Library, Mt. Carmel, IL [*Library symbol Library of Congress*] (LCLS) ... IMtca
Mt. Carmel, TN [*AM radio station call letters*] ... WRVX
Mount Cheaha State Park, AL [*Television station call letters*] ... WCIQ
Mount Clemens, MI [*Location identifier FAA*] (FAAL) ... MTC
Mount Clemens, MI [*Location identifier FAA*] (FAAL) ... NFB
Mount Clemens, MI [*Television station call letters*] ... WADL
Mount Clemens, MI [*AM radio station call letters*] ... WBRB
Mount Clemens, MI [*FM radio station call letters*] ... WDZR
Mount Clemens Public Library, Mount Clemens, MI [*Library symbol Library of Congress*] (LCLS) ... MiMtc
Mount Clemens/Selfridge Air Force Base [*Michigan*] [*ICAO location identifier*] (ICLI) ... KMTC
Mount Constitution [*Washington*] [*Seismograph station code, US Geological Survey*] (SEIS) ... MCW
Mount Cook [*New Zealand*] [*Airport symbol*] (OAG) ... MON
Mt. Cook Airlines [*ICAO designator*] (AD) ... NM
Mount Cook Airlines [*New Zealand*] [*ICAO designator*] (FAAC) ... NZM
Mount Darwin [*Zimbabwe*] [*Seismograph station code, US Geological Survey*] (SEIS) ... MTD
Mount Desert Island Biological Laboratory [*Salsbury Cove, ME*] [*Research center*] ... MDIBL
Mount Diablo [*California*] [*Seismograph station code, US Geological Survey*] (SEIS) ... MDC
Mount Diablo Peace Center (EA) ... MDPC
Mount Dora, FL [*AM radio station call letters*] ... WBGB
Mount Dora, FL [*FM radio station call letters*] ... WMGF
Mount Edgecombe High School, Sitka, AK [*Library symbol*] [*Library of Congress*] (LCLS) ... AkSMH
Mount Emily Exploration Ltd. [*Vancouver Stock Exchange symbol*] ... MEM
Mount Forest District High School, Mount Forest, ON, Canada [*Library symbol*] [*Library of Congress*] (LCLS) ... CaOMfD
Mount Forest District High School, Mount Forest, Ontario [*Library symbol National Library of Canada*] (NLC) ... OMFD
Mount Forest, ON [*ICAO location identifier*] (ICLI) ... CWMN
Mount Fremont [*Washington*] [*Seismograph station code, US Geological Survey*] (SEIS) ... FMW
Mount Gambier [*Australia ICAO location identifier*] (ICLI) ... AMMG
Mount Gambier [*Australia Airport symbol*] (OAG) ... MGB
Mount Garfield Junior High School Library, Clifton, CO [*Library symbol Library of Congress*] (LCLS) ... CoCIM
Mount Gilead, OH [*FM radio station call letters*] ... WVXG
Mount Godwin-Austen [*Initialism denotes that mountain is second highest (to Everest) in the Karakoram range in the Himalayas*] [*Initialism also used as brand name of skiing equipment*] ... K2
Mt. Grant Mines Ltd. [*Vancouver Stock Exchange symbol*] ... MTM

Mount Gunson [*Australia Airport symbol*] (OAG) .... GSN
Mount Hagen [*Papua New Guinea*] [*ICAO location identifier*] (ICLI) .... AYMH
Mount Hagen [*Papua New Guinea*] [*Airport symbol*] (OAG) .... HGU
Mount Hamilton [*Lick Observatory*] [*California*] [*Seismograph station code, US Geological Survey*] (SEIS) .... MHC
Mount Hamilton Road [*California*] [*Seismograph station code, US Geological Survey*] (SEIS) .... MHR
Mount Holly, NJ [*AM radio station call letters*] .... WWJZ
Mount Holyoke College [*South Hadley, MA*] .... MHC
Mount Holyoke College (GAGS) .... Mt Holyoke C
Mount Holyoke College, South Hadley, MA [*Library symbol Library of Congress*] (LCLS) .... MShM
Mount Holyoke College, South Hadley, MA [*OCLC symbol*] (OCLC) .... MTH
Mount Hood Community College, Gresham, OR [*Library symbol Library of Congress*] (LCLS) .... OrGrC
Mount Hood Railway Co. [*AAR code*] .... MH
Mount Hood Railway Co. [*Later, MH*] [*AAR code*] .... MTH
Mount Hope Mineral Railroad Co. [*Absorbed into Consolidated Rail Corp.*] [*AAR code*] .... MHM
Mt. Hope, NY [*FM radio station call letters*] .... WXHD
Mount Hope, WV [*FM radio station call letters*] .... WTNJ
Mount Hopkins Observatory [*Later, FLWO*] [*Smithsonian Institution*] (GRD) .... MHO
Mt. Iron High School, Mt. Iron, MN [*Library symbol*] [*Library of Congress*] (LCLS) .... MnMtiHS
Mount Isa [*Australia ICAO location identifier*] (ICLI) .... ABMA
Mount Isa [*Australia Airport symbol*] (OAG) .... ISA
Mount Jackson, VA [*FM radio station call letters*] .... WSIG
Mount Jackson, VA [*AM radio station call letters*] .... WSVG
Mount John [*New Zealand*] [*Seismograph station code, US Geological Survey*] (SEIS) .... MJZ
Mount John Pukaki [*New Zealand*] [*Seismograph station code, US Geological Survey*] (SEIS) .... MJP
Mount John University Observatory [*New Zealand*] .... MJUO
Mount Juliet, TN [*FM radio station call letters*] (RBYB) .... WAOF
Mount Juliet, TN [*FM radio station call letters*] (RBYB) .... WNPL-FM
Mount Kisco, NY [*FM radio station call letters*] (RBYB) .... WVIB
Mount Kisco, NY [*AM radio station call letters*] .... WVIP
Mount Kisco, NY [*FM radio station call letters*] (RBYB) .... WZZN-FM
Mount Kisco Public Library, Mount Kisco, NY [*Library symbol Library of Congress*] (LCLS) .... NMtK
Mount Magnet [*Australia Airport symbol*] (OAG) .... MMG
Mount Marty College [*South Dakota*] .... MMC
Mount Marty College, Yankton, SD [*OCLC symbol*] (OCLC) .... SDY
Mount Marty College, Yankton, SD [*Library symbol Library of Congress*] (LCLS) .... SdYM
Mount Mary [*New Zealand*] [*Seismograph station code, US Geological Survey*] (SEIS) .... MMP
Mount Mary College [*Wisconsin*] .... MMC
Mount Mary College, Milwaukee, WI [*Library symbol Library of Congress*] (LCLS) .... WMMt
Mount McKinley National Park .... MOMC
Mount Mercy Academy, Grand Rapids, MI [*Library symbol Library of Congress*] (LCLS) .... MiGrMtM
Mount Mercy College [*Iowa; Pennsylvania*] .... MMC
Mount Mercy College, Cedar Rapids, IA [*Library symbol Library of Congress*] (LCLS) .... IaCrMM
Mount Misalignment Data Collection Routine .... MMDC
Mount Morris, IL [*FM radio station call letters*] .... WSEY
Mount Morris Junior/Senior High School Library, Mount Morris, NY [*OCLC symbol*] (OCLC) .... RXA
Mount Olive College, Mount Olive, NC [*Library symbol Library of Congress*] (LCLS) .... NcMtC
Mount Olive, NC [*Location identifier FAA*] (FAAL) .... ONX
Mount Olive, NC [*AM radio station call letters*] .... WDJS
Mount Olive Public Library, Mount Olive, IL [*Library symbol Library of Congress*] (LCLS) .... IMto
Mount Pasian [*Philippines*] [*Seismograph station code, US Geological Survey*] (SEIS) .... MPP
Mount Pearl Public Library, Mount Pearl, NF, Canada [*Library symbol Library of Congress*] (LCLS) .... CaNfMP
Mount Pearl Public Library, Newfoundland [*Library symbol National Library of Canada*] (NLC) .... NFMP
Mount Pleasant [*British ICAO location identifier*] (ICLI) .... EGYP
Mount Pleasant [*Texas*] [*Airport symbol Obsolete*] (OAG) .... MPS
Mount Pleasant [*Utah*] [*Airport symbol*] (OAG) .... MSD
Mount Pleasant, IA [*AM radio station call letters*] .... KILJ
Mount Pleasant, IA [*FM radio station call letters*] .... KILJ-FM
Mount Pleasant, IA [*Location identifier FAA*] (FAAL) .... MPZ
Mount Pleasant, MI [*Location identifier FAA*] (FAAL) .... MOP
Mount Pleasant, MI [*AM radio station call letters*] .... WCEN
Mount Pleasant, MI [*FM radio station call letters*] .... WCEN-FM
Mount Pleasant, MI [*FM radio station call letters*] .... WCMU
Mount Pleasant, MI [*Television station call letters*] .... WCMU-TV
Mount Pleasant, MI [*FM radio station call letters*] .... WCZY
Mount Pleasant, MI [*FM radio station call letters*] .... WMHW
Mount Pleasant News, Mount Pleasant, IA [*Library symbol Library of Congress*] (LCLS) .... IaMpN
Mount Pleasant Public Library, Mount Pleasant, IA [*Library symbol Library of Congress*] (LCLS) .... IaMp
Mount Pleasant Public Library, Mount Pleasant, MI [*Library symbol Library of Congress*] (LCLS) .... MiMtp
Mount Pleasant Public Library, Pleasantville, NY [*Library symbol Library of Congress*] (LCLS) .... NPle
Mt. Pleasant, SC [*FM radio station call letters*] (RBYB) .... WRFQ-FM
Mt. Pleasant, SC [*AM radio station call letters*] .... WZJY
Mount Pleasant, TN [*AM radio station call letters*] .... WXRQ
Mount Pleasant, TX [*AM radio station call letters*] .... KIMP
Mount Pleasant, TX [*FM radio station call letters*] .... KPXI
Mount Pleasant, TX [*Location identifier FAA*] (FAAL) .... MSA
Mount Pocono, PA [*Location identifier FAA*] (FAAL) .... MPO
Mount Pocono, PA [*AM radio station call letters*] (RBYB) .... WILT-AM
Mount Pocono, PA [*AM radio station call letters*] .... WPMR
Mount Prat [*Italy*] [*Seismograph station code, US Geological Survey*] (SEIS) .... MPRI
Mount Rainier National Park .... MORA
Mount Rainier National Park [*Washington*] (AD) .... MRNP
Mount Revelstoke National Park [*British Columbia*] (AD) .... MRNP
Mount Royal College, Calgary, Alberta [*Library symbol National Library of Canada*] (NLC) .... ACMR
Mount Royal Junior College, Calgary, AB, Canada [*Library symbol Library of Congress*] (LCLS) .... CaACMR
Mount Rushmore Memorial Society (EA) .... MRMS
Mount Rushmore National Memorial .... MORU
Mount Saint Agnes College [*Maryland*] [*Merged with Loyola College*] .... MSAC
Mount Saint Agnes College, Baltimore, MD [*Library symbol Library of Congress*] (LCLS) .... MdBMStA
Mount Saint Alphonsus Seminary, Esopus, NY [*Library symbol Library of Congress*] (LCLS) .... NEsM
Mount St. Benedict, Crookston, MN [*Library symbol*] [*Library of Congress*] (LCLS) .... MnCrMS
Mount Saint Clare College, Clinton, IA [*Library symbol Library of Congress*] (LCLS) .... IaCliM
Mount St. Helena [*California*] [*Seismograph station code, US Geological Survey*] (SEIS) .... SHC
Mount St. Helens [*Washington*] [*Geology*] .... MSH
Mount St. Helens [*Washington*] [*Seismograph station code, US Geological Survey*] (SEIS) .... SHW
Mount St. Margaret, NF [*Television station call letters*] CBNAT-9
Mount Saint Mary College, Newburgh, NY [*Library symbol*] [*Library of Congress*] (LCLS) .... NNebgM
Mount St. Mary College, Newburgh, NY [*Library symbol Library of Congress*] (LCLS) .... NNegbM
Mount St. Mary's College (GAGS) .... Mt St Mary's C
Mount St. Mary's College, Emmitsburg, MD [*Library symbol Library of Congress*] (LCLS) .... MdE
Mount St. Mary's College, Emmitsburg, MD [*OCLC symbol*] (OCLC) .... MSM
Mount St. Mary's College, Los Angeles, CA [*Library symbol Library of Congress*] (LCLS) .... CLMSM
Mount St. Mary's College, Los Angeles, CA [*OCLC symbol*] (OCLC) .... CMM
Mount Saint Mary's Hospital, Lewiston, NY [*Library symbol Library of Congress*] (LCLS) .... NLewStM
Mount St. Thomas [*Philippines*] [*Seismograph station code, US Geological Survey*] (SEIS) .... MSP
Mount St. Vincent College [*New York*] .... MSVC
Mount Saint Vincent University, Art Gallery, Halifax, NS, Canada [*Library symbol Library of Congress*] (LCLS) .... CaNSHVA
Mount Saint Vincent University, Halifax, Nova Scotia [*Library symbol National Library of Canada*] (NLC) .... NSHV
Mount Saint Vincent University, Halifax, NS, Canada [*Library symbol Library of Congress*] (LCLS) .... CaNSHV
Mount San Antonio [*New Mexico*] [*Seismograph station code, US Geological Survey*] (SEIS) .... MSA
Mount Saviour Monastery, Elmira, NY [*Library symbol Library of Congress*] (LCLS) .... NElmM
Mount Senario College, Ladysmith, WI [*Library symbol Library of Congress*] (LCLS) .... WLadM
Mount Shasta, CA [*AM radio station call letters*] (RBYB) .... KMJC
Mount Shasta, CA [*FM radio station call letters*] (RBYB) .... KMJC-FM
Mount Shasta, CA [*FM radio station call letters*] .... KNSQ
Mount Shasta, CA [*Location identifier FAA*] (FAAL) .... MHS
Mount Signal [*California*] [*Seismograph station code, US Geological Survey*] (SEIS) .... SGL
Mount Sinai Hospital, Cleveland, OH [*Library symbol Library of Congress*] (LCLS) .... OCIMt
Mount Sinai Hospital, Milwaukee, WI [*Library symbol Library of Congress*] (LCLS) .... WMMS
Mount Sinai Hospital, Minneapolis, MN [*Library symbol Library of Congress*] (LCLS) .... MnMMtS
Mount Sinai Hospital, New York, NY [*Library symbol Library of Congress*] (LCLS) .... NNMtS
Mount Sinai Hospital, Toronto, Ontario [*Library symbol National Library of Canada*] (NLC) .... OTMS
Mount Sinai Medical Center, Media Center, Miami Beach, FL [*Library symbol Library of Congress*] (LCLS) .... FMbMS
Mount Sinai Medical Center, Media Center, Miami Beach, FL [*Library symbol*] [*Library of Congress*] (LCLS) .... FMbMS
Mount Sinai School of Medicine [*New York*] (PDAA) .... MSSM
Mount Sinai School of Medicine of The City University of New York (GAGS) .... Mt Sinai Sch Med
Mount Sinai School of Medicine of the City University of New York, New York, NY [*Library symbol Library of Congress*] (LCLS) .... NNMtSM
Mount Sinai School of Medicine of the City University of New York, New York, NY [*OCLC symbol*] (OCLC) VVL
Mount Sinaid Hospital, Toronto, ON, Canada [*Library symbol*] [*Library of Congress*] (LCLS) .... CaOTMS
Mount Spur [*Alaska*] [*Seismograph station code, US Geological Survey*] (SEIS) .... SPU
Mount Sterling, IL [*FM radio station call letters*] (RBYB) .... WBRJ-FM
Mount Sterling, KY [*AM radio station call letters*] .... WMST

Mount Sterling, KY [*FM radio station call letters*] .... WMST-FM
Mount Tassie [*Australia Seismograph station code, US Geological Survey Closed*] (SEIS) .... MTV
Mount Taylor [*New Mexico*] [*Seismograph station code, US Geological Survey*] (SEIS) .... MTL
Mount Tsukuba [*Japan*] [*Seismograph station code, US Geological Survey*] (SEIS) .... MTJ
Mount Union College [*Alliance, OH*] .... MUC
Mount Union College, Alliance, OH [*Library symbol Library of Congress*] (LCLS) .... OAIM
Mount Union, PA [*Location identifier FAA*] (FAAL) .... MUU
Mount Union, PA [*FM radio station call letters*] .... WXMJ
Mount Vernon [*Illinois*] [*Airport symbol*] (OAG) .... MVN
Mount Vernon [*Washington*] [*Airport symbol*] (OAG) .... MVW
Mount Vernon College, Washington, DC [*Library symbol Library of Congress*] (LCLS) .... DMV
Mount Vernon, IA [*FM radio station call letters*] .... KRNL
Mount Vernon, IL [*Location identifier FAA*] (FAAL) .... VNN
Mount Vernon, IL [*FM radio station call letters*] (RBYB) .... WAJT
Mount Vernon, IL [*FM radio station call letters*] (RBYB) .... WAPO-FM
Mount Vernon, IL [*Television station call letters*] .... WCEE
Mount Vernon, IL [*AM radio station call letters*] .... WMIX
Mount Vernon, IL [*FM radio station call letters*] .... WMIX-FM
Mt. Vernon, IN [*FM radio station call letters*] .... WBLZ
Mount Vernon, IN [*AM radio station call letters*] .... WPCO
Mount Vernon Junior College [*Washington, DC*] .... MVJC
Mount Vernon, KY [*AM radio station call letters*] .... WRVK
Mt. Vernon, KY [*FM radio station call letters*] .... WXJJ
Mount Vernon Ladies' Association of the Union (EA) .... MVLA
Mount Vernon Ladies' Association of the Union, Mount Vernon, VA [*Library symbol Library of Congress*] (LCLS) .... ViMtvL
Mount Vernon, MO [*FM radio station call letters*] .... KHTO
Mount Vernon Nazarene College, Mount Vernon, OH [*OCLC symbol*] (OCLC) .... MZN
Mount Vernon Nazarene College, Mount Vernon, OH [*Library symbol Library of Congress*] (LCLS) .... OMtvN
Mount Vernon, OH [*AM radio station call letters*] .... WMVO
Mount Vernon, OH [*FM radio station call letters*] .... WNZR
Mount Vernon, OH [*FM radio station call letters*] .... WQIO
Mount Vernon Public Library, Mt. Vernon, IL [*Library symbol Library of Congress*] (LCLS) .... IMtv
Mount Vernon Public Library, Mount Vernon, NY [*Library symbol Library of Congress*] (LCLS) .... NMtv
Mount Vernon Public Library, Mount Vernon, OH [*Library symbol Library of Congress*] (LCLS) .... OMtv
Mount Vernon Public Library, Mount Vernon, WA [*Library symbol Library of Congress*] (LCLS) .... WaMtv
Mount Vernon Terminal [*AAR code*] .... MVT
Mount Vernon, WA [*AM radio station call letters*] .... KAPS
Mount Vernon, WA [*AM radio station call letters*] .... KBRC
Mount Vernon, WA [*FM radio station call letters*] .... KSVR
Mount Vernon, WA [*Location identifier FAA*] (FAAL) .... NSR
Mount View Health Facility, Lockport, NY [*Library symbol Library of Congress*] (LCLS) .... NLockMt
Mount View School for Girls, Morrison, CO [*Library symbol Library of Congress*] (LCLS) .... CoMorM
Mount Wachusett Community College, Gardner, MA [*Library symbol Library of Congress*] (LCLS) .... MGaMW
Mount Washington, NH [*Location identifier FAA*] (FAAL) .... MWN
Mount Washington, NH [*FM radio station call letters*] .... WHOM
Mount Washington Railway Co. [*AAR code*] .... MWRC
Mount Wilson [*California*] [*Seismograph station code, US Geological Survey*] (SEIS) .... MWC
Mount Wilson, CA [*Location identifier FAA*] (FAAL) .... MWS
Mount Wilson Observatory (NADA) .... MWO
Mount Wilson Observatory, Pasadena, CA [*Library symbol Library of Congress*] (LCLS) .... CPO
Mount Wilson State Hospital, Mount Wilson, MD [*Library symbol Library of Congress*] (LCLS) .... MdMwH
Mount Zion Church [*South Carolina*] [*Seismograph station code, US Geological Survey Closed*] (SEIS) .... ZIN
Mt. Zion, IL [*FM radio station call letters*] .... WXFM
Mountain .... M
Mountain .... MNT
Mountain [*Commonly used*] (OPSA) .... MNTAIN
Mountain .... MNTN
Mountain [*Commonly used*] (OPSA) .... MOUNTAIN
Mountain [*Commonly used*] (OPSA) .... MOUNTIN
Mountain [*Board on Geographic Names*] .... MT
Mountain (VRA) .... mt
Mountain [*Commonly used*] (OPSA) .... MTIN
Mountain .... MTN
Mountain .... MTN
Mountain Administrative Support Center [*Marine science*] (OSRA) .... MASC
Mountain Administrative Support Center (USDC) .... MASC
Mountain Air Cargo, Inc. [*ICAO designator*] (FAAC) .... MTN
Mountain Air Service, Inc. [*ICAO designator*] (FAAC) .... BRR
Mountain and Arctic Warfare [*British military*] (DMA) .... M & AW
Mountain Area Health Education Center, Health Sciences Library, Asheville, NC [*Library symbol Library of Congress*] (LCLS) .... NcAHE
Mountain Artillery .... MA
Mountain Artillery Training Centre [*British military*] (DMA) .... MATC
Mountain Battery [*British military*] (DMA) .... MB
Mountain Bike Club [*British*] (DBA) .... MBC
Mountain City, GA [*AM radio station call letters*] .... WALH

Mountain City, TN [*Location identifier FAA*] (FAAL) .... JJO
Mountain City, TN [*AM radio station call letters*] .... WMCT
Mountain Commando Units (CINC) .... MCU
Mountain Daylight Saving Time (SSD) .... MDST
Mountain Daylight Time .... MDT
Mountain Empire Community College, Big Stone Gap, VA [*Library symbol Library of Congress*] (LCLS) .... ViBsgM
Mountain Field Exercise [*Military*] (NVT) .... MTFEX
Mountain Gorilla Project (EA) .... MGP
Mountain Grove, MO [*AM radio station call letters*] .... KCMG
Mountain Grove, MO [*FM radio station call letters*] .... KCMG-FM
Mountain Grove, MO [*AM radio station call letters*] (RBYB) .... KELE-AM
Mountain High Aviation [*ICAO designator*] (FAAC) .... MHA
Mountain Home [*Arkansas*] [*Airport symbol*] (OAG) .... WMH
Mountain Home Air Service [*ICAO designator*] (AD) .... YM
Mountain Home, AR [*FM radio station call letters*] .... KCMH
Mountain Home, AR [*FM radio station call letters*] .... KKTZ
Mountain Home, AR [*FM radio station call letters*] .... KPFM
Mountain Home, AR [*AM radio station call letters*] .... KTLO
Mountain Home, AR [*FM radio station call letters*] .... KTLO-FM
Mountain Home, ID [*Location identifier FAA*] (FAAL) .... BRN
Mountain Home, ID [*AM radio station call letters*] .... KLVJ
Mountain Home, ID [*FM radio station call letters*] .... KLVJ-FM
Mountain Home, ID [*Location identifier FAA*] (FAAL) .... MUO
Mountain Home, ID [*Location identifier FAA*] (FAAL) .... STI
Mountain Home/Mountain Home Air Force Base [*Idaho*] [*ICAO location identifier*] (ICLI) .... KMUO
Mountain Home Public Library, Mountain Home, ID [*Library symbol*] [*Library of Congress*] (LCLS) .... IdMh
Mountain Instructor's Certificate [*British*] (DI) .... MIC
Mountain Iron Public Library, Mt. Iron, MN [*Library symbol*] [*Library of Congress*] (LCLS) .... MnMti
Mountain Lake Christian School, Mountain Lake, MN [*Library symbol*] [*Library of Congress*] (LCLS) .... MnMnlCS
Mountain Lake Park, MD [*FM radio station call letters*] .... WKHJ
Mountain Lake Public High School, Mountain Lake, MN [*Library symbol*] [*Library of Congress*] (LCLS) .... MnMnlHS
Mountain Lake Public Library, Mountain Lake, MN [*Library symbol*] [*Library of Congress*] (LCLS) .... MnMnl
Mountain Lake Resources, Inc. [*Vancouver Stock Exchange symbol*] .... MOA
Mountain Lakes Historical Society, Mountain Lakes, NJ [*Library symbol Library of Congress*] (LCLS) .... NjMouHi
Mountain Lakes Public Library, Mountain Lakes, NJ [*Library symbol Library of Congress*] (LCLS) .... NjMou
Mountain Leader [*British military*] (DMA) .... ML
Mountain Leadership Certificate [*British*] (DI) .... MLC
Mountain Meadow Research Center [*Colorado State University*] [*Research center*] (RCD) .... MMRC
Mountain Name (BJA) .... MoN
Mountain Pacific Air Ltd. [*Canada ICAO designator*] (FAAC) .... MPC
Mountain Parks Financial Corp. [*NASDAQ symbol*] (SAG) .... MPFC
Mountain Parks Financial Corp. [*Associated Press*] (SAG) .... MtnPkFn
Mountain Parks Fin'l [*NASDAQ symbol*] (TTSB) .... MPFC
Mountain Pass, CA [*FM radio station call letters*] .... KHYZ
Mountain Pine, AR [*FM radio station call letters*] (RBYB) .... KTDX
Mountain Pine, AR [*AM radio station call letters*] (RBYB) .... KZBR-FM
Mountain Plains Adult Education Association (AEBS) .... MPAEA
Mountain Plains Business Education Association (AEBS) .... MPBEA
Mountain Plains Library Association (AEBS) .... MPLA
Mountain Point [*Guyana*] [*ICAO location identifier*] (ICLI) .... SYMP
Mountain Province [*Vancouver Stock Exchange symbol*] .... MPV
Mountain Province Mining [*NASDAQ symbol*] (TTSB) .... MPVIF
Mountain Province Mining, Inc. [*Associated Press*] (SAG) .... MountPr
Mountain Province Mining, Inc. [*NASDAQ symbol*] (SAG) .... MPVI
Mountain Rescue Association (EA) .... MRA
Mountain Rescue Service (AD) .... MRS
Mountain Standard Time .... MST
Mountain State Tumor Institute Medical Library, Boise, ID [*Library symbol*] [*Library of Congress*] (LCLS) .... IdBTI
Mountain States Employers Council, Information Center, Denver, CO [*Library symbol Library of Congress*] (LCLS) .... CoDMSE
Mountain States Legal Foundation (EA) .... MSLF
Mountain System Digital Automatic Computer .... MODAC
Mountain Time .... MT
Mountain Top, PA [*FM radio station call letters*] .... WBHT
Mountain Valley Air Service, Inc. [*ICAO designator*] (FAAC) .... MTV
Mountain Valley Library System, Sacramento, CA [*Library symbol Library of Congress*] (LCLS) .... CSMV
Mountain Valley Library System, Sacramento, CA [*OCLC symbol*] (OCLC) .... MVL
Mountain View [*Hawaii*] [*Seismograph station code, US Geological Survey*] (SEIS) .... MVH
Mountain View, AR [*Television station call letters*] .... KEMV
Mountain View, AR [*FM radio station call letters*] .... KWOZ
Mountain View, CA [*FM radio station call letters*] .... KSFH
Mountain View, CA [*Location identifier FAA*] (FAAL) .... NUQ
Mountain View College, Dallas, TX [*Library symbol Library of Congress*] (LCLS) .... TxDaMV
Mountain View High School, Bend, OR [*Library symbol*] [*Library of Congress*] (LCLS) .... OrBeMH
Mountain View, MO [*FM radio station call letters*] .... KXOZ
Mountain View, MO [*Location identifier FAA*] (FAAL) .... MNF
Mountain View/Moffett Naval Air Station [*California*] [*ICAO location identifier*] (ICLI) .... KNUQ

Mountain View Public Library, Mountain View, CA [Library symbol Library of Congress] (LCLS) .... CMv

Mountain View Public Library, Mountain View, CA [OCLC symbol] (OCLC) .... MVP

Mountain View School, Helena, MT [Library symbol] [Library of Congress] (LCLS) .... MtHMv

Mountain Village [Alaska] [Airport symbol] (OAG) .... MOU

Mountain War Time .... MWT

Mountain West Airline [Air carrier designation symbol] .... MWAX

Mountain West Airlines [ICAO designator] (AD) .... FX

Mountain West Desegregation Assistance Centers (EDAC) .... MWDAC

Mountaineering Association [British] (BI) .... MA

Mountaineers, Inc., Seattle, WA [Library symbol Library of Congress] (LCLS) .... WaSM

Mountaineers, Inc., Seattle, WA [Library symbol] [Library of Congress] (LCLS) .... WaSMo

Mountains [Commonly used] (OPSA) .... MNTNS

Mountains .... MNTS

Mountains [Commonly used] (OPSA) .... MOUNTAINS

Mountains [Postal Service standard] (OPSA) .... MTNS

Mountains [Board on Geographic Names] .... MTS

Mountain-West Resources [Vancouver Stock Exchange symbol] .... MWR

Mountasia Entertainment [NASDAQ symbol] (TTSB) .... FUNN

Mountasia Entertainment International, Inc. [NASDAQ symbol] (SAG) .... FUNN

Mountasia Entertainment International, Inc. [Associated Press] (SAG) .... MntasiaE

Mountasia Entertainment Intl., Inc. [AMEX symbol] (SAG) .... MBE

Mountbatten, Inc. [Associated Press] (SAG) .... Mountbtn

Mountbatten, Inc. [NASDAQ symbol] (SAG) .... MTBN

Mounted [Technical drawings] .... MT

Mounted .... MTD

Mounted (VRA) .... mtd

Mounted .... MTD

Mounted Infantry .... MI

Mounted Police .... MP

Mounted Ration Heating Device [Army] (INF) .... MRHD

Mounted Warfighting Battlespace Laborarory [Army] (RDA) .... MWBL

Mounting .... MNTG

Mounting .... MTG

Mounting .... MTG

Mounting Azimuth [Weaponry] (INF) .... MAZ

Mounting Bracket (IAA) .... MTGBKT

Mounting Center (MSA) .... MTGC

Mounting Tray .... MT

Mountings [JETDS nomenclature] [Military] (CET) .... MT

Moupoupa [Gabon] [ICAO location identifier] (ICLI) .... FOGU

Mourmelon [France ICAO location identifier] (ICLI) .... LFXM

Mourning (ROG) .... MNG

Mouse [Computer science] (PCM) .... Mou

Mouse Antibody Production [Test for virus] .... MAP

Mouse Biochemical Specific Locus [Test for mutagenesis] .... MBSL

[The] Mouse Club (EA) .... TMC

Mouse Colon Tumor [Pathology] .... MCT

Mouse Duchenne Muscular Dystrophy [Medicine] .... mDMD

Mouse Ear Swelling Test [Analytical biochemistry] .... MEST

Mouse Embryo [Medicine] (DMAA) .... ME

Mouse Embryo Fibroblast .... MEF

Mouse Embryo Tissue Culture .... METC

Mouse Encephalitis .... ME

Mouse Epidermal Growth Factor .... mEGF

Mouse Epidermal Growth Factor - Urogastrone [Endocrinology] .... mEGF-URO

Mouse Epithelial [Cells] [Hematology] (DAVI) .... ME

Mouse Erythroleukemia .... MEL

Mouse Erythroleukemia Cell .... MELC

Mouse Gamma-Globulin .... MGG

Mouse Genome Database .... MGD

Mouse Hepatitis Virus .... MHV

"Mouse in Able" Program .... MIA

Mouse Laminin .... ML

Mouse Leukemia Virus (MAE) .... MLV

Mouse Lymph Node Homing Receptor .... mLNRc

Mouse Lymphoma Cells [Oncology] .... MOLY

Mouse Lysozyme [Biochemistry] .... ML

Mouse Mammary Tumor Virus .... MMTV

Mouse Metallothionein [Biochemistry] .... mMT

Mouse Myeloma Cell [Cell biology] .... MPC

Mouse Myoblast [Cell line] .... MM

Mouse Operating Table [Research instrumentation] .... MOT

Mouse Peritoneal Macrophages .... MPM

Mouse Peroxisome Proliferator-Activated Receptor [Biochemistry] .... MPPAR

Mouse Plasmocytoma [Cell line] .... MOPC

Mouse Red Blood Cell [Medicine] (DMAA) .... MRBC

Mouse Salivary Gland Virus [Medicine] (DMAA) .... MSGV

Mouse Sarcoma Virus .... MSV

Mouse Serum Albumin [Clinical chemistry] .... MSA

Mouse Serum Protein [Biochemistry] (DAVI) .... MSP

Mouse Specific B Lymphocyte Antigen [Immunology] .... MSBLA

Mouse Specific Bone-Marrow-Derived Lymphocyte Antigen [Immunology] .... MBLA

Mouse Specific Lymphocyte Antigen [Immunology] .... MSLA

Mouse Transforming Growth Factor [Biochemistry] .... MTGF

Mouse Unit [Medicine] (DMAA) .... MU

Mouse Urine Protein [Biochemistry] (DAVI) .... MUP

Mouse Uterine Unit [Gynecology] (MAE) .... MUU

Mouse Uterine Weight Unit [Gynecology] .... MUWU

Mouse Visible Specific Locus [Test for mutagenesis] .... MVSL

Moussoro [Chad] [Airport symbol] (AD) .... MXR

Moustache [DSUE] .... MO

MOUT [Military Operations on Urbanized Terrain] Assault Course (INF) .... MAC

MOUT [Military Operations on Urbanized Terrain] Training Complex [Army] (INF) .... MTC

Mouth .... M

Mouth .... MO

Mouth [Maps and charts] .... MO

Mouth Pressure [Dentistry] (DAVI) .... MP

Mouvement Africain de Liberation Nationale [African Movement for National Liberation] .... MALN

Mouvement Anti-Apartheid [France] .... MAA

Mouvement Centrafricain de Liberation Nationale [Central African Movement for National Liberation] (PD) .... MCLN

Mouvement Chretien pour la Paix [Christian Movement for Peace - CMP] [Brussels, Belgium] (EAIO) .... MCP

Mouvement Congolais National [Zaire] [Political party] (EY) .... MCN

Mouvement Contre le Racisme et pour l'Amitie Entre les Peuples [Movement Against Racism and for Friendship between People] (EAIO) .... MRAP

Mouvement Cooperatif National [Haiti] [Political party] (EY) .... MKN

Mouvement d'Action Politique et Sociale [Political and Social Action Movement] [Switzerland Political party] (PPW) .... MNA

Mouvement d'Action pour la Resurrection du Congo [Action Movement for the Resurrection of the Congo] [Zaire] (PD) .... MARC

Mouvement de la Gauche Reformatrice [Movement of the Reformist Left] [France Political party] (PPW) .... MGR

Mouvement de la Jeunesse Djiboutienne [Political party] (EY) .... MJD

Mouvement de la Tendance Islamique [Islamic Trend Movement] [Tunisia] (PD) .... MTI

Mouvement de l'Evolution Democratique de l'Afrique Centrale [Central African Democratic Evolution Movement] .... MEDAC

Mouvement de l'Evolution Sociale de l'Afrique Noire [Black African Social Evolution Movement] .... MESAN

Mouvement de Liberation du Peuple Centrafricain [Movement for the Liberation of the Central African People] (PD) .... MLPC

Mouvement de Liberation Nationale [National Liberation Movement] [Burkina Faso Banned, 1974] [Political party] .... MLN

Mouvement de l'Unite Populaire [Popular Unity Movement] [Tunisia] [Political party] (PD) .... MUP

Mouvement de Redressement National [Gabon] [Political party] (EY) .... MORENA

Mouvement de Regroupement des Populations Congolaises [Movement for the Regrouping of the Congolese People] [Political party] .... MRPC

Mouvement de Regroupement et de Liberation du Peuple Congolais [Movement for the Regroupment and Liberation of the Congolese People] .... MRLPC

Mouvement de Regroupement Voltaique [Upper Volta Regrouping Movement] [Political party] .... MRV

Mouvement d'Ecologie Politique [Ecology Political Movement] [France Political party] (PPW) .... MEP

Mouvement Democrate Socialiste [Democratic Socialist Movement] [France Political party] (PPW) .... MDS

Mouvement Democrate Socialiste de France [Democratic Socialist Movement of France] [Political party] (PPE) .... MDSF

Mouvement Democratique Dahomeen [Dahomean Democratic Movement] [Political party] .... MDD

Mouvement Democratique de Renovation Malgache [Democratic Movement Malagasy Restoration] .... MDRM

Mouvement Democratique et Populaire [Popular Democratic Movement] [Senegal] [Political party] (PPW) .... MDP

Mouvement Democratique Populaire [Popular Democratic Party] [The Comoros] [Political party] (EY) .... MDP

Mouvement Democratique Voltaique [Upper Volta Democratic Movement] .... MDV

Mouvement des Democrates Progressistes [Burkina Faso] [Political party] (EY) .... MDP

Mouvement des Democrates Socialistes [Movement of Socialist Democrats] [Tunisia] [Political party] (PPW) .... MDS

Mouvement des Forces Democratiques de la Casamance [Senegal] [Political party] .... MFDC

Mouvement des Jeunes de l'Union Progressiste Senegalaise [Youth Movement of the Senegalese Progressive Movement] .... MJUPS

Mouvement des Jeunesses Progressistes Soudanaises [Sudanese Progressive Youth Movement] [Mali] .... MJPS

Mouvement des Jeunesses Socialistes Africaines [African Socialist Youth Movement] .... MJSA

Mouvement des Radicaux de Gauche [Left Radical Movement] [Wallis and Futuna Islands] [Political party] (EY) .... MRG

Mouvement des Radicaux de Gauche [Left Radical Movement] [France Political party] (PPE) .... MRG

Mouvement des Renovateurs Communistes [France Political party] (EY) .... MRC

Mouvement des Sociaux-Liberaux [Movement of Social Liberals] [France Political party] (PPW) .... MSL

Mouvement d'Insoumission Bretonne [Breton Insubordination Movement] [France] (PD) .... MIB

Mouvement d'Organisation du Pays [Haiti] [Political party] (EY) .... MOP

Mouvement Europeen [European Movement] .... ME

Mouvement Federaliste Europeen [European Federalist Movement] [France] .... MFE

Mouvement Gaulliste Populaire [Popular Gaullist Movement] [France Political party] (PPW) .... MGP

Mouvement Guyanais de Decolonisation [Guiana Decolonization Movement] [France Political party] (PPW) .... Moguyde

Mouvement Independantiste Martiniquais [Martinique Independance Movement] [Political party] (PD) .... MIM

Mouvement Independent Populaire [Popular Independent Movement] [Luxembourg] [Political party] (PPE) .... MIP

Mouvement International d'Apostolat des Enfants [*International Movement of Apostolate of Children*] [*France*] .... MIDADE
Mouvement International d'Apostolat des Milieux Sociaux Independants [*International Movement of Apostolate in the Independent Social Milieux*] [*Vatican City*] (EAIO) .... MIAMSI
Mouvement International de la Jeunesse Agricole et Rurale Catholique [*International Movement of Catholic Agricultural and Rural Youth - IMCARY*] [*Louvain, Belgium*] (EAIO) .... MIJARC
Mouvement International de la Reconciliation [*International Fellowship of Reconciliation*] .... MIR
Mouvement International des Juristes Catholiques, Pax Romana [*France*] .... MIJC
Mouvement International pour l'Union Fraternelle entre les Races et les Peuples [*International Movement for Fraternal Union among Races and Peoples*] .... UFER
Mouvement Islamique Progressiste [*Islamic Progressive Movement*] [*Tunisia*] [*Political party*] (PD) .... MIP
Mouvement Militant Mauricien [*Mauritian Militant Movement*] [*Political party*] (PPW) .... MMM
Mouvement Militant Mauricien Socialiste Progressiste [*Mauritius Militant Socialist Progressive Movement*] (PPW) .... MMMSP
Mouvement Mondial des Meres [*World Movement of Mothers - WMM*] [*Paris, France*] (EAIO) .... MMM
Mouvement Mondial des Travailleurs Chretiens [*World Movement of Christian Workers - WMCW*] [*Brussels, Belgium*] (EAIO) .... MMTC
Mouvement National [*Morocco*] [*Political party*] (EY) .... MN
Mouvement National Algerien [*National Algerian Movement*] .... MNA
Mouvement National Congolais [*Congolese National Movement*] .... MNC
Mouvement National Congolais - Kalonji [*Congolese National Movement*] [*Kalonji Wing*] .... MNC-K
Mouvement National Congolais - Lumumba [*Congolese National Movement*] [*Lumumba Wing*] .... MNC-L
Mouvement National des Jeunes Travailleurs du Senegal [*National Movement of Young Workers of Senegal*] .... MNJTS
Mouvement National du Congo-Lumumba [*Congo National Movement-Lumumba*] [*Zaire*] (PD) .... MNC
Mouvement National pour la Democratie et le Developpement [*Benin*] [*Political party*] (EY) .... MNDD
Mouvement National pour l'Independance de Madagascar [*National Movement for the Independence of Madagascar*] [*Political party*] (PPW) .... MONIMA
Mouvement National pour l'Union et la Reconciliation au Zaire [*National Movement for Union and Reconciliation in Zaire*] [*Political party*] (PD) .... MNUR
Mouvement National pour une Societe de Developpement [*Niger*] [*Political party*] (EY) .... MNSD
Mouvement Nationale Patriotique [*Haiti*] [*Political party*] (EY) .... MNP
Mouvement Nationaliste Revolutionnaire [*Revolutionary Nationalist Movement*] [*France Political party*] (PD) .... MNR
Mouvement Ouvrier International (BJA) .... MOI
Mouvement Ouvriers-Paysans [*Workers' and Peasants' Movement*] [*Haiti*] (PD) .... MOP
Mouvement Panafricain de la Jeunesse [*Pan-African Youth Movement - PYAM*] [*Algeria*] .... MPJ
Mouvement Patriotique Congolais [*Congo Patriotic Movement*] [*Political party*] .... MPC
Mouvement Patriotique du Salut [*Chad*] [*Political party*] (EY) .... MPS
Mouvement Politique Lulua [*Lulua Political Movement*] [*Political party*] .... MPL
Mouvement Populaire [*Popular Movement*] [*Morocco*] [*Political party*] (PPW) .... MP
Mouvement Populaire Constitutionnel Democratique [*Popular Democratic Constitutional Movement*] [*Morocco*] [*Political party*] (PPW) .... MPCD
Mouvement Populaire de la Revolution [*Popular Revolutionary Movement*] [*Zaire*] [*Political party*] (PD) .... MPR
Mouvement Populaire d'Evolution Africaine [*African People's Evolution Movement*] .... MPEA
Mouvement Populaire Mahorais [*Mayotte People's Movement*] [*Comoros*] [*Political party*] (PPW) .... MPM
Mouvement Populaire pour la Guadeloupe Independante [*Popular Movement for Independent Guadeloupe*] (PD) .... MPGI
Mouvement Populaire pour la Liberation de Djibouti [*Political party*] (EY) .... MPLD
Mouvement Populaire Revolutionnaire [*Popular Revolutionary Movement*] [*Tunisia*] [*Political party*] (PD) .... MPR
Mouvement Populaire Senegalais [*Senegalese Popular Movement*] [*Political party*] .... MPS
Mouvement Populaire Tchadien [*Chadian Popular Movement*] [*Political party*] .... MPT
Mouvement Populaire Togolais [*Togolese Popular Movement*] [*Political party*] .... MPT
Mouvement pour la Defense des Prisonniers Politiques du Quebec [*Movement for the Defense of Political Prisoners of Quebec*] .... MDPPQ
Mouvement pour la Democratie en Algerie [*Algeria*] [*Political party*] (MENA) .... MDA
Mouvement pour la Democratie et le Progres Social [*Benin*] [*Political party*] (EY) .... MDPS
Mouvement pour la Democratie et l'Independance [*Movement for Democracy and Independence*] [*Central Africa*] (PD) .... MDI
Mouvement pour la Democratie Sociale [*Burkina Faso*] [*Political party*] (EY) .... MDS
Mouvement pour la Liberation de Djibouti [*Movement for the Liberation of Djibouti*] (PD) .... MLD
Mouvement pour la Liberation d'Haiti/Parti Revolutionnaire d'Haiti [*Political party*] (EY) .... MODELH/PRDH
Mouvement pour la Reconstruction Nationale [*Haiti*] [*Political party*] (EY) .... MRN
Mouvement pour la Renovation et l'Action Democratique [*The Comoros*] [*Political party*] (EY) .... MOURAD
Mouvement pour la Solidarite, l'Union et le Progres [*Benin*] [*Political party*] (EY) .... MSUP
Mouvement pour le Pouvoir Proletarien [*or aux Petits*] [*Movement for Proletarian Power Malagasy*] [*Political party*] (PPW) .... MFM
Mouvement pour le Progres et la Tolerance [*Burkina Faso*] [*Political party*] (EY) .... MPT
Mouvement pour le Progres National Congolais [*Movement for National Congolese Progress*] .... MPNC
Mouvement pour le Triomphe des Libertes Democratiques [*Movement for the Triumph of Democratic Liberties*] [*Algeria*] .... MTLD
Mouvement pour l'Independance de la Reunion [*Movement for the Independence of Reunion*] [*Political party*] (PD) .... MIR
Mouvement pour l'Instauration de la Democratie en Haiti [*Political party*] (EY) .... MIDH
Mouvement pour l'Ordre et la Paix [*Movement for Order and Peace*] [*New Caledonia*] [*Political party*] (PD) .... MOP
Mouvement pour l'Unification des Forces de Liberation de la Guadeloupe [*Movement for the Unification of National Liberation Forces of Guadeloupe*] [*Political party*] (PD) .... MUFLNG
Mouvement pour l'Unite et la Democratie [*Djibouti*] [*Political party*] (EY) .... MUD
Mouvement pour une Alternative Non-Violente [*Movement for a Nonviolent Alternative*] [*France Political party*] (PPE) .... MAN
Mouvement Progressif [*Cameroon*] [*Political party*] (EY) .... MP
Mouvement Progressiste de Burundi [*Progressive Movement of Burundi*] .... MPB
Mouvement Republicain Populaire [*Popular Republican Movement*] [*France Political party*] (PPE) .... MRP
Mouvement Republicain Senegalais [*Senegalese Republican Movement*] [*Political party*] (PPW) .... MRS
Mouvement Revolutionnaire du Peuple [*Chad*] [*Political party*] (EY) .... MRP
Mouvement Revolutionnaire National pour le Developpement [*National Revolutionary Movement for Development*] [*Rwanda*] [*Political party*] (PPW) .... MRND
Mouvement Revolutionnaire pour la Democratie Nouvelle [*Revolutionary Movement for New Democracy*] [*Senegal*] (PD) .... MRDN
Mouvement Social Mohutu [*Mohutu Social Movement*] .... MSM
Mouvement Social pour la Nouvelle Democratie [*Cameroon*] [*Political party*] (EY) .... MSND
Mouvement Socialiste Africain [*African Socialist Movement*] [*Political party*] .... MSA
Mouvement Socialiste d'Union Senegalaise [*Senegalese Socialist Movement*] [*Political party*] .... MSUS
Mouvement Socialiste Occitan [*Occitanian Socialist Movement*] [*France Political party*] (PPE) .... MSO
Mouvement Socialiste Occitan - Volem Viure al Pais [*Occitanian Socialist Movement*] [*France Political party*] (PPW) .... VVAP
Mouvement Socialiste pour les Etats Unis d'Europe .... MSEUE
Mouvement Solidaire Muluba [*Muluba Solidarity Movement*] [*Political party*] .... MSM
Mouvement Souverainete Association [*Canada*] (PPW) .... MSA
Mouvement Togolais pour la Democratie [*Togolese Movement for Democracy*] [*Political party*] (PD) .... MTO
Mouvement Traditionaliste Congolais [*Congolese Traditionalist Movement*] .... MTC
Mouvement Union Democratique [*Democratic Union Movement*] [*Monaco*] [*Political party*] (PPE) .... MUD
Mouvement Universal pour une Federation Mondiale [*World Association of World Federalists - WAWF*] [*Netherlands*] .... MUFM
Mouvement Universel de la Responsabilite Scientifique [*Universal Movement for Scientific Responsibility - UMSR*] (EAIO) .... MURS
Mouyondzi [*Congo*] [*ICAO location identifier*] (ICLI) .... FCBM
Movable [*Technical drawings*] .... MOV
Movable (AD) .... mov
Movable (MSA) .... MVBL
Movable Appendage Factor [*IOR*] [*Yacht racing*] .... MAF
Movable Closure Valve (NRCH) .... MCV
Movable Core Transformer [*Nuclear energy*] .... MCT
Movable Fine Mesh .... MFM
Movable Head Disc (NITA) .... MHD
Movable In-Core Detector System [*Nuclear energy*] (NRCH) .... MICDS
Movable Instrument Drive System [*Nuclear energy*] (NRCH) .... MIDS
Movable Partition (AD) .... m part
Movable Platform Configuration .... MPC
Movable Search System (MCD) .... MOSES
Movado Group [*NASDAQ symbol*] (TTSB) .... MOVA
Movado Group, Inc. [*NASDAQ symbol*] (SAG) .... MOVA
Movado Group, Inc. [*Associated Press*] (SAG) .... Movado
Move (NASA) .... MO
Move .... MO
Move [*Telecommunications*] (TEL) .... MV
Move Being Made [*Computer science*] .... M
Move Gallery, Inc. [*Associated Press*] (SAG) .... MovieGal
Move In (WDMC) .... MI
[*Time in Days Before*] **Move Operations** .... M
Move Out (WDMC) .... MO
Move Out of Saigon Expeditiously [*or Earliest*] [*Army project, Vietnam*] .... MOOSE
Move Out of Town [*Reduction of troop concentrations in cities*] [*Military*] .... MOOT
Move to End Deception in Advertising [*Student legal action organization*] .... MEDIA
Moved Out of Town (AD) .... moot
Moved, Seconded, and Carried .... MSC
Move-Grow-Learn [*Program for visual perception development*] .... MGL
Move-In Housing Allowance .... MIHA
Movement [*Neurology*] .... M
Movement (AABC) .... MOV
Movement .... MOVMT

Movement [Music] (ROG) .... MOVT
Movement .... MVMNT
Movement (AFM) .... MVMT
Movement (MSA) .... MVT
Movement After-Effect (PDAA) .... MAE
Movement Aftereffect [Optics] .... MAF
Movement Alarm System [Gynecology] .... MAS
Movement and Reinforcement Study (MCD) .... MRS
Movement Capabilities [Military] (CINC) .... MOVECAP
Movement Control [of troops] .... MC
Movement Control Agency [Army] .... MCA
Movement Control Center [Army] .... MCC
Movement Control Officer [Army] .... MCO
Movement Control Organisation [British military] (DMA) .... MOVCO
Movement Control Sub-Committee [IATA] (DS) .... MCSC
Movement Control Team [Air Force] (AFM) .... MCT
Movement Coordinator .... MOVCORD
Movement Designator Code .... MDC
Movement Directive .... MD
Movement Disorder (MAE) .... MD
Movement Echelon [MTMC] (TAG) .... ECH
Movement, Ethyl Chloride, and Elevation [Medicine] .... MECE
Movement for a Better World (EA) .... MBW
Movement for a Democratic Military (EA) .... MDM
Movement for a Democratic Slovakia [Former Czechoslovakia] [Political party] (EY) .... MDS
Movement for a Free Philippines (EA) .... MFP
Movement for a New Society [Defunct] (EA) .... MNS
Movement for All-Macedonian Action [Political party] .... MAAK
Movement for All-Macedonian Action [Political party] .... MAMA
Movement for an Independent and Democratic Cuba (EA) .... CID
Movement for an Independent and Democratic Cuba (EA) .... MIDC
Movement for an Independent Socialist Canada .... MISC
Movement for Autonomous Democracy-Society for Moravia and Silesia [Former Czechoslovakia] [Political party] (EY) .... MAD-SMS
Movement for Democratic Process [Zambia] [Political party] (EY) .... MPD
Movement for Economic Justice (EA) .... MEJ
Movement for Federation of the Americas (EA) .... MFA
Movement for Freedom and Justice [Ghana] [Political party] (EY) .... MFJ
Movement for Human Rights in Vietnam [Defunct] (EA) .... MHRV
Movement for Justice in Africa [Liberia] [Political party] (PPW) .... MOJA
Movement for Justice in Africa-Gambia [Political party] .... MOJA-G
Movement for Liberation and Development [Italy Political party] (EAIO) .... MOLISV
Movement for Multi-Party Democracy [Zambia] [Political party] (EY) .... MMD
Movement for National Liberation [Barbados] [Political party] (PPW) .... MNL
Movement for Political World Union [Blommenslyst, Fyn, Denmark] (EA) .... MPWU
Movement for Rights and Freedoms [Bulgaria] [Political party] .... MRF
Movement for the Advancement of the Zionist Idea [Israel] [Political party] (EY) .... MAZI
Movement for the Liberation of Portuguese Guinea and the Cape Verde Islands .... MLGCV
Movement for the Liberation of Soa Tome and Principe [Political party] .... MLSOP
Movement for the Ordination of Women [British lobbying group] (ECON) .... MOW
Movement for the Redemption of Liberian Muslims [Political party] (EY) .... MRM
Movement for the Restoration of Democracy [Nepal] [Political party] .... MRD
Movement for the Restoration of Democracy [Pakistan] [Political party] (PD) .... MRD
Movement for the Struggle for Political Rights [Uganda] (PD) .... MOSPOR
Movement for the Survival of Ogoni People .... MOSOP
Movement for the Survival of the Ogoni People .... MOSOP
Movement for the Unity of the Left [Ecuador] [Political party] (PPW) .... MUI
Movement Information Distribution Station .... MIDS
Movement Instruction [British military] (DMA) .... MI
Movement Liaison Officer (NATG) .... MLO
Movement of Dependents and Household Goods in Advance of Permanent Change of Station Orders is Authorized [Army] (AABC) .... MOVDHHG
Movement of Dependents and Household Goods to Temporary Station[s] Not Authorized at Government Expense, Except as Prescribed in Joint Travel Regulations [Army] (AABC) .... MDHTSNAGEJTR
Movement of the Assemblies of People [Grenada] .... MAP
Movement of Working Women and Volunteers [Tel Aviv, Israel] (EAIO) .... MWWV
Movement Order [Military] (NVT) .... MOVORD
Movement Order (AD) .... movord
Movement Orders .... MO
Movement Overseas Verification of Enlisted Members [Army] (AABC) .... MOVEM
Movement Overseas Verification of Enlisted Members (AD) .... movem
Movement Priority Designator (DNAB) .... MPD
Movement Protein [Cytology] .... MP
Movement Release Unit [MTMC] (TAG) .... MRU
Movement Report [Military] (NATG) .... MOVEREP
Movement Report (AD) .... moverep
Movement Report [Military] (NVT) .... MOVREP
Movement Report Center [Military] .... MRC
Movement Report Control Center [Military] .... MRCC
Movement Report Office [Military] .... MRO
Movement Report Sheet [Military] .... MRS
Movement Report System [Military] .... MRS
Movement Requirements Generator .... MRG
Movement Research Exchange .... MRX
Movement Shorthand Society (AD) .... Move Short Soc
Movement Shorthand Society [Later, Center for Sutton Movement Writing] (EA) .... MSS
Movement Time [Physical education] .... MT

Movement to Arrest Oppressors (EA) .... MAO
Movement to Restore Decency [Group opposing sex education in schools] .... MOTOREDE
Movement Transfer Order (MCD) .... MTO
Movement-Associates Fetal [Heart rate] Accelerations [Obstetrics] (DAVI) .... MAFAs
Movement-Produced Stimuli .... MPS
Movements and Identification [Military] (AFM) .... M & I
Movements and Transports (NATG) .... M and T
Movements Control Section [British military] (DMA) .... MCS
Movements Identification Officer [Air Force] .... MIO
Movements Identification Technican (SAA) .... MIT
Movements Integration Office .... MIO
Movements Reports Generator (DNAB) .... MORG
Movementu Antiyas Nobo [New Antilles Movement] [Netherlands Political party] (EAIO) .... MAN
Mover' .... MVR
Movers' and Warehousemen's Association of America [Defunct] .... M & WAA
Movers' and Warehousemen's Association of America [Defunct] (EA) .... MWAA
Movers' & Warehousemen's Association of America Inc., Washington DC [STAC] .... MWA
Movers Association of Greater Chicago, Chicago, IL [STAC] .... MGC
Movers Conference of America .... MCA
Moves All Extremities [Medicine] (MAE) .... MAE
Moves All Extremities Equally Well [Neurology] (DAVI) .... MAEEW
Moves All Extremities Well [Medicine] (MEDA) .... MAEW
Movie .... MOV
Movie (AD) .... movi
[The] Movie Channel [Cable-television system] .... TMC
Movie Editor .... ME
Movie Gallery [NASDAQ symbol] (TTSB) .... MOVI
Movie Gallery, Inc. [NASDAQ symbol] (SAG) .... MOVI
Movie Gallery, Inc. [Associated Press] (SAG) .... MovieGal
Movie Going Time .... MGT
Movie Makers Guild (EA) .... MMG
Movie of the Week [Television programming] .... MOW
Movie Projector Operator's School (DNAB) .... MPOS
Movie Star, Inc. [Associated Press] (SAG) .... MovieStr
Movie Star, Inc. (SPSG) .... MSI
MovieFone CI'A' [NASDAQ symbol] (TTSB) .... MOFN
MovieFone, Inc. [NASDAQ symbol] (SAG) .... MOFN
MovieFone, Inc. [Associated Press] (SAG) .... MovieFn
Moviemiento de Integracion Democratica [The Dominican Republic] [Political party] (EY) .... MIDA
Moviment de Defensa de la Terra [Spain Political party] (EY) .... MDT
Movimento [Movement] [Italian] (AD) .... mov
Movimento Academico pela Uniao Democrata [Academic Movement for Democratic Union] [Portugal Political party] (PPE) .... MAUD
Movimento da Resistencia de Mozambique [Mozambique Resistance Movement] .... MRM
Movimento das Forcas Armadas [Armed Forces Movement] [Portugal Political party] (PPE) .... MFA
Movimento de Esquerda Socialista [Movement of the Socialist Left] [Portugal Political party] (PPE) .... MES
Movimento de Libertacao da Guine Portuguesa [Movement for the Liberation of Portuguese Guinea] .... MLGP
Movimento de Libertacao de Sao Tome e Principe [Movement for the Liberation of Sao Tome and Principe] [Portugal] (PPW) .... MLSTP
Movimento de Unidade Nacional Antifacista [National United Antifascist Movement] [Portugal Political party] (PPE) .... MUNAF
Movimento Democratico Brasileiro [Brazilian Democratic Movement] [Political party] (PPW) .... MDB
Movimento Democratico de Mocambique [Democratic Movement of Mozambique] (AF) .... MDM
Movimento Democratico Portugues [Portuguese Democratic Movement] [Political party] (PPE) .... MDP
Movimento di Azione Rivoluzionaria [Revolutionary Action Movement] [Italian] .... MAR
Movimento Independente da Reconstrucao Nacional [Independent Movement of National Reconstruction] [Portugal] (PPE) .... MIRN
Movimento Independente de Reconstrucao Nacional - Partido da Derecha Portuguesa [Independent Movement for National Reconstruction - Party of the Portuguese Right] [Political party] (PPW) .... MIRN-PDP
Movimento Nacional Democratico [National Democratic Movement] [Portugal Political party] (PPE) .... MND
Movimento para Democracia [Cape Verde] [Political party] (EY) .... MPD
Movimento per le Liberta Statuarie [Movement for Statutory Liberty] [Sanmarinese] (PPE) .... MLS
Movimento Politica dei Lavoratori [Workers' Political Movement] [Italy Political party] (PPE) .... MPL
Movimento Popolare Rivoluzionario [Popular Revolutionary Movement] [Italy Political party] (PD) .... MPR
Movimento Popular de Libertacao de Angola [Popular Movement for the Liberation of Angola] [Political party] .... MPLA
Movimento Popular de Libertacao de Angola - Partido do Trabalho [Popular Movement for the Liberation of Angola - Party of Labor] [Political party] (PPW) .... MPLA-PT
Movimento Popular de Libertacao de Cabinda [Popular Movement for the Liberation of Cabinda] [Angola] [Political party] (PD) .... MPLC
Movimento Revolucionario Tiradentes [Revolutionary Tiradentes Movement] [Brazil Political party] (PD) .... MRT
Movimento Sem Terra [Political party] [Brazil] .... MST
Movimento Social Democrata [Social Democrat Movement] [Portugal Political party] (PPE) .... MSD
Movimento Sociale Italiano [Italian Social Movement] [Political party] (PPE) .... MSI

Movimento Sociale Italiano-Destra Nazionale [*Italian Social Movement-National Right*] [*Political party*] (EY) ... MSI-DN
Movimento Socialista Popular [*Popular Socialist Movement*] [*Portugal Political party*] (PPE) ... MSP
Movimentu Antiyas Nobo [*New Antilles Movement*] [*Political party*] (EY) ... MAN
Movimiento 3V [*Nicaragua*] [*Political party*] (EY) ... M-3V
Movimiento 18 de Octubre de Accion Revolucionaria Astra [*Astra 18th October Movement of Revolutionary Action*] [*Ecuador*] [*Political party*] (PD) ... M-18-X
Movimiento Agrario Revolucionario del Campesinado Boliviano [*Revolutionary Movement of Bolivian Indian Peasants*] [*Political party*] (PPW) ... MARC
Movimiento al Socialismo [*Movement towards Socialism*] [*Argentina Political party*] (PPW) ... MAS
Movimiento al Socialismo [*Movement towards Socialism*] [*Venezuela Political party*] (PPW) ... MAS
Movimiento Amplio Colombiano [*Broad-Based Movement of Colombia*] [*Political party*] (PPW) ... MAC
Movimiento Anticomunista Hondureno [*Honduran Anti-Communist Movement*] [*Political party*] (PD) ... Macho
Movimiento Argentino Antiimperialista de Solidaridad Latinoamericana ... MAASLA
Movimiento Autentico Cristiano [*El Salvador*] [*Political party*] (EY) ... MAC
Movimiento Blanco Popular y Progresista [*National Action Movement*] [*Uruguay*] [*Political party*] (EY) ... MBPP
Movimiento Bolivia Libre [*Political party*] (EY) ... MBL
Movimiento Campesino Tupaj Catari [*Bolivia*] [*Political party*] (PPW) ... MCTC
Movimiento Civico Popular [*Panama*] [*Political party*] (EY) ... MCP
Movimiento Colombia Unida [*United Colombian Movement*] [*Political party*] (EY) ... CU
Movimiento da Juventude da Uniao Popular da Guine [*Youth Movement of Guinean People's Union*] ... MJUPG
Movimiento da Unidade Progressiva [*Brazil Political party*] (EY) ... MUP
Movimiento de Accion Nacionalista [*National Action Movement*] [*Uruguay*] [*Political party*] (EY) ... MAN
Movimiento de Accion Popular Unida [*Unified Popular Action Movement*] [*Chile*] [*Political party*] (PD) ... MAPU
Movimiento de Accion Revolucionaria [*Revolutionary Action Movement*] [*Mexico*] (PD) ... MAR
Movimiento de Accion Social Cristiana [*Christian Social Action Movement*] [*Dominican Republic*] [*Political party*] (PPW) ... ASC
Movimiento de Accion Socialista [*Peru*] [*Political party*] (EY) ... MAS
Movimiento de Accion y Unidad Socialista [*Socialist Movement for Action and Unity*] [*Mexico Political party*] (PPW) ... MAUS
Movimiento de Autenticidad Colorada [*Paraguay*] [*Political party*] (EY) ... MAC
Movimiento de Bases Hayistas [*Movement of Hayista Bases*] [*Peru*] [*Political party*] (PPW) ... MBH
Movimiento de Conciliacion Nacional [*National Conciliation Movement*] [*Dominican Republic*] [*Political party*] (PPW) ... MCN
Movimiento de Estudiantes Revolucionarios Salvadorenos [*Revolutionary Movement of Salvadoran Students*] (PD) ... MERS
Movimiento de Independencia Revolucionaria en Armas [*Puerto Rican independence group*] [*Political party*] ... MIRA
Movimiento de Integracion Colorada [*Paraguay*] [*Political party*] (EY) ... MIC
Movimiento de Integracion Democratica [*Democratic Integration Movement*] [*Dominican Republic*] [*Political party*] (PPW) ... MID
Movimiento de Integracion Nacional [*National Integration Movement*] [*Venezuela*] [*Political party*] (PPW) ... MIN
Movimiento de Integracion Nacional [*National Integration Movement*] [*Ecuador*] [*Political party*] (PPW) ... MIN
Movimiento de Izquierda Nacional [*National Left-Wing Movement*] [*Bolivia*] [*Political party*] (PPW) ... MIN
Movimiento de Izquierda Revolucionaria [*Movement of the Revolutionary Left of Peru*] [*Political party*] (PPW) ... MIR-Peru
Movimiento de Izquierda Revolucionario [*Movement of the Revolutionary Left*] [*Bolivia*] [*Political party*] (PPW) ... MIR
Movimiento de Izquierda Revolucionario [*Movement of the Revolutionary Left*] [*Venezuela Political party*] ... MIR
Movimiento de Izquierda Revolucionario [*Movement of the Revolutionary Left*] [*Chile*] [*Political party*] ... MIR
Movimiento de Liberacion del Pueblo [*People's Liberation Movement*] [*El Salvador*] [*Political party*] (PD) ... MLP
Movimiento de Liberacion Nacional [*National Liberation Movement*] [*Guatemala*] [*Political party*] (PPW) ... MLN
Movimiento de Liberacion Nacional [*National Liberation Movement*] [*Uruguay*] [*Political party*] ... MLN
Movimiento de Liberacion Proletaria [*Proletarian Liberation Movement*] [*Mexico Political party*] ... MLP
Movimiento de Liberacion Sebta [*Ceuta Liberation Movement*] [*Spain*] (PD) ... MLS
Movimiento de Patria Socialista [*Venezuela Political party*] (EY) ... MPS
Movimiento de Renovacion Nacional [*National Renewal Movement*] [*Venezuela Political party*] (PPW) ... MORENA
Movimiento de Renovacion Nacional [*Movement for National Renovation*] [*Colorado Political party*] (PPW) ... MRN
Movimiento de Resistencia Armada Puertorriquena [*Puerto Rican Armed Resistance Movement*] [*Political party*] (PD) ... MRAP
Movimiento de Restauracion Nacional [*National Restoration Movement*] [*Colorado Political party*] (EY) ... MORENA
Movimiento de Salvacion Nacional [*National Salvation Movement*] [*Colorado Political party*] (EY) ... MSN
Movimiento de Unidad Revolucionaria [*Guerrilla forces*] [*Honduras*] (EY) ... MUR
Movimiento Democratico del Pueblo [*Paraguay*] [*Political party*] (EY) ... MDP
Movimiento Democratico Nacionalista [*Nationalist Democratic Movement*] [*Guatemala*] [*Political party*] ... MDN
Movimiento Democratico Nicaraguense [*Nicaraguan Democratic Movement*] [*Political party*] (PPW) ... MDN
Movimiento Democratico Peruano [*Peruvian Democratic Movement*] [*Political party*] ... MDP
Movimiento Democratico Popular [*Popular Democratic Movement*] [*Ecuador*] [*Political party*] (PPW) ... MDP
Movimiento Democratico Popular [*Popular Democratic Movement*] [*Chile*] [*Political party*] (PPW) ... MDP
Movimiento Democratico Reformista Peruano [*Peruvian Democratic Reformist Movement*] [*Political party*] (PPW) ... MDRP
Movimiento Electoral del Pueblo [*People's Electoral Movement*] [*Venezuela*] [*Political party*] (PPW) ... MEP
Movimiento Electoral del Pueblo [*People's Electoral Movement*] [*Netherlands Antilles*] [*Political party*] (PPW) ... MEP
Movimiento Emergente de Concordia [*Emerging Movement for Harmony*] [*Guatemala*] [*Political party*] (PPW) ... MEC
Movimiento Estable Republicano Centrista [*El Salvador*] [*Political party*] (EY) ... MERECEN
Movimiento Familiar Cristiano (EA) ... MFC
Movimiento Iberico Libertario [*Spain Political party*] ... MIL
Movimiento Independentista Armado [*Armed Pro-Independence Movement*] [*Puerto Rico*] [*Political party*] (PD) ... MIRA
Movimiento Independiente Democratico [*Independent Democratic Movement*] [*Panama*] [*Political party*] (PPW) ... MID
Movimiento Independiente Peruano [*Peruvian Independent Movement*] [*Political party*] ... MIP
Movimiento Indio Tupaj Katari [*Tupaj Katari Indian Movement*] [*Bolivia*] [*Political party*] (PPW) ... MITKA
Movimiento Juvenil Salesiano [*Salesian Youth Movement - SYM*] (EAIO) ... MJS
Movimiento Liberal Democratico Revolucionario [*Revolutionary Democratic Liberal Movement*] [*Honduras*] [*Political party*] ... MOLIDER
Movimiento Liberal Republicano Nacionalista [*Nationalist Liberal Republican Movement*] [*Panama*] [*Political party*] (PPW) ... Molirena
Movimiento Nacional [*Costa Rica*] [*Political party*] (EY) ... MN
Movimiento Nacional Conservador [*National Conservative Movement*] [*Colorado Political party*] (EY) ... MNC
Movimiento Nacional de Salvacion [*National Movement of Salvation*] [*Dominican Republic*] [*Political party*] (PPW) ... MNS
Movimiento Nacional Reformista [*National Reformist Movement*] [*Honduras*] [*Political party*] ... MNR
Movimiento Nacional Revolucionario [*National Revolutionary Movement*] [*El Salvador*] [*Political party*] (PPW) ... MNR
Movimiento Nacional Tupaj Katari [*Bolivia*] [*Political party*] (PPW) ... MNTK
Movimiento Nacional y Popular [*Paraguay*] [*Political party*] (EY) ... MNP
Movimiento Nacionalista de Izquierda [*Bolivia*] (PPW) ... MNI
Movimiento Nacionalista Justicialista [*Justicialist Nationalist Movement - JNM*] [*Argentina*] (PPW) ... MNJ
Movimiento Nacionalista Popular [*Popular Nationalist Movement*] [*Chile*] [*Political party*] (PD) ... MNP
Movimiento Nacionalista Revolucionario [*National Revolutionary Movement*] [*Bolivia*] [*Political party*] (PPW) ... MNR
Movimiento Nacionalista Revolucionario del Pueblo [*Nationalist Revolutionary People's Movement*] [*Bolivia*] [*Political party*] (PPW) ... MNRP
Movimiento Nacionalista Revolucionario Historico [*Historic Revolutionary Nationalist Movement*] [*Bolivia*] [*Political party*] (PPW) ... MNRH
Movimiento Nacionalista Revolucionario - Vanguardia Revolucionaria 9 de Abril [*Bolivia*] [*Political party*] (EY) ... MNRV
Movimiento Nazionale Pan-Somalo [*Pan-Somali National Movement*] [*Political party*] ... MNPS
Movimiento No Partidarizado [*Peru*] [*Political party*] (EY) ... MNP
Movimiento Obrero Independiente Revolucionario [*Independent Revolutionary Workers' Movement*] [*Colorado Political party*] (PPW) ... MOIR
Movimiento Obrero Izquierdista Revolucionario [*Colorado Political party*] (PPW) ... MOIR
Movimiento Obrero Revolucionario Salvado Cayetano Carpio [*El Salvador*] [*Political party*] (EY) ... MOR
Movimiento para Accion y Solidaridad [*Guatemala*] [*Political party*] (EY) ... MAS
Movimiento para la Autodeterminacion y Independencia del Archipielago Canario [*Movement for the Self-Determination and Independence of the Canary Archipelago*] [*Canary Islands*] [*Spanish*] (PD) ... MPAIAC
Movimiento para la Unificacion Nacional de Guinea Ecuatorial [*Movement for National Unification of Equatorial Guinea*] [*Political party*] (EY) ... MUNGE
Movimiento Paraguayo de Liberacion [*Political party*] (EY) ... MOPALI
Movimiento Patriotica Manuel Rodriguez [*Manuel Rodriguez Patriotic Movement*] [*Chile*] [*Political party*] (EY) ... MPMR
Movimiento Patriotico Cuba Libre [*Free Cuba Patriotic Movement*] [*Political party*] (AD) ... MPCL
Movimiento Patriotico Institucional [*Panama*] [*Political party*] (EY) ... MPI
Movimiento Popular Colorado [*Colorado Popular Movement*] [*Paraguay*] [*Political party*] (PD) ... MOPOCO
Movimiento Popular de Liberacion Cinchonero [*Guerrilla forces*] [*Honduras*] (EY) ... MPLC
Movimiento Popular de Liberacion "Cinchoneros" [*"Cinchoneros" Popular Liberation Movement*] [*Honduras*] [*Political party*] ... MPL
Movimiento Popular Democratico [*Popular Democratic Movement*] [*Ecuador*] [*Political party*] (PPW) ... MPD
Movimiento Popular Dominicano [*Dominican Popular Movement*] [*Dominican Republic*] [*Political party*] (PPW) ... MPD
Movimiento Popular Socialcristiano [*Christian Social Popular Movement*] [*El Salvador*] [*Political party*] (PD) ... MPSC
Movimiento por el Cambio Democratico [*Mexico Political party*] (EY) ... MCD
Movimiento pro Independencia de Puerto Rico (EA) ... MPI
Movimiento Pro-Democracia y Libertad [*Panama*] [*Political party*] (EY) ... MPDL
Movimiento Republicano Progresista [*Progressive Republican Movement*] [*Venezuela Political party*] ... MRP

Movimiento Revolucionario de 13 de Noviembre [*Revolutionary Movement of 13 November*] [*Guatemala*] [*Political party*] (AD) ... MR-13 Movement of 13 NoGuatemala
Movimiento Revolucionario del Pueblo - Ixim [*People's Revolutionary Movement - Ixim*] [*Guatemala*] [*Political party*] (PD) ... MRP
Movimiento Revolucionario Espartaco [*Bolivia*] [*Political party*] (PPW) ... MRE
Movimiento Revolucionario Estudantil [*Colorado Political party*] (EY) ... MRE
Movimiento Revolucionario Popular [*Venezuela Political party*] (EY) ... MRP
Movimiento Revolucionario Tupac Amaru [*Peru*] [*Political party*] (EY) ... MRTA
Movimiento Revolucionario Tupaj Katari [*Tupaj Katari Revolutionary Movement*] [*Bolivia*] [*Political party*] (PPW) ... MRTK
Movimiento Socialista Revolucionario [*Revolutionary Socialist Movement*] [*Panama*] [*Political party*] (PPW) ... MSR
Movimiento Teresiano de Apostolado [*Teresian Apostolic Movement - TAM*] [*Italy*] (EAIO) ... MTA
Movimiento Todos par la Patria [*Argentina Political party*] (EY) ... MTP
Movimiento-20 [*Panama*] [*Political party*] (EY) ... M-20
Moving ... MOVE
Moving ... MVG
Moving Annual Total [*Statistics*] (DCTA) ... MAT
Moving Average [*Statistics*] ... MA
Moving Average Rating Method [*Insurance*] ... MARM
Moving Base Operator ... MBO
Moving Belt Radiator ... MBR
Moving Boundary Electrophoresis [*Analytical biochemistry*] ... MBE
Moving Call for Fire [*Military*] ... MCFF
Moving Coil [*Electronics*] (DEN) ... MC
Moving Coil Galvanometer [*Electronics*] ... MCG
Moving Coil Loudspeaker [*Electronics*] ... MCL
Moving Coil Microphone [*Electronics*] ... MCM
Moving Coil Motor [*Electronics*] (IAA) ... MCM
Moving Deformable Barrier [*NHTSA*] (TAG) ... MDB
Moving Domain Memories [*Computer science*] (MDG) ... MOD
Moving Earth Simulator (MCD) ... MES
Moving Head Disk [*Computer science*] (TEL) ... MHD
Moving Inspection Lot ... MIL
Moving Ion Voltmeter ... MIV
Moving Magnet [*Stereo equipment*] ... MM
Moving Magnetic Feature [*Astronomy*] (OA) ... MMF
Moving Map Display ... MMD
Moving Paper Electrophoresis ... MPE
Moving Part Logic (PDAA) ... MPLAW
Moving [*or Motion*] **Pictures Experts Group** [*Motion video standard*] (PCM) ... MPEG
Moving Presentation Mode ... MPM
Moving Scene Display ... MSD
Moving Target Acquisition RADAR (MCD) ... MTAR
Moving Target Carrier (MCD) ... MTC
Moving Target Detection System (IEEE) ... MOTARDES
Moving Target Detection System ... MOTARDS
Moving Target Detector [*RADAR*] ... MTD
Moving Target Indicator ... MTI
Moving Target Indicator Coherent (IEEE) ... MTIC
Moving Target Indicator Constant False Alarm Rate (CET) ... MTICFAR
Moving Target Indicator Kit ... MTIK
Moving Target Locating RADAR (AABC) ... MTLR
Moving Target Reactor ... MTR
Moving Target Resolver (MCD) ... MTR
Moving Target Screen (MCD) ... MTS
Moving Target Simulator (RDA) ... MTS
Moving Target Video Processor ... MTVP
Moving Terrain Model ... MTM
Moving Time Series ... MTS
Moving Window Display (MCD) ... MWD
Moving-Bed Filter [*Waste*] (DICI) ... MBF
Moving-Withdrawal Chromatography ... MWC
Mowbray's Styles of Deeds [*A publication*] (DLA) ... Mow St
Mower ... MWR
Mower Specialists' Association of Australia Cooperative ... MSAAC
Moxa [*German Democratic Republic*] [*Seismograph station code, US Geological Survey*] (SEIS) ... MOX
Moxalactam [*An antibiotic*] ... MOX
Moxham Bank [*NASDAQ symbol*] (TTSB) ... MOXB
Moxham Bank Corp. [*NASDAQ symbol*] (SAG) ... MOXB
Moxham Bank Corp. [*Associated Press*] (SAG) ... Moxham
Moyale [*Kenya*] [*ICAO location identifier*] (ICLI) ... HKMY
Moyco Technologies [*NASDAQ symbol*] (TTSB) ... MOYC
Moyco Technologies, Inc. [*NASDAQ symbol*] (SAG) ... MOYC
Moyco Technologies, Inc. [*Associated Press*] (SAG) ... MoycoT
Moyer Library, Gibson City, IL [*Library symbol Library of Congress*] (LCLS) ... IGib
Moyle's Criminal Circulars [*India*] [*A publication*] (DLA) ... Moyle
Moyle's Entries [*1658*] [*England*] [*A publication*] (DLA) ... Moyle
Moyobamba [*Peru*] [*ICAO location identifier*] (ICLI) ... SPBB
Moyock, NC [*FM radio station call letters*] ... WMYK
Mozambique [*Aircraft nationality and registration mark*] (FAAC) ... C9
Mozambique [*MARC geographic area code Library of Congress*] (LCCP) ... f-mz--
Mozambique [*ANSI three-letter standard code*] (CNC) ... MOZ
Mozambique (AD) ... Moz
Mozambique (AD) ... Mozam
Mozambique [*MARC country of publication code Library of Congress*] (LCCP) ... mz
Mozambique [*ANSI two-letter standard code*] (CNC) ... MZ
Mozambique [*Mozambique*] [*Airport symbol*] (AD) ... MZQ
Mozambique African National Union [*Later, FRELIMO*] ... MANU
Mozambique, Angola, and Guine Information Center [*British*] ... MAGIC
Mozambique Current (AD) ... Moz Cur
Mozambique Metical [*Monetary unit*] (IMH) ... MM
Mozambique National Resistance [*Political party*] (AD) ... MNR
Mozambique National Resistance Movement ... MNR
Mozambique Solidarity Office (EA) ... MSO
Mozambique Support Network (EA) ... MSN
Mozley and Whiteley's Law Dictionary [*A publication*] (ILCA) ... M & W Law Dic
Mozley and Whiteley's Law Dictionary [*A publication*] (DLA) ... Moz & W
Mozley and Whiteley's Law Dictionary [*A publication*] (DLA) ... Mozley & W
Mozley and Whiteley's Law Dictionary [*A publication*] (DLA) ... Mozley & Whiteley
Mozzarella (AD) ... mozza
Mpacha [*Namibia*] [*ICAO location identifier*] (ICLI) ... FAMP
Mpaka [*Zaire*] [*ICAO location identifier*] (ICLI) ... FZFQ
Mpanda [*Tanzania*] [*ICAO location identifier*] (ICLI) ... HTMP
Mpanda [*Tanzania*] [*Airport symbol*] (AD) ... MPD
MP&L Cap I 8.05% 'QUIPS' [*NYSE symbol*] (TTSB) ... MPLPr
M'Passa [*Congo*] [*ICAO location identifier*] (ICLI) ... FCBP
MPB Technologies, Dorval, PQ, Canada [*Library symbol*] [*Library of Congress*] (LCLS) ... CaQMMPB
MPB Technologies, Dorval, Quebec [*Library symbol National Library of Canada*] (NLC) ... QMMPB
MPG Investment Corp. Ltd. [*Toronto Stock Exchange symbol Vancouver Stock Exchange symbol*] ... MPG
M-Phase Promoting Factor [*Cytology*] ... MPF
m-Phenylenediamine [*Also, MPDA*] [*Organic chemistry*] ... MPD
m-Phenylenediamine [*Also, MPD*] [*Organic chemistry*] ... MPDA
Mpika [*Zambia*] [*ICAO location identifier*] (ICLI) ... FLMP
MPM Launch Right (MCD) ... MLR
MPM Technologies [*NASDAQ symbol*] (TTSB) ... MPMLE
MPM Technologies, Inc. [*Associated Press*] (SAG) ... MPM Tch
MPM Technologies, Inc. [*NASDAQ symbol*] (SAG) ... MPML
Mpongwe [*Zambia*] [*ICAO location identifier*] (ICLI) ... FLGW
Mporokoso [*Zambia*] [*ICAO location identifier*] (ICLI) ... FLPK
M'Pouya [*Congo*] [*ICAO location identifier*] (ICLI) ... FCBO
MPS [*Mucopolysaccharidoses*] **Society** (EA) ... MPS
MPSI Systems, Inc. [*NASDAQ symbol*] (SAG) ... MPSI
MPTER [*Multiple Point Source Model with Terrain*] **Model with Deposition andSettling of Pollutants** [*Environmental Protection Agency*] (GFGA) ... MPTDS
MPTV, Inc. [*NASDAQ symbol*] (SAG) ... MPTV
Mpwapwa [*Tanzania*] [*ICAO location identifier*] (ICLI) ... HTMX
Mr. & Mrs. (VRA) ... M/M
Mr Jay Fashions Intl [*NASDAQ symbol*] (TTSB) ... MRJY
Mr. V Fan Club [*Defunct*] (EA) ... MVFC
Mrs. Gould's Residential Advisory Centre for the Elderly [*British*] (CB) ... GRACE
MRS Technology [*NASDAQ symbol*] (TTSB) ... MRSI
MRS Technology, Inc. [*Associated Press*] (SAG) ... MRS Tch
MRS Technology, Inc. [*NASDAQ symbol*] (SAG) ... MRSI
MRV Communications, Inc. [*Associated Press*] (SAG) ... MRV Cm
MRV Communications, Inc. [*NASDAQ symbol*] (SAG) ... MRVC
MRV Communicatons [*NASDAQ symbol*] (TTSB) ... MRVC
M.S Carriers [*NASDAQ symbol*] (TTSB) ... MSCA
MS Carriers, Inc. [*Associated Press*] (SAG) ... MS Carr
MS Carriers, Inc. [*NASDAQ symbol*] (NQ) ... MSCA
MS Financial [*NASDAQ symbol*] (TTSB) ... MSFI
MS Financial Corp. [*NASDAQ symbol*] (SAG) ... MSFI
MS Financial, Inc. [*Associated Press*] (SAG) ... MS Fncl
Ms. Foundation for Women (EA) ... MFW
Msauli [*South Africa*] [*ICAO location identifier*] (ICLI) ... FAMZ
MSB Bancorp [*NASDAQ symbol*] (TTSB) ... MSBB
MSB Bancorp, Inc. [*AMEX symbol*] (SAG) ... MBB
MSB Bancorp, Inc. [*Associated Press*] (SAG) ... MSB Bcp
MSB Bancorp, Inc. [*NASDAQ symbol*] (SAG) ... MSBB
MSB Financial [*NASDAQ symbol*] (TTSB) ... MSBF
MSB Financial, Inc. [*Associated Press*] (SAG) ... MSB Fn
MSB Financial, Inc. [*NASDAQ symbol*] (SAG) ... MSBF
MSC Industrial Direct'A' [*NYSE symbol*] (TTSB) ... MSM
[*An*] **MSC** [*Military Sealift Command*] **Leased/Controlled Seavan or Milvan** ... MSCVAN
MSC [*Mobile Servicing Center*] **Maintenance Depot** (SSD) ... MMD
MS-DOS, CD-ROM Extension [*Computer science*] ... MSCDEX
Msembe-Ruaha National Park [*Tanzania*] [*ICAO location identifier*] (ICLI) ... HTMR
MSFC [*Marshall Space Flight Center*] **Management Directive** [*NASA*] ... MMD
MSFC [*Marshall Space Flight Center*] **Management Instruction** [*NASA*] ... MMI
MSFC [*Marshall Space Flight Center*] **Mated Element Systems** [*NASA*] (NASA) ... MMES
MSH [*Melanophore-Stimulating Hormone*] **Release Inhibiting Factor** [*Laboratory science*] (DAVI) ... MRIF
MSH [*Melanophore-Stimulating Hormone*] **Releasing Factor** [*Medicine*] (DAVI) ... MRF
MSH [*Melanophore-Stimulating Hormone*] **Releasing Hormone** [*Laboratory Science*] (DAVI) ... MRH
MSR Exploration [*AMEX symbol*] (TTSB) ... MSR
MSR Exploration Ltd. [*AMEX symbol Toronto Stock Exchange symbol*] (SPSG) ... MSR
MSR Exploration Ltd. [*Associated Press*] (SAG) ... MSR
MSU [*Michigan State University*] **and WSU Union List of Serials, Detroit, MI** [*Wayne State University*] [*OCLC symbol*] (OCLC) ... EWM
MSUD [*Maple Syrup Urine Disease*] **Family Support Group** (EA) ... MSUDFSG
M-Sys Flash Disk Pioneers Ltd [*NASDAQ symbol*] (TTSB) ... FLSHF
M-Systems Flash Disk Pioneers Ltd. [*Associated Press*] (SAG) ... M-SysFD
Mt, Pleasant, SC [*FM radio station call letters*] ... WJUK
MTC Electronic [*Vancouver Stock Exchange symbol*] ... MT
MTI Technology [*NASDAQ symbol*] (TTSB) ... MTIG
MTI Technology Corp. [*Associated Press*] (SAG) ... MTI Tch
MTL, Inc. [*Associated Press*] (SAG) ... MTL Inc
MTL, Inc. [*NASDAQ symbol*] (SAG) ... MTLI

MTM [*Methods-Time Measurement*] **Association for Standards and Research** (EA) ... MTM
MTM [*Methods-Time Measurement*] **Association for Standards and Research** [*Later, MTM*] (EA) ... MTMASR
MTM Productions, Inc. [*Named for actress Mary Tyler Moore*] ... MTM
MTMC [*Military Traffic Management Command*] **Automated Transportation Scheduler** (GFGA) ... MATCH
MTS Systems [*NASDAQ symbol*] (TTSB) ... MTSC
MTS Systems Corp. [*Associated Press*] (SAG) ... MTS
MTS Systems Corp. [*NASDAQ symbol*] (NQ) ... MTSC
MTS Systems Corporation, Minneapolis, MN [*Library symbol Library of Congress*] (LCLS) ... MnMMSC
Mtwara [*Tanzania*] [*ICAO location identifier*] (ICLI) ... HTMT
Mtwara [*Tanzania*] [*Airport symbol*] (OAG) ... MYW
Mu [*Twelfth letter of the Greek alphabet*] (DAVI) ... M
Mu Kappa Tau (EA) ... MKT
Muambi [*Zaire*] [*ICAO location identifier*] (ICLI) ... FZUJ
Muan Chon [*Mass Party*] [*Political party*] ... MC
Muanda [*Zaire*] [*ICAO location identifier*] (ICLI) ... FZAG
Muar [*Malaysia*] [*ICAO location identifier*] (ICLI) ... WMAV
Muara Wahau [*Indonesia*] [*ICAO location identifier*] (ICLI) ... WRLW
Muaratewe/Beringin [*Indonesia*] [*ICAO location identifier*] (ICLI) ... WRBM
Much Ado about Nothing [*Shakespearean work*] ... Ado
Much Increased Salary, Hardly Any Pension [*Lifestyle classification*] ... MISHAP
Much Married [*Slang*] ... MM
Much Regret, I Am Unable ... MRU
Muchall's Doctor and Student [*A publication*] (DLA) ... Much D & S
Mucilaginous (ROG) ... MUC
Mucilaginous (ROG) ... MUCILAG
Mucociliary Transport [*Physiology*] ... MCT
Mucocutaneous Leishmaniasis [*Medicine*] ... MCL
Mucocutaneous Lymph Node Syndrome [*Medicine*] ... MCLS
Mucocutaneous Lymph Node Syndrome [*Medicine*] ... MLNS
Mucocutaneous Lymph Node Synrome [*Kawasaki's disease*] (DAVI) ... MCLNS
Mucoid ... M
Mucoid Colony [*Biochemistry*] (DAVI) ... M
Mucoid Exopolysaccharide [*Biochemistry*] ... MEP
Mucolipidosis [*Medicine*] ... ML
Mucolipidosis IV [*A genetic disease*] ... ML IV
Muconate Lactonizing Enzyme ... MLE
Mucopeptide [*Biochemistry*] ... MP
Mucopolysaccaridoses [*Morquio Syndrome*] (PAZ) ... MPS IV
Mucopolysaccharide [*Also, MPS*] [*Clinical chemistry*] ... MP
Mucopolysaccharide [*Also, MP*] [*Clinical chemistry*] ... MPS
Mucopolysaccharidoses [*Hurler Syndrome*] [*Also, Scheie Syndrome and Hurler/Scheie Syndrome*] (PAZ) ... MPS I
Mucopolysaccharidoses [*Hunter Syndrome*] (PAZ) ... MPS II
Mucopolysaccharidosis [*Medicine*] ... MPS
Mucopurulent [*Biochemistry*] (DAVI) ... MP
Mucosa-Associated Lymphoid Tissue [*Anatomy*] ... MALT
Mucosal Disease Virus ... MDV
Mucosal Mast Cell [*Medicine*] ... MMC
Mucosal Ulcerative Colitis [*Medicine*] ... MUC
Mucosubstance (MAE) ... MS
Mucous Cell ... MC
Mucous Glycoproteins [*Biochemistry*] ... MGP
Mucous Membrane ... MM
Mucrones Length [*Of Crustacea*] ... ML
Mucrones Length to Total Body Length Ratio [*Of Crustacea*] ... ML/TL
Mucus Flow Rate (MAE) ... MFR
Mucus-Stimulating Substance ... MSS
Mud ... M
Mud and Snow (AD) ... m & s
Mud and Snow Tire [*Automotive engineering*] ... M & S
MUD [*Multi-User Dungeon*] **Object-Oriented** [*Computer science*] (DOM) ... MOO
Mud, Oil, Hooks, Slings [*Insurance*] (AD) ... mohs
Mud on Airstrip (AD) ... moa
Mud Volcano [*Wyoming*] [*Seismograph station code, US Geological Survey*] (SEIS) ... MVW
Mud Weight [*Well drilling technology*] ... MW
Mudanjiang General Aviation Co. [*China*] [*FAA designator*] (FAAC) ... CMJ
Muddle [*A computer language*] ... MDL
Muddy [*Track condition*] [*Thoroughbred racing*] ... M
Muddy [*Quality of the bottom*] [*Nautical charts*] ... M
Muddy [*Track condition*] [*Thoroughbred racing*] ... MY
Mudgee [*Australia Airport symbol*] (OAG) ... DGE
Mudiad Amdyffyn Cymru [*Welsh Defense Movement*] ... MAC
Mudstone Soil [*Agronomy*] ... Mudst
Mueda [*Mozambique*] [*ICAO location identifier*] (ICLI) ... FQMD
Muehldorf [*Germany ICAO location identifier*] (ICLI) ... EDMY
Mueller Cell [*Eye anatomy*] ... MU
Mueller [*Paul*] **Co.** [*NASDAQ symbol*] (NQ) ... MUEL
Mueller [*Paul*] **Co.** [*Associated Press*] (SAG) ... MuellerP
Mueller Hinton Agar [*Microbiology*] (OA) ... MHA
Mueller Industries [*NYSE symbol*] (SPSG) ... MLI
Mueller Industries [*Associated Press*] (SAG) ... Mueller
Mueller-Hinton [*Agar*] [*Microbiology*] ... M-H
Mueller-Hinton Broth [*Cell growth medium*] ... MHB
Muellerian Inhibiting Substance [*Embryology*] [*Biochemistry*] ... MIS
Muellerian Regression Factor [*Embryology*] (DAVI) ... MRF
Muellerian Repressor Factor [*Embryology*] ... MRF
Muenchen [*Germany ICAO location identifier*] (ICLI) ... EDDM
Muenchen [*Germany ICAO location identifier*] (ICLI) ... EDMM
Muenchen [*Germany ICAO location identifier*] (ICLI) ... EDMU
Muenchen, Hospital, Perlacher Forst [*Germany ICAO location identifier*] (ICLI) ... EDEM
Muenchner Mode-Tage [*Germany*] ... MMT
Muenster [*Germany ICAO location identifier*] (ICLI) ... EDNM
Muenster/Osnabruck [*Germany ICAO location identifier*] (ICLI) ... EDLG
Muenster/Telgte [*Germany ICAO location identifier*] (ICLI) ... EDLT
Muenster, TX [*FM radio station call letters*] ... KXGM
Muenster-Gievenbeck [*Germany ICAO location identifier*] (ICLI) ... EDZM
Muenster-Westfalen [*Federal Republic of Germany*] [*Seismograph station code, US Geological Survey*] (SEIS) ... MWG
Mueo [*New Caledonia*] [*Airport symbol*] (OAG) ... PDC
Mueo/Nickel [*New Caledonia*] [*ICAO location identifier*] (ICLI) ... NWWQ
Muerte a los Secuestradores [*Death to Kidnappers*] [*Colorado*] (PD) ... MAS
Muerto Canyon Virus [*Hantavirus strain*] ... MCV
Muertos Trough [*Geology*] ... MT
Muexins-Length Theory ... MLT
Muffin (ABBR) ... MFN
Muffin-Tin Orbital [*Physics*] ... MTO
Muffler [*Automotive advertising*] ... MFFLR
Muffler ... MUF
Muffler ... MUFLR
Mufulira [*Zambia*] [*ICAO location identifier*] (ICLI) ... FLML
Mug (ABBR) ... MG
Mugera [*Burundi*] [*ICAO location identifier*] (ICLI) ... HBBM
Mugged (ABBR) ... MGD
Mugger (ABBR) ... MGR
Mugginess (ABBR) ... MGINS
Mugging (ABBR) ... MGG
Muggy (ABBR) ... MGY
Muhajir Qaumi Movement [*Pakistan*] [*Political party*] (ECON) ... MQM
Muhammad Ali Amateur Sports ... MAAS
Muhammad Ali Professional Sports [*Commercial firm*] ... MAPS
Muhammadan Anglo-Oriental ... MAO
Muhammadan Era ... ME
Muhl Center Elementary School, Rockford, IL [*Library symbol*] [*Library of Congress*] (LCLS) ... IRoMuE
Muhlenberg College, Allentown, PA [*Library symbol Library of Congress*] (LCLS) ... PAtM
Muhlenberg Hospital, Plainfield, NJ [*Library symbol Library of Congress*] (LCLS) ... NjPlaM
Muhyiddin Ibn Arabi Society ... MIAS
Mui [*Ethiopia*] [*Airport symbol*] (OAG) ... MUJ
Mui River [*Ethiopia*] [*ICAO location identifier*] (ICLI) ... HAMR
Muir Woods National Monument ... MUWO
Muirhea's Institutes of Gaius [*A publication*] (DLA) ... Muir Gai
Mujeres Activas en Letras y Cambio Social (EA) ... MALCS
Mujeres en Accion Sindical [*Organizes national and international conferences on women in the economy*] [*Mexico*] (CROSS) ... MAS
Muk Air Taxi [*Denmark ICAO designator*] (FAAC) ... MUK
Mukah [*Malaysia*] [*Airport symbol*] (OAG) ... MKM
Mukah [*Malaysia*] [*ICAO location identifier*] (ICLI) ... WBGK
Mukalla [*South Arabia*] [*Airport symbol*] (AD) ... MKX
Mukedi [*Zaire*] [*ICAO location identifier*] (ICLI) ... FZDP
Mukeiras [*People's Democratic Republic of Yemen*] [*ICAO location identifier*] (ICLI) ... ODAM
Mukeiras [*South Arabia*] [*Airport symbol*] (AD) ... UKR
Mukerian [*India*] [*Seismograph station code, US Geological Survey Closed*] (SEIS) ... MUK
Mukhrani [*Former USSR ICAO location identifier*] (ICLI) ... UGMM
Mukinge [*Zambia*] [*ICAO location identifier*] (ICLI) ... FLGE
Muko Muko [*Indonesia*] [*ICAO location identifier*] (ICLI) ... WIPU
Mukonchi [*Zambia*] [*ICAO location identifier*] (ICLI) ... FLMI
Mukoy [*Zaire*] [*ICAO location identifier*] (ICLI) ... FZRC
Mukur [*Afghanistan*] [*ICAO location identifier*] (ICLI) ... OAMK
Mulatupo [*Panama*] [*Airport symbol*] (OAG) ... MPP
Mulberry Grove Community Unit, School District 1, Mulberry Grove, IL [*Library symbol Library of Congress*] (LCLS) ... IMulgSD
Mulberry Heart (OA) ... MH
Mulberry Latent Virus [*Plant pathology*] ... MLV
Mulberry Ringspot Virus [*Plant pathology*] ... MRV
Mulege [*Mexico*] [*Airport symbol Obsolete*] (OAG) ... MUG
Mulege [*Mexico*] [*Airport symbol*] (AD) ... MVU
Muleshoe, TX [*FM radio station call letters*] ... KKYC
Muleshoe, TX [*FM radio station call letters*] ... KMUL
Mulgrave, NS [*Television station call letters*] ... CBHFT-2
Mulgrave, NS [*Television station call letters*] ... CBHT-11
Mulheres por um Desenvolvimento Alternativo [*Development Alternatives with women for a New Era - DAWN*] [*Brazil*] (EAIO) ... MUDAR
Mulheres Portuguesas Social-Democratas [*An association*] (EAIO) ... MSPD
Mulholland Library of Conjuring & the Applied Arts, Los Angeles, CA [*Library symbol*] [*Library of Congress*] (LCLS) ... CLMLC
Mulhouse/Basel [*France*] [*Airport symbol*] (OAG) ... MLH
Mulhouse/Habsheim [*France ICAO location identifier*] (ICLI) ... LFGB
Mulia [*Indonesia*] [*Airport symbol*] (OAG) ... LII
Mulia [*Indonesia*] [*ICAO location identifier*] (ICLI) ... WAJM
Mulika [*Kenya*] [*ICAO location identifier*] (ICLI) ... HKMK
Mulitple Association Control Function [*Telecommunications*] (OSI) ... MACF
Mulitple Myeloma [*Hematology*] (DAVI) ... MYEL
Mulka [*Australia Airport symbol Obsolete*] (OAG) ... MVK
Mullan [*Idaho*] [*Seismograph station code, US Geological Survey*] (SEIS) ... MUL
Mullan Pass, ID [*Location identifier FAA*] (FAAL) ... MLP
Mullan Public Library, Mullan, ID [*Library symbol*] [*Library of Congress*] (LCLS) ... IdMu
Mullard Radio Astronomy Observatory (USDC) ... MRAO
Mullard Radio Astronomy Observatory [*Marine science*] (OSRA) ... MRAO

Mullard Space Science Laboratory [*University of London*] (PDAA) ... MSSL
Mullen, NE [*Location identifier FAA*] (FAAL) ... MHN
Mullen Scales of Early Learning [*Child development test*] [*Psychology*] ... MSEL
Mullens, WV [*FM radio station call letters*] ... WPMW
Muller ... MULR
Muller Data Corp. [*Information service or system*] (IID) ... MDC
Muller Industries [*NYSE symbol*] (SAG) ... MLI
Muller Industries [*Associated Press*] (SAG) ... MuellerInd
Mullewa [*Australia Airport symbol Obsolete*] (OAG) ... MXU
Mulliken Approximation for Differential Overlap [*Physics*] ... MADO
Mulliken District Library, Mulliken, MI [*Library symbol Library of Congress*] (LCLS) ... MiMul
Mullins, SC [*AM radio station call letters*] ... WJAY
Mullins, SC [*FM radio station call letters*] (RBYB) ... WWSK
Mullion [*Technical drawings*] ... MULL
Mulobezi [*Zambia*] [*ICAO location identifier*] (ICLI) ... FLMU
MULS [*Minnesota Union List of Serials*], Minneapolis, MN [*OCLC symbol*] (OCLC) ... MUL
Multan [*Pakistan*] [*Airport symbol*] (OAG) ... MUX
Multan [*Pakistan*] [*ICAO location identifier*] (ICLI) ... OPMT
Multi Address Asynchronous Communication System ... MAACS
Multi Column Option (DGA) ... MCO
Multi Disc Reader [*Computer science*] (DGA) ... MDR
Multi/National Business Association (EA) ... M/NBA
Multi Station Boundary Layer Model System (PDAA) ... MSBLMS
Multi-Access Broadcast Unit System (PDAA) ... MABUS
Multi-Access Computer Switch [*Telecommunications*] (TSSD) ... MACS
Multi-Access Computing (NITA) ... MAC
Multiaccess Executive with Fast Interrupt Acceptance [*Computer science*] (MHDI) ... MAFIA
Multi-Access Pointer (PCM) ... MAP
Multiaccess Real-Time Operating System [*AEG Telefunken*] [*Germany*] ... MARTOS
Multi-Access Systems Control Terminal (PDAA) ... MASEC
Multiaction Computer ... MAC
Multi-Adaptive Linear Neuron (PDAA) ... MADALINE
Multi-Additional SCSI [*Small Computer System Interface*] **Subsystem Hot Fix Device** [*Computer science*] ... MASS HFD
Multi-Adversity Resistance [*to root rot*] [*Plant pathology*] ... MAR
Multi-Agent Relevance Linkage Information System (NITA) ... MARLIS
Multiairline [*Type of British pole line construction*] ... MAL
Multiallelic Mating-Type Regulatory Gene ... MAT
Multi-Analyzer Configuration (IAA) ... MAC
Multi-Angle Imaging Spectrometer [*Marine science*] (OSRA) ... MISR
Multi-Angle Imaging Spectrometer (USDC) ... MISR
Multiangle LASER Light-Scattering [*Instrumentation*] ... MALLS
Multi-Anode Microchannel Array (PDAA) ... MAMA
Multiantimicrobial Resistant Hemophilus Influenza B ... MRHIB
Multiaperture Ferrite Logic ... MAFL
Multiaperture Logic Element ... MALE
Multiaperture Reluctance Switch [*Data storage unit*] ... MARS
Multiapertured Device-Resistance (DNAB) ... MAD-R
Multi-Appeal Vehicle ... MAV
Multi-Application Computer (IAA) ... MAC
Multiapplication Monitor ... MAM
Multiarray Gamma Irradiator ... MAGI
Multiaspect Relevance Linkage Information System ... MARLIS
Multiaspect Signaling (IEEE) ... MAS
Multi-Association Policy Advisory Group [*An association*] ... MAPAG
Multi-Attribute Identification and Analysis Program [*Jointly developed by Georgia Tech Research Institute and the US Air Force*] ... MAIDA
Multiattribute Utility (IEEE) ... MAU
Multiattribute Utility Function ... MAUF
Multi-Automatic System for Simulation and Operational Planning (PDAA) ... MASSOP
Multiaxial Radial Circuit (IAA) ... MARC
Multiaxial Stress Field ... MSF
Multi-Axis Spin Test Inertia Facility [*Training device for astronauts*] ... MASTIF
Multibanc Financial Corp. [*Toronto Stock Exchange symbol*] ... MBK
Multibanc NT Financial Corp. [*Toronto Stock Exchange symbol*] ... MIB
Multiband (DEN) ... MB
Multiband Automatic Test Equipment ... MATE
Multiband Direction Finder ... MDF
Multiband Image Scanning System ... MISS
Multiband Infrared Filter Radiometer ... MIFR
Multiband Infrared Radiometer ... MIR
Multi-Band Portable Signal Generator (PDAA) ... MPSG
Multiband Spectral Observation Equipment ... MSOE
Multibank DRAM [*Computer science*] ... MDRAM
Multi-Barrel Smoke Discharger [*Military*] (PDAA) ... MBSD
Multibase Arithmetic Block (ADA) ... MAB
Multibeam Acquisition RADAR (MCD) ... MBAR
Multibeam Antenna ... MBA
Multibeam Multifrequency (CAAL) ... MBMF
Multibeam Radiometer Antenna ... MBRA
Multibeam Steering System ... MSS
Multibit Shifter (IAA) ... MBS
Multiblade Slurry Saw [*Semiconductor technology*] ... MBS
Multiblock Synchronization Signal Unit [*Telecommunications*] (TEL) ... MBS
Multiblock Synchronization Signal Unit [*Telecommunications*] (TEL) ... MSU
Multibomb Rack ... MBR
Multibuoy Mooring [*Oil platform*] ... MBM
Multibus Accounting Package (PDAA) ... MAP
Multibus Interface [*Computer science*] (MCD) ... MBI
Multibutton Electronic Telephone (NITA) ... MET
Multicae Companies [*NYSE symbol*] (SAG) ... MUL
Multicanal Participacoes [*Associated Press*] (SAG) ... MltcPrt
Multicanal Participacoes [*NASDAQ symbol*] (SAG) ... MPAR
Multicare Companies [*Associated Press*] (SAG) ... Multicne
Multicare Companies [*Associated Press*] (SAG) ... Multicre
Multicare Cos. [*NYSE symbol*] (TTSB) ... MUL
Multi-Carrier Station Radio [*or Remote*] **Control Equipment** (PDAA) ... MSR
Multicast Address Resolution Service [*Computer science*] ... MARS
Multicast Backbone [*Computer science*] (DOM) ... M-bone
Multicast Backbone [*Internet*] (WDMC) ... M-Bone
Multicast Backbone [*Internet terminology*] (CDE) ... Mbone
Multicatalytic Proteinase [*An enzyme*] ... MCP
Multicell Compound Tire [*Automotive engineering*] ... MCC
Multicell Test (MCD) ... MCT
Multicenter Acute Stroke Trial-Europe [*Neurology*] ... MAST-E
Multicenter AIDS [*Acquired Immune Deficiency Syndrome*] **Cohort Study** [*National Institutes of Health*] ... MACS
Multicenter Investigation of the Limitation of Infarct Size (MEDA) ... MILIS
Multicenter Isradipine Diuretic Atherosclerosis Study ... MIDAS
Multicenter Study of Perioperative Ischemia ... McSPI
Multicenter Zero Differential Overlap [*Physics*] ... MCZDO
Multicentric Angiofollicular (Lymph Node) Hyperplasia [*Oncology*] ... MAFH
Multichannel (AABC) ... MCHAN
Multichannel Acoustic Relay [*Navy*] (ANA) ... MCAR
Multichannel Analog-to-Digital Data Decoder (IAA) ... MADD
Multichannel Analog-to-Digital Data Encoder (IAA) ... MADE
Multichannel Analyzer ... MCA
Multichannel Astrometric Photometer [*Astronomy*] ... MAP
Multi-Channel Automatic Remote Recording ... MARRC
Multichannel Communication System (IAA) ... MCS
Multichannel Communications Controller ... MCC
Multichannel Communications Program (IEEE) ... MCP
Multi-Channel Communications Software (NITA) ... MCS
Multichannel Connection Protocol Based on the Point-to-Point Protocol [*Computer science*] ... Multilink PPP
Multichannel Data Recorder ... MDR
Multichannel Demultiplexer and Distributor ... MDD
Multichannel DIFAR [*Directional Frequency Analysis and Recording System*] **Relay** (NVT) ... MCDR
Multi-Channel Digital Audio Codec [*Intraplex, Inc.*] ... MDAC
Multichannel Field Effect Transistor (IAA) ... MUCHFET
Multichannel Fixed ... MCF
Multi-Channel In-Band Airborne Relay (PDAA) ... MIBAR
Multichannel Initial System (MCD) ... MCIS
Multichannel Jezebel [*Sonobuoy System*] **Relay** [*Military*] (NG) ... MCJR
Multichannel Memory System [*Computer science*] (AAG) ... MCMS
Multichannel Multipoint Distribution Service [*Broadcasting term*] ... MMDS
Multichannel, Multipoint Distribution System [*Telecommunications*] (ACRL) ... MMDS
Multi-Channel Multi-Port [*Telecommunications*] ... MCMP
Multichannel Ocean Color Sensor [*NASA*] ... MOCS
Multichannel Peak Factor (IAA) ... MCPF
Multichannel Receiver ... MCR
Multichannel Rotary Transformer [*Electronics*] ... MCRT
Multichannel Scaling [*Mode*] ... MCS
Multichannel Sea Surface Temperature [*Algorithms for oceanography*] ... MCSST
Multi-Channel Sea-Surface Temperature [*Marine science*] (OSRA) ... MCSST
Multichannel Seismology [*Geophysics*] ... MCS
Multichannel Signal Averager [*Computer science*] ... MSA
Multichannel Spectrum Analyzer [*Instrumentation*] ... MCSA
Multi-Channel SST [*Sea Surface Temperature*] (USDC) ... MCSST
Multichannel Switch (IAA) ... MCS
Multichannel System (IAA) ... MCS
Multichannel Television Sound [*or Stereo*] ... MTS
Multichannel Triple Bridge ... MTB
Multichannel TV Sound (WDMC) ... MTS
Multichannel TV Stereo (WDMC) ... MTS
Multichannel Voice Frequency [*Telecommunications*] ... MCVF
Multichannel Voice Frequency Telegraphy [*Telecommunications*] (TEL) ... MCVFT
Multichip [*Circuit*] [*Electronics*] ... MC
Multichip Integrated Circuit (NITA) ... MIC
Multichip Integration [*Computer science*] (PDAA) ... MCI
Multichip Module [*Computer science*] ... MCM
Multichromatic ... MC
Multicolor Automatic Projection System (IEEE) ... MAPS
Multi-Color Corp. [*NASDAQ symbol*] (NQ) ... LABL
Multi-Color Corp. [*Associated Press*] (SAG) ... MultClr
Multicolor Graphics Adapter [*Computer technology*] ... MCGA
Multicolor /Graphics Array [*Computer science*] ... MCGA
Multicolor LASER ... MCL
Multicolor LASER Display ... MCLD
Multicolor Spin-Scan Cloudcover Camera ... MSSCC
Multicolored [*Philately*] ... multi
Multicom Publishing [*NASDAQ symbol*] (SAG) ... MNET
Multicom Publishing [*Associated Press*] (SAG) ... MultPb
Multicomet Sample Return [*Space science*] ... MSR
Multicomm Sciences International, Inc. [*Denville, NJ*] (TSSD) ... MSI
Multicomm Telecommunications Corp. [*Formerly, Mutual Satellite Services*] ... MTC
Multicommand Data System ... MCDS
Multi-Company Accounts Payable (MHDB) ... MCOA/P
Multicomponent Boot System [*Army*] (INF) ... MCBS
Multicomponent Circuits ... MCC
Multicomponent Plasma ... MCP
Multicomputing (IAA) ... MC

Multicomputing Multitasking Operating System (NITA) .... MMOS
Multiconfiguration [*Quantum mechanics*] .... MC
Multiconfiguration Paired Excitation Self-Consistent Field [*Physics*] .... MCPESCF
Multiconfiguration Self-Consistent Field [*Physical chemistry*] ...... MCSCF
Multiconfigurational Self-Consistent Field [*Chemical physics*] .... MCSCF
Multi-Console System (NITA) .... MCS
Multi-Contact Relay (IAA) .... MCR
Multiconverter Vector [*Computer science*] (IAA) .... MV
Multicopy Single-Stranded Deoxyribonucleic Acid [*Biochemistry, genetics*] .... MSDNA
Multicore Bar Solder .... MBS
Multicore Extruded Bar Solder .... MEBS
Multi-Corp, Inc. [*NASDAQ symbol*] (SAG) .... MCUAF
Multi-Corp, Inc. [*Associated Press*] (SAG) .... MultiCp
Multi-Corp. [*NASDAQ symbol*] (TTSB) .... MCUAF
Multicoupler .... MUC
Multicoupler Unit [*Antenna*] [*Telecommunications*] (TEL) .... MCU
Multicoverage Account Program [*Insurance*] .... MAP
MULTICS Data Base Manager .... MDBM
Multicultural and Cross-Cultural Supplementation Program [*Australia*].... MASCP
Multicultural Australia Papers [*A publication*] .... MAP
Multicultural Information Strategy .... MIS
Multicultural Network of the American Society for Training and Development (EA) .... MNASTD
Multicultural Psychiatric Center [*Australia*] .... MPC
MultiCultural Review [*A publication*] (BRI) .... MultiCul R
Multicultural Television (ADA) .... MTV
Multicystic Kidney Disease [*Medicine*] .... MCKD
Multidestination [*Carrier*] .... MU
Multidetail Drawing (MSA) .... MUDR
Multi-Differential GPS Receiver .... MDGR
Multidimensional .... MD
Multidimensional Access .... MDA
Multidimensional Analysis (IEEE) .... MDA
Multidimensional Array .... MDA
Multidimensional Attitude Scale on Mental Retardation (EDAC) .... MASMR
Multidimensional Capillary Gas Chromatography .... MDCGC
Multidimensional Compensatory Task .... MDCT
Multidimensional Concept [*Combines robotic combat vehicles with other unmanned systems*] [*Army*] (RDA) .... MDC
Multidimensional Database .... MDD
Multidimensional Gas Chromatography .... MDGC
Multidimensional Health Locus of Control [*Diagnostic scale*] .... MHLC
Multidimensional Personality Questionnaire [*Personality development test*] [*Psychology*] .... MPQ
Multidimensional Query Language [*Computer science*] .... MDQL
Multi-Dimensional Random Sea Facility [*Hydraulics Research Station*] (PDAA) .... MDRSF
Multidimensional Scale for Rating Psychiatric Patients .... MSRPP
Multidimensional Scaling [*Statistics*] .... MDS
Multidimensional Switching System [*Instrumentation*] .... MDSS
Multidimensional Switching System - Packed Column Trap [*Instrumentation*] .... MDSS-PCT
Multidimensional Tasking [*Honeywell, Inc.*] .... MDT
Multidimensional Unfolding [*Model*] [*Statistics*] .... MDU
Multidimensional Warfare [*Military*] (CAAL) .... MDW
Multidimensional-Multiattributional Causality Scale (EDAC) .... MMCS
Multidirectional Category System .... MCS
Multi-Directional Forklift Truck (MCD) .... MDFLT
Multidirectional Harassment (PDAA) .... MDH
Multidirectional Osmotic Drug Absorption System [*Medicine*] .... MODAS
Multi-Disc Reader [*Floppy discs*] (NITA) .... MDR
Multidisciplinary Accident Investigation [*National Accident Sampling System*] .... MDAI
Multidisciplinary Center for Urban and Minority Problems [*Florida State University*] [*Research center Defunct*] (RCD) .... MCUMP
Multi-Disciplinary Counter Intelligence .... MDIC
Multidisciplinary Counterintelligence (MCD) .... MDCI
Multidisciplinary Institute for Neuropsychological Development (EA) .... MIND
Multidisciplinary Integrated Research Activities in Complex Laboratory Environments [*National Science Foundation*] .... MIRACLE
Multidisciplinary Team .... MDT
Multidisciplinary Treatment Plan [*Medicine*] (DAVI) .... MDTP
Multi-Discipline Data Analysis System (GAVI) .... MIDAS
Multidiscipline Engineering Design, Evaluation, and Analysis (RDA) .... MEDEA
Multi-Disperse Latex Reactor .... MLR
Multidocking Adapter (IAA) .... MDA
Multidomain [*Grains in rocks*] [*Geophysics*] .... MD
Multidomain Polymer [*Biology*] .... MDP
Multidrug Resistance [*Medicine*] .... MDR
Multidrug-Resistance Associated [*Genetics*] .... MDRA
Multidrug-Resistant Tuberculosis [*Medicine*] .... MDRTB
Multiduct Fuel Test Assembly [*Nuclear energy*] (NRCH) .... MFTA
Multiechelon Supply Model (AABC) .... MESM
Multiechelon Technique for Recoverable Item Control (MCD) .... METRIC
Multiedge Adaptive Tracker (MCD) .... MEAT
Multieffect Distillation [*Chemical engineering*] .... MED
Multieffect, Multistage .... MEMS
Multi-Effect Multistage Distillation (PDAA) .... MMD
Multielectrolyte Concentrate [*Pharmacology*] (DAVI) MTE-5
Multielectron Photoactive Center [*Physical chemistry*] .... MPC
Multi-Element Articulated Research Vehicle [*Engineering*] (OA) .... MARV
Multielement Assured Tracking Chopper .... MATCH
Multielement Centrifugal Aerowindow .... MECA
Multielement Component Array .... MECA

Multielement RADAR .... MER
Multielement Radio-Linked Interferometer Network [*Astronomy*] .... MERLIN
Multielement Radiometer System .... MERS
Multielliptical Cavity Pump .... MECP
Multielliptical Pump .... MEP
Multiemitter Transistor .... MET
Multiemitter-Coupled Logic (IAA) .... MECL
Multiemployer Pension Plan Amendments Act [*1980*] (GFGA) .... MPPAA
Multiend Item Modification Notice [*NASA*] (KSC) .... MEIMN
Multienergy Californium Assay System [*Nuclear energy*] (NRCH) .... MECAS
Multienergy Gamma Assay System [*Nuclear energy*] (NRCH) .... MEGAS
Multi-Energy X-Ray Holography [*Physics*] .... MEXH
Multiengine .... ME
Multiengine Land [*Pilot rating*] (AIA) .... MEL
Multiengine Sea [*Pilot rating*] (AIA) .... MES
Multiengined .... M-ENG
Multi-Engined Helicopter (MCD) .... MEH
Multienvironment Active RF [*Radio Frequency*] Seeker .... MARFS
Multi-Environment Scheme [*Medicine*] (DMAA) .... MESCH
Multi-Environment Trainer (MCD) .... MET
Multienvironmental Electron Microscope .... MEM
Multi-Factor Productivity .... MFP
Multi-Faith Meal [*Army*] (INF) .... MFM
Multifamily Insurance and Direct Loan Information System [*Department of Housing and Urban Development*] (GFGA) .... MIDLIS
Multifamily Residential Zone (AD) .... MR
Multi-Fiber Arrangement [*International trade*] .... MFA
Multifile Linear Programming .... MFLP
Multiflex Interface Adapter .... MIA
Multifocal and Recurrent Choroidopathy [*Medicine*] (DMAA) .... MARC
Multifocal Atrial Tachycardia [*Cardiology*] .... MAT
Multifocal Atrial Tachycardia [*Cardiology*] (DAVI) .... MFAT
Multifocal Atrial Tachycardia [*Cardiology*] (DMAA) .... MFT
Multifocal Eosinophilic Granuloma [*Medicine*] (DMAA) .... MEG
Multifocal Functional Autonomy [*Medicine*] (DMAA) .... MFA
Multifocal Premature Ventricular Contractions [*Medicine*] (MEDA) .... MFPVC
Multiform Printer .... MFP
Multiformat Electroluminescent Display (PDAA) .... MED
Multi-Format Photointerpretation System (SAA) .... MPS
Multifrequency [*Telecommunications*] .... MF
Multi-Frequency Code [*Telecommunications*] (DA) .... MFC
Multifrequency High-Gain Antenna Configuration (SSD) .... MHAC
Multifrequency Key Pulsing .... MFKP
Multifrequency LASER Sounding (MCD) .... MLS
Multi-Frequency / Local Battery [*Telecommunications*] (DA) .... MFC/LB
Multifrequency Microwave Radiometer (MCD) .... MFMR
Multifrequency Pulsing (MSA) .... MFP
Multifrequency Receiver [*Telecommunications*] .... MFR
Multifrequency Signal Detector [*Telecommunications*] .... MSD
Multifrequency Signaling, Compelled [*Telecommunications*] (TEL) .... MFC
Multi-Frequency Signalling [*Telecommunications*] (NITA) .... MFS
Multi-Frequency Signalling System [*Telecommunications*] (EECA) .... MFSS
Multifunction Adaptive Processor (NITA) .... MAP
Multifunction Antenna .... MFA
Multifunction Array RADAR .... MAR
Multi-Function Array RADAR (MCD) .... MFAR
Multifunction Array RADAR / Missile Site RADAR (SAA) .... MAR/MSR
Multifunction Band Airborne Radio .... MFBAR
Multifunction Card Machine (BUR) .... MFCM
Multifunction Card Unit .... MFCU
Multi-Function Communications Adaptor (NITA) .... MFCA
Multifunction Control/Panel .... MFCP
Multifunction CRT [*Cathode-Ray Tube*] Display System (NASA) .... MCDS
Multifunction CRT [*Cathode-Ray Tube*] Display Unit (NASA) .... MCDU
Multifunction CRT [*Cathode-Ray Tube*] Display Unit .... MCDU
Multifunction Data Set Utility Language .... MFDSUL
Multifunction Display (MCD) .... MFD
Multifunction Display Symbol Generator (MCD) .... MFDSG
Multifunction Display Unit [*Aviation*] .... MFDU
Multifunction Electric Scan Adaptive RADAR [*Military British*] .... MESAR
Multifunction Electronic Display System [*NASA*] .... MEDS
Multi-Function Generator (NITA) .... MFG
Multifunction High-Frequency SONAR (MCD) .... MFHFS
Multifunction Imaging Search/Track Infrared .... MISTIR
Multifunction Microwave Aperture .... MMA
Multi-Function, Multi-Band Airborne Radio System (PDAA) .... MFMBARS
Multifunction Peripheral [*Chip*] [*Computer science*] .... MFP
Multifunction Polis .... MFP
Multifunction Printers (PS) .... MFP
Multifunction Program Keyboard (MCD) .... MFPK
Multifunction Protocol Converter .... MFPC
Multifunction RADAR .... MFR
Multifunction RADAR Signal Processor (MCD) .... MRSP
Multifunction Receiver System .... MFRS
Multifunction Reference Unit (MCD) .... MRU
Multifunction Sensor (MCD) .... MFS
Multi-Function Switch [*Automotive engineering*] .... MFS
Multifunctional (MCD) .... MF
Multifunctional Acrylate [*Organic chemistry*] .... MFA
Multifunctional Automobile Communication System [*Automotive engineering*] .... MAC
Multi-Functional Communications System - Asynchronous (HGAA) .... MCS-A
Multifunctional Inertial Reference Assembly [*Air Force*] (MCD) .... MIRA
Multifunctional Information Distribution System [*NATO*] (MCD) .... MIDS
Multi-functional Information Distribution System .... MIDS

Multifunctional Monomer [*Organic chemistry*] ... MFM
Multifunctional Receiver (NASA) ... MFR
Multifunctional Receiver ... MFR
Multifunctional Review (NASA) ... MFR
Multifunctional Service Vessel [*Off-shore drilling technology*] ... MSV
Multi-functional Transport Satellite ... MTSAT
Multigated Angiogram [*Cardiology*] (DAVI) ... MUGA
Multigated Blood Pool Image at Rest [*Medicine*] (DMAA) ... MUGR
Multigated Blood Pool Image during Exercise [*Hematology*] (DMAA) ... MUGEx
Multigated Blood Pool Scanning [*Medicine*] (DMAA) ... MBPS
Multigauge ... MG
Multigrade Functional Rehabilitation Platform [*Medicine*] ... MFRP
Multigraphic Interface [*XOR Systems*] ... MGI
Multigrid Modulator Multiplier ... MMM
Multigrounded Neutral [*Telecommunications*] (TEL) ... MGN
Multigroup Fourier Transform [*Code*] [*Nuclear energy*] (NRCH) ... MUFT
Multihandicapped ... MH
Multihandicapped Hearing-Impaired ... MHHI
Multihead Disk (NASA) ... MHD
Multi-Housing Laundry Association (EA) ... MLA
Multihundred Watt ... MHW
Multi-Hundred-Watt Radioisotope Thermoelectric Generator (PDAA) ... MHW-RTG
Multi-Impact Signature Register (PDAA) ... MISR
Multi-IMU Operation System [*NASA*] (GFGA) ... MIOS
Multi-IMU [*Internal Measuring Unit*] **Operation System** [*NASA*] ... MIOS
Multi-Indenture NORS [*Not Operationally Ready Status*] **Evaluator** (MCD) ... MINE
Multi-Indexed Sequential Access Method [*Computer science*] ... MSAM
Multi-Industry Interest ... MI
Multi-Information Display [*Automotive engineering*] ... MID
Multi-Input Multi-Output Integrated Injection Logic (IAA) ... MMIIL
Multi-Input Standard Tape ... MIST
Multi-Input-Safety-Shutdown (PDAA) ... MISS
Multi-Institutional Organization [*Generic term*] (DHSM) ... MIO
Multi-International Teacher Education Cooperatives (EDAC) ... MITECS
Multi-Item Multisource (IEEE) ... MIMS
Multi-Item Single Source (IEEE) ... MISS
Multijet Transport ... MJT
Multijunction Semiconductor Rectifier ... MSR
Multijunction Unit [*Computer science*] (BUR) ... MJU
Multi-jurisdictional Automated Pre-clearance System ... MAPS
Multilamellar Cytosome [*Biochemistry*] (MAE) ... MLC
Multilamellar Large Vesicle [*Pharmacy Biochemistry*] ... MLV
Multilaminar Phospholipid Vesicle [*Immunology*] ... MLV
Multi-LAN Storage System [*Computer science*] (HGAA) ... MSS
Multilanguage System [*Computer science*] (IEEE) ... MLS
Multilateral Clearing Facility [*Caribbean Community and Common Market*] (EY) ... MCF
Multilateral Control Board (SSD) ... MCB
Multilateral Development Bank ... MDB
Multilateral Disarmament Information Centre [*British*] ... MDIC
Multilateral Exchange Rate Model (ADA) ... MERM
Multilateral Force [*NATO*] ... MLF
Multilateral Initiative in Malaria ... MIM
Multilateral Investment Guarantee Agency [*World Bank*] ... MIGA
Multilateral Memorandum of Understanding ... MMOU
Multilateral Nuclear Force ... MNF
Multilateral Preparatory Talks (NATG) ... MPT
Multilateral RADAR Strike System [*Air Force*] (MCD) ... MRS
Multilateral RADAR Surveillance/Strike System [*Air Force*] ... MRS3
Multilateral RADAR Surveillance System [*Air Force*] (MCD) ... MRS
Multilateral Staff [*Environmental Protection Agency*] (GFGA) ... MS
Multilateral Trade Agreement (AAGC) ... MTA
Multilateral Trade Negotiations ... MTN
Multilateral Trading Organization (ECON) ... MTO
Multilayer [*Pharmacy*] ... ML
Multilayer Absorbing Bottom Layer ... MABM
Multilayer Actuator Head [*Epson America, Inc.*] [*Computer science*] (PCM) ... MACH
Multilayer Aluminium Oxide-Silicon-Dioxide Combination (IAA) ... MASC
Multilayer Antireflection [*Coating*] ... MLAR
Multilayer Board ... MLB
Multilayer Capacitor [*Electronics*] ... MLC
Multilayer Ceramic [*Materials technology*] ... MLC
Multilayer Ceramic Capacitor (NITA) ... MLC
Multilayer Ceramic Capacitor [*Electronics*] ... MLCC
Multilayer Ceramic Multichip [*Electronics*] ... MCM
Multilayer Ceramic Package [*Electronics*] ... MLCP
Multilayer Ceramic Substrates [*Electronic circuit boards*] ... MLCS
Multilayer Circuit ... MLC
Multilayer Circuit Board ... MLCB
Multilayer Dielectric Coating ... MDC
Multilayer Insulation ... MLI
Multilayer Interconnection Board ... MIB
Multilayer Interference Mirror [*Optical instrumentation*] ... MIM
Multilayer Metalization (IEEE) ... MLM
Multilayer Printed Board ... MPB
Multilayer Printed Circuit ... MLPC
Multilayer Printed Circuit Board ... MPCB
Multilayer Printed-Wiring Board (IEEE) ... MLPWB
Multilayer Printed-Wiring Board ... MPWB
Multilayer Resist [*Lithography*] ... MLR
Multilayer Side-Cladded Ridge Waveguide (PDAA) ... MSCR
Multi-Layer Steel [*Engine gaskets*] [*Automotive engineering*] ... MLS
Multilayer Wiring Board ... MWB
Multi-Layered Packaging (PDAA) ... MLP
Multilayered Structure [*Botany*] ... MLS
Multileaving Remote Job Entry [*IBM Corp.*] ... MRJE
Multileaving Remote Terminal Processor [*Computer science*] (MHDI) ... MLRTP
Multileg Tanker Mooring System (MCD) ... MLTMS
Multi-Legend Display Switch (MCD) ... MLD/S
Multilens Camera ... MLC
Multilevel Academic Skills Inventory [*Educational test*] ... MASI
Multilevel Academic Survey Test [*Educational test*] ... MAST
Multilevel Amplitude Shift Keying ... MASK
Multilevel Informal Language Inventory [*Test*] ... MILI
Multilevel Interconnect Generator ... MIG
Multilevel Large-Scale Integration ... MLSI
Multilevel Marketing ... MLM
Multi-Level Marketing International Association [*Irvine, CA*] (EA) ... MLMIA
Multilevel Multiaccess ... MLMA
Multilevel Precedence ... MLP
Multilevel Precedence and Preemption [*Telecommunications*] (TEL) ... MLPP
Multilevel Procedure (MCD) ... MLP
Multilevel Programmer ... MLP
Multilevel Rail Car ... MLRC
Multilevel Resist [*For microlithography*] ... MLR
Multilevel Security (MCD) ... MLS
Multilevel Security (DOMA) ... MLS
Multilevel Voltage Select (MCD) ... MLVS
Multiline Automatic Calling System (HGAA) ... MACS
Multiline Automatic Network Diagnostic and Transmission Equipment ... MANDATE
Multiline Communications Processor ... MLCP
Multiline Control (BUR) ... MLC
Multi-Line Insurance Rating Bureau [*Later, ISO*] ... MLIRB
Multiline Selection [*Asahi Glass of Japan*] ... MLS
Multilinear Array [*In earth scanning*] ... MLA
Multilinear Events Sequencing [*Engineering*] ... MES
Multilingual [*MARC language code Library of Congress*] (LCCP) ... mul
Multilingual Aphasia Battery [*Medicine*] (DMAA) ... MLAB
Multilingual Aphasia Examination [*Speech and language therapy*] (DAVI) ... MAE
Multilingual Biblioservice, Edmonton, AB, Canada [*Library symbol Library of Congress*] (LCLS) ... CaAEMB
Multilingual Biblioservice, Edmonton, Alberta [*Library symbol National Library of Canada*] (NLC) ... AEMB
Multilingual Biblioservice, National Library of Canada [*Biblioservice Multilingue, Bibliotheque Nationale du Canada*] **Ottawa, Ontario** [*Library symbol National Library of Canada*] (NLC) ... OONLMBS
Multilingual Biblioservice of Alberta, Alberta Culture [*UTLAS symbol*] ... MBS
Multilingual Broadcasting Council of the Northern Territory [*Australia*] ... MBCNT
Multilingual Forestry Terminology ... MFT
Multilingual Publishing Software ... MLPS
Multilingual Services Directorate, Translation Bureau, Department of the Secretary of State [*Direction des Services Multilingues, Bureau des Traductions, Secretariat d'Etat*] **Ottawa, Ontario** [*Library symbol National Library of Canada*] (NLC) ... OOSSTM
MultiLink Advanced [*Local area network*] [*The Software Link, Inc.*] ... MLA
Multilink Control Field [*Telecommunications*] (ACRL) ... MLC
Multilink Point-to-Point Protocol [*Telecommunications*] (ACRL) ... ML-PPP
Multilink PPP [*Point-to-Point Protocol*] (PCM) ... MP
Multilink Procedure [*Computer science*] (TNIG) ... MLP
Multilink Protocol [*Telecommunications*] (ACRL) ... MLP
Multilith ... MULTH
Multi-Longitudinal Mode (ACRL) ... MLM
Multiloop Integral System Test [*Nuclear energy*] (NRCH) ... MIST
Multi-Management Resolution Control Processor ... M-MRCP
Multi-Market Radio ... MMR
Multi-Market Radio, Inc. [*Associated Press*] (SAG) ... MulMR
Multi-Market Radio, Inc. [*Associated Press*] (SAG) ... MulMRad
Multi-Market Radio, Inc. [*Associated Press*] (SAG) ... MultM
Multi-Market Radio, Inc. [*NASDAQ symbol*] (SAG) ... RDIO
Multimaterial Laminate ... MML
Multimechanical Thermal Treatment ... MMTT
MultiMeda Concepts Intl-Wrrt [*NASDAQ symbol*] (TTSB) ... MMCIW
Multi-Media (OICC) ... MM
Multi-Media Access Center [*Cabletron Systems, Inc.*] ... MMAC
Multi-Media Access Center with Flexible Network Bus [*Cabletron Systems, Inc.*] ... MMAC-FNB
Multimedia Access Terminals [*Philips*] [*Electronics*] ... MAT
Multimedia CD [*Computer science*] ... MMCD
Multi-Media Communication Control (DOMA) ... M^2C^2
Multimedia Compact Disc ... MMCD
MultiMedia Concepts International, Inc. [*NASDAQ symbol*] (SAG) ... MMCI
MultiMedia Concepts International, Inc. [*NASDAQ symbol*] (SAG) ... MMCIW
MultiMedia Concepts International, Inc. [*Associated Press*] (SAG) ... MultiMC
MultiMeda Concepts International, Inc. [*Associated Press*] (SAG) ... MultiMed
MultiMedia Concepts International, Inc. [*Associated Press*] (SAG) ... MultMC
Multimedia Concepts International, Inc. [*Associated Press*] (SAG) ... Multmd
MultiMedia Concepts Intl. [*NASDAQ symbol*] (TTSB) ... MMCI
Multimedia Conference Service [*Telecommunications*] (CDE) ... MCS
Multimedia Development Kit [*Microsoft Corp.*] [*Computer science*] ... MDK
Multimedia Environmental Goals [*Environmental Protection Agency*] ... MEG
Multimedia European Center ... MEC
Multimedia Extensions (PCM) ... MMX
Multimedia Games [*NASDAQ symbol*] (TTSB) ... MGAM
Multimedia Games, Inc. [*NASDAQ symbol*] (SAG) ... MGAM
Multimedia Games, Inc. [*Associated Press*] (SAG) ... MltmdG
Multimedia Graphics Architecture [*Computer science*] (PCM) ... MGA
Multimedia, Inc. [*NASDAQ symbol*] (SAG) ... MMED

Multimedia, Inc. (MHDW) ... MMEDC
Multimedia Individualized Instruction [*Army*] ... MMII
Multimedia Individualized Instructional Package [*Army*] ... MMIIP
Multimedia Information Network Exchange [*Computer science*] ... MINX
Multimedia Interactive Control ... MIC
Multimedia Marketing Council (DOM) ... MMC
Multimedia Personal Computer ... MPC
Multimedia Presentation Manager [*IBM Corp.*] (PCM) ... MMPM
Multimedia Publishers Group (EA) ... MPG
Multi-Media Remote Teaching System [*AT & T Co., Illinois Institute of Technology*] ... MRTS
Multimedia Super Corridor [*Proposed, Malaysia*] ... MSC
Multimedia System ... MMS
Multimedia Training Material ... MMTM
Multi-Media Tutorial [*NASDAQ symbol*] (TTSB) ... MMTS
Multi-Media Tutorial Services, Inc. [*NASDAQ symbol*] (SAG) ... MMTS
Multi-Media Tutorial Services, Inc. [*Associated Press*] (SAG) ... MultMT
Multi-Media Tutorial Wrrt [*NASDAQ symbol*] (TTSB) ... MMTSW
Multimedia User Environment [*Computer science*] ... MUSE
Multimedia Video File [*Computer science*] ... MMVF
Multimedia Video Processor [*Texas Instruments*] (PS) ... MVP
Multi-Medium Scale Integration (SAA) ... MMSI
Multimegabit Operation Multiplexer System ... MOMS
Multimegawatt (SDI) ... MMW
Multi-Message Interface (NITA) ... MMI
Multimessage Unit [*Telecommunications*] (TEL) ... MMU
Multimeter ... MM
Multimeter (AAG) ... MULTR
Multimeter Wave Power Source ... MWPS
Multi-Microprocessor Flight Control System (PDAA) ... M^2FCS
Multimini Computer Compiler (MHDI) ... MMCC
Multi-Mirror Reflector [*Lamp*] ... MR
Multi-Missile Fire Control System [*Military*] ... MMFCS
Multimission Advanced Tactical Terminal (DWSG) ... MATT
Multimission Imagery Photographic Interpretation Report (MCD) ... MIPIR
Multimission Modular Spacecraft [*NASA*] (NASA) ... MMS
Multimission Module [*Aerospace*] ... MMM
Multimission Patrol Ship [*Symbol*] ... PSMM
Multi-Mission Redeye Air-Launched Missile [*Military*] (PDAA) ... MRAM
Multimission Ship [*DoD*] ... MMS
Multi-Mission UHF [*Ultra High Frequency*] **SATCOM** [*Satellite Command*] **Terminal** ... MUST
Multimission Weapons Control System ... MMWCS
Multimission-Unique Ground Support Equipment (MCD) ... MUGSE
Multi-Mkt Radio Wrrt'A' [*NASDAQ symbol*] (TTSB) ... RDIOW
Multi-Mkt Radio Wrrt'B' [*NASDAQ symbol*] (TTSB) ... RDIOZ
Multi-Mkt Radio'A' [*NASDAQ symbol*] (TTSB) ... RDIOA
Multimodal Transport Operator ... MTO
Multimodal Traveler Information Systems [*FTA*] (TAG) ... MTIS
Multimodality Evoked Potential [*Neurophysiology*] ... MEP
Multimode ... MM
Multimode Airborne Solid State Array RADAR ... MASSAR
Multimode Airborne Solid-State Array RADAR System [*Military*] (PDAA) ... MASAR
Multimode Aircraft Landing System (MCD) ... M-MALS
Multimode Display ... MMD
Multimode Electro-Optical Weapon System ... MEOWS
Multimode Error Analysis ... MEA
Multimode Fiber (ACRL) ... MMF
Multimode Guidance (MCD) ... MMG
Multimode Hydrophone [*Military*] (CAAL) ... MMH
Multimode Information Distribution System ... MIDS
Multi-Mode International Data Acquisition Service (NITA) ... MIDAS
Multimode Mode Matrix (MCD) ... MMM
Multimode Optical Sensor (NASA) ... MMOS
Multimode RADAR ... MMR
Multimode Radiometer (MCD) ... MMR
Multimode Receiver ... MMR
Multi-Mode Receiver [*Navigation systems*] ... MMR
Multimode Seeker (MCD) ... MMS
Multimode Seeker Deduction (DWSG) ... MMSD
Multimode SONAR Console ... MMSC
Multimode Storage Tube ... MMST
Multimode Storage Tube ... MST
Multimode Tonotron ... MMT
Multimode Tonotron Display ... MMTD
Multimodule Space Station [*NASA*] (KSC) ... MMSS
Multinational Command Systems Working Group (NATG) ... MCSWG
Multinational Communication-Electronics Working Group [*Formerly, SGCEC*] [*NATO*] (NATG) ... MCEWG
Multinational Company [*Business term*] ... MNC
Multinational Computer Models, Inc. [*Information service or system*] (IID) ... MCM
Multinational Coordination Center [*NATO*] ... MNCC
Multinational Corp. ... MNC
Multinational Data Processing (MHDB) ... MNDP
Multinational Enterprise ... MNE
Multinational Fighter Program [*Air Force*] ... MNFP
Multinational Finance Corp. [*Indonesia*] (EY) ... MULTICOR
Multinational Force [*Eleven-nation peace-keeping force for the Sinai*] ... MNF
Multinational Force and Observers [*Eleven-nation peace-keeping force for the Sinai*] ... MFO
Multinational Fuel Cycle Facility ... MFCF
Multinational Instrumentation Conference and Exposition [*China Instrument Society*] ... MICONEX
Multinational Intelligence Cell (MCD) ... MIC
Multinational Meetings Information Services BV [*Netherlands Information service or system*] (IID) ... MMIS
Multinational Mixed Manned Force (NATG) ... MMMF
Multinational Operational Test and Evaluation ... MOT & E
Multinational Resources [*Vancouver Stock Exchange symbol*] ... MUT
Multinational Staged Improvement Program (MCD) ... MSIP
Multinational Trade Negotiations (IAA) ... MTN
Multinational Volunteer Teams ... MVT
Multinetwork Area [*Term used in TV ratings*] ... MNA
Multinodular [*or Multinodulate*] [*Medicine*] ... MN
Multinodular Goiter [*Endocrinology*] (DAVI) ... MNG
Multinomial Distribution [*Statistics*] ... MD
Multinomial Logit [*Statistics*] ... MNL
Multinomial Probit [*Statistics*] ... MNP
Multinozzle Base ... MNB
Multinucleate Nature, Spherical Shape, Unknown History ... MSX
Multinucleated Stromal Giant Cell ... MSGC
Multiobject Phase Tracking and Ranging [*FAA*] ... MOPTAR
Multi-Object Phase-Tracking and Ranging System [*FAA*] (PDAA) ... MOPTARS
Multioccupant Sealed Environment Simulator ... MOSES
Multioptical Reconnaissance Equipment [*Military*] (CAAL) ... MORE
Multi-Option (MCD) ... MO
Multi-Option Facility ... MOF
Multioption Fuze (MCD) ... MOF
Multi-Option Fuze, Artillery ... MOFA
Multioptional Interactive Display and Analytic System (MCD) ... MIDAS
Multiorder Feedback and Compensation Synthesis ... MOFACS
Multi-Outlet Reservoir Study [*Department of the Interior*] (GRD) ... MORS
Multipair Distribution Wire ... MDW
Multipak Heliax Coaxial Cable ... MHCC
Multipara (MAE) ... M
Multiparameter Light Scattering [*Physics*] ... MLS
Multiparameter Pulse Height Analyzer ... MPPHA
Multiparous [*Obstetrics*] ... MP
Multiparous [*Obstetrics*] ... multip
Multipart Memory Controller (NITA) ... MMC
Multi-Part Memory Interface Unit (NITA) ... MMIU
Multi-Part Memory System [*Perkin-Elmer*] (NITA) ... MMS
Multipart, Two Dimensional ... MP2D
Multiparticle Position- and Time- Sensitive Detector ... MUPPATS
Multiparticle Spectrometer [*Brookhaven National Laboratory*] ... MPS
Multipartisan Coalition (EA) ... MC
Multi-Party Conference [*Namibia*] [*Political party*] (PPW) ... MPC
Multiparty Connection Subsystem [*Telecommunications*] (TEL) ... MPCS
Multipath Core ... MPC
Multipath Intersymbol Interference (PDAA) ... MISI
Multipath Reduction Factor [*Electronics*] ... MRF
Multiperil [*Insurance*] ... MP
Multiperil Insurance Conference ... MIC
Multiperson Prisoner's Dilemma [*Statistics*] ... MPD
Multiphase [*Physics*] ... MP
Multi-Phase and Amplitude-Shift-Keying [*Computer science*] (PDAA) ... MPASK
Multiphase Ionization [*Chemical physics*] ... MPI
Multiphase Model for Air, Groundwater, Immiscible Contaminant and Solute Transport [*Computer program for testing water flow*] ... MAGICS
Multiphasic Health Checkup [*Medicine*] (AAMN) ... MHC
Multiphasic Health Screen Test (DAVI) ... MHST
Multiphasic Personality Inventory ... MPI
Multiphasic Personality Inventory (AD) ... mpi
Multiphasic Screening [*Medicine*] ... MPS
Multiphoton Dissociation [*Physical chemistry*] ... MPD
Multiphoton Excitation [*Physics*] ... MPE
Multiphoton Ionization [*Spectrometry*] ... MPI
Multiphoton Ionization (AD) ... mpi
Multiphoton Resonance Ionization [*Spectrometry*] ... MPRI
Multipion Exchange ... MPE
Multiplanar Link Chain ... MLC
Multiplane ... MLTPL
Multi-Plane Programming System (NITA) ... MPS
Multiplant Action [*Nuclear energy*] (NRCH) ... MPA
Multiple [*Missile launch environment symbol*] ... B
Multiple ... MULT
Multiple (DAVI) ... MULTI
Multiple Aberration Region [*Genetics*] ... MAR
Multiple Accelerated Summary Hearing [*Deportation of illegal aliens*] [*Immigration and Naturalization Service*] ... MASH
Multiple Acceleration Sensor Unit (PDAA) ... MASU
Multiple Acceptance Test Criteria [*Lubricant testing*] ... MTAC
Multiple Access (NASA) ... MA
Multiple Access Commercial Satellite (DOMA) ... MACSAT
Multiple Access Communications System [*West German and Dutch*] ... MACS
Multiple Access Computer ... MAC
Multiple Access Control [*Computer science*] (DIT) ... MAC
Multiple Access Demand Assignment (MCD) ... MADA
Multiple Access Device ... MAD
Multiple Access Digital System [*Computer science*] (IAA) ... MADS
Multiple Access - Discrete Address [*Navy tactical voice communication*] ... MADA
Multiple Access Drive (NITA) ... MAD
Multiple Access Facility [*Computer science*] ... MAF
Multiple Access Forward (SSD) ... MAF
Multiple Access Interface ... MAI
Multiple Access Internal Network [*Computer science*] ... MAIN
Multiple Access Relay ... MAR
Multiple Access Retrieval System [*Control Data Corp.*] ... MARS
Multiple Access Return (SSD) ... MAR

Multiple Access Sequential Selection [Computer science] (BUR) .... MASS
Multiple Access Shared Time Executive Routine [Control Data Corp.] [Computer science] .... MASTER
Multiple Access Switching System (NITA) .... MASS
Multiple Access Test .... MAT
Multiple Access Time [Telecommunications] (ECII) .... MAT
Multiple Access to Memory [Computer science] (IEEE) .... MAM
Multiple Access to Memory System [Computer science] .... MAMS
Multiple Access Unit .... MAU
Multiple Access Xerox Computer (NITA) .... MAXC
Multiple Action Raid Simulation [France] .... MARS
Multiple Actuator Test (MCD) .... MAT
Multiple Address .... MX
Multiple Address Code .... MAC
Multiple Address Computer (IAA) .... MAC
Multiple Address Instruction .... MAI
Multiple Address Letter (NOAA) .... MAL
Multiple Address Processing .... MAP
Multiple Address Processing System .... MAPS
Multiple Address Processing Unit [Military] (AABC) .... MAPU
Multiple Address System [Telecommunications] (CDE) .... MAS
Multiple Address Telegrams .... MAT
Multiple Advanced Technique Evaluation [Military] (CAAL) .... MATE
Multiple Aerial Refueling System (PDAA) .... MARS
Multiple Aerial Vehicle Expert [Army] .... MAVE
Multiple Affect Adjective Check List [of Educational and Industrial Testing Service] [Psychology] .... MAACL
Multiple Agency Processing System .... MAPS
Multiple Aim Point [ICBM] .... MAP
Multiple Aim Point System / Alternate Launch Point System (PDAA) .... MAPS/ALPS
Multiple Aim Structure (MCD) .... MAS
Multiple Aim-Point System .... MAPS
Multiple Airborne Reconnaissance Sensors Assessment Model (MCD) .... MARSAM
Multiple Airborne Target Trajectory System .... MATTS
Multiple Aircraft Approach and Landing Techniques (MCD) .... MAALT
Multiple Aircraft Identification Display (PDAA) .... MAID
Multiple Allocation Procedure [PERT] .... MAP
Multiple Aminoglycosides [Antibacterial agents] .... MAGS
Multiple Analytical Isoelectrofocusing Scanning Apparatus .... MAISA
Multiple Angle, Variable Interval, Nonorthogonal [Magnetic resonance imaging] .... MAVIN
Multiple Anodic Stripping Analyzer (PDAA) .... MASA
Multiple Answering Teaching Aid (PDAA) .... MATA
Multiple Application [Military] (AFIT) .... MA
Multiple Application Connector System .... MACS
Multiple Application Phototypesetting System (DGA) .... MAPS
Multiple Applications Control Center (SSD) .... MACC
Multiple Applications Storage Tube .... MAST
Multiple Aptitude Test [Education] (AEBS) .... MAT
Multiple Architecture Control Console (MCD) .... MACC
Multiple Area Technical Information Center .... MATIC
Multiple Array Avionics Subsystem .... MAAS
Multiple Array Correlation (CAAL) .... MAC
Multiple Array Processor .... MAP
Multiple Array RADAR (IAA) .... MAR
Multiple Artillery Rocket System [Army] .... MARS
Multiple Assembly Cooling Cask Test [Nuclear energy] (NRCH) .... MACCT
Multiple Association Application Service Element [Telecommunications] (OSI) .... MA-ASE
Multiple Association Management Institute [Later, IAMC] (EA) .... MAMI
Multiple Audio Distribution [Communications] .... MAD
Multiple Automated Printing Systems (MCD) .... MAPS
Multiple Automated Sample Harvester [for culture systems] .... MASH
Multiple Autonomous Vehicle .... MAUV
Multiple Award Schedule [Government contracting] .... MAS
Multiple Award Schedule Contract [Government contracting] .... MASC
Multiple Ballistic Rocket Launcher .... MBRL
Multiple Basic Channel .... MBC
Multiple Batch Station [Computer science] .... MBS
Multiple Beam Forming Network [Military] (LAIN) .... MBFN
Multiple Beam Interval Scanner .... MUBIS
Multiple Beam Klystron .... MBK
Multiple Beam Switching Tube .... MBST
Multiple Beam Traveling Wave Klystron .... MBTWK
Multiple Berthing Adaptor (SSD) .... MBA
Multiple Birth Association [Australia] .... MBA
Multiple Blinking Jammer (MCD) .... MBJ
Multiple Board Computer (IAA) .... MBC
Multiple Burst Correcting .... MBC
Multiple Business Entity - Accounts Receivable Management System (MHDB) .... MBE-ARMS
Multiple Business System .... MBS
Multiple Carboxylase Deficiency [Medicine] .... MCD
Multiple Cassegrain Feed [Deep Space Instrumentation Facility, NASA] .... MCF
Multiple Central Processing Unit .... MCPU
Multiple Channel Analysis Program .... MCAP
Multiple Channel Control Unit .... MCCU
Multiple Channel Data Acquisition System (NITA) .... MC-DAS
Multiple Channel Oscilloscope .... MCO
Multiple Character Set (CMD) .... MCS
Multiple Chemical Sensitivities [Medicine] .... MCS
Multiple Choice .... MC
Multiple Choice Objective Question (DA) .... MCOQ

Multiple Choice Questions (ADA) .... MCQ
Multiple Cholesterol Emboli Syndrome [Medicine] .... MCES
Multiple Classification Analysis [Aviation] .... MCA
Multiple Column Selector (IAA) .... MCS
Multiple Communications Adapter (DGA) .... MCA
Multiple Communications Control (BUR) .... MCC
Multiple Communications Control Unit [Computer science] .... MCCU
Multiple Comparison Procedure [Statistics] .... MCP
Multiple Compressed Tablet [Pharmacy] .... MCT
Multiple Compression Shear (OA) .... MCS
Multiple Computer Complex .... MCC
Multiple Computer System .... MCS
Multiple Concrete Duct [Telecommunications] (TEL) .... MCD
Multiple Conductor, Heat and Flame Resistant, Armor [Cable] .... MHFA
Multiple Conductor, Marker Buoy (IAA) .... MCMB
Multiple Conductor, Oil-Resistant, Portable [Cable] .... MCOP
Multiple Conductor, Shielded, Pressure-Resistant [Cable] .... MCSP
Multiple Conductor Transmission Line (PDAA) .... MTL
Multiple Congenital Anomalies/Mental Retardation Syndrome [Medicine] (DMAA) .... MCA/MR
Multiple Congenital Anomaly [Syndrome] [Medicine] .... MCA
Multiple Connected Motor .... MCM
Multiple Console Support [Fujitsu Ltd.] [Computer science] (MCD) .... MCS
Multiple Constraint Alternative Selector Program [Bell System] .... MCASP
Multiple Contact .... MC
Multiple Contact Miscible [Physical chemistry] .... MCM
Multiple Control Program [Computer science] .... MCP
Multiple Corridor Identification System [Air Force] .... MCIS
Multiple Cost Factor .... MCF
Multiple Countermeasure System .... MCMS
Multiple Criteria Decision Making .... MCDM
Multiple Critical Root Maximally Flat (PDAA) .... MUCROMAF
Multiple Critical-Pole Equal-Ripple Rational (MCD) .... MCPER
Multiple Data Entry System .... MDES
Multiple Database Management System (NITA) .... MDMS
Multiple Dataset System .... MDS
Multiple Dealer Trading System [Investment term] (DICI) .... MDTS
Multiple Degree of Freedom [Acoustics] .... MDOF
Multiple Delay Code (AFIT) .... MDC
Multiple Deployment System [Military] (IAA) .... MDS
Multiple Device Controller .... MDC
Multiple Dialyzer [Chemical analysis] .... MD
Multiple Digit Absorbing [Telecommunications] (TEL) .... MDA
Multiple Director Train Indicator (MCD) .... MDTI
Multiple Discriminant Analysis [Statistics] .... MDA
Multiple Display Indicator .... MDI
Multiple Dissemination .... MD
Multiple Docking Adapter [Apollo] [NASA] .... MDA
Multiple Document Interface [Computer science] (PCM) .... MDI
Multiple Dose Vial [Pharmacy] .... MDV
Multiple Drive Block .... MDB
Multiple Drone Control (MCD) .... MDC
Multiple Drone Control Strike System (MCD) .... MDC/SS
Multiple Drop Wire [Telecommunications] (TEL) .... MDW
Multiple Earning Statement [Banking] (MHDW) .... MES
Multiple Earthed Neutral (IAA) .... MEN
Multiple Echelon Direct Support System (MCD) .... MEDSS
Multiple ECM [Electronic Countermeasures] Threat Environment [Military] (CAAL) .... METE
Multiple Effect Flash [Evaporator] [Seawater conversion system] .... MEF
Multiple Ejection Rack/Triple Ejection Rack (MCD) .... MER/TER
Multiple Ejector Rack (NG) .... MER
Multiple Electronically Synopsing Hierarchy (RDA) .... MESH
Multiple Electronics Warfare Surveillance [DoD] .... MULTEWS
Multiple Element Directional Universally Steerable Antenna .... MEDUSA
Multiple Employer Trust [Insurance] .... MET
Multiple Employer Welfare Arrangement .... MEWA
Multiple Endocrine Abnormalities [Medicine] .... MEA
Multiple Endocrine Adenomas [Oncology] .... MEA
Multiple Endocrine Adenopathy [Endocrinology] (DAVI) .... MEA
Multiple, Endocrine Deficiency - Addison's Disease - Candidiasis [Syndrome] [Endocrinology] (DAVI) .... MEDAC
Multiple Endocrine Deficiency, Autoimmune-Candidiasis [Syndrome] [Medicine] .... MEDAC
Multiple Endocrine Neoplasia [Medicine] .... MEN
Multiple Endocrine Neoplasia Type I [Medicine] (DMAA) .... MENI
Multiple Endocrine Syndrome [Endocrinology] .... MES
Multiple Engagement Simulation Analyzer [Military] .... MESA
Multiple Engagement Test Environment [Military] (PDAA) .... METE
Multiple Entry Multiple Exit .... MEME
Multiple Environment Threat Emitter (MCD) .... METE
Multiple Epiphyseal Dysplasia [Medicine] (CPH) .... MED
Multiple Event Network .... MEN
Multiple Event Record and Playback System (NTCM) .... MERPS
Multiple Exostoses-Mental Retardation Syndrome [Medicine] (DMAA) .... MEMR
Multiple Experiment Processing Furnace .... MEPF
Multiple Exposure Testing System [Advertising analysis] .... METS
Multiple External Line Control Unit .... MELCU
Multiple Extraction Procedure (GNE) .... MEP
Multiple Facility Organization .... MFO
Multiple Family Dwelling [Real estate] .... MFD
Multiple File Concept (DNAB) .... MFC
Multiple Filer Audit Program .... MFA
Multiple Flight Computer (NASA) .... MFC
Multiple Flight Controller (NASA) .... MFC

Multiple Food Retailers Employers' Association [British]	MFREA
Multiple Fragment Laceration [Shrapnel wound] [Military] (VNW)	MFL
Multiple Fragment Wound (MAE)	MFW
Multiple Frequency Time Division Multiple Access (LAIN)	MFTDMA
Multiple Gas Analyzer	MGA
Multiple Gate Acquisition Analysis [Scan] (DAVI)	MUGA
Multiple Gated Acquisition Exercise [Scan] [Cardiology] (DAVI)	MUGX
Multiple Goal Programming	MGP
Multiple Goal Water Quality Model (PDAA)	MULQUAL
Multiple Gun Motor Carriage	MGMC
Multiple Handicapped Association (NADA)	MHA
Multiple Head Disc (NITA)	MHD
Multiple Headspace Extraction [Analytical chemistry]	MHE
Multiple High-Speed Data Channel	MHSDC
Multiple Hospital System	MHS
Multiple Host Support	MIT
Multiple Incidence Technique [Structure testing]	MIT
Multiple Independently Maneuvering Submunitions (MCD)	MIMS
Multiple Independently-Guided Re-entry Vehicle [NASA] (PDAA)	MIRV
Multiple Independently-Targetable Reentry Vehicle [Military]	MIRV
Multiple Index Data Access System [Prime Computer, Inc.]	MIDAS
Multiple Index Processing System (MCD)	MIPS
Multiple Index Sequential Access Method	MISAM
Multiple Indexing and Console Retrieval Operations (NITA)	MICRO
Multiple Indexing and Console Retrieval Options [Information retrieval Computer science]	MICRO
Multiple Infant Dementia [Neurology] (CPH)	MID
Multiple Infarct Dementia [Neurology]	MID
Multiple Information Retrieval by Parallel Selection	MIRPS
Multiple Infrared Scattered Light Recorder	MIRST
Multiple Input Data Acquisition System [Bell System]	MIDAS
Multiple Input Describing Function (PDAA)	MIDF
Multiple Input Memo Engineering Order (MCD)	MIMEO
Multiple Input/Output (NITA)	MIO
Multiple Input/Output Stream [Computer science]	MIO
Multiple Input Signal Register (NITA)	MISR
Multiple Input Terminal Equipment	MITE
Multiple Instantaneous Response File	MIRF
Multiple Instruction (HGAA)	MI
Multiple Instruction/Multiple Data (NITA)	MIMD
Multiple Instruction, Single Data [Processor configuration] (IEEE)	MISD
Multiple Instruction Stream, Multiple Data Stream (MCD)	MIMD
Multiple Instruction Streams Multiple Data Steams	MISMDS
Multiple Instruction Streams - Single Data Streams [Computer science] (MHDB)	MIS-SDS
Multiple Instrumentation RADAR (MCD)	MIR
Multiple Integrated Document Assembly System [Computer science] (BYTE)	MIDAS
Multiple Integrated LASER Engagement Simulation [or System] [Army]	MILES
Multiple Intercommunications Technical Operations Communications [NASA] (KSC)	MITOC
Multiple Interferometer Determination of Trajectories	MIDOT
Multiple Interior Communications System (MCD)	MINCOMS
Multiple Internal Reflectance Infrared Spectroscopy (MCD)	MIR-IR
Multiple Internal Reflection [Spectroscopy]	MIR
Multiple Internal Reflection Spectroscopy	MIRS
Multiple Investment Sinking Fund Rate of Return (ADA)	MISFROR
Multiple Inward-Turning Scoop (MCD)	MITS
Multiple Ion Detection	MID
Multiple Ion Monitoring [Mass spectrometry]	MIM
Multiple Isomorphous Replacement [Crystallography]	MIR
Multiple Isomorphous Replacement with Anomalous Scattering [Crystallography]	MIRAS
Multiple Item Purchase Order (AAG)	MIPO
Multiple Juxtapositional Fixedness [Tongue-in-cheek description of unusually strong bonding between metal ions and some ligands]	MJF
Multiple Key Hashing	MKH
Multiple Kill [Aerospace]	MK
Multiple Kill Vehicle	MKV
Multiple LASER Source Signature Simulator (MCD)	MULASSS
Multiple Launch Rocket System [DoD] (MCD)	MLRS
Multiple Launch Rocket System Extended Range Rocket [Military]	MLRS ER
Multiple Launch Rocket System Precision Guided Munitions (RDA)	MLRS-PGM
Multiple Launch Rocket System Terminally Guided Warhead	MLRS-TGW
Multiple Length Number	MLN
Multiple Level Indexing Scheme [Computer science]	MLIS
Multiple Line Adaptor (NITA)	MLA
Multiple Line Group [Radiation]	MLG
Multiple Line Printing (CMD)	MLP
Multiple Line Terminal Adapter [Computer science] (BUR)	MLTA
Multiple Linear Regression [Mathematics]	MLR
Multiple Link Interface [Computer science]	MLI
Multiple Link Interface Drive [Telecommunications] (PCM)	MLID
Multiple Link Interface Driver [Telecommunications] (ACRL)	MLID
Multiple Listing Board (BARN)	MLB
Multiple Listing Service [Real estate]	MLS
Multiple Location [Insurance]	ML
Multiple Location Risk [Insurance]	MLR
Multiple Logical Unit	MLU
Multiple Logical Windowing [Computer science]	MLW
Multiple Master [Computer science] (CDE)	MM
Multiple Match Resolver	MMR
Multiple Minor Symptoms Day [Environmental medicine]	MMSD
Multiple Mirror Telescope	MMT

Multiple Mirror Telescope Observatory [Research center] (RCD)	MMTO
Multiple Modality Evoked Potential [Neurophysiology]	MMEP
Multiple Mode Integrated Propulsion System (PDAA)	MMIPS
Multiple Model Adaptive Control [Flight control]	MMAC
Multiple Module Access	MMA
Multiple Myeloma [Medicine]	MM
Multiple Negative [Circuit] (AAG)	MUNE
Multiple Newsagents Association [British] (DBA)	MNA
Multiple Number of Faults per Pass (PDAA)	MNFP
Multiple Object Location System [Army]	MOLS
Multiple Object Parameter Estimation	MOPE
Multiple Object Spectroscopy (PDAA)	MOS
Multiple Objective Linear Programming [Computer science] (PDAA)	MOLP
Multiple Object-Tracking RADAR (MCD)	MOTR
Multiple Occupancy Vehicles (DICI)	MOVE
Multiple Occurrences of Unexplained Symptoms [Medicine]	MOUS
Multiple Online Debugging System [Computer science] (IEEE)	MOLDS
Multiple Online Processing (NITA)	MOP
Multiple On-Line Programming [Computer science] (EECA)	MOL
Multiple Online Programming [Computer science] (DIT)	MOP
Multiple Opening-Closing Net and Environmental Sensing System [For collecting marine samples]	MOCNESS
Multiple Opening-Closing Net Environmental Sampling System (USDC)	MOCNESS
Multiple Operational Data Acquisition Program [Computer science]	MODAP
Multiple Operational Launch Complex (MUGU)	MOLC
Multiple Options Funding Facility [Euronotes]	MOFF
Multiple Orbit - Multiple Satellite	MOMS
Multiple Organ Dysfunction Syndrome [Medicine]	MODS
Multiple Organ Failure [Medicine]	MOF
Multiple Output Control System (ECII)	MOCS
Multiple Output Direct Current Power Supply	MODCPS
Multiple Output Program (MCD)	MOP
Multiple Parameter Analysis	MPA
Multiple Particle Plasma	MPP
Multiple Payload Carrier (SSD)	MPC
Multiple Payload Launcher	MPL
Multiple Payload Program [Military]	MPP
Multiple Peanut-Butter Jars [Unconventional musical instrument used in performance by the "Music for Homemade Instruments" ensemble]	MUPEJARS
Multiple Peptide Analysis [Biochemistry]	MPA
Multiple Peptide Synthesis [Biochemistry]	MPS
Multiple Peril Insurance Rating Organization [Later, Multiperil Insurance Conference]	MPIRO
Multiple Peripheral Adapter	MPA
Multiple Personality Disorder	MPD
Multiple Personality Disorder (AD)	mpd
Multiple Phase Ejector	MPE
Multiple Phase Shift Keying [Computer science] (TEL)	MPSK
Multiple Point Source Model with Terrain [Environmental Protection Agency] (GFGA)	MPTER
Multiple Pool Processor and Computer (PDAA)	MULTIPAC
Multiple Position Letter Sort Machine	MPLSM
Multiple Position Letter Sorting Machine (PDAA)	MPLSM
Multiple Positive [Circuit] (AAG)	MUPO
Multiple Power Input (RDA)	MPI
Multiple Primary Feed [Deep Space Instrumentation Facility, NASA]	MPF
Multiple Primary Feed System [Deep Space Instrumentation Facility, NASA]	MPFS
Multiple Primary Malignant Tumor [Oncology]	MPMT
Multiple Probe Head [Laboratory technology]	MPH
Multiple Problem Youth	MPY
Multiple Process Chart	MPC
Multiple Processor [or Multiprocessing] [Computer science] (BUR)	MP
Multiple Product Announcement (NTCM)	MPA
Multiple Product Announcement (AD)	mpa
Multiple Projected Fibonacci [Microwave circuit]	MUPROF
Multiple Protective Earthing (IAA)	MPE
Multiple Protective Structure [Missile bases]	MPS
Multiple Protective Structure System (AD)	MPSS
Multiple Protocol Architecture [Computer science] (PCM)	MPA
Multiple Protocol Interface [Computer science]	MPI
Multiple Provider Router [Computer science] (ACRL)	MPR
Multiple Pulse Arm Fire Device (MCD)	MPAFD
Multiple Punch (DNAB)	MP
Multiple Punch, Error Release (DNAB)	MP-ER
Multiple Pure Tone [Sound]	MPT
Multiple Pure Tone (AD)	mpt
Multiple Quantum Well [Switch for an optical computer]	MQW
Multiple Quotient (AD)	mq
Multiple RADAR Interrogator (MUGU)	MRI
Multiple RADAR-Integrated Tracking [Military] (PDAA)	MERIT
Multiple Railroad System	MRRS
Multiple Range Alignment Device [Army] (INF)	MRAD
Multiple Rapid Automatic Test of Monolithic Integrated Circuits (PDAA)	MR ATOMIC
Multiple Rate Voice Terminal [Telecommunications] (LAIN)	MRVT
Multiple Reaction Monitoring [Chemistry]	MRM
Multiple Read/Write (AD)	mr/w
Multiple Reading, Writing, Compiling (AD)	mrwc
Multiple Read-Write Compute	MRWC
Multiple Real-Time Commands (NASA)	MRTC
Multiple Real-Time Commands	MRTC
Multiple Recording Accelerometer	MRA
Multiple Reentry Vehicle [Military]	MRV

Multiple Register Counter (IEEE)	MRC
Multiple Regression/Correlation [Statistical analysis]	MRC
Multiple Remote Job Entry (NITA)	MRJE
Multiple Report Creation System	MRCS
Multiple Representative Sections [Pathology] (DAVI)	MRS
Multiple Requesting [IBM Corp.]	MR
Multiple Requests Terminal [Computer science] (HGAA)	MRT
Multiple Resource Area Nomination [National Register of Historic Places]	MRA
Multiple Response Resolver	MRR
Multiple Risk Factor Intervention Trial [Cardiology]	MRFIT
Multiple Rocket Firing Unit	MRFU
Multiple Rocket Launcher	MRL
Multiple Rocket Launcher (AD)	mrl
Multiple RPV [Remotely Piloted Vehicle] Control System (PDAA)	MRCS
Multiple Ruby LASER	MRL
Multiple Sail [Navy] (NVT)	MLTSL
Multiple Scan Correlator	MSC
Multiple Sclerosis [Medicine]	MS
Multiple Sclerosis (AD)	ms
Multiple Sclerosis Association of America	MSAA
Multiple Sclerosis Association of America	MSAA
Multiple Sclerosis Foundation (EA)	MFS
Multiple Sclerosis Society [British]	MSS
Multiple Sclerosis Society of New South Wales [Australia]	MSSNSW
Multiple Sclerosis Society of Queensland [Australia]	MSSQ
Multiple Sclerosis Society of Tasmania [Australia]	MSST
Multiple Sclerosis Society of Victoria [Australia]	MSSV
Multiple Sclerosis Society of Western Australia	MSSWA
Multiple Section (MSA)	MS
Multiple Selling Service (OA)	MSS
Multiple Sensor Display Group (MCD)	MSDG
Multiple Sequential Access Method (NITA)	MSAM
Multiple Shoe Retailers' Association [British] (BI)	MSRA
Multiple Shrapnel Wounds	MSW
Multiple Signal Unit [Telecommunications] (TEL)	MSU
Multiple Simultaneous Engagement (MCD)	MSE
Multiple Single Instruction, Multiple Data (MCD)	MSIMD
Multiple Sleep Latency Test	MSLT
Multiple Small-Angle Neutron Scattering [Surface analysis]	MSANS
Multiple Source Technique	MUST
Multiple Spark Discharge [Autotronic Controls Corp.] [Automotive engineering]	MSD
Multiple Spark Igniter	MSI
Multiple Spindle Chucker	MSC
Multiple Stab Wounds [Emergency medicine] (DAVI)	MSW
Multiple Starters (AD)	ms
Multiple Station Analytical Triangulation (PDAA)	MUSAT
Multiple Steady States [Chemical engineering]	MSS
Multiple Stinger Launcher	MSL
Multiple Stinger Launcher	MUSL
Multiple Stores Ejection Rack [For munitions] (MCD)	MSER
Multiple Stylus Recording System (OA)	MSRS
Multiple Subcutaneous Insulin [Medicine]	MSI
Multiple Sub-Nyquist Subsampling Encoding [Digital recording system introduced 1984]	MUSE
Multiple Subscriber Number [Telecommunications] (DOM)	MSN
Multiple Subsonic Jet	MSJ
Multiple Subsonic Jet	MSSJ
Multiple Sulfatase Deficiency [Medicine] (AAMN)	MSD
Multiple System Atrophy [Medicine]	MSA
Multiple System Intelligent Controller [Computer science]	MUSIC
Multiple System Operator [Cable television]	MSO
Multiple System Operator (WDMC)	MSO
Multiple Systems Coupling [Computer science]	MSC
Multiple Systems Operator (ACRL)	MSO
Multiple Tailors Association [British] (BI)	MTA
Multiple Tap Delay Line	MTDL
Multiple Target Deception (MCD)	MTD
Multiple Target Discrimination (MCD)	MTD
Multiple Target Screen	MTS
Multiple Target Simulation (MCD)	MUTS
Multiple Target Tracker	MTT
Multiple Target Tracking System	MTTS
Multiple Task Management Feature (NITA)	MTMF
Multiple Terminal Emulator	MTE
Multiple Terminal Manager (NITA)	MTM
Multiple Terminal System (NITA)	MTS
Multiple Terminator Emulator (NITA)	MTE
Multiple Test Acceptance Code [Lubricants testing] [Automotive engineering]	MTAC
Multiple Test Acceptance Criteria	MTAC
Multiple Thermocouple Reference	MTR
Multiple Threat Emitter System [Air Force]	MUTES
Multiple Threat Modulation [Military] (CAAL)	MTM
Multiple Tile Duct [Telecommunications] (TEL)	MTD
Multiple Time Around Clutter	MTAC
Multiple Time Scale	MTS
Multiple Token Ring [Telecommunications] (OSI)	MTR
Multiple Track RADAR	MTR
Multiple Tracking Range	MTR
Multiple Transducer Seismic Profiling System	MTSPS
Multiple Transfer	MT
Multiple Transmitter Duplicator	MXD
Multiple Tube Counts	MTC
Multiple Tube Fermentation	MTF
Multiple Tumor Suppressor [Oncology]	MTS
Multiple Tumour Suppressor 1 [Genetics] (ECON)	MTS1
Multiple Twin (IAA)	MT
Multiple Unguided Mine System (MCD)	MUMS
Multiple Unit	MU
Multiple Unit Activity [Neurophysiology]	MUA
Multiple Unit for Transmission Elimination [Military] (CAAL)	MUTE
Multiple Unit Message [Telecommunications] (IEEE)	MUM
Multiple Unit Residential Building [Canada]	MURB
Multiple Unit Steerable Antenna [Electronics]	MUSA
Multiple Unit Steerable Array (NITA)	MUSA
Multiple Unit Terminal Test Set (MCD)	MUTTS
Multiple Unit Training Assembly [Army] (AABC)	MUTA
Multiple Units Link 11 Test and Operational Training System [Navy] (NVT)	MULTOTS
Multiple Universally Programmable Intelligent Decoder [Telecommunications] (TSSD)	MUPID
Multiple Usage Data Sheet (MCD)	MUDS
Multiple Use (IAA)	MU
Multiple Use Counter (IAA)	MUC
Multiple User Dimension [Computer science]	MUD
Multiple User Remote Terminal Supervisor (MHDI)	MURTS
Multiple Utility Peripheral (NITA)	MUP
Multiple Utility Peripheral System [Computer science]	MUPS
Multiple Variate Counter (IEEE)	MVC
Multiple V-Belt Drive	MVBD
Multiple Vertical Protective Shelter [for missiles]	MPS
Multiple Vertical Protective Shelter [for missiles] (MCD)	MVPS
Multiple Vibration System	MVS
Multiple Virtual DOS [Disk Operating System] Machine [Computer science] (PCM)	MVDM
Multiple Virtual Processing (NITA)	MVP
Multiple Virtual Storage [IBM Corp.] [Computer science]	MVS
Multiple Virtual Storage System Extension	MVSSE
Multiple Virtual System [Computer science]	MVS
Multiple Vitamin Infusion [Pharmacology] (DAVI)	MVI
Multiple Water Connector (KSC)	MWC
Multiple Wheel Heavy Gear Loading [Aviation]	MWHGL
Multiple Wine Merchants Association [British] (BI)	MWMA
Multiple Wire Proportional Counter	MWPC
Multiple Wounds	MW
Multiple Yield Defense Weapon	MYDW
Multiple Yield Weapon	MYW
Multiple Zones International, Inc. [Associated Press] (SAG)	MultZns
Multiple Zones International, Inc. [NASDAQ symbol] (SAG)	MZON
Multiple-Access Time Sharing [Computer science] (IAA)	MATS
Multiple-Access Time-Division Experiment (IEEE)	MATE
Multiple-Aircraft Simulation Terminal (DA)	MAST
Multiple-Antenna Moving-Target Surveillance RADAR	MASR
Multiple-Aperture Device (MUGU)	MAD
Multiple-Beam Experiment [In MBE-4, a heavy-ion accelerator at the Lawrence Berkeley Laboratory]	MBE
Multiple-Bit Binary Input	MBBI
Multiple-Bit Binary Output	MBBO
Multiple-Bubble Sonoluminescence [Physics]	MBSL
Multiple-Cause, Systems-Oriented Incident Investigation [Engineering]	MCSOII
Multiple-Chip Carrier [Computer technology]	MCC
Multiple-Chip Package	MCP
Multiple-Conductor Cables [JETDS nomenclature] [Military] (CET)	WM
Multiple-Cue Probability Learning [Psychology]	MCPL
Multiple-Cycle Transient Analysis [Chemistry]	MCTA
Multiple-Electrode Flame Ionization Detector	MFID
Multiple-Employer Welfare Association (WYGK)	MEWA
Multiple-Event Time Recording Apparatus (PDAA)	METRA
Multiple-Exposure Photography	MEP
Multiple-Frequency Shift Keying	MFSK
Multiple-Frequency Synthesizer	MFS
Multiple-Frequency X- and K-Band	MXK
Multiple-Gated Acquisition [Nuclear medicine]	MUGA
Multiple-Input/Multiple-Output [Computer science]	MIMO
Multiple-Input Phase-Variable Canonical Form (PDAA)	MIPVCE
Multiple-Integrated LASER Engagement Simulation / Air Ground Engagement Simulator	MILES/AGES
Multiple-Line [Insurance]	ML
Multiple-Line Encryption System (AABC)	MLES
Multiple-Line Exclusive Agent [Insurance]	MLEA
Multiple-Link Satellite Program	MLSP
Multiple-Locus [Light flashes]	ML
Multiple-Mirror Telescope [Mount Hopkins, AZ] [Jointly operated by Smithsonian Institution and the University of Arizona Astronomy]	MMT
Multiple-Mission Command System [NASA]	MMCS
Multiple-Mission Support Area [Space Flight Operations Facility, NASA]	MMSA
Multiple-Mission Support Equipment [NASA]	MMSE
Multiple-Mission Support Recording [NASA]	MMSR
Multiple-Mission Telemetry [NASA]	MMT
Multiple-Mission Telemetry System [NASA]	MMTS
Multiple-Monitored Electroconvulsive Therapy [Schizophrenia]	MMECT
Multiple-Orbit Bombardment System	MOBS
Multiple-Orifice Valve (AD)	mov
Multiple-Pass Heuristic Procedure (PDAA)	MPHP
Multiple-Period Average (IEEE)	MPA
Multiple-Position Lock (AD)	mpl
Multiple-Pressure Measuring System	MPMS
Multiple-Product Pricing [Business term] (MHDB)	MPP
Multiple-Profile Configuration (MCD)	MPC

Multiple-Purpose Communications (NG)	MPC
Multiple-Purpose Telescope	MPT
Multiple-Response Enable (IEEE)	MRE
Multiples of Background Level [Of environmental contaminants]	MBL
Multiples over the Median [Statistics]	MOM's
Multiple-Sclerosis-Associated Agent [A virus]	MSAA
Multiple-Simultaneous-Target Steerable Telemetry Tracking System [Navy]	MUSTRAC
Multiple-Sine-Slit Microdensitometer (PDAA)	MSSM
Multiple-Start Systematic Sampling [Statistics]	MSSS
Multiple-Task Performance	MTP
Multiple-Technique Analytical Computer System	MACS
Multiple-Terminal Access [Computer science] (IBMDP)	MTA
Multiple-Terminal Communication Adapter [Computer science]	MTCA
Multiple-Trigger Generator	MTG
Multiple-Unit, Moving-Projectile System (MCD)	MUMPS
Multiple-Use Land Alliance (EA)	MULTA
Multiple-Use Linear Engergizer [Automotive engineering]	MULE
Multiple-Use MARC [Machine-Readable Cataloging] System [Online retrieval system] [Information service or system Library of Congress]	MUMS
Multiple-Use Planning Area	MPA
Multiple-Use Sustained-Yield Act of 1960	MUSYA
Multiple-User Dimension Object Oriented [Computer technology]	MOO
Multiple-Valued Logic [Computer science]	MVL
Multiple-Wavelength Anomalous Dispersion [Crystallography]	MAD
Multiple-Weapon Automatic Target and Battery Evaluator (SAA)	MATABE
Multiplex [or Multiplexer] [Telecommunications]	MPX
Multiplex	mpx
Multiplex (AD)	MUX
Multiplex [or Multiplexer] [Telecommunications]	MVX
Multiplex	MX
Multiplex [or Multiplexer]	MX
Multiplex	MBIU
Multiplex Bus Interface Unit (MCD)	MC
Multiplex Channel (IAA)	MDB
Multiplex Data Bus [Computer science] (MCD)	MEDA
Multiplex Electronic Doppler Analyzer	MFISH
Multiplex Fluorescence in Situ Hybridization	MITS
Multiplex Information Transfer System (PDAA)	MIR
Multiplex Intensity Rules	MIA
Multiplex Interface Adapter (NASA)	MIH
Multiplex Interface Handler	MIU
Multiplex Interface Unit (NASA)	MIU
Multiplex Interface Unit	MIFS
Multiplex Interferometric Fourier Spectroscopy	MICS
Multiplex Interior Communications (NG)	MLA
Multiplex Line Adapter	MLIA
Multiplex Loop Interface Adapter	MUXMOD
Multiplex Modulation	MMS
Multiplex Modulation System	MUXIC
Multiplex/Multiple Voice Interior Communications (DNAB)	MRP
Multiplex Recording Photography	MRTU
Multiplex Remote Terminal Unit (MCD)	MTIS
Multiplex Transmitter Input Signals (PDAA)	MAC
Multiplexed Analog Component [Satellite television] [British]	MAC
Multiplexed Analog Components [Satellite television system]	MAC
Multiplexed Analog to Digital, Digital to Analog Multiplexed [Computer science]	MADDAM
Multiplexed Analogue Component, Type B [Satellite television]	B-MAC
Multiplexed Asynchronous Receiver/Transmitter (MCD)	MUXART
Multiplexed Information and Computing Service [Honeywell, Inc.]	MULTICS
Multiplexed Input NHRE [National Hail Research Experiment] Averager	MINA
Multiplexed Matrix Array	MMA
Multiplexed Message Processor	MMP
Multiplexer	MPLX
Multiplexer	MPLXR
Multiplexer	MPXR
Multiplexer	MUL
Multiplexer	MULTI
Multiplexer	MUXER
Multiplexer Analog-to-Digital Converter (MCD)	MADC
Multiplexer and Demultiplexer	MUX/DEMUX
Multiplexer and Terminal Unit	MTU
Multiplexer Channel [Computer science]	MXC
Multiplexer Computer Systems (MCD)	MCS
Multiplexer Control Unit	MCU
Multiplexer/Demultiplexer (NASA)	MDM
Multiplexer/Demultiplexer [Bell Laboratories]	MULDEM
Multiplexer/Demultiplexer	MULDEX
Multiplexer Encoder Unit	MEU
Multiplexer Interface Adapter (NASA)	MIA
Multiplexer/Priority/Second	MUX/PRI/SEC
Multiplexer Regenerator Address [Computer science] (MHDI)	MREGAD
Multiplexer Storage (IAA)	MS
Multiplexer Storage Data Register [Computer science] (IAA)	MSDR
Multiplexer Unit [Telecommunications]	MXU
Multiplexes [or Multiplexers] [Telecommunications]	MUXES
Multiplexing Automatic Error Correction (IAA)	MUXARC
Multiplexing Channel Adapter [Telecommunications] (IAA)	MCA
Multiplexing Identifier [Telecommunications] (ACRL)	MID
Multiplexing Input-Output Processor [Computer science] (BUR)	MIOP
Multiplexing Unit	MU
Multiplexor (AD)	mpxr
Multiplex-Section, Shared-Protection Rings	MS-SPRING
Multiplicand Select Gate (IAA)	MSG
Multiplication (IDOE)	X
Multiplication (IDOE)	x
Multiplication Factor [or Constant]	k
Multiplication Stimulating Activity [Cytochemistry]	MSA
Multiplicative Noise Compensator [Telecommunications] (TEL)	MNC
Multiplicity of Infection	MOI
Multiplicity of Infection (AD)	moi
Multiplier	M
Multiplier	MULTP
Multiplier (NITA)	MULTR
Multiplier	MDG
Multiplier Decoder Gate [Computer science]	MP
Multiplier Phototube	MQ
Multiplier Quotient [Computer science]	MQR
Multiplier Quotient Register [Computer science]	MQU
Multiplier Quotient Unit [Computer science]	MR
Multiplier Register	MTWP
Multiplier Traveling Wave Phototube (IAA)	MLY
Multiply (MDG)	MPY
Multiply (MDG)	mpy
Multiply (AD)	MUL
Multiply (MDG)	MULT
Multiply (NASA)	MACR
Multiply, Accumulate, and Round	MAC
Multiply and Accumulate [Computer science] (PCM)	MAD
Multiply and Add	MLR
Multiply and Round	MTP
Multiply Twinned Particles (DICI)	MD
Multiply-Divide (IAA)	MP-DV
Multiply-Divide (NITA)	MDAC
Multiplying Digital-to-Analog Converter [Computer science] (IEEE)	MF
Multiplying Factor [Microscopy]	MTP
Multipoint (DNAB)	MAFSS
Multipoint Airfield Fuel Support System	MPA
Multi-Point Asynchronous (NITA)	MCU
Multipoint Control Unit [Telecommunications]	MULDEX
Multipoint Cross-Reference Index	MDS
Multipoint Distribution Service [Educational television]	MDS
Multipoint Distribution Services (ACRL)	MDS
Multipoint Distribution System [Line-of-sight relay system for electronic signals]	MFI
Multi-point Fuel Injection	MPFI
Multi-Point Fuel Injection [Automotive engineering]	MPG
Multipoint Grounding (NASA)	MIAC
Multipoint Interactive Audio-Visual Communication (NITA)	MNCS
Multipoint Network-Control System	MRL
Multipoint Recorder/Logger	MPI
Multipoint-Electronic Fuel Injection [Automotive engineering]	MM
Multipolar Magnetic [Sun] (DICI)	MP
Multipole	mp
Multipole (AD)	MEDO
Multipole Expansion of Diatomic Overlap [Physics]	MFI
Multiport Fuel Injection [Automotive technology]	MMB
Multiport Memory Bank [Computer science] (MHDB)	MMC
Multiport Memory Controller	MMI
Multiport Memory Interface [Computer science] (MHDB)	MMIU
Multiport Memory Interface Unit	MPCI
Multiport Programmable Communications Interface	MP/SCM
Multiport Semiconductor Memory (MHDI)	MFT
Multiposition Frequency Telegraphy [Telecommunications] (OA)	MSE
Multi-Position Small Engine [Automotive engineering]	MPPC
Multipotent Hematopoietic Progenitor Cell [Biochemistry]	MSC
Multipotential Stem Cells [Hematology]	mpt
Multipower Transmission (AD)	MPA
Multiprecision Arithmetic	MP
Multiprocessing [Computer science] (CDE)	MPCS
Multiprocessing Control System [Computer science]	MP/M
Multiprocessing Monitor Control Program [Computer science]	MSP
Multiprocessing Server Pack [Computer science] (CDE)	MPS
Multiprocessing System [Computer science]	MCA
Multiprocessor Communications Adapter	MCU
Multiprocessor Communications Unit	MPC
Multiprocessor Computer	MPCC
Multiprocessor Computer Complex	MDM
Multiprocessor Diagnostic Monitor (IAA)	MDS
Multiprocessor Distributed System [Raytheon] (NITA)	MPECC
Multiprocessor Experimental Computer Complex	MPX
Multiprocessor Extension (PCM)	MPC
Multiprogram Control [Computer science]	MGPF
Multiprogram General-Purpose Facilities [Oak Ridge National Laboratory]	MCS
Multiprogrammed Computer System (IEEE)	MQS
Multiprogrammed Queued Tasking System (NITA)	MFT
Multiprogramming (NITA)	MP/M
Multiprogramming Control Program for Microcomputers	MP/M
Multiprogramming Control Program for Microprocessors (NITA)	MPE
Multiprogramming Executive [Hewlett-Packard Co.]	MPX
Multiprogramming Executive [Computer science]	MPE/iX
Multiprogramming Executive / POSIX [Portable Operating System Interface for Unix] [Computer science] (CDE)	MPM
Multiprogramming Monitor	MOPSY
Multi-Programming Operating System [Computer science] (PDAA)	MOS
Multiprogramming Operating System	MPS
Multiprogramming Periodic Tasking System (NITA)	MPS
Multiprogramming System [Computer science]	MPS
Multiprogramming System (AD)	MUS
Multiprogramming Utility System [Regnecentralen] [Denmark]	MUS

Multiprogramming Utility System Interpretive Language [Regnecentralen] [Denmark] .... MUSIL

Multiprogramming with a Finite Amount of Trouble [Computer science] .... MFT

Multiprogramming with a Variable Number of Tasks [IBM Corp.] [Control program] [Computer science] .... MVT

Multiprogramming with Fixed Number of Tasks [Computer science] (BUR) .... MFT

Multiprogramming with Virtual Storage [Computer science] (ECII) .... MVS

Multiproject Automated Control System .... MACS

Multiprotocol Communications Controller .... MPCC

MultiProtocol Router [Novell, Inc.] (PCM) .... MPR

Multiprotocol Transport Network [Telecommunications] (ACRL) .... MPTN

Multi-Protocol Transport Service [Telecommunications] (ACRL) .... MPTS

Multipulse Linear Productive Coding (PDAA) .... MPLPC

Multipulse Observation Sizing Technique [Southwest Research Institute] .... MOST

Multipulse Scaling-Law Code using Data Base Interpolation (PDAA) .... MPLAW

Multipunch Bar (AD) .... mp br

Multipunch Bar .... MPBR

Multipunch Die (AD) .... mp di

Multipunch Die .... MPDI

Multipunch Plate (AD) .... mp pl

Multipunch Plate .... MPPL

Multipurpose .... MP

Multipurpose (AD) .... mp

Multipurpose (AABC) .... MPPS

Multipurpose Acquisition and Control System (IAA) .... MACS

Multipurpose Aero-Space Plane [Russian delta-wing orbiter] .... MAKS

Multipurpose Airmobile Combat-Support Vehicle (SAA) .... MACSV

Multipurpose Airmobile Combat-Support Vehicle .... MACV

Multipurpose All-Terrain Vehicle .... MPAT

Multipurpose Amphibious Assault Ship .... LHD

Multipurpose and Generalized Interface to COBOL [Computer science] .... MAGIC

Multipurpose Application Console (SSD) .... MPAC

Multipurpose Arcade Combat Simulator [Marksmanship training] [Army] (INF) .... MACS

Multipurpose Arthritis and Musculoskeletal Diseases Center [University of Alabama, Birmingham] [Research center] (RCD) .... MAMDC

Multipurpose Arthritis Center [Medical University of South Carolina] [Research center] (RCD) .... MAC

Multipurpose Arthritis Center [Brigham and Women's Hospital] [Research center] (RCD) .... MAC

Multipurpose Automatic Data Analysis Machine .... MADAM

Multipurpose Automatic Inspection and Diagnostic Systems [Army] .... MAIDS

Multipurpose Automatic Test Equipment .... MATE

Multipurpose Automatic Test System (IAA) .... MATS

Multipurpose Bayonet System [Army] (INF) .... MPBS

Multipurpose Carrier (AD) .... mpc

Multipurpose Center .... MPC

Multi-Purpose Central Mount/Module [Military] (LAIN) .... MPCM

Multi-Purpose Close Support Weapon [Military] (AABC) .... MPCSW

Multipurpose Color Display .... MPCD

Multipurpose Communications and Signaling .... MCS

Multipurpose Computer (CMD) .... MPC

Multipurpose Concealed Intrusion Detector [Army] (RDA) .... MCID

Multipurpose Control Display Unit (GAVI) .... MCDU

Multipurpose Data Link (GAVI) .... MDL

Multipurpose Diffractometer .... MPD

Multipurpose Display (MCD) .... MD

Multipurpose Display (MCD) .... MPD

Multipurpose Display Group (MCD) .... MDG

Multi-Purpose Display System (DA) .... MPDS

Multi-Purpose Electric Furnace (PDAA) .... MEF

Multipurpose Electromagnetic Environment Simulator (MCD) .... MEES

Multipurpose Extended Lift Blanket Assembly (IEEE) .... MELBA

Multipurpose Facility (DOMA) .... MPF

Multipurpose Fire Control System .... MPFC

Multipurpose Food [Refers to a specific combination of ingredients used in a food relief program] .... MPF

Multi-Purpose Food (AD) .... mpf

Multi-Purpose Graphic System [Computer science] .... MPGS

Multipurpose High-Speed Vehicle (MCD) .... MHSV

Multipurpose Imaging Radiometer Spectrometer Equipment .... MIRSE

Multipurpose Individual Munition [Weapon] .... MPIM

Multi-Purpose Individual Munition/Short Range Assault Weapon [Military] (RDA) .... MPIM/SRAW

Multipurpose Individual Weapon System (MCD) .... MIWS

Multipurpose Information Processor [Computer science] (MHDB) .... MIP

Multi-purpose Infrared Sight (PDAA) .... MIRS

Multipurpose In-Space Throttleable Engine (MCD) .... MIST

Multipurpose Integrated Chemical Agent Alarm [Army] (DOMA) .... MICAD

Multipurpose International Securities Trading Information (MHDW) .... MISTI

Multipurpose Internet Mail Extension [Computer science] .... MIME

Multipurpose Internet Mail Extensions [Computer science] (ACRL) .... MIME

Multipurpose Light Helicopter (DOMA) .... MPLH

Multipurpose Lightweight Missile .... MLM

Multipurpose Lightweight Missile System .... MLMS

Multipurpose Lightweight Overboot [Army] .... MULO

Multipurpose Limousine .... MPL

Multi-Purpose Lithium Grease .... MPLG

Multipurpose Long Endurance [Aircraft] .... MPLE

Multipurpose Long Endurance Plane .... MLEP

Multipurpose Meal .... MPM

Multipurpose Meal (AD) .... mpm

Multipurpose Missile .... MPM

Multi-Purpose Molybdenum Grease .... MPMG

Multi-Purpose Offshore Industrial Port Islands (NOAA) .... MOIPI

Multipurpose Optimization System [Computer science] .... MPOS

Multipurpose Passenger Vehicle .... MPV

Multipurpose Payload Support Equipment (NASA) .... MPPSE

Multipurpose Payload Support Equipment .... MPPSE

Multipurpose Payload Support Equipment (MCD) .... MPSE

Multipurpose Processing Language [Computer science] (IEEE) .... MPPL

Multipurpose Program that Learns [Computer science] (PDAA) .... MULTIPLE

Multipurpose Programming Language .... MPPL

Multipurpose Rail Transport (NRCH) .... MPRT

Multipurpose Range Complex [Army] (INF) .... MPRC

Multipurpose Range Complex - Heavy [Army] .... MPRC-H

Multipurpose Range Complex - Light [Army] .... MPRC-L

Multipurpose Recorder .... MPR

Multipurpose Research System .... MRS

Multipurpose Reusable Spacecraft (IIA) .... MRS

Multipurpose Sampling System .... MPSS

Multipurpose Semi-Submersible Platform (DNAB) .... MSP

Multipurpose Ship (AABC) .... MPS

Multi-Purpose Special Fund [Asian Development Bank] [United Nations] (EY) .... MPSF

Multipurpose Stores Ship [Navy] .... AOE

Multipurpose Submunition (RDA) .... MPSM

Multipurpose Support Room (MCD) .... MPSR

Multipurpose Support Vessel [Offshore drilling] .... MSV

Multipurpose Target Generator .... MTG

Multipurpose Test Equipment .... MPTE

Multipurpose Test Equipment .... MTE

Multipurpose Test Set (DWSG) .... MPTS

Multipurpose Tool Set (MCD) .... MPTS

Multipurpose, Tracer, Self-Destruct [Army] .... MPT-SD

Multipurpose Training Range [Army] .... MPTR

Multipurpose UHF [Ultra High Frequency] Satellite (IAA) .... MUSAT

Multi-Purpose Universal Programmable Intelligent Decoder (NITA) .... MUPID

Multipurpose User-Oriented Software Technology (MHDI) .... MUST

Multipurpose Vehicle [Automotive engineering] .... MPV

Multipurpose Vehicle (AD) .... mpv

Multipurpose Ventricular Actuating System (NASA) .... MVAS

Multipurpose Weapon (MCD) .... MW

Multiquantum Well (NITA) .... MQW

Multiquantum Well Lasers (NITA) .... MQWL

Multiracial American Scholarship Fund .... MASF

Multi-Racial Education Resources Centre [British] (AIE) .... MERC

Multi-Racial Party [Zambia] [Political party] (EY) .... MRP

Multi-Racial Union of Squatters to Alleviate Racial Discrimination [British] (DI) .... MUSTARD

Multi-RADAR Track Reconstitution [Aviation] (DA) .... MURATREC

Multi-Rail Rocket System (PDAA) .... MRRS

Multireference Configuration Interaction [Quantum chemistry] (MCD) .... MRCI

Multireference Double Excitation [Physics] .... MRD

Multi-Reflecton [Lighting] .... MR

Multi-Region Option (HGAA) .... MRO

Multiregional Input-Output .... MRIO

Multirod Burst Test [Nuclear energy] (NRCH) .... MRBT

Multi-Role Bomber [Program] [DoD] .... MRB

Multirole Combat Aircraft .... MRCA

Multirole Combat Aircraft (AD) .... mrca

Multirole Fighter [Replacement for the F-16] [Air Force] (DOMA) .... MRF

Multirole RADAR .... MRR

Multi-Role Survivable Radar [Army] (DOMA) .... MRSR

Multirole Thermal Imager [Defense electronics] .... MRTI

Multisample Luer Adapter [Medicine] (MEDA) .... MSLA

Multisatellite Attitude Determination [NASA] .... MSAD

Multisatellite Attitude Prediction [NASA] .... MSAP

Multisatellite Attitude Program System [NASA] .... MAPS

Multisatellite Augmentation Program [NASA] .... MUSAP

Multisatellite Dispenser (MCD) .... MSD

Multisatellite Operations Control Center [NASA] .... MSOCC

Multischedule Private Line .... MPL

Multisensor Aided Targeting-Air [Army] (DOMA) .... MSAT-A

Multisensor Correlator (CAAL) .... MSC

Multisensor Display .... MSD

Multisensor Imagery .... MSI

Multisensor Intelligence Correlator (IAA) .... MUSIC

Multisensor Processor (CAAL) .... MSP

Multisensor Stabilized Integrated System .... MSIS

Multisensor Target Acquisition System [Military] (RDA) .... MTAS

Multisensory Disorder .... MSD

Multiservice Center .... MSC

Multiservice Communications Systems (RDA) .... MSCS

Multiservice Electronic Warfare Support Group [Originally Maritime Electronic Warfare Support Group] [NATO] (DOMA) .... MEWSG

Multiservice Test and Evaluation [Military] .... MST & E

Multi-Services, Inc. [FAA designator] (FAAC) .... MPL

Multiservicios Aeronauticos SA de CV [Mexico ICAO designator] (FAAC) .... MUT

Multiset Users Group (EA) .... MUG

Multishare Network Architecture [Mitsubishi Corp.] (BUR) .... MNA

Multishot Grenade Launcher (RDA) .... MSGL

Multishot Portable Flame Weapon (MCD) .... MPFW

Multishot Portable Flame Weapon (DNAB) .... MSPFW

Multisolid Pneumatic Transport Bed [Chemical engineering] .... MPTB

Multi-Solids Fluidized Bed [Chemical engineering] .... MSFB

Multisolvent Delivery System .... MSDS

Multisource Correlation Facility (MCD) .... MSCF

Multisource Intelligence File (MCD) .... MIF

Multisource Processing System (MCD) ... MSPS
Multisource Unified Data Distribution (PDAA) ... MUDD
Multispectral Close Combat Decoy (DWSG) ... MCCD
Multispectral Cloud Radiometer (MCD) ... MCR
Multispectral Image Analyzer (MCD) ... MSIA
Multispectral Imagery (DOMA) ... MSI
Multispectral Linear Array (SSD) ... MLA
Multispectral Measurements Program (MCD) ... MSMP
Multispectral Opium Poppy Sensor System ... MOPS
Multispectral Opium Poppy Sensor System (AD) ... MOPSS
Multispectral Photographic Camera (KSC) ... MPC
Multispectral Photographic Facility ... MPF
Multispectral Photographic Facility ... MSPF
Multispectral Photographic Reconnaissance (MCD) ... MSPRS
Multispectral Scanner [or Sensor] ... MSS
Multispectral Scanner and Data System ... MSDS
Multispectral Scanner and Data System ... MSDS
Multispectral Scanner System ... MSS
Multi-Spectral Thermal Imager Spacecraft [Department of Energy] ... MTI
Multispectral Thermal Infrared Imager (SSD) ... MTIRI
Multispectrum Electronic Self-Scanning Radiometer (MCD) ... MESSR
Multispeed Repeater ... MSR
Multistage Depressed Collector (IAA) ... MDC
Multistage Exercise Test [Medicine] (CPH) ... MSET
Multistage Flash [Desalination method] ... MSF
Multistage Flash Distillation (PDAA) ... MFD
Multi-Stage Force Allocation (SAA) ... MIST-FOAL
Multistage Frequency Multiplexer ... MFM
Multistage Graded Exercise Test [Cardiology] (DAVI) ... M-GXT
Multistage Improvement Program (DOMA) ... MSIP
Multistage Operation (MHDI) ... MSO
Multistart [Optimization method] ... MS
Multistate Atmospheric Power Production Pollution Study [Department of Energy] ... MAP3S
Multistate Bar Examination ... MBE
Multistate Information System [Patient records] ... MSIS
Multistate Tax Commission (EA) ... MTC
Multi-State Teacher Education Project ... M-STEP
Multistatic Sonar System Acoustic Source (DOMA) ... MSS AS
Multistation Access Unit [Telecommunications] (PCM) ... MAU
Multistation Access Unit [Telecommunications] (TSSD) ... MSAU
Multistation Control Unit [Telecommunications] (IAA) ... MSCU
Multistation Interface Unit [Computer science] ... MIU
Multi-Step Industries [Vancouver Stock Exchange symbol] ... MSB
Multi-Step Products [Toronto Stock Exchange symbol] ... MLP
Multistop Time-to-Pulse Height Converter [NASA] ... MSTPHC
Multistring (NASA) ... MS
Multistring ... MS
Multistrip Cesium Contact Thrustor ... MCCT
Multistrip Cesium Thrustor ... MCT
Multistrip Coupler [Telecommunications] (TEL) ... MSC
Multisubscriber Time-Sharing Systems [Computer system] ... MSTS
Multisubsystem Adapter [Sperry UNIVAC] ... MSA
Multisystem Automatic Test Equipment [British] ... MATE
Multi-System Communications Unit (NITA) ... MCU
Multisystem Coupling [Computer science] ... MSC
Multisystem Involvement [Medicine] ... MSI
Multisystem Networking Facility ... MNF
Multisystem Networking Facility [Computer science] ... MSNF
Multisystem Organ Failure [Medicine] (CPH) ... MSOF
Multisystem Test [Military] ... MST
Multisystem Test Equipment [Military] ... MTE
Multisystem Training System ... MSTS
Multisystem Weapon Delivery [Air Force] ... MSWD
Multi-Systems Integration Facility (SSD) ... MSIF
Multi-Taper Method [Spectroscopy] ... MTM
Multitarget Automatic Plotting System ... MAPS
Multitarget Electronic Warfare System ... MULTEWS
Multitarget Frequency ... MTF
Multitarget Instrumentation RADAR [Military] (CAAL) ... MIR
Multitask Single Stream System (NITA) ... MSS
Multitask Terminal System ... MTTS
Multitasking ... MT
Multitasking BASIC [Computer science] ... MTBASIC
Multitasking Extensible Messaging Environment ... MEME
Multi-Tasking Monitor (NITA) ... MTM
Multi-Tasking Operating System (NITA) ... MTOS
Multi-Tech Supervisory Protocol [Telecommunications] (PCM) ... MSP
Multi-Tenant Telecommunications Association (EA) ... MTTA
Multiterminal Adapter (IEEE) ... MTA
Multi-Terminal Modular System (DGA) ... MTMS
Multi-Terminal Monitor (NITA) ... MTM
Multiterminal Unit (TEL) ... MTU
Multitest Evaluation Report [Nuclear energy] (NRCH) ... MTER
Multi-Threat Body Armor [Army] ... MTBA
Multithreshold Element (IAA) ... MTE
Multitier Distributed Application Services [Computer science] ... MIDAS
Multi-Tranche Tap Note [Finance] [British] ... MTTN
Multitumor Antibody [Clinical chemistry] ... MTA
Multitype Branching Process in a Random Environment [Computer science] ... MBPRE
Multiunit Direct Digital Control (IAA) ... MUDDC
Multiunit Space Transport and Recovery Device (MCD) ... MUSTARD
Multiunit Supervisory Control (IAA) ... MUSC
Multi-Use Interagency News [FSS database] (AAGC) ... MUFFIN
Multiuse Manuscript ... MUM
Multiuse Mission Payload Support Equipment (MCD) ... MMPSE
Multiuse Mission Support Equipment ... MMSE
Multiuse Mnemonics (IAA) ... MUM
Multiuse Payload and Mission Support Equipment (MCD) ... MPMSE
Multiuse Terminal Translator (MHDI) ... MUTT
Multiuser Archival and Retrieval System [Computer science] ... MARS
Multi-User Business Operating System (NITA) ... MBOS
Multi-User Domain [Computer science] ... MUD
Multi-User Dungeon [Computer game] ... MUD
Multi-User Engineering Change Proposal Automated Review System (RDA) ... MEARS
Multi-User Message (NITA) ... MUM
Multiuser Monitor ... MUM
Multiuser Terminal Executive (MHDI) ... MUTEX
Multi-User Transaction Executive (NITA) ... MUTEX
Multi-User-Simulated Environment (PS) ... MUSE
Multiutility System (MCD) ... MUS
Multivalue Electronic Circuit Analysis (IAA) ... MECA
Multivalue Program [Computer science] ... MVP
Multivariable Control Unit [Computer science] ... MVCU
Multivariable Frequency Domain ... MFD
Multivariable Internal Model Control [Control engineering] ... MIMC
Multivariable Program [Computer science] (IAA) ... MVP
Multivariable Self-Tuning Regulator [Control technology] ... MSTR
Multivariable Storage [Computer science] ... MVS
Multivariable Task (MCD) ... MVT
Multivariant Discriminant Analysis [Medicine] (DMAA) ... MDA
Multivariate Analysis (GFGA) ... MVA
Multivariate Analysis and Prediction of Schedules ... MAPS
Multivariate Analysis of Variance [Statistics] ... MANOVA
Multivariate Analysis, Participation, and Structure ... MAPS
Multivariate Analysis, Retrieval, and Storage [System] [NASA] ... MARS
Multivariate Exponential Distribution [Statistics] ... MVE
Multivariate Linear Regression Analysis [Advertising marketing] ... MLRA
Multivariate Statistical Process Control ... MSPC
Multivariate Survival Analysis [Statistics] ... MSA
Multivariate, Univariate, and Discriminant Analysis of Irregular Data [Statistics] (IAA) ... MUDAID
Multivariate Variance and Discriminant Analysis [Mathematics] ... MVDA
Multivendor Customer Service [Computer science] (CDE) ... MCS
Multi-Vendor Integration Protocol [Computer science] ... MVIP
Multivesicular Body ... MVB
Multivibrator (IAA) ... MULTIV
Multivibrator ... MV
Multivibrator ... MVB
Multivibrator ... MVBR
Multi-Vintage Wine Growers Society [British] (DBA) ... MVWGS
Multivitamins [Pharmacy] ... multivits
Multivitamins [Nutrition] ... MV
Multivitamins Intravenously [Pharmacology] (DAVI) ... MVI
Multivolume Monographs ... MVM
Multiwall Nanotube [Materials science] ... MWNT
Multiwall Sack Manufacturers Employers Association [British] (DBA) ... MSMEA
Multiwalled Nanotube [Materials science] ... MWNT
Multiwave Italian Key System (NITA) ... MIKE
Multiwavelength Anomalous Diffraction [Physics] ... MAD
Multiway Analysis of Variance (MCD) ... MANOVA
Multiway Principal Components Analysis [Mathematics] ... MPCA
Multiweapons Fire Control System (DNAB) ... MWFCS
Multiwire (IAA) ... MW
Multiwire Proportional Chamber (IAA) ... MWPC
Multiwork Station ... MWS
Multiyear Contract ... MYC
Multi-Year Development Plan [Environmental Protection Agency] (ERG) ... MYDP
Multiyear Operational Plan [Long-range forecast produced by the Canadian government] ... MYOP
Multiyear Procurement [DoD] ... MYP
Multiyear Procurement Objective [DoD] ... MYPO
Multiyear Rescheduling Agreement [Banking] ... MYRA
Multnomah County Law Library, Portland, OR [Library symbol Library of Congress] (LCLS) ... OrPML
Multnomah Literature Ministries [Publisher] [Portland, OR] ... MLM
Multnomah School of the Bible [Oregon] ... MSB
Multnomah School of the Bible, Portland, OR [Library symbol Library of Congress] (LCLS) ... OrPMB
Mulungu [Zaire] [ICAO location identifier] (ICLI) ... FZMC
Mulungwishi [Zaire] [ICAO location identifier] (ICLI) ... FZQD
Mulungwishi [Zaire] [Seismograph station code, US Geological Survey] (SEIS) ... MLN
Mumbwa [Zambia] [Airport symbol] (AD) ... UMW
Mu-Meson [An elementary particle] ... MUON
Mumford's Jamaica Reports [A publication] (DLA) ... Mum Jam
Mumford's Jamaica Reports [A publication] (DLA) ... Mumf
Mumias [Kenya] [Airport symbol Obsolete] (OAG) ... MUM
Mummy Mountain [Arizona] [Seismograph station code, US Geological Survey Closed] (SEIS) ... MMA
Mumps Skin Test Antigen [Clinical chemistry] ... MSTA
MUMPS [Massachusetts General Hospital Utility Multiprogramming System] Users' Group (EA) ... MUG
Mumps-Measles-Rubella Vaccine (ECON) ... MMR
Munchausen Syndrome by Proxy [Medicine] ... MSBP
Muncie [Indiana] [Airport symbol] (OAG) ... MIE
Muncie & Western Railroad Co. [AAR code] ... MWR

Muncie Evening Press, Muncie, IN [*Library symbol Library of Congress*] (LCLS) .... InMuP
Muncie, IN [*Location identifier FAA*] (FAAL) .... MIE
Muncie, IN [*FM radio station call letters*] .... WBST
Muncie, IN [*AM radio station call letters*] .... WERK
Muncie, IN [*FM radio station call letters*] .... WERK-FM
Muncie, IN [*Television station call letters*] .... WIPB
Muncie, IN [*AM radio station call letters*] .... WLBC
Muncie, IN [*FM radio station call letters*] .... WLBC-FM
Muncie, IN [*FM radio station call letters*] .... WWDS
Muncie, IN [*FM radio station call letters*] .... WWHI
Muncie Morning Star-Evening Press, Muncie, IN [*Library symbol Library of Congress*] (LCLS) .... InMuSP
Muncie Public Library, Muncie, IN [*OCLC symbol*] (OCLC) .... IMU
Muncie Public Library, Muncie, IN [*Library symbol Library of Congress*] (LCLS) .... InMu
Muncie-Getrag [*Refers to an automotive transmission designed by Getrag, a West German company, and built by General Motors in Muncie, IN*] .... MG
Muncy, PA [*FM radio station call letters*] .... WHTO
Munda [*Solomon Islands*] [*Airport symbol*] (OAG) .... MUA
Munda, New Georgia Islands [*Solomon Islands*] [*ICAO location identifier*] (ICLI) .... AGGM
Mundaring [*Australia Seismograph station code, US Geological Survey*] (SEIS) .... MUN
Mundee Mines Ltd. [*Vancouver Stock Exchange symbol*] .... MNU
Mundelein College, Chicago, IL [*OCLC symbol*] (OCLC) .... ICM
Mundelein College, Chicago, IL [*Library symbol Library of Congress*] (LCLS) .... ICMund
Munford's Reports [*15-20 Virginia*] [*A publication*] (DLA) .... Mun
Munford's Reports [*15-20 Virginia*] [*A publication*] (DLA) .... Munf
Munford's Reports [*15-20 Virginia*] [*A publication*] (DLA) .... Munf (VA)
Munfordville, KY [*AM radio station call letters*] .... WLOC
Munfordville, KY [*FM radio station call letters*] .... WLOC-FM
Munfordville, KY [*FM radio station call letters*] (RBYB) .... WMCC-FM
Mungbean Yellow Mosaic Virus [*Plant pathology*] .... MYMV
Munger on Application of Payments [*A publication*] (DLA) .... Mung Pay
Muni Insured Fund, Inc. [*Associated Press*] (SAG) .... Muniln
Muniassets Fund [*NYSE symbol*] (SPSG) .... MUA
Muniassets Fund, Inc. [*Associated Press*] (SAG) .... Muniast
Munich [*Germany*] [*Seismograph station code, US Geological Survey Closed*] (SEIS) .... MNH
Munich [*Germany Airport symbol*] (OAG) .... MUC
Municipal .... MNCPL
Municipal .... MUN
Municipal (AFM) .... MUNI
Municipal .... MUNIC
Municipal Advantage Fund [*NYSE symbol*] (SAG) .... MAF
Municipal Advantage Fund [*Associated Press*] (SAG) .... MunAdv
Municipal Airport (MCD) .... MAP
Municipal Analysis Services, Inc. [*Information service or system*] (IID) .... MAS
Municipal and Election Cases [*India*] [*A publication*] (DLA) .... Mun & El Cas
Municipal and Industrial [*Users of water*] .... M & I
Municipal and Industry Strategy for Abatement .... MISA
Municipal and Parish Law Cases [*England*] [*A publication*] (DLA) .... Munic & PL
Municipal Arborist Association [*Later, MAUFS*] (EA) .... MAA
Municipal Arborists and Urban Foresters Society (EA) .... MAUFS
Municipal Assistance Corp. [*New York*] [*Also known as "Big Mac"*] .... MAC
Municipal Association Record [*A publication*] .... MAR
Municipal Automated Geographic Information System [*District of Columbia Office of the Mayor*] [*Information service or system*] (IID) .... MAGIS
Municipal Board Standards Association (NADA) .... MBSA
Municipal Bond .... MB
Municipal Bond Insurance Association (EA) .... MBIA
Municipal Bonds Databank (NITA) .... MUNIDB
Municipal Borough .... MB
Municipal Certificates of Accrual on Tax-Exempt Securities [*Investment term*] (DFIT) .... M-CATS
Municipal Code of the Province of Quebec [*A publication*] (DLA) .... MCPQ
Municipal Compliance Plan [*Environmental Protection Agency*] (GFGA) .... MCP
Municipal Construction Division [*Environmental Protection Agency*] (GFGA) .... MCD
Municipal Corporation Cases [*United States*] [*A publication*] (DLA) .... Mu Corp Ca
Municipal Corporation Cases [*A publication*] (DLA) .... Mun Corp Cas
Municipal Corporation Cases, Annotated [*11 vols.*] [*A publication*] (DLA) .... MC Cas
Municipal Corporation Circular [*England*] [*A publication*] (DLA) .... Mu Corp Cir
Municipal Corporation's Chronicle [*Privately Printed*] [*A publication*] (DLA) .... MCC
Municipal Court (DLA) .... Mun Ct
Municipal Court of Appeals for the District of Columbia (DLA) .... DC Mun App
Municipal Court of Appeals for the District of Columbia (DLA) .... Mun Ct App Dist Col
Municipal Court of Montreal (DLA) .... MCM
Municipal Data Service [*International City Management Association*] [*Information service or system*] (IID) .... MDS
Municipal Development and Loan Board [*Canada*] .... MDLB
Municipal Docks Railway of the Jacksonville Port Authority [*AAR code*] .... MD
Municipal Electricity Undertaking .... MEU
Municipal Employees Association (NADA) .... MEA
Municipal Employees Credit Union (NADA) .... MECU
Municipal Engineering and Environmental Technology [*A publication British*] .... ME
Municipal Environmental Research Laboratory [*Environmental Protection Agency*] (GRD) .... MERL
Municipal Facilities Division [*Environmental Protection Agency*] (GFGA) .... MFD
Municipal Ferrous Scrap .... MFS
Municipal Finance Officers Association of US and Canada [*Later, GFOA*] (EA) .... MFOA
Municipal Financial Corp. [*Toronto Stock Exchange symbol*] .... MFC
Municipal Health Services Program [*Department of Health and Human Services*] (GFGA) .... MHSP
Municipal High Care [*NYSE symbol*] (TTSB) .... MHF
Municipal High Income Fund, Inc. [*NYSE symbol*] (CTT) .... MHF
Municipal High Income Fund, Inc. [*Associated Press*] (SAG) .... MunHi
Municipal Income Op Tr II [*NYSE symbol*] (TTSB) .... OIB
Municipal Income Opp Tr [*NYSE symbol*] (TTSB) .... OIA
Municipal Income Opp Tr III [*NYSE symbol*] (TTSB) .... OIC
Municipal Income Opportunities Trust [*Associated Press*] (SAG) .... MIOT
Municipal Income Opportunities Trust II [*Associated Press*] (SAG) MIOT2
Municipal Income Opportunities Trust III [*Associated Press*] (SAG) MIOT3
Municipal Income Opportunity Trust [*Formerly, Allstate Municipal Income Opportunities Trust*] [*NYSE symbol*] (SPSG) .... OIA
Municipal Income Opportunity Trust [*Formerly, Allstate Municipal Income Opportunities Trust*] [*NYSE symbol*] (SPSG) .... OIB
Municipal Income Opportunity Trust [*Formerly, Allstate Municipal Income Opportunities Trust*] [*NYSE symbol*] (SPSG) .... OIC
Municipal Income Trust [*Associated Press*] (SAG) .... MuIT
Municipal Income Trust [*Formerly, Allstate Municipal Income Trust*] [*NYSE symbol*] (SPSG) .... TFA
Municipal Income Trust [*Formerly, Allstate Municipal Income Trust*] [*NYSE symbol*] (SPSG) .... TFB
Municipal Income Trust [*Formerly, Allstate Municipal Income Trust*] [*NYSE symbol*] (SPSG) .... TFC
Municipal Income Trust II [*Associated Press*] (SAG) MuIT2
Municipal Income Trust II [*NYSE symbol*] (TTSB) .... TFB
Municipal Income Trust III [*Associated Press*] (SAG) MuIT3
Municipal Income Trust III [*NYSE symbol*] (TTSB) .... TFC
Municipal Insured National Trust .... MINT
Municipal Investment Trust .... MIT
Municipal Investment Trust Fund .... MITF
Municipal Law Journal [*A publication*] (DLA) .... Mu LJ
Municipal Law Journal [*A publication*] (DLA) .... Mun LJ
Municipal Law Reporter [*A publication*] (DLA) .... Mun
Municipal Law Reporter [*Pennsylvania*] [*A publication*] (DLA) .... Mun LR
Municipal Law Reporter [*Pennsylvania*] [*A publication*] (DLA) .... Munic LR (PA)
Municipal Law Reports [*1903-13*] [*Scotland*] [*A publication*] (DLA) .... Mun LR
Municipal Leasing Corp. .... MLC
Municipal Library, Shawinigan, PQ, Canada [*Library symbol Library of Congress*] (LCLS) .... CaQSHM
Municipal Library [*Bibliotheque Municipale*] **Shawinigan, Quebec** [*Library symbol National Library of Canada*] (NLC) .... QSHM
Municipal Management Information System [*Civil Defense*] .... MMIS
Municipal Management System (HGAA) .... MMS
Municipal Mortgage & Equity LLC [*AMEX symbol*] (SAG) .... MMA
Municipal Mortgage & Equity LLC [*Associated Press*] (SAG) .... MuniMtg
Municipal Officers' Association (ROG) .... MOA
Municipal Officers' Association of Australia .... MOAA
Municipal Officers' Guild (ROG) .... MOG
Municipal Offices (ROG) .... MO
Municipal Organization Act (DICI) .... MORGA
Municipal Partners Fund [*NYSE symbol*] (SPSG) .... MNP
Municipal Partners Fund [*NYSE symbol*] (SPSG) .... MPT
Municipal Partners Fund [*Associated Press*] (SAG) .... MunPrt
Municipal Partners Fund 2 [*Associated Press*] (SAG) MunPrt2
Municipal Partners Fund II [*NYSE symbol*] (TTSB) .... MPT
Municipal Passenger Transport Association, Inc. [*British*] (BI) .... MPTA
Municipal Police .... MP
Municipal Prem Income Tr [*NYSE symbol*] (TTSB) .... PIA
Municipal Premier Income Trust [*Associated Press*] (SAG) .... MuPIT
Municipal Premises [*Public-performance tariff class*] [*British*] .... M
Municipal Premium Income Trust [*Formerly, Allstate Municipal Premium Fund*] [*NYSE symbol*] (SPSG) .... PIA
Municipal Reference Library, Toronto, ON, Canada [*Library symbol*] [*Library of Congress*] (LCLS) .... CaOTPM
Municipal Reform [*or Reformer*] .... MR
Municipal Reform Group [*Tasmania, Australia*] .... MRG
Municipal Registered Bond Interest Record [*Standard & Poor's Corp.*] [*Information service or system*] (CRD) .... MRBIR
Municipal Reports [*Canada*] [*A publication*] (DLA) .... Mun Rep
Municipal Saleyards Association [*Victoria, Australia*] .... MSA
Municipal Savings & Loan Corp. [*Toronto Stock Exchange symbol*] .... MSL
Municipal, School, and State Tort Liability [*A publication*] (DLA) .... Mun Tort Lib
Municipal Securities Board [*Approved by Congress May 22, 1975*] [*Securities and Exchange Commission*] .... MSB
Municipal Securities Rulemaking Board [*Securities and Exchange Commission*] .... MSRB
Municipal Solid Waste .... MSW
Municipal Solid Waste Landfill .... MSWL
Municipal Solid Waste Landfill .... MSWLF
Municipal Technical Advisory Service, Knoxville, TN [*Library symbol*] [*Library of Congress*] (LCLS) .... TKMT
Municipal Treasurers Association of the United States and Canada .... MTA
Municipal Treasurers Association of the US and Canada (EA) .... MTA US & C
Municipal University of Omaha [*Later, University of Nebraska at Omaha*] .... MUO
Municipal Utility District [*Investment term*] (DFIT) .... MUD
Municipal Valuation Fees Committee [*Victoria, Australia*] .... MVFC
Municipal Waste Combustor (GFGA) .... MWC
Municipal Waste Leachate (GNE) .... MWL
Municipal Wastewater .... MWW
Municipality .... MNCPPLTY

Municipality of East Troy, Wisconsin [*AAR code*] ..... METW
Municipals over Bonds [*Investment term*] ..... MOB
MuniEnhanced Fund [*NYSE symbol*] (SPSG) ..... MEN
MuniEnhanced Fund [*Associated Press*] (SAG) ..... MuniFd
MuniInsured Fund Inc. [*AMEX symbol*] (SPSG) ..... MIF
MuniInsred Fund [*AMEX symbol*] (TTSB) ..... MIF
Muniment (ROG) ..... MUNIMT
Munising, MI [*FM radio station call letters*] ..... WHCH
Munising, MI [*AM radio station call letters*] ..... WQXO
Munising Public Library, Munising, MI [*Library symbol Library of Congress*] (LCLS) ..... MiMun
Munition Accountable Supply Officer [*Air Force*] (AFM) ..... MASO
Munition Data Requirement ..... MDR
Munition Support Squadron ..... MUNSS
Munition Test Vehicle ..... MTV
Munitions (AFM) ..... MUN
Munitions Appeals Reports [*England*] [*A publication*] (DLA) ..... Mun
Munitions Appeals Reports [*England*] [*A publication*] (DLA) ..... Mun App
Munitions Appeals Reports [*England*] [*A publication*] (DLA) ..... Mun App Rep
Munitions Assignment Board [*Anglo-American*] [*World War II*] ..... MAB
Munitions Assignment Board (Washington) [*World War II*] ..... MBW
Munitions Assignments Committee [*World War II*] ..... MAC
Munitions Assignments Committee (Air) [*World War II*] ..... MAC(A)
Munitions Assignments Committee (Ground) [*World War II*] ..... MAC(G)
Munitions Assignments Committee (Navy) [*World War II*] ..... MAC(N)
Munitions Assistance and Standardization Team (MCD) ..... MAST
Munitions Board [*Abolished 1953, functions transferred to Department of Defense*] ..... MB
Munitions Board Cataloging Agency ..... MBCA
Munitions Board Petroleum Committee ..... MBPC
Munitions Board Standards Agency ..... MBSA
Munitions Building [*Washington, DC*] [*Obsolete*] ..... MUNBG
Munitions Building [*Obsolete Washington, DC*] (DNAB) ..... MUNBLDG
Munitions Carriers Conference (EA) ..... MCC
Munitions Command [*Later, Armaments Command*] [*Army*] ..... MC
Munitions Command [*Later, Armaments Command*] [*Army*] (MCD) ..... MU
Munitions Command [*Later, Armaments Command*] [*Army*] ..... MUCOM
Munitions Command [*Later, Armaments Command*] [*Army*] ..... MUNC
Munitions Disposal Technician (SAA) ..... MDT
Munitions Effectiveness ..... ME
Munitions Effectiveness Assessment (DOMA) ..... MEA
Munitions Family Group ..... MFG
Munitions Filling Factory (ADA) ..... MFF
Munitions Handling Equipment (MCD) ..... MHE
Munitions Inventions Department [*British military*] (DMA) ..... MID
Munitions List ..... ML
Munitions List Item (MCD) ..... MLI
Munitions Maintenance (MCD) ..... MM
Munitions Maintenance and Storage ..... MMS
Munitions Maintenance Squadron [*Air Force*] ..... MMS
Munitions Maintenance Squadron [*Air Force*] ..... MMSQ
Munitions Management and Labour Efficiency Committee [*British World War II*] ..... MMLEC
Munitions of War Act [*British*] ..... MWA
Munitions of War Acts, Appeal Reports [*1916-20*] [*Scotland*] [*A publication*] (DLA) ..... Mun App Sc
Munitions Packaging Branch [*Picatinny Arsenal*] [*Army*] (RDA) ..... MPB
Munitions Production Base Modernization, Expansion (RDA) ..... MPBME
Munitions Report [*Worldwide report of location and status of air munitions*] [*Military*] ..... MUNIREP
Munitions Section of Strategic Missile Squadron (AAG) ..... MSSMS
Munitions Support Structure Study [*Army*] MS3
Munitions System Support Structure MS3
Munitions System Support Structure - Extended [*Army*] MS3-X
Munitions Tow Vehicle (MCD) ..... MTV
Munitions Transfer [*or Transporter*] **and Loading System** (MCD) ..... MTLS
Munitions Transfer Truck (MCD) ..... MTT
Munitions Tribunals Appeals, Great Britain High Court of Justice [*A publication*] (DLA) ..... MA
Munitionsanstalt [*Ammunition Depot*] [*German military - World War II*] ..... MA
Munitionskraftwagen [*Ammunition Truck*] [*German military - World War II*] ..... MKW
MuniVest CA Insured Fund [*NYSE symbol*] (TTSB) ..... MVC
Munivest California Insured Fund [*Associated Press*] (SAG) ..... MuvCAIn
MuniVest California Insured Fund [*NYSE symbol*] (SPSG) ..... MVC
MuniVest Florida Fund [*Associated Press*] (SAG) ..... MFLFd
MuniVest Florida Fund [*NYSE symbol*] (SPSG) ..... MVS
MuniVest Fund [*AMEX symbol*] (TTSB) ..... MVF
Munivest Fund II [*Associated Press*] (SAG) Muniv2
MuniVest Fund II [*NYSE symbol*] (SAG) ..... MVT
MuniVest Fund II [*NYSE symbol*] (TTSB) ..... MVT
MuniVest Fund, Inc. [*Associated Press*] (SAG) ..... Munvst
MuniVest Fund, Inc. [*AMEX symbol*] (SPSG) ..... MVF
MuniVest Fund, Inc. [*NYSE symbol*] (SPSG) ..... MVT
MuniVest Michigan Insured Fund [*Associated Press*] (SAG) ..... MuvMIIn
MuniVest Michigan Insured Fund [*NYSE symbol*] (SPSG) ..... MVM
MuniVest New Jersey Fund [*Associated Press*] (SAG) ..... MuvNJFd
MuniVest New Jersey Fund [*NYSE symbol*] (SPSG) ..... MVJ
MuniVest New York Insured Fund [*Associated Press*] (SAG) ..... MuvNYIn
MuniVest New York Insured Fund [*NYSE symbol*] (SPSG) ..... MVY
MuniVest NJ Fund [*NYSE symbol*] (TTSB) ..... MVJ
MuniVest NY Insured Fund [*NYSE symbol*] (TTSB) ..... MVY
MuniVest Pennsylvania Insured Fund [*Associated Press*] (SAG) ..... MuPAIns
MuniVest Pennsylvania Insured Fund [*NYSE symbol*] (SPSG) ..... MVP
Muniyield Arizona Fund [*Associated Press*] (SAG) ..... MunyIAZ
MuniYield Arizona Fund [*AMEX symbol*] (TTSB) ..... MZA
Muniyield Arizona Fund II [*Associated Press*] (SAG) ..... MunyAZ
MuniYield Arizona Fund, Inc. [*AMEX symbol*] (SPSG) ..... MZA
MuniYield CA Insured Fund [*NYSE symbol*] (TTSB) ..... MIC
MuniYield CA Insured Fund II [*NYSE symbol*] (TTSB) ..... MCA
MuniYield California Fund [*Associated Press*] (SAG) ..... MunCA
MuniYield California Fund [*NYSE symbol*] (SPSG) ..... MYC
MuniYield California Insured Fund [*NYSE symbol*] (SPSG) ..... MIC
MuniYield California Insured Fund [*Associated Press*] (SAG) ..... MuCAIns
MuniYield California Insured Fund II [*NYSE symbol*] (SPSG) ..... MCA
Muniyield California Insured Fund II [*Associated Press*] (SAG) MuCA2
MuniYield FL Insured Fund [*NYSE symbol*] (TTSB) ..... MFT
MuniYield Florida Fund [*Associated Press*] (SAG) ..... MunFL
MuniYield Florida Fund [*NYSE symbol*] (SPSG) ..... MYF
MuniYield Florida Insured Fund [*NYSE symbol*] (SPSG) ..... MFT
MuniYield Florida Insured Fund [*Associated Press*] (SAG) ..... MuFLIn
MuniYield Fund [*NYSE symbol*] (SPSG) ..... MYD
MuniYield Fund, Inc. [*Associated Press*] (SAG) ..... Muniyld
Muniyield Insured Fund [*Associated Press*] (SAG) ..... MuInII
MuniYield Insured Fund [*Associated Press*] (SAG) ..... MunIns
MuniYield Insured Fund [*NYSE symbol*] (SPSG) ..... MYI
MuniYield Insured Fund II [*NYSE symbol*] (SPSG) ..... MTI
MuniYield MI Insured Fund [*NYSE symbol*] (TTSB) ..... MIY
MuniYield Michigan Fund [*Associated Press*] (SAG) ..... MunMI
Muniyield Michigan Fund [*NYSE symbol*] (SAG) ..... MYM
MuniYield Michigan Insured Fund [*NYSE symbol*] (SPSG) ..... MIY
MuniYield Michigan Insured Fund [*Associated Press*] (SAG) ..... MunMIIn
MuniYield MY Insured Fund III [*NYSE symbol*] (TTSB) ..... MYY
MuniYield New Jersey Fund [*Associated Press*] (SAG) ..... MunNJ
MuniYield New Jersey Fund [*NYSE symbol*] (SPSG) ..... MYJ
MuniYield New Jersey Insured Fund [*NYSE symbol*] (SPSG) ..... MJI
MuniYield New Jersey Insured Fund [*Associated Press*] (SAG) ..... MuNJIn
MuniYield New York Insured Fund [*Associated Press*] (SAG) ..... MunNY
MuniYield New York Insured Fund [*NYSE symbol*] (SPSG) ..... MYN
Muniyield New York Insured Fund II [*Associated Press*] (SAG) MuNY2
MuniYield New York Insured Fund II [*NYSE symbol*] (SPSG) ..... MYT
Muniyield New York Insured Fund III [*Associated Press*] (SAG) MuNY3
MuniYield New York Insured Fund III [*NYSE symbol*] (SPSG) ..... MYY
MuniYield NJ Insured Fund [*NYSE symbol*] (TTSB) ..... MJI
MuniYield NY Insured Fund [*NYSE symbol*] (TTSB) ..... MYN
MuniYield NY Insured Fund II [*NYSE symbol*] (TTSB) ..... MYT
MuniYield Pennsylvania Fund [*NYSE symbol*] (SPSG) ..... MPA
MuniYield Pennsylvania Fund [*Associated Press*] (SAG) ..... MunPA
MuniYield Quality Fund [*NYSE symbol*] (SPSG) ..... MQY
MuniYield Quality Fund II [*NYSE symbol*] (SPSG) ..... MQT
Muniyield Quality Fund II, Inc. [*Associated Press*] (SAG) MunQ12
MuniYield Quality Fund, Inc. [*Associated Press*] (SAG) ..... MunQlty
Munkfors [*Sweden ICAO location identifier*] (ICLI) ..... ESKO
Munkman's Employer's Liability at Common Law [*8th ed.*] [*1975*] [*A publication*] (DLA) ..... Munk Emp Liab
Munsey Park Elementary School, Manhasset, NY [*Library symbol*] [*Library of Congress*] (LCLS) ..... NManhME
Munsingwear, Inc. [*NYSE symbol*] (SPSG) ..... MUN
Munsingwear, Inc. [*Associated Press*] (SAG) ..... Munsng
Munson, K. G., Weyers Cave VA [*STAC*] ..... MKG
Munson-Williams-Proctor Institute [*Utica, NY*] ..... MWPI
Munson-Williams-Proctor Institute, Library, Utica, NY [*OCLC symbol*] (OCLC) ..... ZUW
Munson-Williams-Proctor Institute, Utica, NY [*Library symbol Library of Congress*] (LCLS) ..... NUtM
Munster (AD) ..... Mnstr
Munster [*Germany Airport symbol*] (OAG) ..... MSR
Munsters and the Addams Family Fan Club (EA) ..... MAFFC
Munta [*Afghanistan*] [*ICAO location identifier*] (ICLI) ..... OAMT
Munte [*Belgium ICAO location identifier*] (ICLI) ..... EBMT
Muntele Rosu [*Romania*] [*Seismograph station code, US Geological Survey*] (SEIS) ..... MLR
Muntinlupa [*Philippines*] [*Geomagnetic observatory code*] ..... MUT
Munz Northern [*ICAO designator*] (AD) ..... XY
Muong Sai [*Laos*] [*Airport symbol*] (AD) ..... UON
Muong Sing [*Laos*] [*Airport symbol*] (AD) ..... MOJ
Mural (VRA) ..... mur
Muramic Acid [*Also, MurA*] [*Biochemistry*] ..... Mur
Muramic Acid [*Also, Mur*] [*Biochemistry*] ..... MurA
Muramyl Dipeptide [*Immunochemistry*] ..... MDP
Muramyl Tripeptide Phosphatidylethanolamine [*Antineoplastic drug*] (CDI) ..... MTP-PE
Murashige-Skoog [*Medium*] [*Botany*] ..... MS
Muratori's Antiquitates Medii Aevi [*A publication*] (DLA) ..... Murat Antiq Med Aevi
Murchison Falls [*Uganda*] [*Airport symbol*] (AD) ..... MUD
Murchison Lyell Township Community Library, Madawaska, Ontario [*Library symbol National Library of Canada*] (NLC) ..... OMMLT
Murcia [*Spain ICAO location identifier*] (ICLI) ..... LESM
Murcia [*Spain*] [*Airport symbol*] (OAG) ..... MJV
Murcia/Alcantarilla [*Spain ICAO location identifier*] (ICLI) ..... LERI
Murcia/San Javier [*Spain ICAO location identifier*] (ICLI) ..... LELC
Murcielago [*Costa Rica*] [*ICAO location identifier*] (ICLI) ..... MRMC
Murder [*FBI standardized term*] ..... MUR
Murder (ROG) ..... MURD
Murder Release Risk Assessment Scale (AD) ..... MRRAS
Murdoch Center, School Library, Butner, NC [*Library symbol Library of Congress*] (LCLS) ..... NcButM
Murdoch University Energy Research Institute [*Australia*] ..... MUERI
Murdoch University, Murdoch, WA, Australia [*Library symbol Library of Congress*] (LCLS) ..... AuMuU
Murdoch's Epitome Canada [*A publication*] (DLA) ..... Murd Epit

Murdock Communications Corp. [*NASDAQ symbol*] (SAG) .... MURC
Murdock Communications Corp. [*Associated Press*] (SAG) .... Murdck
Murdock Communications Corp. [*Associated Press*] (SAG) .... Murdock
Muret/Lherm [*France ICAO location identifier*] (ICLI) .... LFBR
Murexide [*An indicator*] [*Chemistry*] .... MX
Murfree on Official Bonds [*A publication*] (DLA) .... Murfree Off Bonds
Murfreesboro, AR [*FM radio station call letters*] .... KMTB
Murfreesboro, NC [*FM radio station call letters*] .... WBCG
Murfreesboro, NC [*AM radio station call letters*] .... WYCM
Murfreesboro Public Library, Murfreesboro, NC [*Library symbol Library of Congress*] (LCLS) .... NcMf
Murfreesboro, TN [*Location identifier FAA*] (FAAL) .... MBT
Murfreesboro, TN [*AM radio station call letters*] (RBYB) .... WAPB
Murfreesboro, TN [*FM radio station call letters*] (RBYB) .... WFCM
Murfreesboro, TN [*AM radio station call letters*] .... WGNS
Murfreesboro, TN [*Television station call letters*] .... WHTN
Murfreesboro, TN [*FM radio station call letters*] .... WMOT
Murfreesboro, TN [*AM radio station call letters*] .... WMTS
Murfreesboro, TN [*FM radio station call letters*] (RBYB) .... WMTS-FM
Murfreesboro, TN [*FM radio station call letters*] .... WRMX
Murgab [*Former USSR Seismograph station code, US Geological Survey Closed*] (SEIS) .... MUR
Murgold Resources, Inc. [*Toronto Stock Exchange symbol*] .... MGD
Murgor Resources, Inc. [*Vancouver Stock Exchange symbol*] .... MUG
Muriate of Potash [*Fertilizer*] .... MOP
Murine Cytomegalovirus .... MCMV
Murine Erythroleukemia [*Oncology*] .... MEL
Murine Hepatitis .... MH
Murine Hepatitis Virus .... MHV
Murine Leukemia Virus [*Also, MuLV*] .... MLV
Murine Leukemia Virus [*Also, MLV*] .... MuLV
Murine Leukemia Virus (Abelson) .... MLV(A)
Murine Leukemia Virus (Moloney) .... MLV(M)
Murine Leukemia Virus (Rauscher) .... MLV(R)
Murine Mammary Tumor Virus .... MuMTV
Murine Metallothionein [*Biochemistry*] .... MMT
Murine Ovarian Teratocarcinoma [*Animal pathology*] .... MOT
Murine Pathogen Free [*Rats or mice*] .... MPF
Murine Polyomavirus [*Medicine*] .... MuPV
Murine Sarcoma Virus .... MSV
Murine Sarcoma Virus (Moloney) .... MSV(M)
Murine-Acquired Immunodeficiency Syndrome [*Animal pathology*] .... MAIDS
Murlyn [*Record label*] .... Mur
Murmansk [*Former USSR Airport symbol*] (OAG) .... MMK
Murmur [*Heart*] [*Medicine*] .... M
Murmur [*Cardiology*] (DAVI) .... mm
Murmurs [*Medicine*] (DMAA) .... Ms
Murmurs, Gallops, or Rubs [*Cardiology*] (DAVI) .... MGR
Murmurs, Rubs, and Gallops [*Cardiology*] (DAVI) .... MRG
Muroran [*Japan*] [*Seismograph station code, US Geological Survey*] (SEIS) .... MRR
Muroran/Yakumo [*Japan ICAO location identifier*] (ICLI) .... RJCY
Murotomisaki [*Japan*] [*Seismograph station code, US Geological Survey*] (SEIS) .... MRT
Murphey Favre, Inc., Spokane, WA [*Library symbol Library of Congress*] (LCLS) .... WaSpMF
Murphey's Reports [*5-7 North Carolina*] [*A publication*] (DLA) .... Mur
Murphey's Reports [*5-7 North Carolina*] [*A publication*] (DLA) .... Murph
Murphey's Reports [*5-7 North Carolina*] [*A publication*] (DLA) .... Murph (NC)
Murphy and Hurlstone's English Exchequer Reports [*1836-37*] [*A publication*] (DLA) .... M & H
Murphy and Hurlstone's English Exchequer Reports [*1836-37*] [*A publication*] (DLA) .... Mur & H
Murphy and Hurlstone's English Exchequer Reports [*1836-37*] [*A publication*] (DLA) .... Mur & Hurl
Murphy and Hurlstone's English Exchequer Reports [*1836-37*] [*A publication*] (ILCA) .... Murp & H
Murphy and Hurlstone's English Exchequer Reports [*1836-37*] [*A publication*] (DLA) .... Murph & H
Murphy International Transport [*Commercial firm British*] .... MI
Murphy Memorial Library, Monona, IA [*Library symbol Library of Congress*] (LCLS) .... IaMono
Murphy, NC [*Location identifier FAA*] (FAAL) .... TTQ
Murphy, NC [*FM radio station call letters*] .... WCNG
Murphy, NC [*AM radio station call letters*] .... WCVP
Murphy, NC [*AM radio station call letters*] .... WKRK
Murphy Oil [*NYSE symbol*] (TTSB) .... MUR
Murphy Oil Co. Ltd. [*Toronto Stock Exchange symbol*] .... MO
Murphy Oil Corp. [*NYSE symbol*] (SPSG) .... MUR
Murphy Oil Corp. [*Associated Press*] (SAG) .... MurpO
Murphy Public Library, Murphy, NC [*Library symbol Library of Congress*] (LCLS) .... NcMu
Murphysboro, IL [*AM radio station call letters*] .... WINI
Murphysboro, IL [*FM radio station call letters*] .... WTAO
Murray [*Kentucky*] [*Airport symbol*] (OAG) .... CEY
Murray Aviation, Inc. [*ICAO designator*] (FAAC) .... MUA
Murray Bay [*Quebec*] [*Airport symbol*] (AD) .... YML
Murray Darling Basin Initiative [*Australia*] .... MDBI
Murray Grey Beef Cattle Society [*Australia*] .... MGBCS
Murray, KY [*FM radio station call letters*] .... WBLN
Murray, KY [*FM radio station call letters*] .... WKMS
Murray, KY [*Television station call letters*] .... WKMU
Murray, KY [*AM radio station call letters*] .... WNBS
Murray, KY [*AM radio station call letters*] .... WSJP
Murray Public Library, Murray, UT [*Library symbol Library of Congress*] (LCLS) .... UMu
Murray State Agricultural College [*Oklahoma*] .... MSAC
Murray State College [*Later, MSU*] [*Kentucky*] .... MSC
Murray State University [*Kentucky*] .... MSU
Murray State University (GAGS) .... Murray St U
Murray State University, Murray, KY [*OCLC symbol*] (OCLC) .... KMS
Murray State University, Murray, KY [*Library symbol Library of Congress*] (LCLS) .... KyMurT
Murray, UT [*AM radio station call letters*] .... KMGR
Murray Valley Air Service [*Australia*] .... MVAS
Murray Valley Citrus Marketing Board [*Australia*] .... MVCMB
Murray Valley Encephalitis [*Virus*] .... MVE
Murray Valley League [*Australia*] .... MVL
Murray Valley League for Development and Conservation [*Australia*] .... MVLDC
Murray Valley Rural Industry Assistance Group [*Australia*] .... MVRIAG
Murrayaquinone-A [*Biochemistry*] .... MQA
Murray-Darling Basin Ministerial Council [*Australia*] .... MDBMC
Murray's Ceylon Reports [*A publication*] (DLA) .... Mur
Murray's Ceylon Reports [*A publication*] (DLA) .... Murr
Murray's Ceylon Reports [*A publication*] (DLA) .... Murray (Ceylon)
Murray's English Dictionary [*A publication*] (DLA) .... Murray's Eng Dict
Murray's History of Usury [*A publication*] (DLA) .... Mur Us
Murray's Jat Lancers [*British military*] (DMA) .... MJL
Murray's Jury Court Cases [*1815-30*] [*Scotland*] [*A publication*] (DLA) .... Mur
Murray's Jury Court Cases [*1815-30*] [*Scotland*] [*A publication*] (DLA) .... Murr
Murray's Laws and Acts of Parliament [*Scotland*] [*A publication*] (DLA) .... Murr
Murray's Overruled Cases [*A publication*] (DLA) .... Murr Over Cas
Murray's Proceedings in the United States Courts [*A publication*] (DLA) .... Mur US Ct
Murray's Scotch Jury Court Reports [*A publication*] (DLA) .... Murray
Murray's Scotch Jury Trials [*A publication*] (DLA) .... Murray (Scot)
Murray's Table of United States Cases [*A publication*] (DLA) .... Mur Tab Cas
Murrayville, GA [*AM radio station call letters*] .... WKZD
Murrell's Inlet, SC [*FM radio station call letters*] .... WRNN
Murrumbidgee Irrigation Area [*Australia*] (BARN) .... MIA
Murrumbidgee Irrigation Area Tourist Association [*Australia*] .... MIATA
Murrumbidgee Irrigation Area Vine Improvement Society [*Australia*] .... MVIS
Murrysville, PA [*FM radio station call letters*] .... WRWJ
Mursley [*England*] .... MURS
Mururoa [*French Polynesia*] [*ICAO location identifier*] (ICLI) .... NTTX
Musca [*Constellation*] .... Mus
Musca [*Constellation*] .... Musc
Muscarine [*Alkaloid*] .... MUSC
Muscarinic Acetylcholine Receptor [*Biochemistry*] .... m-AChr
Muscarinic Acetylcholine Receptor [*Biochemistry*] .... MAR
Muscat [*Oman*] [*Airport symbol*] (OAG) .... MCT
Muscat [*Oman*] [*ICAO location identifier*] (ICLI) .... OOMM
Muscat and Oman [*Oman*] [*MARC geographic area code Library of Congress*] (LCCP) .... a-mk--
Muscat and Oman [*Oman*] [*MARC country of publication code Library of Congress*] (LCCP) .... mk
Muscat and Oran (AD) .... M & O
Muscat/Seeb International [*Oman*] [*ICAO location identifier*] (ICLI) .... OOMS
Muscatine, IA [*FM radio station call letters*] .... KBOB
Muscatine, IA [*FM radio station call letters*] (RBYB) .... KWCC-FM
Muscatine, IA [*AM radio station call letters*] .... KWPC
Muscatine, IA [*Location identifier FAA*] (FAAL) .... MUT
Muscatine, IA [*Location identifier FAA*] (FAAL) .... RTY
Muscatine Journal, Muscatine, IA [*Library symbol Library of Congress*] (LCLS) .... IaMuJ
Muscatine Junior College [*Iowa*] .... MJC
Muschocho Explorations Ltd. [*Toronto Stock Exchange symbol*] .... MUS
Muscimol [*Biochemistry*] .... MUS
Muscle [*Anatomy*] (DAVI) .... Mu
Muscle Action Potential .... MAP
Muscle Activity (MAE) .... MA
Muscle and Tendon [*Medicine*] (MAE) .... MT
Muscle Calcium Binding Parvalbumin [*Biochemistry*] .... MCBP
Muscle Capillary Basement Membrane [*Medicine*] .... MCBM
Muscle Contraction Headache [*Medicine*] (CPH) .... MCH
Muscle Creatine Kinase [*An enzyme*] .... MCK
Muscle Enhancer Factor [*Genetics*] .... MEF
Muscle Fiber .... MF
Muscle Function Test .... MFT
Muscle Group (MAE) .... MG
Muscle Plasma [*Ratio*] .... M/P
Muscle Receptor [*Medicine*] (DMAA) .... MR
Muscle Receptor Organ [*Neurophysiology*] .... MRO
Muscle Regulatory Factor [*Physiology*] .... MRF
Muscle Relaxant [*Medicine*] (DMAA) .... MR
Muscle Response Test .... MRT
Muscle Shoals [*Alabama*] [*Airport symbol*] (OAG) .... MSL
Muscle Shoals, AL [*AM radio station call letters*] .... WLAY
Muscle Shoals, AL [*FM radio station call letters*] .... WLAY-FM
Muscle Shoals, AL [*FM radio station call letters*] .... WQPR
Muscle Shock Factor .... MSF
Muscle Shortening [*Medicine*] .... MS
Muscle Strength (BABM) .... MM ST
Muscle Strength [*Neurology*] (DAVI) .... mm st
Muscle Strength .... MS
Muscle Strength (AD) .... ms
Muscle Stretch Reflexes [*Medicine*] (DAVI) .... MSR
Muscle Sympathetic Activity [*Medicine*] (DMAA) .... MSA
Muscle Testing System [*Myology*] .... MTS
Muscles [*Medicine*] .... MM
Muscles [*or Muscular*] .... MUSC

Muscle-Specific Enhancer [*Genetics*] ... MSE
Musculactive Substance [*Medicine*] ... MS
Muscular Dystrophy [*Medicine*] ... MD
Muscular Dystrophy Association (EA) ... MDA
Muscular Dystrophy Association of Canada ... MDAC
Muscular Dystrophy Association of New South Wales [*Australia*] ... MDANSW
Muscular Dystrophy Association of South Australia ... MDASA
Muscular Dystrophy Associations of America (EA) ... MDAA
Muscular Subaortic Stenosis [*Cardiology*] ... MSS
Muscularis Mucosa [*Medicine*] (MAE) ... MM
Muscularis Mucosa [*Anatomy*] (DAVI) ... MM
Musculoskeletal [*Medicine*] ... MS
Musculoskeletal [*Orthopedics*] (DAVI) ... MSK
Musculus [*Muscle*] [*Anatomy*] ... M
Musee (VRA) ... mus
Musee Belge [*A publication*] (OCD) ... Mus Belge
Musee Canadien de la Photographie Contemporaine [*Canadian Museum of Contemporary Photography - CMCP*] ... MCPC
Musee d'Art Contemporain, Montreal, PQ, Canada [*Library symbol Library of Congress*] (LCLS) ... CaQMMAC
Musee d'Art Contemporain, Montreal, Quebec [*Library symbol National Library of Canada*] (NLC) ... QMMAC
Musee d'Art de Joliette, Joliette, PQ, Canada [*Library symbol Library of Congress*] (LCLS) ... CaQJMA
Musee d'Art de Joliette, Quebec [*Library symbol National Library of Canada*] (NLC) ... QJMA
Musee de la Gaspesie, Gaspe, PQ, Canada [*Library symbol*] [*Library of Congress*] (LCLS) ... CaQGMG
Musee de la Gaspesie, Gaspe, Quebec [*Library symbol National Library of Canada*] (BIB) ... QGMG
Musee de Madawaska, Edmundston, NB, Canada [*Library symbol*] [*Library of Congress*] (LCLS) ... CaNBEMM
Musee de Madawaska, Edmundston, New Brunswick [*Library symbol National Library of Canada*] (NLC) ... NBEMM
Musee des Augustines de l'Hotel-Dieu de Quebec, Quebec [*Library symbol National Library of Canada*] (NLC) ... QQHDM
Musee des Augustines de l'Hotel-Dieu de Quebec, Quebec, PQ, Canada [*Library symbol Library of Congress*] (LCLS) ... CaQQHDM
Musee du Chatau de Ramezay, Montreal, Quebec [*Library symbol National Library of Canada*] (NLC) ... QMMCR
Musee du Chateau de Ramezay, Montreal, PQ, Canada [*Library symbol Library of Congress*] (LCLS) ... CaQMMCR
Musee du Quebec, Quebec [*Library symbol National Library of Canada*] (NLC) ... QQMQ
Musee du Quebec, Quebec, PQ, Canada [*Library symbol Library of Congress*] (LCLS) ... CaQQMQ
Musee du Royal 22e Regiment et la Regie du Royal 22e Regiment, Quebec, PQ, Canada [*Library symbol Library of Congress*] (LCLS) ... CaQQMR
Musee Oceanographique Monaco [*Monaco Oceanographic Museum*] [*France*] (AD) ... MOM
Museen (VRA) ... mus
Museo (VRA) ... mus
Museo Nacional de Rio de Janeiro [*National Museum of Rio de Janeiro*] [*Portugal*] (AD) ... MNRJ
Museo Oceanografico de Rio Grande [*Oceanographic Museum of Rio Grande*] [*Brazil*] (AD) ... MORG
Musese [*Zaire*] [*ICAO location identifier*] (ICLI) ... FZUO
Museum ... MUS
Museum (VRA) ... mus
Museum ... MUS
Museum and University Data Processing Information Exchange (IAA) ... MUDPIE
Museum and University Storage and Retrieval of Data (NITA) ... MUSTARD
Museum Angkatan Darat [*Indonesia*] ... MUMAD
Museum Applied Science Center for Archeology [*University of Pennsylvania*] ... MASCA
Museum Assessment Program [*National Foundation on the Arts and the Humanities*] ... MAP
Museum Association of the American Frontier (EA) ... MAAF
Museum Association of the Caribbean (EAIO) ... MAC
Museum Board of South Australia ... MBSA
Museum Communication Format (NITA) ... MCF
Museum Computer Network (NITA) ... MCN
Museum Computer Network, Inc. [*American Association of Museums*] [*Research center*] (RCD) ... MCN
Museum Documentation Association [*British*] (DBA) ... MDA
Museum Education Roundtable (EA) ... MER
Museum Exchange for System's Help [*National Museum of Natural History*] (IID) ... MESH
Museum fur Volkerkunde und Schweizerisches Museum fur Volkskunde, Basel, Switzerland [*Library symbol Library of Congress*] (LCLS) ... SzBaM
Museum Manor of Saint George, Center Moriches, NY [*Library symbol Library of Congress*] (LCLS) ... NCmM
Museum Manor of Saint George, Center Moriches, NY [*Library symbol*] [*Library of Congress*] (LCLS) ... NCmMM
Museum Media [*A publication*] ... MM
Museum of African American History (EA) ... MAAH
Museum of African Art - Frederick Douglass Institute [*Smithsonian Institution*] (EA) ... MAA-FDI
Museum of Afro-American History (EA) ... MAAH
Museum of American Financial History (EA) ... MAFH
Museum of Broadcasting ... MB
Museum of Comparative Zoology [*Harvard University*] [*Research center*] ... MCZ
Museum of Contemporary Art [*Los Angeles*] ... MOCA
Museum of Contemporary Art, Chicago, IL [*Library symbol*] [*Library of Congress*] (LCLS) ... ICMCA
Museum of Early Southern Decorative Arts, MESDA Library, Winston-Salem, NC [*Library symbol Library of Congress*] (LCLS) ... NcWsMES
Museum of Fine Arts [*Boston*] (BJA) ... MFA
Museum of Fine Arts, Boston ... MFAB
Museum of Fine Arts, Boston, MA [*Library symbol Library of Congress*] (LCLS) ... MBMu
Museum of Fine Arts, Houston, TX [*Library symbol Library of Congress*] (LCLS) ... TxHM
Museum of Garden History [*British*] ... MGH
Museum of History and Industry, Seattle, WA [*Library symbol*] [*Library of Congress*] (LCLS) ... WaSMHI
Museum of History and Technology [*Smithsonian Institution*] ... MHT
Museum of Holography [*New York City*] ... MOH
Museum of Jurassic Technology ... MJT
Museum of Modern Art [*New York*] ... MOMA
Museum of Modern Art [*New York*] (AD) ... MoMA
Museum of Modern Art, Film Study Center, New York, NY [*Library symbol Library of Congress*] (LCLS) ... NNMMA-F
Museum of Modern Art, New York, NY [*Library symbol Library of Congress*] (LCLS) ... NNMMA
Museum of Modern Art, New York, NY [*Library symbol Library of Congress*] (LCLS) ... NNMoMA
Museum of Natural History [*Smithsonian Institution*] ... MNH
Museum of New Mexico [*Research center*] (RCD) ... MNM
Museum of New Mexico, Laboratory of Anthropology, Santa Fe, NM [*Library symbol Library of Congress*] (LCLS) ... NmSM-A
Museum of New Mexico, Santa Fe, NM [*Library symbol Library of Congress*] (LCLS) ... NmSM
Museum of Northern Arizona, Flagstaff, AZ [*Library symbol Library of Congress*] (LCLS) ... AzFM
Museum of Northern British Columbia, Prince Rupert, British Columbia [*Library symbol National Library of Canada*] (NLC) ... BPRM
Museum of Our National Heritage, Lexington, MA [*Library symbol Library of Congress*] (LCLS) ... MLexM
Museum of Photographic Arts [*San Diego*] (AD) ... MOPA
Museum of Primitive Art, New York, NY [*Library symbol Library of Congress*] (LCLS) ... NNMPA
Museum of Science and Industry [*Chicago, IL*] ... MSI
Museum of Southwestern Biology [*University of New Mexico*] [*Research center*] (RCD) ... MSB
Museum of Sydney [*Australia*] ... MoS
Museum of Television and Radio [*New York*] ... MTR
Museum of Temporary Art [*Washington, DC*] ... MOTA
Museum of the American Indian, New York, NY [*Library symbol Library of Congress*] (LCLS) ... NNMAI
Museum of the City of Mobile, Mobile, AL [*Library symbol Library of Congress*] (LCLS) ... AMobM
Museum of the City of New York ... MCNY
Museum of the City of New York, New York, NY [*Library symbol Library of Congress*] (LCLS) ... NNMus
Museum of the Confederacy, Richmond, VA [*Library symbol Library of Congress*] (LCLS) ... ViRC
Museum of the Great Plains [*Lawton, OK*] ... MGP
Museum of the International College of Surgeons (NADA) ... MICS
Museum of the Moving Image [*London*] (ECON) ... MOMI
Museum of the Plains Indians (AD) ... MPI
Museum of the Rockies [*Montana, USA*] ... MOR
Museum of Transport and Technology (AD) ... MOTAT
Museum of Transport and Technology (NADA) ... MOTAT
Museum of Vertebrate Zoology [*University of California, Berkeley*] ... MVZ
Museum of Western Colorado, Grand Junction, CO [*Library symbol*] [*Library of Congress*] (LCLS) ... CoGjMW
Museum of Zoology (NADA) ... MZ
Museum Plantin Moretus [*Belgium*] (AD) ... MP-M
Museum Publications of America ... MPA
Museum Services Institute [*Department of Education*] (OICC) ... MSI
Museum Store Association (EA) ... MSA
Museum Support Center [*Smithsonian Institution*] ... MSC
Museum Trustee Association (EA) ... MTA
Museums and Art Galleries Board of the Northern Territory [*Australia*] ... MAGBNT
Museums and Art Galleries of the Northern Territory [*Australia*] ... MAGNT
Museums and Galleries Commission [*Government body*] [*British*] ... MGC
Museums Association of Canada ... MAC
Musgrave [*Australia Airport symbol Obsolete*] (OAG) ... MVU
Musgravetown, NF [*AM radio station call letters*] ... CKXB
Mush until No Good [*Describes destruction of computer software*] ... MUNG
Mushandike National Park [*Rhodesia*] (AD) ... MNP
Mushie [*Zaire*] [*ICAO location identifier*] (ICLI) ... FZBJ
Mushroom Body [*Nerve center in insects*] ... MB
Mushroom Canners League (EA) ... MCL
Mushroom Caucus (EA) ... MC
Mushroom Growers Association [*Commercial firm*] (EA) ... MGA
Mushroom Growers Cooperative Association [*Defunct*] (EA) ... MGA
Mushroom Growers Cooperative Association [*Defunct*] ... MGCA
Music [*Films, television, etc.*] ... M
Music ... MUS
Music ... MUSC
Music Advisers' National Association [*British*] ... MANA
Music Alliance [*Defunct*] (EA) ... MA
Music and Arts Society of America (EA) ... MASA
Music and Dance [*American Dance Festival project*] ... MAD
Music and Effects [*Television*] ... M & E

Music and Kodak [Terms combined to coin brand name for canned music] .... MUZAK

Music and Record Library, Canadian Broadcasting Corp. [Musicotheque et Discotheque, Societe Radio-Canada] Halifax, Nova Scotia [Library symbol National Library of Canada] (NLC) .... NSHCB

Music and Record Library, Canadian Broadcasting Corp. [Musicotheque et Discotheque, Societe Radio-Canada] Winnipeg, Manitoba [Library symbol National Library of Canada] (NLC) .... MWC

Music and Sound Effects (WDMC) .... M & E

Music and Sound Effects (WDMC) .... M and E

Music Association of Ireland (DBA) .... MAI

Music Broadcasting Society (NADA) .... MBS

Music Broadcasting Society of Queensland [Australia] .... MBSQ

Music Center Opera Association [Los Angeles] .... MCOA

Music Composition .... MUSICOMP

Music Construction Set [Computer program designed by Will Harvey and published by Electronic Arts] .... MCS

Music Critics Association (EA) .... MCA

Music Director (NTCM) .... MD

Music Distributors Association (EA) .... MDA

Music Editor, Scorer, and Arranger [Computer program] (PCM) .... MESA

Music Editors Association (EA) .... MEA

Music Education League [Defunct] (EA) .... MEL

Music Education Research Council (EA) .... MERC

Music Educators Journal [A publication] (BRI) .... M Ed J

Music Educators National Conference (EA) .... MENC

Music for the Blind [Defunct] (EA) .... MB

Music for the Rights of Man (EA) .... MRM

Music for Youth .... MFY

Music Hall [Record label] .... MH

Music Hall [Record label] [Argentina] .... MusH

Music Industries Association [British] (DBA) .... MIA

Music Industries Golfing Society [British] (BI) .... MIGS

Music Industry Association of Queensland [Australia] .... MIAQ

Music Industry Association of Tasmania [Australia] .... MIAT

Music Industry Conference (EA) .... MIC

Music Industry Council [Later, Music Industry Conference] (EA) .... MIC

Music Industry Educators Association (EA) .... MIEA

Music Industry Manufacturers Association [Defunct] (EA) .... MIMA

Music Information Retrieval [Computer science] .... MIR

Music Information System for Theorists (PDAA) .... MIST

Music Learning System [Trademark] .... MLS

Music Library Association (EA) .... MLA

Music Library, Canadian Broadcasting Corp. [Musicotheque et Discotheque, Societe Radio-Canada], Montreal, Quebec [Library symbol National Library of Canada] (BIB) .... QMCBM

Music Library, Canadian National Institute for the Blind, Toronto, Ontario [Library symbol National Library of Canada] (BIB) .... OTBML

Music Library Records [Record label] .... ML

Music Lovers League (NADA) .... MLL

Music Masters and Mistresses Association (AIE) .... MMMA

Music Masters' Association [British] .... MMA

Music Minus One [Recording label] .... MMO

Music of Modern Art (NADA) .... MMA

Music of the World [American Forces Radio and Television Service] (DNAB) .... MW

Music Operators of America [Later, AMOA] (EA) .... MOA

Music Operators of New York (AD) .... MONY

Music Performance Trust Funds (EA) .... MPTF

Music Power Rating .... MPR

Music Preference Test of Personality [Psychology] .... MPTP

Music Program [Association of Independent Colleges and Schools specialization code] .... MU

Music Publishers Association (NADA) .... MPA

Music Publishers' Association of the United States (EA) .... MPA

Music Publishers' Association of the United States (DGA) .... MPAUS

Music Publishers Contact Employees .... MPCE

Music Publishers Contact Personnel Association [British] (DBA) .... MPCPA

Music Publishers' Protective Association [Later, NMPA] (EA) .... MPPA

Music Reading Software (PCM) .... MRS

Music Records [Record label] .... MR

Music Research Foundation .... MRF

Music Sound Books [Record label] .... MSB

Music, Sport, News [Radio broadcasting format] .... MSN

Music Story Series [A publication] .... MSS

Music Teachers' Association [British] (BI) .... MTA

Music Teachers' Association of South Australia .... MTANSW

Music Teacher's Certificate [British] (DI) .... MTC

Music Teachers National Association (EA) .... MTNA

Music Television [Warner Amex Satellite Entertainment Co.] [Cable-television system] .... MTV

Music Therapist [or Therapy] .... MT

Music Trades' Association [British] (BI) .... MTA

Music Translation (NITA) .... MUSTRAN

Music Treasures of the World [Record label] .... MTW

Music Video Association (EA) .... MVA

Music Wire .... MUW

Music Wire .... MW

Music Wire Gauge .... MWG

Musica Nostra et Vostra, National Corp. of America (EA) .... MNEV

Musica Popular Brasileira [Pop music] .... MPB

Musica sul Velluto (EAIO) .... MSV

Musica Viva (ADA) .... MV

Musicae Baccalaureus [Bachelor of Music] .... MB

Musicae Baccalaureus [Bachelor of Music] [Latin] .... Mus B

Musicae Baccalaureus [Bachelor of Music] [Latin] .... Mus Bac

Musicae Baccalaureus [Bachelor of Music] [Latin] .... Mus Bach

Musicae Doctor [Doctor of Music] (ROG) .... MD

Musicae Doctor [Doctor of Music] [Latin] .... Mus D

Musicae Doctor [Doctor of Music] [Latin] .... Mus Doc

Musicae Graduatus Paedagogus [Graduate Teacher in Music] .... Mus G Paed

Musicae Magister [Master of Music] [Latin] .... Mus M

Musical .... MUSCL

Musical (VRA) .... musi

Musical Appreciation [Record label] .... MA

Musical Appreciation [Record label] .... MApp

Musical Aptitude Profile .... MAP

Musical Arena Theatres Association [Later, PAMI] (EA) .... MATA

Musical Box Society, International (EA) .... MBSI

Musical Box Society of Great Britain .... MBSOGB

Musical Corp. of America (NADA) .... MCA

Musical Director .... MD

Musical Educators Association (NADA) .... MEA

Musical Heritage Society [Commercial firm] (EA) .... MHS

Musical Instruction Composition Oriented Language (NITA) .... MUSICOL

Musical Instrument Digital Interface [Port] [Socket on an electronic synthesizer that permits a direct computer connection] .... MIDI

Musical Majority [Defunct] (EA) .... MM

Musical Masterpiece Society [Record label] [USA, Europe] .... MMS

Musical Performing Arts Association (NTCM) .... MPAA

Musical Quarterly [A publication] (BRI) .... MQ

Musical Series [A publication] .... MUSS

Musical Theatres Association .... MTA

Musical Union [Oberlin College] [Ohio] .... MU

Musically Intelligent Device [Electronic musical instruments] .... MID

Musicassette Quality Committee (NTCM) .... MCQC

Musician [Navy rating] .... MU

Musician [British military] (DMA) .... Musn

Musician, Chief [Navy rating] .... MUC

Musician, First Class [Navy rating] MU1

Musician, Master Chief [Navy rating] .... MUCM

Musician, Second Class [Navy rating] MU2

Musician, Senior Chief [Navy rating] .... MUCS

Musician, Third Class [Navy rating] MU3

Musicians Against Nuclear Arms [Defunct] (EA) .... MANA

Musicians Benevolent Fund [British] (BI) .... MBF

Musicians Club of America (EA) .... MCA

Musicians Emergency Fund (EA) .... MEF

Musicians for Social Responsibility (EA) .... MSR

Musicians Foundation (EA) .... MF

Musicians International Mutual Aid Fund .... MIMAF

Musician's Library [A publication] .... MUSL

Musicians National Hot Line Association (EA) .... MNHLA

Musicians' Union [British] (DCTA) .... MU

Musicians United for Safe Energy (EA) .... MUSE

Musicians United to Stop Exclusion [Defunct] (EA) .... MUSE

Musiciens Amateurs du Canada [Canadian Amateur Musicians] (EAIO) .... MAC

Musicland Stores [NYSE symbol] (SAG) .... MLG

Musicland Stores [Associated Press] (SAG) .... MusicLd

Musik in Geschichte und Gegenwart [A publication] .... MGG

Muskegon [Michigan] [Airport symbol] (OAG) .... MKG

Muskegon Business College, Muskegon, MI [Library symbol Library of Congress] (LCLS) .... MiMuB

Muskegon Community College [Michigan] .... MCC

Muskegon County Library, Muskegon, MI [OCLC symbol] (OCLC) .... EZM

Muskegon County Library, Muskegon, MI [Library symbol Library of Congress] (LCLS) .... MiMuM

Muskegon Heights, MI [FM radio station call letters] .... WMRR

Muskegon Heights, MI [AM radio station call letters] .... WQWQ

Muskegon, MI [Location identifier FAA] (FAAL) .... CJH

Muskegon, MI [Location identifier FAA] (FAAL) .... MKG

Muskegon, MI [AM radio station call letters] .... WKBZ

Muskegon, MI [FM radio station call letters] (RBYB) .... WMHG

Muskegon, MI [AM radio station call letters] .... WMUS

Muskegon, MI [FM radio station call letters] .... WMUS-FM

Muskegon, MI [AM radio station call letters] .... WSFN

Muskegon, MI [FM radio station call letters] (RBYB) .... WSHZ-FM

Muskegon, MI [FM radio station call letters] .... WSNX

Muskegon, MI [Television station call letters] .... WTLJ

Muskies, Inc. (EA) .... MI

Muskinabad [Former USSR Seismograph station code, US Geological Survey Closed] (SEIS) .... MUS

Muskingum College, New Concord, OH [OCLC symbol] (OCLC) .... MSC

Muskingum College, New Concord, OH [Library symbol Library of Congress] (LCLS) .... ONcM

Muskmelon Vein Necrosis Virus [Plant pathology] .... MKVNV

Muskogee [MARC language code Library of Congress] (LCCP) .... mus

Muskogee/Davis [Oklahoma] [ICAO location identifier] (ICLI) .... KMKO

Muskogee, OK [Location identifier FAA] (FAAL) .... HAX

Muskogee, OK [AM radio station call letters] .... KBIX

Muskogee, OK [FM radio station call letters] .... KHTT

Muskogee, OK [FM radio station call letters] .... KMMY

Muskogee, OK [AM radio station call letters] (RBYB) .... KMUS-AM

Muskogee, OK [Location identifier FAA] (FAAL) .... MEE

Muskogee, OK [Location identifier FAA] (FAAL) .... MKO

Muskogee Public Library, Muskogee, OK [Library symbol Library of Congress] (LCLS) .... OkMu

Muskoka, ON [ICAO location identifier] (ICLI) .... CYQA

Muskoka Pioneer Village, Huntsville, ON, Canada [Library symbol] [Library of Congress] (LCLS) .... CaOHuM

Muskoka Pioneer Village, Huntsville, Ontario [*Library symbol National Library of Canada*] (BIB) .... OHUM
Muslim .... Mus
Muslim Almanac [*A publication*] .... MA
Muslim Education Co-Ordinating Council (AIE) .... MECC
Muslim League [*Bangladesh*] [*Political party*] .... ML
Muslim League Assembly Party [*Pakistan*] [*Political party*] (FEA) .... MLAP
Muslim Peoples Republican Party [*Political party*] (AD) .... MPRP
Muslim Society in Great Britain .... MSGB
Muslim Students' Association of the United States and Canada (EA) .... MSAUSC
Muslim Students' Association of the US and Canada (EA) .... MSA
Muslim Teachers' Association (AIE) .... MTA
Muslim World League (BJA) .... MWL
Muslin (ROG) .... MUSL
Muslin (VRA) .... musl
Musoma [*Tanzania*] [*ICAO location identifier*] (ICLI) .... HTMU
Musoma [*Tanzania*] [*Airport symbol*] (OAG) .... MUZ
Musonda Falls [*Zambia*] [*ICAO location identifier*] (ICLI) .... FLMD
Mussau [*Papua New Guinea*] [*Airport symbol*] (OAG) .... MWU
Mussee Acadien, Caraquet, New Brunswick [*Library symbol National Library of Canada*] (NLC) .... NBCMA
Mussee de Kent, Bouctouche, New Brunswick [*Library symbol National Library of Canada*] (NLC) .... NBBMK
Mussels [*Quality of the bottom*] [*Nautical charts*] .... Ms
Musser International Turfgrass Foundation (EA) .... MITF
Mussoorie Volunteer Rifles [*British military*] (DMA) .... MVR
Must Be [*Sold*] [*Classified advertising*] .... MB
Must Be Zero (IAA) .... MBZ
Must Have Reply Here by Tomorrow Morning (AD) .... mrytm
Must Ride Company Material (FAAC) .... RIMAT
Mustang Club of America (EA) .... MCA
Mustang Motorcycle Registry [*Defunct*] (EA) .... MMR
Mustang Owners Club (EA) .... MOC
Mustang Owners Club International (EA) .... MOCI
Mustang Resources, Inc. [*Vancouver Stock Exchange symbol*] .... MUR
Mustang Software [*NASDAQ symbol*] (TTSB) .... MSTG
Mustang Software, Inc. [*NASDAQ symbol*] (SAG) .... MSTG
Mustang Software, Inc. [*Associated Press*] (SAG) .... MustSft
Mustang Software International [*California*] [*Bulletin board system*] .... MSI
Mustard Gas [*Also, HD, HS, HT, M*] [*Poison gas US Chemical Corps symbol*].... H
Mustard Gas [*Also, H, HS, HT, M*] [*Poison gas US Chemical Corps symbol*] ..... HD
Mustard Gas [*Also, H, HD, HS, M*] [*Poison gas US Chemical Corps symbol*] ..... HT
Mustard Gas [*Also, H, HD, HS, HT*] [*Poison gas US Chemical Corps symbol*] .... M
Mustard Information Bureau (EA) .... MIB
Mustard/Lewisite Mix [*Poisonous gas*] [*Army*] .... HL
Mustard, Onions, Pickles [*Restaurant slang*] .... MOP
Mustard Seed (EA) .... MS
Mustargen [*Nitrogen mustard*], Adriamycin, Bleomycin, Oncovin , Prednisone [*Vincristine*] [*Antineoplastic drug regimen*] .... MABOP
Mustargen hydrochloride, Oncovin [*Vincristine*], Procarbazine, Prednisone [*Antineoplastic drug regimen*] .... MOPP
Mustargen [*Nitrogen mustard*], Oncovin , Bleomycin [*Vincristine*] [*Antineoplastic drug regimen*] .... MOB
Mustargen [*Nitrogen mustard*], Oncovin , Methotrexate, Prednisone [*Vincristine*] [*Antineoplastic drug regimen*] .... MOMP
Mustargen [*Nitrogen mustard*], Oncovin , Prednisone [*Vincristine*] [*Antineoplastic drug regimen*] .... MOP
Mustargen [*Nitrogen mustard*], Oncovin , Procarbazine [*Vincristine*] [*Antineoplastic drug regimen*] .... MOPr
Mustargen [*Nitrogen mustard*], Oncovin , Procarbazine, Bleomycin, Adriamycin, Prednisone [*Vincristine*] [*Antineoplastic drug regimen*] .... MOP-BAP
Mustargen [*Nitrogen mustard*], Oncovin , Procarbazine, Prednisone [*Vincristine*] [*Antineoplastic drug regimen*] .... MOPP
Mustargen [*Nitrogen mustard*], Oncovin , Procarbazine, Prednisone, Adriamycin, Bleomycin, Vinblastine [*Vincristine*] [*Antineoplastic drug regimen*] .... MOPP/ABV
Mustargen [*Nitrogen mustard*], Oncovin , Procarbazine, Prednisone, Bleomycin [*Vincristine*] [*Antineoplastic drug regimen*] .... MOPP-BLEO
Mustargen [*Nitrogen mustard*], Oncovin , Procarbazine, Prednisone (for Patients with Compromised Pulmonary Function) [*Vincristine*] [*Antineoplastic drug regimen*] .... MOPPCPF
Mustargen [*Nitrogen mustard*], Oncovin , Procarbazine, Prednisone, High-Dose Bleomycin [*Vincristine*] [*Antineoplastic drug regimen*] .... MOPPHDB
Mustargen [*Nitrogen mustard*], Oncovin , Procarbazine, Prednisone, Low-DoseBleomycin [*Vincristine*] [*Antineoplastic drug regimen*] .... MOPPLDB
Mustargen [*Nitrogen mustard*], Vinblastine, Procarbazine, Prednisone [*Antineoplastic drug regimen*] .... MVPP
Mustargen [*Nitrogen mustard*], Vincristine, Vinblastine, Procarbazine, Prednisone [*Antineoplastic drug regimen*] .... MVVPP
Muster .... M
Muster [*Business term*] (DCTA) .... MU
Muster Report .... MR
Mustered Out [*of military service*] .... MO
Mustered Out (AD) .... mo
Mustering Petty Officer .... MPO
Mustering-Out Pay [*Military*] .... MOP
Mustering-Out Pay (AD) .... mop
Mustine, Oncovin [*Vincristine*] Procarbazine, Prednisone [*Antineoplastic drug regimen*] (DAVI) .... MOPP
Mustine, Vinblastine, Procarbazine, prednisone [*Antineoplastic drug regimen*] (DAVI) .... MVPp
Mustique [*Windward Islands*] [*Airport symbol*] (OAG) .... MQS
Mustique Airways [*Barbados*] [*ICAO designator*] (FAAC) .... MAW
Musto Explorations Ltd. [*Toronto Stock Exchange symbol*] .... MUX
Mutagenic Activity .... MA

Mutagenic Potency Index [*For toxicology*] .... MPI
Mutamycin, Adriamycin, Platinol [*Antineoplastic drug*] (CDI) .... MAP
Mutanda [*Zambia*] [*ICAO location identifier*] (ICLI) .... FLMT
Mutant Hybrid [*Medicine*] (DMAA) .... MH
Mutarara [*Mozambique*] [*ICAO location identifier*] (ICLI) .... FQMU
Mutarara [*Mozambique*] [*Airport symbol*] (AD) .... MUW
Mutare/Grand Reef [*Zimbabwe*] [*ICAO location identifier*] (ICLI) .... FVGR
Mutare/Mutare [*Zimbabwe*] [*ICAO location identifier*] (ICLI) .... FVMU
Mutated in Colorectal Cancer [*Genetics*] .... MCC
Mutating Transformation Converter (IAA) .... MTC
Mutation as Cellular Process .... MCP
Mutation Frequency [*Medicine*] (DMAA) .... MF
Mutatis Mutandis [*With the Necessary Changes*] [*Latin*] .... MM
Mutato Nomine [*The Name Being Changed*] [*Latin*] .... MN
Mutator [*A bacteriophage*] .... Mu
Mutatur Terminatio Versiculi [*The Termination of the Little Verse Is Changed*] .... MTV
Mutena [*Zaire*] [*ICAO location identifier*] (ICLI) .... FZDJ
Mutilated .... MUT
Muting [*Indonesia*] [*Airport symbol*] (OAG) .... MUF
Mutitas [*Dullness*] [*Latin*] .... M
Mutlifunction Communications Adapter .... MFCA
Mutliple Access Remote Computing (PDAA) .... MARC
Mutliple Data Link Controller .... MDLC
Mutoko [*Zimbabwe*] [*ICAO location identifier*] (ICLI) .... FVMT
Mutoto [*Zaire*] [*ICAO location identifier*] (ICLI) .... FZUM
Mutshatsha [*Zaire*] [*ICAO location identifier*] (ICLI) .... FZQN
Muttaburra [*Australia Airport symbol*] (OAG) .... UTB
Mutton [*An em space*] [*Typesetting*] (WDMC) .... mutt
Muttontown Preserve, Muttontown, NY [*Library symbol Library of Congress*] (LCLS) .... NMuP
Mutual (ADA) .... MUT
Mutual (ROG) .... MUTL
Mutual .... MUTL
Mutual Ability for Defense [*Pentagon defense policy*] .... MAD
Mutual Adjustment Bureau of Cloth and Garment Trades [*Defunct*] (EA) .... MABCGT
Mutual Advertising Agency Network [*Grand Forks, ND*] (EA) .... MAAN
Mutual African Press Agency .... MAP
Mutual Age .... MA
Mutual Aid Association of the New Polish Immigration (EA) .... MAANPI
Mutual Aid Centre Managing Agency [*British*] (CB) .... MACMA
Mutual Aid Self-Help Group .... MASH
Mutual Air Board [*Canada World War II*] .... MAB
Mutual and Balanced Force Reduction [*Proposed reduction of forces in central Europe by NATO and Warsaw Pact nations*] .... MBFR
Mutual Assistance Advisory Committee .... MAAC
Mutual Assistance, Executive [*Military appropriation*] (NG) .... MAE
Mutual Assistance of the Latin American Government Oil Companies G2 [*See also ARPEL*] (EA) .... MALAGOC
Mutual Assistance Pact .... MAP
Mutual Assistance Plan (NATG) .... MAP
Mutual Assistance Program .... MAP
Mutual Association of Journeymen Coopers [*A union*] [*British*] .... MAJC
Mutual Assured Destruction [*Nuclear warfare*] .... MAD
Mutual Atomic Energy Liability Underwriters [*Chicago, IL*] (EA) .... MAELU
Mutual Atomic Energy Reassurance Pool .... MAERP
Mutual Bancompany [*NASDAQ symbol*] (TTSB) .... MFSB
Mutual Bancompany, Inc. [*NASDAQ symbol*] (SAG) .... MFSB
Mutual Bancompany, Inc. [*Associated Press*] (SAG) .... MutualB
Mutual Benefit and Aid Society [*Later, WBF*] (EA) .... MBAS
Mutual Black Network (NTCM) .... MBN
Mutual Broadcasting System .... MBS
Mutual Capital Certificate .... MCC
Mutual Coherence Function .... MCF
Mutual Companies .... M
Mutual Conductance .... Gm
Mutual Defense Agency (NADA) .... MDA
Mutual Defense Assistance .... MDA
Mutual Defense Assistance Act .... MDAA
Mutual Defense Assistance, General Area of China .... MDAC
Mutual Defense Assistance, Greece and Turkey .... MDAGT
Mutual Defense Assistance, Iran, Republic of Korea, and Philippines.... MDAIKP
Mutual Defense Assistance, North Atlantic Area .... MDANAA
Mutual Defense Assistance Office (DOMA) .... MDAO
Mutual Defense Assistance Pact [*or Program*] .... MDAP
Mutual Defense Board [*US-Philippines*] (CINC) .... MDB
Mutual Defense Control Staff [*Department of State*] .... MDCS
Mutual Defense Treaty .... MDT
Mutual Educational and Cultural Exchange Act of 1961 .... MECEA
Mutual Federation of Independent Cooperatives [*Later, Northeast Dairy Cooperative Federation*] (EA) .... MFIC
Mutual Force Reductions .... MFR
Mutual Fund [*Business term*] .... MF
Mutual Help and Occupancy Agreement [*Department of Housing and Urban Development*] (GFGA) .... MHOA
Mutual Households Associations Ltd. [*British*] (BI) .... MHA
Mutual Improvement Association [*Mormon Youth Movement*] (BARN) .... MIA
Mutual Improvement Class [*British railroad term*] .... MIC
Mutual Inductance [*Symbol*] [*IUPAC*] .... M
Mutual Inductance .... MI
Mutual Inductance [*Symbol*] (DEN) .... ML
Mutual Inductance Bridge .... MIB
Mutual Information System on Employment Policies in Europe (IID) .... MISEP
Mutual Institutions National Transfer System, Inc. [*Banking*] .... MINTS

Mutual Insurance Advisory Association [Defunct] (EA) ..... MIAA
Mutual Insurance Committee on Federal Taxation (EA) ..... MICOFT
Mutual Insurance Council of Editors [Later, PICA] (EA) ..... MICE
Mutual Insurance National Transfer System, Inc. ..... MINTS
Mutual Insurance Rating Bureau [Defunct] (EA) ..... MIRB
Mutual Interference ..... MI
Mutual Interference Chart (IEEE) ..... MIC
Mutual Interference Report (MCD) ..... MIR
Mutual Loss Research Bureau [Later, Property Loss Research Bureau]
  (EA) ..... MLRB
Mutual Mortgage Insurance Fund [FHA] (EMRF) ..... MMI
Mutual Mortgage Insurance Fund [Federal Housing Administration] ..... MMIF
Mutual Musicians Foundation (EA) ..... MMF
Mutual of New York [Insurance company] ..... MONY
Mutual Permanent Building Society (AD) ..... MPBS
Mutual Real Estate Investment Trust ..... M-REIT
Mutual Recognition ..... MR
Mutual Reduction of Forces and Armaments and Associated
  Measures ..... MURFAAM
Mutual Reduction of Forces and Armaments and Associated Measures in
  Central Europe ..... MURFAAMCE
Mutual Reinsurance Bureau (EA) ..... MRB
Mutual Resources [Vancouver Stock Exchange symbol] ..... MTR
Mutual Responsibility [Movement within Anglican Communion to make its
  mission more efficacious] ..... MR
Mutual Risk Management [NYSE symbol] (SPSG) ..... MM
Mutual Risk Management Ltd. [Associated Press] (SAG) ..... MutRisk
Mutual Savings Bank ..... MSB
Mutual Savings Bank [NASDAQ symbol] (TTSB) ..... MSBK
Mutual Savings Bank FSB [NASDAQ symbol] (SAG) ..... MSBK
Mutual Savings Bank FSB [Associated Press] (SAG) ..... MutSvg
Mutual Security Act [1954] ..... MSA
Mutual Security Agency [Functions transferred to Foreign Operations
  Administration, 1953] ..... MSA
Mutual Security Military Sales ..... MSMS
Mutual Security Objectives Plan (CINC) ..... MSOP
Mutual Security Program ..... MSP
Mutual Security Treaty (MCD) ..... MST
Mutual Sewing Machine Dealers Association (EA) ..... MSMDA
Mutual Society of Arts (NADA) ..... MSA
Mutual Society of the French Community (EA) ..... MSFC
Mutual Support Program ..... MSP
Mutual UFO [Unidentified Flying Object] Network (EA) ..... MUFON
Mutual Weapons Development Data Exchange Agreement [NATO] ..... MWDDEA
Mutual Weapons Development Data Exchange Procedures [NATO] ..... MWDDEP
Mutual Weapons Development Program [NATO] ..... MWDP
Mutual Weapons Development Team [Military] ..... MWDT
Mutual Welfare League (NADA) ..... MWL
Mutually Assured Survival ..... MAS
Mutually Orthogonal Latin Square ..... MOLS
Mutually Owned Society for Songwriters ..... MOSS
Mutually Responsible Facilitation Inventory [Personality development test]
  [Psychology] ..... MRFI
Mutuel Field [Horse racing] ..... F
Mutuelle des Autochtones de la Cote d'Ivoire [Mutual Association of the
  Natives of the Ivory Coast] ..... MUTACI
Mutukisna's Ceylon Reports [A publication] (DLA) ..... Mut
Mutukisna's Ceylon Reports [A publication] (DLA) ..... Mutukisna
Mutwanga [Zaire] [ICAO location identifier] (ICLI) ..... FZNT
MUX [Multiplex] Terminal (MCD) ..... MT
Muyupampa [Bolivia] [ICAO location identifier] (ICLI) ..... SLYP
Muza and Other Labels [Record label] [Poland] ..... Muza
Muzaffarabad [Pakistan] [ICAO location identifier] (ICLI) ..... OPMF
Muzaffarpur [India] [Airport symbol] (AD) ..... MZU
Muzika Esperanto Ligo [Esperantist Music League] (EAIO) ..... MEL
Muzzle (MSA) ..... MZL
Muzzle Bore Sight [British military] (DMA) ..... MBS
Muzzle Boresight Device [Army] (INF) ..... MBD
Muzzle Energy ..... ME
Muzzle Hatch ..... MH
Muzzle Hatch ..... MUZH
Muzzle Hatch Electrical ..... MHE
Muzzle Hatch Electrical Control ..... MHEC
Muzzle Hatch Mechanical ..... MHM
Muzzle Loaders' Association of Great Britain ..... MLA
Muzzle Loaders Association of Great Britain (BI) ..... MLAGB
Muzzle Position Sensor (MCD) ..... MPS
Muzzle Reference System (MCD) ..... MRS
Muzzle Velocity [Ballistics] ..... MV
Muzzle-Loading ..... ML
Muzzle-Loading Rifle ..... MLR
Muzzle-Loading Rifled Gun ..... MLRG
Mvengue [Gabon] [Airport symbol] (OAG) ..... MVB
MVP Capital Corp. [Toronto Stock Exchange symbol] ..... MVP
MVS/Extended Architecture (NITA) ..... MVS/XA
MVS Integrated Control System (NITA) ..... MICS
MVS/System Extension (NITA) ..... MVS/SE
MVS/System Product (NITA) ..... MVS/SP
MVSI, Inc. [NASDAQ symbol] (SAG) ..... MVSI
MVT/Time Sharing Option (NITA) ..... MVT/TSO
Mvula-Sanda [Zaire] [ICAO location identifier] (ICLI) ..... FZAY
Mwadingusha [Zaire] [ICAO location identifier] (ICLI) ..... FZQJ
Mwadui [Tanzania] [ICAO location identifier] (ICLI) ..... HTMD
Mwami [Zambia] [ICAO location identifier] (ICLI) ..... FLMM
Mwanza [Tanzania] [ICAO location identifier] (ICLI) ..... HTMW

Mwanza [Tanzania] [Airport symbol] (OAG) ..... MWZ
M-Wave, Inc. [NASDAQ symbol] (SAG) ..... MWAV
M-Wave Inc. [NASDAQ symbol] (TTSB) ..... MWAV
M-Wave, Inc. [Associated Press] (SAG) ..... M-Wave
Mweka [Zaire] [ICAO location identifier] (ICLI) ..... FZVM
Mwene-Ditu [Zaire] [ICAO location identifier] (ICLI) ..... FZWE
Mweso [Zaire] [ICAO location identifier] (ICLI) ..... FZNM
Mwinilunga [Zambia] [ICAO location identifier] (ICLI) ..... FLMW
MX Information Center [Defunct] (EA) ..... MXIC
M-X [Missile] Renewable Energy System ..... M-X/RES
My Account [Business term] ..... MA
My Compact Operating System [Toshiba] ..... MYCOS
My Eyes Glaze Over [An article, written about an important subject, that resists
  reader interest and has a soporific effect] [Journalistic slang] ..... MEGO
My Favor (ADA) ..... M/F
My Favorite Toy Language [Computer hacker terminology] (NHD) ..... MFTL
My First Hard Drive [Computer science] ..... MFHD
My Old Lady [Wife] [Slang] ..... M-O-L
My Old Man [Husband] [Slang] ..... M-O-M
My Own Bloody Yacht Club [Founded in England; registered with Lloyds of
  London] ..... MOBYC
My Pal [Slang] ..... MP
My Software Co. [Associated Press] (SAG) ..... MySoft
My Very Excellent Mother Just Served Us Nine Pies [Mnemonic guide to the
  nine planets: Mercury, Venus, Earth, Mars, Jupiter, Saturn, Uranus,
  Neptune, Pluto] ..... MVEMJSUNP
Myakka River State Park [Florida] (AD) ..... MRSP
Myalgic Encephalomyelitis [Medicine] ..... ME
Myalgic Encephalomyelitis Association [British] (DBA) ..... MEA
Myanma Airways (EY) ..... MA
Myanmar [Aircraft nationality and registration mark] (FAAC) ..... XY
Myanmar [Aircraft nationality and registration mark] (FAAC) ..... XZ
Myanmar Airways [ICAO designator] (FAAC) ..... UBA
Myanmar International Trust and Investment Co. (ECON) ..... MITIC
Myanmar News Agency (EY) ..... MNA
Myasishchev [Aircraft] [Commonwealth of Independent States] ..... MYA
Myasthenia Gravis [Medicine] ..... MG
Myasthenia Gravis [Medicine] ..... MYG
Myasthenia Gravis Foundation (EA) ..... MG
Myasthenia Gravis Foundation ..... MGF
Myasthenic Syndrome [Neurology] ..... MYS
Myauk U [Myanmar] [ICAO location identifier] (ICLI) ..... VBMU
Mycelial [of fungi] (AAMN) ..... MC
Mycelium [Biology] ..... M
Mycelium Radius Atrovirens [A fungus] ..... MRA
Mycobacteria Other Than Tubercle Bacilli ..... MOTT
Mycobacterial Extracts [Biochemistry] ..... ME
Mycobacterium [Genus of microorganisms] ..... M
Mycobacterium ..... MYCO
Mycobacterium Avium Complex ..... MAC
Mycobacterium Avium-Intracellulare [Medicine] ..... MAI
Mycobacterium Avium-Intracellulare Complex [Bacteriology] ..... MAC
Mycobacterium Avium-Intracellulare-Scrofulaceum [Bacteriology] ..... MAIS
Mycobacterium Tuberculosis [Bacteriology] (CPH) ..... M TUBERC
Mycobacterium Tuberculosis [Bacteriology] ..... Mt
Mycobacterium Tuberculosis [A bacterium] [Medicine] (DAVI) ..... TB
Mycogen Corp. [NASDAQ symbol] (NQ) ..... MYCO
Mycogen Corp. [Associated Press] (SAG) ..... Mycogn
Mycological Society of America (EA) ..... MSA
Mycology (WGA) ..... MYC
Mycology ..... MYCOL
Mycophenolic Acid [Biochemistry] ..... MPA
Mycoplasma [Medicine] (MAE) ..... M
Mycoplasma [A bacterium] (DAVI) ..... Myco
Mycoplasma Pneumonia [Medicine] ..... MP
Mycoplasma Pulmonis [A bacterium] ..... MP
Mycoplasma Synoviae [A pathogen] ..... MS
Mycoplasma-Like Organisms [Microbiology] ..... MLO
Mycoplasmatales Virus ..... MV
Mycoplasmatales Virus [from] Acholeplasma laidlawii ..... MVL
Mycoplasmatales Virus [from] Goat ..... MVG
Mycorrhiza Inoculum Potential [Soil science] ..... MIP
Mycorrhizal Roots [Botany] ..... MR
MYCOS Support System (NITA) ..... MYCOS/SS
Mycosis Fungoides [Dermatology] ..... MF
Myelin [or Myelinated] [Medicine] ..... MYEL
Myelin Basic Protein [Neurology] ..... MBP
Myelin Figure [Medicine] ..... MF
Myelin Oligodendrocyte Glycoprotein [Biochemistry] ..... MOG
Myelin-Associated Glycoprotein [Biochemistry] ..... MAG
Myelinated Fiber [Neuroanatomy] ..... MF
Myeloblastosis-Associated Virus ..... MAV
Myeloblastpromyelocyte Compartment [Hematology] (DAVI) ..... MPC
Myelocyte [Hematology] ..... MYEL
Myelocyte [Hematology] ..... myelo
Myelocytomatosis [Avian disease] ..... MC
Myelodysplasia [Medicine] ..... MDS
Myelodysplastic Syndrome [Medicine] ..... MDS
Myelofibrosis and Myeloid Metaplasia [Hematology] ..... MMM
Myelogenous Leukemia [Oncology] ..... ML
Myelogram (AAMN) ..... MYEL
Myeloid:Erythroid [Ratio] [Hematology] ..... M:E
Myeloid Metaplasia [Medicine] ..... MM
Myeloid Metaplasia with Polycythemia Vera [Hematology] (MAE) ..... PCV-M
Myeloid-Erythrocyte [or Erythroid] [Hematology] (DAVI) ..... MER

Myeloma Cell Growth Factor [*Biochemistry*] ... MCGF

Myeloma Morphology Score [*Oncology*] ... MMS

Myeloma Progression Score [*Oncology*] ... MPS

Myeloma Protein [*Oncology*] (DAVI) ... mp

Myelomeningocele [*Medicine*] ... MM

Myelomonoblastic Leukemia [*Medicine*] (DMAA) ... MMoL

Myelomonocytic Leukemia, Chronic (MAE) ... MLC

Myelomonocytic Leukemia, Subacute (MAE) ... MLS

Myeloperoxidase [*An enzyme*] ... MPO

Myeloproliferative Sarcoma Virus ... MPSV

Myelosclerosis with Myeloid Metaplasia [*Medicine*] (MAE) ... MMM

Myelosuppressive Bleomycin, Adriamycin, Cyclophosphamide, Oncovin [*Vincristine*], Prednisone [*Antineoplastic drug regimen*] ... M-BACOP

Myelotomography [*Medicine*] ... MT

[*The*] **Myers** [*L. E.*] **Co. Group** [*Associated Press*] (SAG) ... MyerL

[*The*] **Myers** [*L. E.*] **Co. Group** [*NYSE symbol*] (SPSG) ... MYR

Myer's Federal Decisions [*A publication*] (DLA) ... Myer Fed Dec

Myer's Federal Decisions [*United States*] [*A publication*] (DLA) ... Myer's Fed Dec

Myers Indus [*AMEX symbol*] (TTSB) ... MYE

Myers Industries, Inc. [*AMEX symbol*] (SPSG) ... MYE

Myers Industries, Inc. [*Associated Press*] (SAG) ... MyersInd

Myer's Texas Digest [*A publication*] (DLA) ... Myer Dig

Myers-Briggs Type Indicator [*Psychology*] ... MBTI

Myers-Briggs Type Indicator: Abbreviated Version [*Personality development test*] [*Psychology*] ... MBTI:AV

Myflug HF [*Iceland*] [*ICAO designator*] (FAAC) ... MYA

Myiare (BARN) ... mya

Myitkyina [*Myanmar*] [*Airport symbol*] (OAG) ... MYT

Myitkyina [*Myanmar*] [*ICAO location identifier*] (ICLI) ... VBMK

Mylan Laboratories, Inc. [*NYSE symbol*] (SPSG) ... MYL

Mylan Laboratories, Inc. [*Associated Press*] (SAG) ... Mylan

Mylan Labs [*NYSE symbol*] (TTSB) ... MYL

Mylan Ventures Ltd. [*Vancouver Stock Exchange symbol*] ... MVL

Mylar Diaphragm Rupture System ... MDRS

Mylar Insulation Material ... MYIM

Mylex Corp. [*Associated Press*] (SAG) ... Mylex

Mylex Corp. [*NASDAQ symbol*] (NQ) ... MYLX

Mylne and Craig's English Chancery Reports [*A publication*] (DLA) ... M & C

Mylne and Craig's English Chancery Reports [*A publication*] (DLA) ... My & C

Mylne and Craig's English Chancery Reports [*A publication*] (DLA) ... My & Cr

Mylne and Craig's English Chancery Reports [*A publication*] (DLA) ... Myl & C

Mylne and Craig's English Chancery Reports [*A publication*] (DLA) ... Myl & C (Eng)

Mylne and Craig's English Chancery Reports [*A publication*] (DLA) ... Myl & Cr

Mylne and Keen's English Chancery Reports [*A publication*] (DLA) ... M & K

Mylne and Keen's English Chancery Reports [*A publication*] (DLA) ... My & K

Mylne and Keen's English Chancery Reports [*A publication*] (DLA) ... Myl & K

Mylne and Keen's English Chancery Reports [*A publication*] (DLA) ... Myl & K (Eng)

Mylne and Keen's English Chancery Reports [*A publication*] (DLA) ... Mylne & K

Mynarski Public Library, Alberta [*Library symbol National Library of Canada*] (NLC) ... AMY

Myoadenylate Deaminase [*An enzyme*] ... MAD

Myoblast Growth Factor [*Biochemistry*] ... MGF

Myocardial [*or Myocardium*] [*Cardiology*] (AAMN) ... MYO

Myocardial Band [*Cardiology*] ... MB

Myocardial Beta Adrenergic Receptor [*Cardiology*] (DMAA) ... MBAR

Myocardial Blood Flow [*Cardiology*] ... MBF

Myocardial Bridging [*Cardiology*] ... MCB

Myocardial Contractile Force [*Cardiology*] ... MCF

Myocardial Contractile State [*Cardiology*] (MAE) ... MCS

Myocardial Damage [*Cardiology*] (MAE) ... MD

Myocardial Depressant Factor ... MDF

Myocardial Depressant Substance [*Cardiology*] (DAVI) ... MDS

Myocardial Disease [*Cardiology*] ... MD

Myocardial Disease of Unknown Origin [*Cardiology*] ... MDUO

Myocardial Efficiency [*Cardiology*] ... M-EFF

Myocardial Efficiency Index [*Cardiology*] ... MEI

Myocardial Fibrosis [*Cardiology*] ... MF

Myocardial Infarction [*Cardiology*] ... MI

Myocardial Infarction [*Cardiology*] (DHSM) ... MIF

Myocardial Infarction Rehabilitation Program [*Cardiology*] (DAVI) ... MIRP

Myocardial Infarction Research Unit [*Cardiology*] (DAVI) ... MIRU

Myocardial Infarction, Triage, and Intervention Project [*or Trial*] [*Cardiology study*] ... MITI

Myocardial Isotopic Perfusion Scan [*Cardiology*] (DAVI) ... MIPS

Myocardial Lactate Extraction [*Clinical chemistry*] ... MLE

Myocardial Metabolic Rate [*Cardiology*] (MAE) ... MMR

Myocardial Oxygen Consumption [*Cardiology*] (MAE) ... MO_2

Myocardial Oxygen Consumption [*Cardiology*] (DAVI) ... MVO_2

Myocardial Oxygen Ventilation Rate [*Cardiology*] (MAE) ... MVo_2

Myocardial Perfusion Imaging [*Cardiology*] ... MPI

Myocardial Stress Perfusion Scintigram [*Medicine*] ... MSPS

Myocardial Vascular Capacity [*Cardiology*] (MAE) ... MVC

Myocardiopathy of Unknown Origin [*Cardiology*] ... MUO

Myocarditis [*Medicine*] ... MC

Myocarditis, Pericarditis [*Cardiology*] (DAVI) ... MYOC-A

Myoclonic Epilepsy Associated with Ragged Red Fibres [*Medicine*] ... MERRF

Myoclonic Twitch Activity [*Neurology*] (DAVI) ... MTA

Myoclonus Families United (EA) ... MFU

Myocyte Enhancing Factor [*Genetics*] ... MEF

Myoelectric Signal ... MES

Myoepithelium [*Cytology*] ... ME

Myofascial Pain [*Medicine*] ... MFP

Myofascial Pain Dysfunction [*Neurology*] ... MPD

Myofascial Pain Dysfunction Syndrome [*Neurology*] (DAVI) ... MPDS

Myofibril Fragmentation Index [*Food technology*] ... MFI

Myofibrillar [*Anatomy*] ... MF

Myogenic Helix-Loop-Helix [*Genetics*] ... MHLH

Myoglobin [*Biochemistry, medicine*] ... Mb

Myoglobin [*Medicine*] (DMAA) ... MG

Myoglobin [*hematology*] (DAVI) ... MYOGLB

Myoglobin, Carboxy [*Biochemistry, medicine*] ... MbCO

Myoglobin, Oxy [*Biochemistry, medicine*] ... MbO_2

Myoglobin Tritium [*Hematology*] (DAVI) ... Mb

Myohemerythrin [*Biochemistry*] ... MHr

Myohemoglobin [*Hematology*] ... MHb

Myo-Inositol [*Chemistry*] [*Dietetics*] (DAVI) ... MI

Myo-inositolphosphate [*Biochemistry*] ... MIP

Myokinetic Psychodiagnosis [*Psychology*] (AEBS) ... MKP

Myoneural [*Medicine*] ... MN

Myoneural Junction [*Medicine*] ... MNJ

Myopia ... M

Myopia ... MY

Myopia [*Ophthalmology*] (DAVI) ... myop

Myopia International Research Foundation (EA) ... MIRF

Myopia Research Foundation [*Later, MIRF*] ... MRF

Myopic Astigmatism [*Ophthalmology*] (DAVI) ... M+Am

Myopic Keratomileusis [*Ophthalmology*] ... MKM

Myosin [*Muscle physiology*] ... M

Myosin Head Fragment [*Biochemistry*] ... MHF

Myosin Heavy Chain [*Muscle biology*] ... MHC

Myosin Light Chain [*Muscle biology*] ... MLC

Myosin Light Chain Kinase [*An enzyme*] ... MLCK

Myotonia Congenita [*Medicine*] ... MC

Myotonic Dystrophy [*See also MyMD*] [*Medicine*] ... MD

Myotonic Muscular Dystrophy [*Medicine Medicine*] (DMAA) ... MMD

Myotonic Muscular Dystrophy [*See also MD*] [*Medicine*] ... MyMD

MYR Group [*NYSE symbol*] (TTSB) ... MYR

Myria [*A prefix meaning multiplied by* 10^4] ... ma

Myria [*A prefix meaning multiplied by* 10^4] ... MY

Myriad Genetics [*NASDAQ symbol*] (TTSB) ... MYGN

Myriad Genetics, Inc. [*NASDAQ symbol*] (SAG) ... MYGN

Myriad Genetics, Inc. [*Associated Press*] (SAG) ... Myriad

Myriagram [*Ten Thousand Grams*] (ROG) ... MG

Myriagram [*Ten Thousand Grams*] ... MYG

Myrialiter [*Unit of measurement*] (ROG) ... ML

Myrialiter [*Unit of measurement*] ... MYL

Myriameter ... MYM

Myriameters [*Metric system*] (ROG) ... MM

Myrias Research Corp., Edmonton, AB, Canada [*Library symbol*] [*Library of Congress*] (LCLS) ... CaAEMR

Myrias Research Corp., Edmonton, Alberta [*Library symbol National Library of Canada*] (NLC) ... AEMR

Myrick's California Probate Court Reports [*1872-79*] [*A publication*] (DLA) ... Myr

Myrick's California Probate Court Reports [*1872-79*] [*A publication*] (DLA) ... Myr Cal Prob

Myrick's California Probate Court Reports [*1872-79*] [*A publication*] (DLA) ... Myr Prob

Myrick's California Probate Court Reports [*1872-79*] [*A publication*] (DLA) ... Myr Prob Rep

Myrick's California Probate Court Reports [*1872-79*] [*A publication*] (DLA) ... Myrick (Cal)

Myrick's California Probate Court Reports [*1872-79*] [*A publication*] (DLA) ... Myrick Prob (Cal)

Myrick's California Probate Court Reports [*1872-79*] [*A publication*] (DLA) ... Myrick's Prob Rep

Myristicin [*or glyceryl trimyristate*] [*Chemical dependency*] (DAVI) ... MMDA

Myristoylated Alanine-Rich C-Kinase Substrate [*Biochemistry*] ... MARCKS

Myristyltrimethylammonium Bromide [*Organic chemistry*] ... MYTAB

Myrnam Public Library, Alberta [*Library symbol National Library of Canada*] (NLC) ... AMYR

Myrnam Public Library, Myrnam, AB, Canada [*Library symbol*] [*Library of Congress*] (LCLS) ... CaAMyr

Myrobalan Latent Ringspot Virus [*Plant pathology*] ... MLRV

Myrtle [*Philately*] ... myr

Myrtle Beach [*South Carolina*] **Myrtle Air Force Base** [*Airport symbol*] (OAG) ... MYR

Myrtle Beach/Myrtle Beach Air Force Base [*South Carolina*] [*ICAO location identifier*] (ICLI) ... KMYR

Myrtle Beach, SC [*Location identifier FAA*] (FAAL) ... BSQ

Myrtle Beach, SC [*TV station call letters*] (RBYB) ... WFXB-TV

Myrtle Beach, SC [*Television station call letters*] ... WGSE

Myrtle Beach, SC [*FM radio station call letters*] ... WJYR

Myrtle Beach, SC [*AM radio station call letters*] ... WKEL

Myrtle Beach, SC [*AM radio station call letters*] ... WKZQ

Myrtle Beach, SC [*FM radio station call letters*] ... WKZQ-FM

Myrtle Mabee Library, Belgrade, MN [*Library symbol*] [*Library of Congress*] (LCLS) ... MnBg

Myrtle Point, OR [*FM radio station call letters*] ... KAHY

Myrtle Point Public Library (Flora M. Laird Library), Myrtle Point, OR [*Library symbol Library of Congress*] (LCLS) ... OrMp

MySoftware Co. [*Associated Press*] (SAG) ... MySoft

MySoftware Co. [*NASDAQ symbol*] (SAG) ... MYSW

Mysoline [*An anticonvulsant*] [*Wyeth-Ayerst Laboratorie*] (DAVI) ... MYSOLN

Mysore [*India*] [*ICAO location identifier*] (ICLI) ... VOMY

Mysore Chief Court Reports [*India*] [*A publication*] (DLA) ... Mys Ch Ct

Mysore High Court Reports [*India*] [*A publication*] (DLA) ... Mys HCR

Mysore Law Journal [*India*] [*A publication*] (DLA) ... My LJ

Mysore Law Journal [*India*] [*A publication*] (DLA) ... Mys LJ

Mysore Law Journal [*India*] [*A publication*] (DLA) .... Mysore LJ
Mysore Law Reports [*India*] [*A publication*] (DLA) .... Mys LR
Mysore Law Reports [*India*] [*A publication*] (DLA) .... Mysore
Mysore Reports (Reprint) [*1878-1923*] [*India*] [*A publication*] (DLA) .... Mys R (R)
Mysore Weekly Notes [*1891-92*] [*India*] [*A publication*] (DLA) .... Mys WN
Mystery .... MYST
Mystery Mountain Minerals [*Vancouver Stock Exchange symbol*] .... MYS
Mystery Science Theater 3000 [*Cable television program*] MST3K
Mystery Writers of America (NADA) .... MWA
Mystery Writers of America Inc. (NADA) .... MWAI
Mystic .... MYSTIC
Mystic, KY [*Location identifier FAA*] (FAAL) .... MYS
Mystic Marinelife Aquarium, New London, CT [*OCLC symbol*] (OCLC) .... MYS
Mystic Seaport, Inc., Mystic, CT [*Library symbol Library of Congress*]
    (LCLS) .... CtMyMHi
Mystic Seaport Museum (EA) .... MSM
Mystic Terminal Co. [*AAR code*] .... MTC
Mystic Valley Railway Society (EA) .... MVRS
Mytec Technology, Inc. [*Vancouver Stock Exchange symbol*] .... MYT
Myth and Ritual. Essays on the Myth and Ritual of the Hebrews in Relation
    to theCulture Pattern of the Ancient East [*A publication*] (BJA) .... MaR
Myth, Legend, Custom in the Old Testament [*A publication*] (BJA) .... MLC
Myth, Ritual, and Kingship [*A publication*] (BJA) .... MRK
Myth, Ritual, and Kingship. Essays on the Theory and Practice of Kingship
    in theAncient Near East and in Israel [*A publication*] (BJA) .... MRaK
Mythadventures Fan Club (EA) .... MAFC
Mythical Operational Environment (SAA) .... MOE
Mythmaking in America [*A publication*] .... MIA
Mythographi Vaticani [*A publication*] (OCD) .... Myth Vat
Mythology .... MYT
Mythology .... MYTH
Mythology (WGA) .... MYTHOL
Mythology of All Races [*A publication*] .... MAR
Mythopoeic Society (EA) .... MS
Mytilene [*Greece*] [*Airport symbol*] (OAG) .... MJT
Myton, UT [*Location identifier FAA*] (FAAL) .... MTU
Myvatn [*Iceland*] [*Airport symbol Obsolete*] (OAG) .... MVA
Myxedematous [*Endocrinology*] (DAVI) .... MY
Myxoid Liposarcoma [*Genetics*] .... MLPS
Myxoma Growth Factor [*Biochemistry*] .... MGF
Myxoma Virus Growth Factor [*Biochemistry*] .... MVGF
Myxomatosis (DSUE) .... MYXO
Mzimba [*Malawi*] [*ICAO location identifier*] (ICLI) .... FWMZ
Mzimba [*Malawi*] [*Airport symbol*] (AD) .... MZY
Mzuzu [*Malawi*] [*ICAO location identifier*] (ICLI) .... FWUU
Mzuzu [*Malawi*] [*Airport symbol*] (AD) .... ZZU

N

By Meaning

N. A. Kovach, Los Angeles, CA [*Library symbol Library of Congress*] (LCLS) .... Kov
N Binary Digits-M Binary Digits (NITA) .... NBMB
N. M. De Rothschild & Co. [*Merchant bank*] [*British*] .... NMR
N. W. Ayer & Son, New York, NY [*Library symbol Library of Congress*] (LCLS) .... NNNWA
N. W. Ayer & Son, Philadelphia, PA [*Library symbol Library of Congress Obsolete*] (LCLS) .... PPNWA
N4 Transportation Systems of Canada Ltd. [*Information service or system*] (IID) CN4
Na Priklad [*For Example*] [*Czech*] (AD) .... na pr
NAACOG [*Nurses Association of the American College of Obstetricians and Gynecologists*] **Certification Corp.** (EA) ...... NCC
NAACOG: the Organization for Obstetric, Gynecologic, and Neonatal Nurses [*Formerly, Nurses Association of the American College of Obstetricians and Gynecologists*] (EA) .... NAACOG
NAACP [*National Association for the Advancement of Colored People*] **Legal Defense and Educational Fund** (EA) .... LDF
Naalehu [*Hawaii*] [*Seismograph station code, US Geological Survey Closed*] (SEIS) .... NAA
Naamloze Vennootschap [*Limited Company, Corporation*] [*Netherlands*] (GPO) .... NV
Naar on Suffrage and Elections [*A publication*] (DLA) .... Naar Elec
NAB Asset Corp. [*Associated Press*] (SAG) .... NAB A
NAB Asset Corp. [*NASDAQ symbol*] (SAG) .... NABC
Nabatean (BJA) .... Nab
Nabb, IN [*Location identifier FAA*] (FAAL) .... ABB
Nabern/Teck [*Germany ICAO location identifier*] (ICLI) ...... EDTN
NABI, Inc. [*Associated Press*] (SAG) .... NABI
NABI, Inc. [*NASDAQ symbol*] (SAG) .... NABI
NABI Inc. [*NASDAQ symbol*] (TTSB) .... NABI
Nabire [*Indonesia*] [*Airport symbol*] (OAG) .... NBX
Nabire [*Indonesia*] [*ICAO location identifier*] (ICLI) .... WABI
Nabisco Brands, Inc. [*Toronto Stock Exchange symbol*] ...... NBI
Nabisco Holdings Corp. [*NYSE symbol*] (SAG) .... NA
Nabisco Holdings Corp. [*Associated Press*] (SAG) .... NabisH
Nabisco Holdings 'A' [*NYSE symbol*] (TTSB) .... NA
Nabonidus (BJA) .... Nbn
Nabonidus and Belshazzar (BJA) .... NB
Nabors Industries [*AMEX symbol*] (TTSB) .... NBR
Nabors Industries, Inc. [*Associated Press*] (SAG) .... Nabors
Nabors Industries, Inc. [*AMEX symbol*] (SPSG) .... NBR
NABU Manufacturing Corp., Ottawa, Ontario [*Library symbol National Library of Canada*] (NLC) .... OONAMC
Nabu Network Corp. [*Toronto Stock Exchange symbol*] ...... NBK
NAC RE Corp. [*Associated Press*] (SAG) .... NAC Re
NAC RE Corp. [*NYSE symbol*] (SAG) .... NRC
Nacala [*Mozambique*] [*ICAO location identifier*] (ICLI) ...... FQNC
Nacala [*Mozambique*] [*Airport symbol*] (AD) .... MNC
NACCO Indus Inc. CI'A' [*NYSE symbol*] (TTSB) .... NC
NACCO Industries, Inc. [*Associated Press*] (SAG) .... NACCO
Nacelle [*Aviation*] .... NAC
Nacelle .... NAC
Nacelle Drag Efficiency [*Factor*] [*Aerospace*] .... NDF
Nacelle Product Development Organization (MCD) .... NPDO
N-Acetylaminophenazone [*Organic chemistry*] .... NAAP
N-Acetylaspartylglutamic Acid [*Biochemistry*] .... NAAG
N-Acetyldopamine [*Biochemistry*] .... NADA
N-Acetylgalactosamine .... GalNac
N-Acetylglucosamine .... GlcNac
N-Acetylglucosamine [*Biochemistry*] .... NAG
N-Acetylglucosaminidase [*An enzyme*] .... NAG
N-Acetylimidazole [*Organic chemistry*] .... NAI
N-Acetyllactopamine [*Biochemistry*] .... NAL
N-Acetyl-L-Cysteine [*Biochemistry*] .... NAC
N-Acetyl-L-Cysteine Ethylenediaminetetra-Acetic Acid [*Biochemistry*] (MAE) .... NAC-EDTA
N-Acetylmannosamine [*Biochemistry*] .... ManNac
N-Acetylmethionine [*Organic chemistry*] .... NAM
N-Acetylmuramate [*Laboratory science*] (DAVI) .... MurNAc
N-Acetylneuraminic Acid [*Also, AcNeu, NANA*] [*Biochemistry*] .. NAN
N-Acetylneuraminic Acid [*Also, AcNeu, NAN*] [*Biochemistry*] .. NANA
N-Acetylneuraminic Acid (AD) .... nana
N-Acetyl-p-aminophenol [*Organic chemistry*] .... NAPA
N-Acetylprocainamide [*Cardiac depressant*] .... NAPA
N-Acetylserotonin [*Biochemistry*] .... NAS

N-Acetyltransferase [*An enzyme*] .... NAT
N-Acetyltryptophan [*Biochemistry*] .... NAT
N-Acetyl-Tryptophan-Amide [*Organic chemistry*] .... NATA
N-Acetyltyramine [*Biochemistry*] .... NATA
Nachalnik Glavnoyo Upravlenia [*Chief of Main Directorate*] [*Soviet military rank*] .... NGU
Nachalnik Otdelenia [*Chief of Department*] [*Soviet military rank*] .. NO
Nachalnik Sektora [*Chief of Sector*] [*Soviet military rank*] ...... NS
Nachalnik Uprovlenia [*Chief of Directorate*] [*Soviet military rank*] . NU
Naches, WA [*FM radio station call letters*] (RBYB) .... KHHK-FM
Naches, WA [*FM radio station call letters*] .... KYKA
Nachingwea [*Tanzania*] [*ICAO location identifier*] (ICLI) ...... HTNA
Nachingwea [*Tanzania*] [*Airport symbol*] (OAG) .... NCH
Nachmittag [*Afternoon*] [*German*] .... NM
Nachmittags [*Afternoon*] [*German*] .... NACHM
Nachrichten der Akademie der Wissenschaften in Goettingen. Philologisch-Historische Klasse [*A publication*] (BJA) .... NAG
Nachrichten von der Gesellschaft der Wissenschaften zu Goettingen [*A publication*] (OCD) .... Gott Nachr
Nachrichtenabteilung [*Signal battalion*] [*German military - World War II*] .... NA
Nachrichten-Aufklaerung [*Signal intelligence*] [*German military - World War II*] .... NA
Nachrichtenregiment [*Signal Regiment*] [*German military - World War II*] .... NR
Nachtjagugeschwader [*Night Fighter*] [*German*] .... NJG
Nacional Financiera [*National Finance Coro.*] [*Spanish*] (AD) .. NAFINSA
Nacionalista [*Nationalist Party*] [*Spain*] [*Political party*] (AD) .. PN
Nacionalista Party [*Philippines*] .... NP
Nacionalna Biblioteka na Makedonija "Kliment Ohridaki", Skopje, Yugoslavia [*Library symbol Library of Congress*] (LCLS) .... YuSkN
Nacionalna i Sveucilisna Biblioteka [*National and University Library of Croatia*], Zagreb, Yugoslavia [*Library symbol Library of Congress*] (LCLS) .... YuZU
Nacka [*Sweden ICAO location identifier*] (ICLI) .... ESHN
Nacogdoches & Southeastern Railroad (IIA) .... N & SE
Nacogdoches, TX [*AM radio station call letters*] .... KEEE
Nacogdoches, TX [*FM radio station call letters*] .... KJCS
Nacogdoches, TX [*Television station call letters*] .... KLSB
Nacogdoches, TX [*FM radio station call letters*] .... KSAU
Nacogdoches, TX [*AM radio station call letters*] .... KSFA
Nacogdoches, TX [*FM radio station call letters*] .... KTBQ
Nacogdoches, TX [*Location identifier FAA*] (FAAL) .... OCH
Nacoia Lda. [*Angola*] [*FAA designator*] (FAAC) .... ANL
N-(Acridinyl)maleimide [*Organic chemistry*] .... NAM
N-Acylethanolamine [*Organic chemistry*] .... NAE
NADGE [*NATO Air Defense Ground Environment*] **Early Warning Program Information Leaflet** (NATG) .... NEWPIL
NADGE [*NATO Air Defense Ground Environment*] **Improvement Plan** (NATG) .... NIP
NADGE [*NATO Air Defense Ground Environment*] **Logistics Committee** (NATG) .... NLC
NADGE [*NATO Air Defense Ground Environment*] **Management Office** [*Belgium*] .... NADGEMO
NADGE [*NATO Air Defense Ground Environment*] **Policy Board** (NATG) ..... NPB
Nadi [*Fiji*] [*Airport symbol*] (OAG) .... NAN
Nadic-Terminated Imide [*Polymer technology*] .... NTI
Nadir (WGA) .... NA
Nadir (WDAA) .... NAD
Nadir (AD) .... nad
Nadir Climate Interferometer Spectrometer (MCD) .... NCIS
Nador [*Morocco*] [*Airport symbol*] (AD) .... NDR
Nador/Taouima [*Morocco*] [*ICAO location identifier*] (ICLI) .... GMFN
Nadym Airlines [*Russian Federation*] [*ICAO designator*] (FAAC) .. NDM
Nadzab [*Papua New Guinea*] [*ICAO location identifier*] (ICLI) .... AYNZ
Naein [*Iran*] [*ICAO location identifier*] (ICLI) .... OIFN
Nafcillin [*An antibiotic*] .... NF
Nafimidone [*Biochemistry*] .... NAF
Naft Air Lines [*Iran*] [*FAA designator*] (FAAC) .... IRG
Naft-E-Shah [*Iran*] [*ICAO location identifier*] (ICLI) ...... OICF
Nag Hammadi Studies [*A publication*] (BJA) .... NagHammSt
Nag Hammadi Studies [*A publication*] (BJA) .... NHS
Naga [*Phillipines*] [*Airport symbol*] (OAG) .... WNP
Naga, Camarines Sur [*Philippines*] [*ICAO location identifier*] (ICLI) .... RPUN
Naga Federal Army [*India*] .... NFA
Naga National Council [*India*] (PD) .... NNC
Naga National Democratic Party [*India*] [*Political party*] (PPW) .. NNDP
Naga Nationalist Organization [*India*] .... NNO

Nagaland Federal Government [*India*] .... NFG
Nagano [*Japan*] [*Seismograph station code, US Geological Survey*] (SEIS) .... NGN
Nagarjunsagar [*India*] [*ICAO location identifier*] (ICLI) .... VONS
Nagasaki [*Japan*] (AD) .... Nag
Nagasaki [*Japan*] (AD) .... Nagas
Nagasaki [*Japan*] [*Seismograph station code, US Geological Survey*] (SEIS) .... NGS
Nagasaki [*Japan*] [*Airport symbol*] (OAG) .... NGS
Nagasaki [*Japan ICAO location identifier*] (ICLI) .... RJFU
Nagase Analbuminemia Rat .... NAR
Nagatsuro [*Irozaki*] [*Japan*] [*Seismograph station code, US Geological Survey*] (SEIS) .... NGT
Naghadeh [*Iran*] [*ICAO location identifier*] (ICLI) .... OITG
Nago [*Ryukyu Islands*] [*Seismograph station code, US Geological Survey*] (SEIS) .... NGO
Nagorno-Karabakh Autonomous Oblast .... NKAO
Nagoya [*Japan*] [*Seismograph station code, US Geological Survey*] (SEIS) .... NAG
Nagoya [*Japan*] (AD) .... Nag
Nagoya [*Japan*] [*Airport symbol*] (OAG) .... NGO
Nagoya [*Japan ICAO location identifier*] (ICLI) .... RJNN
Nagoya Bumpy Torus [*Military*] .... NBT
Nagpur [*India*] [*Airport symbol*] (OAG) .... NAG
Nagpur [*India*] [*ICAO location identifier*] (ICLI) .... VANP
Nagpur, India (AD) .... Nagp
Nagpur Law Journal [*India*] [*A publication*] (DLA) .... Nag LJ
Nagpur Law Journal [*India*] [*A publication*] (DLA) .... NLJ
Nagpur Law Notes [*India*] [*A publication*] (DLA) .... Nag LN
Nagpur Law Reports [*India*] [*A publication*] (DLA) .... Nag LR
Nagpur Law Reports [*India*] [*A publication*] (DLA) .... NLR
Nagpur University. College of Law. Magazine [*1933-34*] [*India*] [*A publication*] (DLA) .... Nag UCL Mag
Nags Head, NC [*FM radio station call letters*] .... WNHW
Naguabo, PR [*FM radio station call letters*] .... WYQE
Nagycenk [*Hungary*] [*Geomagnetic observatory code*] .... NCK
Naha [*Ryukyu Islands*] [*Seismograph station code, US Geological Survey*] (SEIS) .... NAH
Naha [*Ryukyu Islands*] [*Airport symbol*] (OAG) .... NAH
Naha [*Ryukyu Islands*] [*ICAO location identifier*] (ICLI) .... ROAH
Naha [*Ryukyu Islands*] [*ICAO location identifier*] (ICLI) .... RORG
Naha United States Naval Base [*Ryukyu Islands*] [*ICAO location identifier*] (ICLI) .... RONA
Nahal Hever Caves (BJA) .... Hev
Nahanni Air Services Ltd. [*Canada ICAO designator*] (FAAC) .... NAH
Nahanni Mines Ltd. [*Toronto Stock Exchange symbol*] .... NHA
Nahanni National Park, Parks Canada [*Parc National Nahanni, Parcs Canada*] **Fort Simpson, Northwest Territories** [*Library symbol National Library of Canada*] (NLC) .... NWFSPCN
Nahariya to Ashkelon [*Proposed name for possible "super-city" formed by the urban sprawl between these two*] [*Israel*] .... NASH
Nahavand [*Iran*] [*ICAO location identifier*] (ICLI) .... OIHN
NAHB Remodelers Council (EA) .... NAHB/RC
Nahichevan Autonomous Soviet Socialist Republic (AD) .... NASSR
Nahrungs Einheit Milch [*Nahrungsteinheit Milch*] [*Nutritional milk unit*] [*Dietetics*] (DAVI) .... nem
NAHU, an Association of Bull Users [*Formerly, North American Honeywell Users Association*] (EA) .... NAHU
Nahuatlan [*MARC language code Library of Congress*] (LCCP) .... nah
Nahud [*Sudan*] [*ICAO location identifier*] (ICLI) .... HSNH
Nahum [*Old Testament book*] .... Na
[*The Book of*] **Nahum** (AD) .... Nah
Nahum [*Old Testament book*] .... Nah
Nahum [*Bible*] .... NH
NAI Technologies [*Associated Press*] (SAG) .... NAI Tc
NAI Technologies [*Associated Press*] (SAG) .... NAI Tech
NAI Technologies [*NASDAQ symbol*] (SAG) .... NATL
Naiashquan [*Canada*] [*Airport symbol*] (OAG) .... YNA
Naik [*British military*] (DMA) .... Nk
Naikliu [*Indonesia*] [*ICAO location identifier*] (ICLI) .... WRKN
Nail .... N
Nail Manufacturers Council (EA) .... NMC
Nailable [*Technical drawings*] .... NA
Nailable [*Technical drawings*] .... NL
Nailfold Capillary Microscope (DAVI) .... NCM
NAIM [*North American Indian Mission*] **Ministries** (EA) .... NAIM
Nainital (Pantnagar) [*India*] [*ICAO location identifier*] (ICLI) .... VIPT
Naira [*Monetary unit*] [*Nigeria*] .... Na
Nairnshire, Scotland (AD) .... Nairns
Nairobi [*Kenya*] [*ICAO location identifier*] (ICLI) .... HKNC
Nairobi [*Kenya*] [*Seismograph station code, US Geological Survey*] (SEIS) .... NAI
Nairobi [*Kenya*] [*Airport symbol*] (OAG) .... NBO
Nairobi/Eastleigh [*Kenya*] [*ICAO location identifier*] (ICLI) .... HKRE
Nairobi/Jomo Kenyatta International [*Kenya*] [*ICAO location identifier*] (ICLI) .... HKNA
Nairobi Peoples' Convention Party .... NPCP
Nairobi Sheep Disease [*Medicine*] (DMAA) .... NSD
Nairobi/Wilson [*Kenya*] [*ICAO location identifier*] (ICLI) .... HKNW
Nairobi-Wilson [*Kenya*] [*Airport symbol*] (OAG) .... WIL
Naismith Memorial Basketball Hall of Fame (EA) .... NMBHF
Naivasha [*Kenya*] [*ICAO location identifier*] (ICLI) .... HKNV
Najaf Abad [*Iran*] [*ICAO location identifier*] (ICLI) .... OIFJ
Nakano [*Japan*] [*Seismograph station code, US Geological Survey*] (SEIS) .... NNJ
Nakanohara [*Japan*] [*Seismograph station code, US Geological Survey*] (SEIS) .... NKR
Nakashibetsu [*Japan ICAO location identifier*] (ICLI) .... RJCN
Nakashibetsu [*Japan*] [*Airport symbol*] (OAG) .... SHB
Nake [*Tuamotu Archipelago*] [*Seismograph station code, US Geological Survey*] (SEIS) .... NAE
Nake [*Ryukyu Islands*] [*Seismograph station code, US Geological Survey Closed*] (SEIS) .... NKE
Naked Vision .... NV
Naked Weight .... NW
Naked Wire (IAA) .... NW
Nakhichevan [*Former USSR Seismograph station code, US Geological Survey Closed*] (SEIS) .... NAK
Nakhla [*Morocco*] [*Seismograph station code, US Geological Survey*] (SEIS) .... NKM
Nakhon Pathom/Kamphaeng Saen [*Thailand*] [*ICAO location identifier*] (ICLI) .... VTBK
Nakhon Phanom [*Thailand*] [*Airport symbol Obsolete*] (OAG) .... KOP
Nakhon Phanom [*Thailand*] [*ICAO location identifier*] (ICLI) .... VTUP
Nakhon Phanom Royal Thai Air Base [*Leased by USAF during the Vietnam War*] (VNW) .... NKP RTAB
Nakhon Phanom (West) [*Thailand*] [*ICAO location identifier*] (ICLI) .... VTUW
Nakhon Ratchasima [*Thailand*] [*ICAO location identifier*] (ICLI) .... VTUN
Nakhon Ratchasima/Pak Chong [*Thailand*] [*ICAO location identifier*] (ICLI) .... VTUH
Nakhon Sawan [*Thailand*] [*ICAO location identifier*] (ICLI) .... VTPN
Nakhon Sawan/Takhli [*Thailand*] [*ICAO location identifier*] (ICLI) .... VTPI
Nakhon Si Thammarat [*Thailand*] [*ICAO location identifier*] (ICLI) .... VTSN
Nakina, ON [*ICAO location identifier*] (ICLI) .... CYQN
Nakina Public Library, Ontario [*Library symbol National Library of Canada*] (BIB) .... ONA
Naklad [*Edition*] [*Polish*] (AD) .... nakl
Nakladatel [*Edition*] [*Czech*] (AD) .... nakl
Naknek [*Alaska*] [*Airport symbol*] (OAG) .... NNK
Naknek, AK [*FM radio station call letters*] .... KAKN
Nakorn Phanom [*Air base northeast of Bangkok*] .... NKP
Nakskov [*Denmark ICAO location identifier*] (ICLI) .... EKNS
Nakuru [*Kenya*] [*ICAO location identifier*] (ICLI) .... HKNK
Nakusp Museum, British Columbia [*Library symbol National Library of Canada*] (NLC) .... BNAKM
Nakusp Museum, Nakusp, BC, Canada [*Library symbol*] [*Library of Congress*] (LCLS) .... CaBNAKM
Nakusp Public Library, British Columbia [*Library symbol National Library of Canada*] (NLC) .... BNA
Nakusp Public Library, Nakusp, BC, Canada [*Library symbol*] [*Library of Congress*] (LCLS) .... CaBNA
Nakusp Resources Ltd. [*Vancouver Stock Exchange symbol*] .... NKU
NAL Financial Group [*NASDAQ symbol*] (TTSB) .... NALF
NAL Financial Group, Inc. [*Associated Press*] (SAG) .... NAL Fn
NAL Financial Group, Inc. [*NASDAQ symbol*] (SAG) .... NALF
Nalcap Holdings, Inc. [*Vancouver Stock Exchange symbol*] .... NPH
Nalco Chemical [*NYSE symbol*] (TTSB) .... NLC
Nalco Chemical Co. [*Associated Press*] (SAG) .... Nalco
Nalco Chemical Co. [*NYSE symbol*] (SPSG) .... NLC
Nalcus Resources [*Vancouver Stock Exchange symbol*] .... NAU
N-Allylnormetazocine [*Biochemistry*] .... NANM
N-Allylnormorphine [*Narcotic antagonist*] .... NANM
N-Allylnoroxymorphone [*Narcotic antagonist*] .... NALOXONE
Naloxone [*A drug*] .... NAL
Nal-Tel [*Race of maize*] .... N-T
Nalton's Collection of State Papers [*A publication*] (DLA) .... Nal St P
Naltrexone [*A drug*] .... NALT
NAM Corp. [*Associated Press*] (SAG) .... NAM
NAM Corp. [*Associated Press*] (SAG) .... NAM Cp
NAM Corp. [*NASDAQ symbol*] (SAG) .... NAMC
Nam Tai Electronics [*NASDAQ symbol*] (TTSB) .... NTAIF
Nam Tai Electronics, Inc. [*Associated Press*] (SAG) .... NamTai
Nam Tai Electronics, Inc. [*NASDAQ symbol*] (NQ) .... NTAI
Namakwaland Lugdiens [*ICAO designator*] (AD) .... NJ
Namakwaland Lugdiens Bpk [*South Africa*] [*ICAO designator*] (ICDA) .... NJ
Namakwaland Lugdiens (EDMS) BPK [*South Africa ICAO designator*] (FAAC) .... NLD
Namangan [*Former USSR Seismograph station code, US Geological Survey Closed*] (SEIS) .... NAM
Namatanai [*Papua New Guinea*] [*Airport symbol*] (OAG) .... ATN
Namatoni [*Namibia*] [*ICAO location identifier*] (ICLI) .... FANA
NAMBA [*North American Model Boating Association*] **International** (EA) .... NI
Name .... N
Name, Address, and Legal File [*Real estate*] .... NAL
Name and Address .... N/A
Name and Address File [*IRS*] .... NAF
Name and Address Key Index File [*IRS*] .... KIF
Name and Address Update File [*IRS*] .... NAUF
Name Authority Co-Operative (NITA) .... NACO
Name Binding Protocol [*Computer science*] .... NBP
Name Changed To .... NCT
Name Control [*IRS*] .... NC
Name Formula Card .... NFC
Name Index .... NAMDEX
Name Information Correlation Key .... NICK
Name of Publisher (NITA) .... NP
Name on End-Paper [*Antiquarian book trade*] .... N/EP
Name Plate [*Automotive engineering*] .... N/PLT
Name, Rate, and Service Number [*Navy*] .... NARANO
Name, Rate, Service Number, and Expiration of Obligated Service [*Navy*] .... NARANEXOS
Name Registration Scheme [*Telecommunications*] (OSI) .... NRS
Name Removed from End-Paper [*Antiquarian book trade*] .... NREP
Name To (AAG) .... NTO

Name Unknown ... NU
Named ... NAM
Named (ROG) ... ND
Named Areas of Interest [*Army intelligence matrix*] (INF) ... NAI
Namens Trau- und Sterberegister der Judenschaft [*A publication*] (BJA) ... NTS
Nameplate ... NP
Nameplate (MSA) ... NPL
Names (ABBR) ... NN
Names Project Foundation (EA) ... NPF
[*The*] **Names Society** (EA) ... TNS
Namesake (ABBR) ... NMSK
Namib Air [*ICAO designator*] (AD) ... SW
Namib Air (Pty) Ltd. [*Namibia*] [*ICAO designator*] (FAAC) ... NMB
Namibia [*ANSI two-letter standard code*] (CNC) ... NA
Namibia [*ANSI three-letter standard code*] (CNC) ... NAM
Namibia (AD) ... Namib
Namibia [*International vehicle registration*] (ODBW) ... SWA
Namibia Independence Party [*Political party*] (PPW) ... NIP
Namibia National Front [*Political party*] (PPW) ... NNF
Namibie Christelike Demokratiese Party [*Namibian Christian Democratic Party*] [*Political party*] (PPW) ... NCDP
Namlea [*Indonesia*] [*Airport symbol*] (OAG) ... NAM
Namlea [*Indonesia*] [*ICAO location identifier*] (ICLI) ... WAPR
Namligen [*Namely*] [*Swedish*] (AD) ... naml
Namorik [*Marshall Islands*] [*Airport symbol*] (OAG) ... NDK
Nampa, ID [*AM radio station call letters*] ... KFXD
Nampa, ID [*FM radio station call letters*] ... KFXD-FM
Nampa, ID [*Television station call letters*] ... KIVI
Nampa, ID [*FM radio station call letters*] ... KLCI
Nampa, ID [*AM radio station call letters*] ... KTIK
Nampa, ID [*Television station call letters*] ... KTRV
Nampa, ID [*Location identifier FAA*] (FAAL) ... MPA
Nampa Municipal Library, Alberta [*Library symbol National Library of Canada*] (NLC) ... ANM
Nampa Municipal Library, Nampa, AB, Canada [*Library symbol*] [*Library of Congress*] (LCLS) ... CaANM
Nampa Public Library, Nampa, ID [*Library symbol*] [*Library of Congress*] (LCLS) ... IdN
Nampong [*Myanmar*] [*ICAO location identifier*] (ICLI) ... VBNP
Nampula [*Mozambique*] [*Airport symbol*] (OAG) ... APL
Nampula [*Mozambique*] [*ICAO location identifier*] (ICLI) ... FQNP
Namsang [*Myanmar*] [*Airport symbol*] (OAG) ... NMS
Namsang [*Myanmar*] [*ICAO location identifier*] (ICLI) ... VBNS
Namsos [*Norway ICAO location identifier*] (ICLI) ... ENNM
Namsos [*Norway*] [*Airport symbol*] (OAG) ... OSY
Namtu [*Myanmar*] [*ICAO location identifier*] (ICLI) ... VBNT
Namu [*Canada*] [*Airport symbol Obsolete*] (OAG) ... ZNU
Namudi [*Papua New Guinea*] [*Airport symbol*] (OAG) ... NDI
Namulonge Agrometeorology Station [*Uganda*] [*ICAO location identifier*] (ICLI) ... HUNA
Namur-Suarlee [*Belgium ICAO location identifier*] (ICLI) ... EBNM
Namwala [*Zambia*] [*ICAO location identifier*] (ICLI) ... FLNL
Nan [*Phonetic alphabet*] [*World War II*] (DSUE) ... N
Nan [*Thailand*] [*Airport symbol*] (OAG) ... NNT
Nan [*Thailand*] [*ICAO location identifier*] (ICLI) ... VTCN
Nan/Ban Pua [*Thailand*] [*ICAO location identifier*] (ICLI) ... VTCE
Nan/Chiang Klang [*Thailand*] [*ICAO location identifier*] (ICLI) ... VTCD
Nana [*Peru*] [*Seismograph station code, US Geological Survey*] (SEIS) ... NNA
Nanaimo [*Canada*] [*Airport symbol*] (OAG) ... YCD
Nanaimo, BC [*AM radio station call letters*] ... CKEG
Nanaimo, BC [*FM radio station call letters*] ... CKWV
Nanaimo, BC [*ICAO location identifier*] (ICLI) ... CYCD
Nanaimo Centennial Museum, British Columbia [*Library symbol National Library of Canada*] (NLC) ... BNCM
Nanaimo Centennial Museum, Nanaimo, BC, Canada [*Library symbol*] [*Library of Congress*] (LCLS) ... CaBNCM
Nanaimo [*Canada*] **Harbour Airport** [*Airport symbol*] (OAG) ... ZNA
Nanchang [*China*] [*Airport symbol*] (OAG) ... KHN
Nanchang [*China*] [*ICAO location identifier*] (ICLI) ... ZSCN
Nancy [*France*] [*Airport symbol*] (OAG) ... ENC
Nancy (AD) ... Nan
Nancy Ann Story Book [*Doll collecting*] ... NASB
Nancy Aviation [*France ICAO designator*] (FAAC) ... NCY
Nancy/Essey [*France ICAO location identifier*] (ICLI) ... LFSN
Nancy Fisher Fan Club (EA) ... NFFC
Nancy/Ochey [*France ICAO location identifier*] (ICLI) ... LFSO
Nancy Sinatra Fan Club (EA) ... NSFC
Nancy-Azelot [*France ICAO location identifier*] (ICLI) ... LFEX
Nancy-Malzeville [*France ICAO location identifier*] (ICLI) ... LFEZ
Nanded [*India*] [*ICAO location identifier*] (ICLI) ... VAND
Nandi [*Fiji*] [*Seismograph station code, US Geological Survey*] (SEIS) ... NDF
Nandi [*Fiji*] [*ICAO location identifier*] (ICLI) ... NFFF
Nandi/International [*Fiji*] [*ICAO location identifier*] (ICLI) ... NFFN
Nandina Mosaic Virus [*Plant pathology*] ... NANMV
Nandina Stem-Pitting Virus [*Plant pathology*] ... NSPV
Nandrolone Furylpropionate [*Pharmacology*] ... NFP
Naneco Resources Ltd. [*Vancouver Stock Exchange symbol*] ... NRL
Nanette (AD) ... Nan
Nanga Parbat/Haramosh Axis [*Himalayan geology*] ... NPHA
Nangang University, Singapore, Singapore [*Library symbol Library of Congress*] (LCLS) ... SgpNU
Nangapinoh [*Indonesia*] [*ICAO location identifier*] (ICLI) ... WIOG
Nangis/Les Loges [*France ICAO location identifier*] (ICLI) ... LFAI
Nanisivik [*Canada*] [*Airport symbol*] (OAG) ... YSR
Nanisivik/Strathcona Sound, NT [*ICAO location identifier*] (ICLI) ... CYSR
Nanjing [*China*] [*Airport symbol*] (OAG) ... NKG
Nanjing [*China*] [*ICAO location identifier*] (ICLI) ... ZSNJ
Nanjing Airlines [*China*] [*FAA designator*] (FAAC) ... CNJ
Nanjing Institute of Geology and Paleontology [*China*] ... NIG&P
Nanki Shirahama [*Japan*] [*Airport symbol*] (OAG) ... SHM
Nanking [*China*] (AD) ... Nan
Nanking [*Republic of China*] [*Seismograph station code, US Geological Survey*] (SEIS) ... NAN
Nankipoo [*Tennessee*] [*Seismograph station code, US Geological Survey*] (SEIS) ... NKT
Nanki-Shirahama [*Japan ICAO location identifier*] (ICLI) ... RJBD
Nannies Need Nannies Association [*British*] (DBA) ... NNN
Nanning [*China*] [*Airport symbol*] (OAG) ... NNG
Nanning/Wuxu [*China*] [*ICAO location identifier*] (ICLI) ... ZGNN
Nanny Academy of America [*Defunct*] (EA) ... NAA
Nanny Pop-Ins Association [*Defunct*] (EA) ... NPIA
Nano [*A prefix meaning divided by one billion*] [*SI symbol*] ... n
Nano Glass Pellet ... NGP
Nanoampere [*One billionth of an ampere*] ... nA
Nanobar [*One billionth of a bar*] ... nbar
Nanobarn [*Unit of Measure*] ... NB
Nanochannel Glass ... NCG
Nanocurie [*Pne billionth of a curie*] ... nc
Nanocurie [*One billionth of a curie*] ... nCi
Nanofarad [*One billionth of a farad*] ... nF
Nanofiltration ... NF
Nano-Goldblatt Units [*Clinical chemistry*] ... nGU
Nanogram [*One billionth of a gram*] ... ng
Nanogram [*Measurement*] (DAVI) ... ngm
Nanograms [*One billionth of a gram*] **per Milliliter** ... ng/ml
Nanohenry [*One billionth of a henry*] (IEEE) ... nH
Nanojoule [*One billionth of a joule*] ... nJ
Nanoliter [*One billionth of a liter*] (MAE) ... nl
Nanomemory (IAA) ... NM
Nanometer [*One billionth of a meter*] ... nm
Nanometrics, Inc. [*NASDAQ symbol*] (NQ) ... NANO
Nanometrics, Inc. [*Associated Press*] (SAG) ... NanomtR
Nanomole [*One billionth of a mole*] ... nM
Nanomole [*One billionth of a mole*] (MAE) ... nmol
Nanortalik [*Greenland*] [*ICAO location identifier*] (ICLI) ... BGNN
Nanosecond [*One billionth of a second*] [*Also, nsec*] ... ns
Nanosecond [*One billionth of a second*] [*Also, ns*] ... nsec
Nanotec Canada, Inc. [*Vancouver Stock Exchange symbol*] ... NNT
Nanotesla ... nT
Nanounit [*One billionth of a standard unit*] ... nU
Nanovolt [*One billionth of a volt*] (IEEE) ... nV
Nanowatt [*One billionth of a watt*] ... nW
Nantahala Regional Library, Murphy, NC [*Library symbol Library of Congress*] (LCLS) ... NcMuN
Nantes [*France*] [*Airport symbol*] (OAG) ... NTE
Nantes/Chateau Bougon [*France ICAO location identifier*] (ICLI) ... LFRS
Nanticoke, PA [*AM radio station call letters*] ... WNAK
Nanticoke, PA [*FM radio station call letters*] ... WSFX
Nanticoke, PA [*FM radio station call letters*] ... WTZR
Nanton Public Library, Alberta [*Library symbol National Library of Canada*] (NLC) ... ANA
Nantucket [*Massachusetts*] [*Airport symbol*] (OAG) ... ACK
Nantucket [*Massachusetts*] [*ICAO location identifier*] (ICLI) ... KACK
Nantucket Airlines [*ICAO designator*] (AD) ... DV
Nantucket Athenaeum, Nantucket, MA [*Library symbol Library of Congress*] (LCLS) ... MNam
Nantucket Historical Association, Nantucket, MA [*Library symbol Library of Congress*] (LCLS) ... MNanHi
Nantucket Indus [*AMEX symbol*] (TTSB) ... NAN
Nantucket Industries, Inc. [*AMEX symbol*] (SPSG) ... NAN
Nantucket Industries, Inc. [*Associated Press*] (SAG) ... Nantck
Nantucket, MA [*Location identifier FAA*] (FAAL) ... ETZ
Nantucket, MA [*Location identifier FAA*] (FAAL) ... TUK
Nantucket, MA [*Location identifier FAA*] (FAAL) ... TYT
Nantucket, MA [*FM radio station call letters*] ... WRZE
Nantucket Maria Mitchell Association, Nantucket, MA [*Library symbol Library of Congress*] (LCLS) ... MNanMM
Nantucket Whaling Museum, Nantucket, MA [*Library symbol Library of Congress*] (LCLS) ... MNanW
Nanuet Public Library, Nanuet, NY [*Library symbol Library of Congress*] (LCLS) ... NNan
Nanuet Public Library, Nanuet, NY [*Library symbol*] [*Library of Congress*] (LCLS) ... NNanL
Nanumea [*Tuvalu*] [*ICAO location identifier*] (ICLI) ... NGFO
Nanuque [*Brazil*] [*Airport symbol*] (AD) ... NNU
Nanyang [*China*] [*Airport symbol*] (OAG) ... NNY
Nanyang Commercial Bank [*China*] ... NCB
Nanyuki [*Kenya*] [*ICAO location identifier*] (ICLI) ... HKNY
Nanzan University Library [*UTLAS symbol*] ... CUN
Na'or Halutsi Lohem [*Fighting Pioneer Youth*] [*Israel*] (AD) ... Nahal
Naoro [*Papua New Guinea*] [*Airport symbol*] (OAG) ... NOO
Nap of the Earth [*Night helicopter flight*] [*Army*] ... NOE
Napa, CA [*Location identifier FAA*] (FAAL) ... APC
Napa, CA [*AM radio station call letters*] ... KVON
Napa, CA [*Location identifier FAA*] (FAAL) ... SGD
Napa City-County Library, Napa, CA [*Library symbol Library of Congress*] (LCLS) ... CN
Napa College, Napa, CA [*Library symbol Library of Congress*] (LCLS) ... CNC
Napa County Historical Society, Research Library, Napa, CA [*Library symbol*] [*Library of Congress*] (LCLS) ... CNCHi

Napa Resources, Inc. [*Vancouver Stock Exchange symbol*] ... NAP
Napa State Hospital, Imola, CA [*Library symbol Library of Congress*] (LCLS) ... CImoH
Napa Valley Grape Growers Association (EA) ... NVGGA
Napa Valley Vintners Association (EA) ... NVVA
Napa Valley Wine Library Association (EA) ... NVWLA
Napalm (AD) ... nap
NAPALM [*Naphthenic and Palmitic Acids*] (NATG) ... NP
NAPALM [*National ADP Program for AMC Logistics Management*] **Master File Record** ... NMFR
Napan [*West Irian, Indonesia*] [*Airport symbol*] (AD) ... NPA
Napaskiak [*Alaska*] [*Airport symbol*] (OAG) ... PKA
Napaskiak [*Alaska*] [*Airport symbol*] (OAG) ... WNA
Napaskiak, AK [*Location identifier FAA*] (FAAL) ... PKA
Napaskiak, AK [*Location identifier FAA*] (FAAL) ... WNA
Napay [*Former USSR Seismograph station code, US Geological Survey Closed*] (SEIS) ... NAP
Napco Security Sys [*NASDAQ symbol*] (TTSB) ... NSSC
Napco Security Systems, Inc. [*Associated Press*] (SAG) ... Napco
Napco Security Systems, Inc. [*NASDAQ symbol*] (NQ) ... NSSC
Naperian [*or Natural*] **Logarithm Base** [*2.7182818*] ... e
Naperville, IL [*FM radio station call letters*] ... WONC
Naphtali Herz Imber (BJA) ... NHI
Naphtha (AD) ... nap
Naphtha (AD) ... naph
Naphtha (ADA) ... NAPH
Naphthalene Creosote, Iodoform [*Powder for lice*] ... NCI
Naphthalene Dicarboxylate [*Organic chemistry*] ... NDC
Naphthalene Dicarboxylic Acid ... NA
Naphthalene Sulfonic Acid [*Organic chemistry*] ... NSA
Naphthaleneacetamide [*Herbicide*] ... NAD
Naphthaleneacetic Acid [*Biochemistry*] (DAVI) ... NAA
Naphthalenedicarboxaldehyde [*Organic chemistry*] ... NDA
Naphthalenedicarboxylic Acid [*Organic chemistry*] ... NDCA
Naphthalenemethylamine [*Reagent*] [*Organic chemistry*] ... NMA
Naphthene Palmitate (AD) ... napalm
Naphthenic Acid Corrosion Index ... NACI
Naphthenic and Palmitic Acids [*Major constituents of flame thrower*] ... NAPALM
Naphthenic-Palmitic Acid [*Mixture used in flame-throwing weapons and bombs*] [*Also, NAPALM*] (VNW) ... NAPE
Naphthoxyacetic Acid [*Organic chemistry*] ... NOXA
Naphthoyltrifluoroacetone [*Organic chemistry*] ... NTA
Naphthyl [*Organic chemistry*] (MAE) ... NAPH
Naphthyl (AD) ... naph
Naphthylacetamide [*Organic chemistry*] ... NA
Naphthylacetic [*or Napthaleneacetic*] **Acid** [*Organic chemistry*] ... NAA
Naphthylamine [*Organic chemistry*] ... NA
(Naphthyl)ethyl Urea [*Organic chemistry*] ... NEU
Naphthylethylenediamine Dihydrochloride [*Organic chemistry*] ... NED
Naphthylisocyanate [*Organic chemistry*] ... NIC
Naphthylphenyloxazole [*Biochemical analysis*] ... NPO
Naphthylphthalamic Acid [*Organic chemistry*] ... NPA
Napier [*New Zealand*] [*Airport symbol*] (OAG) ... NPE
Napier [*New Zealand*] [*Seismograph station code, US Geological Survey Closed*] (SEIS) ... NPR
Napier [*New Zealand*] [*ICAO location identifier*] (ICLI) ... NZNR
Napier Air Service, Inc. [*ICAO designator*] (FAAC) ... NAP
Napier. Prescription [*A publication*] (ILCA) ... Nap Pres
Napier's Bones [*First slide rule*] (AD) ... Nap's bones
Napierville Junction Railway Co. [*Later, NJ*] [*AAR code*] ... NAJ
Napierville Junction Railway Co. [*AAR code*] ... NJ
Naples [*Florida*] [*Airport symbol*] (OAG) ... APF
Naples [*Italy*] [*Airport symbol*] (OAG) ... NAP
Naples (AD) ... Nap
Naples [*Italy*] [*Seismograph station code, US Geological Survey Closed*] (SEIS) ... NPL
Naples Alcofuel Club [*Defunct*] (EA) ... NAC
Naples, FL [*Location identifier FAA*] (FAAL) ... CCE
Naples, FL [*AM radio station call letters*] ... WARO
Naples, FL [*FM radio station call letters*] (RBYB) ... WARO-FM
Naples, FL [*AM radio station call letters*] ... WNOG
Naples, FL [*FM radio station call letters*] ... WNOG-FM
Naples, FL [*FM radio station call letters*] ... WSGL
Naples, FL [*FM radio station call letters*] ... WSOR
Naples, FL [*FM radio station call letters*] ... WSRX
Naples, FL [*Television station call letters*] (RBYB) ... WTVK
Naples, FL [*Television station call letters*] (RBYB) ... WZVN-TV
Naples Park, FL [*FM radio station call letters*] ... WIXI
Naples Park, FL [*FM radio station call letters*] (RBYB) ... WXRM-FM
Nap-of-the-Earth Communications [*Night helicopter flight*] ... NOECOMM
Napoleon [*or Napoleonic*] ... NAP
Napoleon (AD) ... Nap
Napoleon Exploration [*Vancouver Stock Exchange symbol*] ... NXL
Napoleon, MO [*Location identifier FAA*] (FAAL) ... ANX
Napoleon, OH [*FM radio station call letters*] ... WNDH
Napoleonic Age Philatelists (EA) ... NAP
Napoleonic Association [*Enfield, Middlesex, England*] (EAIO) ... NA
Napoleonic Society of America (EA) ... NSA
Napoli/Capodichino [*Italy ICAO location identifier*] (ICLI) ... LIRN
Nappamerrie [*Queensland*] [*Airport symbol*] (AD) ... NMR
Nappan Experimental Farm, Nappan, NS, Canada [*Library symbol*] [*Library of Congress*] (LCLS) ... CaNSNE
Nappan Experimental Farm, Nova Scotia [*Library symbol National Library of Canada*] (NLC) ... NSNE
Nappanee Advance News, Nappanee, IN [*Library symbol Library of Congress*] (LCLS) ... InNapAN
Nappanee, IN [*FM radio station call letters*] ... WLRX
Nappanee Public Library, Nappanee, IN [*Library symbol Library of Congress*] (LCLS) ... InNap
Napped (ABBR) ... NPD
Napper (ABBR) ... NPR
Napping (ABBR) ... NPG
NaPro Bio Therapeutics [*NASDAQ symbol*] (TTSB) ... NPRO
NaPro BioTherapeutics, Inc. [*Associated Press*] (SAG) ... NaPro
NaPro BioTherapeutics, Inc. [*Associated Press*] (SAG) ... NaProBio
NaPro BioTherapeutics, Inc. [*NASDAQ symbol*] (SAG) ... NPRO
Napro Biotheraputics Wrrts [*NASDAQ symbol*] (TTSB) ... NPROW
Napton's Reports [*4 Missouri*] [*A publication*] (DLA) ... Napt
Napton's Reports [*4 Missouri*] [*A publication*] (DLA) ... Napton
Napuka [*Marquesas Islands*] [*Airport symbol*] (OAG) ... NAU
Napuka [*French Polynesia*] [*ICAO location identifier*] (ICLI) ... NTGN
Nara [*Japan*] [*Seismograph station code, US Geological Survey*] (SEIS) ... NAR
Nara [*Mali*] [*Airport symbol*] (OAG) ... NRM
Nara/Keibane [*Mali*] [*ICAO location identifier*] (ICLI) ... GANK
Naramata Museum, British Columbia [*Library symbol National Library of Canada*] (NLC) ... BNAM
Naramata Museum, Naramata, BC, Canada [*Library symbol*] [*Library of Congress*] (LCLS) ... CaBNAM
Naram-Sin (BJA) ... NS
Naranaup [*India*] [*ICAO location identifier*] (ICLI) ... VINL
Naranjito, PR [*Television station call letters*] ... WECN
Naranjo (Severs) [*Costa Rica*] [*ICAO location identifier*] (ICLI) ... MRNJ
Narathiwat [*Thailand*] [*Airport symbol*] (OAG) ... NAW
Narathiwat [*Thailand*] [*ICAO location identifier*] (ICLI) ... VTSC
Narbonne [*France ICAO location identifier*] (ICLI) ... LFXN
Narcisism (ABBR) ... NRCSM
Narcisist (ABBR) ... NRCST
Narcisistic (ABBR) ... NRSTK
Narcissistic Personality Disorder [*Medicine*] (DMAA) ... NPD
Narcissistic Personality Inventory [*Psychology*] (EDAC) ... NPI
Narcissus Latent Virus ... NLV
Narcissus Mosaic Virus [*Plant pathology*] ... NAMV
Narcissus Tip Necrosis Virus [*Plant pathology*] ... NTNV
Narcissus Yellow Stripe Virus [*Plant pathology*] ... NYSV
Narcolepsy [*Neurology*] (DAVI) ... narco
Narcolepsy and Cataplexy Foundation of America (EA) ... NCFA
Narcolepsy Association [*British*] (DBA) ... NA
Narcotic (ROG) ... NAR
Narcotic (AD) ... narc
Narcotic (AD) ... narco
Narcotic (AD) ... narcot
Narcotic (ABBR) ... NRCTK
Narcotic Addict Rehabilitation Branch [*National Institute of Mental Health*] ... NARB
Narcotic Addict Treatment Act of 1974 ... NATA
Narcotic and Drug Research, Inc., New York, NY [*Library symbol*] [*Library of Congress*] (LCLS) ... NNNDR
Narcotic Drugs Supervisory Body [*UN*] ... NDSB
Narcotic Educational Foundation of America (EA) ... NEFA
Narcotic Traffic Dollars (AD) ... narcodollars
Narcotic-Addict Registration Card (AD) ... narcocard
Narcotics [*FBI standardized term*] ... NARC
Narcotics (AD) ... narcos
Narcotics (AD) ... narcs
Narcotics Addict Rehabilitation Act [*1966*] ... NARA
Narcotics Agent (AD) ... narc
Narcotics Agents (AD) ... narcs
Narcotics and Dangerous Drugs Intelligence File (AD) ... NADDIS
Narcotics Anonymous (EA) ... NA
Narcotics Anonymous [*An association*] (AD) ... Narconon
Narcotics Assistance Unit [*Department of State*] ... NAU
Narcotics Commission [*United Nations*] ... NARCO
Narcotics Commission [*United Nations*] (AD) ... NARCO
Narcotics Coordination Group [*CIA*] ... NARCOG
Narcotics Education [*An association*] (EA) ... NE
Narcotics Education, Inc. (EA) ... NEI
Narcotics Hospital (DAVI) ... narco
Narcotics Hospital (AD) ... narcs
Narcotics Intelligence [*Military*] (ADDR) ... NARCINT
Narcotics Investigation (AD) ... Nar Inv
Narcotics Law Bulletin [*A publication*] (DLA) ... Narcotics L Bull
Narcotics Officer (AD) ... narco
Narcotics Officer ... NO
Narcotics Officers (AD) ... narcs
Narcotics Police Officers (AD) ... narcos
Narcotics Prevention Service (NADA) ... NPS
Narcotics Test (AD) ... narcotest
Narcotics Traffick (AD) ... narco-traf
Narcotics Treatment Administration [*Washington, DC*] ... NTA
Narcotics Treatment Center (DAVI) ... narco
Narcotics Treatment Centers (AD) ... narcs
Narcotism [*Chemical dependency*] (DAVI) ... NARC
Nare [*Colombia*] [*Airport symbol*] (OAG) ... NAR
Nares' Penal Convictions [*1815*] [*A publication*] (DLA) ... Nar Conv
Nargana [*Panama*] [*Airport symbol*] (OAG) ... NGN
N-Arginine Dibasic Convertase [*An enzyme*] ... NRDC
Naringenin [*Organic chemistry*] ... N
Naris [*Nostril*] [*Pharmacy*] ... N
Naristillae [*Nasal Drops*] [*Latin*] (AD) ... narist

Naristillae [*Nasal Drops*] [*Pharmacy*] ..... NARIST
Narmashir [*Iran*] [*ICAO location identifier*] (ICLI) ..... OIKN
Narodna Biblioteka Socijalisticke Republike Srbije, Beograd, Yugoslavia [*Library symbol Library of Congress*] (LCLS) ..... YuBN
Narodna Republika Bulgaria [*Bulgarian People's Republic*] [*Political party*] (AD) ..... Nar Rep Bul
Narodna Stranka [*People's Party*] [*Montenegro*] [*Political party*] (EY) ..... NS
Narodne Biblioteka Bosne i Hercegovine [*National Library of Bosnia and Herzegovina*], Sarajevo, Yugoslavia [*Library symbol Library of Congress*] (LCLS) ..... YuSaN
Narodni Divadlo [*National Theater*] [*Czechoslavakia*] (AD) ..... Nar Div
Narodni Fronta [*National Front*] [*Former Czechoslovakia*] [*Political party*] (PPE) ..... NF
Narodno Trudovoi Soyuz [*People's Labor Union*] [*Frankfurt, Federal Republic of Germany*] (PD) ..... NTS
Narodnoliberalna Partiia [*National Liberal Party*] [*Bulgaria*] [*Political party*] (PPE) ..... NLP
Narodny Komissariat Vneshney Torgovli [*People's Commissariate of Foreign Trade*] [*Russian*] (AD) ..... Narkomvneshtorg
Narodnye Sotsialisty [*Popular Socialists*] [*Former USSR Political party*] (PPE) ..... NS
Narodnyi Komissariat Gosudarstvennoe Bezopasnosti-Narodnyi Komissariat Vnutrennikh Del [*Later, KGB*] ..... NKGB-NKVD
Narodnyi Komissariat Oborony [*People's Commissariat of Defense*] [*Existed until 1946*] [*Former USSR*] ..... NKO
Narodnyi Komissariat Vnutrennikh Del [*People's Commissariat of Internal Affairs (1917-1946)*] [*Also known as NKVD Soviet secret police organization*] ..... NARKOMVNUDEL
Narodnyi Kommissariat Vnutrennikh Del [*People's Commissariat for Internal Affairs*] [*Former USSR*] (NADA) ..... NKVD
Narodnyy Komissariat Inostrannykh Del [*People's Commissariat of Foreign Affairs*] [*Former USSR*] (LAIN) ..... NKID
Narodnyy Komissariat Voyenno-Morskogo Flota [*People's Commissariat of the Navy*] [*Former USSR*] (LAIN) ..... NKVMF
Narodnyy Komissariat Yustitsii [*People's Commissariat of Justice*] [*Former USSR*] (LAIN) ..... NKYu
Narodowa Partia Robotnicza [*National Workers Party*] [*Poland Political party*] (PPE) ..... NPR
Narok [*Kenya*] [*ICAO location identifier*] (ICLI) ..... HKNO
Narrabri [*Australia Airport symbol*] (OAG) ..... NAA
Narragansett (AD) ..... Nar
Narragansett Environmental Research Laboratory [*Narragansett, RI*] [*Environmental Protection Agency*] (GRD) ..... ERL/NARR
Narragansett Marine Laboratory [*University of Rhode Island*] ..... NML
[*The*] **Narragansett Pier Railroad Co., Inc.** [*AAR code*] ..... NAP
[*The*] **Narragansett Pier Railroad Co. Inc.** (IIA) ..... NP
Narragansett Pier, RI [*FM radio station call letters*] ..... WPJB
Narramore Christian Foundation (EA) ..... NCF
Narrandera [*Australia Airport symbol*] (OAG) ..... NRA
Narrated (ABBR) ..... NRRAD
Narrating (ABBR) ..... NRRAG
Narration [*Films, television, etc.*] ..... NAR
Narration (ABBR) ..... NRRAN
Narration, Commentary [*Motion pictures*] ..... NARCOM
Narrationes Modernae [*Style's English King's Bench Reports*] [*1646-55*] [*A publication*] (DLA) ..... Narr Mod
Narrationum Amatoriarum Libellus [*of Parthenius*] [*Classical studies*] (OCD) ..... Amat Narr
Narrative (ABBR) ..... NRRAV
Narrative Accomplishment Reporting System [*Department of Agriculture*] [*Information service or system*] (IID) ..... NARS
Narrative End Item Report [*NASA*] (KSC) ..... NEIR
Narrative Output Vocabulary Editing Language [*Psychiatric test*] ..... NOVEL
Narrator [*or Narration*] ..... NARR
Narrator (ABBR) ..... NRRAR
Narrator [*MARC relator code*] [*Library of Congress*] (LCCP) ..... nrt
Narrogin [*Australia Seismograph station code, US Geological Survey*] (SEIS) ..... NWA
Narrogin [*Australia Seismograph station code, US Geological Survey*] (SEIS) ..... NWAO
Narrow [*Women's shoe width*] [*More than one "A" indicates increasing narrowness, up to AAAAA*] ..... A
Narrow [*Men's shoe width*] ..... B
Narrow ..... N
Narrow (AD) ..... nar
Narrow (AAG) ..... NAR
Narrow Absorption Infrared ..... NAIR
Narrow Angle ..... NA
Narrow Angle Glaucoma [*Medicine*] ..... NAG
Narrow Angle Sun Sensor (SAA) ..... NASS
Narrow Band ..... N/B
Narrow Band Device - Fix ..... NBDF
Narrow Band Digital Voice System [*Telecommunications*] (LAIN) ..... NBDVS
Narrow Band Gaussian Random Noise (PDAA) ..... NBGRN
Narrow Band Nerve [*Neurology*] (DAVI) ..... NBN
Narrow Beam (NATG) ..... NB
Narrow Coverage ..... NC
Narrow Fabrics Institute (EA) ..... NFI
Narrow Field of View ..... NFOV
Narrow Gauge ..... NG
Narrow Gauge Railway Society [*British*] ..... NGRS
Narrow Gauge Railways Ltd. [*Wales*] ..... NGR
Narrow Gauze Roll [*Medicine*] ..... NGR
Narrow Market [*Investment term*] ..... NM
Narrow Resonance [*Nuclear energy*] (NRCH) ..... NR
Narrow Resonance Infinite Absorber (PDAA) ..... NRIA
Narrow Resonance Infinite Mass [*Nuclear energy*] (NRCH) ..... NRIM
Narrow Spectral Band Detection ..... NSBD
Narrow Width Effect (IAA) ..... NWE
Narrow Widths [*Construction*] ..... NW
Narrow-Angle Acquisition ..... NAA
Narrow-Angle Mars Gate [*NASA*] ..... NAMG
Narrow-Angle Sensor ..... NAS
Narrow-Angle Target of Opportunity [*Photography*] [*NASA*] ..... NATO
Narrowband (IDOE) ..... n/b
Narrowband (IDOE) ..... nb
Narrowband ..... NB
Narrowband Allocation ..... NBA
Narrowband Analyzer ..... NBA
Narrowband Beam [*Physics*] ..... NBB
Narrowband Coherent Video (IEEE) ..... NBCV
Narrowband Communicative Services [*Telecommunications*] ..... NC
Narrowband Conducted (IEEE) ..... NBC
Narrowband Data Line ..... NBDL
Narrowband Data Link (IAA) ..... NBDL
Narrowband Detector ..... NBD
Narrowband Dicke-Fix [*Electronics*] (CET) ..... NBDF
Narrowband Dicke-Fix [*Electronics*] (MSA) ..... NBDFX
Narrowband Distributive Services [*Telecommunications*] ..... ND
Narrowband Filter ..... NBF
Narrowband Frequency Modulation [*Radio*] ..... NBFM
Narrowband Frequency Modulation [*Radio*] ..... NFM
Narrowband Frequency Shift Keying (MCD) ..... NFSK
Narrowband Linear Detector (MCD) ..... NBLD
Narrowband Network ..... NBN
Narrowband Noise ..... NBN
Narrow-Band Optimiziation of the Alignment of Highways (PDAA) ..... NOAH
Narrowband Phase Modulation (MCD) ..... NBPM
Narrowband Phase Modulation (DEN) ..... NPM
Narrowband Radiated (IEEE) ..... NBR
Narrowband Search (MCD) ..... NBS
Narrowband Secure Voice System [*Army*] (CAAL) ..... NBSV
Narrowband Secure Voice System [*Army*] (MCD) ..... NBSVS
Narrowband Subscriber Terminal (CET) ..... NBST
Narrowband Tape Recorder ..... NBTR
Narrowband Time Domain Reflectometry (MCD) ..... NBTDR
Narrow-Band Transmission of RADAR Pictures (MCD) ..... NATRAP
Narrowband Trunk Module [*Telecommunications*] ..... NTM
Narrow-Band Voice Modulation (PDAA) ..... NBVM
Narrowband Voice Security ..... NVS
Narrowband Voltage-Controlled Crystal Oscillator ..... NBVCXO
Narrow-Beam Adapter ..... NBA
Narrow-Beam Transducer [*National Ocean Survey*] ..... NBT
Narrowed (ABBR) ..... NRWD
Narrower Term [*Indexing*] ..... NT
Narrowing (ABBR) ..... NRWG
Narrow-Line Radio Galaxy ..... NLRG
Narrow-Minded (ABBR) ..... NRWMDD
Narrow-Mindedness (ABBR) ..... NRWMDDNS
Narrows [*Virginia*] [*Seismograph station code, US Geological Survey*] (SEIS) ..... NAV
Narrows, VA [*AM radio station call letters*] ..... WNRV
Narrows, VA [*FM radio station call letters*] ..... WZFM
Narssaq [*Greenland*] [*ICAO location identifier*] (ICLI) ..... BGNS
Narssarssuaq [*Greenland*] [*ICAO location identifier*] (ICLI) ..... BGBW
Narssarssuaq [*Denmark*] [*Geomagnetic observatory code*] ..... NAQ
Narssarssuaq [*Greenland*] [*Airport symbol*] (OAG) ..... UAK
Narthex (VRA) ..... nhx
Narvik [*Norway*] [*Airport symbol*] (OAG) ..... NVK
Narvik/Framnes [*Norway ICAO location identifier*] (ICLI) ..... ENNK
Naryn [*Former USSR Seismograph station code, US Geological Survey*] (SEIS) ..... NRN
NAS Interfacility Communications System [*FAA*] (TAG) ..... NICS
NAS Management Automation Program [*FAA*] (TAG) ..... NASMAP
NAS/NAE [*National Academy of Sciences/National Academy of Engineering*] **Science and Engineering Committee Advisory to NOAA** [*National Oceanic and Atmospheric Administration*] [*Defunct*] (USDC) ..... NAS/NAE-SECAN
Nas Precision Approach and Landing System [*FAA*] (TAG) ..... NASPALS
NAS System Engineering Service [*FAA*] (TAG) ..... ASE
NAS Transition Implementation Service [*FAA*] (TAG) ..... ANS
NASA Activities [*A publication*] ..... NACT
NASA Aerospace Safety Information System ..... NASIS
NASA Aircrew Oxygen System ..... NAOS
NASA Apollo Trajectory (KSC) ..... NAT
NASA Automated Systems Incident Response Capability ..... NASIRC
NASA Center for Intelligent Robotic System for Space Exploration [*Rensselaer Polytechnic Institute*] [*Research center*] (RCD) ..... CIRSSE
NASA Charging Analyzer Program (MCD) ..... NASCAP
NASA Class Code (NASA) ..... NCC
NASA Communications ..... Nascom
NASA Communications Network ..... NASCOM
NASA Communications Operating Procedures (MCD) ..... NASCOP
Nasa Cotopaxi [*Ecuador*] [*Seismograph station code, US Geological Survey*] (SEIS) ..... NCE
NASA Data Processing Facility (MCD) ..... NDPF
NASA Delta Quotation (MCD) ..... NDQ
NASA Document (KSC) ..... ND
NASA [*National Aeronautics and Space Administration*] **Document** ..... ND
NASA Earth Resources Data Annotation System (MCD) ..... NERDAS
NASA Electronic Research Center (IAA) ..... NASAERC

NASA End-to-End Data Systems .... NEEDS
NASA Energy-Cost Analysis Program .... NECAP
NASA Evaluation with Models of Optimized Nuclear Spacecraft .... NEW MOONS
NASA Expert Simulation System (NITA) .... NESS
NASA Grant Handbook .... NGH
NASA Ground Terminal (MCD) .... NGT
NASA Handbook (KSC) .... NHB
NASA Hazards Identification Committee (KSC) .... NHIC
NASA Headquarters .... NHQ
NASA Headquarters Computer Center .... NHCC
NASA Headquarters Telephone Directory .... NHTD
NASA Industrial Application Center [*University of Southern California*] [*Los Angeles*] [*Information service or system*] (IID) .... NIAC
NASA Industrial Applications Center [*University of Pittsburgh*] [*Pittsburgh, PA*] .... NIAC
NASA Interface Equipment (MCD) .... NIE
NASA Interface System (MCD) .... NIS
NASA Launch Director .... NLD
NASA Launch Vehicle Planning Project (MCD) .... NLVP
NASA Library Network [*NASA Washington, DC Library network*] (MCD) .... NALNET
NASA Management Delegations (MCD) .... NMD
NASA Management Instruction (KSC) .... NMI
NASA Management Issuance (MCD) .... NMI
NASA Management Manual .... NMM
NASA Merritt Island Launch Area (SAA) .... NMILA
NASA Notice .... NN
NASA Part Number (MCD) .... NPN
NASA Pasadena Office .... NAPO
NASA Pasadena Office (MCD) .... NPO
NASA Planning Studies (KSC) .... NPS
NASA Policy Directive .... NPD
NASA Procurement Circular .... NPC
NASA Procurement Regulation .... NAPR
NASA Procurement Regulation (KSC) .... NASPR
NASA Procurement Regulation Directive .... NPRD
NASA Procurement Regulation Supplement .... NPRS
NASA Program Director (SSD) .... NPD
NASA Publication Control (KSC) .... NPC
NASA Quality Control (KSC) .... NQC
NASA Research Announcement .... NRA
NASA Safety Standards Committee .... NSSC
NASA [*or NROSS*] **Scatterometer** [*Instrumentation*] .... NSCAT
NASA Science Internet .... NSI
NASA Scientific and Technical Reports (NITA) .... NASA-STAR
NASA Software Information System (SSD) .... NSIS
NASA Specialized Center for Research and Training .... NSCORT
NASA [*National Aeronautical and Space Administration*] **Standard Indicator** .... NSI
NASA Standard Initiator (NASA) .... NSI
NASA [*National Aeronautics and Space Administration*] **Standard Initiator -Type 1** [*Formerly, SMSI*] (NASA) NSI-1
NASA STI [*Scientific and Technical Information*] **Facility, BWI Airport, MD** [*Baltimore-Washington International*] [*OCLC symbol*] (OCLC) .... NAT
NASA Structural Analysis [*Computer program*] .... NASTRAN
NASA Support Operation (KSC) .... NSO
NASA Support Plan (KSC) .... NSP
NASA Tank Reactor .... NASA-TR
NASA Technology Readiness Level (SSD) .... NTRL
NASA Test Director (MCD) .... NTD
NASA Test Support .... NTS
NASA Test Support Office (KSC) .... NTSO
NASA Unmanned Launch Operations (MCD) .... NULO
NASA [*National Aeronautics and Space Administration*]/VAFB Payload Operati ons Working Group [*Vandenberg Air Force Base*] (NASA) .... NVPOWG
NASA/VAFB [*National Aeronautical and Space Administration/Vandenburg Air Force Base*] **Payload Operations Working Group** .... NVPOWG
NASA Waiver (KSC) .... NW
NASA Washington Office (KSC) .... NWO
NASA Worldwide Communications Network (MCD) .... NASCOM
Nasal .... N
Nasal (AD) .... nas
Nasal .... NAS
Nasal (DAVI) .... NASL
Nasal (ABBR) .... NSL
Nasal Airway Resistance [*Medicine*] .... NAR
Nasal Cannula [*Medicine*] (MEDA) .... NC
Nasal Cannula [*Medicine*] (DAVI) .... NC
Nasal Continuous Positive Airway Pressure [*Medicine*] (DMAA) .... N-CPAP
Nasal Deformity (DAVI) .... ND
Nasal Physical Examination .... NPE
Nasal Prongs [*For administration of oxygen*] (DAVI) .... NP
Nasal Provocation Test [*Immunology*] .... NPT
Nasally (ABBR) .... NSLY
Nasan [*Viet Nam*] [*ICAO location identifier*] (ICLI) .... VVNS
Nasangga [*Fiji*] [*Seismograph station code, US Geological Survey*] (SEIS) .... NAS
NASCAR [*National Association for Stock Car Auto Racing*] **Street Classics** [*Later, WW*] (EA) .... NSC
Nascence (ABBR) .... NSCNC
Nascent (ABBR) .... NSCNT
NASCOM [*NASA Communications Network*] **Assembly** .... NSCA
NASCOM [*Naval Air Systems Command*] **Manual Scheduling System** .... NMSS
NASCOM [*NASA Communications Network*] **Network Scheduling Group** .... NNSG
NASCOM [*NASA Communications Network*] **Simulation Traffic Interface** (SSD) .... NSTI
NASCOM System Control Interface [*NASA*] (MCD) .... NSCI
NASCOM System Development Plan .... NSDP
NASCOM User Traffic Interface [*NASA*] (MCD) .... NUTI
Naselle Youth Camp, Resident Library, Naselle, WA [*Library symbol Library of Congress*] (LCLS) .... WaNasY-R
Naselle Youth Camp, Staff Library, Naselle, WA [*Library symbol Library of Congress*] (LCLS) .... WaNasY
[*The*] **Nash and Cibinic Report** [*A publication*] (AAGC) .... N&CR
Nash Car Club of America (EA) .... NCCA
Nash Finch Co. [*NASDAQ symbol*] (SAG) .... NAFC
Nash Finch Co. [*NASDAQ symbol*] (TTSB) .... NAFC
Nash Finch Co. [*Associated Press*] (SAG) .... NashF
Nash Papyrus (BJA) .... NA
Nash Technical Institute, Rocky Mount, NC [*Library symbol Library of Congress*] (LCLS) .... NcRmN
Nash-Finch Co. [*NASDAQ symbol*] (NQ) .... NAFC
Nash-Healey [*Model of automobile, now out of production*] .... NH
Nash-Healey Car Club (EA) .... N-HCC
Nash-Kelvinator International [*Automobile manufacturer, now out of production*] .... NKI
Nashold Elementary School, Rockford, IL [*Library symbol*] [*Library of Congress*] (LCLS) .... IRoNaE
Nashotah House, Nashotah, WI [*OCLC symbol*] (OCLC) .... WIO
Nashotah House, Nashotah, WI [*Library symbol Library of Congress*] (LCLS) .... WNa
Nash's Ohio Pleading and Practice [*A publication*] (DLA) .... Nash Pl
Nashua Corp. [*Associated Press*] (SAG) .... Nashua
Nashua Corp. [*NYSE symbol*] (SPSG) .... NSH
Nashua, NH [*Location identifier FAA*] (FAAL) .... ASH
Nashua, NH [*FM radio station call letters*] .... WHOB
Nashua, NH [*AM radio station call letters*] .... WMVU
Nashua, NH [*AM radio station call letters*] .... WSMN
Nashua Public Library, Nashua, IA [*Library symbol Library of Congress*] (LCLS) .... IaNas
Nashua Public Library, Nashua, NH [*Library symbol Library of Congress*] (LCLS) .... NhNa
Nashua Reporter, Nashua, IA [*Library symbol Library of Congress*] (LCLS) .... IaNasR
Nashville [*Tennessee*] [*Derived from Berry Field-Nashville*] [*Airport symbol*] .... BNA
Nashville [*Tennessee*] (AD) .... Nash
Nashville [*Diocesan abbreviation*] [*Tennessee*] (TOCD) .... NSH
Nashville, AR [*AM radio station call letters*] .... KBHC
Nashville, AR [*FM radio station call letters*] .... KNAS
Nashville, Chattanooga & St. Louis [*Louisville & Nashville Railroad Co.*] [*AAR code*] .... NC
Nashville, Chattanooga & St. Louis Railway (IIA) .... NC & SL
Nashville, Chattanooga & St. Louis Railway .... NC & ST L
Nashville Community High School District 99, Nashville, IL [*Library symbol Library of Congress*] (LCLS) .... INasSD
Nashville Country Club [*Associated Press*] (SAG) .... NashCtr
Nashville Country Club [*NASDAQ symbol*] (SAG) .... NCCI
Nashville Country Club Wrrt [*NASDAQ symbol*] (TTSB) .... NCCIW
Nashville Entertainment Association (EA) .... NEA
Nashville, GA [*FM radio station call letters*] .... WJYF
Nashville, GA [*AM radio station call letters*] .... WNGA
Nashville High School, Nashville, IL [*Library symbol Library of Congress*] (LCLS) .... INasHS
Nashville, IL [*FM radio station call letters*] .... WNSR
Nashville, IN [*FM radio station call letters*] .... WVNI
Nashville Memorial Hospital, Madison, TN [*Library symbol Library of Congress*] (LCLS) .... TMadH
Nashville/Metropolitan [*Tennessee*] [*ICAO location identifier*] (ICLI) .... KBNA
Nashville Music Association [*Later, NEA*] (EA) .... NMA
[*The*] **Nashville Network** [*Cable-television system*] .... TNN
Nashville Public Library, Nashville, IL [*Library symbol Library of Congress*] (LCLS) .... INas
Nashville Public Library, Nashville, TN [*OCLC symbol*] (OCLC) .... TNN
Nashville Songwriters Association, International (EA) .... NSAI
Nashville State Technical Institute, Educational Resource Center, Nashville, TN [*Library symbol*] [*Library of Congress*] (LCLS) .... TNSTI
Nashville, TN [*Location identifier FAA*] (FAAL) .... PNO
Nashville, TN [*Location identifier FAA*] (FAAL) .... VIY
Nashville, TN [*Television station call letters*] .... WDCN
Nashville, TN [*AM radio station call letters*] .... WENO
Nashville, TN [*FM radio station call letters*] .... WFSK
Nashville, TN [*FM radio station call letters*] .... WJXA
Nashville, TN [*AM radio station call letters*] .... WKDA
Nashville, TN [*FM radio station call letters*] .... WKDF
Nashville, TN [*Television station call letters*] .... WKRN
Nashville, TN [*AM radio station call letters*] .... WLAC
Nashville, TN [*FM radio station call letters*] .... WLAC-FM
Nashville, TN [*AM radio station call letters*] .... WMDB
Nashville, TN [*Television station call letters*] .... WNAB
Nashville, TN [*AM radio station call letters*] .... WNAH
Nashville, TN [*FM radio station call letters*] .... WNAZ
Nashville, TN [*AM radio station call letters*] .... WNQM
Nashville, TN [*FM radio station call letters*] .... WPLN
Nashville, TN [*FM radio station call letters*] .... WRVU
Nashville, TN [*FM radio station call letters*] .... WSIX
Nashville, TN [*AM radio station call letters*] .... WSM
Nashville, TN [*FM radio station call letters*] .... WSM-FM
Nashville, TN [*Television station call letters*] .... WSMV
Nashville, TN [*Television station call letters*] .... WTVF
Nashville, TN [*TV station call letters*] (RBYB) .... WUXP-TV
Nashville, TN [*Television station call letters*] .... WXMT
Nashville, TN [*AM radio station call letters*] .... WYFN
Nashville, TN [*Television station call letters*] .... WZTV

Nashwauk, MN [*AM radio station call letters*] ... WKKQ
Nashwauk-Keewatin Senior High School, Nashwauk, MN [*Library symbol*] [*Library of Congress*] (LCLS) ... MnNaSH
Nasik [*India*] [*Airport symbol*] (OAG) ... ISK
Nasik Road [*India*] [*ICAO location identifier*] (ICLI) ... VANR
Nasion Pogonion [*Anatomy*] (MAE) ... NAP
Nasional, Agama, Kommunist [*Indonesian President Sukarno's policy of unity among National, Religious, and Communist forces*] ... NASAKOM
Nasionale Konserwatiewe Party [*National Conservative Party*] [*South Africa*] [*Political party*] (PPW) ... NKP
Nasionale Party [*National Party*] [*Political party*] (AD) ... Nas Par
Nasionale Party van Suid-Afrika [*National Party of South Africa*] [*Political party*] (PPW) ... NP
Nasionale Party van Suidwesafrika [*National Party of South West Africa*] [*Namibia*] [*Political party*] (PPW) ... NP
Nasionale Pers [*National Press*] [*South Africa*] (AD) ... Nas Pers
Nasion-Sella Line [*Brain anatomy*] ... NSL
Nasir [*Sudan*] [*ICAO location identifier*] (ICLI) ... HSNA
Naskapi School/Public Library, Sops Arm, Newfoundland [*Library symbol National Library of Canada*] (NLC) ... NFSANS
Naskapi School/Public Library, Sops Arms, NF, Canada [*Library symbol Library of Congress*] (LCLS) ... CaNfSANS
Nasmith's Institutes of English Private Law [*1873*] [*A publication*] (DLA) ... Nas Inst
Nasmith's Institutes of English Private Law [*1873*] [*A publication*] (DLA) ... Nas Inst Priv
Nasmith's Institutes of English Public Law [*1873*] [*A publication*] (DLA) ... Nas Inst Pub
Nasoendotracheal Tube [*Medicine*] ... NET
Nasogastric [*Medicine*] ... NG
Nasogastric Replacement [*Medicine*] (DMAA) ... NGR
Nasogastric Tube [*Medicine*] (CPH) ... NGT
Nasojejunal [*Medicine*] ... NJ
Nasolabial Fold [*Medicine*] (DAVI) ... NLF
Nasolacrimal [*Medicine*] (DAVI) ... NL
Nasolacrimal Duct [*Medicine*] (DAVI) ... NLD
Nasolacrimal Occlusion [*Medicine*] ... NLO
Nasopharyngeal [*or Nasopharynx*] [*Medicine*] ... NP
Nasopharyngeal Carcinoma [*Medicine*] ... NPC
Nasopharyngeal Carcinoma [*Medicine*] (MAE) ... NPCa
Nasopharyngeal Culture [*Bacteriology*] (CPH) ... NP Cult
Nasopharynx [*Anatomy*] (DAVI) ... NPhx
Nasoseptal Reconstruction [*Otorhinolaryngology*] (DAVI) ... NSR
Naso-Tracheal [*Medicine*] ... NT
Nasotracheal Suction [*Medical procedure*] (DAVI) ... NTS
Nasotracheal Tube [*Medicine*] (DAVI) ... NTT
Nassau [*Bahamas*] [*ICAO location identifier*] (ICLI) ... MYNA
Nassau [*Bahamas*] [*Airport symbol*] (OAG) ... NAS
Nassau (ROG) ... NASS
Nassau [*Cook Islands*] [*ICAO location identifier*] (ICLI) ... NCNS
Nassau [*Bahamas*] [*Airport symbol*] (OAG) ... WZY
Nassau Academy of Medicine, Garden City, NY [*Library symbol Library of Congress*] (LCLS) ... NGcN
Nassau, Bahamas (AD) ... Nass
Nassau Community College, Garden City, NY [*Library symbol Library of Congress*] (LCLS) ... NGcCC
Nassau Community College, Garden City, NY [*OCLC symbol*] (OCLC) ... VVX
Nassau County Department of Health, Division of Laboratories and Research, Hempstead, NY [*Library symbol Library of Congress*] (LCLS) ... NHemNHR
Nassau County Department of Health, Hempstead, NY [*Library symbol Library of Congress*] (LCLS) ... NHemNH
Nassau County Historical Museum, East Meadow, NY [*Library symbol Library of Congress*] (LCLS) ... NEmNHi
Nassau County Law Library, Mineola, NY [*Library symbol Library of Congress*] (LCLS) ... NMinNCL
Nassau County Medical Center, East Meadow, NY [*Library symbol Library of Congress*] (LCLS) ... NEmMC
Nassau County Medical Center, Plainview Division, Plainview, NY [*Library symbol Library of Congress*] (LCLS) ... NPIMC
Nassau County Research Library, Garden City, NY [*Library symbol Library of Congress*] (LCLS) ... NGcR
Nassau Hospital, Mineola, NY [*Library symbol Library of Congress*] (LCLS) ... NMinH
Nassau/International, New Providence Island [*Bahamas*] [*ICAO location identifier*] (ICLI) ... MYNN
Nassau Library System [*Library network*] ... NLS
Nassau Library System, Garden City, NY [*Library symbol Library of Congress*] (LCLS) ... NGcNLS
Nassi-Schneiderman [*Computer science*] ... N-S
Nasson College, Springvale, ME [*Library symbol Library of Congress*] (LCLS) ... MeSprN
Nastech Pharmaceutical [*NASDAQ symbol*] (TTSB) ... NSTK
Nastech Pharmaceutical Co., Inc. [*Associated Press*] (SAG) ... Nastc
Nastech Pharmaceutical Co., Inc. [*Associated Press*] (SAG) ... Nastech
Nastech Pharmaceutical Wrrt [*NASDAQ symbol*] (TTSB) ... NSTKW
Nastech Pharmaceuticals [*NASDAQ symbol*] (SAG) ... NSTK
Nastily (ABBR) ... NSTY
Nastiness (ABBR) ... NSTNS
NASTRAN [*NASA Structural Analysis*] **Systems Management Office** ... NSMO
Nasty (ABBR) ... NST
Nat Stuckey Fan Club [*Defunct*] (EA) ... NSFC
Nata [*Botswana*] [*ICAO location identifier*] (ICLI) ... FBNT
Natal [*Neonatology*] (DAVI) ... NAT
Natal [*Brazil*] [*Seismograph station code, US Geological Survey*] (SEIS) ... NAT
Natal [*Brazil*] [*Airport symbol*] (OAG) ... NAT
Natal/Augusto Severo [*Brazil ICAO location identifier*] (ICLI) ... SBNT
Natal Carabiniers [*British military*] (DMA) ... NC
Natal Field Artillery [*British military*] (DMA) ... NFA
Natal Field Force [*British military*] (DMA) ... NFF
Natal Law Journal [*South Africa*] [*A publication*] (DLA) ... Nat LJ
Natal Law Journal [*South Africa*] [*A publication*] (DLA) ... Natal LJ
Natal Law Magazine [*South Africa*] [*A publication*] (DLA) ... Nat LM
Natal Law Magazine [*South Africa*] [*A publication*] (DLA) ... Natal LM
Natal Law Quarterly [*South Africa*] [*A publication*] (DLA) ... Nat LQ
Natal Law Quarterly [*South Africa*] [*A publication*] (DLA) ... Natal LQ
Natal Law Reports [*South Africa*] [*A publication*] (ILCA) ... Nat LR
Natal Law Reports [*South Africa*] [*A publication*] (DLA) ... Natal LR
Natal Law Reports [*India*] [*A publication*] (DLA) ... NLR
Natal Law Reports, Old Series [*1867-72*] [*South Africa*] [*A publication*] (DLA) ... NLR (OS)
Natal Medical Corps [*British military*] (DMA) ... NMC
Natal Mounted Rifles [*British military*] (DMA) ... NMR
Natal Museum (AD) ... Nat Mus
Natal Native Contingent [*British military*] (DMA) ... NNC
Natal Native High Court Reports [*1899-1915*] [*South Africa*] [*A publication*] (DLA) ... NNHC
Natal Native Horse [*British military*] (DMA) ... NNH
Natal Reports [*South Africa*] [*A publication*] (DLA) ... NR
Natal Voluntary Ambulance Corps [*British military*] (DMA) ... NVAC
Natalia (AD) ... Nat
Natalie (AD) ... Nat
Natanz [*Iran*] [*ICAO location identifier*] (ICLI) ... OIFZ
Natasha (AD) ... Nat
Natashquan, PQ [*ICAO location identifier*] (ICLI) ... CYNA
Natation (AD) ... natat
Natchez [*Mississippi*] [*Airport symbol*] (OAG) ... HEZ
Natchez (AD) ... Natch
Natchez & Southern Railway Co. [*AAR code Terminated*] ... NASO
Natchez Junior College [*Mississippi*] ... NJC
Natchez, MS [*AM radio station call letters*] ... WMIS
Natchez, MS [*AM radio station call letters*] ... WNAT
Natchez, MS [*Television station call letters*] ... WNTZ
Natchez, MS [*FM radio station call letters*] ... WQNZ
Natchez, MS [*FM radio station call letters*] ... WTRC
Natchez Trace Parkway [*National Park Service designation*] ... NATR
Natchez, Urania & Ruston Railway Co. [*AAR code*] ... NUR
Natchitoches, LA [*Location identifier FAA*] (FAAL) ... ACM
Natchitoches, LA [*Location identifier FAA*] (FAAL) ... IER
Natchitoches, LA [*FM radio station call letters*] ... KDBH
Natchitoches, LA [*AM radio station call letters*] ... KNOC
Natchitoches, LA [*FM radio station call letters*] ... KNWD
Natchitoches, LA [*FM radio station call letters*] ... KZBL
Natchitoches, LA [*Location identifier FAA*] (FAAL) ... TOH
Natchitoches Parish Library, Natchitoches, LA [*Library symbol Library of Congress*] (LCLS) ... LNaNa
Nathalie (AD) ... Nat
Nathan (AD) ... Nat
Nathan Bailey's English Dictionary [*A publication*] (DLA) ... Bailey Dict
Nathan Hale Institute (EA) ... NHI
Nathaniel (AD) ... Nat
Nathaniel (AD) ... Nathl
Nathaniel Bowditch (AD) ... Nath B
Nathaniel Branden Institute ... NBI
Nathaniel Hawthorne Society (EA) ... NHS
Nathan's Common Law of South Africa [*A publication*] (DLA) ... Nathan
Nathan's Famous [*NASDAQ symbol*] (TTSB) ... NATH
Nathan's Famous, Inc. [*NASDAQ symbol*] (NQ) ... NATH
Nathan's Famous, Inc. [*Associated Press*] (SAG) ... Nathans
Nathian [*Pakistan*] [*Seismograph station code, US Geological Survey*] (SEIS) ... NTP
Natick Development Center [*Massachusetts*] [*Army*] ... NDC
Natick Laboratories [*Army*] (MCD) ... NL
Natick Laboratories [*Army*] (AABC) ... NLABS
Natick, MA [*AM radio station call letters*] ... WBIV
Natick Research and Development Center [*Army*] (INF) ... NRDC
Natick Research and Development Command [*Army*] ... NARADCOM
Natick Research Development and Engineering Center [*Army*] (INF) ... NRDEC
Nation (AD) ... nat
Nation [*A publication*] (BRI) ... Nat
Nation ... NAT
Nation Institute (EA) ... NI
Nation of Ishmael [*An association*] (EA) ... NI
Nation of Islam [*Religion*] ... NOI
Nation Party [*Turkey*] [*Political party*] (PPW) ... NP
Nationaal-Socialistische Beweging [*National Socialist Movement*] [*Netherlands Political party*] (PPE) ... NSB
National [*Screw threads*] ... N
National (AD) ... Nat
National (AD) ... nat
National (ODBW) ... Nat
National ... NAT
National (AAG) ... NATL
National (WDMC) ... natl
National (AD) ... natl
National ... NATL
National (DD) ... ntL
National ... NTL
National 4 Wheel Drive Association (EA) ... N4WDA
National 4-H Council (EA) ... N4-HC

National AAU [*Amateur Athletic Union*] Taekwondo Union of the United States of America [*Formerly, NAAUTC*] (EA) .... NAAUTUUSA
National Aboriginal and Torres Strait Islander Education Policy [*Australia*] .... NATSIEP
National Aboriginal Community-Controlled Health Organization [*Australia*] .... NACCHO
National Aboriginal Health Goals and Targets [*Australia*] .... NAHGT
National Aboriginal Health Strategy [*Australia*] .... NAHS
National Aboriginal Health Strategy Working Party [*Australia*] .... NAHSWP
National Aboriginal Literacy and Language Strategy [*Australia*] .... NALLS
National Aboriginal Project Officer Training Scheme [*Australia*] .... NAPOTS
National Aboriginal Sports Foundation (AD) .... NASF
National Aborigine Welfare Fund [*Australia*] (NADA) .... NAWF
National Abortion Campaign [*British*] (DBA) .... NAC
National Abortion Federation (EA) .... NAF
National Abortion Foundation (AD) .... NAF
National Abortion Rights Action League (EA) .... NARAL
National Abstentionalist (AD) .... Nat Absten
National Academic Advising Association (EA) .... NACADA
National Academic Recognition Information Centre (AIE) .... NARIC
National Academician .... NA
National Academies Policy Advisory Group .... NAPAG
National Academy (ROG) .... NA
National Academy for Adult Jewish Studies (EA) .... NAAJS
National Academy for Fire Prevention and Control [*of FEMA*] .... NAFPC
National Academy of American Scholars (EA) .... NAAS
National Academy of Arbitrators (EA) .... NAA
National Academy of Astrology [*Defunct*] (EA) .... NAA
National Academy of Cable Programming (NTCM) .... NACP
National Academy of Clinicians and Holistic Health (EA) .... NACH
National Academy of Code Administration (EA) .... NACA
National Academy of Conciliators (EA) .... NAC
National Academy of Counselors and Family Therapists (EA) .... NACFT
National Academy of Design (EA) .... NAD
National Academy of Economics and Political Science (EA) .... NAEPS
National Academy of Education .... NAE
National Academy of Education (EA) .... NAEd
National Academy of Elder Law Attorneys (EA) .... NAELA
National Academy of Engineering [*Washington, DC*] (GRD) .... NAE
National Academy of Engineering Aeronautics and Space Engineering Board .... NAE-ASEB
National Academy of Engineering Committee on Ocean Engineering .... NAECOE
National Academy of Engineering Marine Board .... NAEMB
National Academy of Engineering Navy Environmental Protection Program Study Group .... NAE-NEPP
National Academy of Foreign Affairs (AD) .... NAFA
National Academy of Geosciences (EA) .... NAG
National Academy of Jazz (EA) .... NAJ
National Academy of Literary Arts (EA) .... NALA
National Academy of Nannies, Inc. (EA) .... NANI
National Academy of Needlearts (EA) .... NAN
National Academy of Neuropsychology (EA) .... NAO
National Academy of Opticianry (EA) .... NAPA
National Academy of Public Administration (EA) .... NAPA
National Academy of Public Administration .... NAPA
National Academy of Recording Arts and Sciences (EA) .... NARAS
National Academy of School Executives [*of American Association of School Administrators*] .... NASE
National Academy of Sciences [*Washington, DC*] .... NAS
National Academy of Sciences Board on Ocean Science Affairs (PDAA) .... NASBOSA
National Academy of Sciences - Chemistry Division .... NAS-CD
National Academy of Sciences Committee on Atmospheric Science .... NASCAS
National Academy of Sciences Committee on Motor Vehicle Emissions (PDAA) .... NASCMVE
National Academy of Sciences Committee on Oceanography .... NASCO
National Academy of Sciences/Committee on Water [*Marine science*] (MSC) .... NAS/COW
National Academy of Sciences/Environmental Studies Board [*Marine science*] (MSC) .... NAS/ESB
National Academy of Sciences/Geophysical Research Board [*Marine science*] (MSC) .... NAS/GRB
National Academy of Sciences, Highway Research Board Library, Washington, DC [*Library symbol Library of Congress*] (LCLS) .... DNAS-HRB
National Academy of Sciences/National Academy of Engineering [*Marine science*] (MSC) .... NAS/NAE
National Academy of Sciences, National Academy of Engineering Library, Washington, DC [*Library symbol Library of Congress*] (LCLS) .... DNAS-NAE
National Academy of Sciences/National Academy of Sciences Engineering Science and Engineering Committee Advisory to NOAA[*National Oceanic and Atmospheric Administration*] [*Marine science*] (OSRA) .... NAS/NAE-SECAN
National Academy of Sciences - National Research Council (EA) .... NAS-NRC
National Academy of Sciences/Ocean Affairs Board [*Marine science*] (MSC) .... NAS/OAB
National Academy of Sciences/Ocean Sciences Board [*Marine science*] (MSC) .... NAS/OSB
National Academy of Sciences' Site Evaluation Committee .... NAS/SEC
National Academy of Sciences/Transportation Board [*Marine science*] (MSC) .... NAS/TRB
National Academy of Songwriters (EA) .... NAS
National Academy of Sports (EA) .... NAS
National Academy of Sports Vision (EA) .... NASV
National Academy of Stationary Engineers [*British*] (DAS) .... NASE
National Academy of Teaching (EA) .... NAT

National Academy of Television Arts and Sciences (EA) .... NATAS
National Academy of Television Arts and Sciences (EA) .... NATVAS
National Academy of Western Art (EA) .... NAWA
National Accelerated Food Production Project [*Agency for International Development*] .... NAFPP
National Accelerator Center [*South Africa*] [*Research center*] .... NAC
National Accelerator Laboratory [*AEC*] .... NAL
National Access Center [*Defunct*] (EA) .... NAC
National Accident Sampling System [*National Highway Traffic Safety Administration*] [*Washington, DC*] .... NASS
National Accordion Organization [*British*] (DBA) .... NAO
National Account Management [*Bell System*] .... NAM
National Account Marketing Association (EA) .... NAMA
National Accounting and Finance Council [*Alexandria, VA*] (EA) .... NAFC
National Accounts Capability Programme [*United Nations*] (EY) .... NACP
National Accreditation Commission for Schools and Colleges of Acupuncture and Oriental Medicine (EA) .... NACSCAOM
National Accreditation Council for Agencies Serving the Blind and Visually Handicapped (EA) .... NAC
National Accreditation Council for Agencies Serving the Blind and Visually Handicapped [*New York, NY*] .... NACAB
National Accreditation Council for Certification Bodies (AIE) .... NACCB
National Accreditation Council for Environmental Health Curricula (EA) .... NACEHC
National Accrediting Agency for Clinical Laboratory Sciences (EA) .... NAACLS
National Accrediting Commission of Cosmetology Arts and Sciences (EA) .... NACCAS
National Achievement Clubs (EA) .... NAC
National Achievement Scholarship Program [*National Merit Scholarship Corp.*] (AEBS) .... NASP
National Acid Deposition Program [*Air pollution*] .... NADP
National Acid Lakes Registry [*Environmental Protection Agency*] .... NALR
National Acid Precipitation Assessment Program [*Council on Environmental Quality*] [*Washington, DC*] .... NAPAP
National Acme [*Thread*] .... NA
National Acoustic Laboratories Hearing Center [*Australia*] .... NALHC
National Acoustical Contractors Association [*Later, CISCA*] (EA) .... NACA
National Acoustical Suppliers Association [*Defunct*] (EA) .... NASA
National Acoustics Board (MUGU) .... NAB
National Acoustics Laboratory [*Australia*] (ECON) .... NAL
National Acquisitions Group [*Libraries*] [*British*] .... NAG
National Action [*Australia*] .... NA
National Action Committee on the Status of Women [*Canada*] (CROSS) .... NAC
National Action Committee on the Status of Women [*Canada*] (AD) .... NACSW
National Action Council for Minorities in Engineering (EA) .... NACME
National Action for Former Military Wives (EA) .... NAFMW
National Action Forum for Midlife and Older Women (EA) .... NAFMOW
National Action Forum for Older Women [*Later, NAFMOW*] (EA) .... NAFOW
National Action Group [*Antibusing organization*] .... NAG
National Action Group for the Prevention and Treatment of Decubitus Ulcers (EA) .... NAGPTDU
National Action Party [*Sierra Leone*] [*Political party*] (EY) .... NAP
National Action Party [*Turkey Political party*] (PD) .... NAP
National Action Party [*Mexico Political party*] (PD) .... PAN
National Action Plan on Breast Cancer .... NAPBC
National Action/Research on the Military Industrial Complex (EA) .... NARMIC
National Activity Education Organization (EA) .... NAEO
National Activity to Test Software .... NATS
National Acupuncture Research Society (EA) .... NARS
National Acute Spinal Cord Injury Study .... NASCIS
National Ad Hoc Committee Against Censorship (AD) .... NAHCAC
National Addison's Disease Foundation (EA) .... NADF
National Administrative Expenses (NATG) .... NAE
National Administrative Expenses (AD) .... nae
National Administrative Information System [*Computer science*] (IID) .... NAIS
National Administrative Rehabilitation Programme [*United Nations program*] .... NARP
National Adoption Assistance Center (EA) .... NAAC
National Adoption Center [*Information service or system*] (IID) .... NAC
National Adoption Exchange (EA) .... NAE
National Adoption Information Clearinghouse (EA) .... NAIC
National Adoption Information Exchange System [*Formerly, ARENA*] (EA) .... NAIES
National Adoption Society (WDAA) .... NAS
National ADP [*Automatic Data Processing*] Program for AMC Logistics Management [*Army Materiel Command*] .... NAPALM
National Adult Education Clearinghouse (NAEC)/National Multimedia Center for Adult Education [*Information service or system Defunct*] (IID) .... NMMC
National Adult School Organisation [*British*] .... NASO
National Adult School Union [*British*] (DAS) .... NASU
National Adult Vocational Education Association (EA) .... AVEA
National Adult Vocational Education Association (EA) .... NAVEA
National Advanced Driver Simulator [*NHTSA*] (TAG) .... NADS
National Advanced Systems (HGAA) .... NAS
National Advanced Technology Management Conference .... NATMC
National Advertised Brands Scanning Reports [*Research project*] .... NABSCAN
National Advertising Agency Network [*New York, NY*] (EA) .... NAAN
National Advertising Benevolent Society [*British*] .... NABS
National Advertising Campaign [*Army*] .... NAC
National Advertising Division [*of the Council of Better Business Bureaus*] .... NAD
National Advertising Golf Association (EA) .... NAGA
National Advertising Lead Tracking System [*Navy*] (NVT) .... NALTS
National Advertising News Association (AD) .... NANA
National Advertising Newspaper Association [*Later, SNA*] (EA) .... NANA

National Advertising Program ... NAP
National Advertising Review Board [*New York, NY*] (EA) ... NARB
National Advertising Sales Association (EA) ... NASA
National Advice and Information Centre for Outdoor Education [*Doncaster Metropolitan Institute of Higher Education*] [*British*] (CB) ... NAIC
National Advisory Board (ACII) ... NAB
National Advisory Board on Science and Technology [*Canada*] ... NABST
National Advisory Body [*British*] ... NAB
National Advisory Cancer Council ... NACC
National Advisory Centre on Careers for Women [*British*] (CB) ... NACCW
National Advisory Commission on Civil Disorders (NADA) ... NACCD
National Advisory Commission on Libraries ... NACL
National Advisory Commission on Libraries ... NACOL
National Advisory Committee ... NAC
National Advisory Committee for Aeronautics [*Functions transferred to NASA, 1958*] ... NACA
National Advisory Committee for Electronics ... NACE
National Advisory Committee for Environmental Policy and Technology [*Environmental Protection Agency*] ... NACEPT
National Advisory Committee for the Flammable Fabrics Act ... NACFFA
National Advisory Committee on Aeronautics [*OST*] (TAG) ... NACA
National Advisory Committee on Farm Labor [*Defunct*] (EA) ... NACFL
National Advisory Committee on Handicapped Children [*Terminated, 1973*] [*HEW*] (EGAO) ... NACHC
National Advisory Committee on Microbiological Criteria for Foods ... NACMCF
National Advisory Committee on Occupational Safety and Health ... NACOSH
National Advisory Committee on Oceanography [*Marine science*] (MSC) ... NACO
National Advisory Committee on Oceans and Atmosphere [*Marine science*] (MSC) ... NACOA
National Advisory Committee on Radiation ... NACOR
National Advisory Committee on Radiation ... NACR
National Advisory Committee on Rhesus Monkey Requirements ... NACRMR
National Advisory Committee on Safety in Agriculture ... NACSA
National Advisory Committee on Scouting for the Handicapped (EA) ... NACOSH
National Advisory Committee on Semiconductors ... NACS
National Advisory Committee on the Education of the Deaf [*Terminated, 1973*] [*HEW*] (EGAO) ... NACED
National Advisory Committee on the Handicapped ... NACH
National Advisory Committee on Uniform Traffic Control Devices [*Terminated, 1979*] [*Department of Transportation*] (EGAO) ... NACUTCD
National Advisory Committee on Water Resources Research [*Canada*] ... NACWRR
National Advisory Committee on Women (AD) ... NACW
National Advisory Committee on Women (NADA) ... NACW
National Advisory Council ... NAC
National Advisory Council for Drug Abuse Prevention [*Terminated, 1975*] (EGAO) ... NACDAP
National Advisory Council for Educational Research and Improvement [*Washington, DC Department of Education*] (GRD) ... NACERI
National Advisory Council for South Asian Affairs (EA) ... NACSAA
National Advisory Council for the Handicapped (NADA) ... NACH
National Advisory Council for Youth Services (AIE) ... NACYS
National Advisory Council on Adult Education [*Washington, DC*] ... NACAE
National Advisory Council on Continuing Education (OICC) ... NACCE
National Advisory Council on Economic Opportunity (EA) ... NACEO
National Advisory Council on Education for Industry and Commerce (MCD) ... NACEIC
National Advisory Council on Education of Disadvantaged Children (OICC) ... NACEDC
National Advisory Council on Education Professions Development [*HEW*] (EGAO) ... NAC/EDP
National Advisory Council on Education Professions Development [*Terminate d, 1976*] [*HEW*] (OICC) ... NACEPD
National Advisory Council on Equality of Educational Opportunity [*Termina ted, 1979*] [*HEW*] (EGAO) ... NACEEO
National Advisory Council on Extension and Continuing Education ... NACECE
National Advisory Council on Indian Education (OICC) ... NACIE
National Advisory Council on Nutrition Education [*British*] ... NACNE
National Advisory Council on Rural Civil Defense ... NACRCD
National Advisory Council on Services and Facilities for the Developmentally Disabled [*Terminated, 1978*] [*HEW*] (EGAO) ... NACDD
National Advisory Council on Supplementary Centers and Services ... NACSCS
National Advisory Council on the Employment of the Disabled [*British*] ... NACED
National Advisory Council on the Teaching of English as a Foreign Language (EA) ... NACTEFL
National Advisory Council on the Training and Supply of Teachers (AD) ... NACTST
National Advisory Council on Vocational Education ... NACVE
National Advisory Council on Women's Educational Programs (OICC) ... NACWEP
National Advisory Drug Committee [*HEW*] ... NADC
National Advisory Eye Council ... NAEC
National Advisory Group, Convenience Stores/Petroleum Companies (EA) ... NAG
National Advisory Health Council ... NAHC
National Advisory Logistics Staff (NATG) ... NALS
National Advocates Society (EA) ... NAS
National Aero Club (EA) ... NAC
National Aero Manufacturing (AD) ... NAM
National Aero Research Laboratory [*Canada*] (PDAA) ... NARL
National Aerobic Fitness Award (AD) ... NAFA
National Aerometric Data Bank (AD) ... NADB
National Aerometric Data Information System [*Environmental Protection Agency*] ... NADIS
National Aeronautic Association (NADA) ... NAA
National Aeronautic Association of the USA (EA) ... NAA
National Aeronautical and Space Administration, Institute for Space Studies, NewYork, NY [*Library symbol Library of Congress*] (LCLS) ... NNNASA
National Aeronautical Corp. ... NAC
National Aeronautical Corp. (MCD) ... NARCO
National Aeronautical Establishment [*Research center Canada*] (IRC) ... NAE
National Aeronautical Laboratory (MCD) ... NAL
National Aeronautical Research Institute [*Netherlands*] (SAA) ... NLL
National Aeronautics and Space Act of 1958 ... NASA
National Aeronautics and Space Administration [*Washington, DC*] ... NASA
National Aeronautics and Space Administration Act (AD) ... NASAA
National Aeronautics and Space Administration, Ames Research Center, Technical Library, Moffett Field, CA [*Library symbol Library of Congress*] (LCLS) ... CMfNASA
National Aeronautics and Space Administration and Atomic Energy Commission (SAA) ... NASA-AEC
National Aeronautics and Space Administration Board of Contract Appeals ... NASABCA
National Aeronautics and Space Administration - Cleveland, Ohio (AD) ... NASA-CO
National Aeronautics and Space Administration - Cocoa Beach, Florida (AD) ... NASA-CF Florida
National Aeronautics and Space Administration - Edwards, California (AD) ... NASA-EC California
National Aeronautics and Space Administration [*NASA*] **Equipment Management System** (AAGC) ... NEMS
National Aeronautics and Space Administration FAR Supplement [*A publication*] (AAGC) ... NASA FAR Supp
National Aeronautics and Space Administration FAR Supplement [*A publication*] (AAGC) ... NFS
National Aeronautics and Space Administration FAR Supplement Directive (AAGC) ... NFSD
National Aeronautics and Space Administration, Goddard Institute for Space Studies, New York, NY [*Library symbol*] [*Library of Congress*] (LCLS) ... NNGI
National Aeronautics and Space Administration - Greenbelt, Maryland (AD) ... NASA-GM Maryland
National Aeronautics and Space Administration - Houston, Texas (AD) ... NASA-HT
National Aeronautics and Space Administration - Huntsville, Alabama (AD) ... NASA-HA Alabama
National Aeronautics and Space Administration, John F. Kennedy Space Center, Kennedy Space Center, FL [*Library symbol*] [*Library of Congress*] (LCLS) ... FKscNA
National Aeronautics and Space Administration, Johnson Space Center, Houston, TX [*OCLC symbol*] (OCLC) ... NAJ
National Aeronautics and Space Administration - Kennedy Space Center ... NASA-KSC
National Aeronautics and Space Administration - Langley Field, Virginia (AD) ... NASA-LV Virginia
National Aeronautics and Space Administration, Langley Research Center, Hampton,VA [*Library symbol Library of Congress*] (LCLS) ... ViHaNASA
National Aeronautics and Space Administration Large Space Telescope (AD) ... NASA LST Telescope
National Aeronautics and Space Administration, Lewis Research Center, Cleveland,OH [*Library symbol Library of Congress*] (LCLS) ... OCINASA
National Aeronautics and Space Administration Library Network [*Information service or system*] (IID) ... ARIN
National Aeronautics and Space Administration - Manned Spacecraft Center ... NASA-MSC
National Aeronautics and Space Administration, Manned Spacecraft Center, Technical Library, Houston, TX [*Library symbol Library of Congress*] (LCLS) ... TxHNASA
National Aeronautics and Space Administration, Marshall Space Flight Center, AL [*Library symbol*] [*Library of Congress*] (LCLS) ... AMscNA
National Aeronautics and Space Administration - Moffett Field, California (AD) ... NASA-MC California
National Aeronautics and Space Administration, NASA/NSTL Research Library, NSTL Station, Bay St. Louis, MS [*Library symbol Library of Congress*] (LCLS) ... MsBsNA
National Aeronautics and Space Administration Procurement Regulation [*A publication*] (AAGC) ... NPR
National Aeronautics and Space Administration Procurement Regulations ... NASAPR
National Aeronautics and Space Administration Procurement Regulations Directive ... NASAPRD
National Aeronautics and Space Administration Remote Console ... NASA/RECON
National Aeronautics and Space Administration - Santa Monica, California (AD) ... NASA-SC California
National Aeronautics and Space Administration/Scientific and Technical Information Facility ... NASA/STIF
National Aeronautics and Space Administration, Scientific and Technical Information Facility, Baltimore/Washington International Airport, MD [*Library symbol*] [*Library of Congress*] (LCLS) ... MdBwiNA
National Aeronautics and Space Administration Tracking Network (AD) ... NASCOM
National Aeronautics and Space Administration, Washington, DC [*OCLC symbol*] (OCLC) ... NAA
National Aeronautics and Space Administration White Sands [*Proving ground*] ... NASWS
National Aeronautics and Space Council [*Terminated, 1973*] ... NASC
National Aerosol Association (EA) ... NAA

National Aerospace and Defense Contractors Accreditation Program [*DoD*] .... NADCAP
National Aerospace Education Association [*Formerly, NAEC*] [*Defunct*] ...... NAEA
National Aerospace Education Council [*Later, NAEA*] (EA) .... NAEC
National Aerospace Electronics Conference [*IEEE*] (MCD) .... NAECON
National Aerospace Laboratory (AD) .... NAL
National Aerospace Plane (AD) .... NAP
National Aero-Space Plane (AD) .... NASP
National Aerospace Plane (AAGC) .... NASP
National Aerospace Plane Joint Programs Office .... NAPJPO
National Aerospace Plane Program [*NASA, DoD*] .... NASP
National Aerospace Services Association [*Defunct*] (MCD) ...... NASA
National Aerospace Services Association [*Defunct*] (EA) .... NASSA
National Aerospace Standards (MCD) .... NAS
National Aerospace Standards Committee (AAGC) .... NA
National Aerospace Standards Industrial Association (AAGC) ...... NAS
National Aerospace Utilization System (NOAA) .... NAUS
National Aesthetician and Nail Artist Association [*Formerly, NANA*] [*WINBA*] [*Absorbed by*] (EA) .... NANAA
National Affiliate of Printing Industries of America (AD) .... NAPIA
National Affiliation for Literacy Advance (EA) .... NALA
National Affiliation of Concerned Business Students [*Defunct*] (EA) .... NACBS
National Afro-American Labor Council [*Later, NALC*] .... NAALC
National Afro-American Labor Council (EA) .... NALC
National Aftermarket Audit Co. .... NAA
National Agency Check [*Security clearance*] .... NAC
National Agency Check and Written Inquiries .... NACI
National Agency Check Center (AFM) .... NACC
National Agency for Finite Element Methods and Standards [*British*] (IRUK) .... NAFEMS
National Agency for Tourism .... NAT
National Agenda for a Multicultural Australia .... NAMA
National Agenda for Women's Grants Program [*Australia*] ...... NAWGP
National Aging Foundation (EA) .... NAF
National Agreement [*Paraguay*] (PD) .... AN
National Agricultural Advertising and Marketing Association [*Later, NAMA*] .... NAAMA
National Agricultural Advisory Commission (NADA) .... NAAC
National Agricultural Advisory Service [*Later, ADAS*] [*British*] ...... NAAS
National Agricultural and Allied Workers' Union of Liberia (IMH) .... NAAWUL
National Agricultural and Industrial Association [*Australia*] ...... NAIA
National Agricultural and Industrial Development Association [*Republic of Ireland*] (BI) .... NAIDA
National Agricultural Aviation Association (EA) .... NAAA
National Agricultural Centre [*British*] (CB) .... NAC
National Agricultural Chemicals Association (EA) .... NACA
National Agricultural Institute [*Later, ACA*] (EA) .... NAI
National Agricultural Legal Fund [*Defunct*] (EA) .... NALF
National Agricultural Libraries Network [*National Agricultural Library*] ...... NALN
National Agricultural Library [*Department of Agriculture*] [*Beltsville, MD*] ...... NAL
National Agricultural Library, Beltsville, MD [*OCLC symbol*] (OCLC) .... AGL
National Agricultural Limestone Association [*Later, National Limestone Institute*] .... NALA
National Agricultural Limestone Institute [*Later, National Limestone Institute*] .... NALI
National Agricultural Marketing Officials [*Richmond, VA*] (EA) ...... NAMO
National Agricultural Pesticide Impact Assessment Program [*Department of Agriculture*] .... NAPIAP
National Agricultural Plastics Association [*Later, ASP*] (EA) ...... NAPA
National Agricultural Press Association (EA) .... NAPA
National Agricultural Research Center .... NARC
National Agricultural Research, Extension, and Teaching Policy Act of 1977 .... NARETPA
National Agricultural Research Organization [*Netherlands*] (ECON) .... NARO
National Agricultural Research Systems (ECON) .... NARS
National Agricultural Society (AD) .... NAS
National Agricultural Society (NADA) .... NAS
National Agricultural Statistics Service [*Department of Agriculture*] [*Information service or system*] (IID) .... NASS
National Agricultural Text-Digitizing Project [*National Agricultural Library*] .... NATDP
National Agricultural Transportation League [*Defunct*] (EA) ...... NATL
National Agricultural Workers Survey .... NAWS
National Agricultural Workers Union .... NAW
National Agricultural Workers Union (EA) .... NAWU
National Agriculture Research Institute (WDAA) .... NARI
National Agri-Marketing Association (EA) .... NAMA
National Aid to Visually Handicapped (AD) .... NAVH
National AIDS Behavioral Survey .... NABS
National AIDS [*Acquired Immune Deficiency Syndrome*] Information Clearinghouse [*Information service or system*] (IID) ...... NAIC
National AIDS [*Acquired Immune Deficiency Syndrome*] Network [*Defunct*] (EA) .... NAN
National AIDS Research Institute [*India*] .... NARI
National Aids Support System [*Military*] (SAA) .... NASS
National AIDS Trust [*British*] .... NAIDST
National Air and Space [*Warfare*] Model [*Air Force*] .... NASM
National Air and Space Museum [*Smithsonian Institution*] [*Formerly, NAM*] .... NASM
National Air and Space Museum Library [*Smithsonian Institute*] (AD) ...... NASML
National Air Audit System [*Environmental Protection Agency*] (GFGA) .... NAAS
National Air Carrier Association (MCD) .... NAC
National Air Carrier Association (EA) .... NACA
National Air Charter PT [*Indonesia*] [*ICAO designator*] (FAAC) ...... NSR
National Air Communications [*British*] .... NAC

National Air Conditioning, Heating, Ventilating, and Refrigeration Officials (EA) .... NACHVRO
National Air Conservation Commission (EA) .... NACC
National Air Data Branch [*Environmental Protection Agency Information service or system*] (IID) .... NADB
National Air Duct Cleaners Association .... NADAC
National Air Filtration Association (EA) .... NAFA
National Air Forwarding Division [*Institute of Freight Forwarders*] (AD) .... NAFD
National Air Material Center (KSC) .... NAMC
National Air Monitoring [*Environmental Protection Agency*] (GNE) ...... NAMS
National Air Monitoring Station [*Environmental Protection Agency*] (ERG) .... NAMS
National Air Museum [*of the Smithsonian Institution*] [*Later, NASM*] ...... NAM
National Air Museum Advisory Board (MUGU) .... NAMAB
National Air Photo Library [*Canada*] (PDAA) .... NAPL
National Air Photo Library, Energy, Mines, and Resources Canada [*BibliothequePhotographie Aerienne Nationale, Energie, Mines, et Ressources Canada*], Otta wa, Ontario [*Library symbol National Library of Canada*] (BIB) .... OOMNA
National Air Pollution Background Network [*Environmental Protection Agency*] (GFGA) .... NAPBN
National Air Pollution Control (KSC) .... NAPC
National Air Pollution Control Administration [*Obsolete*] ...... NAPCA
National Air Pollution Control Administration (AAGC) .... NAPCA
National Air Pollution Control Techniques Advisory Committee [*Environmental Protection Agency*] (GFGA) ...... NAPCTAC
National Air Pollution Manpower Development Advisory Committee [*Terminate d, 1976*] [*HEW*] (EGAO) ...... NAPMDAC
National Air Pollution Technical Information Center [*of National Air Pollution Control Administration*] [*Also, APTIC*] (DIT) ...... NAPTIC
National Air Quality Data Center [*Australia*] .... NAQDC
National Air Quality Index (AD) .... NAQI
National Air Resources Act (GFGA) .... NARA
National Air Rifle and Pistol Association [*British*] .... NARPA
National Air Sampling Network [*Public Health Service*] .... NASN
National Air Surveillance Network [*Environmental Protection Agency*] .... NASN
National Air Taxi Conference (SAA) .... NATC
National Air Toxics Information Clearinghouse [*Environmental Protection Agency*] (GFGA) .... NATICH
National Air Toxics Strategy [*Environmental Protection Agency*] (GFGA) .... NATS
National Air Traffic Control Service (IEEE) .... NATCS
National Air Traffic Control System (NATG) .... NATCS
National Air Traffic Controllers (AD) .... NATC
National Air Traffic Controllers Association (EA) .... NATCA
National Air Traffic Management Advisory Committee [*British*] ...... NATMAC
National Air Traffic Services [*British*] .... NATS
National Air Transport (SAA) .... NAT
National Air Transportation Association (EA) .... NATA
National Air Transportation Conferences [*Later, NATA*] .... NATC
National Aircraft Accident Investigation School [*FAA*] .... NAAIS
National Aircraft Beacon .... NAB
National Aircraft Finance Association (EA) .... NAFA
National Aircraft Noise Abatement Council [*Defunct*] (EA) ...... NANAC
National Aircraft Standards .... NAS
National Aircraft Standards Committee .... NASC
National Aircraft Underwriters' Association (AD) .... NAUA
National Aircraft War Production Council [*World War II*] .... NAWPC
National Airfreight Trucking Alliance (EA) .... NATA
National Airlines (AD) .... NAL
National Airlines (Chile), SA [*FAA designator*] (FAAC) .... NCN
National Airlines, Inc. [*ICAO designator*] .... NA
National Airlines, Inc. [*ICAO designator*] (FAAC) .... NAN
National Air-Monitoring Audit [*Environmental Protection Agency*] (GFGA)..... NAMA
National Airport [*Under control of BAA*] [*British*] .... NA
National Airport Grant Information System [*FAA*] (TAG) .... NAGIS
National Airport System Plans [*Department of Transportation*] ...... NASP
National Airports Authority of India [*FAA designator*] (FAAC) ...... YXA
National Air-Racing Group (EA) .... NAG
National Airspace Analysis [*FAA*] (TAG) .... NAA
National Airspace Communications System .... NASCOM
National Airspace Data Interchange Network [*FAA*] (TAG) ...... NADIN
National Airspace Data Interchange Network II [*National digital message switching network for aeronautical data*] (GAVI) ...... NADIN II
National Airspace Information System [*BTS*] (TAG) .... NAIMS
National Airspace Integrated Logistics Support [*FAA*] (TAG) ...... NAILS
National Airspace Performance Reporting System [*Aviation*] (FAAC) .... NAPRS
National Airspace System [*NASA*] .... NAS
National Airspace System Interfacility Communications System (FAAC) .... NICS
National Airspace System Performance Analysis Capability [*FAA*] (TAG) .... NASPAC
National Airspace System Plan [*FAA*] (TAG) .... NASP
National Airspace System Program Office [*FAA*] (MCD) .... NASPO
National Airways Corp. (Pty) Ltd. [*South Africa ICAO designator*] (FAAC) ...... NTN
National Alarm Association of America (EA) .... NAAA
National Alcohol Fuels Producers Association [*Defunct*] (EA) ...... NAFPA
National Alcohol Tax Coalition (EA) .... NATC
National Alcoholic Beverage Control Association (EA) .... NABCA
National Alcoholism and Drug Abuse Program Inventory [*Department of Health and Human Services*] (GFGA) ...... NADAPI
National All States Hobby Club [*Defunct*] (EA) .... NASHC
National All Terrain Vehicle Association (EA) .... NATVA
National Alliance [*Italy Political party*] (ECON) .... AN
National Alliance (EA) .... NA
National Alliance Against Racist and Political Repression (EA) .... NAARPR
National Alliance Against Violence (EA) .... NAAV

National Alliance Building Trades Society [*A union*] [*British*] .... NABTS
National Alliance Concerned with School-Age Parents [*Defunct*] (EA).... NACSAP
National Alliance for Animal Legislation [*Defunct*] (EA) .... NAAL
National Alliance for Democracy [*Political party*] (AD) .... NAD
National Alliance for Democratic Restoration in Equatorial Guinea [*Switzerland*] (EAIO) .... NADREG
National Alliance for Family Life [*Later, NACFT*] (EA) .... NAFL
National Alliance for Hydroelectric Energy (EA) .... NAHE
National Alliance for Infusion Therapy [*An association*] .... NAIT
National Alliance for Optional Parenthood [*Formerly, NON*] .... NAOP
National Alliance for Optional Parenthood (DAVI) .... NAOP
National Alliance for Reduction of Imprisonment [*Defunct*] (EA) .... NARI
National Alliance for Research on Schizophrenia and the Depressions (EA) .... NARSAD
National Alliance for Rural Action (EA) .... NARA
National Alliance for Safe Schools (EA) .... NASS
National Alliance for Safer Cities (EA) .... NASC
National Alliance for Salvation [*Sudan*] [*Political party*] (MENA) .... NAS
National Alliance for Spiritual Growth (EA) .... NASG
National Alliance for the Advancement of Nodnarbian Philosophy (EA) .... NAANP
National Alliance for the Mentally Ill (EA) .... NAMI
National Alliance for the Prevention and Treatment of Child Abuse (EA) .... NAPTCA
National Alliance of Arts and Industry .... NAAI
National Alliance of Athletic Associations [*Defunct*] (EA) .... NAAA
National Alliance of Black Americans .... NABA
National Alliance of Black Feminists (EA) .... NABF
National Alliance of Black Organizations (EA) .... NABO
National Alliance of Black School Educators (EA) .... NABSE
National Alliance of Black School Superintendents (AEE) .... NABSS
National Alliance of Blind Students (EA) .... NABS
National Alliance of Breast Cancer Organizations (EA) .... NABCO
National Alliance of Business [*Washington, DC*] (EA) .... NAB
National Alliance of Business - Job Opportunities in the Business Sector (OICC) .... NAB-JOBS
National Alliance of Businessmen (NADA) .... NAB
National Alliance of Cardiovascular Technologists (EA) .... NACT
National Alliance of Cleaning Distributors [*Commercial firm*] (EA) .... NACD
National Alliance of Czech Catholics (EA) .... NACC
National Alliance of Financially-Responsible Local Governments (AD) .... NAFRLG
National Alliance of Homebased Businesswomen [*Defunct*] (EA) .... NAHB
National Alliance of Independent Crop Consultants (EA) .... NAICC
National Alliance of Media Arts Centers (EA) .... NAMAC
National Alliance of Mental Patients [*Later, NAPS*] (EA) .... NAMP
National Alliance of Nurse Practitioners (EA) .... NANP
National Alliance of Postal and Federal Employees (EA) .... NAPFE
National Alliance of Postal Employees [*Later, NAPFE*] .... NAPE
National Alliance of Postal Supervisors (AD) .... NAPS
National Alliance of Preservation Commissions (EA) .... NAPC
National Alliance of Senior Citizens (EA) .... NASC
National Alliance of Spanish-Speaking People for Equality (EA) .... NASSPE
National Alliance of Statewide Preservation Organizations (EA) .... NASPO
National Alliance of Supermarket Shoppers (EA) .... NASS
National Alliance of Television and Electronics Services Associations (IAA) .... NATESA
National Alliance of Third World Journalists (EA) .... NATWJ
National Alliance on Shaping Safer Cities [*Later, NASC*] (EA) .... NASSC
National Alliance to End Homelessness (EA) .... NAEH
National Allotments and Gardens Society Ltd. [*British*] (BI) .... NAGS
National Aloe Science Council [*Later, IASC*] (EA) .... NASC
National Alopecia Areata Foundation (EA) .... NAAF
National ALS [*Amyotrophic Lateral Sclerosis*] **Foundation** (EA) .... NALSF
National Alternative Fuel Test (AD) .... NAFT
National Alternative Schools Program .... NASP
National Alumni Association (EA) .... NAA
National Alumni Council of the United Negro College Fund (EA) .... NAC
National Alzheimer's Disease Autopsy and Brain Bank (AD) .... NADABB
National Alzheimer's Disease Foundation (AD) .... NADF
National Alzheimer's Disease Foundation (NADA) .... NADF
National AM Stereophonic Radio Committee .... NAMSRC
National Amalgamated Association of Nut and Bolt Workers [*A union*] [*British*] .... NAANBW
National Amalgamated Association of Sheet Metal Workers and Blaziers [*A union*] [*British*] .... NAASMWB
National Amalgamated Association of Tin Plate Workers and Blaziers [*A union*] [*British*] .... NAATPWB
National Amalgamated Brass Workers' Society [*A union*] [*British*] .... NABWS
National Amalgamated Coal Porters' Union [*British*] .... NACPU
National Amalgamated Coal Porters' Union of Inland and Seaborne Coal Workers [*British*] .... NACPUISCW
National Amalgamated Furnishing Trades Association [*A union*] [*British*] .... NAFTA
National Amalgamated Iron Plate Trade Society [*A union*] [*British*] .... NAIPTS
National Amalgamated Society of Coopers [*A union*] [*British*] .... NASC
National Amalgamated Society of Railway Wagon and Carriage Builders and Lifters [*A union*] [*British*] .... NASRWCBL
National Amalgamated Stevedores and Dockers (AD) .... NASD
National Amalgamated Stevedores' and Dockers' Society [*A union*] [*British*] .... NASDS
National Amalgamated Stevedores and Dockers Union [*British*] (BI) .... NASDU
National Amalgamated Union of Shop Assistants [*A union*] [*British*] .... NAUPA
National Amalgamated Union of Shop Assistants, Warehousemen, and Clerks [*A union*] [*British*] .... NAUSAWC
National Amateur Athletic Union Taekwondo Committee [*Later, NAAUTUUSA*] (EA) .... NAAUTC
National Amateur Baseball Federation (EA) .... NABF
National Amateur Basketball Association (EA) .... NABA
National Amateur Body Building Association [*British*] (BI) .... NABBA
National Amateur Missile Analysis Center .... NAMAC
National Amateur Press Association (EA) .... NAPA
National Amateur Retriever Club (EA) .... NARC
National Amateur Tobacco Growers' Association [*British*] (BI) .... NATGA
National Ambient Air Monitoring Station [*or System*] [*Environmental Protection Agency*] .... NAMS
National Ambient Air Quality Standards [*Environmental Protection Agency*] .... NAAQS
National Ambucs (EA) .... NA
National Ambulatory Medical Care Survey [*National Center for Health Statistics*] .... NAMCS
National American Eskimo Dog Association (EA) .... NAEDA
National American Farmers Association [*Defunct*] (EA) .... NAFA
National American Indian Cattlemen's Association (EA) .... NAICA
National American Indian Court Clerks Association (EA) .... NAICCA
National American Indian Court Judges Association (EA) .... NAICJA
National American Indian Housing Council (EA) .... NAIHC
National American Indian Safety Council (EA) .... NAISC
National American Legion Press Association (EA) .... NALPA
National American Motors Drivers and Racers Association (EA) .... NAMDRA
National American Pit Bull Terrier Association (EA) .... NAPBTA
National American Studies Faculty [*Defunct*] (EA) .... NASF
National American Veterans .... NAV
National Amputation Foundation (EA) .... NAF
National Amputee Golf Association (EA) .... NAGA
National Amusement Park Historical Association (EA) .... NAPHA
National Analysis of Trends in Emergency Systems [*Canada*] (MSC) .... NATES
National Analytical Facility [*National Oceanic and Atmospheric Administration*] .... NAF
National and Aviation Meteorological Facsimile Network [*National Weather Service*] .... NAMFAX
National and Local Government Officers' Association [*British*] .... NALGO
National and Provincial Parks Association of Canada .... NPPAC
National and University Library [*Israel*] (BJA) .... NUL
National Anglers' Council [*British*] .... NAC
National Angling Federation [*British*] .... NAF
National Angora Rabbit Breeders Club (EA) .... NARBC
National Animal Control Association (EA) .... NACA
National Animal Damage Control Association (EA) .... NADCA
National Animal Disease Center [*Ames, IA*] [*Department of Agriculture*] [*Research center*] (GRD) .... NADC
National Animal Disease Laboratory [*Iowa*] .... NADL
National Ankylosing Spondylitis Society [*British*] (DBA) .... NASS
National Annual Report Service [*NYSE*] .... NARS
National Annual Symposium on Reliability [*IEEE*] (MCD) .... NASR
National Anorexic Aid Society (EA) .... NAAS
National Anthropological Film Center [*Smithsonian Institution*] (GRD) .... NAFC
National Antibacterial Residue Minimization Program [*Australia*] .... NARMP
National Antibiotic Minimization Program [*Australia*] .... NAMP
National Anti-Drug Abuse Campaign (AD) .... NADAC
National Anti-Drug Coalition [*Defunct*] (EA) .... NADC
National Antidrug Reorganization and Coordination Act .... NARCA
National Anti-Dumping Committee (EA) .... NADC
National Anti-Fluoridation Campaign [*British*] (DBA) .... NAFC
National Anti-Hunger Coalition (EA) .... NAHC
National Anti-Imperialist Movement in Solidarity with African Liberation (EA) .... NAIMSAL
National Anti-Klan Network (EA) .... NAKN
National Antique and Art Dealers Association of America (EA) .... NAADAA
National Antique Oldsmobile Club (EA) .... NAOC
National Anti-Racist Movement in Education [*British*] (DBA) .... NAME
National Anti-Steel-Trap League (AD) .... NASTL
National Anti-Steel-Trap League (NADA) .... NASTL
National Anti-Vaccination League [*British*] (BI) .... NAVL
National Anti-Vivisection Society (EA) .... NAVS
National Anti-Waste Programme [*British*] (DCTA) .... NAWP
National Anxiety Center (EA) .... NAC
National Apartment Association (EA) .... NAA
National Apartment Owners Association [*Later, NAA*] (EA) .... NAOA
National Apostolate with Mentally Retarded Persons (EA) .... NAMRP
National Appaloosa Pony (EA) .... NAPI
National Apple Institute [*Later, IAI*] (EA) .... NAI
National Apple Month (EA) .... NAM
National Apple Week Association [*Later, NAM*] (EA) .... NAWA
National AppleWorks Users Group (EA) .... NAUG
National Appliance and Radio TV Dealers Association (IAA) .... NARDA
National Appliance Energy Conservation Act [*1987*] .... NAECA
National Appliance Parts Suppliers Association (EA) .... NAPSA
National Appliance Service Association (EA) .... NASA
National Applied Mathematics Laboratory [*National Institute of Standards and Technology*] (MCD) .... NAML
National Apprenticeship Program [*Bureau of Apprenticeship and Training*] [*Department of Labor*] .... NAP
National Appropriate Technology Assistance Service [*Butte, MT*] [*Department of Energy*] (GRD) .... NATAS
National Aquaculture Council (EA) .... NAC
National Aquaculture Information System (NOAA) .... NAIS
National Aquarium Society (EA) .... NAS
National Aquatic Resources Agency [*Sri Lanka*] [*Marine science*] (OSRA) .... NARA

National Aquatic School [Red Cross] .... NAS
National Aquatic Sports Camps (EA) .... NASC
National Arbitration Tribunal [British] .... NAT
National Arbor Day Foundation (EA) .... NADF
National Arborist Association (EA) .... NAA
National Archery Association of the United States (EA) .... NAA
National Archery Association of the United States (NADA) .... NAAUS
National Architect-Engineer Liaison Commission [Defunct] (EA) .... NAELC
National Architectural Accrediting Board (EA) .... NAAB
National Archival Appraisal Board [Canada] .... NAAB
National Archive and Record Service-Automation 1 (NITA) NARS-A1
National Archive for Computerized Data on Aging [Department of Health and Human Services] (GFGA) .... NACDA
[The] National Archives [of the United States] .... NA
National Archives (AD) .... Nat Arc
[The] National Archives [of the United States] .... TNA
National Archives and Historical Foundation of the American GI Fo rum (EA) .... NAHFAGIF
National Archives and Record Service Volunteer Association [Later, NARAVA] (EA) .... NARSVA
National Archives and Records Administration [Independent government agency] [Formerly, NARS] .... NARA
National Archives and Records Administration Volunteer Association (EA) .... NARAVA
National Archives and Records Service (AD) .... NARC
National Archives and Records Service [of GSA] [Washington, DC Later, NARA] .... NARS
National Archives and Records Service, Washington, DC [OCLC symbol] (OCLC) .... NAR
National Archives for Electrical Science and Technology (PDAA) .... NAEST
National Archives of Rhodesia, Salisbury, Rhodesia [Library symbol Library of Congress] (LCLS) .... RhSNA
National Archives Publication .... NAP
National Archives Trust Fund Board .... NATFB
National Archives Volunteers Constitution Study Group [Defunct] (EA) .... NAVCSG
National Archives, Wellington, New Zealand [Library symbol Library of Congress] (LCLS) .... NzWNA
National Armament Directors [NATO] .... NADS
National Armaments Director (NATG) .... NAD
National Armaments Directors Representatives .... NADREPS
National Armed Forces Museum (AD) .... NAFM
National Armed Forces Museum Advisory Board [Smithsonian Institution] .... NAFMAB
National Armored Cable Manufacturers Association (EA) .... NACMA
National Armored Car Association (EA) .... NACA
National Army .... NA
National Army Museum [British military] (DMA) .... NAM
National Army Revolutionary Committee [or Council] [Laos] .... NARC
National Arrangements for Incidents Involving Radioactivity [Nuclear energy] (NUCP) .... NAIR
National Arson Prevention and Action Coalition (EA) .... NAPAC
National Art Dealers Association [Later, ADA] (EA) .... NADA
National Art Education Archive (AIE) .... NAEA
National Art Education Association (EA) .... NAEA
National Art Industry Council [Australia] .... NAIC
National Art Library, Victoria and Albert Museum, London, United Kingdom [Library symbol] [Library of Congress] (LCLS) .... UkLNAL
National Art Materials Trade Association (EA) .... NAMTA
National Art Museum of Sport (EA) .... NAMOS
National Art School Students' Association [Australia] .... NASSA
National Art Workers Community [Later, FCA] (EA) .... NAWC
National Art-Collectors' Fund [British] .... NACF
National Arthritis and Musculoskeletal and Skin Diseases Information Clearinghouse [US Public Health Service] [Information service or system] (IID) .... AMS
National Arthritis and Musculoskeletal and Skin Diseases Information Clearinghouse [Later, NAMSIC] (EA) .... NAMSDIC
National Arthritis and Musculoskeletal and Skin Diseases Information Clearinghouse (EA) .... NAMSIC
National Artists Equity Association (EA) .... NAEA
National Arts and Cultural Development Act of 1964 .... NACDA
National Arts and Handicapped Information Service (EA) .... NAHIS
National Arts Centre [Canada] .... NAC
National Arts Centre, Ottawa, ON, Canada [Library symbol Library of Congress] (LCLS) .... CaOOPA
National Arts Centre [Centre National des Arts] Ottawa, Ontario [Library symbol National Library of Canada] (NLC) .... OOPA
National Arts Club (EA) .... NAC
National Arts Foundation (EA) .... NAF
National Arts Stabilization Fund [Defunct] (EA) .... NASF
National Asbestos Council (EA) .... NAC
National Asbestos Registry [Environmental Protection Agency] (GFGA) .... NAR
National Ash Association (EA) .... NAA
National Asian American Telecommunications Association (EA) .... NAATA
National Asian Pacific American Law Student Association (EA) .... NAPALSA
National Asphalt Pavement Association (EA) .... NAPA
National Asphalt Workers' Union [A union] [British] .... NAWU
National Assault on Illiteracy Program .... NAIP
National Assault Prevention Center (EA) .... NAPC
National Assembly of Chief Livestock Sanitary Officials [Later, United States Animal Health Association] .... NACLSO
National Assembly of Community Arts Agencies (EA) .... NACAA
National Assembly of Local Arts Agencies (EA) .... NALAA

National Assembly of National Voluntary Health and Social Welfare Organizations (AD) .... NANVH&SWO
National Assembly of Religious Brothers (EA) .... NARB
National Assembly of Religious Women (EA) .... NARW
National Assembly of State Arts Agencies (EA) .... NASAA
National Assembly of Women Religious (EA) .... NAWR
National Assessment of Educational Progress (AD) .... NAEP
National Assessment of Educational Progress Information Retrieval System [National Institute of Education] [Database] .... NAEPIRS
National Assessment of Educational Progress, The Nation's Report Card (EA) .... NAEP
National Assessment of Juvenile Correction [University of Michigan] (AD) .... NAJC
National Assessment of Vocational Education [Department of Education] (GFGA) .... NAVE
National Asset Seizure and Forfeiture Office (AD) .... NASFO
National Assistance [British] .... NA
National Assistance League (EA) .... NAL
National Assistance Management Association [Washington, DC] (EA) .... NAMA
National Assocation of Radio Broadcasters (NTCM) .... NARB
National Associated Building Trades Council [A union] [British] .... NABTC
National Associated Businessmen [Defunct] (EA) .... NAB
National Associated Truck Stops and Associates (EA) .... NATSA
National Associates for Informed Depressives [Defunct] (EA) .... NAID
National Association [National Bank] .... NA
National Association (AD) .... Nat Assn
National Association Aerial of Photographic Libraries [British] (DBA) .... NAPLIB
National Association American Balloon Corps Veterans (EA) .... NAABCV
National Association American Business Clubs [High Point, NC] .... NAABC
National Association and Council of Business Schools .... NACBS
National Association Broadcast Employees and Technicians (EA) .... NABET
National Association Diaper Services (EA) .... NADS
National Association Drug and Allied Sales Organizations [Wyncote, PA] (EA) .... NADASO
National Association Executives Club (EA) .... NAEC
National Association for Accreditation in Psychoanalysis (EA) .... NAAP
National Association for Adults with Special Learning Needs (EA) .... NAASLN
National Association for Ambulatory Care (EA) .... NAAC
National Association for Ambulatory Care [Formerly, NAFEC] (EA) .... NAFAC
National Association for American Composers and Conductors (EA) .... NAACC
National Association for Applied Arts and Sciences (EA) .... NAAAS
National Association for Armenian Studies and Research (EA) .... NAASR
National Association for Asian and Pacific American Education (EA) .... NAAPAE
National Association for Association Political Action Committees (EA) .... NAFAPAC
National Association for Bank Auditors and Comptrollers [Later, BAI] (EA) .... NABAC
National Association for Bank Cost Analysis (EA) .... NABCA
National Association for Bank Cost and Management Accounting (EA) .... NABCA
National Association for Better Broadcasting (EA) .... NABB
National Association for Better Radio and Television (NADA) .... NABRT
National Association for Better Radio and Television [Later, NABB] (EA) .... NAFBRAT
National Association for Bilingual Education (EA) .... NABE
National Association for BioMedical Research (EA) .... NABR
National Association for Black Veterans (EA) .... NABV
National Association for Business Organizations [Baltimore, MD] (EA) .... NAFBO
National Association for Business Teacher Education [Reston, VA] (EA) .... NABTE
National Association for Campus Activities (EA) .... NACA
National Association for Career Education (EA) .... NACE
National Association for Cave Diving [Inactive] .... NACD
National Association for Check Safekeeping [Washington, DC] (EA) .... NACS
National Association for Chicano Studies (EA) .... NACS
National Association for Child Care Management [Defunct] (EA) .... NACCM
National Association for Child Development and Education [Later, NACCM] (EA) .... NACDE
National Association for Children of Alcoholism and Other Addictions (EA) .... NACOA
National Association for Church Management Consultants (EA) .... NACMC
National Association for City Drug and Alcohol Coordination [Defunct] (EA) .... NACDAC
National Association for Community Development [Defunct] (EA) .... NACD
National Association for Community Leadership (EA) .... NACL
National Association for Core Curriculum (EA) .... NACC
National Association for Corporate Speaker Activities (EA) .... NACSA
National Association for Corporate Speaker Activities [Reston, VA] (WDMC) .... NASCA
National Association for Court Administration (EA) .... NACA
National Association for Court Management (EA) .... NACM
National Association for Creative Children and Adults (EA) .... NACCA
National Association for Crime Victims Rights (EA) .... NA-CVR
National Association for Curriculum Enrichment and Extension [British] (EAIO) .... NACE
National Association for Design Education [British] .... NADE
National Association for Developmental Education (EA) .... NADE
National Association for Disabled Athletes (EA) .... NADA
National Association for Down Syndrome (EA) .... NADS
National Association for Drama in Education [Australia] .... NADE
National Association for Drama in Education (Victoria) [Australia] .... NADE(V)
National Association for Drama Therapy (EA) .... NADT
National Association for Educational Computing (EA) .... NAEC
National Association for Educational Television (NTCM) .... NAET
National Association for Educational Television [Defunct] .... NAETV

National Association for Environmental Management ... NAEM
National Association for Equal Educational Opportunities (EA) ... NAEEO
National Association for Equal Opportunity in Higher Education (EA) ... NAFEO
National Association for Ethnic Studies (EA) ... NAES
National Association for Families and Addiction Research and Education (PAZ) ... NAFARE
National Association for Family Day Care (EA) ... NAFDC
National Association for Female Executives [*New York, NY*] (EA) ... NAFE
National Association for Film in Education [*British*] ... NAFE
National Association for Foreign Student Affairs (EA) ... NAFSA
National Association for Free Enterprise [*Defunct*] (EA) ... NAFE
National Association for Freedom [*British*] ... NAFF
National Association for Gifted Children (EA) ... NAGC
National Association for Girls and Women in Sport (EA) ... NAGWS
National Association for Hearing and Speech Action (EA) ... NAHSA
National Association for Holocaust Education (EA) ... NAHE
National Association for Home Care (EA) ... NAHC
National Association for Hospital Development (EA) ... NAHD
National Association for Human Development (EA) ... NAHD
National Association for Humane and Environmental Education (EA) ... NAHEE
National Association for Humanities Education (EA) ... NAHE
National Association for Independent Living (EA) ... NAIL
National Association for Industry-Education Cooperation [*Buffalo, NY*] (EA) ... NAIEC
National Association for Information Services (EA) ... NAIS
National Association for Irish Freedom (EA) ... NAIF
National Association for Irish Justice [*Superseded by National Association for Irish Freedom*] (EA) ... NAIJ
National Association for Justice ... NAJ
National Association for Law Placement (EA) ... NALP
National Association for Lay Ministry (EA) ... NALM
National Association for Legal Support of Alternative Schools (EA) ... NALSAS
National Association for Lesbian and Gay Gerontology (AD) ... NALGG
National Association for Loss and Grief [*Australia*] ... NALG
National Association for Mediation in Education (EA) ... NAME
National Association for Mental Health (EA) ... NAMH
National Association for Middle Class Americans (EA) ... NAMCA
National Association for Milk Marketing Reform [*Later, NIDA*] (EA) ... NAMMR
National Association for Minority Education ... NAME
National Association for Multi-Level Marketing (EA) ... NAMLM
National Association for Multiracial Education [*British*] ... NAME
National Association for Music Therapy (EA) ... NAMT
National Association for Native American Children of Alcoholics (EA) ... NANACA
National Association for Neighborhood Schools (EA) ... NANS
National Association for Nursery Education [*Later, NAEYC*] (EA) ... NANE
National Association for Olmsted Parks (EA) ... NAOP
National Association for Outdoor Education [*British*] ... NAOE
National Association for Outlaw and Lawman History (EA) ... NOLA
National Association for Parents of the Visually Impaired (EA) ... NAPVI
National Association for Pastoral Renewal [*Defunct*] (EA) ... NAPR
National Association for Perinatal Addiction Research and Education (EA) ... NAPARE
National Association for Photographic Art [*Canada*] (EAIO) ... NAPA
National Association for Physical Education in Higher Education (EA) ... NAPEHE
National Association for Physical Education of College Women [*Later, NAPEHE*] (EA) ... NAPECW
National Association for Plastic Container Recovery (EA) ... NAPCOR
National Association for Poetry Therapy (EA) ... NAPT
National Association for Practical Nurse Education (DAVI) ... NAPNE
National Association for Practical Nurse Education and Service (EA) ... NAPNES
National Association for Professional Associations and Corporations (EA) ... NAPAC
National Association for Professional Saleswomen (EA) ... NAPS
National Association for Public Accountants (HGAA) ... NASPA
National Association for Public Continuing and Adult Education (EA) ... NAPCAE
National Association for Public Interest Law (EA) ... NAPIL
National Association for Public School Adult Educators [*Later, NAPCAE*] (EA) ... NAPSAE
National Association for Puerto Rican Civil Rights ... NAPCR
National Association for Puerto Rican Civil Rights (EA) ... NAPRCR
National Association for Pupil Transportation (EA) ... NAPT
National Association for Regional Ballet [*Later, RDA*] ... NARB
National Association for Registered Plans (EA) ... NARP
National Association for Released Time Christian Education (EA) ... NARTCE
National Association for Remedial Education [*British*] ... NARE
National Association for Remedial Teaching (AEBS) ... NART
National Association for Remotely Piloted Vehicles (MCD) ... NARPV
National Association for Research and Action in Community Care [*British*] (DI) ... NARACC
National Association for Research in Science Teaching (EA) ... NARST
National Association for Retarded Children (AEBS) ... NARC
National Association for Retarded Citizens [*Later, ARC*] (EA) ... NARC
National Association for Retired Credit Union People (EA) ... NARCUP
National Association for Rights Protection and Advocacy (EA) ... NARPA
National Association for Road Safety Instruction in Schools (AD) ... NARSIS
National Association for Rural Mental Health (EA) ... NARMH
National Association for Safety and Health in the Arts and Crafts (EA) ... NASHAC
National Association for School Magazines [*British*] (BI) ... NASM
National Association for Science, Technology, and Society (EA) ... NASTS
National Association for Search and Rescue (EA) ... NASAR
National Association for Senior Living Industries (EA) ... NASLI
National Association for Sick Child Daycare Centers (PAZ) ... NASCDC
National Association for Sickle Cell Disease (EA) ... NASCD
National Association for Small Schools [*British*] (DI) ... NASS
National Association for Soviet and East European Studies [*British*] ... NASEES
National Association for Special Educational Needs (AIE) ... NASEN
National Association for Speech and Hearing Action (EA) ... NASHA
National Association for Sport and Physical Education (EA) ... NASPE
National Association for Standing Advisory Councils for Religious Education (AIE) ... NASACRE
National Association for State Community Service Programs (EA) ... NASCSP
National Association for State Enrolled Assistant Nurses ... NASEAN
National Association for State Information Systems (EA) ... NASIS
National Association for State-Enrolled Assistant Nurses (AD) ... NASAEN
National Association for Statewide Health and Welfare (EA) ... NASHAW
National Association for Stock Car Advancement and Research (AD) ... NASCAR
National Association for Stock Car Auto Racing (EA) ... NASCAR
National Association for Teachers of Electronics [*Defunct*] (EA) ... NATE
National Association for Teaching English and other Community Languages to Adults [*Formerly, NATELSA*] (AIE) ... NATELCA
National Association for Teaching English as a Secondary Language to Adults [*British*] (DI) ... NATESLA
National Association for the Accreditation of Colleges and Secondary Schools (EA) ... NAACSS
National Association for the Accreditation of Martial Arts Colleges and Curriculum (EA) ... NAAMACC
National Association for the Advancement of Aardvarks in America [*Defunct*] (EA) ... NAAAA
National Association for the Advancement of Black Americans in Vocational Education (EA) ... NAABAVE
National Association for the Advancement of Colored People (EA) ... NAACP
National Association for the Advancement of Humane Education [*LA NAHEE*] (EA) ... NAAHE
National Association for the Advancement of Leboyer's Birth Without Violence (EA) ... NAALBWV
National Association for the Advancement of Native American Composers and Musicians ... NAANACM
National Association for the Advancement of Older People (EA) ... NAAOP
National Association for the Advancement of Orthodox Judaism (EA) ... NAAOJ
National Association for the Advancement of Perry Mason (EA) ... NAAPM
National Association for the Advancement of Private Higher Education [*Later, United Student Association*] (EA) ... NAAPHE
National Association for the Advancement of Psychoanalysis and the American Boards for Accreditation and Certification (EA) ... NAAPABAC
National Association for the Advancement of the Black Aged (EA) ... NAABA
National Association for the Advancement of Time (EA) ... NAFTAT
National Association for the Advancement of White People [*Defunct*] (EA) ... NAAWP
National Association for the Care and Resettlement of Offenders [*British*] ... NACRO
National Association for the Childless [*British*] (DBA) ... NAC
National Association for the Cottage Industry (EA) ... NACI
National Association for the Craniofacially Handicapped (EA) ... NACH
National Association for the Deaf, Blind, and Rubella [*British*] ... NADBR
National Association for the Dually Diagnosed (PAZ) ... NADD
National Association for the Education of Young Children (EA) ... NAEYC
National Association for the Exchange of Industrial Resources (EA) ... NAEIR
National Association for the Mentally Handicapped of Ireland (EAIO) ... NAMHI
National Association for the Paralysed (AD) ... NAP
National Association for the Practice of Anthropology (EA) ... NAPA
National Association for the Preservation and Perpetuation of Storytelling (EA) ... NAPPS
National Association for the Preservation of Baseball (EA) ... NAPB
National Association for the Prevention of Addiction to Narcotics [*Later, NADAP*] ... NAPAN
National Association for the Prevention of Rape by Castration (AD) ... NAPRC
National Association for the Prevention of Tuberculosis [*British*] (DI) ... NAPT
National Association for the Prevention of Venereal Disease (AD) ... NAPVD
National Association for the Relief of Paget's Disease [*British*] ... NARPD
National Association for the Repeal of Abortion Laws ... NARAL
National Association for the Rescue of Animals [*British*] (DI) ... NARA
National Association for the Self-Employed [*Fort Worth, TX*] (EA) ... NASE
National Association for the Self-Employed ... NASE
National Association for the Self-Supporting Active Ministry (EA) ... NASSAM
National Association for the Southern Poor (EA) ... NASP
National Association for the Specialty Food Trade (EA) ... NASFT
National Association for the Study of Epilepsy (DAVI) ... NASE
National Association for the Teaching of English (AD) ... NATE
National Association for the Welfare of Children in Hospital [*British*] ... NAWCH
National Association for Trade and Industrial Education (EA) ... NATIE
National Association for Training the Disabled in Office Work (AD) ... NADOW
National Association for Uniformed Services (EA) ... NAUS
National Association for Variable Annuities ... NAVA
National Association for Ventilator Dependent Individuals (EA) ... NAVDI
National Association for Veterinary Acupuncture (EA) ... NAVA
National Association for Vietnamese American Education (EA) ... NAVAE
National Association for Visually Handicapped (EA) ... NAVH
National Association for Vocational Business Education (AEBS) ... NAVBE
National Association for Widowed People [*Later, IAWP*] (EA) ... NAWP
National Association for Women (NADA) ... NAW
National Association for Women Deans, Administrators, and Counselors (EA) ... NAWDAC
National Association for Women in Careers (EA) ... NAFWIC
National Association for Women in Careers [*Later, NAFWIC*] (EA) ... NAWC
National Association for Women in Careers [*Later, NAFWIC*] (EA) ... NAWiC

National Association for Year-Round Education (EA) ... NAYRE
National Association for Young Writers [*Defunct*] (EA) ... NAYW
National Association Greenhouse Vegetable Growers (EA) ... NAGVG
National Association Legions of Honor (EA) ... NALOH
National Association Medical Staff Services (EA) ... NAMSS
National Association of Academic Advisors for Athletics (EA) ... N4A
National Association of Academies of Science (EA) ... NAAS
National Association of Accordion Wholesalers [*Defunct*] (EA) ... NAAW
National Association of Accountants [*Montvale, NJ*] (EA) ... NAA
National Association of Accountants for the Public Interest [*Later, API*] (EA) ... NAAPI
National Association of Accountants in Insolvencies (EA) ... NAAI
National Association of Accredited Cosmetology Schools (EA) ... NAACS
National Association of Activity Professionals (EA) ... NAAP
National Association of Administrators of State and Federal Education Programs (EA) ... NAASFEP
National Association of Adult College Students (EA) ... NAACS
National Association of Advertising Publishers [*Later, AFCP*] (EA) ... NAAP
National Association of Advertising Representatives (DGA) ... NAAR
National Association of Advisers in Computer Education (AIE) ... NAACE
National Association of Advisors for the Health Professions (EA) ... NAAHP
National Association of Advisory Officers Special Education [*British*] (DBA) ... NAAOSE
National Association of Aeronautical Examiners ... AAE
National Association of Aeronautical Examiners (EA) ... NAAE
National Association of Aeronautical Production Controllers ... APCA
National Association of African American Students of Law (EA) ... NAAASL
National Association of Afro-American Educators ... NAAE
National Association of Agricultural Contractors [*British*] (BI) ... NAAC
National Association of Agricultural Teachers [*Australia*] ... NAAT
National Association of Agriculture Employees (EA) ... NAAE
National Association of Air Forces Women ... NAAFW
National Association of Air National Guard Health Technicians (EA) ... NAANGHT
National Association of Air Traffic Specialists (EA) ... NAATS
National Association of Aircraft and Communications Suppliers [*Defunct*] (EA) ... NAACS
National Association of Alcohol and Tobacco Tax Field Officers ... NAATTFO
National Association of Alcoholic Beverage Importers [*Later, NABI*] (EA) ... NAABI
National Association of Alcoholism and Drug Abuse Counselors (EA) ... NAADAC
National Association of Alcoholism Treatment Programs (EA) ... NAATP
National Association of Aluminum Distributors (EA) ... NAAD
National Association of Amateur Oarsmen [*Later, USRA*] (EA) ... NAAO
National Association of American Academicians (NADA) ... NAAA
National Association of American Business Clubs (EA) ... AMBUCS
National Association of American Community Organizations (EA) ... NAACO
National Association of American School Employees and Retirees (EA) ... NAASER
National Association of American School Employees and Retirees Legal Defense Counsel (EA) ... NAASERLDC
National Association of Americans of Asian Indian Descent (EA) ... NAAAID
National Association of Amusement Parks, Pools, and Beaches [*Later, IAAPA*] ... NAAPPB
National Association of Angling and Casting Clubs [*Later, ACA*] ... NAACC
National Association of Animal Breeders (EA) ... NAAB
National Association of Anorexia Nervosa and Associated Disorders (PAZ) ... ANAD
National Association of Antique Automobile Clubs of Canada ... NAAACC
National Association of Anvil Makers [*A union*] [*British*] ... NAAM
National Association of Apnea Professionals (EA) ... NAAP
National Association of Approved Driving Instructors [*British*] (DBA) ... NAADI
National Association of Arab Americans (EA) ... NAAA
National Association of Arc Welding Equipment Repairers [*British*] (DBA) ... NAAWER
National Association of Architectural Metal Manufacturers (IAA) ... NAAM
National Association of Architectural Metal Manufacturers (EA) ... NAAMM
National Association of Area Agencies on Aging [*Also, NAAAA*] (EA) ... N4A
National Association of Area Agencies on Aging [*Also, N4A*] (EA) ... NAAAA
National Association of Art and Design Companies (EA) ... NAADC
National Association of Art Services [*Later, NAADC*] (EA) ... NAAS
National Association of Artists' Organizations (EA) ... NAAO
National Association of ASCS [*Agricultural Stabilization and Conservation Service*] **County Office Employees** (EA) ... NASCOE
National Association of Asian American Certified Public Accountants (EA) ... NAAACPA
National Association of Asian American Certified Public Accountants (MHDB) ... NAACPA
National Association of Asian-American Professionals (EA) ... NAAAP
National Association of Assessing Officers [*Later, IAAO*] ... NAAO
National Association of Assessors and Collectors of Taxes [*A union*] [*British*] ... NAACT
National Association of Athletic Development Directors ... NAADD
National Association of Atomic Veterans (EA) ... NAAV
National Association of Attorneys General (EA) ... NAAG
National Association of Australian Road Authorities ... AUSTROADS
National Association of Auto Racing Fan Clubs ... NAARFC
National Association of Auto Racing Memorabilia Collectors (EA) ... NAARMC
National Association of Auto Trim Shops (EA) ... NAATS
National Association of Automotive Mutual Insurance Companies [*Later, American Insurers Highway Safety Alliance*] (EA) ... NAAMIC
National Association of Avon Collectors (EA) ... NAAC
National Association of Baby Carriage Manufacturers (EA) ... NABCM
National Association of Baby Sitter Registries [*Later, NASR*] (EA) ... NABR
National Association of Balloon Artists and Suppliers [*Great Britain*] ... NABAS
National Association of Band Instrument Manufacturers (EA) ... NABIM
National Association of Bank Club Organization ... NABOR
National Association of Bank Directors [*Later, ASBD*] (EA) ... NABD
National Association of Bank Servicers (EA) ... NABS
National Association of Bank Women [*Chicago, IL*] (EA) ... NABW
National Association of Bankruptcy Trustees (EA) ... NABT
National Association of Baptist Professors of Religion (EA) ... NABPR
National Association of Bar Executives (EA) ... NABE
National Association of Barber Boards (EA) ... NABB
National Association of Barber Schools [*Later, NABSS*] (EA) ... NABS
National Association of Barber Styling Schools (EA) ... NABSS
National Association of Bar-Related Title Insurers [*San Diego, CA*] (EA) ... NABRTI
National Association of Basketball Coaches of the United States (EA) ... NABC
National Association of Basketball Referees (EA) ... NABR
National Association of Bedding Manufacturers [*Later, ISPA*] (EA) ... NABM
National Association of Bench and Bar Spouses (EA) ... NABBS
National Association of Beverage Importers (EA) ... NABI
National Association of Biblical Instructors [*Later, American Academy of Religion*] (EA) ... NABI
National Association of Bicentennial $2 Cancellation Collectors (EA) ... NAB$2CC
National Association of Bingo Clubs [*British*] (BI) ... NABC
National Association of Bioengineers [*Defunct*] (EA) ... NAB
National Association of Biological Engineering ... NABE
National Association of Biology Teachers (EA) ... NABT
National Association of Black Accountants [*Washington, DC*] (EA) ... NABA
National Association of Black and Minority Chambers of Commerce [*Later, NBCC*] (EA) ... NABMCC
National Association of Black and White Men Together: A Gay Multiracial Organiz ation for All People (EA) ... NABWMT
National Association of Black Catholic Administrators (EA) ... NABCA
National Association of Black Consulting Engineers (EA) ... NABCE
National Association of Black County Officials (EA) ... NABCO
National Association of Black Geologists and Geophysicists (EA) ... NABGG
National Association of Black Hospitality Professionals (EA) ... NABHP
National Association of Black Journalists (EA) ... NABJ
National Association of Black Manufacturers (EA) ... NABM
National Association of Black Media Producers ... NABMP
National Association of Black Owned Broadcasters (EA) ... NABOB
National Association of Black Professors (EA) ... NABP
National Association of Black Real Estate Professionals (EA) ... NABREP
National Association of Black Social Workers (EA) ... NABSW
National Association of Black Students (EA) ... NABS
National Association of Black Television and Film Producers (NTCM) ... NABTFP
National Association of Black Women Attorneys (EA) ... NABWA
National Association of Black Women Entrepreneurs [*Detroit, MI*] (EA) ... NABWE
National Association of Blacks in Criminal Justice (EA) ... NABCJ
National Association of Blacks within Government (EA) ... NABG
National Association of Blind and Visually Impaired Computer Users [*Defunct*] (EA) ... NABVICU
National Association of Blind Teachers (EA) ... NABT
National Association of Blouse Manufacturers (EA) ... NABM
National Association of Blue Shield Plans [*Later, BCBSA*] (EA) ... NABSP
National Association of Blue Shield Plans [*Later, BSA*], Chicago, IL [*Library symbol Library of Congress*] (LCLS) ... ICBS
National Association of Blueprint and Diazotype Coaters [*Later, ARMM*] ... NABDC
National Association of Boards of Barbers Examiners of America [*Later, NABB*] (EA) ... NABBEA
National Association of Boards of Education (EA) ... NABE
National Association of Boards of Examiners for Nursing Home Administrators (EA) ... NAB
National Association of Boards of Pharmacy (EA) ... NABP
National Association of Boards of Pharmacy Licensure Examination ... NABPLEX
National Association of Boat Manufacturers (EA) ... NABM
National Association of Boating Magazines [*Defunct*] (EA) ... NABM
National Association of Bond Lawyers (EA) ... NABL
National Association of Book Editors [*Defunct*] (EA) ... NABE
National Association of Book Manufacturers [*Defunct*] (EA) ... NABM
National Association of Book Publishers (NADA) ... NABP
National Association of Bookmakers Ltd. [*British*] (BI) ... NAB
National Association of Boys' Clubs [*British*] ... NABC
National Association of Brattice Cloth Manufacturers (EA) ... NABCM
National Association of Breeders Services (DBA) ... NABS
National Association of Breweriana Advertising (EA) ... NABA
National Association of Brick Distributors (EA) ... NABD
National Association of British and Irish Millers [*Incorporated*] (DBA) ... NABIM
National Association of British Manufacturers ... NABM
National Association of British Market Authorities ... NABMA
National Association of Broadcast Transmission Standards (PCM) ... NABTS
National Association of Broadcast Unions and Guilds (EA) ... NABUG
National Association of Broadcasters (EA) ... NAB
National Association of Builders' Labourers [*A union*] [*British*] ... NABL
National Association of Building Manufacturers [*Later, HMC*] (EA) ... NABM
National Association of Building Owners and Managers [*Later, BOMA*] (EA) ... NABOM
National Association of Building Service Contractors [*Later, BSCA*] ... NABSC
National Association of Bunco Investigators ... NABI
National Association of Business and Educational Radio (EA) ... NABER
National Association of Business and Industrial Saleswomen [*Denver, CO*] (EA) ... NABIS

National Association of Business Brokers (EA) ... NABB
National Association of Business Economists (EA) ... NABE
National Association of Business Education (IAA) ... NABE
National Association of Business Education State Supervisors [*Stillwater, OK*] (EA) ... NABESS
National Association of Business Law Teachers [*Later, NBLC*] (EA) ... NABLT
National Association of Business Political Action Committees (EA) ... NABPAC
National Association of Business Services [*Baldwin, NY*] (EA) ... NABS
National Association of Business Teacher-Training Institutions ... NABTTI
National Association of Business Travel Agents (EA) ... NABTA
National Association of Buying Services (EA) ... NABS
National Association of Canada Dry Franchise Bottlers (EA) ... NACDFB
National Association of Canadian Race Tracks ... NACRT
National Association of Canadians of Origins in India ... NACOI
National Association of Canoe Liveries and Outfitters (EA) ... NACLO
National Association of Career Development Consultants (EA) ... NACDC
National Association of Careers and Guidance Teachers [*British*] (DBA) ... NACGT
National Association of Careers Teachers (AD) ... NACT
National Association of Carpet Specialists [*Defunct*] ... NACS
National Association of Casual Furniture Retailers (EA) ... NACFR
National Association of Casualty and Surety Agents [*Bethesda, MD*] (EA) ... NACSA
National Association of Casualty and Surety Executives [*New York, NY*] (EA) ... NACSE
National Association of Catalog Showroom Merchandisers (EA) ... NACSM
National Association of Catastrophe Adjusters [*Comfort, TX*] (EA) ... NACA
National Association of Catering Butchers [*British*] (DBA) ... NACB
National Association of Catering Executives (EA) ... NACE
National Association of Catholic Alumni Clubs [*Later, CACI*] (EA) ... NACAC
National Association of Catholic Chaplains (EA) ... NACC
National Association of Catholic Diocesan Family Life Ministers [*Later, NACFLM*] (EA) ... NACDFLM
National Association of Catholic Family Life Ministers (EA) ... NACFLM
National Association of Catholic Publishers and Dealers in Church Goods (EA) ... NACPDCG
National Association of Catholic School Teachers (EA) ... NACST
National Association of Cellular Agents (EA) ... NACA
National Association of Cemeteries [*Later, ACA*] (EA) ... NAC
National Association of Certified Fraud Examiners (EA) ... NACFE
National Association of Certified Mortgage Bankers [*Later, NSREF*] (EA) ... NACMB
National Association of Chain Drug Stores (EA) ... NACDS
National Association of Chain Manufacturers (EA) ... NACM
National Association of Chapter 13 Trustees (MHDB) ... NACT
National Association of Charcoal Manufacturers [*British*] (DBA) ... NACM
National Association of Charitable Estate Counselors (EA) ... NACEC
National Association of Charterboat Operators (EA) ... NACO
National Association of Chemical Distributors (EA) ... NACD
National Association of Chewing Gum Manufacturers (EA) ... NACGM
National Association of Chief Education Social Workers (AIE) ... NACESW
National Association of Chiefs of Police (AD) ... NACP
National Association of Child Care Resource and Referral Agencies (EA) ... NACCRRA
National Association of Childbearing Centers (EA) ... NACC
National Association of Childbirth Assistants (EA) ... NACA
National Association of Childbirth Education [*Defunct*] (EA) ... NACE
National Association of Children's Hospitals and Related Institutions (EA) ... NACHRI
National Association of Chimney Lining Engineers [*British*] (DBA) ... NACLE
National Association of Chimney Sweeps [*British*] (DBA) ... NACS
National Association of Choirs [*British*] (BI) ... NAC
National Association of Christian Marriage Counselors [*Defunct*] (EA) ... NACMC
National Association of Christian Schools [*Defunct*] (EA) ... NACS
National Association of Christian Singles (EA) ... NACS
National Association of Christians in the Arts (EA) ... NACA
National Association of Church and Institutional Financing Organizations [*Atlanta, GA*] (EA) ... NACIFO
National Association of Church Business Administration (EA) ... NACBA
National Association of Church Furnishers [*British*] (BI) ... NACF
National Association of Church Personnel Administrators (EA) ... NACPA
National Association of Cider Makers [*British*] (BI) ... NACM
National Association of Cigarette Machine Operators [*British*] (DBA) ... NACMO
National Association of Citizen Advice Bureaux [*British*] ... NCAB
National Association of Citizens Advice Bureaus [*British*] (DBA) ... NACAB
National Association of Citizens Crime Commissions (EA) ... NACCC
National Association of Civic Secretaries (EA) ... NACS
National Association of Civil Service Employees (EA) ... NACSE
National Association of Civilian Conservation Corps Alumni (EA) ... NACCCA
National Association of Claimants' Compensation Attorneys. Law Journal [*A publication*] (DLA) ... NACCALJ
National Association of Claimants' Counsel of America [*Also known as NACCA Bar Association*] [*Later, ATLA*] ... NACCA
National Association of Claims Assistance Professionals (EA) ... NACAP
National Association of Classroom Educators in Business and Office Education (EA) ... CEBOE
National Association of Classroom Educators in Business Education [*Cambridge City, IN*] (EA) ... NACEBE
National Association of Clergy Hypnotherapists (EA) ... NACH
National Association of Clinical Tutors [*British*] (DBA) ... NACT
National Association of Coal Haulers [*Defunct*] (EA) ... NACH
National Association of Coin Laundry Equipment Operators (EA) ... NACLEO
National Association of Cold Storage Contractors (EA) ... NACSC
National Association of Cold Storage Insulation Contractors (EA) ... NACSIC
National Association of College Admission Counselors (EA) ... NACAC
National Association of College and University Administrators [*Superseded by NEA Higher Education Council*] (EA) ... NACUA
National Association of College and University Attorneys (EA) ... NACUA
National Association of College and University Business Office Associations (AD) ... NACUBO
National Association of College and University Business Officers [*Washington, DC*] (EA) ... NACUBO
National Association of College and University Chaplains and Directors of Religious Life (EA) ... NACUC
National Association of College and University Food Services (EA) ... NACUFS
National Association of College and University Summer Sessions [*Later, NAASS*] ... NACUSS
National Association of College and University Traffic and Security Officers (EA) ... NACUTSO
National Association of College Automotive Teachers (EA) ... NACAT
National Association of College Auxiliary Services (EA) ... NACAS
National Association of College Broadcasters (EA) ... NACB
National Association of College Deans and Registrars [*Later, NACDRAO*] (EA) ... NACDR
National Association of College Deans, Registrars, and Admissions Officers (EA) ... NACDRAO
National Association of College Stores (EA) ... NACS
National Association of College Wind and Percussion Instructors (EA) ... NACWPI
National Association of College Wind and Percussion Instruments (AD) ... NACWPI
National Association of College Women [*Later, NAUW*] (EA) ... NACW
National Association of Colleges and Teachers of Agriculture (EA) ... NACTA
National Association of Colleges and Universities ... NACU
National Association of Collegiate Commissioners [*Later, CCA*] (EA) ... NACC
National Association of Collegiate Directors of Athletics (EA) ... NACDA
National Association of Collegiate Gymnastics Coaches (Men) (EA) ... NACGC
National Association of Collegiate Marketing Administrators ... NACMA
National Association of Colliery Managers [*British*] (DBA) ... NACM
National Association of Colliery Overmen, Deputies, and Shotfirers [*A union*] [*British*] (DCTA) ... NACODS
National Association of Colored Girls Clubs [*Later, NAGC*] (EA) ... NACGC
National Association of Colored Women's Clubs (EA) ... NACWC
National Association of Commercial Broadcasters in Japan (EY) ... MINPOREN
National Association of Commission Lumber Salesmen ... NACLS
National Association of Commissioners, Secretaries, and Directors of Agriculture[*Later, NASDA*] (EA) ... NACSDA
National Association of Commissions for Women (EA) ... NACW
National Association of Commodity Cargo Superintendents and Suveyors [*British*] (DBA) ... NACCSS
National Association of Community Action Agencies (EA) ... NACAA
National Association of Community Development Loan Funds (EA) ... NACDLF
National Association of Community Health Centers (EA) ... NACHC
National Association of Community Leadership Organizations [*Later, National Association for Community Leadership*] (EA) ... NACLO
National Association of Community Legal Centers [*Australia*] ... NACLC
National Association of Community Schools, Colleges, and Centres [*British*] (DBA) ... NACSCC
National Association of Companion Sitter Agencies and Referral Services [*Later, PCA*] (EA) ... NACSARS
National Association of Competitive Mounted Orienteering (EA) ... NACMO
National Association of Composers, USA (EA) ... NAC
National Association of Composers, USA (EA) ... NACUSA
National Association of Computer Consultant Businesses (EA) ... NACCB
National Association of Computer Stores [*Later, IVCI*] [*Defunct*] (EA) ... NACS
National Association of Computer-Assisted Analysis (IAA) ... NACAA
National Association of Computerized Tax Processors (EA) ... NACTP
National Association of Concerned Veterans (EA) ... NACV
National Association of Concession Services (EA) ... NACS
National Association of Concessionaires (EA) ... NAC
National Association of Condominium Owners ... NACO
National Association of Congregational Christian Churches [*Later, CCCNA*] (EA) ... NACCC
National Association of Conservation Districts ... NACD
National Association of Conservative Graduates (AIE) ... NACG
National Association of Consumer Agency Administrators (EA) ... NACAA
National Association of Consumer Credit Administrators (EA) ... NACCA
National Association of Consumer Organizations ... NACO
National Association of Consumers and Travelers (EA) ... NACT
National Association of Container Distributors (EA) ... NACD
National Association of Continuing Medical Education Meetings and Seminars [*Defunct*] (EA) ... NACMEMS
National Association of Convenience Stores (EA) ... NACS
National Association of Convention Bureaus (NADA) ... NACB
National Association of Conveyancers [*British*] (DBA) ... NAC
National Association of Co-Op Advertising Professionals [*Defunct*] (EA) ... NACAP
National Association of Cooperative Officials [*A union*] [*British*] (DCTA) ... NACO
National Association of Coopers [*A union*] [*British*] ... NAC
National Association of Coordinators of State Programs for the Mentally Retarded[*Later, National Association of State Mental Retardation Program Directors*] (EA) ... NACSPMR
National Association of Coroners (EA) ... NAC
National Association of Corporate and Professional Recruiters (EA) ... NACPR
National Association of Corporate Directors [*Washington, DC*] (EA) ... NACD
National Association of Corporate Real Estate Executives (EA) ... NACORE
National Association of Corporate Treasurers [*Washington, DC*] (EA) ... NACT
National Association of Corrosion Engineers (EA) ... NACE
National Association of Corrosion Engineers, Houston, TX [*Library symbol Library of Congress*] (LCLS) ... TxHN

National Association of Cosmetic Boutique Owners (EA) ... NACBO
National Association of Cosmetology Schools (EA) ... NACS
National Association of Cost Accountants [*Later, NAA*] ... NACA
National Association of Costume Jewelers [*Defunct*] (EA) ... NACJ
National Association of Counsel for Children (EA) ... NACC
National Association of Counsellors in Education (AIE) ... NACE
National Association of Counselors (EA) ... NAC
National Association of Counties ... NAC
National Association of Counties (EA) ... NACo
National Association of Counties Research Foundation ... NACORF
National Association of Counties Research Foundation (OICC) ... NACRF
National Association of County 4-H Club Agents [*Later, NAE4-HA*] (EA) ... NACCA
National Association of County Administrators (EA) ... NACA
National Association of County Agricultural Agents (EA) ... NACAA
National Association of County and Prosecuting Attorneys [*Later, NDAA*] ... NACPA
National Association of County Civil Attorneys (EA) ... NACCA
National Association of County Community Development Directors (EA) ... NACCDD
National Association of County Data Processing Administrators (EA) ... NACDPA
National Association of County Employment and Training Administrators [*Later, NACTEP*] (EA) ... NACETA
National Association of County Engineers (EA) ... NACE
National Association of County Governments (OICC) ... NACG
National Association of County Health Facility Administrators (EA) ... NACHFA
National Association of County Health Officials (EA) ... NACHO
National Association of County Human Services Administrators (EA) ... NACHSA
National Association of County Information Officers (EA) ... NACIO
National Association of County Park and Recreation Officials (EA) ... NACPRO
National Association of County Planners (EA) ... NACP
National Association of County Planning Directors [*Later, NACP*] (EA) ... NACPD
National Association of County Recorders and Clerks (EA) ... NACRC
National Association of County Training and Employment Professionals [*Washington, DC*] (EA) ... NACTEP
National Association of County Treasurers and Finance Officers (EA) ... NACTFO
National Association of County Welfare Directors [*Later, NACHSA*] (EA) ... NACWD
National Association of Craftsman Tailors [*British*] (BI) ... NACT
National Association of Crankshaft and Cylinder Grinders [*British*] (BI) ... NACCG
National Association of Credential Evaluation Services (EA) ... NACES
National Association of Credit Management [*New York, NY*] (EA) ... NACM
National Association of Credit Management ... NACM
National Association of Credit Union Presidents (EA) ... NACUP
National Association of Crime Victim Compensation Boards (EA) ... NACVCB
National Association of Criminal Defense Lawyers (EA) ... NACDL
National Association of Criminal Justice Planners [*Defunct*] (EA) ... NACJP
National Association of Crop Insurance Agents [*Anoka, MN*] (EA) ... NACIA
National Association of Cuban Architects (in Exile) [*Defunct*] (EA) ... NACA
National Association of Cuban Women and Men of the United States (EA) ... NACAWM-USA
National Association of Cuban-American Women of the USA (EA) ... NACAW-USA
National Association of Customs Brokers and Forwarders Association of America ... NACBFAA
National Association of Cycle Traders [*British*] (BI) ... NACT
National Association of Cycle Trades (AD) ... NACT
National Association of Dairy Equipment Manufacturers [*Later, DFISA*] (EA) ... NADEM
National Association of Daytime Dress Manufacturers [*Defunct*] ... NADDM
National Association of Dealers in Antiques (EA) ... NADA
National Association of Deans of Women and Advisors to Girls in Negro Schools [*Defunct*] (EA) ... NADWAGNS
[*The*] **National Association of Decorative and Fine Arts Societies** [*British*] ... NADFAS
National Association of Decorative Architectural Finishes (EA) ... NADAF
National Association of Decorative Fabric Distributors (EA) ... NADFD
National Association of Defense Lawyers in Criminal Cases [*Later, NACDL*] (EA) ... NADLCC
National Association of Demolition Contractors (EA) ... NADC
National Association of Dental Assistants (EA) ... NADA
National Association of Dental Laboratories (EA) ... NADL
National Association of Dental Service Plans [*Insurance*] (DHSM) ... NADSP
National Association of Deputising Doctors [*British*] (DBA) ... NADD
National Association of Deputy United States Marshals (EA) ... NADUSM
National Association of Design and Art Service Organizations (EA) ... NADASO
National Association of Design and Fine Art Societies (AD) ... NADFAS
National Association of Desktop Publishers (EA) ... NADP
National Association of Development Companies (EA) ... NADCO
National Association of Development Education Centres [*British*] (DBA) ... NADEC
National Association of Development Organization Research Fund ... NADORF
National Association of Development Organizations (EA) ... NADO
National Association of Developmental Disabilities Councils (EA) ... NADDC
National Association of Diemakers and Diecutters [*Formerly, DDA*] (EA) ... NADD
National Association of Diocesan Altar Guilds of the Protestant Episcopal Church (EA) ... NADAG
National Association of Diocesan Ecumenical Officers (EA) ... NADEO
National Association of Direct Mail Writers ... NADMW
National Association of Direct Selling Companies [*Later, DSA*] (EA) ... NADSC
National Association of Directors of Nursing Administration in Long Term Care (EA) ... NADONA/LTC
National Association of Disability Evaluating Professionals [*Later, IHC*] (EA) ... NADEP
National Association of Disability Examiners (EA) ... NADE
National Association of Discharged Prisoners' Aid Societies [*British*] (DI) ... NADPAS
National Association of Disco Disc Jockeys [*Defunct*] (EA) ... NADD
National Association of Discount Merchants [*Defunct*] (EA) ... NADM
National Association of Display Industries [*New York, NY*] (EA) ... NADI
National Association of Distributive Education Teachers ... NADET
National Association of Distributors and Dealers of Structural Clay Products [*Later, NABD*] (EA) ... NADD
National Association of Diversified Manufacturers Representatives [*Later, NAGMR*] (EA) ... NADMR
National Association of Division Order Analysts (EA) ... NADOA
National Association of Divisional Executives for Education [*British*] ... NADEE
National Association of Doctors in Practice [*British*] (DI) ... NADP
National Association of Doctors in the United States (EA) ... NADUS
National Association of Document Examiners (EA) ... NADE
National Association of Dog Obedience Instructors (EA) ... NADOI
National Association of Doll and Stuffed Toy Manufacturers (EA) ... NADSTM
National Association of Doll Manufacturers [*Later, NADSTM*] (EA) ... NADM
National Association of Domestic and Farm Pump Manufacturers [*Later, WSC*] ... NADFPM
National Association of Drama Advisers [*British*] ... NADA
National Association of Dramatic and Speech Arts (EA) ... NADSA
National Association of Dredging Contractors (EA) ... NADC
National Association of Drop Forgers and Stampers (AD) ... NADFS
National Association of Drug Addiction (AD) ... NADA
National Association of Drug Addiction (NADA) ... NADA
National Association of Ecumenical Staff (EA) ... NAES
National Association of Educational Broadcasters [*Formerly, Association of Collegeand University Broadcasting Stations (1934)*] (EA) ... NAEB
National Association of Educational Buyers [*Woodbury, NY*] (EA) ... NAEB
National Association of Educational Data Systems (IAA) ... NAEDS
National Association of Educational Guidance Services for Adults [*British*] (DBA) ... NAEGS
National Association of Educational Inspectors, Advisers, and Consultants (AIE) ... NAEIAC
National Association of Educational Negotiators (EA) ... NAEN
National Association of Educational Office Personnel (EA) ... NAEOP
National Association of Educational Programs [*Carnegie Foundation*] (AD) ... NAEP
National Association of Educational Secretaries [*Later, NAEOP*] (EA) ... NAES
National Association of Educational Technicians [*British*] ... NAET
National Association of Electric Companies [*Later, EEI*] (EA) ... NAEC
National Association of Electrical Distributors (EA) ... NAED
National Association of Electronic Keyboard Manufacturers (EA) ... NAEKM
National Association of Electronic Organ Manufacturers ... NAEOM
National Association of Elementary School Principals (EA) ... NAESP
National Association of Elevator Contractors (EA) ... NAEC
National Association of Elevator Safety Authorities (EA) ... NAESA
National Association of Emergency Medical Service Physicians (EA) ... NAEMSP
National Association of Emergency Medical Technicians (EA) ... NAEMT
National Association of Employers on Health Care Action ... NAEHCA
National Association of Employers on Health Care Alternatives (EA) ... NAEHCA
National Association of Employers on Health Maintenance Organizations [*Later, NAEHCA*] (EA) ... NAEHMO
National Association of Energy Service Companies (EA) ... NAESC
National Association of Energy Service Companies (EA) ... NAESCO
National Association of Engine and Boat Manufacturers [*Later, NMMA*] (EA) ... NAEBM
National Association of Engineering Companies (EA) ... NAEC
National Association of Engravers and Die-Stampers [*British*] (BI) ... NAEDS
National Association of Enrolled Agents (EA) ... NAEA
National Association of Enrolled Federal Tax Accountants (EA) ... NAEFTA
National Association of Entrepreneurs ... NAE
National Association of Environmental Education [*British*] (DBA) ... NAEE
National Association of Environmental Professionals (EA) ... NAEP
National Association of Episcopal Schools (EA) ... NAES
National Association of Estate Agents [*British*] (EAIO) ... NAEA
National Association of Estate Planning Councils (EA) ... NAEPC
National Association of Evangelicals (EA) ... NAE
National Association of Executive Recruiters (EA) ... NAER
National Association of Executive Secretaries (EA) ... NAES
National Association of Exhibition Contractors [*British*] (BI) ... NAEC
National Association of Export Companies [*New York, NY*] (EA) ... NEXCO
National Association of Exposition Managers (EA) ... NAEM
National Association of Extension 4-H Agents (EA) ... NAE4-HA
National Association of Extension 4-H Agents (EA) ... NAEA
National Association of Extension Home Economists (EA) ... NAEHE
National Association of Extradition Officials (EA) ... NAEO
National Association of Family Planning Doctors [*British*] (DBA) ... NAFPD
National Association of Fan Clubs (EA) ... NAFC
National Association of Fan Manufacturers [*Later, AMCA*] ... NAFM
National Association of Farm and Ranch Trailer Manufacturers [*Defunct*] (EA) ... NAFRTM
National Association of Farm Broadcasters (EA) ... NAFB
National Association of Farm Directors (NTCM) ... NAFD
National Association of Farmer Elected Committeemen (EA) ... NAFEC
National Association of Farmworker Organizations [*Defunct*] (EA) ... NAFO
National Association of Farriers, Blacksmiths, and Agricultural Engineers [*British*] (DBA) ... NAFB & AE
National Association of Fashion and Accessory Designers (EA) ... NAFAD

National Association of Fastener Stockholders [*British*] (DBA) .... NAFS
National Association of Federal Career Employees [*Defunct*] (EA) .... NAFCE
National Association of Federal Credit Unions (EA) .... NAFCU
National Association of Federal Education Program Administrators (EA) .... NAFPA
National Association of Federal Veterinarians (EA) .... NAFV
National Association of Federally Impacted Schools (EA) .... NAFIS
National Association of Federally Licensed Firearms Dealers (EA) .... NAFLFD
National Association of Federations of Syrian and Lebanese American Clubs (EA) .... NAFSLAC
National Association of Field Studies Officers [*British*] (DBA) .... NAFSO
National Association of Financial Consultants (EA) .... NAFC
National Association of Fine Arts [*Defunct*] (EA) .... NAFA
National Association of Finishers of Textile Fabrics [*Later, ATMI*] (EA) .... NAFTF
National Association of Fire Equipment Distributors (EA) .... NAFED
National Association of Fire Investigators (EA) .... NAFI
National Association of Fire Officers [*British*] (DI) .... NAFO
National Association of Fire Science and Administration [*Defunct*] (EA) .... NAFSA
National Association of Fiscally Responsible Cities [*Defunct*] (EA) .... NAFRC
National Association of Flag Manufacturers .... NAFM
National Association of Fleet Administrators [*Iselin, NJ*] (EA) .... NAFA
National Association of Fleet Resale Dealers [*Los Angeles, CA*] (EA) .... NAFRD
National Association of Flight Instructors (EA) .... NAFI
National Association of Flood and Storm Water Management Agencies (EA) .... NAFSWMA
National Association of Floor Covering Distributors (EA) .... NAFCD
National Association of Floor Covering Installers [*Later, AIDS International*] (EA) .... NAFCI
National Association of Flour Distributors (EA) .... NAFD
National Association of Flower Arrangement Societies (AD) .... NAFAS
National Association of Flower Arrangement Societies of Great Britain (BI) .... NAFAS
National Association of FM [*Frequency Modulation*] **Broadcasters** [*Later, NRBA*] (EA) .... NAFMB
National Association of Food Chains [*Later, FMI*] (EA) .... NAFC
National Association of Food Chains (NADA) .... NAFC
National Association of Food Equipment Manufacturers (EA) .... NAFEM
National Association of Food Processors (ECON) .... NAFP
National Association of Foot Specialists (AD) .... NAFS
National Association of Foreign Medical Graduates [*Later, ACIP*] .... NAFMG
National Association of Foreign Student Advisors (AD) .... NAFSA
National Association of Foreign-Trade Zones [*Washington, DC*] (EA) .... NAFTZ
National Association of Forensic Economists (EA) .... NAFE
National Association of Forensic Sciences (AD) .... NAFS
National Association of Formwork Contractors [*British*] (DBA) .... NAFC
National Association of Foster Care Reviewers (EA) .... NAFCR
National Association of Foster Grandparent Program Directors (EA) .... NAFGPD
National Association of Franchise Companies (EA) .... NAFCO
National Association of Franchised Businessmen [*Defunct*] (EA) .... NAFB
National Association of Fraternal Insurance Counsellors [*Sheboygan, WI*] (EA) .... NAFIC
National Association of Freestanding Emergency Centers [*Later, NAAC*] (EA) .... NAFEC
National Association of Freight Payment Banks [*Pittsburgh, PA*] (EA) .... NAFPB
National Association of Freight Transportation Consultants (EA) .... NAFTC
National Association of Fresh Produce Processors (EA) .... NAFPP
National Association of Friendship Centres [*Canada*] .... NAFC
National Association of Frozen Food Packers [*Later, AFFI*] (EA) .... NAFFP
National Association of Frozen Food Producers (AD) .... NAFFP
National Association of Fruits, Flavors, and Syrups (EA) .... NAFFS
National Association of Full Figured Women (EA) .... NAFFW
National Association of Funeral Directors [*British*] (BI) .... NAFD
National Association of Furniture Agents [*Australia*] .... NAFA
National Association of Furniture Manufacturers [*Later, AFMA*] (EA) .... NAFM
National Association of Furniture Warehousemen and Removers (AD) .... NAFWR
National Association of Future Teachers of America [*Later, Student National Education Association*] (AEBS) .... NAFTA
National Association of Future Women [*Later, NAFWIC*] (EA) .... NAFW
National Association of Futures Trading Advisors [*Defunct*] (EA) .... NAFTA
National Association of Gagwriters (EA) .... NAG
National Association of Gambling Regulatory Agencies (EA) .... NAGRA
National Association of Garage Door Manufacturers (EA) .... NAGDM
National Association of Gardeners [*Later, PGMS*] (EA) .... NAG
National Association of Gay Alcoholism Professionals [*Later, NALGAP*] (EA) .... NAGAP
National Association of General Merchandise Representatives [*Chicago, IL*] (EA) .... NAGMR
National Association of Geology Teachers (EA) .... NAGT
National Association of Girls Clubs (EA) .... NAGC
National Association of Glass Container Distributors [*Later, NACD*] (EA) .... NAGCD
National Association of Glove Manufacturers (EA) .... NAGM
National Association of Glue Manufacturers [*Defunct*] (EA) .... NAGM
National Association of Goldsmiths [*British*] .... NAG
National Association of Golf Ball Manufacturers (EA) .... NAGBM
National Association of Golf Club Manufacturers (EA) .... NAGCM
National Association of Government Archives and Records Administrators (EA) .... NAGARA
National Association of Government Communicators (EA) .... NAGC
National Association of Government Deferred Compensation Administrators (EA) .... NAGDCA
National Association of Government Employees (EA) .... NAGE
National Association of Government Engineers [*Defunct*] (EA) .... NAOGE
National Association of Government Inspectors [*Later, National Association of Government Inspectors and Quality Assurance Personnel*] (EA) .... NAGI
National Association of Government Inspectors and Quality Assurance Personnel (EA) .... NAGI/QAP
National Association of Government Secretaries [*Defunct*] .... NAGS
National Association of Government Service Contractors [*Defunct*] (EA) .... NAGSC
National Association of Governmental Labor Officials (EA) .... NAGLO
National Association of Governors and Managers [*British*] (DBA) .... NAGM
National Association of Governors' Highway Safety Representatives (EA) .... NAGHSR
National Association of Grained Plate Makers (AD) .... NAGPM
National Association of Greeting Card Publishers [*Later, GCA*] (EA) .... NAGCP
National Association of Grooms [*British*] (DI) .... NAG
National Association of Groundsmen [*British*] (DI) .... NAG
National Association of Guidance Supervisors and Counselor Trainers .... NAGSCT
National Association of Handwriting Analysts .... NAHA
National Association of Hardwood Wholesalers [*Defunct*] .... NAHW
National Association of Head Teachers [*British*] .... NAHT
National Association of Health and Welfare Ministries of the United Methodist Church [*Later, United Methodist Association of Health and Welfare Ministries - UMA*] (EA) .... NAHWMUMC
National Association of Health Authorities [*British*] (EAIO) .... NAHA
National Association of Health Authorities and Trusts [*British*] (EAIO) .... NAHAT
National Association of Health Authorities in England and Wales (AIE) .... NAHA
National Association of Health Career Schools (EA) .... NAHCS
National Association of Health Data Organizations (EA) .... NAHDO
National Association of Health Estates Managers [*British*] (DBA) .... NAHEM
National Association of Health Service Personnel Officers [*British*] (DBA) .... NAHSPO
National Association of Health Service Security Officers [*British*] (DBA) .... NAHSSO
National Association of Health Services Executives (EA) .... NAHSE
National Association of Health Stores [*British*] (DBA) .... NAHS
National Association of Health Underwriters [*Washington, DC*] (EA) .... NAHU
National Association of Health Unit Clerks-Coordinators (EA) .... NAHUC
National Association of Healthcare Recruitment (EA) .... NAHCR
National Association of Hearing and Speech Agencies (AEBS) .... NAHSA
National Association of Hebrew Day School Administrators (EA) .... NAHDSA
National Association of Hillel Directors [*Later, IAHD*] (EA) .... NAHD
National Association of Hispanic Federal Executives (EA) .... NAHFE
National Association of Hispanic Journalists (EA) .... NAHJ
National Association of Hispanic Nurses (EA) .... NAHN
National Association of Hispanic Publications (EA) .... NAHP
National Association of HMO [*Health Maintenance Organization*] **Regulators** .... NAHMOR
National Association of Holiday Centres [*British*] (DBA) .... NAHC
National Association of Home and Workshop Writers (EA) .... NAHWW
National Association of Home Based Businesses [*Baltimore, MD*] (EA) .... NAHBB
National Association of Home Builders (NADA) .... NAHB
National Association of Home Builders of the United States (EA) .... NAHB
National Association of Home Economics Supervisors [*Later, NASSVHE*] (EA) .... NAHES
National Association of Home Health Agencies [*Later, NAHC*] (EA) .... NAHHA
National Association of Home Manufacturers [*Later, HMC*] (EA) .... NAHM
National Association of Homebuilders (AD) .... NAH
National Association of Homeowners [*British*] (DBA) .... NAHO
National Association of Homes for Boys [*Later, NFCCE*] .... NAHB
National Association of Homes for Children (EA) .... NAHC
National Association of Homoeopathic Groups [*British*] (DBA) .... NAHG
National Association of Horological Schools (EA) .... NAHS
National Association of Horseradish Packers [*Defunct*] (EA) .... NAHP
National Association of Hose and Accessories Distributors (EA) .... NAHAD
National Association of Hosiery Manufacturers (EA) .... NAHM
National Association of Hospital Admitting Managers (EA) .... NAHAM
National Association of Hospital Broadcasting Organizations [*British*] (DBA) .... NAHBO
National Association of Hospital Central Service Personnel [*Later, IAHCSM*] (EA) .... NAHCSP
National Association of Hospital Fire Officers [*British*] (DBA) .... NAHFO
National Association of Hospital Hospitality Houses (EA) .... NAHHH
National Association of Hospital Purchasing Agents [*Later, NAHPMM*] (EA) .... NAHPA
National Association of Hospital Purchasing Management [*Later, NAHPMM*] (EA) .... NAHPM
National Association of Hospital Purchasing Materials Management (EA) .... NAHPMM
National Association of Hospital Supplies Officers [*British*] (BI) .... NAHSO
National Association of Hotel Accountants [*Later, International Association of Hospitality Accountants*] (EA) .... NAHA
National Association of Hotel and Motel Accountants [*Later, International Association of Hospitality Accountants*] .... NAHMA
National Association of Hotel and Restaurant Meat Purveyors [*Later, NAMP*] (EA) .... NAHRMP
National Association of House and Daytime Dress Manufacturers (EA) .... NAHDDM
National Association of House to House Installment Companies [*Later, NAIC*] (EA) .... NAHHIC
National Association of Housing and Redevelopment Officials (EA) .... NAHRO
National Association of Housing Cooperatives (EA) .... NAHC
National Association of Human Rights Workers (EA) .... NAHRW
National Association of Human Services Technologies [*Defunct*] (EA) .... NAHST
National Association of Humanistic Gerontology (EA) .... NAHG

National Association of Hypnotists and Psychotherapists [British] (DBA) .... NAHP
National Association of Ice Cream Vendors [Defunct] (EA) .... NAICV
National Association of Ice Industries [Later, PIA] (EA) .... NAII
National Association of Importers and Exporters of Hides and Skins [Later, USHSLA] (EA) .... NAIEHS
National Association of Income Tax Preparers [Defunct] (EA) .... NAITP
National Association of Independent Business [Defunct] (EA) .... NAIB
National Association of Independent Colleges and Private Schools (EA) .... NAICPS
National Association of Independent Colleges and Universities (EA) .... NAICU
National Association of Independent Computer Companies (EA) .... NAICC
National Association of Independent Fee Appraisers (EA) .... NAIFA
National Association of Independent Food Retailers [Defunct] (EA) .... NAIFR
National Association of Independent Insurance Adjusters [Chicago, IL] (EA) .... NAIIA
National Association of Independent Insurers [Des Plaines, IL] (EA) .... NAII
National Association of Independent Insurers, Des Plaines, IL [Library symbol Library of Congress] (LCLS) .... IDesN
National Association of Independent Life Brokerage Agencies [Washington, DC] (EA) .... NAILBA
National Association of Independent Lighting Distributors (EA) .... NAILD
National Association of Independent Lubes (EA) .... NAIL
National Association of Independent Lumbermen [Defunct] (EA) .... NAIL
National Association of Independent Maritime Educators (EA) .... NAIME
National Association of Independent Music Dealers [Defunct] (EA) .... NAIMD
National Association of Independent Public Finance Advisors .... NAIPFA
National Association of Independent Publishers (EA) .... NAIP
National Association of Independent Record Distributors and Manufacturers (EA) .... NAIRD
National Association of Independent Record Distributors and Manufacturers (EA) .... NAIRDM
National Association of Independent Resurfacers (EA) .... NAIR
National Association of Independent Schools (EA) .... NAIS
National Association of Independent Television Producers and Distributors [Defunct] (EA) .... NAITPD
National Association of Industrial and Office Parks (EA) .... NAIOP
National Association of Industrial and Technical Teacher Educators (EA) .... NAITTE
National Association of Industrial Artists [Later, IG] (EA) .... NAIA
National Association of Industrial Distributors [British] (DBA) .... NAID
National Association of Industrial Parks [Later, NAIOP] (EA) .... NAIP
National Association of Industrial Teacher Educators [Later, NAITTE] (EA) .... NAITE
National Association of Industrial Technology (EA) .... NAIT
National Association of Industries for the Blind and Disabled [British] (DBA) .... NAIBD
National Association of Inland Water Carriers [British] (BI) .... NAIWC
National Association of Inland Waterway Carriers [British] (DBA) .... NAIWC
National Association of Insect Electrocutor Manufacturers (EA) .... NAIEM
National Association of Inspectors and Educational Advisers [British] .... NAIEA
National Association of Inspectors of Schools and Educational Organisers [British] (BI) .... NAIEO
National Association of Inspectors of Schools and Educational Organisers [British] .... NAISEO
National Association of Installation Developers (EA) .... NAID
National Association of Installment Companies [New York, NY] (EA) .... NAIC
National Association of Institutional Laundry Managers [Later, National Association of Institutional Linen Management] (EA) .... NAILM
National Association of Institutional Linen Management (EA) .... NAILM
National Association of Instructional Leaders in Technical Education (EA) .... NAILTE
National Association of Insurance Agents [Later, IIAA] (EA) .... NAIA
National Association of Insurance Brokers [Washington, DC] (EA) .... NAIB
National Association of Insurance Commissioners [Kansas City, MO] (EA) .... NAIC
National Association of Insurance Women (International) [Tulsa, OK] (EA) .... NAIW
National Association of Insured Persons [Defunct] (EA) .... NAIP
National Association of Intercollegiate Athletics (EA) .... NAIA
National Association of Intercollegiate Commissioners (EA) .... NAIC
National Association of Interdisciplinary Ethnic Studies (EA) .... NAIES
National Association of Intergroup Relations Officials [Later, NAHRW] (EA) .... NAIRO
National Association of Interior Designers [Defunct] (EA) .... NAID
National Association of Internal Revenue Employees [Later, NTEU] (EA) .... NAIRE
National Association of Interpretation (EA) .... NAI
National Association of Investigative Specialists (EA) .... NAIS
National Association of Investment Clubs [British] (DBA) .... NAIC
National Association of Investment Companies .... NAIC
National Association of Investment Companies (EA) .... NAIC
National Association of Investors Corp. (EA) .... NAIC
National Association of Iron and Steel Stockholders (AD) .... NAISS
National Association of Jai Alai Frontons (EA) .... NAJF
National Association of Jazz Education (AD) .... NAJE
National Association of Jazz Educators [Later, IAJE] (EA) .... NAJE
National Association of JD/MBA [Juris Doctor/Master of Business Administration] Professionals [Defunct] .... NAJD/MBAP
National Association of Jewelry Appraisers (EA) .... NAJA
National Association of Jewish Center Workers [Later, AJCW] .... NAJCW
National Association of Jewish Family, Children's, and Health Professionals (EA) .... NAJFCHP
National Association of Jewish Homes for the Aged [Later, NAAJHHA] (EA) .... NAJHA

National Association of Jewish Vocational Services (EA) .... NAJVS
National Association of Journalism Directors [Later, JEA] (EA) .... NAJD
National Association of Junior Auxiliaries (EA) .... NAJA
National Association of Juvenile Correctional Agencies (EA) .... NAJCA
National Association of Labor Students [British] (DI) .... NALS
National Association of Laboratory Suppliers [Defunct] (EA) .... NALS
National Association of Labor-Management Committees (EA) .... NALMC
National Association of Labour Student Organisations [British] (BI) .... NALSO
National Association of Lace Curtain Manufacturers [Defunct] .... NALCM
National Association of Ladies Circles [British] (DBA) .... NALC
National Association of Laity (EA) .... NAL
National Association of Land Settlement Association Tenants (AD) .... NALSAT
National Association of Landowners (EA) .... NAL
National Association of Language Advisers [British] .... NALA
National Association of Large City Directors of Vocational Education (EA) .... NALCDVE
National Association of Laryngectomee Clubs [British] (DBA) .... NALC
National Association of Latino Elected and Appointed Officials (AD) .... NALEAO
National Association of Latino Elected and Appointed Officials (EA) .... NALEO
National Association of Launderette Owners Ltd. [British] (BI) .... NALO
National Association of Law Firm Marketing Administrators (EA) .... NALFMA
National Association of Lawn and Garden Manufacturers [Defunct] (EA) .... NALGM
National Association of Leagues of Hospital Friends [British] (DI) .... NALHF
National Association of Leagues, Umpires, and Scorers (EA) .... NALUS
National Association of Learning Laboratory Directors [Later, IALL] .... NALLD
National Association of Leather Glove Manufacturers [Later, NAGM] (EA) .... NALGM
National Association of Left-Handed Golfers (EA) .... NALG
National Association of Legal Assistants (EA) .... NALA
National Association of Legal Investigators (EA) .... NALI
National Association of Legal Secretaries (International) [Tulsa, OK] (EA) .... NALS
National Association of Lesbian/Gay Alcoholism Professionals (EA) .... NALGAP
National Association of Letter Carriers (NADA) .... NALC
National Association of Letter Carriers of the USA (EA) .... NALC
National Association of License Law Officials [Later, NARELLO] (EA) .... NALLO
National Association of Licensed House Managers [Pronounced "nalem"] [A union] [British] (DCTA) .... NALHM
National Association of Licensed Practical Nurses (EA) .... NALPN
National Association of Life Companies [Washington, DC] (EA) .... NALC
National Association of Life Science Industries [Defunct] (EA) .... NALSI
National Association of Life Underwriters [Washington, DC] (EA) .... NALU
National Association of Lift Makers [British] (BI) .... NALM
National Association of Lighting Maintenance Contractors (EA) .... NALMCO
National Association of Lighting Representatives (EA) .... NALR
National Association of Limbless and Disabled [British] (DBA) .... NALD
National Association of Limited Edition Dealers (EA) .... NALED
National Association of Litho Clubs (EA) .... NALC
National Association of Lithographic Plate Manufacturers [Defunct] (EA) .... NALPM
National Association of Livestock Auction Markets .... NALAM
National Association of Local Boards of Health .... NALBOH
National Association of Local Councils [British] .... NALC
National Association of Local Government Officers (AIE) .... NALGO
National Association of Local Governments on Hazardous Wastes (EA) .... NALGHW
National Association of Local Supervisors of Vocational Home Economics (EA) .... NALSVHE
National Association of Loft Insulation Contractors [British] (DI) .... NALIC
National Association of Louisiana Catahoulas (EA) .... NALC
National Association of Lumber Salesmen (EA) .... NALS
National Association of Magazine Publishers [Later, Magazine Publishers Association] .... NAMP
National Association of Mail Service Pharmacies [Later, AMCPA] (EA) .... NAMSP
National Association of Malleable Ironfounders [British] (BI) .... NAMI
National Association of Managed Care Physicians (EA) .... NAMCP
National Association of Management and Technical Assistance Centers [Washington, DC] (EA) .... NAMTAC
National Association of Management Consultants (EA) .... NAMC
National Association of Management/Marketing Educators [Defunct] (EA) .... NAME
National Association of Manufacturers (NTCM) .... NAM
National Association of Manufacturers Law Digest [A publication] (DLA) .... NAML Dig
National Association of Manufacturers of Pressed and Blown Glassware [Defunct] (EA) .... NAMPBG
National Association of Manufacturing Opticians (EA) .... NAMO
National Association of Marble Dealers [Later, MIA] (EA) .... NAMD
National Association of Marble Producers (EA) .... NAMP
National Association of Margarine Manufacturers (EA) .... NAMM
National Association of Marinas and Marine Dealers (EA) .... NAMMD
National Association of Marine Dealers .... NAMD
National Association of Marine Engine Builders (AD) .... NAMEB
National Association of Marine Enginebuilders [British] (BI) .... NAME
National Association of Marine Engineers (AD) .... NAME
National Association of Marine Engineers (NADA) .... NAME
National Association of Marine Engineers of Canada .... NAMEC
National Association of Marine Products and Services (EA) .... NAMPS
National Association of Marine Services (EA) .... NAMS
National Association of Marine Surveyors (EA) .... NAMS
National Association of Market Developers [New York, NY] (EA) .... NAMD
National Association of Married Priests (AD) .... NAMP
National Association of Mass Merchandisers (EA) .... NAMM
National Association of Master Appraisers (EA) .... NAMA
National Association of Master Bakers [British] (DI) .... NAMB

National Association of Master Bakers, Confectioners, and Caterers [*British*] (DBA) ... NAMB
National Association of Master Masons [*British*] (DBA) ... NAMM
National Association of Master Mechanics and Foremen of Naval Shore Establishments ... MMF
National Association of Maternal and Child Welfare [*British*] ... NAMCW
National Association of Mathematics Advisers [*British*] (DBA) ... NAMA
National Association of Mature People (EA) ... NAMP
National Association of MDS [*Multipoint Distribution System*] **Service Companies** [*Later, MDSIA*] (EA) ... NAMSCO
National Association of Meal Programs (EA) ... NAMP
National Association of Meat and Food Seasoning Manufacturers [*Later, NSMA*] (EA) ... NAMFSM
National Association of Meat Processors and Wholesalers (EA) ... NAMPW
National Association of Meat Purveyors (EA) ... NAMP
National Association of Media Brokers (EA) ... NAMB
National Association of Media Educators (EA) ... NAME
National Association of Media Women (EA) ... NAMW
National Association of Medical Equipment Suppliers (EA) ... NAMES
National Association of Medical Examiners (EA) ... NAME
National Association of Medical Legal Nurse Consultants (EA) ... NAMLNC
National Association of Medical Minority Educators (EA) ... NAMME
National Association of Medical-Dental Bureaus [*Later, MDHBA*] ... NAMDB
National Association of Membership Directors of Chambers of Commerce [*Defunct*] (EA) ... NAMD
National Association of Men's and Boys' Apparel Clubs [*Later, Bureau of Wholesale Sales Representatives*] (EA) ... NAMBAC
National Association of Men's Apparel Clubs [*Later, NAMBAC, Bureau of WholesaleSales Representatives*] ... NAMAC
National Association of Men's Sportswear Buyers (EA) ... NAMSB
National Association of Merger and Acquisition Consultants (EA) ... NAMAC
National Association of Metal Finishers (EA) ... NAMF
National Association of Metal Name Plate Manufacturers (AD) ... NAME
National Association of Metal Name Plate Manufacturers ... NAMNPM
National Association of Methodist Hospitals and Homes ... NAMHH
National Association of Midwifery Practitioners [*Defunct*] (EA) ... NAMP
National Association of Military Spouses (EA) ... NAMS
National Association of Military Widows (EA) ... NAMW
National Association of Milk Bottle Collectors (EA) ... NAMBC
National Association of Milliners, Dressmakers, and Tailors (EA) ... NAMDT
National Association of Miniature Enthusiasts (EA) ... NAME
National Association of Mining Groups (EA) ... NAMG
National Association of Mining History Organizations [*British*] (DBA) ... NAMHO
National Association of Ministers' Wives [*Later, NAMWMW*] (EA) ... NAMW
National Association of Ministers' Wives and Ministers' Widows (EA) ... NAMWMW
National Association of Minority Automobile Dealers [*Detroit, MI*] (EA) ... NAMAD
National Association of Minority Businesses (AAGC) ... NAMB
National Association of Minority Certified Public Accounting Firms (EA) ... NAMCPAF
National Association of Minority Consultants and Urbanologists [*Defunct*] (EA) ... NAMCU
National Association of Minority Contractors (EA) ... NAMC
National Association of Minority CPA [*Certified Public Accounting*] **Firms** ... NAMCF
National Association of Minority Engineering Program Administrators (EA) ... NAMEPA
National Association of Minority Entrepreneurs (EA) ... NAME
National Association of Minority Political Women (EA) ... NAMPW
National Association of Minority Students and Educators in Higher Education (EA) ... NAMSE
National Association of Minority Women in Business [*Kansas City, MO*] (EA) ... NAMWB
National Association of Mirror Manufacturers (EA) ... NAMM
National Association of Miscellaneous Ornamental and Architectural Products Contractors (EA) ... NAMOA
National Association of Missing Persons Investigators [*Defunct*] (EA) ... NAMPI
National Association of Modeling and Entertainment (EA) ... NAME
National Association of Mortgage Brokers [*Washington, DC*] (EA) ... NAMB
National Association of Mothers' Centers (EA) ... NAMC
National Association of Motor Bus Operators (AD) ... NAMBO
National Association of Motor Bus Owners [*Later, ABA*] (EA) ... NAMBO
National Association of Multifamily Owners ... NAMO
National Association of Multiple Grocers [*British*] (BI) ... NAMG
National Association of Multiple Shoe Repairers [*British*] (DBA) ... NAMSR
National Association of Municipal Securities Dealers ... NAMS
National Association of Music Executives in State Universities (EA) ... NAMESU
National Association of Music Merchandisers (AD) ... NAMM
National Association of Music Merchants (EA) ... NAMM
National Association of Musical Instrument Mechanics (EA) ... NAMIM
National Association of Musical Merchandise Manufacturers [*Later, GAMA*] (EA) ... NAMMM
National Association of Musical Merchandise Wholesalers [*Later, MDA*] (EA) ... NAMMW
National Association of Mutual Casualty Companies (EA) ... NAMCC
National Association of Mutual Insurance Agents [*Later, PIA*] (EA) ... NAMIA
National Association of Mutual Insurance Companies [*Indianapolis, IN*] (EA) ... NAMIC
National Association of Mutual Savings Banks (EA) ... NAMSB
National Association of Nail Artists [*Later, NANAA*] (EA) ... NANA
National Association of Naturopathic Physicians [*Defunct*] (EA) ... NANP
National Association of Naval Technical Supervisors (EA) ... NANTS
National Association of Negotiated Commissioned Brokers [*Defunct*] (EA) ... NANCB
National Association of Negro Business and Professional Women's Clubs [*Washington, DC*] (EA) ... NANBPWC
National Association of Negro Musicians (EA) ... NANM
National Association of Negro Tailors, Designers, Dressmakers, and Dry Cleaners (EA) ... NANTDDDC
National Association of Neighborhood Health Centers [*Later, NACHC*] (EA) ... NANHC
National Association of Neighborhoods (EA) ... NAN
National Association of Neonatal Nurses (EA) ... NANN
National Association of Nephrology Technologists (EA) ... NANT
National Association of Neuro-Linguistic Programming (EA) ... NA/NLP
National Association of New Careerists (EA) ... NANC
National Association of Newspaper Purchasing Executives [*Later, NPMA*] (EA) ... NANPE
National Association of NIDS [*National Investor Data Service*] **Users** (EA) ... NANU
National Association of Noise Control Officials (EA) ... NANCO
National Association of Non-Smokers (EA) ... NANS
National Association of Nurse Massage Therapists ... NANMT
National Association of Nurse Practitioners in Reproductive Health (EA) ... NANPRH
National Association of Nurse Recruiters [*Later, NAHCR*] (EA) ... NANR
National Association of Nursing Homes and Private Hospitals [*Australia*] ... NANHPH
National Association of Nutrition and Aging Services Programs (EA) ... NANASP
National Association of Off-Track Betting (EA) ... NAOTB
National Association of Oil Equipment Jobbers [*Later, PEI*] (EA) ... NAOEJ
National Association of Oil Heating Service Managers (EA) ... NAOHSM
National Association of Older Americans [*Later, Heartline/National Association of Older Americans*] (EA) ... NAOA
National Association of Older Worker Employment Services [*Washington, DC*] (EA) ... NAOWES
National Association of Oncology Social Workers (EA) ... NAOSW
National Association of Operative Boiler Makers and Iron Ship Builders [*A union*] [*British*] ... NAOBMISB
National Association of Operative Carpenters and Joiners [*A union*] [*British*] ... NAOCJ
National Association of Operative Plasterers ... NAOP
National Association of Operative Plasterers' Labourers [*A union*] [*British*] ... NAOPL
National Association of Operative Plumbers [*A union*] [*British*] ... NAOP
National Association of Optometrists and Opticians (EA) ... NAOO
National Association of Orchestra Leaders (EA) ... NAOL
National Association of Organ Teachers [*Later, IAOT*] ... NAOT
National Association of Orthopaedic Nurses (EA) ... NAON
National Association of Orthopaedic Technologists (EA) ... NAOT
National Association of OTC [*Over-the-Counter*] **Companies** [*Later, APTC*] (EA) ... NAOTC
National Association of Outfitters (AD) ... NAO
National Association of Ovulation Method Instructors [*British*] (DBA) ... NAOMI
National Association of Packaged Fuel Manufacturers [*Defunct*] (EA) ... NAPFM
National Association of Paper and Advertising Collectors (EA) ... NAPAC
National Association of Paper Merchants [*British*] ... NAPM
National Association of Para-Legal Personnel (AD) ... NAPLP
National Association of Para-Legals Personnel (EA) ... NAP-LP
National Association of Parish Coordinators/Directors of Religious Education (EA) ... NPCD
National Association of Parish Councils [*British*] (BI) ... NAPC
National Association of Park Administrators [*British*] (BI) ... NAPA
National Association of Park Rangers (EA) ... NAPR
National Association of Parliamentarians (EA) ... NAP
National Association of Partners in Education ... NAPE
National Association of Partners in Education ... NAPE
National Association of Part-Time and Temporary Employees ... NAPTE
National Association of Party Plan Companies [*Defunct*] (EA) ... NAPPC
National Association of Passenger Vessel Owners (EA) ... NAPVO
National Association of Pastoral Care in Education [*British*] (DBA) ... NAPCE
National Association of Pastoral Counselors [*Defunct*] (EA) ... NAPC
National Association of Pastoral Musicians (EA) ... NPM
National Association of Pat Boone Fan Clubs (EA) ... NAPBFC
National Association of Patient Participation [*British*] (DBA) ... NAPP
National Association of Patients on Hemodialysis and Transplantation [*Later, AAKP*] (EA) ... NAPHT
National Association of Pattern Manufacturers [*LA PPTBA*] (EA) ... NAPM
National Association of Pediatric Nurse Associates and Practitioners (EA) ... NAPNAP
National Association of Pension Consultants and Administrators [*Atlanta, GA*] (EA) ... NAPCA
National Association of Pension Funds [*British*] (DI) ... NAPF
National Association of People with AIDS (EA) ... NAPWA
National Association of Performing Artists ... NAPA
National Association of Performing Artists (AD) ... NAPO
National Association of Performing Arts Managers and Agents (EA) ... NAPAMA
National Association of Perry Makers [*British*] (DBA) ... NAPM
National Association of Personal Financial Advisors (EA) ... NAPFA
National Association of Personnel Consultants [*Defunct*] (EA) ... NAPC
National Association of Personnel Workers (EA) ... NAPW
National Association of Pet Cemeteries [*Later, IAPC*] ... NAPC
National Association of Pet Sitters (EA) ... NAPS
National Association of Petroleum Funds [*British*] ... NAPF
National Association of Pharmaceutical Distributors [*British*] (BI) ... NAPD
National Association of Pharmaceutical Manufacturers (EA) ... NAPM
National Association of Photo Equipment Technicians (EA) ... NAPET
National Association of Photographic Manufacturers (EA) ... NAPM
National Association of Photolithographers (IAA) ... NAPL

National Association of Physical Plant Administrators of Universities and Colleges [*Later, Association of Physical Plant Administrators of Universities and Colleges*] (EA) ... NAPPA
National Association of Physical Therapists (EA) ... NAPT
National Association of Physician Nurses (EA) ... NAPN
National Association of Physician Recruiters (EA) ... NAPR
National Association of Pipe Coating Applicators (EA) ... NAPCA
National Association of Pipe Nipple Manufacturers [*Defunct*] (EA) ... NAPNM
National Association of Pizza Operators [*Commercial firm*] (EA) ... NAPO
National Association of Planners [*Defunct*] (EA) ... NAP
National Association of Planners, Estimators, and Progressmen (EA) ... NAPEP
National Association of Plant Patent Owners (EA) ... NAPPO
National Association of Plasters, Granolithic, and Cement Workers [*A union*] [*British*] ... NAPGCW
National Association of Plastic Fabricators (EA) ... NAPF
National Association of Plastics Distributors (EA) ... NAPD
National Association of Play Publishers ... NAPP
National Association of Plumbing Contractors [*Later, NAPHCC*] ... NAPC
National Association of Plumbing, Heating, and Mechanical Service Contractors [*British*] (DBA) ... NAPH & MSC
National Association of Plumbing/Heating/Cooling Contractors (AD) ... NAPHC
National Association of Plumbing-Heating-Cooling Contractors [*Formerly, NAPC*] (EA) ... NAPHCC
National Association of Police Community Relations Officers (EA) ... NAPCRO
National Association of Police Driving (AD) ... NAPD
National Association of Police Laboratories (EA) ... NAPL
National Association of Police Organizations (EA) ... NAPO
National Association of Polish Americans ... NAPA
National Association of Political Ex-Deportees of the Nazi Camps [*Italy Political party*] (EAIO) ... NAPEDNC
National Association of Pool Owners ... NAPO
National Association of Port Employers [*British*] ... NAPE
National Association of Post Office and General Service Maintenance Employees [*Later, APWU*] [*AFL-CIO*] ... POGS
National Association of Post Office and General Service Maintenance Employees [*Later, APWU*] [*AFL-CIO*] ... POSM
National Association of Post Office Mail Handlers, Watchmen, Messengers, and Group Leaders [*Later, NPOMHWMGL*] (EA) ... NAPOMHWMGL
National Association of Post Office Mail Handlers, Watchmen, Messengers, and Group Leaders [*Later, NPOMHWMGL*] ... POMH
National Association of Postal Supervisors (EA) ... NAPS
National Association of Postmasters (NADA) ... NAP
National Association of Postmasters of the United States ... NAP
National Association of Postmasters of the United States (EA) ... NAPUS
National Association of Postpartum Care Services (PAZ) ... NAPCS
National Association of Postsecondary and Adult Vocational Home Economics Educators (EA) ... NAPAVHEE
National Association of Poultry Packers Ltd. [*British*] (BI) ... NAPP
National Association of Power Engineers (EA) ... NAPE
National Association of Power Loom Overlookers [*British*] (DBA) ... NAPLO
National Association of Precancel Collectors (EA) ... NAPC
National Association of Precancel Collectors, Wildwood, NJ [*Library symbol Library of Congress*] (LCLS) ... NjWwP
National Association of Precollege Directors (EA) ... NAPD
National Association of Premenstrual Syndrome [*British*] (DBA) ... NAPS
National Association of Presbyterian Scouters (EA) ... NAPS
National Association of Pretrial Service Agencies (AD) ... NAPSA
National Association of Priest Pilots (EA) ... NAPP
National Association of Primary Education [*British*] (DBA) ... NAPE
National Association of Principal Agricultural Education Officers [*British*] ... NAPAEO
National Association of Principals of Schools for Girls (EA) ... NAPSG
National Association of Printers and Lithographers (EA) ... NAPL
National Association of Printing Ink Manufacturers (EA) ... NAPIM
National Association of Printing Purchasers [*Defunct*] (EA) ... NAPP
National Association of Prison Officers [*British*] (DI) ... NAPO
National Association of Prison Visitors [*British*] (BI) ... NAPV
National Association of Private Art Foundations [*Defunct*] (EA) ... NAPAF
National Association of Private Enterprise [*Fort Worth, TX*] (EA) ... NAPE
National Association of Private Geriatric Care Managers (EA) ... NAPGCM
National Association of Private Industry Councils [*Washington, DC*] (EA) ... NAPIC
National Association of Private, Nontraditional Schools and Colleges (EA) ... NAPNSC
National Association of Private Placement Syndicators [*Later, California Investment Real Estate Forum*] (EA) ... NAPPS
National Association of Private Process Servers (EA) ... NAPP
National Association of Private Psychiatric Hospitals (EA) ... NAPPH
National Association of Private Residential Facilities for the Mentally Retarded (EA) ... NAPRFMR
National Association of Private Schools for Exceptional Children (EA) ... NAPSEC
National Association of Private Secretaries [*British*] (BI) ... NAPS
National Association of Private Security Vaults (EA) ... NAPSV
National Association of Pro America (EA) ... NAPA
National Association of Probation Officers [*British*] (DI) ... NAPO
National Association of Produce Market Managers [*Hartford, CT*] (EA) ... NAPMM
National Association of Professional Asian-American Women (EA) ... NAPAAW
National Association of Professional Band Instrument Repair Technicians (EA) ... NAPBIRT
National Association of Professional Baseball Leagues (EA) ... NAPBL
National Association of Professional Bureaucrats [*Later, INATAPROBU*] ... NAPB
National Association of Professional Bureaucrats [*Later, INATAPROBU*] ... NATAPROBU
National Association of Professional Contracts Administrators [*Later, NCMA*] (EA) ... NAPCA
National Association of Professional Contracts Administrators (AAGC) ... NAPCA
National Association of Professional Educators (EA) ... NAPE
National Association of Professional Engravers (EA) ... NAPE
National Association of Professional Fund Raisers (EA) ... NAPFR
National Association of Professional Gardeners [*Later, PGMS*] ... NAPG
National Association of Professional Mortgage Women ... NAPMW
National Association of Professional Organizers (EA) ... NAPO
National Association of Professional Print Buyers (EA) ... NAPPB
National Association of Professional Process Servers (EA) ... NAPPS
National Association of Professional Secretarial Services [*Later, PASS*] (EA) ... NAPSS
National Association of Professional Surplus Lines Offices (EA) ... NAPSLO
National Association of Professional Truck Driving Champions (EA) ... NAPTDC
National Association of Professional Upholsterers [*Defunct*] (EA) ... NAPU
National Association of Professional Word Processing Technicians [*Philadelphia, PA*] (EA) ... NAPWPT
National Association of Professors of Christian Education (EA) ... NAPCE
National Association of Professors of Hebrew (EA) ... NAPH
National Association of Progressive Radio Announcers (EA) ... NAPRA
National Association of Property Owners (EA) ... NAPO
National Association of Property Tax Representatives [*Defunct*] (EA) ... NAPTR
National Association of Protection and Advocacy Systems (EA) ... NAPAS
National Association of Psychiatric Survivors (EA) ... NAPS
National Association of Psychiatric Treatment Centers for Children (EA) ... NAPTCC
National Association of Public and Private Employer Negotiators and Administrators (EA) ... NAPPENA
National Association of Public Child Welfare Administrators (EA) ... NAPCWA
National Association of Public Employer Negotiators and Administrators [*Later, NAPPENA*] (EA) ... NAPENA
National Association of Public Exposition Managers [*Later, HGSEI*] (EA) ... NAPEM
National Association of Public Golf Courses [*British*] (BI) ... NAPGC
National Association of Public Hospitals (EA) ... NAPH
National Association of Public Insurance Adjusters [*Baltimore, MD*] (EA) ... NAPIA
National Association of Public School Adult Administrators [*Later, NAPSAE*] ... NAPSAA
National Association of Public Sector Equal Opportunity Officers ... NAPSEO
National Association of Public Service Advertisers [*British*] (DBA) ... NAPSA
National Association of Public Service Organization Executives (EA) ... NAPSOE
National Association of Public Television Stations [*Later, APB*] (EA) ... NAPTS
National Association of Publishers [*Defunct*] (EA) ... NAP
National Association of Publishers' Representatives (EA) ... NAPR
National Association of Punch Manufacturers (EA) ... NAPM
National Association of Pupil Personnel Administrators [*Later, NAPSA*] (EA) ... NAPPA
National Association of Pupil Services Administrators (EA) ... NAPSA
National Association of Purchasing Agents [*Later, NAPM*] (EA) ... NAPA
National Association of Purchasing Agents (AD) ... NAPO
National Association of Purchasing Management (EA) ... NAPM
National Association of Quality Assurance Professionals (EA) ... NAQAP
National Association of Quick Printers (EA) ... NAQP
National Association of Radiation Survivors (EA) ... NARS
National Association of Radiator Specialists [*British*] (DBA) ... NARS
National Association of Radio and Telecommunications Engineers (EA) ... NARTE
National Association of Radio and Television Broadcasters [*Later, NAB*] ... NARTB
National Association of Radio News Directors (IAA) ... NARND
National Association of Radio Telephone Systems [*Later, Telocator Network of America*] (IAA) ... NARTS
National Association of Radiotelephone Systems [*Later, Telocator Network of America*] (EA) ... NARS
National Association of Rail Shippers (EA) ... NARS
National Association of Rail Shippers Advisory Boards (EA) ... NARSAB
National Association of Railroad and Utility Commissioners (NTCM) ... NARCU
National Association of Railroad Passengers (EA) ... NARP
National Association of Railroad Trial Counsel (EA) ... NARTC
National Association of Railway Business Women (EA) ... NARBW
National Association of Ratepayers' Action Groups [*British*] (DI) ... NARAG
National Association of Real Estate Appraisers (EA) ... NAREA
National Association of Real Estate Boards [*Later, National Association of Realtors*] (EA) ... NAREB
National Association of Real Estate Brokers ... NAREB
National Association of Real Estate Buyer Brokers (EA) ... NAREBB
National Association of Real Estate Companies (EA) ... NAREC
National Association of Real Estate Editors (EA) ... NAREE
National Association of Real Estate Investment Funds [*Later, NAREIT*] (EA) ... NAREIF
National Association of Real Estate Investment Trusts (EA) ... NAREIT
National Association of Real Estate License Law Officials (EA) ... NARELLO
National Association of Realtors (EA) ... NAR
National Association of Record Retailer Dealers [*Defunct*] (EA) ... NARRD
National Association of Recording Merchandisers (EA) ... NARM
National Association of Recovered Alcoholics [*Defunct*] (EA) ... NARA
National Association of Recreation Therapists [*Later, NTRS*] (EA) ... NART
National Association of Recruitment Advertising Agencies [*Defunct*] (EA) ... NARAA
National Association of Recycling Industries [*Later, ISRI*] (EA) ... NARI
National Association of Referees in Bankruptcy [*Later, National Conference of Bankruptcy Judges*] (EA) ... NARB

National Association of Refrigerated Warehouses [*Later, IARW*] (EA) .... NARW
National Association of Refunders and Shoppers [*Defunct*] (EA) .... NARS
National Association of Regimental Drummers (AD) .... NARD
National Association of Regional Councils (EA) .... NARC
National Association of Regional Media Centers (EA) .... NARMC
National Association of Registered Nurses (EA) .... NARN
National Association of Regulatory Utility Commission Engineers (IAA) .... NARUCE
National Association of Regulatory Utility Commissioners (EA) .... NARUC
National Association of Rehabilitation Agencies (EA) .... NARA
National Association of Rehabilitation Facilities (EA) .... NARF
National Association of Rehabilitation Instructors (EA) .... NARI
National Association of Rehabilitation Professionals in the Private Sector (EA) .... NARPPS
National Association of Rehabilitation Secretaries (EA) .... NARS
National Association of Reimbursement Officers [*Washington, DC*] (EA).... NARO
National Association of Reinforcing Steel Contractors (EA) .... NARSC
National Association of Relay Manufacturers (EA) .... NARM
National Association of Reporter Training Schools [*Defunct*] (EA) .... NARTS
National Association of Republican Attorneys (EA) .... NARA
National Association of Resale and Thrift Shops (EA) .... NARTS
National Association of Residents and Interns (EA) .... NARI
National Association of Restaurant Managers [*Scottsdale, AZ*] (EA) .... NARM
National Association of Retail Clothiers and Furnishers [*Later, MRA*] (EA) .... NARCF
National Association of Retail Dealers of America (EA) .... NARDA
National Association of Retail Druggists (EA) .... NARD
National Association of Retail Furnishers (AD) .... NARF
National Association of Retail Grocers of Australia (AD) .... NARGA
National Association of Retail Grocers of the United States [*Later, NGA*] (EA) .... NARGUS
National Association of Retail Ice Cream Manufacturers [*Later, NICYRA*] (EA) .... NARICM
National Association of Retail Meat and Food Dealers .... NARMFD
National Association of Retail Merchants (AD) .... NARM
National Association of Retail Merchants (NADA) .... NARM
National Association of Retired and Veteran Railroad Employees (EA) .... NARVRE
National Association of Retired Bankers [*Later, RBA*] (EA) .... NARB
National Association of Retired Catholics (AD) .... NARC
National Association of Retired Civil Employees [*Later, NARFE*] (EA) ...... NARCE
National Association of Retired Federal Employees (EA) .... NARFE
National Association of Retired Police Officers [*British*] (DBA) .... NARPO
National Association of Retired Senior Volunteer Program Directors (EA) .... NARSVPD
National Association of Review Appraisers (EA) .... NARA
National Association of Review Appraisers and Mortgage Underwriters (EA) .... NARA/MU
National Association of River and Harbor Contractors [*Later, NADC*] (EA) .... NARHC
National Association of Rocketry (EA) .... NAR
National Association of Rope and Twine Merchants (AD) .... NARTM
National Association of Royalty Owners (EA) .... NARO
National Association of Rudimental Drummers [*Defunct*] .... NARD
National Association of Sack Merchants and Reclaimers [*British*] (BI) .... NASMAR
National Association of Safety at Home [*British*] (DBA) .... NASH
National Association of Sailing Instructors and Sailing Schools (EA) ..... NASISS
National Association of Sales and Marketing Professionals [*Defunct*] (EA) .... NASMP
National Association of Sandwich Manufacturers [*Defunct*] (EA) .... NASM
National Association of Sanitarians [*Later, NEHA*] (EA) .... NAS
National Association of Sanitary Milk Bottle Closure Manufacturers [*Defunct*] (EA) .... NASMBCM
National Association of Satellite Equipment Manufacturers [*Defunct*] (EA) .... NASEM
National Association of Saw Shops (EA) .... NASS
National Association of Scaffolding Contractors [*British*] (DBA) .... NASC
National Association of Scholars (EA) .... NAS
National Association of School Affiliates (EA) .... NASA
National Association of School Boards (OICC) .... NASB
National Association of School Bus Contract Operators [*Later, NSTA*] (EA) .... NASBCO
National Association of School Counselors [*Defunct*] (EA) .... NASC
National Association of School Meals Organisers [*British*] (DBA) .... NASMO
National Association of School Music Dealers (EA) .... NASMD
National Association of School Nurses (EA) .... NASN
National Association of School Psychologists (EA) .... NASP
National Association of School Security Directors (EA) .... NASSD
National Association of School Superintendents (AD) .... NASS
National Association of School Superintendents (NADA) .... NASS
National Association of Schoolmasters [*British*] .... NAS
National Association of Schoolmasters - Union of Women Teachers [*British*] .... NAS-UWT
National Association of Schools and Colleges of the United Methodist Church (EA) .... NASCUMC
National Association of Schools and Publishers (EA) .... NASP
National Association of Schools of Art (EA) .... NASA
National Association of Schools of Art and Design (EA) .... NASAD
National Association of Schools of Dance (EA) .... NASD
National Association of Schools of Design [*Later, NASA*] .... NASD
National Association of Schools of Music (EA) .... NASM
National Association of Schools of Public Affairs and Administration (EA) .... NASPAA
National Association of Schools of Theatre (EA) .... NAST
National Association of Science Writers (EA) .... NASW
National Association of Scientific Material Managers (EA) .... NAOSMM
National Association of Scissors and Shears Manufacturers (EA) .... NASSM
National Association of Scottish Woollen Manufacturers [*British*] (BI)..... NASWM
National Association of Scuba Diving Schools [*Later, CA*] [*Commercial firm*] (EA) .... NASDS
National Association of Secondary Material Industries [*Later, NARI*] (EA) .... NASMI
National Association of Secondary School Principals (EA) .... NASSP
National Association of Secondary School Principals. Bulletin [*A publication*] (BRI) .... NASSP-B
National Association of Secretarial Services [*St. Petersburg, FL*] (EA) .... NASS
National Association of Secretaries of State (EA) .... NASS
National Association of Secretaries of State Teachers Associations [*Later, NCSEA*] (EA) .... NASSTA
National Association of Securities Administrators .... NASA
National Association of Securities and Commercial Law Attorneys (EA) .... NASCAT
National Association of Securities Dealers [*Washington, DC*] (EA) .... NASD
National Association of Securities Dealers and Investment Managers [*Securities and Investment Board*] [*British*] .... NASDIM
National Association of Securities Dealers Automated Quotations [*Over-the-counter stock quotations*] [*Bunker Ramo Corp. Trumbell, CT*] [*Information service or system*] .... NASDAQ
National Association of Securities Dealers Automated Quotations [*The full name is the Nasdaq Stock Market*] [*Washington, DC*] (WDMC) .... Nasdaq
National Association of Securities Professionals (EA) .... NASP
National Association of Security Dealers Automated Quotation System (AD) .... NASDAQS
National Association of Seed Potato Merchants [*British*] (BI) .... NASPM
National Association of Selective Distributors [*Defunct*] (EA) .... NASD
National Association of Selective Distributors (EA) .... NASDI
National Association of Self-Instructional Language Programs (EA) .... NASILP
National Association of Senior Companion Project Directors (EA) .... NASCPD
National Association of Service and Conservation Corps (EA) .... NASCC
National Association of Service Contractors [*Defunct*] (EA) .... NASC
National Association of Service Dealers (EA) .... NASD
National Association of Service Managers (EA) .... NASM
National Association of Service Merchandising (EA) .... NASM
National Association of Seventh-Day Adventist Dentists (EA) .... NASDAD
National Association of Sewer Service Companies (EA) .... NASSCO
National Association of Sewing Machine Dealers [*Defunct*] (EA) .... NASMD
National Association of Sewing Machine Distributors [*Defunct*] (EA) ...... NASMD
National Association of Sheet Music Dealers [*Later, NAMM*] (EA) .... NASMD
National Association of Sheltered Workshops and Homebound Programs [*Later, NARF*] (EA) .... NASWHP
National Association of Shippers Advisory Boards (EA) .... NASAB
National Association of Shippers' Agents [*Washington, DC*] (EA) .... NASA
National Association of Shirt, Pajama, and Sportswear Manufacturers [*Later, AAMA*] .... NASPSM
National Association of Shoe Chain Stores [*Later, FDRA*] (EA) .... NASCS
National Association of Shooting Range Owners (EA) .... NASRO
National Association of Shopfitters [*British*] (BI) .... NAS
National Association of Shopkeepers [*British*] (DBA) .... NAS
National Association of Sign and Display Advertisers [*Defunct*] .... NASDA
National Association of Single Adult Leaders (EA) .... NASAL
National Association of Single Persons (EA) .... NASP
National Association of Sitter Registries [*Defunct*] (EA) .... NASR
National Association of Slipper and Playshoe Manufacturers (EA) .... NASPM
National Association of Small Business Investment Companies [*Washington, DC*] (EA) .... NASBIC
National Association of Small Government Contractors (EA) .... NASGC
National Association of Small Loan Supervisors (EA) .... NASLS
National Association of Smaller Communities (EA) .... NASCO
National Association of Soap Opera Fans .... NAOSOF
National Association of Social Workers (EA) .... NASW
National Association of Socialist Students' Organizations [*Political party*] (AD) .... NASSO
National Association of Soft Water Service Operators [*Later, WQA*] ..... NASWSO
National Association of Software and Service Companies .... NASSCOM
National Association of Soil Conservation Districts [*Later, National Association of Conservation Districts*] .... NASCD
National Association of Solar Contractors (EA) .... NASC
National Association of Solid Fuel Wholesalers [*British*] (DBA) .... NASFW
National Association of Solvent Recyclers (EA) .... NASR
National Association of Spanish Broadcasters (EA) .... NASB
National Association of Spanish Speaking Librarians (EA) .... NASSL
National Association of Special and Reserve Police [*Defunct*] .... NASRP
National Association of Special Delivery Messengers [*Later, APWU*] [*AFL-CIO*] (EA) .... NASDM
National Association of Special Delivery Messengers [*Later, APWU*] [*AFL-CIO*] .... SDM
National Association of Special Needs State Administrators (EA) .... NASNSA
National Association of Specialized Carriers [*Defunct*] (EA) .... NASC
National Association of Specialized Carriers, Marietta GA [*STAC*] .... NAS
National Association of Specialized Schools [*Defunct*] (EA) .... NASS
National Association of Specialty Food and Confection Brokers (EA) .... NASFCB
National Association of Specimen Hunters (AD) .... NASH
National Association of Sport Aircraft Designers (EA) .... NASAD
National Association of Sporting Goods Wholesalers (EA) .... NASGW
National Association of Sports Car Racing (AD) .... NASCAR
National Association of Sports for Cerebral Palsy [*Later, USCPAA*] (EA) .... NASCP
National Association of Sports Officials (EA) .... NASO

National Association of State Administrators and Supervisors of Private Schools (EA) .... NASASPS

National Association of State Alcohol and Drug Abuse Directors (EA) .... NASADAD

National Association of State and Territorial Apprenticeship Directors [Bureau of Apprenticeship and Training] [Department of Labor] .... NASTD

National Association of State and Territorial Public Health Veterinarians [Later, NASPHV] (EA) .... NASTPHV

National Association of State Approval Agencies (EA) .... NASAA

National Association of State Approved Colleges and Universities (EA) .... NASACU

National Association of State Archeologists (EA) .... NASA

National Association of State Auditors, Comptrollers, and Treasurers (EA) .... NASACT

National Association of State Aviation Officials (EA) .... NASAO

National Association of State Aviation Officials Center for Aviation Research and Education (EA) .... NASAOCARE

National Association of State Boards of Accountancy (AAGC) .... NASB

National Association of State Boards of Accountancy [New York, NY] (EA) .... NASBA

National Association of State Boards of Education (EA) .... NASBE

National Association of State Boating Law Administrators (EA) .... NASBLA

National Association of State Budget Officers (EA) .... NASBO

National Association of State Cable Agencies (EA) .... NASCA

National Association of State Catholic Conference Directors (EA) .... NASCCD

National Association of State Charity Officials (EA) .... NASCO

National Association of State Civil Defense Directors [Later, NEMA] (EA) .... NASCDD

National Association of State Conservation Agencies [Washington, DC] .... NASCA

National Association of State Credit Union Supervisors (EA) .... NASCUS

National Association of State Departments of Agriculture (EA) .... NASDA

National Association of State Development Agencies (EA) .... NASDA

National Association of State Directors and Supervisors of Secondary Education [Later, NASSDSE] (EA) .... NASDSSE

National Association of State Directors for Disaster Preparedness [Later, NEMA] (EA) .... NASDDP

National Association of State Directors of Administration and General Service (EA) .... NASDAGS

National Association of State Directors of Child Development .... NASDCD

National Association of State Directors of Law Enforcement Training .... NASDLET

National Association of State Directors of Migrant Education (EA) .... NASDME

National Association of State Directors of Special Education [Database producer] (EA) .... NASDSE

National Association of State Directors of Teacher Education and Certification (EA) .... NASDTEC

National Association of State Directors of Veterans Affairs (EA) .... NASDVA

National Association of State Directors of Vocational Education (EA) .... NASDVE

National Association of State Drug Abuse Program Coordinators [Later, NASADAD] (EA) .... NASDAPC

National Association of State Education Department Information Officers (EA) .... NASEDIO

National Association of State Educational Media Professionals (EA) .... NASEMP

National Association of State Educational Media Professionals (EA) .... NASTEMP

National Association of State EMS Directors (EA) .... NASEMSD

National Association of State Enrolled Nurses [British] (BI) .... NASEN

National Association of State Environmental Programs Agencies [Marine science] (MSC) .... NASEPA

National Association of State Facilities Administrators (EA) .... NASFA

National Association of State Foresters (EA) .... NASF

National Association of State Human Resource Directors (EA) .... NASHRD

National Association of State Information Resource Executives (AAGC) .... NASIRE

National Association of State Land Reclamationists (EA) .... NASLR

National Association of State Lotteries (EA) .... NASL

National Association of State Mental Health Program Directors (EA) .... NASMHPD

National Association of State Militia (EA) .... NASM

National Association of State Outdoor Recreation Liaison Officers (EA) .... NASORLO

National Association of State Park Directors (EA) .... NASPD

National Association of State Personnel Executives (EA) .... NASPE

National Association of State Public Health Veterinarians (EA) .... NASPHV

National Association of State Purchasing Officials (EA) .... NASPO

National Association of State Racing Commissioners [Later, ARCI] (EA) .... NASRC

National Association of State Radio Networks (EA) .... NASRN

National Association of State Recreation Planners (EA) .... NASRP

National Association of State Retirement Administrators (EA) .... NASRA

National Association of State River Program Managers (EA) .... NASRPM

National Association of State Savings and Loan Supervisors [Later, ACSSS] (EA) .... NASS & LS

National Association of State Social Security Administrators [Later, NCSSSA] (EA) .... NASSSA

National Association of State Supervisors and Directors of Secondary Education (EA) .... NASSDSE

National Association of State Supervisors of Distributive Education (EA) .... NASSDE

National Association of State Supervisors of Home Economics [Later, NASSVHE] .... NASSHE

National Association of State Supervisors of Music (EA) .... NASSM

National Association of State Supervisors of Trade and Industrial Education (EA) .... NASSTIE

National Association of State Supervisors of Vocational Home Economics (EA) .... NASSVHE

National Association of State Telecommunications Directors (EA) .... NASTD

National Association of State Text Book Administrators (EA) .... NASTA

National Association of State Text Book Directors [Later, NASTA] (EA) .... NASTBD

National Association of State Treasurers (EA) .... NAST

National Association of State Units on Aging (EA) .... NASUA

National Association of State Universities [Later, NASULGC] .... NASU

National Association of State Universities and Land-Grant Colleges (EA) .... NASULGC

National Association of State Utility Consumer Advocates (EA) .... NASUCA

National Association of State Veterans Homes (EA) .... NASVH

National Association of Stationary Engineers (AD) .... NASE

National Association of Steel Exporters [Defunct] (EA) .... NASE

National Association of Steel Pipe Distributors (EA) .... NASPD

National Association of Steel Stockholders (MHDB) .... NASS

National Association of Stevedores (EA) .... NAS

National Association of Store Fixture Manufacturers (EA) .... NASFM

National Association of Student Activity Advisers (EA) .... NASAA

National Association of Student Councils (EA) .... NASC

National Association of Student Employment Administrators (EA) .... NASEA

National Association of Student Financial Aid Administrators (EA) .... NASFAA

National Association of Student Personnel Administrators (EA) .... NASPA

National Association of Substance Abuse Trainers and Educators (EA) .... NASATE

National Association of Suggestion Systems (EA) .... NASS

National Association of Summer Sessions [Later, NAASS] .... NASS

National Association of Superintendents of Public Residential Facilities for theMentally Retarded .... NASPRFMR

National Association of Supervisors [Later, Federal Managers Association] (EA) .... NAS

National Association of Supervisors and Administrators of Health Occupations Education (EA) .... NASAHOE

National Association of Supervisors of Agricultural Education (EA) .... NASAE

National Association of Supervisors of Business and Office Education [Later, NASBE] .... NASBOE

National Association of Supervisors of Business Education [Fort Lauderdale, FL] (EA) .... NASBE

National Association of Supervisors of State Banks [Later, CSBS] (EA) .... NASSB

National Association of Support for Small Schools [British] (DBA) .... NASSS

National Association of Surety Bond Producers [Bethesda, MD] (EA) .... NASBP

National Association of Surrogate Mothers (EA) .... NASM

National Association of Swimming Clubs for the Handicapped [British] (DBA) .... NASCH

National Association of Swine Records (EA) .... NASR

National Association of Synagogue Administrators (EA) .... NASA

National Association of System 3 Users (IAA) .... NASU

National Alssociation of Systems Integrators (CDE) .... NASI

National Association of Taurine Clubs (EA) .... NATC

National Association of Tax Accountants [Defunct] (EA) .... NATA

National Association of Tax Administrators (EA) .... NATA

National Association of Tax Consultants (EA) .... NATC

National Association of Tax Practitioners (EA) .... NATP

National Association of Taxicab Owners [Later, ITA] (EA) .... NATO

National Association of Teacher Educators for Business and Office Education [Later, NATEBE] (EA) .... NATEBOE

National Association of Teacher Educators for Business Education [DeKalb, IL] (EA) .... NATEBE

National Association of Teacher Educators for Vocational Home Economics (EA) .... NATEVHE

National Association of Teachers' Agencies (EA) .... NATA

National Association of Teachers in Further and Higher Education [British] .... NATFHE

National Association of Teachers of Agriculture [Australia] .... NATA

National Association of Teachers of Dancing [British] (DBA) .... NATD

National Association of Teachers of English .... NATE

National Association of Teachers of Singing (EA) .... NATS

National Association of Teachers of the Mentally Handicapped [British] .... NATMH

National Association of Teachers of Travellers [British] (DBA) .... NATT

National Association of Telecommunications Dealers (EA) .... NATD

National Association of Telecommunications Officers and Advisors (EA) .... NATOA

National Association of Telemarketing Consultants [Defunct] (EA) .... NATC

National Association of Telephone Operators [A union] [British] .... NATO

National Association of Television and Electronic Servicers of America [N ESSDA] [Absorbed by] (EA) .... NATESA

National Association of Television and Radio Announcers (NTCM) .... NATRA

National Association of Television and Radio Artists [Inactive] .... NATRA

National Association of Television Program Executives (NTCM) .... NATPE

National Association of Television-Radio Farm Directors [Later, NAFB] (EA) .... NATRFD

National Association of Temple Administrators (EA) .... NATA

National Association of Temple Educators (EA) .... NATE

National Association of Temporary Services [Alexandria, VA] (EA) .... NATS

National Association of Tenants and Residents [British] (BI) .... NATR

National Association of Test Directors (EA) .... NATD

National Association of Testing Authorities (IAA) .... NATA

National Association of Texaco Wholesalers (EA) .... NATW

National Association of Textile and Apparel Distributors [Defunct] (EA) .... NATAD

National Association of Textile and Apparel Wholesalers [Later, NATAD] (EA) .... NATAW

National Association of Textile Supervisors (EA) ..... NATS
National Association of the Deaf (EA) ..... NAD
National Association of the Holy Name Society (EA) ..... NAHNS
National Association of the Launderette Industry [*British*] (DBA) ..... NALI
National Association of the Legitimate Theatre [*Defunct*] (EA) ..... NALT
National Association of the Partners of the Alliance [*Later, Partners of the Americas*] (EA) ..... NAPA
National Association of the Pet Industry [*Defunct*] (EA) ..... NAPI
National Association of the Physically Handicapped (EA) ..... NAPH
National Association of the Professions (EA) ..... NAP
National Association of the Remodeling Industry (EA) ..... NARI
National Association of the Sixth Infantry Division (EA) ..... NASID
National Association of the Sixth Infantry/Motorized Division [*Later, NASID*] (EA) ..... NASIMD
National Association of Theatre Nurses [*British*] (BI) ..... NATN
National Association of Theatre Owners (EA) ..... NATO
National Association of Theatrical and Kine Employees (AD) ..... NATKE
National Association of Theatrical and Kinema Employees [*British*] (DI) ..... NATKE
National Association of Theatrical, Television, and Kine Employees [*A union*] [*British*] (DCTA) ..... NATTKE
National Association of Timetable Collectors (EA) ..... NAOTC
National Association of Tobacco & Confectionery Distributors (AC) ..... NATCD
National Association of Tobacco Distributors (EA) ..... NATD
National Association of Tool Dealers [*British*] (BI) ..... NATD
National Association of Toolmakers [*A union*] [*British*] ..... NAT
National Association of Town Watch (EA) ..... NATW
National Association of Towns and Township Officials (EA) ..... NATT
National Association of Towns and Townships (EA) ..... NATaT
National Association of Toy Retailers [*British*] (BI) ..... NATR
National Association of Trade and Industrial Instructors (EA) ..... NATII
National Association of Trade and Technical Schools (EA) ..... NATTS
National Association of Trade Protection Societies [*British*] (DBA) ..... NATPS
National Association of Traffic Accident Reconstructionists and Investigators (EA) ..... NATARI
National Association of Trailer Owners (EA) ..... NATO
National Association of Training Corps for Girls [*British*] (BI) ..... NATCG
National Association of Training Groups [*British*] (DBA) ..... NATG
National Association of Training School and Juvenile Agencies [*Later, NAJCA*] (EA) ..... NATSJA
National Association of Training School Chaplains (EA) ..... NATSC
National Association of Transit Consumer Organizations (EA) ..... NATCO
National Association of Transportation Advertising [*Later, Transit Advertising Association*] ..... NATA
National Association of Trap and Skeet Clubs (EA) ..... NATSC
National Association of Travel Organizations [*Later, TIA*] (EA) ..... NATO
National Association of Traveling Nurses ..... NATN
National Association of Treasurers of Religious Institutes (EA) ..... NATRI
National Association of Trial Court Administrators (EA) ..... NATCA
National Association of Truck Driving Schools (EA) ..... NATDS
National Association of Truck Stop Operators (EA) ..... NATSO
National Association of Unclaimed Property Administrators (EA) ..... NAUPA
National Association of Underwater Instructors (EA) ..... NAUI
National Association of Unemployed Persons [*Defunct*] (EA) ..... NAUP
National Association of Uniform Manufacturers [*Later, NAUMD*] (EA) ..... NAUM
National Association of Uniform Manufacturers and Distributors (EA) ..... NAUMD
National Association of Unions in the Textile Trade [*British*] (DCTA) ..... NAUTT
National Association of University Women (EA) ..... NAUW
National Association of Urban Bankers (EA) ..... NAUB
National Association of Urban Flood Management Agencies [*Later, NAFSWMA*] (EA) ..... NAUFMA
National Association of VA [*Veterans Administration*] **Physicians** (EA) ..... NAVAP
National Association of Van Pool Operators [*Later, Association of Commuter Transportation*] (EA) ..... NAVPO
National Association of Variety Stores [*Defunct*] (EA) ..... NAVS
National Association of Vertical Transportation Professionals ..... NAVTP
National Association of Veterans Program Administrators (EA) ..... NAVPA
National Association of Veterinary Assistants [*Defunct*] (EA) ..... NAVA
National Association of Video Distributors (EA) ..... NAVD
National Association of Videographers [*Defunct*] (EA) ..... NAV
National Association of Vision Professionals (EA) ..... NAVP
National Association of Vision Program Consultants [*Later, NAVP*] (EA) ..... NAVPC
National Association of Visual Education Dealers [*Later, National Audio-Visual Association*] (AEBS) ..... NAVED
National Association of Vocational Education Special Needs Personnel (EA) ..... NAVESNP
National Association of Vocational Home Economics Teachers (EA) ..... NAVHET
National Association of Vocational Homemakers Teachers [*Later, National Association of Vocational Home Economics Teachers*] (EA) ..... NAVHT
National Association of Vocational-Technical Education Communicators (EA) ..... NAVTEC
National Association of Voluntary Help Organisers [*British*] (DBA) ..... NAVHO
National Association of Voluntary Hostels [*British*] (DBA) ..... NAVH
National Association of Volunteer Bureaux [*British*] (EAIO) ..... NAVB
National Association of Volunteer Referral Agencies [*Australia*] ..... NAVRA
National Association of Volvo Owners [*Defunct*] (EA) ..... NAVO
National Association of Warehouse Keepers [*British*] (DBA) ..... NAWK
National Association of Waste Disposal Contractors [*British*] (DCTA) ..... NAWDC
National Association of Waste Material Dealers [*Later, NARI*] ..... NAWMD
National Association of Waste Material Producers [*Defunct*] (EA) ..... NAWMP
National Association of Watch and Clock Collectors (EA) ..... NAWCC
National Association of Water Companies (EA) ..... NAWC
National Association of Water Institute Directors (EA) ..... NAWID
National Association of Water Power Users [*British*] (DBA) ..... NAWPU
National Association of Wheat Growers (EA) ..... NAWG
National Association of Wheat Growers Foundation (EA) ..... NAWGF
National Association of Wheat Weavers (EA) ..... NAWW
National Association of Wholesale Fur Cleaners ..... NAWFC
National Association of Wholesale Newspaper Distributors (DGA) ..... NAWND
National Association of Wholesale Paint Merchants [*British*] (BI) ..... NAWPM
National Association of Wholesale Pie Bakers (EA) ..... NAWPB
National Association of Wholesaler-Distributors [*Washington, DC*] (EA) ..... NAW
National Association of Wholesalers (NADA) ..... NAW
National Association of Widows [*British*] (DI) ..... NAW
National Association of Window Blind Manufacturers [*British*] (BI) ..... NAWBM
National Association of Wine and Beer Makers [*British*] (DBA) ..... NAWB
National Association of Wine Bottlers [*Later, NWA*] (EA) ..... NAWB
National Association of Wine Producers and Bottlers [*Later, NWA*] (EA) ..... NAWPB
National Association of Wiping Cloth Manufacturers [*Later, IAWCM*] (EA) ..... NAWCM
National Association of Women Artists (EA) ..... NAWA
National Association of Women Business Owners [*Chicago, IL*] (EA) ..... NAWBO
National Association of Women Deans and Counselors [*Later, NAWDAC*] (EA) ..... NAWDC
National Association of Women Federal Contractors [*Later, NAWGC*] (EA) ..... NAWFC
National Association of Women Government Contractors [*Defunct*] (EA) ..... NAWGC
National Association of Women Highway Safety Leaders (EA) ..... NAWHSL
National Association of Women in Chambers of Commerce (EA) ..... NAWCC
National Association of Women in Construction (EA) ..... NAWIC
National Association of Women in Criminal Justice (EA) ..... NAWCJ
National Association of Women in Horticulture [*Defunct*] (EA) ..... NAWH
National Association of Women Judges (EA) ..... NAWJ
National Association of Women Lawyers (EA) ..... NAWL
National Association of Women Pharmacists [*British*] (DBA) ..... NAWP
National Association of Women's and Children's Apparel Salesmen [*Later, Bureau of Wholesale Sales Representatives*] (EA) ..... NAWCAS
National Association of Women's Centers [*Defunct*] (EA) ..... NAWC
National Association of Women's Clubs [*British*] (DBA) ..... NAWC
National Association of Wool Manufacturers [*Later, American Textile Manufacturers Institute*] (EA) ..... NAWM
National Association of Woolen and Worsted Overseers [*Later, NATS*] (EA) ..... NAWWO
National Association of Word Processing Specialists [*Later, WPS*] (EA) ..... NAWPS
National Association of World Trade Secretaries [*Later, AWTCE*] (EA) ..... NAWTS
National Association of Writing Instrument Distributors (EA) ..... NAWID
National Association of Young People in Care [*British*] ..... NAYPIC
National Association of Young People's Counselling and Advisory Services [*British*] (DI) ..... NAYPCAS
National Association of Youth and Community Education Officers [*British*] (DI) ..... NAYCEO
National Association of Youth Clubs [*British*] (DI) ..... NAYC
National Association of Youth Orchestras (EAIO) ..... NAYO
National Association of Youth Theatres [*British*] (DBA) ..... NAYT
National Association of Youth Training Agencies (AIE) ..... NAYTA
National Association on Drug Abuse Problems (EA) ..... NADAP
National Association on Service to Unmarried Parents (EA) ..... NASUP
National Association on Standard Medical Vocabulary (EA) ..... NASMV
National Association on Volunteers in Criminal Justice [*Later, IAJV*] (EA) ..... NAVCJ
National Association Practical Refrigerating Engineers [*Later, RETA*] (EA) ..... NAPRE
National Association Rainbow Division Veterans (EA) ..... NARDV
National Association State Agencies for Surplus Property (EA) ..... NASASP
National Association to Advance Fat Acceptance (EA) ..... NAAFA
National Association to Aid Fat Americans [*Bellrose, NY*] ..... NAFA
National Association to Keep and Bear Arms (EA) ..... NAKBA
National Association to Promote Library Services to the Spanish-Speaking ..... REFORMA
National Association to Reform State Liquor Laws [*Later, National Association to Reform State Drinking Ages*] [*Defunct*] (EA) ..... NARSLL
National Associations of Teachers of Home Economics [*British*] ..... NATHE
National Asthma Center [*Later, NJCIRM*] ..... NAC
National Astrological Society [*Defunct*] (EA) ..... NAS
National Astrological Society [*Defunct*] (EA) ..... NASO
National Astronomical League ..... NAL
National Astronomical Observatory [*Japan*] ..... NAO
National Astronomical Observatory of Japan ..... NAOJ
National Astronomical Space Observatory ..... NASO
National Astronomy and Ionosphere Center [*Ithaca, NY*] [*National Science Foundation*] ..... NAIC
National Ataxia Foundation (EA) ..... NAF
National Athletic and Cultural Association [*Ireland*] (EAIO) ..... NACA
National Athletic Health Institute (EA) ..... NAHI
National Athletic Injury/Illness Reporting System [*Pennsylvania State University*] [*Defunct*] ..... NAIRS
National Athletic Steering Committee (EA) ..... NASC
National Athletic Trainers Association (EA) ..... NATA
National Atmospheric Data Bank (GNE) ..... NADB
National Atmospheric Deposition Program [*Department of Agriculture*] ..... NADP
National Atmospheric Deposition Program [*Marine science*] (OSRA) ..... NADP
National Atmospheric Research Institute (AD) ..... NARI
National Atmospheric Sciences Program ..... NASP
National Attack Warning System [*Military*] (IAA) ..... NAWAS
National Auctioneers Association (EA) ..... NAA
National Audience Board [*An association*] (NTCM) ..... NAB

National Audience Composition [*Nielsen Television Index*] (NTCM) ... NAC
National Audience Data Bank [*Newspaper Marketing Bureau*] [*Information service or system*] (CRD) ... NADB
National Audience Demographics Report [*Nielsen Television Index*] (NTCM) ... NAD
National Audio Visual Aids Library (AIE) ... NAVAL
National Audiovisual Aids Centre [*British*] ... NAVAC
National Audio-Visual Association [*Later, ICIA*] (EA) ... NAVA
National Audiovisual Center [*General Services Administration*] ... NAC
National Audit Office [*British*] (ECON) ... NAO
National Audit Plan ... NAP
National Audubon Society (EA) ... NAS
National Audubon Society, New York, NY [*Library symbol Library of Congress*] (LCLS) ... NNAuS
National Australia Bank [*Associated Press*] (SAG) ... NtAust
National Australia Bank ADS [*NYSE symbol*] (SPSG) ... NAB
National Australia Bank. Monthly Summary [*A publication*] (ADA) ... NBS
National Authority for the Ladies Handbag Industry (EA) ... NALHI
National Autism Hotline (EA) ... NAH
National Autistic Society [*British*] ... NAS
National Auto and Flat Glass Dealers Association [*Later, NGA*] ... NAFGDA
National Auto and Truck Wreckers Association [*Later, ADRA*] (EA) ... NATWA
National Auto Auction Association [*Lincoln, NE*] (EA) ... NAAA
National Auto Credit, Inc. [*NYSE symbol*] (SAG) ... NAK
National Auto Credit, Inc. Holding [*Associated Press*] (SAG) ... NatAutoC
National Auto Racing Historical Society (EA) ... NARHS
National Autobody Congress and Exposition [*Precision Planning and Sales, Inc.*] (TSPED) ... NACE
National Automated Accounting Research System [*American Institute of Certified Public Accountants*] [*Database*] [*Information service or system*] (IID) ... NAARS
National Automated Clearing House Association [*Washington, DC*] (EA) ... NACHA
National Automated Highway System Consortium ... NAHSC
National Automated Highway System Consortium ... NAHSC
National Automated Immigration Lookout System [*Immigration and Naturalization Service*] ... NAILS
National Automated Transportation Association (AD) ... NATA
National Automatic Controller for Testing (MUGU) ... NACT
National Automatic Controls Conference ... NACC
National Automatic Data Processing Program for Army Material Command Logistics Management (IAA) ... NAPALM
National Automatic Laundry and Cleaning Council (EA) ... NALCC
National Automatic Merchandising Association [*Chicago, IL*] (EA) ... NAMA
National Automatic Pistol Collectors Association (EA) ... NAPCA
National Automatic Sprinkler and Fire Control Association (AD) ... NAS & FCA
National Automatic Sprinkler and Fire Control Association (EA) ... NASFCA
National Automatic Tool Co. ... NATCO
National Automatic Vendors' Trade Association (EA) ... NAVTA
National Automobile and Truck Museum of the United States ... NATMUS
National Automobile Association (NADA) ... NAA
National Automobile Dealers Association [*McLean, VA*] (EA) ... NADA
National Automobile Safety Belt Association [*British*] ... NASBA
National Automobile Salesmen's Association ... NASA
National Automobile Theft Bureau (EA) ... NATB
National Automobile Theft Bureau ... NATF
National Automobile Transporters Association [*Detroit, MI*] (EA) ... NATA
National Automobile Underwriters Association [*Later, ISO*] (EA) ... NAUA
National Automotive and Truck Model and Toy Museum of the United States ... NATMATMUS
National Automotive and Truck Museum of United States (EA) ... NATMUS
National Automotive Center [*Army*] (RDA) ... NAC
National Automotive Muffler Association [*Defunct*] (EA) ... NAMA
National Automotive Parts Association (EA) ... NAPA
National Automotive Radiator Service Association (EA) ... NARSA
National Automotive Service Co. (AD) ... NASCO
National Automotive Technicians Education Foundation (EA) ... NATEF
National Automotive Trade Association ... NATA
National Autosound Challenge Association [*Later, IASCA*] (EA) ... NACA
National Auxiliary Publications Service [*American Society for Information Science*] ... NAPS
National Average Fuel Consumption ... NAFC
National Average Weekly Male Earning ... NAWME
National Aviation Assistance ... NAAS
National Aviation Club (EA) ... NAC
National Aviation Co. [*Egypt*] [*ICAO designator*] (FAAC) ... GTY
National Aviation Consultants Ltd. [*Canada ICAO designator*] (FAAC) ... TNC
National Aviation Corp. ... NAC
National Aviation Education Council [*Later, National Aerospace Education Council*] (AEBS) ... NAEC
National Aviation Facilities Experimental Center [*of FAA*] [*Atlantic City, NJ*] ... NAFEC
National Aviation Facilities Experimental Center, Atlantic City, NJ [*OCLC symbol*] (OCLC) ... FAA
National Aviation Forum ... NAF
National Aviation Museum [*Musee National de l'Aviation*], Ottawa, Ontario [*Library symbol National Library of Canada*] (NLC) ... OONMA
National Aviation Noise Abatement Council (AD) ... NANAC
National Aviation Safety Data Analysis Center [*FAA*] (TAG) ... NASDAC
National Aviation Safety Inspection Program [*RSPA*] (TAG) ... NASIP
National Aviation System [*FAA*] ... NAS
National Aviation System Plan [*A publication*] ... NASP
National Aviation Trades Association ... NATA
National Aviation Weather Advisory Committee [*Marine science*] (OSRA) ... NAWAC
National Aviation Weather Advisory Committee (USDC) ... NAWAC
National Aviation Weather Advisory Unit [*Federal Aviation Administration*] (USDC) ... NAWAU
National Aviation Weather Advisory Unit [*Marine science*] (OSRA) ... NAWAU
National Aviation Weather Processing Facility [*FAA*] (TAG) ... NAWPF
National Aviation Weather System ... NAWS
National Aviation Weather System Study (NOAA) ... NAVWESS
National Avionics Society (EA) ... NAS
National Awami Party [*Pakistan*] [*Political party*] (PD) ... NAP
National Awami Party-Bashani [*Bangladesh*] [*Political party*] (FEA) ... NAP
National Awami Party-Muzaffar [*Bangladesh*] [*Political party*] (FEA) ... NAP-M
National Award and Trophy Manufacturers Association (EA) ... NATMA
National Awards for Innovation in Local Government [*Australia*] ... NAILG
National Baby Care Council [*Defunct*] (EA) ... NBCC
National Back Pain Association (EAIO) ... NBPA
National Backgammon Players Society [*British*] (DBA) ... NBPS
National Baha'i Museum, Wilmette, IL [*Library symbol*] [*Library of Congress*] (LCLS) ... IWilB
National Bakery School [*British*] (BI) ... NBS
National Bakery Suppliers Association (EA) ... NBSA
National Ballet of America ... NBA
National Ballroom and Entertainment Association (EA) ... NBEA
National Ballroom Operators Association [*Later, National Ballroom and Entertainment Association*] ... NBOA
National Bancorp of Alaska, Inc. [*Associated Press*] (SAG) ... NB Alsk
National Bancorp of Alaska, Inc. [*NASDAQ symbol*] (NQ) ... NBAK
National Bancshares Corp. of Texas [*Associated Press*] (SAG) ... NBcs TX
National Bancshares Corp. of Texas [*AMEX symbol*] (SAG) ... NBT
National Band Association (EA) ... NBA
National Band Council of Australia ... NBCA
National Bank Act of 1863 ... NBA
National Bank Cases [*United States*] [*A publication*] (DLA) ... Nat BC
National Bank for Social and Economical Development [*Cuba*] ... BANDES
National Bank. Monthly Summary [*A publication*] ... Natn Bank Mon Sum
National Bank of Abu Dhabi ... NBAD
National Bank of Australasia. Monthly Summary of Australian Conditions [*A publication*] ... Natn Bank Mon Sum Aust Cond
National Bank of Bahrain (EY) ... NBB
National Bank of Brunei ... NBB
National Bank of Canada [*Toronto Stock Exchange symbol Vancouver Stock Exchange symbol*] ... NA
National Bank of Dubai ... NBD
National Bank of Greece ... NBG
National Bank of Hungary ... NBH
National Bank of Kuwait ... NBK
National Bank of Nigeria Ltd. ... NBN
National Bank of North America [*New York*] ... NBNA
National Bank of Oman Ltd. SAO (EY) ... NBO
National Bank Surveillance System ... NBSS
National BankAmericard, Inc. [*Later, Visa USA, Inc.*] ... NBI
National Bankers Association [*Washington, DC*] (EA) ... NBA
National Bankruptcy Act [*1898*] ... NBA
National Bankruptcy Law [*A publication*] (DLA) ... Nat Bankr Law
National Bankruptcy News and Reports [*A publication*] (DLA) ... Nat Bankr N & R
National Bankruptcy News and Reports [*A publication*] (DLA) ... NBN Rep
National Bankruptcy News and Reports [*A publication*] (DLA) ... NBNR
National Bankruptcy Register [*New York*] [*A publication*] (DLA) ... Bankr Reg
National Bankruptcy Register [*United States*] [*A publication*] (DLA) ... Nat Bankr R
National Bankruptcy Register [*United States*] [*A publication*] (DLA) ... Nat Bankr Reg
National Bankruptcy Register [*United States*] [*A publication*] (DLA) ... Nat BR
National Bankruptcy Register Reports [*A publication*] (DLA) ... Bk Reg
National Bankruptcy Register Reports [*United States*] [*A publication*] (DLA) ... N Bk R
National Bankruptcy Register Reports [*United States*] [*A publication*] (DLA) ... N Bkpt R
National Bankruptcy Register Reports [*United States*] [*A publication*] (DLA) ... N Bkpt Reg
National Bankruptcy Register Reports [*United States*] [*A publication*] (DLA) ... Nat Bank Reg
National Bankruptcy Register Reports [*United States*] [*A publication*] (DLA) ... Nat Bankr Rep
National Bankruptcy Register Reports [*United States*] [*A publication*] (DLA) ... NBR
National Baptist Convention, USA (EA) ... NBC USA
National Baptist Deacons Convention of America (EA) ... NBDCA
National Bar Association (EA) ... NBA
National Bar Journal [*A publication*] (DLA) ... Nat Bar J
National Bar Journal [*A publication*] (DLA) ... Nat BJ
National Bar Journal [*A publication*] (DLA) ... NBJ
National Bar Mitzvah Club [*Later, AZYF*] (EA) ... NBMC
National Barbecue Association ... NBBQA
National Bark Producers Association (EA) ... NBPA
National Barrel and Drum Association [*Later, NABADA - The Association of Container Reconditioners*] (EA) ... NBADA
National Barrel and Drum Association ... NBDA
National Barristers' Wives [*Later, NABBS*] (EA) ... NBW
National Baseball Congress (EA) ... NBC
National Baseball Congress of America (NADA) ... NBCA
National Baseball Fan Association (EA) ... NBFA
National Basic Reference Graphic (MCD) ... NBRG
National Basketball Association (EA) ... NBA
National Basketball Congress (NADA) ... NBC
National Basketball League (NADA) ... NBL
National Basketball Players Association (EA) ... NBPA

National Basketball Trainers Association (EA) ... NBTA
National Bath, Bed, and Linen Association (EA) ... NBBL
National Bath, Bed, and Linen Association [*Later, NBBL*] (EA) ... NBBLA
National Bath, Bed, and Linen Show (ITD) ... NBB & L
National Baton Twirling Association (EA) ... NBTA
National Battery Test Laboratory [*Department of Energy*] ... NBTL
National Battlefield (BARN) ... NB
National Battlefield Park (BARN) ... NBP
National Battlefield Site (BARN) ... NBS
National Battlefields Commission [*See also CCBN*] ... NBC
National Beagle Club (EA) ... NBC
National Beagle Club of America (EA) ... NBCA
National Beauty and Barber Manufacturers Association [*Later, ABA*] (EA) ... NBBMA
National Beauty Career Center (EA) ... NBCC
National Beauty Culturists' League (EA) ... NBCL
National Beauty Salon Chain Association [*Later, ICSA*] (EA) ... NBSCA
National Becaon Code Allocation Plan (FAAC) ... NBCAP
National Bed Federation [*British*] (DBA) ... NBF
National Bed-and-Breakfast Association (EA) ... NB & BA
National Beef Congress ... NBC
National Beefmaster Association (EA) ... NBA
National Beep Baseball Association (EA) ... NBBA
National Beer Wholesalers' Association (EA) ... NBWA
National Belgian Hare Club of America [*Defunct*] (EA) ... NBHCA
National Bellas Hess [*Inc.*] [*Commercial firm*] ... NBH
National Bench Rest Shooters Association (EA) ... NBRSA
National Benevolent Association of the Christian Church [*Disciples of Christ*] (EA) ... NBA
National Benzole and Allied Products Association [*British*] (BI) ... NBA
National Better Business Bureau [*Later, CBBB*] (EA) ... NBBB
National Better Business Bureau (NADA) ... NBBB
National Beverage Corp. [*AMEX symbol*] (SAG) ... FIZ
National Beverage Corp. [*Associated Press*] (SAG) ... NatBev
National Beverage Corp. [*Associated Press*] (SAG) ... NatlBev
National Beverage Corp. [*NASDAQ symbol*] (SAG) ... POPS
National Beverage Dispensing Equipment Association (EA) ... NBDEA
National Beverage Packaging Association (EA) ... NBPA
National Bibliographic Control ... NBC
National Bibliographic Data Base [*Deutsche Bibliothek*] [*Germany*] ... BIBLIODATA
National Bibliography Number ... NBN
National Bicentennial Ethnic-Racial Alliance ... NBERA
National Bicentennial Hospitality Alliance [*American Revolution Bicentennial Administration*] ... NBHA
National Bicycle Dealers Association (EA) ... NBDA
National Bicycle League (EA) ... NBL
National Bidders Control Center ... NBCC
National Bingo Game Association [*British*] (DBA) ... NBGA
National Biographical Association (EA) ... NBA
National Biological Impact Assessment Program [*Computer science*] (IID) ... NBIAP
National Biological Survey ... NABIS
National Biological Survey [*Department of the Interior*] ... NBS
National Biomedical Research Foundation [*Georgetown University*] [*Research center*] ... NBRF
National Biomonitoring Inventory Program [*Department of Energy*] (MSC) ... NBIP
National Biotechnology Advisory Committee [*Canada*] ... NBAC
National Biotechnology Policy Board ... NBPB
National Biotherapy Study Group (EA) ... NBSG
National Bird Cage Week ... NBCW
National Bird-Feeding Society (EA) ... NBFS
National Birman Fanciers (EA) ... NBF
National Birth Control League ... NBCL
National Biscuit Co. [*Acronym now used as company name*] ... NABISCO
National Bituminous Coal Commission [*Functions transferred to Department of the Interior, 1939*] ... NBCC
National Bituminous Concrete Association [*Later, NAPA*] (EA) ... NBCA
National Black Alcoholism Council (EA) ... NBAC
National Black Alliance for Graduate Level Education [*Defunct*] (EA) ... NBAGLE
National Black Anti-War Anti-Draft Union (EA) ... NBAWADU
National Black Association for Speech, Language and Hearing (EA) ... NBASLH
National Black Business Alliance (EA) ... NBBA
National Black Business Council ... NBBC
National Black Catholic Clergy Caucus (EA) ... NBCCC
National Black Catholic Seminarians Association (EA) ... NBCSA
National Black Caucus of Local Elected Officials (EA) ... NBC/LEO
National Black Caucus of State Legislators (EA) ... NBCSL
National Black Chamber of Commerce (EA) ... NBCC
National Black Child Development Institute (EA) ... NBCDI
National Black Coalition of Federal Aviation Employees (EA) ... NBCFAE
National Black Communicators Society (EA) ... NBCS
National Black Economic Development Conference ... NBEDC
National Black Evangelical Association (EA) ... NBEA
National Black Feminist Organization ... NBFO
National Black Health Planners Association (EA) ... NBHPA
National/Black Law Student Association (EA) ... NBLSA
National Black Lay Catholic Caucus (EA) ... NBLCC
National Black Leadership Roundtable (EA) ... NBLR
National Black MBA [*Master of Business Administration*] **Association** [*Chicago, IL*] (EA) ... NBMBAA
National Black McDonald's Operators Association (EA) ... NBMOA
National Black Media Coalition (EA) ... NBMC
National Black Music Caucus - of the Music Educators National Conference (EA) ... NBMC
National Black Network [*A radio network*] ... NBN
National Black Nurses Association (EA) ... NBNA
National Black on Black Love Campaign (EA) ... NBBLC
National Black People's Assembly (EA) ... NBPA
National Black Police Association (EA) ... NBPA
National Black Political Convention [*1972*] ... NBPC
National Black Political Party ... NBPP
National Black Programming Consortium (EA) ... NBPC
National Black Public Relations Society (EA) ... BPRS
National Black Republican Council (EA) ... NBRC
National Black Sisters' Conference (EA) ... NBSC
National Black Survival Fund [*Emergency Black Survival Fund*] [*Acronym is based on former name,*] (EA) ... EBSF
National Black United Front (EA) ... NBUF
National Black United Fund (EA) ... NBUF
National Black Veterans Organization [*Defunct*] (EA) ... NBVO
National Black Women's Consciousness Raising Association (EA) ... BWCR
National Black Women's Health Project (EA) ... NBWHP
National Black Women's Political Leadership Caucus (EA) ... NBWPLC
National Black Youth Leadership Council (EA) ... NBYLC
National Blacksmiths and Welders Association (EA) ... NBWA
National Bladder Cancer Project [*National Cancer Institute*] ... NBCP
National Block and Bridle Club (EA) ... B & B
National Blonde d'Aquitaine Foundation (EA) ... NBAF
National Blood Data Center [*American Blood Commission*] [*Information service or system*] (IID) ... NBDC
National Blood Transfusion Service ... NBTS
National Blue Books, Inc. [*Canoga Park, CA*] [*Publisher*] ... NBBI
National Blue Crab Industry Association (EA) ... NBCIA
National Board ... NB
National Board for Bakery Education [*British*] (BI) ... NBBE
National Board for Cardiovascular and Pulmonary Credentialing [*Later, Cardiovascular Credentialing International - CCI*] (EA) ... NBCPC
National Board for Certification - Certified Dental Technician Program (EA) ... NBC-CDTP
National Board for Certification in Dental Laboratory Technology (EA) ... NBC
National Board for Certification of Dental Laboratories (EA) ... CDL
National Board for Certification of Dental Laboratories [*Later, CDL*] (EA) ... NBCDL
National Board for Certification of Orthopaedic Technologists (EA) ... NBCOT
National Board for Certified Counselors (EA) ... NBCC
National Board for Prices and Incomes [*British*] ... NBPI
National Board for Professional Teaching Standards (EA) ... NBPTS
National Board for Respiratory Care (EA) ... NBRC
National Board for Respiratory Therapy [*Formerly, ARIT*] [*Later, NBRC*] (EA) ... NBRT
National Board for Science and Technology [*Ireland*] (PDAA) ... NBST
National Board for the Promotion of Rifle Practice (EA) ... NBPRP
National Board of Boiler and Pressure Vessel Inspectors (EA) ... NBBPVI
National Board of Catholic Women [*British*] ... NBCW
National Board of Examiners for Osteopathic Physicians and Surgeons [*Later, NBOME*] (EA) ... NBEOPS
National Board of Examiners in Optometry (EA) ... NBEO
National Board of Fire Underwriters [*Later, AIA*] (EA) ... NBFU
National Board of Fur Farm Organizations (EA) ... NBFFO
National Board of Medical Examiners (EA) ... NBME
National Board of Orthopaedic Technologists [*British*] (DAVI) ... NBOT
National Board of Osteopathic Medical Examiners (EA) ... NBOME
National Board of Pediatric Nurse Practitioners and Associates [*Later, NCBPNP/N*] (EA) ... NBPNPA
National Board of Physical Therapy Examiners (EA) ... NBPTE
National Board of Podiatric Medical Examiners (EA) ... NBPME
National Board of Podiatry Examiners ... NBPE
National Board of Polygraph Examiners [*Later, APA*] (EA) ... NBPE
National Board of Review of Motion Pictures ... NBR
National Board of Review of Motion Pictures (EA) ... NBRMP
National Board of the Coat and Suit Industry [*Defunct*] (EA) ... NBCSI
National Board of Trial Advocacy (EA) ... NBTA
National Board of Water and the Environment, Urho Kekkosen Katu, Helsinki, Finland [*Library symbol*] [*Library of Congress*] (LCLS) ... FiHBWE
National Boat Association (EA) ... NBA
National Boating Federation (EA) ... NBF
National Boating Safety Advisory Council [*Department of Transportation*] [*Washington, DC*] (EGAO) ... NBSAC
National Bomb Data Center ... NBDC
National Bone Marrow Donor Registry (EA) ... NBMDR
National Book Awards [*Discontinued*] ... NBA
National Book Committee [*Defunct*] ... NBC
National Book Council [*Later, NBL*] [*United Kingdom*] ... NBC
National Book Critics Circle (EA) ... NBCC
National Book League [*Formerly, NBC*] ... NBL
National Book Number [*British*] ... NBN
National Book Sale [*British*] ... NBS
National Book Trade Provident Institution [*British*] (DGA) ... NBTPI
National Book Trade Provident Society [*British*] (DI) ... NBTPS
National Book Week (NTCM) ... NBW
National Bookkeepers' Society (EA) ... NBS
National Booster Program (AAG) ... NBP
National Boot and Shoe Manufacturers' Association [*Later, FIA*] ... NBSMA
National Border Patrol Council (EA) ... NBPC
National Bowhunter Education Foundation (EA) ... NBEF
National Bowling Association (EA) ... NBA
National Bowling Council (EA) ... NBC
National Boxing Association (NADA) ... NBA
National Boxing Association of America [*Later, WBA*] ... NBA

National Boxing Council [*British*] ... NBC
National Boys' Club (WDAA) ... NBC
National Braille Association (EA) ... NBA
National Braille Club [*Later, NBA*] (EA) ... NBC
National Braille Press (EA) ... NBP
National Brain Injury Research Foundation (EA) ... NBIRF
National Brain Research Association (EA) ... NBRA
National Brands Soft Drinks Institute (EA) ... NBSDI
National Brassfoundry Association [*British*] (BI) ... NBA
National Breast Cancer Coalition ... NBCC
National Bridal Service (EA) ... NBS
National Bridge Inspection Standards [*FHWA*] (TAG) ... NBIS
National Bridge Inventory [*FHWA*] (TAG) ... NBI
National British Softbill Society (BI) ... NBSS
National British Women's Total Abstinence Union (EAIO) ... NBWTAU
National Broadcast Editorial Association (EA) ... NBEA
National Broadcasters' Club (NTCM) ... NBC
National Broadcasting Authority [*Bangladesh*] (EY) ... NBA
National Broadcasting Commission (NADA) ... NBC
National Broadcasting Co., Inc. [*New York, NY*] ... NBC
National Broadcasting Co., Inc., General Library, New York, NY [*Library symbol Library of Congress*] (LCLS) ... NNNBC
National Broadcasting Co., Inc., Information Unit, Research Department, New York, NY [*Library symbol Library of Congress*] (LCLS) ... NNNBC-I
National Broadcasting Service [*Trinidad and Tobago*] (EY) ... NBS
National Broadcasting Service [*New Zealand*] ... NBS
National Broadcasting System ... NBS
National Broiler Association [*Later, NBC*] ... NBA
National Broiler Council (EA) ... NBC
National Broom and Mop Council [*Defunct*] ... NBMC
National Broom Corn and Supply Dealers Association (EA) ... NBCSDA
National Broom Council [*Later, NBMC*] (EA) ... NBC
National Broom Manufacturers and Allied Industries Association [*Later, NBMC*] (EA) ... NBMAIA
National Brotherhood of Packinghouse and Dairy Workers [*Formerly, NBPW*] (EA) ... NBPDW
National Brotherhood of Packinghouse and Industrial Workers (EA) ... NBPIW
National Brotherhood of Packinghouse Workers [*Later, NBPDW*] ... NBPW
National Brotherhood of Skiers (EA) ... NBS
National Buddhist Women's Associations (EA) ... NBWA
National Budget and Consultation Committee [*Defunct*] (EA) ... NBCC
National Buffalo Association (EA) ... NBA
National Buffalo Association Juniors [*Defunct*] (EA) ... NBAJ
National Builders' Hardware Association [*Later, DHI*] (EA) ... NBHA
National Building Agency [*British*] ... NBA
National Building Code ... NBC
National Building Code of Canada (HGAA) ... NBC
National Building Code of Canada ... NBCC
National Building Granite Quarries Association (EA) ... NBGQA
National Building Material Distributors Association (EA) ... NBMDA
National Building Museum (EA) ... NBM
National Building Products Association [*Defunct*] (EA) ... NBPA
National Building Trades Federation [*A union*] [*British*] ... NBTF
National Buildings Record [*British*] ... NBR
National Bulk Commodities Group [*Australia*] ... NBCG
National Bulk Mail System [*Postal Service*] ... NBMS
National Bulk Vendors Association (EA) ... NBVA
National Bureau for Co-Operation in Child Care [*British*] ... NBCC
National Bureau for Co-Operation in Child Care [*British*] (BI) ... NBCCC
National Bureau for Handicapped Students [*British*] (CB) ... NBHS
National Bureau for Lathing and Plastering [*Later, International Institute for Lath and Plaster*] (EA) ... NBLP
National Bureau of Casualty Underwriters [*Later, ISO*] (EA) ... NBCU
National Bureau of Document Examiners (EA) ... NBDE
National Bureau of Economic Research (WDAA) ... NAT BUR ECON RES
National Bureau of Economic Research (AD) ... Nat Bur Econ Res
National Bureau of Economic Research (EA) ... NBER
National Bureau of Engineering Registration ... NBER
National Bureau of Federated Jewish Women's Organizations (EA) ... NBFJWO
National Bureau of Metrology ... NBM
National Bureau of Standards [*Department of Commerce*] [*Later, NIST*] ... NBS
National Bureau of Standards [*Department of Commerce*] (WDAA) ... NT BUR STNDS
National Bureau of Standards - Atomic (SAA) ... NBS-A
National Bureau of Standards Boulder Laboratories ... NBSBL
National Bureau of Standards Center for Computer Sciences and Technology (DIT) ... NBSCCST
National Bureau of Standards Circular [*A publication*] (AD) ... Nat Bur Stand Circ
National Bureau of Standards Frequency Standard (IEEE) ... NBSFS
National Bureau of Standards, Gaithersburg, MD [*OCLC symbol*] (OCLC) ... NBS
National Bureau of Standards Interagency Reports ... NBSIR
National Bureau of Standards Load Determination [*Computer program*] ... NBSLD
National Bureau of Standards Reactor ... NBSR
National Bureau of Standards/Technical Analysis Division (NOAA) ... NBS/TAD
National Burglar and Fire Alarm Association (EA) ... NBFAA
National Burlap Bag Dealers Association [*Later, Textile Bag and Packaging Association*] (EA) ... NBBDA
National Burn Federation (EA) ... NBF
National Burn Information Exchange [*Information service or system*] (CRD) ... NBIE
National Burn Victim Foundation (EA) ... NBVF
National Bus Co. [*British*] ... NBC
National Bus Military Bureau (EA) ... NBMB
National Bus Traffic Association (EA) ... NBTA
National Business Aircraft Association (EA) ... NBAA
National Business and Education Council (OICC) ... NBEC
National Business Association (EA) ... NBA
National Business Career Center (EA) ... NBCC
National Business Circulation Association (EA) ... NBCA
National Business Consortium for the Gifted and Talented [*Defunct*] (EA) ... NBCGT
National Business Council for Consumer Affairs [*Terminated, 1974*] [*Department of Commerce*] (EGAO) ... NBCCA
National Business Education Association [*Reston, VA*] (EA) ... NBEA
National Business Entrance Test [*Education*] (AEBS) ... NBET
National Business Equipment Survey [*British*] ... NBES
National Business Forms Association [*Alexandria, VA*] (EA) ... NBFA
National Business Incubation Association [*Carlisle, PA*] (EA) ... NBIA
National Business Incubation Association ... NBIA
National Business Information Center [*Dun & Bradstreet*] ... NBIC
National Business Law Council [*Formerly, NABLT*] (EA) ... NBLC
National Business League [*Washington, DC*] (EA) ... NBL
National Business Owners Association (EA) ... NBOA
National Business Publications [*Later, ABP*] (EA) ... NBP
National Business Systems, Inc. [*Toronto Stock Exchange symbol*] ... NBS
National Business Teachers Association (NADA) ... NBTA
National Business Travel Association (EA) ... NBTA
National Businessmen's Council [*Defunct*] (EA) ... NBMC
National Businesswomen's Leadership Association [*Defunct*] (EA) ... NBLA
National Butterfly Association (EA) ... NBA
National Button Association ... NBA
National Button Society (EA) ... NBS
National Cable Antenna Television Association of Canada (NTCM) ... NCATA
National Cable Television Association (EA) ... NCTA
National Cable Television Association, Washington, DC [*Library symbol Library of Congress*] (LCLS) ... DNCT
National Cable Television Institute (EA) ... NCTI
National Cactus and Succulent Society [*British*] (BI) ... NCSS
National Cadet Corps (NADA) ... NCC
National Cage Bird Show (EA) ... NCBS
National Cage Bird Week Association [*Defunct*] (EA) ... NCBW
National Calling and Emergency Frequencies (CET) ... NCEF
National Cambodia Crisis Committee [*Defunct*] (EA) ... NCCC
National Cambridge Collectors (EA) ... NCC
National Campaign Against Solvent Abuse [*British*] (DBA) ... NCASA
National Campaign Against Toxic Hazards (EA) ... NCATH
National Campaign for a Peace Tax Fund (EA) ... NCPTF
National Campaign for Firework Reform [*British*] (DBA) ... NCFR
National Campaign for Freedom of Expression ... NCFE
National Campaign for Nursery Education [*British*] ... NCNE
National Campaign for Radioactive Waste Safety (EA) ... NCRWS
National Campaign for the Abolition of Capital Punishment [*Founded in 1955*] [*British*] ... NCACP
National Campaign for the Arts [*British*] (DBA) ... NCA
National Campaign for the Reform of the Obscene Publications Acts [*British*] (DBA) ... NCROPA
National Campaign to Save the ABM [*Antiballistic missile*] **Treaty** [*Defunct*] (EA) ... NCSABMT
National Campaign to Stop the MX [*Defunct*] (EA) ... NCSMX
National Campers and Hikers Association (EA) ... NCHA
National Campground Owners Association (EA) ... NCOA
National Camping Association (EA) ... NCA
National Campus Ministry Association (EA) ... NCMA
National Cancer Advisory Board ... NCAB
National Cancer Advisory Committee [*Australia*] ... NCAC
National Cancer Care Foundation (EA) ... NCCF
National Cancer Center (EA) ... NCC
National Cancer Cytology Center [*Later, NCC*] (EA) ... NCCC
National Cancer Foundation ... NCF
National Cancer Institute [*Database producer*] [*Bethesda, MD*] [*National Institutes of Health*] [*Department of Health and Human Services*] ... NCI
National Cancer Institute [*Research code symbol*] ... NSC
National Cancer Institute of Canada ... NCIC
National Cancer Institute Tissue Culture [*Medium*] ... NCTC
National Cancer Pain Coalition ... NCPC
National Cancer Policy Board ... NCPB
National Cancer Program [*National Institutes of Health*] ... NCP
National Candle Association (EA) ... NCA
National Candy Brokers and Salesmen's Association [*Later, NCBA*] (EA) ... NCBSA
National Candy Brokers Association (EA) ... NCBA
National Candy Wholesalers Association (EA) ... NCWA
National Canine Defence League [*British*] (DI) ... NCDL
National Canners Association [*Later, NFPA*] (EA) ... NCA
National Canners Association Research Laboratory ... NCRL
National Cap and Cloth Hat Institute (EA) ... NCCHI
National Cap and Patch Association (EA) ... CAP
National Capital Administrative Support Center [*Marine science*] (OSRA) ... NCASC
National Capital Administrative Support Center (USDC) ... NCASC
National Capital Association for Cooperative Education (MCD) ... NCACE
National Capital Award ... NCA
National Capital Commission [*Canada*] ... NCC
National Capital Commission, Ottawa, ON, Canada [*Library symbol Library of Congress*] (LCLS) ... CaOONCC
National Capital Commission [*Commission de la Capitale Nationale*] **Ottawa, Ontario** [*Library symbol National Library of Canada*] (NLC) ... OONCC
National Capital Historical Museum of Transportation (EA) ... NCHMT
National Capital Housing Authority ... NCHA
National Capital Management Corp. [*NASDAQ symbol*] (NQ) ... NCMC

National Capital Management Corp. [*Associated Press*] (SAG) .... NtCapit
National Capital Park and Planning Commission [*Later, NCPC*] .... NCPPC
National Capital Planning Commission [*Formerly, NCPPC*] .... NCPC
National Capital Region .... NCR
National Capital Region, District of Columbia (MCD) .... NCRDC
National Capital Region, Maryland (MCD) .... NCRMD
National Capital Region, Virginia (MCD) .... NCRVA
National Capital Regional Planning Council [*Terminated, 1966*] .... NCRPC
National Capital Speakers Association (EA) .... NCSA
National Capital Transportation Agency [*Functions transferred to Washington Metropolitan Area Transit Authority*] .... NCTA
National Capon Council [*Defunct*] (EA) .... NCC
National Captioning Institute (EA) .... NCI
National Captive Nations Committee (EA) .... NCNC
National Car Parks [*British*] .... NCP
National Caravan Council Ltd. [*British*] (BI) .... NCC
National Carbon Co. (MCD) .... NCC
National Cardiovascular Network .... NCN
National Career Center (EA) .... NCC
National Career Development Association (EA) .... NCDA
National Career Information Center [*Defunct*] (EA) .... NCIC
National Cargo Bureau (EA) .... NCB
National Caries Program [*Public Health Service*] (GRD) .... NCP
National Carl Schurz Association [*Defunct*] (EA) .... NCSA
National Carl Schurz Memorial Foundation, Philadelphia, PA [*Library symbol Library of Congress Obsolete*] (LCLS) .... PPCS
National Carousel Association (EA) .... NCA
National Carpenters Craft Board [*Defunct*] (EA) .... NCCB
National Carpet Cleaners Association [*British*] (EAIO) .... NCCA
National Carriers Contract Services [*National Freight Consortium*] [*British*] .... NCCS
National Carriers Ltd. [*British*] (DCTA) .... NCL
National Cartographic and Geographic Information Center [*Geological Survey*] [*Reston, VA Database*] .... NCGIC
National Cartographic Information Center [*United States Geological Survey*] [*Reston, VA*] .... NCIC
National Cartoonists Society (EA) .... NCS
National Carvers Museum Foundation [*Defunct*] (EA) .... NCMF
National Carwash Council [*Later, ICA*] (EA) .... NCC
National Carwash Council .... NCWC
National Cash Register [*Computer science*] (NADA) .... NCR
National Cash Register Applied COBOL [*Common Business-Oriented Language*] **Package** (IAA) .... NACACP
National Cash Register Co. [*Later, NCR Corp.*] [*Computer manufacturer*] .... NCR
National Cash Register Co., Electronics Division, Hawthorne, CA [*Library symbol Library of Congress*] (LCLS) .... CHawN
National Cash Register Co., NCR Library, Dayton, OH [*Library symbol Library of Congress*] (LCLS) .... ODaN
National Cash Register Co., New York, NY [*Library symbol Library of Congress*] (LCLS) .... UmF
National Cash Register Co., Technical Library, Dayton, OH [*Library symbol Library of Congress*] (LCLS) .... ODaNT
National Cash Register Electronic Autocoding Technique [*Computer science*] (IAA) .... NEAT
National Cash Register Electronic Data Processing System (MCD) .... NATRON
National Cashmere Association [*Defunct*] (EA) .... NCA
National Castings Council [*Defunct*] (EA) .... NCC
National Cat Fanciers' Association [*Defunct*] (EA) .... NCFA
National Cat Protection Society (EA) .... NCPS
National Catalog Managers Association (EA) .... NCMA
National Caterers Association [*Later, ICA*] (EA) .... NCA
National Cathedral Association (EA) .... NCA
National Catholic Action Coalition [*Defunct*] (EA) .... NCAC
National Catholic AIDS Network (EA) .... NCAN
National Catholic Bandmasters' Association (EA) .... NCBA
National Catholic Business Education Association [*Emporia, KS*] (EA) .... NCBEA
National Catholic Camping Association [*Defunct*] (EA) .... NCCA
National Catholic Cemetery Conference (EA) .... NCCC
National Catholic Coalition for Responsible Investment (EA) .... NCCRI
National Catholic Commission for Industrial Relations [*Australia*] .... NCCIR
National Catholic Committee on Scouting (EA) .... NCCS
National Catholic Community Service [*Defunct*] (EA) .... NCCS
National Catholic Conference for Interracial Justice (EA) .... NCCIJ
National Catholic Conference for Seafarers (EA) .... NCCS
National Catholic Conference for Total Stewardship (EA) .... NCCTS
National Catholic Conference of Airport Chaplains (EA) .... NCCAC
National Catholic Conference on Family Life (EA) .... NCCFL
National Catholic Development Conference (EA) .... NCDC
National Catholic Disaster Relief Committee (EA) .... NCDRC
National Catholic Educational Association (EA) .... NCEA
National Catholic Educational Exhibitors (EA) .... NCEE
National Catholic Forensic League (EA) .... NCFL
National Catholic Guidance Conference [*Later, ARVIC*] (EA) .... NCGC
National Catholic Kindergarten Association (AEBS) .... NCKA
National Catholic Liturgical Conference (EA) .... NCLC
National Catholic Music Educators Association [*Later, NPM*] (EA) .... NCMEA
National Catholic News Service (EA) .... NANS
National Catholic News Service .... NC
National Catholic News Service (EA) .... NCNS
National Catholic Office for Motion Pictures [*Later, Office for Film and Broadcasting*] .... NCOMP
National Catholic Office for Persons with Disabilities (EA) .... NCOPD
National Catholic Office for Radio and Television [*Later, Office for Film and Broadcasting*] .... NCORT
National Catholic Office for the Deaf (EA) .... NCOD
National Catholic Pharmacists Guild of the United States (EA) .... NCPG
National Catholic Resettlement Council (EA) .... NCRC
National Catholic Rural Life Conference (EA) .... NCRLC
National Catholic Social Action Conference [*Defunct*] (EA) .... NCSAC
National Catholic Society for Animal Welfare [*Later, ISAR*] (EA) .... NCSAW
National Catholic Society of Foresters (EA) .... NCSF
National Catholic Stewardship Council (EA) .... NCSC
National Catholic Theatre Conference (EA) .... NCTC
National Catholic Vocation Council [*Defunct*] (EA) .... NCVC
National Catholic Welfare Conference [*Later, USCC*] (EA) .... NCWC
National Catholic Welfare Conference News Service (NTCM) .... NCWC
National Catholic Women's Union (EA) .... NCWU
National Catholic Youth Association [*British*] (BI) .... NCYA
National Catholic Youth Council .... NCYC
National Cattle Breeders Association [*British*] (DBA) .... NCBA
National Cattle Theft Act .... NCTA
National Cattlemens Association (EA) .... NCA
National Caucus and Center on Black Aged (EA) .... NCBA
National Caucus and Center on Black Aged (EA) .... NCCBA
National Caucus of Gay and Lesbian Counselors (EA) .... NCGLC
National Caucus of Labor Committees .... NCLC
National Cave Rescue Commission .... NCRC
National Caves Association (EA) .... NCA
National Caving Association [*British*] (DBA) .... NCA
National Cavity Installation Association [*British*] .... NCIA
National Cedar Chest Association [*Defunct*] (EA) .... NCCA
National Cellular Resellers' Association (EA) .... NCRA
National Cellulose Insulation Manufacturers Association .... NCIMA
National Cemetery .... NATCEM
National Cemetery (IIA) .... NC
National Cemetery System .... NCS
National Center (IAA) .... NC
National Center Confraternity of Christian Doctrine (EA) .... NCCCD
National Center, Educational Media and Materials for the Handicapped [*Defunct*] (EA) .... NCEMMH
National Center for a Barrier Free Environment (EA) .... NCBFE
National Center for Administrative Justice [*Formerly, CAJ*] (EA) .... NCAJ
National Center for Adult, Continuing, and Manpower Education [*Office of Education*] .... NCACME
National Center for Advanced Materials [*Later, Berkeley Center for A dvanced Materials*] .... NCAM
National Center for Advanced Technology [*Vienna, VA*] .... NCAT
National Center for Air Pollution Control [*Public Health Service*] [*Obsolete*] .... NCAPC
National Center for Alcohol Education [*National Institutes of Health*] .... NCAE
National Center for American Indian Alternative Education (EA) .... NCAIAE
National Center for American Indian and Alaska Native Mental Health Research (EA) .... NCAIANMHR
National Center for American Indian Education [*Later, NCAIAE*] (EA) .... NCAIE
National Center for Analysis of Energy Systems (HGAA) .... NCAES
National Center for Appropriate Technology (EA) .... NCAT
National Center for Association Resources (EA) .... NCAR
National Center for Atmospheric Research [*Boulder, CO*] [*National Science Foundation*] (GRD) .... NCAR
National Center for Atmospheric Research, Boulder, CO [*OCLC symbol*] (OCLC) .... CNR
National Center for Atmospheric Research, Boulder, CO [*Library symbol Library of Congress*] (LCLS) .... CoBA
National Center for Atmospheric Research, High Altitude Observatory, Boulder, CO [*Library symbol Library of Congress*] (LCLS) .... CoBA-HA
National Center for Audio Experimentation [*Defunct*] (EA) .... NCAE
National Center for Audio Tapes Archive (EA) .... NCAA
National Center for Audiotape [*Later, NCATA*] (EA) .... NCAT
National Center for Audiotape Archive [*Defunct*] (EA) .... NCATA
National Center for Automated Information Retrieval (IID) .... NCAIR
National Center for Bilingual Research [*National Institute of Education*] [*Research center*] (RCD) .... NCBR
National Center for Biotechnology Information (IID) .... NCBI
National Center for Business and Economic Communication [*American University*] [*Research center*] (RCD) .... NCBEC
National Center for Charitable Statistics (EA) .... NCCS
National Center for Child Advocacy .... NCCA
National Center for Chronic Disease Control [*Public Health Service*] .... NCCD
National Center for Chronic Disease Control (DAVI) .... NCCDC
National Center for Church Vocations [*Later, NCVC*] (EA) .... NCCV
National Center for Clinical Infant Programs (EA) .... NCCIP
National Center for Community Action (EA) .... NCCA
National Center for Community Crime Prevention (EA) .... NCCCP
National Center for Community Education (EA) .... NCCE
National Center for Computer Crime Data (EA) .... NCCCD
National Center for Constitutional Studies (EA) .... NCCS
National Center for Cross-Cultural Studies in Law [*Monash University*] [*Australia*] .... NCCSL
National Center for Disease Control [*Public Health Service*] .... NCDC
National Center for Dispute Settlement [*American Arbitration Association*] [*Later, CDS*] .... NCDS
National Center for Drug Analysis [*St. Louis*] [*FDA*] .... NCDA
National Center for Drugs and Biologics [*FDA*] .... NCDB
National Center for Earthquake Engineering Research [*Buffalo, NY*] (GRD) .... NCEER
National Center for Earthquake Engineering, Research Information Services, State, Buffalo, NY [*Library symbol*] [*Library of Congress*] (LCLS) .... NBuNCE
National Center for Earthquake Research [*US Geological Survey*] .... NCER
National Center for Economic Alternatives (EA) .... NCEA

National Center for Education and Training in Addictions [*Australia*] .... NCETA
National Center for Education in Maternal and Child Health (EA) .... NCEMCH
National Center for Education in Politics [*Defunct*] (EA) .... NCEP
National Center for Education Statistics [*Office of Education*] [*Later, CES*] .... NCES
National Center for Educational Brokering [*Defunct*] (EA) .... NCEB
National Center for Educational Communication [*Office of Education*] .... NCEC
National Center for Educational Research and Development [*HEW*] .... NCERD
National Center for Educational Technology [*Office of Education*] .... NCET
National Center for Electron Microscopy [*Berkeley, CA*] [*Lawrence Berkeley Laboratory*] [*Department of Energy*] .... NCEM
National Center for Employee Ownership (EA) .... NCEO
National Center for Energy Management and Power .... NCEMP
National Center for Environmental Health Strategies (EA) .... NCEHS
National Center for Excellence in Metalworking Technology [*Navy*] .... NCEMT
National Center for Exploitation of the Oceans .... NCEO
National Center for Family Literacy (PAZ) .... NCFL
National Center for Family Planning Services [*Health Services and Mental Health Administration, HEW*] .... NCFPS
National Center for Film and Video Preservation (EA) .... NCFVP
National Center for Financial Education (EA) .... NCFE
National Center for Fish Protein Concentrate [*Fish and Wildlife Service*].... NCFPC
National Center for Freedom of Information Studies (EA) .... NCFIS
National Center for Genome Resources .... NCGR
National Center for Ground Water Research [*Stillwater, OK*] [*Environmental Protection Agency*] (GRD) .... NCGWR
National Center for Health Care Technology [*US Congress agency*] .... NCHCT
National Center for Health Education (EA) .... NCHE
National Center for Health Promotion and Aging (EA) .... NCHPA
National Center for Health Services Research .... NCHSR
National Center for Health Services Research and Development [*Later, NCHSR*] [*HEW*] .... NCHSR & D
National Center for Health Services Research and Development [*Later, NCHSR*] [*HEW*] .... NCHSRD
National Center for Health Services Research and Health Care Technology Assessment [*Rockville, MD*] [*Public Health Service*] (GRD) .... NCHSR
National Center for Health Statistics [*Public Health Service*] [*Hyattsville, MD Originator and database*] .... NCHS
National Center for Hearing Dog Information [*Later, HDRC*] (EA) .... NCHDI
National Center for Higher Education Management Systems (EA) .... NCHEMS
National Center for HIV [*Human Immunodeficiency Virus*] **Virology Research** [*Australia*] .... NCHVR
National Center for Homecare Education and Research [*Defunct*] (EA)..... NCHER
National Center for Homeopathy (EA) .... NCH
National Center for Housing Management (EA) .... NCHM
National Center for Human Genome Research .... NCHGR
National Center for Human Genome Research [*Renamed*] .... NCHGR
National Center for Immigrants' Rights [*Later, NILC*] (EA) .... NCIR
National Center for Improving Science Education (EA) .... NCISE
National Center for Information and Advice on Educational Disadvantage .... NCIAED
National Center for Initiative Review (EA) .... NCIR
National Center for Initiative Review Foundation [*Defunct*] (EA) .... NCIRF
National Center for Integrated Bioremediation Research & Development [*Initiated in Michigan with government funding, 1994*] .... NCIBRD
National Center for Intermedia Transport Research [*Los Angeles, CA*] (GRD) .... NCITR
National Center for Jewish Film (EA) .... NCJF
National Center for Jewish Policy Studies .... NCJPS
National Center for Job Market Studies [*Commercial firm Washington, DC*] (EA) .... NCJMS
National Center for Jobs and Justice (EA) .... NCJJ
National Center for Juvenile Justice (EA) .... NCJJ
National Center for Law and the Deaf (EA) .... NCLD
National Center for Law and the Handicapped [*Defunct*] (EA) .... NCLH
National Center for Learning Disabilities (EA) .... NCLD
National Center for Legislative Research [*Defunct*] (EA) .... NCLR
National Center for Manufacturing Sciences [*Research center*] .... NCMS
National Center for Mediation Education (EA) .... NCME
National Center for Men (EA) .... NCM
National Center for Missing and Exploited Children (EA) .... NCMEC
National Center for Missing and Exploited Children .... NCMEC
National Center for Municipal Development (EA) .... NCMD
National Center for Neighborhood Enterprise (EA) .... NCNE
National Center for Nonprofit Boards (EA) .... NCNB
National Center for Nursing Research [*Bethesda, MD*] [*Department of Health and Human Services*] (GRD) .... NCNR
National Center for Petroleum Geology and Geophysics [*Australia*] .... NCPGG
National Center for Policy Alternatives [*Later, CPA*] (EA) .... NCPA
National Center for Preservation Law (EA) .... NCPL
National Center for Prevention and Control of Rape [*National Institutes of Health*] .... NCPCR
National Center for Productivity and Quality of Working Life [*Later, National Productivity Council*] .... NCPQWL
National Center for Public Policy Research (EA) .... NCPPR
National Center for Radiological Health [*Public Health Service*] .... NCRH
National Center for Research in Vocational Education (EA) .... NCRVE
National Center for Research into Drug Abuse [*Australia*] .... NCRDA
National Center for Research on Teacher Education [*East Lansing, MI*] [*Department of Education*] (GRD) .... NCRTE
National Center for Research Resources [*National Institutes of Health*] .... NCRR
National Center for Research to Improve Postsecondary Teaching and Learning [*Ann Arbor, MI*] [*Department of Education*] (GRD) .... NCRIPTAL
National Center for Resource Innovations .... NCRI
National Center for Resource Recovery [*Defunct*] .... NCRR
National Center for School and College Television .... NCSCT
National Center for Science Education (EA) .... NCSE
National Center for Science Information Systems [*Japan*] .... NACSIS
[*The*] **National Center for Science Information Systems** [*Computer science*] (TNIG) .... NACSIS
National Center for Service-Learning [*Defunct*] (EA) .... NCSL
National Center for Small-Angle Scattering Research [*Oak Ridge, TN*] [*Department of Energy*] (GRD) .... NCSASR
National Center for Social Policy and Practice (EA) .... NCSPP
National Center for Social Statistics [*HEW*] .... NCSS
National Center for Solid Waste Disposal [*Later, National Center for Resource Recovery*] (EA) .... NCSWD
National Center for Standards and Certification Information [*Gaithersburg, MD*] [*Database*] [*National Institute of Standards and Technology*] .... NCSCI
National Center for State Courts (EA) .... NCSC
National Center for State Courts, Williamsburg, VA [*OCLC symbol*] (OCLC) .... COT
National Center for State Courts, Williamsburg, VA [*Library symbol*] [*Library of Congress*] (LCLS) .... ViWSC
National Center for Statistics and Analysis [*National Highway Traffic Safety Administration*] [*Washington, DC*] (GRD) .... NCSA
National Center for Stuttering (EA) .... NCS
National Center for Supercomputer Applications (NITA) .... NCSA
National Center for Supercomputing Applications [*University of Illinois*] [*National Science Foundation*] [*Research center*] (RCD) .... NCSA
[*The*] **National Center for Supercomputing Applications Network** [*Computer science*] (TNIG) .... NCSAnet
National Center for Surrogate Parenting [*Later, IAI*] [*Commercial firm*] (EA) .... NCSP
National Center for Telephone Research [*Louis Harris and Associates*] [*Commercial firm*] (EA) .... NCTR
National Center for the Advancement of Blacks in the Health Professions (EA) .... NCABHP
National Center for the Analysis of Violent Crime [*Quantico, VA*] [*Department of Justice*] (GRD) .... NCAVC
National Center for the Development of Bilingual Curriculum (EA) .... NCDBC
National Center for the Diaconate [*Later, NAAND*] (EA) .... NCD
National Center for the Exploration of Human Potential (EA) .... NCEHP
National Center for the Improvement of Educational Systems [*Office of Education*] .... NCIES
National Center for the Prevention and Treatment of Child Abuse and Neglect (EA) .... NCPTCAN
National Center for the Prevention of Sudden Infant Death Syndrome (EA) .... NCPSIDS
National Center for the Prosecution of Child Abuse (EA) .... NCPCA
National Center for the Study of Collective Bargaining in Higher Education and the Professions (EA) .... NCSCBHEP
National Center for the Study of Corporal Punishment and Alternatives in the Schools (EA) .... NCSCPAS
National Center for Therapeutic Riding (EA) .... NCTR
National Center for Tourism Studies [*Australia*] .... NCTS
National Center for Toxicological Research [*Department of Health and Human Services*] [*Jefferson, AR*] .... NCTR
National Center for Toxicological Research, Jefferson, AR [*OCLC symbol*] (OCLC) .... HNT
National Center for Urban and Industrial Health [*Public Health Service*] ...... NCUI
National Center for Urban Environmental Studies [*Defunct*] (EA) .... NCUES
National Center for Urban Ethnic Affairs (EA) .... NCUEA
National Center for Vehicle Emissions Control and Safety [*Colorado State University*] .... NCVECS
National Center for Vocational, Occupational, and Technical Education [*Office of Education*] .... NCVOTE
National Center for Voluntary Action [*Later, NVC*] .... NCVA
National Center for Youth Law (EA) .... NCYL
National Center for Youth with Disabilities (EA) .... NCYD
National Center of Afro-American Artists .... NCAAA
National Center of Communication Arts and Sciences (EA) .... NCCAS
National Center of Scientific and Technological Information [*National Council for Research and Development*] [*Israel Also, CSTI*] (IID) .... COSTI
National Center on Arts and the Aging (EA) .... NCAA
National Center on Child Abuse and Neglect [*Department of Health and Human Services*] [*Washington, DC*] .... NCCAN
National Center on Education and Employment [*New York, NY Department of Education*] (GRD) .... NCEE
National Center on Educational Media and Materials for the Handicapped, Columbus, OH [*Inactive*] [*OCLC symbol*] (OCLC) .... NCH
National Center on Educational Media and Materials for the Handicapped, Columbus, OH [*Library symbol Library of Congress*] (LCLS) .... OCoNC
National Center on Employment of the Deaf (EA) .... NCED
National Center on Institutions and Alternatives (EA) .... NCIA
National Center on Missing Children (NADA) .... NCMC
National Center on Occupational Readjustment [*Defunct*] (EA) .... NaCOR
National Center on Rural Aging (EA) .... NCRA
National Center on Women and Family Law (EA) .... NCOWFL
National Centers for Disease Control (NADA) .... NCDC
National Centers for Environmental Prediction [*Marine science*] (OSRA) ..... NCEP
National Centers for Health and Medical Information, Inc. [*Research center*] (RCD) .... NCHMI
National Central American Health Rights Network (EA) .... NCAHRN
National Central Bureau [*INTERPOL term*] .... NCB
National Central Library [*United Kingdom*] .... NCL
National Central Library, Rare Book Collection, Taipei, Taiwan, China [*Library symbol Library of Congress*] (LCLS) .... Ch-R
National Central Office for the Suppression of Counterfeit Currency [*British*] .... NCOSCC

National Centre for Alternative Technology [*British*] ... NCAT
National Centre for Athletic Literature (NITA) ... NATCENTATHLIT
National Centre for Athletics Literature (AIE) ... NCAL
National Centre for Christian Communities and Networks [*Westhill College*] [*British*] (CB) ... NACCCAN
National Centre for Industrial Language Training [*British*] (DI) ... NCILT
National Centre for Orchestral Studies [*Goldsmiths' College*] [*British*] (CB) ... NCOS
National Centre for Ore Deposit and Exploration [*University of Tasmania*] [*Australia*] ... CODES
National Centre for School Biotechnology (AIE) ... NCSB
National Centre for Systems Reliability [*Research center British*] (CB) ... NCSR
National Centre of Tribology [*Risley Nuclear Laboratories*] [*British*] (CB) ... NCT
National Ceramic Association [*Later, ICA*] (EA) ... NCA
National Ceramic Association Educational Foundation (EA) ... NCAEF
National Ceramic Dealers Association (EA) ... NCDA
National Ceramic Manufacturers Association ... NCMA
National Ceramic Teachers Association (EA) ... NCTA
National Certificate (WDAA) ... NC
National Certificate of Agriculture [*British*] ... NCA
National Certification Agency for Medical Laboratory Personnel (EA) ... NCA
National Certification Agency for Medical Laboratory Personnel (MAE) ... NCAMLP
National Certification Board of Pediatric Nurse Practitioners and Nurses (EA) ... NCBPNP/N
National Certification Commission in Chemistry and Chemical Engineering (IAA) ... NCCCHE
National Certification Reciprocity Consortium/Alcoholism and Other Drug Abuse (EA) ... NCRC/AODA
National Certification Skills Test [*Psychiatry*] ... NCST
National Certified Pipe Welding Bureau (EA) ... NCPWB
National Challenged Homeschoolers Associated Network (PAZ) ... NATHHAN
National Chamber Foundation (EA) ... NCF
National Chamber Litigation Center (EA) ... NCLC
National Chamber of Commerce for Women [*New York, NY*] (EA) ... NCCW
National Chamber of Trade [*British*] (BI) ... NCT
National Championship Poker Run [*American Motorcyclists Association*] ... NCPR
National Championship Racing Association [*Auto racing*] ... NCRA
National Championship Stock Car Racing [*Later, NASCAR*] ... NCSCC
National Change of Address Association [*Commercial firm New York, NY*] (EA) ... NCAA
National Change of Address Service [*US Postal Service*] ... NCOA
National Chaplain's Association (EA) ... NCA
National Chaplains Association for Youth Rehabilitation [*Defunct*] ... NCAYR
National Character Laboratory (EA) ... NCL
National Charcoal Association ... NCA
National Charities Information Bureau (EA) ... NCIB
National Chastity Association (EA) ... NCA
National Check Traders Federation [*British*] (BI) ... NCTF
National Cheerleaders Association (EA) ... NCA
National Cheese Institute (EA) ... NCI
National Chemical Credit Association (EA) ... NCCA
National Chemical Emergency Centre [*Atomic Energy Authority*] [*Didcot, Oxon., England*] ... NCEC
National Chemical Information System (DIT) ... NCIS
National Chemical Laboratory (MCD) ... NCHEML
National Chemical Laboratory ... NCL
National Chemical Response and Information Center [*Established by the Chemical Manufacturers Association to provide information and advice during emergencies*] ... NCRIC
National Cherry Growers and Industries Foundation (EA) ... NCGIF
National Chevelle Owners Association (EA) ... NCOA
National Chevy/GMC Truckin' Club [*Defunct*] (EA) ... NCGMCTC
National Chicano Council for Higher Education [*Defunct*] (EA) ... NCCHE
National Chicano Health Organization (EA) ... NCHO
National Child Day Care Association (EA) ... NCDCA
National Child Development Study [*British*] ... NCDS
National Child Health and Education Study [*University of Bristol*] [*British*] ... NCHES
National Child Labor Committee (EA) ... NCLC
National Child Nutrition Project (EA) ... NCNP
National Child Passenger Safety Association [*Later, NPSA*] (EA) ... NCPSA
National Child Safety Council (EA) ... NCSC
National Child Safety Development [*British*] ... NCSD
National Child Support Advocacy Coalition (EA) ... NCSAC
National Child Support Enforcement Association (EA) ... NCSEA
National Childbirth Trust [*British*] ... NCT
National Childminding Association [*British*] (EAIO) ... NCA
National Childminding Association [*British*] (DBA) ... NCMA
National Children and Youth Fitness Study [*HHS*] ... NCYFS
National Children's Bureau [*British*] ... NCB
National Children's Dental Health Month [*American Dental Association*] ... NCDHM
National Children's Eye Care Foundation (EA) ... NCECF
National Children's Home [*British*] ... NCH
National Children's Wear Association [*British*] (EAIO) ... NCWA
National Chile Center [*Formerly, NCCSC*] (EA) ... NCC
National Chimney Sweep Guild (EA) ... NCSG
National China Painting Teachers Organization [*Later, IPAT*] (EA) ... NCPTO
National Chinchilla Breeders of America [*Later, ECBC*] (EA) ... NCBA
National Chinese Curriculum Project [*Australia*] ... NCCP
National Chiropractic Association [*Universal Chiropratic Association and American Chiropratic Association*] [*Later, American Chiropractic Association*] [*Formed by a merger of*] ... NCA
National Cholesterol Education Program Coordinating Committee [*National Institutes of Health*] (EGAO) ... NCEP
National Choreography Project ... NCP
National Christ Child Society (EA) ... NCCS
National Christian Action Coalition [*Defunct*] (EA) ... NCAC
National Christian Association (EA) ... NCA
National Christian College Athletic Association (EA) ... NCCAA
National Christian Education Association (EA) ... NCEA
National Christian Education Council [*Church of England*] ... NCEC
National Christian Leadership Conference for Israel (EA) ... NCLCI
National Christian Network [*Cable-television system*] ... NCN
National Christmas Tree Association (EA) ... NCTA
National Christmas Tree Growers Association [*Later, National Christmas Tree Association*] (EA) ... NCTGA
National Chronic Epstein-Barr Virus Syndrome Association (EA) ... NCEBVS
National Chronic Fatigue Syndrome Association (EA) ... NCFSA
National Chronic Pain Outreach Association (EA) ... NCPO
National Chronic Pain Outreach Association, Inc. (PAZ) ... NCPOA
National Chrysanthemum Society (EA) ... NCS
National Chrysler Products Club (EA) ... NCPC
National Church Goods Association (EA) ... NCGA
National Church Music Fellowship [*Defunct*] ... NCMF
National Church Secretaries Association [*Defunct*] (EA) ... NCSA
National Churches [*A publication*] ... NC
National Cigar and Tobacco Workers' Union [*British*] ... NCTWU
National Cigar Leaf Tobacco Association [*Defunct*] (EA) ... NCLTA
National Cinder Concrete Products Association (EA) ... NCCPA
National Circus Preservation Society (EA) ... NCPS
National Circus Project (EA) ... NCP
National Citizen Communication Lobby (EA) ... NCCL
National Citizens Action Network (EA) ... NCAN
National Citizens' Advice Bureaux Committee [*British*] (BI) ... NCABC
National Citizens Coalition [*Canada*] ... NCC
National Citizens Coalition for Nursing Home Reform (EA) ... NCCNHR
National Citizens Commission for the Public Schools (AEBS) ... NCCPS
National Citizens' Committee [*Poland*] [*Political party*] ... KKO
National Citizens Committee. Bulletin [*A publication*] ... NCC
National Citizens Committee for Broadcasting (EA) ... NCCB
National Citizens Committee for Community Relations [*Defunct*] ... NCCCR
National Citizens Committee for the World Health Organization [*Later, AAWH*] (EA) ... NCCWHO
National Citizens Committee to Save Education and Library Funds ... SELF
National Citizens' Movement for Free Elections [*Philippines*] [*Political party*] ... NAMFREL
National Citizens Participation Council (EA) ... NCPC
National Citizens Radio League (IAA) ... NCRL
National City Bancorp [*NASDAQ symbol*] (NQ) ... NCBM
National City Bancorp [*Associated Press*] (SAG) ... NCtyB
National City Bancshares [*NASDAQ symbol*] (SAG) ... NCBE
National City Bancshares [*Associated Press*] (SAG) ... NCtyBn
National City Corp. [*Associated Press*] (SAG) ... NatlCity
National City Corp. [*NYSE symbol*] (CTT) ... NCC
National City Corp. [*Associated Press*] (SAG) ... NtlCity
National City Public Library, National City, CA [*Library symbol Library of Congress*] (LCLS) ... CNa
National Civic Association ... NCA
National Civic League (EA) ... NCL
National Civic Review [*A publication*] (ILCA) ... Natl Civ Rev
National Civic Review [*A publication*] (BRI) ... NCR
National Civics Federation ... NCF
National Civil Aviation Council [*British*] (BI) ... NCAC
National Civil Defense Advisory Council (EA) ... NCDAC
National Civil Defense Computer Facility ... NCDCF
National Civil Liberties Clearing House [*Defunct*] (EA) ... NCLCH
National Civil Liberties Legal Foundation [*Inactive*] (EA) ... NCLLF
National Civil Service League [*Defunct*] (EA) ... NCSL
National Civilian Community Corps ... NCCC
National C-Lark Association (EA) ... NCLA
National Class E Scow Association (EA) ... NCESA
National Classification Board [*American Trucking Association*] ... NCB
National Classification Management Society (EA) ... NCMS
National Clay Pipe Institute (EA) ... NCPI
National Clay Pot Manufacturers (EA) ... NCPM
National Clayware Federation [*British*] (DBA) ... NCF
National Clean Air Coalition [*Defunct*] (EA) ... NCAC
National Clean Air Fund (GFGA) ... NCAF
National Clean Up - Paint Up - Fix Up Bureau [*Defunct*] (EA) ... CU-PU-FU
National Clearing Corp. [*National Association of Securities Dealers*] ... NCC
National Clearing House of Rehabilitation Training Materials [*Oklahoma State University*] [*Information service or system*] (IID) ... NCHRTM
National Clearinghouse [*Public Health Service*] ... NCH
National Clearinghouse for Alcohol and Drug Abuse Information (PAZ) ... NCADI
National Clearinghouse for Alcohol and Drug Information [*US Public Health Service*] [*Information service or system*] (IID) ... NCADI
National Clearinghouse for Alcohol Information [*Rockville, MD*] [*National Institutes of Health*] ... NCAI
National Clearinghouse for Alcohol Information [*National Institutes of Health*] (IID) ... NCALI
National Clearinghouse for Bilingual Education [*Wheaton, MD*] ... NCBE
National Clearinghouse for Commuter Programs (EA) ... NCCP
National Clearinghouse for Corporate Matching Gift Information (EA) ... NCCMGI
National Clearinghouse for Criminal Justice Planning and Architecture [*Defunct*] (EA) ... NCCJP & A
National Clearinghouse for Drug Abuse Information [*Public Health Service*] [*Rockville, MD*] ... NCDAI

National Clearinghouse for Family Planning Information [*Database*] .... NCFPI
National Clearinghouse for Human Genetic Diseases [*Later, NCEMCH*] [*Public Health Service*] [*Information service or system*] (IID) .... NCHGD
National Clearinghouse for Legal Services [*Legal Services Corp.*] [*Information service or system*] (IID) .... NCLS
National Clearinghouse for Mental Health Information (NITA) .... NCMH
National Clearinghouse for Mental Health Information [*Public Health Service*] [*Rockville, MD Database*] [*HEW*] .... NCMHI
National Clearinghouse for Periodical Title Word Abbreviations [*ANSI*] .... NCPTWA
National Clearinghouse for Poison Control Centers (EA) .... NCPCC
National Clearinghouse for Smoking and Health [*Public Health Service*] .... NCSH
National Clearinghouse for Youth Sports Information [*Operated by the National Alliance for Youth Sports*] (PAZ) .... NCYSI
National Clearinghouse on Child Abuse and Neglect Information (PAZ) .... NCCAN
National Clearinghouse on Child Neglect and Abuse [*HEW*] .... NCCNA
National Clearinghouse on Development Education [*Information service or system*] (IID) .... NCODE
National Clearinghouse on Family Violence, Health and Welfare Canada [*Centre National d'Information sur la Violence dans la Famille, Sante et Bien-Etre Social Canada*], Ottawa, Ontario [*Library symbol National Library of Canada*] (BIB) .... OONHFV
National Clearinghouse on Licensure, Enforcement and Regulation (EA) .... CLEAR
National Clearinghouse on Licensure, Enforcement, and Regulation (EA) .... NCLER
National Clearinghouse on Marital and Date Rape (EA) .... NCOMDR
National Clearinghouse on Marital Rape [*Later, NCOMDR*] (EA) .... NCOMR
National Clearinghouse on Revenue Sharing [*Defunct*] .... NCRS
National Clergy Council on Alcoholism and Related Drug Problems (EA) .... NCCA
National Clients Council (EA) .... NCC
National Climate Program [*Rockville, MD*] [*National Oceanic and Atmospheric Administration*] .... NCP
National Climate Program Coordinating Office .... NCPCO
National Climate Program Office [*National Oceanic and Atmospheric Administration*] .... NCPO
National Climatic Center [*National Oceanic and Atmospheric Administration*] .... NCC
National Climatic Center, Ashville, NC [*OCLC symbol*] (OCLC) .... OAQ
National Climatic Data Center [*National Oceanic and Atmospheric Administration Information service or system*] (IID) .... NCDC
National Climatic Research Program .... NCRP
National Climbing Classification System .... NCCS
National Clogging and Hoedown Council (EA) .... NCHC
National Clonal Germplasm Repository [*Corvallis, OR*] [*Agricultural Research Service*] [*Department of Agriculture*] (GRD) .... NCGR
National Clothing Industry Training Committee [*Australia*] .... NCITC
National Club Association (EA) .... NCA
National Club Cricket Association [*British*] (BI) .... NCCA
National Club Sports Association (EA) .... NCSA
National Coaches Council [*Later, ANCC*] (EA) .... NCC
National Coal Association (EA) .... NCA
National Coal Authority [*Australia*] .... NCA
National Coal Board [*British*] .... NCB
National Coal Council [*Department of Energy*] [*Arlington, VA*] (EGAO) .... NCC
National Coal Model [*Department of Energy*] (GFGA) .... NCM
National Coal Policy Conference [*Defunct*] (EA) .... NCPC
National Coal Policy Project .... NCPP
National Coal Resources Data System [*Geological Survey*] [*Databank*] [*Information service or system*] (IID) .... NCRDS
National Coal Workers Autopsy Study .... NCWAS
National Coalition Against Censorship (EA) .... NCAC
National Coalition Against Domestic Violence (EA) .... NCADV
National Coalition Against Pornography (EA) .... N-CAP
National Coalition Against Sexual Assault (EA) .... NCASA
National Coalition Against Surrogacy (EA) .... NCAS
National Coalition Against the Death Penalty (EA) .... NCADP
National Coalition Against the Misuses of Pesticides (EA) .... NCAMP
National Coalition for a Democratic Constitution [*Political group*] [*South Korea*] .... NCDC
National Coalition for a Free Cuba (EA) .... NCFC
National Coalition for a Just Draft (EA) .... NCJD
National Coalition for a Policy of No-First-Use of Nuclear Weapons (EA) .... NCPNFUNW
National Coalition for Adequate Alcoholism Programs [*Defunct*] (EA) ...... NCAAP
National Coalition for Adult Immunization .... NCAI
National Coalition for Campus Child Care (EA) .... NCCCC
National Coalition for Cancer Research (EA) .... NCCR
National Coalition for Cancer Survivorship (EA) .... NCCS
National Coalition for Consumer Education (EA) .... NCCE
National Coalition for Democracy in Education [*Defunct*] (EA) .... NCDE
National Coalition for Disease Prevention and Environmental Health .... NCDPEH
National Coalition for Enterprise Zones [*San Diego, CA*] (EA) .... NCEZ
National Coalition for Haitian Refugees (EA) .... NCHR
National Coalition for Jail Reform [*Defunct*] (EA) .... NCJR
National Coalition for Land Reform (EA) .... NCLR
National Coalition for Literacy (EA) .... NCL
National Coalition for Marine Conservation (EA) .... NCMC
National Coalition for More Effective School Discipline (EA) .... NCMESD
National Coalition for Parent Involvement in Education .... NCPIE
National Coalition for Public Education and Religious Liberty (EA) ..... NCPEARL
National Coalition for Public Education and Religious Liberty (EA) .... NCPERL
National Coalition for Quality Integrated Education (EA) .... NCQIE
National Coalition for Research in Neurological and Communicative Disorders (EA) .... NCR
National Coalition for Science and Technology [*Defunct*] (EA) .... NCST
National Coalition for Seat Belts on School Buses (EA) .... NCSSB
National Coalition for Sex Equity in Education (EA) .... NCSEE
National Coalition for the Homeless (EA) .... NCH
National Coalition for Universities in the Public Interest [*Defunct*] (EA) .... NCUPI
National Coalition for Women and Girls in Education (EA) .... NCWGE
National Coalition for Women in Defense (EA) .... NCWD
National Coalition of Advocates for Students (EA) .... NCAS
National Coalition of Alternative Community Schools (EA) .... NCACS
National Coalition of American Nuns (EA) .... NCAN
National Coalition of Arts Therapy Associations (EA) .... NCATA
National Coalition of Black Gays (EA) .... NCBG
National Coalition of Black Lesbians and Gays (EA) .... NCBLG
National Coalition of Black Lung and Respiratory Disease Clinics (EA) .... NCBLRDC
National Coalition of Black Meeting Planners (EA) .... NCBMP
National Coalition of Blacks for Reparations in America (ECON) .... N'COBRA
National Coalition of Concerned Legal Professionals (EA) .... CCLP
National Coalition of ESEA [*Elementary and Secondary Education Act*] **Title I Parents** (EA) .... NCTIP
National Coalition of Free Men (EA) .... NCFM
National Coalition of Gay Sexually Transmitted Disease Services [*Defunct*] (EA) .... NCGSTDS
National Coalition of Hispanic Health and Human Services Organizations (EA) .... NCHHHSO
National Coalition of Hispanic Mental Health and Human Services Organizations [*Later, NCHHHSO*] .... NCHMHHSO
National Coalition of Independent College and University Students [*Acronym represents organization's former name*] [*Defunct*] (EA) .... COPUS
National Coalition of Independent Scholars .... NCIS
National Coalition of Patriotic Americans (EA) .... NCPA
National Coalition of Psychiatrists Against Motorcoach Therapy (EA) .... NCPAMT
National Coalition of Redevelopment Agencies (EA) .... NCRA
National Coalition of Title I/Chapter I Parents (EA) .... NCTCP
National Coalition on Black Voter Participation (EA) .... NCBVP
National Coalition on Immune System Disorders (EA) .... NCISD
National Coalition on Television Violence (EA) .... NCTV
National Coalition to Abolish Corporal Punishment in Schools (EA) ..... NCACPS
National Coalition to Ban Handguns [*Later, CSGV*] (EA) .... NCBH
National Coalition to End Racism in America's Child Care System (EA) .... NCERACCS
National Coalition to Expand Charitable Giving [*Defunct*] (EA) .... NCECG
National Coalition to Legalize Freedom (EA) .... NCLF
National Coalition to Prevent Shoplifting (EA) .... NCPS
National Coalition to Stop Food and Water Irradiation (EA) .... NCSFWI
National Coalition to Stop Food Irradiation (EA) .... NCSFI
National Coalition to Support Indian Treaties (EA) .... NCSIT
National Coalition to Support Sexuality Education [*Fact sheet published by the Sexuality Information and Education Coalition of the United States (SIECUS)*] (PAZ) .... NCSSE
National Coarse [*Thread*] .... NC
National Coastal Ecosystems Team [*Office of Biological Services, United States Fish and Wildlife Service*] (MSC) .... NCET
National Coastal Monitoring [*Marine science*] (OSRA) .... NCM
National Coastal Monitoring (USDC) .... NCM
National Coastal Pollution Research Program [*Environmental Protection Agency*] (MSC) .... NCPRP
National Coastal Resources Research and Development Institute [*Newport, OR*] [*Department of Commerce*] (GRD) .... NCRI
National Cocaine Hotline .... NCH
National Codification Bureau [*NATO*] (NATG) .... NCB
National Coffee Association of the United States of America (EA) .... NCA
National Coffee Service Association [*Vienna, VA*] (EA) .... NCSA
National Coil Coaters Association (EA) .... NCCA
National Coin Machine Distributors Association (EA) .... NCMDA
National Coin Machine Institute (EA) .... NCMI
National Coinamatic Auto Wash Association [*Later, ICA/NCC*] .... NCAWA
National Cold Fusion Institute [*Closed June 30, I99I*] .... NCFI
National Cold Storage Federation [*British*] (DBA) .... NCSF
National Collaboration for Youth (EA) .... NCY
National Collection of Fine Arts [*Later, National Mus eum of American Art*] .... NCFA
National Collection of Industrial Bacteria [*British*] .... NCB
National Collection of Industrial Bacteria [*British*] .... NCIB
National Collection of Type Cultures [*British*] .... NCTC
National Collection of Yeast Cultures [*AFRC Institute of Food Research*] [*British Information service or system*] (IID) .... NCYC
National Collection of Yeast Cultures Catalogue [*Norwich Laboratory*] [*Norfolk, England*] [*Information service or system*] [*A publication*] (IID) .... NCYC CAT
National College Education and Admissions Foundation (EA) .... NCEA
National College for Criminal Defense (EA) .... NCCD
National College for Heating, Ventilating, Refrigeration, and Fan Engineering (MCD) .... NCHVRFE
National College for the Training of Youth Leaders [*British*] (BI) .... NCTYL
National College Library, Rapid City, SD [*OCLC symbol*] (OCLC) .... SDT
National College of Agricultural Engineering [*British*] (ARC) .... NCAE
National College of Art and Design, Dublin, Ireland [*Library symbol*] [*Library of Congress*] (LCLS) .... IreDNCA
National College of Business (IAA) .... NCB
National College of Business, Rapid City, SD [*Library symbol Library of Congress*] (LCLS) .... SdRN

National College of Chiropractic, Lombard, IL [Library symbol Library of Congress] (LCLS) ..... ILoC

National College of Chiropractic, Lombard, IL [Library symbol] [Library of Congress] (LCLS) ..... ILoCC

National College of Criminal Defense Lawyers and Public Defenders (DLA) ..... NCCDL

National College of District Attorneys (EA) ..... NCDA

National College of Education [Illinois] ..... NCE

National College of Education, Evanston, IL [Library symbol Library of Congress] (LCLS) ..... IEE

National College of Education, Evanston, IL [OCLC symbol] (OCLC) ..... IGB

National College of Education, Lombard, IL [Library symbol Library of Congress] (LCLS) ..... ILoE

National College of Education, Urban Campus, Chicago, IL [Library symbol Library of Congress] (LCLS) ..... ICNU

National College of Foot Surgeons (EA) ..... NCFS

National College of Music [British] (DI) ..... NCM

National College of Naturopathic Medicine, Portland, OR [Library symbol Library of Congress] (LCLS) ..... OrPCNM

National College of Rubber Technology (PDAA) ..... NCRT

National College of Teachers of the Deaf [British] ..... NCTD

National College of the State Judiciary (DLA) ..... NCSJ

National College of the State Judiciary, Law Library, Reno, NV [Library symbol Library of Congress] (LCLS) ..... NvRNC

National College Physical Education Association [Later, NCPEAM] (EA) ..... NCPEA

National College Physical Education Association for Men [Later, NAPEHE] ..... NCPEAM

National College Student Foundation [Defunct] (EA) ..... NCSF

National College Television [Cable-television system] (WDMC) ..... NCT

National College Television [Cable-television system] ..... NCTV

National Collegiate Association for Secretaries [Defunct] (EA) ..... NCAS

National Collegiate Athletic Association (EA) ..... NCAA

National Collegiate Athletic Bureau [Later, NCSS] (EA) ..... NCAB

National Collegiate Baseball Writers Association (EA) ..... NCBWA

National Collegiate Conference Association (EA) ..... NCCA

National Collegiate Cross Country Coaches Association [Later, USCCCA] (EA) ..... NCCCCA

National Collegiate Football Association (EA) ..... NCFA

National Collegiate Honors Council (EA) ..... NCHC

National Collegiate Parachuting League (EA) ..... NCPL

National Collegiate Players (EA) ..... NCP

National Collegiate Poultry Club ..... NCPC

National Collegiate Ski Association (EA) ..... NCSA

National Collegiate Sports Services (EA) ..... NCSS

National Collegiate Track Coaches Association (EA) ..... NCTCA

National Collegiate Water Ski Association (EA) ..... NCWSA

National Colonialist Party [Australia Political party] ..... NC

National Color-Bred Association (EA) ..... NCA

National Color-Bred Association (EA) ..... NCBA

National Columbia Challenger Association (EA) ..... NCCA

National Combination Storm Window and Door Institute [Defunct] (EA) ..... NCSWDI

National Coming Out Day Campaign (EA) ..... NCOD

National Command and Control System ..... NCCS

National Command Authorities ..... NCA

National Command Authorities and Joint Chiefs of Staff ..... NCA/JCS

National Command Authority Aircraft-747 [MTMC] (TAG) ..... NCAA

National Commemorative Society [Defunct] ..... NCS

National Commerce Bancorp [NASDAQ symbol] (NQ) ..... NCB

National Commerce Bancorp [Associated Press] (SAG) ..... NtCmcBc

National Commercial and Development Bank [Dominica] ..... NCDB

National Commercial Bank [Saudi Arabia] ..... NCB

National Commercial Bank [Jamaica] ..... NCB

National Commercial Finance Association (EA) ..... NCFA

National Commercial Finance Conference [Later, NCFA] (EA) ..... NCFC

National Commercial Refrigeration Sales Association (EA) ..... NCRSA

National Commercial Temperance League [British] (BI) ..... NCTL

National Commission Against Drunk Driving (EA) ..... NCADD

National Commission for Cooperative Education (EA) ..... NCCE

National Commission for Creation of Uniform State Laws ..... NCCUSL

National Commission for Democracy [Ghana] [Political party] ..... NCD

National Commission for Economic Conversion and Disarmament (EA) ..... NCECD

National Commission for Education (AIE) ..... NCE

National Commission for Electrologist Certification (EA) ..... NCEC

National Commission for Full Employment Policy Studies (OICC) ..... NCFEPS

National Commission for Health Certifying Agencies (EA) ..... NCHCA

National Commission for Information and Conscientization on Development Cooperation [Netherlands] ..... NCO

National Commission for Manpower Policy [Department of Labor] ..... NCMP

National Commission for the Certification of Acupuncture (EA) ..... NCCA

National Commission for Women's Equality (EA) ..... CWE

National Commission of Fine Arts (NADA) ..... NCFA

National Commission on a Free and Responsible Media (EA) ..... NCF

National Commission on Accreditation of Alcoholism and Drug Abuse Counselor Credentialing Bodies (EA) ..... NCAADACCB

National Commission on Accrediting [Later, COPA] (EA) ..... NCA

National Commission on Air Quality [Environmental Protection Agency] (ERG) ..... NCAO

National Commission on Air Quality (GNE) ..... NCAQ

National Commission on Allied Health Education [American Occupational Therapy Association] ..... NCAHE

National Commission on Arthritis and Related Musculoskeletal Disease ..... NCARMD

National Commission on Certification of Physician's Assistants (EA) ..... NCCPA

National Commission on Community Public Health Services ..... NCCHS

National Commission on Confidentiality of Health Records [Defunct] (EA) ..... NCCHR

National Commission on Consumer Finance [Terminated] ..... NCCF

National Commission on Coping with Interdependence (EA) ..... NCCI

National Commission on Correctional Health Care (EA) ..... NCCHC

National Commission on Diabetes ..... NCD

National Commission on Egg Nutrition ..... NCEN

National Commission on Electronic Fund Transfers ..... NCEFT

National Commission on Electronic Funds Transfers (MHDW) ..... NCEF

National Commission on Employment and Unemployment Statistics [Bureau of Labor Statistics] (GFGA) ..... NCEUS

National Commission on Fire Prevention and Control ..... NCFPC

National Commission on Food Marketing ..... NCFM

National Commission on Fraudulent Financial Reporting [Defunct] (EA) ..... NCFFR

National Commission on Human Life, Reproduction, and Rhythm (EA) ..... NCHLRR

National Commission on Jobs and Small Business [Defunct] (EA) ..... NCJSB

National Commission on Libraries and Information Science [Washington, DC] ..... NACLIS

National Commission on Libraries and Information Science [Washington, DC] ..... NCLIS

National Commission on Marijuana and Drug Abuse [Presidential advisory committee, terminated 1973] ..... NCMDA

National Commission on Materials Policy ..... NCMP

National Commission on New Technological Uses of Copyrighted Works [Terminated, 1978] [Library of Congress] ..... CONTU

National Commission on New Technological Uses of Copyrighted Works [Terminated, 1978] [Library of Congress] ..... NCNTUCW

National Commission on Organized Crime (NADA) ..... NCOC

National Commission on Orphan Diseases [Department of Health and Human Services] (GFGA) ..... NCOD

National Commission on Product Safety ..... NCPS

National Commission on Productivity [Later, National Productivity Council] ..... NCP

National Commission on Radiological Protection ..... NCRP

National Commission on Reform of Federal Criminal Laws ..... NCRFCL

National Commission on Resources for Youth ..... NCRY

National Commission on Safety Education [Defunct] (EA) ..... NCSE

National Commission on Space [Terminated, 1986] (EGAO) ..... NCOS

National [Presidential] Commission on State Workmen's Compensation Laws ..... NCSWCL

National Commission on Superconductivity [Presidential advisory commission] (EGAO) ..... NCOS

National Commission on Supplies and Shortages [Terminated, 1977] ..... NCSS

National Commission on Teacher Education and Professional Standards [Defunct] (EA) ..... NCTEPS

National Commission on Teacher Education and Professional Standards [Defunct] ..... TEPS

National Commission on the Causes and Prevention of Violence (EA) ..... NCCPV

National Commission on the Indian Canadian ..... NCIC

National Commission on the Public Service [Defunct] (EA) ..... NCPS

National Commission on the Role and Future of State Colleges and Universities [Defunct] (EA) ..... NCRFSCU

National Commission on Unemployment Compensation (NADA) ..... NCUC

National Commission on Water Quality [National Academy of Sciences] ..... NCWQ

National Commission on Working Women (EA) ..... NCWW

National Commission to Prevent Infant Mortality ..... NCPIM

National Committee Against Discrimination in Housing [Defunct] (EA) ..... NCADH

National Committee Against Discrimination in Housing (EA) ..... NCDH

National Committee Against Fluoridation [National Health Federation - NHF] [Absorbed by] (EA) ..... NCAF

National Committee Against Mental Illness [Defunct] (EA) ..... NCAMI

National Committee Against Mental Illness (EA) ..... NCMI

National Committee Against Repressive Legislation (EA) ..... NCARL

National Committee Against War, Racism, and Repression ..... NCAWRR

National Committee, Arts for the Handicapped [Later, VSA] (EA) ..... NCAH

National Committee for a Confrontation with Congress (EA) ..... CWC

National Committee for a Freedom Now Party [Defunct] (EA) ..... NCFNP

National Committee for a Human Life Amendment (EA) ..... NCHLA

National Committee for a Representative Congress (EA) ..... NCRC

National Committee for a Sane Nuclear Policy ["SANE" alone now used as organization name] (EA) ..... SANE

National Committee for Adoption (EA) ..... NCFA

National Committee for Adult Literacy [British] (DI) ..... NCAL

National Committee for Amateur Baseball [Later, USBF] ..... NCAB

National Committee for Amish Religious Freedom ..... NCARF

National Committee for Amnesty Now (EA) ..... NCAN

National Committee for an Effective Congress (EA) ..... NCEC

National Committee for Audio-Visual Aids in Education [British] ..... NCAVAE

National Committee for Careers in Medical Technology [Later, NCCML] (EA) ..... NCCMT

National Committee for Careers in the Medical Laboratory [Defunct] (EA) ..... NCCML

National Committee for Certificates in Office Studies [British] ..... NCCOS

National Committee for Children and Youth [Later, NCOCY] (EA) ..... NCCY

National Committee for Citizens in Education (EA) ..... NCCE

National Committee for Clear Air Turbulence (KSC) ..... NCCAT

National Committee for Clinical Laboratory Standards (EA) ..... NCCLS

National Committee for Cultural Resources ..... NCCR

National Committee for Education in Family Finance (EA) ..... NCEFF

National Committee for Effective Design Legislation (EA) ..... NCEDL

National Committee for Electrical Engineering Films ..... NCEEF

National Committee for Employer Support of the Guard and Reserve (EA) ... NCESGR
National Committee for Employer Support of the Guard and Reserve ... NCESGR
National Committee for Fair Divorce and Alimony Laws (EA) ... NCFDAL
National Committee for Fluid Mechanics Films ... NCFMF
National Committee for Full Employment [*Defunct*] (EA) ... NCFE
National Committee for Geodesy and Geophysics (MCD) ... NCGG
National Committee for Independent Political Action (EA) ... NCIPA
National Committee for Insurance Taxation (EA) ... NCIT
National Committee for International Education through Satellites (EA) ... NCIES
National Committee for Labor Israel [*Later, NCLIIHC*] (EA) ... NCLI
National Committee for Labor Israel-Israel Histadrut Campaign (EA) ... NCLIIHC
National Committee for Latin and Greek (EA) ... NCLG
National Committee for Liberation of Slovakia (EA) ... NCLS
National Committee for Mental Health (DAVI) ... NCMH
National Committee for Mental Hygiene (DAVI) ... NCMH
National Committee for Monetary Reform (EA) ... NCMR
National Committee for Motor Fleet Supervisor Training (EA) ... NCMFST
National Committee for Peace in Central America [*Defunct*] (EA) ... NCPCA
National Committee for Prevention of Child Abuse (EA) ... NCPCA
National Committee for Quality Assurance (EA) ... NCQA
National Committee for Quality Health Care (EA) ... NCQHC
National Committee for Radiation Victims (EA) ... NCRV
National Committee for Rescue from NAZI Terror [*British*] ... NCRNT
National Committee for Research in Neurological Disorders [*Later, NCR*] (EA) ... NCRND
National Committee for Responsible Patriotism (EA) ... NCRP
National Committee for Responsive Philanthropy (EA) ... NCRP
National Committee for Rural Schools [*Defunct*] (EA) ... NCRS
National Committee for Russian Language Study [*American Association for the Advancement of Slavic Studies*] (EDAC) ... NCRLS
National Committee for Sexual Civil Liberties (EA) ... NCSCL
National Committee for Support of the Public Schools [*Later, NCCE*] (EA) ... NCSPS
National Committee for the Berne Convention [*Defunct*] (EA) ... NCBC
National Committee for the Day Care of Children [*Later, DCCA*] ... NCDC
National Committee for the Full Development of Instructional Television Fixed Services [*ITFS regulation*] (NTCM) ... NCFDITFS
National Committee for the Furtherance of Jewish Education (EA) ... NCFJE
National Committee for the In-Service Training of Teachers [*Scotland*] (AIE) ... NCITT
National Committee for the Korean War Memorial [*Later, KWVM*] (EA) ... NCKWM
National Committee for the Prevention of Alcoholism and Drug Dependency [*Later,NCPADD*] (EA) ... NCPA
National Committee for the Prevention of Alcoholism and Drug Dependency (EA) ... NCPADD
National Committee for Theoretical and Applied Mechanics [*British*] ... NCTAM
National Committee for Utilities Radio (MCD) ... NCUR
National Committee for Women in Public Administration (EA) ... NCWPA
National Committee for World Food Day [*Later, USNCWFD*] (EA) ... NCWFD
National Committee of Religious Leaders of Safety (EA) ... NCRLS
National Committee of Shatnez Testers and Researchers (EA) ... NCSTAR
National Committee on American Foreign Policy (EA) ... NCAFP
National Committee on Art Education for the Elderly [*Defunct*] (EA) ... NCAEE
National Committee on Black and Hispanic Concerns (EA) ... NCBHC
National Committee on Central America (EA) ... NCCA
National Committee on Concerns of Hispanics and Blacks [*Defunct*] (EA) ... NCCHB
National Committee on Employment of Youth [*National Child Labor Committee*] (EA) ... NCEY
National Committee on Ethics of the Hearing Aid Industry [*Defunct*] (EA) ... NCEHAI
National Committee on Films for Safety [*Defunct*] (EA) ... NCFS
National Committee on Homemaker Service [*Superseded by NHC*] (EA) ... NCHS
National Committee on Household Employment ... NCHE
National Committee on Housing ... NCH
National Committee on International Trade Documentation [*MARAD*] (TAG) ... NCITD
National Committee on Maternal Health (EA) ... NCMH
National Committee on Paper Stock Conservation ... NCPSC
National Committee on Pay Equity (EA) ... NCPE
National Committee on Pesticide Use in Agriculture [*Canada*] ... NCPUA
National Committee on Planned Giving (NFD) ... NCPG
National Committee on Property Insurance [*Boston, MA*] (EA) ... NCPI
National Committee on Public Employee Pension Systems (EA) ... PEPS
National Committee on Regional Library Cooperation ... NCRLC
National Committee on Safety ... NCS
National Committee on Secondary Education [*of NASSP*] ... NCSE
National Committee on the Education of Migrant Children [*of the National Child Labor Committee*] (EA) ... NCEMC
National Committee on the Emeriti (EA) ... NCE
National Committee on the Observance of Mothers' Day [*Later, MDC*] (EA) ... NCOMD
National Committee on the Treatment of Intractable Pain (EA) ... NCTIP
National Committee on Tunneling Technology ... NCTT
National Committee on Uniform Traffic Laws and Ordinances (EA) ... NCUTLO
National Committee on United States-China Relations (EA) ... NCUSCR
National Committee on Vital and Health Statistics [*Department of Health and Human Services*] (GFGA) ... NCVHS
National Committee on Youth Suicide Prevention (EA) ... NCYSP
National Committee to Abolish the House Un-American Activities Committee [*Later, NCARL*] (EA) ... NCAHUAC
National Committee to Commemorate the Millenium of Christianity in the Ukraine (EA) ... NCCMCU
National Committee to Honor the Fourteenth Centennial of Islam (EA) ... NCHFCI
National Committee to Preserve Social Security and Medicare (EA) ... NCPSSM
National Committee to Reopen the Rosenberg Case (EA) ... NCRRC
National Committee to Repeal the Federal Reserve Act (EA) ... NCRFRA
National Committee to Restore Internal Security (EA) ... NCRIS
National Commodity and Barter Association (EA) ... NCBA
National Commodity Futures Examination ... NCFE
National Commodity-Processing Program [*Department of Agriculture*] (GFGA) ... NCP
National Communicable Disease Center (MCD) ... NCDC
National Communication Agencies (NATG) ... NCA
National Communication System Circulars ... NCSC
National Communication System Instructions ... NCSI
National Communication System Memoranda ... NCSM
National Communications [*System*] ... NACOM
National Communications (AD) ... natcom
National Communications Association (EA) ... NCA
National Communications Club (EA) ... NCC
National Communications Command [*Army*] (RDA) ... NCC
National Communications Commission [*Uganda*] (ECON) ... NCC
National Communications Forum [*National Engineering Consortium, Inc.*] [*Chicago, IL*] [*Telecommunications*] (TSSD) ... NCF
National Communications Network for the Elimination of Violence Against Women [*NCADV*] [*Absorbed by*] (EA) ... NCNEVAW
National Communications Schedule ... NACOS
National Communications Symposium [*IEEE*] ... NATCOM
National Communications System [*DoD*] ... NCS
National Communications Union [*British*] ... NCU
National Communications Union, Engineering Group [*British*] ... NCU(E)
National Communications Working Party [*Australia Political party*] ... NCWP
National Community Action Agency Directors Association [*Formerly, NCAAEDA*] [*Later, NACAA*] (EA) ... NCAADA
National Community Action Agency Executive Directors Association (EA) ... NCAAEDA
National Community Action Foundation (EA) ... NCAF
National Community Crime Prevention League (EA) ... NCCPL
National Community Development Association (EA) ... NCDA
National Community Education Association (EA) ... NCEA
National Community Reinvestment Coalition ... NCRC
National Community Relations Advisory Council [*Later, NJCRAC*] (EA) ... NCRAC
National Community School Education Association [*Later, NCEA*] (EA) ... NCSEA
National Community Services Industry Training Steering Group [*Australia*] ... NCSITSG
National Commuter Airways [*British ICAO designator*] (FAAC) ... NCL
National Company of Crossbowmen [*Defunct*] (EA) ... NCC
National Competitiveness Technology Transfer Act [*1989*] [*Department of Energy*] ... NCTTA
National Compliance Board [*New Deal*] ... NCB
National Compliance Strategy (GNE) ... NCS
National Composition and Prepress Association (EA) ... NCPA
National Composition Association [*Later, NCPA*] (EA) ... NCA
National Comprehensive Cancer Network [*Medical*] ... NCCN
National Computer Association (EA) ... NCA
National Computer Center [*IRS*] ... NCC
National Computer Conference ... NCC
National Computer Council (NADA) ... NCC
National Computer Dealer Forum (EA) ... NCDF
National Computer Exchange ... NACOMEX
National Computer Graphics Association (EA) ... NCGA
National Computer Index [*National Computing Centre Ltd.*] [*British Information service or system*] (CRD) ... NCI
National Computer Institute (MCD) ... NCI
National Computer Network Corp. [*Information service or system*] (IID) ... NCN
National Computer Program Abstract Service, Inc. (IID) ... NCPAS
National Computer Program Index (IAA) ... NCPI
National Computer Security Association [*Computer science*] (PCM) ... NCSA
National Computer Security Council ... NCSC
National Computer Service Network (EA) ... NCSN
National Computer Systems, Inc. ... NCS
National Computer Systems, Inc. [*NASDAQ symbol*] (NQ) ... NLCS
National Computer Systems, Inc. [*Associated Press*] (SAG) ... NtCptr
National Computer User Group in Agricultural Education (NITA) ... NCUGAE
National Computer Users Forum [*National Computing Center*] (PDAA) ... NCUF
National Computing Centre [*Manchester, England*] ... NCC
National Computing Industries (NITA) ... NCI
National Concilio of America (EA) ... NCA
National Concrete Burial Vault Association (EA) ... NCBVA
National Concrete Contractors Association [*Later, ASCC*] (EA) ... NCCA
National Concrete Masonry Association (EA) ... NCMA
National Condominium Owners Association [*Defunct*] ... NCOA
National Confectioners Association of the United States (EA) ... NCA
National Confectionery Salesmen's Association of America (EA) ... NCSA
National Confederation of American Ethnic Groups (EA) ... NCAEG
National Confederation of Parent Teacher Associations [*British*] ... NCPTA
National Confederation of Registered Rest Home Associations [*British*] (DBA) ... NCRRHA
National Conference for New Politics [*Organization formed in 1966 to support peace candidates*] (VNW) ... NCNP
National Conference for Unification [*South Korea Political party*] (PPW) ... NCU
National Conference of Appellate Court Clerks (EA) ... NCACC
National Conference of Artists (EA) ... NCA
National Conference of Bankruptcy Judges (EA) ... NCBJ

National Conference of Bar Examiners (EA) ... NCBE
National Conference of Bar Executives [*Later, NABE*] (EA) ... NCBE
National Conference of Bar Foundations (EA) ... NCBF
National Conference of Bar Presidents (EA) ... NCBP
National Conference of Black Elected Officials (EA) ... COBEO
National Conference of Black Lawyers (EA) ... NCBL
National Conference of Black Mayors (EA) ... NCBM
National Conference of Black Political Scientists (EA) ... NCOBPS
National Conference of Canadian Universities ... NCCU
National Conference of Catholic Art Educators (AEBS) ... NCCAE
National Conference of Catholic Bishops (EA) ... NCCB
National Conference of Catholic Charities (EA) ... NCCC
National Conference of Catholics in Youth Serving Agencies [*Defunct*] (EA) ... NCCYSA
National Conference of Christians and Jews (EA) ... NCCJ
National Conference of Commissioners on Uniform State Laws (EA) ... NCCUSL
National Conference of CPA [*Certified Public Accountant*] **Practitioners** [*New York, NY*] (EA) ... NCCPAP
National Conference of Diocesan Directors of Religious Education - CCD [*Continuing Christian Development*] (EA) ... NCDDRE-CCD
National Conference of Diocesan Vocation Directors (EA) ... NCDVD
National Conference of Editorial Writers (EA) ... NCEW
National Conference of English Teachers (BARN) ... NCET
National Conference of Executives of Higher Education Loan Plans [*Later, NCHELP*] (EA) ... NCEHELP
National Conference of Friendly Societies [*British*] (DBA) ... NCFS
National Conference of Health, Welfare, and Pension Plans, Trustees and Administrators [*Later, International Foundation of Employee Benefit Plans*] (EA) ... NCHWPPTA
National Conference of Insurance Legislators (EA) ... NCOIL
National Conference of Jewish Communal Service [*Later, CJCS*] (EA) ... NCJCS
National Conference of Judicial Councils [*Defunct*] (EA) ... NCJC
National Conference of Law Historians of America (EA) ... NCLHA
National Conference of Lawyers and Scientists [*Joint project of the American Association for the Advancement of Science and the American Bar Association*] ... NCLS
National Conference of Lawyers and Social Workers ... NCL & SW
National Conference of Lieutenant Governors (EA) ... NCLG
National Conference of Local Environmental Health Administrators (EA) ... NCLEHA
National Conference of Non-Profit Shipping Associations (EA) ... NCNPSA
National Conference of Personal Managers (EA) ... NCPM
National Conference of Police Associations (EA) ... NCOPA
National Conference of Professors of Educational Administration [*Later, NAPEHE*] (EA) ... NCPEA
National Conference of Public Youth Agencies [*Defunct*] (EA) ... NCPYA
National Conference of Puerto Rican Women (EA) ... NACOPRW
National Conference of Regulatory Utility Commission Engineers (EA) ... NCRUCE
National Conference of Religious Vocation Directors [*Later, NRVC*] (EA) ... NCRVD
National Conference of Religious Vocation Directors of Men [*Later, NCRVD*] (EA) ... NCRVDM
National Conference of Shomrim Societies (EA) ... NCSS
National Conference of Social Workers ... NCSW
National Conference of Special Court Judges (EA) ... NCSCJ
National Conference of Standards Laboratories (EA) ... NCSL
National Conference of State Criminal Justice Planning Administrators [*Later, NCJA*] (EA) ... NCSCJPA
National Conference of State Fleet Administrators (EA) ... NCSFA
National Conference of State General Service Officers [*Later, NASDAGS*] (EA) ... NCSGSO
National Conference of State Historic Preservation Officers (EA) ... NCSHPO
National Conference of State Legislative Leaders [*Later, NCSL*] (EA) ... NCSLL
National Conference of State Legislatures [*Australia*] ... NCLS
National Conference of State Legislatures (EA) ... NCSL
National Conference of State Liquor Administrators (EA) ... NCSLA
National Conference of State Pharmaceutical Association Secretaries [*Later, NCSPAE*] ... NCSPAS
National Conference of State Retail Associations (EA) ... NCSRA
National Conference of State Social Security Administrators (EA) ... NCSSSA
National Conference of State Societies (EA) ... NCSS
National Conference of State Transportation Specialists (EA) ... NCSTS
National Conference of States on Building Codes and Standards (OICC) ... NCBCS
National Conference of States on Building Codes and Standards (EA) ... NCSBCS
National Conference of Superintendents of Training Schools and Reformatories [*Later, International Conference of Administrators Residential Centers for Youth -ICA*] (EA) ... NCSTSR
National Conference of Synagogue Youth (EA) ... NCSY
National Conference of Tuberculosis Workers [*Later, CLAS*] (EA) ... NCTW
National Conference of University Professors (AIE) ... NCUP
National Conference of Vicars for Religious (EA) ... NCVR
National Conference of Women's Bar Associations (EA) ... NCWBA
National Conference of Yeshiva Principals (EA) ... NCYP
National Conference on Airborne Electronics (MCD) ... NCAE
National Conference on Citizenship (EA) ... NCC
National Conference on Communications (MCD) ... NATCOM
National Conference on Electromagnetic Relays ... NCER
National Conference on Engineering and Training (ACII) ... CONCEET
National Conference on Federal Trial Judges (EA) ... NCFTJ
National Conference on Fluid Power (EA) ... NCFP
National Conference on Industrial Hydraulics ... NCIH
National Conference on Industrial Research ... NCIR
National Conference on International Economic and Social Development [*Later, IDC*] ... NCIESD
National Conference on Interstate Milk Shipments ... NCIMS
National Conference on Law and Poverty ... NCLP
National Conference on Mental Health Statistics [*Department of Health and Human Services*] (GFGA) ... NCMHS
National Conference on Ministry to the Armed Forces (EA) ... NCMAF
National Conference on Parent Involvement (EA) ... NCPI
National Conference on Power Transmission (EA) ... NCPT
National Conference on Prescription Medicine Information and Education ... NCPIE
National Conference on Public Employee Retirement Systems (EA) ... NCPERS
National Conference on Radiation Measurements ... NCRM
National Conference on Research in English (EA) ... NCRE
National Conference on Social Welfare [*Defunct*] (EA) ... NCSW
National Conference on Solicitations ... NCS
National Conference on Soviet Jewry (EA) ... NCSJ
National Conference on State Parks [*Later, NRPA*] (EA) ... NCSP
National Conference on Student Services (EA) ... NCSS
National Conference on the Advancement of Research (EA) ... NCAR
National Conference on the Application of Electrical Insulation ... NCAEI
National Conference on Weights and Measures (EA) ... NCWM
National Conferences on Undergraduate Research [*An association*] ... NCUR
National Congenital Port Wine Stain Foundation (EA) ... NCPWSF
National Congenital Rubella Syndrome Registry [*Centers for Disease Control*] ... NCRSR
National Congress for Community Economic Development (EA) ... NCCED
National Congress for Educational Excellence (EA) ... NCEE
National Congress for Men (EA) ... NCM
National Congress for Men and Children [*An association*] (PAZ) ... NCFC
National Congress for Puerto Rican Rights (EA) ... NCPRR
National Congress of American Indians (EA) ... NCAI
National Congress of Animal Trainers and Breeders (EA) ... NCATB
National Congress of Colored Parents and Teachers (AEBS) ... NCCPT
National Congress of Floor Covering Associations [*Defunct*] (EA) ... NCFCA
National Congress of Inventors Organizations (EA) ... NCIO
National Congress of Italian Canadians ... NCIC
National Congress of Jewish Deaf (EA) ... NCJD
National Congress of Neighborhood Women (EA) ... NCNW
National Congress of Parents and Teachers (PAZ) ... National PTA
National Congress of Parents and Teachers [*Later, National PTA*] (EA) ... NCPT
National Congress of Petroleum Retailers [*Later, SSDA*] (EA) ... NCPR
National Congress of Puerto Rican Veterans (EA) ... NCPRV
National Congress of Women in Music (EA) ... NCWM
National Congress on Volunteerism and Citizenship [*Bicentennial event, 1976*] ... NCVC
National Congressional Analysis Corp. (IID) ... NCA
National Congressional Club (EA) ... NCC
National Consensus Standards (MCD) ... NCS
National Conservation Bureau [*Defunct*] ... NCB
National Conservation Policy Act [*1979*] ... NCPA
National Conservation Strategy (GNE) ... NCS
National Conservative Congressional Committee (EA) ... NCCC
National Conservative Foundation (EA) ... NCF
National Conservative Political Action Committee (EA) ... NCPAC
National Consortium for Black Professional Development (EA) ... NCBPD
National Consortium for Child Mental Health Services (EA) ... NCCMHS
National Consortium for Computer Based Music Instruction [*University of Delaware*] [*Research clearinghouse*] (EA) ... NCCBMI
National Consortium for Education Access (EA) ... NCEA
National Consortium for Graduate Degrees for Minorities in Engineering (EA) ... GEM
National Consortium of Arts and Letters for Historically Black Colleges and Universities (EA) ... NCALHBCU
National Consortium of Chemical Dependency Nurses (EA) ... NCCDN
National Consortium of Universities Preparing Rural Special Educators [*Defunct*] (EA) ... NCUPRSE
National Constables Association (EA) ... NCA
National Construction Employers Council [*Defunct*] (EA) ... NCEC
National Construction Industry Arbitration Committee (EA) ... NCIAC
National Construction Industry Council (EA) ... NCIC
National Construction Machinery Credit Group [*Park Ridge, IL*] (EA) ... NCMCG
National Construction Software Association (EA) ... NCSA
National Constructors Association (EA) ... NCA
National Consumer Advisory Council ... NCAC
National Consumer Affairs Internship Program [*Defunct*] (EA) ... NCAIP
National Consumer Center for Legal Services [*Later, NRCCLS*] (EA) ... NCCLS
National Consumer Cooperative Bank ... NCCB
National Consumer Council [*British*] (ILCA) ... NCC
National Consumer Credit Consultants (EA) ... NCCC
National Consumer Federation (NADA) ... NCF
National Consumer Finance Association (EA) ... NCFA
National Consumer Fraud Task Force (EA) ... NCFTF
National Consumer Law Center (EA) ... NCLC
National Consumer Research Institute (EA) ... NCRI
National Consumer Testing Institute (BARN) ... NCTI
National Consumers Committee for Research and Education [*Later, NCL*] (EA) ... NCCRE
National Consumers Congress [*Later, NCL*] ... NCC
National Consumers League (EA) ... NCL
National Contact Lens Examiners (EA) ... NCLE
National Container Committee [*Later, Uniform Classification Committee*] (EA) ... NCC
National Contesters Association (EA) ... NCA
National Contingency Account (OICC) ... NCA

National Contingency Plan [*Hazardous wastes*] [*Environmental Protection Agency*] ... NCP
National Contract Management Association (EA) ... NCMA
National Contract Management Journal [*A publication*] (AAGC) ... NCMJ
National Contract Sweepers Association [*Later, NCSI*] (EA) ... NCSA
National Contract Sweepers Institute (EA) ... NCSI
National Contractors Group [*British*] (DBA) ... NCG
National Control Data ... NCD
National Control Facility [*FAA*] (TAG) ... NCF
National Convenience Stores [*Associated Press*] (SAG) ... NatConv
National Convenience Stores, Inc. [*NYSE symbol*] (SPSG) ... NCS
National Convenience Stores, Inc. [*NASDAQ symbol*] (SAG) ... NCSI
National Convenience Stores, Inc. [*Associated Press*] (SAG) ... NtCnv
National Convention of Gospel Choirs and Choruses (EA) ... NCGCC
National Convention Party [*Gambia*] [*Political party*] (PPW) ... NCP
National Conversational Software Systems, Inc. ... NCSS
National Cooperative Bank (USGC) ... NCB
National Cooperative Business Association (EA) ... NCBA
National Cooperative Crohn's Disease Study ... NCCDS
National Cooperative Gallstone Study ... NCGS
National Cooperative Highway Research Program ... NCHRP
National Cooperative Refinery Association [*Commercial firm*] (EA) ... NCRA
National Cooperative Research Act [*1984*] ... NCRA
National Cooperative Soil Survey ... NCSS
National Cooperative Transit Research and Development Program [*TRB*] (TAG) ... NCTRP
National Cooperatives [*Later, UNICO*] [*An association*] ... NC
National Coordinated Cataloging Operations [*Library science*] ... NACO
National Coordinated Cataloging Program [*Library science*] ... NCCP
National Coordinating Center for Curriculum Development ... NC^3D
National Coordinating Center in Solidarity with Chile [*Later, NCC*] (EA) ... NCCSC
National Coordinating Committee (USGC) ... NCC
National Coordinating Committee for Aviation Meteorology ... NACCAM
National Coordinating Committee for Multiemployer Plans (EA) ... NCCMP
National Coordinating Committee for the Promotion of History (EA) ... NCC
National Coordinating Committee of the Beverage Industry ... NCCBI
National Coordinating Committee on Large Volume Parenterals (BABM) ... NCCLVP
National Coordinating Committee on Large Volume Parenterals (DAVI) ... NCCLVP
National Coordinating Committee to End the War [*Organization formed in 1965*] (VNW) ... NCC
National Coordinating Committee to End the War in Vietnam [*Defunct*] ... NCCEWV
National Coordinating Council on Drug Abuse Education and Information [*Later, NCCDE*] (EA) ... NCC
National Coordinating Council on Drug Education [*Formerly, NCC*] ... NCCDE
National Coordinating Council on Emergency Management (EA) ... NCCEM
National Coordinating Office for Latin and Greek [*Later, NCLG*] (EA) ... NCOLG
National Coordination Committee [*Responsible for administering the Work Incentive Program*] ... NCC
National Coordination Office for High Performance Computing and Communications ... NCO/HPCC
National Coordinator [*Marine science*] (MSC) ... NATCO
National Copyright Advisory Committee (NADA) ... NCAC
National Corn Growers Association (EA) ... NCGA
National Corporate Cash Management Association (EA) ... NCCMA
National Corporate Fund for Dance (EA) ... NCFD
National Corporate Medical Associates [*An association*] ... NCMA
National Corporate Theatre Fund (EA) ... NCTF
National Corp. for Housing Partnerships ... NCHP
National Corporation for the Care of Old People [*British*] (BI) ... NCCOP
National Correctional Recreational Association (EA) ... NCRA
National Corrosion Service [*British*] (IRUK) ... NCS
National Corrugated Metal Pipe Association [*Later, NCSPA*] (EA) ... NCMPA
National Corrugated Steel Pipe Association (EA) ... NCSPA
National Corvette Museum ... NCM
National Corvette Owners' Association (EA) ... NCOA
National Corvette Restorers Society (EA) ... NCRS
National Cosmetology Association (EA) ... NCA
National Costumers Association (EA) ... NCA
National Cotton Batting Institute (EA) ... NCBI
National Cotton Compress and Cotton Warehouse Association [*Later, CWAA*] (EA) ... NCCCWA
National Cotton Council of America (EA) ... NCC
National Cotton Council of America [*Memphis, TN*] ... NCCA
National Cotton Council of America, Memphis, TN [*Library symbol Library of Congress*] (LCLS) ... TMN
National Cotton Ginners' Association (EA) ... NCGA
National Cottonseed Products Association (EA) ... NCPA
National Council Against Conscription [*World War I*] [*British*] ... NCAC
National Council Against Conscription [*World War I*] [*British*] ... NCC
National Council Against Health Fraud (EA) ... NCAHF
National Council Against Illegal Liquor [*Defunct*] (EA) ... NCAIL
National Council, Daughters of America ... D of A
National Council, Daughters of America [*Harrisburg, OH*] (EA) ... DA
National Council for a Responsible Firearms Policy [*Defunct*] (EA) ... NCRFP
National Council for a World Peace Tax Fund (EA) ... NCWPTF
National Council for a World Peace Tax Fund (EA) ... WPTF
National Council for Accreditation of Teacher Education (EA) ... NCATE
National Council for Adoption [*Formerly National Committee for Adoption*] (PAZ) ... NCFA
National Council for Alternative Work Patterns (EA) ... NCAWP
National Council for Animal Welfare (NADA) ... NCAW
National Council for Aviculture [*British*] (DBA) ... NCA
National Council for Better Education (EA) ... NCBE
National Council for Black Studies (EA) ... NCBS
National Council for Children's Rights (EA) ... NCCR
National Council for Civic Theatres Ltd. [*British*] (BI) ... NCCT
National Council for Civil Liberties [*British*] ... NCCL
National Council for Clean Air and Streams ... NCCAS
National Council for Community Development (EA) ... NCCD
National Council for Community Relations [*Later, NCMPR*] (EA) ... NCCR
National Council for Community Services to International Visitors [*Later, NCIV*] ... COSERV
National Council for Community Services to International Visitors [*Later, NCIV*] ... NCCS
National Council for Criminal Defense (EA) ... NCCD
National Council for Critical Analysis [*Defunct*] (EA) ... NCCA
National Council for Culture and Art (EA) ... NCCA
National Council for Diplomats in Art and Design [*British*] (BI) ... NCDAD
National Council for Drama Training [*British*] ... NCDT
National Council for Educational Awards [*Ireland*] ... NCEA
National Council for Educational Research and Training (WDAA) ... NCERT
National Council for Educational Standards (AIE) ... NCES
National Council for Educational Technology [*British*] ... NCET
National Council for Environmental Balance (EA) ... NCEB
National Council for Families and Television (EA) ... NCFT
National Council for Family Reconciliation (EA) ... NCFR
National Council for Fishing Vessel Safety and Insurance (EA) ... NCFVSI
National Council for Foundation Education in Art and Design (AIE) ... NCFEAD
National Council for GeoCosmic Research (EA) ... NCGR
National Council for Geographic Education (EA) ... NCGE
National Council for History Education (EA) ... NCHE
National Council for Industrial Defense (EA) ... NCID
National Council for Industrial Innovation (EA) ... NCII
National Council for Industrial Peace [*Defunct*] (EA) ... NCIP
National Council for Inordinacy (EA) ... NCI
National Council for Interior Design Qualification (EA) ... NCIDQ
National Council for Interior Horticultural Certification (EA) ... NCIHC
National Council for International Health (EA) ... NCIH
National Council for International Visitors (EA) ... NCIV
National Council for Japanese American Redress [*Defunct*] (EA) ... NCJAR
National Council for Jewish Education [*Later, CJE*] (EA) ... NCJE
National Council for Labor Reform (EA) ... NCLR
National Council for Languages and International Studies (EA) ... NCLIS
National Council for Marketing and Public Relations (EA) ... NCMPR
National Council for Monday Holidays ... NCMH
National Council for Mother Tongue Teaching (AIE) ... NCMTT
National Council for One Parent Families [*British*] ... NCOPF
National Council for Prescription Drug Programs (EA) ... NCPDP
National Council for Preservation Education ... NCPE
National Council for Quality and Reliabiltiy [*British*] (BI) ... NCQR
National Council for Research and Planning (EA) ... NCRP
National Council for Research on Women (EA) ... NCRW
National Council for Resources on Women, New York, NY [*Library symbol*] [*Library of Congress*] (LCLS) ... NNNCR
National Council for School Nurses [*of AAHPER*] ... NCSN
National Council for Small Business Innovation ... NCSBI
National Council for Small Business Management Development [*Later, ICSB*] (EA) ... NCSBMD
National Council for Soviet and East European Research (EA) ... NCSEER
National Council for Special Education [*British*] ... NCSE
National Council for Stream Improvement (EA) ... NCSI
National Council for Teacher-Centred Professional Development [*British*] (DBA) ... NCTPD
National Council for Technological Awards [*British*] ... NCTA
National Council for Textile Education (EA) ... NCTE
National Council for the Accreditation of Nursing Homes (NADA) ... NCANH
National Council for the Church and Social Action (EA) ... NCCSA
National Council for the Conservation of Plants and Gardens (PDAA) ... NCCPG
National Council for the Divorced and Separated [*British*] (DBA) ... NCDS
National Council for the Encouragement of Patriotism (EA) ... NCEP
National Council for the Gifted (EA) ... NCG
National Council for the Observance of Grandparent's Day (EA) ... NCOGD
National Council for the Omnibus Industry [*British*] ... NCOI
National Council for the Public Assessment of Technology [*Defunct*] ... NC/PAT
National Council for the Single Mother and Her Child [*Australia*] ... NCSMHC
National Council for the Single Woman and Her Dependants (EA) ... NCSWD
National Council for the Single Woman and Her Dependants Ltd. [*British*] (BI) ... NCSW
National Council for the Social Studies (EA) ... NCSS
National Council for the Traditional Arts (EA) ... NCTA
National Council for the Training of Journalists [*British*] ... NCTJ
National Council for the Unmarried Mother and Her Child [*British*] (ILCA) ... NCUMC
National Council for the Welfare of Prisoners Abroad [*British*] (DI) ... NCWPA
National Council for Therapeutic Recreation Certification (EA) ... NCTRC
National Council for Therapy and Rehabilitation through Horticulture (EA) ... NCTRH
National Council for Torah Education (EA) ... NCTE
National Council for Universal and Unconditional Amnesty [*For Vietnam-War resisters*] [*Defunct*] (EA) ... NCUUA
National Council for Urban Economic Development (EA) ... CUED
National Council for US-China Trade [*Later, USCBC*] (EA) ... NCUSCT
National Council for Vocational Qualifications [*British*] ... NCVQ
National Council for Voluntary Organisations [*British*] (ILCA) ... NCVO
National Council for Year-Round Education [*Later, NAYRE*] (EA) ... NCYRE
National Council Licensure Examination ... NCLEX

National Council Licensure Examination for Registered Nurses .... NCLEX-RN
National Council of Acoustical Consultants (EA) .... NCAC
National Council of Acupuncture Schools and Colleges (EA) .... NCASC
National Council of Administrative Women in Education (EA) .... NCAWE
National Council of Administrators of Adult Education (EA) .... NCAAE
National Council of Adoptive Parents Organizations [*NACAC*] [*Absorbed by*] .... NCAPO
National Council of Affiliated Advertising Agencies [*Later, First Network of Affiliated Advertising Agencies*] (EA) .... NCAAA
National Council of Agricultural Employers (EA) .... NCAE
National Council of American Importers [*Later, AAEI*] (EA) .... NCAI
National Council of American-Soviet Friendship (EA) .... NCASF
National Council of Architectural Registration Boards (EA) .... NCARB
National Council of Athletic Training [*Athletic Training Council*] [*Acronym is based on former name,*] (EA) .... ATC
National Council of Beth Jacob Schools [*Later, FCBJS*] (EA) .... NCBJS
National Council of BIA [*Bureau of Indian Affairs*] **Educators** (EA) .... NCBIAE
National Council of Bible Believing Churches [*Later, CBBC*] (EA) .... NCBBC
National Council of Building Material Producers [*A union*] [*British*] .... BMP
National Council of Building Material Producers [*A union*] [*British*] .... NCBMP
National Council of Canadian Labour .... NCCL
National Council of Career Women (EA) .... NCCW
National Council of Catholic Employers and Managers (EA) .... NCCEM
National Council of Catholic Laity [*Defunct*] (EA) .... NCCL
National Council of Catholic Men (EA) .... NCCM
National Council of Catholic Nurses [*Defunct*] (EA) .... NCCN
National Council of Catholic Women (EA) .... NCCW
National Council of Catholic Youth [*Defunct*] (EA) .... NCCY
National Council of Chairmen of Graduate Departments of Psychology .... NCCGDP
National Council of Chemical Technician Affiliates .... NCCTA
National Council of Churches Broadcasting Network (NTCM) .... NCCBN
National Council of Churches of Christ in the USA (EA) .... NCC
National Council of Churches of Christ in the USA (NTCM) .... NCC/USA
National Council of Churches of Christ in the USA [*Later, NCC*] (EA) .... NCCC
National Council of Coal Lessors (EA) .... NCCL
National Council of College Publications Advisers (EA) .... NCCPA
National Council of Columbia Associations in Civil Service (EA) .... NCCACS
National Council of Commercial Plant Breeders (EA) .... NCCPB
National Council of Community Churches [*Later, ICCC*] (EA) .... NCCC
National Council of Community Hospitals (EA) .... NCCH
National Council of Community Mental Health Centers (EA) .... NCCMHC
National Council of Community World Affairs Organizations (EA) .... NCCWAO
National Council of Corvette Clubs (EA) .... NCCC
National Council of County Association Executives (EA) .... NCCAE
National Council of Dance Teacher Organizations [*Later, NDCA*] (EA) .... NCDTO
National Council of Educational Opportunity Associations (EA) .... NCEOA
National Council of Elected County Executives (EA) .... NCECE
National Council of Engineering Examiners (EA) .... NCEE
National Council of Erectors, Fabricators, and Riggers (EA) .... NCEFR
National Council of Exchangors (EA) .... NCE
National Council of Farmer Cooperatives (EA) .... NCFC
National Council of Forestry Association Executives (EA) .... NCFAE
National Council of Guilds for Infant Survival (EA) .... NCGIS
National Council of Health Care Services (EA) .... NCHCS
National Council of Health Centers [*Formerly, NCHCS*] [*Later, AHCA*] (EA) .... NCHC
National Council of Higher Education Loan Programs (EA) .... NCHELP
National Council of Hispanic Women (EA) .... NCHW
National Council of Homemakers and Home Health Aides .... NCHHA
National Council of Independent Colleges and Universities [*Later, NAICU*] .... NCICU
National Council of Independent Junior Colleges [*Defunct*] .... NCIJC
National Council of Independent Schools [*Later, National Association of Independent Schools*] (AEBS) .... NCIS
National Council of Independent Truckers [*Defunct*] (EA) .... NCIT
National Council of Individual Investors .... NCII
National Council of Industrial Management Clubs [*Later, IMC*] (EA) .... NCIMC
National Council of Industrial Naval Air Stations (EA) .... NCINAS
National Council of Industrial Naval Air Stations Employee Organizations [*Formerly, NCNASEO*] (EA) .... NCINASEO
National Council of Inland Transport [*British*] (DBA) .... NCIT
National Council of Intellectual Property Law Associations (EA) .... NCIPLA
National Council of Investigation and Security Services (EA) .... NCISS
National Council of Jewish Correctional Chaplains [*Later, AJCCA*] (EA) .... NCJCC
National Council of Jewish Invalids Survivors of Nazism [*Later, CHSD*] (EA) .... NCJISN
National Council of Jewish Women (EA) .... NCJW
National Council of Jewish Women of Australia .... NCJWA
National Council of Junior Outdoorsmen (EA) .... NCJO
National Council of Juvenile and Family Court Judges (EA) .... NCJFCJ
National Council of Juvenile Court Judges [*Later, NCJFCJ*] (EA) .... NCJCJ
National Council of La Raza (EA) .... NCLR
National Council of Labour [*British*] (DCTA) .... NCL
National Council of Labour Colleges .... NCLC
National Council of Local Administrators of Vocational Education and Practical Arts (EA) .... NCLA
National Council of Local Public Welfare Administrators (EA) .... NCLPWA
National Council of Mailing List Brokers [*Later, MLBPA*] (EA) .... NCMLB
National Council of Marine Sciences .... NCMS
National Council of Marine Trade Associations .... NCMTA
National Council of Marriage and Divorce Law Reform and Justice Organizations (EA) .... NCMDLRJO
National Council of Millinery Associations (EA) .... NCMA
National Council of Minority Consulting Engineers (IAA) .... NCMCE
National Council of Moving Associations (EA) .... NCMA
National Council of Music Importers [*Later, NCMIE*] .... NCMI
National Council of Music Importers and Exporters (EA) .... NCMIE
National Council of Naval Air Stations Employee Organizations [*Later, NCINASEO*] (EA) .... NCNASEO
National Council of Negro Women (EA) .... NCNW
National Council of Nigeria and the Cameroons [*Political party*] .... NCNC
National Council of Nonprofit Associations .... NCNA
National Council of Nurses [*British*] (DI) .... NCN
National Council of Obesity (EA) .... NCO
National Council of Officers of State Teachers Associations (EA) .... NCOSTA
National Council of Organizations for Children and Youth (EA) .... NCOCY
National Council of Patent Law Associations [*Later, NCIPLA*] (EA) .... NCPLA
National Council of Patient Information and Education (EA) .... NCPIE
National Council of Physical Distribution Management .... NCPDM
National Council of Preservation Executives (EA) .... NCOPE
National Council of Professional Services Firms [*Later, PSC*] (EA) .... NCPSF
National Council of Psychotherapists and Hypnotherapy Register [*British*] (DBA) .... NCP
National Council of Puerto Rican Volunteers [*Defunct*] (EA) .... NCPRV
National Council of Real Estate Investment Fiduciaries (EA) .... NCREIF
National Council of Refuse Disposal Trade Associations .... NCRDTA
National Council of Research Administrators .... NCRA
National Council of Resistance for Liberty and Independence [*Iran*] (PD) .... NCR
National Council of Returned Peace Corps Volunteers (EA) .... NCRPCV
National Council of Salesmen's Organizations [*New York, NY*] (EA) .... NCSO
National Council of Savings Institutions (EMRF) .... NCSI
National Council of School Press and Advisers Association .... NCSPAA
National Council of Scientific and Technical Art Societies [*Later, IG*] (EA) .... NCSTAS
National Council of Seamen's Agencies [*Later, ICOSA*] (EA) .... NCSA
National Council of Secondary School Athletic Directors (EA) .... NCSSAD
National Council of Self-Insurers [*Chicago, IL*] (EA) .... NCSI
National Council of Senior Citizens (EA) .... NCSC
National Council of Social Security Management Associations (EA) .... NCSSMA
National Council of Social Service [*British*] .... NCSS
National Council of State Agencies for the Blind (EA) .... NCSAB
National Council of State Boards of Engineering Examiners [*Later, NCEE*] (IAA) .... NCBEE
National Council of State Boards of Engineering Examiners [*Later, NCEE*] (EA) .... NCSBEE
National Council of State Boards of Nursing (EA) .... NCSBN
National Council of State Committees for Children and Youth (EA) .... NCSCCY
National Council of State Consultants in Elementary Education [*Defunct*] (EA) .... NCSCEE
National Council of State Education Associations (EA) .... NCSEA
National Council of State Emergency Medical Services Training Coordinators (EA) .... NCSEMSTC
National Council of State Garden Clubs (EA) .... NCSGC
National Council of State Human Service Administrators (EA) .... NCSHSA
National Council of State Pharmaceutical Association Executives (EA) .... NCSPAE
National Council of State Public Welfare Administrators [*Later, NCSHSA*] (EA) .... NCSPWA
National Council of State Self-Insurers Associations [*Later, NCSI*] (EA) .... NCSSIA
National Council of State Supervisors of Foreign Languages (EA) .... NCSSFL
National Council of State Supervisors of Music (EA) .... NCSSM
National Council of State Travel Directors (EA) .... NCSTD
National Council of Stutterers [*Later, NCOS*] (EA) .... NCS
National Council of Supervisors of Mathematics (EA) .... NCSM
National Council of Teachers for Critical Analysis (AEBS) .... NCTCA
National Council of Teachers of English (EA) .... NCTE
National Council of Teachers of Mathematics (EA) .... NCTM
National Council of Technical Schools (EA) .... NCTS
National Council of Technical Service Industries [*Later, Contract Services Association of America - CSA*] .... NCTSI
National Council of the Arts in Education [*Later, ACAE*] (EA) .... NCAIE
National Council of the Housing Industry (EA) .... NCHI
National Council of the Paper Industry for Air and Stream Improvement (EA) .... NCASI
National Council of the Protestant Episcopal Church, New York, NY [*Library symbol Library of Congress*] (LCLS) .... NNPE-NC
National Council of the United States, International Organization of Good Templars (EA) .... NCUSIOGT
National Council of Tourism in Lebanon (EY) .... CNTL
National Council of United Presbyterian Men (EA) .... NCUPM
National Council of University Research Administrators (EA) .... NCURA
National Council of Urban Administrators of Adult Education (OICC) .... NCUAAE
National Council of Urban Education Associations (EA) .... NCUEA
National Council of Women Chiropractors (EA) .... NCWC
National Council of Women of Australia. Quarterly Bulletin [*A publication*] .... Q Bull Natn Counc Women Aust
National Council of Women of Canada .... NCWC
National Council of Women of Free Czechoslovakia (EA) .... NCWFC
National Council of Women of Great Britain (BI) .... NCW
National Council of Women of Great Britain (DI) .... NCWGB
National Council of Women of New South Wales [*Australia*] .... NCWNSW
National Council of Women of Queensland [*Australia*] .... NCWQ
National Council of Women of Tasmania [*Australia*] .... NCWT
National Council of Women of the United States (EA) .... NCW
National Council of Women of the United States (WDAA) .... NCWUS
National Council of Women of the United States of America (DI) .... NCWUSA
National Council of Women of Victoria [*Australia*] .... NCWV

National Council of Women of Western Australia ... NCWWA
National Council of Wool Selling Brokers of Australia ... NCWSBA
National Council of World Affairs Organizations (EA) ... NCWAO
National Council of Yacht Clubs (EA) ... NCYC
National Council of Young Israel (EA) ... NCYI
National Council on Agricultural Life and Labor Research Fund (EA) ... NCALL
National Council on Alcoholism [*Later, NCADD*] (EA) ... NCA
National Council on Alcoholism and Drug Dependence (EA) ... NCADD
National Council on Alcoholism, Inc. (NADA) ... NCAI
National Council on Alternative Health Care Policy (EA) ... NCAHCP
National Council on Art in Jewish Life (EA) ... NCAJL
National Council on Black Aging (EA) ... NCBA
National Council on Business Mail (EA) ... NCBM
National Council on Child Abuse and Family Violence (EA) ... NCCAFV
National Council on City Planning ... NCCP
National Council on Community Foundations [*Later, CF*] (EA) ... NCCF
National Council on Community Services and Continuing Education (EA) ... NCCSCE
National Council on Compensation Insurance [*New York, NY*] (EA) ... NCCI
National Council on Compulsive Gambling [*Later, NAPG*] (EA) ... NCCG
National Council on Crime and Delinquency (EA) ... NCCD
National Council on Crime and Delinquency, Research and Information Division [*Research center*] (RCD) ... NCCD-R & I
National Council on Drug Abuse [*Defunct*] (EA) ... NCDA
National Council on Drugs [*Defunct*] (EA) ... NCD
National Council on Education for the Ceramic Arts (EA) ... NCECA
National Council on Educational Research [*Later, NCERI*] [*Department of Education Washington, DC*] ... NCER
National Council on Employment Policy (EA) ... NCEP
National Council on Family Relations (EA) ... NCFR
National Council on Federal Disaster Assistance ... NCFDA
National Council on Foreign Language and International Studies (EA) ... NCFLIS
National Council on Gene Resources (EA) ... NCGR
National Council on Governmental Accounting (EA) ... NCGA
National Council on Graduate Education in Psychology ... NCGEP
National Council on Health Laboratory Services (EA) ... NCHLS
National Council on Health Planning and Development ... NCHPD
National Council on Independent Living (EA) ... NCIL
National Council on Indian Opportunity (EA) ... NCIO
National Council on International Trade Documentation [*In association name: NCITD - The International Trade Facilitation Council*] (EA) ... NCITD
National Council on Jewish Audio-Visual Materials (EA) ... NCJAVM
National Council on Legal Clinics [*Later, CLEPR*] ... NCLC
National Council on Marine Resources and Engineering Development [*Later, ICMSE*] ... NCMRED
National Council on Measurement in Education (EA) ... NCME
National Council on Measurements Used in Education [*Later, National Council on Measurement in Education*] (AEBS) ... NCMUE
National Council on Medical Technology Education [*Defunct*] ... NCMTE
National Council on Noise Abatement (EA) ... NCNA
National Council on Occupational Licensing [*Formerly, COL*] [*Defunct*] (EA) ... NCOL
National Council on Organized Crime (EA) ... NCOC
National Council on Philanthropy [*Later, IS*] (EA) ... NCOP
National Council on Philanthropy [*Later, IS*] ... NCP
National Council on Private Forests (EA) ... NCPF
National Council on Problem Gambling (EA) ... NCPG
National Council on Psychological Aspects of Disability (EA) ... NCPAD
National Council on Public History [*Database producer*] (EA) ... NCPH
National Council on Public Policy (EA) ... NCPP
National Council on Public Polls (EA) ... NCPP
National Council on Radiation Protection and Measurements [*Later, NCRPM*] ... NCRP
National Council on Radiation Protection and Measurements (EA) ... NCRPM
National Council on Rehabilitation Education (EA) ... NCRE
National Council on Religion and Public Education (EA) ... NCRPE
National Council on Resource Development (EA) ... NCRD
National Council on Schoolhouse Construction [*Later, CEFP*] (EA) ... NCSC
National Council on Student Development (EA) ... NCSD
National Council on Stuttering (EA) ... NCOS
National Council on Synthetic Fuels Production [*Later, CSF*] (EA) ... NCSFP
National Council on Teacher Retirement (EA) ... NCTR
National Council on the Aging [*Washington, DC*] ... NCA
National Council on the Aging (EA) ... NCOA
National Council on the Arts [*of NFAH*] ... NCA
National Council on the Arts and Government (EA) ... NCAG
National Council on the Education of Health Professionals in Health Promotion (DAVI) ... NCEHPHP
National Council on the Evaluation of Foreign Educational Credentials (EA) ... CEC
National Council on the Humanities [*Washington, DC*] ... NCH
National Council on US-Arab Relations (EA) ... NCUSAR
National Council on Vocational Education [*Department of Education Washington, DC*] (EGAO) ... NCVE
National Council on Wholistic Therapeutics and Medicine [*Defunct*] (EA) ... NCWTM
National Council, Sons and Daughters of Liberty (EA) ... SDL
National Council to Combat Blindness [*Also known as Fight for Sight - FS*] (EA) ... NCCB
National Council to Control Handguns [*Later, HCI*] (EA) ... NCCH
National Council to Repeal the Draft [*Defunct*] (EA) ... NCRD
National Counil of Young Men's Christian Associations [*British*] (DBA) ... YMCA
National Counselor Certification [*Psychology*] ... NCC
National Counter Intelligence Corps Association (EA) ... NCICA
National Country Maintenance Index (IAA) ... NCMI
National Country Party of Western Australia [*Political party*] ... NCPW
National Coursing Association [*Later, NGA*] (EA) ... NCA
National Coursing Association of Victoria [*Australia*] ... NCAV
National Court Appointed Special Advocates Association (EA) ... NCASAA
National Court Clubs Association [*Later, IRSA*] (EA) ... NCCA
National CPA [*Certified Public Accountant*] **Group** [*Later, BKR International*] (EA) ... NCPAG
National Cranberry Association ... NCA
National Craniofacial Foundation [*Later, ICF*] (EA) ... NCF
National Crash Severity Study [*National Highway Traffic Safety Administration*] ... NCSS
National Creameries Association [*Later, NMPF*] (EA) ... NCA
National Credential Verification Service (MCD) ... NCVS
National Credit Adjustment Association [*New York, NY*] (EA) ... NCAA
National Credit Association (NADA) ... NCA
National Credit Information Network ... NCIN
National Credit Information Service [*TRW, Inc.*] [*Long Beach, CA Credit-information databank*] (IID) ... NACIS
National Credit Information Service [*TRW, Inc.*] [*Long Beach, CA Credit-information databank*] ... NCIS
National Credit Union Administration ... NCUA
National Credit Union Administration Rules and Regulations ... NCRR
National Credit Union Association (NADA) ... NCUA
National Credit Union Management Association (EA) ... NCUMA
National Credit Union Share Insurance Fund ... NCUSIF
National Cricket Association [*British*] ... NCA
National Crime Commission ... NCC
National Crime Information Center [*FBI*] [*Washington, DC*] ... NCIC
National Crime Prevention Association [*Defunct*] (EA) ... NCPA
National Crime Prevention Council (EA) ... NCPC
National Crime Prevention Institute (EA) ... NCPI
National Crime Stop Program (EA) ... NCSP
National Crime Stoppers [*Later, ACF*] (EA) ... NCS
National Crime Survey [*University of Michigan*] [*Database*] ... NCS
National Crime Victimization Survey [*Department of Justice*] (ECON) ... NCVS
National Criminal Defense College (EA) ... NCDC
National Criminal Justice Association (EA) ... NCJA
National Criminal Justice Information and Statistics Service ... NCJISS
National Criminal Justice Reference Service [*Department of Justice*] [*Information service or system*] ... NCJRS
National Criminal Justice Statistics Center ... NCJSC
National Cristina Foundation (EA) ... NCF
National Critics Institute (EA) ... NCI
National Crop Acreage Program [*Department of Agriculture*] ... NCA
National Crop Insurance Association [*Shawnee Mission, KS*] (EA) ... NCIA
National Crop Insurance Council [*Inactive*] (EA) ... NCIC
National Crop Insurance Services (EA) ... NCIS
National Crop Loss Assessment Network ... NCLAN
National Crossbow Hunters Association (EA) ... NCHA
[*The*] **National Crossbowmen** (EA) ... TNC
National Crusaders Youth Federation (EA) ... NCYF
National Crushed Stone Association [*Later, NSA*] (EA) ... NCSA
National Cryptologic Command [*National Security Agency*] ... NCC
National Cryptologic School [*National Security Agency*] ... NCS
National Cryptologic Training Plan (MCD) ... NCTP
National Cued Speech Association (EA) ... NCSA
National Cultural Center [*Later, John F. Kennedy Center for the Performing Art s*] ... NCC
National Curriculum [*Education*] (AIE) ... NC
National Curriculum Council [*British*] (ECON) ... NCC
National Curriculum Project ... NCP
National Curriculum Study Institute [*Associaton for Supervision and Curriculum Development*] (EDAC) ... NCSI
National Cursillo Movement (EA) ... NCM
National Curtain, Drapery, and Allied Products Association [*Later, HFPA*] ... NCDAPA
National Customs Brokers and Forwarders Association of America [*New York, NY*] (EA) ... NCBFAA
National Customs Service Association [*Later, NTEU*] (EA) ... NCSA
National Cutlery Union [*British*] ... NCU
National Cutting Horse Association (EA) ... NCHA
National Cutting Horse Association of Australia ... NCHAA
National Cycle League (EA) ... NCL
National Cycling Proficiency (BARN) ... NCP
National Cyclists' Union [*British*] ... NCU
National CYO [*Catholic Youth Organizations*] **Federation** (EA) ... NCYOF
National Cystic Fibrosis Research Foundation [*Later, Cystic Fibrosis Foundation*] (EA) ... NCFRF
National Dahlia Society [*British*] (DBA) ... NDS
National Dairy Association (NADA) ... NDA
National Dairy Council (EA) ... NDC
National Dairy Council, Chicago, IL [*Library symbol Library of Congress*] (LCLS) ... ICDC
National Dairymen's Association, Inc. [*British*] (BI) ... NDA
National Dairymen's Benevolent Institution, Inc. [*British*] (BI) ... NDBI
National Damage Assessment Center ... NADAC
National Dance Association (EA) ... NDA
National Dance Council of America (EA) ... NDCA
National Dance Guild [*Later, ADG*] ... NDG
National Dance Institute (EA) ... NDI
National Dance-Exercise Instructor's Training Association (EA) ... NDEITA
National Data Base on Aging (EDAC) ... NDBA
National Data Buoy Center [*National Oceanic and Atmospheric Administration Also, an information service or system*] (IID) ... NDBC

National Data Buoy Development Project [Later, NDBO] [Coast Guard] (MSC) .... NDBDP
National Data Buoy Office [Marine science] (OSRA) .... NDBO
National Data Buoy Office (USDC) .... NDBO
National Data Buoy Program [National Oceanic and Atmospheric Administration] (GFGA) .... NDBP
National Data Buoy System .... NDBS
National Data Communication .... NDC
National Data Corp. [Associated Press] (SAG) .... NData
National Data Corp. [NYSE symbol] (SPSG) .... NDC
National Data Processing Division [Environmental Protection Agency] (GFGA) .... NDPD
National Data Processing Service [British] (DCTA) .... NDPS
National Day of Bread Committee [Defunct] (EA) .... NDBC
National Days Fan Club (EA) .... NDFC
National Deaf Bowling Association (EA) .... NDBA
National Deaf Children's Association [British] .... NDCA
National Deaf Children's Society [British] (BI) .... NDCS
National Deaf Women's Bowling Association (EA) .... NDWBA
National Deaf-Blind League [British] (EAIO) .... NDBL
National Death Index [Department of Health and Human Services] (GFGA) .... NDI
National Debt .... ND
National Debt Commission [Australia] .... NDC
National Debt Management System [Social Security Administration] (GFGA) .... NDMS
National Debt Office [British] .... NDO
National Debt Repayment Foundation (EA) .... NDRF
National Decision Systems [Information service or system] (IID) .... NDS
National Decorated Packaging Association .... NDPA
National Decorating Products Association (EA) .... NDPA
National Defeat Dukakis Campaign (EA) .... NDDC
National Defence College [British] .... NDC
National Defence College [British] .... NDColl
National Defence Committee [Ghana] [Political party] (PPW) .... NDC
National Defence Company [British military] (DMA) .... NDC
National Defence Contribution [British] .... NDC
National Defence Corps [British] .... NDC
National Defence Headquarters [Canada] .... NDHQ
National Defence Headquarters Library [UTLAS symbol] .... NDL
National Defence Medical Centre, Department of National Defence [Centre Medical de la Nationale, Ministere de la Defense Nationale] Ottawa, Ontario [Library symbol National Library of Canada] (NLC) .... OONDM
National Defense Act .... NDA
National Defense Advisory Commission [World War II] .... NDAC
National Defense Advisory Committee (NADA) .... NDAC
National Defense Area (AABC) .... NDA
National Defense Cadet Corps .... NDCC
National Defense Center for Environmental Excellence [DoD] (RDA) .... NDCEE
National Defense College [Australia] .... NDC
National Defense Committee of the Daughters of the American Revolution (EA) .... NDCDAR
National Defense Communications Control Center (MCD) .... NDCCC
National Defense Corps (NADA) .... NDC
National Defense Council (KSC) .... NDC
National Defense Council Foundation (EA) .... NDCF
National Defense Education .... NDE
National Defense Education Act [1958] .... NDEA
National Defense Education Institute .... NDEI
National Defense Emergency [Headquarters] (MCD) .... NDE
National Defense Emergency Authorization .... NDEA
National Defense Executive Reserve .... NDER
National Defense Executive Reserve Roster [of the CSC] .... NDERR
National Defense Foreign Language [Fellowship] .... NDFL
National Defense General Staff (NATG) .... NDGS
National Defense Headquarters [Canada] .... NDH
National Defense Manufacturing Technology Plan .... NDMTP
National Defense Mediation Board [World War II] .... NDMB
National Defense Operations Section [FCC] .... NDOS
National Defense Project Rating Plan .... NDPRP
National Defense Research Committee [of Office of Scientific Research and Development] [World War II] .... NDRC
National Defense Reserve Fleet [Maritime Administration, Department of Commerce] .... NDRF
National Defense Science and Engineering Graduate .... NDSEG
National Defense Sealift Fund (DOMA) .... NDSF
National Defense Service Medal [Military decoration] .... NATDEFSM
National Defense Service Medal [Military decoration] .... NDSM
National Defense Stockpile [Collection of materials essential to the defense industry] .... NDS
National Defense Transportation Association (EA) .... NDTA
National Defense University [DoD] .... NDU
National Defense University, Fort Lesley J. McNair, Washington, DC [Library symbol] [Library of Congress] (LCLS) .... DNDU
National Defense University, Washington, DC [OCLC symbol] (OCLC) .... NDU
National Democracy Party [Thailand] [Political party] (PPW) .... NDP
National Democratic Alliance [Zambia] [Political party] (EY) .... NADA
National Democratic Alliance [Sierra Leone] [Political party] (EY) .... NDA
National Democratic Club (EA) .... NDC
National Democratic Congress [Ghana] [Political party] (ECON) .... NDC
National Democratic Congress [Grenada] [Political party] (EY) .... NDC
National Democratic Front [Pakistan] [Political party] (FEA) .... NDF
National Democratic Front [Philippines] [Political party] (FEA) .... NDF
National Democratic Front [Myanmar] [Political party] (FEA) .... NDF
National Democratic Front [Iran] [Political party] (PD) .... NDF
National Democratic Front [Guyana] [Political party] (EY) .... NDF

National Democratic Front [Yemen] [Political party] (PD) .... NDF
National Democratic Institute for International Affairs (EA) .... NDIIA
National Democratic League [Early British political party] .... NDL
National Democratic Party [Solomon Islands] [Political party] (PPW) .... NADEPA
National Democratic Party [British] .... NDemP
National Democratic Party [Rhodesia and Nyasaland] [Political party] .... NDP
National Democratic Party [Sierra Leone] [Political party] (EY) .... NDP
National Democratic Party [Grenada] [Political party] (PPW) .... NDP
National Democratic Party [India] [Political party] (PPW) .... NDP
National Democratic Party [Morocco] [Political party] (PPW) .... NDP
National Democratic Party [Iraq] [Political party] (BJA) .... NDP
National Democratic Party [Namibia] [Political party] (PPW) .... NDP
National Democratic Party [Egypt] [Political party] (PPW) .... NDP
National Democratic Party [Pakistan] [Political party] (PD) .... NDP
National Democratic Party [Solomon Islands] [Political party] (PPW) .... NDP
National Democratic Party of Liberia [Political party] (EY) .... NDPL
National Democratic Policy Committee (EA) .... NDPC
National Democratic Union [Zimbabwe] [Political party] (PPW) .... NDU
National Democratic United Front [Later, FNDF] [Myanmar] [Political party] (PD) .... NDUF
National Democrats [Political party] (AD) .... Nat Dem
National Demographics & Lifestyles, Inc. .... NDL
National Demonstration Water Project (EA) .... NDWP
National Dental Assistants Association (EA) .... NDAA
National Dental Association (EA) .... NDA
National Dental Hygienists' Association (EA) .... NDHA
National Dental Technicians Association [Defunct] (EA) .... NDTA
National Dentex Corp. [NASDAQ symbol] (SAG) .... NADX
National Dentex Corp. [Associated Press] (SAG) .... NtDentex
National Denturist Association (EA) .... NDA
National Depression Glass Association (EA) .... NDGA
National Depressive and Manic Depressive Association (EA) .... NDMDA
National Derby Rallies (EA) .... NDR
National Design Council [Canada] .... NDC
National Design, Inc. (PCM) .... NDI
National DeSoto Club (EA) .... NDC
National Determination Party (EA) .... NDP
National Development Corp. [Dominica] (EY) .... NDC
National Development Council .... NDC
National Development Party [Montserrat] [Political party] (EY) .... NDP
National Diabetes Data Group [British] .... NDDG
National Diabetes Information Clearinghouse [Public Health Service] (IID) .... NDIC
National Diabetes Research Interchange [Research center] (RCD) .... NDRI
National Diagnostics, Inc. [NASDAQ symbol] (SAG) .... NATD
National Diagnostics, Inc. [Associated Press] (SAG) .... NatDiag
National Diagnostics, Inc. [Associated Press] (SAG) .... NDiag
National Diagnostics Wrrt [NASDAQ symbol] (TTSB) .... NATDW
National Diet Library [Japan] .... NDL
National Dietary Foods Association [Later, NNFA] (EA) .... NDFA
National Diffusion Network [Department of Education] [Information service or system] (IID) .... NDN
National Digestive Diseases Education and Information Clearinghouse [Public Health Service] [Later, NDDIC] (IID) .... NDDEIC
National Digestive Diseases Information Clearinghouse (EA) .... NDDIC
National Dimension Manufacturers Association (EA) .... NDMA
National Dinghy Exhibition [British] .... NDE
National Diocesan Press [Later, Episcopal Communicators] (EA) .... NDP
National Dioxin Study [Environmental Protection Agency] (GFGA) .... NDS
National Diploma [Academic degree] (AIE) .... ND
National Diploma in Agricultural Engineering [British] .... ND Agr E
National Diploma in Agriculture [British] .... NDA
National Diploma in Dairying [British] .... NDD
National Diploma in Design [British] .... NDD
National Diploma in Forestry [British] .... NDF
National Diploma in Horticulture [British] .... NDH
National Diploma in Horticulture (Royal Horticultural Society) [British] (DBQ) .... MHort(RHS)
National Diploma in Poultry Husbandry [British] .... NDP
National Diploma in the Science and Practice of Turfculture and Sports Ground Management [British] .... NDT
National Direct [formerly, Defense] Student Loan [later, Perkins Loan] [Department of Education] .... NDSL
National Directory of Accounting Firms and Accountants [A publication] .... NDAFA
National Directory of Churches, Synagogues, and Other Houses of Worship [A publication] .... NDC
National Directory of Newsletters and Reporting Services [A publication] ..... NDN
National Directory of Nonprofit Organizations [A publication] .... NDNO
National Disability Data System [Social Security Administration] (GFGA) ...... NDDS
National Disabled Law Officers Association (EA) .... NDLOA
National Disaster Medical System .... NDMS
National Disaster Warning System (AD) .... NADWARN
National Disclosure Policy [Military] (MCD) .... NDP
National [Military Information] Disclosure Policy Committee .... NDPC
National Display Equipment Association [British] (BI) .... NDEA
National Disposal Services Association (EA) .... NDSA
National Disposal Site [Environmental Protection Agency] (GFGA) .... NDS
National Distribution Guide [Mailing technique] .... NDG
National District Attorneys Association (EA) .... NDAA
National District Heating Association [Later, IDHCA] (EA) .... NDHA
National Dividend Foundation (EA) .... NDF
National Diving Council .... NDC
National Dock Labour Board [British] .... NDLB
National Document and Information Service [Australia] .... NDIS

National Dog Groomers Association (EA) ... NDGA
National Dog Groomers Association of America (EA) ... NDGAA
National Dog Owners' Association [*British*] (BI) ... NDOA
National Dog Registry (EA) ... NDR
National Dome Association [*Later, NDC*] (EA) ... NDA
National Dome Council (EA) ... NDC
National Domestic Meatworks Wholesalers Council [*Australia*] ... NDMWC
National Domestic Workers Union (EA) ... NDWU
National Door Association [*Defunct*] ... NDA
National Door Manufacturers Association [*Later, NWWDA*] ... NDMA
National Down Syndrome Congress (EA) ... NDSC
National Down Syndrome Society (EA) ... NDSS
National Drain Tile Manufacturers Association [*Defunct*] (EA) ... NDTMA
National Drama Festivals Association [*British*] (BI) ... NDFA
National Dress Manufacturers Association [*Later, AMA*] (EA) ... NDMA
National Dried Fruit Trade Association [*British*] (DBA) ... NDFTA
National Dried (Milk) [*Brand name for the British government's dried milk for babies - manufacturer undisclosed*] ... NDM
National Drilling Contractors Association (EA) ... NDCA
National Drilling Federation [*Later, IDF*] (EA) ... NDF
National Drinking Water Advisory Council [*Environmental Protection Agency*] ... NDWAC
National Driver Register ... NDR
National Driver Register Service [*Department of Transportation*] ... NDRS
National Drivers Association for the Prevention of Traffic Accidents [*Defunct*] (EA) ... NDAPTA
National Dropout Prevention Center (EA) ... NDPC
National Dropout Prevention Network (EA) ... NDPN
National Drowning Prevention Coalition (EA) ... NDPC
National Drug and Alcohol Research Center [*University of New South Wales*] [*Australia*] ... NDARC
National Drug and Alcohol Treatment Utilization Survey [*Department of Health and Human Services*] (GFGA) ... NDATUS
National Drug Code [*FDA*] ... NDC
National Drug Code Directory [*FDA*] [*A publication*] ... NDCD
National Drug Co. [*Research code symbol*] ... NAT
National Drug Co. [*Research code symbol*] ... NDR
National Drug Education Training Program [*HEW*] ... NDETP
National Drug Policy Board [*Department of Justice*] (GFGA) ... NDPB
National Drug Strategy Network (EA) ... NDSN
National Drug Trade Conference (EA) ... NDTC
National Drugs Intelligence Unit [*Metropolitan Police*] [*British*] ... NDIU
National Dry Bean Council (EA) ... NDBC
National Dry Deposition Network (GNE) ... NDDN
National DS Society ... NDSS
National Duck Pin Bowling Congress [*Later, NDBC*] (EA) ... NDPBC
National Duckling Council [*Defunct*] (EA) ... NDC
National Duckpin Bowling Congress (EA) ... NDBC
National Duncan Glass Society (EA) ... NDGS
National E [*Electronic*]-Mail Registry [*Information service or system*] (TSSD) ... NEMR
National Eagle Scout Association (EA) ... NESA
National Early American Glass Club (EA) ... NEAGC
National Early Music Association [*British*] (DBA) ... NEMA
National Earth Observations Center [*National Oceanic and Atmospheric Administration*] ... NEOC
National Earth Science Teachers Association (EA) ... NESTA
National Earth Shelter Builders Association [*Defunct*] (EA) ... NESBA
National Earthquake Early Reporting System (NOAA) ... NEERS
National Earthquake Hazards Reduction Program [*Federal Emergency Management Agency*] [*Washington, DC*] (EGAO) ... NEHRP
National Earthquake Information Center [*US Geological Survey*] ... NEIC
National Earthquake Information Service [*United States Geological Survey*] (IID) ... NEIS
National Earthquake Prediction Evaluation Council [*US Geological Survey*] ... NEPEC
National Easter Seal Society (EA) ... NESS
National Easter Seal Society for Crippled Children and Adults, Chicago, IL [*Library symbol Library of Congress*] (LCLS) ... ICES
National Eclectic Medical Association [*Defunct*] (EA) ... NEMA
National Ecological Research Laboratory [*Environmental Protection Agency*] ... NERL
National Economic and Legislative Report [*Commerce Clearing House*] [*A publication*] (DLA) ... ANR
National Economic Association (EA) ... NEA
National Economic Council [*Defunct*] (EA) ... NEC
National Economic Development and Law Center [*Berkeley, CA*] [*Research center*] (EA) ... NEDLC
National Economic Development Association ... NEDA
National Economic Development Council [*Nickname: Neddie*] [*British*] ... NEDC
National Economic Development Office [*British*] ... NEDO
National Economic Growth and Reconstruction Organization [*Black entrepreneurial organization*] ... NEGRO
National Economic Projections Series [*NPA Data Services, Inc.*] [*Information service or system*] (CRD) ... NEPS
National Economic Research Associates ... NERA
National Economists Club (EA) ... NEC
National Ecumenical Coalition (EA) ... NEC
National Eczema Society [*British*] ... NES
National Edible Oil Distributors Association [*British*] (DBA) ... NEODA
National Editorial Association [*Later, NNA*] (EA) ... NEA
National Education Association (EA) ... NEA
National Education Association, Washington, DC [*Library symbol Library of Congress*] (LCLS) ... DNEA
National Education Center for Paraprofessionals in Mental Health (EA) ... NEC
National Education Computer Center ... NECC
National Education Corp. [*Associated Press*] (SAG) ... NatEdu
National Education Corp. [*NYSE symbol*] (SPSG) ... NEC
National Education Council of the Christian Brothers [*Later, RECCB*] (EA) ... NECCB
National Education Field Service Association [*Defunct*] (EA) ... NEFSA
National Education for Assistance Dog Services [*Formerly, New England Assistance Dog Service*] (PAZ) ... NEADS
National Education Longitudinal Study of 1988 [*Department of Education*] (GFGA) ... NELS:88
National Education Program (EA) ... NEP
National Educational Closed-Circuit Television Association [*British*] ... NECCTA
National Educational Development Test ... NEDT
National Educational Institute for Economic Development (EA) ... NEIED
National Educational Longitudinal Survey ... NELS
National Educational Management Association (EA) ... NEMA
National Educational Radio ... NER
National Educational Radio Network [*Defunct*] (NTCM) ... NERN
National Educational Resources Information Service [*British*] ... NERIS
National Educational Television [*Later, EBC*] ... NET
National Educational Television and Radio Center [*Later, EBC*] (EA) ... NETRC
National Educational Television/Film Service (WGA) ... NETFS
National Educators Fellowship [*Later, CEAI*] ... NEF
National Egg Council [*Later, PEIA*] (EA) ... NEC
National Egg Packers' Association Ltd. [*British*] (BI) ... NEPAL
National Election Studies [*Conducts national surveys of the American electorate*] ... NES
National Electoral Commission [*Nigeria*] (ECON) ... NEC
National Electric Comfort Trade Association [*Defunct*] (EA) ... NECTA
National Electric Light Association ... NELA
National Electric Rate Book by States [*A publication*] ... NERBS
National Electric Safety Code (SAA) ... NESC
National Electric Sign Association (EA) ... NESA
National Electrical and Electronic Industry Training Committee [*Australia*] ... NEEITC
National Electrical Code ... NEC
National Electrical Code Standards ... NECS
National Electrical Contractors Association (EA) ... NECA
National Electrical Effect ... NEE
National Electrical Engineering Department Heads Association (EA) ... NEEDHA
National Electrical Manufacturers Association (EA) ... NEMA
National Electrical Manufacturers Representatives Association (EA) ... NEMRA
National Electrical Safety Code [*Also, NEC*] (NTCM) ... NESC
National Electrical Wholesalers Association ... NEWA
National Electricity Manufacturers' Association (NITA) ... NEMA
National Electricity Market Management Company, Ltd. [*Australia*] [*Commercial firm*] ... NEMMCO
National Electrology Educators (EA) ... NEE
National Electrolysis Organization [*Later, SCME*] (EA) ... NEO
National Electromagnetic Compatibility Analysis Facility [*Department of Commerce*] (PDAA) ... NECAF
National Electron Probe Resource for Analysis of Cells [*Harvard University*] [*Research center*] (RCD) ... NEPRAC
National Electronic Associations [*Later, NESSDA*] ... NEA
National Electronic Autocoding Technique (MHDB) ... NEAT
National Electronic Distributors Association (EA) ... NEDA
National Electronic Industries Procurement Group ... NEIPG
National Electronic Information Corp. [*Information service or system*] (IID) ... NEIC
National Electronic Injury Surveillance System [*Consumer Product Safety Commission*] [*Washington, DC Databank*] ... NEISS
National Electronic Packaging and Production Conference ... NEPCON
National Electronic Reliability Council (NTCM) ... NERC
National Electronic Sales and Service Dealers Association (EA) ... NESSDA
National Electronic Service Dealers Association [*Later, NESSDA*] (EA) ... NESDA
National Electronic Telecommunications System for Surveillance [*Center for Disease Control*] ... NETSS
National Electronics Conference (AEBS) ... NEC
National Electronics Conference, New Zealand [*IEEE*] ... NELCON NZ
National Electronics Council [*British*] (NUCP) ... NEC
National Electronics Council (NITA) ... NEC
National Electronics Facilities Organization ... NEFO
National Electronics Laboratory (IDOE) ... NEL
National Electronics Research Council ... NERC
National Electronics Research Initiative [*British*] ... NERI
National Electronics Teachers' Service [*Defunct*] ... NETS
National Electronics Week ... NEW
National Elephant Collectors Society (EA) ... NECS
National Elevator Industry, Inc. (EA) ... NEII
National Elevator Manufacturing Industry [*Later, NEII*] (EA) ... NEMI
National Emancipation League [*Nigeria*] ... NEL
National Emblem Club (EA) ... NEC
National Emergency ... NE
National Emergency Airborne Command Post [*Pronounced "kneecap"*] [*Modified Boeing 747 jet to be used as a military control center by the President or Vice President during a nuclear war or other crisis*] ... NEACP
National Emergency Alarm Repeater [*Civil defense warning system for homes*] ... NEAR
National Emergency Civil Liberties Committee (EA) ... NECLC
National Emergency Command Post Afloat ... NECPA
National Emergency Coordination Center (BARN) ... NECC
National Emergency Council [*Abolished, 1939*] ... NEC
National Emergency Defense Airlift ... NEDA
National Emergency Equipment Data System (NITA) ... NEEDS

National Emergency Equipment Locator System [*Environment Canada*] [*Information service or system*] (CRD) ... NEELS
National Emergency Management Association (EA) ... NEMA
National Emergency Medicine Association (EA) ... NEMA
National Emergency Planning Establishment [*Canada*] ... NEPE
National Emergency Relief Administration ... NERA
National Emergency Steel Specification [*World War II*] ... NESS
National Emergency Survivable Troop System (AABC) ... NEST
National Emergency Training Center ... NETC
National Emergency Transportation Center ... NETC
National Emission Standards Act [*1967*] ... NESA
National Emission Standards for Hazardous Air Pollutants [*Environmental Protection Agency*] ... NESHAP
National Emissions Data System [*Environmental Protection Agency Information service or system*] ... NEDS
National Emissions Inventory System [*Database*] [*Environment Canada*] [*Information service or system*] (CRD) ... NEIS
National Emissions Report [*Environmental Protection Agency*] (GFGA) ... NER
National Emphasis Program [*Occupational Safety and Health Administration*] ... NEP
National Employ the Handicapped Week ... NETH
National Employ the Handicapped Week (OICC) ... NETHW
National Employee Benefits Institute [*Washington, DC*] (EA) ... NEBI
National Employee Services and Recreation Association (EA) ... NESRA
National Employers Association of Rayon Yarn Producers [*British*] (BI) ... NEARYP
National Employers' Committee ... NEC
National Employment and Training Association [*Upland, CA*] (EA) ... NETA
National Employment Assistance Act (OICC) ... NEAA
National Employment Association [*Later, NAPC*] (EA) ... NEA
National Employment Clearing House [*American Chemical Society*] ... NECH
National Employment Counselors Association (EA) ... NECA
National Employment Law Project [*New York, NY*] (EA) ... NELP
National Employment Lawyers Association (EA) ... NELA
National Employment Lawyers Association ... NELA
National Employment Service Act [*1933*] ... NESA
National Empowerment Consortium [*Investment group*] [*South Africa*] ... NEC
National Empowerment Television ... NET
National EMS [*Emergency Medical Service*] **Pilots Association** (EA) ... NEMSPA
National Endowment for Democracy (EA) ... NED
National Endowment for the Arts ... NEA
National Endowment for the Humanities ... NEH
National Endowment for the Preservation of Liberty [*Foundation created by Carl Channell to collect funds for Nicaraguan CONTRAs*] ... NEPL
National Energy Accounts [*Department of Commerce*] [*Information service or system*] (IID) ... NEA
National Energy Act (GFGA) ... NEA
National Energy Audit Program [*Canada*] ... NEAP
National Energy Board [*Canada*] ... NEB
National Energy Board, Ottawa, ON, Canada [*Library symbol Library of Congress*] (LCLS) ... CaOONE
National Energy Board [*Office National de l'Energie*] **Ottawa, Ontario** [*Library symbol National Library of Canada*] (NLC) ... OONE
National Energy Conservation Policy Act [*1978*] ... NECPA
National Energy Education Development Project (EA) ... NEED
National Energy Extension Service Advisory Board [*Department of Energy Washington, DC*] (EGAO) ... NEESAB
National Energy Foundation (EA) ... NEF
National Energy Group [*Associated Press*] (SAG) ... NatEng
National Energy Group [*NASDAQ symbol*] (SAG) ... NEGX
National Energy Group [*NASDAQ symbol*] (SAG) ... NRGI
National Energy Information Center [*Department of Energy*] [*Washington, DC*] ... NEIC
National Energy Information Center Affiliate [*University of New Mexico*] (IID) ... NEICA
National Energy Management Advisory Committee [*British*] ... NEMAC
National Energy Management Exhibition and Conference (ITD) ... NEMEX
National Energy Office [*Executive Office of the President*] ... NEO
National Energy Policy Act [*Legislation passed in 1992*] [*Department of Energy*] (PS) ... EPACT
National Energy Policy Plan ... NEPP
National Energy Program [*or Plan*] [*Canada*] ... NEP
National Energy Protection Board ... NEPB
National Energy Referal Information System (NITA) ... NERIS
National Energy Resources Organization (EA) ... NERO
National Energy Software [*Department of Energy Information service or system*] (CRD) ... NES
National Energy Software Center [*Department of Energy*] [*Information service or system*] (IID) ... NESC
National Energy Specialist Association (EA) ... NESA
National Energy Strategy [*Department of Energy*] (ECON) ... NES
National Energy Supply Corp. [*Proposed*] ... NESCO
National Energy Watch [*Edison Electric Institute*] ... NEW
National Enforcement Investigations Center [*Environmental Protection Agency*] (EG) ... NEIC
National Engine Parts Manufacturers Association (EA) ... NEPMA
National Engine Use Council [*Defunct*] (EA) ... NEUC
National Engineering and Electrical Trade Union [*Republic of Ireland*] (BI) ... NEETU
National Engineering Aptitude Search ... NEAS
National Engineering Consortium (EA) ... NEC
National Engineering Construction Employers Association [*British*] (DBA) ... NECEA
National Engineering Council for Guidance (EA) ... NECG
National Engineering Information System (BUR) ... NEIS
National Engineering Laboratory [*Superseded IAT*] [*Gaithersburg, MD*] [*National Institute of Standards and Technology*] ... NEL
National Engineering Laboratory [*Scotland*] ... NEL
National Engineering Laboratory's Thermophysical Properties Package [*British Information service or system*] (IID) ... NELPAC
National Engineering Science Co. ... NESCO
National Engineers Commission on Air Resources (PDAA) ... NECAR
National Engineers Register (IAA) ... NER
National Enginemen and Firemen's Protection Society [*A union*] [*British*] ... NEFPS
National Enginemen's Protection Association [*A union*] [*British*] ... NEPA
National English Rabbit Club [*British*] (BI) ... NERC
National Enquiry into Scholarly Communication ... NESC
National Enterprise Bank [*Washington, DC*] (NQ) ... NEBK
National Enterprise Board [*Later, BTG*] [*British*] ... NEB
National Enterprise Education Development and Information Service (AIE) ... NEEDIS
National Entertainment and Campus Activities Association [*Formerly, NEC*] (EA) ... NECAA
National Entertainment Conference [*Later, NECAA*] (EA) ... NEC
National Entertainment Journalists Association [*Defunct*] (EA) ... NEJA
National Environment Laboratory Accreditation Conference [*Environmental Protection Agency*] ... NELAC
National Environment Resource Council [*British*] (NRCH) ... NERC
National Environmental Balancing Bureau (EA) ... NEBB
National Environmental Data and Information Service [*Marine science*] (MSC) ... NEDIS
National Environmental Data Referral Service [*Online database*] [*National Oceanic and Atmospheric Administration Washington, DC*] ... NEDRES
National Environmental Data Referral Service (USDC) ... NESDRES
National Environmental Data Referral Service [*Marine science*] (OSRA) ... NESDRES
National Environmental Development Association (EA) ... NEDA
National Environmental Development Association/Clean Air Act Project [*Defunct*] (EA) ... NEDA/CAAP
National Environmental Development Association/Ground Water Project (EA) ... NEDA/GRND
National Environmental Education and Training Foundation [*An association*] (PS) ... NEETF
National Environmental Education Development [*Program of National Park Service*] [*Defunct*] ... NEED
National Environmental Education Landmarks [*Department of the Interior*] ... NEEL
National Environmental Enforcement Council [*National Association of Attorneys General*] (EPA) ... NEEC
National Environmental Enforcement Journal [*National Association of Attorneys General*] [*A publication*] (EPA) ... NEEJ
National Environmental Engineering Research Institute ... NEERI
National Environmental Health Association (EA) ... NEHA
National Environmental Information Symposium ... NEIS
National Environmental Laboratories [*Proposed*] ... NELS
National Environmental Monitoring and Prediction System (MCD) ... NEMPS
National Environmental Policy Act (EG) ... NEPA
National Environmental Policy Act (DOGT) ... NEPA
National Environmental Policy Act of 1969 ... NEPA
National Environmental Policy Institute [*Washington, D.C.*] ... NEPI
National Environmental Protection Agency [*China*] ... NEPA
National Environmental Research Center [*Later, CERL*] [*Environmental Protection Agency*] ... NERC
National Environmental Research Council (NITA) ... NERC
National Environmental Research Park [*Marine science*] (MSC) ... NERP
National Environmental Satellite Center [*Formerly, National Weather Satellite Center*] [*Later, National Environmental Satellite Service*] ... NESC
National Environmental Satellite Center Technical Memoranda (NOAA) ... NESCTM
National Environmental Satellite, Data, and Information Service [*Washington, DC National Oceanic and Atmospheric Administration*] (GRD) ... NESDIS
National Environmental Satellite Service [*National Oceanic and Atmospheric Administration Telecommunications*] (TEL) ... NESS
National Environmental Services Administration Committee [*Marine science*] (MSC) ... NESAC
National Environmental Specialist Association (EA) ... NESA
National Environmental Specimen Bank [*Energy Research and Development Administration*] ... NESB
National Environmental Studies Project [*Defunct*] (EA) ... NESP
National Environmental Study Areas Program [*National Park Service*] [*Defunct*] ... NESA
National Environmental Svc. [*NASDAQ symbol*] (TTSB) ... NESC
National Environmental Systems Contractors Association [*Later, ACCA*] (EA) ... NESCA
National Environmental Training Association (EA) ... NETA
National Epilepsy League [*Later, EFA*] (EA) ... NEL
National Epilepsy Library and Resource Center [*Epilepsy Foundation of America*] [*Information service or system*] (IID) ... NELRC
National Episcopal Coalition on Alcohol [*Later, NECAD*] (EA) ... NECA
National Episcopal Coalition on Alcohol and Drugs (EA) ... NECAD
National Epson Users Group (EA) ... NEUG
National Equal Rights Council (EA) ... NERC
National Equipment Distributors Association [*Defunct*] (EA) ... NEDA
National Equipment Servicing Dealers Association (EA) ... NESDA
National Equivalence Information Centre (AIE) ... NEIC
National Erectors Association (EA) ... NEA
National Established Repair, Service, and Improvement Contractors Association [*Later, National Remodelers Association*] ... NERSICA

National Estate ..... NE
National Estate Tasmania [*Australia*] ..... NET
National Estimating Society [*Later, SCEA*] (EA) ..... NES
National Estuarine Inventory ..... NEI
National Estuarine Pollution Study [*Federal Water Quality Administration*] (MSC) ..... NEPS
National Estuarine Research Reserve System (USDC) ..... NERRS
National Estuary Program [*Federal government*] ..... NEP
National Euchre Players Association (EA) ..... NEPA
National European American Society (EA) ..... NEAS
National Eutrophication Survey [*Environmental Protection Agency*] ..... NES
National Evangelization Teams (EA) ..... NET
National Event Clearinghouse Database [*National Event Clearinghouse, Inc.*] [*Information service or system*] (CRD) ..... NECH
National Examination Board in Occupational Safety and Health (PDAA) ..... NEBOSH
National Examinations Board in Supervisory Studies [*British*] ..... NEBSS
National Excellence in Teaching Award [*Australia*] ..... NEITA
National Exchange Carrier Association (EA) ..... NECA
National Exchange Club (EA) ..... NEC
National Exchange Club Foundation for the Prevention of Child Abuse (EA) ..... NECF
National Exchange, Inc. [*McLean, VA*] [*Telecommunications*] (TSSD) ..... NEX
National Exchange Market System ..... NEMS
National Exchequer [*British*] ..... NE
National Execution Alert Network (EA) ..... NEAN
National Executive (ADA) ..... NE
National Executive Committee [*British*] (DCTA) ..... NEC
National Executive Compensation Database [*Information service or system*] (IID) ..... EXCOMP
National Executive Housekeepers Association (EA) ..... NEHA
National Executive of Small Business Agencies [*Australia*] ..... NESBA
National Executive Service Corps [*New York, NY*] (EA) ..... NESC
National Exhaust Distributors Association [*Later, NEDA/USA*] (EA) ..... NEDA
National Exhaust Distributors Association/Undercar Specialists Association [*Defunct*] (EA) ..... NEDA/USA
National Exhibition [*British*] ..... NE
National Exhibition Centre [*British*] ..... NEC
National Ex-Offender Grant Alliance [*Defunct*] (EA) ..... NEGA
National Explorers and Collectors Association (EA) ..... NECA
National Export Expansion Council [*Terminated, 1973*] [*Department of Commerce*] ..... NEEC
National Export Meatworks Council [*Australia*] ..... NEMC
National Export Traffic League [*New York, NY*] (EA) ..... NETL
National Exposition of Contract Interior Furnishings ..... NEOCON
National Extension College [*England*] ..... NEC
National Extension Homemakers Council (EA) ..... NEHC
National Extra Fine [*Thread*] ..... NEF
National Eye and Health Foundation (EA) ..... NEHF
National Eye Care Project [*Foundation of the American Academy of Ophthalmology*] (EA) ..... NECP
National Eye Health Education Program [*Information service or system*] (IID) ..... NEHEP
National Eye Institute [*Formerly, NINDB*] [*Department of Health and Human Services Bethesda, MD*] [*National Institutes of Health*] ..... NEI
National Eye Research Foundation [*Later, NEHF*] (EA) ..... NERF
National Facsimile Network [*National Weather Service*] ..... NAFAX
National Faculty Association (NADA) ..... NFA
National Faculty Association of Community and Junior Colleges [*Later, NEA Higher Education Council*] ..... NFA
National Faculty Association of Community and Junior Colleges [*Later, NEA Higher Education Council*] ..... NFACJC
National Faculty Directory [*A publication*] ..... NFD
National Faculty Exchange (EA) ..... NFE
National Faculty of Humanities, Arts, and Sciences (EA) ..... NFHAS
National Fallout Monitoring Network ..... NFMN
National Fallout Shelter Survey [*Civil Defense*] ..... NFSS
National Families in Action (EA) ..... NFA
National Family Association for Deaf-Blind [*Sponsored by the Helen Keller National Center for Deaf-Blind Youths and Adults (HKNC)*] (PAZ) ..... NFADB
National Family Business Association [*Tarzana, CA*] (EA) ..... NFBA
National Family Business Council [*Northbrook, IL*] (EA) ..... NFBC
National Family Conciliation Council [*British*] (DI) ..... NFCC
National Family Council Against Drug Abuse [*Formerly, NFCDA*] (EA) ..... NFCADA
National Family Council on Drug Addiction [*Later, NFCADA*] (EA) ..... NFCDA
National Family Farm Coalition (EA) ..... NFFC
National Family Life Foundation (EA) ..... NFLF
National Family Opinion ..... NFO
National Family Planning and Reproductive Health Association (EA) ..... NFPRHA
National Fancy Rat Society [*British*] ..... NFRS
National Fancy Rat Society [*British*] (DBA) ..... NFRS
National Fantasy Fan Club for Disneyana Enthusiasts ..... NFFC
National Fantasy Fan Federation (EA) N3F
National Fantasy Fan Federation ..... NFFF
National Farm and Power Equipment Dealers Association [*Later, NAEDA*] (EA) ..... NFPEDA
National Farm Borrowers Association (EA) ..... NFBA
National Farm Bureau Federation ..... NFBF
National Farm Coalition [*Defunct*] (EA) ..... NFC
National Farm Home Editors Association [*Defunct*] (EA) ..... NFHEA
National Farm Products Marketing Council [*Canada*] ..... NFPMC
National Farm Products Marketing Council, Ottawa, ON, Canada [*Library symbol*] [*Library of Congress*] (LCLS) ..... CaOONFP
National Farm Products Marketing Council [*Conseil National de Commercialisation des Produits Agricoles*], Ottawa, Ontario [*Library symbol National Library of Canada*] (BIB) ..... OONFP
National Farm Worker Ministry (EA) ..... NFWM
National Farm Workers of America ..... NFWA
National Farm-City Council (EA) ..... NFCC
National Farmer [*A publication*] ..... Natn Farmer
National Farmers' Association [*Republic of Ireland*] (BI) ..... NFA
National Farmers Organization (EA) ..... NFO
National Farmers' Union [*British*] ..... NFU
National Farmers Union Library, Denver, CO [*Library symbol Library of Congress Obsolete*] (LCLS) ..... CoDFU
National Fashion Accessories Association (EA) ..... NHA
National Fashion Accessories Salesmen's Guild (EA) ..... NFASG
National Fastener Distributors Association (EA) ..... NFDA
National Fatherland Front [*Afghanistan*] [*Political party*] (FEA) ..... NFF
National Father's Day Committee (EA) ..... NFDC
National Fathers' Network [*An association*] (PAZ) ..... NFN
National Fats and Oils Brokers Association [*Defunct*] (EA) ..... NFOBA
National Fax Directory [*A publication*] ..... NFD
National Fax Directory [*A publication*] ..... NFXD
National Federated Craft (EA) ..... NFC
National Federated Electrical Association (MHDB) ..... NFEA
National Federation (AD) ..... Nat Fed
National Federation for Biblio/Poetry Therapy (EA) ..... NFBPT
National Federation for Catholic Youth Ministry (EA) ..... NFCYM
National Federation for Decency (EA) ..... NFD
National Federation for Specialty Nursing Organizations (EA) ..... NFSNO
National Federation for the Blind [*British*] (DBA) ..... NFBUK
National Federation for the Self-Employed and Small Businesses [*British*] (DBA) ..... NFSE
National Federation Interscholastic Coaches Association (EA) ..... NFICA
National Federation Interscholastic Music Association (EA) ..... NFIMA
National Federation Interscholastic Officials Association (EA) ..... NFIOA
National Federation Interscholastic Speech and Debate Association (EA) ..... NFISDA
National Federation Music Adjudicator Association (EA) ..... NFMAA
National Federation of Abstracting and Indexing Services (NITA) ..... NFAIS
National Federation of Abstracting and Information Services (EA) ..... NFAIS
National Federation of Advertising Agencies [*Later, IFAA*] (EA) ..... NFAA
National Federation of Agricultural Cooperative Associations [*Japan*] (EAIO) ..... ZEN-NOH
National Federation of American Hungarians (EA) ..... NFAH
National Federation of American Information Services [*International Council of Scientific Unions*] ..... NFAIS
National Federation of Anglers [*British*] (BI) ..... NFA
National Federation of Asian American United Methodists (EA) ..... NFAAUM
National Federation of Asian Indian Organizations in America [*Later, NFIAA*] (EA) ..... NFAIO
National Federation of Badger Groups [*British*] (DBA) ..... NFBG
National Federation of Bakery Students' Societies [*British*] (BI) ..... NFBSS
National Federation of Blind Citizens of Australia ..... NFBCA
National Federation of Buddhist Women's Associations [*Later, BCAFBWA*] (EA) ..... NFBWA
National Federation of Builders' and Plumbers' Merchants [*British*] (BI) ..... NFBPM
National Federation of Building Trades Employers [*British*] (DCTA) ..... NFBTE
National Federation of Building Trades Operatives [*British*] ..... NFBTO
National Federation of Bus Users [*British*] ..... NFBU
National Federation of Business and Professional Women's Clubs (EA) ..... BPW/USA
National Federation of Business and Professional Women's Clubs (WGA) ..... NFBPW
National Federation of Business and Professional Women's Clubs (EA) ..... NFBPWC
National Federation of Canadian University Students ..... NFCUS
National Federation of Catholic College Students [*Defunct*] (EA) ..... NFCCS
National Federation of Catholic Physicians' Guilds (EA) ..... NFCPG
National Federation of Catholic Seminarians [*Defunct*] (EA) ..... NFCS
National Federation of Citizen Band Radio Operators (EA) ..... NFCBRO
National Federation of City Farms [*British*] (EAIO) ..... NFCF
National Federation of Class Teachers (AIE) ..... NFCT
National Federation of Clay Industries [*British*] (BI) ..... NFCI
National Federation of Clubs for Divorced and Separated [*British*] (BI) ..... NFCDS
National Federation of Coffee Growers of Colombia [*See also FNCC*] (EA) ..... NFCGC
National Federation of Cold Storage and Ice Trades [*British*] (BI) ..... NFCSIT
National Federation of Community Associations [*British*] (DI) ..... NFCA
National Federation of Community Broadcasters (EA) ..... NFCB
National Federation of Community Development Credit Unions [*New York, NY*] (EA) ..... NFCDCU
National Federation of Community Organizations [*British*] (EAIO) ..... NFCO
National Federation of Construction Supervisors [*British*] (BI) ..... NFCS
National Federation of Constructional Glass Associations [*British*] (BI) ..... NFCGA
National Federation of Consumer Groups [*British*] (ILCA) ..... NFCG
National Federation of Continuative Teachers' Associations [*British*] ..... NFCTA
National Federation of Corn Trade Associations [*British*] (BI) ..... NFCTA
National Federation of Cuban-American Republican Women (EA) ..... NFCARW
National Federation of Data Processing Manufacturing (NITA) ..... NFDPM
National Federation of Democratic Women (EA) ..... NFDW
National Federation of Demolition Contractors [*British*] (EAIO) ..... NFDC
National Federation of Drapers and Allied Traders Ltd. [*Republic of Ireland*] (BI) ..... NFD
National Federation of Engineering and General Ironfounders [*British*] (BI) ..... NEGI

National Federation of Engineers' Tools Manufacturers (MHDB) .... NFETM
National Federation of Export Associations [*New York, NY*] (EA) .... NFEA
National Federation of Export Management Companies (EA) .... FEMCO
National Federation of Federal Employees (EA) .... NFFE
National Federation of Fish Friers [*British*] (BI) .... NFFF
National Federation of Fishermen [*Inactive*] (EA) .... NFF
National Federation of Fishermen's Organisations (EAIO) .... NFFO
National Federation of Fishmongers [*British*] (DBA) .... NFF
National Federation of Flemish Giant Breeders [*Later, NFFGRB*] .... NFFGB
National Federation of Flemish Giant Rabbit Breeders (EA) .... NFFGRB
National Federation of Freestone Quarry Owners [*British*] (BI) .... NFFQO
National Federation of Fruit and Potato Trades [*British*] (BI) .... NFFPT
National Federation of Furniture Trade Union [*British*] .... NFNTU
National Federation of Furniture Trade Unions [*British*] (BI) .... NFFTU
National Federation of Grain Cooperatives [*Later, NCFC*] (EA) .... NFGC
National Federation of Gramophone Societies (EAIO) .... NFGS
National Federation of Grandmother Clubs of America (EA) .... NFGCA
National Federation of Grange Mutual Insurance Companies [*Glastonbury, CT*] (EA) .... NFGMIC
National Federation of Hebrew Teachers and Principals [*Defunct*] (EA).... NFHTP
National Federation of Hispanics in Communication (EA) .... NFHC
National Federation of Housestaff Organizations (EA) .... NFHO
National Federation of Housing Associations [*British*] (DBA) .... NFHA
National Federation of Housing Coops [*British*] (DBA) .... NFHC
National Federation of Housing Counselors (EA) .... NFHC
National Federation of Independent Business [*San Mateo, CA*] (EA) .... NFIB
National Federation of Independent Scrap Yard Dealers (EA) .... NFISYD
National Federation of Independent Unions (EA) .... NFIU
National Federation of Indian American Associations (EA) .... NFIAA
National Federation of Indian Railwaymen .... NFIR
National Federation of Iron and Steel Merchants [*British*] (BI) .... NFISM
National Federation of Ironmongers' and Builders' Merchants' Staff Associations [*British*] (BI) .... FIBMA
National Federation of Jewish Men's Clubs (EA) .... NFJMC
National Federation of Kidney Patients Association [*British*] (DI) .... NFKPA
National Federation of Land Councils [*Australia*] .... NFLC
National Federation of Laymen (EA) .... NFL
National Federation of Licensed Practical Nurses .... LPN
National Federation of Licensed Practical Nurses (EA) .... NFLPN
National Federation of Local Cable Programmers (EA) .... NFLCP
National Federation of Master Painters and Decorators of England and Wales (BI) .... NFMP
National Federation of Master Window Cleaners [*British*] (DBA) .... NFMWC
National Federation of Meat Traders [*British*] (BI) .... NFMT
National Federation of Milk Hauler Associations (EA) .... NFMHA
National Federation of Modern Language Teachers Associations (EA) .... NFMLTA
National Federation of Music Clubs (EA) .... NFMC
National Federation of Music Societies [*British*] .... NFMS
National Federation of Nurses' Unions [*See also FNSII*] .... NFNU
National Federation of Off-Licence Holders Associations of England and Wales (BI) .... NFOHA
National Federation of Old Age Pensioners' Associations [*British*] (BI) .... NFOAPA
National Federation of Painting and Decorating Contractors [*British*] (DBA) .... NFPDC
National Federation of Paralegal Associations (EA) .... NFPA
National Federation of Parents and Friends of Gays (EA) .... NF/PFOG
National Federation of Parents for Drug-Free Youth (EA) .... NFP
National Federation of Permanent Holiday Camps Ltd. [*British*] (BI) .... NFPHC
National Federation of Plastering Contractors [*British*] (BI) .... NFPC
National Federation of Plumbers and Domestic Heating Engineers [*British*] (BI) .... NFPDHE
National Federation of Post Office Clerks [*Later, APWU*] .... NFPOC
National Federation of Postal and Telegraph Clerks [*A union*] [*British*] ...... NFPTC
National Federation of Press Women (EA) .... NFPW
National Federation of Priests' Councils (EA) .... NFPC
National Federation of Professional Organizations (EA) .... NFPO
National Federation of Professional Workers [*British*] (DI) .... NFPW
National Federation of Property Owners [*British*] (BI) .... NFPO
National Federation of Republican Women (EA) .... NFRW
National Federation of Retail Newsagents [*British*] .... NFRN
National Federation of Roofing Contractors [*British*] (EAIO) .... NFRC
National Federation of Sailing Schools [*British*] .... NFSS
National Federation of Sales Executives [*Later, Sales and Marketing Executives International*] .... NFSE
National Federation of Savings and Cooperative Credit Unions [*British*] (DBA) .... NFSCCU
National Federation of Scale and Weighing Machine Manufacturers [*British*] (DBA) .... NFSWMM
National Federation of Science Abstracting and Indexing Services [*Later, NFAIS*] (EA) .... NFSAIS
National Federation of Sea Anglers [*British*] .... NFSA
National Federation of Self Employed [*British*] .... NFSE
National Federation of Settlements [*Later, UNCA*] .... NFS
National Federation of Settlements and Neighborhood Centers [*Later, UNCA*] (EA) .... NFS & NC
National Federation of Societies for Clinical Social Work (EA) .... NFSCSW
National Federation of Spiritual Directors (EA) .... NFSD
National Federation of Spiritual Healers (EA) .... NFSH
National Federation of Stamp Clubs (EA) .... NFSC
National Federation of State High School Associations (EA) .... NFSHSA
National Federation of State High School Athletic Associations [*Later, NFSHSA*] (EA) .... NFSHSAA
National Federation of State Humanities Councils (EA) .... NFSHC

National Federation of State Poetry Societies (EA) .... NFSPS
National Federation of Students of German (EA) .... NFSG
National Federation of Sub-Postmasters [*British*] (DBA) .... NFSP
National Federation of Taxicab Associations [*British*] (DBA) .... NFTA
National Federation of Telephone Workers [*Later, CWA*] .... NFTW
National Federation of Temple Brotherhoods (EA) .... NFTB
National Federation of Temple Sisterhoods (EA) .... NFTS
National Federation of Terrazzo-Mosaic Specialists [*British*] (BI) .... NFTMS
National Federation of Textiles, New York, NY [*Library symbol Library of Congress*] (LCLS) .... NNFT
National Federation of the Blind (EA) .... NFB
National Federation of the Grand Order of Pachyderm Clubs (EA) .... NFGOPC
National Federation of Tobacco Workers [*A union*] [*British*] .... NFTW
National Federation of Vehicle Trades [*British*] (BI) .... NFVT
National Federation of Voluntary Literacy Schemes [*British*] .... NFVLS
National Federation of Wholesale Grocers and Provision Merchants [*British*] (BI) .... NFWG
National Federation of Wholesalers and Poultry Merchants [*British*] (DBA) .... NFWPM
National Federation of Woman's Exchanges (EA) .... NFWE
National Federation of Women Workers [*British*] .... NFWW
National Federation of Women's Institutes [*British*] .... NFWI
National Federation of Young Farmers' Clubs (EAIO) .... NFYFC
National Federation Party [*Fiji*] [*Political party*] (PPW) .... NFP
National Federation Post Office Motor Vehicle Employees [*Later, APWU*] (EA) .... POMV
National Feed Ingredients Association (EA) .... NFIA
National Feeder Pig Marketing Association (EA) .... NFPMA
National Fellowship of Child Care Executives (EA) .... NFCCE
National Fellowship of Grace Brethren Ministers (EA) .... NFGBM
National Fellowship of Methodist Musicians (EA) .... NFMM
National Feminist Therapist Association (EA) .... NFTA
National Fencing Coaches Association of America (EA) .... NFCAA
National Fenestration Council [*Later, PGMC*] (EA) .... NFC
National Fenestration Rating Council (EA) .... NFRC
National Fenton Glass Society (EA) .... NFGS
National Fertility Center (DAVI) .... NFC
National Fertility Study .... NFS
National Fertilizer Development Center [*Tennessee Valley Authority*] [*Muscle Shoals, AL*] .... NFDC
National Fertilizer Solutions Association (EA) .... NFSA
National Festival of Music for Youth (AIE) .... NFMY
National Fetal Mortality Survey [*Department of Health and Human Services*] (GFGA) .... NFMS
National FFA [*Future Farmers of America*] Organization (EA) .... NFFAO
National Fibre Can and Tube Association [*Later, CCTI*] (EA) .... NFCTA
National Field Archery Association (EA) .... NFAA
National Field Archery Society [*British*] (DBA) .... NFAS
National Field Research [*British*] .... NFR
National Field Service Corp. [*Suffern, NY*] [*Telecommunications*] (TSSD) .... NFS
National Field Volunteer [*Red Cross*] .... NFV
National Fillings Trades Association [*British*] (DBA) .... NFTA
National Film and Television School [*British*] .... NFTS
National Film and Television Sound Archives [*National Film Board of Canada*] [*UTLAS symbol*] .... NFT
National Film and Video Productions [*Australia*] .... NFVP
National Film Archive [*British Film Institute*] .... NFA
National Film Archives, Film Canadiana [*UTLAS symbol*] .... FIL
National Film Archives, Public Archives [*Archives Nationales du Film, Archives Publiques*] Ottawa, Ontario [*Library symbol National Library of Canada*] (NLC) .... OOANF
National Film Board [*Canada*] (WDMC) .... NFB
National Film Board [*Office National du Film*], Halifax, Nova Scotia [*Library symbol National Library of Canada*] (NLC) .... NSHNF
National Film Board, Montreal, PQ, Canada [*Library symbol Library of Congress*] (LCLS) .... CaOONF
National Film Board, Montreal, PQ, Canada [*Library symbol*] [*Library of Congress*] (LCLS) .... CaQMNF
National Film Board, Montreal Quebec [*Formerly, Ottawa*] [*Office National du Film, Montreal (Anciennement Ottawa)*] [*Library symbol*] [*National Library of Canada*] (NLC) .... QMNF
National Film Board, National Information and Distribution System, Montreal, PQ,Canada [*Library symbol Library of Congress*] (LCLS).... CaQMNFNI
National Film Board of Canada [*UTLAS symbol*] .... NFB
National Film Board of Canada .... NFBC
National Film Board, Phototheque, Ottawa, ON, Canada [*Library symbol Library of Congress*] (LCLS) .... CaOOICP
National Film Board, Pretoria, South Africa [*Library symbol Library of Congress*] (LCLS) .... SaPNFB
National Film Board Reference Library [*UTLAS symbol*] .... NFR
National Film Carriers (EA) .... NFC
National Film Finance Corp. [*British*] (BI) .... NFFC
National Film Library (NADA) .... NFL
National Film Music Council [*Defunct*] .... NFMC
National Film Society [*Defunct*] (EA) .... NFS
National Film, Television, and Sound Archives [*Ottawa*] [*UTLAS symbol*] .... NFA
National Film, Television, and Sound Archives [*Canada*] .... NFTSA
National Film Theatre [*British*] .... NFT
National Film Unit (BARN) .... NFU
National Filter Analysis Network [*Environmental Protection Agency*] (GFGA) .... NFAN
National Finals Rodeo Committee (EA) .... NFRC
National Finance Center (USDC) .... NFC
National Finch and Softbill Society (EA) .... NFSS
National Fine [*Thread*] .... NF

National Fire Academy ... NFA
National Fire Academy Library, Emmitsburg, MD [*OCLC symbol*] (OCLC) ... NFP
National Fire Brigades Union (ROG) ... NFBU
National Fire Code ... NFC
National Fire Danger Rating System [*US Forest Service*] ... NFDRS
National Fire Incident Reporting System [*Federal Emergency Management Agency*] (GFGA) ... NFIRS
National Fire Loss Data System [*Military*] (PDAA) ... NFLDS
National Fire Prevention and Control Administration [*Later, United States Fire Administration*] [*Department of Commerce*] ... NFPCA
National Fire Prevention and Control Administration, Washington, DC [*Library symbol Library of Congress*] (LCLS) ... DFCA
National Fire Protection Association (EA) ... NFPA
National Fire Service [*British*] ... NFS
National Fire Sprinkler Association (EA) ... NFSA
National Fire Waste Council ... NFWC
National Firearms Act ... NFA
National Firearms Association [*Canada*] ... NFA
National Firebird Club (EA) ... NFC
National Fireplace Makers Association [*British*] (BI) ... NFMA
National Fish and Wildlife Foundation (EPA) ... NFWF
National Fish Hatchery ... NFH
National Fish Health Research Laboratory [*Department of the Interior*] [*Kearneysville, WV*] (GRD) ... NFHRL
National Fish Meal and Oil Association (EA) ... NFMOA
National Fisheries Adjustment Program Committee [*Australia*] ... NFAPC
National Fisheries Center [*Marine science*] (OSRA) ... NFI
National Fisheries Center (USDC) ... NFI
National Fisheries Center, Kearneysville, WV [*OCLC symbol*] (OCLC) ... UDG
National Fisheries Center - Leetown [*Department of the Interior*] (GRD) ... NFC-L
National Fisheries Contaminant Research Center (EA) ... NFCRC
National Fisheries Education and Research Foundation (EA) ... NFERF
National Fisheries Institute (EA) ... NFI
National Fishermen's Association [*Australia*] ... NFA
National Fishing Lure Collectors Club (EA) ... NFLCC
National Fitness Association [*Later, NHCA*] (EA) ... NFA
National Fitness Foundation (EA) ... NFF
National Fitness Southern Recreation Association [*Australia*] ... NFSRA
National Flag Day Foundation (EA) ... NFDF
National Flag Foundation (EA) ... NFF
National Flaxseed Processors Association (EA) ... NFPA
National Flexible Packaging Association [*Later, FPA*] (EA) ... NFPA
National Flight Data Center [*FAA*] ... NFDC
National Flight Data Digest [*FAA*] (TAG) ... NFDD
National Flight Data Processing System [*ICAO*] (DA) ... NFDPS
National Flight Nurses Association (EA) ... NFNA
National Flight Paramedics Association (EA) ... NFPA
National Flood Frequency Program [*Computer science*] ... NFF
National Flood Insurance Program [*Federal Emergency Management Agency*] ... NFIP
National Flood Insurance Program System [*Federal Emergency Management Agency*] (GFGA) ... NFIPS
National Flood Insurers Association [*Defunct*] (EA) ... NFIA
National Floor Covering Association [*Canada*] (EAIO) ... NFCA
National Floor Products Co., Inc. ... NAFCO
National Florist Association (EA) ... NFA
National Flotation Health Care Foundation (EA) ... NFHCF
National Fluid Power Association (EA) ... NFPA
National Flute Association (EA) ... NFA
National Flying Farmers Association [*Later, International Flying Farmers*] ... NFFA
National Flying Service [*British*] ... NFS
National Focal Points (DCTA) ... NFP
National Folk Festival Association [*Later, National Council for the TraditionalArts*] ... NFFA
National Food Administration ... NFA
National Food and Agricultural Council (NADA) ... NFAC
National Food and Conservation through Swine (EA) ... FACTS
National Food and Energy Council (EA) ... NFEC
National Food and Nutrition Policy [*Australia*] ... NFNP
National Food Bank Network (EA) ... NFBN
National Food Brokers Association (EA) ... NFBA
National Food Conference Association (EA) ... NFC
National Food Distributors Association (EA) ... NFDA
National Food, Drug, and Cosmetic Association of Manufacturers and Distributors [*Defunct*] (EA) ... NFDCAMD
National Food Processors Association (EA) ... NFPA
National Food Service Association (EA) ... NFSA
National Food Situation [*Series*] [*A publication*] ... NFS
National Food Standards Agreement [*Australia*] ... NFSA
National Food Survey [*British*] ... NFS
National Foot Health Council [*Defunct*] (EA) ... NFHC
National Football Conference [*of NFL*] ... NFC
National Football Foundation and Hall of Fame (EA) ... NFF
National Football League (EA) ... NFL
National Football League Alumni (EA) ... NFLA
National Football League Players Association (EA) ... NFLPA
National Footwear Manufacturers Association [*Later, FIA*] ... NFMA
National Foreign Assessment Center [*CIA*] ... NFAC
National Foreign Intelligence Board [*Formerly, USIB*] [*Military*] ... NFIB
National Foreign Intelligence Plan for Human Resources (MCD) ... NPHR
National Foreign Intelligence Program [*DoD*] (MCD) ... NAFIP
National Foreign Intelligence Program [*DoD*] ... NFIP
National Foreign Trade Council (EA) ... NAFTRAC
National Foreign Trade Council [*New York, NY*] (EA) ... NFTC
National Foremen's Association [*A union*] [*British*] ... NFA
National Forensic Association (EA) ... NFA
National Forensic Center (EA) ... NFC
National Forensic League (EA) ... NFL
National Forest (IIA) ... NF
National Forest Industries Association [*Australia*] ... NFIA
National Forest Industries Campaign Association [*Australia*] ... NFICA
National Forest Industries Training Council [*Australia*] ... NFITC
National Forest Management Act (GFGA) ... NFMA
National Forest Products Association [*Washington, DC*] ... NFoPA
National Forest Products Association (EA) ... NFPA
National Forest Recreation Association (EA) ... NFRA
National Forest Reservation Commission [*Terminated, 1976; functions transferred to Department of Agriculture*] ... NFRC
National Forest Service Volunteers Program (EA) ... NFSVP
National Forest System (GNE) ... NFS
National Foresters League (NADA) ... NFL
National Formulary [*A publication listing standard drugs*] ... NF
National Forum [*A publication*] (BRI) ... Nat For
National Forum for Black Public Administrators (EA) ... NFBPA
National Forum for Executive Women [*Washington, DC*] (EA) ... NFEW
National Forum for the Advancement of Aquatics (EA) ... NFAA
National Forum Foundation (EA) ... NFF
National Forum of Catholic Parent Organizations [*Defunct*] (EA) ... NFCPO
National Forum of Greek Orthodox Church Musicians (EA) ... NFGOCM
National Forum on Criminal Justice [*Formerly, NICD*] [*Inactive*] (EA) ... NFCJ
National Foster Care Association [*British*] (EAIO) ... NFCA
National Foster Parent Association (EA) ... NFPA
National Foundation ... NF
National Foundation for Advancement in the Arts (EA) ... NFAA
National Foundation for Affordable Housing Solutions (EA) ... NFAHS
National Foundation for Asthma (EA) ... NFA
National Foundation for Asthmatic Children at Tucson [*Later, NFA*] (EA) ... NFAC
National Foundation for Biomedical Research [*An association*] ... NFBR
National Foundation for Brain Research (EA) ... NFBR
National Foundation for Cancer Research (EA) ... NFCR
National Foundation for Children's Hearing Education and Research (EA) ... CHEAR
National Foundation for Conservation and Environmental Officers [*Defunct*] (EA) ... NFCEO
National Foundation for Consumer Credit [*Silver Spring, MD*] (EA) ... NFCC
National Foundation for Depressive Illness (EA) ... NAFDI
National Foundation for Ectodermal Dysplasias (EA) ... NFED
National Foundation for Education in American Citizenship (EA) ... NFEAC
National Foundation for Educational Research in England and Wales (IID) ... NFER
National Foundation for Environmental Control (EA) ... NFEC
National Foundation for Eye Research (EA) ... NFER
National Foundation for Facial Reconstruction (EA) ... NFFR
National Foundation for Genetics and Neuromuscular Disease [*Later, NGF*] ... NFGND
National Foundation for Happy Horsemanship for the Handicapped (EA) ... HHFTH
National Foundation for Health, Physical Education, and Recreation [*Defunct*] ... NFHPER
National Foundation for History of Chemistry (EA) ... NFHC
National Foundation for Ileitis and Colitis (EA) ... NFIC
National Foundation for Ileitis and Colitis Sports Council (EA) ... NFICSC
National Foundation for Infantile Paralysis [*Later, MDBDF*] ... NFIP
National Foundation for Infectious Diseases (EA) ... NFID
National Foundation for Jewish Culture (EA) ... NFJC
National Foundation for Jewish Genetic Diseases (EA) ... NFJGD
National Foundation for Junior Museums [*Later, NSYF*] ... NFJM
National Foundation for Long Term Health Care [*Defunct*] (EA) ... NFLTHC
National Foundation for Metabolic Research [*Defunct*] (EA) ... NFMR
National Foundation for Muscular Dystrophy ... NFMD
National Foundation for Neuromuscular Diseases [*Later, NGF*] (EA) ... NFND
National Foundation for Non-Invasive Diagnostics (EA) ... NFNID
National Foundation for Peroneal Muscular Atrophy (EA) ... NFPMA
National Foundation for Professional Legal Assistants (EA) ... NFPLA
National Foundation for Research in Medicine (EA) ... NFRM
National Foundation for Rural Medical Care [*Defunct*] (EA) ... NFRMC
National Foundation for the Australian Musical ... NFAM
National Foundation for the Chemically Hypersensitive (EA) ... NFCH
National Foundation for the Handicapped and Disabled [*Defunct*] (EA) ... NFHD
National Foundation for the Improvement of Education (EA) ... NFIE
National Foundation for the March of Dimes (NADA) ... NFMD
National Foundation for the Prevention of Oral Disease [*Defunct*] (EA) ... NFPOD
National Foundation for the Study and Treatment of Pathological Gambling [*Defunct*] (EA) ... NFSTPG
National Foundation for the Study of Equal Employment [*Washington, DC*] (EA) ... NFSEEP
National Foundation for Unemployment Compensation and Workers Compensation (EA) ... NFUCWC
National Foundation for Wholistic Medicine [*Defunct*] (EA) ... NFWH
National Foundation for Women Business Owners ... NFWBO
National Foundation Manufactured Home Owners (EA) ... NFMHO
National Foundation of Arts and Letters (WDAA) ... NFAL
National Foundation of Dentistry for the Handicapped (EA) ... NFDH
National Foundation of Funeral Service (EA) ... NFFS
National Foundation of Wheelchair Tennis (EA) ... NFWT
National Foundation on the Arts and Humanities ... NFAH
National Foundation on the Arts and Humanities Act [*1965*] ... NFAHA
National Foundry and Engineering Training Association [*British*] ... NFETA
National Foundry Association (EA) ... NFA

National Fox Hunters Association (EA) ..... NFHA
National Fragile X Foundation (EA) ..... NFXF
National Frame Builders Association (EA) ..... NFBA
National Franchise Association Coalition (EA) ..... NFAC
National Franchisee Association (EA) ..... NFA
National Fraternal Congress [Later, NFCA] ..... NFC
National Fraternal Congress of America [Naperville, IL] (EA) ..... NFCA
National Fraternal Flag Day Foundation [Defunct] (EA) ..... NFFDF
National Fraternal Society of the Deaf [Mount Prospect, IL] (EA) ..... NFSD
National Fraternity of Student Musicians (EA) ..... NFSM
National Fraud Information Center ..... NFIC
National Free Clinic Council [Superseded by NCAHCP] ..... NFCC
National Free Enterprise Foundation [Australia] ..... NFEF
National Free Lance Photographers Association (EA) ..... NFLPA
National Freedom Academy (EA) ..... NFA
National Freedom Shrine Foundation (EA) ..... NFSF
National Freehold Building Society [British] ..... NFBS
National Freight Consortium (ODBW) ..... NFC
National Freight Corp. [British] ..... NFC
National Freight Group ..... NFG
National Freight Transportation Association [Rocky River, OH] (EA) ..... NFTA
National Fresh Water Fishing Hall of Fame ..... NFWHF
National Friends of Public Broadcasting (EA) ..... NFPB
National Froebel Foundation [British] (BI) ..... NFF
National Front [British Political party] (CDAI) ..... NF
National Front Constitutional Movement [British] ..... NFCM
National Front for the Liberation of Angola ..... NFLA
National Front for the Liberation of South Vietnam ..... NFLSV
National Front of Ahvaz [Iran] ..... NFA
National Front of Zimbabwe (PPW) ..... NFZ
National Frozen Food Association (EA) ..... NFFA
National Frozen Food Distributors Association [Later, NFFA] ..... NFFDA
National Frozen Pizza Institute ..... NFPI
National Frozen Vegetable Council [Later, FVC] (EA) ..... NFVC
National Fructose Center (EA) ..... NFC
National Fruit and Syrup Manufacturers Association (EA) ..... NFSMA
National Frumps of America (EA) ..... NFA
National Fuchsia Society (EA) ..... NFS
National Fuel Credit Association [Defunct] ..... NFCA
National Fuel Gas Co. [Associated Press] (SAG) ..... NatFGs
National Fuel Gas Co. [NYSE symbol] (SPSG) ..... NFG
National Fuelcorp Ltd. [Vancouver Stock Exchange symbol] ..... NLF
National Full-Scale Aerodynamics Complex [Ames Research Center, CA] [NASA] ..... NFAC
National Fund Chairman [or Co-chairman] [Red Cross] ..... NFC
National Fund for Graduate Nursing Education [Defunct] ..... NFGNE
National Fund for Medical Education (EA) ..... NFME
National Fund for Research into Crippling Diseases [British] (DI) ..... NFRCD
National Fund for Research into Poliomyelitis and Other Crippling Diseases [British] (BI) ..... NFPR
National Fund Leadership [Group] [Red Cross] ..... NFL
National Funeral Directors and Morticians Association (EA) ..... NFDMA
National Funeral Directors Association (EA) ..... NFDA
National Furniture Traffic Conference (EA) ..... NFTC
National Furniture Warehousemen's Association [Later, NMSA] (EA) ..... NFWA
National Fusion Energy Computer Center [Lawrence Livermore National Laboratory] (MCD) ..... NFECC
National Futures Association (EA) ..... NFA
National Gadget Manufacturers Association ..... NGMA
National Gallery [London] (WDAA) ..... NAT GAL
National Gallery (AD) ..... Nat Gal
National Gallery [London] ..... NG
National Gallery of Art [Washington, DC] ..... NGA
National Gallery of Art, Washington, DC [Library symbol Library of Congress] (LCLS) ..... DNGA
National Gallery of Art, Washington, DC [OCLC symbol] (OCLC) ..... NGA
National Gallery of Art, Washington, DC ..... NGW
National Gallery of Australia ..... NGA
National Gallery of Canada ..... NGC
National Gallery of Canada Library [UTLAS symbol] ..... NGA
National Gallery of Canada, Ottawa, ON, Canada [Library symbol Library of Congress] (LCLS) ..... CaOONG
National Gallery of Canada [Galerie Nationale du Canada] Ottawa, Ontario [Library symbol National Library of Canada] (NLC) ..... OONG
National Gambling Commission (NADA) ..... NGC
National Gaming Corp. [NASDAQ symbol] (SAG) ..... NAGC
National Gaming Corp. [Associated Press] (SAG) ..... NatGam
National Garden Bureau (EA) ..... NGB
National Garden Institute ..... NGI
National Gardening Association (EA) ..... NGA
National Gardens Scheme Charitable Trust (EAIO) ..... NGS
National Gas & Oil Co. [Associated Press] (SAG) ..... NatGsO
National Gas & Oil Corp. [AMEX symbol] (SPSG) ..... NLG
National Gas & Oil Corp. [Associated Press] (SAG) ..... NtGsO
National Gas Measurement Association (EA) ..... NGMA
National Gas Outlet [Thread] ..... NGO
National Gas Policy Act (GFGA) ..... NGPA
National Gas Straight [Thread] ..... NGS
National Gas Taper [Thread] ..... NGT
National Gas Turbine Establishment [British] ..... NGTE
National Gasohol Commission [Defunct] (EA) ..... NGC
National Gathering [Jordan] [A publication] (BJA) ..... NG
National Gaucher Foundation (EA) ..... NGF
National Gay Alliance for Young Adults (EA) ..... NGAYA
National Gay and Lesbian Task Force (EA) ..... NGLTF

National Gay Health Education Foundation (EA) ..... NGHEF
National Gay Rights Advocates [Defunct] (EA) ..... NGRA
National Gay Student Center [Defunct] (EA) ..... NGSC
National Gay Task Force [Later, NGLTF] (EA) ..... NGTF
National Gay Youth Network (EA) ..... NGYN
National Gender Selection Center (EA) ..... NGSC
National Genealogical Society (EA) ..... NGS
National Genealogical Society Quarterly [A publication] (BRI) ..... NGSQ
National Genealogical Society, Washington, DC [Library symbol Library of Congress] (LCLS) ..... DNGS
National Genetics Foundation [Defunct] (EA) ..... NGF
National Geochemical Data Bank [Natural Environment Research Council] [Information service or system] (IID) ..... NGDB
National Geodetic Information Branch [National Oceanic and Atmospheric Administration] ..... NGIB
National Geodetic Information Center [National Oceanic and Atmospheric Administration] (IID) ..... NGIC
National Geodetic Reference System [National Oceanic and Atmospheric Administration] ..... NGRS
National Geodetic Satellite Program [NASA] ..... NGSP
National Geodetic Survey [National Oceanic and Atmospheric Administration] ..... NGS
National Geodetic Survey Information Center [National Oceanic and Atmospheric Administration] (IID) ..... NGSIC
National Geodetic Survey Operations Center [National Oceanic and Atmospheric Administration] ..... NGSCO
National Geodetic Vertical Datum [National Oceanic and Atmospheric Administration] ..... NGVD
National Geographic Magazine [A publication] (AD) ..... Nat Geog Mag
National Geographic Names Data Base [Geological Survey] [Database] ..... NGN
National Geographic Service ..... NGS
National Geographic Society (EA) ..... NGS
National Geographic Society Education Foundation (EA) ..... NGSEF
National Geographic Society, Washington, DC [Library symbol Library of Congress] (LCLS) ..... DNG
National Geophysical and Solar-Terrestrial Data Center [National Oceanic and Atmospheric Administration] (IID) ..... NGSDC
National Geophysical and Solar-Terrestrial Data Center [National Oceanic and Atmospheric Administration] ..... NGSTDC
National Geophysical Data Center [Later, NGSDC] [Boulder, CO] [National Oceanic and Atmospheric Administration] (MCD) ..... NGDC
National Geoscience Mapping Accord [Australia] ..... NGMA
National Geriatrics Society (EA) ..... NGS
National Ghost Ranch Foundation (EA) ..... NGRF
National GI Pipe Smokers Club of America (EA) ..... NGIPSCA
National Gift and Art Association (EA) ..... NG & A
National Girls Athletic Association [Defunct] ..... NGAA
National Giro Centre [British] (DCTA) ..... NGC
National Gladiolus Society (EA) ..... NGS
National Glass Association (EA) ..... NGA
National Glass Clubs (EA) ..... NGC
National Glass Dealers Association [Later, NGA] (EA) ..... NGDA
National Gliding Association [Later, SSA] ..... NGA
National Gloster Club (EA) ..... NGC
National Goals Research Staff ..... NGRS
National Gold Star Mothers [Defunct] (EA) ..... NGSM
National Goldfish Society ..... NGS
National Golf Clubs Advisory Association [British] (DBA) ..... NGCAA
National Golf Foundation (EA) ..... NGF
National Golf Properties [Associated Press] (SAG) ..... NatGolf
National Golf Properties [NYSE symbol] (SPSG) ..... TEE
National Golf Salesmen Association [Defunct] (EA) ..... NGSA
National Gospel Music Association (EA) ..... NGMA
National Governing Body [United States Olympic Committee] ..... NGB
National Government of the Republic of China ..... NGRC
National Governors' Association (EA) ..... NGA
National Governors Conference [Later, NGA] ..... NGC
National Graduate Fellowship Program [Department of Education] (GFGA) ..... NGFP
National Graduate University, Arlington, VA [Library symbol Library of Congress] (LCLS) ..... ViArNG
National Grain and Feed Association (EA) ..... NGFA
National Grain Exchange [Australia] ..... NGE
National Grain Trade Council (EA) ..... NGTC
National Grand Lodge, International Order of Good Templars [Later, NCUSIOGT] (EA) ..... NGLIOGT
National Grange (EA) ..... NG
National Graniteware Society (EA) ..... NGS
National Grant Agency ..... NGA
National Grants Management Association (AAGC) ..... NGMA
National Graphic Arts Dealers Association (EA) ..... NGADA
National Graphical Association [British printers' union] ..... NGA
National Grassland Demonstration [British] ..... NGD
National Grave's Disease Foundation (EA) ..... NGDF
National Greenhouse Advisory Committee [Australia] ..... NGAC
National Greenhouse Manufacturers Association (EA) ..... NGMA
National Greentown Glass Association (EA) ..... NGGA
National Greyhound Association (EA) ..... NGA
National Greyhound Racing Club [British] (DI) ..... NGRC
National Grid [British Ordnance Survey maps] ..... NG
National Grid Co. [British ICAO designator] (FAAC) ..... GRD
National Grocers Association (EA) ..... NGA
National Ground Water Information Center [National Water Well Association] [Information service or system] (IID) ..... NGWIC
National Group of Unit Trusts [British] (DI) ..... NGUT

National Guard [*or Guardsman*] ... NG
National Guard [*Hawaii*] [*Seismograph station code, US Geological Survey*] (SEIS) ... NGH
National Guard Air Corps (WDAA) ... NGAC
National Guard and Army Reserve Policy ... NGARP
National Guard Association of the United States (EA) ... NGAUS
National Guard Association of the United States, Washington, DC [*Library symbol*] [*Library of Congress*] (LCLS) ... DNGuA
National Guard Bureau [*Army*] ... NGB
National Guard Computer Center ... NGCC
National Guard Intelligence Center [*USA*] ... NGIC
National Guard Not in Federal Service ... NGNF
National Guard of the United States ... NGUS
National Guard Officer Candidate School ... NGOCS
National Guard on Field Training Exercises ... NGFT
National Guard Personnel, Army ... NGPA
National Guard Professional Education Center [*North Little Rock, AR*] ... NGPEC
National Guard Register ... NGR
National Guard Regulations ... NGR
National Guard State of New York (HGAA) ... NGSNY
National Guard Technician (MCD) ... NGT
National Guard Volunteer Corps [*British military*] (DMA) ... NGVC
National Guild of Catholic Psychiatrists (EA) ... NGCP
National Guild of Churchmen (EA) ... NGC
National Guild of Community Music Schools [*Later, NGCSA*] (EA) ... NGCMS
National Guild of Community Schools of the Arts (EA) ... NGCSA
National Guild of Decoupeurs (EA) ... NGD
National Guild of Hypnotists (EA) ... NGH
National Guild of Piano Teachers (EA) ... NGPT
National Guild of Professional Paperhangers (EA) ... NGPP
National Guild of Telephonists [*British*] (BI) ... NGT
National Guilds of St. Paul (EA) ... NGSP
National Guinea Club ... NGC
National Gymnastics Judges Association (EA) ... NGJA
National Gypsum Wrrt [*NASDAQ symbol*] (TTSB) ... NGCOW
National Gypsy Council [*British*] (DBA) ... NGC
National Gypsy Education Council [*British*] ... NGEC
National Hail Research Experiment ... NHRE
National Hairdressers and Cosmetologists Association (EA) ... NHCA
National Hairdressers' Association [*British*] (BI) ... NHA
National Hairdressers' Federation [*British*] (BI) ... NHF
National Hamiltonian Party (EA) ... NHP
National Hand Embroidery and Novelty Manufacturers Association [*Defunct*] (EA) ... NHENMA
National Hand Knitting Yarn Association [*Later, NHKYC*] (EA) ... NHKYA
National Hand Knitting Yarn Committee [*Defunct*] (EA) ... NHKYC
National Handbag and Accessories Salesmen's Association (EA) ... NHASA
National Handbag Association (EA) ... NHA
National Handcraft Society [*Commercial firm*] (EA) ... NHS
National Handicapped Foundation (EA) ... NHF
National Handicapped Skiers Association [*British*] (DBA) ... NHSA
National Handicapped Sports (EA) ... NHS
National Handicapped Sports and Recreation Association [*Later, NHS*] (EA) ... NHSRA
National Handle Manufacturers Association [*Defunct*] (EA) ... NHMA
National Harbours Board [*Canada*] ... NHB
National Harbours Board, Ottawa, ON, Canada [*Library symbol Library of Congress*] (LCLS) ... CaOOHB
National Hardwood Lumber Association (EA) ... NHLA
National Havurah Committee (EA) ... NHC
National Havurah Coordinating Committee (EA) ... NHCC
National Hay Association (EA) ... NHA
National Hay Fever Relief Association [*Defunct*] (EA) ... NHFRA
National Head Injury Foundation (EA) ... NHIF
National Head Start Association (EA) ... NHSA
National Headache Foundation (EA) ... NHF
National Headquarters ... NHQ
National Health Agencies (EA) ... NHA
National Health Agencies for the Combined Federal Campaign [*Formerly, FSCNHA*] [*Later, NVHA*] (EA) ... NHACFC
National Health Agencies Library, New York, NY [*Library symbol Library of Congress Obsolete*] (LCLS) ... NNNH
National Health and Medical Research Council (DAVI) ... NHMRC
National Health and Nutritional Examination Survey ... NHANES
National Health and Safety Awareness Center [*Defunct*] (EA) ... NHSAC
National Health and Welfare Library, Ottawa, ON, Canada [*Library symbol Library of Congress*] (LCLS) ... CaOONH
National Health and Welfare Mutual Life Insurance Association [*Formerly, NHWRA*] (EA) ... NHW
National Health and Welfare Retirement Association [*Later, NHW*] (EA) ... NHWRA
National Health Association ... NHA
National Health Awareness Center [*Later, NHSAC*] (EA) ... NHAC
National Health Board ... NHB
National Health Care Campaign [*Defunct*] (EA) ... NHCC
National Health Care Expenditures Study (DHSM) ... NHCES
National Health Care Foundation for the Deaf [*Later, Deaf-REACH*] (EA) ... NHCFD
National Health Care Survey [*Department of Health and Human Services*] (GFGA) ... NHCS
National Health Club Association (EA) ... NHCA
National Health Council (EA) ... NHC
National Health Education Foundation ... NHEF
National Health Enhancement Systems, Inc. [*NASDAQ symbol*] (NQ) ... NHES
National Health Enhancement Systems, Inc. [*Associated Press*] (SAG) ... NtHlthE
National Health Examination Survey [*Department of Health and Human Services*] (GFGA) ... NHES
National Health Federation (EA) ... NHF
National Health Foundation (NADA) ... NHF
National Health Information Clearinghouse [*Public Health Service*] [*Later, ODPHP Health Information Center*] (IID) ... NHIC
National Health Insurance [*British*] ... NHI
National Health Interview Survey [*Department of Health and Human Services*] (GFGA) ... NHIS
National Health Interview Survey of Child Health [*Department of Health and Human Services*] ... NHISCH
National Health Investors [*NYSE symbol*] (SPSG) ... NHI
National Health Investors [*Associated Press*] (SAG) ... NtHlt
National Health Investors [*Associated Press*] (SAG) ... NtHltI
National Health Law Program (EA) ... NHeLP
National Health Lawyers Association (EA) ... NHLA
National Health Planning and Resource Development Act [*1974*] (DHSM) ... NHRD
National Health Planning Information Center [*Public Health Service*] [*Database*] (IID) ... NHPIC
National Health Policy Forum (EA) ... NHPF
National Health Professions Placement Network ... NHPP
National Health Research and Development Program [*Canada*] ... NHRDP
National Health Research Center (DAVI) ... NHRC
National Health Research Institutes [*Taiwan*] ... NHRI
National Health Resources Advisory Committee [*Terminated, 1978*] [*General Services Administration*] (EGAO) ... NHRAC
National Health Review Board [*Proposed medical-care price regulator*] (ECON) ... NHRB
National Health Screening Council for Volunteer Organizations (EA) ... NHSCVO
National Health Service [*British*] ... NHS
National Health Service Audit Staff [*Department of Health and Social Security*] [*British*] ... NHSAS
National Health Service Corps [*Department of Health and Human Services*] ... NHSC
National Health Survey ... NHS
National Health Survey Division [*of OSG*] ... NHSD
National Healthcare Antifraud Association [*Address unknown*] (EA) ... NHAS
National Healthcare Ltd. [*AMEX symbol*] (SPSG) ... NHC
National Healthcare Ltd. [*Associated Press*] (SAG) ... NHltCre
National Hearing Aid Society (EA) ... NHAS
National Hearing Association (EA) ... NHA
National Hearing Conservation Association (EA) ... NHCA
National Heart and Lung Institute [*Later, NHLBI*] [*National Institutes of Health*] ... NHLI
National Heart Attack Alert Program ... NHAAP
National Heart Education Research Society (EA) ... HERS
National Heart Foundation (NADA) ... NHF
National Heart Institute [*Later, NHLI, NHLBI*] [*National Institutes of Health*] ... NHI
National Heart, Lung, and Blood Advisory Council [*National Institutes of Health*] ... NHLBAC
National Heart, Lung, and Blood Information Center (PAZ) ... NHLBIC
National Heart, Lung, and Blood Institute [*Bethesda, MD*] [*National Institutes of Health*] ... NHLBI
National Heart Research Project (EA) ... NHRP
National Heart Savers Association (EA) ... NHSA
National Hebrew Culture Council (EA) ... NHCC
National Hemi Owners Association (EA) ... NHOA
National Hemophilia Association (DAVI) ... NHA
National Hemophilia Foundation (EA) ... NHF
National Herb Study Society (EA) ... NHSS
National Hereford Hog Record Association (EA) ... NHHRA
National Heritage [*British*] [*An association*] (DBA) ... NH
National Heritage Act [*Protects national treasures from sale out of the country*] [*British*] ... NHA
National Heritage Ltd., Toronto, ON, Canada [*Library symbol Library of Congress*] (LCLS) ... CaOTNH
National Heritage Ltd., Toronto, Ontario [*Library symbol National Library of Canada*] (NLC) ... OTNH
National Heritage Memorial Fund (AIE) ... NHMF
National Hide Association [*Later, USHSLA*] (EA) ... NHA
National High Blood Pressure Coordinating Committee ... NHBPCC
National High Blood Pressure Education Program ... NHBPEP
National High Magnetic Field Laboratory ... NHMEL
National High Magnetic Field Laboratory [*Florida State University*] ... NHMFL
National High School Athletic Coaches Association (EA) ... NHSACA
National High School Band Institute (EA) ... NHSB
National High School Boys Volleyball Association (EA) ... NHSBVA
National High School Rodeo Association (EA) ... NHSRA
National Higher Education Association (EA) ... NHEA
National Higher Education Staff Association [*Defunct*] (EA) ... NHESA
National Highway ... NH
National Highway Accident and Injury Analysis Center ... NHAIAC
National Highway Institute ... NHI
National Highway Needs Report [*Department of Transportation*] ... NHNR
National Highway Planning Network [*FHWA*] (TAG) ... NHPN
National Highway Safety Administration [*Formerly, NHSB; later, NHTSA*] [*Department of Transportation*] ... NHSA
National Highway Safety Advisory Committee ... NHSAC
National Highway Safety Bureau [*Later, NHSA, NHTSA*] [*Department of Transportation*] ... NHSB
National Highway Safety Council (NADA) ... NHSC
National Highway System ... NHS
National Highway System [*Federal transportation planning*] ... NHS

National Highway Traffic Safety Administration [Formerly, NHSB, NHSA] [Department of Transportation] ... NHTSA
National Highway Users Conference [Later, HUF] ... NHUC
National Highway Work Zone Safety Program ... NHWZSP
National Hiking and Ski Touring Association (AD) ... NAHSTA
National Hispanic Association of Construction Enterprises (EA) ... NHACE
National Hispanic Congress on Alcoholism [Defunct] (EA) ... NHCA
National Hispanic Corporate Council (EA) ... NHCC
National Hispanic Council on Aging (EA) ... NHCA
National Hispanic Leadership Agenda (EA) ... NHLA
National Hispanic Leadership Conference (EA) ... NHLC
National Hispanic Media Coalition (EA) ... NHMC
National Hispanic Media Conference (EA) ... NHMC
National Hispanic Psychological Association [Defunct] (EA) ... NHPA
National Hispanic Quincentennial Commission (EA) ... NHQC
National Hispanic Scholarship Fund (EA) ... NHSF
National Historic Communal Societies Association [Later, CSA] (EA) ... NHCSA
National Historic Landmark ... NHL
National Historic Park (BARN) ... NHP
National Historic Park, Cornwall, ON, Canada [Library symbol Library of Congress] (LCLS) ... CaOCN
National Historic Park, Parks Canada [Parc Historique National, Parcs Canada] Coteau-du-Lac, Quebec [Library symbol National Library of Canada] (NLC) ... QCLPC
National Historic Preservation Act (GNE) ... NHPA
National Historic Preservation Act ... NHPA
National Historic Preservation Act of 1966 ... NHPA
National Historic Site (BARN) ... NHS
National Historic Sites, Parks Canada [Lieux Historiques Nationaux, Parcs Canada] Whitehorse, Yukon [Library symbol National Library of Canada] (NLC) ... YWPCN
National Historical Fire Foundation (EA) ... NHFF
National Historical Publications and Records Commission [Formerly, NHPC] [Washington, DC] ... NHPRC
National Historical Publications and Records Commission ... NHPRO
National Historical Publications Commission [Later, NHPRC] ... NHPC
National Historical Society [Commercial firm] (EA) ... NHS
National History Day (EA) ... NHD
National Hobby Institute [Defunct] ... NHI
National Hobo Association (EA) ... NHA
National Hockey Association [to 1917] ... NHA
National Hockey League (EA) ... NHL
National Hockey League Booster Clubs Association (EA) ... NHLBCA
National Hockey League Player's Association (EA) ... NHLPA
National Holiness Association [Later, CHA] (EA) ... NHA
National Holistic Education Network (EA) ... NHEN
National Holography and Imaging Association (EA) ... NHIA
National Home Center Show (ITD) ... NHCS
National Home Centers [Commercial firm Associated Press] (SAG) ... NatHme
National Home Centers [NASDAQ symbol] (SAG) ... NHCI
National Home Demonstration Agents' Association [Later, NAEHE] (EA) ... NHDAA
National Home Demonstration Council [Later, NEHC] (EA) ... NHDC
National Home Education Research Institute (EA) ... NHERI
National Home Enlargement Bureau [British] (DI) ... NHEB
National Home Fashions League (EA) ... NHFL
National Home Furnishings Association (EA) ... NHFA
National Home Health Care Corp. [NASDAQ symbol] (SPSG) ... NHHC
National Home Health Care Corp. [Associated Press] (SAG) ... NtHHlt
National Home Improvement Council [Later, NARI] (EA) ... NHIC
National Home Loans Corp. [British] ... NHLC
National Home Service Association [Defunct] (EA) ... NHSA
National Home Study Council (EA) ... NHSC
National Homecaring Council [Later, FHH] (EA) ... NHC
National Homeowners Association (EA) ... NHA
National Homes Network [British] (DI) ... NHN
National Homeschool Association (EA) ... NHA
National Honey Packers and Dealers Association (EA) ... NHPDA
National Honor Society (EA) ... NHS
National Hook-Up of Black Women (EA) ... NHBW
National Hook-Up of Black Women (EA) ... NHUBW
National Hormone and Pituitary Program (EA) ... NHPP
National Horse Carriers Association, Inc., Frankfort KY [STAC] ... NHC
National Horse Show Association of America (EA) ... NHSA
National Horse Show Association of America (EA) ... NHSAA
National Horse Show Commission (EA) ... NHSC
National Horse Show Foundation (EA) ... NHSF
National Horseshoe Pitchers Association of America (EA) ... NHPA
National Horseshoe Pitchers Association of America (EA) ... NHPAA
National Hose Assemblies Manufacturers Association [Defunct] ... NHAM
National Hospice Organization ... NHO
National Hospital [A publication] ... Natn Hosp
National Hospital Discharge Survey ... NHDS
National Hospital Service Reserve [British] ... NHSR
National Hot Dog and Sausage Council (EA) ... NHDSC
National Hot Rod Association (EA) ... NHRA
National Hotel & Motel Reservations Corp. ... NHMRC
National House Building Council [British] ... NHBC
National Housebuilders' and Plumbers' Merchants [British] (DI) ... NHBPM
National Housebuilders' Registration Association [British] (DI) ... NHBRA
National House-Builders Registration Council [British] (ILCA) ... NHBRC
National Household Survey Capability Program [United Nations] ... NHSCP
National Housewares Manufacturers Association (EA) ... NHMA
National Housewives Association [British] (DBA) ... NHA
National Housewives' League of America ... NHLA

National Housewives Register [British] ... NHR
National Housing Act [1934, 1954] (DLA) ... NH Act
National Housing Act [1934, 1954] ... NHA
National Housing Administration ... NHA
National Housing Agency [Superseded by HHFA, 1947; then by HUD, 1965] ... NHA
National Housing and Economic Development Law Project ... NHEDLP
National Housing and Rehabilitation Association (EA) ... NHRA
National Housing and Town Planning Council [British] ... NHTPC
National Housing Center (EA) ... NHC
National Housing Conference (EA) ... NHC
National Housing Council [of the HHFA] [Abolished, 1965] ... NHC
National Housing Endowment ... NHE
National Housing Law Project (EA) ... NHLP
National Housing Partnership [HUD] ... NHP
National Huguenot Society (EA) ... NHS
National Human Rights Campaign for Political Prisoners in the US (EA) ... NHRCPPUS
National Human Rights Committee (EA) ... NHRC
National Human Rights Congress [Australia] ... NHRC
National Humanitarian Party [Political party Australia] ... NHP
National Humanities Alliance (EA) ... NHA
National Humanities Center (EA) ... NHC
National Humanities Center, Durham, NC [Library symbol Library of Congress] (LCLS) ... NcDurNH
National Humanities Center, Research Triangle Park, NC [OCLC symbol] (OCLC) ... NNH
National Humanities Faculty [Later, NFHAS] (EA) ... NHF
National Humanities Institute (EA) ... NHI
National HUMINT Collection Plan (MCD) ... NHCP
National Hunt [British] ... NH
National Hunt Committee [British] (DI) ... NHC
National Hunt Cup [British] (ROG) ... NHC
National Hunt Rules [British] ... NHR
National Hunter and Jumper Association (EA) ... NHJA
National Hunters Association (EA) ... NHA
National Hunting and Fishing [In "NHF" Day] [National Rifle Association] ... NHF
National Huntington's Disease Association [Later, HDSA] (EA) ... NHDA
National Hurricane and Experimental Meteorology Laboratory [Marine science] (MSC) ... NHEML
National Hurricane Center [National Weather Service] ... NHC
National Hurricane Operations Plan (DNAB) ... NHOP
National Hurricane Research Laboratory [Later, AOML] ... NHRL
National Hurricane Research Project ... NHRP
National Hurricane Warning Service [National Weather Service] ... NHWS
National Hybrid Rice Research Center [China] ... NHRRC
National Hydrocephalus Foundation (EA) ... NHF
National Hydrology Research Centre, Environment Canada [Centre National de Recherche en Hydrologie, Environnement Canada] Saskatoon, Saskatchewan [Library symbol National Library of Canada] (NLC) ... SSEH
National Hydrology Research Institute [Canada] ... NHRI
National Hydropower Association (EA) ... NHA
National Hypertension Association (EA) ... NHA
National Hypoglycemia Association (EA) ... NHA
National Ice Association [Later, PIA] (EA) ... NIA
National Ice Carving Association (EA) ... NICA
National Ice Cream and Yogurt Retailers Association (EA) ... NICYRA
National Ice Cream Mix Association (EA) ... NICMA
National Ice Cream Retailers Association [Later, NICYRA] (EA) ... NICRA
National Iceboat Authority ... NIA
National Ichthyosis Foundation (EA) ... NIF
National Identification Bureau [British] ... NIB
National Identification Program for the Advancement of Women in Higher EducationAdministration (EA) ... NIP
National Ignition Facility [Lawrence Livermore National Laboratory] [Department of Energy] (PS) ... NIF
National Ignition Facility [For nuclear fusion research] ... NIF
National Imagery Exploitation Target Base (MCD) ... NIETB
National Imagery Exploitation Tasking Study ... NIETS
National Imagery Interpretation Rating Scale (MCD) ... NIIRS
National Imagery Transmission Format (DOMA) ... NITF
National Immigration Law Center (EA) ... NILC
National Immigration Project of the National Lawyers Guild (EA) ... NIP/NLG
National Immigration, Refugee and Citizenship Forum (EA) ... NIRCF
National Impact Model [Environmental Protection Agency] (ERG) ... NIM
National Impala Association (EA) ... NIA
National Impatient Profile (MEDA) ... NIP
National Impeachment Coalition [Defunct] (EA) ... NIC
National Imperial Glass Collectors Society (EA) ... NIGCS
National Imported Car Dealers Association (EA) ... NICDA
National Incidence Studies of Missing, Abducted, Runaway, and Thrownaway Children ... NISMART
National Incinerator Testing and Evaluation Program [Environmental Protection Agency] (GFGA) ... NITEP
National Income ... NI
National Income Accounts ... NIA
National Income and Product Account Data by Mailgram [NTIS] ... NIPAGRAM
National Income and Product Accounts [The WEFA Group] [Information service] [Information service or system] (CRD) ... NIPA
National Income and Products [Economics] ... NIAP
National Income Forecasting (ADA) ... NIF
National Income per Person Employed ... NIPPE
National Income Realty Trust [NASDAQ symbol] (NQ) ... NIRTS
National Income Realty Trust [Associated Press] (SAG) ... NtlInco
National Income Statistics [British] ... NIS

National Income Tax Magazine [*A publication*] (DLA) .... Nat Inc Tax Mag
National Income Tax Magazine [*A publication*] (DLA) .... Nat'l Income Tax Mag
National Income Tax Magazine [*A publication*] (DLA) .... NITM
National Income Tax Magazine [*A publication*] (DLA) .... TM
National Incomes Commission [*Nickname: Nicky*] [*British*] .... NIC
National Inconvenienced Sportsmen's Association [*Later, NHSRA*] (EA) .... NISA
National Independence Movement of Latvia [*Political party*] .... NIML
National Independence Party [*Namibia*] [*Political party*] (PPW) .... NIP
National Independent Agents' Association [*Australia*] .... NIAA
National Independent Automobile Dealers Association (EA) .... NIADA
National Independent Bank Equipment and Systems Association [*Park Ridge, IL*] (EA) .... NIBESA
National Independent Bicycle Rep Association [*Defunct*] (EA) .... NIBRA
National Independent Coal Operators Association [*Defunct*] (EA) .... NICOA
National Independent Dairy-Food Association (EA) .... NIDA
National Independent Enginemen's Trade Union [*British*] .... NIETU
National Independent Lynx User Group (NITA) .... NILUG
National Independent Meat Packers Association [*Later, NMA*] (EA) .... NIMPA
National Independent Nursery Furniture Retailers Association (EA) .... NINFRA
National Independent Poultry and Food Distributors Association (EA).... NIPFDA
National Independent Study Center [*Civil Service Commission*] .... NISC
National Independent Teenage Party [*British*] .... NIndTP
National Independent Truckers Unity Council [*Defunct*] (EA) .... NITUC
National Independent Union Council [*Later, NFIU*] .... NIUC
National Independent Vendors Association [*Defunct*] (EA) .... NIVA
National Index of Ecosystems [*Australia*] .... NIE
National Indian Athletic Association (EA) .... NIAA
National Indian Council on Aging (EA) .... NICOA
National Indian Counselors Association (EA) .... NICA
National Indian Education Advisory Committee [*Terminated, 1974*] [*Department of the Interior*] (EGAO) .... NIEAC
National Indian Education Association (EA) .... NIEA
National Indian Health Board (EA) .... NIHB
National Indian Lutheran Board (EA) .... NILB
National Indian Manpower Advisory Board .... NIMAB
National Indian Social Workers Association (EA) .... NISWA
National Indian Training and Research Center (EA) .... NITRC
National Indian Training Center, Brigham City, UT [*Library symbol Library of Congress*] (LCLS) .... UBcI
National Indian Youth Council (EA) .... NIYC
National Indications Center [*Disbanded*] [*DoD*] .... NIC
National Indirect Air Carrier Association [*Defunct*] (EA) .... NIACA
National Indoor Environmental Institute (EPA) .... NIEI
National Indoor Soccer League [*Australia*] .... NISL
National Indoor Tennis Association [*Formerly, ITA*] [*Later, NTA*] (EA) .... NITA
National Indoor Track Meet Directors Association (EA) .... NITMDA
National Industrial Advertisers Association [*Later, B/PAA*] .... NIAA
National Industrial Basic Language (MHDB) .... NIBL
National Industrial Basketball League (EA) .... NIBL
National Industrial Belting Association (EA) .... NIBA
National Industrial Cafeteria Managers Association [*Later, SFM*] (EA) ...... NICMA
National Industrial Competitiveness through Efficiency: Energy, Environment, andEconomics [*Environmental Protection Agency*] .... $NICE^3$
National Industrial Conference Board [*Later, TCB*] (EA) .... NICB
National Industrial Conference Board, Montreal, PQ, Canada [*Library symbol Library of Congress*] (LCLS) .... CaQMNI
National Industrial Conservation Conference .... NICC
National Industrial Council (EA) .... NIC
National Industrial Distributors Association [*Philadelphia, PA*] (EA) .... NIDA
National Industrial Energy Conservation Council (MCD) .... NIECC
National Industrial Engineering Mission (AABC) .... NIEM
National Industrial Equipment Reserve [*of DMS*] .... NIER
National Industrial Fire and Safety Centre (ACII) .... NIFAST
National Industrial Fuel Efficiency Service [*British*] .... NIFES
National Industrial Glove Distributors Association (EA) .... NIGDA
National Industrial Language Training Centre (AIE) .... NILTC
National Industrial Leather Association [*Later, NIBA*] (EA) .... NILA
National Industrial Partner .... NIP
National Industrial Plant Reserve .... NIPR
National Industrial Pollution Control Council [*Terminated, 1973*] [*Department of Commerce*] .... NIPCC
National Industrial Recovery Act [*1933*] .... NIRA
National Industrial Recovery Administration (WDAA) .... NIRA
National Industrial Recovery Board [*Terminated, 1935*] .... NIRB
National Industrial Recreation Association [*Later, NESRA*] (EA) .... NIRA
National Industrial Relations Court [*British*] .... NIRC
National Industrial Reserve Act of 1948 .... NIRA
National Industrial Safety Conference (PDAA) .... NISCON
National Industrial Salvage and Recovery Association [*British*] (BI) .... NISRA
National Industrial Sand Association (EA) .... NISA
National Industrial Security Program [*A publication*] (AAGC) .... NISP
National Industrial Security Program Manual [*A publication*] (AAGC) ...... NISPOM
National Industrial Service Association [*Later, EASA*] .... NISA
National Industrial Space Committee .... NISC
National Industrial Stores Association (EA) .... NISA
National Industrial Television Association [*Later, ITVA*] (EA) .... NITA
National Industrial Traffic League (EA) .... NITL
National Industrial Training Program [*Canada*] .... NITP
National Industrial Transportation League (EA) .... NITL
National Industrial Workers Union .... NIW
National Industrial Workers Union (EA) .... NIWU
National Industrial Zoning Committee (EA) .... NIZC
National Industries for the Blind (EA) .... NIB
National Industries for the Severely Handicapped (EA) .... NISH
National Industry Advisory Committee [*Terminated, 1986*] [*FCC*] .... NIAC
National Industry Associations Anti-Dumping Task Force [*Australia*]..... NIAA-DTF
National Industry Safety Committee (NADA) .... NISC
National Infant Mortality Survey [*Department of Health and Human Services*] (GFGA) .... NIMS
National Infertility Network Exchange [*An association*] (EA) .... NINE
National Informatics Center [*India*] [*Information service or system*] .... NIC
National Information and Analysis Center .... NIAC
National Information and Documentation Center .... NIDOC
National Information Bureau [*Information service or system*] (EA) .... NIB
National Information Bureau for Jewish Life (EA) .... NIBJL
National Information Center for Children and Youth with Disabilities (PAZ) .... NICHCY
National Information Center for Children and Youth with Handicaps (EA) .... NICCYH
National Information Center for Educational Materials (NITA) .... NICEM
National Information Center for Educational Media [*Later, AV Online*] (EA) .... NICEM
National Information Center for Local Government Records [*Canada*]..... NICLOG
National Information Center for Special Education Material/National Instructional Material Information System (EDAC) .... NICSEM/NIMIS
National Information Center for Special Education Materials [*University of Southern California*] [*Los Angeles, CA*] .... NICSEM
National Information Center for the Handicapped (EA) .... NICH
National Information Center on Deafness (EA) .... NICD
National Information Center on Volunteerism [*Later, NVC*] (EA) .... NICOV
National Information Center on Women and the Military [*Later, WMP*] (EA) .... NICWM
National Information Clearinghouse [*for Infants with Disabilities and Life-Threatening Conditions*] (PAZ) .... NIC
National Information Clearinghouse for Infants with Disabilities and Life-Threatening Conditions .... NIC
National Information Conference and Exposition [*Associated Information Managers*] .... NICE
National Information/Distribution System, National Film Board [*Systeme d'Information et de Distribution pour les Produits Audio-Visuels Canadiens, Office National du film*] **Montreal, Quebec** [*Library symbol National Library of Canada*] (NLC) .... QMNFNI
National Information Infrastructure [*Proposed 1992*] [*Telecommunications*] ..... NII
National Information Infrastructure Testbed [*Telecommunications*] (PCM) ..... NIIT
National Information Management System .... NIMS
National Information Network [*ASTIA*] .... NIN
National Information of Software and Services (AIE) .... NISS
National Information Processing System [*Military*] .... NIPS
National Information Research Institute .... NIRI
National Information Retrieval Colloquium [*Later, Benjamin Franklin Colloquium on Information Science*] .... NIRC
National Information Service for Earthquake Engineering (EA) .... NISEE
National Information Services Corp. (IID) .... NISC
National Information Sources on the Handicapped [*Clearinghouse on the Handicapped*] [*Database*] .... NISH
National Information Standards Organization - Z39 (EA) .... NISO
National Information Storage and Retrieval Center .... NISARC
National Information System for Physics and Astronomy (NITA) .... NISPA
National Information System for Psychology .... NISP
National Information System for Science and Technology (NITA) .... NIST
National Information Systems [*Later, GIP*] [*UNESCO*] .... NATIS
National Information Systems [*Later, GIP*] [*UNESCO*] (BUR) .... NIS
National Information Systems, Inc. [*Information service or system*] (IID) .... NIS
National Information Systems Task Force [*Society of American Archivists*] [*Information service or system*] (IID) .... NISTF
National Information Technology in Education Centre (ACII) .... NITEC
National Information Transfer Centre (NITA) .... NITC
National Ingredient Marketing Specialists (EA) .... NIMS
National Inholders Association [*Database producer*] (EA) .... NIA
National Injury Information Clearinghouse [*Consumer Product Safety Commission*] .... NIIC
National Injury Surveillance Unit [*Australia*] .... NISU
National Innovation Fund [*South Africa*] .... NIF
National Inorganic and Radionuclides Survey [*Environmental Protection Agency*] .... NIRS
National Inservice Network .... NIN
National Inshore Union of Fishermen [*British*] .... NIUF
National Inspection Council for Electrical Installation Contracting [*British*] .... NICEIC
National Inspection Plan [*RSPA*] (TAG) .... NIP
National Institute for Advanced Studies (EA) .... NIAS
National Institute for Applied Behavioral Science .... NIABS
National Institute for Architectural Education (EA) .... NIAE
National Institute for Automotive Service Excellence (EA) .... ASE
National Institute for Automotive Service Excellence .... NIASE
National Institute for Biological Standards and Control [*British*] .... NIBSC
National Institute for Burn Medicine (EA) .... NIBM
National Institute for Campus Ministries (EA) .... NICM
National Institute for Careers Education and Counselling [*Research center British*] (IRC) .... NICEC
National Institute for Certification in Engineering Technologies (EA) .... NICET
National Institute for Chemical Studies (EA) .... NICS
National Institute for Child Support Enforcement [*Commercial firm*] (EA) .... NICSE
National Institute for Citizen Education in the Law (EA) .... NICEL
National Institute for Computers in Engineering [*Defunct*] (EA) .... NICE
National Institute for Consumer Education .... NICE
National Institute for Consumer Justice .... NICJ
National Institute for Continuing Education in Developmental Disabilities (EA) .... NICEDD

National Institute for Crime Prevention and Rehabilitation of Offenders ..... NICRO
National Institute for Disaster Mobilization (EA) ..... NIDM
National Institute for Dispute Resolution (EA) ..... NIDR
National Institute for Educational Research (NITA) ..... NIER
National Institute for Farm Safety (EA) ..... NIFS
National Institute for Federal Procurement (AAGC) ..... NIFP
National Institute for Full Employment Research [*Department of Labor*] (OICC) ..... NIFER
National Institute for Global Environmental Change [*University of Southern California and Department of Energy*] ..... NIGEC
National Institute for Higher Education [*Defunct*] (ACII) ..... NIHE
National Institute for Human Genome Research [*National Institutes of Health*] (BARN) ..... NIHGR
National Institute for Jewish Hospice (EA) ..... NIJH
National Institute for Juvenile Justice and Delinquency Prevention ..... NIJJDP
National Institute for Lay Training [*Defunct*] (EA) ..... NILT
National Institute for Low Power Television [*Defunct*] (EA) ..... NILPT
National Institute for Medical Research [*British*] ..... NIMR
National Institute for Medical Research Online Database (PDAA) ..... NIMROD
National Institute for Multicultural Education [*Defunct*] (EA) ..... NIME
National Institute for Music Theater [*Defunct*] (EA) ..... NIMT
National Institute for Nursing Research ..... NINR
National Institute for Occupational Safety and Health [*Public Health Service*] [*Cincinnati, OH Database producer*] ..... NIOSH
National Institute for Occupational Safety and Health, Cincinnati, OH [*Library symbol Library of Congress*] (LCLS) ..... OCNIOS
National Institute for Occupational Safety and Health, Cincinnati, OH [*OCLC symbol*] (OCLC) ..... OSH
National Institute for Occupational Safety and Health, Morgantown, WV [*OCLC symbol*] (OCLC) ..... OSY
National Institute for Occupational Safety and Health, Rockville, MD [*Library symbol Library of Congress*] (LCLS) ..... MdRNIO
National Institute for Occupational Safety and Health, Rockville, MD [*OCLC symbol*] (OCLC) ..... OSI
National Institute for Occupational Safety and Health Technical Information Center [*Database*] [*NIOSH*] [*Information service or system*] (CRD) ..... NIOSHTIC
National Institute for Overseas Koreans (EA) ..... NIOK
National Institute for Petroleum and Energy Research [*Formerly, BETC*] [*Department of Energy Bartlesville, OK*] ..... NIPER
National Institute for Public Policy (EA) ..... NIPP
National Institute for Public Services ..... NIPS
National Institute for Radiological Science [*Japan*] ..... NIRS
National Institute for Rehabilitation Engineering (EA) ..... NIRE
National Institute for Research in Dairying [*British*] ..... NIRD
National Institute for Research in Nuclear Science [*British*] ..... NIRNS
National Institute for Resources in Science and Engineering (EA) ..... RISE
National Institute for Science, Law, and Public Policy (EA) ..... NISLAPP
National Institute for Staff and Organizational Development (OICC) ..... NISOD
National Institute for State Credit Union Examination [*McLean, VA*] (EA) ..... NISCUE
National Institute for the Advancement of Career Education [*Defunct*] (EA) ..... NIACE
National Institute for the Blind (EA) ..... NIB
National Institute for the Deaf (WDAA) ..... NID
National Institute for the Environment [*Proposed government agency*] ..... NIE
National Institute for the Family (EA) ..... NIF
National Institute for the Foodservice Industry (EA) ..... NIFI
National Institute for the Humanities [*Yale University*] [*National Endowment for the Humanities*] ..... NIH
National Institute for the Study of Educational Change ..... NISEC
National Institute for the Word of God (EA) ..... NIWG
National Institute for Trial Advocacy (EA) ..... NITA
National Institute for Uniform Licensing of Power Engineers' ..... NIULPE
National Institute for Urban Wildlife (EA) ..... NIUW
National Institute for Women of Color (EA) ..... NIWC
National Institute for Work and Learning (EA) ..... NIWL
National Institute Northern Accelerator (PDAA) ..... NINA
National Institute of Adult Continuing Education [*British*] ..... NIACE
National Institute of Advertising Management ..... NIAM
National Institute of Aeronautical Sciences ..... NIAS
National Institute of Agricultural Botany [*Research center British*] (IRC) ..... NIAB
National Institute of Agricultural Engineering [*Research center British*] (IRC) ..... NIAE
National Institute of Airworthiness Surveyors [*Australia*] ..... NIAS
National Institute of Allergy and Infectious Diseases [*of National Institutes of Health*] [*Department of Health and Human Services Bethesda, MD*] ..... NIAID
National Institute of American Doll Artists (EA) ..... NIADA
National Institute of Animal Agriculture [*Defunct*] (EA) ..... NIAA
National Institute of Arthritis and Musculoskeletal and Skin Diseases [*Bethesda, MD*] [*Department of Health and Human Services*] (GRD) ..... NIAMS
National Institute of Arthritis and Musculoskeletal and Skin Diseases [*Department of Health and Human Services*] (GFGA) ..... NIAMSD
National Institute of Arthritis, Diabetes, and Digestive and Kidney Diseases [*National Institutes of Health*] (EA) ..... NIADDK
National Institute of Arthritis, Metabolism, and Digestive Diseases [*Formerly, NIAMD*] [*Later, NIADDK*] [*National Institutes of Health*] ..... NIAMDD
National Institute of Arts and Letters [*Later, AAIAL*] (EA) ..... NIAL
National Institute of Atmospheric Research ..... NIAR
National Institute of Biotechnology and Genetic Engineering [*Pakistan*] ..... NIBGE
National Institute of Building Sciences (EA) ..... NIBS
National Institute of Carpet Fitters [*British*] (DBA) ..... NICF
National Institute of Ceramic Engineers (EA) ..... NICE
National Institute of Certified Moving Consultants (EA) ..... CMC
National Institute of Child Health and Human Development [*Bethesda, MD*] [*National Institutes of Health*] (GRD) ..... NICHD
National Institute of Child Health and Human Development [*National Institutes of Health*] ..... NICHHD
National Institute of Comparative Medicine (DAVI) ..... NICM
National Institute of Conveyancing Agents [*British*] (DBA) ..... NICA
National Institute of Corrections [*Department of Justice*] ..... NIC
National Institute of Creativity [*Defunct*] (EA) ..... NIC
National Institute of Credit [*New York, NY*] (EA) ..... NIC
National Institute of Dental Research [*Public Health Service*] [*Bethesda, MD*] ..... NIDR
National Institute of Diabetes and Digestive and Kidney Diseases [*Public Health Service*] [*Also, an information service or system*] (IID) ..... NIDDK
National Institute of Diabetes and Digestive and Kidney Diseases [*Department of Health and Human Services*] (GFGA) ..... NIDDKD
National Institute of Diaper Services [*Defunct*] (EA) ..... NIDS
National Institute of Drycleaning [*Later, IFI*] (EA) ..... NID
National Institute of Dyslexia [*Defunct*] (EA) ..... NID
National Institute of Economic and Social Research [*British*] ..... NIESR
National Institute of Education [*Department of Education*] [*Washington, DC*] ..... NIE
National Institute of Education, Washington, DC [*Library symbol Library of Congress*] (LCLS) ..... DNIE
National Institute of Education, Washington, DC [*OCLC symbol*] (OCLC) ..... NIE
National Institute of Electromedical Information (EA) ..... NIEI
National Institute of Environmental Health Sciences [*Research Triangle Pa rk, NC*] [*National Institutes of Health*] ..... NIEHS
National Institute of Environmental Health Sciences, Research Triangle Park, NC [*OCLC symbol*] (OCLC) ..... HNE
National Institute of Environmental Health Service [*Marine science*] (OSRA) ..... NIEHS
National Institute of Farm and Land Brokers [*Later, FLI*] (EA) ..... NIFLB
National Institute of Farm Brokers [*Later, NIFLB*] (EA) ..... NIFB
National Institute of Fresh Produce [*British*] (DBA) ..... NIFP
National Institute of Furnace and Air Duct Cleaning Specialists (EA) ..... NIFADCS
National Institute of General Medical Sciences [*National Institutes of Health*] [*Bethesda, MD*] ..... NIGMS
National Institute of Governmental Purchasing (EA) ..... NIGP
National Institute of Handicapped Research [*Department of Health and Human Services*] [*Later, NIDRR*] [*Washington, DC*] ..... NIHR
National Institute of Hardware [*British*] (BI) ..... NIH
National Institute of Health and Human Development ..... NIHHD
National Institute of Higher Education (Research, Science, and Technology) [*Spain*] ..... NIHERST
National Institute of Housecraft [*British*] (BI) ..... NIH
National Institute of Hypertension Studies - Institute of Hypertension School ofResearch (EA) ..... NIHS
National Institute of Independent Colleges and Universities (EA) ..... NIICU
National Institute of Industrial Psychology (PDAA) ..... NIIP
National Institute of Infant Services [*Later, NADS*] ..... NIIS
National Institute of Judicial Dynamics [*Defunct*] (EA) ..... NIJD
National Institute of Justice [*Department of Justice*] [*Washington, DC*] ..... NIJ
National Institute of Justice (USGC) ..... NIJ
National Institute of Justice ..... NIJ
National Institute of Labor Education [*Defunct*] (EA) ..... NILE
National Institute of Law Enforcement and Criminal Justice [*Law Enforcement Assistance Administration*] ..... NILE & CJ
National Institute of Law Enforcement and Criminal Justice [*Law Enforcement Assistance Administration*] ..... NILECJ
National Institute of Locker and Freezer Provisioners [*Later, AAMP*] (EA) ..... NILFP
National Institute of Management Counsellors (EA) ..... NIMC
National Institute of Marine Medicine and Pharmacology [*Proposed*] [*National Institutes of Health*] ..... NIMMP
National Institute of Medical Herbalists [*British*] ..... NIMH
National Institute of Mental Health [*Rockville, MD*] [*Department of Health and Human Services*] ..... NIMH
National Institute of Mental Health, Clinical Research Center Medical Library, Fort Worth, TX [*Library symbol Library of Congress*] (LCLS) ..... TxFNIMH
National Institute of Municipal Clerks [*Later, IIMC*] ..... NIMC
National Institute of Municipal Law Officers (EA) ..... NIMLO
National Institute of Municipal Law Officers. Municipal Law Review [*A publication*] (DLA) ..... NIMLO Mun L Rev
National Institute of Neurological and Communicative Disorders and Stroke [*Formerly, NINDS*] [*Public Health Service Bethesda, MD*] ..... NINCDS
National Institute of Neurological Diseases and Blindness [*Later, NEI, NINDS*] [*National Institutes of Health*] ..... NINDB
National Institute of Neurological Diseases and Stroke [*Formerly, NINDB*] [*Later, NINCDS*] [*National Institutes of Health*] ..... NINDS
National Institute of Neurological Disorders and Stroke ..... NINDS
National Institute of Neurology and Blindness (WDAA) ..... NINB
National Institute of Nutrition [*Institut National de la Nutrition*], Ottawa, Ontario [*Library symbol National Library of Canada*] (BIB) ..... OONIN
National Institute of Oceanography [*British*] (IID) ..... NIO
National Institute of Oceanography and Fisheries [*Egypt*] [*Marine science*] (OSRA) ..... NIOF
National Institute of Oilseed Products (EA) ..... NIOP
National Institute of Packaging, Handling, and Logistic Engineers (EA) ..... NIPHLE
National Institute of Pension Administrators [*Santa Ana, CA*] (EA) ..... NIPA
National Institute of Polarology [*Research center British*] (IRUK) ..... NIP
National Institute of Poultry Husbandry [*British*] (BI) ..... NIPH
National Institute of Public Affairs ..... NIPA

National Institute of Public Health ... NIPH
National Institute of Public Management (EA) ... NIPM
National Institute of Real Estate Brokers [*Later, Realtors National Marketing Institute*] (EA) ... NIREB
National Institute of Red Orange Canaries and All Other Cage Birds (EA) ... NIROC
National Institute of Research and Advanced Studies [*Proposed*] ... NIRAS
National Institute of Rug Cleaning [*Superseded by AIDS International*] (EA) ... NIRC
National Institute of Science (EA) ... NIS
National Institute of Science and Technology ... NIST
National Institute of Science and Technology (NADA) ... NIST
National Institute of Senior Centers (EA) ... NISC
National Institute of Senior Housing (EA) ... NISH
National Institute of Social and Behavioral Science (EA) ... NISBS
National Institute of Social Sciences (EA) ... NISS
National Institute of Social Work [*British*] ... NISW
National Institute of Standards and Technology [*Formerly, NBS*] [*Gaithersburg, MD*] [*Department of Commerce*] ... NIST
National Institute of Standards & Technology - Electronics and EE Lab ... NIST-EEEL
National Institute of Steel Detailing (EA) ... NISD
National Institute of Student Governments [*Defunct*] (EA) ... NISG
National Institute of Supply Associations ... NISA
National Institute of Technical Processors, Information Consultants, Keyword Experts, and Retrieval Specialists [*Fictitious organization*] ... NITPICKERS
National Institute of Technology ... NIT
National Institute of Victimology (EA) ... NIV
National Institute of Wood Kitchen Cabinets [*Later, KCMA*] ... NIWKC
National Institute on Adult Daycare (EA) ... NIAD
National Institute on Aging [*Bethesda, MD*] [*National Institutes of Health*] ... NIA
National Institute on Aging, Gerontology Research Center, Baltimore, MD [*Library symbol Library of Congress*] (LCLS) ... MdBNA
National Institute on Aging, Work, and Retirement [*Washington, DC*] (EA) ... NIAWR
National Institute on Alcohol Abuse and Alcoholism [*Rockville, MD*] [*Public Health Service*] [*Department of Health and Human Services*] ... NIAAA
National Institute on Community-Based Long-Term Care (EA) ... NICLC
National Institute on Crime and Delinquency [*Later, NFCJ*] (EA) ... NICD
National Institute on Deafness and Other Communication Disorders [*National Institutes of Health*] (EGAO) ... NIDCD
National Institute on Deafness and Other Communication Disorders [*NIH*] ... NIDOCD
National Institute on Disability and Rehabilitation Research [*Washington, DC Department of Education*] (GRD) ... NIDRR
National Institute on Drug Abuse [*Department of Health and Human Services*] [*Rockville, MD*] ... NIDA
National Institute on Mental Retardation, Toronto, ON, Canada [*Library symbol Library of Congress*] (LCLS) ... CaOTNIMR
National Institute on Mental Retardation [*Institut National pour la Deficience Mentale*] **Toronto, Ontario** [*Library symbol National Library of Canada*] (NLC) ... OTNIMR
National Institute on Park and Grounds Management (EA) ... NIPGM
National Institute on the Holocaust [*Later, AFIP*] (EA) ... NIH
National Institute on Workshop Standards [*Defunct*] (EA) ... NIWS
National Institutes of Health [*Public Health Service*] [*Bethesda, MD*] ... NIH
National Institutes of Health, Bethesda, MD [*OCLC symbol*] (OCLC) ... HNI
National Institutes of Marriage and Family Relations (EA) ... NIMFR
National Institutional Food Distributor Associates (EA) ... NIFDA
National Institutional Teacher Placement Association [*Later, ASCUS*] ... NITPA
National Institutional Training Program [*Canada*] ... NITP
National Instructional Materials Information System ... NIMIS
National Instructional Television [*Superseded by AIT*] (EA) ... NIT
National Instructional Television Association (NTCM) ... NITA
National Instructional Television Center (NTCM) ... NITC
National Instrument Corp. [*NASDAQ symbol*] (SAG) ... NATI
National Instrument Corp. [*Associated Press*] (SAG) ... NatInst
National Insulation and Abatement Contractors Association (EA) ... NIAC
National Insulation Certification Institute (EA) ... NICI
National Insulation Contractors Association [*Later, NIAC*] (EA) ... NICA
National Insulation Manufacturers Association [*Later, Thermal Insulation Manufacturers Association*] (EA) ... NIMA
National Insulator Association (EA) ... NIA
National Insurance [*British*] ... NI
National Insurance Actuarial and Statistical Association [*Later, ISO*] ... NIASA
National Insurance Advisory Committee [*British*] (DCTA) ... NIAC
National Insurance Association [*Chicago, IL*] (EA) ... NIA
National Insurance Brokers' Association of Australia ... NIBAA
National Insurance Buyers Association ... NIBA
National Insurance Certificate [*British*] ... NIC
National Insurance Consumer Organization (EA) ... NICO
National Insurance Contribution [*British*] (ECON) ... NIC
National Insurance Contributions [*British*] ... NIC
National Insurance Contributions System [*Department of Health and Social Security*] [*British*] ... NICS
National Insurance Corp. of Liberia (EY) ... NICOL
National Insurance Development Act of 1975 ... NIDA
National Insurance Development Corp. [*Government-sponsored organization*] ... NIDC
National Insurance Group [*NASDAQ symbol*] (NQ) ... NAIG
National Insurance Group [*Associated Press*] (SAG) ... NtlIns
National Insurance Surcharge [*A separately accounted tax on employment*] [*British*] ... NIS
National Integrated Wage Structure (ADA) ... NIWS
National Integration Party [*Liberia*] [*Political party*] (EY) ... NIP
National Intelligence Authority [*1946-1947*] ... NIA
National Intelligence Committee ... NIC
National Intelligence Estimate ... NIE
National Intelligence Estimates [*Summaries of foreign policy information and advice prepared for the president*] [*Known informally as "knees"*] ... NIES
National Intelligence Officer (MCD) ... NIO
National Intelligence Priorities (MCD) ... NIP
National Intelligence Projection for Planning (AFM) ... NIPP
National Intelligence Service (NADA) ... NIS
National Intelligence Service [*Zaire*] (PD) ... SNI
National Intelligence Situation Report (MCD) ... NISR
National Intelligence Study Center (EA) ... NISC
National Intelligence Summary (MCD) ... NIS
National Intelligence Survey ... NIS
National Intelligence Survey Gazetteer ... NISGAZ
National Intelligence Tasking Center [*CIA*] ... NITC
National Intelligence Test [*Psychology*] ... NIT
National Intelligence Topic (MCD) ... NIT
National Inter Seminary Council ... NISC
National Interactive Video Centre [*British*] ... NIVC
National Interagency Coordination Group [*National Atmospheric Electricity Hazards Program*] (MCD) ... NICG
National Interagency Council on Smoking and Health [*New York, NY*] ... NIC
National Interagency Council on Smoking and Health [*Defunct*] (EA) ... NICSH
National Interagency Counterdrug Institute [*Camp San Luis Obispo, CA*] (DOMA) ... NICI
National Interagency Firefighting Center ... NIFC
National Intercollegiate Boxing Coaches Association (EA) ... NIBCA
National Intercollegiate Flying Association (EA) ... NIFA
National Intercollegiate Rodeo Association (EA) ... NIRA
National Intercollegiate Soccer Officials Association (EA) ... NISOA
National Intercollegiate Squash Racquets Association (EA) ... NISRA
National Intercollegiate Women's Fencing Association (EA) ... NIWFA
National Interdepartmental Seminar [*Military*] ... NIS
National Interest ... NI
National Interfaith Coalition on Aging (EA) ... NICA
National Interfraternity Conference (EA) ... NIC
National Interfraternity Foundation (EA) ... NIF
National Interim Bankruptcy System (AAGC) ... NIBS
National Interim Primary Drinking Water Regulations [*Environmental Protection Agency*] ... NIPDWR
National Interim Primary Drinking Water Standards [*Environmental Protection Agency*] ... NIPDWS
National Intern and Resident Matching Program [*Later, NRMP*] (EA) ... NIRMP
National Intern and Resident Matching Program (DAVI) ... NIRMP
National Intern Matching Program [*Later, NRMP*] (EA) ... NIMP
National Internal Defense Coordination Center [*Army*] (AABC) ... NIDCC
National International Academy ... NIA
National Interreligious Service Board for Conscientious Objectors (EA) ... NISBCO
National Interreligious Task Force on Soviet Jewry (EA) ... NITFSJ
National Interrogation Center [*Military*] ... NIC
National Interscholastic Athletic Administrators Association (EA) ... NIAAA
National Interscholastic Music Activities Commission [*Defunct*] (EA) ... NIMAC
National Interscholastic Swimming Coaches Association of America (EA) ... NISCA
National Interstate Council of State Boards of Cosmetology (EA) ... NIC
National Intervenors [*Defunct*] (EA) ... NI
National Intramural Sports Council ... NISC
National Intramural-Recreational Sports Association (EA) ... NIRSA
National Intravenous Therapy Association [*Later, INS*] (EA) ... NITA
National Inventors Council [*Terminated, 1974*] [*National Institute of Standards and Technology*] ... NIC
National Inventors Foundation (EA) ... NIF
National Inventory Control Center (MCD) ... NICC
National Inventory Control Point [*Military*] ... NICP
National Inventory of Documentary Sources [*British*] ... NIDS
National Inventory of Pollution Sources [*Database*] [*Environment Canada*] [*Information service or system*] (CRD) ... NIPS
National Inventory Programme [*National Museums of Canada*] [*Later, CHIN*] ... NIP
National Inventory Record [*DoD*] ... NIR
National Inventory System [*Department of Agriculture*] (GFGA) ... NIS
National Investigations Committee on Aerial Phenomena [*Defunct*] (EA) ... NICAP
National Investigations Committee on Aerial Phenomena ... NICAP
National Investigations Committee on Unidentified Flying Objects (EA) ... NICUFO
National Investment Bank [*Ghana*] (EY) ... NIB
National Investment Bank for Industrial Development [*Greece*] ... NIBID
National Investment Fund [*Poland*] [*Finance*] ... NIF
National Investor Data Service (EA) ... NIDS
National Investor Relations Institute [*Washington, DC*] (EA) ... NIRI
National Invitation Tournament [*Basketball*] ... NIT
National Involvement Association (EA) ... NIA
National Iranian Front [*Political party*] ... NIF
National Iranian Television (NADA) ... NITV
National Ironfounding Employers Association [*British*] (BI) ... NIEF
National Irrigation Administration (NADA) ... NIA
National ISDN [*Integrated Services Digital Network*] [*Telecommunications*] ... N-ISDN
National Islamic Front [*Sudan*] [*Political party*] ... NIF
National Issues Forums (EA) ... NIF
National Italian American Foundation (EA) ... NIAF

National Item Identification Number (MCD) .... NIIN
National Jail Association [Later, AJA] (EA) .... NJA
National Jail Managers Association [Later, AJA] (EA) .... NJMA
National Japanese Canadian Citizens' Association .... NJCCA
National Jazz Fraternity .... NAJAFRA
National Jazz Service Organization (EA) .... NJSO
National Jet Service, Inc. [ICAO designator] (FAAC) .... AND
National Jewellers' Association [British] (BI) .... NJA
National Jewish Artisans Guild [Defunct] (EA) .... NJAG
National Jewish Center [Australia] .... NJC
National Jewish Civil Service Employees (EA) .... NJCSE
National Jewish Coalition (EA) .... NJC
National Jewish Commission on Law and Public Affairs .... COLPA
National Jewish Committee on Scouting (EA) .... NJCS
National Jewish Community Relations Advisory Council (EA) .... NJCRAC
National Jewish Girl Scout Committee (EA) .... NJGSC
National Jewish Hospital and Research Center, Medical Library, Denver, CO [Library symbol Library of Congress] (LCLS) .... CoDNJ-M
National Jewish Hospital/National Asthma Center [Later, National Jewish Center for Immunology and Respiratory Medicine] (EA) .... NJH/NAC
National Jewish Hospitality Committee (EA) .... NJHC
National Jewish Information Service (for the Propagation of Judaism) [Defunct] (EA) .... NJIS
National Jewish Music Council [Later, Jewish Welfare Board Jewish Music Council] (EA) .... NJMC
National Jewish Resource Center (EA) .... NJRC
National Jewish Television [Cable-television system] .... NJT
National Jewish Welfare Board [Later, JCCANA] (EA) .... JWB
National Jewish Welfare Board [Later, JWB] .... NJWB
National Job Corps Alumni Association [Washington, DC] (EA) .... NJCAA
National Job Sharing Network (EA) .... NJSN
National Jobs with Peace Campaign (EA) .... NJWPC
National Jogging Association [Later, ARFA] (EA) .... NJA
National Joint Advisory Council [on labor-management relations] [British] .... NJAC
National Joint Committee for Learning Disabilities .... NJCLD
National Joint Computer Committee [of ACM, AIEE, IRE] [Superseded by AFIPS] .... NJCC
National Joint Council (AIE) .... NJC
National Joint Council for Administrative, Professional, Technical, and ClericalStaff [British] .... NJCAPT & C
National Joint Council for Handicapped Children [British] .... NJCHC
National Joint Council for Local Authority Fire Brigades [British] .... NJCLAFB
National Joint Council for the Building Industry [British] (DCTA) .... NJCBI
National Joint Fiction Reserve .... NJFR
National Joint Heavy and Highway Construction Committee (EA) .... NJHHCC
National Joint Industrial Council [Pharmacology British] .... NJIC
National Joint Painting, Decorating, and Drywall Apprenticeship and Training Committee (EA) .... NJPDDATC
National Joint Service Delegations (NATG) .... NJSD
National Journal of Legal Education [A publication] (DLA) .... Nat J Leg Ed
National Jousting Association (EA) .... NJA
National Judges Association (EA) .... NJA
National Judicial College (EA) .... NJC
National Judo Black Belt Federation of the USA (EA) .... NJBBF
National Juice Products Association (EA) .... NJPA
National Junior Angus Association (EA) .... NJAA
National Junior College Athletic Association (EA) .... NJCAA
National Junior Honor Society (EA) .... NJHS
National Junior Horticultural Association (EA) .... NJHA
National Junior Polled Hereford Association (EA) .... NJPHA
National Junior Polled Hereford Council [Later, NJPHA] (EA) .... NJPHC
National Junior Santa Gertrudis Association (EA) .... NJSGA
National Junior Science and Humanities Symposium .... NJSHS
National Junior Tennis League (EA) .... NJTL
National Junior Vegetable Growers Association [Later, NJHA] (EA) .... NJVGA
National Jury Project (EA) .... NJP
National Justice Foundation of America (EA) .... NJFA
National Juvenile Court Foundation (EA) .... NJCF
National Juvenile Court Services Association (EA) .... NJCSA
National Juvenile Detention Association (EA) .... NJDA
National Juvenile Law Center [Later, NCYL] (EA) .... NJLC
National Juvenile Restitution Association [Later, ARA] (EA) .... NJRA
National Kangaroo Monitoring Unit [Australia] .... NKMU
National Kerosene Heater Association (EA) .... NKHA
National Kidney and Urologic Diseases Information Clearinghouse (EA) .... NKUDIC
National Kidney Centre [British] (CB) .... NKC
National Kidney Disease Foundation [Later, NKF] (EA) .... NKDF
National Kidney Foundation (EA) .... NKF
National Kindergarten Association [Defunct] (EA) .... NKA
National Kitchen and Bath Association (EA) .... NKBA
National Kitchen Cabinet Association [Later, KCMA] (EA) .... NKCA
National Knife Collectors Association (EA) .... NKCA
National Knitted Outerwear Association [Later, NKSA] (EA) .... NKOA
National Knitwear and Sportswear Association (EA) .... NKSA
National Knitwear Manufacturers Association (EA) .... NKMA
National Korean American Bilingual Educators Association [Defunct] (EA) .... NKABEA
National Korean Studies Center [Australia] .... NKSC
National Kosher Food Trade Association [Defunct] (EA) .... NKFTA
National Kraut Packers Association (EA) .... NKPA
National Labor Board (WDAA) .... NLB
National Labor Committee in Support of Democracy and Human Rights in El Salvador (EA) .... NLCSDHRES
National Labor Law Center (EA) .... NLLC
National Labor Relations Act [1935] .... NLRA
National Labor Relations Board [Department of Labor] [Washington, DC] .... NLRB
National Labor Relations Board Annual Report [A publication] (DLA) .... NLRB Ann Rep
National Labor Relations Board Decisions [A publication] (DLA) .... NLRB Dec
National Labor Relations Board Decisions and Orders [A publication] (DLA) .... NLRB
National Labor Relations Board Field Manual .... LRBFM
National Labor Relations Board Professional Association .... NLRBP
National Labor Relations Board Professional Association (EA) .... NLRBPA
National Labor Relations Board Union (EA) .... NLRBU
National Labor Relations Board, Washington, DC [Library symbol Library of Congress] (LCLS) .... DNLR
National Laboratory Center [Bureau of Alcohol, Tobacco, and Firearms] [Rockville, MD] (GRD) .... NLC
National Laboratory of Psychical Research [British] .... NLPR
National Labor-Management Foundation (EA) .... NLMF
National Labour Congress [Nigeria] (ECON) .... NLC
National Labour Party [Sierra Leone] [Political party] (EY) .... NLP
National Labourers' Union Trade Society [British] .... NLUTS
National Lacrosse League [Disbanded] .... NLL
National Lakes and Rivers Association [Defunct] (EA) .... NLRA
National Lakeshore (BARN) .... NL
National Lamb Feeders Association (EA) .... NLFA
National Lamp and Shade Manufacturers' Association (IAA) .... NLSMA
National Land for People [An association] (EA) .... NLP
National Land Title Reclamation Association (EA) .... NLTRA
National Land Use Classification (PDAA) .... NLUC
National Landscape Association (EA) .... NLA
National Landscape Institute .... NLI
National Landscape Nurserymen's Association [Later, NLA] (EA) .... NLNA
National Landslide Information Center [US Geological Survey] .... NLIC
National Language Interface (NITA) .... NLI
National Language Mediator .... NLM
National Language Support [Computer science] (PCM) .... NLS
National Languages and Literacy Council [Australia] .... NLLC
National Languages Institute of Australia .... NLIA
National LASER Users Facility [Rochester, NY] [Department of Energy] (GRD) .... NLUF
National Latina Health Organization (EAIO) .... NLHO
National Latino Media Coalition [Citizen's group] (NTCM) .... NLMC
National Launch System (ECON) .... NLS
National Law Enforcement Council (EA) .... NLEC
National Law Enforcement Emergency Frequency (LAIN) .... NLEEF
National Law Enforcement Officers Memorial Fund (EA) .... NLEOMF
National Law Enforcement Telecommunications System .... NALECOM
National Law Enforcement Telecommunications System .... NLETS
National Law Firm Marketing Association (EA) .... NLFMA
National Law Record [A publication] (DLA) .... Nat L Rec
National Law Reporter [A publication] (DLA) .... Nat L Rep
National Law Review [A publication] (DLA) .... Nat L Rev
National Lawn and Garden Distributors Association (EA) .... LGDA
National Lawn and Garden Distributors Association (EA) .... NLGDA
National Lawn Tennis Association (WDAA) .... NLTA
National Lawyers Club (EA) .... NLC
National Lawyers Committee for Soviet Jewry (EA) .... NLCSJ
National Lawyers Guild (EA) .... NLG
National Lawyer's Guild Peace and Disarmament Committee [Later, NLGPDS] (EA) .... NLGPDC
National Lawyer's Guild Peace and Disarmament Subcommittee (EA) .... NLGPDS
National Lawyers Guild Quarterly [A publication] (DLA) .... Guild Q
National Lawyers Guild Quarterly [A publication] (DLA) .... Nat L Guild Q
National Lawyers Guild Quarterly [A publication] (DLA) .... Nat Law Guild Q
National Lawyers Guild Quarterly [A publication] (DLA) .... NLGQ
National Lawyers Wives (EA) .... NLW
National Lead Burning Association (EA) .... NLBA
National Lead Co., Research Library, Niagara Falls, NY [Library symbol Library of Congress] (LCLS) .... NNiaN
National Lead Industries, Inc., Baroid Division, Houston, TX [Library symbol Library of Congress] (LCLS) .... TxHBa
National Leadership Coalition on AIDS [Acquired Immune Deficiency Syndrome] (EA) .... NLCOA
National Leadership Committee [Military] .... NLC
National Leadership Council [Defunct] (EA) .... NLC
National Leadership Institute [Defunct] (EA) .... NLI
National League [Baseball] .... N
National League Championship Series [Baseball] .... NLCS
National League for Democracy [Myanmar] [Political party] (EY) .... NLD
National League for Democracy [Political party] [Myanmar] .... NLD
National League for Nursing (EA) .... NLN
National League for Nursing Education (DAVI) .... NLNE
National League for Separation of Church and State (EA) .... NLSCS
National League for Social Understanding (EA) .... NLSU
National League for the Blind and Disabled [British] (DBA) .... NLB & D
National League of American Pen Women (EA) .... NLAPW
National League of Cities (EA) .... NLC
National League of Cuban American Community-Based Centers (EA) .... NLCACBC
National League of Disabled Voters (EA) .... NLDV
National League of Families of Prisoners and Missing in Southeast Asia .... NLF
National League of Insured Savings Associations [Later, NSLL] (EA) .... NLISA
National League of Masonic Clubs (EA) .... NLMC
National League of Nursing Graduate Nursing Examination (GAGS) .... NLNGNE
National League of Postmasters of the United States .... NLP

National League of Postmasters of the United States (EA) .... NLPM
National League of Professional Baseball Clubs (EA) .... NL
National League of Teachers' Associations [*Defunct*] (EA) .... NLTA
National League of the Blind and Disabled [*A union*] [*British*] (DCTA) .... NLBD
National League of the Blind of Ireland (EAIO) .... NLBI
National Learning Disabilities Assistance Project .... NaLDAP
National Leased Housing Association [*Washington, DC*] (EA) .... NLHA
National Leather Association (EA) .... NLA
National Leather Trades Federation [*A union*] [*British*] .... NLTF
National Left-Handers Racquet Sports Association (EA) .... NLHRSA
National Legal Aid and Defender Association (EA) .... NLADA
National Legal Aid and Defender Association Briefcase [*A publication*] (DLA) .... NLADA Brief
National Legal Aid Association .... NLAA
National Legal Center for the Medically Dependent and Disabled (EA) .... NLCMDD
National Legal Center for the Public Interest (EA) .... NLCPI
National Legal Data Center [*Defunct*] (EA) .... NLDC
National Legal Databases (IID) .... NLD
National Legal Foundation (EA) .... NLF
National Legal Magazine [*A publication*] (DLA) .... Nat'l Legal Mag
National Legal Resource Center for Child Advocacy and Protection [*Later, ABACCL*] (EA) .... NLRCCAP
National Legion of Decency [*Later, National Catholic Office for Motion Pictures*] (EA) .... NLD
National Legion of Greek-American War Veterans in America (EA) .... NLGAWVA
National Legislative Conference [*Later, NCSL*] (EA) .... NLC
National Legislative Council [*Later, NCSL*] .... NLC
National Legislative Council for the Handicapped (EA) .... NLCH
National Legislative Education Foundation (EA) .... NLEF
National Legislative Network [*National Conference of State Legislatures*] [*Information service or system*] (IID) .... LEGISNET
National Lending Library for Science and Technology [*Later, BLLD*] [*British Library*] .... NLL
National Lending Library for Science and Technology [*Later, BLL*] [*British*] .... NLLST
National Lesbian and Gay Health Foundation (EA) .... NLGHF
National Lesbian Information Service .... NLIS
National Leukemia Association (EA) .... NLA
National Liberal (AD) .... Nat Lib
National Liberal [*British politics*] .... NL
National Liberal Club [*British*] .... NLC
National Liberal Federation [*British*] .... NLF
National Liberal League [*Later, NLSCS*] (EA) .... NLL
National Liberal Party [*Australia Political party*] .... NatLib
National Liberal Party [*Bermuda*] [*Political party*] (EY) .... NLP
National Liberation Army [*Bolivia*] .... NLA
National Liberation Committee [*South Africa*] .... NLC
National Liberation Council Decree [*1966-69*] [*Ghana*] [*A publication*] (DLA) .... NLCD
National Liberation Front [*Vietnam*] [*Political party*] .... NLF
National Liberation Front [*Myanmar*] [*Political party*] (PD) .... NLF
National Liberation Front [*Aden*] [*Political party*] .... NLF
National Liberation Front [*South Africa*] [*Political party*] (PD) .... NLF
National Liberation Front of South Vietnam [*Political party*] .... NLFSV
National Liberation Front Party Apparatus [*Algeria*] .... NLFPA
National Liberation Movement [*Guatemala*] [*Political party*] (PD) .... MNL
National Liberation Movement of Western Togoland .... NLMWT
National Liberation Party [*Gambia*] [*Political party*] (PPW) .... NLP
National Liberty Committee (EA) .... NLC
National Librarians Association (EA) .... NLA
National Libraries Authority .... NL
National Library [*Canada*] .... NL
National Library Act .... NLA
National Library, Bangkok, Thailand [*Library symbol Library of Congress*] (LCLS) .... ThBNL
National Library, Canadiana Acquisitions, Ottawa, ON, Canada [*Library symbol*] [*Library of Congress*] (LCLS) .... CaOONLC
National Library Division, Canadian National Institute for the Blind, Toronto, Ontario [*Library symbol National Library of Canada*] (NLC) .... OTBNL
National Library for the Blind .... NLB
National Library, Library Systems Centre, Ottawa, ON, Canada [*Library symbol Library of Congress*] (LCLS) .... CaOONLD
National Library Network .... NLN
National Library of Australia (NITA) .... NLA
National Library of Australia, Canberra, ACT, Australia [*Library symbol*] [*Library of Congress*] (LCLS) .... AuNL
National Library of Australia, Canberra, Australia [*Library symbol Library of Congress*] (LCLS) .... Au
National Library of Canada (AD) .... Nat Lib
National Library of Canada (AD) .... NATLIBCAN
National Library of Canada .... NLC
National Library of Canada Advisory Board .... NLCAB
National Library of Canada, Cataloguing Branch [*UTLAS symbol*] .... NLA
National Library of Canada, Locations Division [*UTLAS symbol*] .... NLB
National Library of Canada, Ottawa, ON, Canada [*Library symbol Library of Congress*] (LCLS) .... CaOONL
National Library of Canada, Ottawa, ON, Canada [*OCLC symbol*] (OCLC) .... NLC
National Library of Canada [*Bibliotheque Nationale du Canada*] **Ottawa, Ontario** [*Library symbol National Library of Canada*] (NLC) .... OONL
National Library of Canada, Retrospective Bibliography, Ottawa, ON, Canada [*Library symbol*] [*Library of Congress*] (LCLS) .... CaOONLR
National Library of China .... NLC
National Library of Greenland [*Nunatta Atuagaategarfi*], Nuuk, Greenland [*Library symbol*] [*Library of Congress*] (LCLS) .... Gre
National Library of India, Calcutta, India [*Library symbol Library of Congress*] (LCLS) .... IiCN
National Library of Ireland (AIE) .... NLI
National Library of Ireland, Dublin, Ireland [*Library symbol Library of Congress*] (LCLS) .... IreDNL
National Library of Malaysia, Kuala Lumpur, Malaysia [*Library symbol*] [*Library of Congress*] (LCLS) .... Mly
National Library of Medicine [*Source file*] [*UTLAS symbol*] .... MDE
National Library of Medicine [*Public Health Service*] [*Bethesda, MD Database producer*] .... NLM
National Library of Medicine, Bethesda, MD [*OCLC symbol*] (OCLC) .... NLM
National Library of New Zealand (AD) .... NATLIBNZ
National Library of New Zealand, Wellington, New Zealand [*Library symbol*] [*Library of Congress*] (LCLS) .... Nz
National Library of Science and Invention [*British*] (DIT) .... NLSI
National Library of Scotland (NITA) .... NLS
National Library of Scotland, Edinburgh, United Kingdom [*Library symbol Library of Congress*] (LCLS) .... UkENL
National Library of Scotland Lending Services (NITA) .... NLSLS
National Library, Public Service Branch, Ottawa, ON, Canada [*Library symbol Library of Congress*] (LCLS) .... CaOONLP
National Library Service for the Blind and Physically Handicapped [*Also, NLS /BPH*] [*Library of Congress*] .... NLS
National Library Service for the Blind and Physically Handicapped [*Also, NLS*] [*Library of Congress Computer science*] (IID) .... NLS/BPH
National Library Service for the Blind and Physically Handicapped [*Library of Congress Washington, DC Library network*] .... NSBPH
National Library, Singapore, Singapore [*Library symbol Library of Congress*] (LCLS) .... SgpNL
National Library, Union Catalogue of Books, Ottawa, ON, Canada [*Library symbol Library of Congress*] (LCLS) .... CaOONLB
National Library, Union Catalogue of Serials, Ottawa, ON, Canada [*Library symbol Library of Congress*] (LCLS) .... CaOONLS
National Library Week .... NLW
National Licensed Beverage Association (EA) .... NLBA
National Licensed Practical Nurses Educational Foundation [*Defunct*] (EA) .... NLPNEF
National Licensed Victuallers Association [*British*] (DBA) .... NLVA
National Life Insurance Co., Lincoln National Life Foundation, Louis A. Warren Lincoln Library and Museum, Fort Wayne, IN [*Library symbol Library of Congress*] (LCLS) .... InFWI-F
National Life Share Foundation (EA) .... NLSF
National Lifeguard Championships (EA) .... NLC
National Light Castings Ironfounders' Federation [*British*] (BI) .... NLCIF
National Lighting Bureau (EA) .... NLB
National Lightning Detection Network .... NLDN
National Lilac Rabbit Club of America (EA) .... NLRCA
National Lime Association (EA) .... NLA
National Limestone Institute [*Later, NSA*] (EA) .... NLI
National Limousine Association (EA) .... NLA
National Lincoln Sheep Breeders' Association (EA) .... NLSBA
National Lincoln-Civil War Council (EA) .... NLCWC
National Liquid Reserves Money Market Fund .... NLR
National Liquor Stores Association (EA) .... NLSA
National List of Scientific Plant Names [*Department of Agriculture*] (IID) .... NLSPN
National Listen America Club (EA) .... NLAC
National Lithuanian Society of America (EA) .... NLSA
National Little Britches Rodeo Association (EA) .... NLBRA
National Little College Athletic Association [*Later, NSCAA*] (EA) .... NLCAA
National Liturgical Commission [*Catholic Church*] [*Australia*] .... NLC
National Live Stock and Meat Board (EA) .... NLSMB
National Live Stock Producers Association (EA) .... NLSPA
National Livestock Brand Conference [*Later, International Livestock Brand Conference*] .... NLBC
National Livestock Dealers Association [*Later, Livestock Marketing Association*] (EA) .... NLDA
National Livestock Exchange [*Defunct*] (EA) .... NLE
National Livestock Feeders Association [*Later, NCA*] (EA) .... NLFA
National Livestock Tax Committee [*Later, NCA*] (EA) .... NLTC
National Location Code [*Civil Defense*] .... NLC
National Locksmith Suppliers Association (EA) .... NLSA
National Locksmiths Association (EA) .... NLA
National Logistical Command (MCD) .... NLC
National Logistics Supply Center [*Marine science*] (OSRA) .... NLSC
National Longitudinal Study of Mathematical Abilities .... NLSMA
National Longitudinal Study of Youth .... NLSY
National Longitudinal Survey [*Statistics*] .... NLS
National Longitudinal Surveys of Labor Market Experience [*Ohio State University*] [*Columbus*] [*Information service or system*] (IID) .... NLS
National Long-Lines Agency (NATG) .... NALLA
National Long-Term Care Channeling Demonstration Program [*Department of Health and Human Services*] (GFGA) .... NLTCDP
National Low Income Housing Coalition (EA) .... NLIHC
National Low-Emission Vehicles .... NLEV
National Low-Temperature Neutron Irradiation Facility [*Oak Ridge, TN*] [*Department of Energy*] (GRD) .... NLTNIF
National LP-Gas Association (EA) .... NLPGA
National Lubricating Grease Institute (EA) .... NLGI
National Luggage Dealers Association (EA) .... NLDA
National Lum and Abner Society (EA) .... NLAS
National Lumber and Building Material Dealers Association (EA) .... NLBMDA
National Lumber Exporters Association [*Later, AHEC*] (EA) .... NLEA
National Lumber Grading Agency [*Canada*] .... NLGA
National Lumber Manufacturers Association [*Later, NFPA*] (EA) .... NLMA
National Lupus Erythematosus Foundation [*Defunct*] (EA) .... NLEF

National Lutheran Campus Ministry (EA) ..... NLCM
National Lutheran Commission on Scouting [*Defunct*] (EA) ..... NLCS
National Lutheran Council [*Later, LC/USA*] (EA) ..... NLC
National Lutheran Editors and Managers Association [*Defunct*] (EA) ..... NLEMA
National Lutheran Educational Conference [*Later, LECNA*] (EA) ..... NLEC
National Lutheran Outdoors Ministry Association (EA) ..... NLOMA
National Lutheran Parent-Teacher League (EA) ..... NLPTL
National Macaroni Institute (EA) ..... NMI
National Macaroni Manufacturers Association [*Later, NPA*] (EA) ..... NMMA
National Machine Accountants Association [*Later, DPMA*] ..... NMAA
National Machine Embroidery Instructors Association (EA) ..... NMEIA
National Machine Embroidery Instructors Association of America (EA) ..... NMEIAA
National Machine Tool Builders' Association [*Later, AMT*] (EA) ..... NMTBA
National Magazine Co. ..... NMC
National Magazine Co. Ltd. [*Publisher*] [*British*] ..... NM
National Maglev Initiative [*Department of Transportation*] ..... NMI
National Magnet Laboratory ..... NML
National Magnetic Fusion Energy Computer Center [*Department of Energy*] (MCD) ..... NMFECC
National Mah Jongg League (EA) ..... NMJL
National Mail Centers, Inc. [*Telecommunications service*] (TSSD) ..... NMC
National Mail Order Association [*Los Angeles, CA*] (EA) ..... NMOA
National Mail Order Nurserymen's Association [*Later, MAN*] (EA) ..... NMONA
National Main Street Center (EA) ..... NMSC
National Maintenance Index (IAA) ..... NMI
National Maintenance Management Association [*Defunct*] (EA) ..... NMMA
National Maintenance Point [*Military*] (AABC) ..... NMP
National Maintenance Publications Center [*Army*] (AABC) ..... NMPC
National Malaria Association (DAVI) ..... NMA
National Male Nurse Association [*Later, AAMN*] (EA) ..... NMNA
National Management Association [*Dayton, OH*] (EA) ..... NMA
National Management Award [*GAMC*] ..... NMA
National Management Career Curriculum [*Office of Personnel Management*] (GFGA) ..... NMCC
National Management Systems [*Information service or system*] (IID) ..... NMS
National Manpower Coordinating Committee [*Department of Labor*] ..... NMCC
National Manpower Council ..... NMC
National Manpower Institute [*Later, NIWL*] (EA) ..... NMI
National Manpower Training Association [*Later, NETA*] (EA) ..... NMTA
National Manufactured Housing Federation (EA) ..... NMHF
National Manufactured Housing Finance Association [*Defunct*] (EA) ..... NMHFA
National Manufacturers of Beverage Flavors [*Defunct*] (EA) ..... NMBF
National Map Accuracy Standards (PDAA) ..... NMAS
National Map Collection, Public Archives [*Collection Nationale des Cartes et Plans, Archives Publiques*] **Ottawa, Ontario** [*Library symbol National Library of Canada*] (NLC) ..... OOAMA
National Maple Syrup Council [*Later, NAMSC*] ..... NMSC
National Mapping (AD) ..... NATMAP
National Marble Club of America (EA) ..... NMCA
National Marfan Foundation (EA) ..... NMF
National Marina Association [*Defunct*] (EA) ..... NMA
National Marina Manufacturers Consortium [*Defunct*] (EA) ..... NMMC
National Marine Advisory Service [*National Oceanic and Atmospheric Administration*] (MSC) ..... NMAS
National Marine Bankers Association [*Chicago, IL*] (EA) ..... NMBA
National Marine Board [*British World War II*] ..... NMB
National Marine Center [*Marine science*] (OSRA) ..... NMC
National Marine Center (USDC) ..... NMC
National Marine Data and Information Service [*China*] [*Marine science*] (OSRA) ..... NMDIS
National Marine Data Inventory ..... NAMDI
National Marine Distributors Association (EA) ..... NMDA
National Marine Educators Association (EA) ..... NMEA
National Marine Electronics Association (EA) ..... NMEA
National Marine Engineers' Beneficial Association (EA) ..... NMEBA
National Marine Environmental Forecasting Center [*China*] [*Marine science*] (OSRA) ..... NMEFC
National Marine Fisheries Service [*Formerly, Bureau of Commercial Fisheries*] [*National Oceanic and Atmospheric Administration Washington, DC*] ..... NMFS
National Marine Mammal Laboratory [*National Marine Fisheries Service*] ..... NMML
National Marine Mammal Stranding Network (EA) ..... NMMSN
National Marine Manufacturers Association (EA) ..... NMMA
National Marine Pollution Information System [*Marine science*] (OSRA) ..... NMPIS
National Marine Pollution Information Systems (USDC) ..... NMPIS
National Marine Pollution Program Office (USDC) ..... NMPPO
National Marine Pollution Program Office [*Marine science*] (OSRA) ..... NMPPO
National Marine Representatives Association (EA) ..... NMRA
National Marine Water Quality Laboratory [*Environmental Protection Agency*] (MSC) ..... NMWQL
National Maritime Authority [*Australia*] ..... NMA
National Maritime Board ..... NMB
National Maritime Council [*Defunct*] (EA) ..... NMC
National Maritime Historical Society (EA) ..... NMHS
National Maritime Institute [*British*] ..... NMI
National Maritime Intelligence Center [*Created in 1992 from intelligence activities in the Washington, D.C., area*] [*Navy*] (DOMA) ..... NMIC
National Maritime Museum [*British*] ..... NMM
National Maritime Museum, San Francisco, CA [*OCLC symbol*] (OCLC) ..... UDU
National Maritime Research Center [*Maritime Administration*] [*Also, an information service or system*] (IID) ..... NMRC
National Maritime Resource Center [*MARAD*] (TAG) ..... NMREC
National Maritime System [*MARAD*] (TAG) ..... NMS
National Maritime Union (USDC) ..... NMU
National Maritime Union of America (EA) ..... NMU
National Market Advisory Board [*SEC*] ..... NMAB
National Market System ..... NMS
National Market Traders Federation [*British*] (DBA) ..... NMTF
National Marriage Encounter (EA) ..... NME
National Marriage Guidance Council [*British*] (ILCA) ..... NMGC
National Marrow Donor Program [*Department of Health and Human Services*] ..... NMDP
National Mass Retailing Institute [*New York, NY*] (EA) ..... NMRI
National Master Facility Inventory [*Department of Health and Human Services*] (GFGA) ..... NMFI
National Master Farm Homemakers Guild (EA) ..... NMFHG
National Master Shoe Rebuilders Association (EA) ..... NMSRA
National Master Specification [*Construction Specifications Canada*] [*Information service or system*] (IID) ..... NMS
National Master Tile Fixers Association [*British*] (DBA) ..... NMTFA
National Mastitis Council (EA) ..... NMC
National Match ..... NM
National Match Support Detachment [*Ammunition supplier*] ..... NMSD
National Materials Advisory Board (EA) ..... NMAB
National Materials Handling Centre [*Cranfield Institute of Technology*] [*British*] (CB) ..... NMHC
National Materials Property Data Network (EA) ..... NMPDN
National Maternal and Child Health Clearinghouse (EA) ..... NMCHC
National Maternal and Infant Health Survey [*Department of Health and Human Services*] (GFGA) ..... NMIHS
National Maximum Speed Limit [*NHTSA*] (TAG) ..... NMSL
National Means Test Proposal ..... NMTP
National Measurement Accreditation Service [*Research center British*] (IRC) ..... NAMAS
National Measurement Laboratory [*Gaithersburg, MD*] [*National Institute of Standards and Technology*] (GRD) ..... NML
National Measurement System [*National Institute of Standards and Technology*] ..... NMS
National Meat Association [*Formerly, NIMPA*] (EA) ..... NMA
National Meat Brokers [*Australia*] ..... NMB
National Meat Canners Association (EA) ..... NMCA
National Meat Industry Council (EA) ..... NMIC
National Meat Retail Council [*Australia*] ..... NMRC
National Media Corp. [*NYSE symbol*] (SPSG) ..... NM
National Media Corp. [*Associated Press*] (SAG) ..... NMedia
National Media Liaison Officer ..... NMLO
National Mediation Board [*Department of Labor*] ..... NMB
National Medical and Dental Association (EA) ..... NMDA
National Medical Association (EA) ..... NMA
National Medical Association Foundation [*Defunct*] (EA) ..... NMAF
National Medical Audiovisual Center [*of the National Library of Medicine*] [*LHNCBC*] [*Absorbed by*] (EA) ..... NMAC
National Medical Care ..... NMC
National Medical Care Expenditures Survey [*Department of Health and Human Services*] (GFGA) ..... NMCES
National Medical Care Utilization and Expenditure Survey [*Department of Health and Human Services A publication*] (DHSM) ..... NMCUES
National Medical Expenditure Survey [*Department of Health and Human Services*] (GFGA) ..... NMES
National Medical Fellowships (EA) ..... NMF
National Medical Financial Services Corp. [*Associated Press*] (SAG) ..... NatMFS
National Medical Financial Services Corp. [*NASDAQ symbol*] (SAG) ..... NMFS
National Medical Foundation for Eye Care [*Later, AAO*] (EA) ..... NMFEC
National Medical Library (DAVI) ..... NML
National Medical Organisation (ACII) ..... NMO
National Medical Research Institute (MAE) ..... NMRI
National Medical Utilization Committee [*HEW*] ..... NMUC
National Medic-Card [*Commercial firm*] (EA) ..... NMCS
National Medicinal Chemistry Symposium ..... NMCS
National Medicine Society [*British*] ..... NMS
National Medico-Dental Conference for the Evaluation of Fluoridation [*Later, Medical-Dental Committee on Evaluation of Fluoridation*] (EA) ..... NMDCEF
National Memorials Committee [*Australia*] ..... NMC
National Men's Judo Championships [*British*] ..... NMJC
National Mental Health Association (EA) ..... NMHA
National Mental Health Consumer Self-Help Clearinghouse (EA) ..... NMHCSHC
National Mental Health Consumers' Association (EA) ..... NMHCA
National Mercantile Bancorp [*NASDAQ symbol*] (NQ) ..... MBLA
National Mercantile Bancorp [*Associated Press*] (SAG) ..... NtMerc
National Merit Scholarship Corp. (EA) ..... NMSC
National Merit Scholarship Qualifying Test ..... NMSQT
National Message Center [*Overland Park, KS*] (TSSD) ..... NMC
National Metal Awning Association [*Defunct*] (EA) ..... NMAA
National Metal Decorators Association (EA) ..... NMDA
National Metal Spinners Association (EA) ..... NMSA
National Metal Trades Association [*Later, AAIM*] (EA) ..... NMTA
National Metal Trades Federation [*British*] (DBA) ..... NMTF
National Meteorological Center [*National Oceanic and Atmospheric Administration Information service or system*] (IID) ..... NMC
National Meteorological Rocket Network ..... NMRN
National Meteorological Satellite System (IAA) ..... NMSS
National Meter Programming (NRCH) ..... NMP
National Metric Board ..... NMB
National Metric Conversion Board (NADA) ..... NMCB
National Metric Education Center [*Western Michigan University*] ..... NMEC
National Metrology Laboratory (ACII) ..... NML
National Microelectronics Research Centre (NITA) ..... NMRC
National Microfilm Association [*Later, National Micrographics Association, now AIIM*] [*Trade association*] ..... NMA

National Microfilms Ltd., Dublin, Ireland [*Library symbol*] [*Library of Congress*] (LCLS) ... NmfL
National Microform Association (NITA) ... NMA
National Micrographics Association [*Later, AIIM*] [*Trade association*] (EA) ... NMA
National Microwave Landing System (MCD) ... NMLS
National Midas Dealers Association (EA) ... NMDA
National Middle School Association (EA) ... NMSA
National Middle School Resource Center (EA) ... NMSRC
National Midwives Association (EA) ... NMA
National Migraine Foundation [*Later, National Headache Foundation - NHF*] (EA) ... NMF
National Migrant Clearinghouse (OICC) ... NMC
National Migrant Resource Program (EA) ... NMRP
National Migrant Worker Program [*Department of Labor*] ... NMWP
National Migrant Workers Council [*Farmington Hills, MI*] (EA) ... NMWC
National Military Authority (NATG) ... NMA
National Military Command Authority (NVT) ... NMCA
National Military Command Center [*DoD*] ... NMCC
National Military Command System ... NATMILCOMSYS
National Military Command System ... NMCS
National Military Command System Standards (AFM) ... NMCSS
National Military Command System Support Center (AABC) ... NMCSSC
National Military Council [*Surinam*] (PD) ... NMC
National Military Discharge Review Project (EA) ... NMDRP
National Military Establishment [*Designated Department of Defense, 1949*] ... NME
National Military Family Association (EA) ... NMFA
National Military Fish and Wildlife Association (EA) ... NMFWA
National Military Guidance Association (EA) ... NMGA
National Military Indications System (MCD) ... NMIS
National Military Information Center ... NMIC
National Military Intelligence Association (EA) ... NMIA
National Military Intelligence Support Team [*Defense Intelligence Agency*] (DOMA) ... NMIST
National Military Representatives with SHAPE [*NATO*] ... NMR
National Military Strategy (DOMA) ... NMS
National Military Strategy Document (DOMA) ... NMSD
National Military Vehicle Collectors Association [*Defunct*] ... NMVCA
National Military Wives Association [*Later, NMFA*] (EA) ... NMWA
National Milk Glass Collectors Society ... NMGCS
National Milk Producers Federation (EA) ... NMPF
National Milk Publicity Council [*British*] (BI) ... NMPC
National Milk Record [*British*] (BI) ... NMR
National Milk Testing Service ... NMTS
National Millinery Planning Board [*Defunct*] (EA) ... NMPB
National Mime Association [*Later, NMTA*] (EA) ... NMA
National Mine Health and Safety Academy, Beckley, WV [*OCLC symbol*] (OCLC) ... UDM
National Mine Rescue Association ... NMRA
National Mineral Wool Association [*Later, MIMA*] ... NMWA
National Mineral Wool Insulation Association [*Formerly, NMWA*] [*Later, MIMA*] (EA) ... NMWIA
National Mini-Storage Institute [*Defunct*] (EA) ... NMSI
National Minority AIDS [*Acquired Immune Deficiency Syndrome*] **Council** (EA) ... NMAC
National Minority Business Campaign [*Later, NMBD*] (EA) ... NMBC
National Minority Business Council [*New York, NY*] (EA) ... NMBC
National Minority Business Directories [*Minneapolis, MN*] (EA) ... NMBD
National Minority Health Association (EA) ... NMHA
National Minority Purchasing Council [*Later, NMSDC*] (EA) ... NMPC
National Minority Supplier Development Council (EA) ... NMSDC
National Missile Defense [*DoD*] ... NMD
National Missile Defense-Ground Based RADAR [*Army*] (RDA) ... NMD/GBR
National Missile Industry Conference (AAG) ... NMIC
National Missile Range (KSC) ... NMR
National Mission Operating Procedures (AAG) ... NMOP
National Missionary Council [*Australia*] ... NMC
National Mobile Home Association (EA) ... NMHA
National Mobile/Manufactured Home Owners Foundation [*Later, NFMHO*] (EA) ... NMMHOF
National Mobile Radio Association [*Defunct*] (EA) ... NMRA
National Mobile Radio System [*Later, Telocator Network of America*] (EA) ... NMRS
National Mobility Office [*British*] ... NMO
National Mobility Scheme [*British*] ... NMS
National Mobilization Against AIDS [*Acquired Immune Deficiency Syndrome*] (EA) ... NMAA
National Mobilization for Survival (EA) ... MFS
National Model Cities Community Development Directors Association [*Later, NCDA*] (EA) ... NMCCDDA
National Model Cities Directors Association [*Later, NCDA*] (EA) ... NMCDA
National Model Railroad Association (EA) ... NMRA
National Monument (WDAA) ... NAT MON
National Monument (AD) ... Nat Mon
National Monument (GNE) ... NM
National Moratorium on Prison Construction [*Defunct*] (EA) ... NMPC
National Morgan Cutting and Stock Horse Association (EA) ... NMCSHA
National Mortality Followback Survey [*National Center for Health Statistics*] ... NMFS
National Mossberg Collectors Association (EA) ... NMCA
National Motel Brokers (EA) ... NMB
National Motor Carrier Advisory Committee [*MTMC*] (TAG) ... NMCAC
National Motor Drivers' Association [*A union*] [*British*] ... NMDA
National Motor Freight Classification ... NMFC
National Motor Freight Classification Rules ... NMFCR
National Motor Freight Traffic Association [*Alexandria, VA*] (EA) ... NMFTA
National Motor Freight Traffic Association Inc., Agent, Washington DC [*STAC*] ... NMF
National Motor Vehicle Safety Advisory Council (EA) ... NMVSAC
National Motor Vehicle Theft Act ... NMVTA
National Motor Volunteers [*British military*] (DMA) ... NM
National Motorcycle Commuter Association [*Defunct*] (EA) ... NMCA
National Motorcycle Dealers Association [*Later, NMRA*] (EA) ... NMDA
National Motorcycle Dismantelers Association (EA) ... NMDA
National Motorcycle Racing Association (EA) ... NMRA
National Motorcycle Retailers Association [*Defunct*] (EA) ... NMRA
National Motorists Association (EA) ... NMA
National Motorsports Committee (EA) ... NMC
National Motorsports Press Association (EA) ... NMPA
National Mouse Club [*British*] (BI) ... NMC
National Movement Theatre Association (EA) ... NMTA
National Moving & Storage Association [*MTMC*] (TAG) ... NM&SA
National Moving and Storage Association (EA) ... NMSA
National Moving Image Database [*American Film Institute*] [*Information service or system*] (IID) ... NAMID
National Mud Racing Association ... NMRA
National Multi Housing Council (EA) ... NMHC
National Multiple Sclerosis Society (EA) ... NMSS
National Multiple Sclerosis Society of Australia ... NMSSA
National Multipurpose Space Station ... NMSS
National Municipal League (EA) ... NML
National Municipal Policy [*Environmental Protection Agency*] (EPA) ... NMP
National Munitions Control Board [*World War II*] ... NMCB
National Musclecar Association (EA) ... NMCA
National Museum (AD) ... Nat Mus
National Museum and Gallery Registration Association (EA) ... NMGRA
National Museum of African Art [*Smithsonian Institution*] ... NMAA
National Museum of African Art [*Smithsonian Institution*] (GFGA) ... NMAFA
National Museum of American History, Science, Technology, and Culture [*Smithsonian Institution*] ... NMAHSTC
National Museum of Antiquities in Scotland ... NMA
National Museum of Canada ... NMC
National Museum of Canada Bulletin [*A publication*] ... NMCB
National Museum of Canada, Ottawa, ON, Canada [*Library symbol Library of Congress*] (LCLS) ... CaOONM
National Museum of History and Technology [*Later, National Museum of American History*] (GRD) ... NMHT
National Museum of National History ... NMNH
National Museum of Natural History [*Smithsonian Institution*] ... NMNH
National Museum of Natural Sciences [*National Museums of Canada*] [*Research center*] (RCD) ... NMNS
National Museum of Natural Sciences [*Musee National des Sciences Naturelles*], Ottawa, Ontario [*Library symbol National Library of Canada*] (NLC) ... OONMNS
National Museum of Racing (EA) ... NMR
National Museum of Science and Technology, Ottawa, ON, Canada [*Library symbol Library of Congress*] (LCLS) ... CaOONMS
National Museum of Science and Technology [*Musee National des Sciences et de la Technologie*] **Ottawa, Ontario** [*Library symbol National Library of Canada*] (NLC) ... OONMS
National Museum of Transport [*Later, TMA*] (EA) ... NMT
National Museum of Women in the Arts, Washington, DC [*Library symbol*] [*Library of Congress*] (LCLS) ... DNWM
National Museums of Canada, Canadian Conservation Institute, Ottawa, ON, Canada [*Library symbol Library of Congress*] (LCLS) ... CaOONMCC
National Museums of Canada Library [*UTLAS symbol*] ... NMU
National Museums of Canada, National Museum of Man, Ottawa, ON, Canada [*Library symbol Library of Congress*] (LCLS) ... CaOONMM
National Museums of Canada [*Musees Nationaux du Canada*] **Ottawa, Ontario** [*Library symbol National Library of Canada*] (NLC) ... OONM
National Music Academy [*Australia*] ... NMA
National Music and Disability Information Service [*British*] ... NMDIS
National Music Camp [*Interlochen, MI*] ... NMC
National Music Council (EA) ... NMC
National Music Council of Great Britain (EAIO) ... NMCGB
National Music League (EA) ... NML
National Music Printers and Allied Trades Association (EA) ... NMPATA
National Music Publishers' Association (EA) ... NMPA
National Music Theater Network (EA) ... NMTN
National Mustang Association (EA) ... NMA
National Mutual Benefit [*Madison, WI*] (EA) ... NMB
National Mutual Fund Managers Association [*Defunct*] (EA) ... NMFMA
National Mutual Royal Bank [*Australia*] (ADA) ... NMRB
National Muzzle Loading Rifle Association (EA) ... NMLRA
National Myoclonus Foundation [*Defunct*] (EA) ... NMF
National Namibia Concerns (EA) ... NNC
National Narcotics Border Interdiction System ... NNBIS
National Narcotics Intelligence Consumers Committee [*Drug Enforcement Administration*] [*Washington, DC*] (EGAO) ... NNICC
National Narrowcast Service [*Public Broadcasting Service*] [*Arlington, VA*] [*Telecommunications service*] (TSSD) ... NNS
National Natality Survey ... NNS
National Native Alcohol and Drug Abuse Program [*Canada*] ... NNADAP
National Native American Chamber of Commerce [*Defunct*] (EA) ... NNACC
National Native American Cooperative (EA) ... NNAC
National Nature Reserve [*British*] ... NNR
National Naval Dental Center (DNAB) ... NATNAVDENCEN
National Naval Dental Center ... NNDC
National Naval Medical Center [*Bethesda, MD*] ... NATNAVMEDCEN

National Naval Medical Center [*Maryland*] [*Seismograph station code, US Geological Survey Closed*] (SEIS) ... NHB
National Naval Medical Center [*Bethesda, MD*] ... NNMC
National Naval Officers Association (EA) ... NNOA
National Naval Reserve Master Control Radio Station (DNAB) ... NATNAVRESMASTCONRADSTA
National Naval Volunteers ... NNV
National Navy Notice ... NNN
National Neckwear Association (EA) ... NNA
National Needlecraft Bureau (EA) ... NNB
National Needlework Association (EA) ... NNA
National Negro Business League [*Later, National Business League*] ... NNBL
National Negro County Agents Association (EA) ... NNCAA
National Negro Evangelical Association [*Later, NBEA*] ... NNEA
National Negro Press Association [*Defunct*] (EA) ... NNPA
National Negro Republican Assembly [*Defunct*] ... NNRA
National Neighborhood Coalition (EA) ... NNC
National Neighbors (EA) ... NN
National Nephrosis Foundation [*Later, NKF*] ... NNF
National Network [*Telecommunications British*] ... Natnet
National Network Congestion Signal (NITA) ... NNC
National Network Control Centre [*Communications*] [*British*] ... NNCC
National Network Dialing [*Telecommunications*] (TEL) ... NND
National Network for Curriculum Coordination in Vocational and Technical Education (OICC) ... NNCCVTE
National Network for Immigrant and Refugee Rights (EA) ... NNIRR
National Network for Social Work Managers (EA) ... NNSWM
National Network in Solidarity with the Nicaraguan People (EA) ... NNSNP
National Network in Solidarity with the People of Guatemala (EA) ... NNSPG
National Network of Asian and Pacific Women (EA) ... NNAPW
National Network of Bilingual Centers (EA) ... NNBC
National Network of Episcopal Clergy Associations (EA) ... NNECA
National Network of Graduate Business School Women [*Knoxville, TN*] (EA) ... NNGBSW
National Network of Grantmakers (EA) ... NNG
National Network of Learning Disabled Adults (EA) ... NNLDA
National Network of Libraries of Medicine ... NNLM
National Network of Minority Women in Science (EA) ... MWIS
National Network of Runaway and Youth Services (EA) ... NNRYS
National Network of Women in Sales [*Defunct*] (EA) ... NNWS
National Network of Women Philanthropists (NFD) ... NNWP
National Network of Women's Funds (EA) ... NNWF
National Network of Youth Advisory Boards (EA) ... NNYAB
National Network Operations Center [*Ottawa, ON*] [*Telecommunications*] (TSSD) ... NNOC
National Network Services (NITA) ... NNS
National Neurofibromatosis Foundation (PAZ) ... NNF
National Neurofibromatosis Foundation (EA) ... NNFF
National Neurological Research Bank [*Veterans Administration Medical Center*] [*Research center*] (RCD) ... NNRB
National Neurological Research Foundation (EA) ... NNRF
National Neutron Cross Section Center [*AEC*] (MCD) ... NNCSC
National New Democratic Coalition (EA) ... NNDC
National New Professional Health Workers [*Later, NPSAPHA*] (EA) ... NNPHW
National New Technology Telescope [*Proposed*] [*National Science Foundation*] ... NNTT
National Newman Alumni Association [*Defunct*] (EA) ... NNAA
National Newman Apostolate ... NNA
National Newman Association of Faculty and Staff [*Defunct*] (EA) ... NNAFS
National Newman Chaplains Association [*Later, CCMA*] (EA) ... NNCA
National Newman Club Federation [*Defunct*] (EA) ... NNCF
National Newman Foundation [*Defunct*] (EA) ... NNF
National News Agency [*Lebanon*] ... NNA
National News Bureau [*Commercial firm*] (EA) ... NNB
National News Council (EA) ... NNC
National Newspaper Association (EA) ... NNA
National Newspaper Foundation (EA) ... NNF
National Newspaper Index [*Information Access Co.*] [*Bibliographic database*] [*Information service or system*] (IID) ... NNI
National Newspaper Promotion Association [*Later, INPA*] (EA) ... NNPA
National Newspaper Publishers Association (EA) ... NNPA
National Newspaper Syndicate ... NNS
National Noise Abatement Council [*Defunct*] ... NNAC
National Nomad Club [*Defunct*] (EA) ... NNC
National Nondestructive Testing Centre [*Atomic Energy Authority*] [*Information service or system*] (IID) ... NNDTC
National Nondestructive Testing Centre [*Atomic Energy Authority*] [*Information service or system*] (IID) ... NNTC
National Non-Domestic Rate [*British*] ... NNDR
National Non-Point Source Pollution Program (GNE) ... NNPSPP
National No-Nukes Prison Support Collective (EA) ... NNNPSC
National Nosocomial Infections Surveillance [*Medicine*] ... NNIS
National Nostalgic Nova (EA) ... NNN
National Notary Association (EA) ... NNA
National Nothing Foundation [*Defunct*] (EA) ... NNF
National Notification Disease Surveillance System [*Centers for Disease Control*] ... NNDSS
National Notion Association [*Later, AHSA*] (EA) ... NNA
National Novice Hockey Association [*Later, HNA*] (EA) ... NNHA
National Novice Hockey League [*Later, NNHA*] (EA) ... NNHL
National Nuclear Corp. [*British*] ... NNC
National Nuclear Data Center [*Department of Energy*] [*Database producer*] (IID) ... NNDC
National Nuclear Energy Series [*of AEC-sponsored books*] ... NNES
National Nuclear Rocket Development Center [*Also known as NRDS*] ... NNRDC
National Nuclear Rocket Development Facility (AAG) ... NNRDF
National Nuclear Test Plan [*Later, NNTRP*] ... NNTP
National Nuclear Test Readiness Program [*Formerly, NNTP*] ... NNTRP
National Nudist Council [*Defunct*] (EA) ... NNC
National Number Dialing [*Telecommunications*] (DCTA) ... NND
National Number Group (NITA) ... NNG
National Number Routed [*Telecommunications*] (TEL) ... NNR
National Numismatic Association (EA) ... NNA
National Nursery Examination Board ... NNEB
National Nurses in Business Association (EA) ... NNBA
National Nurses Society on Addictions (EA) ... NNSA
National Nursing Consultative Committee [*Australia*] ... NNCC
National Nursing Home Survey [*Department of Health and Human Services*] (GFGA) ... NNHS
National Nutrition Consortium [*Defunct*] (EA) ... NNC
National Nutrition Education Clearing House [*Society for Nutrition Education*] (IID) ... NNECH
National Nutritional Foods Association (EA) ... NNFA
National Nutrition-Monitoring System [*Department of Agriculture*] (GFGA) ... NNMS
National Oak Flooring Manufacturers Association (EA) ... NOFMA
National Obscenity Law Center (IID) ... NOLC
National Observer [*A publication*] (AD) ... Nat Obs
National Occupant Protection Use Survey [*NHTSA*] (TAG) ... NOPUS
National Occupational Health Survey of Mining [*Department of Health and Human Services*] (GFGA) ... NOHSM
National Occupational Information Coordinating Committee [*Washington, DC*] ... NOICC
National Occupational Information Service ... NOIS
National Occupational Safety Association (NADA) ... NOSA
National Ocean Access Project (EA) ... NOAP
National Ocean Agency Headquarters ... NOAH
National Ocean Communications Network (USDC) ... NOCN
National Ocean Industries Association (EA) ... NOIA
National Ocean Policy Study [*US Senate*] ... NOPS
National Ocean Pollution Planning Act of 1978 ... NOPPA
National Ocean Pollution Program Office (GNE) ... NOPPO
National Ocean Science and Technology Agency ... NOSTA
National Ocean Sediment Coring Program (NOAA) ... NOSCP
National Ocean Service [*Formerly, Coast and Geodetic Survey*] [*Washington, DC National Oceanic and Atmospheric Administration*] ... NOS
National Ocean Survey (NOAA) ... NOS
National Ocean Survey Analytical Plotter [*NOAA*] (PDAA) ... NOSAP
National Ocean Survey Lake Survey Center [*National Oceanic and Atmospheric Administration*] ... NOS-LSCR
National Ocean Survey System [*Cooperative program of governmental agencies*] ... NOSS
National Ocean Survey Tide Station [*Marine science*] (MSC) ... NOSTS
National Oceanic and Atmospheric Administration [*ICAO designator*] (FAAC) ... MAP
National Oceanic and Atmospheric Administration [*Department of Commerce ICAO designator*] (FAAC) ... NAA
National Oceanic and Atmospheric Administration [*Rockville, MD*] [*Pronounced "Noah"*] ... NOAA
National Oceanic and Atmospheric Administration, Boulder, CO [*OCLC symbol*] (OCLC) ... CON
National Oceanic and Atmospheric Administration Joint Tsunami Research Effort ... NOAA-JTRE
National Oceanic and Atmospheric Administration, Miami Branch, Miami, FL [*OCLC symbol*] (OCLC) ... OAL
National Oceanic and Atmospheric Administration, Miami, Miami, FL [*OCLC symbol*] (OCLC) ... OAO
National Oceanic and Atmospheric Administration - National Ocean Service (DNAB) ... NOAA-NOS
National Oceanic and Atmospheric Administration, National Severe Storms Laboratories, Norman, OK [*OCLC symbol*] (OCLC) ... OUE
National Oceanic and Atmospheric Administration - National Weather Service (DNAB) ... NOAA-NWS
National Oceanic and Atmospheric Administration Pacific Marine Environmental Laboratory ... NOAA-PMEL
National Oceanic and Atmospheric Administration, Rockville, MD [*OCLC symbol*] (OCLC) ... OLA
National Oceanic and Atmospheric Administration Technical Report-National MarineFisheries Service-Circular [*A publication*] (PDAA) ... NOAA-TR-NMFS-Circ
National Oceanic and Atmospheric Administration-Technical Report-National MarineFisheries Service-Special Scientific Report Fisheries (PDAA) ... NOAA-TR-NMFS-SSRF
National Oceanic and Atmospheric Data Network ... NOADN
National Oceanic Satellite System (MCD) ... NOSS
National Oceanographic and Atmospheric Research Laboratory (USDC) ... NOARL
National Oceanographic Association ... NOA
National Oceanographic Center [*Marine science*] (MSC) ... NOC
National Oceanographic Council (NADA) ... NOC
National Oceanographic Data Center [*Databank originator*] [*Washington, DC*] [*National Oceanic and Atmospheric Administration*] ... NODC
National Oceanographic Data Center Advisory Board [*National Oceanic and Atmospheric Administration*] (NOAA) ... NODCAB
National Oceanographic Facility [*Marine science*] (OSRA) ... NOF
National Oceanographic Facility (USDC) ... NOF
National Oceanographic Hazard Survey (NITA) ... NOHS
National Oceanographic Instrumentation Center [*National Oceanic and Atmospheric Administration*] ... NOIC
National Oceanographic Laboratory System ... NOLS

National Oceanographic Processing Facility (DOMA) ... NOPF
National Oceanographic Records Center ... NORC
National Oceanographic Reference Station Network (NOAA) ... NORSNET
National Odd Shoe Exchange (EA) ... NOSE
National Off-Campus Housing Association [*Defunct*] (EA) ... NOCHA
National Office ... NO
National Office Computer Facility [*IRS*] ... NOCF
National Office for Black Catholics (EA) ... NOBC
National Office for Decent Literature [*Defunct*] ... NODL
National Office for Social Responsibility (EA) ... NOSR
National Office for the Rights of the Indigent [*Later, LDF*] ... NORI
National Office Furniture Association [*Later, NOPA*] (EA) ... NOFA
National Office Library, Canadian Red Cross Society [*Bibliotheque du Siege Social, Societe Canadienne de la Croix-Rouge*] **Toronto, Ontario** [*Library symbol National Library of Canada*] (NLC) ... OTCRC
National Office Library, Price Waterhouse & Co., Toronto, Ontario [*Library symbol National Library of Canada*] (BIB) ... OTPRW
National Office Machine Dealers Association (EA) ... NOMDA
National Office Machine Service Association [*Paramount, CA*] (EA) ... NOMSA
National Office Management Association [*Later, AMS*] ... NOMA
National Office of Jesuit Social Ministries (EA) ... NOJSM
National Office of Vital Statistics [*Public Health Service*] [*Obsolete*] ... NOVS
National Office, Office of Federal Contract Compliance Programs (AAGC) ... NO
National Office Products Association (EA) ... NOPA
National Office Products Association of Australia ... NOPAA
National Office Resources Management [*IRS*] ... NORM
National Office Staff [*American Occupational Therapy Association*] ... NOS
National Office Support System (NITA) ... NOSS
National Officers Association (EA) ... NOA
National Off-Road Bicycle Association [*Later, USCF*] (EA) ... NORBA
National Off-Road Racing Association ... NORRA
National Offshore Council (EA) ... NOC
National Offshore Operations Industry Advisory Committee [*Coast Guard*] ... NOOIAC
National Offshore Safety Advisory Committee [*Coast Guard*] ... NOSAC
National Oil and Acrylic Painters Society ... NOAPS
National Oil and Hazardous Substances Contingency Plan [*Environmental Protection Agency*] (ERG) ... NOHSCP
National Oil Board (NATG) ... NOB
National Oil Fuel Institute [*Later, NOJC*] (EA) ... NOFI
National Oil Jobbers Council [*Later, PMAA*] (EA) ... NOJC
National Oil Marketers Association [*Defunct*] (EA) ... NOMA
National Oil Products Co. [*Later, NOPCO Chemical Co.*] ... NOPCO
National Oil Recovery Corp. ... NORCO
National Oil Recyclers Association (GNE) ... NORA
National Oil Scouts and Landmen's Association [*Later, IOSA*] ... NOSLA
National Oilseed Processors Association (EA) ... NOPA
National Oilwell, Inc. [*Associated Press*] (SAG) ... NatOilwll
National Oilwell, Inc. [*NYSE symbol*] (SAG) ... NOI
National Old Lacers [*Later, IOL*] (EA) ... NOL
National Old People's Welfare Council (NADA) ... NOPWC
National Old Timers' Association of the Energy Industry (EA) ... NOTAEI
National Old Timers Auto Racing Club (EA) ... NOTARC
National Older Workers Information System [*American Association of Retired Persons*] [*Information service or system Defunct*] (IID) ... NOWIS
National Older Workers Programs - Operation Mainstream [*Department of Labor*] ... NOWP-OM
National Old-Time Fiddlers' Association (EA) ... NO-TFA
National Olympic Committee (NADA) ... NOC
National Olympic Committee of South Africa (ECON) ... NOCSA
National Olympic Committees ... NOC
National Onderzoek Persmedia [*Database*] [*Stichting Nationaal Onderzoek Persmedia*] [*Netherlands*] [*Information service or system*] (CRD) ... NOP
National One Design Racing Association (EA) ... NODRA
National One-Liners Club (EA) ... NOLC
National One-Write Systems Association (EA) ... NOWSA
National Onion Association (EA) ... NOA
National Online Circuit [*Defunct*] (EA) ... NOC
National Online Manpower Information System [*Manpower Services Commission*] [*Information service or system*] (IID) ... NOMIS
National Online Meeting [*Conference*] (IT) ... NOM
National Online Regulatory Access [*Data Development, Inc.*] [*Information service or system*] (CRD) ... NORA
National On-the-Job Training Program [*Department of Labor*] ... NAT-OJT
National Open College Network (AIE) ... NOCN
National Opera Association (EA) ... NOA
National Opera Institute (EA) ... NOI
National Operatic and Dramatic Association (EAIO) ... NODA
National Operating Committee on Standards for Athletic Equipment (EA) ... NOCSAE
National Operational Environmental Satellite Service (MCD) ... NOES
National Operational Environmental Satellite System ... NOESS
National Operational Meteorological Satellite System ... NOMSS
National Operational Satellite ... NOS
National Operations and Automation Conference (HGAA) ... NOAC
National Operations and Intelligence Watch Officers Network (MCD) ... NOIWON
National Ophthalmic Speakers Programme [*Canada*] ... NOSP
National Ophthalmic Treatment Board [*British*] ... NOTB
National Ophthalmic Treatment Board Association [*British*] ... NOTBA
National Opinion Poll ... NOP
National Opinion Research Center [*University of Chicago*] ... NORC
National Opinion Research Center [*The University of Chicago (IL)*] [*Later, NORC: A Social Science Research Center*] (WDMC) ... NORC
National Opportunity Camps for the Pre-Teen Child (EA) ... NOC
National Optical Association [*Later, NAOO*] ... NOA
National Optical Astronomy Observatories [*Tucson, AZ*] [*National Science Foundation*] ... NOAO
National Optical Font [*Typography*] ... NOF
National Option and Futures Society [*Defunct*] (EA) ... NOFS
National Optometric Association (EA) ... NOA
National Oracy Project (AIE) ... NOP
National Oral Health Information Clearinghouse (PAZ) ... NOHIC
National Oratorio Society [*Defunct*] (EA) ... NOS
National Orbiting Space Station ... NOSS
National Orchestral Association (EA) ... NOA
National Order of Battlefield Commissions (EA) ... NOBC
National Order of Trench Rats (EA) ... NOTR
National Order of Women Legislators (EA) ... NOWL
National Order of Women Legislators (EA) ... OWL
National Ordnance Laboratory ... NOL
[*The*] **National Organ Procurement and Transplantation Network** [*Information service or system*] (IID) ... OPTN
National Organ Transplant Act [*1984*] ... NOTA
National Organ Transplant Education Foundation (EA) ... NOTEF
National Organic Standards Board ... NOSB
National Organisation for Women's Management Education [*British*] (DI) ... NOWME
National Organisation of Counselling Adoptees and Their Parents [*British*] (DBA) ... NORCAP
National Organisation of Initiatives for Social Education [*British*] (DBA) ... NOISE
National Organisational Management Database ... NOMAD
National Organization for Advancement of Associate Degree Nursing (EA) ... NOAADN
National Organization for Albinism and Hypopigmentation (EA) ... NOAH
National Organization for an American Revolution (EA) ... NOAR
National Organization for Birthfathers and Adoption Reform (EA) ... NOBAR
National Organization for Changing Men (EA) ... NOCM
National Organization for Continuing Education of Roman Catholic Clergy (EA) ... NOCERCC
National Organization for Improving School Environments [*Defunct*] (EA) ... NOISE
National Organization for Legal Services (EA) ... NOLS
National Organization for Men (EA) ... NOM
National Organization for Men Legal Defense and Education Fund ... NOM
National Organization for Migrant Children [*Later, NCEMC*] (EA) ... NOMC
National Organization for Non-Parents [*Later, NAOP*] ... NON
National Organization for Professional Advancement of Black Chemists and Chemical Engineers ... NOBCChE
National Organization for Professional Advancement of Black Chemists and Chemical Engineers (EA) ... NOPABCCE
National Organization for Public Health Nursing (HGAA) ... NOPHN
National Organization for Rare Disorders (EA) ... NORD
National Organization for Raw Materials (EA) ... NORM
National Organization for Rehabilitation [*British*] ... NOR
National Organization for River Sports (EA) ... NORS
National Organization for Seasonal Affective Disorder (EA) ... NOSAD
National Organization for the Reform of Marijuana Laws (EA) ... NORML
National Organization for the Reinforcement of Marijuana Laws (NADA) ... NORML
National Organization for the Repeal of Marijuana Laws (NADA) ... NORML
National Organization for the Rights of Guide Dogs (EA) ... NORGD
National Organization for Travelers Aid Societies [*Also known as Travelers Aid International*] (EA) ... TAI
National Organization for Victim Assistance (EA) ... NOVA
National Organization for Women (EA) ... NOW
National Organization for Youth Safety [*NHTSA*] (TAG) ... NOYS
National Organization of Adolescent Pregnancy and Parenting (EA) ... NOAPP
National Organization of Bar Counsel (EA) ... NOBC
National Organization of Black Chemists and Chemical Engineers [*Later, NOPABCCE*] (EA) ... NOBCCE
National Organization of Black College Alumni (EA) ... NOBCA
National Organization of Black County Officials (EA) ... NOBCO
National Organization of Black Law Enforcement Executives (EA) ... NOBLE
National Organization of Circumcision Information Resource Centers (EA) ... NO-CIRC
National Organization of Circumcision Information Resource Centers (PAZ) ... NOCIRC
National Organization of Dance and Mime [*British*] (DBA) ... NODM
National Organization of Downsized Employees ... NODE
National Organization of Episcopalians for Life (EA) ... NOEL
National Organization of Gay and Lesbian Scientists and Technical Professionals (EA) ... NOGLSTP
National Organization of Hospital Schools of Nursing [*Defunct*] (EA) ... NOHSN
National Organization of Human Service Education (EA) ... NOHSE
National Organization of Human Services [*Defunct*] (EA) ... NOHS
National Organization of Industrial Trade Unions ... IT
National Organization of Industrial Trade Unions (EA) ... NOITU
National Organization of Italian-American Women (EA) ... NOIAW
National Organization of Liaison for Allocation of Circuit (NATG) ... NOLAC
National Organization of Life and Health Guaranty Associations [*An association*] ... NOLHGA
National Organization of Mall Walkers (EA) ... NOMW
National Organization of Miniaturists and Dollers (EA) ... NOMAD
National Organization of Minority Architects (EA) ... NOMA
National Organization of Mothers of Twins Clubs (EA) ... NOMOTC
National Organization of Poll-Ettes (EA) ... NOPE
National Organization of Social Security Claimants' Representatives (EA) ... NOSSCR
National Organization of Telecommunications Engineers and Scientists [*Washington, DC Telecommunications*] (TSSD) ... NOTES

National Organization of Test, Research, and Training Reactors [Later, TRTR] (EA) .... NOTRTR
National Organization of Tutoring and Mentoring Centers (EA) .... NOTM
National Organization of World War Nurses (EA) .... NOWWN
National Organization on Adolescent Pregnancy, Parenting, and Prevention (PAZ) .... NOAPP
National Organization on Disability .... NOD
National Organization on Disability (EA) .... NOD
National Organization on Legal Problems of Education (EA) .... NOLPE
National Organization Order (USDC) .... NOO
National Organization Taunting Safety and Fairness Everywhere (EA) .... NOT SAFE
National Organization to Halt the Abuse and Routine Mutilation of Males (EA) .... NOHARMM
National Organization to Insure a Sound-Controlled Environment (EA) .... NOISE
National Organization to Insure Survival Economics (EA) .... NOISE
National Organization to Promote English as the Official Language (EA) .... NOPEOL
National Organizational of Mall Walkers .... NOMW
National Organizations of the World [A publication] .... NOW
National Orientation Directors Association (EA) .... NODA
National Origin Minority Education [New Hampshire Department of Education] (EDAC) .... NOME
National Ornament and Electric Lights Christmas Association (EA) .... NOEL
National Ornamental and Miscellaneous Metals Association (EA) .... NOMMA
National Ornamental Goldfish Growers Association (EA) .... NOGGA
National Orthotic and Prosthetic Research Institute (EA) .... NOPRI
National Osteopathic Foundation (EA) .... NOF
National Osteopathic Guild Association (EA) .... NOGA
National Osteopathic Interfraternity Council (EA) .... NOIC
National Osteopathic Women Physician's Association (EA) .... NOWPA
National Osteoporosis Foundation (EA) .... NOF
National Osteoporosis Society [British] .... NOS
National Outboard Association [Defunct] (EA) .... NOA
National Outdoor Advertising Bureau [Defunct] (EA) .... NOAB
National Outdoor Drama Association [Defunct] (EA) .... NODA
National Outdoor Events Association [British] (DBA) .... NOEA
National Outdoor Leadership School .... NOLS
National Outdoor Volleyball Association [Defunct] (EA) .... NOVA
National Outdoorsmen's Association [Defunct] (EA) .... NOA
National Outerwear and Sportswear Association (EA) .... NOSA
National Outlook: an Australian Christian Monthly [A publication] (APTA) ...... NO
National Outpatient Profile [Medicine] (MEDA) .... NOP
National Overhaul Warranty [Automotive engineering] .... NOW
National Overhead Evaluation Assessment [Term for the restructuring process begun at E. F. Hutton after the October 1987 stock market collapse] .... NOVA
National Overseas Airline Co. [Egypt] [ICAO designator] (FAAC) .... NOL
National PAC [Political Action Committee] (EA) .... NAT PAC
National Pacific/Asian Resource Center on Aging (EA) .... NP/ARCA
National Packaging Confederation [British] (DBA) .... NPC
National Paddleball Association (EA) .... NPA
National Paint and Coatings Association (EA) .... NPCA
National Paint Distributors (EA) .... NPD
National Paint, Varnish, and Lacquer Association [Later, NPCA] (EA) .... NPVLA
National Paint, Varnish, and Lacquer Association, Inc., Washington, DC [Library symbol Library of Congress] (LCLS) .... DNPV
National Palace Museum, Wai-shuang-hsi, Shih-lin, Taipei, Taiwan, China [Library symbol] [Library of Congress] (LCLS) .... ChrP
National Palomino Breeders Association [Inactive] .... NPBA
National Panel of Arbitrators .... NPA
National Panhellenic Association of Central Office Executives (EA) ...... NPACOE
National Panhellenic Conference (EA) .... NPC
National Panhellenic Conference of Central Office Executives (EA) .... NPC/COES
National Panhellenic Editors Conference (EA) .... NPEC
National Paper Box Association [Formerly, NPBMA; later NP & PA] (EA) ... NPBA
National Paper Box Manufacturers Association (EA) .... NPBMA
National Paper Box Supplies Association [Defunct] (EA) .... NPBSA
National Paper Marketing Council of Australia .... NPMCA
National Paper Trade Association (EA) .... NPTA
National Paperboard Association [Later, API] .... NPA
National Paperbox and Packaging Association (EA) .... NP & PA
National Parachute Test Range (MCD) .... NPTR
National Paralegal Association (EA) .... NPA
National Paralegal Institute (EA) .... NPI
National Paraplegia Foundation (EA) .... NPF
National Parent Information Network .... NPIN
National Parent to Parent Support & Information Systems, Inc. .... NPPSIS
National Parenthood Association (NADA) .... NPA
National Parents Association .... NPA
National Parents' Resource Institute for Drug Education (EA) .... PRIDE
National Park (BARN) .... Nat Pk
National Park Academy of the Arts (EA) .... NPAA
National Park Board (NADA) .... NPB
National Park Foundation (EA) .... NPF
National Park Service [Department of the Interior] .... NPS
National Park Service Cooperative Park Studies Unit, University of Washington [Research center] (RCD) .... NPS/CPSU/UW
National Park Service, Denver, Denver, CO [OCLC symbol] (OCLC) .... UDP
National Park Service, Harpers Ferry Center, Harpers Ferry, WV [OCLC symbol] (OCLC) .... UDH
National Park Service, National Capital Region, Washington, DC [OCLC symbol] (OCLC) .... UDC
National Park Service, National Register Division, Washington, DC [OCLC symbol] (OCLC) .... UDN

National Park Trust Fund Board [Later, NPF] .... NPTFB
National Parking Association (EA) .... NPA
National Parkinson Foundation (EA) .... NPF
National Parkinson Institute .... NPI
National Parks [A publication] (BRI) .... NP
National Parks Advisory Council [Australia] .... NPAC
National Parks and Access to the Countryside Act [Town planning] [British] .... NPA
National Parks and Access to the Countryside (Grants) Regulations [Town planning] [British] .... NPA(G)R
National Parks and Access to the Countryside Regulations [Town planning] [British] .... NPR
National Parks and Conservation Association (EA) .... NPCA
National Parks and Nature Conservation Authority [Australia] .... NPNCA
National Parks and Primitive Areas .... NPPA
National Parks and Public Lands [Victoria, Australia] .... NPPL
National Parks and Recreation Association (NADA) .... NPRA
National Parks and Wildlife Advisory Council [Tasmania, Australia] .... NPWAC
National Parks and Wildlife Foundation of New South Wales [Australia] .... NPWFNSW
National Parks Association [Later, NPCA] (EA) .... NPA
National Parks Association of the Australian Capital Territory .... NPAACT
National Parks Association of Victoria [Australia] .... NPAV
National Parks Journal [A publication] .... Natn Parks J
National Parole Board [Canada] .... NPB
National Parole Service [Canada] .... NPS
National Particleboard Association (EA) .... NPA
National Particulate Network [Environmental Protection Agency] (GFGA) .... NPN
National Party [Australia Political party] .... Nat
National Party [Papua New Guinea] [Political party] (PPW) .... NP
[The] National Party [Grenada] [Political party] (EY) .... TNP
National Party Boat Owners Alliance (EA) .... NPBOA
National Party for Democracy [Zambia] [Political party] (EY) .... NPD
National Party for Unity and Democracy [Mauritania] [Political party] (EY) .... NPUD
National Party of Nigeria [Political party] (PPW) .... NPN
National Party of Western Australia [Political party] .... NPW
National Passenger Safety Association [Defunct] (EA) .... NPSA
National Passenger Traffic Association [Later, NBTA] (EA) .... NPTA
National Pasta Association (EA) .... NPA
National Patent Council (EA) .... NPC
National Patent Development Corp. [AMEX symbol] (SPSG) .... NPD
National Patent Development Corp. .... NPDC
National Patent Development Corp. [Associated Press] (SAG) .... NtPatnt
National Patents Appeal Tribunal [England] (DLA) .... PAT
National Patio Enclosure Association (EA) .... NPEA
National Patriotic Front of Liberia [Political party] (EY) .... NPFL
National Patriotic Party [Liberia] [Political party] (EY) .... NPP
National Patrolmen's Association .... NPA
National Paving and Kerb Association [British] (DBA) .... NPKA
National Pawnbrokers Association (EA) .... NPA
National Payphone Association (EA) .... NPA
National Peace Academy .... NPA
National Peace Academy Campaign [Formerly, NPA] (EA) .... N-PAC
National Peace Academy Foundation (EA) .... NPAF
National Peace Action Coalition .... NPAC
National Peace Council [British] .... NPC
National Peace Day Celebration (EA) .... NPDC
National Peace Garden .... NPG
National Peace Institute Foundation (EA) .... NPIF
National Peach Council (EA) .... NPC
National Peach Partners [Defunct] (EA) .... NPP
National Peanut Council (EA) .... NPC
National Peanut Festival Association (EA) .... NPFA
National Pecan Marketing Council (EA) .... NPMC
National Pecan Shellers and Processors Association (EA) .... NPSPA
National Pecan Shellers Association (EA) .... NPSA
National Pediatric HIV Resource Center (PAZ) .... NPHRC
National Pediculosis Association (EA) .... NPA
National Pedigree Livestock Council (EA) .... NPLC
National Peer Helpers Association (EA) .... NPHA
National Pegboard Systems Association (EA) .... NPSA
National Pell Grant Coalition (EA) .... NPGC
National Penn Bancshares, Inc. [NASDAQ symbol] (NQ) .... NPBC
National Penn Bancshares, Inc. [Associated Press] (SAG) .... NtPenn
National People Living with AIDS [Acquired Immune Deficiency Syndrome] Coalition [Australia] .... NPLAC
National People's Action (EA) .... NPA
National People's Congress [Nigeria] [Political party] .... NPC
National People's Congress [China] [Political party] (PPW) .... NPC
National People's Party [Pakistan] [Political party] (FEA) .... NPP
National People's Salvation Party [Zambia] [Political party] (EY) .... NPSP
National Performance Network .... NPN
National Performance Review [A publication] .... NPR
National Perinatal Association (EA) .... NPA
National Perinatal Bereavement Association [Defunct] (EA) .... NPBA
National Periodicals Center .... NPC
National Periodicals Publications, Inc. .... NPP
National Periodicals System .... NPS
National Peripheral Association (EA) .... NPA
National Perishable Transportation Association (EA) .... NPTA
National Permit Strategy [Environmental Protection Agency] (GFGA) .... NPS
National Personal Fitness Trainers Association (EA) .... NPFTA
National Personal Robot Association [Later, NSRA] (EA) .... NPRA
National Personnel Associates .... NPA

National Personnel Consultants [*Later, NAPC*] [*Defunct*] (EA) ... NPC
National Personnel Records Center [*National Archives and Records Service*] ... NPRC
National Personnel Records Center (Civilian Personnel Records) [*National Archives and Records Service*] (AFM) ... NPRC (CPR)
National Personnel Records Center (Military Personnel Records) [*National Archives and Records Service*] (AFM) ... NPRC (MPR)
National Pest Control Association (EA) ... NPCA
National Pesticide Information Clearinghouse [*Later, NPTN*] (EA) ... NPIC
National Pesticide Information Retrieval System [*Purdue University*] [*West Lafayette, IN Database*] ... NPIRS
National Pesticide Monitoring Program [*Later, National Contaminant Biomonitoring Program*] [*US Fish and Wildlife Service*] ... NPMP
National Pesticide Survey [*Environmental Protection Agency*] (GFGA) ... NPS
National Pesticide Telecommunication Network (EA) ... NPTN
National Pet Association [*Defunct*] (EA) ... NPA
National Pet Dealers and Breeders Association [*Defunct*] (EA) ... NPDBA
National Petroleum Association [*Later, NPRA*] ... NPA
National Petroleum Corp. Ltd. [*Toronto Stock Exchange symbol*] ... NPT
National Petroleum Council [*Department of Energy*] (EA) ... NPC
National Petroleum Council [*Marine science*] (OSRA) ... NPC
National Petroleum Exploration Database [*Australia*] ... PEDIN
National Petroleum Refiners Association (EA) ... NPRA
National Pharmaceutical Association [*Washington, DC*] ... NPA
National Pharmaceutical Association (EA) ... NPhA
National Pharmaceutical Council (EA) ... NPC
National Pharmaceutical Direct Advertising Association [*Defunct*] (EA) ... NPDAA
National Pharmaceutical Distributors' Association [*Australia*] ... NPDA
National Pharmaceutical Foundation (EA) ... NPF
National Pharmaceutical Union (PDAA) ... NPU
National Pharmacy Insurance Council [*Defunct*] (EA) ... NPIC
National Philanthropy Day (NFD) ... NPD
National Philatelic Center [*Australia*] ... NPC
National Philatelic Collections [*Smithsonian Institution*] ... NPC
National Philatelic Exhibition ... NAPEX
National Philatelic Society [*Defunct*] (EA) ... NPS
National Phlebotomy Association (EA) ... NPA
National Phone Services, Inc. ... NPS
National Photographic Art Archive [*Victoria and Albert Museum*] [*British*] ... NPAA
National Photographic Interpretation Center [*CIA*] ... NPIC
National Photography Instructors Association (EA) ... NPIA
National Physical Laboratory [*Research center British*] (IRC) ... NPL
National Physical Laboratory, Aerodynamics Division [*British*] ... NPL-AERO
National Physics Information System [*American Institute of Physics*] [*New York, NY*] (DIT) ... NPIS
National Physics Laboratory (KSC) ... NPL
National Piano Foundation (EA) ... NPF
National Piano Manufacturers Association of America [*Later, PMAI*] (EA) ... NPMA
National Piano Travelers Association (EA) ... NPTA
National Pickle Packers Association [*Later, PPI*] ... NPPA
National Picture & Frame Co. [*NASDAQ symbol*] (SAG) ... NPAF
National Picture & Frame Co. [*Associated Press*] (SAG) ... NtlPict
National Pig Breeders' Association [*British*] (BI) ... NPBA
National Pig Carvers Association (EA) ... NPCA
National Pig Fair [*British*] (ITD) ... NPF
National Pigeon Association [*Defunct*] (EA) ... NPA
National Piggly Wiggly Operators Association (EA) ... NPWOA
National Pilots Association [*Defunct*] (EA) ... NPA
National Pipe [*Thread*] ... NP
National Pipe Straight Fine [*Mechanical engineering*] ... NPSF
National Pipe Straight Intermediate [*Mechanical engineering*] ... NPSI
National Pipe Taper [*Mechanical engineering*] ... NPT
National Pistol Association [*British*] (DI) ... NPA
National Pituitary Agency [*Later, NHPP*] ... NPA
National Pizza and Pasta Association (EA) ... NPPA
[*A*] **National Plan for Arts in Small Communities** (EA) ... ANPASC
National Plan for Australian Newspapers ... NPAN
National Plan for Australian Newspapers ... NPLAN
National Plan of Action for Women in TAFE [*Technical and Further Education*] [*Australia*] ... NPAWT
National Plan of Integrated Airport Systems [*BTS*] [*FAA*] (TAG) ... NPIAS
National Planning Association (EA) ... NPA
National Planning Board [*Terminated, 1944; superseded by National Resources Board*] ... NPB
National Planning Data Corp. [*Information service or system*] (IID) ... NPDC
National Plant Board (EA) ... NPB
National Plant, Flower, and Fruit Guild (EA) ... NPFFG
National Plant Food Institute [*Later, TFI*] (EA) ... NPFI
National Plant Germplasm System [*Department of Agriculture*] ... NPGS
National Plant Protection Association ... PPA
National Plantation Advisory Committee ... NPAC
National Plastercraft Association (EA) ... NPA
National Plastercraft Association (EA) ... NPCA
National Plastic Exposition ... NPE
National Plastics Products Co., Odenton, MD [*Library symbol Library of Congress Obsolete*] (LCLS) ... MdOdN
National Playbus Association [*British*] (DBA) ... NPA
National Playing Fields Association [*British*] ... NPFA
National Playwrights Conference (EA) ... NPC
National Pledge of Allegiance Foundation (EA) ... NPAF
National Plott Hound Association (EA) ... NPHA
National Plumbing Code ... NPC
National Plywood Distributors Association (EA) ... NPDA
National Pocket Billiards Association (EA) ... NPBA
National Podiatric Medical Association (EA) ... NPMA
National Podiatry Association [*Later, NPMA*] (EA) ... NPA
National Poetry Circle [*Cambridge*] [*British*] ... NPC
National Poetry Day Committee (EA) ... NPDC
National Poetry Foundation (EA) ... NPF
National Poetry Secretariat [*British*] [*An association*] (DBA) ... NPS
National Poetry Series ... NPS
National Point of Contact (PDAA) ... NPOC
National Poison Center Network (EA) ... NPCN
National Poison Control Center (DAVI) ... NPCC
National Poison Prevention Week ... NPPW
National Poisons and Pesticides Board [*Sweden*] ... NPPB
National Poker Association (EA) ... NPA
National Police (CINC) ... NP
National Police and Security Service [*Republic of Vietnam*] ... NPSS
National Police Bloodhound Association (EA) ... NPBA
National Police Field Force [*Military*] ... NPFF
National Police Force [*South Vietnam*] (VNW) ... NPF
National Police Law Enforcement Institute (EA) ... NPLEI
National Police Officers Association of America ... NAPA
National Police Officers Association of America (EA) ... NPOAA
National Police Testing Laboratories (EA) ... NPTL
National Policy Assistance Standards (AAGC) ... NPAS
National Policy Debate [*Nuclear energy*] (NRCH) ... NPD
National Policy Forum ... NPF
National Policy Paper [*Army*] (AABC) ... NPP
National Political Action Committee (EA) ... NPAC
National Political Action Committee for Scientists and Engineers ... NPACSE
National Political Awareness Test [*Sent to all candidates in presidential, congressional, gubernatorial, and most state legislative races*] ... NPAT
National Political Button Exchange [*An association Defunct*] (EA) ... NPBE
National Political Congress of Black Women (EA) ... NPCBW
National Politics [*Behavioral science game*] ... NAPOLI
National Pollutant Discharge Elimination System [*Environmental Protection Agency*] ... NPDES
National Pollutant Discharge Elimination System [*Environmental Protection Agency*] (ERG) ... NPDS
National Pollutant Inventory ... NPI
National Pollution Control Foundation ... NPCF
National Polystyrene Recycling Co. ... NPRC
National Pony Society [*British*] (DI) ... NPS
National Pop Can Collectors (EA) ... NPCC
National Population Control Secretariat [*Australia*] ... NPCS
National Population Enquiry ... NPE
National Pork Council Women (EA) ... NPCW
National Pork Producers Council (EA) ... NPPC
National Porkettes (EA) ... NP
National Poro Beautician Association [*Defunct*] (EA) ... NPBA
National Portage Association [*British*] (DBA) ... NPA
National Portrait Gallery [*Smithsonian Institution*] ... NPG
National Ports Authority [*British*] ... NPA
National Ports Council [*British*] ... NPC
National [*or New*] **Post Office Building** ... NPO
National Post Office Mail Handlers, Watchmen, Messengers, and Group Leaders [*Later, NPMHU*] (EA) ... NPOMHWMGL
National Postal and Travelers Censorship [*Army*] (AABC) ... NPTC
National Postal and Travelers Censorship Organization [*Army*] (AABC) ... NPTCO
National Postal Arts Association (EA) ... NPAA
National Postal Mail Handlers Union (EA) ... NPMHU
National Postal Museum, Ottawa, ON, Canada [*Library symbol Library of Congress*] (LCLS) ... CaOOPM
National Postal Museum [*Musee National des Postes*] **Ottawa, Ontario** [*Library symbol National Library of Canada*] (NLC) ... OOPM
National Postal Transport Association [*Later, APWU*] ... NPTA
National Postal Transport Association [*Later, APWU*] ... PTA
National Postal Union [*Later, APWU*] ... NPU
National Postmasters Auxiliary (EA) ... NPA
National Postsecondary Agriculture Student Organization (EA) ... NPASO
National Postsecondary Agriculture Student Organization (EA) ... PAS
National Postsecondary Student Aid Study [*Department of Education*] (GFGA) ... NPSAS
National Potato Chip Institute [*Later, SFA*] ... NPCI
National Potato Council (EA) ... NPC
National Potato Promotion Board (EA) ... NPPB
National Poultry Association [*Australia*] ... NPA
National Poultry, Butter, and Egg Association [*Defunct*] (EA) ... NPBEA
National Poultry Improvement Plan (EA) ... NPIP
National Poultry Producers Federation [*Defunct*] (EA) ... NPPF
National Power Demonstration (IEEE) ... NPD
National Power PLC [*NYSE symbol*] (SAG) ... NP
National Power PLC [*Associated Press*] (SAG) ... NPwADS
National Power PLC [*Associated Press*] (SAG) ... NtPwADS
National Power PLC [*Associated Press*] (SAG) ... NtPwIntr
National Power Policy Committee [*World War II*] ... NPPC
National Practitioner Data Bank [*Information service or system*] (IID) ... NPDB
National Prairie Grouse Technical Council (EA) ... NPGTC
National Prayer Breakfast (EA) ... NPB
National Precast Concrete Association (EA) ... NPCA
National Precure Retread Dealers Association [*Defunct*] (EA) ... NPRDA
National Premium Incentive Show (ITD) ... NP/IS
National Premium Manufacturers Representatives [*Later, IMRA*] (EA) ... NPMR
National Premium Sales Executives (EA) ... NPSE
National Prepared Frozen Food Association (EA) ... NPFFA

National Prepared Frozen Food Processors Association [*Later, NPFFA*] (EA) ... NPFFPA
National Presbyterian Health and Welfare Association [*Later, PHEWA*] ... NPHWA
National Prescription Audit ... NPA
National Present Volume Method [*Management*] ... NPV
National Preservation Loan Fund [*National Trust for Historic Preservation*] ... NPLF
National Preservers Association [*Later, International Jelly and Preserve Association*] (EA) ... NPA
National Press Club (EA) ... NPC
National Press Club, Washington, DC [*Library symbol Library of Congress*] (LCLS) ... DNPr
National Press Foundation (EA) ... NPF
National Press Photographers Association (EA) ... NPPA
National Press Women's Club (NTCM) ... NPWC
National Presto Industries, Inc. [*NYSE symbol*] (SPSG) ... NPK
National Presto Industries, Inc. [*Associated Press*] (SAG) ... NtPrest
National Pretreatment Program [*Metal finishing technology*] ... NPP
National Pretzel Bakers Institute [*Defunct*] (EA) ... NPBI
National Prevention Network (EA) ... NPN
National Prices Network ... NPN
National Primary Drinking Water Regulations [*Environmental Protection Agency*] ... NPDWR
National Primary Teacher Education Conference (AIE) ... NaPTEC
National Prime Contractor (NATG) ... NPC
National Prime User Group (GNE) ... NPUG
National Printing Equipment and Supply Association (EA) ... NPES
National Printing Equipment Association [*Later, NPES*] (EA) ... NPEA
National Printing Equipment Show ... NPES
National Printing Ink Research Institute (EA) ... NPIRI
National Priorities List [*Hazardous wastes*] [*Environmental Protection Agency*] ... NPL
National Priority Area [*Military*] ... NPA
National Priority Program [*NHTSA*] (TAG) ... NPP
National Priority Reserve Fund [*Australia*] ... NPRF
National Prison Project (EA) ... NPP
National Prisoner of War Information Center (DOMA) ... NPWIC
National Prisoner Statistics [*An association*] ... NPS
National Prisoner Statistics Bulletin [*Department of Justice*] ... NPSB
National Private Circuit Digital Network (PDAA) ... NPCDN
National Private Truck Council ... NPTC
National Privy Diggers Association (EA) ... NPDA
National Probation and Parole Association [*Later, NCCD*] ... NPPA
National Processing Centre [*Marine science*] (MSC) ... NPC
National Processing, Inc. [*NYSE symbol*] (SAG) ... NAP
National Processing, Inc. [*Associated Press*] (SAG) ... NatProc
National Proctologic Association (EA) ... NPA
National Procurement Point [*Military*] (RDA) ... NPP
National Product Liability Council (EA) ... NPLC
National Production Advisory Council on Industry [*British*] ... NPACI
National Production Authority [*Functions merged into BDSA, 1953*] ... NPA
National Productivity Authority (MHDB) ... NPA
National Productivity Board (NADA) ... NPB
National Productivity Council [*Inactive*] ... NPC
National Pro-Family Coalition (EA) ... NPFC
National Professional Driver Education Association (AEBS) ... NPDEA
National Professional Soccer League [*Later, NASL*] ... NPSL
National Professional Squash Racquets Association (EA) ... NPSRA
National Professional Standards Review Council [*Terminated, 1982*] [*HEW*] (EGAO) ... NPSRC
National Proficiency Test Council (AIE) ... NPTC
National Program Director ... NPD
National Program for Acquisitions and Cataloging [*Library of Congress*] ... NAPAC
National Program for Acquisitions and Cataloging [*Library of Congress*] ... NPAC
National Program for Clear Air Turbulence [*Air Force*] ... NCAT
National Program for Dermatology ... NPD
National Program Manager [*Environmental Protection Agency*] (GFGA) ... NPM
National Program Production and Aquisition Grant [*Corporation for Public Broadcasting*] [*Radio*] (NTCM) ... NPPAG
National Progress Association for Economic Development (EA) ... NPAED
National Progressive Broadcast Coalition [*Defunct*] (EA) ... NPBC
National Progressive Consumers Alliance (EA) ... NPCA
National Progressive Front [*Iraq*] [*Political party*] (PPW) ... NPF
National Progressive Party [*Iraq*] [*Political party*] (BJA) ... NPP
National Progressive Unionist Party [*Egypt*] [*Political party*] (PPW) ... NPUP
National Prohibition Act ... NPA
National Prohibition Party (EA) ... NPP
National Project for the Improvement of Televised Instruction [*National Association of Educational Broadcasters*] ... NPITI
National Project in Agricultural Communication (PDAA) ... NPAC
National Project Office ... NPO
National Project on Resource Coordination for Justice Statistics and Information [*Canada*] ... NPRC
National Pro-Life Democrats (EA) ... NPLD
National Pro-Life Political Action Committee [*Defunct*] (EA) ... NP-L PAC
National Propane Gas Association ... NPGA
National Propane Partners LP [*Associated Press*] (SAG) ... NatProp
National Propane Partners LP [*NYSE symbol*] (SAG) ... NPL
National Property Management Association (EA) ... NPMA
National Prostatic Cancer Project ... NPCP
National Provident Institution [*Wales*] ... NPI
National Prune Juice Packers Association (EA) ... NPJPA
National Psoriasis Foundation (EA) ... NPF
National Psychiatric Reform Institute ... NPRI
National Psychic Science Association (EA) ... NPSA
National Psychological Association [*Defunct*] (EA) ... NPA
National Psychological Association for Psychoanalysis (EA) ... NPAP
National Public Affairs Center for Television (NADA) ... NPABC
National Public Affairs Center for Television [*Defunct*] ... NPACT
National Public Domain Software Archive (AIE) ... NPDSA
National Public Education Campaign on Clinical Depression ... NPECCD
National Public Employer Labor Relations Association (EA) ... NPELRA
National Public Employment Reporter [*A publication*] (DLA) ... Nat'l Pub Empl Rep
National Public Employment Reporter Database [*Information service or system*] (IID) ... NPER
National Public Health Program Reporting System [*Department of Health and Human Services*] ... NPHPRS
National Public Interest Research Group (EA) ... NPIRG
National Public Law Training Center (EA) ... NPLTC
National Public Parks Tennis Association (EA) ... NPPTA
National Public Radio [*Washington, DC Telecommunications*] (TSSD) ... NPR
National Public Relations Council of Health and Welfare Services [*Formerly, NPC*] ... NPRC
National Public Relations Roundtable [*Defunct*] ... NPRR
National Public Resources Defense Council (NUCP) ... NPRDC
National Public Services Research Institute ... NPSRI
National Public Switched Telecommunications Network (MHDI) ... NPSTN
National Public Telecomputing Network (TNIG) ... NPTN
National Publicity Council for Health and Welfare Services [*Later, NPRC*] ... NPC
National Publishing Co. [*Philadelphia*] ... NP
National Puerto Rican Coalition (EA) ... NPRC
National Puerto Rican Forum (EA) ... NPRF
National Puerto Rican Women's Caucus [*Defunct*] (EA) ... NPRWC
National Purchasing Institute (EA) ... NPI
National Pure Water Association [*British*] ... NPWA
National Puzzlers' League (EA) ... NPL
National Pygmy Goat Association (EA) ... NPGA
National Pyrotechnic Distributors Association [*APA*] [*Absorbed by*] (EA) ... NPDA
National Quadraphonic Radio Committee ... NQRC
National Quality Award [*LIMRA, NALU*] ... NQA
National Quality Information Centre [*Institute of Quality Assurance*] [*Information service or system*] (IID) ... NQIC
National Quarantine Publicity Program [*Australia*] ... NQPP
National Quarter Horse Registry (EA) ... NQHR
National Quarter Pony Association (EA) ... NQPA
National Quartz Producers Council (EA) ... NQPC
National Quick Lube Ltd. [*Vancouver Stock Exchange symbol*] ... NQL
National Quilting Association (EA) ... NQA
National Quotation Bureau [*Stock market*] ... NQB
National Quotations Committee [*of the National Association of Securities Dealers*] ... NQC
National Racing Authority (NADA) ... NRA
National Racquetball Association of the Deaf (EA) ... NRAD
National Racquetball Association of the Deaf of the USA [*Later, NRAD*] (EA) ... NRADUSA
National Racquetball Club (EA) ... NRC
National Radiator Core Manufacturing Credit Association [*Later, NRMCA*] (EA) ... NRCMCA
National Radiator Manufacturing Credit Association (EA) ... NRMCA
National Radio Astronomy Observatory [*Charlottesville, VA*] [*National Science Foundation*] (GRD) ... NRAO
National Radio Astronomy Observatory [*Charlottesville, VA*] [*National Science Foundation*] (GRD) ... NRAS
National Radio Astronomy Observatory, Charlottesville, VA [*OCLC symbol*] (OCLC) ... RAO
National Radio Astronomy Observatory, Charlottesville, VA [*Library symbol Library of Congress*] (LCLS) ... ViCRA
National Radio Astronomy Observatory, Green Bank, WV [*Library symbol Library of Congress*] (LCLS) ... WvGbN
National Radio Broadcasters Association [*NAB*] [*Absorbed by*] (EA) ... NRBA
National Radio Club [*Defunct*] (EA) ... NRC
National Radio Communications System [*FAA*] (TAG) ... NARACS
National Radio Co., Inc. (IAA) ... NRCI
National Radio Conference [*Broadcast regulations*] (NTCM) ... NRC
National Radio Heritage Association (EA) ... NRHA
National Radio Institute ... NRI
National Radio Station (IAA) ... NRS
National Radio Systems Committee ... NRSC
National Radiological Protection Board [*British*] ... NRPB
National Radiological Protection Board [*British*] ... NRPD
National Rail Freight Initiative [*Australia*] ... NRFI
National Rail Regulatory Authority [*Australia*] ... NRRA
National Railroad Adjustment Board ... NRAB
National Railroad Adjustment Board Awards [*A publication*] (DLA) ... NRAB
National Railroad Construction and Maintenance Association, Inc. (EA) ... NRC
National Railroad Construction and Maintenance Association, Inc. (EA) ... NRC/MAI
National Railroad Freight Committee (EA) ... NRFC
National Railroad Intermodal Association [*Defunct*] (EA) ... NRIA
National Railroad Passenger Corp. [*Government rail transportation*] ... NRPC
National Railroad Pension Forum [*Defunct*] (EA) ... NRPF
National Railway Appliances Association [*Later, REMSA*] (EA) ... NRAA
National Railway Historical Society (EA) ... NRHS
National Railway Labor Conference (EA) ... NRLC
National Railway Labor Panel [*World War II*] ... NRLP
National Rainbow Coalition, Inc. (EA) ... NRCI
National Rally Terminology [*Automotive competition*] ... NRT

National Ramah Commission (EA) ... NRC
National Range ... NR
National Range Division [*Air Force*] ... NRD
National Range Documentation (MUGU) ... NRD
National Range Operations (RDA) ... NRO
National Range Technical Operating Instructions [*NASA*] (KSC) ... NRTOI
National Rare Blood Club [*Later, NRBC/NYBC*] (EA) ... NRBC
National Rare Blood Club/New York Blood Center (EA) ... NRBC/NYBC
National Re Corp. [*Associated Press*] (SAG) ... NatRe
National Reactor Test Station [*INEL*] (NRCH) ... NRTS
National Reactor Testing Station, Technical Library, Phillips Petroleum Co., Idaho Falls, ID [*Library symbol Library of Congress*] (LCLS) ... IdNTS
National Reactor Universal ... NRU
National Readership Survey [*British*] ... NRS
National Reading Conference (EA) ... NRC
National Reading Styles Institute ... NRSI
National Ready Mixed Concrete Association (EA) ... NRMCA
National Real Estate Corp. [*NYSE symbol*] (SPSG) ... NRE
National Real Estate Fliers Association [*Later, Real Estate Aviation Chapter*] (EA) ... NREFA
National Real Estate Service [*Canada*] ... NRS
National Realty Club [*New York, NY*] (EA) ... NRC
National Realty Committee [*Washington, DC*] (EA) ... NRC
National Realty Ltd. [*AMEX symbol*] (SPSG) ... NLP
National Realty Ltd. [*Associated Press*] (SAG) ... NtlRlty
National Reamer Collectors Association (EA) ... NRCA
National Rebel Class Association (EA) ... NRCA
National Reciprocal and Family Support Enforcement Association [*Later, NCSEA*] (EA) ... NRFSEA
National Reclamation Association [*Later, National Water Resources Association*] (EA) ... NRA
National Reconditioning Order [*Marine science*] (OSRA) ... NRC
National Reconditioning Order [*National Weather Service*] (USDC) ... NRC
National Reconnaissance Executive Committee (LAIN) ... NREC
National Reconnaissance Office [*Air Force/CIA*] ... NRO
National Reconnaissance Organization [*CIA*] ... NRO
National Record Mart, Inc. [*Associated Press*] (SAG) ... NatRecd
National Record Mart, Inc. [*NASDAQ symbol*] (SAG) ... NRMI
National Record of Vocational Achievement (AIE) ... NROVA
National Records Center ... NRC
National Records Management Council (EA) ... NAREMCO
National Records Management Council (EA) ... NRMC
National Recovery Act ... NR
National Recovery Act ... NRA
National Recovery Administration [*Voided by Supreme Court, 1935*] ... NR
National Recovery Administration [*Voided by Supreme Court, 1935*] ... NRA
National Recovery and Collection Association (EA) ... NRCA
National Recovery Review Board [*Terminated, 1934*] ... NRRB
National Recreation and Park Association (EA) ... NRPA
National Recreation Area [*National Park Service*] (GFGA) ... NRA
National Recreation Association [*Later, NRPA*] (EA) ... NRA
National Recreation Association [*Later, NRPA*], New York, NY [*Library symbol Library of Congress*] (LCLS) ... NNRecA
National Recycling Coalition (EA) ... NRC
National Red Cherry Institute (EA) ... NRCI
National Redbone Coonhound Association (EA) ... NRCA
National Redemption Council [*Ghana*] ... NRC
National Redemption Council Decree [*Ghana*] [*A publication*] (DLA) ... NRCD
National Reemployment Service ... NRS
National Reference Library [*British*] (NUCP) ... NRL
National Reference Library of Science and Invention [*of the British Museum*] ... NRLSI
National Reference System in Clinical Chemistry (DAVI) ... NRSCC
National Referral Center [*Defunct*] (EA) ... NRC
National Referral Center for Science and Technology (MCD) ... NRCST
National Referral System [*British*] (DCTA) ... NRS
National Reform Association (EA) ... NRA
National Register, Edited by Mead [*1816*] [*A publication*] (DLA) ... Nat Reg
National Register of Archives [*Historical Manuscripts Commission*] [*British*] ... NRA
National Register of Historic Places ... NRHP
National Register of Hypnotherapists and Psychotherapists [*British*] (DBA) ... NRHP
National Register of Industrial Art Designers [*British*] (DAS) ... NRIAD
National Register of Microform Masters [*Library of Congress*] ... NRMM
National Register of Potentially Toxic Chemicals (GNE) ... NRPTC
National Register of Prominent Americans and International Notables (EA) ... NRPAIN
National Register of Scientific and Technical Personnel (IAA) ... NRSTP
National Register Publishing Co. [*Information service or system*] (IID) ... NRPC
National Registered Builders Association [*British*] (DBA) ... NRBA
National Registered Designer [*British*] ... NRD
National Registration Center for Study Abroad (EA) ... NRCSA
National Registry [*Associated Press*] (SAG) ... NatlReg
National Registry [*NASDAQ symbol*] (SAG) ... NRID
National Registry for Librarians (EA) ... NRL
National Registry in Clinical Chemistry (EA) ... NRCC
National Registry of Ambulatory Surgical Facilities (EA) ... NRASF
National Registry of Emergency Medical Technicians (EA) ... NREMT
National Registry of Emergency Medical Technicians - Paramedics (DAVI) ... NREMT-P
National Registry of Environmental Professionals (EA) ... NREP
National Registry of Medical Secretaries (EA) ... NRMS
National Registry of Microbiologists (DAVI) ... NRM
National Registry of Myocardial Infarction ... NRMI
National Registry of Willys-Knight Automobiles [*Later, W-O-KR*] ... NRW-KA
National Registry System for Chemical Compounds (DIT) ... NRSCC
National Regulatory Research Institute [*Ohio State University*] [*Research center*] (RCD) ... NRRI
National Rehabilitation and Service Foundation (EA) ... NRSF
National Rehabilitation Association (EA) ... NRA
National Rehabilitation Counseling Association (EA) ... NRCA
National Rehabilitation Digest [*A publication*] ... Natn Rehab Digest
National Rehabilitation Information Center (EA) ... NARIC
National Rehabilitation Information Center [*Catholic University of America*] [*Bibliographic Database*] [*Washington, DC*] ... NRIC
National Rehabilitation Training Institute [*Defunct*] (EA) ... NRTI
National Reining Horse Association (EA) ... NRHA
National Reliability Evaluation Program [*Nuclear Regulatory Commission*] ... NREP
National Religious Broadcasters (EA) ... NRB
National Religious Party [*Hamiflaga Hadatit Leumit*] [*Israel*] [*Political party*] (PPW) ... NRP
National Religious Vocation Conference (EA) ... NRVC
National Reloading Manufacturers Association (EA) ... NRMA
National Remodelers Association [*Later, NARI*] ... NRA
National Remodelers Council [*Later, NAHB/RC*] (EA) ... NRC
National Remote Sensing Agency [*India*] ... NRSA
National Remote Sensing Centre [*Royal Aircraft Establishment Space Department*] [*British*] (CB) ... NRSC
National Remote Sensing Program [*Marine science*] (OSRA) ... NRSP
National Remote Sensing Programme (USDC) ... NRSP
National Remotivation Therapy Organization (EA) ... NRTO
National Renal Administrators Association (EA) ... NRAA
National Renderers Association (EA) ... NRA
National Renewable Energy Laboratory [*Department of Energy*] ... NREL
National Rental Housing Council [*Later, NMHC*] (EA) ... NRHC
National Rental Service Association (EA) ... NRSA
National Rep/Wholesaler Association (EA) ... NR/WA
National Repertory Theatre Foundation [*Defunct*] (EA) ... NRT
National Report (OICC) ... NR
National Reporter [*Maritime Law Book Co. Ltd.*] [*Canada Information service or system*] (CRD) ... NR
National Reporter System (DLA) ... Nat Rept Syst
National Reporter System (DLA) ... Natl Rep Sys
National Reporter System [*Database*] [*Maritime Law Book Co. Ltd.*] [*Information service or system*] (CRD) ... NRS
National Reporting Program [*National Institute of Mental Health*] [*Department of Health and Human Services*] (GFGA) ... NRP
National Reporting System for Family Planning Services [*National Institutes of Health*] ... NRSFPS
National Representative [*Red Cross*] ... NATR
National Reprographic Centre for Documentation [*British*] ... NRC
National Reprographic Centre for Documentation [*Hatfield Polytechnic Institute*] [*Hertfordshire, England Evaluation and information group*] [*Information service or system*] ... NRCd
National Reprographic Centre for Documentation Study (NITA) ... NRCd
National Republican Alliance [*Australia*] ... NRA
National Republican Club (EA) ... NRC
National Republican Coalition for Choice (EA) ... NRCC
National Republican Congressional Committee (EA) ... NRCC
National Republican Convention [*Nigeria*] [*Political party*] ... NRC
National Republican Foundation (EA) ... NRF
National Republican Heritage Groups (Nationalities) Council (EA) ... NRHGC
National Republican Institute for International Affairs (EA) ... NRIIA
National Republican Party [*Guyana*] [*Political party*] (EY) ... NRP
National Republican Senatorial Committee (EA) ... NRSC
National Research & Development Corp. [*Later, BTG*] [*British*] ... NRDC
National Research and Development Organization (WDAA) ... NRDO
National Research and Education Network [*Federal government*] ... NREN
National Research and Investigations Center [*Zaire*] (PD) ... CNRI
National Research and Manufacturing Co. (AD) ... NARMCO
National Research and Resource Facility for Submicron Structures [*Cornell University*] [*Research center*] (RCD) ... NRRFSS
National Research Bureau [*Commercial firm*] (EA) ... NRB
National Research Center (NATG) ... NRC
National Research Center on Student Learning [*University of Pittsburgh*] [*Research center*] (RCD) ... NRCSL
National Research Corp. ... NRC
National Research Council [*National Academy of Sciences*] [*Washington, DC*] ... NRC
National Research Council Army Countermine Advisory Committee ... NRC-ACAC
National Research Council, Canada [*Research center*] (IRC) ... NRC
National Research Council, Canada Institute for Scientific and Technical Information, Marin Dynamics Branch, St. Johns, NF, Canada [*Library symbol*] [*Library of Congress*] (LCLS) ... CaNfSNM
National Research Council Committee on Salmonella (EA) ... NRCCS
National Research Council - Committee on Toxicology ... NRC-TOX
National Research Council Division of Earth Sciences (USDC) ... NRCDES
National Research Council Division of Earth Sciences [*Marine science*] (OSRA) ... NRCDES
National Research Council, Don Mills, Ontario [*Library symbol National Library of Canada*] (NLC) ... ODMN
National Research Council, Halifax, NS, Canada [*Library symbol Library of Congress*] (LCLS) ... CaNSHM
National Research Council IRAP [*Industrial Research Assistance Program*], St. John's, Newfoundland [*Library symbol National Library of Canada*] (NLC) ... NFSNI
National Research Council Library (DIT) ... NRCL
National Research Council - Mine Advisory Committee ... NRC-MAC

National Research Council - National Academy of Sciences (AAG) ...... NRC-NAS
National Research Council of Canada ...... NRCC
National Research Council of Canada, Division of Mechanical Engineering [*Research center*] (RCD) ...... NRC/DME
National Research Council on Peace Strategy (EA) ...... NRCPS
National Research Experiment [*Canadian reactor*] ...... NRX
National Research Foundation [*Research center*] (RCD) ...... NRF
National Research Foundation [*South Africa*] ...... NRF
National Research Foundation for Business Statistics (EA) ...... NRFBS
National Research Foundation for Fertility [*Inactive*] (EA) ...... NRFF
National Research Institute [*Audience research organization*] (NTCM) ...... NRI
National Research Institute for Mathematical Sciences [*South Africa*] ...... NRIMS
National Research Laboratory [*Netherlands*] (GAVI) ...... NLR
National Research Laboratory ...... NRL
National Research Library [*Canada*] (DIT) ...... NRL
National Research Planning Board ...... NRPB
National Research Service Awards [*Department of Health and Human Services*] ...... NRSA
National Research Universal [*Nuclear reactor*] [*Canada*] ...... NRU
National Reserve [*British military*] (DMA) ...... NR
National Reserve Officers' Training Corps Band Association (AEBS) ...... NROTCBA
National Reservoir Research Program [*Department of the Interior*] (GRD) ...... NRRP
National Resident Matching Program (EA) ...... NRMP
National Residential Appraisers Institute (EA) ...... NRAI
National Residue Database ...... NRDB
National Resistance Army [*Uganda*] (PD) ...... NRA
National Resistance Committee (EA) ...... NRC
National Resistance Movement [*Uganda*] (PD) ...... NRM
National Resistance Party [*Political party*] (BJA) ...... NRP
National Resource Center for Consumers of Legal Services (EA) ...... NRCCLS
National Resource Center for Consumers of Legal Services (DLA) ...... NRCLS
National Resource Center for Minority Contractors (EA) ...... NRCMC
National Resource Center for Paraprofessionals in Special Education and Related Human Services (EA) ...... NRC
National Resource Center on Homelessness and Mental Illness (EA) ...... NRCHMI
National Resource Center on Women and AIDS [*Acquired Immune Deficiency Syndrome*] (EA) ...... NRCWA
National Resource Explorations Ltd. [*Toronto Stock Exchange symbol Vancouver Stock Exchange symbol*] ...... NRE
National Resource for Computation in Chemistry [*Lawrence Berkeley Laboratory*] [*Terminated, 1981*] ...... NRCC
National Resource Institute on Children and Youth with Handicaps [*Defunct*] (EA) ...... NRICH
National Resource Inventory [*US database on erosion*] ...... NRI
National Resource Network [*Commercial firm*] (EA) ...... NRN
National Resource Recovery Association (EA) ...... NRRA
National Resources Analysis Center ...... NRAC
National Resources Board [*Terminated, 1935; functions transferred to National Resources Committee*] ...... NRB
National Resources Committee [*Functions transferred to National Resources Planning Board*] ...... NRC
National Resources Council of America ...... NRCA
National Resources Defence Council (ECON) ...... NRDC
National Resources Evaluation Center [*of OEP*] [*Nuclear effects*] ...... NREC
National Resources Library ...... NRL
National Resources Management Corp. ...... NRMC
National Resources Planning Board [*Abolished, 1943*] ...... NRPB
National Respiratory and Enteric Virus Surveillance System ...... NREVSS
National Respiratory Disease Conference (DAVI) ...... NRDC
National Response Center [*Environmental Protection Agency*] ...... NRC
National Response Team [*RSPA*] (TAG) ...... NRT
National Response Team for Oil and Hazardous Materials Spills [*Environmental Protection Agency Washington, DC*] (EGAO) ...... NRT
National Restaurant Association (EA) ...... NRA
National Restaurant Association Large Independent Operators [*Defunct*] (EA) ...... LIO
National Restaurant Association Market Research Group [*Defunct*] (EA) ...... NRAMRG
National Restaurant Association Marketing Executives Group [*Defunct*] (EA) ...... NRAMEG
National Restaurant Association Quality Assurance Study Group (EA) ...... QA
National Retail Credit Association [*Later, ICA*] ...... NRCA
National Retail Distribution Certificate [*British*] ...... NRDC
National Retail Farm Equipment Association [*Later, NFPEDA*] ...... NRFEA
National Retail Federation (EA) ...... NRF
National Retail Florists Association [*Defunct*] ...... NRFA
National Retail Furniture Association [*Later, NHFA*] (EA) ...... NRFA
National Retail Hardware Association (EA) ...... NRHA
National Retail Lumber Dealers Association [*Later, NLBMDA*] ...... NRLDA
National Retail Merchants Association [*New York, NY*] (EA) ...... NRMA
National Retail Pet Store and Groomers Association (EA) ...... NRPSGA
National Retail Pet Supply Association [*Defunct*] (EA) ...... NRPSA
National Retail Tea and Coffee Merchants Association ...... NRT & CMA
National Retail Trade Centre (EAIO) ...... NRTC
National Retinitis Pigmentosa Foundation [*Later, RPFFB*] (EA) ...... NRPF
National Retired Teachers Association, Division of AARP (EA) ...... NRTA
National Retirees Volunteer Coalition [*An association*] ...... NVRC
National Retirement Association [*Australia*] ...... NRA
National Retreat Centre [*British*] (CB) ...... NRC
National Review [*A publication*] (BRI) ...... Nat R
National Review Panel [*Work Incentive Program*] [*Department of Labor*] ...... NRP
National Revolutionary Movement [*France*] ...... NRM
National Rex Rabbit Club (EA) ...... NRRC
National Reye's Syndrome Foundation (EA) ...... NRSF
National Rice Growers Association [*Defunct*] (EA) ...... NRGA
National Rick Nelson Fan Club (EA) ...... NRNFC
National Riding Committee [*Later, ANRC*] (EA) ...... NRC
National Rifle and Pistol Association of Ireland (EAIO) ...... NRPAI
National Rifle Association (NADA) ...... NRA
National Rifle Association of America (EA) ...... NRA
National Rifle Association of America ...... NRAA
National Right to Life Committee (EA) ...... NRLC
National Right to Life Educational Trust Fund (EA) ...... NRLETF
National Right to Work Committee (EA) ...... NRWC
National Right to Work Legal Defense and Education Foundation [*Also, NRWLDF*] (EA) ...... NRTWLDEF
National Right to Work Legal Defense and Education Foundation [*Later, NRWLDF*] (EA) ...... NRWLDEF
National Right to Work Legal Defense Foundation (EA) ...... NRWLDF
National Risk Retention Association (EA) ...... NRRA
National Rivers and Harbors Congress [*Later, WRC*] ...... NR & HC
National Rivers and Harbors Congress [*Later, WRC*] ...... NRHC
National Rivers Authority [*British*] ...... NRA
National Rivers Inventory (GNE) ...... NRI
National Road Trauma Advisory Council [*Australia*] ...... NRTAC
National Road Traveler, Cambridge City, IN [*Library symbol Library of Congress*] (LCLS) ...... InCcNR
National Roads Board (NADA) ...... NRB
National Roadside Vegetation Management Association (EA) ...... NRVMA
National Rocket Club [*Later, NSC*] ...... NRC
National Roller Canary Society [*British*] (BI) ...... NRCS
National Roller Hockey Association of Great Britain (BI) ...... NRHA
National Roof Deck Contractors Association (EA) ...... NRDCA
National Roofing Contractors Association (EA) ...... NRCA
National Roofing Foundation (EA) ...... NRF
National Roommate Association [*Later, ASRS*] (EA) ...... NRA
National Rose Society of Australia ...... NRSA
National Roster of Scientific and Engineering Personnel (IAA) ...... NRSEP
National Rotorcraft Noise Reduction [*Program to reduce noise of helicopters*] ...... NRNR
National Rounders Association [*British*] (BI) ...... NRA
National Route Program (GAVI) ...... NRP
National Rowing Foundation (EA) ...... NRF
National Rugby Football League (NADA) ...... NRFL
National Runaway Switchboard (EA) ...... NRS
National Running Data Center, Inc. [*Defunct*] (EA) ...... NRDC
National Rural Advisory Council (NADA) ...... NRAC
National Rural and Resources Press Club [*Australia*] ...... NRRPC
National Rural and Small Schools Consortium (EA) ...... NRSSC
National Rural Center (EA) ...... NRC
National Rural Development Institute (EA) ...... NRDI
National Rural Development Leaders School (OICC) ...... NRDLS
National Rural Education Association (EA) ...... NREA
National Rural Education Research Consortium [*Defunct*] (EA) ...... NRERC
National Rural Electric Cooperative Association (EA) ...... NRECA
National Rural Fellows (EA) ...... NRF
National Rural Health Association (EA) ...... NRHA
National Rural Health Care Association [*Formerly, NRPCA*] (EA) ...... NRHCA
National Rural Health Unit [*Australia*] ...... NRHU
National Rural Housing Coalition (EA) ...... NRHC
National Rural Letter Carriers' Association (EA) ...... NRLCA
National Rural Letter Carriers' Association ...... RLCA
National Rural Primary Care Association [*Later, NRHCA*] (EA) ...... NRPCA
National Rural Teacher Education Consortium [*National Rural Development Institute*] [*Later, NRSSC*] (EA) ...... NRTEC
National Rural Utilities Cooperative Finance Corp. [*NYSE symbol*] (SAG) ...... NRU
National Rural Utilities Cooperative Finance Corp. (EA) ...... NRUCFC
National Rural Utilities Cooperative Finance Corp. [*Associated Press*] (SAG) NRurU45
National Rural Water Association (EA) ...... NRWA
National R.V. Holdings, Inc. [*Associated Press*] (SAG) ...... NatlRV
National RV Holdings, Inc. [*NASDAQ symbol*] (SAG) ...... NRVH
National RV [*Recreational Vehicle*] **Owners Club** (EA) ...... NRVOC
National Saanen Breeders Association (EA) ...... NSBA
National Safe Boating Association (EA) ...... NSBA
National Safe Boating Council (EA) ...... NSBC
National Safe Boating Week Committee [*Later, NSBC*] ...... NSBWC
National Safe Kids Campaign (EA) ...... NSKC
National Safe Transit Association (EA) ...... NSTA
National Safe Workplace Institute (EA) ...... NSWI
National Safety Association (NADA) ...... NSA
National Safety Belt Coalition [*NHTSA*] (TAG) ...... NSBC
National Safety Corp. ...... NSC
National Safety Council (EA) ...... NSC
National Safety Council (NADA) ...... NSC
National Safety Council, Chicago, IL [*Library symbol Library of Congress*] (LCLS) ...... ICNS
National Safety Council of Australia, Victoria Division ...... NSCAV
National Safety Management Society (EA) ...... NSMS
National Safflower Council [*Defunct*] (EA) ...... NSC
National Sales Achievement Award [*NALU*] ...... NSAA
National Sales Development Institute ...... NSDI
National Sales Executives ...... NSE
National Salvation Front [*Romania*] [*Political party*] ...... FSN
National Salvation Front [*Romania*] [*Political party*] ...... NSF
National Salvation Party [*Milli Selamet Partisi*] [*Turkey Political party*] (PPW) ...... NSP
National Sample Survey (PDAA) ...... NSS
National Sand and Gravel Association [*Later, NAA*] (EA) ...... NSGA

National SANE Education Fund (EA) ... NSEF
National Sanitary Supply Association [*Later, ISSA*] (EA) ... NSSA
National Sanitary Supply Co. [*NASDAQ symbol*] (NQ) ... NSSX
National Sanitary Supply Co. [*Associated Press*] (SAG) ... NtSanit
National Sanitation Foundation (IAA) ... NSAF
National Sanitation Foundation ... NSanF
National Sanitation Foundation (EA) ... NSF
National Sanitation Foundation Laboratory ... NSFL
National Sanitation Foundation Testing Laboratory, Inc. (MSA) ... NSFTL
National Sash and Door Jobbers Association (EA) ... NSDJA
National Satellite Cable Association [*Defunct*] (EA) ... NSCA
National Save the Family Farm Coalition (EA) ... NSFFC
National Save-a-Life League [*Defunct*] (EA) ... NSLL
National Savings [*British*] ... NS
National Savings and Loan League [*Formerly, NLISA*] (EA) ... NSLL
National Savings Bank [*British*] ... NSB
National Savings Certificates [*British*] (DAS) ... NSC
National Savings Committee [*British*] ... NSC
National Sawmilling Association [*British*] (BI) ... NSA
National Scale Men's Association (EA) ... NSMA
National Schizophrenia Fellowship [*British*] ... NSF
National Scholarship Research Service [*Information service or system*] (IID) ... NSRS
National Scholarship Service and Fund for Negro Students (EA) ... NSSFNS
National Scholarship Trust Fund [*An affiliate of the Graphic Arts Technical Foundation*] ... NSTF
National Scholastic Press Association (EA) ... NSPA
National Scholastic Surfing Association (EA) ... NSSA
National School Band Association [*British*] (DBA) ... NSBA
National School Boards Association (EA) ... NSBA
National School Calendar Study Committee ... NSCSC
National School Curriculum Center for Educational Computing [*Defunct*] (EA) ... NSCEC
National School Development Council (AEE) ... NSCD
National School Development Council (EA) ... NSDC
National School Labor Relations Service [*Later, LMRS*] (EA) ... NSLRS
National School Law Reporter [*A publication*] (DLA) ... Nat'l School L Rptr
National School Lunch Program [*Department of Agriculture*] ... NSLP
National School Orchestra Association (EA) ... NSOA
National School Public Relations Association (EA) ... NSPRA
National School Resource Network [*Defunct*] (EA) ... NSRN
National School Supply and Equipment Association (EA) ... NSSEA
National School Transportation Association (EA) ... NSTA
National School Volunteer Program (EA) ... NSVP
National School Yearbook Association [*Later, NSY/NA*] ... NSYA
National School Yearbook/Newspaper Association [*Defunct*] (EA) ... NSY/NA
National Schools Committee for Economic Education (EA) ... NSCEE
National Science and Technology Advisory Group [*Australia*] ... NSTAG
National Science and Technology Board [*Singapore*] ... NSTB
National Science & Technology Board [*Singapore*] ... NSTB
National Science and Technology Council [*Formerly, FCCSET*] ... NSTC
National Science and Technology Week [*An annual outreach program begun in 1985 by the National Science Foundation*] ... NSTW
National Science Board [*National Science Foundation*] ... NSB
National Science Council [*Irish*] (MSC) ... NSC
National Science Development Board ... NSDB
National Science Fair - International ... NSF-I
National Science Film Library, Ottawa, ON, Canada [*Library symbol Library of Congress*] (LCLS) ... CaOONSF
National Science Film Library [*Cinematheque Nationale Scientifique*] **Ottawa, Ontario** [*Library symbol National Library of Canada*] (NLC) ... OONSF
National Science Foundation (AD) ... Nat Sci Fdn
National Science Foundation (EA) ... NSF
National Science Foundation Acquisition Regulation [*A publication*] (AAGC) ... NSFAR
National Science Foundation Act [*1950*] ... NSFA
National Science Foundation Network ... NSFNET
National Science Foundation Office for the International Decade of Ocean Exploration ... NSF/IDOE
National Science Foundation Procurement Regulation [*A publication*] (AAGC) ... NSFPR
National Science Foundation Program for Science and Technology Aid to the Handicapped ... NSF/STAH
National Science Foundation, Washington, DC [*Library symbol Library of Congress*] (LCLS) ... DNSF
National Science Foundation, Washington, DC [*OCLC symbol*] (OCLC) ... NSF
National Science Laboratories (KSC) ... NSL
National Science Library [*Later, Canada Institute for Scientific and Technical Information*] (DIT) ... NSL
National Science Supervisors Association (EA) ... NSSA
National Science Teachers Association (EA) ... NSTA
National Scientific [*Vancouver Stock Exchange symbol*] ... NS
National Scientific Balloon Facility [*Palestine, TX*] [*NASA*] ... NSBF
National Scientific Committee on Oceanography [*Marine science*] (MSC) ... NASCO
National Scientific Committee on Oceanography ... NSCO
National Scientific Register ... NSR
National Scoliosis Foundation (EA) ... NSF
National Scooter Riders Association [*British*] (DBA) ... NSRA
National Scouting Collectors Society (EA) ... NSCS
National Scrabble Association (EA) ... NSA
National Screw Machine Products Association (EA) ... NSMPA
National Scrip Collectors Association (EA) ... NSCA
National Sculpture Society (EA) ... NSS
National Sea Grant Depository [*National Oceanic and Atmospheric Administration Information service or system*] (IID) ... NSGD
National Sea Grant Depository Library, Pell Marine Science Library, Narragansett, RI [*Library symbol*] [*Library of Congress*] (LCLS) ... RNaNP
National Sea Products Ltd. [*Toronto Stock Exchange symbol*] ... NSP
National Sea Training Schools [*British*] ... NSTS
National Sea Training Trusts [*British*] (DS) ... NSTT
National Seafood Educators (EA) ... NSE
National Seafood Inspection Laboratory [*Pascagoula, MS*] [*Department of Commerce*] (GRD) ... NSIL
National Search and Rescue Plan ... NSRP
National Search and Rescue Secretariat [*Canada*] (DA) ... NSS
National Seashore (BARN) ... NS
National Seasoning Manufacturers Association (EA) ... NSMA
National Seastar [*Vancouver Stock Exchange symbol*] ... NAS
National Second Mortgage Association [*Center Square, PA*] (EA) ... NSMA
National Second Opinion Program (EA) ... NSOP
National Secondary Drinking Water Regualtions (GNE) ... NSDWR
National Secretariat Australia Jaycees ... NSAJ
National Secretaries Association (International) [*Later, PSI*] (EA) ... NSA
National Secs [*NASDAQ symbol*] (TTSB) ... NATS
National Secular Society (AD) ... Nat Sec Soc
National Secular Society [*British*] (DBA) ... NSS
National Securities Clearing Corp. ... NSCC
National Securities Corp. [*NASDAQ symbol*] (NQ) ... NATS
National Securities Corp. [*Associated Press*] (SAG) ... NtlSecs
National Securities Trading System ... NSTS
National Security Act (AAG) ... NSA
National Security Agency [*Acronym is facetiously translated as No Such Agency or Never Say Anything because of staffers' reluctance to give interviews*] [*DoD*] ... NSA
National Security Agency Advisory Board [*Fort George G. Meade, MD*] (EGAO) ... NSAAB
National Security Agency/Central Security Service (AABC) ... NSACSS
National Security Agency, Fort George G. Meade, MD [*Library symbol Library of Congress*] (LCLS) ... MdFmN
National Security Agency, Fort George G. Meade, MD [*OCLC symbol*] (OCLC) ... NSA
National Security Agency Liaison Officer ... NSALO
National Security Agency Memorandum ... NSAM
National Security Agency Pacific (CINC) ... NSAPAC
National Security Agency Scientific Advisory Board [*Ft. George G. Meade, MD*] (EGAO) ... NSASAB
National Security and Emergency Preparedness ... NSEP
National Security and International Affairs [*Office of Management and Budget*] ... NSIA
National Security and International Affairs Division (AAGC) ... NSIAD
National Security Archive ... NSA
National Security Council ... NSC
National Security Council Intelligence Committee [*Inactive*] ... NSCIC
National Security Council Intelligence Directive [*Pronounced "nee-sid"*] (AFM) ... NSCID
National Security Council Interdepartmental Group (MCD) ... NSCIG
National Security Decision Directive ... NSDD
National Security Decision Memorandum [*Air Force*] ... NSDM
National Security Electronic Surveillance ... NSES
National Security Group, Inc. [*NASDAQ symbol*] (SAG) ... NSEC
National Security Group, Inc. [*Associated Press*] (SAG) ... NSecIn
National Security Index of the American Security Council [*A publication*] (DLA) ... NSI
National Security Industrial Association (EA) ... NSIA
National Security Information (NRCH) ... NSI
National Security Management [*Military*] ... NSM
National Security Management Course [*National Defense University*] (GFGA) ... NSMC
National Security Medal ... NATSECM
National Security Medal [*Military decoration*] ... NSM
National Security Office [*or Officer*] (GFGA) ... NSO
National Security Organization [*Royal Thai Government*] ... BSO
National Security Planning Commission ... NSPC
National Security Planning Group ... NSPG
National Security Political Action Committee [*Defunct*] (EA) ... NSPAC
National Security Resources Board [*Functions transferred to ODM, 1953*] ... NSRB
National Security Resources Board [*Functions transferred to ODM, 1953*] (GFGA) ... NSRBD
National Security Resources Development ... NSRD
National Security Review (AAGC) ... NSR
National Security Study Memorandum [*Obsolete*] ... NSSM
National Security Telecommunications Advisory Committee (NITA) ... NSTAC
National Security Traders Association [*Later, STA*] (EA) ... NSTA
National Security Training Commission [*Expired, 1957*] ... NSTC
National Seed and Development Organisation [*British*] ... NSDO
National Seed Storage Laboratory [*Department of Agriculture*] [*Fort Collins, CO*] (GRD) ... NSSL
National Seismic Stations ... NSS
National Selected Morticians (EA) ... NSM
National Selective Service Appeal Board [*of SSS*] [*Inactive since 1975*] ... NSSAB
National Self Government Committee (EA) ... NSGC
National Self-Help Action Center - Food Program (EA) ... NSHAC-FP
National Self-Help Clearinghouse (EA) ... NSHC
National Self-Help Resource Center [*Defunct*] (EA) ... NSHRC
National Semiconductor Corp. ... Nat Semi
National Semiconductor Corp. (IAA) ... NATLSEMICON
National Semiconductor Corp. ... NSC
National Semiconductor Corp. [*Associated Press*] (SAG) ... NSem

National Semiconductor Corp. [*NYSE symbol*] (SPSG) .... NSM
National Semiconductor Corp. [*Associated Press*] (SAG) .... NtSemi
National Semiconductor Inc. (AD) .... NATSEMI
National Semi-Professional Baseball Association (EA) .... NSBA
National Senior Citizens Association [*Commercial firm*] (EA) .... NSCA
National Senior Citizens Law Center (EA) .... NSCLC
National Senior Sports Association (EA) .... NSSA
National Senior Women's Tennis Association (EA) .... NSWTA
National Seniors' Association [*Australia*] .... NSA
National Seniors' Open Golf Association (EA) .... NSOGA
National Seoposengwe Party [*Bophuthatswana*] [*Political party*] (PPW) .... NSP
National Serials Data Centre [*British Library*] (PDAA) .... NSDC
National Serials Data Program [*Library of Congress*] (EA) .... NSDP
National Serials Pilot Project .... NSPP
National Serigraph Society [*Defunct*] .... NSS
National Service [*in the armed forces*] [*British*] .... NS
National Service Acts [*British*] .... NSA
National Service Armed Forces Act [*British*] .... NSAFC
National Service Board for Religious Objectors [*Later, NISBCO*] (EA) ..... NSBRO
National Service Center .... NSC
National Service Conference of the American Ethical Union (EA) .... NSCAEU
National Service Coordinating Committee [*Ministry of Labour and National
Service*] [*British World War II*] .... NSCC
National Service Entertainments Council [*British*] .... NSEC
National Service Industries, Inc. [*NYSE symbol*] (SPSG) .... NSI
National Service Industries, Inc. [*Associated Press*] (SAG) .... NtSvIn
National Service [*Life*] Insurance .... NSI
National Service League [*British military*] (DMA) .... NSL
National Service Life Insurance .... NSLI
National Service Life Insurance .... NSLI
National Service Officer [*Ministry of Labour and National Service*] [*British
World War II*] .... NSO
National Service Robot Association (EA) .... NSRA
National Service Secretariat (EA) .... NSS
National Service Star Legion (EA) .... NSSL
National Serviceman [*British military*] (DMA) .... NSM
National Severe Storms Forecast Center [*National Oceanic and Atmospheric
Administration*] .... NSSFC
National Severe Storms Laboratory [*National Oceanic and Atmospheric
Administration*] [*Research center*] .... NSSL
National Severe Storms Laboratory, Norman, OK [*Library symbol Library of
Congress*] (LCLS) .... OkNNS
National Severe Storms Project [*National Oceanic and Atmospheric
Administration*] .... NSSP
National Sewage Sludge Survey [*Environmental Protection Agency*] ...... NSSS
National Sex Equity Demonstration Project (EDAC) .... NSEDP
National Sex Forum [*Later, ET*] (EA) .... NSF
National Shade Tree Conference [*Later, ISA*] .... NSTC
National Sharecroppers Fund (EA) .... NSF
National Shared Housing Resource Center (EA) .... NSHRC
National Sheep Association [*British*] (DBA) .... NSA
National Sheep Breeders' Association [*British*] (BI) .... NSBA
National Sheet Music Society (EA) .... NSMS
National Shellfish Sanitation Program [*Food and Drug Administration*]
(GFGA) .... NSSP
National Shellfisheries Association (EA) .... NSA
National Sheriffs' Association (EA) .... NSA
National Ship Installations Test Facility .... NSITF
National Shipbuilding Initiative [*MARAD*] (TAG) .... NSI
National Shipping Authority [*Department of Commerce*] .... NSA
National Shipping Report [*NATO*] .... NSR
National Shipping Representative (NATG) .... NSR
National Ships Destination Room (NATG) .... NSDR
National Shoe Institute (EA) .... NSI
National Shoe Manufacturers Association [*Later, FIA*] (EA) .... NSMA
National Shoe Retailers Association (EA) .... NSRA
National Shoe Traveler's Association (EA) .... NSTA
National Shoeboard Conference (EA) .... NSBC
National Shooting Sports Foundation (EA) .... NSSF
National Shoreline Refuse Survey [*British*] .... NSRS
National Shorthand Reporters Association (EA) .... NSRA
National Show Horse Registry (EA) .... NSHR
National Showmen's Association (EA) .... NSA
National Shrimp Breaders and Processors Association (EA) .... NSBPA
National Shrimp Breaders Association (EA) .... NSBA
National Shrimp Canners Association .... NSCA
National Shrimp Congress (EA) .... NSC
National Shrimp Processors Association (EA) .... NSPA
National Shuffleboard Association (EA) .... NSA
National Shut-In Day Society (EA) .... NSIDS
National Shut-In Society (EA) .... NSIS
National Siamese Cat Club (EA) .... NSCC
National Sickle Cell Disease Research Foundation [*Defunct*] (EA) .... NSCDRF
National SIGINT [*Signal Intelligence*] Operations Center (MCD) .... NSOC
National SIGINT [*Signal Intelligence*] Requirements Database (MCD) ... NSRDB
National SIGINT [*Signal Intelligence*] Requirements List (MCD) .... NSRL
National Silage Demonstration [*British*] .... NSD
National Silo Association [*Later, ISA*] (EA) .... NSA
National Silver Dollar Roundtable (EA) .... NSDR
National Silver Fox Rabbit Club (EA) .... NSFRC
National Silver Rabbit Club (EA) .... NSRC
National Silver-Haired Congress (EA) .... NSHC
National Simulation Council (SAA) .... NSC
National Single Service Food Association (EA) .... NSSFA
National Singles Registry (EA) .... NSR

National Sisters Communications Service [*Later, CCM*] (EA) .... NSCS
National Sisters Vocation Conference [*Later, NRVC*] (EA) .... NSVC
National Sjogren's Syndrome Association (EA) .... NSSA
National Skating Association of Great Britain .... NSA
National Skeet Shooting Association (EA) .... NSSA
National Ski Areas Association (EA) .... NSAA
National Ski Association of America [*Later, United States Ski Association*] ..... NSA
National Ski Credit Association (EA) .... NSCA
National Ski Federation (BARN) .... NSF
National Ski Patrol System (EA) .... NSP
National Ski Patrol System (EA) .... NSPS
National Ski Retailers Association (EA) .... NSRA
National Ski Study Group [*Defunct*] .... NSSG
National Ski Touring Operators' Association (EA) .... NSTOA
National Skills Training .... NST
National Skin Cancer Foundation [*Later, SCF*] (EA) .... NSCF
National Slag Association (EA) .... NSA
National Slate Association (EA) .... NSA
National Slavic Convention (EA) .... NSC
National Slavic Honor Society (EA) .... NSHS
National Slovak Society of the USA .... NSS
National Slow Rate (NASA) .... NSR
National Slow Rate .... NSR
National Small Business Association [*Later, NSBU*] .... NSB
National Small Business Association [*Later, NSBU*] .... NSBA
National Small Business Benefits Association (EA) .... NSBBA
National Small Business Government Contractors Association [*Defunct*]
(EA) .... NSBGCA
National Small Business Men's Association [*Later, NSBU*] .... NSBMA
National Small Business United [*Washington, DC*] (EA) .... NSBU
National Small College Athletic Association (EA) .... NSCAA
National Small Craft School [*Red Cross*] .... NSCS
National Small Sailing Yacht Association (EA) .... NSSYA
National Small Shipments Traffic Conference [*Acronym now used as official
name of association*] (EA) .... NASSTRAC
National Small Shipments Traffic Conference (EA) .... NSSTC
National Small Shipments Traffic Council .... NASSTRAC
National Smallbore Rifle Association [*British*] .... NSRA
National Smallgoods Council [*Australia*] .... NSC
National Smokers Alliance .... NSA
National Smooth Dancers (DICI) .... NSD
National Snaffle Bit Association (EA) .... NSBA
National Snapdragon Society (EA) .... NSS
National Snorkellers Club [*British*] (DBA) .... NSC
National Snow and Ice Data Center [*National Oceanic and Atmospheric
Administration*] (GFGA) .... NSIDC
National Snurfing Association (EA) .... NSA
National Soaring Foundation (EA) .... NSF
National Soaring Museum (DICI) .... NSM
National Soccer Coaches Association of America (EA) .... NSCA
National Soccer League (EA) .... NSL
National Social Conditioning Camps [*Later, NOC*] (EA) .... NSCC
National Social Science and Law Center (EA) .... NSSLC
National Social Science and Law Project (EA) .... NSSLP
National Social Science Documentation Centre [*Information service or
system*] (IID) .... NASSDC
National Social Science Documentation Centre [*Information service or
system*] (IID) .... NASSDOC
National Social Science Foundation [*Proposed in 1966*] .... NSSF
National Social Services Consultant and Government Relations Officer,
Salvation Army Library, Ottawa, Ontario [*Library symbol National Library
of Canada*] (BIB) .... OOSA
National Social Welfare Assembly [*Later, National Assembly of National
Voluntary Health and Social Welfare Organizations*] (EA) .... NSWA
National Socialist Action Party [*British*] .... NSAP
National Socialist Board [*Dutch National Socialist Party of 1931; later, Dutch
NAZI Party*] [*Political party*] .... NSB
National Socialist Council of Nagaland [*India*] (PD) .... NSCN
National Socialist Liberation Front (NADA) .... NSLF
National Socialist Movement (EA) .... NSM
National Socialist Nederlandse Arbeiders Partij [*Netherlands group favoring
integration of the Netherlands into the German reich*] [*World War II*] .... NSNA
National Socialist Party [*New Zealand*] [*Political party*] (PD) .... NSP
National Socialist Party of America (EA) .... NSPA
National Socialist Vanguard (EA) .... NSV
National Socialist White American Party [*Political party*] .... NSWAP
National Socialist White People's Party [*Formerly, American NAZI Party*]
(EA) .... NSWPP
National Society .... NS
National Society Against Factory Farming [*British*] (DBA) .... NSAFF
National Society, Daughters of Colonial Wars .... DCW
National Society, Daughters of Founders and Patriots of America (EA) ...... DFPA
National Society, Daughters of the American Colonists (EA) .... DAC
National Society, Daughters of the American Revolution (EA) .... NSDAR
National Society, Daughters of the Barons of Runnemede (EA) .... DBR
National Society, Daughters of the Barons of Runnemede (EA) .... NSDBR
National Society, Daughters of the British Empire (EA) .... NSDBE
National Society, Daughters of the British Empire in the United States of
America (EA) .... DBE
National Society, Daughters of Utah Pioneers (EA) .... DUP
National Society, Daughters of Utah Pioneers (EA) .... NSDUP
National Society, Descendants of Early Quakers (EA) .... NSDEQ
National Society for Animal Protection (EA) .... NSAP
National Society for Art Education [*British*] .... NSAE
National Society for Autistic Children [*British*] .... NSAC

National Society for Business Budgeting [*Later, PEI*] ... NSBB
National Society for Cancer Relief [*British*] ... NSCR
National Society for Cardiopulmonary Technology, Inc. (DAVI) ... NSCTI
National Society for Cardiovascular and Pulmonary Technology (EA) ... NSCPT
National Society for Cardiovascular and Pulmonary Technology (EA) ... NSCVPT
[*The*] **National Society for Children and Adults with Autism 2** [*Formerly, NSAC*] (EA) ... NSCAA
National Society for Clean Air [*British*] (DCTA) ... NSCA
National Society for Crippled Children (DAVI) ... NSCC
National Society for Crippled Children and Adults [*Later, NESS*] (EA) ... NSCCA
National Society for Education in Art and Design (EAIO) ... NSEAD
National Society for Epilepsy [*British*] ... NSE
National Society for Graphology (EA) ... NSG
National Society for Histotechnology (EA) ... NSH
National Society for Internships and Experiential Education (EA) ... NSIEE
National Society for Medical Research (EA) ... NSMR
National Society for Mentally Handicapped Children [*British*] (BI) ... NSMHC
National Society for Park Resources (EA) ... NSPR
National Society for Performance and Instruction (EA) ... NSPI
National Society for Phenylketonuria and Allied Disorders [*British*] (DBA) ... NSPKU
National Society for Prevention of Cruelty to Mushrooms (EA) ... NSPCM
National Society for Programmed Instruction (IAA) ... NSPI
National Society for Real Estate Finance [*Washington, DC*] (EA) ... NSREF
National Society for Research into Allergy [*British*] ... NSRA
National Society for Shut-Ins (EA) ... NSFS
National Society for the Abolition of Cruel Sports [*British*] (BI) ... NSACS
National Society for the Preservation of Covered Bridges (EA) ... NSPCB
National Society for the Prevention of Blindness, New York, NY [*Library symbol Library of Congress*] (LCLS) ... NNNSB
National Society for the Prevention of Cruelty to Animals ... NSPCA
National Society for the Prevention of Cruelty to Children ... NSPCC
National Society for the Promotion of Industrial Education [*Later, AVA*] ... NSPIE
National Society for the Study of Communication [*Later, ICA*] (EA) ... NSSC
National Society for the Study of Education (EA) ... NSSE
National Society of Accountants for Cooperatives (EA) ... NSAC
National Society of Andersonville (EA) ... NSA
National Society of Architectural Engineers (EA) ... NSAE
National Society of Art Directors (EA) ... NSAD
National Society of Artists (EA) ... NSA
National Society of Arts and Letters (EA) ... NSAL
National Society of Asphalt Workers [*A union*] [*British*] ... NSAW
National Society of Auctioneers [*Later, National Auctioneers Association*] ... NSA
National Society of Bank Directors [*Formerly, NABD*] [*Later, ASBD*] (EA) ... NSBD
National Society of Biomedical Equipment Technicians (EA) ... NSBET
National Society of Black Engineers (EA) ... NSBE
National Society of Black Physicists (EA) ... NSBP
National Society of Brushmakers and General Workers [*A union*] [*British*] (DCTA) ... NSBGW
National Society of Certified Public Accountants (EA) ... NSCPA
National Society of Chauffeurs [*A union*] [*British*] ... NSC
National Society of Chief Executive Officers [*Defunct*] (EA) ... NSCEO
National Society of College Teachers of Education [*Later, SPE*] (EA) ... NSCTE
National Society of Colonial Dames of America (EA) ... CDA
National Society of Colonial Dames of America (EA) ... NSCDA
National Society of Colonial Dames of America, Washington, DC [*Library symbol Library of Congress*] (LCLS) ... DNCD
National Society of Commercial Agents [*Australia*] ... NSCA
National Society of Compliance Professionals (EA) ... NSCP
National Society of Computer/Genealogists [*Defunct*] (EA) ... NSC
National Society of Cwens (EA) ... NSC
National Society of Cycle Makers [*A union*] [*British*] ... NSCM
National Society of Cycle Workers [*A union*] [*British*] ... NSCW
National Society of Denture Prosthetists [*Later, ADP*] ... NSDP
National Society of Descendants of Lords of the Maryland Manors (EA) ... NSDLMM
National Society of Electronic Data Processing Machine Operators and Programmers [*Inactive*] ... DPMOAP
National Society of Electrotypers and Stereotypers [*British*] (BI) ... NSES
National Society of Environmental Consultants (EA) ... NSEC
National Society of Fathers for Child Custody and Divorce Law Reform [*Later, FER*] (EA) ... NSFCCDLR
National Society of Film Critics ... NSFC
National Society of Fund Raisers [*Later, NSFRE*] (EA) ... NSFR
National Society of Fund Raisers Institute of Continuing Education [*Former name of the National Society of Fund Raising Executives Foundation*] (NFD) ... NICE
National Society of Fund Raising Executives (EA) ... NSFRE
National Society of Fund Raising Executives Foundation [*Formerly the National Society of Fund Raisers Institute of Continuing Education and the National Society of Fund Raising Executives*] (NFD) ... NSFRE Foundation
National Society of General Tool Makers, Engineers, and Machinists [*A union*] [*British*] ... NSGTMEM
National Society of Genetic Counselors (EA) ... NSGC
National Society of Glass Workers [*A union*] [*British*] ... NSGW
National Society of Hispanic MBAs (EA) ... NSHMBA
National Society of Hypnotherapists (EA) ... NSH
National Society of Insurance Premium Auditors (EA) ... NSIPA
National Society of Interior Designers [*Later, ASID*] ... NSID
National Society of Journeymen Curriers [*A union*] [*British*] ... NSJC
National Society of Literature and the Arts (EA) ... NSLA
National Society of Live Stock Record Associations (EA) ... NSLSRA
National Society of Master Patternmakers [*British*] (BI) ... NSMP
National Society of Master Thatchers [*British*] (DBA) ... NSMT
National Society of Medical Technologists ... NSMT
National Society of Metal Mechanics [*A union*] [*British*] (DCTA) ... NSMM
National Society of Mural Painters (EA) ... NSMP
National Society of New England Women (EA) ... NSNEW
National Society of Old Plymouth Colony Descendants (EA) ... NSOPCD
National Society of Operative Printers and Assistants [*British*] ... NATSOPA
National Society of Painters [*A union*] [*British*] ... NSP
National Society of Painters in Casein (EA) ... NSPC
National Society of Painters in Casein and Acrylic (EA) ... NSPCA
National Society of Painters, Sculptors, and Engravers [*British*] (DI) ... NSPSE
National Society of Patient Representatives of the American Hospital Association (EA) ... NSPR
National Society of Pershing Rifles (EA) ... NSPR
National Society of Pharmaceutical Sales Trainers (EA) ... NSPST
National Society of Professional Engineers (EA) ... NSPE
National Society of Professional Resident Managers (EA) ... NSPRM
National Society of Professional Sanitarians (EA) ... NSPS
National Society of Professional Surveyors (EA) ... NSPS
National Society of Professors [*Later, NEA Higher Education Council*] (EA) ... NSP
National Society of Public Accountants (MCD) ... NASPA
National Society of Public Accountants [*Alexandria, VA*] (EA) ... NSPA
National Society of Quality Circles [*British*] (DBA) ... NSQC
National Society of Sales Training Executives [*Orlando, FL*] (EA) ... NSSTE
National Society of Scabbard and Blade (EA) ... NSSB
National Society of Sons and Daughters of the Pilgrims (EA) ... NSSDP
National Society of Sons and Daughters of the Pilgrims (EA) ... SDP
National Society of State Legislators [*Later, NCSL*] ... NSSL
National Society of Student Film Critics [*Defunct*] (EA) ... NSSFC
National Society of Student Keyboardists (EA) ... NSSK
National Society of Student Organists [*Later, NSSK*] (EA) ... NSSO
National Society of Telephone Employees [*A union*] [*British*] ... NSTE
National Society of the Children of the American Revolution (EA) ... NSCAR
National Society of the Sons of Utah Pioneers (EA) ... NSSUP
National Society of Tole and Decorative Painters (EA) ... NSTDP
National Society of TV Producers (NTCM) ... NSTP
National Society Patriotic Women of America ... NSPWA
National Society, Sons of the American Colonists [*Defunct*] (EA) ... NSSAC
National Society, Sons of the American Revolution (EA) ... SAR
[*The*] **National Society to Discourage Use of the Name Smith for Purposes ofHypothetical Illustration** ... TNSDUNSPHI
National Society to Prevent Blindness (EA) ... NSPB
National Society Women Descendants of the Ancient and Honorable Artillery Company (EA) ... DAH
National Society Women Descendants of the Ancient and Honorable Artillery Company (EA) ... NSWDAHAC
National Society Women Descendants of the Ancient and Honorable Artillery Company (EA) ... WDAHAC
National Society's Religious Education Centre (AIE) ... NSREC
National Soda Dispensing Equipment Association (EA) ... NSDEA
National Soft Drink Association (EA) ... NSDA
National Soft Serve and Fast Food Association (EA) ... NSSFFA
National Soft Wheat Association [*Later, MNF*] (EA) ... NSWA
National Soft Wheat Millers Association [*Later, MNF*] (EA) ... NSWMA
National Softball Association (EA) ... NSA
National Software Works ... NSW
National Software-Testing Laboratories [*Computer science*] ... NSTL
National Soil Dynamics Laboratory [*Auburn, AL*] [*Department of Agriculture*] (GRD) ... NSDL
National Soil Survey Committee [*Canada*] ... NSSC
National Sojourners (EA) ... NS
National Solar Energy Research Institute [*Energy Research and Development Administration*] ... NSERI
National Solar Heating and Cooling Information Center [*Later, CAREIRS*] ... NSHCIC
National Solar Observatory [*Tucson, AZ*] [*National Science Foundation*] (GRD) ... NSO
National Solar Space Observatory [*NASA*] ... NSSO
National Solar Technical Audience File [*Solar Energy Research Institute*] [*Database*] ... NSTAF
National Solar Thermal Test Facility [*Sandia National Laboratories*] ... NSTTF
National Solid Wastes Management Association (EA) ... NSWMA
National Sonic Boom Evaluation Office [*Air Force*] (MCD) ... NSBEO
National Sound and Communications Association (EA) ... NSCA
National Sound Archive [*British Library*] ... NSA
National Sound-Program Center [*Telecommunications*] (TEL) ... NSPC
National Soup Mix Association [*Defunct*] (EA) ... NSMA
National Soybean Crop Improvement Council ... NSCIC
National Soybean Processors Association [*Later, NOPA*] (EA) ... NSPA
National Spa and Pool Institute (EA) ... NSPI
National Space and Aeronautics Agency (MCD) ... NSAA
National Space Club (EA) ... NSC
National Space Council ... NSC
National Space Development Agency [*Japan*] ... NASDA
National Space Institute [*Later, NSS*] (EA) ... NSI
National Space Program (AAG) ... NSP
National Space Science Center [*British*] ... NSSC
National Space Science Data Center [*Greenbelt, MD*] [*NASA*] (MCD) ... NSSDC
National Space Society (EA) ... NSS
National Space Station [*NASA*] (IAA) ... NSS
National Space Surveillance Control Center ... NSSCC
National Space Surveillance System ... NSSS
National Space Technology Laboratories [*Formerly, MTF*] [*Mississippi*] [*NASA*] ... NSTL
National Space Transportation System ... NSTS
National Space Transportation System Program Office (SSD) ... NSTSPO

National Spanish Speaking Housing Development Corp. ... NSSHDC
National Spasmodic Dysphonia Association (EA) ... NSDA
National Spasmodic Torticollis Association (EA) ... NSTA
National Spatial Data Infrastructure [*BTS*] (TAG) ... NSDI
National Spatial Data Infrastructure [*BTS*] (TAG) ... NSPI
National Spatial Reference System [*Marine science*] (OSRA) ... NSRS
National Spatial Reference System (USDC) ... NSRS
National Speakers Association (EA) ... NSA
National Special [*Thread*] ... NS
National Speed Sport News [*A publication*] ... NSSN
National Speleological Society (EA) ... NSS
National Spherical Torus Experiment [*Plasma physics*] ... NSTX
National Spinal Cord Injury Association (EA) ... NSCIA
National Spinal Cord Injury Foundation [*Formerly, NPF*] [*Later, NSCIA*] (EA) ... NSCIF
National Spinal Cord Injury Statistical Center Database [*University of Alabama in Birmingham*] [*Information service or system*] (CRD) ... NSCISC
National Spinal Injuries Centre [*Stoke Mandeville Hospital*] [*British*] (CB) ... NSIC
National Spirit, Metropolitan Club of America (EA) ... NSMCA
[*The*] **National Spiritual Alliance of the United States of America** ... TNSA
National Spiritual Alliance of the USA (EA) ... NSA
National Spiritual Assembly of Baha'is of Australia ... NSABA
National Spiritual Assembly of the Baha'is of the US (EA) ... NSA-US
National Spiritualist Association of Churches (EA) ... NSAC
National Spiritualist Church [*British*] ... NSC
National Spiritualist Teachers Club (EA) ... NSTC
National Spit Tobacco Education Program [*An initiative of Oral Health America*] ... NSTEP
National Split Pea Association [*Defunct*] ... NSPA
National Sport Aviation Council [*Defunct*] (EA) ... NSAC
National Sport Custom Registry (EA) ... NSCR
National Sporting Clays Association ... NSCA
National Sporting Goods Association (EA) ... NSGA
National Sporting Library, Inc., Middleburg, VA [*Library symbol Library of Congress*] (LCLS) ... ViMiNS
National Sports Association (EA) ... NSA
National Sports Car Club of America ... NSCCA
National Sportscasters and Sportswriters Association (EA) ... NSSA
National Spotted Saddle Horse Association (EA) ... NSSHA
National Spotted Swine Record (EA) ... NSSR
National Spray Equipment Manufacturers Association (EA) ... NSEMA
National Spray Painting and Finishing Equipment Association [*Later, NSEMA*] (EA) ... NSPFEA
National Sprayer and Duster Association (EA) ... NSDA
National Sprint Association [*British*] (DBA) ... NSA
National Sprint Car Hall of Fame [*Iowa*] ... NSCHF
National Sprouting Association (EA) ... NSA
National Square Dance Convention (EA) ... NSDC
National Squash Federation [*British*] (DBA) ... NSF
National Squash Tennis Association (EA) ... NSTA
National Staff Committee [*Nurses and midwives*] [*British*] ... NSC
National Staff Development and Training Association (EA) ... NSDTA
National Staff Development Committee [*Australia*] ... NSDC
National Staff Development Council (EA) ... NSDC
National Staff Leasing Association (EA) ... NSLA
National Staff Side [*British*] ... NSS
National Stamp Exhibition [*British*] (ITD) ... STAMPEX
National Standard (IEEE) ... NS
National Standard Co. [*NYSE symbol*] (SAG) ... NSD
National Standard Co. [*Associated Press*] (SAG) ... NStand
National Standard for Common System Component Characteristics (MCD) ... NSCSCC
National Standard Information Resources, Niles, MI [*Library symbol*] [*Library of Congress*] (LCLS) ... MiNiN
National Standard Parts Association [*Later, ASIA*] ... NSPA
National Standard Plumbing Code Committee (EA) ... NSPC
National Standard Race [*Skiing*] ... NASTAR
National Standard Reference Data System [*Gaithersburg, MD*] [*National Institute of Standards and Technology*] ... NSRDS
National Standard Shipping Note (DS) ... NSSN
National Standard Taper (IAA) ... NST
National Standardization Office [*US Army Materiel Command*] ... NSO
National Standards Association (NADA) ... NSA
National Standards Association, Inc. [*Bethesda, MD*] ... NSA
National Standards Authority of Ireland [*Irish Science and Technology Agency*] (IRC) ... NSAI
National Standards Commission (NADA) ... NSC
National Standards Council of American Embroiderers [*Later, CAE*] (EA) ... NSCAE
National Standards Educators Association (EA) ... NSEA
National Standards Laboratory [*Formerly, IBS, IMR*] [*National Institute of Standards and Technology*] ... NSL
National Standards of Performance for Stationary Sources (ACII) ... NSPS
National Standards Reference Data Center ... NSRDC
National Standards Systems Network ... NSSN
National Star Route Mail Contractors Association (EA) ... NSRMCA
National/State Leadership Training Institute on Gifted and Talented (EA) ... N/S-LTI-G/T
National State Printing Association (EA) ... NSPA
National States Rights Party (EA) ... NSRP
National Stationery and Office Equipment Association [*Later, NOPA*] (EA) ... NSOEA
National Status and Trends (GNE) ... NS & T
National STD [*Sexually Transmitted Disease*] **Hotline** (EA) ... NSTDH
National Steam Service Union [*British*] ... NSSU
National Steel [*NYSE symbol*] (SPSG) ... NS
National Steel & Shipbuilding Co. ... NASSCO
National Steel Corp. [*Associated Press*] (SAG) ... NatlStl
National Steel Labor Relations Board [*New Deal*] ... NSLRB
National Steeplechase and Hunt Association (EA) ... NSHA
National Steering Group (AIE) ... NSG
National Stereophonic Radio Committee ... NSRC
National Stereoscopic Association (EA) ... NSA
National Stinson Club (EA) ... NSC
National Stock Car Racing Commission ... NSCRC
National Stock Control and Maintenance Point [*Army*] (AABC) ... NSC & MP
National Stock Control and Maintenance Point [*Army*] (AFIT) ... NSCAMP
National Stock Exchange [*Dissolved, 1975*] ... NATEX
National Stock Exchange [*Dissolved, 1975*] ... NSE
National Stock Exchange [*India*] ... NSE
National Stock Horse Association (EA) ... NSHA
National Stock Number (MCD) ... NSN
National Stock Number Master Data Records (MCD) ... NSNMDR
National Stockbrokers Forum [*Later, CFC*] (EA) ... NSF
National Stockpile Purchase Specification [*for metals*] ... NSPS
National Stockpile Site ... NSS
National Stolen Property ... NSP
National Stone Association (EA) ... NSA
National Storage Industry Consortium ... NSIC
National Story League (EA) ... NSL
National Straight Pipe Threads for Dry Seal Pressure Tight Joints ... NPSF
National Straight Pipe Threads for Hose Couplings and Nipples ... NPSH
National Straight Pipe Threads for Locknuts and Locknut Pipe Threads ... NPSL
National Straight Pipe Threads in Pipe Couplings ... NPSC
National Strategic Target Data Base (CINC) ... NSTDB
National Strategic Target Line [*or List*] (AFM) ... NSTL
National Strategic Targeting and Attack Policy (CINC) ... NSTAP
National Strategy ... NS
National Strategy for Rangeland Management [*Australia*] ... NSRM
National Strategy for Sustainable Development [*Australia*] ... NSSD
National Strategy Information Center (EA) ... NSIC
National Stream Quality Accounting Network [*Department of the Interior*] ... NASQAN
National Street Law Institute (EA) ... NSLI
National Street Rod Association (EA) ... NSRA
National Strength and Conditioning Association (EA) ... NSCA
National Strict Baptist Sunday School Association [*British*] ... NSBSSA
National Strike Force [*Marine science*] (MSC) ... NSF
National Stripper Well Association (EA) ... NSWA
National Stroke Association (EA) ... NSA
National Stroke Recovery Foundation (EA) ... NSRF
National Structured Settlements Trade Association (EA) ... NSSTA
National Student Action Center (EA) ... NSAC
National Student Aid Coalition [*Defunct*] (EA) ... NSAC
National Student Association [*Later, USSA*] ... NSA
National Student Book Club ... NSBC
National Student Campaign Against Hunger [*Later, NSCAHH*] (EA) ... NSCAH
National Student Campaign Against Hunger and Homelessness (EA) ... NSCAHH
National Student Campaign for Voter Registration (EA) ... NSCVR
National Student Christian Federation [*Later, UCM*] (EA) ... NSCF
National Student Consumer Protection Council (EA) ... NSCPC
National Student Drama Festival [*British*] ... NSDF
National Student Educational Fund (EA) ... NSEF
National Student Exchange (EA) ... NSE
National Student Financial Aid Council [*Later, NASFAA*] (EA) ... NSFAC
National Student Involvement Assistance Center [*Boston University*] [*Defunct*] ... NSIAC
National Student Marketing Corp. ... NSMC
National Student Nurses' Association (EA) ... NSNA
National Student Speech and Hearing Association [*Later, NSSLHA*] (EA) ... NSSHA
National Student Speech Language Hearing Association (EA) ... NSSLHA
National Student Strike Information Center [*Brandeis University*] ... NSSIC
National Student Traffic Safety Program [*National Commission on Safety Education*] [*Washington, DC*] (AEBS) ... NSTS
National Student Volunteer Program [*Later, NCSL*] (EA) ... NSVP
National Students Association (NADA) ... NSA
National Students Center for Thailand ... NSCT
National Study Commission on Records and Documents of Federal Officials ... NSCRDFO
National Study of Mathematics Requirements for Scientists and Engineers ... NSMRSE
National Study of School Evaluation (EA) ... NSSE
National Study of Secondary School Evaluation [*Later, NSSE*] (EA) ... NSSSE
National Study Service [*Defunct*] (EA) ... NSS
National Stuttering Project (EA) ... NSP
National Sudden Infant Death Syndrome Clearinghouse (EA) ... NSIDSC
National Sudden Infant Death Syndrome Foundation (EA) ... NSIDSF
National Suffolk Sheep Association (EA) ... NSSA
National Sugar Brokers Association (EA) ... NSBA
National Sulphuric Acid Association [*British*] (DBA) ... NSAA
National Summer Youth Sports Program ... NSYSP
National Sunday School Association [*Defunct*] (EA) ... NSSA
National Sunday School Union [*British*] ... NSSU
National Sunflower Association (EA) ... NSA
National Superannuation (AD) ... Nat Sup
National Superconducting Cyclotron Laboratory [*Michigan State University*] [*National Science Foundation*] [*Research center*] (RCD) ... NSCL
National Supervisory Council for Intruder Alarms [*British*] (DBA) ... NSCIA
National Supervisory Inspectorate [*British*] (EECA) ... NSI

National Suppliers to Food Processors Association (EA) .... NSFPA
National Supply Association of America [Later, NSDA] (EA) .... NSAA
National Supply Class [Military] (AFIT) .... NSC
National Supply Distributors Association [Dayton, OH] (EA) .... NSDA
National Supply Group [Military] (AFIT) .... NSG
National Supply Radio Station (MCD) .... NSRS
National Supply System (MCD) .... NSS
National Support Center for Families of the Aging [Defunct] (EA) .... NSCFA
National Support Elements [British military] (DMA) .... NSE
National Support Group for Dermatomyositis (EA) .... NSGD
National Surf Life Saving Association of America [Later, USLA] (EA) .... NSLSA
National Surface Water Survey (GNE) .... NSWS
National Surgery Centers, Inc. [Associated Press] (SAG) .... NatSurg
National Surgery Centers, Inc. [NASDAQ symbol] (SAG) .... NSCI
National Surgical Adjuvant Breast and Bowel Project (DAVI) .... NSABP
National Surgical Adjuvant Breast Project .... NSABP
National Surplus Dealers Association (EA) .... NSDA
National Survey of Children .... NSC
National Survey of Family Growth .... NSFG
National Survey of Instructional Staff [Department of Education] (GFGA) .... NSIS
National Survey of Oral Health in School Children [Department of Health and Human Services] (GFGA) .... NSOHSC
National Survey of Postsecondary Faculty [Department of Education] (GFGA) .... NSOPF
National Survey of State Laws [A publication] .... NSSL
National Swedish Telecommunications Administration [Stockholm] [Information service or system] (IID) .... Televerket
National Sweet Pea Society [British] (BI) .... NSPS
National Swim and Recreation Association (EA) .... NSRA
National Swim School Association (EA) .... NSSA
National Swimming Pool Foundation (EA) .... NSPF
National Swine Growers Council [Later, NPPC] (EA) .... NSGC
National Swine Improvement Federation (EA) .... NSIF
National Swiss Battle Tank (MCD) .... NSBT
[The] National Switchboard [Phoenix, AZ] [Telecommunications] (TSSD) .... TNS
National Symphony Orchestra .... NSO
National Symphony Orchestra Association (EA) .... NSOA
National Symposium on Reliability and Quality Control in Electronics (MCD) .... NSRQCE
National Symposium on Space Electronics and Telemetry [IEEE] (MCD) .... NSSET
National Symposium on Telemetering (MCD) .... NST
National Synchrotron Light Source [Brookhaven National Laboratory] .... NSLS
National Synthetics Collection [Smithsonian Institution] .... NSC
National Syrian Hamster Council [British] (DBA) .... NSHC
National Syrian Socialist Party [Lebanon] [Political party] .... NSSP
National System Architecture .... NSA
National System of Interstate and Defense Highways (AFIT) .... NSIDH
National Systems Programmers Association (EA) .... NaSPA
National Tabletop Association (EA) .... NTA
National Tactical Force (NATG) .... NTF
National Tactical Interface (MCD) .... NTI
National Tank Co. (AD) .... NATCO
National Tank Manufacturers Association [Defunct] (EA) .... NTMA
National Tank Truck Carriers (AD) .... NATTC
National Tank Truck Carriers [Alexandria, VA] (EA) .... NTTC
National Tap Dance Co. of Canada .... NTD
National Tape Repository (EA) .... NTR
National Taper Pipe [Thread] .... NPT
National Taper Pipe Threads for Dry Seal Pressure Tight Joints .... NPTF
National Taper Pipe Threads for Railing Fixtures .... NPTR
National Taranesc [National Peasant Party] [Romania] [Political party] (PPE) .... NT
National Target Base (MCD) .... NTB
National Targeting and Attack Policy (CINC) .... NTAP
National Task Force on Autocratic Options .... NTFAO
National Task Force on Education for Economic Growth (EA) .... NTFEEG
National Task Force on Prostitution (EA) .... NTFP
National Tasking Center (MCD) .... NTC
National Tasking Plan [Military] .... NTP
National Tattoo Association (EA) .... NTA
National Tax Association [Later, NTA-TIA] .... NTA
National Tax Association. Proceedings [A publication] (DLA) .... NTA Proceedings
National Tax Association - Tax Institute of America (EA) .... NTA-TIA
National Tax Equality Association (EA) .... NTEA
National Tax Magazine [A publication] (DLA) .... Nat Tax Mag
National Tax Strike Coalition (EA) .... NTSC
National Taxi and Car Hire Association [British] (BI) .... NTCHA
National Taxidermists Association [Defunct] (EA) .... NTA
National Tax-Limitation Committee (EA) .... NTLC
National Taxpayers Alliance (EA) .... NTA
National Taxpayers' Investigative Fund (EA) .... NTIF
National Taxpayers Legal Fund (EA) .... NTLF
National Taxpayers Union (EA) .... NTU
National Tay-Sachs and Allied Diseases Association (EA) .... NTSAD
National Tay-Sachs Association [Later, NTSAD] (EA) .... NTSA
National Teacher Examination .... NTE
National Teachers Association (AEE) .... NTA
National Teachers Corps .... NTC
National Teaching Development Grant [Australia] .... NTDG
National Teaching-Family Association (EA) .... NTFA
National Team .... NT
National Team Championship [Swimming] [British] (ROG) .... NTC
National Technical Assistance Center on Family Violence [Defunct] (EA) .... NTAC
National Technical Association (EA) .... NTA

National Technical Information Centre and Library (NITA) .... NTICL
National Technical Information Service (NADA) .... NTIS
National Technical Information Service [Department of Commerce] [Springfield, VA Database producer and database] .... NTIS
National Technical Information Service, Springfield, VA [Library symbol Library of Congress] (LCLS) .... ViSpN
National Technical Institute for the Deaf [Rochester Institute of Technology] [Research center] .... NTID
National Technical Means [For monitoring compliance with the provisions of an agreement] .... NTM
National Technical Processing Center .... NTPC
National Technical Scholarship Foundation (AEBS) .... NTSF
National Technical Services Association (EA) .... NTSA
National Technical Systems .... NTS
National Technical Systems, Inc. [Associated Press] (SAG) .... NTech
National Technical Systems Inc. [Commercial firm] .... NTS
National Technical Systems, Inc. [NASDAQ symbol] (NQ) .... NTSC
National Technical Task Committee on Industrial Wastes .... NTTCIW
National Technological University [Fort Collins, CO] .... NTU
National Technology and Industrial Base (AAGC) .... NTIB
National Technology Initiative [Program introduced by President Bush in February 1992] .... NTI
National Technology Investment Programme [Canada] .... N-TIP
National Technology Ltd. (NITA) .... NTL
National Technology Transfer Center [NASA] .... NTTC
National Technology Transfer Center .... NTTS
National TechTeam, Inc. [Associated Press] (SAG) .... NTeam
National TechTeam, Inc. [NASDAQ symbol] (NQ) .... TEAM
National Teen Age Republican Headquarters (EA) .... NTARH
National Teen Challenge (EA) .... NTC
National TeleAccess Network [Database of physician opportunities] .... NTN
National Telecommunications Agency .... NTA
National Telecommunications and Information Administration [Department of Commerce] [Washington, DC] .... NTIA
National Telecommunications and Information System Security Committee (NITA) .... NTISSC
National Telecommunications & Technology Fund, Inc. [New York, NY] (TSSD) .... TELETECH
National Telecommunications Conference [IEEE] .... NTC
National Telecommunications Education Committee [North American Telecommunications Association] [Washington, DC Telecommunications service] (TSSD) .... NTEC
National Telecommunications Electronics Administration .... NTEA
National Telecommunications Network [Rockville, MD] (TSSD) .... NTN
National Telefilm Associates, Inc. (NTCM) .... NTA
National Telemarketing Fulfillment Center .... NTCF
National Telemarketing Fulfillment Center .... NTFC
National Telemedia Council (EA) .... NTC
National Telephone Cooperative Association (EA) .... NTCA
National Teletypewriter Exchange (IAA) .... NTX
National Television Center [Telecommunications] (TEL) .... NTC
National Television Film Council (EA) .... NTFC
National Television Licensing and Records Office [British] .... NTVLRO
National Television Rental Association [British] .... NTRA
National Television Standard Code [Video equipment] (RDA) .... NTSC
National Television Standards Committee .... NTSC
National Television System Committee [Formed in 1936] .... NTSC
National Temperance and Prohibition Council (EA) .... NTPC
National Temperance League [Later, ACAP] (EA) .... NTL
National Temple Hill Association (EA) .... NTHA
National Temporal Bone Banks Program of the DRF [Deafness Research Foundation] (EA) .... NTBB
National Tenants Organization [Defunct] (EA) .... NTO
National Tenants Union [Defunct] (EA) .... NTU
National Tennis Academy [Commercial firm] (EA) .... NTA
National Tennis Association [Later, IRJA] (EA) .... NTA
National Tennis Center Trust [Australia] .... NTCT
National Tennis Educational Foundation [Later, NTFHF] (EA) .... NTEF
National Tennis Foundation [Formerly, NTEF] [Later, NTFHF] (EA) .... NTF
National Tennis Foundation and Hall of Fame [Later, ITHOF] (EA) .... NTFHF
National Tennis League .... NTL
National Terrazzo and Mosaic Association (EA) .... NTMA
National Territorial Command (MCD) .... NTC
National Test Bed [Military] (SDI) .... NTB
National Test Center (NATG) .... NTC
National Test Facility [Military] (SDI) .... NTF
National Testing Laboratories [Australia] .... NTEA
National Testing Laboratory Accreditation Scheme [Military British] .... NATLAS
National Textile Processors Guild [Defunct] (EA) .... NTPG
National Thanksgiving Commission (EA) .... NTC
National Theater File [Theater Sources, Inc.] [Information service or system Defunct] (IID) .... NTF
National Theatre [Great Britain] .... NT
National Theatre Conference (EA) .... NTC
National Theatre Institute (EA) .... NTI
National Theatre of the Deaf (EA) .... NTD
National Theatre School [Ecole Nationale de Theatre] Montreal, Quebec [Library symbol National Library of Canada] (NLC) .... QMENT
National Theatre Workshop of the Handicapped (EA) .... NTWH
National Therapeutic Recreation Society (EA) .... NTRS
National Thespian Society [Later, ITS] (EA) .... NTS
National Threshers Association (EA) .... NTA
National Thrift and Mortgage News [A publication] .... NTMN
National Thrift Committee [Defunct] (EA) .... NTC
National Tidal Facility [Flinders University] [Australia] .... NTF

National Tile Contractors Association (EA) .... NTCA
National Tile Promotion Federation [*Defunct*] (EA) .... NTPF
National Tile Roofing Manufacturing Association (EA) .... NTRMA
National Tillage Machinery Laboratory [*Department of Agriculture*] [*Research center*] (GRD) .... NTML
National Time Equipment Association (EA) .... NTEA
National Times Magazine [*A publication*] .... Natn Times Mag
National Timesharing Council (EA) .... NTC
National Tire Dealers and Retreaders Association (EA) .... NTDRA
National Tire Svcs [*NASDAQ symbol*] (TTSB) .... NTSI
National Tissue Typing Reference Laboratory (PDAA) .... NTTRL
National Tobacco Tax Association (EA) .... NTTA
National Tool, Die, and Precision Machining Association [*Later, NTMA*] (EA) .... NTDPMA
National Tooling and Machining Association (EA) .... NTMA
National Toothpick Holder Collector's Society (EA) .... NTHCS
National Topographic Map Inventory Control Point .... NTMICP
National Touch Football Leagues (EA) .... NTFL
National Tour Association (EA) .... NTA
National Tour Brokers Association (EA) .... NTBA
National Tourism Administration [*China*] (EY) .... NTA
National Tourism Industry Training Council [*Australia*] .... NTITC
National Tourism Review Commission .... NTRC
National Tourist Association (NADA) .... NTA
National Towing News [*A publication*] (EAAP) .... NTN
National Town Class Association (EA) .... NTCA
National Toxic Campaign Fund [*An association*] .... NTCF
National Toxicology Program [*Department of Health and Human Services*] [*Research Triangle Park, NC*] .... NTP
National Toy Fox Terrier Association (EA) .... NTFTA
National Toy Libraries Association [*British*] (EAIO) .... NTLA
National Track Analysis Program [*Aviation*] (FAAC) .... NTAP
National Track and Field Association [*Superseded by ANG*] (EA) .... NTFA
National Traction Engine Club [*British*] (DBA) .... NTEC
National Traction Engine Trust [*British*] (DBA) .... NTET
National Tractor Pullers Association (EA) .... NTPA
National Trade Data Bank (EGAO) .... NTDB
National Trade Database (ACII) .... NTDB
National Trade Development Association (WDAA) .... NTDA
National Trade Index .... NTI
National Trade Show Exhibitors Association [*Later, IEA*] (EA) .... NTSEA
National Trade Union Congress [*Singapore*] .... NTUC
National Trade Union Council [*Hungary*] .... NTUC
National Trade Union Council for Human Rights (EA) .... NTUC
National Trades and Labour Congress [*Canada*] .... NTLC
National Trades Union Congress (NADA) .... NTUC
National Traditional Country Music Association [*Later, NTMA*] (EA) .... NTCMA
National Traditional Music Association (EA) .... NTMA
National Traditionalist Caucus (EA) .... NTC
National Traffic and Motor Vehicle Safety Act .... NTMVSA
National Traffic Law Center [*MHTSA*] (TAG) .... NTLC
National Traffic Safety Agency [*Federal Highway Administration*] .... NTSA
National Traffic Safety Bureau .... NTSB
National Traffic System [*Amateur radio*] .... NTS
National Trailer Dealers Association (EA) .... NTDA
National Trailer Rental Association (EA) .... NTRA
National Trails Council (EA) .... NTC
National Trainers Federation [*British*] (DBA) .... NTF
National Training and Information Center (EA) .... NTIC
National Training and Operational Technology Center [*Environmental Protection Agency*] (IID) .... NTOTC
National Training Center [*Red Cross*] [*Charlottesville, VA*] .... NTC
National Training Center [*Military*] (INF) .... NTC
National Training Center / Air Warrior System (DWSG) .... NTC/AW
National Training Center - Phase I (MCD) .... NTCI
National Training Institute for Community Economic Development (EA) .... NTICED
National Training Laboratories [*Later, NTLI*] (EA) .... NTL
National Training Systems Association (EA) .... NTSA
National Training Team [*Operated by the Helen Keller National Center for Deaf-Blind Youths and Adults (HKNC)*] (PAZ) .... NTT
National Transcontinental Railway [*Canada*] .... NTR
National Transit Database [*FTA*] (TAG) .... NTD
National Transit Geographic Information System [*FTA*] (TAG) .... NTGIS
National Translations Center [*John Crerar Library*] [*Information service or system*] .... NTC
National Translator Association (EA) .... NTA
National Transonic Facility [*NASA*] .... NTF
National Transport Federation [*Australia*] .... NTF
National Transport, Inc. .... NAT
National Transportation Agency of Canada [*Office National des Transports du Canada*], Ottawa, Ontario [*Library symbol National Library of Canada*] (NLC) .... OOTT
National Transportation Analysis Regions [*FHWA*] (TAG) .... NTARS
National Transportation Apprenticeship and Training Conference [*Bureau of Apprenticeship and Training*] [*Department of Labor*] .... NTATC
National Transportation Center [*Large city situated at a key junction of rail, air, and highway transportation*] [*Postal Service*] .... NTC
National Transportation Policy .... NTP
National Transportation Public Affairs Workshop .... NTPAW
National Transportation Safety Association [*Defunct*] (EA) .... NTSA
National Transportation Safety Board [*Independent government agency*] [*Washington, DC*] .... NTSB
National Transportation Safety Board Decisions [*A publication*] (DLA) .... N Trans S Dec
National Transportation Statistics [*or Survey*] [*Department of Transportation*] .... NTS
National Transportation System [*BTS*] (TAG) .... NTS
National Transsexual-Transvestite Feminization Union (EA) .... NATTFU
National Transuranic Waste Program Office [*Department of Energy*] (GAAI) .... NTPO
National Trappers Association (EA) .... NTA
National Traumatic Occupational Fatalities [*Surveillance system run by National Institute for Occupational Safety and Health*] .... NTOF
National Travel Club [*Commercial firm*] (EA) .... NTC
National Travel Survey [*Census Bureau*] .... NTS
National Travelers Aid Association (EA) .... NTAA
National Traveler's Gasoline Advisory (DICI) .... NTGA
National Treasure Hunters League [*Defunct*] (EA) .... NTHL
National Treasury Employees Union .... NTE
National Treasury Employees Union (EA) .... NTEU
National Treatment Consortium for Alcohol and Other Drugs (EA) .... NTC
National Treatment Improvement Evaluation Study [*Department of Health and Human Services*] .... NTIES
National Trends Network (EPA) .... NTN
National Tribal Chairman's Association [*Defunct*] (EA) .... NTCA
National Tribunal of Second Instance [*Catholic Church*] [*Australia*] .... NTSI
National Triton Association (EA) .... NTA
National Trolleybus Association [*British*] .... NTA
National Troopers Coalition (EA) .... NTC
National Trotting Pony Association [*Later, ITPA*] .... NTPA
National Truck Equipment Association (EA) .... NTEA
National Truck Leasing System (EA) .... NTLS
National Truck Tank and Trailer Tank Institute [*Later, Tank Conference of the Truck Trailer Manufacturers Association*] .... NTTTTI
National Trucking Industrial Relations Association (EA) .... NTIRA
National Trust & Savings Association (MHDB) .... NT & SA
National Trust Closely Held Business Association (EA) .... NTCHBA
National Trust Co. [*Toronto Stock Exchange symbol*] .... NVG
National Trust for Historic Preservation .... NT
National Trust for Historic Preservation (EA) .... NTHP
National Trust for Historic Preservation, Washington, DC [*Library symbol Library of Congress*] (LCLS) .... DNT
National Trust for Places of Historic Interest or Natural Beauty [*British*] (EAIO) .... NTPHINB
National Trust for Scotland (DI) .... NTS
National Trust of Queensland [*Australia*] .... NTQ
National Trust of Western Australia .... NTWA
National Trust Volunteer Unit [*British*] (EAIO) .... NTVU
National T-Shirt Association (EA) .... NTSA
National Tuberculosis and Respiratory Diseases Association [*Later, American Lung Association*] .... NTRDA
National Tuberculosis Association [*Later, American Lung Association*] (EA) .... NTA
National Tuberous Sclerosis Association (EA) .... NTSA
National Tulip Society [*Defunct*] (EA) .... NTS
National Tumor Registrars Association (EA) .... NTRA
National Tung Oil Marketing Cooperative [*Defunct*] (EA) .... NTOMC
National Tunis Sheep Registry (EA) .... NTSR
National Turf Writers Association (EA) .... NTWA
National Turkey Federation (EA) .... NTF
National Turkey Improvement Plan .... NTIP
National Turnover [*Economics*] .... NTO
National Type Approval (PDAA) .... NTA
National Type Evaluation Program [*Environmental Protection Agency*] .... NTEP
National Tyre Distributors Association [*British*] (DBA) .... NTDA
National Tyre Recycling Association [*British*] (DBA) .... NTRA
National UHF [*Ultrahigh Frequency*] **Broadcasters Association** (EA) .... NUBA
National Ulcer Foundation (EA) .... NUF
National Umma Party [*Sudan*] [*Political party*] .... NUP
National Undersea Research Center [*Virgin Islands*] .... NURC
National Undersea Research Program [*Department of Commerce*] (GRD) .... NURP
National Underwater Accident Data Center .... NUADC
National Underwater and Marine Agency (MCD) .... NUMA
National Underwater Laboratory System [*Marine science*] (MSC) .... NULS
National Unemployed Workers Association (NADA) .... NUWA
National Unemployed Workers' Movement [*British*] .... NUMW
National Unemployment Benefit System [*Department of Health and Social Security*] [*British*] .... NUBS
National Unfinished Furniture Institute [*Defunct*] (EA) .... NUFI
National Unification Council [*Philippines*] [*Political party*] (FEA) .... NUC
National Uniform Business Rate [*British*] .... NURB
National Uniform Certification of Building Operators (EA) .... NUCBO
National Uniform-Billing Committee [*Insurance*] (DAVI) .... NUBC
National Unifying Force [*Zimbabwe*] [*Political party*] (PPW) .... NUF
National Union (EA) .... NU
National Union Catalog Author List .... NUCAL
National Union Catalog of Manuscript Collections [*Library of Congress*] .... NUCMC
National Union for Independence and Revolution [*Chad*] [*Political party*] .... NUIR
National Union for Liberation [*Philippines*] [*Political party*] (PPW) .... NUL
National Union for the Homeless (EA) .... NUH
National Union of Agricultural and Allied Workers [*British*] .... NUAAW
National Union of Bank Employees [*Later, Banking, Insurance, and Finance Union*] (DCTA) .... NUBE
National Union of Blastfurnacemen, Ore Miners, Coke Workers, and Kindred Trades [*British*] (DCTA) .... NUBOMCWKT
National Union of Boot and Shoe Operatives [*British*] .... NUBSO
National Union of Boot Top Cutters [*British*] .... NUBTC
National Union of British Fishermen .... NUBF

National Union of Busmen [*British*] ... NUB
National Union of Carriers [*British*] ... NUC
National Union of Certified Officers [*British*] ... NUCO
National Union of Christian Schools [*Later, CSI*] (EA) ... NUCS
National Union of Civil and Public Servants [*British*] (DBA) ... Nucaps
National Union of Civil and Public Servants [*British*] ... NUCPS
National Union of Clerks and Administrative Workers [*British*] ... NUCAW
National Union of Club Stewards [*British*] (DBA) ... NUCS
National Union of Cooperative Insurance Agents [*British*] ... NUCIA
National Union of Cooperative Insurance Society Employees [*British*] ... NUCISE
National Union of Czechoslovak Protestants in America and Canada [*Defunct*] (EA) ... NUCP
National Union of Czechoslovak Students in Exile (EA) ... NUCSE
National Union of Docks, Wharves, and Shipping Staffs [*British*] ... NUDWSS
National Union of Domestic Appliance and General Metal-Workers [*British*] (DCTA) ... NUDAGMW
National Union of Domestic Appliances and General Operatives [*British*] (DBA) ... NUDA & GO
National Union of Dyers, Bleachers, and Textile Workers [*British*] (DCTA) ... NUDBTW
National Union of Elementary Teachers [*British*] ... NUET
National Union of Eritrean Students - North America (EA) ... NUESNA
National Union of Eritrean Women - North America (EA) ... NUEW
National Union of Firemen [*British*] (DAS) ... NUF
National Union of Flint Glassworkers [*British*] (DBA) ... NUFGW
National Union of Footwear, Leather, and Allied Trades [*British*] (DCTA) ... NUFLAT
National Union of Funeral and Cemetery Workers [*British*] (BI) ... NUFCW
National Union of Funeral Service Operatives [*British*] (DI) ... NUFSO
National Union of Furniture Trade Operatives [*British*] ... NUFTO
National Union of General and Municipal Workers [*British*] ... NUGMW
National Union of Glovers [*British*] ... NUG
National Union of Gold, Silver, and Allied Trades [*British*] (DCTA) ... NUGSAT
National Union of Hosiery and Knitwear Workers [*British*] (DCTA) ... NUHKW
National Union of Insurance Workers [*British*] (DCTA) ... NUIW
National Union of Iraqi Students [*British*] (DI) ... NUIS
National Union of Journalists [*British*] ... NUJ
National Union of Labour Organisers [*British*] (DBA) ... NULO
National Union of Liberal Clubs [*British*] (DBA) ... NULC
National Union of Lift and Crane Workers [*British*] ... NULCW
National Union of Lock and Metal Workers [*British*] (DCTA) ... NULMW
National Union of Marine Aviation and Shipping Transport [*British*] ... NUMAST
National Union of Masters and Mates [*British*] ... NUMM
National Union of Metalworkers of South Africa ... NUMSA
National Union of Mineworkers [*South Africa*] ... NUM
National Union of Painters and Decorators Trade Union [*British*] ... NUPDTU
National Union of Press Telegraphists [*British*] (DGA) ... NUPT
National Union of Printing, Bookbinding, and Paperworkers [*British*] (DGA) ... NUPB & PW
National Union of Printing, Bookbinding, and Paperworkers [*British*] ... NUPBP
National Union of Protestants ... NUP
National Union of Provincial Government Employees [*Canada*] ... NUPGE
National Union of Public Employees [*British*] ... NUPE
National Union of Railway Clerks [*British*] ... NURC
National Union of Railwaymen [*British*] ... NUR
National Union of Rate-Payers' Associations [*British*] (BI) ... NURA
National Union of Retail Confectioners [*British*] (BI) ... NURC
National Union of Retail Tobacconists [*British*] (BI) ... NURT
National Union of Scalemakers [*British*] (DCTA) ... NUS
National Union of School Students [*British*] (DI) ... NUSS
National Union of Seamen [*British*] ... NUS
National Union of Sheet Metal Workers, Coppersmiths, Heating and Domestic Engineers [*British*] (DCTA) ... NUSMWCHDE
National Union of Shop Assistants [*British*] (DAS) ... NUSA
National Union of Shop Distributive and Allied Workers [*British*] ... NUDAW
National Union of South African Students ... NUSAS
National Union of Storeworkers, Packers, Rubber and Allied Workers [*Australia*] ... NUSPRAW
National Union of Stove and Grate Workers [*British*] ... NUSGW
National Union of Stove Grate and General Metal Workers [*British*] ... NUSGGMW
National Union of Students [*British*] ... NUS
National Union of Tailors and Garments Workers [*British*] ... NUTGW
National Union of Teachers [*British*] ... NUT
National Union of the Deaf [*British*] ... NUD
National Union of Tin Plate Workers [*British*] ... NUTPW
National Union of Tobacco Trades [*British*] ... NUTT
National Union of Townswomen's Guilds [*British*] ... NUTG
National Union of Trained Nurses [*British*] (DI) ... NUTN
National Union of Uncertified Teachers [*British*] ... NUUT
National Union of United States Forces Employees [*South Korea*] ... NUUSFE
National Union of Vehicle Builders [*British*] ... NUVB
National Union of Vehicular Workers [*British*] ... NUVW
National Union of Wallcoverings, Decorative and Allied Trades [*British*] (DGA) ... NUWDAT
National Union of Women Teachers [*British*] (DAS) ... NUWT
National Union of Women Teachers (AIE) ... NUWT
National Union of Women Workers (MHDB) ... NUWW
National United Affiliated Beverage Association (EA) ... NUABA
National United Church Association of America (EA) ... NUCAA
National United Church Ushers Association of America (EA) ... NUCUAA
National United Democratic Organization [*Namibia*] [*Political party*] (PPW) ... NUDO
National United Front for the Liberation of Vietnam (EA) ... NUFLV
National United Front for the Liberation of Vietnam (EA) ... NUFRONLIV
National United Front of Somalia [*Political party*] (EY) ... NUFS
National United Italian Associations (EA) ... NUIA
National United Law Enforcement Officers Association (EA) ... NULEOA
National United Liberation Front [*Myanmar*] [*Political party*] (FEA) ... NULF
National United Licensees Beverage Association [*Later, NUABA*] (EA) ... NULBA
National United Party [*Vanuatu*] [*Political party*] (EY) ... NUP
National/United Service Agencies ... N/USA
National United States-Arab Chamber of Commerce (EA) ... NUSACC
National United Women's Societies of the Adoration of the Most Blessed Sacrament (EA) ... NUWSAMBS
National Unity Front [*Poland Political party*] (PPW) ... NUF
National Unity Movement [*Sierra Leone*] [*Political party*] (EY) ... NUM
National Unity Party [*British Political party*] ... NU
National Unity Party [*British Political party*] (EA) ... NUP
National Universities Week [*Canada*] ... NUW
National University (AD) ... Nat Uni
National University Consortium for Telecommunications in Teaching (EA) ... NUC
National University Continuing Education Association (EA) ... NUCEA
National University Extension Association [*Later, NUCEA*] (EA) ... NUEA
National University. Law Review [*1921-31*] [*A publication*] (DLA) ... Nat UL Rev
National University Library Cataloging Department, San Diego, CA [*OCLC symbol*] (OCLC) ... CNU
National University of Ireland ... NUI
National University of Mexico [*Mexico*] [*Seismograph station code, US Geological Survey Closed*] (SEIS) ... UNM
National University of Singapore ... NUS
National University Teleconference Network [*Stillwater, OK*] [*Telecommunications*] (TSSD) ... NUTN
National Uranium Resource Evaluation [*Program*] [*Energy Research and Development Administration*] ... NURE
National Uranium Tailings Program [*Canada*] ... NUTP
National Urban Affairs Council (EA) ... NUAC
National Urban Coalition (EA) ... NUC
National Urban Fellows (EA) ... NUF
National Urban Indian Council (EA) ... NUIC
National Urban League (EA) ... NUL
National Urban/Rural Fellows (EA) ... NU/RF
National Used Truck Association ... NUTA
National Utility Contractors' Association (EA) ... NUCA
National Utility Financial Statement Model [*Department of Energy*] (GFGA) ... NUFS
National Utility Reference File [*Department of Energy*] ... NURF
National Utility Services [*British*] ... NUS
National Vaccine Advisory Committee [*Reports to Congress, Health and Human Services*] ... NVAC
National Vaccine Information Center ... NVIC
National Vaccine Injury Compensation Program (PAZ) ... NVICP
National Vaccine Program [*National Institutes of Health*] ... NVP
National Valentine Collectors' Association (EA) ... NVCA
National Van Conversion Association (EA) ... NVCA
National Variety Artists [*Defunct*] (EA) ... NVA
National Vegetable Research Station [*Research center British*] (IRC) ... NVRS
National Vegetable Society [*British*] (DBA) ... NVS
National Vehicle and Fuel Emissions Laboratory ... NVFEL
National Vehicle Conversion Association ... NVCA
National Vehicle Leasing Association (EA) ... NVLA
National Vehicle Population Profile ... NVPP
National Vehicular Traffic Workers' Union of Great Britain and Ireland ... NVTWUGBI
National Velasquista Party [*Ecuador*] [*Political party*] (PPW) ... PNV
National Velthrow Association (EA) ... NVA
National Venture Capital Association [*Arlington, VA*] (EA) ... NVCA
National Vessel Traffic Information System (AD) ... NAVTIS
National Veteran Boxers Association (EA) ... NVBA
National Veterans Association (EA) ... NVA
National Veterans Law Center [*Defunct*] (EA) ... NVLC
National Veteran's Outreach Program (EA) ... NVOP
National Veterinary Medical Association (WDAA) ... NVMA
National Veterinary Services Laboratory [*Ames, IA*] [*Department of Agriculture*] (GRD) ... NVSL
National Viatical Association (ECON) ... NVA
National Victim Center (EA) ... NVC
National Victims of Crime (EA) ... NVC
National Victims of Crime Foundation (EA) ... NVCF
National Victims Resource Centre, Ottawa, ON, Canada [*Library symbol*] [*Library of Congress*] (LCLS) ... CaOONVRC
National Victims Resource Centre [*Centre National de la Documentation sur lesVictimes*] **Ottawa, Ontario** [*Library symbol National Library of Canada*] (NLC) ... OONVRC
National Victoria & Grey Trustco Ltd. [*Toronto Stock Exchange symbol*] ... VGT
National Video Clearinghouse [*Defunct*] (EA) ... NVC
National Video Corp. ... NVC
National Video Resources ... NVR
National Vietnam Veterans Coalition (EA) ... NVVC
National Vietnam Veterans Readjustment Study [*Veterans Administration*] ... NVVRS
National Viewers' and Listeners' Association [*British*] ... NVLA
National Villa Association [*British*] (BI) ... NVA
National Vision Associates [*Associated Press*] (SAG) ... NatVisn
National Vision Associates [*NASDAQ symbol*] (SAG) ... NVAL
National Vision Research Institute of Australia ... NVRIA
National Visiting Teachers Association (EA) ... NVTA
National Vista Alliance (EA) ... NVA
National Visual Presentation Association (EA) ... NVPA

National Vital Statistics Division [National Center for Health Statistics] [Obsolete] .... NVSD

National Vital Statistics System [Department of Health and Human Services] (GFGA) .... NVSS

National Vitamin Distributors Association (EA) .... NVDA

National Vitamin Foundation (EA) .... NVF

National Vitiligo Foundation (EA) .... NVF

National Vitiligo Foundation (PAZ) .... NVFI

National Vocation Qualification [British] .... NVQ

National Vocational Agricultural Teachers' Association (EA) .... NVATA

National Vocational Education and Training System [Australia] .... NVETS

National Vocational Educational Foundation (EA) .... NVEF

National Vocational Educational Professional Development Consortium [Later, NVEPDF] (EA) .... NVEPDC

National Vocational Educational Professional Development Foundation [Later, NVEF] (EA) .... NVEPDF

National Vocational Guidance Association (EA) .... NVGA

National Vocational Training Service .... NVTS

National Vocational-Technical Honor Society (EA) .... NV-THS

National Voice of Iran [Clandestine, Soviet-backed radio station] .... NVOI

National Volkswagen Association .... NVWA

National Voluntary Groups Institute (EA) .... NVGI

National Voluntary Health Agencies (EA) .... NVHA

National Voluntary Laboratory Accreditation Program [Gaithersburg, MD] [National Institute of Standards and Technology] .... NVLAP

National Voluntary Organizations Active in Disaster (EA) .... NVOAD

National Voluntary Organizations for Independent Living for the Aging (EA) .... NVOILA

National Volunteer Brigade [South African equivalent of the British Home Guard] .... NVB

National Volunteer Center (EA) .... NVC

National Volunteer Clearinghouse for the Homeless [Defunct] (EA) .... NVCH

National Volunteer Fire Council .... NVFC

National Volunteer Force (WDAA) .... NVF

National Voter Mobilization [Defunct] (EA) .... NVM

National Vulvodynia Association [Disseminate information about vulvar pain and establish support networks across the country] [Medicine] .... NVA

National Waco Club (EA) .... NWC

National Wage Stabilization Board [Superseded NWLB, 1945; terminated, 1947] .... NWSB

National War College [Later, UND] [DoD] (DNAB) .... NATWARCOL

National War College [Later, UND] [DoD] .... NATWC

National War College [Later, UND] [DoD] .... NWC

National War College Alumni Association .... NWCAA

National War Formulary .... NWF

National War Fund .... NWF

National War Labor Board [World War II] .... NWLB

National War Labor Board [World War II] .... WLB

National War Tax Resistance Coordinating Committee (EA) .... NWTRCC

National Warehouse and General Workers' Union [British] .... NWGWU

National Warm Air Heating and Air Conditioning Association [Later, ACCA] (EA) .... NWAHACA

National Warning Center [Civil Defense] .... NWC

National Warning System [Civil Defense] .... NAWAS

National Waste Minimization and Recycling Strategy [Australia] .... NWMRS

National Waste Terminal Storage [For radioactive wastes] .... NWTS

National Water Alliance .... NWA

National Water and Soil Conservation Agency (BARN) .... NWSCA

National Water Carriers Association .... NWCA

National Water Center (EA) .... NWC

National Water Commission [Terminated, 1973] .... NWC

National Water Co. Conference [Later, NAWC] .... NWCC

National Water Council [British] (DCTA) .... NWC

National Water Data Exchange [United States Geological Survey] [Reston, VA] [Information service or system] .... NAWDEX

National Water Data Storage and Retrieval System [US Geological Survey] [Information service or system] (CRD) .... WATSTORE

National Water Data System [US Geological Survey] [Reston, VA] .... NWDS

National Water Information Clearinghouse [Proposed] [US Geological Survey] .... NWIC

National Water Information System [Department of the Interior] (GFGA) .... NWIS

National Water Lift Co. (MCD) .... NWL

National Water Project [Later, RCAP] .... NWP

National Water Purification Foundation .... NWPF

National Water Quality Data Bank [Environment Canada] [Information service or system] (IID) .... NAQUADAT

National Water Quality Inventory [Environmental Protection Agency] .... NWQI

National Water Quality Laboratory .... NWQL

National Water Quality Surveillance System [Dicontinued, 1981] [Environmental Protection Agency] .... NWQSS

National Water Research Institute [Environment Canada] [Research center] (RCD) .... NWRI

National Water Resources Association (EA) .... NWRA

National Water Safety Congress (EA) .... NWSC

National Water Slide Association (EA) .... NWSA

National Water Supply Improvement Association [Later, IDA] (EA) .... NWSIA

National Water Wall Association, Ground Water Library/Information Center, Worthington, OH [Library symbol] [Library of Congress] (LCLS) .... OWorNW

National Water Well Association [Database producer] (EA) .... NWWA

National Water Well Association, Worthington, OH [OCLC symbol] (OCLC) .... NWA

National Waterbed Retailers Association (EA) .... NWRA

National Watercolor Society (EA) .... NWS

National Waterfowl Alliance, Waterfowl USA [Later, WUSA] (EA) .... NWA

National Waterfowl Council (EA) .... NWC

National Watermen and Lightermen's Federation [A union] [British] .... NWLF

National Watershed Congress (EA) .... NWC

National Waterways Conference (EA) .... NWC

National Waterways Study [Marine science] (MSC) .... NWS

National Waterways Transport Association [British] .... NWTA

National Weather Analysis Center [Air Force, Navy] .... NAWAC

National Weather Analysis Center [Air Force, Navy] .... NWAC

National Weather Association (EA) .... NWA

National Weather Records Center [Later, National Climatic Center] [National Oceanic and Atmospheric Administration] .... NWRC

National Weather Satellite Center [Later, National Environmental Satellite Service] .... NWSC

National Weather Satellite System (KSC) .... NWSS

National Weather Service [Formerly, US Weather Bureau] [Silver Spring, MD] [National Oceanic and Atmospheric Administration] .... NWS

National Weather Service Center (MCD) .... NWSC

National Weather Service Employees Organization (EA) .... NWSEO

National Weather Service Employees Organization .... WSE

National Weather Service Headquarters .... NWSH

National Weather Service River Forecast System (NOAA) .... NWSRFS

National Weather Service Support FAcility (FAAC) .... WSSF

National Weather Service Support Unit (FAAC) .... WSSU

National Weather Service Technical Training Center .... NWSTTC

National Weather Service Telecommunications Gateway .... NWSTG

National Weather Service-Central Region (PDAA) .... NWS-CR

National Weather Service-Eastern Region (PDAA) .... NWS-ER

National Weather Service-Southern Region (PDAA) .... NWS-SR

National Weather Service-Western Region (PDAA) .... NWS-WR

National Welders Association [A union] [British] .... NWA

National Welding Supply Association (EA) .... NWSA

National Welfare Fund (WDAA) .... NWF

National Welfare Rights (WDAA) .... NWR

National Welfare Rights Organization [Defunct] .... NWRO

National Wellness Association (EA) .... NWA

National Western Life Insurance Co. [Associated Press] (SAG) .... NtWnLf

National Western Life Insurance Co. [NASDAQ symbol] (NQ) .... NWLI

National Westminster [Bank] .... NatWest

National Westminster Bancorp, Inc. [NYSE symbol] (SPSG) .... NW

National Westminster Bank Ltd. [Associated Press] (SAG) .... NtlWstA

National Westminster Bank Ltd. [Associated Press] (SAG) .... NtWst

National Westminster Bank Ltd. [Associated Press] (SAG) .... NtWstmin

National Westminster Bank PLC [NYSE symbol] (SAG) .... NWX

National Westminster Investment Bank [British] .... NWIB

National Wetlands Conservation Project [Defunct] (EA) .... NWCP

National Wetlands Inventory .... NWI

National Wetlands Technical Council (EA) .... NWTC

National Wheel and Rim Association (EA) .... NWRA

National Wheelchair Athletic Association (EA) .... NWAA

National Wheelchair Athletic Committee .... NWAC

National Wheelchair Basketball Association (EA) .... NWBA

National Wheelchair Softball Association (EA) .... NWSA

National White American Party (BJA) .... NWAP

National White Wyandotte Club [Defunct] (EA) .... NWWC

National Wholesale Druggists' Association (EA) .... NWDA

National Wholesale Dry Goods Association [Later, NATAD] .... NWDGA

National Wholesale Furniture Association (EA) .... NWFA

National Wholesale Hardware Association (EA) .... NWHA

National Wholesale Jewelers Association [Later, AJDA] (EA) .... NWJA

National Wholesale Lumber Distributing Yard Association (EA) .... NWLDYA

National Wild and Scenic Rivers System .... NWSRS

National Wild Turkey Federation (EA) .... NWTF

National Wilderness Preservation System .... NWPS

National Wildflower Research Center (EA) .... NWRC

National Wildlife Defence Council (USDC) .... NWDC

National Wildlife Defense Council [Marine science] (OSRA) .... NWDC

National Wildlife Federation (EA) .... NWF

National Wildlife Health Foundation .... NWHF

National Wildlife Health Laboratory [Department of the Interior] (GRD) .... NWHL

National Wildlife Refuge (WDAA) .... NWR

National Wildlife Refuge Association (EA) .... NWRA

National Wildlife Refuge System (WDAA) .... NWRS

National Wildlife Rehabilitators Association (EA) .... NWRA

National Wildlife Rescue Team (EA) .... NWRT

National Wildlife Research Centre, Canadian Wildlife Service, Environment Canada[Centre National de Recherche sur la Faune, Service Canadien de la Faune, En vironnement Canada] Ottawa, Ontario [Library symbol National Library of Canada] (NLC) .... OOECWN

National Wilms' Tumor Study [Oncology] .... NWTS

National Wilms' Tumor Study Group [Oncology] .... NWTSG

National Wine Association [Defunct] (EA) .... NWA

National Wine Distributors' Association (EA) .... NWDA

National Winter Convention on Military Electronics [IEEE] (MCD) .... NWCME

National Winter Sports [Association] [Defunct] (EA) .... NWS

National Winter Sports Association .... NWSA

National Wire Gauge .... NWG

National Wireless Holdings, Inc. [Associated Press] (SAG) .... NtlWire

National Wireless Holdings, Inc. [NASDAQ symbol] (SAG) .... NWIR

National Wiretap Commission [Department of Justice] .... NWC

National Wiring Bureau [Defunct] (EA) .... NWB

National Woman Abuse Prevention Project (EA) .... NWAPP

National Woman's Christian Temperance Union (WDAA) .... NWCTU

National Woman's Christian Temperance Union (EA) .... WCTU

National Woman's Christian Temperance Union, Evanston, IL [Library symbol Library of Congress] (LCLS) .... IEWT

National Woman's Party (EA) .... NWP

National Woman's Trucking Association [*Defunct*] (EA) ... NWTA
National Women and the Law Association (EA) ... NWLA
National Women Bowling Writers Association (EA) ... NWBW
National Women's Advisory Council (NADA) ... NWAC
National Women's Association of Allied Beverage Industries (EA) ... WAABI
National Women's Automotive Association [*Defunct*] (EA) ... NWAA
National Women's Business Council ... NWBC
National Women's Coalition [*Defunct*] (EA) ... NWC
National Women's Conference Committee [*Formerly, CCNWC*] (EA) ... NW
National Women's Conference Committee (EA) ... NWCC
National Women's Conference of the American Ethical Union (EA) ... NWCAEU
National Women's Economic Alliance [*Washington, DC*] (EA) ... NWEA
National Women's Education Fund (EA) ... NWEF
National Women's Employment and Education [*Defunct*] (EA) ... NWEE
National Women's Hall of Fame (EA) ... NWHF
National Women's Health Coalition [*Later, IWHC*] ... NWHC
National Women's Health Network (EA) ... NWHN
National Women's Health Resource Center (EA) ... NWHRC
National Women's History Project (EA) ... NWHP
National Women's Insurance Center (EA) ... NWIC
National Women's Law Center (EA) ... NWLC
National Women's League of the United Synagogue of America [*Later, AWL*] (EA) ... NWL
National Women's Mailing List (EA) ... NWML
National Women's Martial Arts Federation (EA) ... NWMAF
National Women's Music Festival (EA) ... NWMF
National Women's Neckwear and Scarf Association (EA) ... NWNSA
National Women's Political Caucus (EA) ... NWPC
National Women's Register [*British*] (DBA) ... NWR
National Women's Rowing Association [*Later, USRA*] (EA) ... NWRA
National Women's Student Coalition (EA) ... NWSC
National Women's Studies Association (EA) ... NWSA
National Women's Suffrage Association (WDAA) ... NWSA
National Wood Energy Association (EA) ... NWEA
National Wood Flooring Association (EA) ... NWFA
National Wood Tank Institute (EA) ... NWTI
National Wood Window and Door Association (EA) ... NWWDA
National Woodcarvers Association (EA) ... NWCA
National Wooden Box Council [*Later, NWPCA*] (EA) ... NWBC
National Wooden Pallet and Container Association (EA) ... NWPCA
National Wooden Pallet Manufacturers Association [*Later, NWPCA*] (EA) ... NWPMA
National Woodie Club (EA) ... NWC
National Woodland Owners Association (EA) ... NWOA
National Woodwork Manufacturers Association [*Formerly, NDMA*] [*Later, NWWDA*] (EA) ... NWMA
National Wool Growers Association [*Later, ASIA*] (EA) ... NWGA
National Wool Marketing Corp. (EA) ... NWMC
National Wool Sorters' Society [*A union*] [*British*] (DCTA) ... NWSS
National Wool Textile Export Corp. [*British*] (BI) ... NWTEC
National Wool Trade Association [*Defunct*] (EA) ... NWTA
National Workers Network [*Defunct*] (EA) ... NWN
National Workers Union (NADA) ... NWU
National Working Group on Screw Fly Worm [*Australia*] ... NWGSFW
National Working Party of Youth Volunteer Organisers (AIE) ... NWPYVO
National Wrestling Alliance (DAVI) ... NWA
National Wrestling Coaches Association (EA) ... NWCA
National Write Your Congressman [*Also known as National Write Your Congressman Club*] (EA) ... NWYCC
National Writers Club (EA) ... NWC
National Writers Union (EA) ... NWU
National Writing Project (EA) ... NWP
National Xeriscape Council, Inc. [*An association*] (EA) ... NXCI
National Yacht Harbour Association [*British*] (BI) ... NYHA
National Yellow Pages Agency Association [*Tucson, AZ*] (EA) ... NYPAA
National Yellow Pages Service ... NYPS
National Yellow Pages Service Association (WDMC) ... NYP-SA
National Yeomen F [*Defunct*] (EA) ... NYF
National Yiddish Book Center (EA) ... NYBC
National Yiddish Book Exchange (EA) ... NYBE
National Yogurt Association (EA) ... NYA
National Yokefellow Prison Ministry [*Later, YPM*] (EA) ... NYPM
National Young Buddhist Association [*Defunct*] (EA) ... NYBA
National Young Christian Students' Movement of Australia ... NYCSMA
National Young Farmer Educational Association (EA) ... NYFEA
National Young Judaea (EA) ... NYJ
National Young Life Campaign [*British*] ... NYLC
National Young Professionals Forum (EA) ... NYPF
National Young Republicans (NADA) ... NYR
National Youth Administration [*Terminated, 1943*] ... NYA
National Youth Advisory Board [*Environmental Protection Agency*] ... NYAB
National Youth Alliance (EA) ... NYA
National Youth Bureau [*British*] ... NYB
National Youth Coalition on Housing [*Australia*] ... NYCH
National Youth Council on Civic Affairs [*Superseded by CCNYA*] (EA) ... YCCA
National Youth Development Foundation [*Defunct*] (EA) ... NYDF
National Youth Development Officer (AIE) ... NYDO
National Youth Employment Coalition (EA) ... NYEC
National Youth Foundation [*Australia*] ... NYF
National Youth Jazz Orchestra [*British*] ... NYJO
National Youth Leadership Council (EA) ... NYLC
National Youth Leadership Training Institute ... NYLTI
National Youth Ministry Organization (EA) ... NYMO
National Youth Orchestra [*British*] (DI) ... NYO
National Youth Pro-Life Coalition (EA) ... NYPLC
National Youth Science Foundation ... NYSF
National Youth Sports Coaches Association (EA) ... NYSCA
National Youth Theatre [*British*] ... NYT
National Youth Work Alliance (EA) ... NYWA
National Yugoslav Army of Liberation [*World War II*] ... NYAL
National Zoning Improvement Plan Code [*US Postal Service*] (AAGC) ... ZIP Code
National Zoological Park ... NZP
National Zoological Park [*Smithsonian Institution*] ... NZP
National-American Wholesale Grocers' Association (EA) ... NAWGA
Nationaldemokratische Partei [*National Democratic Party*] [*Austria Political party*] (PPW) ... NDP
Nationaldemokratische Partei Deutschlands [*German National Democratic Party*] [*Political party*] ... NPD
Nationaldemokratische Partei Deutschlands [*National Democratic Party of Germany*] [*Germany Political party*] (PPE) ... NPD
Nationale Aktion fuer Volk und Heimat [*National Action for People and Homeland*] [*Switzerland Political party*] (PPE) ... NA
Nationale Maatschappij der Belgische Spoorwegen [*Railway*] [*Belgium*] (EY) ... NMBS
Nationale Partij Kombinatie [*National Party Alliance*] [*Surinam*] [*Political party*] (PPW) ... NPK
Nationale Partij Suriname [*Surinam National Party*] [*Political party*] (PPW) ... NPS
Nationale Volksarmee [*National Peoples' Army*] [*Germany*] ... NVA
Nationale Volkspartij - Unie [*National United People's Party*] [*Netherlands Antilles*] [*Political party*] (PPW) ... NVP-U
Nationalen Genossenschaft fuer die Lagerung Radioaktiver Abfaelle [*National Cooperative Society for the Storage of Radioactive Wastes*] [*Germany*] (AD) ... NAGRA
Nationalist (ROG) ... N
Nationalist (ODBW) ... Nat
Nationalist (WDAA) ... NAT
Nationalist Chams Organization (EA) ... NCO
Nationalist Democracy Party [*Turkey Political party*] (PPW) ... NDP
Nationalist Front for Progress [*Solomon Islands*] [*Political party*] (FEA) ... NFP
Nationalist Movement (EA) ... NM
Nationalist Parnellite [*British*] (ROG) ... NP
Nationalist Party [*British Political party*] ... N
Nationalist Party [*Malta*] [*Political party*] (PPE) ... NP
Nationalist Party [*Philippines*] [*Political party*] (PPW) ... NP
Nationalist Party of Puerto Rico (NADA) ... NPPR
Nationalist Unionist Party [*Sudan*] ... NUP
Nationalist-Communist (AD) ... Nasakom
Nationalists (AD) ... Nats
Nationality (AAG) ... NAT
Nationality (AD) ... nation
Nationality Broadcasting Network [*Cable-television system*] ... NBN
Nationalized Industries Computer Committee (NITA) ... NICC
Nationalized Industries Overseas Group [*British*] (DCTA) ... NIOG
National-Louis University (GAGS) ... Nat Louis U
Nationally-Certified Psychiatric Technician ... NCPT
Nationally-Integrated Caring Employees [*Union*] [*British*] (DI) ... NICE
Nationalo Advisory Commission for Aeronautics Board of Contract Appeals (AAGC) ... NACA BCA
Nationalsozialistische Deutsche Arbeiterpartei [*National Socialist German Workers' Party, 1919-45*] [*Political party*] ... NAZI
Nationalsozialistische Deutsche Arbeiterpartei [*National Socialist German Workers' Party, 1919-45*] [*Political party*] (PPW) ... NDAP
Nationalsozialistische Deutsche Arbeiterpartei [*National Socialist German Workers' Party, 1919-45*] [*Political party*] ... NSDAP
National-Standard Co. [*NYSE symbol*] (SPSG) ... NSD
Nationella Samlingspartiet [*National Coalition Party*] [*Finland Political party*] (PPE) ... SAML
Nations Bal Target Mat Fd [*NYSE symbol*] (TTSB) ... NBM
Nations Balanced Target Maturity Fund [*Associated Press*] (SAG) ... NatnsBal
Nation's Balanced Target Maturity Fund [*NYSE symbol*] (SAG) ... NBM
Nations Government Income Term 2003 [*Associated Press*] (SAG) ... NatnGv03
Nations Government Income Term 2004 [*Associated Press*] (SAG) ... NatnGv04
Nations Government Income Term Trust [*NYSE symbol*] (SPSG) ... NGI
Nations Government Income Term Trust 2004 [*NYSE symbol*] (SAG) ... NGF
Nations Gvt Inc. Term Tr 2003 [*NYSE symbol*] (TTSB) ... NGI
Nations Gvt Inc. Term Tr 2004 [*NYSE symbol*] (TTSB) ... NGF
Nations Ministries (EA) ... NM
Nations Unies [*United Nations*] [*French*] (AD) ... Nat U
Nations Unies des Animaux [*United Animal Nations - UAN*] (EA) ... NUA
NationsBank Corp. [*Associated Press*] (SAG) ... NatnsBk
NationsBank Corp. [*NYSE symbol*] (SPSG) ... NB
Nationwide Association of Preserving Specialists [*British*] (DBA) ... NAPS
Nation-Wide Committee on Import-Export Policy [*Defunct*] (EA) ... NWCIEP
Nationwide Demonstration Program ... NDP
Nationwide Educational Computer Service (IEEE) ... NECS
Nationwide Emergency Telecommunications System [*DoD*] ... NETS
Nationwide Evaluation of X-Ray Trends ... NEXT
Nation-Wide Fallout (SAA) ... NWFAL
Nationwide Health Prop [*NYSE symbol*] (TTSB) ... NHP
Nationwide Health Properties, Inc. [*Associated Press*] (SAG) ... NatHP
Nationwide Health Properties, Inc. [*NYSE symbol*] (SPSG) ... NHP
Nationwide Hotel Association ... NHA
Nationwide Housing Trust [*British*] ... NHT
Nationwide Improved Mail Service [*Postal Service*] ... NIMS
Nationwide Integrated Postal Service [*Postal Service*] ... NIPS
Nationwide Investigations Group [*British*] ... NIG
Nationwide Outdoor Recreation Plan [*Bureau of Outdoor Recreation*] ... NWP
Nationwide Permit Program [*Army Corps of Engineers*] (GFGA) ... NWPP
Nationwide Personal Transportation Study [*Department of Transportation*] (GFGA) ... NPTS

Nationwide Personal Transportation Survey [BTS] [FHWA] (TAG) .... NPTS
Nationwide Postal-Strike Contingency Plan (DNAB) .... NWPSC
Nationwide Refrigeration Supplies [British] .... NRS
Nationwide Trailer Rental System .... NTRS
Nationwide Truck Activity Survey [BTS] [FHWA] (TAG) .... NTACS
Nationwide Urban Runoff Program [Water pollution] .... NURP
Nationwide/Worldwide Emergency Ambulance Return .... NEAR
Natitingou [Benin] [ICAO location identifier] (ICLI) .... DBBN
Natitingou [Dahomey] [Airport symbol] (AD) .... DNT
Native [Ecology] .... N
Native (AD) .... nat
Native (AAG) .... NAT
Native American Church (ECON) .... NAC
Native American Community Board (EA) .... NACB
Native American Educational Service [Later, NAESC] (EA) .... NAES
Native American Educational Services College (EA) .... NAESC
Native American Graves Protection and Repatriation Act [Enacted
    1990] .... NAGPRA
Native American Law Students Association (EA) .... NALSA
Native American Legal Defense and Education Foundation (EA) .... NALDEF
Native American Policy Network (EA) .... NAPN
Native American Press Association (EA) .... NAPA
Native American Program (OICC) .... NAP
Native American Program Commission for Multicultural Ministries of ELCA
    [Evangelical Lutheran Church in America] (EA) .... NAPCMM-ELCA
Native American Public Broadcasting Consortium (EA) .... NAPBC
Native American Publishing Program [of Harper & Row, Publishers, Inc.] ..... NAPP
Native American Research Institute (EA) .... NARI
Native American Rights Fund (EA) .... NARF
Native American Scholarship Fund [An association] (EA) .... NASF
Native American Science Education Association [Defunct] (EA) .... NASEA
Native American Studies (AD) .... NAS
Native American Teacher Education (AD) .... NATE
Native Americans for a Clean Environment (EA) .... NACE
Native Americans in Philanthropy .... NAP
Native Appeal Court Reports (Southern Rhodesia) [A publication]
    (ILCA) .... NACR (SR)
Native Appeal Courts [South Africa] [A publication] (DLA) ...... NAC
Native Authority Legal Notice [Northern Nigeria] [A publication] (DLA) .... NALN
Native Authority Public Notice [Nigeria] [A publication] (ILCA) .... NAPN
Native Cavalry [British military] (DMA) .... NC
Native Council of Canada .... NCC
Native Court [Ghana] [A publication] (DLA) .... N Ct
Native Daughters of the Golden West (EA) .... NDGW
Native Egg White .... NEW
Native Employment and Educational Development [Canada] .... NEED
Native Field Hospital [British military] (DMA) .... NFH
Native Forest Council (EA) .... NFC
Native Hawaiian Culture and Arts Program [An association] (EA) .... NHCAP
Native High Court Reports [South Africa] [A publication] (DLA) .... NHC
Native Human Serum Pooled [Hematology] (DAVI) .... NHS
Native Infantry [Indian Armed Forces regiment] .... NI
Native Language (BARN) .... NL
Native Machine Language [Computer science] .... NML
Native North American Almanac [A publication] .... NNAA
Native North American Writers [A publication] .... NNAW
Native Officer [British military] (DMA) .... NO
Native Peoples [A publication] (BRI) .... Nat Peop
Native Pituitary-Derived Somatotropin [Endocrinology] .... NPST
Native Plants Extracts Cooperative [Australia] .... NPEC
Native Porcine Somatotropin [Endocrinology] .... NPST
Native Preacher Co. [An association] (EA) .... NPC
Native Races of the British Empire [A publication] .... NRBE
Native Seeds/SEARCH [Southwestern Endangered Arid-Land Resource
    Clearing House] (EA) .... NS/S
Native Signal Processing [Computer science] (PCM) .... NSP
Native Sons of the Golden West (EA) .... NSGW
Native Sons of the Golden West, Auburn Parlor, Auburn, CA [Library
    symbol Library of Congress] (LCLS) .... CAuN
Native Tribunals' Reports [Egypt] [A publication] (DLA) .... Al Kada
Native Valve Endocarditis [Medicine] .... NVE
Native Vegetation Authority [South Australia] .... NVA
Native Women's Association of Canada .... NWAC
Natividade [Brazil] [Airport symbol] (AD) .... NAV
Nativity [Church calendars] (ROG) .... NAT
Nativity .... NATIV
Nativity (AD) .... Nativ
Nativity of the Virgin Mary .... NVM
Natjonal Samling [National Union] [Norway] (PD) .... NS
Natl Australia Bk ADR [NYSE symbol] (TTSB) .... NAB
Natl Auto Credit [NYSE symbol] (TTSB) .... NAK
Natl Bacshares Texas [AMEX symbol] (TTSB) .... NBT
Natl Bancorp(AK) [NASDAQ symbol] (TTSB) .... NBAK
Natl Beverage [AMEX symbol] (TTSB) .... FIZ
Natl Bk of Canada [MS, exchange symbol] (TTSB) .... NA
Natl Capital Mgmt [NASDAQ symbol] (TTSB) .... NCMC
Natl City Bancorp'n [NASDAQ symbol] (TTSB) .... NCBM
Natl City Bancshares [NASDAQ symbol] (TTSB) .... NCBE
Natl City Corp. [NYSE symbol] (TTSB) .... NCC
Natl Commerce Bancorp [NASDAQ symbol] (TTSB) .... NCBC
Natl Computer Sys [NASDAQ symbol] (TTSB) .... NLCS
Natl Data [NYSE symbol] (TTSB) .... NDC
Natl Dentex [NASDAQ symbol] (TTSB) .... NADX
Natl Diagnostics [NASDAQ symbol] (TTSB) .... NATD
Natl Education [NYSE symbol] (TTSB) .... NEC

Natl Energy Group'A' [NASDAQ symbol] (TTSB) .... NEGX
Natl Fuel Gas [NYSE symbol] (TTSB) .... NFG
Natl Gas & Oil [AMEX symbol] (TTSB) .... NLG
Natl Golf Properties [NYSE symbol] (TTSB) .... TEE
Natl Health Enhacement Sys [NASDAQ symbol] (TTSB) .... NHES
Natl Healthcare L.P. [AMEX symbol] (TTSB) .... NHC
Natl Hlth Inv 8.50%Cv Pfd [NYSE symbol] (TTSB) .... NHIP
Natl Home Health Care [NASDAQ symbol] (TTSB) .... NHHC
Natl Inc. Rlty Tr SBI [NASDAQ symbol] (TTSB) .... NIRTS
Natl Instruments [NASDAQ symbol] (TTSB) .... NATI
Natl Insurance Group [NASDAQ symbol] (TTSB) .... NAIG
Natl Lodging [NASDAQ symbol] (TTSB) .... NALC
Natl Media Corp. [NYSE symbol] (TTSB) .... NM
Natl Medical Finl Svcs [NASDAQ symbol] (TTSB) .... NMFS
Natl Patent Devel [AMEX symbol] (TTSB) .... NPD
Natl Penn Bancshares [NASDAQ symbol] (TTSB) .... NPBC
Natl Power plc [LO, exchange symbol] (TTSB) .... NATP
Natl Power PLC Interim ADS [NYSE symbol] (TTSB) .... NP.PP
Natl Presto Indus [NYSE symbol] (TTSB) .... NPK
Natl Re Corp. [NYSE symbol] (TTSB) .... NRE
Natl Realty L.P. [AMEX symbol] (TTSB) .... NLP
Natl Record Mart [NASDAQ symbol] (TTSB) .... NRMI
Natl R.V.Holding [NASDAQ symbol] (TTSB) .... NRVH
Natl Sanitary Supply [NASDAQ symbol] (TTSB) .... NSSX
Natl Security Group [NASDAQ symbol] (TTSB) .... NSEC
Natl Semiconductor [NYSE symbol] (TTSB) .... NSM
Natl Service Indus [NYSE symbol] (TTSB) .... NSI
Natl Steel 'B' [NYSE symbol] (TTSB) .... NS
Natl Surgery Centers [NASDAQ symbol] (TTSB) .... NSCI
Natl Technical Sys [NQS] (TTSB) .... NTSC
Natl TechTeam Inc. [NASDAQ symbol] (TTSB) .... TEAM
Natl Vision Associates [NASDAQ symbol] (TTSB) .... NVAL
Natl Western Life Ins'A' [NASDAQ symbol] (TTSB) .... NWLIA
Natl Westminister Pref'A'ADS [NYSE symbol] (TTSB) .... NWPrA
Natl Westminster ADS [NYSE symbol] (TTSB) .... NW
Natl Westminster Bk Ex Cap Sec [NYSE symbol] (TTSB) .... NWXPrA
Natl Westminster Pref'B'ADS [NYSE symbol] (TTSB) .... NWPrB
Natl Wireless Hldgs [NASDAQ symbol] (TTSB) .... NWIR
NATO Advisory Group for Aeronautical Research and Development .... NAGARD
NATO AEWC [Airborne Early Warning and Control] Program Management
    Agency .... NAPMA
NATO Air Defense Committee .... NADC
NATO Air Defense Electronic Environment Committee .... NADEEC
NATO Air Defense Ground Environment .... NADGE
NATO Air Defense Ground Environment .... NDGE
NATO Air Defense Ground Environment Consortium .... NADGECO
NATO Air Defense Ground Environment Management Organization
    (NATG) .... NADGEMO
NATO Air Defense Ground Equipment .... NADGE
NATO Air Defense Group Environment (AABC) .... NAGE
NATO Air Doctrine (NATG) .... NAD
NATO Air Force Advisory Group (NATG) .... NAFAG
NATO Air Force Armaments Group .... NAFAG
NATO Air Traffic Service Advisory Agency (NATG) .... NATSAA
NATO Airbase Satellite/Ground Mobile Force (MCD) .... NABS/GMF
NATO Airborne Early Warning .... NAEW
NATO Airborne Early Warning and Control Programme Management
    Organization [Brunssum, Netherlands] .... NAPMO
NATO Airborne Early Warning Program Office (NATG) .... NAPO
NATO Airborne Early Warning System .... NAEWS
NATO Airborne SATCOM (MCD) .... NABS
NATO Aircrew Electronic Warfare Tactics Facility (NATG) .... NAEWTF
NATO and Warsaw Pact [Projects] (NATG) .... NWP
NATO Annual Manpower Plan (NATG) .... NAMP
NATO Anti-Air Warfare System (DOMA) .... NAAWS
NATO Armaments Planning Review (NATG) .... NAPR
NATO Army Advisory Group (NATG) .... NAAG
NATO Army Armaments Group (AABC) .... NAAG
NATO Basic Military Requirements (AABC) .... NBMR
NATO Basic Military Techniques (NATG) .... NBMT
NATO Bullpup Management Office [Missiles] (NATG) .... NABMO
NATO Bullpup Production Organization [Missiles] (NATG) .... NABPO
NATO Bullpup Production Organization [Missiles] (NATG) .... NBPO
NATO Center (NATG) .... NC
NATO Civil Air Augmentation (DOMA) .... NCAA
NATO Civil Communications Planning Committee (NATG) .... NCCPC
NATO Civil Wartime Agency (NATG) .... NCWA
NATO Command and Control Systems Management Agency
    (PDAA) .... NACCSMA
NATO Command, Control, and Information System (NATG) ...... NCCIS
NATO Command, Control, and Information Systems and Automatic Data
    Processing Committee (NATG) .... NCCDPC
NATO Commanders Communications Publication (NATG) .... NCCP
NATO Communication (NATG) .... NATCOM
NATO Communication System Technical Recommendation (NATG) ... NCSTR
NATO Communications and Information Systems Organization
    (EAIO) .... NACISO
NATO Communications Electronics Board .... NCEB
NATO Communications Security Information (NATG) .... NACSIM
NATO Comparative Testing (RDA) .... NCT
NATO Composite Force .... NCF
NATO Confidential (NATG) .... NC
NATO Courier Service (NATG) .... NACOS
NATO Data Exchange (NATG) .... NADEX
NATO Data Requirements and Standards Working Group (NATG) ..... NDRSWG

NATO Data-Buoy System [*National Oceanic and Atmospheric Administration*] ... NDAC
NATO Defense College [*Also, NADEFCOL, NDC*] ... NADC
NATO [*North Atlantic Treaty Organization*] **Defense College** (AD) ... NaDefCo
NATO Defense College [*Also, NADC, NDC*] [*Rome, Italy*] ... NADEFCOL
NATO Defense College [*Also, NADC, NADEFCOL*] (NATG) ... NDC
NATO Defense Data Program (AABC) ... NDDP
NATO Defense Information Complex (NATG) ... NDIC
NATO Defense Information Management Committee (NATG) ... NDIMC
NATO Defense Manpower Committee (NATG) ... NDMC
NATO Defense Planning Review (NATG) ... NDPR
NATO Defense Research Group (NATG) ... NDRG
NATO Electromagnetic Compatibility Agency (NATG) ... NEMCA
NATO Electronic Parts Recommendations (AABC) ... NEPR
NATO Electronic Technical Recommendation (PDAA) ... NETR
NATO Electronic Warfare Advisory Committee (NATG) ... NEWAC
NATO Electronic Warfare Liaison Committee ... NEWLC
NATO English-Speaking Nations ... NESN
NATO Equipment Interpretation Course (MCD) ... NEIC
NATO Equipment Policy Objective (NATG) ... NEPO
NATO Europe Early Warning System Standard Operating Procedures (NATG) ... NEEWSSOP
NATO European Fighter Management Agency ... NAFMA
NATO European Fighter Management Organization (MCD) ... NEFMO
NATO Experimental Tactics (NATG) ... NEXT
NATO Exploratory Conference on Production Logistics (NATG) ... NECPL
NATO Force Planning Exercise (NATG) ... NFPE
NATO French-Speaking Nations ... NFSN
NATO Frigate for the 1990s ... NFR-90
NATO Gazetteer (MCD) ... NGAZ
NATO Guidelines Area (NATG) ... NGA
NATO HAWK Documentation Center [*Missiles*] (NATG) ... NHDC
NATO HAWK Management Office [*Missiles*] (NATG) ... NHMO
NATO HAWK Military Committee [*Missiles*] (AABC) ... NHMILCOM
NATO HAWK Production and Logistics Organization [*France*] (NATG) ... NHPLO
NATO HAWK Production Organization [*Missiles*] ... NHPO
NATO HAWK Support Department [*Missiles*] (NATG) ... NHSD
NATO Helicopter [*NH-90*] (DOMA) ... NH
NATO Identification System ... NIS
NATO Identification System Special Project Office ... NISSPO
NATO Industrial Advisory Group (MCD) ... NIAG
NATO Information Management Control Point (NATG) ... NIMCP
NATO [*North Atlantic Treaty Organization*] **Insensitive Munitions Information Center** ... NIMIC
NATO Integrated Air Defense System (NATG) ... NATINADS
NATO Integrated Communications System (NATG) ... NICS
NATO Integrated Communications System Management Agency (NATG) ... NICSMA
NATO Integrated Communications System Organization [*Brussels, Belgium*] (NATG) ... NICSO
NATO Interface Unit (MCD) ... NIU
NATO Item Identification (NATG) ... NII
NATO Item Identification Guide (NATG) ... NIIG
NATO Joint Communications-Electronics Committee (NATG) ... NJCEC
NATO Letter of Promulgation ... NALOP
NATO Liaison Representative (MCD) ... NLR
NATO Lot Acceptance (MCD) ... NLA
NATO Maintenance and Supply Agency ... NAMSA
NATO Maintenance and Supply Organization [*Formerly, NATO Maintenance Supply Service Agency*] [*Luxembourg*] ... NAMSO
NATO Maintenance and Support Operation (AFM) ... NMSO
NATO Maintenance Supply Service Agency [*Later, NAMSO*] ... NMSSA
NATO Maintenance Supply Service System ... NMSSS
NATO Manual on Codification (NATG) ... NMC
NATO Maritime Defense Zone (NATG) ... NMDZ
NATO Maritime Patrol Aircraft (NATG) ... NMPA
NATO Maritime Patrol Aircraft Agency (NATG) ... NAMPA
NATO Maritime Patrol Aircraft Steering Committee (NATG) ... NMPASC
NATO Military Authorities (NATG) ... NMA
NATO Military Basic Requirement (MCD) ... NMBR
NATO Military Command and Control and Information System (NATG) ... NMCCIS
NATO Military Posture (AABC) ... NAMILPO
NATO Missile Firing Installation ... NAMFI
NATO [*North Atlantic Treaty Organization*] **Multi-Role Combat Aircraft Development a** (AD) ... NAMMO Development a
NATO Multi-Role Combat Aircraft Development and Production Management Agency ... NAMMA
NATO Multi-Role Combat Aircraft Management Organization (PDAA) ... NAMMO
NATO Naval Advisory Group (NATG) ... NNAG
NATO Naval Armaments Group (NATG) ... NNAG
NATO Office of Security (NATG) ... NOS
NATO Oil Authority (NATG) ... NOA
NATO Oil Crisis Contingent (NATG) ... NOCC
NATO Oil Executive Board (NATG) ... NOEB
NATO Oil Executive Board - East ... NOEB-E
NATO Oil Executive Board - West ... NOEB-W
NATO Parliamentarians' Conference ... NPC
NATO Patriot Management Group (MCD) ... NPMG
NATO Patriot Management Office ... NAPATMO
NATO Pipeline Committee ... NPC
NATO Planning Group (NATG) ... NPG
NATO Planning Workshop (NATG) ... NPWS
NATO Production and Logistics Organization (NATG) ... NPLO
NATO Programming Center (NATG) ... NPC
NATO Reference Mobility Model ... NRMM
NATO Refugees Agency (NATG) ... NRA
NATO Request for Air Transport Support [*Military*] ... NARAT
NATO Restricted (NATG) ... NR
NATO [*North Atlantic Treaty Organization*] **Science Committee** (EAIO) ... NSC
NATO Sea Sparrow Missile System ... NSSMS
NATO Sea Sparrow Project Office (MCD) ... NSPO
NATO Secret (NATG) ... NS
NATO Security Board (NATG) ... NSB
NATO Security Bureau Industrial Security Section (NATG) ... NSBISS
NATO Sidewinder Production and Logistics Organization [*Missiles*] (NATG) ... NSPLO
NATO Sidewinder Production Organization [*Missiles*] (NATG) ... NSPO
NATO Sidewinder Program Office [*Missiles*] (NATG) ... NSPO
NATO Small Arms Test (MCD) ... NSAT
NATO Small Arms Test Control Commission (MCD) ... NSMATCC
NATO Staff Requirements (MCD) ... NSR
NATO STANAG International Standards ... NAT-STD
NATO Starfighter Management Office ... NASMO
NATO Starfighter Production Organization ... NASPO
NATO Steering Committee (NATG) ... NSC
NATO Stock Number (NATG) ... NSN
NATO Subject Indicator System (NATG) ... NASIS
NATO Supply Center ... NASC
NATO Supply Center (NATG) ... NSC
NATO Supply Classification ... NSC
NATO Supply Code for Manufacturing (MCD) ... NSCM
NATO Surveillance (NATG) ... NS
NATO Tactical Fighter Center ... NTFC
NATO Tactical Fighter Weapons Training Center ... NTFWTC
NATO Target Data Inventory (MCD) ... NTDI
NATO Unclassified (NATG) ... NU
NATO Wartime Oil Organization (NATG) ... NWOO
NATO Wartime Preliminary Analysis Group (NATG) ... NWPAG
NATO-Wide Communications System (NATG) ... NWCS
NATPE [*National Association of Television Program Executives*] **International** (EA) ... NATPE
Natrium [*Sodium*] [*Chemical element*] ... Na
Natrium [*Sodium*] [*Latin*] (AD) ... natr
Natrium [*Sodium*] [*Pharmacy*] ... NATR
Natriuretic Material [*Physiology*] ... NM
Natriuretic Plasma Dialysate [*Medicine*] (MAE) ... NPD
Natrolite [*A zeolite*] ... NAT
Natrona County Public Library, Casper, WY [*Library symbol Library of Congress*] (LCLS) ... WyCa
Natsionalnyii [*National*] [*Russian*] (AD) ... Nats
Natty (ABBR) ... NT
Natuna/Ransi [*Indonesia*] [*ICAO location identifier*] (ICLI) ... WION
Natura Sanat, Medicus Curat [*Nature Heals, the Doctor Cures*] [*Title of collected talks by Dr. Georg Groddeck, published in 1913*] ... NASAMECU
Natural (AAG) ... NAT
Natural (AD) ... nat
Natural (ODBW) ... Nat
Natural ... NTRL
Natural Actomyosins [*Biochemistry*] ... NAM
Natural Adjuvant Factor Toxoid [*Medicine*] ... NAFT
Natural Alternatives International [*AMEX symbol*] (SPSG) ... NAI
Natural Alternatives International [*NASDAQ symbol*] (SAG) ... NAII
Natural Alternatives International [*Associated Press*] (SAG) ... NatAlt
Natural Alternatives International [*Associated Press*] (SAG) ... NaturlAlt
Natural Alternatives Intl [*AMEX symbol*] (TTSB) ... NAI
Natural and Accelerated Bioremediation Research [*Department of Energy*] ... NABIR
Natural and Synthetic [*Type of long-wearing rubber, which is actually wholly synthetic*] ... NATSYN
Natural Area Council (EA) ... NAC
Natural Areas Association (EA) ... NAA
Natural Areas of Canadian Significance [*NPPAC*] ... NACS
Natural Asphalt Mineowners' and Manufacturers' Council (AD) ... NAMMC
Natural Axial Resonant Frequency (PDAA) ... NARF
Natural Axial-Resonant Frequency (AD) ... narf
Natural Axis ... NA
Natural Background Clutter ... NBC
Natural Bandwidths [*Spectroscopy*] ... NBW
Natural Binary-Coded Decimal ... NBCD
Natural Birth Control ... NBC
Natural Black Slate (MSA) ... NBS
Natural Born Killers [*Movie title*] ... NBK
Natural Bridges National Monument ... NABR
Natural Casing Institute [*Later, International Natural Sausage Casing Institute*] (EA) ... NCI
Natural Cell-Mediated Cytotoxicity [*Immunochemistry*] ... NCMC
Natural Circulation Cooldown [*Nuclear energy*] (NUCP) ... NCC
Natural Circulation Verification Program [*Nuclear energy*] (NRCH) ... NCVP
Natural Clay Mosaic (DICI) ... NCM
Natural Clay Pavers (DICI) ... NCP
Natural Color (AD) ... natcol
Natural Colored Wool Growers Association (EA) ... NCWGA
Natural Convection Boiling Loops ... NCBL
Natural Convection in the Stationary Condition [*Computer program*] ... NAKOSTA
Natural Cytotoxic [*Cells*] [*Immunochemistry*] ... NC
Natural Daylight ... NDL
Natural Death [*Medicine*] ... ND
Natural Disaster Hospitals [*Public Health Service*] ... NDH
Natural Disaster Warning ... NADWARN

Natural Disaster Warning Survey (NOAA) ...... NADWAS
Natural Disaster Warning System (IAA) ...... NADWARN
Natural Distribution Certificate (WDAA) ...... NDC
Natural Division [Geography] ...... N
Natural Draft Cooling Tower [Nuclear energy] (NRCH) ...... NDCT
Natural Draft Heat Exchanger [Nuclear energy] (NRCH) ...... NDHX
Natural Draught ...... ND
Natural Effects Processor ...... NEP
Natural Electronic Business User's Language [International Computers Ltd.] ...... NEBULA
Natural Energy Association [British] ...... NEA
Natural Environment Research Council [Research center British] (IRC) ...... NERC
Natural Environment Support Room (MCD) ...... NESR
Natural Family Planning ...... NFP
Natural Family Planning Association of Connecticut (EA) ...... NFPA
Natural Family Planning National Secretariat [Australia] ...... NFPNS
Natural Flight Indication (MCD) ...... NAFLI
Natural Flight Instrument System ...... NAFLI
Natural Flood (MCD) ...... NF
Natural Flood ...... NF
Natural Food (MCD) ...... NF
Natural Food and Farming [A publication] ...... NF & F
Natural Food Associates (EA) ...... NFA
Natural Food Colours Association [Basel, Switzerland] (EAIO) ...... NATCOL
Natural Food Institute [Defunct] (EA) ...... NFI
Natural Frequency (IAA) ...... NATFREQU
Natural Gas ...... NG
Natural Gas Association (EPA) ...... NGA
Natural Gas Clearinghouse ...... NGC
Natural Gas Consumers Information Center (EA) ...... NGCIC
Natural Gas for Vehicles ...... NGV
Natural Gas Industry [Australia] ...... NGI
Natural Gas Liquids ...... NGL
Natural Gas Pipeline Safety Act [1968] ...... NGPSA
Natural Gas Plant Liquids [DOE] (TAG) ...... NGPL
Natural Gas Policy Act [1978] ...... NGPA
Natural Gas Pressure ...... NGP
Natural Gas Processors Association [Later, GPA] (EA) ...... NGPA
Natural Gas Processors Suppliers Association [Later, GPSA] (EA) ...... NGPSA
Natural Gas Shutoff [NFPA pre-fire planning symbol] (NFPA) ...... NG
Natural Gas Supply Association (EA) ...... NGSA
Natural Gas Tank Pressure ...... NGTP
Natural Gas Tank Temperature ...... NGTT
Natural Gas Temperature ...... NGT
Natural Gas Vehicle ...... NGV
Natural Gas Vehicle Coalition [VDOT] (TAG) ...... NGVC
Natural Gas Vehicle Partnership ...... NGVP
Natural Gasoline Association of America [Later, GPA] ...... NGAA
Natural Gasoline Supply Men's Association [Later, GPSA] ...... NGSMA
Natural, Grazed [Agriculture] ...... NG
Natural Ground Level ...... NGL
Natural Ground Surface ...... NGS
Natural Guard Fund [Defunct] (EA) ...... NGF
Natural Gum Blend [Philately] ...... ngb
Natural Gum Crease [Philately] ...... ngc
Natural Hazards Research and Applications Information Center [University of Colorado - Boulder] [Research center] (RCD) ...... NHRAIC
Natural Health Society of Australia ...... NHSA
Natural Health Trends Corp. [Associated Press] (SAG) ...... NatHlth
Natural Health Trends Corp. [Associated Press] (SAG) ...... NatrlHlth
Natural Health Trends Corp. [NASDAQ symbol] (SAG) ...... NHTC
Natural Health Trends Corp. [Associated Press] (SAG) ...... NtH
Natural Health Trends Corp. [Associated Press] (SAG) ...... NtrlH
Natural Health Trends Wrrt'A' [NASDAQ symbol] (TTSB) ...... NHTCW
Natural Health Trends Wrrt'B' [NASDAQ symbol] (TTSB) ...... NHTCZ
Natural Heritage and Endangered Species Program [Massachusetts State Division of Fisheries and Wildlife] [Also, an information service or system] (IID) ...... NHESP
Natural History (AD) ...... nat hist
Natural History [A publication] (BRI) ...... NH
Natural History Information Retrieval System [Smithsonian Institution] ...... NHIR
Natural History Museum [British] ...... NHM
Natural History Museum Foundation, Los Angeles County, Los Angeles, CA [OCLC symbol] (OCLC) ...... CNH
Natural History Press (DGA) ...... NHP
Natural Human Serum ...... NHS
Natural Hydrocarbon [Organic chemistry] ...... NHC
Natural Image Computer (PDAA) ...... NIC
Natural Interference to Transmission or Reception [Broadcasting] ...... QRS
Natural Killer [Cell] [Immunochemistry] ...... NK
Natural Killer (Cell) Cytotoxic Factor [Immunochemistry] ...... NKCF
Natural Killer Cells [Microbiology] (DAVI) ...... NKC
Natural Killer-Cell Activating Factor [Immunology] ...... NKAF
Natural Killer-Cell Stimulatory Factor [Immunology] ...... NKSF
Natural Language [Computer software] ...... NL
Natural Language Data Base ...... NLDB
Natural Language Mode [Computer science] ...... NLM
Natural Language Operating System ...... NLOS
Natural Language Processing [Computer science] ...... NLP
Natural Language Processing Segment [Computer science] ...... NLPS
Natural Language Processing System for Queuing Problems [Computer science] (PDAA) ...... NLPQ
Natural Language Query [Software] [Battelle Software Products Center] ...... NLQ
Natural Law Party [Australia Political party] ...... NLP
Natural Law Society (EA) ...... NLS

Natural Log [or Logarithm] (WDAA) ...... NL
Natural Logarithm [Mathematics] ...... EXP
Natural Logarithm (IAA) ...... NALOG
Natural Magnetic Remanence [Geophysics] ...... NMR
Natural Marketing Association [Woodland Hills, CA] (EA) ...... NMA
Natural Microsystems [NASDAQ symbol] (TTSB) ...... NMSS
Natural Microsystems Corp. [Associated Press] (SAG) ...... NatMicr
Natural Microsystems Corp. [NASDAQ symbol] (SAG) ...... NMSS
Natural Mortality Schedule [Biology] ...... NMS
Natural, Nongrazed [Agriculture] ...... NN
Natural Number (IDOE) ...... N
Natural Oocyte Retrieval Intravaginal Fertilization [Alternative to traditional in-vitro fertilization (IVF)] (PAZ) ...... NORIF
Natural Orange Aroma ...... NOA
Natural Orbital [Physical chemistry] ...... NO
Natural Order [Botany] (BARN) ...... Nat Ord
Natural Order [Botany] ...... NO
Natural Organic Carbon ...... NOC
Natural Organic Farmers Association (EA) ...... NOFA
Natural Organic Matter ...... NOM
Natural Parity Exchange [Physics] (OA) ...... NPE
Natural Particulate Matter [Oceanography] ...... NPM
Natural Passivation [Metallurgy] ...... NP
Natural Period in Heave ...... NPH
Natural Philosophy (BARN) ...... Nat Phil
Natural Philosophy (AD) ...... nat phil
Natural Processing Language [Computer science] (HGAA) ...... NPL
Natural Product Broker Association [St. Augustine, FL] (EA) ...... NPBA
Natural Products Alert [University of Illinois at Chicago] [Information service or system] (IID) ...... NAPRALERT
Natural Products Quality Assurance Alliance ...... NPQAA
Natural Protamine Hagadorn [Insulin] ...... NPH
Natural Radioactive Nuclides ...... NRN
Natural Rate Hypothesis [Economics] ...... NRH
Natural Rate of Unemployment [Economics] ...... NARU
Natural Remanent Magnetism [or Magnetization] ...... NRM
Natural Resource Damage [Environmental science] ...... NRD
Natural Resource Information System [Department of the Interior] ...... NRIS
Natural Resource Management ...... NRM
Natural Resource Management System [Army Corps of Engineers] [Database] ...... NRMS
Natural Resource Unit [Environmental unit] ...... NRU
Natural Resource-Based Product ...... NRBP
Natural Resources ...... NATR
Natural Resources ...... NS
Natural Resources and Environment Committee [Victoria, Australia] ...... NREC
Natural Resources and Environmental Education Center [Oklahoma State University] [Research center] (RCD) ...... NREEC
Natural Resources Audit Council ...... NRAC
Natural Resources Center [University of Alabama] [Research center] (RCD) ...... NRC
Natural Resources Council of America (EA) ...... NRC
Natural Resources Defense Council (EA) ...... NRDC
Natural Resources Department, Office of Forestry, Baton Rouge, LA [Library symbol Library of Congress] (LCLS) ...... LBrNR-F
Natural Resources Department, Research and Development Library, Baton Rouge, LA [Library symbol Library of Congress] (LCLS) ...... LBrNR
Natural Resources Division [An association] (EAIO) ...... NRD
Natural Resources, Energy, and Environment [Office of Management and Budget] ...... NRES
Natural Resources Institute [University of Greenwich] [British] ...... NRI
Natural Resources International ...... NRI
Natural Resources Journal [A publication] (BRI) ...... NRJ
Natural Resources Library, Ontario Ministry of Natural Resources, Toronto, Ontario [Library symbol National Library of Canada] (NLC) ...... OTLF
Natural Resources Management [Organization of Eastern Caribbean States] ...... NRMU
Natural Resources Research Institute [Research center] (RCD) ...... NRRI
Natural Resources Research Institute, Duluth, MN [Library symbol] [Library of Congress] (LCLS) ...... MnDuNR
Natural Rights Center (EA) ...... NRC
Natural Rubber ...... NR
Natural Rubber Bureau [Later, MRB] (EA) ...... NRB
Natural Rubber Producers' Research Association [British] (BI) ...... NRPRA
Natural Rubber Shippers Association (EA) ...... NRSA
Natural Sausage Casings Association [British] (DBA) ...... NSCA
Natural Science Book Club ...... NSBC
Natural Science for Youth Foundation (EA) ...... NSYF
Natural Science Foudation of China ...... NSFC
Natural Science Foundation of China ...... NSFC
Natural Sciences (WDAA) ...... NAT SC
Natural Sciences ...... NS
Natural Sciences and Engineering Research Council of Canada [Research center] (IRC) ...... NSERC
Natural Sciences and Engineering Research Council of Canada [Conseil de Recherches en Sciences Naturelles et en Genie du Canada], Ottawa, Ontario [Library symbol National Library of Canada] (NLC) ...... OONSE
Natural Sound [Broadcasting] (WDMC) ...... NAT sound
Natural Space Environment ...... NSE
Natural Therapeutic and Osteopathic Society and Register [British] (DBA) ...... NTOS
Natural Thermo Luminescence (IAA) ...... NTL
Natural Toxins Research Center [Public Health Service] (GRD) ...... NTRC
Natural Transition Orbitals [Atomic physics] ...... NTO
Natural Unit (IAA) ...... NAT

Natural Uranium Fuel ... NUF
Natural Wavelength ... NWL
Natural Wonders [*NASDAQ symbol*] (TTSB) ... NATW
Natural Wonders, Inc. [*NASDAQ symbol*] (SAG) ... NATW
Natural Wonders, Inc. [*Associated Press*] (SAG) ... NatWndr
Natural-Colored Yellow [*Diamonds*] ... N-CY
Naturalis Historia [*of Pliny the Elder*] [*Classical studies*] (OCD) ... HN
Naturalism (VRA) ... Natlm
Naturalist (AD) ... nat
Naturalist (AD) ... natur
Naturalist (WDAA) ... NATUR
Naturalist's Library [*A publication*] ... NL
Naturalization (DNAB) ... N
Naturalization (AD) ... nat
Naturalization (AD) ... NT
Naturalization Test ... Nat
Naturalized [*Botany*] ... Natzd
Naturalized [*Biology*] (BARN) ... Natzd
Naturalized United States Citizen ... NATUS
Naturally (AD) ... natch
Naturally (AD) ... naty
Naturally ... NTRLLy
Naturally Aspirated [*Automotive engineering*] ... D
Naturally Aspirated [*Diesel engines*] ... NA
Naturally Commutated Cycloconverter [*Electronics*] (EECA) ... NCC
Naturally Occurring Mutants ... NM
Naturally Occurring or Accelerator-Produced Radioactive Material ... NARM
Naturally Occurring Radioactive Material (FFDE) ... NORM
Naturally Occurring Retirement Community ... NORC
Naturally Occurring Top Component [*Virology*] ... NTC
Naturally Radioactive Product (NRCH) ... NRAP
Natural-Source Vitamin E Association (EA) ... NSVEA
Nature [*or Naturalist*] ... Nat
Nature (AD) ... nat
Nature and Earth United with Science [*Brand of hair products*] ... NEXUS
Nature Conservancy (BARN) ... Nat Con
Nature Conservancy [*NERC*] [*British*] ... NC
[*The*] **Nature Conservancy** (EERA) ... TNC
[*The*] **Nature Conservancy** (EA) ... TNC
Nature Conservancy Council [*British*] ... NCC
Nature Conservation Council of South Australia ... NCCSA
Nature Expeditions International (GNE) ... NEI
Nature Farming International Research Foundation (EAIO) ... NFIRF
Nature of Action [*Military*] (AFM) ... NOA
Nature's Initial Cosmic Kickstart ... NICK
Nature's Sunshine Prod [*NASDAQ symbol*] (TTSB) ... NATR
Natures Sunshine Products [*Associated Press*] (SAG) ... NatrSun
Nature's Sunshine Products, Inc. [*NASDAQ symbol*] (NQ) ... NATR
Naturfreunde-Internationale [*International Friends of Nature - IFN*] (EAIO) ... NFI
Naturist (WDAA) ... NAT
[*The*] **Naturist Society** (EA) ... NS
Naturists and Nudists Opposing Pornographic Exploitation (EA) ... NNOPE
Naturists and Nudists Opposing Pornographic Exploitation (EA) ... NOPE
Naturita Public Library, Naturita, CO [*Library symbol Library of Congress*] (LCLS) ... CoNa
Naturpolitische Volkspartei [*People's Party for Nature Policy*] [*Germany Political party*] (PPW) ... NPV
Naturvetenskapliga forskingsradet [*Swedish Natural Science Research Council*] ... NFR
Natus [*Birth*] [*Latin*] ... N
Natus [*Birth*] [*Latin*] ... NAT
Natuurbestuurvereniging van Suidelike Afrika [*Southern African Wildlife Management Association - SAWMA*] [*Pretoria, South Africa*] (EAIO) ... NVSA
Natuurkunde [*Natural Science*] [*Dutch*] (AD) ... nat
Nat-War Alliance [*Defunct*] (EA) ... NW
Naugahide (AD) ... nauga
Naugatuck, CT [*AM radio station call letters*] ... WFNW
Naughton Branch, Walden Public Library, Ontario [*Library symbol National Library of Canada*] (NLC) ... OWN
NAUI [*National Association of Underwater Instructors*] **Diving Association** (EA) ... NDA
Naukove Tovarystvo Imeni Shevchenka (Shevchenko Scientific Society, Inc.), New York, NY [*Library symbol Library of Congress*] (LCLS) ... NNNTSH
Naungmon [*Myanmar*] [*ICAO location identifier*] (ICLI) ... VBNM
Nauru [*Aircraft nationality and registration mark*] (FAAC) ... C2
Nauru [*Nauru*] [*Airport symbol*] (OAG) ... INU
Nauru [*ANSI two-letter standard code*] (CNC) ... NR
Nauru [*ANSI three-letter standard code*] (CNC) ... NRU
Nauru [*MARC country of publication code Library of Congress*] (LCCP) ... nu
Nauru [*MARC geographic area code Library of Congress*] (LCCP) ... ponu--
Nauru Island [*ICAO location identifier*] (ICLI) ... ANAU
Nauru Island (AD) ... Nau
Nauru Island Council [*Australia*] ... NIC
Nauru Local Government Council [*Australia*] ... NLGC
Nauru Phosphate Commission [*Australia*] ... NPC
Nauruan (AD) ... Nau
Nausea (KSC) ... NSA
Nausea and Vomiting ... N & V
Nausea and Vomiting in Pregnancy ... NVP
Nausea, Vomiting, Diarrhea [*Medicine*] ... NVD
Naushki [*Pakistan*] [*ICAO location identifier*] (ICLI) ... OPNK
Nausori Highlands [*Fiji*] [*Seismograph station code, US Geological Survey*] (SEIS) ... NHF
Nausori/International [*Fiji*] [*ICAO location identifier*] (ICLI) ... NFNA
Nauta [*Peru*] [*ICAO location identifier*] (ICLI) ... SPTA
Nautica [*Nautical*] [*Spanish*] (AD) ... nau
Nautica Enterprises [*NASDAQ symbol*] (TTSB) ... NAUT
Nautica Enterprises, Inc. [*NASDAQ symbol*] (SAG) ... NAUT
Nautica Enterprises, Inc. [*Associated Press*] (SAG) ... Nautica
Nautical ... N
Nautical (AD) ... naut
Nautical (AAG) ... NAUT
Nautical ... NTCL
Nautical Air Miles ... NAM
Nautical Air Miles per Gallon (AD) ... nampg
Nautical Air Miles per Pound of Fuel (AD) ... namppf
Nautical Air Miles per Pound of Fuel (AAG) ... NAMPPF
Nautical Almanac ... NA
Nautical & Aviation Publishing Co. ... N & A
Nautical Archaeology [*Oceanography*] ... NA
Nautical Charting Research and Development Laboratory [*National Oceanic and Atmospheric Administration*] ... NCRDL
Nautical Directional Beacon (IAA) ... NDB
Nautical Institute [*British*] (EAIO) ... NI
Nautical Mile [*6,080 feet*] ... NM
Nautical Mile ... NMI
Nautical Mile ... NML
Nautical Mile/Hour (MCD) ... NM/HR
Nautical Miles (ROG) ... NAUTS
Nautical Miles per Hour ... NMH
Nautical Miles per Pound (MCD) ... NMPP
Nautical Miles per Second ... NMPS
Nautical Research Guild (EA) ... NRG
Nautical Training Corps [*British military*] (DMA) ... NTC
Nautilus Resources Ltd. [*Vancouver Stock Exchange symbol*] ... NUT
Nautla [*Mexico ICAO location identifier*] (ICLI) ... MMNU
Nautophone ... NAUTO
NAVA [*National Audio-Visual Association*] **Materials Council** (EA) ... NMC
Nava Sama Samaja Party [*New Equal Society Party*] [*Sri Lanka*] [*Political party*] (PPW) ... NSSP
Navaho (AD) ... Nav
NAVAIR Advanced Development Plan (MCD) ... NADP
NAVAIR [*Naval Air Systems Command*] **Industrial Finance Management System** (MCD) ... NIFMS
NAVAIR [*Naval Air Systems Command*] **Initial Supply Support Outfitting List** (MCD) ... NISSOL
NAVAIR [*Naval Air Systems Command*] **Naval Aviation Plan** (MCD) ... NNAP
NAVAIR Test Manual (MCD) ... NTM
NAVAIRSYSCOM [*Naval Air Systems Command*] **Integrated Management InformationSystem** (DNAB) ... NAIMIS
Navajo [*MARC language code Library of Congress*] (LCCP) ... nav
Navajo Army Depot [*Arizona*] (AABC) ... NAAD
Navajo Army Depot Activity [*Arizona*] [*Army*] ... NADA
Navajo Code Talkers Association (EA) ... NCTA
Navajo Community College [*Chinle, AZ*] ... NCC
Navajo Community College, Chinle, AZ [*Library symbol Library of Congress*] (LCLS) ... AzCN
Navajo National Monument ... NAVA
Naval ... MVL
Naval [*British military*] (DMA) ... N
Naval (AD) ... Nav
Naval (AD) ... nav
Naval (MSA) ... NAV
Naval Academy ... NA
Naval Academy ... NAC
Naval Academy ... NAVACAD
Naval Academy (DNAB) ... NAVACD
Naval Academy Computer Center ... NACC
Naval Academy Heat Balanced Engine [*Pronounced "knobby"*] ... NAHBE
Naval Academy Midshipmen Branch ... NAMB
Naval Academy Preparatory School ... NAPS
Naval Academy Prepatory Student (DNAB) ... NAP
Naval Accounts [*British*] ... NA
Naval Acoustic Sensor Training Aids Department (DNAB) ... NASTAD
Naval Activities Detachment (DNAB) ... NAVACTDET
Naval Activity ... COMNAVACTS
Naval Administration ... NADM
Naval Administration Unit (MUGU) ... NAVADMINU
Naval Administrative Command ... NAVADCOM
Naval Administrative Command (DNAB) ... NAVADMINCOM
Naval Administrative Unit ... NAU
Naval Administrative Unit ... NAVADUNIT
Naval Administrative Unit Annex (DNAB) ... NAVADMINUANX
Naval Administrator At [*Place*] ... NAVAD
Naval Advanced Base ... NAB
Naval Advanced Base Depot ... NABD
Naval Advanced Base Unit ... NABU
Naval Advanced Undersea Weapons School ... ADVUSWS
Naval Advanced Undersea Weapons School ... NAUWS
Naval Advanced Undersea Weapons School (DNAB) ... NAVADUNSEAWPNSCOL
Naval Advanced Undersea Weapons School (MUGU) ... NAVADVUSEAWPNSCOL
Naval Adviser [*British*] ... NAd
Naval Advisory Group ... NAG
Naval Advisory Group ... NAVADGP
Naval Advisory Group (CINC) ... NAVADGRU
Naval Advisory Group ... NAVGP
Naval Aeronautical Establishment [*Canada*] (AD) ... NAE
Naval Aeronautical Laboratory ... NAL
Naval Aeronautical Material Area (NG) ... NAMA
Naval Aeronautical Medical Center ... NAVAEROMEDCEN
Naval Aeronautical Publications Index (DNAB) ... NAPI

Naval Aeronautical Turbine Laboratory .... NATL
Naval Aeronautics Test Station .... NARTS
Naval Aerospace and Regional Medical Center [*Bureau of Medicine*] .... NARMC
Naval Aerospace Medical Center .... NAMC
Naval Aerospace Medical Center (DNAB) .... NAVAERO(SP)REGMEDCEN
Naval Aerospace Medical Institute .... NAMI
Naval Aerospace Medical Institute .... NAVAEROSPMEDINST
Naval Aerospace Medical Institute (MCD) .... NAVMED
Naval Aerospace Medical Research Institute (DNAB) .... NAMRI
Naval Aerospace Medical Research Institute (DNAB) .... NAVAEROSPMEDRSCHINST
Naval Aerospace Medical Research Laboratory .... NAMRL
Naval Aerospace Medical Research Laboratory (DNAB) .... NAVAERO(SP)OMEDRSCHLAB
Naval Aerospace Recovery Facility .... NAVAERORECOV
Naval Aerospace Recovery Facility (AD) .... NAVAERORECOVF
Naval Aerospace Recovery Facility .... NAVAERORECOVFAC
Naval Aerospace Recovery Facility (DNAB) .... NAVAERO(SP)RECFAC
Naval Aerospace Research Facility .... NARF
Naval Aide .... NAVAIDE
Naval Aide-de-Camp [*British military*] (DMA) .... NADC
Naval Air Advance Training (SAA) .... NAAT
Naval Air Advanced Training Center .... NAVANTRA
Naval Air Advanced Training Command .... NAATC
Naval Air Advanced Training Command .... NAVANTRACOM
Naval Air All Weather Flight Squadron .... NAAWFS
Naval Air Arm [*British*] .... NAA
Naval Air Base .... NAB
Naval Air Base Training Command .... NABTC
Naval Air Basic Training Center .... NABATRA
Naval Air Basic Training Command (DNAB) .... NABTRACOM
Naval Air Center .... NAC
Naval Air Combat Information Office [*or Officer*] .... NACIO
Naval Air Combat Information School .... NACIS
Naval Air Command [*British*] .... NAC
Naval Air Command Instruction (AAGC) .... NavAirInstr
Naval Air Crew Combat Ejection Seat (DWSG) .... NACCES
Naval Air Defense (NATG) .... NAD
Naval Air Depot .... NAD
Naval Air Detachment (MCD) .... NAD
Naval Air Detail .... NAD
Naval Air Development and Material Center .... NADMC
Naval Air Development Center .... NAD
Naval Air Development Center [*Also, NADEVCEN, NAVAIRDEVCEN*] [*Warminster, PA*] .... NADC
Naval Air Development Center [*Marine science*] (OSRA) .... NADC
Naval Air Development Center [*Also, NADC, NAVAIRDEVCEN*] .... NADEVCEN
Naval Air Development Center (AD) .... NaDevCen
Naval Air Development Center [*Also, NADC, NADEVCEN*] (MUGU) .... NAVAIRDEVCEN
Naval Air Development Center - Acoustical Working Group .... NADC-AWG
Naval Air Development Center - Aero Structures Department .... NADC-ST
Naval Air Development Center - Aero-Electronic Technology Department .... NADC-AE
Naval Air Development Center - Aero-Mechanics Department .... NADC-AM
Naval Air Development Center - Aeronautical Computer Laboratory (DNAB) .... NADC-ACL
Naval Air Development Center - Aeronautical Electronic and Electrical Laboratory .... NADC-EL
Naval Air Development Center - Aeronautical Instruments Laboratory .... NADC-AI
Naval Air Development Center - Aeronautical Materials Laboratory (DNAB) .... NADC-AML
Naval Air Development Center - Aeronautical Photographic Experimental Laboratory .... NADC-AP
Naval Air Development Center - Aeronautical Structures Laboratory (DNAB) .... NADC-ASL
Naval Air Development Center - Aerospace Crew Equipment Department .... NADC-AC
Naval Air Development Center - Aerospace Medical Research Department .... NADC-MR
Naval Air Development Center - Air Warfare Research Department .... NADC-AW
Naval Air Development Center - Air Warfare Research Department .... NADC-WR
Naval Air Development Center - Antisubmarine Warfare Laboratory .... NADC-ASW
Naval Air Development Center - Aviation Armament Laboratory .... NADC-AR
Naval Air Development Center - Aviation Medical Acceleration Laboratory .... NADC-ML
Naval Air Development Center - Crew Systems Department .... NADC-CS
Naval Air Development Center - Engineering Development Laboratory .... NADC-ED
Naval Air Development Center - Life Sciences and Bio-Equipment Group .... NADC-LS
Naval Air Development Center - Systems Analysis and Engineering Department .... NADC-SD
Naval Air Development Center - Systems Project Department .... NADC-SY
Naval Air Development Center, Warminster, PA [*OCLC symbol*] (OCLC) .... NAD
Naval Air Development Station .... NADS
Naval Air Development Unit (MUGU) .... NADU
Naval Air Development Unit (MUGU) .... NAVAIRDEVU
Naval Air Division [*British*] .... NAD
Naval Air Effect Model (PDAA) .... NAEM
Naval Air Electronics Shipboard Installation .... NAELSI
Naval Air Emission-Tracking System .... NAETS
Naval Air Engineering Center [*Closed*] .... NAEC
Naval Air Engineering Center [*Closed*] .... NAVAIRENGCEN
Naval Air Engineering Center [*Closed*] .... NAVAIRENGRCEN
Naval Air Engineering Center Aeronautical Engine Laboratory [*Lakehurst, NJ*] .... NAEC-AEL
Naval Air Engineering Center Aeronautical Materials Laboratory [*Lakehurst, NJ*] .... NAEC-AML
Naval Air Engineering Center Aeronautical Structures Laboratory [*Lakehurst, NJ*] .... NAEC-ASL
Naval Air Engineering Center Aerospace Crew Equipment Laboratory [*Lakehurst, NJ*] .... NAEC-ACEL
Naval Air Engineering Center Engineering Department [*Lakehurst, NJ*] .... NAEC-ENG
Naval Air Engineering Center Field Office (DNAB) .... NAECFO
Naval Air Engineering Center Field Office (DNAB) .... NAVAIRENGCENFO
Naval Air Engineering Center Ground Support Equipment Department [*Lakehurst, NJ*] .... NAEC-GSED
Naval Air Engineering Facility (MCD) .... NAEF
Naval Air Engineering Facility (MUGU) .... NAVAIRENGRFAC
Naval Air Engineering Facility Ship Installations Engineering Department [*Philadelphia, PA*] .... NAEF-ENG
Naval Air Engineering Laboratory (MCD) .... NAEL
Naval Air Engineering Laboratory (DNAB) .... NAVAIRENGLAB
Naval Air Engineering Laboratory Ship Installations Engineering Department [*Philadelphia, PA*] .... NAEL-ENG
Naval Air Engineering Support Office [*Norfolk, VA*] .... NESO
Naval Air Experimental Station .... NAES
Naval Air Experimental Station .... NAXSTA
Naval Air Facilities, Atlantic .... NAFLANT
Naval Air Facilities, Pacific .... NAFPAC
Naval Air Facility .... NAF
Naval Air Facility .... NAVAIRFAC
Naval Air Ferry Command [*World War II*] .... NAFC
Naval Air Fighter School .... NAFS
Naval Air Fighting Instructions .... NAFI
Naval Air Force .... NAF
Naval Air Force, Atlantic Fleet .... NAVAIRLANT
Naval Air Force, Pacific Fleet (DNAB) .... NAFP
Naval Air Force, Pacific Fleet .... NAVAIRPAC
Naval Air Forces East Atlantic Area [*NATO*] (NATG) .... AIREASTLANT
Naval Air Forces, Japan (AD) .... NAVFORJAP
Naval Air Forces, Korea (AD) .... NAVFORKOR
Naval Air Ground Center .... NAGCO
Naval Air Gunners School .... NAGS
Naval Air Intelligence Office (MUGU) .... NAVAIRINTO
Naval Air Intelligence Reserve Units .... NAIRU
Naval Air Intercept Training Facility (MUGU) .... NAITF
Naval Air Intermediate Training .... NAIT
Naval Air Intermediate Training (Command) .... NAIT(C)
Naval Air Liaison Officer .... NALO
Naval Air Logistics Command Management Information System for Operating and Support (DNAB) .... NALCOMIS-OS
Naval Air Logistics Control Office .... NALCO
Naval Air Logistics Control Office Atlantic .... NALCOLANT
Naval Air Logistics Control Office Eastern Pacific (DNAB) .... NALCOEASTPAC
Naval Air Logistics Control Office European Representative .... NALCOEURREP
Naval Air Logistics Control Office Pacific .... NALCOPAC
Naval Air Logistics Control Office Pacific Representative .... NALCOPACREP
Naval Air Logistics Control Office Representative .... NALCOREP
Naval Air Logistics Control Office Western Pacific (DNAB) .... NALCOWESTPAC
Naval Air Logistics Control Office Western Pacific Representative (DNAB) .... NALCOWESTPACREP
Naval Air Logistics Office (DOMA) .... NALO
Naval Air Logistics Office (DNAB) .... NAVAIRLOGOFF
Naval Air Logistics Task Force Representative (DNAB) .... NAVAIRLOGTASKFORREP
Naval Air Maintenance Trainer (MUGU) .... NAMT
Naval Air Maintenance Training .... NAMTRA
Naval Air Maintenance Training Detachment (DNAB) .... NAMAINTRADET
Naval Air Maintenance Training Detachment .... NAMTD
Naval Air Maintenance Training Detachment (MCD) .... NAMTRADET
Naval Air Maintenance Training Devices .... NAMTD
Naval Air Maintenance Training Group (DNAB) .... NAMAINTRAGRU
Naval Air Maintenance Training Group (MCD) .... NAMTG
Naval Air Maintenance Training Group (MCD) .... NAMTRAGRU
Naval Air Maintenance Training Group (SAA) .... NAMTRAGRUP
Naval Air Maintenance Training Group (DNAB) .... NAVAIRMAINTRAGRU
Naval Air Maintenance Training Group Detachment (DNAB) .... NAMTGD
Naval Air Maintenance Training Group Detachment (DNAB) .... NAMTRAGRUDET
Naval Air Maintenance Training Type Commander Liaison Office, Fleet (DNAB) .... NAMTRATCLOFLT
Naval Air Maintenance Training Type Commander Liaison Office, Pacific (DNAB) .... NAMTRATCLOPAC
Naval Air Maintenance Training Type Commander Liaison Officer, Atlantic (DNAB) .... NAMTRATCLOLANT
Naval Air Material (SAA) .... NAM
Naval Air Material Center [*Also, NAMC, NAVAIRMATCEN*] .... NAMATCEN
Naval Air Material Center [*Also, NAMATCEN, NAVAIRMATCEN*] .... NAMC
Naval Air Material Center [*Also, NAMATCEN, NAMC*] (MUGU) .... NAVAIRMATCEN
Naval Air Material Center - Aeronautical Engine Laboratory .... NAMC-AEL
Naval Air Material Center - Aeronautical Instruments Laboratory [*Philadelphia, PA*] .... NAMC-AIL
Naval Air Material Center - Aeronautical Materials Laboratory .... NAMC-AML
Naval Air Material Center - Aeronautical Photographic Experimental Laboratory .... NAMC-APEL
Naval Air Material Center - Aeronautical Radio and RADAR Laboratory .... NAMC-ARRL
Naval Air Material Center - Aeronautical Structures Laboratory .... NAMC-ASL

Naval Air Material Command ... NAMATE
Naval Air Materiel Command ... NAMC
Naval Air Mechanic [*British military*] (DMA) ... NAM
Naval Air Mine Defense Development Unit (MUGU) ... NAMDDU
Naval Air Mine Defense Development Unit (MUGU) ... NAVAIRMINDEFDEVU
Naval Air Missile Test Center ... NAMISTESTCEN
Naval Air Missile Test Center ... NAMTC
Naval Air Mobile Training Maintenance ... NAMTM
Naval Air Navigation Facility Advisory Committee ... NANFAC
Naval Air Navigation School ... NANS
Naval Air Operational Training ... NAOT
Naval Air Operational Training Command ... NAOTC
Naval Air Photographic Center (DNAB) ... NAPC
Naval Air Plan (CAAL) ... NAP
Naval Air Primary Training ... NAPT
Naval Air Primary Training Command ... NAPTC
Naval Air Primary Training Command Regional Office ... NAPTCRO
Naval Air Priorities ... NAP
Naval Air Priorities Center (DNAB) ... NAPC
Naval Air Priorities Office ... NAPO
Naval Air Propeller Test Center ... NAVAIRPROPTESTCEN
Naval Air Propulsion Center [*Trenton, NJ*] ... NAPC
Naval Air Propulsion Center (GRD) ... NAVAIRPROPCEN
Naval Air Propulsion Center Measurement and Information Systems Department [*Trenton, NJ*] ... NAPC/MS
Naval Air Propulsion Center Propulsion Engineering Department [*Trenton, NJ*] ... NAPC-PE
Naval Air Propulsion Test Center [*Later, NAPC*] ... NAPTC
Naval Air Propulsion Test Center - Aeronautical Engine Department ... NAPTC-AED
Naval Air Propulsion Test Center - Aeronautical Turbine Department ... NAPTC-ATD
Naval Air Propulsion Test Center - Operations and Plant Engineering Department ... NAPTC-OP
Naval Air Propulsion Test Center - Propulsion Technology and Project EngineeringDepartment ... NAPTC-PE
Naval Air Publication Facility (MCD) ... NAPUBFAC
Naval Air Reconnaissance Technical Support Center ... NAVAIRECONTECHSUPCEN
Naval Air Rescue Service (MUGU) ... NARS
Naval Air Rescue Training Command ... NARSTC
Naval Air Research and Development (MUGU) ... NARAD
Naval Air Research and Development Activities (SAA) ... NARDA
Naval Air Research and Development Activities (MUGU) ... NAVAIRANDACT
Naval Air Research Center (DNAB) ... NARC
Naval Air Research Training Command ... NARTC
Naval Air Reserve ... NAR
Naval Air Reserve ... NAVAIRRES
Naval Air Reserve Center (DNAB) ... NARC
Naval Air Reserve Center (DNAB) ... NAVAIRESCEN
Naval Air Reserve Detachment (DNAB) ... NARDET
Naval Air Reserve Division (Fleet Air) (DNAB) ... NARDIV(FA)
Naval Air Reserve Divisions ... NARDIV
Naval Air Reserve Electronics Training Unit (DNAB) ... NARETU
Naval Air Reserve Force ... NARF
Naval Air Reserve Force Squadron (DNAB) ... NARFS
Naval Air Reserve Force Squadron (DNAB) ... NAVAIRESFORRON
Naval Air Reserve Maintenance Units ... NARMU
Naval Air Reserve Mobile Photographic Unit (DNAB) ... NARMPU
Naval Air Reserve Mobile Photographic Unit (DNAB) ... NAVAIRESMOPIXU
Naval Air Reserve Training Unit ... NARTU
Naval Air Reserve Unit (DNAB) ... NARESU
Naval Air Reserve Unit (NVT) ... NARU
Naval Air Reserve Unit (DNAB) ... NAVAIRESU
Naval Air Rework Facility ... NARF
Naval Air Rework Facility ... NAVAIREWORKF
Naval Air Rework Facility ... NAVAIREWORKFAC
Naval Air Rework Facility (AD) ... NAVAIRREWORKF
Naval Air Rework Facility Field Office (DNAB) ... NARFFO
Naval Air Rocket Test Center (MUGU) ... NARTC
Naval Air Rocket Test Station ... NAROCTESTSTA
Naval Air Rocket Test Station ... NARTS
Naval Air Service ... NAS
Naval Air Signal School ... NASS
Naval Air Software Management Advisory Committee (MCD) ... NASMAC
Naval Air Special Weapons Facility ... NASWF
Naval Air Station ... NAS
Naval Air Station (DNAB) ... NAVAIRSTA
Naval Air Station Annex (DNAB) ... NASANX
Naval Air Station, Bermuda ... NASBERM
Naval Air Station/Command Management Information System (MCD) ... NASCOMIS
Naval Air Station Corpus Christi ... NASCRIST
Naval Air Station Guantanamo ... NASGTMO
Naval Air Station, Imperial Beach (DNAB) ... NASIB
Naval Air Station Jacksonville ... NASJAX
Naval Air Station Lakehurst ... NASLAKE
Naval Air Station North Island ... NASNI
Naval Air Station Pensacola ... NASPENSA
Naval Air Station Quonset Point ... NASQUON
Naval Air Station San Diego ... NASDIEGO
Naval Air Station, Terminal Island (AD) ... NASTI
Naval Air Station Twin Cities (DNAB) ... NASTC
Naval Air [*or Aviation*] **Supply Depot** ... NASD
Naval Air Support Unit ... NAVAIRSUPPU
Naval Air Survivability Program (MCD) ... NASP
Naval Air System Command (DOMA) ... NAVAIR SYSCOM
Naval Air Systems [*Command Headquarters*] [*Marine science*] (OSRA) ... NAVATR
Naval Air Systems Command ... NASC
Naval Air Systems Command (MCD) ... NASCOM
Naval Air Systems Command (AD) ... NASCom
Naval Air Systems Command ... NAVAIR
Naval Air Systems Command (MCD) ... NAVAIRSYSCO
Naval Air Systems Command ... NAVAIRSYSCOM
Naval Air Systems Command ... NW
Naval Air Systems Command Fleet Readiness Representative (DNAB) ... NAVAIRSYSCOMFLEREADREP
Naval Air Systems Command Fleet Supply Representative Center (DNAB) ... NAVAIRSYSCOMFLESUPREPCEN
Naval Air Systems Command Headquarters (AAGC) ... AIR
Naval Air Systems Command Headquarters (USDC) ... NAVAIR
Naval Air Systems Command Headquarters ... NAVAIRSYSCOMHQ
Naval Air Systems Command Instruction ... NAVAIRINST
Naval Air Systems Command Manual ... NA
Naval Air Systems Command, Meteorological Systems Division (DNAB) ... NAVAIRSYSCOMMETSYSDIV
Naval Air Systems Command Representative ... NAVAIRSYSCOMREP
Naval Air Systems Command Representative, Atlantic ... NASCLANT
Naval Air Systems Command Representative, Atlantic ... NASCRL
Naval Air Systems Command Representative, Atlantic ... NAVAIRSYSCOMREPLANT
Naval Air Systems Command Representative, Central ... NASCCEN
Naval Air Systems Command Representative, Central ... NAVAIRSYSCOMREPCENT
Naval Air Systems Command Representative, Naval Air Training Command, Pensacola [*Florida*] ... NASCPNCLA
Naval Air Systems Command Representative, Naval Air Training Command, Pensacola [*Florida*] ... NAVAIRSYSCOMREP PNCLA
Naval Air Systems Command Representative, Pacific ... NASCPAC
Naval Air Systems Command Representative, Pacific ... NAVAIRSYSCOMREPAC
Naval Air Systems Command Representative-Pacific (MCD) ... NASCRP
Naval Air Systems Command Reserve Unit (MCD) ... NASRU
Naval Air Systems Command Target and Range Systems Command (DNAB) ... NAVAIRSYSCOMTARANDSYSDIV
Naval Air Systems Command Technical Representative (DNAB) ... NAVAIRTECHREP
Naval Air Systems Command, Washington, DC [*OCLC symbol*] (OCLC) ... NAS
Naval Air Systems Effectiveness Advisory Board ... NASEAB
Naval Air Tactical Data System (MCD) ... NATDS
Naval Air Technical Evaluation Center (IAA) ... NATEC
Naval Air Technical Services Facility (MUGU) ... NAT
Naval Air Technical Services Facility (MCD) ... NATSF
Naval Air Technical Services Facility (MUGU) ... NAVAIRTECHSERVFAC
Naval Air Technical Services Facility, Quality Assurance Division, Atlantic (DNAB) ... NATSFQADIVLANT
Naval Air Technical Services Facility, Quality Assurance Division, Pacific (DNAB) ... NATSFQADIVPAC
Naval Air Technical Services Unit (NVT) ... NATSU
Naval Air Technical Training (DNAB) ... NATECHTRA
Naval Air Technical Training ... NATT
Naval Air Technical Training Center ... NATECHTRACEN
Naval Air Technical Training Center ... NATTC
Naval Air Technical Training Center ... NAVTECHTRACEN
Naval Air Technical Training Center Detachment (DNAB) ... NATTCDET
Naval Air Technical Training Center, Lakehurst (DNAB) ... NATTCL
Naval Air Technical Training Unit ... NATECHTRAU
Naval Air Technical Training Unit ... NATTU
Naval Air Terminal ... NAT
Naval Air Terminal (DNAB) ... NAVAIRTERM
Naval Air Test Center ... NATC
Naval Air Test Center ... NATESTCEN
Naval Air Test Center (MUGU) ... NAVAIRTESTCEN
Naval Air Test Center (GRD) ... NAVAIRTESTCENT
Naval Air Test Facility ... NATF
Naval Air Test Facility (MUGU) ... NAVAIRTESTFAC
Naval Air Test Facility - Ship Installations ... NATF-SI
Naval Air Test Facility - Ship Installations (DNAB) ... NAVAIRTESTFACSHIPINSTAL
Naval Air Test Station (AD) ... NATS
Naval Air Training ... NAT
Naval Air Training and Experimental Command ... NATEC
Naval Air Training and Operating Procedures Standardization (MCD) ... NATOPS
Naval Air Training Base ... NATB
Naval Air Training Bases ... NATBASES
Naval Air Training Center ... NATC
Naval Air Training Center ... NAVAIRTRACEN
Naval Air Training Command (CAAL) ... NATC
Naval Air Training Command (AFIT) ... NATRA
Naval Air Training Command (DNAB) ... NATRACOM
Naval Air Training Division Engineering Command (DNAB) ... NATDEC
Naval Air Training Division Engineering Command (DNAB) ... NATRADIVENGCOM
Naval Air Training Information System ... NATIS
Naval Air Training Support Facility (AAGC) ... NATMSACT
Naval Air Training Unit (DNAB) ... NAVAIRTU
Naval Air Transport Service ... NATS
Naval Air Transport Service, Atlantic Wing [*World War II*] ... NATSLANT
Naval Air Transport Service, Ferry Command [*World War II*] ... NATSFERRY
Naval Air Transport Service, Pacific Wing [*World War II*] ... NATSPAC
Naval Air Transport Wing, Pacific ... NATWP
Naval Air Turbine Test Station ... NATTS
Naval Air Turbine Test Station ... NATURBTESTSTA
Naval Air Turbine Test Station (MUGU) ... NAVAIRTURBTESTSTA
Naval Air Turbine Test Station - Aeronautical Turbine Laboratory ... NATTS-ATL

Naval Air Warfare Center (DOMA)	NAWC
Naval Air Warfare Center Weapons Division	NAWCWPNS
Naval Air Weapons Meet (MUGU)	NAWM
Naval Air Weapons Station	NAWS
Naval Airborne Project Press Operations Group [Hickam AFB, HI]	NAPOG
Naval Aircraft	NA
Naval Aircraft Delivery Unit	NADU
Naval Aircraft Establishment (AD)	NAE
Naval Aircraft Factory	NAF
Naval Aircraft Inventory Log (AD)	NAIL
Naval Aircraft Investigation Center (AD)	NAIC
Naval Aircraft Maintenance Orders	NAMO
Naval Aircraft Material Utility	NAMU
Naval Aircraft Materials Laboratory (MCD)	NAML
Naval Aircraft Mobile Trainer	NAMT
Naval Aircraft Modification	NAM
Naval Aircraft Modification Unit	NAMU
Naval Aircraft Restorers Association (EA)	NARA
Naval Aircraft Safety Activity (SAA)	NASA
Naval Aircraft Standards Committee (AFIT)	NASC
Naval Aircraft Torpedo Unit	NATU
Naval Aircraft Torpedo Unit (MUGU)	NAVAIRTORPU
Naval Aircraftman [British]	NAC
Naval Airman [Navy rating British]	NA
Naval Airplane Pusher [Slang] (DNAB)	NAP
Naval Airship Association (EA)	NAA
Naval Airship Program for Sizing and Performance (MCD)	NAPSAP
Naval Airship Training and Experimentation Command	NATECOM
Naval Alcohol Rehabilitation Center (DNAB)	NARC
Naval Alcohol Rehabilitation Center (DNAB)	NAVALREHCEN
Naval All Weather Testing Program Detachment	NAWTPD
Naval Ammunition and Net Depot	NAND
Naval Ammunition Depot [Charleston, SC]	NAD
Naval Ammunition Depot [Charleston, SC]	NAMD
Naval Ammunition Depot [Charleston, SC]	NAVAMDEP
Naval Ammunition Depot, Concord [California]	NADC
Naval Ammunition Depot, Concord [California]	NAD-CO
Naval Ammunition Depot, Crane [Indiana]	NAD-CR
Naval Ammunition Depot, Hawaii	NADH
Naval Ammunition Depot Hawthorne Police Records System (DNAB)	NADHPRS
Naval Ammunition Depot, Indiana	NADI
Naval Ammunition Depot - Lwalualei [Hawaii] (DNAB)	NAD-LLL
Naval Ammunition Production Engineering Center	NAPEC
Naval Ammunition Production Engineering Center (DNAB)	NAVAMPROENGCEN
Naval Amphibious Base	NAB
Naval Amphibious Base	NAMB
Naval Amphibious Base (MUGU)	NAVPHIBASE
Naval Amphibious Base Annex	NABA
Naval Amphibious Base Atlantic	NAVPHIBASELANT
Naval Amphibious School (NVT)	NAVPHIBSCOL
Naval Amyloid Component [Medicine]	NAC
Naval Analysis Group (MCD)	NAG
Naval and Maritime Air Communications-Electronics Conference [NATO]	NAVMAIRCOMCON
Naval and Mechanical Co. (AD)	NAMCO
Naval and Military Order of the Spanish-American War (EA)	NMOSAW
Naval Anthropomorphic Teleoperater (DNAB)	NAT
Naval Applications Group	NAG
Naval Applied Science Laboratory	NASL
Naval Applied Science Laboratory (DNAB)	NAVAPSCIENCLAB
Naval Architect	NA
Naval Architect [Academic degree]	Nav Arch
Naval Arctic Research Laboratory	NARL
Naval Area Audit Service	NAAS
Naval Area Audit Service	NAVAREAAUDSVC
Naval Armament Depot [British]	NAD
Naval Armament Depot	NAVARMDEP
Naval Armaments Stores System (PDAA)	NASS
Naval Armed Guard Center	NAGC
Naval Artillery Volunteers [British] (ROG)	NAV
Naval Assistant [Navy rating British]	NA
Naval Assistant to the First Sea Lord [British military] (DMA)	NA 1SL
Naval Assistant to the Military Aide to the President of the United States	NAMAPUS
Naval ASW [Antisubmarine Warfare] Data Center (NVT)	NADAC
Naval Atomic Planning, Support, and Capabilities Report (NG)	NAPSAC
Naval Attache [Canadian Navy]	CANAVAT
Naval Attache (AD)	N Att
Naval Attache (WDAA)	N ATT
Naval Attache [Diplomacy]	NA
Naval Attache for Air	NAA
Naval Audio-Visual Center (DNAB)	NAVAVCEN
Naval Audit Office (DNAB)	NAO
Naval Audit Service (DOMA)	NAS
Naval Audit Service, Capital Area (DNAB)	NAVAUDSVCAP
Naval Audit Service Headquarters (DNAB)	NAVAUDSVCHQ
Naval Audit Service, Northeast Area (DNAB)	NAVAUDSVCNE
Naval Audit Service, Southeast Area (DNAB)	NAVAUDSVCSE
Naval Audit Service, Western Area (DNAB)	NAVAUDSVCWEST
Naval Authority	NAVAUTH
Naval Autonomous Information System-Frigate (DOMA)	NAUTIS-F
Naval Autonomous Intelligent Console (PDAA)	NAUTIC
Naval Auxiliary	NA
Naval Auxiliary Air Facility	NAAF

Naval Auxiliary Air Station	NAAS
Naval Auxiliary Landing Field (NG)	NALF
Naval Auxiliary Patrol [British military] (DMA)	NAP
Naval Auxiliary Reserve	NAR
Naval Aviation [USSR designation]	AVMS
Naval Aviation Cadet	NAVC
Naval Aviation Cadet	NAVCAD
Naval Aviation Cadet Act of 1942	NACA
Naval Aviation Cadet Selection Board	NACSB
Naval Aviation Depot (AAGC)	NAD
Naval Aviation Depot (MCD)	NADEP
Naval Aviation Depot Operations Center (DOMA)	NADOC
Naval Aviation Electronic Service Unit (MCD)	NAESU
Naval Aviation Engineering Service Unit [Philadelphia, PA]	NAESU
Naval Aviation Engineering Service Unit [Philadelphia, PA] (DNAB)	NAVAVNENGRSERVU
Naval Aviation Engineering Service Unit Detachment (DNAB)	NAESUDET
Naval Aviation Engineering Service Unit Detachment (DNAB)	NAVAVENGSERVUDET
Naval Aviation Engineering Services Unit [Philadelphia, PA] (DNAB)	NAVAVENGSERVU
Naval Aviation Evaluation Board	NAEB
Naval Aviation Integrated Logistic Support Center (MCD)	NAILSC
Naval Aviation Integrated Logistic Support Task Force (NG)	NAILS
Naval Aviation Logistics Center (NVT)	NALC
Naval Aviation Logistics Center (NVT)	NAVAVNLOGCEN
Naval Aviation Logistics Center Detachment (DNAB)	NAVAVNLOGCENDET
Naval Aviation Logistics Center Field Service Office (DNAB)	NAVAVNLOGCENFSO
Naval Aviation Logistics Center Meteorology Calibration Laboratory Operations (DNAB)	NAVAVNLOGCENMETALABOPS
Naval Aviation Logistics Command Management Information System (MCD)	NALCOMIS
Naval Aviation Logistics Data Analysis (NVT)	NALDA
Naval Aviation Maintenance Discrepancy Reporting Program (DNAB)	NAMDRP
Naval Aviation Maintenance Program (MCD)	NAMP
Naval Aviation Medical Center (DNAB)	NAMEDCEN
Naval Aviation Medical Center (DNAB)	NAVAVMEDCEN
Naval Aviation Medical Center (DNAB)	NAVAVNMEDCEN
Naval Aviation Museum [Pensacola, FL]	NAM
Naval Aviation Museum [Pensacola, FL] (DNAB)	NAVAVMUSEUM
Naval Aviation Museum Foundation (DNAB)	NAMF
Naval Aviation News	NANEWS
Naval Aviation News [A publication] (DNAB)	NAVAIRNEWS
Naval Aviation News	NAVN
Naval Aviation Observer [Obsolete]	NAO
Naval Aviation Observer Aerology (SAA)	NAOA
Naval Aviation Observer Bombardier (MUGU)	NAOB
Naval Aviation Observer Controller (MUGU)	NAOC
Naval Aviation Observer Intercept (MUGU)	NAOI
Naval Aviation Observer Navigator (MUGU)	NAON
Naval Aviation Observer RADAR (MUGU)	NAOR
Naval Aviation Observer Tactical (SAA)	NAOT
Naval Aviation Officer Candidate	NAOC
Naval Aviation Ordnance Test Station	NAORTS
Naval Aviation Ordnance Test Station	NAOTS
Naval Aviation Pilot	NAP
Naval Aviation Pilot (AD)	nap
Naval Aviation Pilot (Glider)	NAP(G)
Naval Aviation Plan (NVT)	NAP
Naval Aviation Preparatory Program	NAPP
Naval Aviation Publication Facility	NAPF
Naval Aviation Safety Center	AVNSAFCEN
Naval Aviation Safety Center	NAVAVNSAFECEN
Naval Aviation School Command	AVNSCOLCOM
Naval Aviation School Command	NAVAVNSCOLCOM
Naval Aviation School of Medicine	NASM
Naval Aviation Supply Depot (AD)	NASD
Naval Aviation Supply Distribution System (AFIT)	NASDS
Naval Aviation Supply Office	NASO
Naval Aviation Weapons Facilities	NAVAVNWEPSFAC
Naval Aviation Weapons Facilities (DNAB)	NAVAVNWPNSFAC
Naval Aviation Weapons Facility Detachment (DNAB)	NAVAVNWPNSFACDET
Naval Aviation Weapons Maintenance Program (MCD)	NAWMP
Naval Aviator	NA
Naval Aviator/Flight Surgeon (MCD)	NA/FS
Naval Aviator/Naval Flight Officer Reporting Management System (DNAB)	NANFORMS
Naval Aviators Must Energetically Sell Aviation to Keep Effective Strength	NAMESAKES
Naval Aviators' Speech Discrimination Test	NASDT
Naval Avionics Center (MCD)	NAC
Naval Avionics Center (DNAB)	NAVAVIONICSCEN
Naval Avionics Facility [Later, NAC] [Indianapolis, IN]	NAF
Naval Avionics Facility (AD)	NAFI
Naval Avionics Facility [Later, NAC] (MUGU)	NAVAVIONICFAC
Naval Avionics Facility [Later, NAC] (AFIT)	NAVF
Naval Avionics Facility, Indianapolis [Later, NAC]	NAFI
Naval Avionics Support Equipment Appraisal (NG)	NAVSEA
Naval Ballistic Missile (AD)	navbm
Naval Base (AD)	Nav Bs
Naval Base	NAVBASE
Naval Base	NB
Naval Base Consolidated Fire Department (DNAB)	NBCFD

Naval Bases Air Defense ... NBAD
Naval Bases Atlantic ... NAVBASELANT
Naval Bases Pacific ... NAVBASEPAC
Naval Basic Instrument Trainer (PDAA) ... NAVBIT
Naval Beach Group (DNAB) ... NAVBCHGRU
Naval Beach Group (CINC) ... NAVBEACHGRU
Naval Beach Group (NVT) ... NBG
Naval Beach Signal Section ... NBSS
Naval Biodynamics Laboratory (DNAB) ... NAVBIODYNLAB
Naval Biodynamics Laboratory (GRD) ... NBDL
Naval Biological Laboratory (MUGU) ... NAVBIOLAB
Naval Biomedical Research Laboratory ... NBRL
Naval Biosciences Laboratory [*Research center*] ... NBL
Naval Biosciences Research Laboratory (DNAB) ... NAVBIOSCILAB
Naval Blood Research Laboratory [*Bureau of Medicine*] ... NBRL
Naval Boiler and Turbine Laboratory ... NBTL
Naval Bronze (AD) ... nav brz
Naval Bureau of Weapons Reserve Ordnance Plant ... NBWROP
Naval Cadet (AD) ... NavCad
Naval Cadet [*British*] (ROG) ... NC
Naval Campus for Achievement (NVT) ... NCFA
Naval Campus for Achievement Program (MCD) ... NCFAP
Naval Canteen Service [*British military*] (DMA) ... NCS
Naval Capabilities Plan ... NCP
Naval Career Appraisal Team (MUGU) ... NAVCAT
Naval Cargo Handling Battalion ... NAVCARGOHANBN
Naval Center for Cost Analysis ... NCA
Naval Central Torpedo Office ... NCTO
Naval Civil Affairs Officer [*World War II*] ... NCAO
Naval Civil Affairs Staging Area ... NCASA
Naval Civil Engineer Corps Officers School (DNAB) ... NAVSCOLCEOFF
Naval Civil Engineering Laboratory ... NAVCIVENGRLAB
Naval Civil Engineering Laboratory ... NCEL
Naval Civilian Administrators Association [*Later, NCMA*] (EA) ... NCAA
Naval Civilian Manager's Association (EA) ... NCMA
Naval Civilian Personnel Command Instructions (MCD) ... NCPCINST
Naval Clothing Depot ... NAVCLODEP
Naval Coastal Systems Center [*Panama City, FL*] (DNAB) ... NAVCOASTSYSCEN
Naval Coastal Systems Center [*Panama City, FL*] ... NCSC
Naval Coastal Systems Center [*Florida*] ... NSC
Naval Coastal Systems Laboratory [*Later, NCSC*] ... NCSL
Naval Code and Signal Laboratory ... NCSL
Naval College Aptitude Test (NVT) ... NCAT
Naval Combat Air Patrol (DNAB) ... NCAP
Naval Combat Data System ... NCDS
Naval Combat Demolition Training and Experimental Base [*Maui, HI*] (KSC) ... NCDT & E
Naval Combat Demolition Training and Experimental Base [*Maui, HI*] ... NCDT & EBASE
Naval Combat Demolition Unit ... NCDU
Naval Command Assistant ... NCA
Naval Command College (DOMA) ... NCC
Naval Command, Control, and Ocean Surveillance Center [*Formerly, NOSC and other activities*] (DOMA) ... NCCOSC
Naval Command, Control Communications Center (IAA) ... NCCCC
Naval Command Control Communications Laboratory Center ... NCCCLC
Naval Command Control Communications Laboratory Center ... NEL
Naval Command Systems Support Activity (DNAB) ... NAVCOMSYSSUPPACT
Naval Command Systems Support Activity ... NAVCOSSACT
Naval Command Systems Support Activity ... NCSSA
Naval Command Systems Support Center (DNAB) ... NAVCOMSYSSUPPCEN
Naval Command Systems Support Center (DNAB) ... NAVCOSSCEN
Naval Command Systems Support Center ... NCSSC
Naval Commander Western Task Force ... NCWTF
Naval Commercial Traffic Regulations ... NCTR
Naval Communication Area Local Station (NVT) ... NAVCALS
Naval Communication Area Master Station (NVT) ... NAVCAMS
Naval Communication Area Master Station, Atlantic (DNAB) ... NAVCAMSLANT
Naval Communication Area Master Station, Eastern Pacific (DNAB) ... NAVCAMSEASTPAC
Naval Communication Area Master Station, Mediterranean (DNAB) ... NAVCAMSMED
Naval Communication Area Master Station, South America (DNAB) ... NAVCAMSOAM
Naval Communication Area Master Station, Special Communications Division, Atlantic (DNAB) ... NAVCAMSSPECCOMDIVLANT
Naval Communication Liaison Officer (IAA) ... NCLO
Naval Communication Station ... NAVCOMMSTA
Naval Communication Station Detachment (DNAB) ... NAVCOMMDET
Naval Communication Station Detachment, Special Communications Division (DNAB) ... NAVCOMMDETSPECCOMMDIV
Naval Communication Station, Japan ... NCSJ
Naval Communication Station, Philippines (DNAB) ... NCSP
Naval Communication Station, Special Communications Division (DNAB) ... NAVCOMMSTASPECCOMMDIV
Naval Communication System (MUGU) ... NAVCOMMSYS
Naval Communication Unit ... NAVCOMMU
Naval Communications [*System*] ... NAVCOM
Naval Communications [*System*] ... NAVCOMM
Naval Communications Annex ... NCA
Naval Communications Area (NVT) ... NAVCOMMAREA
Naval Communications Board ... NCB
Naval Communications Center (MCD) ... NAVCC
Naval Communications Command ... NAVCOMCOM
Naval Communications Command ... NAVCOMMCOM
Naval Communications Command ... NCOMM
Naval Communications Command Management Information System (MCD) ... NAVCOMMIS
Naval Communications Facility (NVT) ... NAVCOMMFAC
Naval Communications Facility (MUGU) ... NCF
Naval Communications Headquarters (DNAB) ... NAVCOMMHQ
Naval Communications Improvement Review Board (DNAB) ... MCRIB
Naval Communications Improvement Review Board (DNAB) ... NCRIB
Naval Communications Operation Network (DNAB) ... NAVCOMMOPNET
Naval Communications Processing and Routing System (MCD) ... NAVCOMPARS
Naval Communications Station [*or System*] ... NCS
Naval Communications System Headquarters Activity (SAA) ... NCSHA
Naval Communications System Support Activity (DNAB) ... NAVCOMMSYSSUPPACT
Naval Communications Training Center (MUGU) ... NAVCOMMTRACEN
Naval Communications Training Center ... NCTC
Naval Communications Unit ... NAVCOMU
Naval Communications Unit (IAA) ... NCU
Naval Communications Unit, Naval Reserve (IAA) ... NAVCOMMUNR
Naval Compass Stabilizer (PDAA) ... NCS
Naval Component Command (CINC) ... NCC
Naval Comptroller Financial Management Service ... NCFMS
Naval Comptroller Manual ... NAVCOMPTMAN
Naval Computer and Telecommunications Area Master Station (DOMA) ... NCTAMS
Naval Computer and Telecommunications Command (DOMA) ... NCTC
Naval Construction Action Team [*Vietnam*] (VNW) ... NAVCAT
Naval Construction Battalion ... NCB
Naval Construction Battalion Center ... NAVCBCEN
Naval Construction Battalion Center ... NCBC
Naval Construction Force (NVT) ... NCF
Naval Construction Force Support Unit (NVT) ... NCFSU
Naval Construction Regiment (DNAB) ... NAVCONSTREGT
Naval Construction Regiment (NVT) ... NCR
Naval Construction Research Establishment [*British*] (AAG) ... NCRE
Naval Construction Training Center (DNAB) ... NAVCONSTRACEN
Naval Construction Training Center ... NAVCONTRACEN
Naval Construction Training Center ... NCTC
Naval Construction Training Unit (DNAB) ... NAVCONSTRAU
Naval Constructor [*Academic degree*] ... Nav Const
Naval Contract Distribution Center ... NCDC
Naval Control and Protection of Shipping (NVT) ... NCAPS
Naval Control of Shipping [*NATO*] (NATG) ... NCS
Naval Control of Shipping Exercises ... NCSEX
Naval Control of Shipping in Northern European Command Area [*NATO*] (NATG) ... NCSNE
Naval Control of Shipping Liaison Officer ... NCSLO
Naval Control of Shipping Officer ... NCSO
Naval Control of Shipping Operations ... NCSO
Naval Control of Shipping Organization ... NCSORG
Naval Control Service Office [*World War II British Routing Service*] ... NCSO
Naval Convalescent Hospital ... NAVCONVHOSP
Naval Correspondence ... NC
Naval Correspondence Course Center (DNAB) ... NAVCORCOURSECEN
Naval Cost Inspector ... NCI
Naval Counterintelligence Support Center ... NCISC
Naval Countermeasures (CINC) ... NAVCON
Naval Courier Service ... NAVCURSERV
Naval Courier Service Detachment (DNAB) ... NAVCURSERVDET
Naval Courier Service Headquarters ... NAVCURSERVHQ
Naval Courts and Boards ... NC & B
Naval Current Support Group, Atlantic Fleet (DNAB) ... NAVCURRSUPPGRULANTFLT
Naval Current Support Group, Naval Forces, Europe (DNAB) ... NAVCURRSUPPGRUNAVEUR
Naval Current Support Group, Pacific Fleet (DNAB) ... NAVCURRSUPPGRUPACFLT
Naval Dairy Farm ... NDF
Naval Data Automation Command (MCD) ... NAVDAC
Naval Data Center (DNAB) ... NAVDATACEN
Naval Data Center ... NDC
Naval Defence Force [*British military*] (DMA) ... NDF
Naval Defense Acquisition Regulations (MCD) ... NAVDAR
Naval Defense Forces, Eastern Pacific (DNAB) ... NAVDEFEASTPAC
Naval Degaussing Station, Atlantic/Pacific ... NAVDEGSTALANT/PAC
Naval Dental Center ... NAVDENCEN
Naval Dental Clinic ... NAVDENCLINIC
Naval Dental Clinic ... NDC
Naval Dental Research Institute ... NDRI
Naval Dental School ... NAVDENSCOL
Naval Dental School ... NDS
Naval Dental Technicians School ... NAVDENTECHSCOL
Naval Deputy [*NATO*] (NATG) ... DEPNAV
Naval Deputy [*NATO*] (AD) ... Nav Dep
Naval Deputy [*NATO*] (NATG) ... NAVDEP
Naval Deputy National Oceanic and Atmospheric Administration (DNAB) ... NAVDEPNOAA
Naval Deputy to Commander-in-Chief, Allied Forces, Central Europe [*NATO*] (NATG) ... NAVDEPCENT
Naval Despatch Boat Service ... NDBS
Naval Destroyer School (NVT) ... NAVDESCOL
Naval Destroyer School ... NAVDESSCOL
Naval Detachment ... NAVDET
Naval Device Training Center ... NDTC
Naval Disciplinary Barracks ... NAVDISCBAR
Naval Disciplinary Barracks ... NDB

Naval Discipline Act [British military] (DMA) .... NDA
Naval Dispensary .... NAVDISP
Naval Dispensary .... ND
Naval Distillate Fuel (NVT) .... ND
Naval District .... NAVDIS
Naval District .... NAVDIST
Naval District .... ND
Naval District Affairs and Logistics Branch .... NDA & LB
Naval District Washington .... NDW
Naval Diving and Salvage Training Center (DNAB) .... NAVDIVSALVTRACEN
Naval Diving and Salvage Training Center (DNAB) .... NDSTC
Naval Doctrine Publication (DOMA) .... NDP
Naval Draftsman (ROG) .... ND
Naval Drug Rehabilitation Center (DNAB) .... NAVDRUGREHCEN
Naval Dry Dock and Repair Facility .... NDD & RF
Naval Eastern Oceanography Center (DNAB) .... NAVEASTOCEANCEN
Naval Education and Training Center [or Command] (DNAB) .... NAVEDTRACOM
Naval Education and Training Center [or Command] (NVT) .... NETC
Naval Education and Training Command (MCD) .... NAVEDTRA
Naval Education and Training Command (MCD) .... NEDTRA
Naval Education and Training Financial Information Processing Branch (DNAB) .... NETFIPCBR
Naval Education and Training Financial Management System (DNAB) .... NETFMS
Naval Education and Training Information Systems Activity (DNAB) .... NETISA
Naval Education and Training Management Information System (MCD) .... NETMIS
Naval Education and Training Program Development Center [Pensacola, FL] .... NAVEDTRA
Naval Education and Training Program Development Center [Pensacola, FL] (DNAB) .... NAVEDTRAPRODEVCEN
Naval Education and Training Program Development Center [Pensacola, FL] (DNAB) .... NETPDC
Naval Education and Training Program Development Center Coordination Division (DNAB) .... NAVEDTRAPRODEVCENCODIV
Naval Education and Training Program Development Center Detachment (DNAB) .... NAVEDTRAPRODEVCENDET
Naval Education and Training Support Center (DNAB) .... NAVEDTRASUPPCEN
Naval Education and Training Support Center (DNAB) .... NETSC
Naval Education and Training Support Center, Atlantic (DNAB) .... NAVEDTRASUPPCENLANT
Naval Education and Training Support Center, Atlantic (DNAB) .... NETSCL
Naval Education and Training Support Center, Pacific (DNAB) .... NAVEDTRASUPPCENPAC
Naval Education and Training Support Center, Pacific (DNAB) .... NETSCP
Naval Education and Training Support Center, Pacific, Navy Campus for Achievement (DNAB) .... NAVEDTRASUPPCENPACNCFA
Naval Electrical Department [British military] (DMA) .... NLD
Naval Electronic Sensor Operator [Canadian Navy] .... NESO
Naval Electronic Systems Command (SAA) .... NAVELECS
Naval Electronic Systems Command Activities (DNAB) .... NAVELEXACTS
Naval Electronic Systems Command Center Detachment (DNAB) .... NAVELEXSYSCOMCENDET
Naval Electronic Systems Command Detachment (DNAB) .... NAVELEXDET
Naval Electronic Systems Command Division (DNAB) .... NAVELEXSYSCOMDIV
Naval Electronic Systems Command Headquarters (USDC) .... NAVELEX
Naval Electronic Systems Command, Midwest Division (DNAB) .... NAVELEXSYSCOMMIDWESTDIV
Naval Electronic Systems Command, Site Representative (DNAB) .... NAVELEXSITEREP
Naval Electronic Systems Command, Southeast Division (DNAB) .... NAVELEXSYSCOMSEDIV
Naval Electronic Systems Command Technical Representative (DNAB) .... NAVELEXTECHREP
Naval Electronic Systems Command Technician Liaison Representative (DNAB) .... NAVELXSYSCOMTECHLREP
Naval Electronic Systems Command Training and Publications Management Office (DNAB) .... NAVELEXSYSTRAPUBMO
Naval Electronic Systems Engineering Activity .... NESEA
Naval Electronic Systems Test and Evaluation Detachment .... NESTED
Naval Electronic Systems Test and Evaluation Facility .... NESTEF
Naval Electronic Warfare Operator Trainer (MCD) .... NEWOT
Naval Electronic Warfare Simulator .... NEWS
Naval Electronic Warfare Training System .... NEWTS
Naval Electronics Engineering Office (DNAB) .... NAVELEXENGOFF
Naval Electronics Environmental Training System (MCD) .... NEETS
Naval Electronics Laboratory .... NEL
Naval Electronics Laboratory Automatic Tester System (DNAB) .... NELATS
Naval Electronics Laboratory Center [Later, NOSC] .... NELC
Naval Electronics Laboratory International ALGOL Compilers .... NELIAC
Naval Electronics System Command (IAA) .... NAVELEC
Naval Electronics Systems Command .... NAVELECSYSCOM
Naval Electronics Systems Command .... NAVELEX
Naval Electronics Systems Command .... NESC
Naval Electronics Systems Command, Central Atlantic Division .... NAVELECSYSCOMCENLANTDIV
Naval Electronics Systems Command Headquarters .... NAVELECSYSCOMHQ
Naval Electronics Systems Command Headquarters .... NAVSEEC
Naval Electronics Systems Command Headquarters .... NELEX
Naval Electronics Systems Command Instruction .... NAVELEXINST
Naval Electronics Systems Command, Northeast Division .... NAVELECSYSCOMNEDIV
Naval Electronics Systems Command, Southeast Division .... NAVELECSYSCOMSEDIV
Naval Electronics Systems Command, Western Division .... NAVELECSYSCOMWESTDIV

Naval Electronics Systems Command, Western Division, Mare Island, Vallejo, California .... WESTNAVELEX
Naval Electronics Systems Engineering Center (MCD) .... NESEC
Naval Electronics Systems Security Engineering Center (MCD) .... NESSEC
Naval Electronics Systems Test and Evaluation (IAA) .... NESTEV
Naval Emergency Air Cargo Delivery System (CAAL) .... NEACDS
Naval Emergency Fund [A budget category] .... NEF
Naval Emergency Monitoring Teams (PDAA) .... NEMT
Naval Energy and Environmental Support Activity .... NEESA
Naval Engineer [Academic degree] .... Nav E
Naval Engineer (PGP) .... Naval E
Naval Engineer [Academic degree] .... NE
Naval Engineering Experiment Station .... NAVENGRXSTA
Naval Engineering Experiment Station .... NEES
Naval Engineering Service Office (MCD) .... NESO
Naval Engineering Test Establishment [Canadian Armed Forces] (PDAA) .... NETE
Naval Enlisted Reserve Association (EA) .... NERA
Naval Environmental Bulletin Board System .... NEBBS
Naval Environmental Compliance Information System .... NECIS
Naval Environmental Data Network .... NEDN
Naval Environmental Data System (CAAL) .... NEDS
Naval Environmental Display Station (CAAL) .... NEDS
Naval Environmental Prediction Research Facility [Marine science] (MSC) .... ENVPREDRSCHFAC
Naval Environmental Prediction Research Facility (MCD) .... NAVENVPREDRSCHFAC
Naval Environmental Prediction Research Facility .... NEPRF
Naval Environmental Support Office [Marine science] (MSC) .... NESCO
Naval Equerry to the King .... NEK
Naval Equipment Department [British military] (DMA) .... NED
Naval European Research Contract Program (NG) .... NERCP
Naval Examination Service [British military] (DMA) .... NES
Naval Examining Board .... NAVEXAM
Naval Examining Board (DNAB) .... NAVEXAMBD
Naval Examining Center .... NEC
Naval Examining Center Advancement Authorization List (DNAB) .... NAVEXAMCENADVAUTHLIST
Naval Exercise Coordinator (CINC) .... NEC
Naval Exhibit Center .... NAVEXHIBCEN
Naval Exhibit Center .... NEC
Naval Experimental Diving Unit .... XDIVU
Naval Experimental Manned Observatory .... NEMO
Naval Experimental Satellite Terminal (IEEE) .... NEST
Naval Experimenting Station .... NES
Naval Explosive Development Engineering Department (DNAB) .... NEDED
Naval Explosive Laboratory .... NEL
Naval Explosive Ordnance Disposal Association .... NEODA
Naval Explosive Ordnance Disposal Facility .... NAVEODFAC
Naval Explosive Ordnance Disposal Facility .... NEODF
Naval Explosive Ordnance Disposal Technology Center [Indian Head, MD] .... NAVEODTECHCE
Naval Explosive Ordnance Disposal Technology Center [Indian Head, MD] (DNAB) .... NAVEODTECHCEN
Naval Explosive Ordnance Disposal Technology Center [Indian Head, MD] (DNAB) .... NEODTC
Naval Explosive Safety Improvement Program .... NESIP
Naval Explosive Safety Improvement Program / Plan of Action and Milestones (DNAB) .... NESIP/POA & M
Naval Facilites (AD) .... NAVFEC
Naval Facilities Atlantic/Pacific .... NAVFACLANT/PAC
Naval Facilities Engineering Comamnd, Southern Division (DNAB) .... NAVFACSODIV
Naval Facilities Engineering Command [Formerly, Bureau of Yards and Docks] .... NAVFAC
Naval Facilities Engineering Command (CAAL) .... NAVFACENG
Naval Facilities Engineering Command [Formerly, Bureau of Yards and Docks] .... NAVFACENGCOM
Naval Facilities Engineering Command [Formerly, Bureau of Yards and Docks] .... NAVFEC
Naval Facilities Engineering Command (AD) .... NAVFECENGCOM
Naval Facilities Engineering Command (PDAA) .... NAVFECO
Naval Facilities Engineering Command [Formerly, Bureau of Yards and Docks] (IEEE) .... NFEC
Naval Facilities Engineering Command, Alexandria, VA [OCLC symbol] (OCLC) .... NFE
Naval Facilities Engineering Command, Atlantic Division (DNAB) .... NAVFACENGCOMLANTDIV
Naval Facilities Engineering Command, Atlantic Division (DNAB) .... NAVFACLANTDIV
Naval Facilities Engineering Command, Chesapeake Division (DNAB) .... NAVFACCHESDIV
Naval Facilities Engineering Command, Chesapeake Division (DNAB) .... NAVFACENGCOMCHESDIV
Naval Facilities Engineering Command Contracting Manual [A publication] (AAGC) .... NAVFAC P-68
Naval Facilities Engineering Command Contractor (DNAB) .... NAVFACENGCOMCONTR
Naval Facilities Engineering Command Design Manuals .... NAVFACDM
Naval Facilities Engineering Command Headquarters (AAGC) .... FAC
Naval Facilities Engineering Command Headquarters (USDC) .... NAVFAC
Naval Facilities Engineering Command Headquarters .... NAVFACENGCOMHQ
Naval Facilities Engineering Command Headquarters .... NFAC
Naval Facilities Engineering Command Instructions .... NAVFACINST
Naval Facilities Engineering Command, Northern Division (DNAB) .... NAVFACENGCOMNORDIV

Naval Facilities Engineering Command, Northern Division (DNAB) .... NAVFACNORDIV

Naval Facilities Engineering Command, Pacific Division (DNAB) .... NAVFACENGCOMPACDIV

Naval Facilities Engineering Command Publications .... NAVFACP

Naval Facilities Engineering Command, Southern Division (DNAB) .... NAVFACENGCOMSODIV

Naval Facilities Engineering Command Technical Publications - Administration .... NAVFAC-TP-AD

Naval Facilities Engineering Command Technical Publications - Maintenance Operation .... NAVFAC-TP-MO

Naval Facilities Engineering Command Technical Publications - Planning .... NAVFAC-TP-PL

Naval Facilities Engineering Command Technical Publications - Public Utilities .... NAVFAC-TP-PU

Naval Facilities Engineering Command, Western Division (DNAB) .... NAVFACENGCOMWESDIV

Naval Facilities Engineering Command, Western Division (DNAB) .... NAVFACWESDIV

Naval Facilities Engineering Systems Command .... NAVFACENSYSCOM

Naval Facilities .... NAVFAC

Naval Facility Operational Center (DNAB) .... NAVFACOC

Naval Facility Operational Center (DNAB) .... NFOC

Naval Field Contracting System .... NFCS

Naval Field Contracting System (AAGC) .... NLU

Naval Field Liaison Unit (DNAB) .... NAVFLDOPINTO

Naval Field Operational Intelligence Office .... NAVFLDOPINTO

Naval Field Operational Intelligence Office (NVT) .... NFOIO

Naval Field Operational Intelligence Office Detachment (DNAB) .... NFOIODET

Naval Field Operations Support Group .... NAVFLDOPSUPPGRU

Naval Field Operations Support Group .... NFOSG

Naval Fighting Instruction School .... NFIS

Naval Fleet Auxiliary Force .... NFAF

Naval Fleet Missile System Analysis and Evaluation Group .... NFMSAEG

Naval Fleet Missile System Analysis and Evaluation Group Annex (MCD) .... NFMSAEGA

Naval Fleet Training Base .... NFTB

Naval Flight Officer .... NFO

Naval Flight Officer (Bombardier) (DNAB) .... NFO(B)

Naval Flight Officer Candidate (DNAB) .... NFOC

Naval Flight Officer (Controller) (DNAB) .... NFO(C)

Naval Flight Officer (Navigator) (DNAB) .... NFO(N)

Naval Flight Officer (RADAR Intercept) (DNAB) .... NFO(I)

Naval Flight Preparatory School .... NAVFLIGHTPREPSCOL

Naval Flight Preparatory School .... NFPS

Naval Flight Training School .... NFTS

Naval Flying Station [British] .... NFS

Naval Force Status Report (NVT) .... NAVFORSTAT

Naval Forces (AD) .... NAVFOR

Naval Forces Baltic Approaches [NATO] (AD) .... NAVBALTAP

Naval Forces [US] Central [Command] (DOMA) .... NAVCENT

Naval Forces, Europe, Worldwide Military Command Control System, Data Processing (DNAB) .... NAVEURWWMCCS DP

Naval Forces, Europe, Worldwide Military Command Control System, Employment Schedule (DNAB) .... NAVEURWWMCCS EMSKD

Naval Forces, Europe, Worldwide Military Command Control System, Movement Reports (DNAB) .... NAVEURWWMCCS MOVREP

Naval Forces, Europe, Worldwide Military Command Control System, Naval Forces Status (DNAB) .... NAVEURWWMCCS NAVFORSTA

Naval Forces Far East (AD) .... NAVFE

Naval Forces Intelligence Study (MCD) .... NAFIS

Naval Forces, Marianas (AD) .... NAVMAR

Naval Forces, Northern Norway [NATO] (AD) .... NAVNON

Naval Forces - Philippines (AD) .... NAVPHIL

Naval Forces, Scandinavian Approaches [NATO] (AD) .... NAVSCAP

Naval Forces, Southern Europe (AD) .... NAVSOUTH

Naval Forces Vietnam (VNW) .... NFV

Naval Forward Observing Officer [British military] (DMA) .... NFOO

Naval Frontier Base .... NFB

Naval Fuel Annex .... NFA

Naval Fuel Depot .... NAVFUELDEP

Naval Fuel Depot .... NFD

Naval Fuel Facility .... NFF

Naval Fuel Supply Office .... NAVFUELSUPO

Naval Future Policy Staff [British] .... NFPS

Naval Graduate Dental School (DNAB) .... NAVGDENSCOL

Naval Graduate Dental School .... NGDS

Naval Group .... NAVGRU

Naval Gun Factory [Later, NWF] .... NAVGUN

Naval Gun Factory [Later, NWF] .... NGF

Naval Gunfire (SAA) .... NG

Naval Gunfire .... NGF

Naval Gunfire Air Spotting .... NGAS

Naval Gunfire Assistant .... NGA

Naval Gunfire Exercise (NVT) .... NGFEX

Naval Gunfire Liaison Officer .... NGFLO

Naval Gunfire Liaison Officer .... NGLO

Naval Gunfire Liaison Team .... NGFLT

Naval Gunfire Liaison Team (MUGU) .... NGFT

Naval Gunfire Officer .... NGFO

Naval Gunfire Officer .... NGO

Naval Gunfire Operations Center .... NGOC

Naval Gunfire Support (NVT) .... NGFS

Naval Gunfire Support .... NGS

Naval Gunfire Support Forward Observer [British] .... NGSFO

Naval Gunfire Support Liaison Officer .... NGSLO

Naval Gunfire Support Staff Officer .... NGSSO

Naval Headquarters, Ottawa, ON, Canada .... CANAVHED

Naval Health Research Center .... NAVHLTHRSCHC

Naval Health Research Center (DNAB) .... NAVHLTHRSCHCEN

Naval Health Research Center (GRD) .... NHRC

Naval Historical Display Center .... NHDC

Naval Historical Foundation (EA) .... NHF

Naval Historical Society of Australia .... NHSA

Naval History Center (DNAB) .... NAVHISTCEN

Naval History Society, New York, NY [Library symbol Library of Congress Obsolete] (LCLS) .... NNNHi

Naval Home [Philadelphia, PA] .... NAVHOME

Naval Home [Philadelphia, PA] .... NH

Naval Home Resident Information System (DNAB) .... NAVHOMERESINFOSYS

Naval Honor Schools (AFIT) .... NHS

Naval Hospital .... NAVHOSP

Naval Hospital .... NH

Naval Hospital .... NHOS

Naval Hospital Corps School .... NAVHOSPCORPSCOL

Naval Housing Activity (DNAB) .... NAVHOSINGACT

Naval Housing Activity .... NAVHOUSINGACT

Naval Hovercraft Trials Unit .... NHTU

Naval Immediate Area Coordinator (DNAB) .... NAVIMAC

Naval Inactive Ship Maintenance Facility .... NISMF

Naval Industrial Reserve Aircraft Plant (MUGU) .... NIRAP

Naval Industrial Reserve Ordnance Plant (MCD) .... NIROP

Naval Inflatable Life-Saving Equipment [British military] (DMA) .... NILE

Naval Inshore Operations Training Center (NVT) .... NIOTC

Naval In-Shore Warfare (PDAA) .... NISW

Naval Inshore Warfare Command (NVT) .... NIWC

Naval Inshore Warfare Project .... NIW

Naval Inshore Warfare Task Unit (MCD) .... NIWTU

Naval Inspection Certificate (AD) .... navicert

Naval Inspector General .... NAVINSGEN

Naval Inspector General .... NIG

Naval Inspector of Machinery .... NIM

Naval Inspector of Ordnance .... NIO

Naval Institute Press [Publisher] .... NIP

Naval Instructor [British] .... NI

Naval Integrated Flight Training System (MCD) .... NIFTS

Naval Integrated Storage Tracking and Retrieval System .... NISTARS

Naval Integrated Test and Evaluation Working Group (MCD) .... NITEWOG

Naval Intelligence .... NAVINTEL

Naval Intelligence .... NI

Naval Intelligence Activity (DOMA) .... NIA

Naval Intelligence Advisory Board (DNAB) .... NIAB

Naval Intelligence Code [World War II British] .... NIC

Naval Intelligence Command .... NAVINTCOM

Naval Intelligence Command .... NAVINTCOMM

Naval Intelligence Command .... NIC

Naval Intelligence Command Instructions .... NAVINTCOMINST

Naval Intelligence Command - Translation Division .... NIC-TRANS

Naval Intelligence Database (DOMA) .... NID

Naval Intelligence Division [British] .... NID

Naval Intelligence Liaison Officer (NVT) .... NILO

Naval Intelligence Locating Summary (MCD) .... NILS

Naval Intelligence Processing System .... NIPS

Naval Intelligence Processing System Support Activity .... NIPSSA

Naval Intelligence Professionals (EA) .... NIP

Naval Intelligence Publication Register (NVT) .... NIPR

Naval Intelligence School .... NIS

Naval Intelligence Service [Italy] .... SIS

Naval Intelligence Support Center (DNAB) .... NAVINTSUPPCEN

Naval Intelligence Support Center .... NISC

Naval Intelligence Support Center Translation Division .... NISC-TRANS

Naval Intelligence Unit .... NIU

Naval Interservice Liaison Office (DNAB) .... NAVISLO

Naval Investigative Service (DNAB) .... NAVINVSERV

Naval Investigative Service .... NIS

Naval Investigative Service Headquarters (NVT) .... NAVINVSERVHQ

Naval Investigative Service Headquarters .... NISHQ

Naval Investigative Service Office .... NAVINVSERVO

Naval Investigative Service Office (NVT) .... NISO

Naval Investigative Service Office Representative (DNAB) .... NAVINVSERVOREP

Naval Investigative Service Office Representative (DNAB) .... NISOR

Naval Investigative Service Regional Forensic Laboratory (DNAB) .... NISREGFORENSICLAB

Naval Investigative Service Resident Agent (DNAB) .... NAVINVSERVRA

Naval Investigative Service Resident Agent (NVT) .... NISRA

Naval Investigative Service Satellite Unit (DNAB) .... NISSU

Naval Jet Instrument Trainer .... NAVJIT

Naval Joint Services Activity (DNAB) .... NAVJNTSERVACT

Naval Junior Reserve Officer Training Corps .... NJROTC

Naval Justice School .... NAVJUSTSCOL

Naval Laboratory Centers' Employee Association (DNAB) .... NLCEA

Naval Landing Force Equipment Depot .... NLFED

Naval Legal Service Office (DNAB) .... NAVLEGSERVOFF

Naval Legal Service Office Detachment (DNAB) .... NAVLEGSERVOFFDET

Naval Liaison Group (DNAB) .... NAVLIAGRU

Naval Liaison Officer (DNAB) .... NAVLO

Naval Liaison Officer .... NLO

Naval Lighter .... NL

Naval Lighter [Pontoon] Dock .... NLD

Naval Link Station (DNAB) .... NAVLINKSTA

Naval Local Defense Forces .... NLDF

Naval Logistics Engineering Group (DNAB) ..... NAVLOGENGRU
Naval Magazine and Net Depot ..... NMND
Naval Management Program ..... NMP
Naval Management Systems Center (MCD) ..... NAVMGTSYSCEN
Naval Manpower Engineering Center (MCD) ..... NAVMEC
Naval Manpower Information System ..... NMIS
Naval Manpower Shore Survey Team (NVT) ..... NMSST
Naval Manpower Survey Office (NVT) ..... NMSO
Naval Marine Engineering Station ..... NMES
Naval Maritime Intelligence Center [*Formerly, NISC and then NTIC*] (DOMA) ..... NAVMIC
Naval Material Command [*Formerly, NMSE*] (MCD) ..... NAVMAT
Naval Material Command [*Formerly, NMSE*] ..... NAVMATCOM
Naval Material Command [*Formerly, NMSE*] ..... NMC
Naval Material Command [*Formerly, NMSE*] (MCD) ..... NMCOM
Naval Material Command Contingency/Emergency Planning (DNAB) ..... NAVMAT COOPLAN
Naval Material Command Detachment (DNAB) ..... NAVMATDET
Naval Material Command Industrial Resources Detachment (DNAB) ..... NMCIRD
Naval Material Command Instruction ..... NAVMATINST
Naval Material Command Support Activity ..... NAVMATCOMSUPPACT
Naval Material Data Systems Group (DNAB) ..... NAVMATDATASYSGRU
Naval Material Data Systems Group (DNAB) ..... NMDSG
Naval Material Establishment (DOMA) ..... NME
Naval Material Evaluation Unit (DNAB) ..... NAVMATEVALU
Naval Material Evaluation Unit (DNAB) ..... NMEU
Naval Material Industrial Resources Office ..... NAVMIRO
Naval Material Industrial Resources Office ..... NMIRO
Naval Material Support Establishment [*After 1966, NAVMAT, NMCOM, NMC*] ..... NMSE
Naval Material Transportation Office (DNAB) ..... NAVMATRANSOFC
Naval Materials Management (SAA) ..... NML
Naval Mathematics and English Test [*British military*] (DMA) ..... NAMET
Naval Medical Administration Unit (DNAB) ..... NMAU
Naval Medical Center [*Bethesda, MD*] ..... NMC
Naval Medical Command (ANA) ..... NAVMEDCOM
Naval Medical Data Service Center ..... NAVMEDATASERVCEN
Naval Medical Data Service Center (DNAB) ..... NMDSC
Naval Medical Field Research Laboratory [*Camp Lejeune, NC*] ..... NMFRL
Naval Medical Laboratory (DNAB) ..... NAVMEDLAB
Naval Medical Laboratory Detachment (DNAB) ..... NAVMEDLABDET
Naval Medical Materiel Support Command (DNAB) ..... NAVMEDMATSUPPCOM
Naval Medical Neuropsychiatric Research Unit ..... NMNRU
Naval Medical Program for Nuclear Casualties ..... NMPNC
Naval Medical Publication ..... NMP
Naval Medical Research and Development Command (DNAB) ..... NAVMEDRSCHDEVCOM
Naval Medical Research and Development Command (MCD) ..... NMRDC
Naval Medical Research Institute ..... NAVMEDRSCHINST
Naval Medical Research Institute ..... NMRI
Naval Medical Research Institute, Washington, DC [*OCLC symbol*] (OCLC) ..... NMR
Naval Medical Research Laboratory ..... NMRL
Naval Medical Research Unit ..... NAVMEDRSCHU
Naval Medical Research Unit ..... NMRU
Naval Medical Research Unit Detachment (DNAB) ..... NAVMEDRSCHUDET
Naval Medical School ..... NAVMEDSCOL
Naval Medical School (MCD) ..... NMS
Naval Medical Supply Depot ..... NMSD
Naval Medical Supply Unit (DNAB) ..... NMSC
Naval Medicine ..... NAVMED
Naval Member, Canadian Joint Staff ..... NMCJS
Naval Member, Canadian Joint Staff, London, England ..... CANAVBRIT
Naval Memorandum Correction (NVT) ..... NMC
Naval Message Processing (MCD) ..... NMP
Naval Meteorological Branch [*British*] ..... NMB
Naval Meteorological Service ..... NMS
Naval Military Personnel Command (MCD) ..... NAVMILPERSCOM
Naval Military Personnel Command (ANA) ..... NMPC
Naval Military Personnel Command, Recreational Services Division, Regional Office (DNAB) ..... NMPCRECSREDIVREGOFF
Naval Military Transportation Office, Norfolk, Virginia (DNAB) ..... NAVMTONORVA
Naval Military Transportation Office Representative (DNAB) ..... NAVMTOREP
Naval Mine Defense Laboratory [*Naval Facilities Engineering Command*] [*Panama City, FL*] ..... NMDL
Naval Mine Depot ..... NAVMINDEP
Naval Mine Depot ..... NMD
Naval Mine Disposal School ..... NMDS
Naval Mine Engineering Facility ..... NAVMINENGRFAC
Naval Mine Engineering Facility ..... NMEF
Naval Mine Test Facility ..... NMTF
Naval Mine Testing Center (MCD) ..... NMTC
Naval Mine Warfare (DOMA) ..... NMW
Naval Mine Warfare School ..... NAVSCOLMINWARFARE
Naval Mine Warfare School ..... NMWS
Naval Mine Warfare Test Station ..... NMWTS
Naval Mine Warfare Training Center ..... NAVMINWARTRACEN
Naval Mine Warfare Training Center ..... NMWTC
Naval Mine Warfare Training School ..... NMWTS
Naval Minecraft Base ..... NMB
Naval Missile and Astronautics Center ..... NMAC
Naval Missile Center [*Point Mugu, CA*] (MCD) ..... NAVMISCEN
Naval Missile Center (AD) ..... NavMisCen
Naval Missile Center [*Point Mugu, CA*] ..... NMC
Naval Missile Facility [*Also, NMF*] (MUGU) ..... NAVMISFAC
Naval Missile Facility [*Also, NAVMISFAC*] ..... NMF
Naval Missile Facility, Hawaiian Area (MUGU) ..... NMFHAWAREA
Naval Missile Facility, Point Arguello ..... NMFPA
Naval Missile Facility, Point Mugu [*California*] (SAA) ..... NMFPM
Naval Missile Range ..... NMR
Naval Missile Testing Center ..... NMTC
Naval Mission ..... NAVMIS
Naval Mission (AFIT) ..... NM
Naval Mission Center (KSC) ..... NMC
Naval Model Basin ..... NMB
Naval Modular Automated Communications System (NVT) ..... NAVMACS
Naval Mortuary Office (DNAB) ..... NAVMORTOFF
Naval Motion Study Unit [*British*] ..... NMSU
Naval Mutual Aid Association (DNAB) ..... NAVMAA
Naval Net Depot ..... NAVNETDEP
Naval Net Depot ..... NND
Naval Nuclear Evaluation Unit ..... NNEU
Naval Nuclear Power Training Unit (MCD) ..... NAVNUPWRTRAU
Naval Nuclear Power Training Unit (DNAB) ..... NNPTU
Naval Nuclear Power Unit ..... NAVNUPWRU
Naval Nuclear Power Unit [*Obsolete*] ..... NNPU
Naval Nuclear Propulsion Information (MCD) ..... NNPI
Naval Objectives Analysis Group ..... NOAG
Naval Observatory (MUGU) ..... NAVOBS
Naval Observatory [*Navy*] ..... NAVOBSY
Naval Observatory [*Navy*] ..... NO
Naval Observatory [*Navy*] ..... NOBS
Naval Observatory [*Navy*] ..... NOBSY
Naval Observatory Flagstaff [*Arizona*] **Station** ..... NAVOBSYFLAGSTAFFSTA
Naval Observatory Station (DNAB) ..... NAVOBSYSTA
Naval Ocean and Atmosphere Research Laboratory [*USA*] [*Marine science*] (OSRA) ..... NOARL
Naval Ocean Floor Analysis Division (DNAB) ..... NOFAD
Naval Ocean Intelligence Center (DOMA) ..... NOIC
Naval Ocean Processing Facility (DNAB) ..... NAVOCEANPROFAC
Naval Ocean Research and Development Activity [*Bay St. Louis, MS*] ..... NORDA
Naval Ocean Surveillance Information Center (DNAB) ..... NAVOCEANSURVINFOCEN
Naval Ocean Surveillance Information Center ..... NOSIC
Naval Ocean Systems Center [*Formerly, NELC*] (DNAB) ..... NAVOCEANSYSCEN
Naval Ocean Systems Center [*Formerly, NELC*] ..... NOSC
Naval Ocean Systems Center Laboratory (DNAB) ..... NAVOCEANSYSCENLAB
Naval Ocean Systems Center Laboratory (DNAB) ..... NOSCL
Naval Ocean Systems Center Laboratory Detachment (DNAB) ..... NAVOCEANSYSCENLABDET
Naval Ocean Systems Center, San Diego, CA [*OCLC symbol*] (OCLC) ..... CNS
Naval Ocean Transport Service [*Changed to MSTS in 1949 now MSC*] (DOMA) ..... NOTS
Naval Oceanographic Data Distribution System ..... NODDS
Naval Oceanographic Distribution Center ..... NODC
Naval Oceanographic District Office ..... NAVOCEANDISTO
Naval Oceanographic Office (USDC) ..... NAVO
Naval Oceanographic Office [*Marine science*] (OSRA) ..... NAVO
Naval Oceanographic Office [*Also known as NOO; formerly, HO, NHO, USNHO*] [*Bay St. Louis, MS*] ..... NAVOCEANO
Naval Oceanographic Office (DNAB) ..... NAVOCEANOFC
Naval Oceanographic Office [*Also known as NAVOCEANO; formerly, HO, NHO, USNHO*] ..... NOO
Naval Oceanographic Office [*Also known as NOO; formerly, HO, NHO, USNHO*] ..... OO
Naval Oceanographic Office Aircraft Support Squadron (DNAB) ..... NAVOCEANOAIRSUPPGRU
Naval Oceanographic Office Detachment (DNAB) ..... NAVOCEANODET
Naval Oceanographic Office Instruction ..... OCEANAVINST
Naval Oceanographic Office Special Publication ..... NOO-SP
Naval Oceanographic Office, Washington, DC [*Inactive*] [*OCLC symbol*] (OCLC) ..... NOO
Naval Oceanographic Officer (AD) ..... NavOceanO
Naval Oceanographic Processing Center (DOMA) ..... NOPC
Naval Oceanographic Processing Facility (ANA) ..... NOPF
Naval Oceanographic Publication ..... NOP
Naval Oceanographic Research and Development Administration [*USA*] [*Marine science*] (OSRA) ..... NORDA
Naval Oceanography Command [*Marine science*] (MSC) ..... OCEANAV
Naval Oceanography Command Center (DNAB) ..... NAVOCEANCOMCEN
Naval Oceanography Command Center/Joint Typhoon Warning Center ..... NOCC/JTWC
Naval Oceanography Command Detachment (MCD) ..... NAVOCEANCOMDET
Naval Oceanography Command Facility (DNAB) ..... NAVOCEANCOMFAC
Naval Oceanography Command Facility (DNAB) ..... NOCF
Naval Oceanography Command Support System (GFGA) ..... NAVOCEANCOM
Naval Oceanography Communications Detachment (DNAB) ..... NAVOCEANCOMMDET
Naval Office for Occupied Areas [*World War II*] ..... NOFOA
Naval Officer ..... NO
Naval Officer Billet Classifications [*or Code*] ..... NOBC
Naval Officer Candidate School ..... NAVOCS
Naval Officer Personnel Circular Letter ..... NOPCL
Naval Officer Procurement ..... NOP
Naval Officer Record Support Activity (DNAB) ..... NAVORECSUPPACT
Naval Officer-in-Charge ..... NOIC
Naval On-Call Force, Mediterranean [*NATO*] (NATG) ..... NAVOCFORMED
Naval Operating Base ..... NOB
Naval Operating Base, Coco Solo, Canal Zone ..... NOBSOLO
Naval Operating Base, Dutch Harbor, Aleutians ..... NOBDUCHAR
Naval Operating Base, Newport, Rhode Island ..... NOBNEWT

Naval Operating Base, San Francisco, California	NOBFRAN
Naval Operating Base Supplies (DNAB)	NOBS
Naval Operating Base, Trinidad	NOBTRIN
Naval Operating Development Center	NODC
Naval Operating Facility	NAVOPFAC
Naval Operating Facility	NOF
Naval Operational Readiness Reporting Systems	NORRS
Naval Operational Training Unit	NOTU
Naval Operations Center (NVT)	NOC
Naval Operations Network (CINC)	NAVOPNET
Naval Operations Support Group (DNAB)	NAVOPSUPPGRU
Naval Operations Support Group, Atlantic	NAVOPSUPPGRULANT
Naval Operations Support Group, Atlantic	NOSGLANT
Naval Operations Support Group, Pacific	NAVOPSUPPGRUPAC
Naval Operations Support Group, Pacific	NOSGPAC
Naval Operations Support Information Center [Navy]	NOSIC
Naval Ophthalmic Support and Training Activity (DNAB)	NAVOPHTHALSUPPTRACT
Naval Ophthalmic Support and Training Activity	NOSTA
Naval Order of Battle	NOB
Naval Order of Battle Textual Summary (MCD)	NOBTS
Naval Order of the United States [Later, NOUS] [An association] (EA)	NAVOROUS
Naval Order of the United States (EA)	NOUS
Naval Ordnanace Missile Test Station [White Sands Missile Range, NM] (GRD)	NOMTS
Naval Ordnance (MUGU)	NAVORD
Naval Ordnance	NORD
Naval Ordnance Activities, Atlantic	NOACTLANT
Naval Ordnance Activities, Pacific	NOACTPAC
Naval Ordnance Bulletin [A publication]	NOB
Naval Ordnance Chart (MCD)	NAVORDCH
Naval Ordnance Chart	NVORDCH
Naval Ordnance Data Automation Center	NODAC
Naval Ordnance Department [British]	NOD
Naval Ordnance Depot	NOD
Naval Ordnance Electronics Laboratory	NOEL
Naval Ordnance Engineering Facility (DNAB)	NAVORDENGFAC
Naval Ordnance Engineering Facility (DNAB)	NOEF
Naval Ordnance Experimental Unit	NOEU
Naval Ordnance Facility	NAVORDFAC
Naval Ordnance Facility	NOF
Naval Ordnance Gauge Laboratory	NOGL
Naval Ordnance Inspecting Officer	NOIO
Naval Ordnance Inspection Establishment [Ministry of Defence] [British] (PDAA)	NOIE
Naval Ordnance Lab [Maryland] [Seismograph station code, US Geological Survey Closed] (SEIS)	NLM
Naval Ordnance Laboratory [Later, NSWC] (MCD)	NOL
Naval Ordnance Laboratory Corona	NOLC
Naval Ordnance Laboratory Field Division (DNAB)	NAVORDLABFIELDIV
Naval Ordnance Laboratory Miss Distance Indicator	NOL-MDI
Naval Ordnance Laboratory Test Facility (SAA)	NOLTESTFAC
Naval Ordnance Laboratory Test Facility	NOLTF
Naval Ordnance Laboratory, White Oak [Maryland]	NOL/WO
Naval Ordnance Management Information System	NOMIS
Naval Ordnance Missile Test Facility	NAVORDMISTESTFAC
Naval Ordnance Missile Test Facility	NOMTF
Naval Ordnance Plant	NOP
Naval Ordnance Plant, Forest Park [Illinois]	NOPF
Naval Ordnance Plant Institute (MCD)	NOPI
Naval Ordnance Plant, Louisville [Kentucky]	NOPL
Naval Ordnance Research Calculator [or Computer] [Naval Ordnance Proving Ground]	NORC
Naval Ordnance Special Projects	NOSP
Naval Ordnance Station	NAVORDSTA
Naval Ordnance Station	NOS
Naval Ordnance Station Detachment (DNAB)	NAVORDSTADET
Naval Ordnance Station, Indian Head (MCD)	NOSIH
Naval Ordnance Station, Louisville [Kentucky]	NOSL
Naval Ordnance Station, Louisville Quality Assurance Department [Kentucky]	NOSL-QA
Naval Ordnance Supply Office (MUGU)	NOSO
Naval Ordnance Systems Command [Later, Naval Sea Systems Command]	NAVORD
Naval Ordnance Systems Command [Later, Naval Sea Systems Command] (MCD)	NAVORDSYSCO
Naval Ordnance Systems Command [Later, Naval Sea Systems Command]	NAVORDSYSCOM
Naval Ordnance Systems Command [Later, Naval Sea Systems Command]	NOSC
Naval Ordnance Systems Command Headquarters (USDC)	NAVORDSYSCOMHQ
Naval Ordnance Systems Command Instruction	NAVORDINST
Naval Ordnance Systems Command, Integrated Logistics Support / Management Information System (DNAB)	NAVORD ILS/MIS
Naval Ordnance Systems Command, Special Weapons Ordnance Publication	NAVORD-SWOP
Naval Ordnance Systems Support Office	NAVORDSYSSUPPO
Naval Ordnance Systems Support Office (DNAB)	NAVORDSYSSUPPO
Naval Ordnance Systems Support Office (MCD)	NOSSO
Naval Ordnance Systems Support Office, Atlantic (DNAB)	NAVORDSYSSUPPOLANT
Naval Ordnance Systems Support Office, Atlantic	NOSSOLANT
Naval Ordnance Systems Support Office, Pacific (DNAB)	NAVORDSYSSUPPOPAC
Naval Ordnance Systems Support Office, Pacific	NOSSOPAC
Naval Ordnance Systems Support Office Representative (DNAB)	NOSSOREP
Naval Ordnance Technical Representative (MCD)	NAVORDTECHREP
Naval Ordnance Test Center (KSC)	NOTC
Naval Ordnance Test Station	NOTS
Naval Ordnance Test Unit	NAVORDTESTU
Naval Ordnance Test Unit	NOTU
Naval Ordnance Unit	NAVORDU
Naval Ordnance Unit	NOU
Naval Overhaul and Repair Pacific (MUGU)	NORPAC
Naval Overseas Air Cargo Terminal	NOACT
Naval Overseas Air Cargo Terminal, Pearl (MUGU)	NOAP
Naval Overseas Freight Terminal	NOFT
Naval Overseas Transport Service	NOTS
Naval Parachute Facility (MCD)	NPF
Naval Parachute Unit	NPU
Naval Party [British military] (DMA)	NP
Naval Patrol [British military] (DMA)	NP
Naval Pattern [British military] (DMA)	NP
Naval Pension [British] (ROG)	NP
Naval Personnel (AD)	NAVPERS
Naval Personnel and Training Research Laboratory [Formerly, Personnel Research Activity]	NPTRL
Naval Personnel Center	NAVPERSCEN
Naval Personnel Committee [British military] (DMA)	NPC
Naval Personnel Conversion Tables	NP-CT
Naval Personnel Program Support Activity	NAVPERSPROGSUPPACT
Naval Personnel Research Activity	NAVPERSREACT
Naval Personnel Research Activity	NAVPERSRSCHACT
Naval Personnel Research Activity	NPRA
Naval Personnel Research and Development Center	NAVPERSRANDCEN
Naval Personnel Research and Development Center, Washington [DC] Branch (DNAB)	NAVPERSRANDCENWB
Naval Personnel Research and Development Laboratory	NPRDL
Naval Personnel Separation Center	NPSC
Naval Petroleum and Oil Shale Reserve	NP & OSR
Naval Petroleum Reserves	NAVPETRES
Naval Petroleum Reserves	NPR
Naval Petroleum Reserves Office	NAVPETRESO
Naval Petroleum Reserves Office	NPRO
Naval Petroleum Reserves Production Act (AAGC)	NPRPA
Naval Petroleum Training Unit (DNAB)	NAVPETRAU
Naval Petroleum Training Unit (DNAB)	NPTU
Naval Photographic Center	NAVPHOTOCEN
Naval Photographic Center	NPC
Naval Photographic Interpretation Center	NPIC
Naval Photographic Services Depot	NPSD
Naval Pilot Evaluation (MUGU)	NPE
Naval Plant Branch Representative Office	NPBRO
Naval Plant Branch Representative Officer (DNAB)	NAVPBRO
Naval Plant Development Unit (DNAB)	NAVPLANTDEVU
Naval Plant Development Unit (DNAB)	NPDU
Naval Plant Representative	NPR
Naval Plant Representative Office [or Officer] (MCD)	NAVPLANTREP
Naval Plant Representative Office [or Officer]	NAVPLANTREPO
Naval Plant Representative Office [or Officer]	NAVPRO
Naval Plant Technical Representative (DNAB)	NAVPLANTTECHREP
Naval Polar Oceanography Center (DNAB)	NAVPOLAROCEANCEN
Naval Police [British] (ROG)	NP
Naval Port Control Office [or Officer]	NAVPORCO
Naval Port Control Office [or Officer]	NAVPORCOF
Naval Port Control Office [Or officer] (DNAB)	NAVPORTCO
Naval Port Officer	NPO
Naval Postgraduate School	NAVPGSCOL
Naval Postgraduate School	NAVPOSTGRADSCOL
Naval Postgraduate School	NPGS
Naval Postgraduate School	NPS
Naval Postgraduate School	PGS
Naval Postgraduate School	PGSCOL
Naval Postgraduate School Linear Accelerator	NPGLINAC
Naval Potomac Annex	NPANX
Naval Powder Factory	NAVPOWFAC
Naval Powder Factory	NPF
Naval Preflight School	NAVPREFLIGHTSCOL
Naval Preflight School	NPFS
Naval Prison	NAVPRIS
Naval Prison	NP
Naval Prison Farms and Prison Personnel [Budget appropriation title]	NPF & PP
Naval Procurement Account	NPA
Naval Procurement Fund [Budget appropriation title]	NPF
Naval Production Equipment Control Office	NAVPECO
Naval Propellant Plant (DNAB)	NAVPROPLT
Naval Propellant Plant	NPP
Naval Propellant Plant Quality Assurance Department [Indian Head, MD]	NPP/QAS
Naval Proving Ground [Dahlgren, VA]	NAVPROV
Naval Proving Ground [Dahlgren, VA]	NPG
Naval Provost Martial [British]	NPM
Naval Public Affairs Office, East Coast	NAVPAOEASCO
Naval Public Affairs Office, Midwest	NAVPAOMWEST
Naval Public Affairs Office, West Coast	NAVPAOWESCO
Naval Publication (IEEE)	NP
Naval Publications (AD)	NAVPUB
Naval Publications and Forms Center (MCD)	NAVPUBFORMCEN

Naval Publications and Forms Center ..... NPFC
Naval Publications and Printing Service (DNAB) ..... NAVPUBPRINTSERV
Naval Radio Activity ..... NRA
Naval Radio Compass (IAA) ..... NRC
Naval Radio Direction Finder (IAA) ..... NRD
Naval Radio Direction Finder Service ..... NRDFS
Naval Radio Receiving Facility (DNAB) ..... NAVRADRECFAC
Naval Radio Receiving Facility (DNAB) ..... NRRF
Naval Radio Research Observatory (IAA) ..... NRRO
Naval Radio Research Station ..... NRRS
Naval Radio Station ..... NAVRADSTA
Naval Radio Station ..... NRS
Naval Radio Station (Receiving) (DNAB) ..... NRS(R)
Naval Radio Station (Sending) (DNAB) ..... NRS(S)
Naval Radio Transmitting Facility (DNAB) ..... NAVRADTRANSFAC
Naval Radio Transmitting Facility (DNAB) ..... NRTF
Naval Radiological Control ..... NAVRADCON
Naval Radiological Control (DNAB) ..... NRC
Naval Radiological Defense Laboratory ..... NRDL
Naval Radiological Protection Service (PDAA) ..... NRPS
Naval Rating ..... NR
Naval Reactor Branch (MUGU) ..... NRB
Naval Reactor Facility ..... NRF
Naval Reactor Organic Experiment ..... NROE
Naval Reactors (GAAI) ..... NR
Naval Reactors Operations Office ..... NROO
Naval Receiving Station (NVT) ..... NAVRECSTA
Naval Receiving Station ..... NRES
Naval Receiving Station ..... NRS
Naval Reconnaissance and Tactical Support Center, Atlantic (DNAB) ..... NAVRECONTACSUPPCENLANT
Naval Reconnaissance and Technical Support Center ..... NAVRECONTECHSUPPCEN
Naval Reconnaissance and Technical Support Center ..... NRTSC
Naval Reconnaissance and Technical Support Center, Atlantic (DNAB) ..... NAVRECONTECHSUPPCENLANT
Naval Reconnaissance and Technical Support Center, Pacific (DNAB) ..... NAVRECONTECHSUPPCENPAC
Naval Reconnaissance and Technical Support Center, Pacific (DNAB) ..... NRTSCPAC
Naval Records Club [*Later, INRO*] ..... NRC
Naval Records Management Center ..... NRMC
Naval Records Management Center ..... NRMCEN
Naval Recreation Center (DNAB) ..... NAVRECCEN
Naval Recreation Center (DNAB) ..... NRC
Naval Recruiting Department [*British military*] (DMA) ..... NRD
Naval Recruiting Service [*British military*] (DMA) ..... NRS
Naval Recruiting Station ..... NRS
Naval Regional Active Duty Cryptologic Officer (DNAB) ..... NAVRADCO
Naval Regional Contracting Center (AAGC) ..... NRCC
Naval Regional Medical Center (DNAB) ..... NAVREGMEDCEN
Naval Regional Medical Center (NVT) ..... NRMC
Naval Regional Medical Center Branch Clinic (DNAB) ..... NAVREGMEDCENBRCLINIC
Naval Regional Medical Center Branch Hospital (DNAB) ..... NAVREGMEDCENBRHOSP
Naval Regional Medical Center Clinic (DNAB) ..... NAVREGMEDCENCLINIC
Naval Regional Medical Center Detachment (DNAB) ..... NAVREGMEDCENDET
Naval Regional Plant Equipment Office [*or Officer*] (DNAB) ..... NAVREGPEO
Naval Regional Plant Equipment Office [*or Officer*] (DNAB) ..... NRPEO
Naval Regional Procurement Office ..... NRPO
Naval Registered Publications Issuing Office ..... NRPIO
Naval Repair Base ..... NRB
Naval Repair Facility (MCD) ..... NAVREPFAC
Naval Repair Facility ..... NRF
Naval Research Advisory Committee ..... NRAC
Naval Research Advisory Group (KSC) ..... NRAG
Naval Research and Development ..... NAR
Naval Research and Development (KSC) ..... NRD
Naval Research and Development Satellite Communications Group (MUGU) ..... NAVRDSATCOMMGRU
Naval Research and Development Satellite Communications Group (SAA) ..... NRDSCG
Naval Research Center (DNAB) ..... NAVRESCEN
Naval Research Co. - Reserves ..... NRC
Naval Research Electronic Computer ..... NAREC
Naval Research Electronic Computer (AD) ..... narec
Naval Research Establishment ..... NRE
Naval Research Group ..... NRG
Naval Research Laboratory [*ONR*] ..... NAVRESLAB
Naval Research Laboratory [*ONR*] ..... NAVRSCHLAB
Naval Research Laboratory [*Washington, DC Seismograph station code, US Geological Survey Closed*] (SEIS) ..... NRL
Naval Research Laboratory, Chesapeake Bay Detachment (DNAB) ..... NRLCHESBAYDET
Naval Research Laboratory Electro-Optical Technology Program Office [*Washington, DC*] ..... NRL/EOTPO
Naval Research Laboratory, Field Site Detachment (DNAB) ..... NRLSITEDET
Naval Research Laboratory, Flight Support Detachment (DNAB) ..... NRLFLTSUPPDET
Naval Research Laboratory Representative (DNAB) ..... NRLREP
Naval Research Laboratory Shock and Vibration Information Center [*ONR*] ..... NRL/SVIC
Naval Research Laboratory, Special Projects Detachment (DNAB) ..... NRLSPECPROJDET
Naval Research Laboratory, Underwater Sound Reference Detachment (DNAB) ..... NRLUWSREFDET
Naval Research Laboratory, Washington, DC [*OCLC symbol*] (OCLC) ..... NRL
Naval Research Objectives ..... NRO
Naval Research Planning Board (DNAB) ..... NRPB
Naval Research Reactor ..... NRR
Naval Research Requirement ..... NRR
Naval Research Reserve Co. ..... NRRC
Naval Research Section [*Library of Congress*] (MCD) ..... NRS
Naval Reserve ..... NAVRES
Naval Reserve ..... NR
Naval Reserve Association (EA) ..... NRA
Naval Reserve Auxiliary Field ..... NRAF
Naval Reserve Aviation Base ..... NRAB
Naval Reserve Cargo-Handling Battalion ..... NRCHB
Naval Reserve Cargo-Handling Training Battalion ..... NRCHTB
Naval Reserve Center (DNAB) ..... NAVRESCEN
Naval Reserve Commander, Iceland Defense Force (DNAB) ..... NAVRESCOMICEDEFOR
Naval Reserve Evaluation Board (DNAB) ..... NREB
Naval Reserve Fleet [*or Force*] ..... NRF
Naval Reserve Fleet Management Assistance Unit (DNAB) ..... NRFMAU
Naval Reserve Force (DNAB) ..... NAVRESFOR
Naval Reserve Force Study Group (DNAB) ..... NRFS
Naval Reserve Inshore Undersea Warfare (DNAB) ..... NRIUW
Naval Reserve Manpower Center ..... NAVRESMANPOWERCEN
Naval Reserve Manpower Center (DNAB) ..... NAVRESMANPWRCEN
Naval Reserve Manpower Center ..... NRMC
Naval Reserve Medal ..... NRM
Naval Reserve Midshipmen's School ..... NAVRESMIDSCOL
Naval Reserve Midshipmen's School ..... NRMS
Naval Reserve Mobile Inshore Undersea Warfare (DNAB) ..... NRMIUW
Naval Reserve Mobile Mine Assembly Group (DNAB) ..... NRMOMAGU
Naval Reserve Officer Recording Activity (DNAB) ..... NAVRESOREACT
Naval Reserve Officer School ..... NROS
Naval Reserve Officers' Training Corps ..... NROTC
Naval Reserve Officers' Training Corps Unit (DNAB) ..... NROTCU
Naval Reserve Officers' Training Corps Unit and Administrative Unit (DNAB) ..... NROTCUNAVADMINU
Naval Reserve Personnel Center (DNAB) ..... NRPC
Naval Reserve Policy Board (DNAB) ..... NRPB
Naval Reserve Public Affairs Co. ..... NRPAC
Naval Reserve Readiness Command (DNAB) ..... NAVRESREDCOM
Naval Reserve Readiness Command Region (DNAB) ..... NAVRESREDCOMREG
Naval Reserve Readiness Facility (DNAB) ..... NRRF
Naval Reserve Requirement (MCD) ..... NRR
Naval Reserve Security Group (DNAB) ..... NAVRESSECGRP
Naval Reserve Security Group (DNAB) ..... NRSG
Naval Reserve Submarine Detachment (DNAB) ..... NAVRESUBDET
Naval Reserve Supply Company (DNAB) ..... NRSC
Naval Reserve Support Office (DNAB) ..... NAVRESUPPOFC
Naval Reserve Support Office Detachment (DNAB) ..... NAVRESUPPOFCDET
Naval Reserve Training (DNAB) ..... NAVRESTRA
Naval Reserve Training Branch ..... NRTB
Naval Reserve Training Center ..... NAVRESTRACEN
Naval Reserve Training Center ..... NRTC
Naval Reserve Training Command ..... CNRTC
Naval Reserve Training Command ..... NAVRESTRACOM
Naval Reserve Training Command ..... NRTCOMD
Naval Reserve Training Facility ..... NAVRESTRAFAC
Naval Reserve Training in Port (NVT) ..... NRTIPT
Naval Resource Model (MCD) ..... NARM
Naval Retraining Command ..... NAVRETRAINCOM
Naval Retraining Command ..... NRC
Naval Rocket Society (IAA) ..... NRS
Naval Safety Center ..... NAVSAFECEN
Naval Safety Center (MCD) ..... NSC
Naval School (MCD) ..... NS
Naval School Command ..... NSC
Naval School Deep Sea Divers ..... DSDS
Naval School of Aviation Medicine ..... NSAM
Naval School of Cryogenics (DNAB) ..... NAVSCOLCYROGENICS
Naval School of Cryptographic Repair (DNAB) ..... NAVSCOLCRYPTOREP
Naval School of Dental Assisting and Technology (DNAB) ..... NSDAT
Naval School of Explosive Ordnance Disposal (DNAB) ..... NAVSCOLEOD
Naval School of Health Sciences [*Bethesda, MD*] ..... NSHS
Naval School of Health Sciences, Bethesda, MD [*OCLC symbol*] (OCLC) ..... NSH
Naval School of Health Sciences Detachment (DNAB) ..... NSHSDET
Naval School of Hospital Administration (DNAB) ..... NAVSCOLHOSPADMIN
Naval School of Military Government ..... NSMG
Naval School of Military Government and Administration ..... NSMG & A
Naval School of Mine War (DNAB) ..... NAVSCOLMINWAR
Naval School of Music ..... NSM
Naval School of Ordnance Disposal ..... NSOD
Naval School of Physical Distribution Management (DNAB) ..... NAVSCOLPHYDISTMGT
Naval School of Transportation Management (DNAB) ..... NAVSCOLTRANSMGT
Naval School Transportation Management ..... NSTM
Naval Schools Command ..... NAVSCOLCOM
Naval Schools Command, Norfolk, Virginia ..... NAVSCOLCOM NORVA
Naval Schools Construction ..... NAVSCOLCONST
Naval Schools Mine Warfare ..... NSMW
Naval Science Advisor (DNAB) ..... NAVSCIADV
Naval Science and Tactics ..... NS & T
Naval Science and Technology Information Centre (NITA) ..... NSTIC
Naval Science Instructor (DNAB) ..... NSI
Naval Scientific and Technical Group, Far East (DNAB) ..... NAVSCITECHGRUFE

Naval Scientific and Technical Information Centre [Later, DRIC] [British] (MCD) .... NSTIC
Naval Scientific and Technical Intelligence Center .... NAVSCIENTECHINTCEN
Naval Scientific and Technical Intelligence Center .... NAVSTIC
Naval Scientific and Technical Intelligence Center, Atlantic (DNAB) .... NSTICLANT
Naval Scientific and Technical Intelligence Center, Pacific (DNAB) ...... NSTICPAC
Naval Scientist Training and Exchange Program (DNAB) .... NSTEP
Naval Scout Unit .... NSU
Naval Sea Cadet Corps (NVT) .... NSCC
Naval Sea Cadet Corps Liaison Officer (DNAB) .... NSCCLO
Naval Sea Cadets .... NSC
Naval Sea Cargo Coordinator (DNAB) .... NAVSEACARCOORD
Naval Sea Cargo Coordinator (DNAB) .... NSCO
Naval Sea Data Support Activity (NVT) .... NSDSA
Naval Sea Support Center (DNAB) .... NAVSEACEN
Naval Sea Support Center, Atlantic (MCD) .... NAVSEACENLANT
Naval Sea Support Center - Atlantic (AD) .... NAVSEACENLANT
Naval Sea Support Center, Atlantic Detachment (DNAB) .... NAVSEACENFSO
Naval Sea Support Center, Fleet Support Office (DNAB) .... NAVSEACENFSO
Naval Sea Support Center, Hawaii Laboratory (DNAB) .... NAVSEACENHAWLAB
Naval Sea Support Center - Pacific (DNAB) .... NAVSEACENPAC
Naval Sea Support Center, Pacific Detachment (DNAB) .... NAVSEACENPACDET
Naval Sea Support Center Representative (DNAB) .... NAVSEACENREP
Naval Sea [formerly, Ship] Systems Command (MCD) .... NAVSEA
Naval Sea [Formerly, Ship] Systems Command (DNAB) .... NAVSEASYSCOM
Naval Sea [formerly, Ship] Systems Command .... NSSC
Naval Sea Systems Command Automated Data Systems Office (DNAB) .... NAVSEAADSO
Naval Sea Systems Command Automated Data Systems Office Detachment (DNAB) .... NAVSEAADSODET
Naval Sea Systems Command Complex Overhaul Representative (DNAB) .... NAVSEACOHREP
Naval Sea Systems Command Detachment (DNAB) .... NAVSEADET
Naval Sea Systems Command Headquarters (DNAB) .... NAVSEASYSCOMHQ
Naval Sea Systems Command Management Office, Western Pacific (DNAB) .... NAVSEASYSCOMGTOWESTPAC
Naval Sea Systems Command Material Quality Assessment Office (DNAB) .... NAVSEAMQAO
Naval Sea Systems Command Material Representative (DNAB) .... NAVSEAMATREP
Naval Sea Systems Command Technical Representative (DNAB) .... NAVSEATECHREP
Naval Sea Systems Command Technical Representative .... NSTR
Naval Sea Systems Command, Washington, DC [OCLC symbol] (OCLC) ...... NSS
Naval Security and Investigative Command .... NSIC
Naval Security Engineering Facility .... NAVSECENGRFAC
Naval Security Group .... NAVSECGRU
Naval Security Group .... NSG
Naval Security Group Activity .... NSGA
Naval Security Group Activity Field Office (DNAB) .... NAVSECGRUACTFO
Naval Security Group Activity, Special Communications Division (DNAB) .... NAVSECGRUACTSPECOMMDIV
Naval Security Group Command (MCD) .... NAVSECGRUCOM
Naval Security Group Command (DNAB) .... NSGC
Naval Security Group Command Headquarters .... NSGCH
Naval Security Group Command Management Data (DNAB) .... NAVSECGRUMGDAT
Naval Security Group Detachment .... NAVSECGRUDET
Naval Security Group Management Information System (DNAB) .... NAVSECGRU MIS
Naval Security Group Orientation Course (DNAB) .... NSGOC
Naval Security Group Training Publication (DNAB) .... NSGTP
Naval Security Station .... NAVSECSTA
Naval Security Station (NVT) .... NSS
Naval Security Station .... SECSTA
Naval Service Headquarters [Canada] .... NSHQ
Naval Service Headquarters, Ottawa (DNAB) .... NSHO
Naval Service School Command .... NAVSERVSCOLCOM
Naval Service School Command .... SSC
Naval Ship Engineering Center .... NAVSEC
Naval Ship Engineering Center .... NAVSHIPENGCEN
Naval Ship Engineering Center (MCD) .... NSEC
Naval Ship Engineering Center Instruction .... NAVSECINST
Naval Ship Engineering Center Instruction .... NSECINST
Naval Ship Engineering Center, Mechanicsburg [Pennsylvania] Division (DNAB) .... NAVSECMECHSDIV
Naval Ship Engineering Center, Norfolk Division .... NAVSECNORDIV
Naval Ship Engineering Center, Philadelphia Division .... NAVSECPHILA
Naval Ship Engineering Center Philadelphia Division .... NAVSECPHILAD
Naval Ship Engineering Center, Philadelphia Division .... NAVSECPHILADIV
Naval Ship Engineering Center, San Diego [California] Division (DNAB) .... NAVSECSDIEGODIV
Naval Ship Engineering Support Activity .... NAVSHIPENGSUPPACT
Naval Ship Missile System Engineering Station .... NAVSHIPMISYSENGSTA
Naval Ship Missile System Engineering Station .... NSMSES
Naval Ship Missile System Engineering Station Detachment, Atlantic (MUGU) .... NSMSESDETLANT
Naval Ship Production Overseer [British] .... NSPO
Naval Ship Repair Facility .... NAVSHIPREPFAC
Naval Ship Repair Facility (MCD) .... NSRF
Naval Ship Repair Officer (DNAB) .... NAVSHIPREPO
Naval Ship Research and Development Center [Also, DTNSRDC] (DNAB) .... NAVSHIPRSCHDEVCEN
Naval Ship Research and Development Center [Also, DTNSRDC] .... NSRDC

[David W. Taylor] Naval Ship Research and Development Center (AAGC) .... NSRDC
Naval Ship Research and Development Center, Annapolis [Maryland] Division (DNAB) .... NAVSHIPRSCHDEVCENANNA
Naval Ship Research and Development Center, Annapolis [Maryland] Division (DNAB) .... NSRDC/A
Naval Ship Research and Development Center (Annapolis Division) .... NSRDC(AD)
Naval Ship Research and Development Center, Annapolis [Maryland] Division (DNAB) .... NSRDCANNADIV
Naval Ship Research and Development Laboratory (MCD) .... NSRDL
Naval Ship Research and Development Laboratory, Annapolis [Maryland] .... NSRDL/A
Naval Ship Research and Development Laboratory, Panama City [Florida] [Later, NCSC] .... NSRDL/PC
Naval Ship Systems Command [Later, NAVSEA, NSSC] .... NAVSHIP
Naval Ship Systems Command (AD) .... NAVSHIPCOM
Naval Ship Systems Command [Later, NAVSEA, NSSC] .... NAVSHIPS
Naval Ship Systems Command [Later, NAVSEA, NSSC] .... NAVSHIPSYSCOM
Naval Ship Systems Command Headquarters [Formerly, BuShips] (USDC) .... NAVSHIPS
Naval Ship Systems Command Headquarters .... NAVSHIPSYSCOMHQ
Naval Ship Systems Command Instruction .... NAVSHIPSINST
Naval Ship Systems Engineering Station .... NAVSSES
Naval Ship Systems Engineering Station Detachment (DNAB) .... NAVSSESDET
Naval Ship Weapon Systems Engineering Station [Port Hueneme, CA] (DNAB) .... NAVSHIPWPNSYSENGSTA
Naval Ship Weapon Systems Engineering Station [Port Hueneme, CA] .... NSWSES
Naval Ship Weapon Systems Engineering Station Detachment (DNAB) .... NAVSHIPWPNSYSENGSTADET
Naval Ship Weapon Sytems Engineering Station Representative (DNAB) .... NAVSHIPWPNSYSENGSTAREP
Naval Ships Advanced Communications System (SAA) .... NSACS
Naval Ships Missile Systems Engineering System (DNAB) .... NAVSHIPMISENGSYS
Naval Ships Parts Control Center (MCD) .... NSPCC
Naval Shipyard (SAA) .... NAVSHIPY
Naval Shipyard .... NAVSHIPYD
Naval Shipyard (AD) .... NavShipyd
Naval Shipyard .... NAVSYD
Naval Shipyard .... NS
Naval Shipyard .... NSY
Naval Shipyard .... NSYD
Naval Shore Electronics Engineering Activity .... NAVSEEACT
Naval Shore Electronics Engineering Center [Terminated, 1966] (MCD) .... NSEEC
Naval Shore Establishment .... NSE
Naval Shore Patrol Detachment .... NSPD
Naval Simulation System [DoD] .... NSS
Naval Small Craft Facilities .... NSCF
Naval Small Ship Combat Data System (SAA) .... NSSCDS
Naval Space Command (DOMA) .... NAVSPACCOM
Naval Space Command (MCD) .... NSC
Naval Space Projects Office .... NSPO
Naval Space Surveillance [Center or System] .... NAVSPASUR
Naval Space Systems Activity (DNAB) .... NAVSPASYSAC
Naval Special Devices Center (SAA) .... NSDC
Naval Special Warfare (NVT) .... NSW
Naval Special Warfare Group (AABC) .... NAVSPECWARGP
Naval Special Warfare Group (NVT) .... NAVSPECWARGRU
Naval Special Warfare Group (NVT) .... NSWG
Naval Special Warfare Group Detachment (DNAB) .... NAVSPECWARGRAUDET
Naval Special Warfare Task Group (CAAL) .... NSWTG
Naval Special Warfare Unit (DNAB) .... NAVSPECWARU
Naval Special Warfare Unit (DOMA) .... NSWU
Naval Special Warfare Unit Detachment (DNAB) .... NAVSPECWARUDET
Naval Special Weapons Ordnance Publication .... NAVSWOP
Naval Staff College (DOMA) .... NSC
Naval Staff Headquarters [British military] (DMA) .... NSHQ
Naval Staff Officer .... NSO
Naval Standard Flange (MSA) .... NFL
Naval Standardization Agreement [NATO] .... NAVSTAG
Naval Standardization Board .... NSB
Naval Standing Exercises (NATG) .... NAVSEX
Naval Station .... NAVSTA
Naval Station .... NS
Naval Stations Atlantic .... NAVSTALANT
Naval Stations Pacific .... NAVSTAPAC
Naval Status of Forces (MCD) .... NSOF
Naval Stock Account .... NSA
Naval Stock Fund .... NSF
Naval Store Officer [British] .... NSO
Naval Stores [British] .... NS
Naval Stores Conservation Program .... NSCP
Naval Stores Department [British military] (DMA) .... NSD
Naval Stores Officer [Canadian Navy] .... CANAVSTORES
Naval Strategic Communications Simulator (MCD) .... NSCS
Naval Strategic Reserve Fleet .... NSRF
Naval Strategic Study .... NSS
Naval Strategic Systems Navigation Facility .... NSSNF
Naval Strategy Think Tank (DOMA) .... NSTT
Naval Strike Warfare Center (DOMA) .... NAVSTKWARCEN
Naval Studies Board [National Academy of Sciences] (DOMA) .... NSB
Naval Sub-Board of Inspection and Survey (DNAB) .... NAVSUBINSURV
Naval Submarine Base .... NAVSUBBASE
Naval Submarine Base .... NSB

Naval Submarine Base - New London (MCD) ... NSBNL
Naval Submarine League (EA) ... NSL
Naval Submarine Medical Center ... NAVSUBMEDCEN
Naval Submarine Medical Center ... NSMC
Naval Submarine Medical Research Laboratory (DNAB) ... NAVSUBMEDRSCHLAB
Naval Submarine Medical Research Laboratory ... NSMRL
Naval Submarine School ... NAVSUBSCOL
Naval Submarine Support Base (DNAB) ... NAVSUBSUPPBASE
Naval Submarine Support Base Detachment (DNAB) ... NAVSUBSUPPBASEDET
Naval Submarine Training Center, Pacific (DNAB) ... NAVSUBTRACENPAC
Naval Supersonic Facility ... NSF
Naval Supersonic Laboratory ... NSL
Naval Supplement, Manual for Courts-Martial [*United States*] [*A publication*] (DLA) ... NSMCM
Naval Supplies ... NAVSUP
Naval Supply Account ... NSA
Naval Supply Account Fund ... NSAF
Naval Supply [*or Support*] **Activity** ... NAVSUPPACT
Naval Supply Center ... NAVSUPCEN
Naval Supply Center ... NSC
Naval Supply Center Detachment (DNAB) ... NSCDET
Naval Supply Center, Puget Sound [*Bremerton, WA*] (DNAB) ... NSCPS
Naval Supply Corps School ... NAVSCSCOL
Naval Supply Corps School Detachment (DNAB) ... NAVSCSCOLDET
Naval Supply Department (DNAB) ... NAVSUPDEPT
Naval Supply Depot (DNAB) ... NAVSUPDEP
Naval Supply Depot ... NSD
Naval Supply Depot Annex ... NSDA
Naval Supply Depot Aviation Department (DNAB) ... NSDAVNDEPT
Naval Supply Depot Detachment (DNAB) ... NSDDET
Naval Supply Depots, Atlantic/Pacific ... NSDLANT/PAC
Naval Supply Force ... NSF
Naval Supply Office ... NAVSO
Naval Supply Radio Station ... NSRS
Naval Supply Requirement (DNAB) ... NSR
Naval Supply Research and Development Facility ... NAVSUPRANDFA
Naval Supply Research and Development Facility ... NSRDF
Naval Supply System Command Headquarters ... NAVSUPSYSCOMHQ
Naval Supply Systems Command [*Formerly, Bureau of Supplies and Accounts*] (MCD) ... NAVSUP
Naval Supply Systems Command [*Formerly, Bureau of Supplies and Accounts*] ... NAVSUPSYSCOM
Naval Supply Systems Command [*Formerly, Bureau of Supplies and Accounts*] (MCD) ... NSUPSC
Naval Supply Systems Command Headquarters ... NSUP
Naval Supply Systems Command Instruction ... NAVSUPINST
Naval Support Activity (NVT) ... NAVSUPACT
Naval Support Activity [*Vietnam*] ... NSA
Naval Support Activity, Da Nang [*Vietnam*] (VNW) ... NSAD
Naval Support Activity Detachment (DNAB) ... NAVSUPPACTDET
Naval Support Activity Detachment (DNAB) ... NSAD
Naval Support Activity, Saigon [*Vietnam*] (VNW) ... NSAS
Naval Support Element (DOMA) ... NSE
Naval Support Force ... NAVSUPPFOR
Naval Support Force (MCD) ... NSF
Naval Support Force, Antarctica (DNAB) ... NSFA
Naval Support Forces, Antarctic ... NAVSUPPFORANTARCTIC
Naval Support Forces, Antarctica ... NAVSUPFORANT
Naval Support Forces, Antarctica (AD) ... NAVSUPORANT
Naval Support Group (NVT) ... NAVSUPGRU
Naval Surface Force, Atlantic (DNAB) ... NAVSURFLANT
Naval Surface Force, Atlantic Readiness Support Group (DNAB) ... NAVSURFLANTREADSUPPGRU
Naval Surface Force, Pacific ... NAVSURFAC
Naval Surface Force, Pacific Dependents' Assistance Team (DNAB) ... NAVSURFPACDAT
Naval Surface Missile Systems (MCD) ... NAVSURMISYS
Naval Surface Warfare Center [*Silver Spring, MD*] ... NAVSWC
Naval Surface Warfare [*or Weapons*] **Center** [*Dahlgren, VA*] ... NSWC
Naval Surface Weapons Center (PDAA) ... NAVSURFWPNCEN
Naval Surface Weapons Center [*Later, NSWC*] (CAAL) ... NAVSWC
Naval Surface Weapons Center Acoustic Facility (GRD) ... NSWCAF
Naval Surface Weapons Center, Dahlgren Laboratory ... NSWC/DL
Naval Surface Weapons Center Facility (DNAB) ... NAVSWCFAC
Naval Surface Weapons Center Representative (DNAB) ... NAVSWCREP
Naval Surface Weapons Center, White Oak Laboratory ... NSWC/WOL
Naval Tactical Command and Control System (PDAA) ... NTCCS
Naval Tactical Communications Center (MCD) ... NTCC
Naval Tactical Data System / Land-Based Test Site (DNAB) ... NTDS/LBTS
Naval Tactical Data Systems Development and Evaluation Site (DNAB) ... NAVTACDATASYSDEVSITE
Naval Tactical Game ... NAVTAG
Naval Tactical Publication (NVT) ... NTP
Naval Tactical Satellite (DNAB) ... NAVTACSAT
Naval Tactical Standards (MCD) ... NAVTACSTANS
Naval Target Subdivision [*G-2, SHAEF*] ... NTS
Naval Task Force ... NTF
Naval Technical Assistants ... NTA
Naval Technical Data System (IAA) ... NTDS
Naval Technical Intelligence Center [*Pronounced N-tech; Formerly, NISC, now NAVMIC*] (DOMA) ... NTIC
Naval Technical Mission in Europe ... NAVTECMISEU
Naval Technical Mission in Europe ... NTME
Naval Technical Mission to Japan ... NAVTECHJAP
Naval Technical Mission to Japan (DNAB) ... NAVTECHMISJAP
Naval Technical Mission to Japan ... NTMJ
Naval Technical Proficiency Assist (NVT) ... NTPA
Naval Technical Representative ... NAVTECHREP
Naval Technical Training Center ... NTTC
Naval Technical Training Center Detachment (DNAB) ... NAVTECHTRACENDET
Naval Technology Office [*Arlington, VA*] (GRD) ... NTO
Naval Telcommunications System Integration Center (DNAB) ... NAVTELSYSIC
Naval Telecommunications Automation Support Center (DNAB) ... NAVTASC
Naval Telecommunications Automation Support Center, Atlantic (DNAB) ... NAVTASCDETLANT
Naval Telecommunications Automation Support Center, Pacific (DNAB) ... NAVTASCDETPAC
Naval Telecommunications Center (DOMA) ... NTCC
Naval Telecommunications Center Detachment (DNAB) ... NTCCDET
Naval Telecommunications Command ... NAVTELCOM
Naval Telecommunications Command (AAGC) ... TCON
Naval Telecommunications Command Satellite Operations Center (MCD) ... NTCSOC
Naval Telecommunications Operations Center (DNAB) ... NTOC
Naval Telecommunications Operations Center Detachment (DNAB) ... NTOCDET
Naval Telecommunications Procedures (NVT) ... NTP
Naval Telecommunications Publication (NVT) ... NTP
Naval Telecommunications System (NVT) ... NTS
Naval Telecommunications System Architect (MCD) ... NTSA
Naval Telecommunications System Engineer (MCD) ... NTSE
Naval Telecommunications System Test Node (CAAL) ... NTSTN
Naval Teletypewriter Exchange [*Formerly, NTE*] ... NTX
Naval Test Pilot School ... NTPS
Naval Torpedo Station ... NAVTORPSTA
Naval Torpedo Station ... NTORS
Naval Torpedo Station ... NTS
Naval Torpedo Testing Range ... NTTR
Naval Training ... NT
Naval Training Aids Center ... NAVTRAIDSCEN
Naval Training Aids Center (DNAB) ... NTAC
Naval Training Aids Facility (DNAB) ... NTAF
Naval Training and Distribution Center ... NAVTRADISTCEN
Naval Training Bulletin ... NATB
Naval Training Center (DNAB) ... NAVTRACEN
Naval Training Center ... NTC
Naval Training Center, San Diego ... NTCSD
Naval Training Command ... NAVTRA
Naval Training Command ... NAVTRACOM
Naval Training Command ... NTC
Naval Training Department [*British military*] (DMA) ... NTD
Naval Training Device Center ... NAVTRADEV
Naval Training Device Center ... NAVTRADEVCEN
Naval Training Devices Center [*Port Washington, LI*] ... NTDC
Naval Training Devices Supply Center (DNAB) ... NAVTRADEVSUPCEN
Naval Training Equipment Center ... NAVTRAEQUIPC
Naval Training Equipment Center ... NAVTRAEQUIPCEN
Naval Training Equipment Center ... NTEC
Naval Training Equipment Center Field Office (DNAB) ... NAVTRAEQUIPCENFEO
Naval Training Equipment Center, Project Engineer ... NTECPE
Naval Training Equipment Center Representative, Atlantic (DNAB) ... NAVTRAEQUIPCENREPLANT
Naval Training Equipment Center, Representative for the Center (DNAB) ... NAVTRAEQUIPCENREPCEN
Naval Training Equipment Center Representative, Pacific (DNAB) ... NAVTRAEQUIPCENREPPAC
Naval Training Information System (MCD) ... NAVTIS
Naval Training Information System with Automated Data Systems (DNAB) ... NAVTIS ADS
Naval Training Publications Center (MCD) ... NAVTRAPUBCEN
Naval Training Publications Center ... NTPC
Naval Training Research Laboratory (WDAA) ... NTRL
Naval Training School ... NAVTRASCOL
Naval Training School ... NTS
Naval Training School ... NTSCH
Naval Training Station ... NAVTRASTA
Naval Training Station ... NTS
Naval Training Support Command Instruction (MCD) ... NAVTRAINST
Naval Training Systems Center [*Orlando, FL*] ... NAVTRASYSCEN
Naval Training Systems Center [*Orlando, FL*] ... NTSC
Naval Training Unit ... NTU
Naval Transport Officer ... NTO
Naval Transportation Coordinating Office ... NAVTRANSCO
Naval Transportation Service [*Later, MSC*] ... NTS
Naval Travel Instructions ... NTI
Naval Undersea Center [*Later, NOSC*] (MCD) ... NUC
Naval Undersea Research and Development Center (MCD) ... NAVUSEARANDCEN
Naval Undersea Research and Development Center ... NAVUSEARESDEVCEN
Naval Undersea Research and Development Center [*Marine science*] (OSRA) ... NUC
Naval Undersea Research and Development Center (USDC) ... NUC
Naval Undersea Research and Development Center ... NURDC
Naval Undersea Warfare Center ... NAVUSEAWARCEN
Naval Undersea Warfare Center [*Later, NURDC*] ... NUWC
Naval Undersea Warfare Engineering Station (MCD) ... NUWES
Naval Undersea Warfare Museum Foundation (PDAA) ... NUWMF
Naval Underwater Ordnance Laboratory (NOAA) ... NUOL
Naval Underwater Ordnance Station ... NUOS
Naval Underwater Sound Laboratory [*Later, NUSC*] ... NAVUWSOUNDLAB
Naval Underwater Sound Laboratory [*Later, NUSC*] ... NUSL
Naval Underwater Systems Center ... NUSC

Naval Underwater Systems Center/Command (USDC) .... NUSC
Naval Underwater Systems Center Detachment (DNAB) .... NUSCDET
Naval Underwater Systems Center, New London [*Connecticut*] .... NUSC/NL
Naval Underwater Systems Center, Newport [*Rhode Island*] .... NUSC/NPT
Naval Underwater Systems Engineering Center .... NAVUWSES
Naval Underwater Systems Engineering Center (MUGU) .... NUSEC
Naval Underwater Weapons Evaluation Station .... NUWES
Naval Underwater Weapons Research and Engineering Station .... NUWRES
Naval Underwater Weapons Station (MCD) .... NUWS
Naval Underwater Weapons Systems Engineering Center (AD) .... NAVUWSEC
Naval Underwater Weapons Systems Engineering Center .... NUWSEC
Naval Unit Disseminator (RDA) .... NUD
Naval Unit, Fort Detrick [*Maryland*] .... NUFD
Naval Vessel Register (MCD) .... NVR
Naval War College .... NAVWARCOL
Naval War College (MUGU) .... NAWARCOL
Naval War College .... NAWC
Naval War College .... NWC
Naval War College .... PRESNAVWARCOL
Naval War College Advanced Research Program [*Newport, RI*] .... NWC/ARP
Naval War College Center for Advanced Research [*Newport, RI*] .... NWC/CAR
Naval War College / Naval Warfare Course (DNAB) .... NWC/NW
Naval War College, Newport, RI [*Library symbol Library of Congress*] (LCLS) .... RNN
Naval War College, Newport, RI [*OCLC symbol*] (OCLC) .... WNC
Naval War College. Review [*A publication*] (DLA) .... Nav War C Rev
Naval War College Review [*A publication*] .... NWCR
Naval Warfare Analysis (MCD) .... NWA
Naval Warfare Analysis Group .... NAVWAG
Naval Warfare Analysis Group .... NWAG
Naval Warfare Gaming System .... NWGS
Naval Warfare Information Publication .... NWIP
Naval Warfare Intercept Procedures (MCD) .... NWIP
Naval Warfare Planning Chart Bases (MCD) .... NWPCB
Naval Warfare Procedures (MCD) .... NWP
Naval Warfare Publications .... NWP
Naval Warfare Publications Library (NVT) .... NWPL
Naval Warfare Research Center (MCD) .... NWRC
Naval Warfare Tactical Data Base (DOMA) .... NWTDB
Naval Warfare Tactical Publication (DNAB) .... NWTP
Naval Weapon Test Center [*China Lake, California*] [*Navy*] .... NWTC
Naval Weaponeering Information Sheet (MCD) .... NWIS
Naval Weapons Annex .... NWA
Naval Weapons Bulletin .... NWB
Naval Weapons Center (MCD) .... NAVWPNCEN
Naval Weapons Center .... NAVWPNSCEN
Naval Weapons Center .... NWC
Naval Weapons Center, Corona Annex [*California*] .... NWCCA
Naval Weapons Center, Corona Laboratories [*California*] .... NWCCL
Naval Weapons Directory .... NWD
Naval Weapons Engineering Support Activity .... NAVWESA
Naval Weapons Engineering Support Activity (DNAB) .... NAVWPNENGSUPPACT
Naval Weapons Engineering Support Activity (PDAA) .... NAWESA
Naval Weapons Engineering Support Activity (MCD) .... NWESA
Naval Weapons Evaluation Facility [*Kirtland Air Force Base, NM*] (DNAB) .... NAVWEPEVALFAC
Naval Weapons Evaluation Facility [*Kirtland Air Force Base, NM*] .... NAVWPNEVALFAC
Naval Weapons Evaluation Facility [*Kirtland Air Force Base, NM*] .... NWEF
Naval Weapons Factory [*Formerly, NGF*] .... NWF
Naval Weapons Handling Center .... NWHC
Naval Weapons Handling Laboratory .... NWHL
Naval Weapons Industrial Reserve Plant (AFM) .... NWIRP
Naval Weapons Industrial Support Office (DNAB) .... NWISO
Naval Weapons Laboratory [*Later, NSWC*] .... NAVWPNLAB
Naval Weapons Laboratory [*Later, NSWC*] .... NWL
Naval Weapons Laboratory / Dahlgren [*Virginia*] (DNAB) .... NWL/D
Naval Weapons Plant (AAG) .... NWP
Naval Weapons Plant, Washington, DC .... NWPW
Naval Weapons Publications .... NWP
Naval Weapons Quality Assurance Office [*Washington, DC*] .... NAVWPNQAO
Naval Weapons Quality Assurance Office [*Washington, DC*] .... NAVWPNQUALASSURO
Naval Weapons Services Office [*Also, NWSO, WEPSO*] .... NAVWPNSERVO
Naval Weapons Services Office [*Also known as NAVWPNSERVO, WEPSO*] .... NWSO
Naval Weapons Services Office [*Also known as NAVWPNSERVO, NWSO*] .... WEPSO
Naval Weapons Station (MCD) .... NAVWPNSTA
Naval Weapons Station .... NWS
Naval Weapons Station Acceptance Program (MCD) .... NWSAP
Naval Weapons Station, Yorktown [*Virginia*] .... NWSY
Naval Weapons Support Activity (DNAB) .... NAVWPNSUPPACT
Naval Weapons Support Activity .... NWSA
Naval Weapons Support Center (DNAB) .... NAVWPNSUPPCEN
Naval Weapons Support Center (MCD) .... NWSC
Naval Weapons Support Center, Crane [*Indiana*] .... NWSC/CR
Naval Weapons Systems Analysis Office .... NAVWPNSYSANALO
Naval Weapons Test Station .... NWTS
Naval Weapons Training Center (DNAB) .... NAVWPNSTRACEN
Naval Weather and Oceanographic Center (DOMA) .... NWOC
Naval Weather Research Facility .... NWRF
Naval Weather Service Association (EA) .... NWSA
Naval Weather Service Command .... NAVWEASERV
Naval Weather Service Command .... NWSC
Naval Weather Service Detachment [*or Division*] .... NWSD
Naval Weather Service Environmental Detachment [*Navy*] .... NWSED
Naval Weather Service Office .... NWSO
Naval Western Oceanographic Center (DNAB) .... NAVWESTOCEANCEN
Naval Working Fund [*Navy, Coast Guard*] .... NWF
Naval Worldwide Command and Control System (MCD) .... NWCCS
Naval Worldwide Command Support System (MCD) .... NWWCSS
Naval Worldwide Environmental Data Network (MCD) .... NEDN
Navarra (AD) .... Nav
Navarre (AD) .... Nav
Navarre Corp. [*Associated Press*] (SAG) .... Navarre
Navarre Corp. [*NASDAQ symbol*] (SAG) .... NAVR
Navarre Resources [*Vancouver Stock Exchange symbol*] .... NRV
Navarro Junior College [*Texas*] .... NJC
Navarro Junior College, Corsicana, TX [*Library symbol Library of Congress*] (LCLS) .... TxCoN
Navasota, TX [*FM radio station call letters*] .... KMBV
Navasota, TX [*AM radio station call letters*] .... KWBC
Navasota, TX [*Location identifier FAA*] (FAAL) .... TNV
Navassa Island (AD) .... Nav
Navassa Island (AD) .... Nav I
NAVDAC [*Naval Data Automation Command*] **Assembly, Monitor, Executive System** (PDAA) .... NAMES
Navegacion y Servicios Aereos Canarios SA [*Spain ICAO designator*] (FAAC) .... NAY
Navegantes [*Brazil*] [*Airport symbol*] (OAG) .... NVT
Navegantes [*Brazil ICAO location identifier*] (ICLI) .... SBNF
Navel .... NVEL
NAVEUR Intelligence Highlights Summary (MCD) .... NIHS
NAVFAC [*Naval Facilities Engineering Command*] **Technical Training Center** .... NTTC
Navier-Stokes Equation .... NSE
Navigable (AD) .... nav
Navigate (AAG) .... NAV
Navigating Lieutenant [*Navy British*] (ROG) .... NL
Navigating Light System .... NLS
Navigating Sub-Lieutenant [*Navy British*] (ROG) .... NSL
Navigation .... N
Navigation (AD) .... nav
Navigation (GAVI) .... NAV
Navigation .... NAVIG
Navigation .... NVGTN
Navigation Action Cutout (AD) .... navaco
Navigation Action Cutout Switchboard .... NAVACO
Navigation Aid (IAA) .... NA
Navigation Aid .... NAVAID
Navigation Aid (NASA) .... NAVID
Navigation Air RADAR (IAA) .... NAVAR
Navigation Airborne RADAR Scope [*Air Force*] .... NAVASCOPE
Navigation along the East Coast of Asia (AD) .... NavEast
Navigation Analysis Program [*NASA*] (NASA) .... NAP
Navigation and Direction Division [*British military*] (DMA) .... NDD
Navigation and Guidance [*G & N is preferred*] [*NASA*] (KSC) .... N & G
Navigation and Guidance .... N&G
Navigation and Guidance Subsystem [*NASA*] (KSC) .... N & GS
Navigation and Radio Homing [*Aviation*] .... NAVARHO
Navigation and Ranging (IAA) .... NAVAR
Navigation and Sensor Computer .... NSC
Navigation and Timing .... N & T
Navigation and Weapon-Aiming Subsystem (MCD) .... NAVWASS
Navigation/Attack Systems Trainer (PDAA) .... NAST
Navigation Avoidance System (KSC) .... NAS
Navigation Base (NASA) .... NB
Navigation by Visual Observation of Satellites (DNAB) .... NAVOSTAT
Navigation Canal [*Board on Geographic Names*] .... CNLN
Navigation Certificate [*Paper issued by British government to merchant vessel, certifying that cargo was non-contraband, that is, not consigned to Germany*] [*World War II*] .... NAVICERT
Navigation Command (MCD) .... NAVCMD
Navigation Command and Control System .... NC & CS
Navigation Communication (AD) .... navcom
Navigation Computer .... NC
Navigation Computer Control .... NCC
Navigation Computer Unit .... NCU
Navigation Computer Unit .... NCV
Navigation Console .... NC
Navigation Control and Display Unit .... NCDU
Navigation Control and Display Unit (MCD) .... NCU
Navigation Control Console .... NCC
Navigation Control Console Panel .... NCCP
Navigation Control/Display Panel (MCD) .... NCDP
Navigation Control Indicator (MCD) .... NCI
Navigation Control Simulator .... NCS
Navigation Control Systems (RDA) .... NAVCON
Navigation Countermeasure (IAA) .... NAVCM
Navigation Countermeasures and Deception .... NAVCM
Navigation Countermeasures and Deception (AD) .... NavCm
Navigation Data Assimilation Center (AD) .... NAVDAC
Navigation Data Assimilation Computer (IAA) .... NADAC
Navigation Data Assimilation Computer (AD) .... navdac
Navigation Data Assimilation Computer .... NAVDAC
Navigation Development Satellite (MCD) .... NDS
Navigation Display (MCD) .... ND
Navigation Display and Computer (MCD) .... NDC
Navigation Display System .... NDS

Navigation Display Unit [*Military*] ... NDU
Navigation Equipment Capability Analysis (KSC) ... NECAP
Navigation Error Data (MUGU) ... NED
Navigation Exercise [*Navy*] (NVT) ... NAVEX
Navigation Exercise (AD) ... navex
Navigation Flight Test [*Aviation*] (DA) ... NFT
Navigation Guidance Equipment (MCD) ... NGE
Navigation Heading and Altitude Reference System [*Aviation*] (PDAA) ... NAVHARS
Navigation in Australian Waters (AD) ... NavAus
Navigation in the Eastern Atlantic and the Mediterranean (AD) ... NavEams
Navigation in the Indian Ocean (AD) ... NavInd
Navigation in the North Atlantic (AD) ... NavNorlant
Navigation in the North Pacific (AD) ... NavNoPac
Navigation in the South Atlantic (AD) ... NavSat
Navigation Information Bulletin ... NIB
Navigation Information Center ... NIC
Navigation Instrument Development Unit ... NIDS
Navigation Interface Unit [*Navy*] (CAAL) ... NIU
Navigation Light (IAA) ... NAVL
Navigation Light Flasher ... NLF
Navigation/Localizer (IEEE) ... N/L
Navigation Management System (PDAA) ... NMS
Navigation Map Computer ... NMC
Navigation Multiplexer [*Navy*] (CAAL) ... NM
Navigation Network (NVT) ... NAVNET
Navigation of the South Pacific (AD) ... NavSoPac
Navigation Officer ... NO
Navigation Operating Procedure ... NOP
Navigation Operational Checkout Computer ... NOCC
Navigation Operator's Control Console ... NOCC
Navigation Package (DNAB) ... NAVPAC
Navigation Parameter Common Pool (NASA) ... NAVPOOL
Navigation [*Parameter Common*] **Pool** ... NAVPOOL
Navigation Processor Unit (MCD) ... NPU
Navigation RADAR ... NAVAR
Navigation RADAR Screen [*Air Force*] ... NAVASCREEN
Navigation Satellite Executive Steering Group ... NAVSEG
Navigation Satellite Management Office ... NAVSMO
Navigation Satellite System (PDAA) ... NASS
Navigation Satellite Tracking and Ranging [*Later, GPS*] [*Air Force*] ... NAVSTAR
Navigation Satellite Tracking and Ranging Global Positioning System [*Air Force*] (MCD) ... NAVSTAR-GPS
Navigation Star Catalogue ... NSC
Navigation Subsystem (OA) ... NS
Navigation Subsystem Switchboard ... NSS
Navigation Support Equipment ... NSE
Navigation System ... NAVS
Navigation System Using Time and Ranging (AD) ... NAVSTAR
Navigation Tactical (AD) ... navtac
Navigation Tactical (AD) ... NAVTAC
Navigation Technology Satellite (PDAA) ... NTS
Navigation Technology System (IAA) ... NTS
Navigation Tender Maintenance Training (DNAB) ... NTMT
Navigation/Traffic Control Satellite (MCD) ... NAVTRASAT
Navigation/Weapon Delivery Computer (PDAA) ... NWDC
Navigation/Weapons Delivery Computer/System ... NWDC/S
Navigation/Weapons Delivery System ... NWDS
Navigation-Administration [*Inquiry program*] (AFIT) ... NAV-ADMIN
Navigational Aid (DNAB) ... NAVAID
Navigational Aid Flight Inspection System (AFM) ... NAFIS
Navigational Aid Inoperative for Parts ... NAIOP
Navigational Aid Support Base ... NASB
Navigational Aid to Bombing [*Air Force*] ... NAB
Navigational Aids [*JETDS nomenclature*] ... N
Navigational Aids and Landing Systems (MCD) ... NAALS
Navigational Aids/Communications Management Office [*Air Force*] (CET) ... NCMO
Navigational Aids Inoperative for Parts (AD) ... naiop
Navigational Aids Support Unit (DNAB) ... NAVAIDSUPPUNIT
Navigational Aids Technician (DNAB) ... NAT
Navigational and Vessel Inspection Circular [*Coast Guard*] (GFGA) ... NVIC
Navigational Base (KSC) ... NVB
Navigational Bombing and Missile Guidance (MCD) ... NBMG
Navigational Bombing and Missile Guidance System (AAG) ... NBMGS
Navigational Bombing System [*British military*] (DMA) ... NBS
Navigational Computer Set (MCD) ... NCS
Navigational Guidance Support (NVT) ... NAVGSUP
Navigational Information Office ... NIO
Navigational Lane Marking System [*Navy*] (DOMA) ... NLMS
Navigational Microfilm Projector ... NMP
Navigational RADAR ... NR
Navigational Satellite [*NASA*] ... NAVSAT
Navigational Satellite (AD) ... navsat
Navigational Satellite Program [*NASA*] (IAA) ... NSP
Navigational Technology Satellite (MCD) ... NTS
Navigational Time Reference (AAG) ... NTR
Navigational/Traffic-Control Satellite (MCD) ... NAVTRAFSAT
Navigational Warning East Atlantic and Mediterranean [*Navy*] (PDAA) ... NAVEAMS
Navigationally-Derived Air Data (MCD) ... NAVDAD
Navigator (DSUE) ... NAV
Navigator (WGA) ... NAVR
Navigator Bombardier Training [*Air Force*] (AFM) ... NBT
Navigator Training [*Air Force*] ... NAVTNG
Navigator Training Squadron [*Air Force*] ... NAVTNGSq
Navigator Training Squadron [*Air Force*] ... NTS
Navigator Training Wing [*Military*] ... NTW
[*The*] **Navigators** (EA) ... TN
Navigators' and Engineering Officers' Union [*British*] ... NEOU
Navigators Group [*NASDAQ symbol*] (TTSB) ... NAVG
[*The*] **Navigators Group, Inc.** [*NASDAQ symbol*] (NQ) ... NAVG
[*The*] **Navigators Group, Inc.** [*Associated Press*] (SAG) ... NavgGp
Navigator's Yeoman [*British military*] (DMA) ... NAVYEO
Navion Aircraft Co. [*ICAO aircraft manufacturer identifier*] (ICAO) ... NA
Navistar International Corp. [*Associated Press*] (SAG) ... Nav
Navistar International Corp. [*NYSE symbol*] (SPSG) ... NAV
Navistar International Corp. [*Associated Press*] (SAG) ... Navistar
Navistar Intl [*NYSE symbol*] (TTSB) ... NAV
Navistar Intl $6 cm Cv Pfd [*NYSE symbol*] (TTSB) ... NAVPrG
Navistar Intl Cv Jr D Pref [*NYSE symbol*] (TTSB) ... NAVPrD
NAVMAT Instructional Procurement Inventory Monitoring System (MCD) ... NIPIMS
NAVMAT [*Navy Material Command*] **Selected Acquisitions Tracking System** (DNAB) ... NSATS
NAVMAT [*Navy Material Command*] **Special Assistance Team** (DNAB) ... NSAT
Navrongo [*Ghana*] [*ICAO location identifier*] (ICLI) ... DGLN
NAVSEA Data Communications Users Group [*Navy*] ... SEADCUG
NAVSHIPS [*Naval Ship Systems Command*] **Damage Control Diagrams** ... DCD
NAVSHIPS [*Naval Ship Systems Command*] **Damage Control Texts** ... DCT
NAVSHIPS [*Naval Ship Systems Command*] **General Information Book** ... NSGIB
NAVSHIPS [*Naval Ship Systems Command*] **Plant Equipment Support Office** ... NPESO
NAVSHIPS [*Naval Ship Systems Command*] **Propulsion Operating Guides** ... NS-POG
NAVSHIPS [*Naval Ship Systems Command*] **Publication** ... NS
NAVSHIPS [*Naval Ship Systems Command*] **Ship Information Booklets** ... NS-SIB
NAVSHIPS [*Naval Ship Systems Command*] **Technical Manual Index** ... NS-TMI
NAVSHIPS [*Naval Ship Systems Command*] **Training Aid Bulletins** ... NS-TAB
NAVSTAR [*Navigation Satellite Tracking and Ranging*] **Processing Facility** (MCD) ... NPF
Navtech Systems Support, Inc. [*Canada ICAO designator*] (FAAC) ... XNS
NAVWEPS ORDALT Instruction (MCD) ... NOI
Navy ... N
Navy (AAG) ... NAV
Navy Absentee Collection Unit (DNAB) ... NAVABSCOLLU
Navy Accounting and Finance Center ... NAFC
Navy Accounting and Finance Center (DNAB) ... NAVACCTGFINCEN
Navy Accounts Disbursing Office ... NADO
Navy Achievement Medal [*Military decoration*] ... NAM
Navy Acoustical Communication Program (MCD) ... NACP
Navy Acquisition Circular (AAGC) ... NAC
Navy Acquisition Executive (MCD) ... NAE
Navy Acquisition Procedures Supplement [*A publication*] (AAGC) ... NAPS
Navy Acquisition Regulations Supplement ... NARSUP
Navy Acquisition-Contracting Officer (MCD) ... NACO
Navy Activity Control (DNAB) ... NAC
Navy Administrative Group ... NAVADGRU
Navy Administrative Office [*or Officer*] ... NAVADMINO
Navy Adult Basic Skills Training Program (NVT) ... NABSTP
Navy Advanced Concept (CAAL) ... NAC
Navy Advanced SATCOM [*Satellite Communications*] **Program** (ANA) ... NASP
Navy Advanced Tactical Fighter (MCD) ... NATF
Navy Advent Ship Station (SAA) ... NASS
Navy Advent Ship Terminal (SAA) ... NAST
Navy Advisory Section [*Vietnam*] (VNW) ... NAS
Navy Aeroballistics Advisory Committee (MCD) ... NAAC
Navy Aeronautics ... NAVAER
Navy Air Combat Fighter (MCD) ... NACF
Navy Air Control and Identification System ... NACIS
Navy Air Cooperation and Liaison Committee ... NACAL
Navy Air Crew Equipment Laboratory [*Philadelphia, PA*] ... NACEL
Navy Air Navigation Electronic Project ... NANEP
Navy Air Pollution Source Information System ... NAPSIS
Navy Air Support Unit ... NASU
Navy Air Traffic Coordinating Officer ... NATCO
Navy Aircraft (IAA) ... NA
Navy Aircraft Accounting System ... NAAS
Navy Aircraft and Readiness System ... NAIRS
Navy Aircraft Resources Utilization Study ... NARUS
Navy Aircrew Common Ejection Seat [*British*] ... NACES
Navy Alcohol Rehabilitation Drydock (DNAB) ... NARD
Navy Alcohol Rehabilitation Drydock (DNAB) ... NAVALREHDRYDOCK
Navy Alcohol Safety Action Program (DNAB) ... NASAP
Navy Alcohol Safety Action Program Office (DNAB) ... NASAPOFF
Navy Alterations ... NAVALT
Navy Alternate Fuel Reference File [*Battelle Memorial Institute*] [*Information service or system Defunct*] (IID) ... NAFRF
Navy Ammunition Logistics Code ... NALC
Navy Ammunition Reclassification ... NAR
Navy and Army Canteen Board [*British military*] (DMA) ... NACB
Navy and Marine Corps [*Medal*] ... N & MC
Navy and Marine Corps Acquisition Review Committee [*Terminated, 1975*] (MCD) ... NMARC
Navy and Marine Corps Appellate Review Activity (DNAB) ... NAMARA
Navy and Marine Corps Intelligence Training Center (DOMA) ... NMITC
Navy and Marine Corps Medal [*Military decoration*] ... N & MCM
Navy and Marine Corps Medal [*Military decoration*] ... NMCM
Navy and Marine Corps Reserve Training Center ... NAVMARCORESTRACEN
Navy and Marine Corps Reserve Training Center ... NMCRTC

Navy and Marine Corps Reserve Training Center ..... NMRTC
Navy Antenna Computer Tracking and Command ..... NACTAC
Navy Antisubmarine Warfare Data Center ..... NAVASWDATACEN
Navy Antisubmarine Warfare Data Center (DNAB) ..... NAVASWDATCEN
Navy Appellate Review Activity ..... NAVARA
Navy Arctic Research Facility ..... NARF
Navy Area Audit Office [*London*] ..... NAAO
Navy Area Audit Office [*London*] (DNAB) ..... NAVAERAUDOFC
Navy Area Audit Service (DNAB) ..... NAAS
Navy, Army, and Air Force Institutes [*Responsible for clubs, canteens, and provision of some items for messing of British armed forces*] ..... NAAFI
Navy/ARPA [*Advanced Research Projects Agency*] **Chemical LASER** (MCD) ..... NACL
Navy Art Review Board (DNAB) ..... NARB
Navy Assessment and Control of Installation Pollutants ..... NACIP
Navy Astronautics Group (MUGU) ..... NAG
Navy Astronautics Group (MUGU) ..... NAVASTROGRU
Navy Astronautics Group (SAA) ..... NAVASTROGRUP
Navy Astronautics Group Conference [*Navy*] ..... NAGC
Navy Astronautics Group Headquarters, Tracking and Injection Facility (DNAB) ..... NAVASTROGRUHQTRINJFAC
Navy Attitudinal Information System (NVT) ..... NAIS
Navy Audit Office (DNAB) ..... NAVAUDO
Navy Auditor ..... NAVAUD
Navy Authorized Data List (NG) ..... NADL
Navy Automated Civilian Management Information System ..... NACMIS
Navy Automated Pilot Aptitude Measurement System ..... NAPAMS
Navy Automated Research and Development Information System [*Later, NAVWUIS*] ..... NARDIS
Navy Automated Transport Documentation System (DNAB) ..... NAVADS
Navy Automated Transportation Data System (DNAB) ..... NATDS
Navy Automatic Broadcasting, Processing, and Routing System (NG) ..... NABPARS
Navy Automatic Digital Network Switching Center (DNAB) ..... NAVAUTODINSCEN
Navy Automatic RADAR Test Equipment (KSC) ..... NARATE
Navy Auxiliary Air Stations, Atlantic ..... NAASLANT
Navy Auxiliary Air Stations, Pacific ..... NAASPAC
Navy Aviation Maintenance and Material Support System (NG) ..... NAMMIS
Navy Aviation Maintenance and Material Support System ..... NAMMS
Navy Aviation Safety Center (MUGU) ..... NASC
Navy Ballistic Missile ..... NAVBM
Navy Ballistic Missile Committee ..... NAVBMC
Navy Band ..... NB
Navy Basic Logistic [*Plan*] ..... NBL
Navy Basic Modernization [*Plan*] ..... NBM
Navy Beach Amphibious Refresher Training Group (DNAB) ..... NAVBCHPHIBREFTRAGRU
Navy Beach Commando ..... NBC
Navy Board for Production Awards ..... NBPA
Navy Boiler Laboratory ..... NAVBOILAB
Navy Broadcasting Service Detachment (DNAB) ..... NAVBCSTSVCDET
Navy Broadcasting Service Detachment Television Audio Support Activity (DNAB) ..... NAVBCSTSVCDETTASA
Navy Broadcasting Service, Washington, DC (DNAB) ..... NAVBCSTSVCWASHDC
Navy Bureau of Ordnance [*Obsolete*] ..... NBO
Navy Calibration Equipment List ..... NCE
Navy Calibration Laboratory (DNAB) ..... NAVCALAB
Navy Calibration Laboratory ..... NCL
Navy Calibration Laboratory Annex (DNAB) ..... NAVCALABANX
Navy Calibration Laboratory Meteorology Support Group (DNAB) ..... NAVCALABMSG
Navy Calibration Laboratory Operations (DNAB) ..... NAVCALABOPS
Navy Camera Control System ..... NCCS
Navy Capabilities and Mobilization Plan (DOMA) ..... NCMP
Navy Cargo Document (DNAB) ..... NCD
Navy Cargo Handling and Port Group (NVT) ..... NAVCHAPGRU
Navy Cargo Handling and Port Group Detachment (DNAB) ..... NAVCHAPGRUDET
Navy Center for Acquisition Research [*Monterey, CA*] ..... NCAR
Navy Center for Applied Research in Artificial Intelligence [*Washington, DC*] (GRD) ..... NCARAI
Navy Central Clearance Group (DNAB) ..... NCCG
Navy Central Disbursing Office ..... NCDO
Navy Central Freight Control Office ..... NAVCENFRACO
Navy Central Planning Team [*NATO*] (NATG) ..... NCPT
Navy/Chief of Naval Operations (AAG) ..... N/CNO
Navy Civil Engineer [*A publication*] ..... NCE
Navy Civil Engineering Laboratory (DNAB) ..... NAVCIVENGLAB
Navy Civilian Career Management Inventory and Referral System (DNAB) ..... NCCMIRS
Navy Civilian Career Management Program (DNAB) ..... NCCMP
Navy Civilian Personnel Data System ..... NCPDS
Navy Civilian Personnel Instructions ..... NCPI
Navy Civilian Technical Specialist (MCD) ..... NCTS
Navy Clothing and Textile Office (DNAB) ..... NAVCLOTEXTOFC
Navy Clothing and Textile Office (DNAB) ..... NAVCLOTHTEXOFC
Navy Clothing and Textile Research Facility [*Natick, MA*] (DNAB) ..... NAVCLOTEXTRSCHFAC
Navy Clothing and Textile Research Facility [*Natick, MA*] ..... NCTRF
Navy Clothing and Textile Research Unit ..... NAVCLOTEXTRSCHU
Navy Clothing and Textile Research Unit (MCD) ..... NCTRU
Navy Clothing and Textile Supply Office ..... NCTO
Navy Club of the United States of America (EA) ..... NCUSA
Navy Club of the United States of America Auxiliary (EA) ..... NCUSAA
Navy Code Logistic [*Plan*] ..... NCL
Navy Code Room ..... NCR
Navy Combat Art Collection (DNAB) ..... NCAC
Navy Combat Direction System (MCD) ..... NCDS
Navy Command [*Part of North American Air Defense Command*] ..... COMNAV
Navy Command and Control System (DOMA) ..... NCCS
Navy Command and Control System (NVT) ..... NCCS
Navy Command Center (MCD) ..... NCC
Navy Command Support Center (MCD) ..... NCSC
Navy Command Support System (MCD) ..... NCSS
Navy Commendation Medal ..... NCM
Navy Commissary Store (DNAB) ..... NAVCOMSYSTO
Navy Commissary Store ..... NAVCOMSYSTORE
Navy Component ..... NC
Navy Comptroller Budget (NG) ..... NCB
Navy Contract Adjustment Board (AAGC) ..... NAVYCAB
Navy Contract Adjustment Board ..... NCAB
Navy Contract Administrator ..... NCA
Navy Contracting Department (DNAB) ..... NAVCONTDEP
Navy Contracting Directives (MCD) ..... NCD
Navy Contractor Experience List ..... NCEL
Navy Contractor Performance Evaluation Group ..... NCPEG
Navy Control Number (MCD) ..... NCN
Navy Controlled Waste Information System ..... NACWIS
Navy Coolant [*Gunpowder*] ..... NACO
Navy Correctional Custody Unit (DNAB) ..... NAVCORRCUSUNIT
Navy Correspondence Manual ..... NCM
Navy Cost Center ..... NCC
Navy Cost Information System ..... NCIS
Navy Counselor First Class (DNAB) NC1
Navy Counterintelligence Support Activity (DNAB) ..... NAVCINSUPPACT
Navy Counterintelligence Support Center (DNAB) ..... NAVCINTSUPPCEN
Navy Counterintelligence Support Unit (DNAB) ..... NAVCINTSUPPGRU
Navy Cross ..... NC
Navy Current Procurement Directive ..... NCPD
Navy Damage Control Training Center ..... NAVDAMCONTRACEN
Navy Data Automation Center (DNAB) ..... NAVDAF
Navy Data System ..... NDS
Navy Decision Center ..... NADEC
Navy Decision Coordinating Paper ..... NDCP
Navy Deep Sea Oceanographic System ..... NDSOS
Navy Degaussing Station (DNAB) ..... NAVDEGSTA
Navy Department ..... NAVDEPT
Navy Department ..... ND
Navy Department Advisory Committee on Structural Steel ..... NDACSS
Navy Department Board of Contract Appeals [*1944-50*] (AAGC) ..... NBCA
Navy Department Board of Contract Appeals ..... NDBCA
Navy Department Board of Decorations and Medals (DNAB) ..... NDBDM
Navy Department Bulletin [*A publication*] ..... NDB
Navy Department Bulletins, Cumulative Editions [*A publication*] ..... NDBULCUMED
Navy Department Corrosion Committee ..... NDCC
Navy Department Duty Chaplain (DNAB) ..... NDDC
Navy Department Employees Recreation and Welfare Fund (MCD) ..... NDERWF
Navy Department Establishments [*British*] ..... NDE
Navy Department Five Year Plan ..... NDFYP
Navy Department Fuel and Lubricants Advisory Committee [*Ministry of Defense*] [*British*] (PDAA) ..... NAFLAC
Navy Department General Order ..... NDGO
Navy Department Library, Naval Historical Center, Washington, DC [*OCLC symbol*] (OCLC) ..... NHC
Navy Department Mobilization Security Plan (NG) ..... NDMSP
Navy Department Orientation Course (NG) ..... NAVDOC
Navy Department Personnel ..... NDP
Navy Department Program Information Center ..... NDPIC
Navy Department Publications Control Board ..... NAVPUBSCONBD
Navy Dependents School Branch ..... NDSB
Navy Design Selection List ..... NAVDES
Navy Designated Overhaul Point (CAAL) ..... NDOP
Navy Development Center (CAAL) ..... NADEC
Navy Development Concept Paper (CAAL) ..... NDCP
Navy Development Training Center ..... NAVDEVTRACEN
Navy Directive System (NVT) ..... NDS
Navy Disbursing Office ..... NDO
Navy Disciplinary Barracks (DNAB) ..... NAVDISBAR
Navy Disciplinary Command ..... NAVDISCOM
Navy Disease Vector Control Center ..... NAVDISEAVECTORCONCEN
Navy Disease Vector Ecology and Control Center (DNAB) ..... NAVDISVECTTECOLCONCEN
Navy Display Improvement Program ..... NADIP
Navy Display System ..... NDS
Navy Distillate Fuel (DNAB) ..... NDF
Navy Drug Abuse Control Program (DNAB) ..... NDACP
Navy Drug Abuse Counselor School (DNAB) ..... NDACS
Navy Drug and Alcohol Advisory Council (DNAB) ..... NDAAC
Navy Early Warning ..... NEW
Navy Education and Employment Development System (MCD) ..... NEEDS
Navy Educational Tape Catalog (DNAB) ..... NAVETC
Navy EHF [*Extremely High Frequency*] **Satellite Program** (DOMA) ..... NESP
Navy Electromagnetic Spectrum Center (DNAB) ..... NAVEMSCEN
Navy Electromagnetic Spectrum Center (DNAB) ..... NESC
Navy Electronics Application Trainer ..... NEAT
Navy Electronics Laboratory [*San Diego, CA*] ..... NEL
Navy Electronics Laboratory Assembly Tester ..... NELAT
Navy Electronics Laboratory Operating System ..... NELOS
Navy Element (DNAB) ..... NAVELEM
Navy Element Alternate National Military Command Center (MCD) ..... NEANMCC
Navy Embarked Advisory Team ..... NEAT

Navy Employee Appeals Review Board (DNAB) .... NAVEARB
Navy Energy and Environmental Support Activity (DNAB) .... NAVENENVSA
Navy Energy Usage Reporting System (DNAB) .... NEURS
Navy Engineering Technical Services (NG) .... NETS
Navy Enlisted Advanced School Program .... NEASP
Navy Enlisted Classification (NG) .... NEC
Navy Enlisted Code .... NEC
Navy Enlisted Dietetic Education Program .... NEDEP
Navy Enlisted Ground Defense Emergency Force .... NEGDEF
Navy Enlisted Nursing Education Program .... NENEP
Navy Enlisted Occupational Classification System (NVT) .... NEOCS
Navy Enlisted Scientific Education Program .... NESEP
Navy Environmental and Preventive Medicine Unit (DNAB) .... NAVENPVNTMEDU
Navy Environmental and Preventive Medicine Unit (NVT) .... NEPMU
Navy Environmental Health Center (DNAB) .... NAVENVRHLTHCEN
Navy Environmental Protection Data Base [Obsolete] .... NEPDB
Navy Environmental Protection Support Service .... NEPSS
Navy Environmental Remote Sensing Program .... NERSP
Navy Environmental Support Center (DNAB) .... NAVENVSUPPCEN
Navy Environmental Support Office [Obsolete] (DNAB) .... NAVENVSUPPO
Navy Environmental Support Office [Obsolete] .... NESO
Navy Evaluation .... NE
Navy Evaluation of Advanced Reconnaissance Systems .... NEARS
Navy Examination Center .... NAVEXAMCEN
Navy Exchange, England Complex (DNAB) .... NAVEXENGLANDCOM
Navy Exchange Service Command .... NEXCOM
Navy/Executive Offices (AAG) .... N/NAVEXOS
Navy Experimental Diving Unit .... NAVXDIVINGU
Navy Experimental Diving Unit [Panama City, FL] .... NEDU
Navy Extended Electrode Technique (PDAA) .... NEET
Navy Faces (NITA) .... NAVFAC
Navy Facilities System .... NFS
Navy Family Allowance Activity .... NAVFAMALWACT
Navy Federal Credit Union .... NFC
Navy Federal Credit Union .... NFCU
Navy Field Intelligence Office (DNAB) .... NAVFLDINTO
Navy Field Purchase Systems (NG) .... NFPS
Navy Field Safety Association (EA) .... NFSA
Navy Field Service .... NFS
Navy Fighter Weapons School (DNAB) .... NAVFITWEPSCOL
Navy Fighter Weapons School (DNAB) .... NFWS
Navy Finance Center .... NAVFINCEN
Navy Finance Center .... NFC
Navy Finance Center (Allotments Division) (DNAB) .... NFC(ALLOT)
Navy Finance Center (Central Accounts Division) (DNAB) .... NFC(CAD)
Navy Finance Center - Cleveland [Ohio] (DNAB) .... NAVFINCEN-CLEVE
Navy Finance Center - Cleveland [Ohio] (DNAB) .... NFC-CLEVE
Navy Finance Center - Washington, DC (DNAB) .... NAVFINCEN-WASH
Navy Finance Center - Washington, DC (DNAB) .... NFC-WASH
Navy Finance Office .... NAVFINOFF
Navy Finance Office .... NFO
Navy Fleet Material Support (MCD) .... NFMS
Navy Fleet Material Support Office (DNAB) .... NFMSO
Navy Fleet Numerical Weather Facility [Marine science] (MSC) .... NFNWF
Navy Flight Demonstration Squadron (DNAB) .... NAVFLITHTDEMORON
Navy Flight Test (MCD) .... NFT
Navy Food Management Team (DNAB) .... NAVFOODMGTM
Navy Food Management Team (DNAB) .... NFMT
Navy Food Service Systems Office .... NAVFSSO
Navy Food Services Office (DNAB) .... NAVFSSO
Navy Freight Office .... NAVFROF
Navy Frequency Coordinator (DNAB) .... NAVFRCOORD
Navy Fuel Supply Office .... NFSO
Navy General [MCD files] .... NG
Navy General Classification Test (DNAB) .... NGCT
Navy General Publications .... NAVGEN
Navy Good Conduct Medal .... NGCM
Navy Graduate Education Program Select Study Committee [Terminated, 1975] (EGAO) .... NGEPSSC
Navy Guidance Official [British] .... NGO
Navy Guided Missile School .... NAVGMSCHOL
Navy Guided Missile Unit .... NAVGMU
Navy Hazardous Materials Information System (DNAB) .... NHIS
Navy Headquarters Budgeting System (GFGA) .... NHBS
Navy Headquarters Budgeting System/Navy Headquarters Programming System (GFGA) .... NHBS/NHPS
Navy Historical Display Center .... NAVHISTDISPLAYCEN
Navy Hydrographic Office [Later, NOO] .... NHO
Navy Indochina Clearing Office (DNAB) .... NICO
Navy Industrial Association [Later, NSIA] .... NIA
Navy Industrial Fund .... NIF
Navy Industrial Fund-Reporting System (MCD) .... NIFRS
Navy Industrial Management Reviews (NG) .... NIMR
Navy Industrial Readiness Planning List (NG) .... NIRPL
Navy Industrial Relations Activity (DNAB) .... NIRA
Navy Industry Cooperation Plan .... NICOP
Navy/Industry Cooperative Research and Development .... NICRAD
Navy/Industry Cooperative Research and Development Program (MCD) .... NICARD
Navy/Industry Cooperative Research and Development Program .... NICORD
Navy Information Center (MCD) .... NAVIC
Navy Information Center .... NIC
Navy Information Office (DNAB) .... NAVINFO
Navy Information Policy Summaries (NG) .... NIPS
Navy Initial Support Requirement (AFIT) .... NISR

Navy Inspection Service .... NIS
Navy Installation Survey Group .... NISG
Navy Institute of Oceanography .... NIO
Navy Integrated Command Management Information System .... NAICOM/MIS
Navy Integrated Comprehensible Repairable Item Scheduling Program .... NICRISP
Navy Integrated Message Reporting System (MCD) .... NIMRS
Navy Integrated Space Program (NG) .... NISP
Navy Integrated Terminal Evaluation .... NITE
Navy Integrated Training Resources and Administration System (NVT) .... NITRAS
Navy Intelligence Data Network (MCD) .... NIDN
Navy Interceptor Program .... NIP
Navy Interim Surface Ship Model (CAAL) .... NISSM
Navy Internal Relations Activity (DNAB) .... NAVINRELACT
Navy Internal Relations Activity (DNAB) .... NIRA
Navy International Logistics Control Office (MCD) .... NAVILCO
Navy Inventory Control Office .... NICO
Navy Item Control Number (MCD) .... NICN
Navy Jet Trainer (MCD) .... VTXTS
Navy Jet-Propelled-Missile Board .... NJPMB
Navy Job Classification Manual .... NJC
Navy Key Distribution System (CAAL) .... NKDS
Navy Laboratory Computer Network .... NALCON
Navy Laboratory Technical Office for ADP and Communication Systems (GFGA) .... NALTOACS
Navy Law Center (DNAB) .... NLC
Navy League Cadet Corps (EA) .... NLCC
Navy League of Australia .... NLA
Navy League of the United States .... NL
Navy League of the United States (EA) .... NLUS
Navy Liaison Office for Guided Missiles (MCD) .... NLOGM
Navy Liaison Officer for Scouting (DNAB) .... NAVLOS
Navy Library (WDAA) .... NL
Navy List [British military] (DMA) .... NL
Navy Lockheed Service Center .... NLSC
Navy Logistic Support Improvement Plan (NG) .... NAVLOGSIP
Navy Logistics Capabilities Plan .... NLCP
Navy Logistics Capabilities Plan - Fiscal Year (DNAB) .... NLCP-FY
Navy Logistics Information System .... NAVLIS
Navy Logistics Information System .... NLIS
Navy Logistics Management School .... NLMS
Navy Logistics Support Force (DOMA) .... NLSF
Navy Logistics Systems School .... NLSS
Navy Long-Range Guidance .... NLRG
Navy Long-Range Objectives Group (DNAB) .... NLROG
Navy Long-Range Strategic Study .... NLRSS
Navy Mail Clerk .... NMC
Navy Mail Clerk .... NMCLK
Navy Mail Service Veterans Association (EA) .... NMSVA
Navy Maintenance and Material Management System [Also known as MMM, NMMMS, 3M] .... NMMM
Navy Maintenance and Material Management System [Also known as MMM, NMMM, 3M] .... NMMMS
Navy Maintenance and Supply Systems Office (DNAB) .... NAVMASSO
Navy Maintenance and Supply Systems Office (DNAB) .... NMSSO
Navy Maintenance and Supply Systems Office Detachment (DNAB) .... NAVMASSODET
Navy Maintenance and Supply Systems Office Detachment, Pacific (DNAB) .... NAVMASSODETPAC
Navy Maintenance Field Office (NVT) .... NMNFO
Navy Maintenance Management Field Office .... NMMFO
Navy Maintenance Management Field Office (West) (DNAB) .... NMMFO(W)
Navy Maintenance Support Office .... NAMSO
Navy Maintenance Support Office Instruction (MCD) .... NAMSOINST
Navy Management Data File (DNAB) .... NMDF
Navy Management Data List (NG) .... NMDL
Navy Management Fund .... NMF
Navy Management Information System (MCD) .... NAVMIS
Navy Management List (AFIT) .... NML
Navy Management Office .... NMO
Navy Management Review [A publication] .... NMR
Navy Management Systems Center (PDAA) .... NMSC
Navy Management Systems Support Office (AAGC) .... NAVMASSO
Navy Manning Plan (NVT) .... NMP
Navy Manpower and Material Analysis Center (DNAB) .... NAVMAC
Navy Manpower and Material Analysis Center (NVT) .... NAVMMAC
Navy Manpower and Material Analysis Center, Atlantic .... NAVMMACLANT
Navy Manpower and Material Analysis Center, Pacific (DNAB) .... NAVMMACPAC
Navy Manpower and Material Analysis Center, Pacific .... NAVMMACPAC
Navy Manpower Information System Manual (DNAB) .... NMISMAN
Navy Manpower Mobilization System .... NAMMOS
Navy Manpower Planning System (NVT) .... NAMPS
Navy Manpower Requirements System (NVT) .... NMRS
Navy Manpower Survey Board .... NMSB
Navy Manpower Validation Office (DNAB) .... NMVO
Navy Manpower Validation Office, Atlantic (DNAB) .... NMVOLANT
Navy Manpower Validation Office, Pacific (DNAB) .... NMVOPAC
Navy Manpower Validation Program (NG) .... NMVP
Navy Manpower Validation Support Activity .... NMVSA
Navy Marine Diesel Fuel .... NMD
Navy Marine Engineering Laboratory [Later, David W. Taylor Naval Ship Research and Development Center] (KSC) .... NMEL
Navy Material Cataloging Office .... NMCO
Navy Material Command Support Activity .... NMCSA

Navy Material Command Support Activity (PDAA) ... NMSCA
Navy Material Data List ... NMDL
Navy Material Movement Control Plan ... NAVMATMOCON
Navy Material Redistribution and Disposal Office [*or Officer*] ... NMR & DO
Navy Material Redistribution and Disposition Administration ... NMR & DA
Navy Material Redistribution Center ... NMRC
Navy Material Transportation Office ... NAVMTO
Navy Material Transportation Office [*MTMC*] (TAG) ... NAVMTO
Navy Material Transportation Office ... NMTO
Navy Medical Administrative Unit (DNAB) ... NAVMEDADMINU
Navy Medical Center (DNAB) ... NAVMEDCEN
Navy Medical Field Research Laboratory (DNAB) ... NAVMEDFLDRSCHLAB
Navy Medical Information System ... NAVMEDIS
Navy Medical Neuropsychiatric Research Unit (DNAB) ... NAVMEDNPRSCHU
Navy Medical Research Institute Detachment (DNAB) ... NAVMEDRSCHINSTDET
Navy Medical Research Laboratory (DNAB) ... NAVMEDRSHCHLAB
Navy Medical Research Unit [*World War II*] ... NAMRU
Navy Medical Reserve Unit (DAVI) ... NAMRU
Navy Medical Support Unit (DNAB) ... NAVMEDSUPPU
Navy Memorandum Correction ... NMC
Navy Metrication Group (DNAB) ... NMG
Navy Mid-Range Guidance ... NMRG
Navy Mid-Range Objectives ... NMRO
Navy Mid-Range Study ... NMS
Navy Military Assistance Programs ... NMAP
Navy Military Assistance Training Program (NG) ... NMATP
Navy Military Construction Review Board ... NMCRB
Navy Military Government ... NMG
Navy Military Technical Specialist (MCD) ... NMTS
Navy Mine Countermeasures Station ... NAVMINCOMEASTA
Navy Mine Countermeasures Station (MUGU) ... NMCS
Navy Mine Defense Laboratory [*Later, NCSC*] ... NAVMINDEFLAB
Navy Mines (MCD) ... NM
Navy Missile Analysis Program (MCD) ... NAVMAP
Navy Missile Center Laboratory (KSC) ... NMCL
Navy Mobile Construction Battalion ... NAVMOBCONSTBN
Navy Mobile Construction Battalion (CINC) ... NMCB
Navy Mothers' Clubs of America (EA) ... NMCA
Navy Motion Picture Exchange ... NMPX
Navy Motion Picture Office ... NMPO
Navy Motion Picture Service ... NMPS
Navy Motion Picture Service, Motion Picture Distribution Office (DNAB) ... NMPSMOPIXDISTOFF
Navy Movement and Transportation Office ... NAVMTO
Navy Mutual Aid ... NAVMUTAID
Navy Mutual Aid Association (EA) ... NMA
Navy Mutual Aid Association ... NMAA
Navy Navigation Satellite ... NNS
Navy Navigational Satellite System ... NNSS
Navy Network (DOMA) ... NAVNET
Navy News Service (DOMA) ... NNS
Navy Nuclear Power School (DNAB) ... NAVNUPWRSCOL
Navy Nuclear Power School (DNAB) ... NNPS
Navy Nuclear Weapons Bulletin [*A publication*] ... NNWB
Navy Nuclear Weapons Officer (DNAB) ... NNWO
Navy Numerical Weather Prediction [*Computer system*] [*Control Data Corp.*] ... NANWEP
Navy Numerical Weather Problems [*Group*] ... NANWEP
Navy Nurse Corps ... NNC
Navy Nurse Corps Candidate (DNAB) ... NNCC
Navy Objectives Plan ... NOP
Navy Occupation Service Medal ... NOSM
Navy Occupational Development and Analysis Center (DNAB) ... NODAC
Navy Occupational Health Information Management System ... NOHIMS
Navy Occupational Safety and Deficiency Abatement/Management Information System ... NAVOSH DAP/MIS
Navy Occupational Safety and Health (MCD) ... NAVOSH
Navy Occupational Task Analysis Program (NVT) ... NOTAP
Navy Ocean Experimental Acoustic Data Bank (MSC) ... NAVDAB
Navy Ocean Surveillance System ... NOSS
Navy Oceanographic and Meteorological Support System (MCD) ... NOMSS
Navy Oceanographic Meteorological Association [*Marine science*] (OSRA) ... NOMAD
Navy Oceanographic Meteorological Association (USDC) ... NOMAD
Navy Oceanographic Meteorological Automatic Device ... NOMAD
Navy/Office of Naval Intelligence (AAG) ... N/ONI
Navy/Office of Naval Research (AAG) ... N/ONR
Navy Officers Accounts Office (AD) ... NAOA
Navy Officers, Accounts Office (MUGU) ... NOAO
Navy Officer's Classification ... NOC
Navy Oil Analysis Program (NG) ... NOAP
Navy Operation and Maintenance Aviation Deck (MCD) ... NOMAD
Navy Operational Deception (MCD) ... NOD
Navy Operational Global Atmospheric Prediction System ... NOGAPS
Navy Operational Intelligence Center [*Now Naval Maritime Intelligence Center (NAVMIC)*] (DOMA) ... NOIC
Navy Operational Radio and Telephone Switchboard (NVT) ... NORATS
Navy Operational Regional Atmospheric Prediction System (MCD) ... NORAPS
Navy Ordnance List (DNAB) ... NAVORDLIST
Navy Outlying Landing Field (DNAB) ... NAVOLF
Navy Overseas Cargo Terminals ... NOCT
Navy Overseas Dependents School ... NODS
Navy Pacific Missile Test Center (MCD) ... NPMTC
Navy Parachute Team / East Coast (DNAB) ... NPT/E
Navy Parachute Team / West Coast (DNAB) ... NPT/W
Navy Passenger Transportation Office (DNAB) ... NAVPTO
Navy Payroll (DNAB) ... NPR
Navy Pentagon Computer Services Division (DNAB) ... NAVPECOS
Navy Peridontal Screening Examination (DNAB) ... NPSE
Navy Personnel Billeting System (DNAB) ... NPBS
Navy Personnel Management Academy (DNAB) ... NPMA
Navy Personnel Research and Development Center (GRD) ... NPRDC
Navy Personnel Research and Development Laboratory ... NAVPERSRANDLAB
Navy Personnel Survey ... NPS
Navy Petroleum Office ... NAVPETOFF
Navy Planning and Programming System ... NPPS
Navy Plant Representative Office ... NPRO
Navy Pointer Tracker (MCD) ... NPT
Navy Polar Oceanographic Center (DNAB) ... NPOC
Navy Policy Council ... NPC
Navy Post Office ... NPO
Navy Postal Affairs Section Publication ... NPA
Navy Postgraduate College ... NAVPGCOL
Navy Preliminary Evaluation ... NPE
Navy Preliminary Revision (DNAB) ... NPR
Navy Preventive Medicine Unit ... NAVPVNTMEDU
Navy Price Adjustment Board ... NPAB
Navy Primary Standards (MSA) ... NPS
Navy Primary Standards Department (DNAB) ... NAVPRIMSTDEPT
Navy Priorities and Allocations Manual (DNAB) ... NPAM
Navy Procurement Assignment Committee ... NPAC
Navy Procurement Circular ... NPC
Navy Procurement Directives ... NPD
Navy Procurement Regulation ... NPR
Navy Program Decision Meeting (DOMA) ... NPDM
Navy Program Evaluation Procedures ... NAVPEP
Navy Program Language Group ... NPLG
Navy Program Objectives (NG) ... NPO
Navy Program Planning Office ... NPPO
Navy Program Progress Item (CAAL) ... NPPI
Navy Program Progress Report ... NPPR
Navy Programming Manual ... NPM
Navy Programming Planning Council ... NPPC
Navy Propellant Plant (DNAB) ... NPP
Navy Property Redistribution and Disposal (AAGC) ... NPR&D
Navy Prosthetics Research Laboratory ... NPRL
Navy Prototype Optical Interferometer ... NPOI
Navy Prototype Optical Interferometer ... NPOI
Navy Public Affairs Center (DNAB) ... NAVPACEN
Navy Public Affairs Plan (DNAB) ... NPAP
Navy Public Works Center ... NAVPUBWKSCEN
Navy Public Works Center ... NPWC
Navy Public Works Department (DNAB) ... NAVPUBWKSDEPT
Navy Public Works Department ... NPWD
Navy Publications and Printing Office ... NAVPUBPRINTO
Navy Publications and Printing Office ... NPPO
Navy Publications and Printing Service ... NAVPUB
Navy Publications and Printing Service ... NPPS
Navy Publications and Printing Service Branch Office ... NPPSBO
Navy Publications and Printing Service Instruction ... NAVPUBINST
Navy Publications and Printing Service Management Office ... NPPSMO
Navy Publications and Printing Service Office ... NAVPUBPRINTSERVO
Navy Publications and Printing Service Office ... NPPSO
Navy Publications and Printing Service, Southeastern Division (DNAB) ... NPPSSOEASTDIV
Navy Publications and Printing Service, Western Division (DNAB) ... NPPSWESTDIV
Navy Publishing on Demand System (AAGC) ... NPODS
Navy Purchasing Activity (AFIT) ... NPA
Navy Purchasing Department (DNAB) ... NAVPURDEP
Navy Purchasing Office ... NAVPUR
Navy Purchasing Office ... NAVPURO
Navy Purchasing Office ... NPO
Navy Purchasing Office, Los Angeles ... NPOLA
Navy Quality Management ... NQM
Navy Radio (NOAA) ... NRDO
Navy Radio and Sound Laboratory (IAA) ... NRSL
Navy Radio Frequency Spectrum Activity ... NRFSA
Navy Radiological Defense Laboratory ... NAVRADLDEFLAB
Navy Radiological Defense Laboratory (DNAB) ... NRDL
Navy Rapid Delivery Logistics (AFIT) ... NARDELOG
Navy Readiness Analysis System ... NRAS
Navy Readiness Reporting and Analysis System (MCD) ... NRRAS
Navy Reconnaissance Center (MCD) ... NRC
Navy Records Society [*British*] (DBA) ... NRS
Navy Recruit Training Command (DNAB) ... NAVCRUITRACOM
Navy Recruiting Aids Facility (DNAB) ... NRAF
Navy Recruiting Area ... NAVCRUITAREA
Navy Recruiting Area (DNAB) ... NRA
Navy Recruiting Branch Station (DNAB) ... NAVCRUITBRSTA
Navy Recruiting Branch Station (DNAB) ... NRBS
Navy Recruiting Bureau ... NRB
Navy Recruiting Command (DNAB) ... NAVCRUITCOM
Navy Recruiting Command (DNAB) ... NRC
Navy Recruiting Command Instructions ... COMNAVCRUITCOMINST
Navy Recruiting Command Orientation Unit (DNAB) ... NAVCRUITCOMORIENTUNIT
Navy Recruiting Command Standardization and Audit Team (DNAB) ... NAVCRUITCOMSAT
Navy Recruiting Command Youth Programs Field Representative (DNAB) ... NAVCRUITCOMYPFLDREP

Navy Recruiting District (DNAB)	NAVCRUITDIST
Navy Recruiting District (DNAB)	NRD
Navy Recruiting Exhibit Center (DNAB)	NAVCRUITEXHIBCEN
Navy Recruiting Exhibit Center Catalog (DNAB)	NAVCRUITEXHIBCENCAT
Navy Recruiting Station	NAVCRUITSTA
Navy Recruiting Station Commanding Officer	NRSCO
Navy Regional Accounts Office	NRAO
Navy Regional Air Cargo Central [or Control] Office (DNAB)	NAVREGAIRCARCONO
Navy Regional Air Cargo Central [or Control] Office	NRACCO
Navy Regional Airspace Officer (MUGU)	NARASPO
Navy Regional Contracting Office (DNAB)	NAVREGCONTO
Navy Regional Contracting Office Detachment (DNAB)	NAVREGCONTODET
Navy Regional Data Automation Center	NARDAC
Navy Regional Data Automation Center, Washington, DC (DNAB)	NARDACWASHDC
Navy Regional Dental Center (DNAB)	NAVREGDENCEN
Navy Regional Dental Center Branch Facility (DNAB)	NAVREGDENCENBRFAC
Navy Regional Dental Clinic (DNAB)	NAVREGDENCLIN
Navy Regional Finance Center	NAVREGFINCEN
Navy Regional Finance Center	NRFC
Navy Regional Finance Center, Brooklyn [New York] (DNAB)	NAVREGFINCENBRKLN
Navy Regional Finance Center, Brooklyn [New York] (DNAB)	NRFC-B
Navy Regional Finance Center, Great Lakes (DNAB)	NAVREGFINCENGLAKES
Navy Regional Finance Center, Great Lakes (DNAB)	NRFC-GL
Navy Regional Finance Center, Norfolk [Virginia] (DNAB)	NRFC-N
Navy Regional Finance Center, Norfolk, Virginia (DNAB)	NAVREGFINCENNORVA
Navy Regional Finance Center, Pearl Harbor [Hawaii] (DNAB)	NAVREGFINCENPEARL
Navy Regional Finance Center, Pearl Harbor [Hawaii] (DNAB)	NRFC-PH
Navy Regional Finance Center, San Diego [California] (DNAB)	NAVREGFINCENSDIEGO
Navy Regional Finance Center, San Diego [California] (DNAB)	NRFC-SD
Navy Regional Finance Center, San Francisco [California] (DNAB)	NAVREGFINCENSFRAN
Navy Regional Finance Center, San Francisco [California] (DNAB)	NRFC-SF
Navy Regional Finance Office (DNAB)	NAVREGFINOFC
Navy Regional Finance Office	NRFO
Navy Regional Procurement Office (DNAB)	NAVREGPROCO
Navy Regulations	NAVREGS
Navy Regulations	NR
Navy Relief Society	NAVREL
Navy Relief Society (EA)	NRS
Navy Relief Society, Washington, DC, Auxiliary	NRDC
Navy Remote Ocean Sensing System [Proposed]	NROSS
Navy Resale and Services Support Office	NAVRESSO
Navy Resale and Services Support Office (DNAB)	NRSSO
Navy Resale and Services Support Office, Field Office (DNAB)	NAVRESSOFO
Navy Resale System Office (PDAA)	NAVRESO
Navy Resale System Office (PDAA)	NSRO
Navy Resale Systems Field Support Office (DNAB)	NAVRESOFSO
Navy Resale Systems Office (DNAB)	NAVRESO
Navy Resale Systems Office	NRSO
Navy Resale Systems Office Representative (DNAB)	NAVRESOREP
Navy Research and Development (AD)	NARAD
Navy Research and Development Committee	NRDC
Navy Research and Development Information Center	NARDIC
Navy Research and Development Unit - Vietnam (MCD)	NRDU-V
Navy Reservation Bureau	NRB
Navy Reserve Centers (NVT)	NRC
Navy Reserve Intelligence Program (MCD)	NRIP
Navy Reserve Training	NRT
Navy Retail Office (AFIT)	NRO
Navy Routing Office	NAVROUTE
Navy Safety Program (DNAB)	NSP
Navy Satellite Communications Detachment (DNAB)	NAVSATCOMMDET
Navy Satellite Communications Facility (DNAB)	NAVSATCOMMFAC
Navy Satellite Communications Network (DNAB)	NAVSATCOMMNET
Navy Satellite Operations Center (NVT)	NSOC
Navy Scatterometer (MCD)	N-SCATT
Navy Scholarship Information Team (DNAB)	NAVSIT
Navy School, Diving and Salvage (NVT)	NSDS
Navy School for Deep Sea Divers (DNAB)	NAVSCOLDEEPSEADIVER
Navy Science Assistance Program (CAAL)	NSAP
Navy Scientific and Technical Intelligence Center (IEEE)	NSTIC
Navy Sea Cargo Coordinator (NVT)	NAVSEACARCOR
Navy Sea Cargo Coordinator (DNAB)	NSCC
Navy Seabee Veterans of America (EA)	NSVA
Navy Secondary Standards (MSA)	NSS
Navy, Secretary's Office	NAVSO
Navy Security Engineering Facility	NSEF
Navy Security Group Activity	NAVSECGRUACT
Navy Security Group Headquarters	NAVSECGRUHQ
Navy Senior Procurement Executive (AAGC)	NSPE
Navy Service Center	NSC
Navy Ship Technical Manual (DNAB)	NAVSHIPTECHSMAN
Navy Ship Technical Manual (CAAL)	NSTM
Navy Shipboard Terminal	NST
Navy Shipbuilding Office	NAVSHIPLO
Navy Shipbuilding Scheduling Activity	NAVSHIPSA
Navy Shipbuilding Scheduling Office	NAVSHIPSO
Navy Ships' Store Office (DNAB)	NAVSHIPSTO
Navy Ships' Store Office [PX]	NSSO
Navy Shore Patrol Administration (WDAA)	NSPA
Navy Shore Station (IAA)	NSS
Navy Space Project	NSP
Navy Space Systems Activity [Los Angeles, CA] (MCD)	NSSA
Navy Special Fuel	NSF
Navy Special [or Standard] Fuel Oil	NSFO
Navy Special Operations Force (AABC)	NSOF
Navy Special Operations Group [SEALS that operated in Vietnam] (VNW)	NSOG
Navy Special Projects Office	NSPO
Navy Specification (AAGC)	NAVSPEC
Navy Specifications (AAGC)	N-SPECS
Navy Spread Spectrum MODEM (MCD)	NSSM
Navy Staff Offices	NAVSO
Navy Staffing Criteria Program	NSCP
Navy Standard (AAGC)	NAVSTD
Navy Standard Distillate Fuel (NVT)	NSDF
Navy Standard Distribution List (MCD)	NSDL
Navy Standard Part	NSP
Navy Standard Requisitioning and Issuing Procedure	NAVSTRIP
Navy Standard Score (DNAB)	NSS
Navy Standard Teleprinter (DOMA)	NST
Navy Standard Test Model (CAAL)	NSTM
Navy Standard Tracking and Retrieval System (MCD)	NSTARS
Navy Standard Transmission [Dension hydraulics] (CAAL)	NST-D
Navy Standard Transmission [Vickers hydraulics] (CAAL)	NST-V
Navy Standards (AAGC)	N-STDS
Navy Standards Laboratory	NSL
Navy Stock Fund (DOMA)	NSF
Navy Stock List	NSL
Navy Stockpile to Target Sequence	NSTS
Navy Strategic Study	NSS
Navy Study of Transport Aircraft Requirements	NAVSTAR
Navy Submarine Attack Airplane - Experimental (MCD)	VSX
Navy Submarine Support Facility (DNAB)	NAVSUBSUPPFAC
Navy Subsistence Office (DNAB)	NSO
Navy Supply Annex (AFIT)	NSA
Navy Supply Corps School	NSCS
Navy Supply Management Information System	NAVSUPMIS
Navy Supply Office (DNAB)	NAVSUPO
Navy Supply Office Annex (DNAB)	NAVSUPOANX
Navy Supply Research and Development Facility (DNAB)	NAVSUPRANDDFAC
Navy Supply System	NSS
Navy Support and Mobilization Plan (NVT)	NSMP
Navy Support Date (NG)	NSD
Navy Support Plan	NSP
Navy Systems Acquisition Review Council	NSARC
Navy Tactical Action Game	NAVTAG
Navy Tactical Command System Afloat (DOMA)	NTCS-A
Navy Tactical Data System	NTDS
Navy Tactical Doctrine Activity	NAVTACDOCACT
Navy Tactical Doctrine Activity (NVT)	NTDA
Navy Tactical Doctrine Development and Production Activity (DNAB)	NAVTACDOCDEVPRODACT
Navy Tactical Doctrine Development and Production Activity	NTDDPA
Navy Tactical Interoperability Support Activity (DNAB)	NAVTACINTEROPSUPPACT
Navy Tactical Interoperability Support Activity Detachment (DNAB)	NAVTACINTEROPSUPPACTDET
Navy Tactical Support Activity (NVT)	NAVTACSUPPACT
Navy Tactical Support Activity (DNAB)	NTSA
Navy Technical Assessment (MCD)	NTA
Navy Technical Data Office [of the Office of Naval Material]	NTDO
Navy Technical Evaluation (NG)	NTE
Navy Technical Evaluation/Initial Operational Test and Evaluation (MCD)	NTE/IOTE
Navy Technical Information Presentation Program (MCD)	NTIPP
Navy Technical Information Presentation System (MCD)	NTIPS
Navy Technical Information Program	NATIP
Navy Technical Point of Contact (DOMA)	NTPOC
Navy Technical Proficiency Inspection (NG)	NTPI
Navy Technical Proficiency List	NTPL
Navy Technical Representative (MCD)	NTR
Navy Technician Authorization (NG)	NTA
Navy Technological Forecast	NTF
Navy Technological Projections	NTP
Navy Technology Satellite	NTS
Navy Teletypewriter Exchange [Later, NTX]	NTE
Navy Television System	NTVS
Navy Terminal Leave Disbursing Office	NTLDO
Navy Test Controller (DNAB)	NTC
Navy Test Plan for Initial Defense Communications Satellite Program (DNAB)	NTP/IDCSP
Navy Toxicology Unit	NTU
Navy Trainer Advanced Jet - Experimental (MCD)	VTAJX
Navy Training Plan (NVT)	NTP
Navy Training Plan Conference	NTPC
Navy Training Requirements Information	NATRI
Navy Type (MSA)	NT
Navy Underwater Sound Laboratory (MUGU)	NASU
Navy Underwater Sound Reference Laboratory	NUSRL
Navy Underwater Swimmer Assault System (SAA)	NUSAS
Navy Uniform Board (DNAB)	NUB
Navy Uniform Management Information System	NUMIS
Navy Unit Commendation [Military decoration]	NUC
Navy Unit Identification System (NVT)	NUIS

Navy Utility Regulatory Intervention Group (DNAB) .... NURIG
Navy Vocational Interest Inventory (NVT) .... NVII
Navy War Contracts Relief Board .... NWCRB
Navy Weapons Requirement .... NWR
Navy Weather Research Facility .... NAVWEARSCHFA
Navy Weather Service .... NWS
Navy Weight-Control Program (DNAB) .... NWCP
Navy Wifeline Association (EA) .... NWA
Navy with Air Force .... NAWAF
Navy with Army .... NAWAR
Navy Wives Clubs of America (EA) .... NWCA
Navy Work Unit Information Service (IID) .... NAVWUIS
Navy Work Unit Information System (DNAB) .... NWUIS
Navy WWMCCS [*World-Wide Military Command and Control System*] **Standardization Software** .... NWSS
Navy Yard .... NY
Navy Yard .... NYD
Navy Yard, Boston, Massachusetts [*Obsolete*] .... NYBOS
Navy Yard, Charleston, South Carolina .... NYCHARL
Navy Yard, Mare Island, California .... NYMI
Navy Yard, New York, New York .... NYNYK
Navy Yard, Norfolk, Virginia .... NYNOR
Navy Yard, Pearl Harbor, Hawaii .... NYPH
Navy Yard, Philadelphia, Pennsylvania .... NYPHIL
Navy Yard, Portsmouth, New Hampshire .... NYPORT
Navy Yard, Puget Sound [*Bremerton*], Washington .... NYPS
Navy Yard, Washington, DC [*Obsolete*] .... NYWASH
Navy Youth Program Manager (MCD) .... NYPM
Navy-Marine Corps .... NAVMC
Navy-Marine Corps Council [*Defunct*] (EA) .... NMCC
Navy-Marine Corps Exhibit Center (DNAB) .... NAVMAREXHIBCEN
Navy-Marine Corps Exhibit Center .... NMCEC
Navy-Marine Corps Judiciary Activity .... NAVMARJUDACT
Navy-Marine Corps Reserve Center (NVT) .... NMCRC
Navy-Marine Corps Residence Foundation (DNAB) .... NMRF
Navy-Marine Corps Trial Judiciary (DNAB) .... NAVMARTRIJUDIC
Navy-Marine Corps Trial Judiciary Court (DNAB) .... NAVMARTRIJUDCIR
Navy-Marine Corps Trial Judiciary Court Branch Office (DNAB) .... NAVMARTRIJUDCIRBROFF
Navy-Marine Corps-Coast Guard Residence Foundation .... NMCGRF
Nawa Air Transport [*Hungary ICAO designator*] (FAAC) .... NWH
Nawab Shah [*Pakistan*] [*Airport symbol*] (OAG) .... WNS
Nawabshah [*Pakistan*] [*ICAO location identifier*] (ICLI) .... OPNH
Nawapara [*India*] [*ICAO location identifier*] (ICLI) .... VENP
Nawor [*Afghanistan*] [*ICAO location identifier*] (ICLI) .... OANR
Nay [*Vote*] .... N
Nazarene .... NAZ
Nazarene Theological Seminary, Kansas City, MO [*Library symbol Library of Congress*] (LCLS) .... MoKN
Nazarene Theological Seminary, Kansas City, MO [*OCLC symbol*] (OCLC) .... NTM
Nazarene World Mission Society (EA) .... NWMS
Nazareth Academy Library, Rochester, NY [*OCLC symbol*] (OCLC) .... RXB
Nazareth College, Nazareth, MI [*Library symbol Library of Congress*] (LCLS) .... MiNazC
Nazareth College of Rochester, Rochester, NY [*Library symbol Library of Congress*] (LCLS) .... NRNC
Nazareth College of Rochester, Rochester, NY [*OCLC symbol*] (OCLC) .... XNC
Nazareth Mother House Archives, Nazareth, KY [*Library symbol Library of Congress*] (LCLS) .... KyNaM
Nazareth National Motor Speedway [*Pennsylvania*] .... NNMS
Nazca [*Peru*] [*ICAO location identifier*] (ICLI) .... SPZA
Naze [*Ryukyu Islands*] [*Seismograph station code, US Geological Survey*] (SEIS) .... NZJ
NAZI Government (BJA) .... NG
NAZI Oberkommando der Wehrmacht [*NAZI Armed Forces High Command*] [*World War II German*] (BJA) .... NOKW
Nazi Texts in the Semitic Museum [*Harvard*] (BJA) .... SMN
Nazir (BJA) .... Naz
N.B. MacDonald Services Ltd. [*New Zealand*] [*FAA designator*] (FAAC) .... DBK
NBD Bancorp, Inc. [*NYSE symbol*] (SPSG) .... NBD
N-Benzoyl(phenyl)hydroxylamine [*Organic chemistry*] .... NBPHA
N-beta-Alanyldopamine [*Biochemistry*] .... NBAD
N-Bromoacetamide [*Organic chemistry*] .... NBA
N-Bromo(dimethyl)oxazolidinone [*Organic chemistry*] .... NBDMO
N-Bromosuccinimide [*Organic chemistry*] .... NBS
NBSC Corp. [*NASDAQ symbol*] (NQ) .... NSCB
NBS-Standard Information Services (NITA) .... NBS-SIS
NBT Bancorp [*Associated Press*] (SAG) .... NBT Bcp
NBT Bancorp. [*NASDAQ symbol*] (SAG) .... NBTB
NBTY, Inc. [*NASDAQ symbol*] (SAG) .... NBTY
NBU Mines Ltd. [*Toronto Stock Exchange symbol*] .... NBU
N-Butylamine [*Organic chemistry*] .... NBA
NCA Minerals [*Vancouver Stock Exchange symbol*] .... NCA
NCAR [*National Center for Atmospheric Research*] **GARP Task Group** [*Global Atmospheric Research Program*] .... NGTG
N-Carbobenzoxy-Glycyl-L-Phenylalanine (BABM) .... CGP
N-Carboxy Anhydride [*Organic chemistry*] .... NCA
N-(Carboxyethyl)alanine [*Biochemistry*] .... NCEA
N-Carboxymethylchitosan [*Biochemistry*] .... NCMC
NCC [*Navy Command Center*] **Security Test System** .... NSTS
NCH Corp. [*Formerly, National Chemsearch Corp.*] [*NYSE symbol*] (SPSG) .... NCH
Nchalo/Sucoma [*Malawi*] [*ICAO location identifier*] (ICLI) .... FWSU
N-Channel Depletion-Load Triode Inverter .... NDLT
N-Channel Junction Field-Effect Transistor (IDOE) .... NFET
N-Chloroacetamide [*Organic chemistry*] .... NCA
N-Chloroethylnorapomorphine [*Organic chemistry, biochemistry*] .... NCA
N-Chlorosuccinimide [*Organic chemistry*] .... NCS
N-Chlorothiophosphoramide [*Organic chemistry*] .... NCP
N-Cholorpiperidine [*Organic chemistry*] .... NCP
NCI Building Systems [*NASDAQ symbol*] (SAG) .... BLDG
NCI Building Systems [*Associated Press*] (SAG) .... NCI Bldg
NCN Exploration & Development [*Vancouver Stock Exchange symbol*] .... NCX
NCO Group, Inc. [*Associated Press*] (SAG) .... NCO Grp
NCO Group, Inc. [*NASDAQ symbol*] (SAG) .... NCOG
NCO Logistics Program [*Army skill qualification identifier*] (INF) .... K
NCO [*Noncommissioned Officer*] **Professional Development Ribbon** [*Military decoration*] (GFGA) .... NCOPDR
NCO Professional Development Ribbon [*Military decoration*] .... NPDR
NCP Virtual Storage (NITA) .... NCP/VS
NCR [*NCR Corp.*] **Century Software** .... NCS
NCR [*NCR Corp.*] **Electronic Autocoding Technique** [*Computer science*] .... NEAT
NCR [*NCR Corp.*] **Optical Font** (MCD) .... NOF
NCR Telecommunication Services, Inc. (TSSD) .... NCR/TSI
NCS HealthCare 'A' [*NASDAQ symbol*] (TTSB) .... NCSS
NCS Healthcare, Inc. [*Associated Press*] (SAG) .... NCS Hlt
NCS Healthcare, Inc. [*NASDAQ symbol*] (SAG) .... NCSS
NDE Environmental Corp. [*NASDAQ symbol*] (NQ) .... NDEC
N'Dele [*Central African Republic*] [*ICAO location identifier*] (ICLI) .... FEFN
N-Demethylencainide [*Organic chemistry*] .... NDE
N'Dende [*Gabon*] [*ICAO location identifier*] (ICLI) .... FOGE
N'Dende [*Gabon*] [*Airport symbol*] (OAG) .... KDN
N-Desmethylclobazam [*Biochemistry*] .... NDMC
N-Desmethyl-levo-alpha-Acetylmethadol [*Opiate*] .... NLAAM
N-Desmethyl-Methsuximide [*Biochemistry*] (AAMN) .... NDM
N-Dimensional (MCD) .... N-D
N'Djamena [*Chad*] [*ICAO location identifier*] (ICLI) .... FTTJ
N'Djamena [*Chad*] [*ICAO location identifier*] (ICLI) .... FTTT
N'Djamena [*Chad*] [*ICAO location identifier*] (ICLI) .... FTTV
N'Djamena [*Chad*] [*Airport symbol*] (OAG) .... NDJ
Ndjole [*Gabon*] [*ICAO location identifier*] (ICLI) .... FOGJ
Ndola [*Zambia*] [*ICAO location identifier*] (ICLI) .... FLND
Ndola [*Zambia*] [*Airport symbol*] (OAG) .... NLA
NDU Resources [*Vancouver Stock Exchange symbol*] .... NDU
Ne Plus Ultra [*No Further; i.e., the pinnacle of attainment*] [*French*] .... NPU
Ne Tradas sine Nummo [*Cash on Delivery*] [*Latin*] .... NE TR S NUM
Nea Anghialos [*Greece*] [*ICAO location identifier*] (ICLI) .... LGBL
NEA [*Nuclear Energy Agency*] **Data Bank** [*OECD*] [*Information service or system*] (IID) .... NEA-DB
Nea Demokratia [*New Democracy*] [*Greece*] [*Political party*] (PPE) .... ND
Nea Demokratiki Parataxi [*Cyprus*] [*Political party*] (PPE) .... NEDEPA
Nea Demokratiki Parataxi [*Cyprus*] [*Political party*] (PPW) .... NEDIPA
Neah Bay, WA [*Location identifier FAA*] (FAAL) .... EBY
Neah Bay, WA [*Location identifier FAA*] (FAAL) .... TOU
Neanderthal (VRA) .... Ndthl
Neanderthal Conservative [*Slang*] .... NC
Neap Tide .... NP
Neap Tide .... NT
Neapolis [*Greece*] [*Seismograph station code, US Geological Survey*] (SEIS) .... NPS
Near [*Optics*] (WDAA) .... N
Near (VRA) .... nr
Near (EY) .... NR
Near Commercial Breeder Reactor [*Also, PLBR*] .... NCBR
Near Constant Force Suspension .... NCFS
Near Earth Asteroid Returned Samples [*NASA, proposed*] .... NEARS
Near East (BJA) .... NE
Near East Air Force [*British*] .... NEAF
Near East and African Development Service .... NEADS
Near East and South Asia [*Department of State*] .... NESA
Near East Animal Health Institute .... NEAHI
Near East Archaeological Society (EA) .... NEAS
Near East College Association (EA) .... NECA
Near East Emergency Donations .... NEED
Near East Equine Encephalomyelitis [*Medicine*] (DMAA) .... NEEE
Near East Forestry Commission .... NEFC
Near East Foundation (EA) .... NEF
Near East Land Forces [*British military*] (DMA) .... NEARELF
Near East Report [*A publication*] (BJA) .... NER
Near East/South Asia Council of Overseas Schools (EA) .... NE/SA
Near Eastern Affairs [*Department of State*] .... NEA
Near Eastern, African, and South Asian Affairs [*Department of State*] .... NEASA
Near Eastern and Judaistic Studies (BJA) .... NEJS
Near Eastern Society (EA) .... NES
Near Eastern Studies [*A publication*] (BJA) .... NES
Near Face [*Technical drawings*] .... NF
Near Field Scanning Optical Microscopy .... NSOM
Near Galactic Catalog .... NGC
Near Infrared (ECII) .... NIR
Near Infrared Mapping Spectrometer [*Instrument on Galileo spacecraft*] [*NASA*] .... NIMS
Near Infrared Miniaturized Jammer .... NIMJ
Near Infrared Oxygen Sufficiency Scope [*Monitors oxygen delivery to brain during surgery*] (DAVI) .... NIROS
Near Infrared Reflectance Analysis .... NIRA
Near Infrared Reflectance Spectroscopy [*Britton Chance*] .... NIRS
Near Infrared Region .... NIR
Near Infrared Spectral Analysis Software .... NSAS
Near Launch Tracking System .... NLTS
Near Letter Quality [*Computer printer*] .... NLQ

Near Match (MCD)	NM
Near Midair Collision	NMAC
Near Millimeter Wave System [Telecommunications] (TEL)	NMMW
Near Mint [Condition] [Numismatics, deltiology, etc.]	NM
Near Object Probe (SAA)	NOP
Near Obstacle Detection System [General Motors-Delco Co.]	NODS
Near Point	NP
Near Point Accommodation [Ophthalmology]	NPA
Near Point of Convergence [Ophthalmology]	NPC
Near Point of Convergence [Ophthalmology]	PcB
Near Real-Time	NR/T
Near Side [Technical drawings]	NS
Near Space	NS
Near Space Instrumentation Facility [NASA] (KSC)	NSIF
Near Surface Burst (MCD)	NSB
Near Surface Reference Temperature [Oceanography]	NSRT
Near Surface Test Facility [Nuclear energy] (NUCP)	NSTF
Near Term	NT
Near Term Schedule (MCD)	NTS
Near the Nut (or Heel) of the Bow [Music] (ROG)	N
Near Time Processing (IAA)	NTP
Near Ultraviolet	NUV
Near Vertical [Aerospace]	NV
Near Visual Acuity [Medicine]	NVA
Near Zero Field	NZF
Near Zero Gravity	NZG
Near-Coincident Site Lattice [Crystallography]	NCSL
Nearctic Resources, Inc. [Toronto Stock Exchange symbol]	NEA
Near-Death Experience	NDE
Near-Earth Asteroid [Astronomy]	NEA
Near-Earth Asteroid Rendezvous (MCD)	NEAR
Near-Earth Asteroid Tracking	NEAT
Near-Earth Instrumentation Facility [NASA] (KSC)	NEIF
Near-Earth Magnetospheric Satellite	NEMS
Near-Earth Object [Astronomy]	NEO
Near-Earth Orbit	NEO
Near-Earth Phase [NASA]	NEP
Near-Earth Phase Network [NASA] (KSC)	NEPN
Near-Earth Rescue and Operations [NASA]	NERO
Near-Earth Tracking and Data System	NETDS
Near-Edge X-Ray Absorption Fine Structure [For study of surfaces]	NEXAFS
Near-End Crosstalk [Bell System]	NEXT
Near-End Suppressor (IAA)	NES
Nearest Active Upstream Neighbor [Computer science]	NAUN
Nearest Besselian Year	NBY
Nearest Cross Street (ADA)	NCS
Nearest Equivalent Product	NEP
Nearest Grid Point (PDAA)	NGP
Nearest Landing Field	NLF
Nearest Naval District	NEARNAVDIST
Nearest Neighbor [Mathematics] [Computer search term]	NN
Nearest Neighbor Tool [Mathematical method] [Marine science] (OSRA)	NNT
Nearest Neighbor Tool [Mathematical technique] (USDC)	NNT
Nearest-Neighbor Distance Error [Algorithm]	NNDE
Nearest-Neighbor Rule [Mathematics]	NNR
Nearfield Bearing and Range Accuracy Calibration System (PDAA)	NEFBRACS
Near-Field Calibration Array (PDAA)	NFCA
Near-Field Recording [Computer science] (PCM)	NFR
Near-Infrared Camera and Multiobject Spectrograph [Astronomy]	NICMOS
Near-Isotropic Flux Turbulence Instrument [Oceanography]	NIFTI
Nearly (ABBR)	NRY
Nearly Airborne Truck (PDAA)	NAT
Nearly Best Linear Estimator [Statistics]	NBLE
Nearly Certain New Work (MCD)	NCNW
Nearly Commensurate Model [Physics]	NC
Nearly Free Electron [Physics] (OA)	NFE
Nearly Instantaneous Compounding (MCD)	NIC
Nearly Vertical Incident Skywave [Propagation model] (MCD)	NVIS
Near-Metacentric [Botany]	nm
Nearness (ABBR)	NRNS
Near-Object Detection Sensor [Automotive electronics]	NODS
Near-Real Time	NRT
Near-Real-Time Reconnaissance (MCD)	NRTR
Near-Sighted (ABBR)	NRSITD
Near-Sightedness (ABBR)	NRSITNS
Near-Surface Radiation Thermometer	NSRT
Near-Term Construction Permit [Nuclear energy] (NRCH)	NTCP
Near-Term Hybrid Vehicle (PDAA)	NTHV
Near-Term Improvement in Materiel Asset Reporting [Military] (AABC)	TIMAR
Near-Term Improvement Program [For torpedos] (MCD)	NEARTIP
Near-Term Operating License [Nuclear energy] (NRCH)	NTOL
Near-Term Prepositioned Ships	NTPS
Near-Term Prepositioning Forces [Navy]	NTPF
Near-Term Scout Helicopter [Army]	NTSH
Near-Term Swimmer Defense System	NTSDS
Near-Terminal Area [Airports]	NTA
Neat [Plain] [Bookbinding] (ROG)	NT
Neatby Library, Agriculture Canada [Bibliotheque Neatby, Agriculture Canada] Ottawa, Ontario [Library symbol National Library of Canada] (NLC)	OOAGCH
Neath [Welsh depot code]	NEA
Neath and Brecon Railway [Wales]	NB
Nebelkerze [Smoke-Candle] [German military - World War II]	NBK
Nebelwerfer [German six-barrelled mortar] (DSUE)	NEB
Nebenlager [Branch Camp] [German military - World War II]	NL

Neben-Munitionsanstalt [Branch ammunition depot] [German military - World War II]	NEBMA
Nebennieren, Thymus, Quotient [Test] [Medicine]	NTQ
Nebo Air Co. Ltd. [Former USSR] [FAA designator] (FAAC)	NBO
Nebramycin Factor [An antibacterial compound]	NF
Nebraska (IAA)	NB
Nebraska [MARC country of publication code Library of Congress] (LCCP)	nbu
Nebraska [Postal code]	NE
Nebraska	NEB
Nebraska (ODBW)	Neb
Nebraska (ODBW)	Nebr
Nebraska (AAG)	NEBR
Nebraska [MARC geographic area code Library of Congress] (LCCP)	n-us-nb
Nebraska Administrative (Code) Rules and Regulations [A publication] (AAGC)	NAC
Nebraska Administrative Rules and Regulations [A publication] (DLA)	Neb Admin R
Nebraska Calf Diarrhea Virus	NCDV
Nebraska Central College, Central City, NE [Library symbol Library of Congress Obsolete] (LCLS)	NbCenC
Nebraska City, NE [AM radio station call letters]	KNCY
Nebraska City, NE [FM radio station call letters] (RBYB)	KOSJ
Nebraska City Public Library, Nebraska City, NE [Library symbol Library of Congress] (LCLS)	NbNc
Nebraska Educational Television Council for Higher Education, Inc. [Library network]	NETCHE
Nebraska Electronic Transfer System	NETS
Nebraska ETV [Educational Television] Network [Lincoln, NE] [Telecommunications] (TSSD)	NETV
Nebraska HealthNetwork [Information service or system] (IID)	NHN
Nebraska Law Bulletin [A publication] (DLA)	NBLB
Nebraska Law Bulletin [A publication] (DLA)	Neb LB
Nebraska Law Bulletin [A publication] (DLA)	Nebr LB
Nebraska Legal News [A publication] (DLA)	Neb Leg N
Nebraska Legislative Council, Reference Library, Lincoln, NE [Library symbol Library of Congress] (LCLS)	Nb-LR
Nebraska Library Commission, Library for Blind and Physically Handicapped, Lincoln, NE [Library symbol Library of Congress] (LCLS)	Nb-BPH
Nebraska Library Commission, Lincoln, NE [OCLC symbol] (OCLC)	NBL
Nebraska Library Commission, Lincoln, NE [OCLC symbol] (OCLC)	TPB
Nebraska Library Commission, Lincoln, NE [OCLC symbol] (OCLC)	TPC
Nebraska Motor Carriers Association, Petroleum Carriers' Conference, Inc., OmahaNE [STAC]	NMC
Nebraska Natural Resources Information System [Nebraska State Natural Resources Commission] [Lincoln] [Information service or system] (IID)	NNRIS
Nebraska Public Library Commission, Lincoln, NE [Library symbol Library of Congress] (LCLS)	Nb-LC
Nebraska Railway Commission Reports [A publication] (DLA)	Neb RC
Nebraska Reading Retrieval System (EDAC)	NRRS
Nebraska Reports [A publication] (DLA)	Nebr
Nebraska State Historical Society, Lincoln, NE [Library symbol Library of Congress] (LCLS)	NbHi
Nebraska State Library, Lincoln, NE [Library symbol Library of Congress] (LCLS)	Nb
Nebraska State Railway Commission [STAC]	NEC
Nebraska Supreme Court Journal [A publication] (DLA)	Neb Sup Ct J
Nebraska Supreme Court Journal [A publication] (DLA)	SC J
Nebraska Supreme Court Reports [A publication] (DLA)	Neb
Nebraska Test of Learning Aptitude [Education]	NTLA
Nebraska University (MCD)	NU
Nebraska University Disease or N. Underdahl Disease [A disease of swine named both for the place where it was originally identified and for the person who isolated the causative agent]	NUD
Nebraska Unofficial Reports [A publication] (DLA)	Neb (Unof)
Nebraska Unofficial Reports [A publication] (DLA)	Neb Unoff
Nebraska Unofficial Reports [A publication] (DLA)	NU
Nebraska VA Television Network [Telecommunications service] (TSSD)	NEVATV
Nebraska Water Resources Center [University of Nebraska - Lincoln] [Research center] (RCD)	NWRC
Nebraska Wesleyan University	NWU
Nebraska Wesleyan University, Lincoln, NE [Library symbol Library of Congress] (LCLS)	NbLW
Nebraska Wesleyan University, Lincoln, NE [OCLC symbol] (OCLC)	NBW
Nebraska Western College, Scottsbluff, NE [Library symbol Library of Congress] (LCLS)	NbSN
Nebraska Workmen's Compensation Court. Bulletin [A publication] (DLA)	Neb WCC
Nebula [Spray] [Pharmacy]	NEB
Nebula [Spray] [Pharmacy]	NEBUL
NEC Computerised Operation and Maintenance System (NITA)	NCOM
NEC Corp. [Associated Press] (SAG)	NEC
NEC Corp. [NASDAQ symbol] (SAG)	NIPN
NEC Corp. ADR [NASDAQ symbol] (TTSB)	NIPNY
NEC Dataflow Image Processing System (NITA)	NEDIPS
NEC Information Systems, Inc. [Boxborough, MA]	NECIS
NEC/TAMPA Technology Institute, Tampa, FL [Library symbol] [Library of Congress] (LCLS)	FTNT
NEC [Nippon Electric Company]-Toshiba Information Systems, Inc. [Japan]	NTIS
Necessary (AABC)	NEC
Necessary	NECY
Necessary Nuisance [i.e., a husband] [Slang]	NN
Necessity	NEC
Necessity (WDAA)	NECY
Neck	NCK

Neck ... NCK
Neck [*Commonly used*] (OPSA) ... NECK
Neck (AAG) ... NK
Neck Injury Criteria [*Automotive safety testing*] ... NIC
Neck Vein Distention [*Medicine*] ... NVD
Neckarsulm [*Location in Wuerttemberg, Germany, of NSU Werke, automobile manufacturer; initialism used as name of its cars*] ... NSU
Necks with Any Boy [*Slang*] ... NWAB
Neckwear ... NCKWR
Neckwear Association of America (EA) ... NAA
Necochea [*Argentina*] [*Airport symbol*] (OAG) ... NEC
Necochea [*Argentina ICAO location identifier*] (ICLI) ... SAZO
Necocli [*Colombia*] [*Airport symbol*] (OAG) ... NCI
Necrobiosis Lipoidica Diabeticorum [*Medicine*] ... NLD
Necrofile [*A publication*] ... Necro
Necrology (WDAA) ... NECROL
Necrolytic Migratory Erythema [*Dermatology*] ... NME
Necropolis (VRA) ... necrp
Necrosis ... NC
Necrotic ... N
Necrotic Ringspot Virus [*of prunes*] ... NRSV
Necrotizing Enterocolitis [*Medicine*] ... NEC
Necrotizing Ulcerative Gingivitis [*Dentistry*] ... NUG
Nedarim (BJA) ... Ned
Nedarim (BJA) ... Neda
Nederland, TX [*AM radio station call letters*] ... KQHN
Nederlands Bureau voor Bibliotheekwezen en Informatieverzorging [*Netherlands Organization for Libraries and Information Services*] [*Information service or system*] (IID) ... NBBI
Nederlands Instituut voor Onderzoek in de Katalyse [*Netherlands Institute for Catalysis Research*] ... NIOK
Nederlands Luchtvaart Maatschappij [*Airline*] [*Netherlands*] ... NLM
Nederlands Middenstands Partij [*Netherlands Middle Class Party*] [*Political party*] (PPE) ... NMP
Nederlands Tijdschrift voor Internationaal Recht [*Netherlands A publication*] (ILCA) ... NTIR
Nederlandsche Aluminium Maatschappij [*Netherlands Aluminum Co.*] (AD) ... NAM
Nederlandsche Standard Electric Maatschappij (NITA) ... NSEM
Nederlandsche Binnenlandse Strijdkrachten [*Netherlands Forces of the Interior, 1944*] ... BS
Nederlandse Centrale Catalogus/Interbibliothecair Leenverkeer System [*Netherlands Central Catalogue/Interlibrary Loan System*] [*Consortium of the Royal Library and University Libraries*] [*Information service or system*] (IID) ... NCC/IBL
Nederlandse Centrale Organisatie voor Toegepast Natuurwetenschappelijk Onderzoek [*Netherlands Institute for Applied Scientific Research*] ... TNO
Nederlandse Credietbank NV [*Financial institution*] [*Netherlands*] (EY) ... NCB
Nederlandse Dagbladunie ... NDU
Nederlandse Ecologen Vereniging [*Netherlands Ecological Society*] [*Multinational association*] (EAIO) ... NEV
Nederlandse Juristenvereniging [*Netherlands Lawyers Association*] (ILCA) ... NJV
Nederlandse Omroep Stichtung [*Radio and television network*] [*Netherlands*] ... NOS
Nederlandse Organisatie voor Chemische Informatie (NITA) ... NOCI
Nederlandse Spoorwegen [*Netherlands Railways*] ... NS
Nederlandse Vereniging van Gebruikers van Online Informatie-Systemen [*Netherlands Association of Users of Online Information Systems*] (EAIO) ... VOGIN
Nederlandse Volksbeweging [*Dutch People's Movement*] [*Political party*] (PPE) ... NVB
Nederlandse Waterschapsbank NV [*Waterschaps Bank of the Netherlands*] ... NWB
Nedezhda (AD) ... Nad
Need [*Psychology*] ... N
Need Date (MCD) ... N/D
Need for Achievement ... nAch
Need for Affection ... nAff
Need for Affiliation (MHDB) ... NAFF
Need for Affiliation (AD) ... naff
Need International [*An association*] (EA) ... NI
Need Satisfaction of Activity Interview ... NSAI
Need to Know (MCD) ... NTK
Need to Know Only [*Espionage*] ... NKO
Needham, Harper & Steers [*Advertising agency*] ... NH & S
Needham, MA [*Television station call letters*] ... WUNI
Needham's Annual Summary of Tax Cases [*England*] [*A publication*] (DLA) ... Need
Needle (MSA) ... NDL
Needle Aspiration [*Surgery*] ... NA
Needle Aspiration Biopsy [*Surgery*] ... NAB
Needle Biopsy [*Surgical procedure*] (DAVI) ... NB
Needle Catheter Jejunostomy [*Medicine*] (DMAA) ... NCJ
Needle Exchange Program ... NEP
Needle Liver Biopsy [*Medicine*] (DMAA) ... NLB
Needle Makers Association [*British*] (BI) ... NMA
Needle Position [*on dial*] ... NP
Needle Punch Card ... NPC
Needle Stampers' and Filers' Union [*British*] ... NSFU
Needle Valve ... NV
Needle-Nosed Probe ... NNP
Needleroom Felt Manufacturers Association [*British*] (DBA) ... NFMA
Needles, CA [*Location identifier FAA*] (FAAL) ... EED
Needles, CA [*AM radio station call letters*] ... KTOX
Needles, CA [*FM radio station call letters*] ... KWAZ
Needlework (VRA) ... ndlwk
Needlework and Accessories Trade Show (ITD) ... NATS
Needlework and Craft Showcase (ITD) ... NCS
Needlework Guild of America [*Later, NGAI*] (EA) ... NGA
Needs [*Automotive advertising*] ... NDS
Needs Assessment (OICC) ... NA
Needs-Based Goal Attainment Scale (EDAC) ... NGAS
Needs-Based Payment [*Job Training and Partnership Act*] (OICC) ... NBP
Needs-Based Staffing (ADA) ... NBS
Neenah Public Library, Neenah, WI [*Library symbol Library of Congress*] (LCLS) ... WN
Neenah, WI [*Location identifier FAA*] (FAAL) ... EEW
Neenah-Menasha, WI [*AM radio station call letters*] ... WNAM
Neenah-Menasha, WI [*FM radio station call letters*] (RBYB) ... WNCY-FM
Neenah-Menasha, WI [*FM radio station call letters*] ... WROE
Neepawa Collegiate Institute, Manitoba [*Library symbol National Library of Canada*] (NLC) ... MNCI
Neepawa Collegiate Institute, Neepawa, MB, Canada [*Library symbol Library of Congress*] (LCLS) ... CaMNCI
Neerlandia Public Library, Alberta [*Library symbol National Library of Canada*] (NLC) ... AN
Nees Politikes Dynameis [*New Political Forces*] [*Greek Political party*] (PPE) ... NPD
Neesby Delayed Release Mechanism [*Medicine*] ... NDRM
Nefertiti [*ICAO designator*] (AD) ... UZ
Nefteyugansk Aviation Division [*Russian Federation*] [*ICAO designator*] (FAAC) ... NFT
Negage [*Angola*] [*ICAO location identifier*] (ICLI) ... FNNG
Negage [*Angola*] [*Airport symbol*] (OAG) ... GXG
Nega'im (BJA) ... Neg
Negate a Binary Number [*Computer science*] ... NEG
Negate a Binary Number with Extend [*Computer science*] ... NEGX
Negate BCD [*Binary-Coded Decimal*] **Number** [*Computer science*] ... NBCD
Negation (WDAA) ... NEG
Negative [*Crystal*] ... n
Negative (VRA) ... neg
Negative (AAG) ... NEG
Negative [*British naval signaling*] ... NO
Negative Acknowledge [*or Acknowledgment*] [*Data communication*] ... NAK
Negative Acknowledge Character [*Computer science*] (AD) ... nak
Negative Acknowledge Character (ECII) ... NAK
Negative Acknowledgment [*Telecommunications*] ... NACK
Negative Acknowledgment (DOM) ... NAK
Negative Afterwave [*Microelectrode recording*] ... NAW
Negative Air Cushion [*Aviation Air Force*] ... NAC
Negative Authorization Terminal System [*Computer science*] (MHDB) ... NATS
Negative Balance Test (IAA) ... NBT
Negative Binomial Distribution [*Statistics*] ... NB
Negative Binomial Distribution [*Statistics*] ... NBD
Negative Channel [*Computer science*] (IAA) ... NCH
Negative Channel Metal-Oxide Semiconductor (IAA) ... NCHMOS
Negative Channel Metal-Oxide Semiconductor ... NMOS
Negative Channel Self-Aligned Gate (IAA) ... NSAG
Negative Chemical Ionization [*Spectrometry*] ... NCI
Negative Chemical Ionization Mass Spectra ... NCIMS
Negative Declaration (NRCH) ... ND
Negative Differential Conductivity (OA) ... NDC
Negative Differential Mobility (IEEE) ... NDM
Negative Differential Resistance [*Electronics*] ... NDR
Negative Effective Mass Amplifiers and Generators ... NEMAG
Negative Electron Affinity [*Photocathode*] ... NEA
Negative End Expiratory Pressure [*Medicine*] ... NEEP
Negative Entropy Trap ... NET
Negative Equally Probable ... NEP
Negative Expectancy [*Psychometrics*] ... NE
Negative Expected Value ... NEV
Negative Expiratory Pressure [*Medicine*] ... NEP
Negative Factor Counting ... NFC
Negative Feedback (BARN) ... B
Negative Feedback (DEN) ... NFB
Negative Feedback Circuit ... NFC
Negative Flux Rate (IEEE) ... NFR
Negative Glow (IDOE) ... NG
Negative Glucocorticoid Response Element [*Biochemistry*] ... NGRE
Negative Grid Generator ... NGG
Negative Immittance Converter [*Electronics*] ... NIC
Negative Immittance Inverter (PDAA) ... NII
Negative Impedance Booster [*Electronics*] ... NIB
Negative Impedance Converter [*Electronics*] ... NIC
Negative Impedance Transistor [*Electronics*] (IAA) ... NEGIT
Negative Income Tax ... NIT
Negative Input, Positive Output ... NIPO
Negative Inspiratory Force [*Medicine*] ... NIF
Negative Inspiratory Pressure [*Medicine*] (DAVI) ... NIP
Negative Ion Beam ... NIB
Negative Ion Blemish ... NIB
Negative Ion Chamber ... NIC
Negative Ion Chemical Ionization [*Spectrometry*] ... NICI
Negative Ion Chemical Ionization Mass Spectroscopy ... NICIMS
Negative Ion Erosion ... NIE
Negative Ion Generator (ADA) ... NIG
Negative Ion Recombination Chamber ... NIRC
Negative Ion Source ... NIS
Negative Ion Vacancy ... NIV
Negative Knowledge (AD) ... nak

Negative Lens Systems	NLS
Negative Line Transmission [Noise limiter] (IAA)	NLT
Negative Log of Dissociation Constant [Medicine] (DAVI)	pKa
Negative Log of the Dissociation Constant [Medicine]	pK'
Negative Logic Level	NLL
Negative Negabinary Carry-Look-Ahead Adder [Computer science] (MHDI)	NNBCLA
Negative Node Point	NNP
Negative Picture Phase	NPP
Negative Poll Response State (IAA)	NPRS
Negative Population Growth (EA)	NPG
Negative Positive Zero (IAA)	NPO
Negative Potential Shifts [Neurophysiology]	NPS
Negative Predictive Value [Experimentation]	NPV
Negative Prescreening [Marketing]	NP
Negative Pressure (NRCH)	NP
Negative Print	NEGPR
Negative Print (VRA)	NEGPT
Negative Radial Rake (IAA)	NRR
Negative Regulatory Element [Genetics]	NRE
Negative Replies Neither Required nor Desired	NONEG
Negative Report Submitted [Army] (AABC)	NEGRS
Negative Report Submitted [Army] (AABC)	NEGRSBM
Negative Resistance [Electronics]	NR
Negative Resistance (IDOE)	R$_n$
Negative Resistance Amplifier (PDAA)	NRA
Negative Resistance Characteristic [Electrophysiology]	NRC
Negative Resistance Diode	NRD
Negative Resistance Effect	NRE
Negative Resistance Element [Electronics] (IAA)	NRE
Negative Resistance Oscillator [Electronics]	NRO
Negative Resistance Repeater [Electronics] (IAA)	NRR
Negative Resistor (PDAA)	NEGISTOR
Negative Return in Cartridge [Advanced photo system]	NRIC
Negative Run Number [Computer science] (OA)	NRN
Negative Self-Image [Psychology]	NSI
Negative Supply Voltage	NSV
Negative Tax (MHDW)	NEGTAX
Negative Temperature Coefficient	NTC
Negative Thermal Coefficient (IAA)	NTC
Negative Torque Signal (MSA)	NTS
Negative True Rake (IAA)	NTR
Negative Variation [Medicine] (MAE)	NV
Negative Vorticity Advection [NWS] (FAAC)	NVA
Negative Wave in Children [Neurophysiology]	Nc
Negative-Equity Baby Boomer [Lifestyle classification]	Nebby
Negative-Ion Thermal Ionization Mass Spectrometry	NTIMS
Negative-Positive Acknowledgment and Retransmission [Telecommunications] (IAA)	NPAR
Negative-Positive-Intrinsic-Negative [Electron device] (MSA)	NPIN
Negative-Positive-Negative [Transistor] (CET)	N-P-N
Negative-Positive-Negative-Positive [Transistor]	NPNP
Negative-Positive-Zero	NPO
Negative-Regulatory Factor [Genetics]	NEF
Negatives [Film] (WDMC)	negs
Negatives and Deposition (DGA)	ND
Negatives and Etching (DGA)	NE
Negaunee Public Library, Negaunee, MI [Library symbol Library of Congress] (LCLS)	MiNeg
Negginan [Canada] [Airport symbol] (OAG)	ZNG
Neghelle [Ethiopia] [ICAO location identifier] (ICLI)	HANG
Neghelli [Ethiopia] [Airport symbol] (AD)	EGL
Neglect [FBI standardized term]	NEG
Neglect of Core Orbitals [Physical chemistry]	NOCOR
Neglect of Diatomic Differential Overlap [Quantum mechanics]	NDDO
Neglect of Non-Neighbor Differential Overlap [Physics]	NNNDO
Neglected Language Program	NLP
Negligee Manufacturers Association [Later, IAMA]	NMA
Negligence	Negl
Negligence and Compensation Cases, Annotated [A publication] (DLA)	NCCA
Negligence and Compensation Cases, Annotated [A publication] (DLA)	Negl & Comp Cas Ann
Negligence and Compensation Cases, Annotated, New Series [A publication] (DLA)	NCCA NS
Negligence and Compensation Cases, Annotated, New Series [A publication] (DLA)	Negl & Comp Cas Ann (NS)
Negligence and Compensation Cases, Annotated, Third Series [A publication] (DLA)	NCCA 3d
Negligence and Compensation Cases, Annotated, Third Series [A publication] (DLA)	Negl & Comp Cas Ann 3d
Negligence Cases [Commerce Clearing House] [A publication] (DLA)	Neg C
Negligence Cases [Commerce Clearing House] [A publication] (DLA)	Negl Cas
Negligence Cases, Second Series [Commerce Clearing House] [A publication] (DLA)	Negl Cas 2d
Negligible (AAG)	NEG
Negligible Individual Risk Level (GNE)	NIRL
Negotiable (ADA)	NEG
Negotiable	Negb
Negotiable [Legal shorthand] (LWAP)	NEGOT
Negotiable Certificate of Deposit (ADA)	NCD
Negotiable Instrument [Legal term] (DLA)	Neg Inst
Negotiable Instrument	NI
Negotiable Instruments Law (DLA)	NIL
Negotiable Order of Withdrawal [Banking]	NOW
Negotiate Downward Only (MCD)	NDO

Negotiated (ROG)	NEGD
Negotiated Consent Order [Environmental Protection Agency] (ERG)	NCO
Negotiated Critical Dates [Telecommunications] (TEL)	NCD
Negotiated Exit [Telecommunications] (OSI)	NE
Negotiated Search Facility [Information retrieval]	NSF
Negotiation (ROG)	NEGN
Negotiation Decision Document [Environmental Protection Agency] (EPA)	NDD
Negotiation Information System	NIS
Negotiations on Conventional Armed Forces in Europe	CAFE
Negotiations on Conventional Armed Forces in Europe	CFE
Negotiator's Planned Execution Date (MCD)	NEGPED
Negri Body (AAMN)	NB
Negril [Jamaica] [Airport symbol] (OAG)	NEG
Negro	N
Negro	NEG
Negro Actors Guild (NADA)	NAG
Negro Actors Guild of America (EA)	NAG
Negro Airmen International (EA)	NAI
Negro, Anglo-Saxon Protestant	NASP
Negro Education Emergency Drive	NEED
Negro Ensemble Company [A theatre group]	NEC
Negro Female	NF
Negro Heritage Library	NHL
Negro Historical Society of America	NHSA
Negro Industrial and Economic Union	NIEU
Negro Labor Committee [Defunct] (EA)	NLC
Negro Male	NM
Negro Puerto Rican	NPR
Negro Trade Union Leadership Council	NTULC
Negro Universities Press (AEBS)	NUP
Nehbandan [Iran] [ICAO location identifier] (ICLI)	OIMK
Nehemiah [Old Testament book] (BJA)	Ne
Nehemiah [Old Testament book]	Neh
Neher Tetrode Amplifier	NTA
Nehru Memorial Museum and Library, New Delhi, India [Library symbol Library of Congress] (LCLS)	IiNN
Neifu [Republic of China] [Seismograph station code, US Geological Survey] (SEIS)	TWZ
Neighborhood [Slang]	Hood
Neighborhood	NGHBRHD
Neighborhood Action Group (AD)	NAG
Neighborhood Action Program [New York City] (EA)	NAP
Neighborhood Adult Participation Project	NAPP
Neighborhood Arts Program National Organizing Committee (EA)	NAPNOC
Neighborhood Awareness Program (AD)	NAP
Neighborhood Bible Studies (EA)	NBS
Neighborhood Business Revitalization [Program]	NBR
Neighborhood Coalition (EA)	NC
Neighborhood Community Action Program	NCAP
Neighborhood Development Program [Urban renewal]	NDP
Neighborhood Electric Vehicle	NEV
Neighborhood Environmental Evaluation and Decision System [Health Services and Mental Health Administration]	NEEDS
Neighborhood Environmental Workshops (EA)	NEWS
Neighborhood Facilities Program (OICC)	NFP
Neighborhood Family-Care Center (MEDA)	NFCC
Neighborhood Final Fade	NF
Neighborhood Health Center [Generic term] (DHSM)	NHC
Neighborhood Health Program [Generic term]	NHP
Neighborhood Housing Services [Generic term]	NHS
Neighborhood Housing Services of America (EA)	NHSA
Neighborhood Improvement Association (BARN)	NIA
Neighborhood Info Centers Project (EA)	NIC
Neighborhood Information Service	NIS
Neighborhood Information Sharing Exchange [Defunct] (EA)	NISE
Neighborhood Legal Services Program	NLSP
Neighborhood Loan Program	NLP
Neighborhood Patrol Office [or Officer]	NPO
Neighborhood Publication Area Report [Bureau of the Census] (GFGA)	NPA
Neighborhood Service Organization	NSO
Neighborhood Stabilization Unit (LAIN)	NSU
Neighborhood Statistics Program [Bureau of the Census] (GFGA)	NSP
Neighborhood Strategy Area [Program] [HUD]	NSA
Neighborhood Youth Administration (OICC)	NYA
Neighborhood Youth Corps [Department of Labor] [Terminated]	NYC
Neighborhood Youth Development Program	NYDP
Neighborhoods USA (EA)	NUSA
Neighborhoods, Voluntary Associations and Consumer Protection [Environmental Protection Agency] (ERG)	NVACP
Neighborhoods-in-Action [An association] (EA)	NIA
Neighbors in Need [An association]	NIN
Neighbors of Woodcraft [Portland, OR] (EA)	NOW
Neighbors Opposing Smelly Emissions [Student legal action organization]	NOSE
Neighbourhood Advice Council	NAC
Neighbourhood Improvement Program [Canada]	NIP
Neighbours of the Roundtable (EA)	NRT
Neillsville, WI [Location identifier FAA] (FAAL)	VIQ
Neillsville, WI [AM radio station call letters]	WCCN
Neillsville, WI [FM radio station call letters]	WCCN-FM
Neiltown Air Ltd. [Canada ICAO designator] (FAAC)	NLA
Neiman-Marcus	NeimM
Neiman-Marcus Group [Associated Press] (SAG)	NeimM
Neiman-Marcus Group [NYSE symbol] (SPSG)	NMG
Neiman-Marcus Group [NYSE symbol] (TTSB)	NMG

Neimann-Pick Disease (CPH) ..... NPD
Neipperg [*Federal Republic of Germany*] [*Seismograph station code, US Geological Survey*] (SEIS) ..... NEI
Neiriz [*Iran*] [*ICAO location identifier*] (ICLI) ..... OISN
Neishaboor [*Iran*] [*ICAO location identifier*] (ICLI) ..... OIMY
Neisler Laboratories, Inc. [*Research code symbol*] ..... IN
Neisseria [*Medicine*] ..... N
Neither (ROG) ..... NEIR
Neither Confirm nor Deny ..... NCND
Neither Help nor Hinder ..... NHH
Neiva [*Sociedade Construtora Aeronautica Neiva Ltda.*] [*Brazil ICAO aircraft manufacturer identifier*] (ICAO) ..... NE
Neiva [*Colombia*] [*Airport symbol*] (OAG) ..... NVA
Neiva/La Manguila [*Colorado ICAO location identifier*] (ICLI) ..... SKNV
Nejjo [*Ethiopia*] [*ICAO location identifier*] (ICLI) ..... HANJ
Nejo [*Ethiopia*] [*Airport symbol*] (AD) ..... EJO
Nejran [*Saudi Arabia*] [*Airport symbol*] (OAG) ..... EAM
Nejran [*Saudi Arabia*] [*ICAO location identifier*] (ICLI) ..... OENG
Nekempt [*Ethiopia*] [*Airport symbol*] (AD) ..... LKM
Nekemte [*Ethiopia*] [*ICAO location identifier*] (ICLI) ..... HANK
Nekoosa, WI [*AM radio station call letters*] ..... WCAE
Nekoosa, WI [*FM radio station call letters*] ..... WXEC
Nelen Yubu [*A publication*] (APTA) ..... NY
NELINET [*New England Library Information Network*], Newton, MA [*OCLC symbol*] (OCLC) ..... TQK
NELINET [*New England Library Information Network*], Newton, MA [*OCLC symbol*] (OCLC) ..... TQL
NELINET [*New England Library Information Network*], Newton, MA [*OCLC symbol*] (OCLC) ..... XNL
Nellcor, Inc. [*NASDAQ symbol*] (NQ) ..... NELL
Nellcor, Inc. [*Associated Press*] (SAG) ..... Nellcor
Nellcor Puritan Bennett [*NASDAQ symbol*] (TTSB) ..... NELL
Nelle Shean Elementary School, Gilbert, MN [*Library symbol*] [*Library of Congress*] (LCLS) ..... MnGiNSE
Nellie Pederson Civic Library, Clifton, TX [*Library symbol Library of Congress*] (LCLS) ..... TxCli
Nellingen [*Germany ICAO location identifier*] (ICLI) ..... EDIS
Nell's Reports [*1845-55*] [*Ceylon*] [*A publication*] (DLA) ..... Nell
Nelson [*Nevada*] [*Seismograph station code, US Geological Survey*] (SEIS) ..... NEL
Nelson [*New Zealand*] [*Airport symbol*] (OAG) ..... NSN
Nelson [*New Zealand*] [*ICAO location identifier*] (ICLI) ..... NZNS
Nelson Aldrich Rockefeller (AD) ..... NAR
Nelson & Albemarle Railway [*AAR code*] ..... NEA
Nelson Art Gallery, Art Reference Library, Kansas City, MO [*Library symbol Library of Congress*] (LCLS) ..... MoKNG
Nelson Associates [*Also, an information service or system*] (IID) ..... NA
Nelson Aviation College [*New Zealand*] [*ICAO designator*] (FAAC) ..... CGE
Nelson, BC [*AM radio station call letters*] ..... CKKC
Nelson, BC [*Television station call letters*] (RBYB) CKTN-3
Nelson Elementary School, Rockford, IL [*Library symbol*] [*Library of Congress*] (LCLS) ..... IRoNeE
Nelson Holdings International Ltd. [*Toronto Stock Exchange symbol Vancouver Stock Exchange symbol*] ..... NHI
Nelson [*Thomas*], Inc. [*Associated Press*] (SAG) ..... NelsnB
Nelson [*Thomas*], Inc. [*Associated Press*] (SAG) ..... NelsnT
Nelson [*Thomas*], Inc. [*NYSE symbol*] (SAG) ..... TNM
Nelson Lagoon [*Alaska*] [*Airport symbol*] (OAG) ..... NLG
Nelson, Marlborough, and West Coast Regiment [*British military*] (DMA) ..... NMWC
Nelson Museum, British Columbia [*Library symbol National Library of Canada*] (NLC) ..... BNEM
Nelson Museum, Nelson, BC, Canada [*Library symbol*] [*Library of Congress*] (LCLS) ..... CaBNEM
Nelson Public Library, British Columbia [*Library symbol National Library of Canada*] (BIB) ..... BNE
Nelson Tempore Finch [*1673-81*] [*A publication*] (DLA) ..... Nelson's Rep
Nelson Vending Technology Ltd. [*Toronto Stock Exchange symbol*] ..... NVT
Nelson-Atkins Museum of Art, Spencer Art Reference Library, Kansas City, MO [*Library symbol*] [*Library of Congress*] (LCLS) ..... MoKNA
Nelson-Denny Reading Test (EDAC) ..... NDRT
Nelson's Abridgment of the Common Law [*A publication*] (DLA) ..... Nels Abr
Nelson's English Chancery Reports [*A publication*] (DLA) ..... N Ch R
Nelson's English Chancery Reports [*A publication*] (DLA) ..... Nel
Nelson's English Chancery Reports [*A publication*] (DLA) ..... Nel CR
Nelson's English Chancery Reports [*A publication*] (DLA) ..... Nels
Nelson's English Chancery Reports [*A publication*] (DLA) ..... Nels 8vo
Nelson's English Chancery Reports [*A publication*] (DLA) ..... Nelson (Eng)
Nelson's Lex Maneriorum [*A publication*] (DLA) ..... Nels Lex Man
Nelson's Lutwyche, English Common Pleas Reports [*A publication*] (DLA) ..... NL
Nelson's Rights of the Clergy [*A publication*] (DLA) ..... Nels Cler
Nelsonville, OH [*FM radio station call letters*] ..... WSEO
Nelsonville Public Library, Nelsonville, OH [*Library symbol Library of Congress*] (LCLS) ..... ONe
Nelspruit [*South Africa*] [*ICAO location identifier*] (ICLI) ..... FANS
Nelspruit [*South Africa*] [*Airport symbol*] (OAG) ..... NLP
NEM [*N-Ethylmaleimide*]-Sensitive Fusion [*Biochemistry*] ..... NSF
Nema [*Mauritania*] [*Airport symbol*] (OAG) ..... EMN
Nema [*Mauritania*] [*ICAO location identifier*] (ICLI) ..... GQNI
Nematic Curvilinear Aligned Phase [*Emulsion film used in windows*] [*Taliq Corp.*] ..... NCAP
Nematic Liquid Crystal [*Physical chemistry*] ..... NLC
Nematic Phase [*Physical chemistry*] ..... N
Nematocyst [*Zoology*] ..... N
Nematode [*Threadworm*] ..... NEMA
Nematological Society of Southern Africa (EAIO) ..... NSSA
Nematologiese Vereniging van Suidelike Afrika [*Nematological Society of Southern Africa*] (EAIO) ..... NVSA
Nematology ..... NEMATOL
Nematron Corp. [*NASDAQ symbol*] (SAG) ..... NEMA
Nematron Corp. [*Associated Press*] (SAG) ..... Nmatrn
Nemean [*of Pindar*] [*Classical studies*] (OCD) ..... Nem
Nemesis (ABBR) ..... NMSS
Nemeth-Kellner Leukemia ..... NKL
Nemine Contradicente [*No One Contradicting*] [*Latin Legal term*] (DLA) ..... NCD
Nemine Contradicente [*No One Contradicting*] [*Latin Legal term*] ..... NEM CON
Nemine Dissentiente [*No One Dissenting*] [*Latin*] ..... NEM DISS
Nemuro [*Japan*] [*Seismograph station code, US Geological Survey*] (SEIS) ..... NEM
Nemzeti Bank [*National Bank*] [*Hungarian*] ..... NB
Nemzeti Egyseg Partja [*Party of National Unity*] [*Hungary Political party*] (PPE) ..... NEP
Nemzeti Fueggetlensegi Front [*National Independence Front*] [*Hungary Political party*] (PPE) ..... NFF
Nemzeti Paraszt Part [*National Peasant Party*] [*Hungary Political party*] (PPE) ..... NPP
Nemzeti Szabadelvu Part [*National Liberal Party*] [*Hungary Political party*] (PPE) ..... NSZP
Nenana [*Alaska*] [*Seismograph station code, US Geological Survey*] (SEIS) ..... NEA
Nenana, AK [*Location identifier FAA*] (FAAL) ..... ENN
Nenana, AK [*Location identifier FAA*] (FAAL) ..... JUS
Nenana, AK [*AM radio station call letters*] ..... KIAM
Neo Aristero Revma [*Greece*] [*Political party*] (ECED) ..... NAR
NEO [*Neuroticism, Extraversion, Openness to Experience*] **Personality Inventory** [*Personality development test*] [*Psychology*] ..... NEO-PI
Neo Sumerian (BJA) ..... NS
Neo-American Church (EA) ..... NAC
Neoarsphenamine [*or Neosalvarsan*] [*Medicine*] ..... NEO
Neo-Assyrian [*or New Assyrian*] [*Language, etc.*] (BJA) ..... NA
Neo-Babylonian [*or New Babylonian*] (BJA) ..... NB
Neo-Babylonian [*or New Babylonian*] (BJA) ..... NBab
Neocarzinostatin [*Zinostatin*] [*Antineoplastic drug*] ..... NCAS
Neocarzinostatin [*Zinostatin*] [*Antineoplastic drug*] ..... NCS
Neoclassical Radiation Theory ..... NCT
Neoclassical/Rational Planning ..... N/RP
Neocomian [*Paleontology*] ..... NEO
Neoconservative ..... NEOCON
Neodymium [*Chemical element*] ..... Nd
Neodymium ..... Nd
Neodymium, Cerium, Copper, Oxide [*Inorganic chemistry*] ..... NCCO
Neodymium Glass LASER ..... NGL
Neodymium Glass LASER Rod ..... NGLR
Neodymium LASER Illuminator ..... NLI
Neodymium LASER Range-Finder ..... NLR
Neodymium LASER System ..... NLS
Neodymium Pentaphosphate [*Inorganic chemistry*] ..... NPP
Neodymium YAG [*Yttrium Aluminum Garnet*] **LASER** ..... NYL
Neodymium YAG [*Yttrium Aluminum Garnet*] **LASER Range-Finder** ..... NYLR
Neodymium YAG [*Yttrium Aluminum Garnet*] **Range-Finder** ..... NYR
Neodymium-Doped Glass LASER ..... NDGL
Neodymium-Doped YAG [*Yttrium Aluminum Garnet*] **LASER** ..... NDYL
Neodymium-Doped Yttralox [*Ceramic*] ..... NDY
Neodymium-Doped: Yttrium Aluminum Garnet [*LASER technology*] ..... Nd:YAG
Neoga, IL [*FM radio station call letters*] (RBYB) ..... WWGO-FM
Neogen Corp. [*NASDAQ symbol*] (NQ) ..... NEOG
Neogen Corp. [*Associated Press*] (SAG) ..... Neogen
Neo-Hebrew (BJA) ..... NH
Neohemocyte [*An artificial red blood cell*] ..... NHC
Neohesperidin Dihydrochalcone [*Also, NHDC*] [*Sweetening agent*] ..... NEO-DHC
Neohesperidin Dihydrochalcone [*Also, NEO-DHC*] [*Sweetening agent*] ..... NHDC
Neola, IA [*Location identifier FAA*] (FAAL) ..... EOL
Neolens, Inc. [*NASDAQ symbol*] (NQ) ..... NEOL
Neolithic (VRA) ..... Neol
Neologism ..... NEOL
Neomar Resources Ltd. [*Toronto Stock Exchange symbol*] ..... NMR
NeoMedia Technologies, Inc. [*NASDAQ symbol*] (SAG) ..... NEOM
NeoMedia Technologies, Inc. [*Associated Press*] (SAG) ..... NeoMd
NeoMedia Technologies, Inc. [*Associated Press*] (SAG) ..... NeoMdia
Neomenthyldiphenylphosphine [*Organic chemistry*] ..... NMDP
Neomycin [*Antibacterial compound*] ..... NE
Neomycin [*Antibiotic compound*] ..... NEO
Neomycin, Colistin, Nystatin [*Antineoplastic drug regimen*] ..... NEOCON
Neomycin Egg Yolk [*Agar*] [*Microbiology*] ..... NEY
Neomycin Phosphotransferase [*An enzyme*] ..... NPT
Neon [*Chemical element*] ..... NE
Neon (IDOE) ..... ne
Neon [*Chemical element*] (DOG) ..... Ne
Neon [*Chemical element*] (ODBW) ..... Ne
Neon (VRA) ..... ne
Neon Discharge Lighting [*Automotive lighting*] ..... NDL
Neon Globe Tube ..... NGT
Neon Glow Lamp ..... NGL
Neon Indicating Light ..... NEIL
Neon Indicator Functional Test Equipment ..... NIFTE
Neon Komma [*New Party*] [*Greek Political party*] (PPE) ..... NK
Neon Lamp (KSC) ..... NL
Neon Light (IAA) ..... NEL
Neon Pilot Light ..... NPL
Neon Test Light ..... NTL
Neonatal [*Medicine*] ..... NEO
Neonatal (DAVI) ..... NN
Neonatal Abstinence Syndrome (DAVI) ..... NAS

Neonatal Behavioral Assessment Scale-Kansas Revision (EDAC) .... NBAS-K
Neonatal Behavioural Assessment Scale [*Developed by Brazelton*] .... NBAS
Neonatal Calf Diarrhea Coronavirus .... NCDCV
Neonatal Death [*Medicine*] (MAE) .... ND
Neo-Natal Death [*Medicine*] .... NND
Neonatal Hypothyroidism [*Cretinism*] [*Medicine*] .... NH
Neonatal Intensive Care .... NIC
Neonatal Intensive Care Center (DAVI) .... NICC
Neonatal [*or Newborn*] **Intensive Care Unit** .... NICU
Neonatal Lung Fibroblast [*Medicine*] (DMAA) .... NLF
Neonatal Mortality Risk [*Medicine*] .... NMR
Neonatal Narcotic Abstinence Syndrome [*Medicine*] (DMAA) .... NNAS
Neonatal Narcotic Withdrawal Index [*Medicine*] (DMAA) .... NNWI
Neonatal Necrotizing Enterocolitis [*Medicine*] (AAMN) .... NNE
Neonatal Nurse Practitioner (DAVI) .... NNP
Neonatal Society [*British*] (DBA) .... NNS
Neonatal Tetanus .... NT
Neonatal Thymectomy [*Medicine*] .... NTX
Neonatal-Perinatal Medicine [*Medical specialty*] (DHSM) .... NPM
NeoPath, Inc. [*Associated Press*] (SAG) .... NeoPath
NeoPath, Inc. [*NASDAQ symbol*] (SAG) .... NPTH
Neopentyl Glycol [*Organic chemistry*] .... NG
Neopentyl(chloroethyl)nitrosourea [*Biochemistry*] .... NPCNU
Neopentylglycol [*Organic chemistry*] .... NPG
Neopharm, Inc. [*AMEX symbol*] (SAG) .... NEO
Neopharm, Inc. [*Associated Press*] (SAG) .... Neophrm
Neopharm Inc. [*NASDAQ symbol*] (TTSB) .... NPRM
Neopharm Inc. Wrrt [*NASDAQ symbol*] (TTSB) .... NPRMW
Neoplasia, Allergy, Addison's Disease, Collagen Disease, and Parasites [*Medicine*] .... NAACP
Neoplastic Disease [*Medicine*] .... ND
Neoprecipitin Test [*Oncology*] .... NPT
Neoprene [*Synthetic rubber*] .... NPRN
Neoprobe Corp. [*NASDAQ symbol*] (SAG) .... NEOP
Neoprobe Corp. [*Associated Press*] (SAG) .... Neopr
Neoprobe Corp. [*Associated Press*] (SAG) .... Neoprobe
Neoprobe Corp. Wrrt'E' [*NASDAQ symbol*] (TTSB) .... NEOPW
Neoproteolipid [*Hematology*] .... NPL
Neo-Punic (BJA) .... NP
Neopyrithiamine Hydrochloride [*Chemistry*] (DAVI) .... NPT
Neoricans in Puerto Rico (EA) .... NPR
NeoRx $2.4375 Cv Exch Pfd [*NASDAQ symbol*] (TTSB) .... NERXP
NeoRx Corp. [*Associated Press*] (SAG) .... NeoRx
NeoRx Corp. [*NASDAQ symbol*] (NQ) .... NERX
Neorx Corp. Wrrt [*NASDAQ symbol*] (TTSB) .... NERXW
Neose Technologies [*NASDAQ symbol*] (TTSB) .... NTEC
Neosho, MO [*Location identifier FAA*] (FAAL) .... EOS
Neosho, MO [*AM radio station call letters*] .... KBTN
Neosho, MO [*FM radio station call letters*] (RBYB) .... KBTN-FM
Neosho, MO [*FM radio station call letters*] .... KNEO
Neosporin Ointment [*Medicine*] (CPH) .... NSO
NeoStar Retail Group [*NASDAQ symbol*] (SAG) .... NEOS
NeoStar Retail Group [*Associated Press*] (SAG) .... NeoStar
NeoSynthesis Research Centre [*Sri Lanka*] (EAIO) .... NSRC
Neotetrazolium .... NT
Neotetrazolium Chloride [*A dye*] .... NTC
NeoTherapeutics, Inc. [*NASDAQ symbol*] (SAG) .... NEOT
NeoTherapeutics, Inc. [*Associated Press*] (SAG) .... NeoTher
NeoTherapeutics, Inc. [*Associated Press*] (SAG) .... NeoThr
Neotronics Olfactory Sensing Equipment [*Neotronics Scientific*] (PS) .... NOSE
Neoucom Processing Center, Rootstown, OH [*OCLC symbol*] (OCLC) .... TWO
Neovascular Edema [*Ophthalmology*] (DAVI) .... NVE
Neovascular Glaucoma (DAVI) .... NVG
Neovascularization Elsewhere [*Cardiology*] (DAVI) .... NVE
Neovascularization of the Disc [*Ophthalmology*] (DAVI) .... NVD
Neoviridogrisein [*Antibacterial*] .... NVG
Neozyme Corp. [*Associated Press*] (SAG) .... Neoz
Neozyme Corp. [*NASDAQ symbol*] (SAG) .... NIIU
Nepal [*Aircraft nationality and registration mark*] (FAAC) 9N
Nepal [*MARC geographic area code Library of Congress*] (LCCP) .... a-np--
Nepal (VRA) .... Nep
Nepal [*MARC country of publication code Library of Congress*] (LCCP) .... np
Nepal [*ANSI two-letter standard code*] (CNC) .... NP
Nepal [*ANSI three-letter standard code*] (CNC) .... NPL
Nepal Studies Association (EA) .... NSA
Nepal, Tibet, and Bhutan Philatelic Study Circle (EA) .... NTBPSC
Nepalganj [*Nepal*] [*Airport symbol*] (OAG) .... KEP
Nepalgung [*Nepal*] [*ICAO location identifier*] (ICLI) .... VNNG
Nepali [*MARC language code Library of Congress*] (LCCP) .... nep
Nepali Congress Party [*Political party*] (EY) .... NCP
Nepean Public Library [*UTLAS symbol*] .... NEP
Nepean Public Library, Centennial Branch, Centennial, ON, Canada [*Library symbol*] [*Library of Congress*] (LCLS) .... CaONCB
Nepean Public Library, Ruth E. Dickinson Branch, Nepean, ON, Canada [*Library symbol*] [*Library of Congress*] (LCLS) .... CaONRDB
Neper [*A unit on a natural logarithmic scale*] (DEN) .... N
Neper [*A unit on a natural logarithmic scale*] .... Np
Neper per Meter .... Np/m
Nepheline Resources Ltd. [*Vancouver Stock Exchange symbol*] .... NPL
Nephelite [*CIPW classification*] [*Geology*] .... ne
Nephelometric Immunoassay [*Analytical chemistry*] .... NIA
Nephelometric Inhibition Assay [*Analytical chemistry*] (MAE) .... NIA
Nephelometric Inhibition Immunoassay [*Analytical chemistry*] .... NINIA
Nephelometric Turbidity Unit [*Analytical chemistry*] .... NTU
Nephew .... N
Nephi [*Utah*] [*Airport symbol*] (OAG) .... NPH
Nephi Public Library, Nephi, UT [*Library symbol Library of Congress*] (LCLS) .... UN
Nephi, UT [*FM radio station call letters*] .... KYKN
Nephridial Gland .... NG
Nephrite (VRA) .... neph
Nephritic Factor [*Clinical medicine*] .... NeF
Nephritic Factor [*Clinical medicine*] .... NF
Nephrogenic Diabetes Insipidus [*Endocrinology*] .... NDI
Nephrology [*Medical specialty*] (DHSM) .... NEP
Nephrology .... NEPH
Nephrology (DAVI) .... NEPH
Nephron Filtration Rate [*Physiology*] .... NFR
Nephropathia Epidemica [*Medicine*] .... NE
Nephrosclerosis [*Medicine*] .... NS
Nephrostomy Tube [*Nephrology*] (DAVI) .... NT
Nephrotic Syndrome [*Medicine*] (DAVI) .... NS
Nephrotic Syndrome [*Medicine*] .... NS
Nephrotoxic Antibody [*Medicine*] (MAE) .... NTAB
Nephrotoxic Nephritis [*Medicine*] .... NTN
Nephrotoxic Serum Nephritis [*Medicine*] (DMAA) .... NSN
Nepisiguit Centennial Public Library, Bathurst, New Brunswick [*Library symbol National Library of Canada*] (NLC) .... NBBN
Nepisiguit Library Region, Bathurst, NB, Canada [*Library symbol Library of Congress*] (LCLS) .... CaNBBN
Neplanocin A [*Biochemistry*] .... NPC
Neponset Public Library, Neponset, IL [*Library symbol Library of Congress*] (LCLS) .... INep
Neponset Public Library, Neponset, IL [*Library symbol*] [*Library of Congress*] (LCLS) .... INepL
Neponset Public Library, Neponset, IL [*OCLC symbol*] (OCLC) .... ISV
Nepos [*Grandson*] [*Latin*] .... N
Nepos [*First century BC*] [*Classical studies*] (OCD) .... Nep
Nepotism (ABBR) .... NPTSM
Nepotist (ABBR) .... NPTST
Neptune (ROG) .... NEP
Neptune (WDAA) .... NEPT
Neptune Radii [*Astronomy*] .... RN
Neptune Resources Corp. [*Toronto Stock Exchange symbol*] .... NPR
Neptunium [*Chemical element*] .... Np
Nera & Musica [*Record label*] [*Norway*] .... Nera
Nera AS [*Associated Press*] (SAG) .... NeraAS
Nera AS ADS [*NASDAQ symbol*] (TTSB) .... NERAY
Nera-AS [*NASDAQ symbol*] (SAG) .... NERAy
NERCO Minerals Co., Vancouver, WA [*Library symbol*] [*Library of Congress*] (LCLS) .... WaVN
Nereditary Chronic Nephritis [*Medicine*] (DMAA) .... HCN
Neriglissar (BJA) .... Ner
Nerine Latent Virus [*Plant pathology*] .... NELV
Nerine Society [*Defunct*] (EA) .... NS
Nerine Virus X [*Plant pathology*] .... NEVX
Nernst Approximation Formula [*Physics*] .... NAF
Nernst Heat Theorem [*Physics*] .... NHT
Nernst-Thomson Rule [*Physics*] .... NTR
Nero [*of Suetonius*] [*Classical studies*] (OCD) .... Ner
NERVA [*Nuclear Engine for Rocket Vehicle Application*] **Advisory Group** [*NASA*] (KSC) .... NAG
NERVA [*Nuclear Engine for Rocket Vehicle Application*] **Reactor Experiment** .... NRX
NERVA [*Nuclear Engine for Rocket Vehicle Applications*] **Reactor Experiment-EngineSystem Test** (SAA) .... NRX-EST
Nerve (ABBR) .... NRV
Nerve Agent Antidote Kit [*Military*] (RDA) .... NAAK
Nerve Agent Immobilised Enzyme Alarm and Detector (PDAA) .... NAIAD
Nerve Agent Pre-Treatment Set [*A cholinergic drug*] [*Used for protective immunization by the military*] .... NAPS
Nerve and Muscle Stimulating Current .... NMSC
Nerve and Vein [*Medicine*] (DAVI) .... NV
Nerve Cell Food .... NCF
Nerve Center [*An association*] (EA) .... NC
[*The*] **Nerve Center** (EA) .... TNC
Nerve Conduction .... NC
Nerve Conduction Studies [*Neurology*] (DAVI) .... NCS
Nerve Conduction Tests [*Neurology*] (DAVI) .... NCT
Nerve Conduction Time [*neurology*] (DAVI) .... NCT
Nerve Conduction Velocity [*Electrophysiology*] .... NCV
Nerve Conduction Velocity Studies [*Medicine*] (MEDA) .... NCVS
Nerve Ending (MAE) .... NE
Nerve Excitability [*Test*] .... NE
Nerve Fiber Action Potentials [*Neurophysiology*] .... NFAP
Nerve Fiber Layer [*Neurology*] (DAVI) .... NFL
Nerve Fiber Layer Defect [*Medicine*] (DMAA) .... NFLD
Nerve Gas [*US Chemical Corps symbol*] .... GD
Nerve Gas [*US Chemical Corps symbol*] VX
Nerve Growth Factor [*A protein*] [*Biochemistry*] .... NGF
Nerve Growth Factor Receptor [*Neurobiology*] .... NGFR
Nerve Growth Stimulating Activity [*Biochemistry*] .... NGSA
Nerve Impulse Recorder .... NIR
Nerve Net Pulse [*Neurobiology*] .... NNP
Nerve, Vein, and Tendon (DAVI) .... NVT
Nerved (ABBR) .... NRVD
Nerve-Ending Particle (OA) .... NEP
Nerveless (ABBR) .... NRVLS
Nerves .... NN
Nerve-Wracking (ABBR) .... NRVWRKG

Nervi Nerves [*Neurology*] [*Latin*] (DAVI) .... nn	Net Decision Benefit (NUCP) .... NDB
Nervine [*Medicine*] (ROG) .... NER	Net Defence Department [*Navy British*] .... NDD
Nerving (ABBR) .... NRVG	Net Dietary Protein (MAE) .... NDP
Nervous [*Medicine*] .... NERV	Net Difference Report (IAA) .... NDR
Nervous (ABBR) .... NRVU	Net Domestic Product [*Business term*] (PDAA) .... NDP
Nervous (ABBR) .... NRVUS	Net Earnings .... NE
Nervous Debility [*Medicine*] .... ND	Net Economic Value .... NEV
Nervous System .... NS	Net Economic Welfare [*Economic indicator*] .... NEW
Nervous System and Sense Organs .... NS & SO	Net Ecosystem Exchange [*Biology*] .... NEE
Nervous System Sports-Related Injury [*Medicine*] .... NSSRI	Net Ecosystem Production [*Biology*] .... NEP
Nervous Tissue Vaccine (AAMN) .... NTV	Net Energy Thrust .... NET
Nervously (ABBR) .... NRVUSY	Net Equivalent Temperature .... NET
Nervously (ABBR) .... NRVUY	Net Euphotic Zone Production [*Oceanography*] .... NEZP
Nervousness (ABBR) .... NRVUNS	Net Evaluation Subcommittee, National Security Council (AABC) .... NESCNSC
Nervousness (ABBR) .... NRVUSNS	Net Explosive Weight (MSA) .... NET
Nervus [*Nerve*] [*Anatomy*] .... N	Net Explosive Weight (AFM) .... NEW
Nervy (ABBR) .... NRVI	Net Exports .... NX
Nesbitt, Thomson & Co. Ltd., Montreal, PQ, Canada [*Library symbol Library of Congress*] (LCLS) .... CaQMNT	Net Financial Assets (BARN) .... NFA
	Net Financing Requirement .... NFR
Nesbitt, Thomson & Co. Ltd., Montreal, Quebec [*Library symbol National Library of Canada*] (NLC) .... QMNT	Net Flux Radiometer [*Instrumentation*] .... NFR
	Net Free Vent Area [*Roofing*] .... NFVA
Nesbitt Thomson, Inc. [*Toronto Stock Exchange symbol Vancouver Stock Exchange symbol*] .... NTI	Net Fundable Issues (DNAB) .... NFI
	Net Gradability [*Truck specification*] .... GAN
Neshei Ubenos Agudath Israel [*Antwerp*] (BJA) .... NOWAI	Net Histocompatibility Ratio .... NHR
Neshoba County Library, Philadelphia, MS [*Library symbol Library of Congress*] (LCLS) .... MsPh	Net Horsepower [*Engineering*] .... NHP
	Net Imports [*Economics*] .... NM
Nesmont Industry [*Vancouver Stock Exchange symbol*] .... NES	Net in Thirty Days N/30
Nest (ABBR) .... NST	Net Income .... NI
Nestart Library, Richibucto, NB, Canada [*Library symbol Library of Congress*] (LCLS) .... CaNBRN	Net Income per Partner [*Business term*] .... NIPP
	Net Interest .... NI
Nestart Library, Richibucto, New Brunswick [*Library symbol National Library of Canada*] (NLC) .... NBRN	Net Interest Cost [*Investment term*] .... NIC
	Net Interest Income (TDOB) .... NII
Nested [*Freight*] .... N	Net Interest Margin [*Banking*] .... NIM
Nested [*Packaging*] .... NSTD	Net Internal Area .... NIA
Nested Cone Extendable Exit Cone (MCD) .... NCEEC	Net International Investment Position .... NIIP
Nested Grid Model [*Marine science*] (OSRA) .... NGM	Net Laying Light (SAA) .... NL LT
Nested Grid Model [*National Marine Center*] (USDC) .... NGM	Net Laying Ship [*Later, ANL*] [*Navy symbol*] .... AN
Nested or Flat [*Freight*] .... NF	Net Laying Ship [*Formerly, AN*] [*Navy symbol*] .... ANL
Nested Phrase Indexing System [*Automated indexing system*] [*University of Western Ontario*] .... NEPHIS	Net Lettable Area .... NLA
	Net Level Premium [*Insurance*] .... NLP
Nested-Task [*Computer science*] (BYTE) .... NT	Net Liquidity Ratio (PDAA) .... NLR
Nesting [*Ornithology*] .... N	Net Long Ton .... NLT
Nesting (ABBR) .... NSTG	Net Loss .... NL
Nesting Module (MCD) .... NST	Net Matchable Cost .... NMC
Nestled (ABBR) .... NSTL	Net Material Product [*Economics*] .... NMP
Nestling (ABBR) .... NSTLG	Net National Income [*Economics*] .... NNI
Net .... N	Net National Product [*Economics*] .... NNP
Net (WDAA) .... NT	Net National Well Being .... NNWB
Net Acid Flux [*Medicine*] (DMAA) .... NAF	Net Nitrogen Utilization [*Medicine*] (DAVI) .... NNU
Net Acquisition of Financial Assets (ADA) .... NAFA	Net Operating Income .... NOI
Net Ad-Produced Purchases [*Advertising*] .... NETAPPS	Net Operating Loss .... NOL
Net Advertising Circulation (DOAD) .... NAC	Net Operating Profit after Tax .... NOPAT
Net Advertising Revenue [*Television*] [*British*] .... NAR	Net Orders Processed [*Business term*] (DOAD) .... NOP
Net Advertising Revenue after Levy [*Television*] [*British*] .... NARAL	Net Pool Return .... NPR
Net Advertising Revenue before Levy [*Television*] [*British*] .... NARBL	Net Pool Return Rule .... NPRR
Net Aerial Primary Productivity [*Forestry*] .... NAPP	Net Position [*Business term*] .... NP
Net Annual Gain [*Business term*] (PDAA) .... NAG	Net Positive Static Pressure (NASA) .... NPSP
Net Annual Gain (AD) .... nag	Net Positive Suction Head [*Pumps*] .... NPSH
Net Annual Inflow [*Pensions*] .... NAI	Net Positive Suction Head Available [*Pumps*] (PDAA) .... NPSHA
Net Annual Value [*Business term*] (ADA) .... NAV	Net Positive Suction Head Required [*Chemical or food processing*] .... NPSHR
Net Assessment Organization [*Navy*] .... NA	Net Positive Suction Pressure [*Cryogenics*] .... NPSP
Net Asset Backing .... NAB	Net Premium Income [*Insurance*] (AIA) .... NPI
Net Asset Value (AD) .... n/a/v	Net Present Value [*Accounting*] .... NPV
Net Asset Value .... NAV	Net Present Value at the Horizon (PDAA) .... NPVH
Net Asset Value (AD) .... NAVA	Net Present Value for Current Expendable Launch Vehicles [*NASA*] (KSC) .... NPVCE
Net Assets [*Banking*] .... NA	
Net Assimilation Rate (AD) .... nar	Net Present Value for New Expendable Launch Vehicles [*NASA*] (KSC) .... NPVNE
Net Assimilation Rate [*Botany*] .... NAR	
Net Barter Terms of Trade .... NBTT	Net Present Value for Space Shuttle [*NASA*] (KSC) .... NPVSH
Net Book Agreement [*British*] .... NBA	Net Price [*Business term*] (MHDW) .... NP
Net Book Value (TEL) .... NBV	Net Primary Productivity .... NPP
Net Borrowing Requirement [*Banking*] (MHDW) .... NBR	Net Proceeds .... NP
Net Building Area (ADA) .... NBA	Net Profit .... NP
Net Calorific Value (PDAA) .... NCV	Net Propulsion Force (MCD) .... NPF
Net Capital [*Business term*] .... NC	Net Protein Ratio [*Nutrition*] .... NPR
Net Cargo Ship [*Navy symbol Obsolete*] .... AKN	Net Protein Utilization [*Nutrition*] .... NPU
Net Cash Flow .... NCF	Net Public Sector Financing Requirement [*Business term*] .... NPSFR
Net Charter [*Business term*] (DS) .... NC	Net Quick Assets .... NQ
Net Clearing Balance [*Finance*] .... NCB	Net Quick Assets .... NQA
Net Combat Power .... NCP	Net Radio Interface [*Telecommunications*] (TEL) .... NRI
Net Community Productivity (FFDE) .... NCP	Net Rating Point [*Advertising*] (DOAD) .... NRP
Net Control (MCD) .... NC	Net Rating Points [*Media ratings*] (NTCM) .... NRP
Net Control (CAAL) .... NCO	Net Realizable Value .... NRV
Net Control Master (MCD) .... NCM	Net Realizable Value Accounting (ADA) .... NRVA
Net Control Officer, Atlantic [*Navy*] (DNAB) .... NCOLANT	Net Register [*Shipping*] .... NR
Net Control Officer, Mediterranean [*Navy*] (DNAB) .... NCOMED	Net Register Tons [*Shipping*] .... NRT
Net Control Officer, Pacific [*Navy*] (DNAB) .... NCOPAC	Net Registered Tonnage .... NRT
Net Control Outstation [*Military*] (DOMA) .... NCO	Net Rentable Area (ADA) .... NRA
Net Control Procedure .... NCP	Net Replacement Cost [*Accounting*] .... NRC
Net Control Station [*Communications*] [*Amateur radio*] .... NCS	Net Reproductive Rate .... NRR
Net Cost .... NC	Net Requirementes Estimation Model (PDAA) .... NETREM
Net Cost of Transport .... NCT	Net Retail Requirements .... NRR
Net Data Throughout .... NDT	Net Sale Certificate (DGA) .... NSC
Net Debit Balance .... NDB	Net Sales (MHDW) .... NS
Net Debt .... ND	Net Sales Value (BUR) .... NSV

Net Section Fracture Strength (PDAA)	NSFS
Net Social Profitability	NSP
Net Square Feet (MCD)	NSF
Net Surplus	NS
Net Survival Rate	NSR
Net Survival Rate for Monocyclic Process	NSRMP
Net Switching Loss [Telecommunications] (TEL)	NSL
Net Tangible Assets [Business term] (ADA)	NTA
Net Tax [IRS]	NT
Net Technical Assessment (MCD)	NTA
Net Tender [Navy symbol Obsolete]	YN
Net Tender [Tug Class] [Navy symbol Obsolete]	YNT
Net Terms [Business term] (DS)	N/t
Net Ton Mile [Shipping]	NTM
Net Ton of Molten Iron	NTMI
Net Tons [Shipping]	NETT
Net Tons [Shipping]	NT
Net Unduplicated Research	NUR
Net Unit-Load Size (MHDB)	NULS
Net Unrealized Appreciation Tax	NUA
Net Value	NV
Net Weight	N WT
Net Weight	NT WT
Net Weight	NW
Net Working Capital	NWC
Net Worth	NW
Net Yield	NY
NetBIOS [Network Basic Input/Output System] Control Block [Computer science]	NCB
NetBIOS [Network Basic Input/Output System] Extended User Interface [Microsoft Corp.] (PCM)	NetBEUI
NETCM On-Line Comm Svcs [NASDAQ symbol] (TTSB)	NETC
Netcom On-Line Communications Services, Inc. [NASDAQ symbol] (SAG)	NETC
Netcom On-Line Communictions Services, Inc. [Associated Press] (SAG)	Netcom
Netframe Systems [NASDAQ symbol] (SAG)	NETF
Netframe Systems [Associated Press] (SAG)	Netframe
Nether Thorpe [British ICAO location identifier] (ICLI)	EGNF
Netheravon [British ICAO location identifier] (ICLI)	EGDN
Netherland Benevolent Society of New York [Later, Netherlands-America CommunityAssociation] (EA)	NBS
Netherland Club of New York (EA)	NCNY
Netherland-America Foundation [Later, Netherlands-America Community Association] (EA)	NAF
Netherland-America University League [Defunct] (EA)	NAUL
Netherlands [MARC geographic area code Library of Congress] (LCCP)	e-ne--
Netherlands [IYRU nationality code] (IYR)	HA
Netherlands [MARC country of publication code Library of Congress] (LCCP)	ne
Netherlands	NE
Netherlands	NETH
Netherlands (ODBW)	Neth
Netherlands (VRA)	Nethl
Netherlands [ANSI two-letter standard code] (CNC)	NL
Netherlands [ANSI three-letter standard code] (CNC)	NLD
Netherlands Agency for Aerospace Programs	NIVR
Netherlands and Colonial Philately	NCP
Netherlands Antilles [ANSI two-letter standard code] (CNC)	AN
Netherlands Antilles [ANSI three-letter standard code] (CNC)	ANT
Netherlands Antilles [MARC country of publication code Library of Congress] (LCCP)	na
Netherlands Antilles	Neth Ant
Netherlands Antilles [MARC geographic area code Library of Congress] (LCCP)	nwna--
Netherlands Antilles [International civil aircraft marking] (ODBW)	PJ
Netherlands Arbitration Institute (ILCA)	NAI
Netherlands Automated Information Processing Research Centre (NITA)	NAIPRC
Netherlands Board of Tourism (EA)	NBT
Netherlands British Chamber of Commerce (DS)	NBCC
Netherlands Convention Bureau (EA)	NCB
Netherlands East Indies	NEI
Netherlands' Ecological Society [Multinational association] (EAIO)	NES
Netherlands Electrotechnical Committee	NEC
Netherlands Engineering Consultants	NEDECO
Netherlands Flower-Bulb Institute [Defunct] (EA)	NFBI
Netherlands Indies [Later, Republic of Indonesia]	NI
Netherlands Indies Civil Affairs Organization [World War II]	NICA
Netherlands Information Combine [Delft] [Information service or system] (IID)	NIC
Netherlands Information Service, New York, NY [Library symbol Library of Congress] (LCLS)	NNNeI
Netherlands Institute for Sea Research [Marine science] (OSRA)	NIOZ
Netherlands Institute of Ecology	NIE
Netherlands International Law Review [A publication] (DLA)	Neth Int'l L Rev
Netherlands Jurisprudence (NITA)	NJUS
Netherlands Military Administration [World War II]	NMA
Netherlands Museum [Later, HHT] (EA)	NM
Netherlands Offset Industry	NOI
Netherlands Orange Lanyard [Military decoration]	NLOrLanyard
Netherlands Pharmacopoeia [A publication]	Neth P
Netherlands Red Cross	NRC
Netherlands West Indies	NWI
Netherlands Yearbook of International Law [A publication] (DLA)	Neth YB Int'l Law
Netherlands Yearbook of International Law [The Hague, Netherlands] [A publication] (DLA)	Netherl Intl L Rev
Netherlands Yearbook of International Law [A publication] (DLA)	NYIL
Netherlands-America Community Association (EA)	NACA
Netherlands-Australia Trade and Industrial Development Council (AD)	NATIDC
Netherlines [ICAO designator] (AD)	WU
N-Ethylcarboxamide Adenosine [Biochemistry]	NECA
N-ethylinaleimide Sensitive Fusion	NSF
N-Ethylmaleimide [Also, NEMI] [Organic chemistry]	NEM
N-Ethylmaleimide [Also, NEM] [Organic chemistry]	NEMI
N-Ethylmaleimide-Sensitive Fusion (protein) [Organic chemistry]	NSF
N-Ethylmorpholine [Organic chemistry]	NEM
N-Ethyl(phenylisoxazolium)sulfonate [Organic chemistry]	NEPIS
N-Ethylpyrrolidinone [Organic chemistry]	NEP
N-Ethylsuccinimide [Organic chemistry]	NES
NETI Technologies, Inc. [Vancouver Stock Exchange symbol]	NET
Netilmicin-Clindamycin [Antibiotic combination]	NC
Netilmicin-Ticarcillin [Antibiotic combination]	NT
NetLive Communications, Inc. [NASDAQ symbol] (SAG)	NETL
NetLive Communications, Inc. [Associated Press] (SAG)	NetLive
NetManage, Inc. [NASDAQ symbol] (SAG)	NETM
NetManage, Inc. [Associated Press] (SAG)	Netmng
Netmed, Inc. [Associated Press] (SAG)	Netmed
Netmed, Inc. [AMEX symbol] (SAG)	NMD
Net-Net Income [Business term]	NNI
Net-of-Tax Rate (ECON)	NTR
Netrix Corp. [Associated Press] (SAG)	Netrix
Netrix Corp. [NASDAQ symbol] (SAG)	NTRX
Netsah Israel Lo Yeshakker (BJA)	NILI
Netscape Communications [NASDAQ symbol] (TTSB)	NSCP
Netscape Communications Corp. [Associated Press] (SAG)	Netscpe
Netscape Communications Corp. [NASDAQ symbol] (SAG)	NSCP
Netscape Server [Computer science] (PCM)	NSAPI
Netscape Server API [All-Purpose Interface] [Computer science]	NSAPI
Netsmart Technologies, Inc. [Associated Press] (SAG)	Netsmrt
Netsmart Technologies, Inc. [Associated Press] (SAG)	Ntsmrt
Netsmart Technologies, Inc. [NASDAQ symbol] (SAG)	NTST
NetSource Communications, Inc. [Associated Press] (SAG)	NetSrce
NetSource Communications, Inc. [NASDAQ symbol] (SAG)	NSCE
NetStar, Inc. [Associated Press] (SAG)	NetStar
NetStar, Inc. [NASDAQ symbol] (SAG)	NTSR
Nett [Net] [British] (ROG)	NT
Netted Secure Digital Voice (MCD)	NSDV
Netted Secure Voice [Military] (CAAL)	NSV
Netter Digital Entertainment [NASDAQ symbol] (TTSB)	NETT
Netter Digital Entertainment, Inc. [NASDAQ symbol] (SAG)	NETT
Netter Digital Entertainment, Inc. [Associated Press] (SAG)	Netter
Netter Digital Entertainment, Inc. [Associated Press] (SAG)	NetterD
Netter Digital Entm't Wrrt [NASDAQ symbol] (TTSB)	NETTW
Nettleton Elementary School, Duluth, MN [Library symbol] [Library of Congress] (LCLS)	MnDuNE
Netto [Lowest]	NET
Neturei Karta of USA (EA)	NKUSA
NetVantage, Inc. [Associated Press] (SAG)	NetV
NetVantage, Inc. [NASDAQ symbol] (SAG)	NETVA
NetVantage, Inc. [Associated Press] (SAG)	NetVant
NetVantage Inc.'A' [NASDAQ symbol] (TTSB)	NETVA
NetVantage Inc. Unit [NASDAQ symbol] (TTSB)	NETVU
NetVantage Inc. Wrrt'A' [NASDAQ symbol] (TTSB)	NETVW
NetVantage Inc. Wrrt'B' [NASDAQ symbol] (TTSB)	NETVZ
NetWare Access Server [Computer science]	NAS
Netware Application Engine [Networth, Inc.]	NAE
NetWare Asynchronous Communication Service [Novell, Inc.]	NACS
NetWare Asynchronous Services Interface [Computer science] (PCM)	NASI
NetWare Configuration File [Computer science]	NCF
NetWare Console Commander [Frye Computer Systems] [Telecommunications] (PCM)	NCC
NetWare Control Center [Novell, Inc.] [Computer science] (PCM)	NCC
NetWare Core Protocol [Computer science]	NCP
NetWare Directory Services [Novell, Inc.] [Computer science] (PCM)	NDS
Netware Distributed Management Services [Novell, Inc.] (PCM)	NDMS
NetWare Early-Warning System [Frye Computer Systems, Inc.] [Computer science] (PCM)	NEWS
NetWare Global Messaging [Computer science] (CDE)	NGM
NetWare Link Services Protocol [Novell, Inc.] (PCM)	NLSP
NetWare Loadable Module [Computer science] (PCM)	NLM
NetWare Management System [Novell, Inc.] (PCM)	NMS
NetWare Users International	NUI
Network [FCC program source designation] (NTCM)	N
Network (WDMC)	n
Network (WDMC)	net
Network [Telecommunications] (AAG)	NET
Network (MSA)	NTWK
Network	NTWRK
Network (NASA)	NW
Network Access Center [Telecommunications]	NAC
Network Access Controller	NAC
Network Access Device	NAD
Network Access Facility	NAF
Network Access Machine [National Institute of Standards and Technology Computer science]	NAM
Network Access Machine [Computer science] (AD)	nam
Network Access Method [Control Data Corp.] [Telecommunications] (TEL)	NAM
Network Access Point [Telecommunications]	NAP

Network Access Pricing [*Telecommunications*] (TEL)	NAP
Network Access Protocol	NAP
Network Access Switch [*Telecommunications*] (MCD)	NAS
Network Access Switching Subsystem [*Telecommunications*] (MCD)	NASS
Network Access Unit [*Telecommunications*]	NAU
Network Acknowledgment	NAK
Network Action Item Report (MCD)	NAIR
Network Adapter (MCD)	NA
Network Address Translation [*Computer science*]	NAT
Network Address Translation [*Computer science*]	NAT
Network Address Translation [*Computer science*]	NAT
Network Address Translation [*Computer science*]	NAT
Network Address [*or Addressable*] Unit [*Computer science*] (BUR)	NAU
Network Addressable Unit (NITA)	NAU
Network Administration Utilities [*Honeywell*] (NITA)	NAU
Network Advisory Committee [*to Library of Congress and Council on Library Resources*]	NAC
Network Against Psychiatric Assault (EA)	NAPA
Network Analysis (PDAA)	NETANAL
Network Analysis Area [*Space Flight Operations Facility, NASA*]	NAA
Network Analysis Center [*Contel, Inc.*] [*Telecommunications service*] (TSSD)	NAC
Network Analysis Corp., Great Neck, NY [*Library symbol Library of Congress*] (LCLS)	NGrnNA
Network Analysis for Systems Applications Program [*Computer program*] [*NASA*]	NASAP
Network Analysis Model	NAM
Network Analysis System with Optimization Facility [*NASA*] (IAA)	NASOPT
Network Analysis Team	NAT
Network Analysis Technique (IAA)	NAT
Network Analytical Simulator (PDAA)	NEASIM
Network and Evaluation Simulation System (NITA)	NESS
Network and Mixed Model Health Maintenance Organization [*Insurance*] (WYGK)	NMMHMO
Network Appliance [*NASDAQ symbol*] (TTSB)	NTAP
Network Appliance Corp. [*Commercial firm*]	NAC
Network Appliance Corp. [*Associated Press*] (SAG)	NetwkAp
Network Appliance Corp. [*NASDAQ symbol*] (SAG)	NTAP
Network Application Node	NAN
Network Application Support [*Computer science*] (BTTJ)	NAS
Network Aviation Services (NIG) Ltd. [*FAA designator*] (FAAC)	NET
Network Basic Input/Output System [*Computer science*] (DOM)	NetBIOS
Network Basic Input/Output System [*Computer software*]	NETBIOS
Network Booter [*Computer science*] (BYTE)	NB
Network Building Out Capacitor [*Telecommunications*] (TEL)	NBOC
Network Building Out Resistor [*Telecommunications*] (TEL)	NBOR
Network Buildout (IEEE)	NBO
Network Busy Hour [*Telecommunications*] (TEL)	NBH
Network Card [*British Rail*]	NC
Network Career Advancement Institute [*Telecommunications service*] (TSSD)	NCA
Network Cells [*Botany*]	NW
Network Change Request [*NASA*] (KSC)	NCR
Network Channel [*Broadcasting*] (NTCM)	NC
Network Channel Service Unit [*Computer science*] (TNIG)	NCSU
Network Channel Terminating Equipment [*Telecommunications*]	NCTE
Network Common Data Format [*Computer science*]	NET CDF
Network Common Interface Unit	NCIU
Network Common Interference Unit (MCD)	NCIU
Network Communication Access Method	NCAM
Network Communication System (IAA)	NCS
Network Communications	NETCOM
Network Communications Control Facility [*IBM program product*]	NCCF
Network Communications Corp.	NCC
Network Communications Interface, Common (MCD)	NCIC
Network Communications Interface, Unique	NCIU
Network Communications International [*Telecommunications service*] (TSSD)	NCI
Network Communications Server [*J & L Information Systems*]	NCS
Network Communications Services Interface [*Computer science*] (PCM)	NCSI
Network Computer (PCM)	NC
Network Computer [*Computer science*]	NC
Network Computer (PCM)	NC
Network Computer Center (OA)	NCC
Network Computer, Inc.	NCI
Network Computing	NC
Network Computing Architecture [*Computer science*] (TNIG)	NCA
Network Computing Devices [*NASDAQ symbol*] (TTSB)	NCDIE
Network Computing Devices, Inc. [*NASDAQ symbol*] (SAG)	NCDI
Network Computing Devices, Inc. [*Associated Press*] (SAG)	NwkCmp
Network Configuration Utility [*Telecommunications*]	NCU
Network Congestion [*Telecommunications*] (TEL)	NC
Network Connect	NC
Network Connection [*NASDAQ symbol*] (TTSB)	TNCX
Network Connection Element	NCE
Network Connection Handler	NCH
Network Connection, Inc. [*Associated Press*] (SAG)	NtwkC
Network Connection, Inc. [*Associated Press*] (SAG)	NtwkCn
Network Connection, Inc. [*NASDAQ symbol*] (SAG)	TNCX
Network Connection Wrrt [*NASDAQ symbol*] (TTSB)	TNCXW
Network Control (IAA)	NC
Network Control [*Computer science*] (MHDB)	NETCON
Network Control Block	NCB
Network Control Center [*Telecommunications*]	NCC
Network Control Center Data System (SSD)	NCCDS

Network Control Center Representative (SSD)	NCCR
Network Control Communications [*Deep Space Instrumentation Facility, NASA*]	NETCOM
Network Control Computer (HGAA)	NCC
Network Control Elements (MCD)	NCE
Network Control Engine [*Synoptics Communications, Inc.*]	NCE
Network Control Group [*Manned Space Flight Network*]	NCG
Network Control Language	NCL
Network Control Module	NCM
Network Control Node	NCN
Network Control Office [*Telecommunications*] (TEL)	NCO
Network Control Point [*Telecommunications*]	NCP
Network Control Processor [*Telecommunications*] (TSSD)	NCP
Network Control Program [*IBM Corp.*] [*Telecommunications*] (BUR)	NCP
Network Control Program Packet Switching Interface [*Computer science*] (HGAA)	NPSI
Network Control Program Virtual Storage [*Telecommunications*] (IAA)	NCPVS
Network Control Protocol [*Telecommunications*]	NCP
Network Control Room [*Television*]	NCR
Network Control Station (IAA)	NCS
Network Control System	NCS
Network Control Terminal (MCD)	NCT
Network Control Unit [*Computer science*]	NCU
Network Controller	NC
Network Coordination Center [*NASA*]	NCC
Network Coordination Station	NCS
Network Co-ordination System (NITA)	NCS
Network Countdown	NC
Network Cryptographic Device	NCD
Network Data Control (MCD)	NDC
Network Data Link Control	NDLC
Network Data Reduction	NDR
Network Data Representation [*Computer science*]	NDR
Network Data Series (MHDI)	NDS
Network Database Language [*Telecommunications*] (OSI)	NDL
Network Database Management System	NDBMS
Network Definition Language [*Burroughs Corp.*]	NDL
Network Definition Language [*Computer science*] (PDAA)	NEDELA
Network Description Table (MHDI)	NDT
Network Design and Management System	NDMS
Network Development and Implementation Group [*National Research Council of Canada*]	NDI
Network Development Office [*Library of Congress*]	NDO
Network Development System (IAA)	NDS
Network Diagnostic and Control Systems (ADA)	NDACS
Network Diagnostic Control	NDC
Network Directorate (SSD)	ND
Network Driver Interface Specification [*Computer science*] (PCM)	NDIS
Network Electrical Technique System (IAA)	NETS
Network Engineering Administrative Data System [*AT & T*]	NEADS
Network Entry Point (AAGC)	NEP
Network Environmental Technology Transfer [*Europe*] [*An association*]	NETT
Network Equip Tech [*NYSE symbol*] (TTSB)	NWK
Network Equipment Technologies, Inc. (MHDW)	NETX
Network Equipment Technologies, Inc. [*Associated Press*] (SAG)	NtwkEq
Network Equipment Technologies, Inc. [*NYSE symbol*] (SPSG)	NWK
Network Equivalent Analysis	NEA
Network Event Theater [*NASDAQ symbol*] (TTSB)	NETS
Network Event Theater Wrrt [*NASDAQ symbol*] (TTSB)	NETSW
Network Event Theatre, Inc. [*NASDAQ symbol*] (SAG)	NETS
Network Event Theatre, Inc. [*Associated Press*] (SAG)	NetwkE
Network Express [*NASDAQ symbol*] (TTSB)	NETK
Network Express, Inc. [*NASDAQ symbol*] (SAG)	NETK
Network Express, Inc. [*Associated Press*] (SAG)	NtwExp
Network Extensible Window System [*Computer science*]	NEWS
Network Facilities-Development, Edmonton, AB, Canada [*Library symbol*] [*Library of Congress*] (LCLS)	CaAENF
Network Facilities-Development, Edmonton, Alberta [*Library symbol National Library of Canada*] (NLC)	AENF
Network File Access Method	NFAM
Network File Access Protocol	NFAP
Network File System [*Facetious translation: Nightmare File Systems*] [*Sun Microsystems, Inc.*]	NFS
Network File System	NFS
Network for Analysis of Fireball Trajectories (EA)	NAFT
Network for Better Nutrition (EA)	NBN
Network for Community Activities	NCA
Network for Continuing Medical Education (EA)	NCME
Network for Economic Rights [*Defunct*] (EA)	NER
Network for Electronic Transfers System	NETS
Network for Fitness Professionals [*Australia*]	NFP
Network for Informal Adult Learning (AIE)	NIAL
Network for Information Retrieval in Mammology	NIRM
Network for Professional Women [*Hartford, CT*] (EA)	NPW
Network for the Detection of Stratospheric Change [*New Zealand*] [*Marine science*] (OSRA)	NDSC
Network for the Detection of Stratospheric Change [*New Zealand*] (USDC)	NDSC
Network for Work Time Options [*San Francisco, CA*] (EA)	NWTO
Network Front End	NFE
Network General [*NASDAQ symbol*] (TTSB)	NETG
Network General Corp. [*NASDAQ symbol*] (CTT)	NETG
Network General Corp. [*Associated Press*] (SAG)	NtwkG
Network Generation [*Computer science*] (MHDB)	NETGEN
Network Graphics Protocol	NGP

Network Host Protocol .... NHP
Network Identification [*Broadcasting*] (NTCM) .... NI
Network Imaging $2.00 Cv Pfd [*NASDAQ symbol*] (TTSB) .... IMGXP
Network Imaging Corp. [*NASDAQ symbol*] (SAG) .... IMGX
Network Imaging Corp. [*Associated Press*] (SAG) .... NwkIm
Network Imaging Corp. [*Associated Press*] (SAG) .... NwkImg
Network Imaging Wrrt [*NASDAQ symbol*] (TTSB) .... IMGXW
Network in Solidarity with the People of Guatemala (EA) ... NISGUA
[*The*] Network, Inc. [*An association*] (EA) .... TNI
[*The*] Network Inc. of America [*Information service or system*] (IID) .... TNIA
Network Independent File Transfer Program (HGAA) .... NIFTP
Network Independent File Transfer Protocol (PDAA) .... NIFTP
Network In-Dial [*Automatic Voice Network*] (CET) .... NID
Network Information Center [*Advanced Research Projects Agency*] [*DoD*] ...... NIC
Network Information Files [*Burroughs Corp.*] .... NIF
Network Information Management Client-Based User Service (USDC) .... NIMBUS
Network Information Management Client-Based User Service [*Marine science*] (OSRA) .... NIMBUS
Network Information Retrieval .... NIR
Network Information Service .... NIS
Network Information Services (NITA) .... NIS
Network Information System [*AT & T*] .... NIS
Network Injection Molding .... NIM
Network In-Out Dial [*Automatic Voice Network*] (CET) .... NIOD
Network Input Processor [*Computer science*] (MCD) .... NIP
Network Integrity Control System .... NICS
Network Interface Board .... NIB
Network Interface Card [*Computer science*] .... NIC
Network Interface Card [*Computer science*] .... NIC
Network Interface Control .... NIC
Network Interface Data System (MCD) .... NIDS
Network Interface Data System [*NASA*] .... NIDS
Network Interface Definition Language [*Computer science*] .... NIDL
Network Interface Device [*Telecommunications*] .... NID
Network Interface Machine [*Datapac*] .... NIM
Network Interface Message Processing Host [*NERComP*] .... NIMPH
Network Interface Module [*Telecommunications*] (TSSD) .... NIM
Network Interface Monitor .... NIM
Network Interface Processor (MCD) .... NIP
Network Interface System .... NIS
Network Interface Unit [*Computer science*] .... NIU
Network International (EA) .... NI
Network Job Control Language [*Computer science*] .... NJCL
Network Job Entry .... NJE
Network Job Entry, Including Network Job Interface .... NJE/NJI
Network Job Interface .... NJI
Network Job Processing .... NJP
Network Junction [*Telecommunications*] (OA) .... NJ
Network Language Center (MHDB) .... NLC
Network Library System .... NLS
Network Loadable Module (GAVI) .... NLM
Network Logical Data Manager (NITA) .... NLDM
Network Long Distance [*NASDAQ symbol*] (TTSB) .... NTWK
Network Long Distance, Inc. [*NASDAQ symbol*] (SAG) .... NTWK
Network Long Distance, Inc. [*Associated Press*] (SAG) .... NtwkLng
Network Management Center [*Computer science*] .... NMC
Network Management Console [*Industrial Networking, Inc.*] ...... NMC
Network Management Control Center [*Telecommunications*] ...... NMCC
Network Management Directory Services (NITA) .... NMDS
Network Management Protocol [*Computer science*] (TNIG) .... NMP
Network Management Services [*Ohio Bell Communications, Inc.*] [*Cleveland, OH*] [*Telecommunications*] (TSSD) .... NMS
Network Management Signal [*Telecommunications*] (TEL) .... NMS
Network Management System (DA) .... NMS
Network Manager (MCD) .... NM
Network Measurement Center .... NMC
Network Measurement Machine [*Computer Network*] (IAA) .... NMM
Network Measurement System [*Computer network*] .... NMS
Network Mission and Operations Support .... NMOS
Network Monitor Unit [*Telecommunications*] (TSSD) .... NMU
Network Multiplexer (NITA) .... NETMUX
Network News Transport Protocol [*Telecommunications*] .... NNTP
Network Node Interface [*Computer science*] .... NNI
Network of Alternative Technology and Technology Assessment (EAIO) .... NATTA
Network of Concerned Correspondents (EA) .... NCC
Network of Educational Innovation for Development in Africa (EAIO) .... NEIDA
Network of Employees for Traffic Safety [*NHTSA*] (TAG) .... NETS
Network of European CNS [*Central Nervous System*] Transplantation and Restoration .... NECTAR
Network of European Teacher Education (AIE) .... NETE
Network of Gay and Lesbian Alumni Associations (EA) .... NetGALA
Network of Kindred Spirits (EA) .... NKS
Network of Small Businesses [*Lyndhurst, OH*] (EA) .... NSB
[*A*] Network of Social Security Information Resources [*Health and Welfare Canada*] [*Defunct*] (IID) .... ANSSIR
Network of Tropical Fisheries Scientists [*Marine science*] (OSRA) .... NTFS
Network Operating System .... NOS
Network Operating System/Batch Environment .... NOSBE
Network Operating System / Virtual Environment (HGAA) .... NOS/VE
Network Operation Center [*Bell System*] .... NOC
Network Operation Support Program [*Computer science*] .... NOSP
Network Operations and Facilities .... NOF
Network Operations Control [*NASA*] (KSC) .... NOC

Network Operations Control Center [*Manned Space Flight Network, NASA*] .... NOCC
Network Operations Directive [*NASA*] (KSC) .... NOD
Network Operations Forum [*Exchange Carriers Standards Association*] [*Telecommunications*] .... NOF
Network Operations Management System [*Computer science*] .... NOMS
Network Operations Manager [*Manned Space Flight Network, NASA*] .... NOM
Network Operations Performance Analysis [*Manned Space Flight Network, NASA*] .... NOPA
Network Operations Procedure [*Manned Space Flight Network, NASA*] .... NOP
Network Operations Support Plan [*NASA*] (KSC) .... NOSP
Network Operations Trouble Information System [*Telecommunications*] (TEL) .... NOTIS
Network Operator Control Program .... NOCP
Network Operator Process [*Computer science*] (MHDB) .... NETOP
Network Order Wire [*Military*] (CAAL) .... NOW
Network Organization via Advanced Architecture [*Marubeni Corp.*] .... NOVA
Network Out-Dial [*Automatic Voice Network*] (CET) .... NOD
Network Output Multiplexer [*Telecommunications*] (MCD) .... NOM
Network Performance Monitor (NITA) .... NPM
Network Peripherals [*NASDAQ symbol*] (TTSB) .... NPIX
Network Peripherals, Inc. [*NASDAQ symbol*] (SAG) .... NPIX
Network Periphrals, Inc. [*Associated Press*] (SAG) .... NtwkPeri
Network Planning [*Computer science*] .... NP
Network Planning Technique [*Computer science*] (IEEE) .... NPT
Network Power Processor [*Acme Electric Corp.*] [*Computer science*] (PCM) .... NPP
Network Problem Determination Aid (NITA) .... NPDA
Network Problem Determination Application [*Computer science*] .... NPDA
Network Processing and Interface Unit (NITA) .... NPIU
Network Processing Element (NITA) .... NPE
Network Processing Supervisor [*Honeywell, Inc.*] .... NPS
Network Processing Unit .... NPU
Network Processor System (NITA) .... NPS
Network Program (NASA) .... NP
Network Program Analysis by ADI [*Area of Dominant Influence*] [*Arbitron Ratings Co.*] [*Information service or system*] (CRD) .... NPA
Network Project [*An association*] (EA) .... NP
Network Protection Device [*Telecommunications*] (TEL) .... NPD
Network Protective Device (NITA) .... NPD
Network Protocol Addressing Information [*Telecommunications*] (OSI) .... NPAI
Network Protocol Data Unit [*Telecommunications*] (OSI) .... NPDU
Network Protocol Processor .... NPP
Network Pulse Forming .... NPF
Network Quality Tester (NITA) .... NQT
Network Readiness Test (KSC) .... NRT
Network Reliability Assessment Model (PDAA) .... NERAM
Network Reliability Coordinator .... NRC
Network Remote Job Entry [*Telecommunications*] (OSI) .... NETRJE
Network Repair Level Analysis .... NRLA
Network Resolution Area .... NRA
Network Resource Server [*J & L Information Systems*] .... NRS
Network Resource Unit (MHDB) .... NRU
Network Restructuring Language .... NRL
Network Security Module .... NSM
Network Server Management System [*Tylink Corp.*] .... NSMS
Network Service [*Computer science*] (TNIG) .... NS
Network Service Access Point [*Telecommunications*] (OSI) .... NSAP
Network Service Center [*Telecommunications*] .... NSC
Network Service Data Unit [*Telecommunications*] (OSI) .... NSDU
Network Service Element [*Telecommunications*] (OSI) .... NSE
Network Service Provider [*Telecommunications*] .... NSP
Network Service Unit (NITA) .... NSU
Network Services Protocol [*Digital Equipment Corp.*] [*Telecommunications*] (TEL) .... NSP
Network Signal Processor (NASA) .... NSP
[*Traffic*] Network Simulation [*TXDOT*] (TAG) .... NETSIM
Network Simulations Engineer (SSD) .... NSEN
Network Six, Inc. [*Associated Press*] (SAG) .... NtwkSix
Network Six, Inc. [*NASDAQ symbol*] (SAG) .... NWSS
Network Software Associates, Inc. .... NSA
Network Solutions, Inc. .... NSI
Network Solutions Inc. .... NSI
Network Solutions, Inc. .... NSI
Network SouthEast [*British Rail*] (ECON) .... NSE
Network Space Monitor (SAA) .... NSM
Network Status Display .... NSD
Network Status Monitor [*NASA*] (KSC) .... NSM
Network Strategies, Inc. [*Fairfax, VA*] [*Telecommunications*] (TSSD) .... NSI
Network Supervisor System .... NSS
Network Support Group (NITA) .... NSG
Network Support Office [*NASA*] .... NSO
Network Support Plan [*NASA*] (KSC) .... NSP
Network Support Processor (NITA) .... NSP
Network Support System [*Computer science*] .... NSS
Network Support Team [*NASA*] (KSC) .... NST
Network Switching Center [*Telecommunications*] (TEL) .... NSC
Network Synchronization Subsystem [*Telecommunications*] (TEL) .... NSS
Network Synthesis and Evaluation Technique [*Computer science*] .... NETSET
Network Systems and Evaluation Technique (NITA) .... NETSET
Network Systems Corp. [*Brooklyn Park, MN*] [*Telecommunications*] (TSSD) .... NSC
Network Systems Engineer (SSD) .... NSE
Network/TDRSS [*Tracking and Data Relay Satellite System*] [*NASA*] (MCD) .... NTS
Network Technical Architecture Group [*Library of Congress*] .... NTAG
Network Techniques .... NETS

Network Technologies International, Inc. [*Ann Arbor, MI*] [*Telecommunications*] (TSSD) .... NETI
Network Telecommunications, Inc. [*Denver, CO*] [*Telecommunications*] (TSSD) .... NETTEL
Network Terminal (MCD) .... NT
Network Terminal Number [*Telecommunications*] .... NTN
Network Terminal Operator .... NTO
Network Terminal Option [*Computer science*] .... NTO
Network Terminal Protocol .... NTP
Network Terminating Equipment [*Telecommunications*] (IAA) .... NTE
Network Terminating Equipment (NITA) .... NTE
Network Terminating Point [*Telecommunications*] (TEL) .... NTP
Network Terminating [*or Termination*] Unit .... NTU
Network Termination [*Telecommunications*] .... NT
Network Termination Number [*Computer science*] (TNIG) .... NTN
Network Termination Processor .... NTP
Network Terminator Type 1 (PCM) NT-1
Network Test and Training Facility [*Goddard Space Flight Center*] .... NTTF
Network Test Panel [*NASA*] (KSC) .... NTP
Network Test Panel .... NTP
Network Testing Section [*Social Security Administration*] .... NETS
Network Time Protocol .... NTP
Network Transmission Committee [*Video Transmission Engineering Committee*] (NTCM) .... NTC
Network User Address .... NUA
Network User Identifier [*or Identification*] [*Password*] .... NUI
Network User Name [*Telecommunications*] (OSI) .... NUN
Network Users Association [*Defunct*] (EA) .... NUA
Network Virtual Data Management Language [*Telecommunications*] (OSI) .... NVDML
Network Virtual Data Manager [*Computer science*] (IAA) .... NVDM
Network Virtual Terminal .... NVT
Network Wide Directory .... NWD
Network Wide Directory System (MHDI) .... NWDS
Network-Based Project Management (PDAA) .... NBPM
Networked Interactive Multimedia .... NIM
Networking (BARN) .... netwrkg
Networking .... NTWRKNG
Networking Addressing Device [*Computer science*] (AD) .... nad
Networking Advisory Group [*Library of Congress*] .... NAG
Networking Analytical and Computing Information Systems [*National Aeronautics and Space Administration*] .... NACIS
Networking and Expansion [*Computer science*] (PCM) .... NTX
Networking and Telecommunications Task Force [*Computer science*] (TNIG) .... NTTF
Networking and World Information [*Electronic information and communications exchange service*] .... NWI
[*The*] Networking Institute [*Commercial firm*] (EA) .... TNI
Networking Project for Disabled Women and Girls (EA) .... NPDWG
Networking Routing Center (MHDB) .... NRC
NetworkMCI Enterprise Management .... nEM
Network-Oriented Analysis and Transformation Unit [*Computer science*] (MHDB) .... NOA
Network-Oriented Data Acquisition Language .... NODAL
Network-Oriented Data Acquisition System (MHDI) .... NODAS
Network-Oriented Project Management System (PDAA) .... NOPMS
Networks File Transfer .... NFT
Networks for Biotechnology .... NBT
Networks Unlimited, Inc. [*Defunct*] (EA) .... NUI
Networth, Inc. [*Associated Press*] (SAG) .... Networth
Networth, Inc. [*NASDAQ symbol*] (SAG) .... NWTH
Neubabylonische Rechts- und Verwaltungstexte [*A publication*] (BJA) .... NbRVt
Neubabylonische Rechts- und Verwaltungsurkunden [*A publication*] (BJA) .... NRV
Neubabylonische Rechts- und Verwaltungsurkunden Uebersetzt und Erlaeutert [*A publication*] (BJA) .... NbRVu
Neubabylonisches Namenbuch zu den Geschaeftsurkunden [*A publication*] (BJA) .... NBN
Neubabylonisches Namenbuch zu den Geschaeftsurkunden [*A publication*] (BJA) .... NbNb
Neubiberg [*Germany ICAO location identifier*] (ICLI) .... EDSN
Neuburg [*Germany ICAO location identifier*] (ICLI) .... EDSU
Neuchatel [*Switzerland ICAO location identifier*] (ICLI) .... LSGN
Neuchatel [*Switzerland*] [*Seismograph station code, US Geological Survey Closed*] (SEIS) .... NEU
Neue Allgemeine Missions-Zeitschrift [*A publication*] (BJA) .... NAMZ
Neue Ephemeris fuer Semitische Epigraphik [*Wiesbaden*] [*A publication*] (BJA) .... NESE
Neue Folge [*New Series*] [*Bibliography*] [*German*] .... NF
Neue Grosse Partei [*New Great Party*] [*Germany Political party*] (PPW) .... NGP
Neue Justiz. Zeitschrift fuer Recht und Rechtswissenschaft [*Berlin, German Democratic Republic*] [*A publication*] (DLA) .... NJ
Neue Mozart-Ausgabe [*A publication*] .... NMA
Neue Oekonomische Politik [*New Economic Policy*] [*Germany*] .... NOEP
Neue Philologische Rundschau [*A publication*] (BJA) .... NPhR
Neue Sachlichkeit [*New Objectivity*] [*Pre-World War II group of German artists*] .... NS
Neues Goettinger Bibelwerk [*A publication*] (BJA) .... NGB
Neufchateau-Roucaux [*France ICAO location identifier*] (ICLI) .... LFFT
Neufchatel [*Imprint*] (ROG) .... NEUFCH
Neuhausen Ob Eck [*Germany ICAO location identifier*] (ICLI) .... EDPH
Neuhebraeisches Woerterbuch [*A publication*] (BJA) .... NHW
Neuilly, Auteil, and Passy [*Elegant Paris neighborhoods; the term, Nappie, is used as a nickname for French Yuppies*] .... Nappie
Neumann Boundary Conditions .... NBC

Neumann-Electroporation [*Gene technology*] .... NE
Neumarkt, Oberpfalz [*Germany ICAO location identifier*] (ICLI) .... EDQN
Neumuenster [*Germany ICAO location identifier*] (ICLI) .... EDHN
Neuquen [*Argentina*] [*Airport symbol*] (OAG) .... NQN
Neuquen [*Argentina ICAO location identifier*] (ICLI) .... SAZN
Neural Cell Adhesion Molecule [*Medical*] .... NCAM
Neural Cell Adhesion Molecule [*Biochemistry*] .... N-CAM
Neural Crest [*Anatomy*] .... NC
Neural Crest Cell [*Cytology*] .... NCC
Neural Crest Tumor [*Oncology*] .... NCT
Neural Excitation [*neurology*] (DAVI) .... NE
Neural, Informational, and Behavioral Science .... NIBS
Neural Network Simulator .... NNS
Neural Pulse Frequency Modulation (PDAA) .... NPFM
Neural Quantum [*Theory*] [*Sensory discrimination*] .... NQ
Neural Retina [*Ophthalmology*] .... NR
Neural Tube [*Anatomy*] .... NT
Neural Tube (Closure) Defect [*Medicine*] .... NTD
Neuralglial Cell Adhesion Model [*Biochemistry*] .... Ng-CAM
Neuraminic Acid [*Biochemistry*] .... Neu
Neuraminidase [*An enzyme*] .... N
Neuraminidase Activity [*An enzyme*] .... NA
Neuraminidase Inhibition [*Medicine*] (DMAA) .... NI
Neurex Corp. [*Associated Press*] (SAG) .... Neurex
Neurex Corp. [*NASDAQ symbol*] (SAG) .... NXCO
Neurilemma [*Neurology*] (DAVI) .... neu
Neurilemmona [*Oncology*] .... NL
Neurite Outgrowth Factor [*Biochemistry*] .... NOF
Neurite Retraction Factor [*Biochemistry*] .... NRF
Neuritic Plaque [*Pathology*] .... NP
Neuritis of the Cauda Equina [*Medicine*] .... NCE
Neuroallergic Syndrome [*Medicine*] (DMAA) .... NAS
Neurobehavioral Evaluation System .... NES
Neurobehavioral Scale .... NBS
Neurobiological Technologies, Inc. [*Associated Press*] (SAG) .... NeuroTc
Neurobiological Technologies, Inc. [*NASDAQ symbol*] (SAG) .... NTII
Neurobiologist .... NEUROLGST
Neurobiology .... NEUROBIOL
Neurobiotin [*Biochemical labelling compound*] .... NBT
Neuroblast [*Cytology*] .... NB
Neurocirculatory [*Medicine*] (DAVI) .... NC
Neurocirculatory Asthenia [*Medicine*] .... NCA
Neurocirculatory Dystonia [*Medicine*] (DMAA) .... NCD
Neurocrine Biosciences [*NASDAQ symbol*] (TTSB) .... NBIX
Neurocrine Biosciences, Inc. [*NASDAQ symbol*] (SAG) .... NBIX
Neurocrine Biosciences, Inc. [*Associated Press*] (SAG) .... Neucrine
Neuro-Developmental Treatment [*Physical therapy*] .... NDT
Neurodevelopmental Treatment Association (EA) .... NDTA
Neurodysfunction Eye Test System [*Medical*] .... NETS
Neuroelectric Society [*Defunct*] (EA) .... NS
Neuroelectric Therapy [*Substance detoxification*] .... NET
Neuroendocrine Cell [*Cytology*] .... NEC
Neuroepithelial Bodies [*Anatomy*] .... NEB
Neuroepithelial Stem Cells [*Medicine*] .... NESC
Neurofacial-Digitorenal Syndrome [*Medicine*] (DMAA) .... NFDR
Neurofibrillary Degeneration [*Medicine*] .... NFD
Neurofibrillary Tangle [*Brain anatomy*] .... NFT
Neurofibromatosis [*Medicine*] .... NF
Neuro-Fibromatosis Association of Australia .... NFAA
Neurofibromatosis, Inc. [*An association*] (EA) .... NF
Neurofibromatosis Type 1 [*Medicine*] NF1
Neurofilament [*Neurophysiology*] .... NF
Neurofilament Protein [*Neurophysiology*] .... NFP
Neurogen Corp. [*Associated Press*] (SAG) .... Neurgn
Neurogen Corp. [*NASDAQ symbol*] (NQ) .... NRGN
Neuro-Genetic Optimizer (PCM) .... NGO
Neurogenic Battery Acute (DAVI) .... NEUR-A
Neurogenic Bladder Dysfunction [*Medicine*] .... NBD
Neurogenic Element .... N
Neurogenic Intermittent Claudication [*Medicine*] (DMAA) .... NIC
Neurogenic Muscle Weakness, Ataxia, and Retinitis Pigmentosa [*Medicine*] .... NARP
Neurogenic Muscular Atrophy [*Medicine*] .... NMA
Neurogenic Peripheral Intermittent Claudication [*Medicine*] (DMAA) .... NPIC
Neurointermediate Lobe [*Of the pituitary*] .... NI
Neurointermediate Lobe [*Neuroanatomy*] .... NIL
Neurokinin [*Biochemistry*] .... NK
Neurokinin A [*Biochemistry*] .... NKA
Neurokinin B [*Biochemistry*] .... NKB
Neuroleptanalgesia [*Altered state of awareness*] [*Medicine*] (AAMN) .... NLA
Neuroleptic Anesthesia .... NLA
Neuroleptic Malignant Syndrome .... NMS
Neuroleukin [*Biochemistry*] .... NLK
Neurolinguistic Programming .... NLP
Neurologic and Adaptive Capacity Scoring [*System*] .... NACS
Neurologic Check [*Medicine*] .... NC
Neurologic Deficit [*Medicine*] .... ND
Neurologic Disability Score .... NDS
Neurologic Disease Control .... NDC
Neurologic Examination [*Medicine*] .... NS
Neurologic Signs [*Medicine*] (CPH) .... NS
Neurologic Survey [*Medicine*] (MAE) .... NS
Neurological and Related Intervention [*Medicine*] .... NRI
Neurological and Sensory Disease Control Program .... N & SDCP

Neurological Disorders Program [National Institute of Neurological and Communicative Disorders and Stroke] .... NDP
Neurological Dysfunctions of Children [Test] .... NDOC
Neurological Impairment .... NI
Neurological Impress Method (EDAC) .... NIM
Neurological Institute .... NI
Neurological Intensive Care Unit [Medicine] .... NICU
Neurological Resources Center of South Australia .... NRCSA
Neurological Shellfish Poisoning (USDC) .... NSP
Neurological Society of America (DAVI) .... NSA
Neurological Society of Australasia .... NSA
Neurological Soft Signs [Occupational therapy] .... NSS
Neurological Vital Signs [Medicine] .... NVS
Neurologically Intact [Medicine] .... NI
Neurologically Typical [Psychology] .... NT
Neurology .... N
Neurology [Medicine] (MAE) .... neur
Neurology [or Neurological] .... NEURO
Neurology .... NEUROL
Neurology .... NRLGY
Neurology (DAVI) .... NU
NeuROM Technology, Inc. .... NTI
Neuromedical Systems [NASDAQ symbol] (TTSB) .... NSIX
Neuromedical Systems, Inc. [Associated Press] (SAG) .... Neumed
Neuromedical Systems, Inc. [NASDAQ symbol] (SAG) .... NSIX
Neurometric Test Battery [Neurometrics] .... NB
Neuromotor [Neurology] (DAVI) .... NM
Neuromuscular .... NM
Neuromuscular Blockade [Medicine] .... NMB
Neuromuscular Blocking Agent .... NMBA
Neuromuscular Control [Medicine] (DMAA) .... NMC
Neuromuscular Foundation of Western Australia .... NFWA
Neuromuscular Foundation of Western Australia .... NMFWA
Neuromuscular Junction [Anatomy] .... NMJ
Neuromuscular Re-Education Techniques (DAVI) .... NRT
Neuromuscular Research Center [Boston University] .... NMRC
Neuromuscular Stimulator [Neurology] (DAVI) .... NMS
Neuromuscular Tension [Medicine] .... NMT
Neuromuscular Transmission [Physiology] .... NMT
Neuromuscular Unit [Medicine] .... NMU
Neuro-Musculo-Skeletal [Medicine] .... NMS
Neuron Activation Analysis [Neurology] (DAVI) .... NAA
Neuron Location and Ranging .... NULOR
Neuronal Apoptosis Inhibitory Protein [Genetics] .... NAIP
Neuronal Apoptpsos Inhibitory Protein [Cytology] .... NAIP
Neuronal Ceroid Lipofuscinosis [Medicine] .... NCL
Neuronal Correlate of Consciousness .... NCC
Neuronal Nitric Oxide Synthase [An enzyme] .... nNOS
Neuronal Thread Protein [Biology] .... NTP
Neuron-Restrictive Silencer Element [Neurogenesis] .... NRSE
Neuron-Restrictive Silencer Factor [Neurogenesis] .... NRSF
Neuron-Specific Enolase [Formerly, NSP] [An enzyme] .... NSE
Neuron-Specific Protein [Later, NSE] [Biochemistry] .... NSP
Neuropathic Doctor (BARN) .... ND
Neuropathology [Medicine] (DHSM) .... NA
Neuropathology [or Neuropathologist] (DAVI) .... Neuropath
Neuropathology [Medicine] .... NP
Neuropathy [Medicine] (DAVI) .... N
Neuropathy Symptom Score .... NSS
Neuropeptide Y [Biochemistry] .... NPY
Neurophysin [Biochemistry] .... NP
Neurophysin [Biochemistry] .... NPH
Neurophysiological .... NP
Neuropsychiatric .... NP
Neuropsychiatric Hospital, Fargo, ND [Library symbol Library of Congress] (LCLS) .... NdFN
NeuroPsychiatric Institute [UCLA] .... NPI
Neuropsychiatric Interest Checklist .... NTI
Neuropsychiatric Research Unit [Navy] .... NRU
Neuro-Psychiatry [Medical Officer designation] [British] .... N/P
Neuropsychiatry .... NPT
Neuropsychiatry Clerical Procedure [Navy] .... NPC
Neuropsychiatry Clerical Procedure Technician [Navy] .... NP-CLT
Neuropsychiatry Clerical Technician [Navy] .... NPC
Neuropsychiatry Technician [Navy] .... NPT
Neuropsychological Status Examination [Psychology] .... NSE
Neuropsychopharmacology Laboratory [Wayne State University] [Research center] .... NPPL
Neurosciences Institute (BABM) .... NSI
Neurosciences Institute (DAVI) .... NSI
Neurosciences Research Foundation (DAVI) .... NRF
Neurosciences Research Program [Massachusetts Institute of Technology] .... NRP
Neurosecretory .... NS
Neurosecretory Cells .... NSC
Neurosecretory Granules .... NSG
Neurosecretory Material (MAE) .... NSM
Neurosecretory Motoneurons .... NSM
Neurosecretory Vesicle [Neuroanatomy] .... NSV
Neurosensory Center Comprehensive Examination for Aphasia (DAVI) .... NCCEA
Neurosurgeon (BABM) .... Neuro-Surg
Neurosurgery [or Neurosurgeon] (DAVI) .... Neuro-Surg
Neurosurgery [Medicine] .... NS
Neurosurgery [Medicine] .... NSURG
Neurosurgical Society of America (EA) .... NSA
Neuro-Syphilis [Medicine] .... NS

Neurosyphilis [Medicine] (DAVI) .... NS
Neurotensin [Biochemistry] .... NT
Neurotensin-Like Immunoreactivity .... NTLI
Neurotic Depression [Psychiatry] .... ND
Neurotic Personality Factor Test [Psychology] .... NPFT
Neurotic Score [Psychology] .... NS
Neuroticism Scale Questionnaire [Psychology] .... NSQ
Neurotics Anonymous (NADA) .... NA
Neurotics Anonymous International Liaison (EA) .... NAIL
Neurotics Nomine [British] .... NN
Neurotoxic Shellfish Poisoning [Medicine] .... NSP
Neurotoxin [Biochemistry] .... NT
Neurotoxin B .... NXB
Neurotrauma Center [Medicine] (DAVI) .... TC
Neurotrophin [Neurobiology] .... NT
Neurovascular [Anatomy] .... NV
Neustadt Village Public Library, Neustadt, ON, Canada [Library symbol] [Library of Congress] (LCLS) .... CaONEU
Neustadt Village Public Library, Ontario [Library symbol National Library of Canada] (NLC) .... ONEU
Neuter .... N
Neuter .... NEUT
Neuter (WGA) .... NT
Neuter Plural [Grammar] (OCD) .... N PLUR
Neuton Velocity Time (IAA) .... NVT
Neutral .... N
Neutral (AAG) .... NEUT
Neutral Amino Acid [Biochemistry] .... NAA
Neutral and Nonaligned [Nations] .... NN
Neutral Atmosphere Temperature Experiment .... NATE
Neutral Atmospheric Composition Experiment [Geophysics] .... NACE
Neutral Atom Space Engine (AD) .... nase
Neutral Axis .... NA
Neutral Beam Divider .... NBD
Neutral Beam Injection (MCD) .... NBI
Neutral Bitter Principle [Pharmacy] .... NBP
Neutral Buoyancy [Navy] (SSD) .... NB
Neutral Buoyancy Facility [Navy] (MCD) .... NBF
Neutral Buoyancy Simulator [Navy] (MCD) .... NBS
Neutral Buoyancy Trainer [Navy] (MCD) .... NBT
Neutral Contour Technology [Automotive engineering] .... NCT
Neutral Countries Intelligence [of Ministry of Economic Warfare] [British World War II] .... NCI
Neutral Current [Physics] .... NC
Neutral Data Manipulation Language [Computer science] .... NDML
Neutral Density [Photography] .... ND
Neutral Density Filter (WDMC) .... ND
Neutral Density Filter .... NDF
Neutral Detector Assembly .... NDA
Neutral Detergent Fiber [Food analysis] .... NDF
Neutral Detergent Residue [Food analysis] .... NDR
Neutral Endopeptidase [An enzyme] .... NE
Neutral Endopeptidase [An enzyme] .... NEP
Neutral Excitation .... NE
Neutral External Rotation [Sports medicine] .... NER
Neutral Fraction .... NF
Neutral Gear Switch [Automotive engineering] .... NGS
Neutral Grain Spirits .... NGS
Neutral Industry Booking System (AAGC) .... NIBS
Neutral Lipid Fraction [Biochemistry] .... NLF
Neutral Mass Spectrometer [Instrumentation] .... NMS
Neutral Nations Committee [CINCPAC] (CINC) .... NNC
Neutral Nations Supervisory Commission .... NNSC
Neutral/Nonaligned [Countries] .... NNA
Neutral Particle Beam (MCD) .... NPB
Neutral Pressure Switch .... NPS
Neutral Protamine Hagedorn [Insulin suspension] .... NPH
Neutral Red [An indicator] .... NR
Neutral Regular Insulin .... NRI
Neutral Safety Switch [Automotive engineering] .... NSS
Neutral Seat Reference Point (MCD) .... NSRP
Neutral Speed Stability (PDAA) .... NSS
Neutral Sulfite Semichemical [Pulp] .... NSSC
Neutral Time-of-Flight Mass Spectroscopy [Aviation] .... NTOFMS
Neutral Twisted Nematic [Computer science] (PCM) .... NTN
Neutral-Beam Engineering Test Facility [Lawrence Berkeley Laboratory] [Terminated Department of Energy] (GRD) .... NBETF
Neutral-Density Filter [Photography] (WDMC) .... nd filter
Neutral-Drive [Automotive engineering] .... ND
Neutral-Drive Switch [Automotive engineering] .... NDS
Neutral-Equivalent Gasoline Yield [Petroleum chemistry] .... NEGY
Neutrality Zone .... NZ
Neutralization [Electronics] (ECII) .... NEUTN
Neutralization Antigenic Site [Immunogenetics] .... N-Ag
Neutralization Capacitor (IAA) .... NC
Neutralization Equivalent [Chemistry] .... neut equiv
Neutralization Index [Medicine] (DMAA) .... NI
Neutralization Self-Solidification Process (PDAA) .... NSSP
Neutralization Test [Chemistry] .... NT
Neutralization Value (IAA) .... NV
Neutralization-Reionization Mass Spectrometry .... NRMS
Neutralizing (MAE) .... NT
Neutralizing Antibody [Immunochemistry] .... NA
Neutralizing Capacitance [or Coil] (DEN) .... NC
Neutralizing Epitope [Immunogenetics] .... N-Ep

Neutralizing Monoclonal Antibody [*Immunology*] ..... N-MAb
Neutralizing Monoclonal Antibody [*Immunology*] ..... N-McAb
Neutral-Reverse [*Automotive engineering*] ..... NR
Neutral-to-Earth Voltage [*Electrical power transmission*] ..... NEV
Neutraminidase Inhibition (PDAA) ..... NI
Neutron [*A nuclear particle*] ..... n
Neutron [*A nuclear particle*] (MSA) ..... NTN
Neutron Activation Analysis ..... NAA
Neutron Binding Energy ..... NBE
Neutron Bomb ..... N (Bomb)
Neutron Controller [*Nuclear energy*] (NRCH) ..... NC
Neutron Data Under Direct Access (NITA) ..... NEUDATA
Neutron Depth Profiling [*Analytical chemistry*] ..... NDP
Neutron Diffraction (MCD) ..... ND
Neutron Doped Silicon (IAA) ..... NDS
Neutron Dose Monitor ..... NDM
Neutron Flux [*Nuclear energy*] (NRCH) ..... NF
Neutron Flux Density [*Nuclear energy*] ..... NFD
Neutron Flux Spectra [*Nuclear energy*] ..... NFS
Neutron Hardness Assurance Test ..... NHAT
Neutron Inelastic Scattering ..... NIS
Neutron Instrumentation System (IEEE) ..... NIS
Neutron Instruments for Nuclear Analysis (PDAA) ..... NINA
Neutron Intermediate Standard Uranium Source (PDAA) ..... NISUS
Neutron Ionization Effect ..... NIE
Neutron Magnetic Moment ..... NMM
Neutron Monitoring System [*Nuclear energy*] (NRCH) ..... NMS
Neutron Number [*Physics*] (DAVI) ..... N
Neutron Power Spectral Density (OA) ..... NPSD
Neutron Radiation Capture ..... NRC
Neutron Radiography Working Group [*EURATOM*] ..... NRWG
Neutron Resonance Escape Probability [*Nuclear energy*] (NRCH) ..... NREP
Neutron Scattering Facility [*Oak Ridge, TN*] [*Oak Ridge National Laboratory*] [*Department of Energy*] (GRD) ..... NSF
Neutron Scattering Society ..... NSS
Neutron Sensor Testing Facility (IAA) ..... NSTF
Neutron Source Reactor ..... NSR
Neutron Source Thermal Reactor [*British*] (DEN) ..... NESTOR
Neutron Spectrometer Digital System ..... NSDS
Neutron Spectrometer System ..... NSS
Neutron Star X-Ray Binary [*Astrophysics*] ..... NSXB
Neutron Test Reactors (KSC) ..... NTR
Neutron Transient Effect ..... NTE
Neutron Transmitter [*Nuclear energy*] (NRCH) ..... NT
Neutron Transmutation Doped [*Silicon for semiconductor use*] ..... NTD
Neutron Transport Computer Code ..... NTCC
Neutron Velocity Selector ..... NVS
Neutron Well Coincidence Counter [*Nuclear energy*] (NRCH) ..... NWCC
Neutron-Gamma Monte Carlo [*Computer science*] ..... NGM
Neutron-Induced Autoradiography ..... NIAR
Neutron-Induced Gamma Activity (AABC) ..... NIGA
Neutron-Induced Voltagwe (NUCP) ..... NIV
Neutrons per Absorption (DEN) ..... NPA
Neutrons per Fission ..... N/F
Neutrons per Fission (DEN) ..... NPF
Neutrons per Second ..... N/S
Neutrophil [*Hematology*] ..... N
Neutrophil [*Hematology*] ..... neut
Neutrophil Activating Protein ..... NAP
Neutrophil Alkaline Phosphatase [*An enzyme*] ..... NAP
Neutrophil Antibody [*Immunology*] (DAVI) ..... NA
Neutrophil Chemotactic Activity [*Clinical chemistry*] ..... NCA
Neutrophil Chemotactic Factor [*Hematology*] ..... NCF
Neutrophil Complement Rosettes [*Hematology*] ..... NCR
Neutrophil Cytosol Factor [*Cytology*] ..... NCF
Neutrophil Migration Inhibition Factor ..... NIF
Neuvo Rocafuerte [*Ecuador*] [*ICAO location identifier*] (ICLI) ..... SENU
Nevada (ROG) ..... NDA
Nevada (AAG) ..... NEV
Nevada (ODBW) ..... Nev
Nevada [*MARC geographic area code Library of Congress*] (LCCP) ..... n-us-nv
Nevada [*Postal code*] ..... NV
Nevada [*MARC country of publication code Library of Congress*] (LCCP) ..... nvu
Nevada Administrative Code [*A publication*] (DLA) ..... Nev Admin Code
Nevada Agricultural Experiment Station [*University of Nevada - Reno*] [*Research center*] (RCD) ..... NAES
Nevada Applied Ecology Information Center [*Department of Energy*] (IID) ..... NAEIC
Nevada Association Race and Sports Book Operators (EA) ..... NARASO
Nevada City, CA [*FM radio station call letters*] ..... KVMR
Nevada City Free Public Library, Nevada City, CA [*Library symbol Library of Congress*] (LCLS) ..... CNc
Nevada COBOL [*Common Business-Oriented Language*] **Users Group** [*Defunct*] (EA) ..... NCUG
Nevada County Library, Prescott, AR [*Library symbol Library of Congress*] (LCLS) ..... ArPreC
Nevada Dance Theatre ..... NDT
Nevada Desert Experience (EA) ..... NDE
Nevada Division of Environmental Protection ..... NDEP
Nevada Division of Environmental Protection (DOGT) ..... NDEP
Nevada Energy [*NASDAQ symbol*] (TTSB) ..... NNRGA
Nevada Energy Co., Inc. [*Associated Press*] (SAG) ..... NevEngy
Nevada Energy Co., Inc. [*NASDAQ symbol*] (SAG) ..... NNRG
Nevada Evening Journal, Nevada, IA [*Library symbol Library of Congress*] (LCLS) ..... IaNevJ
Nevada Goldfields Corp. [*Toronto Stock Exchange symbol*] ..... NGF
Nevada Goldfields Corp. (MHDW) ..... NGFCF
Nevada, MO [*Location identifier FAA*] (FAAL) ..... EAD
Nevada, MO [*AM radio station call letters*] ..... KNEM
Nevada, MO [*FM radio station call letters*] ..... KNMO
Nevada, MO [*Location identifier FAA*] (FAAL) ..... NVD
Nevada North Resources [*Vancouver Stock Exchange symbol*] ..... NNR
Nevada Northern Railway Co. [*AAR code*] ..... NN
Nevada Nuclear Waste Storage Investigations ..... NNWSI
Nevada Operations Office [*Department of Energy*] ..... NOO
Nevada Operations Office [*Department of Energy*] (MCD) ..... NVO
Nevada Operations Office [*Department of Energy*] ..... NVOO
Nevada Power Co. [*Associated Press*] (SAG) ..... NevPw
Nevada Power Co. [*NYSE symbol*] (SPSG) ..... NVP
Nevada Proving Ground (BARN) ..... NPG
Nevada Public Affairs Institute [*University of Nevada - Reno*] [*Research center*] (RCD) ..... NPAI
Nevada Public Library, Nevada, IA [*Library symbol Library of Congress*] (LCLS) ..... IaNev
Nevada Public Service Commission Opinions [*A publication*] (DLA) ..... Nev PSC Op
Nevada Reports [*A publication*] (DLA) ..... Nevada Rep
Nevada Reports [*A publication*] (DLA) ..... Nevada Repts
Nevada Revised Statutes [*A publication*] (DLA) ..... Nev Rev Stat
Nevada Revised Statutes [*A publication*] ..... NRS
Nevada State Bar Journal [*A publication*] (DLA) ..... Nev SBJ
Nevada State Bar Journal [*A publication*] (DLA) ..... Nev St Bar J
Nevada State Historical Society, Reno, NV [*Library symbol Library of Congress*] (LCLS) ..... NvHi
Nevada State Library, Carson City, NV [*Library symbol Library of Congress*] (LCLS) ..... Nv
Nevada State Library, Division of State Archives, Carson City, NV [*Library symbol Library of Congress*] (LCLS) ..... Nv-Ar
Nevada State Museum, Capital Complex, Carson City, NV [*Library symbol Library of Congress*] (LCLS) ..... NvMus
Nevada Supreme Court Reports [*A publication*] (DLA) ..... Nev
Nevada Territory [*Prior to statehood*] ..... NT
Nevada Test Site [*Department of Energy*] ..... NTS
Nevada Test Site Array [*Nevada*] [*Seismograph station code, US Geological Survey*] (SEIS) ..... NTA
Nevada Test Site Environmental Impact Statement ..... NTS EIS
Nevada Test Site Radiation Victim Association (EA) ..... NTSRVA
Never (ROG) ..... NE'ER
Never Ever Mention Outside [*Secret computer toy project of Axlon, Inc.*] ..... NEMO
Never Hinged [*Philately*] ..... NH
Never Removed from Box [*Doll collecting*] ..... NRFB
NeverEnding Disk [*Computer software*] [*Sytron Corp.*] (PCM) ..... NED
Neverending Program (IAA) ..... NEP
Never-Exceed Redline [*Aerospace*] (AAG) ..... NER
Nevers/Fourchambault [*France ICAO location identifier*] (ICLI) ..... LFQG
Nevertheless (ROG) ..... NEVLESS
Nevertheless (ROG) ..... NVTHLSS
Nevile and Manning's English King's Bench Reports [*A publication*] (DLA) ..... N & M
Nevile and Manning's English King's Bench Reports [*A publication*] (ILCA) ..... Nev & M
Nevile and Manning's English King's Bench Reports [*A publication*] (DLA) ..... Nev & M (Eng)
Nevile and Manning's English King's Bench Reports [*A publication*] (DLA) ..... Nev & Man
Nevile and Manning's English King's Bench Reports [*A publication*] (DLA) ..... Nev & MKB
Nevile and Manning's English Magistrates' Cases [*A publication*] (DLA) ..... N & M Mag
Nevile and Manning's English Magistrates' Cases [*A publication*] (DLA) ..... N & MMC
Nevile and Manning's English Magistrates' Cases [*A publication*] (DLA) ..... Nev & Man Mag Cas
Nevile and Manning's English Magistrates' Cases [*A publication*] (DLA) ..... Nev & MMC
Nevile and Perry's English King's Bench Reports [*1836-38*] [*A publication*] (DLA) ..... N & P
Nevile and Perry's English King's Bench Reports [*1836-38*] [*A publication*] (DLA) ..... Nev & P
Nevile and Perry's English King's Bench Reports [*1836-38*] [*A publication*] (DLA) ..... Nev & PKB
Nevile and Perry's English Magistrates' Cases [*1836-37*] [*A publication*] (DLA) ..... N & P Mag
Nevile and Perry's English Magistrates' Cases [*1836-37*] [*A publication*] (DLA) ..... N & PMC
Nevile and Perry's English Magistrates' Cases [*1836-37*] [*A publication*] (DLA) ..... Nev & P
Nevile and Perry's English Magistrates' Cases [*1836-37*] [*A publication*] (DLA) ..... Nev & P Mag Cas
Nevile and Perry's English Magistrates' Cases [*1836-37*] [*A publication*] (DLA) ..... Nev & PMC
Neville and Macnamara's Railway and Canal Cases [*1855-1950*] [*A publication*] (DLA) ..... N & Macn
Neville and Macnamara's Railway and Canal Cases [*1855-1950*] [*A publication*] (DLA) ..... N & McN
Neville and Macnamara's Railway and Canal Cases [*1855-1950*] [*A publication*] (DLA) ..... Nev & MacN
Neville and Macnamara's Railway Cases [*1855-1950*] [*A publication*] (DLA) ..... Nev & Mac

Neville and Macnamara's Railway Cases [*England*] [*A publication*] (DLA) ..... Nev & Mcn
Neville and Winther's Acid ..... NW
Neville Public Museum, Green Bay, WI [*Library symbol Library of Congress*] (LCLS) ..... WGrNM
Neville Upper Reservoir Buffer [*Medicine*] (DMAA) ..... NURB
Nevirpine [*Organic chemistry*] ..... NVP
Nevis [*Leeward Islands*] [*Airport symbol*] (OAG) ..... NEV
Nevis Island Cultural Center of the US (EA) ..... NICC
Nevis Public School, Nevis, MN [*Library symbol*] [*Library of Congress*] (LCLS) ..... MnNeS
Nevis Reformation Party [*Political party*] ..... NRP
Nevoid Basal Cell Carcinoma Syndrome [*Oncology*] (DMAA) ..... NBCCS
Nevoid Basal Cell Carcinoma Syndrome [*Oncology*] (DMAA) ..... NBS
Nevoid Basal-Cell Carcinoma [*Oncology*] ..... NBCC
New [*Stock exchange term*] (SPSG) ..... N
New ..... NW
New Aalesund [*Norway*] [*Geomagnetic observatory code*] ..... NAL
New Account (ROG) ..... N/C
New Account ..... NA
New Acronyms and Initialisms [*Later, NAIA*] [*A publication*] ..... NAI
New Acronyms, Initialisms, and Abbreviations [*Formerly, NAI*] [*A publication*] ..... NAIA
New Adult Reading Test ..... NART
New Advocate [*A publication*] (BRI) ..... New Ad
New Aeronautical and Nautical Chart Investigations (NOAA) ..... NANCI
New Afrikan People's Organization (EA) ..... NAPO
New Age [*Later, LR*] [*An association*] (EA) ..... NA
New Age Encyclopedia [*A publication*] ..... NAE
New Age Federation (EA) ..... NAF
New Age Journal [*A publication*] (BRI) ..... New Age
New Age Learning Center [*Defunct*] (EA) ..... NALC
New Age Media Fund [*NYSE symbol*] (SPSG) ..... NAF
New Age Media Fund [*Associated Press*] (SAG) ..... NewAge
New Age Patriot [*An association*] (EA) ..... NAP
New Age Professional People in Esoteric Studies [*Lifestyle classification*] ..... Nappies
New Age Publishing and Retailing Alliance (EA) ..... NAPRA
New Age Thinking ..... NAT
New Age World Religious and Scientific Research Foundation (EA) ..... NAWRSRF
New Air Ltd. [*British ICAO designator*] (FAAC) ..... FLS
New Airborne Scatterometer (MCD) ..... NUSCAT
New Aircraft Tool System [*Army*] ..... NATS
New Albany, IN [*FM radio station call letters*] (RBYB) ..... WAJE
New Albany, IN [*FM radio station call letters*] ..... WNAS
New Albany, IN [*FM radio station call letters*] (RBYB) ..... WRVI-FM
New Albany, IN [*AM radio station call letters*] (RBYB) ..... WXLN
New Albany, MS [*AM radio station call letters*] ..... WNAU
New Albany, MS [*FM radio station call letters*] ..... WWKZ
New Albany, MS [*FM radio station call letters*] ..... WWZD
New Albany Tribune and Ledger-Tribune, New Albany, IN [*Library symbol Library of Congress*] (LCLS) ..... InNeaTL
New Albany-Floyd County Public Library, New Albany, IN [*OCLC symbol*] (OCLC) ..... INN
New Albany-Floyd County Public Library, New Albany, IN [*Library symbol Library of Congress*] (LCLS) ..... InNea
New Alchemy Institute [*Defunct*] (EA) ..... NAI
New Alster Energy [*Vancouver Stock Exchange symbol*] ..... NAY
New Alternative Party [*Venezuela Political party*] ..... NA
New Amer Hi Income Fd [*NYSE symbol*] (TTSB) ..... HYB
New America High Income Fund [*Associated Press*] (SAG) ..... NewAm
New America Movement (EA) ..... NAM
New American Bible ..... NAB
New American Community (MHDB) ..... NAC
New American Cyclopaedia [*A publication*] (ROG) ..... New Am Cyc
New American High Income Fund [*NYSE symbol*] (SPSG) ..... HYB
New American Library [*Publisher*] ..... NAL
New American Man [*Lifestyle classification coined by Robert Bly*] (ECON) ..... NAM
New American Standard Bible [*A publication*] (BJA) ..... NASB
New Amino Acid Formula [*Nutrition*] ..... NAAF
New Amsterdam [*Guyana*] [*ICAO location identifier*] (ICLI) ..... SYNA
New Amsterdam Musical Association (AD) ..... NAMA
New and Emerging Sciences and Technologies ..... NEST
New and Expanding Business and Industry Training (OICC) ..... NEBIT
New and Improved Materials and Processes (PDAA) ..... NIMP
New and Improved Technology [*British*] ..... NIMTECH
New and Nonofficial Drugs [*AMA*] ..... NND
New and Nonofficial Remedies [*A publication*] ..... NNR
New and Renewable Energy (PDAA) ..... NRE
New and Unused Equipment (MCD) ..... NAUE
New Animal Drug Application [*Food and Drug Administration*] ..... NADA
New Annual Register [*London*] [*A publication*] (DLA) ..... New Ann Reg
New Antigenic Determinant [*Immunochemistry*] ..... NAD
New Apostolic Church ..... NAC
New Arcadia Explorations [*Vancouver Stock Exchange symbol*] ..... NAX
New Architectural Movement [*British*] (DI) ..... NAM
New Armed Forces of the Philippines (AD) ..... NAFP
New Army Authorization Documents System (AABC) ..... NAADS
New Army Automatic Data System ..... NAADS
New Arrivals Task Force (MCD) ..... NATF
New Art Association (EA) ..... NAA
New Aspiration Party [*Thailand*] ..... NAP
New Assembly Language ..... NAL
New Associations [*Later, NAP*] [*A publication*] ..... NA
New Associations and Projects [*Formerly, NA*] [*A publication*] ..... NAP
New Athens Community Consolidated District 60, New Athens, IL [*Library symbol Library of Congress*] (LCLS) ..... INatCD
New Athens Public Library, New Athens, IL [*Library symbol Library of Congress*] (LCLS) ..... INat
New Atlantean Research Society [*Defunct*] (EA) ..... NARS
New Attainment Target (AIE) ..... NAT
New Australian Republican Party [*Political party*] ..... NARP
New Austrian Tunnel Method [*Civil engineering*] ..... NATM
New Auxiliary Boiler (AD) ..... n aux b
New Balanced File Organization Scheme (MHDB) ..... NBFS
New Basic Logic Unit [*Computer science*] (MHDI) ..... NUBLU
New Bedford [*Massachusetts*] [*Location identifier FAA*] (FAAL) ..... EWB
New Bedford Free Public Library, New Bedford, MA [*Library symbol Library of Congress*] (LCLS) ..... MNBedf
New Bedford Glass Society [*Defunct*] (EA) ..... NBGS
New Bedford Institute of Technology [*Massachusetts*] ..... NBIT
New Bedford, MA [*Location identifier FAA*] (FAAL) ..... DFJ
New Bedford, MA [*AM radio station call letters*] ..... WBSM
New Bedford, MA [*FM radio station call letters*] ..... WCTK
New Bedford, MA [*FM radio station call letters*] ..... WJFD
New Bedford, MA [*Television station call letters*] ..... WLNE
New Bedford, MA [*TV station call letters*] (RBYB) ..... WLWC-TV
New Bedford, MA [*AM radio station call letters*] ..... WNBH
New Beginnings Resources [*Vancouver Stock Exchange symbol*] ..... NBR
New Benloe's Reports, English King's Bench [*1531-1628*] [*A publication*] (DLA) ..... N Ben
New Benloe's Reports, English King's Bench [*1531-1628*] [*A publication*] (DLA) ..... N Benl
New Benloe's Reports, English King's Bench [*1531-1628*] [*A publication*] (DLA) ..... NB
New Benloe's Reports, English King's Bench [*1531-1628*] [*A publication*] (DLA) ..... New Benl
New Berlin Memorial Hospital, New Berlin, WI [*Library symbol Library of Congress*] (LCLS) ..... WNbH
New Berlin, PA [*FM radio station call letters*] (RBYB) ..... WBGM-FM
New Bern [*North Carolina*] [*Airport symbol*] (OAG) ..... EWN
New Bern, NC [*Location identifier FAA*] (FAAL) ..... EWN
New Bern, NC [*FM radio station call letters*] (RBYB) ..... WAAE-FM
New Bern, NC [*AM radio station call letters*] (RBYB) ..... WCOO
New Bern, NC [*Television station call letters*] ..... WCTI
New Bern, NC [*FM radio station call letters*] ..... WIKS
New Bern, NC [*AM radio station call letters*] ..... WLOJ
New Bern, NC [*AM radio station call letters*] ..... WNOS
New Bern, NC [*FM radio station call letters*] ..... WSFL-FM
New Bern, NC [*FM radio station call letters*] ..... WTEB
New Bern/Simmons-Nott [*North Carolina*] [*ICAO location identifier*] (ICLI) ..... KEWN
New Better than Used [*Statistics*] ..... NBU
New Better than Used in Expectation [*Statistics*] ..... NBUE
New Bight, Cat Island [*Bahamas*] [*ICAO location identifier*] (ICLI) ..... MYCB
New Biotechnology Firm ..... NBF
New Birth Party [*Cyprus*] [*Political party*] ..... NBP
New Boiler ..... NB
New Boston, OH [*AM radio station call letters*] ..... WIOI
New Boston Tracking Station (SAA) ..... NBTS
New Boston, TX [*FM radio station call letters*] (RBYB) ..... KEWL
New Boston, TX [*AM radio station call letters*] ..... KNBO
New Boston, TX [*FM radio station call letters*] ..... KZRB
New Bottom [*On ships*] ..... NB
New Brands and Their Companies [*Formerly, NTN*] [*A publication*] ..... NBTC
[*The*] **New Braunfels & Servtex Railroad, Inc.** [*AAR code*] ..... NBST
New Braunfels, TX [*Location identifier FAA*] (FAAL) ..... BAZ
New Braunfels, TX [*AM radio station call letters*] ..... KGNB
New Braunfels, TX [*FM radio station call letters*] ..... KNBT
New Breman Public Library, New Breman, OH [*Library symbol Library of Congress*] (LCLS) ..... ONb
New Britain, CT [*FM radio station call letters*] ..... WFCS
New Britain, CT [*AM radio station call letters*] ..... WNEZ
New Britain, CT [*FM radio station call letters*] ..... WRCH
New Britain, CT [*AM radio station call letters*] ..... WRYM
New Britain, CT [*Television station call letters*] ..... WVIT
New Britain General Hospital, Health Sciences Library, New Britain, CT [*OCLC symbol*] (OCLC) ..... HNB
New Britain Public Library, New Britain, CT [*Library symbol Library of Congress*] (LCLS) ..... CtNb
New British Broadcasting Station (NADA) ..... NBBS
New British Standard [*Imperial wire gauge*] ..... NBS
New Brunswick [*Canadian province*] [*Postal code*] ..... NB
New Brunswick [*MARC geographic area code Library of Congress*] (LCCP) ..... n-cn-nk
New Brunswick [*MARC country of publication code Library of Congress*] (LCCP) ..... nkc
New Brunswick Archives, Beaverbrook Collection, Fredericton, NB, Canada [*Library symbol Library of Congress*] (LCLS) ..... CaNBFB
New Brunswick Area (SAA) ..... NBA
New Brunswick Area Office [*Later, NBL*] [*AEC*] ..... NBAO
New Brunswick Barristers Society, Fredericton, NB, Canada [*Library symbol Library of Congress*] (LCLS) ..... CaNBFBS
New Brunswick Barristers Society, Fredericton, New Brunswick [*Library symbol National Library of Canada*] (NLC) ..... NBFBS
New Brunswick Community College, Edmundston, NB, Canada [*Library symbol Library of Congress*] (LCLS) ..... CaNBECC
New Brunswick Community College, Edmundston, New Brunswick [*Library symbol National Library of Canada*] (NLC) ..... NBECC

New Brunswick Community College, Grand Falls Campus, Grand Falls, NB, Canada [*Library symbol Library of Congress*] (LCLS) .... CaNBGfCC
New Brunswick Community College, Grand Falls, New Brunswick [*Library symbol National Library of Canada*] (NLC) .... NBGFCC
NEw Brunswick Community College, Miramichi Campus, Chatham, NB, Canada [*Library symbol*] [*Library of Congress*] (LCLS) .... CaNBCCC
New Brunswick Community College, Moncton, NB, Canada [*Library symbol Library of Congress*] (LCLS) .... CaNBMoCC
New Brunswick Community College, Moncton, New Brunswick [*Library symbol National Library of Canada*] (NLC) .... NBMOCC
New Brunswick Department of Education, Fredericton, NB, Canada [*Library symbol*] [*Library of Congress*] (LCLS) .... CaNBFED
New Brunswick Department of Education, Fredericton, New Brunswick [*Library symbol National Library of Canada*] (NLC) .... NBFED
New Brunswick Department of Historical Resources, Fredericton, NB, Canada [*Library symbol Library of Congress*] (LCLS) .... CaNBFHR
New Brunswick Department of Historical Resources, Fredericton, New Brunswick [*Library symbol National Library of Canada*] (NLC) .... NBFHR
New Brunswick Department of Lands and Mines, Photogrammetry Branch, Fredericton,NB, Canada [*Library symbol Library of Congress*] (LCLS) .... CaNBFLM
New Brunswick Department of Municipal Affairs, Fredericton, NB, Canada [*Library symbol Library of Congress*] (LCLS) .... CaNBFMA
New Brunswick Department of Natural Resources and Energy, Fredericton, NB, Canada [*Library symbol*] [*Library of Congress*] (LCLS) .... CaNBFNR
New Brunswick Department of Natural Resources and Energy, Fredericton, New Brunswick [*Library symbol National Library of Canada*] (NLC) .... NBFNR
New Brunswick Department of Social Services, Fredericton, NB, Canada [*Library symbol Library of Congress*] (LCLS) .... CaNBFSS
New Brunswick Department of Social Services, Fredericton, New Brunswick [*Library symbol National Library of Canada*] (NLC) .... NBFSS
New Brunswick Department of the Environment, Fredericton, NB, Canada [*Library symbol Library of Congress*] (LCLS) .... CaNBFEn
New Brunswick Department of Transportation, Fredericton, New Brunswick [*Library symbol National Library of Canada*] (NLC) .... NBFTR
New Brunswick Department of Youth, Recreation and Cultural Resources, Fredericton, New Brunswick [*Library symbol National Library of Canada*] (NLC) .... NBFYRC
New Brunswick Equity Cases [*A publication*] (DLA) .... NB Eq Ca
New Brunswick Equity Cases [*A publication*] (DLA) .... New B Eq Ca
New Brunswick Equity Cases [*Canada*] [*A publication*] (DLA) .... New Br Eq Cas (Can)
New Brunswick Equity Reports [*A publication*] (DLA) .... NB Eq
New Brunswick Equity Reports [*A publication*] (DLA) .... NB Eq R
New Brunswick Equity Reports [*A publication*] (DLA) .... NB Eq Rep
New Brunswick Equity Reports [*A publication*] (DLA) .... New B Eq Rep
New Brunswick Equity Reports [*Canada*] [*A publication*] (DLA) .... New Br Eq (Can)
New Brunswick Free Public Library, New Brunswick, NJ [*Library symbol Library of Congress*] (LCLS) .... NjNb
New Brunswick Laboratory [*Formerly, NBAO*] [*Argonne, IL*] [*Department of Energy*] .... NBL
New Brunswick Legislative Library, Fredericton, NB, Canada [*Library symbol Library of Congress*] (LCLS) .... CaNBFL
New Brunswick Library Service, Frederiction, New Brunswick [*Library symbol National Library of Canada*] (NLC) .... NBFC
New Brunswick Library Service, Frederiction, NB, Canada [*Library symbol Library of Congress*] (LCLS) .... CaNBFC
New Brunswick Museum, Saint John, NB, Canada [*Library symbol Library of Congress*] (LCLS) .... CaNBSM
New Brunswick Museum, Saint John, New Brunswick [*Library symbol National Library of Canada*] (NLC) .... NBSM
New Brunswick, NJ [*AM radio station call letters*] .... WCTC
New Brunswick, NJ [*FM radio station call letters*] .... WMGQ
New Brunswick, NJ [*Television station call letters*] .... WNJB
New Brunswick, NJ [*FM radio station call letters*] .... WRSU
New Brunswick Power, Fredericton, NB, Canada [*Library symbol Library of Congress*] (LCLS) .... CaNBFP
New Brunswick Power, Fredericton, New Brunswick [*Library symbol National Library of Canada*] (NLC) .... NBFP
New Brunswick Provincial Archives, Fredericton, NB, Canada [*Library symbol Library of Congress*] (LCLS) .... CaNBFA
New Brunswick Reports [*A publication*] (DLA) .... N Bruns
New Brunswick Reports [*A publication*] (DLA) .... NB
New Brunswick Reports [*A publication*] (DLA) .... NB Rep
New Brunswick Reports [*Maritime Law Book Co. Ltd.*] [*Canada Information service or system A publication*] (CRD) .... NBR
New Brunswick Reports [*A publication*] (DLA) .... New Br
New Brunswick Reports [*A publication*] (DLA) .... New Br R
New Brunswick Reports, Second Series [*A publication*] (DLA) .... NB 2d
New Brunswick Reports, Second Series [*A publication*] (DLA) .... NBR 2d
New Brunswick Research and Productivity Council .... NBRPC
New Brunswick Research and Productivity Council, Fredericton, NB, Canada [*Library symbol Library of Congress*] (LCLS) .... CaNBFRP
New Brunswick Research and Productivity Council, Fredericton, New Brunswick [*Library symbol National Library of Canada*] (NLC) .... NBFRP
New Brunswick Revised Statutes [*Canada*] [*A publication*] (DLA) .... NB Rev Stat
New Brunswick Scient [*NASDAQ symbol*] (TTSB) .... NBSC
New Brunswick Scientific Co., Inc. [*Associated Press*] (SAG) .... NBrunS
New Brunswick Scientific Co., Inc. .... NBS
New Brunswick Scientific Co., Inc. [*NASDAQ symbol*] (NQ) .... NBSC
New Brunswick Spokesman, New Brunswick, NJ [*Library symbol Library of Congress*] (LCLS) .... NjNbSp
New Brunswick Statutes [*Canada*] [*A publication*] (DLA) .... NB Stat
New Brunswick Teachers College .... NBTC
New Brunswick Telephone Co. Ltd. [*Toronto Stock Exchange symbol*] .... NBT

New Brunswick Theological Seminary [*New Jersey*] .... NBTS
New Brunswick Theological Seminary, New Brunswick, NJ [*Library symbol Library of Congress*] (LCLS) .... NjNbS
New Brunswick Vice Admiralty Reports [*A publication*] (DLA) .... NBV Ad
New Buffalo Public Library, New Buffalo, MI [*Library symbol Library of Congress*] (LCLS) .... MiNb
New Business .... NB
New Business Fund Authorization (MCD) .... NBFA
New Business Funds (MCD) .... NBF
New Caledonia .... N Cal
New Caledonia [*ANSI two-letter standard code*] (CNC) .... NC
New Caledonia [*ANSI three-letter standard code*] (CNC) .... NCL
New Caledonia [*MARC country of publication code Library of Congress*] (LCCP) .... nl
New Caledonia [*MARC geographic area code Library of Congress*] (LCCP).... ponl--
New Call to Peacemaking (EA) .... NCP
[*The*] New Cambridge Bibliography of English Literature [*A publication*] .... NCBEL
New Canaan, CT [*FM radio station call letters*] .... WSLX
New Canaan Historical Society, New Canaan, CT [*Library symbol Library of Congress*] (LCLS) .... CtNcHi
New Canaan Library, New Canaan, CT [*Library symbol Library of Congress*] (LCLS) .... CtNc
New Canada Press .... NC
New Car Assessment Program [*Automobile testing*] .... NCAP
New Care Health Corp. [*Associated Press*] (SAG) .... NewCare
New Care Health Corp. [*NASDAQ symbol*] (SAG) .... NWCA
New Careers in Employment Security (OICC) .... NCES
New Carlisle and Olive Township Public Library, New Carlisle, IN [*Library symbol Library of Congress*] (LCLS) .... InNcar
New Carlisle, IN [*FM radio station call letters*] .... WGTC
New Carlisle, PQ [*AM radio station call letters*] .... CHNC
New Cases (Bingham's New Cases) [*A publication*] (DLA) .... New Cas
New Cases (Bingham's New Cases) in Common Pleas [*1834-40*] [*A publication*] (DLA) .... NC
New Cases in Equity [*8, 9 Modern Reports*] [*1721-55*] [*A publication*] (DLA) .... New Cas Eq
New Castle Courier Times, New Castle, IN [*Library symbol Library of Congress*] (LCLS) .... InNcasCT
New Castle Free Public Library, New Castle, PA [*Library symbol Library of Congress*] (LCLS) .... PNc
New Castle Free Public Library, New Castle, PA [*OCLC symbol*] (OCLC) ...... QNC
New Castle - Henry County Public Library, New Castle, IN [*Library symbol Library of Congress*] (LCLS) .... InNcas
New Castle, IN [*Location identifier FAA*] (FAAL) .... UWL
New Castle, IN [*AM radio station call letters*] .... WMDH
New Castle, IN [*FM radio station call letters*] .... WMDH-FM
New Castle, PA [*Location identifier FAA*] (FAAL) .... UCP
New Castle, PA [*AM radio station call letters*] .... WBZY
New Castle, PA [*AM radio station call letters*] .... WKST
New Castle, PA [*FM radio station call letters*] (RBYB) .... WVMN
New Catholic Edition [*Bible*] .... NCE
New Catholic Encyclopedia [*A publication*] .... NCE
New Cavendish Books [*Publisher*] [*British*] .... NC
New Century Bible [*A publication*] (BJA) .... NCB
New Century Bible Commentary [*A publication*] .... NCBC
New Century Cyclopedia of Names [*A publication*] .... NCCN
New Century Gilders Society [*A union*] [*British*] .... NCGS
New Century Policies Educational Programs (EA) .... NCPEP
New Century Resources [*Vancouver Stock Exchange symbol*] .... NCY
New Chancery Cases (Younge and Collyer) [*1841-43*] [*England*] [*A publication*] (DLA) .... NCC
New Charter [*Navigation*] .... N/C
New Chemical Compound [*Food science*] .... NCC
New Chemical Entity .... NCE
New China News Agency .... NCNA
New Choreographers On Point .... NCOP
New Church (ROG) .... NC
New Church Library, Cincinnati, OH [*Library symbol Library of Congress Obsolete*] (LCLS) .... OCNew
New Cinch Uranium [*Vancouver Stock Exchange symbol*] .... NCU
New Cinema Review [*A publication*] .... NCR
New City Free Library, New City, NY [*Library symbol Library of Congress*] (LCLS) .... NNec
New City Free Library, New City, NY [*Library symbol*] [*Library of Congress*] (LCLS) .... NnecL
New City, NY [*AM radio station call letters*] .... WRKL
New College Graduate (BARN) .... NCG
New College of California, San Francisco, CA [*OCLC symbol*] (OCLC) .... NEW
New College, Sarasota, FL [*Library symbol Library of Congress*] (LCLS) .... FSN
New College, University of Toronto, Ontario [*Library symbol National Library of Canada*] (NLC) .... OTUNWC
New Common Carriers .... NCC
New Communities Administration [*HUD*] .... NCA
New Communities Program [*Defunct*] (EA) .... NCP
New Community Development Corp. [*HUD*] .... NCDC
New Community Instrument [*European Community*] (MHDB) .... NCI
New Community Projects [*A publication*] .... NCP
New Component Design (IAA) .... NCD
New Computational Formulas .... NEOCOMP
New Computer Center [*Social Security Administration*] .... NCC
New Computer Family D (SAA) .... NCFD
New Computerized World Information Service [*Information service or system*] (IID) .... NCWIS
New Concord, OH [*FM radio station call letters*] .... WMCO

New Construction [*Navy*] .... NC
New Construction [*Navy*] .... NEWCN
New Construction and Conversion [*Navy*] (AFIT) .... NCC
New Construction and Conversion [*Navy*] .... NCCV
New Construction/Conversion Requirements System [*Navy*] .... NCCR
New Consultants [*A publication*] .... NC
New Consultants [*A publication*] .... NCO
New Consultants and Consulting Organizations Directory [*A publication*] .... NCC
New Creation Institute (EA) .... NCI
New Crime Buffer .... NCB
New Crop .... NC
New Cruzado [*Monetary unit*] [*Brazil*] (BARN) .... NCz
New Cumberland Army Depot [*Pennsylvania*] (AABC) .... NCAD
New Curing Technology .... NCT
New Data Network (IAA) .... NDN
New Dawn [*An association*] (EA) .... ND
New Day Beverage, Inc. [*Associated Press*] (SAG) .... NewDay
New Day Beverage, Inc. [*Associated Press*] (SAG) .... NwDay
New Day Beverage, Inc. [*NASDAQ symbol*] (SAG) .... SUNS
New Deal (DAS) .... ND
New Deck [*On ships*] .... ND
New Delhi [*India*] [*Seismograph station code, US Geological Survey*] (SEIS) .... NDI
New Democracy [*European political movement*] (ECON) .... ND
New Democratic Coalition .... NDC
New Democratic Dimensions (EA) .... NDD
New Democratic Forum (EA) .... NDF
New Democratic Movement (EA) .... NDM
New Democratic Party [*Facetious translations: "Never Dies Politically," "No Dreams of Prosperity"*] [*Canada Political party*] (PPW) .... NDP
New Democratic Party [*South Korea Political party*] (PPW) .... NDP
New Democratic Party [*St. Vincent*] [*Political party*] (PPW) .... NDP
New Democratic Party [*Seychelles*] [*Political party*] (EY) .... NDP
New Democratic Republican Party [*South Korea Political party*] (EY) .... NDRP
New Denmark Historical Museum, New Brunswick [*Library symbol National Library of Canada*] (NLC) .... NBNDH
New Denmark Historical Museum, New Denmark, NB, Canada [*Library symbol Library of Congress*] (LCLS) .... CaNBNdH
New Denver, BC [*FM radio station call letters*] .... CKZX
New Departure Hyatt Division [*General Motors Corp.*] .... NDH
New Desk Accessories [*Utility program*] [*Apple Computers, Inc.*] [*Computer science*] .... NDA
New Developments Human Factors Program [*Navy*] .... NDHFP
New Developments Research Branch [*Bureau of Naval Personnel*] [*Washington, DC*] .... ND
New Developments Research Branch [*Navy*] (MCD) .... NDRB
New Dictionary of Thoughts [*A publication*] .... NDT
New Die Cast [*Honda Motor Co. Ltd.*] .... NDC
New Dimension Software [*NASDAQ symbol*] (TTSB) .... DDDDF
New Dimensions [*Vancouver Stock Exchange symbol*] .... NDT
New Dimensions Foundation (EA) .... NDF
New Dimensions in Medicine .... NDM
New Dimensions Radio (EA) .... NDR
New Directions [*Later, Democratic Alternatives - DA*] (EA) .... ND
New Directions in Biblical Archaeology [*A publication*] (BJA) .... NDBA
New Directions in Creativity Program (EDAC) .... NDC
New Disc Operating System (NITA) .... NDOS
New Disk Access Method [*Computer science*] (MHDI) .... NDAM
New Dosage Form [*Medicine*] (MAE) .... NDF
New Dramatists (EA) .... ND
New Dramatists Committee [*Later, ND*] (EA) .... NDC
New Drug .... ND
New Drug Application [*FDA*] .... NDA
New Drugs [*A publication*] .... ND
New Duty Station [*Navy*] .... NDUSTA
New Earnings Survey [*British*] .... NES
New Economic Policy [*Program of former USSR, 1921-28; also US wage/price freeze and controls of Nixon Administration, 1971*] .... NEP
New Edition .... NE
New Edition / No Date [*of Publication*] (DGA) .... NE/ND
New Edition Pending [*Publishing*] .... NEP
New Editions [*Record label*] .... NE
New Editor [*Computer program*] [*Air Force*] (MCD) .... NED
New Education Fellowship [*Later, WEF*] .... NEF
New Egypt Press, New Egypt, NJ [*Library symbol Library of Congress*] (LCLS) .... NjNeP
New El Salvador Today (EA) .... NEST
New Electric Car [*Daimler-Benz AG*] (PS) .... NECAR
New Electroactive Organic Materials for Electronics [*Esprit*] .... NEOME
New Electronic Media (NTCM) .... NEM
New Ellenton, SC [*FM radio station call letters*] .... WAJY
New Emerging Forces .... NEFOS
New Employment Expansion and Development [*Canada*] .... NEED
New Employment, Transition, and Training [*Department of Labor*] (OICC) .... NETT
New Engine [*On ships*] .... NE
New Englad Rlty Assoc L.P. [*NASDAQ symbol*] (TTSB) .... NEWRZ
New England .... NE
New England .... NENG
New England [*MARC geographic area code Library of Congress*] (LCCP) .... n-usn-
[*The*] **New England Academic and Research Network** [*Computer science*] (TNIG) .... NEARnet
New England Action Research Project .... NEAR
New England Advisory Board for Fish and Game Problems [*Defunct*] (EA) .... NEABFGP
New England Air Express, Inc. [*ICAO designator*] (FAAC) .... NEW
New England Airlines [*ICAO designator*] (AD) .... EJ
New England Airlines, Inc. [*ICAO designator*] (FAAC) .... NEA
New England Albanian Relief Organization .... NEARO
New England and World Missions (EA) .... NEWM
New England Antiquities Research Association (EA) .... NEARA
New England Appalachian Research Project [*University of Maine at Orono*] [*Research center*] (RCD) .... NEARP
New England Association of Colleges and Secondary Schools [*Later, NEASC*] (EA) .... NEACSS
New England Association of School, College, and University Staffing .... NEASCUS
New England Association of Schools and Colleges (EA) .... NEASC
New England Association of Teachers of English (AEBS) .... NEATE
New England Automated Clearing House Association .... NEACH
New England Bibliographic Instruction Collection .... NEBIC
New England Board of Higher Education [*Information service or system*] .... NEBHE
New England Bus Svc [*NYSE symbol*] (TTSB) .... NEB
New England Business Service, Inc. [*NASDAQ symbol*] (NQ) .... NEBS
New England Business Services [*Associated Press*] (SAG) .... NE Bus
New England Business Services [*NYSE symbol*] (SAG) .... NEB
New England Catholic Education Center (AEBS) .... NECEC
New England Center for Organizational Effectiveness (EA) .... NECOE
New England College, Henniker, NH [*OCLC symbol*] (OCLC) .... NEC
New England College, Henniker, NH [*Library symbol Library of Congress*] (LCLS) .... NhHenN
New England College of Optometry, Boston MA [*Library symbol Library of Congress*] (LCLS) .... MBNECO
New England College of Pharmacy .... NECP
New England Comm Bancorp'A' [*NASDAQ symbol*] (TTSB) .... NECB
New England Committee for Nonviolent Action [*Later, CNVA*] (EA) .... NECNVA
New England Community Bancorp, Inc. [*Associated Press*] (SAG) .... NE CBcp
New England Community Bancorp, Inc. [*NASDAQ symbol*] (SAG) .... NECB
New England Confectionery Co. .... NECCO
New England Conference Management [*Australia*] .... NECM
New England Congressional Caucus [*Defunct*] (EA) .... NECC
New England Conservatory of Music (BARN) .... NEC
New England Conservatory of Music [*Boston, MA*] .... NECM
New England Conservatory of Music (GAGS) .... New Eng Cons Music
New England Conservatory of Music, Boston, MA [*Library symbol Library of Congress*] (LCLS) .... MBCM
New England Consumer Development Council .... NECDC
New England Council (EA) .... NEC
New England County Metropolitan Areas .... NECMA
New England Data Film, Inc., Milford, CT [*Library symbol Library of Congress*] (LCLS) .... NeDF
New England Deposit Library .... NEDL
New England Division [*Army Engineers*] .... NED
New England Document Conservation Center [*Information service or system*] (IID) .... NEDCC
New England Document Conservation Center, Andover, MA [*Library symbol Library of Congress*] (LCLS) .... NeDC
New England Economic Project (NITA) .... NEEP
New England Educational Data Systems .... NEEDS
New England El Sys [*NYSE symbol*] (TTSB) .... NES
New England Electric System .... NEES
New England Electric System [*Associated Press*] (SAG) .... NEngEl
New England Electric System [*NYSE symbol*] (SPSG) .... NES
New England Energy Management Information System .... NEEMIS
New England Express [*Steamship*] (MHDW) .... NEE
New England Fish Co. .... NEFCO
New England Fish Exchange (EA) .... NEFE
New England Fisheries Development Association (EA) .... NEFDA
New England Fisheries Development Foundation [*Later, NEFDA*] (EA) .... NEFDF
New England Fisheries Management Council .... NEFMC
New England Free Press [*Publisher*] .... NEFP
New England Fuel Institute .... NEFI
New England Grass Roots Organization .... NEGRO
New England Group (DNAB) .... NEWENGGRU
New England Historic Genealogical Society (EA) .... NEHGS
New England Historic Genealogical Society, Boston, MA [*Library symbol Library of Congress*] (LCLS) .... MBNEH
New England History Resources Center [*University of New England*] [*Australia*] .... NEHRC
New England Information Center [*Information service or system*] .... NEIC
New England Intercollegiate Sailing Association .... NEISA
New England Interstate Environmental Training Center .... NEIETC
New England Interstate Water Pollution Control Commission .... NEIWPCC
New England Inv Cos. L.P. [*NYSE symbol*] (TTSB) .... NEW
New England Investment Companies [*Formerly, Reich & Tang Ltd.*] [*NYSE symbol*] (SPSG) .... NEW
New England Investment Companies Ltd. [*Associated Press*] (SAG) .... NEngInv
New England Journal on Prison Law [*A publication*] (DLA) .... N Eng J Prison L
New England Kiln Drying Association (EA) .... NEKDA
New England Knitted Outerwear Association [*Later, NEKASA*] (EA) .... NEKOA
New England Knitwear and Sportswear Association (EA) .... NEKASA
New England Law Library Consortium, Inc. [*Harvard Law School*] [*Information service or system*] (IID) .... NELLCO
New England Library Association .... NELA
New England Library Board [*Library network*] .... NELB
New England Library Information Network .... NELINET
New England Lumber Women's Association [*Defunct*] (EA) .... NELWA
New England Marine Advisory Service .... NEMAS
New England Marine Resources Information Program [*University of Rhode Island*] [*Later, NEMAS*] .... NEMRIP
New England Materials-Instruction Center .... NEMIC

New England Media Evaluators Association .... NEMEA
New England Medical Center [Boston, MA] .... NEMC
New England Medical Center Hospitals .... NEMCH
New England Methodist Historical Society, Inc., Boston, MA [Library symbol
    Library of Congress] (LCLS) .... MBNMHi
New England MG "T" Register Ltd. (EA) .... NEMG T RL
New England Micrographics, Inc., Waltham, MA [Library symbol Library of
    Congress] (LCLS) .... NeM
New England Modern Language Association (AEBS) .... NEMLA
New England Motor Rate Bureau .... NEMRB
New England Motor Rate Bureau Inc., Burlington MA [STAC] .... NEB
New England Nuclear Corp., Boston, MA [Library symbol Library of
    Congress] (LCLS) .... MBNEN
New England Offshore Mining Experiment Study (NOAA) .... NOMES
New England Order of Protection [Later, Woodmen of the World Life
    Insurance Society] (EA) .... NEOP
New England Plant (NRCH) .... NEP
New England Plant, Soil, and Water Laboratory [Department of Agriculture]
    [Research center] (RCD) .... NEPSWL
New England Power Co. .... NEPC
New England Power Exchange .... NEPEX
New England Power Pool .... NEPOOL
New England Printer and Publisher [A publication] (DGA) .... NEP & P
New England Project on Education of the Aging [Defunct] (EA) .... NEPEA
New England Provision Co. .... NEPCO
New England Quarterly [A publication] (BRI) .... NEQ
New England Reading Association (AEBS) .... NERA
New England Realty Associates Ltd. [Associated Press] (SAG) .... NE Rlty
New England Realty Associates Ltd. [NASDAQ symbol] (NQ) .... NEWR
New England Regional Commission [Terminated, 1981] [Department of
    Commerce] .... NERC
New England Regional Commission [Department of Commerce] [Terminated,
    1981] (EGAO) .... NERCOM
New England Regional Commission [Terminated, 1981] [Department of
    Commerce] (NOAA) .... NERCOMM
New England Regional Computing Program, Inc. [Boston, MA] .... NERComP
New England Regional Medical Library Service (EA) .... NERMLS
New England Regional Primate Research Center [Harvard University]
    [Research center] (RCD) .... NERPRC
New England Regional Primate Research Center, Harvard University,
    Southborough, MA [Library symbol] [Library of Congress] (LCLS) .... MSobPR
New England Reporter [A publication] (DLA) .... N Eng Rep
New England Reporter [A publication] (DLA) .... NE Rep
New England Reporter [A publication] (DLA) .... NER
New England Reporter [A publication] (DLA) .... New Eng
New England Reporter [A publication] (DLA) .... New Eng R
New England Reporter [A publication] (DLA) .... New Eng Rep
New England Research Application Center [University of Connecticut] ...... NERAC
New England Resource Center for Occupational Education .... NERCOE
New England Review [A publication] (BRI) .... New ER
New England River Basin Commission .... NERBC
New England Rural Development Association .... NERDA
New England School Development Council (EA) .... NESDEC
New England School of Art .... NESA
New England School of Law (GAGS) .... New Eng Sch Law
New England School of Law, Boston, MA [Library symbol Library of
    Congress] (LCLS) .... MBNEL
New England School of Law Library, Boston, MA [OCLC symbol] (OCLC) .... NLL
New England Shoe and Leather Association (EA) .... NESLA
New England Small College Athletic Conference .... NESCAC
New England Society of Open Salts Collectors (EA) .... NESOSC
New England Sports Network [Cable-television system] .... NESN
New England Super-Modified Racing Association .... NESMRA
New England Technical Services Librarians .... NETSL
New England Territory Railroad Bureau .... NETRB
New England Territory Railroads Freight Traffic Committee .... NETR-FTC
New England Theatre Conference (EA) .... NETC
New England Trail Conference (EA) .... NETC
New England Trail Rider Association (EA) .... NETRA
New England Trophoblastic Disease Center .... NETDC
New England University. Bulletin [A publication] .... New Engl Univ Bull
New England Wild Flower Society (EA) .... NEWFS
New England Wild Flower Society (EA) .... NEWS
New England Women's Intercollegiate Sailing Association .... NEWISA
New English Art Club [British] .... NEAC
[The] New English Bible [1961] [A publication] (BJA) .... NE
[The] New English Bible [1961] [A publication] .... NEB
New English Dictionary [i.e., the Oxford English Dictionary] .... NED
New English Library [Publishers] [British] .... NEL
New Enhanced Technology .... NEAT
New Enlisted Distribution System (NVT) .... NEDS
New Enlisted System [Navy] (DNAB) .... NES
New Enterprise Institute [University of Southern Maine] [Research center]
    (RCD) .... NEI
New Entitlement Authority .... NEA
New Equipment Introduction [Army] (AABC) .... NEI
New Equipment Introductory Team [Army] (AABC) .... NEIT
New Equipment Personnel Requirements Summary [Army] .... NEPRS
New Equipment Practice .... NEP
New Equipment Resources Requirements Analysis [Army] (AABC) .... NERRA
New Equipment Training [Army] (AABC) .... NET
New Equipment Training Program [Army] (AABC) .... NETP
New Equipment Training Support Package .... NETSP
New Equipment Training Team [Army] .... NETT
New Equipment Training Test Support Package (MCD) .... NETTSP

New Era Development Ltd. [Vancouver Stock Exchange symbol] .... NRA
New Era, Mediapolis, IA [Library symbol Library of Congress] (LCLS) .... IaMediN
New Era Technologies, Inc. [Washington, DC] [Telecommunications]
    (TSSD) .... NET
New European Fighter Aircraft (PS) .... NEFA
New European Wide Warranty System [General Motors Corp.] .... NEWS
New Examiner Training School [Federal Home Loan Bank Board] .... NETS
New Executable [Computer science] (PCM) .... NE
New Executive Office Building [Washington, DC] .... NEOB
New Expanding Shelter Technology [Residential construction] .... NEST
New Experiences in Teaching [Mathematics] .... NExt
New/Experimental Techniques (MCD) .... NEXT
New Extensions for Utilizing Scientists, Inc. .... NEUS
New External Cardiopulmonary Resuscitation .... NECPR
New Eyes for the Needy (EA) .... NEN
New Farmers of America [Later, FFA] (EA) .... NFA
New Federalist Party (EA) .... NFP
New Feminist Talent Associates (EA) .... NFTA
New Fibers International [Vancouver Stock Exchange symbol] .... NFB
New Field Wildcat Drilling [Petroleum technology] .... NFWD
New Fighter Aircraft (MCD) .... NFA
New Forests Fund (EA) .... NFF
New Forests Project (EA) .... NFP
New French [Language, etc.] (ROG) .... NF
New Frontier Party [Japan] [Political party] .... NFP
New Frontier Petroleum Corp. [Vancouver Stock Exchange symbol] .... NFR
New Frontiers in Theology [A publication] (BJA) .... NFT
New Fuel Storage Area (NRCH) .... NFSA
New Games Foundation [Defunct] (EA) .... NGF
New Gatineau Pulp [Pulp and paper technology] .... NGP
New General Catalogue [Astronomy] .... NGC
New Generation Air Traffic Manager (GAVI) .... NGATM
New Generation Truck [Concept vehicle] .... NGT
New Genus [Biology] (BARN) .... n gen
New Genus .... NG
New Germany Fund [NYSE symbol] (SPSG) .... GF
New Glasgow [Nova Scotia] [Airport symbol] (AD) .... ZNG
New Glasgow, NS [AM radio station call letters] .... CKEC
New Glasgow Senior High School, Nova Scotia [Library symbol National
    Library of Canada] (BIB) .... NSNGH
New Gnostics Special Interest Group (EA) .... NG
New Goldcore Ventures [Vancouver Stock Exchange symbol] .... NGV
New Golden Sceptre Minerals Ltd. [Toronto Stock Exchange symbol
    Vancouver Stock Exchange symbol] .... NGD
New Goliath Minerals Ltd. [Toronto Stock Exchange symbol Vancouver Stock
    Exchange symbol] .... NWG
New Governmental Advisory Organizations [A publication] .... NGAO
New Granada .... NG
New Greek [Language, etc.] (ROG) .... N GR
New Greek [Language, etc.] .... NGK
New Group .... NG
New Growth [Medicine] .... NG
New Guinea .... N Guin
New Guinea .... NG
New Guinea Force [Army World War II] .... NGF
New Guinea Island [MARC geographic area code Library of Congress]
    (LCCP) .... a-nw--
New Guinea Territory (WDAA) .... N GUI
New Guinea Volunteer Reserve .... NGVR
New Halfa [Sudan] [ICAO location identifier] (ICLI) .... HSNW
New Halfa [Sudan] [Airport symbol] (OAG) .... NHF
New Hampshire [Postal code] .... NH
New Hampshire [MARC country of publication code Library of Congress]
    (LCCP) .... nhu
New Hampshire [MARC geographic area code Library of Congress]
    (LCCP) .... n-us-nh
New Hampshire Agricultural Experiment Station [University of New
    Hampshire] [Research center] (RCD) .... NHAES
New Hampshire Antiquarian Society, Hopkinton, NH [Library symbol Library
    of Congress] (LCLS) .... NhHopA
New Hampshire Association for Computer Education Statewide
    (EDAC) .... NHACES
New Hampshire Code of Administrative Rules [A publication]
    (DLA) .... NH Admin Code
New Hampshire Code of Administrative Rules Annotated [A publication]
    (AAGC) .... NH Admin Rules Ann
New Hampshire College and University Council, Library Policy Committee
    [Library network] .... NHCUC
New Hampshire Department of Administration and Control, Division of
    Archives andRecords Management, Concord, NH [Library symbol Library
    of Congress] (LCLS) .... Nh-Ar
New Hampshire Historical Society, Concord, NH [Library symbol Library of
    Congress] (LCLS) .... NhHi
New Hampshire International Speedway [Loudon] .... NHIS
New Hampshire Law Reporter [A publication] (DLA) .... NHL Rep
New Hampshire Public Service Commission Reports [A publication]
    (DLA) .... NHPSCR
New Hampshire Reports [A publication] (DLA) .... N Hamp
New Hampshire Reports [A publication] (DLA) .... N Hamp Rep
New Hampshire Reports [A publication] (DLA) .... N Hampshire Rep
New Hampshire Reports [A publication] (DLA) .... New Hamp
New Hampshire Reports [A publication] (DLA) .... New Hamp R
New Hampshire Reports [A publication] (DLA) .... New Hamp Rep
New Hampshire Reports [A publication] (DLA) .... New Hampshire Rep
New Hampshire Reports [A publication] (DLA) .... NH Rep

New Hampshire Reports [*A publication*] (DLA) .... NHR
New Hampshire Reports [*A publication*] (DLA) .... Roc
New Hampshire Reports [*A publication*] (DLA) .... Rock
New Hampshire Revised Statutes [*A publication*] (AAGC) .... NH Rev Stat
New Hampshire Revised Statutes [*A publication*] (DLA) .... NHRS
New Hampshire Revised Statutes, Annotated [*A publication*] (DLA) .... NH Rev Stat Ann
New Hampshire State Library, Concord, NH [*Library symbol Library of Congress*] (LCLS) .... Nh
New Hampshire State Library, Concord, NH [*OCLC symbol*] (OCLC) .... NHS
New Hampshire State Library, Processing Center, Concord, NH [*OCLC symbol*] (OCLC) .... HSA
New Hampshire Supreme Court Reports [*A publication*] (DLA) .... NH
New Hampshire Technical Institute, Concord, NH [*Library symbol Library of Congress*] (LCLS) .... NhCT
New Hampshire Thrift [*NASDAQ symbol*] (TTSB) .... NHTB
New Hampshire Thrift Bancshares, Inc. [*Associated Press*] (SAG) .... NHmpTh
New Hampshire Thrift Bancshares, Inc. [*NASDAQ symbol*] (NQ) .... NHTB
New Hampshire Tracking Station .... NHS
New Hampshire Tracking Station (SAA) .... NHTS
New Hampton Economist, New Hampton, IA [*Library symbol Library of Congress*] (LCLS) .... IaNhE
New Hampton, IA [*FM radio station call letters*] .... KCZE
New Hampton Tribune, New Hampton, IA [*Library symbol*] [*Library of Congress*] (LCLS) .... IaNhT
New Hanover [*South Africa*] [*ICAO location identifier*] (ICLI) .... FANH
New Hanover County Public Library, Carolina Beach Branch Library, Carolina Beach, NC [*Library symbol*] [*Library of Congress*] (LCLS) .... NcWNC
New Hanover County Public Library, Carolina Beach Branch Library, Carolina Beach, NC [*Library symbol Library of Congress*] (LCLS) .... NcWN-C
New Hanover County Public Library, Wilmington, NC [*Library symbol Library of Congress*] (LCLS) .... NcWN
New Harding Group, Inc. [*Toronto Stock Exchange symbol*] .... NHD
New Haven [*Connecticut*] [*Airport symbol*] (OAG) .... HVN
New Haven [*Connecticut*] .... NH
New Haven [*Connecticut*] [*Seismograph station code, US Geological Survey Closed*] (SEIS) .... NHC
New Haven Airways [*ICAO designator*] (AD) .... NB
New Haven Colony Historical Society, New Haven, CT [*Library symbol Library of Congress*] (LCLS) .... CtNhHi
New Haven, CT [*AM radio station call letters*] .... WAVZ
New Haven, CT [*Television station call letters*] .... WEDY
New Haven, CT [*AM radio station call letters*] .... WELI
New Haven, CT [*AM radio station call letters*] .... WNHC
New Haven, CT [*FM radio station call letters*] .... WPLR
New Haven, CT [*Television station call letters*] .... WTNH
New Haven, CT [*Television station call letters*] .... WTVU
New Haven, CT [*FM radio station call letters*] .... WYBC
New Haven Free Public Library, New Haven, CT [*Library symbol Library of Congress*] (LCLS) .... CtNh
New Haven Free Public Library, New Haven, CT [*OCLC symbol*] (OCLC) .... NHP
New Haven, IN [*FM radio station call letters*] .... WJFX
New Haven Railroad .... NHRR
New Head [*Also, NL*] [*News stories*] (NTCM) .... NH
New Health Practitioners [*Nurse practitioners and physician assistants*] .... NHP
New Hebrew [*Language, etc.*] (ROG) .... N HEB
New Hebrides (ROG) .... N HEB
New Hebrides [*MARC country of publication code Library of Congress*] (LCCP) .... nn
New Hebrides [*MARC geographic area code Library of Congress*] (LCCP) .... ponn--
New Hebrides Federal Party [*Political party*] (PPW) .... NHFP
New Hebrides National Party [*Political party*] (FEA) .... NHNP
New Hibernian [*Vancouver Stock Exchange symbol*] .... NHB
New High [*Investment term*] .... NH
New High German [*Language, etc.*] .... NHG
New Hitachi Effective Library for Programming (NITA) .... NHELP
New Holstein, WI [*FM radio station call letters*] .... KFKQ
New Hombre Resources [*Vancouver Stock Exchange symbol*] .... NWH
New Homemakers of America [*Later, FHA*] (EA) .... NHA
New Hope & Ivyland Railroad Co. [*AAR code*] .... NHIR
New Hope, KY [*Location identifier FAA*] (FAAL) .... EWO
New Hope, NC [*AM radio station call letters*] .... WAUG
New Horizon Kids Quest [*NASDAQ symbol*] (TTSB) .... KIDQ
New Horizon Kids Quest, Inc. [*NASDAQ symbol*] (SAG) .... KIDQ
New Horizon Kids Quest, Inc. [*Associated Press*] (SAG) .... NHKidQ
New Horizon Kids Quest, Inc. [*Associated Press*] (SAG) .... NHorizn
New Horizons Savings & Loan Association [*Associated Press*] (SAG) .... NewHrz
New Horizons Savings & Loan Association [*NASDAQ symbol*] (SPSG) .... NHSL
New Horizons Worldwide, Inc. [*NASDAQ symbol*] (SAG) .... NEWH
New Horizons Worldwide, Inc. [*Associated Press*] (SAG) .... NHrzWrld
New Hospital for Women [*1904*] [*British*] (ROG) .... NHW
New Humanity Alliance (EA) .... NHA
New Hyde Park Memorial High School, New Hyde Park, NY [*Library symbol*] [*Library of Congress*] (LCLS) .... NNhpMH
New Hyde Park Memorial High School, Sewanhaka, NY [*Library symbol*] [*Library of Congress*] (LCLS) .... NSewNH
New Hyde Park Public Library, New Hyde Park, NY [*Library symbol Library of Congress*] (LCLS) .... NNhp
New Hyde Park Road School, New Hyde Park, NY [*Library symbol*] [*Library of Congress*] (LCLS) .... NNhpNE
New Iberia Bancorp [*AMEX symbol*] (TTSB) .... NIB
New Iberia Bancorp [*Associated Press*] (SAG) .... NIberiaB
New Iberia Bancorp, Inc. [*AMEX symbol*] (SAG) .... NIB
New Iberia Bancorp, Inc. [*Associated Press*] (SAG) .... NIberia
New Iberia, LA [*Location identifier FAA*] (FAAL) .... ARA
New Iberia, LA [*AM radio station call letters*] .... KANE
New Iberia, LA [*FM radio station call letters*] .... KDEA
New Iberia, LA [*AM radio station call letters*] .... KNIR
New Iberia, LA [*FM radio station call letters*] .... KXKC
New Image Industries [*NASDAQ symbol*] (TTSB) .... NIIS
New Image Industries, Inc. [*NASDAQ symbol*] (NQ) .... NIIS
New Image Industries, Inc. [*Associated Press*] (SAG) .... NwImag
New Impact Resources, Inc. [*Vancouver Stock Exchange symbol*] .... NIP
New Impression [*Publishing*] (DGA) .... N IMP
New Impression [*Publishing*] .... NI
New Incentive Package (ADA) .... NIP
New, Incorporated/Fourth World Movement (EA) .... NI/FWM
New Information Processing Technology Project [*Japan*] (ECON) .... NIPT
New Information Systems and Services [*A publication*] .... NISS
New Information Technology .... NIT
New Initial Commissions [*Business term*] .... NIC
New Inn Hall [*British*] (ROG) .... NIH
New Input/Output Program Status Word Location [*Computer science*] (MHDI) .... NIOPSWL
[*A*] **New Inspiration to Arithmetic** .... ANITA
New Integrated Computer Language .... NICOL
New Integrated Range Timing System .... NIRTS
New Interactive Display [*NEC*] [*Computer science*] (PCM) .... NID
New International Commentary on the New Testament [*A publication*] (BJA) .... NIC
New International Commentary on the New Testament [*A publication*] (BJA) .... NICNT
New International Dictionary [*Webster's*] [*A publication*] .... NID
New International Economic Order .... NIEO
New International Information Order (NITA) .... NIIO
New International Version [*of the Bible*] [*A publication*] .... NIV
New Internationalist [*Australia A publication*] .... NI
New Inventory Pricing Systems (MCD) .... NIPS
New Iowa Bystander, West Des Moines, IA [*Library symbol Library of Congress*] (LCLS) .... IaWdmB
New Iowa Bystander, West Des Moines, IA [*Library symbol Library of Congress*] (LCLS) .... IaWdmNB
New Ireland .... NI
New Ireland Review [*A publication*] (ROG) .... NIR
New Irish Jurist [*A publication*] (DLA) .... NIJ
New Irish Jurist [*A publication*] (DLA) .... NIJR
New Irish Jurist and Local Government Review [*1900-05*] [*A publication*] (DLA) .... New Ir Jur
New Irish Professionals in London [*Lifestyle classification*] .... NIPILS
New Israel Fund (EA) .... NIF
New Issue [*Investment term*] (DFIT) .... N
New Issue [*Publishing*] .... NI
New Item Introductory Schedule (AAGC) .... NIIS
New Jaguar [*Jaguar PLC*] .... NJ
New Japan Aircraft Maintenance Co. Ltd. [*Japan ICAO aircraft manufacturer identifier*] (ICAO) .... NJ
New Jason [*Charter-party clause*] [*Business term*] (DS) .... NJ
New Jersey [*Postal code*] .... NJ
New Jersey [*MARC country of publication code Library of Congress*] (LCCP) .... nju
New Jersey [*MARC geographic area code Library of Congress*] (LCCP) .... n-us-nj
New Jersey Administrative Code [*A publication*] (DLA) .... NJ Admin Code
New Jersey Administrative Code [*A publication*] .... NJAC
New Jersey Administrative Reports [*A publication*] .... NJAR
New Jersey Advance Reports and Weekly Law Review [*A publication*] (DLA) .... Adv Rep NJ
New Jersey Afro-American, Newark, NJ [*Library symbol Library of Congress*] (LCLS) .... NjNAA
New Jersey Airways [*ICAO designator*] (AD) .... OY
New Jersey & New York R. R. [*AAR code*] .... NJNY
New Jersey Asparagus Industry Council (EA) .... NJAIC
New Jersey Board of Railroad Commissioners Annual Reports [*A publication*] (DLA) .... NJRC
New Jersey Business Review, Clifton, NJ [*Library symbol Library of Congress*] (LCLS) .... NjClifB
New Jersey Central Railroad .... NJC
New Jersey College Basic Skills Placement Test (EDAC) .... NJCBSPT
New Jersey College of Medicine and Dentistry, Newark, NJ [*Library symbol Library of Congress*] (LCLS) .... NjNCM
New Jersey Department of Environmental Protection .... NJDEP
New Jersey Department of Environmental Protection (DOGT) .... NJDEP
New Jersey Development Disabilities Council (EDAC) .... NJDDC
New Jersey Devils Fan Club (EA) .... NJDFC
New Jersey Equity Reports [*A publication*] (DLA) .... New Jersey Eq
New Jersey Equity Reports [*A publication*] (DLA) .... New Jersey Equity
New Jersey Equity Reports [*A publication*] (DLA) .... NJ Ch
New Jersey Equity Reports [*A publication*] (DLA) .... NJ Eq
New Jersey Equity Reports [*A publication*] (DLA) .... NJ Eq R
New Jersey Equity Reports [*A publication*] (DLA) .... NJ Equity
New Jersey Equity Reports [*A publication*] (DLA) .... NJE
New Jersey Film Circuit [*Library network*] .... NJLFC
New Jersey Herald, Newton, NJ [*Library symbol Library of Congress*] (LCLS) .... NjNetH
New Jersey Historical Society, Newark, NJ [*Library symbol Library of Congress*] (LCLS) .... NjHi
New Jersey, Indiana & Illinois Railroad Co. [*AAR code*] .... NJII
New Jersey Institute of Technology [*Newark*] .... NJIT
New Jersey Institute of Technology (GAGS) .... NJIT
New Jersey Institute of Technology, Newark, NJ [*OCLC symbol*] (OCLC) .... NJI
New Jersey Institute of Technology, Newark, NJ [*Library symbol Library of Congress*] (LCLS) .... NjNC

New Jersey Labor Herald, Newark, NJ [*Library symbol Library of Congress*] (LCLS) ... NjNLH
New Jersey Law News [*A publication*] (DLA) ... NJ Law N
New Jersey Law Reports [*A publication*] (DLA) ... N Jersey R
New Jersey Law Reports [*A publication*] (DLA) ... New Jersey
New Jersey Law Reports [*A publication*] (DLA) ... NJ Law
New Jersey Law Reports [*A publication*] (DLA) ... NJ Law Rep
New Jersey Law Reports [*A publication*] (DLA) ... NJ Rep
New Jersey Law Reports [*A publication*] (DLA) ... NJL
New Jersey Law Reports [*A publication*] (DLA) ... NJL Rep
New Jersey Law Review [*A publication*] (DLA) ... New Jersey L Rev
New Jersey Law Review [*A publication*] (DLA) ... NJL Rev
New Jersey Legal Record [*A publication*] (DLA) ... New Jersey Leg Rec
New Jersey Legal Record [*A publication*] (DLA) ... NJ Leg Rec
New Jersey Medical School [*Newark*] ... NJMS
New Jersey Miscellaneous Reports [*A publication*] (DLA) ... NJ Mis
New Jersey Miscellaneous Reports [*A publication*] (DLA) ... NJ Mis R
New Jersey Miscellaneous Reports [*A publication*] (DLA) ... NJ Misc
New Jersey Miscellaneous Reports [*A publication*] (DLA) ... NJM
New Jersey Network [*Trenton*] [*Telecommunications service*] (TSSD) ... NJN
New Jersey Realty Title News [*A publication*] (DLA) ... NJ Re Tit N
New Jersey Register [*A publication*] (DLA) ... NJR
New Jersey Resources [*NYSE symbol*] (TTSB) ... NJR
New Jersey Resources [*Associated Press*] (SAG) ... NJRsc
New Jersey Resources [*Associated Press*] (SAG) ... NURsc
New Jersey Resources Corp. [*NYSE symbol*] (SPSG) ... NJR
New Jersey Revised Statutes [*A publication*] (DLA) ... NJ Rev Stat
New Jersey Session Law Service [*A publication*] (DLA) ... NJ Sess Law Serv
New Jersey State Bar Association. Quarterly [*A publication*] (DLA) ... New Jersey SBA Qu
New Jersey State Bar Association. Quarterly [*A publication*] (DLA) ... NJSBAQ
New Jersey State Bar Journal [*A publication*] (DLA) ... NJ St BJ
New Jersey State Bar Journal [*A publication*] (DLA) ... NJSBJ
New Jersey State Board of Tax Appeals, Opinions [*A publication*] (DLA) ... NJSBTA Ops
New Jersey State Data Center [*New Jersey State Department of Labor*] [*Trenton*] [*Information service or system*] (IID) ... NJSDC
New Jersey State Library, Department of Education, Trenton, NJ [*Library symbol Library of Congress*] (LCLS) ... Nj-E
New Jersey State Library, Trenton, NJ [*Library symbol Library of Congress*] (LCLS) ... Nj
New Jersey State Library, Trenton, NJ [*OCLC symbol*] (OCLC) ... NJL
New Jersey Statutes, Annotated [*A publication*] ... NJSA
New Jersey Statutes, Annotated (West) [*A publication*] (DLA).... NJ Stat Ann (West)
New Jersey Steel [*NASDAQ symbol*] (TTSB) ... NJST
New Jersey Steel Corp. [*Associated Press*] (SAG) ... NJ Stl
New Jersey Steel Corp. [*NASDAQ symbol*] (NQ) ... NJST
New Jersey Superior Court Reports [*A publication*] (DLA) ... NJ Sup
New Jersey Superior Court Reports [*A publication*] (DLA) ... NJ Super
New Jersey Superior Court Reports [*A publication*] (DLA) ... NJS
New Jersey Supreme Court Reports [*A publication*] (DLA) ... NJ
New Jersey Zinc Co. [*of Pennsylvania*], Technical Library, Palmerton, PA [*Library symbol Library of Congress*] (LCLS) ... PPalZ
New JEWEL Regime [*Grenada*] ... NJR
New Jewish Agenda (EA) ... NJA
New Jewish Media Project [*JMS*] [*Absorbed by*] (EA) ... NJMP
New Journalism [*Refers to specific style, as that of writer Tom Wolfe*] ... NJ
New Journalist [*A publication*] ... New Journ
New Junior Maudsley Inventory [*Psychology*] ... NJMI
New Keel [*On ships*] ... NKL
New Kelore Mines Ltd. [*Toronto Stock Exchange symbol*] ... NKL
New Kenrell Resources [*Vancouver Stock Exchange symbol*] ... NKR
New Kensington [*Pennsylvania*] [*Seismograph station code, US Geological Survey Closed*] (SEIS) ... NKP
New Kensington, PA [*AM radio station call letters*] ... WGBN
New Kensington, PA [*FM radio station call letters*] ... WZPT
New Kids on the Block [*Music group*] ... NKOTB
New King James Version of the Bible [*A publication*] ... NKJV
New Kingdom [*Egyptology*] (ROG) ... NK
New Kuban Education and Welfare Association (EA) ... NKEWA
New Lao Hak [*Lao Patriotic Front*] [*Vietnam*] [*Political party*] ... NLH
New Lao Hak Sat [*New Life Hamlet*] [*See also NLH Vietnam*] [*Military*] ... NLHS
New Lao Hak Zat [*New Life Hamlet*] [*See also NLH, NLHS Vietnam*] [*Military*] ... NLHZ
New Large Airplane ... NLA
New Largo [*South Africa*] [*ICAO location identifier*] (ICLI) ... FANL
New Latin [*Language, etc.*] ... NL
New Law Journal [*A publication*] (ILCA) ... NLJ
New Law Reports [*Ceylon*] [*A publication*] (DLA) ... NLR
New Law Reports (Ceylon) [*A publication*] (ILCA) ... Ceylon NLR
New Lead [*Also, NH*] [*News stories*] (NTCM) ... NL
New Leader [*A publication*] (BRI) ... NL
New Leadership Fund (EA) ... NLF
New Learning Initiative (AIE) ... NLI
New Least Square (PDAA) ... NLS
New Left Party [*Political party Australia*] ... NLP
New Lexington, OH [*FM radio station call letters*] ... WWJM
New Liberal Club [*Shin Jiyu Club*] [*Japan*] (PPW) ... NLC
New Libertarian Alliance (EA) ... NLA
New Library of Law [*Harrisburg, PA*] [*A publication*] (DLA) ... NLL
New Library of Law and Equity [*England*] [*A publication*] (DLA) ... NLL
New Library of Music [*A publication*] ... NLM
New Library Utility ... NULU
[*A*] **New Life for You, Inc.** ... ALFY
New Life Hamlet [*See also NLHS, NLHZ*] [*Vietnam*] [*Military*] ... NLH
New Life League (EA) ... NLL
New Lightweight Night Sight (INF) ... NLNS
New Line [*Computer science*] ... NL
New Line (WDMC) ... nl
New Line Character [*Keyboard*] [*Computer science*] (MDG) ... NLC
New Lintex Minerals [*Vancouver Stock Exchange symbol*] ... NLN
New Liskeard, ON [*AM radio station call letters*] ... CJTT
New Liskeard Public Library, New Liskeard, ON, Canada [*Library symbol Library of Congress*] (LCLS) ... CaONI
New Liskeard Public Library, Ontario [*Library symbol National Library of Canada*] (NLC) ... ONL
New Location Code [*Military*] ... NLC
New London [*Connecticut*] [*Airport symbol*] (OAG) ... GON
New London Community Hospital, Health Science Library, New London, WI [*Library symbol Library of Congress*] (LCLS) ... WNelH
New London, Connecticut [*Navy*] ... NEWLON
New London, Connecticut [*Navy*] ... NL
New London County Historical Society, New London, CT [*Library symbol Library of Congress*] (LCLS) ... CtNlHi
New London, CT [*Location identifier FAA*] (FAAL) ... NOA
New London, CT [*FM radio station call letters*] ... WCNI
New London, CT [*AM radio station call letters*] ... WNLC
New London, CT [*Television station call letters*] ... WTWS
New London, CT [*FM radio station call letters*] ... WTYD
New London Elementary School, New London, MN [*Library symbol*] [*Library of Congress*] (LCLS) ... MnNIES
New London Journal, New London, IA [*Library symbol Library of Congress*] (LCLS) ... IaNIJ
New London [*Connecticut*] **Laboratory** [*Navy*] (DNAB) ... NLL
New London, MO [*FM radio station call letters*] (RBYB) ... KLSN
New London, MO [*FM radio station call letters*] (RBYB) ... KZZK-FM
New London, NH [*FM radio station call letters*] ... WNTK
New London, NH [*FM radio station call letters*] (RBYB) ... WSCS-FM
New London Public Library, New London, CT [*Library symbol Library of Congress*] (LCLS) ... CtNl
New London Public Library, New London, MN [*Library symbol*] [*Library of Congress*] (LCLS) ... MnNl
New London Submarine School [*Navy*] (MCD) ... NLSS
New London Test and Evaluation Detachment [*Navy*] ... NLONTEVDET
New London Training Unit [*Navy*] ... NLT
New London, WI [*FM radio station call letters*] ... WOZZ
New London-Spicer Junior Senior High School, New London, MN [*Library symbol*] [*Library of Congress*] (LCLS) ... MnNlJSH
New Madrid [*Missouri*] [*Seismograph station code, US Geological Survey Closed*] (SEIS) ... NMM
New Madrid, MO [*Location identifier FAA*] (FAAL) ... EIW
New Madrid, MO [*FM radio station call letters*] ... KMIS
New Madrid Seismic Zone [*Geology*] ... NMSZ
New Magistrates' Cases [*England*] [*A publication*] (DLA) ... N Mag Ca
New Magistrates' Cases (Bittleston, Wise, and Parnell) [*1844-51*] [*A publication*] (DLA) ... New Mag Cas
New Main Battle Tank [*Military*] (RDA) ... NMBT
New Major Investment Program [*Australia*] ... NMIP
New Manning System [*Army*] (MCD) ... NMS
New Market Monitor, New Market, IA [*Library symbol Library of Congress*] (LCLS) ... IaNmM
New Market Public Library, New Market, IA [*Library symbol Library of Congress*] (LCLS) ... IaNm
New Market, VA [*FM radio station call letters*] ... WEZI
New Martinsville, WV [*AM radio station call letters*] ... WETZ
New Martinsville, WV [*FM radio station call letters*] (RBYB) ... WETZ-FM
New Master File ... NMF
New Material [*FAR clauses*] (AAGC) ... NM
New Material Flight Tests ... NMFT
New Material Introductory [*Team*] [*Military*] ... NMI
New Material Introductory Briefing [*Military*] (MCD) ... NMIB
New Material Introductory Briefing Team [*Military*] (MCD) ... NMIBT
New Material Laboratory Tests ... NMLT
New Material Planning Letter (MCD) ... NMPL
New Material/Process (MCD) ... NM/P
New Material Release (MCD) ... NMR
New Materials System Test [*Obsolete Nuclear energy*] ... NMST
New Materiel Introductory Letter [*Army*] (AABC) ... NMIL
New Materiel Introductory Team [*Army*] (AABC) ... NMIT
New Mathematical Library [*School Mathematics Study Group*] ... NML
New Measurement ... NM
New Melleray Abbey, Dubuque, IA [*Library symbol Library of Congress*] (LCLS) ... IaDuN
New Memanbetsu [*Japan ICAO location identifier*] (ICLI) ... RJCM
New Members Round Table [*American Library Association*] ... NMRT
New Methylene Blue [*Organic chemistry*] ... NMB
New Mexico (ROG) ... NEW M
New Mexico [*Postal code*] ... NM
New Mexico ... NMEX
New Mexico [*MARC country of publication code Library of Congress*] (LCCP) ... nmu
New Mexico [*MARC geographic area code Library of Congress*] (LCCP) .... n-us-nm
New Mexico & Arizona Land Co. [*Associated Press*] (SAG) ... NMxAr
New Mexico & Arizona Land Co. [*AMEX symbol*] (SPSG) ... NZ
New Mexico/Ariz Land [*AMEX symbol*] (TTSB) ... NZ
New Mexico Bureau of Mines and Mineral Resources [*New Mexico Institute of Mining and Technology*] [*Research center*] (RCD) ... NMBMMR
New Mexico Court of Appeals (DLA) ... NM App
New Mexico Engineering Research Institute [*University of New Mexico*] [*Research center*] (RCD) ... NMERI

New Mexico Environmental Department (DOGT) .... NMED
New Mexico Environmental Department .... NMED
New Mexico Genealogical Society, Inc., Albuquerque, NM [*Library symbol Library of Congress*] (LCLS) .... NmAGen
New Mexico High School Proficiency Examination (EDAC) .... NMHSPE
New Mexico Highlands [*New Mexico*] [*Seismograph station code, US Geological Survey*] (SEIS) .... NMH
New Mexico Highlands University (GAGS) .... N Mex Highlands U
New Mexico Highlands University [*Las Vegas, NM*] .... NMHU
New Mexico Highlands University, Las Vegas, NM [*OCLC symbol*] (OCLC) .... NMH
New Mexico Highlands University, Las Vegas, NM [*Library symbol Library of Congress*] (LCLS) .... NmLvH
New Mexico Information System [*Library network*] .... NEMISYS
New Mexico Institute of Mining and Technology (GAGS) .... N Mex Inst M&T
New Mexico Institute of Mining and Technology [*Socorro*] .... NMIMT
New Mexico Institute of Mining and Technology Computer Center [*Research center*] (RCD) .... TCC
New Mexico Institute of Mining and Technology, Socorro, NM [*Library symbol Library of Congress*] (LCLS) .... NmSoI
New Mexico Institute of Mining and Technology, Socorro, NM [*OCLC symbol*] (OCLC) .... NMT
New Mexico Junior College, Hobbs, NM [*Library symbol Library of Congress*] (LCLS) .... NmHoC
New Mexico Military Institute [*Roswell*] (MCD) .... NMMI
New Mexico Military Institute, Roswell, NM [*OCLC symbol*] (OCLC) .... NMM
New Mexico Military Institute, Roswell, NM [*Library symbol Library of Congress*] (LCLS) .... NmRM
New Mexico Natural Resources Information System [*New Mexico State Department of Natural Resources*] [*Santa Fe*] (IID) .... NRIS
New Mexico Petroleum Recovery Research Center [*New Mexico Institute of Mining and Technology*] [*Research center*] (RCD) .... PRRC
New Mexico Philatelic Association (EA) .... NMPA
New Mexico Proving Ground [*Army*] .... NMPG
New Mexico Register [*A publication*] (AAGC) .... NM Reg
New Mexico Reports (Gildersleeve) [*1852-89*] [*A publication*] (DLA) .... NM (G)
New Mexico Reports (Johnson) [*A publication*] (DLA) .... NM (J)
New Mexico School of Mines (AAG) .... NMSM
New Mexico State Bar Association, Minutes [*A publication*] (DLA) .... New Mex BA
New Mexico State Bar Association, Report of Proceedings [*A publication*] (DLA) .... New Mex SBA
New Mexico State Hospital, Las Vegas, NM [*Library symbol Library of Congress*] (LCLS) .... NmLvSH
New Mexico State Library, Santa Fe, NM [*Library symbol Library of Congress*] (LCLS) .... Nm
New Mexico State Library, Santa Fe, NM [*OCLC symbol*] (OCLC) .... NMS
New Mexico State Penitentiary Library, Santa Fe, NM [*Library symbol Library of Congress*] (LCLS) .... NmSP
New Mexico State Records Center and Archives, Santa Fe, NM [*Library symbol Library of Congress*] (LCLS) .... Nm-Ar
New Mexico State University (GAGS) .... N Mex St U
New Mexico State University .... NMSU
New Mexico State University, Las Cruces, NM [*OCLC symbol*] (OCLC) .... IRU
New Mexico State University, Las Cruces, NM [*Library symbol Library of Congress*] (LCLS) .... NmLcU
New Mexico Statutes [*A publication*] (DLA) .... NMS
New Mexico Statutes, Annotated [*A publication*] (DLA) .... NM Stat Ann
New Mexico Statutes Annotated [*A publication*] (AAGC) .... NMSA
New Mexico Supreme Court Law Library, Santa Fe, NM [*Library symbol Library of Congress*] (LCLS) .... Nm-L
New Mexico Supreme Court Reports [*A publication*] (DLA) .... NM
New Mexico Territorial Court (DLA) .... NM
New Mexico Western College .... NMWC
New Milford Bank & Trust Co. [*NASDAQ symbol*] (CTT) .... NMBT
New Milford Bank & Trust Co. [*Associated Press*] (SAG) .... NwMilfd
New Milford BK & Tr Conn [*NASDAQ symbol*] (TTSB) .... NMBT
New Milford Elementary School, Rockford, IL [*Library symbol*] [*Library of Congress*] (LCLS) .... IRoNmE
New Milford Savings Bank [*Associated Press*] (SAG) .... NMilBc
New Milford Savings Bank [*NASDAQ symbol*] (NQ) .... NMSB
New Minex Resources Ltd. [*Vancouver Stock Exchange symbol*] .... NWX
New Molecular Entity [*Chemistry*] .... NME
New Mon State Party [*Myanmar*] [*Political party*] .... NMSP
New Montreal International Airport Project [*Canada*] .... NMIAPO
New Moon [*Queensland*] [*Airport symbol*] (AD) .... NCM
New Moon [*Moon phase*] .... NM
New Moon Matchbox and Label Club (EA) .... NMMLC
New Museum of Contemporary Art, New York, NY [*Library symbol*] [*Library of Congress*] (LCLS) .... NNNMCA
New Music Articles [*A publication*] .... NMA
New Music (Australia) [*Record label*] .... ANM
New Music Distribution Service (EA) .... NMDS
New Music Quarterly Review [*Record label*] .... NMQR
New Music Seminar .... NMS
New Music Society [*Australia*] .... NMS
New Nadina Explorations [*Vancouver Stock Exchange symbol*] .... NNA
New Nationals [*Political party Australia*] .... NN
New Natura Brevium [*A publication*] (DLA) .... New Nat Brev
New Natura Brevium [*A publication*] (DSA) .... New NB
New Natura Brevium [*A publication*] (DSA) .... NNB
New Network Architecture .... NNA
New Nickerie [*Surinam*] [*Airport symbol*] (AD) .... NNI
New Nickerie/Nickerie [*Surinam*] [*ICAO location identifier*] (ICLI) .... SMNI
New Obligational Authority .... NOA
New Office and Business Education Learning System .... NOBELS
New Office Education Learning System .... NOELS
New Offshore Dischargement (NATG) .... NOD
New Offshore Dischargement Exercise (NATG) .... NODEX
New Oil Reference Price .... NORP
New Old Replacement Stock [*Automotive parts*] .... NORS
New Old Stock [*Automotive parts*] .... NOS
New Opportunities in Animal Health Sciences .... NOAHS
New Options (EA) .... NO
New Order [*Defunct*] (EA) .... NO
New Order [*Revolutionary group*] [*Italy*] .... ON
New Organization Training .... NOT
New Orleans [*Louisiana*] [*ICAO location identifier*] (ICLI) .... KNEW
New Orleans [*Louisiana*] [*Airport symbol*] .... MSY
New Orleans [*Louisiana*] .... NO
New Orleans [*Louisiana*] [*Mint mark, when appearing on US coins*] [*Obsolete*] .... O
New Orleans [*Mint mark on U.S. coins*] (BARN) .... O
New Orleans/Alvin Callender Naval Air Station [*Louisiana*] [*ICAO location identifier*] (ICLI) .... KNBG
New Orleans & Lower Coast Railroad Co. [*AAR code*] .... NLC
New Orleans & Lower Coast Railroad Co. (IIA) .... NO & LC
New Orleans & Northeastern R. R. [*AAR code*] .... NONE
New Orleans Army Base (SAA) .... NOARB
New Orleans Army Terminal .... NOART
New Orleans Baptist Theological Seminary, New Orleans, LA [*Library symbol Library of Congress*] (LCLS) .... LNB
New Orleans Board of Trade (EA) .... NOBT
New Orleans City Archives, New Orleans, LA [*Library symbol Library of Congress*] (LCLS) .... LNA
New Orleans City Ballet .... NOCB
New Orleans Commodity Exchange (EA) .... NOCE
New Orleans Consortium [*Library network*] .... NOC
New Orleans/International [*Louisiana*] [*ICAO location identifier*] (ICLI) .... KMSY
New Orleans Jazz Club (EA) .... NOJC
New Orleans, LA [*Location identifier FAA*] (FAAL) .... HOX
New Orleans, LA [*Location identifier FAA*] (FAAL) .... HRV
New Orleans, LA [*Location identifier FAA*] (FAAL) .... JFI
New Orleans, LA [*Radio expansion station*] (RBYB) .... KAOA EXP STN
New Orleans, LA [*Location identifier FAA*] (FAAL) .... NBG
New Orleans, LA [*Location identifier FAA*] (FAAL) .... NEW
New Orleans, LA [*Location identifier FAA*] (FAAL) .... NMG
New Orleans, LA [*AM radio station call letters*] .... WBOK
New Orleans, LA [*FM radio station call letters*] .... WBSN
New Orleans, LA [*AM radio station call letters*] .... WBYU
New Orleans, LA [*Television station call letters*] .... WCCL
New Orleans, LA [*Television station call letters*] .... WDSU
New Orleans, LA [*FM radio station call letters*] .... WEZB
New Orleans, LA [*Television station call letters*] .... WGNO
New Orleans, LA [*AM radio station call letters*] .... WGSO
New Orleans, LA [*Television station call letters*] .... WHNO
New Orleans, LA [*Television station call letters*] .... WLAE
New Orleans, LA [*FM radio station call letters*] .... WLMG
New Orleans, LA [*AM radio station call letters*] (RBYB) .... WLNO
New Orleans, LA [*FM radio station call letters*] .... WNOE-FM
New Orleans, LA [*Television station call letters*] .... WNOL
New Orleans, LA [*AM radio station call letters*] (RBYB) .... WODT
New Orleans, LA [*FM radio station call letters*] .... WQUE-FM
New Orleans, LA [*FM radio station call letters*] (RBYB) .... WQUE-FM
New Orleans, LA [*FM radio station call letters*] .... WRBH
New Orleans, LA [*FM radio station call letters*] .... WRNO
New Orleans, LA [*AM radio station call letters*] .... WSHO
New Orleans, LA [*AM radio station call letters*] .... WSMB
New Orleans, LA [*AM radio station call letters*] .... WTIX
New Orleans, LA [*FM radio station call letters*] .... WTKL
New Orleans, LA [*FM radio station call letters*] .... WTUL
New Orleans, LA [*AM radio station call letters*] .... WVOG
New Orleans, LA [*Television station call letters*] .... WVUE
New Orleans, LA [*AM radio station call letters*] .... WWL
New Orleans, LA [*Television station call letters*] .... WWL-TV
New Orleans, LA [*FM radio station call letters*] .... WWNO
New Orleans, LA [*FM radio station call letters*] .... WWOZ
New Orleans, LA [*Television station call letters*] .... WYES
New Orleans, LA [*AM radio station call letters*] .... WYLD
New Orleans, LA [*FM radio station call letters*] .... WYLD-FM
New Orleans - Loyola [*Louisiana*] [*Seismograph station code, US Geological Survey*] (SEIS) .... NOL
New Orleans Museum of Art, New Orleans, LA [*Library symbol Library of Congress*] (LCLS) .... LNMA
New Orleans Police Department [*Initialism also used as title of TV series*] .... NOPD
New Orleans Port of Embarkation .... NOPE
New Orleans Public Belt Railroad [*AAR code*] .... NOPB
New Orleans Public Library, New Orleans, LA [*Library symbol Library of Congress*] (LCLS) .... LN
New Orleans Public Library, New Orleans, LA [*OCLC symbol*] (OCLC) .... LNC
[*The*] **New Orleans Rhythm Kings** [*Jazz band*] .... NORK
New Orleans Steamship Association (EA) .... NOSSA
New Orleans Terminal [*AAR code*] .... NOT
New Orleans, Texas & Mexico [*AAR code*] .... NOTM
New Orleans Times-Picayune, New Orleans, LA [*Library symbol Library of Congress*] (LCLS) .... LNTP
New Oxford English Dictionary [*Proposed*] .... NOED
New Paltz, NY [*FM radio station call letters*] .... WBWZ
New Paradigm Sftwr [*NASDAQ symbol*] (TTSB) .... NPSC
New Paradigm Software [*NASDAQ symbol*] (SAG) .... NPSC
New Paradigm Software [*Associated Press*] (SAG) .... NwPar
New Paradigm Software Wrrt [*NASDAQ symbol*] (TTSB) .... NPSCW

New Paragraph (WDMC) .... np
New Paragraph .... NP
New Parent-Infant Network (AIE) .... NEWPIN
New Party (EA) .... NP
[*The*] **New Party** [*Australia Political party*] .... TNP
New Patient .... NP
New Patriotic Party [*Ghana*] [*Political party*] (ECON) .... NPP
New Pattern [*British military*] (DMA) .... NP
New Pence [*Monetary unit in Great Britain since 1971*] .... np
New Penn Energy [*Vancouver Stock Exchange symbol*] .... NWY
New People's Army [*Philippines*] (PD) .... NPA
New People's Party [*North Korea Political party*] (FEA) .... NPP
New Performance Gallery [*San Francisco*] .... NPG
New Periodical Title Abbreviations [*A publication*] .... NPTA
New Periodical Titles [*of British Union Catalogue of Periodicals*] .... NPT
New Permutations .... NP
New Persian .... N
New Personnel Orientation (MCD) .... NPO
New Philadelphia, OH [*Location identifier FAA*] (FAAL) .... PHD
New Philadelphia, OH [*FM radio station call letters*] .... WKRJ
New Philadelphia, OH [*FM radio station call letters*] .... WNPQ
New Philharmonic Orchestra [*British*] .... NPO
New Physics Project (AIE) .... NPP
New Pioneer Exploration [*Vancouver Stock Exchange symbol*] .... NPX
New Plan Realty Trust [*Associated Press*] (SAG) .... NPlnRl
New Plan Realty Trust SBI [*NYSE symbol*] (SPSG) .... NPR
New Plan Rlty Tr SBI [*NYSE symbol*] (TTSB) .... NPR
New Plymouth [*New Zealand*] [*Airport symbol*] (OAG) .... NPL
New Plymouth [*New Zealand*] [*Seismograph station code, US Geological Survey Closed*] (SEIS) .... NPZ
New Plymouth [*New Zealand*] [*ICAO location identifier*] (ICLI) .... NZNP
New Plymouth, ID [*FM radio station call letters*] .... KZMG
New Plymouth Ventures, Inc. [*Vancouver Stock Exchange symbol*] .... NPV
New Point [*Used in correcting manuscripts, etc.*] .... NP
New Populist Action [*Defunct*] (EA) .... NPA
New Port Richey, FL [*FM radio station call letters*] .... WLPJ
New Port Richey, FL [*AM radio station call letters*] .... WPSO
New Port Richey, FL [*FM radio station call letters*] (RBYB) .... WTBT
New Position .... NP
New [*Corrected*] **Position Report** (NVT) .... NEWPOSITREP
New Practice Cases [*1844-48*] [*A publication*] (DLA) .... New Pr Cases
New Practice Cases [*1844-48*] [*A publication*] (DLA) .... New Pract Case
New Practice Cases [*Legal*] [*British*] .... NPC
New Practice Cases. Bail Court [*1844-48*] [*A publication*] (DLA) .... NPC
New Prague, MN [*AM radio station call letters*] .... KCHK
New Prague, MN [*FM radio station call letters*] .... KCHK-FM
New Preliminary Evaluation (MCD) .... NPE
New Privateer Mines [*Vancouver Stock Exchange symbol*] .... NPM
New Process Line (IAA) .... NPL
New Product Announcements [*Predicasts, Inc.*] [*Cleveland, OH*] [*Information service or system*] (IID) .... NPA
New Product Development [*Business term*] .... NPD
New Product Early Warning System .... NEWS
New Product Evaluation Form .... NPEF
New Product Information Service [*Department of Commerce*] .... NPIS
New Product Line .... NPL
New Product Network [*Television*] .... NPN
New Product Planning (IAA) .... NPP
New Production Reactor [*Department of Energy*] .... NPR
New Professionals Section of the American Public Health Association (EA) .... NPSAPHA
New Program Status Area (IEEE) .... NPSA
New Program Status Word Location .... NPSWL
New Programming Language [*1974*] [*Later, PL/1*] [*Computer science*] .... NPL
New Progressive Party [*Puerto Rico*] [*Political party*] .... NPP
New Providence .... NP
New Providence Development Co. Ltd. [*Toronto Stock Exchange symbol*] .... NPD
New Providence Historical Society, New Providence, NJ [*Library symbol Library of Congress*] (LCLS) .... NjNpHi
New Providence Memorial Library, New Providence, NJ [*Library symbol Library of Congress*] (LCLS) .... NjNp
New Pseudonyms and Nicknames [*A publication*] .... NPN
New Quebec Raglan Mines Ltd. [*Toronto Stock Exchange symbol*] .... NQR
New Range (IAA) .... NR
New Records, Inc. [*Record label*] .... NRI
New Redundancy Benefit [*To reduce unemployment*] [*British*] .... NRB
New Regional Airliner .... NRA
[*The*] **New Repertory** .... TNR
New Reports [*1862-65*] [*England*] [*A publication*] (DLA) .... New Rep
New Reports [*1862-65*] [*England*] [*A publication*] (DLA) .... NR
New Reports of Bosanquet and Puller [*A publication*] (DLA) .... NRBP
New Republic [*A publication*] (BRI) .... New R
New Republic Party [*South Africa*] [*Political party*] (PPW) .... NRP
New Research Centers [*A publication*] .... NRC
New Rhodesia Party [*Political party*] .... NRP
New Rhythm and Blues Quartet [*Rock music group*] .... NRBQ
New Richmond, WI [*Location identifier FAA*] (FAAL) .... RNH
New Richmond, WI [*AM radio station call letters*] .... WIXK
New Richmond, WI [*FM radio station call letters*] .... WIXK-FM
New Riders of the Purple Sage [*Rock music group*] .... NROPS
New Riders of the Purple Sage [*Rock music group*] .... NRPS
New Ridge Resources [*Vancouver Stock Exchange symbol*] .... NGM
New Right Coalition (EA) .... NRC
New Right Watch [*An association*] (EA) .... NRW
New Ring Index [*of chemical compounds*] [*A publication*] .... NRI
New River [*California*] [*Seismograph station code, US Geological Survey*] (SEIS) NW2
New River Area Mental Health, Boone, NC [*Library symbol*] [*Library of Congress*] (LCLS) .... NcBoNM
New Road Map Foundation (EA) .... NRMF
New Roads, LA [*Location identifier FAA*] (FAAL) .... HZR
New Roads, LA [*FM radio station call letters*] .... KQXL
New Rochelle, NY [*FM radio station call letters*] .... WRTN
New Rochelle, NY [*AM radio station call letters*] .... WVOX
New Rochelle Public Library, New Rochelle, NY [*Library symbol Library of Congress*] (LCLS) .... NNer
New Royal Horticultural Society [*British*] .... NRHS
New Rural Society [*HUD project*] .... NRS
New Sabina Resources Ltd. [*Vancouver Stock Exchange symbol*] .... NSA
[*The*] **New Salesmanship** [*Book by Steve Salerno*] .... TNS
New Sarepta Public Library, Alberta [*Library symbol National Library of Canada*] (NLC) .... ANS
[*The*] **New Schaff-Herzog Encyclopaedia of Religious Knowledge** [*A publication*] (BJA) .... NSHE
[*The*] **New Schaff-Herzog Encyclopaedia of Religious Knowledge** [*A publication*] (BJA) .... SHERK
New School .... NS
New School for Democratic Management [*Inactive*] (EA) .... NSDM
[*The*] **New School for Social Research** (GAGS) .... N Sch Social Research
New School for Social Research [*New York, NY*] .... NSSR
New School for Social Research, New York, NY [*Library symbol Library of Congress*] (LCLS) .... NNNS
New School of Family Birthing (EA) .... NSFB
New Schools Movement [*Defunct*] (EA) .... NSM
New Scientist [*A publication*] (BRI) .... New Sci
New Scotland Yard .... NSY
New Senate Office Building .... NSOB
New Serial Titles [*A publication of Library of Congress*] .... NST
New Serial Titles, Library of Congress, Washington, DC [*OCLC symbol*] (OCLC) .... NST
New Series [*Bibliography*] .... NS
New Session Cases [*Scotland*] [*A publication*] (DLA) .... NSC
New Session Cases (Carrow, Hamerton, and Allen) [*1844-51*] [*A publication*] (DLA) .... New Sess Cas
New Sharon, IA [*FM radio station call letters*] .... KCWN
New Sharon Star, New Sharon, IA [*Library symbol*] [*Library of Congress*] (LCLS) .... IaNsS
New Shipborne Aircraft [*Canada*] .... NSA
New Side .... NS
New Signet Resources [*Vancouver Stock Exchange symbol*] .... NFI
New Smoking Material [*A wood cellulose-based tobacco substitute*] .... NSM
New Smyrna Beach, FL [*Television station call letters*] .... WCEU
New Smyrna Beach, FL [*FM radio station call letters*] .... WJLU
New Smyrna Beach, FL [*AM radio station call letters*] .... WSBB
New Smyrna Beach, FL [*AM radio station call letters*] .... WWBH
New Society Educational Foundation (EA) .... NSEF
New Source and Environmental Questionnaire [*Environmental Protection Agency*] (EG) .... NS/EQ
New Source Performance Standards [*Environmental Protection Agency*] .... NSPS
New Source Review [*A publication*] (EPA) .... NSR
New South Africa Fund [*Associated Press*] (SAG) .... NewSAfr
New South Africa Fund [*NYSE symbol*] (SAG) .... NSA
New South African Group Test [*Intelligence test*] .... NSAGT
New South Wales [*MARC geographic area code Library of Congress*] (LCCP) .... u-at-ne
New South Wales Adult Literacy Council [*Australia*] .... NSWALC
New South Wales Amateur Pistol Association [*Australia*] .... NSWAPA
New South Wales Amateur Water Polo Association [*Australia*] .... NSWAWPA
New South Wales Animal Welfare League [*Australia*] .... NSWAWL
New South Wales Arbitration Reports [*A publication*] (DLA) .... NSWAR
New South Wales Assemblies' Evangelic Mission [*Australia*] .... NSWAEM
New South Wales Association of Gifted and Talented Children [*Australia*] .... NSWAGTC
New South Wales Association of Health Professions [*Australia*] .... NSWAHP
New South Wales Association of Sephardim [*Australia*] .... NSWAS
New South Wales Banana Industry Committee [*Australia*] .... NSWBIC
New South Wales Bar Association [*Australia*] .... NSWBA
New South Wales Basketball Association [*Australia*] .... NSWBA
New South Wales Basketball League [*Australia*] .... NSWBL
New South Wales Bloodhorse Breeders' Association [*Australia*] .... NSWBBA
New South Wales Board of Adult and Community Education [*Australia*] .... NSWBACE
New South Wales Board of Jewish Education [*Australia*] .... NSWBJE
New South Wales Board of Surveyors [*Australia*] .... NSWBS
New South Wales Board Sailing Association [*Australia*] .... NSWBSA
New South Wales Bookmakers' Cooperative Society [*Australia*] .... NSWBCS
New South Wales Bowling Greenkeepers' Association [*Australia*] .... NSWBGA
New South Wales Bridge Association [*Australia*] .... NSWBA
New South Wales Bushmen [*British military*] (DMA) .... NSWB
New South Wales Buying Advisory Center [*Australia*] .... NSWBAC
New South Wales Cane Growers' Association [*Australia*] .... NSWCGA
New South Wales Canine Council [*Australia*] .... NSWCC
New South Wales Canning Fruitgrowers' Association [*Australia*] .... NSWCFA
New South Wales Canoe Association [*Australia*] .... NSWCA
New South Wales Chamber of Fruit and Vegetable Industries [*Australia*] .... NSWCFVI
New South Wales Cherry Growers' Association [*Australia*] .... NSWCGA
New South Wales Chicken Growers' Association [*Australia*] .... NSWCGA
New South Wales Chicken Meat Council [*Australia*] .... NSWCMC
New South Wales Child Protection Council [*Australia*] .... NSWCPC

New South Wales Chinese Martial Arts and Cultural Association [*Australia*] .... NSWCMACA
New South Wales Churches Cricket Union [*Australia*] .... NSWCCU
New South Wales Churches Soccer Association [*Australia*] .... NSWCSA
New South Wales Citrus Growers' Council [*Australia*] .... NSWCGC
New South Wales Coal Association [*Australia*] .... NSWCA
New South Wales Coal Mine Owners' Association [*Australia*] .... NSWCMOA
New South Wales Coal Proprietors' Association [*Australia*] .... NSWCPA
New South Wales Cold Storage Association [*Australia*] .... NSWCSA
New South Wales Colliery Officials' Association [*Australia*] .... NSWCOA
New South Wales Cooperative Housing Society [*Australia*] .... NSWCHS
New South Wales Corporate Affairs Commission. Report [*Australia A publication*] .... NSW CAC Report
New South Wales Council for Children's Films and Television [*Australia*] .... NSWCCFT
New South Wales Council of Churches [*Australia*] .... NSWCC
New South Wales Council of Heritage Organizations [*Australia*] .... NSWCOHO
New South Wales Council of the Young Men's Christian Associations [*Australia*] .... NSWCYMCA
New South Wales Council of Tourist Associations [*Australia*] .... NSWCTA
New South Wales Council on the Aging [*Australia*] .... NSWCA
New South Wales Council on the Aging [*Australia*] .... NSWCOTA
New South Wales Credit Union Employers' Association [*Australia*] .... NSWCUEA
New South Wales Credit Unit Association [*Australia*] .... NSWCUA
New South Wales Cricket Umpires' Association [*Australia*] .... NSWCUA
New South Wales Cycling Federation [*Australia*] .... NSWCF
New South Wales Dairy Farmers' Association [*Australia*] .... NSWDFA
New South Wales Dairy Industry Conference [*Australia*] .... NSWDIC
New South Wales Dairy Products Association [*Australia*] .... NSWDPA
New South Wales Dam Safety Committee [*Australia*] .... NSWDSC
New South Wales Debating Union [*Australia*] .... NSWDU
New South Wales Deer Breeders' Association [*Australia*] .... NSWDBA
New South Wales Deer Farmers' Association [*Australia*] .... NSWDFA
New South Wales. Department of Forestry. Bulletin [*Australia A publication*] .... NSW Dept Forestry Bull
New South Wales Domestic Abattoirs Association [*Australia*] .... NSWDAA
New South Wales Dried Fruits Board [*Australia*] .... NSWDFB
New South Wales Drug and Alcohol Authority [*Australia*] .... NSWDAA
New South Wales Education and Training Foundation [*Australia*] .... NSWETF
New South Wales Education Exports Unit [*Australia*] .... NSWEEU
New South Wales Egg Producers' Cooperative [*Australia*] .... NSWEPC
New South Wales Ex-Prisoners of War Association [*Australia*] .... NSWEPOWA
New South Wales Fabian Society [*Australia*] .... NSWFS
New South Wales Farm and Country Holiday Association [*Australia*] .... NSWFCHA
New South Wales Farmers' Association [*Australia*] .... NSWFA
New South Wales Farmers' Industrial Association [*Australia*] .... NSWFIA
New South Wales Federation of Parents and Citizens' Associations [*Australia*] .... NSWFPCA
New South Wales Film and Television Office [*Australia*] .... NSWFTO
New South Wales Fire Brigade Employee's Union [*Australia*] .... NSWFBEU
New South Wales Fire Brigades [*Australia*] .... NSWFB
New South Wales Fishing Industry Council [*Australia*] .... NSWFIC
New South Wales Fitness Council [*Australia*] .... NSWFC
New South Wales Flour Millers' Council [*Australia*] .... NSWFMC
New South Wales Flower Growers' Association [*Australia*] .... NSWFGA
New South Wales Folk Federation [*Australia*] .... NSWFF
New South Wales Food Industry Training Council [*Australia*] .... NSWFITC
New South Wales Forest Products Association [*Australia*] .... NSWFPA
New South Wales Free Growers' Horticultural Council [*Australia*] .... NSWFGHC
New South Wales Friends of the Hebrew University [*Australia*] .... NSWFHU
New South Wales Furniture Guild [*Australia*] .... NSWFG
New South Wales Furniture Industry Training Council [*Australia*] .... NSWFITC
New South Wales. Geological Survey. Mineral Resources [*Australia A publication*] .... NSW Geol Survey Mineral Resour
New South Wales Girls' Marching Association [*Australia*] .... NSWGMA
New South Wales Glass and Ceramic Silica Users' Association [*Australia*] .... NSWGCSUA
New South Wales Glass Merchants' Association [*Australia*] .... NSWGMA
New South Wales Golf Association [*Australia*] .... NSWGA
New South Wales Government Information Service [*Australia*] .... NSWGIS
New South Wales Government Travel Center [*Australia*] .... NSWGTC
New South Wales Grain Corp. [*Australia Commercial firm*] .... GRAINCORP
New South Wales Grains Board [*Australia*] .... NSWGB
New South Wales Greyhound Breeders, Owners and Trainers Association [*Australia*] .... NSWGBOTA
New South Wales Gridiron Football League [*Australia*] .... NSWGFL
New South Wales Group of Cooperative Housing Societies [*Australia*] .... NSWGCHS
New South Wales Guild of Craft Bookbinders [*Australia*] .... NSWGCB
New South Wales Guild of Furniture Manufacturers [*Australia*] .... NSWGFM
New South Wales Gun Club [*Australia*] .... NSWGC
New South Wales Hardcourt Tennis Association [*Australia*] .... NSWHTA
New South Wales Hockey Association [*Australia*] .... NSWHA
New South Wales Homeless Children's Association [*Australia*] .... NSWHCA
New South Wales Horticultural Exporters' Association [*Australia*] .... NSWHEA
New South Wales Hospital Group Apprentices Scheme [*Australia*] .... NSWHGA
New South Wales Hospitals Planning Advisory Center [*Australia*] .... NSWHPAC
New South Wales Hot Rod Association [*Australia*] .... NSWHRA
New South Wales Humanist Society [*Australia*] .... NSWHS
New South Wales Incorporated Acts [*A publication*] (DLA) .... NSW Inc Acts
New South Wales Indo-China Chinese Association .... NSWICCA
New South Wales Industrial Arbitration Cases [*A publication*] (DLA) .... NSW Ind Arbtn
New South Wales Industrial Arbitration Cases [*A publication*] (DLA) .... NSW Ind Arbtn Cas
New South Wales Industrial Arbitration Reports [*A publication*] (DLA) .... NSW Indus Arb R
New South Wales Industrial Gazette [*Australia A publication*] .... NSWIG
New South Wales Institute for Educational Research. Bulletin [*A publication*] .... Bull NSW Inst Ed Res
New South Wales Institute of Dieticians [*Australia*] .... NSWID
New South Wales Institute of Physiotherapy [*Australia*] .... NSWIP
New South Wales Institute of Psychotherapy [*Australia*] .... NSWIP
New South Wales Jersey Herd Society [*Australia*] .... NSWJHS
New South Wales Jewish Board of Deputies [*Australia*] .... NSWJBD
New South Wales Jewish War Memorial [*Australia*] .... NSWJWM
New South Wales Judgements Bulletin [*Australia A publication*] .... NSWJB
New South Wales Junior Cricket Union [*Australia*] .... NSWJCU
New South Wales Ladies Highland Pipe Band [*Australia*] .... NSWLHPB
New South Wales Land Appeal Court Cases [*A publication*] (DLA) .... NSW Land App
New South Wales Land Appeal Courts (DLA) .... NSW Land App Cts
New South Wales Land Tax [*Australia A publication*] .... ANLX
New South Wales Law [*A publication*] (DLA) .... NS Wales L
New South Wales Law Reform Commission [*Australia*] (ILCA) .... NSWLRC
New South Wales Law Reports [*A publication*] .... NSW Law Repts
New South Wales Law Reports, Equity [*A publication*] (DLA) .... NS Wales LR Eq
New South Wales Law Reports, Equity [*A publication*] (DLA) .... NSW Eq Rep
New South Wales Law Reports, Equity [*A publication*] (DLA) .... NSWC Eq
New South Wales Law Reports, Supreme Court [*A publication*] (DLA)..... NSWCRL
New South Wales Leagues Club [*Australia*] .... NSWLC
New South Wales Live Stock Exporters' Association [*Australia*] .... NSWLSEA
New South Wales Local Government Reports [*A publication*] (DLA) .... NSW Local Gov't R
New South Wales Lotteries [*Australia*] .... NSWL
New South Wales Marching Association [*Australia*] .... NSWMA
New South Wales Masonic Hospital [*Australia*] .... NSWMH
New South Wales Meat Exporters' Association [*Australia*] .... NSWMEA
New South Wales Meat Industry Authority [*Australia*] .... NSWMIA
New South Wales Medical Board [*Australia*] .... NSWMB
New South Wales Midwives' Association [*Australia*] .... NSWMA
New South Wales Migrant Employment and Qualifications Board [*Australia*] .... NSWMEQB
New South Wales National Coursing Association [*Australia*] .... NSWNCA
New South Wales National Parks and Wildlife Service [*Australia*] .... NSWNPWS
New South Wales Netball Association [*Australia*] .... NSWNA
New South Wales Nurses' Registration Board [*Australia*] .... NSWNRB
New South Wales Nut Growers' Association [*Australia*] .... NSWNGA
New South Wales Occupational Therapy Association [*Australia*] .... NSWOTA
New South Wales Operating Theatre Association [*Australia*] .... NSWOTA
New South Wales Organic Traders' Association [*Australia*] .... NSWOTA
New South Wales Oyster Distributors' Association [*Australia*] .... NSWODA
New South Wales Parachute Council [*Australia*] .... NSWPC
New South Wales Parents' Council [*Australia*] .... NSWPC
New South Wales Parliamentary Papers [*A publication*] .... NSWPP
New South Wales Physical Education Association [*Australia*] .... NSWPEA
New South Wales Pipe Band Association [*Australia*] .... NSWPBA
New South Wales Poker Association [*Australia*] .... NSWPA
New South Wales Police Aero Club Company [*Australia*] .... NSWPACC
New South Wales Police Legacy [*Australia*] .... NSWPL
New South Wales Polo Association [*Australia*] .... NSWPA
New South Wales Prices Commission [*Australia*] .... NSWPC
New South Wales Privacy Committee. Papers [*Australia A publication*] .... NSW Priv Com Papers
New South Wales Professional Golfers' Association [*Australia*] .... NSWPGA
New South Wales Property Owners' Association [*Australia*] .... NSWPOA
New South Wales Public Acts [*A publication*] (DLA) .... NSW Pub Acts
New South Wales Public Medical Officers' Association [*Australia*] .... NSWPMOA
New South Wales Public Service Professional Officers' Association [*Australia*] .... NSWPSPOA
New South Wales Public Statutes [*A publication*] (DLA) .... NSW Pub Stat
New South Wales Rail Transport Museum [*Australia*] .... NSWRTM
New South Wales Railway and Tramway Magazine [*Australia A publication*] .... NSW Railway & Tramway Mag
New South Wales Railway and Transport Employees' Hospital Fund [*Australia*] .... NSWRTEHF
New South Wales Recreational Fishing Advisory Council [*Australia*].... NSWRFAC
New South Wales Registered Cereal Seedgrowers' Association [*Australia*] .... NSWRCSA
New South Wales Reports, Admiralty [*A publication*] (DLA) .... NSW Adm
New South Wales Reports, Bankruptcy Cases [*A publication*] (DLA) .... NSW Bktcy Cas
New South Wales Reserved Equity Decisions [*A publication*] (DLA) .... RED
New South Wales Revenue Rulings [*Australia A publication*] .... ANRU
New South Wales Rifle Association [*Australia*] .... NSWRA
New South Wales Right to Life Association [*Australia*] .... NSWRTLA
New South Wales Road Transport Association [*Australia*] .... NSWRTA
New South Wales Road Transport Training Council [*Australia*] .... NSWRTTC
New South Wales Rod Fishers' Society [*Australia*] .... NSWRFS
New South Wales Rowing Association [*Australia*] .... NSWRA
New South Wales Rugby Football League [*Australia*] .... NSWRFL
New South Wales Rugby League Insurance Finance Agency [*Australia*] .... NSWRLIFA
New South Wales Rural Assistance Authority [*Australia*] .... NSWRAA
New South Wales Rural Industry Training Committee [*Australia*] .... NSWRITC
New South Wales Sales Representatives and Commercial Travellers' Guild [*Australia*] .... NSWSRCTG
New South Wales School of Hypnotic Sciences [*Australia*] .... NSWSHS

New South Wales School of Therapeutic Massage [*Australia*] ... NSWSTM
New South Wales Science and Technology Council [*Australia*] ... NSWSTC
New South Wales Seed Growers' Association [*Australia*] ... NSWSGA
New South Wales Sheepbreeders' Association [*Australia*] ... NSWSBA
New South Wales Shorinjiryu Karate-do Association [*Australia*] ... NSWSK
New South Wales Show Jumping Council [*Australia*] ... NSWSJC
New South Wales Ski Association [*Australia*] ... NSWSA
New South Wales Soccer Federation [*Australia*] ... NSWSF
New South Wales Society for Crippled Children [*Australia*] ... NSWSCC
New South Wales Soft Drink Association [*Australia*] ... NSWSDA
New South Wales Softball Association [*Australia*] ... NSWSA
New South Wales Standing Advisory Committee on Wheat [*Australia*] ... NSWSACW
New South Wales State Cancer Committee [*Australia*] ... NSWSCC
New South Wales Strata Title Law and Practice [*Australia A publication*] ... ANST
New South Wales Stud Merino Breeders' Association [*Australia*] ... NSWSMBA
New South Wales Superannuation Office [*Australia*] ... NSWSO
New South Wales Supply Service [*Australia*] ... NSWSS
New South Wales Supreme Court Cases [*A publication*] (DLA) ... NSW S Ct Cas
New South Wales Supreme Court Reports [*A publication*] (DLA) ... NSW S Ct R
New South Wales Supreme Court Reports [*A publication*] (DLA) ... NSWSCR
New South Wales Supreme Court Reports [*A publication*] (DLA) ... SCRNSW
New South Wales Swimming Association [*Australia*] ... NSWSA
New South Wales Taxi Council [*Australia*] ... NSWTC
New South Wales Technical and Further Education Commission [*Australia*] ... NSWTAFEC
New South Wales Theatrical Employees' Union [*Australia*] ... NSWTEU
New South Wales Timber Industry Training Council [*Australia*] ... NSWTITC
New South Wales Tobacco Leaf Marketing Board [*Australia*] ... NSWTLMB
New South Wales Tourism Commission [*Australia*] ... NSWTC
New South Wales Travel Center [*Australia*] ... NSWTC
New South Wales Video Retailers' Association [*Australia*] ... NSWVRA
New South Wales Vigoro Association [*Australia*] ... NSVA
New South Wales Water Polo [*Australia An association*] ... NSWWP
New South Wales Water Ski Association [*Australia*] ... NSWWSA
New South Wales Women Justices' Association [*Australia*] ... NSWWJA
New South Wales Women's Advisory Council [*Australia*] ... NSWWAC
New South Wales Wool Selling Brokers' Association [*Australia*] ... NSWWSBA
New South Wales Worker's Compensation Reports [*A publication*] (DLA) ... NSW Worker's Comp R
New South Wales Wrestling Association [*Australia*] ... NSWWA
New Special Libraries [*A publication*] ... NSL
New Species ... NSP
New Spirit Research [*Vancouver Stock Exchange symbol*] ... NSD
New Statesman [*A publication*] (BRI) ... NS
New Statesman & Society [*A publication*] (BRI) ... NS & S
New Statesman and Society [*A publication*] ... NSS
New Stuyahok [*Alaska*] [*Airport symbol*] (OAG) ... KNW
New Style ... NS
New Subiaco Abbey, Subiaco, AR [*Library symbol Library of Congress*] (LCLS) ... ArSuN
New System [*Computer science*] ... NS
New System Training Office [*Army*] ... NSTO
New Systems and Enhancements (MCD) ... NS & E
New Systems Personnel Requirements Data System [*Navy*] ... NSPRDS
New Taiwan ... NT
New Technical and Vocational Education Initiative (AIE) ... NTVEI
New Technical Books [*A publication*] (BRI) ... New TB
New Technical Education Initiative (AIE) ... NTEI
New Technology [*Microsoft operating system*] [*Computer science*] (PCM) ... NT
New Technology Access Centre (AIE) ... NTAC
New Technology Opportunities [*Program*] [*US government*] ... NTO
New Technology Opportunities Program [*US government*] ... NTOP
New Technology Report ... NTR
New Technology Telescopes [*Under development*] ... NTT
New Term Reports [*A publication*] (DLA) ... New Term Rep
New Term Reports, English Queen's Bench [*A publication*] (DLA) ... NT Rep
New Term Reports, English Queen's Bench [*A publication*] (DLA) ... NT Repts
New Terms [*Business term*] ... N/T
New Territories [*Hong Kong*] ... NT
New Testament Apocrypha [*E. Henneke and W. Schneemelcher*] [*A publication*] (BJA) ... HSNTA
New Testament Archaeology Monographs [*A publication*] (BJA) ... NTAM
New Testament Greek (BARN) ... NTGk
New Testament Greek (BJA) ... NTGR
New Testament Handbooks [*A publication*] ... NTH
[*The*] **New Testament in Modern English** [*1958*] [*J. B. Phillips*] [*A publication*] (BJA) ... Ph
[*The*] **New Testament of Our Lord and Saviour Jesus Christ (1937) (Francis Aloysius Spencer)** [*A publication*] (BJA) ... Sp
New Testament Reading Guide [*Collegeville, MN*] [*A publication*] (BJA) ... NTRG
New Thailand Dollar [*Monetary unit*] ... NT
New Threat Upgrade [*Military*] (CAAL) ... NTU
New Threat Warning System [*Military*] ... NTWS
New Town, ND [*Location identifier FAA*] (FAAL) ... ETW
New Towns [*British*] ... NT
New Towns Act [*Town planning*] [*British*] ... NTA
New Trade Names [*Later, NBTC*] [*A publication*] ... NTN
New Translation ... NT
[*A*] **New Translation in Plain English (1963)** [*Charles K. Williams*] [*A publication*] (BJA) ... CKW
New Tribes Mission (EA) ... NTM
New Tube Shelter [*British*] ... NTS
New Tyee Resources [*Vancouver Stock Exchange symbol*] ... NTD
New Ulm [*Diocesan abbreviation*] [*Minnesota*] (TOCD) ... NU
New Ulm [*Minnesota*] [*Airport symbol Obsolete*] (OAG) ... ULM
New Ulm, MN [*AM radio station call letters*] ... KNUJ
New Ulm, MN [*FM radio station call letters*] ... KXLP
New Underwood Public Library, New Underwood, SD [*Library symbol Library of Congress*] (LCLS) ... SdNeu
New Union Party [*Later, IUP*] (EA) ... NUP
New United Motor Manufacturing, Inc. [*Joint venture of Toyota Motor Corp. and General Motors Corp.*] ... NUMMI
New Universal Library [*A publication*] ... NUL
New Universal Terminology Subjects ... NUTS
New Universal Union (EA) ... NUU
New University Conference ... NUC
New University Industrial Unit [*New University of Ulster*] [*Research center British*] ... NUIU
New University of Ulster [*Ireland*] (DI) ... NUU
New Upper Lateral [*Botany*] ... NUL
New Upper Stage [*NASA*] (KSC) ... NUS
New Uses [*Research test*] [*Psychology*] ... NU
New Valley [*Egypt*] [*ICAO location identifier*] (ICLI) ... HENV
New Valley [*Egypt*] [*Airport symbol*] (OAG) ... UVL
New Variant Creutzfeldt-Jakob Disease [*Medicine*] ... NV-CJD
New Vehicle Order ... NVO
New Vehicle Satisfaction with Dealer Service [*Quality research*] ... NVSDS
New Version [*of the Bible*] ... NV
New Virginia Public Library, New Virginia, IA [*Library symbol Library of Congress*] (LCLS) ... IaNv
New Virginian, New Virginia, IA [*Library symbol Library of Congress*] (LCLS) ... IaNvN
New War Department Building [*Obsolete*] ... NWB
New Washington, IN [*FM radio station call letters*] ... WJYL
New Washington, IN [*FM radio station call letters*] (RBYB) ... WSOH-FM
New Waste Calcining Facility [*Nuclear energy*] (NUCP) ... NWCF
New Wave [*Style of music*] ... NW
New Wave of British Heavy Metal [*Rock music type, 1979-81*] ... NWOBHM
New Ways Ministry (EA) ... NWM
New Ways to Work (EA) ... NWW
New West Eyeworks [*NASDAQ symbol*] (TTSB) ... NEWI
New West Eyeworks, Inc. [*NASDAQ symbol*] (SAG) ... NEWI
New West Eyeworks, Inc. [*Associated Press*] (SAG) ... NwWEye
New Westminster, BC [*FM radio station call letters*] ... CFMI
New Westminster, BC [*AM radio station call letters*] ... CKNW
New Westminster Historic Centre and Museum, British Columbia [*Library symbol National Library of Canada*] (NLC) ... BNWHC
New Westminster Historic Centre and Museum, New Westminster, BC, Canada [*Library symbol Library of Congress*] (LCLS) ... CaBNWHC
New Westminster Public Library, British Columbia [*Library symbol National Library of Canada*] (NLC) ... BNW
New Westminster Public Library, New Westminster, BC, Canada [*Library symbol Library of Congress*] (LCLS) ... CaBNW
New Wilderness Foundation (EA) ... NWF
New Wilmington, PA [*FM radio station call letters*] ... WWNW
New Wolcott Enterprise, Wolcott, IN [*Library symbol Library of Congress*] (LCLS) ... InWolE
New Work Authorized (MCD) ... NWA
New Work Opportunities [*A publication*] ... NWO
New Workers Scheme (AIE) ... NWS
New World [*Translation of the Holy Scriptures*] [*A publication*] (BJA) ... NW
New World Alliance [*Defunct*] (EA) ... NWA
New World Club (EA) ... NWC
New World Coalition (EA) ... NWC
New World Coffee [*NASDAQ symbol*] (TTSB) ... NWCI
New World Coffee, Inc. [*NASDAQ symbol*] (SAG) ... NWCI
New World Coffee, Inc. [*Associated Press*] (SAG) ... NwrldCf
New World Coffee, Inc. [*Associated Press*] (SAG) ... NwWCof
New World Communic Grp'A' [*NASDAQ symbol*] (TTSB) ... NWCG
New World Communictions Corp. [*Associated Press*] (SAG) ... NewWrld
New World Communictions Corp. [*NASDAQ symbol*] (SAG) ... NWCG
New World Dictionary [*A publication*] ... NWD
New World Education Fund (EA) ... NWEF
New World Foundation (EA) ... NWF
New World Information and Communications Order [*UNESCO*] ... NWICO
New World Information Order [*Term coined by the Nonaligned Countries at their Fifth Summit Meeting in 1976*] ... NWIO
New World Liberation Front ... NWLF
New World Monkey ... NWM
New World Order [*Bush administration*] ... NWO
New World Power [*NASDAQ symbol*] (TTSB) ... NWPCE
[*The*] **New World Power Corp.** [*Associated Press*] (SAG) ... NWldPwr
[*The*] **New World Power Corp.** [*NASDAQ symbol*] (SAG) ... NWPC
New World Power Corp. (The) [*Associated Press*] (SAG) ... NWldP
New World Radical Liberation Front (NADA) ... NWRLF
New World School of Arts, Music Library, Miami, FL [*Library symbol*] [*Library of Congress*] (LCLS) ... FMNW-Mu
New World Services, Inc. ... NWSI
New World Society (EA) ... NWS
New World Translation (of the Holy Scriptures) [*A publication*] (BJA) ... NWT
New Year ... NY
New Yiddish Theater (BJA) ... NYT
New York [*New York*] [*ICAO location identifier*] (ICLI) ... KRNY
New York [*MARC geographic area code Library of Congress*] (LCCP) ... n-us-ny
New York [*City or state*] [*Postal code*] ... NY
New York [*Naval Shipyard*] ... NY
New York [*City*] ... NYK
New York [*MARC country of publication code Library of Congress*] (LCCP) ... nyu
New York Academy of Medicine ... NYAM

New York Academy of Medicine, New York, NY [*Library symbol Library of Congress*] (LCLS) ... NNNAM
New York Academy of Medicine, New York, NY [*OCLC symbol*] (OCLC) ... VVK
New York Academy of Music ... NYAM
New York Academy of Sciences (EA) ... NYAS
New York Advance Digest Service (Commerce Clearing House), Cited by Year [*A publication*] (DLA) ... NYCCH
New York Advertising Media Planners [*Defunct*] (EA) ... NYAMP
New York Agricultural Experiment Station (Cornell University) [*Research center*] (RCD) ... NYAES-C
New York Air Brake Co. ... NYAB
New York Air Defense Sector (SAA) ... NYADS
New York Air Force Procurement Field Office ... NYPFO
New York Airways, Inc. [*ICAO designator*] ... NY
New York Airways, Inc. [*Air carrier designation symbol*] ... NYA
New York & Erie Railroad ... NY & E
[*The*] **New York & Long Branch Railroad Co.** [*Absorbed into Consolidated Rail Corp.*] [*AAR code*] ... NYLB
New York & New England Railroad [*Nickname: Now You Are Nearing Eternity*] ... NY & NE
New York & New Haven Railroad ... NY & NH
New York and New Jersey Dry Dock Association [*Defunct*] (EA) ... NYNJDDA
New York Annotated Cases [*A publication*] (DLA) ... Ann Cas
New York Annotated Cases [*A publication*] (DLA) ... NY Ann Ca
New York Annotated Cases [*A publication*] (DLA) ... NY Ann Cas
New York Annotated Cases [*A publication*] (DLA) ... NY Anno Cas
New York Annotated Digest [*A publication*] (ILCA) ... NY Anno Dig
New York Annotated Digest [*A publication*] (DLA) ... NY Annot Dig
New York Appellate Division Reports, Second Series [*A publication*] (DLA) ... Ap 2d
New York Assembly Program [*Computer science*] ... NYAP
New York Association for Brain Injured Children ... NYABIC
New York Association for New Americans (EA) ... NYANA
New York Association of Industrial Communicators [*Later, NY/IABC*] (EA) ... NYAIC
New York Attorney General Reports [*A publication*] (DLA) ... New York Att'y Gen Annual Rep
New York Average Price per Share [*Stock market*] ... NYAP
New York Bagel Enterprises, Inc. [*Associated Press*] (SAG) ... NYBagel
New York Bagel Enterprises, Inc. [*NASDAQ symbol*] (SAG) ... NYBS
New York Bancorp [*Associated Press*] (SAG) ... NY Bcp
New York Bancorp [*NYSE symbol*] (SAG) ... NYB
New York Bancorp, Inc. [*Associated Press*] (SAG) ... NY Bcp
New York Bancorp Inc. [*AMEX symbol*] (SPSG) ... NYB
New York Banking Law [*A publication*] (DLA) ... NY Bank Law
New York [*New York*] **Battery Park** [*Airport symbol*] (OAG) ... WTC
New York Bight [*Oceanography*] (MSC) ... NYB
New York Board of Fire Underwriters (BARN) ... NYBFU
New York Board of Trade [*New York, NY*] (EA) ... NYBT
New York, Boston & Montreal Railroad ... NYB & M
New York Botanical Garden ... NYBG
New York Botanical Garden, Bronx, NY [*Library symbol Library of Congress*] (LCLS) ... NNBG
New York Botanical Garden Library, Bronx, NY [*OCLC symbol*] (OCLC) ... VXG
New York Browning Society (EA) ... NYBS
New York Bureau of State Building Codes (BARN) ... NYBSBC
New York Business Communicators [*Later, NY/IABC*] (EA) ... NYBC
New York Business Press Editors [*New York, NY*] (EA) ... NYBPE
New York C. S. Lewis Society (EA) ... NYCSLS
New York Candy Club (EA) ... NYCC
New York Cash Exchange [*Automated teller machine network*] ... NYCE
New York Center Beacon Alphanumerics [*FAA*] ... NYCBAN
New York Central & Hudson River Railroad ... NYC & HR
New York Central & Hudson River Railroad (ROG) ... NYC & HRR
New York Central R. R. [*Later, Penn Central*] [*AAR code*] ... NYC
New York Chamber of Commerce, New York, NY [*Library symbol Library of Congress*] (LCLS) ... NNNC
New York Chancery Sentinel [*A publication*] (DLA) ... NY Ch Sent
New York, Chicago and St. Louis Railroad Co. (IIA) ... NYC & SL
New York, Chicago & St. Louis Railroad Co. ... NYC & STL
New York Chiropractic College, Glen Head, NY [*Library symbol Library of Congress*] (LCLS) ... NGlhC
New York Cipher Society (EA) ... NYCS
New York Circus (EA) ... NYC
New York (City) [*New York*] [*ICAO location identifier*] (ICLI) ... KNYC
New York City ... NYC
New York City Ballet ... NYCB
New York City Bar Association. Bulletin [*A publication*] (DLA) ... NYCBA
New York City Board of Higher Education, New York, NY [*Library symbol Library of Congress*] (LCLS) ... NNHE
New York City Civil Court Act (DLA) ... City Civ Ct Act
New York City Community College ... NYCCC
New York City Community College of the City University of New York, Brooklyn, NY [*Library symbol Library of Congress*] (LCLS) ... NBNC
New York City Court [*A publication*] (DLA) ... NY City Ct
New York City Court Reports [*A publication*] (DLA) ... NY City Ct Rep
New York City Court Reports, Supplement [*A publication*] (DLA) ... NY City Ct Supp
New York City Criminal Court Act (DLA) ... City Crim Ct Act
New York City Hall Recorder [*A publication*] (DLA) ... City H Rec
New York City Hall Recorder [*A publication*] (DLA) ... NY City H Rec
New York City Hall Recorder [*A publication*] (ILCA) ... NY City Hall Rec
New York City Health and Hospitals Corp. (EA) ... HHC
New York City Health and Hospitals Corp. (EA) ... HOSCORP
New York City Human Resources Administration, New York, NY [*Library symbol Library of Congress*] (LCLS) ... NNHR
New York City Metropolitan Area ... NYMA
New York City National Park Service Group ... NEYO
New York City Opera ... NYCO
New York City Public Health Research Laboratory, New York, NY [*Library symbol Library of Congress*] (LCLS) ... NNPHR
New York City Record [*A publication*] (DLA) ... City Rec
New York City Record [*A publication*] (DLA) ... City Rec (NY)
New York City School Library System, Brooklyn, NY [*Library symbol*] [*Library of Congress*] (LCLS) ... NBSL
New York City Technical College ... NYCTC
New York City Technical College, Library, Brooklyn, NY [*OCLC symbol*] (OCLC) ... ZNC
New York City Urban Corps (EA) ... NYCUC
New York City's First [*First beluga whale born at the New York Aquarium, 1981*] [*Pronounced "Nicky"*] ... NYCI
New York Civil Practice [*A publication*] (DLA) ... Civ Prac (NY)
New York Civil Practice Law and Rules [*A publication*] (DLA) ... NY Civ Prac Law & R
New York Civil Procedure [*A publication*] (DLA) ... Civ Proc (NY)
New York Civil Procedure [*A publication*] (DLA) ... NY Civ Pro
New York Civil Procedure [*A publication*] (ILCA) ... NY Civ Proc
New York Civil Procedure, New Series [*A publication*] (DLA) ... NY Civ Proc (NS)
New York Civil Procedure Reports [*A publication*] (ILCA) ... NY Civ Pr Rep
New York Civil Procedure Reports [*A publication*] (ILCA) ... NY Civ Pro R
New York Civil Procedure Reports [*A publication*] (DLA) ... NY Civ Proc R
New York Civil Procedure Reports, New Series [*A publication*] (ILCA) ... NY Civ Pro R NS
New York Civil Procedure Reports, New Series [*A publication*] (DLA) ... NY Civ Proc R NS
New York Clearing House Association [*New York, NY*] (EA) ... NYCHA
New York Clothing Manufacturers Association (EA) ... NYCMA
New York Clothing Manufacturers Exchange [*Later, NYCMA*] (EA) ... NYCME
New York Coat and Suit Association (EA) ... NYCSA
New York Cocoa Clearing Association (EA) ... NYCCA
New York Cocoa Exchange [*Later, CSCE*] ... NYCE
New York Code of Remedial Justice [*A publication*] (DLA) ... NY Co Rem
New York Code Reporter [*A publication*] (DLA) ... NY Code R
New York Code Reporter [*A publication*] (DLA) ... NY Code Rep
New York Code Reporter [*A publication*] (DLA) ... NY Code Report
New York Code Reporter [*A publication*] (DLA) ... NY Code Reptr
New York Code Reporter, New Series [*A publication*] (DLA) ... NY Code Report NS
New York Code Reporter, New Series [*A publication*] (DLA) ... NY Code Reptr NS
New York Code Reports, New Series [*A publication*] (DLA) ... Code Rep NS
New York Code Reports, New Series [*A publication*] (DLA) ... NY Code R NS
New York Code Reports, New Series [*A publication*] (DLA) ... NY Code Rep NS
New York Code Reports, New Series [*A publication*] (DLA) ... NY Code Reports NS
New York Codes, Rules, and Regulations [*A publication*] (DLA) ... NYCRR
New York Coffee and Sugar Exchange [*Later, CSCE*] (EA) ... NYCSE
New York Coffee, Sugar, and Cocoa Exchange ... NYCSCE
New York Coffee, Sugar, and Cocoa Exchange (DFIT) ... NYCSCE
New York Cold Type Composition Group [*Later, TANY*] (EA) ... NYCTCG
New York College of Osteopathic Medicine, Old Westbury, NY [*Library symbol Library of Congress*] (LCLS) ... NOwNC
New York College of Podiatric Medicine, New York, NY [*Library symbol Library of Congress*] (LCLS) ... NNCPM
New York College Stores Association ... NYCSA
New York Condensed Reports [*1881-82*] [*A publication*] (DLA) ... NY Cond
New York Conference on Electronic Reliability (MCD) ... NYCER
New York Connecting Railroad [*AAR code*] ... NYCN
New York Consolidated Laws Service [*A publication*] ... CLS
New York Constitution Study Group (EA) ... NYCSG
New York Contract Management District (SAA) ... NYCMD
New York Corset Club (EA) ... NYCCI
New York Cotton Exchange (EA) ... NYCE
New York Cotton Exchange, Citrus Associates ... NYCTNCA
New York Cotton Exchange, Citrus Associates (DFIT) ... NYCTN,CA
New York Council of Motion Picture and Television Unions (EA) ... COMPTU
New York County Clerk Archives, Division of Old Records, New York, NY [*Library symbol*] [*Library of Congress*] (LCLS) ... NNNCC-Ar
New York County Lawyers Association, New York, NY [*Library symbol Library of Congress*] (LCLS) ... NNNCL
New York Court of Appeals (DLA) ... NY Ct App
New York Court of Appeals Decisions [*A publication*] (DLA) ... NY App Dec
New York Court of Appeals Reports [*A publication*] (DLA) ... New York R
New York Court of Appeals Reports [*A publication*] (DLA) ... New York Rep
New York Court of Appeals Reports [*A publication*] (DLA) ... NY
New York Court of Appeals Reports [*A publication*] (DLA) ... NY Rep
New York Court of Appeals Reports [*A publication*] (DLA) ... NY Reps
New York Court of Appeals Reports [*A publication*] (DLA) ... NYCA
New York Court of Appeals Reports [*A publication*] (DLA) ... NYR
New York Court of Appeals Reports, Second Series [*A publication*] (DLA) ... NY 2d
New York Credit and Financial Management Association [*New York, NY*] (EA) ... NYCFMA
New York Criminal Reports [*A publication*] (DLA) ... N Cr
New York Criminal Reports [*A publication*] (DLA) ... NY Cr
New York Criminal Reports [*A publication*] (DLA) ... NY Cr R
New York Criminal Reports [*A publication*] (DLA) ... NY Cr Rep
New York Criminal Reports [*A publication*] (DLA) ... NY Crim
New York Criminal Reports [*A publication*] (DLA) ... NY Crim R
New York Criminal Reports [*A publication*] (DLA) ... NY Crim Rep
New York Curb Exchange [*Later, AMEX*] ... NYCE
New York Current Court Decisions [*A publication*] (DLA) ... NYCCD

New York Curtain and Drapery Club (EA) .... NYCDC
New York Daily Law Gazette [*A publication*] (DLA) .... NY Daily L Gaz
New York Daily Law Register [*A publication*] (DLA) .... NY Daily L Reg
New York Daily Register [*A publication*] (DLA) .... Dai Reg
New York Daily Register [*A publication*] (DLA) .... NY Daily Reg
New York Daily Register [*A publication*] (DLA) .... NY Reg
New York Daily Transcript [*A publication*] (DLA) .... Daily Transc
New York Daily Transcript, Old and New Series [*A publication*] (DLA) .... Daily Trans
New York Daily Transcript, Old and New Series [*A publication*] (DLA) .... NY Daily Tr
New York Datum (NRCH) .... NYD
New York Department Records [*A publication*] (DLA) .... NY Dep't R
New York Department Reports [*A publication*] (DLA) .... NYDR
New York Disposal Surveillance System [*U.S. Army Corps of Engineers*] .... NYDISS
New York Dock Railway [*AAR code*] .... NYD
New York Drama Critics Circle (EA) .... NYDCC
New York [*New York*] **E. 34th Street** [*Airport symbol*] (OAG) .... TSS
New York [*New York*] **E. 60th Street** [*Airport symbol*] (OAG) .... JRE
New York Election Cases [*A publication*] (DLA) .... NY El Cas
New York Election Cases [*A publication*] (DLA) .... NY Elec Cas
New York Election Cases [*A publication*] (DLA) .... NY Elect Cas
New York Election Cases (Armstrong's) [*A publication*] (DLA) .... El Cas
New York Election Cases (Armstrong's) [*A publication*] (DLA) .... El Cas (NY)
New York Election Cases (Armstrong's) [*A publication*] (DLA) .... Elect Cas NY
New York Estate Tax Reports [*Prentice-Hall, Inc.*] [*A publication*] (DLA) .... NYETR
New York Exchange for Woman's Work [*New York, NY*] (EA) .... NYEWW
New York Fashion Designers [*Later, NYFDF*] (EA) .... NYFD
New York Fashion Designers and Foundation [*Defunct*] (EA) .... NYFDF
New York Federation of Urban Organizations .... NYFUO
New York Fertility Research Foundation [*Later, FRF*] (EA) .... NYFRF
New York Film Board of Trade [*Defunct*] (EA) .... NYFBT
New York Film Critics (EA) .... NYFC
New York Financial Writers' Association (EA) .... NYFWA
New York/Flushing, NY [*Location identifier FAA*] (FAAL) .... FLU
New York Foreign Freight Forwarders and Brokers Association [*New York, NY*] (EA) .... NYFFFBA
New York Foundation .... NYF
New York Futures Clearing Corp. [*New York Futures Exchange*] .... NYFCC
New York Futures Exchange .... NYF
New York Futures Exchange [*Pronounced "knife"*] .... NYFE
New York Genealogical and Biographical Society (EA) .... NYGBS
New York Genealogical and Biographical Society, New York, NY [*Library symbol Library of Congress*] (LCLS) .... NNNGB
New York Governor's Conference .... NYGC
New York Group [*Navy*] .... NYKGRP
New York Guild for Jewish Blind [*Later, JGB*] .... NYGJB
New York Health and Safety Laboratory [*Energy Research and Development Administration*] .... NYHSL
New York Health Care, Inc. [*NASDAQ symbol*] (SAG) .... NYHC
New York Health Care, Inc. [*Associated Press*] (SAG) .... NYHlthC
New York Heart Association [*Classifications I, II, III, and IV*] [*Cardiology*] (DAVI) .... NYHA
New York Heart Associaton (MEDA) .... NYHA
New York Helicopter [*ICAO designator*] (AD) .... HD
New York Helicopter [*ICAO designator*] (AD) .... HQ
New York Helicopter Corp. [*ICAO designator*] (FAAC) .... NYH
New York Herald Tribune [*Defunct newspaper*] .... NYHT
New York Historical Society, New York, NY [*Library symbol Library of Congress*] (LCLS) .... NHi
New York Hospital, Westchester Division, White Plains, NY [*Library symbol Library of Congress*] (LCLS) .... NWhpNH
New York Hospital-Cornell Medical Center Archives, New York, NY [*Library symbol*] [*Library of Congress*] (LCLS) .... NNCorM-A
New York Importers and Distillers Association (EA) .... NYIDA
New York Index - Finance [*Stock market*] .... NYIF
New York Index - Industrials [*Stock market*] .... NYII
New York Index - Transportation [*Stock market*] .... NYIT
New York Index - Utilities [*Stock market*] .... NYIU
New York Institute for Child Development (EA) .... NYICD
New York Institute of Finance (ECON) .... NYIF
New York Institute of Technical, Central Islip, NY [*Library symbol*] [*Library of Congress*] (LCLS) .... NOwNI-CI
New York Institute of Technology .... NYIT
New York Institute of Technology, Commack Center Library, Commack, NY [*Library symbol Library of Congress*] (LCLS) .... NOwNI-C
New York Institute of Technology, New York, NY [*Library symbol Library of Congress*] (LCLS) .... NOwNI-N
New York Institute of Technology, Old Westbury, NY [*Library symbol Library of Congress*] (LCLS) .... NOwNI
New York Insurance Exchange .... NYIE
New York Interbank Official Rate .... NIBOR
New York/International Association of Business Communicators [*New York, NY*] (EA) .... NY/IABC
New York International Ballet Competition .... NYIBC
New York International Bible Society (EA) .... NYIBS
New York Iroquois Conference (EA) .... NYIC
New York Islanders Booster Club (EA) .... NYIBC
New York/John F. Kennedy International [*New York*] [*ICAO location identifier*] (ICLI) .... KJFK
New York Judicial Repository [*A publication*] (DLA) .... Jud Rep
New York Judicial Repository [*A publication*] (DLA) .... NY Jud Rep
New York Judicial Repository [*A publication*] (DLA) .... NY Jud Repos
New York Jurisprudence [*A publication*] (DLA) .... NY Jur
New York Jurist [*A publication*] (DLA) .... NY Jur
New York/La Guardia [*New York*] [*ICAO location identifier*] (ICLI) .... KLGA
New York [*New York*] **La Guardia** [*Airport symbol*] (OAG) .... LGA
New York, Lake Erie & Western Railroad [*Later, EL*] [*Nickname: Now You Lay Easy and Wait*] .... NYLE & W
New York Lamp and Shade Manufacturers Association (EA) .... NYLSMA
New York Law Gazette [*A publication*] (DLA) .... NY Law Gaz
New York Law Gazette [*A publication*] (DLA) .... NYL Gaz
New York Law Group [*Later, BAHRGNY*] (EA) .... NYLG
New York Law Institute, New York, NY [*Library symbol Library of Congress*] (LCLS) .... NNLI
New York Law Record [*A publication*] (DLA) .... NYL Rec
New York Law School (GAGS) .... NY Law Sch
New York Law School .... NYLS
New York Law School Library, New York, NY [*Library symbol Library of Congress*] (LCLS) .... NNLS
New York Law School. Student Law Review [*A publication*] (DLA) .... NYLS Stud L Rev
New York Leading Cases [*A publication*] (DLA) .... NYL Cas
New York Leading Cases, Annotated [*A publication*] (DLA) .... NYLC Ann
New York Leather Exposition [*American European Trade and Exhibition Center*] .... NYLEX USA
New York Legal News [*1880-82*] [*A publication*] (DLA) .... NY Leg N
New York Legal Observer [*A publication*] (DLA) .... Legal Observer
New York Legal Observer [*A publication*] (DLA) .... NYLO
New York Legal Observer (Owen) [*A publication*] (DLA) .... NY Leg Obs
New York Legal Register [*A publication*] (DLA) .... NY Leg Reg
New York Magazine [*A publication*] (BRI) .... New York
New York Medical College [*Valhalla, NY*] .... NYMC
New York Medical College, Flower and Fifth Avenue Hospitals, New York, NY [*Library symbol Library of Congress*] (LCLS) .... NNNM
New York Medical College, New York, NY [*OCLC symbol*] (OCLC) .... VVF
New York Medical College, Westchester Medical Center, Valhalla, NY [*OCLC symbol*] (OCLC) .... VVO
New York Medicine College (GAGS) .... NY Med C
New York Mercantile Exchange .... NYM
New York Mercantile Exchange (EA) .... NYME
New York Mercantile Exchange (EA) .... NYMEX
New York Merchandise Mart .... NYMM
New York Metropolitan Reference and Research Library Agency [*Brooklyn, NY*] [*Library network*] .... METRO
New York Metropolitan Reference and Research Library Agency, Inc., New York, NY [*Library symbol Library of Congress*] (LCLS) .... NNMRR
New York Microscopical Society (EA) .... NYMS
New York Mills High School, New York Mills, MN [*Library symbol*] [*Library of Congress*] (LCLS) .... MnNymH
New York Mills Public Library, New York Mills, MN [*Library symbol*] [*Library of Congress*] (LCLS) .... MnNym
New York Miscellaneous Reports [*A publication*] (DLA) .... Delehanty
New York Miscellaneous Reports [*A publication*] (DLA) .... M
New York Miscellaneous Reports [*A publication*] (DLA) .... Mis
New York Miscellaneous Reports [*A publication*] (DLA) .... Misc Repts
New York Miscellaneous Reports [*A publication*] (DLA) .... Misc Repts
New York Miscellaneous Reports [*A publication*] (DLA) .... Msc
New York Miscellaneous Reports [*A publication*] (DLA) .... NY Misc
New York Miscellaneous Reports. Second Series [*A publication*] (DLA) .... Msc 2d
New York Miscellaneous Reports. Second Series [*A publication*] (DLA) .... NY Misc 2d
New York Monthly Law Bulletin [*A publication*] (DLA) .... Monthly L Bul
New York Monthly Law Bulletin [*A publication*] (DLA) .... NY Law Bul
New York Monthly Law Bulletin [*A publication*] (DLA) .... NY Mo L Bul
New York Monthly Law Bulletin [*A publication*] (DLA) .... NY Mo Law Bul
New York Monthly Law Bulletin [*A publication*] (DLA) .... NY Month L Bul
New York Monthly Law Bulletin [*A publication*] (DLA) .... NY Monthly Law Bul
New York Monthly Law Record [*A publication*] (DLA) .... NY Mo L Rec
New York Monthly Law Reports [*A publication*] (DLA) .... NY Mo LR
New York Monthly Law Reports [*A publication*] (DLA) .... NY Month L Rep
New York Monthly Law Reports [*A publication*] (DLA) .... NY Month LR
New York, Motor Carrier Conference [*STAC*] .... NYC
New York Mounters Association [*New York, NY*] (EA) .... NYMA
New York Movers Tariff Bureau, Inc., New York NY [*STAC*] .... NYM
New York Municipal Gazette [*A publication*] (DLA) .... NY Mun Gaz
New York Naval Shipyard, Material Laboratory (MCD) .... NYNS-ML
New York Naval Shipyard (New York) .... NYSNY
New York Naval Shipyards [*Obsolete*] .... NYNS
New York Navy Yard (DNAB) .... NYNYD
New York New England Exchange [*Telecommunications*] .... NYNEX
New York, New Haven & Hartford R. R. [*AAR code*] .... NH
New York, New Haven & Hartford R. R. .... NYNH & H
New York [*New York*] **Newark** [*Airport symbol*] (OAG) .... EWR
New York [*New York*]/Newark [*New Jersey*] [*Airport symbol*] (OAG) .... NYC
New York, NY [*Location identifier FAA*] (FAAL) .... GDI
New York, NY [*Location identifier FAA*] (FAAL) .... HIQ
New York, NY [*Location identifier FAA*] (FAAL) .... IWY
New York, NY [*Location identifier FAA*] (FAAL) .... JNT
New York, NY [*Location identifier FAA*] (FAAL) .... JOC
New York, NY [*Location identifier FAA*] (FAAL) .... JRA
New York, NY [*Location identifier FAA*] (FAAL) .... JRB
New York, NY [*Location identifier FAA*] (FAAL) .... MOH
New York, NY [*Location identifier FAA*] (FAAL) .... NYC
New York, NY [*Location identifier FAA*] (FAAL) .... PZV
New York, NY [*Location identifier FAA*] (FAAL) .... RTH
New York, NY [*Location identifier FAA*] (FAAL) .... TLK
New York, NY [*Location identifier FAA*] (FAAL) .... URD

New York, NY [*AM radio station call letters*] .... WABC
New York, NY [*Television station call letters*] .... WABC-TV
New York, NY [*AM radio station call letters*] .... WADO
New York, NY [*FM radio station call letters*] .... WAXQ
New York, NY [*FM radio station call letters*] .... WBAI
New York, NY [*AM radio station call letters*] .... WBBR
New York, NY [*TV station call letters*] (RBYB) .... WBIS-TV
New York, NY [*FM radio station call letters*] .... WBLS
New York, NY [*AM radio station call letters*] .... WCBS
New York, NY [*FM radio station call letters*] .... WCBS-FM
New York, NY [*Television station call letters*] .... WCBS-TV
New York, NY [*AM radio station call letters*] .... WEVD
New York, NY [*AM radio station call letters*] .... WFAN
New York, NY [*FM radio station call letters*] .... WFUV
New York, NY [*FM radio station call letters*] .... WHCR
New York, NY [*AM radio station call letters*] .... WINS
New York, NY [*FM radio station call letters*] .... WKCR
New York, NY [*AM radio station call letters*] .... WKDM
New York, NY [*AM radio station call letters*] .... WLIB
New York, NY [*FM radio station call letters*] .... WLTW
New York, NY [*AM radio station call letters*] .... WMCA
New York, NY [*FM radio station call letters*] .... WMXV
New York, NY [*Television station call letters*] .... WNBC
New York, NY [*FM radio station call letters*] .... WNEW
New York, NY [*AM radio station call letters*] .... WNYC
New York, NY [*FM radio station call letters*] .... WNYC-FM
New York, NY [*Television station call letters*] .... WNYC-TV
New York, NY [*FM radio station call letters*] .... WNYE
New York, NY [*Television station call letters*] .... WNYE-TV
New York, NY [*FM radio station call letters*] .... WNYU
New York, NY [*Television station call letters*] .... WNYW
New York, NY [*AM radio station call letters*] .... WOR
New York, NY [*Television station call letters*] .... WPIX
New York, NY [*FM radio station call letters*] .... WPLJ
New York, NY [*FM radio station call letters*] .... WQCD
New York, NY [*AM radio station call letters*] .... WQEW
New York, NY [*FM radio station call letters*] .... WQHT
New York, NY [*FM radio station call letters*] .... WQXR
New York, NY [*FM radio station call letters*] .... WRKS
New York, NY [*FM radio station call letters*] .... WSKQ
New York, NY [*AM radio station call letters*] .... WWRL
New York, NY [*AM radio station call letters*] .... WWRV
New York, NY [*FM radio station call letters*] .... WXRK
New York, NY [*AM radio station call letters*] .... WZRC
New York, NY [*Location identifier FAA*] (FAAL) .... ZNY
New York Ocean Science Laboratory .... NYOSL
New York Ocean Science Laboratory, Montauk, NY [*Library symbol Library of Congress*] (LCLS) .... NMoN
New York Official Department Reports [*A publication*] (DLA) .... NY Off Dept R
New York Oils Ltd. [*Toronto Stock Exchange symbol*] .... NYO
New York On-Line [*Information service or system*] (IID) .... NYOL
New York, Ontario & Western Railway Co. .... NYO & W
New York Operations [*AEC*] (MCD) .... NYO
New York Ordnance District [*Military*] (MUGU) .... NYOD
New York Orthopaedic Hospital, New York, NY [*Library symbol Library of Congress*] (LCLS) .... NNOt
New York Paper Merchants Association (EA) .... NYPMA
New York Philharmonic Symphony Orchestra .... NYPSO
New York Pigment Club (EA) .... NYPC
New York Police Department [*Initialism also used as title of TV series*] .... NYPD
New York Port Authority .... NYPA
New York Port of Embarkation [*Military*] .... NYPE
New York Port of Embarkation [*Military*] .... NYPOE
New York Practice Reports [*A publication*] (DLA) .... NY Pr Rep
New York Practice Reports [*A publication*] (DLA) .... NYPR
New York Press (WDMC) .... NYP
New York Prime Loan Rate [*Finance*] (DS) .... NYPLR
New York Produce Exchange [*Defunct*] (EA) .... NYPE
New York, Providence & Boston Railroad .... NYP & B
New York Psychoanalytic Institute, New York, NY [*Library symbol Library of Congress*] (LCLS) .... NNNPsan
New York Public Interest Research Group .... NYPIRG
New York Public Library [*New York, NY*] .... NYPL
New York Public Library, Albert A. and Henry W. Berg Collection, New York, NY [*Library symbol Library of Congress*] (LCLS) .... NN-B
New York Public Library, Branch Library System, New York, NY [*Library symbol Library of Congress*] (LCLS) .... NN-Br
New York Public Library, Mellon Microfilm Collection, New York, NY [*Library symbol Library of Congress*] (LCLS) .... NN-Mel
New York Public Library, Municipal Reference Library, New York, NY [*Library symbol Library of Congress*] (LCLS) .... NN-M
New York Public Library, New York, NY [*Library symbol Library of Congress*] (LCLS) .... NN
New York Public Library, Public Health Division, New York, NY [*Library symbol Library of Congress*] (LCLS) .... NN-MPH
New York Public Library, Research Library for the Performing Arts at Lincoln Center, New York, NY [*Library symbol Library of Congress*] (LCLS) .... NN-L
New York Public Library, Schomburg Collection, New York, NY [*Library symbol Library of Congress*] (LCLS) .... NN-Sc
New York Public Library, Serials, New York, NY [*OCLC symbol*] (OCLC) .... NYP
New York Publicity Outlet [*A publication*] (WDMC) .... NYPO
New York Publishers Rights and Permissions Group (EA) .... NYPRPG
New York Racing Authority [*Cable-television system*] .... NYRA
New York Railroad Commission Reports [*A publication*] (DLA) .... NYRC
New York Raincoat Manufacturers Association (EA) .... NYRMA
New York Rangers Fan Club (EA) .... NYRFC
New York Record [*A publication*] (DLA) .... NY Rec
New York Reporter [*A publication*] (ILCA) .... NY Reptr
New York Review of Books [*A publication*] (BRI) .... NYRB
New York Revised Laws [*A publication*] (DLA) .... NRE
New York Revised Laws [*A publication*] (DLA) .... NRL
New York Revised Laws [*A publication*] (DLA) .... NYRL
New York Revised Statutes [*A publication*] (DLA) .... NYRS
New York Rights and Permissions Group (EA) .... NYRAPG
New York Road Runners Club (EA) .... NYRRC
New York, Ronkonkoma [*New York*] [*ICAO location identifier*] (ICLI) .... KZNY
New York School of Printing (DGA) .... NYSP
New York Sea Grant Institute [*Albany, NY*] [*Department of Commerce*] (GRD) .... NYSGI
New York Security Dealers Association (EA) .... NYSDA
New York Senate Journal [*A publication*] (DLA) .... NY Sen J
New York Shavians (EA) .... NYS
New York Shipbuilding Corp. .... NYSC
New York Shipping Association (EA) .... NYSA
New York Skirt and Sportswear Association (EA) .... NSSA
New York Society for the Deaf [*Formerly, JSD*] (EA) .... NYSD
New York Society for the Prevention of Cruelty to Children .... NYSPCC
New York Society for the Prevention of Pauperism .... SPP
New York Society Library, New York, NY [*Library symbol Library of Congress*] (LCLS) .... NNS
New York Society of Security Analysts [*New York, NY*] (EA) .... NYSSA
New York State .... NYS
New York State Appellate Division, Law Library, Rochester, NY [*Library symbol Library of Congress*] (LCLS) .... NRAL
New York State Association of Service Stations [*Later, NYSASSRS*] (EA) .... NYSASS
New York State Association of Service Stations and Repair Shops (EA) .... NYSASSRS
New York State Athletic Commission (BARN) .... NYSAC
New York State Bar Association. Bulletin [*A publication*] (DLA) .... NY St Ba A
New York State Bar Association. Bulletin [*A publication*] (DLA) .... NYSBA Bull
New York State Bar Bulletin [*A publication*] (LWAP) .... NY S B BULL
New York State Bulletin (AAGC) .... NY St Bull
New York State Center for Advanced Technology in Computer Applications and Software Engineering [*Syracuse University*] [*Research center*] (RCD) .... CASE
New York State Colonization Society [*Defunct*] (EA) .... NYSCS
New York State Commission on Administration of Justice, Report [*A publication*] (DLA) .... CAJR
New York State Department of Environmental Conservation .... NYSDEC
New York State Department of Environmental Conservation (DOGT) .... NYSDEC
New York State Department of Health, Albany, NY [*OCLC symbol*] (OCLC) .... VXN
New York State Department of Health, Division of Laboratories and Research, Albany, NY [*Library symbol Library of Congress*] (LCLS) .... NAIDH
New York State Department of Labor. Court Decisions of Workmen's Compensation [*A publication*] (DLA) .... NYDLWC Dec
New York State Department of Law Library, Albany, NY [*Library symbol*] [*Library of Congress*] (LCLS) .... NAILL
New York State Department of Mental Hygiene, Institute for Basic Research in Mental Retardation, Staten Island, NY [*Library symbol Library of Congress*] (LCLS) .... NSiIR
New York State Department of Mental Hygiene, Mental Hygiene Research Library, Albany, NY [*Library symbol Library of Congress*] (LCLS) .... NAIMH
New York State Department of Mental Hygiene, Psychiatric Institute, New York, NY [*Library symbol Library of Congress*] (LCLS) .... NNNPsI
New York State Department of Motor Vehicles, Research Library, Albany, NY [*Library symbol Library of Congress*] (LCLS) .... NAIMV
New York State Department of Social Sciences, Social Services and Statistics Library, Albany, NY [*Library symbol Library of Congress*] (LCLS) .... NAISS
New York State Department of State, Community Affairs Library, Albany, NY [*Library symbol Library of Congress*] (LCLS) .... NAIDS
New York State Department Reports [*A publication*] (DLA) .... NY St Dept Rep
New York State Department Reports [*A publication*] (DLA) .... NYSDR
New York State Department Reports [*A publication*] (DLA) .... SDR
New York State Department Reports, Unofficial [*A publication*] (DLA) .... Dept R Un
New York State Division of Criminal Justice Services, Albany, NY [*Library symbol*] [*Library of Congress*] (LCLS) .... NAICJ
New York State E&G [*NYSE symbol*] (TTSB) .... NGE
New York State Education and Research Network, Inc. [*Telecommunications service*] (TSSD) .... NYSERNet
New York State Educational and Research Network .... NYSERNET
New York State Electric & Gas Corp. [*NYSE symbol*] (SPSG) .... NGE
New York State Electric & Gas Corp. [*Associated Press*] (SAG) .... NYEG
New York State Electric & Gas Corp. [*Associated Press*] (SAG) .... NYS
New York State Electric & Gas Corp. [*Associated Press*] (SAG) .... NYSEG
New York State Electric & Gas Corp., Binghamton, NY [*Library symbol Library of Congress*] (LCLS) .... NBiSEG
New York State Energy Research and Development Authority .... NYSERDA
New York State Fruit Testing Cooperative Association (EA) .... NYSFTCA
New York State Historical Association, Cooperstown, NY [*Library symbol Library of Congress*] (LCLS) .... NCooHi
New York State Identification and Intelligence System .... NYSIIS
New York State Institute for Research in Mental Retardation, Staten Island, NY [*OCLC symbol*] (OCLC) .... VVG
New York State Interlibrary Loan [*Network*] .... NYSILL
New York State Inter-Library Loans System (NITA) .... NYSILL

New York State Labor Relations Board Decisions [*A publication*] (DLA)..... NYLRB
New York State Labor Relations Board Decisions and Orders [*A publication*] (DLA) .... NYLRB Dec
New York State Library, Albany, NY [*Library symbol Library of Congress*] (LCLS)............ N
New York State Library, Albany, NY [*OCLC symbol*] (OCLC) .... NYG
New York State Library, General Reference Library, Albany, NY [*Library symbol Library of Congress*] (LCLS) .... N-GR
New York State Library, Law Library, Albany, NY [*Library symbol Library of Congress*] (LCLS) .... N-L
New York State Library, Legislative Reference Library, Albany, NY [*Library symbol Library of Congress*] (LCLS) .... N-LR
New York State Library, Medical Library, Albany, NY [*Library symbol Library of Congress*] (LCLS) .... N-M
New York State Longitudinal Study (EDAC) .... NYLS
New York State Nurses Association, Guilderland, NY [*Library symbol Library of Congress*] (LCLS) .... NGuNA
New York State Psychiatric Institute [*New York State Office of Mental Hygiene*] [*Research center*] (RCD) .... NYSPI
New York State Psychiatric Institute, Medical Library Center of New York, New York, NY [*OCLC symbol*] (OCLC) .... ZPI
New York State Reporter [*A publication*] (DLA) .... NY St
New York State Reporter [*A publication*] (DLA) .... NY St R
New York State Reporter [*A publication*] (DLA) .... NY St Rep
New York State Reporter [*A publication*] (DLA) .... NY St Repr
New York State Reporter [*A publication*] (DLA) .... NY State R
New York State Reporter [*A publication*] (DLA) .... NY State Rep
New York State Reporter [*A publication*] (DLA) .... NYS
New York State Reporter [*A publication*] (DLA) .... NYSR
New York State Reporter [*A publication*] (DLA) .... SR
New York State Reporter [*A publication*] (DLA) .... State R
New York State Reporter [*A publication*] (DLA) .... State Rep
New York State Safe Deposit Association [*New York, NY*] (EA) .... NYSSDA
New York State School of Industrial and Labor Relations, Cornell University, Ithaca, NY [*OCLC symbol*] (OCLC) .... CLR
New York State Science and Technology Foundation (RDA) .... NYSSTF
New York State Supreme Court Law Library, Binghamton, NY [*Library symbol Library of Congress*] (LCLS) .... NBiSC
New York State Supreme Court Law Library, Syracuse, NY [*Library symbol Library of Congress*] (LCLS) .... NSySC
New York State Supreme Court Law Library, Syracuse, NY [*Library symbol Library of Congress*] (LCLS) .... NSySC
New York State Supreme Court Law Library, Utica, NY [*Library symbol Library of Congress*] (LCLS) .... NUtSC
New York State Supreme Court Law Library, White Plains, NY [*Library symbol Library of Congress*] (LCLS) .... NWhpSC
New York State Union Catalog of Film and Video [*Mid-Hudson Library System*] [*Information service or system*] (IID) .... NYSCAT
New York State Union List, Albany, NY [*OCLC symbol*] (OCLC) .... NYS
New York State Union List of Serials, Albany, NY [*Library symbol Library of Congress*] (LCLS) .... NAIULS
New York State Wine Grape Growers, Inc. (EA) .... NYSWGGI
New York Stock Exchange [*New York, NY*] .... N
New York Stock Exchange [*New York, NY*] (EA) .... NYSE
New York Stock Exchange Guide [*Commerce Clearing House*] [*A publication*] (DLA) .... NYSE
New York Superior Court Reports [*A publication*] (DLA) .... NY Super
New York Superior Court Reports [*Various reporters*] [*A publication*] (DLA) .... NY Super Ct
New York Superior Court Reports [*A publication*] (DLA) .... NY Super Ct R
New York Superior Court Reports [*A publication*] (DLA) .... NY Super Ct Rep
New York Superior Court Reports [*A publication*] (DLA) .... NY Supr
New York Superior Court Reports [*A publication*] (DLA) .... NY Supr Ct
New York Superior Court Reports [*A publication*] (DLA) .... NY Supr Ct R
New York Superior Court Reports [*A publication*] (DLA) .... NY Supr Ct Rep
New York Superior Court Reports [*A publication*] (DLA) .... NYS Ct
New York Supplement [*A publication*] (DLA) .... New York Supp
New York Supplement [*A publication*] (DLA) .... NY Supl
New York Supplement [*A publication*] (DLA) .... NY Supp
New York Supplement [*A publication*] (DLA) .... NY Suppl
New York Supplement [*A publication*] (DLA) .... NYS
New York Supplement [*A publication*] (DLA) .... S
New York Supplement Reports [*A publication*] (DLA) .... Supp
New York Supplement, Second Series [*A publication*] (DLA) .... NY Supp 2d
New York Supplement, Second Series [*A publication*] (DLA) .... NYS 2d
New York Supplement, Second Series [*A publication*] (DLA) .... S 2d
New York Supreme Court, Appellate Division Reports [*A publication*] (DLA) .... AD
New York Supreme Court, Appellate Division Reports [*A publication*] (DLA) .... Ap
New York Supreme Court, Appellate Division Reports [*A publication*] (DLA) .... App Div
New York Supreme Court, Appellate Division Reports [*A publication*] (DLA) .... App Div (NY)
New York Supreme Court, Appellate Division Reports [*A publication*] (DLA) .... App Div NY Sup Ct
New York Supreme Court, Appellate Division Reports [*A publication*] (DLA) .... App Div R
New York Supreme Court, Appellate Division Reports [*A publication*] (DLA) .... NY App Div
New York Supreme Court, Appellate Division Reports, Second Series [*A publication*] (DLA) .... AD 2d
New York Supreme Court, Appellate Division Reports, Second Series [*A publication*] (DLA) .... App Div 2d
New York Supreme Court Reports [*A publication*] (DLA) .... Hun

New York Supreme Court Reports [*A publication*] (DLA) .... NY Sup Ct
New York Supreme Court Reports [*A publication*] (DLA) .... NY Suprm Ct
New York Supreme Court Reports [*A publication*] (DLA) .... Sup Ct R (NY)
New York Supreme Court Reports, by Thompson and Cook [*A publication*] (DLA) .... NY Supr Ct Repts (T & C)
New York Supreme Court Reports (Lansing) [*A publication*] (DLA) .... Lansg
New York Supreme Court Reports (Lansing) [*A publication*] (DLA) .... Lansing
New York, Susquehanna & Western Railroad Co. [*AAR code*] .... NYSW
New York Tax Cases [*Commerce Clearing House*] [*A publication*] (DLA) .... NY Tax Cas
New York Tax Exempt Income [*AMEX symbol*] (TTSB) .... XTX
New York Tax Exempt Income Fund [*Associated Press*] (SAG) .... NYTEI
New York Tax Exempt Income Fund [*AMEX symbol*] (SAG) .... XTX
New York Temperance Civic League [*Later, AYE*] (EA) .... NYTCL
New York Term Reports (Caines' Reports) [*A publication*] (DLA) .... NYTR
New York Testing Laboratories, Inc. .... NYT
New York Theatre Annual [*A publication*] .... NYTA
New York Theatre Ballet .... NYTB
New York Theatre Ballet .... NYTB
New York Themis [*New York City*] [*A publication*] (DLA) .... NY Them
New York Theological Seminary .... NYTS
New York Theological Seminary, New York, NY [*Library symbol Library of Congress*] (LCLS) .... NNNT
[*The*] New York Times Biographical File [*The New York Times Co.*] [*Information service or system*] (CRD) .... NYTBIO
New York Times Book Review [*A publication*] (BRI) .... NYTBR
New York Times CI'A' [*AMEX symbol*] (TTSB) .... NYTA
[*The*] New York Times Co. [*Associated Press*] (SAG) .... NY Tim
[*The*] New York Times Co. [*AMEX symbol*] (SPSG) .... NYT
[*The*] New York Times Index [*A publication*] .... TNYTI
New York Times Information Bank .... NYT/IB
New York Times Information Service, Inc. [*Mead Data Central*] [*Database originator and host*] (IID) .... NYTIS
New York Times (Late Edition) [*A publication*] (BRI) .... NYTLa
New York Times, New York, NY [*Library symbol Library of Congress*] (LCLS) .... NNT
New York Times News Service .... NYTNS
New York Transcript [*Numbers 1-11*] [*1861 New York City*] [*A publication*] (DLA) .... NY Trans
New York Transcript Appeals Reports [*A publication*] (DLA) .... NY Trans App
New York Transcript Appeals Reports [*A publication*] (DLA) .... Trans Appeal R
New York Transcript, New Series [*New York City*] [*A publication*] (DLA) .... NY Trans NS
New York Transcript Reports [*A publication*] (DLA) .... NY Trans Rep
New York Turtle and Tortoise Society (EA) .... NYTTS
New York Unconsolidated Laws (McKinney) [*A publication*] (DLA) .... NY Unconsol Laws
New York University .... NYU
New York University, College of Dentistry Library, New York, NY [*OCLC symbol*] (OCLC) .... VXD
New York University, College of Dentistry, New York, NY [*Library symbol Library of Congress*] (LCLS) .... NNU-D
New York University. Conference on Charitable Foundations. Proceedings [*A publication*] (DLA) .... NYU Conf Charitable
New York University. Conference on Charitable Foundations. Proceedings [*A publication*] (DLA) .... NYU Conf Charitable Fdn
New York University, Engineering and Science Library, New York, NY [*Library symbol Library of Congress*] (LCLS) .... NNU-ES
New York University, Fales Collection, New York, NY [*Library symbol Library of Congress*] (LCLS) .... NNU-F
New York University, Fobert F. Wagner Labor Archives, New York Labor Records Survey, New York,NY [*Library symbol*] [*Library of Congress*] (LCLS) .... NNU-LA
New York University, Graduate School of Business Administration, New York, NY [*Library symbol Library of Congress*] (LCLS) .... NNU-B
New York University, Institute of Environmental Medicine, Tuxedo Park, NY [*Library symbol Library of Congress*] (LCLS) .... NNU-IEM
New York University, Institute of Fine Arts, New York, NY [*Library symbol Library of Congress*] (LCLS) .... NNU-FA
New York University, Joe Weinstein Residence Halls Library, New York, NY [*Library symbol Library of Congress*] (LCLS) .... NNU-We
New York University. Law Center. Bulletin [*A publication*] (DLA) .... NYUL Center Bull
New York University, Medical Center, New York, NY [*Library symbol Library of Congress*] (LCLS) .... NNU-M
New York University, Medical Center, New York, NY [*OCLC symbol*] (OCLC) .... VVU
New York University, New York, NY [*Library symbol Library of Congress*] (LCLS) .... NNU
New York University, New York, NY [*OCLC symbol*] (OCLC) .... ZYU
New York University Press (DGA) .... NYUP
New York University Resonance Escape Probability [*Code*] [*Nuclear energy*] (NRCH) .... NUREP
New York University. Review of Law and Social Change [*A publication*] (DLA) .... NYU Rev Law & Soc
New York University, School of Commerce, New York, NY [*Library symbol Library of Congress*] (LCLS) .... NNU-C
New York University School of Continuing Education, Continuing Education in Law and Taxation [*A publication*] (DLA) .... NYULT
New York University, School of Law, New York, NY [*Library symbol Library of Congress*] (LCLS) .... NNU-L
New York University, Tamiment Library, New York, NY [*Library symbol Library of Congress*] (LCLS) .... NNU-T
New York University Tax Institute (DLA) .... NYUTI

New York University, University Heights Library, Bronn, NY [*Library symbol Library of Congress*] (LCLS) .... NNU-H
New York University, Wall Street Library, New York, NY [*Library symbol Library of Congress*] (LCLS) .... NNU-G
New York University, Washington Square Library, New York, NY [*Library symbol Library of Congress*] (LCLS) .... NNU-W
New York Water Color Club [*1890-1941*] (NGC) .... NYWCC
New York Weekly Digest [*A publication*] (DLA) .... NY Week Dig
New York Weekly Digest [*A publication*] (DLA) .... NY Weekly Dig
New York Weekly Digest [*A publication*] (DLA) .... NY Wkly Dig
New York Weekly Digest [*A publication*] (DLA) .... W Dig
New York Weekly Digest [*A publication*] (DLA) .... Week Dig
New York Weekly Digest [*A publication*] (DLA) .... Week Dig (NY)
New York Weekly Digest [*A publication*] (DLA) .... Wkly Dig
New York Wine Council (EA) .... NYWC
New York Wine/Grape Foundation (EA) .... NYWGF
New York World's Fair .... NYWF
New York Yellow Pages, Inc. .... NYYP
New York Zoological Park .... NYZP
New York Zoological Society .... NYZS
New York Zoological Society, New York, NY [*Library symbol Library of Congress*] (LCLS) .... NNZ
New Yorker [*A publication*] (BRI) .... NY
New Yorkers for Abortion Law Repeal (EA) .... NYALR
New York-Pennsylvania League [*Baseball*] .... NYP
New Youth Research Survey [*Religious education test*] .... NYRS
New Yugoslav Law [*A publication*] (DLA) .... New Yugo L
New Zealand [*IYRU nationality code*] (IYR) .... KZ
New Zealand (VRA) .... N Zea
New Zealand [*ANSI two-letter standard code*] (CNC) .... NZ
New Zealand [*MARC country of publication code Library of Congress*] (LCCP) .... nz
New Zealand [*ANSI three-letter standard code*] (CNC) .... NZL
New Zealand [*MARC geographic area code Library of Congress*] (LCCP) .... u-nz--
New Zealand [*International civil aircraft marking*] (ODBW) .... ZK
New Zealand Air Charter [*ICAO designator*] (AD) .... NX
New Zealand Air Force (DAS) .... NZAF
New Zealand Air Services Ltd. [*ICAO designator*] (FAAC) .... ENZ
New Zealand Appeal Reports [*A publication*] (DLA) .... NZ App Rep
New Zealand Army Detachment (CINC) .... NEWZAD
New Zealand Associated Press (BARN) .... NZAP
New Zealand Awards, Recommendations, Agreements, Etc. [*A publication*] (DLA) .... NZ Awards
New Zealand Black [*Mice hybrids*] .... NZB
New Zealand Broadcasting Corp. .... NZBC
New Zealand Broadcasting Service .... NZBS
New Zealand Colonial Law Journal [*A publication*] (DLA) .... NZ Col LJ
New Zealand Consulate General, Library, New York, NY [*Library symbol*] [*Library of Congress*] (LCLS) .... NNZCG
New Zealand Court of Appeals (DLA) .... NZ Ct App
New Zealand Court of Arbitration (DLA) .... NZ Ct Arb
New Zealand Cross (DAS) .... NZC
New Zealand Department of Scientific and Industrial Research, Antarctic Division, Christchurch, New Zealand [*Library symbol*] [*Library of Congress*] (LCLS) .... NzCSI-A
New Zealand Employers' Federation (ODBW) .... NZEF
New Zealand Federation of Labor (ODBW) .... NZFL
New Zealand Gazette Law Reports [*A publication*] (DLA) .... Gaz LR (NZ)
New Zealand Gazette Law Reports [*A publication*] (DLA) .... NZ Gaz LR
New Zealand Gazette Law Reports [*A publication*] (DLA) .... NZGLR
New Zealand Industrial Arbitration Awards [*A publication*] (DLA) .... NZ Ind Arb
New Zealand Institute of Chemistry .... NZIC
New Zealand Institute of Economic Research .... NZIER
New Zealand Jurist [*1873-78*] [*A publication*] (DLA) .... NZ Jur
New Zealand Jurist, New Series [*A publication*] (DLA) .... NZ Jur NS
New Zealand Jurist Reports [*A publication*] (DLA) .... New Zeal Jur R
New Zealand Justice of the Peace [*1876-77*] [*A publication*] (DLA) .... NZJP
New Zealand Kiwifruit Marketing Board .... NZKMB
New Zealand Labour Party [*Political party*] (PPW) .... NZLP
New Zealand Law Journal, Magistrates' Court Decisions [*A publication*] (DLA) .... NZLJMC
New Zealand Law Reports [*A publication*] (DLA) .... Law Rep
New Zealand Law Reports [*A publication*] (DLA) .... LR
New Zealand Law Reports [*A publication*] (DLA) .... New Zeal L
New Zealand Law Reports [*A publication*] (DLA) .... New Zeal LR
New Zealand Law Reports [*A publication*] (DLA) .... NZLR
New Zealand Law Reports, Court of Appeal [*A publication*] (DLA) .... NZLRCA
New Zealand Law Society. Newsletter [*A publication*] (DLA) .... NZ Law Soc N
New Zealand Liaison Officer .... NZLO
New Zealand Merchant Navy (DAS) .... NZMN
New Zealand Meteorological Service [*Marine science*] (OSRA) .... NZMS
New Zealand Ministry of Works and Development, Head Office Library, Wellington, New Zealand [*Library symbol Library of Congress*] (LCLS) .... NzWMW
New Zealand National Airways Corp. [*ICAO designator*] .... NZ
New Zealand National Committee for UNICEF (EAIO) .... UNICEF-NZ
New Zealand Naval Board [*Wellington*] .... NZNB
New Zealand Obese [*Mouse*] [*Medicine*] (DMAA) .... NZO
New Zealand Oceanographic Institute .... NZOI
New Zealand Post Office [*Telecommunications*] .... NZPO
New Zealand Press Association .... NZPA
New Zealand Privy Council Cases [*A publication*] (DLA) .... NZPC Cas
New Zealand Privy Council Cases [*A publication*] (DLA) .... NZPCC
New Zealand Red [*Rabbit*] [*Medicine*] (DMAA) .... NZR
New Zealand Reports [*A publication*] (DLA) .... NZ
New Zealand Reports, Court of Appeals [*A publication*] (DLA) .... NZ Rep
New Zealand Rough Riders [*Military*] (ROG) .... NZRR
New Zealand Sea Frontier .... NZSEAFRON
New Zealand Statutory Regulations [*A publication*] (DLA) .... NZ Stat Regs
New Zealand Supreme Court [*A publication*] (DLA) .... NZSC
New Zealand Taxation Board of Review Decisions [*A publication*] (DLA) .... NZTBR
New Zealand Tourism Office (EA) .... NZTO
New Zealand Tourist and Publicity Office [*Later, NZTO*] (EA) .... NZTP
New Zealand Treaty Series [*A publication*] (DLA) .... NZTS
New Zealand White [*Mice hybrids*] .... NZW
New Zealand-Australia Free Trade Agreement (AD) .... NAFTA
Newair [*Denmark ICAO designator*] (FAAC) .... NAW
Newair [*ICAO designator*] (AD) .... NC
Newair, Inc. [*ICAO designator*] (FAAC) .... HVA
Newalta Corp. [*Toronto Stock Exchange symbol*] .... NAL
Newari [*MARC language code Library of Congress*] (LCCP) .... new
Newark [*New Jersey*] [*Airport symbol*] (AD) .... EWR
Newark [*Delaware*] [*Seismograph station code, US Geological Survey*] (SEIS) .... NED
Newark [*Diocesan abbreviation*] [*New Jersey*] (TOCD) .... NEW
Newark (ABBR) .... NRK
Newark Air Force Station [*Ohio*] .... NAFS
Newark, AR [*Television station call letters*] .... KLEP
Newark, AR [*FM radio station call letters*] .... KLLN
Newark College of Engineering [*New Jersey*] .... NCE
Newark Contract Management District (SAA) .... NECMD
Newark, DE [*AM radio station call letters*] .... WNRK
Newark, DE [*FM radio station call letters*] .... WVUD
Newark Free Library, Newark, DE [*Library symbol Library of Congress*] (LCLS) .... DeN
Newark/International [*New Jersey*] [*ICAO location identifier*] (ICLI) .... KEWR
Newark Island Layered Intrusion [*Geology*] [*Canada*] .... NILI
Newark, NJ [*Location identifier FAA*] (FAAL) .... EWR
Newark, NJ [*Location identifier FAA*] (FAAL) .... EZA
Newark, NJ [*Location identifier FAA*] (FAAL) .... GKQ
Newark, NJ [*Location identifier FAA*] (FAAL) .... LSQ
Newark, NJ [*FM radio station call letters*] .... WBGO
Newark, NJ [*FM radio station call letters*] .... WFME
Newark, NJ [*Television station call letters*] .... WHSE
Newark, NJ [*FM radio station call letters*] .... WHTZ
Newark, NJ [*Television station call letters*] .... WNET
Newark, NJ [*AM radio station call letters*] .... WNJR
Newark, NJ [*FM radio station call letters*] .... WNWK
Newark, NJ [*AM radio station call letters*] (RBYB) .... WXLX
Newark, NY [*AM radio station call letters*] .... WACK
Newark, OH [*Location identifier FAA*] (FAAL) .... HEH
Newark, OH [*Location identifier FAA*] (FAAL) .... RXK
Newark, OH [*AM radio station call letters*] .... WCLT
Newark, OH [*FM radio station call letters*] .... WCLT-FM
Newark, OH [*FM radio station call letters*] .... WNKO
Newark, OH [*Television station call letters*] .... WSFJ
Newark Public Library, Newark, NJ [*Library symbol Library of Congress*] (LCLS) .... NjN
Newark Public Library, Newark, OH [*Library symbol Library of Congress*] (LCLS) .... ONew
Newaygo Carnegie Public Library, Newaygo, MI [*Library symbol Library of Congress*] (LCLS) .... MiNew
Newberg Library Association, Newberg, OR [*Library symbol Library of Congress*] (LCLS) .... OrN
Newberg, OR [*Location identifier FAA*] (FAAL) .... UBG
Newberry Bancorp [*NASDAQ symbol*] (TTSB) .... NEWB
Newberry Bancorp, Inc. [*NASDAQ symbol*] (SAG) .... NEWB
Newberry Bancorp, Inc. [*Associated Press*] (SAG) .... NwbBc
Newberry College, Newberry, SC [*OCLC symbol*] (OCLC) .... NCW
Newberry College, Newberry, SC [*Library symbol Library of Congress*] (LCLS) .... ScNC
Newberry, FL [*FM radio station call letters*] .... WNFQ
Newberry Library, Chicago, IL [*OCLC symbol*] (OCLC) .... IBV
Newberry Library, Chicago, IL [*Library symbol Library of Congress*] (LCLS) .... ICN
Newberry Library/D'Arcy McNickle Center for the History of the American Indian [*Research center*] (RCD) .... CHAI
Newberry Library Family and Community History Center [*Research center*] (RCD) .... FCHC
Newberry, MI [*Location identifier FAA*] (FAAL) .... ERY
Newberry, MI [*FM radio station call letters*] (RBYB) .... WIHC
Newberry, MI [*AM radio station call letters*] .... WNBY
Newberry, MI [*FM radio station call letters*] .... WNBY-FM
Newberry, SC [*Location identifier FAA*] (FAAL) .... EOE
Newberry, SC [*FM radio station call letters*] (RBYB) .... WDXZ
Newberry, SC [*AM radio station call letters*] .... WKDK
Newberry, SC [*AM radio station call letters*] .... WKMG
Newberry's United States District Court, Admiralty Reports [*A publication*] (DLA) .... Newb
Newberry's United States District Court, Admiralty Reports [*A publication*] (DLA) .... Newb Adm
Newberry's United States District Court, Admiralty Reports [*A publication*] (DLA) .... Newberry
Newberry's United States District Court, Admiralty Reports [*A publication*] (DLA) .... Newberry Adm (F)
Newberry's United States District Court, Admiralty Reports [*A publication*] (DLA) .... Newberry's Ad Rep
Newberry-Saluda Regional Library, Newberry, SC [*Library symbol*] [*Library of Congress*] (LCLS) .... ScN

Newbon's Private Bills Reports [*1895-99*] [*England*] [*A publication*] (DLA) ... Newbon
Newborn ... NB
Newborn Calf Serum [*Immunology*] ... NCS
Newborn Convalescent Care Unit [*Medicine*] ... NCCU
Newborn Nursery [*Medicine*] ... NBN
Newborn Rights Society (EA) ... NRS
Newborn, Term, Normal, Female [*Obstetrics*] ... NBTNF
Newborn, Term, Normal, Male [*Obstetrics*] ... NBTNM
Newbridge Communication Network Corp., Kanata, Ontario [*Library symbol National Library of Canada*] (BIB) ... OKNC
Newbridge Communication Neywork Corp., Kanata, ON, Canada [*Library symbol*] [*Library of Congress*] (LCLS) ... CaOKanNC
Newbridge Networks [*NYSE symbol*] (TTSB) ... NN
Newbridge Networks, Inc. [*Associated Press*] (SAG) ... NewbNk
Newbridge Networks, Inc. [*NYSE symbol*] (SAG) ... NN
Newbridge Road Elementary School, North Bellmore, NY [*Library symbol*] [*Library of Congress*] (LCLS) ... NNbeNE
Newbrook Public Library, Alberta [*Library symbol National Library of Canada*] (NLC) ... ANE
Newbrook Public Library, Newbrook, AB, Canada [*Library symbol*] [*Library of Congress*] (LCLS) ... CaANE
Newburg, KY [*AM radio station call letters*] ... WXKN
Newburgh [*New York*] [*Airport symbol*] (OAG) ... SWF
[*The*] **Newburgh & South Shore Railway Co.** [*AAR code*] ... NSS
Newburgh Branch, Lennox and Addington County, Ontario [*Library symbol National Library of Canada*] (BIB) ... ONELAC
Newburgh Free Library, Newburgh, NY [*Library symbol Library of Congress*] (LCLS) ... NNebg
Newburgh, IN [*AM radio station call letters*] ... WGAB
Newburgh, IN [*FM radio station call letters*] ... WJPS
Newburgh, NY [*Location identifier FAA*] (FAAL) ... SKU
Newburgh, NY [*AM radio station call letters*] ... WGNY
Newburgh, NY [*FM radio station call letters*] ... WGNY-FM
Newburgh/Stewart [*New York*] [*ICAO location identifier*] (ICLI) ... KSWF
Newburgh-Ohio Township Public Library, Newburgh, IN [*Library symbol Library of Congress*] (LCLS) ... InNeb
Newbury [*Municipal borough in England*] ... NEWB
Newbury International Ventures, Inc. [*Vancouver Stock Exchange symbol*] ... NIV
Newburyport Birders' Exchange (EA) ... NBE
Newburyport Historical Society, Newburyport, MA [*Library symbol Library of Congress*] (LCLS) ... MNeHi
Newburyport, MA [*AM radio station call letters*] ... WNBP
Newburyport Public Library, Newburyport, MA [*Library symbol Library of Congress*] (LCLS) ... MNe
Newbyth's Manuscript Decisions, Scotch Session Cases [*A publication*] (DLA) ... Newbyth
Newcan Minerals [*Vancouver Stock Exchange symbol*] ... NWN
NewCare Health [*NASDAQ symbol*] (TTSB) ... NWCA
Newcastle [*British ICAO location identifier*] (ICLI) ... EGNT
Newcastle [*British ICAO location identifier*] (ICLI) ... EGRT
Newcastle [*South Africa*] [*ICAO location identifier*] (ICLI) ... FANC
Newcastle [*England*] [*Airport symbol*] (OAG) ... NCL
Newcastle [*South Africa*] [*Airport symbol*] (OAG) ... NCS
Newcastle [*Name of two cities in England*] ... NEWC
Newcastle [*Australia Airport symbol*] (OAG) ... NTL
Newcastle Broadcasting Network [*Australian company broadcasting in Papua New Guinea*] (FEA) ... NBN
Newcastle Business School [*British*] (ODBW) ... NBS
Newcastle Conservatorium of Music [*Australia*] ... NCM
Newcastle Disease [*Virus*] [*Also, NDV*] ... ND
Newcastle Disease Virus [*Also, ND*] ... NDV
Newcastle Disease Virus, L-Kansas Strain ... LK-NDV
Newcastle Public Library Board, Bowmanville, ON, Canada [*Library symbol Library of Congress*] (LCLS) ... CaOBoN
Newcastle Public Library Board, Bowmanville, Ontario [*Library symbol National Library of Canada*] (NLC) ... OBON
Newcastle Public Library, Civic Center, Newcastle, NSW, Australia [*Library symbol Library of Congress*] (LCLS) ... AuNc
Newcastle University Mountaineering Club [*Australia*] ... NUMC
Newcastle Virus Disease [*Veterinary medicine*] (MAE) ... NVD
Newcastle, WY [*Location identifier FAA*] (FAAL) ... ECS
Newcastle, WY [*AM radio station call letters*] ... KASL
Newcastle-Under-Lyme [*City in England*] (ROG) ... NEWC L
Newcastle-Upon-Tyne [*City in England*] (ROG) ... NEW T
Newcastle-Upon-Tyne [*City in England*] ... N-U-T
Newcoast Silver Mines [*Vancouver Stock Exchange symbol*] ... NWV
Newcombe, KY [*Location identifier FAA*] (FAAL) ... ECB
Newcomen Society for the Study of the History of Engineering and Technology [*British*] (EAIO) ... NSSHET
Newcomen Society in North America (EA) ... NSNA
Newcomen Society in North America, Downingtown, PA [*Library symbol Library of Congress*] (LCLS) ... PDowN
Newcomen Society of the United States (EA) ... NSUS
Newcomerstown, OH [*Location identifier FAA*] (FAAL) ... CTW
Newcor, Inc. [*NASDAQ symbol*] (SAG) ... NEWC
Newcor, Inc. [*Associated Press*] (SAG) ... Newcor
Newell Co. [*Associated Press*] (SAG) ... Newell
Newell Co. [*NYSE symbol*] (SPSG) ... NWL
Newell Mirror, Newell, IA [*Library symbol Library of Congress*] (LCLS) ... IaNewM
Newell on Defamation, Slander, and Libel [*A publication*] (DLA) ... Newell Defam
Newell on Slander and Libel [*A publication*] (DLA) ... Newell Sland & L
Newell Public Library, Newell, SD [*Library symbol Library of Congress*] (LCLS) ... SdNe
Newell's Appeals Reports [*48-90 Illinois*] [*A publication*] (DLA) ... Newell
Newell's Illinois Appeal Reports [*A publication*] (DLA) ... New
Newell's Treatise on Malicious Prosecution [*A publication*] (DLA) ... Newell Mal Pros
Newell's Treatise on the Action of Ejectment [*A publication*] (DLA) ... Newell Eject
Newfane Free Library, Newfane, NY [*Library symbol*] [*Library of Congress*] (LCLS) ... NNefL
Newfane Public Library, Newfane, NY [*Library symbol Library of Congress*] (LCLS) ... NNef
Newfield Exploration [*Associated Press*] (SAG) ... NewfEx
Newfield Exploration [*NYSE symbol*] (TTSB) ... NFX
Newfield Exploration Co. [*NYSE symbol*] (SPSG) ... NFX
Newfields Minerals Ltd. [*Toronto Stock Exchange symbol*] ... NWM
Newfoundland [*MARC geographic area code Library of Congress*] (LCCP) ... n-cn-nf
Newfoundland [*with Labrador, a Canadian province*] ... NEWF
Newfoundland [*with Labrador, a Canadian province*] ... NEWFLD
Newfoundland [*with Labrador, a Canadian province*] ... NEWFO
Newfoundland [*with Labrador, a Canadian province*] [*Postal code*] ... NF
Newfoundland [*MARC country of publication code Library of Congress*] (LCCP) ... nfc
Newfoundland [*with Labrador, a Canadian province*] ... NFD
Newfoundland [*with Labrador, a Canadian province*] ... NFLD
Newfoundland [*Canada*] (DD) ... Nfld
Newfoundland & Labrador Corp. ... NALCO
Newfoundland and Labrador Development Corp., St. John's, Newfoundland [*Library symbol National Library of Canada*] (NLC) ... NFSNLD
Newfoundland & Labrador Development Corp., St. John's, NF, Canada [*Library symbol Library of Congress*] (LCLS) ... CaNfSNLD
Newfoundland and Labrador Hydro, St. John's, Newfoundland [*Library symbol National Library of Canada*] (NLC) ... NFSNL
Newfoundland and Labrador Hydro, St. John's, NF, Canada [*Library symbol Library of Congress*] (LCLS) ... CaNfSNL
Newfoundland and Labrador Institute of Fisheries and Marine Technology (Marine Institute), St. John's, New Foundland [*Library symbol National Library of Canada*] (NLC) ... NFSCF
[*The*] **Newfoundland and Labrador Network** [*Canada*] [*Computer science*] (TNIG) ... NLnet
Newfoundland and Prince Edward Island Reports [*Maritime Law Book Co. Ltd.*] [*Canada Information service or system*] (CRD) ... NFL
Newfoundland Archives, St. John's, NF, Canada [*Library symbol Library of Congress*] (LCLS) ... CaNfSA
Newfoundland Base Command [*Army World War II*] ... NBC
Newfoundland Base Command [*Army World War II*] ... NFBC
Newfoundland Capital Corp. Ltd. [*Toronto Stock Exchange symbol*] ... NCC
Newfoundland Club of America (EA) ... NC of A
Newfoundland Club of America (EA) ... NCA
Newfoundland Department of Consumer Affairs and Environment, Environment Division, St. John's, NF, Canada [*Library symbol Library of Congress*] (LCLS) ... CaNfSCAEE
Newfoundland Department of Forest Resources and Lands, Corner Brook, New Foundland [*Library symbol National Library of Canada*] (NLC) ... NFCBF
Newfoundland Department of Forest Resources and Lands, Corner Brook, NF, Canada [*Library symbol*] [*Library of Congress*] (LCLS) ... CaNfCBF
Newfoundland Department of Health, Health Education Division, St. John's, NF, Canada [*Library symbol Library of Congress*] (LCLS) ... CaNfSHE
Newfoundland Department of Health, Public Health Nursing Division, St. John's, NF, Canada [*Library symbol Library of Congress*] (LCLS) ... CaNfSHPH
Newfoundland Department of Justice, Law Library, St. John's, NF, Canada [*Library symbol Library of Congress*] (LCLS) ... CaNfSJL
Newfoundland Department of Mines and Energy, Mineral Development Division, St. John's, NF, Canada [*Library symbol Library of Congress*] (LCLS) ... CaNfSMEM
Newfoundland Department of Mines and Energy, St. John's, Newfoundland [*Library symbol National Library of Canada*] (NLC) ... NFSME
Newfoundland Department of Mines and Energy, St. John's, NF, Canada [*Library symbol Library of Congress*] (LCLS) ... CaNfSME
Newfoundland Department of Municipal Affairs, St. John's, NF, Canada [*Library symbol Library of Congress*] (LCLS) ... CaNfSMA
Newfoundland Department of Rural Development, St. John's, Newfoundland [*Library symbol National Library of Canada*] (NLC) ... NFSRD
Newfoundland Department of Rural Development, St. John's, NF, Canada [*Library symbol Library of Congress*] (LCLS) ... CaNfSRD
Newfoundland Department of Tourism, St. John's, Newfoundland [*Library symbol National Library of Canada*] (NLC) ... NFST
Newfoundland Department of Tourism, St. John's, NF, Canada [*Library symbol Library of Congress*] (LCLS) ... CaNfST
Newfoundland Forest Research Centre, Environment Canada [*Centre de RecherchesForestieres de Terre-Neuve, Environnement Canada*] **St. John's, Newfoundland** [*Library symbol National Library of Canada*] (NLC) ... NFSEC
Newfoundland Forest Service, St. John's, Newfoundland [*Library symbol National Library of Canada*] (NLC) ... NFSFS
Newfoundland Institute for Cold Ocean Science [*Memorial University of Newfoundland*] [*Canada Research center*] (RCD) ... NICOS
Newfoundland Labrador Air Transport Ltd. [*Canada ICAO designator*] (FAAC) ... NLT
Newfoundland Law Reports [*A publication*] (DLA) ... Newf LR
Newfoundland Law Reports [*A publication*] (DLA) ... Newfld LR
Newfoundland Law Reports [*A publication*] (DLA) ... Newfoundl LR
Newfoundland Law Reports [*A publication*] (DLA) ... Nfld LR
Newfoundland Law Reports [*A publication*] (DLA) ... NLR
Newfoundland Light & Power Co., Central Records Library, St. John's, NF, Canada [*Library symbol Library of Congress*] (LCLS) ... CaNfSLP
Newfoundland Light & Power Co. Ltd. [*Toronto Stock Exchange symbol*] ... NFL

Newfoundland Public Libraries Board, St. John's, NF, Canada [*Library symbol Library of Congress*] (LCLS) .... CaNfSG
Newfoundland Public Library Services [*UTLAS symbol*] .... NPL
Newfoundland Public Library Services, St. John's, Newfoundland [*Library symbol National Library of Canada*] (NLC) .... NFSG
Newfoundland Reports [*A publication*] (DLA) .... Nd
Newfoundland Reports [*A publication*] (DLA) .... Newfoundl R
Newfoundland Reports [*A publication*] (DLA) .... NF
Newfoundland Reports [*A publication*] (DLA) .... Nfld R
Newfoundland Revised Statutes [*Canada*] [*A publication*] (DLA) .... Nfld Rev Stat
Newfoundland Select Cases [*A publication*] (DLA) .... Newf Sel Cas
Newfoundland Select Cases [*A publication*] (DLA) .... Newfoundl Sel Cas
Newfoundland Select Cases [*A publication*] (DLA) .... Nfld Sel Cas
Newfoundland Standard Time [*Aviation*] (AIA) .... NST
Newfoundland Status of Women Council, St. John's, Newfoundland [*Library symbol National Library of Canada*] (NLC) .... NFSSW
Newfoundland Status of Women Council, St. John's, NF, Canada [*Library symbol Library of Congress*] (LCLS) .... CaNfSSW
Newfoundland Statutes [*Canada*] [*A publication*] (DLA) .... Nfld Stat
Newfoundland Supreme Court Decisions [*A publication*] (DLA) .... Newf S Ct
Newfoundland Supreme Court Decisions [*Canada*] [*A publication*] (DLA) ...... Nfld
Newfoundland Teachers' Association, St. John's, Newfoundland [*Library symbol National Library of Canada*] ·(NLC) .... NFSTA
Newfoundland Teachers' Association, St. John's, NF, Canada [*Library symbol Library of Congress*] (LCLS) .... CaNfSTA
Newfoundland Telephone Co. Ltd. [*Toronto Stock Exchange symbol*] .... NFT
Newfoundland Tracking Station .... FLD
Newfoundland Tracking Station .... NFD
Newgate Resources [*Vancouver Stock Exchange symbol*] .... NWW
Newhall Land & Farming Co. [*Associated Press*] (SAG) .... Newhal
Newhall Land & Farming Co. [*NYSE symbol*] (SPSG) .... NHL
Newhall Land/Farming [*NYSE symbol*] (TTSB) .... NHL
Newhawk Gold Mines Ltd. [*Toronto Stock Exchange symbol Vancouver Stock Exchange symbol*] .... NHG
Newhouse News Service (WDMC) .... NNS
Newington Branch, Stormont, Dundas, and Glengarry County Library, Ontario [*Library symbol National Library of Canada*] (BIB) .... ONSDG
Newjay Resources Ltd. [*Vancouver Stock Exchange symbol*] .... NJY
Newland, NC [*AM radio station call letters*] (RBYB) .... WECR-AM
Newland, NC [*AM radio station call letters*] .... WJTP
Newland on Contracts [*1806*] (DLA) .... Newl Cont
Newland's Chancery Practice [*A publication*] (DLA) .... Newl Ch PR
Newland's Chancery Practice [*A publication*] (DLA) .... Newl Ch Prac
Newlands Field Laboratory [*University of Nevada - Reno*] [*Research center*] (RCD) .... NFL
Newline Development [*Vancouver Stock Exchange symbol*] .... NWL
Newline Resources Ltd. [*Vancouver Stock Exchange symbol*] .... NWE
Newly Founded Nest [*Ornithology*] .... NFN
Newly Generated .... NG
Newly Industrialized Countries (DFIT) .... NICS
Newly Industrialized Developing Country .... NIDC
Newly Industrializing Country (ECON) .... NIC
Newly Maturing Economy [*Business term*] .... NME
Newly Molded .... NM
Newly Presented (DMAA) .... NP
Newly Qualified to Teach (GFGA) .... NQT
Newly-Independent States [*Of former Soviet Union*] .... NIS
Newly-Industrialized Economy .... NIE
Newman [*Australia Airport symbol*] (OAG) .... ZNE
Newman Ecumenical Seminary, Kansas City, MO [*Library symbol Library of Congress*] (LCLS) .... MoKNE
Newman on Conveyancing [*A publication*] (DLA) .... Newm Conv
Newman Township Library, Newman, IL [*Library symbol Library of Congress*] (LCLS) .... INew
Newman Township Library, Newman, IL [*Library symbol*] [*Library of Congress*] (LCLS) .... INewm
Newman, TX [*Location identifier FAA*] (FAAL) .... EWM
Newman's Electronic Rhyming Dictionary [*Computer software*] (PCM) .... NERD
Newmarket [*Urban district in England*] .... NWMKT
Newmarket, ON [*AM radio station call letters*] .... CKDX
Newmarket Public Library, Newmarket, ON, Canada [*Library symbol Library of Congress*] (LCLS) .... CaOne
Newmarket Public Library, Ontario [*Library symbol National Library of Canada*] (NLC) .... ONE
NewMil Bancorp [*NASDAQ symbol*] (TTSB) .... NMSB
Newmont Gold [*NYSE symbol*] (TTSB) .... NGC
Newmont Gold Co. [*NYSE symbol*] (SPSG) .... NGC
Newmont Gold Co. [*Associated Press*] (SAG) .... NwmtG
Newmont Mining [*NYSE symbol*] (TTSB) .... NEM
Newmont Mining [*Associated Press*] (SAG) .... NewmtM
Newmont Mining Corp. [*NYSE symbol*] (SPSG) .... NEM
Newnan, GA [*Location identifier FAA*] (FAAL) .... CCO
Newnan, GA [*AM radio station call letters*] .... WCOH
Newnan, GA [*FM radio station call letters*] .... WMKJ
Newnan, GA [*AM radio station call letters*] .... WNEA
Newnan Savings Bank [*Associated Press*] (SAG) .... NewSvg
Newnan Savings Bank [*NASDAQ symbol*] (NQ) .... NFSL
Newnan Svgs Bank FSB [*NASDAQ symbol*] (TTSB) .... NFSL
Neworld Bancorp, Inc. [*NASDAQ symbol*] (NQ) .... NWOR
Newpark Resources [*NYSE symbol*] (TTSB) .... NR
Newpark Resources, Inc. [*NASDAQ symbol*] (SAG) .... NPRS
Newpark Resources, Inc. [*Associated Press*] (SAG) .... NwpkRs
Newport [*Vermont*] [*Airport symbol*] (AD) .... EFK
Newport [*Quebec*] [*Geomagnetic observatory code*] .... NEW

Newport [*Washington*] [*Seismograph station code, US Geological Survey*] (SEIS) .... NEW
Newport [*England*] .... NEWP
Newport [*Rhode Island*] .... NP
Newport [*Rhode Island*] [*Airport symbol*] (OAG) .... NPT
Newport [*Oregon*] [*Airport symbol Obsolete*] (OAG) .... ONP
Newport, AR [*Location identifier FAA*] (FAAL) .... EWP
Newport, AR [*AM radio station call letters*] .... KNBY
Newport, AR [*FM radio station call letters*] .... KOKR
Newport Army Ammunition Plant (AABC) .... NAAP
Newport Beach, CA [*Location identifier FAA*] (FAAL) .... JNP
Newport Beach, CA [*FM radio station call letters*] .... KBCD
Newport Beach Public Library, Newport Beach, CA [*Library symbol Library of Congress*] (LCLS) .... CNb
Newport Corp. [*NASDAQ symbol*] (NQ) .... NEWP
Newport Corp. [*Associated Press*] (SAG) .... Newpt
Newport Dock [*British depot code*] .... PILL
Newport Ebbw Junction [*British depot code*] .... NPT
Newport Historical Society, Newport, RI [*Library symbol Library of Congress*] (LCLS) .... RNHi
Newport, KY [*AM radio station call letters*] .... WNOP
Newport, KY [*Television station call letters*] .... WXIX
Newport, NC [*FM radio station call letters*] .... WKQT
Newport, NC [*FM radio station call letters*] (RBYB) .... WMGV-FM
Newport News [*Virginia*] [*Airport symbol*] (OAG) .... PHF
Newport News/Patrick Henry [*Virginia*] [*ICAO location identifier*] (ICLI) .... KPHF
Newport News Public Library, Newport News, VA [*Library symbol Library of Congress*] (LCLS) .... ViNe
Newport News Shipbuilding (DOMA) .... NNS
Newport News Shipbuilding & Dry Dock Co. (DNAB) .... NNSB & DDCO
Newport News Shipbuilding & Dry Dock Co., Newport News, VA [*Library symbol Library of Congress*] .... ViNeN
Newport News, VA [*Location identifier FAA*] (FAAL) .... PJS
Newport News, VA [*AM radio station call letters*] .... WGH
Newport News, VA [*FM radio station call letters*] .... WGH-FM
Newport News, VA [*AM radio station call letters*] .... WTJZ
Newport, NH [*AM radio station call letters*] .... WNTK
Newport, NH [*FM radio station call letters*] .... WXXK
Newport, OR [*Location identifier FAA*] (FAAL) .... JNW
Newport, OR [*FM radio station call letters*] .... KCLM
Newport, OR [*FM radio station call letters*] (RBYB) .... KCRF
Newport, OR [*AM radio station call letters*] .... KLCO
Newport, OR [*AM radio station call letters*] .... KNPT
Newport, OR [*FM radio station call letters*] .... KYTE
Newport Public Library, Newport, NC [*Library symbol*] [*Library of Congress*] (LCLS) .... NcNep
Newport Public Library, Newport, OR [*Library symbol Library of Congress*] (LCLS) .... OrNep
Newport Public Library, Newport, RI [*Library symbol Library of Congress*] (LCLS) .... RN
Newport Restoration Foundation (EA) .... NRF
Newport, RI [*Location identifier FAA*] (FAAL) .... ILZ
Newport, RI [*Location identifier FAA*] (FAAL) .... OTI
Newport, RI [*AM radio station call letters*] .... WADK
Newport, TN [*AM radio station call letters*] .... WLIK
Newport, TN [*AM radio station call letters*] .... WNPC
Newport, TN [*FM radio station call letters*] .... WNPC-FM
Newport, VT [*Location identifier FAA*] (FAAL) .... EFK
Newport, VT [*AM radio station call letters*] .... WIKE
Newport, WA [*AM radio station call letters*] .... KMJY
Newport, WA [*FM radio station call letters*] .... KMJY-FM
Newport, WA [*AM radio station call letters*] .... KUBS
Newport-Vermillion County Library, Newport, IN [*Library symbol Library of Congress*] (LCLS) .... InNep
Newquay [*Urban district in England*] .... NEWQ
Newquay [*England*] [*Airport symbol*] (OAG) .... NQY
News .... N
News (WDMC) .... n
News [*A radio station format*] (WDMC) .... NS
News Agency of Burma .... NAB
News Agency of Nigeria (EY) .... NAN
News and Feature Assistant (WDMC) .... NFA
News and Feature Assistant [*An employee of a TV network*] (WDMC) .... nfa
News and Information Service [*National Broadcasting Co.*] .... NIS
News and Letters Committee (EA) .... NLC
News and Observer Publishing Co., Raleigh, NC [*Library symbol*] [*Library of Congress*] (LCLS) .... NcRNO
News Bank, Inc., Greenwich, CT [*Library symbol Library of Congress*] (LCLS) .... CtGreN
News Communications [*NASDAQ symbol*] (TTSB) .... NCOM
News Communications, Inc. [*NASDAQ symbol*] (SAG) .... NCOM
News Communications, Inc. [*Associated Press*] (SAG) .... NwCm
News Communictions, Inc. [*Associated Press*] (SAG) .... NewsCm
News Corp Ltd. [*Associated Press*] (SAG) .... NewsCorp
[*The*] News Corp. Ltd. [*Associated Press*] (SAG) .... NewsCp
[*The*] News Corp. Ltd. [*NYSE symbol*] (SPSG) .... NWS
News Corp. Ltd ADS [*NYSE symbol*] (TTSB) .... NWS
News Corp. Ltd Pfd ADS [*NYSE symbol*] (TTSB) .... NWSPr
News Director (WDMC) .... ND
News Director (NTCM) .... ND
News Dispatch, Saddle Brook, NJ [*Library symbol Library of Congress*] (LCLS) .... NjSabN
News Editing and Layout System of Newspapers (DGA) .... NELSON
News Editor (ADA) .... NE

News Election Service [*Vote-counting consortium of the major TV networks and two wire services*] ... NES
News Features of India [*Press agency*] ... NFI
News for Farmer Cooperatives [*A publication*] ... NFC
News from Saudi Arabia [*A publication*] (BJA) ... NFSA
News from the Ukraine [*A publication*] ... NFO
News Group Newspapers [*British*] ... NGN
News Information Weekly Service ... NIWS
News International [*An association*] (EA) ... NI
[*The*] **News Is the News** [*Television comedy program*] ... TN^2
News Leader, Netcong, NJ [*Library symbol Library of Congress*] (LCLS) ... NjNetcN
News of the World [*A publication*] (DGA) ... NOW
News, Paterson, NJ [*Library symbol Library of Congress*] (LCLS) ... NjPatNe
News Print Service Bureau ... NPSB
News Program (NTCM) ... N
News Publishing Co., Hammonton, NJ [*Library symbol Library of Congress*] (LCLS) ... NjHamN
News/Retrieval for Your Information [*Dow Jones & Co., Inc.*] [*Information service or system*] (CRD) ... FYI
News/Talk [*Radio programming format*] (WDMC) ... NT
Newsagency Council of South Australia ... NCSA
Newsagency Council of Western Australia ... NCWA
Newsagents' Association of New South Wales and the Australian Capital Territory,Inc. ... NANA
Newscope Resources Ltd. [*NASDAQ symbol*] (SAG) ... NNEXF
Newscope Resources Ltd. [*Toronto Stock Exchange symbol*] ... NSC
Newscope Resources Ltd. [*Associated Press*] (SAG) ... Nwscop
Newscorp Overseas Ltd. [*Associated Press*] (SAG) ... NewOv
Newscorp Overseas Ltd. [*NYSE symbol*] (SPSG) ... NOP
Newscp Overseas Ltd Adj Pref [*NYSE symbol*] (TTSB) ... NOPPrB
Newscp Pverseas Ltd Pref [*NYSE symbol*] (TTSB) ... NOPPrA
Newsday, Garden City, NY [*Library symbol Library of Congress*] (LCLS) ... NGcNe
News-Gazette, Champaign, IL [*Library symbol*] [*Library of Congress*] (LCLS) ... IChamNG
Newsletter ... NEWSL
Newsletter ... NEWSLTR
Newsletter (WDMC) ... NL
Newsletter Association (EA) ... NA
Newsletter Association of America (EA) ... NAA
Newsletter Editors' Association [*Australia*] ... NEA
Newsletter of Engineering Analysis Software [*A publication*] (MCD) ... NEAS
Newsletter of International Labour Studies [*Netherlands*] ... NILS
Newsletter of the Army Medical Department ... NAMD
Newsletter on Legislative Activities [*Council of Europe*] [*A publication*] (DLA) ... Newsl Leg Act
Newsletters Directory [*Later, NIP*] [*A publication*] ... ND
Newsletters in Print [*Formerly, ND*] [*A publication*] ... NIP
Newsline Fan Club (EA) ... NFC
Newspaper ... N
Newspaper ... N/P
Newspaper ... NSWPR
Newspaper (VRA) ... nwspa
Newspaper Advertising Bureau [*New York, NY*] (EA) ... NAB
Newspaper Advertising Co-Op Network (EA) ... NACN
Newspaper Advertising Co-Op Network (EA) ... NACON
Newspaper Advertising Executives Association [*Later, INAME*] (EA) ... NAEA
Newspaper Advertising Executives' Associaton (DOAD) ... NAEA
Newspaper Advertising Sales Association (EA) ... NASA
Newspaper and Mail Deliverers Union of New York and Vicinity (EA) ... NMDU
Newspaper and Printing Industries Pension Fund [*British*] (BI) ... NPIPF
Newspaper Archive Developments Ltd., New Haven, CT [*Library symbol Library of Congress*] (LCLS) ... NewAD
Newspaper Association Managers (EA) ... NAM
Newspaper Association of America [*Reston, VA*] (WDMC) ... NAA
Newspaper Bag (ROG) ... NPB
Newspaper Benevolent and Provident Institution [*British*] (DGA) ... NBPI
Newspaper Collectors Society of America (EA) ... NCSA
Newspaper Comics Council [*Later, NFC*] (EA) ... NCC
Newspaper Composition (PDAA) ... NEWSCOMP
Newspaper Credit Managers' Association (EA) ... NCMA
Newspaper Design Award (DGA) ... NDA
Newspaper Designated Market (WDMC) ... NDM
Newspaper Division, National Library of Canada [*Division des Journaux Bibliotheque Nationale du Canada*] **Ottawa, Ontario** [*Library symbol National Library of Canada*] (NLC) ... OONLN
Newspaper Editor's Course [*Defense Information School*] (DNAB) ... NEC
Newspaper Enterprise Association [*A syndicate*] ... NEA
Newspaper Farm Editors of America (EA) ... NFEA
Newspaper Features Council (EA) ... NFC
Newspaper Food Editors and Writers Association (EA) ... NFEWA
Newspaper Food Editors Conference (EA) ... NFEC
Newspaper Fund (EA) ... NF
[*The*] **Newspaper Guild** (EA) ... TNG
Newspaper in Education Program ... NIE
Newspaper Index [*Bell & Howell Co.*] [*Database*] ... NDEX
Newspaper Indexing Center [*Flint, MI*] ... NIC
Newspaper Institute of America (EA) ... NIA
Newspaper Lines per Minute (DGA) ... NLPM
Newspaper News [*A publication*] ... NN
Newspaper Pagination System [*Typography*] (DGA) ... NPS
Newspaper Personnel Relations Association (EA) ... NPRA
Newspaper Press Directory [*A publication*] (DGA) ... NPD
Newspaper Press Fund (DGA) ... NPF
Newspaper Press Union (DGA) ... NPU
Newspaper Production and Research Center ... NPRC
Newspaper Publishers' Association [*British*] (DCTA) ... NPA
Newspaper Purchasing Management Association (EA) ... NPMA
Newspaper Research Council (EA) ... NRC
Newspaper Society [*British*] ... NS
Newspaper Systems Group (EA) ... NSG
Newspapers in Microform (NITA) ... NIM
Newspapers Mutual Insurance Society Ltd. [*British*] (BI) ... NMIS
Newspapers on Microfilm ... NOM
Newsprint Information Committee [*Defunct*] (EA) ... NIC
Newsprint Service Bureau [*Later, API*] (EA) ... NSB
Newsreel Access Systems, Inc. [*Also, an information service or system*] (IID) ... NAS
Newsstand [*Also N/S*] (WDMC) ... n/s
News-Tribune, Woodbridge, NJ [*Library symbol Library of Congress*] (LCLS) ... NjWooN
Newsweek [*A publication*] (BRI) ... NW
Newswomen's Club of New York (EA) ... NCNY
Newtec Industries Ltd. [*Vancouver Stock Exchange symbol*] ... NEW
NewTel Enterprises Ltd. [*Toronto Stock Exchange symbol*] ... NEL
Newtex SS [*Steamship company*] [*AAR code*] ... NSC
Newtok [*Alaska*] [*Airport symbol*] (OAG) ... WWT
Newtok, AK [*Location identifier FAA*] (FAAL) ... WWT
Newton [*British ICAO location identifier*] (ICLI) ... EGXN
Newton [*Symbol*] [*SI unit of force*] ... N
Newton ... NEW
Newton [*England*] ... NEWT
Newton (NASA) ... nt
Newton ... NT
Newton [*Diocesan abbreviation*] [*Melkite United States*] (TOCD) ... NTN
Newton Abbot [*British depot code*] ... NA
Newton College, Newton, MA [*Inactive*] [*OCLC symbol*] (OCLC) ... NTN
Newton College of the Sacred Heart [*Later, Newton College*] [*Massachusetts*] ... NCSH
Newton College of the Sacred Heart [*Later, Newton College*], **Newton, MA** [*Library symbol Library of Congress*] (LCLS) ... MNtSH
Newton County Enterprise, Kentland, IN [*Library symbol Library of Congress*] (LCLS) ... InKentE
Newton County Recorder's Office, Kentland, IN [*Library symbol Library of Congress*] (LCLS) ... InKentCR
Newton Daily News, Newton, IA [*Library symbol Library of Congress*] (LCLS) ... IaNewtN
Newton Emission Theory [*Physics*] ... NET
Newton Extrapolation Ploynominal (IAA) ... NEP
Newton Free Library, Newton, MA [*Library symbol Library of Congress*] (LCLS) ... MNt
Newton Historical Society, Newton, IA [*Library symbol Library of Congress*] (LCLS) ... IaNewtHi
Newton, IA [*AM radio station call letters*] ... KCOB
Newton, IA [*FM radio station call letters*] ... KCOB-FM
Newton, IA [*Location identifier FAA*] (FAAL) ... TNU
Newton, IL [*FM radio station call letters*] ... WIKK
Newton Junior College [*Massachusetts*] ... NJC
Newton K. Gregg, Novato, CA [*Library symbol Library of Congress*] (LCLS) ... NkG
Newton, KS [*Location identifier FAA*] (FAAL) ... CAC
Newton, KS [*Location identifier FAA*] (FAAL) ... EWK
Newton, KS [*AM radio station call letters*] ... KJRG
Newton, KS [*FM radio station call letters*] ... KOEZ
Newton, MA [*AM radio station call letters*] ... WNTN
Newton, MA [*FM radio station call letters*] ... WZBC
Newton, MS [*AM radio station call letters*] (RBYB) ... WMYQ
Newton, MS [*FM radio station call letters*] (RBYB) ... WMYQ-FM
Newton, NC [*AM radio station call letters*] ... WNNC
Newton, NJ [*Television station call letters*] ... WMBC
Newton, NJ [*AM radio station call letters*] ... WNNJ
Newton, NJ [*FM radio station call letters*] ... WNNJ-FM
Newton per Meter ... N/m
Newton Public Library, Newton, IA [*Library symbol Library of Congress*] (LCLS) ... IaNewt
Newton Public Library, Newton, IL [*Library symbol Library of Congress*] (LCLS) ... INewt
Newton Public Library, Newton, MS [*Library symbol Library of Congress*] (LCLS) ... MsNe
Newton Second per Square Meter (WDAA) ... N-S/M^2
Newton Tool Kit [*Computer science*] ... NTK
Newtonbrook Secondary School, Willowdale, ON, Canada [*Library symbol Library of Congress*] (LCLS) ... CaOTN
Newtonbrook Secondary School, Willowdale, Ontario [*Library symbol National Library of Canada*] (NLC) ... OTN
Newton-Cotes Formula [*Mathematics*] ... NCF
Newton-Evans Research Co., Inc. [*Ellicott City, MD*] [*Information service or system*] (TSSD) ... NERC
Newtonian Potential Function [*Mathematics*] ... NPF
Newtons per Square Meter [*Pascals*] (IDOE) ... N/m^2
Newtown Library Co., Newtown, PA [*Library symbol Library of Congress Obsolete*] (LCLS) ... PNt
Newtown Public Library, Newtown Square, PA [*Library symbol Library of Congress*] (LCLS) ... PNts
Newtownards [*British ICAO location identifier*] (ICLI) ... EGAD
Newvariant Creutzfeldt-Jakob Disease [*Medicine*] ... NVCJD
NewWest Airlines, Inc. [*FAA designator*] (FAAC) ... FGY
NexGen, Inc. [*Associated Press*] (SAG) ... NexGen
NexGen, Inc. [*NASDAQ symbol*] (SAG) ... NXGN
NEXRAD [*Next Generation Weather Radar*] **Product Interface** (USDC) ... NPI
NEXRAD [*Next Generation Weather Radar*] **Product Interface** [*Marine science*] (OSRA) ... NPI

NeXstar Pharmaceutical [*NASDAQ symbol*] (SAG) ..... NXTR
NeXstar Pharmaceuticals [*Associated Press*] (SAG) ..... Nexstar
NeXstar Pharmaceuticals [*NASDAQ symbol*] (TTSB) ..... NXTR
Next [*Computer science*] [*Telecommunications*] ..... n
Next ..... NXT
Next Action (NASA) ..... NA
Next Assembly ..... N/A
Next Assembly ..... NA
Next Assembly Support Table Index [*Aerospace*] (MCD) ..... NASTI
Next Brochure ..... NB
Next Day [*Stock exchange term*] (SPSG) ..... ND
Next Day's Delivery ..... ND
Next European Torus [*Formerly, Joint European Torus (JET)*] ..... NET
Next Full Moon [*Freemasonry*] (ROG) ..... NFM
Next Generation Advanced Vehicle [*Nippon Steel Corp.*] ..... NAV
Next Generation Computer Resources (DWSG) ..... NGCR
Next Generation Internet [*Computer science*] ..... NGI
Next Generation Internet [*A governmental research initiative*] ..... NGI
Next Generation/Notional System [*Army*] ..... NG/NS
Next Generation Space Telescope [*Proposed, 1996*] [*NASA*] ..... NGST
Next Generation Space Telescope [*NASA*] ..... NGST
Next Generation Trainer [*Air Force*] ..... NGT
Next Generation Trainer Aircraft (MCD) ..... NGTA
Next Generation Upper Air System [*National Weather Service*] ..... NEXAIR
Next Generation Weather RADAR [*National Weather Service*] ..... NEXRAD
Next Higher Assembly [*Engineering*] ..... N/H
Next Higher Assembly [*Engineering*] ..... NHA
Next Higher Assembly Removal Frequency [*Engineering*] (MCD) ..... NHAR
Next Higher Authority (MUGU) ..... NHA
Next Higher Repairable Assembly (MCD) ..... NHRA
Next Hop Resolution Protocol [*Computer science*] ..... NHRP
Next In, First Out [*Queuing technique*] ..... NIFO
Next Inferior Rank ..... NIR
Next Instruction Register (NITA) ..... NIR
Next Linear Collider [*Proposed*] ..... NLC
Next Lower Assembly (MCD) ..... NLA
Next Most Significant Digit [*Computer science*] ..... NMSD
Next Most Significant Digit [*Computer science*] ..... NSD
Next Nearest Neighbor [*Chemical physics*] ..... NNN
Next of Kin ..... NK
Next of Kin ..... NOK
Next (or Nearest) New Moon [*Freemasonry*] (ROG) ..... NNM
Next Renewal ..... NR
Next Senior in Command [*Navy*] ..... NSIC
Next Sequential Instruction ..... NSI
Next Standing Order ..... NSO
[*The*] Next Step [*Physics*] ..... TNS
Next System [*Computer science*] ..... NS
Next Task Register ..... NTR
Next to Reading Matter [*Also, NRM*] [*Advertising*] (NTCM) ..... NR
Next to Reading Matter [*Advertising*] (WDMC) ..... NRM
[*The*] Next Trend ..... TNT
Next Visit [*Medicine*] ..... NV
Next Word Request ..... NWR
Nextel Communications [*NASDAQ symbol*] (SAG) ..... CALL
Nextel Communications [*Commercial firm Associated Press*] (SAG) ..... NextelCm
NEXTEL Communic'ns'A' [*NASDAQ symbol*] (TTSB) ..... CALL
Next-Generation GOES [*Geostationary Operational Environmental Satellite*] (USDC) ..... GOES-Next
Next-Generation Internet [*Proposed*] ..... NGI
NextHealth, Inc. [*NASDAQ symbol*] (SAG) ..... NEXT
NextHealth, Inc. [*Associated Press*] (SAG) ..... NextHlth
Nexus Resources Corp. [*Vancouver Stock Exchange symbol Toronto Stock Exchange symbol*] ..... NXS
Nexus Telecomm Sys Wrrt [*NASDAQ symbol*] (TTSB) ..... NXULF
Nexus Telecommns Sys Ltd [*NASDAQ symbol*] (TTSB) ..... NXUSF
Nexus Telecommunication Systems Ltd. [*Associated Press*] (SAG) ..... NexT
Nexus Telecommunication Systems Ltd. [*Associated Press*] (SAG) ..... NexusTel
Nexus Telecommunication Systems Ltd. [*NASDAQ symbol*] (SAG) ..... NXSPC
Nexus Telecommunication Systems Ltd. [*NASDAQ symbol*] (SAG) ..... NXUL
Nexus Telecommunication Systems Ltd. [*NASDAQ symbol*] (SAG) ..... NXUS
Nexus Telecommunication Systems Ltd. [*NASDAQ symbol*] (SAG) ..... NXUW
Nexus Telecommunication Systems Ltd. [*NASDAQ symbol*] (SAG) ..... NXUZ
Nexus Telecommunication Systems Ltd. [*NASDAQ symbol*] (SAG) ..... NXWPC
Nexus Telecommunication Systems Ltd. [*NASDAQ symbol*] (SAG) ..... NXZPC
Nexus Telecommuns Sys Wrrt'A' [*NASDAQ symbol*] (TTSB) ..... NXUWF
Nexus Telecommuns Sys Wrrt'B' [*NASDAQ symbol*] (TTSB) ..... NXUZF
Ney-Allen [*Astronomy*] ..... NA
Neylan Conference (EA) ..... NC
Neyland [*British depot code*] ..... NEY
Nez Perce County District Library, Culdesac Branch, Culdesac, ID [*Library symbol*] [*Library of Congress*] (LCLS) ..... IdLNP-Cu
Nez Perce County District Library, Lapwai Branch, Lapwai, ID [*Library symbol*] [*Library of Congress*] (LCLS) ..... IdLNP-L
Nez Perce County District Library, Nez Perce Branch, Nez Perce, ID [*Library symbol*] [*Library of Congress*] (LCLS) ..... IdLNP-N
Nez Perce County District Library, Peck Branch, Peck, ID [*Library symbol*] [*Library of Congress*] (LCLS) ..... IdLNP-P
Nez Perce County District Library, Winchester Branch, Winchester, ID [*Library symbol*] [*Library of Congress*] (LCLS) ..... IdLNP-W
Nez Perce County Free Library District, Lewiston, ID [*Library symbol Library of Congress*] (LCLS) ..... IdLNP
Nez Perce National Historical Park ..... NEPE
Nezavisna Radnicka Partija Jugoslavije [*Independent Labor Party of Yugoslavia*] [*Political party*] ..... NRPJ

Nezperce Railroad Co. [*AAR code*] ..... NEZP
NFC Ltd. [*Associated Press*] (SAG) ..... NFC
NFC PLC [*AMEX symbol*] (SPSG) ..... NFC
NFC plc ADS [*AMEX symbol*] (TTSB) ..... NFC
NFO Research [*NASDAQ symbol*] (TTSB) ..... NFOR
NFO Research, Inc. [*Associated Press*] (SAG) ..... NFO Rs
NFO Research, Inc. [*NASDAQ symbol*] (SAG) ..... NFOR
N-Formimidoylthienamycin [*Biochemistry*] ..... NFT
N-Formylmethionylphenylalanine [*Biochemistry*] ..... NFP
NFS Financial Corp. [*NASDAQ symbol*] (NQ) ..... NFSF
NGA [*Needlework Guild of America*], Inc. (EA) ..... NGAI
N'Gaoundere [*Cameroon*] [*ICAO location identifier*] (ICLI) ..... FKKN
N'Gaoundere [*Cameroon*] [*Airport symbol*] (OAG) ..... NGE
Ngare Nairobi [*Tanzania*] [*ICAO location identifier*] (ICLI) ..... HTWK
Ngau [*Fiji*] [*ICAO location identifier*] (ICLI) ..... NFNG
Ngau [*Fiji*] [*Airport symbol*] (OAG) ..... NGI
NGC Corp. [*Associated Press*] (SAG) ..... NGC Cp
NGC Corp. [*NYSE symbol*] (TTSB) ..... NGL
Ngebolobo [*Zaire*] [*ICAO location identifier*] (ICLI) ..... FZBP
Ngerengere [*Tanzania*] [*ICAO location identifier*] (ICLI) ..... HTNG
Ngi [*Zaire*] [*ICAO location identifier*] (ICLI) ..... FZDH
N'Giva [*Angola*] [*ICAO location identifier*] (ICLI) ..... FNGI
N-Glycidylpyrrolidone [*Organic chemistry*] ..... NGP
Ngoma [*Zambia*] [*ICAO location identifier*] (ICLI) ..... FLNA
Ngoma [*Zambia*] [*Airport symbol*] (AD) ..... ZGM
N'Gongo [*Congo*] [*ICAO location identifier*] (ICLI) ..... FCMN
N'Guigmi [*Niger*] [*ICAO location identifier*] (ICLI) ..... DRZN
N'Guigmi [*Niger*] [*Airport symbol*] (AD) ..... GUG
Ngukurr [*Airport symbol*] ..... RPM
Ngultrum [*Monetary unit*] [*Bhutan*] (BARN) ..... N
Ngultrum [*Monetary unit*] [*Bhutan*] (BARN) ..... Nu
N'Gunza [*Angola*] [*ICAO location identifier*] (ICLI) ..... FNGU
Ngwane National Liberatory Congress [*Swaziland*] ..... NNLC
NHANES [*National Health and Nutritional Examination Survey*] Epidemiologic Follow-Up Study [*Department of Health and Human Services*] (GFGA) ..... NHEFS
Nhatrang [*Vietnam*] [*Seismograph station code, US Geological Survey Closed*] (SEIS) ..... NHA
Nhatrang [*Viet Nam*] [*ICAO location identifier*] (ICLI) ..... VVNT
N-Hexylcarborane [*Rocket fuel*] (RDA) ..... NHC
Nhill [*Victoria, Australia*] [*Airport symbol*] (AD) ..... ANH
Nhlangano [*Swaziland*] [*ICAO location identifier*] (ICLI) ..... FDGD
NHP, Inc. [*Associated Press*] (SAG) ..... NHP
NHP, Inc. [*NASDAQ symbol*] (SAG) ..... NHPI
NHS Financial [*NASDAQ symbol*] (TTSB) ..... NHSL
N-Hydroxysuccinimide [*Organic chemistry*] ..... NHS
N-Hydroxysuccinimidyl Palmitate [*Organic chemistry*] ..... NHSP
NIACET Corporation, Niagara Falls, NY [*Library symbol Library of Congress*] (LCLS) ..... NNiaNC
Niacin Equivalent ..... NE
Niafunke [*Mali*] [*ICAO location identifier*] (ICLI) ..... GANF
Niag Moh Pwr 3.40% Pfd [*NYSE symbol*] (TTSB) ..... NMKPrA
Niag Moh Pwr 3.60% Pfd [*NYSE symbol*] (TTSB) ..... NMKPrB
Niag Moh Pwr 3.90% Pfd [*NYSE symbol*] (TTSB) ..... NMKPrC
Niag Moh Pwr 4.10% Pfd [*NYSE symbol*] (TTSB) ..... NMKPrD
Niag Moh Pwr 4.85% Pfd [*NYSE symbol*] (TTSB) ..... NMKPrE
Niag Moh Pwr 5.25% Pfd [*NYSE symbol*] (TTSB) ..... NMKPrG
Niag Moh Pwr 7.72% Pfd [*NYSE symbol*] (TTSB) ..... NMKPrI
Niagar Corp. Wrrt [*NASDAQ symbol*] (TTSB) ..... NIAGW
Niagara (ROG) ..... NIAG
Niagara College of Applied Arts and Technology, Library Technician Program, Welland, ON, Canada [*Library symbol*] [*Library of Congress*] (LCLS) ..... CaOWeNL
Niagara College of Applied Arts and Technology, Welland, ON, Canada [*Library symbol Library of Congress*] (LCLS) ..... CaOWeN
Niagara College of Applied Arts and Technology, Welland, Ontario [*Library symbol National Library of Canada*] (NLC) ..... OWEN
Niagara Corp. [*NASDAQ symbol*] (SAG) ..... NIAG
Niagara Corp. [*Associated Press*] (SAG) ..... Niag
Niagara Corp. [*NASDAQ symbol*] (TTSB) ..... NIAG
Niagara Corp. [*Associated Press*] (SAG) ..... NiagCp
Niagara County Community College [*UTLAS symbol*] ..... NCC
Niagara County Community College, Niagara Falls, NY [*Library symbol Library of Congress*] (LCLS) ..... NNiaC
Niagara County Community College, Sanborn, NY [*OCLC symbol*] (OCLC) ..... YIN
Niagara County Historical Society, Lockport, NY [*Library symbol Library of Congress*] (LCLS) ..... NLockNHi
Niagara Falls/International [*New York*] [*ICAO location identifier*] (ICLI) ..... KIAG
Niagara Falls Memorial Medical Center, Medical Library, Niagara Falls, NY [*Library symbol Library of Congress*] (LCLS) ..... NNiaMed
Niagara Falls, NY [*Location identifier FAA*] (FAAL) ..... IAG
Niagara Falls, NY [*AM radio station call letters*] ..... WHLD
Niagara Falls, NY [*AM radio station call letters*] ..... WJJL
Niagara Falls, NY [*FM radio station call letters*] ..... WKSE
Niagara Falls, ON [*AM radio station call letters*] ..... CJRN
Niagara Falls Public Library, Niagara Falls, NY [*Library symbol Library of Congress*] (LCLS) ..... NNia
Niagara Falls Public Library, Niagara Falls, ON, Canada [*Library symbol Library of Congress*] (LCLS) ..... CaONf
Niagara Falls Public Library, Ontario [*Library symbol National Library of Canada*] (NLC) ..... ONF
Niagara Frontier Tariff Bureau ..... NFTB
Niagara Frontier Tariff Bureau, Inc., Buffalo NY [*STAC*] ..... NFB
Niagara Historical Society, Niagara-On-The-Lake, ON, Canada [*Library symbol Library of Congress*] (LCLS) ..... CaONHi

Niagara Historical Society, Niagara-On-The-Lake, Ontario [*Library symbol National Library of Canada*] (NLC) .... ONHI
Niagara Institute (EA) .... NI
Niagara Institute for International Studies [*Canada*] .... NIIS
Niagara Junction Railway Co. [*Absorbed into Consolidated Rail Corp.*] [*AAR code*] .... NIAJ
Niagara Moh Pwr 9.50% Pfd [*NYSE symbol*] (TTSB) .... NMKPrM
Niagara Moh Pwr Adj Rt A Pfd [*NYSE symbol*] (TTSB) .... NMKPr
Niagara Mohawk Power Corp. [*Associated Press*] (SAG) .... NiaM
Niagara Mohawk Power Corp. [*Associated Press*] (SAG) .... NiaMP
Niagara Mohawk Power Corp. [*NYSE symbol*] (SPSG) .... NMK
Niagara Mohawk Pwr [*NYSE symbol*] (TTSB) .... NMK
Niagara Mohawk Pwr Adj C Pfd [*NYSE symbol*] (TTSB) .... NMKPrK
Niagara Regional Library, Saint Catharines, ON, Canada [*Library symbol Library of Congress Obsolete*] (LCLS) .... CaOStCNR
Niagara, St. Catharines & Toronto [*AAR code*] .... NSCT
Niagara University (GAGS) .... Niagara U
Niagara University, Niagara University, NY [*Library symbol Library of Congress*] (LCLS) .... NNiaU
Niagara University, Niagara University, NY [*OCLC symbol*] (OCLC) .... VVN
Niagara-On-The-Lake [*Ontario*] .... N-O-T-L
Niagara-on-the-Lake Public Library, Niagara-on-the-Lake, ON, Canada [*Library symbol*] [*Library of Congress*] (LCLS) .... CaONOL
Niagara-On-The-Lake Public Library, Ontario [*Library symbol National Library of Canada*] (BIB) .... ONOL
Niamey [*Niger*] [*ICAO location identifier*] (ICLI) .... DRRR
Niamey [*Niger*] [*ICAO location identifier*] (ICLI) .... DRRV
Niamey [*Niger*] [*Airport symbol*] (OAG) .... NIM
Niamey Airport [*Niger*] [*ICAO location identifier*] (ICLI) .... DRRN
Niamtougou [*Togo*] [*ICAO location identifier*] (ICLI) .... DXNG
Nibbling Template .... NITP
NIC [*Naval Intelligence Center*] Analyst Support Facility .... NASF
Ni-Cal Developments Ltd. [*Vancouver Stock Exchange symbol*] .... NDL
Ni-Cal Developments Ltd. (MHDW) .... NICLF
Nicander [*Second century BC*] [*Classical studies*] (OCD) .... Nic
Nicaragua [*MARC geographic area code Library of Congress*] (LCCP) .... ncnq--
Nicaragua [*ANSI two-letter standard code*] (CNC) .... NI
Nicaragua [*ANSI three-letter standard code*] (CNC) .... NIC
Nicaragua (VRA) .... Nic
Nicaragua .... NICAR
Nicaragua [*MARC country of publication code Library of Congress*] (LCCP) .... nq
Nicaragua [*License plate code assigned to foreign diplomats in the US*] .... QU
Nicaragua [*International civil aircraft marking*] (ODBW) .... YN
Nicaragua Interfaith Committee for Action (EA) .... NICA
Nicaragua Medical Aid (EA) .... NMA
Nicaragua Network (EA) .... NN
Nicaragua Peace Fleet [*Defunct*] (EA) .... NPF
Nicaragua Solidarity Campaign (EAIO) .... NSC
Nicaragua-Honduras Education Project (EA) .... NHEP
Nicaraguan Campaign Medal .... NCM
Nicaraguan Exile Relocation Program [*CIA*] .... NERP
Nicaraguan Humanitarian Coalition (EA) .... NHC
Nicaraguan Information Center (EA) .... NIC
Nicaraguan International Rescue from Communism (PD) .... SINC
Nicaraguan Resistance [*An association*] (EA) .... NR
Nicaraguan Telecommunication by Satellite [*Commercial firm*] .... NICATELSAT
Nicaraguense de Aviacion SA [*Nicaragua*] [*ICAO designator*] (FAAC) .... NICA
Nicaraguense de Aviacion SA [*Nicaragua*] [*ICAO designator*] (FAAC) .... NIS
Nicaro [*Cuba*] [*Airport symbol Obsolete*] (OAG) .... ICR
Nicaro [*Cuba ICAO location identifier*] (ICLI) .... MUNC
Nice [*France*] [*Airport symbol*] (OAG) .... NCE
Nice/Cote D'Azur [*France ICAO location identifier*] (ICLI) .... LFMN
Nice Jewish Girl [*Slang*] .... NJG
Nice/Mont Agel [*France ICAO location identifier*] (ICLI) .... LFMJ
Nice Safe Man [*Slang*] .... NSM
NICE-Systems ADR [*NASDAQ symbol*] (TTSB) .... NICEY
Niceville, FL [*FM radio station call letters*] .... WNCV
Nichibei Fujinkai [*An association*] .... NF
Nichiren Shoshu of the UK [*Buddhist organization*] (DI) .... NSUK
Nichiren Shoshu Soka Gakkai of America [*Buddhist organization*] (EA) .... NSA
Nicholas Data [*Vancouver Stock Exchange symbol*] .... NDS
Nicholas de Aquila [*Flourished, 1197-1217*] [*Authority cited in pre-1607 legal work*] (DSA) .... N de Aqi
Nicholas on Adulterine Bastardy [*A publication*] (DLA) .... Nich Adult Bast
Nicholasville, KY [*AM radio station call letters*] .... WCGW
Nicholasville, KY [*FM radio station call letters*] (RBYB) .... WLTO
Nicholasville, KY [*AM radio station call letters*] .... WNVL
Nicholl, Hare, and Carrow [*1835-55*] [*A publication*] (DLA) .... Nicholl H & C
Nicholl, Hare, and Carrow's Railway and Canal Cases [*1835-55*] [*A publication*] (ILCA) .... Nic H & C
Nicholl, Hare, and Carrow's Railway and Canal Cases [*1835-55*] [*A publication*] (DLA) .... Nic Ha C
Nicholl, Hare, and Carrow's Railway and Canal Cases [*1835-55*] [*A publication*] (DLA) .... Nich H & C
Nicholl, Hare, and Carrow's Railway Cases [*1835-55*] [*A publication*] (DLA) .... RC
Nicholls and Stops' Reports [*1897-1904*] [*Tasmania*] [*A publication*] [*A publication*] (DLA) .... N & S
Nicholls State University, Ellender Memorial Library, Thibodaux, LA [*OCLC symbol*] (OCLC) .... LNS
Nicholls State University, Thibodaux, LA [*Library symbol Library of Congress*] (LCLS) .... LTF
Nichols Air Service, Inc. [*ICAO designator*] (FAAC) .... CBL
Nichols Library, Naperville, IL [*Library symbol Library of Congress*] (LCLS) .... INap
Nichols Research [*NASDAQ symbol*] (TTSB) .... NRES
Nichols Research Corp. [*Associated Press*] (SAG) .... NichRs

Nichols Research Corp. [*NASDAQ symbol*] (NQ) .... NRES
Nichols-Cahill's Annotated New York Civil Practice Acts [*A publication*] (DLA) .... Nichols-Cahill
Nicholson Memorial Library, Garland, TX [*Library symbol Library of Congress*] (LCLS) .... TxGar
Nicholson Peninsula, NT [*ICAO location identifier*] (ICLI) .... CYUC
Nicholson's Manuscript Decisions, Scotch Session Cases [*A publication*] (DLA) .... Nicholson
Nichrome (IAA) .... N
Nickajack Dam [*TVA*] .... ND
Nickel [*Chemical element*] .... Ni
Nickel (VRA) .... ni
Nickel [*Watchmaking*] (ROG) .... NIK
Nickel .... NKL
Nickel Alkaline Battery .... NAB
Nickel Cadmium (IAA) .... NC
Nickel Cadmium (NG) .... NICAD
Nickel Cadmium (MCD) .... NICD
Nickel Chromium [*Alloy*] [*Trade name*] .... NICHROME
Nickel Clad .... NC
Nickel Copper .... NICOP
Nickel Copper [*Freight*] .... NKL C
Nickel Development Institute (EAIO) .... NiDI
Nickel Electroformed Mold .... NEM
Nickel Equivalent [*Coinage*] .... NE
Nickel Faced (DGA) .... NF
Nickel Faced (DGA) .... NKL FCD
Nickel Offsets Ltd. [*Toronto Stock Exchange symbol*] .... NOF
Nickel Plated [*Guns*] .... NP
Nickel Producers Environmental Research Association .... NIPERA
Nickel Rim Mines Ltd. [*Toronto Stock Exchange symbol*] .... NIK
Nickel Silver [*Used in minting coins*] .... NS
Nickel Steel .... NS
Nickel Titanium Naval Ordnance Laboratory [*An alloy named by William Buehler of the NOL*] (KSC) .... NITINOL
Nickel-Base Alloy .... NBA
Nickel-Cadmium .... Ni-Cd
Nickel-Cadmium Battery .... NCB
Nickel-Cadmium Rechargeable Cell .... NCRC
Nickel-Chromium Honeycomb Panel .... NCHP
Nickel-Chromium Panel .... NCP
Nickel-Coated Graphite [*Materials technology*] .... NCG
Nickel-Copper Alloy (MSA) .... NCA
Nickel-Iron Alloy .... NIA
Nickel-Iron Film .... NIF
Nickel-Iron System .... NIS
Nickel-Metal Hydride [*Organic chemistry*] (PS) .... NiMH
Nickelodeon [*Cable television channel*] .... NICK
Nickelodeon Industries Corp. [*Vancouver Stock Exchange symbol*] .... NCK
Nickel-Silver .... NI-SIL
Nickerson, C. R., San Francisco CA [*STAC*] .... NCR
Nickerson RPB Ltd. [*British*] (IRUK) .... NRPB
Nickling Resources, Inc. [*Vancouver Stock Exchange symbol*] .... NIC
Nickname .... nick
Nic-Nik Resources [*Vancouver Stock Exchange symbol*] .... NNK
Nicola Valley Museum-Archives, Merritt, British Columbia [*Library symbol National Library of Canada*] (NLC) .... BMNV
Nicolas' Adulterine Bastardy [*1836*] [*A publication*] (DLA) .... Nic Adult Bast
Nicolaus Bellonus [*Flourished, 1542-47*] [*Authority cited in pre-1607 legal work*] (DSA) .... Nic Bel
Nicolaus Boerius [*Authority cited in pre-1607 legal work*] (DSA) .... Nic Boe
Nicolaus de Alexandria [*Authority cited in pre-1607 legal work*] (DSA) .... Nico Alex
Nicolaus de Tudeschis [*Deceased, 1445*] [*Authority cited in pre-1607 legal work*] (DSA) .... Ni
Nicolaus de Tudeschis [*Deceased, 1445*] [*Authority cited in pre-1607 legal work*] (DSA) .... Nic
Nicolaus de Tudeschis [*Deceased, 1445*] [*Authority cited in pre-1607 legal work*] (DSA) .... Nico
Nicolaus Furiosus [*Flourished, 12th century*] [*Authority cited in pre-1607 legal work*] (DSA) .... N
Nicolaus Furiosus [*Flourished, 12th century*] [*Authority cited in pre-1607 legal work*] (DSA) .... Ni
Nicolaus Rufulus [*Flourished, 13th century*] [*Authority cited in pre-1607 legal work*] (DSA) .... N Ru
Nicolaus Rufulus [*Flourished, 13th century*] [*Authority cited in pre-1607 legal work*] (DSA) .... Nic R
Nicolaus Rufulus [*Flourished, 13th century*] [*Authority cited in pre-1607 legal work*] (DSA) .... NR
Nicolaus Rufulus [*Flourished, 13th century*] [*Authority cited in pre-1607 legal work*] (DSA) .... Nic R
Nicolaus (Siculus Doctor) de Tudeschis [*Deceased, 1445*] [*Authority cited in pre-1607 legal work*] (DSA) .... Nic Sic Do
Nicolet College, Learning Resources Center, Rhinelander, WI [*OCLC symbol*] (OCLC) .... WNL
Nicolet Federated Library System [*Library network*] .... NFLS
Nicoll and Flaxman on Registration [*A publication*] (DLA) .... Nic & Fl Reg
Nicolle-Novy-MacNeal [*Medium*] [*Microbiology*] (DAVI) .... NNM
Nicolle-Novy-MacNeal [*Medium*] [*Medicine*] (MEDA) .... NNN
Nicollet Process Engineering, Inc. [*Associated Press*] (SAG) .... Nicollet
Nicollet Process Engineering, Inc. [*NASDAQ symbol*] (SAG) .... NPET
Nicollet Process Engr [*NASDAQ symbol*] (TTSB) .... NPET
Nicolson's Elections in Scotland [*A publication*] (DLA) .... Nic Elec
NICOR, Inc. [*Formerly, Northern Illinois Gas Co.*] [*NYSE symbol*] (SPSG) .... GAS
NICOR, Inc. [*Formerly, Northern Illinois Gas Co.*] [*Associated Press*] (SAG) .... NICOR

Nicorandil [*Biochemistry*] ... NCR
Nicosia [*Cyprus*] [*ICAO location identifier*] (ICLI) ... LCCC
Nicosia [*Cyprus*] [*ICAO location identifier*] (ICLI) ... LCNC
Nicosia [*Cyprus*] [*ICAO location identifier*] (ICLI) ... LCRR
Nicosia [*Cyprus*] [*Airport symbol*] (AD) ... NIC
Nicotiana mesophilia [*Tobacco*] ... Nm
Nicotiana tabacum [*Tobacco*] ... Nt
Nicotiana Velutina Mosaic Virus [*Plant pathology*] ... NVMV
Nicotinamide [*Also, NAA*] [*Vitamin*] ... N
Nicotinamide Adenine Dinucleotide (AD) ... NAD/NADH
Nicotinamide Adenine Dinucleotide Glycohydrolase [*An enzyme*] (DMAA) ... NADG
Nicotinamide Adenine Dinucleotide Phosphate (AD) ... nadp
Nicotinamide Adenine Dinucleotide Phosphate [*An enzyme*] (DMAA) ... NAPH
Nicotinamide Cytosine Dinucleotide [*Biochemistry*] ... NCD
Nicotinamide-Adenine Dinucleotide [*Preferred form, but also see ARPPRN, DPN, NADH*] [*Biochemistry*] ... NAD
Nicotinamide-Adenine Dinucleotide Glycohydrolase [*Also, DPNase*] [*An enzyme*] ... NADase
Nicotinamide-Adenine Dinucleotide Phosphate [*Preferred form, but see also TPN*] [*Biochemistry*] ... NADP
Nicotinamide-Adenine Dinucleotide Phosphate (Reduced) [*Preferred form, but see also TPNH*] [*Biochemistry*] ... NADPH
Nicotinamide-Adenine Dinucleotide (Reduced) [*See also NAD*] [*Biochemistry*] ... NADH
Nicotinamide-Mononucleotide [*Biochemistry*] ... NMN
Nicotinamidenucleotide Phosphoribohydrolase [*An enzyme*] ... NMNase
Nicotine Chewing Gum (PDAA) ... NCG
Nicotine-Replacement Therapy [*Medicine*] ... NRT
Nicotine-Stimulated Neurophysin [*Biochemistry*] ... NSN
Nicotinic Acetylcholine Receptor [*Immunology*] ... NAChR
Nicotinic Acid [*Biochemistry*] ... NA
Nicotinic Acid Adenine Dinucleotide [*Biochemistry*] ... NAAD
Nicotinic Acid Amide [*Also, N*] ... NAA
Nicotinic Acid Dehydrogenase [*An enzyme*] (AAMN) ... NAD
Nicotinyl Alcohol [*Biochemistry*] (MAE) ... Nic
Nicoya [*Costa Rica*] [*Seismograph station code, US Geological Survey*] (SEIS) ... AR8
Nicoya [*Costa Rica*] [*ICAO location identifier*] (ICLI) ... MRNC
Nicoya [*Costa Rica*] [*Airport symbol*] (AD) ... NCT
Nictitating Membrane [*Animal anatomy*] ... NM
Nictitating Membrane Response [*Neurophysiology*] ... NMR
Niddah (BJA) ... Nid
Niece (ADA) ... N
Niederfrequenz [*Audio Frequency*] [*German military - World War II*] ... NF
Niedersachsische Staats- und Universitatsbibliothek, Gottingen, Germany [*Library symbol Library of Congress*] (LCLS) ... GyGoN
Niedersachsische Staatsarchiv, Wolfenbuttel, Germany [*Library symbol Library of Congress*] (LCLS) ... GyWoS
Niedersachsischer Zeitschriftennachweis [*Deutsches Bibliotheksinstitut*] [*Germany Information service or system*] (CRD) ... NZN
Niederstetten/Bad Mergentheim [*Germany ICAO location identifier*] (ICLI) ... EDPT
Niedzica [*Poland*] [*Seismograph station code, US Geological Survey*] (SEIS) ... NIE
Nieghborhood Electric Vehicle ... NEV
Niello (VRA) ... niel
Nielsbohrium [*Proposed name and symbol for recently-discovered element*] ... Ns
Nielsen Broadcast Index [*A. C. Nielsen Co.*] (NTCM) ... NBI
Nielsen [*A. C.*] **Co.** [*Commercial firm*] (WDMC) ... ACN
Nielsen Coverage Service [*A.C. Nielson Co.*] (DOAD) ... NCS
Nielsen Drug Index [*Marketing*] (DOAD) ... NDI
Nielsen Engineering & Research, Inc. ... NEAR
Nielsen Food Index [*Marketing*] (DOAD) ... NFI
Nielsen Home Video Index [*A. C. Nielsen Co.*] (NTCM) ... NHI
Nielsen Station Index [*Nielsen Media Research*] [*Information service or system*] ... NSI
Nielsen Television Area (WDAA) ... NTA
Nielsen Television Index [*Nielsen Media Research*] [*Information service or system*] ... NTI
Nielsen-Kellerman ... NK
Nielson Audience Composition ... NAC
Nielson Audience Demographic Report [*A publication*] (DOAD) ... NAD
Nielson Clearing House [*A.C. Nielson Co.*] (DOAD) ... NCH
Nieman Foundation (EA) ... NF
Niemann-Pick Disease [*Medicine*] ... NPD
Niemann-Pick Type C [*Disease*] [*Medicine*] ... NP-C
Niemegk [*German Democratic Republic*] [*Geomagnetic observatory code*] ... NGK
Nient Culpable [*Not Guilty*] [*Latin Legal term*] (DLA) ... Nient Cul
Nies Babylonian Collection [*Yale University*] (BJA) ... NBC
Nietzsche Society (EA) ... NS
Nieuw Front [*New Front*] [*Suriname*] [*Political party*] (EY) ... NF
Nieuw Milligen [*Netherlands ICAO location identifier*] (ICLI) ... EHMC
Nieuw Milligen [*Netherlands ICAO location identifier*] (ICLI) ... EHML
Nieuw Nickerie [*Surinam*] [*Airport symbol*] (OAG) ... ICK
Nieuwe Internationale Orde [*Netherlands*] ... NIO
Nieuwe Vertaling Nederlands Bijbelgenootschap [*A publication*] (BJA) ... NBG
Nieuwoudtville [*South Africa*] [*ICAO location identifier*] (ICLI) ... FANV
Nieve [*Bolivia*] [*ICAO location identifier*] (ICLI) ... SLNV
Nieves M. Flores Memorial Library, Agana, Guam [*Library symbol Library of Congress*] (LCLS) ... GuaAF
Nifedipine [*Pharmacology*] ... N
Nifedipine [*Pharmacology*] ... NIF
Niger [*MARC geographic area code Library of Congress*] (LCCP) ... f-ng--
Niger [*ANSI two-letter standard code*] (CNC) ... NE
Niger [*ANSI three-letter standard code*] (CNC) ... NER
Niger [*MARC country of publication code Library of Congress*] (LCCP) ... ng
Niger [*Black*] [*Pharmacy*] ... NIG
Niger River and Basin [*MARC geographic area code Library of Congress*] (LCCP) ... fi----
Niger-Congo [*MARC language code Library of Congress*] (LCCP) ... nic
Nigeria [*MARC geographic area code Library of Congress*] (LCCP) ... f-nr--
Nigeria [*ANSI two-letter standard code*] (CNC) ... NG
Nigeria [*ANSI three-letter standard code*] (CNC) ... NGA
Nigeria ... NIG
Nigeria (VRA) ... Nigr
Nigeria [*MARC country of publication code Library of Congress*] (LCCP) ... nr
Nigeria Airways [*ICAO designator*] (AD) ... WT
Nigeria America Line (AD) ... NAL
Nigeria International Bank Ltd. ... NIB
Nigeria Law Quarterly Review [*A publication*] (DLA) ... NLQR
Nigeria Law Reports [*A publication*] (DLA) ... Nig LR
Nigeria Law Reports [*A publication*] (DLA) ... Nigeria LR
Nigeria Law Reports [*A publication*] (DLA) ... NLR
Nigeria Lawyer's Quarterly [*A publication*] (DLA) ... Nig Lawy Q
Nigeria Lawyer's Quarterly [*A publication*] (ILCA) ... Nig LQ
Nigeria Lawyer's Quarterly [*A publication*] (DLA) ... NLQ
Nigeria Regiment [*British military*] (DMA) ... NR
Nigeria Trade Journal [*A publication*] ... NTJ
Nigeria-Arab Bank Ltd. ... NAB
Nigerian Agip Oil Co. (AD) ... NAOC
Nigerian Annual of International Law [*A publication*] (DLA) ... Nig Ann Int'l L
Nigerian Annual of International Law [*A publication*] (DLA) ... Nigerian Ann Int'l L
Nigerian Army School of Infantry ... NASI
Nigerian Bank for Commerce and Industry ... NBCI
Nigerian Bar Journal [*A publication*] (DLA) ... Nig Bar J
Nigerian Bar Journal [*A publication*] (DLA) ... Nig BJ
Nigerian Bar Journal. Annual Journal of the Nigeria Bar Association [*Lagos, Nigeria*] [*A publication*] (DLA) ... Nigeria Bar J
Nigerian British Chamber of Commerce [*London*] (DCTA) ... NBCC
Nigerian Broadcasting Corp. ... NBC
Nigerian Electricity Supply Corp. African Workers' Union ... NESCO
Nigerian Embassy, Washington, DC [*Library symbol Library of Congress*] (LCLS) ... DNigE
Nigerian External Telecommunications Ltd. [*Lagos*] ... NET Ltd
Nigerian Geographical Journal [*A publication*] ... NGJ
Nigerian International Air Services Ltd. [*ICAO designator*] (FAAC) ... HMZ
Nigerian Journal of Economic and Social Studies [*A publication*] ... NJESS
Nigerian Law Journal [*A publication*] (DLA) ... Nig LJ
Nigerian Law Journal [*A publication*] (DLA) ... Nigerian LJ
Nigerian Law Quarterly Review [*A publication*] (DLA) ... Nig LQR
Nigerian Monthly Law Reports [*1964-65*] [*A publication*] (DLA) ... NMLR
Nigerian National Petroleum Corp. (ECON) ... NNPC
Nigerian Navy ... NN
Nigerian People's Party [*Political party*] (PPW) ... NPP
Nigerian Students Union in the Americas (EA) ... NSUA
Nigerian Trade Union Congress ... NTUC
Nigerian Trust Fund [*African Development Bank*] ... NTF
Nigerian-American Alliance (EA) ... NAA
Nigerum [*Papua New Guinea*] [*Airport symbol*] (OAG) ... NGR
Niggers with Attitude [*Rap recording group*] ... NWA
Night [*Approach and landing charts*] [*Aviation*] ... N
Night [*Broadcasting term*] ... N
Night (WDMC) ... n
Night ... NGT
Night (AABC) ... NI
Night (ROG) ... NT
Night Action [*American diplomat's jargon*] ... NIACT
Night Adoration in the Home (EA) ... NAH
Night/Adverse Weather Evaluator (IEEE) ... N/AW
Night Aerial Photographic System ... NAPS
Night Air Defence [*British World War II*] ... NAD
Night Alarm [*Telecommunications*] (TEL) ... NA
Night Alarm Cutoff (AAG) ... NACO
Night and morning (DAVI) ... NM
Night Answer (WDMC) ... NA
Night Attack Combat Training Unit [*Navy*] ... NACTU
Night Attack Interdiction System ... NAIS
Night Attack Program [*Military*] ... NAP
Night Bombardment - Long Distance [*Air Force*] ... NBL
Night Bombardment - Short Distance [*Air Force*] ... NBS
Night Bombardment - Short Distance [*Air Force*] (IEEE) ... NBSD
Night Carrier Landing Trainer [*Navy*] ... NCLT
Night Closing Trunks [*Telecommunications*] (TEL) ... NCT
Night Coach [*Airline designation*] ... NC
Night Coach [*Airline fare code*] ... YN
Night Combat Air Patrol [*Military*] ... NCAP
Night Combat Air Patrol [*Military*] (NVT) ... NIGHTCAP
Night Defense Fire (DNAB) ... NDF
Night Defensive Position [*Military*] ... NDP
Night Development Squadron ... NITEDEVRON
Night Experimental [*British military*] (DMA) ... NE
Night Express [*Germany*] [*FAA designator*] (FAAC) ... EXT
Night Fighter [*When suffix to plane designation*] [*Navy*] ... N
Night Fighter Aircraft ... NF
Night Fighter Association ... NFA
Night Fighter Squadrons [*Navy symbol*] ... VF(N)
Night Fighting Training Facility [*Army*] (INF) ... NFTF
Night First Class [*Airline fare code*] ... FN
Night Forward Air Controller [*Aircraft*] ... NIFAC
Night Frequency [*Aviation*] (IAA) ... NF
Night Frequency (FAAC) ... NFQ

Night Game [*Baseball*] .... N
Night Hawk Resources Ltd. [*Vancouver Stock Exchange symbol*] .... NHW
Night Illumination System .... NIS
Night Imaging Thermal Equipment [*Army*] (INF) .... NITE
Night Imaging Through Electro-Optic Package [*Military British*] .... NITEOP
Night Intruder Mission [*Air Force*] .... NIM
Night Law School Bulletin. University of Omaha [*A publication*]
   (DLA) .... U of Omaha Bull
Night Letter .... NL
Night Letter [*Telegraphic communications*] .... NLT
Night Message .... NM
Night Message (MSA) .... NTM
Night Missile Flash Simulator (MCD) .... NMFS
Night Navigation and Pilotage System .... NNAPS
Night Noise Group C [*Aircraft*] .... NN/C
Night Observation Device .... NOD
Night Observation Device, Long-Range [*Army*] (RDA) .... NODLR
Night Observation Device, Medium-Range [*Army*] .... NODMR
Night Observation Gunship (MCD) .... NOGS
Night Observation Helicopter (MCD) .... NOH
Night Observation Sight [*Air Force*] .... NOS
Night Observation System [*Navy*] (CAAL) .... NOS
Night Observation Television in a Pod .... NOTIP
Night Only Calligraphic Image Generator .... NOCIG
Night Operation System [*Aviation*] .... NOS
Night Operational Vision and the Individual Combat Engineer (MCD) ..... NOVICE
Night Perimeter Defense .... NPD
Night Photographic System .... NPS
Night Plane Guard Station (NVT) .... NPLG
Night Plane Landing Guard (NVT) .... NPLG
Night Press Rate [*of newspapers*] .... NPR
Night Ration Locker (MSA) .... NRL
Night Reconnaissance System .... NRS
Night Sky Radiation .... NSR
Night Sleep Deprivation [*Medicine*] (DMAA) .... NSD
Night Telegram .... NT
Night Telegraph Letter .... NTL
Night Torpedo Bomber Squadron [*Navy symbol*] .... VT(N)
Night Trunk [*Business term*] (DCTA) .... NT
Night Visibility Measuring Set .... NVMS
Night Vision Aerial Surveillance Device .... NVASD
Night Vision Airborne Surveillance System .... NVASS
Night Vision and Electro Optics Directorate [*Army*] (RDA) .... NVEOD
Night Vision and Electronic Sensors Directorate [*Army*] (RDA) ...... NVESD
Night Vision and Electro-Optics Center [*Fort Belvoir, VA*] [*US Army
   Communications-Electronics Command*] (RDA) .... NVEOC
Night Vision and Electro-Optics Laboratory [*Army*] (RDA) ...... NV & EOL
Night Vision and Electro-Optics Laboratory [*Army*] (GRD) .... NVEOL
Night Vision Attack System .... NVAS
Night Vision Binocular .... NVB
Night Vision Device [*Optics*] .... NV
Night Vision Device [*Optics*] .... NVD
Night Vision Equipment (MCD) .... NVE
Night Vision Equipment for Armor .... NIVEA
Night Vision Goggle Sensor (DWSG) .... NVGS
Night Vision Goggles .... NVG
Night Vision Group .... NVG
Night Vision Imaging (DWSG) .... NVI
Night Vision Laboratory [*Army*] .... NVL
Night Vision Net Technical Assessment (MCD) .... NVNTA
Night Vision Pilotage System [*Military*] .... NVPS
Night Vision Reconnaissance System .... NVRS
Night Vision Safety [*Automotive rear-view mirrors*] .... NVS
Night Vision System .... NVS
Night Vision System Development [*Military*] .... NVSD
Night Visual Flight Rating .... NVFR
Night-Alarm Cutoff (AD) .... nacro
Nightcap (ABBR) .... NTCP
Night-Day Optical Survey of Lightning [*NASA*] .... NOSL
Night-Fire [*Rifle*] Control Sight [*Army*] .... NFCS
Night-Fire [*Rifle*] Training Aid [*Army*] (INF) .... NFTA
Nightingale-Conant [*Audio publisher*] .... N-C
[*The*] Nightly Business Reports [*Television program*] .... NBR
Nightmute [*Alaska*] [*Airport symbol*] (OAG) .... NME
Nightmute, AK [*Location identifier FAA*] (FAAL) .... IGT
Nighttime (NTCM) .... N
Nighttime Fatal Crash .... NFC
Night-Time Marine Air Temperature .... NMAT
Nigrinus [*of Lucian*] [*Classical studies*] (OCD) .... Nigr
NIH [*National Institutes of Health*]-EPA Chemical Information System [*Falls
   Church*] [*Environmental Protection Agency Information service or system*]
   (IID) .... CIS
Nihil Obstat [*Official Approval*] [*Latin*] .... N Obs
Niho Fukushi University [*UTLAS symbol*] .... NFU
Nihon Aeroplane Manufacturing Co. (AD) .... NAMC
Nihon Aeroplane Manufacturing Co. Ltd. [*Japan ICAO aircraft manufacturer
   identifier*] (ICAO) .... YS
Nihon Keizai Shimbun, Inc. [*Tokyo, Japan*] (IID) .... NIKKEI
Nihon Kinkyori Airways [*ICAO designator*] (AD) .... EL
Nihon Shinbun Kyokai [*Japanese Newspaper Association*], Tokyo, Japan
   [*Library symbol Library of Congress*] (LCLS) .... JTNS
Nihon University [*UTLAS symbol*] .... NUL
NII Norsat International, Inc. [*Associated Press*] (SAG) .... NII Nor
NII Norsat International, Inc. [*NASDAQ symbol*] (SAG) .... NSAT
Niigata [*Japan*] [*Airport symbol*] (OAG) .... KIJ

Niigata [*Japan*] [*Seismograph station code, US Geological Survey*] (SEIS) .... NII
Niigata [*Japan ICAO location identifier*] (ICLI) .... RJSN
Niihama [*Japan*] [*Seismograph station code, US Geological Survey Closed*]
   (SEIS) .... NHM
Niijima [*Japan*] [*Seismograph station code, US Geological Survey Closed*]
   (SEIS) .... NJJ
Nijmegen Breakage Syndrome [*Medicine*] (DMAA) .... NBS
Nike Hercules [*Surface-to-air missile system*] (MCD) .... NH
Nike, Inc. [*Associated Press*] (SAG) .... NikeB
Nike, Inc. Class B [*NYSE symbol*] (SPSG) .... NKE
NIKE, Inc. Cl'B' [*NYSE symbol*] (TTSB) .... NKE
Nike Operator Proficiency Scale [*Army*] .... NOPS
Nike Target Measurements Program .... NTMP
Nike-Iroquois [*Rockets*] .... NIRO
Nike-X Development Office [*Army*] (AABC) .... NXDO
Nike-X Management Information System [*Army*] .... NXMIS
Nike-X Program [*or Project*] Office [*Army*] .... NXPO
Nike-X Program Review Group [*Army*] (AABC) .... NXPRG
Nike-X Project Manager [*Army*] (AABC) .... NXPM
Nike-X Support Office [*Army*] .... NXSO
Nike-X System Manager [*Army*] (AABC) .... NXSM
Nike-X System Manager's Office [*Army*] .... NXSMO
Nike-Zeus [*Missiles*] (AAG) .... N-Z
Nike-Zeus at Point Mugu [*Missile defense*] (SAA) .... ZM
Nike-Zeus at White Sands [*Missile defense*] (SAA) .... ZW
Nike-Zeus Automatic Programming System [*Missiles*] .... NZAPS
Nike-Zeus Target Joint Working Group [*Missiles*] (MUGU) ...... NZTJWG
Nike-Zeus Target Vehicle [*Missiles*] (IAA) .... NZTV
Nikiskha [*Alaska*] [*Seismograph station code, US Geological Survey*] (SEIS) .... NKA
NIKKEI Economic Electronic Databank Service - Information Retrieval
   [*Information service or system Japan*] (IID) .... NEEDS-IR
NIKKEI Economic Electronic Databank Service - Time Sharing [*Information
   service or system Japan*] (IID) .... NEEDS-TS
Nikolai Andreyvich Rimsky-Korsakov (AD) .... NARK
Nikolski [*Alaska*] [*Airport symbol*] (OAG) .... IKO
Nikolski [*Alaska*] [*Seismograph station code, US Geological Survey Closed*]
   (SEIS) .... NIK
Nikolski [*Alaska*] [*Seismograph station code, US Geological Survey*] (SEIS) ..... NKI
Nikon Historical Society (EA) .... NHS
Nikon Intracellular Calcium Ion System .... NICIS
Nik-Shahr [*Iran*] [*ICAO location identifier*] (ICLI) .... OIZY
Nikunau [*Kiribati*] [*ICAO location identifier*] (ICLI) .... NGNU
Nikunau [*Kiribati*] [*Airport symbol*] (OAG) .... NIG
Nil per Os [*Nothing by Mouth*] [*Medicine*] .... NPO
Nil-Ductility Temperature [*Metallurgy*] .... NDT
Nil-Ductility Transition [*Metallurgy*] (IEEE) .... NDT
Nil-Ductility Transition Temperature [*Metallurgy*] .... NDTT
Nile River and Basin [*MARC geographic area code Library of Congress*]
   (LCCP) .... fl----
Nile Safaris Aviation [*Sudan*] [*ICAO designator*] (FAAC) .... NSA
Nile Valley Aviation Co. [*Egypt*] [*ICAO designator*] (FAAC) ...... NVA
Niles Community Library, Niles, MI [*Library symbol Library of Congress*]
   (LCLS) .... MiNi
Niles, MI [*FM radio station call letters*] .... WAOR
Niles, MI [*AM radio station call letters*] .... WNIL
Niles, OH [*FM radio station call letters*] .... WNCD
Niles, OH [*AM radio station call letters*] (RBYB) .... WNIO
Niles' Weekly Register [*A publication*] (DLA) .... Nil Reg
Niles' Weekly Register [*A publication*] (DLA) .... Niles Reg
Nilore [*Pakistan*] [*Seismograph station code, US Geological Survey*] (SEIS) ...... NIL
Nimba [*Liberia*] [*ICAO location identifier*] (ICLI) .... GLNA
Nimbostratus [*Cloud*] [*Meteorology*] (AIA) .... NbSt
Nimbostratus [*Cloud*] [*Meteorology*] .... NS
Nimbus [*Cloud*] [*Meteorology*] .... NB
Nimbus Arctic Ice Reconnaissance [*Canadian project*] .... NAIREC
Nimbus Automatic Programming System (IEEE) .... NAPS
Nimbus Aviation [*British ICAO designator*] (FAAC) .... NBS
Nimbus Beacon Transmitter .... NBT
Nimbus CD International, Inc. [*Associated Press*] (SAG) .... Nimbus
Nimbus CD International, Inc. [*NASDAQ symbol*] (SAG) .... NMBS
Nimbus CD Intl. [*NASDAQ symbol*] (TTSB) .... NMBS
Nimbus Data Handling System .... NDHS
Nimbus Data Utilization Center .... NDUC
Nimbus E Microwave Spectrometer [*Meteorology*] .... NEMS
Nimbus Experiment Team [*NASA*] .... NET
Nimbus Integration and Test [*NASA*] (KSC) .... NIMIT
Nimbus Meteorological Radiation Tape [*NASA*] .... NMRT
Nimbus Operational Satellite System [*GSFC/USWB*] .... NOSS
Nimbus Operational System .... NOS
Nimbus Technical Control Center .... NTCC
Nimbus Weather Satellite .... NWS
Nimes [*France*] [*Airport symbol*] (OAG) .... FNI
Nimes [*Frances*] [*Airport symbol*] (AD) .... FNI
Nimes/Courbessac [*France ICAO location identifier*] (ICLI) ...... LFME
Nimes/Garons [*France ICAO location identifier*] (ICLI) .... LFTW
Nimule/Nimule [*Sudan*] [*ICAO location identifier*] (ICLI) .... HSNM
Nincompoop (AD) .... poop
Nine Inch Nails [*Rock music group*] .... NIN
Nine Lives Associates (EA) .... NLA
Nine Mile Canyon [*California*] [*Seismograph station code, US Geological
   Survey*] (SEIS) .... NMC
Nine Mile Point Nuclear Station (NRCH) .... NMPNS
Nine Pin Association [*Schauenburg, Federal Republic of Germany*] (EAIO) ..... NPA
Nine West Group [*NYSE symbol*] (TTSB) .... NIN
Nine West Group, Inc. [*NYSE symbol*] (SPSG) .... NIN

Nine West Group, Inc. [Associated Press] (SAG) .... NineWest
Nineteen Thirty-Two Buick Registry (EA) .... NTTBR
Nineteen-Hundred Commercial Language .... NICOL
Nineteen-Hundred Indexing and Cataloging (DIT) .... NIC
Nineteen-Hundred Integrated Modular Management System .. NIMMS
Nineteen-Hundred [Computer] Management and Recovery of
   Documentation (PDAA) .... NIMROD
Nineteenth Century Literary Criticism [A publication] .... NCLC
Nineteenth Century Series [A publication] .... NCS
Nineteenth Century Short Title Catalogue [Avero Publications Ltd.]
   [Information service or system British] (CRD) .... NSTC
Nineteenth-Century Literature [A publication] (BRI) ...... Nine-C Lit
Ninety Pound Charge .... NPC
Ninety-Nine Cent Only Stores [Associated Press] (SAG) .... 99 Cents
Ninety-Nine Cent Only Stores [NYSE symbol] (SAG) ...... NDN
Ningsia Hui Autonomous Region [China, Mainland] [MARC geographic area
   code Library of Congress] (LCCP) .... a-cc-nn
Ninhydrine [Chemical agent used in espionage] .... NIN
Ninilchik [Alaska] [Seismograph station code, US Geological Survey Closed]
   (SEIS) .... NIN
Ninilchik [Alaska] [Seismograph station code, US Geological Survey] (SEIS) .... NNL
Ninilchik, AK [Location identifier FAA] (FAAL) .... NIN
Ninos de las Americas [Children of the Americas] (EAIO) .... NDA
Nintendo Entertainment System [Video game] .... NES
Ninth Coast Guard District [Cleveland, OH] [USCG] (TAG) D9
Ninth Judicial District Law Library, Newburgh, NY [Library symbol Library of
   Congress] (LCLS) .... NNebgL
Ninth to Twelfth Cranial Nerves [Anatomy] (DMAA) ...... CIX-CXII
Ninth United States Army .... NUSA
Ninth-Plate (VRA) .... NINE
Niobium [See Cb] [Chemical element] .... Nb
Niobium [See Cb] [Chemical element] (ROG) .... NIO
Niobium Zinc Alloy .... NZA
Niobrara County Library, Lusk, WY [Library symbol Library of Congress]
   (LCLS) .... WyLu
N-Iodosuccinimide [Organic chemistry] .... NIS
Nioga Library System, Niagara Falls, NY [Library symbol Library of
   Congress] (LCLS) .... NNiaNL
Nioga Library System, Niagara Falls, NY [OCLC symbol] (OCLC) ...... ZNM
Nioki [Zaire] [ICAO location identifier] (ICLI) .... FZBI
Nioki [Zaire] [Airport symbol] (OAG) .... NIO
Niokolo Koba [Senegal] [ICAO location identifier] (ICLI) .... GOTN
Nioro [Mali] [ICAO location identifier] (ICLI) .... GANR
Nioro [Mali] [Airport symbol] (OAG) .... NIX
Niort/Souche [France ICAO location identifier] (ICLI) ...... LFBN
NIOSH Technical Information Center (NITA) .... NIOSHTIC
Nipawin, SK [Television station call letters] CKBI-4
Nipigon Public Library, Ontario [Library symbol National Library of Canada]
   (NLC) .... ONI
Nipigon-Red Rock, ON [FM radio station call letters] .... CFJQ
Nipissing University College, North Bay, ON, Canada [Library symbol Library
   of Congress] (LCLS) .... CaONbNU
Nipissing University College, North Bay, Ontario [Library symbol National
   Library of Canada] (NLC) .... ONBNU
Nipple (AAG) .... NIP
Nipple .... NIP
Nipple Areolar Complex [Oncology] .... NAC
Nippon Advanced Ship Design (AD) .... NASD
Nippon Air Brake Co. Ltd. [Tokyo, Japan] .... NABCO
Nippon Atomic Industry Group [Japan] .... NAIG
Nippon Australian Relations Agreement (AD) .... NARA
Nippon Aviatronics Corp. Ltd. [Japan] .... NACL
Nippon Calculating Machine Co. [Japan] (PDAA) .... NCM
Nippon Cargo Airlines [Japan] .... NCA
Nippon Cargo Airlines Co. Ltd. [Japan ICAO designator] (FAAC) .. NCA
Nippon Club (EA) .... NC
Nippon Credit Bank [Japan] .... NCB
Nippon Decimal Classification [Library science] .... NDC
Nippon Electric Automatic Computer (IEEE) .... NEAC
Nippon Electric Co. [Japan] .... NEC
Nippon Electric Co. (IAA) .... NECO
Nippon Hoso Kyokai [Japanese national broadcasting system] (NTCM) ...... NHK
Nippon Information and Communication [Joint venture of IBM Corp. Japan
   and Nippon Telegraph and Telephone] .... NI & C
Nippon Information Processing System [Nippon Shuppan Hanbai, Inc.]
   [Database] .... NIPS
Nippon Institute of Biological Sciences (DAVI) .... NIBS
Nippon Investment Corp. [Vancouver Stock Exchange symbol] ...... NP
Nippon Kaiji Kyokai [Japanese ship classification society] (DS) .... NK
Nippon Seiko Kabushiki Kaisha [Japan] .... NSK
Nippon Steel Corp. [Japan] .... NSC
Nippon Tel & Tel ADS [NYSE symbol] (TTSB) .... NTT
Nippon Telegraph & Telephone Co. [Associated Press] (SAG) .... NippnTT
Nippon Telegraph & Telephone Co. [NYSE symbol] (SAG) .... NTT
Nippon Telegraph & Telephone Corp. [Telecommunications and videotex
   company] [Japan] .... NTT
Nippon Telegraph & Telephone Public Corp. [Telecommunications]
   (IAA) .... NTTPC
Nippon Television Network Corp. [Japan] .... NTV
Nippondenso Co. [Toyota Motor Corp.] .... ND
Nipponese .... NIP
NIPSCO Cap Mkt 7.75% Debt Sec [NYSE symbol] (TTSB) .. NIC
NIPSCO Capital Markets [NYSE symbol] (SAG) .... NIC
NIPSCO Capital Markets [Associated Press] (SAG) .... NIPS
NIPSCO Industries [NYSE symbol] (TTSB) .... NHY

NIPSCO Industries [NYSE symbol] (SPSG) .... NI
NIPSCO Industries [Associated Press] (SAG) .... NIPSCO
Nirvana Industries Ltd. [Vancouver Stock Exchange symbol] ...... NVN
Nisab [South Arabia] [Airport symbol] (AD) .... ISB
Nisbet of Dirleton's Scotch Session Cases [1665-77] [A publication]
   (DLA) .... Nisbet
Nisei Mass Evacuation Group .... NMEG
Nisi Aliter Notetur [Unless Otherwise Noted] [Latin] ...... NAN
Nisi Aliter Notetur [Unless It is Otherwise Noted] [Latin] (AD) .... nan
Nisi Prius [Unless Before] [Legal term Latin] (WGA) ...... ni pr
Nisi Prius [Unless Before] [Legal term Latin] .... NI PRI
Nisi Prius [Unless Before] [Legal term Latin] .... NP
Nisi Prius and General Term Reports [Ohio] [A publication]
   (DLA) .... Nisi Prius & Gen T Rep
Nisi Prius and General Term Reports [Ohio] [A publication] (DLA) ...... NP & GT Rep
Nisi Prius Cases [England] [A publication] (DLA) .... NPC
Nisi Prius Reports [A publication] (DLA) .... NPR
Nisley Elementary School, Grand Junction, CO [Library symbol Library of
   Congress] (LCLS) .... CoGjNE
N-Isopropylacrylamide [Organic chemistry] .... NIPA
N-Isopropylcarbazole [Organic chemistry] .... NIPC
Nissan Air Pollution System (AD) .... NAPS
Nissan Design International .... NDI
Nissan Direct Ignition System [Automotive engineering] .... NDIS
Nissan Island [Papua New Guinea] [Airport symbol] (OAG) .... IIS
Nissan Motor Acceptance Corp. .... NMAC
Nissan Motor Co. ADR [NASDAQ symbol] (TTSB) .... NSANY
Nissan Motor Co. Ltd. [Associated Press] (SAG) .... Nissan
Nissan Motor Co. Ltd. [NASDAQ symbol] (NQ) .... NSAN
Nissan Motorsports .... NISMO
Nissan Motorsports Europe .... NME
Nissan Motorsports International [Automotive competition] .... NMI
Nissan Performance Technology, Inc. .... NPTI
Nissan Safety Device Advisor [Driver information system] .... NSDA
Nissan Technical Center [Automobile manufacturing] ...... NTC
Nissan Valve Control System [Automotive engineering] .... NVCS
Nissan Valve Timing Control System .... NVTCS
Nissan's Induction Control System [Automotive engineering] .... NICS
Nissim Ezra Benjamin [Shanghai] (BJA) .... NEB
Nisswa Elementary School, Nisswa, MN [Library symbol] [Library of
   Congress] (LCLS) .... MnNisE
Nistransair [Republic of Moldova] [FAA designator] (FAAC) .... NTP
Nit [Unit of luminance] .... nt
Nitchequon, PQ [ICAO location identifier] (ICLI) .... CYNI
Nitches, Inc. [NASDAQ symbol] (SAG) .... NICH
Nitches Inc. [NASDAQ symbol] (TTSB) .... NICH
Nitches, Inc. [Associated Press] (SAG) .... Nitches
Nite-Lite, Newark, NJ [Library symbol Library of Congress] (LCLS) ...... NjNN
Nitinol Medical Technologies, Inc. [Associated Press] (SAG) .... Nitinol
Nitinol Medical Technologies, Inc. [NASDAQ symbol] (SAG) .... NMTI
Niton (ABBR) .... NT
Nitra Air [Slovakia] [FAA designator] (FAAC) .... NRA
Nitrate (GNE) .... NO_3
Nitrate Ester Plasticized Polyethylene (PDAA) .... NEPE
Nitrate Motion Picture (VRA) .... NTMP
Nitrate Negative (VRA) .... NTNG
Nitrate Reductase [An enzyme] .... NR
Nitrated Polycyclic Aromatic Hydrocarbons [Automotive emissions] [Organic
   chemistry] .... NPAH
Nitric Acid [Chemistry] (DAVI) .... HNO_3
Nitric Acid Concentrator (MCD) .... NAC
Nitric Acid Dihydrate [Inorganic chemistry] .... NAD
Nitric Acid Trihydrate [Inorganic chemistry] .... NAT
Nitric Oxide (GNE) .... NO
Nitric Oxide .... NO
Nitric Oxide Myoglobin [Food technology] .... NOMb
Nitric Oxide Optical Detector .... NOOD
Nitric Oxide Synthase [An enzyme] .... NOS
Nitride Forming Element [Metal treating] .... NFE
Nitride Steel .... NITSTL
Nitride-Barrier Avalanche Injection Missile (MCD) .... NAMIS
Nitrigin Eireann Teoranta [Nationalized industry] [Ireland] (EY) .. NET
Nitrile Rubber [Organic chemistry] .... NR
Nitrile Silicone Rubber [Organic chemistry] .... NSR
Nitrile-Butadiene Rubber .... NBR
Nitrile-Chloroprene Rubber .... NCR
Nitrilotriacetic Acid [Organic chemistry] .... NTA
Nitrilotriacetonitrile [Organic chemistry] .... NTAN
Nitrilotrimethylenephosphonic Acid [Organic chemistry] .... NTPO
Nitrite Positive [Organic chemistry] (DAVI) .... NPOS
Nitrite Reductase [An enzyme] .... NIR
Nitro Proved [Rifle mark] (DICI) .... NP
Nitro-(amino)butyric Acid .... NABA
Nitroaminophenol [Organic chemistry] .... NAP
Nitroanthranilic Acid [Organic chemistry] .... NAA
Nitroarginine Methyl Ester [Organic chemistry] .... NAME
Nitrobenzene [Organic chemistry] .... NB
Nitrobenzene Association [Defunct] (EA) .... NA
Nitrobenzenediazonium Tetrafluoroborate [Organic chemistry] .... NBDFB
Nitrobenzenesulfenyl Chloride [Organic chemistry] .... NBSC
Nitrobenzenesulfonyl Fluoride [Organic chemistry] .... NBSF
Nitro(benzothiazolo)quinolinium Perchlorate [Antineoplastic drug] .... NBQ
Nitrobenzoxadiazole [Organic chemistry] .... NBD
Nitrobenzoxadiazole Phosphatidylserine [Biochemistry] .... NBD-PS
(Nitrobenzyl)(Diethylaminophenylazo)-pyridinium Bromide [Reagent] .... NDPP

(Nitrobenzyl)pyridine [*Organic chemistry*]	NBP
Nitrobenzylthioinosine [*Organic chemistry*]	NBTI
Nitroblue Tetrazolium [*A stain*] [*Hematology*]	NBT
Nitroblue Tetrazolium Diformazan [*A stain*] [*Hematology*]	NBT-DF
Nitroblue Tetrazolium Dye [*Test*] [*Laboratory science*] (DAVI)	NTD
Nitro(carboxyphenyl)diphenylcarbamate [*Biochemistry*]	NCDC
Nitrocellulose [*Organic chemistry*]	NC
Nitrocellulose (WDAA)	NITRO
Nitrocellulose (WDAA)	NCM
Nitrocellulose Membrane	NDD
Nitro(dimethyl)dihydrobenzofuran [*Organic chemistry*]	NF
Nitrofluoranthene [*Organic chemistry*]	NBM
Nitro-Form Bind Medium [*Analytical biochemistry*]	NFS
Nitrofuraldehyde Semicarbazone [*Germicide*]	NFZ
(Nitro)furfuralsemicarbazone [*Organic chemistry*]	N
Nitrogen [*Chemical element*]	N2
Nitrogen	NI
Nitrogen [*Chemical element*]	NITRO
Nitrogen [*Chemical element*]	NB
Nitrogen Base (NASA)	NCP
Nitrogen Charge Panel [*Later, MRAC*] (AAG)	NCC
Nitrogen Charging Console	NCU
Nitrogen Control Unit (AAG)	NO2
Nitrogen Dioxide	NFA
Nitrogen Filling Assembly	
Nitrogen Fixing Tree Association [*University of Hawaii*] [*Research center*] (RCD)	NFTA
Nitrogen Flow Measuring System	NFMS
Nitrogen Flow System	NFS
Nitrogen Gauge (MCD)	NG
Nitrogen Generation Module (NASA)	NGM
Nitrogen Generation Module	NGM
Nitrogen Heat Exchange	NHE
Nitrogen, Helium, and Oxygen Experiment (DNAB)	NIHOE
Nitrogen High Pressure	NHP
Nitrogen Inerting Line (IEEE)	NIL
Nitrogen Manual Valve (MCD)	NMV
Nitrogen Measuring System	NMS
, Nitrogen Mustard [*Vincristine*] [*Antineoplastic drug regimen*]	BACON
Nitrogen Mustard [*Also, M, MBA, NM*] [*Antineoplastic drug, war-gas base Army symbol used with numerals, as HN1*]	HN
Nitrogen Mustard [*Antineoplastic drug*] (DAVI)	HN_2
Nitrogen Mustard [*Also, HN, M, MBA*] [*Antineoplastic drug, war-gas base*]	NM
Nitrogen Mustard [*Mustargen*], Adriamycin, CCNU [*Lomustine*] [*Antineoplastic drug regimen*]	NAC
Nitrogen ohne Radikal [*Chemical prefix*]	nor
Nitrogen Oxide [*Emission control*] [*Automotive engineering*]	NO
Nitrogen Oxide Reduction [*Research in automotive air pollution*]	NOR
Nitrogen, Phosphorus Gas Chromatographic Detector [*Spectroscopy*]	NPD
Nitrogen, Phosphorus, Potassium [*Fertilizer components*]	NPK
Nitrogen Phosphorus Thermionic Detector [*Instrumentation*]	NPTD
Nitrogen Pressure Relief Valve (MCD)	NPRV
Nitrogen Pressure Unit (MCD)	NPU
Nitrogen Pressure Valve (KSC)	NPV
Nitrogen Purge Control (NASA)	NPC
Nitrogen Purge Control	NPC
Nitrogen Purge Unit (MCD)	NPU
Nitrogen Recharge Station	NRS
Nitrogen Rejection Facility [*Process engineering*]	NRF
Nitrogen Rejection Unit [*Process engineering*]	NRU
Nitrogen Solubility Index [*Analytical chemistry*]	NSI
Nitrogen, Sulfur, and Oxygen [*In chemical compounds*]	NSO
Nitrogen Supply	NS
Nitrogen Supply Flask	NSF
Nitrogen Supply Subsystem	NSS
Nitrogen Supply System [*or Subsystem*] (AAG)	NSS
Nitrogen Supply Unit (AAG)	NSU
Nitrogen System	NS
Nitrogen Tetroxide [*Inorganic chemistry*]	NTO
Nitrogen Utilization Efficiency [*Ecology*]	NUE
Nitrogen Vent Header [*Nuclear energy*] (NRCH)	NVH
Nitrogen-Fixing [*Biology*] (BARN)	nif
Nitrogen-Free Extract [*Analytical chemistry*]	NFE
Nitrogen-Phosphorus [*Chemistry*] (MAE)	NP
Nitrogen-Phosphorus Detector [*Analytical instrumentation*]	NPD
Nitrogen-Phosphorus-Flame Ionization Detector [*Instrumentation*]	NPFID
Nitrogen-Tillage-Residue Management (GNE)	NTRM
Nitroglycerin [*Also, GTN, NTG*] [*Explosive, vasodilator*]	NG
Nitroglycerin [*Pharmacy*]	nitro
Nitroglycerin [*Also, GTN, NG*] [*Explosive, vasodilator*]	NTG
Nitroglycerin Ointment [*Pharmacy*] (CPH)	NGO
Nitroglycerin Sublingual [*Pharmacology*] (DAVI)	NTG SL
Nitroglycerin Transdermal System [*Pharmacy*]	NTS
Nitroglycerine Ointment [*Pharmacy*]	NTGO
Nitroguanidine [*Organic chemistry*]	NG
Nitroguanidine Support Element (MCD)	NSE
Nitrohippuric Acid [*Organic chemistry*]	NHA
Nitro(hydroxy)benzoic Acid [*Organic chemistry*]	NHB
Nitroisatoic Anhydride [*Organic chemistry*]	NIA
Nitroisobutametriol Trinitrate [*An explosive*]	NIBTN
Nitrol Paste [*Pharmacology*] (DAVI)	NTP
Nitromethane [*Organic chemistry*]	NM
Nitromethylpropanediol [*Organic chemistry*]	NMPD
Nitrophenide [*Pharmacology*]	NP
Nitrophenoacetylamino Caproate	NP
Nitrophenyl Butyl Ether [*Organic chemistry*]	NPBE

Nitrophenyl Dodecyl Ether [*Organic chemistry*]	NPDDE
Nitrophenyl Hexyl Ether [*Organic chemistry*]	NPHE
Nitrophenyl Hydroxyoctyl Ether [*Organic chemistry*]	NPHOE
Nitrophenyl Octyl Ether [*Organic chemistry*]	NPOE
Nitrophenyl Pentyl Ether [*Organic chemistry*]	NPPE
Nitrophenyl Phosphate [*Biochemical analysis*]	NPP
Nitrophenyl Propyl Ether [*Organic chemistry*]	NPPRE
Nitrophenyl Sulfenyl [*Organic chemistry*]	NPS
Nitrophenyl Sulfenyl Chloride	NPS-CL
(Nitrophenyl)guanidinobenzoate [*Organic chemistry*]	NPGB
(Nitrophenyl)pentadienal [*Tracer chemical*] [*Organic chemistry*]	NPPD
Nitrophenylprolinol [*Organic chemistry*]	NPP
Nitro(Phenylpropylamino) Benzoate [*Organic chemistry*]	NPPB
Nitrophenylthio(nitrophenylsulfonyl) [*Biochemistry*]	Nps
Nitropropane [*Organic chemistry*]	NP
Nitropropenyl Pivalate [*Organic chemistry*]	NPP
Nitroprusside [*A vasodilator*]	NP
Nitroprusside [*A vasodilator*]	NTP
Nitropyrene [*Organic chemistry*]	NP
Nitroquinoline Oxide [*Organic chemistry*]	NQO
Nitrosamide [*Biochemistry*]	Nad
Nitrosamine [*Biochemistry*]	Nan
Nitrosoanabasine [*Organic chemistry*]	NAB
Nitrosoanatabine [*Also, NAtB*] [*Organic chemistry*]	NAT
Nitrosoanatabine [*Organic chemistry*]	NAtB
Nitrosobenzamide [*Organic chemistry*]	NOBA
Nitrosobenzopyrone [*Organic chemistry*]	NOBP
Nitrosodibutylamine [*Organic chemistry*]	NDBA
Nitrosodiethanolamine [*Also, NDEOL*] [*Organic chemistry*]	NDELA
Nitrosodiethanolamine [*Also, NDELA*] [*Organic chemistry*]	NDEOL
Nitrosodiethylamine [*Organic chemistry*]	NDEA
Nitrosodimethylaniline [*Chemistry*] (DAVI)	NDMA
Nitrosodimethylpiperazinium Iodide [*Organic chemistry*]	NDMPI
Nitrosodipropylamine [*Also, DPN, DPNA*] [*Organic chemistry*]	NDPA
Nitrosoguanidine [*Biochemistry*]	Ngd
Nitrosoguanidine [*Organic chemistry*]	NTG
Nitrosohexamethyleneimine [*Organic chemistry*]	NHM
Nitrosohydroxyproline [*Organic chemistry*]	NHPRO
Nitrosohydroxypyrrolidine [*Organic chemistry*]	NHPYR
(Nitrosomethylamino) Butyric Acid [*Organic chemistry*]	NMBA
(Nitrosomethylamino) Propionic Acid [*Organic chemistry*]	NMPA
Nitrosomethylpropylamine [*Organic chemistry*]	NMPA
Nitrosomethylurea [*Also, MNU*] [*Organic chemistry*]	NMU
Nitrosomorpholine [*Also, NNM*] [*Organic chemistry*]	NMOR
Nitrosonornicotine [*Organic chemistry*]	NNN
Nitrosooxazolidinecarboxylic Acid [*Organic chemistry*]	NOCA
Nitroso(oxopropyl)propylamine [*Organic chemistry*]	NOPPA
Nitrosopipecolic Acid [*Organic chemistry*]	NPIC
Nitrosopiperidine [*Organic chemistry*]	NP
Nitrosopiperidine [*Also, NP*] [*Organic chemistry*]	NPIP
Nitrosoprolylalanine [*Organic chemistry*]	NPROA
Nitrosoprolylglycine [*Organic chemistry*]	NPROG
Nitrosopyrrolidine [*Also, NYPYR*] [*Organic chemistry*]	NPYR
Nitrosopyrrolidine [*Also, NPYR*] [*Organic chemistry*]	NYPYR
Nitrososarcosine [*Organic chemistry*]	NSAR
Nitrosourea [*Biochemistry*]	Nur
Nitrostarch (AAG)	NITROS
Nitrosyl Fluoride (SAA)	NOF
Nitrosylsulfuric Acid [*Inorganic chemistry*]	NSA
(Nitro)thiocyanatobenzoic Acid [*Organic chemistry*]	NTCB
Nitro(thiocyano)benzoic Acid [*Organic chemistry*]	NTCD
Nitrous Oxide [*An Anesthetic*] (DAVI)	N_2O
Nitrous Oxide [*Laughing gas*] (AAMN)	NIT OX
Nitrous Oxide [*Laughing gas*]	NOX
Nitrous Oxide to Oxygen Ratio [*Anesthesiology*] (DAVI)	$N_2O:O_2$
Nitrous Oxide-Barbiturate [*Organic chemistry*] (MAE)	NB
Nitroveratryloxycarbonyl [*Organic radical*]	NVOC
Nitroxide Stable Free Radical [*For tissue NMR*]	NSFR
Nitroxyperoxypropyl Nitrate [*Environmental chemistry*]	NPPN
Nitrum [*Chemistry*] (ROG)	NIT
Nitsanim [*Israel*] [*Later, AMT*] [*Geomagnetic observatory code*]	NSM
Nittenau/Bruck [*Germany ICAO location identifier*] (ICLI)	EDYN
Nitty Gritty Dirt Band Fan Club (EA)	NGDBFC
Niuafo'Ou [*Tonga*] [*ICAO location identifier*] (ICLI)	NFTO
Niuatoputapu [*Tonga*] [*ICAO location identifier*] (ICLI)	NFTP
Niue [*ANSI three-letter standard code*] (CNC)	NIU
Niue [*ANSI two-letter standard code*] (CNC)	NU
Niue [*Niue Island*] [*Seismograph station code, US Geological Survey*] (SEIS)	NUE
Niue [*MARC geographic area code Library of Congress*] (LCCC)	poxh--
Niue [*MARC country of publication code Library of Congress*] (LCCP)	xh
Niue Airways Ltd. (EY)	NAL
Niue Island [*Niue*] [*Airport symbol*] (OAG)	IUE
Niue People's Action Party [*Political party*] (EY)	NPAP
Niumate [*Tonga*] [*Seismograph station code, US Geological Survey Closed*] (SEIS)	
Nivalenol [*A mycotoxin*]	NIV
Nixa [*Record label*] [*Great Britain, etc.; including Vanguard label re-issues*]	Nix
Nixa, MO [*FM radio station call letters*]	KGBX
Nixdorf Broadband Network [*Communications*] [*British*]	NBN
Nixdorf Communications Network [*Nixdorf*] [*Germany*]	NCN
Nixdorf Computer (IAA)	NC
Nixdorf Integrated Office System (HGAA)	NIOS
Nixdorf Real-Time Operating System (NITA)	NIROS
Nixon Family Association (EA)	NFA

Nixon, Hargrave, Devans & Doyle, Rochester, NY [Library symbol] [Library of Congress] (LCLS) .... NRNHD
Nixon's Digest of Laws [New Jersey] [A publication] (DLA) .... Nix Dig
Nixon's Forms [A publication] (DLA) .... Nix F
Nix-O-Tine Pharmaceuticals Ltd. [Vancouver Stock Exchange symbol] .... NIX
Nizam's Own Golgonda Lancers [British military] (DMA) .... NOGL
Nizamut Adalat Reports [India] [A publication] (DLA) .... NA
Nizhne-Angarsk [Former USSR Seismograph station code, US Geological Survey] (SEIS) .... NIZ
Nizhneudinsk [Former USSR ICAO location identifier] (ICLI) .... UINN
Nizhnevartovsk [Former USSR ICAO location identifier] (ICLI) .... USRN
Nizwa [Oman] [ICAO location identifier] (ICLI) .... OONZ
Njdole [Gabon] [Airport symbol] (AD) .... KDJ
Njoeng Jakob Kondre [Surinam] [ICAO location identifier] (ICLI) .... SMJK
Njombe [Tanzania] [ICAO location identifier] (ICLI) .... HTNJ
Njombe [Tanzania] [Airport symbol] (AD) .... JOM
Nkaus [Lesotho] [ICAO location identifier] (ICLI) .... FXNK
Nkaus [Lesotho] [Airport symbol] (OAG) .... NKU
N'Kay/Yokangassi [Congo] [ICAO location identifier] (ICLI) .... FCBY
Nkhotakota [Malawi] [ICAO location identifier] (ICLI) .... FWKK
Nkolo [Zaire] [Airport symbol] (AD) .... NKL
Nkolo-Fuma [Zaire] [ICAO location identifier] (ICLI) .... FZAR
N'Komo [Congo] [ICAO location identifier] (ICLI) .... FCPK
N'Kongsamba [Cameroon] [ICAO location identifier] (ICLI) .... FKAN
NL Industries, Inc. [Formerly, National Lead Co.] [NYSE symbol] (SPSG) .... NL
NL Industries, Inc. [Formerly, National Lead Co.] [Associated Press] (SAG) .... NL Ind
NL Industries, Inc., Hightstown, NJ [Library symbol Library of Congress] (LCLS) .... NjHigN
n-Laurylpyridinium Chloride [Detergent] .... NLPC
NII Norsat Intl. [NASDAQ symbol] (TTSB) .... NSATE
NLM-Dutch Airlines [ICAO designator] (AD) .... HN
NLX Resources, Inc. [Toronto Stock Exchange symbol] .... NLX
NMCS [Nuclear Material Control System] Automatic Control .... NAC
NMCS Information Processing System (NITA) .... NIPS
NMCSSC [National Military Command System Support Center] Automated ControlExecutive .... NACE
N-Methyl Fucosamine [Organic chemistry] .... NMF
N-Methylaspartate [Organic chemistry] .... NMA
N-Methylaspartic Acid [An amino acid] .... NMA
N-Methyl-D-Aspartic Acid [An amino acid] .... NMDA
N-Methyl-D-Aspartic Acid Receptor [Neurochemistry] .... NMDAR
N-Methyl-D-Glucamine [Biochemistry] .... NMDG
N-Methylformamide [Antineoplastic compound] .... NMF
N-Methylglucamine [USAN] [Organic chemistry] .... MEGLUMINE
N-Methylhydroxylamine [Organic chemistry] .... NMH
N-Methyliminodiacetic Acid [Organic chemistry] .... NMIDA
N-Methylmorpholine [Organic chemistry] .... NMM
N-Methylmorpholine N-Oxide [Organic chemistry] .... NMO
N-Methylnitroanisole [Organic chemistry] .... NMSO
N-Methylolacrylamide [Organic chemistry] .... NMA
N-Methylphenazium [Organic chemistry] .... NMP
N-Methyl(phenyl)tetrahydropyridine [Biochemistry] .... NMPTP
N-Methylphthalimide [Organic chemistry] .... NMP
N-Methylpyrrolidone [Organic chemistry] .... NMP
N-Methylspiperone [Biochemistry] .... NMSP
N-methyl-triazolinedione .... MTAD
NMFS [National Marine Fisheries Service] Northeast Fisheries Center, WoodsHole, MA [OCLC symbol] (OCLC) .... OAP
NMFS [National Marine Fisheries Service] Southeast Fisheries Center, Beaufort Laboratory, Beaufort, NC [OCLC symbol] (OCLC) .... OAN
NMIC [National Military Intelligence Center] Control Subsystem .... NCS
NMIC [National Military Information Center] Support System (MCD) .... NMICSS
NMIC [National Military Information Center] Support System (MCD) .... NSS
N-Monochloro(amino)butyric Acid [Organic chemistry] .... NMAB
N-Monochloroglycine [Dental caries treatment named for patent holders, Goldman and Kronman] GK-101
N-Monomethyltryptamine [Organic chemistry] .... NMT
NMR of America [NASDAQ symbol] (TTSB) .... NMRR
NMR of America, Inc. [Associated Press] (SAG) .... NMR
NMR of America, Inc. [NASDAQ symbol] (NQ) .... NMRR
N-Myristoyl Acyltransferase [An enzyme] .... NMT
NN Ball & Roller [NASDAQ symbol] (TTSB) .... NNBR
NN Ball & Roller, Inc. [Associated Press] (SAG) .... NN Ball
NN Ball & Roller, Inc. [NASDAQ symbol] (SAG) .... NNBR
N-Nitrosamine [Organic chemistry] .... NNA
N-Nitrosodimethylamine [Also, DMN, DMNA] [Organic chemistry] .... NDMA
N-Nitrosodiphenylamine [Organic chemistry] .... NDPhA
N-Nitrosodiphenylamine [Organic chemistry] .... NNDPA
N-Nitrosomorpholine [Also, NMOR] [Organic chemistry] .... NNM
N-Nitrosonornicotine [Organic chemistry] .... NNN
N-Nitrosoproline [Organic chemistry] .... NPRO
N-Nitrosopyrrolidine [Also, NYPR] [Biochemistry, organic chemistry] .... NO-PYR
N-Nitrosopyrrolidine [Organic chemistry] .... NPYRR
N-Nitrosopyrrolidine [Also, NO-PYR] [Biochemistry, organic chemistry] .... NYPR
N-Nitrosothiazolidine [Organic chemistry] .... NTHZ
N-Nitrosothioazolidine Carboxylic Acid [Organic chemistry] .... NTCA
No .... N
No Abnormal Findings [Medicine] .... NAF
No Abnormality [Medicine] (MAE) .... NA
No Abnormality Detected [Medicine] .... NAD
No Access [Telecommunications] (TEL) .... NA
No Account [Banking] .... NA
No Action .... N/A
No Action (MUGU) .... NOACT

No Action Indicated .... NAI
No Action Indicated (AD) .... nai
No Action Necessary [Military] (CINC) .... NAN
No Action [or Answer] Required (NVT) .... NAR
No Action Taken .... NAT
No Action, Talk Only (DICI) .... NATO
No Active Disease (DAVI) .... NAD
No Activity Log (MCD) .... NAL
No Acute Distress [Medicine] .... NAD
No Added Salt (AD) .... n-a-s
No Added Salt [Medicine] .... NAS
No Additional Charge .... NAC
No Additional Traffic Reported [Aviation] .... NATR
No Address Instruction (AD) .... nai
No Adverse Response Level [Medicine] (HCT) .... NARL
No Advice [Business term] .... N/A
No After Duty Action Required [Military] .... NADAR
No Airborne Intercept [Fighter aircraft lacking airborne intercept RADAR] .... NAI
No Alternative (DAVI) .... N/A
No American Equivalent [Language] .... NAE
No American Equivalent (AD) .... nAe
No American Flag Shipping Available .... NAFSA
No Answer (WDMC) .... NA
No Apparent Abnormalities [Medicine] .... NAA
No Apparent Change (MCD) .... NAC
No Apparent Defect [Shipping] .... NAD
No Apparent Defect (AD) .... nad
No Apparent Distress [Medicine] .... NAD
No Apparent Rate (AD) .... nar
No Appreciable Difference (AD) .... nad
No Appreciable Disease (AD) .... nad
No Appreciable Disease [Medicine] .... NAD
No Approval Required (MHDW) .... NA
No Arrival Report [Aviation] (FAAC) .... NORIV
No Assets (AFIT) .... NA
No Attack Area [Military] (NVT) .... NOTACK
No Bacteria Seen [Clinical microbiology] .... NBS
No Ball [Cricket] .... NB
No Berth List [Shipping] (DS) .... NBL
No Bias [Relay] [Electronics] .... NB
No Bias [Relay] .... NB
No Bid [or Bidders] .... NB
No Big Deal [Internet language] [Computer science] .... nbd
No Blasted Good [Slang] .... NBG
No Bloody Good [British slang] .... NBG
No Bone Injury [Medicine] .... NBI
No Bowel Movement [Gastroenterology] (DAVI) .... NB
No Bowel Movement [Medicine] (DMAA) .... NBM
No Business as Usual (EA) .... NBAU
No Caffeine [or] Pepper (DAVI) .... NCP
No Calibration Required (MCD) .... NCR
No Can Do [From pidgin English] .... NCD
No Canadian Rights .... NCR
No Carbon Required (NG) .... NCR
No Cardiopulmonary Resuscitation [For terminal patients] (DAVI) .... NCPR
No Casualty (MAE) .... NC
No Change (AAGC) .... N/C
No Change .... NC
No Change in Estimates .... NCE
No Change in Price (MCD) .... NCIP
No Change in the Due Date (AFM) .... NCDD
No Charge .... NC
No Charge Storage Agreement (AAGC) .... NCSA
No Checking Signal [Telecommunications] (TEL) .... NCS
No Children under 17 Admitted [Movie rating] NC-17
No Christian Name .... NXN
No Circuits .... NC
No Claim Bonus [Insurance] (ADA) .... NCB
No Claim Bonus on Renewal [Insurance] (AIA) .... NCBOR
No Claim Discount [Insurance] (AIA) .... NCD
No Clean Flux Process [Computer manufacturing] (PCM) .... NCF
No Code Blue [For terminal cases] [Medicine] (DAVI) .... NCB
No Coil (MSA) .... NC
No Collaterals [Medicine] .... NC
No Comment (NASA) .... NC
No Commercial Value [Business term] .... NCV
No Commission until Paid .... NCUP
No Common Interest .... NCI
No Complaints [Medicine] .... N/C
No Compromise Majority [An association] (EA) .... NCM
No Concentrated Sweets [Medicine] (DMAA) .... NCS
No Connection [Valve pins] [Radio] [Technical drawings] .... NC
No Connection (IDOE) .... nc
No Connection (IDOE) X
No Conscription Fellowship [England, World War I] .... NCF
No Contact .... NC
No Contest [Sports] .... NC
No Continuing Interest (NG) .... NOCONIT
No Control Circuit Contacts (MSA) .... NOCCC
No Copies Available (ADA) .... NCA
No Core Value [Business term] .... NCV
No Cost (AAG) .... NC
No Coupons Attached (DLA) .... NCA
No Credit (WGA) .... NC
No Customs Value (DS) .... NCV

No Data	ND
No Data Accepted [Computer science] (IAA)	NDAC
No Data Available [Computer science]	NDA
No Date [of publication]	ND
No Date (WDMC)	nd
No Date (VRA)	nd
No Date Club [Brooklyn girls - no dates for the duration] [World War II]	NDC
No Date Established	NDE
No Date Given (AFM)	NDG
No Decision [Sports]	ND
No Decompression Limit	NDL
No Defect Found	NDF
No Defect Found	N/D
No Defects	NDE
No Delay Expected	NDA
No Demonstrable Antibody [Medicine] (MAE)	ND
No Detect	NDA
No Detectable Activity	nDEA
No Deviation of Electrical Axis [On electrocardiogram] [Cardiology] (DAVI)	NDA
No Diagnosis of Anything	NDT
No Dial Tone [Of a telephone] (WDMC)	NDD
No Dialysis Days [Nephrology] (DAVI)	NDC
No Direct Charge	ND
No Discount [Business term] (DS)	ND
No Disease [Medicine]	NDF
No Disease Found (DAVI)	ND
No Distribution [Military security classification] (AFM)	NODIS
No Drawing [Engineering]	NDC-PS
No Drawing Change Project Slip	NET/NLT
No Earlier Than/No Later Than (MCD)	NE
No Earthly Chance (DSUE)	NEBM
No Eating between Meals	NE
No Ectopy [Medicine] (MEDA)	NEL
No Effect Level (ADA)	NE
No Effects	NOEC
No Effects Concentration [British environmental standard]	NEDEL
No Epidemiologically Detectable Exposure Level [Medicine] (HCT)	
No Erasures, No Leaves Torn Out, No Blank Spaces, No Overturning, No Writing between Lines, Statements to Be in Exact Words [Directions for written reports] [Scotland Yard]	ELBOWS
No Essential Traffic Reported [Aviation]	NETR
No Evidence of Disease	NED
No Evidence of Distal Metastasis [Oncology] (DAVI)	MO
No Evidence of Failure (MCD)	NEOF
No Evidence of Primary Tumor [Oncology] (DAVI)	TO
No Evidence of Pulmonary Disease (DAVI)	NEPD
No Evidence of Pulmonary Tuberculosis [Medicine]	NEPT
No Evidence of Recurrence [Medicine] (MAE)	NER
No Evidence of Recurrent Disease [Medicine] (MAE)	NERD
No Evidence of Tumor [Medicine]	NET
No Expiration Date	NED
No Explosion of the Total Contents [Business term] (DCTA)	NETC
No Eye Contact [Psychology]	NEC
No Fault Found (MCD)	NFF
No Feed Back (AEBS)	NFB
No Field Lubrication (PDAA)	NFL
No Fighter Suitably Located (SAA)	NFSL
No Filing Time [Aviation]	NFT
No Fire Area [Military] (INF)	NFA
No Fire Line [Military]	NFL
No Fire Zone [Military]	NFZ
No Fixed Abode	NFA
No Fixed Date	NFD
No Flash [Phototypesetting] (DGA)	NF
No Fly [Shrewd tradesman] [Slang British] (DSUE)	NF
No Fool	NF
No Foreign Dissemination [Intelligence classification] (MCD)	NFD
No Foreign Dissemination [Intelligence classification]	NOFODIS
No Form (AAG)	NF
No Form Necessary	NFN
No Frills Fund	NFF
No Funds (WDMC)	n/f
No Funds [Banking]	NF
No Further Action	NFA
No Further Action Required (DAVI)	NFAR
No Further Clearance Required [Aviation] (FAAC)	NEF
No Further Clearance Required (KSC)	NFC
No Further Consequences (NRCH)	NFC
No Further Information	NOFIN
No Further Need (MUGU)	NFN
No Further Requirement	NFR
No Further Service (Inspections)	NFI
No Further Visits [Medicine]	NFV
No Gallstones [Medicine]	NGS
No Gammopathy Detected [Biochemistry] (DAVI)	NOGM
No Gift Wrap [Mail-order catalogs]	NGW
No Gimbal Lock	NGL
No Go [i.e., an unacceptable arrangement]	NG
No Good [Similar to IC - Inspected and Condemned]	NG
No Greater Love (EA)	NGL
No Gum [Philately]	NG
No Hepatosplenomegaly [On physical examination] [Gastroenterology] (DAVI)	NHSM
No Hot Metal [Photocomposition]	NHM

No Immediate Miracles [Acronym and facetious translation derived from turning President Gerald Ford's anti-inflation WIN buttons upside down] [See WIN entry]	NIM
No Imprint (ADA)	NI
No Income, Lots of Kids [Lifestyle classification]	NILKY
No Income, No Kids [Lifestyle classification]	Nink
No Increase in Contract Price	NIICP
No Independence before Majority African Rule [British policy in regard to Rhodesia]	NIBMAR
No Individual Requirement (MSA)	NIR
No Information	NI
No Information Available	NIA
No Input Acknowledge [Computer science]	NIA
No Inspector, No Operator (ODBW)	NINO
No Interaction [Medicine]	NI
No Intermediate Storage [Industrial engineering]	NIS
No Irish Need Apply [Classified advertising]	NINA
No Issue	NI
No Ketones [Organic chemistry] (DAVI)	NK
No Kidding [An association Canada] (EAIO)	NK
No Known Allergies [Medicine]	NKA
No Known Drug Allergies [Medicine]	NKDA
No Known Medication Allergies (DAVI)	NKMA
No Known Relatives or Concerned	NKRC
No Ledger (SAA)	N/L
No Liability (ADA)	NL
No License [Traffic offense charge]	NL
No Light Perception [Ophthalmology]	NLP
No Limit (NASA)	NIL
No Limit (NASA)	NL
No Liner (DS)	NL
No Live Operator (NG)	NOLO
No Load	NL
No Load (MSA)	NLD
No Location (AABC)	NOLOC
No Longer Needed (AABC)	NLN
No Lunch Break	NLB
No Maintenance Requirement (NVT)	NMR
No Man's Land [Medical slang, cardiology]	NML
No Mark	NM
No Master Record [Military] (AFIT)	NMR
No Message	NM
No Middle Initial	NMI
No Middle Name	NMN
No Military Branch	NMB
No More Credit [Business term] (ADA)	NMC
No More Than [Pharmacy] (DAVI)	NMT
No More to Be Done [Medicine]	NMTBD
No More Trouble [Coates' brand of cotton thread] (ROG)	NMT
No Name	NN
No Name, No Address	NNNA
No National Name	NNN
No National Stock Number (AABC)	NNSN
No Net Loss	NNL
No Neutral Mode	NNM
No New Orders [Medical Records] (DAVI)	NNO
No No Nanette [Broadway musical]	NNN
No Observed Adverse Effect Level [Toxicology] (EG)	NOAEL
No Observed Effect Concentration [Toxicology]	NOEC
No Observed Effect Level [Toxicology]	NOEL
No Obvious Value Mail [Postal service]	NOVM
No One Else Has It [Lexicography]	NOEHI
No Operating Zone (DA)	NOZ
No Operation [Computer science]	NOOP
No Operation [Computer science]	NOP
No Operator [Telemarketing] (WDMC)	no-op
No Ophthalmologic Examination [Medicine]	NOE
No Option Offered [Investment term] (DFIT)	S
No Orders [Business term]	N/O
No Other Entry (ADA)	NOE
No Paging	NP
No Palpable Nodes [Oncology]	NO
No Par Value [Stock exchange term]	NPV
No Parity	NP
No Part on Order (MCD)	NPO
No Party with the Name of the Recipient of the Message [International telex abbreviation] (WDMC)	NP
No Passed Proof	NPP
No Pathologic Diagnosis [Medicine] (BARN)	NPD'
No Pay Due [Military] (ADDR)	NPD
No Payroll Division	NPD
No Perception of Light [Ophthalmology] (CPH)	NPL
No Periodic Calibration Required (MCD)	NPCR
No Periodic Inspection Required [Military] (AFIT)	NPIR
No Phone Listed [Cablegram marking] [British]	NFL
No Pilot Balloon Observation Due to High, or Gusty, Surface Wind [NWS] (FAAC)	PIWI
No Pilot Balloon Observation Due to Snow [Meteorology] (FAAC)	PISO
No Pilot Balloon Observation Due to Unfavorable Sea Conditions [NWS] (FAAC)	PISE
No Pilot Balloon Observation Will Be Filed Next Collection Unless Weather Changes Siginificantly [NWS] (FAAC)	NORPI
No Pin [Electronics] (OA)	NP
No Place [of publication] [Bibliography]	NP
No Place (WDMC)	np

No Place [*or Unknown*] [*MARC country of publication code Library of Congress*] (LCCP) ... xx
No Place or Date ... NP or D
No Pollution ... NOPOL
No Predators [*Ecology*] ... NP
No Present Illness ... NPI
No Previous Admission [*Medicine*] (MEDA) ... NPA
No Previous Carrier [*Insurance*] ... NPC
No Previous Complaint [*Medicine*] (DAVI) ... NPC
No Previous History [*Medicine*] (DAVI) ... NPH
No Previous Information [*to tip off a US Customs Service seizure*] ... NPI
No Price Available [*Business term*] (ADA) ... NPA
No Primary Staff Responsibility [*Army*] (AABC) ... NPSR
No Print [*Telecommunications*] (TEL) ... NP
No Printer Listed (NTCM) ... NP
No Prior or Current Federal Service (AABC) ... NPFS
No Prior Service [*Military*] ... NPS
No Procedure Turn Required [*Aviation*] ... NOPT
No Profit Here [*Business term*] ... NPH
No Programmed Calibration Required (MCD) ... NPCR
No Promotion [*Refers to lack of publicity in the record business*] ... NOPE
No Prospect [*In sports*] ... NP
No Protest [*Banking*] ... NP
No Protest [*Banking*] ... X
No Protest Nonacceptance [*Banking*] ... NPNA
No Publisher Listed (NTCM) ... NP
No Qualified Bidders [*Investment term*] (DFIT) ... NQB
No Radiation (MAE) ... NR
No Radio ... NORDO
No Radio [*Military*] ... RADNOS
No Radio Contact [*Aviation*] ... NORAC
No Record (AAG) ... N/R
No Record ... NOREC
No Record of Destination [*Aviation*] ... NRD
No Record of Mustering-Out Payment (DNAB) ... NOMOP
No Redeeming Features ... NRF
No Reference ... NOREF
No Refill [*Pharmacy*] ... NR
No Reflight ... NRF
No Reinforcement [*Psychology*] ... NRF
No Release (AAG) ... NR
No Remaining Radiation Service [*Unit*] [*Military*] ... NRRS
No Remittance ... NR
No Repair Action [*Military*] ... NRA
No Reply Heard [*ICAO designator*] (FAAC) ... NRH
No Reply Received ... NOREP
No Reply Received (FAAC) ... NORR
No Reply Received (NOAA) ... NORRD
No Report [*Medicine*] ... NR
No Requirement ... NR
No Residency Requirement [*Voter registration*] ... NR
No Response [*Medicine*] ... NR
No Response Required ... NRR
No Restrictions (FAAC) ... NORST
No Resume Required ... NRR
No Returns Permitted [*Business term*] ... XR
No Risk [*Business term*] ... NR
No Risk After Discharge [*Shipping*] ... NRAD
No Salt Added ... NSA
No Sample (MAE) ... NS
No Scramble (IAA) ... NS
No Separate Billing Price (MCD) ... NSP
No Sequelae [*Aftereffects*] [*Medicine*] (MAE) ... ns
No Serious Abnormality (DAVI) ... NSA
No Shop Order Required ... NSOR
No Significant Abnormalities [*Medicine*] ... NSA
No Significant Change [*Used to qualify weather phenomena*] ... NOSIG
No Significant Change [*Medicine*] ... NSC
No Significant Cloud [*Meteorology*] (FAAC) ... NSC
No Significant Defects [*or Deficiency*] [*Medicine*] ... NSD
No Significant Deviation [*Medicine*] ... NSD
No Significant Difference [*Medicine*] ... NSD
No Significant Disease [*Medicine*] ... NSD
No Small Craft or Storm Warnings are Being Displayed [*Weather*] ... NSCSWD
No Sound [*Script notation*] (NTCM) ... NS
No Space, No Print [*Computer science*] (MHDI) ... NSNP
No Spares Ordered (AAG) ... NSO
No Sparring (DS) ... NS
No Special Observation Taken [*NWS*] (FAAC) ... NOSPL
No Specific Working Hours [*ICAO*] (FAAC) ... HX
No Specimen [*Medicine*] ... NS
No Staff Responsibility [*Army*] (AABC) ... NSR
No Stamp [*Deltiology*] ... N/S
No Stimulation [*Neurophysiology*] ... NS
No Stock Number ... NSN
No Surgery Performed ... NS
No Talent Bum [*Slang*] ... NTB
No Terms [*Shipping*] ... N/T
No Test ... NT
No Texts Required [*Education*] ... NTR
No Tillage [*Agriculture*] ... NT
No Time Lost [*Military*] ... NTL
No Title Page [*Bibliography*] ... NTP
No Tool (SAA) ... NT
No Toxic Incinerator Group [*Political party*] ... NOTOX
No Trace [*Counterintelligence*] ... NT
No Traditions [*Internet*] ... Notrad
No Traffic Reported [*Air Traffic Control*] (FAAC) ... NTC
No Traffic Reported [*Aviation*] ... NTR
No Traffic Reported [*Aviation*] (FAAC) ... NTRP
No Transmission [*Telecommunications*] ... NT
No Travel Involved [*Military*] ... NTI
No Travel Involved for Officer Concerned [*Military*] ... NTIOC
No Trouble Found ... NTF
No Trouble Found [*Aviation*] (FAAC) ... NTFND
No Trump [*in game of bridge*] ... NT
No Try On [*Purchaser did not have a fitting*] [*Merchandising slang*] ... NTO
No Uniform [*For schoolgirls*] [*British*] ... N
No Upper Limit (MHDW) ... NUL
No Value [*Legal term*] (DLA) ... N/V
No Value Declared [*Business term*] (DCTA) ... NVD
No Venous Distention [*Medicine*] (MEDA) ... NVD
No Verification Required (NASA) ... NVR
No Voltage Amplification [*Electronics*] (IAA) ... NVA
No Voltage Release [*Electronics*] ... NVR
No Wait [*Industrial engineering*] ... NW
No Weight-Bearing [*orthopedics*] (DAVI) ... NWB
No Wind [*Air*] **Position** [*Navigation*] ... NW
No Work - No Woo [*Slogan adopted by women war workers in Albina shipyards in Portland, Oregon, who agreed not to date men who were absent from work*] [*World War II*] ... NW-NW
No Year [*of publication*] [*Bibliography*] ... NY
NOAA [*National Oceanic and Atmospheric Administration*] **Accounting Manual** (NOAA) ... NAM
NOAA [*National Oceanic and Atmospheric Administration*] **Administrative Order** (USDC) ... NAO
NOAA [*National Oceanic and Atmospheric Administration*] **Administrative Order** [*Marine science*] (OSRA) ... NAO
NOAA [*National Oceanic and Atmospheric Administration*] **Corps** [*Marine science*] (OSRA) ... NC
NOAA [*National Oceanic and Atmospheric Administration*] **Corps** (USDC) ... NC
NOAA [*National Oceanic and Atmospheric Administration*] **Data Buoy Office** [*or Operation*] (IID) ... NDBO
NOAA [*National Oceanic and Atmospheric Administration*] **Directives Manual** (NOAA) ... NDM
NOAA [*National Oceanic and Atmospheric Administration*]-Forecast Systems Lab ... NOAA-FSL
NOAA [*National Oceanic and Atmospheric Administration*] **Geophysical Fluid Dynamics Laboratory, Princeton, NJ** [*OCLC symbol*] (OCLC) ... OAY
NOAA [*National Oceanic and Atmospheric Administration*] **Interoceanic Canal Project** (NOAA) ... NICP
NOAA [*National Oceanic and Atmospheric Administration*] **Library and Information Network** [*Marine science*] (OSRA) ... NLIN
NOAA [*National Oceanic and Atmospheric Administration*] **Library and Information Network** (USDC) ... NLIN
NOAA [*National Oceanic and Atmospheric Administration*]-LISD Seattle Center, Seattle, WA [*OCLC symbol*] (OCLC) ... OAE
NOAA [*National Oceanic and Atmospheric Administration*] **Operational Telecommunications Coordinator** (NOAA) ... NOTC
NOAA [*National Oceanic and Atmospheric Administration*] **Operational Telecommunications System** (NOAA) ... NOTS
NOAA [*National Oceanic and Atmospheric Administration*] **Satellite** (USDC) ... NIMBUS-7
NOAA [*National Oceanic and Atmospheric Administration*] **Undersea Research Program** (USDC) ... NURP
NOAA [*National Oceanic and Atmospheric Administration*] **Undersea Research Program** [*Marine science*] (OSRA) ... NURP
NOAA [*National Oceanic and Atmospheric Administration*] **Weather Radio** (NOAA) ... NWR
NOAA [*National Oceanic and Atmospheric Administration*] **Weather Wire Service** (NOAA) ... NWWS
No-Acid Descaling (IEEE) ... NAD
No-Acronym Sort of Guy [*Term coined by William F. Doescher, publisher of "D & B Reports"*] [*Lifestyle classification*] ... Nag
No-Address Instruction (AAG) ... NAI
No-Adjust Car Building Process [*Ford Motor Co.*] [*Automotive engineering*] ... NACBP
Noah (ABBR) ... NO
Noah Worcester Dermatological Society (EA) ... NWDS
Noan Mizrachi [*American Zionist organization*] ... NOAM
No-Antihalation Film ... NAH
Noar Halutzi Lohem [*Pioneering Fighting Youth*] [*Israel*] ... NAHAL
Noatak [*Alaska*] [*Airport symbol*] (OAG) ... WTK
Noatak, AK [*Location identifier FAA*] (FAAL) ... WTK
Nobel Ed Dynamics [*NASDAQ symbol*] (TTSB) ... NEDI
Nobel Education Dynamics, Inc. [*NASDAQ symbol*] (SAG) ... NEDI
Nobel Education Dynamics, Inc. [*Associated Press*] (SAG) ... NobelEd
Nobel Foundation (EA) ... NF
Nobel Insurance [*NASDAQ symbol*] (TTSB) ... NOBLF
Nobel Insurance Ltd. [*Associated Press*] (SAG) ... Nobel
Nobel Insurance Ltd. [*NASDAQ symbol*] (NQ) ... NOBL
Nobel Prize ... NP
Nobelair [*Turkey*] [*ICAO designator*] (FAAC) ... NAD
Nobelium [*Chemical element*] ... No
Nobelstiftelsen [*Nobel Foundation - NF*] (EAIO) ... NS
Nobeoka [*Japan*] [*Seismograph station code, US Geological Survey*] (SEIS) ... NOB
Nobeyama Radio Observatory ... NRO
Nobile [*Nobly*] [*Music*] (ROG) ... NOB
Nobility (ABBR) ... NOB

Nobility (ABBR) ... NOBT
Nobility Homes [*NASDAQ symbol*] (TTSB) ... NOBH
Nobility Homes [*Associated Press*] (SAG) ... NobltyH
Nobility Homes, Inc. [*NASDAQ symbol*] (NQ) ... NOBH
Nobility Homes, Inc. [*Associated Press*] (SAG) ... NobiltyH
Nobis [*With Us*] [*Latin*] (ROG) ... NOB
Noble (ABBR) ... NOB
Noble Affiliates [*NYSE symbol*] (TTSB) ... NBL
Noble Affiliates, Inc. [*NYSE symbol*] (SPSG) ... NBL
Noble Affiliates, Inc. [*Associated Press*] (SAG) ... NoblAf
Noble County Public Library, Albion, IN [*Library symbol Library of Congress*] (LCLS) ... InAlb
Noble Drilling $1.50 Cv Pfd [*NYSE symbol*] (TTSB) ... NEPr
Noble Drilling Corp. [*Associated Press*] (SAG) ... NblD
Noble Drilling Corp. [*Associated Press*] (SAG) ... NbleDr
Noble Gas Activity Monitor (IEEE) ... NGAM
Noble Gas Storage Facility (NRCH) ... NGSF
Noble Gases [*Nuclear energy*] (NRCH) ... NG
Noble Grand ... NG
Noble Guard [*Freemasonry*] (ROG) ... NG
Noble Metal Catalyst [*Automotive engineering*] ... NMC
Noble Mines & Oils Ltd. [*Toronto Stock Exchange symbol*] ... NMO
Noble Order, Descendants of the Conqueror and His Companions (EA) ... NODCC
Noble Peak Resources Ltd. [*Vancouver Stock Exchange symbol*] ... NPK
Noble Roman's, Inc. [*Associated Press*] (SAG) ... NobleR
Noble Roman's, Inc. [*NASDAQ symbol*] (NQ) ... NROM
Noble Romns [*NASDAQ symbol*] (TTSB) ... NROM
Noble-Collip Drum Trauma [*Physiology*] ... NCDT
Nobleman (ABBR) ... NOBMN
Noble-Metal-Coated Titanium [*Anode*] ... NMT
Nobler (ABBR) ... NOBR
Nobles County Library, Worthington, MN [*Library symbol Library of Congress*] (LCLS) ... MnWoN
Noble's Current Court Decisions [*New York*] [*A publication*] (DLA) ... Noble
Noblest (ABBR) ... NOBST
Noblesville Daily Ledger, Noblesville, IN [*Library symbol Library of Congress*] (LCLS) ... InNobL
Noblesville, IN [*FM radio station call letters*] (RBYB) ... WGLD-FM
Noblesville, IN [*FM radio station call letters*] ... WXTZ
Noblesville Public Library, Noblesville, IN [*Library symbol Library of Congress*] (LCLS) ... InNob
Noblewomen (ABBR) ... NOBWN
Nobly (ABBR) ... NOBY
Nobody Don't Say Nothing ... NDSN
Nobody Ever Tells Me Anything [*Executive complaint*] ... NETMA
Nobody Gives a Damn ... NGAD
Nocardia [*Genus of bacteria*] (MAE) ... N
Nockian Society (EA) ... NS
No-Claim Bonus as Earned [*Insurance*] (ODBW) ... NCBAE
No-Copy Paper ... NCP
No-Cost Item (AAG) ... NCI
No-Cost Time Extension (MCD) ... NCTE
Nocte [*At Night*] [*Pharmacy*] ... N
Nocte [*At Night*] [*Pharmacy*] (ROG) ... NOCT
Nocte et Mane [*Night and Morning*] [*Pharmacy*] ... N et M
Nocte et Mane [*Night and Morning*] [*Latin*] [*Pharmacy*] (DAVI) ... n et m
Nocte et Mane [*Night and Morning*] [*Pharmacy*] ... NM
Nocte Maneque [*Night and Morning*] [*Pharmacy*] ... NMQUE
Nocte Maneque [*Night and Morning*] [*Pharmacy*] ... NOCT MANEQ
Noctes Atticae [*of Gellius*] [*Classical studies*] (OCD) ... NA
Noctilucent Cloud Particles ... NCP
Noctilucent Clouds ... NLC
Noctis [*Night*] [*Medicine*] ... noc
Nocturia [*Urology*] (DAVI) ... No
Nocturnal (CPH) ... noct
Nocturnal Acid Accumulation [*Botany*] ... NAA
Nocturnal Adoration Society (EA) ... NAS
Nocturnal Penile Tumescence [*Psychiatry*] ... NPT
Nodal [*Oncology*] ... N
Nodal Exchange (MCD) ... NE
Nodal Exchange Area (MHDB) ... NXA
Nodal Point Keying ... NPK
Nodal Premature Beat [*Cardiology*] ... NPB
Nodal Premature Contraction [*Cardiology*] (MAE) ... NPC
Nodal Rhythm [*Cardiology*] (DAVI) ... NR
Nodal Switching Center ... NSC
Nodal-His [*Medicine*] (MEDA) ... NH
Nodamura Virus ... NOV
NODC [*National Oceanographic Data Center*] **Index to Instrument Measures Subsurface Current Observations** [*Marine science*] (MSC) ... NIMSCO
Nodding Image Motion Compensation [*Instrumentation*] ... NIMC
Nodding Subdish System ... NSS
Node [*Lymphatic*] [*Anatomy*] ... N
Node Administration (NITA) ... NAD
Node Compatibility List [*Telecommunications*] (TEL) ... NCL
Node Dissection [*Medicine*] ... ND
Node Initialization Block [*Computer science*] (IBMDP) ... NIB
Node Location Code (PDAA) ... NLC
Node of First-Fruiting Branch [*Botany*] (OA) ... NFB
Node Operator Interface (NITA) ... NOI
Node Switching Assembly (SSD) ... NSA
Node Tracker [*Frye Computer Systems*] [*Telecommunications*] (PCM) ... NT
Nodes Above White Flower [*Botany*] ... NAWF
No-Dig International [*A publication*] ... NDI
Nodine, MN [*Location identifier FAA*] (FAAL) ... ODI
Nodular and Diffuse Lymphoma [*Oncology*] ... N & D
Nodular Histiocytic [*Lymphoma*] [*Oncology*] (DAVI) ... NH
Nodular Histiocytic Lymphoma [*Oncology*] ... NHL
Nodular Liquifying Panniculitis [*Dermatology*] (DAVI) ... NLP
Nodular Lymphoma [*Oncology*] (DAVI) ... NL
Nodular Melanoma [*Oncology*] ... NM
Nodular Mixed Lymphoma [*Onocology*] (DAVI) ... NM
Nodular Mixed Lymphoma [*Onocology*] (DAVI) ... NML
Nodular Poorly Differentiated Lymphocyte ... NPDL
Nodular Poorly Differentiated Lymphoma [*Oncology*] (DAVI) ... NPL
Nodular Regenerative Hyperplasia [*of liver*] [*Medicine*] ... NRH
Nodular Sclerosing Hodgkin's Disease [*Medicine*] (DMAA) ... NSHD
Nodular Sclerosis [*Medicine*] (AAMN) ... NS
Nodular Subepidermal Fibrosis [*Dermatology*] ... NSF
Nodular Subepidermal Fibrosis [*Dermatology*] (DAVI) ... NSF
Nodule-Inducing Virus ... NIV
Nodulocystic Acne [*Medicine*] (DMAA) ... NCA
Noel Group [*NASDAQ symbol*] (TTSB) ... NOEL
Noel Group, Inc. [*NASDAQ symbol*] (SAG) ... NOEL
Noel Group, Inc. [*Associated Press*] (SAG) ... NoelGp
Noemfoor [*New Guinea*] [*Airport symbol*] (AD) ... FOO
No-Error Check (IAA) ... NEC
Nogales, AZ [*Location identifier FAA*] (FAAL) ... ENZ
Nogales, AZ [*FM radio station call letters*] (RBYB) ... KNOG-FM
Nogales, AZ [*FM radio station call letters*] (RBYB) ... KZNO
Nogales, AZ [*Location identifier FAA*] (FAAL) ... OLS
Nogales/Internacional [*Mexico ICAO location identifier*] (ICLI) ... MMNG
Nogales/International [*Arizona*] [*ICAO location identifier*] (ICLI) ... KOLS
Nogales Public Library, Nogales, AZ [*Library symbol Library of Congress*] (LCLS) ... AzN
Nogaro [*France ICAO location identifier*] (ICLI) ... LFCN
Nohanas [*Lesotho*] [*ICAO location identifier*] (ICLI) ... FXNH
Noise [*Broadcasting*] ... N
Noise (ABBR) ... NSE
Noise Abatement Office (AD) ... NAO
Noise Abatement Procedure (AAG) ... NAP
Noise Abatement Society (AD) ... N A S
Noise Abatement Society [*British*] ... NAS
Noise Abatement Society of Great Britain (AD) ... NAS-GB
Noise Abatement Test System (FAAC) ... NATS
Noise Acoustic Emitter [*Military*] (CAAL) ... NAE
Noise Advisory Council [*British*] ... NAC
Noise Amplitude Distribution ... NAD
Noise Amplitude Distribution Measuring Equipment (PDAA) ... NADME
Noise Analysis Program ... NAP
Noise and Number Exposure (PDAA) ... NNE
Noise and Number Index ... NNI
Noise and Vibration Monitor Analyzer [*Military*] (CAAL) ... NVMA
Noise Augmentation Unit [*Military*] (CAAL) ... NAU
Noise Balancing Circuit (DEN) ... NBC
Noise Balancing Control (IAA) ... NBC
Noise Bandwidth ... NBW
Noise Bandwidth (IDOE) ... nbw
Noise Blanker ... NB
Noise Canceling Microphone ... NCM
Noise Cancellation Tech [*NASDAQ symbol*] (TTSB) ... NCTI
Noise Cancellation Technologies, Inc. [*NASDAQ symbol*] (SAG) ... NCTI
Noise Cancellation Technologies, Inc. [*Associated Press*] (SAG) ... NoiseCT
Noise Cancellation Technology (PS) ... NCT
Noise Com, Inc. (SPSG) ... NOI
Noise Control Act (EG) ... NCA
Noise Control Association (EA) ... NCA
Noise Control Committee ... NCC
Noise Control Laboratory [*Pennsylvania State University*] [*Research center*] (RCD) ... NCL
Noise Control Product and Materials Association [*Later, NCA*] (IAA) ... NCPAMA
Noise Control Products and Materials Association [*Later, NCA*] (EA) ... NCPMA
Noise Correlation (MSA) ... NC
Noise Correlation ... NOCO
Noise Criterion ... NC
Noise Deficiency Management System ... NDMS
Noise Depreciation Index ... NDI
Noise Diode [*Electronics*] (IAA) ... NODE
Noise Diotic, Signal Monaural (PDAA) ... NOSM
Noise Dose Count (IAA) ... NDC
Noise Equivalent Exposure [*Photonics*] ... NEE
Noise Evaluation Test (IAA) ... NET
Noise Exposure Computer Integrator (PDAA) ... NECI
Noise Exposure Forecast [*Aircraft*] ... NEF
Noise Factor ... NF
Noise Figure ... NF
Noise Figure Indicator ... NFI
Noise Figure Meter ... NFM
Noise Figure Meter System ... NFMS
Noise Frequency (MSA) ... NF
Noise Frequency Spectrum ... NFS
Noise Fuse (MCD) ... NF
Noise Generation Mechanism ... NGM
Noise Generator (MSA) ... NGEN
Noise Generator (CET) ... NSGN
Noise Generator Card ... NGC
Noise Generator Tube ... NGT
Noise Improvement Factor (IEEE) ... NIF
Noise Index ... NI

Noise Information Service .... NOISE
Noise Information System [*Environmental Protection Agency*] (IID) .... NIS
Noise Isolation Class (PDAA) .... NIC
Noise Jammer Simulator [*Telecommunications*] (TEL) .... NJS
Noise Library, Air Navigation Systems Requirements, Transport Canada [*Bibliotheque Normes de Bruit, Exigences du Systeme de Navigation Aerienne, Transports Canada*], Vancouver, British Columbia [*Library symbol National Library of Canada*] (NLC) .... BVATAN
Noise Limit Indicator .... NLI
Noise Limiter (IAA) .... NLT
Noise Load Ratio .... NLR
Noise, Measurement Buoy .... NMB
Noise Measurement Test Set .... NMTS
Noise Measuring Set [*Telecommunications*] (TEL) .... NMS
Noise Meter (MSA) .... NM
Noise Nuisance Index (PDAA) .... NNI
Noise Output Device .... NOD
Noise Pollution and Abatement Act (GFGA) .... NPAA
Noise Pollution Level .... NPL
Noise Power/Bandwidth .... N/B
Noise Power Ratio .... NPR
Noise Power Spectra [*Spectrometry*] .... NPS
Noise Power Spectre Density .... NPSD
Noise Prediction and Reduction .... NPR
Noise Preferential Route [*Aviation*] (DA) .... NPR
Noise Rating (NASA) .... NR
Noise Ratio .... NR
Noise Ration .... NR
Noise Reduction (IAA) .... NR
[*Dolby*] **Noise Reduction** (WDMC) .... NR
Noise Reduction Coefficient [*of insulation*] .... NRC
Noise Reduction Rating [*Audio technology*] (EG) .... NRR
Noise Regulation Reporter [*Bureau of National Affairs*] [*A publication*] (DLA) .... Noise Reg Rep
Noise Review Program [*Navy*] (DNAB) .... NRP
Noise Sensitivity (IAA) .... NS
Noise, Shock, and Vibration (PDAA) .... NSV
Noise Source Instrumentation .... NSI
Noise Source Meter .... NSM
Noise Source Tube .... NST
Noise, Spikes, and Transients (PDAA) .... NST
Noise Substest of the Goldman-Fristoe-Woodcock Auditory Skills Test Battery (EDAC) .... NS-GFW
Noise Suppression Circuit (DEN) .... NSC
Noise Suppression Device .... NSD
Noise Suppression Oscillator (MCD) .... NSO
Noise Suppressor Assembly .... NSA
Noise Suppressor System (MCD) .... NSS
Noise Supressor [*Radio*] (NTCM) .... NS
Noise Temperature Ratio (AAG) .... NTR
Noise to Interference Ratio [*Telecommunications*] (TEL) .... N/I
Noise Transmission Impairment [*Telecommunications*] .... NTI
Noise, Vibration, Harshness [*Automotive technology*] .... NVH
Noise-Adding Radiometer .... NAR
Noise-Equivalent (IAA) .... NE
Noise-Equivalent Angle (MCD) .... NEA
Noise-Equivalent Bandwidth .... NEB
Noise-Equivalent Charge (PDAA) .... NEC
Noise-Equivalent Differential Temperature .... NEDT
Noise-Equivalent Energy (MCD) .... NEE
Noise-Equivalent Flux .... NEF
Noise-Equivalent Flux Density .... NEFD
Noise-Equivalent Input .... NEI
Noise-Equivalent Intensity .... NEI
Noise-Equivalent Power .... NEP
Noise-Equivalent Power Density .... NEPD
Noise-Equivalent Radiance .... NER
Noise-Equivalent Signal (IEEE) .... NES
Noise-Equivalent Spectral Radiance [*Physics*] .... NESR
Noise-Equivalent Temperature .... NET
Noise-Equivalent Temperature Difference [*Thermography*] .... NETD
Noise-Induced Hearing Damage [*Medicine*] (MEDA) .... NIHD
Noise-Induced Hearing Loss .... NIHL
Noise-Induced Permanent Hearing Loss (PDAA) .... NIPHL
Noise-Induced Permanent Threshold Shift [*Hearing*] .... NIPTS
Noiseless (ABBR) .... NSELS
Noiseless Camera (NTCM) .... NC
Noise-Level Cable .... NLC
Noise-Level Frequency Monitor .... NLFM
Noise-Level Gain Control (MCD) .... NLGC
Noise-Level Monitor [*SONAR*] .... NLM
Noise-Measuring Equipment .... NME
Noise-Operated Automatic Level Adjustment .... NOALA
Noise-Operated Device for Antinoise [*Telecommunications*] (TEL) .... NODAN
Noise-Operated Gain-Adjusting Device .... NOGAD
Noise-Rating Curve (OA) .... NRC
Noise-to-Signal Ratio (IAA) .... NSR
Noisily (ABBR) .... NSLY
Noisiness (ABBR) .... NSENS
Noisy (ABBR) .... NSY
Nokaneng [*Botswana*] [*ICAO location identifier*] (ICLI) .... FBNN
Nokes' Mortgages and Receiverships [*3rd ed.*] [*1951*] [*A publication*] (DLA) .... Nok Mort
Nokia Corp. [*NYSE symbol*] (SAG) .... NOK
Nokia Corp. [*Associated Press*] (SAG) .... Nokia
Nokomis Community Unit, School District 22, Nokomis, IL [*Library symbol Library of Congress*] (LCLS) .... INokSD
Nokomis Public Library, Nokomis, IL [*Library symbol Library of Congress*] (LCLS) .... INok
Nolan, Norton & Co., Inc., Lexington, MA [*OCLC symbol*] (OCLC) .... NNC
Nolan on the Poor Laws [*A publication*] (DLA) .... Nol PL
Nolan on the Poor Laws [*A publication*] (DLA) .... Nolan
Nolan Resources Ltd. [*Vancouver Stock Exchange symbol*] .... NLR
Noland Co. [*Associated Press*] (SAG) .... Noland
Noland Co. [*NASDAQ symbol*] (NQ) .... NOLD
Nolan's English Magistrates' Cases [*A publication*] (DLA) .... Nol
Nolan's English Magistrates' Cases [*A publication*] (DLA) .... Nol Mag
Nolan's English Magistrates' Cases [*A publication*] (DLA) .... Nolan
Nolan's English Settlement Cases [*A publication*] (DLA) .... Nol
Nolanville, TX [*FM radio station call letters*] (RBYB) .... KLFX
Nolichucky Regional Library Center, Morristown, TN [*Library symbol Library of Congress*] (LCLS) .... TMorNR
No-Limit Order .... NLO
Nolisair International, Inc. [*Canada ICAO designator*] (FAAC) .... NXA
Nolle Prosequi [*Unwilling to Prosecute*] [*Legal term Latin*] .... NOL PROS
Nolo Contendere [*I Do Not Wish to Contend*] [*Legal term*] [*Latin*] (BARN) .... nol con
No-Load Frame Time .... NLFT
No-Load Funds .... NLF
No-Load Mutual Fund Association (EA) .... NLMFA
No-Load Speed .... NLS
No-Load Start .... NLS
NOLPE [*National Organization on Legal Problems of Education*] **School Law Journal** [*A publication*] (DLA) .... NOLPE Sch LJ
NOLPE [*National Organization on Legal Problems of Education*] **School Law Journal** [*A publication*] (DLA) .... NOLPE School LJ
NOLPE [*National Organization on Legal Problems of Education*] **School Law Reporter** [*A publication*] (DLA) .... NOLPE School L Rep
Noludar [*A hypnotic*] [*Roche laboratories*] (DAVI) .... NOLDAR
Noma Industries Ltd. [*Toronto Stock Exchange symbol*] .... NMA
Nomad Energy & Resources [*Vancouver Stock Exchange symbol*] .... NDM
Nomad River [*Papua New Guinea*] [*Airport symbol*] (OAG) .... NOM
Nomadic Computing Environment .... NCE
Nomads' Charitable and Educational Foundation [*Australia*] .... NCEF
Nome [*Alaska*] [*Seismograph station code, US Geological Survey Closed*] (SEIS) .... NOM
Nome [*Alaska*] [*Airport symbol*] (OAG) .... OME
Nome [*Alaska*] [*ICAO location identifier*] (ICLI) .... PAOM
Nome, AK [*Location identifier FAA*] (FAAL) .... FDV
Nome, AK [*AM radio station call letters*] .... KICY
Nome, AK [*FM radio station call letters*] .... KICY-FM
Nome, AK [*FM radio station call letters*] .... KNOM
Nome, AK [*FM radio station call letters*] .... KNOM-FM
Nomemklatur Kommission [*Commission on Nomenclature*] [*Germany*] (DAVI) .... NK
Nomen [*Name*] [*Latin*] .... N
Nomen Conservandum [*Retained Name*] [*Latin*] .... nom cons
Nomen Dubium [*Doubtful Name*] [*Latin*] .... nom dub
Nomen Illegitimum [*Illegitimate Name*] [*Latin*] .... nom illeg
Nomen Invalidum [*Name Not Valid*] [*Latin*] .... nom inval
Nomen Masculinam [*Masculine Name*] [*Latin*] (ROG) .... NM
Nomen Nescio [*Unknown*] [*Latin*] (GPO) .... nn
Nomen Novum [*New Name*] [*Latin*] (BABM) .... N NOV
Nomen Novum [*New Name*] [*Latin*] [*Pharmacy*] (DAVI) .... n nov
Nomen Novum [*New Name*] [*Latin*] (DAVI) .... nn
Nomen Novum [*New Name*] [*Latin*] .... nom nov
Nomen Nudum [*A Name without Designation*] [*Latin*] (BABM) .... NOM MUD
Nomen Nudum [*Invalid Name*] [*Biology, taxonomy*] [*Latin*] .... nom nud
Nomen Proprium [*Proper Name*] [*Latin*] .... NP
Nomen Provisiorum [*Provisional Name*] [*Latin*] .... nom prov
Nomen Rejiciendum [*Rejected Name*] [*Latin*] .... nom rej
Nomen Superfluum [*Superfluous Name*] [*Latin*] .... nom superfl
Nomenclature (AAG) .... NOM
Nomenclature (AFM) .... NOMEN
Nomenclature Board [*Tasmania, Australia*] .... NB
Nomenclature Control Index (MCD) .... NCI
Nomenclature for Imports and Exports [*European Community*] (PDAA) .... NIMEX
Nomenclature Sequence Code [*Navy*] (AFIT) .... NSC
Nomenclature-in-Federal Employment .... NIFE
Nomina [*Names*] [*Probably a misprint for NN, by some supposed to denote St. Mary, patron saint of girls*] [*Latin*] (ROG) .... M
Nomina [*Names*] [*Latin*] .... NN
Nomina Anatomica [*System of anatomical terminology*] .... NA
Nomina Anatomica (Paris) [*Anatomical Nomenclature*] (DAVI) .... PNA
Nomina Anatomica Parisiensia [*Medicine*] .... NAP
Nominal [*Stock exchange term*] (SPSG) .... N
Nominal (AAG) .... NOM
Nominal (ROG) .... NOML
Nominal Band Edge .... NBE
Nominal Bore [*Tubing*] .... NB
Nominal Characteristics File (IEEE) .... NCF
Nominal Correction .... NC
Nominal Correction I [*Phasing maneuver*] (MCD) .... NCI
Nominal Corrective Combination (MCD) .... NCC
Nominal Defendant (Queensland) [*Australia*] .... ND(Q)
Nominal Detectable Signal (IAA) .... NDS
Nominal Gross National Product .... Y
Nominal Group [*Linguistics*] .... Ngp
Nominal Grouping Technique .... NGT
Nominal Guidance Scheme (OA) .... NGS
Nominal Height (MCD) .... NH

Nominal Horsepower	NHP
Nominal Horsepower (IAA)	NP
Nominal Line Width	NLW
Nominal Operating Cell [Photovoltaic energy systems]	NOC
Nominal [or Normal] Operating Cell Temperature [Photovoltaic energy systems]	NOCT
Nominal Percent Defective	NPD
Nominal Pipe Size (SAA)	NPS
Nominal Protection Coefficient [Business term]	NPC
Nominal Rim Diameter [Automotive engineering]	NRD
Nominal Root Mean Square (IAA)	NRMS
Nominal Single Dose [Pharmacology] (DAVI)	NSC
Nominal Slow Rate [NASA] (KSC)	NSR
Nominal Stagnation Point	NSP
Nominal Standard Dose [Medicine]	NSD
Nominal Stress Approach (PDAA)	NSA
Nominal Ultimate Strength (IAA)	NUS
Nominal Velocity of Propagation [Electronics] (PCM)	NVP
Nominal Width (NATG)	NW
Nominalism (ABBR)	NOMLM
Nominalist (ABBR)	NOMLT
Nominally (ABBR)	NOMLY
Nominally Labeled [Compound, with radioisotope]	N
Nominate (AFM)	NOM
Nominated (ABBR)	NOMD
Nominated Air Traffic Service Unit (DA)	NATSU
Nominating (ABBR)	NOMG
Nominating Committee [American Occupational Therapy Association]	NC
Nomination	NOMN
Nomination	N
Nominative	NOM
Nominative	NOMIN
Nominative (WDAA)	NOMV
Nominative (ABBR)	NOMR
Nominator (ABBR)	NOMEE
Nominee (ABBR)	NOMEE
Nominee [Legal shorthand] (LWAP)	NOMEE
NOMOS Verlagskatalog [NOMOS Datapool] [Information service or system] (IID)	NOVE
Noms Propres Sud-Semitiques [A publication] (BJA)	NPSS
Nomura Research Institute (NITA)	NRI
Non Absorbing Mirror Constricted Double Heterostructure (NITA)	NAM-CDH
Non Alibi Occurrit [It Occurs in No Other Place] [Latin] (ROG)	NON AL OCC
Non Allocatur [Legal] [Latin] (ROG)	NA
Non Compliance Order [Environmental Protection Agency]	NCO
Non Compos Mentis [Not of Sound Mind] [Latin] (LWAP)	NCM
Non Compos Mentis [Not in Sound Mind] [Latin] (ROG)	NON COM
Non Culpabilis [Not Guilty] [Latin] (ROG)	NON CUL
Non Detected [Laboratory science] (DAVI)	NOND
Non Disponible [Not Available] [French]	ND
Non Domestic Substances List [Canada]	NDSL
Non Est Inventus [It Has Not Been Found or Discovered] [Latin]	NEI
Non Est Mortale Quod Opto [It Is No Mortal Thing I Desire] [Motto of Friedrich III, Duke of Schleswig-Holstein-Gottorp (1597-1659)] [Latin]	NEMQO
Non Free Trade Zone (DS)	NFTZ
Non Justifying [Typography] (DGA)	NJ
Non Licet [It Is Not Permitted] [Latin]	NL
Non Liquet [It Is Not Clear] [Latin]	NL
Non Longe [Not Far] [Latin]	NL
Non Obstante [Notwithstanding] [Latin]	NON OBS
Non Obstante [Notwithstanding] [Latin] (ROG)	NON OBST
Non Obstante Veredicto [Judgment Notwithstanding] [Latin Legal term] (DLA)	NOV
Non Per Os [Nothing by Mouth] [Latin] (BABM)	NPO
Non Prosequitur [Does Not Prosecute] [Latin]	NON PROS
No'n Pwr Minn,$4.10 Pfd [NYSE symbol] (TTSB)	NSPPrC
Non Recedet Malum a Domo Ingrati [Evil Shall Not Depart from the House of the Ungrateful] [(After Prov., XVII. 13) Motto of Julius, Duke of Braunschweig-Wolfenbuttel (1529-89)] [Latin]	NRMADI
Non Repetatur [Do Not Repeat] [Pharmacy]	NON REP
Non Repetatur [Do Not Repeat] [Pharmacy]	Non Repetat
Non Repetatur [Do Not Repeat] [Pharmacy]	NR
Non Self-Representing Primary Sampling Unit [Bureau of the Census] (GFGA)	NSR PSU
Non Sequitur [It Does Not Follow] [Latin]	NON SEQ
No'n St Pwr Minn,$4.08 Pfd [NYSE symbol] (TTSB)	NSPPrB
No'n St Pwr Minn,$4.11 Pfd [NYSE symbol] (TTSB)	NSPrD
No'n St Pwr Minn,$4.56 Pfd [NYSE symbol] (TTSB)	NSPPrG
No'n St Pwr Minn,$6.80 Pfd [NYSE symbol] (TTSB)	NSPPrH
No'n St Pwr Minn,$7.00 Pfd [NYSE symbol] (TTSB)	NSPPrI
Non Statutory Training Organisation [British]	NSTO
Non Theatrical Film Distributors Council (EA)	NTFDC
Non Vidi [Not Seen] [Latin]	nv
Non Zero Binary	NZB
Non-A, Non-B [Hepatitis] [Infectious diseases] (DAVI)	NAB
Non-A, Non-B [Hepatitis] [Medicine] (DAVI)	NANB
Non-A, Non-B [Virology]	NANB
Non-A, Non-B Hepatic Virus	NANBV
Non-A, Non-B Hepatitis [Medicine]	NANBH
Non-Accelerating-Inflation Rate of Unemployment	NAIRU
Nonaccelerating-Unemployment Rate of Inflation [Economics]	NAURI
Nonacceptance [Business term]	N/A
Nonaccidental Injury	NAI
Nonaccounting Majors Program	NAMP
Nonacknowledgment Character [Computer science]	NACK
Nonacoustic Antisubmarine Warfare [Military]	NAASW
Nonacoustic Sensor Operator [Military] (CAAL)	NASO
Nonacoustic Submarine Effects (NVT)	NASE
Nonacquiescence [Legal term] (DLA)	NA
Nonacquiescence by Commissioner in a Tax Court or Board of Tax Appeals Decision [United States] [Legal term] (DLA)	Nonacq
Non-Acquisition Program Definition Document [Navy] (DOMA)	NAPDD
Nonacquisition Project [Military] (CAAL)	NAP
Nonactivated	NA
Nonadditive Mixing (DICI)	NAM
Nonadditive Operational Project [Military]	NAOP
Nonadditivity [Statistics]	NONADD
Nonadecanoic Acid [Organic chemistry]	NDA
Non-Adherent Peritoneal Cell (PDAA)	NAPC
Non-Adherent Peritoneal Cells (AD)	napc
Nonadjusting Ball-Up [A hopeless state of confusion] [Military slang]	NABU
Non-Adrenergic, Non-Cholinergic [Neurology]	NANC
Non-Advanced Further Education [British]	NAFE
Nonadvertising Promotion [Public relations] (WDMC)	NAP
Nonaffiliated Reserve Section	NARS
Nonagency Purchase	NAP
Non-Agency Purchase (AD)	nap
Nonagglutinable [or Nonagglutinating] [Immunochemistry]	NAG
Nonaggression Pact	NAP
Nonairline Carrier [Aerospace]	NAC
Nonalcoholic	NA
Nonalcoholic Volunteers	NAV
Non-Aligned [Political group] [EC] (ECED)	NI
Nonaligned Movement	NAM
Non-Aligned Movement (AD)	nam
Non-All-Weather (CINC)	NAW
Non-Ammonia-Nitrogen (PDAA)	NAN
Nonanoyloxybenzene Sulfonate [Laundry bleach activator]	NOBS
Nonappropriated Fund [or Funds]	NAF
Nonappropriated Fund Accounting System [Military] (DNAB)	NAFAS
Nonappropriated Fund Activity (CINC)	NAFA
Nonappropriated Fund Instrumentalities [DoD] (MCD)	NAFI
Nonappropriated Fund Instrumentalities Act	NFIA
Nonappropriated Fund Statement of Operations and Net Worth	NAFSONW
Nonappropriated Funds (AD)	naf
Nonappropriated Funds (DNAB)	NAPF
Nonappropriated Funds Information Standard System [Army]	NAFISS
Nonappropriated Funds Management Information System	NAFMIS
Nonappropriated Funds, Marine Corps (DNAB)	NAFMC
Nonaqueous Phase Liquid [Chemistry]	NAPL
Nonaqueous Reversed Phase [Chromatography]	NARP
Nonaqueous-Phase Liquid [Environmental Science]	NAPL
Nonarteritic Anterior Ischemic Optic Neuropathy	NAION
Nonarteritic Anterior Ischemic Optic Neuropathy	NAION
Non-Asbestos Organic [Friction materials]	NAO
Non-Assessable Stock [Investment term] (MHDW)	NAS
Non-Atomic Military Research and Development [Subcommittee]	NAMRAD
Non-Attached [European political movement] (ECON)	NA
Nonattainment Area [Environmental Protection Agency] (EPA)	NAA
Nonattainment Plan Provision [Environmental Protection Agency]	NAPP
Nonattendance	NA
Nonautomatic Relay Center (AABC)	NARC
Nonautomatic Self-Verification [Computer science] (MDG)	NSV
Nonavailability Statement [Military]	NAS
Non-Avionics Common Support Equipment (MCD)	NACSE
Nonazeotropic Refrigerant Blend	NARB
NonBacterial Prostatis [Medicine]	NBP
Nonbacterial Thrombotic Endocarditis [Cardiology]	NBTE
Non-Bank Financial Institutions [Ghana]	NBFI
Non-Bank Financial Intermediary (ADA)	NBFI
Nonbaseline Software Library (MCD)	NBS
Nonbattle [Army] (AABC)	NB
Nonbattle Casualty (NVT)	NBC
Nonbattle Injuries	NBI
Nonbed Occupancy (AAMN)	NBO
Nonbinding Preliminary Allocation of Responsibility [Environmental Protection Agency] (FFDE)	NBAR
Nonbonding Molecular Orbital [Physical chemistry]	NBMO
Nonbook Materials (ADA)	NBM
Non-Book Materials Cataloguing Rules (NITA)	NBMCR
Nonborrowed Reserve [Banking]	NBR
Nonbreathing	NBR
Nonbridging Oxygen [Materials science]	NBO
Nonbuffered Pyrophosphatase Activity	NPA
Nonbusiness [IRS]	NB
Nonbusiness [IRS]	NON-BUS
Noncallable Bond [Investment term]	NC
Noncallable Bond [Investment term]	NCB
Noncallable Deposit [Investment term]	NCD
Noncallable Security [Investment term]	NCS
Noncancelable Commitment (SDI)	NCC
Noncancellable [Insurance]	NONCAN
Noncancerous Skin Fibroblast [Medicine]	NSF
Noncapsid Viral Protein [Biochemistry]	NCVP
Noncarbohydrate Craver [Nutrition]	NCC
Noncarbon Paper (IAA)	NCP
Noncardiac Pulmonary Edema [Medicine]	NCPE
Non-Casein Nitrogen (OA)	NCN
Noncathode Ray Tube Indicators [JETDS nomenclature] [Military] (CET)	ID
Non-Chargeable Downtime	NCDT
Non-Chargeable Time (DGA)	NCT

Non-Chemical Shift Anisotropy [*Physical chemistry*] .... NCSA
Non-Cholera Vibrios [*Microbiology*] .... NCV
Non-Circumcision Educational Foundation (EA) .... NCEF
Non-Circumcision Information Center (EA) .... NCIC
Noncircumferential Stenosis [*Medicine*] (DMAA) .... NCS
Noncitizen (AABC) .... NONCIT
Nonclosed Shell Many Electron Theory [*Physics*] .... NCMET
Noncoded Information [*Computer science*] (IBMDP) .... NCI
Noncoding Region [*Genetics*] .... NCR
Noncoherent Carrier Keying (IAA) .... NCCK
Noncoherent Frequency Shift Keying .... NCFSK
Noncoherent Integration .... NCI
Noncoherent Moving Target Indicator (MCD) .... NCMTI
Noncoherent Optical Processing System .... NOPS
Noncoherent Optical Processor .... NOP
Noncoherent Oscillator (MCD) .... NONCOHO
Noncoin (IAA) .... NC
Noncold Front [*Meteorology*] .... NCF
Noncollagen Protein .... NCP
Noncollectable .... NC
Non-Collimated Source (PDAA) .... NCS
Noncollinear (MHDI) .... noncoll
Non-Color Sensitized Emulsion [*Also called color-blind emulsion*] (WDMC) .... NC
Noncombat Aircraft [*Military*] (MCD) .... NCA
Non-Combat Development Item .... NDI
Noncombat Operations [*Military*] (CAAL) .... NCO
Non-Combat Ready [*Military*] (SAA) .... NCR
Noncombatant Corps [*British*] .... NCC
Noncombatant Emergency and Evacuation Plan (NVT) .... NEMVAC
Noncombatant Evacuation Operation [*Army*] (INF) .... NEO
Noncombatant Evacuation Order [*Navy*] (CINC) .... NCO
Noncombatant Evacuation Order [*Army*] (AABC) .... NEO
Noncombatant Labour Corps [*British*] .... NCLC
Noncombustible (MSA) .... NCOMBL
Noncommercial [*Rate*] [*Value of the English pound*] .... NC
Noncommercial Education [*FCC*] (NTCM) .... NCE
Noncommercial Spot Announcement [*Public service announcement*] (NTCM) .... NCSA
Noncommissioned .... NC
Noncommissioned Officer [*Military*] .... NCO
Noncommissioned Officer [*Military*] .... NONCOM
Noncommissioned Officer Academy [*Military*] (AABC) .... NCOA
Noncommissioned Officer Bachelor Quarters [*Military*] (AFM) .... NCOBQ
Noncommissioned Officer Course (VNW) .... NCOC
Noncommissioned Officer Development Program [*Army*] (INF) .... NCODP
Noncommissioned Officer Education System [*Military*] (AABC) .... NCOES
Noncommissioned Officer Evaluation Reporting [*Army*] (INF) .... NCO-ER
Noncommissioned Officer Logistics Program [*Army*] (AABC) .... NCOLP
Noncommissioned Officer Professional Development Program [*Army*] (INF) .... NCOPDP
Noncommissioned Officer-in-Charge [*Military*] .... NCOIC
Non-Commissioned Officers Association of the United States of America (EA) .... NCOA
Noncommissioned Officers' Leadership School [*Air Force*] (AFM) .... NCOLS
Noncommissioned Officers' Open Mess [*Military*] (AFM) .... NCOOM
Non-Communicable Disease .... NCD
Noncommunications Detection System (MCD) .... NDS
Noncommunications Electronics Countermeasures [*Military*] (AABC) .... NONCOMECM
Noncommunications Emitter Location and Identification System (MCD) .... NELIS
Noncommunications Emitter Location and Identification System - Airborne .... NELIS-A
Noncommunications Jamming [*Military*] (AABC) .... NONCOMJAM
Non-Community Water System [*Environmental Protection Agency*] .... NCWS
Non-Competitive Tenders [*Business term*] (MHDW) .... NCT
Noncomplex (MCD) .... NC
Noncompliance [*Noncompliant*] (DAVI) .... NC
Noncompliance Penalty [*Environmental Protection Agency*] (EPA) .... NCP
Noncompliance Report [*Environmental Protection Agency*] (EPA) .... NCR
Non-Concurrent Operating System [*Sperry UNIVAC*] .... NCOS
Noncondensible Gases .... NCG
Nonconformance and Corrective Action Reporting System [*NASA*] (KSC) .... NCAR
Nonconformance Event Record [*NASA*] (KSC) .... NER
Non-Conformance Penalties [*Automotive emissions standards*] .... NCP
Nonconformance Record [*NASA*] (KSC) .... NCR
Nonconformance Report [*Nuclear energy*] (NRCH) .... NCR
Nonconformance Report [*Nuclear energy*] (NRCH) .... NR
Nonconformance Reporting System (NASA) .... NRS
Nonconformance Review Board [*Nuclear Regulatory Commission*] (NRCH) .... NRB
Nonconforming .... NC
Nonconforming Material Report .... NCMR
Nonconforming Material Report (MCD) .... NMR
Nonconforming Reporting System .... NRS
Nonconforming Use (ADA) .... NCU
Nonconformist [*Indicating religious preference*] [*Military British*] .... NC
Nonconformist .... NONCON
Nonconsent .... NONCNST
Nonconserved Region [*Genetics*] .... NCR
Nonconsumable Item Materiel Support Code [*Military*] (AFIT) .... NIMSC
Nonconsumable Item Materiel Support Request [*Military*] (AFIT) .... NIMSR
Nonconsumable Item Subgroup [*Military*] (AFIT) .... NIS
Non-Contact Time (AIE) .... NCT
Noncontingent Footshock .... NCFS
Non-Continuous Liner [*Shipping*] (DS) .... NC
Noncontractual Authorization .... NCA
Noncontributory [*Medicine*] .... NC
Noncontributory (DAVI) .... NC
Non-Contributory Invalid Pension [*British*] (DI) .... NCIP
Non-Contributory Pension Scheme (DLA) .... NCPS
Non-Conventional Brake Fluid [*Automotive engineering*] .... NCBF
Non-Conventional System [*Post coordinate indexing*] (NITA) .... NCS
Nonconversational (IAA) .... NC
Nonconvulsive Epilepsy [*Medicine*] .... NCE
Noncooperative Identification Friend or Foe Technology Evaluation (RDA) .... NIFFTE
Noncooperative Target Recognition (MCD) .... NCTR
Noncoronary Sinus [*Cardiology*] (AAMN) .... NCS
Noncorrosive Metal .... NCM
Noncoupled .... NCPLD
Noncrew Member .... NCM
Noncritical Phase Matching (IAA) .... NCPM
Noncritical Sensitive [*DoD*] .... NCS
Noncrossing Rule .... NXR
Non-Crystalline (OA) .... NC
Noncrystalline Solid [*Physics*] .... NCS
Noncrystallographic Symmetry [*Chemistry*] .... NCS
Noncumulative (ABBR) .... NON-CM
Non-Cumulative [*Business term*] .... NON-CUM
Non-Cumulative Dividend [*Business term*] (MHDW) .... NCD
Noncumulative Preferred Stock [*Investment term*] (MHDW) .... NPS
Non-Curling [*Photographic film*] (ROG) .... NC
Non-Custodial Parent .... NCP
Nondalton [*Alaska*] [*Airport symbol*] (OAG) .... NNL
Nondeferred Development (MCD) .... NDD
Nondefinitive Pattern [*Laboratory science*] (DAVI) .... NOD
Nondelay [*Military*] .... ND
Nondeliverable Support Equipment .... NDSE
Nondelivery [*Shipping*] .... ND
Non-Denominational .... ND
Non-Denominational Bible Prophecy Study Association (EA) .... NDBPSA
Non-Departmental Public Body [*British*] .... NDPB
Nondeployment Mobilization Troop Basis (AABC) .... NDMTB
Non-Descript (WDMC) .... ND
Nondestructible Aiming Target .... NDAT
Nondestructive .... N/D
Nondestructive Assay .... NDA
Non-Destructive Assay Technique [*Military*] (PDAA) .... NDAT
Nondestructive Evaluation .... NDE
Non-Destructive Evaluation Laboratory [*NASA*] .... NDEL
Nondestructive Examination [*Nuclear energy*] (NRCH) .... NDE
Nondestructive Inspection (AFM) .... NDI
Nondestructive Read [*Computer science*] .... NDR
Nondestructive Read Only [*Computer science*] (IAA) .... NDRO
Nondestructive Read/Write [*Computer science*] .... NDRW
Nondestructive Readout [*Computer science*] .... NDRO
Nondestructive Test Facility (MCD) .... NDTF
Nondestructive Test Laboratory (MCD) .... NDTL
Nondestructive Testing .... NDT
Nondestructive Testing and Evaluation Programs [*Pennsylvania State University*] [*Research center*] (RCD) .... NDT & E
Nondestructive Testing and Inspection .... NDTI
Nondestructive Testing and Inspection Building .... NDTIB
Non-Destructive Testing Association of Australia .... NDTA
Nondestructive Testing Center (IEEE) .... NDTC
Nondestructive Testing Data Support Center [*DoD*] (MCD) .... NTDSC
Nondestructive Testing Information Analysis Center [*Army Materials and Mechanics Research Center*] [*Watertown, MA*] .... NTIAC
Non-Destructive Testing Information Center [*Army Materials and Mechanics Research Center*] (PDAA) .... NDTIAC
Nondestructive Testing Information Center [*Battelle Memorial Institute*] [*Databank*] [*Information service or system*] (IID) .... NTIC
Nondestructive Testing Information System (SAA) .... NTIS
Nondeterministic (IAA) .... ND
Nondeterministic Finite Automaton .... NFA
Non-Deterministic Incomplete Sequential Machine (PDAA) .... NISM
Nondeterministic Polynomial [*Mathematics*] .... NP
Nondeterministic Polynomial Complete Problem [*Mathematics*] .... N-P, Complete
Nondeterministic Sequential Machine (IAA) .... NSM
Nondeterministic Time Variant Automation [*Mathematics*] (IAA) .... NTVA
Non-Development [*or Developmental*] **Issue** [*or Item*] .... NDI
Nondevelopment Item (MCD) .... NDI
Non-Developmental Item [*Military*] (INF) .... NDI
Non-Developmental Items Candidate Evaluation .... NDICE
Non-Developmental Software .... NDS
Nondiabetic [*Medicine*] .... ND
Nondifferentiated Cell [*Medicine*] (DMAA) .... NDC
Nondimensional Analysis .... NDA
Nondipole Field [*Electromagnetism*] .... NDF
Nondirectional (IAA) .... ND
Nondirectional Antenna .... ND
Nondirectional Beacon .... NBD
Nondirectional Beacon (AFM) .... NDB
Nondirectional Cross-Country (MCD) .... NDCC
Nondirectional Microphone (WDMC) .... ND
Non-Directional Mud-and-Snow (PDAA) .... NDMS
Nondirectional Radio Beacon [*ITU designation*] (CET) .... RC
Nondirectional Radio Homing Beacon [*Navigation charts*] .... H
Nondirector (IAA) .... ND

Nondisabling [*Medicine*] ... ND
Non-Disclosure Agreement (WDMC) ... NDA
Nondispersive Infrared [*Analyzer*] ... NDIR
Nondispersive Ultraviolet ... NDUV
Non-Double-Couple [*Seismology*] ... NDC
Nondramatic Literary Works [*US Copyright Office class*] ... TX
Non-Drinker [*Medicine*] ... N/D
Nonduplicate ... NDUP
Nonduty [*Military*] ... ND
Non-Dwelling Floor Space (SAA) ... NDFS
None ... N
None ... O
None (DAVI) ... N/D/U
None Done Up [*Bookselling*] ... NF
None Found [*Medicine*] ... N/T
None in Town [*Bookselling*] ... NIT
None in Town [*Bookselling*] ... NKT
None Kept in Town ... n/o
None Obtained [*Medicine*] ... NAB
None of the Above ... NOTA
None of the Above [*Politics*] ... NE
Nonelastic [*Medicine*] (MAE) ... NELEC
Nonelectric ... NEST
Nonelectric Stimulus Transfer ... NESTS
Nonelectric Stimulus Transfer System ... NEM
Nonelectronic Maintenance ... NEP
Nonelectronic Part ... NEDCO
Non-Electronic Part Data Collection (PDAA) ... NPRD
Nonelectronic Parts Reliability Data (MCD) ... NEP
Nonelutable Polar Compounds [*Analytical chemistry*] ... NEMO
Nonempirical Molecular Orbitals [*Atomic physics*] ... NEVE
Nonempirical Valence-Electron [*Physics*] ... NENCL
Nonenclosure ... NEC
Nonengineering Change (DNAB) ... NECP
Nonengineering Change Proposal ... NEL
Non-English Language ... NE
Non-English Speaker [*Airline notation*] ... NEP
Non-English-Proficient ... NES
Non-English-Speaking (ADA) ... NESB
Non-English-Speaking Background (ADA) ... NESC
Non-English-Speaking Country ... NONTT
Nonentity (ABBR) ... NED
Nonenzymatic Glycosylation [*Biochemistry*] (DAVI) ... NEB
Nonenzymatic Maillard Browning [*Food technology*] ... NEX
Nonepoxide Xanthophyll [*Organic chemistry*] ... NID
Nonequilibrium Ionospheric Disturbance [*Geophysics*] ...
Nonequilibrium Molecular Dynamics [*Chemical property simulation technique*] ... NEMD
Nonequilibrium pH Gradient Gel Electrophoresis ... NEPHGE
Nonerasable Storage [*Computer science*] ... NES
Nonerasing Deterministic Stack Automation [*Computer science*] (IAA) ... NEDSA
Nonessential ... NE
Non-Essential Amino Acid N [*Biochemistry*] (PDAA) ... NEAAN
Nonessential Motor Control Center (AAG) ... NEMCC
Nonessential Service Water Relay Pump [*Nuclear energy*] (IAA) ... NESW
Nonessential Services Chilled Water System [*Nuclear energy*] (NRCH) ... NESCWS
Nonesterified Fatty Acid [*Biochemistry*] ... NEFA
Non-European Unity Movement [*South Africa*] (PD) ... NEUM
Non-Existent Memory (MHDB) ... NXM
Non-Extraction Steam Rate (PDAA) ... NXSR
Nonextrusion Texturized Soy Concentrate ... NTSC
Nonextrusion Texturized Soy Flour ... NTSF
Nonextrusion Texturized Soy Isolate ... NTSI
Nonfamilial Hematuria [*Medicine*] (DMAA) ... NFH
Non-Faradaic Electrochemical Modification of Catalytic Activity [*Chemistry*] ... NEMCA
Nonfasting [*Laboratory science*] (DAVI) ... NONF
Nonfat Dry Milk ... NFDM
Nonfat Milk (OA) ... NFM
Nonfat Milk Solids (OA) ... NFMS
Nonfavorably Considered (DAVI) ... NFC
Nonfederal Control Tower [*For chart use only*] ... NFCT
Nonfermenting Bacteria ... NFB
Nonferrous ... NF
Nonferrous ... NFER
Non-Ferrous Founders Society (EA) ... NFFS
Nonferrous Metal ... NFM
Nonferrous Metal Powder ... NFMP
Non-Ferrous Metals Producers Committee (EA) ... NFMPC
Nonferrous Smelter Order [*Environmental Protection Agency*] ... NSO
Nonfiction (NTCM) ... NF
Nonfiler [*IRS*] ... NF
Nonfiltered ... NF
Non-Financial Agreement (OICC) ... NFA
Non-Financial Public Enterprise [*British*] ... NFPE
Non-Firing Test [*Military*] ... NFT
Nonflammable ... NONFLMB
Nonflammable Cellulosic Foam ... NCF
Nonflare Proton ... NFP
Non-Fleet Experienced Aviator (NVT) ... NFEA
Nonflight Switch Panel (NASA) ... NFSP
Non-Flight Switch Panel ... NFSP
Nonflying Support Unit ... NFSU
Non-Food Agricultural [*Commodity Price Index*] (ECON) ... NFA
Nonformal Education ... NFE
Non-Fossil Fuel Obligation [*Pronounced "Noffo"*] [*Nuclear power*] ... NFFO
Non-Fragmentation [*Bomb*] ... NON-FRAG
Non-Fragments (NITA) ... NF
Nonfriendly Submarines (MCD) ... NFS
Nonfuel Core Array [*Nuclear energy*] (NRCH) ... NFCA
Non-Fuel-Wasting (MCD) ... NFW
Nonfunction (AAMN) ... NF
Non-Functional Test (SAA) ... NFT
Nonfundable ... NF
Nonfused (MSA) ... NFSD
Nongkhai [*Thailand*] [*ICAO location identifier*] (ICLI) ... VTUM
Nonglycosylated Serum Protein ... NGSP
Nongonococcal Urethritis [*Medicine*] ... NGU
Non-Government Non-Catholic [*School*] ... NGNC
Nongovernment Quarters (AFM) ... NGQ
Non-Government Schools' Secretariat [*South Australia*] ... NGSS
Non-Governmental Liaison Service [*World Resources Institute*] ... NGLS
Nongovernmental Observer ... NGO
Nongovernmental Organization [*Generic term*] ... NGO
Non-Governmental Organization Committee on Disarmament (EA) ... NGOCD
Nongraduate ... NG
Non-Grain-Raising [*Coating technology*] ... NGR
Non-GSE [*Ground Support Equipment*] **Utilization List** [*NASA*] (NASA) ... NUL
Nonguaranteed Trade Arrears (IMH) ... NGTA
Nonhandicapped ... NH
Nonhazardous Dry Solid [*Shipping classification*] ... NHDS
Nonhazardous Oil Field Waste [*Environmental Protection Agency*] (FFDE) ... NOW
Non-Heatset Web Unit (EA) ... NHWU
Nonhigh Density Lipoprotein [*Medicine*] (DMAA) ... NHDL
Non-Highly Compensated Employee ... NHCE
Nonhistone Chromosomal Protein [*Genetics*] (MAE) ... NHC
Nonhistone Chromosomal Protein [*Genetics*] ... NHCP
Nonhistone Nucleoprotein Antibodies [*Immunochemistry*] ... NNA
Non-Hodgkin's Lymphoma [*Oncology*] ... NHL
Non-Hodgkin's Malignant Lymphoma [*Oncology*] (DMAA) ... NHML
Nonhostile Missing [*Military*] (CINC) ... NHM
Nonhuman (MAE) ... NH
Nonhuman Primate ... NHP
Nonhydrogen Atom [*Chemistry*] ... NHA
Nonhydroxylated Fatty Acid [*Organic chemistry*] ... NFA
Nonhygroscopic ... NH
Nonillusion Direction [*Ophthalmology*] ... NID
Non-Immune [*or Normal*] **Goat Serum** ... NGS
Nonimmune Hydrops [*Medicine*] ... NIH
Nonimmune Hydrops Fetalis [*Medicine*] ... NIHF
Nonimmune Renal Disease [*Medicine*] (DMAA) ... NIRD
Nonimmune Transfer Utensil [*i.e., spoon*] [*Slang*] ... NTU
Nonimpact Off-Line Operating System [*Computer science*] ... NIPOLOS
Nonimpact Printer ... NIP
Nonimpact Printing (DGA) ... NIPPING
Nonimpact Printing Process (MCD) ... NIPP
Non-Indexable Address Tag (SAA) ... NIAT
Non-Indigenous Aquatic Species [*Marine science*] (OSRA) ... NAS
Non-indigenous Aquatic Species (USDC) ... NAS
Noninductive (DEN) ... NI
Noninductive Resistor ... NIR
Non-Inertial Guidance Set (SAA) ... NIGS
Noninherited Maternal Antigen [*Genetics*] [*Immunology*] ... NIMA
Noninherited Paternal Antigen [*Genetics*] [*Immunology*] ... NIPA
Non-Inhibitable Interrupt (MHDB) ... NI
Non-Injurious Free-on-Board ... NIFOB
Non-Innovator Multiple Source Drug Product ... NIMSDP
Non-Instrument Runway [*Aviation*] (DA) ... NINST
Noninsulin-Dependent [*Diabetes*] [*Endocrinology*] (DAVI) ... NID
Non-Insulin-Dependent Diabetes [*Medicine*] ... NIDD
Non-Insulin-Dependent Diabetes Mellitus [*Medicine*] ... NIDDM
Noninsulin-Dependent Diabetes Mellitus [*Endocrinology*] (DAVI) ... NIDM
Non-Insulin-Requiring [*Medicine*] ... NIR
Nonintegrated RADAR (MCD) ... NIRDR
Non-Intel [*Corp.*]-Compatible Chips [*Computer science*] ... NIC
Non-Intelligent Terminal (NITA) ... NIT
Non-Interest-Bearing Negotiable Order of Withdrawal [*Banking*] ... NINOW
Noninterference Basis ... NIB
Noninterference Performance Assessment ... NIPA
Non-Interlaced (CDE) ... NI
Non-Internal Development [*DoD*] ... NID
Noninterrupt Mode ... NIM
Nonintervention ... NI
Non-Intervention in Chile [*An association*] (EA) ... NIC
Non-Intervention in Chile [*An association*] (EA) ... NICH
Noninvasive Carotid [*Study*] [*Cardiology*] (DAVI) ... NIC
Noninvasive Carotid Examination [*Cardiology*] (DAVI) ... NICE
Noninvasive Cerebrovascular Examination [*Cardiology*] (DAVI) ... NICE
Noninvasive Index [*Medicine*] ... NI
Noninvasive Neurovascular Study [*Medicine*] (DAVI) ... NINVS
Noninvasive Peripheral Vascular Examination [*or Evaluation*] (DAVI) ... NIPE
Noninverted Hand Position [*Neuropsychology*] ... NHP
Noninverting Amplifier Pair ... NIAP
Nonionic Organic Compound [*Organic chemistry*] ... NOC
Nonionic Organic Contaminant [*Environmental chemistry*] ... NOC
Non-Ionic Organic Contaminant [*Environmental chemistry*] ... NOC
Nonionizing Electromagnetic Radiation ... NER
Non-Irradiated Fuel Handling Equipment [*Nuclear energy*] (NRCH) ... NFHE
Nonisotopic In Situ Hybridization [*Analytical biochemistry*] ... NISH
Nonisotropic Immunoassay ... NIIA

Noniterative Partial Least Squares [*Algorithm*] ... NIPALS
Nonjob Routed [*Military*] (AFIT) ... NJR
Nonjudicial Punishment [*Military*] ... NJP
Nonketotic Diabetic Coma [*Medicine*] (CPH) ... NKDC
Nonketotic Hyperglycemia [*Endocrinology*] (DAVI) ... NKH
Nonketotic Hyperosmolar Acidosis [*Medicine*] ... NKHA
Nonketotic Hyperosmolar Hyperglycemis Coma [*Also, HHNK*] [*Medicine*] ... NKHHC
Nonketotic Hyperosmolar Syndrome [*Biochemistry*] (DAVI) ... NKHS
Nonketotic Hyperosmotic [*Medicine*] (MAE) ... NKH
Non-Labeled [*Tape*] [*Computer science*] ... NL
Nonlanguage Qualification Test ... NQT
Non-Lethal Disabling Technology ... NDT
Nonlethal Entanglement Technology ... NET
Nonlethal Incapacitating Weapon ... NIW
Nonline of Sight ... NLOS
Nonlinear ... NL
Nonlinear ... NLin
Nonlinear (MSA) ... NLNR
Nonlinear (IAA) ... NONLIN
Nonlinear Amplifier ... NLA
Non-Linear Analysis Program (PDAA) ... NOLAP
Nonlinear Antenna System ... NAS
Nonlinear Capacitance ... NC
Non-Linear Charge Storage Element (PDAA) ... NLCSE
Nonlinear Circuit Analysis Program (MCD) ... NCAP
Nonlinear Control Design [*Computer science*] ... NCD
Nonlinear Differential Equations ... NDE
Nonlinear Distortion Analysis Program [*Bell System*] ... NODAP
Nonlinear Distortion Factor [*Telecommunications*] (OA) ... NDF
Nonlinear Element ... NLE
Non-Linear Ferromagnetic Resonance (PDAA) ... NFMR
Nonlinear Grain Analysis Program (MCD) ... NONGAP
Nonlinear Inertialess Three-Pole [*Telecommunications*] (OA) ... NIT
Nonlinear Interference Filter [*Electronics*] ... NLIF
Nonlinear Interpolating (IEEE) ... NLI
Nonlinear, Iterative Constrained Estimator (MCD) ... NICE
Nonlinear Kalman Filter ... NLKF
Nonlinear Least Square [*Mathematics*] ... NLLS
Nonlinear Least Squares [*Computer program*] ... NLLSQ
Non-Linear Least Squares [*Statistics*] ... NLS
Nonlinear Mapping (MCD) ... NLM
Non-Linear Material Effect (PDAA) ... NLME
Nonlinear Optical Loop Mirror [*Optical computing*] ... NOLM
Nonlinear Optical Polymer ... NLOP
Nonlinear Optics (IEEE) ... NLO
Nonlinear Partial Differential Equation ... NPDE
Nonlinear Poisson-Boltzmann Equation [*Physical chemistry*] ... NPBE
Nonlinear Programming [*Algorithm*] ... NLP
Nonlinear Quantization [*Telecommunications*] (NTCM) ... NLQ
Nonlinear Regression [*Mathematics*] ... NLR
Nonlinear Resistance (IDOE) ... NLR
Nonlinear Resistance (IAA) ... NR
Nonlinear Resistive ... NLR
Nonlinear Resistor [*Electronics*] (ECII) ... NLR
Nonlinear Sea Surface Temperature (USDC) ... NLSST
Nonlinear Smoothing ... NLS
Nonlinear Structural Analysis Program [*Computer science*] ... NONSAP
Nonlinear Systems ... NLS
Nonlinear Transient Fuel Film Compsensation [*Automotive fuel system*] ... NTFC
Nonlinear Vacuum Regulator Valve [*Automotive engineering*] ... NLVR
Nonline-of-Sight Antitank/Air Defense Vehicle [*Army*] ... NLOS-AT/AD
Nonline-of-Sight / Internal Operator Equipment (DWSG) ... NLOS/IOE
Non-Line-of-Sight-Combined Arms System (INF) ... NLOS-CA
Non-Line-of-Sight-Rear [*Army*] (DOMA) ... NLOS-R
Nonlisted Name [*Telecommunications*] (TEL) ... NLST
Non-Loaded (NITA) ... NL
Nonlocal Thermodynamic Equilibrium ... NLTE
Non-Locating Head [*Engineering*] (OA) ... NLH
Nonlocking ... NL
Nonmagnetic (IAA) ... NM
Nonmagnetic (MSA) ... NMAG
Nonmagnetic (IAA) ... NOMAG
Nonmagnetic Cast Iron (IAA) ... NONMAGCI
Nonmagnetic Drill Collar [*Well drilling technology*] ... NMDC
Nonmajor Item (MCD) ... NMI
Nonmajor System (MCD) ... NMS
Nonmalignant [*Of tumors*] [*Medicine*] ... N
Non-Marine Association [*Lloyd's Underwriters*] (AIA) ... NMA
Nonmasking [*or Nonmaskable*] **Interrupt** ... NMI
Nonmass Analyzed [*Photovoltaic energy systems*] ... NMA
Nonmaster File [*Computer science*] ... NMF
[*The*] **Nonmateriel Objectives Coordinating Document** [*Army*] (RDA) ... NMOCOD
Nonmeasured Time ... N/T
Nonmechanized Artillery Transport [*Navy symbol Obsolete*] ... APN
Nonmedical Attendant (AABC) ... NMA
Nonmedical Science Category (DAVI) ... NMS
Nonmelanoma Skin Cancer [*Medicine*] ... NMSC
Non-Melanoma Skin Cancer ... NMSC
Nonmember Firm [*of NYSE*] ... NMF
Nonmetalic [*Technical drawings*] ... NMT
Nonmetallic ... NM
Nonmetallic (ABBR) ... NMTLK
Nonmetastatic Trophoblastic Disease [*Medicine*] (DMAA) ... NMTD
Nonmethane Hydrocarbons [*Organic chemistry*] ... NMHC
Non-Methane Organic Compound [*Environmental chemistry*] ... NMOC
Non-Methane Organic Gas [*Organic chemistry*] ... NMOG
Nonmethane Total Hydrocarbons [*Organic chemistry*] ... NMTHC
Nonmethane Volatile Organic Carbon [*Environmental chemistry*] ... NMVOC
Nonmetric Multidimensional Scaling [*Statistics*] ... NMDS
Non-Metric Multidimensional Scaling (PDAA) ... NMS
Non-Metropolitan Counties [*British*] ... NMC
Nonmigrating Fraction [*of spermatozoa*] [*Medicine*] ... NMF
Non-Military Supplies Committee [*Combined Production and Resources Board*] [*British World War II*] ... NMSC
Nonmine Bottom Objects [*Navy*] (NVT) ... NOMBOS
Non-Mission Capable [*Military*] (INF) ... NMC
Nonmonetary Determination [*Unemployment insurance*] (OICC) ... NMD
Nonmotile [*Microbiology*] ... NM
Nonmotile [*Laboratory science*] (DAVI) ... O
Non'n St Pwr Minn,$3.60 Pfd [*NYSE symbol*] (TTSB) ... NSPPrA
Non-Native Speakers (EDAC) ... NNS
Nonne [*Globulin test*] ... N
Nonnegative Unbiased Variance Estimator [*Statistics*] ... NNUVE
Nonneuron-Specific Enolase [*An enzyme*] ... NNE
Non-Noise Certificated Aircraft (DA) ... NNC
Nonnormal Working Hours ... NNWH
Nonnuclear Armament Plan (MCD) ... NAP
Nonnuclear Consumable Annual Analysis (MCD) ... NCAA
Nonnuclear Instrumentation (NRCH) ... NNI
Nonnuclear Instrumentation System (NRCH) ... NNIS
Nonnuclear Kill ... NNK
Non-Nuclear Kill Requirements and Applications Study [*Military*] ... NNKRAS
Non-Nuclear Lance (MCD) ... NN
Non-Nuclear Lance Missile (PDAA) ... NNL
Non-Nuclear Munitions Safety Board ... NMMSB
Nonnuclear Munitions Safety Board [*Military*] ... NNMSB
Nonnuclear Munitions Safety Control Program [*Military*] ... NNMSCP
Nonnuclear Munitions Safety Group [*Air Force*] (AFM) ... NNMSG
Nonnuclear Munitions Safety Group [*Air Force*] ... NNMSGP
Nonnuclear Munitions Storage Area [*Air Force*] (DOMA) ... NMSA
Nonnuclear Ordnance Requirement (MCD) ... NNOR
Nonnuclear Safety (NRCH) ... NNS
Nonnuclear Strategic Warfare ... NNSW
Nonnuclear Survivability Technology Working Group (AFIT) ... NNSTWG
Nonnuclear Weapons Country ... NNWC
Nonnuclear Weapons State ... NNWS
Non-Nucleoside Reverse Transcriptase [*Biochemistry*] ... NNRT
Non-Nucleoside Reverse Transcriptase Inhibitor [*Biochemistry*] ... NNRTI
Nonnutritive Sweetener ... NNS
Nonobese [*A diabetic mouse strain*] ... NOB
Nonobese Diabetic [*Mouse strain*] ... NOD
Nonoccluded Virus ... NOV
Non-Occlusive Intestinal Ischemia [*Medicine*] (DMAA) ... NOII
Nonocclusive Mesenteric Infarction [*Medicine*] (AAMN) ... NOMI
Nonocclusive Mesenteric Ischemia [*Medicine*] ... NOMI
Non-Occupational Pesticide Exposure Study [*Environmental Protection Agency*] (GFGA) ... NOPES
Non-Ocular Source [*Physiology*] ... NOS
Nonofficial ... NO
Non-Official Trade Organisation [*British*] ... NOTO
Non-Oil Less-Developed Country ... NOLDC
Non-OPEC [*Oil producing countries which are not members of OPEC*] ... NOPEC
Non-OPEC Developing Country (NUCP) ... NODC
Nonoperating (KSC) ... NOP
Nonoperating Aircraft Authorization ... NOAA
Nonoperational Intelligence ... NOI
Nonoperational Ready (NVT) ... NOR
Non-Ordinary Resident [*British*] ... NOR
Nonorganic Ceramic Adhesive ... NCA
Nonorganic Failure to Thrive [*Neonatology*] [*Pediatrics*] (DAVI) ... NFTT
Nonorganic Failure-to-Thrive [*Medicine*] (DMAA) ... NOFT
Nonorganic Failure-to-Thrive [*Medicine*] (MEDA) ... NOFTT
Nonoriented Satellite ... NOS
Nonoriginal ... NO
Nonorthogonal Analysis of Variance (ADA) ... NANOVA
Non-Orthogonal Analysis of Variance (AD) ... nanova
Nonorthogonal Timing Error (IAA) ... NTO
Nonoscillating ... NOSC
Nonouti [*Kiribati*] [*ICAO location identifier*] (ICLI) ... NGTO
Nonouti [*Kiribati*] [*Airport symbol*] (OAG) ... NON
Nonpackaged ... NONP
Non-Packet Mode Terminal (MHDB) ... NPT
Nonpaired Spatial Orbitals [*Atomic physics*] ... NPSO
Nonpapillate [*Type of seed*] [*Botany*] ... NP
Non-Par Approved ... NPA
Non-Par Not Approved ... NPN
Nonparametric Detection Scheme [*Communication signal*] ... NDS
Nonparametric Empirical Bayes [*Statistics*] ... NPEB
Nonparametric Multipoint Linkage [*Mathematics*] ... NPL
Nonpareil (ADA) ... NONP
Nonpareil, Council Bluffs, IA [*Library symbol Library of Congress*] (LCLS) ... IaCbN
Nonparental Ditype [*Genetics*] ... NPD
Nonparoxysmal Atrioventricular Junction Tachycardia [*Cardiology*] ... NPJT
Nonparticipating [*Insurance*] ... NONPAR
Nonparticipating [*Insurance or finance*] ... NP
Non-Participating Provider ... Non-Par
Nonpartisan (ABBR) ... NPRTSN
Nonpartisan League [*Political party in North Dakota opposed by the IVA*] ... NPL
Nonpartisanship (ABBR) ... NPRTSNSP

Non-Patents (NITA) ... NP
Nonpayment (ROG) ... N/P
Nonpayment (ROG) ... NONPAYT
Non-Penetrating Periscope [*DARPA*] ... NPP
Nonperforated (ABBR) ... NONPERF
Nonperformance of Duty because Imprisoned [*Navy*] ... NPDI
Nonperishable Subsistence ... NPS
Nonpermanent Active Militia ... NPAM
Nonpersistent (FAAC) ... NPRS
Nonperson ... NP
Nonpersonal Liability ... NPL
Nonperturbative Open-Shell Theory [*Physics*] ... NPOST
Nonpetroleum ... NPET
Nonphased Color [*Television signals*] (NTCM) ... NPC
Nonphotochemical Hole Burning [*Spectrometry*] ... NPHB
Nonplasminogen Binding [*Hematology*] ... NPB
Nonplayer Characters [*Computer science*] ... NPC
Nonplus (ABBR) ... NPLS
Nonplused (ABBR) ... NPLSD
Non-Pneumatic Spare [*Automotive engineering*] ... NPS
Nonpoint Source Pollution [*Agricultural engineering*] ... NPS
Nonpolarized [*Computer science*] ... NP
Nonpolarized Return-to-Zero Recording [*Computer science*] (IBMDP) ... RZ(NP)
Nonpolice (BARN) ... NP
Nonpolio Enterovirus [*Infectious Diseases*] (DAVI) ... NPEV
Nonpolluting Engine [*Rocketdyne/Commonwealth Edison Co.*] ... NPE
Nonpolychrome (VRA) ... nonpoly
Nonpotential Energy [*of molecules*] ... NPE
Non-Powder Gun Products Association (EA) ... NPGPA
Nonpractising Member [*Chiropody*] [*British*] ... NP
Non-Precision Approach Runway [*Aviation*] (DA) ... NONP
Nonprescription Drug Manufacturers Association (EA) ... NDMA
Non-Pressure Thermit Welding (PDAA) ... NTW
Nonprimate Biosatellite ... NPB
Non-Principal Axis ... NPA
Nonprint [*Computer science*] (IAA) ... NP
Non-Print Media [*Advertising*] ... NPM
Nonprinting Character [*Computer science*] ... NPC
Non-Prior Service (MCD) ... NPS
Nonprocedural Interface [*Computer science*] ... NPI
Nonprocedural Referencing Language ... NPRL
Nonprocessor Grant (IAA) ... NPG
Nonprocessor Request (IAA) ... NPR
Nonprocurable ... NP
Nonproduction Release (MCD) ... NPR
Nonproductive Cough [*Medicine*] (MEDA) ... NPC
Nonproductive Cough [*Medicine*] (DAVI) ... NPC
Nonproductive Procurement Directive ... NPPR
Non-Productive Standard Minute (PDAA) ... NPSM
Nonprofessional ... NONPROF
Nonprofit (BARN) ... NP
Nonprofit (ABBR) ... NPRFT
Non-Profit Distributing Organization (PDAA) ... NPDO
Nonprofit International Consortium for Eiffel (EA) ... NICE
Nonprofit Mailers Federation (EA) ... NMF
Nonprofit Management Association (EA) ... NMA
Nonprofit Management Strategies [*A publication*] ... NMS
Nonprogrammer Language [*Computer science*] (PDAA) ... NL
Nonprogramming Language (IAA) ... NPL
Nonproliferation Alternative Systems Assessment Program [*Nuclear energy*] (NRCH) ... NASAP
Nonproliferation Program Review Committee [*US, multiagency*] ... NPRC
Nonproliferative Diabetic Retinopathy [*Medicine*] (MAE) ... NPDR
Nonpropelled (AAG) ... NP
Nonpropulsive Vent (KSC) ... NPV
Non-Protein Bound [*Medicine*] (DMAA) ... NPB
Nonprotein Nitrogen [*Analytical chemistry*] ... NPN
Nonprotein Sulfhydryl [*Biochemistry*] ... NPSH
Nonpublic Funds [*Canadian Forces*] ... NPF
Non-Public School Section [*American Association of School Librarians*] ... NPSS
Nonpurgeable Organic Carbon ... NPOC
Nonpyramidal Tract ... NPT
Nonquaded [*Telecommunications*] (TEL) ... NQD
Non-Quadratic Residues (MHDB) ... NQR
Nonqualified Stock Options (WYGK) ... NQSO
Non-Q-Wave Myocardial Infarction [*Cardiology*] (CPH) ... NQWMI
Nonradiating Target ... NRT
Nonradiative Energy Transfer [*Physics*] ... NET
Nonradio Frequency Cable Assemblies [*JETDS nomenclature*] [*Military*] (CET) ... CX
Nonradioactive Waste [*Nuclear energy*] (NRCH) ... NRW
Nonradioactive Waste Vent [*Nuclear energy*] (NRCH) ... NRWV
Non-Random Two-Liquid [*Equation of state*] ... NRTL
Nonrapid Eye Movement [*Type of sleep*] (MAE) ... Non-REM
Nonrapid Eye Movement [*Type of sleep*] ... NREM
Nonrapid Eye Movement Sleep [*Neurology*] (DAVI) ... NREMS
Nonrated ... NR
Nonrationed (AABC) ... NRAT
Nonreactive [*Relay*] ... NR
Nonreading Aptitude Test Battery [*US Employment Service*] [*Department of Labor*] ... NATB
Nonready Hours ... NRH
Nonreal Time ... NRT
Nonreal-Time Conversion Subsystem [*Space Flight Operations Facility, NASA*] ... NRTC
Nonreal-Time Data Automation System [*NASA*] (IAA) ... NRTDAS
Nonrebreathing [*Medicine*] (AAMN) ... NR
Non-Rebreathing ... NR
Nonrebreathing System [*Medicine*] (DAVI) ... NRBS
Nonreceptor Tyrosine Kinase [*An enzyme*] ... NRTK
Non-Reciprocal Impedance Converter (PDAA) ... NRIC
Non-Reciprocal Junction (PDAA) ... NRJ
Nonrecoverable (IEEE) ... NR
Nonrecurring Costs (AAGC) ... NC
Nonrecurring Costs [*Accounting*] (KSC) ... NRC
Nonrecurring Engineering Expense ... NRE
Nonrecurring Finished Intelligence (MCD) ... NRFI
Nonrecurring Installation Charge [*Telecommunications*] (TEL) ... NRI
Nonrecurring Investment (NASA) ... NRI
Nonrecurring Maintenance [*NASA*] (KSC) ... NRM
Non-Recurrrence Action (SAA) ... NRA
Non-Recursive Digital File (NITA) ... NRDF
Nonrecursive Digital Filter [*Navy*] (IAA) ... NDF
Nonrecursive Digital Filter [*Navy*] ... NRDF
Nonredundant Array ... NRA
Non-Redundant Pinhole Array (PDAA) ... NRPA
Nonrefundable [*Airline fare code*] ... NR
Nonregenerative Heat Exchanger [*Nuclear energy*] (NRCH) ... NRHE
Nonregenerative Heat Exchanger [*Nuclear energy*] (NRCH) ... NRHX
Nonregistered (AABC) ... NR
Nonregistered Accountable [*Military*] ... NRA
Nonregistered Publication ... NRP
Nonregistered Publications Memoranda ... NRPM
Nonreinforced Concrete Pipe [*Technical drawings*] ... NRCP
Nonrenal Death (MAE) ... NRD
Nonrepairable Item (MCD) ... NRI
Nonreplaceable Unit (IAA) ... NRU
Nonreplenishable Demand ... NRD
Non-Reportable Birth [*Medicine*] (MEDA) ... NRB
Nonreportable Property [*Military*] ... NRP
Nonreporting Secondary Stock Point (AFIT) ... NSSP
Nonrequestor Terminal (IAA) ... NRT
Non-Resetting Data Reconstruction (PDAA) ... NRDR
Non-Resetting Data Reconstruction with Continuous Feedback (PDAA) ... NRDR-CF
Non-Resetting Data Reconstruction with Discrete Feedback (PDAA) ... NRDR-DF
Nonresidence (ABBR) ... NRSDNC
Nonresident (WDAA) ... NON RES
Nonresident [*British*] ... NR
Nonresident (ABBR) ... NRSDNT
Nonresident Alien ... NRA
Nonresident Instruction (MCD) ... NRI
Nonresident Interprovince Motor Vehicle Liability Insurance Card [*For travel in Canada*] ... NRIPMVLIC
Nonresidential Building Energy Consumption Survey [*Department of Energy*] (GFGA) ... NBECS
Nonresidential Fixed Business Investment (MCD) ... NFBI
Nonresident-Owned Funds [*Investment term*] ... NRO
Nonresonant (IAA) ... NONRSNT
Nonresonant Deflection Amplifier ... NDA
Nonresonant Deflection Yoke ... NDY
Nonresonant Magnetic Amplifier ... NMA
Nonresonant Magnetic Deflection Amplifier ... NMDA
Nonresonant Magnetic Deflection Yoke ... NMDY
Nonresonant Magnetic Yoke ... NMY
Non-Respiratory Infection [*Medicine*] (DMAA) ... NRI
Nonresponder [*Strain of mice*] ... NR
Non-Response (WDMC) ... NR
Nonresponse Follow-Up [*Bureau of the Census*] (GFGA) ... NRFU
Nonrestrictive (ABBR) ... NRSTCTV
Nonreturn ... NRETN
Nonreturn to Zero [*Data transmission*] ... NRZ
Nonreturn to Zero Change ... NRZC
Nonreturn to Zero Change on One (BUR) ... NRZ1
Nonreturn to Zero Inverted [*Recording method*] ... NRZI
Nonreturn to Zero Level ... NRZL
Nonreturn to Zero Logic (MCD) ... NRZL
Nonreturn to Zero Mark ... NRZM
Non-Return to Zero-Space (MCD) ... NRZ-S
Nonreturnable [*Beverage bottles*] ... NR
Nonreturn-to-Zero (Change) Recording ... NRX(C)
Non-Reusable Containers (GNE) ... NRC
Nonrevenue [*Passengers or cargo*] [*Transportation*] ... NRV
Nonreversible ... NRVSBL
Nonreversing (IAA) ... NR
Nonreversing, Dynamic Braking (IAA) ... NRDB
Nonrigid Observation Airship [*Navy symbol*] ... ZNO
Nonrigid Patrol Airship [*Navy symbol*] ... ZNP
Nonrigid Scouting Airship [*Navy symbol*] ... ZNS
Nonrigid Training Airship [*Navy symbol*] ... ZNN
Non-Rising Stem [*Valve*] (DICI) ... NRS
Nonrotating Earth (NATG) ... NRE
Non-Salt Sensitive ... NSS
Nonsan [*South Korea ICAO location identifier*] (ICLI) ... RKTO
Nonsatellite Identification ... NSI
Nonsaturating Inverter Logic (IAA) ... NSIL
Nonscheduled (ABBR) ... NONSKED
Nonscheduled ... NS
Nonscheduled Air Services (AAG) ... NSAS
Nonschizophrenic [*Psychology*] ... NS

Non-Sea Salt	NSS
Nonsectarian (ABBR)	NSCTRN
Non-Sectarian Anti-NAZI League (EA)	NSANL
Non-Secure Data Communication Terminal (DWSG)	NDCT
Nonsecurity Exemption [Military]	NSE
Nonsegmented Neutrophils [Medicine] (CPH)	non segs
Non-Selective Catalyst Reduction [Diesel engine emissions]	NCR
Non-Selective Catalytic Reduction [Chemistry]	NSCR
Nonself	NSLF
Non-Self-Deployable Aircraft and Boats (MCD)	NSDAB
Non-Self-Destroying	NSD
Non-Self-Governing Territories [United Nations]	NSGT
Non-Self-Propelled	NSP
Non-Self-Sustaining [Container ship] (MCD)	NSS
Nonseminomatous Germ Cell Tumors of the Testes	NSGCTT
Nonsense (ABBR)	NSNS
Nonsensical (ABBR)	NSNCL
Nonsensically (ABBR)	NSNSCLY
Nonsequenced (IAA)	NS
Nonsequenced Acknowledgement (IAA)	NSA
Nonsequenced Information (IAA)	NSI
Nonsequential Disk [Computer science] (IAA)	NSD
Nonseries Parallel (IAA)	NSP
Nonserviceable (MSA)	NS
Non-Service-Connected	NSC
Nonservice-Connected Disability (MAE)	NSCD
Non-Sexist Child Development Project (EA)	NSCDP
Nonshivering Thermogenesis [Physiology]	NST
Nonshorting (IAA)	NS
Nonsiminomatous Germ Cell Turmors [Medicine] (MEDA)	NSGCT
Nonskew (IAA)	NS
Nonslip (ABBR)	NS
Nonslip Tread [Technical drawings]	NST
Non-Small-Cell Lung Cancer [Oncology]	NSCLC
Nonsmokers' Travel Club [Defunct] (EA)	NSTC
Nonsmoking Attributable Lung Cancer	NSALC
Nonsmutted [Plant pathology]	NS
Non-Social Security Equivalent Benefit	NSSEB
Non-Sodium Fire Protection [Nuclear energy] (NRCH)	NSFP
Non-Soviet Warsaw Pact (NATG)	NSWP
Nonspecific [Laboratory science] (DAVI)	NONS
Nonspecific Air Pollution Syndrome	NAPS
Nonspecific Binder	NSB
Nonspecific Cross-Reacting Antigen [Immunology]	NCA
Nonspecific Esophageal Motility Disorder [Gastroenterology] (DAVI)	NEMD
Nonspecific Esophageal Motor Dysfunction [Medicine]	NEMD
Nonspecific Esterase [An enzyme]	NSE
Nonspecific Excitability Level [Animal behavior]	NEL
Nonspecific Gene Resistance [Genetics]	NR
Nonspecific Hepatocellular Abnormality [Medicine] (MAE)	NHA
Nonspecific Prostatitis [Medicine] (ADA)	NSP
Nonspecific Reaction [Medicine] (DMAA)	NSR
Nonspecific Sexually Transmitted Infection [Medicine]	NSI
Nonspecific ST and T [Wave on electrocardiogram] [Cardiology] (DAVI)	NSSTT
Nonspecific ST Segment Changes [On electroencephalogram] [Cardiology] (DAVI)	NSST
Nonspecific Urethritis [Medicine]	NSU
Nonspecific Vaginitis [Medicine]	NSV
Nonspecified	NS
Non-Speech Language Initiation Program	NON-SLIP
Nonspinning Vehicle	NSV
Nonstandard (WDAA)	NONSTAND
Nonstandard	NONSTD
Nonstandard (AABC)	NS
Nonstandard Facilities Setup [Computer science]	NSS
Non-Standard FORTRAN [Computer science] (PDAA)	NSFORT
Nonstandard Item	NSI
Nonstandard Label [Computer science]	NSL
Nonstandard Line Item Number [Army] (AABC)	NSLIN
Nonstandard Metropolitan Statistical Area	NMSA
Non-Standard Metropolitan Statistical Area (OICC)	NON-MSA
Nonstandard Negro English	NNE
Nonstandard Part	NSP
Nonstandard Part Approval Request (MCD)	NPAR
Nonstandard Part Approval Request	NSPAR
Nonstandard Part Approval Request	NSPR
Nonstandard Part Request	NSRP
Nonstandard Parts List (MCD)	NPL
Nonstandard Telephone Number [Telecommunications] (TEL)	NSTN
Non-Standard Yiddish (BJA)	NONStY
Nonstationary Random Process	NRP
Nonstatus Candidates May Apply [Civil Service]	NS
Non-Statutory Body	NSB
Nonsterile Field Soil [Agronomy]	NSF
Non-Sterling Area (PDAA)	NSA
Nonsteroid Dependent Asthmatic [Medicine] (DAVI)	NSDA
Nonsteroidal Anti-Inflammatory [Pharmacochemistry]	NSAI
Nonsteroidal Anti-Inflammatory Agent	NSAIA
Nonsteroidal Anti-Inflammatory Drug	NSAID
Nonstimulation	NS
Nonstock Fund	NSF
Nonstock Numbered Repair Parts	NSNRP
Nonstockage List	NSL
Nonstocked Item	NSI
Non-Stockpile Chemical Materiel [Military] (RDA)	NSCM
Nonstop [Aviation]	NS
Nonstorage Protein [Food technology]	NSP
Nonstorage Protein Isolate [Food technology]	NSPI
Non-Store Marketing Report [A publication]	NSMR
Nonstrategic Nuclear Forces (MCD)	NSNF
Nonstress Test [Gynecology]	NST
Nonsubmarine [Navy] (NVT)	NONSUB
Nonsupervisory Manufacturing Engineer	NME
Nonsupport (ABBR)	NSPRT
Nonsuppressible Insulin-Like Activity [Cytochemistry]	NSILA
Nonsuppurative Destructive Cholangitis [Medicine]	NSDC
Nonsustained Breakdown (IAA)	NSB
Nonsustained Polymorphic Ventricular Tachycardia [Cardiology] (DAVI)	NSPVT
Nonsustained Ventricular Tachycardia [Medicine] (CPH)	NSVT
Nonsymmetric Gravitational Theory	NGT
Nonsymptomatic [Medicine] (MAE)	NS
Nonsymptomatic, Nondisabling (MAE)	NSND
Nonsynaptic Diffusion Neurotransmission [Neurology]	NDN
Nonsynchronous	NONSYN
Nonsynchronous Pulse Suppression (MCD)	NSPS
Non-Syncytium-Inducing [Medicine]	NSI
Non-Syncytium-Inducing [Cytology]	NSI
Non-System Training Devices [USA]	NSTD
Non-T Cell [Cytology]	NT
Nontactical [Military]	N
Nontactical Equipment	NTE
Nontactical Generator (RDA)	NTG
Nontactical Generator, Southeast Asia	NOTACGENSEA
Nontactical Instrumentation Kit [Military] (DWSG)	NTIK
Nontactical Kit [Military] (DWSG)	NTK
Non-Tactical Peripheral Equipment [Military]	NTPE
Nontactical Support Equipment (MCD)	NTSE
Non-Tactical Tape [Military]	NTT
Nontactical Telecommunications Requirement [Army] (AABC)	NTTR
Non-Tactical Training Equipment [Military]	NTTE
Nontactical Vehicle [Army]	NTV
Nontariff Barrier [Kennedy Round]	NTB
Nontariff Measures	NTM
Nontariff Size	NTS
Non-Technical Generator [Army]	NTG
Nontechnical Intelligence Report	NTIR
Nontechnical Services Real Property	NTSRP
Nontechnical Support Real Property	NSRP
Nontemporary Storage [Personal property]	NTS
Nontemporary Storage System (MCD)	NOTEMPS
Nontender (DAVI)	NT
Nonthreshold Logic (IAA)	NTL
Nonthyroidal Illness [Medicine]	NTI
Nontight (AAG)	NT
Nontight Door	NTD
Nontoxic Goiter [Medicine]	NTG
Nontoxic, Multinodular Goiter [Medicine] (DAVI)	NTMNG
Non-Toxic Vinyl Tubing	NTVT
Nontrack while Scan	NTWS
Non-Traditional Casting Project (EA)	NTCP
Non-Traditional Employment for Women	NEW
Nontraditional Occupations	NTO
Non-Traffic Sensitive [Costs] [Telecommunications]	NTS
Nontranscribed Spacer [Genetics]	NTS
Non-Transient Non-Community Water System [Environmental Protection Agency]	NTNCWS
Non-Transition Metal (MCD)	NTM
Nontranslated Region [Genetics]	NTR
Nontransmural Myocardial Infarction [Cardiology] (CPH)	NTMI
Non-Transposed Loop Sensor (PDAA)	NTLS
Nontreatment Group [Medical research] (DAVI)	NTG
Nontryptophan [Protein-bound fluorescence]	NT
Nontuberculous [Medicine] (DAVI)	N/TBC
Nontuberculous Mycobacterium [A bacterium] (DAVI)	NTMB
Nontumor-Bearing	NTB
Nontypeable (MAE)	NT
Nontypesetting Runoff [Computer science] (CDE)	nroff
Nonulcer Dyspepsia [Gastroenterology] (DAVI)	NUD
Nonuniform Linear Array	NLA
Nonuniform Magnetic Field	NMF
Nonuniform - Memory - Access [Computer science]	NUMA
Nonuniform Progressive Phase Shift (IAA)	NUPPS
Nonuniform Rational B-Spline [A type of spline] [Computer science]	NURBS
Nonuniform Relational B-Spline [Micro Cadam 3-D] [Computer science]	NURBS
Nonuniform Simple Surface Evaporated Model (MCD)	NUSSE
Nonuniform Transmission Line [Computer science] (IAA)	NTL
Nonuniform Transmission Line (IAA)	NUTL
Non-Uniformity Correction	NUC
Nonuniformity Ratio	NUR
Nonuniformly Spaced (IAA)	NUS
Nonunit Personnel Generator (DOMA)	NPG
Non-unit Related Personnel [Military] (DOMA)	NRP
Non-United States Coalition Partner (DOMA)	NCP
Non-unit-Related Cargo (DOMA)	NRC
Non-urea Adducting Fatty Acid [Food science]	NAF
Nonutility Generating Source	NUGS
Nonutility Generator	NUG
Nonvaccinated	NV
Nonvacuum Electron Beam Welding	NEBW

Non-Vacuum Electron Beam Welding (PDAA) .... NVEBW
Non-Value Indicator [*Type of postage stamp*] (ODBW) .... NVI
Nonvalvular Heart Disease (MAE) .... NVD
Nonvenereal [*Medicine*] .... NV
Non-Verbal Ability Tests [*Intelligence test*] .... NAT
Nonverbal Classification Test .... NVCT
Nonverbal Communication (ADA) .... NVC
Nonverbal Operation .... NVO
Non-Verbal Scale of Suffering [*Personality development test*]
  [*Psychology*] .... N-VSOS
Nonverbal Test of Cognitive Skills [*Intelligence test*] .... NTCS
Nonvessel Operating Common Carrier [*Shipping*] .... NVOCC
Non-Vessel Operating Container Carrier .... NVOCC
Nonvessel Operator [*Shipping*] .... NVO
Nonvessel-Owning Carrier [*Shipping*] (DS) .... NVOC
Nonvessel-Owning Common Carrier [*Shipping*] (DS) ...... NVOCC
Nonveteran .... NV
Nonvintage [*Wine*] .... NV
Non-Violent Alternatives [*An association*] (EA) .... NVA
Non-Violent Anarchist Network (EA) .... NVAN
Nonviolent Explosive Destructive System (MCD) .... NEDS
Nonviolent Techniques Against Rape [*An association*] (EA) .. NTAR
Nonvirulent [*Pathology*] .... nv
Nonvisual Eyepiece .... NVE
Nonvisualization (DAVI) .... non-vis
Nonvocal Severely Handicapped .... NVSH
Nonvolatile .... NV
Nonvolatile Charge-Addressed Memory [*Computer science*] (PDAA) ... NOVCAM
Nonvolatile Electrically Alterable Memory .... NEAM
Non-Volatile Field-Effect-Transistor [*Electronics*] ...... NVFET
Nonvolatile Matter .... NVM
Nonvolatile Memory [*Computer science*] (HGAA) .... NVM
Nonvolatile Metal-Oxide Semiconductor (MCD) .... NMOS
Non-Volatile Nitrosamine [*Organic chemistry*] .... NVNA
Nonvolatile Organic [*Residue of thermal processing*] ...... NVO
Non-Volatile Random Access Memory [*Computer science*] .. NOVRAM
Non-Volatile Random Access Memory [*Computer science*] ... NRAM
Non-Volatile Random Access Memory [*Computer science*] ... NVM
Nonvolatile Random-Access Memory [*Computer science*] .. NVRAM
Nonvolatile Residue (NASA) .... NVR
Nonvolatile Semiconductor Memory (MCD) .... NVSM
Nonvolatile Semiconductor Memory Device (PDAA) .... NVSMD
Nonvolatile Suspended Solids [*Environmental chemistry*] .. NVSS
Nonvolatile Total Organic Carbon [*Environmental chemistry*] .. NVTOC
Nonvolatile Whole Smoke Condensate [*Environmental chemistry*]
  (AAMN) .... NVWSC
Nonvolotile Static RAM (NITA) .... NOVRAM
Non-Von Neumann [*Experimental computer, not based on the principles of Von Neumann computer design, under construction at Columbia University*] .... NON-VON
Non-Von Neumann .... NVN
Non-Voting [*Business term*] .... NON-VTG
Nonvoting [*Investment term*] .... NV
Nonvoting Stock [*Investment term*] .... NVS
Nonwater Cooling System .... NCS
Nonwatertight [*Packaging*] (AAG) .... NWT
Nonwatertight Door (ADA) .... NWTD
Nonweightbearing .... NWB
Non-Weight-Bearing [*Orthopedics and physical therapy*] (DAVI) .. NWB
Non-Weight-Bearing Ambulation [*Orthopedics*] (DAVI) .... NBA
Nonwhite Female .... NF
Nonwhite Male .... NM
Nonwhite Noise .... NWN
Nonwireline Multiple-Access Communications Exchange System
  (PDAA) .... NMAX
Non-Woven Fabrics Institute [*Defunct*] (EA) .... NWFI
Nonwoven Oriented .... NWO
Nonwoven Polyester Fabric .... NWPF
Nonylphenol [*Organic chemistry*] .... NP
Nonylphenol Ethoxylate [*Organic chemistry*] .... NPE
Nonylphenol Polyethoxylate [*Organic chemistry*] .... NPEO
Nonylsuccinic Acid [*Organic chemistry*] .... NSA
Nonzero Binary (NASA) .... NZB
Nonzero Digit (ECII) .... NZD
Nonzero Sum [*Genetics*] .... NZS
Nonzero Temperature Plasma .... NTP
Nonzero Test (IAA) .... NZT
Nonzero Transfer .... NZT
Non-Zero-Sum Game (MHDW) .... NZSG
Noodle Kidoodle [*NASDAQ symbol*] (TTSB) .... NKID
Noodle Kidoodle, Inc. [*NASDAQ symbol*] (SAG) .... NKID
Noodle Kidoodle, Inc. [*Associated Press*] (SAG) ...... NoodKid
Noon [*Meridies*] .... M
Noon .... N
Noon (WDMC) .... n
Noon .... NN
Nooney Realty Trust [*NASDAQ symbol*] (TTSB) .... NRTI
Nooney Realty Trust, Inc. [*Associated Press*] (SAG) .... Nooney
Nooney Realty Trust, Inc. [*NASDAQ symbol*] (NQ) .... NRTI
Noor [*Iran*] [*ICAO location identifier*] (ICLI) .... OINO
Noorduyn Aviation Ltd. [*Canada ICAO aircraft manufacturer identifier*]
  (ICAO) .... NY
Noorvik [*Alaska*] [*Airport symbol*] (OAG) .... ORV
Noosa [*Australia Airport symbol*] (OAG) .... NSA
Noosa Air [*ICAO designator*] (AD) .... OF

Noosa Air Sunstate Airlines [*Australia ICAO designator*] (FAAC) ..... SSQ
Nootka Sound Historical Society, Gold River, BC, Canada [*Library symbol*]
  [*Library of Congress*] (LCLS) .... CaBGRNS
Nootka Sound Historical Society, Gold River, British Columbia [*Library symbol National Library of Canada*] (NLC) ...... BGRNS
Nopaline Synthase [*An enzyme*] .... NOS
No-Par Stock [*Investment term*] (MHDW) .... NPS
No-Par-Value Stock [*Stock exchange term*] .... NPVS
Nor Antizana [*Ecuador*] [*ICAO location identifier*] (ICLI) ... SENA
Nor Cayambe [*Ecuador*] [*ICAO location identifier*] (ICLI) ... SENC
Nor Iliniza [*Ecuador*] [*ICAO location identifier*] (ICLI) ... SENI
Nora, AK [*Location identifier FAA*] (FAAL) .... OAA
Nora Alice [*DoD satellite*] .... NA
Nora Eccles Harrison Cardiovascular Research and Training Center
  [*University of Utah*] [*Research center*] (RCD) .... CVRTC
Nora Springs Advertiser, Nora Springs, IA [*Library symbol Library of Congress*] (LCLS) .... IaNosA
Nora-2000 [*Bulgaria*] [*ICAO designator*] (FAAC) .... ANE
Nor-Acme Gold Mines Ltd. [*Toronto Stock Exchange symbol*] ... NAG
NORAD Alert System (MCD) .... NAS
NORAD Attack Alert System (MCD) .... NAAS
NORAD Attack Warning System (MCD) .... NAWS
NORAD Automated Forward Tell Output to Canada (MCD) .... NAFTOC
NORAD Automatic Attack Warning System (TEL) .... NAAWS
NORAD Cheyenne Mountain Complex [*Military*] (AABC) ..... NCMC
NORAD Combat Operations System (MCD) .... NOCOPS
NORAD/CONAD Airborne Command Post .... NACP
NORAD Control Center [*Military*] .... NCC
NORAD Cost Factors and System Data [*Military*] (MCD) ... NCFSD
NORAD Direction Center [*Military*] .... NDC
NORAD Division Direction Center [*Military*] (AABC) ...... NDDC
NORAD Forward Automated Reporting System (MCD) .... NFARS
NORAD Intelligence Indications Center (MCD) .... NIIC
NORAD Intelligence Memorandum (MCD) .... NIM
NORAD Intelligence Plan [*Military*] (AABC) .... NORIP
NORAD Joint Manual Direction Center [*Military*] .... NJMDC
NORAD Office of Operational Analysis (IAA) .... NOOOA
NORAD Operational Employment Concept [*Military*] (AABC) . NOROEC
NORAD Operational Evaluation (MCD) .... NOE
NORAD Operational Evaluation (IAA) .... NOEV
NORAD Qualitative Requirement [*Military*] (AABC) .... NORQR
NORAD Region (IAA) .... NR
NORAD Region Combat Center [*Military*] .... NRCC
NORAD Sector Direction Center [*Military*] .... NSDC
NORAD Sector Direction Center Manual [*Military*] .... NSDCM
NORAD Space Intelligence Bulletin [*DoD*] .... NORSIB
NORAD Surveillance and Tactical Network (MCD) .... SURTAC
NORAD [*North American Aerospace Defense Command*] **Technical Intelligence Center** (DOMA) .... NORTIC
Noradrenaline [*Also known as NE: Norepinephrine*] [*Biochemistry*] ... NA
Noradrenaline [*or Norepinephrine*] [*Endocrinology*] (DAVI) .. NOR
Noradrenaline [*Norepinephrine*] [*Endocrinology*] (DAVI) ... Noradr
Norair Science Report (SAA) .... NSR
Noram Energy $3 Cv Ex A Pfd [*NYSE symbol*] (TTSB) ...... NAEPrA
Noram Energy Corp. [*Formerly, Arkla, Inc.*] [*NYSE symbol*] (SAG) ... NAE
Noram Energy Corp. [*Associated Press*] (SAG) .... Noram
Noram Energy Corp. [*Formerly, Arkla, Inc.*] [*Associated Press*] (SAG) ... NoramE
Noram Environment [*Vancouver Stock Exchange symbol*] ... NEM
Noram Financing I [*NYSE symbol*] (SAG) .... NAE
Noram Financing I [*Associated Press*] (SAG) .... Noram
Noramco Mining Corp. [*Toronto Stock Exchange symbol Vancouver Stock Exchange symbol*] .... NNN
Noramex Minerals [*Vancouver Stock Exchange symbol*] .... NXM
Norand Corp. [*Associated Press*] (SAG) .... Norand
Norand Corp. [*NASDAQ symbol*] (SAG) .... NRND
Noranda Forest, Inc. [*Toronto Stock Exchange symbol Vancouver Stock Exchange symbol*] .... NF
Noranda, Inc. [*Toronto Stock Exchange symbol Vancouver Stock Exchange symbol*] .... NOR
Noranda Research Centre, Montreal, PQ, Canada [*Library symbol Library of Congress*] (LCLS) .... CaQMNR
Noranda Research Centre, Pointe-Claire, Quebec [*Library symbol National Library of Canada*] (NLC) .... QMNR
Norbaska Mines Ltd. [*Toronto Stock Exchange symbol*] .... NBL
Norbeau Mines, Inc. [*Toronto Stock Exchange symbol*] .... NOM
Norbornadiene [*Organic chemistry*] .... NBD
Norbornadiene [*Also, NBD*] [*Organic chemistry*] .... NOR
Norbornene Spiroorthocarbonate [*Organic chemistry*] .... NSOC
Norcanair [*Canada ICAO designator*] (FAAC) .... NKA
Norcen Energy Resources Ltd., Calgary, AB, Canada [*Library symbol Library of Congress*] (LCLS) .... CaACNER
Norcen Energy Resources Ltd., Calgary, Alberta [*Library symbol National Library of Canada*] (NLC) .... ACNER
Norchenodeoxycholic Acid [*Biochemistry*] .... NCDC
Norco, LA [*AM radio station call letters*] .... WADU
Norco, LA [*AM radio station call letters*] (RBYB) ... WFNO-AM
Norco Nuclear Power Station (NRCH) .... NNPS
Norco Resources [*Vancouver Stock Exchange symbol*] ...... NRC
Norcross, GA [*Location identifier FAA*] (FAAL) .... OCR
Norcross' Reports [*23-24 Nevada*] [*A publication*] (DLA) ... Norc
Nord [*Greenland*] [*Seismograph station code, US Geological Survey Closed*]
  (SEIS) .... NOR
Nord Africa Aviazione .... NAA
Nord Amerikanischer Sangerbund (EA) .... NAS
Nord Pacific Ltd. [*Associated Press*] (SAG) .... NordPac

Nord Pacific Ltd. [*Associated Press*] (SAG) .... NordPc
Nord Pacific Ltd. [*NASDAQ symbol*] (SAG) .... NORP
Nord Pacific Ltd ADR [*NASDAQ symbol*] (TTSB) .... NORPY
Nord Resources [*NYSE symbol*] (TTSB) .... NRD
Nord Resources Corp. [*Associated Press*] (SAG) .... NordRs
Nord Resources Corp. [*NYSE symbol*] (SPSG) .... NRD
Nordair [*ICAO designator*] (AD) .... ND
Nordair Ltd. [*Canada ICAO designator*] (OAG) .... ND
Nordair Ltd. [*Toronto Stock Exchange symbol*] .... NDA
Nord-Aviation 262 [*Airplane code*] Nd2
Norddeutscher Lloyd [*German steamship company*] .... NDL
Norddeutscher Rundfunk [*Radio network*] [*Germany*] .... NDR
Nordegg Public Library, Alberta [*Library symbol National Library of Canada*] (NLC) .... ANO
Norden/Norddeich [*Germany ICAO location identifier*] (ICLI) .... EDWS
Norden Optics Setting, Mechanized Operation [*Air Force bombsight*] .... NOSMO
Norden Search Terrain Avoidance RADAR (SAA) .... NORSTAR
Nordenbeck [*Germany ICAO location identifier*] (ICLI) .... EDGN
Norden-Hage [*Germany ICAO location identifier*] (ICLI) .... EDWA
Nordenham-Einswarden [*Germany ICAO location identifier*] (ICLI) .... EDWT
Norden-Norddeich [*Germany*] [*Airport symbol*] .... NOE
Nordens Institut pa Aland [*Nordic Institute in Aland - NIA*] [*Finland*] (EAIO) .... NIPA
Nordens Liberale og Radikale Ungdom [*Nordic Liberal and Radical Youth*] (EAIO) .... NLRU
Norderney [*Germany ICAO location identifier*] (ICLI) .... EDWY
Norderney [*Germany Airport symbol*] (OAG) .... NRD
Nordeste, Linhas Aereas Regionais SA [*Brazil*] [*ICAO designator*] (FAAC) .... NES
Nordeste-Lineas Aereas Regionais [*ICAO designator*] (AD) .... JH
Nordfjordur [*Iceland*] [*ICAO location identifier*] (ICLI) .... BINF
Nordfjordur [*Iceland*] [*Airport symbol*] (OAG) .... NOR
Nordholz [*Germany ICAO location identifier*] (ICLI) .... EDCN
Nordhorn/Klausheide [*Germany ICAO location identifier*] (ICLI) .... EDWN
Nordhorn Range [*Germany ICAO location identifier*] (ICLI) .... EDUN
Nordic Academic Council [*Defunct*] (EA) .... NAC
Nordic Actors' Council (EAIO) .... NAC
Nordic Agricultural Research Workers Association (EA) .... NARWA
Nordic Amateur Theatre Council (EAIO) .... NATC
Nordic Amer Tanker Ship Wrrt [*AMEX symbol*] (TTSB) .... NAT WS
Nordic American Tanker Shipping Ltd. [*AMEX symbol*] (SAG) .... NAT
Nordic American Tanker Shipping Ltd. [*Associated Press*] (SAG) .... Nordic
Nordic Association for Adult Education (EAIO) .... NAAE
Nordic Association for American Studies (EAIO) .... NAAS
Nordic Association for Campanology (EA) .... NAC
Nordic Association for Hydrology (EA) .... NAH
Nordic Association for Rehabilitation [*Denmark*] (EAIO) .... NAR
Nordic Association for Study and Vocational Guidance [*See also NRSY*] (EAIO) .... NASVG
Nordic Association for the Handicapped (EA) .... NAH
Nordic Association of Applied Geophysics (EA) .... NAAG
Nordic Association of Hairdressers [*Sweden*] (EAIO) .... NAH
Nordic Association of Journalists' Unions (EA) .... NAJU
Nordic Association of Non-Commercial Phonogram Producers (EA) .... NANNP
Nordic Association of Plumbers and Tinsmiths (EAIO) .... NAPT
Nordic Atomic Libraries Joint Secretariat [*Information service or system*] (IID) .... NALJS
Nordic Automobile Technical Committee [*Defunct Denmark*] (EAIO) .... NATC
Nordic Boat Council (EA) .... NBC
Nordic Child and Youth Welfare Alliance (EA) .... NCYWA
Nordic Choral Committee (EAIO) .... NCC
Nordic Church Council for Seamen [*Denmark*] (EAIO) .... NCCS
Nordic Committee for Central Africa [*Defunct*] (EA) .... NCCA
Nordic Committee for Commercial Education [*See also NKH*] [*Odense, Denmark*] (EAIO) .... NCCE
Nordic Committee for Soviet and East European Studies (EA) .... NCSEES
Nordic Committee of Journalism Teachers (EA) .... NCJT
Nordic Committee of Schools of Social Work (EAIO) .... NCSSW
Nordic Committee of the Research Councils for the Humanities (EA) .... NCRCH
Nordic Committee on Disability (EAIO) .... NCD
Nordic Committee on Salaries and Personnel [*Nordic Council of Ministers*] [*Copenhagen, Denmark*] (EAIO) .... NCSP
Nordic Confederation of Supervisors, Technicians, and Other Managers [*Formerly, Nordic Union of Foremen*] (EA) .... NAU
Nordic Cooperation Committee for International Politics, Including Conflict and Peace Research (EA) .... NCCIP
Nordic Cooperation on Telecommunications (EAIO) .... NCT
Nordic Council .... NC
Nordic Council for Adult Studies in Church [*See also NKS*] (EAIO) .... NCASC
Nordic Council for Alcohol and Drug Research (EA) .... ECADR
Nordic Council for Animal Protection (EA) .... NCAP
Nordic Council for Arctic Medical Research (EA) .... NCAMR
Nordic Council for Church Studies (EA) .... NCCS
Nordic Council for Music Conservatories (EA) .... NCMC
Nordic Council for Physical Oceanography (EA) .... NCPO
Nordic Council for Railway Music (EA) .... NCRM
Nordic Council for Tax Research (EA) .... NCTR
Nordic Council for the Deaf [*See also DNR*] (EAIO) .... NCD
Nordic Council for Wildlife Research (EAIO) .... NCWR
Nordic Council of Ministers (EAIO) .... NCM
Nordic Council of Reindeer Research (EAIO) .... NCRR
Nordic Council of Ski Schools (EAIO) .... NCSS
Nordic Council on Medicines [*See also NLN*] (EAIO) .... NCM
Nordic Customs Administrative Council (EA) .... NCAC
Nordic Demographic Society (EA) .... NDS
Nordic Documentation Center for Mass Communication Research [*Database ori ginator*] [*Finland Information service or system*] (IID) .... NORDICOM
Nordic East International Aircraft, AB [*Sweden ICAO designator*] (FAAC) .... ELN
Nordic Economic Research Council (EA) .... NERC
Nordic Energy Index [*Database*] [*Nordic Atomic Libraries Joint Secretariat*] [*Denmark*] [*Information service or system*] (IID) .... NEI
Nordic Energy Index [*Database*] [*Nordic Atomic Libraries Joint Secretariat*] [*Information service or system*] (CRD) .... NEIX
Nordic Energy Index, Literature [*Database*] [*Nordic Atomic Libraries Joint Secretariat*] [*Information service or system*] (CRD) .... NEIL
Nordic Engineer Officers' Federation (EA) .... NEOF
Nordic Ergonomic Society (EAIO) .... NES
Nordic Federation for Medical Education [*Denmark*] (EAIO) .... NFME
Nordic Federation of Building and Wood Workers (EA) .... NFBWW
Nordic Federation of Factory Workers Unions (EA) .... NFFWU
Nordic Federation of Heart and Lung Associations (EA) .... NHL
Nordic Forwarding Agents Association [*Defunct*] (EA) .... NFAA
Nordic Geodetic Commission (EA) .... NGC
Nordic Institute for Theoretic Atomic Physics [*Later, NIIP*] (EY) .... NORDITA
Nordic Investment Bank (GNE) .... NIB
Nordic Joint Committee for Domestic Education (EA) .... NJCDE
Nordic Joint Committee of Commercial and Office Executives (EA) .... NJCCOE
Nordic Joint Group for Forest Entomology (EA) .... NJGFE
Nordic Judo Union (EAIO) .... NJU
Nordic Labour Market Committee (EAIO) .... NLMC
Nordic Language Secretariat [*See also SLN*] [*Norway*] (EAIO) .... NLS
Nordic Leather Chemists Society [*Formerly, IVLIC Scandinavian Section*] (EA) .... NLCS
Nordic Literature Committee [*Copenhagen, Denmark*] (EAIO) .... NLC
Nordic Master Painters' Organization (EA) .... NMPO
Nordic Meat Industry Union (EA) .... NMIU
Nordic Metalworkers Secretariat (EA) .... NMS
Nordic Mobile Telephone [*Radio-telephone system for car users*] [*Denmark, Finland, Norway, Sweden*] .... NMT
Nordic Mobile Telephone Network (NITA) .... NMT
Nordic Musicians' Union (EA) .... NMU
Nordic Narrow/16mm Film Society (EA) .... NNFS
Nordic Numismatic Union (EAIO) .... NNU
Nordic Optical Telescope .... NOT
Nordic Packet Switched Data Network (NITA) .... NPSDN
Nordic Pharmacopoeia [*A publication*] .... Nord P
Nordic Pool for Marine Insurance [*Helsinki, Finland*] (EA) .... NPMI
Nordic Postal Union (EA) .... NPU
Nordic Public Data Network [*Denmark, Finland, Iceland, Norway and Sweden*] (PDAA) .... NPDN
Nordic Road Safety Council [*See also NTR*] [*Helsinki, Finland*] (EAIO) .... NRSC
Nordic Shooting Region (EAIO) .... NSR
Nordic Society Against Painful Experiments on Animals (EA) .... NSAPEA
Nordic Society for Cell Biology (EA) .... NSCB
Nordic Society for Radiation Protection [*See also NSFS*] [*Helsinki, Finland*] (EAIO) .... NSRP
Nordic Society of Space Research .... NSSR
Nordic Swimming Federations Association (EA) .... NSFA
Nordic Temperance Council (EA) .... NTC
Nordic Theater Committee [*Later, NTDC*] (EAIO) .... NTC
Nordic Theatre and Dance Committee (EAIO) .... NTDC
Nordic Transportworkers' Federation [*See also NT*] (EAIO) .... NTF
Nordic Union of Private Schools (EA) .... NUPS
Nordic Union of Young Conservatives (EA) .... NUYC
[*The*] **Nordic University Network** (TNIG) .... NORDUnet
Nordic Working Group on Development Education [*Nordic Council of Ministers*] [*Denmark*] (EAIO) .... NWGDE
Nordihydroguaiaretic Acid [*Antioxidant, food additive*] .... NDGA
Nordischer Amator Theater Rat [*Nordic Amateur Theatre Council - NATC*] (EAIO) .... NATR
Nordischer Friseurverband [*Nordic Association of Hairdressers*] [*Sweden*] (EAIO) .... NFV
Nordisk Anaestesiologisk Forening [*Scandinavian Society of Anaesthesiologists - SSA*] (EA) .... NAF
Nordisk Avisteknisk Samarbetsnamnd [*Nordic Joint Technical Press Board*] [*Sweden*] (EAIO) .... NATS
Nordisk Barnkirurgisk Forening [*Scandinavian Association of Paediatric Surgeons - SAPS*] [*Denmark*] (EAIO) .... NBF
Nordisk Bilteknisk Kommitte [*Nordic Automobile Technical Committee - NATC*] [*Defunct Denmark*] (EAIO) .... NBK
Nordisk Forening for Cellforskning [*Nordic Society for Cell Biology - NSCB*] (EAIO) .... NFC
Nordisk Forening for Folkendansforskning [*Nordic Association for Folk Dance Research*] [*Sweden*] (EAIO) .... Nff
Nordisk Forening for Klinisk Kemi [*Scandinavian Society for Clinical Chemistry - SSCC*] [*Finland*] (EAIO) .... NFKK
Nordisk Forening for Medisinsk Radiologi [*Scandinavian Radiological Society - SRS*] (EAIO) .... NFMR
Nordisk Forening for Rehabilitering [*Nordic Association for Rehabilitation*] (EAIO) .... NFR
Nordisk Herpetologisk Forening [*Scandinavian Herpetological Society - SHS*] (EAIO) .... NHF
Nordisk Hydrologisk Forening [*Nordic Association for Hydrology - NAH*] [*Denmark*] (EAIO) .... NHF
Nordisk Kirkelig Studierad [*Nordic Council for Adult Studies in Chruch - NCASC*] (EAIO) .... NKS
Nordisk Kollegium for Fysisk Oceanografi [*Nordic Council for Physical Oceanography - NCPO*] (EAIO) .... NKFO

Nordisk Kollegium for Marinbiologi [*Nordic Council for Marine Biology - NCMB*] (EAIO) .... NKMB

Nordisk Komite for Handelsundervisning [*Nordic Committee for Commercial Education - NCCE*] [*Odense, Denmark*] (EAIO) .... NKH

Nordisk Konservatorierad [*Nordic Council for Music Conservatories - NCMC*] (EAIO) .... NKR

Nordisk Konstforbund [*Nordic Art Association*] [*Norway*] (EAIO) ... NKF

Nordisk Kontaktorgan for Atomenergisporgsmal [*Nordic Liaison Committee for Atomic Energy*] (EAIO) .... NKA

Nordisk Metodikkommitte for Livsmedel [*Nordic Committee on Food Analysis*] (EAIO) .... NMKL

Nordisk Musikkomite [*Nordic Music Committee*] (EAIO) .... NOMUS

Nordisk Neurokirurgisk Forening [*Scandinavian Neurosurgical Society - SNS*] (EAIO) .... NNF

Nordisk Neurologisk Forening [*Scandinavian Neurological Association - SNA*] (EAIO) .... NNF

Nordisk Organ for Reinforskning [*Nordic Council of Reindeer Research*] [*Norway*] (EAIO) .... NOR

Nordisk Plastikkirurgisk Forening [*Scandinavian Association of Plastic Surgeons - SAPS*] (EAIO) .... NPF

Nordisk Samarbeidskomite for Husstellundervisning [*Nordic Joint Committee for Domestic Education - NJCDE*] (EAIO) .... NSH

Nordisk Samkatalog foer Seriella Medicinska Publikationer [*Karolinska Institutets Bibliotek och Informationscentral*] [*Sweden Information service or system*] (CRD) .... Nordser

Nordisk Sammanslutning for Barnavard [*Nordic Child and Youth Welfare Alliance - NCYWA*] (EA) .... NSB

Nordisk Sekretariat for Gartneri- Land-, og Skovarbejderforbund [*Nordic Secretariat for Agricultural and Horticultural Workers - NSAHW*] [*Denmark Defunct*] (EAIO) .... NSGLS

Nordisk Skuespillerrad [*Nordic Actors' Council - NAC*] [*Sweden*] (EAIO) .... NSR

Nordisk Speditorforbund [*Nordic Forwarding Agents Association - NFAA*] [*Defunct*] (EAIO) .... NS

Nordisk Svommeforbund [*Nordic Swimming Federations Association - NSFA*] (EAIO) .... NS

Nordisk Teaterkomite [*Nordic Theater Committee - NTC*] (EAIO) ... NTK

Nordisk Thoraxkirurgisk Forening [*Scandinavian Association for Thoracic and Cardiovascular Surgery - SATCS*] (EAIO) .... NTF

Nordisk Tolladministrativt Rad [*Nordic Customs Administrative Council - NCAC*] (EAIO) .... NTR

Nordisk Traebeskyttelsesrad [*Nordic Wood Preservation Council - NWPC*] (EAIO) .... NT

Nordisk Trafikskoleunion [*Nordic Union of Motor Schools Associations - NUMSA*] [*Finland*] (EAIO) .... NTU

Nordisk Union for Alkoholfri Trafikk [*Scandinavian Union for Non-Alcoholic Traffic - SUNAT*] (EA) .... NUAT

Nordisk Urologisk Forening [*Scandinavian Association of Urology - SAU*] (EAIO) .... NUF

Nordisk Vejteknisk Forbund [*Nordic Association of Road and Traffic Engineering*] (EAIO) .... NVF

Nordisk Verbane Musik Rad [*Nordic Council for Railway Music - NCRM*] (EAIO) .... NJMR

Nordisk Vetenskapliga Bibliotekarie-Forbundet [*Scandinavian Federation of Research Librarians*] (EA) .... NVBF

Nordiska Akademiker Radet [*Nordic Academic Council - NAC*] [*Defunct*] (EA) .... NAR

Nordiska Akademiska Idrottsforbund [*Scandinavian Federation for University Sport*] (EA) .... NAIF

Nordiska Bankmannaunionen [*Confederation of Nordic Bank Employees' Unions*] (EA) .... NBU

Nordiska Batradet [*Nordic Boat Council*] [*Sweden*] (EAIO) .... NB

Nordiska Byggforskningsorgans Samarbetsgrupp [*Nordic Building Research Cooperation Group*] [*Iceland*] (EAIO) .... NBS

Nordiska Ekonomiska Forskningsradet [*Nordic Economic Research Council - NERC*] (EAIO) .... NEF

Nordiska Ergonomisallskapet [*Nordic Ergonomic Society*] (EAIO) ... NES

Nordiska Fabriksarbetarefederationen [*Nordic Federation of Factory Workers Unions - NFFWU*] (EAIO) .... NF

Nordiska Forbundet for Statskunskap [*Nordic Political Science Association - NPSA*] [*Norway*] (EAIO) .... NFS

Nordiska Forbundet for Studie- och Yrkesvagledning [*Nordic Association for Study and Vocational Guidance - NASVG*] (EAIO) .... NRSY

Nordiska Handikappforbundet [*Nordic Association for the Handicapped - NAH*] (EAIO) .... NHF

Nordiska Ickekommersielles Fonogramproducenters Forening [*Nordic Association of Non-Commercial Phonogram Producers - NANPP*] (EAIO) .... NIFF

Nordiska Journalistforbundet [*Nordic Association of Journalists Unions - NAJU*] (EAIO) .... NJF

Nordiska Kemistradet [*Chemical Societies of the Nordic Countries*] (EAIO) .... NK

Nordiska Kommitten for Byggbestammelser [*Nordic Committee on Building Regulations - NCBR*] [*Finland*] (EAIO) .... NKB

Nordiska Kommitten for Samordning av Elektriska Sakerhetsfragor [*Nordic Committee for Coordination of Electrical Safety Matters*] (EAIO) ..... NSS

Nordiska Kooperativa och Allmannyttiga Bostadsforetags Organisation [*Organization of Cooperative and Non-Profit Making Housing Enterprises in the Nordic Countries*] (EAIO) .... NBO

Nordiska Lakemedelsnamnden [*Nordic Council on Medicines - NCM*] (EAIO) .... NLN

Nordiska Maskinbefalsfederationen [*Nordic Engineer Officers' Federation - NEOF*] (EAIO) .... NMF

Nordiska Metallarbetaresekretariatet [*Nordic Metalworkers Secretariat - NMS*] (EAIO) .... NM

Nordiska Namden for Alkohol- och Drogforskning [*Nordic Council for Alcohol and Drug Research - NCADR*] (EAIO) .... NAD

Nordiska Namnden for Handikappfragor [*Nordic Committee on Disability - NCD*] [*Sweden*] (EAIO) .... NNH

Nordiska Nykterhetsradet [*Nordic Temperance Council - NTC*] (EAIO) ... NNR

Nordiska Publiceringsnamnden for Naturvetenskap [*Nordic Publishing Board in Science*] (EAIO) .... NOP-N

Nordiska Samarbetskommitten for Internationell Politik [*Nordic Cooperation Committee for International Politics, Including Conflict and Peace Research*] (EAIO) .... NSKIP

Nordiska Samarbetsnamnden for Humanistisk Forskning [*Nordic Committee of the Research Councils for the Humanities - NCRCH*] (EA) ... NOS-H

Nordiska Samarbetsorganet for Vetenskaplig Information [*Nordic Council for Scientific Information and Research Libraries*] [*Finland*] (EAIO) ... NORDINFO

Nordiska Samarbetsradet for Kriminologi [*Scandinavian Research Council for Criminology - SRCC*] [*Finland*] (EAIO) .... NSfK

Nordiska Samfundet for Latinamerika Forskning [*Nordic Association for Research on Latin America*] [*Sweden*] (EAIO) .... NOSALF

Nordiska Sjoforsakringspoolen [*Nordic Pool for Marine Insurance - NPMI*] (EA) .... NSP

Nordiska Skattevetenskapliga Forskningradet [*Nordic Council for Tax Research - NCTR*] (EAIO) .... NSF

Nordiska Skeppstekniska Mote [*Joint Committee of Nordic Marine Technology - JCNMT*] (EAIO) .... NSTM

Nordiska Skidskolans Rad [*Nordic Council of Ski Schools - NCSS*] [*Finland*] (EAIO) .... NSR

Nordiska Skogsarbetsstudiernas Rad [*Nordic Research Council on Forest Operations*] [*Sweden*] (EAIO) .... NSR

Nordiska Statistiska Sekretariatet [*Nordic Statistical Secretariat*] (EAIO) ... NSS

Nordiska Tele-Satelit Kommitton [*Norway*] .... NTSK

Nordiska Trafiksakerhetsradet [*Nordic Road Safety Council - NRSC*] [*Finland*] (EAIO) .... NTR

Nordiska Transportarbetarefederationen [*Nordic Transportworkers' Federation - NTF*] (EAIO) .... NT

Nordiska Unionen for Arbetsledare, Tekniska Funktionarer och andra Chefer [*Nordic Confederation of Supervisors, Technicians and Other Managers*] (EAIO) .... NUATFAC

Nordiske Jordbrugsforskeres Forening [*Nordic Agricultural Research Workers Association - NARWA*] (EAIO) .... NJF

Nordiske Kvinners Fredsnettverk [*Nordic Women's Peace Network*] [*Denmark, Finland, Norway, and Sweden*] (EAIO) .... NKF

Nordiske Laererorganisationers Samrad [*Council of Nordic Teachers' Association*] [*Sweden*] (EAIO) .... NLS

Nordiske Teleansattes Samarbeidsorgan [*Nordic Telecommunications Association*] (EAIO) .... NTS

Nordiskt Samarbete Inom Telekommunikation [*Nordic Cooperation on Telecommunications*] [*Finland*] (EAIO) .... NORDTEL

Nordkalottkommitten [*North Calotte Committee - NCC*] [*Finland*] (EAIO) ... NKK

Nordlands Bank [*Norway*] .... NB

NORDLEK Council (EAIO) .... NC

Nordlingen [*Federal Republic of Germany*] [*Seismograph station code, US Geological Survey Closed*] (SEIS) .... NRD

Nordmaling [*Sweden*] [*Airport symbol*] (AD) .... OLG

Nordman [*Idaho*] [*Seismograph station code, US Geological Survey Closed*] (SEIS) .... NTI

Nordmanns-Forbunder [*Norsemen's Federation*] (EA) .... NF

Nord-Nord-Ouest [*North-Northwest*] [*French*] .... NNO

Nordoff-Robbins Music Therapy Centre Ltd. [*British*] (CB) .... NRMTC

Nord-Ouest [*Northwest*] [*French*] .... NO

Nordson Corp. [*NASDAQ symbol*] (NQ) .... NDSN

Nordson Corp. [*Associated Press*] (SAG) .... Nordsn

Nordstress (Australia) Pt Ltd. [*FAA designator*] (FAAC) .... NDS

Nordstrom, Inc. [*NASDAQ symbol*] (NQ) .... NOBE

Nordstrom, Inc. [*Associated Press*] (SAG) .... Nordst

Nordstrom Personal Touch America [*E-mail shopping service*] ..... NPTA

Nord-Sud [*Benin*] [*ICAO designator*] (FAAC) .... NSB

Nord-Viscount Corp. .... NV

Nor-East Commuter Airlines [*ICAO designator*] (AD) .... YN

Norein [*Geology*] .... N

Norepinephrine [*Also known as NA: Noradrenaline*] [*Biochemistry*] .... NE

Norethindrone/Ethinyl Estradiol [*Oral contraceptive*] .... NEE

Norethisterone [*Oral contraceptive ingredient*] .... NET

Norex America [*AMEX symbol*] (TTSB) .... NXA

Norex America, Inc. [*Associated Press*] (SAG) .... Norex

Norex America, Inc. [*AMEX symbol*] (SPSG) .... NXA

Norfolk [*Virginia*] [*Navy Yard*] .... NF

Norfolk [*County in England*] .... NORF

Norfolk [*County in England*] (ODBW) .... Norf

Norfolk [*County in England*] .... NORFLK

Norfolk [*Nebraska*] [*Airport symbol*] (OAG) .... OFK

Norfolk & Portsmouth Belt Line Railroad Co. [*AAR code*] .... NPB

Norfolk & Western Railway Co. .... N & W

Norfolk & Western Railway Co. [*AAR code*] .... NW

Norfolk & Western Railway Co., Roanoke, VA [*Library symbol Library of Congress*] (LCLS) .... ViRoNW

Norfolk, Baltimore & Carolina Line [*Steamship*] (MHDB) .... NB & C

Norfolk County Medical Society, Inc., Norfolk, VA [*Library symbol Library of Congress*] (LCLS) .... ViNM

Norfolk, Franklin & Danville Railway Co. [*The Atlantic & Danville Railway Co.*] [*AAR code*] .... AD

Norfolk, Franklin & Danville Railway Co. [*AAR code*] .... NFD

Norfolk Historical Society, Simcoe, ON, Canada [*Library symbol Library of Congress*] (LCLS) .... CaOSiNH

Norfolk Historical Society, Simcoe, Ontario [*Library symbol National Library of Canada*] (NLC) .... OSINH

Norfolk Howard [*Refers to a bed-bug*] [*Slang*] (DSUE) .... NH

Norfolk Information Exchange Scheme (NITA) .... NINES

Norfolk Island [*Australia ICAO location identifier*] (ICLI) .... ASNF
Norfolk Island [*ANSI two-letter standard code*] (CNC) .... NF
Norfolk Island [*ANSI three-letter standard code*] (CNC) .... NFK
Norfolk Island [*Australia Seismograph station code, US Geological Survey Closed*] (SEIS) .... NIA
Norfolk Island [*Airport symbol*] (OAG) .... NLK
Norfolk Island [*MARC country of publication code Library of Congress*] (LCCP) .... nx
Norfolk Island Airlines [*Australia ICAO designator*] (FAAC) .... NIA
Norfolk Island Airlines [*Australia ICAO designator*] (ICDA) .... UG
Norfolk Junior College [*Nebraska*] .... NJC
Norfolk, MA [*AM radio station call letters*] .... WDIS
Norfolk Naval Hospital, Portsmouth, VA [*Library symbol Library of Congress*] (LCLS) .... ViPoN
Norfolk Naval Shipyard [*Portsmouth, VA*] (MCD) .... NNS
Norfolk Naval Shipyard [*Portsmouth, VA*] .... NNSY
Norfolk Navy Yard [*Virginia*] [*Later, Norfolk Naval Shipyard*] .... NNYD
Norfolk, NE [*FM radio station call letters*] .... KEXL
Norfolk, NE [*FM radio station call letters*] .... KNEN
Norfolk, NE [*FM radio station call letters*] .... KPNO
Norfolk, NE [*FM radio station call letters*] .... KXNE
Norfolk, NE [*Television station call letters*] .... KXNE-TV
Norfolk, NE [*Location identifier FAA*] (FAAL) .... OFK
Norfolk, NE [*AM radio station call letters*] .... WJAG
Norfolk/Norfolk Naval Air Station [*Virginia*] [*ICAO location identifier*] (ICLI) .... KNGU
Norfolk/Norfolk Regional Airport [*Virginia*] [*ICAO location identifier*] (ICLI) .... KORF
Norfolk Petroleum Ltd. [*Vancouver Stock Exchange symbol*] .... NFP
Norfolk Public Library, Norfolk, NE [*Library symbol Library of Congress*] (LCLS) .... NbNf
Norfolk Public Library, Norfolk, VA [*Library symbol Library of Congress*] (LCLS) .... ViN
Norfolk Rangers [*British military*] (DMA) .... NR
Norfolk Sample Drug Program .... NSDP
Norfolk Southern [*NYSE symbol*] (TTSB) .... NSC
Norfolk Southern Corp. [*Associated Press*] (SAG) .... NflkSo
Norfolk Southern Railway [*NYSE symbol*] (SPSG) .... NSC
Norfolk Southern Railway Co. [*AAR code*] .... NS
Norfolk Southern Railway Co. [*NYSE symbol*] (SAG) .... NSR
Norfolk Southern Railway Co. [*Associated Press*] (SAG) .... NSRy
Norfolk State College, Norfolk, VA [*Library symbol Library of Congress*] (LCLS) .... ViNS
Norfolk State College, Norfolk, VA [*OCLC symbol*] (OCLC) .... VNS
Norfolk Testing Laboratories, Norfolk, VA [*Library symbol Library of Congress*] (LCLS) .... ViNT
Norfolk, VA [*Location identifier FAA*] (FAAL) .... JZQ
Norfolk, VA [*Location identifier FAA*] (FAAL) .... NCL
Norfolk, VA [*Location identifier FAA*] (FAAL) .... NGU
Norfolk, VA [*Location identifier FAA*] (FAAL) .... NIY
Norfolk, VA [*Location identifier FAA*] (FAAL) .... NWV
Norfolk, VA [*AM radio station call letters*] (RBYB) .... WCKO
Norfolk, VA [*AM radio station call letters*] .... WCMS
Norfolk, VA [*FM radio station call letters*] .... WCMS-FM
Norfolk, VA [*FM radio station call letters*] .... WHRO
Norfolk, VA [*FM radio station call letters*] .... WHRV
Norfolk, VA [*Television station call letters*] .... WJCB
Norfolk, VA [*FM radio station call letters*] (RBYB) .... WJCD
Norfolk, VA [*FM radio station call letters*] .... WLTY
Norfolk, VA [*AM radio station call letters*] .... WNIS
Norfolk, VA [*AM radio station call letters*] .... WNOR
Norfolk, VA [*FM radio station call letters*] .... WNOR-FM
Norfolk, VA [*FM radio station call letters*] .... WNSB
Norfolk, VA [*FM radio station call letters*] .... WNVZ
Norfolk, VA [*FM radio station call letters*] .... WOWI
Norfolk, VA [*AM radio station call letters*] .... WTAR
Norfolk, VA [*Television station call letters*] .... WTKR
Norfolk, VA [*Television station call letters*] .... WTVZ
Norfolk, VA [*FM radio station call letters*] .... WYFI
Norfolk, Virginia [*Navy*] .... NORVA
Norfolk/Virginia Beach [*Virginia*] [*Airport symbol*] (OAG) .... ORF
Norfolk, Virginia Group [*Navy*] .... NORVAGRP
Norfolk Volunteer Regiment [*British military*] (DMA) .... NVR
NorfolkSo'nRy$2.60cmPfd [*NYSE symbol*] (TTSB) .... NSRPr
Norges Allmennvitenskapelige Forskningsrad [*Norwegian Research Council for Science and the Humanities*] [*Information service or system*] (IID) .... NAVF
Norges Automobil Fornund [*Norway Automobile Association*] (AD) .... NAF
Norges Geologiske Undersoekelse Biblioteket [*Geological Survey of Norway*], Trondheim, Norway [*Library symbol*] [*Library of Congress*] (LCLS) .... NoTNG
Norges Kommunalbank [*Bank*] [*Norway*] .... NKB
Norges Kommunistiske Parti [*Norwegian Communist Party*] [*Political party*] (PPE) .... NKP
Norges Statsbaner [*Norwegian State Railways*] .... NSB
Norges Tekniske Vitenskapsakademi [*Norwegian Academy for Technical Sciences*], Trondheim, Norway [*Library symbol Library of Congress*] (LCLS) .... NoTN
Norges Teknisk-Naturvitenskapelige Forskningsraad [*Online database*] ..... NTNF
Norges Unge Venstre [*Norway*] .... NUV
Norgold Resources [*Vancouver Stock Exchange symbol*] .... NGR
Norgold Russet Potato .... NR
Norgulf Lines (North Atlantic & Gulf) (AD) .... NA & G
Noril'sk [*Former USSR Geomagnetic observatory code*] .... NOK
Noril'sk [*Former USSR Seismograph station code, US Geological Survey*] (SEIS) .... NRI
Norimberge [*Nuremberg*] [*Imprint*] (ROG) .... NORIMB
Norland Medical Systems [*NASDAQ symbol*] (TTSB) .... NRLD
Norland Medical Systems, Inc. [*Associated Press*] (SAG) .... Norland
Norland Medical Systems, Inc. [*NASDAQ symbol*] (SAG) .... NRLD
Norland Potato .... N
Norlaudanosolinecarboxylic Acid [*Biochemistry*] .... NLCA
Norleucine [*A nonessential amino acid*] [*Biochemistry*] .... Nle
Norleucine [*A nonessential amino acid*] [*Biochemistry*] .... NORLEU
Norleucine [*Biochemistry*] (DAVI) .... norleu
Norlink Air Ltd. [*British ICAO designator*] (FAAC) .... NLK
Norlithocholic Acid [*Biochemistry*] .... NLCA
Norm (WDAA) .... N
Norma [*Constellation*] .... Nor
Norma [*Constellation*] .... Norm
Norma Jean Fan Club (EA) .... NJFC
Norma Zimmer National Fan Club (EA) .... NZNFC
Normal .... N
Normal [*Solute concentration*] [*Chemistry*] .... N
Normal [*Molecular structure*] [*Chemistry*] .... n
Normal (DAVI) .... NL
Normal .... NML
Normal (KSC) .... NOR
Normal .... NOR
Normal .... NORM
Normal [*or Normalize*] (AAG) .... NORM
Normal (DAVI) .... NORML
Normal (MAE) .... NR
Normal (WGA) .... NRML
Normal Abdominal Bowel Sound [*Medicine*] (CPH) .... NABS
Normal Acceleration .... NZ
Normal Administrative Practice .... NAP
Normal Adult .... NA
Normal Alarm (SAA) .... NA
Normal Allowed Time (AD) .... nat
Normal Allowed Time (IEEE) .... NAT
Normal Analytical Zone [*Chemistry*] .... NAZ
Normal Approach Course [*Navy*] (NVT) .... NAC
Normal Atmosphere (DAVI) .... A_n
Normal Axis Deviation [*Medicine*] .... NAD
Normal Binocular Experience [*Ophthalmology*] .... NBE
Normal Birth Weight .... NBW
Normal Blood Serum (MAE) .... NBS
Normal Boiling Point .... NBP
Normal Bone Marrow [*Medicine*] (DMAA) .... NBM
Normal Bowel Movement [*Gastroenterology*] (DAVI) .... NB
Normal Bowel Movement [*Medicine*] (DMAA) .... NBM
Normal Bowel Sounds [*Gastroenterology*] (DAVI) .... NBS
Normal Burro Serum [*Biochemistry*] (DAVI) .... NBS
Normal Calomel Electrode [*Electrochemistry*] .... NCE
Normal Cephalic Atraumatic [*Medicine*] (DMAA) .... NC/AT
Normal Charge (MHDB) .... N CHG
Normal Chick Embryo .... NCE
Normal Childhood Diseases (DAVI) .... NCD
Normal Childhood Disorders [*Medicine*] .... NCD
Normal Children .... NC
Normal Circular Pitch (MSA) .... NCP
Normal Control .... NC
Normal Coordinate Analysis .... NCA
Normal Copy [*Oncology*] .... NC
Normal Crop Acreage Farm Base .... NCAFB
Normal Curve [*Laboratory science*] (DAVI) .... NORC
Normal Curve Equivalent [*Testing*] (EDAC) .... NCE
Normal Curve Equivalent Scores [*Testing*] (EDAC) .... NCES
Normal Daily Requirement [*Military*] .... NDR
Normal Delivery [*Obstetrics*] .... ND
Normal Depth [*Earthquakes*] .... N
Normal Development [*Pediatrics*] (DAVI) .... ND
Normal Diametral Pitch (MSA) .... NDP
Normal Digital Echo Suppressor [*Telecommunications*] (TEL) .... NDES
Normal Dog Serum [*Medicine*] (DMAA) .... NDS
Normal Engineered Safety Features [*Nuclear energy*] (NRCH) .... NESF
Normal Entry Point (MCD) .... NEP
Normal Equivalent Deviation .... NED
Normal Error Model Analysis Chart .... NEMAC
Normal Excitability [*Medicine*] .... NE
Normal Extraocular Movements [*Ophthalmology*] (DAVI) .... NOM
Normal Failure Period .... NFP
Normal Female Liver [*Hepatology*] .... NFL
Normal Flow [*Medicine*] .... NF
Normal Form [*Database design rule*] [*Computer science*] (PCM) .... NF
Normal Formula .... NF
Normal Frequency [*Telecommunications*] (NTCM) .... NF
Normal Fuel Oil (DNAB) .... NFO
Normal Fuel-Oil Tank (MSA) .... NFT
Normal, Full Term Delivery [*Obstetrics*] .... NFTD
Normal Full-Term Spontaneous Delivery [*Obstetrics*] (DAVI) .... NFTSD
Normal Graduate .... NG
Normal Hair Distribution [*Medicine*] (DAVI) .... NHD
Normal Hearing Peer [*of the hearing-impaired*] .... NHP
Normal Horse Serum .... NHS
Normal Horsepower .... N
Normal Hourly Space Velocity [*Emission control*] .... NHSV
Normal Human Bronchial Epithelial [*Cells*] .... NHBE
Normal Human Colon Mucosal [*Cells*] .... NCM
Normal Human Diploid Fibroblast [*Medicine*] (DMAA) .... NHDF
Normal Human Epidermal Keratinocyte .... NHEK
Normal Human Epidermal Melanocyte [*Cytology*] .... NHEM

Normal Human Gastric Juice [*Medicine*] (DMAA)	NHGJ
Normal Human Globulin [*or anticancer substance derived from NHG*] [*Biochemistry*]	NHG
Normal Human Lymphocyte	NHL
Normal Human Mammary Cell	NHMC
Normal Human Milk	NHM
Normal Human Serum	NHS
Normal Human-Pooled Plasma	NHP
Normal Hydrogen Electrode	NHE
Normal, IL [*FM radio station call letters*]	WGLT
Normal, IL [*FM radio station call letters*]	WIHN
Normal Impact Point	NIP
Normal Impurity [*Metals*]	NI
Normal Incidence Pyrheliometer (PDAA)	NIP
Normal Incidence Spectrometer (PDAA)	NIS
Normal Incidence Technique [*Structural testing*]	NIT
Normal Incidence X-Ray Telescope	NIXT
Normal Inferior	NI
Normal Input-Output Control Executive [*Computer science*]	NICE
Normal Integration Mode	NIM
Normal Intraocular Pressure [*Ophthalmology*] (DAVI)	Tn
Normal Intraocular Tension [*Ophthalmology*] (DAVI)	Tn
Normal Investment Practice	NIP
Normal Lactase Activity [*Medicine*] (DMAA)	NLA
Normal Light Perception [*Physiology*] (MAH)	NLP
Normal Limits	n/l
Normal Liquid Level [*Engineering*]	NLL
Normal Lube-Oil Tank (MSA)	NLT
Normal Lungs	NL
Normal Lymphocyte Transfer [*Immunochemistry*]	NLT
Normal Magnitude Probability Function	NMPF
Normal Manual Operation (KSC)	NMO
Normal Manual Operation	NMO
Normal Market Size Transaction	NMS
Normal Menstrual Period [*Gynecology*] (MAE)	NMP
Normal Method of Acquisition (MCD)	NMA
Normal Mode Operation	NMO
Normal Mode Rejection	NMR
Normal Molecular Weight	NMW
Normal Molecular Weight, Low in Extractables	NMWL
Normal Mouse Serum	NMS
Normal Muscle Development (DAVI)	NMD
Normal Operating Procedure (NRCH)	NOP
Normal Operation with Unscram [*Nuclear energy*] (NRCH)	NOWUS
Normal Operational Loss [*Nuclear energy*]	NOL
Normal Overload	NOL
Normal Paraffin Hydrocarbon	NPH
Normal Phase [*Chromatography*]	NP
Normal Phase Chromatography	NPC
Normal Phase Liquid Chromatography	NPLC
Normal Pipe Size	NPS
Normal Pitch (ADA)	NP
Normal Plasma [*Medicine*] (MAE)	NP
Normal Pool Plasma [*Clinical chemistry*]	NPP
Normal Power Level (KSC)	NPL
Normal Pregnancy [*Medicine*]	NP
Normal Pressure	NP
Normal Pressure and Temperature	NPT
Normal Pressure Angle	NPA
Normal Pressure Hydrocephalus [*Medicine*]	NPH
Normal Priority Exit (IAA)	NPEX
Normal Probability Distribution Function	NPDF
Normal Probability Frequency Function	NPFF
Normal Profit [*Business term*] (MHDW)	NP
Normal Propyl Nitrate (MCD)	NPN
Normal Rabbit Serum [*Culture medium*]	NRS
Normal Range	NR
Normal Rat Kidney	NRK
Normal Rat Kidney Fibroblast [*Cytology*]	NRKF
Normal Rat Serum [*Hematology*]	NRS
Normal Rated Load	NRL
Normal Rated Power	NRP
Normal Rated Thrust (AAG)	NRT
Normal Record [*Medicine*] (DAVI)	NR
Normal Reference Serum (MAE)	NRS
Normal Renin Essential Hypertension [*Medicine*] (DMAA)	NREH
Normal Responder	NR
Normal Response Level	NRL
Normal Response Mode	NRM
Normal Retinal Correspondence	NRC
Normal Retirement Age	NRA
Normal Retirement Date	NRD
Normal Return Point (MCD)	NORMRP
Normal Saline	NS
Normal Saline Nose Drops [*Pharmacology*] (DAVI)	NSND
Normal Saline Solution	NSS
Normal Segment	NS
Normal Serum	NS
Normal Serum Albumin [*Clinical chemistry*]	NSA
Normal Serum Pool	NSP
Normal Sinus Rate and Rhythm [*Cardiology*] (DAVI)	NSRR
Normal Sinus Rhythm [*Medicine*] (DMAA)	NSR
Normal Size, Shape, and Position [*On examination*] [*Anatomy*] (DAVI)	NSSP
Normal Size, Shape, and Position Anteverted, and Anteflexed [*Uterus*] [*On examination*] [*Gynecology*] (DAVI)	NSSPAVAF
Normal Slow Rate Maneuver (NASA)	NSR
Normal Solution (DOG)	N
Normal Sphincter Tone [*Gastroenterology*] (DAVI)	NST
Normal, Spontaneous Delivery [*Obstetrics*]	NSD
Normal, Spontaneous, Full Term Delivery [*Obstetrics*]	NSFTD
Normal Spontaneous Vaginal Delivery [*Obstetrics*] (DMAA)	NSVD
Normal Standard Dose [*Oncology radiation*]	NSD
Normal Superphosphate [*Fertilizer*]	NSP
Normal Takeoff and Landing [*Aviation*] (MCD)	NTOL
Normal Temperature (ADA)	NT
Normal Temperature and Pressure [*Medicine*]	NTP
Normal Temperature, Pressure Differential (MCD)	NTPD
Normal Terminate Interrupt Handler (MCD)	NTIH
Normal Throat Flora [*Medicine*] (DMAA)	NTF
Normal through Patch Panel (MCD)	NTPP
Normal to X-Axis (MCD)	NX
Normal to Y-Axis (MCD)	NY
Normal to Z-Axis (MCD)	NZ
Normal Tour	NT
Normal Tour of Duty Completed	NTC
Normal Tour of Shore Duty	NORMSHOR
Normal Trading Unit	NTU
Normal Transmitting Male [*Genetics*]	NTM
Normal Value [*Clinical chemistry*]	NV
Normal Waste [*Nuclear energy*] (NRCH)	NW
Normal Water Leg [*Nuclear energy*] (NRCH)	NWL
Normal Water Level (IAA)	NWL
Normal Water Surface (ADA)	NWS
Normal Working Hours	NWH
Normalair-Garrett Ltd. [*British*] (IRUK)	NGL
Normal-Branch Oscillation [*Astronomy*]	NBO
Normal-Control Children [*Psychology*]	NCC
Normalcy (ABBR)	NRMLC
Normal-Hexylcarbane (MCD)	NHC
Normalisation, Automatisation de la Terminologie [*Standardization and Automation of Terminology*] [*Databank*] [*France*] [*Information service or system*] (IID)	NORMATERM
Normality (ABBR)	NRMLT
Normalization (ABBR)	NRMLZN
Normalize (DEN)	NRM
Normalize (ABBR)	NRMLZ
Normalized (ABBR)	NRMLZD
Normalized Abundance Pattern [*Geochemistry*]	NAP
Normalized Alignment Score	NAS
Normalized and Tempered (MCD)	NT
Normalized Critical View	NCV
Normalized Cumulative Deviation	NCD
Normalized Device Coordinates [*Computer science*]	NDC
Normalized Difference Vegetation Index [*Plant biota*]	NDVI
Normalized Electron-Peak to Gamma-Peak [*Electronics*] (OA)	NPG
Normalized Integral Squared Error	NISE
Normalized Load Access (NITA)	NLA
Normalized Mass Loss Coefficient [*Nuclear energy*] (NUCP)	NMLC
Normalized Peak Filling Rate [*Cardiology*]	NPFR
Normalized Photoacoustic Signal [*Instrumentation*]	NPAS
Normalized Plateau Slope	NPS
Normalized Programming Generator (IAA)	NPG
Normalized RADAR Cross Section	NRCS
Normalized Transmission Energy Requirement	NTER
Normalized Variance (PDAA)	NVAR
Normalized Vegetation Index [*Meteorology*]	NVI
Normalized Volt-Ampere	NVa
Normalizer (ABBR)	NRMLZR
Normalizing (ABBR)	NRMLZG
Normally (ABBR)	NRMLY
Normally Aspirated [*Automotive engineering*]	NA
Normally Closed	N/C
Normally Closed [*Switch*]	NC
Normally Closed [*Switch*] [*Electronics*] (IAA)	NORMCLSD
Normally Closed Contact [*Switch*] (IAA)	NCC
Normally Energized (NRCH)	NE
Normally Occurring Retirement Community	Norc
Normally Open	N/O
Normally Open [*Switch*]	NO
Normally Open [*Switch*]	NOPN
Normally Open [*Switch*] [*Electronics*] (IAA)	NORMOPN
Normally Open [*Ship's fittings classification*]	Z
Normally Open Contact [*Switch*] (IAA)	NOC
Normally Shut (NRCH)	NS
Normal-Mode Rejection Ratio [*Electronics*] (BARN)	NMRR
Normalnull [*Mean Sea Level*] [*German*]	NN
Normal-Octyl & -Deyl Adipate [*Organic chemistry*]	NODA
Normal-Variant Short Stature [*Medicine*]	NVSS
Norman [*Oklahoma*] [*Seismograph station code, US Geological Survey Closed*] (SEIS)	NMO
Norman	NOR
Norman [*or Normandy*]	NORM
Norman Conquest [*of England, 1066*]	NC
Norman County West High School, Halstad, MN [*Library symbol*] [*Library of Congress*] (LCLS)	MnHaH
Norman, Craig & Kummel [*Advertising agency*]	NCK
Norman French [*Language, etc.*]	NF
Norman French [*Language, etc.*] (DLA)	Nor Fr
Norman Junior College, Norman Park, GA [*Library symbol Library of Congress*] (LCLS)	GNpN

Norman. Letters Patent [*1853*] [*A publication*] (DLA) ..... Nor Pat
Norman MacKenzie Art Gallery, University of Regina, Saskatchewan [*Library symbol National Library of Canada*] (NLC) ..... SRUNM
Norman, OK [*FM radio station call letters*] ..... KGOU
Norman, OK [*AM radio station call letters*] ..... KNOR
Norman, OK [*Location identifier FAA*] (FAAL) ..... OUN
Norman, OK [*Location identifier FAA*] (FAAL) ..... PHY
Norman Resources Ltd. [*Vancouver Stock Exchange symbol*] ..... NMZ
Norman Rockwell Memorial Society (EA) ..... NRMS
Norman Wells [*Canada*] [*Airport symbol*] (OAG) ..... YVQ
Norman Wells, NT [*ICAO location identifier*] (ICLI) ..... CYVQ
Normanby Township Community & School Library, Ayton, ON, Canada [*Library symbol*] [*Library of Congress*] (LCLS) ..... CaOANT
Normanby Township Community and School Library, Ayton, Ontario [*Library symbol National Library of Canada*] (NLC) ..... OANT
Normandale Community College, Bloomington, MN [*OCLC symbol*] (OCLC) ..... NOR
Normandale Community College, Minneapolis, MN [*Library symbol Library of Congress*] (LCLS) ..... MnMN
Normandy Base Section [*World War II*] ..... NBS
Norman's Cay, Exuma Island [*Bahamas*] [*ICAO location identifier*] (ICLI) ..... MYEN
Normanton [*Australia Airport symbol*] (OAG) ..... NTN
Normative (ABBR) ..... NRMV
Normative Operating Reporting Method ..... NORM
Normatively (ABBR) ..... NRMVY
Norme Europeene de Telecommunications [*Telecommunications*] (OSI) ..... NET
Normes et Reglements Informations Automatisees Accessibles en Ligne [*Automated Standards and Regulations Information Online*] [*Database French Association for Standardization*] [*Information service or system*] (IID) ..... NORIANE
Normetadrenaline [*Biochemistry*] (DAVI) ..... NM
Normetal [*AAR code*] ..... NORM
Normetanephrine [*Also, Methylnorepinephrine*] [*Biochemistry*] ..... NMN
Normetanephrine [*Biochemistry*] (DAVI) ..... NMN
Normetanephrine [*Also, Methylnorepinephrine*] [*Biochemistry*] (AAMN) ..... NORMET
Normick Perron, Inc. [*Toronto Stock Exchange symbol*] ..... NPI
Normine Resources Ltd. [*Vancouver Stock Exchange symbol*] ..... NON
Normoactive Bowel Sounds [*Gastroenterology*] (DAVI) ..... NABS
Normoblast [*Hematology*] (AAMN) ..... NB
Normoblast [*Hematology*] ..... nbl
Normocephalic [*On physical examination*] [*Medicine*] (DAVI) ..... NC
Normochromic Normocytic [*Medicine*] (MEDA) ..... NCNC
Normochromic, Normocytic Anemia [*Hematology*] (DAVI) ..... NCNC
Normochromic, Normocytic Anemia [*Hematology*] (DAVI) ..... NCNCA
Normochromic, Normocytic Anemia (DAVI) ..... NNA
Normocytic/Normochromic Anemia (DAVI) ..... N/N
Normotensive Donor Rat ..... NDR
Normotensive Group [*Cardiology*] ..... NG
Normotensive Rat [*Medicine*] (DMAA) ..... NR
Normotensive Rat Kidney ..... NRK
Norm-Referenced Measurement [*Education*] ..... NRM
Norm-Referenced Testing [*Education*] ..... NRT
Noront Resources Ltd. [*Vancouver Stock Exchange symbol*] ..... NOT
Norontair [*Canada ICAO designator*] (FAAC) ..... NOA
Norpet Resources Ltd. [*Toronto Stock Exchange symbol*] ..... NPO
Nor-Quest Resources Ltd. [*Vancouver Stock Exchange symbol*] ..... NQT
Norrell Corp. [*Associated Press*] (SAG) ..... Norrell
Norrell Corp. [*NYSE symbol*] (SAG) ..... NRL
Norridgewock, ME [*Location identifier FAA*] (FAAL) ..... OWK
Norris and Leach on Rule Against Perpetuities [*A publication*] (DLA) ..... Norris & L Perpetuities
Norris Arm Public Library, Newfoundland [*Library symbol National Library of Canada*] (NLC) ..... NFNA
Norris Arm Public Library, Norris Arm, NF, Canada [*Library symbol Library of Congress*] (LCLS) ..... CaNfNA
Norris Communications [*NASDAQ symbol*] (TTSB) ..... NORRF
Norris Communications Corp. [*NASDAQ symbol*] (SAG) ..... NCRRF
Norris Communications Corp. [*Vancouver Stock Exchange symbol*] ..... NOC
Norris Communications Corp. [*Associated Press*] (SAG) ..... NorrisC
Norris Cotton Cancer Center [*Dartmouth-Hitchcock Medical Center*] [*Research center*] (RCD) ..... NCCC
Norris Dam [*TVA*] ..... NOD
Norris' Edition of Peake's Law of Evidence [*A publication*] (DLA) ..... Norr Peake
Norris Junction [*Wyoming*] [*Seismograph station code, US Geological Survey*] (SEIS) ..... NJW
Norris' Law of Seamen [*A publication*] (DLA) ..... Norris Seamen
Norris Point Public Library, Newfoundland [*Library symbol National Library of Canada*] (NLC) ..... NFNP
Norris Point Public Library, Norris Point, NF, Canada [*Library symbol Library of Congress*] (LCLS) ..... CaNfNP
Norris Public Library, Rutherfordton, NC [*Library symbol Library of Congress*] (LCLS) ..... NcRu
Norris' Reports [*82-96 Pennsylvania*] [*A publication*] (DLA) ..... Norr
Norris' Reports [*82-96 Pennsylvania*] [*A publication*] (DLA) ..... Norris
Norris-LaGuardia Act (MHDB) ..... NLA
Norristown, PA [*AM radio station call letters*] ..... WNAP
Norristown State Hospital, Norristown, PA [*OCLC symbol*] (OCLC) ..... PHN
Norristown State Hospital, Norristown, PA [*Library symbol Library of Congress*] (LCLS) ..... PNoH
Norrkoping [*Sweden ICAO location identifier*] (ICLI) ..... ESKL
Norrkoping [*Sweden ICAO location identifier*] (ICLI) ..... ESWI
Norrkoping [*Sweden*] [*Airport symbol*] (OAG) ..... NRK
Norrkoping/Bravalla [*Sweden ICAO location identifier*] (ICLI) ..... ESCK
Norrkoping/Kungsangen [*Sweden ICAO location identifier*] (ICLI) ..... ESSP
Norsar Array Site 01A00 [*Norway*] [*Seismograph station code, US Geological Survey*] (SEIS) ..... NAO
Norsar Array Site 01B00 [*Norway*] [*Seismograph station code, US Geological Survey*] (SEIS) ..... NBO
Norsar Array Site 01C00 [*Norway*] [*Seismograph station code, US Geological Survey*] (SEIS) ..... NCO
Norsar Array Site 02B00 [*Norway*] [*Seismograph station code, US Geological Survey*] (SEIS) NB2
Norsar Array Site 03B00 [*Norway*] [*Seismograph station code, US Geological Survey*] (SEIS) NB3
Norsar Array Site 03C00 [*Norway*] [*Seismograph station code, US Geological Survey*] (SEIS) NC3
Norsar Array Site 04B00 [*Norway*] [*Seismograph station code, US Geological Survey*] (SEIS) NB4
Norsar Array Site 05B00 [*Norway*] [*Seismograph station code, US Geological Survey*] (SEIS) NB5
Norsar Array Site 05C00 [*Norway*] [*Seismograph station code, US Geological Survey*] (SEIS) NC5
Norsat International, Inc. [*Vancouver Stock Exchange symbol*] ..... NIN
Norse [*Language, etc.*] ..... N
Norse Oriental Lines (MHDW) ..... NOL
Norseman [*Australia Airport symbol*] (OAG) ..... NSM
Norsemont Mining [*Vancouver Stock Exchange symbol*] ..... NMM
Norsk Data (NITA) ..... NORD
Norsk Front [*Norwegian Front*] (PD) ..... NF
Norsk Hydro [*Associated Press*] (SAG) ..... Norsk
Norsk Hydro AS [*NYSE symbol*] (SPSG) ..... NHY
Norsk Luftambulanse AS [*Norway ICAO designator*] (FAAC) ..... DOC
Norsk Rikskringkasting [*Norwegian Broadcasting Corporation*] ..... NRK
Norsk Samfunnsvitenskapelig Datatjeneste [*Norwegian Social Science Data Services*] [*Information service or system*] (IID) ..... NSD
Norsk Senter for Informatikk [*Norwegian Center for Informatics*] [*Information service or system*] (IID) ..... NSI
Norsk Telegrambyra [*Norwegian News Agency*] ..... NTB
Norskair [*Norway ICAO designator*] (FAAC) ..... NIR
Norsk-Data AS (MHDW) ..... NORKZ
Norske Reindriftsamers Lansforbund [*Norway*] ..... NRL
Norske Samers Riksforbund [*Norway*] ..... NSR
Norske Veritas [*Norwegian ship classification society*] (ROG) ..... N
Norske Veritas [*Norwegian ship classification society*] (DS) ..... NV
Norstan, Inc. [*Associated Press*] (SAG) ..... Norstan
Norstan, Inc. [*NASDAQ symbol*] (NQ) ..... NRRD
Norsup [*Vanuatu*] [*Airport symbol*] (OAG) ..... NUS
Norsup [*Vanuatu*] [*ICAO location identifier*] (ICLI) ..... NVSP
Nort Jet [*Spain ICAO designator*] (FAAC) ..... ENJ
Nortech Systems [*NASDAQ symbol*] (TTSB) ..... NSYS
Nortech Systems, Inc. [*Associated Press*] (SAG) ..... NorSys
Nortech Systems, Inc. [*NASDAQ symbol*] (SAG) ..... NSYS
Nortek Capital Corp. [*Formerly, Nortek Energy Corp.*] [*Vancouver Stock Exchange symbol*] ..... NKE
Nortek, Inc. [*Associated Press*] (SAG) ..... Nortek
Nortek, Inc. [*NYSE symbol*] (SPSG) ..... NTK
Nortel Inversora 10%'MEDS' [*NYSE symbol*] (TTSB) ..... NRT
Nortel Inversora SA [*Associated Press*] (SAG) Nortel100
Nortel Inversora SA [*NYSE symbol*] (SAG) ..... NRT
North [*or Northern*] ..... N
North ..... NO
North ..... NOR
North (ABBR) ..... NRTH
North Adams, MA [*FM radio station call letters*] ..... WJJW
North Adams, MA [*FM radio station call letters*] ..... WMNB
North Adams, MA [*AM radio station call letters*] ..... WNAW
North Adams State College (GAGS) ..... No Adams St C
North Adams State College, North Adams, MA [*Library symbol Library of Congress*] (LCLS) ..... MNoadT
North Africa ..... N Afr
North Africa ..... NA
North Africa, Near East, Asia, and Pacific Region [*Program of ACTION, an independent government agency*] ..... NANEAP
North African Adjutant General [*World War II*] ..... NAAG
North African Adjutant General, Analysis and Control Division [*World War II*] ..... NAAGA
North African Adjutant General, Casualty Branch [*World War II*] ..... NAAGC
North African Adjutant General, Executive Division [*World War II*] ..... NAAGG
North African Adjutant General, Operations Division [*World War II*] ..... NAAGO
North African Adjutant General, Personnel Division [*World War II*] ..... NAAGE
North African Adjutant General, Postal Division [*World War II*] ..... NAAGP
North African Adjutant General, Statistical Division [*World War II*] ..... NAAGS
North African Air Force [*World War II*] ..... NAAF
North African Antiaircraft Section [*World War II*] ..... NACAC
North African Army Exchange Service [*World War II*] ..... NAES
North African Censorship Section, US [*World War II*] ..... NACRS
North African Chaplain's Section [*World War II*] ..... NACHP
North African Chemical Warfare Section [*World War II*] ..... NACWS
North African Chief of Staff [*World War II*] ..... NACOS
North African Claims Section [*World War II*] ..... NACLM
North African Commanding General [*World War II*] ..... NACG
North African Economic Board [*World War II*] ..... NAEB
North African Engineer Section [*World War II*] ..... NAENG
North African Finance Section [*World War II*] ..... NAFIN
North African Inspector General's Section [*World War II*] ..... NAOIG
North African Joint Economic Mission [*World War II*] ..... NAJEM
North African Joint Rearmament Committee [*World War II*] ..... NAJRC
North African Judge Advocate General's Section [*World War II*] ..... NAJAG
North African Liaison Section [*World War II*] ..... NALN

North African Medical Section [*World War II*] ... NAMED
North African Military Mission [*World War II*] ... NAMM
North African Ordnance Section [*World War II*] ... NAORD
North African Provost Marshal General [*World War II*] ... NAPMG
North African Quartermaster Section [*World War II*] ... NAQMC
North African Secretary General Staff [*World War II*] ... NASGS
North African Shipping Board [*World War II*] ... NASBO
North African Signal Section [*World War II*] ... NASIG
North African Special Service Section [*World War II*] ... NASS
North African Theater [*World War II*] ... NAT
North African Theater of Operations [*World War II*] ... NATO
North African Theater of Operations (AD) ... NATUSA
North African Theater of Operations, United States Army [*World War II*] ... NATOUSA
North African Theater, United States Army [*World War II*] ... NATUSA
North African Transportation Section [*World War II*] ... NATPN
North African War Shipping [*World War II*] ... NAWS
North African Waters ... NAW
North Alabama Cooperative Library System [*Library network*] ... NACLS
North Amer Palladium [*NASDAQ symbol*] (TTSB) ... PDLCF
North Amer Svgs Bk [*NASDAQ symbol*] (TTSB) ... NASB
North Amer Technologies Group [*NASDAQ symbol*] (TTSB) ... NATK
North America [*MARC geographic area code Library of Congress*] (LCCP) ... n-----
North America (AD) ... N Am
North America (ODBW) ... N Am
North America ... NA
North America ... NAM
North America/Caribbean ... NAMCAR
North America Coordinating Center for Responsible Tourism (EA) ... NACCRT
North America Engineering Parts Inquiry System ... NAEPIS
North America Mtge [*NYSE symbol*] (TTSB) ... NAC
North America Regional Test Center (NATG) ... NARTC
North America Supply Council ... NASC
North America Taiwanese Professors' Association (EA) ... NATPA
North America Trail Complex (EA) ... NOAMTRAC
North American Academy of Ecumenists (EA) ... NAAE
North American Academy of Liturgy (EA) ... NAAL
North American Academy of Musculoskeletal Medicine (EA) ... NAAMM
North American Academy of the Spanish Language (EA) ... NAASL
North American Adoption Congress (EA) ... NAAC
North American Aero Dynasty [*Vancouver Stock Exchange symbol*] ... NAD
North American Aerodynamic Laboratory [*Wind tunnel*] (NASA) ... NAAL
North American Aerospace Defense Command [*FAA*] (TAG) ... NORAD
North American Air Defense [*Integrated United States-Canada command*] ... NORAD
North American Air Defense Combat Operations Center [*Military*] (AFM) ... NORADCOC
North American Air Defense Command (AAG) ... NAADC
North American Air Defense Command (AAGC) ... NORAD
North American Air Defense Command Post Exercise (SAA) ... NORAD CPX
North American Air Defense Exercise (NVT) ... NORADEX
North American Air Defense Orientation Cruise (NVT) ... NORADCRU
North American Airlines, Inc. [*ICAO designator*] (FAAC) ... NAO
North American Airlines, Inc. [*Canada ICAO designator*] (FAAC) ... NTM
North American Aliyah Movement (EA) ... NAAM
North American Antisubmarine Defense Force, Atlantic (NATG) ... NORASDEFLANT
North American Apiotherapy Society (EA) ... NAAS
North American Association for Environmental Education (EA) ... NAEE
North American Association for the Diaconate (EA) ... NAAD
North American Association for the Diaconate (EA) ... NAAND
North American Association for the Study of Jean-Jacques Rousseau (EA) ... NAASR
North American Association of Alcoholism Programs [*Later, ADPA*] (EA) ... NAAAP
North American Association of Christians in Social Work [*Later, NACSW*] (EA) ... NAACSW
North American Association of Christians in Social Work (EA) ... NACSW
North American Association of Environmental Educators ... NAAEE
North American Association of Hunter Safety Coordinators ... NAAHSC
North American Association of Inventory Services [*Greensboro, NC*] (EA) ... NAAIS
North American Association of Jewish Homes and Housing for the Aging (EA) ... NAAJHHA
North American Association of State and Provincial Lotteries (EA) ... NAASPL
North American Association of Summer Sessions (EA) ... NAASS
North American Association of the ICIF [*International Cooperative Insurance Federation*] [*Detroit, MI*] (EA) ... NAA-ICIF
North American Association of Ventriloquists (EA) ... NAAV
North American Association of Wardens and Superintendents (EAIO) ... NAAWS
North American Automotive Operations [*Ford Motor Co.*] ... NAAO
North American Aviation, Inc. [*Later, Rockwell International Corp.*] ... NAA
North American Aviation, Inc. [*Later, Rockwell International Corp.*] [*Acronym also used to refer to light aircraft of World War II*] ... NAVION
North American Aviation Rocketdyne Division (SAA) ... NAARD
North American Aviation Science Center (SAA) ... NAASC
North American Aviation Space Division (SAA) ... NAASD
North American Ballet Association [*Defunct*] (EA) ... NABA
North American Band Directors Coordinating Committee (EA) ... NABDCC
North American Baptist College and Divinity School, Edmonton, AB, Canada [*Library symbol Library of Congress*] (LCLS) ... CaAENABC
North American Baptist College and Divinity School, Edmonton, Alberta [*Library symbol National Library of Canada*] (NLC) ... AENABC
North American Baptist Fellowship (EA) ... NABF
North American Baptist Seminary, Sioux Falls, SD [*OCLC symbol*] (OCLC) ... SDN
North American Baptist Seminary, Sioux Falls, SD [*Library symbol Library of Congress*] (LCLS) ... SdSifB
North American Basic Teletext Specification (WDMC) ... NABTS
North American Benefit Association [*Port Huron, MI*] (EA) ... NABA
North American Benthological Society (EA) ... NABS
North American Bicycle Exhibitor Association [*Defunct*] (EA) ... NABEA
North American Biologicals, Inc. ... NAB
North American Biologicals, Inc. [*Associated Press*] (SAG) ... NABio
North American Biologicals, Inc. [*NASDAQ symbol*] (NQ) ... NBIO
North American Blueberry Council (EA) ... NABC
North American Blue-Bird Society (EA) ... NABS
North American Boxing Federation (EA) ... NABF
North American Braodcast Teletext Standard (OSI) ... NABTS
North American Brass Band Association (EA) ... NABBA
North American Broadcast Teletext Standard (NTCM) ... NABTS
North American Bungee Association (EA) ... NABA
North American Butterfly Association ... NABA
North American Car Corp. [*AAR code*] ... RCSX
North American Cartographic Information Society (EA) ... NACIS
North American Center on Adoption [*Defunct*] (EA) ... NACA
North American Christian Peace Conference (EA) ... NACPC
North American Clear Air Turbulence Tracking System [*Aviation*] ... NACATS
North American Clinical Dermatologic Society (EA) ... NACDS
North American Clun Forest Association (EA) ... NACFA
North American Coalition for Human Rights in Korea (EA) ... NACHRK
North American Coalition on Religion and Ecology (EA) ... NACRE
North American Collections Inventory Project [*Established 1982*] [*Library science*] ... NCIP
North American Collectors (EA) ... NAC
North American College of Acupuncture ... NACA
North American Commercial Gladiolus Growers [*Later, CGD-NAGC*] (EA) ... NACGG
North American Commission on the Environment ... NACE
North American Committee for IME [*Institut Medical Evangelique*] [*Defunct*] (EA) ... NACIME
North American Committee for Reconciliation in Ulster (EA) ... NACRU
North American Committee of Enamel Creators (EA) ... NACEC
North American Computer Service Association (EA) ... NACSA
North American Conference of Separated and Divorced Catholics (EA) ... NACSDC
North American Conference on British Studies (EA) ... NACBS
North American Conference on Christianity and Ecology (EA) ... NACCE
North American Conference on Ethiopian Jewry (EAIO) ... NACOEJ
North American Congress on Latin America (EA) ... NACLA
North American Corriente Association (EA) ... NACA
North American Council for Muslim Women (EA) ... NACMW
North American Council on Adoptable Children (EA) ... NACAC
North American Currach Association (EA) ... NACA
North American Cycle Exhibitor Association (EA) ... NACE
North American Data Airborne Recorder ... NADAR
North American Data Airborne Recorder (IAA) ... NAMDAR
North American Datamanager Users Group (EA) ... NADUG
North American Datum ... NAD
North American Datum of 1983 [*Marine science*] (OSRA) ... NAD83
North American Datum of 1983 (USDC) ... NAD83
North American Deep Drawing Research Group [*Automotive metal stampings*] ... NADDRG
North American Deer Farmers Association (EA) ... NADFA
North American Defense Industrial Base ... NADIB
North American Defense Industrial Base Organization ... NADIBO
North American Defense Operation Plan [*NORAD*] ... NADOP
North American Directory Forum ... NADF
North American District Heating and Cooling Institute [*Defunct*] (EA) ... NADHCI
North American District of the Belgian Warmblood Breeding Association (EA) ... BWBA
North American Dr. Who Appreciation Society (EA) ... NADWAS
North American Dostoevsky Society (EA) ... NADS
North American Draft Cross Association (EA) ... NADCA
North American Economic Studies Association (EA) ... NAESA
North American Economics and Finance Association (EA) ... NAEFA
North American Electric Reliability Council (EA) ... NAERC
North American Electric Reliability Council (EA) ... NERC
North American English Ford Registry (EA) ... NAEFR
North American Equipment Dealers Association (EA) ... NAEDA
North American Export Grain Association (EA) ... NAEGA
North American Falconers Association (EA) ... NAFA
North American Family Campers Association (EA) ... NAFCA
North American Farm Alliance (EA) ... NAFA
North American Federation of Temple Youth (EA) ... NFTY
North American Federation of Third Order Franciscans (EA) ... NAF
North American Fire [*Vancouver Stock Exchange symbol*] ... NAF
North American Fishing Club (EA) ... NAFC
North American Flowerbulb Wholesalers Association (EA) ... NAFWA
North American Forestry Commission [*UN Food and Agriculture Organization*] ... NAFC
North American Forum on the Catechumenate (EA) ... NAFC
North American Free Trade Agreement [*Passed in 1993*] ... NAFTA
North American Free-Trade Area (ECON) ... NAFTA
North American Friends of Palestinian Universities [*Defunct*] (EA) ... NAFPU
North American Fruit Explorers (EA) ... NAFEX
North American Fuzzy Information Processing Society (EA) ... NAFIPS
North American Game Breeders and Shooting Preserve Association [*Later, NAGA*] (EA) ... NAGB & SPA

North American Gamebird Association (EA) .... NAGA
North American Gasoline Tax Conference (EA) .... NAGTC
North American Ginseng Association [*Defunct*] (EA) .... NAGA
North American Gladiolus Council (EA) .... NAGC
North American Gladiolus Council, Commercial Growers Division [*Defunct*] (EA) .... CGD-NAGC
North American Great Plains/North China Plain Project [*Agriculture*].... NAGP/NCP
North American Guild of Change Ringers (EA) .... NAGCR
North American Gunnery Instruction Monitor .... NAGIM
North American Habitat Preservation Society (EA) .... NAHPS
North American Heather Society (EA) .... NAHS
North American Heating and Airconditioning Wholesalers Association .... NAHAWA
North American Highway Association .... NAHA
North American Hockey League .... NAHL
North American Horticultural Supply Association (EA) .... NAHSA
North American Hunting Club (EA) .... NAHC
North American Hunting Club .... NAHC
North American Indian [*MARC language code Library of Congress*] (LCCP) ..... nai
North American Indian Association (EA) .... NAIA
North American Indian Landmarks [*A publication*] .... NAIL
North American Indian Museums Association (EA) .... NAIMA
North American Indian Women's Association (EA) .... NAIWA
North American Industry Classification System [*BTS*] (TAG) .... NAICS
North American Industry Classification System (AAGC) .... NAICS
North American Internet Co. .... NAI
North American Islamic Trust (EA) .... NAIT
North American Iterative Weighted Least Squares (SAA) .... NAWL
North American Jewish Students Appeal (EA) .... NAJSA
North American Jewish Students' Network (EA) .... NAJSN
North American Jewish Youth Council [*Defunct*] (EA) .... NAJYC
North American Judges Association [*Later, AJA*] .... NAJA
North American Junior Limousin Association (EA) .... NAJLA
North American Kant Society (EA) .... NAKS
North American Lake Management Society (EA) .... NALMS
North American Land Mammal Age [*Geological epoch*] .... NALMA
North American Land Sailing Association (AD) .... NALSA
North American Life Union Assurance Society (EA) .... NALUAS
North American Lighting [*Automotive industry supplier*] .... NAL
North American Lily Society (EA) .... NALS
North American Limousin Foundation (EA) .... NALF
North American Log Builders Association (EA) .... NALBA
North American Log Homes Council (EA) .... NALHC
North American Loon Fund (EA) .... NALF
North American Man-Boy Love Association .... NAMBLA
North American Manufacturing Research Institution of SME [*Society of Manufacturing Engineers*] (EA) .... NAMRI/SME
North American Manx Association (EA) .... NAMA
North American Maple Syrup Council (EA) .... NAMSC
North American Maritime Agencies (AD) .... NAMA
North American Marten Rabbit Club (EA) .... NAMRC
North American Medical/Dental Association (EA) .... NAMDA
North American Membrane Society (EA) .... NAMS
North American Menopause Society (EA) .... NAMS
North American Metals Corp. [*Vancouver Stock Exchange symbol*] .... NAM
North American MGA [*Morris Garage Automobile*] **Register** (EA) .... NAMGAR
North American Mini Moke Registry (EA) .... NAMMR
North American Mini-Champ Racing Association (EA) .... NAMRA
North American Monogrammers and Embroiderers [*Defunct*] (EA) .... NAME
North American Morab Horse Association (EA) .... NAMHA
North American Mortgage Co. [*NYSE symbol*] (SPSG) .... NAC
North American Mortgage Co. [*Associated Press*] (SAG) .... NAMtge
North American Movement (AD) .... NAM
North American Multihull Sailing Association (EA) .... NAMSA
North American Mustang Association and Registry (EA) .... NAMAR
North American Mycological Association (EA) .... NAMA
North American National Broadcasters Association (EA) .... NANBA
North American Native Fishes Association (EA) .... NANFA
North American Natural Casing Association (EA) .... NANCA
North American Nature Photography Association .... NANPA
North American NCR [*National Cash Register Co.*] **Financial Users Group** (EA) .... NANCRFUG
North American Network of Women Runners (EA) .... NANWR
North American Newspaper Alliance .... NANA
North American Nietzsche Society (EA) .... NANS
North American Nippon Technologies Corp. [*Vancouver Stock Exchange symbol*] .... NAN
North American Normande Association (EA) .... NANA
North American Nursing Diagnosis Association (EA) .... NANDA
North American Nutrition and Preventive Medicine Association (EA) .... NANPMA
North American Offshore One-Design Association (EA) .... NAOODA
North American Opel GT [*Gran Turismo*] **Club** (EA) .... NAOGTC
North American Paleontological Convention .... NAPC
North American Palladium [*Associated Press*] (SAG) .... NAPall
North American Palladium [*NASDAQ symbol*] (SAG) .... PDLC
North American Patristic Society (EA) .... NAPS
North American Pediatric Pseudo-Obstruction Society (EA) .... NAPPS
North American Philips Corp. (IAA) .... NAP
North American Photonics Association [*Defunct*] (EA) .... NAPA
North American Photonics Association (EA) .... NAPhA
North American Pizza Association [*Defunct*] .... NAPA
North American Poetry Network (EA) .... NAPN
North American Police Work Dog Association (EA) .... NAPWDA
North American Poultry Cooperative Association [*Defunct*] .... NAPCA
North American Power [*Vancouver Stock Exchange symbol*] .... NPP
North American Power Systems Interconnection Committee [*US and Canada*] [*Electric power*] .... NAPSIC
North American Precis Syndicate .... NAPS
North American Presentation Level Protocol Standard (DOM) .... NAPLPS
North American Presentation Level Protocol Syntax [*Computer display system*] [*Pronounced "naplips"*] .... NAPLPS
North American Primary Care Research Group (EA) .... NAPCRG
North American Pro Series [*Auto racing*] .... NAPS
North American Professional Driver Education Association (EA) .... NAPDEA
North American Professional Driver's Association [*Defunct*] (EA) .... NAPDA
North American Racing Team [*Auto racing*] .... NART
North American Radio Archives (EA) .... NARA
North American Radon Association [*Defunct*] (EA) .... NARA
North American Region [*USTTA*] (TAG) .... NAM
North American Regional Alliance of IATA [*International Amateur Theatre Association*] (EA) .... NARA
North American Regional Broadcasting Agreement [*To minimize interference between AM stations*] .... NARBA
North American Regional Office (AD) .... NARO
North American Regional World Anti-Communist League (AD) .... NARWACL
North American Research Group on Management (PDAA) .... NARGOM
North American Restaurant and Tavern Alliance (EA) .... NARTA
North American Review [*A publication*] (BRI) .... NAR
North American Riders Club (EA) .... NARC
North American Riding for the Handicapped Association (EA) .... NARHA
North American Rockwell Corp. [*Later, Rockwell International Corp.*] (MCD) .... NAR
North American Rockwell Corp. [*Later, Rockwell International Corp.*]..... NAR CORP
North American Rockwell Corp. [*Later, Rockwell International Corp.*] (MCD) .... NARC
North American Rockwell Corp., A. R. Rechnitzer Oceanographic Collection, Anaheim, CA [*Library symbol Library of Congress*] (LCLS) .... CAnaA-R
North American Rockwell Corp., Autonetics Technical Library, Anaheim, CA [*Library symbol Library of Congress*] (LCLS) .... CAnaA
North American Rockwell Corp., Downey, CA [*Library symbol Library of Congress*] (LCLS) .... CDoN
North American Rockwell Corp., Solid Rocket Division, McGregor, TX [*Library symbol Library of Congress*] (LCLS) .... TxMcgR
North American Rockwell Information Systems Co. .... NARISCO
North American Rockwell Microelectronics Co. [*Obsolete*] .... NRMEC
North American Rockwell Training and Services [*Obsolete*] .... NARTRANS
North American Route [*Aviation*] .... NAR
North American Royalties (AD) .... NAR
North American Sailing Association (AD) .... NASA
North American Sailing Association (NADA) .... NASA
North American Salmon Research Center [*Later, Atlantic Salmon Research Institute*] [*Canada Research center*] (RCD) .... NASRC
North American Savings Bank [*Associated Press*] (SAG) .... NAmSv
North American Savings Bank FSB [*NASDAQ symbol*] (SAG) .... NASB
North American Saxophone Alliance (EA) .... NASA
North American Search and Range RADAR [*Military*] .... NASARR
North American Search and Range RADAR [*Military*] .... NASRR
North American Securities Administrators Association [*Also, NASAA*] (EA) .... NASA
North American Securities Administrators Association [*Topeka, KS*] (EA) .... NASAA
North American Securities Administrators Association .... NASAA
North American Serials Group (EA) .... NASIG
North American Shagya-Arabian Society (EA) .... NASS
North American Shale [*Geology*] .... NAS
North American Shale Composite [*Geology*] .... NASC
North American Sheep Dog Society (EA) .... NASDS
North American Shippers Association (EA) .... NASA
North American Shortwave Association (EA) .... NASWA
North American Simulation and Gaming Association (EA) .... NASAGA
North American Singer Owners Club (EA) .... NASOC
North American Singers Association (EA) .... NASA
North American Singers Union (EA) .... NASU
North American Ski Journalists Association (EA) .... NASJA
North American Slope Water [*Oceanography*] (MSC) .... NASW
North American Soccer Foundation [*Defunct*] (EA) .... NASF
North American Soccer League [*Defunct*] (EA) .... NASL
North American Soccer League Players Association [*Defunct*] (EA) .... NASLPA
North American Soccer Players Association [*Later, NASLPA*] (EA) .... NASPA
North American Society for Corporate Planning [*Later, PF*] (EA) .... NASCP
North American Society for Dialysis and Transplantation (EA) .... NASDT
North American Society for Oceanic History (EA) .... NASOH
North American Society for Pediatric Gastroenterology [*Later, NASPGN*] (EA) .... NASPG
North American Society for Pediatric Gastroenterology and Nutrition (EA) .... NASPGN
North American Society for Social Philosophy (EA) .... NASSP
North American Society for Sport History (EA) .... NASSH
North American Society for Sport Management (EA) .... NASSM
North American Society for the Psychology of Sport and Physical Activity (EA) .... NASPSPA
North American Society for the Sociology of Sport (EA) .... NASSS
North American Society for Trenchless Technology (EA) .... NASTT
North American Society of Adlerian Psychology [*Later, NASAP*] (EA) .... ASAP
North American Society of Adlerian Psychology (EA) .... NASAP
North American Society of Pacing and Electrophysiology (EA) .... NASPE
North American Society of Teachers of the Alexander Technique (EA) .... NASTAT

North American South Devon Association (EA) .... NASDA
North American Spine Society (EA) .... NASS
North American Sporting Clays [An association] .... NASC
North American Stock Market [I. P. Sharp Associates] [Canada Information service or system] .... NASTOCK
North American Strawberry Growers Association (EA) .... NASGA
North American Student Cooperative League .... NASCL
North American Student Humanist Organizing Committee [Defunct] (EA) .... NASHOC
North American Students of Cooperation (EA) .... NASCO
North American Study Center for Polish Affairs (EA) .... NASCPA
North American Super Sports [Defunct] (EA) .... NASS
North American Supply [World War II] .... NAS
North American Supply Committee, Miscellaneous [World War II] .... NAS(MISC)
North American Supply Committee, Scientific Subcommittee [World War II] .... NAS(S)
North American Survival and Homesteading Association (AD) .... NASHA
North American Swing Club Association (EA) .... NASCA
North American Swiss Alliance (EA) .... NASA
North American Tasar Association (EA) .... NATA
North American Technologies Corp. [Associated Press] (SAG) .... NAmTch
North American Technologies Corp. [NASDAQ symbol] (SAG) .... NATK
North American Telecommunications Association (EA) .... NATA
North American Telephone Association (EA) .... NATA
North American Test Instrument Vehicle [Air Force test rocket] .... NATIV
North American Test Instrument Vehicle [Air force test rocket] (IAA) .... NATIVE
North American Thermal Analysis Society (EA) .... NATAS
North American Tiddlywinks Association (EA) .... NATwA
North American Toyah Fan Club (EA) .... NATFC
North American Trackless Trolley Association (EA) .... NATTA
North American Trail Ride Conference (EA) .... NATRC
North American Trakehner Association (EA) .... NATA
North American Transplant Coordinators Organization (EA) .... NATCO
North American Transvestite/Transsexual Society [Defunct] (EA) .... NATTS
North American Trap Collector Association (EA) .... NATCA
North American Travel Association [Defunct] (EA) .... NATA
North American Treat Organization [AIA] (TAG) .... NATO
North American Truffling Society (EA) .... NATS
North American Tug of War Federation (EA) .... NATWF
North American UFO Federation [Defunct] (EA) .... NAUFOF
North American Union Life Assurance Society [Chicago, IL] (EA) .... NAULAS
North American Union of Sisters of Our Lady of Charity (TOCD) .... NAU-OLC
North American Vaccine [AMEX symbol] (TTSB) .... NVX
North American Vaccine, Inc. [Associated Press] (SAG) .... NA Vacc
North American Vaccine, Inc. [AMEX symbol] (SAG) .... NVX
North American Vane Jump Angle Computer .... NAVJAC
North American Vegetarian Society (EA) .... NAVS
North American Ventures, Inc. [Vancouver Stock Exchange symbol] .... NAV
North American Vertical Datum [National Oceanic and Atmospheric Administration] .... NAVD
North American Vertical Datum of 1988 [Marine science] (OSRA) NAVD88
North American Vertical Datum of 1988 (USDC) NAVD88
North American Vexillological Association (EA) .... NAVA
North American Voltage and Phase Indicator (IEEE) .... NAVAPI
North American Voyageur Council (EA) .... NAVC
North American Warmblood Association (EA) .... NAWA
North American Watch Corp. [Associated Press] (SAG) .... NAWatch
North American Watch Corp. [NASDAQ symbol] (SAG) .... NAWC
North American Water and Power Alliance .... NAWAPA
North American Water and Power Alliance .... NAWPA
North American Water and Power Alliance (NADA) .... NOWAPA
North American Waterfowl Federation .... NAWF
North American Wholesale Lumber Association (EA) .... NAWLA
North American Wilderness Survival School .... NAWSS
North American Wildlife Foundation (EA) .... NAWF
North American Wildlife Park Foundation (EA) .... NAWPF
North American Wolf Society (EA) .... NAWF
North American Wolf Society (EA) .... NAWS
North American Working Dog Association (EA) .... NAWDA
North American Yacht Racing Union (EA) .... NAYRU
North American Yngling Association (EA) .... NAYA
North American Youth Glider Training Association .... NAYGTA
North American Youth Sport Institute (EA) .... NAYSI
North American-Chilean Chamber of Commerce (EA) .... NACC
North and Guthrie's Appeals Reports [68-80 Missouri] [A publication] (DLA) .... North & G
North Anna [Virginia] [Seismograph station code, US Geological Survey Closed] .... NV
North Anna Power Station [Virginia] [Nuclear energy] (NRCH) .... NAPS
North Arizona University (AD) .... NAU
North Arkansas Regional Library, Harrison, AR [Library symbol Library of Congress] (LCLS) .... ArHN
North Arlington Free Public Library, North Arlington, NJ [Library symbol Library of Congress] (LCLS) .... NjNoa
North Arlington Free Public Library, North Arlington, NJ [Library symbol] [Library of Congress] (LCLS) .... NjNoaP
North [European] Army Group [NATO] .... NORTHAG
North Atlanta, GA [AM radio station call letters] .... WCNN
North Atlantic (AD) .... N Atl
North Atlantic .... NORTLANT
North Atlantic Air, Inc. [ICAO designator] (FAAC) .... NAT
North Atlantic Airways and Air Communications Service (SAA) .... NORLANTAACS
North Atlantic Alliance .... NAA
North Atlantic & Gulf Steamship Co. (MHDW) .... NA & G
North Atlantic and Neighboring Seas .... NANS
North Atlantic Area (MUGU) .... NORLANT
North Atlantic Assembly .... NAA
North Atlantic Biocultural Organization [A research cooperative] .... NABO
North Atlantic Coast .... NAC
North Atlantic Communications and Information Systems Agency [NATO] .... NACISA
North Atlantic Consultive Process (OSI) .... NACP
North Atlantic Cooperation Council .... NACC
North Atlantic Council .... NAC
North Atlantic Council Memorandum [NATO] .... C-M
North Atlantic Current (AD) .... N Atl Cur
North Atlantic Current [Oceanography] .... NAC
North Atlantic Current System [Oceanography] .... NACS
North Atlantic Deep Water [Oceanography] .... NADW
North Atlantic Deepwater Oil Terminal (PDAA) .... NADOT
North Atlantic Defense Production Board (NATG) .... NADPB
North Atlantic Defense System .... NADS
North Atlantic Division [Army Engineers] .... NAD
North Atlantic Fisheries Research Center (PDAA) .... NAFRC
North Atlantic Free Trade Area .... NAFTA
North Atlantic Industries .... NA
North Atlantic Institute for Defense Studies [NATO] (AD) .... NAIDS
North Atlantic Institute for Defense Study [NATO] (NATG) .... AIDS
North Atlantic Lobster Institute (EA) .... NALI
North Atlantic Mediterranean Freight Conference (EA) .... NAMFC
North Atlantic Mid-Ocean-Ridge Basalt [Geology] .... NAMORB
North Atlantic Military Committee .... NAMC
North Atlantic Military Committee .... NAMILCOM
North Atlantic Military Committee (AD) .... NAMilCom
North Atlantic Naval Coastal Frontier .... NANCF
North Atlantic Navigation .... NATNAV
North Atlantic Network (EA) .... NAN
North Atlantic Ocean [MARC geographic area code Library of Congress] (LCCP) .... ln----
North Atlantic Ocean Regional Planning Board [NATO] .... NAORPB
North Atlantic Ocean Regional Planning Group [NATO] (NATG) .... NAORPG
North Atlantic Ocean Station [WMO] .... NAOS
North Atlantic Ocean Stations Program (MUGU) .... NAOSP
North Atlantic Oscillation [Climatology] .... NAO
North Atlantic Ports Association (EA) .... NAPA
North Atlantic Quality Figure .... NAQF
North Atlantic Radio System .... NARS
North Atlantic Radio Telephone Committee .... NARTEL
North Atlantic Region [USTTA] (TAG) .... NAT
North Atlantic Regional Area [Aviation] .... NAT
North Atlantic Regional Business Law Review [A publication] (DLA) .... N Atlantic Reg Bus L Rev
North Atlantic Regional Experiment [Ozone measurement] .... NARE
North Atlantic Relay Communication Satellite .... NARCOM
North Atlantic Salmon Conservation Organization [Edinburgh, Scotland] (EAIO) .... NASCO
North Atlantic Salmon Convention (USDC) .... NASC
North Atlantic Salmon Convention [Marine science] (OSRA) .... NASC
North Atlantic Salmon Research Center [Marine science] (MSC) .... NASRC
North Atlantic Seafood Association [Defunct] (EA) .... NASA
North Atlantic Shippers Association (DS) .... NASA
North Atlantic Shipping Conference (DS) .... NAC
North Atlantic Systems Planning Group [Military] (WDAA) .... NATSPG
North Atlantic - Training Exercise (MCD) .... NORLANTEX
North Atlantic Treaty .... NAT
North Atlantic Treaty Alliance .... NATA
North Atlantic Treaty Council (NATG) .... NATC
North Atlantic Treaty Information Service (NATG) .... NATIS
North Atlantic Treaty Organization [Facetious translation: "No Action, Talk Only"] [Brussels, Belgium] .... NATO
North Atlantic Treaty Organization - Advisory Group for Aeronautical Research and Development .... NATO-AGARD
North Atlantic Treaty Organization Airborne Early Warning Program .... NATO AEW
North Atlantic Treaty Organization Defense College (DNAB) .... NATODC
North Atlantic Treaty Organization Defense College (DNAB) .... NATODEFCOL
North Atlantic Treaty Organization - European Long Lines Agency .... NATOELLA
North Atlantic Treaty Organization - Long-Range Scientific Studies .... NATO-LRSS
North Atlantic Treaty Organization Military Committee .... NATO MC
North Atlantic Treaty Organization - Military Oceanography Group (NATG) .... NATOMILOCGRP
North Atlantic Treaty Organization - Multilateral Research and Development Production Program .... NATO-RDPP
North Atlantic Treaty Organization [NATO] Multi-Role Combat Aircraft Development and Production Management Organization (AAGC) .... NAMMO
North Atlantic Treaty Organization [NATO] Mutual Support Act (AAGC) .... NMSA
North Atlantic Treaty Organization Satellite .... NATOSAT
North Atlantic Treaty Organization - Science Committee .... NATO-SC
North Atlantic Treaty Regional Planning Group (NATG) .... NAT-RPG
North Atlantic Treaty Regional Planning Group .... PLANAT
North Atlantic Westbound Freight Association (DS) .... NAWFA
North Augusta, SC [AM radio station call letters] .... WGUS
North Augusta, SC [AM radio station call letters] .... WKZK
North Augusta Senior High School, North Augusta, SC [Library symbol Library of Congress] (LCLS) .... ScNoaSH
North Australia Program .... NAP
North Australia Railway .... NAR
North Australian Canine Association .... NACA
North Australian Research Unit (AD) .... NARU

North Babylon High School, North Babylon, NY [*Library symbol*] [*Library of Congress*] (LCLS) .... NNbHS
North Babylon Public Library, North Babylon, NY [*Library symbol Library of Congress*] (LCLS) .... NNb
North Babylon Public Library, North Babylon, NY [*Library symbol*] [*Library of Congress*] (LCLS) .... NNbL
North Baltimore, OH [*FM radio station call letters*] .... WHMQ
North Bancshares [*NASDAQ symbol*] (TTSB) .... NBSI
North Bancshares, Inc. [*NASDAQ symbol*] (SAG) .... NBSI
North Bancshares, Inc. [*Associated Press*] (SAG) .... NoBncshs
North Battleford, SK [*Television station call letters*] CFQC-2
North Battleford, SK [*AM radio station call letters*] .... CJNB
North Battleford, SK [*ICAO location identifier*] (ICLI) .... CYQW
North Bay [*Hawaii*] [*Seismograph station code, US Geological Survey Closed*] (SEIS) .... NBH
North Bay [*Canada*] [*Airport symbol*] (OAG) .... YYB
North Bay Canadian Forces Base, ON [*ICAO location identifier*] (ICLI) .... CZNB
North Bay Cooperative Library System, Santa Rosa, CA [*Library symbol*] [*Library of Congress*] (LCLS) .... CStrNB
North Bay Cooperative Library System, Santa Rosa, CA [*OCLC symbol*] (OCLC) .... NOB
North Bay, ON [*Station begun by Lord Roy Thomson in March, 1931*] [*AM radio station call letters*] .... CFCH
North Bay, ON [*Television station call letters*] .... CHNB
North Bay, ON [*AM radio station call letters*] .... CHUR
North Bay, ON [*FM radio station call letters*] (RBYB) .... CHUR-FM
North Bay, ON [*FM radio station call letters*] .... CKAT
North Bay, ON [*FM radio station call letters*] (RBYB) .... CKFX-FM
North Bay, ON [*Television station call letters*] .... CKNY
North Bay, ON [*ICAO location identifier*] (ICLI) .... CYYB
North Bay Public Library, North Bay, ON, Canada [*Library symbol Library of Congress*] (LCLS) .... CaONB
North Bay Public Library, Ontario [*Library symbol National Library of Canada*] (NLC) .... ONB
North Bellmore Public Library, North Bellmore, NY [*Library symbol Library of Congress*] (LCLS) .... NNbe
North Bend [*Oregon*] [*Airport symbol*] (OAG) .... OTH
North Bend, OR [*FM radio station call letters*] .... KACW
North Bend, OR [*AM radio station call letters*] .... KBBR
North Bend, OR [*FM radio station call letters*] .... KOOS
North Bend Public Library, North Bend, OR [*Library symbol Library of Congress*] (LCLS) .... OrNb
North Bergen Federation of Public Libraries [*Library network*] .... NBF
North Borneo Law Reports [*A publication*] (DLA) .... NBLR
North Branch Area Library, North Branch, MN [*Library symbol*] [*Library of Congress*] (LCLS) .... MnNob
North Branch High School, North Branch, MN [*Library symbol*] [*Library of Congress*] (LCLS) .... MnNobH
North Branch Middle School, North Branch, MN [*Library symbol*] [*Library of Congress*] (LCLS) .... MnNobM
North Brevard Public Library, Titusville, FL [*Library symbol Library of Congress*] (LCLS) .... FTi
North Britain [*i.e., Scotland*] .... NB
North British Academy .... NBA
North British Airlines Ltd. [*ICAO designator*] (FAAC) .... NBN
North British Railway .... NBR
North by East .... NbE
North by West .... NbW
North Caicos [*Turks and Caicos Islands*] [*ICAO location identifier*] (ICLI) .... MBNC
North Caicos [*British West Indies*] [*Airport symbol*] (OAG) .... NCA
North Calotte Committee [*See also NKK*] [*Nordic Council of Ministers*] [*Finland*] (EAIO) .... NCC
North Canadian Oils Ltd. [*Toronto Stock Exchange symbol*] .... NCO
North Canterbury Mounted Rifles [*British military*] (DMA) .... NCMR
North Cape May, NJ [*FM radio station call letters*] .... WJNN
North Caribou Flying Service Ltd. [*Canada ICAO designator*] (FAAC) .... NCB
North Carolina (DLA) .... N Car
North Carolina [*Postal code*] .... NC
North Carolina [*MARC country of publication code Library of Congress*] (LCCP) .... ncu
North Carolina [*MARC geographic area code Library of Congress*] (LCCP) .... n-us-nc
North Carolina Administrative Code [*A publication*] (DLA) .... NC Admin Code
North Carolina Administrative Code [*A publication*] (AAGC) .... NCAC
North Carolina Advance Legislative Service (Michie) [*A publication*] (DLA) .... NC Adv Legis Serv
North Carolina Agricultural & Technical State University (GAGS) .... No Car Ag & Tech
North Carolina Agricultural and Technical State University, Greensboro, NC [*Library symbol Library of Congress*] (LCLS) .... NcGA
North Carolina Agricultural and Technical State University, Greensboro, NC [*OCLC symbol*] (OCLC) .... NQA
North Carolina Appellate Reports [*A publication*] (AAGC) .... NC App
North Carolina Association for Institutional Research (EDAC) .... NCAIR
North Carolina Attorney General Reports [*A publication*] (DLA).... Rep NC Att'y Gen
North Carolina Biotechnology Center [*Research center*] (RCD) .... NCBC
North Carolina Center for Laws Affecting Women, Inc. [*Research center*] (RCD) .... NCC-LAW
North Carolina Central University [*Durham*] .... NCCU
North Carolina Central University (GAGS) .... No Car Cent U
North Carolina Central University, Durham, NC [*Library symbol Library of Congress*] (LCLS) .... NcDurC
North Carolina Central University, Durham, NC [*OCLC symbol*] (OCLC) .... NCX
North Carolina Central University, School of Library Science, Durham, NC [*Library symbol Library of Congress*] (LCLS) .... NcDurCL
North Carolina Central University, School of Library Science, Durham, NC [*OCLC symbol*] (OCLC) .... NLS
North Carolina College Law Journal [*A publication*] (DLA) .... North Carolina College LJ
North Carolina Conference Reports [*A publication*] (DLA) .... NC Conf
North Carolina Conference Reports [*A publication*] (DLA) .... NC Conf Rep
North Carolina Court of Appeals Reports [*A publication*] (DLA) .... NC App
North Carolina Court of Appeals Reports [*A publication*] (DLA) .... NCA
North Carolina Dance Theater .... NCDT
North Carolina Department of Corrections, Central Prison School, Raleigh, NC [*Library symbol Library of Congress*] (LCLS) .... NcRDC
North Carolina Department of Corrections, Eastern Correctional Center Library, Maury, NC [*Library symbol*] [*Library of Congress*] (LCLS) .... NcMauDC
North Carolina Department of Corrections, Troy, NC [*Library symbol*] [*Library of Congress*] (LCLS) .... NcTrDC
North Carolina Department of Human Resources, Dorothea Dix Hospital, F. T. Fuller Staff Library, Raleigh, NC [*Library symbol Library of Congress*] (LCLS) .... NcRDD
North Carolina Department of Human Resources, Eastern North Carolina School for the Deaf, Wilson, NC [*Library symbol Library of Congress*] (LCLS) .... NcWilE
North Carolina Department of Human Resources, Public Health Library, Raleigh, NC [*Library symbol Library of Congress*] (LCLS) .... NcRHR
North Carolina Department of Human Resources, The Governor Morehead School, Raleigh, NC [*Library symbol Library of Congress*] (LCLS) .... NcRGM
North Carolina Department of Natural Resources and Community Development, Raleigh, NC [*Library symbol*] [*Library of Congress*] (LCLS) .... NcRNR
North Carolina Department of Public Instruction, Education Information Services, Raleigh, NC [*Library symbol*] [*Library of Congress*] (LCLS) .... NcRPI
North Carolina Department of Transportation, Raleigh, NC [*OCLC symbol*] (OCLC) .... NCO
North Carolina Educational Computing Services (NITA) .... NCECS
North Carolina Industrial Commission Advance Sheets [*A publication*] (DLA) .... NCIC Ops
North Carolina Information Network [*Library network*] .... NCIN
North Carolina Journal of International Law and Commercial Regulation [*A publication*] (DLA) .... North Car J Int'l L & Comm
North Carolina Journal of Law [*A publication*] (DLA) .... NCJ of L
North Carolina Justice Academy, Salemburg, NC [*Library symbol Library of Congress*] (LCLS) .... NcSbJ
North Carolina Law Journal [*A publication*] (DLA) .... NCLJ
North Carolina Law Repository [*A publication*] (DLA) .... NC Law Repos
North Carolina Law Repository [*A publication*] (DLA) .... NCL Rep
North Carolina Law Repository (Reprint) [*A publication*] (DLA) .... NC Law Repository
North Carolina Law Repository (Reprint) [*A publication*] (DLA) .... NCL Reps
North Carolina Library for the Blind and Physically Handicapped, Raleigh, NC [*Library symbol Library of Congress*] (LCLS) .... Nc-BPH
North Carolina Marine Resources Center, Bogue Banks Library, Atlantic Beach, NC [*Library symbol Library of Congress*] (LCLS) .... NcAbMR
North Carolina Marine Resources Center, Fort Fisher, Kure Beach, NC [*Library symbol Library of Congress*] (LCLS) .... NcKbMR
North Carolina Marine Resources Center, Roanoke Island Resource Library, Manteo,NC [*Library symbol Library of Congress*] (LCLS) .... NcManMR
North Carolina Motor Carriers Association [*STAC*] .... NCM
North Carolina Museum of Art in Raleigh, Raleigh, NC [*Library symbol Library of Congress*] (LCLS) .... NcRMA
North Carolina Nat Gas [*NYSE symbol*] (TTSB) .... NCG
North Carolina Natural Gas [*NYSE symbol*] (SAG) .... NOG
North Carolina Natural Gas Corp. [*Associated Press*] (SAG) .... NCarNG
North Carolina Online User Group (NITA) .... NCOLUG
North Carolina Railroad .... NC
North Carolina Register [*A publication*] (AAGC) .... NC Reg
North Carolina Register [*A publication*] (AAGC) .... NCR
North Carolina Reports [*A publication*] (DLA) .... N Car
North Carolina Reports [*A publication*] (DLA) .... N Car Rep
North Carolina Reports [*A publication*] (DLA) .... N Carolina Cases
North Carolina Reports [*A publication*] (DLA) .... NC
North Carolina Reports [*A publication*] (AAGC) .... NC
North Carolina Reports [*A publication*] (DLA) .... NC Rep
North Carolina Reports [*A publication*] (DLA) .... NC Reports
North Carolina Reports, Appendix [*A publication*] (DLA) .... NC Rep Appendix
North Carolina School of Science and Mathematics [*Free, residential public high school for gifted students*] .... NCSSM
North Carolina School of Science and Mathematics, Durham, NC [*Library symbol Library of Congress*] (LCLS) .... NcDurSci
North Carolina School of the Arts, Winston-Salem, NC [*Library symbol Library of Congress*] (LCLS) .... NcWsN
North Carolina School of the Arts, Winston-Salem, NC [*OCLC symbol*] (OCLC) .... NZG
North Carolina Science and Technology Research Center [*North Carolina Department of Commerce*] [*Research center*] (RCD) .... NC/STRC
North Carolina Science and Technology Research Center, Durham, NC [*Library symbol Library of Congress*] (LCLS) .... NcDurST
North Carolina State Agency for Public Telecommunications [*Raleigh*] (TSSD) .... APT
North Carolina State College .... NCSC
North Carolina State College Reactor .... NCSCR
North Carolina State Department of Archives and History, Raleigh, NC [*Library symbol Library of Congress*] (LCLS) .... Nc-Ar
North Carolina State Library, Raleigh, NC [*Library symbol Library of Congress*] (LCLS) .... Nc
North Carolina State Library, Raleigh, NC [*OCLC symbol*] (OCLC) .... NCS

North Carolina State Museum of Natural History, H. H. Brimley Memorial Library, Raleigh, NC [Library symbol Library of Congress] (LCLS)..... NcRMNH-B
North Carolina State Museum of Natural History, Raleigh, NC [Library symbol Library of Congress] (LCLS) .... NcRMNH
North Carolina State Occupational Information Coordinating Committee (EDAC) .... NCSOICC
North Carolina State Supreme Court, Raleigh, NC [Library symbol Library of Congress] (LCLS) .... Nc-SC
North Carolina State University [Raleigh] .... NCSU
North Carolina State University at Raleigh, Photocopy Services, Raleigh, NC [Library symbol] [Library of Congress] (LCLS) .... NcRS-P
North Carolina State University at Raleigh, Raleigh, NC [Library symbol Library of Congress] (LCLS) .... NcRS
North Carolina State University (Raleigh) (GAGS) .... No Car St U (Raleigh)
North Carolina State University, Raleigh, NC [OCLC symbol] (OCLC) .... NRC
North Carolina State University, School of Veterinary Medicine, Raleigh, NC [Library symbol Library of Congress] (LCLS) .... NcRS-V
North Carolina State University, School of Veterinary Medicine, Raleigh, NC [OCLC symbol] (OCLC) .... NRV
North Carolina Supreme Court Reports [A publication] (DLA) .... NC
North Carolina Term Reports [A publication] (DLA) .... NC Term R
North Carolina Term Reports [A publication] (DLA) .... NC Term Rep
North Carolina Term Reports [A publication] (DLA) .... NCT Rep
North Carolina Union List of Serials for Community Colleges [Library network] .... LRA
North Carolina Utilities Commission Reports [A publication] (DLA) .... NCUC
North Carolina Wesleyan College, Rocky Mount, NC [Library symbol] [Library of Congress] (LCLS) .... NcRmW
North Cascades National Park .... NOCA
North Castle Library, Armonk, NY [Library symbol Library of Congress] (LCLS) .... NArmN
North Caucasus, RSFSR [MARC geographic area code Library of Congress] (LCCP) .... e-urr-
North Celestial Pole [Astronomy] .... NCP
North Celestial Pole (AD) .... Pn
North Central .... NCEN
North Central Airlines, Inc. [ICAO designator] (OAG) .... NC
North Central Airlines, Inc. .... NO
North Central Airlines, Inc. .... NOR
North Central Alaskan Seasonal Earned Premium Scale [Aviation] (AIA) .... NCASEPS
North Central Association of Colleges and Schools (EA) .... NCACS
North Central Association of Colleges and Secondary Schools [Later, NCACS] .... NCA
North Central Bancshares [NASDAQ symbol] (TTSB) .... FFFD
North Central Bancshares, Inc. [NASDAQ symbol] (SAG) .... FFFD
North Central Bancshares, Inc. [Associated Press] (SAG) .... NCentBsh
North Central Bible College, Minneapolis, MN [Library symbol Library of Congress] (LCLS) .... MnMNC
North Central Bible College, Minneapolis, MN [OCLC symbol] (OCLC) .... NCA
North Central Business Education Association (AEBS) .... NCBEA
North Central College [Naperville, IL] .... NCC
North Central College, Naperville, IL [OCLC symbol] (OCLC) .... ICN
North Central College, Naperville, IL [Library symbol Library of Congress] (LCLS) .... INapN
North Central Computer Institute [Research center] (RCD) .... NCCI
North Central Conference on Summer Schools (EA) .... NCCSS
North Central Dairy Forwarders Tariff Bureau, Minneapolis MN [STAC] .... NCD
North Central Division [Army Engineers] .... NCD
North Central Experiment Station [University of Minnesota] [Research center] (RCD) .... NCES
North Central Field Area .... NCFA
North Central Forest Experiment Station [St. Paul, MN] [Department of Agriculture] (GRD) .... NCFES
North Central Kansas Libraries, Manhattan, KS [Library symbol Library of Congress] (LCLS) .... KMNC
North Central Kansas Libraries System [Library network] .... NCKL
North Central Kansas Library, Manhattan, KS [OCLC symbol] (OCLC) .... KKM
North Central Michigan College, Petoskey, MI [Library symbol Library of Congress] (LCLS) .... MiPetN
North Central Name Society (EA) .... NCNS
North Central Regional Center for Rural Development [Iowa State University] [Research center] (RCD) .... NCRCRD
North Central Regional Educational Laboratory [Elmhurst, IL] [Department of Education] (GRD) .... NCREL
North Central Regional Library, Community Information Directory Project [UTLAS symbol] .... CID
North Central Regional Library, Ojibway Cree Project [UTLAS symbol] .... OJC
North Central Regional Library, Sudbury, ON, Canada [Library symbol Library of Congress] (LCLS) .... CaOSuN
North Central Regional Library, Sudbury, Ontario [Library symbol National Library of Canada] (NLC) .... OSUN
North Central Regional Library System [Library network] .... NCIRLS
North Central Regional Library, Wenatche, WA [Library symbol Library of Congress] (LCLS) .... WaWeN
North Central School Law Review [A publication] (DLA) .... N Cent School L Rev
North Central States [MARC geographic area code Library of Congress] (LCCP) .... n-usc-
North Central Texas Film Cooperative [Library network] .... NCTFC
North Central Turfgrass Exposition [Illinois Turfgrass Foundation] (TSPED) .... NCTE
North Central Watershed Research Unit [Department of Agriculture] (GRD) .... NCWRU
North Central Yiddish (BJA) .... NCY
North Charleston, SC [FM radio station call letters] .... WBUB

North Charleston, SC [FM radio station call letters] .... WXLY
North Charleston, SC [FM radio station call letters] .... WYFH
North Coast (ADA) .... NC
North Coast Air Services Ltd. [Canada ICAO designator] (FAAC) .... NCC
North Coast Airlines [Australia] .... NCA
North Coast Aviation, Inc. [ICAO designator] (FAAC) .... AOH
North Coast Energy [NASDAQ symbol] (TTSB) .... NCEB
North Coast Energy [NASDAQ symbol] (SAG) .... NCEB
North Coast Energy [Associated Press] (SAG) .... NthCsE
North Coast Energy [Associated Press] (SAG) .... NthCstE
North Coast Energy Cv'B'Pfd [NASDAQ symbol] (TTSB) .... NCEBP
North Coast Energy, Inc. [Associated Press] (SAG) .... NthCst
North Coast Energy Wrrt [NASDAQ symbol] (TTSB) .... NCEBW
North Coast Export Co. [An association Defunct] (EA) .... NCEC
North Coast Industries Ltd. [Vancouver Stock Exchange symbol] .... NCT
North Coast Life Ins Cv'A'Pfd [NASDAQ symbol] (TTSB) .... NCLIP
North Coast Life Insurance Co. [NASDAQ symbol] (SAG) .... NCLIP
North Coast Life Insurance Co. [Associated Press] (SAG) .... NCstLf
North Coast Railroad Historical Society (EA) .... NCRH
North Conway Institute (EA) .... NCI
North Conway, NH [Location identifier FAA] (FAAL) .... CWN
North Country (ROG) .... NC
North Country Community College, Saranac Lake, NY [Library symbol Library of Congress] (LCLS) .... NSINC
North Country Community College, Saranac Lake, NY [OCLC symbol] (OCLC) .... ZNO
North Country Educational Services [Library network] .... NCES
North Country Library System [Library network] .... NCLS
North Country Library System, Watertown, NY [Library symbol Library of Congress] (LCLS) .... NWattN
North Country Library System, Watertown, NY [OCLC symbol] (OCLC) .... RTN
North Country Reference and Research Resources Council [Information service or system] (IID) .... NCRRRC
North Country Reference and Research Resources Council, Canton, NY [Library symbol Library of Congress] (LCLS) .... NCaN
North Country Reference and Research Resources Council, Canton, NY [Library symbol Library of Congress Obsolete] (LCLS) .... NCaRC
North Country Reference and Research Resources Council, Canton, NY [OCLC symbol] (OCLC) .... VWR
North Country Reference and Research Resources Council, Union List of Serials, Canton, NY [OCLC symbol] (OCLC) .... VNC
North Country Trail Association (EA) .... NCTA
North Creek, NY [FM radio station call letters] .... WXLG
North Crosby Union Library, Westport, ON, Canada [Library symbol] [Library of Congress] (LCLS) .... CaOWNC
North Crossett, AR [FM radio station call letters] .... KWLT
North Cumberland Historical Society, Pugwash, Nova Scotia [Library symbol National Library of Canada] (NLC) .... NSPNC
North Cumberland Historical Society, Pugwash, NS, Canada [Library symbol] [Library of Congress] (LCLS) .... CaNSPNC
North Dakota (AAG) .... N DAK
North Dakota [Postal code] .... ND
North Dakota [MARC country of publication code Library of Congress] (LCCP) .... ndu
North Dakota [MARC geographic area code Library of Congress] (LCCP) .... n-us-nd
North Dakota Administrative Code [A publication] (DLA) .... ND Admin Code
North Dakota Administrative Code [A publication] (AAGC) .... NDAC
North Dakota Agricultural College .... NDAC
North Dakota Bar Brief [A publication] (DLA) .... NDBB
North Dakota Century Code [A publication] (DLA) .... ND Cent Code
North Dakota Century Code [A publication] .... NDCC
North Dakota Farmers Union Resource Library, Jamestown, ND [Library symbol Library of Congress] (LCLS) .... NdJF
North Dakota Industrial School, Mandan, ND [Library symbol Library of Congress] (LCLS) .... NdManN
North Dakota Memorial Mental Health and Retardation Center, Mandan, ND [Library symbol Library of Congress] (LCLS) .... NdManMH
North Dakota Natural Heritage Inventory [North Dakota State Department of Natural Resources] [Bismarck] [Information service or system] (IID) .... NDNHI
North Dakota Reports [A publication] (DLA) .... N Dak
North Dakota Research Foundation Bulletin [A publication] ...... ND Res Found Bull
North Dakota School of Forestry .... NDSF
North Dakota State Department of Public Instruction, Bismarck, ND [Library symbol Library of Congress] (LCLS) .... NdBPI
North Dakota State Health Department, Bismarck, ND [Library symbol Library of Congress] (LCLS) .... NdBHD
North Dakota State Highway Department, Bismarck, ND [Library symbol Library of Congress] (LCLS) .... NdBHwy
North Dakota State Industrial School .... NDIS
North Dakota State Law Library, Bismarck, ND [Library symbol Library of Congress] (LCLS) .... Nd-L
North Dakota State Library, Bismarck, ND [Library symbol Library of Congress] (LCLS) .... Nd
North Dakota State Library Commission, Bismarck, ND [Library symbol Library of Congress] (LCLS) .... NdLibC
North Dakota State Library Commission, Bismarck, ND [OCLC symbol] (OCLC) .... NDS
North Dakota State Public Welfare Board, Bismarck, ND [Library symbol Library of Congress] (LCLS) .... NdBPW
North Dakota State School of Science, Mildred Johnson Library, Wahpeton, ND [OCLC symbol] (OCLC) .... NDW
North Dakota State School of Science, Wahpeton, ND [Library symbol Library of Congress] (LCLS) .... NdWahS
North Dakota State University .... NDSU
North Dakota State University (GAGS) .... No Dak St U

North Dakota State University, Bottineau Branch, Bottineau, ND [Library symbol Library of Congress] (LCLS) .... NdBoU

North Dakota State University, Fargo, ND [Library symbol Library of Congress] (LCLS) .... NdFA

North Dakota Supreme Court Reports [1890-1953] [A publication] (DLA) .... ND

North Dakota Tracer Experiment (USDC) .... NDTE

North Dakota Tracer Experiment [Marine science] (OSRA) .... NTDE

North Dakota Water Resources Research Institute [Fargo, ND] [Department of the Interior] (GRD) .... NDWRRI

North Dartmouth, MA [FM radio station call letters] .... WSMU

North Davidson Public Library, Welcome, NC [Library symbol Library of Congress] (LCLS) .... NcWelc

North Devon Imperial Yeomanry [British military] (DMA) .... NDIY

North Durham Militia [British military] (DMA) .... NDM

North, East, and Down .... NED

North East Asian Treaty Organization (NATG) .... NEATO

North East Bolivian Airways [ICAO designator] (FAAC) .... NBA

North East Bolivian Airways [ICAO designator] (FAAC) .... NEBA

North East Coast Institution of Engineers and Shipbuilders (EAIO) .... NECIES

North East Corner [Freemasonry] .... NEC

North East Insurance [NASDAQ symbol] (TTSB) .... NEIC

North East Insurance Co. [Associated Press] (SAG) .... NE Ins

North East Insurance Co. [NASDAQ symbol] (NQ) .... NEIC

North East Iowa Academic Libraries [Library network] .... NEIAL

North East London Polytechnic [School] [England] .... NELP

North East, PA [AM radio station call letters] .... WEYZ

North East, PA [FM radio station call letters] .... WRKT

North East Pacific Culture Collection [of marine organisms] [University of British Columbia] .... NEPCC

North East States for Coordinated Air Use Management .... NESCAUM

North Eastern Electricity Board [British] .... NEEB

North Eastern Railway [British] .... NER

North Eastern Reporter [A publication] (DLA) .... NE

North Eastern Reporter [Commonly cited NE] [A publication] (DLA) .... NE Rep

North Eastern Reporter [Commonly cited NE] [A publication] (DLA) ...... NE Reporter

North Eastern Reporter [Commonly cited NE] [A publication] (DLA) ...... NE Repr

North Eastern Reporter [Commonly cited NE] [A publication] (DLA) ...... NER

North Eastern Reporter, Second Series [West] [A publication] (AAGC) .... NE 2d

North Eastern Vecturists Association .... NEVA

North Elementary School, Staples, MN [Library symbol] [Library of Congress] (LCLS) .... MnStNE

North Elementary School, Talmoon, MN [Library symbol] [Library of Congress] (LCLS) .... MnTalE

North Eleuthera [Bahamas] [Airport symbol] (OAG) .... ELH

North Eleuthera, Eleuthera Island [Bahamas] [ICAO location identifier] (ICLI) .... MYEH

North English Record, North English, IA [Library symbol Library of Congress] (LCLS) .... IaNoengR

North Equatorial Belt [Planet Jupiter] .... NEB

North Equatorial Countercurrent [Oceanography] .... NECC

North Equatorial Current [Oceanography] (MSC) .... NEC

North European and Mediterranean Routing Information [Naval Oceanographic Office] .... NEMEDRI

North European Oil Royalty Trust [NYSE symbol] (SPSG) .... NET

North European Oil Royalty Trust [Associated Press] (SAG) .... NEurO

North European Region Air Information Center (NATG) .... NERAIC

North Europn Oil Rty Tr [NYSE symbol] (TTSB) .... NET

North Face, Inc. (The) [Associated Press] (SAG) .... NrthFce

North Face, Inc. (The) [NASDAQ symbol] (SAG) .... TNFI

North Florida Junior College, Madison, FL [Library symbol Library of Congress] (LCLS) .... FMadN

North Flying AS [Denmark ICAO designator] (FAAC) .... NFA

North Following [Astronomy] .... NF

North Fork Bancorp [NYSE symbol] (SPSG) .... NFB

North Fork Bancorp (MHDW) .... NFBC

North Fork Bancorp [Associated Press] (SAG) .... NoFkBc

North Fort Myers, FL [AM radio station call letters] .... WWCN

North Fort Polk, LA [FM radio station call letters] .... KCIJ

North Fort Riley, KS [FM radio station call letters] .... KBLS

North Galactic Pole .... NGP

North Gasline [Alaska] [Seismograph station code, US Geological Survey] (SEIS) .... NGL

North Georgia College [Dahlonega] .... NGC

North Georgia College, Dahlonega, GA [Library symbol Library of Congress] (LCLS) .... GDahN

North Georgia College, Stewart Library, Dahlonega, GA [OCLC symbol] (OCLC) .... GND

North German Coal Control [Post-World War II] .... NGCC

North German Coal Distribution Organization [Post-World War II] .... NGCDO

North German Oil Control [Post-World War II] .... NGOC

North Gower Branch, Rideau Township Library, Ontario [Library symbol National Library of Canada] (BIB) .... ONGRT

North Greene Community Unit, School District 3, White Hall, IL [Library symbol Library of Congress] (LCLS) .... IWhhSD

North Greenville College, Tigerville, SC [Library symbol] [Library of Congress] (LCLS) .... ScTvC

North Greenville Junior College [South Carolina] .... NGJC

North Hampton [South Carolina] [Seismograph station code, US Geological Survey Closed] (SEIS) .... NHS

North Harris County College, Houston, TX [Library symbol Library of Congress] (LCLS) .... TxHNH

North Hart Resources [Vancouver Stock Exchange symbol] .... NHR

North Haven, ME [Location identifier FAA] (FAAL) .... TJW

North Hennepin Community College Library, Brooklyn Park, MN [OCLC symbol] (OCLC) .... NHE

North Hennepin Community College, Minneapolis, MN [Library symbol Library of Congress] (LCLS) .... MnMNHe

North High School, Commack, NY [Library symbol] [Library of Congress] .... NCoHS-N

North Highlands, CA [FM radio station call letters] .... KEBR

North Highlands Museum, Dingwall, Nova Scotia [Library symbol National Library of Canada] (NLC) .... NSDNHM

North Highlands Museum, Dingwall, NS, Canada [Library symbol] [Library of Congress] (LCLS) .... CaNSDiNHM

North Hills School District Instructional Materials Center, Pittsburgh, PA [OCLC symbol] (OCLC) .... PNH

North Himsworth Township Public Library, Callander, Ontario [Library symbol National Library of Canada] (NLC) .... OCNHT

North Idaho College, Coeur d'Alene, ID [Library symbol Library of Congress] (LCLS) .... IdCN

North Indiana Public Service Co. [AMEX symbol] (SAG) .... NI

North Iowa Area Community College, Mason City, IA [Library symbol Library of Congress] (LCLS) .... IaMcNC

North Iowa Area Community College, Mason City, IA [OCLC symbol] (OCLC) .... IWN

North Iowa Cooperative Library Extension, Mason City, IA [Library symbol Library of Congress] (LCLS) .... IaMcN

North Iowa Times, McGregor, IA [Library symbol Library of Congress] (LCLS) .... IaMcgN

North Irish Horse [Military unit] [British] .... NIH

North Irish Militia [Military unit] [British] .... NIM

North Island [New Zealand] (BARN) .... NI

North Island (MUGU) .... NORIS

North Island College, Comox, BC, Canada [Library symbol Library of Congress] (LCLS) .... CaBComN

North Island College, Courtenay, British Columbia [Library symbol National Library of Canada] (NLC) .... BCOMN

North Jersey Suburbanite, Englewood, NJ [Library symbol Library of Congress] (LCLS) .... NjEnS

North Judson-Wayne Township Public Library, North Judson, IN [Library symbol Library of Congress] (LCLS) .... InNoj

North Junior-Senior High School, Franklin Square, NY [Library symbol] [Library of Congress] .... NFsNH

North Kalimantan Communist Party [Malaysia] [Political party] (PD) .... NKCP

North Kanaga [Alaska] [Seismograph station code, US Geological Survey] (SEIS) AD7

North Kansas City Memorial Hospital, North Kansas City, MO [Library symbol Library of Congress] (LCLS) .... MoNMH

North Kansas City Public Library, North Kansas City, MO [Library symbol Library of Congress] (LCLS) .... MoN

North Kingstown Free Library, North Kingstown, RI [Library symbol Library of Congress] (LCLS) .... RNk

North Kingstown, RI [Location identifier FAA] (FAAL) .... OQU

North Korea [License plate code assigned to foreign diplomats in the US] .... GQ

North Korean .... NK

North Korean Air Force .... NKAF

North Korean Army .... NKA

North Korean Navy .... NKN

North Korean People's Army .... NKPA

North Lake Tahoe Historical Society, Tahoe City, CA [Library symbol] [Library of Congress] (LCLS) .... CTcHi

North Las Vegas, NV [FM radio station call letters] .... KJUL

North Las Vegas, Nv [AM radio station call letters] (RBYB) .... KKDD

North Las Vegas, NV [AM radio station call letters] .... KSHP-AM

North Las Vegas, NV [AM radio station call letters] .... KVEG

North Las Vegas, NV [AM radio station call letters] .... KXNO

North Latitude .... NL

North Lee County Historical Society, Fort Madison, IA [Library symbol Library of Congress] (LCLS) .... IaFmLHi

North Lilly Mining Co. [NASDAQ symbol] (NQ) .... NLMC

North Lilly Mining Co. [Associated Press] (SAG) .... NthLily

North Lilly Mining [NASDAQ symbol] (TTSB) .... NLMC

North Little Rock, AR [FM radio station call letters] .... KDRE

North Little Rock, AR [AM radio station call letters] .... KLRG

North Little Rock, AR [AM radio station call letters] (RBYB) .... KPAL-AM

North Little Rock, AR [AM radio station call letters] (RBYB) .... KRNN-AM

North London [Postcode] (ODBW) .... N

North London Railway [British] .... NLR

North Louisiana & Gulf Railroad Co. [AAR code] .... NLG

North Luffenham [British ICAO location identifier] (ICLI) .... EGWL

North Luzon Force [Army World War II] .... NLF

North Manchester, IN [FM radio station call letters] .... WBKE

North Manchester News-Journal, North Manchester, IN [Library symbol Library of Congress] .... InNomanNJ

North Manchester Public Library, North Manchester, IN [Library symbol] [Library of Congress] (LCLS) .... InNom

North Manchester Public Library, North Manchester, IN [Library symbol Library of Congress] (LCLS) .... InNoman

North Mankato, MN [FM radio station call letters] .... KDOG

North Marysburgh Museum, Picton, ON, Canada [Library symbol] [Library of Congress] (LCLS) .... CaOPiNM

North Marysburgh Museum, Picton, Ontario [Library symbol National Library of Canada] (BIB) .... OPINM

North Memorial Hospital, Minneapolis, MN [Library symbol Library of Congress] (LCLS) .... MnMNH

North Merrick Public Library, North Merrick, NY [Library symbol Library of Congress] (LCLS) .... NNm

North Merrick Public Library, North Merrick, NY [Library symbol] [Library of Congress] (LCLS) .... NNmN

North Metropolitan Tramways Co. [British] (ROG) .... NMTC

North Miami, FL [*AM radio station call letters*] .... WKAT
North Middle School, Lynbrook, NY [*Library symbol*] [*Library of Congress*] (LCLS) .... NLynNM
North Muskegon, MI [*FM radio station call letters*] .... WLCS
North Myrtle Beach, SC [*Location identifier FAA*] (FAAL) .... CRE
North Myrtle Beach, SC [*FM radio station call letters*] (RBYB) .... WAPV-FM
North Myrtle Beach, SC [*AM radio station call letters*] .... WGSN
North Myrtle Beach, SC [*FM radio station call letters*] .... WNMB
North Newton, KS [*FM radio station call letters*] .... KBCU
North Norway (NATG) .... NON
North Of [*In outdoor advertising*] (WDMC) .... N/O
North of England Biotechnology Information Service [*University of Newcastle-Upon-Tyne Medical School*] [*England*] [*Information service or system*] (IID) .... NEBIS
North of England Institute for Christian Education .... NEICE
North of Houston Street [*Artists' colony in New York City*] [*See also SoHo, SoSo, TriBeCa*] .... NoHo
North of Scotland Hydro-Electric Board (ECON) .... NSHEB
North Olympic Library System, Port Angeles, WA [*Library symbol Library of Congress*] (LCLS) .... WaPoN
North Oscura Peak [*White Sands Missile Range*] [*Army*] .... NOP
North Pacific [*Aviation*] (FAAC) .... NOPAC
North Pacific [*Military*] .... NORPAC
North Pacific [*MARC geographic area code Library of Congress*] (LCCP) .... pn----
North Pacific Central Mode Water [*Marine science*] (OSRA) .... NPCMW
North Pacific Coast Freight Bureau .... NPCFB
North Pacific Coast Freight Bureau, Seattle WA [*STAC*] .... NPC
North Pacific Coast Line (MHDB) .... NPCL
North Pacific Deep Water [*Oceanography*] .... NPDW
North Pacific Division [*Army World War II*] .... NPD
North Pacific Drift [*Oceanography*] .... NPD
North Pacific Experiment [*National Science Foundation*] .... NORPAX
North Pacific Fisheries Commission (NOAA) .... NPFC
North Pacific Fisheries Project (NOAA) .... NORFISH
North Pacific Fisheries Research Center [*National Oceanic and Atmospheric Administration*] .... NPFRC
North Pacific Fishery Management Council [*National Oceanic and Atmospheric Administration*] (GFGA) .... NPFMC
North Pacific Fur Seal Commission [*Defunct*] .... NPFC
North Pacific Fur Seal Commission [*Defunct*] .... NPFSC
North Pacific Industry [*Vancouver Stock Exchange symbol*] .... NPC
North Pacific Intermediate Water [*Marine science*] (OSRA) .... NPIW
North Pacific Marine Science Organization (USDC) .... PICES
North Pacific Ocean Monitoring for Climate Research [*Japan-USA*] [*Marine science*] (OSRA) .... TRANSPAC
North Pacific Trade Winds Zone Investigation (NOAA) .... NPTWZI
North Pacific Transition Zone [*Marine science*] (OSRA) .... NPTZ
North Pacific Transition Zone (USDC) .... NPTZ
North Pahute Mesa [*Nevada*] [*Seismograph station code, US Geological Survey*] (SEIS) .... NPM
North Park College and Theological Seminary, Chicago, IL [*Library symbol Library of Congress*] (LCLS) .... ICNPT
North Park College and Theological Seminary, Chicago, IL [*OCLC symbol*] (OCLC) .... ICZ
North Peralta Community College [*California*] .... NPCC
North Pit [*Hawaii*] [*Seismograph station code, US Geological Survey*] (SEIS) .... NPH
North Platte [*Nebraska*] [*Airport symbol*] (OAG) .... LBF
North Platte, NE [*Location identifier FAA*] (FAAL) .... BGN
North Platte, NE [*FM radio station call letters*] .... KELN
North Platte, NE [*AM radio station call letters*] .... KJLT
North Platte, NE [*FM radio station call letters*] .... KJLT-FM
North Platte, NE [*Television station call letters*] .... KNOP
North Platte, NE [*AM radio station call letters*] .... KODY
North Platte, NE [*AM radio station call letters*] .... KOOQ
North Platte, NE [*Television station call letters*] .... KPNE
North Platte, NE [*FM radio station call letters*] .... KPNE-FM
North Platte, NE [*FM radio station call letters*] .... KXNP
North Platte, NE [*Location identifier FAA*] (FAAL) .... LBF
North Platte, NE [*Location identifier FAA*] (FAAL) .... LED
North Platte, NE [*Location identifier FAA*] (FAAL) .... PNB
North Platte Public Library, North Platte, NE [*Library symbol Library of Congress*] (LCLS) .... NbNp
North Pocatello Valley [*Idaho*] [*Seismograph station code, US Geological Survey*] (SEIS) .... NPI
North Polar Cap [*A filamentary mark on Mars*] .... NPC
North Polar Distance .... NPD
North Polar Region .... NPR
North Polar Sequence .... NPS
North Pole [*Also, PN*] .... NP
North Pole [*Also, NP*] .... PN
North Pole, AK [*AM radio station call letters*] .... KJNP
North Pole, AK [*FM radio station call letters*] .... KJNP-FM
North Pole, AK [*Television station call letters*] .... KJNP-TV
North Pole High School, North Pole, AK [*Library symbol*] [*Library of Congress*] (LCLS) .... AkNpHS
North Pole, NY [*Television station call letters*] .... WPTZ
North Pyrenean Fault [*Geology*] .... NPF
North Pyrenean Fault Zone [*Geology*] .... NPFZ
North Pyrenean Zone [*Geology*] .... NPZ
North Queens Heritage Society, Caledonia, Nova Scotia [*Library symbol National Library of Canada*] (NLC) .... NSCNQH
North Queens Historical Society, Caledonia, NS, Canada [*Library symbol*] [*Library of Congress*] (LCLS) .... CaNSCaNQH
North Queensland Libraries: A Directory [*Australia A publication*] .... NQL
North Queensland Logging Association [*Australia*] .... NQLA
North Queensland Multifunction Polis [*Australia*] .... NQMFP
North Queensland Newspaper Co. Ltd., Townsville, QLD, Australia [*Library symbol Library of Congress*] (LCLS) .... AuTNQ
North Queensland Television [*Australia*] .... NQTV
North Queensland Tobacco Growers Cooperative Association [*Australia*] .... NQTGCA
North Rainier Mesa [*Nevada*] [*Seismograph station code, US Geological Survey*] (SEIS) .... NRM
North Region Cooperative Development Agency [*British*] .... NRCDA
North Reno [*Nevada*] [*Seismograph station code, US Geological Survey*] (SEIS) .... NRR
North Research Stillwater Pioneers, Dayton, OH [*Library symbol Library of Congress*] (LCLS) .... ODaNR
North Ridge Elementary School, Commack, NY [*Library symbol*] [*Library of Congress*] (LCLS) .... NCoNE
North Ridgeville, OH [*AM radio station call letters*] .... WJTB
North Riding [*England*] (ROG) .... NR
North River [*New York, New Jersey*] .... NR
North River [*Alaska*] [*Seismograph station code, US Geological Survey*] (SEIS) .... NRA
North Ronaldsay [*Scotland*] [*Airport symbol*] (OAG) .... NRL
North Russia Expeditionary Force [*World War I*] [*Canada*] .... NREF
North Salem Free Library, North Salem, NY [*Library symbol Library of Congress*] (LCLS) .... NNs
North Salopian Yeomanry [*British military*] (DMA) .... NSY
North Salt Lake City, UT [*AM radio station call letters*] .... KFAM
North, SC [*Location identifier FAA*] (FAAL) .... XNO
North Scott Press, Eldridge, IA [*Library symbol Library of Congress*] (LCLS) .... IaEldrN
North Sea Assets [*Investment firm*] [*British*] .... NSA
North Sea Hydrographic Commission [*of the International Hydrographic Organization*] [*Belgium*] .... NSHC
North Sea Mine Force Association (EA) .... NSMFA
North Sea - Nonrigid Airship [*Royal Naval Air Service*] [*British*] .... NS
North Sea Oceanographical Study Group [*British*] .... NSOSG
North Sea Subarea (NATG) .... NORSEACENT
North Sea Working Group [*Advisory Committee on Pollution of the Sea*] .... NSWG
North Seattle Community College, Seattle, WA [*Library symbol Library of Congress*] (LCLS) .... WaSC-N
North Seeking Gyro .... NSG
North Shore Aero Club, Inc. [*New Zealand*] [*ICAO designator*] (FAAC) .... SHO
North Shore Community College [*Beverly, MA*] .... NSCC
North Shore Community College, Beverly, MA [*Library symbol Library of Congress*] (LCLS) .... MBevN
North Shore Elementary School, Duluth, MN [*Library symbol*] [*Library of Congress*] (LCLS) .... MnDuNSE
North Shore High School, Glen Head, NY [*Library symbol*] [*Library of Congress*] (LCLS) .... NGlhNH
North Shore Hospital, Manhasset, NY [*Library symbol Library of Congress*] (LCLS) .... NManhH
North Shore Junior High School, Glen Head, NY [*Library symbol Library of Congress*] (LCLS) .... NGlhNJ
North Shore Junior High School, North Shore, NY [*Library symbol*] [*Library of Congress*] (LCLS) .... NnosJH
North Shore Senior High School, North Shore, NY [*Library symbol*] [*Library of Congress*] (LCLS) .... NNosSH
North Shore Women Writers Alliance [*Later, NSWA*] (EA) .... NSWWA
North Shore Writers Alliance (EA) .... NSWA
North Side [*In outdoor advertising*] (WDMC) .... N/S
North Side Elementary School, East Williston, NY [*Library symbol Library of Congress*] (LCLS) .... NEawNE
North Side Elementary School, East Williston, NY [*Library symbol*] [*Library of Congress*] (LCLS) .... NEwNE
North Side Savings Bank [*Associated Press*] (SAG) .... NoSdeSv
North Side Savings Bank [*NASDAQ symbol*] (NQ) .... NSBK
North Slope, AK [*Location identifier FAA*] (FAAL) .... CNR
North Slope Borough School District, Barrow, AK [*Library symbol*] [*Library of Congress*] (LCLS) .... AkBarN
North Solomon Trench [*Geoscience*] .... NST
North Somerset Imperial Yeomanry [*British military*] (DMA) .... NS
North Somerset Imperial Yeomanry [*British military*] (DMA) .... NSIY
North Somerset Yeomanry [*British military*] (DMA) .... NSY
North South Roundtable (EAIO) .... NSRT
North Staffordshire Railway [*British*] (ROG) .... NSR
North Stansbury [*Utah*] [*Seismograph station code, US Geological Survey*] (SEIS) .... NSU
North Star Christian Academy, Little Falls, MN [*Library symbol*] [*Library of Congress*] (LCLS) .... MnLfN
North Star Computer Society (EA) .... NSCS
North Star Network [*Defunct*] (EA) .... NSN
North Star Universal [*NASDAQ symbol*] (TTSB) .... NSRU
North Star Universal, Inc. [*NASDAQ symbol*] (NQ) .... NSRU
North Star Universal, Inc. [*Associated Press*] (SAG) .... NStarU
North State Cooperative Library System [*Library network*] .... NSCLS
North State Cooperative Library System, Willows, CA [*Library symbol Library of Congress*] (LCLS) .... CWiN
North State Cooperative Library System, Willows, CA [*OCLC symbol*] (OCLC) .... NSO
North Steaming Error (SAA) .... NSE
North Stonington [*Connecticut*] [*Seismograph station code, US Geological Survey*] (SEIS) .... NSC
North Stratford Railroad Corp. [*AAR code*] .... NSRC
North. Study of the Laws [*1824*] [*A publication*] (DLA) .... North St L
North Suburban Library System, Wheeling, IL [*OCLC symbol*] (OCLC) .... IEE

North Suburban Library System, Wheeling, IL [*Library symbol Library of Congress*] (LCLS) ... IWhN
North Suburban Library System, Wheeling, IL [*Library network*] ... NSLS
North Syracuse, NY [*AM radio station call letters*] ... WKRL
North Syracuse, NY [*FM radio station call letters*] ... WKRL-FM
North Syracuse, NY [*AM radio station call letters*] (RBYB) ... WTLA
North Tanaga [*Alaska*] [*Seismograph station code, US Geological Survey*] (SEIS) ... AK3
North Tanaga [*Alaska*] [*Seismograph station code, US Geological Survey*] (SEIS) ... AK5
North Tanaga [*Alaska*] [*Seismograph station code, US Geological Survey Closed*] (SEIS) ... AT3
North Temperate Zone [*Planet Jupiter*] ... NTeZ
North Temperate Zone [*Planet Jupiter*] ... NTZ
North Texas State College [*Later, North Texas State University*] ... NTSC
North Texas State University, Denton, TX [*OCLC symbol*] (OCLC) ... INT
North Texas State University, Denton, TX [*Library symbol Library of Congress*] (LCLS) ... TxDN
North Texas State University, State Historical Collection, Denton, TX [*Library symbol Library of Congress*] (LCLS) ... TxDN-Hi
North Tonawanda Public Library, North Tonawanda, NY [*Library symbol Library of Congress*] (LCLS) ... NNot
North Tonawanda Public Library, North Tonawanda, NY [*Library symbol*] [*Library of Congress*] (LCLS) ... NNotP
North Tropical Zone [*Planet Jupiter*] ... NTrZ
North Up [*Automotive engineering*] ... NU
North Up Cursor Centered [*Automotive engineering*] ... NUCC
North Up Cursor Moving [*Automotive engineering*] ... NUCM
North Vancouver City Library, British Columbia [*Library symbol National Library of Canada*] (NLC) ... BNV
North Vancouver City Library, North Vancouver, BC, Canada [*Library symbol Library of Congress*] (LCLS) ... CaBNv
North Vancouver District Public Library [*UTLAS symbol*] ... NVD
North Vandenberg Air Force Base (NASA) ... NVAFB
North Vernon, IN [*Location identifier FAA*] (FAAL) ... OVO
North Vernon, IN [*FM radio station call letters*] ... WINN
North Vernon, IN [*AM radio station call letters*] ... WKRP
North Vernon Sun-Plain Dealer, North Vernon, IN [*Library symbol*] [*Library of Congress*] (LCLS) ... InNovSP
North Vietnam (VNW) ... NVN
North Vietnamese Air Force ... NVAF
North Vietnamese Air Force ... NVNAF
North Vietnamese and Viet Cong Collecting Group [*Defunct*] (EA) ... NVVCCG
North Vietnamese Army ... NVA
North Vietnamese Army Captured ... NVAC
North Vietnamese Army Suspect ... NVAS
North Vietnamese Navy ... NVNN
North Wales ... NW
North Wales Independent Press ... NWIP
North Wales Weekly News, Conway, United Kingdom [*Library symbol Library of Congress*] (LCLS) ... UkCwN
North Walworth School District Number Five, Walworth, WI [*Library symbol Library of Congress*] (LCLS) ... WWalSD
North Warning System (MCD) ... NWS
North Warren Town and County News, Norwalk, IA [*Library symbol Library of Congress*] (LCLS) ... IaNowkN
North West Airline [*Australia ICAO designator*] (FAAC) ... NWW
North West Atlantic Fisheries, Memorial University [*UTLAS symbol*] ... NAF
North West College, Terrace, BC, Canada [*Library symbol Library of Congress*] (LCLS) ... CaBTeNW
North West College, Terrace, British Columbia [*Library symbol National Library of Canada*] (NLC) ... BTENW
North West Community College Library [*UTLAS symbol*] ... NWC
North West Cooperative Development Council [*British*] ... NWCDC
North West Frontier Fellowship (EA) ... NWFF
North West Frontier, Pakistan (ILCA) ... NWF Pak
North West Geomatics Ltd. [*Canada ICAO designator*] (FAAC) ... PTO
North West Intercollegiate Yacht Racing Association ... NWIYRA
North West London Press Ltd., London, United Kingdom [*Library symbol Library of Congress*] (LCLS) ... UkLNw
North West Regional Health Board [*Tasmania, Australia*] ... NWRHB
North West Regional Water Authority [*Tasmania, Australia*] ... NWRWA
North West Santo [*Vanuatu*] [*ICAO location identifier*] (ICLI) ... NVSZ
North West Territories Law Reports [*A publication*] (DLA) ... NWTLR
North West Territories Reports [*1885-1907*] [*Canada*] [*A publication*] (DLA) ... NWTR
North West Territory Alliance (EA) ... NWTA
North West Token Kai [*An association*] (EA) ... NWTK
North West Tourist Board [*British*] (DCTA) ... NWTB
North Western Bell (HGAA) ... NWB
North Western Employes Transportation Corp. [*Successor to Chicago & North Western Railway*] ... NETCO
North Western Expeditionary Force [*Norway*] [*World War II*] ... NWEF
North Western Law Review [*Chicago*] [*A publication*] (DLA) ... NWL Rev
North Western Railway [*India*] ... NWR
North Western Reporter [*National Reporter System*] [*A publication*] (DLA) ... NW
North Western Reporter [*A publication*] (DLA) ... NW Repr
North Western Reporter [*Legal*] ... NWR
North Western Reporter, Second Series [*A publication*] (DLA) ... NW 2d
North Western Reporter, Second Series [*West*] [*A publication*] (AAGC) ... NW 2d
North Wilkesboro, NC [*AM radio station call letters*] ... WKBC
North Wilkesboro, NC [*FM radio station call letters*] ... WKBC-FM
North Windham, ME [*FM radio station call letters*] (RBYB) ... WLAM-FM
North Windham, ME [*FM radio station call letters*] ... WVYH
North York Board of Education [*UTLAS symbol*] ... NYB
North York Board of Education, F. W. Minkler Library, Willowdale, Toronto, ON, Canada [*Library symbol Library of Congress*] (LCLS) ... CaOTNYE
North York Public Library [*UTLAS symbol*] ... NYK
North York Public Library, Toronto, ON, Canada [*Library symbol Library of Congress*] (LCLS) ... CaOTNY
North York Public Library, Willowdale, Ontario [*Library symbol National Library of Canada*] (NLC) ... OTNY
North Zenith East ... NZE
Northair Aviation Ltd. [*British ICAO designator*] (FAAC) ... NTL
Northair Mines Ltd. [*Toronto Stock Exchange symbol Vancouver Stock Exchange symbol*] ... NRM
Northaire Freight Lines Ltd. [*ICAO designator*] (FAAC) ... NFL
Northamerican Association of Sheet Metal Distributors [*Later, division of NHAW*] (EA) ... NASMD
Northamerican Heating and Airconditioning Wholesalers Association (EA) ... NHAW
Northampton [*Postcode*] (ODBW) ... NN
Northampton [*City in England*] (ROG) ... NORTH'N
Northampton [*England*] [*Airport symbol*] (AD) ... ORM
Northampton Activity Rating Scale [*Psychology*] ... NARS
Northampton & Bath Railroad Co. [*AAR code*] ... NB
Northampton County Area Community College, Bethlehem, PA [*Library symbol Library of Congress*] (LCLS) ... PBN
Northampton County Area Community College, Bethlehem, PA [*OCLC symbol*] (OCLC) ... PNC
Northampton County Historical and Genealogical Society, Mary Illick Memorial Library, Easton, PA [*Library symbol Library of Congress*] (LCLS) ... PEHi
Northampton County Law Reporter [*Pennsylvania*] [*A publication*] (DLA) ... Northam Law Rep
Northampton County Memorial Library, Jackson, NC [*Library symbol Library of Congress*] (LCLS) ... NcJac
Northampton County Memorial Library, Jackson, NC [*Library symbol*] [*Library of Congress*] (LCLS) ... NcJacL
Northampton County Reporter [*Pennsylvania*] [*A publication*] (DLA) ... North
Northampton County Reporter [*Pennsylvania*] [*A publication*] (DLA) ... North Co
Northampton County Reporter [*Pennsylvania*] [*A publication*] (DLA) ... North Co R (PA)
Northampton County Reporter [*Pennsylvania*] [*A publication*] (DLA) ... North Co Rep
Northampton County Reporter [*Pennsylvania*] [*A publication*] (DLA) ... Northamp Co Repr
Northampton County Reporter [*Pennsylvania*] [*A publication*] (DLA) ... Northampton Co Rep
Northampton Law Reporter [*Pennsylvania*] [*A publication*] (DLA) ... Northam
Northampton Law Reporter [*Pennsylvania*] [*A publication*] (DLA) ... Northam L Rep
Northampton, MA [*Location identifier FAA*] (FAAL) ... FAW
Northampton, MA [*FM radio station call letters*] ... WEIB
Northampton, MA [*AM radio station call letters*] ... WHMP
Northampton, MA [*FM radio station call letters*] ... WHMP-FM
Northampton, MA [*FM radio station call letters*] ... WOZQ
Northampton/Sywell [*British ICAO location identifier*] (ICLI) ... EGBK
Northamptonshire [*County in England*] ... NORTHANTS
Northamptonshire Imperial Yeomanry [*British military*] (DMA) ... NIY
Northamptonshire Rifle Volunteer Corps [*British military*] (DMA) ... NRV
Northamptonshire Yeomanry [*British military*] (DMA) ... NY
Northanger Abbey [*Novel by Jane Austen*] ... NA
Northbay Financial Corp. [*AMEX symbol*] (SPSG) ... NBF
Northbay Financial Corp. [*Associated Press*] (SAG) ... Northbay
Northbound ... NB
Northbrook Elementary School, Mendota, IL [*Library symbol Library of Congress*] (LCLS) ... IMenN
Northbrook, IL [*Location identifier FAA*] (FAAL) ... OBK
Northbrook Public Library, Northbrook, IL [*Library symbol Library of Congress*] (LCLS) ... INb
Northbrook Public Library, Northbrook, IL [*OCLC symbol*] (OCLC) ... INO
Northcal Resources [*Vancouver Stock Exchange symbol*] ... NHL
Northcoast Executive Airlines [*ICAO designator*] (FAAC) ... NCE
Northcor Resources Ltd. [*Vancouver Stock Exchange symbol*] ... NC
Northeast ... NE
Northeast ... NORE
Northeast ... NTHEST
Northeast Academic Science Information Center ... NASIC
Northeast Air Command ... NAC
Northeast Air Command ... NEAC
Northeast Airlines, Inc. [*Obsolete*] ... NE
Northeast Airlines, Inc. [*Obsolete*] ... NEA
North-East Airlines Ltd. [*Nigeria*] [*FAA designator*] (FAAC) ... NEN
Northeast Asia (CINC) ... NEA
Northeast Asia Association of Theological Schools ... NEAATS
Northeast Asia Tactical Information Communications Center (DNAB) ... NEATICC
Northeast Atlantic Deep Water [*Oceanography*] ... NEADW
Northeast Atlantic Dynamics Studies [*Marine science*] (MSC) ... NEADS
North-East Atlantic Fisheries Commission [*British*] (EAIO) ... NEAFC
Northeast Aviation Services Ltd. [*British ICAO designator*] (FAAC) ... NAS
Northeast by East ... NEbE
Northeast by North ... NEbN
North-East Cargo Airlines [*Russian Federation*] [*ICAO designator*] (FAAC) ... MGD
Northeast Club for Pre-War Austins [*British*] (EAIO) ... NECPWA
Northeast Colorado Regional Library, Wray, CO [*Library symbol Library of Congress*] (LCLS) ... CoWrN
Northeast Computer Center [*Military*] (AABC) ... NECC
Northeast Computer Institute (HGAA) ... NCI
Northeast Conference on the Teaching of Foreign Languages (EA) ... NEC

Northeast Corridor [*Railroad line*] (EGAO) .... NEC
Northeast Corridor Improvement Project [*Department of Transportation*] .... NECIP
Northeast Corridor Regional Modeling Project [*Environmental Protection Agency*] (GFGA) .... NECRMP
Northeast Corridor Transportation Project .... NECTP
Northeast Corridor Transportation System [*Boston to Washington high-speed transportation*] .... NCTS
Northeast Dairy Cooperative Federation [*Defunct*] (EA) .... NEDCO
Northeast Dallas County Record, Woodward, IA [*Library symbol Library of Congress*] (LCLS) .... IaWowN
Northeast Division Naval Facilities Engineering Command .... NOREASTNAVFACENGCOM
Northeast Document Conservation Center .... NEDCC
Northeast Electronics Research and Engineering Meeting .... NEREM
Northeast Express Regional Airlines, Inc. [*ICAO designator*] (FAAC) .... NEE
Northeast Fisheries Center [*Department of Commerce*] [*Woods Hole, MA*] .... NEFC
Northeast Fisheries Center [*National Marine Fisheries Service*] (USDC) .... NEFEC
Northeast Graphics Conference and Printing Show [*Printing Industry Association of Connecticut and Western Massachusetts*] (TSPED) .... NORGRAPH
Northeast Gulf of Alaska [*Marine science*] (MSC) .... NEGOA
Northeast Hazardous Waste Project [*Environmental Protection Agency*] (GFGA) .... NHWP
Northeast Indiana Banc [*NASDAQ symbol*] (TTSB) .... NEIB
Northeast Indiana Bancorp, Inc. [*NASDAQ symbol*] (SAG) .... NEIB
Northeast Indiana Bancorp, Inc. [*Associated Press*] (SAG) .... NeINBc
Northeast Interagency Motor Equipment Advisory Committee [*Terminated, 1981*] [*General Services Administration*] (EGAO) .... IMEAC
Northeast Iowa Union List of Serials .... NEIULS
Northeast Kansas Library System [*Library network*] .... NEKL
Northeast Library Service Area [*Library network*] .... NELSA
Northeast Louisiana University (GAGS) .... No E La U
Northeast Louisiana University, Monroe, LA [*Library symbol Library of Congress*] (LCLS) .... LMN
Northeast Louisiana University, Monroe, LA [*OCLC symbol*] (OCLC) .... LNE
Northeast Management, Inc. [*ICAO designator*] (FAAC) .... DSH
Northeast Mediterranean Area [*NATO*] (NATG) .... MEDNOREAST
Northeast Minnesota Historical Center Library, Duluth, MN [*Library symbol*] [*Library of Congress*] (LCLS) .... MnDuHi
Northeast Missouri State University (GAGS) .... No E Mo St U
Northeast Missouri State University, Kirksville, MO [*OCLC symbol*] (OCLC) .... MKN
Northeast Missouri State University, Kirksville, MO [*Library symbol Library of Congress*] (LCLS) .... MoKiU
Northeast Ohio Major Academic and Research Libraries [*Library network Information service or system*] (IID) .... NEOMARL
Northeast Oklahoma R. R. [*AAR code*] .... NEO
Northeast Pacific Area .... NEPA
Northeast Parallel Architectures Center [*Syracuse University*] [*Research center*] (RCD) .... NPAC
Northeast Power Coordinating Council [*Regional power council*] .... NPCC
Northeast Radio Observatory Corp. .... NEROC
Northeast Rail Service Act [*1981*] [*Also, NRSA*] .... NERSA
Northeast Rail Service Act [*1981*] [*Also, NERSA*] .... NRSA
Northeast Rat and Mouse Club (EA) .... NRMC
Northeast Regional Coastal Information Center [*Marine science*] (MSC) .... NERCIC
Northeast Regional Data Center [*University of Florida*] [*Research center*] (RCD) .... NERDC
Northeast Regional Implementation Team [*Army Corps of Engineers*] .... NERIT
Northeast Regional Library, Corinth, MS [*Library symbol Library of Congress*] (LCLS) .... MsCor
Northeast Regional Library System [*Library network*] .... NEIRLS
Northeast Regional Oxidant Study [*Environmental Protection Agency*] (GFGA) .... NEROS
Northeast Satellite Systems [*Avoca, PA*] [*Telecommunications*] (TSSD) .... NESS
Northeast Shipbuilders Ltd. [*Commercial firm British*] .... NESL
Northeast Subarea Channel (NATG) .... NORECHAN
Northeast Technical Community College, Norfork, NE [*Library symbol Library of Congress*] (LCLS) .... NbNfN
Northeast Test Area [*Military*] (MCD) .... NETA
Northeast Texas Community College, Mount Pleasant, TX [*Library symbol*] [*Library of Congress*] (LCLS) .... TxMtpN
Northeast Texas Library System [*Library network*] .... NETLS
Northeast Texas Library System/Dallas Public Library Film Service [*Library network*] .... NETLS/DPL
Northeast Transportation Coalition .... NETC
Northeast (United States) [*MARC geographic area code Library of Congress*] (LCCP) .... n-use-
Northeast Utilities [*Associated Press*] (SAG) .... NestU
Northeast Utilities [*Associated Press*] (SAG) .... NoestUt
Northeast Utilities [*NYSE symbol*] (SPSG) .... NU
Northeast Utilities [*NASDAQ symbol*] (SAG) .... NUWT
Northeast Utils Wrrt [*NASDAQ symbol*] (TTSB) .... NUWTW
Northeast Waste Management Officials Association .... NEWMOA
Northeast Water Resources Information Terminal (IID) .... NEWRIT
Northeast Watershed Research Center [*University Park, PA*] [*Department of Agriculture*] (GRD) .... NWRC
Northeast Wisconsin Intertype Libraries [*Library network*] .... NEWIL
Northeast Wood Products Expo [*In company name, NEWPEX, Inc.*] (TSPED) .... NEWPEX
North-Eastbound [*Aviation*] (FAAC) .... NEB
Northeastern .... NTHESTN
Northeastern Air Procurement District .... NEAPD
Northeastern Bird-Banding Association [*Later, AFO*] (EA) .... NEBBA
Northeastern Colorado Hail Experiment .... NECHE

Northeastern Consortium for Health Information [*Library network*] .... NECHI
North-Eastern Electronic Peak Tracing Unit and Numerical Evaluator (IEEE) .... NEPTUNE
Northeastern Forest Experiment Station [*Department of Agriculture*] [*Broomall, PA*] (GRD) .... NEFES
Northeastern Illinois University (GAGS) .... No E Ill U
Northeastern Illinois University, Chicago, IL [*OCLC symbol*] (OCLC) .... IAO
Northeastern Illinois University, Chicago, IL [*Library symbol Library of Congress*] (LCLS) .... ICNE
Northeastern Industrial Developers Association .... NIDA
Northeastern Junior College of Colorado [*Sterling*] .... NJCC
Northeastern Junior College of Colorado, Sterling, CO [*Library symbol Library of Congress*] (LCLS) .... CoStN
Northeastern Law Review [*A publication*] (DLA) .... NL Rev
Northeastern Loggers Association (EA) .... NELA
Northeastern Louisiana State College .... NLSC
Northeastern Lumber Manufacturers Association (EA) .... NELMA
Northeastern Lumber Manufacturers Association .... NLMA
Northeastern Minnesota Development Association .... NEMDA
Northeastern Mississippi Junior College [*Senatobia*] .... NMJC
Northeastern Nevada Historical Society, Elko, NV [*Library symbol Library of Congress*] (LCLS) .... NvEHi
Northeastern Ohio Library Association [*Library network*] .... NOLA
Northeastern Ohio Major Academic Libraries [*The College of Wooster*] [*Wooster, OH Later, NEOMARL*] [*Library network*] .... NEOMAL
Northeastern Ohio Universities, College of Medicine, Basic Medical Sciences Library, Rootstown, OH [*Library symbol Library of Congress*] (LCLS) .... ORootN
Northeastern Ohio University (GAGS) .... No E Ohio U
Northeastern Ohio University, College of Medicine, Rootstown, OH [*OCLC symbol*] (OCLC) .... ONE
Northeastern Oklahoma State University, Tahlequah, OK [*OCLC symbol*] (OCLC) .... OKN
Northeastern Ontario Oncology Program [*Programme d'Oncologie du Nord-Est de l'Ontario*], Sudbury, Ontario [*Library symbol National Library of Canada*] (NLC) .... OSUOP
Northeastern Operations Office [*NASA*] .... NEO
Northeastern Pacific Hurricane Analog Tracker .... NEPHAT
Northeastern Pennsylvania Bibliographic Center [*King's College*] [*Wilkes-Barre, PA*] [*Library network*] .... NEPBC
Northeastern Poultry Producers Council [*Later, PEIA*] (EA) .... NEPPCO
Northeastern Radiological Health Laboratory [*Massachusetts*] .... NERHL
Northeastern Regional Library, Cimarron, NM [*OCLC symbol*] (OCLC) .... NER
Northeastern Regional Library, Cimarron, NM [*Library symbol Library of Congress*] (LCLS) .... NmCiN
Northeastern Regional Library, Cimarron, NM [*Library symbol*] [*Library of Congress*] (LCLS) .... NmCiN
Northeastern Regional Library, Kirkland Lake, ON, Canada [*Library symbol Library of Congress*] (LCLS) .... CaOKlN
Northeastern Regional Library, Kirkland Lake, Ontario [*Library symbol National Library of Canada*] (NLC) .... OKLN
Northeastern Reporter [*Commonly cited NE*] [*A publication*] (DLA) .... N
Northeastern Reporter [*Commonly cited NE*] [*A publication*] (DLA) .... No East Rep
Northeastern Reporter, Second Series [*A publication*] (DLA) .... NE 2d
Northeastern Retail Lumbermen's Association (EA) .... NRLA
Northeastern Saengerbund of America (EA) .... NSA
Northeastern Spoon Collectors Guild (EA) .... NSCG
Northeastern State College [*Oklahoma*] .... NSC
Northeastern State College, Tahlequah, OK [*Library symbol Library of Congress*] (LCLS) .... OkTahN
Northeastern State University (GAGS) .... No E St U
Northeastern United States .... NEUS
Northeastern United States Seismic Network (NRCH) .... NEUSSN
Northeastern University (GAGS) .... No E U
Northeastern University, Boston, MA [*Library symbol Library of Congress*] (LCLS) .... MBNU
Northeastern University, Boston, MA [*OCLC symbol*] (OCLC) .... NED
Northeastern University Center for Urban and Regional Economic Studies [*Research center*] (RCD) .... NUCURES
Northeastern University, Law School, Boston, MA [*Library symbol Library of Congress*] (LCLS) .... MBNU-L
Northeastern Weed Control Conference [*Later, NEWSS*] (EA) .... NEWCC
Northeastern Weed Science Society [*Formerly, NEWCC*] (EA) .... NEWSS
Northeastern Wisconsin Technical Institute, Green Bay, WI [*Library symbol Library of Congress*] (LCLS) .... WGrN
Northeastern Yiddish [*Language, etc.*] (BJA) .... NEY
Northeast-Midwest Congressional Coalition (EA) .... NMCC
Northeast-Midwest Institute (EA) .... NMI
Northeast-Midwest Senate Coalition (EA) .... NMSC
Northeim [*Germany ICAO location identifier*] (ICLI) .... EDVN
Northerly .... NLY
Northerly (ABBR) .... NORTH
Northern (ABBR) .... NO
Northern (ABBR) .... NORTH
Northern .... NRN
Northern .... NTHN
Northern .... NTHRN
Northern Advanced Technologies Corp. [*Research center*] (RCD) .... NATCO
Northern Agricultural Development Corp. (AD) .... NADC
Northern Agricultural Energy Center .... NAEC
Northern Air Cargo, Inc. [*ICAO designator*] (FAAC) .... NAC
Northern Air Cargo, Inc. [*Air carrier designation symbol*] .... NACX
Northern Air Materiel Area, Europe [*Army*] .... NAMAE
Northern Air Materiel Area, Pacific [*Army*] .... NAMAP
Northern Air Service, Inc. [*ICAO designator*] (FAAC) .... NTX

Northern Airlines [British ICAO designator] (FAAC) .... TLR
Northern Airlines Sanya Lts. [China] [FAA designator] (FAAC) .... BYC
Northern Airways, Inc. [ICAO designator] (FAAC) .... NDA
Northern Alberta Institute of Technology [UTLAS symbol] ... NAI
Northern Alberta Institute of Technology [Edmonton, AB] .... NAIT
Northern Alberta Institute of Technology, Edmonton, AB, Canada [Library symbol Library of Congress] (LCLS) .... CaAENA
Northern Alberta Institute of Technology, Edmonton, Alberta [Library symbol National Library of Canada] (NLC) .... AENA
Northern Alberta Railways Co. (IIA) .... NA
Northern Alberta Railways Co. [AAR code] .... NAR
Northern Area Command .... NACOM
Northern Area Communications System (MCD) .... NACS
Northern Area Maintenance Unit [British ICAO location identifier] (ICLI) .... EGCN
Northern Area Ultrahigh Frequency Radio System [Green Pine] (MCD) .... NAUHF
Northern Arizona University (GAGS) .... No Ariz U
Northern Arizona University, Flagstaff, AZ [Library symbol Library of Congress] (LCLS) .... AzFU
Northern Arizona University, Flagstaff, AZ [OCLC symbol] (OCLC) .... AZN
Northern Arkansas Regional Library, Harrison, AR [OCLC symbol] (OCLC) .... ANA
Northern Army Group (NATG) .... NAG
Northern Attack Area .... NAA
Northern Attack Force [Navy] .... NAF
Northern Attack Force Commander [Navy] .... NAFC
Northern Australia Jockey Club (AD) .... NAJC
Northern Auto Racing Association [Sanctioning organization] .... NARA
Northern Automobile Racing Club [Sanctioning organization] .... NARC
Northern Ballet Theatre [England] .... NBT
Northern Bank of Commerce [Associated Press] (SAG) .... NBkCmce
Northern Bank of Commerce [NASDAQ symbol] (SAG) .... NBOC
Northern Baptist Theological Seminary [Lombard, IL] .... NBTS
Northern Base Section [Corsica] .... NORBS
Northern Bengal Mounted Rifles [British military] (DMA) .... NBMR
Northern Bk Comm Ore [NASDAQ symbol] (TTSB) .... NBOC
Northern Border Partners Ltd. [NYSE symbol] (SPSG) .... NBP
Northern Border Partners Ltd. [Associated Press] (SAG) .... NoBordr
Northern Border Ptnrs L.P. [NYSE symbol] (TTSB) .... NBP
Northern Business Information, Inc. [New York, NY] [Information service or system] (TSSD) .... NBI
Northern California Cancer Program [Research center] (RCD) .... NCCP
Northern California Earthquake Data Center .... NCEDC
Northern California Occupational Health Center [University of California] [Research center] (RCD) .... NCOHC
Northern California Section, Western Sea Frontier .... NORCALSEC
Northern Canada Mines Ltd. [Toronto Stock Exchange symbol] .... NH
Northern Carpet Trades Union [British] (DCTA) .... NCTU
Northern Central Railway [British] (ROG) .... NCR
Northern Cereal Mosaic Virus [Plant pathology] .... NCMV
Northern College, Kirkland Lake Campus, Kirkland Lake, ON, Canada [Library symbol Library of Congress] (LCLS) .... CaOKINC
Northern College of Applied Arts and Technology, Porcupine Campus, South Porcupine, ON, Canada [Library symbol Library of Congress] (LCLS) .... CaOSpNC
Northern Colorado Educational Board of Cooperative Services, Longmont, CO [Library symbol Library of Congress] (LCLS) .... CoLoN
Northern Colorado Research-Demonstration Center [Colorado State University] [Research center] (RCD) .... NCRDC
Northern Combat Area Command [Myanmar] .... NCAC
Northern Command .... NC
Northern Communications Area [Military] .... NCA
Northern Commuter Airlines [New Zealand] [ICAO designator] (FAAC) .... NLE
Northern Conservatory of Music [Maine] .... NCM
Northern Consolidated Airlines, Inc. .... NC
Northern Consolidated Airlines, Inc. .... NCA
Northern Counties Motor & Engineering Co. Ltd. [British] (DCTA) .... NCME
Northern Counties Textile Trades' Federation [British] (DCTA) .... NCTTF
Northern Cross Society (EA) .... NCS
Northern Cruise Master (SAA) .... NCM
Northern Cultural Trust [South Australia] .... NCT
Northern Cyclist Battalion [British military] (DMA) .... N CYC BN
Northern Development Co. [British] (ECON) .... NDC
Northern District (DLA) .... ND
Northern Dynasty Explorations Ltd. [Toronto Stock Exchange symbol Vancouver Stock Exchange symbol] .... NDX
Northern Eagle Mines [Vancouver Stock Exchange symbol] .... NTE
Northern Electric Co., Belleville, ON, Canada [Library symbol Library of Congress] (LCLS) .... CaOBNE
Northern Electric Co. Ltd., Montreal, Quebec [Library symbol National Library of Canada] (NLC) .... QMNE
Northern Electric Co., Montreal, PQ, Canada [Library symbol Library of Congress] (LCLS) .... CaQMNE
Northern Electric Industries [British] .... NEI
Northern Electricity Authority of Queensland [Australia] .... NEAQ
Northern Elementary School, Bemidji, MN [Library symbol] [Library of Congress] (LCLS) .... MnBemNE
Northern Elements Progression Union [Nigeria] [Political party] .... NEPU
Northern Engineering Industries [Commercial firm British] .... NEI
Northern Engineering Services Co. Ltd., Calgary, AB, Canada [Library symbol Library of Congress] (LCLS) .... CaACNE
Northern Engineering Services Co. Ltd., Calgary, Alberta [Library symbol National Library of Canada] (NLC) .... ACNE
Northern Environmental Council [Defunct] (EA) .... NOREC
Northern Essex Community College [Haverhill, MA] .... NECC
Northern Essex Community College [Haverhill, MA] .... NECCO

Northern Essex Community College, Haverhill, MA [OCLC symbol] (OCLC) .... ESS
Northern Essex Community College, Haverhill, MA [Library symbol Library of Congress] (LCLS) .... MHaNE
Northern Europe Committee [NATO] (NATG) .... NEC
Northern European Chiefs of Staff [NATO] (NATG) .... NECOS
Northern European Command [NATO] (NATG) .... NEC
Northern European Countries .... NEC
Northern European Regional Planning Group [NATO] (NATG) .... NERPG
Northern European Transhipment Organization [NATO] (NATG) .... NETSO
Northern European Universities Computer Centre [Denmark] (PDAA) .... NEUCC
Northern Examinations and Assessment Board (AIE) .... NEAB
Northern Examining Association [British] .... NEA
Northern Executive Aviation Ltd. [British ICAO designator] (FAAC) .... NEX
Northern Extratropical Land [Geography] .... NEL
Northern Federation of Advertisers Associations [Stockholm, Sweden] (EAIO) .... NFAA
Northern Fishing Vessel Owners Association [Defunct] (EA) .... NFVOA
Northern Forest Fire Laboratory [Later, Intermountain Fire Sciences Laboratory] [Research center] (RCD) .... NFFL
Northern Forest Research Centre [Canadian Forestry Service of Agriculture Canada] [Research center] (RCD) .... NOFRC
Northern Forest Research Centre, Environment Canada [Centre de Recherches Forestieres du Nord, Environnement Canada] Edmonton, Alberta [Library symbol National Library of Canada] (NLC) .... AEF
Northern Foundation [Canada] (EAIO) .... NF
Northern Fowl Mite [Immunology] .... NFM
Northern Fraternal Life Insurance (EA) .... NFLI
Northern French [Language, etc.] (ROG) .... N FR
Northern French [Language, etc.] (ROG) .... NF
Northern Frontier District [Kenya] .... NFD
Northern Frontier Province [Kenya] .... NFP
Northern Galactic Pole .... NGP
Northern General Transport Co. [British] (DCTA) .... NGT
Northern Great Lakes Area Council .... NORGLAC
Northern Great Plains Research Center [Department of Agriculture] [Research center] (RCD) .... NGPRS
Northern Great Plains Resource Program [Dept. of the Interior, Dept. of Agriculture and Environmental Protection Agency] (PDAA) .... NGPRP
Northern Group of Forces [Commonwealth of Independent States] (NATG) .... NGF
Northern Hardwood and Pine Manufacturers Association [Defunct] (EA) .... NHPMA
Northern Hemisphere .... NH
Northern Hemisphere Glaciation .... NHG
Northern Hemisphere Observatory [Canary Islands] (PDAA) .... NHO
Northern Hemisphere Reference Line [Geology] .... NHRL
Northern Hogsucker [Ichthyology] .... Nh
Northern Horizon [Vancouver Stock Exchange symbol] .... NHN
Northern Illinois Commuter [ICAO designator] (FAAC) .... NIC
Northern Illinois Learning Resources Cooperative [Library network] .... NILRC
Northern Illinois Library for Mental Health, Rockford, IL [Library symbol Library of Congress] (LCLS) .... IRoN
Northern Illinois Library System [Library network] .... NILS
Northern Illinois Library System, Rockford, IL [OCLC symbol] (OCLC) .... INS
Northern Illinois Meteorological Research on Downbursts [National Center for Atmospheric Research] .... NIMROD
Northern Illinois University [Dekalb, IL] .... NIU
Northern Illinois University (GAGS) .... No Ill U
Northern Illinois University, College of Law, De Kalb, IL [Library symbol] [Library of Congress] (LCLS) .... IDeKN-L
Northern Illinois University, De Kalb, IL [Library symbol Library of Congress] (LCLS) .... IDeKN
Northern Illinois University, De Kalb, IL [OCLC symbol] (OCLC) .... JNA
Northern Illinois University, Department of Library Science, De Kalb, IL [OCLC symbol] (OCLC) .... ILH
Northern Illinois University, Department of Library Sciences, De Kalb, IL [Library symbol Library of Congress] (LCLS) .... IDeKN-LS
Northern Illinois University, Law Library, Glen Ellyn, IL [OCLC symbol] (OCLC) .... ILY
Northern Independent Steel Training Association (AIE) .... NISTA
Northern Indiana Consortium for Education [Library network] .... NICE
Northern Indiana Muck Crop Growers Association [Defunct] (EA) .... NIMCGA
Northern Indiana Public Service Co. [NYSE symbol] (SAG) .... NI
Northern Indiana Public Service Co. [Associated Press] (SAG) .... NIPS
Northern Indiana Railway .... NI
Northern Indiana State Historical Society, South Bend, IN [Library symbol Library of Congress] (LCLS) .... InSNHi
Northern Information Technology Centre Consultancy Unit [NITA] .... NITCCU
Northern Institute of Technology, Prince Albert, Saskatchewan [Library symbol National Library of Canada] (NLC) .... SPANI
Northern Institute of Technology, Prince Albert, SK, Canada [Library symbol] [Library of Congress] (LCLS) .... CaSPANI
Northern Iowan, Cedar Falls, IA [Library symbol Library of Congress] (LCLS) .... IaCfNI
Northern Ireland [MARC geographic area code Library of Congress] (LCCP) .... e-uk-ni
Northern Ireland .... N IRE
Northern Ireland .... NI
Northern Ireland [MARC country of publication code Library of Congress] (LCCP) .... nik
Northern Ireland Association for the Care and Resettlement of Offenders (DI) .... NIACRO
Northern Ireland Automation Centre [Queen's University of Belfast] (CB) ..... NIAC
Northern Ireland Base Command [World War II] .... NIBC
Northern Ireland Civil Rights Association .... NICRA

Northern Ireland Council for Educational Research (AIE) .... NICER
Northern Ireland District .... NID
Northern Ireland Economic Research Centre .... NIERC
Northern Ireland Further Education Guidance Service (AIE) ...... NIFEGS
Northern Ireland Head Teachers' Association .... NIHTA
Northern Ireland Hotels and Caterers Association (ODBW) ...... NIHCA
Northern Ireland House of Commons .... NIHC
Northern Ireland Korfball Association (EAIO) .... NIKA
Northern Ireland Labour Party [*Political party Defunct*] .... NILab
Northern Ireland Labour Party [*Political party Defunct*] (PPW) .. NILP
Northern Ireland Law Reports [*A publication*] (DLA) .... N
Northern Ireland Law Reports [*A publication*] (DLA) .... N Ir
Northern Ireland Law Reports [*A publication*] (DLA) .... N Ir LR
Northern Ireland Law Reports [*A publication*] (DLA) .... NI
Northern Ireland Law Reports [*A publication*] (DLA) .... NILR
Northern Ireland Local Government Officers Superannuation
    Committee .... NILGOSC
Northern Ireland Mixed Marriage Association .... NIMMA
Northern Ireland News Service [*Information service or system*] (IID) .... NINS
Northern Ireland Office .... NIO
Northern Ireland Orchid Society (EAIO) .... NIOS
Northern Ireland Peace Forum .... NIPF
Northern Ireland Ploughing Association (EAIO) .... NIPA
Northern Ireland Police Authority .... NIPA
Northern Ireland Postal and Telecommunications Board .... NIP & TB
Northern Ireland Public General Acts [*A publication*] (DLA) .... N Ir Pub Gen Acts
Northern Ireland Public Service Alliance (EAIO) .... NIPSA
Northern Ireland Railways Co. Ltd. .... NIR
Northern Ireland Schools Examination Council (AIE) .... NISEC
Northern Ireland Statutes [*A publication*] (DLA) .... N Ir Stat
Northern Ireland Tourist Board .... NITB
Northern Jiaotong Univeristy [*China*] .... NJU
Northern Kentucky State Law Forum [*A publication*] (DLA) .... N Ky St LF
Northern Kentucky State Law Review [*A publication*] (DLA) .... North Ken'y SL Rev
Northern Kentucky University (GAGS) .... No Kent U
Northern Kentucky University, B. P. Chase College of Law, Covington, KY
    [*Library symbol Library of Congress*] (LCLS) .... KyHhN-L
Northern Kentucky University, Highland Heights, KY [*OCLC symbol*]
    (OCLC) .... KHN
Northern Kentucky University, Highland Heights, KY [*Library symbol Library*
    of Congress] (LCLS) .... KyHhN
Northern Libraries Colloquy (EA) .... NLC
Northern Library Services, Saskatchewan Library, Regina, Saskatchewan
    [*Library symbol National Library of Canada*] (NLC) .... SRNLS
Northern Lights College, Dawson Creek, BC, Canada [*Library symbol Library*
    of Congress] (LCLS) .... CaBDCNL
Northern Lights College, Dawson Creek, British Columbia [*Library symbol*
    National Library of Canada] (NLC) .... BDCNL
Northern Lights College Library [*UTLAS symbol*] .... NLI
Northern Lights Library Co-Operative, Grand Centre, AB, Canada [*Library*
    symbol Library of Congress] (LCLS) .... CaAGcNL
Northern Limit Line [*Korea*] .... NLL
Northern Mariana Islands [*Postal code*] .... CM
Northern Mariana Islands [*ANSI three-letter standard code*] (CNC) ...... MNP
Northern Mariana Islands [*ANSI two-letter standard code*] (CNC) .... MP
Northern Materials Resource Centre, Alberta Education, Edmonton, Alberta
    [*Library symbol National Library of Canada*] (NLC) .... AEEM
Northern Michigan University [*Marquette*] .... NMU
Northern Michigan University (GAGS) .... No Mich U
Northern Michigan University, Marquette, MI [*OCLC symbol*] (OCLC) .... EZN
Northern Michigan University, Marquette, MI [*Library symbol Library of*
    Congress] (LCLS) .... MiMarqN
Northern Michigan University, University Archives and Historical
    Collections, Marquette, MI [*Library symbol*] [*Library of Congress*]
    (LCLS) .... MiMarqNA
Northern Mines, Toronto, ON, Canada [*Library symbol Library of Congress*]
    (LCLS) .... CaOTNM
Northern Mines, Toronto, Ontario [*Library symbol National Library of*
    Canada] (NLC) .... OTNM
Northern Montana College [*Havre*] .... NMC
Northern Montana College, Havre, MT [*Library symbol Library of Congress*]
    (LCLS) .... HtHaN
Northern Montana College, Havre, MT [*Library symbol*] [*Library of*
    Congress] (LCLS) .... MtHaN
Northern Navigation Co. Ltd. [*AAR code*] .... NNC
Northern New York Health Information Cooperative, Canton, NY [*Library*
    symbol Library of Congress] (LCLS) .... NCaNNH
Northern Nigeria Case Notes [*A publication*] (DLA) .... NNCN
Northern Nigeria Law Reports [*A publication*] (DLA) .... NNLR
Northern Nigeria Legal Notes [*A publication*] (DLA) .... NNLN
Northern Nigeria Teacher Education Project [*University of Wisconsin*]
    (AEBS) .... NNTEP
Northern NORAD [*North American Air Defense*] **Region** (SAA) .... NNR
Northern Nurses Federation [*Norway*] .... NNF
Northern Nut Growers Association (EA) .... NNGA
Northern Ohio Data and Information Service [*Cleveland State University*]
    [*Information service or system*] (IID) .... NODIS
Northern Oklahoma Junior College .... NOJC
Northern Ontario Public School Principals' Association, Burks Falls, ON,
    Canada [*Library symbol Library of Congress*] (LCLS) .... CaOBfNO
Northern Ontario Public School Principals' Association, Burks Falls,
    Ontario [*Library symbol National Library of Canada*] (NLC) ...... OBFNO
Northern Operations of Rail Transportation and Highways [*Alaska*] .... NORTH
Northern Orion Explorations [*Vancouver Stock Exchange symbol*] .... NNO

Northern Outreach Library Service, University of Western Ontario, London,
    Ontario [*Library symbol National Library of Canada*] (BIB) .... OLUNO
Northern Pacific Railway Co. .... NORPAC
Northern Pacific Railway Co. (MHDW) .... NP
Northern Parkway Elementary School, Uniondale, NY [*Library symbol*]
    [*Library of Congress*] (LCLS) .... NUnNE
Northern Phoenician (BJA) .... NPh
Northern Pine [*Utility pole*] [*Telecommunications*] (TEL) .... NP
Northern Pipeline Agency [*Ottawa, ON*] .... NPA
Northern Pipeline Agency, Calgary, AB, Canada [*Library symbol Library of*
    Congress] (LCLS) .... CaACNP
Northern Pipeline Agency, Calgary, Alberta [*Library symbol National Library*
    of Canada] (NLC) .... ACNP
Northern Pipeline Agency Canada [*See also APNC*] .... NPAC
Northern Platinum [*Vancouver Stock Exchange symbol*] .... NTH
Northern Polk County News, Johnston, IA [*Library symbol Library of*
    Congress] (LCLS) .... IaJoN
Northern Prairie Wildlife Research Center [*Jamestown, ND*] [*Department of*
    the Interior] (GRD) .... NPWRC
Northern Prairie Wildlife Research Center, Jamestown, ND [*Library symbol*
    Library of Congress] (LCLS) .... NdJN
Northern Prairie Wildlife Research Center, Jamestown, ND [*OCLC symbol*]
    (OCLC) .... UDJ
Northern Prawn Fishery Management Committee [*Australia*] ...... NPFMC
Northern Program, Indian and Northern Affairs Canada [*Programme du*
    Nord, Affaires Indiennes et du Nord Canada] [*Library symbol National*
    Library of Canada] (BIB) .... YWIN
Northern Range [*Navigation*] .... NR
Northern Region Information System (NORIS), Canada Department of
    National Defence [*Reseau d'Information de la Region du Nord (NORIS),*
    Ministere de la DefenseNationale] **Yellowknife, Northwest Territories**
    [*Library symbol National Library of Canada*] (NLC) .... NWYND
Northern Region of Nigeria Law Reports [*A publication*] (DLA) .... NRNLR
Northern Regional Legal Notice [*1954-61*] [*Nigeria*] [*A publication*] (DLA) .... NRLN
Northern Regional Library, Espanola, NM [*Library symbol Library of*
    Congress] (LCLS) .... NmEN
Northern Regional Research Center [*Formerly, NRRL*] [*Peoria, IL*]
    [*Department of Agriculture*] .... NRRC
Northern Regional Research Laboratory [*Later, NRRC*] [*Department of*
    Agriculture] .... NRRL
Northern Rhodesia [*Later, Zambia*] .... NR
Northern Rhodesia European Mineworkers' Union .... NRMU
Northern Rhodesia Gazette [*A publication*] (DLA) .... NRG
Northern Rhodesia Law Reports [*A publication*] (DLA) .... NRLR
Northern Rhodesia Mine Officials and Salaried Staff Association .... MOSSA
Northern Rhodesia Regiment .... NRR
Northern Rivers Energy Action Network [*Australia*] .... NREAN
Northern Rivers Hydrophonic Association [*Australia*] .... NRHA
Northern Rockies Cancer Center, Billings, MT [*Library symbol*] [*Library of*
    Congress] (LCLS) .... MtBilNC
Northern Rocky Mountain Trench [*Geology*] .... NRMT
Northern Rocky Mountains .... NRM
Northern Sea Route (NATG) .... NSR
Northern Security Exhibition [*British*] (ITD) .... NORSEC
Northern Shipowners' Defence Club [*See also NORDISK*] (EAIO) .... NSDC
Northern Solomons Area .... NORSOLS
Northern Sotho [*MARC language code Library of Congress*] (LCCP) .... nso
Northern Soviet Boundary .... NSB
Northern State College, Aberdeen, SD [*Library symbol Library of Congress*]
    (LCLS) .... SdAbN
Northern State College Library, Aberdeen, SD [*OCLC symbol*] (OCLC) .... NOS
Northern State College (South Dakota) (GAGS) .... No St C
Northern State Multi-Service Center, Sedro Woolley, WA [*Library symbol*]
    [*Library of Congress*] (LCLS) .... WaSwN
Northern States Financial Corp. [*NASDAQ symbol*] (SAG) .... NSFC
Northern States Financial Corp. [*Associated Press*] (SAG) .... NthStat
Northern States Finl [*NASDAQ symbol*] (TTSB) .... NSFC
Northern States Power Co. [*Associated Press*] (SAG) .... NoStPw
Northern States Power Co. [*NYSE symbol*] (SPSG) .... NSP
Northern States Power Co. [*Associated Press*] (SAG) .... NSPw
Northern States Pwr [*NYSE symbol*] (TTSB) .... NSP
Northern Student Movement [*Defunct*] (EA) .... NSM
Northern Teacher Education Program, Inc., La Ronge, Saskatchewan
    [*Library symbol National Library of Canada*] (NLC) .... SLPRF
Northern Technol Intl. [*AMEX symbol*] (TTSB) .... NTL
Northern Technologies International [*Associated Press*] (SAG) ...... NthnTch
Northern Technology International [*AMEX symbol*] (SPSG) .... NTI
Northern Telecom [*Canada*] .... Nortel
Northern Telecom, Brampton, ON, Canada [*Library symbol Library of*
    Congress] (LCLS) .... CaOBraNT
Northern Telecom, Brampton, Ontario [*Library symbol National Library of*
    Canada] (NLC) .... OBRANT
Northern Telecom Canada Ltd., Montreal, PQ, Canada [*Library symbol*]
    [*Library of Congress*] (LCLS) .... CaQMNOT
Northern Telecom Canada Ltd., Montreal, Quebec [*Library symbol National*
    Library of Canada] (NLC) .... QMNOT
Northern Telecom Data Systems (NITA) .... NTDS
Northern Telecom Ltd. [*Associated Press*] (SAG) .... NorTel
Northern Telecom Ltd. [*NYSE symbol*] (SPSG) .... NT
Northern Telecom Ltd. [*Toronto Stock Exchange symbol Vancouver Stock*
    Exchange symbol] .... NTL
Northern Telecom, Mississauga, ON, Canada [*Library symbol Library of*
    Congress] (LCLS) .... CaOMNT
Northern Telecom, Mississauga, Ontario [*Library symbol National Library of*
    Canada] (NLC) .... OMNT

Northern Territorial Ordinances [*Australia A publication*] (DLA) ..... N Terr Austl Ord
Northern Territory .... N Terr
Northern Territory [*Australia MARC geographic area code Library of Congress*] (LCCP) .... u-at-no
Northern Territory AIDS [*Acquired Immune Deficiency Syndrome*] **Council** [*Australia*] .... NTAIDSC
Northern Territory Anti-Cancer Foundation .... NTACF
Northern Territory Architects' Board [*Australia*] .... NTAB
Northern Territory Archives Service [*Australia*] .... NTAS
Northern Territory Board of Studies [*Australia*] .... NTBS
Northern Territory Bowls Association [*Australia*] .... NTBA
Northern Territory Buffalo Industry Council [*Australia*] .... NTBIC
Northern Territory Building Referees' Board [*Australia*] .... NTBRB
Northern Territory Chamber of Mines and Petroleum [*Australia*] ... NTCMP
Northern Territory Clay Target Association [*Australia*] .... NTCTA
Northern Territory Commercial Fishermen's Association [*Australia*] ... NTCFA
Northern Territory Community Government Association [*Australia*] ... NTCGA
Northern Territory Conservation Commission [*Australia*] ...... NTCC
Northern Territory Convention Bureau [*Australia*] .... NTCB
Northern Territory Council of Social Service [*Australia*] .... NTCOSS
Northern Territory Council on the Aging [*Australia*] .... NTCOTA
Northern Territory Counter Disaster Council [*Australia*] .... NTCDC
Northern Territory Country Liberal Party [*Australia Political party*] ... NTCLP
Northern Territory Crab Fishermen's Association [*Australia*] ... NTCFA
Northern Territory Cricket Association [*Australia*] .... NTCA
Northern Territory Drug and Alcohol Board [*Australia*] .... NTDAB
Northern Territory Electoral Office [*Australia*] .... NTEO
Northern Territory Emergency Service [*Australia*] .... NTES
Northern Territory Field Naturalists' Club [*Australia*] .... NTFNC
Northern Territory Fire Service [*Australia*] .... NTFS
Northern Territory Fishing Industry Council [*Australia*] .... NTFIC
Northern Territory Fishing Industry Training Committee [*Australia*] ... NTFITC
Northern Territory Girls' Marching Association [*Australia*] ..... NTGMA
Northern Territory Government Pipeline Executive [*Australia*] ... NTGPE
Northern Territory Government Printing Office [*Australia*] ..... NTGPO
Northern Territory Government Publications [*Australia*] .... NTGP
Northern Territory Grain Marketing Board [*Australia*] .... NTGMB
Northern Territory Hockey Association [*Australia*] .... NTHA
Northern Territory Housing Commission [*Australia*] .... NTHC
Northern Territory Interpreter and Translator Service [*Australia*] ... NTITS
Northern Territory Land Acquisition Tribunal [*Australia*] ...... NTLAT
Northern Territory Land Board [*Australia*] .... NTLB
Northern Territory Library [*Australia*] .... NTL
Northern Territory Live Stock Exporters' Association [*Australia*] ... NTLSEA
Northern Territory Local Government Association [*Australia*] ... NTLGA
Northern Territory Local Government Grants Commission [*Australia*] .... NTLGGC
Northern Territory Marine and Ports Authority [*Australia*] .... NTMPA
Northern Territory News [*A publication*] .... NTN
Northern Territory Nurserymen's Association [*Australia*] .... NTNA
Northern Territory Place Names Committee [*Australia*] .... NTPNC
Northern Territory Planning Appeals Committee [*Australia*] ... NTPAC
Northern Territory Planning Authority [*Australia*] .... NTPA
Northern Territory Plumbers and Drainers Licensing Board [*Australia*] .... NTPDLB
Northern Territory Police Association [*Australia*] .... NTPA
Northern Territory Power and Water Authority [*Australia*] .... NTPWA
Northern Territory Racing, Gaming and Liquor Board [*Australia*] ... NTRGLB
Northern Territory Rifle Association [*Australia*] .... NTRA
Northern Territory Rugby Union [*Australia*] .... NTRU
Northern Territory Rural College [*Australia*] .... NTRC
Northern Territory School Sports Council [*Australia*] .... NTSSC
Northern Territory Softball Association [*Australia*] .... NTSA
Northern Territory Surveyor Board [*Australia*] .... NTSB
Northern Territory Totalizator Agency Board [*Australia*] .... NTTAB
Northern Territory Trades and Labor Council [*Australia*] ...... NTTLC
Northern Textile Association (EA) .... NTA
Northern Thunderbird Air Ltd. [*Canada ICAO designator*] (FAAC) ... NTA
Northern Transgressive Zone [*Geology*] .... NTZ
Northern Troops and Landing Force .... NTLF
Northern Trust [*NASDAQ symbol*] (TTSB) .... NTRS
Northern Trust Co., Chicago, IL [*Library symbol Library of Congress*] (LCLS) .... ICNT
Northern Trust Corp. [*Associated Press*] (SAG) .... NorTrst
Northern Trust Corp. [*Associated Press*] (SAG) .... NorTst
Northern Trust Corp. [*NASDAQ symbol*] (NQ) .... NTRS
Northern UFO Network [*British*] .... NUFON
Northern Union [*Rugby*] [*British*] (DAS) .... NU
Northern Union of Operative Masons [*British*] .... NUOM
Northern Universities Joint Matriculation Board (AIE) .... NUJMB
Northern Utah Satellite .... NUSAT
Northern Valley Private Industry Council [*Sunnyvale, CA*] (ECON) ... NOVA
Northern Virginia Community College .... NVCC
Northern Virginia Community College, Annandale, VA [*Library symbol Library of Congress*] (LCLS) .... ViAnN
Northern Virginia Community College, Springfield, VA [*OCLC symbol*] (OCLC) .... VAN
Northern Warfare Training Center [*Army*] (MCD) .... NWTC
Northern Wings [*ICAO designator*] (AD) .... WS
Northern Wisconsin Colony and Training School, Chippewa Falls, WI [*Library symbol Library of Congress*] (LCLS) ... WCfNC
Northern Wisconsin Health Science Library Cooperative [*Library network*] .... NWHSLC
Northern Woods Logging Association (EA) .... NWLA
Northern Wyoming Mental Health Center, Sheridan, WY [*Library symbol Library of Congress*] (LCLS) .... WyShMH

Northern-Southern Hybrid [*Hemoglobin phenotype of Rana pipiens*] ... NSH
Northern-Tier Integration Project [*Military*] (DNAB) .... NOTIP
Northfield [*Vermont*] [*Seismograph station code, US Geological Survey Closed*] (SEIS) .... NRT
Northfield Laboratories [*NASDAQ symbol*] (TTSB) .... NFLD
Northfield Laboratories, Inc. [*NASDAQ symbol*] (SAG) .... NFLD
Northfield Laboratories, Inc. [*Associated Press*] (SAG) .... NthfldLb
Northfield, MA [*FM radio station call letters*] .... WNMH
Northfield, MN [*FM radio station call letters*] .... KRLX
Northfield, MN [*AM radio station call letters*] .... KYMN
Northfield, MN [*FM radio station call letters*] .... WCAL
Northfield, VT [*FM radio station call letters*] .... WNUB
North-Finding Module (RDA) .... NFM
Northgate Explor [*NYSE symbol*] (TTSB) .... NGX
Northgate Exploration Ltd. [*Gold producer*] [*Canada*] ...... N
Northgate Exploration Ltd. [*NYSE symbol Toronto Stock Exchange symbol*] (SPSG) .... NGX
Northgate Exploration Ltd. [*Associated Press*] (SAG) .... Nthgat
Northgate Universal Floppy Drive Controller [*Computer science*] ... NUFDC
Northhampton, MA [*Location identifier FAA*] (FAAL) .... LFV
Northlake Public Library District, Northlake, IL [*Library symbol Library of Congress*] (LCLS) .... INol
Northland Aviation, Inc. [*ICAO designator*] (FAAC) .... KOE
Northland Bank [*Toronto Stock Exchange symbol Vancouver Stock Exchange symbol*] .... NLD
Northland College, Ashland, WI [*Library symbol Library of Congress*] (LCLS) .... WAsN
Northland Cranberries [*Associated Press*] (SAG) .... NorCran
Northland Cranberries, Inc. [*NASDAQ symbol*] (NQ) .... CBRY
Northland Cranberries, Inc. [*Associated Press*] (SAG) .... NorldCr
Northland Cranberries'A' [*NASDAQ symbol*] (TTSB) .... CBRYA
Northland High School, Remer, MN [*Library symbol*] [*Library of Congress*] (LCLS) .... MnRemH
Northland Library System [*Library network*] .... NLC
Northland Oils Ltd. [*Toronto Stock Exchange symbol*] .... NOL
Northland State Junior College, Thief River Falls, MN [*Library symbol Library of Congress*] (LCLS) .... MnTN
Northleach [*England*] .... NLEACH
North'n Ind Pub Sv Adj RtA Pfd [*NYSE symbol*] (TTSB) ... NIPrA
North'n Ind Pub Sv.4 1/4%cmPfd [*AMEX symbol*] (TTSB) .. NIPr
North-Northeast .... NNE
North-Northeastward (FAAC) .... NNEWD
North-Northwest .... NNW
North-Norwestern (FAAC) .... NNWRN
Northolt [*British ICAO location identifier*] (ICLI) .... EGVC
Northolt [*British ICAO location identifier*] (ICLI) .... EGWU
Northome School, Northome, MN [*Library symbol*] [*Library of Congress*] (LCLS) .... MnNoS
Northop University (GAGS) .... Northop U
Northport, AL [*FM radio station call letters*] .... WLXY
Northport High School, Northport, NY [*Library symbol*] [*Library of Congress*] (LCLS) .... NNopoHS
Northport Junior High School, Northport, NY [*Library symbol*] [*Library of Congress*] (LCLS) .... NNopoJH
Northport Public Library, East Northport Branch, East Northport, NY [*Library symbol Library of Congress*] (LCLS) .... NNopo-E
Northport Public Library, Northport, NY [*Library symbol Library of Congress*] (LCLS) .... NNopo
Northridge, CA [*FM radio station call letters*] .... KCSN
Northrim Bank [*Associated Press*] (SAG) .... Northrim
Northrim Bank [*NASDAQ symbol*] (SAG) .... NRIM
Northrop Aeronautical Institute [*Later, Northrop University*] ... NAI
Northrop Aircraft, Inc. (MCD) .... NAI
Northrop Automatic RADAR Test System (SAA) .... NARATE
Northrop Corp. (KSC) .... NC
Northrop Corp. [*NYSE symbol*] (SPSG) .... NOC
Northrop Corp., Aircraft Division, Hawthorne, CA [*Library symbol Library of Congress*] (LCLS) .... CHawNo
Northrop Grumman [*NYSE symbol*] (TTSB) .... NOC
Northrop Grumman Corp. [*NYSE symbol*] (SAG) .... NOC
Northrop Grumman Corp. [*Formerly, Northrup Corp.*] [*Associated Press*] (SAG) .... NortrpG
Northrop Institute of Technology, Inglewood, CA [*Library symbol Library of Congress*] (LCLS) .... CIngN
Northrop Overhead Rail Assembly and Installation Line (SAA) ... NORAIL
Northrop Pulse Radiation Facility .... NPRF
Northrop Resource Room, Thief River Falls, MN [*Library symbol*] [*Library of Congress*] (LCLS) .... MnTNo
Northrop Terminal Attrition Model (SAA) .... NORTAM
Northrop Unit [*Of hydrolytic enzyme activity*] .... NU
Northrop University. Law Journal of Aerospace, Energy, and the Environment [*A publication*] (DLA) .... Northrop ULJ
Northrop-Ventura (SAA) .... N-V
Northrup Space Laboratories (KSC) .... NSL
Northrup Voice Interruption Priority System (MUGU) .... NORVIPS
North's Probate Practice [*Illinois*] [*A publication*] (DLA) ... Nor Pro Pr
North's Probate Practice [*Illinois*] [*A publication*] (DLA) ... North Pr
Northside .... NRTHSD
Northside Aviation Ltd. [*British ICAO designator*] (FAAC) ... NSD
Northside Elementary School, Farmingdale, NY [*Library symbol*] [*Library of Congress*] (LCLS) .... NFarNE
Northside Elementary School, Levittown, NY [*Library symbol*] [*Library of Congress*] (LCLS) .... NLevNE
Northside Hospital, Atlanta, GA [*Library symbol Library of Congress*] (LCLS) .... GANH

Northside Reporter, Evansville, IN [*Library symbol Library of Congress*] (LCLS) ... InENR
North-South ... NS
North-South Acceleration ... NSA
North-South Fine, Hundreds ... NSFH
North-South Fine, Tens ... NSFT
North-South Fine, Units ... NSFU
North-South Institute [*Canada*] (EAIO) ... NSI
North-South Institute [*L'Institut Nord-Sud*], Ottawa, Ontario [*Library symbol National Library of Canada*] (NLC) ... OONSI
North-South Map [*Via orbiter*] ... NSM
North-South Skirmish Association (EA) ... N-SSA
North-South Station-Keeping (PDAA) ... NSSK
Northstar Aviation, Inc. [*ICAO designator*] (FAAC) ... NSS
Northstar Computer Forms [*NASDAQ symbol*] (TTSB) ... NSCF
Northstar Computer Forms, Inc. [*NASDAQ symbol*] (SAG) ... NSCF
Northstar Computer Forms, Inc. [*Associated Press*] (SAG) ... NthstCF
Northstar Energy Corp. [*Toronto Stock Exchange symbol*] ... NEN
Northstar Health Services, Inc. [*NASDAQ symbol*] (SAG) ... NSTR
Northstar Health Services, Inc. [*Associated Press*] (SAG) ... NthstrHl
Northstar Health Svcs [*NASDAQ symbol*] (TTSB) ... NSTRE
Northstar Resources Ltd. [*Toronto Stock Exchange symbol*] ... NOS
Northumberland [*County in England*] (ROG) ... NORTHD
Northumberland (ABBR) ... NORTHM
Northumberland [*County in England*] ... NORTHUM
Northumberland [*County in England*] (ROG) ... NORTHUMB
Northumberland [*County in England*] (ODBW) ... Northumb
Northumberland [*County in England*] (ROG) ... NRTHUM
Northumberland [*County in England*] (WGA) ... Nthmb
Northumberland and Newcastle Board of Education [*UTLAS symbol*] ... NNB
Northumberland and Newcastle Board of Education, Cobourg, ON, Canada [*Library symbol*] [*Library of Congress*] (LCLS) ... CaOCoN
Northumberland and Newcastle Board of Education, Cobourg, Ontario [*Library symbol National Library of Canada*] (NLC) ... OCON
Northumberland County Legal News [*Pennsylvania*] [*A publication*] (DLA) ... Northum
Northumberland County Legal News [*Pennsylvania*] [*A publication*] (ILCA) ... Northum Co Leg N
Northumberland County Legal News [*Pennsylvania*] [*A publication*] (DLA) ... Northum Leg N (PA)
Northumberland County Legal News [*Pennsylvania*] [*A publication*] (DLA) ... Northumb Co
Northumberland County Public Library, Garden Hill Branch, Campbellcroft, ON, Canada [*Library symbol*] [*Library of Congress*] (LCLS) ... CaOCNGH
Northumberland County Public Library, Hastings Branch, Hastings, ON, Canada [*Library symbol*] [*Library of Congress*] (LCLS) ... CaOHasN
Northumberland County Public Library, Warkworth, Ontario [*Library symbol National Library of Canada*] (NLC) ... OTREN
Northumberland Fusiliers [*British military*] (DMA) ... NF
Northumberland Hussars [*British military*] (DMA) ... NH
Northumberland Hussars Imperial Yeomanry [*British military*] (DMA) ... NHIY
Northumberland Hussars Yeomanry [*British military*] (DMA) ... NHY
Northumberland Imperial Yeomanry [*British military*] (DMA) ... NIY
Northumberland Legal Journal [*Pennsylvania*] [*A publication*] (DLA) ... Northum Leg J
Northumberland Legal Journal [*Pennsylvania*] [*A publication*] (DLA) ... Northum Leg J (PA)
Northumberland Legal Journal [*Pennsylvania*] [*A publication*] (DLA) ... Northumb Legal J
Northumberland Legal Journal [*Pennsylvania*] [*A publication*] (DLA) ... Northumb LN
Northumberland Legal Journal [*Pennsylvania*] [*A publication*] (DLA) ... Northumberland Co Leg Jour
Northumberland Legal Journal [*Pennsylvania*] [*A publication*] (DLA) ... Northumberland LJ
Northumberland Legal Journal News [*Pennsylvania*] [*A publication*] (DLA) ... Northumb LJ
Northumberland Mines Ltd. [*Toronto Stock Exchange symbol*] ... NUB
Northumberland, PA [*FM radio station call letters*] ... WKOK
Northumberland Yeomanry [*British military*] (DMA) ... NY
Northumbria Tourist Board [*British*] (DCTA) ... NTB
Northumbrian Universities Multiple Access Computer (NITA) ... NUMAC
Northumbrian Water Authority [*British*] (DCTA) ... NWA
Northward (ABBR) ... NOWD
Northward Aviation Ltd. (MHDW) ... NR
Northway [*Alaska*] [*ICAO location identifier*] (ICLI) ... PAOR
Northway, AK [*Location identifier FAA*] (FAAL) ... AES
Northway, AK [*Location identifier FAA*] (FAAL) ... ORT
Northway Aviation Ltd. [*Canada ICAO designator*] (FAAC) ... NAL
Northway Explorations Ltd. [*Toronto Stock Exchange symbol*] ... NOW
Northwest ... NTHWST
Northwest ... NW
Northwest African Air Forces [*World War II*] ... NWAAF
Northwest African Air Service Command [*World War II*] ... NAASC
Northwest African Coastal Air Force [*World War II*] ... NACAF
Northwest African Photographic Reconnaissance Wing [*World War II*] ... NAPRW
Northwest African Strategic Air Force [*British military*] (DMA) ... NASAF
Northwest African Tactical Air Force [*World War II*] ... NATAF
Northwest African Tactical Bomber Force [*World War II*] ... NATBF
Northwest African Training Command [*World War II*] ... NATC
Northwest African Troop Carrier Command [*World War II*] ... NATCC
Northwest African Waters ... NAW
Northwest AHEC [*Area Health Education Center*] **- Bowman Gray School of Medicine, Taylorsville, NC** [*OCLC symbol*] (OCLC) ... NBF
North-West AHEC Library at Winston-Salem, Bowman-Gray School of Medicine, Winston-Salem, NC [*Library symbol*] [*Library of Congress*] (LCLS) ... NcWsA
North-West Air Command Headquarters, Edmonton, Alberta, Canada ... CANAIRNORWEST
Northwest Air Services Ltd. [*Nigeria*] [*ICAO designator*] (FAAC) ... NWD
Northwest Airlines (MHDB) ... NWA
Northwest Airlines Corp. [*NASDAQ symbol*] (SAG) ... NWAC
Northwest Airlines Corp. [*Associated Press*] (SAG) ... NwstAirl
Northwest Airlines, Inc. [*ICAO designator*] (FAAC) ... NWA
Northwest Airlines'A' [*NASDAQ symbol*] (TTSB) ... NWAC
Northwest Alabama Junior College (AD) ... NAJC
Northwest Alaska Native Association [*Later, MA*] ... NANA
Northwest America Civil Air Routes Manual ... NACARM
Northwest and Alaska Fisheries Center [*National Marine Fisheries Service*] [*Department of Commerce*] [*Research center*] (RCD) ... NWAFC
Northwest Area Health Education Center, Boone, NC [*Library symbol*] [*Library of Congress*] (LCLS) ... NcBoHE
Northwest Association of Horticulturists, Entomologists, and Plant Pathologists [*Defunct*] (EA) ... HEPP
Northwest Association of Private Colleges and Universities [*Library network*] (EA) ... NAPCU
Northwest Association of Private Colleges and Universities, Microform Center, Portland, OR [*Library symbol Library of Congress*] (LCLS) ... OrPNA
Northwest Association of Schools and Colleges (EA) ... NASC
Northwest Atlantic [*Military*] ... NORWESTLANT
Northwest Atlantic Fisheries Act of 1950 ... NAFA
North-West Atlantic Fisheries Centre, Fisheries and Oceans Canada [*Centre de Pecheries de l'Atlantique du Nord-Ouest, Peches et Oceans Canada*] **St. John's,Newfoundland** [*Library symbol National Library of Canada*] (NLC) ... NFSF
Northwest Atlantic Fisheries Organization (EA) ... NAFO
Northwest Bank of Commerce [*Oregon*] [*Associated Press*] (SAG) ... NBkCmce
Northwest Bank of Commerce [*Oregon*] [*NASDAQ symbol*] (SAG) ... NBOC
Northwest Bible College, Minot, ND [*Library symbol Library of Congress*] (LCLS) ... NdMinN
Northwest by North ... NWbN
Northwest by West ... NWbW
Northwest Cape ... NWC
Northwest Cherry Briners Association (EA) ... NCB
Northwest Cherry Briners Association ... NWCA
Northwest Christian College [*Oregon*] ... NCC
Northwest Christian College [*Oregon*] ... NWCC
Northwest Christian College, Eugene, OR [*Library symbol Library of Congress*] (LCLS) ... OrENC
Northwest Coalition for Alternatives to Pesticides [*An association*] ... NCAP
Northwest Coalition for Alternatives to Pesticides (GNE) ... NCAP
Northwest Coastal Information Center [*Marine science*] (MSC) ... NCIC
Northwest College [*Washington*] ... NWC
Northwest College and University Association for Science [*Richland, WA*] [*Department of Energy*] (GRD) ... NORCUS
Northwest College, Kirkland, WA [*Library symbol Library of Congress*] (LCLS) ... WaKiN
Northwest Community College, Nome, AK [*Library symbol*] [*Library of Congress*] (LCLS) ... AkNNC
Northwest Community College, Powell, WY [*Library symbol Library of Congress*] (LCLS) ... WyPN
Northwest Computing Association ... NCA
Northwest Digital Ltd. [*Toronto Stock Exchange symbol*] ... NWQ
Northwest Division Naval Facilities Engineering Command ... NORWESTNAVFACENGCOM
Northwest Drama Conference (EA) ... NDC
Northwest Drama Conference (EA) ... NWDC
Northwest Dried Fruit Export Association [*Defunct*] (EA) ... NDFEA
Northwest Drug Co. Ltd. [*Toronto Stock Exchange symbol*] ... NWD
Northwest Education Cooperative Service Unit, Thief River Falls, MN [*Library symbol*] [*Library of Congress*] (LCLS) ... MnTEC
Northwest Educators of the Hearing Impaired (EDAC) ... NEHI
Northwest Elementary School, LaSalle, IL [*Library symbol Library of Congress*] (LCLS) ... ILasN
Northwest Equity Corp. [*NASDAQ symbol*] (TTSB) ... NWEQ
Northwest Equity Corp. [*NASDAQ symbol*] (SAG) ... NWEQ
Northwest Equity Corp. [*Associated Press*] (SAG) ... NwstEqty
Northwest Farm Managers Association (EA) ... NFMA
Northwest Farm Managers Association (EA) ... NWFA
Northwest Farm Managers Association ... NWFMA
Northwest Festivals Association (EA) ... NFA
Northwest Fisheries Association (EA) ... NFA
Northwest Fisheries Association (EA) ... NWFA
Northwest Forest Workers Association [*Defunct*] (EA) ... NWFWA
Northwest Forestry Association (EA) ... NFA
North-West Frontier Province [*Pakistan*] (PD) ... NWFP
Northwest Fruit Growers (EA) ... NFG
Northwest General Hospital, Milwaukee, WI [*Library symbol Library of Congress*] (LCLS) ... WMNG
Northwest Guides Association [*Defunct*] ... NWGA
Northwest Hardwood Association [*Later, WHA*] (EA) ... NHA
Northwest History Collection, Vancouver Public Library, British Columbia [*Library symbol National Library of Canada*] (NLC) ... BVANHC
Northwest Horticultural Council (EA) ... NHC
Northwest Hospital, Effie M. Storey Learning Center, Seattle, WA [*Library symbol Library of Congress*] (LCLS) ... WaSNH
Northwest Indiana Area Library Services Authority [*Library network*] ... NIALSA
Northwest Indiana Health Science Library Consortium [*Library network*] ... INUMRC

Northwest Kansas Library System [*Library network*] .... NWKLS
Northwest Library District [*Library network*] .... NORWELD
Northwest Marine Iron Works (AAGC) .... NMIW
Northwest Marine Trade Association (EA) .... NMT
Northwest Medical Team International .... NWMTI
Northwest Michigan College .... NWMC
Northwest Microfilm, Inc. [*Information service or system*] (IID) .... NMI
Northwest Mining Association (EA) .... NMA
Northwest Mining Association (EA) .... NWMA
Northwest Mississippi Junior College .... NMJC
Northwest Missouri Library Network [*Library network*] .... NLN
Northwest Missouri State College [*Later, Northwest Missouri State University*] .... NMSC
Northwest Missouri State University, Maryville, MO [*OCLC symbol*] (OCLC) .... MNW
Northwest Missouri State University, Maryville, MO [*Library symbol Library of Congress*] (LCLS) .... MoMaryU
Northwest Monsoon .... NWM
North-West Mounted Police [*Later, RCMP*] [*Canada*] .... NWMP
Northwest Natural Gas [*NASDAQ symbol*] (TTSB) .... NWNG
Northwest Natural Gas Co. [*NASDAQ symbol*] (NQ) .... NWNG
Northwest Nazarene College [*Nampa, ID*] .... NNC
Northwest Nazarene College, Nampa, ID [*Library symbol Library of Congress*] (LCLS) .... IdNN
Northwest Ohio Consortium [*Library network*] .... NOC
Northwest Orient Airlines, Inc. .... NOA
Northwest Orient Airlines, Inc. [*ICAO designator*] .... NW
Northwest Orient Airlines, Inc. (MCD) .... NWA
Northwest Pacific Oceanographers [*An association*] (NOAA) .... NWPO
Northwest Passage (ROG) .... NWP
Northwest Pipe [*NASDAQ symbol*] (TTSB) .... NWPX
Northwest Provinces .... NWP
Northwest Provinces Code [*India*] [*A publication*] (DLA) .... NWPC
Northwest Provinces, High Court Reports [*India*] [*A publication*] (DLA) .... NWPHC
Northwest Quoin Key Association [*Defunct*] (EA) .... NQKA
North-West Recording Society [*Record label*] .... NWRS
Northwest Region Spinners Association (EA) .... NwRSA
Northwest Regional Educational Laboratory [*Portland, OR*] [*Research center*] .... NWREL
Northwest Regional Educational Laboratory, Information Center Library, Portland,OR [*Library symbol Library of Congress*] (LCLS) .... OrPNR
Northwest Regional Library, Panama City, FL [*Library symbol Library of Congress*] (LCLS) .... FPcN
North-West Regional Library, Swan River, Manitoba [*Library symbol National Library of Canada*] (NLC) .... MSRNW
North-West Regional Library, Swan River, MB, Canada [*Library symbol Library of Congress*] (LCLS) .... CaMSrNW
Northwest Regional Library System, Sioux City, IA [*Library symbol Library of Congress*] (LCLS) .... IaScNR
Northwest Regional Library, Thief River Falls, MN [*Library symbol Library of Congress*] (LCLS) .... MnTNR
Northwest Salmon Canners Association (EA) .... NSCA
Northwest Savings Bank [*NASDAQ symbol*] (SAG) .... NWSB
Northwest Savings Bank [*Associated Press*] (SAG) .... NwstSBk
Northwest Sea Frontier .... NWSF
North-West Semitic (BJA) .... NWS
Northwest Skyways [*ICAO designator*] (AD) .... BV
Northwest Sports Enterprises Ltd. [*Vancouver Stock Exchange symbol*] .... NSE
Northwest State School, Bossier City, LA [*Library symbol Library of Congress*] (LCLS) .... LBocNS
Northwest States (ROG) .... NWS
Northwest Steam Society (EA) .... NSS
Northwest Teleprod'ns [*NASDAQ symbol*] (TTSB) .... NWTL
Northwest Teleproductions, Inc. [*Associated Press*] (SAG) .... NTelpd
Northwest Teleproductions, Inc. [*NASDAQ symbol*] (NQ) .... NWTL
Northwest Territorial Airways [*ICAO designator*] (AD) .... NV
Northwest Territorial Airways [*Canada ICAO designator*] (FAAC) .... NWT
Northwest Territories [*MARC geographic area code Library of Congress*] (LCCP) .... n-cn-nt
Northwest Territories [*Postal code*] [*Canada*] .... NT
Northwest Territories [*MARC country of publication code Library of Congress*] (LCCP) .... ntc
Northwest Territories [*Canada*] .... NWT
Northwest Territories Ordinances [*Canada*] [*A publication*] (DLA) .... NWT Ord
Northwest Territories Public Library Services, Hay River, Northwest Territories [*Library symbol National Library of Canada*] (NLC) .... NWHRN
Northwest Territories Public Library Services, Hay River, NT, Canada [*Library symbol Library of Congress*] (LCLS) .... CaNWHRN
Northwest Territories Revised Ordinances [*Canada*] [*A publication*] (DLA) .... NW Rev Ord
Northwest Territories Revised Ordinances [*Canada A publication*] (DLA) .... NWT Rev Ord
Northwest Territories, Supreme Court Reports [*A publication*] (DLA) .... NW Terr
Northwest Territory Alliance (EA) .... NTA
Northwest Territory Genealogical Society (EA) .... NTGS
Northwest Towboat Tariff Bureau, Inc., Seattle WA [*STAC*] .... NWB
Northwest (United States) [*MARC geographic area code Library of Congress*] (LCCP) .... n-usw-
North-West Water Authority [*British*] (DCTA) .... NWWA
Northwest Wisconsin Library System [*Library network*] .... NWLS
Northwestbound [*ICAO designator*] (FAAC) .... NWB
Northwestern .... NTHWSTN
Northwestern .... NWN
Northwestern (FAAC) .... NWRN
Northwestern Air Lease Ltd. [*Canada ICAO designator*] (FAAC) .... PLR
Northwestern Alumni Players .... NORAP
Northwestern College, Orange City, IA [*Library symbol Library of Congress*] (LCLS) .... IaOcN
Northwestern College, Orange City, IA [*OCLC symbol*] (OCLC) .... IOO
Northwestern College, Roseville, MN [*Library symbol Library of Congress*] (LCLS) .... MnRoN
Northwestern College, Watertown, WI [*Library symbol Library of Congress*] (LCLS) .... WWatN
Northwestern Community Unit, School District 2, Palmyra, IL [*Library symbol Library of Congress*] (LCLS) .... IPalmSD
Northwestern Electricity Board (NADA) .... NORWEB
Northwestern Electricity Board [*British*] .... NWEB
Northwestern Hawaiian Islands .... NWHI
Northwestern Law Journal [*A publication*] (DLA) .... North WLJ
Northwestern Law Review [*A publication*] (DLA) .... NW Law Rev
Northwestern Lumbermen's Association (EA) .... NLA
Northwestern Lutheran Theological Seminary, St. Paul, MN [*Library symbol Library of Congress Obsolete*] (LCLS) .... MnSN
Northwestern Michigan College [*Traverse City*] .... NMC
Northwestern Michigan College, Traverse City, MI [*Library symbol Library of Congress*] (LCLS) .... MiTN
Northwestern Oklahoma Railroad Co. [*AAR code*] .... NOKL
Northwestern Oklahoma State University (GAGS) .... No W Okla St U
Northwestern Oklahoma State University, Library, Alva, OK [*OCLC symbol*] (OCLC) .... OUF
Northwestern Online Total Integrated System [*Northwestern University Library*] [*Library automation project*] [*Information service or system*] (IID) .... NOTIS
Northwestern Pacific Railroad Co. [*AAR code*] .... NWP
North-Western Provinces, High Court Reports [*India*] [*A publication*] (DLA).... NW
North-Western Provinces, High Court Reports [*India*] [*A publication*] (DLA) .... NWP
Northwestern Pub Svc [*NYSE symbol*] (TTSB) .... NPS
Northwestern Public Service Co. [*NYSE symbol*] (SPSG) .... NPS
Northwestern Public Service Co. [*Associated Press*] (SAG) .... NWPS
Northwestern Region, RSFSR [*MARC geographic area code Library of Congress*] (LCCP) .... e-urn-
Northwestern Regional Library, Belen, NM [*Library symbol Library of Congress*] (LCLS) .... NmBeN
Northwestern Regional Library System, Thunder Bay, ON, Canada [*Library symbol Library of Congress*] (LCLS) .... CaOFWN
Northwestern Reporter [*Commonly cited NW*] [*A publication*] (DLA) .... N
Northwestern Reporter [*Commonly cited NW*] [*A publication*] (DLA) .... No West Rep
Northwestern Reporter [*Commonly cited NW*] [*A publication*] (DLA) ..... Northw Rep
Northwestern Reporter [*A publication*] (DLA) .... NW
Northwestern Reporter [*Commonly cited NW*] [*A publication*] (DLA) .... NW Rep
Northwestern Reporter [*Commonly cited NW*] [*A publication*] (DLA) .... NWR
Northwestern School of Law, Lewis and Clark College, Portland, OR [*OCLC symbol*] (OCLC) .... ONS
Northwestern School of Law, Lewis and Clark College, Portland, OR [*Library symbol Library of Congress*] (LCLS) .... OrPL-L
Northwestern Sea Frontier .... NORWESSEAFRON
Northwestern Sector, Western Sea Frontier .... NORWESSEC
Northwestern State College, Alva, OK [*Library symbol Library of Congress*] (LCLS) .... OkAlvN
Northwestern State University of Louisiana (GAGS) .... No W St U La
Northwestern State University of Louisiana, Natchitoches, LA [*Library symbol Library of Congress*] (LCLS) .... LNaN
Northwestern States Network [*Computer science*] (TNIG) .... NWNet
Northwestern Steel & Wire Co. [*Associated Press*] (SAG) .... NwStlWr
Northwestern Steel & Wire Co. [*NASDAQ symbol*] (SAG) .... NWSW
Northwestern Syntax Screening Test [*Education*] .... NSST
Northwestern Tariff Bureau .... NWTB
Northwestern Terminal R. R. [*AAR code*] .... NWT
Northwestern United States .... NWUS
Northwestern University (GAGS) .... Northwestern U
Northwestern University, Dental School, Chicago, IL [*Library symbol Library of Congress*] (LCLS) .... IEN-D
Northwestern University, Evanston, IL [*Library symbol Library of Congress*] (LCLS) .... IEN
Northwestern University, Joseph Schaffner Library of Commerce, Chicago, IL [*Library symbol Library of Congress*] (LCLS) .... IEN-C
Northwestern University, Law Library, Chicago, IL [*Library symbol Library of Congress*] (LCLS) .... IEN-L
Northwestern University Library Computer-Assisted Information Service (OLDSS) .... NULCAIS
Northwestern University, Medical School, Chicago, IL [*Library symbol Library of Congress*] (LCLS) .... IEN-M
Northwestern University, Music Library, Evanston, IL [*Library symbol*] [*Library of Congress*] (LCLS) .... IEN-Mu
Northwestern University School of Law (DLA) .... NWU
Northwestern University, Technological Institute, Evanston, IL [*Library symbol Library of Congress*] (LCLS) .... IEN-T
Northwestern University, Transportation Library, Evanston, IL [*Library symbol Library of Congress*] (LCLS) .... IEN-Tr
Northwestern Utilities Ltd. [*Toronto Stock Exchange symbol*] .... NWT
North-Westward (FAAC) .... NNWWD
Northwick Park Heart Study (DAVI) .... NPHS
Northwinds Northern Ltd. [*Canada ICAO designator*] (FAAC) .... NWN
Northwood Anchor, Northwood, IA [*Library symbol Library of Congress*] (LCLS) .... IaNowdA
Northwood, IA [*FM radio station call letters*] .... KYTC
Northwood Institute, Midland, MI [*Library symbol Library of Congress*] (LCLS) .... MiMidN

Northwood Institute of Texas, Cedar Hill, TX [Library symbol Library of Congress] (LCLS) .... TxCeN
North-Wright Air Ltd. [ICAO designator] (AD) .... HW
Nortland Air Manitoba [Canada ICAO designator] (FAAC) .... NAM
Norton Administrator for Networks [Symantec Corp.] [Telecommunications] (PCM) .... NAFN
Norton Administrator for Networks [Computer software] [Symantec Corp.] (PCM) .... NAN
Norton Air Force Base [California] .... NAFB
Norton AntiVirus for Firewalls [Symantec] [Computer science] .... NAVFW
Norton Change Directory [Computer science] .... NCD
Norton Co., Coated Abrasive Division, R and D Department, Troy, NY [Library symbol Library of Congress] (LCLS) .... NTN
Norton Co. Electric, Chippewa, Ontario [Library symbol National Library of Canada] (NLC) .... OCHIN
Norton Desktop for Windows [Symantec Corp.] [Computer science] (PCM) .... NDW
Norton Disk Doctor [Computer science] .... NDD
Norton Electric Co., Chippewa, ON, Canada [Library symbol Library of Congress] (LCLS) .... CaOChiN
Norton, KS [AM radio station call letters] .... KQNK
Norton, KS [FM radio station call letters] .... KQNK-FM
Norton McNaughton [NASDAQ symbol] (TTSB) .... NRTY
Norton McNaughton, Inc. [Associated Press] (SAG) .... NortMc
Norton McNaughton, Inc. [NASDAQ symbol] (SAG) .... NRTY
Norton Micro Images, Inc., Trenton, NJ [Library symbol Library of Congress] (LCLS) .... NtM
Norton State Hospital, Norton, KS [Library symbol Library of Congress] (LCLS) .... KNoSH
Norton, VA [AM radio station call letters] .... WNVA
Norton, VA [FM radio station call letters] .... WNVA-FM
Norton, VA [Television station call letters] .... WSBN
Norton Villiers Triumph [Automobile manufacturer] [British] .... NVT
Norton Villiers Triumph Group [Automobile manufacturer] [British] .... NVTG
Norton-Children's Hospital Medical Library, Louisville, KY [OCLC symbol] (OCLC) .... KLN
Norton's Cases on Hindu Law of Inheritance [1870-71] [India] [A publication] (DLA) .... Norton
Norton's Leading Cases on Inheritance [India] [A publication] (DLA) .... Nort LC
Nortriptyline [Antidepressant drug] .... NT
Nortronics Automatic Test Equipment Language [Computer science] .... NATEL
Nortronics Corp. .... NORTR
Nortronics Corp., Anaheim, CA [Library symbol Library of Congress] (LCLS) .... CAnaN-N
Nortronics System Support .... NSS
Nortwest Missouri State University (GAGS) .... No W Mo St U
Norvaline [Biochemistry] .... NORVAL
Norvaline [Biochemistry] .... Nva
Norvell Family Organization (EA) .... NFO
Norvenich [Germany ICAO location identifier] (ICLI) .... EDNN
Norvicensis [Norwich] [Imprint] (ROG) .... NORVIC
Norving [ICAO designator] (AD) .... RT
Norwalk, CT [Location identifier FAA] (FAAL) .... ORQ
Norwalk, CT [FM radio station call letters] .... WEFX
Norwalk, CT [AM radio station call letters] .... WNLK
Norwalk, OH [FM radio station call letters] .... WLKR
Norwalk, OH [AM radio station call letters] .... WVAC
Norwalk Public Library, Norwalk, CT [Library symbol Library of Congress] (LCLS) .... CtNowa
Norwalk Public Library, Norwalk, CT [Inactive] [OCLC symbol] (OCLC) .... NWK
Norwalk Savings Society [Associated Press] (SAG) .... NorwlkSv
Norwalk Savings Society [NASDAQ symbol] (SAG) .... NSSY
Norway [MARC geographic area code Library of Congress] (LCCP) .... e-no--
Norway [IYRU nationality code] .... N
Norway [ANSI two-letter standard code] (CNC) .... NO
Norway [MARC country of publication code Library of Congress] (LCCP) .... no
Norway [ANSI three-letter standard code] (CNC) .... NOR
Norway (VRA) .... Nor
Norway [or Norwegian] .... NORW
Norway Airlines [ICAO designator] (FAAC) .... NOS
Norway, Canada, United Kingdom, United States (DOMA) .... NORCANUKUS
Norway, Denmark, Finland, Sweden [Nordic Economic Community] [Trade bloc] .... NORDEK
Norway House [Canada] [Airport symbol] (OAG) .... YNE
Norway, ME [FM radio station call letters] .... WOXO
Norway, MI [FM radio station call letters] .... WZNL
Norway Station [South Africa] [Later, SNA] [Geomagnetic observatory code] .... NWS
Norway Technical Science Academy .... NTSA
Norway-America Association (EA) .... NAA
NORWEB PLC [Associated Press] (SAG) .... Norweb
NORWEB PLC [NASDAQ symbol] (SAG) .... NORWY
Nor-Weberine [Biochemistry] .... NW
Norwegian .... NG
Norwegian [MARC language code Library of Congress] (LCCP) .... nor
Norwegian (ABBR) .... NRW
Norwegian Adapted HAWK [Hughes Aircraft Co.] .... NOAH
Norwegian Advanced Surface to Air Missile System .... NSAM
Norwegian Agency for International Development .... NORAD
Norwegian Agency for International Development .... NORAID
Norwegian Air Shuttle, AS [FAA designator] (FAAC) .... NAX
Norwegian America Line .... NAL
Norwegian American Chamber of Commerce .... NACC
Norwegian American Museum Corp. (EA) .... NAM
Norwegian Antarctic Expedition [1956-] .... NorAE

Norwegian Caribbean Lines .... NCL
Norwegian Club (EA) .... NC
Norwegian Consulate General, New York, NY [Library symbol] [Library of Congress] (LCLS) .... NNCG
Norwegian Defense Research Establishment .... NDRE
Norwegian Elkhound Association of America (EA) .... NEAA
Norwegian Fjord Association of North America (EA) .... NFANA
Norwegian Fjord Horse Association of North America [Later, NFANA] (EA) .... NFHANA
Norwegian Government Office of Culture [Record label] .... NOC
Norwegian Krone [Monetary unit] .... N KR
Norwegian Lutheran Church of America (IIA) .... NLCA
Norwegian MARC (NITA) .... NORMARC
Norwegian Method of Tunnelling [Civil engineering] .... NMT
Norwegian Refugee Council .... NRC
Norwegian Regional Seismic Array .... NORESS
Norwegian Remote Sensing Experiment [in marginal ice zone] .... NORSEX
Norwegian Research Centre for Computers and Law (NITA) .... NRCCL
Norwegian Satellite System .... NORSAT
Norwegian Seamen's Association (EA) .... NSA
Norwegian Seismic Array [Royal Norwegian Council for Scientific and Industrial Research] .... NORSAR
Norwegian Singers Association of America (EA) .... NSAA
Norwegian Telecommunications Administration [or Agency] [Oslo] .... NTA
Norwegian Telecommunications Users Group .... NORTEB
Norwegian Zero Power Reactor Assembly .... NORA
Norwegian-American Historical Association (EA) .... NAHA
Norwegian-American Historical Association, Northfield, MN [Library symbol Library of Congress] (LCLS) .... MnNHi
Norwegian-American Historical Museum (AD) .... NAWH
Norwegian-American Historical Museum and Library, Decorah, IA [Library symbol Library of Congress] (LCLS) .... IaDN
Norwegian-British-Swedish Antarctic Expedition [1949-52] .... NBSAE
Norwegium [Chemistry] (ROG) .... NG
Norwell District Secondary School, Palmerston, ON, Canada [Library symbol] [Library of Congress] (LCLS) .... CaOpalN
Norwell District Secondary School, Palmerston, Ontario [Library symbol National Library of Canada] (NLC) .... OPN
Norwell, MA [Television station call letters] .... WHRC
Norwest Corp. [NYSE symbol] (SPSG) .... NOB
Norwest Corp. [Associated Press] (SAG) .... Norwest
Norwest Corp. [Associated Press] (SAG) .... Norwt
Nor'Wester Brewing [NASDAQ symbol] (TTSB) .... ALES
Norwich [British ICAO location identifier] (ICLI) .... EGRN
Norwich [British ICAO location identifier] (ICLI) .... EGSH
Norwich [Diocesan abbreviation] [Connecticut] (TOCD) .... NOR
Norwich [City in England] (ROG) .... NOR
Norwich [City in England] (ROG) .... NORW
Norwich [England] [Airport symbol] (OAG) .... NWI
Norwich and District Archives, Norwich, Ontario [Library symbol National Library of Canada] (BIB) .... ONDA
Norwich and Norfolk Terrier Club (EA) .... NNTC
Norwich, CT [Location identifier FAA] (FAAL) .... ORW
Norwich, CT [FM radio station call letters] .... WCTY
Norwich, CT [Television station call letters] .... WEDN
Norwich, CT [AM radio station call letters] .... WICH
Norwich, CT [FM radio station call letters] .... WNPR
Norwich Financial [NASDAQ symbol] (TTSB) .... NSSB
Norwich Financial Corp. [Associated Press] (SAG) .... NorwFn
Norwich Financial Corp. [NASDAQ symbol] (NQ) .... NSSB
Norwich Free Academy, Norwich, CT [Library symbol Library of Congress] (LCLS) .... CtNwchA
Norwich nd District Archives, Norwich, ON, Canada [Library symbol] [Library of Congress] (LCLS) .... CaONoDA
Norwich, NY [Location identifier FAA] (FAAL) .... OIC
Norwich, NY [AM radio station call letters] .... WCHN
Norwich, NY [FM radio station call letters] .... WKXZ
Norwich Pharmacal Co. [Research code symbol] .... Eu
Norwich Pharmacal Co., Norwich, NY [Library symbol Library of Congress] (LCLS) .... NNorP
Norwich Public Libraries, Norwich, United Kingdom [Library symbol Library of Congress] (LCLS) .... UkNr
Norwich Terrier Club [Later, NNTC] (EA) .... NTC
Norwich University, Northfield, VT [Library symbol Library of Congress] (LCLS) .... VtNN
Norwood & St. Lawrence Railroad Co. [AAR code] .... NSL
Norwood, MA [Location identifier FAA] (FAAL) .... OWD
Norwood, NY [Television station call letters] .... WNPI
Norwood Promotional Prd [NASDAQ symbol] (TTSB) .... NPPI
Norwood Promotional Products [Associated Press] (SAG) .... Norwood
Norwood Promotional Products [NASDAQ symbol] (SAG) .... NPPI
Norwood Public Library, Norwood, CO [Library symbol Library of Congress] (LCLS) .... CoNo
Norwood Public Library, Norwood, NJ [Library symbol Library of Congress] (LCLS) .... NjNor
Norwood Public Library, Ontario [Library symbol National Library of Canada] (BIB) .... ONO
No's St Pwr Minn.$4.16 Pfd [NYSE symbol] (TTSB) .... NSPPrE
Nosara [Costa Rica] [ICAO location identifier] (ICLI) .... MRNS
Nose [Horse racing] .... NO
Nose [Horse racing] .... NS
Nose Alone Reference [Aviation] (MCD) .... NAR
Nose and Throat [Medicine] .... N & T
Nose Cone [Aviation] (AFM) .... NC
Nose Cone Protective Covering [Aviation] .... NCPC

Nose Cone Warhead [*Aviation*] (NATG) .... NCW
Nose Creek School, Grovedale, Alberta [*Library symbol National Library of Canada*] (BIB) .... AGNCS
Nose Down [*Aviation*] .... ND
Nose Drops [*Pharmacy*] (DAVI) .... ND
Nose Fairing [*Missiles*] .... NF
Nose Fairing Container [*Missiles*] .... NFC
Nose Fairing Exit [*Missiles*] .... NFE
Nose Fuse [*Aviation*] .... NF
Nose Gear [*Aviation*] (MCD) .... NG
Nose Gear Launch (MCD) .... NGL
Nose Impact Rocket (NATG) .... NIR
Nose Instantaneous [*Aerospace*] .... NINST
Nose Landing Gear [*Aviation*] .... NLG
Nose Left [*Aviation*] (MCD) .... NL
Nose Right [*Aviation*] (MCD) .... NR
Nose Shipping Plug .... NSP
Nose, Tail, Waist [*Aviation*] .... NTW
Nose to Ear to Xiphoid [*Medicine*] .... NEX
Nose to X-Axis (MCD) .... NX
Nose to Y-Axis (NASA) .... NY
Nose to Y-Axis .... NY
Nose to Z-Axis (MCD) .... NZ
Nose Up [*Aviation*] .... NU
Nose Wheel [*Aviation*] (MCD) .... NW
Nose Wheel Steering [*Aviation*] .... NWS
Nose Wheel Steering Amplifier [*Aviation*] (MCD) .... NWSA
Nose Wheel Up [*Aviation*] .... NWU
Nose Wheel Well [*Aviation*] (MCD) .... NWW
Nosed (ABBR) .... NOSD
Nosed One Edge [*Lumber*] (DAC) N1E
Nosed Two Edges [*Lumber*] (DAC) N2E
Noshahr [*Iran*] [*ICAO location identifier*] (ICLI) .... OINN
Nosier (ABBR) .... NSIR
Nosiness (ABBR) .... NOSINS
Nosing (ABBR) .... NOS
Nosing (ABBR) .... NOSG
Nosocomial Infections Surveillance System [*Center for Disease Control*] .... NNISS
No-son Dependency Ratio [*Demographics*] .... NSDR
Nossi-Be [*Madagascar*] [*Airport symbol*] (OAG) .... NOS
Nostalgia [*A radio station format*] (WDMC) .... NOS
Nostalgia (ABBR) .... NSTLG
Nostalgia Book Club .... NBC
Nostalgia Drag Race Association (EA) .... NDRA
Nostalgic (ABBR) .... NSTLGC
Noster [*Our*] [*Latin*] .... N
Noster Salvator Iesus Christus [*Our Savior, Jesus Christ*] [*Latin*] .... NSIC
Noster Salvator Jesus Christus [*Our Savior, Jesus Christ*] [*Latin*] .... NSJC
Nostra Aetate [*Declaration on the Relationship of the Church to the Non-Christian Religions*] [*Vatican II document*] .... NA
Nostra Domina [*Our Lady*] [*Latin*] .... ND
Nostril (AAMN) .... N
Nostro Account [*Our Account*] [*An account maintained by a bank with a bank in a foreign country*] .... NA
Nostro Signore [*Our Lord*] .... NS
Nosy-Be/Fascene [*Madagascar*] [*ICAO location identifier*] (ICLI) .... FMNN
Not (DAVI) .... N
Not a Bean [*Penniless*] [*Facetious translation of NB, Nota Bene (Note Well)*] (DSUE) .... NB
Not a Number [*Computer programming*] (BYTE) .... NaN
Not a Priori .... NAP
Not Above .... N/A
Not Above [*Aviation*] .... NAB
Not According to Routine .... NAR
Not Acidified [*Biochemistry*] (DAVI) .... NACD
Not Admitted [*Medicine*] (MAE) .... NA
Not Affected (AAG) .... N/A
Not Allowed .... NA
Not Always Afloat [*Shipping*] .... NAA
Not Always Afloat [*Shipping*] (ODBW) .... naa
Not Always Afloat but Safe Aground [*Shipping*] .... NAABSA
Not Always Excused (AD) .... nae
Not an A-List Writer [*Screenwriter's lexicon*] .... NALW
Not And [*Logical operator*] [*Computer science*] .... NA
Not And [*Logical operator*] [*Computer science*] .... NAND
'Not' and 'And' (NITA) .... NAND
Not Applicable .... NA
Not Appropriated .... NA
Not Assigned .... NA
Not Assigned a National Stock Number .... NON-NSN
Not at All .... NOTAL
Not at Home .... NAH
Not at Present .... NAP
Not at Present (AD) .... nap
Not Attending Training .... NAT
Not Authorized .... NA
Not Authorized If Issued Under [*Army*] .... NAIIU
Not Available .... NA
Not Available (NOAA) .... NTAVL
Not Available .... NVAL
Not Available Status Report System [*DoD*] .... NASRS
Not Before [*ICAO designator*] (FAAC) .... NBFR
Not Bent [*Freight*] .... NB
Not Blind [*Experimental conditions*] .... NB
Not Bloody Likely [*British slang*] .... NBL
Not Carried .... NC
Not Coded (MCD) .... NC
Not Commissioned [*Military*] .... NOTCOMM
Not Competitive [*Rejected research proposals*] [*National Institutes of Health*] .... NC
Not Completed [*Medicine*] (DMAA) .... NC
Not Complied With [*Military*] .... NCW
Not Connected [*Electronics*] (DEN) .... NC
Not Considered Disabling [*Medicine*] (MAE) .... NCD
Not Considered Disqualifying .... NCD
Not Controlled [*Experimental conditions*] .... NC
Not Critical (NASA) .... N/C
Not Critical .... N/C
Not Crushed or Not Ground .... NCNGD
Not Cultured (MAE) .... NC
Not Dated [*Banking, bibliography*] .... ND
Not Detected [*or Detectable*] [*Medicine*] .... ND
Not Determined [*Medicine*] .... ND
Not Diagnosed [*Medicine*] .... ND
Not Directly (DGA) .... ND
Not Done .... ND
Not Dressed nor Tanned .... NDNT
Not Earlier Than .... NET
Not Economically Repairable .... NER
Not Elevated [*Laboratory science*] (DAVI) .... NE
Not Elsewhere Classified (ODBW) .... nec
Not Elsewhere Classified .... NEC
Not Elsewhere Indicated .... NEI
Not Elsewhere Mentioned .... NEM
Not Elsewhere Specified .... NES
Not Emanating Main Office [*Remote broadcast*] (NTCM) .... NEMO
Not Employed .... NE
Not Enameled [*Freight*] .... N ENMLD
Not Engaged .... NE
Not Enlarged [*Medicine*] .... NE
Not Entailing Excessive Cost [*Environmental technology*] .... NEEC
Not Entitled [*British military*] (DMA) .... NE
Not Equal [*Relational operator*] .... NE
Not Equal (EECA) .... NEQ
Not Equal To (NITA) .... NE
Not Evaluated (INF) .... NE
Not Examined [*Medicine*] .... NE
Not Exceeding .... N/E
Not Exceeding [*Freight*] .... N EX
Not Exceeding .... NX
Not Expendable (MUGU) .... NX
Not Explosive .... NE
Not Favorably Considered .... NFC
Not Fertilized .... NF
Not Finished [*Freight*] .... N FNSHD
Not Fit for Issue [*Navy*] .... NFFI
Not for Attribution [*Military*] .... NFA
Not for Profit (ADA) .... NFP
Not for Publication (ADA) .... NFP
Not for Resuscitation [*Hospital patient classification*] .... NFR
Not for Sale .... NFS
Not for Us [*Communications*] .... NFU
Not Fordable [*Maps and charts*] .... NF
Not Forgotten Association [*British*] (DBA) .... NFA
Not Found [*Telephone listing*] [*Telecommunications*] (TEL) .... NF
Not Fully Equipped [*of aircraft*] [*Air Force*] .... NFE
Not Fully Open (MCD) .... NFO
Not Further Identified (MCD) .... NFI
Not Given (DAVI) .... n giv
Not Given (ADA) .... NG
Not Glazed [*Freight*] .... N GLZD
Not Good .... NG
Not Greater Than .... NGT
Not Guilty .... NG
Not Guilty by Reason of Insanity .... NGBRI
Not Guilty by Reason of Insanity .... NGI
Not Guilty by Reason of Insanity .... NGRI
Not Heard [*Communications*] .... NHD
Not Held .... NH
Not Holding [*a given course or altitude*] [*Aviation*] .... NOHOL
Not Identified .... NI
Not Illustrated [*Publishing*] .... NI
Not In .... NI
Not In Active Labor [*Obstetrics*] (DAVI) .... NIAL
Not in Contact [*Electronics*] (DEN) .... NIC
Not in Contract [*Technical drawings*] .... NIC
Not in File .... NIF
Not in Labor [*Medicine*] .... NIL
Not in Labor Force (GFGA) .... NILF
Not in Line of Duty [*as of an injury*] [*Military*] .... NLD
Not in My Back Yard [*i.e., garbage incinerators, prisons, roads, etc.*] .... NIMBY
Not in My Election Year [*Slang*] .... NIMEY
Not in My Front Yard [*i.e., Garbage incinerators, landfills, etc.*] .... NIMFY
Not in My Insurance Company [*Insurance slang*] .... NIMIC
Not in My Term of Office [*Government slang*] .... NIMTOF
Not in Stock .... NIS
Not in the Public Domain .... NIPD
Not Included Elsewhere .... NIE
Not Included in Technical Service Demand Stockage Lists [*Army*] (AABC) .... NONTSDSL

Not Indicated [*Laboratory science*] (DAVI) ... NI
Not Industrially Funded [*Military*] ... NIF
Not Informed ... NI
Not Inoculated ... NI
Not Interested ... NI
Not Invented Here (NITA) ... NIH
Not Invented Here Syndrome [*Business Management*] ... NIH
Not Isolated ... NI
Not Issued (AAG) ... NI
Not Knocked Out (DAVI) ... XKO
Not Known ... NK
Not Later Than ... NLT
Not Less Than ... NLT
Not Letter Quality (NITA) ... NLQ
Not Listed (AFM) ... NL
Not Located ... NL
Not Machine Pressed ... NMP
Not Made in Canada [*Business term*] ... NMIC
Not Marked [*Business term*] ... N/M
Not Married ... NM
Not Measurable [*or Measured*] ... NM
Not Member of a Branch ... NMB
Not Mentioned [*Medicine*] ... n/m
Not Mission Capable (MCD) ... NMC
Not Mission Capable, Maintenance (NVT) ... NMCM
Not Mission Capable, Supply (MCD) ... NMCS
Not More Than ... NMT
Not Necessarily the News [*Cable television comedy program*] ... NNTN
Not Nested [*Freight*] ... NN
Not Nested or Folded Flat [*Freight*] ... NNFF
Not Normal ... NN
Not North Of ... N/N
Not on Active Duty ... NAD
Not on Active Duty [*Military*] (AD) ... nad
Not on Bonus ... NOB
Not on Drawing List (MCD) ... NODL
Not on Flying Status ... NFS
Not on Planet Earth [*Waste management slang*] ... NOPE
Not on Shelf (ADA) ... NOS
Not One of Us [*Slang*] ... NOOU
Not Operational Ready Materiel [*Military*] (AFIT) ... NORM
Not Operationally Assigned ... NOA
Not Operationally Ready [*Military*] (AFM) ... NOR
Not Operationally Ready, Aircraft Intermediate Maintenance [*Military*] (DNAB) ... NORAIM
Not Operationally Ready for Service [*Military*] (VNW) ... NORS
Not Operationally Ready for Service - Grounded (VNW) ... NORS-G
Not Operationally Ready Maintenance [*Military*] (NG) ... NORM
Not Operationally Ready Maintenance - Flyable [*Military*] (MCD) ... NORM(F)
Not Operationally Ready Maintenance - Grounded [*Military*] (MCD) ... NORM(G)
Not Operationally Ready Other [*Military*] (AFM) ... NORO
Not Operationally Ready Supply [*Military*] ... NORS
Not Operationally Ready Supply Aviation Items Report [*Military*] ... NORSAIR
Not Operationally Ready Supply Flyable [*Military*] (MCD) ... NORSF
Not Operationally Ready Supply Grounded [*Military*] (NG) ... NORSG
Not Operationally Ready Supply Nongrounded [*Military*] (NG) ... NORSN
Not Operationally Ready System [*Military*] ... NORS
Not Or [*Logical operator*] [*Computer science*] ... NO
Not Or [*Logical operator*] [*Computer science*] ... NOR
Not Ordered, This Part of Package (DAVI) ... NORD
Not Otherwise ... N/O
Not Otherwise Authorized ... NOA
Not Otherwise Classified ... NOC
Not Otherwise Coded (GFGA) ... NOC
Not Otherwise Enumerated ... NOE
Not Otherwise Herein Provided ... NOHP
Not Otherwise Identified (NG) ... NOI
Not Otherwise Identified [*or Indicated*] **by Name** [*Military*] (AABC) ... NOIBN
Not Otherwise Indexed ... NOI
Not Otherwise Indexed by Name [*Tariffs*] ... NOIBN
Not Otherwise Provided ... NOP
Not Otherwise Specified (AFM) ... NOS
Not Otherwise Stated ... NOS
Not Our Class, Dear [*Slang*] ... NOCD
Not Our Kind, Dear [*Slang*] ... NOKD
Not Our Publication ... NO
Not Our Publication ... NOP
Not Our Title [*Publishing*] (WDMC) ... NOT
Not Out [*Bookselling*] ... N/O
Not Out of Bed [*Medicine*] (DAVI) ... NOOB
Not Out Yet ... NOY
Not Paged [*Publishing*] ... NPG
Not Paid on Prior Rolls ... NPOPR
Not Passed Urine [*Medicine*] ... NPU
Not Perceptible [*Medicine*] ... NP
Not Performed ... NP
Not Pickled Ordinary [*Metal industry*] ... NPO
Not Planned ... NP
Not Practiced [*Medicine*] ... NP
Not Preferred ... NP
Not Present (DAVI) ... NP
Not Pressed or Glazed [*Paper*] (DGA) ... NP
Not Printed (ILCA) ... NP
Not Provided (KSC) ... N/P
Not Provided ... N/P
Not Provided For (ODBW) ... npf
Not Provided For ... NPF
Not Quite Our Sort (IIA) ... NQOS
Not Quite Us [*Lower in social status*] [*Slang British*] ... NQU
Not RAM [*Reliability, Availability, and Maintainability*] **Oriented** ... NRO
Not Rated ... NR
Not Readable ... NR
Not Ready for Data ... NRFD
Not Ready for Issue ... NRFI
Not Receiving Additional Irrigation [*Agriculture*] ... NRE
Not Recently Used [*Replacement algorithm*] [*Computer science*] (BYTE) ... NRU
Not Recommended for Children (ADA) ... NRC
Not Recorded ... NR
Not Releasable to Contractors (MCD) ... NOCONTRACT
Not Releasable to Foreign Nationals [*Military security classification*] ... NOFORN
Not Releasable to Foreign Nationals ... NORFORM
Not Remarkable [*Medicine*] ... N/R
Not Repairable This Ship [*Navy*] (AFIT) ... NRTS
Not Reparable This Station ... NRTS
Not Reportable ... NOREP
Not Reported ... NR
Not Required ... NR
Not Required, but Desired ... NR/D
Not Required to Take New Physical Provided No Material Change since Recent Retirement Physical [*Military*] ... NOPHYSRET
Not Resolved (MAE) ... NR
Not Responsible For ... N/R
Not Routine Care [*Medicine*] ... NRC
Not Running at Finish [*Automobile racing*] ... NRAF
Not Running at the Finish [*Automobile racing term*] ... NRF
Not Safe in Taxis ... NSIT
Not Seasonally Adjusted [*US Census terminology*] ... NSA
Not Seen ... NS
Not Seen Regularly [*Medicine*] (DAVI) ... NSR
Not Separately Billed ... NSB
Not Separately Priced (NG) ... NSP
Not Series by Title (MCD) ... NSBT
Not Service-Connected [*Medicine*] (MEDA) ... NSC
Not Significant ... NS
Not So Good ... NSG
Not So Hot [*Slang*] ... NSH
Not So Much a Programme, More a Way of Life [*British television program*] ... NSMAPMAWOL
Not Sooner Than ... NST
Not Specifically Provided For ... NSPF
Not Specified ... NS
Not Specified (WDMC) ... ns
Not Specified by Kind (MHDI) ... NSK
Not Sprinklered [*Insurance*] ... NS
Not Stated ... NS
Not Statistically Significant (MAE) ... NSS
Not Stock Listed ... NSL
Not Stocked ... NS
Not Stung ... NS
Not Subject to Call (MHDB) ... NSTC
Not Sufficient (WDMC) ... n/s
Not Sufficient ... NS
Not Sufficient Funds [*Banking*] ... NSF
Not Sufficient Funds [*Banking*] (ODBW) ... nsf
Not Sufficient Quantity [*Clinical chemistry*] ... NSQ
Not Suitable ... NS
Not Suppressed ... NS
Not Switchable (MCD) ... NS
Not Taken Out [*Insurance*] ... NTO
Not Taken Up ... NTU
Not Tender (DAVI) ... NT
Not Tested ... NT
Not the New York Times [*A publication*] ... NTNYT
Not Titled [*Accounting*] ... NT
Not to Be Noted [*Business term*] ... N/N
Not to Be Resuscitated ... NTBR
Not to Delay ... NODEL
Not to Delay Delivery ... NDV
Not to Delay Vessel ... NDV
Not to Descend Below [*Aviation*] (FAAC) ... NDBLO
Not to Exceed (NOAA) ... NOTOX
Not to Exceed [*Aviation*] ... NTE
Not to Interface Base ... NIB
Not to My Knowledge ... NTM
Not to, nor Needed by, All ... NOTAL
Not to Scale [*Drafting*] ... NTS
Not Typical ... NT
Not Under the Act ... NUA
Not Used ... NU
Not Used for Production (AAG) ... NUFP
Not Used on Next Assembly (AAG) ... NUNA
Not Vaccinated [*Medicine*] ... NV
Not Yet Answered ... NYA
Not Yet Diagnosed [*Facetious translation: "Not Yet Dead"*] [*Medicine*] ... NYD
Not Yet in Library of Congress [*Suggested name for the Library of Congress computer system*] ... NYET LC
Not Yet Operating (DA) ... NYO
Not Yet Published ... NYP
Not Yet Reported [*Air Force*] ... NYR
Not Yet Required (MUGU) ... NYR

Not Yet Returned [*Military*] .... NYR
Not Yet Specified .... NYS
Nota Bene [*Note Well*] [*Latin*] .... NB
Nota Bene [*Note Well*] [*Latin*] (WDMC) .... nb
Notable (ABBR) .... NTAB
Notable (ABBR) .... NTB
Notable Asian Americans [*A publication*] .... NAA
Notable Black American Women [*A publication*] .... NBAW
Notable Hispanic American Women [*A publication*] .... NHAW
Notably (ABBR) .... NTABY
Notably (ABBR) .... NTBY
No-Tail Rotor [*Helicopters*] .... NOTAR
NOTAM Office .... NOF
NOTAMS International, Inc. [*ICAO designator*] (FAAC) .... XNT
Notarial (ROG) .... NOTL
Notaries Journal [*A publication*] (DLA) .... Not J
Notary (WDAA) .... NOT
Notary (ROG) .... NOTY
Notary (ABBR) .... NTARY
Notary Public .... NP
Notation (ROG) .... NOT
Notation (ABBR) .... NTATN
Notation of Content [*Aerospace*] .... NOC
Notation of Content .... NOC
Notational (ABBR) .... NTATNL
Notative Speed (WDAA) .... N
Notch Die [*Tool*] (AAG) .... NHDI
Notch Root Contraction (OA) .... NRC
Notch Tensile Strength (OA) .... NTS
Notch-Bend (PDAA) .... NB
Notched .... NCH
Notched, Returned, and Mitred Ends [*Construction*] .... NRME
Notcutt on Factories and Workshops [*2nd ed.*] [*1879*] [*A publication*] (DLA) .... Notc on Fac
Note .... N
Note (WDMC) .... n
Note [*Online database field identifier*] .... NT
Note, Record, Report [*Medical records and nursing*] (DAVI) .... NRR
Notebook (ABBR) .... NTBK
Notebook User Interface [*Penpoint*] [*Computer science*] .... NUI
Noted .... NOT
Noted but Not Corrected (MCD) .... NBNC
Note-Issuance Facility [*Banking*] .... NIF
Notes [*Finance*] .... NN
Notes [*Online database field identifier*] .... NO
Notes [*Finance*] .... NTS
Notes from Hume's Lectures [*A publication*] (DLA) .... NHL
Notes (Music Library Association) [*A publication*] (BRI) .... Notes
Notes of Cases [*England*] [*A publication*] (DLA) .... Notes of Ca
Notes of Cases at Madras (Strange) [*A publication*] (DLA) .... N of Cas
Notes of Cases at Madras (Strange) [*A publication*] (DLA) .... NC
Notes of Cases at Madras (Strange) [*A publication*] (DLA) .... No of Cas Madras
Notes of Cases at Madras (Strange) [*A publication*] (DLA) .... Not Cas
Notes of Cases at Madras (Strange) [*A publication*] (DLA) .... Not Cas Madras
Notes of Cases, English Ecclesiastical and Maritime Courts [*1844-50*] [*A publication*] (DLA) .... Ec & Mar
Notes of Cases, English Ecclesiastical and Maritime Courts [*1841-50*] [*A publication*] (DLA) .... N of Cas
Notes of Cases, English Ecclesiastical and Maritime Courts [*1841-50*] [*A publication*] (DLA) .... NC
Notes of Cases, English Ecclesiastical and Maritime Courts [*1841-50*] [*A publication*] (DLA) .... NC Ecc
Notes of Cases, English Ecclesiastical and Maritime Courts [*1841-50*] [*A publication*] (DLA) .... No Ca Ecc & Mar
Notes of Cases, English Ecclesiastical and Maritime Courts [*1841-50*] [*A publication*] (DLA) .... Not Cas
Notes of Cases, English Ecclesiastical and Maritime Courts [*1841-50*] [*A publication*] (DLA) .... Not Cas Ecc & M
Notes of Cases, English Ecclesiastical and Maritime Courts [*1841-50*] [*A publication*] (DLA) .... Notes of Cas
Notes of Cases, English Ecclesiastical and Maritime Courts [*1841-50*] [*A publication*] (DLA) .... Notes of Cases
Notes of Cases in Smoult's Collection of Orders [*Calcutta, India*] [*A publication*] (DLA) .... Smoult
Notes of Cases, Law Journal [*A publication*] (DLA) .... No Cas LJ
Notes of Decisions [*Martin's North Carolina Reports*] [*A publication*] (DLA) .... Not Dec
Notes of Decisions of Appeal Court of Registration at Inverness [*1835-53*] [*Scotland*] [*A publication*] (DLA) .... Inv Reg Cas
Notes of English Ecclesiastical Cases [*A publication*] (DLA) .... NEC
Notes of Unreported Cases, Supreme Court of Canada (Coutlee) [*A publication*] (DLA) .... Cout SC
Notes on Higher Education [*A publication*] .... Notes Higher Ed
Notes on United States Reports [*A publication*] (DLA) .... Notes on US
Notes Payable .... N/P
Notes Payable [*Finance*] (DFIT) .... N/P
Notes Receivable .... N/R
Not-for-Profit Corp. Law [*New York, NY A publication*] .... N-PCL
Nothin' Worth Askin' [*Rap recording group*] .... NWA
Nothing Abnormal Detected (AD) .... nad
Nothing Abnormal Detected [*or Discovered*] [*Medicine*] .... NAD
Nothing Adverse Known (AD) .... nak
Nothing Adverse Known (ADA) .... NAK
Nothing Before Something [*Library cataloguing*] (DGA) .... NBS
Nothing but Initials [*Initialism is name of commercial word processor firm*] .... NBI
Nothing by Mouth .... NBM
Nothing Doing [*Amateur radio slang*] .... ND
Nothing in Light Disease [*Nephrotic Syndrome*] (DAVI) .... NIL
Nothing in Mind [*Acronym and facetious translation derived from turning President Gerald Ford's anti-inflation WIN buttons upside down*] [*See WIN entry*] .... NIM
Nothing per Mouth [*Medicine*] (DMAA) .... NPM
Nothing Recorded Against [*Security investigation result*] [*British*] .... NRA
Nothing So Called [*Bookselling*] .... NSC
Nothing to Report .... NTR
Nothing Unsatisfactory (MHDB) .... NU
Nothwestern Steel & Wire [*NASDAQ symbol*] (TTSB) .... NWSW
Notice (ROG) .... NOT
Notice .... NTC
Notice Number Tracking (MCD) .... NNT
Notice of Adverse Finding [*Food and Drug Administration*] .... NAF
Notice of Ammunition Reclassification [*Navy*] (NG) .... NAR
Notice of Availability (MCD) .... NOA
Notice of Availability .... NTCAVAL
Notice of Award .... NAWD
Notice of Award (AAGC) .... NAWD
Notice of Cancellation (AAGC) .... NOC
Notice of Cancellation at Anniversary Date [*Insurance*] (DCTA) .... NCAD
Notice of Change (MCD) .... NOC
Notice of Change Inception (MCD) .... NCI
Notice of Change Incorporation (MCD) .... NCI
Notice of Commencement (EPA) .... NOC
Notice of Commencement of Manufacture [*Toxic Substances Control Act*] [*Environmental Protection Agency*] (EPA) .... NCM
Notice of Contents [*Indexing*] .... NOC
Notice of Credit Due .... NCD
Notice of Deficiency (EPA) .... NOD
Notice of Delayed [*or Delinquent*] **Item** .... NODI
Notice of Drawing Change [*Navy*] (DNAB) .... NDC
Notice of Exception (MCD) .... NE
Notice of Exception .... NOE
Notice of Execution .... NOE
Notice of Funding Availability [*Department of Housing and Urban Development*] (GFGA) .... NOFA
Notice of Information [*Computer science*] .... NI
Notice of Initiation of Procurement Action (NRCH) .... NIPA
Notice of Inquiry (IEEE) .... NOI
Notice of Intelligence Potential [*Military*] (AFM) .... NIP
Notice of Intent (MCD) .... NOI
Notice of Intent to Purchase [*DoD*] .... NIP
Notice of Intention .... NOI
Notice of Interim Trail Use [*Interstate Commerce Commission*] .... NITU
Notice of Judgment (Official) [*Legal term*] (DLA) .... NJ
Notice of Nonavailability .... NONA
Notice of Noncompliance (EPA) .... NNC
Notice of Noncompliance (EPA) .... NON
Notice of Obligation [*Military*] (AFM) .... NOO
Notice of Procurement [*Navy*] (NG) .... NOP
Notice of Program Reimbursement (MEDA) .... NPR
Notice of Proposed Amendment (DA) .... NPA
Notice of Proposed Rule Making [*Federal agencies*] .... NOPR
Notice of Proposed Rule Making [*Federal agencies*] (GFGA) .... NPR
Notice of Proposed Rule Making [*Federal agencies*] .... NPRM
Notice of Quality Discrepancy .... NQD
Notice of Rating Required [*Civil Service*] .... NR
Notice of Readiness [*Shipping*] .... N/R
Notice of Readiness [*Shipping*] .... NOR
Notice of Research Project .... NRP
Notice of Revision .... NOR
Notice of Structural or Functional Deficiency .... NSFD
Notice of Unreliability .... NOTUN
Notice of Violation [*Nuclear energy*] (NRCH) .... NOV
Notice of Violation / Compliance Demand (EPA) .... NOV/CD
Notice to Airmen .... NOTAM
Notice to Airmen Address .... NOTAD
Notice to Airmen Office .... NOTOF
Notice to Airmen Summary .... NOTAS
Notice to Law Enforcement Officials .... NOLEO
Notice to Mariner .... NM
Notice to Mariner (NVT) .... NOTMAR
Notice to Mariners (DOMA) .... NOTAM
Notice to Mariners .... NTM
Notice to Proceed (KSC) .... NTP
Noticeable (ABBR) .... NTCB
Noticeably (ABBR) .... NTCBY
Noticed (ABBR) .... NTCD
Notices of Judgment, Federal Insecticide, Fungicide, and Rodenticide Act [*A publication*] (DLA) .... NJIFR
Notices of Judgment, United States Food and Drug Administration [*A publication*] (DLA) .... NJFD
Notices of Noncompliance/Notices of Violation [*Navy*] .... NON/NOV
Notices to Airmen Publication [*A publication*] (FAAC) .... NTAP
Noticias Argentinas SA [*News agency*] [*Argentina*] (EY) .... NA
Noticing (ABBR) .... NTCG
Notification .... NOTIF
Notification (ROG) .... NOTIN
Notification of Change Report (NRCH) .... NCR
Notification of Foreign Travel (AFM) .... NOFT
Notification of Master Tool (NASA) .... NMT
Notified [*Telecommunications*] (TEL) .... NFYD

Notify [Telecommunications] (TEL) .... NFY
Notify (AFM) .... NTFY
Notify of Death (DAVI) .... NOD
Notion .... NOT
Notion (ABBR) .... NOTN
Notion Round Table (EA) .... NRT
Notional Number (NVT) .... NONUM
Notional Number (NVT) .... NOTNO
Notitia Dignitatum [Classical studies] (OCD) .... Not Dign
Notodden [Norway ICAO location identifier] (ICLI) .... ENNO
Notodden [Norway] [Airport symbol] (AD) .... NDE
Not-Or-And [Computer science] .... N-O-A
Notre Cause Commune [Benin] [Political party] (EY) .... NCC
Notre Dame College [Missouri, New Hampshire, Ohio] .... NDC
Notre Dame College, Cleveland, OH [Library symbol Library of Congress]
(LCLS) .... OCIND
Notre Dame College, Manchester, NH [Inactive] [OCLC symbol] (OCLC) .... NDC
Notre Dame College, Manchester, NH [Library symbol Library of Congress]
(LCLS) .... NhMND
Notre Dame College of Staten Island, Staten Island, NY [Library symbol
Library of Congress] (LCLS) .... NSiND
Notre Dame College, Wilcox, Saskatchewan [Library symbol National Library
of Canada] (NLC) .... SWN
Notre Dame College, Wilcox, SK, Canada [Library symbol Library of
Congress] (LCLS) .... CaSWN
Notre Dame du BonConseil (Quebec) (TOCD) .... BC
Notre Dame Estate Planning Institute. Proceedings [A publication]
(DLA) .... Notre Dame Est Plan Inst
Notre Dame Hospital, Medical Library, Montreal, PQ, Canada [Library
symbol Library of Congress] (LCLS) .... CaQMHND
Notre Dame, IN [FM radio station call letters] .... WSND
Notre Dame Institute, Middleburg, VA [Library symbol Library of Congress]
(LCLS) .... ViMiN
Notre Dame Journal of Legislation [A publication] (DLA) .... Notre Dame J Leg
Notre Dame Radiation Laboratory [University of Notre Dame] [Research
center] (RCD) .... NDRL
Notre Dame Seminary, New Orleans, LA [Library symbol Library of
Congress] (LCLS) .... LNND
Notre Dame Sisters (TOCD) .... ND
Notre Dame Translator [Programming language] [1977] [Computer science]
(CSR) .... NDTRAN
Notre Seigneur [Our Lord] [French] .... NS
Notre Seigneur Jesus Christ [Our Lord, Jesus Christ] [French] .... NSJC
Nott and Hopkins' Reports [United States Court of Claims] [A publication]
(DLA) .... N & H
Nott and Hopkins' Reports [United States Court of Claims] [A publication]
(DLA) .... N & Hop
Nott and Hopkins' Reports [United States Court of Claims] [A publication]
(DLA) .... Nott & Hop
Nott and Huntington's Reports [1-7 United States Court of Claims]
[A publication] (DLA) .... N & H
Nott and Huntington's Reports [1-7 United States Court of Claims]
[A publication] (DLA) .... N & Hunt
Nott and Huntington's Reports [1-7 United States Court of Claims]
[A publication] (DLA) .... Nott & Hunt
Nott and McCord's South Carolina Reports [A publication] (DLA) .... N & Mc
Nott and McCord's South Carolina Reports [A publication] (DLA) .... N & McC
Nott and McCord's South Carolina Reports [A publication] (DLA) .... Nott & McC
Nott and M'Cord's South Carolina Reports [A publication]
(DLA) .... Nott & M'C (SC)
Nott on the Mechanics' Lien Law [A publication] (DLA) .... Nott Mech L
Nottawa Township Library, Centerville, MI [Library symbol Library of
Congress] (LCLS) .... MiCe
Nottignham and Nottinghamshire Technical Information Service [British]
(AD) .... NANTIS
Nottingham [British ICAO location identifier] (ICLI) .... EGBN
Nottingham [British ICAO location identifier] (ICLI) .... EGRW
Nottingham [Postcode] (ODBW) .... NG
Nottingham [County in England] .... NOTTM
Nottingham, MD [Location identifier FAA] (FAAL) .... OTT
Nottinghamshire [County in England] .... NOTTS
Nottinghamshire [County in England] (ODBW) .... Notts
Nottoway County Library, Nottoway, VA [Library symbol Library of
Congress] (LCLS) .... ViNott
Notus Public Library, Notus, ID [Library symbol] [Library of Congress]
(LCLS) .... IdNo
Notwithstanding .... NOTWG
Notwithstanding .... NOTWSTG
Nouadhibou [Mauritania] [ICAO location identifier] (ICLI) .... GQPP
Nouadhibou [Mauritania] [Airport symbol] (OAG) .... NDB
Nouadhibou [Mauritania] [Airport symbol] (AD) .... PTE
Nouakchott [Mauritania] [ICAO location identifier] (ICLI) .... GQNN
Nouakchott [Mauritania] [ICAO location identifier] (ICLI) .... GQNV
Nouakchott [Mauritania] [Airport symbol] (OAG) .... NKC
N'Oubliez Pas Vos Decorations Maconniques [Do Not Forget Your Masonic
Regalia] [Freemasonry] [French] .... NoPVDM
Noumbi [Congo] [ICAO location identifier] (ICLI) .... FCPN
Noumea [New Caledonia] [Airport symbol] (OAG) .... NOU
Noumea [New Caledonia] [Seismograph station code, US Geological Survey]
(SEIS) .... NOU
Noumea [New Caledonia] [ICAO location identifier] (ICLI) .... NWBB
Noumea [New Caledonia] [ICAO location identifier] (ICLI) .... NWWN
Noumea/La Tontouta [New Caledonia] [ICAO location identifier] (ICLI) .... NWCC
Noumea/La Tontouta [New Caledonia] [ICAO location identifier] (ICLI) .... NWWW
Noumea/Magenta [New Caledonia] [ICAO location identifier] (ICLI) .... NWWM

Noumea [New Caledonia] Magenta Airport [Airport symbol] (OAG) .... GEA
Noun .... N
Noun (WDMC) .... n
Noun Modifier [Linguistics] .... NM
Noun Phrase [Linguistics] .... NP
Noun, Plural [Grammar] (CDAI) .... npl
Noun Substantive [Grammar] (ROG) .... NS
Nouna [Burkina Faso] [ICAO location identifier] (ICLI) .... DHON
Nouns .... NN
Noun-Verb-Noun [Education of the hearing-impaired] .... NVN
Nourish (ABBR) .... NOUR
Nourish (ABBR) .... NRSH
Nourished (ABBR) .... NOURD
Nourished (ABBR) .... NRSHD
Nourishing (ABBR) .... NOURG
Nourishing (ABBR) .... NRSHG
Nourishing Stout [Brewing] (ROG) .... NS
Nourishment (ABBR) .... NOURT
Nourishment (ABBR) .... NRSHNT
Nourishment [Dietetics] (DAVI) .... nx
Nouveau Franc [New Franc] [Monetary unit Introduced in 1960] [France] .... NF
Nouveau Parti Democratique [New Democratic Party] [Canada Political
party] (EAIO) .... NPD
Nouveau Quartier Latin [Paris bookstore] .... NQL
Nouvel Ordre Social [New Social Order] [Switzerland] (PD) .... NOS
Nouvelle Action Francaise [New French Action] [Political party] (PPE) .... NAF
Nouvelle Front NAZI [New NAZI Front] [French] (PD) .... NFN
Nouvelle Revue de Droit Francais [Paris] [A publication] (DLA) .... Nouv Rev
Nouvelles (NITA) .... NOU
Nouvelles Equipes Internationales [Later, European Christian Democratic
Union] .... NEI
Nouvelles Messageries de la Presse Parisienne [Paris press distribution
agency] .... NMPP
Nova, an Alberta Corp., Calgary, AB, Canada [Library symbol] [Library of
Congress] (LCLS) .... CaACNA
Nova, An Alberta Corp., Calgary, Alberta [Library symbol National Library of
Canada] (NLC) .... ACNA
Nova, an Alberta Corp., Edmonton, Alberta [Library symbol National Library
of Canada] (BIB) .... AENAC
Nova Beaucage Mines Ltd. [Toronto Stock Exchange symbol] .... NBE
NOVA Corp. [NYSE symbol] (TTSB) .... NIS
Nova Corp. [Associated Press] (SAG) .... Nova
NOVA Corp.(Cda) [NYSE symbol] (TTSB) .... NVA
Nova Corp. (Georgia) [NYSE symbol] (SAG) .... NIS
Nova Corp. of Alberta [Later, Nova Corp.] [NYSE symbol Toronto Stock
Exchange symbol] (SPSG) .... NVA
Nova Freixo [Mozambique] [Airport symbol] (AD) .... FXO
Nova/Husky Research Corp. Ltd. [UTLAS symbol] .... NHR
Nova/Husky Research Corp. Ltd., Calgary, Alberta [Library symbol National
Library of Canada] (NLC) .... ACNH
Nova Lisboa [Angola] [Airport symbol] (AD) .... NOV
Nova Marketing Ltd. [Vancouver Stock Exchange symbol] .... NVM
Nova Omega Ventura Apollo [General Motors automobiles] .... NOVA
Nova Scotia [MARC geographic area code Library of Congress] (LCCP) ...... n-cn-ns
Nova Scotia [Canadian province] [Postal code] .... NS
Nova Scotia [MARC country of publication code Library of Congress] (LCCP) .... nsc
Nova Scotia Agricultural College .... NSAC
Nova Scotia Agricultural College Library [UTLAS symbol] .... NAG
Nova Scotia Agricultural College, Truro, Nova Scotia [Library symbol
National Library of Canada] (NLC) .... NSTA
Nova Scotia Agricultural College, Truro, NS, Canada [Library symbol Library
of Congress] (LCLS) .... CaNSTA
Nova Scotia Barristers Society, Halifax, Nova Scotia [Library symbol
National Library of Canada] (NLC) .... NSHBS
Nova Scotia Barristers Society, Halifax, NS, Canada [Library symbol Library
of Congress] (LCLS) .... CaNSHBS
Nova Scotia College of Art .... NSCA
Nova Scotia College of Art and Design, Halifax, Nova Scotia [Library symbol
National Library of Canada] (NLC) .... NSHCA
Nova Scotia College of Art and Design Library [UTLAS symbol] .... NCD
Nova Scotia College of Art, Halifax, NS, Canada [Library symbol Library of
Congress] (LCLS) .... CaNSHCA
Nova Scotia Commission on Drug Dependency, Halifax, Nova Scotia
[Library symbol National Library of Canada] (NLC) .... NSHCDD
Nova Scotia Commission on Drug Dependency, Halifax, NS, Canada
[Library symbol Library of Congress] (LCLS) .... CaNSHCDD
Nova Scotia Communications and Information Centre, Halifax, Nova Scotia
[Library symbol National Library of Canada] (NLC) .... NSHCIC
Nova Scotia Communications and Information Centre, Halifax, NS, Canada
[Library symbol Library of Congress] (LCLS) .... CaNSHCIC
Nova Scotia Decisions [A publication] (DLA) .... N Sc Dec
Nova Scotia Decisions [A publication] (DLA) .... Nov Sc Dec
Nova Scotia Decisions [A publication] (DLA) .... NS Dec
Nova Scotia Decisions, by Geldert and Oxley [A publication] (DLA) .... Geld & O
Nova Scotia Decisions, by Geldert and Oxley [A publication] (DLA) .... Geld & Ox
Nova Scotia Department of Advanced Education and Job Training, Halifax,
Nova S cotia [Library symbol National Library of Canada] (NLC) .... NSHVTT
Nova Scotia Department of Community Services, Halifax, Nova Scotia
[Library symbol National Library of Canada] (NLC) .... NSHSS
Nova Scotia Department of Consumer Affairs, Halifax, Nova Scotia [Library
symbol National Library of Canada] (NLC) .... NSHDCA
Nova Scotia Department of Consumer Affairs, Halifax, NS, Canada [Library
symbol Library of Congress] (LCLS) .... CaNSHDCA
Nova Scotia Department of Development, Halifax, NS, Canada [Library
symbol Library of Congress] (LCLS) .... CaNSHDD

Nova Scotia Department of Education, Adult Education Division, Halifax, NS, Canada [*Library symbol Library of Congress*] (LCLS) .... CaNSHAE
Nova Scotia Department of Fisheries, Halifax, Nova Scotia [*Library symbol National Library of Canada*] (NLC) .... NSHDF
Nova Scotia Department of Fisheries, Halifax, NS, Canada [*Library symbol Library of Congress*] (LCLS) .... CaNSHDF
Nova Scotia Department of Health, Halifax, Nova Scotia [*Library symbol National Library of Canada*] (NLC) .... NSHH
Nova Scotia Department of Health, Halifax, NS, Canada [*Library symbol Library of Congress*] (LCLS) .... CaNSHH
Nova Scotia Department of Highways, Halifax, NS, Canada [*Library symbol Library of Congress*] (LCLS) .... CaNSHDH
Nova Scotia Department of Industry, Trade, and Technology, Halifax, Nova Scotia [*Library symbol National Library of Canada*] (NLC) .... NSHDD
Nova Scotia Department of Labour and Manpower, Halifax, Nova Scotia [*Library symbol National Library of Canada*] (NLC) .... NSHDOL
Nova Scotia Department of Labour, Halifax, NS, Canada [*Library symbol Library of Congress*] (LCLS) .... CaNSHDOL
Nova Scotia Department of Lands and Forests [*Canada*] [*FAA designator*] (FAAC) .... PTR
Nova Scotia Department of Mines, Halifax, Nova Scotia [*Library symbol National Library of Canada*] (NLC) .... NSHDOM
Nova Scotia Department of Mines, Halifax, NS, Canada [*Library symbol Library of Congress*] (LCLS) .... CaNSHDOM
Nova Scotia Department of Municipal Affairs, Halifax, Nova Scotia [*Library symbol National Library of Canada*] (NLC) .... NSHMA
Nova Scotia Department of Municipal Affairs, Halifax, NS, Canada [*Library symbol Library of Congress*] (LCLS) .... CaNSHMA
Nova Scotia Department of Recreation, Halifax, NS, Canada [*Library symbol Library of Congress*] (LCLS) .... CaNSHDR
Nova Scotia Department of Social Services, Halifax, NS, Canada [*Library symbol Library of Congress*] (LCLS) .... CaNSHSS
Nova Scotia Department of the Attorney-General, Halifax, Nova Scotia [*Library symbol National Library of Canada*] (NLC) .... NSHDAG
Nova Scotia Department of the Attorney-General, Halifax, NS, Canada [*Library symbol Library of Congress*] (LCLS) .... CaNSHDAG
Nova Scotia Department of the Environment, Halifax, Nova Scotia [*Library symbol National Library of Canada*] (NLC) .... NSHDE
Nova Scotia Department of the Environment, Halifax, NS, Canada [*Library symbol Library of Congress*] (LCLS) .... CaNSHDE
Nova Scotia Department of Tourism, Halifax, NS, Canada [*Library symbol Library of Congress*] (LCLS) .... CaNSHDT
Nova Scotia Department of Transportation, Halifax, Nova Scotia [*Library symbol National Library of Canada*] (NLC) .... NSHDH
Nova Scotia Department of Vocational and Technical Training, Halifax, NS, Canada [*Library symbol*] [*Library of Congress*] (LCLS) .... CaNSHVTT
Nova Scotia Hospital, Dartmouth, Nova Scotia [*Library symbol National Library of Canada*] (NLC) .... NSDNSH
Nova Scotia Hospital, Dartmouth, NS, Canada [*Library symbol Library of Congress*] (LCLS) .... CaNSDNSH
Nova Scotia Human Rights Commission, Halifax, Nova Scotia [*Library symbol National Library of Canada*] (NLC) .... NSHHR
Nova Scotia Human Rights Commission, Halifax, NS, Canada [*Library symbol Library of Congress*] (LCLS) .... CaNSHHR
Nova Scotia Institute of Technology, Halifax, Nova Scotia [*Library symbol National Library of Canada*] (NLC) .... NSHTI
Nova Scotia Institute of Technology, Halifax, NS, Canada [*Library symbol Library of Congress*] (LCLS) .... CaNSHTI
Nova Scotia Land Survey Institute, Lawrencetown, Nova Scotia [*Library symbol National Library of Canada*] (NLC) .... NSLAL
Nova Scotia Law Reports [*A publication*] (DLA) .... LRNS
Nova Scotia Law Reports [*A publication*] (DLA) .... Nov Sc LR
Nova Scotia Law Reports [*A publication*] (DLA) .... NSLR
Nova Scotia Legal Aid, Halifax, Nova Scotia [*Library symbol National Library of Canada*] (BIB) .... NSHLA
Nova Scotia Museum, Halifax, Nova Scotia [*Library symbol National Library of Canada*] (NLC) .... NSHMS
Nova Scotia Museum of Science, Halifax, NS, Canada [*Library symbol Library of Congress*] (LCLS) .... CaNSHMS
Nova Scotia Nautical Institute, Halifax, Nova Scotia [*Library symbol National Library of Canada*] (NLC) .... NSHNI
Nova Scotia Newspaper Project, Halifax [*Library symbol National Library of Canada*] (BIB) .... NSHNP
Nova Scotia Normal College .... NSNC
Nova Scotia Power Corp., Halifax, NS, Canada [*Library symbol Library of Congress*] (LCLS) .... CaNSHPC
Nova Scotia Provicial Library, Public Library Services, Halifax, NS, Canada [*Library symbol*] [*Library of Congress*] (LCLS) .... CaNSHPLP
Nova Scotia Provincial Library [*UTLAS symbol*] .... NSR
Nova Scotia Provincial Library, Nova Scotia Union Catalogue, Halifax, NS, Canada [*Library symbol Library of Congress*] (LCLS) .... CaNSHPL
Nova Scotia Provincial Library, Reference Services, Halifax, NS, Canada [*Library symbol Library of Congress*] (LCLS) .... CaNSHPLX
Nova Scotia Provincial Library, Teachers' Library, Halifax, NS, Canada [*Library symbol Library of Congress*] (LCLS) .... CaNSHE
Nova Scotia Public Archives, Halifax, Nova Scotia [*Library symbol National Library of Canada*] (NLC) .... NSHP
Nova Scotia Public Archives, Halifax, NS, Canada [*Library symbol Library of Congress*] (LCLS) .... CaNSHP
Nova Scotia Regiment [*Canada*] (DMA) .... NSR
Nova Scotia Regional Libraries, Halifax, Nova Scotia [*Library symbol National Library of Canada*] (NLC) .... NSHRL
Nova Scotia Regional Libraries, Halifax, NS, Canada [*Library symbol Library of Congress*] (LCLS) .... CaNSHRL
Nova Scotia Rehabilitation Centre, Halifax, Nova Scotia [*Library symbol National Library of Canada*] (NLC) .... NSHRC
Nova Scotia Rehabilitation Centre, Halifax, NS, Canada [*Library symbol Library of Congress*] (LCLS) .... CaNSHRC
Nova Scotia Reports, by Geldert and Oxley [*A publication*] (DLA) .... NSRG & O
Nova Scotia Reports, by Geldert and Russell [*A publication*] (DLA) .... NSRG & R
Nova Scotia Reports (James) [*Canada*] [*A publication*] (DLA) .... NSR (James)
Nova Scotia Reports (James) [*A publication*] (DLA) .... NSRJ
Nova Scotia Research Foundation Corp. [*Crown Corp.*] [*Canada*] (IRC) .... NSRFC
Nova Scotia Research Foundation, Dartmouth, Nova Scotia [*Library symbol National Library of Canada*] (NLC) .... NSHR
Nova Scotia Research Foundation, Halifax, NS, Canada [*Library symbol Library of Congress*] (LCLS) .... CaNSHR
Nova Scotia Research Foundation, Photogrammetry Division, Halifax, NS, Canada [*Library symbol Library of Congress*] (LCLS) .... CaNSHRP
Nova Scotia Revised Statutes [*Canada*] [*A publication*] (DLA) .... NS Rev Stat
Nova Scotia Sanatorium, Kentville, NS, Canada [*Library symbol Library of Congress*] (LCLS) .... CaNSKS
Nova Scotia Savings & Loans Co. [*Toronto Stock Exchange symbol*] .... NSV
Nova Scotia Society of Artists [*1922-72*] [*Canada*] (NGC) .... NSSA
Nova Scotia Statutes [*Canada*] [*A publication*] (DLA) .... NS Stat
Nova Scotia Teachers College [*Canada*] .... NSTC
Nova Scotia Teachers' College, Truro, Nova Scotia [*Library symbol National Library of Canada*] (NLC) .... NSTT
Nova Scotia Teachers' College, Truro, NS, Canada [*Library symbol Library of Congress*] (LCLS) .... CaNSTT
Nova Scotia Teachers Union, Halifax, Nova Scotia [*Library symbol National Library of Canada*] (NLC) .... NSHTU
Nova Scotia Teachers Union, Halifax, NS, Canada [*Library symbol Library of Congress*] (LCLS) .... CaNSHTU
Nova Scotia Technical College .... NSTC
Nova Scotia Technical College, Halifax, NS, Canada [*Library symbol Library of Congress*] (LCLS) .... CaNSHT
[*The*] **Nova Scotia Technology Network** [*Canada*] [*Computer science*] (TNIG) .... NSTN
Nova Scotia Union Catalogue, Nova Scotia Provincial Library, Halifax, Nova Scotia [*Library symbol National Library of Canada*] (NLC) .... NSHPL
Nova University (GAGS) .... Nova U
Nova University, Fort Lauderdale, FL [*Library symbol Library of Congress*] (LCLS) .... FFIN
Nova University, Law Library, Fort Lauderdale, FL [*Library symbol Library of Congress*] (LCLS) .... FFIN-L
Nova University, Law Library, Fort Lauderdale, FL [*Library symbol*] [*Library of Congress*] (LCLS) .... FFIN-L
Nova University, Physical Oceanographic Laboratory Library, Dania, FL [*Library symbol Library of Congress*] (LCLS) .... FFIN-O
NovaCare [*NYSE symbol*] (SPSG) .... NOV
NovaCare [*Associated Press*] (SAG) .... NovaCre
Nova-Cogesco Resources, Inc. [*Toronto Stock Exchange symbol*] .... NCG
Novacor Chemicals Ltd., Calgary, AB, Canada [*Library symbol*] [*Library of Congress*] (LCLS) .... CaACNC
Novacor Chemicals Ltd., Calgary, Alberta [*Library symbol National Library of Canada*] (NLC) .... ACNC
Novadigm, Inc. [*Associated Press*] (SAG) .... Novadig
Novadigm, Inc. [*NASDAQ symbol*] (SAG) .... NVDM
Novae Comoediae Fragmenta in Papyris Reperta Exceptis Menandreis [*A publication*] (OCD) .... Nov Com Fragm
Novae Narrationes [*New Counts*] [*1516*] [*A publication*] (DLA) .... No N
Novagold Resources, Inc. [*Toronto Stock Exchange symbol*] .... NRI
Novair-Aviacao Geral SA [*Portugal ICAO designator*] (FAAC) .... NOP
Noval Air Test Center (IAA) .... NATC
Novametrics Medical Systems [*NASDAQ symbol*] (SAG) .... NMTX
Novametrics Medical Systems [*Associated Press*] (SAG) .... Novmtx
Novametrics Medical Systems [*Associated Press*] (SAG) .... Nvmt
Novametrix Med Sys [*NASDAQ symbol*] (TTSB) .... NMTX
Novametrix Med Sys Wrrt'B' [*NASDAQ symbol*] (TTSB) .... NMTXZ
Novametrix Med Sys Wrt'A' [*NASDAQ symbol*] (TTSB) .... NMTXW
Novametrix Medical Systems, Inc. [*NASDAQ symbol*] (NQ) .... NMTX
Novametrix Medical Systems, Inc. [*Associated Press*] (SAG) .... Novmtx
Novametrix Medical Systems, Inc. [*Associated Press*] (SAG) .... Nvmt
Novamin, Inc. [*Toronto Stock Exchange symbol*] .... NOV
Novantrone, Oncovin, Vinblastine, Prednisone [*Antineoplastic drug*] (CDI) .... NOVP
Novara [*Sicily*] [*Seismograph station code, US Geological Survey*] (SEIS) .... NOV
Novatek International, Inc. [*Associated Press*] (SAG) .... Novatk
Novatek International, Inc. [*NASDAQ symbol*] (SAG) .... NVTK
NovAtel Communications Ltd. [*UTLAS symbol*] .... NTL
Novatel Communications Ltd., Technical Library, Calgary, AB, Canada [*Library symbol*] [*Library of Congress*] (LCLS) .... CaACNOC
Novation [*Legal term*] (DLA) .... NOV
Novavax, Inc. [*Associated Press*] (SAG) .... Novavx
Novavax, Inc. [*AMEX symbol*] (SAG) .... NOX
Novavax Inc. [*AMEX symbol*] (TTSB) .... NOX
Novel (ROG) .... NOV
Novel Architectures Computing Committee [*British*] .... NACC
Novel Plasminogen Activator [*Anticlotting agent*] .... NPA
Novelist (ABBR) .... NOV
Novelist (ABBR) .... NOVST
Novell Application Launcher [*Computer science*] .... NAL
Novell Application Launcher [*Computer science*] .... NAL
Novell Asynchronous Services Interface .... NASI
Novell Directory Service [*Computer Networking*] (PCM) .... NDS
Novell Distributed Print Services [*Computer science*] .... NDPS
Novell Distributed Print Services [*Computer science*] .... NDPS
Novell Embedded Systems Technology [*Novell, Inc.*] [*Computer science*] .... NEST

Novell, Inc. [*Associated Press*] (SAG) .... Novell
Novell, Inc. [*NASDAQ symbol*] (NQ) .... NOVL
Novell Inc. [*NASDAQ symbol*] (TTSB) .... NOVL
Novell Virtual Terminal [*Novell, Inc.*] [*Computer science*] (PCM) .... NVT
Novellae [*Novels*] [*New Constitutions of Justinian*] [*A publication*] (DLA) .... N
Novellae [*Classical studies*] (OCD) .... Nov
Novellus Systems [*NASDAQ symbol*] (TTSB) .... NVLS
Novellus Systems, Inc. [*Associated Press*] (SAG) .... Novlus
Novellus Systems, Inc. [*NASDAQ symbol*] (CTT) .... NVLS
Novelty [*Insulation*] .... N
Novelty .... NOVLT
Novelty (ABBR) .... NOVT
November [*Phonetic alphabet*] [*International*] (DSUE) .... N
November (ADA) .... NO
November (AAG) .... NOV
November (ODBW) .... Nov
November (CDAI) .... Nvb
November and May [*Denotes semiannual payments of interest or dividends in these months*] [*Business term*] .... N & M
November, February, May, and August [*Denotes quarterly payments of interest or dividends in these months*] [*Business term*] .... NFMA
Noven Pharmaceuticals [*NASDAQ symbol*] (TTSB) .... NOVN
Noven Pharmaceuticals, Inc. [*Associated Press*] (SAG) .... Noven
Noven Pharmaceuticals, Inc. [*NASDAQ symbol*] (NQ) .... NOVN
Noverco, Inc. [*Toronto Stock Exchange symbol*] .... NVC
Novi et Veteris Testamenti (DSA) .... No et Vet Test
Novi Ligure [*Italy ICAO location identifier*] (ICLI) .... LIMR
Novi, MI [*FM radio station call letters*] .... WOVI
Novice (ABBR) .... NOVC
Novice Agility .... NA
Novice Amateur Operator's Certificate of Proficiency [*Radio*] .... NAOCP
Novice Slope [*Skiing*] .... N
Novice, Society of St. Francis .... N/SSF
Novitiate (ROG) .... NOV
Novitiate of Los Gatos, Los Gatos, CA [*Library symbol Library of Congress*] (LCLS) .... CLgN
Novitiate of Saint Andrew-On-Hudson, Poughkeepsie, NY [*Library symbol Library of Congress*] (LCLS) .... NPSA
Novitron International, Inc. [*NASDAQ symbol*] (SAG) .... NOVI
Novitron International, Inc. [*Associated Press*] (SAG) .... Novitrn
Novo Cruzado [*Brazilian currency*] .... NC
Novo Nordisk A/S ADR [*NYSE symbol*] (SPSG) .... NVO
Novo Nordisk AS [*Associated Press*] (SAG) .... NovoNdk
Novo Redondo [*Angola*] [*Airport symbol*] (AD) .... NDD
Novo-Kazalinsk [*Former USSR Geomagnetic observatory code*] .... NKK
Novokuznetsk [*Former USSR ICAO location identifier*] (ICLI) .... UNCE
Novolazarevskaya [*Antarctica*] [*Seismograph station code, US Geological Survey*] (SEIS) .... NVL
Novosibirsk [*Former USSR Seismograph station code, US Geological Survey*] (SEIS) .... NVS
Novosibirsk [*Former USSR Airport symbol*] (OAG) .... OVB
Novosibirsk/Tolmachevo [*Former USSR ICAO location identifier*] (ICLI) .... UNNN
Novoste Corp [*NASDAQ symbol*] (TTSB) .... NOVT
Novoste Corp. [*Associated Press*] (SAG) .... Novoste
Novoste Corp. [*NASDAQ symbol*] (SAG) .... NOVT
Novosti Tehnikskoi Literatury (NITA) .... NTL
Novotech Services Ltd., Sidney, British Columbia [*Library symbol National Library of Canada*] (NLC) .... BSN
Novum [*New*] [*Latin*] (MAE) .... nov
Novum Nomen [*New Name*] [*Latin*] (BABM) .... NOV N
Novum Nomen [*New Name*] [*Latin*] (DAVI) .... nov n
Novum Species [*New species*] [*Latin*] (DAVI) .... nov sp
Novum Species [*New Species*] [*Latin*] (BABM) .... NOV SP
Novum Testamentum (DSA) .... No Test
Novum Testamentum [*New Testament*] [*of the Bible*] .... NT
Novy, MacNeal, and Nicolle's Medium [*Medicine*] (MAE) .... NNN
Novy Vasyugan [*Former USSR ICAO location identifier*] (ICLI) .... UNCW
Novye Inostrannyye Knigi [*New Foreign Books*] [*A publication*] .... NIK
Novye Torit [*Newly Flattened*] [*KGB term for newly recruited agent abroad*] .... NOVATOR
Now .... NW
Now Available (NOAA) .... NWAVL
Now I Have You, Son of a Bitch [*Term coined by Kenneth Blanchard, author of "The One-Minute Manager"*] .... NIHYSOB
Now Known As (DLA) .... NKA
NOW [*National Organization for Women*] **Legal Defense and Education Fund** (EA) .... NOW LDEF
Nowata [*Papua New Guinea*] [*Airport symbol*] (OAG) .... NWT
Nowata, OK [*FM radio station call letters*] (RBYB) .... KQSY
Nowata, OK [*FM radio station call letters*] .... KRIG
Nowra [*Australia ICAO location identifier*] (ICLI) .... ASNW
Nowsco Well Service Ltd. [*Toronto Stock Exchange symbol*] .... NWS
Nowsco Well Service Ltd., Calgary, AB, Canada [*Library symbol Library of Congress*] (LCLS) .... CaACNWS
Nowsco Well Service Ltd., Calgary, Alberta [*Library symbol National Library of Canada*] (NLC) .... ACNWS
Nowsco Well Services [*NASDAQ symbol*] (SAG) .... NWSLF
Nowsco Well Services Ltd. [*Associated Press*] (SAG) .... Nowsc
Nowsco WellService [*NASDAQ symbol*] (TTSB) .... NWSLF
Noxe Resources Corp. [*Vancouver Stock Exchange symbol*] .... NXP
Noxious (ABBR) .... NOX
Noxious Stimuli .... NS
Noxiously (ABBR) .... NOXY
Noxon Public School, Noxon, MT [*Library symbol*] [*Library of Congress*] (LCLS) .... MtNxPS
Noxso Corp. [*NASDAQ symbol*] (NQ) .... NOXO
Noxso Corp. [*Associated Press*] (SAG) .... Noxso
Noxubee County Library, Macon, MS [*Library symbol Library of Congress*] (LCLS) .... MsMac
Noyack, NY [*FM radio station call letters*] .... WSUF
Noyaux Armes pour l'Autonomie Populaire [*Armed Cells for Popular Autonomy*] [*France*] (PD) .... NAPAP
Noyes Data Corp. .... NDC
Noyes on Charitable Uses [*A publication*] (DLA) .... Noy Ch U
Noy's English King's Bench Reports [*1559-1649*] [*A publication*] (DLA) .... Noy
Noy's English King's Bench Reports [*1559-1649*] [*A publication*] (DLA) .... Noy (Eng)
Noy's Maxims [*A publication*] (DLA) .... Noy Max
Nozzle (AAG) .... NOZ
Nozzle .... NOZ
Nozzle Actuating System [*Aerospace*] (MCD) .... NAS
Nozzle Actuator Auxiliary Power Supply (SAA) .... NAAPS
Nozzle Area Control .... NAC
Nozzle Assembly .... NA
Nozzle Control Unit [*NASA*] .... NCU
Nozzle Flow Sensor (MCD) .... NFS
Nozzle Gap Control [*Aerospace*] (AAG) .... NGC
Nozzle Guide Vanes [*Aviation*] (AIA) .... NGV
Nozzle Hinge Moment .... NHM
Nozzle Jetevator Assembly .... NJA
Nozzle Materials Application and Design (MCD) .... NOMAD
Nozzle Pressure Ratio [*Aviation*] .... NPR
Nozzle Vanes (AAG) .... NV
Nozzleless Center-Perforated Grain (MCD) .... NCPG
Nozzleless Performance Program Module (MCD) .... NPP
N-Paraffins, iso-Paraffins, Naphthenes and Aromatics [*Gasoline analysis*] .... NPiPNA
N-Para-Isopropylacetanilide-Iminodiacetic Acid [*Scan*] [*Radiology*] (DAVI) .... PIPIDA
NPC International, Inc. [*Associated Press*] (SAG) .... NPC
NPC International, Inc. [*Associated Press*] (SAG) .... NPC Intl
NPC International, Inc. [*NASDAQ symbol*] (SAG) .... NPCI
NPC Intl. [*NASDAQ symbol*] (TTSB) .... NPCI
N-Pentylpalmitamide [*Organic chemistry*] .... NPP
N-Phenylglycine [*Organic chemistry*] .... NPG
N-Phenylglycine Glycidyl Methacrylate [*Organic chemistry*] .... NPG-GMA
N-Phenylselenenylphthalimide [*Organic chemistry*] .... NPSP
N-(Phosphoacetyl)-L-aspartate [*Biochemistry*] .... PALA
NPIC [*National Photographic Interpretation Center*] **Data System** (MCD) .... NDS
N-Player Prisoneris Dilemma .... NPD
N-Propylamine [*Organic chemistry*] .... NPA
NPS Pharmaceutical, Inc. [*Associated Press*] (SAG) .... NPS Phm
NPS Pharmaceutical, Inc. [*NASDAQ symbol*] (SAG) .... NPSP
NPS Pharmaceuticals [*NASDAQ symbol*] (TTSB) .... NPSP
NRA [*National Restaurant Association*] **Management Information Services** [*Defunct*] (EA) .... MIS
NRA [*National Restaurant Association*] **Marketing Executives Group** [*Chicago, IL*] (EA) .... MEG
NRA [*National Restaurant Association*] **Multi-Unit Architects, Engineers, and Construction Officers** (EA) .... MAECO
NRC Master File (NITA) .... NRCMF
NRD Mining Ltd. [*Vancouver Stock Exchange symbol*] .... NMN
NRDS [*Nevada*] [*Seismograph station code, US Geological Survey Closed*] (SEIS) .... ADM
NRG Resources Ltd. [*Vancouver Stock Exchange symbol*] .... NGN
NRL [*Naval Research Laboratory*] **Satellite Image Processing System** (USDC) .... NSIPS
NRL [*Naval Research Laboratory*] **Satellite Image Processing System** [*Marine science*] (OSRA) .... NSIPS
NRP, Inc [*NASDAQ symbol*] (SAG) .... ATCT
NRP, Inc. [*Associated Press*] (SAG) .... NRP
NRZ Indicator (NITA) .... NRZI
NS & L Bancorp, Inc. [*Associated Press*] (SAG) .... NS & L
NS & L Bancorp, Inc. [*NASDAQ symbol*] (SAG) .... NSLB
NS Bancorp, Inc. [*Associated Press*] (SAG) .... NS Bcp
NS Bancorp, Inc. [*NASDAQ symbol*] (SAG) .... NSBI
NS Group [*NYSE symbol*] (SPSG) .... NSS
NS Group, Inc. [*Associated Press*] (SAG) .... NS Grp
NSA International [*NASDAQ symbol*] (TTSB) .... NSAI
NSA International, Inc. [*Associated Press*] (SAG) .... NSA Int
NSA International, Inc. [*NASDAQ symbol*] (SAG) .... NSAI
NSAC, the National Society for Children and Adults with Autism (EA) .... NSAC
NS&L Bancorp [*NASDAQ symbol*] (TTSB) .... NSLB
Nsangi [*Zaire*] [*ICAO location identifier*] (ICLI) .... FZAF
Nsanje [*Malawi*] [*ICAO location identifier*] (ICLI) .... FWSJ
NSAPAC Operations Group .... NOG
NSC Corp. [*Associated Press*] (SAG) .... NSC
NSC Corp. [*NASDAQ symbol*] (SAG) .... NSCC
NSD Bancorp [*Associated Press*] (SAG) .... NSD Bc
NSD Bancorp [*NASDAQ symbol*] (SAG) .... NSDB
NSDAP Auslands- und Aufbauorganisation (EA) .... NSDAP-AO
NSF [*National Science*] **Network Service Center** [*Internet*] (TNIG) .... NNSC
N'shei Agudath Israel (BJA) .... NAI
NSP Status Word [*NASA*] (GFGA) .... NSW
NSP [*National Aeronautical and Space Administration Support Plan*] **Status Word** .... NSW
NSR Resources, Inc. [*Toronto Stock Exchange symbol*] .... NSR
NT [*New Technology*] **File System** [*Microsoft Corp.*] .... NIFS
NT File System [*Computer science*] .... NTFS
Ntchisi [*Malawi*] [*ICAO location identifier*] (ICLI) .... FWCS

NTID [*National Technical Institute for the Deaf*] **Center on Employment** (PAZ) .... NCE
NTL Institute (EA) .... NTLI
NTN Canada, Inc. [*Associated Press*] (SAG) .... NTN
NTN Canada, Inc. [*Associated Press*] (SAG) .... NTN Cda
NTN Canada, Inc. [*NASDAQ symbol*] (SAG) .... NTNC
NTN Cda [*NASDAQ symbol*] (TTSB) .... NTNC
NTN Communications [*AMEX symbol*] (TTSB) .... NTN
NTN Communications, Inc. [*AMEX symbol*] (SPSG) .... NTN
NTN Communications, Inc. [*Associated Press*] (SAG) .... NTNCom
N-Tolylglycine [*Organic chemistry*] .... NTG
N-Tone International Ltd. [*Vancouver Stock Exchange symbol*] .... NTD
NTV Oil Services Industries, Inc. [*Vancouver Stock Exchange symbol*] .... NTV
Nu [*Thirteenth letter of the Greek alphabet*] (DAVI) .... N
Nu Horizons Electronics [*NASDAQ symbol*] (TTSB) .... NUHC
Nu Pacific Resources Ltd. [*Vancouver Stock Exchange symbol*] .... NEP
Nuance (ABBR) .... NNC
Nubes [*Clouds*] [*of Aristophanes*] [*Classical studies*] (OCD) .... Nub
Nubian [*MARC language code Library of Congress*] (LCCP) .... nub
Nucal Resources Ltd. [*Vancouver Stock Exchange symbol*] .... NCR
Nucha [*Nape of the Neck*] [*Latin*] (ROG) .... NUCH
Nuchal Rigidity [*Medicine*] .... NR
Nucla, CO [*Location identifier FAA*] (FAAL) .... HPL
Nucla Public Library, Nucla, CO [*Library symbol Library of Congress*] (LCLS) .... CoNu
Nuclear .... N
Nuclear (AAG) .... NCR
Nuclear (AFM) .... NUC
Nuclear .... NUC
Nuclear .... NUCL
Nuclear .... NUCLE
Nuclear .... NUKE
Nuclear Accident and Incident Control [*Army*] (AABC) .... NAIC
Nuclear Accident and Incident Control Center [*Army*] (AABC) .... NAICC
Nuclear Accident and Incident Control Officer [*Army*] (AABC) .... NAICO
Nuclear Accident and Incident Control Plan [*Army*] .... NAICP
Nuclear Accident Dosimetry .... NAD
Nuclear Accident Response Capability Listing (MCD) .... NARCL
Nuclear Accident Support Team [*Canada*] .... NAST
Nuclear Acoustic Resonance .... NAR
Nuclear Activation Analysis (PDAA) .... NAA
Nuclear Aerospace Research Facility (IEEE) .... NARF
Nuclear Aerospace Research Institute [*Air Force*] .... NARI
Nuclear Age (AD) .... N-age
Nuclear Age Peace Foundation (EA) .... NAPF
Nuclear Age Resource Center (EA) .... NARC
Nuclear Agency [*Army*] .... NUA
Nuclear Air Burst .... NAB
Nuclear Air Burst Effect .... NABE
Nuclear Aircraft Research Facility (AD) .... NARF
Nuclear Alternative System Assessment Program .... NASAP
Nuclear Amplification by Stimulated Isomer Radiation (SAA) .... NASIR
Nuclear and Chemical Agency [*Army*] .... NCA
Nuclear and Plasma Science Symposium (MCD) .... NPSS
Nuclear and Plasma Sciences (MCD) .... NPS
Nuclear and Space Talks (DOMA) .... NST
Nuclear Androgen Receptor [*Endocrinology*] .... NAR
Nuclear Armament (AD) .... N-arm
Nuclear Arms Alert Network [*Defunct*] (EA) .... NAAN
Nuclear Assembly Building .... NAB
Nuclear Assessment Routine (MCD) .... NAR
Nuclear Attack (AD) .... N-attack
Nuclear Attack Hazards in the Continental United States .... NAHICUS
Nuclear Attack Preparedness Evaluation .... NAPE
Nuclear Auditing and Testing Co. .... NATCO
Nuclear Authentication System .... NUCAS
Nuclear Auxiliary Power .... NAP
Nuclear Auxiliary Power Unit .... NAPU
Nuclear Auxiliary Power Unit System .... NAPUS
Nuclear Ballistic Missile .... NBM
Nuclear Beta Gauge .... NBG
Nuclear Binding Energy .... NBE
Nuclear, Biological, and Chemical [*Warfare*] .... NBC
Nuclear, Biological, and Chemical Contamination (DOMA) .... NBCC
Nuclear, Biological, and Chemical Defense (NATG) .... NBCD
Nuclear, Biological, and Chemical Defense Control Element [*Military*] ..... NBCDCE
Nuclear, Biological, and Chemical Defense Exercise [*NATO*] (NATG) .... NBCDX
Nuclear, Biological, and Chemical Element .... NBCE
Nuclear, Biological, and Chemical Warfare Operations [*Military*] .... NUBICWOPS
Nuclear, Biological, and Chemical Warning and Reporting System ...... NBCWRS
Nuclear, Biological, Chemical, Conventional [*Warfare*] .... NBCC
Nuclear Blank (NRCH) .... NB
Nuclear Boiler (NRCH) .... NB
Nuclear Boiler Rated (NRCH) .... NBR
Nuclear Bomb Line (CINC) .... NBL
Nuclear Bunkered Instrumentation Center (MCD) .... NUBIC
Nuclear Burst Detection Systems (MCD) .... NBDS
Nuclear Burst Indicator (NATG) .... NBI
Nuclear Cannon Projectile [*Army*] .... NUCAP
Nuclear Capability .... NC
Nuclear Capability [*Military*] .... NUCAP
Nuclear Capability Evaluation .... NCE
Nuclear Capability Exercise [*Army*] (AABC) .... NCE
Nuclear Capability Inspection (CINC) .... NCI
Nuclear Capability Report (CINC) .... NUCAP

Nuclear Capable Forces (MCD) .... NCF
Nuclear Certification Test Team (MCD) .... NCTT
Nuclear Certified Equipment List (DNAB) .... NCEL
Nuclear Chemical Accident Incident Control (MCD) .... NCAIC
Nuclear/Chemical Environment [*Battlefield condition*] (RDA) .... NCE
Nuclear Chemistry Users Committee .... NCUC
Nuclear Commission Date (DNAB) .... NCD
Nuclear Complex .... NUPLEX
Nuclear Components Spare (IAA) .... NCS
Nuclear Congress .... NC
Nuclear Contingency Plan (MCD) .... NCP
Nuclear Contingency Planning System (MCD) .... NCPS
Nuclear Contour Index [*Cytology*] .... NCI
Nuclear Control Institute (EA) .... NCI
Nuclear Cratering Group [*Later, EERA*] [*Army*] .... NCG
Nuclear Criteria Group Secretariat [*Air Force Weapons Laboratory*] [*Kirtland Air Force Base, NM*] .... NCGS
Nuclear Criticality Information System [*Lawrence Livermore National Laboratory*] [*Information service or system*] (IID) .... NCIS
Nuclear Criticality Safety (NRCH) .... NCS
Nuclear Cross Section Advisory Group (NRCH) .... NCSAG
Nuclear Cross Sections Advisory Committee .... NCSAC
Nuclear Cruise Missile Submarine (MCD) .... SSCN
Nuclear Cytoplasmic Ratio [*Cytology*] .... NCR
Nuclear Damage Report (AABC) .... NUCREP
Nuclear Data Center (IAA) .... NUDAC
Nuclear Data Committee (NRCH) .... NDC
Nuclear Data Information Center [*ORNL*] .... NDIC
Nuclear Data Link System [*Nuclear Regulatory Commission*] .... NDL
Nuclear Data Sheets [*National Academy of Sciences*] .... NDS
Nuclear Data Tape Program .... NDTP
Nuclear Data Unit [*International Atomic Energy Agency*] (DIT) .... NDU
Nuclear Defense (AABC) .... NUCDEF
Nuclear Defense Affairs Committee [*NATO*] .... NDAC
Nuclear Defense Laboratory [*Army*] .... NDL
Nuclear Definition and Reporting System (AAG) .... NDRS
Nuclear Delivery Vehicle .... NDV
Nuclear Depth Bomb (NVT) .... NDB
Nuclear Depth/Strike Bomb (DOMA) .... ND/SB
Nuclear Desalination Information Center .... NDIC
Nuclear Desalination Plant .... NDP
Nuclear Design and Construction [*British*] .... NDC
Nuclear Design Calculations [*Program*] .... NDC
Nuclear Detection (MCD) .... NUDET
Nuclear Detection [*Radiation monitoring device*] (WDAA) .... NU-TEC
Nuclear Detection and Reporting System .... NUDETS
Nuclear Detection Device (MCD) .... NDD
Nuclear Detection Satellite .... NDS
Nuclear Detection System (MCD) .... NDS
Nuclear Detection Test (IAA) .... NDT
Nuclear Detonating Data Points (MCD) .... NUDAP
Nuclear Detonation Detection and Reporting System (AABC) ...... NUCDETS
Nuclear Detonation Detection and Reporting System .... NUDETS
Nuclear Detonation Detection System (DOMA) .... NDDS
Nuclear Detonation Detection System .... NDS
Nuclear Detonation Evaluation Technique (MCD) .... NUDET
Nuclear Detonation Summary (NVT) .... NUSUM
Nuclear Development Corp. of America .... NDCA
Nuclear Device (AAG) .... ND
Nuclear Device Association (AAG) .... NDA
Nuclear Directed-Energy Weapon .... NDEW
Nuclear Disarmament Party [*Australia Political party*] .... NDP
Nuclear Doctrine Organization and Equipment (MCD) .... NUDORE
Nuclear Double Resonance [*Analytical chemistry*] .... NDR
Nuclear Duty Position Roster (MCD) .... NDPR
Nuclear Effects from Analysis of Residual Signatures .... NEFARS
Nuclear Effects Handbook .... NEH
Nuclear Effects on Joint Force Communications (MCD) .... NUCOM
Nuclear Effects Rocket Operations .... NERO
Nuclear Effects Simulation Study .... NESS
Nuclear Effects Support Team .... NEST
Nuclear Effects Test .... NET
Nuclear Electric Propulsion [*System*] .... NEP
Nuclear Electric Resonance (PDAA) .... NER
Nuclear Electromagnetic Propagation .... NEMP
Nuclear Electromagnetic Pulse (AABC) .... NEMP
Nuclear Electronics Effects Program .... NEEP
Nuclear Emergency Recovery Vehicle (NUCP) .... NERV
Nuclear Emergency Search Team [*Department of Energy*] .... NEST
Nuclear Emergency Team Operations (AFM) .... NETOPS
Nuclear Emergency Teams [*DASA*] .... NET
Nuclear Emulsion Recovery Vehicle (MUGU) .... NERV
Nuclear Energy Agency [*See also AEN*] [*Organization for Economic Cooperation and Development*] (EAIO) .... NEA
Nuclear Energy Agency Committee on Reactor Physics [*OECD*] (EY) .... NEACRP
Nuclear Energy Agency Nuclear Data Committee [*OECD*] (EY) .... NEANDC
Nuclear Energy Board [*Republic of Ireland*] (NUCP) .... NEB
Nuclear Energy Center (NRCH) .... NEC
Nuclear Energy Center Site Survey (NRCH) .... NECSS
Nuclear Energy Commission (USDC) .... NEC
Nuclear Energy Commission [*Marine science*] (OSRA) .... NEC
Nuclear Energy Division [*General Electric Co.*] .... NED
Nuclear Energy for Propulsion of Aircraft .... NEPA
Nuclear Energy Information Service [*An association*] (EA) .... NEIS
Nuclear Energy Laboratory [*Research center*] (RCD) .... NEL

Nuclear Energy Liability Insurance Association [*Later, ANI*] (EA) .... NELIA
Nuclear Energy Liability Property Insurance Association [*Later, ANI*] ...... NELPIA
Nuclear Energy Property Insurance Association [*Later, ANI*] (EA) .... NEPIA
Nuclear Energy Research Center [*Also, CEEN, SCK*] [*Belgium*] .... NERC
Nuclear Energy Research Vehicle .... NERV
Nuclear Energy Team .... NET
Nuclear Energy Test Facility (AFM) .... NETF
Nuclear Energy Trade Associations' Conference .... NETAC
Nuclear Energy Waste Space Transportation and Removal (GFGA) .... NEWSAR
Nuclear Energy Women [*Defunct*] (EA) .... NEW
Nuclear Energy Writers Association [*Defunct*] .... NEWA
Nuclear Engine for Rocket Vehicle Application [*NASA*] .... NERVA
Nuclear Engine Reactor Critical Assembly (SAA) .... NRX-CX
Nuclear Engine Reactor Experiment (NRCH) .... NRX
Nuclear Engineer .... NE
Nuclear Engineer .... Nuc E
Nuclear Engineer Trainee .... NET
Nuclear Engineering and Scientific Congress (MCD) .... NESC
Nuclear Engineering Co., Inc. .... NECO
Nuclear Engineering Directorate [*Army*] .... NED
Nuclear Engineering Laboratory [*University of Utah*] [*Research center*]
  (RCD) .... NEL
Nuclear Engineering Teaching Laboratory [*University of Texas at Austin*]
  [*Research center*] (RCD) .... NETL
Nuclear Engineering Test Facility (AAG) .... NETF
Nuclear Engineering Test Reactor [*Air Force*] .... NETR
Nuclear Envelope [*Cytology*] .... NE
Nuclear Envelope Breakdown [*Also, NEBD*] [*Cytology*] .... NEB
Nuclear Envelope Breakdown [*Also, NEB*] [*Cytology*] .... NEBD
Nuclear Exchange Model .... NEMO
Nuclear Exercise [*Also, NUKEX*] (NVT) .... NUCEX
Nuclear Exercise [*Also, NUCEX*] (NVT) .... NUKEX
Nuclear Explosion Effects Center .... NEEC
Nuclear Explosion Pulse Reaction (AAG) .... NEPR
Nuclear Explosion Warning and Radiological Data System .... NEWRADS
Nuclear Explosive .... NE
Nuclear Explosive Simulation Technique .... NEST
Nuclear Export Signal [*Biochemistry*] .... NES
Nuclear Export Signal [*Immunochemistry*] .... NES
Nuclear Extended Range Aircraft [*Proposed*] [*Air Force*] .... NUERA
Nuclear Extract [*Cytology*] .... NE
Nuclear Factor [*Cytology*] .... NF
Nuclear Factor Interleukin [*Genetics*] .... NFIL
Nuclear Factor of Activated T-Cells [*Genetics*] .... NFAT
Nuclear Fire Planning and Assessment Model (MCD) .... NUFAM
Nuclear Fission Reactor .... NFR
Nuclear Flight Propulsion Module (KSC) .... NFPM
Nuclear Flight Propulsion System (AAG) .... NFPS
Nuclear Flight Test Base .... NFTB
Nuclear Force Posture .... NUCFO
Nuclear Forces Communications Satellite .... NFCS
Nuclear Free America (EA) .... NFA
Nuclear Free Australia Party [*Political party*] .... NFAP
Nuclear Free Zone (AFM) .... NFZ
Nuclear Free Zone Registry [*Defunct*] (EA) .... NFZR
Nuclear Freeze Foundation [*Defunct*] (EA) .... NFF
Nuclear Fuel Assurance Act .... NFAA
Nuclear Fuel Cost (PDAA) .... NUFUCO
Nuclear Fuel Cycle (NUCP) .... NFC
Nuclear Fuel Cycle Information System [*Database*] [*International Atomic
  Energy Agency*] [*United Nations*] (DUND) .... NFCIS
Nuclear Fuel Recovery and Receiving Center (NRCH) .... NFRRC
Nuclear Fuel Services Fuel Fabrication Plant .... NFS
Nuclear Fuel Services Plant (NRCH) .... NFS
Nuclear Fuels Technology Information Center (DIT) .... NUFTIC
Nuclear Galaxy (BARN) .... NG
Nuclear Generating Station (BARN) .... NGS
Nuclear Hardening and Survivability .... NH & S
Nuclear Hardening Interceptor Structure .... NHIS
Nuclear Heart Pacer .... NHP
Nuclear Helicopter Air Density Indicating [*System*] [*Army*] .... NUHADI
Nuclear Helicopter Lift Indicator (KSC) .... NUHELI
Nuclear Hyperfine Magnetic [*Rare-earth alloy*] .... NHM
Nuclear Hyperfine Quadrupolar [*Rare-earth alloy*] .... NHQ
Nuclear Immediate Photo Interpretation Report (MCD) .... NIPIR
Nuclear Incident Control Plan .... NICP
Nuclear Industries Exhibition .... NUCLEX
Nuclear Industry Radioactive Waste Executive [*British*] (ECON) .... NIREX
Nuclear Information and Records Management Association (EA) .... NIRMA
Nuclear Information and Resource Service (EA) .... NIRS
Nuclear Information File (AFM) .... NIF
Nuclear Installation Services Co. (NRCH) .... NISCO
Nuclear Installations Inspectorate [*British*] .... NII
Nuclear Instrument Landing System .... NILS
Nuclear Instrumentation (NRCH) .... NI
Nuclear Instrumentation Modular Bin .... NIMBIN
Nuclear Instrumentation Modular System (MCD) .... NIMS
Nuclear Instrumentation Module .... NIM
Nuclear Instrumentation System (NRCH) .... NIS
Nuclear Instruments and Detectors [*IEEE*] (MCD) .... NID
Nuclear Insurance Association of Canada .... NIAC
Nuclear Insurance Rating Bureau .... NIRB
Nuclear Integrated Data System .... NIDS
Nuclear Intelligence (MCD) .... NUCINT
Nuclear Irradiation Test .... NIT

Nuclear Island (NRCH) .... NI
Nuclear Isotope Monopropellant Hydrazine Engine .... NIMPHE
Nuclear Issues Information Service (IID) .... NIIS
Nuclear Kill .... NK
Nuclear Killing Zone [*Military British*] .... NKZ
Nuclear Law Bulletin [*A publication*] (ILCA) .... Nuc L Bull
Nuclear Level Mixing [*Physics*] .... NLM
Nuclear Light Bulb .... NLB
Nuclear Liquid Air Cycle Engine .... NULAC
Nuclear Liquid Air Cycle Engine .... NULACE
Nuclear Loadout Exercise [*Military*] (NVT) .... NUCLEX
Nuclear Localization Signal [*Biochemistry*] .... NLS
Nuclear Location Sequence [*Cytology*] .... NLS
Nuclear Magnetic .... NM
Nuclear Magnetic Double Resonance .... NMDR
Nuclear Magnetic Imaging .... NMI
Nuclear Magnetic Logging (IAA) .... NML
Nuclear Magnetic Relaxation .... NMR
Nuclear Magnetic Relaxation Dispension [*Physics*] .... NMRD
Nuclear Magnetic Resonance [*Also, NUMAR*] [*Atomic physics*] .... NMR
Nuclear Magnetic Resonance [*Also, NMR*] .... NUMAR
Nuclear Magnetic Resonance Imaging .... NMRI
Nuclear Magnetic Resonance Literature System [*Chemical Information
  Systems, Inc.*] [*Information service or system*] .... NMRLIT
Nuclear Magnetic Resonance Program .... NMRP
Nuclear Magnetism Log (PDAA) .... NML
Nuclear Magnetron (MSA) .... NM
Nuclear Management and Resources Council (EA) .... NUMARC
Nuclear Material Control Center (NUCP) .... NMEC
Nuclear Material Report and Analysis System [*Energy Research and
  Development Administration*] .... NMRAS
Nuclear Materials Accounting and Control .... NMAC
Nuclear Materials Accounting Control Team [*British*] (NUCP) .... NMACT
Nuclear Materials & Equipment Corp. .... NUMEC
Nuclear Materials Control System (IEEE) .... NMCS
Nuclear Materials Information System .... NMIS
Nuclear Materials Inventory System (NRCH) .... NMIS
Nuclear Materials Management .... NMM
Nuclear Materials Management and Safeguards System (NRCH) .... NMMSS
Nuclear Materials Safeguards .... NMS
Nuclear Materials Security (NRCH) .... NUMS
Nuclear Materials Transfer Document .... NMTD
Nuclear Materials Transfer Report .... NMTR
Nuclear Measurement (IAA) .... NM
Nuclear Medicine .... NM
Nuclear Medicine Technology .... NMT
Nuclear Medicine Technology Certification Board (EA) .... NMTCB
Nuclear Metal Conference .... NMC
Nuclear Metals [*NASDAQ symbol*] (TTSB) .... NUCM
Nuclear Metals, Inc. .... NMI
Nuclear Metals, Inc. [*NASDAQ symbol*] (NQ) .... NUCM
Nuclear Metals, Inc. [*Associated Press*] (SAG) .... NucMet
Nuclear Missile Safety Office [*or Officer*] (AFM) .... NMSO
Nuclear Munitions (RDA) .... NUCMUN
Nuclear Network (EA) .... NN
Nuclear Nitrogen Fixation Plant .... NNFP
Nuclear Nonfirst Use .... NNFU
Nuclear Nonproliferation Act [*1975*] .... NNPA
Nuclear Non-Proliferation Treaty [*United Nations*] (ECON) .... NPT
Nuclear Operational Readiness Exercise (NVT) .... NOREX
Nuclear Operational Readiness Maneuver (NVT) .... NORM
Nuclear Operational Status Report (NATG) .... NUCSTAT
Nuclear Operational Systems Test .... NOST
Nuclear Operations Analysis Center [*Department of Energy*] [*Information
  service or system*] (IID) .... NOAC
Nuclear Operations and Maintenance Information Service (IID) .... NOMIS
Nuclear Operations Center (MCD) .... NOC
Nuclear Operations Concept II [*Military*] .... NOC II
Nuclear Operations Monitoring System (MCD) .... NOMS
Nuclear Operations Plan (MCD) .... NOP
Nuclear Orbit Transfer Stage (PDAA) .... NOTS
Nuclear Orbit-to-Orbit Shuttle [*NASA*] .... NOOS
Nuclear Order of Battle (AFM) .... NOB
Nuclear Ordnance Air Force Materiel [*Military*] (AFIT) .... NOAM
Nuclear Ordnance Catalog Office [*DoD*] .... NOCO
Nuclear Ordnance Cataloging Officer [*Military*] .... NOCO
Nuclear Ordnance Commission [*Military*] (AFIT) .... NOC
Nuclear Ordnance Commodity Manager (AFM) .... NOCM
Nuclear Ordnance Group [*Air Force*] (MCD) .... NOG
Nuclear Ordnance Platoon [*Marine Corps*] (NVT) .... NOP
Nuclear Ordnance Readiness Manpower .... NORM
Nuclear Ordnance Readiness Test (NVT) .... NORT
Nuclear Ordnance Record Card (NVT) .... NORC
Nuclear Ordnance War Reserve [*Military*] (AFIT) .... NOWR
Nuclear Overhauser Effect .... NOE
Nuclear Overhauser Effect Spectroscopy .... NOESY
Nuclear Overhauser Enhancement Difference Spectrometry .... NOEDS
Nuclear Paramagnetic Resonance (MCD) .... NPR
Nuclear Particle Detection System (KSC) .... NPDS
Nuclear Photographic Emulsion .... NPE
Nuclear Physics (WDAA) .... NUC PHY
Nuclear Planning and Execution (Service) (DOMA) .... NPE(S)
Nuclear Planning and Execution System (MCD) .... NPE
Nuclear Planning Group [*NATO*] .... NPG
Nuclear Plant Analyzer (NRCH) .... NPA

Nuclear Plant Databank (NRCH) ... NPDB
Nuclear Plant Island Structure (NRCH) ... NPIS
Nuclear Plant Operator (NRCH) ... NPO
Nuclear Plant Reliability Data ... NPRD
Nuclear Plant Reliability Data System (NRCH) ... NPRDS
Nuclear Polyhedrosis Virus ... NPV
Nuclear Pore Complex [*Protein*] ... NPC
Nuclear Posture Review [*DoD*] ... NPR
Nuclear Power [*or Powered*] (DNAB) ... NUPWR
Nuclear Power Advisory Board (PDAA) ... NPAB
Nuclear Power Co. (NRCH) ... NPC
Nuclear Power Corp. of India Ltd. ... NPCIL
Nuclear Power Demonstration [*of a reactor*] ... NPD
Nuclear Power Division (SAA) ... NPD
Nuclear Power Engineering (IAA) ... NPE
Nuclear Power Engineering Committee [*Nuclear Regulatory Commission*] (NRCH) ... NPEC
Nuclear Power Engineering Test Center (NRCH) ... NUPEC
Nuclear Power Facility (NRCH) ... NPF
Nuclear Power Field Office (IEEE) ... NPFO
Nuclear Power for Marine Purposes Committee (MCD) ... NUMARCOM
Nuclear Power Generating Station (NRCH) ... NPGS
Nuclear Power Group [*British Defunct*] (NUCP) ... NPG
[*The*] **Nuclear Power Group** [*British*] ... TNPG
Nuclear Power Information Group [*British*] (NUCP) ... NPIG
Nuclear Power Plant (IEEE) ... NPP
Nuclear Power Plant Co. Ltd. ... NPPC
Nuclear Power Plant Training Simulator (PDAA) ... NPPTS
Nuclear Power Propulsion Evaluation (NG) ... NPPE
Nuclear Power Range Channel (IEEE) ... NPRC
Nuclear Power Reactor ... NPR
Nuclear Power Source ... NPS
Nuclear Power System ... NPS
Nuclear Power Task Force ... NPTF
Nuclear Power Task Group [*Navy*] (MCD) ... NPTG
Nuclear Power Unit (DNAB) ... NUPWRU
Nuclear Powered (NVT) ... NUCPWR
Nuclear Powered Guided Missile Destroyer [*Navy symbol*] ... DDGN
Nuclear Products Department, Westinghouse Canada, Inc., Port Hope, Ontario [*Library symbol National Library of Canada*] (NLC) ... OPHWA
Nuclear Proof Test Facility [*Proposed, but never built*] (NRCH) ... NPTF
Nuclear Propelled [*When following vessel classification, as CAG(N)*] [*Navy*] ... N
Nuclear Propulsion Mobile Training Team [*Military*] (CAAL) ... NPMTT
Nuclear Propulsion Office ... NPO
Nuclear Propulsion Officer Candidate [*Navy*] ... NUPOC
Nuclear Propulsion Officer Candidate - Submarine (DNAB) ... NUPOC-S
Nuclear Public Relations Contact Group ... NPRCG
Nuclear Pulse Rocket [*NASA*] ... NPR
Nuclear Quadrupole Coupling Constant [*Physics*] ... NQCC
Nuclear Quadrupole Interaction [*Physics*] ... NQL
Nuclear Quadrupole Resonance [*Frequencies*] ... NQR
Nuclear Quadrupole Resonance Response ... NQRR
Nuclear Quality Assurance Agency ... NQAA
Nuclear Quality Control (DNAB) ... NQC
Nuclear Quality Engineering (DNAB) ... NQE
Nuclear Radiation ... NR
Nuclear Radiation Absorber ... NRA
Nuclear Radiation Center [*Washington State University*] [*Research center*] (RCD) ... NRC
Nuclear Radiation Detector ... NRD
Nuclear Radiation Effect ... NRE
Nuclear Radiation Effects Handbook (SAA) ... NREH
Nuclear Radiation Shield ... NRS
Nuclear Radiation-Resistant Oils (NRCH) ... NRRO
Nuclear Radiology [*Medical specialty*] (DHSM) ... NR
Nuclear RADWASTE (IEEE) ... NRW
Nuclear RADWASTE [*Radioactive Waste*] **Operator** (IAA) ... NRWO
Nuclear Reaction Analysis ... NRA
Nuclear Reaction Spectrometry (BARN) ... NRS
Nuclear Reactor ... NR
Nuclear Reactor, Experimental ... NRX
Nuclear Reactor Laboratory [*Massachusetts Institute of Technology*] [*Research center*] (RCD) ... NRL
Nuclear Reactor Operator, Basic Badge [*Military decoration*] (GFGA) ... NRBBAS
Nuclear Reactor Operator, Basic Badge [*Military decoration*] (AABC) ... NucReaOpBasBad
Nuclear Reactor Operator, First-Class Badge [*Military decoration*] (GFGA) ... NRB1CL
Nuclear Reactor Operator, First-Class Badge [*Military decoration*] (AABC) ... NucReaOpFCBad
Nuclear Reactor Operator, Second-Class Badge [*Military decoration*] (GFGA) ... NRB2CL
Nuclear Reactor Operator, Second-Class Badge [*Military decoration*] (AABC) ... NucReaOpSCBad
Nuclear Reactor Operator, Shift Supervisor Badge [*Military decoration*] (GFGA) ... NRBSUPV
Nuclear Reactor Operator, Shift Supervisor Badge [*Military decoration*] (AABC) ... NucReaOpSftSupvBad
Nuclear Reactor Systems Safety Group [*Air Force*] ... NRSSG
Nuclear Reactor Systems Safety Group [*Air Force*] ... NRSSGP
Nuclear Reactors Branch [*AEC*] ... NRB
Nuclear Receptor Element [*Biochemistry*] ... NRE
Nuclear Records Management Association (EA) ... NRMA
Nuclear Recycling Consultants (EA) ... NRC
Nuclear Red Fast [*A dye*] ... NF
Nuclear Reform Project (EA) ... NRP
Nuclear Regulation Reports (Commerce Clearing House) [*A publication*] (DLA) ... Nuclear Reg Rep (CCH)
Nuclear Regulatory Agency ... NRA
Nuclear Regulatory Commission [*Washington, DC*] ... NRC
Nuclear Regulatory Commission ... NUREG
Nuclear Regulatory Commission Acquisition Regulation (AAGC) ... NRCAR
Nuclear Regulatory Commission Issuances [*A publication*] (DLA) ... NRCI
Nuclear Regulatory Commission Procurement Regulation (AAGC) ... NRCPR
Nuclear Release Authentication System [*Seventh Army*] (AABC) ... NRAS
Nuclear Requirements [*Military*] ... NUREQ
Nuclear Requirements Determination [*Military*] ... NURED
Nuclear Requirements Extrapolation [*Model*] (MCD) ... NUREX
Nuclear Requirements Methodology [*Military*] ... NUREM
Nuclear Research Council ... NRC
Nuclear Research Information Center [*American Nuclear Center*] [*Information service or system*] (IID) ... NRIC
Nuclear Research Submarine (MCD) ... NR
Nuclear Resonance Fluorescence (IAA) ... NRF
Nuclear Ribonucleoprotein [*Medicine*] (DMAA) ... NRNP
Nuclear Risk Reduction Center (DOMA) ... NRRC
Nuclear River Service Water (IEEE) ... NRSW
Nuclear Rocket Detection System [*NASA*] ... NRDS
Nuclear Rocket Development Station ... NRDS
Nuclear Rocket Engine (AAG) ... NRE
Nuclear Rocket Project (SAA) ... NUROC
Nuclear Rocket Reactor ... NRR
Nuclear Rocket Shuttle (KSC) ... NRS
Nuclear Safety Advisory Committee (NUCP) ... NSAC
Nuclear Safety Analysis Center [*Electric Power Research Institute*] (NRCH) ... NSAC
Nuclear Safety Analysis Document (KSC) ... NSAD
Nuclear Safety and Licensing Commission ... NSLC
Nuclear Safety Cross-Check Analysis (DOMA) ... NSCCA
Nuclear Safety Facility ... NSF
Nuclear Safety Information Center ... NSIC
Nuclear Safety Inspection (NVT) ... NSI
Nuclear Safety Institute ... NSI
Nuclear Safety Line ... NSL
Nuclear Safety Office [*or Officer*] [*Air Force*] (AFM) ... NSO
Nuclear Safety Operational Analysis (NRCH) ... NSOA
Nuclear Safety Pilot Plant [*ORNL*] ... NSPP
Nuclear Safety Protection System (NRCH) ... NSPS
Nuclear Safety Research Association [*See also GAKK*] [*Japan*] (NRCH) ... NSRA
Nuclear Safety Research Reactors (NRCH) ... NSRR
Nuclear Safety Review Board (NRCH) ... NSRB
Nuclear Safety Standard (PDAA) ... NUSS
Nuclear Safety Working Group (CINC) ... NSWG
Nuclear Science ... NS
Nuclear Science and Engineering [*A publication*] ... NSE
Nuclear Science and Technology Facility [*State University of New York at Buffalo*] [*Research center*] (RCD) ... NSTF
Nuclear Science Association (NADA) ... NSA
Nuclear Science Center [*Louisiana State University*] [*Research center*] (RCD) ... NSC
Nuclear Science Center Reactor ... NSCR
Nuclear Science Foundation (IAA) ... NSF
Nuclear Science Symposium (PDAA) ... NSS
Nuclear Sciences Advisory Committee [*Department of Energy/National Science Foundation*] ... NUSAC
Nuclear Sclerosis [*Ophthalmology*] ... NS
Nuclear Sealed Authentication System (AABC) ... NSAS
Nuclear Sediment Density Meter (PDAA) ... NSDM
Nuclear Service Control Date (DNAB) ... NSCD
Nuclear Service Raw Water (IEEE) ... NSRW
Nuclear Service Raw Water Pump [*Electronics*] (IAA) ... NSRWP
Nuclear Service Vessel ... NSV
Nuclear Service Water System (NRCH) ... NSWS
Nuclear Services and Training Laboratory [*Ohio State University*] [*Research center*] (RCD) ... NSTL
Nuclear Services Closed Cooling (IEEE) ... NSCC
Nuclear Services International ... NSI
Nuclear Ship ... NS
Nuclear Shuttle (NASA) ... NS
Nuclear Spin Relaxation [*Physics*] ... NSR
Nuclear Statistical Equilibrium [*Physics*] ... NSE
Nuclear Status Indicator (DNAB) ... NSI
Nuclear Steam Supply Shutoff System (NRCH) ... NSSSS
Nuclear Steam Supply System [*Vendor*] (NRCH) ... NSSS
Nuclear Steam System (NRCH) ... NSS
Nuclear Stock Association [*British*] (DBA) ... NSA
Nuclear Strike Alternate Control Group (NATG) ... NSACG
Nuclear Strike Information Center ... NSIC
Nuclear Strike Plan [*Army*] (AABC) ... NSP
Nuclear Strike Planning System (MCD) ... NSPS
Nuclear Strike Target Graphic (MCD) ... NSTG
Nuclear Structure Facility [*British*] ... NSF
Nuclear Structure References [*Brookhaven National Laboratory*] [*Information service or system*] ... NSR
Nuclear Structure Research Laboratory (NRCH) ... NSRL
Nuclear Submarine ... NS
Nuclear Submarine Control Trainer (PDAA) ... NUSCOT
Nuclear Submarine Maneuvering Room Training Simulator (PDAA) ... NSMRTS
Nuclear Superheat Critical Experiment (SAA) ... NUSU-CX
Nuclear Superheating (SAA) ... NUSU

Nuclear Suppliers Association (EA) .... NSA
Nuclear Suppliers' Group [*Australia*] (ECON) .... NSG
Nuclear Support Equipment .... NSE
Nuclear Support Services, Inc. [*NASDAQ symbol*] (NQ) .... NSSI
Nuclear Surety Inspection .... NSI
Nuclear Surface Warfare Officer [*Navy*] (DOMA) .... NSWO
Nuclear Surface-to-Air Missile (NVT) .... NUCSAM
Nuclear Survivability and Hardening .... NV & H
Nuclear Sweep and RADAR (IAA) .... NUSAR
Nuclear Systems .... NS
Nuclear Systems Analysis .... NSA
Nuclear Systems Engineering .... NSE
Nuclear Systems Material Handbook (NRCH) .... NSMH
Nuclear Systems Project Office [*Air Research and Development Command*] [*Air Force*] (AAG) .... NSPO
Nuclear Tactical Exercise .... NUTEX
Nuclear Targeting Policy Review (MCD) .... NTPR
Nuclear Technical Advisory Board [*American National Standards Institute*] .... NTAB
Nuclear Technology Laboratory [*Stanford University*] (MCD) .... NTL
Nuclear Test Aircraft .... NTA
Nuclear Test Ban .... NTB
Nuclear Test Directorate [*Air Force*] .... NTD
Nuclear Test Facility .... NTF
Nuclear Test Monitoring Working Group [*Military*] .... NTMWG
Nuclear Test Plant .... NTP
Nuclear Test Reactor [*Also known as GETR*] .... NTR
Nuclear Test Site (MCD) .... NTS
Nuclear Test Stage (AAG) .... NTS
Nuclear Testing (WDAA) .... N-TEST
Nuclear Thermionics Laboratory .... NTL
Nuclear Training Proficiency Inspection [*Navy*] (DOMA) .... NTPI
Nuclear Training Unit (MCD) .... NTU
Nuclear Transfer .... NT
Nuclear Transport Ltd. [*British*] (IRUK) .... NTL
Nuclear Transportation Project (EA) .... NTP
Nuclear Underwater Sound Source (NG) .... NUSOS
Nuclear Uranium Materials and Equipment Corp. (GAAI) .... NUMEC
Nuclear Uses Technology Reaction Analysis Team .... NUTRAT
Nuclear Utility Services .... NUS
Nuclear Vehicle Projects Office [*NASA*] .... NVPO
Nuclear War .... NUCWAR
Nuclear War Capability (AAG) .... NWC
Nuclear War Graphics Project [*Defunct*] (EA) .... NWGP
Nuclear War Study Group (EA) .... NWSG
Nuclear Warfare .... NW
Nuclear Warfare Status Branch (CINC) .... NWSB
Nuclear Warning Message [*Military*] (ADDR) .... NUCWARN
Nuclear Waste Fund (NUCP) .... NWF
Nuclear Waste Isolation Technology (NUCP) .... NWIT
Nuclear Waste News [*Business Publishers, Inc.*] [*No longer available online*] [*Information service or system*] (CRD) .... NWN
Nuclear Waste Policy Act (NRCH) .... NWPA
Nuclear Waste Policy Act of 1982 (GAAI) .... NWPA
Nuclear Waste Project [*Defunct*] (EA) .... NWP
Nuclear Waste Technical Review Board [*Nuclear energy*] (EGAO) .... NWTRB
Nuclear Weapon (AABC) .... NUCWPN
Nuclear Weapon (NG) .... NW
Nuclear Weapon Accident Investigation Board (AABC) .... NWAIB
Nuclear Weapon Burst Height Indicator .... NWBHI
Nuclear Weapon Effects Development .... NWED
Nuclear Weapon Effects Office [*DoD*] (RDA) .... NWEO
Nuclear Weapon Effects Test .... NWET
Nuclear Weapon Employment Officer (AABC) .... NWEO
Nuclear Weapon Employment Policy (MCD) .... NUWEP
Nuclear Weapon State .... NWS
Nuclear Weapon Systems Surety Group [*Army*] .... NWSG
Nuclear Weapons Acceptance Inspection (NG) .... NWAI
Nuclear Weapons Accident Exercises .... NUWAX
Nuclear Weapons Accident Report Procedures (AD) .... NARP
Nuclear Weapons Accounting (MCD) .... NUCWA
Nuclear Weapons Command, Control, and Security Requirements (MCD) .... CC & S
Nuclear Weapons Complex .... Complex
Nuclear Weapons Control .... NWC
Nuclear Weapons Control System .... NWCS
Nuclear Weapons Coordinating Group .... NWCG
Nuclear Weapons Correction Report [*Army*] (AABC) .... NWCR
Nuclear Weapons Education Fund (EA) .... NWEF
Nuclear Weapons Effect Planning .... NUWEP
Nuclear Weapons Effects .... NWE
Nuclear Weapons Effects Course (MCD) .... NWEC
Nuclear Weapons Effects Laboratory .... NWEL
Nuclear Weapons Effects Panel .... NWEP
Nuclear Weapons Effects Research [*Army*] .... NWER
Nuclear Weapons Effects Research and Testing [*Army*] (RDA) .... NWER/T
Nuclear Weapons Electronic Specialist (AABC) .... NWES
Nuclear Weapons Emergency Destruct System [*Navy*] (ANA) .... NUWEDS
Nuclear Weapons Fire Planning (MCD) .... NWFP
Nuclear Weapons Freeze Campaign (EA) .... NWFC
Nuclear Weapons Inventory (SSD) .... NWI
Nuclear Weapons Maintenance Foreman (AABC) .... NWMF
Nuclear Weapons Maintenance Specialist (AABC) .... NWMS
Nuclear Weapons Officer .... NWO
Nuclear Weapons Report [*Army*] (AABC) .... NWR
Nuclear Weapons Requirements Study (CINC) .... NWRS
Nuclear Weapons State .... NWS
Nuclear Weapons Stockpile Memorandum .... NWSM
Nuclear Weapons Storage Facility [*Army*] (AABC) .... NWSF
Nuclear Weapons Supply Annex .... NUWPNSUPANX
Nuclear Weapons Supply Annex .... NWSA
Nuclear Weapons Support Section [*Army*] (AABC) .... NWSS
Nuclear Weapons System Control Console (MCD) .... NWSCC
Nuclear Weapons System Safety Group .... NWSSG
Nuclear Weapons System Safety Group .... NWSSGP
Nuclear Weapons System Satellite Group [*Military*] (IAA) .... NWSSG
Nuclear Weapons Technical Inspections .... NWTI
Nuclear Weapons Technician/Specialist (AAG) .... NWT/S
Nuclear Weapons Training Center .... NUCWPNSTRACEN
Nuclear Weapons Training Center (MCD) .... NUWPNSTRACEN
Nuclear Weapons Training Center .... NUWPNTRACEN
Nuclear Weapons Training Center .... NWTC
Nuclear Weapons Training Center, Atlantic .... NUWPNTRACENLANT
Nuclear Weapons Training Center, Atlantic (DNAB) .... NWTCL
Nuclear Weapons Training Center, Pacific .... NUWPNTRACENPAC
Nuclear Weapons Training Center, Pacific (DNAB) .... NWTCP
Nuclear Weapons Training Group (DNAB) .... NWTG
Nuclear Weapons Training Group, Atlantic (DNAB) .... NWTGL
Nuclear Weapons Training Group, Pacific (DNAB) .... NWTGP
Nuclear Weapons-Free Zone .... NWFZ
Nuclear Work Authorization Technical Instruction (DNAB) .... NUWATI
Nuclear Yellow [*A fluorescent dye*] .... NY
Nuclear Yield .... NY
Nuclear Yield Requirement (NATG) .... NYR
Nuclear Zone .... NZ
Nuclear-Active Particles [*Astrophysics*] .... NAP
Nuclear-Armed (AD) .... N-armed
Nuclear-Armed Bombardment Satellite [*Study*] [*Air Force*] (AAG) .... NABS
Nuclear-Biological-Chemical Reconnaissance System [*Military*] .... NBCRS
Nuclear-Chicago Solubilizer .... NCS
Nuclear-Cytoplasmic [*Ratio*] [*Cytology*] (MAE) .... NC
Nuclear-Driven Directed-Energy Weapon .... NDEW
Nuclear-Electric Unmanned Spacecraft .... NEUS
Nuclear-Induced Ground Radioactivity (NATG) .... NIGA
Nuclear-Induced Lightning .... NIL
Nuclear-Powered Active Detection System .... NUPAD
Nuclear-Powered Container Ship (PDAA) .... NCS
Nuclear-Powered Energy Depot .... NPED
Nuclear-Powered Guided Aviation Destroyer [*Navy symbol*] .... DDHGN
Nuclear-Powered Guided Missile Aircraft Carrier [*Navy symbol*] .... CVGN
Nuclear-Powered Guided Missile Light Aircraft Carrier (MCD) .... CVLGN
Nuclear-Powered Light Aircraft Carrier (MCD) .... CVLN
Nuclear-Powered Merchant Ship (PDAA) .... NMS
Nuclear-Powered Ocean Engineering Vehicle [*Minisub*] .... NPOEV
Nuclear-Powered Ship (NVT) .... NPS
Nuclear-Powered Strike Cruiser .... CSGN
Nuclear-Powered V/STOL [*Vertical / Short Take-off and Landing*] **Aircraft Carrier** [*Navy symbol*] .... CVHN
Nuclease-Hypersensitive Element [*Biochemistry*] .... NHE
Nucleated .... NUC
Nucleated Red Blood Cell .... NRBC
Nuclei Armati Proletari [*Armed Proletarian Nuclei*] [*Italian*] (PD) .... NAP
Nuclei Armati Rivoluzionari [*Armed Revolutionary Nuclei*] [*Italian*] (PD) .... NAR
Nucleic Acid [*Biochemistry*] .... NA
Nucleic Acid Binding Protein [*Biochemistry*] .... NBP
Nucleic Acid Chromatography System .... NACS
Nucleic Acid Phosphorus [*Biochemistry*] .... NAP
Nucleic Acid Sequence-Based Amplification [*Biochemistry*] .... NASBA
Nucleic Acids Research [*A publication*] .... NAR
Nucleoacidic Protein [*Cytochemistry*] .... NAP
Nucleohistone Deoxyribonucleic Acid .... NHDNA
Nucleolar Channel System .... NCS
Nucleolar Organizer Region [*in chromosomes*] .... NOR
Nucleolus [*Cytology*] .... Nu
Nucleolus Organizer Region [*Genetics*] (DOG) .... NOR
Nucleon Transport Code .... NTC
Nucleonic Gauging System .... NGS
Nucleonic Oil Quantity Indication System [*Air Force*] .... NOQUIS
Nucleonics Calibration Facility (RDA) .... NCF
Nucleon-Meson Transport Code .... NMTC
Nucleon-Nucleon .... NN
Nucleon-Nucleon Interaction .... NNI
Nucleon-Nucleon Scattering .... NNS
Nucleoplasmic [*Index*] [*Cytology*] .... NP
Nucleoprotamine Deoxyribonucleic Acid .... NPDNA
Nucleoprotein [*Biochemistry*] .... NP
[*A*] **Nucleoside** [*One-letter symbol; see Nuc*] .... N
[*A*] **Nucleoside** [*Also, N*] .... Nuc
Nucleoside Diphosphate [*Biochemistry*] .... NDP
Nucleoside Diphosphate Kinase [*An enzyme*] .... NDK
Nucleoside Diphosphokinase [*An enzyme*] .... NDPK
Nucleoside Monophosphate [*Biochemistry*] .... NMP
Nucleoside Phosphorylase [*An enzyme*] .... NP
Nucleoside Revenue Transcript Inhibitor [*Biochemistry*] .... NRTI
Nucleoside Triphosphate [*Biochemistry*] .... NTP
Nucleosidetriphosphate Pyrophosphatase [*An enzyme*] .... NTPH
Nucleosome Remodeling Factor [*Analytical biochemistry*] .... NURF
Nucleotidase [*An enzyme*] (DAVI) .... NT
Nucleotide [*Genetics*] (DOG) .... nt
Nucleotide Binding Domain [*Biochemistry*] .... NBD

Nucleotide Binding Fold [Genetics] ... NBF
Nucleotide Binding Site [Genetics] ... NBS
Nucleotide Column Affinity for Purification [Biochemical analysis] ... NCAP
Nucleotide Diphosphate Kinase [An enzyme] ... NDPK
Nucleotide Pair [Genetics] (DOG) ... np
Nucleotide Sequencing Search System [NIH/EPA Chemical Information System] [Database] ... NUCSEQ
Nucleotide-Excision Repair ... NER
Nucleus [Psychology] ... n
Nucleus [of a cell] [Biology] ... N
Nucleus (WDAA) ... NUC
Nucleus ... NUCL
Nucleus Accumbens [Neuroanatomy] ... NA
Nucleus Ambiguus [Neuroanatomy] ... NA
Nucleus Average Optical Density [Microscopy] ... NUAD
Nucleus Basalis [Brain anatomy] ... NB
Nucleus Basalis Magnocellularis [Cytology] ... NBM
Nucleus Basalis of Meynert [Brain anatomy] ... nbM
Nucleus Expert User System (NITA) ... NEXUS
Nucleus Fleet Scientific Support ... NFSS
Nucleus Fleet Sealift ... NFSL
Nucleus Initialization Program [Computer science] ... NIP
Nucleus Landing Force Staff (DNAB) ... NLFS
Nucleus of Basal Optic Root [Neuroanatomy] ... NBOR
Nucleus of Ciliated Cell ... NC
Nucleus of Epidermal Cell ... NEC
Nucleus of Longitudinal Muscle Fiber ... NLMF
Nucleus (of Syllable) [Linguistics] ... N
Nucleus of the Optic Tract [Eye anatomy] ... NOT
Nucleus Pulposus [Medicine] (DAVI) ... NP
Nucleus Raphe Alatus [Neurology] ... NRA
Nucleus Raphe Dorsalis [Neuroanatomy] ... NRD
Nucleus Reticularis Gigantocellularis [Brain anatomy] ... NGC
Nucleus Reticularis Gigantocellularis [Neuroanatomy] ... NRGC
Nucleus Reticularis Tegmenti Pontis [Neuroanatomy] ... NRTP
Nucleus Reticularis Thalami [Neuroanatomy] ... NRT
Nucleus Retroambigualis [Neurology] (DAVI) ... NRA
Nucleus Shape [Microscopy] ... NUSH
Nucleus Size [Microscopy] ... NUSZ
Nucleus Sum Optical Density [Microscopy] ... NUSD
Nucleus Support Crew [Navy] (DNAB) ... NCS
Nucleus Texture [Microscopy] ... NUTX
Nucleus Tractus Solitarii [Brain anatomy] ... NTS
NuCo2 Inc. [NASDAQ symbol] (TTSB) ... NUCO
NuCo2, Inc. [NASDAQ symbol] (SAG) ... NUCO
NuCo2, Inc. [Associated Press] (SAG) ... NuCo2
Nucor Corp. [Associated Press] (SAG) ... Nucor
Nucor Corp. [NYSE symbol] (SPSG) ... NUE
Nucorr Petroleums Ltd. [Toronto Stock Exchange symbol] ... NUC
Nu-Dawn Resources, Inc. [Vancouver Stock Exchange symbol] ... NDN
Nude [Mouse] [Medicine] (DMAA) ... nu
Nude Ionization Gauge ... NIG
Nudist Information Center [Defunct] (EA) ... NIC
Nudist National Committee (EA) ... NNC
NUDO [Namibia United Democratic Organization] Progressive Party of Namibia [Political party] (PPW) ... NPPN
Nueces County Historical Society, La Retama Public Library, Corpus Christi, TX [Library symbol Library of Congress] (LCLS) ... TxCcNHi
Nuernberg [Germany ICAO location identifier] (ICLI) ... EDDN
Nuernberg, Hospital [Germany ICAO location identifier] (ICLI) ... EDIT
Nuernberger [ICAO designator] (AD) ... NS
Nuestra Cuenta [Our Account] [Business term Spanish] ... NC
Nuestra Orden [Our Order] [Spanish Business term] ... NO
Nuestra Remesa [Our Remittance] [Spanish Business term] ... NR
Nuestro Senor Jesucristo [Our Lord, Jesus Christ] [Spanish] ... NSJ
Nueva Alternativa [Venezuela Political party] (EY) ... NA
Nueva Asuncion [Paraguay] [ICAO location identifier] (ICLI) ... SGNA
Nueva Casas Grandes [Mexico] [Airport symbol] (AD) ... NCG
Nueva Concepcion [El Salvador] [Seismograph station code, US Geological Survey Closed] (SEIS) ... NCS
Nueva Era [Bolivia] [ICAO location identifier] (ICLI) ... SLNE
Nueva Esperanza [Bolivia] [ICAO location identifier] (ICLI) ... SLNP
Nueva Esperanza (Marban) [Bolivia] [ICAO location identifier] (ICLI) ... SLNQ
Nueva Fuerza Democratica [New Democratic Force] [Colorado Political party] (EY) ... NFD
Nueva Gerona [Cuba] [Airport symbol] (OAG) ... GER
Nueva Gerona [Cuba ICAO location identifier] (ICLI) ... MUNG
Nueva Organizacion Antiterrorista [New Anti-Terrorist Organization] [Guatemala] (PD) ... NOA
Nueve De Julio [Argentina ICAO location identifier] (ICLI) ... SAZX
Nuevo Casas Grandes [Mexico ICAO location identifier] (ICLI) ... MMCG
Nuevo Energy [NYSE symbol] (TTSB) ... NEV
Nuevo Energy Co. [NYSE symbol] (SPSG) ... NEV
Nuevo Energy Co. [Associated Press] (SAG) ... NuevEn
Nuevo Financing I [NYSE symbol] (SAG) ... NEV
Nuevo Financing I [Associated Press] (SAG) ... NvoFn
Nuevo Laredo [Mexico ICAO location identifier] (ICLI) ... MMNL
Nuevo Laredo [Mexico] [Airport symbol] (OAG) ... NLD
Nuevo Mundo [Bolivia] [ICAO location identifier] (ICLI) ... SLNO
Nuevo Ocotepeque [Honduras] [ICAO location identifier] (ICLI) ... MHNV
"Nuff Ced" [Enough Said] [Slang] ... NC
Nuffield Service Teaching Project ... NSTP
Nufort Resources, Inc. [Toronto Stock Exchange symbol] ... NR
Nugget Coombs Foundation for Indigenous Studies [Australia] ... NCF
Nugold Enterprises Corp. [Vancouver Stock Exchange symbol] ... NUO

Nu-Gro Corp. [Toronto Stock Exchange symbol] ... NU
Nuh [India] [ICAO location identifier] (ICLI) ... VINH
Nu-Horizons Electronics Corp. [NASDAQ symbol] (SAG) ... NUHC
Nu-Horizons Electronics Corp. [Associated Press] (SAG) ... NuHoriz
NUI Corp. [NYSE symbol] (SPSG) ... NUI
Nuiatoputapu [Tonga] [Airport symbol] (OAG) ... NTT
Nuinsco Resources Ltd. [Toronto Stock Exchange symbol] ... NWI
Nuiqsut [Alaska] [Airport symbol] (OAG) ... NUI
Nuiqsut Village, AK [Location identifier FAA] (FAAL) ... UQS
Nuisance (ABBR) ... NSNCE
Nuisance Tax (MHDW) ... NT
Nuisance Value (MHDB) ... NV
Nuisance Valve Tactics ... NVT
Nuits-Saint-Georges [France ICAO location identifier] (ICLI) ... LFGZ
Nuko Information Sys [NASDAQ symbol] (TTSB) ... NUKO
Nuko Information Systems, Inc. [NASDAQ symbol] (SAG) ... NUKO
Nuko Information Systems Inc. [Associated Press] (SAG) ... NukoInfo
Nu-Kote Holding, Inc. [NASDAQ symbol] (SAG) ... NKOT
Nu-Kote Holding, Inc. [Associated Press] (SAG) ... NuKote
Nu-kote Holding 'A' [NASDAQ symbol] (TTSB) ... NKOT
Nuku [Papua New Guinea] [Airport symbol] (OAG) ... UKU
Nuku Hiva [French Polynesia] [Airport symbol] (OAG) ... NHV
Nuku Hiva [French Polynesia] [ICAO location identifier] (ICLI) ... NTMD
Nuku'Alofa [Tonga] [ICAO location identifier] (ICLI) ... NFTN
Nukutavake [French Polynesia] [ICAO location identifier] (ICLI) ... NTGW
Nukutavake [French Polynesia] [Airport symbol] (OAG) ... NUK
Nu-Lady Gold Mines [Vancouver Stock Exchange symbol] ... NUL
Nulato [Alaska] [Airport symbol] (OAG) ... NUL
Nulato, AK [Location identifier FAA] (FAAL) ... NUL
Nulead [Journalism] [Slang] (WDMC) ... NL
Null (OSI) ... NUL
Null Balance Recorder ... NBR
Null Character [Keyboard] [Computer science] ... NUL
Null Command Generator ... NCG
Null Error Amplifier ... NEA
Null Filter Mobile RADAR (PDAA) ... NFMRAD
Null Line Gap ... NLG
Null Operation [Computer science] ... NOP
Null Reception Zone ... NRZ
Null Voltage Test Set (MCD) ... NVTS
Nulla Bona [No Goods] [Latin Legal term] (DLA) ... NB
Nulla per Os Hora Somni [Nothing by Mouth at Bedtime] [Latin Pharmacy] (MAH) ... NPO/HS
Nullagine [Australia Airport symbol] (OAG) ... NLL
Null-Balance Transmissometer (IEEE) ... NBT
Nullified Unpostable [Computer science] ... NU
Nullipara [obstetrics] (DAVI) ... nullip
Nullity [Divorce cases] [British] (ROG) ... N
Numa [of Plutarch] [Classical studies] (OCD) ... Num
Numac Energy [AMEX symbol] (SPSG) ... NMC
Numac Energy [Associated Press] (SAG) ... Numac
Numadu [Japan] [Seismograph station code, US Geological Survey Closed] (SEIS) ... NUM
Numar Corp. [Associated Press] (SAG) ... Numar
Numar Corp. [NASDAQ symbol] (SAG) ... NUMR
Number ... N
Number (IDOE) ... N
Number [Usually integer] (IDOE) ... n
Number (KSC) ... NBR
Number (EY) ... NO
Number (IDOE) ... No
Number (WDMC) ... no
Number (AAG) ... NR
[Reynolds] Number [Aerodynamics] (BARN) ... NRe
Number [or Numerator, or Numeric] ... NUM
Number (DAVI) ... NUMBR
Number 3 Common [Lumber] ... 3COM
No. 6 Elementary School, Woodmere, NY [Library symbol] [Library of Congress] (LCLS) ... NWdmE
No. 32 (The Royal) Squadron [British] [FAA designator] (FAAC) ... KRF
Number Allocation and Inspection Module (PDAA) ... NAIM
Number Base Conversion ... NBC
Number [or Name] Changed [Telephone Listing] (BARN) ... NCH
Number Connection Test ... NCT
Number Cruncher Statistical System [Computer software] (PCM) ... NCSS
Number Crunching Unit (MHDB) ... NCU
Number Needed to Treat ... NNT
Number Nine Visual Tech [NASDAQ symbol] (TTSB) ... NINE
Number Nine Visual Technology, Inc. [NASDAQ symbol] (SAG) ... NINE
Number Nine Visual Technology, Inc. [Associated Press] (SAG) ... No9Vis
Number of Aimpoints [Military] ... NA
Number of Bids Received [DoD] ... NBR
Number (of Bits) [Computer science] (ECII) ... N
Number of Bursts ... NOB
Number of Carriers (IDOE) ... x
Number of Critical Micro-Operations [Computer science] (MHDI) ... NMO
Number of Dissimilar Matches ... Nd
Number of Document [Online database field identifier] ... ND
Number of Element Types ... NET
Number of Elements Loaded [Army] ... NELTS
Number of Engine Revolutions per Minute per Vehicle Miles per Hour [Automotive engineering] ... N/V
Number of Equally Strong Beams [Military] (CAAL) ... NESB
Number of Inverters Along Any Loop is Even (MHDI) ... NILE
Number of Module Types ... NMT

Number of Molecules [Symbol] [IUPAC] .... N
Number of Observations [Statistics] (DAVI) .... n
Number of Open Microphones .... NOM
Number of Openings [Technical drawings] .... NOP
Number of Passes (MSA) .... NOP
Number of Primary Turns (IAA) .... NP
Number of Primary Turns (IDOE) .... N_p
Number of Records Ignored (SAA) .... NRI
Number of Rejected Initial Pickups .... NRIP
Number of Remaining Words .... NRW
Number of Rounds [Military] (CINC) .... NOR
Number of Rounds between Failures [Quality control] (MCD) .... NRBF
Number of Runs .... NR
Number of Scans per Vehicle (OA) .... NSPV
Number of Secondary Turns (IAA) .... NS
Number of Secondary Turns (IDOE) .... N_s
Number of Similar Negative Matches .... Nsn
Number of Similar Positive Matches .... Nsp
Number of Simultaneous Engagements [Military] .... NSE
Number of Steps, Polynomial Time [Mathematics] .... NP
Number of Stops (IAA) .... NOS
Number of Terminals per Failure [Computer science] .... NTPF
Number of Theoretical Plates .... NTP
Number of Theoretical Stages [Chemical engineering] .... NTS
Number of Transfer Units .... NTU
Number (of Turns) [Electronics] (ECII) .... N
Number of Turns (IAA) .... NOT
Number of Uncorrected Flight Plans (SAA) .... NUFP
Number of Video Samples .... NVS
Number of Words (MSA) .... NWD
Number of Words .... NWDS
Number of Words per Entry (MSA) .... NWDEN
Number of Words per Entry .... NWDSEN
Number Theoretic Transform (MHDI) .... NTT
Number Unobtainable [Telecommunications] .... NU
Number Unobtainable Tone [Telecommunications] (TEL) .... NUT
Number-Controlled Oscillator .... NCO
Numbered .... NUMB
Numbered Air Force (AFM) .... NAF
Numbered Fleet Commander (DOMA) .... NFC
Numbered Fleet Flagship [Navy] .... NFF
Numbering .... NOG
Numbering Counter [Computer science] (OA) .... NC
Numbering Plan Area [Bell System] [Telecommunications] .... NPA
Numbering Plan Indicator [Computer science] (TNIG) .... NPI
Numbering Tool (AAG) .... NOTO
Numbering Transmitter .... NT
Numbers [Old Testament book] (BJA) .... Nb
Numbers [Old Testament book] .... Nm
Numbers (AAG) .... NOS
Numbers (WDMC) .... nos
Numbers [Old Testament book] (BJA) .... Nu
Numbers [Old Testament book] .... Num
Numbers [Old Testament book] .... Numb
Numbers Rabbah .... NumR
Numed Home Health Care, Inc. [Associated Press] (SAG) .... Numd
Numed Home Health Care, Inc. [NASDAQ symbol] (SAG) .... NUMD
Numed Home Health Care, Inc. [Associated Press] (SAG) .... Numed
Numed Home Health Care, Inc. [Associated Press] (SAG) .... NumedH
NuMED Home Health Care Wrrt [NASDAQ symbol] (TTSB) .... NUMDW
NuMED Home Hlth Care [NASDAQ symbol] (TTSB) .... NUMD
Nu-Media Industry International [Vancouver Stock Exchange symbol] .... NMD
Numeral [or Numerical] .... NUM
Numerex Corp. [NASDAQ symbol] (SAG) .... NMRX
Numerex Corp. [Associated Press] (SAG) .... Numerex
Numeric .... N
Numeric Backspace Character [Computer science] .... NBS
Numeric Data Base [INPADOC] [Computer science] .... NDB
Numeric Data Processor .... NDP
Numeric Indicator Performance .... NIP
Numeric Meta Language Processing System (PDAA) .... NUMEPS
Numeric Parts Preference Code [Military] (AFIT) .... NPPC
Numeric Space Character [Computer science] .... NSP
Numeric Stockage Objective [Items] [DoD] .... NSO
Numerical Aerodynamic Simulation [NASA supercomputer system] .... NAS
Numerical Aerodynamic Simulation Facility .... NASF
Numerical [formerly, Nottingham] Algorithms Group .... NAG
Numerical Analysis [Computer science] (BUR) .... NA
Numerical Analysis Laboratory (MCD) .... NAL
Numerical Analysis of Semiconductor Devices and Integrated Circuits [Computer science] .... NASECODE
Numerical Analysis Problem Solving System .... NAPSS
Numerical Analysis Research (MCD) .... NAR
Numerical Analysis Subroutines [Computer science] (BUR) .... NAS
Numerical Analysis System (BUR) .... NUMERALS
Numerical and Atmospheric Sciences Network [NASA] .... NAS
Numerical and Textile Information System (PDAA) .... NUTIS
Numerical Aperture [Microscopy] .... NA
Numerical Assignment Number [Computer science] .... NAM
Numerical Category Scaling .... NCS
Numerical Code (NATG) .... NUCO
Numerical Contouring Mechanism .... NUCOM
Numerical Control (IDOE) .... N/C
Numerical Control [Computer science] .... NC
Numerical Control Code .... NCC

Numerical Control Distribution System [Computer science] (MHDI) .... NCDS
Numerical Control Graphics (MCD) .... NCG
Numerical Control Information Management System (MCD) .... NCIMS
Numerical Control Inspection Tape (MCD) .... NCIT
Numerical Control Language [Computer science] (PDAA) .... NUCOL
Numerical Control Society [Later, NCS/AIMTECH] (EA) .... NCS
Numerical Control Society/AIMTECH [Association for Integrated Manufacturing Technology] (EA) .... NCS/AIMTECH
Numerical Control System (IAA) .... NCS
Numerical Controlled Machine .... NCM
Numerical Data Advisory Board [National Academy of Sciences] [Information service or system] (IID) .... NDAB
Numerical Designation Index (IEEE) .... NDI
Numerical Drawing List .... NDL
Numerical Engineering Society [British] (DBA) .... NES
Numerical Examination of Urban Smog (IAA) .... NEXUS
Numerical Experimentation Group [Marine science] (OSRA) .... NEG
Numerical Index (BUR) .... NI
Numerical Index and Requirement Table (MCD) .... NI & RT
Numerical Integration of the Boltzmann Transport Equation .... NIOBE
Numerical Largeness of More Significant [Statistics] .... NLMS
Numerical Master Geometry [System] .... NMG
Numerical Multifactor Assessment System (ADA) .... NUMAS
Numerical Oceanographic Prediction (PDAA) .... NOP
Numerical Optimisation Centre [British] .... NOC
Numerical Parts List (MCD) .... NPL
Numerical Plotting System (NRCH) .... NPS
Numerical Position Readout (IAA) .... NPR
Numerical Preference List [Military] (AFIT) .... NPL
Numerical Processing and Interface Unit [Computer science] (MHDB) .... NPIU
Numerical Production Analysis (IEEE) .... NPA
Numerical Rating System [Insurance] .... NRS
Numerical Sequence Code .... NSC
Numerical Summary Report [Military] (AFM) .... NUSUM
Numerical Surveying Technique (PDAA) .... NST
Numerical Tape Punch .... NTP
Numerical Value Rating System [Navy] .... NVRS
Numerical Weather and Oceanographic Forecasting Center [Marine science] (MSC) .... NWOFC
Numerical Weather Facility .... NWF
Numerical Weather Prediction .... NWP
Numerical Weather Prediction Operational Grid (SAA) .... NWPOG
Numerical Weather Prediction Unit (DNAB) .... NWPU
Numerically Controlled Drafting (MCD) .... NCD
Numerically Controlled Drafting Machine (MCD) .... NCDM
Numerically Controlled Lathe .... NCL
Numerically Controlled Line Plotter .... NCLP
Numerically Controlled Machine Equipment .... NCME
Numerically Controlled Machine Tool .... NCMT
Numerically Integrated Differential Analyzer [Computer science] .... NIDA
Numerically Integrated Elements for System Analysis (MCD) .... NISA
Numerically-Controlled Machine Center (IAA) .... NCMC
Numerically-Controlled Machine System (IAA) .... NCMS
Numerically-Controlled Manufacture System (IAA) .... NCMS
Numerically-Controlled Measuring and Evaluating System (IAA) .... NCMES
Numerically-Controlled Peripheral (IAA) .... NCP
Numero [In Number] [Pharmacy] (ROG) .... NO
Numero d'Identification Personnel [Personal Identification Number - PIN] .... NIP
Numerous (FAAC) .... NMRS
Numerous (ROG) .... NUMS
Numfor [Indonesia] [Airport symbol] (OAG) .... FOO
Numfor/Jemburwo [Indonesia] [ICAO location identifier] (ICLI) .... WABF
Numidian .... Numid
Numismatic (ABBR) .... NMSMK
Numismatic and Antiquarian Society, Philadelphia, PA [Library symbol Library of Congress Obsolete] (LCLS) .... PPN
Numismatic Bibliomania Society (EA) .... NBS
Numismatic Error Collectors of America (EA) .... NECA
Numismatic Literary Guild (EA) .... NLG
Numismatic Society .... NS
Numismaticist (ABBR) .... NMSMTST
Numismatics .... NUMIS
Numismatics .... NUMISM
Numismatics International (EA) .... NI
Nummela [Finland ICAO location identifier] (ICLI) .... EFNU
Nun [Buoy] .... N
Nuna Air AS [Denmark ICAO designator] (FAAC) .... NUA
Nunapitchuk [Alaska] [Airport symbol] (OAG) .... NUP
Nunasi-Central Airlines Ltd. [Canada ICAO designator] (FAAC) .... NUN
Nunatak [Alaska] [Seismograph station code, US Geological Survey] (SEIS) .... NTK
Nunnery .... NNRY
Nunnery (ABBR) .... NNRY
Nuns of Perpetual Adoration of Blessed Sacrament (TOCD) .... AP
Nuova Sinistra Unita [New United Left] [Italy Political party] (PPE) .... NSU
Nupta [Married] [Latin] .... N
Nuptial (ABBR) .... NPTL
Nuqui [Colombia] [Airport symbol] (OAG) .... NQU
Nur Advanced Technologies [NASDAQ symbol] (TTSB) .... MURTF
Nur Advanced Technologies Ltd. [Associated Press] (SAG) .... NuraTL
Nur Advanced Technologies Ltd. [NASDAQ symbol] (SAG) .... NURTE
Nurek [Former USSR Seismograph station code, US Geological Survey Closed] (SEIS) .... NRK
Nuremberg [Germany Airport symbol] (OAG) .... NUE
Nuriootpa Viticulture Center [Australia] .... NVC

Nurmijarvi [*Finland*] [*Seismograph station code, US Geological Survey*] (SEIS) ... NUR
Nurse (ADA) ... N
Nurse ... NR
Nurse (ABBR) ... NRS
Nurse (ABBR) ... NRSE
Nurse (AABC) ... NUR
Nurse ... NUR
Nurse Aide/Orderly (OICC) ... NAO
Nurse Anesthetist (AAMN) ... NA
Nurse Competency Inventory ... NCI
Nurse Consultants Association (EA) ... NCA
Nurse Corps [*Military*] ... NC
Nurse Detachments [*Army*] ... NURSEDETS
Nurse Education Support Program ... NESP
Nurse Healers - Professional Association (EA) ... NHPA
Nurse Managed Center (MEDA) ... NMC
Nurse Practitioner ... NP
Nurse Practitioner Project ... NPP
Nurse Satisfaction Questionnaire ... NSQ
Nurse Technician ... NT
Nurse Training Act ... NTA
Nurse Unit Manager ... NUM
Nursed (ABBR) ... NRSD
Nursed (ABBR) ... NRSED
Nursed Fairly Well [*Medicine*] (DMAA) ... NFW
Nursed Poorly [*Medicine*] (DMAA) ... NP
Nursemaid (ABBR) ... NRSEMD
Nursery ... nrsry
Nursery ... NRSY
Nursery (DAVI) ... NSY
Nursery ... NURS
Nursery Association Executives [*Later, NAENA*] (EA) ... NAE
Nursery Association Executives of North America (EA) ... NAENA
Nursery Association Secretaries [*Later, Nursery Association Executives*] (EA) ... NAS
Nursery Education Week (AEBS) ... NEW
Nursery Industry Association of New South Wales [*Australia*] ... NIANSW
Nursery Industry Association of Tasmania [*Australia*] ... NIAT
Nursery Industry Association of Western Australia [*Australia*] ... NIAWA
Nursery Marketing Council (EA) ... NMC
Nursery School Association [*British*] (BARN) ... NSA
Nurses Against Misrepresentation (EA) ... NAM
Nurse's Aide ... NA
Nurses Alliance for the Prevention of Nuclear War [*Defunct*] (EA) ... NAPNW
Nurses Almanac ... NA
Nurses and Army Medical Specialists ... NAMS
Nurses' Board of South Australia ... NBSA
Nurses' Central Clearing House (AIE) ... NCCH
Nurses Christian Fellowship (EA) ... NCF
Nurses' Christian Fellowship of Australia ... NCFA
Nurses Coalition for Action in Politics ... N-CAP
Nurses Educational Funds (EA) ... NEF
Nurses for Environmental Health Education (DAVI) ... NEHE
Nurses for Laughter ... NFL
Nurses for Laughter [*Defunct*] (EA) ... NL
Nurses in Transition (EA) ... NIT
Nurses' Library, Montreal General Hospital [*Bibliotheque des Infirmieres, Hopital General de Montreal*], Quebec [*Library symbol National Library of Canada*] (NLC) ... QMGHN
Nurses' Notes (MAE) ... N/N
Nurses Observation Scale for Inpatient Evaluation [*Psychiatry*] ... NOSIE
Nurses Organization of Veterans Affairs (EA) ... NOVA
Nurses' Registration Board of Queensland [*Australia*] ... NRBQ
Nurses Support Network [*Later, NIT*] (EA) ... NSN
Nurses Underrepresented in Social Equality (BABM) ... NURSE
Nurses Underrepresented in Social Equality (DAVI) ... NURSE
Nursing (ABBR) ... NRSEG
Nursing ... NRSG
Nursing ... NSG
Nursing ... NURS
Nursing ... NURSE
Nursing and Personal Care ... NPC
Nursing Assistant ... NA
Nursing Audit Committee (MEDA) ... NAC
Nursing Auxiliary [*British*] ... NA
Nursing Auxiliary Service [*British*] ... NAS
Nursing Boards Review [*Course*] [*American Journal of Nursing*] ... NBR
Nursing Care Integration [*Medicine*] (DMAA) ... NCI
Nursing Care Plan ... NCP
Nursing Citation Index ... NCI
Nursing Clerical Coordinator ... NCC
Nursing Doctorate ... ND
Nursing Education, General Hospital Corp., St. John's, Newfoundland [*Library symbol National Library of Canada*] (NLC) ... NFSGHN
Nursing Education Module Authoring System ... NEMAS
Nursing Education Research Unit ... NERU
Nursing Educator (AAMN) ... NE
Nursing Field Representative [*Red Cross*] ... NFR
Nursing Home ... NH
Nursing Home Advisory and Research Council (EA) ... NHARC
Nursing Home Care Unit [*Veterans Administration*] ... NHCU
Nursing Home Improvement Program [*National Institute of Mental Health*] ... NHIP
Nursing Home Information Service (EA) ... NHIS
Nursing Home Placement (DAVI) ... NHP
Nursing Home Quality Reform Act ... NHQRA
Nursing Home Type (ADA) ... NHT
Nursing Home-Type Patient ... NHTP
Nursing Mothers' Association of Australia ... NMAA
Nursing Officer [*British*] ... NO
Nursing Performance Simulation Instrument ... NPSI
Nursing Policy Studies Centre [*University of Warwick*] [*British*] (CB) ... NPSC
Nursing Procedure ... NP
Nursing Representative [*Red Cross*] ... NR
Nursing Sentence Completions [*Nursing school test*] ... NSC
Nursing Services (HCT) ... NR
Nursing Services ... NS
Nursing Sister [*Navy British*] ... NS
Nursing/Social Work Library, McGill University, Montreal, Quebec [*Library symbol National Library of Canada*] (NLC) ... QMMN
Nursing Station (DAVI) ... Nsg Sta
Nursing System-Wide ... NURSW
Nursing the Environment ... NTE
Nurturant-Authoritative [*Psychotherapy*] ... NA
Nurture (ABBR) ... NRTR
Nurtured (ABBR) ... NRTRD
Nurture-Outreach-Witness [*Religion*] ... NOW
Nurturing (ABBR) ... NRTRG
Nurturing Network [*An association*] (EA) ... NN
NUS Corp. (GAAI) ... NUS
NUS [*National University of Singapore*] **Financial Database** [*Information service or system*] (IID) ... NUSFDB
Nuspar Resources [*Vancouver Stock Exchange symbol*] ... NUR
Nusselt Number [*IUPAC*] ... Nu
Nu-Start Resource Corp. [*Vancouver Stock Exchange symbol*] ... NUS
Nut and Bolt ... NAB
Nut Plate (AAG) ... NTPL
Nutation Control System (MCD) ... NCS
Nutcracker (ABBR) ... NTCKR
Nu-Tech Bio Med, Inc. [*NASDAQ symbol*] (SAG) ... NTBM
Nu-Tech Bio Med, Inc. [*Associated Press*] (SAG) ... Nu-Tech
NU-Tech Bio-Med [*NASDAQ symbol*] (TTSB) ... NTBM
Nutlet Length [*Botany*] ... NTLEN
Nutley Free Public Library, Nutley, NJ [*Library symbol Library of Congress*] (LCLS) ... NjNu
Nutley Historical Society, Nutley, NJ [*Library symbol Library of Congress*] (LCLS) ... NjNuHi
Nutmeg (ADA) ... NM
Nutmeg Electric Companies Atomic Project ... NECAP
Nutmeg Federal Savings & Loan Association [*NASDAQ symbol*] (SAG) ... NTMG
Nutmeg Federal Savings & Loan Association [*Associated Press*] (SAG) ... NutmgFd
Nutmeg Fedl Svgs & Loan [*NASDAQ symbol*] (TTSB) ... NTMG
Nutmeg Industries, Inc. (MHDW) ... NUTM
NutraMax Products, Inc. [*NASDAQ symbol*] (SAG) ... NMPC
NutraMax Products, Inc. [*Associated Press*] (SAG) ... Nutrmax
Nu-Trans Cooperative (EA) ... NTC
Nutrient Agar [*Microbiology*] ... NA
Nutrient Broth Yeast [*Microbiology*] ... NBY
Nutrient Data Table ... NUTTAB
Nutrient Film Technique ... NFT
Nutrient Gelatin Agar [*Microbiology*] ... NGA
Nutrient Sporulation Medium [*Medicine*] (DMAA) ... NSM
Nutrient Starch Cycloheximide Agar [*Microbiology*] ... NSCA
Nutrient Starch Cycloheximide Antibiotic Agar [*Microbiology*] ... NSCAA
Nutrient Supply Rate [*Oceanography*] ... NSR
Nutrient-Enhanced Coastal Ocean Productivity [*Marine science*] (OSRA) ... NECOP
Nutrient-Enhanced Coastal Ocean Productivity [*Program*] (USDC) ... NECOP
Nutrilite Products, Inc., Technical Library, Buena Park, CA [*Library symbol Library of Congress*] (LCLS) ... CBpN
Nutrition ... NTR
Nutrition (AABC) ... NUTR
Nutrition ... NUTRI
Nutrition ... NUTRI
Nutrition Education Association (EA) ... NEA
Nutrition, Exercise, Relaxation, Sleep, and Enjoyment ... NERSE
Nutrition For Life International, Inc. [*NASDAQ symbol*] (SAG) ... NFLI
Nutrition For Life International, Inc. [*Associated Press*] (SAG) ... NutrLf
Nutrition for Life International, Inc. [*Associated Press*] (SAG) ... NutrLfe
Nutrition For Life Intl. [*NASDAQ symbol*] (TTSB) ... NFLI
Nutrition For Life Intl. Wrrt [*NASDAQ symbol*] (TTSB) ... NFLIW
Nutrition for Optimal Health Association (EA) ... NOHA
Nutrition Foundation [*Later, ILSI-NF*] ... NF
Nutrition Institute of America [*Inactive*] (EA) ... NIA
Nutrition Labeling and Education Act [*1990*] [*Food and Drug Administration*] ... NLEA
Nutrition Management [*NASDAQ symbol*] (SAG) ... NMSC
Nutrition Management [*Associated Press*] (SAG) ... NutrMg
Nutrition Management [*Associated Press*] (SAG) ... NutrMgt
Nutrition Mgmt Svcs Wrrt [*NASDAQ symbol*] (TTSB) ... NMSCW
Nutrition Mgmt Svcs'A' [*NASDAQ symbol*] (TTSB) ... NMSCA
Nutrition Monitoring Division [*Department of Agriculture*] (GFGA) ... NMD
Nutrition Research Foundation [*Australia*] ... NRF
Nutrition Society [*British*] (EAIO) ... NS
Nutrition Today Society [*Defunct*] (EA) ... NTS
Nutritional ... NUTRL
Nutritional Foods Association [*Australia*] ... NFA
Nutritional Health Alliance ... NHA

Nutritional Information and Analysis Center [*Illinois Institute of Technology and Institute of Food Technologists*] (IID) .... NIAC
Nutritional Oncology Vascular Access .... NOVA
Nutritional Support Panel [*Dietetics*] (DAVI) .... NSP
Nutritional Support Team [*Dietetics*] (DAVI) .... NST
Nutrition-Related Complications [*Medicine*] .... NRC
Nutritive Ratio .... NR
Nuts [*Phonetic alphabet*] [*Royal Navy World War I Pre-World War II*] (DSUE) ...... N
Nuttall Ornithological Club (EA) .... NOC
Nuuk [*Greenland*] [*Airport symbol*] (OAG) .... GOH
Nuveen [*John*] & Co. [*NYSE symbol*] (SPSG) .... JNC
Nuveen Arizona Premium Income [*NYSE symbol*] (SAG) .... NAZ
Nuveen Arizona Premium Income [*Associated Press*] (SAG) .... NuvAZ
Nuveen AZ Prem Inc. Muni Fd [*NYSE symbol*] (TTSB) .... NAZ
Nuveen CA Inv Qual Muni [*NYSE symbol*] (TTSB) .... NQC
Nuveen CA Muni Mkt Oppt [*NYSE symbol*] (TTSB) .... NCO
Nuveen CA Muni Val Fd [*NYSE symbol*] (TTSB) .... NCA
Nuveen CA Perf Plus Muni [*NYSE symbol*] (TTSB) .... NCP
Nuveen CA Prem Inc. Muni [*AMEX symbol*] (TTSB) .... NCU
Nuveen CA Qual Income Muni [*NYSE symbol*] (TTSB) .... NUC
Nuveen CA Select Qual Muni [*NYSE symbol*] (TTSB) .... NVC
Nuveen California Investment Quality Municipal Fund [*NYSE symbol*] (SPSG) .... NQC
Nuveen California Investment Quality Municipal Fund [*Associated Press*] (SAG) .... NvCIQ
Nuveen California Municipal Fund [*NYSE symbol*] (SPSG) .... NCA
Nuveen California Municipal Income [*NYSE symbol*] (SPSG) .... NCM
Nuveen California Municipal Income Fund [*Associated Press*] (SAG) .... NvCMI
Nuveen California Municipal Market Opportunities [*NYSE symbol*] (SPSG) .... NCO
Nuveen California Municipal Market Opportunity Fund [*Associated Press*] (SAG) .... NCMM
Nuveen California Municipal Value Fund [*Associated Press*] (SAG) .... NuvCal
Nuveen California Performance Plus Municipal [*NYSE symbol*] (SPSG) .... NCP
Nuveen California Performance Plus Municipal Fund [*Associated Press*] (SAG) .... NVCPP
Nuveen California Premium Income Municipal (SPSG) .... NCU
Nuveen California Premium Income Municipal Fund [*Associated Press*] (SAG) .... NCAPI
Nuveen California Premium Income Municipal Fund [*AMEX symbol*] (SAG) .... NCU
Nuveen California Quality Income Municipal [*NYSE symbol*] (SPSG) .... NUC
Nuveen California Quality Income Municipal [*Associated Press*] (SAG) .... NvCAQI
Nuveen California Select Quality Municipal [*NYSE symbol*] (SPSG) .... NVC
Nuveen California Select Quality Municipal Fund [*Associated Press*] (SAG) .... NvCSQ
Nuveen [*John*] Co. [*Associated Press*] (SAG) .... JNuveen
Nuveen Connecticut Premium Income Municipal Fund [*Associated Press*] (SAG) .... NCTPI
Nuveen Connecticut Premium Income Municipal Fund [*NYSE symbol*] (SPSG) .... NTC
Nuveen CT Prem Inc. Muni [*NYSE symbol*] (TTSB) .... NTC
Nuveen FL Inv Qua Muni [*NYSE symbol*] (TTSB) .... NQF
Nuveen FL Qual Income Muni [*NYSE symbol*] (TTSB) .... NUF
Nuveen Florida Investment Quality Municipal [*NYSE symbol*] (SPSG) .... NQF
Nuveen Florida Investment Quality Municipal Fund [*Associated Press*] (SAG) .... NvFL
Nuveen Florida Quality Income Municipal [*NYSE symbol*] (SPSG) .... NUF
Nuveen Florida Quality Income Municipal Fund [*Associated Press*] (SAG) .... NFLQI
Nuveen GA Prem Inc. Muni [*AMEX symbol*] (TTSB) .... NPG
Nuveen Georgia Premium Income Municipal Fund [*Associated Press*] (SAG) .... NGAPI
Nuveen Georgia Premium Income Municipal Fund [*AMEX symbol*] (SPSG) .... NPG
NuVeen Ins CA Prem Inc Muni 2 [*NYSE symbol*] (TTSB) .... NCL
Nuveen Ins CA Prem Inc. Muni [*NYSE symbol*] (TTSB) .... NPC
Nuveen Ins CA Sel Tax-Free Inc. [*NYSE symbol*] (TTSB) .... NXC
Nuveen Ins FL Prem Inc. Muni [*NYSE symbol*] (TTSB) .... NFL
Nuveen Ins Muni Oppt Fd [*NYSE symbol*] (TTSB) .... NIO
Nuveen Ins. NY Prem Inc. Muni [*NYSE symbol*] (TTSB) .... NNF
Nuveen Ins NY Sel Tax-Free Inc. [*NYSE symbol*] (TTSB) .... NXN
Nuveen Ins Prem Inc. Muni [*NYSE symbol*] (TTSB) .... NPE
Nuveen Ins Prem Inc. Muni 2 [*NYSE symbol*] (TTSB) .... NPX
Nuveen Ins Qual Muni [*NYSE symbol*] (TTSB) .... NQI
Nuveen Insurance Municipal Opportunity Fund [*Associated Press*] (SAG) .... NvIMO
Nuveen Insured California Premium Income Municipal [*Associated Press*] (SAG) .... NICAP
Nuveen Insured California Premium Income Municipal [*NYSE symbol*] (SPSG) .... NPC
Nuveen Insured California Premium Income Municipal Fund 2 [*Associated Press*] (SAG) NICAP2
Nuveen Insured California Premium Income Municipal II [*NYSE symbol*] (SPSG) .... NCL
Nuveen Insured California Select Tax Free [*Associated Press*] (SAG) ... NICAS
Nuveen Insured California Select Tax-Free Income [*NYSE symbol*] (SPSG) .... NXC
Nuveen Insured Florida Premium Income Municipal [*NYSE symbol*] (SPSG) .... NFL
Nuveen Insured Florida Premium Income Municipal Fund [*Associated Press*] (SAG) .... NIFLP
Nuveen Insured Municipal Opportunity Fund [*NYSE symbol*] (SPSG) .... NIO
Nuveen Insured New York Premium Income Municipal [*Associated Press*] (SAG) .... NINYP

Nuveen Insured New York Premium Income Municipal [*NYSE symbol*] (SPSG) .... NNF
Nuveen Insured New York Select Tax Free Income [*Associated Press*] (SAG) .... NINYS
Nuveen Insured New York Select Tax-Free Income [*NYSE symbol*] (SPSG) .... NXN
Nuveen Insured Premium Income Municipal [*NYSE symbol*] (SPSG) .... NPE
Nuveen Insured Premium Income Municipal Fund [*Associated Press*] (SAG) .... NIPIMn
Nuveen Insured Premium Income Municipal Fund [*NYSE symbol*] (SPSG).... NPX
Nuveen Insured Premium Income Municipal Fund 2 [*Associated Press*] (SAG) NIPIM2
Nuveen Insured Quality Fund [*Associated Press*] (SAG) .... NvInQI
Nuveen Insured Quality Municipal [*NYSE symbol*] (SPSG) .... NQI
Nuveen Inv Quality Muni [*NYSE symbol*] (TTSB) .... NQM
Nuveen Investment Quality Municipal [*NYSE symbol*] (SPSG) .... NQM
Nuveen Investment Quality Municipal Fund [*Associated Press*] (SAG) .... NvIQI
Nuveen MA Prem Inc. Muni Fd [*NYSE symbol*] (TTSB) .... NMT
Nuveen Maryland Premium Income Municipal Fund [*Associated Press*] (SAG) .... NMDPI
Nuveen Maryland Premium Income Municipal Fund [*NYSE symbol*] (SPSG) .... NMY
Nuveen Massachusetts Premium Income Municipal Fund [*NYSE symbol*] (SPSG) .... NMT
Nuveen Massachusetts Premium Income Municipal Fund [*Associated Press*] (SAG) .... NvMAP
Nuveen MD Prem Inc. Muni Fd [*NYSE symbol*] (TTSB) .... NMY
Nuveen MI Prem Inc. Muni [*NYSE symbol*] (TTSB) .... NMP
Nuveen MI Qual Income Muni [*NYSE symbol*] (TTSB) .... NUM
Nuveen Michigan Premium Income Municipal [*NYSE symbol*] (SPSG) .... NMP
Nuveen Michigan Premium Income Municipal [*Associated Press*] (SAG) .... NvMIPI
Nuveen Michigan Quality Income Municipal [*NYSE symbol*] (SPSG) .... NUM
Nuveen Michigan Quality Income Municipal Fund [*Associated Press*] (SAG) .... NMIQI
Nuveen Missouri Premium Income Municipal Fund [*Associated Press*] (SAG) .... NMOPI
Nuveen Missouri Premium Income Municipal Fund [*AMEX symbol*] (SPSG) .... NOM
Nuveen MO Prem, Inc. Muni [*AMEX symbol*] (TTSB) .... NOM
Nuveen Muni Advantage Fd [*NYSE symbol*] (TTSB) .... NMA
Nuveen Muni Mkt Oppt [*NYSE symbol*] (TTSB) .... NMO
Nuveen Muni Value Fd [*NYSE symbol*] (TTSB) .... NUV
Nuveen Municipal Advantage Fund [*NYSE symbol*] (SPSG) .... NMA
Nuveen Municipal Advantage Fund [*Associated Press*] (SAG) .... NvMAd
Nuveen Municipal Income Fund [*NYSE symbol*] (SPSG) .... NMI
Nuveen Municipal Income Fund [*Associated Press*] (SAG) .... NvMul
Nuveen Municipal Market Opportunities [*NYSE symbol*] (SPSG) .... NMO
Nuveen Municipal Opportunity Fund [*Associated Press*] (SAG) .... NvMO
Nuveen Municipal Value Fund, Inc. [*NYSE symbol*] (SPSG) .... NUV
Nuveen Municipal Value Fund, Inc. [*Associated Press*] (SAG) .... NuvMu
Nuveen NC Prem Inc. Muni [*NYSE symbol*] (TTSB) .... NNC
Nuveen New Jersey Investment Quality Municipal [*NYSE symbol*] (SPSG).... NQJ
Nuveen New Jersey Investment Quality Municipal Fund [*Associated Press*] (SAG) .... NvNJ
Nuveen New Jersey Premium Income Municipal [*NYSE symbol*] (SPSG) ...... NNJ
Nuveen New Jersey Premium Income Municipal [*Associated Press*] (SAG) .... NvNJPI
Nuveen New York Investment Quality Municipal Fund [*Associated Press*] (SAG) .... NNYIQ
Nuveen New York Investment Quality Municipal Fund [*NYSE symbol*] (SPSG) .... NQN
Nuveen New York Municipal Fund [*NYSE symbol*] (SPSG) .... NNY
Nuveen New York Municipal Income [*AMEX symbol*] (SPSG) .... NNM
Nuveen New York Municipal Income Fund [*Associated Press*] (SAG) .... NNYMI
Nuveen New York Municipal Value Fund [*Associated Press*] (SAG) .... NNYMV
Nuveen New York Performance Plus Municipal [*NYSE symbol*] (SPSG) .... NNP
Nuveen New York Performance Plus Municipal Fund [*Associated Press*] (SAG) .... NvNYP
Nuveen New York Quality Income Municipal [*NYSE symbol*] (SPSG) .... NUN
Nuveen New York Quality Income Municipal [*Associated Press*] (SAG) .... NvNYQI
Nuveen New York Select Quality Municipal [*NYSE symbol*] (SPSG) .... NVN
Nuveen New York Select Quality Municipal Fund [*Associated Press*] (SAG) .... NNYSQ
Nuveen NJ Inv Qua Muni [*NYSE symbol*] (TTSB) .... NQJ
Nuveen NJ Prem Inc. Muni [*NYSE symbol*] (TTSB) .... NNJ
Nuveen North Carolina Premium Income Municipal Fund [*NYSE symbol*] (SPSG) .... NNC
Nuveen North Carolina Premium Income Municipal Fund [*Associated Press*] (SAG) .... NNCPI
Nuveen NY Inv Qual Muni [*NYSE symbol*] (TTSB) .... NQN
Nuveen NY Muni Val Fd [*NYSE symbol*] (TTSB) .... NNY
Nuveen NY Perform Plus Muni [*NYSE symbol*] (TTSB) .... NNP
Nuveen NY Qual Income Muni [*NYSE symbol*] (TTSB) .... NUN
Nuveen NY Selct Qual Muni [*NYSE symbol*] (TTSB) .... NVN
Nuveen OH Qual Incme Muni [*NYSE symbol*] (TTSB) .... NUO
Nuveen Ohio Quality Income Municipal [*NYSE symbol*] (SPSG) .... NUO
Nuveen Ohio Quality Income Municipal Fund [*Associated Press*] (SAG) .... NOHQI
Nuveen PA Inv Qua Muni [*NYSE symbol*] (TTSB) .... NQP
Nuveen PA Prem Inc. Muni 2 [*NYSE symbol*] (TTSB) .... NPY
Nuveen Pennsylvania Investment Quality Municipal [*NYSE symbol*] (SPSG) .... NQP
Nuveen Pennsylvania Investment Quality Municipal Fund [*Associated Press*] (SAG) .... NvPA
Nuveen Pennsylvania Premium Income Municipal [*NYSE symbol*] (SPSG) .... NPY

Nuveen Pennsylvania Premium Income Municipal Fund [*Associated Press*] (SAG) NvPAP2
Nuveen Perform Plus Muni [*NYSE symbol*] (TTSB) .... NPP
Nuveen Performance Plus Municipal [*NYSE symbol*] (SPSG) .... NPP
Nuveen Performance Plus Municipal Fund [*Associated Press*] (SAG) .... NuvPP
Nuveen Prem Income Muni [*NYSE symbol*] (TTSB) .... NPI
Nuveen Prem Income Muni 2 [*NYSE symbol*] (TTSB) .... NPM
Nuveen Prem Income Muni 4 [*NYSE symbol*] (TTSB) .... NPT
Nuveen Prem Insured Muni Inc. [*NYSE symbol*] (TTSB) .... NIF
Nuveen Prem Muni Income [*NYSE symbol*] (TTSB) .... NPF
Nuveen Premier Insured Municipal Income Fund [*Associated Press*] (SAG) .... NvPIM
Nuveen Premium Income Municipal 2 [*NYSE symbol*] (SPSG) .... NPM
Nuveen Premium Income Municipal Fund 2 [*Associated Press*] (SAG) NuvPI2
Nuveen Premium Income Municipal Fund 4 [*Associated Press*] (SAG) NuvPI4
Nuveen Premium Income Municipal Fund, Inc. [*NYSE symbol*] (SPSG) .... NPI
Nuveen Premium Income Municipal Fund, Inc. [*Associated Press*] (SAG) .... NuvPI
Nuveen Premium Income Municipal Fund IV [*NYSE symbol*] (SPSG) .... NPT
Nuveen Premium Insured Municipal Income [*NYSE symbol*] (SPSG) .... NIF
Nuveen Premium Municipal Income [*NYSE symbol*] (SPSG) .... NPF
Nuveen Premium Municipal Income Fund [*Associated Press*] (SAG) .... NvPMI
Nuveen Qual Income Muni Fd [*NYSE symbol*] (TTSB) .... NQU
Nuveen Quality Income Municipal Fund [*NYSE symbol*] (SPSG) .... NQU
Nuveen Quality Income Municipal Fund [*Associated Press*] (SAG) .... NuvQInc
Nuveen Selct Tax-Free Inc. 2 [*NYSE symbol*] (TTSB) .... NXQ
Nuveen Selct Tax-Free Inc. 3 [*NYSE symbol*] (TTSB) .... NXR
Nuveen Select Maturities Muni [*NYSE symbol*] (TTSB) .... NIM
Nuveen Select Maturities Municipal [*NYSE symbol*] (SPSG) .... NIM
Nuveen Select Maturities Municipal Fund [*Associated Press*] (SAG) .... NvSMM
Nuveen Select Qual Muni [*NYSE symbol*] (TTSB) .... NQS
Nuveen Select Quality [*Associated Press*] (SAG) .... NuvSel
Nuveen Select Quality Municipal [*NYSE symbol*] (SPSG) .... NQS
Nuveen Select Tax Free Income Portfolio [*Associated Press*] (SAG) .... NSTFI
Nuveen Select Tax Free Income Portfolio 2 [*Associated Press*] (SAG) NSTFI2
Nuveen Select Tax Free Income Portfolio 3 [*Associated Press*] (SAG) NSTFI3
Nuveen Select Tax-Free Income [*NYSE symbol*] (SPSG) .... NXP
Nuveen Select Tax-Free Income 2 [*NYSE symbol*] (SPSG) .... NXQ
Nuveen Select Tax-Free Income 3 [*NYSE symbol*] (SPSG) .... NXR
Nuveen Select Tax-Free Inc. [*NYSE symbol*] (TTSB) .... NXP
Nuveen Texas Quality Income [*NYSE symbol*] (SPSG) .... NTX
Nuveen Texas Quality Income [*Associated Press*] (SAG) .... NTXQI
Nuveen TX Qual Income Muni [*NYSE symbol*] (TTSB) .... NTX
Nuveen VA Prem Inc. Muni Fd [*NYSE symbol*] (TTSB) .... NPV
Nuveen Virginia Premium Income Municipal Fund [*NYSE symbol*] (SPSG) .... NPV
Nuveen Virginia Premium Income Municipal Fund [*Associated Press*] (SAG) .... NVAPI
Nuveen WA Prem Inc. Muni Fd [*AMEX symbol*] (TTSB) .... NPW
Nuveen Washington Premium Income Municipal Fund [*AMEX symbol*] (SPSG) .... NPW
Nuveen Washington Premium Income Municipal Fund [*Associated Press*] (SAG) .... NuvWA
Nuwe Republiekparty [*New Republic Party*] [*Political party Afrikaans*] .... NRP
NUWEP [*Nuclear Weapon*] **Intelligence Support Plan** [*Military*] .... NISP
Nu-West Group Ltd. [*Toronto Stock Exchange symbol*] .... NUW
Nu-West Industries [*NASDAQ symbol*] (SAG) .... FERTP
Nu-West Industries, Inc. [*Associated Press*] (SAG) .... NuWt
Nux Moschata [*Nutmeg*] [*Pharmacology*] (ROG) .... NM
Nux Vomica Strychnia [*Strychnine-producing plant*] [*Pharmacy*] (ROG) .... VOM
[*The*] **Nuzi Dialect of Akkadian** [*A publication*] (BJA) .... NDA
NV Luchtvaartmaatschappij Twente [*Netherlands ICAO designator*] (FAAC) .... LTW
NVA [*North Vietnam Army*] **Regulars** (VNW) .... NVR
NVIEW Corp. [*Associated Press*] (SAG) .... NVIEW
NVIEW Corp. [*NASDAQ symbol*] (SAG) .... NVUE
N-Vinylacetamide [*Organic chemistry*] .... NVA
N-Vinylcarbazole [*Organic chemistry*] .... NVCZ
N-Vinylpyrrolidone [*Organic chemistry*] .... NVP
N-Viro International [*NASDAQ symbol*] (TTSB) .... NVIC
N-Viro International Corp. [*NASDAQ symbol*] (SAG) .... NVIC
N-Viro International Corp. [*Associated Press*] (SAG) .... N-ViroInt
N-Vision, Inc. [*Associated Press*] (SAG) .... nVision
N-Vision, Inc. [*NASDAQ symbol*] (SAG) .... NVSN
n-Vision Inc. [*NASDAQ symbol*] (TTSB) .... NVSN
n-Vision Inc. Wrrt [*NASDAQ symbol*] (TTSB) .... NVSNW
NVR, Inc. [*AMEX symbol*] (SPSG) .... NVR
NVR Inc. Wrrt [*AMEX symbol*] (TTSB) .... NVR.WS
N-W Group, Inc. [*Toronto Stock Exchange symbol*] .... NGI
NWFS Capital Financing Trust [*NYSE symbol*] (SAG) .... NFS
NWP Resources [*Vancouver Stock Exchange symbol*] .... NWP
NWPS Cap Fin 8.125% Tr Sec 1 [*NYSE symbol*] (TTSB) .... NPSPrA
NWPS Capital Financing Tr PERCS [*NYSE symbol*] (SAG) .... NPS
NWPS Capital Financing Tr PERCS [*Associated Press*] (SAG) .... NWPS
NWS Capital Financing Trust [*Associated Press*] (SAG) .... NWFS
NWS [*National Weather Service*] **Forecast Office** [*Marine science*] (OSRA) .... NWSFO
NWS [*National Weather Service*] **Forecast Office** (USDC) .... NWSFO
NWS [*National Weather Service*] **Telecommunications Gateway** (USDC) .... NWSTG
NWS [*National Weather Service*] **Telecommunications Gateway** [*Marine science*] (OSRA) .... NWSTG
NWSA Journal [*A publication*] (BRI) .... NWSA Jnl
Ny Alesund (Svalbard) [*Norway ICAO location identifier*] (ICLI) .... ENAS
Ny Demokrati [*New Democracy*] [*Sweden Political party*] (EY) .... ND
N.Y. State E&G, 3.75% Pfd [*NYSE symbol*] (TTSB) .... NGEPr
N.Y. State E&G 7.40% Pfd [*NYSE symbol*] (TTSB) .... NGEPrE
N.Y. State E&G Adj Rt B Pfd [*NYSE symbol*] (TTSB) .... NGEPrD
Nyack, AK [*Location identifier FAA*] (FAAL) .... ZNC
Nyack Library, Nyack, NY [*Library symbol Library of Congress*] (LCLS) .... NNy
Nyack Missionary College, Nyack, NY [*Library symbol Library of Congress*] (LCLS) .... NNyM
Nyack, NY [*FM radio station call letters*] .... WNYK
Nyakagunda [*Burundi*] [*ICAO location identifier*] (ICLI) .... HBBN
Nyala [*Sudan*] [*ICAO location identifier*] (ICLI) .... HSNL
Nyala [*Sudan*] [*Airport symbol*] (OAG) .... UYL
Nyamwezi [*MARC language code Library of Congress*] (LCCP) .... nym
Nyanga [*Congo*] [*ICAO location identifier*] (ICLI) .... FCMS
Nyanga [*Zaire*] [*ICAO location identifier*] (ICLI) .... FZDG
Nyanja [*MARC language code Library of Congress*] (LCCP) .... nya
Nyanza-Lac [*Burundi*] [*ICAO location identifier*] (ICLI) .... HBBL
Nyasaland (ROG) .... NY
Nyasaland Law Reports [*A publication*] (DLA) .... NLR
Nyasaland Law Reports [*South Africa*] [*A publication*] (DLA) .... Ny LR
Nyasaland Protectorate Law Reports [*A publication*] (ILCA) .... NPLR
Nyasaland Trade Union Congress .... NTUC
Nyaung U [*Myanmar*] [*ICAO location identifier*] (ICLI) .... VBNU
Nyaung-U [*Myanmar*] [*Airport symbol*] (OAG) .... NYU
NYC Parents of Lesbians and Gay Men (EA) .... PLGM
Nycomed ASA ADS [*NYSE symbol*] (TTSB) .... NYD
NYCOR, Inc. [*NASDAQ symbol*] (NQ) .... NYCO
NYCOR, Inc. [*Associated Press*] (SAG) .... Nycor
NYCOR Inc.'A' [*NASDAQ symbol*] (TTSB) .... NYCOA
Nyer Med Group [*NASDAQ symbol*] (TTSB) .... NYER
Nyer Medical Group [*NASDAQ symbol*] (SAG) .... NYER
Nyer Medical Group [*Associated Press*] (SAG) .... NyerMd
Nyeri [*Kenya*] [*ICAO location identifier*] (ICLI) .... HKNI
Nye's Reports [*18-21 Utah*] [*A publication*] (DLA) .... Nye
Nyge Aero AB [*Sweden ICAO designator*] (FAAC) .... NYG
Nyimba [*Zambia*] [*ICAO location identifier*] (ICLI) .... FLNY
Nykoping/Oxelosund [*Sweden ICAO location identifier*] (ICLI) .... ESKN
Nylon (AAG) .... N
Nylon (MSA) .... NYL
Nylon Full-Line Filter .... NFLF
Nylon Insert Lock Nut .... NILN
Nylon Insulation Material .... NIM
Nylon Jacket .... NJ
Nylon Suture [*Medicine*] .... NS
Nylon Wire Tie .... NWT
Nylstroom [*South Africa*] [*ICAO location identifier*] (ICLI) .... FANY
NYMAGIC, Inc. [*Formerly, New York Marine & General Insurance Co.*] [*NYSE symbol*] (SPSG) .... NYM
NYMAGIC, Inc. [*Formerly, New York Marine & General Insurance Co.*] [*Associated Press*] (SAG) .... NYMAGC
Nymph [*Entomology*] .... N
Nymphaeum (VRA) .... nymphm
Nymphomaniac (DSUE) .... NYMPH
Nymphomaniac (DSUE) .... NYMPHO
Nynex Cable Communications Group PLC [*NASDAQ symbol*] (SAG) .... NYNCY
Nynex Cable Communications Group PLC [*Associated Press*] (SAG) .... NynxCbl
NYNEX CableCommsGrpADS Unit [*NASDAQ symbol*] (TTSB) .... NYNCY
NYNEX Corp. [*NYSE symbol*] (SPSG) .... NYN
NYNEX Corp. [*Associated Press*] (SAG) .... Nynex
Nynex Corp., White Plains, NY [*Library symbol*] [*Library of Congress*] (LCLS) .... NWhpNC
Nyngan [*Australia Airport symbol*] (OAG) .... NYN
Nyoro [*MARC language code Library of Congress*] (LCCP) .... nyo
Nyssa, OR [*FM radio station call letters*] .... KGZH
Nystagmus [*Medicine*] .... NYST
Nystagmus Action Group [*British*] (DBA) .... NAG
Nystagmus Recorder .... NR
Nystatin [*Antifungal antibiotic*] .... N
Nytest Environmental [*NASDAQ symbol*] (TTSB) .... NYTS
NYTEST Environmental, Inc. [*Associated Press*] (SAG) .... Nytest
NYTEST Environmental, Inc. [*NASDAQ symbol*] (NQ) .... NYTS
Nyunzu [*Zaire*] [*ICAO location identifier*] (ICLI) .... FZRN
Nyutabaru [*Japan ICAO location identifier*] (ICLI) .... RJFN
NZ Warbirds Association, Inc. [*New Zealand*] [*ICAO designator*] (FAAC) .... WAR
N'Zabi [*Congo*] [*ICAO location identifier*] (ICLI) .... FCMZ
Nzamba [*Zaire*] [*ICAO location identifier*] (ICLI) .... FZDF
Nzerekore [*Guinea*] [*Airport symbol*] (AD) .... NZE
N,Zerekore/Konia [*Guinea*] [*ICAO location identifier*] (ICLI) .... GUNZ
N'Zeto [*Angola*] [*Airport symbol*] (OAG) .... ARZ
N'Zeto/N'Zeto [*Angola*] [*ICAO location identifier*] (ICLI) .... FNZE
N'Ziba [*Congo*] [*ICAO location identifier*] (ICLI) .... FCMB
Nzingha Society (EA) .... NS

O
By Meaning

O Estado de Sao Paulo [*State of Sao Paulo*] [*Brazil*] [*A publication*] (AD) ..... OESP
O/ET [*Orbiter/External Tank*] **Separation System** [*NASA*] (MCD) ...... OESS
O. J. Noer Research Foundation (EA) ...... OJNRF
O Negative [*Blood type*] [*Hematology and laboratory*] (DAVI) ...... ONEG
O Sapientia, O Radix, O Adonai [*Three anthems sung in Roman Catholic churches before Christmas*] (ROG) ...... OOO
O-Acetylhomoserine (thiol)-lyase [*An enzyme*] ...... OAHS
O-Acetylserine (thiol)-lyase [*An enzyme*] ...... OAS
Oacis Healthcare Holdings Corp. [*NASDAQ symbol*] (SAG) ...... OCIS
Oacis Healthcare Holdings Corp. [*Associated Press*] (SAG) ...... OcisHlth
Oacis Heathcare Hldgs [*NASDAQ symbol*] (TTSB) ...... OCIS
Oahu [*Hawaii*] [*ICAO location identifier*] (ICLI) ...... PHFF
Oahu Education Association [*Hawaii*] (AD) ...... OEA
Oahu Metropolitan Planning Organization [*Hawaii*] (AD) ...... OMPO
Oak Bark Tanners' Association (AD) ...... OBTA
Oak Creek, CO [*FM radio station call letters*] ...... KFMU
Oak Creek Public Library, Oak Creek, CO [*Library symbol Library of Congress*] (LCLS) ...... CoOc
Oak Forest Hospital, Oak Forest, IL [*Library symbol Library of Congress*] (LCLS) ...... IOfH
Oak Grove [*Tennessee*] [*Seismograph station code, US Geological Survey*] (SEIS) ...... OKG
Oak Grove, LA [*FM radio station call letters*] ...... KWCL
Oak Harbor [*Washington*] [*Airport symbol*] (OAG) ...... ODW
Oak Harbor [*Washington*] [*Seismograph station code, US Geological Survey*] (SEIS) ...... OHW
Oak Harbor, OH [*FM radio station call letters*] ...... WJZE
Oak Harbor, WA [*AM radio station call letters*] ...... KJTT
Oak Harbor, WA [*Location identifier FAA*] (FAAL) ...... NXI
Oak Harbor, Whidbey Island, WA [*Naval base*] ...... WI
Oak Hill Financial [*NASDAQ symbol*] (TTSB) ...... OAKF
Oak Hill Financial, Inc. [*NASDAQ symbol*] (SAG) ...... OAKF
Oak Hill Financial, Inc. [*Associated Press*] (SAG) ...... OakHill
Oak Hill Financial, Inc. [*Associated Press*] (SAG) ...... OakHillF
Oak Hill Sportswear [*NASDAQ symbol*] (TTSB) ...... OHSC
Oak Hill Sportswear Corp. [*Associated Press*] (SAG) ...... OakHill
Oak Hill Sportswear Corp. [*NASDAQ symbol*] (NQ) ...... OHSC
Oak Hill, WV [*FM radio station call letters*] ...... WAXS
Oak Hill, WV [*AM radio station call letters*] ...... WOAY
Oak Hill, WV [*Television station call letters*] ...... WOAY-TV
Oak Hills Bible College, Bemidji, MN [*Library symbol*] [*Library of Congress*] (LCLS) ...... MnBemOH
Oak Indus [*NYSE symbol*] (TTSB) ...... OAK
Oak Industries, Inc. [*NYSE symbol*] (SPSG) ...... OAK
Oak Industries, Inc. [*Associated Press*] (SAG) ...... OakInds
Oak Lawn Public Library, Oak Lawn, IL [*Library symbol Library of Congress*] (LCLS) ...... IOl
Oak Lawn Public Library, Oak Lawn, IL [*OCLC symbol*] (OCLC) ...... IVJ
Oak Leaf Cluster [*Military decoration*] ...... OLC
Oak Park, IL [*AM radio station call letters*] ...... WPNA
Oak Park, IL [*FM radio station call letters*] ...... WVAZ
Oak Park Public Library, Dole Branch, Oak Park, IL [*Library symbol Library of Congress*] (LCLS) ...... IOa-D
Oak Park Public Library, Maze Branch, Oak Park, IL [*Library symbol Library of Congress*] (LCLS) ...... IOa-M
Oak Park Public Library, Oak Park, IL [*Library symbol Library of Congress*] (LCLS) ...... IOa
Oak Park-River Forest High School, Oak Park, IL [*Library symbol Library of Congress*] (LCLS) ...... IOaHS
Oak Ridge [*Tennessee*] [*Seismograph station code, US Geological Survey*] (SEIS) ...... ORT
Oak Ridge Analytical Systems ...... ORANS
Oak Ridge Associated Universities (EA) ...... ORAU
Oak Ridge Associated Universities, Oak Ridge, TN [*Library symbol Library of Congress*] (LCLS) ...... TOU
Oak Ridge Automatic Computer and Logical Engine ...... ORACLE
Oak Ridge Binary Internal-Translator ...... ORBIT
Oak Ridge Boys International Fan Club (EA) ...... ORBIFC
Oak Ridge Complex [*Department of Energy*] [*Oak Ridge National Laboratory*] (GAAI) ...... OR
Oak Ridge Computerized Hierarchical Information System [*AEC*] (IID) ...... ORCHIS
Oak Ridge Data Evaluation and Analysis Language [*Department of Energy*] (PDAA) ...... ORDEAL
Oak Ridge Electron Linear Accelerator [*Oak Ridge, TN*] [*Department of Energy*] ...... ORELA

Oak Ridge Full Matrix Least Squares ...... ORFLS
Oak Ridge Gaseous Diffusion Plant [*Department of Energy*] ...... ORGDP
Oak Ridge Graduate School of Biomedical Sciences [*Tennessee*] ...... ORGSBS
Oak Ridge Hospital, Oak Ridge, TN [*Library symbol Library of Congress*] (LCLS) ...... TOH
Oak Ridge Institute for Science and Education [*Oak Ridge Associated Universities*] [*Research center*] (RCD) ...... ORISE
Oak Ridge Institute of Nuclear Studies [*Later, ORAU*] (EA) ...... ORINS
Oak Ridge Isochronous Cyclotron [*Department of Energy*] ...... ORIC
Oak Ridge Isotope Generation and Depletion Code [*Department of Energy*] (GAAI) ORIGEN2
Oak Ridge K-25 Site [*Department of Energy*] [*Oak Ridge, TN*] (GAAI) K-25
Oak Ridge Military Institute ...... ORMI
Oak Ridge National Laboratory [*Oak Ridge, TN*] [*Department of Energy*] ...... ORNL
Oak Ridge National Laboratory Nuclear Data Project [*Database producer*] ...... ORNLY-NDP
Oak Ridge National Laboratory, Oak Ridge, TN [*OCLC symbol*] (OCLC) ...... ORN
Oak Ridge National Laboratory Pool Critical Assembly (SAA) ...... ORNL-PCA
Oak Ridge Operations Office (DOGT) ...... OR
Oak Ridge Operations Office (MCD) ...... ORO
Oak Ridge Public Library, Oak Ridge, TN [*Library symbol Library of Congress*] (LCLS) ...... TO
Oak Ridge Regional Modeling Information System ...... ORRMIS
Oak Ridge Research Reactor [*ORNL*] (NRCH) ...... ORR
Oak Ridge Research Reactor [*Department of Energy*] (NRCH) ...... ORRR
Oak Ridge Reservation (DOGT) ...... ORR
Oak Ridge Reservation ...... ORR
Oak Ridge Reservation ...... ORR
Oak Ridge School of Reactor Technology [*Department of Energy*] ...... ORSORT
Oak Ridge Selective Dissemination of Information [*Department of Energy*] (NASA) ...... ORSDI
Oak Ridge Systems Analysis Code ...... ORSAC
Oak Ridge Technical Enterprises Corp. ...... ORTEC
Oak Ridge, TN [*AM radio station call letters*] ...... WATO
Oak Ridge, TN [*FM radio station call letters*] ...... WNFZ
Oak Ridge, TN [*FM radio station call letters*] ...... WOKI
Oak Ridge TOKAMAK [*Energy Research and Development Administration*] ...... ORMAK
Oak Ridge Uranium Separation Plant [*Code designation*] (DEN) K25
Oak Ridge Y-12 Plant [*Department of Energy*] [*Oak Ridge, TN*] (GAAI) Y-12
Oak Satellite Corp. (NITA) ...... OSC
Oak, Sunk, and Weathered [*Construction*] ...... OS & W
Oak Technology [*NASDAQ symbol*] (TTSB) ...... OAKT
Oak Technology, Inc. [*NASDAQ symbol*] (SAG) ...... OAKT
Oak Technology, Inc. [*Associated Press*] (SAG) ...... OakTch
Oakdale, CA [*FM radio station call letters*] ...... KDJK
Oakdale, LA [*AM radio station call letters*] ...... KICR
Oakdale, LA [*FM radio station call letters*] ...... KICR-FM
Oakdale, LA [*AM radio station call letters*] ...... KREH
Oakdale-Bohemia Junior High School, Oakdale, NY [*Library symbol Library of Congress*] (LCLS) ...... NOaJH
Oakes, ND [*AM radio station call letters*] ...... KDDR
Oakey [*Australia ICAO location identifier*] (ICLI) ...... ABOK
Oakey [*Queensland*] [*Airport symbol*] (AD) ...... OKY
Oakfield [*New York*] [*Seismograph station code, US Geological Survey Closed*] (SEIS) ...... OAK
Oakfield Public Library (Haxton Memorial), Oakfield, NY [*Library symbol Library of Congress*] (LCLS) ...... NOaf
Oakhurst, CA [*FM radio station call letters*] ...... KAAT
Oakhurst, CA [*AM radio station call letters*] ...... KTNS
Oakhurst Capital, Inc. [*NASDAQ symbol*] (SAG) ...... OAKC
Oakhurst Capital, Inc. [*Associated Press*] (SAG) ...... Oakhurst
Oakhurst Co. [*NASDAQ symbol*] (TTSB) ...... OAKC
Oakhurst Co., Inc. [*NASDAQ symbol*] (SAG) ...... OAKC
Oakhurst Co., Inc. [*Associated Press*] (SAG) ...... Oakhurst
Oakington [*British ICAO location identifier*] (ICLI) ...... EGUO
Oakland [*California*] [*Airport symbol*] ...... OAK
Oakland Acorn, Oakland, IA [*Library symbol Library of Congress*] (LCLS) .... IaOakA
Oakland [*California*] Army Base (VNW) ...... OAB
Oakland Army Base [*California*] (AABC) ...... OARB
Oakland Army Terminal [*California*] ...... OART
Oakland, CA [*Location identifier FAA*] (FAAL) ...... AAZ
Oakland, CA [*Location identifier FAA*] (FAAL) ...... EZB
Oakland, CA [*Location identifier FAA*] (FAAL) ...... INB
Oakland, CA [*AM radio station call letters*] ...... KABL
Oakland, CA [*AM radio station call letters*] ...... KDIA

Oakland, CA [*AM radio station call letters*] ... KNEW
Oakland, CA [*Television station call letters*] ... KTVU
Oakland, CA [*Location identifier FAA*] (FAAL) ... ZOA
Oakland City College, Oakland City, IN [*Library symbol Library of Congress*] (LCLS) ... InOcC
Oakland Community College, Auburn Heights, MI [*Library symbol Library of Congress*] (LCLS) ... MiAhO
Oakland County Law Library, Clark J. Adams-Philip Pratt Library, Pontiac, MI [*Library symbol Library of Congress*] (LCLS) ... MiPonO
Oakland, Freemont [*California*] [*ICAO location identifier*] (ICLI) ... KZOA
Oakland Growth Study [*1932-1964*] [*Sociology*] ... OGS
Oakland, MD [*Television station call letters*] ... WGPT
Oakland, MD [*AM radio station call letters*] ... WMSG
Oakland, MD [*FM radio station call letters*] (RBYB) ... WWHC
Oakland/Metropolitan Oakland International [*California*] [*ICAO location identifier*] (ICLI) ... KOAK
Oakland, MI [*FM radio station call letters*] ... WXOU
Oakland Museum, Oakland, CA [*Library symbol Library of Congress*] (LCLS) ... COMus
Oakland, NJ [*AM radio station call letters*] ... WVNJ
Oakland Operations Office (DOGT) ... OAK
Oakland Public Library, Oakland, CA [*Library symbol Library of Congress*] (LCLS) ... CO
Oakland Public Library, Oakland, CA [*Library symbol*] [*Library of Congress*] (LCLS) ... COPL
Oakland Public Library, Oakland, NJ [*Library symbol Library of Congress*] (LCLS) ... NjOak
[*The*] **Oakland Terminal Railway** [*Later, OTR*] [*AAR code*] ... OKT
[*The*] **Oakland Terminal Railway** [*Formerly, OKT*] [*AAR code*] ... OTR
Oakland Township Public Library, Scotland, Ontario [*Library symbol National Library of Canada*] (BIB) ... OSOT
Oakland Tribune, Oakland, CA [*Library symbol Library of Congress*] (LCLS) ... COOT
Oakland Unit School District, Oakland, IL [*Library symbol*] [*Library of Congress*] (LCLS) ... IOakSD
Oakland University (GAGS) ... Oakland U
Oakland University, Rochester, MI [*OCLC symbol*] (OCLC) ... EYR
Oakland University, Rochester, MI [*Library symbol Library of Congress*] (LCLS) ... MiRochOU
Oakland-Pontiac Enthusiast Organization (EA) ... OPEO
Oak-Leaf Roller [*Moth*] [*Entomology*] ... OLR
Oakley District Library, Oakley, ID [*Library symbol*] [*Library of Congress*] (LCLS) ... IdOa
Oakley, KS [*Location identifier FAA*] (FAAL) ... OEL
Oakly, Inc. [*Associated Press*] (SAG) ... Oakly
Oakly, Inc. [*NYSE symbol*] (SAG) ... OO
Oakridge Group Home, Tacoma, WA [*Library symbol Library of Congress*] (LCLS) ... WaTO
Oakridge, OR [*FM radio station call letters*] ... KAVE
Oakridge Public Library, Oakridge, OR [*Library symbol Library of Congress*] (LCLS) ... OrOa
Oakridge Secondary School, London, ON, Canada [*Library symbol Library of Congress*] (LCLS) ... CaOLOS
Oakridge Secondary School, London, Ontario [*Library symbol National Library of Canada*] (NLC) ... OLOS
Oakton Community College, Morton Grove, IL [*OCLC symbol*] (OCLC) ... IAP
Oakton Community College, Morton Grove, IL [*Library symbol Library of Congress*] (LCLS) ... IMgO
Oakton Community Colleges, Learning Resources Center, Des Plaines, IL [*Library symbol Library of Congress*] (LCLS) ... IMgO-Dp
Oaktown, IN [*Location identifier FAA*] (FAAL) ... OTN
Oakville Museums, Ontario [*Library symbol National Library of Canada*] (BIB) ... OOAKM
Oakville, ON [*AM radio station call letters*] ... CHWO
Oakville Public Library, Oakville, ON, Canada [*Library symbol Library of Congress*] (LCLS) ... CaOOak
Oakville Public Library, Ontario [*Library symbol National Library of Canada*] (NLC) ... OOAK
Oakwood College, Huntsville, AL [*Library symbol Library of Congress*] (LCLS) ... AHO
Oakwood College, Huntsville, AL [*OCLC symbol*] (OCLC) ... OAK
Oakwood Elementary School, Huntington Station, NY [*Library symbol*] [*Library of Congress*] (LCLS) ... NHsOE
Oakwood Homes [*NYSE symbol*] (TTSB) ... OH
Oakwood Homes Corp. [*Associated Press*] (SAG) ... Oakwood
Oakwood Homes Corp. [*NYSE symbol*] (SPSG) ... OH
Oakwood Hospital, Dearborn, MI [*Library symbol*] [*Library of Congress*] (LCLS) ... MidbO
Oakwood Petroleums Ltd. [*Toronto Stock Exchange symbol*] ... OAK
Oamaru [*New Zealand*] [*ICAO location identifier*] (ICLI) ... NZOU
Oamaru [*New Zealand*] [*Airport symbol*] (OAG) ... OAM
Oamaru [*New Zealand*] [*Seismograph station code, US Geological Survey*] (SEIS) ... OMZ
o-Aminoacetanilide [*Organic chemistry*] ... OAA
Oasis ... O
Oasis [*Board on Geographic Names*] ... OAS
Oasis Bungera [*Antarctica*] [*Seismograph station code, US Geological Survey Closed*] (SEIS) ... OBA
Oasis International Airlines [*Spain ICAO designator*] (FAAC) ... AAN
Oasis Residential [*NYSE symbol*] (SPSG) ... OAS
Oasis Residential $2.25'A' Pfd [*NYSE symbol*] (TTSB) ... OASPrA
Oasis Residential, Inc. [*Associated Press*] (SAG) ... OasisR
Oasis Residential, Inc. [*Associated Press*] (SAG) ... OasisRsd
Oat Blue Dwarf Virus [*Plant pathology*] ... OBDV
Oat Mosaic Virus [*Plant pathology*] ... OMV
Oat Sterile Dwarf Virus [*Plant pathology*] ... OSDV
Oat Striate Mosaic Virus [*Plant pathology*] ... OSMV
Oath ... O
Oath and Acceptance Date [*Date from which a military officer's commissioned service runs*] ... O & A (Date)
Oatmeal [*Freight*] ... OTML
OAU [*Organization of African Unity*] **Coordinating Committee for the Liberation o f Africa** [*Tanzania*] (EAIO) ... AFLICO
OAU [*Organization of African Unity*] **Liberation Committee** [*Addis Ababa, Ethiopia*] (EAIO) ... OAULC
Oaxaca [*Mexico ICAO location identifier*] (ICLI) ... MMOX
Oaxaca [*Mexico*] [*Seismograph station code, US Geological Survey*] (SEIS) ... OAX
Oaxaca [*Mexico*] [*Airport symbol*] (OAG) ... OAX
OB [*Out-of-the-Body*] **Experient** [*Parapsychology*] ... OBEr
Obadiah [*Old Testament book*] ... Ob
Obadiah [*Old Testament book*] ... Obad
Obadiah [*Old Testament book*] (BJA) ... Obd
Oban [*Scotland*] [*Airport symbol*] (OAG) ... OBN
Oban-Heliport [*Scotland*] [*Airport symbol*] (OAG) ... OHP
Obbia [*Somalia*] [*ICAO location identifier*] (ICLI) ... HCMO
Obbligatissimo [*Your Obedient Servant*] [*Italian*] ... Obbmo
Obbligato [*Essential*] [*Music*] ... OBB
Obbligato [*Essential*] [*Music*] ... Obbl
Obedience Champion [*Dog show term*] ... OCH
Obedience Stewards Club (EA) ... OSC
Obedience Trial Champion [*Dog training*] ... OTCH
Obedience Trial Champion [*Prefix*] ... OTCh
Obedient ... OBDT
Obedient ... OBT
Obedient (AD) ... obt
Obeh [*Afghanistan*] [*ICAO location identifier*] (ICLI) ... OAOB
Obenteni [*Peru*] [*ICAO location identifier*] (ICLI) ... SPBT
Ober Ramstadt Depot Activity [*Germany*] [*Army*] ... ORDA
Obera [*Argentina ICAO location identifier*] (ICLI) ... SATO
Oberbefehlshaber Suedost [*Headquarters, Commander-in-Chief, South*] [*Southern Germany and several army groups on the Eastern Front*] [*German military - World War II*] ... OBSUED
Obere Winkelgruppe [*Angles above 45*] [*German military - World War II*] ... OW
Oberfeldkommandantur [*Military government area headquarters*] [*German military - World War II*] ... OFK
Oberg Industries Ltd. [*Vancouver Stock Exchange symbol*] ... OBG
Obergericht [*Court of Appeal*] [*German*] (DLA) ... Ob G
Obergericht [*Court of Appeal*] [*German*] (DLA) ... OG
Obergurgl [*Austria*] [*Seismograph station code, US Geological Survey*] (SEIS) ... OGA
Oberhasli Breeders of America (EA) ... OBA
Oberkommando der Kriegsmarine [*Navy High Command*] [*German military - World War II*] ... OKM
Oberkommando der Luftwaffe [*Air Force High Command*] [*German military - World War II*] ... OKL
Oberkommando der Marine [*Naval High Command*] [*Germany*] (AD) ... OKM
Oberkommando der Wehrmacht [*Armed Forces High Command*] [*German military - World War II*] ... OKW
Oberkommando des Heeres [*Army High Command*] [*German military - World War II*] ... OKH
Oberlandesgericht [*District Court of Appeal*] [*German*] (DLA) ... OLG
Oberlerchner [*Joseph Oberlerchner Holzindustrie*] [*Austria ICAO aircraft manufacturer identifier*] (ICAO) ... OB
Oberlin College (AD) ... OC
Oberlin College, Conservatory of Music, Library, Oberlin, OH [*OCLC symbol*] (OCLC) ... OBM
Oberlin College, Conservatory of Music, Oberlin, OH [*Library symbol Library of Congress*] (LCLS) ... OOC
Oberlin College, Oberlin, OH [*OCLC symbol*] (OCLC) ... OBE
Oberlin College, Oberlin, OH [*Library symbol Library of Congress*] (LCLS) ... OO
Oberlin, KS [*FM radio station call letters*] ... KFNF
Oberlin, KS [*Location identifier FAA*] (FAAL) ... OIN
Oberlin, OH [*FM radio station call letters*] ... WOBC
Oberlin, OH [*AM radio station call letters*] ... WOBL
Oberlin Public Library, Oberlin, OH [*Library symbol Library of Congress*] (LCLS) ... OOL
Oberlin Public Library, Oberlin, OH [*OCLC symbol*] (OCLC) ... OPL
Obermanual [*Upper Manual*] [*Music*] ... OM
Oberpfaffenhofen [*Germany ICAO location identifier*] (ICLI) ... EDMO
O'Berry Center, Professional Library, Goldsboro, NC [*Library symbol Library of Congress*] (LCLS) ... NcGoO
Oberschleissheim [*Germany ICAO location identifier*] (ICLI) ... EDMX
Oberst [*Colonel*] [*German military - World War II*] ... O
Oberste Herresleitung [*Supreme Headquarters*] [*German*] (AD) ... OHL
Oberstes Gericht [*Supreme Court*] [*German*] ... OG
Oberstimme [*Upper Part*] [*Music*] ... OBERST
Oberverwaltungsgericht [*Provincial Administrative Court of Appeal*] [*German*] (DLA) ... OVG
Oberwerk [*Upper Work*] [*Music*] ... OBERW
Oberwerk [*Upper Work*] [*Music*] ... OBW
Oberwerk [*Highest Organ Bank*] [*German*] (AD) ... Obw
Obese ... ob
Obese Strain [*White leghorn*] ... OS
[*The*] **Obesity Foundation** (EA) ... TOF
Obesity Hypoventilation Syndrome ... OHS
Obesity Research Foundation [*British*] (DI) ... ORF
Obeum [*Nickname for toilets at Cambridge University*] [*Slang British*] (DSUE) ... OB
Obidiah [*Old Testament*] ... OB
Obidos [*Brazil*] [*Airport symbol*] (AD) ... OBI
Obie Media Corp. [*NASDAQ symbol*] (SAG) ... OBIE

Obie Media Corp. [*Associated Press*] (SAG) ... ObieMed
Obiedinennoye Gosudartsvennoye Politicheskoye Upravlenie [*United State Political Administration*] [*Russian*] (AD) ... OGPU
Obigarm [*Former USSR Seismograph station code, US Geological Survey Closed*] (SEIS) ... OBG
Obihiro [*Japan*] [*Seismograph station code, US Geological Survey*] (SEIS) ... OBI
Obihiro [*Japan*] [*Airport symbol*] (OAG) ... OBO
Obihiro [*Japan ICAO location identifier*] (ICLI) ... RJCB
Obiit [*He, or She, Died*] [*Latin*] ... O
Obiit [*He, or She, Died*] [*Latin*] ... OB
Obiit [*He, or She, Died*] [*Latin*] ... OBIT
Obiit [*He, or She, Died*] [*Latin*] ... OBT
Obiit [*He Died*] [*Latin*] (AD) ... obt
Obiit in Christo [*Died in Christ*] [*Latin*] ... OBINXTO
Obiit sine Prole [*Died without Issue*] [*Latin*] ... OBSP
Obiit sine Prole [*Died without Issue*] [*Latin*] ... OSP
Obiit sine Prole Masculus [*He, or She, Died without Male Issue*] [*Latin*] ... OBSPM
Obiit Vita Patris [*He, or She, Died in the Lifetime of His, or Her, Father*] [*Latin*] ... OBVP
Obiter [*Incidentally*] [*Latin*] (GPO) ... ob
Obiter [*A publication*] ... Obit
Obiter Dicta [*Legal term Latin*] (DLA) ... OD
Obituary [*Journalism*] [*Also, ob*] (WDMC) ... obit
Obituary Notice (DSUE) ... OB
Obituary Notice (DSUE) ... OBIT
Object ... O
Object (AAG) ... OBJ
Object (VRA) ... obj
Object Average Optical Density [*Microscopy*] ... OBAD
Object Behavior Analysis [*Computer science*] ... OBA
Object Class [*Military*] ... OC
Object Class Code [*Military*] (AFM) ... OCC
Object Classification (NG) ... O/C
Object Code Only (HGAA) ... OCO
Object Database Management Group [*Computer science*] (CDE) ... ODMG
Object Definition Language [*Computer science*] ... ODL
Object Design, Inc. [*Associated Press*] (SAG) ... ObjDes
Object Design, Inc. [*NASDAQ symbol*] (SAG) ... ODIS
Object Exchange [*Computer science*] (PCM) ... OBEX
Object Film Distance [*Optics*] ... OFD
Object Free Area [*FAA*] (TAG) ... OFA
Object Glass (MSA) ... OG
Object Identification Test ... OIT
Object Identifier [*Computer science*] ... OID
Object Interface Definition Language [*Computer science*] ... OIDL
Object Linking and Embedding [*Windows*] [*Computer science*] ... OLE
Object Location and Small Object Recovery [*Military*] (DNAB) ... OLSOR
Object Management Architecture [*Computer science*] (CDE) ... OMA
Object Management Architecture [*Computer science*] ... OMB
Object Management Extension ... OME
Object Management Facility [*Computer science*] ... OMF
Object Management Group [*Computer science*] ... OMG
Object Management Group ... OMG
Object Manipulation Speed Test ... OMST
Object Model Working Group ... OMWG
Object Modeling Technology [*Ungermann-Bass, Inc.*] ... OMT
Object Module Assembly Program ... OMAP
Object Module File [*Computer science*] (IAA) ... OMF
Object Module Format ... OMF
Object of Affections [*Slang*] ... OOA
Object Oriented Structured Design [*Computer science*] ... OOSD
Object Program (IAA) ... OP
Object Program Utility Routine ... OPUR
Object Relations Technique [*Psychology*] ... ORT
Object Request Broker [*Computer science*] ... ORB
Object Shape [*Microscopy*] ... OBSH
Object Size [*Microscopy*] ... OBSZ
Object Snap [*Auto CAD*] [*Computer science*] ... OSNAP
Object Sorting Scales [*Psychology*] ... OSS
Object Sorting Test [*Psychology*] ... OST
Object Sum Optical Density [*Microscopy*] ... OBSD
Object/Surface/Special Effect ... OSSE
Object Technology [*Computer science*] (CDE) ... OT
Object Texture [*Microscopy*] ... OBTX
Object Time System (MHDB) ... OTS
Object Unit (NITA) ... OU
Object Windows Library [*Borland International*] [*Computer science*] (PCM) ... OWL
Object-Attribute-Value ... O-A-V
Objection (ROG) ... OB
Objection (WDAA) ... OBJ
Objection ... OBJN
Objective ... O
Objective [*Microscopy*] ... OB
Objective ... OBJ
Objective (MSA) ... OBJV
Objective Analytic Batteries [*Personality development test*] [*Psychology*] ... O-A
Objective Aperture [*Microscopy*] ... OA
Objective Area [*Military*] ... OA
Objective Benefit (MAE) ... OB
Objective Capability ... OC
Objective Crew-Served Weapon ... OCSW
Objective End Time ... OET
Objective Family of Weapons ... OFW
Objective Force Designator (MCD) ... OFD
Objective Force Gross Requirement [*Army*] (AABC) ... OFGR
Objective Individual Combat Weapon ... OIC
Objective Individual Combat Weapon [*USA*] ... OICW
Objective Individual Combat Weapon [*Army*] (INF) ... OICW
Objective Judgment Quotient ... OJQ
Objective Loudness Rating [*of telephone connections*] (IEEE) ... OLR
Objective Personal Weapon ... OPW
[*The*] **Objective Personnel Inventory - Civilian** [*Air Force*] ... TOPIC
Objective Quality Evidence (MCD) ... OQE
Objective Rally [*or Rallying*] **Point** [*Military*] ... ORP
Objective Reference Equivalent Measurement (IAA) ... OREM
Objective Release Point [*Army*] (INF) ... ORP
Objective Reliability (MCD) ... OR
Objective Start Time ... OST
Objective Supply Capability [*Army*] (RDA) ... OSC
Objective Supply System [*Army*] ... OSS
Objective Sys Integrators [*NASDAQ symbol*] (TTSB) ... OSII
Objective Systems Integrators, Inc. [*Associated Press*] (SAG) ... ObjSys
Objective Systems Integrators, Inc. [*NASDAQ symbol*] (SAG) ... OSII
Objective Test [*Psychology*] ... OT
Objective, Time, and Cost ... OTC
Objective-Analytic Anxiety Battery [*Psychology*] ... OAAB
Objectives, Strategy, and Tactics [*Management system*] ... OST
Objectives-Based Management System (ADA) ... OBMS
Object-Kowal [*Object in the solar system*] ... O-K
Object-Oriented (BYTE) ... OO
Object-Oriented Analysis [*Computer science*] ... OOA
Object-Oriented Analysis & Design [*Computer science*] (CDE) ... OOAD
Object-Oriented Database [*Computer science*] (CDE) ... OODB
Object-Oriented Database Management System [*Objectivity, Inc.*] [*Computer science*] ... OODBMS
Object-Oriented Design [*Computer science*] ... OOD
Object-Oriented Dynamic Language [*Computer science*] (PCM) ... OODL
Object-Oriented Graphical User Interface [*Computer science*] ... OOGUI
Object-Oriented Language [*Computer science*] (BYTE) ... OOL
Object-Oriented Operating System [*Computer science*] (CDE) ... OOOS
Object-Oriented Pieces of Something [*Computer science*] ... OOPS
Object-Oriented Programming [*Computer science*] ... OOP
Object-Oriented Programming (BYTE) ... OOPS
Object-Oriented Programming Language [*Computer science*] (PCM) ... OOPL
Object-Oriented Programming Systems, Languages, and Applications [*Computer conference*] ... OOPSLA
Object-Oriented Technology [*Computer science*] (CDE) ... OOT
Object-Oriented User Interface [*Computer science*] ... OOUI
Object-Oriented Z Environment [*Computer science*] ... OOZE
Objects of Verification [*Arms control*] (DOMA) ... OOV
ObjectSoft Corp. [*Associated Press*] (SAG) ... ObjSoft
ObjectSoft Corp. [*NASDAQ symbol*] (SAG) ... OSFT
Object-Subject [*Education of the hearing-impaired*] ... OS
Object-to-Image Receptor Distance [*Radiology*] (DAVI) ... OIRD
Oblast [*Governmental subdivision in USSR corresponding to a province or state*] ... O
Oblast [*Governmental subdivision in USSR corresponding to a province or state*] ... OBL
Oblate Archives of Alberta-Saskatchewan, Edmonton, AB, Canada [*Library symbol Library of Congress*] (LCLS) ... CaAEO
Oblate Archives of Alberta-Saskatchewan, Edmonton, Alberta [*Library symbol National Library of Canada*] (NLC) ... AEO
Oblate College (AD) ... OC
Oblate College of the Southwest, San Antonio, TX [*Library symbol Library of Congress*] (LCLS) ... TxSaOC
Oblate College, Washington, DC [*Library symbol Library of Congress*] (LCLS) ... DOC
Oblate Conference of the United States (EA) ... OCUS
Oblate Education Association [*Defunct*] (EA) ... OEA
Oblate Missionaries of Mary Immaculate (TOCD) ... OMMI
Oblate Radial (PDAA) ... OBRAD
Oblate Resource Center and Archives, Vancouver, BC, Canada [*Library symbol*] [*Library of Congress*] (LCLS) ... CaBVAOCA
Oblate Resource Centre and Archives, Vancouver, British Columbia [*Library symbol National Library of Canada*] (NLC) ... BVAOCA
Oblate Sisters of Providence [*Roman Catholic religious order*] ... OSP
Oblate Sisters of the Assumption [*Roman Catholic religious order*] ... OA
Oblate Sisters of the Blessed Sacrament [*Roman Catholic religious order*] ... OSBS
Oblate Sisters of the Sacred Heart of Jesus [*Roman Catholic religious order*] ... OSHJ
Oblate Spherical Coordinates ... OSC
Oblate Spheroid (PDAA) ... OSPRDS
Oblates of Mary Immaculate (TOCD) ... OMI
Oblates of Mary Immaculate (TOCD) ... omi
Oblates of St. Francis de Sales (TOCD) ... osfs
Oblates of St. Francis de Sales (TOCD) ... OSFS
Oblates of St. Joseph (TOCD) ... osj
Oblates of St. Joseph [*Roman Catholic religious order*] ... OSJ
Oblates of St. Martha (TOCD) ... OSM
Oblates of the Most Holy Redeemer (TOCD) ... OSSR
Oblates [*or Order*] **of the Most Holy Redeemer** [*Roman Catholic women's religious order*] ... OSSR
Oblates of the Mother of Orphans (TOCD) ... OMO
Oblates of the Virgin Mary (TOCD) ... omv
Oblates of the Virgin Mary (TOCD) ... OMV
Oblati Sacratissimi Cordis [*Oblate Fathers of the Sacred Heart*] [*Roman Catholic religious order*] ... OSSC
Oblati Sancti Caroli [*Oblate Fathers of St. Charles*] [*Roman Catholic religious order*] ... OSC

Oblati Sancti Francisci Salesii [*Oblate Fathers or Sisters of St. Francis of Sales*] [*Roman Catholic religious orders*] ... OSFS
Oblats de Marie Immaculee [*Oblates of Mary Immaculate*] [*Rome, Italy*] (EAIO) ... OMI
Oblatum [*Cachet*] [*Pharmacy*] ... OBLAT
Obligate (AABC) ... OBLG
Obligated Involuntary Officer [*Military*] ... OBI
Obligated Involuntary Officers [*Used in movie "Spies Like Us"*] ... OIO
Obligated Position [*Civil Service*] ... OP
Obligated Reserve Section [*Air Force*] (AFM) ... ORS
Obligated Services of [*numbers of months indicated*] **Required** [*Navy*] ... OBLISERV
Obligated to Serve on Active Duty a Period of Two Years [*Navy*] ... OBLISERVTWOYR
Obligated to Serve on Active Duty a Period Three Times the Length of Period of Education [*Navy*] ... OBLISERVTHREETIME
Obligated to Serve on Active Duty One Year for Each Six Months Schooling or Fraction Thereof [*Navy*] ... OBLISERVONEASIX
Obligated to Serve Three and One-Half Years Following Date of Completion of Training within the Naval Air Training Command ... OBLISERVNATRA
Obligated Volunteer Officer [*Military*] ... OBV
Obligated War Reserves [*Army*] (AABC) ... OWR
Obligation (ROG) ... OB
Obligation (ADA) ... OBL
Obligation (ROG) ... OBLIGN
Obligation (AFM) ... OBLN
Obligation Authority [*Army*] ... OA
Obligation Authority [*Army*] (AABC) ... OBLAUTH
Obligation Bond ... OB
Obligations (ROG) ... OBS
Obligato [*Obbligato*] [*Music*] (ROG) ... OBL
Oblique (AABC) ... OBL
Oblique Anterior Gauche [*Left Anterior Oblique Position*] [*Medicine*] ... OAG
Oblique Photo Sketcher ... OPS
Oblique Photography (WDAA) ... OB PH
Oblique Shock Wave ... OSW
Oblique Sounding [*Telecommunications*] (OA) ... OS
Oblique Tape Wound Refrasil ... OTWR
Oblique-Incidence Transmission ... OIT
Obliteration ... OB
Obliterative Pulmonary Hypertension [*Medicine*] ... OPH
Oblong ... OB
Oblong [*Bookbinding*] (WDMC) ... ob
Oblong [*Bookbinding*] (WDMC) ... obl
Oblong ... OBL
Obninsk [*Former USSR Seismograph station code, US Geological Survey*] (SEIS) ... OBN
Obo [*Central African Republic*] [*ICAO location identifier*] (ICLI) ... FEFB
Obock [*Djibouti*] [*Airport symbol*] (OAG) ... OBC
Obock [*Djibouti*] [*Seismograph station code, US Geological Survey*] (SEIS) ... OBO
Oboe [*Phonetic alphabet*] [*World War II*] (DSUE) ... O
Oboe ... OB
Obokote [*Zaire*] [*ICAO location identifier*] (ICLI) ... FZOJ
Obolus [*Coin*] [*Latin*] (ADA) ... OB
Oboz Narodowo-Radykalny [*Radical Nationalist Camp*] [*Poland Political party*] (PPE) ... ONR
Oboz Polski Walczacej [*A publication*] (BJA) ... OPW
Oboz Wielkiej Polski [*Camp of Great Poland*] (PPE) ... OWP
Obras de Teatro Estrenadas en Espana [*Ministerio de Cultura*] [*Spain Information service or system*] (CRD) ... TEAT
O'Brien County Bell, Primghar, IA [*Library symbol Library of Congress*] (LCLS) ... IaPriB
O'Brien Energy & Resources Ltd. [*Toronto Stock Exchange symbol*] ... OB
O'Brien's Lawyer's Rule of Holy Life [*A publication*] (DLA) ... O'Bri Lawy
O'Brien's Military Law [*A publication*] (DLA) ... O'Bri ML
O'Brien's Oil Pollution Service of New Orleans [*Oil spill cleanup service*] ... OOPS
O'Brien's Upper Canada Reports [*A publication*] (DLA) ... O'Brien
Obscene [*Legal term*] ... Obs
Obscene Publications Act [*British*] ... OPA
Obscene Publications Squad [*British*] (DI) ... OPS
Obscura (VRA) ... obs
Obscurant ... OBS
Obscure (KSC) ... OB
Obscure (ADA) ... OBS
Obscure ... OBSC
Obscure Glass ... OG
Obscure Glass (AAG) ... OGL
Obscure Glass (AD) ... ogl
Obscure Wire Glass ... OWGL
Obscured Light [*Navigation signal*] ... OBSC
Observable Difference ... OD
Observable Differences/Functionally Related Observable Differences (MCD) ... ODS/FRODS
Observable Evidence of Good Teaching (AD) ... oegt
Observable Evidences of Good Teaching ... OEGT
Observation (WGA) ... OB
Observation (ROG) ... OBS
Observation (AAG) ... OBSN
Observation ... OBSR
Observation (IAA) ... OBSV
Observation (AD) ... obsv
Observation Aircraft [*Designation for all US military aircraft*] ... O
Observation Amphibian Plane [*Coast Guard*] ... OAP
Observation and Assessment [*Medicine*] ... O & A
Observation and Evaluation [*Medicine*] (DAVI) ... O & E
Observation and Examination [*Medicine*] ... O & E
Observation and Fields of Fire, Cover and Concealment, Obstacles, Key Terrain, Avenues of Approach (MCD) ... OCOKA
Observation Balloon ... OBBO
Observation Balloon [*Navy symbol*] ... ZKO
Observation Car [*British*] ... OC
Observation Care Unit [*Medicine*] (DAVI) ... OCU
Observation/Command Post (DNAB) ... OB/CP
Observation Deck (WDAA) ... OB DK
Observation Fighter Squadron [*Navy symbol*] ... VOF
Observation File Maintenance ... OFM
Observation Flight (IAA) ... OBSNFL
Observation Helicopter ... HO
Observation Helicopter ... OH
Observation Landplane [*Coast Guard*] ... OLP
Observation/Losing [*Army*] (ADDR) ... O/L
Observation Officer [*Military*] ... OO
Observation Plane ... OP
Observation Plane [*Navy symbol*] ... VO
Observation Plane Squadron [*Navy symbol*] ... VOG
Observation Point [*or Post*] ... OP
Observation Post [*Military*] ... OP
Observation Post Royal Artillery [*British military*] (DMA) ... OPRA
Observation Report Conversion [*Program*] ... ORCON
Observation Requirements Data Sheet (IAA) ... ORDS
Observation Research and Classroom Learning Evaluation (AIE) ... ORACLE
Observation Schedule and Records ... OSCAR
Observation Scout Plane [*Navy symbol*] ... VOS
Observation Skills Test ... OST
Observation Spot [*Control point*] [*Nautical charts*] ... Obs Spot
Observation Spotter Squadron [*Navy symbol*] ... VOC
Observation Squadron ... OBSRON
Observation Unit ... OU
Observation Ward [*British*] ... OW
Observation Window ... OBW
Observation Window (AD) ... obw
Observational Test and Development Center [*National Weather Service*] (NOAA) ... OTDC
Observation-Measurement-Balancing and Installation [*Production analysis*] ... OMBI
Observation-Scouting Plane [*When first two letters in Navy designation*] ... OS
Observatorio Astronomico de Quito [*Ecuador*] [*Seismograph station code, US Geological Survey*] (SEIS) ... OAQ
Observatory ... OBS
Observatory ... OBSERV
Observatory ... OBSRVTRY
Observatory (AD) ... obsv
Observatory (IAA) ... OBSV
Observatory (AABC) ... OBSY
Observe ... OBS
Observe ... OBS
Observe (ROG) ... OBSVE
Observed ... OBSD
Observed Altitude ... Ho
Observed Bearing [*Navigation*] ... OB
Observed Bombing of Enemy ... OBOE
Observed Drift ... OD
Observed Effect Concentration [*Environmental science*] (ERG) ... OEC
Observed Fire Trainer [*Army*] (RDA) ... OFT
Observed Intrinsic Frequency [*Medicine*] (DMAA) ... OIF
Observed Man [*or Mass*] **Point Trajectory** [*NASA*] (KSC) ... OMPT
Observed Position [*Navigation*] ... OP
Observed Position Data ... OPD
Observed Quality Level ... OQL
Observed Range Limit ... ORL
Observed Ratio (MCD) ... OR
Observed Temperature Rise ... OTR
Observed Vehicle (WDAA) ... OV
Observed versus Expected ... O/E
Observed Vertical Detection Range ... OVDR
Observed Zenith Distance [*Navigation*] ... OZD
Observer ... O
Observer ... OBSV
Observer (AD) ... obsv
Observer Air Lock System (OA) ... OALS
Observer Corps [*Became ROC, 1941*] [*British*] ... OC
Observer, De Witt, IA [*Library symbol Library of Congress*] (LCLS) ... IaDewO
Observer Foreign News Service (AD) ... OFNS
Observer Group Egypt [*UN Truce Supervisor Organization*] ... OGE
Observer Group in El Salvador ... OGELS
Observer, Hasbrouck Heights, NJ [*Library symbol Library of Congress*] (LCLS) ... NjHasO
Observer Impression Assessment Scale ... OIAS
Observer Lieutenant [*British military*] (DMA) ... Obs Lt
Observer (London) [*A publication*] (BRI) ... Obs
Observer (Radio) [*British military*] (DMA) ... RO
Observer Single-Handed Transatlantic Race [*Sailing*] ... OSTAR
Observer Target [*Army*] ... OT
Observer Target Acquisition Subsystem (MCD) ... OTAS
Observer Target Line (NVT) ... OTL
Observer Training [*Army*] ... OBT
Observer Training [*Army*] (AABC) ... OTNG
Observer-Controller [*Army*] (INF) ... OC
Observer's Assessment of Alertness / Sedation Scale [*Medicine*] ... OAA/S

Observer's Mate [*British military*] (DMA) .... OM
Observer's Thermal Imaging System (PDAA) .... OTIS
Observer-Tribune, Mendham, NJ [*Library symbol Library of Congress*] (LCLS) .... NjMenO
Observing Simulation System (USDC) .... OSS
Observing Station [*Marine science*] (MSC) .... OS
Observing Stimulation System [*Marine science*] (OSRA) .... OSS
Observing Systems Simulation Experiments [*National Center for Atmospheric Research*] .... OSSE
Obsessive Compulsive (PAZ) .... OC
Obsessive Compulsive Disorder [*Medicine*] (AD) .... ocd
Obsessive Compulsive Foundation (EA) .... OCF
Obsessive Compulsive Scale [*Psychology*] (EDAC) .... OCS
Obsessive Compulsive Spectrum Disorder [*Psychology*] .... OCSD
Obsessive-Compulsive Anonymous (EA) .... OCA
Obsessive-Compulsive Disorder [*Psychology*] .... OCD
Obsessive-Deductive Disorder [*Facetious term for a malady affecting some taxpayers*] .... ODD
Obsidian Butte [*California*] [*Seismograph station code, US Geological Survey*] (SEIS) .... OBB
Obsidian Junior High School, Redmond, OR [*Library symbol*] [*Library of Congress*] (LCLS) .... OrRedOJ
Obsolescent (AFIT) .... O
Obsolescent .... OBSOL
Obsolescent .... Obsoles
Obsolete (AABC) .... OB
Obsolete (AAG) .... OBS
Obsolete General Supplies [*Military*] .... OGS
Obstacle (AABC) .... OBS
Obstacle (AFM) .... OBST
Obstacle Assessment Surface [*Aviation*] (DA) .... OAS
Obstacle Avoidance (MCD) .... OA
Obstacle Avoidance System [*Army*] (RDA) .... OASYS
Obstacle Breaching Vehicle [*Military*] .... OBV
Obstacle Clearance (PDAA) .... OC
Obstacle Clearance Altitude [*Aviation*] (DA) .... OCA
Obstacle Clearance Height [*Aviation*] (FAAC) .... OCH
Obstacle [*or Obstruction*] Clearance Panel [*Aviation*] (OA) .... OCP
Obstacle Clearance Surface [*ICAO*] (FAAC) .... OCS
Obstacle Clearance Surface (AD) .... ocs
Obstacle Detection Device .... ODD
Obstacle Detection System .... ODS
Obstacle Free Zone .... OFZ
Obstacle Height .... OBSHT
Obstacle Identification Surface [*Aviation*] (DA) .... OIS
Obstacle Light [*Aviation*] (DA) .... Obs
Obstacle Planner Software (RDA) .... OPS
Obstacle-Dominance [*Medicine*] (DMAA) .... O-D
Obstetric .... OBST
Obstetric Anaesthetists Association [*British*] (DBA) .... OAA
Obstetric Conjugate [*Pelvic measurement*] [*Gynecology*] .... OC
Obstetric, Gynecologic, and Neonatal .... OGN
Obstetric Ultrasound [*Microcomputer system dealing with results of obstetric ultrasound examinations*] .... OBUS
Obstetrical Conjugate [*Medicine*] (AD) .... oc
Obstetrical Service [*Medicine*] (MAE) .... OBS
Obstetrician .... OB
Obstetrician [*Medicine*] .... OBSTRN
Obstetrician-Gynecologist (PAZ) .... OB-GYN
Obstetrics [*Medicine*] (MAE) .... O
Obstetrics [*Medicine*] .... OB
Obstetrics [*Medicine*] .... OBS
Obstetrics [*Medicine*] .... OBST
Obstetrics [*Medicine*] .... OBSTET
Obstetrics and Gynaecology [*Medical Officer designation*] [*British*] .... G
Obstetrics-Gynecology [*Medicine*] .... OBG
Obstetrics-Gynecology [*Medicine*] .... OB-GYN
Obstetrics-Gynecology [*Medicine*] .... OG
Obstruction (WGA) .... OBS
Obstruction (AFM) .... OBST
Obstruction (MSA) .... OBSTN
Obstruction .... Obstr
Obstruction (AD) .... obstr
Obstruction Chart .... OC
Obstruction Light (AD) .... obstl
Obstruction of Justice .... OOJ
Obstructive Airway Disease [*Medicine*] .... OAD
Obstructive Asymmetrical Septal Hypertrophy [*Medicine*] (CPH) .... OASH
Obstructive Sleep Apnea [*Medicine*] .... OSA
Obstructive Sleep Apnea Syndrome [*Medicine*] (DMAA) .... OSAS
Obtain (ROG) .... OBTN
Obtain by Local Manufacture [*Military*] .... GETMA
Obtain by Local Purchase [*Military*] .... GETLO
Obtain Endorsement to Transport (DNAB) .... OBTAINDORSETRANS
Obtain Increased Productivity through Improved Modernization of Facilities and Updating Maintenance Tools, Equipment, and Methods [*Military*] .... OPTIMUM
Obtain Service From [*Navy*] (NVT) .... OSF
Obtained .... OBTD
Obtained (AD) .... obtd
Obtained Radiation Emittance .... ORE
Obtaining (ROG) .... OBTG
Obtaining Goods by False Pretense .... OGFP
Obtaining Money by False Pretense .... OMFP
Obtaining Money by False Pretenses (AD) .... omfp

Obtuse Bisectrix [*Crystallography*] .... OB
Obtuse Marginal [*Medicine*] (MAE) .... OM
Obverse .... OBV
Obverse (AD) .... obv
Obvious (AD) .... obv
Obvious (AAMN) .... OV
Obviously (AD) .... obvy
OC [*Overseas Crusades*] International (EA) .... OCI
Ocal Inc. [*NASDAQ symbol*] (TTSB) .... OCAL
Ocal, Inc. [*NASDAQ symbol*] (SAG) .... OCAL
Ocal, Inc. [*Associated Press*] (SAG) .... Ocal
Ocala [*Florida*] [*Airport symbol*] (OAG) .... OCF
Ocala, FL [*Location identifier FAA*] (FAAL) .... OCF
Ocala, FL [*FM radio station call letters*] .... WHIJ
Ocala, FL [*FM radio station call letters*] .... WMFQ
Ocala, FL [*AM radio station call letters*] .... WMOP
Ocala, FL [*FM radio station call letters*] .... WOCA
Ocala, FL [*FM radio station call letters*] .... WOGK
Ocala, FL [*Television station call letters*] .... WOGX
Ocala, FL [*AM radio station call letters*] .... WTMC
O'Callaghan's History of New Netherland [*A publication*] (DLA) .... O'Callaghan New Neth
Ocana [*Spain ICAO location identifier*] (ICLI) .... LEOC
Ocana [*Colombia*] [*Airport symbol*] (OAG) .... OCV
Ocana/Aguas Claras [*Colorado ICAO location identifier*] (ICLI) .... SKOC
Ocarina (AD) .... oca
Occasion .... OCCN
Occasion (AD) .... ocsn
Occasional [*Concerning occurrence of species*] .... O
Occasional .... OCCAS
Occasional (AD) .... occas
Occasional .... OCCASL
Occasional .... OCNL
Occasional (AD) .... ocnl
Occasional .... ocsnl
Occasional Light [*Navigation signal*] .... Occas
Occasional Newsletter [*American Bar Association, Committee on Environmental Law*] [*A publication*] (ILCA) .... Occ Newsl
Occasional Notes, Canada Law Times [*A publication*] (DLA) .... Occ N
Occasional Paper .... OP
Occasionally .... OCC
Occasionally (AD) .... occ
Occasionally .... OCNLY
Occasionally (AD) .... ocsnly
Occidental .... O
Occidental .... OC
Occidental Chemical Corp., Technical Information Center, Niagra Falls, NY [*Library symbol*] [*Library of Congress*] (LCLS) .... NNiaO
Occidental College (AD) .... OC
Occidental College (GAGS) .... Occidental C
Occidental College, Los Angeles, CA [*OCLC symbol*] (OCLC) .... CCO
Occidental College, Los Angeles, CA [*Library symbol Library of Congress*] (LCLS) .... CLO
Occidental Petr $3 Cv Pfd [*NYSE symbol*] (TTSB) .... OXYPrA
Occidental Petroleum Corp. [*Associated Press*] (SAG) .... OcciPet
Occidental Petroleum Corp. [*Associated Press*] (SAG) .... OcciPt
Occidental Petroleum Corp. [*NYSE symbol Toronto Stock Exchange symbol*] (SPSG) .... OXY
Occidental Petrol'm [*NYSE symbol*] (TTSB) .... OXY
Occidental Research Corp., La Verne, CA [*Library symbol Library of Congress*] (LCLS) .... CLavO
Occidental Society of Metempiric Analysis (EA) .... OSMA
Occidentale Afrique Francaise [*French West Africa*] .... OAF
Occipital [*or Occiput*] [*Anatomy*] (MAE) .... occ
Occipital (AD) .... occip
Occipital Artery [*Anatomy*] .... OA
Occipital Cortex [*Brain anatomy*] .... OC
Occipital Horn [*Brain anatomy*] .... OH
Occipital Temporal Sulcus [*Medicine*] (DMAA) .... OTS
Occipitalfrontal [*Diameter of skull*] .... OF
Occipitodextra Anterior [*A fetal position*] [*Medicine*] (AAMN) .... ODA
Occipito-Dextra Anterior (AD) .... oda
Occipito-Dextra Posterior (AD) .... odp
Occipitodextra Posterior [*A fetal position*] [*Medicine*] (AAMN) .... ODP
Occipitodextra Transversa [*A fetal position*] [*Medicine*] (AAMN) .... ODT
Occipito-Dextra Transverse (AD) .... odt
Occipitofrontal Circumference [*Anatomy*] .... OFC
Occipitofrontal Diameter [*of the skull*] .... OFD
Occipitolaeva Anterior [*A fetal position*] [*Medicine*] (AAMN) .... OLA
Occipito-Laeva Anterior (AD) .... ola
Occipito-Laeva Posterior (AD) .... olp
Occipitolaeva Posterior [*A fetal position*] [*Medicine*] (AAMN) .... OLP
Occipitolaeva Transversa [*A fetal position*] [*Medicine*] (AAMN) .... OLT
Occipito-Laeva Transverse (AD) .... olt
Occipitomental [*Diameter of skull*] .... OM
Occipitoparietal [*Medicine*] (AAMN) .... OP
Occipitotransverse [*Obstetrics*] .... OT
Occiput [*Medicine*] .... OA
Occiput [*Anatomy*] (WDAA) .... OCCIP
Occiput Anterior [*Medicine*] .... OA
Occiput Posterior [*Medicine*] .... OP
Occiput Posterior Position (DAVI) .... OPP
Occlude (AD) .... occl
Occlude (DA) .... OCI
Occluded Corrosion Cell (PDAA) .... OCC

Occluded Eye Gunsight [*Military*] (INF) ... OEG
Occlusal [*Dentistry*] ... O
Occlusal Vertical Dimension [*Dentistry*] ... OVD
Occlusion ... OCC
Occlusion Time (MAE) ... OT
Occlusocervical [*Dentistry*] ... OC
Occlusogingival [*Dentistry*] ... OG
Occulentum [*Medicine*] (CPH) ... OC
Occult Bleeding [*Medicine*] ... OB
Occult Blood [*Medicine*] (DAVI) ... OCC-BL
Occult Blood Negative [*Medicine*] (DAVI) ... OBN
Occult Blood Positive [*Medicine*] (DAVI) ... OB +
Occult Blood Positive [*Medicine*] (DAVI) ... OBP
Occult Constrictive Pericardial Disease [*Cardiology*] (CPH) ... OCPD
Occult Gastrointestinal Bleeding [*Medicine*] ... OGIB
Occult Papillary Carcinoma [*Oncology*] ... OPC
Occult Primary Malignancy [*Oncology*] ... OPM
Occultation [*Astronomy*] ... OCC
Occulting (AD) ... Occ
Occulting Light [*Navigation signal*] ... Oc
Occulting Light [*Navigation signal*] ... OCC
Occuluded Front [*NWS*] (FAAC) ... OCFNT
Occupant Safety Research Partnership ... OSRP
Occupation (ADA) ... O
Occupation (AFM) ... OCC
Occupation (AD) ... occ
Occupation (AD) ... occup
Occupation (ROG) ... OCCUPON
Occupation ... OCCUPTN
Occupation Centres for Defectives [*British*] ... OCD
Occupational ... OCCUP
Occupational ... OCCUPTNL
Occupational Accidents Analysis and Reporting ... OCAAR
Occupational, Adult, and Vocational Education (OICC) ... OAVE
Occupational Analysis Field Center ... OAFC
Occupational and Adult Education [*Office of Education*] (OICC) ... OAE
Occupational & Environment Health Unit, Science and Medicine Library, Universityof Toronto, Ontario [*Library symbol National Library of Canada*] (NLC) ... OTUHO
Occupational and Environmental Health Laboratory [*Brooks Air Force Base, TX*] [*Air Force*] ... OEHL
Occupational and Environmental Health Unit, University of Toronto [*UTLAS symbol*] ... KOC
Occupational and Environmental Medicine ... OEM
Occupational Aptitude Pattern [*US Employment Service*] [*Department of Labor*] ... OAP
Occupational Aptitude Survey and Interest Schedule ... OASIS
Occupational Aptitude Survey and Interest Schedule - Aptitude Survey [*Vocational guidance test*] ... OASIS-AS
Occupational Aptitude Survey and Interest Schedule - Interest Schedule [*Vocational guidance test*] ... OASIS-IS
Occupational Area Defense Grouping (DNAB) ... OA-DG
Occupational Aspiration Scale [*Education*] ... OAS
Occupational Back Pain ... OBP
Occupational Behavior ... OB
Occupational Changes in a Generation [*Socioeconomics*] ... OCG
Occupational Cluster Program (OICC) ... OCP
Occupational Demand Schedule (ADA) ... ODS
Occupational Disease ... OD
Occupational Education Project ... OEP
Occupational Employment Statistics [*Department of Labor*] ... OES
Occupational Exploration Program (OICC) ... OEP
Occupational Exposure Limit ... OEL
Occupational Exposure Limit ... OEL
Occupational Exposure Standard [*Environmental chemistry*] ... OES
Occupational Guidance Unit [*Department of Employment*] [*British*] ... OGU
Occupational Health ... OH
Occupational Health Administration (AD) ... OHA
Occupational Health & Rehabilitation, Inc. [*Associated Press*] (SAG) ... OccuHlt
Occupational Health & Rehabilitation, Inc. [*NASDAQ symbol*] (SAG) ... OHRI
Occupational Health and Safety ... OHAS
Occupational Health and Safety ... OHS
Occupational Health and Safety Authority [*Victoria, Australia*] ... OHSA
Occupational Health and Safety Commission of South Australia ... OHSCSA
Occupational Health and Safety Library, Alberta Workers' Health, Safety and Compensation, Calgary, Alberta [*Library symbol National Library of Canada*] (NLC) ... ACOHS
Occupational Health and Safety Staff [*Environmental Protection Agency*] (GFGA) ... OHSS
Occupational Health and Safety Technologist ... OHST
Occupational Health Australia and New Zealand [*A publication*] ... Occ Heal ANZ
Occupational Health Center (KSC) ... OHC
Occupational Health Facility [*NASA*] (KSC) ... OHF
Occupational Health Hazard Assessment ... OHHA
Occupational Health Institute [*Defunct*] (EA) ... OHI
Occupational Health Labels [*Army*] ... OC-HLTHLB
Occupational Health Library, Regina, SK, Canada [*Library symbol Library of Congress*] (LCLS) ... CaSROH
Occupational Health Management Information System [*Military*] (GFGA) ... OHMIS
Occupational Health Monitoring and Evaluation System (PDAA) ... OHMES
Occupational Health Nurse [*Government classification*] ... OHN
Occupational Health Nursing Certificate [*British*] ... OHNC
Occupational Health Nursing Officer (AD) ... OHNO
Occupational Health Nursing Sister (AD) ... OHNS
Occupational Health Safety and Rehabilitation Council [*New South Wales, Australia*] ... OHSRC
Occupational Health Services, Inc. [*Secaucus, NJ*] [*Medical databank originator*] [*Information service or system*] ... OHS
Occupational Health Services Material Safety Data Sheets [*Database*] ... OHS MSDS
Occupational Health-Safety-Programs Accreditation Commission (AD) ... OHSPAC
Occupational Hearing Service ... OHS
Occupational History [*Medicine*] ... OH
Occupational Information Access System (WDAA) ... OIAS
Occupational Information System [*Department of Labor*] ... OIS
Occupational Interest Rating Scale [*Vocational guidance test*] ... OIRS
Occupational Interest Survey [*Aptitude test*] ... OIS
Occupational Level ... OL
Occupational Measurement Center [*Air Force*] ... OCMCEN
Occupational Measurement Squadron [*Air Force*] ... OCCMS
Occupational Measurement Squadron [*Air Force*] ... OCMSq
Occupational Medal [*as used with special reference to Germany or Japan*] [*Military decoration*] ... OM
Occupational Medical Administrators' Association (EA) ... OMAA
Occupational Medicine (AABC) ... OCCMED
Occupational Medicine ... OM
Occupational Medicine and Hygiene Laboratory [*British*] (IRUK) ... OMHL
Occupational Medicine/Environmental Health Evaluation Center [*Emory University*] ... OM/EH
Occupational Outlook Handbook [*A publication*] (OICC) ... OOH
Occupational Overuse Syndrome ... OOS
Occupational Pensions Board [*British*] (DCTA) ... OPB
Occupational Personality Questionnaires [*Employment test*] ... OPQ
Occupational Preparation Scheme (AIE) ... OPS
Occupational Program Consultants Association (EA) ... OPCA
Occupational Projections and Training Information for Michigan [*Information service or system*] (IID) ... OPTIM
Occupational Psychologist ... OP
Occupational Radiation Exposure (NRCH) ... ORE
Occupational Research and Development Coordinating Unit ... ORDCU
Occupational Research Centre [*Hatfield Polytechnic*] [*British*] (CB) ... ORC
Occupational Role History [*Psychology*] ... ORH
Occupational Safety (DAVI) ... OS
Occupational Safety Aid ... OSA
Occupational Safety and Health [*Department of Labor*] ... OSH
Occupational Safety and Health Act [*1970*] ... OSHA
Occupational Safety and Health Administration [*Department of Labor*] [*Washington, DC*] ... OSHA
Occupational Safety and Health Administration, Technical Data Center, Washington, DC [*OCLC symbol*] (OCLC) ... ULO
Occupational Safety and Health Branch, Labour Canada [*Direction de la Securite et de l'Hygiene, Travail Canada*] **Ottawa, Ontario** [*Library symbol National Library of Canada*] (NLC) ... OOLAP
Occupational Safety and Health Cases [*A publication*] (DLA) ... OSH Cas
Occupational Safety and Health Control Report [*Navy*] ... OCR
Occupational Safety and Health Decisions [*A publication*] (DLA) ... OSH Dec
Occupational Safety and Health Decisions [*A publication*] (DLA) ... OSHD
Occupational, Safety, and Health Institute [*University of Houston*] [*Research center*] (RCD) ... OSHI
Occupational Safety and Health Review Commission [*Department of Labor*] ... OSAHRC
Occupational Safety and Health Review Commission [*Department of Labor*] ... OSHRC
Occupational Safety and Health Statistics [*Bureau of Labor Statistics*] (GFGA) ... OSHS
Occupational Specialities [*A publication*] (DNAB) ... OCCSPEC
Occupational Standards Council (AIE) ... OSC
Occupational Superannuation Standard ... OSS
Occupational Supplies and Equipment [*Red Cross*] ... OSE
Occupational Survey Report ... OSR
Occupational Therapist [*or Therapy*] [*Medicine*] ... OT
Occupational Therapist in Independent Practice ... OTIP
Occupational Therapist, Registered ... OTR
Occupational Therapist Registered [*Canada*] (BABM) ... OTReg
Occupational Therapist Registered [*Canada*] (DAVI) ... OTReg
Occupational Therapists Association (NADA) ... OTA
Occupational Therapists' Board of Queensland [*Australia*] ... OTBQ
Occupational Therapists' Registration Board of South Australia ... OTRBSA
Occupational Therapy (AD) ... occ th
Occupational Therapy [*or Therapist*] (DAVI) ... OccTh
Occupational Therapy Association of Western Australia ... OTAWA
Occupational Therapy Comprehensive Functional Assessment ... OTCFA
Occupational Therapy Technician [*Navy*] ... OT
Occupational Training (AIE) ... OT
Occupational Training Information System ... OTIS
Occupational Wage Survey ... OWS
Occupationally Induced Lung Disease ... OILD
Occupational-Vocational-Technical Training ... OVT
Occupations for Patients in Mental Hospitals [*British*] ... OPMH
Occupations Study Group [*British*] ... OSG
Occupied [*International telex abbreviation*] (WDMC) ... OC
Occupied (IAA) ... OCC
Occupied (AD) ... occd
Occupied Area News Service [*Military*] (IAA) ... OANS
Occupied Areas Section [*Military government*] ... OAS
Occupied Command Center [*Military*] ... OCC
Occupied Enemy Territory Administration [*World War II*] ... OETA
Occupied Japan Club (EA) ... OJC

Occupied Territories (BJA) ... OT
Occupied Territory Administration [*World War II*] ... OTA
Occupiers' Liability Act [*1957*] [*British*] (DCTA) ... OLA
Occupying Public Quarters [*Military*] ... OPQ
Occurrence ... O
Occurrence ... OCC
Occurs (MDG) ... OC
Occurs (ILCA) ... Occ
OccuSystems, Inc. [*Associated Press*] (SAG) ... OccuSys
OccuSystems, Inc. [*NASDAQ symbol*] (SAG) ... OSYS
Oce Copy Control System (NITA) ... OCCS
Ocean [*Maps and charts*] ... O
Ocean ... OC
Ocean (AD) ... Oc
Ocean (AD) ... oc
Ocean ... OCN
Ocean Acoustic Tomography ... OAT
Ocean Acre [*Marine science*] (MSC) ... OA
Ocean Acre Project [*Marine science*] (MSC) ... OCAC
Ocean Acres, NJ [*FM radio station call letters*] ... WQNJ
Ocean Affairs Advisory Committee [*Department of State*] (MSC) ... OAAC
Ocean Affairs Board [*National Academy of Sciences*] (MSC) ... OAB
Ocean Aids to Navigation [*Coast Guard*] ... OAN
Ocean Airways [*ICAO designator*] (AD) ... VM
Ocean All-Source Information System ... OASIS
Ocean and Coastal Resource Management (GNE) ... OCRM
Ocean and Lake Surveys [*Budget appropriation title*] [*Navy*] ... O & LS
Ocean and Rail [*Shipping*] ... O & R
Ocean and Science Engineering Inc. ... OSE
Ocean Area Reconnaissance Satellite [*Antisubmarine warfare*] ... OARS
Ocean Atmosphere Response Studies [*Marine science*] (MSC) ... OARS
Ocean Beach (AD) ... Ocn Bch
Ocean Bill of Lading (AD) ... oc b/l
Ocean Bill of Lading [*Shipping*] ... OC/B/L
Ocean Bio-Chem [*NASDAQ symbol*] (TTSB) ... OBCI
Ocean Bio-Chem, Inc. [*NASDAQ symbol*] (NQ) ... OBCI
Ocean Bio-Chem, Inc. [*Associated Press*] (SAG) ... OceanB
Ocean Biogeochemical Model ... OBM
Ocean Boarding Vessel (AD) ... obv
Ocean Boarding Vessel ... OBV
Ocean Bottom ... OB
Ocean Bottom Scanning SONAR ... OBSS
Ocean Bottom Seismometer [*California*] [*Seismograph station code, US Geological Survey Closed*] (SEIS) ... OBS
Ocean Bottom Station ... OBS
Ocean Cargo Clearance Authority (DOMA) ... OCCA
Ocean Cargo Line (AD) ... OCL
Ocean Cay, Bimini Island [*Bahamas*] [*ICAO location identifier*] (ICLI) ... MYBO
Ocean Chemistry Division [*Marine science*] (OSRA) ... OCD
Ocean Chemistry Division [*Atlantic Oceanographic and Meteorological Laboratory*] (USDC) ... OCD
Ocean City [*Maryland*] [*Airport symbol*] (OAG) ... OCE
Ocean City College [*Maryland*] ... OCC
Ocean City Historical Museum, Ocean City, NJ [*Library symbol Library of Congress*] (LCLS) ... NjOcM
Ocean City, MD [*Location identifier FAA*] (FAAL) ... OIK
Ocean City, MD [*AM radio station call letters*] ... WETT
Ocean City, MD [*FM radio station call letters*] ... WRXS
Ocean City, MD [*FM radio station call letters*] ... WWFG
Ocean City, NJ [*AM radio station call letters*] ... WIBG
Ocean City, NJ [*FM radio station call letters*] ... WKOE
Ocean City, NJ [*FM radio station call letters*] ... WKTU
Ocean City, NJ [*FM radio station call letters*] ... WRTQ
Ocean City, NJ [*FM radio station call letters*] (RBYB) ... WTKU-FM
Ocean City-Salisbury, MD [*FM radio station call letters*] ... WQHQ
Ocean Climate Research Division [*Pacific Marine Environmental Laboratory*] (USDC) ... OCRD
Ocean Climate Research Division [*Marine science*] (OSRA) ... OCRD
Ocean Color Experiment [*NASA*] ... OCE
Ocean Color Imager [*Meteorology*] [*NASA*] ... OCI
Ocean Color Scanner (PDAA) ... OCS
Ocean Construction Equipment Inventory (DNAB) ... OCEI
Ocean Container Zebrugge (AD) ... OCZ
Ocean Control Authority ... OCA
Ocean Coordinating Committee [*IEEE*] (MSC) ... OCC
Ocean County Citizen, Lakewood, NJ [*Library symbol Library of Congress*] (LCLS) ... NjLakC
Ocean County Clerk, Toms River, NJ [*Library symbol Library of Congress*] (LCLS) ... NjTrCoC
Ocean County College, Toms River, NJ [*Library symbol Library of Congress*] (LCLS) ... NjTrO
Ocean County Daily Times, Lakewood, NJ [*Library symbol Library of Congress*] (LCLS) ... NjLakT
Ocean County Leader, Point Pleasant Beach, NJ [*Library symbol Library of Congress*] (LCLS) ... NjPoiO
Ocean County Public Library, Toms River, NJ [*Library symbol Library of Congress*] (LCLS) ... NjTrCo
Ocean County Review, Seaside Heights, NJ [*Library symbol Library of Congress*] (LCLS) ... NjShO
Ocean Covered Earth (OA) ... OCE
Ocean Cruising Club [*British*] (DI) ... OCC
Ocean Culture Product ... OCP
Ocean Culture System ... OCS
Ocean Data Acquisition Systems ... ODAS
Ocean Data Acquisition Systems, Aids and Devices [*Marine science*] (OSRA) ... ODAS
Ocean Data Buoy [*Marine science*] (MSC) ... ODB
Ocean Data Environmental Science Services Acquisition [*Buoy*] ... ODESSA
Ocean Data Station [*Marine science*] (MSC) ... ODS
Ocean Data Station Buoy ... ODSB
Ocean Data Systems, Inc. [*Information service or system*] (IID) ... ODSI
Ocean Data Transmitter ... ODT
Ocean Design Engineering Corp. (AD) ... ODEC
Ocean Disposal Database [*US Army Corps of Engineers*] ... ODD
Ocean Drilling and Exploration Co. (AD) ... ODECO
Ocean Drilling Program [*Texas A & M University*] [*Research center*] (RCD) ... ODP
Ocean Dumping Ban Act [*1988*] ... ODBA
Ocean Dumping Control Act [*Canada*] (MSC) ... ODCA
Ocean Dumping Permits [*Database*] [*Environment Canada*] [*Information service or system*] (CRD) ... ODUMP
Ocean Dumping Surveillance System [*Coast Guard*] (MSC) ... ODSS
Ocean Dynamics Advisory Subcommittee [*NASA*] (MSC) ... ODAS
Ocean Dynamics Information System [*Marine science*] (MSC) ... ODIS
Ocean Economics and Technology Branch [*United Nations*] (MSC) ... OETB
Ocean Education Project (EA) ... OEP
Ocean Engineer (PGP) ... Ocean E
Ocean Engineering Centre, Memorial University, St. John's, Newfoundland [*Library symbol National Library of Canada*] (NLC) ... NFSMO
Ocean Engineering Division [*Coast Guard*] ... OED
Ocean Engineering Information Centre [*Memorial University of Newfoundland*] [*Information service or system*] (IID) ... OEIC
Ocean Engineering System Development ... OESD
Ocean Environment Research Division [*Formerly, MARD, Marine Assessment Research Division and MRRD, Marine Resources Research Division*] [*Marine science*] (OSRA) ... OERD
Ocean Environment Research Division [*Formerly, Marine Resources Research Division*] (USDC) ... OERD
Ocean Falls [*Canada*] [*Airport symbol Obsolete*] (OAG) ... ZOF
Ocean Financial Corp. [*Associated Press*] (SAG) ... OceanF
Ocean Financial Corp. [*NASDAQ symbol*] (SAG) ... OCFC
Ocean Floor Analysis Division [*Later, Sea Floor Division*] [*NORDA*] (EA) ... OFAD
Ocean Floor Drilling ... OFD
Ocean Freight Differential [*MARAD*] (TAG) ... OFD
Ocean General Circulation Model [*Atmospheric science*] ... OGCM
Ocean Grove Times, Ocean Grove, NJ [*Library symbol Library of Congress*] (LCLS) ... NjOgT
Ocean Heat Convergence ... OHC
Ocean Heat Transport ... OHT
Ocean Heat Transport Experiment [*Japan*] [*Marine science*] (OSRA) ... OHTEX
Ocean Hill-Brownsville (AD) ... OH-B
Ocean Industries Association (AD) ... OIA
Ocean Instrumentation Engineering Office [*National Oceanic and Atmospheric Administration*] (MSC) ... OIEO
Ocean Letter ... OL
Ocean Living Institute [*Defunct*] (EA) ... OLI
Ocean Management [*A publication*] (ILCA) ... Ocean Man
Ocean Map [*Marine science*] (OSRA) ... OCNMAP
Ocean Map (USDC) ... OCNMAP
Ocean Margin Drilling [*Program*] [*National Science Foundation*] ... OMD
Ocean Margin Drilling Program [*National Science Foundation*] ... OMDP
Ocean Marine Technology [*Vancouver Stock Exchange symbol*] ... OMT
Ocean Measurement and Array Technology [*Navy*] (CAAL) ... OMAT
Ocean Microwave Package (SSD) ... OMP
Ocean Minelayer [*NATO*] ... CMO
Ocean Minesweeper ... OMS
Ocean Mining Administration (AD) ... OMA
Ocean Mining Administration (NADA) ... OMA
Ocean Movement Designator ... OMD
Ocean Network Information Center [*Information service or system*] (IID) ... OCEANIC
Ocean Observing System [*Marine science*] (OSRA) ... OOS
Ocean Observing System Development Panel [*Marine science*] (OSRA) ... OOSPD
Ocean Optique Distributors, Inc. [*Associated Press*] (SAG) ... OceanOpt
Ocean Optique Distributors, Inc. [*NASDAQ symbol*] (SAG) ... OPTQ
Ocean Optique Dstr [*NASDAQ symbol*] (TTSB) ... OPTQ
Ocean Outlook (EA) ... OO
Ocean Pearl Button Manufacturers Association [*Defunct*] ... OPBMA
Ocean Pines, MD [*FM radio station call letters*] ... WLFX
Ocean Platform Station [*National Data Buoy Office*] (NOAA) ... OPS
Ocean Policy Committee [*Marine science*] (MSC) ... OPC
Ocean Pollution Data and Information Network [*Washington, DC Department of Commerce*] (GRD) ... OPDIN
Ocean Pollution Data Center (USDC) ... OPDIN
Ocean Pollution Data Center [*Marine science*] (OSRA) ... OPDIN
Ocean Prediction through Observation, Modeling, and Analysis [*Experimental program*] ... OPTOMA
Ocean Pressure Laboratory ... OPL
Ocean Process Analysis Laboratory [*University of New Hampshire*] [*Research center*] (RCD) ... OPAL
Ocean Products Center [*Marine science*] (OSRA) ... OPC
Ocean Products Center (USDC) ... OPC
Ocean RADAR Station Ship [*Navy symbol Obsolete*] ... YAGR
Ocean Range Vessel [*Air Force*] ... ORV
Ocean Reconnaissance Submarine [*NATO*] (LAIN) ... OARS
Ocean Reef Club [*Florida*] [*Airport symbol*] (OAG) ... OCA
Ocean Research and Engineering Laboratory (SAA) ... OREL
Ocean Research Buoy (IAA) ... ORB
Ocean Research Institute (WDAA) ... ORI

Ocean Resource Coordination and Assessment [*National Oceanic and Atmospheric Administration*] .... ORCA
Ocean Resource Utilization Program (ASF) .... ORUP
Ocean Resources Conservation Association [*British*] .... ORCA
Ocean Resources Institute (NADA) .... ORI
Ocean Sampling and Environmental Analysis System (PDAA) .... OSEAS
Ocean Science and Technology Division [*Office of Naval Research*] (DNAB) .... OS & TD
Ocean Science and Technology Group [*Navy*] (MCD) .... OSTG
Ocean Science Committee [*National Academy of Sciences/Ocean Affairs Board*] (NOAA) .... OSC
Ocean Science in Relation to Non-Living Resources [*Marine science*] (OSRA) .... OSNLR
Ocean Science Information Center [*University of Hawaii*] (NOAA) .... OSIC
Ocean Science Laboratory [*Oceanography*] .... OSCILAB
Ocean Science News [*Marine science*] (OSRA) .... OSN
Ocean Science News (USDC) .... OSN
Ocean Science Technology Advisory Committee [*Terminated, 1976*] [*National Security Industrial Association*] (MSC) .... OSTAC
Ocean Sciences Board [*NASA*] (MSC) .... OSB
Ocean Sciences Center [*Memorial University of Newfoundland*] [*Canada*] .... OSC
Ocean Sediment Coring Program [*National Science Foundation*] .... OSCP
Ocean Ship Surveillance Training .... OSST
Ocean Shipping Procedures .... OSPRO
Ocean Shipping Requirements and Capabilities .... OSRAC
Ocean Simulation Facility [*Naval Coastal Systems Laboratory*] (DNAB) .... OSF
Ocean Springs, MS [*FM radio station call letters*] .... WOSM
Ocean Springs, MS [*FM radio station call letters*] .... WXOR
Ocean Station [*Maps and charts*] .... OS
Ocean Station Vessel .... OSV
Ocean Station Vessel Charlie [*British ICAO location identifier*] (ICLI) .... EGRU
Ocean Station Vessel Lima [*British ICAO location identifier*] (ICLI) .... EGRL
Ocean Station Vessel Mike [*British ICAO location identifier*] (ICLI) .... EGRM
Ocean Station Vessel Romeo [*British ICAO location identifier*] (ICLI) .... EGRK
Ocean Subarea (Atlantic) [*NATO*] (NATG) .... OCEANLANT
Ocean Surface Current RADAR .... OSCR
Ocean Surface Temperature [*Marine science*] (OSRA) .... OST
Ocean Surveillance Air Patrol (CINC) .... OSAP
Ocean Surveillance Information System [*Navy*] (MCD) .... OSIS
Ocean Surveillance Product (DOMA) .... OSP
Ocean Surveillance Satellite (MCD) .... OSS
Ocean Surveillance Ship [*Navy*] (CAAL) .... AGOS
Ocean Surveillance System [*Navy*] (SAA) .... OSS
Ocean Survey Advisory Panel [*Marine science*] (MSC) .... OSAP
Ocean Survey Plan [*or Program*] [*Navy*] .... OSP
Ocean Survey Ship (NOAA) .... OSS
Ocean Swell Powered Renewable Energy [*United Kingdom*] .... OSPREY
Ocean Systems, Atlantic .... OCEANSYSLANT
Ocean Systems Operation [*NASA*] .... OSO
Ocean Systems, Pacific .... OCEANSYSPAC
Ocean Systems Technician [*Navy*] (DNAB) .... OT
Ocean Systems Technician, Master Chief [*Navy rating*] (DNAB) .... OTCM
Ocean Systems Technician, Seaman [*Navy rating*] (DNAB) .... OTSN
Ocean Systems Technician, Seaman Apprentice [*Navy rating*] (DNAB) .... OTSA
Ocean Systems Technician, Senior Chief [*Navy rating*] (DNAB) .... OTCS
Ocean Test Platform [*Marine science*] (MSC) .... OTP
Ocean Testing Ranges and Instrumentation Conference .... OTRAN
Ocean Thermal Boundary Analysis Charts [*Marine science*] (MSC) .... OTBA
Ocean Thermal Energy Conversion .... OTEC
Ocean Thermal Energy Conversion Act of 1980 .... OTECA
Ocean Thermal Energy Conversion Systems [*Department of Energy*] .... OTECS
Ocean Thermal Gradient Hydraulic Power Plant .... OTGHPP
Ocean Thermal Gradient System [*National Science Foundation*] .... OTGS
Ocean Thermal Power Plant .... OTPP
Ocean Topography Experiment [*Marine science*] (OSRA) .... TOPEX
Ocean Transport and Trading [*British*] .... OTT
Ocean Transportation [*Military*] .... OT
Ocean Travel Development (DS) .... OTD
Ocean Tug, Old [*Navy symbol*] .... ATO
Ocean View (AD) .... oc vu
Ocean View, DE [*FM radio station call letters*] .... WRKE
Ocean Wave Profile Recorder (IEEE) .... OWPR
Ocean Weather Ship .... OWS
Ocean Weather Station (MCD) .... OWS
Ocean Weather Vessel [*Shipping*] (AIA) .... OWV
Oceana, VA [*Location identifier FAA*] (FAAL) .... NTU
Oceanair [*ICAO designator*] (AD) .... TJ
Oceanair-Transportes Aeroes Regional SA [*Portugal ICAO designator*] (FAAC) .... OCN
Ocean-Atmosphere Carbon Exchange Study [*Marine science*] (OSRA) .... OACES
Ocean-Atmosphere Carbon Exchange Study (USDC) .... OACES
Ocean-Atmosphere Exchange Processes [*Marine science*] (MSC) .... OAMEX
Ocean-Atmosphere General Circulation Model [*Oceanography*] .... OAGCM
Ocean-Atmospheric Climatic Interaction Studies .... OACIS
Oceaneering International, Inc. [*Associated Press*] (SAG) .... Oceaner
Oceaneering International, Inc. [*NYSE symbol*] (SPSG) .... OII
Oceaneering Intl. [*NYSE symbol*] (TTSB) .... OII
Oceania Amateur Athletic Association (EAIO) .... OAAA
Oceania Basketball Confederation [*Australia*] (EA) .... OBC
Oceania Football Confederation .... OFC
Oceania National Olympic Committee [*Australia*] .... ONOC
Oceania Olympic Training Center [*Australia*] .... OOTC
Oceania Weightlifting Federation [*Australia*] (EA) .... OWF
Oceanic [*Record label*] .... Oce
Oceanic Air Traffic Center .... OATC

Oceanic Air Traffic Control [*ICAO designator*] (ICDA) .... ZO
Oceanic Air Traffic Control [*FAA designator*] (FAAC) .... ZOZ
Oceanic and Atmospheric Management Advisory Committee [*National Oceanic and Atmospheric Administration*] (EGAO) .... OAMAC
Oceanic and Atmospheric Scientific Information System [*National Oceanic and Atmospheric Administration*] (MCD) .... OASIS
Oceanic Area Control [*Aviation*] (FAAC) .... OAC
Oceanic Area Control Centre .... OACC
Oceanic Automation Program [*FAA*] (TAG) .... OAP
Oceanic Boundary Layer .... OBL
Oceanic Control Area [*ICAO*] .... OCA
Oceanic Control Area [*Aviation*] (DA) .... OCTA
Oceanic Control Center (OA) .... OCC
Oceanic Data Link [*FAA*] (TAG) .... ODL
Oceanic Display and Planning System [*Air traffic control*] .... ODAPS
Oceanic Educational Foundation (EA) .... OEF
Oceanic Flight Information Region (IAA) .... OFIR
Oceanic Gamefish Investigations [*National Oceanic and Atmospheric Administration*] (MSC) .... OGI
Oceanic Institute of Hawaii .... OIH
Oceanic Island Basalt [*Geology*] .... OIB
Oceanic Navigation Research Society (EA) .... ONRS
Oceanic Navigational Error Report [*Aviation*] (FAAC) .... ONER
Oceanic Research Foundation [*Australia*] .... ORF
Oceanic Ridge Basalts .... ORB
Oceanic Scanning Spectrophotometer .... OSS
Oceanic Society (EA) .... OS
Oceanic Society Expeditions (EA) .... OSE
Oceanic Space Subcommittee [*Congressional committee*] (MSC) .... OSS
Oceanic System Development and Support [*FAA*] (TAG) .... OSDA
Oceanic Trade Alliance Council International .... OTAC
Oceanic Traffic Planning System [*FAA*] (TAG) .... OTPS
Oceanic Transition Route [*FAA*] (TAG) .... OTR
Oceanica [*MARC geographic area code Library of Congress*] (LCCP) .... po----
Oceanografiska Institute [*Oceanographic Institute*] [*Goeteborg, Sweden*] (AD) .... Ocean Inst
Oceanographer of the Navy .... OCEANAV
Oceanographic Advisory Committee [*Marine science*] (OSRA) .... OAC
Oceanographic Advisory Committee [*Navy Oceanographer*] (USDC) .... OAC
Oceanographic Air Survey Unit .... OASU
Oceanographic and Environmental Service Laboratory [*Raytheon Co.*] .... OESL
Oceanographic, Boarding, and Diving Officer [*Navy British*] .... OBDO
Oceanographic Coordination, Evaluation, and Analysis Network .... OCEAN
Oceanographic Data Center (MCD) .... ODC
Oceanographic Data for the Environmental Science Services Administration (GFGA) .... ODESSA
Oceanographic Data in Subtrial Areas .... ODISTA
Oceanographic Data Processing and Control System (OA) .... ODPCS
Oceanographic Datastation [*Telecommunications*] (TEL) .... OD
Oceanographic Development Squadron [*Navy*] (DNAB) .... OCEANDEVRON
Oceanographic Development Squadron [*Navy symbol*] (DNAB) .... VNX
Oceanographic Devices [*JETDS nomenclature*] [*Military*] (CET) .... OC
Oceanographic Digital Data System [*Navy*] .... ODDS
Oceanographic Equipment Evaluation Range (NOAA) .... OEER
Oceanographic Experiment in the North-East Atlantic [*Former USSR*] [*Marine science*] (OSRA) .... POLYGON
Oceanographic Facility .... OF
Oceanographic Institute of Washington [*Marine science*] (MSC) .... OIW
Oceanographic Institute Wellington New Zealand (AD) .... OIW
Oceanographic Instrumentation Center [*Navy*] .... OIC
Oceanographic Observations of the Pacific .... OOP
Oceanographic Office .... OO
Oceanographic Plans and Policy Board (SAA) .... OP & PB
Oceanographic Research Buoy .... ORB
Oceanographic Research Equipment .... ORE
Oceanographic Research Ship .... AGOR
Oceanographic Research Ship .... ORS
Oceanographic Research Vessel .... ORV
Oceanographic Technical Data Handling Committee .... OTDHC
Oceanography .... OCEANOG
Oceanography (AD) .... oceanog
Oceanography and Fisheries Committee (ASF) .... OFC
Oceanography and Marine Assessment [*Marine science*] (OSRA) .... OMA
Oceanography and Marine Assessment (USDC) .... OMA
Oceanography and Marine Technology [*Defunct*] (USDC) .... OMT
Oceanography and Meteorology .... OM
Oceanologist (AD) .... oceano
Oceanroutes, Inc., Palo Alto, CA [*OCLC symbol*] (OCLC) .... OCU
Oceans and Coastal Areas .... OCA
Oceans Institute of Canada (IRC) .... OIC
Oceanside, CA [*FM radio station call letters*] .... KIOZ
Oceanside, CA [*AM radio station call letters*] (RBYB) .... KKLQ
Oceanside, CA [*AM radio station call letters*] (RBYB) .... KKSM-AM
Oceanside, CA [*FM radio station call letters*] (RBYB) .... KXST-FM
Oceanside, CA [*Location identifier FAA*] (FAAL) .... NFG
Oceanside, CA [*Location identifier FAA*] (FAAL) .... OCN
Oceanside Free Library, Oceanside, NY [*Library symbol Library of Congress*] (LCLS) .... NOc
Oceanside Middle School, Oceanside, NY [*Library symbol*] [*Library of Congress*] (LCLS) .... NocMS
Oceanside Public Library, Oceanside, CA [*Library symbol Library of Congress*] (LCLS) .... COc
Oceanside Senior High School, Oceanside, NY [*Library symbol*] [*Library of Congress*] (LCLS) .... NocSH
Oceanus Procellarum [*Lunar area*] .... OP

Ocellus	OCL
Ocellus Width	OW
Ocellus Width Index	OWI
Ocelot Chemicals, Kitimat, British Columbia [*Library symbol National Library of Canada*] (NLC)	BKOCH
Ocelot Industries Ltd. [*Toronto Stock Exchange symbol*]	OIL
Oce-van der Grinten ADR [*NASDAQ symbol*] (TTSB)	OCENY
Oce-Van der Grinten NV [*Netherlands NASDAQ symbol*]	OCEN
Oce-Van der Grinten NV [*Associated Press*] (SAG)	Oce-NY
OCG Technology [*NASDAQ symbol*] (TTSB)	OCGT
OCG Technology, Inc. [*Associated Press*] (SAG)	OCG
OCG Technology, Inc. [*NASDAQ symbol*] (NQ)	OCGT
Och Dylika [*And the Like*] [*Swedish*] (AD)	od
O'Charley's, Inc. [*NASDAQ symbol*] (SAG)	CHUX
OCharleys, Inc. [*Associated Press*] (SAG)	OCharlys
Ocheyedan Press, Ocheyedan, IA [*Library symbol Library of Congress*] (LCLS)	IaOchP
Ocheyedan Public Library, Ocheyedan, IA [*Library symbol Library of Congress*] (LCLS)	IaOch
Ochlocknee, GA [*AM radio station call letters*]	WJEP
Ocho Rios [*Jamaica*] [*Airport symbol*] (OAG)	OCJ
Ochotnicza Brygada Robotnicza Obrony Warszawy [*A publication*] (BJA)	OBROW
Ochre [*Philately*] (ROG)	OCH
Ochre (AD)	och
Ochsner-Mahorner [*Echocardiogram*] (DAVI)	OM
Ocilla, GA [*FM radio station call letters*]	WKAA
Ocilla, GA [*FM radio station call letters*]	WLPF
OCLC [*Online Computer Library Center*] Europe, Birmingham, England [*OCLC symbol*] (OCLC)	EQA
OCLC [*Online Computer Library Center*] Library, Columbus, OH [*OCLC symbol*] (OCLC)	OCC
OCLC Microcomputer Program Exchange (NITA)	OMPX
OCLC Online Computer Library Center, Dublin, OH [*Library symbol*] [*Library of Congress*] (LCLS)	OCoLC
OCLC Pacific Network [*Claremont, CA*] [*Information service or system*] (IID)	PACNET
OCLC [*Online Computer Library Center*] Training Symbol, Columbus, OH [*OCLC symbol*] (OCLC)	TRN
OCLC [*Online Computer Library Center*] Western Services Center, Claremont, CA [*OCLC symbol*] (OCLC)	TQM
OCLC [*Online Computer Library Center*] Western Services Center, Claremont, CA [*OCLC symbol*] (OCLC)	TQN
O'Clock (ROG)	O/C
Ocmulgee National Monument	OCMU
Ocmulgee Regional Library System, Eastman, GA [*Library symbol*] [*Library of Congress*] (LCLS)	GEaO
Ocoee, FL [*AM radio station call letters*]	WUNA
Oconee County Library, Walhalla, SC [*Library symbol Library of Congress*] (LCLS)	ScWal
Oconee Nuclear Station (NRCH)	ONS
O'Connell Ranch [*California*] [*Seismograph station code, US Geological Survey*] (SEIS)	OCR
O'Connor, Cavanagh, Anderson, Westover, Killingsworth & Beshears, Law Library, Phoenix, AZ [*Library symbol*] [*Library of Congress*] (LCLS)	AzPhOC
Oconto, WI [*Location identifier FAA*] (FAAL)	OCQ
Oconto, WI [*AM radio station call letters*]	WOCO
Oconto, WI [*FM radio station call letters*]	WOCO-FM
Ocracoke, NC [*Location identifier FAA*] (FAAL)	OUC
Ocracoke, NC [*FM radio station call letters*] (RBYB)	WAHL
Octacalcium Phosphate [*Inorganic chemistry*]	OCP
Octachlorocyclopentene [*Organic chemistry*]	OCCP
Octachlorodibenzodioxin [*Organic chemistry*]	OCDD
Octachlorostyrene [*Organic chemistry*]	OCS
Octadecylsilane [*Organic chemistry*]	ODS
Octadecyltrichlorosilane [*Organic chemistry*]	OTS
Octadeyl(dimethyl)chlorosilane [*Organic chemistry*]	ODS
Octagon (AAG)	OCT
Octagon (AD)	oct
Octagon Car Club [*Later, MOCC*] (EAIO)	OCC
Octahedral [*Molecular geometry*]	Oc
Octahedral [*Molecular geometry*] (IAA)	OCT
Octahedral	OCTAHDR
Octahedral Molecular Sieve [*Inorganic chemistry*]	OMS
Octahedral Research Satellite [*NASA*]	ORS
Octal [*Number system with a base of eight*] [*Computer science*] (BUR)	O
Octal [*Number system with a base of eight*] [*Computer science*] (CET)	OCT
Octal (AD)	oct
Octal (IDOE)	oct
Octal	OCT
Octal Correction Cards [*Computer science*]	OCC
Octal Debugging Aid [*Computer science*]	ODA
Octal Debugging Technique [*Computer science*] (IEEE)	ODT
Octal Debugging Technique (AD)	odt
Octal Editor [*Computer science*] (MHDI)	OEDIT
Octal Identifier [*Computer science*] (KSC)	OID
Octal Print Punch [*Computer science*]	OPP
Octal Program Updating System [*Computer science*]	OPUS
Octal Track Number [*Computer science*]	OTN
Octal-to-Binary [*Computer science*] (BUR)	OB
Octal-to-Decimal [*Computer science*] (BUR)	OD
Octal-to-Hexadecimal [*Computer science*] (IEEE)	O-H
Octamer Transcription Factor [*Genetics*]	OTF
Octamethylcyclotetrasiloxane [*Organic chemistry*]	OMCTS
Octamethylnaphthalene [*Organic chemistry*]	OMN

Octamethylpyrophosphoramide [*Insecticide*]	OMPA
Octamethyltetrabenzporphyrin [*Organic chemistry*]	OMTBP
Octane (AAG)	OCT
Octane (AD)	oct
Octane Blending Value (AD)	obv
Octane Blending Value (PDAA)	OBV
Octane Number [*Fuel terminology*]	ON
Octane Number (AD)	on
Octane Number Barrel [*Fuel terminology*]	ONB
Octane Number Requirement [*Automotive engineering*]	ONR
Octane Number Requirement Increase [*Automotive engineering*]	ONRI
Octane Rating [*Automotive engineering*]	OR
Octane Requirement [*Mechanical engineering*]	OR
Octane Requirement Increase [*Mechanical engineering*]	ORI
Octane Weekly Cost Ledger (MCD)	OWCL
Octanol [*Organic chemistry*]	OCT
Octanol Dehydrogenase [*An enzyme*]	ODH
Octanol (AD)	Oct
Octanucleotide [*Biochemistry*]	OCTA
Octanus [*Constellation*]	Oct
Octanus [*Constellation*]	Octn
Octapentadiene [*Toxic chemical*]	OCTA
Octapeptide [*Biochemistry*]	OP
Octaploidy [*State of having eight sets of chromosomes*] [*Genetics*] (DAVI)	8n
Octarios Duobus cum Semisse [*Two and a Half Pints*] [*Pharmacy*] (ROG)	OIJSS
Octarios Quatior [*Four Pints*] [*Pharmacy*] (ROG)	OIV
Octarius [*Pint*] [*Pharmacy*]	O
Octarius [*Pint*] [*Pharmacy*]	OCT
Octarius Duos [*Two Pints*] [*Pharmacy*] (ROG)	OIJ
Octava Pars [*Eighth Part*] [*Latin*] (AD)	oct pars
Octave (AD)	oct
Octave	OCT
Octave (ADA)	OCT
Octave Band	OB
Octave Band Analyzer	OBA
Octave Band Automatic Data Reduction System	OBADRS
Octave Band Filter	OBF
Octave Band Filter Set	OBFS
Octave Band Sound Pressure Level	OBSPL
Octave Filter Set	OFS
Octavian Society (EA)	OS
Octavius (AD)	Oct
Octavo [*A 16-page book*] (WDMC)	8vo
Octavo [*Book from 20 to 25 centimeters in height*] [*Bibliography*]	O
Octavo [*Book from 20 to 25 centimeters in height*] [*Bibliography*]	OCT
Octavo (AD)	oct
Octavo Strange [*Strange's Select Cases on Evidence*] [*A publication*] (DLA)	Oct Str
Octel Communications [*Associated Press*] (SAG)	Octel
Octel Communications [*NASDAQ symbol*] (TTSB)	OCTL
Octel Communications Corp. [*NASDAQ symbol*] (NQ)	OCTL
Octet (AD)	oct
Octipara [*Having borne eight children*] [*Gynecology and obstetrics*] (DAVI)	para VIII
Octo Archives, Inc., Laurel, MD [*Library symbol*] [*Library of Congress*] (LCLS)	Ocal
October	O
October (ADA)	OC
October (EY)	OCT
October (ODBW)	Oct
October (CDAI)	Otb
October 4th Organization (EA)	O40
October and April [*Denotes semiannual payments of interest or dividends in these months*] [*Business term*]	O & A
October, January, April, and July [*Denotes quarterly payments of interest or dividends in these months*] [*Business term*]	OJAJ
October League (AD)	OL
Octodecimo [*Book from 12-1/2 to 15 centimeters in height*] [*Bibliography*]	T
Octopine Dehydrogenase [*An enzyme*]	ODH
Octopine Synthase [*An enzyme*]	OCS
Octoraro Railway, Inc. [*AAR code*]	OCTR
Octrooi Protectie [*Patent Protected*] [*Dutch*] (AD)	octr prot
Octuple (MSA)	OCT
Octuplicate (AD)	octupl
Octuplus [*Eightfold*] [*Latin*] (MAE)	octup
Octupole [*Physics*] (OA)	O
Octyl [*Biochemistry*]	Oc
Octyl Glucoside [*Organic chemistry*]	OG
Octyl Isocyanate [*Organic chemistry*]	OIC
Octyl Isodecyl Phthalate [*Organic chemistry*]	ODP
Octylphenol Polyethoxylate [*Organic chemistry*]	OPEO
Octylpyrophosphoric Acid [*Organic chemistry*]	OPPA
Octylthio(trifluoro)propanone [*Biochemistry*]	OTFP
Ocular [*Microscopy*]	OC
Ocular Cicatricial Pemphigoid [*Ophthalmology*]	OCP
Ocular Density [*Ophthalmology*]	OD
Ocular Dominance [*Opthalmology*]	OD
Ocular Following Reflex [*Ophthalmology*]	OFR
Ocular Herpes [*Medicine*] (AD)	OH
Ocular Hypertension Indicator (AD)	ohi
Ocular Hypertension Indicator	OHI
Ocular Hypertensive [*Ophthalmology*]	OHT
Ocular Muscle Dystrophy [*Ophthalmology*] (MAE)	OMD

Ocular Tension [*Medicine*] ... OT
Oculentum [*Eye Ointment*] [*Pharmacy*] ... OC
Oculentum [*Eye Ointment*] [*Pharmacy*] ... OCULENT
Oculentum [*Eye Ointment*] [*Latin*] (AD) ... oculent
Oculi Unitas [*Both Eyes Together*] [*Ophthalmology*] ... OU
Oculis [*To the Eyes*] [*Latin*] (AD) ... ocul
Oculo [*To the Eye*] [*Pharmacy*] ... OCUL
Oculoauriculovertebral Dysplasia [*Medicine*] (MAE) ... OAV
Oculoauriculovertebral Dysplasia [*Medicine*] (MEDA) ... OAVD
Oculocardiac Reflex [*Physiology*] ... OCR
Oculocutaneous Albinism [*Medicine*] (DAVI) ... OCA
Oculodentodigital Dysplasia [*Medicine*] (MAE) ... ODD
Oculogyral Illusion [*NASA*] ... OGI
Oculomotor Delayed Response [*Performance test task*] ... ODR
Oculomotor Nucleus [*Eye anatomy*] ... OCN
Oculonasal [*Anatomy*] ... ON
Oculoparalytic Illusion [*Ophthalmology*] ... OPI
Oculoplethysmograph [*Instrumentation*] ... OPG
Oculoplethysmography/Carotid Phonoangiography [*Medicine*] (DAVI) ... OPG/CPA
Oculopneumoplethysmography (DAVI) ... OPPG
Oculus [*Eye*] [*Latin*] ... O
Oculus Dexter [*Right Eye*] [*Ophthalmology*] ... OD
Oculus Dexter [*Right Eye*] [*Latin*] (AD) ... od
Oculus Laevus [*Left Eye*] [*Latin*] (AD) ... ol
Oculus Laevus [*Left Eye*] [*Ophthalmology*] ... OL
Oculus Sinister [*Left Eye*] [*Ophthalmology*] ... OS
Oculus Uterque [*Each Eye*] [*Ophthalmology*] ... OU
Ocurest Laboratories, Inc. [*Associated Press*] (SAG) ... OcrstLb
Ocurest Laboratories, Inc. [*NASDAQ symbol*] (SAG) ... OCUL
Ocurrence of Reinforcing Information (PDAA) ... ORI
Ocutech Canada [*Vancouver Stock Exchange symbol*] ... OCC
Ocwen Financial Corp. [*NASDAQ symbol*] (SAG) ... OCWN
Ocwen Financial Corp. [*Associated Press*] (SAG) ... OcwnFin
ODA Natural Resources Office ... ONRO
Odalisque (VRA) ... odlsq
Odd Discrete Fourier Transform (MCD) ... ODFT
Odd Fellows [*An association*] ... OF
Odd Fellows Hall (ROG) ... OFH
Odd Fellows Temple, Des Moines, IA [*Library symbol Library of Congress*] (LCLS) ... IaDmOF
Odd Lot [*Stock exchange term*] ... OL
Odd Lot Dealer ... OLD
Odd Positive Acknowledgment [*Computer science*] (IBMDP) ... ACK1
Odd Side Flat ... OSF
Odd Symmetric ... OS
Odd Transversal Magnetic (IAA) ... OTM
Odd-Even Check ... OEC
Odd-Even Nuclei ... OEN
Odd-Even Predominance [*Organic chemistry*] ... OEP
Odd-Even Rule ... OER
Oddity-Learning Task [*Psychology*] ... OLT
Odd-Lot Broker [*Finance*] (MHDW) ... OLB
Odd-Odd Nuclei ... OON
Odds and Ends Input/Output (MCD) ... OEIO
Odds for Effectiveness [*Navy*] ... OFE
Odds Ratio [*Statistics*] ... OR
O'Dea's Medical Experts [*A publication*] (DLA) ... O'Dea Med Exp
Odebolt Chronicle, Odebolt, IA [*Library symbol Library of Congress*] (LCLS) ... IaOdC
O'Dedy's Principal and Accessory [*1812*] [*A publication*] (DLA) ... O'D Pr & Acc
Odem, TX [*FM radio station call letters*] ... KKHQ
Odem, TX [*FM radio station call letters*] (RBYB) ... KLHB-FM
Odendaalsrus [*South Africa*] [*ICAO location identifier*] (ICLI) ... FAOD
Odeneal's Reports [*9-11 Oregon*] [*A publication*] (DLA) ... Odeneal
Odense [*Denmark*] [*Airport symbol*] (OAG) ... ODE
Odense (AD) ... Odn
Odense/Beldringe [*Denmark ICAO location identifier*] (ICLI) ... EKOD
Odense Universitet [*Odense University*], Odense, Denmark [*Library symbol Library of Congress*] (LCLS) ... DnOU
Odeon [*Record label*] [*Europe, etc.*] ... Od
Odericus [*Flourished, 1166-1200*] [*Authority cited in pre-1607 legal work*] (DSA) ... O
Odericus [*Flourished, 1166-1200*] [*Authority cited in pre-1607 legal work*] (DSA) ... Od
Odericus [*Flourished, 1166-1200*] [*Authority cited in pre-1607 legal work*] (DSA) ... Oderi
Odes of Solomon (BJA) ... OSol
Odessa (AD) ... Oda
Odessa [*Former USSR Geomagnetic observatory code*] ... ODE
Odessa [*Ukraine*] [*Airport symbol*] (OAG) ... ODS
Odessa [*Washington*] [*Seismograph station code, US Geological Survey*] (SEIS) ... ODS
Odessa Branch, Lennox and Addington County Library, Ontario [*Library symbol National Library of Canada*] (NLC) ... OODLAC
Odessa College (AD) ... OC
Odessa College, Odessa, TX [*Library symbol Library of Congress*] (LCLS) ... TxOC
Odessa Commodity Exchange [*Ukraine*] (EY) ... OCE
Odessa Explorations Ltd. [*Vancouver Stock Exchange symbol*] ... ODS
Odessa/Tsentralny [*Former USSR ICAO location identifier*] (ICLI) ... UKOO
Odessa, TX [*FM radio station call letters*] ... KADM
Odessa, TX [*AM radio station call letters*] ... KENT
Odessa, TX [*FM radio station call letters*] ... KENT-FM
Odessa, TX [*FM radio station call letters*] ... KKKK
Odessa, TX [*Television station call letters*] ... KMLM
Odessa, TX [*FM radio station call letters*] ... KMRK
Odessa, TX [*FM radio station call letters*] ... KOCV
Odessa, TX [*Television station call letters*] ... KOCV-TV
Odessa, TX [*FM radio station call letters*] ... KODM
Odessa, TX [*Television station call letters*] ... KOSA
Odessa, TX [*AM radio station call letters*] ... KOZA
Odessa, TX [*Television station call letters*] ... KPEJ
Odessa, TX [*FM radio station call letters*] ... KQIP
Odessa, TX [*FM radio station call letters*] (RBYB) ... KQLM-FM
Odessa, TX [*AM radio station call letters*] ... KRIL
Odessa, TX [*Television station call letters*] ... KWES-TV
Odetics, Inc. [*NASDAQ symbol*] (SAG) ... ODET
Odetics, Inc. [*Associated Press*] (SAG) ... Odetics
Odetics,Inc.'A' [*NASDAQ symbol*] (TTSB) ... ODETA
Odetics,Inc.'B' [*NASDAQ symbol*] (TTSB) ... ODETB
Odgers on Libel and Slander [*A publication*] (DLA) ... Odg Lib
Odgers on Libel and Slander [*A publication*] (DLA) ... Odgers
Odgers on Principles of Pleading [*20th ed.*] [*1975*] [*A publication*] (DLA) ... Odg Pl
Odienne [*Ivory Coast*] [*ICAO location identifier*] (ICLI) ... DIOD
Odienne [*Ivory Coast*] [*Airport symbol*] (OAG) ... KEO
Odiham [*British ICAO location identifier*] (ICLI) ... EGVO
Odiham FTU [*British ICAO designator*] (FAAC) ... ODM
Odin (AD) ... Odn
Odin Industry Ltd. [*Vancouver Stock Exchange symbol*] ... ODI
O'Dochartaigh Family Research Association (EA) ... OFRA
Odofredus [*Deceased, 1265*] [*Authority cited in pre-1607 legal work*] (DSA) ... Od
Odofredus [*Deceased, 1265*] [*Authority cited in pre-1607 legal work*] (DSA) ... Odf
Odofredus [*Deceased, 1265*] [*Authority cited in pre-1607 legal work*] (DSA) ... Odo
Odofredus [*Deceased, 1265*] [*Authority cited in pre-1607 legal work*] (DSA) ... Odof
Odofredus [*Deceased, 1265*] [*Authority cited in pre-1607 legal work*] (DSA) ... Odofr
Odofredus [*Deceased, 1265*] [*Authority cited in pre-1607 legal work*] (DSA) ... Odofre
Odometer [*Automotive engineering*] ... ODO
Odometer (AAG) ... ODOM
Odometer (AD) ... odom
Odometer Data Computer [*Developed by Mileage Validator, Inc.*] ... ODC
Odometer Disclosure Statement ... ODS
Odon Journal, Odon, IN [*Library symbol Library of Congress*] (LCLS) ... InOdJ
Odon Winkelpeck Memorial Library, Odon, IN [*Library symbol Library of Congress*] (LCLS) ... InOd
Odonellus Mercandilis [*Authority cited in pre-1607 legal work*] (DSA) ... Odonel Mercandil
O'Donnell and Brady's Irish Equity Digest [*A publication*] (DLA) ... O'D & Br Eq Dig
Odontoblast ... ODB
Odontoglossum Ringspot Virus [*Plant pathology*] ... ORSV
Odontology ... ODONT
Odontology (AD) ... odont
Odor Control (AD) ... oc
Odor Control ... OC
Odor Detection Threshold (PDAA) ... ODT
Odor Detection Threshold (AD) ... odt
Odor Unit [*Air pollution*] ... OU
Odoramentum [*Perfume*] [*Latin*] (MAE) ... odoram
Odorant-Binding Protein [*Biochemistry*] ... OBP
Odoratus [*Odorous*] [*Latin*] (MAE) ... odorat
Odorless (AD) ... odorl
Odorless Kerosene ... OK
O'Dowd's Merchant Shipping Act [*A publication*] (DLA) ... O'Dowd Sh
ODPHP Health Information Center (EA) ... OHIC
ODPHP [*Office of Disease Prevention and Health Promotion*] **National Health Information Center** (IID) ... ONHIC
Oduma Magazine [*A publication*] ... OM
Odur [*or*] [*German*] (AD) ... od
Odwalla, Inc. [*NASDAQ symbol*] (SAG) ... ODWA
Odwalla, Inc. [*Associated Press*] (SAG) ... Odwalla
Odyssey [*of Homer*] [*Classical studies*] (OCD) ... Od
Odyssey House McGrath Foundation [*Australia*] ... OHMcGF
Odyssey Industries, Inc. [*Toronto Stock Exchange symbol*] ... ODY
Odyssey Institute [*Later, OIC*] (EA) ... OI
Odyssey Institute Corp. (EA) ... OIC
Odyssey International [*Canada ICAO designator*] (FAAC) ... ODY
Odyssey of the Mind ... OM
Odyssey Resources Ltd. [*Vancouver Stock Exchange symbol*] ... OSY
OE, Inc. [*Toronto Stock Exchange symbol*] ... OE
OEA, Inc. [*NYSE symbol*] (SPSG) ... OEA
OEC Medical [*Associated Press*] (SAG) ... OEC Md
OEC Medical Sys [*NYSE symbol*] (TTSB) ... OXE
OEC Medical Systems [*Formerly, Diasonics, Inc.*] [*NYSE symbol*] (SPSG) ... OXE
OECD Main Economics Indicators (NITA) ... OECD/MEI
OECD National Income Accounts (NITA) ... OECD/NIA
Oeconomica [*of Aristotle*] [*Classical studies*] (OCD) ... Oec
Oeconomicus [*of Xenophon*] [*Classical studies*] (OCD) ... Oec
Oecussi [*East Timor*] [*ICAO location identifier*] (ICLI) ... WPOC
Oedheim [*Germany ICAO location identifier*] (ICLI) ... EDGO
Oedipus Coloneus [*of Sophocles*] [*Classical studies*] (OCD) ... OC
Oedipus Tyrannus [*of Sophocles*] [*Classical studies*] (OCD) ... OT
OEEC [*Organization for European Economic Cooperation*] **Petroleum Industry Emergency Group** (NATG) ... OPGE
OEF [*Overseas Educational Fund*] **International** (EA) ... OEFI
Oekologisch-Demokratische Partei [*Ecological Democratic Party*] [*Germany Political party*] (PPW) ... ODP
Oelemari [*Surinam*] [*ICAO location identifier*] (ICLI) ... SMOL
Oelwein, IA [*AM radio station call letters*] ... KOEL
Oelwein, IA [*FM radio station call letters*] ... KOEL-FM

Oelwein, IA [*Location identifier FAA*] (FAAL) ... OLZ
Oelwein Public Library, Oelwein, IA [*Library symbol Library of Congress*] (LCLS) ... IaOe
Oenanthic (AD) ... oen
Oenanthyl (AD) ... oen
oenomancy (AD) ... oen
oenomel (AD) ... oen
oenometer (AD) ... oen
oenophilist (AD) ... oen
oenophobist (AD) ... oen
oenopoetic (AD) ... oen
Oerlikon-Buehrle [*Switzerland*] ... O-B
Oerlinghausen [*Germany ICAO location identifier*] (ICLI) ... EDLO
Oersted [*Unit of magnetizing force*] [*Physics*] (DMAA) ... H
Oersted (AD) ... oe
Oersted [*Unit of magnetizing intensity*] ... Oe
Oersted [*Unit of magnetizing intensity*] ... OER
Oertlicher Landwirtschaftsbetrieb [*Local Agricultural Enterprise*] [*German*] ... OELB
Oertlicher Landwirtschaftsbetrieb [*Local Agricultural Enterprise*] [*German*] ... OLB
Oesophagus ... OESOPH
Oesophagus (AD) ... oesoph
Oesterreichische Bundesbahnen [*Austrian Federal Railways*] ... OBB
Oesterreichische Computer Gesellscahft [*Austrian Computer Society*] [*German*] (AD) ... OCG
Oesterreichische Galerie [*Austrian Gallery*] (AD) ... OG
Oesterreichische Gesellschaft fur Akupunktur [*Austrian Society of Acupuncture and Auricular Therapy*] (EAIO) ... OGA
Oesterreichische Gesseleschaft fuer Informatik [*Austrian Society for Information Processing*] [*German*] (AD) ... OGI
Oesterreichische Luftverkehrs Aktiengesellschaft [*Austrian Airlines*] ... OLAG
Oesterreichische Monatsschrift fuer den Orient (BJA) ... OM
Oesterreichische Nationalbibliothek, Vienna, Austria [*Library symbol Library of Congress*] (LCLS) ... As
Oesterreichische Schuhmusterschau [*Austrian Footwear Exhibition*] [*Wiener Messen und Kongress GmbH*] (TSPED) ... OSMU
Oesterreichische Volkspartei [*Austrian People's Party*] [*Political party*] (PPW) ... OVP
Oesterreichischer Aero-Club [*Austrian Aero Club*] [*German*] (AD) ... OEC
Oesterreichischer Gewerkschaftsbund [*Austrian Trade Union Federation*] [*German*] (AD) ... OGB
Oesterreichischer Rundfunk [*Radio and television network*] [*Austria*] ... ORF
Oesterreichisches Bundesinstitut fuer Gesundheitswesen [*Austrian National Institute for Public Health*] [*Information service or system*] (IID) ... OBIG
Oeuvres de Pothier [*A publication*] (DLA) ... Poth Oeuv
OEX [*Orbiter Experiments*] **Support System** [*NASA*] (NASA) ... OSS
OEX [*Orbiter Experiments*] **Support System** [*NASA*] ... OSS
Of a Like Mind [*An association*] (EA) ... OALM
Of Concern to Air Passengers [*Group affiliated with PATCO*] (EA) ... OCTAP
Of Course ... OC
Of Human Rights (EA) ... OHR
Of This Parish ... OTP
Of True Position (MSA) ... OTP
O'Fallon Community Consolidated District 90, O'Fallon, IL [*Library symbol Library of Congress*] (LCLS) ... IOfaCD
O'Fallon Public Library, O'Fallon, IL [*Library symbol Library of Congress*] (LCLS) ... IOfa
O'Fallon Township High School District 203, O'Fallon, IL [*Library symbol Library of Congress*] (LCLS) ... IOfaSD
OFCCP Federal Contract Compliance Manual [*A publication*] (AAGC) ... OFCCP Fed Cont Compl Man
Ofensiva de Izquierda Democratica [*Offensive of the Democratic Left*] [*Bolivia*] (PPW) ... OID
Off ... O
Off Boresight Angle (MCD) ... OBA
Off Boresight Correction [*Military*] (CAAL) ... OBC
Off Center (WGA) ... OC
Off Course Target/Remote Reference Display (NG) ... OCT/RR
Off Frequency Rejection [*Radio communications*] ... OFR
Off Frequency Rejection (AD) ... ofr
Off Hook [*Computer science*] ... OH
Off Load Route [*Aviation*] (DA) ... OLR
Off Normal ... ON
Off Ocean (SAA) ... O/O
Off Off Broadway Alliance [*Later, ART/NY*] ... OOBA
Off Our Backs [*A publication*] (BRI) ... OOB
Off Peak (WDAA) ... O/P
Off Reservation Boarding School (EDAC) ... ORBS
Off Scale (IAA) ... OS
Off Screen [*or Stage*] ... OS
Off Service Note [*Medicine*] (DAVI) ... OSN
Off the Board [*Investment term*] ... OTB
Off the Shelf ... OTS
Off the Wall [*Slang*] ... OTW
Off the Wall Street Journal [*Parody of the Wall Street Journal*] ... OWSJ
Off Time (WDAA) ... OT
Off Watch [*Aviation*] (FAAC) ... OFW
Offaly (AD) ... Ofly
Offa's Dyke Association [*British*] (DBA) ... ODA
Off-Axis LASER Detection System (MCD) ... OLDS
Offboard Deception Device [*Navy*] (CAAL) ... ODD
Offboard Targeting Experiments (GAVI) ... OBTEX
Off-Broadway (WGA) ... OB
Off-Camera [*Film*] (WDMC) ... OC
Off-Diagonal Long-Range Order [*Physics*] ... ODLRO
Offenbach [*Germany ICAO location identifier*] (ICLI) ... EDZW
Offenburg/Baden [*Germany ICAO location identifier*] (ICLI) ... EDTO
Offender Aid and Restoration (EA) ... OAR
Offender Base Transaction Statistical System [*Department of Justice*] [*Database*] [*Information service or system*] (IID) ... OBTS
Offender Based State Corrections Information System (OICC) ... OBSCIS
Offender Rehabilitation Division of the Public Defender Service (EA) ... ORDPDS
Offender-Based Transaction Statistics (AD) ... obts
Offenders' Review Board [*New South Wales, Australia*] ... ORB
Offene Handelsgesellschaft [*General Partnership*] [*German*] ... OHG
Offense Only Fighter (MCD) ... OOF
Offense Variable [*Criminal sentencing*] ... OV
Offensive ... OFF
Offensive [*Ammunition*] (AAG) ... OFFEN
Offensive (AD) ... offen
Offensive ... OFFENS
Offensive Air Support (MCD) ... OAS
Offensive Air Support Mission Analysis (MCD) ... OASMA
Offensive Attack System (DOMA) ... OAS
Offensive Avionics System ... OAS
Offensive Back [*Football*] ... OB
Offensive Burst Operating Environment ... OBOE
Offensive Center [*Football*] ... OC
Offensive Counterair [*Army*] (ADDR) ... OCA
Offensive Counterintelligence Operations (MCD) ... OFCO
Offensive Efficiency Ratio [*Basketball*] ... OER
Offensive End [*Football*] ... OE
Offensive Guard [*Football*] ... OG
Offensive Missile Order of Battle (MCD) ... OMOB
Offensive Tackle [*Football*] ... OT
Offer ... OFF
Offer Accepted (ADA) ... O/A
Offer in Compromise [*IRS*] ... OIC
Offer Parent-Adolescent Questionnaire [*Personality development test*] [*Psychology*] ... OPAQ
Offer Self-Image Questionnaire ... OSIQ
Offer Self-Image Questionnaire for Adolescents (EDAC) ... OSIQA
Offer Teacher-Student Questionnaire [*Personality development test*] [*Psychology*] ... OTSQ
Offer Therapist-Adolescent Questionnaire [*Personality development test*] [*Psychology*] ... OTAQ
Offer Wanted ... OW
Offered [*Stock exchange term*] (SPSG) ... O
Offered [*Stock exchange term*] ... Ofd
Offeree [*Legal shorthand*] (LWAP) ... OFFEE
Offering (AD) ... offg
Offering Price ... OP
Offeror [*Legal shorthand*] (LWAP) ... OFFOR
Offertories (AD) ... offer
Offertory ... OFF
Off-Frequency Decoupling Resonance [*Physical chemistry*] ... OFDR
Off-Gas [*Nuclear energy*] (NRCH) ... OG
Off-Gas Isolation [*Nuclear energy*] (NRCH) ... OGI
Off-Gas System [*Nuclear energy*] (NRCH) ... OGS
Off-Highway Vehicle ... OHV
Off-Hook Service [*Telecommunications*] (TEL) ... OHS
Office [*or Officer*] ... O
Office [*or Officer*] (AFM) ... OFC
Office (AD) ... ofc
Office ... OFC
Office [*or Officer*] ... OFCE
Office [*or Officer*] (AFM) ... OFF
Office (DD) ... off
Office ... OFFC
Office Address (WDAA) ... OA
Office Administration Simulation Study ... OASIS
Office & Factory, Rochevert Industrie, Inc., Lindsay, Ontario [*Library symbol National Library of Canada*] (NLC) ... OLRI
Office and Industrial Records Management (AD) ... OIRM
Office and Professional Employees International Union (EA) ... OPEIU
Office and Technical Employees (International) Union ... OTEU
Office Appliance and Business Equipment Trades Association (HGAA) ... OABETA
Office Audit [*IRS*] ... OA
Office Automation ... OA
Office Automation / Distributed Data Processing (MHDI) ... OA/DDP
Office Automation Management Association (EA) ... OAMA
Office Automation Reporting Service (NITA) ... OARS
Office Automation Society International (EA) ... OASI
Office Automation Specialist Group (NITA) ... OASG
Office Automation System ... OAS
Office Automation System (NASA) ... OAS
Office Automation System ... OASYS
Office Balancing Network [*Telecommunications*] (TEL) ... OBN
Office Busy Hour [*Telecommunications*] (TEL) ... OBH
Office Call [*Medicine*] ... OC
Office Canadien de Commercialisation des Oeufs ... OCCO
Office Canadien du Poisson Sale [*Canadian Saltfish Corporation*] ... OCPS
Office Canadien pour un Renouveau Industriel [*Canadian Office for Industrial Revival*] ... OCRI
Office Central des Transports Internationaux par Chemins de Fer [*Central Office for International Railway Transport*] (EAIO) ... OCTI
Office Channel Unit (IAA) ... OCU
Office, Chief, Chemical Corps [*Army*] ... OCCMLC
Office, Chief of Aerospace (SAA) ... OCAF

Office, Chief of Army Field Forces ... OCAFF
Office, Chief of Chaplains [*Later, OCCH*] [*Army*] (AABC) ... OC of Ch
Office, Chief of Chaplains [*Formerly, OC of Ch*] [*Army*] (AABC) ... OCCH
Office, Chief of Civil Affairs ... OCCA
Office, Chief of Engineers [*Army*] ... OCE
Office, Chief of Finance and Accounting [*Army*] (AABC) ... OCF & A
Office, Chief of Legislative Liaison [*Military*] ... OCLL
Office, Chief of Ordnance [*Army*] ... OC of ORD
Office, Chief of Ordnance [*Army*] ... OCO
Office, Chief of Ordnance [*Army*] ... OCORD
Office, Chief of Public Affairs [*Army*] ... OCPA
Office, Chief of Research and Development [*Army*] ... OCRD
Office, Chief of Staff [*Army*] ... OCS
Office, Chief of Staff, Army (AABC) ... OC of SA
Office, Chief of Staff, Army ... OCSA
Office, Chief of Transportation [*Army*] ... OC of T
Office, Chief of Transportation [*Army*] ... OCOT
Office, Chief of Transportation [*Army*] ... OCT
Office, Chief of Transportation, Historical Branch [*Army*] ... OCTHB
Office Cleaning Service [*Commercial firm British*] ... OCS
Office, Comptroller of the Army ... OCA
Office Computer System (IAA) ... OCS
Office, Computing, and Accounting Machinery ... OCAM
Office Consultation (AD) ... OC
Office Contents Special Form [*Inventor*] (AD) ... ocsf
Office Contents Special Form [*Insurance*] ... OCSF
Office, Coordinator of Army Studies (AABC) ... OCAS
Office Copy ... OC
Office de Biologie, Ministere du Loisir, de la Chasse et de la Peche, Montreal, Quebec [*Library symbol Obsolete National Library of Canada*] (NLC) ... QMOB
Office de Commercialisation du Poisson d'Eau Douce [*Freshwater Fish Marketing Corp. - FFMC*] ... OCPED
Office de la Construction du Quebec, Montreal, PQ, Canada [*Library symbol Library of Congress*] (LCLS) ... CaQMOCQ
Office de la Construction du Quebec, Montreal, Quebec [*Library symbol National Library of Canada*] (NLC) ... QMOCQ
Office de la Langue Francaise, Montreal, PQ, Canada [*Library symbol Library of Congress*] (LCLS) ... CaQMOLF
Office de la Langue Francaise, Montreal, PQ, Canada [*Library symbol National Library of Canada*] (NLC) ... QMOLF
Office de la Langue Francaise, Quebec, PQ, Canada [*Library symbol Library of Congress*] (LCLS) ... CaQQOLF
Office de la Langue Francaise, Quebec, Quebec [*Library symbol National Library of Canada*] (NLC) ... QQOLF
Office de la Propriete Industrielle [*Department of Industrial Property*] [*Ministry of Economic Affairs*] (IID) ... OPRI
Office de la Protection du Consommateur [*Quebec, PQ*] ... OPC
Office de la Protection du Consommateur, Quebec, PQ, Canada [*Library symbol Library of Congress*] (LCLS) ... CaQQOPC
Office de la Protection du Consommateur, Quebec, Quebec [*Library symbol National Library of Canada*] (NLC) ... QQOPC
Office de la Radio et de la Television Francaise [*State-owned radio and television network*] [*France*] ... ORTF
Office de la Recherche Scientifique et Technique Outre-Mer (USDC) ... ORSTOM
Office de Planification et de Developpement du Quebec, Quebec, PQ, Canada [*Library symbol Library of Congress*] (LCLS) ... CaQQOP
Office de Planification et de Developpement du Quebec, Trois-Rivieres, PQ, Canada [*Library symbol Library of Congress*] (LCLS) ... CaQTOPDQ
Office de Promotion et d'Animation Touristique de Tahiti et ses Iles (EY) ... OPATTI
Office de Protection contre les Rayonnements Ionisants [*France*] ... OPRI
Office de Protection contre les Rayonnements Ionisants [*Office for Protecti on Against Ionizing Radiation*] [*France*] ... ORPL
Office de Radiodiffusion-Television Francaise [*National Broadcasting Organization*] [*France*] (NTCM) ... ORTF
Office de Repartition des Approvisionnements d'Energie [*Canada*] ... ORAE
Office Decision [*United States Internal Revenue Bureau*] [*A publication*] (DLA) ... OD
Office Depot [*NYSE symbol*] (TTSB) ... ODP
Office Depot [*Associated Press*] (SAG) ... OffcDpt
Office Depot, Inc. [*NYSE symbol*] (SPSG) ... ODP
Office, Deputy Under Secretary for Manpower [*Navy*] ... ODUSM
Office, Deputy Under Secretary of the Navy ... ODUSN
Office des Normes Generales du Canada ... ONGC
Office des Personnes Handicapees du Quebec, Drummondville, PQ, Canada [*Library symbol Library of Congress*] (LCLS) ... CaQDOPH
Office des Personnes Handicapees du Quebec, Drummondville, Quebec [*Library symbol National Library of Canada*] (NLC) ... QDOPH
Office des Promotions du Quebec, Direction de la Documentation, Quebec, PQ, Canada [*Library symbol Library of Congress*] (LCLS) ... CaQQOPD
Office des Services de Garde a l'Enfance, Montreal, PQ, Canada [*Library symbol Library of Congress*] (LCLS) ... CaQMSGE
Office des Services de Garde a l'Enfance, Montreal, Quebec [*Library symbol National Library of Canada*] (NLC) ... QMSGE
Office Dialog System [*Computer science*] ... ODS
Office, Director of Personnel [*Air Force*] ... ODIRP
Office Document Architecture [*Telecommunications*] (TSSD) ... ODA
Office Document Architecture/Office Document Interchange Format (DOMA) ... ODA/ODIF
Office Document Index ... ODI
Office Document Interchange Format (HGAA) ... ODIF
Office Document Language [*Telecommunications*] ... ODL
Office du Baccalaureat International [*International Baccalaureate Office - IBO*] (EAIO) ... OBI
Office Education Association (EA) ... OEA
Office Employes International Union [*Later, OPEIU*] ... OEIU
Office Equipment ... OE
Office Equipment (AD) ... offeq
Office Equipment Industry Association of Australia ... OEIAA
Office Equipment Maintenance ... OEM
Office Equipment Manufacturers Association (AD) ... OEMA
Office Equipment Manufacturers Association (NADA) ... OEMA
Office Equipment Manufacturers Institute [*Later, CBEMA*] ... OEMI
Office Executives Association (AD) ... OEA
Office Federal de l'Aviation Civile [*Sweden ICAO designator*] (FAAC) ... FOC
Office for Accreditation [*American Library Association*] ... OA
Office for Advanced Studies (AAG) ... OAS
Office for Advanced Technology [*Air Force*] ... OAT
Office for Advancement of Public Black Colleges [*of the National Association of State Universities and Land Grant Colleges*] (EA) ... OAPBC
Office for Analysis and Evaluation of Operational Data [*Nuclear Regulatory Commission*] ... AEOD
Office for Battlefield Technical Vulnerability Reduction [*Army*] (RDA) ... OBTVR
Office for Church in Society (EA) ... OCIS
Office for Civil Rights [*Department of Education*] ... OCR
Office for Communication in the Humanities (NITA) ... OCH
Office for Consumer Services [*HEW*] ... OCS
Office for Dependents' Medical Care [*Army*] (AABC) ... ODMC
Office for Domestic Shipping [*Department of Commerce*] ... ODS
Office for Economic and Business Affairs [*Department of State*] ... OEBA
Office for Emergency Management [*World War II*] ... OEM
Office for Emergency Operations in Africa [*United Nations*] (EY) ... OEOA
Office for Families (DICI) ... OFF
Office for Gifted and Talented [*Education*] ... OGT
Office for Improvements in the Administration of Justice (AD) ... OIAJ
Office for Information Technology Policy [*American Library Association*] ... OITP
Office for Intellectual Freedom [*American Library Association*] ... OIF
Office for Jewish Population Research [*Defunct*] (EA) ... OJPR
Office for Laboratory Management [*DoD*] (MCD) ... OLM
Office for Library Education [*American Library Association*] ... OLE
Office for Library Outreach Service [*American Library Association*] ... OLOS
Office for Library Service to the Disadvantaged [*American Library Association*] ... OLSD
Office for National Statistics [*British*] ... ONS
Office for Network Development [*Ottawa, ON*] [*National Library of Canada Telecommunications service*] (TSSD) ... OND
Office for Ocean Affairs and the Law of the Sea [*United Nations*] (GNE) ... OALOS
Office for Official Publications of the European Communities (ECED) ... OOPEC
Office for Operations in Political Systems ... OOPS
Office for Ordnance Research [*Later, Army Research Office*] ... OOR
Office for Protection from Research Risks [*Bethesda, MD*] [*National Institutes of Health*] (GRD) ... OPRR
Office for Recruitment [*American Library Association*] ... OFR
Office for Relations with Military and Occupation Authorities ... ORMOA
Office for Remote Sensing of Earth Resources [*Pennsylvania State University*] [*Research center*] ... ORSER
Office for Research [*American Library Association*] ... OFR
Office for Research (AD) ... OfR
Office for Research and Development [*American Library Association*] (AEBS) ... ORD
Office for Research & Statistics [*American Library Association*] ... ORS
Office for Standards in Education (AIE) ... OFSTED
Office for the Aged [*Australia*] ... OFTA
Office for the Aging (BARN) ... OFA
Office for the Civilian Health and Medical Program of the Uniformed Services (AABC) ... OCHAMPUS
Office for the Sahelian Relief Operation [*UN Food and Agriculture Organization*] ... OSRO
Office for the Study of Automotive Transportation [*Department of Transportation*] ... OSAT
Office for Victims of Crime [*Department of Justice*] ... OVC
Office Francais d'Exportation de Materiel Aeronautique [*French Office for theExportation of Aeronautical Materiel*] (AD) ... OFEMA
Office Franco-Quebecois pour la Jeunesse, Montreal, PQ, Canada [*Library symbol Library of Congress*] (LCLS) ... CaQMOFJ
Office Franco-Quebecois pour la Jeunesse, Montreal, Quebec [*Library symbol National Library of Canada*] (NLC) ... QMOFJ
Office Furniture Distribution Association (EA) ... OFDA
Office Group/Office Branch [*IRS*] ... OG/OB
Office Hours ... OH
Office Hours (AD) ... oh
Office Information System (NITA) ... OFIS
Office Instruction (AFM) ... OI
Office Interconnect Facility [*Computer science*] (BTTJ) ... OIF
Office International de la Vigne et du Vin [*International Vine and Wine Office*] (EAIO) ... OIV
Office International de l'Enseignement Catholique [*Catholic International Education Office - CIEO*] (EAIO) ... OIEC
Office International des Epizooties [*International Office of Epizootics*] [*Research center France*] (IRC) ... OIE
Office International d'Hygiene Publique [*United Nations*] ... OIHP
Office Internationale de Documentation de Medecine Militaire [*International Office of Documentation on Military Medicine - IODMM*] (EAIO) ... OIDMM
Office Internationale de la Vigne et du Vin [*International Office of Vines and Wines*] [*French*] (AD) ... OIVV
Office Lady [*Japan*] (ECON) ... OL
Office Landscape Users Group [*Later, OPUG*] (EA) ... OLUG
Office Loop Repeater (MHDB) ... OLR

Office Machines and Equipment Federation [*British*] (DIT) .... OMEF
Office Machines Group [*Business Equipment Manufacturers Association*] ...... OMG
Office Management System [*Computer science*] (IAA) .... OMS
Office Manager .... OM
Office Master Frequency Supply [*Telecommunications*] (TEL) .... OMFS
Office Messenger [*Military*] .... OM
Office Methods Research .... OMR
Office Methods Research (AD) .... omr
Office Motor Vehicle Transportation Officer [*Army*] (AABC) .... OMVTO
Office National Centrafricain du Tourisme (EY) .... OCATOUR
Office National de l'Energie [*National Energy Board - NEB*] [*Canada*] .... ONE
Office National d'Edition, de Presse, et d'Imprimerie [*Publisher*] [*Benin*] (EY) .... ONEPI
Office National d'Edition et de Presse [*News agency*] [*Niger*] (EY) .... ONEP
Office National des Chemins de Fer [*Moroccan Railways*] .... ONCF
Office National des Chemins de Fer du Maroc [*Moroccan Railways*] (DCTA) .... ONCFM
Office National du Film du Canada [*National Film Board of Canada - NFB*].......... ONF
Office Nationale du Tourisme [*Algeria*] (EY) .... ONT
Office Network Exchange [*Honeywell, Inc.*] .... ONE
Office Nurse .... ON
Office of Aboriginal Health [*Australia*] .... OAH
Office of Academic Computing [*Research center*] (RCD) .... OAC
Office of Acid Deposition, Environmental Monitoring, and Quality Assurance [*Washington, DC Environmental Protection Agency*] (GRD) .... ADEMQA
Office of Acid Deposition, Environmental Monitoring, and Quality Assurance [*Environmental Protection Agency*] (GFGA) .... OADEMQA
Office of Administration [*NASA*] .... OA
Office of Administration .... OAD
Office of Administration and Management [*Employment and Training Administration*] [*Department of Labor*] .... OAM
Office of Administration and Management Services [*Employment and Training Administration*] [*Department of Labor*] .... OA & MS
Office of Administration and Resources Management [*Environmental Protection Agency*] (GFGA) .... OARM
Office of Administrative Analysis, Information, and Statistics [*Red Cross*] .... OAAIS
Office of Administrative and Management Systems [*Social Security Administration*] .... OAMS
Office of Administrative Appeals [*U.S. Department of Labor*] (BARN) .... OAA
Office of Administrative Law Judges [*Department of Agriculture*] (GFGA) .... OALJ
Office of Administrative Systems [*Department of Agriculture*] (GFGA) .... OAS
Office of Adolescent Pregnancy [*Medicine*] (BABM) .... OAP
Office of Adolescent Pregnancy (DAVI) .... OAP
Office of Adolescent Pregnancy Programs [*HEW*] .... OAPP
Office of Adult, Vocational, Technical, and Manpower Education [*Office of Education*] .... OAVTME
Office of Advanced Research and Technology [*Later, OAST*] [*NASA*] .... OART
Office of Advanced Research Programs [*Later, OART*] [*NASA*] .... OARP
Office of Advanced Scientific Computing [*National Science Foundation*] .... OASC
Office of Aerial Phenomena [*Air Force*] .... OAP
Office of Aeronautical and Space Research [*Later, OART*] [*NASA*] .... OASR
Office of Aeronautical and Space Technology [*Formerly, OART*] [*NASA*].......... OAST
Office of Aerospace Medicine [*NASA*] (MCD) .... OAM
Office of Aerospace Medicine [*NASA*] (KSC) .... OASM
Office of Aerospace Research [*Air Force*] .... OAR
Office of Aerospace Research [*Air Force*] (AD) .... OER
Office of Agricultural and Chemical Development [*of TVA*] .... OACD
Office of Agricultural Defense Relations [*New Deal*] .... OADR
Office of Agricultural War Relations [*World War II*] .... OAWR
Office of AIDS Research [*National Institute of Health*] .... OAR
Office of Air and Radiation [*Environmental Protection Agency*] (GFGA) .... OAR
Office of Air and Water Measurement [*National Institute of Standards and Technology*] .... OAWM
Office of Air and Water Programs (OICC) .... OAWP
Office of Air Force Chaplains .... OAFC
Office of Air, Noise, and Radiation [*Environmental Protection Agency*] (ERG) .... OANR
Office of Air Programs [*Obsolete Environmental Protection Agency*] .... OAP
Office of Air Quality Planning and Standards [*Environmental Protection Agency*] .... OAQPS
Office of Air Research Automatic Computer .... OARAC
Office of Air Transportation Security [*FAA*] .... OATS
Office of Aircraft Operations [*Miami, FL*] [*National Oceanic and Atmospheric Administration*] (GRD) .... OAO
Office of Aircraft Production [*World War II*] .... OAP
Office of Airline Statistics [*U.S. Department of Transportation*] (BARN) .... OAS
Office of Airport Planning and Programming [*FAA*] (TAG) .... APP
Office of Alcohol and Other Drug Abuse Programming [*University of Minnesota*] [*Research center*] (RCD) .... AODAP
Office of Alcohol Fuels [*Department of Energy*] .... AF
Office of Alcohol Fuels [*Department of Energy*] .... OAF
Office of Alcoholism and Drug Abuse Prevention [*Department of Health and Human Services*] .... OADAP
Office of Alcoholism and Substance Abuse Services [*U.S. Department of Health and Human Services*] (BARN) .... OASAS
Office of Alien Property [*World War II*] (DLA) .... OAP
Office of Alien Property Custodian [*World War II*] .... OAPC
Office of Alternative Medicine [*National Institutes of Health*] .... OAM
Office of Analysis and Evaluation [*Environmental Protection Agency*] (EPA) .... OAE
Office of Analysis and Inspections [*Department of Health and Human Services*] (GFGA) .... OAI
Office of Analysis and Review [*Army, Navy*] .... OAR

Office of Analysis and Review, Navy (MUGU) .... OAR-N
Office of Animal Care and the A. J. Carlson Animal Research Facility [*University of Chicago*] [*Research center*] (RCD) .... AJCARF
Office of Antarctic Programs [*National Science Foundation*] [*Later, Division of Polar Programs*] .... OAP
Office of Applications [*NASA*] .... OA
Office of Applied Research, Evaluation, and Planning [*West Virginia University*] [*Research center*] (RCD) .... AREP
Office of Arid Land Studies [*University of Arizona*] (AD) .... OLAS
Office of Arid Lands Studies [*University of Arizona*] [*Research center*] (RCD) .... OALS
Office of Armed Forces Information and Education .... OAFIE
Office of Arts and Libraries [*British*] .... OAL
Office of Asbestos and Small Business Ombudsman [*Environmental Protection Agency*] .... OASBO
Office of Assistant Secretary of Air Force .... OASAF
Office of Assistant Secretary of Defense (Manpower-Reserve Affairs and Logistics) (MCD) .... OASD (MRA & L)
Office of Atmospheric Water Resources [*Bureau of Reclamation*] .... OAWR
Office of Atomic Programs [*DoD*] .... OAP
Office of Attorney General, State of Washington, Bellingham Regional Office, Bellingham, WA [*Library symbol*] [*Library of Congress*] (LCLS) .... WaBeAG
Office of Audit and Inspection [*Energy Research and Development Administration*] .... OAI
Office of Audit and Investigation [*United States Geological Survey*] .... OAI
Office of Automated Data Management Services [*General Services Administration*] .... OADMS
Office of Automatic Data Processing Services (AAGC) .... OADPS
Office of Automation and Manpower [*Department of Labor*] [*See also OMAT*] .... OAM
Office of Aviation Affairs [*Army*] .... OAA
Office of Aviation Information Management [*Department of Transportation*] [*Information service or system*] (IID) .... OAIM
Office of Aviation Medicine [*FAA*] .... OAM
Office of Aviation Policy and Plans [*FAA*] (TAG) .... APO
Office of Bank Customer Affairs [*FDIC*] .... OBCA
Office of Basic Energy Science/Geosciences [*Department of Energy*] .... OBESG
Office of Basic Energy Services [*Department of Energy*] .... OBES
Office of Basic Instrumentation [*National Bureau of Standards*] .... OBI
Office of Bilingual Education and Minority Language Affairs [*Department of Education*] (GFGA) .... OBEMLA
Office of Biochemical Nomenclature [*NAS-NRC*] .... OBN
Office of Biological Education (DAVI) .... OBE
Office of Biological Service [*Marine science*] (MSC) .... OBS
Office of Boating Safety [*Coast Guard*] .... OBS
Office of Budget and Program Analysis [*Department of Agriculture*] (GFGA) .... OB & PA
Office of Budget and Reports .... OBR
Office of Buildings and Community Systems [*Department of Energy*] .... BCS
Office of Buildings Energy Research and Development [*Department of Energy*] .... BERD
Office of Business Administration [*Later, Office of Administration*] [*NASA*] .... OBA
Office of Business Affairs [*Northern Territory, Australia*] .... OBA
Office of Business Analysis [*Information service or system*] (IID) .... OBA
Office of Business Development [*Economic Development Administration*] .... OBD
Office of Business Economics [*Later, Office of Economic Analysis*] [*Department of Commerce*] .... OBE
Office of Business Economics Research Service (NRCH) .... OBERS
Office of Business Loans [*Economic Development Administration*] .... OBL
Office of Business Research and Analysis [*Department of Commerce*] .... OBRA
Office of Cabinet and Government Management [*Australia*] .... OCGM
Office of Cable Signal Theft [*National Cable Television Association*] (NTCM) .... OCST
Office of Cancer and Toxic Substances Research, Trenton, NJ [*OCLC symbol*] (OCLC) .... NJE
Office of Cancer Communications [*Department of Health and Human Services*] (GFGA) .... OCC
Office of Career Education [*Office of Education*] .... OCE
Office of Carrier Accounts and Statistics [*of CAB*] .... OCAS
Office of Censorship [*Terminated, 1945*] [*Military*] .... OC
Office of Censorship [*Terminated, 1945*] [*Military*] .... OOC
Office of Census and Population Studies [*British*] .... OCPS
Office of Central Operations [*Bureau of Health Insurance*] .... OCO
Office of Challenge Grants [*National Endowment for the Humanities*] (BARN) .... OCG
Office of Charting and Geodetic Services [*National Ocean Service*] (USDC) .... C&GS
Office of Chief of Counsel, War Crimes [*Allied German Occupation Forces*] .... OCCWC
Office of Chief of Psychological Warfare (LAIN) .... OCPW
Office of Chief Quartermaster [*Military*] .... OCQM
Office of Child Development [*HEW*] .... OCD
Office of Child Support Enforcement [*Department of Health and Human Services*] .... OCSE
Office of Child Support Enforcement (USGC) .... OSCE
Office of Civil and Defense Mobilization [*Merged with Office of Emergency Planning*] .... OCDM
Office of Civil Aviation Security (AD) .... OCAS
Office of Civil Defense .... OCD
Office of Civil Operations [*Coordinated US civilian pacification efforts in Vietnam*] (VNW) .... OCO
Office of Civil Rights [*Environmental Protection Agency*] (GFGA) .... OCR
Office of Civilian Defense [*Within Office of Emergency Management*] [*World War II*] .... OCD

Office of Civilian Health and Medical Program of the Uniformed Services (USGC) OCHAMPUS
Office of Civilian Manpower Management [*Later, Office of Civilian Personnel*] [*Navy*] OCMM
Office of Civilian Manpower Management Instruction [*Navy*] OCMMINST
Office of Civilian Manpower Management - Navy OCMM-N
Office of Civilian Personnel [*Military*] OCP
Office of Civilian Personnel Instruction [*Navy*] (MCD) OCPINST
Office of Civilian Personnel Operations [*Air Force*] OCPO
Office of Civilian Radioactive Waste Management [*Oak Ridge National Laboratory*] OCRWM
Office of Civilian Requirements [*Division of War Production Board*] [*World War II*] OCR
Office of Civilian Supply [*Division of War Production Board*] OCS
Office of Claims and Payments Requirements [*Social Security Administration*] OCPR
Office of Coal Research [*Energy Research and Development Administration*] OCR
Office of Coastal Environment [*National Oceanic and Atmospheric Administration*] OCE
Office of Coastal Resource Management (USDC) OCRM
Office of Coastal Resource Management [*Marine science*] (OSRA) OCRM
Office of Coastal Zone Management [*National Oceanic and Atmospheric Administration*] OCZM
Office of Collateral Development Responsibility (AFM) OCDR
Office of Collateral Policy Responsibility (AFM) OCPR
Office of Collateral Responsibility (AFM) OCR
Office of Combat Indentification Technology [*Army*] OCRIT
Office of Combined Chiefs of Staff [*World War II*] OCCS
Office of Commercial and Financial Policy [*Department of Commerce*] OCFP
Office of Commercial Communications Management (AFM) OCCM
Office of Commercial Programs [*NASA*] OCP
Office of Commercial Services [*Department of Commerce*] OCS
Office of Commercial Space Transportation [*NASA*] OCST
Office of Communication and Research Utilization (AD) OCRU
Office of Communication Systems [*Air Force*] OCS
Office of Community and Intergovernmental Liaison [*Environmental Protection Agency*] (GFGA) OCIL
Office of Community Development [*HUD*] OCD
Office of Community Employment Programs [*Department of Labor*] OCEP
Office of Community Investment [*Federal Home Loan Bank Board*] OCI
Office of Community Services [*Military*] OCOMS
Office of Community Services (AD) OComS
Office of Community Services [*Family Support Administration*] [*Department of Health and Human Services*] (GFGA) OCS
Office of Community Services [*Bureau of Indian Affairs*] OCS
Office of Competitive Assessment [*Department of Commerce*] OCA
Office of Compliance Analysis and Program Operations [*Environmental Protection Agency*] (GFGA) OCAPO
Office of Compliance Monitoring [*Environmental Protection Agency*] (GFGA) OCM
Office of Comprehensive Employment Development [*Department of Labor*] OCED
Office of Computer and Communication Systems (NITA) OCCS
Office of Computer Information [*Department of Commerce*] [*Originator and database*] OCI
Office of Computer Processing Operations [*Social Security Administration*] OCPO
Office of Computing Activities [*Later, DCR*] [*National Science Foundation*] OCA
Office of Computing and Information Services [*University of Georgia*] [*Research center*] (RCD) OCIS
Office of Computing Services [*Georgia Institute of Technology*] [*Research center*] (RCD) OCS
Office of Congressional Affairs [*Energy Research and Development Administration*] (NRCH) CA
Office of Congressional Affairs [*Energy Research and Development Administration*] OCA
Office of Congressional and Legislative Affairs [*U.S. Department of Interior*] (BARN) OCLA
Office of Congressional and Public Affairs [*FCC*] (TSSD) OCPA
Office of Congressional, Community, and Consumer Affairs OCCCA
Office of Congressional Liaison [*Environmental Protection Agency*] (GFGA) OCL
Office of Consumer Advisor [*USDA*] OCA
Office of Consumer Affairs [*US Postal Service ombudsman*] OCA
Office of Consumer Affairs and Special Impact [*Federal Energy Administration*] CA/SI
Office of Consumer Protection (AD) OCP
Office of Contract Compliance [*NASA*] (NASA) OCC
Office of Contract Settlement [*Functions transferred to GSA, 1949; now obsolete*] OCS
Office of Contract Settlement Appeal Board [*Abolished, 1952*] OCSAB
Office of Contract Settlement, Appeal Board Decisions [*A publication*] (DLA) App Bd OCS
Office of Coordinating Responsibility [*Air Force*] OCR
Office of Coordinator of Inter-American Affairs [*World War II*] OCIAA
Office of Corollary Interest [*DoD*] OCI
Office of Corrections [*Victoria, Australia*] OOC
Office of Corrections Network OOCNET
Office of Country Marketing [*Department of Commerce*] (IMH) OCM
Office of Crime Prevention and Criminal Justice Research (AD) OCPCJR
Office of Criminal Enforcement [*Environmental Protection Agency*] (EPA) OCE
Office of Criminal Investigation [*Environmental Protection Agency*] (EPA) OCI
Office of Criminal Justice Planning (AD) OCJP
Office of Criminal Justice Program (OICC) OCJP
Office of Critical Tables [*NAS-NRC*] OCT
Office of Cued Speech Programs [*Gallaudet College*] [*Research center*] (RCD) OCSP
Office of Cultural Exchange [*Department of State*] OCE
Office of Cultural Presentations (AD) OCP
Office of Current Intelligence (MCD) OCI
Office of Curriculum Frameworks and Textbooks (AD) OCFT
Office of Data Collection and Survey Operations [*Bureau of Labor Statistics*] ODCSO
Office of Debt [*or Depreciation*] **Analysis** [*Department of the Treasury*] ODA
Office of Defender Services (AD) ODS
Office of Defense and Civilian Mobilization [*See also OCDM*] (MUGU) ODCM
Office of Defense Cooperation (DOMA) ODC
Office of Defense Health and Welfare Services [*World War II*] ODHWS
Office of Defense Lending [*Department of the Treasury*] ODL
Office of Defense Management and Organization [*Military*] ODMO
Office of Defense Mobilization [*Transferred to Office of Defense and Civilian Mobilization, 1958*] ODM
Office of Defense Planning [*of FRS*] ODP
Office of Defense Representative, Pakistan [*Army*] ODRP
Office of Defense Resources [*Civil Defense*] ODR
Office of Defense Trade Controls (AAGC) ODTC
Office of Defense Transportation [*Within Office for Emergency Management*] [*World War II*] ODT
Office of Defense Waste and Transportation Management [*Washington, DC Department of Energy*] (GRD) DWTM
Office of Dependency Benefits ODB
Office of Dependent Area Affairs [*Department of State*] ODAA
Office of Deputy Chief of Staff Programs and Resources [*Air Force*] ODC
Office of Deputy Director for Administration [*Marshall Space Flight Center*] (KSC) ODDA
Office of Deputy Director for Research and Development [*Marshall Space Flight Center*] (KSC) ODDRD
Office of Development Information and Utilization [*Agency for International Development*] [*Information service or system*] (IID) DIU
Office of Director of Intelligence [*Military*] ODI
Office of Director Public Information [*Military*] ODPI
Office of Disability [*Department of Health and Human Services*] (GFGA) OD
Office of Disability [*Australia*] OOD
Office of Disability Operations [*Social Security Administration*] [*Began in 1979*] (OICC) ODO
Office of Disability Programs [*Social Security Administration*] (OICC) ODP
Office of Disaster Preparedness (AD) ODP
Office of Disaster Relief Coordinator [*United Nations*] (WDAA) ODRC
Office of Disease Prevention and Health Promotion [*US Public Health Service*] [*Information service or system*] (IID) ODPHP
Office of Dissemination and Resources [*HEW*] ODR
Office of Domestic Gold and Silver Operations [*Department of the Treasury*] ODGSO
Office of Drinking Water [*Environmental Protection Agency*] ODW
Office of Drug Abuse (AD) ODA
Office of Drug Abuse Law Enforcement [*Later, Drug Enforcement Administration*] [*Department of Justice*] ODALE
Office of Earth Sciences Applications [*Department of the Interior*] (GRD) OESA
Office of Earthquakes, Volcanoes, and Engineering [*US Geological Survey*] (AD) OEVE
Office of Economic Adjustment [*Air Force*] (AFM) OEA
Office of Economic Analysis [*Formerly, Office of Business Economics*] [*Department of Commerce*] OEA
Office of Economic Development [*Bureau of Indian Affairs*] OED
Office of Economic Liaison and Regulatory Review [*Western Australia*] OELRR
Office of Economic Opportunity [*Functions transferred to other federal agencies, 1973-75*] OEO
Office of Economic Programs [*of BDSA*] OEP
Office of Economic Research [*Department of Commerce*] OER
Office of Economic Security, Department of Economic Security, St. Paul, MN [*OCLC symbol*] (OCLC) DES
Office of Economic Stabilization [*World War II*] OES
Office of Economic Trends and Labor Conditions [*Department of Labor*] OETLC
Office of Economic Warfare [*World War II*] OEW
Office of Education [*HEW*] OE
Office of Education and Training (AD) OET
Office of Education for the Gifted and Talented [*HEW*] OEGT
Office of Educational and Manpower Assistance (OICC) OEMA
Office of Educational Exchange [*Department of State*] OEE
Office of Educational Exchange [*Department of State*] OEX
Office of Educational Programs and Services [*NASA*] OEPS
Office of Educational Research and Improvement [*Department of Education Washington, DC*] OERI
Office of Electricity Regulation [*British*] OFFER
Office of Electronic Machines [*Commercial firm British*] OEM
Office of Elementary and Secondary Education [*Department of Education*] OESE
Office of Emergency and Remedial Response [*Environmental Protection Agency*] (GFGA) OERR
Office of Emergency Communications [*FCC*] (NTCM) OEC
Office of Emergency Planning (AD) OEP
Office of Emergency Preparedness [*formerly, Planning*] [*Terminated, 1973*] OEP
Office of Emergency Service [*Federal disaster planning*] OES
Office of Emergency Transportation [*FAA*] OET
Office of Employee Benefits Security [*Department of Labor*] OEBS
Office of Employment [*Victoria, Australia*] OOE
Office of Employment Development Programs (AD) OEDP

Office of Employment Security [*Department of Labor*] .... OES
Office of Employment Service Administration [*US Employment Service*] [*Department of Labor*] .... OESA
Office of Endangered Species [*Department of the Interior*] .... OES
Office of Energy [*Department of Agriculture*] (GFGA) .... OE
Office of Energy [*New South Wales, Australia*] .... OOE
Office of Energy Conservation [*Functions transferred to Federal Energy Administration*] .... OEC
Office of Energy Data and Analysis [*Functions transferred to Federal Energy Administration*] .... OEDA
Office of Energy Information Services [*Department of Energy*] (IID) .... OEIS
Office of Energy, Minerals, and Industry [*Environmental Protection Agency*] .... OEMI
Office of Energy Planning (NADA) .... OEP
Office of Energy Programs [*NASA*] .... OEP
Office of Energy Research [*Department of Energy Washington, DC*] (GRD) .... OER
Office of Energy Research [*University of Illinois*] [*Research center*] (RCD) .... OER
Office of Energy-Related Inventions [*Gaithersburg, MD*] [*National Institute of Standards and Technology*] .... OERI
Office of Enforcement [*Environmental Protection Agency*] (GFGA) .... OE
Office of Enforcement and Compliance Monitoring [*Environmental Protection Agency*] (GFGA) .... OECM
Office of Engineering and Information Processing Standards [*National Bureau of Standards*] .... OEIPS
Office of Engineering and Technology [*Washington, DC FCC*] (GRD) .... OET
Office of Engineering Design and Construction [*Tennessee Valley Authority*] .... OEDC
Office of Engineering Infrastructure Development [*Washington, DC National Science Foundation*] (GRD) .... OEID
Office of Engineering Standards Liaison and Analysis [*National Bureau of Standards*] (IAA) .... OESLA
Office of Engineering Standards Services [*National Bureau of Standards*] .... OESS
Office of Environment, Safety, and Health .... ES&H
Office of Environment (US Department of) State/Office of Cooperative Science and Technology Programs (GNE) .... OES/SCT
Office of Environmental Affairs (AD) .... OEA
Office of Environmental Analysis [*Oak Ridge National Laboratory*] .... OEA
Office of Environmental Engineering and Technology [*Environmental Protection Agency*] (EPA) .... OEET
Office of Environmental Engineering and Technology Demonstration [*Washington, DC Environmental Protection Agency*] (GRD) .... OEETD
Office of Environmental Mediation .... OEM
Office of Environmental Monitoring and Prediction [*Marine science*] (OSRA) .... OEMP
Office of Environmental Monitoring and Prediction [*National Oceanic and Atmospheric Research Laboratory*] (USDC) .... OEMP
Office of Environmental Policy [*White House*] (USDC) .... OEP
Office of Environmental Policy [*White House*] [*Marine science*] (OSRA) .... OEP
Office of Environmental Processes and Effects Research [*Environmental Protection Agency Washington, DC*] (GRD) .... OEPER
Office of Environmental Project Review [*Department of the Interior*] .... OEPR
Office of Environmental Quality Control (NADA) .... OEQC
Office of Environmental Quality Control (AD) .... OEQC
Office of Environmental Restoration and Waste Management [*U.S. Department of Energy*] (BARN) .... OERWM
Office of Equal Educational Opportunities [*Office of Education*] .... OEEO
Office of Equal Employment Opportunity [*Department of Labor*] (OICC) .... OEEO
Office of Equal Opportunity [*NASA*] .... OEO
Office of Ethnic Affairs [*Victoria, Australia*] .... OEA
Office of Evaluation Research [*University of Illinois at Chicago*] [*Research center*] (RCD) .... OER
Office of Examinations and Supervision [*Federal Home Loan Bank Board*] .... OES
Office of Executive Director for Operations [*Nuclear energy*] (NRCH) .... EDO
Office of Executive Director of Regional Operations [*Nuclear energy*] (NRCH) .... EDRO
Office of Executive Management .... OEM
Office of Executive Support [*Environmental Protection Agency*] (GFGA) .... OES
Office of Exploration [*NASA*] .... OEXP
Office of Exploratory Research [*Environmental Protection Agency Washington, DC*] (GRD) .... OER
Office of Exploratory Research and Problem Assessment [*National Science Foundation*] .... ERPA
Office of Exploratory Research and Problem Assessment [*National Science Foundation*] (AD) .... OERPA
Office of Export Administration [*Formerly, OEC*] [*Department of Commerce*] .... OEA
Office of Export Control [*Later, OEA*] [*World War II*] .... OEC
Office of Export Marketing Assistance [*Department of Commerce*] .... OEMA
Office of External Affairs [*Environmental Protection Agency*] (GFGA) .... OEA
Office of External Programs [*Environmental Protection Agency*] (GFGA) .... OEP
Office of Extramural Program Review [*Department of Health and Human Services*] (GRD) .... OEPR
Office of Facts and Figures [*Later, Office of War Information*] [*Military*] .... OFF
Office of Fair Trading [*British*] .... OFT
Office of Family Assistance [*Department of Health and Human Services*] (GFGA) .... OFA
Office of Federal Activities [*Environmental Protection Agency*] (GFGA) .... OFA
Office of Federal Contract Compliance [*Later, OFCCP*] [*Department of Labor*] .... OFCC
Office of Federal Contract Compliance Programs [*Formerly, OFCC*] [*Department of Labor*] .... OFCCP
Office of Federal Elections [*Later, FEC*] .... OFE
Office of Federal Employees Compensation [*Department of Labor*] .... OFEC
Office of Federal Procurement Policy [*Executive Office of the President*] (MCD) .... OFPP
Office of Federal Statistical Policy [*Later, OFSPS*] [*Department of Commerce*] .... OFSP
Office of Federal Statistical Policy and Standards [*Formerly, OFSP*] [*Department of Commerce*] .... OFSPS
Office of Field Operations [*Employment and Training Administration*] [*Department of Labor*] .... OFO
Office of Field Service [*OSRD*] [*World War II*] .... OFS
Office of Field Services [*Later, Bureau of Domestic Commerce*] [*Department of Commerce*] .... OFS
Office of Finance and Management [*Department of Agriculture*] (GFGA) .... OFM
Office of Financial Analysis [*Department of the Treasury*] .... OFA
Office of Financial and Administrative Management [*Department of Labor*] .... OFAM
Office of Financial and Management Information Systems (OICC) .... OFMIS
Office of Financial and Management Services [*Department of Labor*] .... OFMS
Office of Financial Management [*Bureau of the Budget; later, OMB*] .... OFM
Office of Fiscal Plans and Management [*Bureau of Indian Affairs*] .... OFPM
Office of Fisheries [*National Oceanic and Atmospheric Administration*] (GFGA) .... OOF
Office of Fishery Coordination [*World War II*] .... OFC
Office of Flight Missions [*NASA*] (MCD) .... OFM
Office of Flight Operations [*NASA*] .... OFO
Office of Flight Tracking and Data Acquisition [*NASA*] .... OFTDA
Office of Foreign Agricultural Relations [*Department of Agriculture*] .... OFAR
Office of Foreign Commercial Services [*Abolished 1970, functions transferred to Bureau of International Commerce*] .... OFCS
Office of Foreign Direct Investments [*Department of Commerce*] .... OFDI
Office of Foreign Economic Administration [*Lend-Lease*] [*World War II*] .... OFEA
Office of Foreign Economic Coordination [*World War II*] .... OFEC
Office of Foreign Economic Relief and Rehabilitation Administration .... OFERRA
Office of Foreign Investment [*Department of Commerce*] .... OFI
Office of Foreign Labor and Trade [*Department of Labor*] .... OFLT
Office of Foreign Liquidation Commission .... OFLC
Office of Foreign Liquidation Commission .... OFLIC
Office of Foreign Missions [*Department of State*] .... OFM
Office of Foreign Relief and Rehabilitation [*Obsolete*] .... OFRR
Office of Foreign Relief and Rehabilitation Operation [*Obsolete*] .... OFRRO
Office of Fossil Energy .... FE
Office of Fuel and Fuel Additive Registration [*Environmental Protection Agency*] .... OFFAR
Office of Fuels and Engergy (AD) .... OFE
Office of Fusion Energy [*Oak Ridge National Laboratory*] .... OFE
Office of Gambling [*Victoria, Australia*] .... OOG
Office of Gas Service [*Government body*] [*British*] .... OFGAS
Office of General Counsel .... OGC
Office of General Counsel - NASA .... OGC-N
Office of Geography [*Functions transferred to Geographic Names Division of Army Topographic Command*] [*Department of the Interior*] .... OG
Office of Global Programs [*Marine science*] (OSRA) .... OGP
Office of Global Programs [*National Oceanic and Atmospheric Administration*] (USDC) .... OGP
Office Of Global Programs [*Marine science*] (OSRA) .... OPG
Office of Government Contract Wage Standards (AAGC) .... OGCWS
Office of Government Ethics .... OGE
Office of Government Relations [*Environmental Protection Agency*] (GFGA) .... OGR
Office of Government Reports [*New Deal*] .... OGR
Office of Governmental and Public Affairs [*Department of Agriculture*] (GFGA) .... OGPA
Office of Graduate Studies and Research (AD) .... OGSR
Office of Grants and Program Systems [*Department of Agriculture*] .... OGPS
Office of Grants and Research Contracts [*NASA*] .... OGRC
Office of Grants Management [*Public Health Service*] .... OGM
Office of Ground Water Protection [*Environmental Protection Agency*] (GFGA) .... OGWP
Office of Guided Missile (IAA) .... OGM
Office of Hazardous Materials [*Department of Transportation*] .... OHM
Office of Hazardous Materials Exemptions and Approvals [*RSPA*] (TAG) .... OHMEA
Office of Hazardous Materials Operations [*Department of Transportation*] (DLA) .... OHMO
Office of Hazardous Materials Regulation [*Department of Transportation*] (OICC) .... OHMR
Office of Hazardous Materials Standards [*RSPA*] (TAG) .... OHMS
Office of Hazardous Materials Transportation [*Department of Transportation*] (GFGA) .... OHMT
Office of Health and Environmental Assessment [*Environmental Protection Agency*] (GFGA) .... OHEA
Office of Health and Environmental Research [*Department of Energy Washington, DC*] .... OHER
Office of Health and Medical Affairs (GHCT) .... OHMA
Office of Health Economics [*British*] .... OHE
Office of Health Maintenance Organization [*Insurance*] (DHSM) .... OHMO
Office of Health Research [*Environmental Protection Agency Washington, DC*] (GRD) .... OHR
Office of Health Technology Assessment [*HHS*] .... OHTA
Office of Hearings and Appeals [*In various federal departments*] .... OHA
Office of High-Speed Ground Transportation [*Department of Transportation*] .... OHSGT
Office of Highway Safety [*of BPR*] .... OHS
Office of Home Care Services (AD) .... OHCS
Office of Housing Technology [*National Bureau of Standards*] .... OHT
Office of Human Development [*Later, OHDS*] [*HEW*] .... OHD
Office of Human Development Services [*Department of Health and Human Services*] .... HDS

Office of Human Development Services [*Formerly, OHD*] [*Department of Health and Human Services*] ... OHDS
Office of Human Resource Information Management [*Department of Health and Human Services*] (GFGA) ... OHRIM
Office of Human Resources Management [*Environmental Protection Agency*] (GFGA) ... OHRM
Office of Humanities Communication (AD) ... OHC
Office of HUMINT [*Human Intelligence*] **Collection** [*Military*] ... OHC
Office of Impact Analysis [*Environmental Protection Agency*] (BARN) ... OIA
Office of Import Programs [*Functions transferred to Domestic and International Business Administration*] [*Department of Commerce*] ... OIP
Office of Independent Counsel [*U.S. Department of Justice*] (BARN) ... OIC
Office of Indian Education [*Department of Education*] (GFGA) ... OIE
Office of Indian Rights [*Department of Justice*] ... OIR
Office of Indian Water Rights [*Bureau of Indian Affairs*] ... OIWR
Office of Indigenous Women [*Australia*] ... OIW
Office of Industrial Associates (AD) ... OIA
Office of Industrial Base Assessment (DOMA) ... OIBA
Office of Industrial Cooperation [*AEC*] ... OIC
Office of Industrial Growth and Research [*of BDSA*] ... OIGR
Office of Industrial Management [*Navy*] (DNAB) ... OFINDMAN
Office of Industrial Managers [*Navy*] ... OIM
Office of Industrial Mobilization [*of BDSA*] ... OIM
Office of Industrial Personnel Access Authorization Review [*Army*] (AABC) ... OIPAAR
Office of Industrial Programs [*Department of Energy*] ... OIP
Office of Industrial Relations [*Superseded, 1966, by Office of Civilian Manpower*] [*Navy*] ... OIR
Office of Industrial Relations, Navy [*Superseded, 1966, by Office of Civilian Manpower*] ... OIR-N
Office of Industrial Research [*University of Manitoba*] [*Canada Research center*] (RCD) ... OIR
Office of Industrial Resource Administration (AAGC) ... OIRA
Office of Industrial Security [*DoD*] ... OIS
Office of Industrial Security, Europe [*DoD*] ... OISE
Office of Industrial Security, International [*DoD*] (MCD) ... OISI
Office of Industry Affairs and Technology Utilization [*NASA*] ... OIA & TU
Office of Industry Affairs and Technology Utilization [*NASA*] ... OIATU
Office of Industry and State and Local Government Relations [*Energy Research and Development Administration*] ... OISLGR
Office of Information (DNAB) ... OFCOFINFO
Office of Information (AFM) ... OI
Office of Information and Regulatory Affairs [*Office of Management and Budget*] ... OIRA
Office of Information for the Armed Forces (AABC) ... IAF
Office of Information for the Armed Forces (DNAB) ... OIAF
Office of Information, Navy ... OI-N
Office of Information Programmes and Services [*UNESCO*] (IID) ... IPS
Office of Information, Publications, and Reports [*Department of Labor*] ... OIPR
Office of Information Resources Management [*General Services Administration*] ... OIRM
Office of Information Services (AAGC) ... OIMC
Office of Information Services [*Council of State Governments*] [*Lexington, KY*] ... OIS
Office of Information Systems [*Social and Rehabilitation Service, HEW*] ... OIS
Office of Information Systems and Services (AAGC) ... OISS
Office of Information Systems and Telecommunications [*Veterans Administration*] (TSSD) ... OIS & T
Office of Inspection and Enforcement [*Nuclear Regulatory Commission*] ... OIE
Office of Inspection and Enforcement. Bulletin [*A publication*] (NRCH) ... IEB
Office of Inspection and Enforcement. Circular [*A publication*] (NRCH) ... IEC
Office of Inspection and Enforcement Information Notice [*Nuclear energy*] (NRCH) ... IN
Office of Inspector and Auditor [*Nuclear Regulatory Commission*] (NRCH) ... OIA
Office of Institutional Relations [*Energy Research and Development Administration*] ... OIR
Office of Integration and Checkout ... OICO
Office of Intelligence Policy and Review [*U.S. Department of Justice*] (BARN) ... OIPR
Office of Inter-American Affairs [*Later, BIAA*] ... OIAA
Office of Inter-American Radio (AD) ... OIR
Office of Intergovernmental Liaison [*Environmental Protection Agency*] (GFGA) ... OIL
Office of Intergovernmental Management (OICC) ... OIM
Office of Intergovernmental Relations [*US Congress*] [*Washington, DC*] (GRD) ... OIGR
Office of Intergovernmental Science and Research Utilization [*National Science Foundation*] ... OISRU
Office of Interim Space Station Program [*NASA*] (NASA) ... OISSP
Office of Interim Space Station Program [*NASA*] ... OISSP
Office of International Activities [*American Chemical Society*] ... OIA
Office of International Administration [*Department of State*] ... OIA
Office of International Affairs [*NASA, HUD*] ... OIA
Office of International Aviation Affairs [*FAA*] ... OIAA
Office of International Commercial Relations [*Department of State*] ... OICR
Office of International Communications Policy (NITA) ... OICP
Office of International Conferences [*Department of State*] ... OIC
Office of International Cooperation [*in CAA*] ... OIC
Office of International Cooperation and Development [*Department of Agriculture*] ... OICD
Office of International Criminal Justice (AD) ... OICJ
Office of International Economic and Social Affairs [*Department of State*] ... OIESA
Office of International Economic Research (AD) ... OIER
Office of International Epizootics (AD) ... OIE
Office of International Finance [*Department of the Treasury*] ... OIF
Office of International Health [*Department of Health and Human Services*] ... OIH
Office of International Investment [*Department of Commerce*] ... OII
Office of International Labor Affairs [*Department of Labor*] ... OILA
Office of International Operations [*of IRS*] ... OIO
Office of International Programs [*Nuclear energy National Science Foundation*] (NRCH) ... IP
Office of International Programs [*National Science Foundation*] ... OIP
Office of International Public Health (AD) ... OIPH
Office of International Research [*National Institutes of Health*] ... OIR
Office of International Resources [*Department of State*] ... OIR
Office of International Science Activities [*National Science Foundation*] ... OISA
Office of International Scientific Affairs (AD) ... OISA
Office of International Services [*Red Cross*] ... OIS
Office of International Tax Affairs [*Department of the Treasury*] ... OITA
Office of International Trade [*Department of Commerce*] ... OIT
Office of International Trade and Finance [*Department of State*] ... OITF
Office of International Trade Fairs [*Department of Commerce*] ... OITF
Office of International Trade Promotion [*Department of State*] ... OITP
Office of Interoceanic Canal Studies [*National Oceanic and Atmospheric Administration*] (NOAA) ... OICS
Office of Interstate Land Sales Registration (AD) ... OILSR
Office of Interstate Sales Registration [*HUD*] ... OISR
Office of Invention and Innovation [*Disbanded*] [*National Institute of Standards and Technology*] ... OI & I
Office of Invention and Innovation (AD) ... OII
Office of Investigation and Compliance [*Employment and Training Administration*] [*Department of Labor*] ... OI & C
Office of Investigations [*Environmental Protection Agency*] (GFGA) ... OI
Office of Job Corps [*Department of Labor*] ... OJC
Office of Justice Assistance, Research, and Statistics [*Department of Justice*] ... OJARS
Office of Justice Programs [*Department of Justice*] ... OJP
Office of Juvenile Delinquency and Youth Development [*Later, Youth Development Bureau*] [*HEW*] ... OJDYD
Office of Juvenile Justice (AD) ... OJJ
Office of Juvenile Justice and Delinquency Prevention [*Department of Justice*] [*Washington, DC*] ... OJJDP
Office of Labor Management Relations (AD) ... OLMR
Office of Labor Production [*WPB*] [*World War II*] ... OLP
Office of Labor Racketeering [*Department of Labor*] ... OLR
Office of Labor-Management and Welfare-Pension Reports [*Department of Labor*] ... OLMWPR
Office of Labor-Management Standards [*Department of Labor*] ... OLMS
Office of Land Use and Water Planning [*Abolished, 1976*] [*Department of the Interior*] ... OLUWP
Office of Land Use Coordination [*Abolished, 1944*] [*Department of Agriculture*] ... OLUC
Office of Launch Vehicle Programs [*Obsolete NASA*] ... OLVP
Office of Law Enforcement and Planning (AD) ... OLEP
Office of Law Enforcement and Planning (NADA) ... OLEP
Office of Law Enforcement Assistance (AD) ... OLEA
Office of Law Enforcement Programs [*Federal government*] ... OLEP
Office of Legal Affairs [*Navy*] (DNAB) ... OFOFLEGAFFAIRS
Office of Legal Aid Administration ... OLAA
Office of Legal Aid and Family Services ... OLAFS
Office of Legal Counsel [*Department of Justice*] ... OLC
Office of Legal Enforcement Policy [*Environmental Protection Agency*] (EPA) ... OLEP
Office of Legal Services [*of Office of Economic Opportunity*] ... OLS
Office of Legislative Affairs ... OLA
Office of Legislative Affairs, Navy (MUGU) ... OLA-N
Office of Legislative Analysis [*Environmental Protection Agency*] (GFGA) ... OLA
Office of Legislative Development [*Bureau of Indian Affairs*] ... OLD
Office of Legislative Liaison (AD) ... OLL
Office of Legislative Reference [*Bureau of the Budget; later, OMB*] ... OLR
Office of Lend-Lease Administration [*World War II*] ... OLLA
Office of Libraries and Learning Technologies (NITA) ... OLLT
Office of Library Personnel Resources [*American Library Association*] ... OLPR
Office of Library Services (AAGC) ... OLS
Office of Life Science Programs [*Obsolete NASA*] ... OLSP
Office of Management Analysis and Audit [*Civil Service Commission*] ... OMAA
Office of Management and Administration [*Social Security Administration*] (OICC) ... OMA
Office of Management and Budget [*Executive Office of the President*] [*Formerly, Bureau of the Budget Washington, DC*] ... OMB
Office of Management and Budget Circular (AAGC) ... OMB Circular
Office of Management and Budget/Federal Procurement Policy Office (OICC) ... OMB/FPPO
Office of Management and Finance (NADA) ... OMF
Office of Management and Finance (AD) ... OMF
Office of Management and Information Systems (USGC) ... OMIS
Office of Management and Technical Assessment [*Environmental Protection Agency*] (GFGA) ... OMTA
Office of Management Development [*Later, OMPR*] [*NASA*] ... OMD
Office of Management Engineer ... OME
Office of Management Improvement [*Department of Agriculture*] ... OMI
Office of Management Information [*Military*] (AFIT) ... OMI
Office of Management Information Systems [*Office of Administration and Management*] [*Department of Labor*] ... OMIS
Office of Management Planning and Evaluation [*Environmental Protection Agency*] (EPA) ... OMPE
Office of Management Planning and Review [*Formerly, OMD*] [*NASA*] ... OMPR
Office of Management Services [*Department of Agriculture*] ... OMS
Office of Management Studies (EA) ... OMS

Office of Management Support [*Environmental Protection Agency*] (EPA) ...... OMS
Office of Management Systems and Evaluation [*Environmental Protection Agency*] (GFGA) .... OMSE
Office of Manned Space Flight [*NASA*] .... OMSF
Office of Manpower, Automation, and Training [*See also OAM*] [*Department of Labor*] .... OMAT
Office of Manpower Economics [*Department of Employment*] [*British*] .... OME
Office of Manpower Policy, Evaluation, and Research [*Department of Labor*] .... OMPE & R
Office of Manpower Policy, Evaluation, and Research [*Department of Labor*] .... OMPER
Office of Manpower Research and Development [*National Academy of Sciences*] .... OMRD
Office of Manufacturing Technology [*DARCOM*] [*Army*] (RDA) .... OMT
Office of Marine and Estuarine Protection [*Environmental Protection Agency*] (EPA) .... OMEP
Office of Marine Geology [*United States Geological Survey*] .... OMG
Office of Marine Minerals .... OMM
Office of Marine Operations (USDC) .... OMO
Office of Marine Operations [*Marine science*] (OSRA) .... OMO
Office of Marine Pollution Assessment [*National Oceanic and Atmospheric Administration*] (ASF) .... OMPA
Office of Marine Resources [*Department of the Interior*] (NOAA) .... OMR
Office of Maritime Administration [*Navy*] .... OMA
Office of Maritime Affairs (AD) .... OMA
Office of Marketing Services [*of BDSA*] .... OMS
Office of Medical Applications of Research [*Bethesda, MD*] [*Department of Health and Human Services National Institutes of Health*] .... OMAR
Office of Medical Education Research and Development [*Michigan State University*] [*Research center*] (RCD) .... OMERAD
Office of Mental Health (AD) .... OMH
Office of Merchant Marine Safety [*Coast Guard*] .... OMMS
Office of Metric Programs [*Department of Commerce*] .... OMP
Office of Military Affairs .... OMA
Office of Military Applications [*Department of Energy*] .... OMA
Office of Military Assistance .... OMA
Office of Military Cooperation [*Foreign Service*] .... OMC
Office of Military Government .... OMG
Office of Military Government for Bavaria [*US Military Government, Germany*] .... OMGB
Office of Military Government for Berlin Sector [*US Military Government, Germany*] .... OMGBS
Office of Military Government for Hesse [*US Military Government, Germany*] .... OMGH
Office of Military Government for Wuerttemberg-Baden [*US Military Government, Germany*] .... OMGWB
Office of Military Government, United States .... OMGUS
Office of Mineral Policy Development [*Department of the Interior*] .... OMPD
Office of Minerals and Solid Fuels [*Formerly, OMM*] [*Abolished, 1971 Department of the Interior*] .... OMSF
Office of Minerals Exploration [*Functions transferred to Geological Survey*] [*Department of the Interior*] .... OME
Office of Minerals Mobilization [*Later, OMSF*] [*Department of the Interior*]..... OMM
Office of Minerals Policy and Research Analysis (AD) .... OMPRA
Office of Minority Affairs [*Department of Agriculture*] (GFGA) .... OMA
Office of Minority Business Enterprise [*Later, MBDA*] [*Department of Commerce*] .... OMBE
Office of Minority Economic Impact [*Department of Energy*] .... OMEI
Office of Minority Health Resource Center .... OMH-RC
Office of Minority Institutions Program [*U.S. Department of the Interior*] (BARN) .... OMIP
Office of Missile Electronic Warfare [*Army*] (RDA) .... OMEW
Office of Mobile Source Air Pollution Control [*Environmental Protection Agency*] .... OMSAPC
Office of Mobile Sources [*Environmental Protection Agency*] (GFGA) .... OMS
Office of Modeling, Monitoring Systems, and Quality Assurance [*Environmental Protection Agency*] .... OMMSQA
Office of Monitoring Systems and Quality Assurance [*Environmental Protection Agency*] (EPA) .... OMSQA
Office of Motor Carrier Standards [*Federal Highway Administration*] .... OMCS
Office of Motor Carrier Transportation [*Federal Highway Administration*] .... OMCT
Office of Motor Carriers [*FHWA*] [*NHSTA*] [*RSPA*] (TAG) .... OMC
Office of Multicultural and Ethnic Affairs [*Australia*] .... OMEA
Office of Multicultural Interests [*Western Australia*] .... OMI
Office of Municipal Pollution Control [*Environmental Protection Agency*] (GFGA) .... OMPC
Office of Munitions Control [*Department of State*] .... OMC
Office of Narcotics Coordinator [*Later, NARCOG*] [*CIA*] .... ONC
Office of National Assessments [*Australia*] .... ONA
Office of National Cost Estimates [*Department of Health and Human Services*] (GFGA) .... ONCE
Office of National Drug Control Policy [*Executive Office of the President*] .... ONDCP
Office of National Geodetic Survey [*National Ocean Survey*] .... ONGS
Office of National Industry Promotion [*Bureau of Apprenticeship and Training*] [*Department of Labor*] .... ONIP
Office of National Narcotics Intelligence [*Later, Drug Enforcement Administration*] [*Department of Justice*] .... ONNI
Office of National Programs [*Employment and Training Administration*] [*Department of Labor*] .... ONP
Office of National Projects Administration [*Department of Labor*] .... ONPA
Office of National Range Support (SAA) .... ONRS
Office of Navajo Economic Opportunity .... ONEO
Office of Naval Disability Evaluation (NVT) .... ONDE
Office of Naval History [*Also, ONH*] .... OFFNAVHIST

Office of Naval History [*Also, OFFNAVHIST*] .... ONH
Office of Naval Inspectors of Ordnance .... ONIO
Office of Naval Intelligence .... ONI
Office of Naval Intelligence Publications .... NNI
Office of Naval Liaison [*NASA*] (KSC) .... ONL
Office of Naval Material [*Later, NMCOM*] .... ONM
Office of Naval Material - Permanent Cadre .... ONMPC
Office of Naval Material Publication Type Instruction .... ONMINST
Office of Naval Officer Procurement .... ONOP
Office of Naval Operations .... ONO
Office of Naval Petroleum and Oil Shale Reserves .... ONPOSR
Office of Naval Research [*Arlington, VA*] .... ONR
Office of Naval Research and Development .... NRD
Office of Naval Research, Area Research Office (DNAB) .... ONRARO
Office of Naval Research Branch Research Office .... ONRBRO
Office of Naval Research, Chicago .... ONRC
Office of Naval Research Detachment (DNAB) .... ONRDET
Office of Naval Research, East Coast Regional Office (DNAB) .... ONREAST
Office of Naval Research, Far East Regional Office (DNAB) .... ONRFE
Office of Naval Research, London .... ONRL
Office of Naval Research Resident Representative .... ONRRR
Office of Naval Research, Tokyo .... ONRT
Office of Naval Research, West Coast Regional Office (DNAB) .... ONRWEST
Office of Naval Technology (MCD) .... ONT
Office of Naval Weapons .... ONW
Office of Naval Weather Service .... OFFNAVWEASERV
Office of Naval Weather Service .... ONWS
Office of Neighborhood Development (OICC) .... OND
Office of New Careers [*HEW*] .... ONC
Office of New Concepts and Initiatives [*Air Force*] (TEL) .... NCI
Office of New Production Reactors [*U.S. Department of Energy*] (BARN) .... ONPR
Office of NOAA [*National Oceanic and Atmospheric Administration*] Corps Operations (USDC) .... ONCO
Office of NOAA [*National Oceanic and Atmospheric Administration*] Corps Operations [*Marine science*] (OSRA) .... ONCO
Office of Noise Abatement and Control [*Environmental Protection Agency*] .... ONAC
Office of Nuclear Materials Safety and Safeguards [*Nuclear Regulatory Commission*] .... NMSS
Office of Nuclear Materials Safety and Safeguards [*Nuclear Regulatory Commission*] .... ONMSS
Office of Nuclear Reactor Regulation [*Nuclear Regulatory Commission*] .... NRR
Office of Nuclear Regulatory Research [*Nuclear Regulatory Commission*] ..... RES
Office of Nuclear Systems (SAA) .... ONS
Office of Nuclear Waste Isolation (MCD) .... ONWI
Office of Ocean Affairs [*Navy*] .... OOA
Office of Ocean Engineering [*National Oceanic and Atmospheric Administration*] (MSC) .... OOE
Office of Ocean Management [*Marine science*] (MSC) .... OOM
Office of Oceanic and Atmospheric Research [*National Oceanic and Atmospheric Administration*] .... OAR
Office of Oceanic and Atmospheric Services [*National Oceanic and Atmospheric Administration*] (MSC) .... OAS
Office of Oceanographic Facilities and Support [*Marine science*] (OSRA) ..... OFS
Office of Oceanographic Facilities and Support [*National Science Foundation*] (USDC) .... OFS
Office of Oceanography and Limnology [*Smithsonian Institution*] (MCD) .... OOL
Office of Oil and Gas [*Functions transferred to Energy Research and Development Administration*] [*Department of the Interior*] .... OOG
Office of Oil Spill Prevention and Response .... OSPR
Office of Olympic Coordination [*New South Wales, Australia*] .... OOC
Office of Operational Planning and Control [*Social Security Administration*] .... OOPC
Office of Operations [*Coast Guard*] .... O
Office of Operations [*Department of Agriculture*] (GFGA) .... OO
Office of Operations Analysis [*Arms Control and Disarmament Agency*] (GRD) .... OA
Office of Operations Support [*Law Enforcement Assistance Administration*].... OOS
Office of Organization and Management [*NASA*] .... OOM
Office of Organization Planning .... OOP
Office of Origin (AFM) .... O/O
Office of Overseas Dependent Education [*Military*] .... OODE
Office of Passenger Rail Franchising [*British*] (ECON) .... OPRAF
Office of Patents and Inventions .... OP & I
Office of Personnel [*Department of Agriculture*] (GFGA) .... OP
Office of Personnel [*Coast Guard*] .... P
Office of Personnel Management [*Supersedes Civil Service Commission*] ..... OPM
Office of Personnel Management Evaluation (DNAB) .... OPME
Office of Personnel Management Procurement Regulations [*A publication*] (AAGC) .... OPMPR
Office of Personnel Operations [*Army*] .... OPO
Office of Personnel Operations Standards and Systems Office [*Army*] .... OPOSS
Office of Pesticide Programs [*Environmental Protection Agency*] .... OPP
Office of Pesticides [*Public Health Service*] .... OP
Office of Pesticides and Toxic Substances [*Environmental Protection Agency*] .... OPTS
Office of Petroleum Allocation [*Federal Energy Administration*] .... OPA
Office of Petroleum Coordination for War [*New Deal*] .... OPCW
Office of Physical Measurement Services [*Gaithersburg, MD*] [*National Institute of Standards and Technology*] (GRD) .... OPMS
Office of Pipeline Safety [*Department of Transportation*] .... OPS
Office of Pipeline Safety Operations [*Department of Transportation*] (DLA) .... OPSO
Office of Pipeline Safety Regulation [*Department of Transportation*] (OICC) .... OPSR

Office of Placement Support and Development [*US Employment Service*] [*Department of Labor*] .... OPSD

Office of Planning and Evaluation [*Office of Personnel Management*] (GRD) .... OPE

Office of Planning and Management [*DoD*] .... OPM

Office of Planning and Program Services [*Office of Field Operations*] [*Department of Labor*] .... OPPS

Office of Planning and Research [*International Trade Administration*] (GRD) .... OPR

Office of Planning, Budgeting, and Evaluation [*National Institute of Education*] .... OPBE

Office of Planning, Control, and Validation [*Social Security Administration*] .... OPCV

Office of Planning Standards and Coordination [*HUD*] .... OPSC

Office of Planning, Technical Assistance, Research, and Evaluation [*Washington, DC Department of Commerce*] (GRD) .... OPTARE

Office of Plans and Policy (LAIN) .... OPP

Office of Plans and Program Evaluation (SAA) .... OPPE

Office of Polar Programs [*Later, Division of Polar Programs*] [*National Science Foundation*] .... OPP

Office of Policy [*NASA*] .... OP

Office of Policy Analysis [*Environmental Protection Agency*] (GFGA) .... OPA

Office of Policy Analysis and Review [*Environmental Protection Agency*] (GFGA) .... OPAR

Office of Policy and Economic Research [*Federal Home Loan Bank Board*] [*Washington, DC*] (GRD) .... OPER

Office of Policy and Management [*Environmental Protection Agency*] (GFGA) .... OPM

Office of Policy and Planning [*Office of Policy, Evaluation, and Research*] [*Department of Labor*] .... OPP

Office of Policy and Program Management [*Environmental Protection Agency*] (GFGA) .... OPPM

Office of Policy Coordination (LAIN) .... OPC

Office of Policy Development [*Executive Office of the President*] .... OPD

Office of Policy Development Planning and Evaluation [*Pronounced "opey dopey"*] [*NIMH*] .... OPDPE

Office of Policy Evaluation [*Nuclear energy*] (NRCH) .... OPE

Office of Policy, Evaluation, and Research [*Employment and Training Administration*] [*Department of Labor*] .... OPER

Office of Policy, Planning, and Evaluation [*Environmental Protection Agency*] (GFGA) .... OPPE

Office of Policy, Planning, and Information [*Environmental Protection Agency*] (GFGA) .... OPPI

Office of Population Affairs [*HEW*] .... OPA

Office of Population Census and Surveys [*British*] (ECON) .... OPCS

Office of Population Censuses and Surveys [*Department of Employment*] [*British*] .... OPCS

Office of Population Surveys [*British*] .... OPS

Office of Postsecondary Education [*Department of Education*] (GFGA) .... OPE

Office of Pre-Claims Requirements [*Social Security Administration*] .... OPR

Office of Prepaid Health Care [*Department of Health and Human Services*] (GFGA) .... OPHC

Office of Preparedness (DNAB) .... OP

Office of Preparedness, General Services Administration [*Later, Federal Preparedness Agency*] .... OP/GSA

Office of Preparedness, General Services Administration [*later, Federal Preparedness Agency*], Special Facility .... OP SF

Office of Preschool and Child Care [*Victoria, Australia*] .... OPCC

Office of Presidential Libraries [*National Archives*] (BARN) .... OPL

Office of Price Administration [*World War II*] .... OPA

Office of Price Administration and Civilian Supply [*Name changed to Office of Price Administration*] [*World War II*] .... OPACS

Office of Price Control [*World War II*] .... OPC

Office of Price Stabilization [*Terminated, 1953*] .... OPS

Office of Primary Concern [*DoD*] .... OPC

Office of Primary Development Responsibility (AFM) .... OPDR

Office of Primary Interest .... OPI

Office of Primary Responsibility [*Air Force*] .... OPR

Office of Private and Public Sector Liaison [*Environmental Protection Agency*] (GFGA) .... OPPSL

Office of Private Cooperation [*Department of State*] .... OPC

Office of Private Resources [*Department of State*] .... OPR

Office of Procurement and Contracts [*Department of Housing and Urban Development*] (GFGA) .... OPC

Office of Procurement and Materiel [*Army*] .... OPM

Office of Producer Affairs [*Federal Telecommunications Commission*] .... OPA

Office of Product Standards [*Department of Commerce*] (WDAA) .... OPS

Office of Product Standards Policy [*Gaithersburg, MD*] [*Department of Commerce*] (GRD) .... OPSP

Office of Production [*National Security Agency*] .... PROD

Office of Production and Defense Lending [*Department of the Treasury*] .... OPDL

Office of Production Management [*Superseded by WPB, 1942*] .... OPM

Office of Production Research and Development .... OPRD

Office of Productivity Programs [*Office of Personnel Management*] (GRD) .... OPP

Office of Productivity, Technology, and Innovation [*Department of Commerce*] .... OPTI

Office of Products Safety [*FDA*] .... OPS

Office of Professional Research Services [*American Occupational Therapy Association*] .... OPRS

Office of Professional Responsibility [*Department of Justice*] .... OPR

Office of Professional Standards Review [*Medicare and Medicaid*] [*HEW*] .... OPSR

Office of Professional Standards Review [*Medicare and Medicaid*] **Organization** [*HEW*] .... OPSRO

Office of Program Analysis [*Department of Energy Washington, DC*] .... OPA

Office of Program Analysis and Evaluation [*DoD*] .... OPAE

Office of Program and Budget Development and Review [*Bureau of Apprenticeship and Training*] [*Department of Labor*] .... OPBDR

Office of Program and Fiscal Integrity (USGC) .... OPFI

Office of Program and Technical Services [*Employment and Training Administration*] [*Department of Labor*] .... OPTS

Office of Program Appraisal [*Navy*] .... OPA

Office of Program Development [*Environmental Protection Agency*] (GFGA) .... OPD

Office of Program Development [*NASA*] .... OPD

Office of Program Eligibility (AAGC) .... OPE

Office of Program Evaluation [*Office of Policy, Evaluation, and Research*] [*Department of Labor*] .... OPE

Office of Program Management [*Unemployment Insurance Service*] [*Department of Labor*] .... OPM

Office of Program Management [*Environmental Protection Agency*] (GFGA) .... OPM

Office of Program Management and Evaluation [*Environmental Protection Agency*] (GFGA) .... OPME

Office of Program Management and Support [*Environmental Protection Agency*] (GFGA) .... OPMS

Office of Program Management Operations [*Environmental Protection Agency*] (GFGA) .... OPMO

Office of Program Planning (AAGC) .... OPP

Office of Program Planning and Evaluation [*National Institutes of Health*] .... OPPE

Office of Program Policy and Planning [*Social Security Administration*] (OICC) .... OPPP

Office of Program Services [*US Employment Service*] [*Department of Labor*] .... OPS

Office of Program Support and Advanced Systems (SAA) .... OPSAS

Office of Programmatic Systems [*Social Security Administration*] .... OPS

Office of Programs Integration [*Energy Research and Development Administration*] .... OPI

Office of Propulsion and Power Generation (SAA) .... OPPG

Office of Public Affairs [*in various government agencies*] .... OPA

Office of Public Affairs [*DoD*] .... PA

Office of Public Education and Information [*NASA*] .... OPEI

Office of Public Information [*UNESCO*] .... OPI

Office of Public Information [*NASA*] .... OPI

Office of Public Information [*Formerly, OPR*] [*Navy*] .... PUBINFO

Office of Public Library and Interlibrary Cooperation, St. Paul, MN [*OCLC symbol*] (OCLC) .... MIL

Office of Public Programs [*National Archives*] (BARN) .... OPP

Office of Public Prosecutions [*Northern Territory, Australia*] .... OPP

Office of Public Relations [*Later, PUBINFO*] [*Navy*] .... OPR

Office of Public Roads and Rural Engineering [*Later, Bureau of Public Roads*] .... OPRRE

Office of Public Sector Management [*Australian Capital Territory*] .... OPSM

Office of Public Trustee Information Management User System [*Canada*] .... OPTIMUS

Office of Public Works (WDAA) .... OPW

Office of Publications and Information [*Department of Commerce*] .... OP & I

Office of Publications and Public Affairs [*National Endowment for the Humanities*] (BARN) .... OPPA

Office of Publishing Services (AAGC) .... OPS

Office of Quality Control [*Social and Rehabilitation Service, HEW*] .... OQC

Office of Racing and Gaming [*Western Australia*] .... ORG

Office of Radiation Programs [*Environmental Protection Agency*] .... ORP

Office of Radiation Standards [*AEC*] .... ORS

Office of Rail Public Counsel [*Terminated, 1979*] [*Affiliated with Interstate Commerce Commission*] .... ORPC

Office of Ready Reserve [*Army*] .... ORR

Office of Recombinant DNA Activities [*Bethesda, MD*] [*National Institute of Allergy and Infectious Diseases*] .... ORDA

Office of Record (AFM) .... O/R

Office of Records Administration [*National Archives*] (BARN) .... ORA

Office of Recruitment-American Library Association (AD) .... OFR-ALA

Office of Recycled Materials [*National Bureau of Standards*] .... ORM

Office of Redress Administration [*Department of Justice*] .... ORA

Office of Refugee and Migration Affairs [*Department of State*] .... ORMA

Office of Refugee Relief [*Department of Health and Human Services*] .... ORR

Office of Refugee Resettlement (USGC) .... ORR

Office of Regional Counsel [*Environmental Protection Agency*] (GFGA) .... ORC

Office of Regional Development [*Organization of American States*] .... ORD

Office of Regional Economics [*Department of Commerce*] .... ORE

Office of Regional Management [*Employment and Training Administration*] .... ORM

Office of Regional Operations [*Office of Field Operations*] [*Department of Labor*] .... ORO

Office of Regional Operations [*Environmental Protection Agency*] (GFGA) .... ORO

Office of Regulated Material [*Environmental Protection Agency*] (GFGA) .... ORM

Office of Regulatory Analysis [*Federal Energy Regulatory Commission*] .... ORA

Office of Regulatory Information Systems [*Energy Regulatory Commission*] (IID) .... ORIS

Office of Regulatory Policy, Oversight, and Supervision [*Federal Home Loan Bank Board*] .... ORPOS

Office of Regulatory Programs [*Federal Energy Administration*] [*Obsolete*] .... ORP

Office of Regulatory Support [*Environmental Protection Agency*] (GFGA) .... ORS

Office of Rent Stabilization [*Functions transferred to Office of Defense Mobilization, 1953*] .... ORS

Office of Research [*Bureau of Intelligence and Research*] [*Department of State*] [*Washington, DC*] (GRD) .... RES

Office of Research Administration [*University of Pennsylvania*] [*Research center*] (RCD) .... ORA

Office of Research Administration [*North Carolina A & T State University*] [*Research center*] (RCD) .... ORA

Office of Research Administration [*St. Louis University*] [*Research center*] (RCD) ... ORA
Office of Research Administration [*University of Hawaii*] [*Research center*] (RCD) ... ORA
Office of Research Analysis [*Air Force*] ... ORA
Office of Research and Development [*Washington, DC Environmental Protection Agency*] (GRD) ... ORD
Office of Research and Development [*National Oceanic and Atmospheric Administration*] (GFGA) ... ORD
Office of Research and Evaluation [*Bureau of Labor Statistics*] (GRD) ... ORE
Office of Research and Evaluation Methods [*National Institute of Justice*] (GRD) ... OREM
Office of Research and Inventions ... ORI
Office of Research and Reports, Intelligence Memoranda [*CIA*] ... RR-IM
Office of Research and Sponsored Programs [*Research center*] (RCD) ... OR & SP
Office of Research and Statistics [*Social Security Administration*] ... ORS
Office of Research and Technology Applications [*Gaithersburg, MD*] [*National Institute of Standards and Technology*] (GRD) ... ORTA
Office of Research and Technology Applications [*Berkeley, CA*] [*Lawrence Berkeley Laboratory*] [*Department of Energy*] (GRD) ... ORTA
Office of Research and Technology Applications [*Army*] (RDA) ... ORTA
Office of Research, Demonstrations, and Statistics [*Health Care Financing Administration*] ... ORDS
Office of Research, Demonstrations, and Training [*Social and Rehabilitation Service, HEW*] ... ORDT
Office of Research Development [*Office of Policy, Evaluation, and Research*] [*Department of Labor*] ... ORD
Office of Research, Development, and Demonstrations [*Federal Railroad Administration*] ... ORDD
Office of Research Integrity [*Department of Health and Human Services*] ... ORI
Office of Research, Legislation, and Program Policies [*Unemployment Insurance Service*] [*Department of Labor*] ... ORLPP
Office of Research Program Management [*Environmental Protection Agency*] (GFGA) ... ORPM
Office of Research, Statistics, and International Policy [*Later, ORS*] [*Social Security Administration*] (IID) ... ORSIP
Office of Reserve Components [*Army*] ... ORC
Office of Resource Management [*Nuclear energy*] (NRCH) ... RM
Office of Revenue Sharing [*Department of the Treasury*] ... ORS
Office of Road Inquiry [*Later, Bureau of Public Roads*] ... ORI
Office of Rubber Director [*WPB*] [*World War II*] ... ORD
Office of Rural Affairs [*Victoria, Australia*] ... ORA
Office of Rural Areas Development [*Later, Rural Community Development Service*] [*Department of Agriculture*] ... ORAD
Office of Rural Development Policy [*Department of Agriculture*] ... ORDP
Office of Rural Health (MEDA) ... ORH
Office of Safeguards and Materials Management [*AEC*] ... OSMM
Office of Safeguards and Security [*Department of Energy Washington, DC*] (GRD) ... OSS
Office of Saline Water [*Later, OWRT*] [*Department of the Interior*] ... OSW
Office of Samoa Information [*Press agency*] ... OSI
Office of Saver and Consumer Affairs [*Federal Reserve Board*] ... OSCA
Office of Savings Associations [*Formerly, FHLIC*] ... OSA
Office of Savings Bonds [*Navy*] ... OSB
Office of Science and Technology [*Terminated 1973, functions transferred to National Science Foundation*] [*Later, CSTD*] ... OST
Office of Science and Technology Policy [*Executive Office of the Presiden t*] [*Washington, DC*] ... OSTP
Office of Science Information Service [*National Science Foundation*] ... OSIS
Office of Science Policy [*National Science Foundation*] ... OSP
Office of Scientific and Engineering Personnel [*National Academy of Sciences*] [*Information service or system*] (IID) ... OSEP
Office of Scientific and Technical Information [*Later, BLR & DD*] [*British Library*] ... OSTI
Office of Scientific and Technical Information [*Department of Energy*] [*Information service or system*] (IID) ... OSTI
Office of Scientific Information [*National Science Foundation*] (MCD) ... OSI
Office of Scientific Integrity [*National Institutes of Health*] ... OSI
Office of Scientific Integrity Review [*US Secretary of Health*] ... OSIR
Office of Scientific Intelligence [*Fictitious government agency on TV series "The Six Million Dollar Man"*] ... OSI
Office of Scientific Personnel [*NAS-NRC*] ... OSP
Office of Scientific Research [*AFSC*] ... OSR
Office of Scientific Research and Development [*World War II*] ... OSRD
Office of Sea Grant [*National Oceanic and Atmospheric Administration*] ... OSG
Office of Sea Grant Development [*National Oceanic and Atmospheric Administration*] (MSC) ... OSGD
Office of Sea Grant Programs [*National Oceanic and Atmospheric Administration*] ... OSGP
Office of Secretary of War [*Obsolete*] ... OSW
Office of Security Review [*Obsolete DoD*] ... OSR
Office of Senate Security [*Congress*] ... OSS
Office of Senior Citizens Affairs (NADA) ... OSCA
Office of Seniors' Interests [*Australia*] ... OSI
Office of Servicemen's Group Life Insurance ... OSGLI
Office of Servicemen's Life Insurance (OICC) ... OSLI
Office of Services to the Aging (DAVI) ... OSA
Office of Small and Disadvantaged Business Utilization (AAGC) ... OSADBU
Office of Small and Disadvantaged Business Utilization [*See also SDBU/CR*] [*Agency for International Development*] ... OSDBU
Office of Small Business Research and Development [*National Science Foundation*] (GRD) ... OSBRD
Office of Small Manufacturers Assistance [*FDA*] ... OSMA
Office of Software Development and Information Technology [*General Services Administration*] ... OSDIT
Office of Software Improvement and Engineering [*Social Security Administration*] ... OSIE
Office of Solid Fuels Coordinator [*Military*] (DNAB) ... OSFCO
Office of Solid Fuels Coordinator for War [*World War II*] ... OSFCW
Office of Solid Waste [*Environmental Protection Agency*] (EPA) ... OSW
Office of Solid Waste and Emergency Response [*Environmental Protection Agency Washington, DC*] ... OSWER
Office of Solid Waste Management Programs [*Environmental Protection Agency*] ... OSWMP
Office of Space and Terrestrial Applications [*NASA*] (GRD) ... OSTA
Office of Space Biology and Medicine [*Proposed for NASA*] ... OSBM
Office of Space Communications [*NASA*] (BARN) ... OSC
Office of Space Flight [*NASA*] ... OSF
Office of Space Flight [*NASA Washington, DC*] (NASA) ... OSF
Office of Space Flight Development [*Obsolete NASA*] ... OSFD
Office of Space Flight Programs [*Obsolete NASA*] ... OSFP
Office of Space Science [*NASA*] ... OSS
Office of Space Science and Applications [*Washington, DC NASA*] ... OSSA
Office of Space Systems [*Air Force*] ... OSS
Office of Space Systems Development [*NASA*] ... OSSD
Office of Space Tracking and Data Systems [*NASA*] (NASA) ... OSTDS
Office of Space Transportation Operations [*NASA*] (NASA) ... OSTO
Office of Space Transportation System [*NASA*] ... OSTS
Office of Space Transportation Systems [*NASA*] (GRD) ... OSTS
Office of Space Vehicles ... OSV
Office of Spacecraft and Flight Missions [*NASA*] ... OSFM
Office of Special Activities (CINC) ... OSA
Office of Special Assistant, Secretary of the Navy ... OSASN
Office of Special Counsel [*Federal agency*] ... OSC
Office of Special Education and Rehabilitative Services [*Department of Education*] ... OSERS
Office of Special Education Programs [*Also, SEP*] [*Department of Education*] ... OSEP
Office of Special Housing Assistance [*HUD*] ... OSHA
Office of Special Investigation [*Air Force*] ... OSI
Office of Special Technology [*Formerly, Office of Special Projects*] [*Washington, DC Department of Energy*] (GRD) ... OSP
Office of Special Weapons Development [*Army*] ... OSWD
Office of Spectrum Management [*US National Telecommunications and Information Administration*] (TSSD) ... OSM
Office of Sponsored Program Development [*State University of New York at Binghamton*] [*Research center*] (RCD) ... OSPD
Office of Sport and Recreation [*Australian Capital Territory*] ... OSR
Office of Staffing Policy [*Office of Personnel Management*] [*Washington, DC*] (GRD) ... OSP
Office of Standard Reference Data [*Gaithersburg, MD*] [*National Institute of Standards and Technology*] ... OSRD
Office of Standard Reference Data Bibliography [*National Institute of Standards and Technology*] ... OSRDB
Office of Standard Reference Materials [*Gaithersburg, MD*] [*National Institute of Standards and Technology*] (GRD) ... OSRM
Office of Standards and Regulations [*Environmental Protection Agency*] (GFGA) ... OSR
Office of Standards Development [*Abolished*] [*Nuclear Regulatory Commission*] ... OSD
Office of State Administration [*Australia*] ... OSA
Office of State and Local Assistance Programs [*Department of Energy*] ... SLAP
Office of State Corporate Affairs [*Western Australia*] ... OSCA
Office of State Programs [*Nuclear energy*] (NRCH) ... SP
Office of State Systems Operations [*Social and Rehabilitation Service, HEW*] ... OSSO
Office of State Technical Services [*Also, STS*] [*Abolished, 1970 Department of Commerce*] ... OSTS
Office of State Technical Services [*Also, OSTS*] [*Abolished, 1970 Department of Commerce*] ... STS
Office of Statistical Standards [*Bureau of the Budget; later, OMB*] ... OSS
Office of Strategic Information [*DoD*] ... OSI
Office of Strategic Intelligence [*Air Force*] (INF) ... OSI
Office of Strategic Offensive and Defensive Systems [*Navy*] ... OSODS
Office of Strategic Research, Intelligence Memoranda [*CIA*] ... SR-IM
Office of Strategic Services [*Facetiously translated as "Oh So Social" because some of its staff were socially prominent*] [*World War II*] ... OSS
Office of Student Detachment [*Navy*] ... OSD
Office of Student Financial Assistance [*Department of Education*] (GFGA) ... OSFA
Office of Substance Abuse Prevention [*Department of Agriculture*] (EGAO) ... OSAP
Office of Supersonic Transport Development [*Department of Transportation*] [*Obsolete*] ... OSTD
Office of Supervisory Jurisdiction [*Investment term*] ... OSJ
Office of Support Services [*Army*] ... OSS
Office of Surface Mining [*Department of the Interior*] (AAGC) ... OSM
Office of Surface Mining Reclamation and Enforcement [*Department of the Interior*] ... OSM
Office of Surface Mining Reclamation and Enforcement [*Also, OSM*] [*Department of the Interior*] ... OSMRE
Office of Surface Mining Reclamation and Enforcement, Region V, Denver, CO [*OCLC symbol*] (OCLC) ... UDS
Office of Surface Mining Reclamation and Enforcement, Washington, DC [*OCLC symbol*] (OCLC) ... UDX
Office of Surplus Property [*Superseded by War Assets Corporation*] [*World War II*] ... OSP
Office of System Capacity and Requirements [*FAA*] (TAG) ... ASC

Office of Systems [*NASA*] (KSC) .... OS
Office of Systems Analysis and Information [*Department of Transportation*] .... OSAI
Office of Systems and Financial Management [*DoD*] .... OS & FM
Office of Systems Development [*Social Security Administration*] .... OSD
Office of Systems Engineering [*Social Security Administration*] .... OSE
Office of Systems Engineering Management [*Department of Transportation*] .... OSEM
Office of Systems Integration [*Social Security Administration*] .... OSI
Office of Systems Modernization Requirements [*Social Security Administration*] .... OSMR
Office of Systems Operations [*Social Security Administration*] .... OSO
Office of Systems Operations [*National Weather Service*] (USDC) .... OSS
Office of Systems Operations [*Marine science*] (OSRA) .... OST
Office of Systems Requirements [*Social Security Administration*] .... OSR
Office of Talented Identification and Development [*Johns Hopkins University*] (EDAC) .... OTID
Office of Talented Indentification and Development [*Johns Hopkins Institute*] (WDAA) .... OTID
Office of Tax Analysis [*Department of the Treasury*] .... OTA
Office of Technical and Special Services [*Office of Field Operations*] [*Department of Labor*] .... OTSS
Office of Technical Assistance (USGC) .... OTA
Office of Technical Cooperation [*United Nations*] .... OTC
Office of Technical Cooperation and Research [*Department of State*] .... OTCR
Office of Technical Information (MUGU) .... OTI
Office of Technical Information Agency [*Army*] (MCD) .... OTIA
Office of Technical Information and Educational Programs [*Terminated NASA*] .... OTIEP
Office of Technical Resources .... OTR
Office of Technical Service, Selective Bibliographies [*US government*] .... OTS SB
Office of Technical Services (AD) .... OFTS
Office of Technical Services [*Later, CFSTI, NTIS*] [*National Institute of Standards and Technology*] .... OTS
Office of Technical Support [*US Employment Service*] [*Department of Labor*] .... OTS
Office of Technology Assessment [*Congressional study group*] [*Washington, DC*] .... OTA
Office of Technology Assessment and Forecast [*Patent and Trademark Office*] [*Washington, DC*] .... OTAF
Office of Technology Assessment and Forecasts Data Base (NITA) .... OTAF Data Base
Office of Technology Assistance [*General Services Administration*] .... OTA
Office of Technology Support Programs [*Washington, DC Department of Energy*] (GRD) .... OTSP
Office of Technology Transfer [*University of Illinois*] .... OTT
Office of Technology Utilization [*NASA*] .... OTU
Office of Telecommunications [*Independent government agency*] [*British*] .... OFTEL
Office of Telecommunications [*Department of Commerce*] .... OT
Office of Telecommunications Applications [*US National Telecommunications and Information Administration*] (TSSD) .... OTA
Office of Telecommunications Institute for Telecommunication Sciences [*Boulder, CO*] [*Department of Commerce*] .... OT/ITS
Office of Telecommunications Management [*Later, OTP*] [*FCC*] .... OTM
Office of Telecommunications Policy [*Terminated, 1978*] [*Executive Office of the President*] .... OTP
Office of Telecommunications Systems Operations [*Social Security Administration*] .... OTSO
Office of Temporary Controls .... OTC
Office of Territories [*Department of the Interior*] .... OT
Office of Terrorism and Narcotics Analysis [*Bureau of Intelligence and Research*] [*Department of State*] [*Washington, DC*] (GRD) .... TNA
Office of Textiles and Apparel [*Department of Commerce*] (GFGA) .... OTEXA
Office of the Actuary [*Department of Health and Human Services*] (GFGA) .... OACT
Office of the Adjutant General [*Military*] (MCD) .... OAG
Office of the Adjutant General [*Military*] .... OTAG
Office of the Administrative Assistant to the Secretary of the Army .... OAASA
Office of the Administrative Assistant to the Secretary of the Navy .... OAASN
Office of the Administrator .... OA
Office of the Administrator of Norfolk Island [*Australia*] .... OANI
Office of the Admiral Commanding Reserves [*Navy British*] .... OACR
Office of the Air Force Assistant for Atomic Energy, Section 1 (LAIN) AFOAT-1
Office of the Americas [*An association*] (EA) .... OOA
Office of the Assisant Secretary of Defense (Health Affairs) (DNAB) .... OASD(HA)
Office of the Assistant Administrator for Research and Development [*HEW*] .... OAARD
Office of the Assistant Chief of Staff [*Military*] .... OAC of S
Office of the Assistant Chief of Staff [*Military*] (AAG) .... OACS
Office of the Assistant Chief of Staff for Automation and Communications [*Military*] (MCD) .... OACSA
Office of the Assistant Chief of Staff for Automation and Communications [*Military*] .... OACSAC
Office of the Assistant Chief of Staff for Communications-Electronics (AABC) .... OACSC-E
Office of the Assistant Chief of Staff for Force Development [*Army*] .... OACSFOR
Office of the Assistant Chief of Staff for Information Management [*Military*] .... OACSIM
Office of the Assistant Chief of Staff for Intelligence [*Army*] .... OACSI
Office of the Assistant Comptroller General (AAGC) .... OACG
Office of the Assistant Director of the Army Budget .... OADAB
Office of the Assistant for Study Support [*Air Force*] .... OAS
Office of the Assistant for Weather [*Air Force*] .... OWX
Office of the Assistant Secretary [*Defense*] [*Navy*] .... OAS
Office of the Assistant Secretary for Administration and Management [*Department of Labor*] .... OASAM
Office of the Assistant Secretary for Employment and Training [*Department of Labor*] .... OASET
Office of the Assistant Secretary for Export Enforcement [*Department of Commerce*] (GFGA) .... OEE
Office of the Assistant Secretary for Health [*Department of Health and Human Services*] .... OASH
Office of the Assistant Secretary for International Affairs [*Department of the Treasury*] .... OASIA
Office of the Assistant Secretary for Technology Policy [*U.S. Department of Commerce*] (BARN) .... OASTP
Office of the Assistant Secretary of Defense .... OASD
Office of the Assistant Secretary of Defense (Applications Engineer) (MCD) .... OASD(AE)
Office of the Assistant Secretary of Defense - Comptroller .... OASD-C
Office of the Assistant Secretary of Defense for International Security Policy (SDI) .... OASD/ISP
Office of the Assistant Secretary of Defense/Installations and Logistics (MCD) .... OASD/IL
Office of the Assistant Secretary of Defense/International Security Affairs (CINC) .... OASD/ISA
Office of the Assistant Secretary of Defense (Manpower and Reserve Affairs) .... OASD(MRA)
Office of the Assistant Secretary of Defense (Public Affairs) (NTCM) .... OASD(PA)
Office of the Assistant Secretary of Defense (Research and Development) (MCD) .... OASD(R & D)
Office of the Assistant Secretary of Defense (Supply and Logistics) [*Obsolete*] (MCD) .... OASD(S & L)
Office of the Assistant Secretary of Defense (Systems Analysis) (CINC) .... OASD(SA)
Office of the Assistant Secretary of Defense (Telecommunications) .... OASD(T)
Office of the Assistant Secretary of the Army (Financial Management) (MUGU) .... OASA (FM)
Office of the Assistant Secretary of the Army (Installations and Logistics) (MUGU) .... OASA (I & L)
Office of the Assistant Secretary of the Army (Manpower and Reserve Affairs) .... OASA(M & RA)
Office of the Assistant Secretary of the Army (Research and Development) (MUGU) .... OASA (R & D)
Office of the Assistant Secretary of the Army (Research, Development and Aquisition) (RDA) .... OASARDA
Office of the Assistant Secretary of the Navy .... OASN
Office of the Assistant Secretary of the Navy (DNAB) .... OFCOFASSTSECNAV
Office of the Assistant Secretary of the Navy (Financial Management) (DNAB) .... OFCOFASSTSECNAV(FINMGMT)
Office of the Assistant Secretary of the Navy for Financial Management .... OASN(FM)
Office of the Assistant Secretary of the Navy for Installations and Logistics .... OASN(I & L)
Office of the Assistant Secretary of the Navy for Personnel and Reserve Force .... OASN(P & RF)
Office of the Assistant Secretary of the Navy for Research and Development .... OASN(R & D)
Office of the Assistant Secretary of the Navy (Installations and Logistics) (DNAB) .... OFCOFASSTSECNAV(INSTALLOG)
Office of the Assistant Secretary of the Navy (Manpower and Reserve Affairs) .... OASN(M/RA)
Office of the Assistant Secretary of the Navy (Manpower, Reserve Affairs, and Logistics) .... OASN(M/RA/L)
Office of the Assistant Secretary of the Navy (Personnel and Reserve Force) (DNAB) .... OFCOFASSTSECNAV(PERSRESFOR)
Office of the Assistant Secretary of the Navy (Research and Development) (DNAB) .... OFCOFASSTSECNAV(RSCHDEV)
Office of the Assistant Secretary of War [*World War II*] .... OASW
Office of the Assistant Vice Chief of Staff, Army [*Later, OAVCSA*] (AABC) .... OAVC of SA
Office of the Assistant Vice Chief of Staff, Army [*Formerly, OAVC of SA*] (AABC) .... OAVCSA
Office of the Attorney General (State of Washington) Opinions [*A publication*] (DLA) .... Op Wash Att'y Gen
Office of the Attorney-General .... OAG
Office of the Auditor General, Ottawa, ON, Canada [*Library symbol Library of Congress*] (LCLS) .... CaOOOAG
Office of the Auditor General [*Bureau du Verificateur General*] Ottawa, Ontario [*Library symbol National Library of Canada*] (NLC) .... OOOAG
Office of the Auditor General, Springfield, IL [*Library symbol Library of Congress*] (LCLS) .... ISAG
Office of the Chairman, Joint Chiefs of Staff (MCD) .... OCJCS
Office of the Chemical Industry Trade Advisor .... OCITA
Office of the Chief, Air Defense Artillery .... OCADA
Office of the Chief, Army Reserve (AABC) .... OCAR
Office of the Chief Chemical Officer (AD) .... Oc C Cm O
Office of the Chief Chemical Officer [*Military*] .... OCCMLO
Office of the Chief Chemical Officer [*Military*] (AAG) .... OCCO
Office of the Chief Economist (AAGC) .... OCE
Office of the Chief of Air Corps [*World War II*] .... OC of AC
Office of the Chief of Air Corps [*World War II*] .... OCAC
Office of the Chief of Air Service [*World War II*] .... OCAS
Office of the Chief of Air Staff [*World War II*] .... OC of AS
Office of the Chief of Communications-Electronics [*Army*] (AABC) .... OCC-E
Office of the Chief of Engineers [*Army*] (RDA) .... OCOE
Office of the Chief of Finance [*Military*] .... OC of F
Office of the Chief of Finance [*Military*] .... OCF

Office of the Chief of Information [*Military*] ... OCINFO
Office of the Chief of Military History [*Army*] ... OCMH
Office of the Chief of Naval Operations ... OCNO
Office of the Chief of Naval Operations ... OPN
Office of the Chief of Naval Operations ... OPNAV
Office of the Chief of Naval Operations ... OPNAVO
Office of the Chief of Naval Operations, Communications Office (DNAB) ... OPNAVCOMMO
Office of the Chief of Naval Operations Instruction ... OPNAVINST
Office of the Chief of Naval Operations, Support Activity (DNAB) ... OPNAVSUPPACT
Office of the Chief of Naval Operations, Support Activity Detachment (DNAB) ... OPNAVSUPPACTDET
Office of the Chief of Naval Operations, Support Activity Flight Information Group (DNAB) ... OPNAVSUPPACT FIG
Office of the Chief of Naval Operations, Support Activity Telecommunications Center (DNAB) ... OPNAVSUPPACT TCC
Office of the Chief of Naval Operations, Support Activity, Worldwide Military Command Control System, Data Processing (DNAB) ... OPNAVSUPPACT WWMCCS DP
Office of the Chief of Naval Operations, Support Activity, Worldwide Military Command Control System, Employment Schedule (DNAB) ... OPNAVSUPPACT WWMCCS EMPSKED
Office of the Chief of Naval Operations, Support Activity, Worldwide Military Command Control System, Force Status (DNAB) ... OPNAVSUPPACT WWMCCS FORSTAT
Office of the Chief of Naval Operations, Support Activity, Worldwide Military Command Control System, Movement Reports (DNAB) ... OPNAVSUPPACT WWMCCS MOVREP
Office of the Chief of Protocol [*US Department of State*] (AD) ... OCP
Office of the Chief of Special Warfare [*Army*] ... OCSPWAR
Office of the Chief of Support Services [*Army*] (AABC) ... OC of SptS
Office of the Chief of Support Services [*Army*] ... OCSS
Office of the Chief Scientist ... OCS
Office of the Chief Signal Officer ... OCSIGO
Office of the Chief Signal Officer ... OCSO
Office of the Chief Signal Officer ... OSIGO
Office of the Chief Surgeon [*Military*] ... OCS
Office of the City Attorney (AD) ... OCA
Office of the Civilian Health and Medical Program of the Uniformed Services in Europe (DNAB) ... OCHAMPUSEUR
Office of the Commanding General [*Army*] ... OCG
Office of the Commission [*Nuclear energy*] (NRCH) ... OCM
Office of the Commissioner [*Office of Education*] ... OC
Office of the Commissioner for Equal Opportunity [*Australia*] ... OCEO
Office of the Commissioner for Federal Judicial Affairs [*Bureau du Commissaire a la Magistrature Federale*], Ottawa, Ontario [*Library symbol National Library of Canada*] (BIB) ... OOCMF
Office of the Commissioners of Inquiry for Environment and Planning [*Australia*] ... OCIEP
Office of the Community Advocate [*Australian Capital Territory*] ... OCA
Office of the Comptroller ... OC
Office of the Comptroller General (AAGC) ... OCG
Office of the Comptroller of the Currency [*Department of the Treasury*] ... OCC
Office of the Comptroller of the Currency, Washington, DC [*Library symbol Library of Congress*] (LCLS) ... DOCC
Office of the Comptroller of the Navy ... NAVCOMPT
Office of the Comptroller of the Navy ... OC-N
Office of the Comptroller of the Navy Instruction ... NAVCOMPTINST
Office of the Coordinator of Information (AD) ... OCI
Office of the Coordinator, Regulatory Reform [*Canada*] ... OCRR
Office of the County Recorder (AD) ... OCR
Office of the Defense Attache [*Foreign Service*] ... ODA
Office of the Deputy Assistant Secretary of Defense ... ODASD
Office of the Deputy Chief of Staff [*World War II*] ... ODC of S
Office of the Deputy Chief of Staff [*World War II*] ... ODCS
Office of the Deputy Chief of Staff, Combat Developments [*Army*] ... ODCSCD
Office of the Deputy Chief of Staff for Intelligence ... ODCSI
Office of the Deputy Chief of Staff for Logistics [*Army*] (AABC) ... ODCSLOG
Office of the Deputy Chief of Staff for Operations and Plans [*Army*] ... ODCSOPS
Office of the Deputy Chief of Staff for Personnel [*Army*] ... ODCSPER
Office of the Deputy Chief of Staff for Research, Development, and Acquisition [*Army*] (AABC) ... ODCSRDA
Office of the Deputy Director of Defense Research and Engineering (RDA) ... ODDDR & R
Office of the Deputy Under Secretary of Defense (Environmental Security) [*DoD*] (RDA) ... ODUSD(ES)
Office of the Deputy Under Secretary of Defense for Research and Advanced Technology [*DoD*] (RDA) ... ODUSD (R & AT)
Office of the Director ... OD
Office of the Director, Joint Staff (MCD) ... ODJS
Office of the Director of Aerospace Programs [*Air Force*] ... OAP
Office of the Director of Civil Engineering [*Air Force*] ... OCE
Office of the Director of Command, Control, and Communications [*Air Force*] ... OCC
Office of the Director of Defense Research and Engineering [*Later, Office of the Under Secretary of Defense for Research and Engineering*] [*Army*] ... ODDR & E
Office of the Director of Defense Research and Engineering [*Later, Office of the Under Secretary of Defense for Research and Engineering*] [*Army*] ... ODDRE
Office of the Director of Development Planning [*Air Force*] (MCD) ... ODDP
Office of the Director of Industrial Demobilization ... ODID
Office of the Director of Law Reform, Northern Ireland (DLA) ... NIDLR
Office of the Director of Manpower and Organization [*Air Force*] ... OMO
Office of the Director of Military Assistance [*Air Force*] (AFM) ... ODMA
Office of the Director of Military Training ... ODMT
Office of the Director of Public Prosecutions [*Australia*] ... ODPP
Office of the Director of Scientific Research (AD) ... ODSR
Office of the Director (Program Analysis and Evaluation) (MCD) ... OD (PA & E)
Office of the Director, Telecommunications, and Command and Control Systems [*DoD*] (PDAA) ... ODTACCS
Office of the Directorate of Weapon Systems Analysis [*Army*] (AABC) ... ODWSA
Office of the District Administrator (AD) ... ODA
Office of the District Attorney (AD) ... ODA
Office of the Division Quartermaster ... ODQM
Office of the Duchy of Lancaster [*British*] ... ODL
Office of the Economic Planning Advisory Council [*Australia*] ... OEPAC
Office of the Environment (US Department of) State/Environment, Health and Natural Resources (GNE) ... OES/E
Office of the Environment (US Department of) State/Nuclear Energy and Energy Technology Affairs (GNE) ... OES/N
Office of the Environment (US Department of) State/Oceans and Fisheries Affairs (GNE) ... OES/O
Office of the Environment (US Department of) State/Office of Advanced Technology (GNE) ... OES/SAT
Office of the Environment (US Department of) State/Office of Ecology, Health and Conservation (GNE) ... OES/EHC
Office of the Environment (US Department of) State/Office of Environmental Protection (GNE) ... OES/ENV
Office of the Environment (US Department of) State/Office of Export and Import Control (GNE) ... OES/NED
Office of the Environment (US Department of) State/Office of Fisheries Affairs (GNE) ... OES/OFA
Office of the Environment (US Department of) State/Office of Global Change (GNE) ... OES/EGC
Office of the Environment (US Department of) State/Office of Marine Science and Polar Affairs (GNE) ... OES/OSP
Office of the Environment (US Department of) State/Office of Non-Proliferation and Export Policy (GNE) ... OES/NEP
Office of the Environment (US Department of) State/Office of Nuclear Technology and Safeguards (GNE) ... OES/NTS
Office of the Environment (US Department of) State/Office of Ocean Law and Policy (GNE) ... OES/OLP
Office of the Environment (US Department of) State/Science and Technology Affairs (GNE) ... OES/S
Office of the Executive Legal Director [*Nuclear energy*] (NRCH) ... ELD
Office of the Executive Legal Director [*Nuclear Regulatory Commission*] (GFGA) ... OELD
Office of the Family [*Western Australia*] ... OOF
Office of the Federal Coordinator for Meteorological Services and Research ... OFCM
Office of the Federal Inspector (AD) ... OFI
Office of the Federal Register ... OFR
Office of the Field Directorate of Ammunition Plants ... OFDAP
Office of the Future (IAA) ... OOF
Office of the Future Information Exchange (NITA) ... OFIX
Office of the General Purchasing Agent [*Military*] ... OGPA
Office of the General Sales Manager [*Department of Agriculture*] ... OGSM
Office of the Handicapped ... OH
Office of the Housing Expediter [*Terminated, 1951*] (GPO) ... OHE
Office of the Inspector General [*Army*] ... OIG
Office of the Inspector General [*Army*] (AABC) ... OTIG
Office of the Inspector General Instructions [*Navy*] ... INGENINST
Office of the Inspector-General of Intelligence and Security [*Australia*] ... OIGIS
Office of the Insurance Commissioner (AD) ... OIC
Office of the Joint Chiefs of Staff (AFM) ... OJCS
Office of the Judge Advocate General [*British*] ... OJA-G
Office of the Judge Advocate General [*Army*] (AABC) ... OTJAG
Office of the Judge Advocate General Instructions [*Navy*] ... JAGINST
Office of the Liquor Licensing Commissioner [*South Australia*] ... OLLC
Office of the Manager National Communications System [*GSA*] ... OMNCS
Office of the Medical Examiner (DAVI) ... OME
Office of the Mining Warden [*Victoria, Australia*] ... OMW
Office of the Nominal Defendant [*Australia*] ... OND
Office of the Oceanographer of the Navy ... OCNAV
Office of the Ombudsman ... OOO
Office of the Pardon Attorney [*Department of Justice*] ... OPA
Office of the Postmaster General [*Obsolete*] ... OPG
Office of the Project Manager for Training Devices [*Military*] (RDA) ... PM TRADE
Office of the Project Manager Selected Ammunition [*DoD*] ... PMSA
Office of the Protective Commissioner [*Australia*] ... OPC
Office of the Provost Marshal General [*Army*] ... OPMG
Office of the Provost Marshal General [*Army*] ... OTPMG
Office of the Provost Marshal General [*Army*] ... PMGO
Office of the Public Service Commissioner [*Australia*] ... OPSC
Office of the Public Trustee [*Australian Capital Territory*] ... OPT
Office of the Publication Board [*Department of Commerce*] ... OPB
Office of the Quartermaster [*Military*] ... OQM
Office of the Quartermaster General [*Military*] ... OQMG
Office of the Regional Commissioner [*Social Security Administration*] (OICC) ... ORC
Office of the Registrar of Restrictive Trading Agreements (PDAA) ... ORRTA
Office of the Secretary ... OS
Office of the Secretary ... OSEC
Office of the Secretary General [*United Nations*] ... OSG
Office of the Secretary of Defense ... OSD
Office of the Secretary of Defense, Ballistic Missile Committee ... OSDBMC
Office of the Secretary of Defense, Defense Security Assistance Agency (MCD) ... OSD/DSAA

Office of the Secretary of Defense for International Security Affairs ...... OSD/ISA
Office of the Secretary of Defense for Program Analysis and Evaluation (MCD) .... OSD(PA & E)
Office of the Secretary of Defense Identification Badge [*Military decoration*] (GFGA) .... OSDIDBAD
Office of the Secretary of Defense Identification Badge (AABC) .... OSDIdentBad
Office of the Secretary of Defense Productivity Investment Funding ...... OS-PIF
Office of the Secretary of Defense, Scientific Advisory Committee .... OSDSAC
Office of the Secretary of Defense - Systems Analysis .... OSD-SA
Office of the Secretary of State, Boise, ID [*Library symbol Library of Congress*] (LCLS) .... Id-S
Office of the Secretary of State, State Papers Division, Montpelier, VT [*Library symbol Library of Congress*] (LCLS) .... VtMS
Office of the Secretary of State, Vermont State Archives, Montpelier, VT [*Library symbol*] [*Library of Congress*] (LCLS) .... VtMS-Ar
Office of the Secretary of the Air Force (AD) .... OFST
Office of the Secretary of the Air Force .... OSAF
Office of the Secretary of the Army .... OSA
Office of the Secretary of the Army for Development / Acquisition and Logistics .... OSAD A & L
Office of the Secretary of the General Staff .... OSGS
Office of the Secretary of the Navy .... OSN
Office of the Secretary of Transportation [*Department of Transportation*] .... OST
Office of the Secretary of Transportation Continuity of Operations Plan .... OSTCOOP
Office of the Secretary of Transportation Office of Noise Abatement .... OST-ONA
Office of the Secretary to the Staff [*NATO*] (NATG) .... OSECY
Office of the Security Council .... OSC
Office of the Sheriff of New South Wales [*Australia*] .... OSNSW
Office of the Solicitor [*Department of Labor*] .... OSOL
Office of the Solicitor General [*Department of Justice*] .... OSG
Office of the Special Assistant for Field Operations [*Formerly, CORDS*] (VNW) .... OSAFO
Office of the Special Assistant for Training [*Army*] (RDA) .... OSAT
Office of the Special Assistant to the Ambassador .... OSA
Office of the Special Prosecutor [*Queensland, Australia*] .... OSP
Office of the Special Representative for Trade Negotiations [*Later, Office of the United States Trade Representative*] [*Executive Office of the President*] .... OSRTN
Office of the State Training Board [*Australia*] .... OSTB
Office of the Superintendent of Financial Institutions [*Department of Insurance*] [*Ottawa, ON*] [*Information service or system*] (IID) ...... OSFI
Office of the Superintendent of Financial Institutions Canada [*Bureau du Surintendant des Institutions Financieres Canada*] **Ottawa, Ontario** [*Library symbol National Library of Canada*] (NLC) .... OOIN
Office of the Surgeon General [*of Public Health Service; later, absorbed by office of Assistant Secretary for Health and Scientific Affairs*] .... OSG
Office of the Surgeon General [*Public Health Service*] .... OTSG
Office of the Theater Chief Quartermaster [*World War II*] .... OTCQM
Office of the Treasurer of the United States .... OTUS
Office of the Under Secretary of Defense (MCD) .... OUSD
Office of the Under Secretary of Defense (Acquisition and Technology) (RDA) .... OUSD(A & T)
Office of the Under Secretary of Defense for Acquisition .... OUSDA
Office of the Under Secretary of Defense for Research and Engineering .... OUSDRE
Office of the Under Secretary of Defense for Research and Engineering .... USDRE
Office of the Under Secretary of Defense (Policy) (MCD) .... OUSD(P)
Office of the Under Secretary of the Air Force .... OUNSAF
Office of the Under Secretary of the Air Force .... OUSAF
Office of the Under Secretary of the Army .... OUSA
Office of the Under Secretary of the Army .... OUSOFA
Office of the Under Secretary of the Navy .... OUSN
Office of the Under Secretary of War [*Obsolete*] .... OUSW
Office of the United States Air Attache (CINC) .... OUSAIRA
Office of the United States Army Attache .... OUSARMA
Office of the Valuer-General [*Northern Territory, Australia*] .... OVG
Office of the Vice President of the United States (BARN) .... OVPUS
Office of the Vice-President .... OVP
Office of Thrift Supervision [*Department of the Treasury*] [*Superseded Federal Home Loan Bank Board, 1989*] .... OTS
Office of Toxic Substances [*Environmental Protection Agency*] .... OTS
Office of Tracking and Data Acquisition [*NASA*] .... OTADA
Office of Tracking and Data Acquisition [*NASA*] .... OTDA
Office of Trade Adjustment Assistance [*Department of Labor*] .... OTAA
Office of Trade and Investment [*Victoria, Australia*] .... OTI
Office of Trade Promotion [*Department of Commerce*] .... OTP
Office of Transport, Policy and Planning [*South Australia*] .... OTPP
Office of Transportation [*Department of Agriculture*] .... OT
Office of Transportation Energy Policy [*Department of Transportation*] .... OTEP
Office of Transportation Security (AD) .... OFTS
Office of Transportation Security [*Department of Transportation*] .... OTS
Office of Transportation Systems and Planning [*Battelle Memorial Institut e*] [*Department of Energy Also, an information service or system*] (IID) .... OTSP
Office of Treatment Improvement [*U.S. Public Health Service*] (BARN) .... OTI
Office of Tributary Area Development [*Tennessee Valley Authority*] .... OTAD
Office of Underground Storage Tanks [*Environmental Protection Agency*] .... OUST
Office of Unemployment Insurance [*Employment and Training Administration*] [*Department of Labor*] .... OUI
Office of United Nations Political and Security Affairs [*Department of State*] .... OUNPSA
Office of United States Defense Representative, India [*Army*] (AABC) .... ODRI
Office of United States Foreign Disaster Assistance [*Agency for International Development*] .... OFDA

Office of University Affairs [*NASA*] .... OUA
Office of Urban Neighborhood Services [*HUD*] .... OUNS
Office of Urban Studies and Clearinghouse Services [*HUD*] .... OUSCS
Office of Vehicle Systems Research [*Later, Safety System Laboratory*] [*National Institute of Standards and Technology*] .... OVSR
Office of Veterans' Affairs .... OVA
Office of Veterans Reemployment Rights [*Department of Labor*] .... OVRR
Office of Vice Chancellor for Research and Advanced Study [*University of Alaska*] [*Research center*] (RCD) .... VCRAS
Office of Visas and Registrations [*Former USSR*] .... OVIR
Office of Vocational and Adult Education [*Department of Education*] (OICC) .... OVAE
Office of Vocational Rehabilitation [*Later, Vocational Rehabilitation Administration*] [*HEW*] .... OVR
Office of Volunteer Liaison [*ACTION*] .... OVL
Office of Volunteerism Initiatives (BARN) .... OVI
Office of Volunteers [*Red Cross*] .... OV
Office of Vulnerability Assessment and Management Services [*Department of Commerce*] .... OVAMS
Office of War Information [*World War II*] .... OWI
Office of War Mobilization [*Succeeded by OWMR, 1944*] .... OWM
Office of War Mobilization and Reconversion [*Succeeded OWM, 1944; became part of Office of Temporary Controls, 1946*] .... OWMR
Office of War Utilities [*War Production Board*] .... OWU
Office of Waste Isolation [*Department of Energy*] .... OWI
Office of Waste Programs Enforcement [*Environmental Protection Agency*] (EPA) .... OWPE
Office of Water [*Environmental Protection Agency*] (GFGA) .... OW
Office of Water and Hazardous Materials (OICC) .... OWHM
Office of Water and Waste Management (ERG) .... OWWM
Office of Water Data Coordination [*US Geological Survey*] [*Reston, VA*] .... OWDC
Office of Water Enforcement [*Environmental Protection Agency*] (ERG) .... OWE
Office of Water Enforcement and Permits [*Environmental Protection Agency*] (GFGA) .... OWEP
Office of Water Policy [*Department of the Interior*] .... OWP
Office of Water Program Operations [*Environmental Protection Agency*] (EPA) .... OWPO
Office of Water Programs [*Abolished*] [*Environmental Protection Agency*] ...... OWP
Office of Water Regulations and Standards [*Environmental Protection Agency*] (GFGA) .... OWRS
Office of Water Research and Technology [*Formerly, OSW, OWRR*] [*Abolished, 1982 Department of the Interior*] .... OWRT
Office of Water Resources Research [*Later, OWRT*] [*Department of the Interior*] .... OWRR
Office of Water Services [*British*] .... OFWAT
Office of Water Services [*British*] (ODBW) .... Ofwat
Office of Weather Research and Modification [*National Oceanic and Atmospheric Administration*] (GRD) .... OWRM
Office of Weights and Measures [*National Institute of Standards and Technology*] .... OWM
Office of Welfare and Pension Plans [*Department of Labor*] .... OWPP
Office of Women's Business Enterprise [*Federal government*] .... OWBE
Office of Women's Business Ownership [*Small Business Administration*] .... OWBO
Office of Work Incentive Program [*Office of Comprehensive Employment Development*] [*Department of Labor*] .... OWIN
Office of Work-Based Learning [*U.S. Department of Labor*] (BARN) .... OWBL
Office of Worker Retraining and Adjustment Programs [*U.S. Department of Labor*] (BARN) .... OWRAP
Office of Workers' [*formerly, Workmen's*] Compensation Programs [*Formerly, Bureau of Employees' Compensation*] [*Department of Labor*] .... OWCP
Office of Worship Resources [*Later, WRO*] (EA) .... OWR
Office of Youth Programs [*Department of Labor*] .... OYP
Office of Youth, Sport, Recreation and Ethnic Affairs [*Northern Territory, Australia*] .... OYSREA
Office, Ogden Air Material Area [*AFLC*] .... OOAMA
Office on Educational Credit [*Later, OECC*] (EA) .... OEC
Office on Educational Credit and Credentials (EA) .... OECC
Office on Smoking and Health Database [*Centers for Disease Control*] [*Information service or system*] (CRD) .... OSH
Office Operations Department .... OOD
Office Pass (AAG) .... OP
Office, Personnel Manager [*Army*] (MUGU) .... OPM
Office Product (IAA) .... OP
Office Productivity Network [*Computer science*] .... OPN
Office Products Manufacturers Association (EA) .... OPMA
Office Products Reps Association (EA) .... OPRA
Office Professional Development System (MCD) .... OPDS
Office Publications (AD) .... Office Pubns
Office Research Institute (NADA) .... ORI
Office Research into Buildings and IT (NITA) .... ORBIT
Office, Secretary of the Army (Army Board for Correction of Military Records) .... OSA (ABCMR)
Office, Services and Information Agency [*Military*] (AABC) .... OSIA
Office Space Allocation Plan (MCD) .... OSAP
Office, Special Assistant for Logistical Support of Army Aircraft (AABC) .... OSALSAA
Office, Special Assistant for Logistical Support of Tactical Communications (AABC) .... OSALSTC
Office Statistique des Communautes Europeennes [*Statistical Office of the European Communities - EUROSTAT*] [*Commission of the European Communities*] .... OSCE
Office System .... OS
Office Systems Education and Counseling (HGAA) .... OSEC
Office Systems Family (HGAA) .... OSF
Office Systems Interconnection [*Telecommunications*] (TSSD) .... OSI

Office Systems Owners Group (HGAA) .... OSOG
Office Systems Research Association [*Cleveland, OH*] (EA) .... OSRA
Office Technology Ltd. (NITA) .... OTL
Office Technology Management Association [*Defunct*] (EA) .... OTMA
Office Technology Plus [*General Services Administration*] .... OTP
Office Technology Research Group [*Defunct*] (EA) .... OTRG
Office Visit [*Medicine*] .... OV
Office Workers Link Shift [*After-hours production workers*] [*World War II*] .... OWLS
Office Workstations Ltd. (NITA) .... OWL
Officeholders Expense Funds [*Slush money*] .... OEF
Officemax, Inc. [*Associated Press*] (SAG) .... Officmx
Officemax, Inc. [*NYSE symbol*] (SAG) .... OMX
Officer .... OFCR
Officer (AD) .... Off
Officer .... OFFR
Officer Accession/Separation System (MCD) .... OAS^2
Officer Advanced Course [*Army*] (INF) .... OAC
Officer, Airman, Civilian, and Total (MCD) .... OACT
Officer Assignment Folder [*Military*] (AFM) .... OAF
Officer Basic Course [*Military*] .... OBC
Officer Battery Flight Aptitude Selection Test [*Military*] (INF) .... FAST-OB
Officer Cadet [*British military*] (DMA) .... O/C
Officer Cadet [*Military*] (WDAA) .... O/CDT
Officer Cadet Training Unit [*Military British*] .... OCTU
Officer Candidate [*Military*] .... OC
Officer Candidate Airman .... OCAN
Officer Candidate Preparatory School (DNAB) .... OCPS
Officer Candidate Programme [*British military*] (DMA) .... OCP
Officer Candidate School [*Military*] .... OCS
Officer Candidate Test [*Army*] .... OCT
Officer Career Brief [*Resume*] [*Military*] .... OCB
Officer Career Counseling System [*Army*] (RDA) .... OCCS
Officer Classification Test .... OCT
Officer Commanding [*Military*] .... OC
Officer Commanding Administrative Centre [*World War I*] [*British*] .... OCAC
Officer Commanding Exercises [*Military*] .... OCE
Officer Commanding in Charge [*Facetious acronym*] [*Army British*] (DSUE) .... OCIC
Officer Commanding Royal Marines [*British military*] (DMA) .... OCRM
Officer Conducting the Exercise [*Navy, Coast Guard*] [*Military*] .... OCE
Officer Control Distribution Report .... OCDR
Officer Corps Engineers .... OCE
Officer Data Card .... ODC
Officer Deficiency Letter [*Navy*] (NVT) .... ODL
Officer Distribution Control Report [*Navy*] (NG) .... ODCR
Officer Distribution Plan [*Army*] .... ODP
Officer Dual Specialty Allocation System .... ODSAS
Officer Education and Training Branch [*BUPERS*] .... OE & TB
Officer Education Research Laboratory [*Air Force*] .... OERL
Officer Education System [*Army*] (RDA) .... OES
Officer Effectiveness Report [*Air Force*] (AFM) .... OER
Officer Efficiency Report [*Military*] .... OER
Officer Engineering Reserve (AD) .... OER
Officer Evaluation Report [*Military*] (INF) .... OER
Officer Evaluation Reporting System [*Army*] .... OERS
Officer Exercising General Court-Martial Jurisdiction .... OEGCMJ
Officer Exercising Special Court-Martial Jurisdiction .... OESPCMJ
Officer Fitness Report [*Navy*] (NVT) .... FITREP
Officer Fitness Report [*Navy*] (NVT) .... OFR
Officer Front End Analysis (MCD) .... OFEA
Officer Grade Limitations Act of 1954 .... OGLA
Officer Grade Objectives .... OGO
Officer in Charge (AD) .... OC
Officer in Tactical Command [*Air Force*] .... OTC
Officer in Tactical Command Information Exchange Subsystem [*Navy*] (ANA) .... OTCIXS
Officer in Training (AD) .... O i T
Officer Job/Task Analysis [*Military*] .... OJTA
Officer Master File [*Army*] (INF) .... OMF
Officer Master File Automated System (DNAB) .... OFFMAUTSYS
Officer Master Record [*Air Force*] (AFM) .... OMR
Officer Master Tape Record [*Army*] (AABC) .... OMTR
Officer Message Mail [*Military*] .... OMM
Officer Message Mail Center [*Military*] .... OMMC
Officer Messenger Mail (Sub) Center [*Navy*] .... OMM(S)C
Officer of Arms Extraordinary [*College of Arms/Heralds' College*] [*British*] .... OAE
Officer of Merit, Order of St. Lazarus of Jerusalem (DD) .... OMLJ
Officer of the Day [*or Deck*] [*Also, OOD*] [*Navy*] .... OD
Officer of the Day [*or Deck*] [*Also, OD*] [*Navy*] .... OOD
Officer of the Guard [*Army*] .... OG
Officer of the Guard [*Navy British*] .... OOG
Officer of the Order of Canada .... OC
Officer of the Order of Canada (DD) .... OC
Officer of the Order of Leopold .... OL
Officer of the Order of Military Merit .... OMM
Officer of the Order of Military Merit [*Canada*] (DD) .... OMM
Officer of the Order of Niger .... OON
Officer of the Order of St. John of Jerusalem [*British*] .... OStJ
Officer of the Order of the British Empire (NGC) .... OBE
Officer of the Post Office [*British*] .... OPO
Officer of the Quarters .... OOQ
Officer of the Watch [*Navigation*] .... OOW
Officer Personnel Act .... OPA
Officer Personnel Course [*Air Force*] .... OPERSCRS
Officer Personnel Directorate [*Army*] .... OPD
Officer Personnel Division [*Coast Guard*] .... PO
Officer Personnel Management Directorate [*Military*] .... OPMD
Officer Personnel Management System [*Army*] .... OPMS
Officer Personnel Office (DNAB) .... O-PERS
Officer Personnel Record Review Board [*Air Force*] (AFM) .... OPRRB
[*The*] **Officer Personnel System, The Army Reserve** (AABC) .... TOPSTAR
Officer Professional Development [*Military*] (INF) .... OPD
Officer Professional Development Program [*Pronounced "opey-dopey"*] [*Canadian Navy*] .... OPDP
Officer Program [*Military*] (DNAB) .... OP
Officer Promotion System (DNAB) .... OFFPROMSYS
Officer Qualification Questionnaire [*Navy*] (DOMA) .... OQQ
Officer Qualification Test .... OQT
Officer Record Brief [*Army*] (AABC) .... ORB
Officer Records [*Military*] (AFM) .... OR
Officer Requirements Plan (DNAB) .... ORP
Officer Responsible for the Exercise [*Navy*] (NVT) .... ORE
Officer Scheduling the Exercise [*Navy*] (NVT) .... OSE
Officer Selection Battery [*Military*] .... OSB
Officer Selection Battery Test [*Military*] .... OSBT
Officer Selection Board .... OSB
Officer Selection Office (DNAB) .... OSO
Officer Separation Questionnaire (DNAB) .... OSQ
Officer Service Date [*Air Force*] (AFM) .... OSD
Officer Specialty Code [*Army*] (INF) .... OSC
Officer Status (DNAB) .... OFF STA
Officer Student Quarters (DNAB) .... OSQ
Officer Supervising Yardcraft [*Canadian Navy*] .... OSYC
Officer Training Allowance [*Naval Reserve*] .... OTA
Officer Training Center [*Navy*] .... OTC
Officer Training Program Examining Center [*Air Force*] .... OTPEC
Officer Training School Alumni Association (EA) .... OTSAA
Officer Undergraduate Degree Program [*Army*] (AABC) .... OUDP
Officer-Cadet (AD) .... O/Cdt
Officer-in-Charge [*Army*] .... O/C
Officer-in-Charge .... O in C
Officer-in-Charge .... OIC
Officer-in-Charge (AD) .... O-i-C
Officer-in-Charge [*Navy*] .... OINC
Officer-in-Charge, Advanced Base Combat Communication Training Center [*Pearl Harbor*] [*Navy*] .... OINCABCCTC
Officer-in-Charge, Branch Office of Naval Officer Procurement (DNAB) .... ONOP
Officer-in-Charge, Marine Air Traffic Control Unit (DNAB) .... OICMATU
Officer-in-Charge, Marine Inspection Office [*Coast Guard*] .... OCMI
Officer-in-Charge, Military Department (DNAB) .... OICMILDEPT
Officer-in-Charge of Armament Supply .... OCAS
Officer-in-Charge of Civilian Affairs [*in newly occupied countries*] [*Army World War II*] .... OCCA
Officer-in-Charge of Construction [*Navy*] .... OICC
Officer-in-Charge of Construction, Far East [*Navy*] .... OICCFE
Officer-in-Charge of Construction, South Western Pacific (DNAB) .... OICCSOWESPAC
Officer-in-Charge of National Guard Affairs .... OCNGA
Officer-in-Charge Police District (AD) .... OCPD
Officer-Like Qualities (AD) .... olq
Officer-Like Qualities [*British military*] (DMA) .... OLQ
Officer-of-the-Deck (Fleet Task Force Operations) [*Navy*] (DNAB) .... OODF
Officer-of-the-Deck (Independent) [*Navy*] (DNAB) .... OODI
Officers' Accounts Division [*Navy*] .... OAD
Officers' Assignment Division, The Adjutant General's Office [*Army*] .... OAD
Officers Association [*British military*] (DMA) .... OA
Officers' Basic Military Corps [*Air Force*] .... OBMC
Officers' Cadet Battalion [*British*] .... OCB
Officers' Caterer [*Navy British*] .... OCA
Officers' Chief Cook .... OCC
Officers' Chief Steward [*Navy*] .... OCS
Officers' Christian Fellowship of the USA (EA) .... OCF
Officers' Cook .... OC
Officers' Emergency Reserve [*British*] .... OER
Officers' Eyes Only [*Military*] (NVT) .... OEO
Officer's Eyes Only (AD) .... oeo
Officers' Family Fund .... OFF
Officers for Temporary Service [*Navy British*] (ROG) .... TEM
Officers' Home Advance (ADA) .... OHA
Officer's Mess [*Military*] (AD) .... O-Mess
Officer's Name (NITA) .... ON
Officers' Open Mess [*Military*] (AFM) .... OOM
Officers' Organization for Economic Benefits [*Commercial firm*] (EA) .... OEB
Officer's Qualification Record [*Army*] .... OQR
Officers' Quarters [*Military*] .... OQ
Officers' Recreation Facility .... ORF
Officer's Reports [*1-9 Minnesota*] [*A publication*] (DLA) .... Officer
Officers' Reserve Corps [*Later, Army Reserve*] .... ORC
Officers Service Dress [*British military*] (DMA) .... OSD
Officers' Steward [*Ranking title*] [*British Women's Royal Naval Service*] .... OS
Officers' Tactical School [*Navy*] (NVT) .... OTS
Officers' Training Camp [*World War I*] .... OTC
Officers' Training Corps .... OTC
Officers Training School (AD) .... OFTS
Officers' Training School .... OTS
Officers' Training Unit [*Air Force British*] .... OTU
Officers Transit Camp [*British military*] (DMA) .... OTC
Officers' Wives Club [*Military*] .... OWC
Officer's Writer [*British military*] (DMA) .... OW

Offices of the Information and Privacy Commissioners of Canada, Ottawa, ON, Canada [*Library symbol*] [*Library of Congress*] (LCLS) .... CaOOIPC
Offices of the Information and Privacy Commissioners of Canada [*Bureaux des Commissaires a l'Information et a la Protection de la Vie Privee du Canada*] **Ottawa, Ontario** [*Library symbol National Library of Canada*] (NLC) .... OOIPC
Offices, Shops, and Railway Premises Act [*1963*] [*British*] .... OSRPA
Officeworker Reader Information Services [*British*] .... ORIS
Official [*Rate*] [*Value of the English pound*] .... O
Official (DAVI) .... Of
Official (AD) .... ofcl
Official .... OFCL
Official .... OFCL
Official .... OFF
Official .... OFFI
Official .... OFFIC
Official (AD) .... offic
Official (AFM) .... OFFL
Official (AABC) .... OFL
Official (AD) .... ofl
Official 3 Stooges Fan Club [*Defunct*] (EA) .... OTFC
Official Aerrage Fan Club [*Defunct*] (EA) .... OAFC
Official Air Freight Tariffs .... OAFT
Official Airline Guide, Inc. [*ICAO designator*] (FAAC) .... OAG
Official Airline Guide-Electronic Edition [*Official Airline Guides, Inc.*] [*Database*] .... OAG-EE
Official Airline Guides, Inc. [*Information service or system*] (IID) .... OAG
Official Assignee (ROG) .... OA
Official Betty Boop Fan Club (EA) .... OBBFC
Official Board of Ballroom Dancing [*British*] (BI) .... OB
Official Board of Ballroom Dancing [*British*] .... OBBD
Official Bobby Hart Fan Club (EA) .... OBHFC
Official Bulletin. International Commission for Air Navigation [*A publication*] (DLA) .... OB
Official Bulletin Station [*Amateur radio*] .... OBS
Official Business Only (AFM) .... OBO
Official Business Only (DNAB) .... OFF BUS ONLY
Official Circular [*Poor Law Board, etc.*] [*A publication*] (DLA) .... OC
Official Classification .... OC
Official Code of Georgia, Annotated [*A publication*] (DLA) .... OCGA
Official Committee on Armistice Terms and Civil Administration [*British World War II*] .... ACAO
Official Committee on Service Attaches and Advisers [*British*] .... OCSAA
Official Compilation of Codes, Rules, and Regulations of the State of New York [*A publication*] (DLA) .... NY Admin Code
Official Compilation of the Rules and Regulations of the State of Georgia [*A publication*] (DLA) .... GA Admin Comp
Official Compilation of the Rules and Regulations of the State of Tennessee [*A publication*] (DLA) .... Tenn Admin Comp
Official Crude Prices [*Petroleum Intelligence Weekly*] [*Information service or system*] (CRD) .... OCP
Official Custodian of Charities [*British*] .... OCC
Official Development Aid [*or Assistance*] .... ODA
Official Development Finance .... ODF
Official Discount Rate [*Finance*] (ECON) .... ODR
Official Elvis Presley Fan Club (EAIO) .... OEPFC
Official English Title .... OET
Official Establishments Trust [*Australia*] .... OET
Official Experimental Station [*Amateur radio*] .... OES
Official Failure Rate [*Military*] (AFIT) .... OFR
Official Files .... OF
Official First Day Cover [*Canada Post Corp.*] .... OFDC
Official Flight Kit [*NASA*] (NASA) .... OFK
Official Flight Kit .... OFK
Official Gary Lewis and the Playboys Fan Club (EA) .... OGLPFC
Official Gazette [*PTO*] [*A publication*] (AAGC) .... OG
Official Gazette Reports, British Guiana [*A publication*] (DLA) .... OGBG
Official Gazette. United States Patent and Trademark Office [*A publication*] (DLA) .... Off Gaz Pat Office
Official Gazette. United States Patent and Trademark Office [*A publication*] (DLA) .... OGTM
Official Guide of the Railways [*A publication*] (AD) .... OGR
Official Gumby Fan Club (EA) .... OGFC
Official Hostess (BARN) .... OH
Official Hotel and Resort Guide [*A publication*] (AD) .... OHRG
Official Information Base .... OIB
Official Intermodal Equipment Register [*Intermodal Publishing Co.*] [*Information service or system*] (IID) .... OIER
Official International Michael York Fan Club (EA) .... OIMYFC
Official International Peter Coyote Fan Club (EA) .... OIPCFC
Official Irish FORTH [*Programming language*] **Interest Group** (EAIO) .... OIFIG
Official Journal of Industrial and Commercial Property [*Eire*] [*A publication*] (DLA) .... Official J Ind Comm Prop
Official Journal of the European Communities [*A publication*] (AD) .... OJEC
Official Kate Linder Fan Club (EA) .... OKLFC
Official Lane Brody Global Fan Club (EA) .... OLBGFC
Official Languages Act [*Canada*] .... OLA
Official Latin Title .... OLT
Official Liquidator [*British*] (ROG) .... OL
Official Log Book [*Ship's diary*] (DS) .... OLB
Official Mail Center [*Air Force*] (AFM) .... OMC
Official Mail Control Officer (MCD) .... OMCO
Official Mail Study Group [*Defunct*] (EA) .... OMSG
Official Martin Landau-Barbara Bain Fan Association (EA) .... LBFA
Official Military Personnel File [*Army*] (AABC) .... OMPF
Official Munitions Production United States .... OMPUS
Official Naval Reporter [*British*] .... ONR
Official Number (DS) .... ON
Official Opinions of the Attorney General of Nevada [*A publication*] (DLA) .... Op Nev Att'y Gen
Official Opinions of the Solicitor for the Post Office Department [*A publication*] (DLA) .... Op Solic PO Dep't
Official Personnel File (MCD) .... OPF
Official Personnel Folder [*Military*] .... OPF
Official Phone Station [*Amateur radio*] .... OPS
Official Production System [*Production-system language*] .... OPS
Official Public Service Reports [*New York*] [*A publication*] (DLA) .... OPS
Official Publication (ADA) .... OP
Official Publications Library [*The British Library*] .... OPL
Official Publications, National Library of Canada [*Publications Officielles, Bibliotheque Nationale du Canada*] **Ottawa, Ontario** [*Library symbol National Library of Canada*] (NLC) .... OONLG
Official Railway Equipment Register [*National Railway Publication Co.*] [*Information service or system*] (IID) .... ORER
Official Receiver .... OR
Official Receiver's Office [*Australia*] .... ORO
Official Records .... OR
[*The*] **Official Recreation Guide** [*Applied Information Services, Inc.*] [*Whitefish, MT*] [*Information service or system*] (IID) .... ORG
Official Referee .... OR
Official Register of the United States .... ORUS
Official Relay Station [*Amateur radio*] .... ORS
Official Reports, Illinois Courts Commission [*A publication*] (DLA) .... Official Rep Ill Courts Commission
Official Reports of the Court of Claims [*GPO*] (AAGC) .... Ct Cl
Official Reports of the High Court of the Transvaal [*A publication*] (DLA) .... Off Rep
Official Reports, South Africa [*A publication*] (DLA) .... OR
Official Reports, South African Republic [*A publication*] (DLA) .... ORSAR
Official Rocky Horror Fan Club (EA) .... ORHFC
Official Secrets Act [*British*] .... OSA
Official Seed Testing Station (WDAA) .... OSTS
Official Station .... OS
Official Summary of Security Transactions and Holdings .... OSST
Official Table of Distances (AFM) .... OTD
Official Test Insecticide .... OTI
Official Tim Topper Fan Club [*Defunct*] (EA) .... OTTFC
Official Unionist Party [*Northern Ireland*] (PPW) .... OUP
Official Use (WDAA) .... OU
Official Use Only .... OUO
Official Visitors' Scheme .... OVS
Official Visitors to Departmental Facilities [*New South Wales, Australia*] .... OVDF
Officials of the Irish Republican Army [*Northern Ireland*] .... OIRA
Officiate .... OFFIC
Officiating .... OFFG
Officiating Chaplain to the Forces [*Military British*] .... OCF
Officiating Minister to the Troops [*British*] .... OMT
Officie Radiodiffusion Television du Niger [*Radio and television network*] [*Niger*] .... ORTN
Officina Brevium [*1679*] [*A publication*] (DLA) .... Off Br
Officina Brevium [*1679*] [*A publication*] (DLA) .... Off Brev
Officine Meccaniche [*Italian auto manufacturer*] .... OM
Officium Clerici Pacis [*A publication*] (DLA) .... Of Cl Pac
Offizierlager [*Officer's Prison Camp*] [*German*] (AD) .... Oflag
Offizierslager [*Permanent Prison Camp for Captured Officers*] [*German military - World War II*] .... OFLAG
Offline Adaptive Computer [*Computer science*] .... OLAC
Offline Data Generator .... ODG
Off-Line Express [*Mustang Software, Inc.*] (PCM) .... OLX
Off-Line Operating Simulator [*Computer science*] .... OOPS
Offline Orthophoto Printer [*Computer science*] (PDAA) .... OOP
Off-Line Program [*Computer science*] .... OLP
Offline Reader [*Bulletin board*] .... OLR
Offline Recovery [*Telecommunications*] (TEL) .... OLR
Off-Line Selectric Analyser [*Computer science*] (IAA) .... OLSA
Off-Line Universal Command History [*Computer science*] (KSC) .... OUCH
Off-Load (NVT) .... OFLD
Off-Load Control Officer [*Navy*] (ANA) .... OCO
Off-Load Preparation Party [*Navy*] (ANA) .... OPP
Off-Machine Coated [*Paper*] (DGA) .... OC
Off-Machine Coated [*Paper*] (DGA) .... OMC
Off-Machine Coated Board [*Paper*] (DGA) .... OCB
Off-Machine Coated Board [*Paper*] (DGA) .... OMCB
Off-Magic-Angle-Spinning [*Spectroscopy*] .... OMAS
Off-Market Date (AD) .... omd
Off-Market Date Received (AD) .... omdr
Off-Net Access Line [*Telecommunications*] (TEL) .... ONAL
Off-Normal Switch .... ONS
Off-Off Broadway [*Theater*] .... OOB
Off-On Control .... OOC
Off-Premise Extension [*Nuclear energy*] (NRCH) .... OPX
Off-Premise Station [*Telecommunications*] (TEL) .... OPS
Off-Price [*A retail outlet selling discounted merchandise*] .... O-P
Off-Radial (RDA) .... OR
Off-Range Distance (MCD) .... ORD
Offretite [*A zeolite*] .... OFF
Off-Road Mobility .... ORM
Off-Road Mobility Evaluation and Generalized Analysis [*Army*] .... OMEGA
Off-Road Recreation Vehicle .... ORRV
Off-Road Vehicle .... ORV

Off-Route Antitank Mine System (MCD) ORATMS
Off-Route Mine ORM
Off-Route [*Smart*] **Mine Clearance** [*Military*] ORMC
Off-Screen Model [*Computer science*] OSM
Offscreen Voice [*Films, television, etc.*] OSV
Offset (MSA) OFS
Offset (VRA) ofst
Offset OS
Offset Aiming Point (AFM) OAP
Offset Doppler ODOP
Offset Doppler (AD) odop
Offset Doppler Tracking System (KSC) ODTS
Offset Printing and Reprographics [*A publication*] (DGA) OP & R
Offset Printing Press OPPR
Offset Printing Program [*Association of Independent Colleges and Schools specialization code*] OF
Offset QPSK (NITA) O-QPSK
Offset Target Indicator System (MCD) OTIS
Offset, Tilted Dipole [*Model of Uranus' magnetic field*] OTD
Offsets Review Board [*New South Wales, Australia*] ORB
Off-Shift Work Authorization (AAG) OSWA
Offshore (NVT) OFFSHR
Offshore Acquisition [*Army*] (AABC) OSA
Offshore and Coastal Dispersion (GNE) OCD
Offshore Banking Unit OBU
Offshore Bulk Fuel System OBFS
Offshore Buoy-Observing Equipment (PDAA) OBOE
Offshore Certification Bureau [*British*] (CB) OCB
Offshore Commercial Loan OCL
Offshore Discharge of Container-Ships (RDA) OSDOC
Offshore Drilling and Production Exhibition (PDAA) ODPEX
Offshore Drilling Platform ODP
Offshore Ecology Investigation [*Oil study*] OEI
Offshore Energy Development Corp. [*NASDAQ symbol*] (SAG) OEDC
Offshore Energy Development Corp. [*Associated Press*] (SAG) OffshEnr
Offshore Energy Technology Board [*British*] OETB
Offshore Engineering Conference (MCD) OECON
Offshore Exploration Conference OECON
Offshore Fossil-Fueled Electric Generators OFFEG
Offshore Funds [*Investment term*] OF
Offshore Installations Technical Advisory Committee [*British Marine science*] (MSC) OFINTAC
Offshore Islands (CINC) OSI
Offshore Lease Data System [*Department of the Interior*] [*Information service or system*] (IID) OLDS
Offshore Logistics [*NASDAQ symbol*] (TTSB) OLOG
Offshore Logistics, Inc. [*ICAO designator*] (FAAC) ALG
Offshore Logistics, Inc. [*Associated Press*] (SAG) OffsLog
Offshore Logistics, Inc. [*NASDAQ symbol*] (NQ) OLOG
Offshore Logistics, Inc. (MHDW) OLOGP
Offshore Marine Service Association [*New Orleans, LA*] (EA) OMSA
Offshore Mechanics and Polar Engineering Council OMPEC
Offshore Patrol Vessel (DOMA) OPV
Offshore Persistent Upwelling Structure OPUS
Offshore Petroleum Distribution System OPDS
Offshore Pollution Liability Association Ltd. (EA) OPOL
Offshore Power Systems (NRCH) OPS
Offshore Power Systems, Jacksonville, FL [*Library symbol Library of Congress*] (LCLS) FJO
Offshore Procurement [*Army*] OSP
Offshore Procurement, Japan OSPJ
Offshore Racing Council ORC
Offshore Shrimp Fisheries Act of 1973 OSFA
Offshore Storage Tank OSST
Offshore Suppliers Office [*British*] OSO
Offshore Supply Vessel [*Coast Guard*] (GFGA) OSV
Offshore Surf Zone OSZ
Offshore Surveillance System OSS
Offshore Survival Centre [*Robert Gordon's Institute of Technology*] [*British*] (CB) OSC
Offshore Survival Craft Emergency Radiotelephone [*Telecommunications*] (PDAA) OSCER
Offshore Technology Board [*British*] OFTB
Offshore Technology Conference OTC
Offshore Valve Association (EA) OVA
Offshore Vessels Availability System [*Alpha Asia Systems Pte. Ltd.*] [*Defunct Information service or system*] (CRD) OVAS
Offshore Windpower System [*Proposed system to generate electricity by wind turbines mounted on offshore platforms*] OWPS
Offshore-Installation Manager [*Oil well drilling*] OIM
Off-Site Dose Calculation Manual [*Nuclear energy*] (NRCH) ODCM
Off-Site Operations Plan (SSD) OSOP
Off-Site Originated Change (AAG) OSOC
Offsite Procurement Request (IEEE) OPR
Off-Site Procurement Request (NRCH) OPR
Off-Site Production Inspection (AAG) OPI
Off-Site Radiation Exposure Review Project [*Department of Energy*] ORERP
Off-Site Repair and Support (MCD) ORS
Off-Site Surveillance Data [*Military*] OSSD
Off-Site Technical Director (MHDI) OSTD
Off-Site Vital Area (MCD) OSVA
Offsites/Infrastructure/Establishment [*Engineering*] O/I/E
Off-station Housing Allowance (DOMA) OHA
Off-Street Parking (AD) off-st pkg
Off-Street Parking (WDAA) O-SP
Off-the-Air Record Club [*Record label*] OTA
Off-the-Film [*Photography*] (WDMC) OTF
Off-the-Film Metering [*Olympus cameras*] OTF
Off-the-Job OTJ
Off-the-Road OTR
Off-the-Shelf System [*Bell System*] OTSS
Off-Track Betting OTB
Offutt Air Force Base [*Nebraska*] (AAG) OAFB
Offutt Air Force Base, Omaha [*Nebraska*] [*ICAO location identifier*] (ICLI) KGWC
Offutt Air Force Base, Omaha [*Nebraska*] [*ICAO location identifier*] (ICLI) KOFF
Offutt Air Force Base Processing and Correlation Center (MCD) OPCC
Ofice of the Chief of Naval Operations, Telecommunications Center (DNAB) OPNAVTCC
Oficial [*Official*] [*Spanish*] (AD) ofic
Oficina Alemania [*Chile*] [*Seismograph station code, US Geological Survey*] (SEIS) OFA
Oficina Central de Organizacion y Metodos [*Central Office of Organization and Methods*] [*Spain*] (AD) OCOM
Oficina Central de Personal [*Central Personnel Office*] [*Spain*] (AD) OCP
Oficina de Educacion Iberoamericana [*Ibero-American Bureau of Education - IABE*] [*Madrid, Spain*] (EAIO) OEI
Oficina de Planificacion Nacional [*Office of National Planning*] [*Spain*] (AD) ODEPLAN
Oficina del Coordinador de las Naciones Unidas para la Ayuda en los Desastres [*Office of the Coordinator of the United Nations for Help in Disasters*] [*Spanish*] (AD) OCNAUD
Oficina Internacional Catolica de la Infancia [*International Catholic Child Bureau*] OICI
Oficina Internacional de Informacion del Frente Democratico Revolucionario de ElSalvador [*International Information Office of the Democratic Revolutionary Front of El Salvador - IIODRFES*] [*San Jose, Costa Rica*] (EAIO) OIIFDRES
Oficina Municipale de Planeamiento Urbano [*Municipal Office of Urban Planning*] [*Spain*] (AD) OMPU
Oficina Nacional de Informacion [*National Information Office*] [*Press agency Peru*] ONI
Oficina Permanente Internacional de la Carne [*Permanent International Meat Office*] (EAIO) OPIC
Oficina Regional de Educacion para America Latina y el Caribe [*Regional Office for Education in Latin America and the Caribbean-Chile*] (IID) OEALC
Oficina Sanitaria Panamericana [*Pan-American Sanitary Bureau - PASB*] [*Washington, DC*] OSP
OFS [*Orbital Flight System*] **Retransmission Processor** [*NASA*] (GFGA) ORP
OFS [*Orbiter Functional Simulator*] **Retransmission Processor** [*NASA*] ORP
OFS [*Orbiter Functional Simulator*] **Uplink Processor** [*NASA*] OUP
OFS [*Orbital Flight System*] **Uplink Processor** [*NASA*] (GFGA) OUP
Often OFT
Ofu Island [*American Samoa*] [*Airport symbol*] (OAG) OFU
Ofunato [*Japan*] [*Seismograph station code, US Geological Survey*] (SEIS) OFU
Ogallala, NE [*FM radio station call letters*] KMCX
Ogallala, NE [*AM radio station call letters*] KOGA
Ogallala, NE [*FM radio station call letters*] KOGA-FM
Ogallala, NE [*Location identifier FAA*] (FAAL) OGA
Ogallala, NE [*Location identifier FAA*] (FAAL) SAE
OGara Co. (The) [*NASDAQ symbol*] (SAG) OGAR
OGara Co. (The) [*Associated Press*] (SAG) OGaraCo
Ogasawara Trench OG
Ogden [*Utah*] [*Airport symbol*] (AD) OGD
Ogden Air Logistics Center (MCD) OALC
Ogden Air Logistics Center (MCD) ODALC
Ogden Air Material Area [*AFLC*] OAMA
Ogden Air Material Area [*AFLC*] OGAMA
Ogden Bay [*Utah*] [*Seismograph station code, US Geological Survey*] (SEIS) OGU
Ogden Contract Management District (SAA) OGCMD
Ogden Corp. [*NYSE symbol*] (SPSG) OG
Ogden Corp. [*Associated Press*] (SAG) Ogden
Ogden Corp. [*Associated Press*] (SAG) Ogdn
Ogden Corp. $1.875 cm Cv Pfd [*NYSE symbol*] (TTSB) OGPr
Ogden Elementary School, Hewlett, NY [*Library symbol Library of Congress*] (LCLS) NHewOE
Ogden Elementary School, Valley Stream, NY [*Library symbol*] [*Library of Congress*] (LCLS) NVsOE
Ogden/Hill Air Force Base [*Utah*] [*ICAO location identifier*] (ICLI) KHIF
Ogden, KS [*FM radio station call letters*] KQLA
Ogden Nash (AD) ON
Ogden Public Library, Ogden, IA [*Library symbol Library of Congress*] (LCLS) IaOgd
Ogden Reporter, Ogden, IA [*Library symbol Library of Congress*] (LCLS) IaOgdR
Ogden [*Utah*] **Service Center** [*IRS*] OSC
Ogden Technology Laboratories [*NASA*] (KSC) OTL
Ogden Test Unit (SAA) OTU
[*The*] **Ogden Union Railway & Depot Co.** [*AAR code*] OURD
Ogden, UT [*Location identifier FAA*] (FAAL) HIF
Ogden, UT [*FM radio station call letters*] KBER
Ogden, UT [*FM radio station call letters*] KBZN
Ogden, UT [*FM radio station call letters*] KKAT
Ogden, UT [*AM radio station call letters*] KLO
Ogden, UT [*Television station call letters*] KOOG
Ogden, UT [*AM radio station call letters*] KSVN
Ogden, UT [*Television station call letters*] KULC
Ogden, UT [*FM radio station call letters*] KWCR
Ogden, UT [*AM radio station call letters*] KYFO
Ogden, UT [*FM radio station call letters*] KYFO-FM
Ogden, UT [*Location identifier FAA*] (FAAL) OGD

Ogden's Reports [12-15 Louisiana] [A publication] (DLA) .... Ogd
Ogden's Reports [12-15 Louisiana] [A publication] (DLA) .... Ogden
Ogdensburg [New York] [ICAO location identifier] (ICLI) .... KOGS
Ogdensburg [Diocesan abbreviation] [New York] (TOCD) .... OG
Ogdensburg (AD) .... Ogd
Ogdensburg [New Jersey] [Seismograph station code, US Geological
Survey] (SEIS) .... OGD
Ogdensburg [New York] [Airport symbol] (OAG) .... OGS
Ogdensburg Bridge & Port Authority [AAR code] .... ONRY
Ogdensburg, NY [Location identifier FAA] (FAAL) .... OGS
Ogdensburg, NY [FM radio station call letters] .... WPAC
Ogdensburg, NY [AM radio station call letters] .... WSLB
Ogdensburg Public Library, Ogdensburg, NY [Library symbol Library of
Congress] (LCLS) .... NOg
Ogdensburg Public Library, Ogdensburg, NY [OCLC symbol] (OCLC) .... VNE
OGE Energy Corp. [NYSE symbol] (SAG) .... OGE
OGE Energy Corp. [Associated Press] (SAG) .... OGE Engy
Ogee [A molding] [Architecture] (ROG) .... OG
Ogemaw District Library, Rose City, MI [Library symbol Library of
Congress] (LCLS) .... MiRsc
Oggetto [Object] [Italian] (AD) .... ogg
Ogilvie Flour Mills Co. Ltd., Montreal, PQ, Canada [Library symbol Library of
Congress] (LCLS) .... CaQMOF
Ogilvie Flour Mills Co. Ltd., Montreal, Quebec [Library symbol National
Library of Canada] (NLC) .... QMOF
Ogilvie Public School, Ogilvie, MN [Library symbol] [Library of Congress]
(LCLS) .... MnOgS
Ogilvie's Imperial Dictionary of the English Language [A publication]
(DLA) .... Ogilvie Dict
Ogilvy & Mather [Advertising agency] .... O & M
Ogilvy, Renaud Law Library, Montreal, Quebec [Library symbol National
Library of Canada] (BIB) .... QMOR
Oglala Sioux Community College, Learning Resources Center, Pine Ridge,
SD [OCLC symbol] (OCLC) .... SDO
Oglala Sioux Community College, Pine Ridge, SD [Library symbol Library of
Congress] (LCLS) .... SdPiO
Ogle [Guyana] [ICAO location identifier] (ICLI) .... SYGO
Oglebay Institute, Wheeling, WV [Library symbol Library of Congress]
(LCLS) .... WvWO
Oglebay Norton [NASDAQ symbol] (TTSB) .... OGLE
Oglebay Norton Co. [Associated Press] (SAG) .... Oglbay
Oglebay Norton Co. [NASDAQ symbol] (NQ) .... OGLE
Oglesby, IL [FM radio station call letters] (RBYB) .... WALS
Oglesby Public Library, Oglesby, IL [Library symbol Library of Congress]
(LCLS) .... IOg
Oglesby Public Schools, Oglesby, IL [Library symbol Library of Congress]
(LCLS) .... IOgPS
Oglethorpe University (GAGS) .... Oglethorpe U
Oglethorpe University, Atlanta, GA [Library symbol Library of Congress]
(LCLS) .... GAOC
Oglethorpe University, Atlanta, GA [OCLC symbol] (OCLC) .... GOU
Ogooue Air Cargo [Gabon] [ICAO designator] (FAAC) .... GBO
Ogren, Paul C., South Bend IN [STAC] .... OPC
Ogston's Medical Jurisprudence [1878] [A publication] (DLA) .... Ogs Med Jur
OGY Petroleum [Vancouver Stock Exchange symbol] .... OGY
O'Gyalla [Later, HRB] [Czechoslovakia] [Geomagnetic observatory code] .... OGY
OH Aviationa [France ICAO designator] (FAAC) .... OHA
Oh, By the Way [Computer hacker terminology] (NHD) .... OBTW
Oh, Gee [Slang] .... OG
Oh Gee (AD) .... og
Oh, I See [Computer science] (DOM) .... OIC
Ohakea [New Zealand] [ICAO location identifier] (ICLI) .... NZOH
Ohaloth (BJA) .... Oha
O'Hara Resources Ltd. [Vancouver Stock Exchange symbol] .... OHR
Ohashi Institute (EA) .... OI
O'Higgins [Antarctica] [Seismograph station code, US Geological Survey]
(SEIS) .... OHC
Ohio [MARC geographic area code Library of Congress] (LCCP) .... n-us-oh
Ohio .... O
Ohio [Postal code] .... OH
Ohio [MARC country of publication code Library of Congress] (LCCP) .... ohu
[The] Ohio Academic Resources Network [Computer science] (TNIG) .... OARnet
Ohio Academy of Science (PDAA) .... OAS
Ohio Administrative Code [A publication] (AAGC) .... OAC
Ohio Administrative Code [Official compilation published by Banks-Baldwin]
[A publication] (DLA) .... Ohio Admin Code
Ohio Aerospace Institute .... OAI
Ohio Agricultural Research and Development Center [Ohio State University]
[Research center] (RCD) .... OARDC
Ohio Agricultural Research and Development Center, Wooster, OH [Library
symbol Library of Congress] (LCLS) .... OWoA
Ohio & Morenci Railroad (IIA) .... O & M
Ohio Appellate Reports [A publication] (DLA) .... App
Ohio Appellate Reports [A publication] (DLA) .... O App
Ohio Appellate Reports [A publication] (DLA) .... OA
Ohio Appellate Reports [A publication] (DLA) .... OAR
Ohio Appellate Reports [A publication] (DLA) .... Oh A
Ohio Appellate Reports [A publication] (DLA) .... Oh Ap
Ohio Appellate Reports [A publication] (DLA) .... Ohio App
Ohio Appellate Reports [A publication] (DLA) .... Ohio Apps
Ohio Appellate Reports, Second Series [A publication] (DLA) .... O App 2d
Ohio Appellate Reports, Second Series [A publication] (DLA) .... OA 2d
Ohio Appellate Reports, Second Series [A publication] (DLA) .... Oh A 2d
Ohio Appellate Reports, Second Series [A publication] (DLA) .... Ohio App 2d
Ohio Art [AMEX symbol] (TTSB) .... OAR

[The] Ohio Art Co. [AMEX symbol] (SPSG) .... OAR
[The] Ohio Art Co. [Associated Press] (SAG) .... OhArt
Ohio Bar (NITA) .... OBAR
Ohio Bell Communications, Inc. [Cleveland] [Telecommunications] (TSSD) ..... OBC
Ohio Board of Tax Appeals Reports [A publication] (DLA) .... Ohio BTA
Ohio Carriers Tariff Service Inc., Cleveland OH [STAC] .... OTS
Ohio Casualty [NASDAQ symbol] (TTSB) .... OCAS
Ohio Casualty Corp. [NASDAQ symbol] (NQ) .... OCAS
Ohio Casualty Corp. [Associated Press] (SAG) .... OhioCa
Ohio Casualty Corp. [Associated Press] (SAG) .... OhioCas
Ohio Circuit Court Decisions [A publication] (DLA) .... OA & C
Ohio Circuit Court Decisions [A publication] (DLA) .... OCD
Ohio Circuit Court Decisions [A publication] (DLA) ...... Ohio CC Dec
Ohio Circuit Court Decisions [A publication] (DLA) .... Ohio Cir Ct
Ohio Circuit Court Decisions [A publication] (DLA) ...... Ohio Circuits
Ohio Circuit Court Decisions, New Series [A publication] (DLA) ...... CD (NS)
Ohio Circuit Court Reports [A publication] (DLA) CC
Ohio Circuit Court Reports [A publication] (DLA) .... Cir Ct Ohio
Ohio Circuit Court Reports [A publication] (DLA) .... Oh Cir Ct
Ohio Circuit Court Reports [A publication] (DLA) .... Ohio CC
Ohio Circuit Court Reports [A publication] (DLA) .... Ohio CCR
Ohio Circuit Court Reports [A publication] (DLA) .... Ohio Cir Ct R
Ohio Circuit Court Reports, New Series [A publication] (DLA) .... CCNS
Ohio Circuit Court Reports, New Series [A publication] (DLA) .... OCC NS
Ohio Circuit Court Reports, New Series [A publication] (DLA) .... Oh Cir Ct NS
Ohio Circuit Court Reports, New Series [A publication] (DLA) .... Ohio CC NS
Ohio Circuit Court Reports, New Series [A publication] (DLA) .... Ohio CCR NS
Ohio Circuit Court Reports, New Series [A publication] (DLA) .... Ohio Cir Ct (NS)
Ohio Circuit Court Reports, New Series [A publication] (DLA) .... Ohio Cir Ct R NS
Ohio Circuit Decisions [A publication] (DLA) .... CD
Ohio Circuit Decisions [A publication] (DLA) .... Circ Dec
Ohio Circuit Decisions [A publication] (DLA) .... Oh Cir Dec
Ohio Circuit Decisions [A publication] (DLA) .... Ohio C Dec
Ohio Circuit Decisions [A publication] (DLA) .... Ohio CD
Ohio Circuit Decisions [A publication] (DLA) .... Ohio Cir Dec
Ohio Circuit Decisions [A publication] (DLA) .... Ohio Circ Dec
Ohio Circuit Reports [or Decisions] [A publication] (DLA) .... OCC
Ohio College (AD) .... OC
Ohio College Association (AD) .... OCA
Ohio College Library Center (BARN) .... OCLC
Ohio College Library Center, Columbus, OH [Library symbol Library of
Congress] (LCLS) .... OCoLC
Ohio College of Applied Science .... OCAS
Ohio College of Chiropody .... OCC
Ohio College of Podiatric Medicine, Cleveland, OH [OCLC symbol]
(OCLC) .... OPD
Ohio Conservation Consortium [Library network] .... OCC
Ohio Correctional and Court Services Association (AD) .... OCCSA
Ohio County Historical Society, Rising Sun, IN [Library symbol Library of
Congress] (LCLS) .... InRisHi
Ohio County News, Rising Sun, IN [Library symbol Library of Congress]
(LCLS) .... InRisCN
Ohio County Public Library, Rising Sun, IN [Library symbol Library of
Congress] (LCLS) .... InRis
Ohio County Public Library, Wheeling, WV [Library symbol Library of
Congress] (LCLS) .... WvW
Ohio County Recorder's Office, Rising Sun, IN [Library symbol Library of
Congress] (LCLS) .... InRisCR
Ohio Courts of Appeals Reports [A publication] (DLA) .... OCA
Ohio Courts of Appeals Reports [A publication] (DLA) .... Oh
Ohio Courts of Appeals Reports [A publication] (DLA) .... Ohio CA
Ohio Courts of Appeals Reports [A publication] (DLA) .... Ohio Ct App
Ohio Data Users Center [Columbus] [Information service or system] (IID) ..... ODUC
Ohio Decisions [A publication] (DLA) .... Dec O
Ohio Decisions [A publication] (DLA) .... OD
Ohio Decisions [A publication] (DLA) .... ODNP
Ohio Decisions [A publication] (DLA) .... Oh Dec
Ohio Decisions [A publication] (DLA) .... Ohio Dec
Ohio Decisions [A publication] (DLA) .... S & CP Dec
Ohio Decisions, Circuit Court [Properly cited Ohio Circuit Decisions]
[A publication] (DLA) .... ODCC
Ohio Decisions Nisi Prius [A publication] (DLA) .... Ohio Dec NP
Ohio Decisions Reprint [A publication] (DLA) .... Dec R
Ohio Decisions Reprint [A publication] (DLA) .... Dec Re
Ohio Decisions Reprint [A publication] (DLA) .... Dec Rep
Ohio Decisions Reprint [A publication] (DLA) .... Dec Repr
Ohio Decisions Reprint [A publication] (DLA) .... DRep
Ohio Decisions Reprint [A publication] (DLA) .... DRepr
Ohio Decisions Reprint [A publication] (DLA) .... O Dec Rep
Ohio Decisions Reprint [A publication] (DLA) .... OD Re
Ohio Decisions Reprint [A publication] (DLA) .... OD Rep
Ohio Decisions Reprint [A publication] (DLA) .... Oh Dec Rep
Ohio Decisions Reprint [A publication] (DLA) .... Ohio Dec R
Ohio Decisions Reprint [A publication] (DLA) .... Ohio Dec Re
Ohio Decisions Reprint [A publication] (DLA) .... Ohio Dec Rep
Ohio Decisions Reprint [A publication] (DLA) .... Ohio Dec Repr
Ohio Decisions Reprint [A publication] (DLA) .... Re
Ohio Department Reports [A publication] (DLA) .... O Dep Rep
Ohio Department Reports [A publication] (DLA) .... Ohio Dep't
Ohio Division of Wildlife .... ODOW
Ohio Dominican College, Columbus, OH [Library symbol Library of
Congress] (LCLS) .... OCoD
Ohio Dominican College, Columbus, OH [OCLC symbol] (OCLC) .... ODC
Ohio Edison [NYSE symbol] (TTSB) .... OEC
Ohio Edison 3.90% Pfd [NYSE symbol] (TTSB) .... OECPrA

Ohio Edison, 4.40% Pfd [*NYSE symbol*] (TTSB) .... OECPrB
Ohio Edison 4.44% Pfd [*NYSE symbol*] (TTSB) .... OECPrC
Ohio Edison 4.56% Pfd [*NYSE symbol*] (TTSB) .... OERCPrD
Ohio Edison Co. [*NYSE symbol*] (SPSG) .... OEC
Ohio Edison Co. [*Associated Press*] (SAG) .... OhEd
Ohio Edison Co. [*Associated Press*] (SAG) .... OhioEd
Ohio Edison Fin Tr 9.00% Pfd [*NYSE symbol*] (TTSB) .... OECPrT
Ohio Edison Financing Trust [*NYSE symbol*] (SAG) .... OEC
Ohio Edison Financing Trust [*Associated Press*] (SAG) .... OhEd
Ohio Education Association (AD) .... OEA
Ohio Educational Library/Media Association (AD) .... OEL/MA
Ohio Educational Library Media Association (EDAC) .... OELMA
Ohio Environmental Protection Agency .... OEPA
Ohio Environmental Protection Agency (DOGT) .... OEPA
Ohio Environmental Protection Agency Library, Columbus, OH [*OCLC symbol*] (OCLC) .... OEN
Ohio Federal Decisions [*A publication*] (DLA) .... OFD
Ohio Federal Decisions [*A publication*] (DLA) .... Oh F Dec
Ohio Federal Decisions [*A publication*] (DLA) .... Ohio F Dec
Ohio Federal Decisions [*A publication*] (DLA) .... Ohio FD
Ohio Federal Decisions [*A publication*] (DLA) .... Ohio Fed Dec
Ohio Federation of Teachers (AD) .... OFT
Ohio Foundation of Independent Colleges (AD) .... OFIC
Ohio Genealogical Society (EA) .... OGS
Ohio Government Reports [*A publication*] (DLA) .... Ohio Gov't
Ohio Historical Society, Columbus, OH [*Library symbol Library of Congress*] (LCLS) .... OHi
Ohio Historical Society, Columbus, OH [*OCLC symbol*] (OCLC) .... OHT
Ohio Household Goods Carriers Bureau Inc., Warren OH [*STAC*] .... OHH
Ohio Improved Chesters [*Initialism itself now used as name of breed of swine*] .... OIC
Ohio Inspection Bureau (AD) .... OIB
Ohio Jurisprudence [*A publication*] (DLA) .... O Jur
Ohio Jurisprudence [*A publication*] (DLA) .... Oh Jur
Ohio Jurisprudence [*A publication*] (DLA) .... Ohio Jur
Ohio Jurisprudence, Second Series [*A publication*] (DLA) .... Ohio Jur 2d
Ohio Kache Systems Corp. .... OKS
Ohio Law Abstract [*A publication*] (DLA) .... Abs
Ohio Law Abstract [*A publication*] (DLA) .... Ohio Abs
Ohio Law Abstract [*A publication*] (DLA) .... Ohio Abstract
Ohio Law Abstract [*A publication*] (DLA) .... Ohio L Abs
Ohio Law Abstract [*A publication*] (DLA) .... Ohio Law Abs
Ohio Law Abstract [*A publication*] (DLA) .... Ohio Law Abst
Ohio Law Abstract [*A publication*] (DLA) .... OL Abs
Ohio Law Abstract [*A publication*] (DLA) .... OLA
Ohio Law Bulletin [*A publication*] (DLA) .... Oh L Bul
Ohio Law Bulletin [*A publication*] (DLA) .... Ohio L Bull
Ohio Law Bulletin [*A publication*] (DLA) .... OLB
Ohio Law Journal [*A publication*] (DLA) .... Oh LJ
Ohio Law Journal [*A publication*] (DLA) .... Ohio Law J
Ohio Law Journal [*A publication*] (DLA) .... Ohio LJ
Ohio Law Journal [*A publication*] (DLA) .... OL Jour
Ohio Law Journal [*A publication*] (DLA) .... OLJ
Ohio Law Reporter [*A publication*] (DLA) .... Law Rep
Ohio Law Reporter [*A publication*] (DLA) .... LR
Ohio Law Reporter [*A publication*] (DLA) .... Oh L Rep
Ohio Law Reporter [*A publication*] (DLA) .... Ohio L Rep
Ohio Law Reporter [*A publication*] (DLA) .... Ohio Law R
Ohio Law Reporter [*A publication*] (DLA) .... Ohio Law Rep
Ohio Law Reporter [*A publication*] (DLA) .... Ohio Law Repr
Ohio Law Reporter [*A publication*] (DLA) .... Ohio LR
Ohio Law Reporter [*A publication*] (DLA) .... OL Rep
Ohio Law Reporter [*A publication*] (DLA) .... OLR
Ohio Law Reporter and Weekly Bulletin [*A publication*] (DLA) .... Ohio LR & Wk Bul
Ohio Laws [*A publication*] (DLA) .... OL
Ohio Legal News [*A publication*] (DLA) .... O Legal News
Ohio Legal News [*A publication*] (DLA) .... Oh Leg N
Ohio Legal News [*A publication*] (DLA) .... Ohio Leg N
Ohio Legal News [*A publication*] (DLA) .... Ohio Leg News
Ohio Legal News [*A publication*] (DLA) .... Ohio Legal N
Ohio Legal News [*A publication*] (DLA) .... OLN
Ohio Legislative Bulletin (Anderson) [*A publication*] (DLA) .... Ohio Legis Bull
Ohio Legislative Reference Bureau, Columbus, OH [*Library symbol Library of Congress*] (LCLS) .... O-LR
Ohio Legislative Service [*A publication*] (DLA) .... Ohio Legis Serv
Ohio Legislative Service Commission, Columbus, OH [*OCLC symbol*] (OCLC) .... OLG
Ohio Library Association (AD) .... OLA
Ohio Library Foundation (AD) .... OLF
Ohio Lower Court Decisions [*A publication*] (DLA) .... LCD
Ohio Lower Court Decisions [*A publication*] (DLA) .... Lower Ct Dec
Ohio Lower Court Decisions [*A publication*] (DLA) .... O Lower D
Ohio Lower Court Decisions [*A publication*] (DLA) .... Oh L Ct D
Ohio Lower Court Decisions [*A publication*] (DLA) .... Ohio Low Dec
Ohio Lower Court Decisions [*A publication*] (DLA) .... Ohio Lower Dec
Ohio Lower Court Decisions [*A publication*] (DLA) .... OLD
Ohio Magazine [*A publication*] (ROG) .... OHIO M
Ohio Mechanics Institute .... OMI
Ohio Medical Education Network [*Ohio State University*] [*Columbus*] (TSSD) .... OMEN
Ohio Midland Light & Power [*AAR code*] .... OMLP
Ohio Miscellaneous Decisions [*A publication*] (DLA) .... Ohio Misc Dec
Ohio Miscellaneous Decisions (Gottschall) [*1865-73*] [*A publication*] (DLA) .... Misc Dec
Ohio Miscellaneous Reports [*A publication*] (DLA) .... M
Ohio Miscellaneous Reports [*A publication*] (DLA) .... O Misc
Ohio Miscellaneous Reports [*A publication*] (DLA) .... Oh Misc
Ohio Miscellaneous Reports [*A publication*] (DLA) .... Ohio Misc
Ohio Miscellaneous Reports, Second Series [*A publication*] (DLA) .... Ohio Misc 2d
Ohio Miscellaneous Reports, Third Series [*A publication*] (DLA) .... Ohio Misc 3d
Ohio Modern Language Teachers Association (EDAC) .... OMLTA
Ohio Monthly Record [*A publication*] (DLA) .... Ohio Monthly Rec
Ohio Motor Freight Tariff Committee Inc., Columbus OH [*STAC*] .... OTC
Ohio Network (NITA) .... OHIONET
Ohio Nisi Prius Reports [*A publication*] (DLA) .... Nisi Prius Rep
Ohio Nisi Prius Reports [*A publication*] (DLA) .... NP
Ohio Nisi Prius Reports [*A publication*] (DLA) .... NP Ohio
Ohio Nisi Prius Reports [*A publication*] (DLA) .... Oh NP
Ohio Nisi Prius Reports [*A publication*] (DLA) .... Ohio Nisi Prius
Ohio Nisi Prius Reports [*A publication*] (DLA) .... Ohio NP
Ohio Nisi Prius Reports [*A publication*] (DLA) .... ONP
Ohio Nisi Prius Reports, New Series [*A publication*] (DLA) .... NP NS
Ohio Nisi Prius Reports, New Series [*A publication*] (DLA) .... Oh NP (NS)
Ohio Nisi Prius Reports, New Series [*A publication*] (DLA) .... Ohio Nisi Prius (NS)
Ohio Nisi Prius Reports, New Series [*A publication*] (DLA) .... Ohio NP NS
Ohio Nisi Prius Reports, New Series [*1903-13*] [*A publication*] (DLA) .... ONPNS
Ohio Northern University (GAGS) .... Ohio No U
Ohio Northern University [*Ada, OH*] .... ONU
Ohio Northern University, Ada, OH [*Library symbol Library of Congress*] (LCLS) .... OAdN
Ohio Northern University, Ada, OH [*OCLC symbol*] (OCLC) .... ONU
Ohio Northern University. Intramural Law Review [*A publication*] (DLA) .... Oh NU Intra LR
Ohio Northern University. Intramural Law Review [*A publication*] (DLA) .... ONU Intra LR
Ohio Northern University, Law Library, Ada, OH [*OCLC symbol*] (OCLC) .... ONL
Ohio Opinions [*A publication*] (DLA) .... Ohio O
Ohio Opinions [*A publication*] (DLA) .... Ohio Op
Ohio Opinions [*A publication*] (DLA) .... Ohio Ops
Ohio Opinions [*A publication*] (DLA) .... OO
Ohio Opinions, Annotated [*A publication*] (DLA) .... Ohio O
Ohio Opinions, Second Series [*A publication*] (DLA) .... Ohio O 2d
Ohio Opinions, Second Series [*A publication*] (DLA) .... Ohio Op 2d
Ohio Opinions, Second Series [*A publication*] (DLA) .... OO 2d
Ohio Opinions, Third Series [*A publication*] (DLA) .... Ohio Op 3d
Ohio Penal Racing Association (EA) .... OPRA
Ohio Power 8.16% Jr Sub Debs [*NYSE symbol*] (TTSB) .... OPJ
Ohio Power Co. [*NYSE symbol*] (SAG) .... DPJ
Ohio Power Co. [*Associated Press*] (SAG) OhP25
Ohio Power Co. [*NYSE symbol*] (SAG) .... ORJ
Ohio Probate [*A publication*] (DLA) .... Oh Prob
Ohio Probate Reports, by Goebel [*A publication*] (DLA) .... Ohio Prob
Ohio Program of Intensive English (EDAC) .... OPIE
Ohio Project for Research in Information Service (NITA) .... OPRIS
Ohio Regional Library, Braille and Talking Books Division, Cleveland Public Library, Cleveland, OH [*Library symbol Library of Congress*] (LCLS) .... OCl-BPH
Ohio Report [*A publication*] (DLA) .... Ohio R
Ohio Reports [*A publication*] (DLA) .... O
Ohio Reports [*A publication*] (DLA) .... O Rep
Ohio Reports Condensed [*A publication*] (DLA) .... Ohio R Cond
Ohio Resources Corp. [*Vancouver Stock Exchange symbol*] .... OHO
Ohio Revised Code, Annotated [*A publication*] (DLA) .... Ohio Rev Code Ann
Ohio Revised Code, Annotated (Anderson) [*A publication*] (DLA) .... Ohio Rev Code Ann (Anderson)
Ohio Revised Code, Annotated (Baldwin) [*A publication*] (DLA) .... Ohio Rev Code Ann (Baldwin)
Ohio Revised Code, Annotated (Page) [*A publication*] (DLA) .... Ohio Rev Code Ann (Page)
Ohio River and Basin [*MARC geographic area code Library of Congress*] (LCCP) .... n-uso-
Ohio River Division [*Army Corps of Engineers*] .... ORD
Ohio River Division Laboratory [*Army Corps of Engineers*] (KSC) .... ORDL
Ohio River Division Laboratory, Engineer Corps [*Army*] (MCD) .... ORDL-EC
Ohio River Valley Water Sanitation Commission .... ORSANCO
Ohio Social Acceptance Scale (EDAC) .... OSAS
Ohio State Archives, Columbus, OH [*Library symbol Library of Congress*] (LCLS) .... O-Ar
Ohio State Bar Association. Bulletin [*A publication*] (DLA) .... Ohio SBA Bull
Ohio State Bar Association. Bulletin [*A publication*] (DLA) .... OSBA Bull
Ohio State Inventory of Guidance Awareness .... OSIGA
Ohio State Library, Columbus, OH [*Library symbol Library of Congress*] (LCLS) .... O
Ohio State Reports [*A publication*] (DLA) .... O St
Ohio State Reports [*A publication*] (DLA) .... O St R
Ohio State Reports [*A publication*] (DLA) .... O St Rep
Ohio State Reports [*A publication*] (DLA) .... O State
Ohio State Reports [*A publication*] (DLA) .... Oh St
Ohio State Reports [*A publication*] (DLA) .... Ohio S
Ohio State Reports [*A publication*] (DLA) .... Ohio S Rep
Ohio State Reports [*A publication*] (DLA) .... Ohio SR
Ohio State Reports [*A publication*] (DLA) .... Ohio St
Ohio State Reports [*A publication*] (DLA) .... Ohio St R
Ohio State Reports [*A publication*] (DLA) .... Ohio St Rep
Ohio State Reports [*A publication*] (DLA) .... Ohio St Report
Ohio State Reports [*A publication*] (DLA) .... Ohio State
Ohio State Reports [*A publication*] (DLA) .... Ohio State Rep
Ohio State Reports [*A publication*] (DLA) .... OS
Ohio State Reports [*A publication*] (DLA) .... OS Rep
Ohio State Reports [*A publication*] (DLA) .... OSR

Ohio State Reports, New Series [*A publication*] (DLA) .... Ohio (New Series)
Ohio State Reports, New Series [*A publication*] (DLA) .... Ohio NS
Ohio State Reports, New Series [*A publication*] (DLA) .... Ohio St R (NS)
Ohio State Reports, New Series [*A publication*] (DLA) .... Ohio State R (NS)
Ohio State Reports, Second Series [*A publication*] (DLA) .... Ohio St 2d
Ohio State Reports, Second Series [*A publication*] (DLA) .... OS 2d
Ohio State Reports, Third Series [*A publication*] (DLA) .... Ohio St 3d
[*The*] Ohio State University (GAGS) .... Ohio St U
Ohio State University [*Columbus*] .... OSU
Ohio State University, Byrd Polar Research Center, Goldthwait Polar
   Library, Columbus, OH [*Library symbol*] [*Library of Congress*] (LCLS) .... OU-BP
Ohio State University, College of Law, Columbus, OH [*Library symbol
   Library of Congress*] (LCLS) .... OU-L
Ohio State University, Columbus, OH [*OCLC symbol*] (OCLC) .... OSU
Ohio State University, Columbus, OH [*Library symbol Library of Congress*]
   (LCLS) .... OU
Ohio State University, Health Sciences Library, Columbus, OH [*Library
   symbol Library of Congress*] (LCLS) .... OU-H
Ohio State University Libraries (NITA) .... OSUL
Ohio State University, Mansfield Regional Campus, Mansfield, OH [*Library
   symbol Library of Congress*] (LCLS) .... OMansU
Ohio State University, Marion Campus, Marion, OH [*Library symbol Library of
   Congress*] (LCLS) .... OMarionU
Ohio State University Museum of Zoology [*Research center*] (RCD) .... OSUM
Ohio State University, Newark Campus, Newark, OH [*Library symbol Library
   of Congress*] (LCLS) .... ONewU
Ohio State University, Pharmacy and Bacteriology Library, Columbus, OH
   [*Library symbol Library of Congress*] (LCLS) .... OU-P
Ohio State University Press (DGA) .... OSUP
Ohio State University Psychological Exam (EDAC) .... OSUPE
Ohio State University Radio Observatory .... OSURO
Ohio State University Reactor .... OSUR
Ohio State University Research Foundation .... OSURF
Ohio Superior and Common Pleas Decisions [*A publication*] (DLA) ..... Oh S & CP
Ohio Superior and Common Pleas Decisions [*A publication*] (DLA).... Ohio S & CP
Ohio Superior and Common Pleas Decisions [*A publication*]
   (DLA) .... Ohio S & CP Dec
Ohio Superior and Common Pleas Decisions [*A publication*]
   (DLA) .... Ohio Sup & CP Dec
Ohio Superior and Common Pleas Decisions [*A publication*]
   (DLA) .... OS & CP Dec
Ohio Supplement [*A publication*] (DLA) .... O Su
Ohio Supplement [*A publication*] (DLA) .... O Supp
Ohio Supplement [*A publication*] (DLA) .... Ohio Supp
Ohio Supreme Court, Columbus, OH [*Library symbol Library of Congress*]
   (LCLS) .... O-SC
Ohio Supreme Court Decisions, Unreported Cases [*A publication*]
   (DLA) .... Oh SCD
Ohio Supreme Court Decisions, Unreported Cases [*A publication*]
   (DLA) .... Ohio SU
Ohio Supreme Court Decisions, Unreported Cases [*A publication*]
   (DLA) .... Ohio Unrep
Ohio Supreme Court Decisions, Unreported Cases [*A publication*]
   (DLA) .... Ohio Unrept Cas
Ohio Supreme Court Decisions, Unreported Cases [*A publication*] (DLA).... OSCD
Ohio Supreme Court Decisions, Unreported Cases [*A publication*] (DLA) ..... OSU
Ohio Supreme Court Reports [*1821-51*] [*A publication*] (DLA) .... Ohio
Ohio Tank Truck Carriers Bureau, Worthington OH [*STAC*] .... OHT
Ohio Theological Librarians [*Library network*] .... OTL
Ohio Township Library, Ohio, IL [*Library symbol Library of Congress*]
   (LCLS) .... IOh
Ohio Turnpike (AD) .... Ohio Turn
Ohio University (GAGS) .... Ohio U
Ohio University [*Athens*] .... OU
Ohio University, Athens, OH [*Library symbol Library of Congress*] (LCLS) ...... OAU
Ohio University, Athens, OH [*OCLC symbol*] (OCLC) .... OUN
Ohio University, Belmont County Branch Campus, St. Clairsville, OH
   [*Library symbol Library of Congress*] (LCLS) .... OStcU
Ohio University Cartographic Center [*Research center*] (RCD) .... OUCC
Ohio University, Chillicothe Branch Campus, Chillicothe, OH [*Library
   symbol Library of Congress*] (LCLS) .... OChU
Ohio University, Chillicothe Branch Campus, Chillicothe, OH [*OCLC
   symbol*] (OCLC) .... OUC
Ohio University, Lancaster Branch Campus, Lancaster, OH [*Library symbol
   Library of Congress*] (LCLS) .... OLanU
Ohio University, Lancaster Branch Campus, Lancaster, OH [*OCLC
   symbol*] (OCLC) .... OUL
Ohio University, Portsmouth Branch Campus, Portsmouth, OH [*Library
   symbol Library of Congress Obsolete*] (LCLS) .... OPosmU
Ohio University Press (AD) .... Ohio U Pr
Ohio University, Zanesville Branch Campus, Zanesville, OH [*Library symbol
   Library of Congress*] (LCLS) .... OZavU
Ohio Valley .... OV
Ohio Valley Banc Corp. [*Associated Press*] (SAG) .... OhioVal
Ohio Valley Banc Corp. [*NASDAQ symbol*] (SAG) .... OVBC
Ohio Valley Banc Corp. [*NASDAQ symbol*] (TTSB) .... OVBC
Ohio Valley College, Parkersburg, WV [*Library symbol Library of Congress*]
   (LCLS) .... WvPO
Ohio Valley Conference [*Collegiate sports*] .... OVC
Ohio Valley Electric Railroad .... OVE
Ohio Valley Local District Free Public Library, Manchester, OH [*Library
   symbol Library of Congress*] (LCLS) .... OMancO
Ohio Valley Local District Free Public Library, Peebles Branch, Peebles,
   OH [*Library symbol Library of Congress*] (LCLS) .... OPeeO
Ohio Vocational Education Achievement Test Program (EDAC) .... OVEATP

Ohio Vocational Interest Survey [*Vocational guidance test*] .... OVIS
Ohio Wesleyan University [*Delaware, OH*] .... OWU
Ohio Wesleyan University, Delaware, OH [*Library symbol Library of
   Congress*] (LCLS) .... ODW
Ohio Wesleyan University, Delaware, OH [*OCLC symbol*] (OCLC) .... OWU
Ohioana Library, Columbus, OH [*Library symbol Library of Congress*]
   (LCLS) .... OCoO
Ohio-Kentucky-Indiana Regional Planning Authority .... OKI
OHIONET, Columbus, OH [*OCLC symbol*] (OCLC) .... OHN
OHIONET, Columbus, OH [*OCLC symbol*] (OCLC) .... TQO
OHIONET, Columbus, OH [*OCLC symbol*] (OCLC) .... TQP
Ohlinger's Federal Practice [*A publication*] (DLA) .... Ohlinger Fed Practice
Ohm [*Electricity*] .... O
Ohm Centimeter (IAA) .... OCM
OHM Corp. [*NYSE symbol*] (SPSG) .... OHM
OHM Corp. [*Associated Press*] (SAG) .... OHM Cp
Ohm-Ampere-Second Meter [*System of units*] .... OASM
Ohm-Centimeter (AAG) .... OHM-CM
Ohm-Centimeter (AD) .... ohm-cm
Ohmic Heating .... OH
Ohmic Heating Toroidal Experiment [*Nuclear fusion device*] .... OHTE
Ohmine [*Japan*] [*Seismograph station code, US Geological Survey*] (SEIS) ..... OMJ
Ohmmeter [*Engineering*] (AAG) .... OHM
Ohmmeter (AD) .... ohm
Ohmmeter .... OHMM
Ohmmeter [*Engineering*] .... OHMM
Ohms per Volt .... OPV
Ohne [*Antigen*] [*Immunology*] .... O
Ohne Jahr [*Without Date of Publication*] [*Bibliography*] [*German*] .... OJ
Ohne Jahr [*Without Year*] [*German*] (AD) .... oJ
Ohne Kosten [*Without Cost*] [*German*] (AD) .... ok
Ohne Kosten [*Without Cost*] [*German*] .... OK
Ohne Ort [*Without Place of Publication*] [*Bibliography*] [*German*] .... OO
Ohne Pedal [*Without Pedal*] [*Music*] .... OH PED
Ohne Pedale [*Without Pedals*] [*German*] (AD) .... oh Ped
Ohne Wert [*Without Value*] [*German*] .... OW
Oholoth (BJA) .... Oh
Oholoth (BJA) .... Oho
Oholoth (BJA) .... Ohol
Ohoopee Regional Library, Vidalia, GA [*Library symbol Library of Congress*]
   (LCLS) .... GVidO
Ohrid [*Former Yugoslavia*] [*ICAO location identifier*] (ICLI) .... LYOH
Ohrid [*Former Yugoslavia*] [*Airport symbol*] (OAG) .... OHD
Ohrid [*Yugoslavia*] [*Seismograph station code, US Geological Survey*]
   (SEIS) .... OHR
OHSL Financial Corp. [*NASDAQ symbol*] (SAG) .... OHSL
OHSL Financial Corp. [*Associated Press*] (SAG) .... OHSL Fn
Ohsweken, ON [*FM radio station call letters*] .... CKRZ
OI Corp. [*Associated Press*] (SAG) .... OI Corp
OI Corp. [*NASDAQ symbol*] (NQ) .... OICO
Oiapoque [*Brazil*] [*Airport symbol*] (AD) .... OYK
Oiapoque [*Brazil ICAO location identifier*] (ICLI) .... SBOI
Oil (VRA) .... o
Oil .... O
Oil [*Pharmacy*] (CPH) .... ol
Oil Analysis Program [*Military*] (AFIT) .... OAP
Oil and Chemical Plant Constructors' Association [*British*] .... OCPCA
Oil and Colour Chemists' Association .... OCCA
Oil and Gas Development Corp. (AD) .... OGDC
Oil and Gas Field Study [*Department of the Interior*] .... OGFS
Oil and Gas Journal [*A publication*] (AD) .... OGJ
Oil and Gas Law Review [*A publication*] (DLA) .... Oil & Gas LR
Oil and Gas/Pipeline Facilities .... O & G/PF
Oil and Gas Reporter [*A publication*] (DLA) .... Oil & Gas
Oil and Gas Reporter [*A publication*] (DLA) .... Oil & Gas Reptr
Oil and Gas Reporter [*A publication*] (DLA) .... Oil & Gas Rptr
Oil and Hazardous Materials Incidence .... OHM
Oil and Hazardous Materials Simulated Environmental Test Tank [*Leonardo,
   NJ*] [*Environmental Protection Agency*] .... OHMSETT
Oil and Hazardous Materials Spills Branch [*Environmental Protection
   Agency*] (GRD) .... OHMSB
Oil and Hazardous Materials Technical Assistance Data System [*Databank*]
   [*Environmental Protection Agency*] (IID) .... OHM-TADS
Oil Appliance Manufacturers' Association [*British*] (BI) .... OAMA
Oil Bath Heater .... OBH
Oil Bearing (DCTA) .... OB
Oil Bomb .... OB
Oil Breather Pressure .... OBP
Oil/Bulk/Ore Carrier [*Multipurpose bulk carrier*] (DS) .... OBO
Oil Burner .... OBRNR
Oil Catcher .... OCHR
Oil Check Valve .... OCV
Oil, Chemical, and Atomic Workers (AD) .... OCAW
Oil, Chemical, and Atomic Workers International Union (EA) .... OCAW
Oil [*Operated*] Circuit Breaker .... OCB
Oil Circuit Breaker (AD) .... ocb
Oil Circuit Recloser .... OCR
Oil City Library, Oil City, PA [*Library symbol Library of Congress*] (LCLS) .... PO
Oil City Lubricants Ltd. [*Vancouver Stock Exchange symbol*] .... OCL
Oil City, PA [*Location identifier FAA*] (FAAL) .... OIL
Oil City, PA [*AM radio station call letters*] .... WKQW
Oil City, PA [*FM radio station call letters*] .... WKQW-FM
Oil City, PA [*AM radio station call letters*] .... WOYL
Oil City, PA [*FM radio station call letters*] .... WRJS
Oil Cleaner .... OCLNR

Oil Collection Basin (NRCH) ... OCB
Oil Companies' European Organization for Environmental and Health Protection (EA) ... CONCAWE
Oil Companies International Marine Forum [*British*] (EAIO) ... OCIMF
Oil Companies' Materials Association [*British*] (BI) ... OCMA
Oil Company of Australia (AD) ... OCA
Oil Content Monitor (AD) ... ocm
Oil Content Monitor [*Navy*] (CAAL) ... OCM
Oil Control ... OCONT
Oil Control Board [*British*] ... OCB
Oil Control Board, Supply [*British*] ... OCB(S)
Oil Control Coordination Committee (AD) ... OCCC
Oil Control Valve - Low-Speed ... OCV-L
Oil Cooler ... OC
Oil Cooler ... OCLR
Oil Country Tubular Goods [*Metal industry*] ... OCTG
Oil Debris Monitor ... ODM
Oil Desurger ... OD
Oil Differential ... ODIFF
Oil Dipstick ... ODPSK
Oil Distribution (DNAB) ... OD
Oil Drainage ... OD
Oil Drilling and Exploration (AD) ... ODE
Oil Emersion Field [*Biochemistry*] (DAVI) ... OEF
Oil Emulsion [*Microbiology*] ... OE
Oil Engineering Apprentices Association (AD) ... OEAA
Oil Equivalent ... OE
Oil Exporting Countries (AD) ... OEC
Oil Extended Styrene Butadiene Rubber (PDAA) ... OESBR
Oil Extended Synthetic Rubber (PDAA) ... OESR
Oil Facility [*International Monetary Fund*] ... OF
Oil Field Haulers Association (EA) ... OFHA
Oil Field Haulers Association Inc., Austin TX [*STAC*] ... OFH
Oil Filter ... OFLTR
Oil Filter Pack ... OFP
Oil Fired (ADA) ... OF
Oil Forced Blast (IAA) ... OFB
Oil Free Compressor ... OFC
Oil from Sludge ... OFS
Oil Fuel [*British military*] (DMA) ... OF
Oil Gauge [*Automotive engineering*] ... O/GA
Oil Gauge ... OG
Oil Gland (AD) ... og
Oil Glands [*In propeller shaft*] ... OG
Oil Heat Institute (AD) ... OHI
Oil Hydraulic Power Switch ... OHPS
Oil Immersion Field (MAE) ... OIF
Oil Import Administration [*Later, Office of Oil and Gas*] [*Department of the Interior*] ... OIA
Oil Import Appeals Board (AD) ... OIAB
Oil Importing and Developing Country ... OIDC
Oil in Place (AD) ... oip
Oil in Water ... O/W
Oil Industry Commission (AD) ... OIC
Oil Industry Industrial Committee [*Australia*] ... OIIC
Oil Industry International Exploration and Production Forum (EAIO) ... E & P
Oil Industry International Exploration and Production Forum (EA) ... E & P Forum
Oil Industry Working Party (AD) ... OIWP
Oil Insurance Association [*Later, Industrial Risk Insurance*] (EA) ... OIA
Oil Interceptor Trap ... OIT
Oil Investment Institute [*Washington, DC*] (EA) ... OII
Oil Lands Leasing Act ... OLLA
Oil Level (AAG) ... OL
Oil Level (AD) ... ol
Oil Level ... OLVL
Oil Lighter [*Shipping*] [*British*] ... OL
Oil Market Module [*Department of Energy*] (GFGA) ... OMM
Oil Market Simulation Model [*Department of Energy*] (GFGA) ... OMS
Oil Mill Machinery Manufacturers and Supply Association (EA) ... OMMMSA
Oil Nozzle ... ONOZ
Oil of Vitriol ... OV
Oil on Board (VRA) ... o/bd
Oil on Burlap (VRA) ... o/bur
Oil on Canvas (VRA) ... o/c
Oil on Cardboard (VRA) ... o/cdbd
Oil on Panel (VRA) ... o/p
Oil on Paper (VRA) ... o/pa
Oil/Ore [*Ship*] (DS) ... O/O
Oil Out Temperature ... OOT
Oil Pan ... OPN
Oil Patch Group, Inc. [*Toronto Stock Exchange symbol*] ... OPI
Oil Plug ... OPLG
Oil Point [*Alaska*] [*Seismograph station code, US Geological Survey*] (SEIS) ... OPT
Oil Policy Committee [*Office of Emergency Preparedness*] [*Obsolete*] ... OPC
Oil Pollution Act of 1990 [*MARAD*] (TAG) ... OPA
Oil Pollution Research Unit [*British*] (ARC) ... OPRU
Oil Pressure ... OP
Oil Pressure ... OPRS
Oil Pressure Indicator ... OPI
Oil Pressure Out ... OPO
Oil Pressure Switch ... OPS
Oil Pressure Transmitter ... OPT
Oil Producers' Economic Cartel (NADA) ... OPEC
Oil Production Stock ... OPS
Oil Pump ... OP
Oil Pump Assembly Housing (MCD) ... OPAH
Oil Quality Assessment Program [*Society of Automotive Engineers, Inc.*] ... OQAP
Oil Quantity Indicator ... OQI
Oil Quench (IAA) ... OQ
Oil Recovery and Separation Technology [*Jastram Werke*] ... ORAS
Oil Recovery System ... ORS
Oil Red O [*A stain*] ... ORO
Oil Refiners Association (NADA) ... ORA
Oil Rehabilitation Committee [*British*] ... OR
Oil Remaining after Waterflooding [*Petroleum technology*] ... ORAW
Oil Retention [*Enema*] [*Medicine*] ... OR
Oil Ring (MSA) ... OR
Oil Ripoff (AD) ... oiloff
Oil Sands Environmental Study Group [*Canada*] ... OSESG
Oil Sands Research Centre [*Alberta*] ... OSRC
Oil Screen ... OSCRN
Oil Seal ... OSL
Oil Shale Corp., Research Center Library, Golden, CO [*Library symbol Library of Congress*] (LCLS) ... CoGO
Oil Shale Environmental Advisory Panel [*Department of the Interior*] ... OSEAP
Oil Slick Detection RADAR ... OSDR
Oil Solenoid ... OS
Oil Spill Clean-Up Technology (ASF) ... OSCUT
Oil Spill Control Association of America [*Later, SCAA*] (EA) ... OSCAA
Oil Spill Information Center [*Santa Barbara, CA*] ... OSIC
Oil Spill Intelligence Report ... OSIR
Oil Spill Response Plan [*Pollution prevention*] ... OSRP
Oil Spill Simulation Model ... OSSM
Oil Spillage Analytical and Identification Service [*Laboratory of the Government Chemist*] (PDAA) ... OSAIS
Oil Spillage Analytical Information Service (NITA) ... OSAIS
Oil Springs, ON [*Television station call letters*] ... CIII-29
Oil Storage Barge [*Non-self-propelled*] [*Navy symbol*] ... YOS
Oil Suction Pump (MSA) ... OSP
Oil Switch ... OS
Oil Tank ... OTK
Oil Temperature [*Automotive engineering*] ... OT
Oil Temperature Gauge (MSA) ... OTG
Oil Temperature Out ... OTO
Oil Trades Association of New York (EA) ... OTA
Oil Trades Association of New York (EA) ... OTANY
Oil Turbine Drive ... OTD
Oil, Water, Gas ... OWG
Oil Water Separator [*Navy*] (CAAL) ... OWS
Oil Workers International Union [*Later, OCAW*] ... OWIU
Oil-Cooled ... OCLD
Oildale, CA [*FM radio station call letters*] ... KLLY
Oil-Degrading Bacteria ... ODB
Oil-dispersed-in-Water [*Emulsion*] ... O/W
Oil-Dri Corp. of America [*NYSE symbol*] (SPSG) ... ODC
Oil-Dri Corp. of America [*Associated Press*] (SAG) ... OilDri
Oil-Emulsion Mud (AD) ... oem
Oiler [*Fuel tanker*] [*Navy ship symbol*] ... AO
Oil-Extended Natural Rubber ... OENR
Oil-Extended Polymer (IAA) ... OEP
Oil-Extended Styrene-Butadiene Rubber (AD) ... oesbr
Oilfield Production Equipment Manufacturers Association [*Defunct*] (EA) ... OPEMA
Oilfield Tank Manufacturers Association (EA) ... OTMA
Oil-Filled (IAA) ... OF
Oil-Filled Resistor ... OFR
[*The*] **Oilgear Co.** [*Associated Press*] (SAG) ... Oilgear
[*The*] **Oilgear Co.** [*NASDAQ symbol*] (NQ) ... OLGR
Oil-Hardened Tool Steel ... OHTS
Oil-Heat Institute of America [*Later, PMAA*] ... OHI
Oil-Heat Institute of America [*Later, PMAA*] (KSC) ... OHIA
Oil-Immersed ... OI
Oil-Immersed (AD) ... oi
Oil-Immersed Forced-Air-Cooled [*Transformer*] (IEEE) ... OFA
Oil-Immersed Forced-Oil-Cooled [*Transformer*] (IEEE) ... FO
Oil-Immersed Forced-Oil-Cooled with Forced-Air Cooler [*Transformer*] (IEEE) ... FOA
Oil-Immersed Forced-Oil-Cooled with Forced-Water Cooler [*Transformer*] (IEEE) ... FOW
Oil-Immersed Natural-Colled Transformer (IAA) ... ON
Oil-Immersed Self-Cooled [*Transformer*] (IEEE) ... OA
Oil-Immersed Water-Cooled [*Transformer*] (IEEE) ... OW
Oil-in-Place ... OIP
Oil-Insulated ... OI
Oil-Insulated, Fan-Cooled ... OIFC
Oil-Insulated, Self-Cooling ... OISC
Oil-Insulated, Water-Cooled ... OIWC
Oil-in-Water Dispersion [*Pollution*] ... OWD
Oilproof ... OP
Oilseeds Research Council [*Australia*] ... ORC
Oilskin Manufacturers' Association of Great Britain Ltd. (BI) ... OMA
Oilstick (VRA) ... ostk
Oil-Tempered (IAA) ... OT
Oiltex International Ltd. [*Toronto Stock Exchange symbol*] ... OTX
Oil-Tight ... OT
Oil-Tight Hatch [*Shipfitting*] ... OTH
Oil-Tight Light ... OTL
Oil-Vapor Pump ... OVP
Oil-Water [*Ratio*] [*Laboratory science*] (DAVI) ... O/W

Ointment (AD) ... oint
Ointment ... OINT
OIS Optical Imaging Sys [*NASDAQ symbol*] (TTSB) ... OVON
OIS Optical Imaging Systems, Inc. [*Associated Press*] (SAG) ... OIS
OIS Optical Imaging Systems, Inc. [*NASDAQ symbol*] (SAG) ... OVON
Oiseau-Lyre [*Record label*] [*France*] ... OL
Oiselet [*Record label*] [*France*] ... DO
Oishiyama [*Japan*] [*Seismograph station code, US Geological Survey*] (SEIS) ... OIS
Oishiyama A [*Japan*] [*Seismograph station code, US Geological Survey*] (SEIS) ... OIA
Oishiyama B [*Japan*] [*Seismograph station code, US Geological Survey*] (SEIS) ... OIB
Oishiyama C [*Japan*] [*Seismograph station code, US Geological Survey*] (SEIS) ... OIC
Oita [*Japan*] [*Seismograph station code, US Geological Survey*] (SEIS) ... OIT
Oita [*Japan*] [*Airport symbol*] (OAG) ... OIT
Oita [*Japan ICAO location identifier*] (ICLI) ... RJFO
Oiwake [*Japan*] [*Seismograph station code, US Geological Survey Closed*] (SEIS) ... OIW
Ojai, CA [*FM radio station call letters*] (RBYB) ... KTND
Ojai Valley Museum, Ojia, CA [*Library symbol*] [*Library of Congress*] (LCLS) ... COjOVM
Ojibwa [*MARC language code Library of Congress*] (LCCP) ... oji
Ojika [*Japan ICAO location identifier*] (ICLI) ... RJDO
Okaba [*Indonesia*] [*Airport symbol*] (OAG) ... OKQ
Okaba [*Indonesia*] [*ICAO location identifier*] (ICLI) ... WAKO
Okada Airlines Ltd. [*Nigeria*] [*ICAO designator*] (FAAC) ... OKJ
Okahandja [*Namibia*] [*ICAO location identifier*] (ICLI) ... FAON
Okakarara [*Namibia*] [*ICAO location identifier*] (ICLI) ... FAOK
Okaloosa-Walton Junior College, Niceville, FL [*Library symbol Library of Congress*] (LCLS) ... FNiO
Okanagan College, Kelowna, BC, Canada [*Library symbol Library of Congress*] (LCLS) ... CaBKOC
Okanagan College, Kelowna, British Columbia [*Library symbol National Library of Canada*] (NLC) ... BKOC
Okanagan College Learning Resources Centre [*UTLAS symbol*] ... OKC
Okanagan Regional Library, Kelowna, BC, Canada [*Library symbol Library of Congress*] (LCLS) ... CaBKO
Okanagan Regional Library, Kelowna, British Columbia [*Library symbol National Library of Canada*] (NLC) ... BKO
Okanagan Skeena Group Ltd. [*Vancouver Stock Exchange symbol Toronto Stock Exchange symbol*] ... OKS
Okara [*Pakistan*] [*ICAO location identifier*] (ICLI) ... OPOK
Okaukuejo [*Namibia*] [*ICAO location identifier*] (ICLI) ... FAOO
Okay [*International telex abbreviation*] (WDMC) ... OK
Okay Except for [*with*] **the Corrections** [*Proofreading*] (WDMC) ... OK W/C
Okayama [*Japan*] [*Seismograph station code, US Geological Survey*] (SEIS) ... OKA
Okayama [*Japan*] [*Airport symbol*] (OAG) ... OKJ
Okayama [*Japan ICAO location identifier*] (ICLI) ... RJOB
Oke. Fisher Laws [*4th ed.*] [*1924*] [*A publication*] (DLA) ... Oke Fish L
Oke. Game Laws [*5th ed.*] [*1912*] [*A publication*] (DLA) ... Oke Game L
Oke. Magisterial Formulist [*19th ed.*] [*1978*] [*A publication*] (DLA) ... Oke Mag Form
Oke. Magisterial Synopsis [*14th ed.*] [*1893*] [*A publication*] (DLA) ... Oke Mag Syn
Oke. Turnpike Laws [*2nd ed.*] [*1861*] [*A publication*] (DLA) ... Oke Turn
Okeechobee, FL [*Location identifier FAA*] (FAAL) ... OBE
Okeechobee, FL [*AM radio station call letters*] ... WOKC
Okeechobee, FL [*FM radio station call letters*] ... WWFR
O'Keefe Ranch and Interior Heritage Society, Vernon, BC, Canada [*Library symbol*] [*Library of Congress*] (LCLS) ... CaBVOR
O'Keefe Ranch and Interior Heritage Society, Vernon, British Columbia [*Library symbol National Library of Canada*] (NLC) ... BVOR
O'Keefe's Order in Chancery [*Ireland*] [*A publication*] (DLA) ... O'Keefe Ord
Okehampton [*England*] ... OKEH
Okemah Public Library, Okemah, OK [*Library symbol*] [*Library of Congress*] (LCLS) ... OkOke
Okha [*Former USSR Seismograph station code, US Geological Survey*] (SEIS) ... OKH
Oki [*Japan ICAO location identifier*] (ICLI) ... RJNO
Oki Island [*Japan*] [*Airport symbol*] (OAG) ... OKI
Okierabu [*Japan ICAO location identifier*] (ICLI) ... RJKB
Okijuku [*Japan*] [*Seismograph station code, US Geological Survey Closed*] (SEIS) ... OKI
Okinawa [*Japan*] ... OK
Okinawa [*Japan*] [*Airport symbol*] (OAG) ... OKA
Okinawa (AD) ... Okin
Okinawa Interboard Committee [*Absorbed by Interboard Committee for Christian Work in Japan*] (EA) ... OIC
Okino Erabu [*Japan*] [*Airport symbol*] (OAG) ... OKE
Okla Gas & Elec,4% Pfd [*NYSE symbol*] (TTSB) ... OGEPrA
Oklahoma [*MARC geographic area code Library of Congress*] (LCCP) ... n-us-ok
Oklahoma (DLA) ... O
Oklahoma [*Postal code*] ... OK
Oklahoma (DLA) ... Okl
Oklahoma (AFM) ... OKLA
Oklahoma (ODBW) ... Okla
Oklahoma (AD) ... Okla
Oklahoma [*MARC country of publication code Library of Congress*] (LCCP) ... oku
Oklahoma Appellate Court Reporter [*A publication*] (DLA) ... Okla Ap Ct Rep
Oklahoma Baptist University ... OBU
Oklahoma Baptist University, Shawnee, OK [*OCLC symbol*] (OCLC) ... OKB
Oklahoma Baptist University, Shawnee, OK [*Library symbol Library of Congress*] (LCLS) ... OkShB
Oklahoma Bar Association. Journal [*A publication*] (DLA) ... OBJ
Oklahoma Children's Memorial Hospital, Library, Oklahoma City, OK [*OCLC symbol*] (OCLC) ... OUG
Oklahoma Christian College, Oklahoma City, OK [*Library symbol*] [*Library of Congress*] (LCLS) ... OkOkC
Oklahoma Citizen's Commission on Education (EDAC) ... OCCE
Oklahoma City [*Oklahoma*] [*ICAO location identifier*] (ICLI) ... KOEX
Oklahoma City [*Oklahoma*] [*Airport symbol*] (OAG) ... OKC
Oklahoma City [*Diocesan abbreviation*] [*Oklahoma*] (TOCD) ... OKL
Oklahoma City (AD) ... OklaC
Oklahoma City Air Defense Sector (SAA) ... OCADS
Oklahoma City Air Logistic Center [*Formerly, OCAMA*] (MCD) ... OCALC
Oklahoma City Air Materiel Area [*Later, OCALC*] ... OCAMA
Oklahoma City Air Materiel Area [*later, OCALC*] **Service Engineering Division** ... OCAMA-SED
Oklahoma City Community College, Learning Resources Center, Oklahoma City, OK [*Library symbol Library of Congress*] (LCLS) ... OkOkSO
Oklahoma City Community College, Oklahoma City, OK [*OCLC symbol*] (OCLC) ... OKJ
Oklahoma City Community Foundation (AD) ... OCCF
Oklahoma City Geological Survey, Inc., Oklahoma City, OK [*Library symbol*] [*Library of Congress*] (LCLS) ... OkOkCGS
Oklahoma City NORAD [*North American Air Defense*] **Sector** (SAA) ... OCNS
Oklahoma City, OK [*Location identifier FAA*] (FAAL) ... FRJ
Oklahoma City, OK [*Location identifier FAA*] (FAAL) ... JTZ
Oklahoma City, OK [*FM radio station call letters*] ... KATT
Oklahoma City, OK [*AM radio station call letters*] ... KBYE
Oklahoma City, OK [*FM radio station call letters*] ... KEBC
Oklahoma City, OK [*Television station call letters*] ... KETA
Oklahoma City, OK [*Television station call letters*] ... KFOR-TV
Oklahoma City, OK [*FM radio station call letters*] ... KJYO
Oklahoma City, OK [*FM radio station call letters*] ... KMGL
Oklahoma City, OK [*Television station call letters*] ... KMNZ
Oklahoma City, OK [*FM radio station call letters*] (RBYB) ... KNRX-FM
Oklahoma City, OK [*Television station call letters*] ... KOCB
Oklahoma City, OK [*FM radio station call letters*] ... KOCC
Oklahoma City, OK [*Television station call letters*] ... KOCO
Oklahoma City, OK [*Television station call letters*] ... KOKH
Oklahoma City, OK [*AM radio station call letters*] ... KOMA
Oklahoma City, OK [*FM radio station call letters*] ... KOMA-FM
Oklahoma City, OK [*AM radio station call letters*] ... KQCV
Oklahoma City, OK [*FM radio station call letters*] ... KRXO
Oklahoma City, OK [*Television station call letters*] ... KSBI
Oklahoma City, OK [*Television station call letters*] ... KTBO
Oklahoma City, OK [*Television station call letters*] ... KTLC
Oklahoma City, OK [*AM radio station call letters*] ... KTOK
Oklahoma City, OK [*FM radio station call letters*] (RBYB) ... KTST
Oklahoma City, OK [*AM radio station call letters*] ... KVSP
Oklahoma City, OK [*Television station call letters*] ... KWTV
Oklahoma City, OK [*AM radio station call letters*] ... KXXY
Oklahoma City, OK [*FM radio station call letters*] ... KXXY-FM
Oklahoma City, OK [*FM radio station call letters*] ... KYIS
Oklahoma City, OK [*Location identifier FAA*] (FAAL) ... OEX
Oklahoma City, OK [*Location identifier FAA*] (FAAL) ... PWA
Oklahoma City, OK [*Location identifier FAA*] (FAAL) ... RGR
Oklahoma City, OK [*Location identifier FAA*] (FAAL) ... TIK
Oklahoma City, OK [*AM radio station call letters*] ... WKY
Oklahoma City Public Library (AD) ... OCPL
Oklahoma City/Tinker Air Force Base [*Oklahoma*] [*ICAO location identifier*] (ICLI) ... KTIK
Oklahoma City University ... OCU
Oklahoma City University (GAGS) ... Okla City U
Oklahoma City University, Law Library, Oklahoma City, OK [*Library symbol Library of Congress*] (LCLS) ... OkOkU-L
Oklahoma City University, Law Library, Oklahoma City, OK [*OCLC symbol*] (OCLC) ... OKY
Oklahoma City University. Law Review [*A publication*] (DLA) ... Okl City UL Rev
Oklahoma City University. Law Review [*A publication*] (DLA) ... Okla CULR
Oklahoma City University, Oklahoma City, OK [*Library symbol Library of Congress*] (LCLS) ... OkOkU
Oklahoma City/Will Rogers World [*Oklahoma*] [*ICAO location identifier*] (ICLI) ... KOKC
Oklahoma City-Ada-Atoka Railway Co. [*AAR code*] ... OCAA
Oklahoma College for Women ... OCW
Oklahoma College of Liberal Arts, Chickasha, OK [*Library symbol Library of Congress*] (LCLS) ... OkChicW
Oklahoma College of Osteopathic Medicine and Surgery, Library, Tulsa, OK [*OCLC symbol*] (OCLC) ... OUH
Oklahoma County Libraries, Oklahoma City, OK [*Library symbol Library of Congress*] (LCLS) ... OkOk
Oklahoma Court of Appeals (DLA) ... Okl App
Oklahoma Crime Commission (AD) ... OCC
Oklahoma Criminal Justice Association (AD) ... OCJA
Oklahoma Criminal Reports [*A publication*] (DLA) ... O Cr
Oklahoma Criminal Reports [*A publication*] (DLA) ... Okl Cr
Oklahoma Criminal Reports [*A publication*] (DLA) ... Okl Cr R
Oklahoma Criminal Reports [*A publication*] (DLA) ... Okla
Oklahoma Criminal Reports [*A publication*] (DLA) ... Okla Cr
Oklahoma Criminal Reports [*A publication*] (DLA) ... Okla Crim
Oklahoma Department of Libraries, Oklahoma City, OK [*Library symbol Library of Congress*] (LCLS) ... Ok
Oklahoma Department of Libraries, Oklahoma City, OK [*OCLC symbol*] (OCLC) ... OKD
Oklahoma Department of Transportation ... ODT
Oklahoma Electronics (AD) ... Oktronics
Oklahoma Executive Jet Charter, Inc. [*FAA designator*] (FAAC) ... EFT

Oklahoma Federation of Republican Women ... OFRW
Oklahoma Gas & Elec [*NYSE symbol*] (TTSB) ... OGE
Oklahoma Gas & Electric Co. [*NYSE symbol*] (SPSG) ... OGE
Oklahoma Gas & Electric Co. [*Associated Press*] (SAG) ... OklaG
Oklahoma Gas & Electric Co. [*Associated Press*] (SAG) ... OklaGE
Oklahoma Gazette [*A publication*] (DLA) ... Okla Gaz
Oklahoma Historical Society, Oklahoma City, OK [*Library symbol Library of Congress*] (LCLS) ... OkHi
Oklahoma Independent College Foundation (AD) ... OICF
Oklahoma Industrial Commission Reports [*A publication*] (DLA) ... Okla ICR
Oklahoma Information Lines [*Oklahoma State Department of Libraries*] [*Oklahoma City*] [*Information service or system*] (IID) ... OIL
Oklahoma Inspection Bureau (AD) ... OIB
Oklahoma Law Journal [*A publication*] (DLA) ... Okla LJ
Oklahoma Lawyer [*A publication*] (DLA) ... Okla Lawy
Oklahoma Library Association (AD) ... OLA
Oklahoma Library for the Blind and Physically Handicapped, Oklahoma City, OK [*Library symbol Library of Congress*] (LCLS) ... OkOkB
Oklahoma Machismo [*Term coined by author Mark Singer*] ... OKIESMO
Oklahoma Medical Research Foundation [*University of Oklahoma*] [*Research center*] ... OMRF
Oklahoma Medical Research Institute ... OMRI
Oklahoma Military Academy ... OMA
Oklahoma On Line Users Group (NITA) ... OOLUG
Oklahoma Osteopathic Hospital, Library, Tulsa, OK [*OCLC symbol*] (OCLC) ... OUI
Oklahoma Register [*A publication*] (AAGC) ... Ok Reg
Oklahoma Reports [*A publication*] (DLA) ... Okl
Oklahoma Reports [*A publication*] (DLA) ... Oklahoma
Oklahoma Resources Integrated General Information Network System ... ORIGINS
Oklahoma Session Law Service (West) [*A publication*] (DLA) ... Okla Sess Law Serv
Oklahoma Session Laws [*A publication*] (DLA) ... Okla Sess Laws
Oklahoma State Bar Journal [*A publication*] (DLA) ... Okla SBJ
Oklahoma State University (GAGS) ... Okla St U
Oklahoma State University ... OSU
Oklahoma State University, Stillwater, OK [*Library symbol Library of Congress*] (LCLS) ... OkS
Oklahoma State University Technical Branch, Okmulgee, OK [*Library symbol*] [*Library of Congress*] (LCLS) ... OkS-TBO
Oklahoma State University Technical Institute Library, Oklahoma City, OK [*Library symbol Library of Congress*] (LCLS) ... OkS-T
Oklahoma State University, Technical Institute Library, Oklahoma City, OK [*OCLC symbol*] (OCLC) ... OUJ
Oklahoma Statutes [*A publication*] (DLA) ... Okla Stat
Oklahoma Statutes, Annotated [*A publication*] (DLA) ... Okl St Ann
Oklahoma Statutes Annotated [*A publication*] (DLA) ... OSA
Oklahoma Statutes, Annotated (West) [*A publication*] (DLA) ... Okla Stat Ann (West)
Oklahoma Statutes, Supplement [*A publication*] (DLA) ... OS Supp
Oklahoma Supreme Court Reports [*A publication*] (DLA) ... Okla
Oklahoma Teletype Interlibrary System [*Library network*] ... OTIS
Oklahoma Union List of Serials Project, Stillwater, OK [*OCLC symbol*] (OCLC) ... OUS
Oklahoma University ... OU
Oklahoma University Health Sciences Center ... OUHSC
Oklahoma University Research Institute ... OURI
Oklahoma Water Resources Research Institute [*Stillwater, OK*] [*Department of the Interior*] (GRD) ... OWRRI
Oklahoma-Arkansas-Kansas League [*Old baseball league*] ... OAK
Oklahomans for Indian Opportunity (AD) ... OIO
Oklee Public School, Oklee, MN [*Library symbol*] [*Library of Congress*] (LCLS) ... MnOkS
Okmulgee Northern Railway Co. [*AAR code*] ... OKN
Okmulgee, OK [*Television station call letters*] ... KGLB
Okmulgee, OK [*AM radio station call letters*] ... KOKL
Okmulgee, OK [*FM radio station call letters*] ... KTHK
Okmulgee, OK [*Location identifier FAA*] (FAAL) ... OKM
Okolona College (AD) ... OC
Okolona, KY [*FM radio station call letters*] ... WJIE
Okondja [*Gabon*] [*ICAO location identifier*] (ICLI) ... FOGQ
Okondja [*Gabon*] [*Airport symbol*] (OAG) ... OKN
Okonite (IAA) ... OK
Okotoks Municipal Library, Alberta [*Library symbol National Library of Canada*] (NLC) ... AOM
Okotoks Municipal Library, Okotoks, AB, Canada [*Library symbol Library of Congress*] (LCLS) ... CaAOM
Okoyo [*Congo*] [*Airport symbol*] (OAG) ... OKG
Okra Mosaic Virus [*Plant pathology*] ... OKMV
Oksapmin [*Papua New Guinea*] [*Airport symbol*] (OAG) ... OKP
Oksibil [*Indonesia*] [*ICAO location identifier*] (ICLI) ... WAJO
Oktal (IAA) ... OK
Oktibbeha County Library System, Starkville, MS [*Library symbol Library of Congress*] (LCLS) ... MsSt
Oktibbeha County Library System, Starkville, MS [*Library symbol*] [*Library of Congress*] (LCLS) ... MsStL
Oktober [*October*] [*GRM*] (AD) ... okt
Oktyab [*October*] [*Russian*] (AD) ... okt
Oktyabrsky [*Former USSR ICAO location identifier*] (ICLI) ... UTDO
Okumenische Vereinigung der Akademien und Tagungzentren in Europa [*Ecumenical Association of Laity Centres and Academies in Europe - EALCAE*] [*Bad Boll, Federal Republic of Germany*] (EAIO) ... OVATE
Okumenischer Jugendrat in Europa [*Ecumenical Youth Council in Europe - EYCE*] (EAIO) ... OJE
Okushiri [*Japan*] [*Airport symbol*] (OAG) ... OIR
Okushiri [*Japan ICAO location identifier*] (ICLI) ... RJEO
Okwa [*Botswana*] [*ICAO location identifier*] (ICLI) ... FBOK
Ola District Library, Ola, ID [*Library symbol*] [*Library of Congress*] (LCLS) ... IdOl
Ola Kala [*All is Fine*] [*Greek*] (AD) ... ok
Ola Kala [*All Is Well*] [*Greek*] ... OK
Olafsfjordur [*Iceland*] [*Airport symbol*] (OAG) ... OFJ
Olafsvik [*Iceland*] [*Airport symbol*] (OAG) ... OLI
Olana State Historic Site, Hudson, NY [*Library symbol*] [*Library of Congress*] (LCLS) ... NhudO
Olanchito [*Honduras*] [*ICAO location identifier*] (ICLI) ... MHOA
Olanda [*Sweden ICAO location identifier*] (ICLI) ... ESMZ
Olathe [*Kansas*] [*Airport symbol*] (OAG) ... JCI
Olathe Community Hospital, Olathe, KS [*Library symbol Library of Congress*] (LCLS) ... KOIH
Olathe, KS [*Location identifier FAA*] (FAAL) ... IXD
Olathe, KS [*FM radio station call letters*] ... KCCV-FM
Olathe, KS [*Location identifier FAA*] (FAAL) ... OJC
Olathe Public Library, Olathe, KS [*Library symbol Library of Congress*] (LCLS) ... KOI
Olav Trygvason (AD) ... Olav Tryg
Olavarria [*Argentina ICAO location identifier*] (ICLI) ... SAZF
Olbia [*Italy*] [*Airport symbol*] (OAG) ... OLB
Olbia/Costa Smeralda [*Italy ICAO location identifier*] (ICLI) ... LIEO
Olcott's United States District Court Reports [*A publication*] (DLA) ... Bett's Dec
Olcott's United States District Court Reports, Admiralty [*A publication*] (DLA) ... Olc
Olcott's United States District Court Reports, Admiralty [*A publication*] (DLA) ... Olc Adm
Olcott's United States District Court Reports, Admiralty [*A publication*] (DLA) ... Olcott
Olcott's United States District Court Reports, Admiralty [*A publication*] (DLA) ... Olcott Adm (F)
Olcott's United States District Court Reports, Admiralty [*A publication*] (DLA) ... Olcott's Adm
Old ... O
Old Abandoned Well (WDAA) ... OAW
Old Account [*Banking*] ... OA
Old Age ... OA
Old Age and Survivors' Insurance (IAA) ... OAS
Old Age Survivors Health and Disability Program [*Health insurance*] (GHCT) ... OASHDI
Old Aircraft Carrier [*Navy symbol*] ... OCV
Old Akkadian (BJA) ... OAkk
Old Alliance Society of French Polishers [*A union*] [*British*] ... OASFP
Old America Stores [*NASDAQ symbol*] (TTSB) ... OASI
Old America Stores, Inc. [*Associated Press*] (SAG) ... OldAmer
Old Americia Stores, Inc. [*NASDAQ symbol*] (SAG) ... OASI
Old Antarctic Explorer ... OAE
Old Assyrian (BJA) ... OA
Old Assyrian (BJA) ... OAss
Old Babylonian (BJA) ... OB
Old Babylonian Grammatical Texts [*A publication*] (BJA) ... OBGT
Old Babylonian Inscriptions [*A publication*] (BJA) ... OBI
Old Babylonian Sumerian (BJA) ... OBS
Old Babylonian Version of Lu [*A publication*] (BJA) ... OBLu
[*The*] **Old Bailey** [*London court*] ... OB
Old Bailey Chronicle [*A publication*] (DLA) ... Old Bailey Chr
Old Bailey's Sessions Papers [*A publication*] (DLA) ... OBS
Old Bailey's Sessions Papers [*Legal term British*] ... OBSP
Old Bailey's Sessions Papers [*A publication*] (DLA) ... Sess Pap OB
Old Battleship [*Navy*] ... OBB
Old Benloe's Reports, English Common Pleas [*1486-1580*] [*A publication*] (DLA) ... O Ben
Old Benloe's Reports, English Common Pleas [*1486-1580*] [*A publication*] (DLA) ... O Benl
Old Berkeley Hunt [*British*] ... OBH
Old Berkshire Hounds [*British*] ... OBH
Old Bethpage Elementary School, Plainview, NY [*Library symbol Library of Congress*] (LCLS) ... NPIBE
Old Bonded [*Whiskey*] (ROG) ... OB
Old Books of Entries [*A publication*] (DLA) ... Lib Ent
Old Boy [*Communications operators' colloquialism*] ... OB
Old Boys' Corps [*Military British*] ... OBC
Old Boys Network Turtle Club (EA) ... OBNTC
Old Breton [*Language, etc.*] ... OBRET
Old British [*Language, etc.*] ... OBRIT
Old Buffer over Forty [*Elderly recruits*] [*World War I*] [*British*] ... OBOF
Old Buildings [*British Admiralty*] ... OB
Old Bulgarian (AD) ... O Bul
Old Bulgarian [*Language*] (BARN) ... OBulg
Old Byblian (BJA) ... OBy
Old Canada Investment Corp. Ltd. [*Toronto Stock Exchange symbol*] ... OCI
Old Cars Weekly [*A publication*] ... OCW
Old Carthusian ... OC
Old Catalan (AD) ... O Cat
Old Category Code (NITA) ... OC
Old Catholic ... OC
Old Celtic (AD) ... O Celt
Old Charter [*Business and trade*] ... O/C
Old Cheltonian [*British*] (ROG) ... OC
Old Church Slavonic [*Language, etc.*] ... OCS
Old Code [*Louisiana Code of 1808*] [*A publication*] (DLA) ... OC
Old Colony Historical Society (AD) ... OCHS
Old Colony Historical Society, Taunton, MA [*Library symbol Library of Congress*] (LCLS) ... MTaHi
Old Comrades Association [*British military*] (DMA) ... OCA

Old Cornish (AD) ... O Corn
Old Cornish [*Language, etc.*] ... OCO
Old Corrugated Container [*Paper recycling*] ... OCC
Old Country Elementary School, Hicksville, NY [*Library symbol Library of Congress*] (LCLS) ... NHickCE
Old Court House Museum, Guysborough, Nova Scotia [*Library symbol National Library of Canada*] (NLC) ... NSGOC
Old Court House Museum, Guysborough, NS, Canada [*Library symbol*] [*Library of Congress*] (LCLS) ... CaNSGuOC
Old Court House Museum Library, Vicksburg, MS [*Library symbol Library of Congress*] (LCLS) ... MsVO
Old Crop ... OC
Old Crow [*Canada*] [*Airport symbol*] (OAG) ... YOC
Old Crow, YT [*ICAO location identifier*] (ICLI) ... CYOC
Old Danish (AD) ... ODa
Old Danish [*Language, etc.*] ... ODAN
Old Dartmouth Historical Society, Dartmouth, MA [*Library symbol Library of Congress*] (LCLS) ... MDarHi
Old Dartmouth Historical Society, New Bedford Whaling Museum, New Bedford, MA [*Library symbol Library of Congress*] (LCLS) ... MNBedfHi
Old Destroyer [*Navy symbol*] ... ODD
Old Dominion College Technical Institute (AD) ... ODCTI
Old Dominion Foundation (AD) ... ODF
Old Dominion Freight Line [*NASDAQ symbol*] (TTSB) ... ODFL
Old Dominion Freight Lines, Inc. [*NASDAQ symbol*] (SPSG) ... ODFL
Old Dominion Freight Lines, Inc. [*Associated Press*] (SAG) ... OldDom
Old Dominion Speedway [*Auto racing*] ... ODS
Old Dominion University [*Virginia*] ... ODU
Old Dominion University (GAGS) ... Old Dom U
Old Dominion University, Norfolk, VA [*Library symbol Library of Congress*] (LCLS) ... ViNO
Old Dominion University, Norfolk, VA [*OCLC symbol*] (OCLC) ... VOD
Old Dominion University Research Foundation [*Old Dominion University*] [*Research center*] (RCD) ... ODURF
Old Dutch [*Language, etc.*] ... OD
Old Dutch [*Language, etc.*] ... ODU
Old East Scandinavian [*Language, etc.*] ... OESCAND
Old English [*Language, etc.*] [*i.e., before 1150 or 1200*] ... OE
Old English [*Typeface*] (WDMC) ... OE
Old English Game Club of America (EA) ... OEGCA
Old English Sheepdog Club of America (EA) ... OESCA
Old Established Forces [*Military*] (CINC) ... OLDFOS
Old Established Forces (AD) ... Oldfos
Old Etonian [*British*] ... OE
Old Executive Office Building [*Washington, DC*] ... OEOB
Old Face [*Typography*] ... OF
Old Face (AD) ... of
Old Farms Elementary School, Commack, NY [*Library symbol*] [*Library of Congress*] (LCLS) ... NCoOE
Old Fashioned (AD) ... old-fash
Old Field [*Botany*] ... OF
Old Fired Copper [*Initialism once used as brand name for bourbon*] ... OFC
Old Flemish [*Language, etc.*] (BARN) ... OFlem
Old Folks Association (AD) ... OFA
Old Fort, NC [*FM radio station call letters*] ... WDLF
Old Fort Niagara Association, Youngstown, NY [*Library symbol Library of Congress*] (LCLS) ... NYoOF
Old Frankish (AD) ... O Frk
Old Free Order of Chaldeans [*Freemasonry*] (ROG) ... OFOC
Old French (AD) ... O Fr
Old French [*Language, etc.*] ... OF
Old French [*Language, etc.*] ... OFR
Old French Canadian [*Initialism used in Schenley brand of Canadian whisky*] ... OFC
Old Frisian [*Language, etc.*] ... OFRIS
Old Frisian (AD) ... OFris
Old Gaelic (AD) ... O Gael
Old Gaelic (AD) ... OG
Old Garden Rose [*Pre-1870*] [*Horticulture*] ... OGR
Old German [*Language, etc.*] ... OG
Old Girl [*A wife*] [*Slang*] ... OG
Old Girl (AD) ... og
Old Granulomatus Disease (DAVI) ... OGD
Old Greasybeard: Tales from the Cumberland Gap [*A publication*] ... OG
Old Harbor [*Alaska*] [*Airport symbol*] (OAG) ... OLH
Old Harbor, AK [*Location identifier FAA*] (FAAL) ... OLH
Old Hickory Dam [*TVA*] ... OHD
Old High German [*Language, etc.*] ... OHG
Old Highland Blend [*Whisky*] (ROG) ... OBH
Old Icelandic [*Language, etc.*] (ROG) ... O ICE
Old Icelandic [*Language*] (BARN) ... OI
Old Icelandic [*Language*] (BARN) ... OIcel
Old Input/Output Program Status Word Location [*Computer science*] (MHDB) ... OIOPSWL
Old Irish [*Language, etc.*] ... OIR
Old Irish (AD) ... OIr
Old Italian (AD) ... O It
Old Italian [*Language, etc.*] (ROG) ... O IT
Old Italian (AD) ... OIt
Old Jamaica Rum (AD) ... oJr
Old Jamaica Rum (ROG) ... OJR
Old Kent Financial Corp. [*NASDAQ symbol*] (NQ) ... OKEN
Old Kent Financial Corp. [*Associated Press*] (SAG) ... OldKent
Old Kent Finl [*NASDAQ symbol*] (TTSB) ... OKEN
Old Kinderhook (IIA) ... OK
Old Kingdom [*Egyptology*] (ROG) ... OK
Old Kings Courthouse Heritage Museum, Kentville, Nova Scotia [*Library symbol National Library of Canada*] (NLC) ... NSKOK
Old Kings Courthouse Heritage Museum, Kentville, NS, Canada [*Library symbol*] [*Library of Congress*] (LCLS) ... CaNSKOK
Old King's Scholars Association [*Canterbury, England*] ... OKS
Old Latin [*Language, etc.*] ... OL
Old Latin Version (BJA) ... La
Old Lesbians Organizing for Change [*An association*] (EA) ... OLOC
Old Light Cruiser [*Navy symbol*] ... OCL
Old Lighthouse Museum, Michigan City, IN [*Library symbol Library of Congress*] (LCLS) ... InMicLM
[*The*] **Old Log Church Museum, Whitehorse, Yukon** [*Library symbol National Library of Canada*] (NLC) ... YWOM
Old Low Franconian [*Language, etc.*] ... OLF
Old Low German [*Language, etc.*] ... OLG
Old Lyme Holding Corp. [*NASDAQ symbol*] (SAG) ... OLHC
Old Maid's Day [*June 4*] (AD) ... Old Maid's
Old Man (AD) ... om
Old Man [*Communications operators' colloquialism*] ... OM
[*The*] **Old Man** ... TOM
Old Man, AK [*Location identifier FAA*] (FAAL) ... OLN
Old Man's Out [*Facetious translation of Omo, a brand of detergent*] [*British*] ... OMO
Old Manse Library, Newcastle, NB, Canada [*Library symbol Library of Congress*] (LCLS) ... CaNBN
Old Manse Library, Newcastle, New Brunswick [*Library symbol National Library of Canada*] (NLC) ... NBN
Old Master File ... OMF
Old Measurement ... OM
Old Measurement (AD) ... om
Old Merchant Taylors [*School*] [*British*] (ROG) ... OMT
Old Mill Road Elementary School, North Merrick, NY [*Library symbol*] [*Library of Congress*] (LCLS) ... NnmOE
Old Mine Lamp Collectors Society of America (EA) ... OMLCSA
Old Mission Beach Athletic Club (AD) ... OMBAC
Old Mission Santa Barbara Seminary, Santa Barbara, CA [*Library symbol Library of Congress*] (LCLS) ... CStbOM
Old Myocardial Infarction [*Medicine*] ... OMI
Old National Bancorp [*NASDAQ symbol*] (NQ) ... OLDB
Old National Bancorp Industries [*Associated Press*] (SAG) ... OldNB
Old Natl Bancorp(Ind) [*NASDAQ symbol*] (TTSB) ... OLDB
Old Natura Brevium [*A publication*] (DLA) ... Old Nat Brev
Old Natura Brevium [*A publication*] (DLA) ... ONB
Old Natura Brevium [*A publication*] (ILCA) ... Vet N Br
Old Natura Brevium [*A publication*] (DLA) ... Vet Na B
Old Newspaper [*Recycling*] ... ONP
Old Norman French [*Language, etc.*] ... ONF
Old Norse [*Language, etc.*] ... ON
Old Northern French [*Language, etc.*] ... ONF
Old Northern French [*Language, etc.*] ... ONFR
Old Old Timers Club (EA) ... OOTC
Old Orkney [*Whisky*] (ROG) ... OO
Old Parliamentary Hand [*Political*] [*British*] ... OPH
Old Particular [*Marsala*] ... OP
Old [*Previously seen*] **Patient** ... OP
Old Pattern [*British military*] (DMA) ... OP
Old Perlican Public Library, Newfoundland [*Library symbol National Library of Canada*] (NLC) ... NFOP
Old Perlican Public Library, Old Perlican, NF, Canada [*Library symbol Library of Congress*] (LCLS) ... CaNfOP
Old Persian [*Language, etc.*] ... OP
Old Persian [*Language*] (BARN) ... OPer
Old Persian [*Language*] (BARN) ... OPers
Old Persian Grammar Texts Lexicon [*A publication*] (BJA) ... OPersLex
Old Phoenician (BJA) ... OPh
Old Price [*Riots*] [*Occurred for 67 nights, beginning December 30, 1808, opening night of rebuilt Covent Garden Theatre, London, because of new and higher prices*] ... OP
Old Product Line (IAA) ... OPL
Old Program Status Word Location ... OPSWL
Old Provencal [*Language*] (BARN) ... OProv
Old Prussian [*Language, etc.*] ... OPR
Old Prussian [*Language*] (BARN) ... OPruss
Old Radio Program Collectors Club (EA) ... ORPC
Old Red Sandstone ... ORS
Old Repertory (AD) ... old rep
Old Republic Int 8.75% Pfd'H' [*NYSE symbol*] (TTSB) ... ORIPrH
Old Republic International Corp. [*Associated Press*] (SAG) ... OldRep
Old Republic International Corp. [*Associated Press*] (SAG) ... OldRp
Old Republic International Corp. [*NYSE symbol*] (SPSG) ... ORI
Old Republic Intl. [*NYSE symbol*] (TTSB) ... ORI
Old Roman (ADA) ... OR
Old Russian [*Language*] (BARN) ... ORuss
Old Sarum [*British ICAO location identifier*] (ICLI) ... EGLS
Old Saxon [*Language, etc.*] ... OS
Old Saybrook, CT [*AM radio station call letters*] ... WLIS
Old Scandinavian [*Language, etc.*] ... OSCAND
Old School ... OS
Old Scientific Technical Aerospace Reports Extended ... OSTARE
Old Second Bancorp [*NASDAQ symbol*] (TTSB) ... OSBC
Old Second Bancorp, Inc. [*Associated Press*] (SAG) ... OldSecBc
Old Second Bancorp, Inc. [*NASDAQ symbol*] (SAG) ... OSBC
Old Select Cases [*Oudh, India*] [*A publication*] (DLA) ... Old SC
Old Senate Office Building [*Also, RSOB*] [*Washington, DC*] (DLA) ... OSOB

Old Series ... OS
Old Side ... OS
Old Slave Mart Museum, Charleston, SC [*Library symbol Library of Congress*] (LCLS) ... ScCSM
Old [*Church*] **Slavic** [*Language*] (BARN) ... O Slav
Old [*Church*] **Slavonic** [*Language, etc.*] ... OSL
Old Sleepy Eye Collectors' Club of America (EA) ... OSECCA
Old Songs Library, Kenosha, WI [*Library symbol Library of Congress*] (LCLS) ... WKenOS
Old South Arabic (BJA) ... OSA
Old Spaghetti Warehouse, Inc. (MHDW) ... OSWI
Old Standard [*Currency*] (ROG) ... OS
Old Sturbridge Village Library, Sturbridge, MA [*Library symbol Library of Congress*] (LCLS) ... MStuO
Old Style [*Printing*] (NTCM) ... OS
Old Style [*Calendar, previous to 1752*] ... OS
Old Style Antique [*British*] ... OSA
Old Style Latin (ADA) ... OSL
Old Style Roman (ADA) ... OSR
Old Submarine [*Navy symbol*] ... OSS
Old Swedish [*Language, etc.*] ... OSW
Old Term ... OT
Old Terminology ... OT
Old Testament (AD) ... Old Test
Old Testament [*of the Bible*] ... OT
Old Testament Abstracts [*A publication*] (BJA) ... OTA
[*The*] **Old Testament and Modern Study** [*A publication*] (BJA) ... OTMS
Old Testament Commentary [*A publication*] (BJA) ... OTC
[*The*] **Old Testament in the Light of the Ancient East** [*A publication*] (BJA) ... OTAE
[*The*] **Old Testament Library** [*A publication*] (BJA) ... OTL
Old Testament Reading Guide [*Collegeville, MN*] [*A publication*] (BJA) ... OTRG
Old Teutonic [*Language, etc.*] ... O TEUT
Old Time Country Music Club of Canada (EA) ... OTCMCC
Old Time Radio ... OTR
Old Time Western Film Club (EA) ... OTWFC
Old Timer [*Communications operators' colloquialism*] ... OT
Old Timer Assay Commissioners Society [*Defunct*] (EA) ... OTACS
Old Timers' Club (EA) ... OTC
Old Tired Broads ... OTB
Old Tom [*British slang term for gin*] (ROG) ... OT
Old Top [*Communications operators' colloquialism*] ... OT
Old Town, ME [*Location identifier FAA*] (FAAL) ... OLD
Old Town, ME [*FM radio station call letters*] ... WBZN
Old [*or Original*] **Tuberculin** [*Also, TO*] [*Medicine*] ... OT
Old Water Colour Society's Club (EA) ... OWCSC
Old Wellingtonian [*Wellington College*] [*British*] ... OW
Old Welsh [*Language, etc.*] ... OW
Old West Regional Commission [*Department of Commerce*] ... OWRC
Old West Saxon [*Language, etc.*] (ROG) ... OWS
Old West Scandinavian [*Language, etc.*] ... OWSC
Old Westbury School of the Holy Child, Upper School, Old Westbury, NY [*Library symbol*] [*Library of Congress*] (LCLS) ... NOwHC-U
Old Woman [*A wife*] [*Slang*] ... OW
Old World Archaeological Study Unit (EA) ... OWASU
Old Yellow Enzyme [*Biochemistry*] ... OYE
Old York Historical Society, York, ME [*Library symbol*] [*Library of Congress*] (LCLS) ... MeYoO
Old-Age and Survivors Insurance [*Program*] [*Social Security Administration*] ... OASI
Old-Age Assistance [*Superseded by SSI*] [*HEW*] ... OAA
Old-Age Benefits ... OAB
Old-Age Insurance Benefit (MHDB) ... OAIB
Old-Age Pension [*or Pensioner*] ... OAP
Old-Age Security ... OAS
Old-Age, Survivors, and Disability Insurance [*Program*] [*Social Security Administration*] ... OASDI
Old-Age, Survivors, Disability, and Health Insurance [*Program*] [*Social Security Administration*] ... OASDHI
Old-Age-Pensioner CBer [*Experienced citizens band radio operator*] ... OAPCB
Oldenburg [*Germany ICAO location identifier*] (ICLI) ... EDNO
Oldenburg [*Germany ICAO location identifier*] (ICLI) ... EDZG
Oldenburg/Hatten [*Germany ICAO location identifier*] (ICLI) ... EDWH
Older Adult Offender Project [*of the Alston Wilkes Society*] (EA) ... OAOP
Older American Community Service Employment Act [*1975*] ... OACSEA
Older Americans Act [*1965*] ... OAA
Older Americans Advocacy Commission [*HEW*] ... OAAC
Older Americans Almanac [*A publication*] ... OAA
Older Americans Consumer Cooperative [*Washington, DC*] (EA) ... OACC
Older Americans Corps [*Proposed*] ... OAK
Older Americans Information Directory [*A publication*] ... OAID
Older Americans' Legal Action Center (DICI) ... OALAC
Older Americans Volunteer Program [*ACTION*] ... OAVP
Older Metamorphic Group [*Geology*] ... OMG
Older People with Active Lifestyles [*Lifestyle classification*] ... OPAL
Older People with Active Lifestyles [*Lifestyle classification*] ... OPALs
Older People with an Active Lifestyle [*Lifestyle classification*] ... Opals
Older Woman / Younger Man (WDAA) ... OW/YM
Older Women's League (EA) ... OWL
Older Women's League Educational Fund (EA) ... OWLEF
Older Women's Liberation [*Feminist group*] [*Defunct*] ... OWL
Older Worker ... OW
Older Worker Specialists Group ... OWSG
Older Workers Benefit Protection Act of 1990 (WYGK) ... OWBPA
Older-Worker Service Unit [*US Employment Service*] [*Department of Labor*] ... OSU
Oldest and Wisest [*Nickname for President Ronald Reagan*] ... O & W
Oldest English Texts ... OET
Oldest Finest Canadian [*Whiskey*] (IIA) ... OFC
Oldfield Middle School, Harborfield, NY [*Library symbol*] [*Library of Congress*] (LCLS) ... NHaOM
Oldham [*Postcode*] (ODBW) ... OL
Oldham [*City in England*] ... OLDHM
Oldham and White's Digest of Laws [*Texas*] [*A publication*] (DLA) ... O & W Dig
Old-House Journal [*A publication*] ... OHJ
Oldie but Goodie [*Music*] ... OBG
Oldnall's Sessions Practice [*A publication*] (DLA) ... Oldn Pr
Oldradus da Ponte de Laude [*Deceased, 1335*] [*Authority cited in pre-1607 legal work*] (DSA) ... Ol
Oldradus da Ponte de Laude [*Deceased, 1335*] [*Authority cited in pre-1607 legal work*] (DSA) ... Old
Oldradus da Ponte de Laude [*Deceased, 1335*] [*Authority cited in pre-1607 legal work*] (DSA) ... Oldr
Oldradus da Ponte de Laude [*Deceased, 1335*] [*Authority cited in pre-1607 legal work*] (DSA) ... Oldra
Oldradus da Ponte de Laude [*Deceased, 1335*] [*Authority cited in pre-1607 legal work*] (DSA) ... Oldra de Lau
Oldright's Nova Scotia Reports [*A publication*] (DLA) ... NSR Old
Oldright's Nova Scotia Reports [*A publication*] (DLA) ... Old
Oldright's Nova Scotia Reports [*A publication*] (DLA) ... Oldr
Oldright's Nova Scotia Reports [*A publication*] (DLA) ... Oldr NS
Olds Agricultural College, Olds, AB, Canada [*Library symbol Library of Congress*] (LCLS) ... CaAOAC
Olds College, Alberta [*Library symbol National Library of Canada*] (NLC) ... AOAC
Olds Public Library, Alberta [*Library symbol National Library of Canada*] (NLC) ... AOL
Oldsmobile [*Automotive engineering*] ... OLDS
Oldsmobile (AD) ... Olds
Oldsmobile Club of America (EA) ... OCA
Oldsmobile Motor Division [*General Motors Corp.*] ... OMD
Oldsmobile Performance Chapter (EA) ... OPC
Oldtime Radio Collectors and Traders Society (EA) ... ORCATS
Oldtime Radio-Show Collector's Association (EA) ... ORCA
Olduvai Hominid [*Paleoanthropology*] ... OH
OLE Database [*Computer science*] ... OLE DB
OLE [*Object Linking and Embedding*] **for Process Control** (ACII) ... OPC
Olean [*New York*] [*Airport symbol*] (AD) ... OLE
Olean General Hospital, Olean, NY [*Library symbol Library of Congress*] (LCLS) ... NOIH
Olean, NY [*Location identifier FAA*] (FAAL) ... LYS
Olean, NY [*Location identifier FAA*] (FAAL) ... OLE
Olean, NY [*AM radio station call letters*] ... WHDL
Olean, NY [*AM radio station call letters*] ... WMNS
Olean, NY [*FM radio station call letters*] ... WMXO
Olean, NY [*FM radio station call letters*] ... WOLN
Olean, NY [*FM radio station call letters*] ... WPIG
Olean Public Library, Olean, NY [*Library symbol Library of Congress*] (LCLS) ... NOI
O'Leary Brothers Fan Club (EA) ... OBFC
Oleck's Modern Corporation Law [*A publication*] (DLA) ... Oleck Corporations
Olefin Strain Energy [*Organic chemistry*] ... OSE
Oleic Acid [*Medicine*] (DMAA) ... OA
Oleic Acid, Albumin, Dextrose, Catalase ... OADC
Olema [*California*] [*Seismograph station code, US Geological Survey*] (SEIS) ... OLC
Oleomargarine [*Dietetics*] (DAVI) ... oleo
Oleoresin (AD) ... ol res
Oleoresin [*Also, OR*] [*Pharmacy*] ... Ol Res
Oleoresin [*Also, Ol Res*] [*Pharmacy*] ... OR
Oleoresin Capsicum (BARN) ... OC
Oleoresins (AD) ... oleo
Oleoyl Methyl Taurate [*Organic chemistry*] ... OMT
Oleoyl(acetyl)glycerol [*Organic chemistry*] ... OAG
Olericulture ... OLER
Olericulture (AD) ... olericult
Oleum [*Oil*] [*Latin*] (AD) ... ol
Oleum [*Oil*] [*Pharmacy*] ... OL
Oleum Lini sine Igne [*Cold-Drawn Linseed Oil*] [*Pharmacy*] (ROG) ... OL LINI SI
Oleum Olivae [*Olive Oil*] [*Pharmacy*] ... ol oliv
Oleum Olivae [*Olive Oil*] [*Pharmacy*] (ROG) ... OLIV
Oleum Olivae Optimum [*Best Olive Oil*] [*Pharmacy*] (ROG) ... OOO
Oleum Ricini [*Castor Oil*] [*Pharmacy*] (ROG) ... OL RIC
Olfactory [*Medicine*] (DAVI) ... olf
Olfactory G Protein [*Physiology*] ... Golf
Olfactory Marker Protein [*Biochemistry*] ... OMP
Olfactory Nerve [*Neuroanatomy*] ... ON
Olfactory Peduncle [*Medicine*] (DMAA) ... OP
Olfactory Receptor [*Biochemistry*] ... OR
Olfactory Receptor Neuron [*Biochemistry*] ... ORN
Olfactory Reference Syndrome [*Medicine*] (DMAA) ... ORS
Olfactory Research Fund ... ORF
Olfactory Threshold ... OT
Olfactory Tubercle [*Neuroanatomy*] ... OT
Olga Bay [*Alaska*] [*Airport symbol*] (OAG) ... KOY
Olicom A/S [*NASDAQ symbol*] (TTSB) ... OLCMF
Olicom AS [*NASDAQ symbol*] (SAG) ... OLCM
Olicom AS [*Associated Press*] (SAG) ... Olicom
Olifants River Bridge [*South Africa*] [*ICAO location identifier*] (ICLI) ... FAOR
Oligoblastic Leukemia [*Oncology*] ... OL
Oligocene (AD) ... Olig

Oligoclonal Band [*Analytical biochemistry*] ... OB
Oligoclonal Immunoglobulin Bands [*Clinical chemistry*] ... OIB
Oligodendrocyte [*Also, OLG*] [*Cytology*] ... ODC
Oligodendrocyte [*Also, ODC*] [*Cytology*] ... OLG
Oligodendrocytes and Type 2 Astrocytes [*Neurology*] ... O-2A
Oligodeoxynucleotide [*Biochemistry*] ... ODN
Oligomer Restriction [*Genetics*] ... OR
Oligo-N-methylmorpholinopropylene Oxide [*Pharmacology*] ... OMP
Oligonucleotide [*Chemistry*] ... ON
Oligonucleotide Ligation Assay [*Analytical biochemistry*] ... OLA
Oligonucleotide Purification Cartridge [*Chromatography*] ... OPC
Oligophranic Detail [*Psychology*] ... Do
Oliktok, AK [*Location identifier FAA*] (FAAL) ... OLI
Olimpiadas [*Ministerio de Cultura*] [*Spain Information service or system*] (CRD) ... OLIM
Olimpo [*Paraguay*] [*ICAO location identifier*] (ICLI) ... SGOL
Olin Corp. [*Associated Press*] (SAG) ... Olin
Olin Corp. [*NYSE symbol*] (TTSB) ... OLN
Olin Corp., D. B. Beene Technical Information Center, Charleston, TN [*Library symbol Library of Congress*] (LCLS) ... TChO
Olin Corp., Ecusta-Film Technical Library, Pisgah Forest, NC [*Library symbol Library of Congress*] (LCLS) ... NcPfO
Olin Corp., New Haven, CT [*Library symbol Library of Congress*] (LCLS) ... CtNhO
Oliphant Washington Service [*Information service or system*] (IID) ... OWS
Oliphant's Law of Horses [*6th ed.*] [*1908*] [*A publication*] (DLA) ... Ol Horse
Oliphant's Law of Horses [*6th ed.*] [*1908*] [*A publication*] (DLA) ... Oliph Hor
Olivaceous (AD) ... olv
Olivary [*Neurology*] ... OL
Olive [*Philately*] ... ol
Olive [*Political party*] (AD) ... Ol
Olive (AD) ... olv
Olive Advisory Board [*Defunct*] (EA) ... OAB
Olive [*Geo S.*] **& Co.** [*Indianapolis, IN*] (TSSD) ... GSO
Olive Branch, MS [*Location identifier FAA*] (FAAL) ... OLV
Olive Branch, MS [*FM radio station call letters*] ... WRXQ
Olive Brown (AD) ... OlBr
Olive Drab ... OD
Olive Drab [*Color often used for military clothing and equipment*] ... OD
Olive Free Library Association, West Shokan, NY [*Library symbol Library of Congress*] (LCLS) ... NWes
Olive Green [*Army*] (ADDR) ... OG
Olive Green (AD) ... OlG
Olive Hill, TN [*FM radio station call letters*] ... WDNX
Olive Latent Ringspot Virus [*Plant pathology*] ... OLRV
Olive Oil (AD) ... ol ol
Olive Oil Association (EA) ... OOA
Olive Oil Association of America [*Later, OOA*] (EA) ... OOAA
Olive Oil Group [*Later, OOA*] (EA) ... OOG
Olivebridge, NY [*FM radio station call letters*] (RBYB) ... WFSO-FM
Olive-Drab (AD) ... od
Olive-Harvey College Library, City Colleges of Chicago, Chicago, IL [*Library symbol*] [*Library of Congress*] (LCLS) ... ICOH
Oliver (AD) ... Oli
Oliver, Beavan, and Lefroy's English Railway and Canal Cases [*A publication*] (DLA) ... Oliv B & L
Oliver Gold Corp. [*Vancouver Stock Exchange symbol*] ... OGO
Oliver Heritage Society Museum and Archives, British Columbia [*Library symbol National Library of Canada*] (NLC) ... BOH
Oliver Organization Description Questionnaire [*Test*] ... OODQ
Oliver, PA [*FM radio station call letters*] ... WASP
Oliver Resources [*Vancouver Stock Exchange symbol*] ... OLV
Oliver Springs, TN [*FM radio station call letters*] ... WXVO
Oliver Township Public Library, Murillo, Ontario [*Library symbol National Library of Canada*] (BIB) ... OMOL
Oliver Wendell Holmes Association ... OWHA
Olivera (AD) ... Olive
Oliver-Osoyoos, BC [*Television station call letters*] ... CKKM
Oliver's Conveyancing [*A publication*] (DLA) ... Ol Conv
Oliver's Conveyancing [*A publication*] (DLA) ... Oliv Conv
Oliver's Precedents [*A publication*] (DLA) ... Ol Prec
Oliver's Precedents [*A publication*] (DLA) ... Oliv Prec
Olivet College (AD) ... OC
Olivet College, Olivet, MI [*OCLC symbol*] (OCLC) ... EXO
Olivet College, Olivet, MI [*Library symbol Library of Congress*] (LCLS) ... MiOC
Olivet, MI [*FM radio station call letters*] ... WOCR
Olivet Nazarene College [*Kankakee, IL*] ... ONC
Olivet Nazarene College, Kankakee, IL [*Library symbol Library of Congress*] (LCLS) ... IKON
Olivet Nazarene University (GAGS) ... Olivet Naz U
Olivetan Benedictine Sisters (TOCD) ... OSB
Olivetti Personal Computers ... OPC
Olivetti Research Laboratory Ltd. [*British*] (IRUK) ... ORL
Olivia Elementary School, Olivia, MN [*Library symbol*] [*Library of Congress*] (LCLS) ... MnOlES
Olivia, MN [*FM radio station call letters*] ... KOLV
Olivia Newton-John [*Singer*] ... ONJ
Olivia Public Library, Olivia, MN [*Library symbol*] [*Library of Congress*] (LCLS) ... MnOl
Olivine [*CIPW classification*] [*Geology*] ... ol
Olivine [*Philately*] ... olvn
Olivine Subgroup [*Fayalite, forsterite*] [*CIPW classification Geology*] ... O
Olivopontocerebellar Atrophy [*Neurology*] ... OPCA
Ollague [*Chile*] [*Seismograph station code, US Geological Survey Closed*] (SEIS) ... OLL
Ollennu's Principles of Customary Land Law in Ghana [*A publication*] (DLA) ... PCLLG
Olley Air Service Ltd. ... OAS
Ollivier, Bell, and Fitzgerald's Court of Appeal Reports [*1878-80*] [*New Zealand*] [*A publication*] (DLA) ... OB & F
Ollivier, Bell, and Fitzgerald's Court of Appeal Reports [*1878-80*] [*New Zealand*] [*A publication*] (DLA) ... OB & F (CA)
Ollivier, Bell, and Fitzgerald's New Zealand Reports [*A publication*] (DLA) ... OB & FNZ
Ollivier, Bell, and Fitzgerald's New Zealand Reports [*A publication*] (DLA) ... Oll B & F
Ollivier, Bell, and Fitzgerald's New Zealand Reports [*A publication*] (DLA) ... Olliv B & F
Ollivier, Bell, and Fitzgerald's Supreme Court Reports [*New Zealand*] [*A publication*] (DLA) ... OB & F (SC)
Olmedo [*Ecuador*] [*ICAO location identifier*] (ICLI) ... SEOL
Olmsted's Privy Council Decisions [*1867-1954*] [*A publication*] (DLA) ... Olmsted
Olney Carnegie Public Library, Olney, IL [*Library symbol Library of Congress*] (LCLS) ... IOln
Olney Communication College (AD) ... OCC
Olney, IL [*FM radio station call letters*] ... WPTH
Olney, IL [*FM radio station call letters*] ... WSEI
Olney, IL [*FM radio station call letters*] ... WUSI
Olney, IL [*Television station call letters*] ... WUSI-TV
Olney, IL [*AM radio station call letters*] ... WVLN
Olney Springs Public Library, Olney Springs, CO [*Library symbol Library of Congress*] (LCLS) ... CoOs
Olney, TX [*Location identifier FAA*] (FAAL) ... ONY
Olney-Noble, IL [*Location identifier FAA*] (FAAL) ... LZW
Olney-Noble, IL [*Location identifier FAA*] (FAAL) ... OLY
Olofsson Corp. [*Associated Press*] (SAG) ... Olofson
Olofsson Corp. [*NASDAQ symbol*] (SAG) ... OLOFV
Olomouc [*Czechoslovakia*] [*Airport symbol*] (AD) ... OLO
Oloron/Herrere [*France ICAO location identifier*] (ICLI) ... LFCO
Olotillo [*Race of maize*] ... OLO
OLS Asia Hlds ADS [*NASDAQ symbol*] (TTSB) ... OLSAY
OLS Asia HLDS ADS Wrrt [*NASDAQ symbol*] (TTSB) ... OLSWF
OLS Asia Holdings Ltd. [*Associated Press*] (SAG) ... OLS
OLS Asia Holdings Ltd. [*Associated Press*] (SAG) ... OLS AH
OLS Asia Holdings Ltd. [*NASDAQ symbol*] (SAG) ... OLSA
Olsen Line (AD) ... OL
Olsen's Biomass Energy [*G. V. Olsen Associates*] [*Information service or system*] (CRD) ... OLBIEN
Olso [*Norway ICAO location identifier*] (ICLI) ... ENMI
Olsobip [*Papua New Guinea*] [*Airport symbol*] (OAG) ... OLQ
Olson 30 Class Association (EA) ... OTCA
Olsten Corp. [*NYSE symbol*] (SAG) ... OLS
Olsten Corp. [*Associated Press*] (SAG) ... Olsten
Olwine's Law Journal [*Pennsylvania*] [*A publication*] (DLA) ... Olwine's LJ (PA)
Olymbiaki Aeroporia [*Olympic Airlines*] ... OA
Olympia [*Washington*] [*Airport symbol*] (AD) ... OLM
Olympia (AD) ... Oly
Olympia (AD) ... Olym
Olympia & York [*Commercial firm Canada*] (ECON) ... O & Y
Olympia Technical Community College, Olympia, WA [*Library symbol Library of Congress*] (LCLS) ... WaOTC
Olympia, WA [*FM radio station call letters*] ... KAOS
Olympia, WA [*AM radio station call letters*] ... KCPL
Olympia, WA [*AM radio station call letters*] (RBYB) ... KGHO-AM
Olympia, WA [*AM radio station call letters*] ... KGY
Olympia, WA [*FM radio station call letters*] ... KXXO
Olympia, WA [*Location identifier FAA*] (FAAL) ... OLM
Olympiad ... OLYM
Olympian [*of Pindar*] [*Classical studies*] (OCD) ... Ol
Olympic ... OL
Olympic (AD) ... Oly
Olympic Airways [*Greece*] [*ICAO designator*] (OAG) ... OA
Olympic Airways SA [*Greece*] [*ICAO designator*] (FAAC) ... OAL
Olympic Aviation SA [*Greece*] [*ICAO designator*] (FAAC) ... OLY
Olympic Center, Bremerton, WA [*Library symbol Library of Congress*] (LCLS) ... WaBrOC
Olympic College (AD) ... OC
Olympic College, Bremerton, WA [*Library symbol Library of Congress*] (LCLS) ... WaBrO
Olympic Committee Congress ... OCC
Olympic Council of Asia [*Hawalli, Kuwait*] (EAIO) ... OCA
Olympic Council of Ireland (EAIO) ... OCI
Olympic Dam [*Australia Airport symbol*] (OAG) ... OLP
Olympic Financial Ltd. [*NASDAQ symbol*] (NQ) ... OLYM
Olympic Financial Ltd. [*Associated Press*] (SAG) ... OlymF
Olympic Financial Ltd. [*Associated Press*] (SAG) ... OlymFn
Olympic Financial Ltd [*NYSE symbol*] (TTSB) ... OLM
Olympic Finl Cv Exch Pfd [*NASDAQ symbol*] (TTSB) ... OLYMP
Olympic Games ... OG
Olympic Installations Board ... OIB
Olympic Job Opportunities Program ... OJOP
Olympic Lift [*Sports*] ... OL
Olympic Media Information (AD) ... OMI
Olympic National Park ... OLYM
Olympic National Park, Washington (AD) ... Olympic
[*The*] **Olympic Programme** (ECON) ... TOP
Olympic Project for Human Rights ... OPHR
Olympic Savings & Loan Association, Berwyn, IL [*Library symbol Library of Congress*] (LCLS) ... IBerO
Olympic Steel [*NASDAQ symbol*] (TTSB) ... ZEUS

Olympic Steel, Inc. [*Associated Press*] (SAG) ... OlympStl
Olympic Steel, Inc. [*NASDAQ symbol*] (SAG) ... ZEUS
Olympic Technology Trailer Operations ... OTTO
Olympic Training Center Outreach Program ... OTCOP
Olympics Radio and Television Organization [*Organisme de Radio-Television des Olympiques*] [*Canada*] ... ORTO
Olympics Research Group [*University of Calgary*] [*Canada Research center*] (RCD) ... ORG
Olympic-Wallowa Lineament [*Geology*] ... OWL
Olympus Endoscopy System [*Gastroenterology*] (DAVI) ... OES
Olympus Mons [*A filamentary mark on Mars*] ... OM
Olyphant, PA [*FM radio station call letters*] ... WKQV
Olyphant, PA [*AM radio station call letters*] ... WMXH
OM Group [*NASDAQ symbol*] (TTSB) ... OMGI
OM Group, Inc. [*Associated Press*] (SAG) ... OM Grp
OM Group, Inc. [*NASDAQ symbol*] (SAG) ... OMGI
OM Group, Inc. [*NYSE symbol*] (SAG) ... OMP
Omaezaki [*Japan*] [*Seismograph station code, US Geological Survey*] (SEIS) ... OMA
Omaha [*Diocesan abbreviation*] [*Nebraska*] (TOCD) ... OM
Omaha (AD) ... Om
Omaha [*Nebraska*] [*Airport symbol*] ... OMA
Omaha/Eppley Air Field [*Nebraska*] [*ICAO location identifier*] (ICLI) ... KOMA
Omaha Grain Exchange [*Defunct*] (EA) ... OGE
Omaha, Lincoln & Beatrice Railway Co. [*AAR code*] ... OLB
Omaha, NE [*Location identifier FAA*] (FAAL) ... ENF
Omaha, NE [*Location identifier FAA*] (FAAL) ... GWC
Omaha, NE [*AM radio station call letters*] ... KBBX
Omaha, NE [*AM radio station call letters*] ... KCRO
Omaha, NE [*FM radio station call letters*] ... KEFM
Omaha, NE [*FM radio station call letters*] ... KESY
Omaha, NE [*Television station call letters*] ... KETV
Omaha, NE [*AM radio station call letters*] ... KEZO
Omaha, NE [*FM radio station call letters*] ... KEZO-FM
Omaha, NE [*AM radio station call letters*] ... KFAB
Omaha, NE [*FM radio station call letters*] ... KGBI
Omaha, NE [*FM radio station call letters*] ... KGOR
Omaha, NE [*FM radio station call letters*] ... KIOS
Omaha, NE [*AM radio station call letters*] ... KKAR
Omaha, NE [*FM radio station call letters*] ... KKCD
Omaha, NE [*Television station call letters*] ... KMTV
Omaha, NE [*FM radio station call letters*] (RBYB) ... KNOS-FM
Omaha, NE [*AM radio station call letters*] (RBYB) ... KOSR-AM
Omaha, NE [*Television station call letters*] ... KPTM
Omaha, NE [*FM radio station call letters*] ... KVNO
Omaha, NE [*Television station call letters*] (RBYB) ... KXVO
Omaha, NE [*Television station call letters*] ... KYNE
Omaha, NE [*Location identifier FAA*] (FAAL) ... MLE
Omaha, NE [*Location identifier FAA*] (FAAL) ... OFF
Omaha, NE [*Location identifier FAA*] (FAAL) ... SWC
Omaha, NE [*AM radio station call letters*] ... WOW
Omaha, NE [*FM radio station call letters*] ... WOW-FM
Omaha, NE [*Television station call letters*] ... WOWT
Omaha, Nebraska (AD) ... Oma
Omaha Public Library, Omaha, NE [*Library symbol Library of Congress*] (LCLS) ... NbO
Omaha Public Library, Omaha, NE [*OCLC symbol*] (OCLC) ... NBO
Omaha Public Power District ... OPPD
Omak [*Washington*] [*Seismograph station code, US Geological Survey*] (SEIS) ... OMW
Omak, WA [*AM radio station call letters*] ... KOMW
Omak, WA [*FM radio station call letters*] ... KOMW-FM
Omak, WA [*Location identifier FAA*] (FAAL) ... OMK
O'Malley and Hardcastle's Election Cases [*England*] [*A publication*] (DLA) ... O'M & H
O'Malley and Hardcastle's Election Cases [*England*] [*A publication*] (DLA) ... O'M & H El Cas
O'Malley and Hardcastle's Election Cases [*England*] [*A publication*] (DLA) ... O'Mal & H
Oman [*Aircraft nationality and registration mark*] (FAAC) ... A40
Oman (AD) ... Om
Oman [*IYRU nationality code*] [*ANSI two-letter standard code*] (CNC) ... OM
Oman [*ANSI three-letter standard code*] (CNC) ... OMN
Oman Aviation Services Co. [*ICAO designator*] (FAAC) ... OAS
Oman Royal Flight [*ICAO designator*] (FAAC) ... ORF
Omani Rial [*Monetary unit*] (IMH) ... RO
Omarbetad [*Revised*] [*Swedish*] (AD) ... omarb
OMB [*Office of Management and Budget*] **Watch** (EA) ... OMBW
Omboue [*Gabon*] [*ICAO location identifier*] (ICLI) ... FOOH
Omboue [*Gabon*] [*Airport symbol*] (OAG) ... OMB
Ombudsman (AD) ... Omb
Ombudsman for Business [*Department of Commerce*] ... OB
Ombudsman of the Northern Territory [*Australia*] ... ONT
Omdring [*About*] [*Norwegian*] (AD) ... omkr
Omega [*Namibia*] [*ICAO location identifier*] (ICLI) ... FAOE
Omega [*Record label*] [*Belgium, etc.*] ... Ome
Omega [*Namibia*] [*Airport symbol*] (OAG) ... OMG
Omega Arts Network (EA) ... OAN
Omega Chi Epsilon [*Honor society*] (EA) ... OCE
Omega Dropwindsonde [*Meteorology*] ... ODW
Omega Environmental [*NASDAQ symbol*] (SPSG) ... OMEG
Omega Environmental, Inc. [*Associated Press*] (SAG) ... OmegaEn
Omega Financial [*NASDAQ symbol*] (TTSB) ... OMEF
Omega Financial Corp. [*NASDAQ symbol*] (SAG) ... OMEF
Omega Financial Corp. [*Associated Press*] (SAG) ... OmegFn
Omega First Amendment Legal Fund (EA) ... OFALF
Omega, GA [*FM radio station call letters*] ... WTIF
Omega Gamma Delta [*Fraternity*] (EA) ... OGD
Omega Health Systems [*NASDAQ symbol*] (TTSB) ... OHSI
Omega Health Systems, Inc. [*NASDAQ symbol*] (SAG) ... OHSI
Omega Health Systems, Inc. [*Associated Press*] (SAG) ... OmgaHl
Omega Healthcare Investors [*NYSE symbol*] (SPSG) ... OHI
Omega Healthcare Investors [*Associated Press*] (SAG) ... OmegHlt
Omega House (AD) ... OH
Omega Hydrocarbons Ltd. [*Toronto Stock Exchange symbol*] ... OMH
Omega Hyperbolic Grid System ... OHGS
Omega Ltd. [*Ukraine*] [*FAA designator*] (FAAC) ... OGA
Omega Navigation (PDAA) ... ON
Omega Navigation System ... ONS
Omega Navigation System Operations Detail ... ONSOD
Omega Neuron [*Neuroanatomy*] ... ON
Omega Position Location Experiment [*NASA*] ... OPLE
Omega Project (EA) ... OP
Omega Society [*Defunct*] (EA) ... OS
Omega West Reactor [*Los Alamos, NM*] [*Department of Energy*] ... OWR
O'Melveny & Myers, Los Angeles, CA [*Library symbol Library of Congress*] (LCLS) ... CLOM
O'Melveny & Myers, Los Angeles, CA [*Library symbol*] [*Library of Congress*] (LCLS) ... CLOMM
Ometepe [*Nicaragua*] [*Seismograph station code, US Geological Survey*] (SEIS) ... OME
O-Methyldopa [*Biochemistry*] ... OMD
O-Methylthreonine [*Biochemistry*] ... OMT
OMGUS [*Office of Military Government, United States*] **Civilian Employees Association** [*Post-World War II, Germany*] ... OCE
OMI Corp. [*Associated Press*] (SAG) ... OMI
OMI Corp. [*NYSE symbol*] (SAG) ... OMM
OMI Corp. [*NYSE symbol*] (TTSB) ... OMM
Omicron ... O
Omicron [*Fifteenth letter of the Greek alphabet*] (NASA) ... O
Omicron Delta Epsilon [*Fraternity*] ... ODE
Omicron Delta Kappa [*Fraternity*] ... ODK
Omicron Kappa Upsilon [*Fraternity*] ... OKU
Omidyeh [*Iran*] [*ICAO location identifier*] (ICLI) ... OIAJ
Ominato [*Japan ICAO location identifier*] (ICLI) ... RJSO
Omission (AAG) ... OMIS
Omission Excepted (IAA) ... OE
Omissions Excepted ... OE
Omissions Expected (AD) ... oe
Omit ... om
Omittatur [*Let It Be Omitted*] [*Pharmacy*] (ROG) ... OMITT
Ommatidium [*Arthropod eye anatomy*] ... OMM
Omnes Dies [*Every Day*] [*Pharmacy*] ... OD
Omni Bidus [*Every Two Days*] [*Pharmacy*] (ROG) ... O BID
Omni Bidus [*Every Two Days*] [*Pharmacy*] (ROG) ... OMN BID
Omni Bihora [*Every Two Hours*] [*Pharmacy*] (ROG) ... O BIH
Omni Bihora [*Every Two Hours*] [*Pharmacy*] ... OMN BIH
Omni Bihora [*Every Two Hours*] [*Latin*] (AD) ... omn bih
Omni Hora [*Hourly*] [*Latin*] (AD) ... oh
Omni Hora [*Every Hour*] [*Pharmacy*] ... OH
Omni Hora [*Every Hour*] [*Pharmacy*] ... OMN H
Omni Hora [*Every Hour*] [*Pharmacy*] ... OMN HOR
Omni Insurance Group [*NASDAQ symbol*] (TTSB) ... OMGR
Omni Insurance Group, Inc. [*NASDAQ symbol*] (SAG) ... OMGR
Omni Insurance Group, Inc. [*Associated Press*] (SAG) ... OmniIns
Omni Mane [*Every Morning*] [*Pharmacy*] ... OM
Omni Mane [*Every Morning*] [*Latin*] (AD) ... om
Omni Mane [*Every Morning*] [*Latin*] (AD) ... omn man
Omni Mane [*Every Morning*] [*Pharmacy*] ... OMN MAN
Omni MultiMedia Group [*AMEX symbol*] (TTSB) ... OMG
Omni Multimedia Group, Inc. [*AMEX symbol*] (SAG) ... OMG
Omni Multimedia Group, Inc. [*Associated Press*] (SAG) ... Omni
Omni Multimedia Group, Inc. [*Associated Press*] (SAG) ... OmniMult
Omni Nocte [*Every Night*] [*Latin*] (AD) ... omn noct
Omni Nocte [*Every Night*] [*Pharmacy*] ... OMN NOCT
Omni Nocte [*Every Night*] [*Pharmacy*] ... ON
Omni Nocte [*Every Night*] [*Latin*] (AD) ... on
Omni Quadrante Hora [*Every quarter of An Hour*] [*Latin*] [*Pharmacy*] (DAVI) ... omn quad hor
Omni Quadrante Horae [*Every Quarter of an Hour*] [*Pharmacy*] (ROG) ... OMN QUADR HOR
Omni Quarta Hora [*Every Quarter of An Hour*] [*Latin*] [*Pharmacy*] (DAVI) ... OM QUAR HOR
Omni Resources, Inc. [*Vancouver Stock Exchange symbol*] ... ORI
Omni Secunda Hora [*Every Two Hours*] [*Latin*] [*Pharmacy*] (DAVI) ... omn 2 hor
Omni Singula Hora [*Every Hour*] [*Pharmacy*] ... OSH
OMNI U.S.A. [*NASDAQ symbol*] (TTSB) ... OUSA
Omni USA, Inc. [*Associated Press*] (SAG) ... OmniUSA
Omni USA, Inc. [*NASDAQ symbol*] (SAG) ... OUSA
Omnia ad Majorem Dei Gloriam [*All to the Greater Glory of God*] [*Latin*] ... OAMDG
Omniantenna ... OA
Omni-Aviacao e Tecnologia Lda. [*Portugal ICAO designator*] (FAAC) ... OAV
Omnibearing Distance ... OBD
Omnibearing Indicator [*Radio*] ... OBI
Omnibearing Selector [*Radio*] ... OBS
Omnibus Alternis Horis [*Every Other Hour*] [*Pharmacy*] (ROG) ... O ALT HOR
Omnibus Bidendis [*Every Two Days*] [*Latin*] (AD) ... om bid
Omnibus Budget Reconciliation Act [*1987*] ... OBRA
Omnibus Computer Graphics, Inc. [*Toronto Stock Exchange symbol*] ... OMI

Omnibus Conference on Experimental Aspects of NMR [Nuclear Magnetic Resonance] Spectroscopy (MUGU) .... OCEANS
Omnibus Crime Control Act of 1970 (OICC) .... OCCA
Omnibus Crime Control and Safe Streets Act [1968] .... OCC
Omnibus Education Reconciliation Act of 1981 .... OERA
Omnibus Personality Inventory [Psychology] .... OPI
Omnibus Program with Tabular Numerical Functions [Programming language] [1965] (CSR) .... OMNITAB
Omnibus Society [British] .... OS
Omnibus Society of America (EA) .... OSA
Omnicardiogram [Medicine] (DMAA) .... OCG
Omnicardiogram [Medicine] (AD) .... ocg
Omnicare, Inc. [NYSE symbol] (SPSG) .... OCR
Omnicare, Inc. [Associated Press] (SAG) .... Omncre
Omnicom Group [NYSE symbol] (TTSB) .... OMC
Omnicom Group, Inc. [NYSE symbol] (SPSG) .... OMC
Omnicom Group, Inc. (MHDW) .... OMCM
Omnicom Group, Inc. [Associated Press] (SAG) .... Omnicm
Omnidirection Transmission (NVT) .... ODT
Omnidirectional .... OMNI
Omnidirectional [Microphone] (WDMC) .... omni
Omnidirectional Air Data Computer (MCD) .... ODADC
Omnidirectional Air Data System .... OADS
Omnidirectional Antenna .... ODA
Omnidirectional Approach Lighting System [FAA] (TAG) .... ODALS
Omnidirectional Approach Lighting System [Aviation] (FAAC) .... ODALS
Omnidirectional Point Source (PDAA) .... OPS
Omnidirectional RADAR Range (IAA) .... ORR
Omnidirectional Radio Beacon .... ORB
Omnidirectional Radio Range (MSA) .... OMNIRANGE
Omnidirectional Radio Range (MCD) .... Or
Omnidirectional Radio Range (IAA) .... ORR
Omnidirectional Range .... ODR
Omnidirectional Range Station [ITU designation] (CET) .... RLO
Omnidirectional Transmitter Antenna .... OTA
Omniflys SA de CV [Mexico ICAO designator] (FAAC) .... OMF
Omniforce Spatial Environment (AAG) .... OSE
Omnipoint Corp. [Associated Press] (SAG) .... Omnipt
Omnipoint Corp. [NASDAQ symbol] (SAG) .... OMPT
Omnipoint Corp. [NASDAQ symbol] (TTSB) .... OMPT
Omnipol Foreign Trade Corp. [Former Czechoslovakia] [ICAO aircraft manufacturer identifier] (ICAO) .... O
Omnipotent Overseer of the Quest for Unsurpassable Excellence [Rank in the Junior Woodchucks organization mentioned in Donald Duck comic by Carl Barks] .... OOOTQFUE
Omnirange (AD) .... omni
Omnirange Antenna (IAA) .... OA
Omnirange Antenna .... OMNITENNA
Omnirange Digital RADAR .... ORDIR
Omnirange Zero (IAA) .... ORZ
Omnirange Zone .... ORZ
Omnispace Environments Ltd., Toronto, ON, Canada [Library symbol] [Library of Congress] (LCLS) .... CaOTOE
Omnispace Environments Ltd., Toronto, Ontario [Library symbol National Library of Canada] (NLC) .... OTOE
Omnispectra Miniature .... OSM
Omnivisual (AD) .... omni
Omnivore .... O
Omnivorous .... OMN
Omniwest Corporation, Salt Lake City, UT [Library symbol Library of Congress] (LCLS) .... OwC
Omoco Holdings [Vancouver Stock Exchange symbol] .... OMO
Omond's Law of the Sea [1916] [A publication] (DLA) .... Om Sea
Omond's Merchant Shipping Acts [1877] [A publication] (DLA) .... Om Mer Sh
Ompah Branch, Frontenac County Library, Ontario [Library symbol National Library of Canada] (BIB) .... OOMFC
Omphaloskepsis (AD) .... ompf
Omro, WI [FM radio station call letters] .... WPKR
OMS [Orbital Maneuvering Subsystem] Cutoff .... OCO
OMS [Orbital Maneuvering Subsystem] Cutoff [NASA] (NASA) .... OCO
Omsk [Former USSR Airport symbol] (OAG) .... OMS
Omsk Hemorrhagic Fever [Medicine] .... OHF
Omsk Hemorrhagic Fever (AD) .... ohf
On a Track [Rail] [Shipping] (DCTA) .... OT
On Acceptance [Business term] .... OA
On Account [Business and trade] .... OA
On Account Of .... OAS
On Active Service .... OAS
On Air Ltd. [Canada ICAO designator] (FAAC) .... ORL
On and Off Instruments [Aviation] .... OAOI
On Application (NITA) .... O/A
On Approved Credit .... OAC
On Arrival (ADA) .... OA
On Assignment [NASDAQ symbol] (TTSB) .... ASGN
On Assignment, Inc. [NASDAQ symbol] (SAG) .... ASGN
On Assignment, Inc. [Associated Press] (SAG) .... OnAssign
On Being: the Servant's Servant [A publication] (APTA) .... OB
On Board .... O/B
On Board .... OB
On Board .... OB
On Board (NASA) .... ONBD
On Board (NASA) .... ONBD
On Board a Submarine [Navy] .... ONBOSUB
On Board Hard Copier (NASA) .... OHC
On Call (BUR) .... OC

On Camera (WDMC) .... O/C
On Camera (AD) .... oc
On Camera (WDMC) .... OC
On Cards .... OC
On Center [Technical drawings] .... OC
On Center (AD) .... oc
On Command Corp. [NASDAQ symbol] (SAG) .... ONCO
On Command Corp. [Associated Press] (SAG) .... OnCo
On Command Corp. [Associated Press] (SAG) .... OnCom
On Command Corp. [Associated Press] (SAG) .... OnComm
On Company Service (AD) .... ocs
On Consignment (MHDB) .... OC
On Course [Navigation] .... OC
On Deck (KSC) .... O/D
On Demand [Business term] .... OD
On Demand (AD) .... od
On Demand Analyzer Computer .... ODAC
On Display Racks [Freight] .... ODR
On Dock (MCD) .... O/D
On Duty .... OD
On Equipment Materiel [Army] (AABC) .... OEM
On Equipment Training (MCD) .... OET
On Examination (AD) .... o/e
On Examination [Medicine] .... OE
On Farm Research Advisory Committee [Australia] .... OFRAC
On Gard Systems [NASDAQ symbol] (SAG) .... OGSI
On Gard Systems [Associated Press] (SAG) .... OnGrd
On Gard Systems [Associated Press] (SAG) .... OnGrdSy
On Grade (DAC) .... OG
On Ground [Aviation] .... OG
On Ground (AD) .... og
On Guard (AD) .... og
On Hand (AD) .... oh
On Hand .... OH
On His [or Her] Britannic Majesty's Service .... OHBMS
On His [or Her] Majesty's Service .... OHMS
On Instruments [Aviation] .... OI
On Its Merits [British] (ROG) .... OIM
On Location Repair (MCD) .... OLR
On Margin [Investment term] .... OM
On or About (WDAA) .... O/A
On or About (WDMC) .... o/a
On or About (WDAA) .... OOA
On or After Full Moon [Freemasonry] (ROG) .... OAFM
On or After New Moon [Freemasonry] (ROG) .... OANM
On or Before Full Moon [Freemasonry] (ROG) .... OBFM
On or Before New Moon [Freemasonry] (ROG) .... OBNM
On or Nearest Full Moon [Freemasonry] (ROG) .... ONFM
On or Nearest New Moon [Freemasonry] (ROG) .... ONNM
On Orbit (MCD) .... O/O
On Order .... OO
On Probation [Navy British] .... p
On Proof [Publishing] (DGA) .... O/P
On Request .... O/R
On Reserved List [Army British] (ROG) .... RES
On Return .... OR
On Sale .... OS
On Same Terms (WDAA) .... OST
On Sample .... OS
On Schedule .... OS
On Sea [In place names] [British] (ROG) .... O/S
On Service [A publication] .... On Serv
On Sheet (WGA) .... OS
On Shore [NWS] (FAAC) .... ONSHR
On Side .... OS
On Spot (ROG) .... OS
On Station [Military] .... OSM
On Station Mode .... OSP
On Station Position (MUGU) .... OSV
On Station Vehicle (MCD) .... OS
On Switch .... OT
On Target [Military] (CAAL) .... OT
ON Technology [NASDAQ symbol] (TTSB) .... ONTC
ON Technology Corp. [Associated Press] (SAG) .... ON Tch
ON Technology Corp. [Associated Press] (SAG) .... ON Tch
ON Technology Corp. [NASDAQ symbol] (SAG) .... ONTC
ON Technology Corp. [NASDAQ symbol] (SAG) .... ONTC
On Thames [In place names] [British] (ROG) .... O/T
On the Bow [Nautical] .... OTB
On the Deck .... OTD
On the Floor [Computer language] [Computer science] .... OTF
On the Hatch Cover [Stowage] (DNAB) .... ON/H
On the Issues [A publication] (BRI) .... OnIssues
On the Job .... OTJ
On the Job Training .... OTJT
On the Lighter Side, International Lighter Collectors (EA) .... OLSILC
On the Mark - Mark Hamill Fan Club (EA) .... OTM
On the One Hand, On the Other Hand .... OOH-OOH
On the Other Hand [Internet language] [Computer science] .... OTOH
On the Quarter .... OTQ
On the Shoulders of Giants [Literature] .... OTSOG
On Time .... OT
On Top [Aviation] .... OTP
On Top and Smooth [NWS] (FAAC) .... OTAS
On Top Position Indicator [Navy] (NG) .... OTPI

On Trak Systems, Inc. [*NASDAQ symbol*] (SAG) ... ONTK
On Trent [*In place names*] [*British*] (ROG) ... O/T
On Truck [*Shipping*] ... OT
On Vehicle Equipment ... OVE
On Vehicle Materiel [*Military*] ... OVM
On Watch ... ONW
On Weight of Fiber ... OWF
On Work Order [*Military*] (AFIT) ... OWO
Onafhankelijke Partij [*Independent Party*] [*Netherlands Political party*] (PPW) ... OPA
Onahama [*Japan*] [*Seismograph station code, US Geological Survey*] (SEIS) ... ONA
On-Air Test [*Telecommunications*] (DOAD) ... OAT
On-Aircraft Test Procedure (MCD) ... OATP
Onamia Elementary School, Onamia, MN [*Library symbol*] [*Library of Congress*] (LCLS) ... MnOnE
Onamia High School, Onamia, MN [*Library symbol*] [*Library of Congress*] (LCLS) ... MnOnH
Onaping Branch, Onaping Falls Public Library, Ontario [*Library symbol National Library of Canada*] (NLC) ... OOOF
Onarga Public Library, Onarga, IL [*Library symbol Library of Congress*] (LCLS) ... IOna
Onawa Democrat, Onawa, IA [*Library symbol Library of Congress*] (LCLS) ... IaOnD
Onawa, IA [*FM radio station call letters*] (RBYB) ... KOLK-FM
Onawa Public Library, Onawa, IA [*Library symbol Library of Congress*] (LCLS) ... IaOn
Onawa Sentinel, Onawa IA [*Library symbol Library of Congress*] (LCLS) ... IaOnS
On-Axis Pointing (PDAA) ... OAP
On-Balance Volume [*Measurement devised by stock market technician Joseph Granville*] ... OBV
ONBANCorp 6.75% Cv 'B' Pfd [*NASDAQ symbol*] (TTSB) ... ONBKP
ONBANCorp, Inc. [*Associated Press*] (SAG) ... Onbcp
Onbancorp, Inc. [*NASDAQ symbol*] (NQ) ... ONBK
On-Base Percentage [*Baseball*] ... OBP
On-Board Acoustic Tracking System [*Navy*] (CAAL) ... OATS
On-Board Aircraft Weighing System (MCD) ... OBAWS
Onboard at Site Invoicing System [*IBM Computer Program*] ... OASIS
On-Board Checkout [*Aircraft*] ... OBC
On-Board Checkout [*NASA*] (KSC) ... OBCO
On-Board Checkout and Data Management System (MCD) ... OCDMS
On-Board Checkout and Monitoring System [*NASA*] (KSC) ... OCMS
On-Board Checkout Equipment (MCD) ... OBCE
On-Board Checkout Subsystem [*NASA*] (NASA) ... OBCS
On-Board Checkout [*Instrumentation*] **System** ... OBCS
On-Board Checkout System [*NASA*] ... OCS
On-Board Checkout System Test Language [*NASA*] (KSC) ... OCSTL
On-Board Computational Facility [*NASA*] (NASA) ... OCF
On-Board Computer (MCD) ... OBC
On-Board Controller [*Telecommunications*] ... OBC
On-Board Controller Interface [*Telecommunications*] ... OBCI
On-Board Data Bank (DNAB) ... OBDB
On-Board Database Management System (SSD) ... ODBMS
On-Board Diagnostics [*Chrysler Corp.'s computer system*] ... OBD
On-Board Digital Computer Control ... ODCC
On-Board Digital Data Handling ... ODDH
On-Board Electronic Warfare Simulation [*Air Force*] ... OBEWS
On-Board Equipment ... OBE
On-Board Experimental Data Support Facility ... OEDSF
On-Board Gunnery Simulator (PDAA) ... OBGS
Onboard Hard Copier ... OHC
Onboard Health Monitoring System (AD) ... OHMS
On-Board Inert Gas Generator System [*Aviation*] (MCD) ... OBIGGS
On-Board In-Flight Checkout (MCD) ... OBIFCO
On-Board Information Compression Device [*Aerospace*] ... OICD
On-Board Interface Unit (DWSG) ... OBIU
On-Board Local Area Network [*Aviation*] ... OLAN
On-Board Maintenance System [*Aviation*] ... OMS
On-Board Microwave MODEM [*Telecommunications*] (LAIN) ... ONMM
On-Board Navigation ... OBN
On-Board Navigation (MCD) ... O-NAV
On-Board Oxygen Generating System [*Navy*] (CAAL) ... OBOGS
On-Board Oxygen-Generation [*For military aviation*] ... OBOG
On-Board Pilot-Observer Camera (SAA) ... OPOC
On-Board Processor ... OBP
On-Board Refueling Vapor Recovery [*Automotive engineering*] ... ORVR
On-Board Refueling Vapor Recovery ... ORVR
On-Board Repair Parts [*Navy*] ... OBRP
On-Board Spares [*Army*] ... OBS
On-Board Spares and Repair Parts [*Navy*] (DNAB) ... OS & RP
On-Board System [*Navy*] (CAAL) ... OBS
On-Board Trainer [*Navy*] (CAAL) ... OBT
On-Camera Meteorologist ... OCM
Once a Day [*or Daily*] (DAVI) ... OD
Once a Week [*Every Week*] [*Pharmacy*] (DAVI) ... qwk
Once Over [*To examine cursorily*] [*Slang*] ... OO
Once Through, Then Out [*Fuel management system*] ... OTTO
Once upon a Time (The Prisoner Fan Club) (EA) ... OUAT
Once-Over [*Theater*] [*Slang*] (WDMC) ... o-o
Once-Run Distillate (PDAA) ... ORD
Once-Through [*Nuclear reactor technology*] ... OT
Once-Through Cooling [*Nuclear energy*] (NRCH) ... OTC
Once-Through Integral System [*Nuclear energy*] (NRCH) ... OTIS
Once-Through Steam Generating System [*Nuclear energy*] (IEEE) ... OTSGS
Once-Through Steam Generator [*Nuclear energy*] ... OTSG
Once-Through Superheat Reactor [*Nuclear energy*] ... OTSR
Once-through-Methanol [*Fuel technology*] ... OTM
Onchocerciasis Chemotherapy Project [*WHO*] ... OCP
Oncofetal Antigen [*Immunology*] ... OFA
Oncogen Library, Seattle, WA [*Library symbol*] [*Library of Congress*] (LCLS) ... WaSOnc
Oncogene Science [*NASDAQ symbol*] (TTSB) ... ONCS
Oncogene Science, Inc. [*Associated Press*] (SAG) ... Oncogn
Oncogene Science, Inc. [*NASDAQ symbol*] (NQ) ... ONCS
Oncogenic Virus Battery - Acute [*Oncology*] (DAVI) ... ONCG-A
Oncologist ... ONCOL
Oncology [*Medical specialty*] (DHSM) ... ON
Oncology (DAVI) ... ONC
Oncology Information Service [*University of Leeds*] [*England*] [*Information service or system*] (IID) ... OIS
Oncology Nursing Society (EA) ... ONS
On-Command Restartable (MCD) ... ONCORE
On-Condition (NASA) ... OC
On-Condition Maintenance (AABC) ... OCM
On-Condition Maintenance Rate (MCD) ... OCMR
Oncor, Inc. [*AMEX symbol*] (SAG) ... ONC
Oncor, Inc. [*Associated Press*] (SAG) ... Oncor
OncorMed, Inc. [*Associated Press*] (SAG) ... Oncormd
OncorMed, Inc. [*AMEX symbol*] (SAG) ... ONM
OncoRx, Inc. [*NASDAQ symbol*] (SAG) ... OCRX
OncoRx, Inc. [*Associated Press*] (SAG) ... Onco
OncoRx, Inc. [*Associated Press*] (SAG) ... OncoRx
Oncostatin [*Antibiotic*] ... OSM
Oncovin [*Leurocristine, Vincristine*] [*Also, LCR, V, VC, VCR*] [*Antineoplastic drug*] ... O
Oncovin [*Vincristine*], Ara-C, Prednisone [*Antineoplastic drug regimen*] ... OAP
Oncovin [*Vincristine*] **ARA-C** [*Cytarabine or cytosine arabinoside*] **Prednisone, Bleomycin** [*Antineoplastic drug regimen*] (DAVI) ... OAP-BLEO
Oncovin [*Vincristine*] **Cyclophosphamide, Adriamycin** [*Doxorubicin*] [*Antineoplastic drug regimen*] (DAVI) ... OCA
Oncovin [*Vincristine*], Dianhydrogalactitol, Adriamycin, Platinol [*Cisplatin*] [*Antineoplastic drug regimen*] ... O-DAP
Oncovin [*Vincristine*], Methotrexate, Adriamycin, Dactinomycin [*Actinomycin D*] [*Antineoplastic drug regimen*] ... OMAD
Oncovin [*Vincristine*], Prednisolone, Adriamycin, L-Asparaginase [*Antineoplastic drug regimen*] ... OPAL
Oncovin, Prednisone, Etopside, Mitoxantrone [*Antineoplastic drug*] (CDI) ... OPEN
Oncovin [*Vincristine*], Procarbazine, Prednisone [*Antineoplastic drug regimen*] ... OPP
Ondangua [*Namibia*] [*ICAO location identifier*] (ICLI) ... FAOA
Ondangua [*Namibia*] [*Airport symbol*] (OAG) ... OND
One [*Roman numeral*] ... I
One (IDOE) ... uni-
One and Only (IIA) ... O & O
One and Only [*A favorite girl or boy friend*] ... OAO
One and Only Parents Association (EA) ... OOPA
[*The*] **One and Only Tom Jones Fan Club** (EA) ... TOOTJFC
One at a Time ... OAT
One Australian Movement [*Political party*] ... OAM
One Big Computer [*Proposed model for automation of the New York and American stock exchanges*] ... OBC
One Big Union [*A reference to Canada*] ... OBU
One Billion (WDMC) ... giga
One Billion [*British thermal units*] (GNE) ... Q
One Billion Floating Point Operations per Second (ACRL) ... GFLOPS
One billionth [*From the Latin nanus*] (WDMC) ... nano
One Block Look-Ahead [*Computer science*] ... OBL
One Damn Thing After Another [*Title of book by John Masefield*] ... ODTAA
One Day (SAA) ... OD
One Day at a Time (AD) ... odat
One Day Event [*Horse-riding*] [*British*] (DI) ... ODE
One Day Mission [*NASA*] (KSC) ... ODM
One Engine Inoperative [*Aviation*] ... OEI
One Finger breadth above the Umbilicus [*Obstetrics*] (DAVI) ... 1/U
One Finger Breadth below the Umbilicus [*Obstetrics*] (DAVI) ... U/1
One Flow Cascade Cycle (IAA) ... OFC
One Gene One Disorder [*Hypothesis*] ... OGOD
One Hundred [*Roman numeral*] ... C
One Hundred Call Seconds [*A unit of television call measurement*] (WDMC) ... CCC
One Hundred Call-Seconds [*Also, UC*] [*Bell System*] (TSSD) ... CCS
One Hundred Dollar Bill [*C Note*] [*Slang*] ... C
One Hundred Mile House, BC [*Television station call letters*] ... CITM
One Hundred Mile House, BC [*AM radio station call letters*] ... CKBX
One Income, No Kids [*Lifestyle classification*] ... Oink
One Income plus Inheritance [*Lifestyle classification*] ... Oipi
ONE, Inc. (EA) ... OI
One Kind Kiss Before We Part [*Slang*] ... OKKBWP
One Liberty Prop $1.60 Cv Pfd [*AMEX symbol*] (TTSB) ... OLPP
One Liberty Properties [*AMEX symbol*] (TTSB) ... OLP
One Liberty Properties, Inc. [*AMEX symbol*] (SPSG) ... OLP
One Liberty Properties, Inc. [*Associated Press*] (SAG) ... OneLb
One Liberty Properties, Inc. [*Associated Press*] (SAG) ... Onelibt
One Life to Live [*Television program*] ... OLTL
One Man, One Responsibility (AD) ... omor
One Man Operation [*Railroad*] [*British*] ... OMO
One Member, One Vote [*System to select parliamentary candidates*] [*British*] ... OMOV
One of the Firm [*Telecommunications*] (TEL) ... OF
One Per Desk (NITA) ... OPD
One Person's Impact [*An association*] (EA) ... OPI
One Player Median Competitive (PDAA) ... OPMC

One Pound Charge (MCD) ... OPC
One Price Clothing Stores, Inc. [*Associated Press*] (SAG) ... OnePrice
One Price Clothing Stores, Inc. [*NASDAQ symbol*] (NQ) ... ONPR
One Price Clothing Strs [*NASDAQ symbol*] (TTSB) ... ONPR
One Price Only (WDAA) ... OPO
One Shoe Crew [*An association*] (EA) ... OSC
One Shot ... OS
One Shot Multivibrator (MSA) ... OSMV
One Side (WDMC) ... 1S
One Side ... OS
One Sky, the Saskatchewan Cross Cultural Centre, Saskatoon, Saskatchewan [*Library symbol National Library of Canada*] (NLC) ... SSOS
One Sky, the Saskatchewan Cross Culture Centre, Saskatoon, SK, Canada [*Library symbol*] [*Library of Congress*] (LCLS) ... CaSSOS
One Stop Shop [*Small business advice*] [*British*] (ECON) ... OSS
One Term In-Service Course (AIE) ... OTIS
One Thousand (NASA) ... K
One Thousand [*Roman numeral*] ... M
One Thousand Pulses per Second (KSC) ... KPS
One Time ... OT
One Touch Recording ... OTR
One Turn Right [*Dance terminology*] ... 1TR
One Valley Bancorp [*NASDAQ symbol*] (TTSB) ... OVWV
One Valley Bancorp of West Virginia, Inc. [*Associated Press*] (SAG) ... OneVall
One Valley Bancorp of West Virginia, Inc. [*NASDAQ symbol*] (NQ) ... OVWV
One Village [*An association*] (EAIO) ... OV
One Voice: a Magazine about Church Music [*A publication*] (APTA) ... OV
One Way [*Fare*] ... OW
O'Neal's Negro Law of South Carolina [*A publication*] (DLA) ... O'Neal Neg L
One-Arm Dove Hunt Association (EA) ... OADH
One-Bar Function (OA) ... OBF
One-Base Hit [*Baseball*] ... 1B
One-Base Hit [*Baseball*] ... 1BH
One-Boson Exchange [*Physics*] (OA) ... OBE
One-Boson Exchange Model ... OBEM
One-Boson Exchange Potential ... OBEP
One-Button-Recording [*Video technology*] ... OBR
One-Cancels-the-Other Order [*Business term*] ... OCO
One-Channel Map [*Computer science NASA*] ... OCM
OneComm Corp. [*NASDAQ symbol*] (SAG) ... ONEC
OneComm Corp. [*Associated Press*] (SAG) ... OneCm
One-Component Plasma ... OCP
One-Day Event (AD) ... ode
One-Day One-Trial System (AD) ... ODOTS
(One-Day) Tactical Deception [*Orientation*] (DOMA) ... TACDEP
One-Day Trials (AD) ... odt
One-Design Class Council (EA) ... ODCC
One-Digit Code Point [*Telecommunications*] (TEL) ... ODCP
One-Dimension Flow ... ODF
One-Dimensional Equilibrium (MCD) ... ODE
One-Dimensional Kinetics [*Computer program*] (MCD) ... ODK
One-Dimensional LASER and Mixing Program ... ODLAMP
One-Directional Control [*Engineering*] ... ODC
One-Function Diagram (AD) ... ofd
One-Function Diagram ... OFD
One-Function Sketch ... OFS
One-Function Sketch (AD) ... ofs
One-Hour Duty (IAA) ... OHD
Oneida & Western Railroad (IIA) ... O & W
Oneida County District Library, Malad City, ID [*Library symbol*] [*Library of Congress*] (LCLS) ... IdMa
Oneida Historical Society, Utica, NY [*Library symbol Library of Congress*] (LCLS) ... NUtHi
Oneida Library, Oneida, NY [*Library symbol Library of Congress*] (LCLS) ... NO
Oneida Ltd. [*NYSE symbol*] (SPSG) ... OCQ
Oneida Ltd. [*Associated Press*] (SAG) ... Oneida
Oneida, NY [*AM radio station call letters*] ... WMCR
Oneida, NY [*FM radio station call letters*] ... WMCR-FM
Oneida Resources, Inc. [*Vancouver Stock Exchange symbol*] ... ORJ
Oneida, TN [*Location identifier FAA*] (FAAL) ... BPO
Oneida, TN [*Location identifier FAA*] (FAAL) ... OLC
Oneida, TN [*Location identifier FAA*] (FAAL) ... SCX
Oneida, TN [*FM radio station call letters*] ... WBNT
Oneida, TN [*AM radio station call letters*] ... WOCV
[*An*] **O'Neill Concordance** [*A publication*] ... ONCN
O'Neill Educational Ideologies Inventory (EDAC) ... OEII
O'Neill, NE [*AM radio station call letters*] ... KBRX
O'Neill, NE [*FM radio station call letters*] ... KBRX-FM
O'Neill, NE [*Location identifier FAA*] (FAAL) ... ONL
One-in-a-Thousand Society (EA) ... OATHS
Oneita Industries [*NYSE symbol*] (SAG) ... ONA
Oneita Industries [*Associated Press*] (SAG) ... Oneita
One-Lung Ventilation [*Medicine*] ... OLV
One-Man Atmospheric Submersible (PDAA) ... OMAS
One-Man Control (DNAB) ... OMC
One-Man Live Interception Test (SAA) ... OMLIT
One-Man Pension Arrangement [*Management*] ... OMPA
One-Man Pension Arrangement (AD) ... ompa
One-Man Propulsion Research Apparatus [*NASA*] ... OMPRA
One-Man-LAN [*Linked Access Network*] [*PC Interconnect, Inc.*] [*Telecommunications*] (PCM) ... OML
One-Man-Operated Bus [*London, England*] ... OMO
One-Minute Superstar [*Actor whose bit part in a television series results in instant stardom*] ... OMS
ONEOK, Inc. [*NYSE symbol*] (SPSG) ... OKE
ONEOK, Inc. [*Associated Press*] (SAG) ... ONEOK
Oneonta [*New York*] [*Airport symbol*] (OAG) ... ONH
Oneonta, AL [*AM radio station call letters*] ... WCRL
Oneonta, AL [*FM radio station call letters*] ... WKLD
Oneonta, NY [*Location identifier FAA*] (FAAL) ... OZX
Oneonta, NY [*AM radio station call letters*] ... WDOS
Oneonta, NY [*FM radio station call letters*] ... WONY
Oneonta, NY [*FM radio station call letters*] ... WRHO
Oneonta, NY [*FM radio station call letters*] ... WSQC
Oneonta, NY [*FM radio station call letters*] ... WSRK
Oneonta, NY [*FM radio station call letters*] ... WZOZ
One-Page Four-Color [*Advertising*] (WDMC) ... 1p4c
One-Pass Cold-Rolled [*Steel sheets*] ... OPCR
One-Person Library ... OPL
One-Person Operation [*Slang Business term*] (DCTA) ... OPO
One-Piece Folder [*Publishing*] (WDMC) ... OPF
One-Pion Exchange [*Nuclear energy*] ... OPE
One-Pion Exchange Model [*Nuclear energy*] ... OPEM
Onepusu [*Solomon Islands*] [*Airport symbol Obsolete*] (OAG) ... ONE
Onerahi [*Whangarei*] [*New Zealand*] [*Seismograph station code, US Geological Survey*] (SEIS) ... ONE
One-Sided Height Balanced [*Telecommunications*] ... OSHB
One-Statement Banking (MHDB) ... OSB
One-Station Training ... OST
One-Station-Unit Training [*Army*] ... OSUT
One-Station-Unit Training - Conduct of Fire Trainer [*Army*] (MCD) ... OSUT-COFT
One-Stop [*Aviation*] ... OS
One-Stop Tour Charter [*Airline fare*] ... OTC
One-Time Carbon [*Paper*] (PDAA) ... OTC
One-Time Mortgage Insurance Premium (GFGA) ... OTMIP
One-Time Pad [*Navy British*] ... OTP
One-Time Programmable [*Computer science*] ... OTP
One-Time Programmable Read Only Memory [*Computer science*] ... OTPROM
One-Time Source (MCD) ... OTS
One-Time Tape ... OTT
One-Time Use ... OTU
One-Time-Only ... OTO
OneWave, Inc. [*Associated Press*] (SAG) ... OneWve
OneWave, Inc. [*NASDAQ symbol*] (SAG) ... OWAV
One-Way ... 1/W
One-Way Doppler (MCD) ... OWD
One-Way Doppler Extraction ... OWDE
One-Way Polar [*Telegraph*] ... OWP
One-Way Radio Link [*Telecommunications*] (LAIN) ... OWRL
OneWorld Internet [*Global Village Communication*] [*Internet gateway service*] ... OWI
One-Write Plus [*Computer software*] ... OWP
Onex Corp. [*Toronto Stock Exchange symbol*] ... OCX
Onex Packaging, Inc. [*Toronto Stock Exchange symbol*] ... ONP
On-Flight Origin and Destination [*International Civil Aviation Organizati on*] [*Information service or system*] (DUND) ... OFOD
On-Frequency Repeater (IEEE) ... OFR
Ongar [*England*] ... ONG
Ongard Sys [*NASDAQ symbol*] (TTSB) ... OGSI
Ongko Asa [*Indonesia*] [*ICAO location identifier*] (ICLI) ... WRLO
Ongoing ... O
Ongoing (ADA) ... OG
On-Going Thing (AD) ... ogt
Ongoro [*Peru*] [*Seismograph station code, US Geological Survey Closed*] (SEIS) ... ONG
Ongwanada Hospital, Penrose Division, Kingston, ON, Canada [*Library symbol*] [*Library of Congress*] (LCLS) ... CaOKOH
On-Hudson (AD) ... o-H
Oni [*Former USSR Seismograph station code, US Geological Survey*] (SEIS) ... ONI
Onida Public Library, Onida, SD [*Library symbol Library of Congress*] (LCLS) ... SdO
Onion, Tomato, or Lettuce [*Notation on restaurant checks*] ... ONTOLT
Onion Yellow Dwarf Virus [*Plant pathology*] ... OYDV
Onions (ROG) ... ON
Onitap Resources, Inc. [*Toronto Stock Exchange symbol*] ... TAP
O-Nitrophenyl Galactoside (DOG) ... ONPG
O-Nitrophenyl-beta-D-galactopyranoside [*Test*] [*Microbiology*] ... ONPG
Onklos-Jonathan Aramaic (BJA) ... OJA
Onley-Onancock, VA [*AM radio station call letters*] ... WESR
Onley-Onancock, VA [*FM radio station call letters*] ... WESR-FM
Online ... OL
On-Line Acquisitions Systems [*Brodart, Inc.*] [*Book acquisition system*] [*Information service or system*] (IID) ... OLAS
Online Administrative Information System [*Computer science*] (IAA) ... OASIS
Online Airlines Guide [*A publication*] ... OAG
Online Analytical Processing [*Computer science*] (CDE) ... OLAP
On-Line Analytical Processing [*Computer science*] ... OLAR
Online Associative Query System (NITA) ... OAQS
Online Audiovisual Catalogers [*An association*] (EA) ... OLAC
On-Line Automated Reference Service [*Library science*] ... OARS
Online Automotive Service Information System [*Ford Motor Co.*] ... OASIS
Online Batch (NITA) ... OLB
On-Line Benefits Processing ... OBP
Online Book Initiative [*Trademark name*] [*Internet*] ... OBI
Online BookStore [*Commercial firm*] ... OBS
OnLine Bookstore ... OLBS
On-Line Business Systems, Inc. [*Information service or system*] (IID) ... OBS
Online Chronicle (NITA) ... OC
Online Circuit Analysis [*System*] [*Computer science*] ... OLCA
Online Communications Drive [*or Driver*] [*Computer science*] (WDAA) ... OCD

On-Line Communications Driver [*Computer science*] (AD) .... ocd
Online Complex Processing [*Computer science*] (CDE) .... OLCP
On-Line Computer (AD) .... olc
Online Computer [*System*] [*Computer science*] .... OLC
Online Computer Library Center [*Formerly, Ohio College Library Center. Initialism used in reference to cataloging system it developed*] [*Information service or system*] .... OCLC
Online Computer Library Center (BARN) .... OCLC
On-Line Computer System (AD) .... OLCS
On-Line Corporation Tax Assessment [*British*] .... OCTA
Online Cryptanalytic Aid Language [*Computer science*] .... OCAL
On-Line Cryptanalytic Aid Language [*Computer science*] (AD) .... ocal
Online Cryptanalytic Aid System [*Computer science*] (IEEE) .... OCAS
Online Dakota Information Network [*Information service or system*] (IID) ...... ODIN
Online Data Capture .... ODC
Online Data Collection [*Computer science*] (MCD) .... OLDC
Online Data Compression System (PDAA) .... ODCS
Online Data Entry (ADA) .... ODE
Online Data Entry and Display System [*Job Service*] (OICC) .... ODDS
Online Data Entry System [*Burroughs Corp.*] .... ODESY
Online Data Interchange (DA) .... OLDI
Online Data Processor (PDAA) .... OLDAP
Online Database [*or Data Bank*] .... OLDB
Online Database Search Assistance Machine [*Franklin Institute*] [*Information service or system Defunct*] (IID) .... OL'SAM
Online Database Search Services Directory [*A publication*] .... OLDSS
Online Debug [*Computer science*] (IAA) .... OLD
Online Debugging Technique .... ODT
On-Line Debugging Technique [*Computer science*] (AD) .... odt
On-Line Detection System [*Nuclear energy*] .... OLDS
Online Display System [*Computer science*] .... OLDS
Online Diver Monitoring System .... OMDS
Online Dokumentations und Informationsnetz (NITA) .... ODIN
Online Dokumentations- und Informationsverbund [*Online Documentation and Information Affiliation*] .... ODIN
Online Editorial System [*Computer science*] (DGA) .... OLES
On-Line Encyclopedia [*Hypergraphics Corp.*] .... OLE
Online Enquiry [*System*] .... OLE
On-Line Executive [*Computer science*] (MHDB) .... OLX
Online Executive for Real Time [*Computer science*] (IEEE) .... OLERT
On-Line Executive for Real-Time [*Computer science*] (MHDB) .... OLDERT
Online Filing [*Computer science*] (PDAA) .... OLF
On-Line Filing (AD) .... olf
On-Line Free Form Input [*Computer science*] (MHDI) .... OFI
On-line Guitar Archive [*Internet site*] .... OLGA
On-Line Hospital Management Information System [*Computer science*] .... OLHMIS
Online Image Forming Light Modulator .... OLIFLM
Online Information .... OLI
Online Information Centre (NITA) .... OLIC
Online Information Retrieval Ltd. [*Information service or system Defunct*] (IID) .... OIR
Online Information Search Service [*Computer science*] (AD) .... OISS
Online Information Services [*Mercer County Community College Library*] (OLDSS) .... OLIS
Online Instrument and Control Program [*Computer science*] (NRCH) .... OIC
Online Instrument Package [*Computer science*] (NRCH) .... OLIP
Online Instrumentation via Energetic Radioisotopes [*Computer science*] (PDAA) .... OLIVER
Online Interactive Variable Editing Reporter [*Computer science*] (IAA) ..... OLIVER
Online Librarian's Microcomputer User Group [*Teleconferencing system*] .... OLMUG
Online Library Index [*Western Michigan University*] .... OLLI
Online Logical Simulation System [*Computer science*] (KSC) .... OLLS
On-Line Mainframe Testing System [*Computer science*] (IAA) .... OLTS
Online Manufacturing, Accounting, and Control System .... OMAC
Online Manufacturing and Control System [*Computer science*] (PDAA) ..... OMACS
Online Manufacturing Control (NITA) .... OMAC
Online Medical Record (HCT) .... OMR
Online Mendelian Inheritance in Man [*Genetics*] .... OMIM
Online Monitor [*Computer science*] .... OLM
[*The*] On-Line Multi-User System [*Carlyle Systems, Inc.*] [*Information service or system*] (IID) .... TOMUS
Online News (NITA) .... OLN
Online Object Patching System [*Computer science*] (PDAA) .... OOPS
Online Operation [*Computer science*] .... OLO
Online Order Entry .... OLOE
On-Line Order Entry System [*Computer science*] (MHDB) .... ORDER
Online Patient Billing and Accounts Receivable System [*Computer science*] (PDAA) .... OL/PBAR
Online Pattern Analysis and Recognition System [*Computer science*] (MCD) .... OLPARS
Online Peripheral Test System .... OPTS
Online Plotter Controller [*California Computer Products, Inc.*] .... OPC
On-Line Process Synthesis [*Computer science*] .... OPS
Online Processor (TEL) .... OLP
On-Line Program Development [*Computer science*] (MHDB) .... ONLP
Online Program Testing System [*Computer science*] (IAA) .... OPTS
Online Programming .... OLP
Online Programming System [*Computer science*] .... OLPS
Online Public Access Catalog [*Silicon Valley Information Center - SVIC*] [*San Jose, CA*] [*Information service or system*] (IID) .... OPAC
Online Public Education Network .... OPEN
Online Query Language .... OQL
On-Line Reactivity Computer [*Nuclear energy*] (NRCH) .... ORC

Online Real Time [*Computer science*] .... OLRT
On-Line Real Time [*Computer science*] (AD) .... olrt
Online Real Time [*Computer science*] (ADA) .... ONRT
On-Line, Real-Time, Branch Information Transmission [*IBM Corp.*] [*Computer science*] .... ORBIT
On-Line Reduced Bandwidth Information Transfer [*Computer science*] ..... ORBIT
Online Reference Service [*Thunder Bay Public Library*] [*Canada*] (OLDSS) ..... ORS
On-Line Remote Job Entry Terminal System [*Computer science*] .... ORJETS
On-Line Replacement Unit [*Computer science*] (MCD) .... ORU
On-Line Research, Inc. [*Information service or system*] (IID) .... OLR
Online Research Systems [*Information service or system*] (IID) .... ORS
Online Resource Control Aid [*Computer science*] (HGAA) .... ORCA
Online Resources Communications Co. .... ORCC
On-Line Retrieval and Computational Language for Economists [*Computer science*] .... ORACLE
On-Line Retrieval of Bibliographic Text [*Search system*] [*Computer science*] .... ORBIT
Online Retrieval of Information over a Network .... ORION
Online Scan [*Computer science*] (CAAL) .... OLS
Online Scientific Computer [*Computer science*] .... OLSC
On-Line Scientific Computer (AD) .... olsc
Online Search (NITA) .... OLS
Online Search Assistance Machine (NITA) .... OL'SAM
Online Search Information Retrieval Information Storage [*Computer science*] (PDAA) .... OSIRIS
On-Line Search Service [*Lockheed*] (DLA) .... DIALOG
Online Serials Control at Ratcliffe (NITA) .... OSCAR
Online Shared Cataloging System [*Computer science*] .... ONLICATS
Online Software System [*Computer science*] (IEEE) .... OLSS
Online Subsystem Facility [*Computer science*] (MCD) .... OLSF
On-Line System [*Stanford Research Institute*] [*Computer science*] .... NLS
Online System [*Computer science*] .... OLS
Online System Availability and Service Simulation [*Computer science*] (PDAA) .... OLSASS
Online System Drivers [*NCR Corp.*] .... OSD
Online System Svcs [*NASDAQ symbol*] (TTSB) .... WEBB
Online System Svcs Wrrt [*NASDAQ symbol*] (TTSB) .... WEBBW
Online System Use Statistics (NITA) .... OLSUS
Online Task Loader .... OTL
Online Telecommunications Information Service [*Connections Telecommunications, Inc.*] [*West Bridgewater, MA*] [*Telecommunications service*] (TSSD) .... OTIS
Online Teller Terminal .... OLTT
On-Line Teller Terminal [*Computer science*] (AD) .... oltt
On-Line Terminal System [*Computer science*] (MHDB) .... OTS
Online Terminal Test [*Computer science*] (IBMDP) .... OLTT
Online Test [*Computer science*] .... OLT
Online Test (NITA) .... OLTE
Online Test Executive Program [*Computer science*] (PDAA) .... OLTE
On-Line Test Executive Program [*IBM Corp.*] [*Computer science*] .... OLTEP
Online Test Section (NITA) .... OLTS
Online Test System [*Computer science*] (BUR) .... OLTS
Online Time Share [*Computer science*] .... OLTS
Online Training and Practice (NITA) .... ONTAP
On-Line Training and Practice File [*Lockheed*] [*Computer science*] .... ONTAP
On-Line Transaction Processing [*Tandem Computers*] .... OLTP
Online Transaction System [*Computer science*] (IAA) .... OLTS
Online Union Catalog [*Online Computer Library Center, Inc.*] [*Information service or system*] (CRD) .... OLUC
Online Update (TEL) .... OLUD
Online Update Control Module (TEL) .... OLUM
Online Update System (RDA) .... OLUS
Online Users' Group/Ireland (EAIO) .... OUG/I
On-Line Validation [*Computer science*] (AD) .... olv
Online Version Storage [*Computer science*] (PDAA) .... OVS
On-Line Voltammetric Wastewater Analyzer [*Biochemistry*] .... OVWA
On-Line Wholesale Distribution System [*Computer science*] (BUR) .... OWD
Online without Limits .... OWL
Online Writing Lab [*Purdue University*] [*Computer science*] .... OWL
Online X-ray Evaluation over Video-Display Including Documentation (PDAA) .... ORVID
Online Yield [*Computer science*] .... ONLY
Only .... O
Only But Not All (NITA) .... OBNA
Only Child .... OC
Only Input Line (MHDI) .... OIL
Only Living Father [*of Newfoundland's confederation with Canada in 1949*] [*Epithet for Joseph R. Smallwood*] .... OLF
Only Loadable [*Computer science*] (IAA) .... OL
Only Official Peggy Lee Fan Club and Archives (EA) .... OOPLFC & A
Only Official Rolling Stones Fan Club (EAIO) .... OORSFC
Only Son .... OS
Only to Order (DGA) .... O/O
Onmidirectional (AD) .... omni
On-oard Diagnostics-Second Generation .... OBDII
On-Off Keying [*Computer science*] (IEEE) .... OOK
Ono-I-Lau [*Fiji*] [*Airport symbol Obsolete*] (OAG) .... ONU
Onomasticon [*of Eusebius*] (BJA) .... Onom
Onomastikon [*Lexicon*] [*Greek*] (AD) .... on
Onomatopoeia (ROG) .... ONOMAT
Onondaga Community College (AD) .... OCC
Onondaga Community College, Syracuse, NY [*Library symbol Library of Congress*] (LCLS) .... NSyOC
Onondaga Community College, Syracuse, NY [*OCLC symbol*] (OCLC) .... VOC

Onondaga County Public Library, Syracuse, NY [*Library symbol Library of Congress*] (LCLS) .... NSy
Onondaga Historical Association, Syracuse, NY [*Library symbol Library of Congress*] (LCLS) .... NSyOHi
Onondaga Library System [*Library network*] .... OCPL
Onondaga Library System, Syracuse, NY [*Library symbol Library of Congress*] (LCLS) .... NSyOL
Onondaga Library System, Syracuse, NY [*OCLC symbol*] (OCLC) .... YVO
Onondaga, MI [*Television station call letters*] .... WILX
Onondaga-Courtland-Madison Board of Cooperative Education Service, Syracuse, NY [*Library symbol*] [*Library of Congress*] (LCLS) .... NSyOB
Ononis Yellow Mosaic Virus [*Plant pathology*] .... OYMV
On-Orbit Assembly, Maintenance, and Service [*NASA*] (SSD) .... OOAM & S
On-Orbit Flight Technique Meeting [*NASA*] (MCD) .... OFTM
On-Orbit Repair Experiment [*NASA*] (NASA) .... ORE
On-Orbit Repairs Experiment .... ORE
On-Orbit Station [*NASA*] (NASA) .... OOS
On-Orbit Station [*NASA*] (MCD) .... OS
On-Orbit Station Distribution Panel [*NASA*] (MCD) .... OOSDP
On-Orbit Support .... OOS
Onorevole [*Honorable*] (EY) .... ON
Onorevole [*Honorable*] [*Italian*] (AD) .... On
Onotoa [*Kiribati*] [*ICAO location identifier*] (ICLI) .... NGON
Onotoa [*Kiribati*] [*Airport symbol*] (OAG) .... OOT
Onoway Public Library, Alberta [*Library symbol National Library of Canada*] (NLC) .... AO
On-Point Technology Systems, Inc. [*Associated Press*] (SAG) .... OnPointT
On-Point Technology Systems, Inc. [*NASDAQ symbol*] (SAG) .... ONPT
Onrechtmatige Daad [*Tort or Tortious Act*] [*Netherlands*] (ILCA) .... OD
On-Road Costs [*Motor vehicles*] .... ORC
Onsager Reciprocal Relations [*Thermodynamics*] .... ORR
Onsala Space Observatory [*Sweden*] .... OSO
On-Scene Commander [*Navy*] (NVT) .... OSC
On-Scene Coordinator [*Environmental Protection Agency*] (FFDE) .... OSC
On-Screen Manager [*Computer science*] .... OSM
On-Screen Manager [*Computer science*] .... OSM
Onsdag [*Wednesday*] [*Danish*] (AD) .... On
Onset and Course [*Medicine*] (AD) .... o & c
Onset and Course [*of a disease*] [*Medicine*] .... O & C
Onset of Blood Lactose Accumulation [*Metabolism*] .... OOBLA
On-Shift Test (IEEE) .... OST
On-Sight Surveys Division .... ONSIDIV
On-Site .... OS
On-Site Change Control Board [*Military*] (CAAL) .... OSCCB
On-Site Computer Assisted Research [*Oscar, Inc.*] [*Information service or system*] (IID) .... OSCAR
On-Site Container (DOMA) .... ONC
On-Site Data Processing [*or Processor*] [*NASA*] .... OSDP
On-Site Inspection .... OSI
On-Site Inspection Agency [*DoD ICAO designator*] (FAAC) .... OPS
On-Site Inspection Agency [*DoD*] .... OSIA
On-Site Integrated Energy System .... OS/IES
On-Site Logistics Team (MCD) .... OSLT
On-Site Maintenance .... OSM
On-Site Multiple Network Installation [*Thomas & Betts Corp.*] .... OMNI
On-Site/On-Line Maintenance .... OS/OLM
Onsite Review [*Military*] .... OSR
On-Site Safety Committee (IAA) .... OSC
On-Site Sourcing, Inc. [*Associated Press*] (SAG) .... OnSiteS
On-Site Sourcing, Inc. [*NASDAQ symbol*] (SAG) .... ONSS
On-Site Test (IAA) .... OST
On-Site Test Procedure .... OSTP
On-Site User Evaluation (MCD) .... OSUE
On-Site User Test .... OSUT
On-Site User Training .... OSUT
Onslow [*Australia Airport symbol Obsolete*] (OAG) .... ONS
Onslow County Public Library, Jacksonville, NC [*Library symbol Library of Congress*] (LCLS) .... NcJa
Onslow's Nisi Prius [*A publication*] (DLA) .... Onsl NP
Onstage [*Theater*] (WDMC) .... on
On-Target Earnings [*Sales industry*] (ODBW) .... OTE
On-Target Fire Control System (MCD) .... OTFCS
Ontario [*MARC geographic area code Library of Congress*] (LCCP) .... n-cn-on
Ontario (DLA) .... O
Ontario [*Canadian province*] [*Postal code*] .... ON
Ontario [*MARC country of publication code Library of Congress*] (LCCP) .... onc
Ontario [*Oregon*] [*Airport symbol*] (AD) .... ONO
Ontario [*Canada*] (DD) .... Ont
Ontario (ODBW) .... Ont
Ontario [*California*] [*Airport symbol*] .... ONT
Ontario [*Canadian province*] .... ONT
Ontario Agricultural College [*Canada*] .... OAC
Ontario Agricultural Museum, Milton, Ontario [*Library symbol National Library of Canada*] (NLC) .... OMOAM
Ontario & Western Railroad [*Nickname: Old and Weary*] .... O & W
Ontario and Western Railroad Historical Society (EA) .... OWRHS
Ontario Appeal Cases [*Database*] [*Maritime Law Book Co. Ltd.*] [*Information service or system*] (CRD) .... OAC
Ontario Appeal Reports [*A publication*] (DLA) .... App Rep
Ontario Appeal Reports [*A publication*] (DLA) .... App Rep Ont
Ontario Appeal Reports [*A publication*] (DLA) .... AR
Ontario Appeal Reports [*A publication*] (DLA) .... AR (Ont)
Ontario Appeal Reports [*A publication*] (DLA) .... OAR
Ontario Appeal Reports [*A publication*] (DLA) .... Ont App
Ontario Appeals [*A publication*] (DLA) .... Ont A

Ontario Arts Council .... OAC
Ontario Assessment Instrument Pool [*Educational test*] [*Canada*] .... OAIP
Ontario Association of Architects [*1890*] [*Canada*] (NGC) .... OAA
Ontario Bible College-Ontario Theological College, J. William Horsey Library, Willowdale, ON, Canada [*Library symbol*] [*Library of Congress*] (LCLS) .... CaOWdOBC
Ontario Building Officials Association [*Canada*] (AAGC) .... OBOA
Ontario, CA [*Location identifier FAA*] (FAAL) .... AOD
Ontario, CA [*Location identifier FAA*] (FAAL) .... JIO
Ontario, CA [*Television station call letters*] .... KHSC
Ontario, CA [*AM radio station call letters*] .... KNSE
Ontario, CA [*FM radio station call letters*] .... KREA
Ontario, CA [*Location identifier FAA*] (FAAL) .... PDZ
Ontario, CA [*Location identifier FAA*] (FAAL) .... TWO
Ontario CAD/CAM Centre, Cambridge, ON, Canada [*Library symbol*] [*Library of Congress*] (LCLS) .... CaOCaOCC
Ontario CAD/CAM Centre, Cambridge, Ontario [*Library symbol National Library of Canada*] .... OCOCC
Ontario Cancer Clinic, London, ON, Canada [*Library symbol*] [*Library of Congress*] (LCLS) .... CaOLCC
Ontario Cancer Clinic, London, Ontario [*Library symbol National Library of Canada*] (NLC) .... OLCC
Ontario Cancer Foundation, Alta Vista Branch, Ottawa, ON, Canada [*Library symbol Library of Congress*] (LCLS) .... CaOOACF
Ontario Cancer Foundation, Ottawa Clinic, Ottawa, ON, Canada [*Library symbol Library of Congress*] (LCLS) .... CaOOOCF
Ontario Cancer Institute [*UTLAS symbol*] .... OCI
Ontario Cancer Institute, Toronto, ON, Canada [*Library symbol Library of Congress*] (LCLS) .... CaOTOC
Ontario Cancer Institute, Toronto, Ontario [*Library symbol National Library of Canada*] (NLC) .... OTOC
Ontario Cancer Treatment and Research Foundation, Thunder Bay, ON, Canada [*Library symbol Library of Congress*] (LCLS) .... CaOTBOC
Ontario Cancer Treatment and Research Foundation, Thunder Bay, Ontario [*Library symbol National Library of Canada*] (NLC) .... OTBOC
Ontario Center for Machinery and Food Processing Technology, Chatham, ON, Canada [*Library symbol*] [*Library of Congress*] (LCLS) .... CaOChaFMFP
Ontario Centre for Farm Machinery and Food Processing Technology, Chatham, Ontario [*Library symbol National Library of Canada*] (NLC) .... OCFMFP
Ontario Centre for Materials Research [*Canada Research center*] (RCD) .... OCMR
Ontario Centre for Microelectronics, Information Services, Ottawa, ON, Canada [*Library symbol*] [*Library of Congress*] (LCLS) .... CaOOOCM
Ontario Centre for Remote Sensing [*Canada*] .... OCRS
Ontario City Library, Ontario, CA [*OCLC symbol*] (OCLC) .... ONT
Ontario College of Agriculture .... OCA
Ontario College of Art .... OCA
Ontario College of Art, Toronto, ON, Canada [*Library symbol Library of Congress*] (LCLS) .... CaOTCA
Ontario College of Art, Toronto, Ontario [*Library symbol National Library of Canada*] (NLC) .... OTCA
Ontario College of Education .... OCE
Ontario College of Education, Toronto, ON, Canada [*Library symbol Library of Congress*] (LCLS) .... CaOTC
Ontario College of Ophthalmology [*Canada*] (AD) .... OCO
Ontario College of Pharmacy .... OCP
Ontario Community College Librarians [*Canada*] (AD) .... OCCL
Ontario Confederation of University Facility Associations [*Canada*] (AD) .... OCUFA
Ontario Consolidated Regulations [*Canada*] [*A publication*] (DLA) .... Ontario Cons Reg
Ontario Cooperative Program in Latin American and Caribbean Studies [*Research center*] (RCD) .... OCPLACS
Ontario Council on University Affairs [*Canada*] (AD) .... OCUA
Ontario County Historical Society, Canandaigua, NY [*Library symbol Library of Congress*] (LCLS) .... NCanHi
Ontario Department of Education, Curriculum Division, Toronto, ON, Canada [*Library symbol Library of Congress*] (LCLS) .... CaOTDE
Ontario Department of Education, Provincial Library Service, Toronto, ON, Canada [*Library symbol Library of Congress*] (LCLS) .... CaOTEP
Ontario Department of Energy and Resources Management, Toronto, ON, Canada [*Library symbol Library of Congress Obsolete*] (LCLS) .... CaOTERM
Ontario Department of Health [*Canada*] (AD) .... ODH
Ontario Department of Health, Laboratories Branch, Toronto, ON, Canada [*Library symbol Library of Congress*] (LCLS) .... CaOTDHL
Ontario Department of Highways, Planning and Design Branch, Toronto, ON, Canada [*Library symbol Library of Congress Obsolete*] (LCLS) .... CaOTHP
Ontario Department of Labour, Toronto, ON, Canada [*Library symbol Library of Congress*] (LCLS) .... CaOTDL
Ontario Department of Public Records and Archives, Toronto, ON, Canada [*Library symbol Library of Congress*] (LCLS) .... CaOTAr
Ontario Department of Public Works, Toronto, ON, Canada [*Library symbol Library of Congress Obsolete*] (LCLS) .... CaOTDP
Ontario Economic Council, Toronto, ON, Canada [*Library symbol Library of Congress*] (LCLS) .... CaOTOEC
Ontario Education Resources Information System [*Ontario Ministry of Education*] [*Toronto*] [*Information service or system*] (IID) .... ONTERIS
Ontario Educational Communications Authority [*Canada*] .... OECA
Ontario Educational Communications Authority, Toronto, ON, Canada [*Library symbol Library of Congress*] (LCLS) .... CaOTET
Ontario Educational Communications Authority, Toronto, Ontario [*Library symbol National Library of Canada*] (NLC) .... OTET
Ontario Educational Research Council [*Canada*] (EDAC) .... OERC
Ontario Election Cases [*1884-1900*] [*Canada*] [*A publication*] (DLA) .... EC
Ontario Election Cases [*1884-1900*] [*Canada A publication*] (DLA) .... Ont El Cas

Ontario Election Cases [*1884-1900*] [*Canada A publication*] (DLA) .... Ont Elec
Ontario Election Cases [*1884-1900*] [*Canada A publication*] (DLA) .... Ont Elec C
Ontario Election Cases [*1884-1900*] [*Canada A publication*] (DLA) .... Ont Elect
Ontario Election Decisions [*A publication*] (DLA) .... OEC
Ontario Energy Board, Toronto, ON, Canada [*Library symbol*] [*Library of Congress*] (LCLS) .... CaOTOEB
Ontario Energy Board, Toronto, Ontario [*Library symbol National Library of Canada*] (NLC) .... OTOEB
Ontario Express Ltd. [*Canada ICAO designator*] (FAAC) .... OEL
Ontario Federation of Construction Associations [*Canada*] (AD) .... OFCA
Ontario Federation of Students [*Canada*] (AD) .... OFS
Ontario Film Development Corp. [*Canada*] .... OFDC
Ontario Film Institute, Ontario Science Centre Library, Don Mills, Ontario [*Library symbol National Library of Canada*] (NLC) .... OTSTF
Ontario Film Institute, Science Centre Library, Toronto, ON, Canada [*Library symbol Library of Congress*] (LCLS) .... CaOTSTF
Ontario Geological Survey [*Ontario Ministry of Northern Development and Mines*] [*Canada*] (IRC) .... OGS
Ontario Geriatrics Research Society, Toronto, ON, Canada [*Library symbol Library of Congress*] (LCLS) .... CaOTOGR
Ontario Government Information [*Database*] [*Ministry of Culture and Communications*] [*Information service or system*] (CRD) .... OGI
Ontario Government Railway [*Canada*] (AD) .... OGR
Ontario Health-Services Insurances Plan [*Canada*] (AD) .... OHSIP
Ontario Hospital Insurance Plan [*Canada*] (AD) .... OHIP
Ontario Housing Corp., Toronto, ON, Canada [*Library symbol Library of Congress*] (LCLS) .... CaOTOH
Ontario Humane Society [*Canada*] (AD) .... OHS
Ontario Hydro, Central Records, Toronto, ON, Canada [*Library symbol Library of Congress*] (LCLS) .... CaOTOHOR
Ontario Hydro, Central Records, Toronto, ON, Canada [*Library symbol Library of Congress*] (LCLS) .... CaTOHOR
Ontario Hydro Library [*UTLAS symbol*] .... OHL
Ontario Hydro Research, Toronto, Ontario [*Library symbol National Library of Canada*] (NLC) .... OTHR
Ontario Hydro, Toronto, Ontario [*Library symbol National Library of Canada*] (NLC) .... OTH
Ontario Hydroelectric [*Canada*] .... OH
Ontario Institute for Studies in Education [*University of Toronto*] [*Research center*] (RCD) .... OISE
Ontario Institute for Studies in Education Library [*UTLAS symbol*] .... KOI
Ontario Institute for Studies in Education, Toronto, ON, Canada [*Library symbol Library of Congress*] (LCLS) .... CaOTER
Ontario Institute for Studies in Education, Toronto, Ontario [*Library symbol National Library of Canada*] (NLC) .... OTER
Ontario Institute of Chartered Accountants [*Canada*] (DD) .... OICA
Ontario Institute of Painters, Toronto [*1958*] [*Canada*] (NGC) .... OIP
Ontario/International [*California*] [*ICAO location identifier*] (ICLI) .... KONT
Ontario Judicature Act [*A publication*] (DLA) .... OJ Act
Ontario Labor Relations Board [*Canada*] (AD) .... OLRB
Ontario Labour Relations Board Monthly Report [*A publication*] (DLA) .... OLRB
Ontario Labour Relations Board [*Commission des Relations de Travail de l'Ontario*], Toronto, Ontario [*Library symbol National Library of Canada*] (NLC) .... OTOLR
Ontario Ladies College .... OLC
Ontario Land Economist [*Canada*] (DD) .... OLE
Ontario Land Surveyor [*Canada*] (DD) .... OLS
Ontario Law Journal [*A publication*] (DLA) .... Ont LJ
Ontario Law Journal, New Series [*A publication*] (DLA) .... Ont LJ (NS)
Ontario Law Reform Commission, Toronto, Ontario [*Library symbol National Library of Canada*] (BIB) .... OTOLRC
Ontario Law Reporter [*A publication*] (DLA) .... OLR
Ontario Law Reports [*A publication*] (DLA) .... OLR
Ontario Law Reports [*A publication*] (DLA) .... Ont L
Ontario Law Reports [*A publication*] (DLA) .... Ont L Rep
Ontario Legislative Library, Toronto, ON, Canada [*Library symbol Library of Congress*] (LCLS) .... CaOTL
Ontario Libraries Service Escarpment, Hamilton, ON, Canada [*Library symbol*] [*Library of Congress*] (LCLS) .... CaOHESC
Ontario Library Association [*Canada*] (AD) .... OLA
Ontario Library Co-Operative [*UTLAS symbol*] .... OLC
Ontario Library Co-Operative, Wyoming, ON, Canada [*Library symbol*] [*Library of Congress*] (LCLS) .... CaOWyOL
Ontario Library Co-Operative, Wyoming, Ontario [*Library symbol National Library of Canada*] (NLC) .... OWOL
Ontario Library Service - Escarpment, Hamilton [*UTLAS symbol*] ILL
Ontario Library Service - Escarpment, Hamilton, Ontario [*Library symbol National Library of Canada*] (NLC) .... OHESC
Ontario Library Service - James Bay, Kirkland Lake, Ontario [*Library symbol National Library of Canada*] (NLC) .... OKLN
Ontario Library Service - Nipigon, Thunder Bay, Ontario [*Library symbol National Library of Canada*] (NLC) .... OFWN
Ontario Library Service Nipigon/Thunder Bay Public Library [*UTLAS symbol*] .... NPG
Ontario Library Service - Rideau, Ottawa, Ontario [*Library symbol National Library of Canada*] (NLC) .... OOEO
Ontario Library Service - Saugeen, Kitchener, Ontario [*Library symbol National Library of Canada*] (NLC) .... OKITM
Ontario Library Service - Thames, London, Ontario [*Library symbol National Library of Canada*] (NLC) .... OLLE
Ontario Library Service - Trent, Richmond Hill, Ontario [*Library symbol National Library of Canada*] (NLC) .... ORCO
Ontario Library Service - Voyageur [*UTLAS symbol*] .... NCR
Ontario Library Service - Voyageur, Sudbury, Ontario [*Library symbol National Library of Canada*] (NLC) .... OSUN
Ontario Library Services Center, Waterloo, ON, Canada [*Library symbol*] [*Library of Congress*] (LCLS) .... CaOWtO
Ontario Library Services Center, Waterloo, Ontario [*Library symbol National Library of Canada*] (NLC) .... OWTO
Ontario Library Service-Trent, Richmond Hill, ON, Canada [*Library symbol*] [*Library of Congress*] (LCLS) .... CaORhT
Ontario Lottery Corporation, Toronto, Ontario [*Library symbol National Library of Canada*] (BIB) .... OTOL
Ontario Medical Association [*Canada*] (AD) .... OMA
Ontario Medical Association, Toronto, ON, Canada [*Library symbol Library of Congress*] (LCLS) .... CaOTOMA
Ontario Medical Association, Toronto, Ontario [*Library symbol National Library of Canada*] (NLC) .... OTOMA
Ontario Medical Surgical Insurance Plan [*Canada*] (AD) .... OMSIP
Ontario Milks Marketing Board, Toronto, ON, Canada [*Library symbol Library of Congress*] (LCLS) .... CaOTMMB
Ontario Milks Marketing Board, Toronto, Ontario [*Library symbol National Library of Canada*] (NLC) .... OTMMB
Ontario Ministry of Agriculture and Food [*UTLAS symbol*] .... OAF
Ontario Ministry of Agriculture and Food, Home Economics Branch, Toronto, ON, Canada [*Closed*] [*Library symbol Library of Congress*] (LCLS) .... CaOTAH
Ontario Ministry of Agriculture and Food, Horticultural Research Institute, Vineland Station, ON, Canada [*Library symbol Library of Congress*] (LCLS) .... CaOVAg
Ontario Ministry of Agriculture and Food, Kemptville, ON, Canada [*Library symbol Library of Congress*] (LCLS) .... CaOKemAF
Ontario Ministry of Agriculture and Food, Kemptville, Ontario [*Library symbol National Library of Canada*] (NLC) .... OKEMAF
Ontario Ministry of Agriculture and Food, Toronto, ON, Canada [*Library symbol Library of Congress*] (LCLS) .... CaOTAF
Ontario Ministry of Agriculture and Food, Toronto, Ontario [*Library symbol National Library of Canada*] (NLC) .... OTAF
Ontario Ministry of Colleges and Universities, Toronto, ON, Canada [*Library symbol Library of Congress*] (LCLS) .... CaOTDU
Ontario Ministry of Colleges and Universities, Toronto, Ontario [*Library symbol National Library of Canada*] (NLC) .... OTDU
Ontario Ministry of Community and Social Services, Children's Psychiatric Research Institute, London, ON, Canada [*Library symbol Library of Congress*] (LCLS) .... CaOLCSSCP
Ontario Ministry of Community and Social Services Library [*UTLAS symbol*] .... CSS
Ontario Ministry of Community and Social Services, Toronto, ON, Canada [*Library symbol Library of Congress*] (LCLS) .... CaOTPW
Ontario Ministry of Community and Social Services, Toronto, Ontario [*Library symbol National Library of Canada*] (NLC) .... OTPW
Ontario Ministry of Consumer and Commercial Relations, Toronto, ON, Canada [*Library symbol Library of Congress*] (LCLS) .... CaOTFC
Ontario Ministry of Consumer and Commercial Relations, Toronto, Ontario [*Library symbol National Library of Canada*] (NLC) .... OTFC
Ontario Ministry of Correctional Services, Toronto, Ontario [*Library symbol National Library of Canada*] (NLC) .... OTCS
Ontario Ministry of Culture and Communications (TSSD) .... MCC
Ontario Ministry of Culture and Communications, Toronto, Ontario [*Library symbol National Library of Canada*] (NLC) .... OTCR
Ontario Ministry of Culture and Recreation, Toronto, ON, Canada [*Library symbol Library of Congress*] (LCLS) .... CaOTCR
Ontario Ministry of Education, Colleges and Universities, Toronto, ON, Canada [*Library symbol*] [*Library of Congress*] (LCLS) .... CaOTECU
Ontario Ministry of Education, Information Centre, Research Branch [*UTLAS symbol*] .... MOE
Ontario Ministry of Education, Sudbury, Ontario [*Library symbol National Library of Canada*] (BIB) .... OSUME
Ontario Ministry of Education, Thunder Bay, Ontario [*Library symbol National Library of Canada*] (NLC) .... OTBE
Ontario Ministry of Education, Toronto, Ontario [*Library symbol National Library of Canada*] (NLC) .... OTDE
Ontario Ministry of Energy, Toronto, ON, Canada [*Library symbol Library of Congress*] (LCLS) .... CaOTME
Ontario Ministry of Energy, Toronto, Ontario [*Library symbol National Library of Canada*] (NLC) .... OTME
Ontario Ministry of Government Services, Bibliographic Centre, Toronto, ON, Canada [*Library symbol Library of Congress*] (LCLS) .... CaOTGSB
Ontario Ministry of Health, Toronto, ON, Canada [*Library symbol Library of Congress*] (LCLS) .... CaOTDH
Ontario Ministry of Health, Toronto, Ontario [*Library symbol National Library of Canada*] (NLC) .... OTDH
Ontario Ministry of Industry and Tourism, Toronto, ON, Canada [*Library symbol Library of Congress*] (LCLS) .... CaOTTI
Ontario Ministry of Industry and Trade, Toronto, Ontario [*Library symbol National Library of Canada*] (NLC) .... OTTI
Ontario Ministry of Industry, Trade, and Technology [*UTLAS symbol*] .... OIT
Ontario Ministry of Labour Library [*UTLAS symbol*] .... OML
Ontario Ministry of Labour, Toronto, Ontario [*Library symbol National Library of Canada*] (NLC) .... OTDL
Ontario Ministry of Municipal Affairs and Housing, Toronto, Ontario [*Library symbol National Library of Canada*] (NLC) .... OTOH
Ontario Ministry of Natural Resources, Information Section, Reference Library, Toronto, ON, Canada [*Library symbol Library of Congress*] (LCLS) .... CaOTLC
Ontario Ministry of Natural Resources, Lands and Surveys Branch, Toronto, ON, Canada [*Library symbol Library of Congress*] (LCLS) .... CaOTLL
Ontario Ministry of Natural Resources, Maple, Ontario [*Library symbol National Library of Canada*] (NLC) .... OMAPFW

Ontario Ministry of Natural Resources, Mines Library, Toronto, ON, Canada [*Library symbol Library of Congress*] (LCLS) .... CaOTDM

Ontario Ministry of Natural Resources, Natural Resources Library, Toronto, ON, Canada [*Library symbol Library of Congress*] (LCLS) .... CaOTLF

Ontario Ministry of Natural Resources, Research Branch, Toronto, ON, Canada [*Library symbol Library of Congress*] (LCLS) .... CaOTLR

Ontario Ministry of Northern Affairs, Toronto, ON, Canada [*Library symbol Library of Congress*] (LCLS) .... CaOTNA

Ontario Ministry of Northern Development and Mines, Toronto, Ontario [*Library symbol National Library of Canada*] (NLC) .... OTNA

Ontario Ministry of Northern Development and Mines, Tweed [*Library symbol National Library of Canada*] (BIB) .... OTWEN

Ontario Ministry of Revenue, Toronto, ON, Canada [*Library symbol Library of Congress*] (LCLS) .... CaOTOMR

Ontario Ministry of Revenue, Toronto, Ontario [*Library symbol National Library of Canada*] (NLC) .... OTOMR

Ontario Ministry of the Attorney General, Judges Library, Toronto, ON, Canada [*Library symbol Library of Congress*] (LCLS) .... CaOTJL

Ontario Ministry of the Attorney General [*Ministere du Procureur-General*], Toronto [*Library symbol National Library of Canada*] (BIB) .... OTMAG

Ontario Ministry of the Attorney General, Toronto, ON, Canada [*Library symbol*] [*Library of Congress*] (LCLS) .... CaOTMAG

Ontario Ministry of the Environment, Laboratory, Toronto, ON, Canada [*Library symbol Library of Congress*] (LCLS) .... CaOTMENL

Ontario Ministry of the Environment, Toronto, ON, Canada [*Library symbol Library of Congress*] (LCLS) .... CaOTMEN

Ontario Ministry of the Environment, Toronto, Ontario [*Library symbol National Library of Canada*] (NLC) .... OTMEN

Ontario Ministry of Transportation and Communications [*Canada*] (TSSD) .... MTC

Ontario Ministry of Transportation and Communications [*Downsview, ON*] [*Telecommunications*] (TSSD) .... OMTC

Ontario Ministry of Transportation and Communications, Toronto, ON, Canada [*Library symbol Library of Congress*] (LCLS) .... CaOTDT

Ontario Ministry of Transportation and Communications, Toronto, Ontario [*Library symbol National Library of Canada*] (NLC) .... OTDT

Ontario Ministry of Treasury and Economics Library [*UTLAS symbol*] .... OTE

Ontario Ministry of Treasury and Economics, Toronto, Ontario [*Library symbol National Library of Canada*] (NLC) .... OTDRE

Ontario Ministry of Treasury, Economics, and Inter-governmental Affairs, Toronto, ON, Canada [*Library symbol Library of Congress*] (LCLS) ..... CaOTDRE

Ontario Motor Coach Association .... OMCA

Ontario Motor League [*Canada*] (AD) .... OML

Ontario Municipal Board Reports [*A publication*] (DLA) .... OMBR

Ontario New Universities Library Project .... ONULP

Ontario Northland Railway [*Canada*] (AD) .... ON

Ontario Northland Railway .... ONR

Ontario Northland Railway [*AAR code*] .... ONT

Ontario Nurses Association, Toronto, Ontario [*Library symbol National Library of Canada*] (NLC) .... OTONA

Ontario, OH [*AM radio station call letters*] .... WRGM

Ontario, OR [*AM radio station call letters*] .... KSRV

Ontario, OR [*FM radio station call letters*] .... KSRV-FM

Ontario, OR [*Location identifier FAA*] (FAAL) .... ONO

Ontario Paper Co. Ltd., Thorold, ON, Canada [*Library symbol Library of Congress*] (LCLS) .... CaOThoP

Ontario Police College, Aylmer West, Ontario [*Library symbol National Library of Canada*] (NLC) .... OAWOP

Ontario Police Commission, Technical Services Branch, Planning and Research Library, Toronto, ON, Canada [*Library symbol*] [*Library of Congress*] (LCLS) .... CaOTOPCT

Ontario Practice [*A publication*] (DLA) .... Ont Pr

Ontario Practice Reports [*A publication*] (DLA) .... Ont PR

Ontario Practice Reports [*A publication*] (DLA) .... Ont Pr Rep

Ontario Practice Reports [*A publication*] (DLA) .... OPR

Ontario Provincial Police [*UTLAS symbol*] .... OPP

Ontario Provincial Police College, Toronto, ON, Canada [*Library symbol Library of Congress*] (LCLS) .... CaOTPPC

Ontario Provincial Police College, Toronto, Ontario [*Library symbol National Library of Canada*] (NLC) .... OTPPC

Ontario Provincial Police, Toronto, ON, Canada [*Library symbol Library of Congress*] (LCLS) .... CaOTPP

Ontario Provincial Police, Toronto, Ontario [*Library symbol National Library of Canada*] (NLC) .... OTPP

Ontario Public Library, Ontario, CA [*Library symbol Library of Congress*] (LCLS) .... COn

Ontario Regiment [*Canada*] (DMA) .... Ont Rgt

Ontario Region, Canadian Air Transportation Administration, Transport Canada [*Region de l'Ontario, Administration Canadienne des Transports Aeriens, Transports Canada*] **Toronto, Ontario** [*Library symbol National Library of Canada*] (NLC) .... OTTOA

Ontario Region Library, Employment and Immigration Canada [*Bibliotheque de laRegion de l'Ontario, Emploi et Immigration Canada*], **North York, Ontario** [*Library symbol National Library of Canada*] (NLC) .... OTMIO

Ontario Regional Library, Public Works Canada [*Bibliotheque Regionale de l'Ontario, Travaux Publics Canada*] **Toronto, Ontario** [*Library symbol National Library of Canada*] (NLC) .... OTPWC

Ontario Regional Library, Secretary of State Canada [*Bibliotheque Regionale de l'Ontario, Secretariat d'Etat*], **Toronto, Ontario** [*Library symbol National Library of Canada*] (NLC) .... OTSS

Ontario Regional Network [*Canada*] [*Computer science*] (TNIG) .... Onet

Ontario Regulations [*Canada*] [*A publication*] (DLA) .... Ont Reg

Ontario Regulations [*Canada A publication*] (DLA) .... Ont Regs

Ontario Reports [*A publication*] (DLA) .... O

Ontario Reports [*A publication*] (DLA) .... Ont

Ontario Reports [*A publication*] (DLA) .... Ont LR

Ontario Reports [*A publication*] (DLA) .... Ont R

Ontario Reports [*A publication*] (DLA) .... OR

Ontario Reports and Ontario Weekly Notes [*Canada*] [*A publication*] (DLA) .... Ont R & WN

Ontario Reports, Second Series [*Canada*] [*A publication*] (DLA) .... Ont 2d

Ontario Research Foundation [*Canada Research center*] (RCD) .... ORF

Ontario Research Foundation, Sheridan Park, Mississauga, Ontario [*Library symbol National Library of Canada*] (NLC) .... OTRF

Ontario Research Foundation, Toronto, ON, Canada [*Library symbol Library of Congress*] (LCLS) .... CaOTRF

Ontario Revised Regulations [*Canada A publication*] (DLA) .... Ont Rev Regs

Ontario Revised Statutes [*Canada*] [*A publication*] (DLA) .... Ont Rev Stat

Ontario Science Centre, Toronto, ON, Canada [*Library symbol Library of Congress*] (LCLS) .... CaOTST

Ontario Science Centre, Toronto, Ontario [*Library symbol National Library of Canada*] (NLC) .... OTST

Ontario Secondary School Teachers' Federation [*UTLAS symbol*] .... OSS

Ontario Secondary School Teachers Federation, Toronto, ON, Canada [*Library symbol*] [*Library of Congress*] (LCLS) .... CaOTOSS

Ontario Secondary School Teachers Federation, Toronto, Ontario [*Library symbol National Library of Canada*] (NLC) .... OTOSS

Ontario Securities Commission (HGAA) .... OSC

Ontario Securities Commission Decisions [*QL Systems Ltd.*] [*Information service or system Canada*] (CRD) .... OSCD

Ontario Securities Commission, Toronto, ON, Canada [*Library symbol*] [*Library of Congress*] (LCLS) .... CaOTOSC

Ontario Securities Commission, Toronto, Ontario [*Library symbol National Library of Canada*] (NLC) .... OTOSC

Ontario Society for Training and Development [*Canada*] (EDAC) .... OSTD

Ontario Society of Artists [*Canada*] (BARN) .... OSA

Ontario Statutes [*Canada*] [*A publication*] (DLA) .... Ont Stat

Ontario Tax Reporter (Commerce Clearing House) [*A publication*] (DLA) .... Ont Tax Rep (CCH)

Ontario Teachers Federation (AEBS) .... OTF

Ontario University Libraries Cooperative System (NITA) .... OULCS

Ontario Veterinary College .... OVC

Ontario Weekly Notes [*A publication*] (DLA) .... Ont Week N

Ontario Weekly Notes [*A publication*] (DLA) .... Ont Wkly N

Ontario Weekly Notes [*A publication*] (DLA) .... Ont WN

Ontario Weekly Notes [*A publication*] (DLA) .... OWN

Ontario Weekly Reporter [*A publication*] (DLA) .... Ont Week R

Ontario Weekly Reporter [*A publication*] (DLA) .... Ont Wkly Rep

Ontario Weekly Reporter [*A publication*] (DLA) .... Ont WR

Ontario Weekly Reporter [*A publication*] (DLA) .... OWR

Ontario Weekly Reporter. Opinions of United States Attorneys General [*A publication*] (DLA) .... Ont WR Op

Ontario Workers' Compensation Appeals Tribunal [*UTLAS symbol*] .... OWC

Ontario Workers' Compensation Appeals Tribunal, Toronto, ON, Canada [*Library symbol*] [*Library of Congress*] (LCLS) .... CaOTWCA

Ontario Workers' Compensation Appeals Tribunal, Toronto, Ontario [*Library symbol National Library of Canada*] (NLC) .... OTWCA

Ontario Workmen's Compensation Board, Toronto, Ontario [*Library symbol National Library of Canada*] (NLC) .... OTWC

Ontatio Police College, Aylmer West, ON, Canada [*Library symbol*] [*Library of Congress*] (LCLS) .... CaOAwOP

On-the-Bottom Sonobuoy (MCD) .... OTBS

On-the-Fly [*Computer compression program*] (PCM) .... OTF

On-the-Fly Printer .... OFP

On-the-Job Education .... OJE

On-the-Job Evaluation (OICC) .... OJE

On-the-Job Experience .... OJE

On-the-Job Injuries .... OJI

On-the-Job Injuries (AD) .... oji

On-the-Job Training (AD) .... ojt

On-the-Job Training .... OJT

On-Time Marker [*Computer science*] .... OTM

Ontonagon, MI [*Location identifier FAA*] (FAAL) .... OGM

Ontonagon, MI [*FM radio station call letters*] .... WOAS

Ontonagon, MI [*FM radio station call letters*] .... WUPY

Ontonagon Township Library, Ontonagon, MI [*Library symbol Library of Congress*] (LCLS) .... MiOnt

Ontong Java Plateau [*Geology*] .... OJP

Ontrack Data International, Inc. [*NASDAQ symbol*] (SAG) .... ONDI

Ontrack Data International, Inc. [*Associated Press*] (SAG) .... OntrDta

OnTrak Systems [*NASDAQ symbol*] (TTSB) .... ONTK

OnTrak Systems, Inc. [*Associated Press*] (SAG) .... OnTrak

Onuphrius. De Interpretatione Vocum Ecclesiae [*A publication*] (DLA) .... Onuphr De Interp Voc Eccles

Onur Hava Tasimacilik AWMS [*Turkey*] [*ICAO designator*] (FAAC) .... OHY

O'Nyong-Nyong Virus .... ONN

Onyx (VRA) .... onx

Onyx Acceptance [*NASDAQ symbol*] (TTSB) .... ONYX

Onyx Acceptance Corp. [*NASDAQ symbol*] (SAG) .... ONYX

Onyx Acceptance Corp. [*Associated Press*] (SAG) .... OnyxAcc

Onyx Petroleum Exploration Co. Ltd. [*Toronto Stock Exchange symbol*] .... ONX

ONYX Pharmaceuticals [*NASDAQ symbol*] (TTSB) .... ONXX

Onyx Pharmaceuticals, Inc. [*NASDAQ symbol*] (SAG) .... ONXX

Onyx Pharmaceuticals, Inc. [*Associated Press*] (SAG) .... OnyxPh

Onze Alma Mater (BJA) .... OAM

Onze Lieve Vrouw [*Our Lady*] [*Dutch*] (AD) .... OLV

Oocyte Maturation Inhibitor [*Endocrinology*] .... OMI

Oocyte-Corona-Cumulus Complex .... OCCC

Oodnadatta [*Australia Airport symbol*] (OAG) .... ODD

O'okiep Copper ADR [*AMEX symbol*] (TTSB) .... OKP

O'Okiep Copper Co. Ltd. [AMEX symbol] (SPSG) .... OKP
O'Okiep Copper Co. Ltd. [Associated Press] (SAG) .... OOkiep
Oologah [Oklahoma] [Seismograph station code, US Geological Survey Closed] (SEIS) .... OLO
Oomiya [Japan] [Seismograph station code, US Geological Survey Closed] (SEIS) .... OOM
Oophorectomized [Gynecology] .... OO
Oostende [Belgium ICAO location identifier] (ICLI) .... EBOS
Ootomari [Former USSR Seismograph station code, US Geological Survey Closed] (SEIS) .... OOT
Ooty Radio Telescope [India] .... ORT
Ooze [Quality of the bottom] [Nautical charts] .... Oz
OP Resources Ltd. [Vancouver Stock Exchange symbol] .... OPR
Opa Locka, FL [Location identifier FAA] (FAAL) .... NOM
Opacity (MCD) .... O
Opacity Distribution Function [Spectroscopy] .... ODF
Opal Air [ICAO designator] (AD) .... OB
Opal Air Pty Ltd. [Australia] [FAA designator] (FAAC) .... OPA
Opal Air Pty Ltd. [Australia ICAO designator] (FAAC) .... OPA
Opal, Inc. [NASDAQ symbol] (SAG) .... OPAL
Opalescent Indicating Light .... OPIL
Opalotype (VRA) .... OPTYP
Opana [Hawaii] [Seismograph station code, US Geological Survey] (SEIS) .... OPA
Opaque [Envelopes] .... OP
Opaque [Type of ice formation] .... OPA
Opaque Media [X-ray microscopy] .... OM
Opawica Explorations, Inc. [Toronto Stock Exchange symbol] .... OPW
Opcode MIDI [Musical Instrument Digital Interface] System .... OMS
Ope Consilio [By Aid and Counsel] [Latin Legal term] (DLA) .... OC
OPEC [Organization of Petroleum Exporting Countries] Fund for International Development (EAIO) .... OFID
OPEC [Organization of Petroleum Exporting Countries] News Agency [See also APOPEC] [Vienna, Austria] (EAIO) .... OPECNA
Opel Motorsport Club AG (EA) .... OMC
Opelika, AL [AM radio station call letters] .... WJHO
Opelika, AL [FM radio station call letters] .... WMXA
Opelika, AL [Television station call letters] .... WSWS
Opelika, AL [AM radio station call letters] .... WZMG
Opelousas, LA [FM radio station call letters] .... KOGM
Opelousas, LA [AM radio station call letters] .... KSLO
Opelousas, LA [FM radio station call letters] .... KVOL
Opelousas, LA [Location identifier FAA] (FAAL) .... OPL
Opelousas-Eunice Public Library, Opelousas, LA [Library symbol Library of Congress] (LCLS) .... LO
Open [Dancing position] .... O
Open [Stock exchange term] .... OP
Open .... OP
Open (AAG) .... OPN
Open Access [Library shelves] (DGA) .... O/A
Open Access Satellite Education Services (EDAC) .... OASES
Open Account .... OA
Open Agility .... OA
Open Air Campaigners, US (EA) .... OAC
Open Air Factor .... OAF
Open Allotments/Navy-Wide Operating Budgets (MCD) .... OA/NWOB
Open and Distance Learning (AIE) .... ODL
Open Angle Glaucoma [Ophthalmology] .... OAG
Open Annealed [Metal industry] .... OA
Open Application Interface .... OAI
Open Architecture [Telecommunications] (IAA) .... OA
Open Architecture Development Group [IBM Corp.] (CDE) .... OADG
Open Architecture Receiver [Telecommunications] .... OAR
Open Architecture Test System (MCD) .... OATS
Open Bay [Papua New Guinea] [Airport symbol] (OAG) .... OPB
Open Blade Damper (OA) .... OBD
Open Break Position [Dancing] .... OBP
Open Broadcasting Authority [Noncommercial TV channel] [British] .... OBA
Open Burning/Open Detonation [Military] .... OB/OD
Open Buying on the Internet [Computer science] .... OBI
Open Canalicular System [Hematology] .... OCS
Open Cargo Lighter [Navy ship symbol] [Obsolete] .... YCK
Open Channel Air Preheater [Heat exchanger] .... OCAP
Open Channel Cooperative .... OCC
Open Channel Flow .... OCF
Open Charter [Business term] .... OC
Open Charter (AD) .... oc
Open Chest Cardiac Compression [Cardiology] (DAVI) .... OCCC
Open Chest Cardiac Massage [Cardiology] (DAVI) .... OCCM
Open Chock [Shipfitting] .... OC
Open Circuit .... O
Open Circuit (IDOE) .... o/c
Open Circuit .... OC
Open Circuit Characteristic (IAA) .... OCC
Open Circuit Inductance (IAA) .... OCI
Open Circuit Potential (PDAA) .... OCP
Open Circular [Configuration of DNA] [Microbiology] .... OC
Open/Closed [Mouth] [Doll collecting] .... O/C
Open Collaborative Environment [Apple Computer, Inc.] .... OCE
Open Collector (IAA) .... OC
Open College (AIE) .... OC
Open College Network (AIE) .... OCN
Open College of Arts [British] .... OCA
Open Communications Architecture (AD) .... OCA
Open Computing Facility .... OCF
Open Contract .... OC

Open Cooperative Test System [Trademark of NCR Corp.] .... OCTS
Open Court Language Development Program: Kindergarten (EDAC) .... OCLDP-K
Open Cover [Shipping] .... O/C
Open Cover (AD) .... o/c
Open Cup (AD) .... oc
Open Cup [Electronics] .... OC
Open Data Link Interface [Computer science] .... ODLI
Open Data Path (MCD) .... ODP
Open Database Applications Program Interface [Microsoft Corp.] .... ODAPI
Open Database Connectivity [Computer science] .... ODBC
Open Database Connectivity .... ODBC
Open Database Connectivity .... ODBC
Open Database Server [Computer science] .... ODS
Open Datalink Interface [Computer science] .... ODI
Open DeviceNet Vendors Association (ACII) .... ODVA
Open Diapason [Organ stop] [Music] .... OP DIAP
Open Die Forging Institute (EA) .... ODFI
Open Distributed Processing [Telecommunications] (OSI) .... ODP
Open Distributed Systems Architecture [British] .... ODSA
Open Document Management API [Application Programming Interface] [Computer science] .... ODMA
Open Door Bible School, Granite Falls, MN [Library symbol] [Library of Congress] (LCLS) .... MnGfODS
Open Door International for the Economic Emancipation of the Woman Worker [Brussels, Belgium] (EAIO) .... ODI
Open Door Policy .... ODP
Open Door Student Exchange (EA) .... ODSE
Open Drain (IAA) .... OD
Open Dripproof .... ODP
Open Dripproof Protected .... ODPP
Open Drop .... OD
Open End (MSA) .... OE
Open End (AD) .... oe
Open Entry/Open Exit (OICC) .... OE/OE
Open Environment [NASDAQ symbol] (TTSB) .... OPEN
Open Environment Corp. [NASDAQ symbol] (SAG) .... OPEN
Open Environment Corp. [Associated Press] (SAG) .... OpnEnv
Open Failure Report [NASA] (KSC) .... OFR
Open Fault Locater .... OFL
Open File Report (MCD) .... OFR
Open Financial Connectivity [Microsoft Computer Software] [Computer Science] .... OFC
Open Financial Exchange [Computer science] .... OFX
Open Financial Exchange [Computer science] .... OFX
Open Fireplace [Classified advertising] (ADA) .... OFP
Open for Public Inspection [Patent applications] .... OPI
Open Forum [An association] (EA) .... OF
Open Frame Linear Power Supply [Electronics] (EECA) .... OFLINPS
Open Frame Power Supply [Electronics] (EECA) .... OFPS
Open Frame Switch Mode Power Supply [Electronics] (EECA) .... OFSMPS
Open Full [Container] (DCTA) .... OF
Open General Import Licence [British] (DS) .... OGIL
Open General License [Import license] (DS) .... OGL
Open Geographic Information System .... OGIS
Open Government Document (PDAA) .... OGD
Open Head Injury [Medicine] (PAZ) .... OHI
Open Heart Recovery Room [Cardiology] (DAVI) .... OHRR
Open Heart Surgery [Medicine] .... OH
Open Heart Surgery [Medicine] .... OHS
Open Heart World Mission (EA) .... OHWM
Open Hearth .... OH
Open Hearth (AD) .... oh
Open Item Review (KSC) .... OIR
Open Item Status Report (NASA) .... OISR
Open Landing Lighter [Navy symbol] .... YLA
Open Learning (AIE) .... OL
Open Learning Electronic Support Services [Australia] .... OLESS
Open Learning Federation [British] (DI) .... OLF
Open Learning Information and Materials Clearing House [Australia] ..... OLIMCH
Open Learning Institute [UTLAS symbol] .... OLI
Open Learning Institute, Richmond, BC, Canada [Library symbol] [Library of Congress] (LCLS) .... CaBVaOL
Open Learning Institute, Richmond, British Columbia [Library symbol National Library of Canada] (NLC) .... BVAOL
Open Learning Programme (AIE) .... OLP
Open Lighter [Non-self-propelled] [Navy symbol] .... YC
Open Link Interface (TNIG) .... OLI
Open Liver Biopsy [Medicine] (DMAA) .... OLB
OPEN LOOK Intrinsic Toolkit .... OLIT
Open Loop .... OL
Open Loop Insulin Delivery System [Medicine] (DMAA) .... OLIDS
Open Lung Biopsy .... OLB
Open Macrodefinition .... OMD
Open Mail System [Raindrop Software Co.] (PCM) .... OMS
Open Management System [Vitalink Communicatons Corp.] .... OMS
Open Market .... OM
Open Market [NASDAQ symbol] (TTSB) .... OMKT
Open Market Committee [Also, FOMC] [Federal Reserve System] .... OMC
Open Market, Inc. [NASDAQ symbol] (SAG) .... OMKT
Open Market, Inc. [Associated Press] (SAG) .... OpenMkt
Open Market Operations [Economics] .... OMO
Open Marsh Water Managed [Ecology] .... OMWM
Open Matching [Parapsychology] .... OM
Open Measurement Solution .... OMS
Open Media Framework (DOM) .... OMF

Open Media Research Institute ... OMRI
Open Media Research Institute [*Non-profit news and analysis organization covering Eastern Europe and the former Soviet Union*] (ECON) ... OMRI
Open Messaging Environment [*Computer science*] (CDE) ... OME
Open Messaging Interface [*Lotus Development Corp.*] (PCM) ... OMI
Open Minded Comics Club [*Defunct*] (EA) ... OMCC
Open Mitral Valve Commissurotomy [*Medicine*] ... OMVC
Open Modular Architecture Controller (ACII) ... OMAC
Open Mouth [*Doll collecting*] ... OM
Open Network Architecture [*Computer science*] ... ONA
Open Network Computing [*Computer science*] (PCM) ... ONC
Open Network Computing Plus [*Computer science*] (PCM) ... ONC+
Open Network Environment [*Netscape network*] [*Computer science*] ... ONE
Open Network Provision ... ONP
Open Network Server [*Tylink Corp.*] ... ONS
Open Ocean Area (SAA) ... OOA
Open Ocean Mining ... OOM
Open Ocean Release ... OOR
Open Ocean Zone [*Oceanography*] ... OOZ
Open Order ... OO
Open Order Master (MCD) ... OOM
Open Pan Sulphitation [*Sugar production*] ... OPS
Open Perfusion Micro-Incubator ... OPMI
Open Pilot Warranty [*Insurance*] (AIA) ... OPW
Open Pit Mining Association (EA) ... OPMA
Open Plan Systems [*NASDAQ symbol*] (TTSB) ... PLAN
Open Plan Systems, Inc. [*Associated Press*] (SAG) ... OpenPln
Open Plan Systems, Inc. [*NASDAQ symbol*] (SAG) ... PLAN
Open Point Expanding [*Bullet*] (DICI) ... OPE
Open Policy ... OP
Open Pool Reactor [*Nuclear energy*] (NRCH) ... OPR
Open Position [*Dancing*] ... OP
Open Prepress Interface [*Computer science*] (PCM) ... OPI
Open Printed Circuit (IAA) ... OPC
Open Problem List (NASA) ... OPL
Open Problem List ... OPL
Open Profiling Standard [*Firefly Network*] [*Computer science*] ... OPS
Open Profiling Standard [*Computer science*] ... OPS
Open Promoter Complex [*Genetics*] ... OPC
Open Protocol Enhanced Network [*Northern Telecom communications network*] [*Canada*] ... OPEN
Open Protocol Interface [*Telecommunications*] ... OPI
Open Reading Frame [*Genetics*] ... ORF
Open Reciprocating Brayton Engine (PDAA) ... ORBE
Open Reduction [*Orthopedics*] (DAVI) ... OR
Open Reduction with Internal Fixation [*Medicine*] ... ORIF
Open Registry [*Flag of convenience*] [*Shipping*] (DS) ... OR
Open Road Camper Clubs of America [*Later, ORSAC*] (EA) ... ORCCA
Open Road "See America" Club [*Defunct*] (EA) ... ORSAC
Open Shelter Deck [*Shipping*] (DS) ... OSD
Open Shelter Deck/Closed Shelter Deck [*Shipping*] (DS) ... OSD/CSD
Open/Short Locator ... OSL
Open Shortest Path First [*Communications routing protocol*] ... OSPF
Open Signal Coprocessing Architecture [*Computer science*] ... OSPA
Open Software Description [*Computer science*] ... OSD
Open Software Foundation ... OSF
Open Space Institute (EA) ... OSI
Open Standards Interconnection [*International Standards Organisation*] ... OSI
Open Steel Flooring Institute [*Defunct*] ... OSFI
Open System Interconnections [*Networking technique*] ... OSI
Open Systems Accounting Software [*Computer science*] ... OSAS
Open Systems Architecture [*Computer science*] ... OSA
Open Systems Foundation ... OSF
Open Systems Interconnect ... OSI
Open Systems Interconnect Network Management Forum [*Computer science*] (BTTJ) ... OSI/NMF
Open Systems Interconnection Division (ACII) ... OSID
Open Systems Interconnection Environment [*Telecommunications*] (OSI) ... OSIE
Open Systems Interconnection Technical and Office Protocols [*Telecommunications*] (OSI) ... OSITOP
Open Systems Interconnections Division [*Now Open Systems Interconnection Division*] (ACII) ... OSICOM
Open Systems Technology Transfer Programme [*British*] ... OSTT
Open Systems Unit [*British*] ... OSU
Open Tech Training Support Unit (AIE) ... OTTSU
Open Test Assembly [*Nuclear energy*] (NRCH) ... OTA
Open Text [*NASDAQ symbol*] (TTSB) ... OTEXF
Open Text Corp. [*Associated Press*] (SAG) ... OpenTxt
Open Text Corp. [*NASDAQ symbol*] (SAG) ... OTEX
Open to Buy ... OTB
Open Token Foundation (BTTJ) ... OTF
Open Top [*Freight*] ... OTP
Open Top Vapor Cleaner [*Engineering*] ... OTVC
Open Topped [*Container*] [*Packaging*] (DCTA) ... OT
Open Transport [*Computer science*] ... OT
Open Transport and Session Support (NITA) ... OTSS
Open Tubular Column [*For gas chromatography*] ... OTC
Open Tubular Heterogeneous Enzyme Reactor [*Biochemical engineering*] ... OTHER
Open Tubular Liquid Chromatography ... OTLC
Open Two Seater [*Style of automobile*] ... OTS
Open Type Control Circuit Contacts (MSA) ... OTCCC
Open University [*British*] ... OU
Open University Business School [*British*] ... OUBS
Open University Students' Association [*British*] ... OUSA
Open Ventilated (MSA) ... OV
Open Vision Technology [*NASDAQ symbol*] (TTSB) ... OPVN
Open Water Disposal Area Management Simulation [*US Army Corps of Engineers*] ... ODAMS
Open Web Joist [*Technical drawings*] ... OJ
Open Wedge [*Osteotomy*] [*Orthopedics*] (DAVI) ... OW
Open Wheel [*A publication*] ... OW
Open Wire (NATG) ... OW
Open Work Items (KSC) ... OWI
Open-Air Mission ... OAM
Open-Air Places [*Parks, pools, etc.*] [*Public-performance tariff class*] [*British*] ... O
Open-Air Theater ... OAT
Open-Back Inclinable ... OBI
Open-Back Inclinable Press [*Manufacturing term*] ... OBI
Open-Back Stationary Press [*Manufacturing term*] ... OBS
Opencast Coal Act [*Town planning*] [*British*] ... OCA
Open-Chest Cardiopulmonary Resuscitation ... OCCPR
Open-Circuit Television ... OCTV
Open-Circuit Television (AD) ... octv
Open-Circuit Voltage (AD) ... ocv
Open-Circuit Voltage ... OCV
Open-Circuit Voltage Decay [*In silicon devices*] ... OCVD
Open-Circuited Terminating Line (IAA) ... OCTL
Open-Circuited Transmission Line ... OCTL
Open-Circuit-Stable ... OCS
Open-Close-Open [*Technical drawings*] ... OCO
Open-Close-Open (AD) ... oco
Open-Cycle Gas Turbine (PDAA) ... OCGT
Open-Door International [*An association*] (AD) ... ODI
Opened [*Stock exchange term*] (SPSG) ... OPD
Opened Edges [*Publishing*] (DGA) ... OE
Open-End Company [*Business term*] (MHDW) ... OEC
Open-End Contract Information Circulars (AAGC) ... OECIC
Open-End Credit [*Business term*] (MHDW) ... OEC
Open-End Funds [*Investment term*] ... OEF
Open-End Investment Co. [*Investment term*] ... OEIC
Open-End Investment Trust [*Investment term*] ... OEIT
Open-End Marriage ... OEM
Open-End Wrench ... OEW
Open-Ended Health Maintenance Organization [*Insurance*] (WYGK) ... OEHMO
Open-Ended Plan [*Human resources*] (WYGK) ... OEP
Open-Ended Spinning [*Textile industry*] ... OES
Open-Ended System [*Computer science*] ... OES
Open-Ended Systems Corp. ... OESC
Open-Ended Working Group (NATG) ... OEWG
Opener (MSA) ... OPR
Opener Inhibitor ... OI
Open-Face Dectector [*Instrumentation*] ... OFD
Open-Frame Low Voltage (IEEE) ... OLV
Open-Hearth Acid Steel ... OAS
Open-Hearth Basic Steel ... OBS
Open-Hearth Steel ... OHS
Open-Hearth Steel (AD) ... ohs
Opening ... O
Opening ... OPG
Opening (AAG) ... OPNG
Opening Altitude Judgement [*Parachuting*] (DICI) ... OAJ
Opening Automated Report Service [*NYSE*] ... OARS
Opening Doors Wider in Nursing [*Project*] ... ODWIN
Opening Filled Other State [*Employment*] ... OFOS
Opening of Anterior Digestive [*Gland*] ... OAD
Opening of Books ... OB
Opening of Business (MCD) ... OOB
Opening of Intestine ... OI
Opening of Oesophagus ... OOE
Opening of Salivary [*Gland*] ... OSAL
Opening Posterior Digestive [*Gland*] ... OPD
Opening Pressure [*Medicine*] ... OP
Opening Price [*Stock exchange term*] ... OP
Opening Purchase [*Stock exchange term*] ... OP
Opening Snaps [*Cardiology*] ... OS
Open-Joint (AD) ... oj
Open-Joisted [*Technical drawings*] ... OJ
Open-Loop Bandwidth [*Also, OLBW*] ... OLB
Open-Loop Bandwidth [*Also, OLB*] ... OLBW
Open-Loop Damping ... OLD
Open-Loop Feedback Optimal (PDAA) ... OLFO
Open-Loop Gain ... OLG
Open-Loop Oxygen-Generating System [*Air Force*] ... OLOGS
Open-Loop Receiver [*or Response*] ... OLR
Open-Loop System [*Chemical engineering*] ... OLS
Open-Loop Voltage Gain ... OLVG
Open-Pore Foam [*Plastic*] ... OPF
Open-Pore Polyurethan [*Plastic*] ... OPP
Openside ... OPSD
Open-Tubular Reactor ... OTR
OpenVision Technologies, Inc. [*Associated Press*] (SAG) ... OpenVis
OpenVision Technologies, Inc. [*NASDAQ symbol*] (SAG) ... OPVN
Open-Window Unit (MSA) ... OWU
Opeongo High School, Douglas, ON, Canada [*Library symbol Library of Congress*] (LCLS) ... CaODO
Opeongo High School, Douglas, Ontario [*Library symbol National Library of Canada*] (NLC) ... ODO
Opera [*Works*] [*Italian*] ... op
Opera ... OP

Opera America [*An association*] (EA) ... OA

Opera Ballet School (DICI) ... OBS

Opera Company (AD) ... OC

Opera di Maria [*Work of Mary*] [*An association*] (EAIO) ... OM

Opera et Dies [*of Hesiod*] [*Classical studies*] (OCD) ... Op

Opera Guilds International (AD) ... OGI

Opera House (AD) ... OH

Opera Mundi [*Book-packaging firm based in Paris*] ... OM

Opera News [*A publication*] (BRI) ... ON

Opera of the Month Club [*Record label*] ... Opa

Operability Testing [*Military*] (CAAL) ... OPT

Opera-Comique [*Comic Opera*] [*French*] (AD) ... OC

Opera-Comique [*Comic Opera*] [*Music*] ... OP-COM

Operado de Terminal de Contenedores [*Container Terminal Operator*] [*Shipping*] [*Spanish*] ... OTC

Operador de Transporte Combinado [*Combined Transport Operator*] [*Spanish Business term*] ... OTC

Operand [*Computer science*] ... O

Operand [*Computer science*] ... OP

Operand [*Computer science*] ... OPD

Operand (ECII) ... OPND

Operand [*Computer science*] ... OPR

Operand Address (NITA) ... OA

Operand Address [*Computer science*] (IAA) ... OPADR

Operand Address Register [*Computer science*] ... OA

Operand Address Register [*Computer science*] (IAA) ... OAR

Operand Buffering System [*Computer science*] (IAA) ... OBS

Operand Execution Pipeline [*Computer science*] ... OEP

Operand Select Gate [*Computer science*] ... OSG

Operand Storage Register [*Computer science*] ... OSR

Operarios del Reina de Cristo (TOCD) ... ORC

Operarios del Reina de Cristo (TOCD) ... orc

Operate (IDOE) ... op

Operate ... OP

Operate [*or Operator*] (AAG) ... OPR

Operate (WGA) ... OPT

Operated Preference Controls ... OPC

Operating [*Automotive engineering*] ... OPER

Operating (MDG) ... OPERG

Operating ... OPG

Operating a Motor Vehicle Intoxicated (MEDA) ... OMVI

Operating a Vehicle while under the Influence of Liquor [*Traffic offense charge*] ... OUIL

Operating Agency ... OA

Operating Agency [*Military*] ... OPAGY

Operating Agency Code (AFM) ... OAC

Operating Aircraft ... OA

Operating Ambient Temperature ... OAT

Operating and Maintenance [*USCG*] (TAG) ... O&M

Operating and Maintenance Costs ... OMC

Operating and Maintenance Division, Alberta Government Services, Edmonton, Alberta [*Library symbol National Library of Canada*] (NLC) ... AEAGS

Operating and Repair Instruction ... ORI

Operating and Support Cost Reduction [*Army*] ... OSCR

Operating and Support Costs Management Information System ... O & SCMIS

Operating and Support Costs Management Information System (MCD) ... OASCMIS

Operating and Support Costs Management Information System (MCD) ... OSCMIS

Operating and Support Hazard Analysis ... O & S HA

Operating and Support Hazard Analysis (MCD) ... OASHA

Operating Area (CAAL) ... OPAREA

Operating Assemblies [*JETDS nomenclature*] [*Military*] (CET) ... OA

Operating Authorization ... OA

Operating Base [*Navy*] ... OB

Operating Basis Earthquake [*Nuclear reactor*] (NRCH) ... OBE

Operating Basis Event (IEEE) ... OBE

Operating Budget (AFM) ... OB

Operating Budget ... OPBU

Operating Budget Account Number [*Air Force*] ... OBAN

Operating Budget Authority (MCD) ... OBA

Operating Budget Authority Document [*Military*] (AFIT) ... OBAD

Operating Budget Review Committee [*Military*] ... OBRC

Operating Characteristic ... OC

Operating Characteristics Curve ... OCC

Operating Code [*Computer science*] ... OP-COD

Operating Coil (IAA) ... OC

Operating Company ... OC

Operating [*or Operational*] **Control Procedure** (MSA) ... OCP

Operating Cost Model ... OCMODL

Operating Curve (NRCH) ... OC

Operating Engineer (NRCH) ... OE

Operating Expense ... OE

Operating Facilities [*Coast Guard publication*] ... OPFAC

Operating Flight Strength Diagram ... OFSD

Operating Force Plan ... OFP

Operating Forces [*Navy*] ... OF

Operating Forces Support Equipment (DNAB) ... OFSE

Operating [*or Operational*] **Ground Equipment** ... OGE

Operating Ground Equipment/Real Property Installed Equipment (AFM) ... OGE/RPIE

Operating Ground Equipment Specification [*Italian*] (AD) ... OGES

Operating Hour/Flight Hour [*Ratio*] ... OH/FH

Operating Hours (MCD) ... OH

Operating House of Ill Repute ... OHIR

Operating Impedance Bridge (IAA) ... OIB

Operating Income [*Accounting*] ... OI

Operating Information System [*Army*] ... OIS

Operating Instructions ... OI

Operating Internal Pressure [*Nuclear energy*] (NRCH) ... OIP

Operating Level (IEEE) ... OL

Operating Level Days ... OLD

Operating License ... OL

Operating License (AD) ... ol

Operating Location [*Army*] ... OL

Operating Location-Iceland (DNAB) ... OL-IC

Operating Log ... OL

Operating Loss ... OL

Operating, Maintenance, Interest, and Adaptability ... OMIA

Operating Maintenance Panel (IAA) ... OMP

Operating Maintenance Procedure (IAA) ... OMP

Operating Material Review Board [*NASA*] (NASA) ... OMRB

Operating Memorandum ... OM

Operating Memorandum - Information ... OMI

Operating Memorandum - Personnel Assignment ... OMPA

Operating Memorandum - Policy ... OMP

Operating Memory (KSC) ... OM

Operating Motor Vehicle under the Influence of Liquor [*Traffic offense charge*] ... OMVUIL

Operating Motor Vehicle while Intoxicated [*Traffic offense charge*] ... OMVWI

Operating Network Advisory Committee [*NERComP*] ... ONAC

Operating Nursing Procedure ... ONP

Operating Plan [*Management term*] (MCD) ... OP

Operating Plan Change Orders [*Coast Guard publication*] ... OPCO

Operating Plane Months [*Navy*] (NG) ... OPM

Operating Point (IAA) ... OP

Operating Policy [*Military*] ... OP

Operating Procedure [*Management term*] (KSC) ... OP

Operating Procedure for Ministers ... OPM

Operating Profit [*DoD*] ... OP

Operating Program ... OPPR

Operating Reactor [*Nuclear energy*] (NRCH) ... OR

Operating Resources (AFM) ... OR

Operating Room [*Medicine*] ... OR

Operating Room Attendant [*Ranking title*] [*British Royal Navy*] ... O

Operating Room Attendant [*British military*] (DMA) ... ORA

Operating Room Nurse [*Medicine*] ... ORN

Operating Room Technician (DAVI) ... OR tech

Operating Room Technician [*Medicine*] ... ORT

Operating Schedule [*Field stations*] (MCD) ... OS

Operating Schedule/Virtual System ... OS/VS

Operating Sequence Control Array [*NASA*] ... OSCAR

Operating Service Month ... OSM

Operating Software (MCD) ... OS

Operating Space/Allowance Equipage List ... OS/AEL

Operating Space Item [*Military*] (CAAL) ... OSI

Operating Steam Pressure (MSA) ... OSP

Operating Strength [*Army*] (AABC) ... OPSTR

Operating System [*Computer science*] ... OPSYS

Operating System [*Computer science*] (BUR) ... OS

Operating System 2 [*Computer science*] ... OS/2

Operating System/Application Program Interface [*Computer science*] ... OSAPI

Operating System Command and Response Language ... OSCRL

Operating System Communication Application Program [*Computer science*] ... OSCAP

Operating System Control Language (NITA) ... OSCL

Operating System/Disk Operating System [*Software*] ... OS/DOS

Operating System/Environment [*Computer science*] (BYTE) ... OS/E

Operating System Implementation Language ... OSIL

Operating System Interface ... OSI

Operating System/Inter-Process Communications (DOMA) ... OS/IPC

Operating System Language ... OSL

Operating System Manual (MCD) ... OSM

Operating System Monitor ... OSM

Operating System/Multiprogramming Fixed Task (NITA) ... OS/MFT

Operating System/Multiprogramming with a Fixed Number of Tasks [*IBM Corp.*] [*Computer science*] ... OS/MFT

Operating System/Multiprogramming with a Variable Number of Tasks [*Computer science*] ... OS/MVT

Operating System/Multiprogramming with Virtual Storage [*Computer science*] ... OS/MVS

Operating System Plan (SAA) ... OSP

Operating System Simulation Language [*1971*] [*Computer science*] (CSR) ... OSSL

Operating System Software [*Personal computers*] ... OSS

Operating System Supervisor ... OSS

Operating System Support (NITA) ... OSS

Operating System Support Facility (MHDI) ... OSSF

Operating System Table Loader [*Telecommunications*] (TEL) ... OSTL

Operating System Test [*Telecommunications*] (TEL) ... OSTEST

Operating System/Virtual Storage [*Computer science*] (MDG) ... OS/VS

Operating System Workstation [*Computer science*] ... OSWS

Operating Systems, Inc. (MCD) ... OSI

Operating Target ... OPTAR

Operating Telephone Co. [*Bell System*] (TEL) ... OTC

Operating Temperature [*Nuclear energy*] ... OT

Operating Temperature Limit ... OTL

Operating Temperature Range ... OTR

Operating Temporaries ... OTEMPO

Operating Theater .... OT
Operating Time .... OT
Operating Time at Failure (MCD) .... OTAF
Operating Time Log (AAG) .... OTL
Operating Time Record Tag (AAG) .... OTRT
Operating Time Update .... OTU
Operating Vehicle under Influence of Liquor or Narcotic Drugs [*FBI standardized term*] .... OVUIL
Operating Vehicle while Drunk [*Traffic offense charge*] .... OVWD
Operating Vehicle while Intoxicated [*Traffic offense charge*] .... OWI
Operating Vehicle without Owner's Consent [*Traffic offense charge*] .... OOC
Operating Weight [*Air Force*] .... OPW
Operating Weight Empty [*of space shuttle*] [*NASA*] .... OWE
Operating Year Guidance (GFGA) .... OYG
Operating-Differential Subsidy [*Authorized by Merchant Marine Act of 1936*] .... ODS
Operating-Differential Subsidy Agreement [*MARAD*] (TAG) .... ODSA
Operation .... O
Operation .... OP
Operation (AFM) .... OPER
Operation [*or Operational*] (KSC) .... oper
Operation (DD) .... OPN
Operation .... OPRN
Operation Acknowledge [*Computer science*] (MHDI) .... OPACK
Operation Alert [*Designed to test ability to recover from an enemy attack*] .... OPAL
Operation Analysis [*or Analyst*] (WDAA) .... OA
Operation Analysis Strategic Interaction Simulator [*Nuclear war games*] .... OASIS
Operation and Checkout [*NASA*] .... O & C
Operation and Checkout [*O & C is preferred*] [*NASA*] (KSC) .... O & C/O
Operation and Checkout [*NASA*] (IAA) .... OACO
Operation and Conservation of Naval Petroleum Reserves [*Budget appropriation title*] .... OCNPR
Operation and Conversion of Naval Petroleum Reserves (DNAB) .... OCPR
Operation and Inspection Record (KSC) .... O & IR
Operation and Inspection Route Sheet (DNAB) .... OIRS
Operation and Maintainability Data Record .... OMDR
Operation and Maintenance (DOMA) .... O & M
Operation and Maintenance (AD) .... O & M
Operation and Maintenance .... O & M
Operation and Maintenance Activities (AAG) .... O & MA
Operation and Maintenance, Army (AAGC) .... O&MA
Operation and Maintenance, Army National Guard (AABC) .... OMARNG
Operation and Maintenance, Defense Agencies [*DoD*] .... O & M-DA
Operation and Maintenance Facilities (MUGU) .... O & MF
Operation and Maintenance, Family Housing [*Army*] (AABC) .... O & MFH
Operation and Maintenance Instruction Summary Sheet [*NASA*] (MCD) .... OMISS
Operation and Maintenance Manual .... OMM
Operation and Maintenance, Naval Reserve (NVT) .... O & MNR
Operation and Maintenance, Navy .... O & MN
Operation and Maintenance of Facilities [*Army*] .... OMF
Operation and Maintenance of Facilities Budget Activity Account [*Army*] (AABC) .... OMFBAA
Operation and Maintenance of Facilities Cost Account [*Army*] (AABC) .... OMFCA
Operation and Maintenance of Facilities Summary Cost Account [*Army*] (AABC) .... OMFSCA
Operation and Regulation .... OANDR
Operation and Regulation (FAAC) .... OANDR
Operation and Support (MCD) .... OPS
Operation and Support Funds [*DoD*] (RDA) .... O & S
Operation Angel Plane (EA) .... OAP
Operation Anti-Christ (EA) .... OAC
Operation Appreciation (EA) .... OA
Operation Bahamas, Antilles, and Turks [*Air Force*] .... OPBAT
Operation Better Block .... OBB
Operation Big Vote (EA) .... OBV
Operation Blessing International [*An association*] .... OBI
Operation Brotherhood .... OB
Operation Buckle Down [*NHTSA*] (TAG) .... OBD
Operation Buster-Jangle [*Atomic weapons testing*] .... OBJ
Operation California (EA) .... OP-CAL
Operation Child Identification [*Defunct*] (EA) .... OCI
Operation Code (IAA) .... OC
Operation Code (IDOE) .... op code
Operation Code .... OPC
Operation Completion Notice (AAG) .... OCN
Operation Control [*Military*] (VNW) .... OPCON
Operation Control Key [*Computer science*] (IAA) .... OCK
Operation Control Language [*Computer programming*] .... OCL
Operation CORK [*Joan B. Kroc Foundation*] [*CORK is derived from the foundation name*] [*Defunct*] (EA) .... OC
Operation Counter (IAA) .... OPCTR
Operation Crossroads [*Atomic weapons testing*] .... OC
Operation Crossroads Africa (EA) .... OCA
Operation Data Analysis Program (IAA) .... ODAP
Operation Description .... OD
Operation Description Distribution Order .... ODDO
Operation Desert Capture [*DoD*] .... ODC
Operation Desert Storm [*Military*] (RDA) .... ODS
Operation Design Criteria (MCD) .... ODC
Operation Effectiveness Demonstration (RDA) .... OED
Operation Enterprise [*Hamilton, NY*] (EA) .... OE
Operation Enterprise Newsletter [*A publication*] .... OE
Operation, Evaluation Wartime Group (NATG) .... OEWG
Operation Everest II [*Army*] (RDA) .... OEII
Operation Eyesight Universal [*Canada*] (EAIO) .... OEU
Operation Fish Watch [*National Oceanic and Atmospheric Administration*] (MSC) .... OFW
Operation Grass Roots [*Small communities employment service*] .... OGR
Operation Greenhouse [*Atomic weapons testing*] .... OG
Operation Hours (DA) .... Op Hrs
Operation Identity (EA) .... OI
Operation Inspection Log (AAG) .... OIL
Operation Instruction Block (NITA) .... OIB
Operation Joshua (EA) .... OJ
Operation Last Laugh Independence Expenditure [*Political Action Committee opposed to Oliver North's candidacy for United States Senator of Virginia*] .... OLLIE
Operation Liftoff (EA) .... OL
Operation Load Code (MCD) .... OLC
Operation Mainstream (OICC) .... OM
Operation Management Room [*NASA*] (KSC) .... OMR
Operation Medicare Alert .... OMA
Operation Microscope [*Surgery*] .... OPMI
Operation Military Aid to the Civil Community [*British military*] (DMA) .... OPMACC
Operation Missouri Plan [*Program for five-day state funeral planned several years in advance for ex-President Harry Truman*] [*Army*] .... OPMOPLAN
Operation Mobilisation [*Religious movement*] [*British*] .... OM
Operation Model Evaluation Group, Air Force (MCD) .... OMEGA
Operation Monkees (EA) .... OM
Operation Move-In [*New York City*] .... OMI
Operation Notice (AAG) .... ON
Operation Oceanography Center [*Marine science*] (OSRA) .... OOC
Operation of Aircraft Costs (DNAB) .... OAC
Operation Order [*Military*] .... OO
Operation Overlord Preparations [*World War II*] .... OP
Operation Overlord Preparations, Inland Transport [*World War II*] .... OP(IT)
Operation Overlord Preparations, Service Leave and Travel [*World War II*] .... OP(ST)
Operation: Peace of Mind [*Later, Runaway Hotline*] [*An association*] (EA) .... POM
Operation Plan [*Army*] .... OPLAN
Operation Plan Analysis Logic [*Search technology*] .... OPAL
Operation Plan Package Appraisal (AFM) .... OPPA
Operation Plan, Southeast Asia [*Military*] .... OPLAN SEA
Operation Planning and Execution System for Railway Unified Network (PDAA) .... OPERUN
Operation Plans .... OP
Operation Plans Steering Group (DOMA) .... OPSG
Operation Prime Time [*Television*] .... OPT
Operation Protocol Data Unit [*Telecommunications*] (OSI) .... OPDU
Operation Reach-Out [*Department of Labor*] .... OR
Operation Record .... OR
Operation Register (IAA) .... OPREG
Operation Register (IAA) .... OREG
Operation Request [*Computer science*] (MHDI) .... OPREQ
Operation Rescue (EA) .... OR
Operation Rescue Saint Bernard [*Test given to Junior Woodchucks in Donald Duck comic by Carl Barks*] .... OR St B
Operation Response Area (MCD) .... ORA
Operation Sandstone [*Atomic weapons testing*] .... OS
Operation Sciences Appliquees [*Quebec*] .... OSA
Operation Sisters United (EA) .... OSU
Operation Smile (EA) .... OS
Operation Snapper [*Atomic weapons testing*] .... OS
Operation Status Equipment .... OSE
Operation Suburbia [*Defunct*] (EA) .... OS
Operation Support Facility [*National Weather Service*] (USDC) .... OSF
Operation Support Facility [*Marine science*] (OSRA) .... OSF
Operation Test Readiness Review [*Army*] .... OTRR
Operation Town Affiliations [*An association*] (EA) .... OTA
Operation, Transport, Inspection, Storage (MHDB) .... OTIS
Operation Unit .... OU
Operation Upshot-Knothole [*Atomic weapons testing*] .... OUK
Operation USA [*An association*] (EA) .... OUSA
Operation Venus (EA) .... OV
Operation Work Load Scheduling (MCD) .... OWLS
Operational (CAAL) .... OP
Operational (IDOE) .... op
Operational (AFM) .... OPL
Operational .... OPNL
Operational (AAG) .... OPRNL
Operational .... OPRNTL
Operational Acceptable Level of Traffic [*FAA*] (TAG) .... OALT
Operational Acceptance Test .... OAT
Operational Acceptance Test Procedure (NRCH) .... OATP
Operational Active Data [*Navy*] .... OAD
Operational Address Register [*Computer science*] (IAA) .... OAR
Operational Advice .... OA
Operational Aerospace Vehicle .... OAV
Operational Aft (MCD) .... OA
Operational Agreement (DNAB) .... OPAGREE
Operational Air Traffic (NATG) .... OAT
Operational Aircraft Not Fully Equipped (NG) .... OANFE
Operational Amplifier [*Telecommunications*] (TEL) .... OA
Operational Amplifier [*Computer science*] .... OP AMP
Operational Amplifier (IDOE) .... op amp
Operational [*or operations*] **Analysis** .... OA
Operational Analysis (IAA) .... OPERA
Operational Analysis and System Interface System .... OASIS

Operational Analysis Code Package (PDAA) .... OACP
Operational Analysis Division [*Air Force*] .... OAD
Operational and Organizational (RDA) .... O & O
Operational and Organizational (MCD) .... OAO
Operational and Safety Improvement Program (NVT) .... OSIP
Operational and Supportability Implementation System [*FAA*] (TAG) .... OASIS
Operational Announcing System (IAA) .... OAS
Operational Applications Laboratory [*Air Force*] .... OAL
Operational Applications of Satellite Snowcover Observations [*NASA*] .... OASSO
Operational Applications of Special Intelligence System (MCD) .... OASIS
Operational Approved Configuration Identification Index (SAA) .... OACII
Operational Area Industry Advisory Committee [*Civil Defense*] .... OAIAC
Operational Assignment (DA) .... OPAS
Operational Assist Project/Shipborne Application .... O/S
Operational Assistance [*United Nations Development Program*] .... OPAS
Operational Assistance and Instructive Data Equipment .... OAIDE
Operational Assurance/Fault Isolation (MCD) .... OA/FI
Operational Automatic Scheduling Information System (MUGU) .... OASIS
Operational Availability .... Ao
Operational Availability (AAGC) .... Ao
Operational Availability and Reliability [*Military*] .... OAR
Operational Availability Data [*Military*] .... OAD
Operational Availability Date [*Nuclear Regulatory Commission*] (GFGA) .... OAD
Operational Aviation Services - Australia [*ICAO designator*] (FAAC) .... OAX
Operational Base .... O/B
Operational Base [*Navy*] .... OB
Operational Base Development (AAG) .... OBD
Operational Base Facility .... OBF
Operational Base Launch [*Air Force*] .... OBL
Operational Base Unit [*British military*] (DMA) .... OBU
Operational Baseline Cost Estimate [*Army*] .... OBCE
Operational Battery Effectiveness Model (MCD) .... OBEM
Operational Bioinstrumentation System [*NASA*] .... OBS
Operational Biomedical Harness .... OBH
Operational Biomedical Sensors (NASA) .... OBS
Operational Biomedical Systems (KSC) .... OBS
Operational Call Sign (IAA) .... OCS
Operational Capability (AAG) .... OC
Operational Capability Date (AAG) .... OCD
Operational Capability Date (AD) .... ocd
Operational Capability Demonstration (AAGC) .... OCD
Operational Capability Development .... OCD
Operational Capability Development (NASA) .... OCD
Operational Capability Improvement Request Out of Commission, In Reserve [*Vesselstatus*] (DNAB) .... OCIR
Operational Capability Objective [*Army*] .... OCO
Operational Capability Plan [*Army*] .... OCP
Operational Capability Release .... OCR
Operational Change Report [*Military*] (NVT) .... OCR
Operational Characteristics (NATG) .... OCS
Operational Check (MCD) .... OC
Operational Check List (MUGU) .... OCL
Operational Checkout (AAG) .... OCO
Operational Checkout Instruction (AD) .... OCI
Operational Checkout Procedure [*NASA*] (KSC) .... OCP
Operational Climate Prediction and Services [*Marine science*] (OSRA) .... OCLIPS
Operational Climate Prediction and Services (USDC) .... OCLIPS
Operational Climatic Testing (MCD) .... OCT
Operational Command [*Military*] (MCD) .... OPCOM
Operational Command and Control Intelligence System [*Army*] (AABC) .... OCCIS
Operational Command and Control System [*Army*] (AABC) .... OCCS
Operational Command Center [*Navy*] (NVT) .... OPCOMCTR
Operational Communications Plan (MCD) .... OCP
Operational Computer (IEEE) .... OC
Operational Computer Complex (KSC) .... OCC
Operational Concept Document .... OCD
Operational Configuration Control Board (AFM) .... OCCB
Operational Control [*Army*] (NVT) .... OPCON
Operational Control Authority [*NATO*] .... OCA
Operational Control Center [*Navy*] .... OPCONCEN
Operational Control Center [*Navy*] (NVT) .... OPCONCTR
Operational Control Equipment (AD) .... oce
Operational Control Facility (SAA) .... OCF
Operational Control Level .... OCL
Operational Control Panel .... OCP
Operational Control Record [*Nuclear energy*] (NRCH) .... OCR
Operational Control Segment (SSD) .... OCS
Operational Control Unit .... OCU
Operational Control Zone (MCD) .... OCZ
Operational Conversion Unit (NATG) .... OCU
Operational Conversion Unit (AD) .... ocu
Operational Cycle Time .... OCT
Operational Data Analysis .... ODA
Operational Data and Notices to Airmen [*FAA*] .... ODNA
Operational Data Book [*NASA*] (KSC) .... ODB
Operational Data Center [*Deep Space Network, NASA*] .... ODC
Operational Data Delivery Services (MCD) .... ODDS
Operational Data Group (MCD) .... ODG
Operational Data Management (KSC) .... ODM
Operational Data Management System [*FAA*] (TAG) .... ODMS
Operational Data Processing Squadron .... ODPS
Operational Data Summary (AAG) .... ODS
Operational Database (SSD) .... ODB
Operational Deception [*Navy*] (NVT) .... OPDEC
Operational Demand Time [*Military*] (CAAL) .... ODT
Operational Demonstration Test .... ODT
Operational Deployment Force (AD) .... ODF
Operational Design and Analysis (IEEE) .... ODA
Operational Design Group .... ODG
Operational Design Resolution (SAA) .... ODR
Operational Detachment (MCD) .... OPDET
Operational Detachment Delta [*Antiterrorist unit*] [*Military*] (LAIN) .... ODD
Operational Development Forces .... OPDEVFOR
Operational Development Ground Support Equipment (AAG) .... ODGSE
Operational Development Inspection (SAA) .... ODI
Operational Development Memorandum (AAG) .... ODM
Operational Development Plan [*or Program*] .... ODP
Operational Development Team (IAA) .... ODT
Operational Development Test Facility (AAG) .... ODTF
Operational Development Test Site (AAG) .... ODTS
Operational Direction and Management Control (NATG) .... OD and MC
Operational Display Information Network (MCD) .... ODIN
Operational Display Procedure (MCD) .... ODP
Operational Display System .... Z/S
Operational Document Control .... ODC
Operational Documentation [*Military*] .... OPDOC
Operational Downlink/Downlist (NASA) .... OD
Operational DownList .... OD
Operational Drawing Revision Advance Notice (NASA) .... ODRAN
Operational Effectiveness Analysis (MCD) .... OEA
Operational ELINT Requirements (MCD) .... OER
Operational Employment Concept [*Army*] (AABC) .... OEC
Operational Employment Plan [*Army*] .... OEP
Operational Employment Testing and Evaluation (AFM) .... OET & E
Operational Empty Weight [*Aviation*] .... OEW
Operational Engineering Detachment (MCD) .... OED
Operational Engineering Division [*Central Electricity Generating Board*] [*British*] (IRUK) .... OED
Operational Equipment Requirement (AAG) .... OER
Operational Equipment Requirement (IAA) .... OR
Operational Error Analysis Program .... OEAP
Operational Evaluation [*Army*] .... OE
Operational Evaluation [*Navy*] (NG) .... OPEVAL
Operational Evaluation and Training Squadron [*Air Force*] .... OPNSEVAL & TNGSq
Operational Evaluation Command [*Army*] (DOMA) .... OEC
Operational Evaluation Demonstration (MCD) .... OED
Operational Evaluation of Armed Helicopters (MCD) .... OPENAH
Operational, Executive, and Administrative Personnel Program [*United Nations*] .... OPEX
Operational Exercise [*NATO*] (NATG) .... OPREX
Operational Exposure Guidance [*Military*] (INF) .... OEG
Operational Extension .... OPEX
Operational Facilities Branch [*NASA*] (MCD) .... OFB
Operational Facility (RDA) .... OPFAC
Operational Failure Report (IAA) .... OFR
Operational Feasibility Testing (MCD) .... OFT
Operational Figure of Merit [*Military*] (CAAL) .... OFOM
Operational Fixed .... OF
Operational Fixed Microwave Council (IAA) .... OFMC
Operational Fleet Requirements (MCD) .... OFR
Operational Flight and Tactics Simulator (MCD) .... OFTS
Operational Flight and Tactics Trainer (MCD) .... OFTT
Operational Flight Control [*NASA*] .... OFC
Operational Flight Control System [*NASA*] (KSC) .... OFCS
Operational Flight Information Service [*ICAO*] (DA) .... OFIS
Operational Flight Instrumentation [*NASA*] (NASA) .... OFI
Operational Flight Profile [*NASA*] (NASA) .... OFP
Operational Flight Profit .... OFP
Operational Flight Program [*NASA*] (NASA) .... OFP
Operational Flight Safety Monitor (SAA) .... OFSM
Operational Flight Trainer .... OFT
Operational Flight Transfer Airframe .... OFTA
Operational Flight/Weapons System Trainer (NG) .... OF/WST
Operational Forces Interface Group [*US Army Natick Research, Development, and Engineering Center*] [*Natick, MA*] (RDA) .... OFIG
Operational Format Program [*NASA*] (KSC) .... OFP
Operational Ground Equipment (AD) .... oge
Operational Ground Support Equipment (AAG) .... OGSE
Operational Ground Support Equipment List (AAG) .... OGSEL
Operational Ground Support Equipment Systems Specification (SAA) .... OGSESS
Operational Ground-Support Equipment (AD) .... ogse
Operational Group [*World War II*] .... OG
Operational Handbook [*Marine Corps*] (INF) .... OH
Operational Hardware (KSC) .... OH
Operational Hazard Analysis (NASA) .... OHA
Operational Hazard Report [*Air Force*] (AFM) .... OHR
Operational Hydrology Program [*World Meteorological Organization*] (GFGA) .... OHP
Operational Hydromet Data Management System (PDAA) .... OHDMS
Operational Improvement Plan [*or Program*] [*Navy*] .... OIP
Operational Independent Evaluator .... OIE
Operational Insertion System .... OIS
Operational Instruction Pamphlet .... OIP
Operational Instrumentation (NASA) .... OI
Operational Instrumentation System .... OIS
Operational Intelligence .... OI
Operational Intelligence .... OPINTEL
Operational Intelligence Centre [*British military*] (DMA) .... OIC
Operational Intelligence Collection System .... OICS

Operational Intelligence Crisis Center [Defense Intelligence Adgency] (DOMA) ... OICC
Operational Intelligence Support System (MCD) ... OISS
Operational Intercommunication System [NASA] (KSC) ... OIS
Operational Issue [Military] ... OI
Operational LASER Beam Recorder ... OLBR
Operational Launch Station (AAG) ... OLS
Operational Left ... OL
Operational Lines of Succession [Defense readiness] ... OLS
Operational Linescan System [Navy] (ANA) ... OLS
Operational Logistic Support Plan ... OLSP
Operational Logistic Support Summary [Military] (CAAL) ... OLSS
Operational Maintainability Problem Reporting (NASA) ... OMPR
Operational Maintainability Reporting Systems Document [NASA] (NASA) ... OMRSD
Operational Maintenance Activity (NVT) ... OMA
Operational Maintenance Battalion [Army] (DOMA) ... OMB
Operational Maintenance Instruction (AAG) ... OMI
Operational Maintenance Requirements and Specifications Document [NASA] (NASA) ... OMRSD
Operational Maintenance Requirements Catalog [NASA] (MCD) ... OMRC
Operational Maintenance Support Plan [NASA] (MCD) ... OMSP
Operational Maintenance System ... OMS
Operational Management [Computer science] (IAA) ... OM
Operational Management Information System [Computer science] ... OMIS
Operational Maneuver from the Sea [Marine Corps] (DOMA) ... OMFTS
Operational Maneuvering Reentry Vehicle (MCD) ... OMRV
Operational Maneuvering Reentry Vehicle (MCD) ... OPMARV
Operational Meteorological Information [ICAO] (FAAC) ... OPMET
Operational Meteorological Satellite [NASA] ... OMS
Operational Miscellaneous Audio Subsystem ... OMAS
Operational Mission Environment (MCD) ... OME
Operational Mission Failure (MCD) ... OMF
Operational Mission Summary [Army] ... OMS
Operational Mock-Up ... OMU
Operational Mode Summary ... OMS
Operational Mode Summary/Mission Profiles (MCD) ... OMS/MP
Operational Modification Report (IAA) ... OMR
Operational Monitor (IAA) ... OM
Operational Monitor (AD) ... om
Operational Monitoring System (MCD) ... OMS
Operational Navigation Charts [Air Force] ... ONC
Operational Needs Statement [Army] ... ONS
Operational NonRADAR Directed Flights (NATG) ... ONR
Operational Note (MCD) ... OPNOTE
Operational Nuclear Planning Group [Military] ... ONPG
Operational Oceanography Center (USDC) ... OOC
Operational OGE [Operational Ground Equipment] Data Acquisition and Patch Subsystem (GAVI) ... ODAPS
Operational Operating System [Telecommunications] (TEL) ... OOS
Operational Paging System [NASA] (KSC) ... OPS
Operational Performance Analysis Language [Computer science] ... OPAL
Operational Performance Data System ... OPDATS
Operational Performance Goals ... OPG
Operational Performance Recording and Evaluation Data System [Military] (CAAL) ... OPREDS
Operational Performance Standard [Aviation] (DA) ... OPS
Operational Performance Unit (ADA) ... OPU
[The] Operational PERT System ... TOPS
Operational Plan Data Document [Military] (AFM) ... OPDD
Operational Planning and Control System [Department of Labor] (OICC) ... OPCS
Operational Planning and Review Systems [Employment and Training Administration] [Department of Labor] ... OPRS
Operational Planning Estimate ... OPE
Operational Planning Grant (OICC) ... OPG
Operational Planning Identification File [Military] ... OPDIF
Operational Planning Identification File (MCD) ... OPIDF
Operational Planning Identification File ... OPIDF
Operational Power Supply ... OPS
Operational Preference (DA) ... OPR
Operational Pressure Transducer (MCD) ... OPT
Operational Priority ... OP
Operational Priority Indicating System (NATG) ... OPIS
Operational Procedure (MCD) ... OP
Operational Procedures Interface Document (MCD) ... OPID
Operational Proficiency Training Equipment [Roland International Corp.] (MCD) ... OPTE
Operational Program Functional Checkout (MCD) ... OPFCO
Operational Program Time Base [NASA] (MCD) ... OPTB
Operational Programming Department [Telecommunications] (TEL) ... OPD
Operational Project [Army] (AABC) ... OP
Operational Project Requirements (AABC) ... OPR
Operational Propellant Handling [NASA] (AAG) ... OPH
Operational Propellant Handling System [NASA] (AAG) ... OPHS
Operational Propellant Handling Test Site [NASA] (AAG) ... OPHTS
Operational Propulsion Plant Examination [Navy] (NVT) ... OPPE
Operational Protection System [Nuclear energy] (NRCH) ... OPS
Operational Public Address System ... OPAS
Operational Qualification (ACII) ... OQ
Operational Qualifications Test Deficiency [Air Force] ... OQTD
Operational RADAR Directed Flights (NATG) ... ORA
Operational Radiation Instrumentation Equipment (SAA) ... ORIE
Operational Radio Interferometry Observing Network (MCD) ... ORION
Operational Reactor Safeguard Examination (NVT) ... ORSE
Operational Reactor Safeguards (DNAB) ... ORS
Operational Readiness [Army] ... OR
Operational Readiness [Navy] (NG) ... ORE
Operational Readiness and Confidence Test ... ORACT
Operational Readiness and Reliability Test ... ORRT
Operational Readiness Assessment ... ORA
Operational Readiness Assessment and Training System (MCD) ... ORATS
Operational Readiness Check ... ORC
Operational Readiness Date ... ORD
Operational Readiness Demonstration [FAA] (TAG) ... ORD
Operational Readiness Evaluation [Army] ... ORE
Operational Readiness Exercise (MCD) ... ORE
Operational Readiness Float (AABC) ... ORF
Operational Readiness Inspection [Army] ... ORI
Operational Readiness Inspection Committee [NASA] ... ORIC
Operational Readiness Inspection Team [Air Force] ... ORIT
Operational Readiness Inspection Test [Air Force] ... ORIT
Operational Readiness Instruction [Military] ... ORI
Operational Readiness Management System ... ORMS
Operational Readiness Monitoring System (MCD) ... ORMONS
Operational Readiness Panel ... ORP
Operational Readiness Platform [Aviation] (DA) ... ORP
Operational Readiness Report (Nonatomic) (CINC) ... REDNON
Operational Readiness Reporting ... ORR
Operational Readiness Review (NASA) ... ORR
Operational Readiness Test ... ORT
Operational Readiness Test System [Military] (CAAL) ... ORTS
Operational Readiness Training [Army] ... ORT
Operational Readiness Training - Combat Training Launch [Military] (SAA) ... ORT/CTL
Operational Readiness Training Equipment [Military] (SAA) ... ORTE
Operational Readiness Training Program [Military] (AABC) ... ORTP
Operational Readiness Training Test [Army] (AABC) ... ORTT
Operational Readiness Unit ... ORU
Operational Readiness-Oriented Supply System [Army] (PDAA) ... OROSS
Operational Ready [or Readiness] Data [NASA] (GFGA) ... ORD
Operational Ready Data ... ORD
Operational Ready Rate (MCD) ... ORR
Operational Reentry Systems Evaluation Program (SAA) ... ORSEP
Operational Reliability [Army] (AABC) ... OR
Operational Replenishment Ship [Canadian Navy] ... AOR
Operational Report (AAG) ... OR
Operational Reporting [Army] ... OPREP
Operational Reporting System [Military] ... OPREPS
Operational Reports Control [Military] (AFM) ... ORC
Operational Reports - Lessons Learned [Army] (AABC) ... ORLL
Operational Requirement ... OR
Operational Requirements Committee [Ministry of Defence] [British] ... ORC
Operational Requirements Handbook ... ORH
Operational Requirements/Military Characteristics (NG) ... OR/MC
Operational Requirements Working Group (DOMA) ... ORWG
Operational Research ... OR
Operational Research and Analysis Establishment (MCD) ... ORAE
Operational Research and Analysis Establishment, Department of National Defence [Centre d'Analyse et de Recherche Operationnelle, Ministere de la Defense Nationale] Ottawa, Ontario [Library symbol National Library of Canada] (NLC) ... OONDORAE
Operational Research and Systems Analysis (PDAA) ... ORASA
Operational Research Branch [Canada] ... ORB
Operational Research Co., Universal Systems ... ORCUS
Operational Research Division [Department of National Defence] [Canada] ... ORD
Operational Research in Electrical Power Systems (PDAA) ... OREPS
Operational Research Section (Bomber Command) [British World War II] ... ORS(BC)
Operational Research Section (Singapore) [Military] ... ORS(S)
Operational Research Society [British] ... ORS
Operational Research Society [British] (DBA) ... ORSoc
Operational Research Society (ACII) ... ORSociety
Operational Research Station [Air Ministry] [British World War II] ... ORS
Operational Research Unit, Far East ... ORUFE
Operational Resource Management Assessment System [Military] ... ORMAS
Operational Right ... OR
Operational Safety Review Team [International Atomic Energy Agency] ... OSART
Operational Satellite Active Archive (USDC) ... OSAA
Operational Satellite Active Archive [Marine science] (OSRA) ... OSAA
Operational Scanning Recognition ... OSR
Operational Sea Vehicle Diagram (MCD) ... OSD
Operational Search Lower Bound [RADAR] ... OSLB
Operational Security ... OPSEC
Operational Security Evaluation (MCD) ... OSE
Operational Sequence (KSC) ... OS
Operational Sequence Diagram (IEEE) ... OSD
Operational Service Fee (WDAA) ... OSF
Operational Sheets ... OS
Operational Silo Test Facility ... OSTF
Operational Simulation Subsystem (MCD) ... OPSIMS
Operational Simulator [Coast Guard] ... OPSIM
Operational Simulator Console ... OSC
Operational Specialist [Navy] ... OS
Operational Specialist Supervisor, Night [Navy] ... OSSN
Operational Standoff Range (NVT) ... OSOR
Operational Station (SAA) ... OPS
Operational Status [Navy] (NVT) ... OPSTAT
Operational Status BIT [Binary Digit] ... OSB
Operational Status Indicator (MUGU) ... OSI
Operational Status Recording Subsystem ... OSRS

Operational Status Release [*Navy*] (NG) .... OSR
Operational Storage Site [*Army*] .... OSS
Operational SUBPAY (DNAB) .... OPSUB
Operational Suitability .... OS
Operational Suitability Improvement Program [*Aviation*] .... OSIP
Operational Suitability Test [*Aviation*] .... OST
Operational Suitability Test Facility [*Aviation*] .... OSTF
Operational Suitability Test Site [*Aviation*] (AAG) .... OSTS
Operational Summary [*Navy*] (NVT) .... OPSUM
Operational Summary Console .... OSC
Operational Supplements [*Air Force*] (MCD) .... OS
Operational Supply Support Plan (MCD) .... OSSP
Operational Support (MCD) .... OPS
Operational Support Aircraft [*or Airlift*] .... OSA
Operational Support Airlift [*Air Force*] (DOMA) .... OSA
Operational Support Area .... OSA
Operational Support Area (NASA) .... OSA
Operational Support Center (NRCH) .... OSC
Operational Support Chart [*Nuclear energy*] (NUCP) .... OSC
Operational Support Directive [*Military*] (AFM) .... OSD
Operational Support Equipment .... OSE
Operational Support Equipment Design Specification .... OSEDS
Operational Support Facility (MCD) .... OPSUPPFAC
Operational Support Integration Engineering .... OSIE
Operational Support Maintenance Plan [*NASA*] (MCD) .... OSMP
Operational Support Readiness .... OSR
Operational Support Requirement [*Military*] .... OSR
Operational Support System [*Computer science*] .... OSS
Operational Support Television [*Military*] (AFM) .... OSTV
Operational Surveillance Program [*Nuclear Regulatory Commission*] (NRCH) .... OSP
Operational Survival Plan [*Civil Defense*] .... OSP
Operational Switching Cabinet .... OSC
Operational Switching Unit .... OSU
Operational Switching Unit .... OSW
Operational Synchronous Earth Observatory Satellite [*Telecommunications*] (TEL) .... OSEOS
Operational System Characteristics .... OSCAR
Operational System Development Program .... OSDP
Operational System Interface Document (MCD) .... OSID
Operational System Test (KSC) .... OST
Operational System Test Facility [*Air Force*] .... OSTF
Operational Systems Development (MCD) .... OSD
Operational Tasking (DOMA) .... OPTASK
Operational Taxonomic Unit [*Numerical taxonomy*] .... OTU
Operational Technical Documentation [*NASA*] (NASA) .... OTD
Operational Technical Managerial System (NVT) .... OTMS
Operational Techniques Conference .... OTC
Operational Technology [*Nuclear energy*] (NRCH) .... OT
Operational Teletype Communications Subsystem .... OTCS
Operational Teletype Message .... OPS-X
Operational Teletype Network .... OTN
Operational Television (KSC) .... OTV
Operational Test (AFM) .... OT
Operational Test Agency (DOMA) .... OTA
Operational Test and Evaluation [*Military*] .... OPTEV
Operational Test and Evaluation [*Military*] (AFM) .... OT & E
Operational Test and Evaluation [*Army*] (AABC) .... OTE
Operational Test and Evaluation Agency [*Army*] .... OTEA
Operational Test and Evaluation Command [*Army*] (RDA) .... OPTEC
Operational Test and Evaluation Command [*Army*] (AAGC) .... OTEC
Operational Test and Evaluation Force [*Norfolk, VA*] [*Navy*] .... OPTEVFOR
Operational Test and Evaluation Force Detachment (DNAB) .... OPTEVFORDET
Operational Test and Evaluation Plan [*Military*] (AFM) .... OTEP
Operational Test and Evaluation Squadron [*Military*] .... OTES
Operational Test Center [*NASA*] (KSC) .... OTC
Operational Test Coordinator [*Military*] (CAAL) .... OTC
Operational Test, Development Test .... OTDT
Operational Test Director [*Navy*] .... OTD
Operational Test Equipment [*NASA*] (KSC) .... OTE
Operational Test/Follow-On Operational Test .... OT/FOT
Operational Test/Follow-On Test [*Missiles*] (DOMA) .... OT/FT
Operational Test Incident Report (MCD) .... OTIR
Operational Test Instrumentation Ship [*Navy*] .... OTIS
Operational Test, Non-Major Systems (MCD) .... OTN
Operational Test Plan .... OTP
Operational Test Procedure (KSC) .... OTP
Operational Test Program Instruction (MCD) .... OTPI
Operational Test Program Set (MCD) .... OTPS
Operational Test Program Tape (MCD) .... OTPT
Operational Test Readiness Statement .... OTRS
Operational Test Site (AAG) .... OTS
Operational Test Support System .... OTSS
Operational Test Supportability Demonstration .... OTSD
Operational Test Unit (KSC) .... OTU
Operational Test Vehicle (IAA) .... OTV
Operational Testing and Evaluation (USDC) .... OT&E
Operational Testing, Training, and Evaluation .... OTTE
Operational Time Record (AAG) .... OTR
Operational Time Sync .... OTS
Operational TIROS [*NASA*] .... OT
Operational Traffic Flow Planning (GAVI) .... OTFP
Operational Training (DNAB) .... OPTRA
Operational Training (MCD) .... OT
Operational Training and Evaluation Facility .... OTEF

Operational Training Capability [*Air Force*] (AFM) .... OTC
Operational Training Command (MCD) .... OTC
Operational Training Squadron (DNAB) .... OPTRARON
Operational Training Squadron (MCD) .... OTS
Operational Training System [*HAWK*] .... OTS
Operational Training Test (NVT) .... OTT
Operational Training, Test, and Evaluation RADAR .... OTTER
Operational Training Unit [*Military*] .... OTU
Operational Trajectory [*Aerospace*] (KSC) .... OT
Operational Transconductance Amplifier (IEEE) .... OTA
Operational Transit (GAAI) .... OPTRAN
Operational Unit Transportable System (MCD) .... OUTS
Operational Use Data .... OUD
Operational Utility Evaluation .... OUE
Operational Validation Inspection (MCD) .... OVI
Operational Verification/Demonstration .... OV/D
Operational Verification Test .... OVT
Operational Video Tape Recorder [*Air Force*] (MCD) .... OVTR
Operational Voice Communication Office [*NASA*] (MCD) .... OVCO
Operational Voice Communication Subsystem .... OVCS
Operational Voice Recording Subsystem .... OVRS
Operational Voice System (MCD) .... OVS
Operational Weather Support .... OWS
Operationally Available (NATG) .... OA
Operationally Ready [*Army*] (AABC) .... OPRDY
Operationally Ready (MCD) .... OR
Operationally Ready Time .... ORT
Operational-Maneuver Group [*Military*] .... OMG
Operation...Life Support [*Online lobbying for the television show "My So-Called Life"*] .... OLS
Operations (KSC) .... OP
Operations (NASA) .... OPNS
Operations (MCD) .... OPS
Operations/Administration (SSD) .... O/A
Operations, Administration, and Maintenance [*Telecommunications*] .... OA & M
Operations Advisor [*NASA*] .... OA
Operations/Air Intelligence Photography Division (DNAB) .... OP DIV
Operations Analysis [*Navy*] (NG) .... OPANAL
Operations Analysis Center .... OAC
Operations Analysis Chief [*Air Force*] .... OAC
Operations Analysis Office, Air Force (MCD) .... OAOAF
Operations Analysis Office, Air Force Logistics Command (MCD) .... OAOAFLC
Operations Analysis Report .... OAR
Operations Analysis Working Paper [*NASA*] (KSC) .... OAWP
Operations and Control System (IAA) .... OPCON
Operations and Engineering .... O & E
Operations and Engineering (AD) .... o & e
Operations and Engineering Squadron .... OES
Operations and Equipment Section (SAA) .... OES
Operations and Flight Support [*NASA*] (NASA) .... O & FS
Operations and Food Analysis .... OF
Operations and Intelligence [*Section*] [*Army*] (INF) .... O & I
Operations and Intelligence Tactical Data Systems (MCD) .... OITDS
Operations and Liquidations Division [*Federal Savings and Loans Insurance Corporation*] .... OLD
Operations and Logistics (IAA) .... OAL
Operations and Maintainer Decision .... OMD
Operations and Maintenance, Air Force .... OMAF
Operations and Maintenance Application Part [*Telecommunications*] .... OMAP
Operations and Maintenance Appopriation [*Army*] .... OMA
Operations and Maintenance, Army .... OMA
Operations and Maintenance, Army Reserve (AABC) .... OMAR
Operations and Maintenance Control File [*NASA*] (NASA) .... OMCF
Operations and Maintenance Data Record [*NASA*] (KSC) .... OMDR
Operations and Maintenance Documentation [*NASA*] (NASA) .... OMD
Operations and Maintenance, Marine Corps .... O & MMC
Operations and Maintenance, National Guard [*Army*] .... OMNG
Operations and Maintenance, Navy (AFIT) .... OAMN
Operations and Maintenance Plan [*NASA*] (NASA) .... OMP
Operations and Maintenance Requirements (NASA) .... OMR
Operations and Maintenance Requirements and Specification Documentation (NASA) .... OMRSD
Operations and Maintenance Requirements and Specifications Documentation .... OMRSD
Operations and Maintenance Requirements/Plan [*NASA*] (NASA) .... OMR/P
Operations and Maintenance Requirements Specifications (NASA) .... OMRS
Operations and Maintenance Security Working Group (SSD) .... OMSWG
Operations and Management .... O & M
Operations and Management (MCD) .... OAM
Operations and Procedures (KSC) .... O & P
Operations and Procedures (IAA) .... OAP
Operations and Regulations (IAA) .... OAR
Operations and Support (MCD) .... O & S
Operations and Sustainment Cost Reduction Strategy (RDA) .... OSCR
Operations and Technical Data [*Engineering*] .... OTD
Operations and Telling (SAA) .... OPT
Operations and Training [*Military*] .... O & T
Operations and Training Section [*of an air staff; also, officer in charge of this section*] [*Air Force*] A-3
Operations and Training Section [*of an Army or Marine Corps division general staff or Marine brigade or aircraft wing general staff; also, the officer in charge of this section*] G-3
Operations and Training Section [*of a joint military staff; also, the officer in charge of this section*] J-3

Operations and Training Section [*in Army brigades or smaller units, and in Marine Corps units smaller than a brigade; also, the officer in charge of this section*] S-3
Operations Area .... OA
Operations Capability Reference (SSD) .... OCR
Operations Cargo Passenger Office (DNAB) .... OCPO
Operations Center [*Military*] .... OC
Operations Center [*INTELSAT*] .... OPCEN
Operations Center [*Military*] .... OPCTR
Operations Chief [*Deep Space Network, NASA*] .... OC
Operations Code [*Army*] (IAA) .... OPC
Operations Code [*Army*] (AABC) .... OPCODE
Operations/Combat Information Center Division (DNAB) .... OI DIV
Operations Command and Control Information System [*Military*] .... OCCIS
Operations, Commitments, and Requirements [*Military*] .... OC & R
Operations Communications (MCD) .... OPSCOMM
Operations Concept Document .... OCD
Operations Conductor (MUGU) .... OC
Operations Console Operator (MUGU) .... OCO
Operations Control .... OC
Operations Control (IAA) .... OPC
Operations Control [*NASA*] (KSC) .... OPSCON
Operations, Control, and Analysis Center (DOMA) .... OCAC
Operations Control and Display Facility [*Military*] (RDA) .... OCDF
Operations Control Center [*or Console*] (AFM) .... OCC
Operations Control Plan (AAG) .... OCP
Operations Control [*Monitor*] **Program** .... OPSCOP
Operations Control Room [*Military*] (CAAL) .... OCR
Operations Control System .... OCS
Operations Control Team [*Deep Space Network, NASA*] .... OCT
Operations Control Technique for Actuals Number Extraction (MCD) .... OCTANE
Operations Coordinating Board [*Terminated, 1961*] [*National Security Council*] .... OCB
Operations Coordinator [*Marine science*] (MSC) .... OPECO
[*The*] **Operations Council of the American Trucking Associations** (EA) .... TOC
Operations Critical (MCD) .... O/C
Operations Data Message (MCD) .... ODM
Operations Deputy [*In JCS system*] [*Military*] .... OPSDEP
Operations Design Reference Mission (MCD) .... ODRM
Operations Directive [*or Director*] .... OD
Operations Directorate Station (SAA) .... ODS
Operations Division .... OD
Operations Division [*War Department General Staff*] [*World War II*] .... OPD
Operations Division [*NATO*] (NATG) .... OPS
Operations Division of Naval Staff [*British*] .... ODNS
Operations Division, War Department General Staff [*World War II*] .... OPD WDGS
Operations Duty Officer (MUGU) .... ODO
Operations Engineering (AAG) .... OE
Operations Engineering Report (AAG) .... OER
Operations Evaluation Group [*Military*] .... OEG
Operations Experimental Test Plan (IAA) .... OETP
Operations Fixed Service [*Microwave service*] (NTCM) .... OFS
Operations Flight [*Military*] .... OPF
Operations Following (MCD) .... OF
Operations for Military Assistance to the Community (PDAA) .... OPMAC
Operations in a Nuclear Environment [*DoD*] .... OPINE
Operations Instrumentation Coordinator [*NASA*] (KSC) .... OIC
Operations Integration Branch [*NASA*] (KSC) .... OIB
Operations Integration Instruction [*NASA*] (NASA) .... OII
Operations Integration Officer [*NASA*] (MCD) .... OIO
Operations Integration Review (NASA) .... OIR
Operations Interface (MCD) .... OI
Operations Interface Control Chart (KSC) .... OICC
Operations Knowledge Data Base Management System [*NASA*] .... OKDBMS
Operations Launch Order (MUGU) .... OLO
Operations Library, Syncrude Canada Ltd., Fort McMurray, Alberta [*Library symbol National Library of Canada*] (NLC) .... AFMS
Operations/Logistics .... O/L
Operations/Logistics (AD) .... o/l
Operations/Lookout and Recognition Division (DNAB) .... OLDIV
Operations Maintenance .... OM
Operations Maintenance Area (NASA) .... OMA
Operations Management Application (SSD) .... OMA
Operations Management Education and Research Foundation (EA) .... OMER
Operations Management Education and Research Foundation [*Formerly, OFMP*] (EA) .... OMERF
Operations Management Ground Application (SSD) .... OMGA
Operations Management Room [*NASA*] .... OMR
Operations Management System (SSD) .... OMS
Operations Manager .... OM
Operations Manager [*The assistant manager at some radio stations*] (WDMC) .... OM
Operations Manager's Report .... OMR
Operations Manual (NITA) .... OM
Operations Manual Letter [*National Weather Service*] (NOAA) .... OML
Operations Memorandum [*Department of Agriculture*] (GFGA) .... OM
Operations Message (SSD) .... OPM
Operations Monitor Alarm .... OMA
Operations Monitoring Computer .... OMC
Operations Normal (FAAC) .... OPNML
Operations Office [*Environmental Protection Agency*] (GFGA) .... OO
Operations Officer [*Navy British*] .... OO
Operations Officer [*Navy*] (DOMA) .... OPS O
Operations Operating Budget [*Military*] (AFIT) .... OOB
Operations Order (MCD) .... OP

Operations Order [*Army*] .... OPORD
Operations Orientation Director [*NASA*] .... OOD
Operations Other Than War [*Army*] (INF) .... OOTW
Operations Panel [*ICAO*] (DA) .... OPSP
Operations per Minute [*Performance measure*] .... OPM
Operations per Second (IAA) .... OPS
Operations per Second (IAA) .... OPSEC
Operations Plan (IAA) .... OP
Operations Plan (KSC) .... OPL
Operations Plan (KSC) .... OPPLAN
Operations Planning Analysis [*NASA*] (MCD) .... OPA
Operations Planning Division [*Manned Spacecraft Center*] .... OPD
Operations Planning Group [*Military*] .... OPG
Operations Planning Project Engineer [*Deep Space Instrumentation Facility, NASA*] .... OPPE
Operations Planning Review (NASA) .... OPR
Operations Planning Team [*Air Force*] (DOMA) .... OPT
Operations Priority Unit .... OPU
Operations Procedure (MUGU) .... OPR
Operations Project Engineer [*NASA*] (KSC) .... OPE
Operations Quality Assurance [*Nuclear energy*] (NRCH) .... OQA
Operations Readiness (MCD) .... OPSRDY
Operations Record Book [*Air Ministry*] [*British World War II*] .... ORB
Operations Reduction [*Government term*] .... OPRED
Operations Report [*NATO*] (NATG) .... OPSREP
Operations Request [*Military*] .... OR
Operations [*or Operational*] **Requirement Document** .... ORD
Operations Requirements .... OR
Operations Requirements Review (NASA) .... ORR
Operations Research [*Computer science*] .... OR
Operations Research Analyst [*Army*] (AABC) .... ORA
Operations Research and Development Management (PDAA) .... OPRAD
Operations, Research and Facilities (USDC) .... OR&F
Operations, Research and Facilities [*Marine science*] (OSRA) .... OR&F
Operations Research Center [*Massachusetts Institute of Technology*] [*Research center*] (KSC) .... ORC
Operations Research Group .... ORG
Operations Research, Inc. [*Information service or system*] .... ORI
Operations Research Office .... ORO
Operations Research or Management Science .... OR/MS
Operations Research Service [*FAA*] (TAG) .... AOR
Operations Research Society of America (EA) .... ORSA
Operations Research/Systems Analysis [*Army*] .... OR/SA
Operations Research/Systems Analysis Executive Course [*Army*] .... OR/SAEC
Operations Research Technical Assistance Group [*Army*] (PDAA) .... ORTAG
Operations Review [*NASA*] (MCD) .... OR
Operations Room .... OR
Operations, Scheduling, Control, and Reporting (MCD) .... OSCAR
Operations Scheduling Office (SSD) .... OSO
Operations Security Program (AAGC) .... OPSEC
Operations Sequence [*NASA*] (MCD) .... OPS
Operations Sequence Chart (MCD) .... OSC
Operations Shop/Laboratory Manager [*NASA*] (MCD) .... OSLM
Operations Shop/Laboratory Manager .... OSLM
Operations Specialist [*Navy*] (DNAB) .... OPS
Operations Squadron .... OPS
Operations Staff [*Military British*] .... OPS
Operations Stations Book [*Navy*] .... OSB
Operations Status Report (NATG) .... OPSTATUSREP
Operations Subdirective .... OSD
Operations Suitability Assessment Report (SSD) .... OSAR
Operations Supervisor [*NASA*] (MCD) .... OPSR
Operations Support Building [*NASA*] (KSC) .... OSB
Operations Support Computing Facility (MCD) .... OSCF
Operations Support Group [*Nuclear energy*] (NRCH) .... OSG
Operations Support Plan [*Navy*] (NG) .... OSP
Operations Support Requirements Office [*NASA*] (KSC) .... OSRO
Operations Support Room [*NASA*] (KSC) .... OSR
Operations Support Room [*NASA*] .... OSR
Operations Support System (DOMA) .... OSS
Operations Support Team [*NASA*] (MCD) .... OST
Operations Support Wing [*NASA*] .... OSW
Operations System Development Program [*Marine science*] (OSRA) .... OSDP
Operations Systems Engineering Support (MCD) .... OSES
Operations Tactical Data Systems [*Army*] (RDA) .... OPTADS
Operations Target Analysis [*of strike missions in North Vietnam*] .... OPTAN
Operations Team (MCD) .... OT
Operations Training and Technical Services [*Nuclear Regulatory Commission*] (NRCH) .... OTTS
Operations Training Certification Management System [*NASA*] .... OTCMS
Operations Training Development Team [*Air Force*] .... OTDT
Operations Turnaround Plan (NASA) .... OTP
Operations Work Procedure [*Nuclear energy*] (NRCH) .... OWP
Operations-Communications .... OP-COM
Operation-Triggered Architecture [*Computer science*] .... OTA
Operative .... OPTV
Operative Bakers' Union of Victoria [*Australia*] .... OBUV
Operative Bootmakers Union (AD) .... OBU
Operative Builders' Union [*British*] .... OBU
Operative Coachmakers' and Wheelwrights' Federal Labour Union [*British*] .... OCWFLU
Operative Crate Makers' Society [*A union*] [*British*] .... OCMS
Operative Dentistry (BABM) .... OpDent
Operative Dentistry (DAVI) .... Opdent
Operative Federal Plasterers [*A union*] [*British*] .... OFP

Operative Glovers' Society [A union] [British] .... OGS
Operative Ironmoulders' Association [A union] [British] .... OIA
Operative Machine Needle Makers' Protection Society [A union]
   [British] .... OMNMPS
Operative Mechanics' Union [British] .... OMU
Operative Morality Rate [Statistics] [Medicine] (DAVI) .... OMR
Operative Painters amd Decorators' Union of Australia .... OPDUA
Operative Personenkontrolle [Operational Person Control] [German] .... OPK
Operative Plasterers and Cement Masons International Association of the
   US and Canada .... OPCM
Operative Plasterers and Cement Masons International Association of US
   and Canada (EA) .... OPCMIA
Operative Plasteres amd Plaster Workers' Federation of Australia ...... OPPWFA
Operative Procedure .... OP
Operative Roller Makers' Society [A union] [British] .... ORMS
Operative Society of Bricklayers [A union] [British] .... OSB
Operative Society of Spring Knife Cutlers [A union] [British] .... OSSKC
Operative United Painters [A union] [British] .... OUP
Operative United Plumbers [A union] [British] .... OUP
Operator 0
[Telephone] Operator (WDMC) 0
Operator (IDOE) .... op
Operator [Computer science] .... OP
Operator (IAA) .... OPER
Operator .... OPER
Operator .... OPR
Operator .... OPR
Operator (IAA) .... OR
Operator Accelerated Retraining Program [Nuclear energy] (NRCH) ...... OARP
Operator Access (IAA) .... OA
Operator Assistance Unit (NITA) .... OAU
Operator Authorization Record [Computer science] (IBMDP) .... OAR
Operator Call Handling Center [Telecommunications] (TEL) .... OCHC
Operator Circuit [Telecommunications] (IAA) .... OC
Operator Command (NITA) .... OC
Operator Command Function Processor [Computer science] (MHDI) .... OCFP
Operator Communication and Control Facility [IBM Corp.] .... OCCF
Operator Console Facility [Computer science] (IBMDP) .... OCF
Operator Control Command (BUR) .... OCC
Operator Control Console [Canadian Navy] .... OCC
Operator Control Element [Computer science] (IBMDP) .... OPCE
Operator Control Interface (OA) .... OCI
Operator Control Language (AD) .... ocl
Operator Data Register [Telecommunications] (TEL) .... ODR
Operator Distance Dialing .... ODD
Operator Distance Dialing (AD) .... odd
Operator Error Analysis .... OEA
Operator Fault (AAG) .... OPRFLT
Operator Fault [Computer science] (MHDI) .... OPRLFT
Operator Fractionation Decision Guide [Process control] .... OFDG
[Meteorological Information Extraction Center] Operator Guide .... MIEC
Operator in Charge (IAA) .... OPRIC
Operator Input .... OI
Operator Integration Shakedown Test .... OIST
Operator Interface (ACII) .... OI
Operator Interface Rolling Loop .... OPIRL
Operator Interface Table (MCD) .... OPIT
Operator Interface Terminal (MCD) .... OIT
Operator Interface Unit [Computer science] .... OIU
Operator/Maintenance Task Description (DNAB) .... OMTD
Operator Measures and Criteria (MCD) .... OMAC
Operator Need Date (NASA) .... OND
Operator Number Identification [Bell System] .... ONI
Operator Override [Telecommunications] (TEL) .... OOR
Operator Please Deliver Immediately .... OPDI
Operator Position Controller [Telecommunications] .... OPC
Operator Preparation Program (IAA) .... OPP
Operator Priority Access (NITA) .... OPA
Operator Programming Method [Computer science] .... OPM
Operator Quality Control [RADAR] .... OQC
Operator Services Complex [Telecommunications] (TEL) .... OSC
Operator Services Switching Unit [Telecommunications] (TEL) ...... OSSU
Operator Set Loop [Electronics] (ECII) .... OSL
Operator System Program [Manufacturing engineering] [Computer science] .... OPS
Operator Table .... OPRT
Operator Tactics Trainer [Patriot air defense system] (MCD) .... OTT
Operator Test Control Console (MCD) .... OTCC
Operatore di Trasporto Combinato [Combined Transport Operator] [Italian
   Business term] .... OTC
Operator-Level Chart (AFIT) .... OLC
Operator-Oriented Language [Computer science] .... OOL
Operator's Computer Console .... OCC
Operator's Connection Set (IAA) .... OCS
Operator's Console .... OPCON
Operators Control Language [Computer science] (BUR) .... OCL
Operator's Control Transfer Channel [Electronics] (ECII) .... OCTC
Operator's Handbook .... OH
Operator's Instruction Chart .... OIC
Operator's License (AD) .... O-license
Operator's Local Representative (AIA) .... OLR
Operator's Manual .... OM
Operators Reference Manual (IAA) .... ORM
Operator's Service Manual .... OSM
Operator's Set .... OS
Operator's Subsystem [Telecommunications] (TEL) .... OPS

Operator's Training New Equipment Training [Army] (INF) .... OPNET
Operator-to-General Support [Maintenance] (MCD) .... O-GS
Operator-to-Operator [Military] (CAAL) .... OTO
Opercular Nerve .... OPN
Operculum Ridge .... OR
Opere Citato [In the Work Cited] [Latin] (WDAA) .... OC
Opere Citato [In the Work Cited] [Latin] (AD) .... oc
Opere Citato [In the work cited] [Latin] (WDMC) .... op cit
Opere Citato [In the Work Cited] [Latin] .... OP CIT
Operon [Genetics] .... O
Opetus-ja Tutkimusalan Unioni [Teaching and Research Employees Union]
   [Finalnd] (EY) .... OTU
Opferfuersorgegesetz (BJA) .... OFG
o-Phenanthroline [Organic chemistry] .... phen
Ophicleide [Musical instrument] .... OPH
Ophiuchus [Constellation] .... Oph
Ophiuchus [Constellation] .... Ophi
O-Phthalaldehyde .... OPA
Ophthalmic .... OPHT
Ophthalmic (ROG) .... OPTH
Ophthalmic Arterial Pressure [Medicine] .... OAP
Ophthalmic Exhibitors' Association [British] (DBA) .... OEA
Ophthalmic Imaging Sys [NASDAQ symbol] (TTSB) .... OISI
Ophthalmic Imaging Systems [Associated Press] (SAG) .... OphtImg
Ophthalmic Imaging Systems, Inc. [NASDAQ symbol] (SAG) ...... OISI
Ophthalmic Medical Assistant (DAVI) .... OMT
Ophthalmic Medical Technician [or Technologist] (HCT) .... OMT
Ophthalmic Nurse (DAVI) .... OPN
Ophthalmic Nursing Diploma .... OND
Ophthalmic Photographers' Society (EA) .... OPS
Ophthalmic Prescription Manufacturers Association [British] (DBA) .... OPMA
Ophthalmic Research Institute (EA) .... ORI
Ophthalmic Rete [Bird anatomy] .... OR
Ophthalmodynamometry [Ophthalmology] (MAE) .... ODM
Ophthalmodynamometry [Ophthalmology] (AD) .... odm
Ophthalmodynamometry [Ophthalmology] .... ODN
Ophthalmodynamometry [Ophthalmology] .... OPH
Ophthalmodynamometry [Ophthalmology] .... OPM
Ophthalmolgist .... OPH
Ophthalmological Foundation [Later, NSPB] .... OF
Ophthalmological Products Trade and Industry Conference [British]
   (DBA) .... OPTIC
Ophthalmological Society of the United Kingdom .... OSUK
Ophthalmology [Medical Officer designation] [British] .... O
Ophthalmology .... OP
Ophthalmology [or Ophthalmoscopy] .... OPH
Ophthalmology (AABC) .... OPHTH
Ophthalmology .... OPHTHAL
Ophthalmology, Otology, Laryngology, Rhinology .... OOLR
[The] Ophthalmoscope [London] [A publication] (ROG) .... OPH
Ophthalmoscope [or Ophthalmoscopic] [Ophthalmology] (DAVI) .... Oph
Opiate Analgesia .... OA
Opiate-Directed Behavior .... ODB
Opiate-Directed Behavior (AD) .... odb
Opiates [Chemical dependency] [Pharmacology] (DAVI) .... OPIAT
Opimian California Vineyards Corp. [Toronto Stock Exchange symbol] ...... OCV
Opinion (ADA) .... OP
Opinion (ROG) .... OPN
Opinion (ROG) .... OPON
Opinion, Attitude, and Interest Survey [Psychology] .... OAIS
Opinion, Chief Counsel, United States Coast Guard [A publication]
   (DLA) .... Op CCCG
Opinion, General Counsel, United States Treasury Department
   [A publication] (DLA) .... Op GCT
Opinion, Judge Advocate General, United States Air Force [A publication]
   (DLA) .... Op JAGAF
Opinion, Judge Advocate General, United States Navy [A publication]
   (DLA) .... Op JAGN
Opinion Letter [A publication] (DLA) .... Op Let
Opinion of Attorney General, State of Kentucky [A publication]
   (DLA) .... Op KY Att'y Gen
Opinion of the Judge Advocate General (AAGC) .... Op Judge Adv Gen
Opinion of the Solicitor of Labor (AAGC) .... Sol Labor Op
Opinion Research [NASDAQ symbol] (TTSB) .... ORCI
Opinion Research Center .... ORC
Opinion Research Corp. [Associated Press] (SAG) .... OpinRsh
Opinion Research Corporation Youth (NITA) .... ORC youth
Opinion Research Crop. [NASDAQ symbol] (SAG) .... ORCI
Opinions [Legal term] (DLA) .... Ops
Opinions about Mental Illness [A questionnaire] .... OMI
Opinions and Orders of the Railroad Commission of California
   [A publication] (DLA) .... Cal R Com
Opinion(s) of the Army Judge Advocate General .... OP(S)ARMYJAG
Opinions of the Attorney General .... OAG
Opinions of the Attorney General [A publication] (DLA) .... Op AG
Opinions of the Attorney General [A publication] (DLA) .... Op Att'y Gen
Opinions of the Attorney General [A publication] (DLA) .... Ops AG
Opinions of the Attorney General [A publication] (DLA) .... Ops Atty Gen
Opinions of the Attorney General and Report to the Governor of Virginia
   [A publication] (DLA) .... Op VA Att'y Gen
Opinions of the Attorney General of California [A publication]
   (DLA) .... Op Cal Att'y Gen
Opinions of the Attorney General of Georgia [A publication]
   (DLA) .... Op GA Att'y Gen

Opinions of the Attorney General of Kansas [*A publication*] (DLA) ... Op Kan Att'y Gen
Opinions of the Attorney General of Louisiana [*A publication*] (DLA) ... Op LA Att'y Gen
Opinions of the Attorney General of Minnesota [*A publication*] (DLA) ... Op Minn Att'y Gen
Opinions of the Attorney General of New York [*A publication*] (DLA) ... NY Ops Atty Gen
Opinions of the Attorney General of North Dakota [*A publication*] (DLA) ... Op ND Att'y Gen
Opinions of the Attorney General of Ohio [*A publication*] (DLA) ... Op Ohio Att'y Gen
Opinions of the Attorney General of Oklahoma [*A publication*] (DLA) ... Op Okla Att'y Gen
Opinions of the Attorney General of Oregon [*A publication*] (DLA) ... Op Or Att'y Gen
Opinions of the Attorney General of Pennsylvania [*A publication*] (DLA) ... Op PA Att'y Gen
Opinions of the Attorney General of Tennessee [*A publication*] (DLA) ... Op Tenn Att'y Gen
Opinions of the Attorney General of Texas [*A publication*] (DLA) ... Op Tex Att'y Gen
Opinions of the Attorney General of Wisconsin [*A publication*] (DLA) ... Op Wis Att'y Gen
Opinions of the Attorney General of Wyoming [*A publication*] (DLA) ... Op Wyo Att'y Gen
Opinions of the Attorneys-General [*United States*] [*A publication*] (DLA) ... Op Att Gen
Opinions of the Attorneys-General [*United States*] [*A publication*] (DLA) ... Op Attys Gen
Opinions of the Attorneys-General [*United States*] [*A publication*] (DLA) ... Opin
Opinions of the Attorneys-General of New York [*A publication*] (DLA) ... NY Op Att Gen
Opinions of the Attorneys-General of New York [*A publication*] (DLA) ... Op NY Atty Gen
Opinions of the Judge Advocate General, United States Army [*A publication*] (DLA) ... Ops JAG
Opinions of the Office of Legal Counsel [*A publication*] (DLA) ... Op Off Legal Counsel
Opinions of the Solicitor for the Department of Labor [*United States*] [*A publication*] (DLA) ... Op Sol Dept
Opinions of the Solicitor for the Department of Labor Dealing with Workmen's Compensation [*A publication*] (DLA) ... Op Sol Dept Labor
Opinions of the Solicitor for the Post Office Department [*United States*] [*A publication*] (DLA) ... Op Sol POD
Opinion-Tribune, Glenwood, IA [*Library symbol Library of Congress*] (LCLS) ... IaGleOT
Opisu Struktur Mikroprogramownych [*Programming language*] (CSR) ... OSM
Opium [*Slang*] ... O
Opium and Belladonna [*Pharmacy*] (MAE) ... O & B
Opium Joint [*Slang*] ... OJ
Opium Poppy Control Act of 1942 ... OPCA
Oporto [*Portugal*] [*Airport symbol*] (OAG) ... OPO
Opp, AL [*AM radio station call letters*] ... WAMI
Opp, AL [*FM radio station call letters*] ... WAMI-FM
Opp, AL [*FM radio station call letters*] ... WJIF
Opp, AL [*AM radio station call letters*] ... WOPP
Oppenheimer Cap L.P. [*NYSE symbol*] (TTSB) ... OCC
Oppenheimer Capital Ltd. [*NYSE symbol*] (SPSG) ... OCC
Oppenheimer Capital Ltd. [*Associated Press*] (SAG) ... OpnhCa
Oppenheimer Multi-Government Trust [*NYSE symbol*] (SPSG) ... OGT
Oppenheimer Multi-Government Trust [*Associated Press*] (SAG) ... OpMG
Oppenheimer Multi-Gvt Tr [*NYSE symbol*] (TTSB) ... OGT
Oppenheimer Multi-Sector [*NYSE symbol*] (TTSB) ... OMS
Oppenheimer Multi-Sector Income Trust [*NYSE symbol*] (SPSG) ... OMS
Oppenheimer Multi-Sector Income Trust [*Associated Press*] (SAG) ... OppMS
Oppenheimer World Bond Fund [*Associated Press*] (SAG) ... OpWldBd
Oppenheimer World Bond Fund [*NYSE symbol*] (SAG) ... OWB
Oppenheimer-Phillips [*Process*] ... O-P
Oppenheim's International Law [*A publication*] (DLA) ... Opp Int L
Opponens Digiti Quinti [*Muscle*] [*Anatomy*] (DAVI) ... ODQ
Opponent ... OPP
Opponents' Runs [*Baseball*] ... OR
Opportunistic Infection [*Medicine*] ... OI
Opportunities for Professional Transition [*An association*] (EA) ... OPT
Opportunities for Youth [*Canada*] (AD) ... OFY
Opportunities for Youth Program [*Canada*] ... OFY
Opportunities for Youth Program [*Canada*] ... OYP
Opportunities Industrialization Center (OICC) ... OIC
Opportunities Industrialization Centers of America (EA) ... OIC/A
Opportunities to See [*Business term*] ... OTS
Opportunity (ADA) ... OPP
Opportunity ... OPP
Opportunity (AABC) ... OPPOR
Opportunity (ADA) ... OPPORT
Opportunity (ROG) ... OPPY
Opportunity ... OPRTNTY
Opportunity Cost (MHDB) ... OC
[*The*] **Opportunity Prospector** [*A publication*] ... TOP
Opportunity Resources for the Arts (EA) ... ORA
Opportunity to Confront the Best Opposing Force [*Army*] (INF) ... OPFOR
Opportunity, WA [*AM radio station call letters*] ... KKPL
Opportunity, WA [*AM radio station call letters*] (RBYB) ... KMAX-AM
Opportunity, WA [*FM radio station call letters*] ... KNFR
Opportunity, WA [*AM radio station call letters*] ... KSVY
Oppose Entry [*Navy*] (NVT) ... OPOSENT
Oppose Replenishment [*Navy*] (NVT) ... OPORPL
Oppose Sortie [*Navy*] (NVT) ... OPOSORT
Oppose Sortie [*Navy*] (ANA) ... OPOSTOR
Opposed (NVT) ... OP
Opposed (DAVI) ... opp
Opposed To ... OPP
Opposed Zone Reheating Furnace (PDAA) ... OZRF
Opposing Force [*Military*] (INF) ... OPFOR
Opposing Force Component (MCD) ... OFC
Opposing Forces Vehicle [*Military*] ... OFV
Opposite ... OP
Opposite (WDMC) ... op
Opposite (WDMC) ... opp
Opposite ... OPP
Opposite (AAG) ... OPP
Opposite Commutator End (IEEE) ... OPPCE
Opposite Editorial Page [*in a newspaper*] [*Usually consists of opinion columns by various guest writers or syndicated columnists*] ... OP-ED
Opposite Hand (OA) ... OH
Opposite Hand [*Technical drawings*] ... OPH
Opposite Hand (MSA) ... OPP HND
Opposite Prompt [*i.e., the left side*] [*A stage direction*] ... OP
Opposite Prompters' Side [*i.e., the left side*] [*Stage direction*] (ROG) ... OPS
Opposite Surface [*Technical drawings*] ... OPS
Opposite - the Editorial Page [*Newspapers*] (WDMC) ... op ed
Oppositely-Directed Travelling Wave (PDAA) ... ODTW
Opposition Unie [*United Opposition*] [*The Comoros*] [*Political party*] (EY) ... OU
Oppositional Defiant Disorder ... ODD
Oppure [*Otherwise*] [*Music*] ... OPP
Opsconic Index [*Laboratory science*] (DAVI) ... OI
OPSEC [*Operations Security*] **Professional Society** (EA) ... OPS
OPSEC Professionals Society [*Later, OPS*] (EA) ... OPSEC
Opsonic Index (AD) ... o/i
Opsonic Index [*Medicine*] ... OI
Opsonized Zymosan [*Biochemistry*] ... OPZ
Opta Food Ingredients [*NASDAQ symbol*] (TTSB) ... OPTS
Opta Food Ingredients, Inc. [*Associated Press*] (SAG) ... Opta
Opta Food Ingredients, Inc. [*NASDAQ symbol*] (SAG) ... OPTS
Optand [*Sweden ICAO location identifier*] (ICLI) ... ESNM
Optatam Totius [*Decree on Priestly Formation*] [*Vatican II document*] ... OT
Optative [*Grammar*] ... OPT
Optek Technology [*NASDAQ symbol*] (TTSB) ... OPTT
Optelecom, Inc. [*NASDAQ symbol*] (NQ) ... OPTC
Optelecom, Inc. [*Associated Press*] (SAG) ... Optlcm
OPTEVFOR [*Operational Test and Evaluation Force*] **Air Test and Evaluation Squadron Five, Naval Weapons Center, China Lake, CA** (CAAL) ... VX-5
OPTEVFOR [*Operational Test and Evaluation Force*] **Air Test and Evaluation Squadron Four, Naval Air Station, Pt. Mugu, CA** (CAAL) ... VX-4
OPTEVFOR [*Operational Test and Evaluation Force*] **Air Test and Evaluation Squadron One, Naval Air Station, Patuxent River, MD** (CAAL) ... VX-1
OPTEVFOR [*Operational Test and Evaluation Force*] **Detachment, Patuxent River, MD** [*Navy*] (CAAL) ... PAX
OPTEVFOR [*Operational Test and Evaluation Force*] **Detachment, Sunnyvale, CA** [*Navy*] (CAAL) ... SUN
OPTEVFOR [*Operational Test and Evaluation Force*] **Tactics Guide** [*Navy*] (CAAL) ... OTG
Optex Biomedical [*NASDAQ symbol*] (TTSB) ... OPTX
Opthalmology Medical Group (AD) ... OMG
OPTI, Inc. [*NASDAQ symbol*] (SAG) ... OPTI
Optic (IAA) ... OPT
Optic Atrophy (CPH) ... OA
Optic Chiasm [*Anatomy*] ... OC
Optic Display Test Chamber ... ODTC
Optic Fiber Layer ... OFL
Optic Ganglion ... OG
Optic Memory Disk Recorder ... OMDR
Optic Nerve [*Anatomy*] ... ON
Optic Nerve Decompression Surgery ... ONDS
Optic Nerve Fiber [*Anatomy*] ... ONF
Optic Support Table ... OST
Optic Tectum [*Anatomy*] ... OT
Optical (AAG) ... OPT
Optical ... OPTIC
Optical Acceleration Cancellation [*Vision*] ... OAC
Optical Acquisition Aid [*Deep Space Instrumentation Facility, NASA*] ... OAA
Optical Acquisition and Tracking Aid Assembly ... OATA
Optical Active Surface Approach Fuze ... OASAF
Optical Activity Detection ... OAD
Optical Adaptive Technique ... OAT
Optical Address Light Modulator [*Instrumentation*] ... OALM
Optical Adjunct ... OA
Optical Aimpoint Guidance System [*Weaponry*] ... OPTAG
Optical Alignment Equipment ... OAE
Optical Alignment Group ... OAG
Optical Alignment Kit (MCD) ... OAK
Optical Alignment, Monitoring, and Calibration Equipment ... OAMCE
Optical Alignment Sights [*NASA*] ... OAS
Optical Alignment Unit ... OAU
Optical Analog Matrix Processing ... OAMP
Optical Angle Readout ... OAR
Optical Angular Motion Sensor ... OAMS
Optical Area Correlator ... OAC
Optical Array Spectrometer ... OAS
Optical Art (ODBW) ... op art

Optical Art (WDMC) ... op art
Optical Associates Inc. (NITA) ... OAI
Optical Atmospheric Quality in Europe (MCD) ... OPAQUE
Optical Attitude Transfer System (SSD) ... OATS
Optical Augmentation Project ... OAP
Optical Augmentation System ... OAS
Optical Automatic Car Identification ... OACI
Optical Automatic Ranging ... OAR
Optical Automatic Ranging ... OPTAR
Optical Band Imager and Photometer System [*Aerospace*] ... OBIPS
Optical Bar Camera [*NASA*] (LAIN) ... OBC
Optical Bar Code ... OBR
Optical Bar Code Reader (NITA) ... OBCR
Optical Bar Code Reader (MHDB) ... OBR
Optical Bar Recognition [*Commonly known as a bar code*] (WDMC) ... OBR
Optical Base Assembly (KSC) ... OBA
Optical Beam Deflection ... OBD
Optical Beam Scanner ... OBS
Optical Beam Steering ... OBS
Optical Beam Steering Device ... OBSD
Optical Brightening Agents ... OBA
Optical Cable [*NASDAQ symbol*] (TTSB) ... OCCF
Optical Cable Corp. [*NASDAQ symbol*] (SAG) ... OCCF
Optical Cable Corp. [*Associated Press*] (SAG) ... OptCble
Optical Cable Interface Unit (MCD) ... OCIU
Optical Cable Signal Repeater (MCD) ... OCSR
Optical Cable Transmission System (MCD) ... OCTS
Optical Cavity [*LASER technology*] (EECA) ... OC
Optical Character Definition [*Computer science*] (AD) ... ocd
Optical Character Printing ... OCP
Optical Character Reader [*Computer science*] ... OCR
Optical Character Reader [*Computer science*] (AD) ... ocr
Optical Character Recognition [*Computer science*] (AD) ... ocr
Optical Character Recognition [*Computer science*] ... OCR
Optical Character Recognition - ANSI Standard (Font A) [*Computer science*] ... OCRA
Optical Character Recognition - ANSI Standard (Font B) [*Computer science*] ... OCRB
Optical Character Recognition Bar [*Computer science*] (IAA) ... OCRB
Optical Character Recognition Engine (PDAA) ... OCHRE
Optical Character Recognition Equipment [*Computer science*] (AABC) ... OCRE
Optical Character Recognition Equipment [*Computer science*] (AD) ... ocre
Optical Character Recognition System (NITA) ... OCRS
Optical Character Recognition Users Association [*Later, RTUA*] (EA) ... OCRUA
Optical Character Recognizing Intelligent Terminal [*Computer science*] (IAA) ... OCRIT
Optical Character Resolution [*Ligature Co.*] (PCM) ... OCR
Optical Character Scanner [*Computer science*] ... OCS
Optical Character-Recognizing Intelligent Terminal [*Computer science*] (AD) ... ocrit
Optical Circuit and Component (NITA) ... OCC
Optical Coating Evaluation Laboratory (AD) ... OCEL
Optical Coating Lab [*NASDAQ symbol*] (TTSB) ... OCLI
Optical Coating Laboratories, Inc. (PCM) ... OCLI
Optical Coating Laboratory, Inc. [*NASDAQ symbol*] (NQ) ... OCLI
Optical Coating Laboratory, Inc. [*Associated Press*] (SAG) ... OpticC
Optical Coherence Tomography [*Medicine*] ... OCT
Optical Coincidence Coordinate Indexing (PDAA) ... OCCI
Optical Communications Linkage (AD) ... ocl
Optical Communicator System (MCD) ... OCS
Optical Component Testing and Evaluation (AD) ... octe
Optical Computer System (IAA) ... OCS
Optical Contact Sensor ... OCS
Optical Contour Maximization [*Chemistry*] ... OCM
Optical Contract Seeker (MCD) ... OCT
Optical Contrast Contour Seeker ... OCCS
Optical Contrasting Seeker (MCD) ... OCS
Optical Counter-Countermeasures ... OCCM
Optical Countermeasures ... OCM
Optical Covert Communications Using LASER Transceivers (MCD) ... OCCULT
Optical Data Converter (NOAA) ... OPDAC
Optical Data Digitizer [*Computer science*] ... ODD
Optical Data Disc (NITA) ... ODD
Optical Data Processing ... ODP
Optical Data Recognition [*Computer science*] ... ODR
Optical Data Systems [*NASDAQ symbol*] (TTSB) ... ODSI
Optical Data Systems [*Associated Press*] (SAG) ... OptclData
Optical Data Systems, Inc. [*NASDAQ symbol*] (SAG) ... ODSI
Optical Data Systems, Inc. [*Associated Press*] (SAG) ... OptclDt
Optical Data Transmission ... ODT
Optical Data Transmission System ... ODTS
Optical Density ... OD
Optical Density (AD) ... od
Optical Density Unit ... ODU
Optical Designation Evaluation (MCD) ... ODE
Optical Detection and Ranging (DNAB) ... ODAR
Optical Detection and Ranging ... OPDAR
Optical Detection and Ranging System (IAA) ... OPDARS
Optical Device [*JETDS nomenclature*] [*Military*] (CET) ... SU
Optical Diffraction Analysis [*Microscopy*] ... ODA
Optical Diffractogram ... ODM
Optical Digital Data Disk ... OD3
Optical Digital Data Disk ... ODD
Optical Digital Data Disk ... ODDD
Optical Digital Disc (NITA) ... ODD
Optical Digital Imagery ... ODI
Optical Disc Controller (NITA) ... ODC
Optical Discrimination and Tracking System [*Army*] ... ODTS
Optical Discrimination Evaluation Study [*NASA*] (NASA) ... ODES
Optical Disk Data System (NITA) ... ODDS
Optical Disk Interface System [*Computer science*] ... ODIS
Optical Disk Memory ... ODM
Optical Dispensers' Licensing Board [*New South Wales, Australia*] ... ODLB
Optical Display Memory [*Computer science*] ... ODM
Optical Display Unit [*Computer science*] (MCD) ... ODU
Optical Distributors and Manufacturers Association (AD) ... ODMA
Optical Docking System ... ODS
Optical Effect Code ... OEC
Optical Effects Module Electronic Controller and Processor [*NASA*] ... OEMCP
Optical Effects Module Electronic Controller and Processor (AD) ... oemcp
Optical/Electrical Conversion [*Telecommunications*] ... OE
Optical Electron Microscope (PDAA) ... OEM
Optical Electron Microscope (AD) ... oem
Optical Electronic Microscope (WDAA) ... OEM
Optical Emission (MCD) ... OE
Optical Emission Spectroscopy ... OES
Optical Emission Spectroscopy [*Laboratory science*] (DAVI) ... OES
Optical Evaluation Facility (RDA) ... OEF
Optical Fiber Production Unit ... OFPU
Optical Fiber Sensor ... OFS
Optical Fiber Thermometry [*Instrumentation*] ... OFT
Optical Fiber Time-Domain Reflectometer [*Computer science*] ... OTDR
Optical Fiber Tube ... OFT
Optical Fiber-Pulling Facility (SSD) ... OFPF
Optical Fibre (EECA) ... OF
Optical Fibre Technology ... OFT
Optical Fibre Transfer Function (EECA) ... OFTF
Optical Fibre Transmission System (NITA) ... OFTS
Optical File Cabinet [*Computer science*] ... OFC
Optical Fire Detector (AD) ... ofd
Optical Flight Evaluation ... OFE
Optical Flight Kit (NASA) ... OFK
Optical Formatter Controller (NITA) ... OFC
Optical Fourier Transform ... OFT
Optical Frame Importers' Association [*British*] (DBA) ... OFIA
Optical Frequency ... OF
Optical Frequency Conversion ... OFC
Optical Frequency Generator ... OFG
Optical Fuzing System ... OFS
Optical Glass and Macromolecular Materials [*Imaging*] ... OGAMM
Optical Glide Path Indicator ... OGPI
Optical Grating Reflectance Evaluator (PDAA) ... OGRE
Optical Gravitational Lens Experiment [*Astronomy*] ... OGLE
Optical Groundwire [*Telecommunications*] (TSSD) ... OPGW
Optical Guidance System ... OGS
Optical Gun Fire Director [*Military*] (PDAA) ... OFD
Optical Heterodyne Detection ... OHD
Optical Image Processing System ... OIPS
Optical Image Processor ... OIP
Optical Image Sensor ... OIS
Optical Imaging Systems (RDA) ... OIS
Optical Immunoassay [*Clinical chemistry*] ... OIA
Optical Improvement Program [*Army*] ... OIP
Optical Incremental Encoder ... OIE
Optical Information System [*Computer science*] ... OIS
Optical Infrared Equipment ... OIE
Optical Infrared Equipment ... OIRE
Optical Integrated Circuit (IEEE) ... OIC
Optical Intelligence ... OPINT
Optical Intelligence (MCD) ... OPTINT
Optical Isolator [*Nuclear energy*] (NRCH) ... OI
Optical Jammer Source ... OJS
Optical Kerr Effect [*Birefringence induced in an electrical field*] ... OKE
Optical Key Reader [*Automotive engineering*] ... OKR
Optical Klystron (PDAA) ... OK
Optical Klystron (AD) ... ok
Optical Laboratories Association (EA) ... OLA
Optical Landing System ... OLS
Optical LASER Ranging System ... OLRS
Optical Line Pair ... OLP
Optical Link in the Atmosphere (PDAA) ... OLA
Optical Manufacturers Association (EA) ... OMA
Optical Mark and Automatic Dialing [*Facsimile transmission*] (DGA) ... OMAD
Optical Mark Page Reader [*Computer science*] (AABC) ... OMPR
Optical Mark Page Reader (AD) ... ompr
Optical Mark Printer (NITA) ... OMP
Optical Mark Reader [*Computer science*] ... OMAR
Optical Mark Reader [*Computer science*] ... OMR
Optical Mark Reader (AD) ... omr
Optical Mark Reader Card [*Computer science*] (MHDI) ... OMRC
Optical Mark Reader Sheet [*Computer science*] (MHDI) ... OMRS
Optical Mark Recognition [*Computer science*] (MCD) ... OMR
Optical Mark Recognition (AD) ... omr
Optical MASER [*Microwave Amplification by Stimulated Emission of Radiation*] **Radiation Weapon** (AAG) ... OMRW
Optical MASER [*Microwave Amplification by Stimulated Emission of Radiation*] **System** ... OMS
Optical Master (KSC) ... OM
Optical Matched Filter ... OMF
Optical Matched Filter Technique ... OMFT

Optical Measurement Instrument (SAA) ..... OMI
Optical Measuring Unit (KSC) ..... OMU
Optical Media [Computer graphics] ..... OM
Optical Memory Disc Recorder (DOM) ..... OMDR
Optical Meter Relay ..... OM
Optical Microscope (ECII) ..... OM
Optical Microscopy ..... OM
Optical Modulation System ..... OMS
Optical Multichannel Analyzer [Spectrometry] ..... OMA
Optical Navigation Attachment (WDAA) ..... ONA
Optical Network Unit [Telecommunications] ..... ONU
Optical Night Landing Approach System [Aviation] (PDAA) ..... ONLAS
Optical Page Reader [Computer science] ..... OPR
Optical Parametric Oscillator [Tunable LASER device] ..... OPO
Optical Partial Decoy (IAA) ..... OPADEC
Optical Particle Counter (PDAA) ..... OPC
Optical Particle Decoy ..... OPADEC
Optical Particle Detector [for evaluating film quality] ..... OPD
Optical Path Difference (MCD) ..... OPD
Optical Path Length ..... OPL
Optical Path-Length Variation (PDAA) ..... OPV
Optical Pattern Recognition ..... OPR
Optical Phase Conjugator [LASER-aiming device] ..... OPC
Optical Phase Distortion (PDAA) ..... OPD
Optical Photo Coupler ..... OPC
Optical Photoconductor (PCM) ..... OPC
Optical Pickoff Two-Axis Gyroscope (SAA) ..... OPTAG
Optical Platform Alignment Linkage ..... OPAL
Optical Plotting Attachment (WDAA) ..... OPA
Optical Point Transfer ..... OPT
Optical Pointing Error ..... OPE
Optical Power Meter ..... OPM
Optical Power Spectrum (PDAA) ..... OPS
Optical Prism Uniformity System ..... OPUS
Optical Probe (AAG) ..... OP
Optical Procedural Task Instruction Compiler ..... OPTIC
Optical Processing System ..... OPS
Optical Product Code Council (EA) ..... OPCC
Optical Programmable Read-Only Memory [Disk] (BYTE) ..... OPROM
Optical Propagation Facility ..... OPF
Optical Properties Technical Evaluation Center ..... OPTEC
Optical Property of Orbiting Satellite [NASA] (PDAA) ..... OPOS
Optical Propulsion Management Interface System ..... OPMIS
Optical Proximity Detector ..... OPD
Optical Publishing Association (EA) ..... OPA
Optical Publishing, Inc. [Information service or system] (IID) ..... OPI
Optical Pulse Transmitter Using LASER ..... OPTUL
Optical Quality ..... OQ
Optical Quantum Amplifier (PDAA) ..... OQA
Optical Quantum Detector ..... OQD
Optical Quantum Generator ..... OQG
Optical Quick Access Recorder (GAVI) ..... O-QAR
Optical Radiation Corp. ..... ORC
Optical Radiation Weapon Program (AAG) ..... ORWP
Optical Ranging and Detection System ..... ORADS
Optical Ratio Reflector ..... ORR
Optical Reader [Computer science] (BUR) ..... OR
Optical Reading Direct Input System (IAA) ..... ORDIS
Optical Read-Only Memory [Computer science] ..... OROM
Optical Read-Only Storage [Computer science] ..... OROS
Optical Readout Cherenkov Imaging Detector [Computer science] (PDAA) ..... ORCID
Optical Reception of Announcements by Coded Line Electronics ..... ORACLE
Optical Recognition of Chemical Structures Program [IBM Almaden Research Center] [San Jose, CA] ..... OROCS
Optical Recording Corp. ..... ORC
Optical Reference Axis ..... ORA
Optical Reference Device ..... ORD
Optical Reference Manual ..... ORM
Optical Reference Unit ..... ORU
Optical Relay Tube (MCD) ..... ORT
Optical Relay Tube Assembly (MCD) ..... ORTA
Optical Research Radiometrical Analysis System (IEEE) ..... ORRAS
Optical Rotary Dispersion ..... ORD
Optical Rotary Power ..... ORP
Optical Rotary Table ..... ORT
Optical Satellite Communications (MCD) ..... OPSATCOM
Optical Satellite Communications ..... OPSTACOM
Optical Scanning [Computer science] (WDAA) ..... OPSCAN
Optical Scanning [Computer science] ..... OS
Optical Scanning Device [Computer science] ..... OSD
Optical Scanning Recognition [Computer science] ..... OSR
Optical Scanning Unit (DNAB) ..... OSU
Optical Sciences Center [University of Arizona] [Research center] (RCD) ..... OSC
Optical Section Microscope ..... OSM
Optical Security Group [NASDAQ symbol] (TTSB) ..... OPSC
Optical Security Group, Inc. [NASDAQ symbol] (SAG) ..... OPSC
Optical Security Group, Inc. [Associated Press] (SAG) ..... OptiSG
Optical Sensing Trigger ..... OST
Optical Sensor and Tracker ..... OSAT
Optical Sensor Subsystem [Military] (CAAL) ..... OSS
Optical Sensors [NASDAQ symbol] (TTSB) ..... OPSI
Optical Sensors Collaborative Association [British] (DBA) ..... OSCA
Optical Sensors, Inc. [NASDAQ symbol] (SAG) ..... OPSI
Optical Sensors, Inc. [Associated Press] (SAG) ..... OptSens

Optical Sensors Research Unit (NITA) ..... OSRU
Optical Service Unit [Telecommunications] ..... OSU
Optical Sight System ..... OSS
Optical Signature Code ..... OSC
Optical Signature Program [Military] (CAAL) ..... OSP
Optical Society (NADA) ..... OS
Optical Society of America (EA) ..... OSA
Optical Solar Reflector ..... OSR
Optical Sound Recorder ..... OSR
Optical Space Surveillance Subsystem (AAG) ..... OSSS
Optical Space Surveillance System [or Subsystem] (IAA) ..... OSSS
Optical Space-Division Multiplexing (EECA) ..... OSDM
Optical Spectrometric Multichannel Analyzer [Instrumentation] ..... OSMA
Optical Star Tracker ..... OST
Optical Still Recorder [LASER-disc technology] ..... OSR
Optical Storage Access Method [Computer science] (PDAA) ..... OPSAM
Optical Storage and Retrieval [Computer science] ..... OSAR
Optical Storage Ltd. ..... OSL
Optical Storage Technology Association (CDE) ..... OSTA
Optical String Switch Controller (NITA) ..... OSC
Optical Submarine Communications by Aerospace Relay ..... OSCAR
Optical Subsystem (KSC) ..... OSS
Optical Surveillance System (AAG) ..... OSS
Optical Systems Working Group (MUGU) ..... OSWG
Optical Target Designation Computer ..... OTDC
Optical Target Detecting Device ..... OTDD
Optical Technician Program [Association of Independent Colleges and Schools specialization code] ..... OP
Optical Technology Experiment System ..... OTES
Optical Technology Satellite ..... OTS
Optical Technology Satellite - Apollo Extension System (DNAB) ..... OTS-AES
Optical Telescope Assembly [NASA] ..... OTA
Optical Telescope Technology Workshop [NASA] (PDAA) ..... OTTW
Optical Terminal Flight Evaluation ..... OTFE
Optical Time Domain (EECA) ..... OTD
Optical Time Domain Reflectometer (NITA) ..... OTDR
Optical Time History (MCD) ..... OTH
Optical Tool ..... OT
Optical Tool Master (MCD) ..... OTM
Optical Tracker Operator (MUGU) ..... OTO
Optical Tracking [NASA] (KSC) ..... OT
Optical Tracking [NASA] (KSC) ..... OTR
Optical Tracking Aid [Deep Space Instrumentation Facility, NASA] ..... OTA
Optical Tracking and Ranging Kit (PDAA) ..... OPTRAK
Optical Tracking Device ..... OTD
Optical Tracking Electronics ..... OTE
Optical Tracking Satellite [NASA] (IAA) ..... OTS
Optical Tracking Servo ..... OTSS
Optical Transfer Function ..... OTF
Optical Transient Current Spectroscopy ..... OTCS
Optical Transient Detector ..... OTD
Optical Transition Radiation [Physics] ..... OTR
Optical Transport Systems (IEEE) ..... OTS
Optical Van Trailer ..... OVT
Optical Video Disk ..... OVD
Optical Viewing System ..... OVS
Optical Warning Locator/Detector (MCD) ..... OWL/D
Optical Wholesalers Association [Later, OLA] (EA) ..... OWA
Optical Window ..... OPW
Optical Window (NASA) ..... OW
Optical-Density Units (AD) ..... od units
Optically Active Polymer ..... OAP
Optically Connected Parallel Machines [Computer science] ..... OCPM
Optically Coupled Isolator ..... OCI
Optically Detected Electron Nuclear Double Resonance [Spectroscopy] ..... OD-ENDOR
Optically Detected Electron Spin Resonance [Spectroscopy] ..... OD-ESR
Optically Detected Magnetic Resonance [Spectroscopy] ..... ODMR
Optically Isolated Digital Input ..... OIDI
Optically Isolated Gate (IEEE) ..... OIG
Optically Projected Map ..... OPM
Optically Pumped Nuclear Magnetic Resonance [Physics] ..... OPNMR
Optically Scanned Character Automatic Reader [Computer science] (DIT) ..... OSCAR
Optically Stimulated Electron Emission [Also, PEE] [Physics] ..... OSEE
Optically Stimulated Luminescence [Analytical Chemistry] ..... OSL
Optically Transparent Electrode ..... OTE
Optically Transparent Thin-Layer Electrode ..... OTTLE
Optically Variable Device ..... OVD
Optically Violently Variable [QUASAR] ..... OVV
Optically Void Liquid ..... OVL
Optically-Coupled Insulator (IAA) ..... OCI
Optically-Coupled Oscillator [Instrumentation] ..... OCO
Optically-Detected Nuclear Magnetic Resonance [Spectroscopy] ..... ODNMR
Optically-Shaped Film ..... OSF
Optically-Thin Thermal Bremsstrahlung [Astrophysics] ..... OTTB
Opticalman [Navy rating] ..... OM
Opticalman [Navy] (DAVI) ..... OM
Opticalman, Chief [Navy rating] (DNAB) ..... OMC
Opticalman, First Class [Navy rating] OM1
Opticalman, Second Class [Navy rating] OM2
Opticalman, Third Class [Navy rating] OM3
Optical-Mechanical Assembly [Apollo] [NASA] ..... OMA
Optical-Optical Double Resonance Multiphonton Ionization [Spectrocopy] ..... OODR-MPI

Optical-Pan-Tilt-Zoom Unit (SAA) .... OPTZU
Optical-Probe Experiment [*Giotto probe of Halley's comet*] [*European Space Agency*] .... OPE
Optical-to-Optical (IAA) .... OTTO
Optical-to-Tactile Converter [*Electronic reader for the blind*] .... OPTACON
Optical-Transient [*Astronomy*] .... OT
Optic-Electronic Corp. (RDA) .... OEC
Optician .... OPT
Optician .... OPTCN
Opticians Association of America (EA) .... OAA
Optico-Electronic Device for Registering Coincidences (PDAA) .... OEDRC
Optics .... OPT
Optics .... OPT
Optics and Sensors [*Program*] (MCD) .... OAS
Optics and Sensors Program .... O & S
Optics Automation and Management (RDA) .... Opticam
Optics Coupling Data [*or Display*] Unit [*Guidance and navigation*] (KSC) .... OCDU
Optics Hand Controller (KSC) .... OHC
Optics Inertial Analyzer (SAA) .... OIA
Optics Subsystem (NASA) .... OS
Optics Subsystem .... OS
Optika Imaging Systems, Inc. [*Associated Press*] (SAG) .... OptImag
Optika Imaging Systems, Inc. [*NASDAQ symbol*] (SAG) .... OPTK
Optima Energy Corp. [*Vancouver Stock Exchange symbol*] .... OAE
Optima Petroleum [*NASDAQ symbol*] (TTSB) .... OPPCF
Optima Petroleum Corp. [*NASDAQ symbol*] (SAG) .... OPPC
Optima Petroleum Corp. [*Associated Press*] (SAG) .... Optima
Optimal Amplitude and Phase Modulation .... OAPM
Optimal Automatic Control .... OAC
Optimal Body Mass [*Ecology*] .... OBM
Optimal Channel Network [*Physics*] .... OCN
Optimal Climate Normals [*Climatology*] .... OCN
Optimal Code Generation .... OCG
Optimal Control Theory .... OCT
Optimal Cutting Temperature [*Material for tissue fixation*] .... OCT
Optimal Decision Function .... ODF
Optimal Decisions System .... ODS
Optimal [*or Orbital*] Design Integration [*Computer program*] .... ODIN
Optimal Digital Voice Processor (MCD) .... ODVP
Optimal Financial Decision Strategy (MHDI) .... OFDS
Optimal Foraging Theory [*Animal behavior*] .... OFT
Optimal Missile Engagement Guidance Algorithm (AD) .... OMEGA
Optimal Performance Theoretically Attainable (IEEE) .... OPTA
Optimal Pneumatic Systems Analysis (PDAA) .... OPSA
Optimal Real Storage (CMD) .... ORS
Optimal Replaceable Unit (IAA) .... ORU
Optimal Robotics Corp. [*NASDAQ symbol*] (SAG) .... OPMR
Optimal Robotics Corp. [*Associated Press*] (SAG) .... OpRobt
Optimal Set [*of Parameters*] [*Hydrology*] .... OPSET
Optimal Terminal Descent (PDAA) .... OTD
Optimally Designed Experiments .... ODE
Optimally Localized Averages [*Mathematics*] .... OLA
Optimax Inds Wrrt'BB' [*NQS*] (TTSB) .... OPMXZ
Optimax Industries, Inc. [*NASDAQ symbol*] (SAG) .... OPMX
Optimax Industries, Inc. [*Associated Press*] (SAG) .... Optimax
Optimax Industries, Inc. [*Associated Press*] (SAG) .... Optmx
Optime [*Best*] [*Latin*] (ROG) .... OP
Optimises Rectangles [*AERE Harwell*] [*Software package*] (NCC) .... OREC
Optimist International (EA) .... OI
Optimists National Corps [*British military*] (DMA) .... ONC
Optimization by Simulated Annealing [*Mathematics*] .... OSA
Optimization of a Production Process by an Ordered Simulation and Iteration Technique (IEEE) .... OPPOSIT
Optimization of Subcarrier Information Capacity .... OSIC
Optimization of Systems for Data Processing and Transmission (PDAA) .... OSDPT
Optimization Program for Economical Remote Trunk Arrangement and TSPS [*Traffic Service Positions System*] Operator Arrangements [*Telecommunications*] (TEL) .... OPERATORS
Optimization Study [*Nuclear energy*] (NRCH) .... OPT
Optimization-Oriented Language .... OPOL
Optimized Aftercooled [*Truck engineering*] .... OAC
Optimized Air-to-Surface Infrared Seeker .... OASIS
Optimized Delivery Model [*Compaq*] [*Computer science*] .... ODM
Optimized Distribution Model [*Compaq Computer Corp.*] [*Computer science*] .... ODM
Optimized Fuel Assembly [*Nuclear energy*] (NRCH) .... OFA
Optimized Image Compression (PCM) .... OIC
Optimized Kill Probability .... OKP
Optimized Magnetohydrodynamic Conversion .... OMACON
Optimized Microminiature Electronic Circuit .... OMEC
Optimized Optical Link .... OOL
Optimized Optical Link Helmet-Mounted Display .... OOLHMD
Optimized Palette Reduction [*Algorithm*] [*Computer Presentations, Inc.*] (PCM) .... OPR
Optimized Portable Life-Support System [*NASA*] .... OPLSS
Optimized Processing Element .... OPE
Optimized Production Technology .... OPT
Optimized Reliability and Component Life Estimate .... ORACLE
Optimized Systems Software [*San Jose, CA*] .... OSS
Optimized Test-Oriented Language [*Computer science*] (PDAA) .... OPTOL
Optimized Valence Configuration [*Air Force*] .... OVC
Optimizing Control [*Military*] .... OPCON
Optimum (AAG) .... OPT
Optimum .... OPT

Optimum Aerial Target Sensor .... OATS
Optimum Allocation of Test and Equipment Manpower Against Logistics .... OATMEAL
Optimum Approach Course [*Navy*] (NVT) .... OAC
[*The*] Optimum Army Materiel Command (RDA) .... TOAMAC
Optimum Artillery Mix (SAA) .... OAM
Optimum Burn-In Screening .... OBIS
Optimum Charge Regulator .... OCR
Optimum Coordinated Shipboard [*or Shorebased*] Allowance List (DNAB) .... OCS
Optimum Coordinated Shipboard [*or Shorebased*] Allowance List .... OPCOSAL
Optimum Earth Reentry Corridor [*Aerospace*] .... OERC
Optimum Earth-Reentry Corridor (AD) .... oerc
Optimum Gradient Method .... OGM
Optimum Guidance [*Technique*] (NASA) .... OPGUID
Optimum Insect Pest Management Trial [*Department of Agriculture*] .... OIPMT
Optimum Installation Position Only (MCD) .... OIPO
Optimum Insulation Thickness (DICI) .... OIT
Optimum Interpolation [*Marine science*] (OSRA) .... OI
Optimum Life Cycle Costing (PDAA) .... OLCC
Optimum Life-Cycle Costing (AD) .... olcc
Optimum Metric Fastener System .... OMFS
Optimum Mix of Short Range Air Defense Systems .... OMSRADS
Optimum Mode Selector (CAAL) .... OMS
Optimum Nutritional Effectiveness [*Brand name of dog food*] [*Ralston Purina Co.*] .... ONE
Optimum Optical Pump .... OOP
Optimum Orbital Altitude (AAG) .... OOA
Optimum Phase Shift Keyed Signals [*Telecommunications*] .... OPSKS
Optimum Private Trunk Network Embodying Tandems (PDAA) .... OPTNET
[*The*] Optimum Publishing System [*IBM Corp.*] .... TOPS
Optimum Qualification Procedure .... OQP
Optimum Record Automation for Court and Law Enforcement .... ORACLE
Optimum Repair Level Analysis .... ORL
Optimum Repair Level Analysis [*Air Force*] .... ORLA
Optimum Repair Level Authorization (MCD) .... ORLA
Optimum Report Level Analysis [*Military*] .... ORLA
Optimum Resolution Technique .... ORT
Optimum Resource Extraction (PDAA) .... ORE
Optimum Ship Routing [*Obsolete*] .... OSR
Optimum Step Size Random Search [*Computer science*] (IAA) .... OSSRS
Optimum Supply and Maintenance Model [*Army*] (RDA) .... OSAMM
Optimum Supply and Maintenance Model .... OSMM
Optimum Survival Containment and Recovery (AAG) .... OSCAR
Optimum Sustainable Population [*Marine science*] (MSC) .... OSP
Optimum System for the Control of Aircraft Retardation .... OSCAR
Optimum Systems Covariance Analysis Results (IEEE) .... OSCAR
Optimum Technical Operational Concept to Accomplish .... OTOCTA
Optimum Time Invariant (IAA) .... OTI
Optimum Time Varying (IAA) .... OTV
Optimum Track Ship Routing [*Navy*] (NVT) .... OTSR
Optimum Traffic Condition [*Radio*] (IAA) .... OTF
Optimum Traffic Frequency [*Radio*] .... OTF
Optimum Usual Frequency Radio (IAA) .... OUF
Optimum Value Engineered (Home) .... OVE
Optimum Vehicle for Effective Reconnaissance [*Air Force*] (PDAA) .... OVER
Optimum Working Efficiency .... OWE
Optimum Working Facility (NITA) .... OWF
Optimum Working Frequency [*Telecommunications*] .... OWF
Optimum Yaw Control Vertical (SAA) .... OYCV
Optimum Yield .... OY
Optimus [*Best*] [*Latin*] .... O
Optimus [*Best*] [*Latin*] .... OPT
Optimus Maximus [*Greatest and Best*] [*Latin*] .... OM
Option (ADA) .... OPN
Option [*Shares*] .... OPT
Option .... OPT
Option [*Legal shorthand*] (LWAP) .... OPTN
OPTION CARE [*NASDAQ symbol*] (TTSB) .... OPTN
Option Care, Inc. [*NASDAQ symbol*] (SAG) .... OPTN
Option Care, Inc. [*Associated Press*] (SAG) .... OptnCr
Option Clearing Corp. .... OCC
Option Growth Fund (AD) .... ogf
Option Income [*Business term*] .... Opine
Option Not Traded [*Investment term*] (DFIT) .... R
[*The*] Option Process [*HUD*] .... TOP
Option Select Mode [*Computer science*] (OA) .... OSM
Option Spreading [*Investment term*] .... OS
Option Table Generator .... OTG
Optional .... OP
Optional (AAG) .... OPT
Optional (IDOE) .... opt
Optional (MSA) .... OPTL
Optional Calling Measured Service [*Telecommunications*] (TEL) .... OCMS
Optional Calling Plans [*Telecommunications*] (TEL) .... OPC
Optional Character Reader [*Computer science*] (DA) .... OCR
Optional Claiming Race (WGA) .... Opt Clm
Optional Construction Joint .... OCJ
Optional County Government [*A publication*] (DLA) .... Opt County Gov't
Optional Delivery Dispenser System (MCD) .... ODDS
Optional Dishes [*School meals*] [*British*] .... O
Optional Educational Programs (AD) .... OEP
Optional Exchange [*Dietetics*] .... OptEx
Optional Feature (IAA) .... OF
Optional Flag [*Navy British*] .... OP
Optional Form .... OF

Optional Form (AD) .... of
Optional Ground Equipment (AAGC) .... OGE
Optional Parts Request (SAA) .... OPR
Optional Reception of Announcements by Coded Line Electronics [*Independent Television "newspaper"*] [*British*] (DI) .... ORACLE
Optional Recovery of Announcements by Coded Line Electronics (NITA) .... ORACLE
Optional Residential Telephone Service [*Telecommunications*] (TEL) .... ORTS
Optional Team Targeting (MCD) .... OTT
Optional With [*Automotive engineering*] .... O/W
Optioned [*Automotive advertising*] .... OPT'D
Options [*Computer science*] [*Telecommunications*] .... o
Options Exchange [*Finance*] .... OEX
Options Exchange Index .... OEI
Options for Animals Foundation (EA) .... OAF
Options for Men [*A publication*] .... OM
Options for Women [*Later, Options*] (EA) .... OW
Options Income (BARN) .... Opinc
Options Market [*Finance*] .... OM
Options Price Reporting Authority [*Information service or system*] (IID) .... OPRA
Options Pricing Model .... OPM
Options to Purchase or Sell Specific Mortgage-Backed Securities [*Merrill Lynch & Co.*] [*Finance*] .... OPOSSMS
Optiram, St. Helier, Jersey, Channel Islands, United Kingdom [*Library symbol*] [*Library of Congress*] (LCLS) .... O+R
Opto/Graphic (AD) .... O/G
Optoacoustic [*Cell*] .... OA
Optoacoustic Spectrometry [*Also, PAS*] .... OAS
Optoelectronic Imaging Device .... OID
Optoelectronic Industry and Technology Development Association [*Japan*] .... OITDA
Optoelectronic Integrated Circuit [*Computer science*] .... OEIC
Opto-Electronic Integrated Circuits .... OEIC
Optoelectronic Isolator .... OEI
Optoelectronic Pulse Amplifier .... OPA
Optoelectronic Systems Programme [*British*] .... OSP
Opto-Electronics Center (MCD) .... OEC
Optoelectronics Joint Research Laboratory [*Japan*] .... OJRL
Optoelectronics Technology Consortium [*Sponsored by the Department of Defense*] .... OETC
Optofiber Metric Switch .... OFM
Optogalvanic Effect (MCD) .... OGE
Opto-Graphic (AD) .... o/g
Optokinetic .... OPK
Optokinetic After-After-Nystagmus [*Ophthalmology*] .... OKAAN
Optokinetic After-Nystagmus [*Ophthalmology*] .... OKAN
Optokinetic Nystagmus [*Ophthalmology*] .... OKN
Optomechanical Display Module .... OMDM
Optometric .... OPTMTRC
Optometric College Aptitude Test (WDAA) .... OCAT
Optometric Corp. (AD) .... OC
Optometric Editors Association (EA) .... OEA
Optometric Extension Program Foundation (EA) .... OEPF
Optometric Historical Society (EA) .... OHS
Optometrist .... OPTOM
Optometrists' Board [*Australian Capital Territory*] .... OB
Optometrists' Board of Queensland .... OBQ
Optometrists' Registration Board [*Victoria, Australia*] .... ORB
Optometrists' Registration Board of the Australian Capital Territory .... ORBACT
Optometrists' Registration Board of Victoria [*Australia*] .... ORBV
Optometrists' Registration Board of Western Australia .... ORBWA
Optometry .... OPTM
Optometry .... Optom
Optometry Admissions Test (GAGS) .... OAT
Optometry College Admissions Test (WDAA) .... OCAT
Optonics Devices Incorporated .... ODI
Optotek Ltd., Ottawa, Ontario [*Library symbol National Library of Canada*] (NLC) .... OOOL
Opus [*Work*] [*Latin*] .... OP
Opus (WDMC) .... op
Opus Citatum (IAA) .... OPCIT
Opus Dei (EA) .... OD
Opuscula [*Minor Works*] [*Latin*] (ROG) .... OPUSC
Opuscula Archaeologica [*A publication*] (OCD) .... Op Arch
Opuwa [*Namibia*] [*ICAO location identifier*] (ICLI) .... FAOP
Opuwa [*Namibia*] [*Airport symbol*] (OAG) .... OPW
Opytnyi Reaktivnyi Motor [*Experimental Reaction Motor*] [*Former USSR*] .... ORM
Or Best Offer [*Classified advertising*] .... OBO
Or Better [*Business term*] .... OB
Or Gate [*Computer science*] .... OG
OR Gate [*Electronics*] (ECII) .... OG
Or Less (AD) .... ol
Or Less .... OL
Or Nearest [*or Near*] **Offer** [*Business term*] (ADA) .... ONO
or WSMR [*Hugh L. Dryden Flight Research Center*] [*White Sands Missile Range*] (NASA) .... GOM
Ora pro Nobis [*Pray for Us*] [*Latin*] .... OPN
Ora pro Nobis Jesu Christe [*Pray for Us, Jesus Christ*] [*Motto of Ernst, Duke of Bavaria (1554-1612)*] [*Latin*] .... OPNJC
Oracle, AZ [*FM radio station call letters*] .... KLQB
ORACLE Binary Internal Translator [*Algebraic programming system*] .... ORBIT
Oracle Corp. [*NASDAQ symbol*] (TTSB) .... ORCL
Oracle Parallel Server [*Computer science*] .... OPS
Oracle Public Library, Oracle, AZ [*Library symbol Library of Congress*] (LCLS) .... AzO
Oracle Resources [*Vancouver Stock Exchange symbol*] .... OCR
Oracle Systems Corp. [*Associated Press*] (SAG) .... Oracle
Oracle Systems Corp. [*NASDAQ symbol*] (NQ) .... ORCL
Oracle Teletext Ltd. (NITA) .... OTL
Orad [*Romania*] [*Airport symbol*] (OAG) .... OMR
Oradea [*Romania*] [*ICAO location identifier*] (ICLI) .... LROD
Oradell Public Library, Oradell, NJ [*Library symbol Library of Congress*] (LCLS) .... NjOrd
Orah Hayyim Shulhan 'Arukh (BJA) .... OH
Oral [*Medicine*] .... O
Oral Access to Library .... ORAL
Oral Alimentation [*Gastroenterology*] (DAVI) .... OA
Oral and Maxillofacial Surgery .... OMS
Oral and Maxillofacial Surgery In-Training Examination .... OMSITE
Oral and Pharyngeal Development [*Section*] [*National Institute of Dental Research*] .... OPD
Oral Apparatus [*Zoology*] .... OA
Oral Care [*Denistry*] (DAVI) .... OC
Oral Cholecystography [*or Cholecystogram*] [*Radiology*] .... OCG
Oral Contraceptive [*Endocrinology*] .... OC
Oral Contraceptive [*Medicine*] (AD) .... oc
Oral Contraceptive Agent [*Endocrinology*] .... OCA
Oral Contraceptive Council [*Defunct*] (EA) .... OCC
Oral Contraceptive Pill [*Gynecology*] [*Pharmacology*] (DAVI) .... OCP
Oral Contraceptive Therapy [*Endocrinology*] (AAMN) .... OCT
Oral Deaf Adults Section [*Later, OHIS*] (EA) .... ODAS
Oral Electrolyte Solution [*Nutrition*] .... ORS
Oral Glucose Loading [*Endocrinology*] .... OGL
Oral Glucose Tolerance Test [*Medicine*] .... OGTT
Oral Hairy Leukoplakia [*Medicine*] .... OHL
Oral Health Maintenance Program [*Army*] (AABC) .... OHMP
Oral Health Research Institute [*Indiana University*] [*Research center*] (RCD) .... OHRI
Oral Health Status Index [*Dentistry*] .... OHSI
Oral Hearing-Impaired Section [*of the Alexander Graham Bell Association for the Deaf*] (EA) .... OHIS
Oral History Association (EA) .... OHA
Oral History in the Mid-Atlantic Region [*An association*] .... OHMAR
Oral Hygiene [*Dentistry*] (DAVI) .... OH
Oral Hygiene Index-Simplified .... OHI-S
Oral Hygiene Service (AD) .... OHS
Oral Hygiene Society (NADA) .... OHS
Oral Hypoglycemic [*Endocrinology*] (DAVI) .... OHG
Oral Hypoglycemic Agent [*Medicine*] (CPH) .... OHA
Oral Language Evaluation [*English and Spanish test*] .... OLE
Oral Language Sentence Imitation Diagnostic Inventory - Format Revised [*Educational test*] .... OLSIDI-F
Oral Language Sentence Imitation Screening Test - Format Revised [*Educational test*] .... OLSIST-F
Oral Lichen Plannus [*Medicine*] .... OLP
Oral Mucosal Transudate [*Clinical chemistry*] .... OMT
Oral Nitroglycerine [*Medicine*] .... ONTG
Oral Osmotic [*System for delivering drugs into the bloodstream*] [*Alza Corp. trademark*] .... OROS
Oral Polio Vaccine [*Also, Sabin vaccine*] (PAZ) .... OPV
Oral Polio Virus Vaccine .... OPV
Oral Poliovirus [*Infectious diseases*] (DAVI) .... OPV
Oral Rehydration Fluid .... ORF
Oral Rehydration Salts [*or Solution*] .... ORS
Oral Rehydration Therapy .... ORT
Oral Roberts University (GAGS) .... Oral Roberts U
Oral Roberts University [*Oklahoma*] .... ORU
Oral Roberts University Educational Fellowship (EA) .... ORUEF
Oral Roberts University, Learning Resources Center, Tulsa, OK [*Library symbol Library of Congress*] (LCLS) .... OkTOR
Oral Roberts University, Tulsa, OK [*OCLC symbol*] (OCLC) .... OKO
Oral Speech Mechanism Screening Examination [*Educational test*] .... OSME
Oral Surgeon .... ORS
Oral Surgery .... OS
Oral Suspension [*Pharmacy*] .... OS
Oral Temperature (DAVI) .... O/T
Oral Temperature Device (MCD) .... OTD
Oral Testimony (BJA) .... OT
Oral Thrush [*Medicine*] (MEDA) .... OT
Oral Trade Tests [*Department of Labor*] .... OTT
Oral Transfer Factor [*Virology*] .... OTF
Oral-Facial-Digital [*Genetics*] (DAVI) .... OFD
Oran [*Argentina*] [*Airport symbol*] (AD) .... ORA
Oran [*Algeria*] [*Airport symbol*] (OAG) .... ORN
Oran [*Algeria*] [*ICAO location identifier*] (ICLI) .... SASO
Oran/Es Senia [*Algeria*] [*ICAO location identifier*] (ICLI) .... DAOO
Oran/Tafaroui [*Algeria*] [*ICAO location identifier*] (ICLI) .... DAOL
Orange [*Color*] [*Medicine*] (DMAA) .... O
Orange [*Maps and charts*] .... O
Orange [*Phonetic alphabet*] [*Royal Navy World War I Pre-World War II*] (DSUE) .... O
Orange [*Australia Airport symbol*] (OAG) .... OAG
Orange .... OR
Orange [*Laboratory science*] (DAVI) .... ORAN
Orange [*Diocesan abbreviation*] [*California*] (TOCD) .... ORG
Orange [*Philately*] .... org
Orange (AAG) .... ORN
Orange .... ORNG
Orange & Rockland Utilities, Inc. [*Associated Press*] (SAG) .... OranRk
Orange & Rockland Utilities, Inc. [*NYSE symbol*] (SPSG) .... ORU

Orange Badge Scheme [*Disabled parking permit*] [*British*] ... OBS
Orange Beach, AL [*FM radio station call letters*] (RBYB) ... WCSN-FM
Orange Beach, AL [*FM radio station call letters*] ... WXAH
Orange, CA [*AM radio station call letters*] ... KPLS
Orange/Caritat [*France ICAO location identifier*] (ICLI) ... LFMO
Orange Carpet Crowd [*An association*] ... OCC
Orange City, IA [*Location identifier FAA*] (FAAL) ... ORC
Orange Coast College [*Formerly, OCJC*] [*Costa Mesa, CA*] ... OCC
Orange Coast College, Costa Mesa, CA [*Library symbol Library of Congress*] (LCLS) ... CCmO
Orange Coast Junior College [*California*] [*Later, OCC*] ... OCJC
Orange Co. [*NYSE symbol*] (SPSG) ... OJ
Orange County [*California*] [*Airport symbol*] (OAG) ... SNA
Orange County California Genealogical Society, Orange, CA [*Library symbol Library of Congress*] (LCLS) ... COrGS
Orange County Community College (AD) ... OCCC
Orange County Community College, Middletown, NY [*Library symbol Library of Congress*] (LCLS) ... NMiOC
Orange County General Hospital, Orange, CA [*Library symbol Library of Congress*] (LCLS) ... COrGH
Orange County Historical Society, Santa Ana, CA [*Library symbol*] [*Library of Congress*] (LCLS) ... CStaHi
Orange County Law Library, Santa Ana, CA [*Library symbol Library of Congress*] (LCLS) ... CStaOL
Orange County Public Library [*Florida*] ... OCPL
Orange County Public Library, Orange, CA [*Library symbol Library of Congress*] (LCLS) ... COrCL
Orange County Public Library, Orange, VA [*Library symbol Library of Congress*] (LCLS) ... ViOr
Orange Cove, CA [*FM radio station call letters*] ... KMAK
Orange Cyan Wideband (IAA) ... OCW
Orange Field Naturalist and Conservation Society [*Australia*] ... OFNCS
Orange Free Public Library, Orange, CA [*Library symbol Library of Congress*] (LCLS) ... COr
Orange Free State [*South Africa*] ... OFS
Orange Free State (DAS) ... OrFS
Orange Free State Reports, High Court [*1879-83*] [*South Africa*] [*A publication*] (DLA) ... OFS
Orange Free State, South Africa (ILCA) ... OFSSA
Orange Green [*Stain*] [*Medicine*] ... OG
Orange Indicating Light (MSA) ... OIL
Orange Juice ... OJ
Orange Juice (AD) ... oj
Orange Juice ... OrJ
Orange Light ... OLT
Orange, MA [*Location identifier FAA*] (FAAL) ... ORE
Orange, MA [*FM radio station call letters*] (RBYB) ... WJDF
Orange National Bancorp [*NASDAQ symbol*] (SAG) ... OGNB
Orange National Bancorp [*Associated Press*] (SAG) ... OrangN
Orange Natl Bancorp [*NASDAQ symbol*] (TTSB) ... OGNB
Orange Park, FL [*AM radio station call letters*] ... WAYR
Orange Park, FL [*TV station call letters*] (RBYB) ... WYDP-TV
Orange Pekoe [*Tea*] ... OP
Orange Pigment Cell ... OPC
Orange PLC [*Associated Press*] (SAG) ... Orange
Orange PLC [*NASDAQ symbol*] (SAG) ... ORNG
Orange PLC ADR [*NASDAQ symbol*] (TTSB) ... ORNGY
Orange Public Library, Orange, TX [*Library symbol Library of Congress*] (LCLS) ... TxOr
Orange River Colony [*Later, Orange Free State*] [*South Africa*] ... ORC
Orange River Colony, South Africa (ILCA) ... ORCSA
Orange/Rockland Util [*NYSE symbol*] (TTSB) ... ORU
Orange, TX [*FM radio station call letters*] ... KIOC
Orange, TX [*FM radio station call letters*] ... KKMY
Orange, TX [*AM radio station call letters*] ... KOGT
Orange, TX [*Location identifier FAA*] (FAAL) ... ORG
Orange, VA [*AM radio station call letters*] ... WJMA
Orange, VA [*FM radio station call letters*] ... WJMA-FM
Orange Walk [*British Honduras*] [*Airport symbol*] (AD) ... ORW
Orange Walk [*Belize*] [*Airport symbol Obsolete*] (OAG) ... ORZ
Orange Washed Pulp [*Citrus processing*] ... OWP
Orange Yellow ... OY
Orange-Athol, MA [*AM radio station call letters*] ... WCAT
Orangeburg [*South Carolina*] [*Seismograph station code, US Geological Survey*] (SEIS) ... OSB
Orangeburg [*South Carolina*] [*Seismograph station code, US Geological Survey Closed*] (SEIS) ... OSC
Orangeburg County Free Library, Orangeburg, SC [*Library symbol*] [*Library of Congress*] (LCLS) ... ScOr
Orangeburg Public Library, Orangeburg, NY [*Library symbol Library of Congress*] (LCLS) ... NOrb
Orangeburg, SC [*Location identifier FAA*] (FAAL) ... EDS
Orangeburg, SC [*Location identifier FAA*] (FAAL) ... OGB
Orangeburg, SC [*FM radio station call letters*] ... WIGL
Orangeburg, SC [*AM radio station call letters*] ... WJZS
Orangeburg, SC [*FM radio station call letters*] ... WKSO
Orangeburg, SC [*AM radio station call letters*] ... WPJK
Orangeburg, SC [*FM radio station call letters*] ... WSSB
Orangeburg, SC [*FM radio station call letters*] ... WTCB
Orangeburg-Calhoune Technical College, Orangeburg, SC [*Library symbol*] [*Library of Congress*] (LCLS) ... ScOrTC
Orangeburgh German Swiss Genealogical Society (EA) ... OGSGS
Orange-Co. [*NYSE symbol*] (TTSB) ... OJ
Orange-Co., Inc. [*Associated Press*] (SAG) ... OrngCo
Orange-Cudal [*Australia Airport symbol*] (OAG) ... CUG
Orange-Green (AD) ... o-g
Orange-Green Stain (AD) ... o-g stain
Orangeville, ON [*FM radio station call letters*] ... CIDC
Orangeville Public Library, Ontario [*Library symbol National Library of Canada*] (NLC) ... OORA
Orangutan Recovery Service [*Later, IUCN*] ... OURS
Oranjemund [*Namibia*] [*ICAO location identifier*] (ICLI) ... FAOG
Oranjestad/F. D. Roosevelt, Sint Eustatius Island [*Netherlands Antilles*] [*ICAO location identifier*] (ICLI) ... TNCE
Oranjestad/Reina Beatrix, Aruba Island [*Netherlands Antilles*] [*ICAO location identifier*] (ICLI) ... TNCA
Oran-Tafaraoui [*Algeria*] [*Airport symbol*] (OAG) ... TAF
Orapa [*Botswana*] [*ICAO location identifier*] (ICLI) ... FBOR
Orapa [*Botswana*] [*Airport symbol Obsolete*] (OAG) ... ORP
Orapouche [*An arbovirus*] [*Medicine*] (BABM) ... ORO
Orapouche [*An arbovirus*] [*Laboratory science*] (DAVI) ... ORO
Oratio [*A publication*] (OCD) ... Or
Oratio in Senatu in Toga Candida [*of Cicero*] [*Classical studies*] (OCD) ... Tog Cand
Oration [*or Orator or Oratorio*] ... Orat
Orationes [*of Julian*] [*Classical studies*] (OCD) ... Or
Orationes [*of Dio Chrysostomus*] [*Classical studies*] (OCD) ... Or
Orationes Philippicae [*of Cicero*] [*Classical studies*] (OCD) ... Phil
Oratoire Saint-Joseph du Mont-Royal, Montreal, PQ, Canada [*Library symbol Library of Congress*] (LCLS) ... CaQMO
Oratoire Saint-Joseph, Montreal, Quebec [*Library symbol National Library of Canada*] (NLC) ... QMO
Orator ad M. Brutum [*of Cicero*] [*Classical studies*] (OCD) ... Orat
Orator Verbis Electric (IAA) ... OVE
Oratorians (TOCD) ... co
Oratorians (TOCD) ... CO
Oratorians ... OR
Oratorical ... ORAT
Oratorum Romanorum Fragmenta [*A publication*] (OCD) ... ORF
Oratory of the Good Shepherd [*British*] ... OGS
OraVax, Inc. [*Associated Press*] (SAG) ... OraVax
OraVax, Inc. [*NASDAQ symbol*] (SAG) ... ORVX
Orbe [*Switzerland*] [*Seismograph station code, US Geological Survey Closed*] (SEIS) ... ORB
Orbex Industries, Inc. [*Vancouver Stock Exchange symbol*] ... OXI
Orbi [*Former USSR ICAO designator*] (FAAC) ... DVU
Orbis [*Record label*] [*Germany, etc.*] ... Orb
Orbit [*Medicine*] (DAVI) ... O
Orbit ... ORB
Orbit Adjust Propulsion Subsystem [*NASA*] ... OAPS
Orbit Analysis ... OA
Orbit Analyst (MCD) ... OA
Orbit and Attitude Tracking (GAVI) ... OATS
Orbit, Ballistic Impact, and Trajectory [*Computer*] (MUGU) ... ORBIT
Orbit Computation System (MCD) ... OCS
Orbit Correction Subsystem (NOAA) ... OCS
Orbit Data Editor Assembly [*Space Flight Operations Facility, NASA*] ... ODE
Orbit Data Generator [*NASA*] ... ODG
Orbit Determination ... OD
Orbit Determination and Vehicle Attitude Reference ... ODVAR
Orbit Determination Facility (MCD) ... ODF
Orbit Determination Group ... ORDET
Orbit Determination Program ... ODP
Orbit [*or Orbital*] **Insertion** ... OI
Orbit Insertion Maneuver ... OIM
Orbit International [*NASDAQ symbol*] (TTSB) ... ORBT
Orbit International Corp. [*Associated Press*] (SAG) ... Orbit
Orbit International Corp. [*NASDAQ symbol*] (NQ) ... ORBT
Orbit Maneuvering Propulsion System [*NASA*] (KSC) ... OMPS
Orbit Modification (IAA) ... OM
Orbit Navigation Analysis Program ... ONAP
Orbit Oil & Gas Ltd. [*Toronto Stock Exchange symbol*] ... ORB
Orbit/Payload Recorder [*NASA*] (MCD) ... OPR
Orbit Rate Display - Earth and Lunar [*NASA*] ... ORDEAL
Orbit Readiness Test [*NASA*] (NASA) ... ORT
Orbit Semiconductor [*NASDAQ symbol*] (SAG) ... ORRA
Orbit Semiconductor Co. [*Associated Press*] (SAG) ... OrbtSemi
Orbit Shift Coil ... OSC
Orbit Stay Time ... OST
Orbit Test Direction [*or Directive*] (IAA) ... OTD
Orbital (KSC) ... ORB
Orbital Altitude and Maneuvering System (IAA) ... OAMS
Orbital Analysis ... ORAN
Orbital Antenna Farm (PDAA) ... OAF
Orbital Assembly (MCD) ... OA
Orbital Assembly Module (MCD) ... OAM
Orbital Assembly Support Vehicle ... OASV
Orbital Attitude and Maneuvering Electronics ... OAME
Orbital Attitude and Maneuvering System [*NASA*] ... OAMS
Orbital Bombardment Guidance System ... OBGS
Orbital Bombardment System ... OBS
Orbital Bomber (IAA) ... OBO
Orbital Check (MCD) ... OC
Orbital Circularization Technique ... OCT
Orbital Combustion Process (PDAA) ... OCP
Orbital Control Program (SAA) ... OCP
Orbital Correction Program [*NASA*] (KSC) ... OCP
Orbital Curve of Growth [*Mathematics*] ... OCG
Orbital Data Collector ... ODC
Orbital Design Integration System ... ODIS

Orbital Determination Module .... ODM
Orbital Doppler (IAA) .... ODOP
Orbital Electron Capture .... OEC
Orbital Emergency Arresting System [*NASA*] (NASA) .... OEAS
Orbital Engine ADS [*NYSE symbol*] (SPSG) .... OE
Orbital Engine Corp. Ltd. [*Associated Press*] (SAG) .... OrbEng
Orbital Facility (IAA) .... OF
Orbital Flight [*NASA*] (KSC) .... O/F
Orbital [*or Orbiter*] **Flight System** [*NASA*] (MCD) .... OFS
Orbital Flight Test [*NASA*] (NASA) .... OFT
Orbital Flight Test Data System [*NASA*] (MCD) .... OFTDS
Orbital Flight Test Requirement [*NASA*] (NASA) .... OFTR
Orbital Height Adjustment Maneuver (MCD) .... OHA
Orbital Horizontal Ground Vibration Test [*NASA*] (NASA) .... OHGVT
Orbital Improvement Program .... OIP
Orbital International Laboratory .... OIL
Orbital Launch .... OL
Orbital Launch Facility .... OLF
Orbital Launch Operation .... OLO
Orbital Launch Vehicle .... OLV
Orbital Launched Balistic Missile (AD) .... olbm
Orbital Launched Ballistic Missile [*Military*] (WDAA) .... OLBM
Orbital Lock Assembly .... OLA
Orbital [*or Orbiter*] **Main Engine** [*NASA*] (NASA) .... OME
Orbital Maintenance Mission [*NASA*] (SSD) .... OMM
Orbital Maneuvering Engine [*NASA*] (KSC) .... OME
Orbital Maneuvering System [*or Subsystem*] [*NASA*] .... OMS
Orbital Maneuvering Vehicle [*NASA*] .... OMV
Orbital Maneuvering Vehicle Control Center [*NASA*] (SSD) .... OMVCC
Orbital Multifunction Satellite .... OMS
Orbital Period (AAG) .... OP
Orbital Period [*of a comet*] [*In years*] .... P
Orbital Polarized Hartree-Fock [*Atomic physics*] .... OPHF
Orbital Position Indicator .... OPI
Orbital Probe [*NASA*] .... OP
Orbital Propellant Storage Facility (MCD) .... OPSF
Orbital Propellant Storage Subsystem (MCD) .... OPSS
Orbital Rate Drive Electronics for Apollo and LM [*NASA*] .... ORDEAL
Orbital Reentry Vehicle [*NASA*] (IAA) .... ORV
Orbital Refueling System [*NASA*] (NASA) .... ORS
Orbital Remote Maneuvering Unit .... ORMU
Orbital Rendezvous Base System .... ORBS
Orbital Rendezvous Positioning, Indexing, and Coupling System .... ORPICS
Orbital Rendezvous Procedure (AAG) .... ORP
Orbital Rendezvous RADAR (AAG) .... ORR
Orbital Rendezvous Technique (AAG) .... ORT
Orbital Replaceable Unit (SSD) .... ORU
Orbital Replacement Unit (MCD) .... ORU
Orbital Requirements Document .... ORD
Orbital Rescue Vehicle [*NASA*] (KSC) .... ORV
Orbital Research Centrifuge [*NASA*] (KSC) .... ORC
Orbital Research Laboratory [*NASA*] .... ORL
Orbital Return Vehicle [*NASA*] (IAA) .... ORV
Orbital Sciences Corp. [*NASDAQ symbol*] (SAG) .... ORBI
Orbital Sciences Corp. [*Associated Press*] (SAG) .... OrbSci
Orbital Sciences Corp. .... OSC
Orbital Sequence of Events [*NASA*] (IAA) .... OSE
Orbital Service Module [*NASA*] (MCD) .... OSM
Orbital Solar Observation (IAA) .... OSB
Orbital Space Station Study [*NASA*] (IAA) .... OSS
Orbital Space Station Study .... OSSS
Orbital Space Station System [*of NASA*] .... OSSS
Orbital Stabilization System (MCD) .... OSS
Orbital Support Plan (MCD) .... OSP
Orbital Support Vehicle .... OSV
Orbital Test Flight (MCD) .... OTF
Orbital Test Satellite [*Communications satellite*] [*European Space Agency*] .... OTS
Orbital Transport Systems (MCD) .... OTS
Orbital Transport- und Raketen-Aktiengesellschaft [*Rocket company*] [*Germany*] .... OTRAG
Orbital Uncertainty Estimate .... OUE
Orbital Utility Light .... OUL
Orbital [*or Orbiter*] **Vehicle** [*NASA*] .... OV
Orbital Vehicle Assembly Mode [*NASA*] .... OVAM
Orbital Vehicle Reentry Simulator [*NASA*] .... OVERS
Orbital Very-Long Baseline Interferometer [*Communications satellite*] [*Telecommunications*] (IEEE) .... OVLBI
Orbital Weapon System (AAG) .... OWS
Orbital, Weightless Flight (IAA) .... OWF
Orbital Workshop [*NASA*] .... OWS
Orbital-Escape System [*NASA*] .... OES
Orbital-Plane Experiment Package [*NASA*] .... OPEP
Orbited Assembly Operation .... OAO
Orbiter [*NASA*] (NASA) .... ORB
Orbiter .... ORB
Orbiter Access Arm [*NASA*] .... OA
Orbiter Access Arm [*NASA*] (NASA) .... OAA
Orbiter Aeroflight Simulator [*NASA*] (NASA) .... OAS
Orbiter Air Flight Deck [*NASA*] (MCD) .... OAFD
Orbiter Alternate Airfield [*NASA*] (MCD) .... OAA
Orbiter Antenna Test Model [*NASA*] .... OATM
Orbiter Atmospheric Drag [*NASA*] .... OAD
Orbiter Atmospheric Flight Test Office [*NASA*] (NASA) .... OAFTO
Orbiter Atmospheric Simulator [*NASA*] (MCD) .... OAS
Orbiter Automatic Landing System (MCD) .... OALS
Orbiter Avionics Software Control Board [*NASA*] (NASA) .... OASCB
Orbiter Avionics System [*NASA*] (NASA) .... OAS
Orbiter CEI [*Contract End Item*] **Specification** [*NASA*] (NASA) .... OS
Orbiter Cloud Photopolarimeter [*NASA*] .... OCPP
Orbiter Common Hardware [*NASA*] (NASA) .... OCH
Orbiter Computational Facility [*NASA*] (NASA) .... OCF
Orbiter Crash and Rescue Manuals [*NASA*] (NASA) .... OCRM
Orbiter Crash and Rescue Manuals [*NASA*] .... OCRM
Orbiter Critical Design Review [*NASA*] (NASA) .... OCDR
Orbiter Data Reduction Center [*NASA*] (MCD) .... ODRC
Orbiter Data Reduction Center [*NASA*] .... ORDC
Orbiter Delta CDR [*NASA*] (GFGA) .... ODCDR
Orbiter Dynamic Simulator [*NASA*] .... ODS
Orbiter Dynamic Test Model [*NASA*] .... ODTM
Orbiter Electric Field Detector [*NASA*] .... OEFD
Orbiter Electrical Interface Simulator [*NASA*] .... OEIS
Orbiter Electron Temperature Probe [*NASA*] .... OETP
Orbiter Emergency Site [*NASA*] (NASA) .... OES
Orbiter Experiments [*NASA*] (MCD) .... OEX
Orbiter/External Tank [*NASA*] (NASA) .... O/ET
Orbiter Flight Dynamics Simulator [*NASA*] (NASA) .... OFDS
Orbiter Flight Program [*NASA*] (NASA) .... OFP
Orbiter Functional Simulator (NASA) .... OFS
Orbiter Functional Simulator .... OFS
Orbiter Functional Simulator Control Center (MCD) .... OFSCC
Orbiter Gamma Burst Detecter [*NASA*] .... OGBD
Orbiter Greenwich Mean Time [*NASA*] (MCD) .... OGMT
Orbiter Infrared Radiometer [*NASA*] .... OIR
Orbiter Instrumentation [*NASA*] (NASA) .... OI
Orbiter Instrumentation Systems [*NASA*] (MCD) .... OIS
Orbiter Integrated Checkout [*NASA*] (NASA) .... OIC
Orbiter Integrated Test [*NASA*] (NASA) .... OIT
Orbiter Interface Adapter [*NASA*] (NASA) .... OIA
Orbiter Interface Box [*NASA*] (NASA) .... OIB
Orbiter Interface Box .... OIB
Orbiter Interface Verification Set .... OIVS
Orbiter Interface Verification Set [*NASA*] (NASA) .... OIVS
Orbiter Ion Mass Spectrometer [*NASA*] .... OIMS
Orbiter Landing Facility [*NASA*] (NASA) .... OLF
Orbiter Landing Instrumentation Facilities [*NASA*] (NASA) .... OLIF
Orbiter Lift-Off Mass [*NASA*] (KSC) .... OLOM
Orbiter Lift-Off Weight [*NASA*] .... OLOW
Orbiter Liftoff Weight (AD) .... olow
Orbiter Logistics Support Plan [*NASA*] .... OLSA
Orbiter Logistics Support Plan [*NASA*] (NASA) .... OLSP
Orbiter Logistics Support Plan .... OLSP
Orbiter/LPS [*Launch Processing System*] **Signal Adapter** [*NASA*] (NASA) .... OLSA
Orbiter Magnetometer [*NASA*] .... OMAG
Orbiter Maintenance and Checkout [*NASA*] (NASA) .... OMC
Orbiter Maintenance and Checkout .... OMC
Orbiter Maintenance and Checkout Facility [*NASA*] (NASA) .... OMCF
Orbiter Maintenance Area [*NASA*] (MCD) .... OMA
Orbiter Maintenance Engineering Working Group [*NASA*] (NASA) .... OMEWG
Orbiter Maintenance Man-Hours [*NASA*] (NASA) .... OMMH
Orbiter Management Review [*NASA*] (NASA) .... OMR
Orbiter Mating Device [*NASA*] (NASA) .... OMD
Orbiter Mating Device [*NASA*] .... OMD
Orbiter Midbody Umbilical Unit [*NASA*] (NASA) .... OMBUU
Orbiter Mission Elapsed Time [*NASA*] (MCD) .... OMET
Orbiter Mold Line [*NASA*] (NASA) .... OML
Orbiter Neutral Buoyancy Trainer [*NASA*] (MCD) .... ONBT
Orbiter Neutral Mass Spectrometer [*NASA*] .... ONMS
Orbiter on Dock [*NASA*] (KSC) .... OOD
Orbiter One-G Trainer [*NASA*] (NASA) .... ORB 1-G
Orbiter (Operational) Downlink [*NASA*] .... OD
Orbiter Payload Interrogator [*NASA*] (MCD) .... OPI
Orbiter Payload Work Station (MCD) .... OPWS
Orbiter Plasma Analyzer [*NASA*] .... OPA
Orbiter Preflight Checklist [*NASA*] (MCD) .... OPFC
Orbiter Prime Item Specification [*NASA*] (NASA) .... OPIS
Orbiter Processing and Landing Facility [*NASA*] (MCD) .... OPLF
Orbiter Processing Facility [*NASA*] (NASA) .... OPF
Orbiter Processing Support Building [*NASA*] (NASA) .... OPSB
Orbiter Processing Support Building .... OPSB
Orbiter Project Office [*NASA*] (MCD) .... OPO
Orbiter Project Parts Authorization Request [*NASA*] (NASA) .... OPPAR
Orbiter Project Parts List [*NASA*] (NASA) .... OPPL
Orbiter Project Schedules [*NASA*] (NASA) .... OPS
Orbiter RADAR [*NASA*] .... ORAD
Orbiter Refueling System [*NASA*] .... ORS
Orbiter Relay Simulator [*NASA*] .... ORS
Orbiter Retarding Potential Analyzer [*NASA*] .... ORPA
Orbiter Subsystem Requirements Handbook [*NASA*] (NASA) .... OSSRH
Orbiter Support Equipment [*NASA*] (NASA) .... OSE
Orbiter Support Trolley [*NASA*] (NASA) .... OST
Orbiter System Definition Handbook [*NASA*] (NASA) .... OSDH
Orbiter Systems Operating Procedures [*NASA*] (NASA) .... OSOP
Orbiter Test Conductor [*NASA*] (NASA) .... OTC
Orbiter Test Director [*NASA*] (NASA) .... OTD
Orbiter Thermal Control Model [*NASA*] .... OTCM
Orbiter Thermal Effects Simulator [*NASA*] .... OTES
Orbiter Timeline Constraints [*NASA*] (NASA) .... OTLC
Orbiter Transfer Vehicle [*NASA*] .... OTV
Orbiter Ultraviolet Spectrometer [*NASA*] .... OUVS
Orbiter Utilities Tray [*NASA*] (NASA) .... OUT

Orbiting and Launch Approach Flight Simulator ... OLAFS
Orbiting Astronomical Explorer [*NASA*] (IIA) ... OAE
Orbiting Astronomical Observatory [*NASA*] ... OAO
Orbiting Astronomical Support Facility (MCD) ... OASF
Orbiting Data Relay Network ... ODRN
Orbiting Data Relay Satellite System (MCD) ... ODRSS
Orbiting Data Relay System (MCD) ... ODRS
Orbiting Deep Space Relay Station (MCD) ... ODSRS
Orbiting Energy Depot ... OED
Orbiting Experimental Capsule ... OEC
Orbiting Far and Extreme Ultraviolet Spectrometer [*Telescope*] ... ORFEUS
Orbiting Frog Otolith [*NASA experimental spacecraft*] ... OFO
Orbiting Geophysical Observatory [*NASA*] ... OGO
Orbiting Lunar Station [*NASA*] ... OLS
Orbiting Military Laboratory (AAG) ... OML
Orbiting Planetary Observatory ... OPO
Orbiting Primate Experiment (MCD) ... OPE
Orbiting Primate Spacecraft (MCD) ... OPS
Orbiting Propellant Depot [*NASA*] ... OPD
Orbiting Radio Beacon Ionosphere Satellite for Calibration [*NASA*] (PDAA) ... ORBIS CAL
Orbiting Radio Beacon Ionospheric Satellite [*NASA*] ... ORBIS
Orbiting Radio Emission Observatory [*Satellite*] ... OREO
Orbiting Research Satellite [*NASA*] ... ORS
Orbiting Satellite Carrying Amateur Radio [*Telecommunications*] (TEL) ... OSCAR
Orbiting Satellite Observer (IEEE) ... OSO
Orbiting Scientific Observatory (IAA) ... OSO
Orbiting Solar Observatory [*A satellite*] ... OSO
Orbiting Space Laboratory ... OSL
Orbiting Space Station [*NASA*] ... OSS
Orbiting Space Station [*NASA*] ... OSS
Orbiting Surveillance and Target Acquisition Relay [*Army*] (RDA) ... OSTARS
Orbiting System Test Plan [*NASA*] (NASA) ... OSTP
Orbiting Tanker Base [*NASA*] (NASA) ... OTB
Orbiting Trajectory Computations ... OTC
Orbiting Transition State-Phase Space Theory [*Physical chemistry*] ... OTS-PST
Orbiting Vehicle Assembly Building [*Later, OVSB*] ... OVAB
Orbiting Vehicle Checkout Procedure ... OVCP
Orbiting Vehicle Integrating Contractor ... OVIC
Orbiting Vehicle Limited Maintenance Area ... OVLMA
Orbiting Vehicle Requirements ... OVR
Orbiting Vehicle Support Building [*Formerly, OVAB*] ... OVSB
Orbiting Vehicle System ... OVS
Orbiting Velocity Meter ... OVM
Orbiting X-Ray Observatory [*NASA*] ... OXO
Orbiting Zoological Observatory to Track Animals ... OZO
Orbitofrontal ... OF
Orbit-on-Demand Vehicle ... OODV
Orbitor Avionics Simulator [*NASA*] ... OAS
Orbit-to-Air Intercept (IAA) ... ORTAI
Orbit-to-Orbit Shuttle [*NASA*] ... OOS
Orbit-to-Orbit Stage [*NASA*] (NASA) ... OOS
Orbit-to-Orbit Stage [*NASA*] (MCD) ... OTOS
Orbit-to-Orbit Vehicle (MCD) ... OOV
Orbotech [*Associated Press*] (SAG) ... Orbotch
Orbotech Ltd. [*Formerly, Optrotech Ltd.*] [*NASDAQ symbol*] (SPSG) ... ORBK
Orbotech Ltd Ord [*NASDAQ symbol*] (TTSB) ... ORBKF
OrCAD Inc. [*NASDAQ symbol*] (TTSB) ... OCAD
Orcad, Inc. [*NASDAQ symbol*] (SAG) ... OCAD
Orcad, Inc. [*Associated Press*] (SAG) ... Orcad
Orcadas Del Sur [*Argentina*] [*Geomagnetic observatory code*] ... ORC
Orcale Data Publishing, Bellevue, WA [*Library symbol*] [*Library of Congress*] (LCLS) ... WaBODP
Orcana Resources Ltd. [*Vancouver Stock Exchange symbol*] ... OCN
Orcas Island Library, East Sound, WA [*Library symbol*] [*Library of Congress*] (LCLS) ... WaOrc
Orcatech, Inc. [*Toronto Stock Exchange symbol*] ... ORC
Orchard ... ORCH
Orchard ... ORCH
Orchard [*Commonly used*] (OPSA) ... ORCHARD
Orchard [*Commonly used*] (OPSA) ... ORCHRD
Orchard Avenue Elementary School, Grand Junction, CO [*Library symbol Library of Congress*] (LCLS) ... CoGjOAE
Orchard Lake, MI [*FM radio station call letters*] ... WBLD
Orchard Mesa Junior High School, Grand Junction, CO [*Library symbol Library of Congress*] (LCLS) ... CoGjOMJ
Orchard, NE [*FM radio station call letters*] ... KGRD
Orchard Park Public Library, Orchard Park, NY [*Library symbol Library of Congress*] (LCLS) ... NOrc
Orchard Supply Hardware Stores Corp. [*Associated Press*] (SAG) ... OrchSHw
Orchard Supply Hardware Stores Corp. [*NASDAQ symbol*] (SAG) ... OSHC
Orchard Supply Hardware Strs [*NYSE symbol*] (TTSB) ... ORH
Orchard Valley, WY [*AM radio station call letters*] ... KUUY
Orchardists and Fruit Cool Stores Association of Victoria [*Australia*] ... OFCSAV
Orchestra ... ORCH
Orchestra (ODBW) ... orch
Orchestra of the Age of Enlightenment [*British*] ... OAE
Orchestral [*Music*] ... ORCHL
Orchestral Employers' Association [*British*] (BI) ... OEA
Orchestral Manoeuvres in the Dark [*Pop music group*] ... OMD
Orchestrated (By) [*Music*] ... ORCHD
Orchestre des Jeunes de la Communaute Europeenne [*European Community Youth Orchestra - ECYO*] (EAIO) ... OJCE
Orchid Beach [*Australia Airport symbol*] ... OKB
Orchid Fleck Virus [*Plant pathology*] ... OFV
Orchid Flowering [*Horticulture*] ... O
Orchid Society of Great Britain (EAIO) ... OSGB
Orchid Society of South Australia ... OCSA
Orchid Society of Western Australia ... OSWA
Orckit Communications Ltd. [*Associated Press*] (SAG) ... OrckitCo
Orckit Communications Ltd. [*NASDAQ symbol*] (SAG) ... ORCT
Orcutt, CA [*AM radio station call letters*] ... KGDP
Ord, NE [*AM radio station call letters*] ... KNLV
Ord, NE [*FM radio station call letters*] ... KNLV-FM
Ord, NE [*Location identifier FAA*] (FAAL) ... ODX
Ord on Usury [*A publication*] (DLA) ... Ord Us
Ordained ... O
Ordained ... ORD
ORDALT [*Ordnance Alterations*] **Accomplishment Requirement** (NG) ... OAR
ORDALT [*Ordnance Alterations*] **Deficiency Review** (MCD) ... ODR
ORDALT [*Ordnance Alterations*]/SHIPALT Inspector [*Ship Alteration*] (MCD) ... OSI
Orde des Technologistes de Laboratoire Medical de l'Ontario (AC) ... OTLMO
Ordean Junior High School, Duluth, MN [*Library symbol*] [*Library of Congress*] (LCLS) ... MnDuOJ
Order ... O
Order (AD) ... odr
Order ... ORB
Order ... ORD
Order ... ORDR
Order, Accounting, Stock, Invoicing and Statistics (MHDB) ... OASIS
Order Action List [*Military*] (DNAB) ... OAL
Order Allocation System ... OASYS
Order and Change Control (AAG) ... O & CC
Order and Change Control (AD) ... o & cc
Order and Schedules Input System (MCD) ... OASIS
Order and Shipping Time [*Military*] (MCD) ... O & ST
Order and Shipping Time [*Military*] (AFIT) ... OAST
Order Authority (MCD) ... O/A
Order Bill of Lading [*Shipping*] ... OBL
Order Billing Inventory Technique (PDAA) ... ORBIT
Order Book Official [*Investment term*] ... OBO
Order by Order ... OBO
Order Canceled ... OC
Order Card ... OC
Order Code Processor [*International Computers Ltd.*] ... OCP
Order Control Number (NASA) ... OCN
Order Control Number ... OCN
Order Control Record (SAA) ... OCR
Order Delivery Schedule Summary (MCD) ... ODSS
Order Dienst [*Netherlands first organized resistance group, 1940*] [*World War II*] ... OD
Order/Entry System [*Computer science*] (DHSM) ... O/E
Order/Entry System [*Computer science*] (OA) ... OES
Order for Assignment [*Military*] (CAAL) ... OFA
Order for Correction of Defect of Nonconformance ... OCDN
Order for Engagement [*Military*] (CAAL) ... OFE
Order for Reinforced Alert (NATG) ... ORA
Order for Simple Alert (NATG) ... OSA
Order Holding Office ... OHO
Order in Council [*A publication*] (DLA) ... OC
Order Initiated Distribution ... OID
Order Location and Control (MCD) ... OLC
Order Materials For ... OMF
Order Notify [*Bill of lading*] [*Shipping*] ... O/N
Order Number (NITA) ... ON
Order Of [*Business term*] ... O/O
Order of AHEPA [*Also known as American Hellenic Educational Progressive Association*] (EA) ... OA
Order of Amaranth (EA) ... O of A
Order of Americans of Armorial Ancestry (EA) ... OAAA
Order of Ancient Lights ... OAL
Order of Ancient Maccabees (BJA) ... OAM
Order of Architects of Quebec [*1974, founded 1890 as PQAA*] [*Canada*] (NGC) ... OAQ
Order of Australia Association ... OAA
Order of Battle [*Military*] ... OB
Order of Battle [*Military*] (NVT) ... OOB
Order of Battle Report [*Military*] (NATG) ... ORBAT
Order of Battle Summary [*Military*] (MCD) ... OBSUM
Order of British Columbia [*Canada*] (DD) ... OBC
Order of British India ... OBI
Order of Brothers of the Blessed Virgin Mary of Mount Carmel [*Rome, Italy*] (EAIO) ... OCARM
Order of Burma [*British military*] (DMA) ... OB
Order of Calced Carmelites [*Roman Catholic religious order*] (DICI) ... OCC
Order of Carthusians [*Roman Catholic religious order*] ... OCart
Order of Carthusians (TOCD) ... ocart
Order of Christian Unity [*British*] ... OCU
Order of Cistercian Nuns of the Strict Observance [*Roman Catholic religious order*] ... OCSO
Order of Cistercians [*Roman Catholic religious order*] ... OC
Order of Cistercians of the Strict Observance [*Trappists*] [*Roman Catholic men's religious order*] ... OCSO
Order of Corporate Reunion [*British*] ... OCR
Order of Daedalians (EA) ... OD
Order of De Molay (AD) ... ODM
Order of DeMolay (EA) ... OD
Order of Deportation ... O/D
Order of Descendants of Colonial Physicians and Chirurgiens [*Defunct*] (EA) ... ODCPC

Order of Discalced Carmelites [*Roman Catholic religious order*] ... ODC
Order of Engineers of Quebec [*Canada*] (PDAA) ... OEQ
Order of First Families of Virginia, 1607-1624/5 (EA) ... OFFV
Order of Friars Minor Capuchin [*Capuchins*] [*Roman Catholic religious order*] ... OFM Cap
Order of Friars Minor Conventual [*Conventuals*] [*Roman Catholic religious order*] ... OFM Conv
Order of Friars Minor Conventual [*Conventuals*] [*Roman Catholic religious order*] ... OFMC
Order of Friars Preachers [*Dominicans*] (ADA) ... OFP
Order of Jacques-Cartier [*Canada*] (BARN) ... OJC
Order of Jamaica ... OJ
Order of Japan (DD) ... OJapan
Order of Job's Daughters ... OJD
Order of Knights (ADA) ... OK
Order of Lafayette (EA) ... OL
Order of Mercedarians [*Also, MMB*] [*Roman Catholic women's religious order*] ... OMerc
Order of Merit ... OM
Order of Merit List [*Army*] (AABC) ... OML
Order of Ontario [*Canada*] (DD) ... OOnt
Order of Our Lady of Mercy (TOCD) ... odem
Order of Our Lady of Mercy (TOCD) ... OdeM
Order of Owls (EA) ... OOO
Order of Preachers, Dominican Fathers (TOCD) ... op
Order of Preachers (Dominicans) (TOCD) ... OP
Order of Preceptors ... OP
Order of Railroad Telegraphers [*Later, Transportation-Communication Employees Union*] (EA) ... ORT
Order of Railway Conductors and Brakemen [*Later, United Transportation Union*] (EA) ... ORCB
Order of Recollects of St. Augustine ... ORSA
Order of Saint Andrew the Apostle (EA) ... OSATA
Order of St. Anne [*Anglican religious community*] ... OSA
Order of St. Augustine [*See also OFSA*] [*Rome, Italy*] (EAIO) ... OSA
Order of St. Basil the Great (TOCD) ... osbm
Order of St. Camillus [*Camillians*] [*Roman Catholic religious order*] ... OS Cam
Order of St. Clare [*Roman Catholic women's religious order*] ... OSC
Order of St. Clare (TOCD) ... PCC
Order of St. Elizabeth of Hungary [*Anglican religious community*] ... OSEH
Order of St. Francis [*Franciscans*] [*Roman Catholic religious order*] ... OSF
Order of St. Lazarus of Jerusalem [*British*] ... OLJ
Order of St. Luke the Physician of America (EA) ... OSL
Order of St. Paul [*Anglican religious community*] ... OSP
Order of St. Paul the First Hermit [*Pauline Fathers*] [*Roman Catholic religious order*] ... OSP
Order of St. Ursula [*Roman Catholic women's religious order*] ... OSU
Order of St. Vincent (EA) ... OSV
Order of Servites ... OS
Order of Shepherds of Bethlehem (EA) ... OSB
Order of the Alhambra (EA) ... OA
Order of the Arrow (EA) ... OA
Order of the Augustinian Recollects [*Roman Catholic men's religious order*] ... OAR
Order of the Augustinian Recollects (TOCD) ... oar
Order of the Bath ... OB
Order of the British Empire [*Facetious translations: Old Boiled Egg, Other Buggers' Efforts*] ... OBE
Order of the Chief of the Army Air Forces ... OCAAF
Order of the Compassionate Heart (EA) ... OCH
Order of the Cross Society (EA) ... OCS
Order of the Crown in America [*Later, TOCA*] (EA) ... OCA
[*The*] **Order of the Crown in America** (EA) ... TOCA
Order of the Crown of Rumania ... OCR
Order of the Eastern Star [*Freemasonry*] (EA) ... OES
Order of the Founder [*Salvation Army*] ... OF
Order of the Founders and Patriots of America (EA) ... OFPA
Order of the Golden Chain (EA) ... OGC
Order of the Golden Rule (EA) ... OGR
Order of the Holy Cross [*Episcopalian religious order*] ... OHC
Order of the Holy Paraclete [*Anglican religious community*] ... OHP
Order of the Holy Trinity (TOCD) ... OSST
Order of the Imitation of Christ (TOCD) ... OIC
Order of the Imitation of Christ (TOCD) ... oic
Order of the Indian Wars (EA) ... OIW
Order of the Most Holy Redeemer (TOCD) ... OSSR
Order of the Most Holy Savior [*Bridgettine Sisters*] [*Roman Catholic religious order*] ... OSSS
Order of the Most Holy Trinity, Trinitarian Fathers (TOCD) ... osst
Order of the Red Cross ... ORC
Order of the Republic of Sierra Leone ... ORSL
Order of the Road [*British*] (DBA) ... OR
Order of the Sacred Word [*Affiliate of the magical society, Aurum Solis*] ... OSW
Order of the Societies of Mary and Joseph (ROG) ... OSSMJ
Order of the Sons of Divine Providence ... ODP
Order of the Star in the East [*A theosophical organization*] ... OSE
Order of the Stars and Bars [*Later, MOSB*] (EA) ... OSB
Order of the Trinity Cross [*Trinidad and Tobago*] ... TC
Order of the White Rose of Finland (DD) ... OWR
Order of Three Crusades (EA) ... OTC
Order of United American Mechanics ... OUAM
Order of United Americans (NADA) ... OUA
Order of United Commercial Travelers of America (EA) ... OUCTA
Order of United Commercial Travelers of America [*Columbus, OH*] (EA) ... UCT
Order of Use File (MCD) ... OUF
Order of Woodcraft Chivalry [*British*] (DBA) ... OWC
Order Pennant [*Navy British*] ... OR
Order Planning and Control System (MCD) ... OPACS
Order Point Recognition (ADA) ... OPR
Order Point Technique for Inventory Management (BUR) ... OPTIM
Order Policy [*Insurance*] ... OP
Order Processing and Inventory Monitoring [*Computer science*] ... OPIM
Order Quantity (DNAB) ... OQ
Order [*or Ordering*] **Register** (SAA) ... OR
Order Scheduled Shipment Analysis (MCD) ... OSSA
Order Secular of St. Augustine [*See also ASAS*] [*Rome, Italy*] (EAIO) ... OSSA
Order Sheet ... OS
Order Ship Time [*DoD*] ... OST
Order Sons of Italy in America (EA) ... OSIA
Order Sons of Italy in America Supreme Lodge [*Later, OSIA*] (EA) ... OSIASL
Order Status Control and Reporting [*Telecommunications*] (TEL) ... OSCAR
Order Status Control and Reporting System [*Telecommunications*] ... OSCARS
Order to Show Cause ... OSC
Order Trunk Line [*Telecommunications*] (OA) ... OTL
Order Wire [*Military*] (AABC) ... OW
Order Writing (IAA) ... OW
Order-Despatched (AD) ... odp
Order-Disorder Transformation ... ODT
Ordered (ROG) ... ORDD
Ordered, Adjudged, and Decreed (WDAA) ... OAD
Ordered Back ... OB
Ordered Bicontinuous Double Diamond [*Phase structure*] ... OBDD
Ordered Computer Collation of Unprepared Literary Texts ... OCCULT
Ordered Multistate [*Botany*] ... M
Ordered Random Access Talking Equipment ... ORATE
Ordered Recorded ... OR
Ordered to Active Duty (AABC) ... OAD
Order-in-Council [*Canada*] ... O-I-C
Ordering ... ORDNG
Ordering and Billing System ... ORBIS
Ordering and Distributing (IAA) ... OAD
Ordering as Required (MHDB) ... OAR
Ordering Function Register ... OFR
Ordering Register (IAA) ... OR
Orderly [*Medicine*] (DAVI) ... O
Orderly (WGA) ... ODLY
Orderly ... ORD
Orderly Corporal [*British*] ... OC
Orderly Departure Program [*for Vietnamese refugees*] [*United Nations*] ... ODP
Orderly Marketing Agreement ... OMA
Orderly Marketing Arrangement (AD) ... oma
Orderly Officer [*British*] ... OO
Orderly Room ... OR
Orderly Room Corporal [*British*] ... ORC
Orderly Room Quartermaster-Corporal [*British military*] (DMA) ... ORQMC
Orderly Room Quartermaster-Sergeant [*British military*] (DMA) ... ORQMS
Orderly Room Sergeant [*British*] ... ORS
Orders and Medals Research Society (EA) ... OMRS
Orders and Medals Society of America (EA) ... OMSA
Orders Canceled [*Air Force*] ... ORDCAN
Orders Considered Canceled [*Air Force*] ... ORDCONCAN
Orders Corrected [*Air Force*] ... ORDCOR
Orders for Correction of Nonconformance [*Navy*] (NG) ... OCON
Orders Further Modified [*Navy*] (DNAB) ... FURORDMOD
Orders Group [*British military*] (DMA) ... O
Orders Modified [*Navy*] ... ORDMOD
Orders Not to Resuscitate [*Medicine*] ... ONTR
Order-Sorting Aperture [*Instrumentation*] ... OSA
Orderwire Operator Control Unit (MCD) ... OCU
Ordinal ... ORD
Ordinal Memory Inspecting Binary Automatic Computer (IEEE) ... OMIBAC
Ordinance ... O
Ordinance ... ORD
Ordinance ... ORD
Ordinance Lieutenent-Commander (AD) ... O L Cr
Ordinance Map (AD) ... Om
Ordinance of Amsterdam [*A publication*] (DLA) ... Ord Amst
Ordinance of Antwerp [*A publication*] (DLA) ... Ord Antw
Ordinance of Bilboa [*A publication*] (DLA) ... Ord Bilb
Ordinance of Copenhagen [*A publication*] (DLA) ... Ord Copen
Ordinance of Florence [*A publication*] (DLA) ... Ord Flor
Ordinance of Genoa [*A publication*] (DLA) ... Ord Gen
Ordinance of Hamburg [*A publication*] (DLA) ... Ord Hamb
Ordinance of Konigsberg [*A publication*] (DLA) ... Ord Konigs
Ordinance of Leghorn [*A publication*] (DLA) ... Ord Leg
Ordinance of Portugal [*A publication*] (DLA) ... Ord Port
Ordinance of Prussia [*A publication*] (DLA) ... Ord Prus
Ordinance of Rotterdam [*A publication*] (DLA) ... Ord Rott
Ordinance of Sweden [*A publication*] (DLA) ... Ord Swe
Ordinances of Bilboa [*A publication*] (DLA) ... Bilb Ord
Ordinances of the Legislative Council of New Zealand [*A publication*] (DLA) ... NZ Ords
Ordinances of the Legislative Council of New Zealand [*A publication*] (DLA) ... Ords NZ
Ordinario [*Ordinarily*] [*Music*] (ROG) ... ORDO
Ordinary ... O
Ordinary (MSA) ... ORD
Ordinary (AABC) ... ORDY
Ordinary Administrative Radio Conference ... OARC
Ordinary Alterations Plan [*Navy*] (OAG) ... OAP

Ordinary Capital Account [*Inter-American Development Bank*] .... OC
Ordinary Chondrite [*A type of meteorite*] .... OC
Ordinary Combustibles [*Fire classification*] .... A
Ordinary Conversational Voice [*Medicine*] .... OCV
Ordinary Decent Criminal [*British prison slang for other than a political prisoner*] .... ODC
Ordinary Differential Equation [*Mathematics*] .... ODE
Ordinary Discharge [*Military*] .... ORDDIS
Ordinary Electromagnetic Wave .... OEW
Ordinary General Meeting .... OGM
Ordinary High Current Configuration [*Magnetic field*] .... OHCC
Ordinary Hydrodynamic .... OHD
Ordinary Interest [*Banking*] .... OI
Ordinary Least Squares [*Statistics*] .... OLS
Ordinary Least-Squares Estimators [*Statistics*] .... OLSE
Ordinary Leave [*Military*] (AFM) .... OL
Ordinary Level [*School graduating grade*] [*British*] .... O
Ordinary Level (ODBW) .... O level
Ordinary Levels [*of educational tests*] (AD) .... O-levels
Ordinary Linear Differential Equations with Constant Coefficients [*Mathematics*] .... OLD ECC
Ordinary Low Current Configuration [*Magnetic field*] .... OLCC
Ordinary Member of the Order of St. John of Jerusalem .... M ST J
Ordinary Mode (MCD) .... OMODE
Ordinary Money Order .... OMO
Ordinary Multiple Regression [*Statistics*] .... OREG
Ordinary National Certificate [*British*] .... ONC
Ordinary National Certificate/Diploma (ACII) .... ONC/D
Ordinary National Diploma [*British*] .... OND
Ordinary Neap Tide (WDAA) .... ONT
Ordinary Portland Cement .... OPC
Ordinary Ray [*Direction of*] .... O
Ordinary, Reasonable, and Prudent [*Legal term*] (BARN) .... ORP
Ordinary Seaman [*British*] (DMA) .... OD
Ordinary Seaman [*British*] .... ORD
Ordinary Seaman [*British*] .... OS
Ordinary Seamen Under Training [*Canadian Navy*] .... OSUT
Ordinary Shareholders Fund (WDAA) .... OSF
Ordinary Shares (WDAA) .... ORDS
Ordinary Spring Tides .... OST
Ordinary Warfare .... OW
Ordinary Wave (MCD) .... O-W
Ordinary Wave (MSA) .... OWAVE
Ordinary Wave Component .... OWC
Ordinary Welfare (BABM) .... OW
Ordinary Welfare (DAVI) .... OW
Ordinate [*Mathematics*] (MSA) .... O
Ordinate (IDOE) .... y
Ordinator .... ORDNTR
Ordinis [*By the Order Of*] [*Latin*] .... O
Ordinis Cisterciensis [*Cistercian Order*] (ROG) .... O CIST
Ordinis Praedicatorum [*Of the Order of Preachers, or Dominicans*] [*Latin*] .... OP
Ordinis Sancti Bernardi [*Order of St. Bernard*] [*Latin*] (ROG) .... OSB
Ordinis Sancti Dominici [*Order of St. Dominic*] [*Latin*] (ROG) .... OSD
Ordinis Sancti Francisci Capuccini [*Franciscan Capuchins*] [*Roman Catholic men's religious order*] .... OSFC
Ordinis Sancti Joannis de Deo [*Order of St. John of God*] .... OSJD
Ordnance .... O
Ordnance (AAG) .... ORD
Ordnance (KSC) .... ORDN
Ordnance Aerophysics Laboratory .... OAL
Ordnance Allowance Report [*Navy*] .... OAR
Ordnance Alteration (MCD) .... O/A
Ordnance Alteration Installation Plan [*Navy*] .... ORDIP
Ordnance Alteration Reporting .... OAR
Ordnance Alteration Requirement (NG) .... OAR
Ordnance Alterations .... ORDALT
Ordnance Ammunition Command [*Merged with Munitions Command*] [*Army*] .... OAC
Ordnance Ammunition Surveillance and Maintenance School [*Army*] ... OASMS
Ordnance and Chemical Center and School [*Army*] (MCD) .... OCCS
Ordnance and Explosive Waste [*Military*] .... OEW
Ordnance and Facilities - Navy .... O & FN
Ordnance and Ordnance Stores [*Navy*] .... O & OS
Ordnance and Ordnance Stores [*Coast Guard*] .... OANDOS
Ordnance and Terminal Ballistics .... OTB
Ordnance Artificer [*Obsolete Navy British*] .... OA
Ordnance Assembly Building (MUGU) .... OAB
Ordnance Battalion [*Navy*] .... OB
Ordnance Battalion .... ORDBN
Ordnance Bench Mark (IAA) .... OBM
Ordnance Board [*Navy*] .... OB
Ordnance Board [*Military*] (WDAA) .... ORD BD
Ordnance Board [*British*] .... OrdBrd
Ordnance Calibration [*Navy*] (NVT) .... ORDCAL
Ordnance Calibration Management Information System [*Navy*] (DNAB) .... ORCALMIS
Ordnance Center and School [*Army*] (RDA) .... OC & S
Ordnance Chart (MCD) .... OC
Ordnance Circular Letter .... OCL
Ordnance Classification of Defects [*Navy*] .... OCD
Ordnance College [*Military British*] (ROG) .... OC
Ordnance Command Converter [*Military*] (IAA) .... OCC
Ordnance Command Management System .... OCMS
Ordnance Committee Meeting (AAG) .... OCM

Ordnance Committee Meeting Standards (AAG) .... OCMS
Ordnance Committee Minutes [*Military*] .... OCM
Ordnance Configuration Accounting System [*Navy*] .... OCAS
Ordnance Control Technician (DNAB) .... ORDCONTECH
Ordnance Corps [*Army*] (GFGA) .... OD
Ordnance Corps [*Army*] .... ORDC
Ordnance Corps [*Army*] .... ORDCORPS
Ordnance Corps Manual (AAG) .... ORDM
Ordnance Corps Order (AAG) .... OCO
Ordnance Corps Pamphlet [*Army*] (MCD) .... ORDP
Ordnance Corps Technical Instruction .... OCTI
Ordnance Data [*Inspection and test data*] .... OD
Ordnance Delivery Schedule [*Navy*] (NG) .... ODS
Ordnance Department [*or Division*] .... OD
Ordnance Department [*Military*] (WDAA) .... ORD DEPT
Ordnance Department and California Institute of Technology [*Army*] (RDA) .... ORDCIT
Ordnance Dial Reader and Translator .... ORDRAT
Ordnance Difficulty Report (MCD) .... ODR
Ordnance Discharge (DNAB) .... ORDIS
Ordnance Document [*Navy*] .... OD
Ordnance Drawing .... OD
Ordnance Electrical Artificer [*British military*] (DMA) .... OEA
Ordnance Electrical Mechanic [*British military*] (DMA) .... OEM
Ordnance Electrical Mechanician [*British military*] (DMA) .... OEMN
Ordnance Electrical Mechanician (Air) [*British military*] (DMA) .... OELMN(A)
Ordnance Electrician [*British military*] (DMA) .... OE
Ordnance Engineer [*British military*] (DMA) .... OE
Ordnance Engineer Overseer (AD) .... OEO
Ordnance Engineering .... ORDENG
Ordnance Engineering Duty Officer .... OEDO
Ordnance Engineering Laboratory .... OEL
Ordnance Equipment Chart .... OEC
Ordnance Equipment List [*Navy*] (NG) .... OEL
Ordnance Executive Officer [*Military British*] .... OEO
Ordnance Facility .... ORDFAC
Ordnance Field Manual [*Military*] .... OFM
Ordnance Field Park [*British*] .... OFP
Ordnance Field Service Bulletin [*Military*] .... OFSB
Ordnance Field Service Circular [*Military*] .... OFSC
Ordnance Guided Missile Center (MCD) .... OGMC
Ordnance Guided Missile School .... OGMS
Ordnance, Gunnery, and Readiness Division [*Coast Guard*] .... OGR
Ordnance Handling Instructions .... OHI
Ordnance Handling Officer [*Navy*] (DOMA) .... OHO
Ordnance Historical Files [*Military*] .... OHF
Ordnance Industrial Data Agency .... OIDA
Ordnance Installation Plan (MCD) .... OIP
Ordnance Instruction .... ORDINST
Ordnance Investigation Laboratory .... OIL
Ordnance Job Guide .... OJG
Ordnance Lieutenant [*Navy British*] .... OL
Ordnance Lieutenant-Commander [*Navy British*] .... OLCR
Ordnance Logistics Information System [*Navy*] .... ORDLIS
Ordnance Machine Shop .... OMS
Ordnance Maintenance Bulletin .... OMB
Ordnance Maintenance Company [*Navy*] (DNAB) .... ORDMAINTCO
Ordnance Maintenance Management Information Center [*Navy*] ... OMMIC
Ordnance Maintenance Truck [*British*] .... OMT
Ordnance Management Engineering Training Agency [*Army*] .... OMETA
Ordnance Master Publication Index (MCD) .... OMPI
Ordnance Material Letter (SAA) .... OML
Ordnance Material Research Reactor [*Nuclear energy*] .... OMRR
Ordnance Materials Research Office [*Later, AMMRC*] [*Army*] (MCD) .... OMRO
Ordnance Mechanical Engineer [*British military*] (DMA) .... OME
Ordnance Medical Department [*British military*] (DMA) .... OMD
Ordnance Middle East Tasks [*Military*] .... OMET
Ordnance Missile and Munitions Center and School [*Army*] .... OMMCS
Ordnance Missile Command [*Later, Missile Command*] .... OMC
Ordnance Missile Laboratories (KSC) .... OML
Ordnance Missile Support Agency (SAA) .... OMSA
Ordnance Mission (AAG) .... OM
Ordnance Modifications Instructions .... OMI
Ordnance Multiple-Purpose Tactical Satellite System .... OMTSS
Ordnance Muzzle Loading [*British military*] (DMA) .... OML
Ordnance Office [*or Officer*] .... OO
Ordnance Office Bulletin [*Military*] .... OOB
Ordnance Pamphlets .... OP
Ordnance Personnel .... OP
Ordnance Personnel Office [*Army*] .... OPO
Ordnance Procedure Instrumentations (AAG) .... OPI
Ordnance Procedures Review [*Military*] (NVT) .... ORDREV
Ordnance Procurement Center [*Army*] .... OPC
Ordnance Procurement Instructions [*Army*] .... OPI
Ordnance Proof Manual (SAA) .... OPM
Ordnance Publications [*Navy*] (MCD) .... OP
Ordnance Publications for Supply Index [*Military*] .... OPSI
Ordnance Pulses Experimental Research Assembly [*Nuclear reactor*] ...... OPERA
Ordnance Rapid Area Clearance [*Military*] (CAAL) .... ORACLE
Ordnance Repair Truck [*British*] .... ORT
Ordnance Report .... OR
Ordnance Report .... ORDRPT
Ordnance Requirement .... OR
Ordnance Research and Development Center [*Aberdeen Proving Ground, Maryland*] [*Navy*] .... ORDC

Ordnance Research Laboratory [*Later, Applied Research Laboratory*] [*Pennsylvania State University*] (MCD) ... ORL
Ordnance Rocket Center (KSC) ... ORC
Ordnance Safety Manual [*Military*] ... OSM
Ordnance Safety Switch [*Military*] (IAA) ... OSS
Ordnance Safing Device ... OSD
Ordnance School [*Army*] (MCD) ... OS
Ordnance Sergeant [*Military*] (DMA) ... Ord Sgt
Ordnance Services [*Military British*] ... OS
Ordnance Shock Test [*Military*] ... OST
Ordnance Special Training (AAG) ... OST
Ordnance Special Weapons Ammunition Command [*Later, Weapons Command*] ... OSWAC
Ordnance Special Weapons Command [*Merged with Missile Command*] [*Army*] ... OSWC
Ordnance Specifications [*Navy*] ... OS
Ordnance Standard Technical Directives [*Obsolete*] ... OSTD
Ordnance Standards ... OSTD
Ordnance Station ... ORDSTA
Ordnance Status Report (NG) ... OSR
Ordnance Storage and Shipment Chart [*Army*] (MCD) ... OSSC
Ordnance Storage Facility (KSC) ... OSF
Ordnance Store Corps [*British military*] (DMA) ... OSC
Ordnance Store Department [*British*] (ROG) ... OSD
Ordnance Sub-Lieutenant [*British military*] (DMA) ... OSL
Ordnance Suitability Test ... OST
Ordnance Supply Bulletin ... OSB
Ordnance Supply Depot ... OSD
Ordnance Supply Office ... OSO
Ordnance Supply Office Illustrated Parts Breakdown [*Navy*] ... OSOIPB
Ordnance Supply Segment of the Navy Supply System ... OSSNSS
Ordnance Support Element Review (NVT) ... ORDSER
Ordnance Survey ... OS
Ordnance Systems Command [*Formerly, Bureau of Naval Weapons; later, Naval Sea Systems Command*] ... ORDSYSCOM
Ordnance Systems Command [*Formerly, Bureau of Naval Weapons; later, Naval Sea Systems Command*] ... OSC
Ordnance Systems Command Hydroballistics Advisory Committee [*Obsolete Navy*] ... ORDHAC
Ordnance Tank-Automotive Command [*Merged with Weapons and Mobility Command*] [*Army*] ... OTAC
Ordnance Technical Committee [*Military*] (MUGU) ... OTC
Ordnance Technical Committee Minutes [*Military*] ... OTCM
Ordnance Technical Instructions [*Navy*] ... OTI
Ordnance Technical Intelligence Agency (AAG) ... OTIA
Ordnance Telemetry Instrumentation Station [*Army*] (AABC) ... OTIS
Ordnance Test Laboratory (NASA) ... OTL
Ordnance Training Command [*Army*] ... OTC
Ordnance Unit Training Center [*Military*] ... OUTC
Ordnance Variable Automatic Computer ... ORDVAC
Ordnance Weapon Systems [*Army*] ... OWS
Ordnance Weapons Command [*Later, Weapons Command*] ... OWC
Ordnungsdienst [*Military Police Service*] [*German military - World War II*] ... OD
Ordo ab Chao [*Order Out of Chaos*] [*Freemasonry*] [*Latin*] ... OAC
Ordo Canonicorum Regularium Praemonstatenstium [*Order of the Canons Regular of Premontre*] [*Norbertines*] [*Roman Catholic men's religious order*] ... OPraem
Ordo Carmelitarum Calceatorum [*Carmelites*] [*Roman Catholic religious order*] ... OCC
Ordo Carmelitarum Discalceatorum [*Order of Discalced, or Barefoot, Carmelites*] [*Roman Catholic religious order*] ... OCD
Ordo Charitatis [*Fathers of the Order of Charity*] [*Roman Catholic religious order*] ... OC
Ordo Clericorum Regularium Pauperum Matris Dei Scholarum Piarum [*Roman Catholic men's religious order*] ... SchP
Ordo Constantini Magni [*International Constantinian Order*] (EA) ... OCM
Ordo Fratrum Minorum [*Order of Friars Minor*] [*Observant Franciscans*] [*Roman Catholic religious order*] (EA) ... OFM
Ordo Fratrum Sancti Augustini [*Order of St. Augustine - OSA*] [*Rome, Italy*] (EAIO) ... OFSA
Ordo [*Fratrum*] **Minimorum** [*Minims of St. Francis of Paul*] [*Roman Catholic men's religious order*] ... OM
Ordo Minorum Cappucinorum [*Capuchins*] [*Roman Catholic men's religious order*] ... OMC
Ordo Minorum Conventualium [*Conventual Franciscans*] [*Roman Catholic men's religious order*] ... OMC
Ordo Nobilium Urbium [*of Ausonius*] [*Classical studies*] (OCD) ... Ordo Nob Urb
Ordo Praedicatorum [*Order of Preachers*] [*Dominicans*] [*Roman Catholic religious order*] ... OP
Ordo Reformatorum Cisterciensium [*Cistercians, Trappists*] [*Roman Catholic men's religious order*] ... OCR
Ordo Sancti Basil Magni [*Order of St. Basil the Great*] [*Roman Catholic religious order*] ... OSBM
Ordo Sancti Benedicti [*Order of St. Benedict*] [*Roman Catholic religious order*] ... OSB
Ordo Sancti Hieronymi [*Hieronymites*] ... OSH
Ordo Sanctissimae Trinitatis Redemptionis Captivorum [*Order of the Most Holy Trinity*] [*Trinitarians*] [*Roman Catholic religious order*] ... OSsT
Ordo Servorum Mariae [*Order of Servants of Mary*] [*Servites*] [*Roman Catholic religious order*] ... OSM
Ordo Templi Orientis [*Order of the Oriental Templars*] [*A mystical lodge*] [*Latin*] (ADA) ... OTO
Ordonnanzoffizier [*Special-Missions Staff Officer*] [*German military - World War II*] ... O
Ordovician [*Period, era, or system*] [*Geology*] ... ORD
Ordre de Comptables Agrees du Quebec [*Canada*] (DD) ... OCAQ
Ordre de l'Etoile de l'Europe [*Huy, Belgium*] (EAIO) ... OEE
Ordre de Premontre [*Order of the Canons Regular of Premontre*] [*Rome, Italy*] (EAIO) ... OPrem
Ordre des Chevaliers du Verseau [*Knights of Aquarius Order*] (EAIO) ... OCV
Ordre des Infirmieres et Infirmiers du Quebec, Montreal, PQ, Canada [*Library symbol Library of Congress*] (LCLS) ... CaQMOI
Ordre des Infirmieres et Infirmiers du Quebec, Montreal, Quebec [*Library symbol National Library of Canada*] (NLC) ... QMOI
Ordre des Ingenieurs du Quebec [*Canada*] (DD) ... OIQ
Ordre du Quebec [*Order of Quebec*] [*Canada*] (DD) ... OQ
Ordronaux on Judicial Aspects of Insanity [*A publication*] (DLA) ... Ordr Jud Ins
Ordronaux's Medical Jurisprudence [*A publication*] (DLA) ... Ord Med Jur
Ordronaux's Medical Jurisprudence [*A publication*] (DLA) ... Ordr Med Jur
Ordway Public Library, Ordway, CO [*Library symbol Library of Congress*] (LCLS) ... CoOrd
Ore/Bulk/Oil [*Bulk carrier vessel*] ... O/B/O
Ore Deposits Research Section [*Pennsylvania State University*] [*Research center*] (RCD) ... ODRS
Ore/Slurry/Oil [*Supertanker*] ... O/S/O
Orebro [*Sweden ICAO location identifier*] (ICLI) ... ESOE
Orebro [*Sweden*] [*Airport symbol*] (OAG) ... ORB
Oredicorp Ltd. [*NYSE symbol*] (SAG) ... BAP
Oregon [*MARC geographic area code Library of Congress*] (LCCP) ... n-us-or
Oregon (ROG) ... O
Oregon [*Obsolete*] (ROG) ... ON
Oregon [*Postal code*] ... OR
Oregon (AAG) ... ORE
Oregon (ODBW) ... Ore
Oregon (ODBW) ... Oreg
Oregon (AFM) ... OREG
Oregon [*MARC country of publication code Library of Congress*] (LCCP) ... oru
Oregon Administrative Code [*A publication*] (AAGC) ... OAC
Oregon Administrative Rules [*A publication*] (DLA) ... Or Admin R
Oregon Administrative Rules Bulletin [*A publication*] (DLA) ... Or Admin R Bull
Oregon Advanced Computing Institute [*Research center*] (RCD) ... OACIS
Oregon & Northwestern Railroad Co. (IIA) ... O & N
Oregon & Northwestern Railroad Co. [*AAR code*] ... ONW
Oregon Ballet ... OB
Oregon Bar Bulletin [*A publication*] (DLA) ... Or Bar Bull
Oregon Bulletin [*A publication*] (AAGC) ... Or Bull
Oregon Business Education Association (EDAC) ... OBEA
Oregon Business Information System [*Oregon State Economic Development Department*] [*Information service or system Defunct*] (IID) ... ORBIS
Oregon, California, and Eastern Railroad (AD) ... OC & E
Oregon, California & Eastern Railway Co. [*AAR code*] ... OCE
Oregon Caves National Monument (AD) ... OCNM
Oregon Caves National Monument ... ORCA
Oregon City, OR [*AM radio station call letters*] ... KFXX
Oregon City Public Library, Oregon City, OR [*Library symbol Library of Congress*] (LCLS) ... OrO
Oregon City Senior High School, Oregon City, OR [*Library symbol Library of Congress*] (LCLS) ... OrOHS
Oregon Coastal Conservation and Development Commission (AD) ... OCCDC
Oregon College of Education ... OCE
Oregon College of Education, Monmouth, OR [*Library symbol Library of Congress*] (LCLS) ... OrMonO
Oregon Compiled Laws Annotated [*A publication*] ... OCLA
Oregon Corrections Association (AD) ... OCA
Oregon Court of Appeals Reports [*A publication*] (DLA) ... Or A
Oregon Court of Appeals Reports [*A publication*] (DLA) ... Ore App
Oregon Daily Journal, Portland, OR [*Library symbol*] [*Library of Congress*] (LCLS) ... OrPOj
Oregon Department of Energy (AD) ... ODOE
Oregon Department of Fish and Wildlife Research and Development Section [*Oregon State University*] [*Research center*] (RCD) ... ODFW
Oregon Department of Transportation, Salem, OR [*Library symbol*] [*Library of Congress*] (LCLS) ... OrSaT
Oregon Draymen & Warehousemen's Association, Portland OR [*STAC*] ... ODW
Oregon Education Association (AD) ... OEA
Oregon Educational Broadcasting (AD) ... OEB
Oregon Educational Computing Consortium (EDAC) ... OECC
Oregon Electric Railway Co. [*AAR code*] ... OE
Oregon Graduate Center, Beaverton, OR [*OCLC symbol*] (OCLC) ... OGE
Oregon Graduate Center, Beaverton, OR [*Library symbol Library of Congress*] (LCLS) ... OrBG
Oregon Graduate Center for Study and Research [*Research center*] (RCD) ... OGC
Oregon Health Sciences University (IID) ... OHSU
Oregon Health Sciences University (GAGS) ... Ore Health Sci U
Oregon Health Sciences University, Dental Library, Portland, OR [*Library symbol Library of Congress*] (LCLS) ... OrPHS-D
Oregon High Desert Museum, Bend, OR [*Library symbol*] [*Library of Congress*] (LCLS) ... OrBeOHM
Oregon Highland Bentgrass Commission (EA) ... OHBC
Oregon Historical Society, Portland, OR [*Library symbol Library of Congress*] (LCLS) ... OrHi
Oregon, IL [*FM radio station call letters*] (RBYB) ... WOXM
Oregon Independent College Foundation (AD) ... OICF
Oregon Institute of Technology, Klamath Falls, OR [*OCLC symbol*] (OCLC) ... OIT
Oregon Insurance Rating Bureau (AD) ... OIRB
Oregon Law School Journal [*1902-03*] [*A publication*] (DLA) ... Or LSJ
Oregon Laws Advance Sheets [*A publication*] (DLA) ... Or Laws Adv Sh
Oregon Laws and Resolutions [*A publication*] (DLA) ... Or Laws

Oregon Laws and Resolutions [*A publication*] (DLA) ... Or Laws Spec Sess
Oregon Legislative Information System [*Information service or system*] ... OLIS
Oregon Masonic Grand Lodge, Forest Grove, OR [*Library symbol Library of Congress*] (LCLS) ... OrFFM
Oregon Metallurgical [*NASDAQ symbol*] (TTSB) ... OREM
Oregon Metallurgical Corp. [*Associated Press*] (SAG) ... OregMt
Oregon Metallurgical Corp. [*NASDAQ symbol*] (NQ) ... OREM
Oregon Museum of Science and Industry ... OMSI
Oregon Odd Fellows Grand Lodge, Portland, OR [*Library symbol Library of Congress*] (LCLS) ... OrPOF
Oregon Office of the Public Utilities Commissioner. Opinions and Decisions [*A publication*] (DLA) ... Or PUC Ops
Oregon Online User Group (NITA) ... OOUG
Oregon, Pacific & Eastern Railway Co. [*AAR code*] ... OPE
Oregon Railroad & Navigation Co. ... OR & N
Oregon Regional Primate Research Center, Beaverton, OR [*Library symbol Library of Congress*] (LCLS) ... OrBP
Oregon Reports [*A publication*] (DLA) ... O
Oregon Reports [*A publication*] (DLA) ... Or Rep
Oregon Reports [*A publication*] (DLA) ... Oregon
Oregon Reports, Court of Appeal [*A publication*] (DLA) ... Or App
Oregon Research Institute ... ORI
Oregon Resources Corp. [*Vancouver Stock Exchange symbol*] ... ORE
Oregon Revised Statutes [*A publication*] (DLA) ... Or Rev Stat
Oregon Revised Statutes [*A publication*] (DLA) ... Ore Rev Stat
Oregon Revised Statutes [*A publication*] (DLA) ... Oreg Rev Stat
Oregon Revised Statutes [*A publication*] (AAGC) ... ORS
Oregon Revised Statutes Annotated [*A publication*] ... ORSA
Oregon Royal Arch Masons Grand Chapter Archives, Portland, OR [*Library symbol Library of Congress*] (LCLS) ... OrPRAM
Oregon Ryegrass Growers Seed Commission (EA) ... ORGSC
Oregon Short Line Law Department, Salt Lake City, UT [*Library symbol Library of Congress Obsolete*] (LCLS) ... USlOr
Oregon Short Line R. R. [*of Union Pacific Railroad Co.*] [*AAR code*] ... UP
Oregon Short Line Railroad [*of Union Pacific Railroad Co.*] ... OSL
Oregon State Archives, Salem, OR [*Library symbol Library of Congress*] (LCLS) ... Or-Ar
Oregon State Bar. Bulletin [*A publication*] (ILCA) ... Or SB Bull
Oregon State Bar Bulletin [*A publication*] (DLA) ... Or St B Bull
Oregon State Bar Bulletin [*A publication*] (DLA) ... Ore St B Bull
Oregon State Bar Bulletin [*A publication*] (DLA) ... Oreg SB Bull
Oregon State College [*Later, OSU*] ... OSC
Oregon State Conversational Aid to Research [*Computer science*] (CSR) ... OSCAR
Oregon State Hospital, Medical Library, Salem, OR [*Library symbol*] [*Library of Congress*] (LCLS) ... OrSaSH
Oregon State Library, Salem, OR [*Library symbol Library of Congress*] (LCLS) ... Or
Oregon State Library, Salem, OR [*OCLC symbol*] (OCLC) ... OSO
Oregon State Library, Services for the Blind and Physically Handicapped, Salem, OR [*Library symbol Library of Congress*] (LCLS) ... Or-BPH
Oregon State Public Interest Research Group [*Research center*] (RCD) ... OSPIRG
Oregon State University (GAGS) ... Ore St U
Oregon State University [*Formerly, OSC*] ... OSU
Oregon State University Archives, Corvallis, OR [*Library symbol Library of Congress*] (LCLS) ... OrCS-Ar
Oregon State University, Corvallis, Corvallis, OR [*OCLC symbol*] (OCLC) ... ORE
Oregon State University, Corvallis, OR [*Library symbol Library of Congress*] (LCLS) ... OrCS
Oregon State University, Hatfield Marine Science Center, Newport, OR [*Library symbol*] [*Library of Congress*] (LCLS) ... OrCS-MSC
Oregon State University, Institute of Marine Biology, Coos Bay, OR [*Library symbol Library of Congress*] (LCLS) ... OrCS-MB
Oregon Steel Mills [*Associated Press*] (SAG) ... OreStl
Oregon Steel Mills [*NYSE symbol*] (SPSG) ... OS
Oregon Supreme Court Reports [*A publication*] (DLA) ... Or
Oregon Supreme Court, Salem, OR [*Library symbol Library of Congress*] (LCLS) ... Or-SC
Oregon Tax Court Reports [*A publication*] (DLA) ... Ore Tax Ct
Oregon Tax Reporter [*A publication*] (ILCA) ... Or T Rep
Oregon Tax Reporter [*A publication*] (DLA) ... Or TR
Oregon Tax Reports [*A publication*] (DLA) ... OTR
Oregon Technical Institute ... OTI
Oregon Technical Institute, Klamath Falls, OR [*Library symbol Library of Congress*] (LCLS) ... OrKT
Oregon Territory [*Prior to statehood*] ... OT
Oregon Total Information System [*Eugene*] [*Information service or system*] (IID) ... OTIS
Oregon Trunk Railway [*AAR code*] ... OT
Oregon-California Trails Association (EA) ... OCTA
Oregonian Publishing Co. Library, Portland, OR [*Library symbol Library of Congress*] (LCLS) ... OrPO
Oregon-Nevada-California [*Truck line*] (IIA) ... ONC
Oregon-Washington R. R. & Navigation [*of Union Pacific Railroad Co.*] [*AAR code*] ... UP
O'Reilly Automotive [*Associated Press*] (SAG) ... OReilyAu
O'Reilly Automotive [*NASDAQ symbol*] (SAG) ... ORLY
Orem City Library, Orem, UT [*Library symbol Library of Congress*] (LCLS) ... UOr
Orem, UT [*FM radio station call letters*] (RBYB) ... KENZ-FM
Orem, UT [*FM radio station call letters*] ... KMXB
Orem, UT [*FM radio station call letters*] ... KOHS
Orenstein & Koppel (AD) ... O & K
Orenthal James [*Given names of football player O. J. Simpson*] ... OJ
Orenthal James Simpson [*Sports personality*] (ECON) ... OJ
Orestes [*of Euripides*] [*Classical studies*] (OCD) ... Or
Orfeo [*Record label*] ... Ofo
Orfeo [*Record label*] ... Orf
Orfila's Medecine Legale [*A publication*] (DLA) ... Orf ML
Organ ... O
Organ ... ORG
Organ and Piano Teachers Association [*Defunct*] (EA) ... OPTA
Organ Blood Flow [*Physiology*] ... OBF
Organ Builders' Amalgamated Society [*A union*] [*British*] ... OBAS
Organ Builders' United Trade Society [*A union*] [*British*] ... OBUTS
Organ Clearing House (EA) ... OCH
Organ Historical Society (EA) ... OHS
Organ Historical Trust of Australia ... OHTA
Organ Literature Foundation (EA) ... OLF
Organ of Consultation ... OC
Organ Pipe Cactus National Monument ... ORPI
Organ Procurement Agency [*Department of Health and Human Services*] (GFGA) ... OPA
Organ Procurement Organization [*Generic term*] [*Medicine*] ... OPO
Organ Procurement Organizations (USGC) ... OPO
Organ Recovery (EA) ... OR
Organ Recovery Program (EA) ... ORP
Organ Society of Western Australia ... OSWA
Organ System Failure [*Medicine*] ... OSF
Organ Tolerance Dose ... OTD
Organe de Controle des Stupefiants [*Narcotic Drug Control Organization*] [*France*] (AD) ... OCS
Organe International de Controle des Stupefiants [*International Narcotics Control Board*] (EAIO) ... OICS
Organic [*Soil*] ... O
Organic ... ORG
Organic Ablative Insulative Plastic ... OAIP
Organic Ablative Plastic ... OAP
Organic Acid Labile Fluoride [*Chemistry*] (AAMN) ... OALF
Organic Acid Soluble Phosphorus ... OASP
Organic Acidemia Association (EA) ... OAA
Organic and Atmospheric Mass Spectrometer (KSC) ... OAMS
Organic Anion Binding Protein [*Biochemistry*] ... OABP
Organic Anionic Dye [*Medicine*] (DMAA) ... OAD
Organic Brain Disease ... OBD
Organic Brain Syndrome [*Medicine*] (AD) ... ob syn
Organic Brain Syndrome [*Psychiatry*] ... OBS
Organic Carbon ... OC
Organic Carbon Cycle ... OCC
Organic Chemical, Plastic, and Synthetic Fiber ... OCPSF
Organic Chemical Producers Data Base (NITA) ... OCPDB
Organic Compound - Coenzyme A Ester [*Biochemistry*] (DAVI) ... Acyl-Co A
Organic Consultative Committee [*Victoria, Australia*] ... OCC
Organic Content Monitor (NASA) ... OCM
Organic Content Monitor ... OCM
Organic Control ... ORCON
Organic Crop Improvement Association (EA) ... OCIA
Organic Development Problem (SAA) ... ODP
Organic Dry Weight ... ODW
Organic Dust Toxic Syndrome [*Medicine*] ... ODTS
Organic Electrolyte Battery ... OEB
Organic Electrolyte Battery System ... OEBS
Organic Failure to Thrive [*Medicine*] (MEDA) ... OFTT
Organic Farming and Gardening Society of Australia ... OFGSA
Organic Farming and Gardening Society of Tasmania [*Australia*] ... OFGST
Organic Farming Research Foundation ... OFRF
Organic Food Alliance (EA) ... OFA
Organic Foods Production Act ... OFPA
Organic Foods Production Association of North America (EA) ... OFPANA
Organic Gardening [*A publication*] ... OG
Organic Gaseous Mercury [*Environmental chemistry*] ... OGM
Organic Geochemistry Group ... OGG
Organic Growers Association [*British*] (DBA) ... OGA
Organic Growers' Association of New South Wales [*Australia*] ... OGANSW
Organic Growers' Association of Western Australia [*Australia*] ... OGAWA
Organic Hearing Disease [*Medicine*] (AD) ... ohd
Organic Heart Disease [*Medicine*] (AD) ... ohd
Organic Heart Disease [*Medicine*] ... OHD
Organic Insulating Material ... OIM
Organic Insulative Plastic ... OIP
Organic Integrity Test [*Psychology*] ... OIT
Organic Leach Model [*Landfill technology*] ... OLM
Organic Light Emitting Diode [*Electronics*] ... OLED
Organic Light-Emitting Device [*Photonics*] ... OLED
Organic Liquid LASER ... OLL
Organic Liquid Moderated Reactor ... OLMR
Organic Liquid-Moderator Reactor (AD) ... olmr
Organic Magnetic Resonance ... OMR
Organic Mass Spectroscopy ... OMS
Organic Material Hydrocarbon Equivalent [*Materials science*] ... OMCHE
Organic Material Hydrocarbon Equivalent [*Automotive emissions control*] ... OMHCE
Organic Materials Laboratory [*Watertown, MA*] [*Army*] (GRD) ... OML
Organic Matter ... OM
Organic Matter (AD) ... om
Organic Mental Disorder [*Neurology*] (CPH) ... OMD
Organic Mental Syndrome [*Medicine*] (DMAA) ... OMS
Organic Molecular Crystal ... OMC
Organic Phosphates (GNE) ... OP
Organic Photoconductor ... OPC

Organic/Polymer Crystal Growth Experiment (SSD) ..... OPCGE
Organic/Polymer Crystal Growth Facility (SSD) ..... OPCGF
Organic Power and Heat Industrial Reactor ..... OPHIR
Organic Process Research & Development [*A publication*] ..... OPRD
Organic Rankine Cycle ..... ORACLE
Organic Rankine Cycle [*for power generation*] (PDAA) ..... ORC
Organic Rankine Cycle System [*For power generation*] ..... ORCS
Organic Reactions Catalysis Society (EA) ..... ORCS
Organic Sign Index [*Psychology*] ..... OSI
Organic Sulfur Compound [*Organic chemistry*] ..... OSC
Organic Test Reactor [*Nuclear energy*] ..... OTR
Organic Thermal Control Coating ..... OTCC
Organic Trade Association ..... OTA
Organic Vapor Analyzer [*Chromatography*] ..... OVA
Organic Weather Team ..... OWT
Organic-Cooled Deuterium Reactor Experiment [*Nuclear energy*] ..... OCDRE
Organic-Cooled Reactor [*Nuclear energy*] (OA) ..... OCR
Organic-Moderated Cooled Reactor ..... OMCR
Organic-Moderated Critical Assembly [*Nuclear energy*] (NRCH) ..... OMCA
Organic-Moderated Fluidized Bed Reactor ..... OMFBR
Organic-Moderated Reactor [*Nuclear energy*] ..... OMR
Organic-Moderated Reactor Critical Assembly [*Nuclear energy*] ..... OMRCA
Organic-Moderated Reactor Experiment [*Nuclear energy*] ..... OMRE
Organics-in-Water Analyzer [*Instrumentation*] ..... OWA
Organik Tech Wrrt [*NASDAQ symbol*] (TTSB) ..... ORGKL
Organik Technologies [*NASDAQ symbol*] (TTSB) ..... ORGK
Organik Technologies, Inc. [*Associated Press*] (SAG) ..... Organik
Organik Technologies, Inc. [*NASDAQ symbol*] (SAG) ..... ORGK
Organik Technologies, Inc. [*Associated Press*] (SAG) ..... Orgnik
Organik Technologies Wrrt'A' [*NASDAQ symbol*] (TTSB) ..... ORGKW
Organik Technologies Wrrt'B' [*NASDAQ symbol*] (TTSB) ..... ORGKZ
Organique et Eau Lourde [*Organic liquid and heavy water nuclear reactor*] ..... ORGEL
Organisasi Papua Merdeka [*Papua Independent Organization*] [*Indonesia*] (PD) ..... OPM
Organisation Africaine de Cartographie et de Teledetection [*Algeria*] (EAIO) ..... OACT
Organisation Africaine du Bois [*African Timber Organization*] (EAIO) ..... OAB
Organisation Arabe des Pays Exportateurs de Petrole [*Organization of Arab Petroleum Exporting Countries*] ..... OAPEP
Organisation Catholique Internationale du Cinema et de l'Audiovisuel [*International Catholic Organization for Cinema and Audiovisual*] (EAIO) ..... OCIC
Organisation Clandestine de la Revolution Algerienne [*Secret Organization of the Algerian Revolution*] [*France*] (AD) ..... OCRA
Organisation Combat Anarchiste [*Anarchist Combat Organization*] [*France Political party*] (PPW) ..... OCA
Organisation Combat Communiste [*Communist Combat Organization*] [*France Political party*] (PPW) ..... OCC
Organisation Commune Africaine et Mauricienne [*African and Mauritian Common Organization*] [*Formerly, Organisation Commune Africaine et Malgache*] ..... OCAM
Organisation Commune Africaine, Malgache, et Mauricienne [*African, Malagasy, and Mauritian Common Organization*] [*Formerly, Organisation Commune Africaine et Malgache Later, OCAM*] ..... OCAMM
Organisation Commune des Regions Sahariennes [*Common Organization of the Saharan Regions*] ..... OCRS
Organisation Communiste de France - Marxiste-Leniniste [*Communist Organization of France - Marxist-Leninist*] (PPW) ..... OCF-ML
Organisation Communiste des Travailleurs [*Communist Organization of Workers*] [*France Political party*] (PPW) ..... OCT
Organisation Communiste Internationaliste [*Internationalist Communist Organization*] [*France Political party*] (PPW) ..... OCI
Organisation Communiste Marxiste-Leniniste de la Reunion [*Reunionese Communist Organization, Marxist-Leninist*] [*Political party*] (PPW) ..... OCMLR
Organisation de Cooperation et de Developpement Economiques [*Organization for Economic Cooperation and Development - OECD*] [*France*] (EAIO) ..... OCDE
Organisation de Coordination et de Cooperation pour la Lutte Contre les Grandes Endemies [*Organization for Co-Ordination and Co-Operation in the Control of Major Endemic Diseases*] (EAIO) ..... OCCGE
Organisation de Coordination pour la Lutte Contre les Endemies en Afrique Centrale [*Organization for Co-Ordination in Control of Endemic Diseases in Central Africa - OCCEDCA*] (EAIO) ..... OCEAC
Organisation de la Communaute Europeenne des Avitailleurs des Navires [*Ship Suppliers' Organization of the European Community - SSOEC*] [*Hague, Netherlands*] (EAIO) ..... OCEAN
Organisation de la Conference Islamique [*Organization of the Islamic Conference - OIC*] [*Jeddah, Saudi Arabia*] (EAIO) ..... OCI
Organisation de l'Armee Secrete [*Secret Army Organization*] [*France*] (PD) ..... OAS
Organisation de l'Aviation Civile Internationale [*International Civil Aviation Organization*] [*French United Nations*] ..... OACI
Organisation de l'Unite Africaine [*Organization of African Unity - OAU*] (EAIO) ..... OUA
Organisation de l'Unite Guineenne [*Organization of Guinean Unity*] (PD) ..... OUG
Organisation de l'Unite Syndicale Africaine [*Organisation of African Trade Union Unity - OATUU*] [*Accra, Ghana*] (EAIO) ..... OUSA
Organisation de Resistance de l'Armee [*France*] ..... ORA
Organisation der Ehemaligen Schutzstaffel Angehoeriggen [*Organization of Former Members of the Elite Guard*] [*Founded after World War II to smuggle war criminals out of Germany and provide them with false identities*] ..... ODESSA
Organisation des Fabricants de Produits Cellulosiques Alimentaires de la CEE [*Organization of Manufacturers of Cellulose Products for Foodstuffs in the European Economic Community*] ..... OFCA
Organisation des Musiciens d'Orchestres Symphoniques du Canada [*Organization of Canadian Symphony Musicans - OCSM*] ..... OMOSC
Organisation des Nations Unies [*United Nations French*] ..... ONU
Organisation des Nations Unies au Congo [*United Nations Organization in the Congo*] ..... ONUC
Organisation des Nations Unies pour l'Alimentation et l'Agriculture [*Food and Agriculture Organization of the United Nations*] ..... OAA
Organisation des Nations Unies pour le Developpement Industriel [*United Nations Industrial Development Organization*] ..... ONUDI
Organisation des Pays Arabes Exportateurs de Petrole [*Organization of Arab Petroleum Exporting Countries*] (EAIO) ..... OPAEP
Organisation des Producteurs d'Energie Nucleaire [*Paris, France*] (EAIO) ..... OPEN
Organisation du Baccalaureat International [*International Baccalaureate Organisation - IBO*] (EAIO) ..... OBI
Organisation du Traite de l'Atlantique Nord [*North Atlantic Treaty Organization - NATO*] [*Brussels, Belgium*] ..... OTAN
Organisation Europaischer Aluminium Schmelzhutten [*Organization of European Aluminium Foundries*] (PDAA) ..... OEAS
Organisation Europeene pour la Controle de la Qualite GG1European Quality-Control OrganizationGG2 [*France*] (AD) ..... OECQ
Organisation Europeenne de Cooperation Economique [*Organization for European Economic Cooperation - OEEC*] [*Later, OECD See also OCDE France*] (MSC) ..... OECE
Organisation Europeenne de Recherches Spatiales ..... OERS
Organisation Europeenne des Industries Transformatrices de Fruits et Legumes [*European Organization of Fruit and Vegetable Processing Industries*] [*Common Market*] [*Belgium*] ..... OEITFL
Organisation Europeenne des Scieries [*European Sawmills Organization*] [*EC*] (ECED) ..... OES
Organisation Europeenne d'Etudes Photogrammetriques Experimentales [*European Organisation for Experimental Photogrammetric Research*] [*Research Center Netherlands*] (PDAA) ..... OEEPE
Organisation Europeenne et Mediterraneenne pour la Protection des Plantes [*European and Mediterranean Plant Protection Organization - EPPO*] (EAIO) ..... OEPP
Organisation Europeenne pour des Recherches Astronomiques dans l'Hemisphere Austral [*European Southern Observatory - ESO*] (EAIO) ..... OERAHA
Organisation Europeenne pour la Qualite [*European Organization for Quality -EOQC*] [*Switzerland*] ..... OECQ
Organisation Europeenne pour la Qualite [*Switzerland*] (EAIO) ..... OEQ
Organisation Europeenne pour la Recherche Nucleaire [*European Organization for Nuclear Research*] [*Acronym represents previous name, Conseil Europeen pour la Recherche Nucleaire*] (EAIO) ..... CERN
Organisation for Black Arts Advancement and Learning Activities [*British*] ..... OBAALA
Organisation for Security and Co-Operation in Europe (ECON) ..... OSCE
Organisation for Sickle Cell Anemia Research [*British*] ..... OSCAR
Organisation for the Collaboration of Railways [*See also OSShD*] [*Warsaw, Poland*] (EAIO) ..... OCR
Organisation fur die Zusammenarbeit der Eisenbahnen [*Organisation for the Collaboration of Railways - OCR*] (EAIO) ..... OSShD
Organisation Gestosis [*Basel, Switzerland*] (EAIO) ..... OG
Organisation Hydrographique Internationale [*International Hydrographic Organization - IHO*] [*Monte Carlo, Monaco*] ..... OHI
Organisation Interafricaine du Cafe [*Inter-African Coffee Organization*] [*French*] (AD) ..... O-I-C
Organisation Intergouvernementale [*Inter-Governmental Organization*] [*French*] (AD) ..... OIG
Organisation Intergouvernementale pour les Transports Internationaux Ferrovaires [*Intergovernmental Organization for International Carriage by Rail*] (EAIO) ..... OTIF
Organisation Intergouvernementale pour les Transports Internationaux Ferroviaires [*Intergovernmental Organization for International Carriage by Rail*] (EAIO) ..... OITF
Organisation Internationale Catholique ..... OIC
Organisation Internationale Contre le Criquet Migrateur Africain [*International African Migratory Locust Organization*] (EAIO) ..... OICMA
Organisation Internationale de la Paleobotanique [*International Organization of Paleobotany*] ..... OIP
Organisation Internationale de Lutte Biologique Contre les Animaux et les Plantes Nuisibles [*International Organization for Biological Control of Noxious Animals and Plants - IOBC*] (EAIO) ..... OILB
Organisation Internationale de Metrologie Legale [*International Organization of Legal Metrology*] (EAIO) ..... OIML
Organisation Internationale de Normalisation [*International Organization for Standardization*] ..... OIN
Organisation Internationale de Police Criminelle [*International Criminal Police Organization*] [*French*] (AD) ..... OIPC
Organisation Internationale de Protection Civile [*International Civil Defense Organization - ICDO*] (EAIO) ..... OIPC
Organisation Internationale de Psychophysiologie [*International Organization of Psychophysiology - IOP*] (EAIO) ..... OIP
Organisation Internationale de Radiodiffusion [*International Radio Organization*] [*Later, OIRT*] ..... OIR
Organisation Internationale de Radiodiffusion et Television [*International Radio and Television Organization*] [*Formerly, OIR*] (EAIO) ..... OIRT
Organisation Internationale des Constructeurs d'Automobiles (EAIO) ..... OICA
Organisation Internationale des Employeurs [*International Organization of Employers*] ..... OIE
Organisation Internationale des Journalistes [*International Organization of Journalists - IOJ*] (EAIO) ..... OIJ

Organisation Internationale d'Etudes Statistiques pour les Maladies de l'Oesophage [*International Organization for Statistical Studies on Diseases of the Esophagus*] (EAIO) ... OESO
Organisation Internationale du Commerce [*International Organization for Commerce*] [*France*] ... OIC
Organisation Internationale du Travail [*International Labor Organization*] [*French United Nations*] (EAIO) ... OIT
Organisation Internationale Non-Gouvernementale [*Non-Governmental International Organization*] [*French*] (AD) ... OING
Organisation Internationale pour la Cooperation Medicale [*International Organization for Medical Cooperation*] ... OICM
Organisation Internationale pour la Science et la Technique du Vide [*International Organization for Vacuum Science and Technology*] [*French*] (AD) ... OISTV
Organisation Internationale pour le Progres [*Austria*] (EAIO) ... OIP
Organisation Internationale pour l'Etude de l'Endurance des Cables [*International Organization for the Study of the Endurance of Wire Ropes - IOSEWR*] (EAIO) ... OIPEEC
Organisation Juive de Combat [*Jewish Combat Organization*] [*French*] (AD) ... OJC
Organisation Maritime Consultatif Intergouvernementale [*Intergovernmental Maritime Consultative Organization*] ... OMCI
Organisation Maritime Internationale [*International Maritime Organization - IMO*] (EAIO) ... OMI
Organisation Meteorologique Internationale ... OMI
Organisation Meteorologique Mondiale [*World Meteorological Organization - WMO*] (EAIO) ... OMM
Organisation Mondiale Agudath Israel [*Agudas Israel World Organization - AIWO*] (EAIO) ... OMAI
Organisation Mondiale Contre la Torture [*World Organization Against Torture*] [*Switzerland*] (EAIO) ... OMCT
Organisation Mondiale Contre la Torture/SOS-Torture [*World Organization Against Torture/SOS-Torture*] [*Geneva, Switzerland*] (EAIO) ... OMCT/SOST
Organisation Mondiale de Gastroenterologie [*World Organization of Gastroenterology - WOG*] [*Edinburgh, Scotland*] (EAIO) ... OMGE
Organisation Mondiale de la Propriete Intellectuelle [*World Intellectual Property Organization - WIPO*] [*Information service or system*] (IID) ... OMPI
Organisation Mondiale de la Sante [*World Health Organization - WHO*] [*Switzerland*] ... OMS
Organisation Mondiale de l'Emballage [*World Packaging Organization - WPO*] (EAIO) ... OME
Organisation Mondiale des Anciens et Anciennes Eleves de l'Enseignement Catholique [*World Organization of Former Pupils of Catholic Schools*] (EAIO) ... OMAAEEC
Organisation Mondiale des Medicins Independants [*International Organization of Private and Independent Doctors*] (EAIO) ... IATROS
Organisation Mondiale du Tourisme et de l'Automobile [*World Touring and Automobile Organization*] ... OTA
Organisation Mondiale pour la Systemique et la Cybernetique [*World Organization of Systems and Cybernetics*] (EAIO) ... OMSC
Organisation Mondiale pour le Promotion Sociale des Aveugles [*World Council for the Welfare of the Blind - WCWB*] (EAIO) ... OMPSA
Organisation Mondiale pour l'Education Prescolaire [*World Organization for Early Childhood Education*] (EAIO) ... OMEP
Organisation Nationale d'Anti-Pauvrete [*Canada*] ... ONAP
Organisation of African Trade Union Unity [*Formerly, AATUF, ATUC*] [*See also OUSA Accra, Ghana*] (EAIO) ... OATUU
Organisation of Eastern Caribbean States (EAIO) ... OECS
Organisation of Eastern Caribbean States, Economic Affairs Secretariat [*St. Johns, Antigua*] (EAIO) ... OECSEAS
Organisation of Professional Users of Statistics ... OPUS
Organisation of Teachers of Transport Studies [*British*] ... OTTS
Organisation of Women of Asian and African Descent [*British*] (DI) ... OWAAD
Organisation Pan-Africaine de la Profession Enseignante [*All Africa Teachers' Organization*] (EAIO) ... OPAPE
Organisation Panamericaine de la Sante [*Pan American Health Organization*] (MSC) ... OPS
Organisation pour la Conservation du Saumon de l'Atlantique Nord [*North Atlantic Salmon Conservation Organization*] [*Scotland*] (EAIO) ... OCSAN
Organisation pour la Democratie Populaire/Mouvement du Travail [*Burkina Faso*] [*Political party*] (EY) ... ODP/MT
Organisation pour la Liberation du Rwanda [*Organization for the Liberation of Rwanda*] ... OLR
Organisation pour la Mise en Valeur du Fleuve Gambie [*Gambia River Basin Organisation*] (EAIO) ... OMVG
Organisation pour l'Amenagement et le Developpement du Bassin de la Riviere Kagera [*Organization for the Management and Development of the Kagera River Basin - KBO*] (EAIO) ... OBK
Organisation Regionale Africaine de Normalisation [*African Regional Organization for Standardization - AROS*] (EAIO) ... ORAN
Organisation Regionale Africaine de Normalisation [*African Regional Organization for Standardization - AROS*] (EA) ... ORGAN
Organisation Regionale de la Federation Internationale Dentaire pour l'Europe [*European Regional Organization of the International Dental Federation*] (EAIO) ... ORE/ERO
Organisation Regionale Europeenne de la Federation Internationale des Employes, Techniciens et Cadres [*European Regional Organization of the International Federation of Commercial, Clerical, Professional and Technical Employees*] [*EC*] (ECED) ... EURO-FIET
Organisation Revolutionnaire Anarchiste [*Revolutionary Anarchist Organization*] [*France Political party*] (PPE) ... ORA
Organisation Scientifique et Technique Internationale du Vol a Voile [*International Technical and Scientific Organization for Soaring Flight*] ... OSTIV
Organisation Socialiste des Travailleurs [*Socialist Workers' Organization*] [*Senegal*] [*Political party*] (PPW) ... OST
Organisation Universitaire Interamericaine [*Inter-American Organization for Higher Education*] (EAIO) ... OUI
Organisation Value Analysis Chart (PDAA) ... OVAC
Organisations Nationales Volontaires [*Canada*] ... ONV
Organised Science Series [*A publication*] ... OSS
Organising Bureau of European School Student Unions (EAIO) ... OBESSU
Organism [*Psychology*] ... O
Organism (ADA) ... ORG
Organism Identification Number [*Medicine*] (BABM) ... OID
Organism Identification Number [*Microbiology*] (DAVI) ... OID
Organisme de Liaison des Industries Metalliques Europeennes [*Liaison Group for the European Engineering Industries*] [*Brussels, Belgium*] (EAIO) ... ORGALIME
Organisme Europeen de Recherche sur la Carie [*European Organization for Caries Research*] (EAIO) ... ORCA
Organismes de Radiodiffusion des Pays NonAlignes [*Broadcasting Organizations of Non-Aligned Countries - BONAC*] (EAIO) ... ORDNA
Organismo Coordinador de Operaciones Antisubversivas [*Coordinating Organism of Antisubversive Operations*] [*Uruguay*] (AD) ... OCOA
Organismo Internacional de Energia Atomica [*International Atomic Energy Agency*] [*Spanish United Nations*] (DUND) ... OIEA
Organismo Internacional Regional de Sanidad Agropecuaria [*Regional International Organization of Plant Protection and Animal Health*] [*El Salvador*] ... OIRSA
Organismo para la Proscripcion de las Armas Nucleares en la America Latina [*Agency for the Prohibition of Nuclear Weapons in Latin America*] (EAIO) ... OPANAL
Organismos Tilepikoinonion Ellados [*Hellenic Telecommunications Organization*] [*Greek*] ... OTE
Organist ... ORGT
Organist and Choir Master (ROG) ... O & CM
Organizacao Comunista Marxista-Leninista Portuguesa [*Portuguese Communist Organization, Marxist-Leninist*] [*Political party*] (PPE) ... OCM-LP
Organizacao do Tratado da Asia Sul-Oriental [*South-East Asia Treaty Organization*] [*Portuguese*] ... OTASO
Organizacao do Tratado do Atlantico Norte [*North Atlantic Treaty Organization*] [*Portuguese*] ... OTAN
Organizacao Revolucionaria Armada [*Terrorist group*] [*Portugal*] (EY) ... ORA
Organizacao Unida de Trabalhadores [*United Organization of Workers*] [*Portugal Political party*] (PPE) ... OUT
Organizacion Continental Latinoamericana de Estudiantes [*Latin American Continental Students' Organization*] (EAIO) ... OCLAE
Organizacion de Aviacion Civil Internacional [*International Civil Aviation Organization*] [*Spanish United Nations*] (DUND) ... OACI
Organizacion de Cooperacion y Desarrollo Economicos [*Organization for Economic Cooperation and Development - OECD*] [*Spain*] (MSC) ... OCDE
Organizacion de Estados Americanos [*Organization of American States*] [*Spain*] (AD) ... OES
Organizacion de Estados Iberoamericanos para la Educacion, la Ciencia, y la Cultura [*Organization of Ibero-American States for Education, Science, and Culture*] (EAIO) ... OEI
Organizacion de las Cooperativas de America [*Organization of the Cooperatives of America - OCA*] (EAIO) ... OCA
Organizacion de las Naciones Unidas [*United Nations*] [*Spanish*] (DUND) ... ONU
Organizacion de las Naciones Unidas para el Desarrollo Industrial [*United Nations Industrial Development Organization*] [*Spanish*] (DUND) ... ONUDI
Organizacion de los Estados Americanos [*Organization of American States - OAS*] [*Spanish*] ... OEA
Organizacion de los Estados Centroamericanos [*Organization of Central American States - OCAS*] [*San Salvador, El Salvador*] (EAIO) ... ODECA
Organizacion de Unidad Revolucionaria [*Organization of Revolutionary Unity*] [*Bolivia*] [*Political party*] (PPW) ... OUR
Organizacion de Voluntarios para la Revolucion Puertorriquena [*Organization of Volunteers for the Puerto Rican Revolution*] (PD) ... OVRP
Organizacion Democrata Cristiana de America [*Christian Democratic Organization of America - CDOA*] [*Caracas, Venezuela*] ... ODCA
Organizacion Deportiva Panamericana [*Pan American Sports Organization - PASO*] [*Mexico City, Mexico*] (EAIO) ... ODEPA
Organizacion Deportiva Sudamericana [*An association*] (EAIO) ... ODESUR
Organizacion Europea de Cooperacion Economica [*Organization for European Economic Cooperation - OEEC*] [*Later, OECD Spain*] ... OECE
Organizacion Ibero-Americana de Cooperacion Intermunicipal [*Ibero-American Municipal Organization*] (EAIO) ... OICI
Organizacion Iberoamericana de Pilotos [*Ibero-American Organization of Pilots - IOP*] [*Mexico City, Mexico*] (EAIO) ... OIP
Organizacion Iberoamericana de Seguridad Social [*Ibero-American Social Security Organization*] ... OISS
Organizacion Interamericana de Cooperacion [*Inter-American Cooperation Organ ization*] [*Spanish*] (AD) ... OICI
Organizacion Interamericana de Cooperacion Intermunicipal [*Interamerican Municipal Organization*] ... OICI
Organizacion Internacional de la Aviacion Civil [*International Civil AviationOrganization*] [*Spanish*] (AD) ... OIAC
Organizacion Internacional del Azucar [*International Sugar Organization - ISO*] (EAIO) ... OIA
Organizacion Internacional del Trabajo [*International Labor Organization*] [*Spanish United Nations*] (DUND) ... OIT
Organizacion Latin-Americana de Energia [*Latin American Energy Organization*] [*Spanish*] (AD) ... OLADE
Organizacion Latino-Americana de Solidaridad [*Latin American Solidarity Organization*] [*Spanish*] (AD) ... OLAS
Organizacion Maritima Internacional [*International Maritime Organization*] [*Spanish*] (AD) ... OMI
Organizacion Maritima Internacional [*International Maritime Organization*] [*Spanish United Nations*] (DUND) ... OMI

Organizacion Meteorologica Mundial [*World Meteorological Organization - WMO*] [*Spanish*] .... OMM

Organizacion Mundial de la Propiedad Intelectual [*World Intellectual Property Organization*] [*Spanish United Nations*] (DUND) .... OMPI

Organizacion Mundial de la Salud [*World Health Organization*] [*Spanish United Nations*] (DUND) .... OMS

Organizacion para Estudios Tropicales [*Organization for Tropical Studies*] (EAIO) .... OET

Organizacion para la Educacion la Ciencia, y la Cultura [*Organization for Education, Science, and Culture*] [*United Nations*] (AD) .... OECCNU

Organizacion para la Liberacion de Cuba [*Organization for the Liberation of Cuba*] (PD) .... OPLC

Organizacion para la Liberacion Palestina [*Palestinian Liberation Organization*] [*Political party*] (AD) .... OLP

Organizacion Politico-Militar [*Politico-Military Organization*] [*Paraguay*] (PD) .... OPM

Organizacion Regional del Oriente para la Administracion Publica [*Eastern Regional Organization for Public Administration*] (EAIO) ...... OROAP

Organizacion Regional Gallega Autonoma [*Regional Galician Autonomy Organization*] [*Spain Political party*] (PPE) .... ORGA

Organizacion Revolucionaria del Pueblo en Armas [*Revolutionary Organization of the People in Arms*] [*Guatemala*] [*Political party*] (PD) ..... ORPA

Organizacion Socialista de los Trabajadores [*Socialist Workers' Organization*] [*Costa Rica*] [*Political party*] (PPW) .... OST

Organizacion Socialista de los Trabajadores [*Socialist Workers' Organization*] [*Bolivia*] [*Political party*] (PPW) .... OST

Organization .... O

Organization [*or Organizational*] (AAG) .... ORG

Organization (AAGC) .... Org

Organization .... ORGAN

Organization [*or Organizational*] (DAVI) .... organiz

Organization .... ORGN

Organization (AFM) .... ORGN

Organization and Equipment Guide [*Army*] (AABC) .... OEG

Organization and Finance Subcommittee .... OFSC

Organization and Management .... O & M

Organization and Management User Parts [*Telecommunications*] (OSI) ...... OMUP

Organization and Methods (AABC) .... O & M

Organization and Methods [*Military*] (AFIT) .... OAM

Organization and Operation .... O & O

Organization and Personnel Plan [*Army*] .... OPP

Organization and Staffing Guide [*Department of Labor*] (OICC) .... OSG

Organization and Training [*Military*] .... O & T

Organization and Training Division [*Supreme Headquarters Allied Powers Europe*] (NATG) .... OANDT

Organization Breakdown Structure [*Computer science*] (PCM) .... OBS

Organization Change Notice .... OCN

Organization Change Request .... OCR

Organization Conflict of Interest (AD) .... oci

Organization Development [*Human resources*] (WYGK) .... OD

Organization Development .... OD

Organization Development Council [*Defunct*] (EA) .... ODC

Organization Development Network (EA) .... ODN

Organization Field Maintenance .... OFM

Organization for African Unity (NADA) .... OAU

Organization for Afro-Asian Peoples Solidarity .... OAAPS

Organization for American-Soviet Exchanges (EA) .... OASES

Organization for Applied Science in Society .... OASIS

Organization for Black Designers .... OBD

Organization for Collectors of Covered Bridge Postcards (EA) .... OCCBP

Organization for Cooperation in Overseas Development [*Canada*] (EAIO) ... OCOD

Organization for Cooperation in the Roller Bearings Industry [*Warsaw, Poland*] (EAIO) .... OCRBI

Organization for Cooperation of Socialist Countries in the Domain of Posts and Telecommunications [*Defunct*] (EAIO) .... OSS

Organization for Coordination and Cooperation in the Control of Major Endemic Diseases .... OCCCE

Organization for Co-Ordination in Control of Endemic Diseases in Central Africa (EA) .... OCCEDCA

Organization for Defense of Four Freedoms for Ukraine (EA) .... ODFFU

Organization for Economic Cooperation and Development [*Formerly, OEEC*] .... OECD

Organization for Economic Cooperation and Development/Environment Committee [*Marine science*] (MSC) .... OECD/ENC

Organization for Equal Education of the Sexes (EA) .... OEES

Organization for European Economic Cooperation [*Later, OECD*] .... OEEC

Organization for European Nuclear Research .... OENR

Organization for European Research (AD) .... OER

Organization for Femininity .... OFF

Organization for Flora Neotropica (EA) .... OFN

Organization for Getting Legs Exposed [*Group opposing below-the-knee fashions introduced in 1970*] .... OGLE

Organization for Industrial, Spiritual, and Cultural Advancement International [*Tokyo, Japan*] (EAIO) .... OISCA

Organization for International Cooperation (EA) .... OIC

Organization for International Economic Relations [*Vienna, Austria*] (EAIO) .... IER

Organization for Microinformation .... OMI

Organization for Nordic Electrical Cooperation (EA) .... NORDEL

Organization for Rebirth of Ukraine (EA) .... ORU

Organization for Rehabilitation through Training [*Acronym is used in names of several Jewish social welfare organizations*] .... ORT

Organization for Scientific Coordination in AIDS [*Acquired Immune Deficiency Syndrome*] **Research, Inc.** [*New York, NY*] .... OSCAR

Organization for Social and Technical Innovation .... OSTI

Organization for the Advancement of Knowledge (EA) .... OAK

Organization for the Enforcement of Child Support (EA) .... OECS

Organization for the Lifelong Establishment of Paternity (EA) .... OLEP

Organization for the Management and Development of the Kagera River Basin (EA) .... KBO

Organization for the Phyto-Taxonomic Investigation of the Mediterranean Area [*Berlin, Federal Republic of Germany*] (EAIO) .... OPTIMA

Organization for the Prohibition of Chemical Weapons [*Proposed, 1992*] .... OPCW

Organization for the Protection and Advancement of Small Telephone Companies (EA) .... OPASTCO

Organization for the Rational Guidance of Youth [*Fictitious organization in film, "The Man from ORGY"*] .... ORGY

Organization for the Recovery of Allied Prisoners of War and Internees [*Initially in Headquarters of Allied Land Forces, Southeast Asia*] [*World War II*] .... RAPWI

Organization for the Support of Democratic Movement of Taiwan (EA) .... OSDMT

Organization for Trade Cooperation [*GATT*] .... OTC

Organization for Tropical Studies (EA) .... OTS

Organization for Unemployed Teachers .... OUT

Organization for United Response [*Later, AFA (Adoptive Families of America)*] (PAZ) .... OURS

Organization for Use of the Telephone (EA) .... OUT

Organization for West African Economic Co-operation .... OWAEC

Organization Forecast Authorization Equipment Data [*Military*] (AFIT) .... OFAED

Organization Health Program Officer (AFM) .... OHPO

Organization Health Survey [*Test*] .... OHS

Organization Iberoamericaine de Television (NTCM) .... OIT

Organization Integration [*Military*] .... OI

Organization List (MCD) .... OL

Organization Manning Equipment Table (MCD) .... OMET

Organization Not Allocated Exclusive Designator [*FAA designator*] (FAAC) .... YYY

Organization of Advanced Disabled Hobbyists (EA) .... OADH

Organization of African Unity .... OAU

Organization of African Unity Scientific and Technical Research Commission [*Marine science*] (MSC) .... OAU/STRC

Organization of African-American Veterans (EA) .... OAAV

Organization of Afro-American Unity .... OAAU

Organization of American Historians (EA) .... OAH

Organization of American Kodaly Educators (EA) .... OAKE

Organization of American States (EA) .... OAS

Organization of American States Electoral Observation Mission .... OAS/EOM

Organization of American States, Washington, DC [*OCLC symbol*] (OCLC) .... DOA

Organization of American States, Washington, DC [*Library symbol*] [*Library of Congress*] (LCLS) .... DOAS

Organization of American States, Washington, DC [*Library symbol Library of Congress Obsolete*] (LCLS) .... DPU

Organization of American States-Observer Group in Nicaragua .... OAS-OGN

Organization of Arab Petroleum Exporting Countries [*See also OPAEP*] [*OPEC Kuwait*] [*Absorbed by*] .... OAPEC

Organization of Arab Students in the USA and Canada (EA) .... OAS

Organization of Architectural Employees .... OAE

Organization of Asia-Pacific News Agencies [*Malaysia*] (EY) .... OANA

Organization of Athletic Administrators [*Defunct*] (EA) .... OAA

Organization of Biological Field Stations (EA) .... OBFS

Organization of Black Airline Pilots (EA) .... OBAP

Organization of Bricklin Owners (EA) .... OBO

Organization of Canadian Symphony Musicians [*See also OMOSC*] .... OCSM

Organization of Central American Armies (AD) .... OCAA

Organization of Central American States [*See also ODECA*] [*San Salvador, El Salvador*] (EAIO) .... OCAS

Organization of Chinese American Women (EA) .... OCAW

Organization of Chinese Americans (EA) .... OCA

Organization of Communist Action in Lebanon (PD) .... OCAL

Organization of East Caribbean States (NADA) .... OECS

Organization of European States (AD) .... OES

Organization of Facility Managers and Planners [*Later, OMERF*] (EA) ...... OFMP

Organization of Fitness and Personal Care Professionals [*Defunct*] (EA) .... OFPCP

Organization of Gas Exporting Countries [*Proposed gas cartel*] .... OGEC

Organization of Generally Rotten Enterprises [*Evil organization in television cartoon series "The Drak Pack"*] .... OGRE

Organization of Historical Studies (EA) .... OHS

Organization of Historical Studies (AD) .... OHS

Organization of International Numismatists .... OIN

Organization of Islamic Capitals and Cities (EA) .... OICC

Organization of Islamic Countries [*Intergovernmental group*] .... OIC

Organization of Latin American Petroleum Exporting Countries (AD) .... OLAPEC

Organization of Latin American Students (AD) .... OLAS

Organization of Mineral Exporting Countries [*Proposed*] .... OMEC

Organization of News Ombudsmen (EA) .... ONO

Organization of North American Indian Students [*Defunct*] (EA) .... ONAIS

Organization of Pan Asian American Women (EA) .... PANASIA

Organization of Pan Asian-American Women (EA) .... OPAAW

Organization of Petroleum Exporting Countries [*Also, OAPEC*] [*Vienna, Austria*] .... OPEC

Organization of Petroleum Exporting Countries (NADA) .... OPEC

[*The*] Organization of Plastics Processors .... OPP

[*The*] Organization of Plastics Processors [*Defunct*] (EA) .... TOPP

Organization of Professional Acting Coaches and Teachers (EA) .... OPACT

Organization of Professional Employees of the United States Department of Agriculture (EA) ... OPEDA
Organization of Progressive Socialists of the Mediterranean Basin ... OPSMB
Organization of Revolutionaries of the North [*Lebanon*] (PD) ... ORN
Organization of Solidarity of the Peoples of Africa, Asia, and Latin America ... OSPAAAL
Organization of Spanish Marxist-Leninists (PD) ... OMLE
Organization of Teachers of Oral Diagnosis (EA) ... OTOD
Organization of the Islamic Conference [*See also OCI*] [*Jeddah, Saudi Arabia*] (EAIO) ... OIC
Organization of the Joint Chiefs of Staff ... OJCS
Organization of Wildlife Planners (EA) ... OWP
Organization of Women for Legal Awareness (EA) ... OWLA
Organization, Personnel Equipment and Training [*Group*] ... OPET
Organization Radio Television France (IAA) ... ORTF
Organization Rating Scale ... ORS
Organization Regional Interamericana de Trabdjadores [*Inter-American Labor Organization*] [*Spanish*] (BARN) ... ORIT
Organization Requirements Clerk [*Defense Supply Agency*] ... ORC
Organization Resources Counselors (MCD) ... ORC
Organization Table ... OT
Organizational (AFM) ... ORGL
Organizational ... ORGNL
Organizational ... ORGNL
Organizational Accounting Structure (IAA) ... OAS
Organizational Analysis ... OA
Organizational and Intermediate (AD) ... o & i
Organizational and Operational Plan [*Army*] ... O & OP
Organizational Assessment ... OA
Organizational Behavior Teaching Society (EA) ... OBTS
Organizational Behaviour (DD) ... OrgBehav
Organizational Chart ... OC
Organizational Climate Description Questionnaire ... OCDQ
Organizational Climate Index [*Test*] ... OCI
Organizational Clothing and Individual Equipment [*Military*] ... OCIE
Organizational Competitiveness Program [*Motivational program*] ... OCP
Organizational Conflict of Interest (AAGC) ... OCI
Organizational Development (AD) ... od
Organizational Development/Organizational Effectiveness (MCD) ... OD/OE
Organizational Effectiveness ... OE
Organizational Effectiveness (AD) ... oe
Organizational Effectiveness Center and School [*Army*] ... OEC & S
Organizational Effectiveness Consultants (INF) ... OEC
Organizational Effectiveness General Officer Steering Committee (MCD) ... OBEGOSC
Organizational Effectiveness Noncommissioned Officer [*Military*] ... OENCO
Organizational Effectiveness Staff Officer [*Military*] ... OESO
Organizational Effectiveness Staff Officer Course [*Army*] ... OESOC
Organizational Effectiveness Survey System [*Army*] ... OESS
Organizational Effectiveness Training Center [*Army*] (MCD) ... OETC
Organizational Element Model ... OEM
Organizational Entity ... OE
Organizational Entity Code ... OEC
Organizational Entity Code (AD) ... oec
Organizational Entity Identity (AD) ... oei
Organizational Entity Identity ... OEI
Organizational Entity Name ... OEN
Organizational Equipment List [*Army*] ... OEL
Organizational Error [*Engineering*] ... OE
Organizational Expense Accounts [*Army*] ... OEA
Organizational Governance Advisory Committee [*NERComP*] ... OGAC
Organizational/Intermediate (MCD) ... OI
Organizational Intermediate Maintenance [*Military*] (AFIT) ... OIM
Organizational Leadership for Executives [*Military*] (RDA) ... OLE
Organizational Level (MCD) ... O-LVL
Organizational Level Maintenance Timer ... OLMT
Organizational Level Test Equipment (MCD) ... OLTE
Organizational Maintenance (MCD) ... OM
Organizational Maintenance Activity ... OMA
Organizational Maintenance Level (NVT) ... OML
Organizational Maintenance Level Activity (MCD) ... OMLA
Organizational Maintenance New Equipment Training [*Army*] (INF) ... OMNET
Organizational Maintenance Shop [*Army*] ... OMS
Organizational Maintenance Squadron [*Air Force*] (MCD) ... OMS
Organizational Maintenance Squadron [*Air Force*] (AFM) ... OMSq
Organizational Maintenance Support ... OMS
Organizational Maintenance Technician [*Army*] (AABC) ... OMT
Organizational Maintenance Test Station [*Army*] ... OMTS
Organizational Maintenance Trainer (MCD) ... OMT
Organizational Manual and Management Guide ... OM & MG
Organizational Master File [*Army*] ... OMF
Organizational Missile Maintenance Squadron [*Air Force*] ... OMMS
Organizational Missile Maintenance Squadron [*Air Force*] ... OMSLMSq
Organizational Operations and Maintenance Manual (NASA) ... OOMM
Organizational Project Plan [*Civil Defense*] ... OPP
Organizational Records Branch [*Army*] ... ORB
Organizational Role Analysis (PDAA) ... ORA
Organizational Source [*Online database field identifier*] [*Computer science*] ... OS
Organizational Source Code (NITA) ... OSCO
Organizational Spare Parts and Equipment [*Army*] ... OSPE
Organizational Structure Code [*Air Force*] (AFIT) ... OSC
Organizational Supply Code [*Army*] (AABC) ... OSC
Organizational Supply Management System [*Army*] (INF) ... OSMS
Organizational Support Equipment [*Army*] ... OSE
Organizational Table ... OT
Organizational Vehicle Automatic Tester ... ORVAT
Organizations and Agencies Directories Series [*A publication*] ... OAD
Organizations and Functions (MCD) ... O & F
Organizations and Systems Research Laboratory [*Army*] (RDA) ... OSRL
Organizations Concerned about Rural Education (AD) ... OCRE
Organizations, Functions, and Programs [*IRS*] ... OFP
Organizations Master Index [*A publication*] ... OMI
Organizations System (IAA) ... OS
Organize Training Center (EA) ... OTC
Organized ... ORGD
Organized Adoption Search Information Services (EA) ... OASIS
Organized Air Reserve ... OAR
Organized Behavioral System (WDMC) ... OBS
Organized Crime (AD) ... o/c
Organized Crime and Racketeering Section [*Department of Justice*] (DLA) ... OCR
Organized Crime and Racketeering Section [*Department of Justice*] ... OCRS
Organized Crime and Racketeering Strike Force (AD) ... OCRSF
Organized Crime Control Act of 1970 ... OCCA
Organized Crime Control Bureau (LAIN) ... OCCB
Organized Crime Drug Enforcement Task Force ... OCDETF
Organized Crime Information System [*Federal Bureau of Investigation*] [*Information service or system*] (IID) ... OCIS
Organized Crime Intelligence Bureau (AD) ... OCIB
Organized Crime Intelligence Unit [*Law Enforcement Assistance Administration*] ... OCI
Organized Crime Narcotics Program [*Department of Justice*] ... OCN
Organized Crime-Control Commission [*California*] (AD) ... OCCC
Organized Flying Adjusters (EA) ... OFA
Organized Marine Corps Reserve ... OMCR
Organized Migrants in Community Action [*Florida*] [*Defunct*] ... OMICA
Organized Naval Reserve ... O
Organized Naval Reserve Aviation ... O2
Organized Naval Reserve Seagoing ... O1
Organized Occupational Curricula ... OOC
Organized Organic Monolayer [*Organic chemistry*] ... OOM
Organized Projected Hypotheses for Innovations in Curriculum [*Educational planning*] ... ORPHIC
Organized Reserve Corps [*Later, Army Reserve*] ... ORC
Organized Reserve Port Security Unit [*Military*] ... ORPSU
Organized Reserve Training Center [*Military*] ... ORTC
Organized Reserve Training Unit [*Military*] ... ORTU
Organized Reserve Training Unit, Administration of Mobilization [*Military*] ... ORTUAM
Organized Reserve Training Unit, Aviation Support [*Military*] ... ORTUAV
Organized Reserve Training Unit, Coastal Force [*Military*] ... ORTUF
Organized Reserve Training Unit, Electronics [*Military*] ... ORTUEL
Organized Reserve Training Unit, Port Security [*Military*] ... ORTUPS
Organized Reserve Training Unit, Port Security (Operational) [*Military*] ... ORTUPS(O)
Organized Reserve Training Unit, Rescue Coordination Center [*Military*] ... ORTUR
Organized Reserve Training Unit, Vessel Augmentation [*Military*] ... ORTUAG
Organized Reserves [*Military*] ... OR
Organized Reservists in Drill Pay Status [*Military*] ... ODP
Organized Resistance to Capture in Alaska [*Defunct*] (EA) ... ORCA
Organized Track System [*Aviation*] ... OTS
Organizer Programming Language [*Computer science*] ... OPL
Organizing Committee for a Fifth Estate (AD) ... OC-5
Organizing Committee for a National Writers Union (EA) ... OCNWU
Organizing Committee of the World Congress on Implantology and Bio-Materials [*See also COCMIB*] [*Rouen, France*] (EAIO) ... OCWCIB
Organizing District Delegate [*British labor*] ... ODD
Organizing Interstitial Pneumonia [*Medicine*] ... OIP
Organizzazione Internazionale dei Trasporti a Fune [*International Organization for Transportation by Rope*] **- North American Continental Section** (EA) ... OITAF-NACS
Organizzazione Nazioni Unite [*United Nations*] [*Italian*] ... ONU
Organo [*Organ*] [*Music*] (ROG) ... ORGO
Organo Corale [*Choir Organ*] [*Latin*] (AD) ... OC
Organo Espressivo [*Swell Organ*] [*Italian*] (AD) ... oe
Organo Espressivo [*Swell Organ*] [*Music*] ... OE
Organo Espressivo [*Swell Organ*] [*Music*] ... Org Exp
Organochlorine [*Also, OCL*] [*Organic chemistry*] ... OC
Organochlorine [*Also, OC*] [*Organic chemistry*] ... OCL
Organogenesis, Inc. [*AMEX symbol*] (SPSG) ... ORG
Organogenesis, Inc. [*Associated Press*] (SAG) ... Orgngn
Organometallic Chemical Vapor Deposition [*Also, OM-VPE, MO-CVD, MO-VPE*] [*Semiconductor technology*] ... OM-CVD
Organometallic Material ... OMM
Organometallic Polymer (CAAL) ... OMP
Organo-Metallic Polymer (AD) ... omp
Organometallic Vapor Phase Epitaxy [*Also, OM-CVD, MO-CVD, MO-VPE*] [*Semiconductor technology*] ... OM-VPE
Organon [*Netherlands*] [*Research code symbol*] ... ORG
Organon, Inc. [*Research code symbol*] ... NA
Organon Laboratories Ltd. [*Great Britain*] [*Research code symbol*] ... BTC
Organophosphate Induced Delayed Neural Toxicity ... OPIDN
Organophosphate Insecticide ... OPI
Organophosphorous Acid [*Organic chemistry*] ... OPA
Organophosphorous Acid Anhydrase [*An enzyme*] ... OPAA
Organophosphorus [*Organic chemistry*] ... OP
Organophosphorus Hydrolase [*An enzyme*] ... OPH
Organotin Antifouling Paint Control Act of 1988 ... OAPCA
Organotin Compound [*Organic chemistry*] ... OTC
Organo-Transition-Metal (PDAA) ... OTM

Organum Vasculosum of the Lamina Terminalis [Medicine] .... OVLT
Orgasmic Impairment [Medicine] .... OI
Orgasmic Impairment (AD) .... o-i
Orgelbuechlein [Little Organ Book] [Bach Music] .... OB
Orghologic Corp. [Associated Press] (SAG) .... Orthlog
Orgue Expressif [Swell Organ] [Music] .... EXP
Orgue Expressif [Swell Organ] [Music] .... EXPR
Oria [Papua New Guinea] [Airport symbol Obsolete] (OAG) .... OTY
Orialsa [Bolivia] [ICAO location identifier] (ICLI) .... SLOI
Oribi Gorge Nature Reserve [South Africa] (AD) .... OGNR
Oriel College (AD) .... OCS
Oriel Computer Services Ltd. (NITA) .... OCSL
Oriel Computer Services Limited (NITA) .... KZ
Oriens & King [ICAO designator] (AD) .... O
Orient [Freemasonry] .... OR
Orient .... ORI
Orient Air Ltd. [British ICAO designator] (FAAC) .... OAA
Orient Airlines Association (EA) .... ORN
Orient Airways [Pakistan] [ICAO designator] (FAAC) .... OMEL
Orient Mid-East Lines (AD) .... OP
Orient Press [Press agency] [South Korea]
Orient, Spell Out, Nail Down [Method for organizing and communicating information, proposed by Barry Tarshis in his book "How to Write without Pain"] .... ORSON
Oriental .... OR
Oriental (ROG) .... O
Oriental Airlines (Gambia) Ltd. [ICAO designator] (FAAC) .... ORG
Oriental Airlines Ltd. [Nigeria] [ICAO designator] (FAAC) .... OAC
Oriental and African Studies .... OAS
Oriental and Biblical Studies [A publication] (BJA) .... OBS
Oriental Bank & Trust [NYSE symbol] (SAG) .... OBT
Oriental Bank & Trust [NYSE symbol] (TTSB) .... OBT
Oriental Bank & Trust [Associated Press] (SAG) .... OrientB
Oriental Boat Mission [Later, International Missions] (EA) .... OBM
Oriental Ceramic Society (EA) .... OCS
Oriental Chair of Solomon [Freemasonry] .... OCS
Oriental Fruit Moth [Entomology] .... OFM
Oriental Herb Association (AD) .... OHA
Oriental Institute (AD) .... OI
Oriental Institute Museum [University of Chicago] (AD) .... OIM
Oriental Medicine Doctor [Medicine] .... OMD
Oriental Merchants Association [Defunct] (EA) .... OMA
Oriental Missionary Society [Later, OMS International] (EA) .... OMS
Oriental, NC [FM radio station call letters] .... WNBR
Oriental Nocturnal Death Syndrome [Neurology] (DAVI) .... ONDS
Oriental Numismatic Society [Reading, Berkshire, England] (EAIO) .... ONS
Oriental Pearl Airways Ltd. [British ICAO designator] (FAAC) .... OJA
Oriental Rug Importers Association of America (EA) .... ORIA
Oriental Rug Retailers of America (EA) .... ORRA
Oriental Shorthairs International (EA) .... OSI
Orientalische Bibliographie [A publication] (BJA) .... OB
Orientalium Ecclesiarum [Decree on the Eastern Catholic Churches] [Vatican II document] .... OE
Orientation (AABC) .... ORIEN
Orientation .... ORIENT
Orientation and Access to Information and Documentation Sources in France [Commission de Coordination de la Documentation Administrative] [Database] .... ORIADOC
Orientation and Mobility [for the blind] .... O & M
Orientation Distribution Function .... ODF
Orientation Group [Air Force] .... OG
Orientation Inventory [Psychology] .... OI
Orientation Inventory [Vocational guidance test] .... ORI
Orientation Linkage for a Solar Cell Array .... OLSCA
Orientation Program in American Law [of AALS] .... OPAL
Orient-Avia [Former USSR] [FAA designator] (FAAC) .... ORT
Oriented Cellular Structure .... OCS
Oriented Polyethylene Terephthalate [Organic chemistry] .... OPET
Oriented Polypropylene [Plastics technology] .... OPP
Oriented Polystyrene [Plastics technology] .... OPS
Oriented Scintillation Spectrometer Experiment [Instrumentation in Gamma Ray Observatory] [NASA] .... OSSE
Oriented Space Vehicle .... OSV
Oriented-Strand Board [A plywood panel composition] .... OSB
Orienteering Federation of Australia .... OFA
Orienteering Tasmania [Australia An association] .... OT
Orienting Response [Psychology] .... OR
Orientis Graeci Inscriptiones Selectae [A publication] (OCD) .... OGI
Orientos [Queensland] [Airport symbol] (AD) .... OXO
Orient-Pacific Line [Shipping] (ROG) .... OPL
Orifice (NASA) .... ORF
Orifice .... ORF
Orifice (AAG) .... ORFC
Orifice Rod Assembly [Nuclear energy] (NRCH) .... ORA
Orifice Spark Advance Control [Valve] [Automotive technology] .... OSAC
Orifice Tube [Automobile air conditioning system]
Origanum [Marjoram] [Pharmacology] (ROG) .... ORIGAN
Origen [Deceased circa 254] [Authority cited in pre-1607 legal work] (DSA) .... Or
Origen [Deceased circa 254] [Authority cited in pre-1607 legal work] (DSA) ..... Orig
Origin .... o
Origin (IDOE) .... ORG
Origin (MDG) .... ORIG
Origin [or Original] (AAG) .... orig
Origin (VRA) .... O
Origin Address Field [Computer science] (IBMDP) .... OAF

Origin and Destination [Aviation] .... O & D
Origin and Destination (AD) .... o & d
Origin and Destination [OST] (TAG) .... O/D
Origin and Destination [NITA] .... OAND
Origin and Destination [Aviation] (AFM) .... OD
Origin Destination Information System [US Postal Service] .... ODIS
Origin of Columellar Muscle .... OCM
Origin Rail Freight [MARAD] (TAG) .... ORFS
Origin Recognition Complex [Genetics] .... ORC
Original .... O
Original .... OR
Original (ADA) .... ORIGL
Original (ROG) .... OAC
Original Acquisition Cost (AAGC) .... OAR
Original Action Record .... OAC
Original Air Conditioning (IIA) .... OAD
Original Air Date [of program's first telecast] .... OATS
Original Article Tear Sheets .... OATS
Original Article Tearsheet Service (NITA) .... OATS
Original Article Text Service .... ORIG BDS
Original Boards [Graphic arts] (DGA) .... ORICAT
Original Cataloguing System (NITA) .... OC
Original Claim (MAE) .... OC
Original Cosmopolitans [Defunct] (EA) .... OC
Original Cover .... ODF
Original Data File (NITA) .... ODR
Original Data Record .... ODP
Original Departure Point .... OD
Original Design .... od
Original Design (AD) .... ODC
Original Design Cutoff (AAG) .... OD
Original Dirac [Vacuum model] [Physics] .... ODJB
Original Dixieland Jazz Band .... ODP
Original Document Processing .... ODACA
Original Doll Artists Council of America (EA) .... OEP
Original Element Processor (MHDB) .... OE
Original Entry [Computer science] .... OE
Original Equipment [Automobile industry] .... OEM
Original Equipment Manufacturer .... OEM
Original Equipment Manufacturer (AD) .... oem
Original Equipment Manufacturer (AD) .... oer
Original Equipment Replacement (AD) .... OER
Original Equipment Request (AAG) .... OE
Original Error [Navigation] .... OFP
Original Flight Plan .... OGIP
Original Gas in Place [Natural resources] .... OGIFC
Original Gilligan's Island Fan Club (EA) .... OG
Original Gravity (BARN) .... OGP
Original Gross Premium [Insurance] (AIA) .... OGR
Original Gross Rate [Insurance] (AIA) .... OGS
Original Ground Surface .... OG
Original Gum [Philately] .... og
Original Gum (AD) .... oid
Original Issue Discount (AD) .... OID
Original Issue Discount [Business term] .... OID
Original Issue Discount Obligations (TDOB) .... OL
Original Learning [Psychometrics] .... OLS
Original Line of Sight .... olp
Original List Price (AD) .... omiom
Original Meaning is the Only Meaning (AD) .... OMIOM
Original Meaning Is the Only Meaning [Writing term] .... ON
Original Negative (MCD) .... ONP
Original Net Premium [Insurance] (AIA) .... ONR
Original Net Rate [Insurance] (AIA) .... ORG
Original New York Seltzer of Canada Ltd. [Vancouver Stock Exchange symbol] .... ORG
Original Oil in Place [Petroleum] .... OOIP
Original Online Module [Computer science] (PDAA) .... OOM
Original Pack Dispensing [For drugs] [Packaging] .... OPD
Original Paper Doll Artists Guild (EA) .... OPDAG
Original Policy (ADA) .... OP
Original Premium [Insurance] .... OP
Original Print Collectors Group (EA) .... OPCG
Original Proof Gallon .... OPG
Original Running Time [Movies] (CDAI) .... ORT
Original Series .... OS
Original Set Pattern [Ice dancing] .... OSP
Original Sixteen To One Mine [PC, exchange symbol] (TTSB) .... OAU
Original Society of Painters and Glaziers [A union] [British] .... OSPG
Original Title [Online database field identifier] .... OTI
Original Transmission Density (OA) .... OTD
Original Trenton Cracker Co. [Maker of Chowder & Oyster Crackers, claimed by some to be the oldest continuously manufactured American food product] .... OTC
Original Tuberculin [Medicine] (DMAA) .... OT
Original Turkey Mill [Paper] (DGA) .... OTM
Original-Abfuellung [On estate-bottled German wine labels] .... O/A
Originally Cultured Formulation (AD) .... ocf
Originally Derived .... OOPS
Originals on Permanent Sale .... ORIGINATG
Originating (ROG) .... OA
Originating Agency (SAA) .... OADR
Originating Agency Determination Required (MCD) .... OH
Originating Hospital [Aeromedical evacuation] .... OJ
Originating Junctor [Telecommunications] (TEL) .... ORS
Originating Register Sender

Originating Station Routing Identifier .... OSRI
Originating Station Treatment [*Telecommunications*] (TEL) .... OST
Originating Toll Center [*Telecommunications*] (TEL) .... OTC
Originating Toll Circuit [*Telecommunications*] (IAA) .... OTC
Originating Trunk Center [*Telecommunications*] (IAA) .... OTC
Origination Screening Office [*Telecommunications*] (TEL) .... OSO
Originator [*MARC relator code*] [*Library of Congress*] (LCCP) .... org
Originator (MSA) .... ORIG
Originator Controlled [*Information dissemination*] .... ORCON
Originator Controlled [*CIA terminology*] .... ORCON
Originator or Recipient [*Telecommunications*] (OSI) .... O/R
Originator-Controlled Information (MCD) .... ORCON
Originators Status Report [*Army*] .... OSR
Origin-of-Assembly Sequence [*Genetics*] .... OAS
Origins of Plasma in the Earth's Neighborhood [*Ad Hoc Advisory Committee terminated, 1981*] .... OPEN
Orilla Soldiers' Memorial Hospital, Health Sciences Library, Orilla, ON, Canada [*Library symbol*] [*Library of Congress*] (LCLS) .... CaOOrSMH
Orillia, ON [*FM radio station call letters*] CICX
Orillia Public Library, Ontario [*Library symbol National Library of Canada*] (NLC) .... OORI
Orillia Public Library, Orillia, ON, Canada [*Library symbol Library of Congress*] (LCLS) .... CaOOr
Orinduik [*Guyana*] [*Airport symbol*] (OAG) .... ORJ
Orinduik [*Guyana*] [*ICAO location identifier*] (ICLI) .... SYOR
O-Ring [*Automotive engineering*] .... OR
Orinthine-Decarboxylase, Motility, Indole, Trytophandeaminase (AD) .... omit
Oriol Avia [*Russian Federation*] [*ICAO designator*] (FAAC) .... OAU
Oriole [*Record label*] [*Great Britain*] .... Ori
Oriole Communication [*Vancouver Stock Exchange symbol*] .... OLE
Oriole Homes 'B' [*AMEX symbol*] (TTSB) .... OHC.B
Oriole Homes Corp. [*AMEX symbol*] (SPSG) .... OHC
Oriole Homes Corp. [*Associated Press*] (SAG) .... OriolH
Oriole HomesCv'A' [*AMEX symbol*] (TTSB) .... OHC.A
Orion [*Constellation*] .... Ori
Orion [*Constellation*] .... Orio
Orion Air [*Bulgaria*] [*ICAO designator*] (FAAC) .... BOR
Orion Air, Inc. [*ICAO designator*] (FAAC) .... TAG
Orion Capital [*NYSE symbol*] (TTSB) .... OC
Orion Capital Corp. [*NYSE symbol*] (SPSG) .... OC
Orion Capital Corp. [*Associated Press*] (SAG) .... OrionCap
Orion Molecular Cloud [*Astronomy*] .... OMC
Orion Molecular Cloud 1 [*Astronomy*] OMC1
Orion Network Systems [*NASDAQ symbol*] (TTSB) .... ONSI
Orion Network Systems, Inc. [*NASDAQ symbol*] (SAG) .... ONSI
Orion Network Systems, Inc. [*Associated Press*] (SAG) .... OrionNS
Orion Resources Ltd. [*Vancouver Stock Exchange symbol*] .... ORL
Orion SpA [*Italy ICAO designator*] (FAAC) .... MTT
Oripaa [*Finland ICAO location identifier*] (ICLI) .... EFOP
Oritkari [*Finland ICAO location identifier*] (ICLI) .... EFOR
Oriximina [*Brazil*] [*Airport symbol*] (AD) .... ORX
Oriya [*MARC language code Library of Congress*] (LCCP) .... ori
Orkney [*South Africa*] [*ICAO location identifier*] (ICLI) .... FAOY
Orkney [*County in Scotland*] (ROG) .... ORK
'Orlah (BJA) .... 'Or
'Orlah (BJA) .... 'Orl
Orland [*Norway ICAO location identifier*] (ICLI) .... ENOL
Orland [*Norway*] [*Airport symbol*] (OAG) .... OLA
Orland, CA [*FM radio station call letters*] .... KDIG
Orland Free Library, Orland, CA [*Library symbol Library of Congress*] (LCLS) .... COrl
Orland Free Library, Orland, CA [*Library symbol*] [*Library of Congress*] (LCLS) .... COrlL
Orland Park Public Library, Orland Park, IL [*Library symbol Library of Congress*] (LCLS) .... IOp
Orlando [*Florida*] [*ICAO location identifier*] (ICLI) .... KORL
Orlando [*Florida*] [*Airport symbol*] (OAG) .... ORL
Orlando Aerospace [*Martin Marietta*] (RDA) .... OA
Orlando Bridgman's English Common Pleas Reports [*A publication*] (DLA) .... Bridg O
Orlando Bridgman's English Common Pleas Reports [*A publication*] (DLA) .... O Bridg
Orlando Bridgman's English Common Pleas Reports [*A publication*] (DLA) .... O Bridg (Eng)
Orlando Bridgman's English Common Pleas Reports [*A publication*] (DLA) .... O Bridgm
Orlando Bridgman's English Common Pleas Reports [*A publication*] (DLA) .... Orl Bridg
Orlando Bridgman's English Common Pleas Reports [*A publication*] (DLA) .... Orl Bridgman
Orlando College (AD) .... OC
Orlando Contract Management District (SAA) .... ORCMD
Orlando, FL [*Location identifier FAA*] (FAAL) .... DWS
Orlando, FL [*Location identifier FAA*] (FAAL) .... MCO
Orlando, FL [*Location identifier FAA*] (FAAL) .... OJP
Orlando, FL [*Location identifier FAA*] (FAAL) .... TFE
Orlando, FL [*Television station call letters*] .... WCPX
Orlando, FL [*AM radio station call letters*] .... WDBO
Orlando, FL [*FM radio station call letters*] .... WDIZ
Orlando, FL [*Television station call letters*] .... WFTV
Orlando, FL [*AM radio station call letters*] .... WHOO
Orlando, FL [*AM radio station call letters*] .... WHTQ
Orlando, FL [*FM radio station call letters*] .... WMFE
Orlando, FL [*Television station call letters*] .... WMFE-TV
Orlando, FL [*FM radio station call letters*] .... WMMO

Orlando, FL [*Television station call letters*] .... WOFL
Orlando, FL [*FM radio station call letters*] .... WOMX-FM
Orlando, FL [*Television station call letters*] .... WRBW
Orlando, FL [*AM radio station call letters*] .... WRMQ
Orlando, FL [*FM radio station call letters*] .... WUCF
Orlando, FL [*FM radio station call letters*] .... WWKA
Orlando, FL [*AM radio station call letters*] .... WWNZ
Orlando, FL [*AM radio station call letters*] (RBYB) .... WZKD
Orlando, FL [*Television station call letters*] .... WZWY
Orlando [*Florida*] International [*Airport symbol*] (OAG) .... MCO
Orlando Junior College [*Florida*] .... OJC
Orlando/McCoy Air Force Base [*Florida*] [*ICAO location identifier*] (ICLI) ...... KMCO
Orlando Public Library, Orlando, FL [*Library symbol Library of Congress*] (LCLS) .... FO
Orlando Public Library, Orlando, FL [*OCLC symbol*] (OCLC) .... ORL
Orleans [*France ICAO location identifier*] (ICLI) .... LFLF
Orleans/Bricy [*France ICAO location identifier*] (ICLI) .... LFOJ
Orleans County Historical Society, Kendall, NY [*Library symbol Library of Congress*] (LCLS) .... NKendOHi
Orleans Court of Appeals [*Louisiana*] (DLA) .... Orleans App
Orleans, MA [*AM radio station call letters*] .... WKPE
Orleans, MA [*FM radio station call letters*] .... WKPE-FM
Orleans Parish Medical Society, New Orleans, LA [*Library symbol Library of Congress*] (LCLS) .... LNOP
Orleans Progress-Examiner, Orleans, IN [*Library symbol Library of Congress*] (LCLS) .... InOrPE
Orleans Public Library, Orleans, IN [*Library symbol Library of Congress*] (LCLS) .... InOr
Orleans/Saint-Denis-De-L'Hotel [*France ICAO location identifier*] (ICLI) .... LFOZ
Orleans Term Reports [*1, 2 Martin*] [*Louisiana*] [*A publication*] (DLA) .... Or T Rep
Orleans Term Reports [*1, 2 Martin*] [*Louisiana*] [*A publication*] (DLA) .... Orl TR
Orleans Term Reports [*1, 2 Martin*] [*Louisiana*] [*A publication*] (DLA) .... Orleans TR
Orleans-Hanna Algebra Prognosis Test (EDAC) .... OHAPT
Orleans-Niagara Board of Cooperative Educational Services, Associates Special Educational Instruction Materials Center, Sanborn, NY [*Library symbol Library of Congress*] (LCLS) .... NSanO
Orleans-Niagara Board of Cooperative Educational Services, Educational Communications Center, Sanborn, NY [*Library symbol Library of Congress*] (LCLS) .... NSanO-C
Orleans-Niagara Board of Cooperative Educational Services, Sanborn, NY [*Library symbol*] [*Library of Congress*] (LCLS) .... NSanO-S
Ormara [*Pakistan*] [*ICAO location identifier*] (ICLI) .... OPOR
Ormara [*Pakistan*] [*Airport symbol*] (AD) .... ORP
Ormec Serro Analyst (NITA) .... OSA
Ormetoprim [*Potentiator for antibacterials*] [*Veterinary medicine*] .... OMP
Ormoc, Leyte [*Philippines*] [*ICAO location identifier*] (ICLI) ...... RPVO
Ormolu (VRA) .... orm
Ormond Beach, FL [*Location identifier FAA*] (FAAL) .... OMN
Ormond Beach, FL [*AM radio station call letters*] .... WELE
Ormond Beach Public Library, Ormond Beach, FL [*Library symbol Library of Congress*] (LCLS) .... FOb
Ormond-by-the-Sea, FL [*FM radio station call letters*] (RBYB) .... WHOG-FM
Ormond's Reports [*19-107 Alabama*] [*A publication*] (DLA) .... Ormond
Ormone Adrenocorticotropina [*Italian Medicine*] .... OACT
Ormont Explorations Ltd. [*Vancouver Stock Exchange symbol*] .... OME
Ormsby Public Library, Carson City, NV [*Library symbol Library of Congress*] (LCLS) .... NvC
Ornament (MSA) .... ORN
Ornament (VRA) .... ornam
Ornament .... ORNMT
Ornamental .... ORNAM
Ornamental .... ORNTL
Ornamental Fish International (EAIO) .... OFI
Ornamental Growers Association (EA) .... OGA
Ornamental Pool and Fountain Constructors Association [*British*] (DBA) .... OPFCA
Ornamental Stitching (DNAB) .... OS
OrNda Healthcorp [*NYSE symbol*] (TTSB) .... ORN
Ornda Healthcorp [*Formerly, Republic Health Corp.*] [*NASDAQ symbol*] (SPSG) .... ORND
Ornda Healthcorp [*Associated Press*] (SAG) .... Ornda
Ornithine [*Same as DAV*] [*An amino acid*] .... Orn
Ornithine Carbamoyltransferase [*Also, OTC*] [*An enzyme*] .... OCT
Ornithine Carbamoyltransferase Deficiency [*Medicine*] .... OCTD
Ornithine Decarboxylase [*An enzyme*] .... ODC
Ornithine Transcarbamoylase [*Also, OCT*] [*An enzyme*] .... OTC
Ornithine Transcarbamylase [*An enzyme*] (DAVI) .... OTC
Ornithineaminotransferase [*An enzyme*] .... OAT
Ornithodoros Coriaceus Spirochete [*Entomology*] .... OCS
Ornithological Society of the Middle East (EAIO) .... OSME
Ornithology .... ORN
Ornithology .... ORNITH
Ornithology .... ORNITHOL
Ornithyl-Beta-Alanine [*Biochemistry*] .... OBA
Ornitologia Rondo Esperantlingva [*Esperantist Ornithologists' Association*] (EAIO) .... ORE
ORNL [*Oak Ridge National Laboratory*] Graphite Reactor .... OGR
Ornskoldsvik [*Sweden ICAO location identifier*] (ICLI) .... ESNO
Ornskoldsvik [*Sweden*] [*Airport symbol*] (OAG) .... OER
Oro [*Ecuador*] [*ICAO location identifier*] (ICLI) .... SEOR
Oro Americano [*American Gold*] [*Spanish Business term*] .... OA
Oro Sellado [*Standard Gold*] [*Business term Spanish*] .... OS
Oro Valley, AZ [*FM radio station call letters*] .... KCDI
Oro Valley, AZ [*FM radio station call letters*] (RBYB) .... KSJM-FM
Oro Valley, AZ [*AM radio station call letters*] .... KVOI

Oroamerica, Inc. [*NASDAQ symbol*] (SAG) ... OROA
Oroamerica, Inc. [*Associated Press*] (SAG) ... Oroamer
Orodara [*Burkina Faso*] [*ICAO location identifier*] (ICLI) ... DHOR
Orofacial Malformation ... OFM
Oro-Facio-Digital [*Syndrome*] [*Medicine*] ... OFD
Orofino High School Library, Orofino, ID [*Library symbol*] [*Library of Congress*] (LCLS) ... IdOrHS
Orofino, ID [*AM radio station call letters*] ... KLER
Orofino, ID [*FM radio station call letters*] ... KLER-FM
Orofino Resources Ltd. [*Toronto Stock Exchange symbol Vancouver Stock Exchange symbol*] ... ORO
Orogastric [*Feeding*] [*Gastroenterology*] (DAVI) ... OG
Orogastric Aspirate [*Medicine*] (AAMN) ... OGA
Orogastric Feeding [*Gastroenterology*] (DAVI) ... OGF
Oromo Abo Liberation Front [*Ethiopia*] [*Political party*] (EY) ... OALF
Oromo Liberation Front [*Ethiopia*] [*Political party*] (PD) ... OLF
Oromo People's Democratic Organization [*Ethiopia*] [*Political party*] (EY) ... OPDO
Oromocto Public Library, New Brunswick [*Library symbol National Library of Canada*] (NLC) ... NBO
Oromocto Public Library, Oromocto, NB, Canada [*Library symbol Library of Congress*] (LCLS) ... CaNBO
Oronite Fuel Additive ... OFA
Orono, ME [*FM radio station call letters*] ... WMEB
Orono, ME [*Television station call letters*] ... WMEB-TV
Oropa [*Italy*] [*Seismograph station code, US Geological Survey Closed*] (SEIS) ... ORO
Oropouche [*An arbovirus*] ... ORO
Orosomucoid [*Biochemistry*] ... OR
Orotate [*Biochemistry*] ... Oro
Orotek Resources Corp. [*Vancouver Stock Exchange symbol*] ... OTR
Orotic Acid [*Biochemistry*] ... Oro
Orotidine [*One-letter symbol; see Ord*] ... O
Orotidine [*Also, O*] [*A nucleoside*] ... Ord
Orotidine Monophosphate [*Organic chemistry*] ... OMP
Orotracheal [*Medicine*] ... OT
Orotracheal Suction [*Medicine*] (DAVI) ... OTS
Orotracheal Tube [*Medicine*] (DAVI) ... OTT
Oroville [*California*] [*Seismograph station code, US Geological Survey*] (SEIS) ... ORV
Oroville, CA [*FM radio station call letters*] ... KEWE
Oroville, CA [*AM radio station call letters*] ... KORV
Oroville, CA [*FM radio station call letters*] (RBYB) ... KZCO-FM
Oroville, CA [*Location identifier FAA*] (FAAL) ... OVE
Oroville Public Library, Oroville, CA [*Library symbol Library of Congress*] (LCLS) ... COro
Orpen's Light Horse [*British military*] (DMA) ... OLH
Orphan [*or Orphanage*] ... ORPH
Orphan Drug Ace [*1983*] (BARN) ... ODA
Orphan Foundation [*Later, OFA*] (EA) ... OF
Orphan Foundation of America (EA) ... OFA
Orphan Med Inc. [*NASDAQ symbol*] (TTSB) ... ORPH
Orphan Medical, Inc. [*NASDAQ symbol*] (SAG) ... ORPH
Orphan Medical, Inc. [*Associated Press*] (SAG) ... OrphanM
Orphan Train Heritage Society of America (EA) ... OTHSA
Orphan Voyage (EA) ... OV
Orphans' Court (DLA) ... OC
Orpheon [*Record label*] [*Poland*] ... Ophn
Orpheus Island [*Australia Airport symbol*] ... ORS
Orphica Fragmenta [*A publication*] (OCD) ... Orph Frag
Orr, MN [*Location identifier FAA*] (FAAL) ... ORB
Orr Public School, Orr, MN [*Library symbol*] [*Library of Congress*] (LCLS) ... MnOrS
Orroval Valley, Australia, Tracking Station [*NASA*] (NASA) ... ORR
Orrville, AL [*FM radio station call letters*] ... WJAM
Orsa [*Sweden ICAO location identifier*] (ICLI) ... ESNR
Orsett [*England*] ... ORS
Orsina Resources [*Vancouver Stock Exchange symbol*] ... ORS
Orssuiorssuaq [*Greenland*] [*ICAO location identifier*] (ICLI) ... BGOS
Orsta/Volda [*Norway*] [*Airport symbol*] (OAG) ... HOV
Orsta-Volda/Hovden [*Norway ICAO location identifier*] (ICLI) ... ENOV
Orszagos Muszaki Informacios Kozpont es Konyvtar [*National Technical Information Center and Library*] [*Information service or system*] (IID) ... OMIKK
Orszagos Muszaki Konyvtar es Dokumentacios Kozpont, Budapest, Hungary [*Library symbol Library of Congress*] (LCLS) ... HuBM
Orszagos Szechenyi Konyvtar [*National Szechenyi Library*] [*Information service or system*] (IID) ... OSzK
Orszagos Szechenyi Konyvtar [*National Szechenyi Library*], Budapest, Hungary [*Library symbol Library of Congress*] (LCLS) ... HuOSzK
Ortanova [*Italy ICAO location identifier*] (ICLI) ... LIBO
Ortec International, Inc. [*NASDAQ symbol*] (SAG) ... ORTC
Ortec International, Inc. [*Associated Press*] (SAG) ... OrtecInt
Ortec International, Inc. [*Associated Press*] (SAG) ... OrtInt
Ortec Intl. [*NASDAQ symbol*] (TTSB) ... ORTC
Ortec Intl. Wrrt'A' [*NASDAQ symbol*] (TTSB) ... ORTCW
Ortec Intl. Wrrt'B' [*NASDAQ symbol*] (TTSB) ... ORTC
Ortel Corp. [*Associated Press*] (SAG) ... Ortel
Ortel Corp. [*NASDAQ symbol*] (SAG) ... ORTL
Orthagonal ... ORTHOG
Orthicon Read-Out ... ORO
Ortho [*Chemistry*] ... o
Ortho Diagnostics ... Ort
Ortho Diagnostics, Raritan, NJ [*Library symbol Library of Congress*] (LCLS) ... NjRarOD
Ortho, Para-Dichloro-Diphenyldichlorethane [*Mitotane*] [*Antineoplastic drug regimen*] (DAVI) ... O,p-DDD
Ortho Pharmaceutical Canada Ltd., Don Mills, Ontario [*Library symbol National Library of Canada*] (NLC) ... OTOPC
Ortho Pharmaceutical Canada Ltd., Don Mills, Toronto, ON, Canada [*Library symbol Library of Congress*] (LCLS) ... CaOTOPC
Ortho Pharmaceutical Corp. [*Research code symbol*] ... ORF
Ortho Pharmaceutical Corp., Raritan, NJ [*Library symbol Library of Congress*] (LCLS) ... NjRarO
Ortho Tolidine (PDAA) ... OT
Ortho-Aminoacetophenone [*Organic chemistry*] ... OAP
Ortho-Aminoazotoluene [*A dye*] [*Organic chemistry*] ... OAAT
Ortho-Aminobenzenethiol [*Organic chemistry*] ... OABT
Ortho-Benzyl-para-chlorophenol [*Disinfectant*] ... OBCP
Ortho-Chlorobenzoic Acid [*Organic chemistry*] ... OCBA
Ortho-Chlorobenzonitrile [*Organic chemistry*] ... OCBN
Ortho-Chlorobenzyl Chloride [*Organic chemistry*] ... OCBC
Ortho-Chloro-para-nitroaniline [*Organic chemistry*] ... OCPNA
Ortho-Chlorophenol [*Organic chemistry*] ... OCP
Ortho-Chlorophenoxyacetic Acid [*Organic chemistry*] ... OCPA
(Ortho-Chlorophenoxy)propionic Acid [*Organic chemistry*] ... OCPP
Ortho-Chlorophenylacetic Acid [*Organic chemistry*] ... OCPA
Ortho-Chlorotoluene [*Organic chemistry*] ... OCT
Orthochromatic [*Photography*] (ROG) ... ORTHO
Orthochromatic Film [*Photography*] (DGA) ... OF
Orthoclase [*CIPW classification*] [*Geology*] ... or
Ortho-Cyclohexanediaminetetraacetic Acid [*Also, DCTA*] [*Organic chemistry*] ... OCTA
Ortho-Demethylencainide [*Biochemistry*] ... ODE
Ortho-Demethylfortimicin [*Biochemistry*] ... ODMF
Orthodontic Centers of Amer [*NASDAQ symbol*] (TTSB) ... OCAI
Orthodontic Centers of America, Inc. [*NASDAQ symbol*] (SAG) ... OCAI
Orthodontic Centers of America, Inc. [*Associated Press*] (SAG) ... Orthodon
Orthodontic Education and Research Foundation (EA) ... OERF
Orthodontic Technicians Association [*British*] (DBA) ... OTA
Orthodox [*Judaism*] ... O
Orthodox ... ORTH
Orthodox and Anglican Fellowship (EA) ... OAF
Orthodox Black Jews (BJA) ... OBJ
[*The*] **Orthodox Church of America** ... OCA
Orthodox Job Enrichment (PDAA) ... OJE
Orthodox Theological Society in America (EA) ... OTSA
Orthodox Youth of America [*Later, SOYO*] ... OYA
Orthoenstatite [*Mineral*] ... OE
Orthofix International [*NASDAQ symbol*] (SAG) ... OFIX
Orthofix International [*NASDAQ symbol*] (TTSB) ... OFIXF
Orthofix International [*Associated Press*] (SAG) ... Orthfx
Orthogonal (NASA) ... ORTHOG
Orthogonal Array Arithmetic Unit [*Computer science*] ... OAAU
Orthogonal Array Processor [*Computer*] ... OAP
Orthogonal Memory (MHDB) ... OM
Orthogonal Mini-Embedment (MHDI) ... OMEN
Orthogonal Mode Transducer (IAA) ... OMT
Orthogonal Polynomial (OA) ... OP
Orthogonal Row Computer ... ORC
Orthogonal-Field-Alternation Gel Electrophoresis [*Analytical biochemistry*] ... OFAGE
Orthogonalized Atomic Orbital (OA) ... OAO
Orthogonalized Linear Combination of Atomic Orbitals [*Optics*] ... OLCAO
Orthogonalized Plane Wave ... OPW
Orthogonals (VRA) ... orthg
Orthographic RADAR Restitutor ... ORR
Orthography ... ORTH
Orthohombic-Tetragonal [*Temperature transition*] ... O-T
Ortho-Iodobenzoic (Acid) [*Biochemistry*] ... OIB
Ortho-Iodohippurate [*Clinical chemistry*] (AAMN) ... OIH
Orthoiodohippuric Acid [*Clinical chemistry*] (DAVI) ... OIHA
Ortho-Isopropylaniline [*Organic chemistry*] ... OIPA
Orthokeratology [*Medicine*] ... Ortho-K
Orthologic Corp. [*NASDAQ symbol*] (SAG) ... OLGC
Orthomat Plot (MCD) ... OP
Ortho-Methylfluorescein Phosphate [*Biochemistry*] ... OMFP
Orthomin ... OMN
Orthomode Junction [*Electronics*] ... OJ
Orthomode Junction [*Electronics*] ... OMJ
Orthomode Junction and Switching Assembly [*Electronics*] ... OJSA
Orthomode Transducer [*Electronics*] ... OMT
Orthomode Transducer (AD) ... omt
Ortho-Mycaminosyltylonolide [*Antibacterial compound*] ... OMT
Orthonitroaniline (DICI) ... ONA
Ortho-Nitrobiphenyl [*Organic chemistry*] ... ONB
Ortho-Nitrophenol [*Organic chemistry*] ... ONP
Ortho-Nitrophenyl-B-Galactosidase [*Organic chemistry*] (MAE) ... ONP-GAL
Orthonormal Basis of an Error Space [*Statistics*] ... OBES
Ortho-Novum [*A contraceptive*] [*Ortho Pharmaceutical Corp.*] (DAVI) ... ON
Orthopaedic Nursing Diploma [*British*] ... OND
Orthopaedic Surgery [*Medical Officer designation*] [*British*] ... O/S
Orthopaedics Overseas (EA) ... OO
Orthopedic ... OR
Orthopedic ... ORTH
Orthopedic ... ORTHO
Orthopedic ... ORTHO
Orthopedic Appliance and Limb Manufacturers Association [*Later, AOPA*] ... OALMA
Orthopedic Appliance Mechanic [*Navy*] ... OAM
Orthopedic Appliance Service ... OAS
Orthopedic Casting Laboratory (DAVI) ... OCL

Orthopedic Foundation for Animals *(EA)* .... OFA
Orthopedic Nurse .... ON
Orthopedic Nurse .... ORN
Orthopedic Nursing Certificate .... ONC
Orthopedic Research *[Medicine]* .... OR
Orthopedic Research and Education Foundation *[Medicine]* *(DMAA)* .... OREF
Orthopedic Research Society *(EA)* .... ORS
Orthopedic Surgeon .... ORS
Orthopedic Surgery *(DAVI)* .... OS
Orthopedic Surgical Manufacturers Association *(EA)* .... OSMA
Orthopedic Technology, Inc. *[NASDAQ symbol]* *(SAG)* .... ORTH
Orthopedic Technology, Inc. *[Associated Press]* *(SAG)* .... OrthopT
Orthopedic Transcription Unit .... OTU
Orthopedically Impaired .... OI
Orthopedics *(DAVI)* .... OS
Orthopedist *[Orthopedic Physician]* *(DAVI)* .... orthopod
Ortho-Phenylenediamine *[Organic chemistry]* .... OPD
Ortho-Phenylphenol *[Disinfectant]* .... OPP
Ortho-Phosphoserine *[Biochemistry]* .... OPS
Orthophoto Resolution Enhancer *[Army]* .... ORE
Ortho-Phthaldehyde *[Organic chemistry]* .... OPA
Orthoplast Jacket *[Orthopedics]* *(DAVI)* .... OJ
Orthopnea *[Medicine]* *(DAVI)* .... orthop
Ortho-Propylaniline .... OPA
Orthopyroxene *[A silicate mineral]* .... OPX
Orthorhombic *[Crystallography]* .... o-rh
Orthorhombic Enstatite *[Geology]* .... OREN
Orthostatic Hypotension *[Medicine]* .... OH
Ortho-Tolidine Arsenite *[Organic chemistry]* .... OTA
Ortho-Tolidine Manganese Sulphate .... OTM
Ortho-Toluenediamine *[Organic chemistry]* .... OTD
Ortho-Toluenesulfonamide *[Used in manufacture of saccharin]* .... OTS
Ortho-Toluidine Boric Acid *[Organic chemistry]* .... OTB
Orthotopic Liver Transplantation *[Medicine]* .... OLT
Orthotropic Multicell Tank .... OMT
Ortiz *[New Mexico]* *[Seismograph station code, US Geological Survey]* *(SEIS)* .... OTZ
Ortner Air Service *[Air carrier designation symbol]* .... ORTX
Ortolan's History of the Roman Law *[A publication]* *(DLA)* .... Ort Hist
Ortolan's History of the Roman Law *[A publication]* *(DLA)* .... Ort Rom Law
Ortolan's Justinian's Institutes *[A publication]* *(DLA)* .... Ort Inst
Orton Dyslexia Society *(EA)* .... ODS
Orton Society *[Later, ODS]* *(EA)* .... OS
Ortonville Hospital, Ortonville, MN *[Library symbol]* *[Library of Congress]* *(LCLS)* .... MnOrvH
Ortonville, MN *[FM radio station call letters]* *(RBYB)* .... KAHF-FM
Ortonville, MN *[FM radio station call letters]* .... KCGN-FM
Ortonville, MN *[AM radio station call letters]* .... KDIO
Ortonville, MN *[Location identifier FAA]* *(FAAL)* VVV
Ortonville Public Library, Ortonville, MN *[Library symbol]* *[Library of Congress]* *(LCLS)* .... MnOrv
Ortonville Public School, Ortonville, MN *[Library symbol]* *[Library of Congress]* *(LCLS)* .... MnOrvPS
Orts-, Regional-, und Landesplanung Literaturinformationssystem *[Literature Information System for Town and Regional Planning]* *[1974-1978 Database]* .... ORLIS
Ortsbatterie *[Local Battery]* *[German military - World War II]* .... OB
Orumieh *[Iran]* *[Airport symbol Obsolete]* *(OAG)* .... OMH
Oruro *[Bolivia]* *[Airport symbol]* *(AD)* .... ORU
Oruro *[Bolivia]* *[ICAO location identifier]* *(ICLI)* .... SLOR
Orwell Resources Ltd. *[Vancouver Stock Exchange symbol]* .... ORW
Orwex *[Poland ICAO designator]* *(FAAC)* .... ORW
Oryx Aviation *[South Africa ICAO designator]* *(FAAC)* .... ORX
Oryx Energy Co. *[NYSE symbol]* *(SPSG)* .... ORX
Oryx Energy Co. *[Associated Press]* *(SAG)* .... Oryx
Oryx Pecos Test Inquiry and Control System *(NITA)* .... OPTIC
Oryx Technology *[NASDAQ symbol]* *(TTSB)* .... ORYX
Oryx Technology Corp. *[NASDAQ symbol]* *(SAG)* .... ORYX
Oryx Technology Corp. *[Associated Press]* *(SAG)* .... OryxTc
Oryx Technology Wrrt *[NASDAQ symbol]* *(TTSB)* .... ORYXW
Oryzacystatins I *[Biochemistry]* .... OCI
Oryzacystatins II *[Biochemistry]* .... OCII
Orzeck Aphasia Evaluation *[Psychology]* .... OAE
Os *[Bone]* *[Latin]* .... O
Osage *[MARC language code Library of Congress]* *(LCCP)* .... osa
Osage Beach *[Missouri]* *[Airport symbol Obsolete]* *(OAG)* .... OSB
Osage Beach, MO *[AM radio station call letters]* .... KRMS
Osage Beach, MO *[FM radio station call letters]* .... KYLC
Osage City, KS *[FM radio station call letters]* *(RBYB)* .... KANS
Osage, IA *[FM radio station call letters]* .... KCZY
Osage Tribal Education Committee *[Department of the Interior]* *[Muskogee, OK]* *(EGAO)* .... OTEC
Osaka *[Japan]* *[Seismograph station code, US Geological Survey]* *(SEIS)* .... OSA
Osaka *[Japan]* *[Airport symbol]* *(OAG)* .... OSA
Osaka *[Takayasuyama]* *[Japan]* *[Seismograph station code, US Geological Survey]* *(SEIS)* .... OSK
Osaka Bioscience Institute *[Japan]* .... OBI
Osaka/International *[Japan ICAO location identifier]* *(ICLI)* .... RJOO
Osaka International Textile Machinery Show .... OTEMAS
Osaka Prefecture. University. Bulletin *[A publication]* *(DLA)* .... Osaka Pref Bull
Osaka Stock Exchange *[Japan]* .... OSE
Osaka Stock Futures *[Japan]* *(ECON)* .... OSF
Osaka University, Kita-ku, Osaka, Japan *[Library symbol Library of Congress]* *(LCLS)* .... JOU
Osaka University. Law Review *[A publication]* *(DLA)* .... Osaka UL Rev

Osaka University. Law Review *[A publication]* *(DLA)* .... Osaka ULR
Osaka University. Law Review *[Osaka, Japan]* *[A publication]* *(DLA)* .... Osaka Univ L Rev
Osaka University, Nakanishima Library, Osaka, Japan *[Library symbol Library of Congress]* *(LCLS)* .... JOU-N
Osaka/Yao *[Japan ICAO location identifier]* *(ICLI)* .... RJOY
Osakeyhtioe *[Limited Company]* *[Finland]* .... Oy
Osakis, MN *[FM radio station call letters]* .... KBHL
Osakis School, Osakis, MN *[Library symbol]* *[Library of Congress]* *(LCLS)* .... MnOsS
Osan *[South Korea ICAO location identifier]* *(ICLI)* .... RKSO
Osawatomie State Hospital, Osawatomie, KS *[Library symbol Library of Congress]* *(LCLS)* .... KOSH
OSB Financial *[Associated Press]* *(SAG)* .... OSB Fn
OSB Financial *[NASDAQ symbol]* *(SAG)* .... OSBF
OSB Finl Corp. *[NASDAQ symbol]* *(TTSB)* .... OSBF
Osborn Communications *[NASDAQ symbol]* *(TTSB)* .... OSBN
Osborn Communications *[Associated Press]* *(SAG)* .... Osborn
Osborn Communications Corp. *[NASDAQ symbol]* *(NQ)* .... OSBN
Osborn Laboratories of Marine Sciences *[New York Zoological Society]* *[Research center]* *(RCD)* .... OLMS
Osborne & Chappel Goldfields US *[Toronto Stock Exchange symbol]* .... OCG
Osborne Association *(EA)* .... OA
Osborne Communications Corp. *[Associated Press]* *(SAG)* .... Osborn
Osborne Computer Corporation *(NITA)* .... OCC
Osborne Mendel Rat *[Medicine]* *(DMAA)* .... OM
Osborno/Canal Bajo *[Chile]* *[ICAO location identifier]* *(ICLI)* .... SCJO
Osburn Public Library, Osburn, ID *[Library symbol Library of Congress]* *(LCLS)* .... IdO
Oscar *[Phonetic alphabet]* *[International]* *(DSUE)* .... O
Oscar Adolphson Primary School, Valleyview, Alberta *[Library symbol National Library of Canada]* *(BIB)* .... AVVOS
Oscar Resources Ltd. *[Vancouver Stock Exchange symbol]* .... OSR
Oscar Rose Junior College Library, Midwest City, OK *[OCLC symbol]* *(OCLC)* .... OUK
Oscar Rose Junior College, Midwest City, OK *[Library symbol Library of Congress]* *(LCLS)* .... OkMcO
Osceola, AR *[AM radio station call letters]* .... KOSE
Osceola, AR *[FM radio station call letters]* .... KOSE-FM
Osceola County Courthouse, Sibley, IA *[Library symbol]* *[Library of Congress]* *(LCLS)* .... IaSibCoC
Osceola, IA *[FM radio station call letters]* .... KJJC
Osceola, MO *[FM radio station call letters]* .... KBUG
Osceola Public Library, Osceola, IA *[Library symbol Library of Congress]* *(LCLS)* .... IaOsc
Osceola Public Library, Osceola, NE *[Library symbol Library of Congress]* *(LCLS)* .... NbOsc
Osceola Sentinel, Osceola, IA *[Library symbol Library of Congress]* *(LCLS)* .... IaOscS
Osceola Township Public and School Library, Dollar Bay, MI *[Library symbol Library of Congress]* *(LCLS)* .... MiDolb
Osceola, WI *[Location identifier FAA]* *(FAAL)* .... OEO
Oscillate *[or Oscillation, Oscillator, Oscillograph, Oscilloscope]* *(KSC)* .... OSC
Oscillating .... OSCG
Oscillating Current Element .... OCE
Oscillating Doublet Antenna .... ODA
Oscillating Limiter *(IAA)* .... OL
Oscillating Output Geneva .... OOG
Oscillating Pressure Method .... OPM
Oscillating Secondary Mirror *[Telescope]* .... OSM
Oscillating-Analyzer Ellipsometer *(PDAA)* .... OAE
Oscillating-Compensator Oscillating-Analyzer Polarimeter *(PDAA)* .... OCOAP
Oscillation or Fluctuation in Behavior *[Psychology]* .... O
Oscillation Test Point *[British military]* *(DMA)* .... OTP
Oscillation Transformer *[Radio]* .... OT
Oscillator *(IDOE)* .... osc
Oscillator Activity Monitor *[Telecommunications]* *(TEL)* .... OAM
Oscillator and Clock Module .... OCM
Oscillator/Doubler/Amplifier .... ODA
Oscillator Frequency *[Telecommunications]* *(IAA)* .... OF
Oscillator Housing Assembly .... OHA
Oscillator Instability Measurement System .... OIMS
Oscillator Single Gain Region *(PDAA)* .... OSGR
Oscillator-Multiplier *[Telecommunications]* *(TEL)* .... OSC-MULT
Oscillators *[JETDS nomenclature]* *[Military]* *(CET)* .... O
Oscillatory Magnetic Field .... OMF
Oscillatory, Nonoscillatory Flip-Flop *[Computer science]* .... ON-OFF
Oscillogram *[Engineering]* .... OSCGRM
Oscillogram Scan and Recorder System *(PDAA)* .... OSCAR
Oscillogram Trace Reader *[Non-Linear Systems, Inc.]* *[Computer science]* .... OTRAC
Oscillograph, String .... OSCG
Oscillographic Recording System .... ORS
Oscillopolarograph .... PO
Oscilloscope *(IAA)* .... OSCILLOSC
Oscilloscope *(AAG)* .... OSCP
Oscilloscope Digital Control .... ODC
Oscilloscope Face Plane .... OFP
Oscilloscope Panel .... OSCP
Oscoda County Public Library, Mio, MI *[Library symbol Library of Congress]* *(LCLS)* .... MiMio
Oscoda, MI *[Location identifier FAA]* *(FAAL)* .... ASP
Oscoda, MI *[Location identifier FAA]* *(FAAL)* .... LJU
Oscoda, MI *[Location identifier FAA]* *(FAAL)* .... OSC
Oscoda, MI *[FM radio station call letters]* .... WCLS

Oscoda/Wurtsmith Air Force Base [*Michigan*] [*ICAO location identifier*]
(ICLI) .... KOSC
OSD [*Office of the Secretary of Defense*] **Developmental Test and
Evaluation** (RDA) .... DDTE
OSD [*Office of the Secretary of Defense*] **Operational Test and Evaluation**
(RDA) .... DOTE
Osec Petroleum [*Vancouver Stock Exchange symbol*] .... OSE
'Osef Piskei Din shel ha-Rabanut ha-Rashit le-'Erets Yisrael (BJA) .... OPD
Osfriends (EA) .... OF
Osgood Journal, Osgood, IN [*Library symbol Library of Congress*] (LCLS) .... InOsJ
Osgood Semantic Differential [*Occupational therapy*] .... OSD
Osgoode Public Library, Ontario [*Library symbol National Library of
Canada*] (BIB) .... OOSGO
Osgoode Township High School Library, Metcalfe, Ontario [*Library symbol
National Library of Canada*] (BIB) .... OMOTH
Osgood-Schlatter's Disease [*Medicine*] .... OS
OSHA [*Occupational Safety and Health Administration*] **Computerized
Information System** [*Environmental science*] .... OCIS
Oshakati [*Namibia*] [*ICAO location identifier*] (ICLI) .... FAOS
OSHAP Technologies Ltd. [*Associated Press*] (SAG) .... Oshap
OSHAP Technologies Ltd. [*NASDAQ symbol*] (NQ) .... OSHS
Oshap Technologies Ltd. [*NASDAQ symbol*] (TTSB) .... OSHSF
Oshawa General Hospital, Eduction Resource Centre, Oshawa, ON,
Canada [*Library symbol*] [*Library of Congress*] (LCLS) .... CaOOSHH
Oshawa Group Ltd. [*Toronto Stock Exchange symbol*] .... OSH
Oshawa, ON [*AM radio station call letters*] .... CKDO
Oshawa, ON [*FM radio station call letters*] .... CKGE
Oshawa Public Library, Ontario [*Library symbol National Library of Canada*]
(NLC) .... OOSH
Oshawa Public Library, Oshawa, ON, Canada [*Library symbol Library of
Congress*] (LCLS) .... CaOOsh
Oshima [*Japan*] [*Seismograph station code, US Geological Survey*] (SEIS) .... OSH
Oshima [*Japan ICAO location identifier*] (ICLI) .... RJTO
Oshima Island [*Japan*] [*Airport symbol*] (OAG) .... OIM
Oshima Island [*Japan*] [*Airport symbol*] (OAG) .... OSH
Oshkosh [*Wisconsin*] [*Airport symbol*] (OAG) .... GOSH
Oshkosh B Gosh, Inc. [*NASDAQ symbol*] (SAG) .... GOSHA
Oshkosh B'Gosh Cl'A' [*NASDAQ symbol*] (TTSB) .... GOSHB
Oshkosh B'Gosh Cl'B' [*NASDAQ symbol*] (TTSB) .... OshB
Oshkosh B'Gosh, Inc. [*Associated Press*] (SAG) .... OKS
Oshkosh, NE [*Location identifier FAA*] (FAAL) .... GZK
Oshkosh Public Library, Oshkosh, WI [*OCLC symbol*] (OCLC) .... WOsh
Oshkosh Public Library, Oshkosh, WI [*Library symbol Library of Congress*]
(LCLS) .... OshkT
Oshkosh Truck Corp. [*Associated Press*] (SAG) .... OTC
Oshkosh Truck Corp. .... OTRK
Oshkosh Truck Corp. [*Oshkosh, WI*] [*NASDAQ symbol*] (NQ) .... OTRKB
Oshkosh Truck'B' [*NASDAQ symbol*] (TTSB) .... WOSH
Oshkosh, WI [*AM radio station call letters*] .... WRST
Oshkosh, WI [*FM radio station call letters*] .... WUSW
Oshkosh, WI [*FM radio station call letters*] .... WVBO
Oshkosh, WI [*FM radio station call letters*] .... WVCY
Oshkosh, WI [*AM radio station call letters*] (RBYB) .... OSH
Oshman's Sporting Gds [*AMEX symbol*] (TTSB) .... OSH
Oshman's Sporting Goods, Inc. [*AMEX symbol*] (SAG) .... Oshmn
Oshman's Sporting Goods, Inc. [*Associated Press*] (SAG) .... DNOS
Oshogbo [*Nigeria*] [*ICAO location identifier*] (ICLI) .... FZBD
Oshwe [*Zaire*] [*ICAO location identifier*] (ICLI) ....
OSI [*Open Systems Interconnection*] **Applications Kernel** [*Computer
science*] (TNIG) .... OSAK
Osicom Technologies, Inc. [*NASDAQ symbol*] (SAG) .... FIBR
Osicom Technologies, Inc. [*Associated Press*] (SAG) .... Osicom
Osijek [*Former Yugoslavia*] [*ICAO location identifier*] (ICLI) .... LYOS
Osijek [*Former Yugoslavia*] [*Airport symbol*] (OAG) .... OSI
OSIS [*Ocean Surveillance Information System*] **Baseline System** [*Navy*] .... OBS
OSIS [*Ocean Surveillance Information System*] **Baseline Upgrade** [*Navy*] .... OBU
Osisko Lake Mines Ltd. [*Toronto Stock Exchange symbol*] .... OSS
Oskaloosa Daily Herald, Oskaloosa, IA [*Library symbol Library of Congress*]
(LCLS) .... IaOskH
Oskaloosa, IA [*AM radio station call letters*] .... KBOE
Oskaloosa, IA [*FM radio station call letters*] .... KBOE-FM
Oskaloosa, IA [*FM radio station call letters*] .... KIGC
Oskaloosa, IA [*Location identifier FAA*] (FAAL) .... OOA
Oskaloosa Public Library, Oskaloosa, IA [*Library symbol Library of
Congress*] (LCLS) .... IaOsk
Oskar Kokoschka [*Austrian painter*] [*1886-1980*] .... OK
Oskarshamn [*Sweden ICAO location identifier*] (ICLI) .... ESMO
Oskarshamn [*Sweden*] [*Airport symbol*] (OAG) .... OSK
Osler Library, McGill University, Montreal, Quebec [*Library symbol National
Library of Canada*] (NLC) .... QMMO
Osler Resources, Inc. [*Vancouver Stock Exchange symbol*] .... OSL
Oslo [*Norway ICAO location identifier*] (ICLI) .... ENOS
Oslo [*Norway*] [*Airport symbol*] (AD) .... FBU
Oslo [*Norway*] [*Airport symbol*] (OAG) .... OSL
Oslo [*Norway*] **Ardermoen Airport** [*Airport symbol*] (OAG) .... GEN
Oslo Caa [*Norway ICAO location identifier*] (ICLI) .... ENCA
Oslo Commission (EAIO) .... OSCOM
Oslo/Fornebu [*Norway ICAO location identifier*] (ICLI) .... ENFB
Oslo/Gardermoen [*Norway ICAO location identifier*] (ICLI) .... ENGM
Oslo Kommune Tunnelbanekontoret [*Oslo Subway System*] (AD) .... OKT
OSMH Health Sciences Library, Orillia Soldiers' Memorial Hospital, Ontario
[*Library symbol National Library of Canada*] (NLC) .... OORISMH
Osmiophilic Layer [*Botany*] .... OM
Osmiridium (IDOE) .... Os-Ir
Osmium [*Chemical element*] .... Os
Osmium Tetroxide [*Inorganic chemistry*] .... OT

Osmolality [*Chemistry*] .... osmo
Osmolality Urin-Spot [*Test*] [*Biochemistry*] (DAVI) .... OS-SPT
Osmolar [*Chemistry*] (DAVI) .... osM
Osmolarity Serum [*Biochemistry*] (DAVI) .... OSM S
Osmolarity Urine [*Biochemistry*] (DAVI) .... OSM U
Osmole [*Physical chemistry*] .... Osm
Osmole [*Measurement*] (DAVI) .... osmol
Osmond Boys International Fan Club (EA) .... OBIFC
Osmonics, Inc. [*NYSE symbol*] (SPSG) .... OSM
Osmonics, Inc. [*Associated Press*] (SAG) .... Osmonic
Osmotic .... OSM
Osmotic Erythrocyte Resistance .... OER
Osmotic Fragility Test .... OF
Osmotic Permeability [*Biochemistry*] (DAVI) .... Posmo
Osmotic Pressure .... OP
Osmotic Shock .... OS
Osmotically Active Substance [*Medicine*] (DMAA) .... OAS
Osmotically Sensitive Cell .... OSC
Osnabruck/Atterheide [*Germany ICAO location identifier*] (ICLI) .... EDWO
Osnaburgh, ON [*FM radio station call letters*] .... CBQN
Osobyi Otdel [*Counterintelligence surveillance unit in military formation until
1943*] [*Former USSR*] .... OO
Osorno [*Chile*] [*Airport symbol*] (AD) .... ZOS
Osoyoos, BC [*AM radio station call letters*] .... CJOR
Osoyoos Museum, British Columbia [*Library symbol National Library of
Canada*] (NLC) .... BOM
Osoyoos Museum, Osoyoos, BC, Canada [*Library symbol*] [*Library of
Congress*] (LCLS) .... CaBOM
Osphradial Ganglion [*In mollusks*] .... OSG
Osphradial Nerve [*In mollusks*] .... OSN
Osphradium [*An organ in mollusks*] .... O
Osric Dining Society (EA) .... ODS
Osrodek Informacji Naukowej [*Scientific Information Center*] [*Polish Academy
of Sciences Warsaw*] [*Information service or system*] (IID) .... OIN
Ossa Resources, Inc. [*Vancouver Stock Exchange symbol*] .... OSA
Osseous Defect [*Medicine*] .... OD
Ossetic [*MARC language code Library of Congress*] (LCCP) .... oss
Ossian Bee, Ossian, IA [*Library symbol Library of Congress*] (LCLS) .... IaOssB
Ossian Journal, Ossian, IN [*Library symbol Library of Congress*] (LCLS) .... InOssJ
Ossian Public Library, Ossian, IA [*Library symbol Library of Congress*]
(LCLS) .... IaOss
Ossification of Posterior Longitudinal Ligament [*Orthopedics*] (DAVI) .... OPLL
Ossining Correctional Facility [*Sing Sing*] (AD) .... OCF
Ossining, NY [*FM radio station call letters*] .... WDFH
Ossining, NY [*FM radio station call letters*] .... WOSS
Ossining Public Library, Ossining, NY [*Library symbol Library of Congress*]
(LCLS) .... NOss
Ossory [*Ireland*] (ROG) .... OSS
Ostacalcium Phosphate [*A fertilizer*] .... OCP
Osteitis Fibrosa [*Medicine*] (MAE) .... OF
Osteitis Fibrosa Cystica [*Medicine*] (DMAA) .... OFC
Osten [*East*] [*German*] .... O
Ostend [*Belgium*] [*Airport symbol*] (OAG) .... OST
Osteoarthritis [*Medicine*] .... OA
Osteoarthritis [*Medicine*] .... osteo
Osteoarthropathy [*Medicine*] (MAE) .... OAP
Osteocalcin [*Biochemistry*] .... OC
Osteochondritis Dissecans [*Medicine*] .... OCD
Osteoclast Activating Factor [*Endocrinology*] .... OAF
Osteogenesis Imperfecta [*Brittle bone disease*] .... OA
Osteogenesis Imperfecta [*Medicine*] .... OI
Osteogenesis Imperfecta Foundation (EA) .... OIF
Osteogenic Sarcoma [*Medicine*] .... OS
Osteoinductive Factor [*Biochemistry*] .... OIF
Osteomalacia [*Medicine*] (MAE) .... OM
Osteomyelitis [*Medicine*] .... OM
Osteomyelitis [*Medicine*] .... OSTEO
Osteomyelitis [*Orthopedics*] (DAVI) .... Osteo
Osteopath .... OST
Osteopathic (WGA) .... OSTEO
Osteopathic .... ONG
Osteopathic and Naturopathic Guild [*British*] (DBA) .... OAGB
Osteopathic Association of Great Britain .... OCOA
Osteopathic College of Ophthalmology and Otorhinolaryngology (EA) .... OCA
Osteopathic Cranial Association [*Later, CA*] .... OEF
Osteopathic Educational Foundation (AD) .... OF
Osteopathic Foundation [*Later, NOF*] .... OH
Osteopathic Hospital (DAVI) .... OLA
Osteopathic Libraries Association [*Defunct*] (EA) .... OMT
Osteopathic Manipulative Therapy (CPH) .... OM & S
Osteopathic Medicine and Surgery .... OP
Osteopoetin [*Biochemistry*] .... OP
Osteoporosis [*Orthopedics*] (DAVI) .... OS
Osteosarcoma [*Oncology*] .... OS
Osteosarcoma-Derived Growth Factor [*Biochemistry*] .... ODGF
Osteosclerosis [*Medicine*] (DAVI) .... OS
Osteotech, Inc. [*NASDAQ symbol*] (SAG) .... OSTE
Osteotech, Inc. [*Associated Press*] (SAG) .... Osteotch
Osteotomy [*Orthopedics*] (DAVI) .... Ost
Osterhout Free Library [*Library network*] .... DLC
Osterhout Free Library, Wilkes-Barre, PA [*OCLC symbol*] (OCLC) .... OST
Osterhout Free Library, Wilkes-Barre, PA [*Library symbol Library of
Congress*] (LCLS) .... PWb
Osterogenic Protein .... OP
Ostersund [*Sweden*] [*Airport symbol*] (OAG) .... OSD

Ostersund/Froson [*Sweden ICAO location identifier*] (ICLI) .... ESPC
Osteryoung Square Wave Voltammogram [*Electrochemistry*] .... OSWV
Osteuropaeische Zeit [*East European Time*] [*German*] (AD) .... OEZ
Osteuropeiska Solidaritetskommitten [*East European Solidarity Committee*] (EAIO) .... OESK
Ostex International, Inc. [*Associated Press*] (SAG) .... Ostex
Ostex International, Inc. [*NASDAQ symbol*] (SAG) .... OSTX
Ostex Intl. [*NASDAQ symbol*] (TTSB) .... OSTX
Ostfriesische Lufttransport GmbH [*Germany ICAO designator*] (ICDA) .... OL
Ostfriesische Lufttransport GmbH [*Germany ICAO designator*] (FAAC) .... OLT
Ostiole [*Biology*] .... O
Ostmark [*Monetary unit*] [*Germany*] .... OM
Ostrava [*Former Czechoslovakia*] [*ICAO location identifier*] (ICLI) .... LKMT
Ostrava [*Former Czechoslovakia*] [*Airport symbol*] (OAG) .... OSR
Ostrich Eggshell [*Archeological material*] .... OES
Ostwald Dilution Law [*Chemistry*] .... ODL
O'Sullivan Corp. [*AMEX symbol*] (SPSG) .... OSL
O'Sullivan Corp. [*Associated Press*] (SAG) .... OSullvnC
O'Sullivan Industries Hldg [*NYSE symbol*] (TTSB) .... OSU
O'Sullivan Industries Holding [*NYSE symbol*] (SPSG) .... OSU
O'Sullivan Industries Holdings [*Associated Press*] (SAG) .... OSulvInd
Oswego City Library, Oswego, NY [*Library symbol Library of Congress*] (LCLS) .... NOs
Oswego County BOCES [*Boards of Cooperative Educational Services*], Mexico, NY [*OCLC symbol*] (OCLC) .... VBO
Oswego County Historical Society, Oswego, NY [*Library symbol Library of Congress*] (LCLS) .... NOsHi
Oswego County Library System, Oswego, NY [*Library symbol*] [*Library of Congress*] (LCLS) .... NOsC
Oswego Hospital, Oswego, NY [*Library symbol*] [*Library of Congress*] (LCLS) .... NOsH
Oswego, KS [*Location identifier FAA*] (FAAL) .... OSW
Oswego, NY [*FM radio station call letters*] .... WGES
Oswego, NY [*FM radio station call letters*] .... WNYO
Oswego, NY [*FM radio station call letters*] .... WRVO
Oswego, NY [*AM radio station call letters*] .... WSGO
Oswego, NY [*FM radio station call letters*] (RBYB) .... WTKV-FM
Oswego, NY [*FM radio station call letters*] .... WZOS
Oswego Township Library, Oswego, IL [*Library symbol Library of Congress*] (LCLS) .... IOs
Oswestry [*British depot code*] .... OSW
Oswestry Rangers [*British military*] (DMA) .... OR
OT Industries, Inc. [*Vancouver Stock Exchange symbol*] .... OTI
Ota [*Portugal ICAO location identifier*] (ICLI) .... LPOT
Otago Daily Times [*A publication*] (AD) .... ODT
Otago Hussars [*British military*] (DMA) .... OH
Otago Police Gazette [*1861-64*] [*New Zealand*] [*A publication*] (DLA) .... Otago Pol Gaz
Otago University Medical Corps [*British military*] (DMA) .... OUMC
Otavi [*Namibia*] [*ICAO location identifier*] (ICLI) .... FAOV
Otavi [*South-West Africa*] [*Airport symbol*] (AD) .... OTV
OTC [*Overseas Telecommunications Commission*] **International Ltd.** [*Australia Telecommunications service*] (TSSD) .... OTCI
Otdelenie Gosudarstvenni Politcheskoi Upravi [*Special Government Political Administration*] [*Former Soviet secret service organization, also known as GPU Later, KGB*] .... OGPU
Ote Iwapo [*All That Is Must Be Considered*] [*of OI Committee International, a third-world lobby opposing systematic birth control Swahili*] .... OI
Otepa [*Tuamotu Archipelago*] [*Seismograph station code, US Geological Survey*] (SEIS) .... OTP
Otero College (AD) .... OC
Otero Junior College [*La Junta, CO*] .... OJC
Otero Junior College, La Junta, CO [*Library symbol Library of Congress*] (LCLS) .... CoLjO
Othello [*Shakespearean work*] .... Oth
Othello [*Washington*] [*Seismograph station code, US Geological Survey*] (SEIS) .... OTH
Othello, WA [*AM radio station call letters*] .... KRSC
Othello, WA [*FM radio station call letters*] .... KZLN
Other .... O
Other (ROG) .... OR
Other (VRA) .... oth
Other (DAVI) .... OTH
Other Abnormal Morphology [*On differential*] [*Biochemistry*] (DAVI) .... DESCR
Other Acquisition War Reserve Material Requirements (MCD) .... OAWRMR
Other Acronymic Agencies .... OAA
Other Active Military Service (DNAB) .... OAS
Other Administrative Reasons [*Medicine*] (MAE) .... OAR
Other Appointments .... OA
Other Approved Studies (ADA) .... OAS
Other Arms and Services [*Military*] .... OA & S
Other Articles .... OA
Other Checkable Deposits [*Federal Reserve system*] (GFGA) .... OCD
Other Common Carrier [*Telecommunications*] .... OCC
Other Comprehensive Bases of Accounting (ADA) .... OCBOA
Other Connective Tissue Diseases [*Medicine*] .... OCTD
Other Controllable Expenses (MEDA) .... OCE
Other Denomination [*British military*] (DMA) .... OD
Other Design Activity (MSA) .... ODA
Other Direct Costs [*Accounting*] .... ODC
Other Direct Costs (AD) .... odc
[*The*] **Other Economic Summit** [*of North America*] (CROSS) .... TOES
[*The*] **Other Economic Summit of North America** (EA) .... TOES-NA
Other Equipment Manufacturer (IAA) .... OEM
Other Equipment Manufacturers (CMD) .... OEM
Other Equipment Manufacturer's Information (IAA) .... OEMI
Other Essays [*Literature*] (ROG) .... OE
Other Further Education .... OFE
Other Health Impaired [*Education*] .... OHI
Other Intelligence File (MCD) .... OIF
Other Intelligence Requirements [*Army*] (MCD) .... OIR
Other Large Phased-Array RADAR (AD) .... olpar
Other Line [*Telecommunications*] (TEL) .... OL
Other Loans Especially Mentioned (TDOB) .... OLEM
Other Major End Item [*Military*] (AFIT) .... OMEI
Other Manufacturing Industries [*Department of Employment*] [*British*] .... OMI
Other Medical/Surgical Facility (MEDA) .... OF
Other Military Target .... OMT
Other Military Teletypewriter Network (CET) .... OMTN
Other Music for Urban Gormandizers [*Acronym used as subtitle to the New York City nightclub name, CBGB*] .... OMFUG
Other Neurological Disorders .... OND
Other Papers (ROG) .... OP
Other Pay Entry Date [*Army*] (AABC) .... OPED
Other People's [*Borrowed money, cigarettes, etc.*] [*Slang*] .... OP
Other People's Butts [*Cigarette butts garnered from ash trays*] [*Slang*] .... OPB
Other People's Money .... OPM
Other People's Tobacco [*Slang*] .... OPT
Other Personal Services .... OPS
Other Physical Principles [*Defense system*] .... OPP
Other Plant Equipment [*DoD*] .... OPE
Other Procurement .... OP
Other Procurement, Army (AABC) .... OPA
Other Procurement, Navy .... OPN
Other Program (NTCM) .... O
Other Programmed Operations (IAA) .... OPO
Other Project Element (NASA) .... OPE
Other Project Element .... OPE
Other Provisions Basic Orders Remain in Effect .... PROVMAIN
Other Ranks [*Ranks other than officers*] [*Military*] .... OR
Other Real Estate Owned (TDOB) .... OREO
Other Regulated Material .... ORM
Other Regulated Materials (GNE) .... ORMS
Other Side [*A publication*] (BRI) .... OS
Other Sources .... OS
Other Specialty Serial Numbers [*Air Force*] .... OSSN
Other Support Items .... OSI
Other Talk Address (IAA) .... OTA
Other Technical Effort .... OTE
Other Than .... OT
Other than Air (CINC) .... OTA
Other than Automatic [*Freight*] .... O T AUTIC
Other than Cost Base Review [*DoD*] .... OCBR
Other than Flat [*Freight*] .... OTF
Other than Full Paid [*IRS*] .... OTFP
Other than Hand [*Freight*] .... OTH
Other than Honorable Conditions [*Military*] (AABC) .... OTH
Other than Iron or Steel [*Freight*] .... OTIS
Other than Knocked Down Flat [*Freight*] .... OTKDF
Other than Mexican [*Term applied by US Border Patrol to certain illegal immigrants*] .... OTM
Other than New Procurement [*Navy*] (DNAB) .... OTNP
Other than Permanent Full-Time (GFGA) .... OPFT
Other than Permanent Full-Time Equivalent (GFGA) .... OPFTE
Other than Portable [*Freight*] .... OTP
Other than Psychotic .... OP
Other than Regular Army (AABC) .... OTRA
Other than Regular Army .... OTRAR
Other than Ship or Squadron Reinforcement Unit [*Naval Reserve*] (DNAB) .... ORU
Other than Special Consultants [*Military*] .... O/TSC
Other than Steel or Zinc Heads [*Freight*] .... OTSZH
Other Time .... OT
Other Valuable Considerations [*Commerce*] (BARN) .... ovc
[*The*] **Other Victims of Alcoholism** (EA) .... TOVA
Other War Materiel Requirements [*Army*] .... OWMR
Other War Reserve Materiel .... OWRM
Other War Reserve Materiel Requirement (AFIT) .... OWRMR
Other War Reserve Materiel Stocks [*Army*] (AABC) .... OWRMS
Other Woman Limited [*An association*] .... OWL
Others .... ORS
Otherwise .... ORSE
Otherwise (ROG) .... ORWISE
Otherwise .... OWSE
Otherwise Known As .... OKA
Otherwise Known As (AD) .... oka
Otherwise Specified (MSA) .... OS
Otiai [*Former USSR Seismograph station code, US Geological Survey Closed*] (SEIS) .... OTI
Otimax Industries [*NASDAQ symbol*] (TTSB) .... OPMX
Otis Art Institute of Parsons School of Design (GAGS) .... Otis Art Inst
Otis Art Institute of Parsons School of Design, Los Angeles, CA [*Library symbol*] [*Library of Congress*] (LCLS) .... CLOA
Otis Lennon Mental Ability Test (EDAC) .... OLMAT
Otis Library, Norwich, CT [*Library symbol*] [*Library of Congress*] (LCLS) .... CtNwch
Otis Public Library, Otis, CO [*Library symbol Library of Congress*] (LCLS) .... CoOt
Otis Quick Scoring Mental Abilities Tests [*Psychology*] (DAVI) .... OQSMAT
Otis Test [*Psychiatry*] (DAVI) .... OT
Otis-Lennon School Ability Test [*Education*] .... OLSAT
Otitis Externa (AD) .... o/e

Otitis Externa [*Medicine*] ... OE
Otitis Media [*Medicine*] ... OM
Otitis Media, Catarrhal, Acute [*Medicine*] (MAE) ... OMCA
Otitis Media, Purulent, Acute [*Medicine*] ... OMPA
Otitis Media, Secretory, Chronic [*Medicine*] (DAVI) ... OMSC
Otitis Media, Suppurative, Acute [*Medicine*] ... OMSA
Otitis Media, Suppurative, Chronic [*Medicine*] ... OMSC
Otitis Media with Effusion [*Medicine*] ... OME
Otjiwarongo [*Namibia*] [*ICAO location identifier*] (ICLI) ... FAOW
Otjiwarongo [*South-West Africa*] [*Airport symbol*] (AD) ... OJW
Otolaryngology [*Medicine*] ... OT
Otolaryngology [*Medicine*] ... Oto
Otolaryngology [*Medicine*] (DAVI) ... Otolar
Otolith Test Goggles [*NASA*] (KSC) ... OTG
Otolitic Membrane [*Otology*] ... OM
Otology [*Medicine*] ... OT
Otology [*Medicine*] ... OTO
Otology ... OTO
Otology [*Medicine*] ... OTOL
Otomian [*MARC language code Library of Congress*] (LCCP) ... oto
Otonabee Airways [*ICAO designator*] (AD) ... OU
Otonabee Township Library, Keen, Ontario [*Library symbol National Library of Canada*] (NLC) ... OKOT
O'Toole's Group, Inc. [*Toronto Stock Exchange symbol*] ... OT
Oto-Palato-Digital [*Syndrome*] ... OPD
Otorhinolaryngology [*Medicine*] (DAVI) ... ENT
Otorhinolaryngology [*Medicine*] ... ORL
Otorhinolaryngology [*Medicine*] (DHSM) ... OTO
Otorhinolaryngology ... OTRHNLRGYNGY
Otorhinolaryngology and Head/Neck Nurses (EA) ... OHNN
Otosclerosis Study Group (EA) ... OSG
Otospondylomegaepiphyseal Dystrophy [*Medicine*] (DAVI) ... OSMED
OTR Express [*NASDAQ symbol*] (TTSB) ... OTRX
OTR Express, Inc. [*Associated Press*] (SAG) ... OTR Ex
OTR Express, Inc. [*NASDAQ symbol*] (SAG) ... OTRX
Otsar Yehude Sefarad (BJA) ... OYS
Otsego District Public Library, Otsego, MI [*Library symbol Library of Congress*] (LCLS) ... MiOt
Otsego, MI [*AM radio station call letters*] ... WQXC
Otsego, MI [*FM radio station call letters*] ... WQXC-FM
Ottava [*Octave*] [*Music*] ... OTT
Ottava [*Octave*] [*Music*] ... OVA
Ottawa [*Ontario*] [*Seismograph station code, US Geological Survey*] (SEIS) ... OTT
Ottawa [*Canada*] [*Airport symbol*] (OAG) ... YOW
Ottawa Board of Education, Library Services Centre [*UTLAS symbol*] ... OBE
Ottawa Board of Education, Library Services Centre (Films) [*UTLAS symbol*] ... OBF
Ottawa Board of Education, Library Services Centre (Software) [*UTLAS symbol*] ... OBS
Ottawa Board of Education, Ontario [*Library symbol National Library of Canada*] (NLC) ... OOBE
Ottawa Board of Education, Ottawa, ON, Canada [*Library symbol Library of Congress*] (LCLS) ... CaOOBE
Ottawa Citizen, Ontario [*Library symbol National Library of Canada*] (NLC) ... OOCZ
Ottawa Citizen, Ottawa, ON, Canada [*Library symbol Library of Congress*] (LCLS) ... CaOOCz
Ottawa Civic Hospital, Ontario [*Library symbol National Library of Canada*] (NLC) ... OOOCH
Ottawa Civic Hospital, Ottawa, ON, Canada [*Library symbol Library of Congress*] (LCLS) ... CaOOOCH
Ottawa Clinic, Ontario Cancer Foundation, Ontario [*Library symbol National Library of Canada*] (NLC) ... OOOCF
Ottawa Financial [*NASDAQ symbol*] (TTSB) ... OFCP
Ottawa Financial Corp. [*NASDAQ symbol*] (SAG) ... OFCP
Ottawa Financial Corp. [*Associated Press*] (SAG) ... OttawFn
Ottawa Fundraisers Network [*Ontario, Canada*] ... OFN
Ottawa Fundraising Executives [*Ontario, Canada*] ... OFE
Ottawa General Hospital [*Hopital General d'Ottawa*] **Ontario** [*Library symbol National Library of Canada*] (NLC) ... OOHG
Ottawa General Hospital, Ottawa, IL [*Library symbol Library of Congress*] (LCLS) ... IOtGH
Ottawa, IL [*Location identifier FAA*] (FAAL) ... OIX
Ottawa, IL [*AM radio station call letters*] ... WCMY
Ottawa, IL [*FM radio station call letters*] ... WRKX
Ottawa, IL [*FM radio station call letters*] ... WWGN
Ottawa/International, ON [*ICAO location identifier*] (ICLI) ... CYOW
Ottawa, KS [*FM radio station call letters*] (RBYB) ... KCHZ-FM
Ottawa, KS [*AM radio station call letters*] ... KOFO
Ottawa, KS [*FM radio station call letters*] ... KTJO
Ottawa, KS [*FM radio station call letters*] ... KZTO
Ottawa, KS [*Location identifier FAA*] (FAAL) ... OWI
Ottawa, OH [*Location identifier FAA*] (FAAL) ... OWX
Ottawa, OH [*FM radio station call letters*] ... WQTL
Ottawa, ON [*FM radio station call letters*] ... CBO
Ottawa, ON [*AM radio station call letters*] ... CBOF
Ottawa, ON [*FM radio station call letters*] ... CBOF-FM
Ottawa, ON [*Television station call letters*] ... CBOFT
Ottawa, ON [*FM radio station call letters*] ... CBOQ
Ottawa, ON [*Television station call letters*] ... CBOT
Ottawa, ON [*FM radio station call letters*] ... CBOX
Ottawa, ON [*AM radio station call letters*] ... CFGO
Ottawa, ON [*AM radio station call letters*] ... CFRA
Ottawa, ON [*FM radio station call letters*] ... CHEZ
Ottawa, ON [*FM radio station call letters*] (RBYB) ... CHRI-FM
Ottawa, ON [*FM radio station call letters*] ... CHUO
Ottawa, ON [*Television station call letters*] ... CICO-24
Ottawa, ON [*Television station call letters*] ... CIII-6
Ottawa, ON [*AM radio station call letters*] ... CIWW
Ottawa, ON [*FM radio station call letters*] ... CJMJ
Ottawa, ON [*Television station call letters*] ... CJOH
Ottawa, ON [*FM radio station call letters*] ... CKBY
Ottawa, ON [*FM radio station call letters*] ... CKCU
Ottawa, ON [*FM radio station call letters*] (RBYB) ... CKDJ
Ottawa, ON [*FM radio station call letters*] ... CKKL
Ottawa, ON [*FM radio station call letters*] ... CKQB
Ottawa, ON [*ICAO location identifier*] (ICLI) ... CYAA
Ottawa, ON [*ICAO location identifier*] (ICLI) ... CYHQ
Ottawa Public Library [*UTLAS symbol*] ... OPL
Ottawa Public Library [*Bibliotheque Publique d'Ottawa*] **Ontario** [*Library symbol National Library of Canada*] (NLC) ... OOC
Ottawa Public Library, Ottawa, ON, Canada [*Library symbol Library of Congress*] (LCLS) ... CaOOC
Ottawa Roman Catholic Separate School Board, Ontario [*Library symbol National Library of Canada*] (NLC) ... OORCS
Ottawa Roman Catholic Seperate School Board, Ottawa, ON, Canada [*Library symbol*] [*Library of Congress*] (LCLS) ... CaOORCS
Ottawa Teachers' College, Ottawa, ON, Canada [*Library symbol Library of Congress*] (LCLS) ... CaOOTEC
Ottawa Township High School District 140, Ottawa, IL [*Library symbol Library of Congress*] (LCLS) ... IOtHS
Ottawa University, Ottawa, KS [*OCLC symbol*] (OCLC) ... KKO
Ottawa University, Ottawa, KS [*Library symbol Library of Congress*] (LCLS) ... KOtU
Ottawa/Uplands, Canadian Forces Base ON [*ICAO location identifier*] (ICLI) ... CUUP
Ottawa Valley Historical Society, Pembroke, ON, Canada [*Library symbol*] [*Library of Congress*] (LCLS) ... CaOPemO
Ottawa Valley Historical Society, Pembroke, Ontario [*Library symbol National Library of Canada*] (BIB) ... OPEMO
Otter Creek Elementary School District 56, Streator, IL [*Library symbol Library of Congress*] (LCLS) ... IStrOSD
Otter Hound Club of America [*Later, OCA*] (EA) ... OHCA
Otter Tail County Historical Society, Fergus Falls, MN [*Library symbol*] [*Library of Congress*] (LCLS) ... MnFfHi
Otter Tail Power [*NASDAQ symbol*] (TTSB) ... OTTR
Otter Tail Power Co. [*NASDAQ symbol*] (NQ) ... OTTR
Otter Tail Power Co. [*Associated Press*] (SAG) ... OttrTP
Otter Tail Power Co., Fergus Falls, MN [*Library symbol*] [*Library of Congress*] (LCLS) ... MnFfO
Otterbein College, Westerville, OH [*OCLC symbol*] (OCLC) ... OTC
Otterbein College, Westerville, OH [*Library symbol Library of Congress*] (LCLS) ... OWeO
Otterhound Club of America (EA) ... OCA
Otterville, MO [*FM radio station call letters*] ... KOTT
Ottery Saint Mary [*Urban district in England*] ... OTT
Otto Erich Deutsch [*Music cataloger*] ... OED
Otto Fuel II [*Military*] (DNAB) ... OFII
Otto, NM [*Location identifier FAA*] (FAAL) ... OTO
Otto Papiensis [*Flourished, 12th century*] [*Authority cited in pre-1607 legal work*] (DSA) ... Ot
Otto Papiensis [*Flourished, 12th century*] [*Authority cited in pre-1607 legal work*] (DSA) ... Ot P
Otto Papiensis [*Flourished, 12th century*] [*Authority cited in pre-1607 legal work*] (DSA) ... Ot Pp
Otto Pre-Marital Counseling Schedules [*Psychology*] ... OPMCS
Ottobrunn [*Germany ICAO location identifier*] (ICLI) ... EDMR
Ottoman Turkish [*MARC language code Library of Congress*] (LCCP) ... ota
Otto's United States Supreme Court Reports [*91-107 United States*] [*A publication*] (DLA) ... O
Otto's United States Supreme Court Reports [*91-107 United States*] [*A publication*] (DLA) ... Ot
Otto's United States Supreme Court Reports [*91-107 United States*] [*A publication*] (DLA) ... Ott
Otto's United States Supreme Court Reports [*91-107 United States*] [*A publication*] (DLA) ... Otto
Otto's United States Supreme Court Reports [*91-107 United States*] [*A publication*] (DLA) ... Ott's US Sup Ct R
Ottumwa [*Iowa*] [*Airport symbol*] (OAG) ... OTM
Ottumwa Courier, Ottumwa, IA [*Library symbol Library of Congress*] (LCLS) ... IaOtCo
Ottumwa Heights College [*Iowa*] ... OHC
Ottumwa Heights College, Ottumwa, IA [*Library symbol Library of Congress*] (LCLS) ... IaOtC
Ottumwa, IA [*AM radio station call letters*] ... KBIZ
Ottumwa, IA [*AM radio station call letters*] ... KLEE
Ottumwa, IA [*FM radio station call letters*] ... KOTM
Ottumwa, IA [*FM radio station call letters*] ... KTWA
Ottumwa, IA [*Television station call letters*] ... KYOU-TV
Ottumwa Public Library, Ottumwa, IA [*Library symbol Library of Congress*] (LCLS) ... IaOt
Otu [*Colombia*] [*Airport symbol*] (OAG) ... OTU
Otu/Otu [*Colorado ICAO location identifier*] (ICLI) ... SKOT
O-Type Backward-Wave Oscillator (IDOE) ... OBWO
Ouachita Baptist College [*Arkadelphia, AR*] [*Later, OBU*] ... OBC
Ouachita Baptist University [*Arkadelphia, AR*] [*Formerly, OBC*] ... OBU
Ouachita Baptist University, Arkadelphia, AR [*OCLC symbol*] (OCLC) ... AKO
Ouachita Baptist University, Arkadelphia, AR [*Library symbol Library of Congress*] (LCLS) ... ArAO

Ouachita Parish Public Library, Monroe, LA [Library symbol Library of Congress] (LCLS) .... LMO
Ouaco/Paquiepe [New Caledonia] [ICAO location identifier] (ICLI) .... NWWY
Ouadda [Central African Republic] [Airport symbol] (AD) .... ODA
Ouagadougou [Burkina Faso] [ICAO location identifier] (ICLI) .... DHHV
Ouagadougou [Burkina Faso] [Airport symbol] (OAG) .... OUA
Ouagadougou (Airport) [Burkina Faso] [ICAO location identifier] (ICLI) .... DHHH
Ouahigouya [Burkina Faso] [ICAO location identifier] (ICLI) .... DHCC
Ouahigouya [Upper Volta] [Airport symbol] (AD) .... OUG
Ouallam [Niger] [ICAO location identifier] (ICLI) .... DRRU
Ouanaham [Loyalty Islands] [Seismograph station code, US Geological Survey] (SEIS) .... OUA
Ouanda Djalle [Central African Republic] [Airport symbol] (AD) .... ODJ
Ouango Fitini [Ivory Coast] [ICAO location identifier] (ICLI) .... DIOF
Ouargaye [Burkina Faso] [ICAO location identifier] (ICLI) .... DHEY
Ouargla [Algeria] [ICAO location identifier] (ICLI) .... DAUU
Ouargla [Algeria] [Airport symbol] (OAG) .... OGX
Ouarzazate [Morocco] [Airport symbol] (OAG) .... OZZ
Oubain-Like Compound [Biochemistry] .... OLC
Ouchterlony Double Diffusion Test [Immunogel assay] .... ODD
Oudh and Rohilkand Railway Rifles [British military] (DMA) .... ORR
Oudh Appeals [India] [A publication] (DLA) .... OA
Oudh Cases [India] [A publication] (DLA) .... OC
Oudh Code [India] [A publication] (DLA) .... Oud C
Oudh Code [India] [A publication] (DLA) .... Oudh C
Oudh Criminal Cases [India] [A publication] (DLA) .... O Cr C
Oudh Law Journal [India] [A publication] (DLA) .... OL Jour
Oudh Law Journal [India] [A publication] (DLA) .... OLJ
Oudh Law Journal [India] [A publication] (DLA) .... Oudh LJ
Oudh Law Reports [India] [A publication] (DLA) .... OLR
Oudh Law Reports [India] [A publication] (DLA) .... Oudh LR
Oudh Select Cases [India] [A publication] (DLA) .... SC Oudh
Oudh Weekly Notes [India] [A publication] (DLA) .... Oudh Wkly N
Oudh Weekly Notes [India] [A publication] (DLA) .... Oudh WN
Oudh Weekly Notes [India] [A publication] (DLA) .... OWN
Oudomsay [Laos] [ICAO location identifier] (ICLI) .... VLOS
Oudtshoorn [South Africa] [ICAO location identifier] (ICLI) .... FAOH
Oudtshoorn [South Africa] [Airport symbol] (OAG) .... OUH
Oudtshoorn Volunteer Rifles [British military] (DMA) .... OVR
Oued Fodda [Algeria] [Seismograph station code, US Geological Survey] (SEIS) .... OFD
Ouessant [France ICAO location identifier] (ICLI) .... LFEC
Ouesso [Congo] [ICAO location identifier] (ICLI) .... FCOU
Ouesso [Congo] [Airport symbol] (OAG) .... OUE
Ouest [West] [French] .... O
Ouezzane [Morocco] [ICAO location identifier] (ICLI) .... GMFA
Ought (ROG) .... OT
Oughton's Ordo Judiciorum [Order of Judgments] [A publication] (DLA) .... Ought
Ouguiya [Monetary unit] (ODBW) .... UM
Oujda [Morocco] [Airport symbol] (OAG) .... OUD
Oujda/Angads [Morocco] [ICAO location identifier] (ICLI) .... GMFO
Oulton's Index to Irish Statutes [A publication] (DLA) .... Oult Ind
Oulton's Laws of Ireland [A publication] (DLA) .... Oult Laws Ir
Oulu [Finland ICAO location identifier] (ICLI) .... EFOU
Oulu [Finland] [Airport symbol] (OAG) .... OUL
Oulu [Finland] [Seismograph station code, US Geological Survey] (SEIS) .... OUL
Oulun Yliopisto [Oulu University], Oulu, Finland [Library symbol Library of Congress] (LCLS) .... FiOU
Ounce [Unit of weight] (CDAI) .... ou
Ounce [Unit of weight] (AAG) .... oz
Ounce (IDOE) .... oz
Ounce Foot (AAG) .... OZ-FT
Ounce Inch (AAG) .... OZ-IN
Ounce of Prevention [A publication] .... OOP
Ounce-Inch (IDOE) .... oz-in
Ounce-Inches (IDOE) .... oz-in
Ounce-Inches per Second (IAA) .... OIS
Ounces per Cubic Inch .... OZ/IN³
Ounces per Gallon .... OZ/GAL
Ounces per Pint .... OZ/PT
Ounces per Square Foot .... OZ/FT²
Ounces per Square Inch .... OZ/IN²
Ounces per Square Yard .... OZ/YD²
Ounces Troy [Unit of weight] .... OZT
Our Account [Business term] .... O/A
Our Bodies Ourselves [A publication] .... OBOS
Our Developing World [An association] (EA) .... ODW
Our First Men [Slang] .... OFM
Our Helpless Millions Saved [Title of early film] .... OHMS
Our Lady of Angels College, Aston, PA [OCLC symbol] (OCLC) .... LAD
Our Lady of Angels College, Aston, PA [Library symbol Library of Congress] (LCLS) .... PAstO
Our Lady of Carey Seminary, Carey, OH [Library symbol Library of Congress] (LCLS) .... OCareyS
Our Lady of Charity of Refuge (TOCD) .... ROLC
Our Lady of Cincinnati College [Ohio] .... OLCC
Our Lady of Deliverance Syriac, Union City [Diocesan abbreviation] [New Jersey] (TOCD) .... OLD
Our Lady of Guadalupe Parish Library, Hebbronville, TX [Library symbol Library of Congress] (LCLS) .... TxHebO
Our Lady of Lebanon of Los Angeles [Diocesan abbreviation] [California] (TOCD) .... OLL
Our Lady of Light Catholic Library, Santa Barbara, CA [Library symbol Library of Congress] (LCLS) .... CStbOL

Our Lady of Lourdes Hospital, Binghamton, NY [Library symbol Library of Congress] (LCLS) .... NBiL
Our Lady of Lourdes School, Little Falls, MN [Library symbol] [Library of Congress] (LCLS) .... MnLfO
Our Lady of Mercy Academy, Syosset, NY [Library symbol] [Library of Congress] (LCLS) .... NSyoOL
Our Lady of Mercy High School Library, Rochester, NY [OCLC symbol] (OCLC) .... RXC
Our Lady of Mercy School, Hicksville, NY [Library symbol] [Library of Congress] (LCLS) .... NHickOL
Our Lady of the Lake College [Texas] .... OLLC
Our Lady of the Lake College, San Antonio, TX [Library symbol Library of Congress] (LCLS) .... TxSaO
Our Lady of the Lake University [Texas] .... OLLU
Our Lady of the Lake University (GAGS) .... Our Lady Lake U
Our Lady of the Most Holy Trinity Convent (TOCD) .... SOLT
Our Lady of the Sacred Heart (ADA) .... OLSH
Our Lady of Victory Hospital, Lackawanna, NY [Library symbol Library of Congress] (LCLS) .... NLacOH
Our Lady of Victory Missionary Sisters [Roman Catholic religious order] .... OLVM
Our Lady of Victory School, Lucan, MN [Library symbol] [Library of Congress] (LCLS) .... MnLucOLS
Our Main Interest (LAIN) .... OMI
Our Material Returned (AAG) .... OMR
Our Memo (AD) .... om
Our Message .... OM
Our Message [Aviation] (FAAC) .... OMSG
Our Neighbours [A publication] .... ON
Our New Thread [Clark thread designation] .... ONT
Our Telegram (NATG) .... OURTEL
Our Torah Institutions of Israel (EA) .... OTII
Our Town, Maywood, NJ [Library symbol Library of Congress] (LCLS) .... NjMayO
Our World-Underwater Scholarship Society (EA) .... OW-USS
Ouray, CO [FM radio station call letters] .... KURA
Ouray Public Library, Ouray, CO [Library symbol Library of Congress] (LCLS) .... CoOu
Ourinhos [Brazil] [Airport symbol] (OAG) .... OUS
Ourinhos [Brazil ICAO location identifier] (ICLI) .... SBOU
Ourobourus Institute (EA) .... OII
Ours, Inc. (EA) .... OI
Out (NASA) .... O
Out .... O
Out Board .... OB
Out Card in File .... OCIF
Out Cold [Slang] .... OC
Out for Maintenance [Aviation] (FAAC) .... OFM
Out Home [Men's lacrosse position] .... OH
Out Home (AD) .... oh
Out Island Airways (OAG) .... OE
Out of Action (MCD) .... OOA
Out of Area (NVT) .... OOA
Out of Band [Telecommunications] (TEL) .... OOB
Out of Bed [Medicine] .... OOB
Out of Bed with Bathroom Privileges [Medicine] (DAVI) .... OOBBRP
Out of Body [Parapsychology] .... OOB
Out of Bounds (IIA) .... OOB
Out of Charge [Customs] .... O/C
Out of Collector's District [Bookselling] (ROG) .... O/C/D
Out of Commission (NVT) .... OOC
Out of Commission for Parts (AFM) .... OCP
Out of Commission, Special [Vessel status] (DNAB) .... OCSP
Out of Control .... OOC
Out of Controlled Airspace [Aviation] (FAAC) .... OCAS
Out of Gauge [Shipping] (DCTA) .... OOG
Out of Line of Sight (NATG) .... OLOS
Out of Line of Sight (AD) .... olos
Out of Orbit Launch [NASA] (LAIN) .... OOL
Out of Order [International telex abbreviation] (WDMC) .... DER
Out of Order [Telecommunications] (TEL) .... OOO
Out of Oxygen Tent .... OOT
Out of Pelvis [Obstetrics] (DAVI) .... OOP
Out of Place Artifact [Archeology] .... OOPART
Out of Plane .... OOP
Out of Plant .... OOP
Out of Plaster [Orthopedics] (DAVI) .... OOP
Out of Position (MCD) .... OOP
Out of Print [Also, OP] [Publishing] .... OOP
Out of Print [Also, OOP] [Publishing] .... OP
Out of Print [Publishing] (WDMC) .... op
Out of Print and Cancelled [Publishing] (WDMC) .... opc
Out of Print and Searching [Publishing] (WDMC) .... ops
Out of Print at Present [Publishing] (WDMC) .... opp
Out of Print at Present [Publishing] .... OPP
Out of Print, Canceled [Publishing] .... OPC
Out of Print, Searching [Publishing] .... OPS
Out of Production Spares (MCD) .... OPS
Out of Range .... OR
Out of Room (DAVI) .... OOR
Out of School (OICC) .... OOS
Out of School Hours .... OOSH
Out of Sequence (NRCH) .... OOS
Out of Service (AFM) .... O/S
Out of Service (NRCH) .... OOS
Out of Service in Reserve [Military] (CINC) .... OSIR
Out of Stock .... OOS

Out of Stock (NTCM) .... OS
Out of Stock, Canceled [*Business term*] .... OSC
Out of Stock for the Duration [*Business term*] (DGA) .... OSD
Out of Stock, Indefinite [*Business term*] .... OSI
Out of Stock, Temporary [*Business term*] .... OST
Out of Stock, To Follow [*Business term*] .... OSF
Out of the Body Experiences [*Parapsychology*] (ECON) .... OTBE
Out of Tolerance (FAAC) .... OOT
Out of Tolerance .... OT
Out of Use (IAA) .... OOU
Out of View .... OOV
Out of Vision [*Films, television, etc.*] .... OOV
Out of Wedlock .... OW
Out on Pass (DAVI) .... OOP
Out, See Copy [*Proofreader's note*] .... OSC
Out Stealing [*Baseball*] .... OS
Out Temperature (MCD) .... OT
Out the Door (DAVI) .... OTD
Out to Lunch .... OTL
Out to Out [*Technical drawings*] .... O to O
Out Year Costs (MCD) .... OYC
Outagamie County Health Center, Appleton, WI [*Library symbol*] [*Library of Congress*] (LCLS) .... WAOH
Outagamie County Hospital, Appleton, WI [*Library symbol Library of Congress*] (LCLS) .... WAO
Outagamie-Waupaca Counties Federated Library System [*Library network*] .... OWLS
Outage (KSC) .... OUTG
Outback Areas Community Developmnent Trust [*Australia*] .... OACDT
Outback Steakhouse [*NASDAQ symbol*] (TTSB) .... OSSI
Outback Steakhouse, Inc. [*NASDAQ symbol*] (SPSG) .... OSSI
Outback Steakhouse, Inc. [*Associated Press*] (SAG) .... OutbkStk
Outboard (DS) .... O
Outboard .... OB
Outboard (ADA) .... OTBD
Outboard .... OTBD
Outboard .... OUTBD
Outboard (AAG) .... OUTBD
Outboard Boat Manufacturers Association [*Later, NMMA*] (EA) .... OBMA
Outboard Boating Club of America [*Defunct*] (EA) .... OBC
Outboard Data Manager [*Computer science*] (BUR) .... ODM
Outboard Engine Cutoff [*NASA*] (KSC) .... OBECO
Outboard Engine Cutoff [*NASA*] .... OECO
Outboard Engine Cutoff (AD) .... oeco
Outboard Engine Cutoff (AD) .... oecu
Outboard Industry Association [*Later, NMMA*] (EA) .... OIA
Outboard Marine [*NYSE symbol*] (TTSB) .... OM
Outboard Marine Corp. .... OMC
Outboard Marine Corp. [*Associated Press*] (SAG) .... OutbdM
Outboard Message Format Conversion Unit (MCD) .... OMFCU
Outboard Motor Manufacturers Association [*Later, MEMA*] (EA) .... OMMA
Outboard Motorboat .... OMB
Outboard Recorder [*Computer science*] (BUR) .... OBR
Outboard Rotating Shield .... ORS
Outbound (WDAA) .... OB
Outbound [*ICAO designator*] (FAAC) .... OUBD
Outbound .... OUTBD
Outbound Midcourse Correction [*NASA*] (KSC) .... OBMC
Outbound RADAR Control .... ORC
Outbuildings (ROG) .... OUTBGS
Outcare Civil Rehabilitation Council of Western Australia .... OCRCWA
Outcome-Based Education [*School reform*] .... OBE
Outcomes Management System Information Board .... OMSB
Outdoing Line Unit (IAA) .... OLU
Outdoor .... OTDR
Outdoor Adventure Online [*America Online*] .... OAO
Outdoor Advertising Association (BARN) .... OAA
Outdoor Advertising Association of America [*Washington, DC*] (EA) .... OAAA
Outdoor Advertising Total System (PDAA) .... OATS
Outdoor Amusement Business Association (EA) .... OABA
Outdoor Biology Instructional Strategies [*National Science Foundation project*] .... OBIS
Outdoor Club of New South Wales [*Australia*] .... OCNSW
Outdoor Education (AD) .... oe
Outdoor Education Association (EA) .... OEA
Outdoor Educators' Association of Queensland [*Australia*] .... OEAQ
Outdoor Ethics Guild (EA) .... OEG
Outdoor Girl [*Max Factor cosmetic line*] .... OG
Outdoor Microphone System .... OMS
Outdoor Officer [*Customs*] [*British*] .... ODO
Outdoor Power Equipment Aftermarket Association (EA) .... OPEAA
Outdoor Power Equipment Distributors Association (EA) .... OPEDA
Outdoor Power Equipment Institute (EA) .... OPEI
Outdoor Recreation Center Victoria [*Australia*] .... ORCV
Outdoor Recreation Grants-in-Aid Manual .... ORGM
Outdoor Recreation Institute (EA) .... ORI
Outdoor Recreation Resources Review Commission [*Terminated, 1962*] [*Department of the Interior*] .... ORRRC
Outdoor Systems [*NASDAQ symbol*] (TTSB) .... OSIA
Outdoor Systems, Inc. [*Associated Press*] (SAG) .... OdoorS
Outdoor Systems, Inc. [*NASDAQ symbol*] (SAG) .... OSIA
Outdoor Unit Substation .... OUS
Outdoor Writers Association of America (EA) .... OWAA
Outdoors Unlimited (EA) .... OUI
Outer (MSA) .... OTR
Outer .... OTR
Outer Air Battle [*Navy*] (ANA) .... OAB
Outer Anchorage [*Navigation*] .... O/A
Outer Approach Channel .... OAC
Outer Atmospheric Temperature (IAA) .... OAT
Outer Banks Protection Act (AAGC) .... OBPA
Outer Border Zone [*Geology*] .... OBZ
Outer Continental Shelf .... OCS
Outer Continental Shelf Advisory Board [*Marine science*] (MSC) .... OCSAB
Outer Continental Shelf Committee [*Congressional committee*] (MSC) .... OCSC
Outer Continental Shelf Energy Program [*Marine science*] (MSC) .... OCSEP
Outer Continental Shelf Environmental Assessment [*Marine science*] (MSC) .... OCSEA
Outer Continental Shelf Environmental Assessment Program [*Department of Commerce, Department of the Interior*] .... OCSEAP
Outer Continental Shelf Environmental Studies Advisory Commission [*Department of the Interior*] (MSC) .... OCSEAC
Outer Continental Shelf Events File [*Department of the Interior*] (MSC) .... OCSEF
Outer Continental Shelf Lands Act .... OCSLA
Outer Continental Shelf Oil and Gas Supply Model [*Department of Energy*] (GFGA) .... OCSM
Outer Continental Shelf Policy Committee [*California*] (AD) .... OCSPC
Outer Critics Circle (EA) .... OCC
Outer Dead Center (DNAB) .... ODC
Outer Dead Center (AD) .... odc
Outer Defense Zone .... ODZ
Outer Diameter [*Mechanical engineering*] .... OD
Outer (Edge of) Basal Piece .... OBP
Outer Enamel Epithelium [*Dentistry*] .... OEE
Outer Enamel Epithelium (AD) .... oee
Outer Fix Time [*FAA*] (TAG) .... OFT
Outer Fix Time [*Aviation*] (FAAC) .... OFXT
Outer Gimbal .... OG
Outer Gimbal Angle (NASA) .... OGA
Outer Gimbal Assembly (NASA) .... OGA
Outer Gimbal Axis [*NASA*] (IAA) .... OGA
Outer Glide Slope [*Aviation*] (NASA) .... OGS
Outer Glidescope .... OGS
Outer Grid Injection .... OGI
Outer Hair Cells [*of cochlea*] [*Anatomy*] .... OHC
Outer Hair Cells (AD) .... ohc
Outer Harbor Dock and Wharf (AD) .... OHD & W
Outer Head Temperature Control System [*Nuclear energy*] (NRCH) .... OHTCS
Outer Helmholtz Plane [*Physics*] .... OHP
Outer Integument [*Botany*] .... OUI
Outer Jacket .... OJ
Outer Keel .... OK
Outer Keel (AD) .... ok
Outer Lead Bond [*Integrated circuit technology*] .... OLB
Outer Marker [*Part of an instrument landing system*] [*Aviation*] .... OM
Outer Marker (AD) .... om
Outer Marker [*Part of an instrument landing system*] [*Aviation*] .... OMKR
Outer Marker Beacon [*Part of an instrument landing system*] [*Aviation*] .... OMB
Outer Membrane [*Biochemistry*] .... OM
Outer Membrane Protein [*Biochemistry*] .... OMP
Outer Membrane Protein A [*Biochemistry*] .... OMPA
Outer Mitochondrial Membrane [*Also, OMM*] [*Cytology*] .... OMiM
Outer Mitochondrial Membrane [*Also, OMiM*] [*Cytology*] .... OMM
Outer Mold Line (NASA) .... OML
Outer Nuclear Layer [*Anatomy*] .... ONL
Outer Pane [*Aerospace*] (IAA) .... OTPNL
Outer Panel (AAG) .... OP
Outer Passenger Cabin .... OPC
Outer Planet Mission .... OPM
Outer Planet Project .... OPP
Outer Planets Explorer [*NASA*] .... OPE
Outer Planets Grand Tour [*NASA*] .... OPGT
Outer Plexiform Layer [*Retina*] .... OPL
Outer Proliferative Center [*Brain anatomy*] .... OPC
Outer Radiation Belt .... ORB
Outer Radiation Zone .... ORZ
Outer Roll [*Aviation*] (MCD) .... OR
Outer Sheath [*Botany*] .... OS
Outer Shell Photoelectron Spectroscopy .... OSPES
Outer Solar System .... OSS
Outer Solar System Probe .... OSSP
Outer Space Contact .... OSC
Outer Spiral Fibers [*Ear anatomy*] .... OSF
Outer Surface Protein [*Cytology*] .... OSP
Outer Table (MCD) .... OT
Outer Target Azimuth Datum Line .... OTADL
Outer Transport Area .... OTA
Outer Tube .... OT
Outer Tube Centerline .... OTC
Outer Tube Equipment .... OTE
Outer Tube Limit [*Chemical engineering*] .... OTL
Outer Tube Vertical Centerline Target .... OTVCT
Outer Upper Right Quadrant [*Anatomy*] .... OURQ
Outer Vapor Phase Deposition [*Coating technology*] .... OVD
Outer Window Envelope [*Business stationery*] .... OWE
Outer Wing .... OW
Outer Wing Canted Station (MCD) .... OWCS
Outer Wing Panel .... OWP
Outer Wing Station (MCD) .... OWS
Outer Zone Electron .... OZE

Outer Zone Electron Precipitation	OZEP
Outerback End	OBE
Outerbridge's State Reports [97, 98 Pennsylvania] [A publication] (DLA)	Out
Outer-Perimeter Fleet Air Defense	OPFAD
Outfield [Baseball]	O
Outfield [Baseball]	OF
Outfit [Doll collecting]	O/F
Outfit (MSA)	OFT
Outfit	OT
Outfit Supply Activity (MCD)	OSA
Outfits	OTFTS
Outfitting Stock Point	OSP
Outflow Channels [A filamentary mark on Mars]	OC
Outgoing [Computer science]	O/G
Outgoing (AD)	o/g
Outgoing	OUT
Outgoing Calls Barred [Telecommunications] (TEL)	OCB
Outgoing Correspondence Log (AAG)	OCL
Outgoing/Delay Dial [Telecommunications] (TEL)	OGDD
Outgoing Echo Suppressor [Telecommunications] (TEL)	OES
Outgoing/Immediate Dial [Telecommunications] (TEL)	OGID
Outgoing Junction [Telecommunications] (TEL)	OGJ
Outgoing Letter	OL
Outgoing Line	OGL
Outgoing Line Circuit	OLC
Outgoing Long-Wave Radiation [Satellite sensed]	OLR
Outgoing Matching Loss [Telecommunications] (TEL)	OML
Outgoing Message [Telecommunications]	OGM
Outgoing Message Process [Telecommunications] (TEL)	OGP
Outgoing Quality Level	OQL
Outgoing Quality Limit	OQL
Outgoing Relay Set [Telecommunications] (IAA)	OGRS
Outgoing Repeater	OGR
Outgoing Rural Line [Telecommunications] (IAA)	OGRL
Outgoing Rural Selector [Telecommunications] (IAA)	OGRS
Outgoing Secondary Switch (IAA)	OGS
Outgoing Secondary Switches (SAA)	OGS
Outgoing Teletype	OTT
Outgoing Toll Center [Telecommunications] (IAA)	OGTC
Outgoing Toll Circuit [Telecommunications] (IAA)	OGTC
Outgoing Trunk	OGT
Outgoing Trunk Message Junction [Telecommunications] (OA)	OTMJ
Outgoing Trunk Terminal [Telecommunications] (IAA)	OTT
Outgoing Trunk Testing System [Telecommunications] (TEL)	OTTS
Outgoing Unit [Telecommunications] (IAA)	OGU
Outgoing Unit [Military]	OGU
Outgoing Wide-Area Telephone Service [Telecommunications] (TEL)	OUTWATS
Outgoing/Wink Start [Telecommunications] (TEL)	OGWS
Outgrowth Medium [Microbiology] (DAVI)	OGM
Outhouse (ROG)	OUTHO
Outing (ROG)	OUT
Outing Club	OC
Outjo [Namibia] [ICAO location identifier] (ICLI)	FAOJ
Outland Resources [Vancouver Stock Exchange symbol]	OTL
Outlaw HAWK [Naval Air Development Center]	OH
Outlaw Motorcycle Gang	OMG
Outlaw Shark [RADAR surveillance] [Naval Electronic Systems Command]	OS
Outlay (GFGA)	O
Outler Continental Shelf (AD)	ocs
Outlet	O
Outlet [Hawaii] [Seismograph station code, US Geological Survey] (SEIS)	OUT
Outlet	OUTL
Outlet	OUTLT
Outlet	OUTRAN
Outlet Absolute Pressure	OAP
Outlet and Switch Box Association [Defunct] (EA)	OSBA
Outlet Communications, Inc. [NASDAQ symbol] (NQ)	OCOM
Outlet Communications, Inc. [Associated Press] (SAG)	Outlet
Outlet Contact	OC
Outlet Gas Temperature (MSA)	OGT
Outlet Gas Temperature (AD)	ogt
Outlet Guide Vane (AD)	ogv
Outlet Guide Vane	OGV
Outlet Plenum Feature Model [Nuclear energy] (NRCH)	OPFM
Outlet Region Feature Model [Nuclear energy] (NRCH)	ORFM
Outline (VRA)	outl
Outline Acquisition Plan [Army]	OAP
Outline and Installation (MCD)	O & I
Outline and Installation Drawing	OID
Outline Development Plan [Army] (AFIT)	ODP
Outline Feasibility Test [Army]	OFT
Outline Font [Computer science] (PCM)	OLF
Outline Font Demonstration [Computer science]	OLFDEMO
Outline Individual and Collective Training Plan [Army]	OICTP
Outline NATO Operational Objective (MCD)	ONOO
Outline NATO Staff Target	ONST
Outline of Cultural Materials [Human Relations Area Files] [Information retrieval]	OCM
Outline of World Cultures [Human Relations Area Files] [Information retrieval]	OWC
Outline Square Condition [Vision]	OS
Outline Test Plan [Army]	OTP
Outline Test Plan/Resume Sheet (MCD)	OTP/RS
Outlook (AD)	o/l
Outlook [NWS] (FAAC)	OTLK

Outlook and Situation Information System [Department of Agriculture] [Defunct] (IID)	OASIS
Outlook Express [Computer science] (PCM)	OE
Outlook Group [NASDAQ symbol] (TTSB)	OUTL
Outlook Group Corp [NASDAQ symbol] (SPSG)	OUTL
Outlook Group Corp. [Associated Press] (SAG)	OutlkGrp
Outlying Field [Army]	OLF
Out-of-Band Noise	OBN
Out-of-Body Experience [Parapsychology]	OBE
Out-of-Body Experience [Parapsychology]	OOBE
Out-Of-Box Experience [Computer hacker's terminology] (PCM)	OOBE
Out-of-Business (OICC)	OB
Out-of-Date	OD
Out-of-Detent Pitch [Aviation] (MCD)	OODP
Out-of-Detent Roll [Aviation] (MCD)	OODR
Out-of-Ecliptic Mission [NASA] (EGAO)	OOE
Out-Off-On-In [Telecommunications]	OOOI
Out-of-Ground Effect	OGE
Out-of-Home Measurement Bureau [Later, TABMM] (EA)	OMB
Out-of-House Operation (AD)	oho
Out-of-Kilter Algorithm [Mathematics]	OKA
Out-of-Line Igniter [Military] (CAAL)	OLI
Out-of-Line Interrupter (MCD)	OLI
Out-of-Phase [Gynecology]	OOP
Out-of-Phase Loading	OPL
Out-of-Pile Expulsion and Reentry Apparatus [Nuclear energy]	OPERA
Out-of-Pile Systems Test [Nuclear energy] (NRCH)	OPST
Out-of-Pocket (MHDW)	OOP
Out-of-Pocket [Costs/expenses]	OOP
Out-of-Press [Recordings]	OP
Out-of-Roundness [Manufacturing term]	OOR
Out-of-Shot [Photography]	O/S
Out-of-Shot [Photography] (ADA)	OOS
Out-of-Sight Control (MUGU)	OOSC
Out-of-Site Control Center (SAA)	OOSCC
Out-of-Town [Word processing]	OOT
Out-of-Town Executive	OOTE
Outpatient [Medicine]	OP
Outpatient [Medicine] (AAMN)	OPT
Outpatient Appointment Scheduling and Information System	OASIS
Outpatient Basis [Medicine]	OPB
Outpatient Clinci Substation [Medicine] (DAVI)	OCS
Outpatient Clinic [Medicine]	OPC
Outpatient Clinic (Hospital) [Veterans Administration]	OCH
Outpatient Clinic (Independent) [Veterans Administration]	OCI
Outpatient Clinic Substation [Veterans Administration]	OCS
Outpatient Department [or Dispensary] [Medicine]	OPD
Outpatient Hospital [Medicine]	OH
Outpatient Nonavailability Statement [DoD]	ONAS
Outpatient Ophthalmic Surgery Society (EA)	OOSS
Outpatient Physical Therapy [Health insurance] (GHCT)	OPT
Outpatient Physical Therapy/Outpatient Speech Pathology Services [Department of Health and Human Services] (GFGA)	OPT/OSP
Outpatient Professional Psychiatric Clinic [Health insurance] (GHCT)	OPPC
Outpatient Psychiatric Care [Health insurance] (GHCT)	OPC
Outpatient Psychiatric Care Coverage	OPCC
Outpatient Rate [Medicine] (AFM)	OPR
Outpatient Section (DAVI)	OPS
Outpatient Service [Medicine]	OPS
Outpatient Surgery [Health insurance] (GHCT)	OPS
Outpatient Therapy (DAVI)	OPT
Outpatient Treatment [Medicine]	OPT
Outpatient Treatment/Nonservice-Connected [Veterans Administration] (DAVI)	OPT-NSC
Outpatient Treatment/Service Connected [Veterans Administration] (DAVI)	OPT-SC
Outplant Procurement Manufacturing Specification (SAA)	OPMS
Outpost	OP
Outpost Line	OPL
Outpost Line of Resistance	OPLR
Outpulser, Identifier, Trunk Test	OITT
Output (BUR)	O
Output (IDOE)	o
Output (AAG)	OP
Output [Computer science] (IAA)	OT
Output (KSC)	OTPT
Output (AAG)	OUPT
Output (NASA)	OUT
Output	OUTRAN
Output [Business term]	Q
Output Amplitude	OA
Output Amplitude Stability	OAS
Output Axis	OA
Output Blocking Factor [Computer science] (IBMDP)	BO
Output Buffer [Computer science]	OB
Output Buffer Full [Computer science] (IAA)	OBF
Output Bus [Computer science]	OB
Output Capacitance (IDOE)	C_0
Output Channel Buffer Register [Computer science] (IAA)	OCBR
Output Circuit Check [Electronics]	OCC
Output Clock Trigger (IAA)	OCT
Output Computer	OC
Output Control Program	OCP
Output Control Pulse (NASA)	OCP
Output Control Pulses (AD)	ocp

Output Control Register ... OCR
Output Control Subsystem ... OCS
Output Current Booster ... OCB
Output Data (IEEE) ... OD
Output Data Buffer ... ODB
Output Data Control ... ODC
Output Data File ... ODF
Output Data Redundancy (MCD) ... ODR
Output Data Strobe ... ODS
Output Definition Register ... ODR
Output Disable ... OD
Output Discrete Word (MCD) ... ODW
Output Display [*Computer science*] (IAA) ... OD
Output Display Branch [*Computer science*] (IAA) ... ODB
Output Display Unit [*Computer science*] ... ODU
Output Enable [*Semiconductor memory*] (IEEE) ... OE
Output Factor [*Computer science*] (IEEE) ... OF
Output Feedback (NITA) ... OFB
Output Format Table Modification Submodule ... OFTMS
Output Gate [*Computer science*] (IAA) ... OG
Output Impedance ... OI
Output Latch ... OL
Output Limiting Facility [*Computer science*] (MDG) ... OUTLIM
Output Logic Level ... OLL
Output Logic Macrocell [*Computer science*] ... OLMC
Output Makeup ... OMP
Output Measures for Public Libraries [*Clarion University of Pennsylvania*] [*Information service or system*] (IID) ... OUTPUTM
Output Module ... OM
Output Multiplex Synchronizer ... OMS
Output per Man (ODBW) ... OPM
Output per Man Shift (AD) ... oms
Output per Man Shift ... OMS
Output Plate Assembly (MCD) ... OPA
Output Position Map [*Computer science*] (OA) ... OPM
Output Primary [*Electronics*] ... OP
Output Processor Module (MCD) ... OPM
Output Productivity Index ... OPI
Output Reference Axis (IAA) ... ORA
Output Register (MSA) ... OR
Output Register (IAA) ... OUTREG
Output Register Address ... ORA
Output Register Empty (MHDB) ... ORE
Output Resistance (IDOE) ... R_o
Output Resistance (IDOE) ... R_{OUT}
Output Secondary [*Electronics*] ... OS
Output Sequence Number ... OSN
Output Serving Voltage ... OSV
Output Shift Register ... OSR
Output Signal Distribution Unit (MCD) ... OSDU
Output Signal Range ... OSR
Output State Check [*Electronics*] ... OSC
Output Status Register ... OSR
Output Switch Module [*Automotive engineering*] ... OSM
Output Terminal ... OT
Output Terminal Unit (SSD) ... OTU
Output to Display Buffer [*Computer science*] ... ODB
Output to Display Buffer [*Computer science*] (AD) ... odb
Output Transformer (IAA) ... OPT
Output Transformerless Amplifier (DICI) ... OTA
Output Translator [*IBM Corp.*] ... OUTRAN
Output Translator [*IBM Corp.*] (MSA) ... OUTXLTR
Output Unit [*Computer science*] (IAA) ... OU
Output Voltage ... OV
Output Voltage (IDOE) ... V_o
Output Voltage (IDOE) ... V_{OUT}
Output-to-Display Parity Error [*Computer science*] (SAA) ... ODP
Output-Transformerless (SAA) ... OTL
Outside ... OS
Outside Air Intake (NRCH) ... OAI
Outside Air Temperature [*Aviation*] ... OAT
Outside Back Cover [*Publishing*] (WDMC) ... OBC
Outside Battery Limits [*Chemical engineering*] ... OSBL
Outside Broadcast (EY) ... OB
Outside Bugs [*Nonresident staff at a school*] [*British*] (DSUE) ... OB
Outside Cable Rehabilitation II [*Army*] (RDA) ... OSCAR II
Outside Circumference (MSA) ... OC
Outside Communications Cable Plant (CET) ... OCCP
Outside Continental Limits of the United States (AD) ... OConUS
Outside Continental Limits of the United States [*Military*] (DNAB) ... OUTCONUS
Outside Continental Limits of United States [*Military*] ... OCLUS
Outside Continental United States [*Military*] (AFIT) ... EXTRACONUS
Outside Continental United States [*Military*] ... OCONUS
Outside Cylinders [*Trains*] [*British*] ... O
Outside Design and Development ... ODD
Outside Diameter (AD) ... od
Outside Diameter ... OD
Outside Diameter of Female Coupling (AD) ... odfc
Outside Diameter of Inner Conductor ... ODIC
Outside Diameter of Male Coupling (AD) ... odmc
Outside Diameter Tube (MSA) ... ODT
Outside Dimension ... OD
Outside Dimension (AD) ... od
Outside Edge [*Skating*] ... O
Outside Engineering Personnel (MCD) ... OEP
Outside Face [*Technical drawings*] ... OF
Outside Face (AD) ... of
Outside Front Cover [*Publishing*] (NTCM) ... OFC
Outside Gage Marks (SAA) ... OGM
Outside Guard ... OG
Outside Guardian [*Freemasonry*] (ROG) ... OG
Outside Helix Angle ... OHA
Outside Helix Angle (AD) ... oha
Outside Left [*Soccer position*] ... OL
Outside Left Position [*Dancing*] ... OLP
Outside Linebacker [*Football*] ... OLB
Outside Location Engineer (MCD) ... OLE
Outside Mail (AFM) ... OSM
Outside Manufacturing ... OM
Outside Mold Line [*Technical drawings*] ... OML
Outside Mold Line (AD) ... oml
Outside of Metal (MSA) ... O/M
Outside of Metal ... OSM
Outside of the Battery Limits [*Engineering economics*] ... OBL
Outside Plant [*Telecommunications*] (TEL) ... OSP
Outside Plant Planning, Engineering, and Construction Operations System (MCD) ... OPEOS
Outside Procured Stores (AAG) ... OSP
Outside Procurement [*or Purchase*] **Inspection** (AAG) ... OPI
Outside Production ... OP
Outside Production Consignment Order ... OPCO
Outside Production Group ... OPG
Outside Production Material Sales Order ... OPMSO
Outside Production Operation Sheet (MCD) ... OPOS
Outside Production Order (SAA) ... OPO
Outside Production Requirement Record (SAA) ... OPRR
Outside Production Service (SAA) ... OPS
Outside Purchase (WDAA) ... OSP
Outside Purchase Order (SAA) ... OPO
Outside Quality Control (KSC) ... OQC
Outside Radius [*Technical drawings*] ... OR
Outside Reactor Building [*Nuclear energy*] (NRCH) ... ORB
Outside Rear View [*Mirrors*] [*Automotive features*] ... OSRV
Outside Right [*Soccer position*] ... OR
Outside Right Position [*Dancing*] ... ORP
Outside School Hours Care ... OSHC
Outside Screw and Yoke ... OS & Y
Outside Screw and Yoke (IAA) ... OSAY
Outside Sentinel ... OS
Outside Temperature Sensor [*Automotive engineering*] ... OTS
Outside the United States ... OUTUS
Outside Trim Template (MSA) ... OTT
Outside Vapor Deposition [*Coating technology*] ... OVD
Outside Vapor Phase Oxidation [*Glass technology*] ... OVPO
Outside Vendor Personnel ... OVP
Outsiders Club (EAIO) ... OC
Outside-Wheel Turning Angle [*Automotive engineering*] ... OTA
Outsize [*Of clothes*] ... OS
Outsized Cargo Tanker Aircraft ... OCTA
Outstanding ... O/S
Outstanding [*Business term*] ... OUTSTDG
Outstanding [*Business term*] (MHDW) ... outstg
Outstanding Airman of the Year Ribbon [*Military decoration*] (AFM) ... OAYR
Outstanding Balance List [*IRS*] ... OBL
Outstanding Civil Engineering Achievement [*Award*] [*American Society of Civil Engineers*] ... OCEA
Outstanding Civilian Service Award ... OCSA
Outstanding Claims Advance [*Insurance*] (AIA) ... OCA
Outstanding Debt [*Finance*] (MHDB) ... OD
Outstanding Hardware Problem Report (MCD) ... OHPR
Outstanding Leg [*NASA*] (KSC) ... OSL
Outstanding Media Advertising by Restaurants (AD) ... OMARS
Outstanding Merchandising Achievement Award ... OMA
Outstanding Performance Rating [*Military*] (RDA) ... OPR
Outstanding Performance Rating with Quality Step Increase [*Military*] (DNAB) ... ORQ
Outstanding Requisition System (DNAB) ... ORS
Outstanding Requisitions Defeat Endurance Readiness (DNAB) ... ORDER
Outstanding Reserve Airman Appointment Program ... ORAAP
Outstanding Resource Waters [*Water quality standards*] [*Environmental Protection Agency*] ... ORW
Outstanding Superior Kitchen All-Rounder [*Trademark of Sunbeam Corp.*] ... OSKAR
Outstanding Young American Pianist ... OYAP
Outstanding Young Man (DICI) ... OYM
Outstate Facility Network Planning System [*Telecommunications*] (TEL) ... OFNPS
Outstation (MCD) ... OS
Out-to-Out (AAG) ... OTO
Outward (ROG) ... OUTWD
Outward Bound (EA) ... OB
Outward Bound Australia ... OBA
Outward Grade of Service (DNAB) ... OGOS
Outward-Rectifying Chloride Channel [*Biochemistry*] ... ORCC
Ouvea [*Loyalty Islands*] [*Airport symbol*] (OAG) ... UVE
Ouvea/Ouloup, Iles Loyaute [*New Caledonia*] [*ICAO location identifier*] (ICLI) ... NWWV
Ouvriers Unis de l'Electricite, de la Radio, et de la Machinerie d'Amerique [*United Electrical, Radio, and Machine Workers of America - UE*] ... OUE
Ouvriers Unis des Textiles d'Amerique [*United Textile Workers of America - UTWA*] ... OUTA

Ouzinkie, AK [Location identifier FAA] (FAAL)	KOZ
Ova and Parasites [Medicine]	O & P
Ova, Blood, and Parasites [Medicine] (MAE)	OBP
Ova, Cysts, Parasites [Medicine] (MEDA)	OCP
Ova, Cysts, Parasites [Gastroenterology] (DAVI)	OCP
Oval	OV
Oval [Postal Service standard] (OPSA)	OVAL
Oval [Commonly used] (OPSA)	OVL
Oval Head (AD)	oh
Oval Head	OVHD
Oval Paint	OVP
Oval Ring Seal	ORS
Oval Track Equipment Association (EA)	OTEA
Ovalbumin [Also, OV, OVA, OVAL] [Biochemistry]	OA
Ovalbumin [Also, OA, OVA, OVAL] [Biochemistry]	OV
Ovalbumin [Also, OA, OV, OVAL] [Biochemistry]	OVA
Ovalbumin [Also, OA, OV, OVA]	OVAL
Oval-Headed Screw (DAC)	OHS
Ovalocytes [Laboratory science] (DAVI)	OVAL
Ovalocytosis [Laboratory science] (DAVI)	OVALO
Ovarian Androgenic Hyperfunction [Medicine] (DMAA)	OAH
Ovarian Ascorbic Acid Depletion [Test]	OAAD
Ovarian Ascorbic Acid Depletion Material	OAADM
Ovarian Carcinoma [Oncology]	OVCA
Ovarian Cholesterol Depletion [Test]	OCD
Ovarian Cholesterol Depletion [Medicine] (AD)	ocd
Ovarian Follicular Fluid Peptide [Endocrinology]	OFFP
Ovarian Growth Factor [Medicine]	OGF
Ovarian Hyperstimulation Syndrome [Medicine] (DMAA)	OHS
Ovarian Papillary Adenocarcinoma [Oncology]	OPA
Ovarian Tumor Registry [Medicine]	OTR
Ovarian Vein Plasma [Endocrinology]	OVP
Ovarian Vein Serum [Endocrinology]	OVS
Ovarian Volume [Gynecology]	OV
Ovariectomized [Gynecology]	OVAX
Ovariectomized [Gynecology]	OVX
Ovariectomized [Gynecology] (DAVI)	OVX
Ovary	O
Ovary (ADA)	OV
Ovary Pubescence - Curly [Botany]	OVPC
Ovary Pubescence, Glandular [Botany]	OVPG
Ovary Style Length [Botany]	OSTL
Ovation (WGA)	O
Ovda [Israel] [ICAO location identifier] (ICLI)	LLOV
Oven	O
Oven [Refers to the open space below the stage in a theater] [Slang] (DSUE)	OV
Oven Dried (AD)	od
Oven Dry	OD
Oven Dry Basis	ODB
Oven-Controlled Crystal Oscillator	OCXO
Oven-Dried Weight	ODW
Ovenstone Factor [Medicine] (MAE)	Of
Ovenstone Factor (AD)	Of
Over	O
Over (ROG)	O'ER
Over (AAG)	OV
Over (VRA)	ov
Over All Rate [Real estate] (DICI)	OAR
Over and Short Account [Business term]	O & S
Over Armor Technology Synthesis (RDA)	OATS
Over Bath [Classified advertising] (ADA)	OB
Over Burner Air	OBA
Over Castle Rock [New York] [Seismograph station code, US Geological Survey] (SEIS)	OCN
Over Center [Automotive engineering]	O/CTR
Over Consolidated Ratio [Nuclear energy] (NUCP)	OCR
Over Current	OC
Over Drive [Automotive engineering]	O/DRV
Over Fifties Association [Australia]	OFA
Over Fire Air [Combustion technology]	OFA
Over Fire Air Port	OAP
Over Frequency Relay	OFR
Over Mountains [NWS] (FAAC)	OMTNS
Over My Dead Body	OMDB
Over Pressure (AAG)	OP
Over Run (MHDW)	OR
Over, Short, and Damaged [Report] [Shipping] (MSA)	OS & D
Over, Short, and Damaged [Report] [Shipping] (MCD)	OSD
Over, Short, and Damaged Report [Shipping]	OS & DR
Over Stress Testing	OST
Over the Hill Gang, International (EA)	OHGI
Over the Hill in October [Used prior to the bombing of Pearl Harbor to typify a recruit's view of US Army life]	OHIO
Over the Line (WDAA)	OTL
Over the Nose [Aviation]	OTN
Over the Shoulder Shot [Also, OS] [Cinematography] (NTCM)	X/S
Over the State [Regarding distribution]	OS
Over the Top [British Slang]	OTT
Over the Wing [Aircraft]	OTW
Over There (ADA)	OT
Over Thirty but Still Swinging Club	OTBSSC
Over Voltage	O/V
Over Voltage - Under Voltage (MCD)	O/V-U/V
Over Water (WDAA)	OW
Overachievers Anonymous (EA)	OA

Over-Achieving Women	OW
Overall (IAA)	O
Overall	O/A
Overall [Technical drawings]	OA
Overall	OA
Overall Absolute Deviation [Mathematics]	OAD
Overall Average Percentage (DNAB)	OAP
Overall Combat Systems Operability Test (NVT)	OCSOT
Overall Connection Loss [Telecommunications] (TEL)	OCL
Overall Depth (WDAA)	OAD
Overall Depth [Typography] (DGA)	OD
Overall Dimensions (IAA)	OAD
Overall Distance Standard [for golf balls] [Adopted by the United States Golf Association in 1976]	ODS
Overall Documentation Plan [NATO] (NATG)	ODP
Overall Echo Return Loss	OERL
Overall Economic Development Program [Bureau of Indian Affairs]	OEDP
Overall Efficiency Index	OEI
Overall Height [Automotive specifications]	OAH
Overall Height [of the Vehicle] [TII] (TAG)	OH
Overall Length [Automotive specifications]	OAL
Overall Level (NASA)	OAL
Overall Manufacturers' Association (AD)	OMA
Overall Manufacturers' Association of Great Britain (BI)	OMA
Overall Missile Guidance Tests (MCD)	OMGT
Overall Modernity [Sociological scale]	OM
Overall NATO Command (NATG)	ONC
Overall Objective Loudness Rating [of telephone connections] (IEEE)	OOLR
Overall Performance Appraisal Certification [Environmental Protection Agency] (GFGA)	OPAC
Overall Performance Category	OPC
Overall Performance Index [Finance]	OPI
Overall Planning and Optimization and Machining Process (MHDI)	OPOMP
Overall Plume Enhancement Factor [Space Shuttle] [NASA]	OPEF
Overall Position [Tertiary entrance]	OP
Overall Power Watt Level (PDAA)	OAPWL
Overall Pressure Ratio	OPR
Overall Probability of Attack (DNAB)	OPA
Overall Program Design (OICC)	OPD
Overall Rating [Broadcasting]	O
Overall Reading Grade Level (MCD)	ORGL
Overall Reference Equivalent (NITA)	ORE
Overall Report	OR
Overall Resistance (IAA)	OR
Over-All Sound Pressure (PDAA)	OASP
Overall Sound Pressure Level	OASPL
Overall System Effectiveness (IAA)	OSE
Overall Systems Combat Operability Test [Navy] (ANA)	OSCOT
Overall Test	OAT
Overall Test (KSC)	OT
Overall Test Set	OATS
Overall Transfer Function Response	OTFR
Overall Width	OAW
Overall Width [of the Vehicle] [TII] (TAG)	OW
Overalls [Freight]	OVAL
Overarching Integrated Product Team [Army]	OIPT
Overboard (AAG)	OB
Overboard (AAG)	OVBD
Overburden Drill (PDAA)	OD
Overcast	OC
Overcast (AABC)	OCST
Overcast (AD)	ocst
Overcast	OVC
Overcast (AFM)	OVCST
Overcharge	O/C
Overcharge (AD)	o/c
Overcome [or Overtaken] by Events	OBE
Overcoming Mobility Barriers International (EA)	OMBI
Overcurrent	OC
Overcurrent Relay (MSA)	OCR
Overdeduction	OVDED
Overdose [of narcotics]	OD
Overdose (AD)	od
Overdraft [or Overdrawn] [Banking]	OD
Overdraft Charge [Banking] (AD)	oc
Overdrive [TII] (TAG)	O/D
Overdrive (AD)	od
Overdrive (AAG)	OD
Overdue	Od
Overeaters Anonymous (EA)	OA
Overfill (NASA)	OVF
Overfill	OVF
Overfill Shutoff Sensor (KSC)	OFSO
Overfire Airport [Combustion technology]	OA
Overflight Traffic [Aviation] (FAAC)	OTFC
Overflow	OF
Overflow [Computer science]	OFL
Overflow	OV
Overflow [Computer science]	OVF
Overflow (AAG)	OVFL
Overflow (HGAA)	ovflo
Overflow Heat Removal System [Nuclear energy] (NRCH)	OHRS
Overflow Level	OL
Overflow Sequential Access Method [Computer science]	OSAM
Overfrequency (MSA)	OF

Overfull Employment [Economics]	OFN
Overgrowth Stimulating Factor [Cancer cause]	OSF
Overhandled [Freight]	OVHDLD
Overhanging	o/h
Overhaul (AD)	OH
Overhaul	OHL
Overhaul (AAG)	OVHL
Overhaul Alignment Kit (MCD)	OAK
Overhaul and Maintenance, Navy (MCD)	O & MN
Overhaul and Repair	O & R
Overhaul and Repair	OAR
Overhaul and Repair	OR
Overhaul and Repair	ORI
Overhaul and Repair Instruction	ORM
Overhaul and Repair Manual	OCR
Overhaul Component Requirement [NASA] (KSC)	OCD
Overhaul Consumption Data	OCL
Overhaul Cycle Limit	ohf
Overhaul Factor (AD)	OMR
Overhaul, Maintenance, and Repair (MCD)	OM
Overhaul Manual (MCD)	ORT
Overhaul RADAR Technology	ORE
Overhaul, Rebuild, and Exchange (MCD)	OHRI
Overhaul Recurrent Item (CINC)	OHRI
Overhaul Removal Interval [Military] (AFIT)	OHRI
Overhaul Removal Item (CINC)	ohrf
Overhaul Replacement Factor (AD)	ORF
Overhaul Replacement Factor (MCD)	ORR
Overhaul Replacement Rate	OVS
Overhaul Specification (NG)	OTRO
Overhaul Test Requirement Outline	OH
Overhead	oh
Overhead (AD)	OVHD
Overhead (AAG)	OVRHD
Overhead	OAH
Overhead Air Hoist	ohc
Overhead Cam (AD)	OHC
Overhead Camshaft [Automotive term]	OCR
Overhead Component Requirement (IAA)	OHC
Overhead Cupboards [Classified advertising] (ADA)	OHD
Overhead Display	OER
Overhead Expenditure Request	OHF
Overhead Fire (MCD)	OHF
Overhead Frame (MEDA)	OGW
Overhead Ground Wire	OHLH
Overhead Heavy Load Handling [Nuclear energy] (NRCH)	OIV
Overhead Inlet Valve [Automotive engineering]	OL
Overhead Line	OHMS
Overhead Machine Screw [Technical drawings]	O-MAN
Overhead Manipulator [For handling loads in a nuclear environment]	OMR
Overhead Materials Requirement [Manufacturing]	OPS
Overhead Positioning System [AEC]	OVHD PWR CAB
Overhead Power Cable [Nautical charts]	OPA
Overhead Precautionary Approach	ohp
Overhead Projection (AD)	OPT
Overhead Projection Transparency (MCD)	OHP
Overhead Projector (ADA)	OSS
Overhead Speaker System [Automotive engineering]	OHST
Overhead Storage Tank [Nuclear energy] (NRCH)	OSI
Overhead Supply Inventory (MCD)	OSAR
Overhead Systems Appraisance Research (IAA)	OT
Overhead Transparencies	OTP
Overhead Trickle Purification (PDAA)	OVA
Overhead Value Analysis (ADA)	OHV
Overhead Valve	ohv
Overhead Valve (AD)	OHV
Overhead Vent (WDAA)	OWAP
Overhead Warning Annunciator Panel (MCD)	OHWS
Overhead Wood Screw [Technical drawings]	OHC
Over-Head-Cam [TII] (TAG)	oheat
Overheat (AD)	OHEAT
Overheat	OVHT
Overheat (NASA)	OVHT
Overheat	oht
Overheating Temperature (AD)	OHT
Overheating Temperature (PDAA)	
Overlake Hospital, Medical Library, Bellevue, WA [Library symbol Library of Congress] (LCLS)	WaBOH
Overland	O/LAND
Overland [A publication]	Overl
Overland Air Superiority Training [Navy] (DOMA)	OAST
Overland Common Point [Imported item] [Business term]	OCP
Overland Common Points (AD)	ocp
Overland Flow Research Facility [Army]	OFRF
Overland, MO [FM radio station call letters]	KRHS
Overland Monthly [A publication] (ROG)	OM
Overland Park, KS [AM radio station call letters]	KCCV
Overland RADAR Technology (MCD)	ORT
Overlanded	O/LANDED
Overlap	OL
Overlap (IAA)	OVL
Overlap Shear	OLS
Overlap Slotted Container [Packaging]	OSC
Overlap Technician	OT
Overlap Technician Supervisor (SAA)	OTS

Overlap Telling (MCD)	OT
Overlap Telling and Surveillance (SAA)	OTS
Overlapping Resolution Mapping [Computer science]	ORM
Overlapping Spreading Centers [Geology]	OSC
Overlay (NASA)	OL
Overlay (IAA)	OVL
Overlay	OVLAY
Overlay Battle Manager	OLBM
Overlay Demonstration Program [Military]	ODP
Overlay File [Computer science]	OVL
Overlay File [Computer science]	OVR
Overlay Interceptor	OLI
Overlay Reproducer System	ORS
Overload	O/L
Overload	OL
Overload	OL
Overload (AAG)	OVLD
Overload	OVLD
Overload Control Process [Telecommunications] (TEL)	OCP
Overload Control Subsystem [Telecommunications] (TEL)	OCS
Overload Detection [Telecommunications] (TEL)	OD
Overload Gross Weight (NG)	OGW
Overload Relay	OLR
Overload Relay (AD)	olr
Overload Relay (KSC)	OR
Overload Relay (IEEE)	ORLY
Overload Warning System (MCD)	OWS
Overload Warning Unit (MCD)	OWU
Overload-Reverse Current (NASA)	O/L-RC
Overlong Sentence [Used in correcting manuscripts, etc.]	OVNGT
Overnight (FAAC)	OCL
Over-Night Cargo Ltd. [Nigeria] [ICAO designator] (FAAC)	ONL
Overnight Loan (ADA)	
Overnight Message Service [Diversified Data Processing and Consulting, Inc.] [Oak Park, MI] [Telecommunications] (TSSD)	OMS
Overnight Statewide Customer Accounting Reporting (IAA)	OSCAR
Over-Ocean Communications	OOC
Overpaid (ROG)	O/PD
Overpaid (AFM)	OVPD
Overpaid Entry Certificate (DS)	OEC
Overpaid Last Account	OPL
Overpass	OPAS
Overpass [Postal Service standard] (OPSA)	OPAS
Overpass [Commonly used] (OPSA)	OVERPASS
Overplus (DGA)	OVERS
Overpower	OVPWR
Overpressure Layer Chromatography	OPLC
Overpressure [or Overpressurization] Protection System [Nuclear energy] (NRCH)	OPS
Overpressurization Protection Switch (IEEE)	OPPS
Overpressurization Protection System (IEEE)	OPPS
Overpressurized	OVPRESS
Overpressurized Thin-Layer Chromatography	OPTLC
Overpriced (WDAA)	O/P
Overprint	OP
Overprint [Journalism] (WDMC)	op
Overproof [Distilling]	OP
Overrange [System or element] (IEEE)	O/R
Overrange Detection and Correction [Analytical chemistry]	ORDAC
Overreaching Transfer Trip (IAA)	ORTT
Override (KSC)	O/R
Override (KSC)	ORIDE
Override (AAG)	OVRD
Override	OVRD
Override Control BITS [Binary Digits] [Computer science]	OCB
Overriding Cam Valve	OCV
Overriding Cam Valve	ORCV
Overruled [Ruling in cited case expressly overruled] [Used in Shepard's Citations] [Legal term] (DLA)	o
Overruled [Legal shorthand] (LWAP)	OV
Overruled In [or Overruling] [Legal term] (DLA)	Overr
Overrun (AFM)	OVRN
Overrun Clutch	ORC
Overrun Standard Approach Lighting System [Aviation] (DA)	OVRN
Overrunning [Automotive engineering]	O/RUNN
Overrunning (DA)	OVRNG
Over-Sand Vehicle	OSV
Overscene [Films, television, etc.]	OS
Oversea [Military]	OS
Oversea Duty Selection Date [Air Force]	ODSD
Oversea Employment Office [Air Force] (AFM)	OEO
Oversea Intelligence Data Processing System	OIDPS
Oversea Internal Defense Policy [Army] (AABC)	OIDP
Oversea Replacement [Army]	OSREPL
Oversea Returnee [Military]	OSR
Oversea Returnee [Army]	OSRET
Oversea Terminal Arrival Date [Army] (AABC)	OTAD
Oversea Theater Requisitioning Authority [Military]	OTRA
Overseas	O/SEAS
Overseas [Aviation] (FAAC)	OVSEA
Overseas Affairs Branch [Army]	OAB
Overseas Air Preparation Unit [British military] (DMA)	OAPU
Overseas Air Traffic Control	OATC
Overseas Air Weapons Control System	OAWCS

Overseas Appointments Bureau [Christian Education Movement] [British] (AEBS) .... OAB
Overseas Automotive Club (EA) .... OAC
Overseas Bankers' Club [British] .... OBC
Overseas Base Facilities Summary [Navy] .... OBFS
Overseas Book Centre .... OBC
Overseas Booksellers' Clearing House (DGA) .... OBCH
Overseas Branch Transfer (AD) .... OBT
Overseas Brats [Commercial firm] (EA) .... OB
Overseas Broadcast [or Broadcasting] (IAA) .... OB
Overseas Broadcasting Representatives Association (IAA) .... OBRA
Overseas Chinese (AD) .... OC
Overseas Chinese Association of South Australia .... OCASA
Overseas Chinese Banking Corp. (AD) .... OCBC
Overseas Christian Fellowship Australia .... OCFA
Overseas Citizens Voting Rights Act .... OCVRA
Overseas Civil Servants (AD) .... OCS
Overseas College of Defence Studies [British] .... OCDS
Overseas Combined Federal Campaign [Red Cross] .... OCFC
Overseas Command Records Holding Area [Army] .... OCRHA
Overseas Commands [Air Force] .... OC
Overseas Common Point [Exported item] [Business term] .... OCP
Overseas Company Registration Agents Ltd. (ECON) .... OCRA
Overseas Container Line (AD) .... OCL
Overseas Container Line Unit (AD) .... OCLU
Overseas Container Lines and Associated Container Transport (AD) .... OCL/ACT
Overseas Containers Ltd. (AD) .... OCL
Overseas Containers of Australia, Ltd. (AD) .... OCAL
Overseas Countries and Territories [Common Market] .... OCT
Overseas Country (ODBW) .... OC
Overseas Courier Service (AD) .... OCS
Overseas Currency Loan .... OCL
Overseas Custody (Child Removal) .... OCCR
Overseas Deployment Data [Military] .... ODD
Overseas Deployment Training [Army] .... ODT
Overseas Development Administration [British] (EAIO) .... ODA
Overseas Development Agency [British] .... ODA
Overseas Development Aid .... ODA
Overseas Development Assistance (AD) .... ODA
Overseas Development Bank [Investors' Overseas Services] .... ODB
Overseas Development Corp. (AD) .... ODC
Overseas Development Corporation (NADA) .... ODC
Overseas Development Council (EA) .... ODC
Overseas Development Institute (EA) .... ODI
Overseas Development Institute Ltd. (AD) .... ODIL
Overseas Development Ministry [British] .... ODM
Overseas Development Natural Resources Institute [British Information service or system] (IID) .... ODNRI
Overseas Development Network (EA) .... ODN
Overseas Diplomacy Coordinator (DNAB) .... ODC
Overseas Discharge and Replacement Depot .... OD & RD
Overseas Doctors Association in the United Kingdom [British] .... ODA
Overseas Duty .... OSD
Overseas Duty Selection Date (AD) .... odsd
Overseas Economic Cooperation Fund (AD) .... OECF
Overseas Economic Intelligence Committee [Military] .... OEIC
Overseas Education Association (EA) .... OEA
Overseas Education Fund [Later, OEFI] (EA) .... OEF
Overseas Educational Service [Defunct] .... OES
Overseas Employment Program [DoD] .... OEP
Overseas Exchange Transactions (AD) .... OET
Overseas Expenditure Reduction Program [Military] (AFM) .... OERP
Overseas Family Allowance [British military] (DMA) .... OFA
Overseas Family Residence Program [Military] (NVT) .... OFRP
Overseas Finance and Trade Corp. (AD) .... OFTC
Overseas Fixed Telecommunications System (AD) .... OFTS
Overseas Flight Assistance Service .... OFAS
Overseas Food Corp. (AD) .... OFC
Overseas Food Corp. (NADA) .... OFC
Overseas Fuel Region (AFIT) .... OFR
Overseas Ground Station (MCD) .... OGS
Overseas Headquarters [British military] (DMA) .... OHQ
Overseas Homeported Units [Navy] (NVT) .... OHU
Overseas Hotel Corp. (AD) .... OHC
Overseas Housing Allowance .... OHA
Overseas Indian Congress of North America [Defunct] (EA) .... OICNA
Overseas Internal Security Program [Army] .... OISP
Overseas Investment [Economics] .... O/I
Overseas Investment Commission (AD) .... OIC
Overseas Investors Services (AD) .... OIS
Overseas Issues Identification Meeting (DNAB) .... OIIM
Overseas Jazz Club (EA) .... OJC
Overseas Labour Consultative Committee [British] (DCTA) .... OLCC
Overseas Liaison and Consultancy Department (NITA) .... OLCD
Overseas Liaison Committee [of the American Council on Education] [Later, Division of International Educational Relations of the American Council on Education] (EA) .... OLC
Overseas Limited Storage Site [Army] .... OLSS
Overseas Mail [British] .... OM
Overseas Manpower [British] .... OMP
Overseas Media Visitor .... OMV
Overseas Military Forces of Canada [World War I] .... OMFC
Overseas Military Personnel Charter (MCD) .... OMPC
Overseas Mineral Resource Development (AD) .... OMRD
Overseas Minister [World War I] [Canada] .... OM

Overseas Mission Society [Defunct] (EA) .... OMS
Overseas Missionary Fellowship, USA Headquarters (EA) .... OMF
Overseas National Airways [Belgium ICAO designator] (FAAC) .... ONA
Overseas National Airways (GAVI) .... OV
Overseas National Airways, Inc. .... ONA
Overseas National Airways, Inc. [Air carrier designation symbol] .... ONAX
Overseas News Agency .... ONA
Overseas Number Group Analysis [Telecommunications] (TEL) .... ONGA
Overseas Operating Committee [World War II] .... OOC
Overseas Operational Storage Site [Army] .... OOSS
Overseas Plexiglas Unit .... OPU
Overseas Policy Defence Committee [British] .... OPD
Overseas Policy Defence Committee [British] (DI) .... OPDC
Overseas Post (ADA) .... OP
Overseas Press and Media Association [British] (EAIO) .... OPMA
Overseas Press Club (NADA) .... OPO
Overseas Press Club of America (EA) .... OPC
Overseas Press Club of America (WDAA) .... OPCA
Overseas Private Enterprise Development Corp. [Proposed successor to Agency for International Development] .... OPEDC
Overseas Private Investment Corp. [US International Development Cooperation Agency] [Washington, DC] .... OPIC
Overseas Private Investment Corp. .... OPIC
Overseas Private Investment Corp., Washington, DC [Library symbol Library of Congress] (LCLS) .... DOPI
Overseas Private Investment Corp., Washington, DC [OCLC symbol] (OCLC) .... OVP
Overseas Products Group [Department of Trade] [British] .... OPG
Overseas Project Fund [British Overseas Trade Board] (DS) .... OPF
Overseas Reconstruction Committee [British World War II] .... ORC
Overseas Records Center [Military] .... ORCEN
Overseas Replacement [Military] .... OR
Overseas Replacement [Military] .... ORPL
Overseas Replacement Depot [Military] .... ORD
Overseas Research Center [Wake Forest University] [Research center] (RCD) .... ORC
Overseas Return Placement System [Military] .... ORPS
Overseas Sales and Marketing Association of America [Lake Bluff, IL] (EA) .... OSMA
Overseas Schools Advisory Council [Department of State] [Washington, DC] (EGAO) .... OSAC
Overseas Security Advisory Council [Department of State] [Washington, DC] (EGAO) .... OSAC
Overseas Security Eligibility [DoD] .... OSE
Overseas Service Aid Scheme .... OSAS
Overseas Service Ribbon [Military decoration] .... OSR
Overseas Services Storage Facility .... OSSF
Overseas Settlement Committee [World War I] [British] .... OSC
Overseas Settlement Department [World War I] [British] .... OSD
Overseas Shiphldg [NYSE symbol] (TTSB) .... OSG
Overseas Shipholding Group, Inc. [NYSE symbol] (SPSG) .... OSG
Overseas Shipholding Group, Inc. [Associated Press] (SAG) .... OvShip
Overseas Staff College [British] .... OSC
Overseas Standards Digest [A publication] (ADA) .... OSD
Overseas Student Health Coverage .... OSHC
Overseas Students Trust [British] (AEBS) .... OST
Overseas Supply Agency [Military] .... OSA
Overseas Supply Agency, San Francisco [Military] (CINC) .... OSASF
Overseas Supply Committee [World War II] .... OSC
Overseas Supply Division [Military] .... OSD
Overseas Switch [Military] .... OSS
Overseas Tariffs and Regulations (DS) .... OTAR
Overseas Technical Information Unit [Department of Trade] [British] .... OTIU
Overseas Telecommunications Commission (NITA) .... OTC
Overseas Telecommunications Commission of Australia (BARN) .... OTC
Overseas Telegraph Superintending Officers' Association [A union] [British] .... OTSOA
Overseas Telephone Services (DAS) .... OTS
Overseas Territories (MCD) .... OT
Overseas Trade .... OT
Overseas Trading [A publication] .... OT
Overseas Transportation Office, Naval Support Activity (DNAB) .... OTO NAVSUPPACT
Overseas Trust Bank [Hong Kong] .... OTB
Overseas Unit Replacement [System] [Army] .... OVUREP
Overseas Unit Replacement System [Military] (AFIT) .... OSUREP
Overseas Visitors Bureau [Department of Trade] [British] .... OVB
Overseas Visual Aids Centre [British] .... OVAC
Overseas Weapons, Logistically Supported (MCD) .... OWLS
Overseas Writers (EA) .... OW
Overseas-Foreign Aeronautical Communications Station (MUGU) .... OFACS
Overseas-Foreign Aeronautical Receiver Station .... OFARS
Overseas-Foreign Aeronautical Transmitter Station .... OFATS
Overseas-Trained Doctors .... OTD
Overseer .... O
Overseer .... O/SEER
Overshipped (MCD) .... O/S
Overside Drainage [Medicine] (DAVI) .... OSD
Oversight .... OVRSGHT
Oversight of Resources and Capability for Logistics Effectiveness (PDAA) .... ORACLE
Oversize (AAG) .... OS
Oversize .... OVS
Overspecificity [Psychometrics] .... OS
Overspeed (AAG) .... OVSP

Overspeed Control System (AAG) ... OCS
Overspenders Anonymous (EA) ... OSA
Overstayer Tracing and Intelligence System [*British*] ... OTIS
Overstuffed [*Freight*] ... OVSTFD
Overt Meditation ... OM
Overtake (FAAC) ... OVTK
Overtaken by Events [*Military*] ... OTBE
Overtaken by Events [*US Congress*] ... OTE
Overtemperature (KSC) ... O/T
Overtemperature (NASA) ... OTEMP
Overtemperature ... OTEMP
Over-the-Calf [*Women's fashions*] (IIA) ... OTC
Over-the-Capacitor [*Sockets*] ... OTC
Over-the-Counter [*Also, OTC*] [*Stock exchange term*] ... O/C
Over-the-Counter [*Pharmacy*] ... OTC
Over-the-Counter [*Also, O/C*] [*Stock exchange term*] ... OTC
Over-the-Counter Batch [*Stock exchange term*] (MHDW) ... OCB
Over-the-Counter Control Unit [*Stock exchange term*] (MHDW) ... OCU
Over-the-Counter Drug (MEDA) ... OTCRx
Over-the-Counter-Drug (MEDA) ... OTCD
Over-the-Horizon [*RADAR*] ... OTH
Over-the-Horizon Airborne Sensor Information System [*Navy*] (DOMA) ... OASIS
Over-the-Horizon Back-Scatter [*RADAR*] ... OTHB
Over-the-Horizon Compressed (MCD) ... OC
Over-the-Horizon/Damage Assessment [*Navy*] (CAAL) ... OTH/DA
Over-the-Horizon Detection [*RADAR*] (SAA) ... OHDET
Over-the-Horizon Detection, Classification, and Targeting (NVT) ... OTHDC & T
Over-the-Horizon Detection RADAR-Backscatter (MCD) ... OHD-B
Over-the-Horizon Detection System [*RADAR*] ... OHDETS
Over-the-Horizon Detector [*RADAR*] ... OHD
Over-the-Horizon Expanded (MCD) ... OE
Over-the-Horizon - Expanded ... OTH-E
Over-the-Horizon - Forward Scatter ... OTH-F
Over-the-Horizon RADAR ... OHR
Over-the-Horizon RADAR (MCD) ... OTHR
Over-the-Horizon Ship-to-Ship Missile ... OTHSSM
Over-the-Horizon Targeting (NVT) ... OTHT
Over-the-Horizon Targeting System (MCD) ... OS
Over-the-Horizon Targeting System Digital Interface Unit ... OSDIU
Over-the-Horizon Transmission ... O/H
Over-the-Nose Vision Line (PDAA) ... ONVL
Over-the-Road [*Automotive engineering*] ... OTR
Over-the-Shore Discharge of Cargo [*Navy*] (CAAL) ... OSDOC
Over-the-Shoulder [*Cinematography*] ... OTS
Over-the-Shoulder Cinematography (NTCM) ... OS
Over-the-Shoulder Rating ... OSR
Over-the-Shoulder Shot [*Photography*] (WDMC) ... OSS
Over-the-Side [*Navy*] (CAAL) ... OTS
Over-the-Top [*Marshall-MacIntosh knee operation*] ... OTT
Over-Thirty-Never-Married [*Lifestyle classification*] ... OTNM
Overthread Guide Sleeve Tool [*Nuclear energy*] (NRCH) ... OGST
Overtime ... OT
Overtime Authorization (AAG) ... OA
Overtime Authorization Request (MCD) ... OAR
Overtime Pay (MHDB) ... OP
Overtime Premium (MCD) ... OTP
Overtly Diabetic [*Medicine*] ... OD
Overton [*Nevada*] [*Seismograph station code, US Geological Survey Closed*] (SEIS) ... OVE
Overtone ... OT
Overtone [*Record label*] ... Over
Overton's Iowa and Wisconsin Practice [*A publication*] (DLA) ... Overt Pr
Overton's Tennessee Supreme Court Reports [*1791-1816*] [*A publication*] (DLA) ... Over
Overton's Tennessee Supreme Court Reports [*1791-1816*] [*A publication*] (DLA) ... Overt
Overtraining Reversal Effect ... ORE
Overtravel ... OVTR
Overture (ROG) ... OV
Overturning Moment ... OM
Overventilation [*Medicine*] ... OV
Overview Latin America (EA) ... OLA
Overvoltage ... OV
Overvoltage ... OVV
Overvoltage Factor (IAA) ... OVF
Over-Voltage Factor (PDAA) ... OVF
Overvoltage Load Protection ... OVLP
Overvoltage Protection ... OVP
Over-Voltage Protection Relay [*Electrical engineering*] ... OVPR
Over-Voltage Protection Unit [*Computer science*] (EECA) ... OVPU
Overvoltage Relay ... OVR
Overvoltage Sensing (MCD) ... OVS
Over-Water Jet Transport (MCD) ... OJT
Overwear Syndrome [*Of contact lens*] ... OWS
Overwhelming Post-Splenectomy Infection [*Medicine*] ... OPSI
Overwintered Nest [*Ornithology*] ... OWN
Overzuche Handels Maatschappij [*Foreign Trade Company*] [*Dutch*] (ILCA) ... O/H
Ovid [*Roman poet, 43BC-17AD*] [*Classical studies*] (ROG) ... OV
Ovid Public Library, Ovid, CO [*Library symbol Library of Congress*] (LCLS) ... CoOv
Ovid Public Library, Ovid, MI [*Library symbol Library of Congress*] (LCLS) ... MiOv
Ovid Technologies [*NASDAQ symbol*] (SAG) ... OVID
Ovid Technoloiges [*Associated Press*] (SAG) ... OvidTec
Ovid-Elsie, MI [*FM radio station call letters*] ... WOES
Oviedo [*Spain ICAO location identifier*] (ICLI) ... LEOV
Oviedo [*Spain*] [*Airport symbol*] (OAG) ... OVD
Oviedo, FL [*AM radio station call letters*] ... WONQ
Ovine Corticotrophin Releasing Factor [*Endocrinology*] ... oCRF
Ovine Lactogenic Hormone [*Endocrinology*] (MAE) ... OLH
Ovine Luteinizing Hormone [*Endocrinology*] ... OLH
Ovine Placental Lactogen [*Medicine*] (DMAA) ... OPL
Ovine Prolactin [*Endocrinology*] ... OP
Ovine Prolactin [*Endocrinology*] ... OPRL
Ovine Submaxillary Mucin [*Medicine*] (DMAA) ... OSM
Ovine Testicular Lymph [*Endocrinology*] ... OTL
Ovine Trophoblast Protein [*Biochemistry*] ... OTP
Oviposition-Determining Pheromone ... ODP
Ovomucoid Trypsin Inhibitor [*Medicine*] (DMAA) ... OTI
Ovonic Memory Switch (PDAA) ... OMS
Ovonic Threshold Switch ... OTS
Ovotransferrin [*Biochemistry*] ... OT
Ovshinsky and Electronic [*Excitation processing term formed by combining name of Stanford Ovshinsky, energy researcher, and "electronic"*] ... OVONIC
Ovulate [*Gynecology*] (DAVI) ... OV
Ovulation Method [*Birth control*] ... OM
Ovulation Method Teachers Association (EA) ... OMTA
Ovulation Predictor Kit ... OPK
Ovulation-Inducing Hormone [*Endocrinology*] ... OIH
Ovulation-Producing Hormone [*Medicine*] (AD) ... OIH
Ovule [*Botany*] ... O
Ovum [*Egg*] [*Latin*] ... OV
Ovvero [*Otherwise*] [*Music*] ... OVV
Owando [*Congo*] [*ICAO location identifier*] (ICLI) ... FCOO
Owando [*Congo*] [*Airport symbol*] (OAG) ... FTX
Owasco River [*AAR code*] ... OR
Owase [*Japan*] [*Seismograph station code, US Geological Survey*] (SEIS) ... OWA
Owasso, OK [*FM radio station call letters*] ... KQLL
Owatonna Free Public Library, Owatonna, MN [*Library symbol Library of Congress*] (LCLS) ... MnO
Owatonna, MN [*AM radio station call letters*] ... KRFO
Owatonna, MN [*FM radio station call letters*] ... KRFO-FM
Owatonna, MN [*Location identifier FAA*] (FAAL) ... OWA
Owego, NY [*AM radio station call letters*] ... WEBO
Owego, NY [*FM radio station call letters*] ... WGRG
Owen Electric Pictures [*Telecommunications service*] (TSSD) ... OEP
Owen Harrison Harding [*of the James W. Ellison novel, "I'm Owen Harrison Harding"*] ... OHH
Owen Hart Fan Club (EA) ... OHFC
Owen Healthcare [*NYSE symbol*] (TTSB) ... OWN
Owen Healthcare, Inc. [*NASDAQ symbol*] (SAG) ... OWEN
Owen Healthcare, Inc. [*Associated Press*] (SAG) ... OwenHlt
Owen on Bankruptcy [*A publication*] (DLA) ... Owen Bankr
Owen Sound Museum, County of Grey, Ontario [*Library symbol National Library of Canada*] (BIB) ... OOWM
Owen Sound, ON [*AM radio station call letters*] ... CFOS
Owen Sound, ON [*Television station call letters*] ... CIII-4
Owen Sound, ON [*FM radio station call letters*] ... CIXK
Owen Sound Public Library, Ontario [*Library symbol National Library of Canada*] (NLC) ... OOW
Owen Sound Public Library, Owen Sound, ON, Canada [*Library symbol Library of Congress*] (LCLS) ... CaOOw
Owen Vapor Engine ... OVE
Owen Ventures Ltd. [*Vancouver Stock Exchange symbol*] ... OWN
Owena Bank [*Nigeria*] ... OB
Owens & Minor [*NYSE symbol*] (TTSB) ... OMI
Owens & Minor, Inc. [*NYSE symbol*] (SPSG) ... OMI
Owens & Minor Inc. Holding Co. [*Associated Press*] (SAG) ... OwensM
Owens, B. R., Montebello CA [*STAC*] ... OBR
Owen's English Common Pleas Reports [*A publication*] (DLA) ... Ow
Owen's English King's Bench Reports [*1556-1615*] [*A publication*] (DLA) ... Ow
Owen's English King's Bench Reports [*1556-1615*] [*A publication*] (DLA) ... Owen
Owens Group Ltd. [*New Zealand*] [*ICAO designator*] (FAAC) ... OWN
Owens Illinois [*NYSE symbol*] (SAG) ... OI
Owens Illinois [*Associated Press*] (SAG) ... OwensIll
Owens Technical College, Learning Resource Media Center, Toledo, OH [*OCLC symbol*] (OCLC) ... MJO
Owens Valley Radio Observatory [*California Institute of Technology*] [*Research center*] (RCD) ... OVRO
Owensboro [*Kentucky*] [*Airport symbol*] (OAG) ... OWB
Owensboro [*Kentucky*] [*Airport symbol*] (AD) ... OWB
Owensboro [*Diocesan abbreviation*] [*Kentucky*] (TOCD) ... OWN
Owensboro Community College, Owensboro, KY [*Library symbol*] [*Library of Congress*] (LCLS) ... KyOwC
Owensboro, KY [*FM radio station call letters*] ... WBKR
Owensboro, KY [*Television station call letters*] ... WKOH
Owensboro, KY [*FM radio station call letters*] ... WKWC
Owensboro, KY [*AM radio station call letters*] ... WOMI
Owensboro, KY [*FM radio station call letters*] ... WSTO
Owensboro, KY [*AM radio station call letters*] ... WVJS
Owensboro-Daviess County Public Library, Owensboro, KY [*Library symbol Library of Congress*] (LCLS) ... KyOw
Owens-Corning [*NYSE symbol*] (TTSB) ... OCF
Owens-Corning Fiberglas Corp. [*NYSE symbol*] (SPSG) ... OCF
Owens-Corning Fiberglas Corp. [*Associated Press*] (SAG) ... OwenC
Owens-Corning Fiberglas Corp., Granville, OH [*Library symbol Library of Congress*] (LCLS) ... OGraO
Owens-Illinois [*NYSE symbol*] (TTSB) ... OI
Owens-Illinois, Inc. [*NYSE symbol*] (SPSG) ... OI
Owens-Illinois, Inc., Technical and Business Information Services, Toledo, OH [*OCLC symbol*] (OCLC) ... OWI

Owens-Illinois, Inc., Technical Information Service-NTC, Toledo, OH [*Library symbol Library of Congress*] (LCLS) .... OTO
Owensville, MO [*FM radio station call letters*] .... KLZE
Owensville Public Library, Owensville, IN [*Library symbol Library of Congress*] (LCLS) .... InOw
Owensville Star-Echo, Owensville, IN [*Library symbol Library of Congress*] (LCLS) .... InOwSE
Owenton, KY [*Television station call letters*] .... WKON
Owingsville, KY [*FM radio station call letters*] .... WKCA
Owl and the Pussy Cat [*Poem by Edward Lear, 1871*] .... O & PC
Owl Monkey Kidney [*Cell line*] .... OMK
Own Brand (MHDB) .... OB
Own Doppler Nullifer (AD) .... odn
Own Doppler Nullifier .... ODN
Own Equipment Material .... OEM
Own Exchange [*Telecommunications*] (TEL) .... OE
Own Name .... O/N
Own Name (AD) .... o/n
Own Number Dialing [*Telecommunications*] (OA) .... OND
Own Occupation [*Banking*] .... OO
Own Recognizance [*Legal term*] .... OR
Own Ship [*Navy*] (CAAL) .... OS
Own Ship's Centerline [*Navy*] .... OSCL
Own Ship's Course [*Navy*] .... OSC
Own Ship's Distance [*Navy*] (MCD) .... OSD
Own Ship's Heading [*Navy*] .... OSH
Own Ship's Motion Simulator [*Navy*] .... OSMOS
Own Ship's Motion System [*Navy*] .... OSMOS
Own Ship's Position [*Navy*] (MCD) .... OSP
Own Ship's Roll [*Navy*] .... OSR
Own Ship's Speed [*Navy*] .... OSS
Own Ship's Speed Repeater [*Navy*] .... OSSR
Own Ship's Use [*Navy*] (DNAB) .... OSU
Own Time Switch [*Connection or call*] [*Telecommunications*] (TEL) .... OTS
Owned and Operated .... O & O
Owner .... O
Owner (MCD) .... OWN
Owner .... OWNR
Owner Handler Association of America (EA) .... OHA
Owner, Officer, Director, or Executive Personnel (MCD) .... OODEP
Owner/Operator .... O/O
Owner Operators of America [*Boston, NY*] (EA) .... OOA
Owner President Management Program (DD) .... OPM
Owner Will Carry [*Banking*] .... OWC
Owner-Operator Independent Drivers Association .... OOIDA
Owners Abroad Aviation Ltd. [*British ICAO designator*] (FAAC) .... OAB
Owners and Contractors Protective [*Insurance*] .... OCP
Owners & Officers of Private Companies [*A publication*] .... OOPC
Owners, Landlords, and Tenants [*Liability insurance*] .... OL & T
Owners, Landlords, and Tenants (AD) .... ol & t
Owners Manual .... OM
Owner's Risk [*Shipping*] .... OR
Owner's Risk of Becoming Wet [*Shipping*] .... ORW
Owner's Risk of Breaking [*Shipping*] .... ORB
Owner's Risk of Chafing [*Shipping*] .... ORC
Owner's Risk of Damage [*Shipping*] .... ORD
Owner's Risk of Deterioration [*Shipping*] .... ORDet
Owner's Risk of Fire [*Shipping*] .... ORF
Owner's Risk of Freezing [*Shipping*] .... ORF
Owner's Risk of Leakage [*Shipping*] .... ORL
Owner's Risk of Shifting [*Shipping*] .... ORS
Owner's Risk Rates [*Shipping*] .... ORR
Owner's Tank Wagons [*Shipping*] .... OTW
Owners, Traders, Breeders Association (NADA) .... OTBA
Owner's Vans [*Shipping*] .... OV
Owner's Wagons [*Shipping*] .... OW
Ownership Accountability of Selected Secondary Items Stocked .... OASIS
Ownership Purpose and Condition Code [*Navy*] (DNAB) .... OPC
Ownership Purpose Code [*Army*] (AABC) .... O/P
Ownership Reporting System [*Securities and Exchange Commission*] (GFGA) .... ORS
Owning the Weather [*Army*] (RDA) .... OTW
Owning Work Center [*Military*] (AFIT) .... OWC
Own-the-Night [*Technology*] [*Army*] (INF) .... OTN
Owosso Corp. [*NASDAQ symbol*] (SAG) .... OWOS
Owosso Corp. [*Associated Press*] (SAG) .... Owosso
Owosso, MI [*FM radio station call letters*] (RBYB) .... WAHV-FM
Owosso, MI [*FM radio station call letters*] .... WMZX
Owosso, MI [*AM radio station call letters*] .... WOAP
Owosso Public Library, Owosso, MI [*Library symbol Library of Congress*] (LCLS) .... MiOw
Owyhee, NV [*Location identifier FAA*] (FAAL) .... OWY
Ox Red Blood Cell [*Medicine*] (DMAA) .... ORBC
Oxacillin [*Antibacterial compound*] .... OX
Oxaero [*British*] [*FAA designator*] (FAAC) .... OXE
Oxalate [*Laboratory science*] (DAVI) .... OXLAT
Oxalic Acid [*Organic chemistry*] (AAMN) .... OA
Oxalic Acid [*Organic chemistry*] .... OXA
Oxaloacetic [*or Oxalacetic*] Acid [*Organic chemistry*] .... OAA
Oxalosis and Hyperoxaluria Foundation (EA) .... OHF
Oxalyl Thiolester [*Biochemistry*] .... OTE
Oxapentamethylenediethylenephosphoramide [*Pharmacology*] .... ODEPA
Oxazolinylphenoxy [*Organic radical*] .... OP
Oxboro Med Intl. [*NASDAQ symbol*] (TTSB) .... OMED
Oxboro Medical International, Inc. [*NASDAQ symbol*] (SAG) .... OMED

Oxboro Medical International, Inc. [*Associated Press*] (SAG) .... OxboroM
Oxbow Falls (AD) .... OF
Oxbridge Directory of Newsletters [*A publication*] .... ODN
Oxenstierna Foundation (AD) .... OF
Oxford [*County borough in England*] .... O
Oxford [*England*] .... OX
Oxford [*Record label*] .... Ox
Oxford [*England*] [*Seismograph station code, US Geological Survey Closed*] (SEIS) .... OXD
Oxford [*England*] .... OXF
Oxford [*British depot code*] .... OXF
Oxford [*Mississippi*] [*Seismograph station code, US Geological Survey Closed*] (SEIS) .... OXF
Oxford [*England*] [*Airport symbol*] (AD) .... OXF
Oxford Advanced Learner's Dictionary of Current English .... OALDCE
Oxford, AL [*AM radio station call letters*] .... WOXR
Oxford, AL [*FM radio station call letters*] .... WTBJ
Oxford, AL [*FM radio station call letters*] .... WVOK
Oxford American Dictionary [*A publication*] .... OAD
Oxford and Bucks Light Infantry [*Military unit*] [*British*] .... OBLI
Oxford and Cambridge Schools Examination Board [*British*] (DCTA) .... O & C
Oxford and Cambridge Universities Club [*British*] (DAS) .... OCUC
Oxford Annotated Bible [*New York*] [*A publication*] (BJA) .... OAB
Oxford Applied Research [*Software manufacturer*] [*British*] .... OAR
Oxford Bible Warehouse [*British*] (ROG) .... OBW
Oxford Bibliographical Society (DGA) .... OBS
Oxford Biographies [*A publication*] .... OB
Oxford/Cambridge [*England*] .... OXBRIDGE
Oxford Centre for Islamic Studies [*British*] .... OCIS
Oxford Church Textbooks [*A publication*] .... OCTB
Oxford Classical Texts [*A publication*] (OCD) .... OCT
Oxford Committee for Family Relief [*British*] (AD) .... OCFR
Oxford Committee for Famine Relief [*British*] (DI) .... OCFR
Oxford Committee for Famine Relief [*Acronym is now organization's official name British*] (EA) .... OXFAM
[*The*] Oxford Companion to American Literature [*A publication*] .... OCAL
Oxford Companion to English Literature [*A publication*] (AD) .... OCEL
Oxford Companion to Music [*A publication*] (AD) .... OCM
Oxford Concordance Project (NITA) .... OCP
Oxford Consolidated, Inc. [*NASDAQ symbol*] (NQ) .... OXCI
Oxford Consolidated, Inc. [*Associated Press*] (SAG) .... OxfrdC
Oxford County Public Library, Woodstock, ON, Canada [*Library symbol Library of Congress*] (LCLS) .... CaOWoO
Oxford County Public Library, Woodstock, Ontario [*Library symbol National Library of Canada*] (NLC) .... OWOO
Oxford, CT [*Location identifier FAA*] (FAAL) .... OXC
Oxford, CT [*Location identifier FAA*] (FAAL) .... TBY
Oxford Decimal Classification .... ODC
[*The*] Oxford Dictionary of English Etymology [*A publication*] .... ODEE
Oxford Dictionary of Nursery Rhymes [*A publication*] .... ODNR
[*The*] Oxford Dictionary of Quotations [*A publication*] .... ODQ
Oxford Dictionary of the Christian Church .... ODCC
Oxford Down Sheep Breeders Association [*British*] (DBA) .... ODSBA
Oxford Economic Research Associates Ltd .... OXERA
Oxford Editions of Cuneiform Texts [*A publication*] (BJA) .... OECT
Oxford English Dictionary [*Information service or system A publication*] .... OED
Oxford English Dictionary Inputting, Proofing, and Updating Service .... OEDIPUS
Oxford Forestry Institute [*University of Oxford*] [*British*] (IRUK) .... OFI
Oxford Foundation (AD) .... OF
Oxford Gazette, Oxford, IN [*Library symbol Library of Congress*] (LCLS) .... InOxG
Oxford Health Plans [*NASDAQ symbol*] (SPSG) .... OXHP
Oxford Health Plans, Inc. [*Associated Press*] (SAG) .... OxfdHlt
Oxford Higher Local Examination [*British*] (ROG) .... OHL
Oxford House [*Canada*] [*Airport symbol*] (OAG) .... YOH
Oxford India Paper (AD) .... oip
Oxford Indus [*NYSE symbol*] (TTSB) .... OXM
Oxford Industries, Inc. [*Associated Press*] (SAG) .... Oxford
Oxford Industries, Inc. [*NYSE symbol*] (SPSG) .... OXM
Oxford Institute for Energy Studies [*British*] .... OIES
Oxford/Kidlington [*British ICAO location identifier*] (ICLI) .... EGTK
Oxford Latin Dictionary [*A publication*] .... OLD
Oxford Lawyer [*1958-61*] [*A publication*] (DLA) .... Oxf Lawy
Oxford Lawyer [*1958-61*] [*A publication*] (DLA) .... Oxford Law
Oxford Library Information System (TNIG) .... OLIS
Oxford Library of Practical Theology [*A publication*] .... OLPT
Oxford Library of Translations [*A publication*] .... OLT
Oxford Medical Manuals [*A publication*] .... OMM
Oxford Medical Publications [*A publication*] .... OMP
Oxford Memorial Library, Oxford, NY [*Library symbol Library of Congress*] (LCLS) .... NOx
Oxford Military College (ROG) .... OMC
Oxford Mills Branch, Oxford-On-Rideau Township Public Library [*Library symbol National Library of Canada*] (BIB) .... OOMO
Oxford Mission Brotherhood of the Epiphany [*Anglican religious community*] .... OMBE
Oxford Mission to Calcutta [*British*] (ROG) .... OMC
Oxford, MS [*Location identifier FAA*] (FAAL) .... UOX
Oxford, MS [*FM radio station call letters*] .... WMAV
Oxford, MS [*Television station call letters*] .... WMAV-TV
Oxford, MS [*FM radio station call letters*] .... WOXD
Oxford, MS [*FM radio station call letters*] .... WQLJ
Oxford, MS [*AM radio station call letters*] .... WSUH
Oxford, MS [*FM radio station call letters*] .... WWMS
Oxford, NC [*Location identifier FAA*] (FAAL) .... HXO

Oxford, NC [*AM radio station call letters*] .... WCBQ
Oxford, OH [*Location identifier FAA*] (FAAL) .... OXD
Oxford, OH [*FM radio station call letters*] .... WMUB
Oxford, OH [*FM radio station call letters*] .... WOXY
Oxford, OH [*Television station call letters*] .... WPTO
Oxford Orthopaedic Engineering Centre [*British*] (IRUK) ...... OOEC
Oxford [*J. B.*] Oxford Holdings [*NASDAQ symbol*] (SAG) ...... JBOH
Oxford Paperback Dictionary [*A publication*] .... OPD
Oxford Pocket Classics [*A publication*] (ROG) .... OPC
Oxford Poets [*A publication*] .... OXP
Oxford Policy Management [*British*] .... OPM
Oxford Properties Canada Ltd. [*Toronto Stock Exchange symbol*] ... OXF
Oxford Public Library, Oxford, IN [*Library symbol Library of Congress*]
  (LCLS) .... InOx
Oxford Quarter Sessions Records [*Oxford Record Society, No. 16*]
  [*A publication*] (DLA) .... Gretton
Oxford Resources CI'A' [*NASDAQ symbol*] (TTSB) .... OXFD
Oxford Resources Corp. [*NASDAQ symbol*] (SAG) .... OXFD
Oxford Resources Corp. [*Associated Press*] (SAG) .... OxfdRsc
Oxford Superconductive Technology [*Manufacturing company*] [*British*] .... OST
Oxford Text System (NITA) .... OU
Oxford University [*England*] .... OU
Oxford University Air Squadron [*British*] (DI) .... OUAS
Oxford University, All Souls College, Oxford, United Kingdom [*Library
  symbol Library of Congress*] (LCLS) .... UkOxU-AS
Oxford University, Bodleian Library, Oxford, United Kingdom [*Library
  symbol Library of Congress*] (LCLS) .... UkOxU
Oxford University, Bodleian Library, Rhodes House, Oxford, United
  Kingdom [*Library symbol Library of Congress*] (LCLS) ...... UkOxU-Rh
Oxford University Dramatic Society [*British*] (AIE) .... OUDS
Oxford University, Nuffield College, Oxford, United Kingdom [*Library
  symbol Library of Congress*] (LCLS) .... UkOxU-N
Oxford University Press (NADA) .... OUP
Oxford University Press, Inc. [*New York, NY*] .... OUP
Oxford University Volunteer Battalion [*British military*] (DMA) ... OUVB
Oxford Word and Language Service [*A service of the Oxford English
  Dictionary group*] .... OWLS
Oxford Word and Language Service [*British*] (DAVI) .... OWLS
Oxford-on-Rideau Township Public Library, Burritt's Rapids, ON, Canada
  [*Library symbol*] [*Library of Congress*] (LCLS) .... CaOBRO
Oxford-On-Rideau Township Public Library, Burritt's Rapids, Ontario
  [*Library symbol National Library of Canada*] (BIB) .... OBRO
Oxfordshire [*County in England*] .... OXON
Oxfordshire Light Horse [*British military*] (DMA) .... OLH
Oxfordshire Light Infantry [*Military unit*] [*British*] .... OLI
Oxfordshire Modern Languages Achievement Certificate [*British*]
  (AIE) .... OMLAC
Oxfordshire Project for the Training of Instructors and Supervisors
  [*British*] (AIE) .... OPTIS
Oxfordshire Record Society [*British*] (DBA) .... ORS
Oxidant [*Photochemical*] (ERG) .... OX
Oxidation .... OXIDN
Oxidation Catalyst [*Automotive engineering*] .... OC
Oxidation/Fermentation (AD) .... o/f
Oxidation Number (IAA) .... ON
Oxidation-Fermentation [*Growth medium*] .... O-F
Oxidation-Fluorination Ratio (MCD) .... OFR
Oxidation-Induced Stacking Fault (PDAA) .... OSF
Oxidation-Reduction .... O-R
Oxidation-Reduction Potential [*Symbol*] (MAE) .... eH
Oxidation-Reduction Potential .... ORP
Oxidation-Resistant Coating .... ORC
Oxidative Coupling of Methane [*Chemistry*] .... OCM
Oxidative Pentose Phosphate (PDAA) .... OPP
Oxidative Phosphorylation [*Medicine*] .... OXPHOS
Oxidative-Desulfurization [*Fuel technology*] .... ODS
Oxidatively Solubilized Coal [*Fuel technology*] .... OSC
Oxide [*or Oxidizer*] (AAG) .... OX
Oxide Control and Indication (NRCH) .... OCI
Oxide Dispersion Strengthened [*Metallurgy*] .... ODS
Oxide Dispersion Strengthened (AD) .... ods
Oxide Dispersion Strengthened [*Ferrous metallurgy*] .... ODS
Oxide Isolated (NITA) .... OXIS
Oxide Isolation (IAA) .... OXIS
Oxide Layer Isolation Structure .... OLIS
Oxide Throat Insert .... OTI
Oxide-Aligned Transistor [*Electronics*] (PDAA) .... OAT
Oxide-Coated Brush Cathode .... OBC
Oxide-Isolated Monolith .... OXIM
Oxides (VRA) .... ox
Oxide-Stable Resin .... OSR
Oxidizable Carbon Ratio .... OCR
Oxidized (MSA) .... OXD
Oxidized Metal Explosive (AD) .... mox
Oxidized Porous Silicon [*Materials science*] .... OPS
Oxidized Regenerated Cellulose [*Hemostatic*] [*Organic chemistry*] ... ORC
Oxidizer (NASA) .... OXDZR
Oxidizer .... OXDZR
Oxidizer (AAG) .... OXID
Oxidizer Bleed Valve (NASA) .... OBV
Oxidizer Fill Line (AAG) .... OFL
Oxidizer Heat Exchange (MCD) .... OHE
Oxidizer Isolation Valve (MCD) .... OIV
Oxidizer Particle Size .... OPS
Oxidizer Preburner (KSC) .... OPB

Oxidizer Preburner Oxidizer Valve (NASA) .... OPBOV
Oxidizer Preburner Oxidizer Valve (MCD) .... OPOV
Oxidizer Tank (MCD) .... OTK
Oxidizer Tanking Panel (AAG) .... OTP
Oxidizer to Fuel Ratio (AD) .... o/f
Oxidizer Topping Line (AAG) .... OTL
Oxidizer Turbine Bypass Valve (KSC) .... OTBV
Oxidizer Vent Control .... OVC
Oxidizer-to-Fuel [*Ratio*] .... O/F
Oxidizing Catalyst [*Automotive engineering*] .... OXC
Oxidizing Flame .... OF
Oxidizing Flame (AD) .... of
Oxigene, Inc. [*NASDAQ symbol*] (SAG) .... OXGN
Oxigene, Inc. [*Associated Press*] (SAG) .... Oxigene
Oxigene, Inc. [*Associated Press*] (SAG) .... Oxign
OXIGENE Inc. Wrrt [*NASDAQ symbol*] (TTSB) .... OXGNW
Oxin Industries Ltd. [*Vancouver Stock Exchange symbol*] .... OXN
OXIS International [*NASDAQ symbol*] (TTSB) .... OXIS
Oxis International, Inc. [*NASDAQ symbol*] (SAG) .... OXIS
Oxley [*British depot code*] .... OXY
Oxley Airlines [*ICAO designator*] (AD) .... VQ
Oxley Aviation [*Australia ICAO designator*] (FAAC) .... OAA
Oxley's Railway Cases [*1897-1903*] [*A publication*] (DLA) ... Oxley
Oxnard [*California*] [*Airport symbol*] (OAG) .... OXR
Oxnard, CA [*Location identifier FAA*] (FAAL) .... CMA
Oxnard, CA [*Television station call letters*] .... KADY
Oxnard, CA [*FM radio station call letters*] .... KCAQ
Oxnard, CA [*FM radio station call letters*] .... KCRU
Oxnard, CA [*FM radio station call letters*] .... KDAR
Oxnard, CA [*AM radio station call letters*] .... KOXR
Oxnard, CA [*FM radio station call letters*] .... KXLM
Oxnard, CA [*Location identifier FAA*] (FAAL) .... VTU
Oxnard Public Library, Oxnard, CA [*Library symbol Library of Congress*]
  (LCLS) .... COx
Oxogenic Steroid (MAE) .... OGS
Oxoglutarate Dehydrogenase [*An enzyme*] .... OGDH
Oxo(mercaptoethyl)(phenyl)imidazolidine [*Biochemistry*] ... OMPI
Oxonia [*Oxford University*] [*Latin*] .... OXON
Oxoniensis [*Of Oxford University*] [*Latin*] .... OXON
Oxothiazolidine [*Biochemistry*] .... OTZ
Oxothiazolidinecarboxylic Acid [*Biochemistry*] .... OTCA
Oxotremorine [*Cholinergic agent*] .... OTMN
Oxprenolol [*Vasodilator*] .... OXP
Oxtotitlan [*Mexico*] [*Seismograph station code, US Geological Survey*]
  (SEIS) .... OXM
Oxy Metal Industries International (AD) .... OMII
Oxyacetylene Welding .... OAW
Oxybisbenzene [*Organic chemistry*] .... OBB
Oxybis(benzenesulfonylhydrazine) [*Organic chemistry*] ...... OBSH
Oxybisphenoxarsine [*Organic chemistry*] .... OBPA
Oxychloride Cement Association [*Defunct*] .... OCA
Oxydianiline [*Organic chemistry*] .... ODA
Oxydibenzil [*Organic chemistry*] .... ODB
Oxydizer-to-Fuel [*Ratio*] .... OF
Oxyfuel Cutting - Natural Gas [*Welding*] .... OFC-N
Oxyfuel-Gas Cutting [*Welding*] .... OFC
Oxyfuel-Gas Cutting - Acetylene [*Welding*] .... OFC-A
Oxyfuel-Gas Cutting - Hydrogen [*Welding*] .... OFC-H
Oxyfuel-Gas Cutting - Propane [*Welding*] .... OFC-P
Oxyfuel-Gas Welding .... OFW
Oxygen [*Chemical element*] .... O
Oxygen (IDOE) .... O_2
Oxygen (IDOE) .... ox
Oxygen [*Chemical element*] (IAA) .... OX
Oxygen [*Chemical element*] [*Symbol is O*] (AAG) .... OXY
Oxygen .... OXY
Oxygen [*Chemical element*] [*Symbol is O*] .... OXYG
Oxygen Activated Sludge (DICI) .... OAS
Oxygen Adsorption, Out-gassing, and Chemical Reduction (PDAA) ... OAOR
Oxygen Alternate Fill .... OAF
Oxygen at Atmospheric Pressure .... OAP
Oxygen at High Pressure (AD) .... obp
Oxygen at High Pressure [*Also, HBO, HPO*] (MCD) .... OHP
Oxygen at High Temperature (OA) .... OHT
Oxygen at Low Pressure (KSC) .... OLP
Oxygen Breathing Apparatus .... OBA
Oxygen Cabin Pressurization Section [*NASA*] (KSC) .... OCPS
Oxygen Capacity (MAE) .... O_2 Cap
Oxygen Consumed .... OC
Oxygen Consumption [*Biochemistry*] (DAVI) .... QO
Oxygen Consumption Gauge .... OCG
Oxygen Consumed .... OC
Oxygen Cutting [*Welding*] .... ODS
Oxygen Depletion Sensor .... ODS
Oxygen Diffusion Rate (OA) .... ODR
Oxygen Dissociation Curve [*Medicine*] (DMAA) .... ODC
Oxygen Drain (MCD) .... OD
Oxygen Enchancement Ratio (IAA) .... OR
Oxygen Enhancement Ratio .... OER
Oxygen Enriched Air System (MCD) .... OEAS
Oxygen Evolution Reaction (PDAA) .... OER
Oxygen Extraction Fraction [*Medicine*] (DMAA) .... OEF
Oxygen Fill (NASA) .... OF
Oxygen Fill to Missile (AAG) .... OFM
Oxygen Fluid Distribution System [*NASA*] (NASA) .... OFDS
Oxygen Free Hard Copper (IAA) .... OFHC

Oxygen Furnace Tilt Drive ..... OFTD
Oxygen Gauge (NASA) ..... OG
Oxygen Gauge Valve (NASA) ..... OGV
Oxygen Generation System (NASA) ..... OGS
Oxygen Generation System ..... OGS
Oxygen Heat Exchanger (KSC) ..... OXH
Oxygen Hemoglobin Affinity (OA) ..... OHA
Oxygen Income [or Intake] [Medicine] ..... OI
Oxygen Index [Medicine] (DAVI) ..... OI
Oxygen Intact [Medicine] (DAVI) ..... OI
Oxygen Lance Powder ..... OLP
Oxygen Lime Powder [Steelmaking process] ..... OLP
Oxygen Manual Valve (NASA) ..... OMV
Oxygen/Ozone Indicator ..... OOI
Oxygen/Ozone Recorder ..... OOR
Oxygen Partial Pressure ..... OPP
Oxygen Partial Pressure Sensor ..... OPPS
Oxygen Pressure (DAVI) ..... pO_2
Oxygen Pressure on Room Air [Medicine] (DAVI) ..... pAO_2
Oxygen Pressure Process [Ore leach process] ..... OP
Oxygen Pressure Regulator (MCD) ..... OPR
Oxygen Pressure Relief Valve (MCD) ..... OPRV
Oxygen Production Rate [Biochemistry] ..... OPR
Oxygen Purge [NASA] (NASA) ..... OP
Oxygen Purge System [or Subsystem] [NASA] ..... OPS
Oxygen Quotient (AAMN) ..... QO_2
Oxygen Radical Absorbance Capacity [Analytical Chemistry] ..... ORAC
Oxygen Relief ..... O/R
Oxygen Relief (NASA) ..... OR
Oxygen Replacement Bottles ..... OXRB
Oxygen Saturation (MAE) ..... O_2sat
Oxygen Saturation Meter (MAE) ..... OSM
Oxygen Scavenging Cell Membrane Fragment [Biochemistry] ..... OSCMF
Oxygen Selective Detector [Chromatography] ..... OSD
Oxygen Sensor [Automotive engineering] ..... OS
Oxygen Service (DNAB) ..... OS
Oxygen Sleep Starvation ..... OSS
Oxygen Steel Making ..... OSM
Oxygen Supply and Cabin Pressurization Section [Apollo] [NASA] ..... OSCPS
Oxygen Test Stand (KSC) ..... OTS
Oxygen Tolerance Test ..... OTT
Oxygen Transfer Compressor ..... OTC
Oxygen Transfer Rate [Chemical engineering] ..... OTR
Oxygen under Hyperbaric Pressure [For hyperbaric oxygen therapy] [Medicine] (DAVI) ..... OHP
Oxygen Uptake Rate [Biochemistry] ..... OUR
Oxygen Utilization Factor ..... OUF
Oxygen Utilization Rate [Photosynthesis] ..... OUR
Oxygen Vent (NASA) ..... OV
Oxygen Vent Fill ..... OVF
Oxygen Ventilation Equivalent [Laboratory science] (DAVI) ..... O_2V
Oxygenated Fuels Association (EA) ..... OFA
Oxygenated Fuels Program Reformulated Gasoline ..... OPRG
Oxygenated Sterol Compound [Biochemistry] ..... OSC
Oxygen-Derived Free Radicals [Biochemistry] ..... ODFR
Oxygen-Dope Polysilicon (PDAA) ..... O-POS
Oxygen-Evolving Complex [Photosynthesis] ..... OEC
Oxygen-Flame Ionization Detector ..... O-FID
Oxygen-Free High Conductivity (AD) ..... ofhc
Oxygen-Free High-Carbon (AD) ..... ofhc
Oxygen-Free, High-Conductivity [Copper] ..... OFHC
Oxygen-Minimum Zone [Oceanography] ..... OMZ
Oxygen-Regulated Protein [Biochemistry] ..... ORP
Oxygen-to-Metal [Ratio] (NRCH) ..... O/M
Oxyhaemoglobin Dissociation Curve (PDAA) ..... ODC
Oxyhydrogen Welding ..... OHW
Oxymel [Syrup of vinegar and honey] [Pharmacy] ..... OX
Oxymel [Syrup of vinegar and honey] [Pharmacy] (ROG) ..... OXYM
Oxymorphonazine [An analgesic] ..... OMZ
Oxypneumocardiogram [Cardiology] (DAVI) ..... OPC
Oxypolygelatin [Plasma extender] ..... OPG
Oxyquinoline [Organic chemistry] ..... OXINE
Oxytetracycline [Antibiotic] ..... OTC
Oxytocin [Endocrinology] ..... OT
Oxytocin [Endocrinology] ..... OXY
Oxytocin Challenge Test [Medicine] ..... OCT
Oy Rekolid, Mikrofilmipalvelu, Helsinki, Finland [Library symbol Library of Congress] (LCLS) ..... FiHR
Oyama [Japan] [Seismograph station code, US Geological Survey] (SEIS) ..... OYM

Oyem [Gabon] [ICAO location identifier] (ICLI) ..... FOGO
Oyem [Gabon] [Airport symbol] (OAG) ..... OYE
Oyen Municipal Library, Alberta [Library symbol National Library of Canada] (NLC) ..... AOYM
Oyen Municipal Library, Oyen, AB, Canada [Library symbol Library of Congress] (LCLS) ..... CaAOyM
Oyer and Terminer [Hear and Determine] [Legal term] (DLA) ..... O & T
OYO Geospace Corp. [NASDAQ symbol] (SAG) ..... OYOG
OYO Geospace Corp. [Associated Press] (SAG) ..... OYOGeo
Oyonnax/Arbent [France ICAO location identifier] (ICLI) ..... LFLK
Oyster Bay High School, Oyster Bay, NY [Library symbol Library of Congress] (LCLS) ..... NOyHS
Oyster Bay-East Norwich Public Library, Oyster Bay, NY [Library symbol Library of Congress] (LCLS) ..... NOy
Oyster Creek Nuclear Generating Station (NRCH) ..... OCNGS
Oyster Creek Nuclear Power Plant (NRCH) ..... OCNPP
Oyster Farmers' Association of Australia ..... OFAA
Oyster Farmers' Association of New South Wales [Australia] ..... OFANSW
Oyster Growers and Dealers Association (EA) ..... OGDA
Oyster Institute of North America [Later, SINA] (EA) ..... OINA
Oyster Pond Historical Society, Orient Point, NY [Library symbol Library of Congress] (LCLS) ..... NOrpOHi
Oyster Shell Institute (EA) ..... OSI
Oysters [Quality of the bottom] [Nautical charts] ..... Oys
Ozamis City [Philippines] [Airport symbol] (OAG) ..... OZC
Ozamis, Misamis Oriental [Philippines] [ICAO location identifier] (ICLI) ..... RPWI
Ozar Hatorah (EA) ..... OH
Ozark (MCD) ..... OZA
Ozark Academy, Gentry, AR [Library symbol Library of Congress] (LCLS) ..... ArGeO
Ozark Airlines (MHDB) ..... OZA
Ozark Airlines, Inc. [ICAO designator] (OAG) ..... OZ
Ozark, AL [Location identifier FAA] (FAAL) ..... SHA
Ozark, AL [FM radio station call letters] (RBYB) ..... WAQG-FM
Ozark, AL [Television station call letters] (RBYB) ..... WDFX-TV
Ozark, AL [FM radio station call letters] ..... WOAB
Ozark, AL [AM radio station call letters] ..... WOZK
Ozark, AL [AM radio station call letters] ..... WQLS
Ozark, AL [FM radio station call letters] ..... WQLS-FM
Ozark, AL [Location identifier FAA] (FAAL) ..... XBR
Ozark, AL [Location identifier FAA] (FAAL) ..... XMD
Ozark, AR [AM radio station call letters] ..... KDYN
Ozark, AR [FM radio station call letters] ..... KDYN-FM
Ozark, AR [Location identifier FAA] (FAAL) ..... OZZ
Ozark/Fort Rucker, AL [Location identifier FAA] (FAAL) ..... HEY
Ozark, Fort Rucker, AL [Location identifier FAA] (FAAL) ..... LOR
Ozark, Fort Rucker, AL [Location identifier FAA] (FAAL) ..... OZR
Ozark, Fort Rucker, AL [Location identifier FAA] (FAAL) ..... XWB
Ozark, MO [FM radio station call letters] (RBYB) ..... KCTG
Ozark National Scenic Riverways [National Park Service designation] ..... OZAR
Ozark Society (EA) ..... OSI
Ozarks Regional Commission [Department of Commerce] ..... ORC
Ozarks Regional Library, Fayetteville, AR [Library symbol Library of Congress] (LCLS) ..... ArFO
OZEmail Ltd. [Associated Press] (SAG) ..... OzEmail
OzEmail Ltd ADR [NASDAQ symbol] (TTSB) ..... OZEMY
Ozenji Critical Facility [Nuclear reactor] [Japan] ..... OCF
OzMail Ltd. [NASDAQ symbol] (SAG) ..... OZEM
Ozona Microfilm, Inc., Ozona, FL [Library symbol Library of Congress] (LCLS) ..... FOzM
Ozona, TX [FM radio station call letters] ..... KYXX
Ozona, TX [Location identifier FAA] (FAAL) ..... OZA
Ozone (PS) ..... O_3
Ozone O3
Ozone (IDOE) ..... oz
Ozone ..... OZ
Ozone ARCAS [All-Purpose Rocket for Collecting Atmospheric Soundings] [Navy] ..... OZARC
Ozone Depletion Potential [Meteorology] ..... ODP
Ozone Forming Potential [Exhaust emissions] [Automotive engineering] ..... OFP
Ozone Isopleth Plotting Package (GFGA) ..... OZIPP
Ozone Isopleth Plotting Package, Modified (GFGA) ..... OZIPPM
Ozone Transport Commission [State environmental agencies] ..... OTC
Ozone Trends Panel [NASA] ..... OTP
Ozone-Depleting Compound [Environmental chemistry] ..... ODC
Ozone-Depleting [or Depletion] Potential [Environmental science] ..... ODP
Ozone-Depleting Substance (AAGC) ..... ODS
Ozone-Forming Potential-Maximum Incremental Reactivity [Exhaust emissions] [Automotive engineering] ..... OFP-MIR
Ozuki [Japan ICAO location identifier] (ICLI) ..... RJOZ